MW01200448

YOUR WORD IS A LAMP TO MY FEET AND A LIGHT FOR MY PATH. PS 119:105

PRESENTED

TO

____

____

____

BY

____

____

ON

____

YOU KNIT ME TOGETHER IN MY MOTHER'S WOMB. PS 139:13

BIRTHS

NAME

BORN TO DATE

NAME

BORN TO DATE

NAME

BORN TO DATE

NAME

BORN TO DATE

NAME

BORN TO DATE

NAME

BORN TO DATE

NAME

BORN TO DATE

SPECIAL EVENTS

EVENT

PLACE DATE

EVENT

PLACE DATE

EVENT

PLACE DATE

EVENT

PLACE DATE

EVENT

PLACE DATE

EVENT

PLACE DATE

A MAN WILL... BE UNITED TO HIS WIFE, AND THEY WILL BECOME ONE FLESH. GE 2:24

THIS CERTIFIES THAT

and

were united in

HOLY MATRIMONY

on *the*

day of *A.D.*

at

in accordance with the laws of

Officiating

Witness

Witness

MARRIAGES

HUSBAND

WIFE

PLACE DATE

HUSBAND

WIFE

PLACE DATE

HUSBAND

WIFE

PLACE DATE

HUSBAND

WIFE

PLACE DATE

HUSBAND

WIFE

PLACE DATE

HUSBAND

WIFE

PLACE DATE

*BLESSED IS THE MAN
WHO FEARS THE LORD. PS 112:1*

HUSBAND'S FAMILY TREE

NAME

BIRTHPLACE DATE

BROTHERS AND SISTERS

PARENTS

FATHER

NAME

BIRTHPLACE DATE

MOTHER

NAME

BIRTHPLACE DATE

GRANDPARENTS

PATERNAL

GRANDFATHER

BIRTHPLACE DATE

GRANDMOTHER

BIRTHPLACE DATE

MATERNAL

GRANDFATHER

BIRTHPLACE DATE

GRANDMOTHER

BIRTHPLACE DATE

GREAT-GRANDPARENTS

PATERNAL

GRANDFATHER'S FATHER

BIRTHPLACE DATE

GRANDFATHER'S MOTHER

BIRTHPLACE DATE

GRANDMOTHER'S FATHER

BIRTHPLACE DATE

GRANDMOTHER'S MOTHER

BIRTHPLACE DATE

MATERNAL

GRANDFATHER'S FATHER

BIRTHPLACE DATE

GRANDFATHER'S MOTHER

BIRTHPLACE DATE

GRANDMOTHER'S FATHER

BIRTHPLACE DATE

GRANDMOTHER'S MOTHER

BIRTHPLACE DATE

A WOMAN WHO FEARS THE LORD IS TO BE PRAISED. PR 31:30

WIFE'S FAMILY TREE

NAME

BIRTHPLACE DATE

BROTHERS AND SISTERS

PARENTS

FATHER

NAME

BIRTHPLACE DATE

MOTHER

NAME

BIRTHPLACE DATE

GRANDPARENTS

PATERNAL

GRANDFATHER

BIRTHPLACE DATE

GRANDMOTHER

BIRTHPLACE DATE

MATERNAL

GRANDFATHER

BIRTHPLACE DATE

GRANDMOTHER

BIRTHPLACE DATE

GREAT-GRANDPARENTS

PATERNAL

GRANDFATHER'S FATHER

BIRTHPLACE DATE

GRANDFATHER'S MOTHER

BIRTHPLACE DATE

GRANDMOTHER'S FATHER

BIRTHPLACE DATE

GRANDMOTHER'S MOTHER

BIRTHPLACE DATE

MATERNAL

GRANDFATHER'S FATHER

BIRTHPLACE DATE

GRANDFATHER'S MOTHER

BIRTHPLACE DATE

GRANDMOTHER'S FATHER

BIRTHPLACE DATE

GRANDMOTHER'S MOTHER

BIRTHPLACE DATE

DEATHS

NAME

DATE

NAME

DATE

NAME

DATE

NAME

DATE

NAME

DATE

NAME

DATE

NAME

DATE

THE FULL LIFE STUDY BIBLE

THE FULL LIFE STUDY BIBLE

KING JAMES VERSION

General Editor
DONALD C. STAMPS

Associate Editor
J. WESLEY ADAMS

ZONDERVAN PUBLISHING HOUSE

GRAND RAPIDS, MICHIGAN 49530, U.S.A.

Requests for information should be addressed to
The Zondervan Corporation
Grand Rapids, MI 49530

Library of Congress Catalog Card Number 92–060909

Published by ZondervanPublishingHouse
Grand Rapids, Michigan 49530, U.S.A.
http://www.zondervan.com

Printed in the United States of America

00 01 02 03 04 13 12 11 10 9

The Full Life Study Bible

General Editor

Donald C. Stamps, M.A., M. Div.

Writer of study notes and articles

Associate Editor

J. Wesley Adams, Ph.D.

Writer of introductions to books of the Bible

Editorial Committee

Stanley M. Horton, Th.D., Chairman

William W. Menzies, Ph.D., Co-chairman

French Arrington, Ph.D.

Robert Shank, A.B., D.H.L.

Roger Stronstad, M.C.S.

Richard Waters, D.Min.

Bishop Roy L. H. Winbush, M.Div., D.D.

Zondervan Editors

Verlyn D. Verbrugge, Ph.D.

Dirk R. Buursma, M.Div.

Dedication

On November 7, 1991, after a year-long struggle with cancer, Donald C. Stamps went to be with his Lord and Savior (Philippians 1:21,23). Though he did not live to see the complete Full Life Study Bible published, he did persevere to finish writing the notes. We gratefully acknowledge that his vision, his love for God and the Word, his zeal for truth and righteousness, and his persevering faith enabled God to use him in a crucial way for the realization of this Study Bible. Thus we dedicate in his memory this edition of God's Word to the glory of God and the advancement of His kingdom, righteousness and truth throughout the world.

Table of Contents

Contents: Articles

Contents: Maps and Charts

Abbreviations

BOOKS OF THE BIBLE

Genesis	Gen.
Exodus	Ex.
Leviticus	Lev.
Numbers	Num.
Deuteronomy	Deut.
Joshua	Josh.
Judges	Judg.
Ruth	Ruth
1 Samuel	1 Sam.
2 Samuel	2 Sam.
1 Kings	1 Ki.
2 Kings	2 Ki.
1 Chronicles	1 Chr.
2 Chronicles	2 Chr.
Ezra	Ezra
Nehemiah	Neh.
Esther	Esth.
Job	Job
Psalms	Ps.
Proverbs	Prov.
Ecclesiastes	Eccl.
Song of Solomon	Sol.
Isaiah	Is.
Jeremiah	Jer.
Lamentations	Lam.
Ezekiel	Ezek.
Daniel	Dan.
Hosea	Hos.
Joel	Joel
Amos	Amos
Obadiah	Obad.
Jonah	Jonah
Micah	Mic.
Nahum	Nah.
Habakkuk	Hab.
Zephaniah	Zeph.
Haggai	Hag.
Zechariah	Zech.
Malachi	Mal.
Matthew	Mat.
Mark	Mark
Luke	Luke
John	John
Acts	Acts
Romans	Rom.
1 Corinthians	1 Cor.
2 Corinthians	2 Cor.
Galatians	Gal.
Ephesians	Eph.
Philippians	Phil.
Colossians	Col.
1 Thessalonians	1 Thes.
2 Thessalonians	2 Thes.
1 Timothy	1 Tim.
2 Timothy	2 Tim.
Titus	Tit.
Philemon	Philem.
Hebrews	Heb.
James	Jas.
1 Peter	1 Pet.
2 Peter	2 Pet.
1 John	1 John
2 John	2 John
3 John	3 John
Jude	Jude
Revelation	Rev.

GENERAL

i.e.	that is
e.g.	for example
ch., chs.	chapter(s)
v., vv.	verse(s)
etc.	and so forth
c.	about (with dates)
f., ff.	and the following verse(s)
Gk.	Greek
Heb.	Hebrew

The Full Life Study Bible

Author's Preface

The vision, call, and urgency from God for this study Bible came to me while serving as a missionary in Brazil. I realized how much Christian workers were in need of a Bible that would give them direction in their thinking and preaching. Thus, ten years ago I began writing the notes and articles for this work. Later, when I came back to the United States for a short period of time, I also discovered a similar desire among both pastors and lay people for a study Bible with notes that have a Pentecostal emphasis.

During the past number of years I have written with an increasing assurance that the Holy Spirit is not confined to just the pages of Scripture, but that He wants to act today as He did in Bible times. The Spirit has come to abide personally with God's people, and His abiding presence is to be manifested in righteousness and power (Mat. 6:33; Rom. 14:17; 1 Cor. 2:4; 4:20; Heb. 1:8). In and through the church, God's Spirit desires to work in the same manner as He began to do in the earthly ministry of Jesus and continued to do in the apostolic church of the first century.

This study Bible is called *The Full Life Study Bible.* It has been so named because it is founded on three fundamental convictions:

(1) The original revelation of Christ and the apostles as recorded in the Bible is fully inspired by the Holy Spirit; along with the O.T., it is the inerrant and infallible truth of God and the ultimate authority for the church of Jesus Christ today. All believers throughout history are dependent on the words and teachings of Biblical revelation for determining God's standard of truth and practice. In other words, we must view the N.T. message, standards, and experience as God's pre-eminent pattern for the church, valid for all times.

(2) It is the task of every generation of believers not only to accept the N.T. as God's inspired Word, but also to sincerely seek to reproduce in our personal lives and congregations the same faith, devotion, and power that were demonstrated in and through the faithful in the early church. I am persuaded that the full and complete life in the Spirit as promised by Christ and experienced by the N.T. believers is still available for God's people today (John 10:10; 17:20; Acts 2:38-39; Eph. 3:20-21; 4:11-13). It is the divine inheritance of all God's children to receive the fullness of Christ in the original power of the Holy Spirit.

(3) The church will fully experience the original kingdom power and life in the Holy Spirit only as it seeks with all its heart the righteousness and holiness set forth by God in the N.T. as His standard and will for all believers (2 Cor. 6:14-18). That is, kingdom power and kingdom righteousness go together. They cannot be separated. Jesus states that we are to seek both "the kingdom of God, and his righteousness" (Mat. 6:33). The apostle Paul states that the kingdom of God consists of both "power" (1 Cor. 4:20) and "righteousness" (Rom. 14:17). Thus the way to the fullness of God's kingdom with all its redemptive power is found in sincere faith and devotion to the Lord Jesus Christ and in a separation from all unrighteousness that offends Him and the Holy Spirit whom He has poured forth (Acts 2:17,38-40).

In summary, the major purpose of this study Bible is to lead you, the reader, to an abiding faith in holy Scripture, and especially a deeper faith in the N.T.'s apostolic message that will lead you to a greater expectancy for a N.T. experience made possible by the fullness of Christ dwelling in the church (Eph. 4:13) and by the fullness of the Holy Spirit dwelling in the believer (Acts 2:4; 4:31).

It is our sincere hope and prayer that all readers will earnestly seek the N.T. church's devotion to God, its longing for the nearness of the risen Christ, its unshakeable trust in and love for God's Word, its zeal for truth and righteousness, its mutual care for other believers, its compassion for the lost, its dedication to a life of fervent prayer, its passion for holiness, its fullness in the Spirit, its manifestation of spiritual gifts, its urgency to preach the gospel to all nations, and its hope for the imminent return of our Lord and Savior Jesus Christ.

I gratefully acknowledge that a great debt is owed to those who served on the Editorial Committee for this study Bible. Their help, evaluations, comments, and suggestions have been invaluable in its preparation. They gave of themselves and sacrificially took time from their own tasks to help in this work. What will be accomplished in God's kingdom through this work is in no small measure due to their help in the Lord. Also, I have benefited from the learning and labor of godly writers of the past and present who have produced a vast amount of literature and commentaries on the Holy Scriptures. I have thankfully entered into their labor, research, and learning, and have reaped where they have sown.

Throughout these years of labor I have felt a profound sense of weakness and unworthiness to expound on God's holy Word. Many times I have been driven to my knees in need of special grace and help. I can testify that God, who is rich in mercy and whose grace is sufficient, has sustained me by His Spirit. Through all the long days and hours His Word has spoken to my heart. My desire for a full manifestation of Biblical Christianity has deepened and developed into an intense longing that is surpassed only by my longing for that Day of the appearing of our Lord and Savior. With thanks to God—the Father, the Son, and the Holy Spirit—for the privilege of laboring in the Scriptures. I send forth this work unto Him who loves us and gave Himself for us, that we might have life, and have it more abundantly (John 10:10).

Donald C. Stamps
November, 1991

Note: The author's and editor's royalties from *The Full Life Study Bible* will go entirely to missions for the translating and printing of additional copies of *The Full Life Study Bible* in foreign languages.

How to Use The Full Life Study Bible

The Full Life Study Bible is designed to help you gain a more thorough understanding of the truths of God's Word, whereby you may grow in love, purity, and faith toward the Lord Jesus Christ (1 Tim. 1:5). The special features and study helps of *The Full Life Study Bible* are the following:

Sectional headings

The entire Bible is provided with sectional headings within the Bible text in order to help you more easily understand the subject and content of each section.

Cross-reference system

The center column reference system is designed to help you connect one text of the Bible with others that have a similar theme. By using this system, difficult or obscure passages are clarified by Scripture itself. Cross references are indicated by raised light-italic letters. A corresponding letter in the center column under the designated verse is followed by a list of appropriate Scripture verses.

Study Notes

The study notes at the bottom of nearly every page are written from a Pentecostal perspective and with the belief that the full message, standard, and experience testified to by Christ and the apostles is forever valid and available for His people today.

The study notes fall into five classes:

(1) Expositional. The notes explain the meaning of words, phrases, and verses of many important passages in the Word of God.

(2) Theological. The notes define and explain the great doctrines and truths of the Bible, such as what the Bible teaches about baptism, forgiveness, salvation, perseverance, repentance, sanctification, etc.

(3) Devotional. The notes emphasize the importance of maintaining a close and devoted relationship with God—the Father, the Son, and the Holy Spirit—through faith, obedience, prayer, and the many means of grace.

(4) Ethical. The notes direct you to unreservedly commit yourself to the kingdom of God and its righteousness. They emphasize the importance of the Biblical principles of self-denial, godly conduct, following Christ, separation from sin, discernment of good and evil, and obligation to God and others.

(5) Practical. The notes present useful information on the believer's daily walk. They contain practical instruction concerning baptism in the Spirit, raising godly children, resisting temptations, healing, spiritual welfare, overcoming worry, etc.

The study notes provide extensive Scripture references (usually in parentheses) which confirm comments made in the notes and which will help you in further in-depth Bible study. If the Scripture reference in parentheses is from the same chapter, it will normally appear first in the list, with the symbol "v." or "vv." Next will come Scripture references from the same book, usually without the book's name being mentioned. Last in the parentheses are passages from other Bible books, given in Bible-book order. In many cases, other notes and articles are also cross-referenced.

Articles

The articles deal with important and critical subjects in a more comprehensive manner than do the notes. They usually appear close to one of the major texts related to the subject of the article. For a complete list of the articles, see the Table of Contents for Articles on p. viii.

The articles, like the study notes, provide extensive Biblical references in parentheses. In the case of the articles, the name of each Bible book, in Bible-book order, is usually given for each reference. If there is no book mentioned before a Scripture reference, it means that that reference is found in the same book as the previous reference.

Introductions

Each book of the Bible has an introduction which includes (1) an outline of the book; (2) an explanation of the book's background and historical setting, including information about the author, circumstances, and date of writing; (3) a statement of the original purpose of the book; (4) a survey of its contents; (5) a list of the book's special features and emphases; and (6) a suggested reading plan for covering the entire Bible in two years (one year for the O.T. and one year for the N.T.). Careful reading of the introductions will help you understand the book and its applications more fully. At the end of each introduction, space is provided for you to write personal notes on that book.

Themefinders

On many pages of this Bible you will see one of twelve symbols in the margin, next to a vertical line. Each of these symbols represents a specific theme of importance in the Pentecostal tradition. They are:

— Baptized in/Filled with the Holy Spirit (begin at Exodus 31:1-6)

— Gifts of the Holy Spirit (begin at Exodus 35:30-35)

 — Fruit of the Holy Spirit (begin at Genesis 50:19-21)

 — Healing (begin at Genesis 20:17-18)

 — Faith that moves mountains (begin at Genesis 15:3-6)

— Witnessing (begin at Exodus 10:1-2)

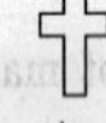 — Salvation (begin at Genesis 12:1-3)

 — Second Coming (begin at Psalm 98:8-9)

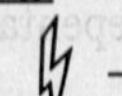 — Victory over Satan and demons (begin at Genesis 3:15)

 — Overcoming the world and worldliness (begin at Genesis 19:15-26)

 — Praise (begin at Exodus 15:1-21)

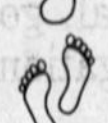 — Walking in obedience and righteousness (begin at Genesis 5:22)

The symbol informs you which theme is contained in accompanying verses; at the bottom of each vertical line is a Bible text, directing you to the next text on that particular theme.

Charts

Throughout *The Full Life Study Bible* are various charts that will help you at a glance to learn more about the Bible and its teachings, on such topics as the ministry of Jesus, the kingdom of God versus the kingdom of Satan, the last days of history, the gifts of the Holy Spirit, etc. See the Table of Contents for Maps and Charts on p. ix for a list of these charts.

Maps

A number of maps have been included within the Bible text to help you understand where the events written about in the Bible occurred. See the Table of Contents for Maps and Charts on p. ix for a list of these maps. At the back of this book are 16 full-color maps.

Subject Index

The subject index directs you to the most important notes and articles on the many topics and great doctrines of Scripture. Under each entry in this index, you will find texts of the Bible that have notes on that particular subject; next to the text is the page number on which that note is found. Articles and introductions are also included in this index.

Themefinder™ Index

The Themefinder Index at the back of this Bible lists the Scripture passages assigned to the 12 key themes described earlier in the Themefinder section. Under each pertinent Themefinder you will find the passages in the order in which they are linked.

Reading Plan

The Reading Plan outlined in the back gives you the flexibility of choosing a method of reading through the Bible either in one year or in two years. The reading plan found at the end of each book introduction follows the two-year design, listing Old Testament readings for one year and New Testament readings for the second year.

Concordance

A concordance is included to help you find Bible verses quickly and easily. By looking up key words in a Bible verse, you can find a verse for which you remember a word or two but not its location. For example, if you wanted to find out where the Bible says, "the word of God *is* quick, and powerful, and sharper than any twoedged sword," you would look up the word "sword" in the concordance and find that it is located at Heb. 4:12.

We trust that you will receive a rich blessing from using *The Full Life Study Bible.* It is our prayer that your knowledge of God's Word, your experience of the presence and power of the Holy Spirit, and your daily walk with Christ in truth and righteousness will increase through this book.

TO THE MOST HIGH AND MIGHTY PRINCE

JAMES

BY THE GRACE OF GOD

KING OF GREAT BRITAIN, FRANCE, AND IRELAND

DEFENDER OF THE FAITH, &c.

The Translators of the Bible wish Grace, Mercy, and Peace through JESUS CHRIST our Lord

Great and manifold were the blessings, most dread Sovereign, which Almighty God, the Father of all mercies, bestowed upon us the people of *England,* when first he sent Your Majesty's Royal Person to rule and reign over us. For whereas it was the expectation of many, who wished not well unto our *Sion,* that upon the setting of that bright *Occidental Star,* Queen *Elizabeth* of most happy memory, some thick and palpable clouds of darkness would so have overshadowed this Land, that men should have been in doubt which way they were to walk; and that it should hardly be known, who was to direct the unsettled State; the appearance of Your Majesty, as of the *Sun* in his strength, instantly dispelled those supposed and surmised mists, and gave unto all that were well affected exceeding cause of comfort; especially when we beheld the Government established in Your Highness, and Your hopeful Seed, by an undoubted Title, and this also accompanied with peace and tranquility at home and abroad.

But among all our joys, there was no one that more filled our hearts, than the blessed continuance of the preaching of God's sacred Word among us; which is that inestimable treasure, which excelleth all the riches of the earth; because the fruit thereof extendeth itself, not only to the time spent in this transitory world, but directeth and disposeth men unto that eternal happiness which is above in heaven.

Then not to suffer this to fall to the ground, but rather to take it up, and to continue it in that state, wherein the famous Predecessor of Your Highness did leave it: nay, to go forward with the confidence and resolution of a Man in maintaining the truth of Christ, and propagating it far and near, is that which hath so bound and firmly knit the hearts of all Your Majesty's loyal and religious people unto You, that Your very name is precious among them: their eye doth behold You with comfort, and they bless You in their hearts, as that sanctified Person who, under God, is the immediate Author of their true happiness. And this their contentment doth not diminish or decay, but every day increaseth and taketh strength, when they observe, that the zeal of Your Majesty toward the house of God doth not slack or go backward, but is more and more kindled, manifesting itself abroad in the farthest parts of *Christendom,* by writing in defence of the Truth, (which hath given such a blow unto that man of sin, as will not be healed,) and every day at home, by religious and learned discourse, by frequenting the house of God, by hearing the Word preached, by cherishing the Teachers thereof, by caring for the Church, as a most tender and loving nursing Father.

There are infinite arguments of this right Christian and religious affection in Your Majesty; but none is more forcible to declare it to others than the vehement and perpetuated desire of accomplishing and publishing of this work, which now with all humility we present unto Your Majesty. For when Your Highness had once out of deep judgment apprehended how convenient it was, that out of the Original Sacred Tongues, together with comparing of the labours, both in our own, and other foreign Languages, of many worthy men who went before us, there should be one more exact Translation of the holy Scriptures into the *English Tongue;* Your Majesty did never desist to urge and to excite those to whom it was commended, that the work might be hastened, and that the business might be expedited in so decent a manner, as a matter of such importance might justly require.

And now at last, by the mercy of God, and the continuance of our labours, it being brought unto such a conclusion, as that we have great hopes that the Church of *England* shall reap good fruit thereby; we hold it our duty to offer it to Your Majesty, not only as to our King and Sovereign, but as to the principal Mover and Author of the work: humbly craving of Your most Sacred Majesty, that since things of this quality have ever been subject to the censures of illmeaning and

discontented persons, it may receive approbation and patronage from so learned and judicious a Prince as Your Highness is, whose allowance and acceptance of our labours shall more honour and encourage us, than all the calumniations and hard interpretations of other men shall dismay us. So that if, on the one side, we shall be traduced by Popish Persons at home or abroad, who therefore will malign us, because we are poor instruments to make God's holy Truth to be yet more and more known unto the people, whom they desire still to keep in ignorance and darkness; or if, on the other side, we shall be maligned by self-conceited Brethren, who run their own ways, and give liking unto nothing, but what is framed by themselves, and hammered on their anvil; we may rest secure, supported within by the truth and innocency of a good conscience, having walked the ways of simplicity and integrity, as before the Lord; and sustained without by the powerful protection of Your Majesty's grace and favour, which will ever give countenance to honest and Christian endeavours against bitter censures and uncharitable imputations.

The Lord of heaven and earth bless Your Majesty with many and happy days, that, as his heavenly hand hath enriched Your Highness with many singular and extraordinary graces, so You may be the wonder of the world in this latter age for happiness and true felicity, to the honour of that great GOD, and the good of his Church, through Jesus Christ our Lord and only Saviour.

THE OLD TESTAMENT

GENESIS

Outline

I. The Beginnings of Human History (1:1—11:26)
  A. Origin of the Universe and Life (1:1—2:25)
    1. Summary of all Creation (1:1—2:4)
    2. Expanded Creation Account of Adam and Eve (2:5–25)
  B. Origin of Sin (3:1–24)
    1. Temptation and the Fall (3:1–6)
    2. Consequences of the Fall (3:7–24)
  C. Origins of Civilization (4:1—5:32)
    1. Cain: Pagan Culture (4:1–24)
    2. Seth: A Righteous Remnant (4:25–26)
    3. Genealogical History of Pre-flood Patriarchs (5:1–32)
  D. The Great Flood: God's Judgment on Primeval Civilization (6:1—8:19)
    1. Universal Depravity (6:1–8,11–12)
    2. Noah: Preparation to Save a Righteous Remnant (6:9–22)
    3. Final Instructions and the Flood (7:1—8:19)
  E. Humanity's New Beginning (8:20—11:26)
    1. The Posterity of Noah (8:20—10:32; esp. Shem, 11:10–26)
    2. The Tower of Babel (11:1–9)
    3. Genealogical Links Between Shem and Abraham (11:10–26)

II. The Beginnings of the Hebrew People (11:27—50:26)
  A. Abraham (11:27—25:18)
    1. Abram's Family Background (11:27–32)
    2. Abram's Call and Journey of Faith (12:1—14:24)
    3. God's Formal Covenant with Abram (15:1–21)
    4. Hagar and Ishmael (16:1–16)
    5. Abrahamic Covenant Sealed by a New Name and Circumcision (17:1–27)
    6. Abraham's Promise and Lot's Tragedy (18:1—19:38)
    7. Abraham and Abimelech (20:1–18)
    8. Abraham and Isaac, the Son of Promise (21:1—24:67)
    9. The Posterity of Abraham (25:1–18)
  B. Isaac (25:19—28:9)
    1. Birth of Esau and Jacob (25:19–26)
    2. Esau Selling his Birthright to Jacob (25:27–34)
    3. Isaac, Rebekah, and Abimelech II (26:1–17)
    4. Dispute about Wells and the Move to Beersheba (26:18–33)
    5. The Patriarchal Blessing (26:34—28:9)
  C. Jacob (28:10—37:2a)
    1. Jacob's Dream and Journey (28:10–22)
    2. Jacob with Laban in Haran (29:1—31:55)
    3. Jacob and Esau Reconciled (32:1—33:17)
    4. Jacob's Return to the Promised Land (33:18—35:20)
    5. The Posterity of Jacob and Esau (35:21—37:2a)
  D. Joseph (37:2b—50:26)
    1. Joseph and his Brothers in Canaan (37:2b–36)

2. Judah and Tamar (38:1–30)
3. Joseph's Testing and Promotion in Egypt (39:1—41:57)
4. Joseph and his Brothers in Egypt (42:1—45:28)
5. Joseph's Father and Brothers Settle in Egypt (46:1—47:26)
6. Jacob's Last Days, Final Prophecies, and Death (47:27—50:14)
7. The Joseph Summary (50:15–26)

Author: Moses

Theme: Beginnings

Date of Writing: c. 1445–1405 B.C.

Background

Genesis appropriately stands as the first book of the O.T. and serves as an essential introduction to the whole Bible. The book's title in Hebrew is derived from the first word of the book, *bereshith* ("in the beginning"). "Genesis," the title in our English Bible, is the Greek translation of the Hebrew title and means "the origin, source, creation, or beginning of something." Genesis is "the book of beginnings."

The author of Genesis is nowhere designated in the book itself. The testimony of the rest of the Bible, however, is that Moses was the author of the entire Pentateuch (i.e., the first five books of the O.T.) and thus of Genesis (e.g., 1 Ki. 2:3; 2 Ki. 14:6; Ezra 6:18; Neh. 13:1; Dan. 9:11–13; Mal. 4:4; Mark 12:26; Luke 16:29,31; John 7:19–23; Acts 26:22; 1 Cor. 9:9; 2 Cor. 3:15). Also, ancient Jewish writers and the early church fathers unanimously testify that Moses was the author/editor of Genesis. Insofar as the entire history of Genesis antedates Moses' life, his role in writing Genesis was largely to integrate, under the inspiration of the Holy Spirit, all the available written and oral records from Adam to the death of Joseph that are now preserved in Genesis. Perhaps an indication of the historical records used by Moses when writing Genesis is found in the eleven occurrences of the phrase, "these are the generations of" (Heb. *'elleh toledoth*), which also may be translated as "these are the histories by" (see 2:4; 5:1; 6:9; 10:1; 11:10,27; 25:12,19; 36:1,9; 37:2).

Genesis accurately records creation, the beginnings of human history, and the origin of the Hebrew people and God's covenant with them through Abraham and the other patriarchs. Its historical reliability as inspired Scripture is certified in the N.T. by the Lord Jesus (Mat. 19:4–6; 24:37–39; Luke 11:51; 17:26–32; John 7:21–23; 8:56–58) and by the apostles (Rom. 4; 1 Cor. 15:21–22,45–47; 2 Cor. 11:3; Gal. 3:8; 4:22–24,28; 1 Tim. 2:13–14; Heb. 11:4–22; 2 Pet. 3:4–6; Jude 7,11). Its historicity continues to be confirmed by modern archaeological discoveries. Moses was remarkably prepared by education (Acts 7:22) and by God to write this unique first book of the Bible.

Purpose

Genesis provides an essential foundation for the remainder of the Pentateuch and all subsequent Biblical revelation. It preserves the only trustworthy record about the beginnings of the universe, humankind, marriage, sin, cities, languages, nations, Israel, and redemptive history. It was written in accordance with God's purpose to give His covenant people in both the O.T. and N.T. a foundational understanding of Himself, creation, the human race, the fall, death, judgment, covenant, and the promise of redemption through the seed of Abraham.

Survey

Genesis divides naturally into two major parts. (A) Chs. 1—11 provide an overview of human beginnings from Adam to Abraham and focus on five epochal events. (1) Creation: God created all things, including Adam and Eve whom He placed in the Garden of Eden (chs. 1—2). (2) The Fall: Adam and Eve by their transgression introduced the curse of sin and death into human history (ch. 3). (3) Cain and Abel: This tragedy set in motion the two basic streams of history: humanistic civilization and a redemptive remnant (chs. 4—5). (4)

The Great Flood: The ancient world had become so evil by the time of Noah's generation that God destroyed it by a universal flood, sparing only righteous Noah and his family as a remnant (chs. 6—10). (5) Tower of Babel: When the post-flood world unified in idolatry and rebellion, God dispersed it by fragmenting language and culture and by scattering the human race throughout the earth (ch. 11).

(B) Chs. 12—50 record the beginnings of the Hebrew people and focus on God's ongoing redemptive purpose through the lives of Israel's four great patriarchs—Abraham, Isaac, Jacob, and Joseph. God's call of Abraham (ch. 12) and His covenantal dealings with him and his seed form the pivotal beginning of the outworking of God's purpose concerning a Redeemer and redemption in history. Genesis concludes with the death of Joseph and the impending bondage of Israel in Egypt.

Special Features

Seven major features or emphases characterize Genesis. (1) It was the first book of the Bible written (with the possible exception of Job) and records the beginning of human history, sin, the Hebrew people, and redemption. (2) The history in Genesis spans a larger period of time than the rest of the Bible combined, beginning with the first human couple, broadening to pre-flood world history, and then narrowing to Hebrew history as the redemptive stream that is traced throughout the remainder of the O.T. (3) Genesis reveals that the material universe and life on earth are distinctly God's work and not an independent process of nature. Fifty times in chs. 1—2 God is the subject of verbs showing what He did as Creator. (4) Genesis is a book of firsts—recording the first marriage, first family, first birth, first sin, first murder, first polygamist, first musical instruments, first promise of redemption, and the like. (5) The covenant of God with Abraham, which began with his call (12:1–3), was made formal in ch. 15, and was ratified in ch. 17, is central to all of Scripture. (6) Genesis alone explains the origin of the twelve tribes of Israel. (7) It reveals how the descendants of Abraham ended up in Egypt (for 430 years) and thus sets the stage for the exodus, the central redemptive event in the O.T.

New Testament Fulfillment

Genesis reveals the prophetic history of redemption and a Redeemer as coming through the seed of the woman (3:15), through the line of Seth (4:25–26), through the line of Shem (9:26–27), and through the seed of Abraham (12:3). The N.T. applies 12:3 directly to God's provision of redemption in Jesus Christ (Gal. 3:16,29). Numerous persons and events from Genesis are mentioned in the N.T. in relation to faith and righteousness (e.g., Rom. 4; Heb. 11:1–22), God's judgment (e.g., Luke 17:26–29,32; 2 Pet. 3:6; Jude 7,11a), and the person of Christ (e.g., Mat. 1:1; John 8:58; Heb. 7).

Reading Genesis

In order to read the entire Old Testament in one year, the book of Genesis should be read in 21 days, according to the following schedule: ☐ 1–2 ☐ 3–5 ☐ 6–8 ☐ 9–11 ☐ 12–14 ☐ 15–17 ☐ 18–19 ☐ 20–22 ☐ 23–24 ☐ 25–26 ☐ 27–28 ☐ 29–30 ☐ 31–33 ☐ 34–35 ☐ 36–37 ☐ 38–39 ☐ 40–41 ☐ 42–43 ☐ 44–45 ☐ 46–48 ☐ 49–50

NOTES

The Great Flood: The ancient world had become so evil by the time of Noah's generation that God destroyed it by a universal flood, sparing only righteous Noah and his family as a remnant (chs. 6—10). (3) Tower of Babel: When the post-flood world unified in idolatry and rebellion, God dispersed it by fragmenting language and culture and by scattering the human race throughout the earth (ch. 11).

(B) Chs. 12—50 record the beginnings of the Hebrew people and focus on God's ongoing redemptive purpose through the lives of Israel's four great patriarchs—Abraham, Isaac, Jacob, and Joseph. God's call of Abraham (ch. 12) and His covenantal dealings with him and his seed form the pivotal beginning of the outworking of God's purpose concerning a Redeemer and redemption in history. Genesis concludes with the death of Joseph and the impending bondage of Israel in Egypt.

Special Features

Seven major features or emphases characterize Genesis. (1) It was the first book of the Bible written (with the possible exception of Job) and records the beginning of human history, sin, the Hebrew people, and redemption. (2) The history in Genesis spans a larger period of time than the rest of the Bible combined, beginning with the first human couple, broadening to the pre-flood world history, and then narrowing to Hebrew history as the redemptive stream that is traced throughout the remainder of the O.T. (3) Genesis reveals that the material universe and life on earth are distinctly God's work and not an independent process of nature. Fifty times in chs. 1—2 God is the subject of verbs showing what He did as Creator. (4) Genesis is a book of firsts—recording the first marriage, first family, first birth, first sin, first murder, first polygamist, first musical instruments, first promise of redemption, and the like. (5) The covenant of God with Abraham, which began with his call (12:1–3), was made formal in ch. 15, and was ratified in ch. 17, is central to all of Scripture. (6) Genesis alone explains the origin of the twelve tribes of Israel. (7) It reveals how the descendants of Abraham ended up in Egypt (for 430 years) and thus sets the stage for the exodus, the central redemptive event in the O.T.

New Testament Fulfillment

Genesis reveals the prophetic history of redemption and a Redeemer as coming through the seed of the woman (3:15), through the line of Seth (4:25–26), through the line of Shem (9:26–27), and through the seed of Abraham (12:3). The N.T. applies 12:3 directly to God's provision of redemption in Jesus Christ (Gal. 3:16,29). Numerous persons and events from Genesis are mentioned in the N.T. in relation to faith and righteousness (e.g., Rom. 4; Heb. 11:1–22), God's judgment (e.g., Luke 17:26–29,32; 2 Pet. 3:6; Jude 7,11a), and the person of Christ (e.g., Mat. 1:1; John 8:58; Heb. 7).

Reading Genesis

In order to read the entire Old Testament in one year, the book of Genesis should be read in 21 days, according to the following schedule: ☐ 1–2 ☐ 3–5 ☐ 6–8 ☐ 9–11 ☐ 12–14 ☐ 15–17 ☐ 18–19 ☐ 20–22 ☐ 23–24 ☐ 25–26 ☐ 27–28 ☐ 29–30 ☐ 31–33 ☐ 34–35 ☐ 36–37 ☐ 38–39 ☐ 40–41 ☐ 42–43 ☐ 44–45 ☐ 46–48 ☐ 49–50

NOTES

The creation

1 IN THE [a]beginning [b]God created
the heaven and the earth.
2 And the earth was [c]without
form, and void; and darkness *was* upon
the face of the deep. [d]And the spirit of
God moved upon the face of the waters.
3 [e]And God said, [f]Let there be
light: and there was light.
4 And God saw the light, that *it was*
good: and God divided [a]the light from
the darkness.
5 And God called the light [g]Day,
and the darkness he called Night.
[b]And the evening and the morning
were the first day.
6 ¶ And God said, [h]Let there be a
[c]firmament in the midst of the waters,
and let it divide the waters from the
waters.
7 And God made the firmament,
[i]and divided the waters which *were*
under the firmament from the waters
which *were* [j]above the firmament: and
it was so.
8 And God called the firmament
Heaven. And the evening and the
morning were the second day.
9 ¶ And God said, [k]Let the waters
under the heaven be gathered together
unto one place, and let the dry *land* ap-
pear: and it was so.
10 And God called the dry *land*
Earth; and the gathering together of
the waters called he Seas: and God saw
that *it was* good.
11 And God said, Let the earth
[l]bring forth [d]grass, the herb yielding
seed, *and* the fruit tree yielding [m]fruit
after his kind, whose seed *is* in itself,
upon the earth: and it was so.
12 And the earth brought forth

1:1 [a]John 1:1,2 Heb. 1:10 [b]Ps. 8:3 Is. 44:24 Acts 17:24 Rev. 4:11
1:2 [c]Jer. 4:23 [d]Ps. 33:6 Is. 40:13,14
1:3 [e]Ps. 33:9 [f]2 Cor. 4:6
1:5 [g]Ps. 74:16
1:6 [h]Job 37:18 Jer. 10:12
1:7 [i]Prov. 8:28 [j]Ps. 148:4
1:9 [k]Job 26:10 Prov. 8:29 Jer. 5:22 2 Pet. 3:5
1:11 [l]Heb. 6:7 [m]Luke 6:44

[a] Heb. *between the light and between the darkness* [b] Heb. *And the evening was, and the morning was* [c] Heb. *expansion* [d] Heb. *tender grass*

1:1 IN THE BEGINNING GOD CREATED. "In the beginning" here is emphatic and draws attention to the fact of a real beginning. Other ancient religions, when speaking of creation, indicate that it came about out of something that was already there. They see history as occurring forever in cycles. The Bible looks at history in a linear way, with a God-given goal. God had a plan in creation and He will carry it out. For comments on God and His role as Creator, see article on CREATION, p. 6.

Several implications flow from the truth contained in the first verse of the Bible. (1) Since God is the source of all that exists, human beings and nature are not self-existent, but owe their being and continuance to Him. (2) All existence and life is good if it is related rightly to God and dependent upon Him. (3) All life and creation can be eternally meaningful and purposeful. (4) God has sovereign rights over all creation by virtue of being its Creator. In a fallen world, He lays claim to those rights through redemption (Ex. 6:6; 15:13; Deut. 21:8; Luke 1:68; Rom. 3:24; Gal. 3:13; 1 Pet. 1:18).

1:2 EARTH WAS WITHOUT FORM, AND VOID. This verse describes both the process God used in creating and the role of the Holy Spirit in creation (see article on CREATION, p. 6).

1:3 LET THERE BE LIGHT. The Hebrew word for "light" is *'or*, referring to the initial waves of light energy coming upon the earth. Later God placed "lights" (Heb. *ma'or*, literally "light-bearers," v. 14) in the heavens as permanent generators and reflectors of light waves. The primary purpose of these light-bearers was to serve for signs and seasons, and to mark days and years (vv. 5, 14). For comments about the role of God's word or speech in creation, see article on CREATION, p. 6.

1:5 THE EVENING AND THE MORNING WERE THE FIRST DAY. This designation is repeated six times in this chapter (vv. 5,8,13, 19,23,31). The Hebrew word for day is *yom*. It normally means a twenty-four hour day (cf. 7:17; cf. Mat. 17:1) or the daylight portion of the twenty-four hours ("day" as distinct from "night"). But it also can refer to a time period of undetermined length (e.g., "time of harvest," Prov. 25:13). Notice that 2:4 puts all six creation days together as "the day." Many believe the creation days were twenty-four hour days because they are described as consisting of an "evening" and "morning" (v. 5; cf. Ex. 20:11). Others believe "evening" and "morning" simply mean that a particular evening brought an end to that step of creation and the next morning brought a new beginning.

1:7 THE FIRMAMENT. The "firmament" refers to the atmosphere between the water on earth and the clouds above.

1:10 IT WAS GOOD. Seven times God states that what He created was "good" (vv. 4,10, 12,18,21,25,31). Each part of God's creation completely fulfilled His will and intended purpose. God created the world to reflect His glory and to be a place where humankind could share in His joy and life. Notice how God created according to a plan and order:

Day 1	light	bringing order to creation
Day 2	firmament	
Day 3	dry land	
Day 4	light-bearers	giving life to creation
Day 5	fish and birds	
Day 6	animals and humans	
Day 7	rest	creation is complete and good

CREATION

Gen. 1:1 "In the beginning God created the heaven and the earth."

THE GOD OF CREATION. (1) God is revealed in the Bible as an infinite, eternal, self-existent Being who is the First Cause of all that is. Never was there a moment when God did not exist. As Moses affirms, "Before the mountains were brought forth, or ever thou hadst formed the earth and the world, even from everlasting to everlasting, thou *art* God" (Ps. 90:2). In other words, God existed eternally and infinitely before creating the finite universe. He is above, independent of, and prior to all that has been created in heaven and on earth (see 1 Tim. 6:16, note; cf. Col. 1:16).

(2) God is revealed as a personal Being who created Adam and Eve "in his *own* image" (Gen. 1:27; see 1:26, note). Because Adam and Eve were created in God's image, they could respond to and have fellowship with God in a loving and personal way.

(3) God is also revealed as a moral Being who created everything good and therefore without sin. After God had finished creating and was surveying what He had made, He observed that it was "very good" (Gen. 1:31). Since Adam and Eve were created in God's image and likeness, they were also without sin (see Gen. 1:26, note). Sin entered human existence when Eve was tempted by the serpent, or Satan (Gen. 3; cf. Rom. 5:12; Rev. 12:9).

THE ACTIVITY OF CREATION. (1) God created all things in "the heaven and the earth" (Gen. 1:1; cf. Is. 40:28; 42:5; 45:18; Mark 13:19; Eph. 3:9; Col. 1:16; Heb. 1:2; Rev. 10:6). The word "created" (Heb. *bara'*) is used exclusively of an activity that only God can do. It means that at a specific moment God called into existence matter and substance which had no prior existence (see Gen. 1:3, note).

(2) The Bible describes God's creation as formless, empty, and covered with darkness (Gen. 1:2). At that time the universe and the world did not have the ordered form it has now. It was empty, barren of all living creatures, and void of all light. After this initial stage, God created light to dispel the darkness (Gen. 1:3–5), gave form to the universe (Gen. 1:6–13), and filled the earth with living things (Gen. 1:20–28).

(3) The method God used in creation was the power of His word. Over and over it is stated, "And God said. . . ." (Gen. 1:3,6,9,11,14,20,24,26). In other words, God spoke the heavens and earth into being; before God's creative word went forth, they had no prior existence (cf. Ps. 33:6,9; 148:5; Is. 48:13; Rom. 4:17; Heb. 11:3).

(4) The entire Trinity, not just the Father, had a role in creation. (a) The Son Himself is the powerful Word through whom God created all things. In the prologue to John's Gospel, Christ is revealed as the eternal Word of God (John 1:1). "All things were made made by him; and without him was not any thing made that was made" (John 1:3). Likewise, the apostle Paul affirms that by Christ "were all things created, that are in heaven, and that are in earth, visible and invisible . . . all things were created by him, and for him" (Col. 1:16). Finally, the author of the letter to the Hebrews asserts emphatically that by His Son, God made the worlds (Heb. 1:2).

(b) Likewise, the Holy Spirit had an active role in the work of creation. He is pictured as "moving" over the creation, preserving and preparing it for God's further creative activity. The Hebrew word for "Spirit" (*ruah*) may also be translated as "wind" and "breath." Thus, the psalmist affirms the role of the Spirit when he states: "By the word of the LORD were the heavens made; and all the host of them by the breath [*ruah*] of his mouth" (Ps. 33:6). Also, the Holy Spirit continues to be involved in sustaining creation (Job 33:4; Ps. 104:30).

THE PURPOSE AND GOAL OF CREATION. God had specific reasons for creating the world. (1) God created the heavens and the earth as a manifestation of His glory, majesty, and power. David says, "The heavens declare the glory of God; and the firmament showeth his handiwork" (Ps. 19:1; cf. Ps. 8:1). By looking at the entire

created cosmos—from the immense expanse of the created universe to the beauty and order of nature—we cannot help but stand in awe of the majesty of the Lord God, our Creator.

(2) God created the heavens and the earth in order to receive back the glory and honor due Him. All the elements of nature—e.g., sun and moon, trees of the forest, rain and snow, rivers and streams, hills and mountains, animals and birds—shout out praise to the God who made them (Ps. 98:7–8; 148:1–10; Is. 55:12). How much more God desires and expects to receive glory and praise from human beings!

(3) God created the earth in order to provide a place where His purpose and goals for humankind might be fulfilled. (a) God created Adam and Eve in His own image so that He could have a loving, personal relationship for all eternity. God designed humankind as a triune being (body, soul, spirit), possessing mind, emotion, and will with which they can respond to Him freely as Lord and worship and serve Him out of faith, loyalty, and gratitude. (b) God so desired this intimate relationship with the human race that, when Satan succeeded in tempting Adam and Eve to rebel against and disobey God's command, He promised to send a Savior to redeem humankind from sin's consequences (see Gen. 3:15, note). In this way God would have a people for His own possession who would enjoy Him, glorify Him, and live in righteousness and holiness before Him (Is. 60:21; 61:1–3; Eph. 1:11–12; 1 Pet. 2:9). (c) The culmination of God's purpose in creation is recorded in the book of Revelation, where John describes the end of history with these words: "He will dwell with them, and they shall be his people, and God himself shall be with them, *and be* their God" (Rev. 21:3).

CREATION AND EVOLUTION. Evolution is the predominant view regarding the origin of life and the universe proposed in the scientific and educational community of the contemporary world. Bible-believing Christians should consider these four observations about evolution.

(1) Evolution is a *naturalistic effort* to account for the origin and development of the universe. This view begins with the assumption that there is no personal, divine Creator who made and fashioned the world; rather, everything came into existence by a series of chance happenings that occurred over billions of years. Proponents of evolution claim to have scientific data that support their hypothesis.

(2) The teaching of evolution is *not truly scientific*. According to the scientific method, all conclusions must be based on indisputable evidence gathered from experiments that can be duplicated in any laboratory. However, no experiments have been or can be devised to test and substantiate theories about the origin of matter from some supposed "big bang" beginning or about the gradual development of living beings from their simplest to their most complex form. Consequently, evolution is a hypothesis without scientific "evidence"; therefore, to accept it one must have faith in a human theory. The faith of God's people, in contrast, is in the Lord and in His inspired revelation, which states that He is the one who made all things out of nothing (Heb. 11:3).

(3) It is undeniable that change and development within various species of living things occur. For example, some varieties of species are becoming extinct; on the other hand, we occasionally see new strains forming within species. But there is no evidence, not even in the geologic record, which supports the theory that one "kind" of living thing ever evolved from another "kind." Rather, existing evidence supports the Bible's declaration that God created each living creature "after his kind" (Gen. 1:21,24–25).

(4) Bible-believing Christians must also reject the theory called *theistic evolution*. This theory adopts most of the conclusions of naturalistic evolution, adding only that God started the evolutionary process. Such a theory denies the Biblical revelation that ascribes to God an active role in *all* aspects of creation. For example, every main verb in Gen. 1 has God as its subject, except for Gen. 1:12 (which fulfills the command of God in v. 11) and the recurring phrase "there was evening and there was morning." God is not a passive supervisor of an evolutionary process; rather, He is the active Creator of all things (cf. Col. 1:16).

grass, *and* herb yielding seed after his kind, and the tree yielding fruit, whose seed *was* in itself, after his kind: and God saw that *it was* good.

13 And the evening and the morning were the third day.

14 ¶ And God said, Let there be lights in the firmament of the heaven to divide [e]the day from the night; and let them be for signs, and for seasons, and for days, and years:

15 And let them be for lights in the firmament of the heaven to give light upon the earth: and it was so.

16 And God made two great lights; the [n]greater light [f]to rule the day, and the [o]lesser light to rule the night: *he made* [p]the stars also.

17 And God set them in the firmament of the heaven to give light upon the earth,

18 And to [q]rule over the day and over the night, and to divide the light from the darkness: and God saw that *it was* good.

19 And the evening and the morning were the fourth day.

20 And God said, Let the waters bring forth abundantly the [g]moving creature that hath [h]life, and [i]fowl *that* may fly above the earth in the [j]open firmament of heaven.

21 And [r]God created great whales, and every living creature that moveth, which the waters brought forth abundantly, after their kind, and every winged fowl after his kind: and God saw that *it was* good.

22 And God blessed them, saying, [s]Be fruitful, and multiply, and fill the waters in the seas, and let fowl multiply in the earth.

23 And the evening and the morning were the fifth day.

24 ¶ And God said, Let the earth bring forth the living creature after his kind, cattle, and creeping thing, and beast of the earth after his kind: and it was so.

25 And God made the beast of the earth after his kind, and cattle after their kind, and every thing that creepeth upon the earth after his kind: and God saw that *it was* good.

26 ¶ And God said, [t]Let us make man in our image, after our likeness:

1:16 [n]Ps. 136:8 [o]Ps. 8:3 [p]Job 38:7
1:18 [q]Jer. 31:35
1:21 [r]Ps. 104:26
1:22 [s]ch. 8:17
1:26 [t]Ps. 100:3 Eccl. 7:29 Eph. 4:24 Jas. 3:9

[e] Heb. *between the day and between the night* [f] Heb. *for the rule of the day* [g] Or, *creeping* [h] Heb. *soul* [i] Heb. *let fowl fly* [j] Heb. *face of the firmament of heaven*

1:14 BE FOR SIGNS. God intended that the sun, moon, and stars serve as signs that point to Him as well as mark the advancing days, seasons, and years. Astrology has twisted these intended purposes for the stars by proposing instead the false theory that the stars and planets guide the lives of people.

1:22 GOD BLESSED THEM. God blessed living creatures and declared nature and animals good (vv. 12,21–22). (1) God delighted in His work and valued it for itself. Likewise, the believer should regard nature and its beauty and animals as good, something to be enjoyed, and of immense value. (2) Although nature is now marred by sin, it still has great value as an expression of God's glory and love for humankind (cf. Ps. 19:1). Believers should pray for the complete liberation of creation from its bondage to sin and decay (Rom. 8:21; Rev. 21:1).

1:26 GOD SAID, LET US. This expression contains an early implication of the triune God. The use of the plural "us" suggests that God has a certain plurality (cf. Ps. 2:7; Is. 48:16). Revelation of the tri-unity of God does not become clear, however, until the N.T. (see Mat. 3:17, note; Mark 1:11, note).

1:26 LET US MAKE MAN. In vv. 26–28 we read about the creation of human beings; 2:4–25 gives more specific details about their creation and environment. These two accounts are complementary and teach several things. (1) Both man and woman were a special creation of God, not a product of evolution (v. 27; Mat. 19:4; Mark 10:6).

(2) Man and woman were both created in the "image" and "likeness" of God. On the basis of this image, they could respond to and have fellowship with God and uniquely reflect His love, glory, and holiness. They were to do this by knowing God and obeying Him (2:15–17). (a) They possessed a *moral* likeness to God, for they were sinless and holy, possessing wisdom, a heart of love, and the will to do the right (cf. Eph. 4:24). They lived in a personal fellowship with God that involved moral obedience (2:16–17) and intimate communion. When Adam and Eve sinned, their moral likeness to God was corrupted (6:5). In redemption believers must be renewed to the original moral likeness (cf. Eph. 4:22–24; Col. 3:10). (b) Adam and Eve possessed a *natural* likeness to God. They were created personal beings with spirit, mind, emotions, self-consciousness, and power of choice (2:19–20; 3:6–7; 9:6). (c) In some sense man and woman's *physical* makeup is in God's image in a way not true of animals. God gave to human beings the image in which He was to appear visibly to them (18:1–2) and the form that His Son would one day assume (Luke 1:35; Phil. 2:7; Heb. 10:5).

(3) That human beings were made in the image of God does not mean they are divine. They have been created on a lower order and are dependent on God (Ps. 8:5).

(4) All human life is derived initially from Adam and Eve (Gen. 3:20; Rom. 5:12).

and [u]let them have dominion over the
fish of the sea, and over the fowl of the
air, and over the cattle, and over all
the earth, and over every creeping thing
that creepeth upon the earth.
27 So God created man in his *own*
image, [v]in the image of God created
he him; [w]male and female created he
them.
28 And God blessed them, and God
said unto them, [x]Be fruitful, and mul-
tiply, and replenish the earth, and sub-
due it: and have dominion over the fish
of the sea, and over the fowl of the air,
and over every living thing that
[k]moveth upon the earth.
29 ¶ And God said, Behold, I have
given you every herb [l]bearing seed,
which *is* upon the face of all the earth,
and every tree, in the which *is* the fruit
of a tree yielding seed; [y]to you it shall
be for meat.
30 And to [z]every beast of the
earth, and to every [a]fowl of the air,
and to every thing that creepeth upon
the earth, wherein *there is* [m]life, *I have*
given every green herb for meat: and it
was so.
31 And [b]God saw every thing that
he had made, and, behold, *it was* very
good. And the evening and the morning
were the sixth day.

1:26 [u]ch. 9:2 Ps. 8:6 **1:27** [v]1 Cor. 11:7 [w]ch. 5:2 Mat. 19:4 **1:28** [x]ch. 9:1,7 Lev. 26:9 **1:29** [y]ch. 9:3 Ps. 104:14,15 **1:30** [z]Ps. 145:15 [a]Job 38:41 **1:31** [b]Ps. 104:24

2:1 [c]Ps. 33:6 **2:2** [d]Ex. 20:11 Heb. 4:4 **2:3** [e]Is. 58:13 **2:4** [f]ch. 1:1 **2:5** [g]ch. 1:12 [h]Job 38:26-28 [i]ch. 3:23 **2:7** [j]ch. 3:19,23 Ps. 103:14

2 THUS THE heavens and the earth
were finished, and [c]all the host of
them.
2 [d]And on the seventh day God
ended his work which he had made;
and he rested on the seventh day from
all his work which he had made.
3 And God [e]blessed the seventh
day, and sanctified it: because that in
it he had rested from all his work
which God [n]created and made.

Adam and Eve

4 ¶ [f]These *are* the generations of
the heavens and of the earth when they
were created, in the day that the LORD
God made the earth and the heavens,
5 And every [g]plant of the field be-
fore it was in the earth, and every herb
of the field before it grew: for the LORD
God had not [h]caused it to rain upon
the earth, and *there was* not a man [i]to
till the ground.
6 But [o]there went up a mist from
the earth, and watered the whole face
of the ground.
7 And the LORD God formed man
[p]*of* the [j]dust of the ground, and

[k]Heb. *creepeth* [l]Heb. *seeding seed* [m]Heb. *a living soul* [n]Heb. *created to make* [o]Or, *a mist which went up from* [p]Heb. *dust of the ground*

1:28 BE FRUITFUL, AND MULTIPLY. Man and woman were charged with being fruitful and ruling over the earth and animal kingdom. (1) They were created to form family relationships. This stated purpose of God in creation indicates that He considers a godly family and the raising of children of utmost priority in the world (see Eph. 5:21, note; Tit. 2:4–5, note; see article on PARENTS AND CHILDREN, p. 1880).

(2) God expected them to consecrate all things in the earth to Him and to manage it in a God-glorifying way, fulfilling the divine purpose (cf. Ps. 8:6–8; Heb. 2:7–9).

(3) The future of the earth was placed under their dominion. When they sinned, they brought ruin, futility, and suffering to God's creation (cf. 3:14–24; Rom. 8:19–22).

(4) It is the work of Jesus Christ alone to restore the earth to its perfect place and function at His coming at the end of this age (Rom. 8:19–25; 1 Cor. 15:24–28; Heb. 2:5–8; see Rev. 21:1, note).

2:3 GOD BLESSED THE SEVENTH DAY. God blessed the seventh day (i.e., Sabbath) and designated it both as a sacred and special day of rest and as a memorial to the completion of all His created work. God later made the Sabbath a day of blessing for His faithful people (Ex. 20:8). He designed it as a day of rest, service, and communion with Him (Ex. 16:29; 31:12–17; see Mat. 12:1, note).

2:4 THE GENERATIONS. This second account of creation (2:4–25) is not contradictory to 1:1—2:3. It explains in greater detail the creation of man and woman, their environment, and their probation. Ch. 2 gives details in a topical fashion, whereas ch. 1 gives the chronological order.

2:4 THE LORD GOD. Another name for God is introduced in 2:4, the name "LORD" (Heb. *YHWH*, "Yahweh" or "Jehovah"). Whereas *Elohim* (e.g., 1:1) is the general name for God, emphasizing His greatness and power (see article on CREATION, p. 6), "LORD" is the personal and covenant name by which God reveals Himself to His own people. Inherent in the revelation of God's covenant name is His lovingkindness, His redemptive concern for the human race, and His nearness to and faithful presence with His people. This personal name is used in situations where He is seen in direct relationship to His people or nature. Where the words "LORD God" are coupled together, it points to God as the all-powerful Creator who has entered into a caring covenant relationship with humankind (see vv. 9–25; Ex. 6:6; Lev. 11:44–45; Is. 53:1,5–6; see Ex. 3:14, note).

2:7 A LIVING SOUL. The giving of life to human beings is described as the result of a special act of God in distinction from the creation of all other living things. God specifically imparted life and breath to the first man, indicating that human life stands higher and in a different category from

[k]breathed into his [l]nostrils the
breath of life; and [m]man became a liv-
ing soul.
8 ¶ And the LORD God planted [n]a
garden [o]eastward in [p]Eden; and
there he put the man whom he had
formed.
9 And out of the ground made the
LORD God to grow [q]every tree that is
pleasant to the sight, and good for
food; [r]the tree of life also in the midst
of the garden, and the tree of knowl-
edge of good and evil.
10 And a river went out of Eden to
water the garden; and from thence it
was parted, and became into four
heads.
11 The name of the first *is* Pison:
that *is* it which compasseth [s]the
whole land of Havilah, where *there is*
gold;
12 And the gold of that land *is* good:
[t]there *is* bdellium and the onyx stone.
13 And the name of the second river
is Gihon: the same *is* it that com-
passeth the whole land of [q]Ethiopia.
14 And the name of the third river
is [u]Hiddekel: that *is* it which goeth
[r]toward the east of Assyria. And the
fourth river *is* Euphrates.
15 And the LORD God took [s]the

2:7 [k]Job 33:4 [l]ch. 7:22 [m]1 Cor. 15:45
2:8 [n]Is. 51:3 [o]ch. 3:24 [p]ch. 4:16
2:9 [q]Ezek. 31:8 [r]ch. 3:22 Rev. 2:7
2:11 [s]ch. 25:18
2:12 [t]Num. 11:7
2:14 [u]Dan. 10:4
2:17 [v]ch. 3:1,3,11,17 [w]ch. 3:3,19 Rom. 6:23
2:18 [x]1 Cor. 11:9 1 Tim. 2:13
2:19 [y]ch. 1:20,24 [z]Ps. 8:6
2:21 [a]1 Sam. 26:12

man, and put him into the garden of
Eden to dress it and to keep it.
16 And the LORD God commanded
the man, saying, Of every tree of the
garden [t]thou mayest freely eat:
17 But of the tree of the knowledge
of good and evil, [v]thou shalt not eat of
it: for in the day that thou eatest there-
of [w]thou[u] shalt surely die.
18 ¶ And the LORD God said, *It is* not
good that the man should be alone; [x]I
will make him an help [v]meet for him.
19 [y]And out of the ground the LORD
God formed every beast of the field,
and every fowl of the air; and [z]brought
them unto [w]Adam to see what he
would call them: and whatsoever
Adam called every living creature, that
was the name thereof.
20 And Adam [x]gave names to all
cattle, and to the fowl of the air, and to
every beast of the field; but for Adam
there was not found an help meet for
him.
21 And the LORD God caused a
[a]deep sleep to fall upon Adam, and he

[q] Heb. *Cush* [r] Or, *eastward to Assyria* [s] Or, *Adam* [t] Heb. *eating thou shalt eat* [u] Heb. *dying thou shalt die* [v] Heb. *as before him* [w] Or, *the man* [x] Heb. *called*

all other forms of life and that there is a unique relationship of divine life to human life (cf. 1:26–27). God is the ultimate source of human life.

2:8 A GARDEN EASTWARD IN EDEN. The garden was located near the Tigris (called "Hiddekel" here) and Euphrates flood plain (see v. 14). Some believe it was located in what is now known as southern Iraq; others maintain that there is not sufficient data given in the Biblical account (vv. 10–14) to determine a specific location.

2:9 THE TREE OF LIFE. Two trees in the garden had special importance. (1) The "tree of life" was probably intended to make physical death impossible. It is related to eternal life in 3:22 (cf. Rev. 2:7). God's people will have access to the tree of life in the new heaven and new earth (Rev. 2:7; 22:2). (2) The "tree of knowledge of good and evil" was designed to test Adam's faith and obedience to God and His word (see v. 16, note). God created humans as moral beings with the ability to choose freely to love and obey their Creator, or to disobey Him and rebel against His will.

2:15 PUT HIM INTO THE GARDEN OF EDEN. At this time Adam as the first man was holy, free from sin, and in perfect communion with God. He was the pinnacle of God's creation and was given the responsibility of working under the direction of God in caring for His creation. This harmonious relationship between God and the human race was lost because of Adam and Eve's disobedience (3:6,14–19).

2:16 THE LORD GOD COMMANDED THE MAN. From the very beginning of history the human race has been bound to God through belief in and obedience to His word as absolute truth. (1) Life through faith and obedience is presented as the governing principle in Adam's relationship to God in Eden. Adam was warned that he would die if he transgressed God's will and partook of the tree of the knowledge of good and evil (v. 17). This threat of death had to be accepted by faith based on what God said, since Adam had not yet seen human death.

(2) The command of God (vv. 16–17) was given to Adam as a moral test. It placed before him a conscious, deliberate choice to believe and obey, or to disbelieve and disobey his Creator's will.

(3) As long as Adam believed God's word and obeyed, he would continue in eternal life and in blessed fellowship with God (see article on FAITH AND GRACE, p. 1738). If he sinned by disobeying, he would reap moral disaster and a harvest of death (v. 17).

2:18 AN HELP MEET FOR HIM. Woman was created to be a loving companion for man and a helper for him. As such she was to share his responsibility and cooperate with him in fulfilling God's purpose for his life and the life of their family (see Eph. 5:22, note; see Ps. 33:20; 70:5; 115:9, where the term "helper" is also used to describe God).

slept: and he took one of his ribs, and
closed up the flesh instead thereof;
22 And the rib, which the LORD God
had taken from man, [y]made he a
woman, and [b]brought her unto the
man.
23 And Adam said, This *is* now
[c]bone of my bones, and flesh of my
flesh: she shall be called [z]Woman, be-
cause she was [d]taken out of [a]Man.
24 [e]Therefore shall a man leave
his father and his mother, and shall
cleave unto his wife: and they shall be
one flesh.
25 [f]And they were both naked, the
man and his wife, and were not
[g]ashamed.

The fall of man

3 NOW [h]THE serpent was [i]more
subtle than any beast of the field
which the LORD God had made. And he
said unto the woman, [b]Yea, hath God
said, Ye shall not eat of every tree of
the garden?
2 And the woman said unto the ser-
pent, We may eat of the fruit of the
trees of the garden:
3 But of the fruit of the tree which
is in the midst of the garden, God hath
said, Ye shall not eat of it, neither shall
ye touch it, lest ye die.
4 [j]And the serpent said unto the
woman, Ye shall not surely die:
5 For God doth know that in the day
ye eat thereof, then your eyes shall be
opened, and ye shall be as gods, know-
ing good and evil.
6 And when the woman saw that the

2:22 [b]Heb. 13:4
2:23 [c]ch. 29:14 Eph. 5:30 [d]1 Cor. 11:8
2:24 [e]Mat. 19:5 Eph. 5:31
2:25 [f]ch. 3:7,10 [g]Is. 47:3
3:1 [h]Rev. 12:9 [i]2 Cor. 11:3
3:4 [j]2 Cor. 11:3

[y]Heb. *builded* [z]Heb. *Isha* [a]Heb. *Ish*
[b]Heb. *Yea, because*

2:24 LEAVE HIS FATHER AND HIS MOTHER. God in the beginning ordained marriage and the family unit as the first and most important institution on earth (see 1:28, note). God's plan for marriage consists of one male and one female who become "one flesh" (i.e., united physically and spiritually). This instruction excludes adultery, polygamy, homosexuality, immoral living, and unscriptural divorce (Mark 10:7–9; see Mat. 19:9, note).

3:1 THE SERPENT. In this episode the serpent attacked God through His creation. He stated that what God had said to Adam was not true (vv. 3–4); he ultimately caused God to curse His creation, including the human race whom He had made in His image (vv. 16–19). The "serpent" is later identified with Satan or the devil (cf. Rev. 12:9; 20:2). Satan evidently took control of the serpent and used it as an instrument in his work of temptation (cf. 2 Cor. 11:3,14; Rev. 20:2; see Mat. 4:10, note on Satan).

3:4 YE SHALL NOT SURELY DIE. The human race is bound to God by faith in His word as absolute truth (see 2:16, note). (1) Because he knew this, Satan sought to destroy the woman's faith in what God had said by raising doubts about that word. Satan suggested that God did not really mean what He said (cf. 2:16–17). In other words, the first lie proposed by Satan was a form of antinomianism, denying the judgment of death for sin and apostasy.

(2) One of the basic sins of humankind is unbelief in God's word. It is believing that somehow God does not really mean what He says about salvation, righteousness, sin, judgment, and death. Satan's most persistent lie is that unrepentant, deliberate sin and rebellion against God will not necessarily bring separation from God and eternal condemnation (see 1 Cor. 6:9, note; Gal. 5:21, note; 1 John 2:4, note).

3:5 YE SHALL BE AS GODS. Satan, from the beginning of the human race, has tempted humans to believe that they can be like God and decide for themselves what is good and what is evil. (1) Humanity, in seeking to be "as gods," became independent from God Almighty and as such became false gods (see v. 22, note; John 10:34, note). Humans now seek to derive moral knowledge and ethical discernment from their own minds and desire independence from God's word. Nevertheless, only God has the right to determine what is good and evil. (2) The Scripture declares that all who seek to be gods "shall perish from the earth, and from under these heavens" (Jer. 10:10–11). This will likewise be the fate of the antichrist, who will claim "that he is God" (2 Thes. 2:4).

3:6 WHEN THE WOMAN SAW . . . SHE TOOK. See Mat. 4:1–11, note on how to overcome temptation.

3:6 THE WOMAN . . . DID EAT, AND . . . HER HUSBAND WITH HER. When Adam and Eve sinned, moral and spiritual death came immediately (cf. 2:17), while physical death came later (5:5). (1) God had said, "In the day that thou eatest thereof thou shalt surely die" (2:17). Thus spiritual and moral death occurred at once when they sinned (cf. John 17:3, note). Moral death consisted in the death of God's life in them and their nature becoming sinful; spiritual death meant that their former relationship to God was destroyed. Since the sin of Adam and Eve, every person born comes into the world with a sinful nature (Rom. 8:5–8). This corruption of human nature involves the innate desire to go one's own selfish way without concern for God or others, and is passed on to all human beings (5:3; 6:5; 8:21; see Rom. 3:10–18, note; Eph. 2:3).

(2) It should be noted, however, that nowhere does Scripture teach that all sinned when Adam sinned, or that his guilt was imputed to the whole human race (see Rom. 5:12, note). The Bible does teach that Adam introduced the law of sin and death to the whole human race (cf. Rom. 5:12; 8:2; 1 Cor. 15:21–22).

tree *was* good for food, and that it *was*
[c]pleasant to the eyes, and a tree to be
desired to make *one* wise, she took of
the fruit thereof, [k]and did eat, and
gave also unto her husband with her;
and he did eat.
7 And the eyes of them both were
opened, [l]and they knew that they
were naked; and they sewed fig leaves
together, and made themselves
[d]aprons.
8 And they heard [m]the voice of the
LORD God walking in the garden in the
[e]cool of the day: and Adam and his
wife [n]hid themselves from the pres-
ence of the LORD God amongst the trees
of the garden.
9 And the LORD God called unto
Adam, and said unto him, Where *art*
thou?
10 And he said, I heard thy voice in
the garden, [o]and I was afraid, because
I *was* naked; and I hid myself.
11 And he said, Who told thee that
thou *wast* naked? Hast thou eaten of
the tree, whereof I commanded thee
that thou shouldest not eat?
12 And the man said, [p]The woman
whom thou gavest *to be* with me, she
gave me of the tree, and I did eat.
13 And the LORD God said unto the
woman, What *is* this *that* thou hast
done? And the woman said, [q]The ser-
pent beguiled me, and I did eat.
14 And the LORD God said unto the
serpent, Because thou hast done this,
thou *art* cursed above all cattle, and
above every beast of the field; upon thy
belly shalt thou go, and [r]dust shalt
thou eat all the days of thy life:
15 And I will put enmity between
thee and the woman, and between
[s]thy seed and [t]her seed; [u]it shall
bruise thy head, and thou shalt bruise Ex. 7:10-12
his heel.
16 Unto the woman he said, I will
greatly multiply thy sorrow and thy

3:6 [k]1 Tim. 2:14
3:7 [l]ch. 2:25
3:8 [m]Job 38:1 [n]Job 31:33 Jer. 23:24
3:10 [o]ch. 2:25 1 John 3:20
3:12 [p]Prov. 28:13
3:13 [q]ver. 4 2 Cor. 11:3 1 Tim. 2:14
3:14 [r]Is. 65:25
3:15 [s]John 8:44 Acts 13:10 1 John 3:8 [t]Is. 7:14 Luke 1:31,34,35 [u]Rom. 16:20 Rev. 12:7

[c] Heb. *a desire* [d] Or, *things to gird about*
[e] Heb. *wind*

3:7 THEY KNEW THAT THEY *WERE* NAKED. When Adam and Eve lived in moral innocence (i.e., before the fall), nakedness was not wrong nor did it bring a feeling of shame (2:25). However, after they sinned, the awareness of nakedness became associated with sin and the fallen and depraved condition of humankind. Because of the evil that nakedness would cause in the world, God Himself made garments and clothed Adam and Eve (v. 21), and now He commands all people to dress discreetly and modestly (see 1 Tim. 2:9, note).

3:8 HID THEMSELVES. The guilt and consciousness of sin caused Adam and Eve to shun God. They felt afraid and uncomfortable in His presence, knowing that they were sinful and under His displeasure. In this condition they found it impossible to draw near to Him with confidence (see Acts 23:1, note; 24:16, note). In our sinful condition, we too are like Adam and Eve. However, God has provided us a way to cleanse our guilty conscience, free us from sin, and restore us to His fellowship—the "way" called Jesus Christ (John 14:6). Through the redemption God provided in His Son, we can draw near to Him in order to receive His love, mercy, grace, and help in time of need (see Heb. 4:16, note; 7:25, note).

3:13 THE SERPENT BEGUILED ME. Satan caused the downfall of the human race through deception. This is one of his chief methods for leading people away from God's way and truth. (1) The Bible teaches that Satan deceives and blinds the minds of the unbelieving of this world in order that they may not understand the gospel (see 2 Cor. 4:4, note). (2) According to Paul, it is through Satan's deception that some within the church will believe they can live immoral lives and still inherit the kingdom of God (see 1 Cor. 6:9, note; Gal. 5:21, note). (3) Deception will be Satan's chief means of leading many into rebellion against God at history's end (2 Thes. 2:8–12; Rev. 20:8). (4) All Christians must be prepared for, and committed to, a continuous life-and-death struggle against the deception of Satan as it relates to their personal lives, marriages, families, schools, churches, and work (see Mat. 24:4,11,24; Eph. 6:11, note).

3:15 IT SHALL BRUISE THY HEAD, AND THOU SHALT BRUISE HIS HEEL. This verse contains the first implicit promise of God's plan of redemption for the world. It predicts the ultimate victory for humankind and God over Satan and evil by prophesying of a spiritual conflict between the "seed" of the woman (i.e., the Lord Jesus Christ) and the "seed" of the serpent (i.e., Satan and his followers; see v. 1, note). God promised here that Christ would be born of a woman (cf. Is. 7:14) and would be "bruised" through His crucifixion. Yet, He would rise from the dead to completely destroy (i.e., "bruise") Satan, sin, and death for the sake of the salvation of the human race (cf. Is. 53:5; Mat. 1:20–23; John 12:31; Acts 26:18; Rom. 5:18–19; 16:20; 1 John 3:8; Rev. 20:10).

3:16–19 I WILL GREATLY MULTIPLY THY SORROW. The punishment placed upon man and woman (vv. 16–19), as well as the effect of sin upon nature, were meant to remind humankind of the terrible consequences of sin and cause them to depend upon God in faith and obedience. God intended the present condition of the human race on earth to be redemptive. (1) Eve's attempt to liberate herself from God and act independently from her husband would be counteracted by a strong desire for her husband. Her deep attraction towards Adam and his headship over her would bring trouble and suffering along with joy and

conception; [v]in sorrow thou shalt
bring forth children; [w]and thy desire
shall be [f]to thy husband, and he shall
[x]rule over thee.
17 And unto Adam he said, [y]Be-
cause thou hast hearkened unto the
voice of thy wife, and hast eaten of the
tree, [z]of which I commanded thee,
saying, Thou shalt not eat of it:
[a]cursed *is* the ground for thy sake;
[b]in sorrow shalt thou eat *of* it all the
days of thy life;
18 Thorns also and thistles shall it
[g]bring forth to thee; and [c]thou shalt
eat the herb of the field;
19 [d]In the sweat of thy face shalt
thou eat bread, till thou return unto the
ground; for out of it wast thou taken:
[e]for dust thou *art,* and [f]unto dust
shalt thou return.
20 And Adam called his wife's name
[h]Eve; because she was the mother of
all living.
21 Unto Adam also and to his wife
did the LORD God make coats of skins,
and clothed them.
22 ¶ And the LORD God said, Behold,
the man is become as one of us, to
know good and evil: and now, lest he
put forth his hand, and take also of the
tree of life, and eat, and live for ever:
23 Therefore the LORD God sent him
forth from the garden of Eden, [g]to till
the ground from whence he was taken.

3:16 [v]Is. 13:8 John 16:21 [w]ch. 4:7 [x]1 Cor. 11:3 Eph. 5:22
3:17 [y]1 Sam. 15:23 [z]ch. 2:17 [a]Rom. 8:20 [b]Eccl. 2:23
3:18 [c]Ps. 104:14
3:19 [d]2 Thes. 3:10 [e]ch. 2:7 [f]Job 21:26 Eccl. 3:20
3:23 [g]ch. 4:2 & 9:20
3:24 [h]ch. 2:8 [i]Ps. 104:4 Heb. 1:7
4:3 [j]Num. 18:12
4:4 [k]Num. 18:17 [l]Lev. 3:16 [m]Heb. 11:4
4:5 [n]ch. 31:2

24 So he drove out the man; and he
placed [h]at the east of the garden of
Eden [i]Cherubims, and a flaming
sword which turned every way, to keep
the way of the tree of life.

Cain and Abel

4 AND ADAM knew Eve his wife;
and she conceived, and bare
[i]Cain, and said, I have gotten a man
from the LORD.
2 And she again bare his brother
[j]Abel. And Abel was [k]a keeper of
sheep, but Cain was a tiller of the
ground.
3 And [l]in process of time it came
to pass, that Cain brought [j]of the fruit
of the ground an offering unto the LORD.
4 And Abel, he also brought of [k]the
firstlings of his [m]flock and of [l]the fat
thereof. And the LORD had [m]respect
unto Abel and to his offering:
5 But unto Cain and to his offering
he had not respect. And Cain was very
wroth, [n]and his countenance fell.
6 And the LORD said unto Cain, Why
art thou wroth? and why is thy counte-
nance fallen?
7 If thou doest well, shalt thou not

[f] Or, *subject to thy husband* [g] Heb. *cause to bud* [h] Heb. *Chavah* i.e. *Living* [i] i.e. *Gotten* [j] Heb. *Hebel* [k] Heb. *a feeder* [l] Heb. *at the end of days* [m] Heb. *sheep,* or, *goats*

blessing (cf. 1:26–27; 1 Cor. 11:7–9; Eph. 5:22–25; 1 Tim. 2:11–14). (2) Because of God's curse upon nature, Adam and Eve would experience physical hardships, toil, struggle, and eventually death for themselves and all their offspring.

3:20 CALLED HIS WIFE'S NAME EVE. Adam called his wife "Eve," meaning "life," because she was the first mother of all humanity of all generations.

3:22 TO KNOW GOOD AND EVIL. Adam and Eve had attempted to set themselves up as God's equal and to determine their own standards (see v. 5, note). Through their fall, human beings became to some extent independent of God and began to distinguish for themselves between good and evil. (1) In this world, imperfect and perverted human judgment often decides what is good or evil. This was never God's will, for He intended us to know only good in dependence on Him and His word. (2) All who confess Christ as Lord return to God's original purpose for humankind. They rely on God's word to determine what is good.

3:24 HE DROVE OUT THE MAN. Adam's perfect relationship to God had been lost. He was now driven from the garden, and a life of dependence on God in the midst of trials began. In addition, Satan in some sense gained power over the world through the fall of Adam and Eve, for the N.T. speaks of Satan as being "the prince of this world" (John 14:30; cf. 2 Cor. 4:4; 1 John 5:19). However, God so loved the human race that He determined to conquer Satan by reconciling them and the world to Himself at the cost of the life of His Son (see v. 15, note; John 3:16; Rev. 21:1–8).

4:1 KNEW EVE HIS WIFE. The word "knew" is commonly used in the Bible for marital and sexual intimacy. It should be noted that when Eve gave birth to her son, she gave sincere praise to the Lord for the child. She was seeking to be rightly related to God in thankfulness for His love, forgiveness, and help.

4:3–5 AN OFFERING UNTO THE LORD. The Lord accepted the offering of Abel because he came before God in true faith and dedication to righteousness (cf. Heb. 11:4; 1 John 3:12; cf. John 4:23–24). Cain's offering was rejected because he lacked a sincerely obedient faith and because his deeds were evil (vv. 6–7; 1 John 3:12). God takes pleasure in our offerings and thanksgivings only when we are striving to live a righteous life according to His will (see Deut. 6:5, note).

4:7 UNTO THEE *SHALL BE* HIS DESIRE. A better translation of this verse might be: "Sin is crouching at the door; its desire is to possess you, but you must master it." God pictures sin as a tempting force or power which, like a wild beast

[n]be accepted? and if thou doest not
well, sin lieth at the door. And
[o]unto[o] thee *shall be* his desire, and
thou shalt rule over him.
8 And Cain talked with Abel his
brother: and it came to pass, when they
were in the field, that Cain rose up
against Abel his brother, and [p]slew
him.
9 ¶ And the LORD said unto Cain,
Where *is* Abel thy brother? And he
said, [q]I know not: *Am* I my brother's
keeper?
10 And he said, What hast thou
done? the voice of thy brother's
[p]blood [r]crieth unto me from the
ground.
11 And now *art* thou cursed from
the earth, which hath opened her
mouth to receive thy brother's blood
from thy hand;
12 When thou tillest the ground, it
shall not henceforth yield unto thee
her strength; a fugitive and a vagabond
shalt thou be in the earth.
13 And Cain said unto the LORD,
[q]My punishment *is* greater than I can
bear.
14 Behold, thou hast driven me out
this day from the face of the earth; and
[s]from thy face shall I be hid; and I
shall be a fugitive and a vagabond in
the earth; and it shall come to pass,
[t]*that* every one that findeth me shall
slay me.

4:7 [o]ch. 3:16
4:8 [p]Mat. 23:35
4:9 [q]John 8:44
4:10 [r]Heb. 12:24 Rev. 6:10
4:14 [s]Ps. 51:11 [t]ch. 9:6 Num. 35:19,21,27
4:15 [u]Ps. 79:12
4:16 [v]2 Ki. 13:23 & 24:20 Jer. 23:39 & 52:3
4:17 [w]Ps. 49:11

15 And the LORD said unto him,
Therefore whosoever slayeth Cain,
vengeance shall be taken on him [u]sev-
enfold. And the LORD set a mark upon
Cain, lest any finding him should kill
him.
16 ¶ And Cain [v]went out from the
presence of the LORD, and dwelt in the
land of Nod, on the east of Eden.
17 And Cain knew his wife; and she
conceived, and bare [r]Enoch: and he
builded a city, [w]and called the name of
the city, after the name of his son,
Enoch.
18 And unto Enoch was born Irad:
and Irad begat Mehujael: and Mehujael
begat Methusael: and Methusael begat
[s]Lamech.
19 ¶ And Lamech took unto him two
wives: the name of the one *was* Adah,
and the name of the other Zillah.
20 And Adah bare Jabal: he was the
father of such as dwell in tents, and *of
such as have* cattle.
21 And his brother's name *was* Ju-
bal: he was the father of all such as
handle the harp and organ.
22 And Zillah, she also bare Tubal-
cain, an [t]instructor of every artificer
in brass and iron: and the sister of Tu-
bal-cain *was* Naamah.

[n] Or, *have the excellency?* [o] Or, *subject unto thee,* [p] Heb. *bloods* [q] Or, *Mine iniquity* is *greater than* that it may *be forgiven* [r] Heb. *Chanoch* [s] Heb. *Lemech* [t] Heb. *whetter*

or demon, is ready to attack and to devour. Yet God also ascribes to human beings the capacity to overcome and resist sin by submitting to His word, with the assistance of His grace. It is their choice whether they will yield to sin or will conquer it (cf. Rom. 6).

4:10 THE VOICE OF THY BROTHER'S BLOOD CRIETH UNTO ME. The death of Abel and God's concern for him show that God throughout the ages cares for all who suffer because of their commitment to righteousness. Their suffering is known to God, and He will one day act on their behalf to render justice and destroy all evil (cf. Heb. 12:24).

4:11 NOW *ART* THOU CURSED. Cain was cursed by God in the sense that God would no longer bless his efforts to gain his living from the ground (cf. vv. 2–3). Evidently Cain did not humble himself in godly sorrow and repentance, for he separated himself from the Lord and sought to live without His help (v. 16).

4:15 A MARK UPON CAIN. This should probably be understood in the sense of a sign given to Cain to assure him of God's promise. The death penalty was not carried out on Cain. Capital punishment came later when the wickedness and violence of humankind became very great on the earth (6:5–7,11; 9:6).

4:16 CAIN WENT OUT FROM THE PRESENCE OF THE LORD. Cain and his descendants were the pioneers of God-estranged human civilization. A basic motivation in all humanistic societies is the attempt to overcome the curse, find pleasure, and regain "Paradise" without submission to God. In other words, the world's system is founded upon the principle of self-redemption for the human race in its revolt against God (see 1 John 5:19, note).

4:17 CAIN . . . HIS WIFE. Adam and Eve had other sons and daughters (5:4). Hence, Cain must have married one of his sisters. Such a relationship was necessary in the beginning. Later, because the results of the fall increased and interfamily marriages multiplied the biological weaknesses in the children, this type of marriage was forbidden (Lev. 18:6,9).

4:19 TOOK UNTO HIM TWO WIVES. Lamech was the first to reject God's ordained principle of monogamy (2:21–24). Inherited depravity was progressively manifesting itself in the home and family.

23 And Lamech said unto his wives,
Adah and Zillah, Hear my voice; ye
wives of Lamech, hearken unto my
speech: for [u]I have slain a man to
my wounding, and a young man [v]to my
hurt.
24 [x]If Cain shall be avenged seven-
fold, truly Lamech seventy and seven-
fold.
25 ¶ And Adam knew his wife
again; and she bare a son, and [y]called
his name [w]Seth[x]: For God, *said she,*
hath appointed me another seed in-
stead of Abel, whom Cain slew.
26 And to Seth, [z]to him also there
was born a son; and he called his name
[y]Enos: then began men [a]to[z] call
upon the name of the LORD.

The descendants of Adam

5 THIS *IS* the book of the genera-
tions of Adam. In the day that God
created man, in [b]the likeness of God
made he him;
2 [c]Male and female created he
them; and blessed them, and called
their name Adam, in the day when they
were created.
3 ¶ And Adam lived an hundred and
thirty years, and begat *a son* in his own
likeness, after his image; and [d]called
his name Seth:
4 [e]And the days of Adam after he
had begotten Seth were eight hundred
years: [f]and he begat sons and daugh-
ters:
5 And all the days that Adam lived
were nine hundred and thirty years:
[g]and he died.
6 And Seth lived an hundred and
five years, and [h]begat Enos:
7 And Seth lived after he begat
Enos eight hundred and seven years,
and begat sons and daughters:
8 And all the days of Seth were nine
hundred and twelve years: and he died.
9 ¶ And Enos lived ninety years,
and begat [a]Cainan:
10 And Enos lived after he begat
Cainan eight hundred and fifteen
years, and begat sons and daughters:
11 And all the days of Enos were
nine hundred and five years: and he
died.
12 ¶ And Cainan lived seventy
years, and begat [b]Mahalaleel:
13 And Cainan lived after he begat
Mahalaleel eight hundred and forty
years, and begat sons and daughters:
14 And all the days of Cainan were
nine hundred and ten years: and he
died.
15 ¶ And Mahalaleel lived sixty and
five years, and begat [c]Jared:
16 And Mahalaleel lived after he be-
gat Jared eight hundred and thirty
years, and begat sons and daughters:
17 And all the days of Mahalaleel

4:24 [x]ver. 15
4:25 [y]ch. 5:3
4:26 [z]ch. 5:6 [a]1 Ki. 18:24 Ps. 116:17 1 Cor. 1:2
5:1 [b]ch. 1:26 Eph. 4:24 Col. 3:10
5:2 [c]ch. 1:27
5:3 [d]ch. 4:25
5:4 [e]1 Chr. 1:1 [f]ch. 1:28
5:5 [g]ch. 3:19 Heb. 9:27
5:6 [h]ch. 4:26

[u]Or, *I would slay a man in my wound* [v]Or, *in my hurt* [w]Heb. *Sheth* [x]i.e. *Appointed,* or, *Put* [y]Heb. *Enosh* [z]Or, *to call themselves by the name of the LORD* [a]Heb. *Kenan* [b]Gk. *Maleleel* [c]Heb. *Jered*

4:26 CALL UPON THE NAME OF THE LORD. Under the encouragement of Enos, public prayer and worship began (see 2 Sam. 6:2; 1 Chr. 13:6; Ps. 79:6; Jer. 10:25, where calling on the name of the Lord refers to public worship). The ungodly family of Cain developed and centered their lives around the secular arts and business, establishing a way of self-reliance. The family of Seth, in contrast, called "upon the name of the LORD" in order to express their dependence upon Him. Thus, two fundamentally different family groups were developing on the earth—the godly people and the ungodly.

5:1 THE GENERATIONS OF ADAM. This chapter gives a list of the descendants of Adam down to the flood. The names reflect the godly line who stood for God in an increasingly corrupt age (see ch. 6). (1) Heb. 11 selects two individuals (Abel and Enoch) for special mention from this period as those who pleased God by their faith (Heb. 11:4–5). These two were among the remnant, the faithful few who refused to go the way of Cain. By the time of the flood the hearts of nearly everyone were evil; only eight individuals remained who were saved (6:5,11,18; 7:1,7; 1 Pet. 3:20).

(2) There will always be some, at times only a few, who will worship God, remain faithful to Him, follow His word, and wait for His promises. These people will be a minority (Mat. 7:13–14). Yet God marks their names as He did the people in this chapter. Today, if we feel we are standing alone in our faith in God and His word, we must remember we are really never alone. God still has His thousands throughout the earth who remain faithful to Him and His cause (cf. 1 Ki. 19:18).

5:5 NINE HUNDRED AND THIRTY YEARS. The reason that humankind lived a great number of years may be because sin had only just begun to work its corrupting influence upon the environment and one's physical body. By Abraham's time life expectancy had fallen to less than two hundred years.

5:6 SETH . . . BEGAT ENOS. The word "begat" can also mean "became the ancestor of." Thus these genealogies, like other genealogies in the Bible, were not intended to name every individual in the line.

were eight hundred ninety and five
years: and he died.
18 ¶ And Jared lived an hundred six-
ty and two years, and he begat
[i]Enoch:
19 And Jared lived after he begat
Enoch eight hundred years, and begat
sons and daughters:
20 And all the days of Jared were
nine hundred sixty and two years: and
he died.
21 ¶ And Enoch lived sixty and five
years, and begat [d]Methuselah:
22 And Enoch [j]walked with God
after he begat Methuselah three hun-
dred years, and begat sons and daugh-
ters:
(Gen. 6:9-10)
23 And all the days of Enoch were
three hundred sixty and five years:
24 And [k]Enoch walked with God:
and he *was* not; for God took him.
25 And Methuselah lived an hun-
dred eighty and seven years, and begat
[e]Lamech:
26 And Methuselah lived after he
begat Lamech seven hundred eighty
and two years, and begat sons and
daughters:
27 And all the days of Methuselah
were nine hundred sixty and nine
years: and he died.
28 ¶ And Lamech lived an hundred
eighty and two years, and begat a son:
29 And he called his name
[f] [g]Noah, saying, This *same* shall
comfort us concerning our work and
toil of our hands, because of the
ground [l]which the LORD hath cursed.
30 And Lamech lived after he begat
Noah five hundred ninety and five
years, and begat sons and daughters:
31 And all the days of Lamech were
seven hundred seventy and seven
years: and he died.
32 And Noah was five hundred
years old: and Noah begat [m]Shem,
Ham, [n]and Japheth.

5:18 [i]Jude 14,15
5:22 [j]ch. 6:9 & 17:1 2 Ki. 20:3 Ps. 16:8 Mic. 6:8 Mal. 2:6
5:24 [k]2 Ki. 2:11 Heb. 11:5
5:29 [l]ch. 3:17
5:32 [m]ch. 6:10 [n]ch. 10:21
6:1 [o]ch. 1:28
6:2 [p]Deut. 7:3
6:3 [q]Gal. 5:16 1 Pet. 3:19 [r]Ps. 78:39

The flood

6 AND IT came to pass, [o]when men
began to multiply on the face of the
earth, and daughters were born unto
them,
2 That the sons of God saw the
daughters of men that they *were* fair;
and they [p]took them wives of all
which they chose.
3 And the LORD said, [q]My spirit
shall not always strive with man, [r]for
that he also *is* flesh: yet his days shall
be an hundred and twenty years.
4 There were giants in the earth in
those days; and also after that, when
the sons of God came in unto the

[d] Gk. *Mathusala* [e] Heb. *Lemech* [f] Gk. *Noe;* see Luke 3:36; Heb. 11:7; 1 Pet. 3:20 [g] i.e. *Rest,* or, *Comfort*

5:22 ENOCH WALKED WITH GOD. Enoch undoubtedly excelled in godliness. Notice what the Bible says about him. (1) He "walked with God" (vv. 22,24)—i.e., he lived by faith in God, trusted in His word and promises (Heb. 11:5–6), endeavored to live a holy life (cf. 1 John 1:5–7), and embraced God's ways (cf. Amos 3:3), while standing firm against the ungodliness of his generation (Jude 14–15).

(2) Enoch was a preacher of righteousness who denounced sin and the unrighteous lifestyle of his generation. Referring to Enoch, Jude 14–15 tell us that he cried out against ungodliness and immorality by warning people of God's coming in judgment to punish men and women for their ungodly deeds: "And Enoch also, the seventh from Adam, prophesied of these, saying, Behold, the Lord cometh with ten thousands of his saints, to execute judgment upon all, and to convince all that are ungodly among them of all their ungodly deeds which they have ungodly committed, and of all their hard *speeches* which ungodly sinners have spoken against him."

(3) Enoch pleased God (Heb. 11:5). His life, message, and sympathy with God so pleased Him that the Lord honored him by taking him away from the earth to be in His presence forever without experiencing death.

Believers today should ponder the life of Enoch as an example, for we too live in an evil and ungodly generation. Do we walk with God, live in true holiness, denounce sin, and warn people to flee the wrath to come (Acts 3:19–20; 1 Thes. 1:10); and do we wait for the return of Jesus Christ to take us away from this earth to be with Him forever (1 Thes. 4:16–17)?

5:24 GOD TOOK HIM. Enoch's being taken directly to heaven without experiencing death implies that righteous men and women before Abraham possessed a hope for future life with God (Heb. 11:5; cf. Job 19:25–26; 2 Ki. 2:10–11).

6:2 THE SONS OF GOD. The "sons of God" most likely refer to men who were descendants of the godly line of Seth (cf. Deut. 14:1; 32:5; Ps. 73:15; Hos. 1:10); they began to intermarry with the "daughters of men," i.e., women from the ungodly family of Cain (see 4:16, note). The theory that the "sons of God" were angels is less likely in view of Jesus' words that angels do not marry (Mat. 22:30; Mark 12:25). This union of the godly with the unrighteous led to "wickedness" (v. 5), i.e., the godly became preoccupied with evil. As a result the earth became corrupt and filled with violence (vv. 11–13; see article on SPIRITUAL SEPARATION FOR BELIEVERS, p. 1814).

daughters of men, and they bare *chil-*
dren to them, the same *became* mighty
men which *were* of old, men of renown.
5 ¶ And GOD saw that the wicked-
ness of man *was* great in the earth, and
that [h]every [s]imagination of the
thoughts of his heart *was* only evil
[i]continually.
6 And [t]it repented the LORD that he
had made man on the earth, and it
[u]grieved him at his heart.
7 And the LORD said, I will destroy
man whom I have created from the face
of the earth; [j]both man, and beast,
and the creeping thing, and the fowls
of the air; for it repenteth me that I
have made them.
8 But Noah [v]found grace in the
eyes of the LORD.
9 ¶ These *are* the generations of
Noah: [w]Noah was a just man *and*
[k]perfect in his generations, *and* Noah
[x]walked with God.
Gen. 17:1-2
10 And Noah begat three sons,
[y]Shem, Ham, and Japheth.
11 The earth also was corrupt [z]be-
fore God, and the earth was [a]filled
with violence.
12 And God [b]looked upon the
earth, and, behold, it was corrupt; for
all flesh had corrupted his way upon
the earth.
13 And God said unto Noah, [c]The
end of all flesh is come before me; for
the earth is filled with violence through
them; [d]and, behold, I will destroy
them [l]with the earth.
14 ¶ Make thee an ark of gopher
wood; [m]rooms shalt thou make in the
ark, and shalt pitch it within and with-
out with pitch.
15 And this *is the fashion* which thou
shalt make it *of:* The length of the ark
shall be three hundred cubits, the
breadth of it fifty cubits, and the height
of it thirty cubits.
16 A window shalt thou make to the

6:5 [s]ch. 8:21
6:6 [t]1 Sam. 15:11,29; 2 Sam. 24:16; Mal. 3:6; Jas. 1:17; [u]Is. 63:10
6:8 [v]ch. 19:19; Ex. 33:12; Luke 1:30; Acts 7:46
6:9 [w]ch. 7:1; Ezek. 14:14,20; Heb. 11:7; 2 Pet. 2:5; [x]ch. 5:22
6:10 [y]ch. 5:32
6:11 [z]Rom. 2:13; [a]Ezek. 8:17
6:12 [b]Ps. 14:2 & 53:2,3
6:13 [c]Jer. 51:13; 1 Pet. 4:7; [d]ver. 17

[h] Or, *the whole imagination:* the Hebrew word signifieth not only *the imagination,* but also *the purposes and desires* [i] Heb. *every day*
[j] Heb. *from man unto beast* [k] Or, *upright*
[l] Or, *from the earth* [m] Heb. *nests*

6:5 THE WICKEDNESS OF MAN *WAS* GREAT. In Noah's day the character of human sin was blatantly manifested in two primary ways: sexual lust (v. 2) and violence (v. 11). Human depravity has not changed; it is still through lust and violence that evil finds unrestrained expression. Today immorality, ungodliness, pornography, and violence dominate our societies (see Mat. 24:37–39; Rom. 1:32, note).

6:6 AND IT REPENTED THE LORD. God is revealed in these early chapters of the Bible as a God who deals with people personally and is capable of emotion, disappointment, and reaction against the willful sin and rebellion of humankind. (1) The word "repented" indicates that because of the tragic sin of the human race, God's disposition was changed towards them; his attitude of mercy and longsuffering turned to one of judgment.

(2) Although God's existence, character, and ultimate purposes remain changeless (1 Sam. 15:29; Jas. 1:17), He remains open and responsive in His dealings with humans. God does alter his feelings, attitudes, actions, and mind in accordance with a changing response to His will (cf. Ex. 32:14; 2 Sam. 24:16; Jer. 18:7,8; 26:3,13,19; Ezek. 18; Jonah 3:10).

(3) This revelation of God as a God who can have regret and grief makes clear that God exists in a personal and intimate relationship to His creation. He possesses an intense love for human beings and a divine attentiveness to the plight of the human race (Ps. 139:7–18).

6:9 NOAH WAS A JUST MAN *AND* PERFECT IN HIS GENERATIONS. Amidst the widespread wickedness and evil of those days (v. 5), God found in Noah one man who still sought communion with Him and who was a righteous man. (1) "Perfect in his generations" indicates that he kept himself separate from the moral evil of the society around him. Because he was a righteous man who feared God and set his face against popular public opinion and conduct, Noah found favor with God (v. 8; 7:1; Heb. 11:7; 2 Pet. 2:5).

(2) This righteousness in Noah's life came by God's grace, through Noah's faith and walk with God (v. 9). Salvation in the N.T. era must be found in exactly the same way, namely, by God's mercy and grace received through a faith so vital that it results in a sincere effort to walk with God and remain separated from a perverse generation (v. 22; 7:5,9,16). Heb. 11:7 states that Noah "became heir of the righteousness which is by faith."

(3) The N.T. also states that Noah was not only a just man, but also a preacher of righteousness (2 Pet. 2:5). In this he is an example of what preachers ought to be.

6:14 AN ARK. The Hebrew word "ark" means a vessel for floating and occurs only here and in Ex. 2:3,5 (where it is used of the basket in which the baby Moses was placed). It resembled a barge, but not necessarily with square corners. Its dimensions are given in "cubits" (v. 15). An ancient cubit equaled about eighteen inches. Thus, the ark was approximately 450 feet long, seventy-five feet wide, and forty-five feet high. Its carrying capacity was equal to more than 300 railroad stock cars. It is calculated that the ark could hold some 7,000 kinds of animals. Heb. 11:7 suggests that the ark is a type of Christ, He who is the means of the believer's salvation from judgment and death (cf. 1 Pet. 3:20–21).

ark, and in a cubit shalt thou finish it above; and the door of the ark shalt thou set in the side thereof; *with* lower, second, and third *stories* shalt thou make it.

17 [e]And, behold, I, even I, do bring a flood of waters upon the earth, to destroy all flesh, wherein *is* the breath of life, from under heaven; *and* every thing that *is* in the earth shall die.

18 But with thee will I establish my covenant; and [f]thou shalt come into the ark, thou, and thy sons, and thy wife, and thy sons' wives with thee.

19 And of every living thing of all flesh, [g]two of every *sort* shalt thou bring into the ark, to keep *them* alive with thee; they shall be male and female.

20 Of fowls after their kind, and of cattle after their kind, of every creeping thing of the earth after his kind, two of every *sort* [h]shall come unto thee, to keep *them* alive.

21 And take thou unto thee of all food that is eaten, and thou shalt gather *it* to thee; and it shall be for food for thee, and for them.

22 [i]Thus did Noah; [j]according to all that God commanded him, so did he.

7 AND THE LORD said unto Noah, [k]Come thou and all thy house into the ark; for [l]thee have I seen righteous before me in this generation.

2 Of every [m]clean beast thou shalt take to thee by [n]sevens, the male and his female: [n]and of beasts that *are* not clean by two, the male and his female.

3 Of fowls also of the air by sevens, the male and the female; to keep seed alive upon the face of all the earth.

4 For yet seven days, and I will cause it to rain upon the earth [o]forty days and forty nights; and every living substance that I have made will I [o]destroy from off the face of the earth.

5 [p]And Noah did according unto all that the LORD commanded him.

6 And Noah *was* six hundred years old when the flood of waters was upon the earth.

7 ¶ [q]And Noah went in, and his sons, and his wife, and his sons' wives with him, into the ark, because of the waters of the flood.

8 Of clean beasts, and of beasts that *are* not clean, and of fowls, and of every thing that creepeth upon the earth,

9 There went in two and two unto Noah into the ark, the male and the female, as God had commanded Noah.

10 And it came to pass [p]after seven days, that the waters of the flood were upon the earth.

11 ¶ In the six hundredth year of Noah's life, in the second month, the seventeenth day of the month, the

[n] Heb. *seven seven* [o] Heb. *blot out* [p] Or, *on the seventh day*

6:17 [e]ch. 7:4,21-23 2 Pet. 2:5
6:18 [f]ch. 7:1,7,13 1 Pet. 3:20 2 Pet. 2:5
6:19 [g]ch. 7:8,9,15,16
6:20 [h]ch. 7:9,15
6:22 [i]Heb. 11:7 See Ex. 40:16 [j]ch. 7:5,9,16
7:1 [k]Mat. 24:38 Luke 17:26 Heb. 11:7 1 Pet. 3:20 2 Pet. 2:5 [l]ch. 6:9 Ps. 33:18 Prov. 10:9 2 Pet. 2:9
7:2 [m]Lev. ch. 11 [n]Lev. 10:10 Ezek. 44:23
7:4 [o]ver. 12,17
7:5 [p]ch. 6:22
7:7 [q]ver. 1

6:18 WITH THEE WILL I ESTABLISH MY COVENANT. Through His covenant, God promised Noah that he would be saved from the judgment to be meted out through the flood. Noah responded to God's covenant by believing in Him and His word (v. 13; Heb. 11:7). His faith was demonstrated by being "moved with fear" (Heb. 11:7) and by preparing and entering the ark (v. 22; 7:7; see 1 Pet. 3:21, note; see article on GOD'S COVENANT WITH ABRAHAM, ISAAC, AND JACOB, p. 48).

7:6 THE FLOOD OF WATERS WAS UPON THE EARTH. The flood was God's universal judgment upon an ungodly and unrepentant world. The apostle Peter refers to the flood to remind his readers that God will again judge the whole world at the end of time, then by fire (2 Pet. 3:10). That judgment will involve the outpouring of God's wrath upon the ungodly in a way unequaled in history (Mat. 24:21; see article on THE GREAT TRIBULATION, p. 1456). God calls believers today, as He did Noah of old, to warn the unsaved about this terrible day and to call them to repent of their sins, turn to God through Christ, and be saved.

7:11–12 THE GREAT DEEP BROKEN UP. Two cataclysmic events precipitated the flood: the eruption of great reservoirs of subterranean waters, perhaps caused by earthquakes with subsequent great tidal waves from the oceans, and torrential rains which fell on the earth for forty days (v. 12). (1) Thus, all living creatures outside the ark who normally lived on dry land died, both human and animal life (vv. 21–22; Mat. 24:37–39; 1 Pet. 3:20; 2 Pet. 2:5).

(2) Water rose to such height that it covered "all the high hills, that *were* under the whole heaven" (vv. 19–20); i.e., the entire earth was covered with water. This indicates a universal flood and not simply a local one confined to a small portion of earth (cf. 2 Pet. 3:6). The water began to recede only after 150 days (v. 24). Noah's ark finally came to rest on one of the mountains of Ararat (Armenia), 500 miles from where it started (8:4).

(3) The earth dried up, and Noah left the ark 377 days after the flood began (8:13–14).

(4) The apostle Peter states that the pre-flood world "perished" (2 Pet. 3:6). This suggests that due to the enormous topographical upheaval, the pre-flood earth changed radically, both physically and geologically, into the earth that now exists.

same day were all [r]the fountains of
the great deep broken up, and the
[s]windows[q] of heaven were opened.
12 [t]And the rain was upon the
earth forty days and forty nights.
13 In the selfsame day entered
Noah, and Shem, and Ham, and Ja-
pheth, the sons of Noah, and Noah's
wife, and the three wives of his sons
with them, into the ark;
14 [u]They, and every beast after his
kind, and all the cattle after their kind,
and every creeping thing that creepeth
upon the earth after his kind, and every
fowl after his kind, every bird of every
[r]sort.
15 And they [v]went in unto Noah
into the ark, two and two of all flesh,
wherein *is* the breath of life.
16 And they that went in, went in
male and female of all flesh, [w]as God
had commanded him: and the LORD
shut him in.
17 [x]And the flood was forty days
upon the earth; and the waters in-
creased, and bare up the ark, and it
was lift up above the earth.
18 And the waters prevailed, and
were increased greatly upon the earth;
[y]and the ark went upon the face of the
waters.
19 And the waters prevailed ex-
ceedingly upon the earth; and all the
high hills, that *were* under the whole
heaven, were covered.
20 Fifteen cubits upward did the
waters prevail; and the mountains
were covered.
21 [z]And all flesh died that moved
upon the earth, both of fowl, and of cat-
tle, and of beast, and of every creeping
thing that creepeth upon the earth, and
every man:
22 All in [a]whose nostrils *was* [s]the
breath of life, of all that *was* in the dry
land, died.
23 And every living substance was

7:11 [r]ch. 8:2 Prov. 8:28 Ezek. 26:19 [s]ch. 8:2 Ps. 78:23
7:12 [t]ver. 4,17
7:14 [u]ch. 6:19
7:15 [v]ch. 6:20
7:16 [w]ver. 2,3
7:17 [x]ver. 4,12
7:18 [y]Ps. 104:26
7:21 [z]ch. 6:13,17
7:22 [a]ch. 2:7
7:23 [b]1 Pet. 3:20 2 Pet. 2:5
7:24 [c]ch. 8:3 & 8:4 compared with ver. 11 of this chapter
8:1 [d]ch. 19:29 Ex. 2:24 1 Sam. 1:19 Ps. 106:4 [e]Ex. 14:21
8:2 [f]ch. 7:11 [g]Job 38:37
8:3 [h]ch. 7:24
8:6 [i]ch. 6:16

destroyed which was upon the face of
the ground, both man, and cattle, and
the creeping things, and the fowl of the
heaven; and they were destroyed from
the earth: and [b]Noah only remained
alive, and they that *were* with him in the
ark.
24 [c]And the waters prevailed upon
the earth an hundred and fifty days.
8 AND GOD [d]remembered Noah,
and every living thing, and all the
cattle that *was* with him in the ark:
[e]and God made a wind to pass over
the earth, and the waters assuaged;
2 [f]The fountains also of the deep
and the windows of heaven were
stopped, and [g]the rain from heaven
was restrained;
3 And the waters returned from off
the earth [t]continually: and after the
end [h]of the hundred and fifty days the
waters were abated.
4 And the ark rested in the seventh
month, on the seventeenth day of the
month, upon the mountains of Ararat.
5 And the waters [u]decreased con-
tinually until the tenth month: in the
tenth *month,* on the first *day* of the
month, were the tops of the mountains
seen.
6 ¶ And it came to pass at the end
of forty days, that Noah opened [i]the
window of the ark which he had made:
7 And he sent forth a raven, which
went forth [v]to and fro, until the wa-
ters were dried up from off the earth.
8 Also he sent forth a dove from
him, to see if the waters were abated
from off the face of the ground;
9 But the dove found no rest for the
sole of her foot, and she returned unto
him into the ark, for the waters *were* on
the face of the whole earth: then he put

[q] Or, *floodgates* [r] Heb. *wing* [s] Heb. *the breath of the spirit of life* [t] Heb. *in going and returning* [u] Heb. *were in going and decreasing* [v] Heb. *in going forth and returning*

7:23 AND NOAH ONLY REMAINED *ALIVE*. The flood story tells of both judgment and salvation. (1) The flood with its total destruction of all human life outside the ark was necessary in order to blot out the extreme moral corruption of men and women and to give the human race a new chance for fellowship with God. (2) The apostle Peter states that Christian baptism corresponds to Noah's salvation through the flood waters (see 1 Pet. 3:21, note).

8:1 AND GOD REMEMBERED NOAH. Noah had not heard from God for 150 days (cf. 7:24). His faith was being tested, for he had no idea when the waters would subside or when God would intervene again. Then God acted out of concern and love for Noah and his family. God's dealings with Noah are recorded to give all God's faithful people hope and trust in His ways. If God has not acted in your life for a long time, you can be confident He will act again and manifest His loving care toward you. At the present time your task is to draw near to the Lord and continue in faithful obedience to His word and Spirit (Prov. 3:5–6; 16:3; Phil. 2:13).

forth his hand, and took her, and [w]pulled her in unto him into the ark.

10 And he stayed yet other seven days; and again he sent forth the dove out of the ark;

11 And the dove came in to him in the evening; and, lo, in her mouth *was* an olive leaf plucked off: so Noah knew that the waters were abated from off the earth.

12 And he stayed yet other seven days; and sent forth the dove; which returned not again unto him any more.

13 ¶ And it came to pass in the six hundredth and first year, in the first *month,* the first *day* of the month, the waters were dried up from off the earth: and Noah removed the covering of the ark, and looked, and, behold, the face of the ground was dry.

14 And in the second month, on the seven and twentieth day of the month, was the earth dried.

15 ¶ And God spake unto Noah, saying,

16 Go forth of the ark, [j]thou, and thy wife, and thy sons, and thy sons' wives with thee.

17 Bring forth with thee every living thing that *is* with thee, of all flesh, *both* of fowl, and of cattle, and of every creeping thing that creepeth upon the earth; that they may breed abundantly in the earth, and [k]be fruitful, and multiply upon the earth.

18 And Noah went forth, and his sons, and his wife, and his sons' wives with him:

19 Every beast, every creeping thing, and every fowl, *and* whatsoever creepeth upon the earth, after their [x]kinds, went forth out of the ark.

20 ¶ And Noah builded an altar unto the LORD; and took of [l]every clean beast, and of every clean fowl, and offered burnt offerings on the altar.

21 And the LORD smelled [m]a[y] sweet savour; and the LORD said in his heart, I will not again [n]curse the ground any more for man's sake; [z]for the [o]imagination of man's heart *is* evil from his youth; [p]neither will I again smite any more every thing living, as I have done.

22 [q]While[a] the earth remaineth, seedtime and harvest, and cold and heat, and summer and winter, and [r]day and night shall not cease.

The covenant with Noah

9 AND GOD blessed Noah and his sons, and said unto them, [s]Be fruitful, and multiply, and replenish the earth.

2 [t]And the fear of you and the dread of you shall be upon every beast of the earth, and upon every fowl of the air, upon all that moveth *upon* the earth, and upon all the fishes of the sea; into your hand are they delivered.

3 [u]Every moving thing that liveth shall be meat for you; even as the [v]green herb have I given you [w]all things.

4 [x]But flesh with the life thereof, *which is* the blood thereof, shall ye not eat.

5 And surely your blood of your lives will I require; [y]at the hand of every beast will I require it, and [z]at the hand of man; at the hand of every [a]man's brother will I require the life of man.

6 [b]Whoso sheddeth man's blood, by man shall his blood be shed: [c]for in the image of God made he man.

7 And you, [d]be ye fruitful, and multiply; bring forth abundantly in the earth, and multiply therein.

8 ¶ And God spake unto Noah, and to his sons with him, saying,

9 And I, [e]behold, I establish [f]my

8:16 [j]ch. 7:13
8:17 [k]ch. 1:22
8:20 [l]Lev. ch. 11
8:21 [m]Lev. 1:9 Ezek. 20:41 2 Cor. 2:15 Eph. 5:2
[n]ch. 3:17 & 6:17
[o]ch. 6:5 Job 14:4 Jer. 17:9
[p]ch. 9:11,15
8:22 [q]Is. 54:9
[r]Jer. 33:20,25
9:1 [s]ver. 7,19 ch. 1:28 & 10:32
9:2 [t]ch. 1:28 Hos. 2:18
9:3 [u]Deut. 12:15 & 14:3,9,11 Acts 10:12,13
[v]ch. 1:29
[w]Rom. 14:14,20 1 Cor. 10:23,26 Col. 2:16 1 Tim. 4:3,4
9:4 [x]Lev. 17:10,11,14 Deut. 12:23 1 Sam. 14:33
9:5 [y]Ex. 21:28
[z]ch. 4:9,10 Ps. 9:12
[a]Acts 17:26
9:6 [b]Ex. 21:12,14 Lev. 24:17 Mat. 26:52
[c]ch. 1:27
9:7 [d]ver. 1,19
9:9 [e]ch. 6:18
[f]Is. 54:9

[w]Heb. *caused her to come* [x]Heb. *families* [y]Heb. *a saviour of rest* [z]Or, *though* [a]Heb. *As yet all the days of the earth*

8:21 MAN'S HEART *IS* EVIL FROM HIS YOUTH. The Lord states the truth about the corruption and depravity of human nature. The tendency toward evil is innate in a person from birth and is expressed early in childhood or youth (see Rom. 3:10–18, note).

9:6 WHOSO SHEDDETH MAN'S BLOOD, BY MAN SHALL HIS BLOOD BE SHED. Because of the desire for violence and bloodshed that arises within the human heart (cf. 6:11; 8:21), God sought to guard the sanctity of human life by restraining murder in society. He did this in two ways: (1) By emphasizing that humans have been created in His image (1:26) and that their lives are sacred in His sight; (2) by instituting capital punishment, commanding that every murderer be punished with death (cf. Ex. 21:12,14; 22:2; Num. 35:6–34; Deut. 19:1–13; see Rom. 13:4, note). The authority of governments to use the "sword" for capital punishment is reaffirmed in the N.T. (Acts 25:11; Rom. 13:4; cf. Mat. 26:52).

9:9–17 I ESTABLISH MY COVENANT. These verses speak of God's covenant with humanity and nature, in which He promised never again to de-

covenant with you, and with your seed after you;

10 [g]And with every living creature that *is* with you, of the fowl, of the cattle, and of every beast of the earth with you; from all that go out of the ark, to every beast of the earth.

11 And [h]I will establish my covenant with you; neither shall all flesh be cut off any more by the waters of a flood; neither shall there any more be a flood to destroy the earth.

12 And God said, [i]This *is* the token of the covenant which I make between me and you and every living creature that *is* with you, for perpetual generations:

13 I do set [j]my bow in the cloud, and it shall be for a token of a covenant between me and the earth.

14 And it shall come to pass, when I bring a cloud over the earth, that the bow shall be seen in the cloud:

15 And [k]I will remember my covenant, which *is* between me and you and every living creature of all flesh; and the waters shall no more become a flood to destroy all flesh.

16 And the bow shall be in the cloud; and I will look upon it, that I may remember [l]the everlasting covenant between God and every living creature of all flesh that *is* upon the earth.

17 And God said unto Noah, This *is* the token of the covenant, which I have established between me and all flesh that *is* upon the earth.

18 ¶ And the sons of Noah, that went forth of the ark, were Shem, and Ham, and Japheth: [m]and Ham *is* the father of [b]Canaan.

19 [n]These *are* the three sons of Noah: [o]and of them was the whole earth overspread.

Canaan cursed; Shem blessed

20 And Noah began *to be* [p]an husbandman, and he planted a vineyard:

21 And he drank of the wine, [q]and was drunken; and he was uncovered within his tent.

22 And Ham, the father of Canaan, saw the nakedness of his father, and told his two brethren without.

23 [r]And Shem and Japheth took a garment, and laid *it* upon both their shoulders, and went backward, and covered the nakedness of their father; and their faces *were* backward, and they saw not their father's nakedness.

24 And Noah awoke from his wine, and knew what his younger son had done unto him.

25 And he said, [s]Cursed *be* Canaan; [t]a servant of servants shall he be unto his brethren.

26 And he said, [u]Blessed *be* the LORD God of Shem; and Canaan shall be [c]his servant.

27 God shall [d]enlarge Japheth, [v]and he shall dwell in the tents of Shem; and Canaan shall be his servant.

28 ¶ And Noah lived after the flood three hundred and fifty years.

29 And all the days of Noah were nine hundred and fifty years: and he died.

9:10 [g]Ps. 145:9
9:11 [h]Is. 54:9
9:12 [i]ch. 17:11
9:13 [j]Rev. 4:3
9:15 [k]Lev. 26:42,45
9:16 [l]ch. 17:13,19 Is. 55:3 Jer. 32:40 Heb. 13:20
9:18 [m]ch. 10:6
9:19 [n]ch. 5:32 [o]ch. 10:32 1 Chr. 1:4
9:20 [p]ch. 3:19,23 & 4:2 Prov. 12:11
9:21 [q]Prov. 20:1 1 Cor. 10:12
9:23 [r]Ex. 20:12 Gal. 6:1
9:25 [s]Deut. 27:16 Josh. 9:23,27 [t]Josh. 9:23 1 Ki. 9:20,21
9:26 [u]Ps. 144:15 Heb. 11:16
9:27 [v]Eph. 2:13,14 & 3:6

[b] Heb. *Chenaan* [c] Or, *servant to them* [d] Or, *persuade*

---

stroy the earth and all living creatures with a flood (vv. 11,15).

9:13 MY BOW IN THE CLOUD. The rainbow was God's sign and ongoing reminder of His promise never again to destroy all inhabitants on the earth by a flood. The rainbow should remind us of God's mercy and His faithfulness to His word.

9:21 HE DRANK OF THE WINE, AND WAS DRUNKEN. This first mention of wine in Scripture is connected with drunkenness, sin, shame, and a curse (vv. 21–25). Because of the accompanying evils of intoxicating beverages, God has made total abstinence the high standard for His people (cf. Lev. 10:9; Judg. 13:4–7; Prov. 31:4; see Num. 6:3, note; Prov. 23:31, note; 1 Thes. 5:6, note; Tit. 2:2, note; see articles on WINE IN THE OLD TESTAMENT, p. 220, and WINE IN NEW TESTAMENT TIMES (1) and (2), p. 1538 and p. 1594).

9:22 HAM. Ham's sin consisted in his failure to honor and respect his father; rather than covering him, he exposed his shameful condition.

9:25 CURSED *BE* CANAAN. When Noah learned of Ham's shameful action, he pronounced a curse on Ham's son Canaan (though not on Ham himself). (1) Perhaps Canaan was in some way involved in Ham's sin or possessed the same character faults of his father. The curse indicated that Canaan's descendants (who were not black) would be oppressed and under the control of other nations. In contrast, Shem and Japheth's descendants would be blessed by God (vv. 26–27). (2) This prophecy of Noah was conditional for all concerned. Any descendants of Canaan who turned to God would also receive the blessing of Shem (Josh. 6:22–25; Heb. 11:31), while any descendants of Shem and Japheth who departed from God would experience the curse of Canaan (cf. Jer. 18:7–10).

Descendants of Noah's sons

10:2–5pp — 1 Chr. 1:5–7
10:6–20pp — 1 Chr. 1:8–16
10:21–31pp — Gen. 11:10–27; 1 Chr. 1:17–27

10 NOW THESE *are* the genera-
tions of the sons of Noah,
Shem, Ham, and Japheth: [w]and unto
them were sons born after the flood.
2 [x]The sons of Japheth; Gomer,
and Magog, and Madai, and Javan, and
Tubal, and Meshech, and Tiras.
3 And the sons of Gomer; Ashke-
naz, and Riphath, and Togarmah.
4 And the sons of Javan; Elishah,
and Tarshish, Kittim, and [e]Dodanim.
5 By these were [y]the isles of the
Gentiles divided in their lands; every
one after his tongue, after their fami-
lies, in their nations.
6 ¶ [z]And the sons of Ham; Cush,
and Mizraim, and Phut, and Canaan.
7 And the sons of Cush; Seba, and
Havilah, and Sabtah, and Raamah, and
Sabtecha: and the sons of Raamah;
Sheba, and Dedan.
8 And Cush begat Nimrod: he began
to be a mighty one in the earth.
9 He was a mighty [a]hunter [b]be-
fore the LORD: wherefore it is said,
Even as Nimrod the mighty hunter be-
fore the LORD.
10 [c]And the beginning of his king-
dom was [f]Babel, and Erech, and Ac-
cad, and Calneh, in the land of Shinar.
11 Out of that land [g]went forth As-
shur, and builded Nineveh, and [h]the
city Rehoboth, and Calah,
12 And Resen between Nineveh and
Calah: the same *is* a great city.
13 And Mizraim begat Ludim, and
Anamim, and Lehabim, and Naph-
tuhim,
14 And Pathrusim, and Casluhim,
([d]out of whom came Philistim,) and
Caphtorim.
15 ¶ And Canaan begat [i]Sidon his
firstborn, and Heth,
16 And the Jebusite, and the Amo-
rite, and the Girgasite,

10:1 [w]ch. 9:1,7,19
10:2 [x]1 Chr. 1:5
10:5 [y]Ps. 72:10 Jer. 2:10 & 25:22
10:6 [z]1 Chr. 1:8
10:9 [a]Jer. 16:16 Mic. 7:2 [b]ch. 6:11
10:10 [c]Mic. 5:6
10:14 [d]1 Chr. 1:12
10:19 [e]ch. 13:12,14,15, 17 & 15:18-21
10:22 [f]1 Chr. 1:17
10:24 [g]ch. 11:12
10:25 [h]1 Chr. 1:19
10:32 [i]ver. 1

17 And the Hivite, and the Arkite,
and the Sinite,
18 And the Arvadite, and the Zema-
rite, and the Hamathite: and afterward
were the families of the Canaanites
spread abroad.
19 [e]And the border of the Canaan-
ites was from Sidon, as thou comest to
Gerar, unto [j]Gaza; as thou goest,
unto Sodom, and Gomorrah, and Ad-
mah, and Zeboim, even unto Lasha.
20 These *are* the sons of Ham, after
their families, after their tongues, in
their countries, *and* in their nations.
21 ¶ Unto Shem also, the father of
all the children of Eber, the brother of
Japheth the elder, even to him were
children born.
22 The [f]children of Shem; Elam,
and Asshur, and [k]Arphaxad, and Lud,
and Aram.
23 And the children of Aram; Uz,
and Hul, and Gether, and Mash.
24 And Arphaxad begat [g]Salah;[l]
and Salah begat Eber.
25 [h]And unto Eber were born two
sons: the name of one *was* [m]Peleg; for
in his days was the earth divided; and
his brother's name *was* Joktan.
26 And Joktan begat Almodad, and
Sheleph, and Hazarmaveth, and Jerah,
27 And Hadoram, and Uzal, and
Diklah,
28 And Obal, and Abimael, and
Sheba,
29 And Ophir, and Havilah, and Jo-
bab: all these *were* the sons of Joktan.
30 And their dwelling was from Me-
sha, as thou goest unto Sephar a
mount of the east.
31 These *are* the sons of Shem, after
their families, after their tongues, in
their lands, after their nations.
32 [i]These *are* the families of the
sons of Noah, after their generations,

[e] Or, *Rodanim* [f] Gk. *Babylon* [g] Or, *he went out* into *Assyria* [h] Or, *the streets of the city* [i] Heb. *Tzidon* [j] Heb. *Azzah* [k] Heb. *Arpachshad* [l] Heb. *Shelah* [m] i.e. *Division*

10:1 THE GENERATIONS OF THE SONS OF NOAH. The purpose of ch. 10 was to reveal how all the nations and people of the earth stemmed from Noah and his sons after the flood (v. 32).

10:2–5 THE SONS OF JAPHETH. These verses list the descendants of Japheth, who went north and settled around the coast lands of the Black and Caspian Seas. They became the progenitors of the Medes, Greeks, and the Caucasian races of Europe and Asia.

10:6–20 THE SONS OF HAM. These verses list the descendants of Ham, who settled in southern Arabia, southern Egypt, the east shore of the Mediterranean, and north coast of Africa. Canaan's descendants (vv. 15–19) settled in a territory that was given the name of Canaan, a territory that was later to become the home of the Jewish people.

10:21–31 UNTO SHEM. These verses list the descendants of Shem, who settled in Arabia and the Middle East Valley. They include Jews, Assyrians, Syrians, and Elamites.

in their nations: [j]and by these were
the nations divided in the earth after
the flood.

The tower of Babel

11 AND THE whole earth was of
one [n]language, and of one
[o]speech.
2 And it came to pass, as they journeyed
[p]from the east, that they found
a plain in the land of Shinar; and they
dwelt there.
3 And [q]they said one to another,
Go to, let us make brick, and [r]burn
them thoroughly. And they had brick
for stone, and slime had they for mortar.
4 And they said, Go to, let us build
us a city and a tower, [k]whose top *may*
reach unto heaven; and let us make us
a name, lest we be scattered abroad
upon the face of the whole earth.
5 [l]And the LORD came down to see
the city and the tower, which the children
of men builded.
6 And the LORD said, Behold, [m]the
people *is* one, and they have all [n]one
language; and this they begin to do:
and now nothing will be restrained
from them, which they have [o]imagined
to do.
7 Go to, [p]let us go down, and there
confound their language, that they may

10:32 [j]ch. 9:19
11:4 [k]Deut. 1:28
11:5 [l]ch. 18:21
11:6 [m]ch. 9:19 Acts 17:26 [n]ver. 1 [o]Ps. 2:1
11:7 [p]ch. 1:26

[n] Heb. *lip* [o] Heb. *words* [p] Or, *eastward*
[q] Heb. *a man said to his neighbour* [r] Heb. *burn them to a burning*

11:2 THE LAND OF SHINAR. The land of Shinar is the O.T. name for the territory of ancient Sumer and later of Babylonia or Mesopotamia.

11:4 LET US BUILD . . . LET US MAKE US A NAME. The sin of the people in the land of Shinar was the desire to dominate the world and their own destiny apart from God through man-centered organizational unity, power, and great accomplishments. This purpose was based on pride and rebellion against God. God destroyed this effort by multiplying languages so that some could no longer communicate with others (v. 7). This explains the diversity of race and language in the world. At this time the human race turned from God to idolatry, sorcery, and astrology (cf. Is. 47:12; see Ex. 22:18, note; Deut. 18:10, note). The spiritual condition of humans is described in Rom. 1:21–28. As a result, God gave them up to the impurity of their own hearts (Rom. 1:24,26,28), and He turned to Abram to begin a way of salvation for humanity (see v. 31, note).

TABLE OF NATIONS

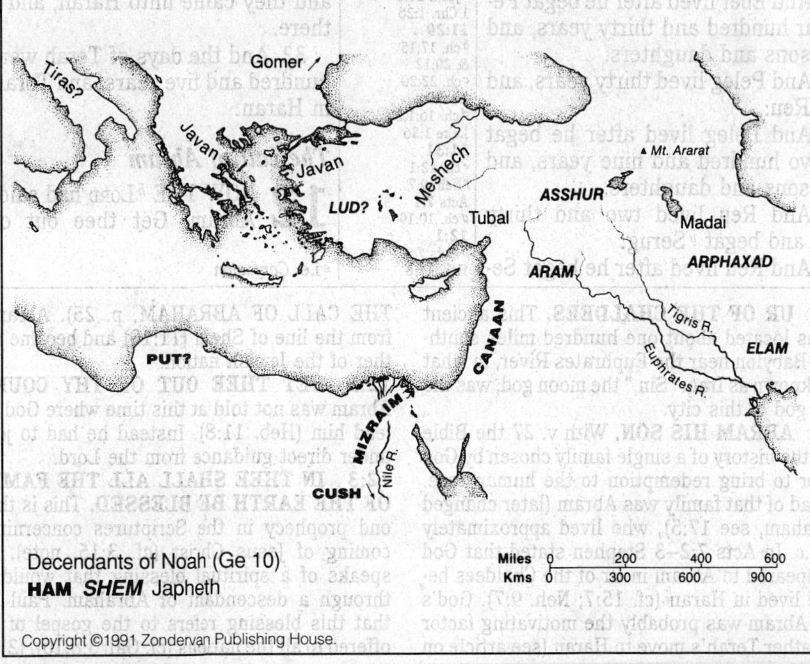

[q]not understand one another's
speech.
8 So [r]the LORD scattered them
abroad from thence [s]upon the face of
all the earth: and they left off to build
the city.
9 Therefore is the name of it called
[s]Babel; [t]because the LORD did there
confound the language of all the earth:
and from thence did the LORD scatter
them abroad upon the face of all the
earth.

The descendants of Shem

11:10–27pp — Gen. 10:21–31; 1 Chr. 1:17–27

10 ¶ [u]These *are* the generations of
Shem: Shem *was* an hundred years old,
and begat Arphaxad two years after
the flood:
11 And Shem lived after he begat
Arphaxad five hundred years, and be-
gat sons and daughters.
12 And Arphaxad lived five and
thirty years, [v]and begat Salah:
13 And Arphaxad lived after he be-
gat Salah four hundred and three
years, and begat sons and daughters.
14 And Salah lived thirty years, and
begat Eber:
15 And Salah lived after he begat
Eber four hundred and three years, and
begat sons and daughters.
16 [w]And Eber lived four and thirty
years, and begat [x]Peleg:
17 And Eber lived after he begat Pe-
leg four hundred and thirty years, and
begat sons and daughters.
18 And Peleg lived thirty years, and
begat Reu:
19 And Peleg lived after he begat
Reu two hundred and nine years, and
begat sons and daughters.
20 And Reu lived two and thirty
years, and begat [y]Serug:
21 And Reu lived after he begat Se-

11:7 [q]ch. 42:23 1 Cor. 14:2,11
11:8 [r]Luke 1:51 [s]ch. 10:25,32
11:9 [t]1 Cor. 14:23
11:10 [u]ch. 10:22 1 Chr. 1:17
11:12 [v]See Luke 3:36
11:16 [w]1 Chr. 1:19 [x]Called, Luke 3:35, *Phalec*
11:20 [y]Luke 3:35, *Saruch*
11:24 [z]Luke 3:34, *Thara*
11:26 [a]Josh. 24:2 1 Chr. 1:26
11:29 [b]ch. 17:15 & 20:12 [c]ch. 22:20
11:30 [d]ch. 16:1,2 Luke 1:36
11:31 [e]ch. 12:1 [f]Neh. 9:7 Acts 7:4 [g]ch. 10:19
12:1 [h]Acts 7:3 Heb. 11:8

rug two hundred and seven years, and
begat sons and daughters.
22 And Serug lived thirty years, and
begat Nahor:
23 And Serug lived after he begat
Nahor two hundred years, and begat
sons and daughters.
24 And Nahor lived nine and twenty
years, and begat [z]Terah:
25 And Nahor lived after he begat
Terah an hundred and nineteen years,
and begat sons and daughters.
26 And Terah lived seventy years,
and [a]begat Abram, Nahor, and Haran.
27 ¶ Now these *are* the generations
of Terah: Terah begat Abram, Nahor,
and Haran; and Haran begat Lot.
28 And Haran died before his father
Terah in the land of his nativity, in Ur
of the Chaldees.
29 And Abram and Nahor took them
wives: the name of Abram's wife *was*
[b]Sarai; and the name of Nahor's wife,
[c]Milcah, the daughter of Haran, the
father of Milcah, and the father of Is-
cah.
30 But [d]Sarai was barren; she *had*
no child.
31 And Terah [e]took Abram his
son, and Lot the son of Haran his son's
son, and Sarai his daughter-in-law,
his son Abram's wife; and they went
forth with them from [f]Ur of the Chal-
dees, to go into [g]the land of Canaan;
and they came unto Haran, and dwelt
there.
32 And the days of Terah were two
hundred and five years: and Terah died
in Haran.

The call of Abram

12 NOW THE [h]LORD had said unto
Abram, Get thee out of thy

[s]i.e. *Confusion*

11:28 UR OF THE CHALDEES. This ancient city was located about one hundred miles southeast of Babylon near the Euphrates River, in what is now known as Iraq. "Sin," the moon god, was the patron god of this city.

11:31 ABRAM HIS SON. With v. 27 the Bible begins the history of a single family chosen by God in order to bring redemption to the human race. The head of that family was Abram (later changed to Abraham, see 17:5), who lived approximately 2100 B.C. In Acts 7:2–3 Stephen stated that God first appeared to Abram in Ur of the Chaldees before he lived in Haran (cf. 15:7; Neh. 9:7). God's call to Abram was probably the motivating factor in his father Terah's move to Haran (see article on THE CALL OF ABRAHAM, p. 25). Abram was from the line of Shem (11:10) and became the father of the Jewish nation.

12:1 GET THEE OUT OF THY COUNTRY. Abram was not told at this time where God would lead him (Heb. 11:8). Instead he had to journey under direct guidance from the Lord.

12:3 IN THEE SHALL ALL THE FAMILIES OF THE EARTH BE BLESSED. This is the second prophecy in the Scriptures concerning the coming of Jesus Christ (cf. 3:15, note). (1) It speaks of a spiritual blessing that would come through a descendant of Abraham. Paul states that this blessing refers to the gospel of Christ offered to all the nations (cf. Gal. 3:8,16). (2) God's

THE CALL OF ABRAHAM

Gen. 12:1–3 "Now the LORD had said unto Abram, Get thee out of thy country, and from thy kindred, and from thy father's house, unto a land that I will show thee: And I will make of thee a great nation, and I will bless thee, and make thy name great; and thou shalt be a blessing: And I will bless them that bless thee, and curse him that curseth thee: and in thee shall all families of the earth be blessed."

The call of Abram as recorded in Gen. 12 (later Abraham, see Gen. 17:5) begins a new chapter in the O.T. revelation of God's purpose to redeem and save humanity. God intended to have a man who would know and serve Him with devoted faith. From this man would come a family who would know, teach, and keep the ways of the Lord (see Gen. 18:19, note). From this family would come forth a chosen nation of people who would be separated from the ungodly ways of other nations to do God's will. From this nation would come Jesus Christ, the Savior of the world, the promised seed of the woman (see Gen. 3:15, note; Gal. 3:8,16,18). Several important principles can be deduced from Abraham's call.

(1) Abraham's call involved separating himself from his country, his kinsmen, and his father's house (Gen 12:1) in order to become a stranger and pilgrim upon the earth (Heb. 11:13). In Abraham God was establishing the important principle that His people were to separate themselves from all that hinders His purpose for their lives (see articles on SPIRITUAL SEPARATION FOR BELIEVERS, p. 1814, and THE CHRISTIAN'S RELATIONSHIP TO THE WORLD, p. 2004).

(2) God promised Abraham a land, a great nation through his descendants, and a blessing that would affect all the nations of the earth (Gen.12:2–3). The N.T. clearly teaches that the last element of this promise is being fulfilled in the missionary proclamation of the gospel of Christ (Acts 3:25; Gal. 3:8).

(3) Moreover, Abraham's call involved not only an earthly land, but also a heavenly one. His vision came to encompass an ultimate home no longer on earth but in heaven, and a city whose builder and maker was God Himself. Abraham henceforth desired and sought a heavenly country where he would dwell forever with his God in righteousness, joy, and peace (see Heb. 11:9–10,14–16; cf. Rev. 21:1–4; 22:1–5). Until then he would be a stranger and pilgrim upon the earth (Heb. 11:9,13).

(4) The call of Abraham contained not only promises, but also obligations. God required both obedience from Abraham and personal commitment to Him as Lord in order to receive what was promised. Obedience and commitment entailed: (a) trust in God's word, even when the realization of the promises appeared humanly impossible (Gen. 15:1–6; 18:10–14), (b) obedience to God's command to leave his home (Gen. 12:4; Heb. 11:8), and (c) a sincere endeavor to live a righteous life (Gen. 17:1–2).

(5) God's promise to and blessing upon Abraham extend not only to his physical descendants (i.e., believing Jews), but also to all who in true faith (Gen. 12:3) embrace and follow Jesus Christ, the true "seed" of Abraham (see Gal. 3:14,16). All who possess faith like Abraham's are "children of Abraham" (Gal. 3:7) and are blessed with him (Gal. 3:9). They become Abraham's offspring, heirs according to promise (Gal. 3:29), which includes "the promise of the Spirit through faith" in Christ Jesus (see Gal. 3:14, note).

(6) Because Abraham possessed a faith in God that expressed itself in obedience, he is declared a foremost example of true saving faith (cf. Gen. 15:6; Rom. 4:1–5,16–24; Gal. 3:6–9; Heb. 11:8–19; Jas. 2:21–23; see Gen. 15:6, note). Biblically, any profession of faith in Jesus Christ as Savior that does not involve obedience to Him as Lord is not the kind of faith Abraham possessed and hence is not true saving faith (see John 3:36, note; see article on FAITH AND GRACE, p. 1738).

country, and from thy kindred, and
from thy father's house, unto a land
that I will show thee:
2 [i]And I will make of thee a great
nation, [j]and I will bless thee, and
make thy name great; [k]and thou shalt
be a blessing:
3 [l]And I will bless them that bless
thee, and curse him that curseth thee:
Ex. 12:29-42 [m]and in thee shall all families of the
earth be blessed.
4 So Abram departed, as the LORD
had spoken unto him; and Lot went
with him: and Abram *was* seventy and
five years old when he departed out of
Haran.
5 And Abram took Sarai his wife,
and Lot his brother's son, and all their
substance that they had gathered, and
[n]the souls that they had gotten [o]in
Haran; and they went forth to go into
the land of Canaan; and into the land
of Canaan they came.
6 ¶ And Abram [p]passed through
the land unto the place of Sichem,
[q]unto the plain of Moreh. [r]And the
Canaanite *was* then in the land.
7 [s]And the LORD appeared unto
Abram, and said, [t]Unto thy seed will
I give this land: and there builded he an
[u]altar unto the LORD, who appeared
unto him.

12:2 [i]ch. 17:6 & 18:18 Deut. 26:5 1 Ki. 3:8 [j]ch. 24:35 [k]ch:28:4 Gal. 3:14
12:3 [l]ch. 27:29 Ex. 23:22 Num. 24:9 [m]ch. 18:18 & 22:18 & 26:4 Ps. 72:17 Acts 3:25 Gal. 3:8
12:5 [n]ch. 14:14 [o]ch. 11:31
12:6 [p]Heb. 11:9 [q]Deut. 11:30 Judg. 7:1 [r]ch. 10:18,19
12:7 [s]ch. 17:1 [t]ch. 13:15 & 17:8 Ps. 105:9,11 [u]ch. 13:4
12:8 [v]ch. 13:4
12:9 [w]ch. 13:3
12:10 [x]ch. 26:1 [y]Ps. 105:13 [z]ch. 43:1
12:11 [a]ver. 14 ch. 26:7
12:12 [b]ch. 20:11 & 26:7
12:13 [c]ch. 20:5,13

8 And he removed from thence unto
a mountain on the east of Beth-el, and
pitched his tent, *having* Beth-el on the
west, and Hai on the east: and there he
builded an altar unto the LORD, and
[v]called upon the name of the LORD.
9 And Abram journeyed, [w]going[t]
on still toward the south.

Abram goes to Egypt

12:10–20Ref — Gen. 20:1–18; 26:1–11

10 ¶ And there was [x]a famine in
the land: and Abram [y]went down into
Egypt to sojourn there; for the famine
was [z]grievous in the land.
11 And it came to pass, when he
was come near to enter into Egypt, that
he said unto Sarai his wife, Behold
now, I know that thou *art* [a]a fair wom-
an to look upon:
12 Therefore it shall come to pass,
when the Egyptians shall see thee,
that they shall say, This *is* his wife: and
they [b]will kill me, but they will save
thee alive.
13 [c]Say, I pray thee, thou *art* my
sister: that it may be well with me for
thy sake; and my soul shall live be-
cause of thee.
14 ¶ And it came to pass, that, when

[t] Heb. *in going and journeying*

promise to Abram reveals that from the very beginning the purpose of the gospel was to bless all the nations with salvation and goodness. God is now accomplishing this purpose through Jesus Christ and His faithful people who share His burden by sending forth preachers who proclaim the gospel to all the families of the earth. This verse, in other words, serves as a foundation for mission work throughout the world (see article on THE CALL OF ABRAHAM, p. 25).

12:4 ABRAM DEPARTED, AS THE LORD HAD SPOKEN. The narrative from the very beginning emphasizes the truth that obedience to God is essential to a saving relationship with Him. (1) Abram obeyed the word of the Lord. His obedience included leaving his home and country and trusting in God's care, guidance, and promises (see v. 1, note; Jas. 2:17, note; 1 John 2:4, note). (2) Like Abram, all believers in Christ are called to leave their "country . . . kindred, and . . . father's house" (12:1) to follow Jesus in the sense of seeking "a better country, that is, an heavenly" (Heb. 11:16; see article on THE CALL OF ABRAHAM, p. 25).

12:7 THE LORD APPEARED UNTO ABRAM. This is the first time Scripture explicitly states that God "appeared" to someone, though it is reasonable to assume that God had already appeared to Adam and others (cf. 2:15–16,22; 3:8). That this appearance was an objective, visible manifestation of God in the likeness of a human being is indicated in 18:1–3,9–33 (cf. Ex. 33:18–23). Visible appearances of the Lord are called "theophanies"—i.e., God-manifestations (see Ex. 3:2, note). The land that God promised to give to Abram was the land of Canaan (the ancient name for Palestine), along the southeast coast of the Mediterranean Sea.

12:10 A FAMINE IN THE LAND. Obedience to God does not mean that we will never encounter serious problems and trials. (1) Abram had barely arrived at his destination when he faced bitter disappointment. His problems included a barren wife (11:30), separation from his family (12:1), and a famine that was bringing him to starvation and driving him from the land. (2) As Abram's example teaches, believers who are seeking to serve God and obey His word must not think it strange if they encounter great obstacles, hardships, and problems. It is often God's way with those whom He has called to obey Him. In such cases we must go forward with obedience and trust that God is still working on our behalf to accomplish His purpose (see Mat. 2:13, note).

12:13 SAY . . . THOU *ART* MY SISTER. Abram's trust in God momentarily failed, resulting in sinful deception and shameful deportation from Egypt (12:19—13:1). These verses show how honest God's Word is regarding the saints. Although Abram repented, his moral failure was not covered up. Such failure solemnly reminds all believers to

Abram was come into Egypt, the Egyp-
tians beheld the woman that she *was*
very fair.
15 The princes also of Pharaoh saw
her, and commended her before Phar-
aoh: and the woman was taken into
Pharaoh's house.
16 And he [d]entreated Abram well
for her sake: and he had sheep, and
oxen, and he asses, and menservants,
and maidservants, and she asses, and
camels.
17 And the LORD [e]plagued Pharaoh
and his house with great plagues be-
cause of Sarai Abram's wife.
18 And Pharaoh called Abram, and
said, [f]What *is* this *that* thou hast done
unto me? why didst thou not tell me
that she *was* thy wife?
19 Why saidst thou, She *is* my sis-
ter? so I might have taken her to me to
wife: now therefore behold thy wife,
take *her*, and go thy way.
20 [g]And Pharaoh commanded *his*
men concerning him: and they sent him
away, and his wife, and all that he had.

Abram and Lot part

13 AND ABRAM went up out of
Egypt, he, and his wife, and all
that he had, and Lot with him, [h]into
the south.
2 [i]And Abram *was* very rich in cat-
tle, in silver, and in gold.
3 And he went on his journeys
[j]from the south even to Beth-el, unto
the place where his tent had been at
the beginning, between Beth-el and
Hai;
4 Unto the [k]place of the altar,
which he had made there at the first:
and there Abram [l]called on the name
of the LORD.
5 ¶ And Lot also, which went with
Abram, had flocks, and herds, and
tents.
6 And [m]the land was not able to
bear them, that they might dwell to-
gether: for their substance was great,
so that they could not dwell together.
7 And there was [n]a strife between
the herdmen of Abram's cattle and the
herdmen of Lot's cattle: [o]and the Ca-
naanite and the Perizzite dwelled then
in the land.
8 And Abram said unto Lot, [p]Let
there be no strife, I pray thee, between
me and thee, and between my herdmen
and thy herdmen; for we *be* [q]breth-
ren.[u]
9 [r]*Is* not the whole land before
thee? separate thyself, I pray thee,
from me: [s]if *thou wilt take* the left
hand, then I will go to the right; or if
thou depart to the right hand, then I will
go to the left.
10 And Lot lifted up his eyes, and
beheld all [t]the plain of Jordan, that it
was well watered every where, before
the LORD [u]destroyed Sodom and Go-
morrah, [v]*even* as the garden of the
LORD, like the land of Egypt, as thou
comest unto [w]Zoar.
11 Then Lot chose him all the plain
of Jordan; and Lot journeyed east: and
they separated themselves the one
from the other.
12 Abram dwelled in the land of Ca-
naan, and Lot [x]dwelled in the cities of
the plain, and [y]pitched *his* tent toward
Sodom.
13 But the men of Sodom [z]*were*
wicked and [a]sinners before the LORD
exceedingly.
14 ¶ And the LORD said unto Abram,
after that Lot [b]was separated from
him, Lift up now thine eyes, and look

12:16 [d]ch. 20:14
12:17 [e]ch. 20:18; 1 Chr. 16:21; Ps. 105:14
12:18 [f]ch. 20:9 & 26:10
12:20 [g]Prov. 21:1
13:1 [h]ch. 12:9
13:2 [i]ch. 24:35; Ps. 112:3; Prov. 10:22
13:3 [j]ch. 12:8,9
13:4 [k]ch. 12:7,8 [l]Ps. 116:17
13:6 [m]ch. 36:7
13:7 [n]ch. 26:20 [o]ch. 12:6
13:8 [p]1 Cor. 6:7 [q]See ch. 11:27,31
13:9 [r]ch. 20:15 & 34:10 [s]Rom. 12:18
13:10 [t]ch. 19:17 [u]ch. 19:24 [v]ch. 2:10; Is. 51:3 [w]ch. 14:2,8 & 19:22
13:12 [x]ch. 19:29 [y]ch. 14:12 & 19:1
13:13 [z]ch. 18:20; 2 Pet. 2:7 [a]ch. 6:11
13:14 [b]ver. 11

[u] Heb. *men brethren*

look not at circumstances but at the promises and faithfulness of God. His failure also encourages us in that it reveals how God in mercy worked to bring Abram back into His will and purpose.

13:10 LOT LIFTED UP HIS EYES. Scripture states that "*the LORD seeth* not as man seeth" (1 Sam. 16:7). Lot saw only the well-watered valley. God saw the people of Sodom who were "wicked . . . exceedingly" (v. 13). Lot's failure to discern and abhor evil brought death and tragedy to his family (see next note).

13:12 PITCHED *HIS* TENT TOWARD SODOM. Lot's great failure was that he loved personal gain more than he hated the wickedness of Sodom (vv. 10–13). (1) If he had loved righteousness sufficiently (see Heb. 1:9, note), it would have caused him to remain separate from the wicked ways of sinful people. Instead he tolerated evil and chose to live in wicked Sodom (v. 13). Perhaps he reasoned that the material advantages, culture, and pleasures of Sodom outweighed the dangers, and that he was strong enough spiritually to remain faithful to God. Thus, he exposed himself and his family to the immorality and ungodliness of Sodom, only to learn the bitter lesson that his family was not strong enough to resist its evil influences (see 19:24–26,30–38). (2) Parents must be careful not to place themselves or their children in any "Sodom," lest they come to spiritual ruin as did the family of Lot.

from the place where thou art [c]northward, and southward, and eastward, and westward:

15 For all the land which thou seest, [d]to thee will I give it, and [e]to thy seed for ever.

16 And [f]I will make thy seed as the dust of the earth: so that if a man can number the dust of the earth, *then* shall thy seed also be numbered.

17 Arise, walk through the land in the length of it and in the breadth of it; for I will give it unto thee.

18 Then Abram removed *his* tent, and came and [g]dwelt in the [v]plain of Mamre, [h]which *is* in Hebron, and built there an altar unto the LORD.

The wars of the kings

14 AND IT came to pass in the days of Amraphel king [i]of Shinar, Arioch king of Ellasar, Chedorlaomer king of [j]Elam, and Tidal king of nations;

2 *That these* made war with Bera king of Sodom, and with Birsha king of Gomorrah, Shinab king of [k]Admah, and Shemeber king of Zeboiim, and the king of Bela, which is [l]Zoar.

3 All these were joined together in the vale of Siddim, [m]which is the salt sea.

4 Twelve years [n]they served Chedorlaomer, and in the thirteenth year they rebelled.

5 And in the fourteenth year came Chedorlaomer, and the kings that *were* with him, and smote [o]the Rephaims in Ashteroth Karnaim, and [p]the Zuzims in Ham, [q]and the Emims in [w]Shaveh Kiriathaim,

6 [r]And the Horites in their mount Seir, unto [x]El-paran, which *is* by the wilderness.

7 And they returned, and came to En-mishpat, which *is* Kadesh, and smote all the country of the Amalekites, and also the Amorites, that dwelt [s]in Hazezon-tamar.

8 And there went out the king of Sodom, and the king of Gomorrah, and the king of Admah, and the king of Zeboiim, and the king of Bela (the same *is* Zoar;) and they joined battle with them in the vale of Siddim;

9 With Chedorlaomer the king of Elam, and with Tidal king of nations, and Amraphel king of Shinar, and Arioch king of Ellasar; four kings with five.

10 And the vale of Siddim *was full of* [t]slimepits; and the kings of Sodom and Gomorrah fled, and fell there; and they that remained fled [u]to the mountain.

11 And they took [v]all the goods of Sodom and Gomorrah, and all their victuals, and went their way.

12 And they took Lot, Abram's [w]brother's son, [x]who dwelt in Sodom, and his goods, and departed.

13 ¶ And there came one that had escaped, and told Abram the Hebrew; for [y]he dwelt in the plain of Mamre the Amorite, brother of Eshcol, and brother of Aner: [z]and these *were* confederate with Abram.

14 And when Abram heard that [a]his brother was taken captive, he [y]armed his [z]trained *servants,* [b]born in his own house, three hundred and eighteen, and pursued *them* [c]unto Dan.

15 And he divided himself against them, he and his servants, by night, and [d]smote them, and pursued them unto Hobah, which *is* on the left hand of Damascus.

16 And he brought back all the goods, and also brought again his brother Lot, and his goods, and the women also, and the people.

Melchizedek blesses Abram

17 ¶ And the king of Sodom [e]went out to meet him [f]after his return from the slaughter of Chedorlaomer, and of the kings that *were* with him, at the valley of Shaveh, which *is* the [g]king's dale.

18 And [h]Melchizedek king of Sa-

13:14 [c]ch. 28:14
13:15 [d]ch. 12:7 & 15:18 Deut. 34:4 Acts 7:5 [e]2 Chr. 20:7 Ps. 37:22
13:16 [f]ch. 22:17 Ex. 32:13
13:18 [g]ch. 14:13 [h]ch. 35:27
14:1 [i]ch. 10:10 & 11:2 [j]Is. 11:11
14:2 [k]Deut. 29:23 [l]ch. 19:22
14:3 [m]Num. 34:12 Deut. 3:17 Josh. 3:16
14:4 [n]ch. 9:26
14:5 [o]ch. 15:20 [p]Deut. 2:20 [q]Deut. 2:10
14:6 [r]Deut. 2:12,22
14:7 [s]2 Chr. 20:2
14:10 [t]ch. 11:3 [u]ch. 19:17,30
14:11 [v]ver. 16,21
14:12 [w]ch. 12:5 [x]ch. 13:12
14:13 [y]ch. 13:18 [z]ver. 24
14:14 [a]ch. 13:8 [b]ch. 15:3 [c]Deut. 34:1
14:15 [d]Is. 41:2,3
14:17 [e]1 Sam. 18:6 [f]Heb. 7:1 [g]2 Sam. 18:18
14:18 [h]Heb. 7:1

[v] Heb. *plains* [w] Or, *The plain of Kiriathaim* [x] Or, *The plain of Paran* [y] Or, *led forth* [z] Or, *instructed*

14:13 ABRAM THE HEBREW. The term "Hebrew" may have initially referred to any people who wandered from place to place, crossing over lands and property as nomads. It later came to refer specifically to Abraham and his descendants (cf. Ex. 3:18; 5:3).

14:14 HE ARMED HIS TRAINED *SERVANTS*. Abram was not a solitary nomad but a wealthy leader of a large clan. His 318 armed men shows that he probably had a total company of about one thousand.

14:18 MELCHIZEDEK KING OF SALEM. Melchizedek (meaning "king of righteousness") was both "king of Salem" (possibly ancient Jerusa-

lem brought forth bread and wine: and he *was* [i]the priest of [j]the most high God.

19 And he blessed him, and said, [k]Blessed *be* Abram of the most high God, [l]possessor of heaven and earth:

20 And [m]blessed be the most high God, which hath delivered thine enemies into thy hand. And he gave him tithes [n]of all.

21 And the king of Sodom said unto Abram, Give me the [a]persons, and take the goods to thyself.

22 And Abram said to the king of Sodom, I [o]have lift up mine hand unto the LORD, the most high God, [p]the possessor of heaven and earth,

23 That [q]I will not *take* from a thread even to a shoelatchet, and that I will not take any thing that *is* thine, lest thou shouldest say, I have made Abram rich:

24 Save only that which the young men have eaten, and the portion of the men which went with me, Aner, Eshcol, and Mamre; let them take their portion.

The covenant with Abram

15 AFTER THESE things the word of the LORD came unto Abram [r]in a vision, saying, [s]Fear not, Abram: I *am* thy [t]shield, *and* thy exceeding [u]great reward.

2 And Abram said, Lord GOD, what wilt thou give me, [v]seeing I go childless, and the steward of my house *is* this Eliezer of Damascus?

3 And Abram said, Behold, to me thou hast given no seed: and, lo, [w]one born in my house is mine heir.

4 And, behold, the word of the LORD *came* unto him, saying, This shall not be thine heir; but he that [x]shall come forth out of thine own bowels shall be thine heir.

5 And he brought him forth abroad, and said, Look now toward heaven, and [y]tell the [z]stars, if thou be able to number them: and he said unto him, [a]So shall thy seed be.

6 And he [b]believed in the LORD; and he [c]counted it to him for righteousness.

Gen. 22:1-14

7 And he said unto him, I *am* the LORD that [d]brought thee out of [e]Ur of the Chaldees, [f]to give thee this land to inherit it.

8 And he said, Lord GOD, [g]whereby shall I know that I shall inherit it?

9 And he said unto him, Take me an heifer of three years old, and a she goat of three years old, and a ram of three years old, and a turtledove, and a young pigeon.

10 And he took unto him all these,

[a] Heb. *souls*

14:18 [i]Ps. 110:4 Heb. 5:6 [j]Acts 16:17
14:19 [k]Ruth 3:10 [l]ver. 22
14:20 [m]ch. 24:27 [n]Heb. 7:4
14:22 [o]Dan. 12:7 [p]ver. 19
14:23 [q]See Esth. 9:15, 16
15:1 [r]Dan. 10:1 [s]ch. 26:24 Dan. 10:12 [t]Ps. 3:3 & 84:11 & 91:4 [u]Prov. 11:18
15:2 [v]Acts 7:5
15:3 [w]ch. 14:14
15:4 [x]2 Sam. 7:12
15:5 [y]Ps. 147:4 [z]Jer. 33:22 [a]Ex. 32:13 Heb. 11:12
15:6 [b]Rom. 4:3,9,22 Gal. 3:6 [c]Ps. 106:31
15:7 [d]ch. 12:1 [e]ch. 11:28,31 [f]Ps. 105:42,44
15:8 [g]See ch. 24:13,14 1 Sam. 14:9,10

---

lem) and "priest of the most high God." He served the one true God as did Abram. Melchizedek was a Canaanite, and thus, like Job, an example of a godly non-Israelite. Melchizedek is a type or figure of the royalty and eternal priesthood of Jesus Christ (cf. Ps. 110:4; see Heb. 7:1,3, notes).

14:20 HE GAVE HIM TITHES OF ALL. Abram gave Melchizedek a tenth of the spoils he had retrieved (cf. Heb. 7:4) in gratitude for the help and grace of God. This is the first time tithing is mentioned in the Bible.

14:23 I WILL NOT TAKE ANY THING THAT *IS* THINE. Abram's refusal to take the riches of the Canaanites reveals his dependence on God and on His blessing alone (v. 19; see Mat. 14:19, note).

15:1 THY SHIELD, *AND* . . . GREAT REWARD. After his battle with the kings, Abram became troubled and fearful. Thus God reassured him in a vision that He was Abram's shield and reward. Abram responded to these comforting words by recalling that he had no children and thus no heir (v. 2), so he suggested that he adopt one of his servants to become his heir. God rejected the idea, promising Abram that he would father a son with his barren wife Sarai (cf. 11:30) and have countless descendants. The incredible thing—and Abram's greatness—is that he believed God. It is this faith in God which was counted for righteousness (see next note).

15:6 HE BELIEVED . . . HE COUNTED IT TO HIM FOR RIGHTEOUSNESS. For the first time faith and righteousness are mentioned together in Scripture. (1) In the O.T., faith had a twofold designation: (a) "trust in" or "reliance upon," and (b) "fidelity to" or "faithfulness." Thus, "believe" (Heb. *'aman*) means to persevere in trust and belief by manifesting an obedient faithfulness. This was the kind of faith Abram possessed. His heart was turned toward God in an enduring trust, obedience, and submission.

(2) God saw Abram's heart-attitude of faith and counted it as righteousness. The term "righteousness" means being in a right relationship to God and His will (cf. 6:9; Job 15:14–16). Furthermore, God entered into covenant fellowship with Abram, whereby he received God as his shield and reward (v. 1), many descendants (v. 5), and the promise of the land (v. 7; see article on GOD'S COVENANT WITH ABRAHAM, ISAAC, AND JACOB, p. 48).

(3) Under the new covenant, God's blessing, a right relationship with Him, and fellowship with Him also come through faith. This is a foundational truth in the N.T. (Rom. 4:3; Gal. 3:6; Jas. 2:23; see article on FAITH AND GRACE, p. 1738). As such Abraham is the "father of all them that believe" (Rom. 4:11).

and [h]divided them in the midst, and laid each piece one against another: but [i]the birds divided he not.

11 And when the fowls came down upon the carcases, Abram drove them away.

12 And when the sun was going down, [j]a deep sleep fell upon Abram; and, lo, an horror of great darkness fell upon him.

13 And he said unto Abram, Know of a surety [k]that thy seed shall be a stranger in a land *that is* not theirs, and shall serve them; and [l]they shall afflict them four hundred years;

14 And also that nation, whom they shall serve, [m]will I judge: and afterward [n]shall they come out with great substance.

15 And [o]thou shalt go [p]to thy fathers in peace; [q]thou shalt be buried in a good old age.

16 But [r]in the fourth generation they shall come hither again: for the iniquity [s]of the Amorites [t]*is* not yet full.

17 And it came to pass, that, when the sun went down, and it was dark, behold a smoking furnace, and [b]a burning lamp that passed between those pieces.

18 In the same day the LORD [u]made a covenant with Abram, saying, [v]Unto thy seed have I given this land, from the river of Egypt unto the great river, the river Euphrates:

19 The Kenites, and the Kenizzites, and the Kadmonites,

20 And the Hittites, and the Perizzites, and the Rephaims,

21 And the Amorites, and the Canaanites, and the Girgashites, and the Jebusites.

Hagar and Ishmael

16 NOW SARAI Abram's wife [w]bare him no children: and she had an handmaid, [x]an Egyptian, whose name *was* [y]Hagar.

2 [z]And Sarai said unto Abram, Behold now, the LORD [a]hath restrained me from bearing: I pray thee, [b]go in unto my maid; it may be that I may [c]obtain children by her. And Abram [c]hearkened to the voice of Sarai.

3 And Sarai Abram's wife took Hagar her maid the Egyptian, after Abram [d]had dwelt ten years in the land of Canaan, and gave her to her husband Abram to be his wife.

4 ¶ And he went in unto Hagar, and she conceived: and when she saw that she had conceived, her mistress was [e]despised in her eyes.

5 And Sarai said unto Abram, My wrong *be* upon thee: I have given my maid into thy bosom; and when she saw that she had conceived, I was despised in her eyes: [f]the LORD judge between me and thee.

6 [g]But Abram said unto Sarai, Behold, thy maid *is* in thy hand; do to her [d]as it pleaseth thee. And when Sarai [e]dealt hardly with her, [h]she fled from her face.

7 ¶ And the angel of the LORD found

15:10 [h]Jer. 34:18 [i]Lev. 1:17 **15:12** [j]ch. 2:21 **15:13** [k]Ex. 1:11 Acts 7:6 [l]Ex. 12:40 **15:14** [m]Ex. 6:6 [n]Ex. 12:36 **15:15** [o]Job 5:26 [p]Acts 13:36 [q]ch. 25:8 **15:16** [r]Ex. 12:41 [s]1 Ki. 21:26 [t]Mat. 23:32 **15:18** [u]ch. 24:7 [v]ch. 12:7 Ex. 23:31 Num. 34:3 Deut. 11:24 Josh. 1:4

16:1 [w]ch. 15:2,3 [x]ch. 21:9 [y]Gal. 4:24 **16:2** [z]ch. 30:3 [a]ch. 20:18 [b]ch. 30:3,9 [c]ch. 3:17 **16:3** [d]ch. 12:5 **16:4** [e]Prov. 30:21,23 **16:5** [f]ch. 31:53 **16:6** [g]1 Pet. 3:7 [h]Ex. 2:15

b Heb. *a lamp of fire* c Heb. *be builded by her*
d Heb. that which is *good in thine eyes*
e Heb. *afflicted her*

15:13 A LAND THAT IS NOT THEIRS. God told Abram that his descendants would go into Egypt and be oppressed for four hundred years. This figure is a round number for the actual 430 years (cf. Ex. 12:40).

15:18 THE LORD MADE A COVENANT WITH ABRAM. The making of a covenant is described in vv. 9–17. (1) It consisted in taking slaughtered animals, cutting them in half, and the halves separated and placed opposite each other (v. 10). After this the two parties entering into the agreement would walk between the two halves of the slain animal, symbolizing that if they did not keep the promises of the covenant, they would perish just like the slain animals (v. 17; cf. Jer. 34:18). The "smoking furnace, and a burning lamp" represented God's presence (v. 17; cf. Ex. 3:2; 14:24).

(2) Note that although a covenant usually established responsibilities for both parties (cf. 17:9–14), in this instance only God passed between the pieces of the animal (v. 17). God alone established the promises and obligations of the covenant; Abram had only to accept them in obedient faith (see 17:2, note).

16:2 THE LORD HATH RESTRAINED ME FROM BEARING. It was customary among the people of Mesopotamia for a barren wife to have her handmaid provide children. Such children were considered as belonging to the wife. (1) Regardless of this custom, Abram and Sarai's attempt to provide a way for God to bring a child into the family through Abram's union with Hagar was not God's way (cf. 2:24). (2) The N.T. likens Hagar's son to the product of human effort—"after the flesh" and not "after the Spirit" (Gal. 4:29). In other words, it is never right to attempt to accomplish God's purpose in ways not according to the Spirit, patient hope, and fervent prayer.

16:7 THE ANGEL OF THE LORD. As this story progresses, the "angel of the LORD" is revealed to be God Himself speaking to Hagar (v. 13; cf. 18:1; Judg. 6:12,14).

her by a fountain of water in the wilder-
ness, [i]by the fountain in the way to
[j]Shur.
8 And he said, Hagar, Sarai's maid,
whence camest thou? and whither wilt
thou go? And she said, I flee from the
face of my mistress Sarai.
9 And the angel of the LORD said
unto her, Return to thy mistress, and
[k]submit thyself under her hands.
10 And the angel of the LORD said
unto her, [l]I will multiply thy seed ex-
ceedingly, that it shall not be num-
bered for multitude.
11 And the angel of the LORD said
unto her, Behold, thou *art* with child,
and shalt bear a son, [m]and shalt call
his name [f]Ishmael; because the LORD
hath heard thy affliction.
12 [n]And he will be a wild man; his
hand *will be* against every man, and ev-
ery man's hand against him; [o]and he
shall dwell in the presence of all his
brethren.
13 And she called the name of the
LORD that spake unto her, Thou God
seest me: for she said, Have I also here
looked after him [p]that seeth me?
14 Wherefore the well was called
[q]Beer-lahai-roi;[g] behold, *it is* [r]be-
tween Kadesh and Bered.
15 ¶ And [s]Hagar bare Abram a
son: and Abram called his son's name,
which Hagar bare, Ishmael.

16:7 [i]ch. 25:18 [j]Ex. 15:22 **16:9** [k]Tit. 2:9 **16:10** [l]ch. 17:20 **16:11** [m]Luke 1:13,31 **16:12** [n]ch. 21:20 [o]ch. 25:18 **16:13** [p]ch. 31:42 **16:14** [q]ch. 24:62 [r]Num. 13:26 **16:15** [s]Gal. 4:22
17:1 [t]ch. 28:3 Ex. 6:3 [u]2 Ki. 20:3 [v]Deut. 18:13 **17:2** [w]ch. 12:2 **17:4** [x]Rom. 4:11,12,16 **17:5** [y]Neh. 9:7 [z]Rom. 4:17 **17:6** [a]ch. 35:11 [b]Mat. 1:6 **17:7** [c]Gal. 3:17

16 And Abram *was* fourscore and
six years old, when Hagar bare Ishma-
el to Abram.

The covenant of circumcision

17 AND WHEN Abram was ninety
years old and nine, the LORD ap-
peared to Abram, and said unto him,
[t]I *am* the Almighty God; [u]walk be-
fore me, and be thou [v]perfect.[h]
2 And I will make my covenant be-
tween me and thee, and [w]will multiply
thee exceedingly. Gen. 26:2-5
3 And Abram fell on his face: and
God talked with him, saying,
4 As for me, behold, my covenant *is*
with thee, and thou shalt be [x]a father
of [i]many nations.
5 Neither shall thy name any more
be called Abram, but [y]thy name shall
be [j]Abraham; [z]for a father of many
nations have I made thee.
6 And I will make thee exceeding
fruitful, and I will make [a]nations of
thee, and [b]kings shall come out of
thee.
7 And I will [c]establish my cov-
enant between me and thee and thy
seed after thee in their generations for

[f] i.e. *God shall hear* [g] i.e. *The well of him that liveth* and *seeth me* [h] Or, *upright*, or, *sincere* [i] Heb. *multitude of nations* [j] i.e. *Father of a great multitude*

16:11 ISHMAEL. The name "Ishmael" means "God hears" and signifies that God saw and responded to Abram and Sarai's unjust treatment of Hagar. That name is a judgment against Abram, revealing that God hates any injustice within His community. That God will punish a person because of wrong done toward those within the church is emphasized in the N.T. (see Col. 3:25, note).

16:12 AGAINST EVERY MAN. Ishmael, along with his descendants, would be a man of conflict, power, and courage. His desire for conflict could be used in a struggle for God or against Him. The choice would be his.

17:1 NINETY YEARS OLD AND NINE. Abram was now ninety-nine years old and Sarai long past the age of having children. But thirteen years after Ishmael's birth and twenty-four years after God's original promise, the Lord appeared to Abram with a message and a demand. (1) God revealed Himself as "Almighty God" (Heb. *El Shaddai*), meaning that He was all-powerful and that nothing was impossible with Him. As Almighty God, He could fulfill His promises when no natural way seemed to exist to fulfill them. Hence, God would bring Abram's promised son into the world by a miracle (cf. vv. 15–19; 35:11; Is. 13:6; Rom. 4:19; Heb. 11:12).

(2) God demanded that Abram walk before Him and be "perfect" (i.e., wholly dedicated to performing His will). Just as Abram's faith was necessary to receive God's covenant, so a sincere effort to please God was required for the continuation of God's covenant blessings (cf. 22:16–18). Abram's faith had to be accompanied by obedience (see Rom. 1:5), or he would disqualify himself from participation in God's eternal purposes. In other words, God's promises and miracles will only occur when His people seek to live blameless lives and keep their hearts turned toward Him (cf. 5:24; 6:9; Deut. 13:4; see Mat. 17:20, note).

17:2 MY COVENANT. God had earlier covenanted to give Abram the promised land (ch. 15); now He renewed that promise by stating that from Abram would come many nations and kings (v. 6), that the Lord would be God of his descendants, and that Sarai, his wife, would bear a son and be the mother of nations and kings (vv. 15–16). Abram and his descendants would see the fulfillment of the covenant as they bound themselves to God and the obligations of the covenant (vv. 9–14; see 15:6, note).

17:5 ABRAM . . . ABRAHAM. Abram means "exalted father"; Abraham means "father of a multitude" (see next note; cf. Neh. 9:7; Rom. 4:17). A new relationship with God often required a new name to signify that new relationship.

an everlasting covenant, [d]to be a God unto thee, and to [e]thy seed after thee.

8 And [f]I will give unto thee, and to thy seed after thee, the land [g]wherein[k] thou art a stranger, all the land of Canaan, for an everlasting possession; and [h]I will be their God.

9 ¶ And God said unto Abraham, Thou shalt keep my covenant therefore, thou, and thy seed after thee in their generations.

10 This *is* my covenant, which ye shall keep, between me and you and thy seed after thee; [i]Every man child among you shall be circumcised.

11 And ye shall circumcise the flesh of your foreskin; and it shall be [j]a token of the covenant betwixt me and you.

12 And [l]he that is eight days old [k]shall be circumcised among you, every man child in your generations, he that is born in the house, or bought with money of any stranger, which *is* not of thy seed.

13 He that is born in thy house, and he that is bought with thy money, must needs be circumcised: and my covenant shall be in your flesh for an everlasting covenant.

14 And the uncircumcised man child whose flesh of his foreskin is not circumcised, that soul [l]shall be cut off from his people; he hath broken my covenant.

15 ¶ And God said unto Abraham, As for Sarai thy wife, thou shalt not call her name Sarai, but [m]Sarah *shall* her name *be*.

17:7 [d]ch. 26:24 & 28:13 [e]Rom. 9:8
17:8 [f]ch. 12:7 [g]ch. 23:4 & 28:4 [h]Ex. 6:7 Lev. 26:12
17:10 [i]Acts 7:8
17:11 [j]Rom. 4:11
17:12 [k]Lev. 12:3 Luke 2:21
17:14 [l]Ex. 4:24
17:16 [m]ch. 18:10 [n]ch. 35:11 Gal. 4:31 1 Pet. 3:6
17:17 [o]ch. 18:12 & 21:6
17:19 [p]ch. 18:10 & 21:2 Gal. 4:28
17:20 [q]ch. 16:10 [r]ch. 25:12,16 [s]ch. 21:18
17:21 [t]ch. 21:2

16 And I will bless her, [m]and give thee a son also of her: yea, I will bless her, and [n]she shall be *a mother* [n]of nations; kings of people shall be of her.

17 Then Abraham fell upon his face, [o]and laughed, and said in his heart, Shall *a child* be born unto him that is an hundred years old? and shall Sarah, that is ninety years old, bear?

18 And Abraham said unto God, O that Ishmael might live before thee!

19 And God said, [p]Sarah thy wife shall bear thee a son indeed; and thou shalt call his name Isaac: and I will establish my covenant with him for an everlasting covenant, *and* with his seed after him.

20 And as for Ishmael, I have heard thee: Behold, I have blessed him, and will make him fruitful, and [q]will multiply him exceedingly; [r]twelve princes shall he beget, [s]and I will make him a great nation.

21 But my covenant will I establish with Isaac, [t]which Sarah shall bear unto thee at this set time in the next year.

22 And he left off talking with him, and God went up from Abraham.

23 ¶ And Abraham took Ishmael his son, and all that were born in his house, and all that were bought with his money, every male among the men of Abraham's house; and circumcised the flesh of their foreskin in the selfsame day, as God had said unto him.

[k] Heb. *of thy sojournings* [l] Heb. *a son of eight days* [m] i.e. *Princess* [n] Heb. *she shall become nations*

17:7 TO BE A GOD UNTO THEE. The very essence and reality of the Abrahamic covenant was God giving Himself to Abraham and his descendants (vv. 7–8). God's promise "to be a God unto thee" is the greatest promise in Scripture. It is the first and fundamental promise on which all other promises rest. It means that God unreservedly binds Himself to His faithful people to be their God, their shield, and their reward (cf. 15:1, note). It also means that God's grace, pardon, promises, protection, guidance, goodness, help, and blessing are given to them in love (cf. Jer. 11:4; 24:7; 30:22; 32:38; Ezek. 11:20; 36:28; Zech. 8:8). All Christians inherit this same promise through faith in Christ (Gal. 3:16).

17:8 EVERLASTING POSSESSION. Abraham and his physical descendants were promised the land of Canaan (12:7; 13:15; 15:7,18–21). The covenant was "everlasting" from God's point of view. It could be broken only by Abraham's descendants (Is. 24:5; Jer. 31:32), so that possession of the land was conditional on obedience to God (v. 9, see v. 1, note; see article on GOD'S COVENANT WITH ABRAHAM, ISAAC, AND JACOB, p. 48).

17:11 CIRCUMCISE. Circumcision was to be a sign and seal of God's covenant with Abraham and his offspring. (1) It was a sign or mark that they had accepted God's covenant and God Himself as their Lord. (2) It was a seal of the righteousness they had by faith (15:6; Rom. 4:11). (3) It was to remind the people of God's promises to them and their own personal obligations of the covenant (cf. v. 14).

17:15 SARAH. Sarah means "princess" and points to her place as "*a mother* of nations" and kings (v. 16).

17:17 LAUGHED. Abraham probably experienced a temporary measure of disbelief (cf. 18:12). We should understand that even people of great faith may at times undergo momentary periods of doubt. When this occurs in our lives, we must nevertheless press on in obedience, calling on God to renew our faith.

24 And Abraham *was* ninety years old and nine, when he was circumcised in the flesh of his foreskin.

25 And Ishmael his son *was* thirteen years old, when he was circumcised in the flesh of his foreskin.

26 In the selfsame day was Abraham circumcised, and Ishmael his son.

27 And [u]all the men of his house, born in the house, and bought with money of the stranger, were circumcised with him.

The three visitors

18 AND THE LORD appeared unto him in the [v]plains of Mamre: and he sat in the tent door in the heat of the day;

2 [w]And he lift up his eyes and looked, and, lo, three men stood by him: [x]and when he saw *them*, he ran to meet them from the tent door, and bowed himself toward the ground,

3 And said, My Lord, if now I have found favour in thy sight, pass not away, I pray thee, from thy servant:

4 Let [y]a little water, I pray you, be fetched, and wash your feet, and rest yourselves under the tree:

5 And [z]I will fetch a morsel of bread, and [a]comfort[o] ye your hearts; after that ye shall pass on: [b]for therefore [p]are ye come to your servant. And they said, So do, as thou hast said.

6 And Abraham hastened into the tent unto Sarah, and said, [q]Make ready quickly three measures of fine meal, knead *it*, and make cakes upon the hearth.

7 And Abraham ran unto the herd, and fetched a calf tender and good, and gave *it* unto a young man; and he hasted to dress it.

8 And [c]he took butter, and milk, and the calf which he had dressed, and set *it* before them; and he stood by them under the tree, and they did eat.

9 ¶ And they said unto him, Where *is* Sarah thy wife? And he said, Behold, [d]in the tent.

10 And he said, I [e]will certainly return unto thee [f]according to the time of life; and, lo, [g]Sarah thy wife shall have a son. And Sarah heard *it* in the tent door, which *was* behind him.

11 Now [h]Abraham and Sarah *were* old *and* well stricken in age; *and* it ceased to be with Sarah [i]after the manner of women.

12 Therefore Sarah [j]laughed within herself, saying, [k]After I am waxed old shall I have pleasure, my [l]lord being old also?

13 And the LORD said unto Abraham, Wherefore did Sarah laugh, saying, Shall I of a surety bear a child, which am old?

14 [m]Is any thing too hard for the LORD? [n]At the time appointed I will return unto thee, according to the time of life, and Sarah shall have a son.

15 Then Sarah denied, saying, I laughed not; for she was afraid. And he said, Nay; but thou didst laugh.

Abraham pleads for Sodom

16 ¶ And the men rose up from thence, and looked toward Sodom: and Abraham went with them [o]to bring them on the way.

17 And the LORD said, [p]Shall I hide from Abraham that thing which I do;

18 Seeing that Abraham shall surely become a great and mighty nation, and all the nations of the earth shall be [q]blessed in him?

19 For I know him, [r]that he will command his children and his household after him, and they shall keep the way of the LORD, to do justice and judgment; that the LORD may bring upon Abraham that which he hath spoken of him.

20 And the LORD said, Because

17:27 [u]ch. 18:19
18:1 [v]ch. 13:18 & 14:13
18:2 [w]Heb. 13:2 [x]ch. 19:1 1 Pet. 4:9
18:4 [y]ch. 19:2 & 43:24
18:5 [z]Judg. 6:18 & 13:15 [a]Judg. 19:5 Ps. 104:15 [b]ch. 19:8 & 33:10
18:8 [c]ch. 19:3
18:9 [d]ch. 24:67
18:10 [e]ver. 14 [f]2 Ki. 4:16 [g]ch. 17:19,21 & 21:2 Rom. 9:9
18:11 [h]ch. 17:17 Rom. 4:19 Heb. 11:11,12,19 [i]ch. 31:35
18:12 [j]ch. 17:17 [k]Luke 1:18 [l]1 Pet. 3:6
18:14 [m]Num. 11:23 Jer. 32:17 Zech. 8:6 Mat. 3:9 Luke 1:37 [n]ver. 10 ch. 17:21 2 Ki. 4:16
18:16 [o]Acts 15:3 Rom. 15:24 3 John 6
18:17 [p]Ps. 25:14 Amos 3:7 John 15:15
18:18 [q]ch. 12:3 & 22:18 Acts 3:25 Gal. 3:8
18:19 [r]Deut. 4:9,10 & 6:7 Josh. 24:15 Eph. 6:4

o Heb. *stay* p Heb. *you have passed* q Heb. *Hasten*

18:2 THREE MEN. One of the three men was most likely a manifestation of God in human form and the other two were angels appearing as men. Abraham may not have initially recognized the visitors as God and angels.

18:14 IS ANY THING TOO HARD FOR THE LORD? God wants us to understand that He has the power to accomplish what He has promised. Jesus emphasized this truth when He said, "With God all things are possible" (Mat. 19:26).

18:19 HE WILL COMMAND HIS CHILDREN . . . KEEP THE WAY OF THE LORD. Essential in the calling of Abraham was God's purpose that he be a spiritual leader at home and teach his children the way of the Lord. With the call of Abraham, God established the father as the one responsible to train his children to "keep the way of the LORD, to do justice and judgment" (see Deut. 6:7, note; see article on PARENTS AND CHILDREN, p. 1880).

18:20 THEIR SIN IS VERY GRIEVOUS. God does not overlook sin; He sees every evil, injustice,

[s]the cry of Sodom and Gomorrah is great, and because their sin is very grievous;

21 [t]I will go down now, and see whether they have done altogether according to the cry of it, which is come unto me; and if not, [u]I will know.

22 And the men turned their faces from thence, [v]and went toward Sodom: but Abraham [w]stood yet before the LORD.

23 ¶ And Abraham [x]drew near, and said, [y]Wilt thou also destroy the righteous with the wicked?

24 [z]Peradventure there be fifty righteous within the city: wilt thou also destroy and not spare the place for the fifty righteous that *are* therein?

25 That be far from thee to do after this manner, to slay the righteous with the wicked: and [a]that the righteous should be as the wicked, that be far from thee: [b]Shall not the Judge of all the earth do right?

26 And the LORD said, [c]If I find in Sodom fifty righteous within the city, then I will spare all the place for their sakes.

27 And Abraham answered and said, [d]Behold now, I have taken upon me to speak unto the Lord, which *am* [e]*but* dust and ashes:

28 Peradventure there shall lack five of the fifty righteous: wilt thou destroy all the city for *lack of* five? And he said, If I find there forty and five, I will not destroy *it*.

29 And he spake unto him yet again, and said, Peradventure there shall be forty found there. And he said, I will not do *it* for forty's sake.

30 And he said *unto him*, Oh let not the Lord be angry, and I will speak: Peradventure there shall thirty be found there. And he said, I will not do *it*, if I find thirty there.

31 And he said, Behold now, I have taken upon me to speak unto the Lord: Peradventure there shall be twenty found there. And he said, I will not destroy *it* for twenty's sake.

32 And he said, [f]Oh let not the Lord be angry, and I will speak yet but this once: Peradventure ten shall be found there. [g]And he said, I will not destroy *it* for ten's sake.

33 And the LORD went his way, as soon as he had left communing with Abraham: and Abraham returned unto his place.

Sodom and Gomorrah destroyed

19 AND THERE [h]came two angels to Sodom at even; and Lot sat in the gate of Sodom: and [i]Lot seeing *them* rose up to meet them; and he bowed himself with his face toward the ground;

2 And he said, Behold now, my lords, [j]turn in, I pray you, into your servant's house, and tarry all night, and [k]wash your feet, and ye shall rise up early, and go on your ways. And they said, [l]Nay; but we will abide in the street all night.

3 And he pressed upon them greatly; and they turned in unto him, and entered into his house; [m]and he made them a feast, and did bake unleavened bread, and they did eat.

4 ¶ But before they lay down, the men of the city, *even* the men of Sodom, compassed the house round, both old and young, all the people from every quarter:

5 [n]And they called unto Lot, and

18:20 [s]ch. 4:10 **18:21** [t]ch. 11:5 [u]Deut. 8:2 & 13:3 Josh. 22:22 Luke 16:15 2 Cor. 11:11 **18:22** [v]ch. 19:1 [w]ver. 1 **18:23** [x]Heb. 10:22 [y]Num. 16:22 **18:24** [z]Jer. 5:1 **18:25** [a]Job 8:20 Is. 3:10,11 [b]Job 8:3 & 34:17 Ps. 58:11 & 94:2 Rom. 3:6 **18:26** [c]Jer. 5:1 Ezek. 22:30 **18:27** [d]Luke 18:1 [e]ch. 3:19 Job 4:19 Eccl. 12:7 1 Cor. 15:47,48 2 Cor. 5:1 **18:32** [f]Judg. 6:39 [g]Jas. 5:16 **19:1** [h]ch. 18:22 [i]ch. 18:1 **19:2** [j]Heb. 13:2 [k]ch. 18:4 [l]See Luke 24:28 **19:3** [m]ch. 18:8 **19:5** [n]Is. 3:9

---

and immorality that are committed (cf. 4:10; Ps. 34:17; Jas. 5:4). At the right time, if there is no repentance from sin, God will judge and condemn. The very nature of God requires that wickedness be punished.

18:22 ABRAHAM STOOD YET BEFORE THE LORD. Out of concern for Lot and his relatives, Abraham prayed that God would not destroy the cities (vv. 22–33). God answered the prayer of Abraham, though not in the way he expected. God did not destroy the righteous with the wicked. He saved the righteous, yet destroyed the guilty. In the day of God's future wrath that is coming upon the world (see 1 Thes. 5:2, note; 2 Thes. 2:2, note), God has promised to rescue the righteous (see Luke 21:36, note; Rev. 3:10, note; see article on THE RAPTURE, p. 1889).

19:1 LOT SAT IN THE GATE OF SODOM. Although Lot was distressed by the filthy deeds he saw and heard (2 Pet. 2:7–8), he still was willing to tolerate the wickedness of Sodom for social and material advantages (see 13:12, note). This compromise brought tragedy to his family (v. 24). Likewise, believers today who expose their families to ungodly environments and evil influences for social or material gain are setting themselves up for family tragedies.

19:5 THAT WE MAY KNOW THEM. The term "know them" indicates that the men of the city wanted to sexually abuse the male strangers. It is from this incident that the word "sodomy" gains its meaning; it primarily refers to homosexuality and homosexual lust. Sodomy is severely condemned in the Bible (Lev. 20:13; Deut. 23:17; 1 Cor. 6:9; 1 Tim. 1:8–10; see Rom. 1:27, note).

said unto him, Where *are* the men which came in to thee this night? [o]bring them out unto us, that we [p]may know them.

6 And [q]Lot went out at the door unto them, and shut the door after him,

7 And said, I pray you, brethren, do not so wickedly.

8 [r]Behold now, I have two daughters which have not known man; let me, I pray you, bring them out unto you, and do ye to them as *is* good in your eyes: only unto these men do nothing; [s]for therefore came they under the shadow of my roof.

9 And they said, Stand back. And they said *again*, This one *fellow* [t]came in to sojourn, [u]and he will needs be a judge: now will we deal worse with thee, than with them. And they pressed sore upon the man, *even* Lot, and came near to break the door.

10 But the men put forth their hand, and pulled Lot into the house to them, and shut to the door.

11 And they smote the men that *were* at the door of the house with blindness, both small and great: so that they wearied themselves to find the door.

12 ¶ And the men said unto Lot, Hast thou here any besides? son-in-law, and thy sons, and thy daughters, and whatsoever thou hast in the city, [v]bring *them* out of this place:

13 For we will destroy this place, because the [w]cry of them is waxen great before the face of the LORD; and [x]the LORD hath sent us to destroy it.

14 And Lot went out, and spake unto his sons in law, [y]which married his daughters, and said, [z]Up, get you out of this place; for the LORD will destroy this city. [a]But he seemed as one that mocked unto his sons in law.

15 ¶ And when the morning arose, then the angels hastened Lot, saying, [b]Arise, take thy wife, and thy two daughters, which [r]are here; lest thou be consumed in the [s]iniquity of the city.

16 And while he lingered, the men laid hold upon his hand, and upon the hand of his wife, and upon the hand of his two daughters; [c]the LORD being merciful unto him: [d]and they brought him forth, and set him without the city.

17 ¶ And it came to pass, when they had brought them forth abroad, that he said, [e]Escape for thy life; [f]look not behind thee, neither stay thou in all the plain; escape to the mountain, lest thou be consumed.

18 And Lot said unto them, Oh, [g]not so, my Lord:

19 Behold now, thy servant hath found grace in thy sight, and thou hast magnified thy mercy, which thou hast shown unto me in saving my life; and I cannot escape to the mountain, lest some evil take me, and I die:

20 Behold now, this city *is* near to flee unto, and it *is* a little one: Oh, let me escape thither, (*is* it not a little one?) and my soul shall live.

21 And he said unto him, See, [h]I have accepted [t]thee concerning this thing also, that I will not overthrow this city, for the which thou hast spoken.

22 Haste thee, escape thither; for [i]I cannot do any thing till thou be come thither. Therefore [j]the name of the city was called [u]Zoar.

23 ¶ The sun was [v]risen upon the earth when Lot entered into Zoar.

24 Then [k]the LORD rained upon Sodom and upon Gomorrah brimstone and fire from the LORD out of heaven;

25 And he overthrew those cities, and all the plain, and all the inhabitants of the cities, and [l]that which grew upon the ground.

26 ¶ But his wife looked back from

19:5 [o]Judg. 19:22 [p]ch. 4:1 Rom. 1:24,27 Jude 7 **19:6** [q]Judg. 19:23 **19:8** [r]See Judg. 19:24 [s]See ch. 18:5 **19:9** [t]2 Pet. 2:7,8 [u]Ex. 2:14 **19:12** [v]ch. 7:1 2 Pet. 2:7,9 **19:13** [w]ch. 18:20 [x]1 Chr. 21:15 **19:14** [y]Mat. 1:18 [z]Num. 16:21,45 [a]Ex. 9:21 Luke 17:28 & 24:11 **19:15** [b]Num. 16:24,26 Rev. 18:4

19:16 [c]Luke 18:13 [d]Ps. 34:22 **19:17** [e]1 Ki. 19:3 [f]ver. 26 Mat. 24:16-18 Luke 9:62 Phil. 3:13,14 **19:18** [g]Acts 10:14 **19:21** [h]Job 42:8,9 Ps. 145:19 **19:22** [i]See ch. 32:25,26 Ex. 32:10 Deut. 9:14 Mark 6:5 [j]ch. 13:10 & 14:2 **19:24** [k]Deut. 29:23 Is. 13:19 Jer. 20:16 Ezek. 16:49,50 Hos. 11:8 Luke 17:29 2 Pet. 2:6 Jude 7 **19:25** [l]ch. 14:3 Ps. 107:34

[r] Heb. *are found* [s] Or, *punishment* [t] Heb. *thy face* [u] i.e. *Little* [v] Heb. *gone forth*

19:8 I HAVE TWO DAUGHTERS. It is difficult to believe that Lot was truly willing to allow his two daughters to be defiled and abused by a mob of sexual perverts, merely in order to protect two strangers he had never met. It may have been that in desperation he was stalling for time, believing that his friends in the city would not allow the others to brutalize him or his family.

19:26 HIS WIFE LOOKED BACK . . . AND SHE BECAME A PILLAR OF SALT. Lot's wife did not take the specific command of the angel seriously (v. 17) and was struck dead. Evidently her heart was still clinging to the pleasures of Sodom. Jesus in the N.T. warns believers to "remember Lot's wife" (Luke 17:32), meaning that those whose hearts are attached to the world's present corrupt system will not be spared God's wrath and destruction which is coming upon the ungodly (cf. Ezek. 3:20; Rom. 8:13; Heb. 4:1; see articles on PERSONAL APOSTASY, p. 1946, and THE CHRISTIAN'S RELATIONSHIP TO THE WORLD, p. 2004).

Ex. 23:23-24

behind him, and she became [m]a pillar of salt.

27 ¶ And Abraham gat up early in the morning to the place where [n]he stood before the LORD:

28 And he looked toward Sodom and Gomorrah, and toward all the land of the plain, and beheld, and, lo, [o]the smoke of the country went up as the smoke of a furnace.

29 ¶ And it came to pass, when God destroyed the cities of the plain, that God [p]remembered Abraham, and sent Lot out of the midst of the overthrow, when he overthrew the cities in the which Lot dwelt.

The sin of Lot's daughters

30 ¶ And Lot went up out of Zoar, and [q]dwelt in the mountain, and his two daughters with him; for he feared to dwell in Zoar: and he dwelt in a cave, he and his two daughters.

31 And the firstborn said unto the younger, Our father *is* old, and *there is* not a man in the earth [r]to come in unto us after the manner of all the earth:

32 Come, let us make our father drink wine, and we will lie with him, that we [s]may preserve seed of our father.

33 And they made their father drink wine that night: and the firstborn went in, and lay with her father; and he perceived not when she lay down, nor when she arose.

34 And it came to pass on the morrow, that the firstborn said unto the younger, Behold, I lay yesternight with my father: let us make him drink wine this night also; and go thou in, *and* lie with him, that we may preserve seed of our father.

35 And they made their father drink wine that night also: and the younger arose, and lay with him; and he perceived not when she lay down, nor when she arose.

36 Thus were both the daughters of Lot with child by their father.

37 And the firstborn bare a son, and called his name Moab: [t]the same *is* the father of the Moabites unto this day.

38 And the younger, she also bare a son, and called his name Ben-ammi: [u]the same *is* the father of the children of Ammon unto this day.

Abraham and Abimelech

20:1–18Ref — Gen. 12:10–20; 26:1–11

20 AND ABRAHAM journeyed from [v]thence toward the south country, and dwelled between [w]Kadesh and Shur, and [x]sojourned in Gerar.

2 And Abraham said of Sarah his wife, [y]She *is* my sister: and Abimelech king of Gerar sent, and [z]took Sarah.

3 But [a]God came to Abimelech [b]in a dream by night, and said to him, [c]Behold, thou *art but* a dead man, for the woman which thou hast taken; for she *is* [w]a man's wife.

4 But Abimelech had not come near her: and he said, Lord, [d]wilt thou slay also a righteous nation?

5 Said he not unto me, She *is* my sister? and she, even she herself said, He *is* my brother: [e]in the [x]integrity of my heart and innocency of my hands have I done this.

6 And God said unto him in a dream, Yea, I know that thou didst this in the integrity of thy heart; for [f]I also withheld thee from sinning [g]against me:

[w] Heb. *married to an husband* [x] Or, *simplicity*, or, *sincerity*

19:26 [m]Luke 17:32
19:27 [n]ch. 18:22
19:28 [o]Rev. 18:9
19:29 [p]ch. 8:1 & 18:23
19:30 [q]ver. 17,19
19:31 [r]ch. 16:2,4 & 38:8,9 Deut. 25:5
19:32 [s]Mark 12:19
19:37 [t]Deut. 2:9
19:38 [u]Deut. 2:19
20:1 [v]ch. 18:1 [w]ch. 16:7,14 [x]ch. 26:6
20:2 [y]ch. 12:13 & 26:7 [z]ch. 12:15
20:3 [a]Ps. 105:14 [b]Job 33:15 [c]ver. 7
20:4 [d]ch. 18:23
20:5 [e]2 Ki. 20:3
20:6 [f]ch. 31:7 & 35:5 Ex. 34:24 1 Sam. 25:26,34 [g]ch. 39:9 Lev. 6:2 Ps. 51:4

19:28 SMOKE OF A FURNACE. The apostle Peter states that the destruction of Sodom and Gomorrah is an example of what is going to happen to all the ungodly (2 Pet. 2:6,9). The N.T. warns that the final day of God's wrath is approaching (see article on THE GREAT TRIBULATION, p. 1456).

19:33 THEY MADE THEIR FATHER DRINK WINE. Lot's daughters were guilty of the sin of incest and Lot the sin of drunkenness. (1) Evidently, the girls' close association with the ungodly Sodomites, tolerated by their father (v. 14), had caused them to adopt low moral standards for their lives. Because of Lot's toleration of the ungodly, he lost his family and his descendants became pagans. (2) Lot remains an example of a believing father whose faith and commitment to God were enough to save himself, but not enough to save his family. He learned too late that the true way of faith is to teach one's family to stand apart and "love not the world" (1 John 2:15,17; see 2 Cor. 6:14, note).

20:2 SHE *IS* MY SISTER. Once again Abraham's faith failed and he jeopardized God's plan for Sarah. God intervened in order to preserve Sarah's participation in the history of redemption as the mother of the covenant people (vv. 3–7). God in His grace will at times deliver His normally faithful children from situations which are the result of their failure in faith and obedience.

therefore suffered I thee not to touch her.

7 Now therefore restore the man *his* wife; [h]for he *is* a prophet, and he shall pray for thee, and thou shalt live: and if thou restore *her* not, [i]know thou that thou shalt surely die, thou, [j]and all that *are* thine.

8 Therefore Abimelech rose early in the morning, and called all his servants, and told all these things in their ears: and the men were sore afraid.

9 Then Abimelech called Abraham, and said unto him, What hast thou done unto us? and what have I offended thee, [k]that thou hast brought on me and on my kingdom a great sin? thou hast done deeds unto me [l]that ought not to be done.

10 And Abimelech said unto Abraham, What sawest thou, that thou hast done this thing?

11 And Abraham said, Because I thought, Surely [m]the fear of God *is* not in this place; and [n]they will slay me for my wife's sake.

12 And yet indeed [o]*she is* my sister; she *is* the daughter of my father, but not the daughter of my mother; and she became my wife.

13 And it came to pass, when [p]God caused me to wander from my father's house, that I said unto her, This *is* thy kindness which thou shalt show unto me; at every place whither we shall come, [q]say of me, He *is* my brother.

14 And Abimelech [r]took sheep, and oxen, and menservants, and womenservants, and gave *them* unto Abraham, and restored him Sarah his wife.

15 And Abimelech said, Behold, [s]my land *is* before thee: dwell [y]where it pleaseth thee.

16 And unto Sarah he said, Behold, I have given thy brother a thousand *pieces* of silver: [t]behold, he *is* to thee [u]a covering of the eyes, unto all that *are* with thee, and with all *other:* thus she was reproved.

17 ¶ So Abraham [v]prayed unto God: and God healed Abimelech, and his wife, and his maidservants; and they bare *children.*

18 For the LORD [w]had fast closed up all the wombs of the house of Abimelech, because of Sarah Abraham's wife. [Ex. 15:26]

The birth of Isaac

21 AND THE LORD [x]visited Sarah as he had said, and the LORD did unto Sarah [y]as he had spoken.

2 For Sarah [z]conceived, and bare Abraham a son in his old age, [a]at the set time of which God had spoken to him.

3 And Abraham called the name of his son that was born unto him, whom Sarah bare to him, [b]Isaac.

4 And Abraham [c]circumcised his son Isaac being eight days old, [d]as God had commanded him.

5 And [e]Abraham was an hundred years old, when his son Isaac was born unto him.

6 ¶ And Sarah said, [f]God hath made me to laugh, *so that* all that hear [g]will laugh with me.

7 And she said, Who would have said unto Abraham, that Sarah should have given children suck? [h]for I have born *him* a son in his old age.

Hagar and Ishmael cast out

8 And the child grew, and was weaned: and Abraham made a great feast the *same* day that Isaac was weaned.

9 ¶ And Sarah saw the son of Hagar [i]the Egyptian, [j]which she had born unto Abraham, [k]mocking.

10 Wherefore she said unto Abraham, [l]Cast out this bondwoman and her son: for the son of this bondwoman shall not be heir with my son, *even* with Isaac.

11 And the thing was very grievous in Abraham's sight [m]because of his son.

12 ¶ And God said unto Abraham, Let it not be grievous in thy sight because of the lad, and because of thy bondwoman; in all that Sarah hath said unto thee, hearken unto her voice; for [n]in Isaac shall thy seed be called.

13 And also of the son of the bondwoman will I make [o]a nation, because he *is* thy seed.

14 And Abraham rose up early in

20:7 [h]1 Sam. 7:5 2 Ki. 5:11 Job 42:8 Jas. 5:14,15 [i]ch. 2:17 [j]Num. 16:32,33
20:9 [k]ch. 26:10 Ex. 32:21 Josh. 7:25 [l]ch. 34:7
20:11 [m]ch. 42:18 Ps. 36:1 Prov. 16:6 [n]ch. 12:12 & 26:7
20:12 [o]See ch. 11:29
20:13 [p]ch. 12:1,9,11 Heb. 11:8 [q]ch. 12:13
20:14 [r]ch. 12:16
20:15 [s]ch. 13:9
20:16 [t]ch. 26:11 [u]ch. 24:65
20:17 [v]Job 42:9
20:18 [w]ch. 12:17

21:1 [x]1 Sam. 2:21 [y]ch. 17:19 Gal. 4:23,28
21:2 [z]Acts 7:8 Gal. 4:22 Heb. 11:11 [a]ch. 17:21
21:3 [b]ch. 17:19
21:4 [c]Acts 7:8 [d]ch. 17:10,12
21:5 [e]ch. 17:1,17
21:6 [f]Ps. 126:2 Is. 54:1 [g]Luke 1:58
21:7 [h]ch. 18:11,12
21:9 [i]ch. 16:1 [j]ch. 16:15 [k]Gal. 4:29
21:10 [l]Gal. 4:30 See ch. 25:6 & 36:6,7
21:11 [m]ch. 17:18
21:12 [n]Rom. 9:7,8 Heb. 11:18
21:13 [o]ver. 18 ch. 16:10 & 17:20

y Heb. *as is good in thine eyes*

21:5 HIS SON ISAAC WAS BORN. Isaac, the son of promise, was finally born to Abraham and Sarah. Through Isaac God would continue His covenant with Abraham (v. 12; 17:19). Twenty-five years had passed before God's promise was fulfilled to Abraham (cf. 12:4). "The LORD *is* good unto them that wait for him" (Lam. 3:25); in His own time He faithfully brings His promises to pass.

the morning, and took bread, and a bottle of water, and gave *it* unto Hagar, putting *it* on her shoulder, and the child, and [p]sent her away: and she departed, and wandered in the wilderness of Beer-sheba.

15 And the water was spent in the bottle, and she cast the child under one of the shrubs.

16 And she went, and sat her down over against *him* a good way off, as it were a bowshot: for she said, Let me not see the death of the child. And she sat over against *him,* and lift up her voice, and wept.

17 And [q]God heard the voice of the lad; and the angel of God called to Hagar out of heaven, and said unto her, What aileth thee, Hagar? fear not; for God hath heard the voice of the lad where he *is.*

18 Arise, lift up the lad, and hold him in thine hand; for [r]I will make him a great nation.

19 And [s]God opened her eyes, and she saw a well of water; and she went, and filled the bottle with water, and gave the lad drink.

20 And God [t]was with the lad; and he grew, and dwelt in the wilderness, [u]and became an archer.

21 And he dwelt in the wilderness of Paran: and his mother [v]took him a wife out of the land of Egypt.

Covenant with Abimelech

22 ¶ And it came to pass at that time, that [w]Abimelech and Phichol the chief captain of his host spake unto Abraham, saying, [x]God *is* with thee in all that thou doest:

23 Now therefore [y]swear unto me here by God [z]that thou wilt not deal falsely with me, nor with my son, nor with my son's son: *but* according to the kindness that I have done unto thee, thou shalt do unto me, and to the land wherein thou hast sojourned.

21:14 [p]John 8:35
21:17 [q]Ex. 3:7
21:18 [r]ver. 13
21:19 [s]Num. 22:31
21:20 [t]ch. 28:15 & 39:2,3,21 [u]ch. 16:12
21:21 [v]ch. 24:4
21:22 [w]ch. 20:2 & 26:26 [x]ch:26:28
21:23 [y]Josh. 2:12 1 Sam. 24:21
21:25 [z]See ch. 26:15,18, 20-22
21:27 [a]ch. 26:31 & 31:44 1 Sam. 18:3
21:29 [b]ch. 33:8
21:30 [c]ch. 31:48,52
21:31 [d]ch. 26:33
21:33 [e]ch. 4:26 [f]Deut. 33:27
22:1 [g]1 Cor. 10:13 Heb. 11:17 Jas. 1:12 1 Pet. 1:7
22:2 [h]Heb. 11:17

24 And Abraham said, I will swear.

25 And Abraham reproved Abimelech because of a well of water, which Abimelech's servants [z]had violently taken away.

26 And Abimelech said, I wot not who hath done this thing: neither didst thou tell me, neither yet heard I *of it,* but today.

27 And Abraham took sheep and oxen, and gave them unto Abimelech; and both of them [a]made a covenant.

28 And Abraham set seven ewe lambs of the flock by themselves.

29 And Abimelech said unto Abraham, [b]What *mean* these seven ewe lambs which thou hast set by themselves?

30 And he said, For *these* seven ewe lambs shalt thou take of my hand, that [c]they may be a witness unto me, that I have digged this well.

31 Wherefore he [d]called that place [a]Beer-sheba; because there they sware both of them.

32 Thus they made a covenant at Beer-sheba: then Abimelech rose up, and Phichol the chief captain of his host, and they returned into the land of the Philistines.

33 ¶ And *Abraham* planted a [b]grove in Beer-sheba, and [e]called there on the name of the LORD, [f]the everlasting God.

34 And Abraham sojourned in the Philistines' land many days.

God tests Abraham

22 AND IT came to pass after these things, that [g]God did tempt Abraham, and said unto him, Abraham: and he said, [c]Behold, *here* I *am.*

2 And he said, Take now thy son, [h]thine only *son* Isaac, whom thou lov-

[z] Heb. *if thou shalt lie unto me* [a] i.e. *The well of the oath* [b] Or, *tree* [c] Heb. *Behold me*

21:17 GOD HATH HEARD. God knew it was best that Hagar and Ishmael leave Abraham. Nevertheless, God did not forsake those two, for they remained in His presence and care (vv. 17–21). God had a purpose for Ishmael, paralleling His purpose for Isaac, namely, that He would "make him a great nation" (v. 18).

22:1 GOD DID TEMPT ABRAHAM. Abraham's faith in and commitment to God were tested to the maximum. God commanded him to do something completely contrary to common sense, his fatherly love, and his lifelong hope (v. 2). In the Abraham story, we read of three great tests of his faith: (1) the call to separate himself from his kinsmen and country (12:1) and to go forth, not knowing where he was going (cf. Heb. 11:8); (2) the requirement to trust God for the promise of the covenant without seeing the fulfillment of that promise for twenty-five years (12:1–3; 15:6,8; 18:9–14; Heb. 11:8–13); (3) the command that he offer up Isaac, the promised son (ch. 22). In a manner similar to Abraham, the true faith of all believers will be tested.

22:2 TAKE NOW THY SON. Abraham was com-

est, and get thee [i]into the land of Mo-
riah; and offer him there for a burnt
offering upon one of the mountains
which I will tell thee of.
3 ¶ And Abraham rose up early in
the morning, and saddled his ass, and
took two of his young men with him,
and Isaac his son, and clave the wood
for the burnt offering, and rose up, and
went unto the place of which God had
told him.
4 Then on the third day Abraham
lifted up his eyes, and saw the place
afar off.
5 And Abraham said unto his young
men, Abide ye here with the ass; and
I and the lad will go yonder and wor-
ship, and come again to you.
6 And Abraham took the wood of
the burnt offering, and [j]laid *it* upon
Isaac his son; and he took the fire in
his hand, and a knife; and they went
both of them together.
7 And Isaac spake unto Abraham
his father, and said, My father: and he
said, [d]Here *am* I, my son. And he said,
Behold the fire and the wood: but
where *is* the [e]lamb for a burnt offer-
ing?
8 And Abraham said, My son, God
will provide himself a lamb for a burnt
offering: so they went both of them to-
gether.
9 And they came to the place which
God had told him of; and Abraham
built an altar there, and laid the wood
in order, and bound Isaac his son,
and [k]laid him on the altar upon the
wood.
10 And Abraham stretched forth his
hand, and took the knife to slay his
son.
11 And the angel of the LORD called
unto him out of heaven, and said, Abra-
ham, Abraham: and he said, Here *am* I.
12 And he said, [l]Lay not thine
hand upon the lad, neither do thou any
thing unto him: for [m]now I know that
thou fearest God, seeing thou hast not
withheld thy son, thine only *son*
from me.
13 And Abraham lifted up his eyes,
and looked, and behold behind *him* a
ram caught in a thicket by his horns:
and Abraham went and took the ram,
and offered him up for a burnt offering
in the stead of his son.
14 And Abraham called the name of

22:2 [i]2 Chr. 3:1
22:6 [j]John 19:17
22:9 [k]Heb. 11:17; Jas. 2:21
22:12 [l]1 Sam. 15:22; [m]ch. 26:5; Jas. 2:22

[d] Heb. *Behold me* [e] Or, *kid*

manded to sacrifice his son Isaac. (1) The central issue lay in two areas that illustrate God's measure in dealing with all believers. (a) Was Abraham's love for God greater than his love for others, even his beloved son? (b) Were Abraham's hope and expectation of the fulfillment of the promise still in God, or did he now hope in something else, i.e., in Isaac? (2) Through this test God forced Abraham to face these questions and to make clear whether he indeed feared God with all his heart (v. 12). (3) God did not really desire the physical death of Isaac (cf. vv. 12–13), for He later condemned human sacrifice as a terrible sin (Lev. 20:1–5). But He did want to test the commitment of Abraham.

22:5 I AND THE LAD WILL ... COME AGAIN. Abraham's statement that he and Isaac would return from the sacrifice was a testimony to his faith and conviction that God's promises concerning Isaac would be fulfilled (i.e., "in Isaac shall thy seed be called," 21:12). In this story, Isaac is a type of Christ: (1) in his giving himself to his father for a sacrifice unto death (v. 16; cf. John 10:17–18), and (2) in his being saved from death, an act which corresponds to the resurrection of Christ (v. 12; see Heb. 11:17–19).

22:8 GOD WILL PROVIDE. "God will provide" ("Jehovah-jireh," v. 14) is prophetic and points to God providing a substitute sacrifice, a ram (v. 13). The ultimate fulfillment of Abraham's statement is found in God providing His only begotten Son as an atoning sacrifice on Calvary for the redemption of humankind. Thus, the heavenly Father Himself did what He had asked Abraham to do (John 3:16; Rom. 3:24–25; 8:32).

22:9 BOUND ISAAC HIS SON. Isaac was probably a young adult who was well able to resist his father, had he so desired. But in complete submission to God and obedience to his father, he allowed himself to be bound and laid on the altar, just as Jesus voluntarily went to the cross.

22:10 ABRAHAM STRETCHED FORTH HIS HAND. Scripture states that Abraham was "justified by works, when he had offered Isaac his son upon the altar" (Jas. 2:21). That is, Abraham's faith manifested itself in sincere obedience to God (see 15:6, note). The hidden life of true saving faith will inevitably become a manifested life of obedience (see Rom. 1:5, note; 2:7, note; Jas. 2:21, note; see article on FAITH AND GRACE, p. 1738).

22:12 FOR NOW I KNOW THAT THOU FEAREST GOD. As Abraham began to perform the sacrifice (v. 10), God saw that he had made the ultimate surrender in his heart. The Lord now knew that Abraham was a God-fearing man whose chief concern was to do God's will.

22:14 JEHOVAH-JIREH. This name means "the LORD will provide." From God's test of Abraham we learn that: (1) God sometimes tests the faith of His children (cf. 1 Pet. 1:6–7; Heb. 11:35, note). Testing must be considered an honor in God's kingdom (1 Pet. 4:12–14).

(2) God may be trusted to provide His presence, grace, and all that is necessary for any circum-

Ex. 17:8-13

that place [f]Jehovah-jireh: as it is said *to* this day, In the mount of the LORD it shall be seen.

15 ¶ And the angel of the LORD called unto Abraham out of heaven the second time,

16 And said, [n]By myself have I sworn, saith the LORD, for because thou hast done this thing, and hast not withheld thy son, thine only *son:*

17 That in blessing I will bless thee, and in multiplying I will multiply thy seed [o]as the stars of the heaven, [p]and as the sand which *is* upon the sea [g]shore; and [q]thy seed shall possess [r]the gate of his enemies;

18 [s]And in thy seed shall all the nations of the earth be blessed; [t]because thou hast obeyed my voice.

19 So Abraham returned unto his young men, and they rose up and went together to [u]Beer-sheba; and Abraham dwelt at Beer-sheba.

20 ¶ And it came to pass after these things, that it was told Abraham, saying, Behold, [v]Milcah, she hath also born children unto thy brother Nahor;

21 [w]Huz his firstborn, and Buz his brother, and Kemuel the father [x]of Aram,

22 And Chesed, and Hazo, and Pildash, and Jidlaph, and Bethuel.

23 And [y]Bethuel begat [z]Rebekah: these eight Milcah did bear to Nahor, Abraham's brother.

24 And his concubine, whose name *was* Reumah, she bare also Tebah, and Gaham, and Thahash, and Maachah.

The death of Sarah

23 AND SARAH was an hundred and seven and twenty years old: *these were* the years of the life of Sarah.

2 And Sarah died in [a]Kirjath-arba; the same *is* [b]Hebron in the land of Canaan: and Abraham came to mourn for Sarah, and to weep for her.

3 ¶ And Abraham stood up from before his dead, and spake unto the sons of Heth, saying,

4 [c]I *am* a stranger and a sojourner with you: [d]give me a possession of a buryingplace with you, that I may bury my dead out of my sight.

5 And the children of Heth answered Abraham, saying unto him,

6 Hear us, my lord: thou *art* [e]a [h]mighty prince among us: in the choice of our sepulchres bury thy dead; none of us shall withhold from thee his sepulchre, but that thou mayest bury thy dead.

7 And Abraham stood up, and bowed himself to the people of the land, *even* to the children of Heth.

8 And he communed with them, saying, If it be your mind that I should bury my dead out of my sight; hear me, and entreat for me to Ephron the son of Zohar,

9 That he may give me the cave of Machpelah, which he hath, which *is* in the end of his field; for [i]as much money as it is worth he shall give it me for a possession of a buryingplace amongst you.

10 And Ephron dwelt among the children of Heth: and Ephron the Hittite answered Abraham in the [j]audience of the children of Heth, *even* of all that [f]went in at the gate of his city, saying,

11 [g]Nay, my lord, hear me: the field give I thee, and the cave that *is* therein, I give it thee; in the presence of the sons of my people give I it thee: bury thy dead.

12 And Abraham bowed down himself before the people of the land.

22:16 [n]Ps. 105:9 Luke 1:73 Heb. 6:13,14
22:17 [o]ch. 15:5 Jer. 33:22 [p]ch. 13:16 [q]ch. 24:60 [r]Mic. 1:9
22:18 [s]ch. 12:3 & 18:18 & 26:4 Acts 3:25 Gal. 3:8,9,16,18 [t]ver. 3,10 ch. 26:5
22:19 [u]ch. 21:31
22:20 [v]ch. 11:29
22:21 [w]Job 1:1 [x]Job 32:2
22:23 [y]ch. 24:15 [z]Called, Rom. 9:10, *Rebecca*
23:2 [a]Josh. 14:15 [b]ver. 19 ch. 13:18
23:4 [c]ch. 17:8 1 Chr. 29:15 Ps. 105:12 Heb. 11:9,13 [d]Acts 7:5
23:6 [e]ch. 13:2 & 14:14 & 24:35
23:10 [f]ch. 34:20,24 Ruth 4:4
23:11 [g]See 2 Sam. 24:21-24

[f]i.e. *The LORD will see,* or *provide* [g]Heb. *lip* [h]Heb. *a prince of God* [i]Heb. *full money* [j]Heb. *ears*

stance that lies within His will (Ps. 46:1–23 2 Cor. 9:8; 12:9; Eph. 3:20).

(3) God often works His redemptive purpose through the death of a vision; i.e., He may allow things to happen in our lives that seem to destroy our hopes and dreams (17:15–17; 22:1–12; 37:5–7,28; Mark 14:43–50; 15:25,37).

(4) After a trial of faith, God will confirm, strengthen, establish, and reward the believer (vv. 16–18; 1 Pet. 5:10).

(5) The way to find true life in God is through the willingness to sacrifice all that God requires (cf. Mat. 10:37–39; 16:24–25; John 12:25).

(6) After a test of suffering and faith, the outcome of all the Lord's dealings toward the believer is "very pitiful, and of tender mercy" (Jas. 5:11).

22:18 BECAUSE THOU HAST OBEYED MY VOICE. Because of Abraham's sincere obedience from the heart, demonstrated by his willingness to sacrifice his son, Abraham was told that God would continue His covenant promise with him (see article on GOD'S COVENANT WITH ABRAHAM, ISAAC, AND JACOB, p. 48). The "seed" that would bless the nations ultimately refers to Christ Jesus (Gal. 3:8,16,18; see article on THE CALL OF ABRAHAM, p. 25).

13 And he spake unto Ephron in the audience of the people of the land, saying, But if thou *wilt give it,* I pray thee, hear me: I will give thee money for the field; take *it* of me, and I will bury my dead there.

14 And Ephron answered Abraham, saying unto him,

15 My lord, hearken unto me: the land *is worth* four hundred [h]shekels of silver; what *is* that betwixt me and thee? bury therefore thy dead.

16 And Abraham hearkened unto Ephron; and Abraham [i]weighed to Ephron the silver, which he had named in the audience of the sons of Heth, four hundred shekels of silver, current *money* with the merchant.

17 ¶ And [j]the field of Ephron, which *was* in Machpelah, which *was* before Mamre, the field, and the cave which *was* therein, and all the trees that *were* in the field, that *were* in all the borders round about, were made sure

18 Unto Abraham for a possession in the presence of the children of Heth, before all that went in at the gate of his city.

19 And after this, Abraham buried Sarah his wife in the cave of the field of Machpelah before Mamre: the same *is* Hebron in the land of Canaan.

20 And the field, and the cave that *is* therein, [k]were made sure unto Abraham for a possession of a buryingplace by the sons of Heth.

Isaac and Rebekah

24 AND ABRAHAM [l]was old, *and* [k]well stricken in age: and the LORD [m]had blessed Abraham in all things.

2 And Abraham said [n]unto his eldest servant of his house, that [o]ruled over all that he had, [p]Put, I pray thee, thy hand under my thigh:

3 And I will make thee [q]swear by the LORD, the God of heaven, and the God of the earth, that [r]thou shalt not take a wife unto my son of the daughters of the Canaanites, among whom I dwell:

4 [s]But thou shalt go [t]unto my country, and to my kindred, and take a wife unto my son Isaac.

5 And the servant said unto him, Peradventure the woman will not be willing to follow me unto this land: must I needs bring thy son again unto the land from whence thou camest?

6 And Abraham said unto him, Beware thou that thou bring not my son thither again.

7 ¶ The LORD God of heaven, which [u]took me from my father's house, and from the land of my kindred, and which spake unto me, and that sware unto me, saying, [v]Unto thy seed will I give this land; [w]he shall send his angel before thee, and thou shalt take a wife unto my son from thence.

8 And if the woman will not be willing to follow thee, then [x]thou shalt be clear from this my oath: only bring not my son thither again.

9 And the servant put his hand under the thigh of Abraham his master, and sware to him concerning that matter.

10 ¶ And the servant took ten camels of the camels of his master, and departed; [y]for[1] all the goods of his master *were* in his hand: and he arose, and went to Mesopotamia, unto [z]the city of Nahor.

11 And he made his camels to kneel down without the city by a well of water at the time of the evening, *even* the time [a]that[m] women go out to draw *water.*

12 And he said, [b]O LORD God of my master Abraham, I pray thee, [c]send

23:15 [h]Ex. 30:13 Ezek. 45:12 **23:16** [i]Jer:32:9 **23:17** [j]ch. 25:9 & 49:30-32 & 50:13 Acts 7:16 **23:20** [k]Jer. 32:10,11 **24:1** [l]ch. 21:5 [m]ver. 35 ch. 13:2 Ps. 112:3 Prov. 10:22 **24:2** [n]ch. 15:2 [o]ver. 10 ch. 39:4-6 [p]ch. 47:29 1 Chr. 29:24 **24:3** [q]ch. 14:22 Deut. 6:13 Josh. 2:12 [r]ch. 26:35 & 28:2 Ex. 34:16 Deut. 7:3 **24:4** [s]ch. 28:2 [t]ch. 12:1 **24:7** [u]ch. 12:1 [v]ch. 12:7 & 13:15 & 17:8 Ex. 32:13 Deut. 1:8 & 34:4 Acts 7:5 [w]Ex. 23:20,23 & 33:2 Heb. 1:14 **24:8** [x]Josh. 2:17,20 **24:10** [y]ver. 2 [z]ch. 27:43 **24:11** [a]Ex. 2:16 1 Sam. 9:11 **24:12** [b]ver. 27 ch. 26:24 & 32:9 Ex. 3:6,15 [c]Neh. 1:11 Ps. 37:5

k Heb. *gone into days* **1** Or, *and* **m** Heb. *that women which draw* water *go forth*

23:20 THE FIELD . . . FOR A POSSESSION. The Scriptures reveal that the only piece of land in Canaan that Abraham ever possessed in fulfillment of God's promise was a grave (Heb. 11:8–9). His descendants did not begin to possess the promised land until the time of Joshua. This fact points to the life of faith that waits till the end of life for the full reward of one's trust in God (Heb. 11:13). Believers, like Abraham, must not set their hearts ultimately on things of this earth, but must desire a heavenly country where God "has prepared a city for them" (Heb. 11:16; see 11:10, note).

24:3 NOT TAKE A WIFE. Abraham knew that God had called him and his descendants to live a life separated from the people around him (see article on THE CALL OF ABRAHAM, p. 25). Their separation was God's method of preserving a holy people for Himself. For this reason Isaac was not permitted to marry a Canaanite woman or to return to the land from where Abraham came (vv. 3,5; see article on SPIRITUAL SEPARATION FOR BELIEVERS, p. 1814).

24:12 O LORD GOD . . . I PRAY THEE. Abra-

me good speed this day, and show kindness unto my master Abraham.

13 Behold, [d]I stand *here* by the well of water; and [e]the daughters of the men of the city come out to draw water:

14 And let it come to pass, that the damsel to whom I shall say, Let down thy pitcher, I pray thee, that I may drink; and she shall say, Drink, and I will give thy camels drink also: *let the same be* she *that* thou hast appointed for thy servant Isaac; and [f]thereby shall I know that thou hast shown kindness unto my master.

15 ¶ And it came to pass, before he had done speaking, that, behold, Rebekah came out, who was born to Bethuel, son of [g]Milcah, the wife of Nahor, Abraham's brother, with her pitcher upon her shoulder.

16 And the damsel [h]*was* [n]very fair to look upon, a virgin, neither had any man known her: and she went down to the well, and filled her pitcher, and came up.

17 And the servant ran to meet her, and said, Let me, I pray thee, drink a little water of thy pitcher.

18 [i]And she said, Drink, my lord: and she hasted, and let down her pitcher upon her hand, and gave him drink.

19 And when she had done giving him drink, she said, I will draw *water* for thy camels also, until they have done drinking.

20 And she hasted, and emptied her pitcher into the trough, and ran again unto the well to draw *water,* and drew for all his camels.

21 And the man wondering at her held his peace, to wit whether [j]the LORD had made his journey prosperous or not.

22 And it came to pass, as the camels had done drinking, that the man took a golden [k]earring[o] of half a shekel weight, and two bracelets for her hands of ten *shekels* weight of gold;

23 And said, Whose daughter *art* thou? tell me, I pray thee: is there room *in* thy father's house for us to lodge in?

24 And she said unto him, [l]I *am* the daughter of Bethuel the son of Milcah, which she bare unto Nahor.

25 She said moreover unto him, We have both straw and provender enough, and room to lodge in.

26 And the man [m]bowed down his head, and worshipped the LORD.

27 And he said, [n]Blessed *be* the LORD God of my master Abraham, who hath not left destitute my master of [o]his mercy and his truth: I *being* in the way, the LORD [p]led me to the house of my master's brethren.

28 And the damsel ran, and told *them of* her mother's house these things.

29 ¶ And Rebekah had a brother, and his name *was* [q]Laban: and Laban ran out unto the man, unto the well.

30 And it came to pass, when he saw the earring and bracelets upon his sister's hands, and when he heard the words of Rebekah his sister, saying, Thus spake the man unto me; that he came unto the man; and, behold, he stood by the camels at the well.

31 And he said, Come in, [r]thou blessed of the LORD; wherefore standest thou without? for I have prepared the house, and room for the camels.

32 ¶ And the man came into the house: and he ungirded his camels, and [s]gave straw and provender for the camels, and water to wash his feet, and the men's feet that *were* with him.

33 And there was set *meat* before him to eat: but he said, [t]I will not eat,

24:13 [d]ver. 43 [e]Ex. 2:16 **24:14** [f]See Judg. 6:17,37 1 Sam. 6:7 & 14:10 & 20:7 **24:15** [g]ch. 11:29 & 22:23 **24:16** [h]ch. 26:7 **24:18** [i]1 Pet. 3:8 **24:21** [j]ver. 12,56 **24:22** [k]Ex. 32:2,3 Is. 3:19-21

24:24 [l]ch. 22:23 **24:26** [m]ver. 52 Ex. 4:31 **24:27** [n]Ex. 18:10 Ruth 4:14 1 Sam. 25:32,39 [o]ch. 32:10 Ps. 98:3 [p]ver. 48 **24:29** [q]ch. 29:5 **24:31** [r]ch. 26:29 Judg. 17:2 Ruth 3:10 Ps. 115:15 **24:32** [s]ch. 43:24 Judg. 19:21 **24:33** [t]Job 23:12 John 4:34 Eph. 6:5-7

[n] Heb. *good of countenance* [o] Or, *jewel for the forehead*

ham's servant (probably Eliezer, 15:2) was a devout man who sought the Lord through prayer. This narrative indicates that each step of his journey was marked by seeking God for His blessing and guidance (cf. 1 Thes. 5:17). Notice also that after Rebekah responded favorably, he praised God immediately (vv. 26–27). The servant's prayer and his faith in God reveal that Abraham's obedient faith was not merely private; it was also active in the lives of other members of his household.

24:14 I WILL GIVE THY CAMELS DRINK. Abraham's servant asked for a sign from God as to which girl God had chosen. Watering camels would be a difficult and laborious task. Any young woman who would voluntarily agree to such a task would be demonstrating an inner spirit of submission, helpfulness, and willingness to serve.

24:27 THE LORD LED ME. Because the servant had devoutly sought the Lord, the Lord guided him along the way. This accords with the Scriptural teaching that "the steps of a *good* man are ordered by the LORD: and he delighteth in his way" (Ps. 37:23). Again, "in all thy ways acknowledge him, and he shall direct thy paths" (Prov. 3:6). In a similar manner, all believers should expect God to guide them faithfully as He did Abraham's servant (see v. 40, note; cf. John 7:17; Rom. 12:2).

until I have told mine errand. And he said, Speak on.

34 And he said, I *am* Abraham's servant.

35 And the LORD [u]hath blessed my master greatly; and he is become great: and he hath given him flocks, and herds, and silver, and gold, and menservants, and maidservants, and camels, and asses.

36 And Sarah my master's wife [v]bare a son to my master when she was old: and [w]unto him hath he given all that he hath.

37 And my master [x]made me swear, saying, Thou shalt not take a wife to my son of the daughters of the Canaanites, in whose land I dwell:

38 [y]But thou shalt go unto my father's house, and to my kindred, and take a wife unto my son.

39 [z]And I said unto my master, Peradventure the woman will not follow me.

40 [a]And he said unto me, The LORD, [b]before whom I walk, will send his angel with thee, and prosper thy way; and thou shalt take a wife for my son of my kindred, and of my father's house:

41 [c]Then shalt thou be clear from *this* my oath, when thou comest to my kindred; and if they give not thee *one,* thou shalt be clear from my oath.

42 And I came this day unto the well, and said, [d]O LORD God of my master Abraham, if now thou do prosper my way which I go:

43 [e]Behold, I stand by the well of water; and it shall come to pass, that when the virgin cometh forth to draw *water,* and I say to her, Give me, I pray thee, a little water of thy pitcher to drink;

44 And she say to me, Both drink thou, and I will also draw for thy camels: *let* the same *be* the woman whom the LORD hath appointed out for my master's son.

45 [f]And before I had done [g]speaking in mine heart, behold, Rebekah came forth with her pitcher on her shoulder; and she went down unto the well, and drew *water:* and I said unto her, Let me drink, I pray thee.

46 And she made haste, and let down her pitcher from her *shoulder,* and said, Drink, and I will give thy camels drink also: so I drank, and she made the camels drink also.

47 And I asked her, and said, Whose daughter *art* thou? And she said, The daughter of Bethuel, Nahor's son, whom Milcah bare unto him: and I [h]put the earring upon her face, and the bracelets upon her hands.

48 [i]And I bowed down my head, and worshipped the LORD, and blessed the LORD God of my master Abraham, which had led me in the right way to take [j]my master's brother's daughter unto his son.

49 And now if ye will [k]deal kindly and truly with my master, tell me: and if not, tell me; that I may turn to the right hand, or to the left.

50 Then Laban and Bethuel answered and said, [l]The thing proceedeth from the LORD: we cannot [m]speak unto thee bad or good.

51 Behold, Rebekah [n]*is* before thee, take *her,* and go, and let her be thy master's son's wife, as the LORD hath spoken.

52 And it came to pass, that, when Abraham's servant heard their words, he [o]worshipped the LORD, *bowing himself* to the earth.

53 And the servant brought forth [p]jewels[p] of silver, and jewels of gold, and raiment, and gave *them* to Rebekah: he gave also to her brother and to her mother [q]precious things.

54 And they did eat and drink, he and the men that *were* with him, and tarried all night; and they rose up in the morning, and he said, [r]Send me away unto my master.

55 And her brother and her mother said, Let the damsel abide with us [q]*a few* days, at the least ten; after that she shall go.

56 And he said unto them, Hinder me not, seeing the LORD hath prospered

24:35 [u]ver. 1 ch. 13:2 **24:36** [v]ch. 21:2 [w]ch. 21:10 & 25:5 **24:37** [x]ver. 3 **24:38** [y]ver. 4 **24:39** [z]ver. 5 **24:40** [a]ver. 7 [b]ch. 17:1 **24:41** [c]ver. 8 **24:42** [d]ver. 12 **24:43** [e]ver. 13 **24:45** [f]ver. 15 [g]1 Sam. 1:13

24:47 [h]Ezek. 16:11,12 **24:48** [i]ver. 26 [j]ch. 22:23 **24:49** [k]ch. 47:29 Josh. 2:14 **24:50** [l]Ps. 118:23 Mat. 21:42 [m]ch. 31:24 **24:51** [n]ch. 20:15 **24:52** [o]ver. 26 **24:53** [p]Ex. 3:22 & 11:2 & 12:35 [q]2 Chr. 21:3 Ezra 1:6 **24:54** [r]ver. 56,59

p Heb. *vessels* q Or, *a full year,* or, *ten months*

24:40 THE LORD . . WILL SEND HIS ANGEL WITH THEE. This verse reveals one of the ways that God protects His children and guides them on their way. He may send angels to operate behind the scenes to make their way successful. Heb. 1:14 states that angels are "ministering spirits, sent forth to minister for them who shall be heirs of salvation" (see Mat. 18:10, note; see article on ANGELS AND THE ANGEL OF THE LORD, p. 368.

my way; send me away that I may go to my master.

57 And they said, We will call the damsel, and inquire at her mouth.

58 And they called Rebekah, and said unto her, Wilt thou go with this man? And she said, I will go.

59 And they sent away Rebekah their sister, and [s]her nurse, and Abraham's servant, and his men.

60 And they blessed Rebekah, and said unto her, Thou *art* our sister, be thou [t]*the mother* of thousands of millions, and [u]let thy seed possess the gate of those which hate them.

61 ¶ And Rebekah arose, and her damsels, and they rode upon the camels, and followed the man: and the servant took Rebekah, and went his way.

62 And Isaac came from the way of the [v]well Lahai-roi; for he dwelt in the south country.

63 And Isaac went out [w]to[r] meditate in the field at the eventide: and he lifted up his eyes, and saw, and, behold, the camels *were* coming.

64 And Rebekah lifted up her eyes, and when she saw Isaac, [x]she lighted off the camel.

65 For she *had* said unto the servant, What man *is* this that walketh in the field to meet us? And the servant *had* said, It *is* my master: therefore she took a veil, and covered herself.

66 And the servant told Isaac all things that he had done.

67 And Isaac brought her into his mother Sarah's tent, and took Rebekah, and she became his wife; and he loved her: and Isaac [y]was comforted after his mother's *death.*

The death of Abraham

25:1–4pp — 1 Chr. 1:32–33

25 THEN AGAIN Abraham took a wife, and her name *was* Keturah.

2 And [z]she bare him Zimran, and Jokshan, and Medan, and Midian, and Ishbak, and Shuah.

3 And Jokshan begat Sheba, and Dedan. And the sons of Dedan were Asshurim, and Letushim, and Leummim.

4 And the sons of Midian; Ephah, and Epher, and Hanoch, and Abidah, and Eldaah. All these *were* the children of Keturah.

5 ¶ And [a]Abraham gave all that he had unto Isaac.

6 But unto the sons of the concubines, which Abraham had, Abraham gave gifts, and [b]sent them away from Isaac his son, while he yet lived, eastward, unto [c]the east country.

7 And these *are* the days of the years of Abraham's life which he lived, an hundred threescore and fifteen years.

8 Then Abraham gave up the ghost, and [d]died in a good old age, an old man, and full *of years;* and [e]was gathered to his people.

9 And [f]his sons Isaac and Ishmael buried him in the cave of Machpelah, in the field of Ephron the son of Zohar the Hittite, which *is* before Mamre;

10 [g]The field which Abraham purchased of the sons of Heth: [h]there was Abraham buried, and Sarah his wife.

11 ¶ And it came to pass after the death of Abraham, that God blessed his son Isaac; and Isaac dwelt by the [i]well Lahai-roi.

The descendants of Ishmael

25:12–16pp — 1 Chr. 1:29–31

12 ¶ Now these *are* the generations of Ishmael, Abraham's son, [j]whom Hagar the Egyptian, Sarah's handmaid, bare unto Abraham:

13 And [k]these *are* the names of the sons of Ishmael, by their names, according to their generations: the first-

[r] Or, *to pray*

24:59 [s]ch. 35:8
24:60 [t]ch. 17:16 [u]ch. 22:17
24:62 [v]ch. 25:11
24:63 [w]Josh. 1:8 Ps. 1:2 & 77:12 & 119:15 & 143:5
24:64 [x]Josh. 15:18
24:67 [y]ch. 38:12
25:2 [z]1 Chr. 1:32
25:5 [a]ch. 24:36
25:6 [b]ch. 21:14 [c]Judg. 6:3
25:8 [d]ch. 15:15 [e]ch. 35:29 & 49:33
25:9 [f]ch. 35:29 & 50:13
25:10 [g]ch. 23:16 [h]ch. 49:31
25:11 [i]ch. 16:14
25:12 [j]ch. 16:15
25:13 [k]1 Chr. 1:29

25:5 ABRAHAM GAVE ALL HE HAD TO ISAAC. Abraham's last act was to insure that God's covenant promise would pass on to Isaac. His concern and action provide an example to all family and church leaders, who must do all they can to ensure that the full reality of the believer's fellowship with God in truth, purity, power, and blessing is passed on to the next generation. To allow God's people to drift gradually into worldliness and away from God's way is the ultimate failure in spiritual leadership (see Eph. 4:11–13; see article on THE MINISTRY GIFTS OF THE CHURCH, p. 1852).

25:6 CONCUBINES. See 29:28, note.

25:6 GIFTS. Most likely the gifts were an adequate inheritance for each one to establish his own flocks and herds.

25:8 THEN ABRAHAM . . . WAS GATHERED TO HIS PEOPLE. This O.T. expression signifies more than mere burial, for it refers to life with one's people after death (cf. 15:15; 47:30; 2 Sam. 12:23; Mat. 22:31–32; Heb. 11:13–16).

born of Ishmael, Nebajoth; and Kedar, and Adbeel, and Mibsam,

14 And Mishma, and Dumah, and Massa,

15 [s]Hadar, and Tema, Jetur, Naphish, and Kedemah:

16 These *are* the sons of Ishmael, and these *are* their names, by their towns, and by their castles; [l]twelve princes according to their nations.

17 And these *are* the years of the life of Ishmael, an hundred and thirty and seven years: and [m]he gave up the ghost and died; and was gathered unto his people.

18 [n]And they dwelt from Havilah unto Shur, that *is* before Egypt, as thou goest toward Assyria: *and* he [t]died [o]in the presence of all his brethren.

Jacob and Esau

19 ¶ And these *are* the generations of Isaac, Abraham's son: [p]Abraham begat Isaac:

20 And Isaac was forty years old when he took Rebekah to wife, [q]the daughter of Bethuel the Syrian of Padan-aram, [r]the sister to Laban the Syrian.

21 And Isaac entreated the LORD for his wife, because she *was* barren: [s]and the LORD was entreated of him, and [t]Rebekah his wife conceived.

22 And the children struggled together within her; and she said, If *it be* so, why *am* I thus? [u]And she went to inquire of the LORD.

25:16 [l]ch. 17:20
25:17 [m]ver. 8
25:18 [n]1 Sam. 15:7 [o]ch. 16:12
25:19 [p]Mat. 1:2
25:20 [q]ch. 22:23 [r]ch. 24:29
25:21 [s]1 Chr. 5:20 2 Chr. 33:13 Ezra 8:23 [t]Rom. 9:10
25:22 [u]1 Sam. 9:9 & 10:22

25:23 [v]ch. 17:16 & 24:60 [w]2 Sam. 8:14 [x]ch. 27:29 Mal. 1:3 Rom. 9:12
25:25 [y]ch. 27:11,16,23
25:26 [z]Hos. 12:3 [a]ch. 27:36
25:27 [b]ch. 27:3,5 [c]Job 1:1,8 [d]Heb. 11:9
25:28 [e]ch. 27:19,25,31 [f]ch. 27:6

23 And the LORD said unto her, [v]Two nations *are* in thy womb, and two manner of people shall be separated from thy bowels; and [w]*the one* people shall be stronger than *the other* people; and [x]the elder shall serve the younger.

24 ¶ And when her days to be delivered were fulfilled, behold, *there were* twins in her womb.

25 And the first came out red, [y]all over like an hairy garment; and they called his name Esau.

26 And after that came his brother out, and [z]his hand took hold on Esau's heel; and [a]his name was called Jacob: and Isaac *was* threescore years old when she bare them.

27 And the boys grew: and Esau was [b]a cunning hunter, a man of the field; and Jacob *was* [c]a plain man, [d]dwelling in tents.

28 And Isaac loved Esau, because [u]he did [e]eat of *his* venison: [f]but Rebekah loved Jacob.

29 ¶ And Jacob sod pottage: and Esau came from the field, and he *was* faint:

30 And Esau said to Jacob, Feed me, I pray thee, [v]with that same red *pottage;* for I *am* faint: therefore was his name called [w]Edom.

31 And Jacob said, Sell me this day thy birthright.

[s] Or, *Hadad* [t] Heb. *fell* [u] Heb. *venison* was *in his mouth* [v] Heb. *with that red,* with that *red* pottage [w] i.e. *Red*

25:17 ISHMAEL . . . WAS GATHERED UNTO HIS PEOPLE. This suggests that Ishmael trusted in God and received the spiritual inheritance of his father and of all who die in faith (cf. previous note).

25:21 AND ISAAC ENTREATED THE LORD. Rebekah, like Sarah, was barren for many years, and Isaac had to ask the Lord for the next child of promise from whose seed the Redeemer eventually would be born. In this way God emphasizes the spiritual principle that redemption, spiritual inheritance, and the fulfillment of the covenant are not realized through natural means, but by God's action and grace in response to prayer and seeking Him. In other words, prayer is the means by which God chooses to grant His promises and blessings.

25:23 TWO NATIONS. The two nations are the Israelites (Jacob's descendants) and the Edomites (Esau's descendants). Hostility and conflict subsequently characterized the relationship between these two nations (e.g., Num. 20:14–21; 2 Sam. 8:14; Ps. 137:7).

25:23 THE ELDER SHALL SERVE THE YOUNGER. It was customary that the younger of two sons would serve the older. In this case, however, God reversed this pattern. This too illustrates the principle that one's place in God's redemptive purpose is not determined by natural development but by God's grace and will (cf. 48:13ff; 1 Sam. 16:1; Rom. 9:11–12).

25:26 ISAAC *WAS* THREESCORE YEARS OLD. Because Rebekah was barren, Isaac and Rebekah had to wait twenty years for the promised seed (cf. v. 20). The fulfillment of God's purposes in their lives came through prayer and the endurance of faith (see v. 21, note).

25:31 BIRTHRIGHT. The birthright (i.e., the inheritance of the firstborn) consisted of: (1) leadership in worship and headship in the family; (2) a double portion of the inheritance (at least in later times, cf. Deut. 21:17); and (3) the title to the covenant blessing that God had promised to Abraham. That Esau sold his birthright reveals how little value he placed on God's blessings and covenant promises. He foolishly chose to trade future long-range blessings for present momentary pleasures. Thus, he "despised *his* birthright" (v. 34; cf. Heb. 12:16). Jacob, on the other hand, desired the spiritual blessings of the future, and from

32 And Esau said, Behold, I *am* [x]at the point to die: and what profit shall this birthright do to me?

33 And Jacob said, Swear to me this day; and he sware unto him: and [g]he sold his birthright unto Jacob.

34 Then Jacob gave Esau bread and pottage of lentiles; and [h]he did eat and drink, and rose up, and went his way: thus Esau despised *his* birthright.

Isaac and Abimelech

26:1–11Ref — Gen. 12:10–20; 20:1–18

26 AND THERE was a famine in the land, beside the [i]first famine that was in the days of Abraham. And Isaac went unto [j]Abimelech king of the Philistines unto Gerar.

2 And the LORD appeared unto him, and said, Go not down into Egypt; dwell in [k]the land which I shall tell thee of:

3 [l]Sojourn in this land, and [m]I will be with thee, and [n]will bless thee; for unto thee, and unto thy seed, [o]I will give all these countries, and I will perform [p]the oath which I sware unto Abraham thy father;

4 And [q]I will make thy seed to multiply as the stars of heaven, and will give unto thy seed all these countries; [r]and in thy seed shall all the nations of the earth be blessed;

5 [s]Because that Abraham obeyed my voice, and kept my charge, my commandments, my statutes, and my laws.

Ex. 19:3-6

6 ¶ And Isaac dwelt in Gerar:

7 And the men of the place asked *him* of his wife; and [t]he said, She *is* my sister: for [u]he feared to say, *She is* my wife; lest, *said he,* the men of the place should kill me for Rebekah; because she [v]*was* fair to look upon.

8 And it came to pass, when he had been there a long time, that Abimelech king of the Philistines looked out at a window, and saw, and, behold, Isaac *was* sporting with Rebekah his wife.

9 And Abimelech called Isaac, and said, Behold, of a surety she *is* thy wife: and how saidst thou, She *is* my sister? And Isaac said unto him, Because I said, Lest I die for her.

10 And Abimelech said, What *is* this thou hast done unto us? one of the people might lightly have lain with thy wife, and [w]thou shouldest have brought guiltiness upon us.

11 And Abimelech charged all *his* people, saying, He that [x]toucheth this man or his wife shall surely be put to death.

12 Then Isaac sowed in that land, and [y]received in the same year [y]an hundredfold: and the LORD [z]blessed him.

13 And the man [a]waxed great, and [z]went forward, and grew until he became very great:

14 For he had possession of flocks, and possession of herds, and great store of [a]servants: and the Philistines [b]envied him.

15 For all the wells [c]which his father's servants had digged in the days of Abraham his father, the Philistines had stopped them, and filled them with earth.

16 And Abimelech said unto Isaac, Go from us; for [d]thou art much mightier than we.

17 ¶ And Isaac departed thence, and pitched his tent in the valley of Gerar, and dwelt there.

18 And Isaac digged again the wells of water, which they had digged in the days of Abraham his father; for the Philistines had stopped them after the death of Abraham: [e]and he called

25:33 [g]Heb. 12:16 **25:34** [h]Eccl. 8:15 Is. 22:13 1 Cor. 15:32 **26:1** [i]ch. 12:10 [j]ch. 20:2 **26:2** [k]ch. 12:1 **26:3** [l]ch. 20:1 Ps. 39:12 Heb. 11:9 [m]ch. 28:15 [n]ch. 12:2 [o]ch. 13:15 [p]ch. 22:16 Ps. 105:9 **26:4** [q]ch. 15:5 & 22:17 [r]ch. 12:3 & 22:18 **26:5** [s]ch. 22:16,18 **26:7** [t]ch. 12:13 & 20:2,13 [u]Prov. 29:25 [v]ch. 24:16 **26:10** [w]ch. 20:9 **26:11** [x]Ps. 105:15 **26:12** [y]Mat. 13:8 Mark 4:8 [z]ver. 3 Job 42:12 **26:13** [a]ch. 24:35 Prov. 10:22 **26:14** [b]ch. 37:11 Eccl. 4:4 **26:15** [c]ch. 21:30 **26:16** [d]Ex. 1:9 **26:18** [e]ch. 21:31

[x] Heb. *going to die* [y] Heb. *found* [z] Heb. *went going* [a] Or, *husbandry*

him came the twelve tribes of Israel.

26:3–4 I WILL BE WITH THEE. God appeared to Isaac and passed on to him the promises made with Abraham (12:1–3,7; 13:14–18; 15; 17:1–8,15–22; 22:15–18). Like his father, Isaac had to learn to live by the promises of God. An important part of the covenant promise was the personal relationship with God described in the words, "I *am* with thee" (v. 24; see 17:7, note; see article on GOD'S COVENANT WITH ABRAHAM, ISAAC, AND JACOB, p. 48).

26:5 BECAUSE THAT ABRAHAM OBEYED. God lifted up Abraham as a model of the obedience of faith (cf. Rom. 1:5; 16:26). He had made a sincere endeavor to keep the laws and commandments of the Lord. Because of this, God blessed him. Isaac and all believers must emulate Abraham's faith and obedience if they hope to participate in God's covenant promises and salvation (cf. Lev. 26:14–15,46; Deut. 11:1).

26:12 THE LORD BLESSED HIM. In the O.T., wealth was sometimes given as a reward for faithfulness. In the N.T., by contrast, wealth is usually viewed as a potential hindrance to spiritual life and commitment to God (see 1 John 2, note; see article on RICHES AND POVERTY, p. 1568).

their names after the names by which
his father had called them.
19 And Isaac's servants digged in
the valley, and found there a well of
[b]springing water.
20 And the herdmen of Gerar [f]did
strive with Isaac's herdmen, saying,
The water *is* ours: and he called the
name of the well [c]Esek; because they
strove with him.
21 And they digged another well,
and strove for that also: and he called
the name of it [d]Sitnah.
22 And he removed from thence,
and digged another well; and for that
they strove not: and he called the name
of it [e]Rehoboth; and he said, For now
the LORD hath made room for us, and
we shall [g]be fruitful in the land.
23 And he went up from thence to
Beer-sheba.
24 And the LORD appeared unto him
the same night, and said, [h]I *am* the
God of Abraham thy father: [i]fear not,
for [j]I *am* with thee, and will bless
thee, and multiply thy seed for my ser-
vant Abraham's sake.
25 And he [k]builded an altar there,
and [l]called upon the name of the
LORD, and pitched his tent there: and
there Isaac's servants digged a well.
26 ¶ Then Abimelech went to him
from Gerar, and Ahuzzath one of his
friends, [m]and Phichol the chief cap-
tain of his army.
27 And Isaac said unto them,
Wherefore come ye to me, seeing [n]ye
hate me, and have [o]sent me away
from you?
28 And they said, [f]We saw certain-
ly that the LORD [p]was with thee: and
we said, Let there be now an oath be-
twixt us, *even* betwixt us and thee, and
let us make a covenant with thee;
29 [g]That thou wilt do us no hurt,
as we have not touched thee, and as we
have done unto thee nothing but good,
and have sent thee away in peace:
[q]thou *art* now the blessed of the LORD.
30 [r]And he made them a feast, and
they did eat and drink.
31 And they rose up betimes in the
morning, and [s]sware one to another:
and Isaac sent them away, and they de-
parted from him in peace.
32 And it came to pass the same
day, that Isaac's servants came, and
told him concerning the well which
they had digged, and said unto him, We
have found water.
33 And he called it [h]Shebah:
[t]therefore the name of the city *is*
[i]Beer-sheba unto this day.
34 ¶ [u]And Esau was forty years old
when he took to wife Judith the daugh-
ter of Beeri the Hittite, and Bashemath
the daughter of Elon the Hittite:
35 Which [v]were [j]a grief of mind
unto Isaac and to Rebekah.

Jacob's stolen blessing

27 AND IT came to pass, that
when Isaac was old, and [w]his
eyes were dim, so that he could not
see, he called Esau his eldest son, and
said unto him, My son: and he said
unto him, Behold, *here am* I.
2 And he said, Behold now, I am
old, I [x]know not the day of my death:
3 [y]Now therefore take, I pray thee,
thy weapons, thy quiver and thy bow,
and go out to the field, and [k]take me
some venison;
4 And make me savoury meat, such
as I love, and bring *it* to me, that I may
eat; that my soul [z]may bless thee be-
fore I die.
5 And Rebekah heard when Isaac
spake to Esau his son. And Esau went
to the field to hunt *for* venison, *and* to
bring *it*.

26:20 [f]ch. 21:25 **26:22** [g]ch. 17:6 & 28:3 & 41:52 Ex. 1:7 **26:24** [h]ch. 17:7 & 24:12 [i]ch. 15:1 [j]ver. 3,4 **26:25** [k]ch. 12:7 & 13:18 [l]Ps. 116:17 **26:26** [m]ch. 21:22 **26:27** [n]Judg. 11:7 [o]ver. 16 **26:28** [p]ch. 21:22,23 **26:29** [q]ch. 24:31 Ps. 115:15 **26:30** [r]ch. 19:3 **26:31** [s]ch. 21:31 **26:33** [t]ch. 21:31 **26:34** [u]ch. 36:2 **26:35** [v]ch. 27:46 & 28:1,8 **27:1** [w]ch. 48:10 1 Sam. 3:2 **27:2** [x]Prov. 27:1 Jas. 4:14 **27:3** [y]ch. 25:27,28 **27:4** [z]ver. 27 ch. 48:9,15 & 49:28 Deut. 33:1

[b] Heb. *living* [c] i.e. *Contention* [d] i.e. *Hatred* [e] i.e. *Room* [f] Heb. *Seeing we saw* [g] Heb. *If thou shalt* [h] i.e. *An oath* [i] i.e. *The well of the oath* [j] Heb. *bitterness of spirit* [k] Heb. *hunt*

26:35 A GRIEF . . . UNTO ISAAC AND TO REBEKAH. Esau was indifferent to the righteous standards of his parents, for he married two women who were not followers of the true God. This action also demonstrated his lack of interest in God's covenant blessing.

27:1 WHEN ISAAC WAS OLD. Ch. 27 portrays Isaac and his family pursuing God's blessing in an unrighteous way. Personal preference of Isaac for Esau, contrary to God's will, and deceptive manipulation by Rebekah and Jacob took preeminence over the spiritual good of God's covenant. Whenever God's work is undertaken in unrighteous ways, damage is done to God's purpose and to all those involved.

27:4 MY SOUL MAY BLESS THEE. The birthright blessing and oral declaration of the father were legally binding in ancient Near Eastern law (cf. 49:28–33). Isaac appeared to have forgotten or ignored God's word that Esau would serve Jacob, the younger (25:23). He also disregarded the fact that Esau had married two heathen women (cf. 26:34–35). Furthermore, Isaac made no attempt to seek or consider God's will in the matter.

GOD'S COVENANT WITH ABRAHAM, ISAAC, AND JACOB

***Gen. 26:3–5** "Sojourn in this land, and I will be with thee, and will bless thee; for unto thee, and unto thy seed, I will give all these countries, and I will perform the oath which I sware unto Abraham thy father; And I will make thy seed to multiply as the stars of the heaven, and will give unto thy seed all these countries; and in thy seed shall all the nations of the earth be blessed; Because that Abraham obeyed my voice, and kept my charge, my commandments, my statutes, and my laws."*

THE NATURE OF A COVENANT. God's relationship with His people is described throughout the Bible in terms of "covenant." The word first occurs in Gen. 6:18 and extends into the N.T., where God made a new covenant with humankind in Jesus Christ (see article on THE OLD COVENANT AND THE NEW COVENANT, p. 1954). By understanding God's covenant with the patriarchs (Abraham, Isaac, and Jacob), we learn about how God wants us to live in our covenantal relationship with Him.

(1) God's special covenant name as revealed in the Bible is *Yahweh* (translated as "LORD"; see Gen. 2:4, note; Ex. 3:14, note). Inherent in this covenant name is God's lovingkindness, His redemptive concern for the human race, His faithful presence with His people, and His desire to be in fellowship with them and to be their Lord.

(2) The fundamental promise of the covenant is the Lord's promise "to be a God unto thee, and to thy seed after thee" (see Gen. 17:7, note). On this promise rest all the other promises that are a part of the covenant. It means that God firmly binds Himself to His faithful people to be their God, and that His grace, protection, goodness, and blessing are given to them in love (cf. Jer. 11:4; 24:7; 30:22; 32:38; Ezek. 11:20; 36:28; Zech. 8:8).

(3) The ultimate goal of God's covenant with humankind was to bring salvation, not just to one nation (Israel), but to the whole human race. Already with Abraham God promised that in him "all families of the earth" would be blessed (Gen. 12:3; 18:18; 22:18; cf. 26:4). God extended His covenant grace to the nation of Israel in order that they might be "a light to the Gentiles" (Is. 49:6; cf. 42:6). This covenant was fulfilled through the coming of the Lord Jesus Christ as Redeemer, when Christians began to spread the message of the gospel throughout the world (see Luke 2:32; Acts 13:46–47; Gal. 3:8–14).

(4) In the various covenantal arrangements that God made with humans throughout the Scriptures, two principles are operative: (a) God alone established the promises and obligations of His covenant, and (b) human beings were expected to accept them in obedient faith. On some occasions God outlined fully ahead of time the promises and responsibilities for both parties (see article on GOD'S COVENANT WITH THE ISRAELITES, p. 314); at no time, however, were people in a situation where they could bargain with God about the stipulations of the covenant.

GOD'S COVENANT WITH ABRAHAM. (1) When God entered into covenant fellowship with Abraham (see Gen. 15), He explicitly offered several promises that He had in store for him: God as Abraham's shield and reward (Gen. 15:1), many descendants (Gen. 15:5), and the land of Canaan as his inheritance (Gen. 15:7; see Gen. 15:6, note; 17:8, note; cf. also 12:1–3; see article on THE CALL OF ABRAHAM, p. 25).

(2) God called upon Abraham to respond in faith to these promises, to accept them, and to trust in God as his Lord. Because he did so, Abraham was accepted by God as righteous (Gen. 15:6) and was confirmed in a personal relationship with Him.

(3) Not only was faith necessary to receive the covenant initially, but God also required that if the covenant blessings were to continue, Abraham had to make a sincere effort to please Him by an obedient life. (a) God demanded that Abraham walk before Him and be "perfect" (see Gen. 17:1, note). In other words, if his faith were not ac-

companied by obedience (cf. Rom. 1:5), Abraham would disqualify himself from participation in God's eternal purposes. (b) In one specific instance, God tested Abraham by commanding him to sacrifice his son Isaac (Gen. 22:1–2). Abraham passed the test, and consequently God promised to continue His covenant with him (see Gen. 22:18, note). (c) God specifically informed Isaac that the blessings of the covenant were still valid and would be passed on to him *because* Abraham had obeyed His voice and kept His commandments (Gen. 26:4–5).

(4) God specifically commanded Abraham and his descendants to see to it that every male child born in his household be circumcised (Gen. 17:9–13). The Lord went on to stipulate that any male who was not circumcised would be cut off from the people of God (Gen. 17:14), for he had broken the covenant. In other words, refusal to obey God would lead to the removal of covenant blessings.

(5) God's covenant with Abraham was called an "everlasting covenant" (Gen. 17:7). God intended that the covenant be a permanent arrangement. However, it could be broken by Abraham's descendants, so that God would no longer be bound to His promises. For example, His promise that the land of Canaan would be an everlasting possession for Abraham and his descendants (Gen. 17:8) was broken by Israel's apostasy and Judah's unfaithfulness and their refusal to obey God's law (Is. 24:5; Jer. 31:32); thus Israel was carried away into exile in Assyria (2 Ki. 17), while Judah was later carried away captive to Babylon (see 2 Ki. 25; 2 Chr. 36; Jer. 11:1–17; Ezek. 17:16–21).

GOD'S COVENANT WITH ISAAC. (1) God sought to establish the Abrahamic covenant with each succeeding generation, beginning with Abraham's son Isaac (see Gen. 17:21). In other words, it was not enough that Isaac had Abraham as his father; he too had to accept God's promises by faith. Only then would God say, "I *am* with thee, and will bless thee, and multiply thy seed" (Gen. 26:24).

(2) For the first twenty years of their marriage, Isaac and Rebekah had no children (cf. Gen. 25:20,26). Rebekah's womb was not opened until Isaac earnestly prayed to the Lord for his wife to conceive (Gen. 25:21). This answer of prayer demonstrates that the fulfillment of the covenant is not realized through natural means, but only by God's gracious action in response to prayer and seeking Him (see Gen. 25:21, note).

(3) Isaac also had to be obedient to the Lord in order to continue receiving the covenant blessings. When a famine appeared in the land of Canaan, for example, God told Isaac not to go down to Egypt but to remain where he was. If he obeyed God, God promised to "perform the oath which I sware unto Abraham thy father" (Gen. 26:3; see 26:5, note).

GOD'S COVENANT WITH JACOB. (1) Isaac and Rebekah had two children, Esau and Jacob. Normally one would expect the blessings of the covenant to be passed on through the firstborn, i.e., Esau. But God revealed to Rebekah that her older twin would serve the younger, and Esau himself despised his birthright (see Gen. 25:31, note). Furthermore, he showed indifference to the righteous standards of his parents by marrying two women who were not followers of the true God. In summary, Esau showed no interest in God's covenant blessings. Consequently, Jacob, who did desire the spiritual blessings of the future, received the promises rather than Esau (Gen. 28:13–15).

(2) As with Abraham and Isaac, the covenant with Jacob required the obedience of faith for its continuance. For much of his life, this patriarch depended on his own ingenuity to survive and succeed. It was not until Jacob finally obeyed the command and will of the Lord (Gen. 31:13) to leave Haran and return to the promised land of Canaan, and more specifically, to go to Bethel (Gen. 35:1–7), that God renewed with him the covenant promises made to Abraham (Gen. 35:9–13).

For more on the covenant, see article on GOD'S COVENANT WITH THE ISRAELITES, p. 314.

6 ¶ And Rebekah spake unto Jacob her son, saying, Behold, I heard thy father speak unto Esau thy brother, saying,

7 Bring me venison, and make me savoury meat, that I may eat, and bless thee before the LORD before my death.

8 Now therefore, my son, [a]obey my voice according to that which I command thee.

9 Go now to the flock, and fetch me from thence two good kids of the goats; and I will make them [b]savoury meat for thy father, such as he loveth:

10 And thou shalt bring *it* to thy father, that he may eat, and that he [c]may bless thee before his death.

11 And Jacob said to Rebekah his mother, Behold, [d]Esau my brother *is* a hairy man, and I *am* a smooth man:

12 My father peradventure will [e]feel me, and I shall seem to him as a deceiver; and I shall bring [f]a curse upon me, and not a blessing.

13 And his mother said unto him, [g]Upon me *be* thy curse, my son: only obey my voice, and go fetch me *them.*

14 And he went, and fetched, and brought *them* to his mother: and his mother [h]made savoury meat, such as his father loved.

15 And Rebekah took [i]goodly[1] raiment of her eldest son Esau, which *were* with her in the house, and put them upon Jacob her younger son:

16 And she put the skins of the kids of the goats upon his hands, and upon the smooth of his neck:

17 And she gave the savoury meat and the bread, which she had prepared, into the hand of her son Jacob.

18 ¶ And he came unto his father, and said, My father: and he said, Here *am* I; who *art* thou, my son?

19 And Jacob said unto his father, I *am* Esau thy firstborn; I have done according as thou badest me: arise, I pray thee, sit and eat of my venison, [j]that thy soul may bless me.

20 And Isaac said unto his son, How *is it* that thou hast found *it* so quickly, my son? And he said, Because the LORD thy God brought *it* [m]to me.

21 And Isaac said unto Jacob, Come near, I pray thee, that I [k]may feel thee, my son, whether thou *be* my very son Esau or not.

22 And Jacob went near unto Isaac his father; and he felt him, and said, The voice *is* Jacob's voice, but the hands *are* the hands of Esau.

23 And he discerned him not, because [l]his hands were hairy, as his brother Esau's hands: so he blessed him.

24 And he said, *Art* thou my very son Esau? And he said, I *am.*

25 And he said, Bring *it* near to me, and I will eat of my son's venison, [m]that my soul may bless thee. And he brought *it* near to him, and he did eat: and he brought him wine, and he drank.

26 And his father Isaac said unto him, Come near now, and kiss me, my son.

27 And he came near, and kissed him: and he smelled the smell of his raiment, and blessed him, and said, See, [n]the smell of my son *is* as the smell of a field which the LORD hath blessed:

28 Therefore [o]God give thee of [p]the dew of heaven, and [q]the fatness of the earth, and [r]plenty of corn and wine:

29 [s]Let people serve thee, and nations bow down to thee: be lord over thy brethren, and [t]let thy mother's sons bow down to thee: [u]cursed *be* ev-

27:8 [a]ver. 13
27:9 [b]ver. 4
27:10 [c]ver. 4
27:11 [d]ch. 25:25
27:12 [e]ver. 22 [f]ch. 9:25 Deut. 27:18
27:13 [g]ch. 43:9 1 Sam. 25:24 2 Sam. 14:9 Mat. 27:25
27:14 [h]Prov. 23:3 Luke 21:34
27:15 [i]ver. 27
27:19 [j]ver. 4
27:21 [k]ver. 12
27:23 [l]ver. 16
27:25 [m]ver. 4,10,19,31
27:27 [n]Sol. 4:11 Hos. 14:6
27:28 [o]Heb. 11:20 [p]Deut. 33:13,28 2 Sam. 1:21 Ps. 133:3 Mic. 5:7 [q]ch. 45:18 [r]Deut. 33:28
27:29 [s]ch. 9:25 & 25:23 [t]ch. 49:8 [u]ch. 12:3 Num. 24:9 Zeph. 2:8

[1]Heb. *desirable* [m]Heb. *before me*

27:6–17 REBEKAH SPAKE UNTO JACOB. Rebekah and Jacob sought to fulfill God's covenant purposes by deception and manipulation. They had lost sight of the basic reason for God's blessing—to bring about a godly and just people who walked with God in faith and obedience. Rebekah suffered greatly for her deceitful scheme, for Jacob had to flee, and she never saw her son again (v. 43; 28:5).

27:19 JACOB SAID UNTO HIS FATHER. If Jacob had trusted God and committed his way to the Lord, he would have gained the blessing in God's own time. Yet he lied twice to obtain the blessing in his own way (vv. 19–20). (1) He got what he wanted, yet it cost him dearly. He had to flee for his life and to give up his possessions and the comforts of home. He reaped deceitful treatment himself (29:20–25; 31:7; 37:32–36) and lived many years in exile (31:41). All his life he had one misfortune after another until he finally stated: "Few and evil have the days . . . of my life been" (47:9). (2) Jacob's actions and experiences should be pondered by all who misrepresent facts and deceive others in the work of the kingdom of God. Spiritual success must be gained by righteous means, not by manipulation and deception.

ery one that curseth thee, and blessed *be* he that blesseth thee.

30 ¶ And it came to pass, as soon as Isaac had made an end of blessing Jacob, and Jacob was yet scarce gone out from the presence of Isaac his father, that Esau his brother came in from his hunting.

31 And he also had made savoury meat, and brought it unto his father, and said unto his father, Let my father arise, and [v]eat of his son's venison, that thy soul may bless me.

32 And Isaac his father said unto him, Who *art* thou? And he said, I *am* thy son, thy firstborn Esau.

33 And Isaac [n]trembled very exceedingly, and said, Who? where *is* he that hath [o]taken venison, and brought *it* me, and I have eaten of all before thou camest, and have blessed him? yea, [w]*and* he shall be blessed.

34 And when Esau heard the words of his father, [x]he cried with a great and exceeding bitter cry, and said unto his father, Bless me, *even* me also, O my father.

35 And he said, Thy brother came with subtlety, and hath taken away thy blessing.

36 And he said, [y]Is not he rightly named [p]Jacob? for he hath supplanted me these two times: [z]he took away my birthright; and, behold, now he hath taken away my blessing. And he said, Hast thou not reserved a blessing for me?

37 And Isaac answered and said unto Esau, [a]Behold, I have made him thy lord, and all his brethren have I given to him for servants; and [b]with corn and wine have I [q]sustained him: and what shall I do now unto thee, my son?

38 And Esau said unto his father, Hast thou but one blessing, my father? bless me, *even* me also, O my father. And Esau lifted up his voice, [c]and wept.

39 And Isaac his father answered and said unto him, Behold, [d]thy dwelling shall be [r]the fatness of the earth, and of the dew of heaven from above;

40 And by thy sword shalt thou live, and [e]shalt serve thy brother; and [f]it shall come to pass when thou shalt have the dominion, that thou shalt break his yoke from off thy neck.

Isaac sends Jacob to Laban

41 ¶ And Esau [g]hated Jacob because of the blessing wherewith his father blessed him: and Esau said in his heart, [h]The days of mourning for my father are at hand; [i]then will I slay my brother Jacob.

42 And these words of Esau her elder son were told to Rebekah: and she sent and called Jacob her younger son, and said unto him, Behold, thy brother Esau, as touching thee, doth [j]comfort himself, *purposing* to kill thee.

43 Now therefore, my son, obey my voice; and arise, flee thou to Laban my brother [k]to Haran;

44 And tarry with him a few days, until thy brother's fury turn away;

45 Until thy brother's anger turn away from thee, and he forget *that* which thou hast done to him: then I will send, and fetch thee from thence: why should I be deprived also of you both in one day?

46 And Rebekah said to Isaac, [l]I am weary of my life because of the daughters of Heth: [m]if Jacob take a wife of the daughters of Heth, such as these *which are* of the daughters of the land, what good shall my life do me?

28 AND ISAAC called Jacob, and [n]blessed him, and charged him, and said unto him, [o]Thou shalt not take a wife of the daughters of Canaan.

2 [p]Arise, go to [q]Padan-aram, to the house of [r]Bethuel thy mother's father; and take thee a wife from thence of the daughters of [s]Laban thy mother's brother.

3 [t]And God Almighty bless thee, and make thee fruitful, and multiply thee, that thou mayest be [s]a multitude of people;

4 And give thee [u]the blessing of Abraham, to thee, and to thy seed with

27:31 [v]ver. 4
27:33 [w]ch. 28:3,4 Rom. 11:29
27:34 [x]Heb. 12:17
27:36 [y]ch. 25:26 [z]ch. 25:33
27:37 [a]Fulfilled 2 Sam. 8:14 [b]ver. 28
27:38 [c]Heb. 12:17
27:39 [d]ver. 28 Heb. 11:20
27:40 [e]ch. 25:23 2 Sam. 8:14 Obad. 18-20 [f]2 Ki. 8:20
27:41 [g]ch. 37:4,8 [h]ch. 50:3,4,10 [i]Obad. 10
27:42 [j]Ps. 64:5
27:43 [k]ch. 11:31
27:46 [l]ch. 26:35 & 28:8 [m]ch. 24:3
28:1 [n]ch. 27:33 [o]ch. 24:3
28:2 [p]Hos. 12:12 [q]ch. 25:20 [r]ch. 22:23 [s]ch. 24:29
28:3 [t]ch. 17:1,6
28:4 [u]ch. 12:2

[n] Heb. *trembled with a great trembling greatly* [o] Heb. *hunted* [p] i.e. *A supplanter* [q] Or, *supported* [r] Or, *of the fatness* [s] Heb. *an assembly of people*

27:38 ESAU ... WEPT. According to Heb. 12:16–17, Esau lost his blessing because he was a godless person who had disdained the sacredness of the blessing (cf. 25:31–34). Now he changed his mind and sought the blessing with tears, yet his tears were tears of disappointment and anger, not of sorrow for his own sinful choice. Esau's experience warns us about wrong choices in life that bring terrible consequences that cannot be undone (see 2 Sam. 12:7–14).

thee; that thou mayest inherit the land [v]wherein[t] thou art a stranger, which God gave unto Abraham.

5 And Isaac sent away Jacob: and he went to Padan-aram unto Laban, son of Bethuel the Syrian, the brother of Rebekah, Jacob's and Esau's mother.

6 ¶ When Esau saw that Isaac had blessed Jacob, and sent him away to Padan-aram, to take him a wife from thence; and that as he blessed him he gave him a charge, saying, Thou shalt not take a wife of the daughters of Canaan;

7 And that Jacob obeyed his father and his mother, and was gone to Padan-aram;

8 And Esau seeing [w]that the daughters of Canaan [u]pleased not Isaac his father;

9 Then went Esau unto Ishmael, and took unto the wives which he had [x]Mahalath the daughter of Ishmael Abraham's son, [y]the sister of Nebajoth, to be his wife.

Jacob's dream at Beth-el

10 ¶ And Jacob [z]went out from Beer-sheba, and went toward [a]Haran.

11 And he lighted upon a certain place, and tarried there all night, because the sun was set; and he took of the stones of that place, and put *them for* his pillows, and lay down in that place to sleep.

12 And he [b]dreamed, and behold a ladder set up on the earth, and the top of it reached to heaven: and behold [c]the angels of God ascending and descending on it.

13 [d]And, behold, the LORD stood above it, and said, [e]I *am* the LORD God of Abraham thy father, and the God of Isaac: [f]the land whereon thou liest, to thee will I give it, and to thy seed;

14 And [g]thy seed shall be as the dust of the earth, and thou shalt [v]spread abroad [h]to the west, and to the east, and to the north, and to the south: and in thee and [i]in thy seed shall all the families of the earth be blessed.

15 And, behold, [j]I *am* with thee, and will [k]keep thee in all *places* whither thou goest, and will [l]bring thee again into this land; for [m]I will not leave thee, [n]until I have done *that* which I have spoken to thee of.

16 ¶ And Jacob awaked out of his sleep, and he said, Surely the LORD is in [o]this place; and I knew *it* not.

17 And he was afraid, and said, How dreadful *is* this place! this *is* none other but the house of God, and this *is* the gate of heaven.

18 And Jacob rose up early in the morning, and took the stone that he had put *for* his pillows, and [p]set it up *for* a pillar, [q]and poured oil upon the top of it.

19 And he called the name of [r]that place [w]Beth-el: but the name of that city *was called* Luz at the first.

20 [s]And Jacob vowed a vow, saying, If [t]God will be with me, and will keep me in this way that I go, and will give me [u]bread to eat, and raiment to put on,

21 So that [v]I come again to my father's house in peace; [w]then shall the LORD be my God:

22 And this stone, which I have set *for* a pillar, [x]shall be God's house: [y]and of all that thou shalt give me I will surely give the tenth unto thee.

Jacob meets Rachel

29 THEN JACOB [x]went on his journey, [z]and came into the land of the [y]people of the east.

2 And he looked, and behold a well in the field, and, lo, there *were* three flocks of sheep lying by it; for out of

28:4 [v]ch. 17:8 **28:8** [w]ch. 24:3 & 26:35 **28:9** [x]ch. 36:3, she is called *Bashemath* [y]ch. 25:13 **28:10** [z]Hos. 12:12 [a]Called, Acts 7:2 *Charran* **28:12** [b]ch. 41:1 [c]John 1:51 Heb. 1:14 **28:13** [d]ch. 35:1 & 48:3 [e]ch. 26:24 [f]ch. 13:15 & 35:12 **28:14** [g]ch. 13:16 [h]ch. 13:14 Deut. 12:20 [i]ch. 12:3 & 18:18 & 22:18 & 26:4 **28:15** [j]See ver. 20,21 [k]ch. 48:16 [l]ch. 35:6 [m]Deut. 31:6,8 Josh. 1:5 1 Ki. 8:57 Heb. 13:5 [n]Num. 23:19 **28:16** [o]Ex. 3:5 Josh. 5:15 **28:18** [p]ch. 31:13,45 [q]Lev. 8:10-12 **28:19** [r]Judg. 1:23,26 Hos. 4:15 **28:20** [s]ch. 31:13 Judg. 11:30 2 Sam. 15:8 [t]ver. 15 [u]1 Tim. 6:8 **28:21** [v]Judg. 11:31 2 Sam. 19:24,30 [w]Deut. 26:17 2 Sam. 15:8 **28:22** [x]ch. 35:7,14 [y]Lev. 27:30 **29:1** [z]Num. 23:7 Hos. 12:12

[t]Heb. *of thy sojournings* [u]Heb. were *evil in the eyes* [v]Heb. *break forth* [w]i.e. *The house of God* [x]Heb. *lift up his feet* [y]Heb. *children*

28:4 THE BLESSING OF ABRAHAM. The blessing of Abraham here is the land: "that thou mayest inherit the land . . . which God gave unto Abraham." Note that when Paul applies this to N.T. believers ("Abraham's seed," Gal. 3:29), he does so concerning spiritual rather than material blessings—specifically, the promise of the Spirit through faith (Gal. 3:14).

28:12 THE ANGELS OF GOD. The vision of the angels suggests that they played an important part in God's protection, care, and guidance of His people. Under the new covenant, angels are also active in the lives of believers (see 24:40, note).

28:13–15 THE LORD STOOD ABOVE IT. God came to Jacob with the message that the blessing promised to Abraham would be carried on through him (cf. 12:3; 13:14–17). With this blessing came the promise of God's presence, guidance, and protection.

28:19 BETH-EL. "Beth-el" means "the house of God" and may represent any place where God is present in a very special sense.

that well they watered the flocks: and a great stone *was* upon the well's mouth.

3 And thither were all the flocks gathered: and they rolled the stone from the well's mouth, and watered the sheep, and put the stone again upon the well's mouth in his place.

4 And Jacob said unto them, My brethren, whence *be* ye? And they said, Of Haran *are* we.

5 And he said unto them, Know ye Laban the son of Nahor? And they said, We know *him*.

6 And he said unto them, [a]*Is*[z] he well? And they said, *He is* well: and, behold, Rachel his daughter cometh with the sheep.

7 And he said, Lo, [a]*it is* yet high day, neither *is it* time that the cattle should be gathered together: water ye the sheep, and go *and* feed *them*.

8 And they said, We cannot, until all the flocks be gathered together, and *till* they roll the stone from the well's mouth; then we water the sheep.

9 ¶ And while he yet spake with them, [b]Rachel came with her father's sheep: for she kept them.

10 And it came to pass, when Jacob saw Rachel the daughter of Laban his mother's brother, and the sheep of Laban his mother's brother, that Jacob went near, and [c]rolled the stone from the well's mouth, and watered the flock of Laban his mother's brother.

11 And Jacob [d]kissed Rachel, and lifted up his voice, and wept.

12 And Jacob told Rachel that he *was* [e]her father's brother, and that he *was* Rebekah's son: [f]and she ran and told her father.

13 And it came to pass, when Laban heard the [b]tidings of Jacob his sister's son, that [g]he ran to meet him, and embraced him, and kissed him, and brought him to his house. And he told Laban all these things.

14 And Laban said to him, [h]Surely thou *art* my bone and my flesh. And he abode with him [c]the space of a month.

29:6 [a]ch. 43:27
29:9 [b]Ex. 2:16
29:10 [c]Ex. 2:17
29:11 [d]ch. 33:4 & 45:14,15
29:12 [e]ch. 13:8 & 14:14,16 [f]ch. 24:28
29:13 [g]ch. 24:29
29:14 [h]ch. 2:23 Judg. 9:2 2 Sam. 5:1 & 19:12,13
29:18 [i]ch. 31:41 2 Sam. 3:14
29:20 [j]ch. 30:26 Hos. 12:12
29:21 [k]Judg. 15:1
29:22 [l]Judg. 14:10 John 2:1,2
29:27 [m]Judg. 14:12

Jacob marries Leah and Rachel

15 ¶ And Laban said unto Jacob, Because thou *art* my brother, shouldest thou therefore serve me for nought? tell me, what *shall* thy wages *be?*

16 And Laban had two daughters: the name of the elder *was* Leah, and the name of the younger *was* Rachel.

17 Leah *was* tender eyed; but Rachel was beautiful and wellfavoured.

18 And Jacob loved Rachel; and said, [i]I will serve thee seven years for Rachel thy younger daughter.

19 And Laban said, *It is* better that I give her to thee, than that I should give her to another man: abide with me.

20 And Jacob [j]served seven years for Rachel; and they seemed unto him *but* a few days, for the love he had to her.

21 ¶ And Jacob said unto Laban, Give *me* my wife, for my days are fulfilled, that I may [k]go in unto her.

22 And Laban gathered together all the men of the place, and [l]made a feast.

23 And it came to pass in the evening, that he took Leah his daughter, and brought her to him; and he went in unto her.

24 And Laban gave unto his daughter Leah Zilpah his maid *for* an handmaid.

25 And it came to pass, that in the morning, behold, it *was* Leah: and he said to Laban, What *is* this thou hast done unto me? did not I serve with thee for Rachel? wherefore then hast thou beguiled me?

26 And Laban said, It must not be so done in our [d]country, to give the younger before the firstborn.

27 [m]Fulfil her week, and we will give thee this also for the service which thou shalt serve with me yet seven other years.

28 And Jacob did so, and fulfilled

[z] Heb. Is there *peace to him?* [a] Heb. *yet the day is great* [b] Heb. *hearing* [c] Heb. *a month of days* [d] Heb. *place*

29:5 LABAN. Laban was Jacob's uncle. Jacob was seeking his mother's family near Haran (v. 10; cf. 24:15,50).

29:25 WHEREFORE THEN HAST THOU BEGUILED ME? Perhaps God allowed Jacob to be deceived by Laban and Leah in order to chastise him and to make him aware of the evil and hurt that he had caused when he deceived his own father and brother (cf. ch. 27). We must understand that although God forgives us for a certain sin and restores us to His favor, He may at the same time discipline us for that sin (see 2 Sam. 12:7–14). God's principle remains: "Be not deceived . . . whatsoever a man soweth, that shall he also reap" (Gal. 6:7; cf. Prov. 22:8; Hos 8:7; 10:12–13).

29:28 HE GAVE HIM RACHEL HIS DAUGH-

her week: and he gave him Rachel his daughter to wife also.

29 And Laban gave to Rachel his daughter Bilhah his handmaid to be her maid.

30 And he went in also unto Rachel, and he [n]loved also Rachel more than Leah, and served with him [o]yet seven other years.

The sons of Jacob

31 ¶ And when the LORD [p]saw that Leah *was* hated, he [q]opened her womb: but Rachel *was* barren.

32 And Leah conceived, and bare a son, and she called his name [e]Reuben: for she said, Surely the LORD hath [r]looked upon my affliction; now therefore my husband will love me.

33 And she conceived again, and bare a son; and said, Because the LORD hath heard that I *was* hated, he hath therefore given me this *son* also: and she called his name [f]Simeon.

34 And she conceived again, and bare a son; and said, Now this time will my husband be joined unto me, because I have born him three sons: therefore was his name called [g]Levi.

35 And she conceived again, and bare a son: and she said, Now will I praise the LORD: therefore she called his name [s]Judah;[h] and [i]left bearing.

30 AND WHEN Rachel saw that [t]she bare Jacob no children, Rachel [u]envied her sister; and said unto Jacob, Give me children, [v]or else I die.

2 And Jacob's anger was kindled against Rachel: and he said, [w]*Am* I in God's stead, who hath withheld from thee the fruit of the womb?

3 And she said, Behold [x]my maid Bilhah, go in unto her; [y]and she shall bear upon my knees, [z]that I may also [j]have children by her.

4 And she gave him Bilhah her handmaid [a]to wife: and Jacob went in unto her.

5 And Bilhah conceived, and bare Jacob a son.

6 And Rachel said, God hath [b]judged me, and hath also heard my voice, and hath given me a son: therefore called she his name [k]Dan.

7 And Bilhah Rachel's maid conceived again, and bare Jacob a second son.

8 And Rachel said, With [l]great wrestlings have I wrestled with my sister, and I have prevailed: and she called his name [c]Naphtali.[m]

9 When Leah saw that she had left bearing, she took Zilpah her maid, and [d]gave her Jacob to wife.

10 And Zilpah Leah's maid bare Jacob a son.

11 And Leah said, A troop cometh: and she called his name [n]Gad.

12 And Zilpah Leah's maid bare Jacob a second son.

13 And Leah said, [o]Happy am I, for the daughters [e]will call me blessed: and she called his name [p]Asher.

14 ¶ And Reuben went in the days of wheat harvest, and found mandrakes in the field, and brought them unto his mother Leah. Then Rachel said to Leah, [f]Give me, I pray thee, of thy son's mandrakes.

29:30 [n]Deut. 21:15 [o]ch. 30:26 & 31:41 Hos. 12:12 **29:31** [p]Ps. 127:3 [q]ch. 30:1 **29:32** [r]Ex. 4:31 Deut. 26:7 Ps. 25:18 **29:35** [s]Mat. 1:2 **30:1** [t]ch. 29:31 [u]ch. 37:11 [v]Job 5:2 **30:2** [w]ch. 16:2 1 Sam. 1:5 **30:3** [x]ch. 16:2 [y]ch. 50:23 Job 3:12 [z]ch. 16:2 **30:4** [a]ch. 16:3 **30:6** [b]Lam. 3:59 **30:8** [c]Called, Mat. 4:13, *Nephthalim* **30:9** [d]ver. 4 **30:13** [e]Prov. 31:28 Luke 1:48 **30:14** [f]ch. 25:30

[e]i.e. *See a son* [f]i.e. *Hearing* [g]i.e. *Joined* [h]i.e. *Praise* [i]Heb. *stood from bearing* [j]Heb. *be built by her* [k]i.e. *Judging* [l]Heb. *wrestlings of God* [m]i.e. *My wrestling* [n]i.e. *A troop,* or, *company* [o]Heb. *In my happiness* [p]i.e. *Happy*

TER TO WIFE. Jacob's marriage to two sisters conflicted with God's creation ordinance that marriage should consist of only one man and one woman (see 2:24, note; cf. Ex. 20:17; Deut. 5:21). Later, in the Mosaic Law, God specifically forbade Jacob's type of marriage (Lev. 18:18). The N.T. revelation regards monogamy (one wife and one husband) as the only rightful form of marriage (Mat. 19:4–6; Mark 10:4–5). God may have tolerated polygamy in the O.T. because the people lacked a full understanding of God's will regarding marriage and because their hearts were hard. The evil effects of polygamy are described in v. 30; 30:1; 35:22; 1 Ki. 11:1–12.

29:31 WHEN THE LORD SAW THAT LEAH *WAS* HATED. God allowed Leah to have a child. From her was born Judah, and from Judah's line was born the Christ (Mat. 1:3,16). God often takes the side of those who are oppressed or treated wrongfully (cf. Ps. 9:18; 22:24; Luke 4:18). Injustice is intolerable to God, especially among His covenant people (see Col. 3:25, note).

30:1–24 GIVE ME CHILDREN. These verses record the forming of the family of Jacob, the founders of the tribes of Israel. The narrative shows that God worked to accomplish His ultimate purpose in spite of weaknesses, struggles, and human faults in Jacob's family.

30:1 OR ELSE I DIE. In the ancient East, a childless woman was looked upon with disdain (cf. 16:2; 30:2); hence, Rachel's despairing comment.

15 And she said unto her, [g]*Is it* a small matter that thou hast taken my husband? and wouldest thou take away my son's mandrakes also? And Rachel said, Therefore he shall lie with thee tonight for thy son's mandrakes.

16 And Jacob came out of the field in the evening, and Leah went out to meet him, and said, Thou must come in unto me; for surely I have hired thee with my son's mandrakes. And he lay with her that night.

17 And God hearkened unto Leah, and she conceived, and bare Jacob the fifth son.

18 And Leah said, God hath given me my hire, because I have given my maiden to my husband: and she called his name [q]Issachar.

19 And Leah conceived again, and bare Jacob the sixth son.

20 And Leah said, God hath endued me *with* a good dowry; now will my husband dwell with me, because I have born him six sons: and she called his name [h]Zebulun.[r]

21 And afterwards she bare a daughter, and called her name [s]Dinah.

22 ¶ And God [i]remembered Rachel, and God hearkened to her, and [j]opened her womb.

23 And she conceived, and bare a son; and said, God hath taken away [k]my reproach:

24 And she called his name [t]Joseph; and said, [l]The LORD shall add to me another son.

Jacob's bargain with Laban

25 ¶ And it came to pass, when Rachel had born Joseph, that Jacob said unto Laban, [m]Send me away, that I may go unto [n]mine own place, and to my country.

26 Give *me* my wives and my children, [o]for whom I have served thee, and let me go: for thou knowest my service which I have done thee.

27 And Laban said unto him, I pray thee, if I have found favour in thine eyes, *tarry: for* [p]I have learned by experience that the LORD hath blessed me [q]for thy sake.

28 And he said, [r]Appoint me thy wages, and I will give *it.*

29 And he said unto him, [s]Thou knowest how I have served thee, and how thy cattle was with me.

30 For *it was* little which thou hadst before I *came,* and it is *now* [u]increased unto a multitude; and the LORD hath blessed thee [v]since my coming: and now when shall I [t]provide for mine own house also?

31 And he said, What shall I give thee? And Jacob said, Thou shalt not give me any thing: if thou wilt do this thing for me, I will again feed *and* keep thy flock.

32 I will pass through all thy flock today, removing from thence all the speckled and spotted cattle, and all the brown cattle among the sheep, and the spotted and speckled among the goats: and [u]*of such* shall be my hire.

33 So shall my [v]righteousness answer for me [w]in time to come, when it shall come for my hire before thy face: every one that *is* not speckled and spotted among the goats, and brown among the sheep, that shall be counted stolen with me.

34 And Laban said, Behold, I would it might be according to thy word.

35 And he removed that day the he goats that were ringstraked and spotted, and all the she goats that were speckled and spotted, *and* every one that had *some* white in it, and all the brown among the sheep, and gave *them* into the hand of his sons.

36 And he set three days' journey betwixt himself and Jacob: and Jacob fed the rest of Laban's flocks.

37 ¶ And [w]Jacob took him rods of green poplar, and of the hazel and chestnut tree; and pilled white strakes in them, and made the white appear which *was* in the rods.

38 And he set the rods which he had pilled before the flocks in the gutters in the watering troughs when the flocks came to drink, that they should conceive when they came to drink.

39 And the flocks conceived before

30:15 [g]Num. 16:9,13 **30:20** [h]Called, Mat. 4:13, *Zabulon* **30:22** [i]1 Sam. 1:19 [j]ch. 29:31 **30:23** [k]1 Sam. 1:6 Is. 4:1 Luke 1:25 **30:24** [l]ch. 35:17 **30:25** [m]ch. 24:54,56 [n]ch. 18:33 **30:26** [o]ch. 29:20,30 **30:27** [p]ch. 39:3,5 [q]See ch. 26:24

30:28 [r]ch. 29:15 **30:29** [s]ch. 31:6,38-40 Mat. 24:45 Tit. 2:10 **30:30** [t]1 Tim. 5:8 **30:32** [u]ch. 31:8 **30:33** [v]Ps. 37:6 **30:37** [w]See ch. 31:9-12

[q] i.e. *An hire* [r] i.e. Dwelling [s] i.e. *Judgment* [t] i.e. *Adding* [u] Heb. *broken forth* [v] Heb. *at my foot* [w] Heb. *tomorrow*

30:18 GOD HATH GIVEN ME. Leah's declaration that God had rewarded her because she had given her handmaiden to Jacob reflects her own feeling about the matter, not necessarily God's. The narrative here only tells us what Leah said. God tolerated this situation for a time and worked through the kind of marriages into which Jacob entered (see 29:28, note).

the rods, and brought forth cattle ringstraked, speckled, and spotted.

40 And Jacob did separate the lambs, and set the faces of the flocks toward the ringstraked, and all the brown in the flock of Laban; and he put his own flocks by themselves, and put them not unto Laban's cattle.

41 And it came to pass, whensoever the stronger cattle did conceive, that Jacob laid the rods before the eyes of the cattle in the gutters, that they might conceive among the rods.

42 But when the cattle were feeble, he put *them* not in: so the feebler were Laban's, and the stronger Jacob's.

43 And the man [x]increased exceedingly, and [y]had much cattle, and maidservants, and menservants, and camels, and asses.

Jacob flees from Laban

31 AND HE heard the words of Laban's sons, saying, Jacob hath taken away all that *was* our father's; and of *that* which *was* our father's hath he gotten all this [z]glory.

2 And Jacob beheld [a]the countenance of Laban, and, behold, it *was* not [b]toward him [x]as before.

3 And the LORD said unto Jacob, [c]Return unto the land of thy fathers, and to thy kindred; and I will be with thee.

4 And Jacob sent and called Rachel and Leah to the field unto his flock,

5 And said unto them, [d]I see your father's countenance, that it *is* not toward me as before; but the God of my father [e]hath been with me.

6 And [f]ye know that with all my power I have served your father.

7 And your father hath deceived me, and [g]changed my wages [h]ten times; but God [i]suffered him not to hurt me.

8 If he said thus, [j]The speckled shall be thy wages; then all the cattle bare speckled: and if he said thus, The ringstraked shall be thy hire; then bare all the cattle ringstraked.

9 Thus God hath [k]taken away the cattle of your father, and given *them* to me.

10 And it came to pass at the time that the cattle conceived, that I lifted up mine eyes, and saw in a dream, and, behold, the [y]rams which leaped upon the cattle *were* ringstraked, speckled, and grisled.

11 And [l]the angel of God spake unto me in a dream, *saying,* Jacob: And I said, Here *am* I.

12 And he said, Lift up now thine eyes, and see, all the rams which leap upon the cattle *are* ringstraked, speckled, and grisled: for [m]I have seen all that Laban doeth unto thee.

13 I *am* the God of Beth-el, [n]where thou anointedst the pillar, *and* where thou vowedst a vow unto me: now [o]arise, get thee out from this land, and return unto the land of thy kindred.

14 And Rachel and Leah answered and said unto him, [p]*Is there* yet any portion or inheritance for us in our father's house?

15 Are we not counted of him strangers? for [q]he hath sold us, and hath quite devoured also our money.

16 For all the riches which God hath taken from our father, that *is* ours, and our children's: now then, whatsoever God hath said unto thee, do.

17 ¶ Then Jacob rose up, and set his sons and his wives upon camels;

18 And he carried away all his cattle, and all his goods which he had gotten, the cattle of his getting, which he had gotten in Padan-aram, for to go to Isaac his father in the land of Canaan.

19 And Laban went to shear his sheep: and Rachel had stolen the [r]images [s]that[z] *were* her father's.

20 And Jacob stole away [a]unawares to Laban the Syrian, in that he told him not that he fled.

21 So he fled with all that he had;

30:43 [x]ver. 30 [y]ch. 13:2 & 24:35 & 26:13,14
31:1 [z]Ps. 49:16
31:2 [a]ch. 4:5 [b]Deut. 28:54
31:3 [c]ch. 28:15,20,21 & 32:9
31:5 [d]ver. 2 [e]ver. 3
31:6 [f]ver. 38-41 ch. 30:29
31:7 [g]ver. 41 [h]Num. 14:22 Neh. 4:12 Job 19:3 Zech. 8:23 [i]ch. 20:6 Job 1:10 Ps. 37:28 & 105:14
31:8 [j]ch. 30:32
31:9 [k]ver. 1,16
31:11 [l]ch. 48:16
31:12 [m]Ex. 3:7 Ps. 139:3 Eccl. 5:8
31:13 [n]ch. 28:18-20 [o]ver. 3 ch. 32:9
31:14 [p]ch. 2:24
31:15 [q]ch. 29:15,27 Neh. 5:8
31:19 [r]ch. 35:2 [s]Judg. 17:5; 1 Sam. 19:13; Hos. 3:4

[x] Heb. *as yesterday and the day before* [y] Or, *he goats* [z] Heb. *teraphim* [a] Heb. *the heart of Laban*

30:39 THE FLOCKS ... BROUGHT FORTH ... SPOTTED. The breeding process of the flocks was influenced not by the rods, but by the intervention of God. Jacob acknowledged God's work in increasing his flock (31:7–9).

31:19 RACHEL HAD STOLEN THE IMAGES. Rachel stole "the images that *were* her father's" and then lied to keep them (vv. 34–35). Archaeological discoveries in that area show that the possession of those images were thought to guarantee a double portion of the inheritance when the father died. Rachel and Leah felt cheated out of any inheritance (v. 15). Thus, Rachel took the images, not for worship but for financial gain. They did her no good, however, for Jacob later ordered his household to put away all the idols and symbols of foreign gods, and they were buried before going back to Bethel (35:2–4; see 35:2, note).

JACOB'S JOURNEYS

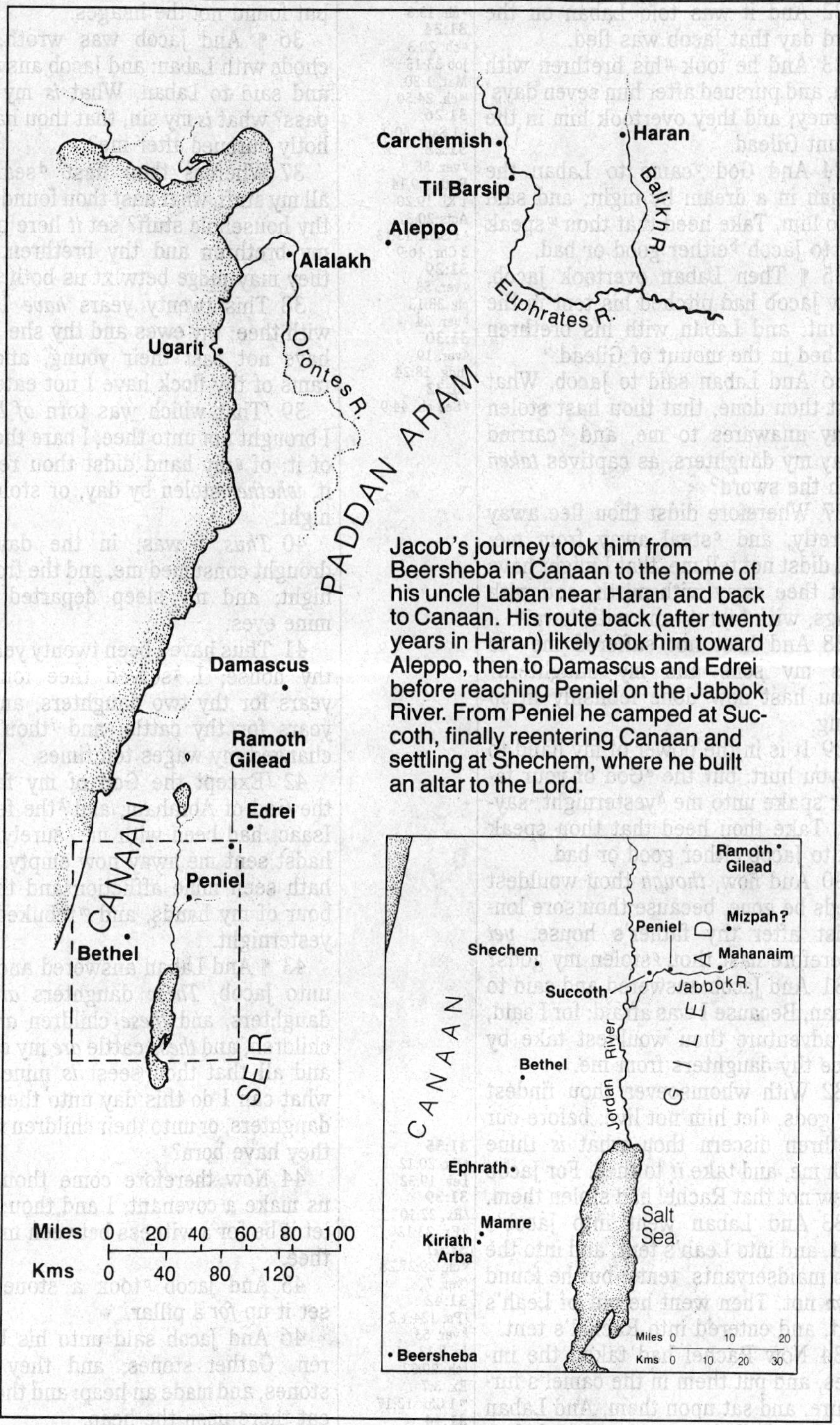

Jacob's journey took him from Beersheba in Canaan to the home of his uncle Laban near Haran and back to Canaan. His route back (after twenty years in Haran) likely took him toward Aleppo, then to Damascus and Edrei before reaching Peniel on the Jabbok River. From Peniel he camped at Succoth, finally reentering Canaan and settling at Shechem, where he built an altar to the Lord.

and he rose up, and passed over the river, and [t]set his face *toward* the mount Gilead.

22 And it was told Laban on the third day that Jacob was fled.

23 And he took [u]his brethren with him, and pursued after him seven days' journey; and they overtook him in the mount Gilead.

24 And God [v]came to Laban the Syrian in a dream by night, and said unto him, Take heed that thou [w]speak not to Jacob [b]either good or bad.

25 ¶ Then Laban overtook Jacob. Now Jacob had pitched his tent in the mount: and Laban with his brethren pitched in the mount of Gilead.

26 And Laban said to Jacob, What hast thou done, that thou hast stolen away unawares to me, and [x]carried away my daughters, as captives *taken* with the sword?

27 Wherefore didst thou flee away secretly, and [c]steal away from me; and didst not tell me, that I might have sent thee away with mirth, and with songs, with tabret, and with harp?

28 And hast not suffered me [y]to kiss my sons and my daughters? [z]thou hast now done foolishly in *so* doing.

29 It is in the power of my hand to do you hurt: but the [a]God of your father spake unto me [b]yesternight, saying, Take thou heed that thou speak not to Jacob either good or bad.

30 And now, *though* thou wouldest needs be gone, because thou sore longedst after thy father's house, *yet* wherefore hast thou [c]stolen my gods?

31 And Jacob answered and said to Laban, Because I was afraid: for I said, Peradventure thou wouldest take by force thy daughters from me.

32 With whomsoever thou findest thy gods, [d]let him not live: before our brethren discern thou what *is* thine with me, and take *it* to thee. For Jacob knew not that Rachel had stolen them.

33 And Laban went into Jacob's tent, and into Leah's tent, and into the two maidservants' tents; but he found *them* not. Then went he out of Leah's tent, and entered into Rachel's tent.

34 Now Rachel had taken the images, and put them in the camel's furniture, and sat upon them. And Laban [d]searched all the tent, but found *them* not.

35 And she said to her father, Let it not displease my lord that I cannot [e]rise up before thee; for the custom of women *is* upon me. And he searched, but found not the images.

36 ¶ And Jacob was wroth, and chode with Laban: and Jacob answered and said to Laban, What *is* my trespass? what *is* my sin, that thou hast so hotly pursued after me?

37 Whereas thou hast [d]searched all my stuff, what hast thou found of all thy household stuff? set *it* here before my brethren and thy brethren, that they may judge betwixt us both.

38 This twenty years *have* I *been* with thee; thy ewes and thy she goats have not cast their young, and the rams of thy flock have I not eaten.

39 [f]That which was torn *of beasts* I brought not unto thee; I bare the loss of it; of [g]my hand didst thou require it, *whether* stolen by day, or stolen by night.

40 *Thus* I was; in the day the drought consumed me, and the frost by night; and my sleep departed from mine eyes.

41 Thus have I been twenty years in thy house; I [h]served thee fourteen years for thy two daughters, and six years for thy cattle: and [i]thou hast changed my wages ten times.

42 [j]Except the God of my father, the God of Abraham, and [k]the fear of Isaac, had been with me, surely thou hadst sent me away now empty. [l]God hath seen mine affliction and the labour of my hands, and [m]rebuked *thee* yesternight.

43 ¶ And Laban answered and said unto Jacob, *These* daughters *are* my daughters, and *these* children *are* my children, and *these* cattle *are* my cattle, and all that thou seest *is* mine: and what can I do this day unto these my daughters, or unto their children which they have born?

44 Now therefore come thou, [n]let us make a covenant, I and thou; [o]and let it be for a witness between me and thee.

45 And Jacob [p]took a stone, and set it up *for* a pillar.

46 And Jacob said unto his brethren, Gather stones; and they took stones, and made an heap: and they did eat there upon the heap.

31:21 [t]ch. 46:28 2 Ki. 12:17 Luke 9:51,53
31:23 [u]ch. 13:8
31:24 [v]ch. 20:3 Job 33:15 Mat. 1:20 [w]ch. 24:50
31:26 [x]1 Sam. 30:2
31:28 [y]ver. 55 Ruth 1:9,14 1 Ki. 19:20 Acts 20:37 [z]1 Sam. 13:13 2 Chr. 16:9
31:29 [a]ver. 53 ch. 28:13 [b]ver. 24
31:30 [c]ver. 19 Judg. 18:24
31:32 [d]See ch. 44:9
31:35 [e]Ex. 20:12 Lev. 19:32
31:39 [f]Ex. 22:10 [g]Ex. 22:12
31:41 [h]ch. 29:27,28 [i]ver. 7
31:42 [j]Ps. 124:1,2 [k]ver. 53 Is. 8:13 [l]ch. 29:32 Ex. 3:7 [m]1 Chr. 12:17
31:44 [n]ch. 26:28 [o]Josh. 24:27
31:45 [p]ch. 28:18

[b] Heb. *from good to bad* [c] Heb. *hast stolen me*
[d] Heb. *felt*

47 And Laban called it [e]Jegar-sahadutha: but Jacob called it [f]Galeed.

48 And Laban said, [q]This heap *is* a witness between me and thee this day. Therefore was the name of it called Galeed;

49 And [r]Mizpah;[g] for he said, The LORD watch between me and thee, when we are absent one from another.

50 If thou shalt afflict my daughters, or if thou shalt take *other* wives beside my daughters, no man *is* with us; see, God *is* witness betwixt me and thee.

51 And Laban said to Jacob, Behold this heap, and behold *this* pillar, which I have cast betwixt me and thee;

52 This heap *be* witness, and *this* pillar *be* witness, that I will not pass over this heap to thee, and that thou shalt not pass over this heap and this pillar unto me, for harm.

53 The God of Abraham, and the God of Nahor, the God of their father, [s]judge betwixt us. And Jacob [t]sware by [u]the fear of his father Isaac.

54 Then Jacob [h]offered sacrifice upon the mount, and called his brethren to eat bread: and they did eat bread, and tarried all night in the mount.

55 And early in the morning Laban rose up, and kissed his sons and his daughters, and [v]blessed them: and Laban departed, and [w]returned unto his place.

Jacob prepares to meet Esau

32 AND JACOB went on his way, and [x]the angels of God met him.

2 And when Jacob saw them, he said, This *is* God's [y]host: and he called the name of that place [i]Mahanaim.

3 And Jacob sent messengers before him to Esau his brother [z]unto the land of Seir, [a]the [j]country of Edom.

4 And he commanded them, saying, [b]Thus shall ye speak unto my lord Esau; Thy servant Jacob saith thus, I have sojourned with Laban, and stayed there until now:

5 And [c]I have oxen, and asses, flocks, and menservants, and womenservants: and I have sent to tell my lord, that [d]I may find grace in thy sight.

6 ¶ And the messengers returned to Jacob, saying, We came to thy brother Esau, and also [e]he cometh to meet thee, and four hundred men with him.

7 Then Jacob was greatly afraid and [f]distressed: and he divided the people that *was* with him, and the flocks, and herds, and the camels, into two bands;

8 And said, If Esau come to the one company, and smite it, then the other company which is left shall escape.

9 ¶ [g]And Jacob said, [h]O God of my father Abraham, and God of my father Isaac, the LORD [i]which saidst unto me, Return unto thy country, and to thy kindred, and I will deal well with thee:

10 [k]I am not worthy of the least of all the [j]mercies, and of all the truth, which thou hast shown unto thy servant; for with [k]my staff I passed over this Jordan; and now I am become two bands.

11 [l]Deliver me, I pray thee, from the hand of my brother, from the hand of Esau: for I fear him, lest he will come and smite me, *and* [m]the mother [l]with the children.

12 And [n]thou saidst, I will surely do thee good, and make thy seed as the sand of the sea, which cannot be numbered for multitude.

13 ¶ And he lodged there that same night; and took of that which came to

31:48 [q]Josh. 24:27 **31:49** [r]Judg. 11:29 1 Sam. 7:5 **31:53** [s]ch. 16:5 [t]ch. 21:23 [u]ver. 42 **31:55** [v]ch. 28:1 [w]ch. 18:33 & 30:25 Num. 24:25 **32:1** [x]Ps. 91:11 Heb. 1:14 **32:2** [y]Josh. 5:14 Ps. 103:21 & 148:2 Luke 2:13 **32:3** [z]ch. 33:14,16 [a]ch. 36:6-8 Deut. 2:5 Josh. 24:4 **32:4** [b]Prov. 15:1 **32:5** [c]ch. 30:43 [d]ch. 33:8,15 **32:6** [e]ch. 33:1 **32:7** [f]ch. 35:3 **32:9** [g]Ps. 50:15 [h]ch. 28:13 [i]ch. 31:3,13 **32:10** [j]ch. 24:27 [k]Job 8:7 **32:11** [l]Ps. 59:1,2 [m]Hos. 10:14 **32:12** [n]ch. 28:13-15

[e] i.e. *The heap of witness* Chald. [f] i.e. *The heap of witness* Heb. [g] i.e. *A beacon*, or, *watchtower* [h] Or, *killed beasts* [i] i.e. *Two hosts*, or, *camps* [j] Heb. *field* [k] Heb. *I am less than all* [l] Heb. *upon*

32:1 THE ANGELS OF GOD MET HIM. Jacob had obeyed God's instruction by leaving Laban and returning to the land of Canaan (31:13), the region where his hostile brother, Esau, lived. God sent angels to assure Jacob of His continued protection.

32:9 O GOD OF MY FATHER. Jacob was fearful and distressed as he approached Esau's territory. Would he and his family suffer violence at Esau's hand because of Jacob's deception of more than twenty years earlier? In that situation Jacob prayed to God for help. His prayer is a pattern for all believers in life-threatening circumstances. (1) He reminded God of His promise of care and protection for those who follow God's will (v. 9); (2) in awareness of his unworthiness, he expressed his gratitude for all God's past blessing and help (v. 10); (3) he prayed for God's deliverance (v. 11); and (4) he stated the ultimate reason for requesting God's protection, i.e., to fulfill God's covenant purpose in his life (v. 12).

his hand [o]a present for Esau his brother;

14 Two hundred she goats, and twenty he goats, two hundred ewes, and twenty rams,

15 Thirty milch camels with their colts, forty kine, and ten bulls, twenty she asses, and ten foals.

16 And he delivered *them* into the hand of his servants, every drove by themselves; and said unto his servants, Pass over before me, and put a space betwixt drove and drove.

17 And he commanded the foremost, saying, When Esau my brother meeteth thee, and asketh thee, saying, Whose *art* thou? and whither goest thou? and whose *are* these before thee?

18 Then thou shalt say, *They be* thy servant Jacob's; it *is* a present sent unto my lord Esau: and, behold, also he *is* behind us.

19 And so commanded he the second, and the third, and all that followed the droves, saying, On this manner shall ye speak unto Esau, when ye find him.

20 And say ye moreover, Behold, thy servant Jacob *is* behind us. For he said, I will [p]appease him with the present that goeth before me, and afterward I will see his face; peradventure he will accept [m]of me.

21 So went the present over before him: and himself lodged that night in the company.

Jacob's wrestling at Peniel

22 And he rose up that night, and took his two wives, and his two womenservants, and his eleven sons, [q]and passed over the ford Jabbok.

23 And he took them, and [n]sent them over the brook, and sent over that he had.

24 ¶ And Jacob was left alone; and there [r]wrestled a man with him until the [o]breaking of the day.

25 And when he saw that he prevailed not against him, he touched the hollow of his thigh; and [s]the hollow of Jacob's thigh was out of joint, as he wrestled with him.

26 And [t]he said, Let me go, for the day breaketh. And he said, [u]I will not let thee go, except thou bless me.

27 And he said unto him, What *is* thy name? And he said, Jacob.

28 And he said, [v]Thy name shall be called no more Jacob, but [p]Israel: for as a prince hast thou [w]power with God and [x]with men, and hast prevailed.

29 And Jacob asked *him*, and said, Tell *me*, I pray thee, thy name. And he said, [y]Wherefore *is* it *that* thou dost ask after my name? And he blessed him there.

30 And Jacob called the name of the place [q]Peniel: for [z]I have seen God face to face, and my life is preserved.

31 And as he passed over Penuel the sun rose upon him, and he halted upon his thigh.

32 Therefore the children of Israel eat not *of* the sinew which shrank, which *is* upon the hollow of the thigh, unto this day: because he touched the hollow of Jacob's thigh in the sinew that shrank.

32:13 [o]ch. 43:11 Prov. 18:16
32:20 [p]Prov. 21:14
32:22 [q]Deut. 3:16
32:24 [r]Hos. 12:3,4
32:25 [s]See Mat. 26:41 2 Cor. 12:7
32:26 [t]See Luke 24:28 [u]Hos. 12:4
32:28 [v]ch. 35:10 2 Ki. 17:34 [w]Hos. 12:3,4 [x]ch. 25:31 & 27:33
32:29 [y]Judg. 13:18
32:30 [z]ch. 16:13 Ex. 24:11 Deut. 5:24 Judg. 6:22 Is. 6:5

[m]Heb. *my face* [n]Heb. *caused to pass* [o]Heb. *ascending of the morning* [p]i.e. *A prince of God* [q]i.e. *The face of God*

32:24 WRESTLED A MAN WITH HIM. The "man" who wrestled with Jacob was probably the "angel of the LORD" (see 16:7ff; 21:17; 22:11; 31:11; Hos. 12:4), who is often identified with God Himself (cf. vv. 28,30; Judg. 6:12–14,22; see Ex. 3:2, note). As Jacob desperately wrestled with God for the promised blessing, God let him prevail (v. 28). However, God smote Jacob's hip (v. 25) as a reminder that he must no longer walk in his own strength but must rely entirely on God and walk in dependence on Him (vv. 30–32).

32:28 CALLED . . . ISRAEL. The name Jacob, which implied a crafty deceiver, was now changed to "Israel," which means "one who strives with God" (see next note). Followers of Christ are sometimes called the "Israel of God" (Gal. 6:16)—i.e., the God-strivers. God does not want His people to be passive but earnestly to seek Him for His blessing and grace (Mat. 5:6; 6:33; 7:7–8; 11:12; Luke 11:5–10).

32:29 HE BLESSED HIM THERE. Jacob's night of wrestling with God resulted in God's blessing on his life. (1) From then on, he knew that his life and well-being were dependent not on his own devices, but on God's help, guidance, and blessing. Later God reminded the descendants of Israel of this truth: "Not by might, nor by power, but by my spirit, saith the LORD of hosts" (Zech. 4:6). (2) Victory and blessing in the lives of all God's people come the same way. While we may not wrestle physically with God, we can seek Him earnestly and persistently in prayer (Luke 11:5–10), confess our sin and ask His forgiveness (Luke 11:4), hunger and thirst for His kingdom and close presence (Luke 11:2), desire the reality and power of the Holy Spirit (Acts 1:8; 2:4), and pursue a life of true faith and righteousness (Mat. 6:30–33).

Jacob and Esau meet

33 AND JACOB lifted up his eyes, and looked, and, behold, [a]Esau came, and with him four hundred men. And he divided the children unto Leah, and unto Rachel, and unto the two handmaids.

2 And he put the handmaids and their children foremost, and Leah and her children after, and Rachel and Joseph hindermost.

3 And he passed over before them, and [b]bowed himself to the ground seven times, until he came near to his brother.

4 [c]And Esau ran to meet him, and embraced him, [d]and fell on his neck, and kissed him: and they wept.

5 And he lifted up his eyes, and saw the women and the children; and said, Who *are* those [r]with thee? And he said, The children [e]which God hath graciously given thy servant.

6 Then the handmaidens came near, they and their children, and they bowed themselves.

7 And Leah also with her children came near, and bowed themselves: and after came Joseph near and Rachel, and they bowed themselves.

8 And he said, [s]What *meanest* thou by [f]all this drove which I met? And he said, *These are* [g]to find grace in the sight of my lord.

9 And Esau said, I have enough, my brother; [t]keep that thou hast unto thyself.

10 And Jacob said, Nay, I pray thee, if now I have found grace in thy sight, then receive my present at my hand: for therefore I [h]have seen thy face, as though I had seen the face of God, and thou wast pleased with me.

11 Take, I pray thee, [i]my blessing that is brought to thee; because God hath dealt graciously with me, and because I have [u]enough. [j]And he urged him, and he took *it*.

12 And he said, Let us take our journey, and let us go, and I will go before thee.

13 And he said unto him, My lord knoweth that the children *are* tender, and the flocks and herds with young *are* with me: and if men should overdrive them one day, all the flock will die.

14 Let my lord, I pray thee, pass over before his servant: and I will lead on softly, [v]according as the cattle that goeth before me and the children be able to endure, until I come unto my lord [k]unto Seir.

15 And Esau said, Let me now [w]leave with thee *some* of the folk that *are* with me. And he said, [x]What needeth it? [l]let me find grace in the sight of my lord.

16 ¶ So Esau returned that day on his way unto Seir.

17 And Jacob journeyed to [m]Succoth, and built him an house, and made booths for his cattle: therefore the name of the place is called [y]Succoth.

18 ¶ And Jacob came to [n]Shalem, a city of [o]Shechem,[z] which *is* in the land of Canaan, when he came from Padan-aram; and pitched his tent before the city.

19 And [p]he bought a parcel of a field, where he had spread his tent, at the hand of the children of [a]Hamor, Shechem's father, for an hundred [b]pieces of money.

20 And he erected there an altar, and [q]called it [c]El-elohe-Israel.

The defiling of Dinah

34 AND [r]DINAH the daughter of Leah, which she bare unto Ja-

33:1 [a]ch. 32:6 **33:3** [b]ch. 18:2 & 42:6 **33:4** [c]ch. 32:28 [d]ch. 45:14,15 **33:5** [e]ch. 48:9 Ps. 127:3 Is. 8:18 **33:8** [f]ch. 32:16 [g]ch. 32:5 **33:10** [h]ch. 43:3 2 Sam. 3:13 & 14:24,28,32 **33:11** [i]Judg. 1:15 1 Sam. 25:27 & 30:26 [j]2 Ki. 5:23

33:14 [k]ch. 32:3 **33:15** [l]ch. 34:11 & 47:25 Ruth 2:13 **33:17** [m]Josh. 13:27 Judg. 8:5 Ps. 60:6 **33:18** [n]John 3:23 [o]Josh. 24:1 Judg. 9:1 **33:19** [p]Josh. 24:32 John 4:5 **33:20** [q]ch. 35:7 **34:1** [r]ch. 30:21

[r] Heb. *to thee?* [s] Heb. *What is all this band to thee?* [t] Heb. *be that to thee that is thine* [u] Heb. *all things* [v] Heb. *according to the foot of the work, &c. and according to the foot of the children* [w] Heb. *set,* or, *place* [x] Heb. *Wherefore is this?* [y] i.e. *Booths* [z] Called *Sychem* in Acts 7:16 [a] Called *Emmor* in Acts 7:16 [b] Or, *lambs* [c] i.e. *God the God of Israel*

33:4 ESAU ... KISSED HIM: AND THEY WEPT. God had dealt with Esau and placed within him the desire for reconciliation with his brother. Esau's friendly attitude was God's answer to Jacob's prayer (32:11).

34:1 DINAH ... THE DAUGHTERS OF THE LAND. Jacob settled near the pagan city of Shechem rather than the home of his father, Isaac, where God had commanded him to go (cf. 31:13; 35:1). He later bitterly regretted his choice. Only after the tragic incident involving Dinah did Jacob finally go to Beth-el and destroy all the foreign idols in his home (see next note; 35:2, note).

34:2 HE TOOK HER ... AND DEFILED HER. Both Dinah and her parents were at fault. (1) Jacob failed by choosing to live in close association with evil and immoral people, just as Lot had done (cf. 13:12–13). He failed to establish correct boundaries and rules for his children concerning their interaction with unbelievers and to supervise his

cob, [s]went out to see the daughters of the land.

2 And when Shechem the son of Hamor the Hivite, prince of the country, [t]saw her, he [u]took her, and lay with her, and [d]defiled her.

3 And his soul clave unto Dinah the daughter of Jacob, and he loved the damsel, and spake kindly unto the damsel.

4 And Shechem [v]spake unto his father Hamor, saying, Get me this damsel to wife.

5 And Jacob heard that he had defiled Dinah his daughter: now his sons were with his cattle in the field: and Jacob [w]held his peace until they were come.

6 ¶ And Hamor the father of Shechem went out unto Jacob to commune with him.

7 And the sons of Jacob came out of the field when they heard *it:* and the men were grieved, and they [x]were very wroth, because he [y]had wrought folly in Israel in lying with Jacob's daughter; [z]which thing ought not to be done.

8 And Hamor communed with them, saying, The soul of my son Shechem longeth for your daughter: I pray you give her him to wife.

9 And make ye marriages with us, *and* give your daughters unto us, and take our daughters unto you.

10 And ye shall dwell with us: and [a]the land shall be before you; dwell and [b]trade ye therein, and [c]get you possessions therein.

11 And Shechem said unto her father and unto her brethren, Let me find grace in your eyes, and what ye shall say unto me I will give.

12 Ask me never so much [d]dowry and gift, and I will give according as ye shall say unto me: but give me the damsel to wife.

13 And the sons of Jacob answered Shechem and Hamor his father [e]deceitfully, and said, because he had defiled Dinah their sister:

14 And they said unto them, We cannot do this thing, to give our sister to one that is uncircumcised; for [f]that *were* a reproach unto us:

15 But in this will we consent unto you: If ye will be as we *be,* that every male of you be circumcised;

16 Then will we give our daughters unto you, and we will take your daughters to us, and we will dwell with you, and we will become one people.

17 But if ye will not hearken unto us, to be circumcised; then will we take our daughter, and we will be gone.

18 And their words pleased Hamor, and Shechem Hamor's son.

19 And the young man deferred not to do the thing, because he had delight in Jacob's daughter: and he *was* [g]more honourable than all the house of his father.

20 ¶ And Hamor and Shechem his son came unto the gate of their city, and communed with the men of their city, saying,

21 These men *are* peaceable with us; therefore let them dwell in the land, and trade therein; for the land, behold, *it is* large enough for them; let us take their daughters to us for wives, and let us give them our daughters.

22 Only herein will the men consent unto us for to dwell with us, to be one people, if every male among us be circumcised, as they *are* circumcised.

23 *Shall* not their cattle and their substance and every beast of theirs *be* ours? only let us consent unto them, and they will dwell with us.

24 And unto Hamor and unto Shechem his son hearkened all that [h]went out of the gate of his city; and every male was circumcised, all that went out of the gate of his city.

25 ¶ And it came to pass on the

34:1 [s]Tit. 2:5
34:2 [t]ch. 6:2 Judg. 14:1 [u]ch. 20:2
34:4 [v]Judg. 14:2
34:5 [w]1 Sam. 10:27 2 Sam. 13:22
34:7 [x]ch. 49:7 2 Sam. 13:21 [y]Josh. 7:15 Judg. 20:6 [z]Deut. 23:17 2 Sam. 13:12
34:10 [a]ch. 13:9 & 20:15 [b]ch. 42:34 [c]ch. 47:27
34:12 [d]Ex. 22:16,17 Deut. 22:29 1 Sam. 18:25
34:13 [e]See 2 Sam. 13:24
34:14 [f]Josh. 5:9
34:19 [g]1 Chr. 4:9
34:24 [h]ch. 23:10,18

d Heb. *humbled her*

children properly. For her part, Dinah appears to have been seeking companionship with the ungodly "daughters of the land." The end result was tragedy, hurt, and shame for Jacob, his daughter, and his family.

(2) Parents who fail to maintain a strict separation of their family from evil companions put their children in a place of temptation and compromise, along with potential shame and disaster (see article on PARENTS AND CHILDREN, p. 1880).

34:7 THE SONS OF JACOB . . . WERE GRIEVED. The sons of Jacob were justifiably angry about the sexual violation of their sister, and they knew that such a disgraceful deed could not be tolerated. They sinned, however, by retaliating in an excessive, unjust, and ruthless manner.

34:15 BE CIRCUMCISED. Jacob's sons wrongfully used the sign of their covenant relationship with God in a deceptive manner.

34:25 SIMEON AND LEVI . . . CAME UPON THE CITY. Simeon and Levi not only killed the males of the city, but also looted the city of its

third day, when they were sore, that
two of the sons of Jacob, [i]Simeon and
Levi, Dinah's brethren, took each man
his sword, and came upon the city bold-
ly, and slew all the males.
26 And they slew Hamor and She-
chem his son with the [e]edge of the
sword, and took Dinah out of She-
chem's house, and went out.
27 The sons of Jacob came upon the
slain, and spoiled the city, because
they had defiled their sister.
28 They took their sheep, and their
oxen, and their asses, and that which
was in the city, and that which *was* in
the field,
29 And all their wealth, and all their
little ones, and their wives took they
captive, and spoiled even all that *was*
in the house.
30 And Jacob said to Simeon and
Levi, [j]Ye have [k]troubled me [l]to
make me to stink among the inhabi-
tants of the land, among the Canaan-
ites and the Perizzites: [m]and I *being*
few in number, they shall gather them-
selves together against me, and slay
me; and I shall be destroyed, I and my
house.
31 And they said, Should he deal
with our sister as with an harlot?

Jacob returns to Beth-el

35 AND GOD said unto Jacob,
Arise, go up to [n]Beth-el, and
dwell there: and make there an altar
unto God, [o]that appeared unto thee
[p]when thou fleddest from the face of
Esau thy brother.
2 Then Jacob said unto his [q]house-
hold, and to all that *were* with him, Put
away [r]the strange gods that *are*
among you, and [s]be clean, and change
your garments:
3 And let us arise, and go up to
Beth-el; and I will make there an altar
unto God, [t]who answered me in the
day of my distress, [u]and was with me
in the way which I went.
4 And they gave unto Jacob all the
strange gods which *were* in their hand,
and *all their* [v]earrings which *were* in
their ears; and Jacob hid them under
[w]the oak which *was* by Shechem.
5 And they journeyed: and [x]the ter-
ror of God was upon the cities that *were*
round about them, and they did not
pursue after the sons of Jacob.
6 ¶ So Jacob came to [y]Luz, which
is in the land of Canaan, that *is*, Beth-
el, he and all the people that *were* with
him.
7 And he [z]built there an altar, and
called the place [f]El-beth-el: because
[a]there God appeared unto him, when
he fled from the face of his brother.
8 But [b]Deborah Rebekah's nurse
died, and she was buried beneath Beth-
el under an oak: and the name of it was
called [g]Allon-bachuth.
9 ¶ And [c]God appeared unto Jacob
again, when he came out of Padan-
aram, and blessed him.
10 And God said unto him, Thy
name *is* Jacob: [d]thy name shall not be
called any more Jacob, [e]but Israel
shall be thy name: and he called his
name Israel.
11 And God said unto him, [f]I *am*
God Almighty: be fruitful and multiply;
[g]a nation and a company of nations
shall be of thee, and kings shall come
out of thy loins;
12 And the land [h]which I gave
Abraham and Isaac, to thee I will give
it, and to thy seed after thee will I
give the land.

[e] Heb. *mouth* [f] i.e. *The God of Beth-el*
[g] i.e. *The oak of weeping*

34:25 [i] ch. 49:5-7
34:30 [j] ch. 49:6 [k] Josh. 7:25 [l] Ex. 5:21 1 Sam. 13:4 [m] Deut. 4:27 Ps. 105:12
35:1 [n] ch. 28:19 [o] ch. 28:13 [p] ch. 27:43
35:2 [q] ch. 18:19 Josh. 24:15 [r] ch. 31:19,34 Josh. 24:2,23 1 Sam. 7:3 [s] Ex. 19:10
35:3 [t] ch. 32:7,24 [u] ch. 28:20 & 31:3,42
35:4 [v] Hos. 2:13 [w] Josh. 24:26 Judg. 9:6
35:5 [x] Ex. 15:16 Deut. 11:25 Josh. 2:9 1 Sam. 14:15
35:6 [y] ch. 28:19,22
35:7 [z] Eccl. 5:4 [a] ch. 28:13
35:8 [b] ch. 24:59
35:9 [c] Hos. 12:4
35:10 [d] ch. 17:5 [e] ch. 32:28
35:11 [f] ch. 17:1 & 48:3,4 Ex. 6:3 [g] ch. 17:5,6,16 & 28:3 & 48:4
35:12 [h] ch. 12:7 & 13:15 & 26:3,4 & 28:13

property and captured the women and children. This cruel action resulted in Simeon and Levi losing the leadership of the nation. God distinguishes between justifiable war and ruthless cruelty (see 49:5–7).

35:2 PUT AWAY THE STRANGE GODS. After the terrible events of ch. 34, God directed Jacob's family to go to Bethel in order to bring them into closer obedience to His word. Jacob, realizing the depth of spiritual deterioration in his family, commanded all the members of his household to "put away the strange gods that *are* among you." This spiritual renewal in the life of Jacob's family consisted in: (1) removing from their home everything that offended God (v. 2); (2) committing themselves to personal holiness (v. 2); (3) renewing vows to God in devotion and worship (v. 7; 28:20–22); (4) entering fellowship with God (v. 9); (5) and leading lives based on God's word (vv. 10–15) and spiritual sacrifice (v. 14). Because of Jacob's renewal, he again experienced God's protection, presence, revelation, and blessing (vv. 5, 9–13).

35:9–13 GOD APPEARED UNTO JACOB AGAIN . . . AND BLESSED HIM. Now that Jacob was finally back in the land of promise and allied with God's will, the covenant promise made to Abraham (17:1–8) was renewed (see article on GOD'S COVENANT WITH ABRAHAM, ISAAC, AND JACOB, p. 48).

13 And God [i]went up from him in the place where he talked with him.

14 And Jacob [j]set up a pillar in the place where he talked with him, *even* a pillar of stone: and he poured a drink offering thereon, and he poured oil thereon.

15 And Jacob called the name of the place where God spake with him, [k]Beth-el.

The deaths of Rachel and Isaac

35:23–26pp — 1 Chr. 2:1–2

16 ¶ And they journeyed from Beth-el; and there was but **h**a little way to come to Ephrath: and Rachel travailed, and she had hard labour.

17 And it came to pass, when she was in hard labour, that the midwife said unto her, Fear not; [l]thou shalt have this son also.

18 And it came to pass, as her soul was in departing, (for she died) that she called his name **i**Ben-oni: but his father called him **j**Benjamin.

19 And [m]Rachel died, and was buried in the way to [n]Ephrath, which *is* Beth-lehem.

20 And Jacob set a pillar upon her grave: that *is* the pillar of Rachel's grave [o]unto this day.

21 ¶ And Israel journeyed, and spread his tent beyond [p]the tower of Edar.

22 And it came to pass, when Israel dwelt in that land, that Reuben went and [q]lay with Bilhah his father's concubine: and Israel heard *it.* Now the sons of Jacob were twelve:

23 The sons of Leah; [r]Reuben, Jacob's firstborn, and Simeon, and Levi, and Judah, and Issachar, and Zebulun:

24 The sons of Rachel; Joseph, and Benjamin:

25 And the sons of Bilhah, Rachel's handmaid; Dan, and Naphtali:

26 And the sons of Zilpah, Leah's handmaid; Gad, and Asher: these *are* the sons of Jacob, which were born to him in Padan-aram.

27 ¶ And Jacob came unto Isaac his father unto [s]Mamre, unto the [t]city of Arbah, which *is* Hebron, where Abraham and Isaac sojourned.

28 And the days of Isaac were an hundred and fourscore years.

29 And Isaac gave up the ghost, and died, and [u]was gathered unto his people, *being* old and full of days: and [v]his sons Esau and Jacob buried him.

The descendants of Esau

36:10–14pp — 1 Chr. 1:35–37
36:20–28pp — 1 Chr. 1:38–42

36 NOW THESE *are* the generations of Esau, [w]who *is* Edom.

2 [x]Esau took his wives of the daughters of Canaan; Adah the daughter of Elon the Hittite, and [y]Aholibamah the daughter of Anah the daughter of Zibeon the Hivite;

3 And [z]Bashemath Ishmael's daughter, sister of Nebajoth.

4 And [a]Adah bare to Esau Eliphaz; and Bashemath bare Reuel;

5 And Aholibamah bare Jeush, and Jaalam, and Korah: these *are* the sons of Esau, which were born unto him in the land of Canaan.

6 And Esau took his wives, and his sons, and his daughters, and all the **k**persons of his house, and his cattle, and all his beasts, and all his substance, which he had got in the land of Canaan; and went into the country from the face of his brother Jacob.

7 [b]For their riches were more than that they might dwell together; and [c]the land wherein they were strangers could not bear them because of their cattle.

8 Thus dwelt Esau in [d]mount Seir: [e]Esau *is* Edom.

35:13 [i]ch. 17:22
35:14 [j]ch. 28:18
35:15 [k]ch. 28:19
35:17 [l]ch. 30:24; 1 Sam. 4:20
35:19 [m]ch. 48:7; [n]Ruth 1:2; Mic. 5:2; Mat. 2:6
35:20 [o]1 Sam. 10:2
35:21 [p]Mic. 4:8
35:22 [q]ch. 49:4; 1 Chr. 5:1
35:23 [r]ch. 46:8; Ex. 1:2
35:27 [s]ch. 13:18; [t]Josh. 14:15
35:29 [u]ch. 15:15 & 25:8; [v]See ch. 25:9 & 49:31
36:1 [w]ch. 25:30
36:2 [x]ch. 26:34; [y]ver. 25
36:3 [z]ch. 28:9
36:4 [a]1 Chr. 1:35
36:7 [b]ch. 13:6,11; [c]ch. 17:8 & 28:4
36:8 [d]ch. 32:3; Deut. 2:5; Josh. 24:4; [e]ver. 1

h Heb. *a little piece of ground* **i** i.e. *The son of my sorrow* **j** i.e. *The son of the right hand* **k** Heb. *souls*

35:18 SHE CALLED HIS NAME BEN-ONI: BUT HIS FATHER CALLED HIM BENJAMIN. Leah and Rachel named all of Jacob's children. However, Ben-oni ("son of my sorrow") would have put a terrible burden of guilt on the boy, for it would make him think he was responsible for his mother's death. Jacob changed his name to the honorable name of Benjamin, meaning "son of my right hand" and indicating that he was happy to have Benjamin as his son even though Rachel was gone. Children need to be protected from guilt and trouble that comes through no fault of their own.

35:22 REUBEN. Because of Reuben's sexual immorality, his rights as the firstborn were taken away from him. He lost his inheritance and place of leadership forever (see 49:3–4; 1 Chr. 5:1).

36:6–7 ESAU . . . RICHES. In many ways Esau prospered materially, yet he did not prosper spiritually. His life was characterized by little regard for spiritual things (25:34; 26:34–35; 36:2). Consequently, the nation he founded (Edom) was ungodly and became a special object of God's wrath (see Is. 11:14; Amos 9:12; Obad. 1–4).

9 ¶ And these *are* the generations of Esau the father of [1]the Edomites in mount Seir:

10 These *are* the names of Esau's sons; [f]Eliphaz the son of Adah the wife of Esau, Reuel the son of Bashemath the wife of Esau.

11 And the sons of Eliphaz were Teman, Omar, [m]Zepho, and Gatam, and Kenaz.

12 And Timna was concubine to Eliphaz Esau's son; and she bare to Eliphaz [g]Amalek: these *were* the sons of Adah Esau's wife.

13 And these *are* the sons of Reuel; Nahath, and Zerah, Shammah, and Mizzah: these were the sons of Bashemath Esau's wife.

14 ¶ And these were the sons of Aholibamah, the daughter of Anah the daughter of Zibeon, Esau's wife: and she bare to Esau Jeush, and Jaalam, and Korah.

15 ¶ These *were* dukes of the sons of Esau: the sons of Eliphaz the firstborn *son* of Esau; duke Teman, duke Omar, duke Zepho, duke Kenaz,

16 Duke Korah, duke Gatam, *and* duke Amalek: these *are* the dukes *that came* of Eliphaz in the land of Edom; these *were* the sons of Adah.

17 ¶ And these *are* the sons of Reuel Esau's son; duke Nahath, duke Zerah, duke Shammah, duke Mizzah: these *are* the dukes *that came* of Reuel in the land of Edom; these *are* the sons of Bashemath Esau's wife.

18 ¶ And these are the sons of Aholibamah Esau's wife; duke Jeush, duke Jaalam, duke Korah: these *were* the dukes *that came* of Aholibamah the daughter of Anah, Esau's wife.

19 These *are* the sons of Esau, who *is* Edom, and these *are* their dukes.

20 ¶ [h]These *are* the sons of Seir [i]the Horite, who inhabited the land; Lotan, and Shobal, and Zibeon, and Anah,

21 And Dishon, and Ezer, and Dishan: these *are* the dukes of the Horites, the children of Seir in the land of Edom.

22 And the children of Lotan were Hori and [n]Hemam; and Lotan's sister *was* Timna.

23 And the children of Shobal *were* these; [o]Alvan, and Manahath, and Ebal, [p]Shepho, and Onam.

24 And these *are* the children of Zibeon; both Ajah, and Anah: this *was that* Anah that found [j]the mules in the wilderness, as he fed the asses of Zibeon his father.

25 And the children of Anah *were* these; Dishon, and Aholibamah the daughter of Anah.

26 And these *are* the children of Dishon; [q]Hemdan, and Eshban, and Ithran, and Cheran.

27 The children of Ezer *are* these; Bilhan, and Zaavan, and [r]Akan.

28 The children of Dishan *are* these; Uz, and Aran.

29 These *are* the dukes *that came* of the Horites; duke Lotan, duke Shobal, duke Zibeon, duke Anah,

30 Duke Dishon, duke Ezer, duke Dishan: these *are* the dukes *that came* of Hori, among their dukes in the land of Seir.

The kings of Edom

36:31–43pp — 1 Chr. 1:43–54

31 ¶ And [k]these *are* the kings that reigned in the land of Edom, before there reigned any king over the children of Israel.

32 And Bela the son of Beor reigned in Edom: and the name of his city *was* Dinhabah.

33 And Bela died, and Jobab the son of Zerah of Bozrah reigned in his stead.

34 And Jobab died, and Husham of the land of Temani reigned in his stead.

35 And Husham died, and Hadad the son of Bedad, who smote Midian in the field of Moab, reigned in his stead: and the name of his city *was* Avith.

36 And Hadad died, and Samlah of Masrekah reigned in his stead.

37 And Samlah died, and Saul of [l]Rehoboth *by* the river reigned in his stead.

38 And Saul died, and Baal-hanan the son of Achbor reigned in his stead.

39 And Baal-hanan the son of Achbor died, and [m]Hadar reigned in his stead: and the name of his city *was* Pau; and his wife's name *was* Mehetabel, the daughter of Matred, the daughter of Mezahab.

40 And these *are* the names of [n]the dukes *that came* of Esau, according to

36:10 [f]1 Chr. 1:35
36:12 [g]Ex. 17:8,14 Num. 24:20 1 Sam. 15:2,3
36:20 [h]1 Chr. 1:38 [i]ch. 14:6 Deut. 2:12,22
36:24 [j]See Lev. 19:19
36:31 [k]1 Chr. 1:43
36:37 [l]ch. 10:11
36:39 [m]1 Chr. 1:50, *Hadad Pai*
36:40 [n]1 Chr. 1:51

[1] Heb. *Edom* [m] Or, *Zephi;* see 1 Chr. 1:36
[n] Or, *Homam;* see 1 Chr. 1:39 [o] Or, *Alian;* see 1 Chr. 1:40 [p] Or, *Shephi;* see 1 Chr. 1:40
[q] Or, *Amram;* see 1 Chr. 1:41 [r] Or, *Jakan;* see 1 Chr. 1:42

their families, after their places, by
their names; duke Timnah, duke [s]Al-
vah, duke Jetheth,
41 Duke Aholibamah, duke Elah,
duke Pinon,
42 Duke Kenaz, duke Teman, duke
Mibzar,
43 Duke Magdiel, duke Iram: these
be the dukes of Edom, according to
their habitations in the land of their
possession: he *is* Esau the father of
[t]the Edomites.

Joseph's dream

37 AND JACOB dwelt in the land
[o]wherein[u] his father was a
stranger, in the land of Canaan.
2 These *are* the generations of Ja-
cob. Joseph, *being* seventeen years old,
was feeding the flock with his breth-
ren; and the lad *was* with the sons of
Bilhah, and with the sons of Zilpah, his
father's wives: and Joseph brought
unto his father [p]their evil report.
3 Now Israel loved Joseph more
than all his children, because he *was*
[q]the son of his old age: and he made
him a coat of *many* [r]colours.[v]
4 And when his brethren saw that
their father loved him more than all his
brethren, they [s]hated him, and could
not speak peaceably unto him.
5 ¶ And Joseph dreamed a dream,
and he told *it* his brethren: and they
hated him yet the more.
6 And he said unto them, Hear, I
pray you, this dream which I have
dreamed:
7 For, [t]behold, we *were* binding
sheaves in the field, and, lo, my sheaf
arose, and also stood upright; and, be-
hold, your sheaves stood round about,
and made obeisance to my sheaf.

37:1 [o]ch. 17:8 & 23:4 & 28:4 & 36:7 Heb. 11:9
37:2 [p]1 Sam. 2:22-24
37:3 [q]ch. 44:20 [r]Judg. 5:30 2 Sam. 13:18
37:4 [s]ch. 27:41 & 49:23
37:7 [t]ch. 42:6,9 & 43:26 & 44:14
37:9 [u]ch. 46:29
37:10 [v]ch. 27:29
37:11 [w]Acts 7:9 [x]Dan. 7:28 Luke 2:19,51
37:12 [y]ch. 33:18
37:14 [z]ch. 13:18 & 35:27

8 And his brethren said to him,
Shalt thou indeed reign over us? or
shalt thou indeed have dominion over
us? And they hated him yet the more
for his dreams, and for his words.
9 ¶ And he dreamed yet another
dream, and told it his brethren, and
said, Behold, I have dreamed a dream
more; and, behold, [u]the sun and the
moon and the eleven stars made obei-
sance to me.
10 And he told *it* to his father, and
to his brethren: and his father rebuked
him, and said unto him, What *is* this
dream that thou hast dreamed? Shall I
and thy mother and [v]thy brethren in-
deed come to bow down ourselves to
thee to the earth?
11 And [w]his brethren envied him;
but his father [x]observed the saying.

Joseph sold to merchants

12 ¶ And his brethren went to feed
their father's flock in [y]Shechem.
13 And Israel said unto Joseph, Do
not thy brethren feed *the flock* in She-
chem? come, and I will send thee unto
them. And he said to him, Here *am I*.
14 And he said to him, Go, I pray
thee, [w]see whether it be well with thy
brethren, and well with the flocks; and
bring me word again. So he sent him
out of the vale of [z]Hebron, and he
came to Shechem.
15 ¶ And a certain man found him,
and, behold, *he was* wandering in the
field: and the man asked him, saying,
What seekest thou?

[s] Or, *Aliah* [t] Heb. *Edom* [u] Heb. *of his father's sojournings* [v] Or, *pieces,* [w] Heb. *see the peace of thy brethren*

37:2 JOSEPH. The story of Joseph reveals how Jacob's descendants became a nation that sojourned in Egypt. This section of Genesis not only prepares us for the narrative of the exodus, but also reveals the loyalty that Joseph showed toward his God and the many ways by which God protected and directed his life for the good of others. It emphasizes the truth that the righteous may suffer in an evil and unjust world, but ultimately the purpose of God for the righteous will triumph.

37:3 A COAT OF *MANY* COLOURS. The tunic that Joseph received from his father was bright-colored and full-length, in contrast to the plainer tunics worn by his brothers. It represented a position of special favoritism and honor with his father.

37:5 A DREAM. God sometimes reveals His will to us through prophetic dreams (cf. 28:10–17; Num. 12:6–8; Dan. 7; Mat. 1:20–24). Today, under the new covenant, God may yet speak to us through dreams (cf. Acts 2:17), although His primary revelation and guidance come through Scripture (John 15:7; 1 Tim. 4:6; Jas. 1:21) and the indwelling Holy Spirit (Rom. 8:1–17; Gal. 5:16–25).

37:6 HEAR . . . THIS DREAM. Joseph showed insensitivity and immaturity in telling his brothers his dream. Its purpose was to provide him revelation and faith for his difficult future, not to give him an occasion to exalt himself over his brothers. God may have chosen Joseph for the task of protecting Jacob's family in Egypt because his moral standards and dedication to God and His laws were clearly superior to those of his brothers (see 2 Tim. 2:20–21).

37:7 MADE OBEISANCE. Later this dream was literally fulfilled (42:6; 43:26; 44:14).

16 And he said, I seek my brethren:
[a]tell me, I pray thee, where they feed
their flocks.
17 And the man said, They are de-
parted hence; for I heard them say, Let
us go to Dothan. And Joseph went after
his brethren, and found them in [b]Do-
than.
18 And when they saw him afar off,
even before he came near unto them,
[c]they conspired against him to slay
him.
19 And they said one to another,
Behold, this [x]dreamer cometh.
20 [d]Come now therefore, and let
us slay him, and cast him into some pit,
and we will say, Some evil beast hath
devoured him: and we shall see what
will become of his dreams.
21 And [e]Reuben heard *it,* and he
delivered him out of their hands; and
said, Let us not kill him.
22 And Reuben said unto them,
Shed no blood, *but* cast him into this pit
that *is* in the wilderness, and lay no
hand upon him; that he might rid him
out of their hands, to deliver him to his
father again.
23 ¶ And it came to pass, when Jo-
seph was come unto his brethren, that
they stripped Joseph out of his coat, *his*
coat of *many* [y]colours that *was* on
him;
24 And they took him, and cast him
into a pit: and the pit *was* empty, *there*
was no water in it.
25 [f]And they sat down to eat
bread: and they lifted up their eyes and
looked, and, behold, a company of
[g]Ishmeelites came from Gilead with
their camels bearing spicery and
[h]balm and myrrh, going to carry *it*
down to Egypt.
26 And Judah said unto his breth-
ren, What profit *is it* if we slay our
brother, and [i]conceal his blood?
27 Come, and let us sell him to the
Ishmeelites, and [j]let not our hand be
upon him; for he *is* [k]our brother *and*
[l]our flesh. And his brethren [z]were
content.

37:16 [a]Sol. 1:7
37:17 [b]2 Ki. 6:13
37:18 [c]1 Sam. 19:1 Mat. 27:1 Mark 14:1 Acts 23:12
37:20 [d]Prov. 1:11
37:21 [e]ch. 42:22
37:25 [f]Prov. 30:20 [g]See ver. 28,36 [h]Jer. 8:22
37:26 [i]ver. 20
37:27 [j]1 Sam. 18:17 [k]ch. 42:21 [l]ch. 29:14
37:28 [m]Judg. 6:3 [n]Ps. 105:17 Acts 7:9 [o]See Mat. 27:9
37:29 [p]Job 1:20
37:30 [q]ch. 42:13,36
37:31 [r]ver. 23
37:33 [s]ver. 20
37:34 [t]2 Sam. 3:31
37:35 [u]2 Sam. 12:17 [v]ch. 42:38
37:36 [w]ch. 39:1
38:1 [x]2 Ki. 4:8
38:2 [y]ch. 34:2

28 Then there passed by [m]Midian-
ites merchantmen; and they drew and
lifted up Joseph out of the pit, [n]and
sold Joseph to the Ishmeelites for
[o]twenty *pieces* of silver: and they
brought Joseph into Egypt.
29 ¶ And Reuben returned unto the
pit; and, behold, Joseph *was* not in the
pit; and he [p]rent his clothes.
30 And he returned unto his breth-
ren, and said, The child [q]*is* not; and I,
whither shall I go?
31 And they took [r]Joseph's coat,
and killed a kid of the goats, and
dipped the coat in the blood;
32 And they sent the coat of *many*
colours, and they brought *it* to their fa-
ther; and said, This have we found:
know now whether it *be* thy son's coat
or no.
33 And he knew it, and said, *It is* my
son's coat; an [s]evil beast hath de-
voured him; Joseph is without doubt
rent in pieces.
34 And Jacob [t]rent his clothes,
and put sackcloth upon his loins, and
mourned for his son many days.
35 And all his sons and all his
daughters [u]rose up to comfort him;
but he refused to be comforted; and he
said, For [v]I will go down into the
grave unto my son mourning. Thus his
father wept for him.
36 And [w]the Midianites sold him
into Egypt unto Potiphar, an [a]officer
of Pharaoh's, *and* [b] [c]captain of the
guard.

Judah and Tamar

38 AND IT came to pass at that
time, that Judah went down
from his brethren, and [x]turned in to a
certain Adullamite, whose name *was*
Hirah.
2 And Judah [y]saw there a daughter

[x]Heb. *master of dreams* [y]Or, *pieces* [z]Heb. *hearkened* [a]Heb. *eunuch:* But the word doth signify not only *eunuchs,* but also *chamberlains, courtiers,* and *officers* [b]Heb. *chief of the slaughtermen,* or, *executioners* [c]Or, *chief marshal*

37:21 REUBEN. Reuben was Jacob's firstborn and as such was supposed to be the leader of the brothers. However, after his immorality with Bilhah (see 35:22, note), he forever lost his effective spiritual leadership and could not influence his brothers sufficiently (vv. 22–29; cf. 42:37–38).

37:28 THEY BROUGHT JOSEPH INTO EGYPT. Though Joseph was treated cruelly by his brothers and sold into slavery, yet in all this God used the evil action of humans to work out His will in Joseph's life (see article on THE PROVIDENCE OF GOD, p. 80).

37:35 DOWN INTO THE GRAVE. The word "grave" here is the Hebrew word *Sheol* (see Ps. 16:10, note, for comments on this important word).

38:2 A CERTAIN CANAANITE. Holy Scripture records this shameful story of Judah for at least

of a certain Canaanite, whose name
was [z]Shuah; and he took her, and
went in unto her.
3 And she conceived, and bare a
son; and he called his name Er.
4 And she conceived again, and
bare a son; and she called his name
[a]Onan.
5 And she yet again conceived, and
bare a son; and called his name [b]She-
lah: and he was at Chezib, when she
bare him.
6 And Judah [c]took a wife for Er his
firstborn, whose name *was* Tamar.
7 And [d]Er, Judah's firstborn, was
wicked in the sight of the LORD; [e]and
the LORD slew him.
8 And Judah said unto Onan, Go in
unto [f]thy brother's wife, and marry
her, and raise up seed to thy brother.
9 And Onan knew that the seed
should not be [g]his; and it came to
pass, when he went in unto his broth-
er's wife, that he spilled *it* on the
ground, lest that he should give seed to
his brother.
10 And the thing which he did [d]dis-
pleased the LORD: wherefore he slew
[h]him also.
11 Then said Judah to Tamar his
daughter-in-law, [i]Remain a widow at
thy father's house, till Shelah my son
be grown: for he said, Lest peradven-
ture he die also, as his brethren *did*.
And Tamar went and dwelt [j]in her fa-
ther's house.
12 ¶ And [e]in process of time the
daughter of Shuah Judah's wife died;
and Judah [k]was comforted, and went
up unto his sheepshearers to Timnath,
he and his friend Hirah the Adullamite.
13 And it was told Tamar, saying,
Behold thy father-in-law goeth up [l]to
Timnath to shear his sheep.
14 And she put her widow's gar-
ments off from her, and covered her
with a veil, and wrapped herself, and
[m]sat in [f]an open place, which *is* by
the way to Timnath; for she saw [n]that
Shelah was grown, and she was not
given unto him to wife.
15 When Judah saw her, he thought
her *to be* an harlot; because she had
covered her face.
16 And he turned unto her by the
way, and said, Go to, I pray thee, let me
come in unto thee; (for he knew not
that she *was* his daughter-in-law.) And
she said, What wilt thou give me, that
thou mayest come in unto me?
17 And he said, [o]I will send *thee*
[g]a kid from the flock. And she said,
[p]Wilt thou give *me* a pledge, till thou
send *it?*
18 And he said, What pledge shall I
give thee? And she said, [q]Thy signet,
and thy bracelets, and thy staff that *is*
in thine hand. And he gave *it* her, and
came in unto her, and she conceived by
him.
19 And she arose, and went away,
and [r]laid by her veil from her, and put
on the garments of her widowhood.
20 And Judah sent the kid by the
hand of his friend the Adullamite, to

38:2 [z]1 Chr. 2:3
38:4 [a]Num. 26:19
38:5 [b]Num. 26:20
38:6 [c]ch. 21:21
38:7 [d]Num. 26:19 [e]1 Chr. 2:3
38:8 [f]Deut. 25:5
38:9 [g]Deut. 25:6
38:10 [h]ch. 46:12
38:11 [i]Ruth 1:13 [j]Lev. 22:13
38:12 [k]2 Sam. 13:39
38:13 [l]Josh. 15:10,57
38:14 [m]Prov. 7:12 [n]ver. 11,26
38:17 [o]Ezek. 16:33 [p]ver. 20
38:18 [q]ver. 25
38:19 [r]ver. 14

[d]Heb. *was evil in the eyes of the LORD* [e]Heb. *the days were multiplied* [f]Heb. *the door of eyes,* or, *of Enajim* [g]Heb. *a kid of the goats*

four reasons. (1) It reveals the loose morals of that day against which Joseph's purity stands out in sharp contrast. Notice the contrast between "Judah went down" (of his own accord, v. 1) and "Joseph was brought down" (39:1). (2) It shows why it was necessary for Israel's family to leave Canaan and go to Egypt. If Jacob had remained among the Canaanites, his descendants would have lost their identity through mixed marriages (see vv. 1–2). In Egypt Jacob's descendants were segregated from the Egyptians and thereby were able to become a distinctly separate people devoted only to God (see note on 46:34). (3) It illustrates that the sins of everyone, even prominent people in God's redemptive plan, will ultimately be exposed (see article on THE JUDGMENT OF BELIEVERS, p. 1811). (4) It shows that leadership of God's people goes to those who are morally pure. Joseph was faithful to God and His laws, while Judah failed. The same standard applies in the N.T. for those appointed to spiritual leadership (see article on MORAL QUALIFICATIONS FOR OVERSEERS, p. 1908).

38:6 TAMAR. When Tamar's husband died (v. 7), she was left a childless widow. She longed for a child by which to carry on her family name and to produce descendants (v. 8).

38:9 ONAN. Ancient laws of the Near East required that a brother should marry his brother's widow if she had no children and thus produce a child in the name of his deceased brother (v. 8; Deut. 25:5–10). Onan's sin was his refusal to fulfill this responsibility. God took his life because he would not give Tamar a son (v. 10).

38:15 THOUGHT HER *TO BE* A HARLOT. Although Tamar was wrong in her action, Judah was the greater sinner whose conduct was hypocritical and corrupt (v. 26). In the times before the coming of Christ, God overlooked some evils until full redemption was made available in Christ (see Acts 17:30).

receive *his* pledge from the woman's hand: but he found her not.

21 Then he asked the men of that place, saying, Where *is* the harlot, that *was* [h]openly by the way side? And they said, There was no harlot in this *place*.

22 And he returned to Judah, and said, I cannot find her; and also the men of the place said, *that* there was no harlot in this *place*.

23 And Judah said, Let her take *it* to her, lest we [i]be shamed: behold, I sent this kid, and thou hast not found her.

24 ¶ And it came to pass about three months after, that it was told Judah, saying, Tamar thy daughter-in-law hath [s]played the harlot; and also, behold, she *is* with child by whoredom. And Judah said, Bring her forth, [t]and let her be burnt.

25 When she *was* brought forth, she sent to her father-in-law, saying, By the man, whose these *are*, *am* I with child: and she said, [u]Discern, I pray thee, whose *are* these, [v]the signet, and bracelets, and staff.

26 And Judah [w]acknowledged *them*, and said, [x]She hath been more righteous than I; because that [y]I gave her not to Shelah my son. And he knew her again [z]no more.

27 ¶ And it came to pass in the time of her travail, that, behold, twins *were* in her womb.

28 And it came to pass, when she travailed, that *the one* put out *his* hand: and the midwife took and bound upon his hand a scarlet thread, saying, This came out first.

29 And it came to pass, as he drew back his hand, that, behold, his brother came out: and she said, [j]How hast thou broken forth? *this* breach *be* upon thee: therefore his name was called [a]Pharez.[k]

30 And afterward came out his brother, that had the scarlet thread upon his hand: and his name was called Zerah.

38:24 [s]Judg. 19:2 [t]Lev. 21:9 Deut. 22:21
38:25 [u]ch. 37:32 [v]ver. 18
38:26 [w]ch. 37:33 [x]1 Sam. 24:17 [y]ver. 14 [z]Job 34:31,32
38:29 [a]ch. 46:12 Num. 26:20 1 Chr. 2:4 Mat. 1:3

Joseph and Potiphar's wife

39 AND JOSEPH was brought down to Egypt; and [b]Potiphar, an officer of Pharaoh, captain of the guard, an Egyptian, [c]bought him of the hands of the Ishmeelites, which had brought him down thither.

2 And [d]the LORD was with Joseph, and he was a prosperous man; and he was in the house of his master the Egyptian.

3 And his master saw that the LORD *was* with him, and that the LORD [e]made all that he did to prosper in his hand.

4 And Joseph [f]found grace in his sight, and he served him: and he made him [g]overseer over his house, and all *that* he had he put into his hand.

5 And it came to pass from the time *that* he had made him overseer in his house, and over all that he had, that [h]the LORD blessed the Egyptian's house for Joseph's sake; and the blessing of the LORD was upon all that he had in the house, and in the field.

6 And he left all that he had in Joseph's hand; and he knew not aught he had, save the bread which he did eat. And Joseph [i]was *a* goodly *person*, and wellfavoured.

7 ¶ And it came to pass after these things, that his master's wife cast her eyes upon Joseph; and she said, [j]Lie with me.

8 But he refused, and said unto his master's wife, Behold, my master wotteth not what *is* with me in the house, and he hath committed all that he hath to my hand;

9 *There is* none greater in this house

39:1 [b]ch. 37:36 Ps:105:17 [c]ch. 37:28
39:2 [d]ver. 21 ch. 21:22 & 26:24,28 & 28:15 1 Sam. 16:18 & 18:14,28 Acts 7:9
39:3 [e]Ps. 1:3
39:4 [f]ver. 21 [g]ch. 24:2
39:5 [h]ch. 30:27
39:6 [i]1 Sam. 16:12
39:7 [j]2 Sam. 13:11

[h] Or, *in Enajim* [i] Heb. *become a contempt*
[j] Or, *Wherefore hast thou made* this *breach against thee?* [k] i.e. *A breach*

39:1 JOSEPH WAS BROUGHT DOWN TO EGYPT. Joseph was taken to Egypt approximately 1900 B.C. This would have been about two hundred years after the call of Abraham (12:1–3). Joseph faced three great tests in Egypt: the test of personal purity, a test that often comes to young people away from home; the test of the opportunity for revenge, a test that often comes to people who have been mistreated; and the test of facing death. In each case he overcame the test through his trust in God and His promises.

39:2 THE LORD WAS WITH JOSEPH. Scripture is clear that Joseph's separation from his people was under God's direction. God was working through Joseph and Joseph's circumstances to preserve Israel's family and unite them again according to God's promise (cf. 45:5–15; 50:17–20,24; see article on THE PROVIDENCE OF GOD, p. 80).

39:9 SIN AGAINST GOD? All sin, including sin against the integrity of marriage (i.e., adultery), is fundamentally a sin against God (cf. Ps. 51:4). King David later learned this the hard way through God's continued judgment upon his life and home (see Ex. 20:14, note).

than I; neither hath he kept back any thing from me but thee, because thou *art* his wife: [k]how then can I do this great wickedness, and [l]sin against God?

10 And it came to pass, as she spake to Joseph day by day, that he hearkened not unto her, to lie by her, *or* to be with her.

11 And it came to pass about this time, that *Joseph* went into the house to do his business; and *there was* none of the men of the house there within.

12 And [m]she caught him by his garment, saying, Lie with me: and he left his garment in her hand, and fled, and got him out.

13 And it came to pass, when she saw that he had left his garment in her hand, and was fled forth,

14 That she called unto the men of her house, and spake unto them, saying, See, he hath brought in an Hebrew unto us to mock us; he came in unto me to lie with me, and I cried with a [1]loud voice:

15 And it came to pass, when he heard that I lifted up my voice and cried, that he left his garment with me, and fled, and got him out.

16 And she laid up his garment by her, until his lord came home.

17 And she [n]spake unto him according to these words, saying, The Hebrew servant, which thou hast brought unto us, came in unto me to mock me:

18 And it came to pass, as I lifted up my voice and cried, that he left his garment with me, and fled out.

19 And it came to pass, when his master heard the words of his wife, which she spake unto him, saying, After this manner did thy servant to me; that his [o]wrath was kindled.

20 And Joseph's master took him, and [p]put him into the [q]prison, a place where the king's prisoners *were* bound: and he was there in the prison.

21 ¶ But the LORD was with Joseph, and [m]showed him mercy, and [r]gave him favour in the sight of the keeper of the prison.

22 And the keeper of the prison [s]committed to Joseph's hand all the prisoners that *were* in the prison; and whatsoever they did there, he was the doer *of it.*

23 The keeper of the prison looked not to any thing *that was* under his hand; because [t]the LORD was with him, and *that* which he did, the LORD made *it* to prosper.

Joseph interprets dreams

40 AND IT came to pass after these things, *that* the [u]butler of the king of Egypt and *his* baker had offended their lord the king of Egypt.

2 And Pharaoh was [v]wroth against two *of* his officers, against the chief of the butlers, and against the chief of the bakers.

3 [w]And he put them in ward in the house of the captain of the guard, into the prison, the place where Joseph *was* bound.

4 And the captain of the guard charged Joseph with them, and he

39:9 [k]Prov. 6:29,32 [l]ch. 20:6
39:12 [m]Prov. 7:13
39:17 [n]Ex. 23:1 Ps. 120:3
39:19 [o]Prov. 6:34,35
39:20 [p]Ps. 105:18 1 Pet. 2:19 [q]See ch. 40:3,15 & 41:14
39:21 [r]Ex. 3:21 Prov. 16:7 Dan. 1:9 Acts 7:9,10
39:22 [s]ch. 40:3,4
39:23 [t]ver. 2,3
40:1 [u]Neh. 1:11
40:2 [v]Prov. 16:14
40:3 [w]ch. 39:20,23

[1]Heb. *great* [m]Heb. *extended kindness unto him*

39:12 HE . . . FLED. Joseph, both out of loyalty and faithfulness to his God and out of loyalty to Potiphar, continued to resist sin (cf. Prov. 7:6–27). He was victorious over the temptation because he had previously made up his mind to remain obedient to his Lord and not to sin (v. 9). Believers under the new covenant emerge victorious over temptation the same way. We must make a firm and determined decision not to sin against God. Given this purpose, there can be no room for evasion, exception, or compromise.

39:20 PUT HIM INTO THE PRISON. Victory over temptation and faithfulness to God do not always result in immediate reward. Joseph suffered for his righteousness. Christ speaks of His followers also being persecuted for the sake of righteousness (Mat. 5:10) and reminds us that such people will be considered blessed and receive a great reward in heaven (Mat. 5:11–12).

39:21 THE LORD WAS WITH JOSEPH. Four times in ch. 39 it is said that "the LORD was with Joseph" (vv. 2,3,21,23). Because Joseph honored God, God honored him. Those who fear God and acknowledge Him in all their ways have the promise that God will direct all their steps (Prov. 3:5–7).

40:1 IT CAME TO PASS. Joseph maintained his faith in God while being unjustly confined to prison for at least two years. His interpretations of Pharaoh's dreams through the revelation of God's Spirit provided the opportunity for his later release and ascendancy in authority. This narrative emphasizes that although God does not cause all things that happen (see 39:7–23), He nevertheless can use adverse circumstances to work His will for our good according to His purposes (see Rom. 8:28, note).

40:2 PHARAOH. This was the general term used for all the kings of Egypt. It was commonly attached to the monarch's name.

served them: and they continued a sea-
son in ward.
5 ¶ And they dreamed a dream both
of them, each man his dream in one
night, each man according to the inter-
pretation of his dream, the butler and
the baker of the king of Egypt, which
were bound in the prison.
6 And Joseph came in unto them in
the morning, and looked upon them,
and, behold, they *were* sad.
7 And he asked Pharaoh's officers
that *were* with him in the ward of his
lord's house, saying, Wherefore [n]look
ye *so* sadly today?
8 And they said unto him, [x]We
have dreamed a dream, and *there is* no
interpreter of it. And Joseph said unto
them, [y]*Do* not interpretations *belong*
to God? tell me *them,* I pray you.
9 And the chief butler told his
dream to Joseph, and said to him, In my
dream, behold, a vine *was* before me;
10 And in the vine *were* three
branches: and it *was* as though it bud-
ded, *and* her blossoms shot forth; and
the clusters thereof brought forth ripe
grapes:
11 And Pharaoh's cup *was* in my
hand: and I took the grapes, and
pressed them into Pharaoh's cup, and
I gave the cup into Pharaoh's hand.
12 And Joseph said unto him,
[z]This *is* the interpretation of it: The
three branches [a]*are* three days:
13 Yet within three days shall Phar-
aoh [b]lift[o] up thine head, and restore
thee unto thy place: and thou shalt de-
liver Pharaoh's cup into his hand, after
the former manner when thou wast his
butler.
14 But [c]think[p] on me when it
shall be well with thee, and [d]show
kindness, I pray thee, unto me, and
make mention of me unto Pharaoh, and
bring me out of this house:
15 For indeed I was stolen away out
of the land of the Hebrews: [e]and here
also have I done nothing that they
should put me into the dungeon.
16 When the chief baker saw that
the interpretation was good, he said
unto Joseph, I also *was* in my dream,
and, behold, *I had* three [f]white bas-
kets on my head:
17 And in the uppermost basket

40:8
[x]ch. 41:15
[y]See ch. 41:16
Dan. 2:11,28,47
40:12
[z]ver. 18
ch. 41:12,25
Judg. 7:14
Dan. 2:36
& 4:19
[a]ch. 41:26
40:13
[b]2 Ki. 25:27
Ps. 3:3
Jer. 52:31
40:14
[c]Luke 23:42
[d]Josh. 2:12
1 Sam. 20:14,15
2 Sam. 9:1
1 Ki. 2:7
40:15
[e]ch. 39:20
40:16
[f]Or *full of holes*

40:18
[g]ver. 12
40:19
[h]ver. 13
40:20
[i]Mat. 14:6
[j]Mark 6:21
[k]ver. 13,19
Mat. 25:19
40:21
[l]ver. 13
[m]Neh. 2:1
40:22
[n]ver. 19
40:23
[o]Job 19:14
Eccl. 9:15,16
Amos 6:6

there was of all manner of [q]bakemeats
for Pharaoh; and the birds did eat them
out of the basket upon my head.
18 And Joseph answered and said,
[g]This *is* the interpretation thereof:
The three baskets *are* three days:
19 [h]Yet within three days shall
Pharaoh [r]lift up thy head from off
thee, and shall hang thee on a tree; and
the birds shall eat thy flesh from off
thee.
20 ¶ And it came to pass the third
day, *which was* Pharaoh's [i]birthday,
that he [j]made a feast unto all his ser-
vants: and he [k]lifted[s] up the head of
the chief butler and of the chief baker
among his servants.
21 And he [l]restored the chief but-
ler unto his butlership again; and [m]he
gave the cup into Pharaoh's hand:
22 But he [n]hanged the chief baker:
as Joseph had interpreted to them.
23 Yet did not the chief butler re-
member Joseph, but [o]forgat him.

Pharaoh's dreams

41 AND IT came to pass at the end
of two full years, that Pharaoh
dreamed: and, behold, he stood by the
river.
2 And, behold, there came up out of
the river seven wellfavoured kine and
fatfleshed; and they fed in a meadow.
3 And, behold, seven other kine
came up after them out of the river, ill
favoured and leanfleshed; and stood by
the *other* kine upon the brink of the
river.
4 And the ill favoured and lean-
fleshed kine did eat up the seven well-
favoured and fat kine. So Pharaoh
awoke.
5 And he slept and dreamed the sec-
ond time: and, behold, seven ears of
corn came up upon one stalk, [t]rank
and good.
6 And, behold, seven thin ears and
blasted with the east wind sprung up
after them.
7 And the seven thin ears devoured
the seven rank and full ears. And Phar-

[n] Heb. are *your faces evil?* [o] Or, *reckon* [p] Heb. *remember me with thee* [q] Heb. *meat of Pharaoh, the work of a baker,* or, *cook* [r] Or, *reckon thee,* and take thy office *from thee* [s] Or, *reckoned* [t] Heb. *fat*

41:1 AT THE END OF TWO FULL YEARS . . . PHARAOH DREAMED. Ch. 41 shows God working in the lives of the Pharaoh and Joseph in order to control the destinies of the nations and to provide a place for His chosen people. All nations are subject to God's interventions and direct control.

aoh awoke, and, behold, *it was* a dream.

8 And it came to pass in the morning [p]that his spirit was troubled; and he sent and called for all [q]the magicians of Egypt, and all the [r]wise men thereof: and Pharaoh told them his dream; but *there was* none that could interpret them unto Pharaoh.

9 ¶ Then spake the chief butler unto Pharaoh, saying, I do remember my faults this day:

10 Pharaoh was [s]wroth with his servants, [t]and put me in ward in the captain of the guard's house, *both* me and the chief baker:

11 And [u]we dreamed a dream in one night, I and he; we dreamed each man according to the interpretation of his dream.

12 And *there was* there with us a young man, an Hebrew, [v]servant to the captain of the guard; and we told him, and he [w]interpreted to us our dreams; to each man according to his dream he did interpret.

13 And it came to pass, [x]as he interpreted to us, so it was; me he restored unto mine office, and him he hanged.

14 ¶ [y]Then Pharaoh sent and called Joseph, and they [z]brought[u] him hastily [a]out of the dungeon: and he shaved *himself,* and changed his raiment, and came in unto Pharaoh.

15 And Pharaoh said unto Joseph, I have dreamed a dream, and *there is* none that can interpret it: [b]and I have heard say of thee, *that* [v]thou canst understand a dream to interpret it.

16 And Joseph answered Pharaoh, saying, [c]*It is* not in me: [d]God shall give Pharaoh an answer of peace.

17 And Pharaoh said unto Joseph, [e]In my dream, behold, I stood upon the bank of the river:

18 And, behold, there came up out of the river seven kine, fatfleshed and wellfavoured; and they fed in a meadow:

19 And, behold, seven other kine

41:8 [p]Dan. 2:1 & 4:5,19 [q]Ex. 7:11,22 Is. 29:14 Dan. 1:20 & 2:2 & 4:7 [r]Mat. 2:1
41:10 [s]ch. 40:2,3 [t]ch. 39:20
41:11 [u]ch. 40:5
41:12 [v]ch. 37:36 [w]ch. 40:12
41:13 [x]ch. 40:22
41:14 [y]Ps. 105:20 [z]Dan. 2:25 [a]1 Sam. 2:8 Ps. 113:7,8
41:15 [b]ver. 12 Dan. 5:16
41:16 [c]Dan. 2:30 Acts 3:12 2 Cor. 3:5 [d]ch. 40:8 Dan. 2:22,28,47 & 4:2
41:17 [e]ver. 1
41:24 [f]ver. 8 Dan. 4:7
41:25 [g]Dan. 2:28,29,45 Rev. 4:1
41:27 [h]2 Ki. 8:1
41:28 [i]ver. 25
41:29 [j]ver. 47
41:30 [k]ver. 54 [l]ch. 47:13

came up after them, poor and very ill favoured and leanfleshed, such as I never saw in all the land of Egypt for badness:

20 And the lean and the ill favoured kine did eat up the first seven fat kine:

21 And when they had [w]eaten them up, it could not be known that they had eaten them; but they *were* still ill favoured, as at the beginning. So I awoke.

22 And I saw in my dream, and, behold, seven ears came up in one stalk, full and good:

23 And, behold, seven ears, [x]withered, thin, *and* blasted with the east wind, sprung up after them:

24 And the thin ears devoured the seven good ears: and [f]I told *this* unto the magicians; but *there was* none that could declare *it* to me.

25 ¶ And Joseph said unto Pharaoh, The dream of Pharaoh *is* one: [g]God hath shown Pharaoh what he *is* about to do.

26 The seven good kine *are* seven years; and the seven good ears *are* seven years: the dream *is* one.

27 And the seven thin and ill favoured kine that came up after them *are* seven years; and the seven empty ears blasted with the east wind shall be [h]seven years of famine.

28 [i]This *is* the thing which I have spoken unto Pharaoh: What God *is* about to do he showeth unto Pharaoh.

29 Behold, there come [j]seven years of great plenty throughout all the land of Egypt:

30 And there shall [k]arise after them seven years of famine; and all the plenty shall be forgotten in the land of Egypt; and the famine [l]shall consume the land;

31 And the plenty shall not be known in the land by reason of that

[u] Heb. *made him run* [v] Or, when *thou hearest a dream thou canst interpret it* [w] Heb. *come to the inward parts of them* [x] Or, *small*

41:8 THE MAGICIANS OF EGYPT. Magicians (people who practiced magic) were common in Egypt (cf. Ex. 7:11; 8:7,18–19; 9:11). Magic consisted in practicing divination (i.e., the attempt to discover hidden knowledge by means of spirits), attempting to forecast the future, and trying to control the course of nature, humans, or circumstances by the aid of supernatural powers or spirits. The Mosaic Law strictly condemned all contact with magic (Deut. 18:9–14), as does the N.T. (Acts 19:17–20; Rev. 9:20–21; 22:15).

41:16 GOD SHALL GIVE . . . AN ANSWER. Joseph insisted that his God would give the interpretation of Pharaoh's dream. His outspoken faith in the Lord God could have cost him his life in the presence of an Egyptian king who was considered a god himself.

famine following; for it *shall be* very [y]grievous.

32 And for that the dream was doubled unto Pharaoh twice; *it is* because the [m]thing *is* [z]established by God, and God will shortly bring it to pass.

33 Now therefore let Pharaoh look out a man discreet and wise, and set him over the land of Egypt.

34 Let Pharaoh do *this,* and let him appoint [a]officers over the land, and [n]take up the fifth part of the land of Egypt in the seven plenteous years.

35 And [o]let them gather all the food of those good years that come, and lay up corn under the hand of Pharaoh, and let them keep food in the cities.

36 And that food shall be for store to the land against the seven years of famine, which shall be in the land of Egypt; that the land [p]perish[b] not through the famine.

Pharaoh makes Joseph a ruler

37 ¶ And [q]the thing was good in the eyes of Pharaoh, and in the eyes of all his servants.

38 And Pharaoh said unto his servants, Can we find *such a one* as this *is,* a man [r]in whom the spirit of God *is?*

39 And Pharaoh said unto Joseph, Forasmuch as God hath shown thee all this, *there is* none so discreet and wise as thou *art:*

40 [s]Thou shalt be over my house, and according unto thy word shall all my people [c]be ruled: only in the throne will I be greater than thou.

41 And Pharaoh said unto Joseph, See, I have [t]set thee over all the land of Egypt.

42 And Pharaoh [u]took off his ring from his hand, and put it upon Joseph's hand, and [v]arrayed him in vestures of [d]fine linen, [w]and put a gold chain about his neck;

43 And he made him to ride in the second chariot which he had; [x]and they cried before him, [e] [f]Bow the knee: and he made him *ruler* [y]over all the land of Egypt.

44 And Pharaoh said unto Joseph, I *am* Pharaoh, and without thee shall no man lift up his hand or foot in all the land of Egypt.

45 And Pharaoh called Joseph's name [g]Zaphnath-paaneah; and he gave him to wife Asenath the daughter of Poti-pherah [h]priest of On. And Joseph went out over *all* the land of Egypt.

46 ¶ And Joseph *was* thirty years old when he [z]stood before Pharaoh king of Egypt. And Joseph went out from the presence of Pharaoh, and went throughout all the land of Egypt.

47 And in the seven plenteous years the earth brought forth by handfuls.

48 And he gathered up all the food of the seven years, which were in the land of Egypt, and laid up the food in the cities: the food of the field, which *was* round about every city, laid he up in the same.

49 And Joseph gathered corn [a]as the sand of the sea, very much, until he left numbering; for *it was* without number.

50 [b]And unto Joseph were born two sons before the years of famine came, which Asenath the daughter of Poti-pherah [i]priest of On bare unto him.

51 And Joseph called the name of the firstborn [j]Manasseh: For God, *said he,* hath made me forget all my toil, and all my father's house.

52 And the name of the second called he [k]Ephraim: For God hath caused me to be [c]fruitful in the land of my affliction.

53 ¶ And the seven years of plenteousness, that was in the land of Egypt, were ended.

54 [d]And the seven years of dearth began to come, [e]according as Joseph had said: and the dearth was in all lands; but in all the land of Egypt there was bread.

55 And when all the land of Egypt

41:32 [m]Num. 23:19 Is. 46:10,11 **41:34** [n]Prov. 6:6-8 **41:35** [o]ver. 48 **41:36** [p]ch. 47:15,19 **41:37** [q]Ps. 105:19 Acts 7:10 **41:38** [r]Num. 27:18 Job 32:8 Prov. 2:6 Dan. 4:8,18 & 5:11,14 & 6:3 **41:40** [s]Ps. 105:21 Acts 7:10 **41:41** [t]Dan. 6:3 **41:42** [u]Esth. 3:10 [v]Esth. 8:15 [w]Dan. 5:7,29 **41:43** [x]Esth. 6:9 [y]ch. 42:6 Acts 7:10 **41:46** [z]1 Sam. 16:21 1 Ki. 12:6,8 Dan. 1:19 **41:49** [a]ch. 22:17 Judg. 7:12 1 Sam. 13:5 **41:50** [b]ch. 46:20 & 48:5 **41:52** [c]ch. 49:22 **41:54** [d]Ps. 105:16 Acts 7:11 [e]ver. 30

[y] Heb. *heavy* [z] Or, *prepared of God* [a] Or, *overseers* [b] Heb. *be not cut off* [c] Heb. *be armed,* or, *kiss* [d] Or, *silk* [e] Or, *Tender father* [f] Heb. *Abrech* [g] Which in the Coptic signifies, *A revealer of secrets,* or, *The man to whom secrets* are *revealed* [h] Or, *prince;* see Ex. 2:16; 2 Sam. 8:18 & 20:26 [i] Or, *prince* [j] i.e. *Forgetting* [k] i.e. *Fruitful*

41:46 JOSEPH *WAS* THIRTY YEARS OLD WHEN HE STOOD BEFORE PHARAOH. Joseph was seventeen years old when he was sold into slavery by his brothers (37:2). He then spent thirteen years as a slave and at least three of those were spent in prison. When God exalted him to a position of honor and rulership at age thirty, Joseph continued to be faithful to his God. This commitment to God is signified in the Hebrew names of his two sons (vv. 50–52).

was famished, the people cried to Pharaoh for bread: and Pharaoh said unto all the Egyptians, Go unto Joseph; what he saith to you, do.

56 And the famine was over all the face of the earth: and Joseph opened [l]all the storehouses, and [f]sold unto the Egyptians; and the famine waxed sore in the land of Egypt.

57 [g]And all countries came into Egypt to Joseph for to buy *corn;* because that the famine was *so* sore in all lands.

Joseph's brethren visit Egypt

42 NOW WHEN [h]Jacob saw that there was corn in Egypt, Jacob said unto his sons, Why do ye look one upon another?

2 And he said, Behold, I have heard that there is corn in Egypt: get you down thither, and buy for us from thence; that we may [i]live, and not die.

3 ¶ And Joseph's ten brethren went down to buy corn in Egypt.

4 But Benjamin, Joseph's brother, Jacob sent not with his brethren; for he said, [j]Lest peradventure mischief befall him.

5 And the sons of Israel came to buy *corn* among those that came: for the famine was [k]in the land of Canaan.

6 And Joseph *was* the governor [l]over the land, *and* he *it was* that sold to all the people of the land: and Joseph's brethren came, and [m]bowed down themselves before him *with* their faces to the earth.

7 And Joseph saw his brethren, and he knew them, but made himself strange unto them, and spake [m]roughly unto them; and he said unto them, Whence come ye? And they said, From the land of Canaan to buy food.

8 And Joseph knew his brethren, but they knew not him.

9 And Joseph [n]remembered the dreams which he dreamed of them, and said unto them, Ye *are* spies; to see the nakedness of the land ye are come.

10 And they said unto him, Nay, my lord, but to buy food are thy servants come.

11 We *are* all one man's sons; we *are* true *men,* thy servants are no spies.

12 And he said unto them, Nay, but to see the nakedness of the land ye are come.

13 And they said, Thy servants *are* twelve brethren, the sons of one man in the land of Canaan; and, behold, the youngest *is* this day with our father, and one [o]*is* not.

14 And Joseph said unto them, That *is it* that I spake unto you, saying, Ye *are* spies:

15 Hereby ye shall be proved: [p]By the life of Pharaoh ye shall not go forth hence, except your youngest brother come hither.

16 Send one of you, and let him fetch your brother, and ye shall be [n]kept in prison, that your words may be proved, whether *there be any* truth in you: or else by the life of Pharaoh surely ye *are* spies.

17 And he [o]put them all together into ward three days.

18 And Joseph said unto them the third day, This do, and live; [q]*for* I fear God:

19 If ye *be* true *men,* let one of your brethren be bound in the house of your prison: go ye, carry corn for the famine of your houses:

20 But [r]bring your youngest brother unto me; so shall your words be verified, and ye shall not die. And they did so.

21 ¶ And they said one to another, [s]We *are* verily guilty concerning our

41:56 [f]ch. 42:6
41:57 [g]Deut. 9:28
42:1 [h]Acts 7:12
42:2 [i]ch. 43:8; Is. 38:1
42:4 [j]ver. 38
42:5 [k]Acts 7:11
42:6 [l]ch. 41:41; [m]ch. 37:7
42:9 [n]ch. 37:5,9
42:13 [o]ch. 37:30; Lam. 5:7; See ch. 44:20
42:15 [p]See 1 Sam. 1:26 & 17:55
42:18 [q]Lev. 25:43; Neh. 5:15
42:20 [r]ver. 34; ch. 43:5 & 44:23
42:21 [s]Job 36:8,9; Hos. 5:15

[l] Heb. *all wherein* was *with them* [m] Heb. *hard things* [n] Heb. *bound* [o] Heb. *gathered*

42:4 BENJAMIN. Benjamin was one of Rachel's two sons and thus a full brother of Joseph. Having already lost one son of Rachel, Jacob carefully protected Benjamin by keeping him at home.

42:8 JOSEPH KNEW HIS BRETHREN. Joseph concealed his identity until he determined whether his brothers would show sorrow for what they had done to him and his father years ago (ch. 37).

42:9 YE *ARE* SPIES. While Joseph recognized his brothers and knew they were not spies, he tested them in order to determine if they had changed in character and had come to a point of remorse over the evil they had done to him and his father, Jacob.

42:21 WE *ARE* VERILY GUILTY. The brothers were brought to a realization of their guilt for their unmerciful treatment of Joseph twenty years earlier (37:2; 41:46,53–54). They believed God was justly punishing them for their crime (vv. 21–22). Often with concealed sin in our lives, God will work in order to open our consciences to our guilt. We can either harden our hearts or humble ourselves before God, confess our sin, and resolve to act righteously.

brother, in that we saw the anguish of his soul, when he besought us, and we would not hear; [t]therefore is this distress come upon us.

22 And Reuben answered them, saying, [u]Spake I not unto you, saying, Do not sin against the child; and ye would not hear? therefore, behold, also his blood is [v]required.

23 And they knew not that Joseph understood *them;* for [p]he spake unto them by an interpreter.

24 And he turned himself about from them, and wept; and returned to them again, and communed with them, and took from them Simeon, and bound him before their eyes.

25 ¶ Then Joseph commanded to fill their sacks with corn, and to restore every man's money into his sack, and to give them provision for the way: and [w]thus did he unto them.

26 And they laded their asses with the corn, and departed thence.

27 And as [x]one of them opened his sack to give his ass provender in the inn, he espied his money; for, behold, it *was* in his sack's mouth.

28 And he said unto his brethren, My money is restored; and, lo, *it is* even in my sack: and their heart [q]failed *them,* and they were afraid, saying one to another, What *is* this *that* God hath done unto us?

29 ¶ And they came unto Jacob their father unto the land of Canaan, and told him all that befell unto them; saying,

30 The man, *who is* the lord of the land, [y]spake [r]roughly to us, and took us for spies of the country.

31 And we said unto him, We *are* true *men;* we are no spies:

32 We *be* twelve brethren, sons of our father; one *is* not, and the youngest *is* this day with our father in the land of Canaan.

33 And the man, the lord of the country, said unto us, [z]Hereby shall I know that ye *are* true *men;* leave one of your brethren *here* with me, and take *food for* the famine of your households, and be gone:

34 And bring your youngest brother unto me: then shall I know that ye *are* no spies, but *that* ye *are* true *men: so* will I deliver you your brother, and ye shall [a]traffic in the land.

35 ¶ And it came to pass as they emptied their sacks, that, behold, [b]every man's bundle of money *was* in his sack: and when *both* they and their father saw the bundles of money, they were afraid.

36 And Jacob their father said unto them, Me have ye [c]bereaved *of my children:* Joseph *is* not, and Simeon *is* not, and ye will take Benjamin *away:* all these things are against me.

37 And Reuben spake unto his father, saying, Slay my two sons, if I bring him not to thee: deliver him into my hand, and I will bring him to thee again.

38 And he said, My son shall not go down with you; for [d]his brother is dead, and he is left alone: [e]if mischief befall him by the way in the which ye go, then shall ye [f]bring down my gray hairs with sorrow to the grave.

The second trip to Egypt

43 AND THE famine *was* [g]sore in the land.

2 And it came to pass, when they had eaten up the corn which they had brought out of Egypt, their father said unto them, Go again, buy us a little food.

3 And Judah spake unto him, saying, The man [s]did solemnly protest unto us, saying, Ye shall not see my face, except your [h]brother *be* with you.

4 If thou wilt send our brother with us, we will go down and buy thee food:

5 But if thou wilt not send *him,* we will not go down: for the man said unto us, Ye shall not see my face, except your brother *be* with you.

6 And Israel said, Wherefore dealt ye *so* ill with me, *as* to tell the man whether ye had yet a brother?

7 And they said, The man [t]asked us straitly of our state, and of our kindred, saying, *Is* your father yet alive? have ye *another* brother? and we told him according to the [u]tenor of these

42:21 [t]Prov. 21:13 Mat. 7:2
42:22 [u]ch. 37:21 [v]ch. 9:5 1 Ki. 2:32 2 Chr. 24:22 Ps. 9:12 Luke 11:50,51
42:25 [w]Mat. 5:44 Rom. 12:17,20,21
42:27 [x]See ch. 43:21
42:30 [y]ver. 7
42:33 [z]ver. 15,19,20
42:34 [a]ch. 34:10
42:35 [b]See ch. 43:21
42:36 [c]ch. 43:14
42:38 [d]ver. 13 ch. 37:33 & 44:28 [e]ver. 4 ch. 44:29 [f]ch. 37:35 & 44:31
43:1 [g]ch. 41:54,57
43:3 [h]ch. 42:20 & 44:23

[p] Heb. *an interpreter* was *between them* [q] Heb. *went forth* [r] Heb. *with us hard things* [s] Heb. *protesting protested* [t] Heb. *asking asked us* [u] Heb. *mouth*

42:37 SLAY MY TWO SONS. Vv. 29–38 show that Joseph's brothers had changed for the better. Reuben, for example, was willing to give up his own sons rather than bring any more sorrow upon his father.

words: [v]could we certainly know that he would say, Bring your brother down?

8 And Judah said unto Israel his father, Send the lad with me, and we will arise and go; that we may live, and not die, both we, and thou, *and* also our little ones.

9 I will be surety for him; of my hand shalt thou require him: [i]if I bring him not unto thee, and set him before thee, then let me bear the blame for ever:

10 For except we had lingered, surely now we had returned [w]this second time.

11 And their father Israel said unto them, If *it must be* so now, do this; take of the best fruits in the land in your vessels, and [j]carry down the man a present, a little [k]balm, and a little honey, spices, and myrrh, nuts, and almonds:

12 And take double money in your hand; and the money [l]that was brought again in the mouth of your sacks, carry *it* again in your hand; peradventure it *was* an oversight:

13 Take also your brother, and arise, go again unto the man:

14 And God Almighty give you mercy before the man, that he may send away your other brother, and Benjamin. [m]If[x] I be bereaved *of my children,* I am bereaved.

15 ¶ And the men took that present, and they took double money in their hand, and Benjamin; and rose up, and went down to Egypt, and stood before Joseph.

16 And when Joseph saw Benjamin with them, he said to the [n]ruler of his house, Bring *these* men home, and [y]slay, and make ready; for *these* men shall [z]dine with me at noon.

17 And the man did as Joseph bade; and the man brought the men into Joseph's house.

18 And the men were afraid, because they were brought into Joseph's house; and they said, Because of the money that was returned in our sacks at the first time are we brought in; that he may [a]seek occasion against us, and fall upon us, and take us for bondmen, and our asses.

19 And they came near to the steward of Joseph's house, and they communed with him at the door of the house,

20 And said, O sir, [o]we[b] came indeed down at the first time to buy food:

21 And [p]it came to pass, when we came to the inn, that we opened our sacks, and, behold, *every* man's money *was* in the mouth of his sack, our money in full weight: and we have brought it again in our hand.

22 And other money have we brought down in our hands to buy food: we cannot tell who put our money in our sacks.

23 And he said, Peace *be* to you, fear not: your God, and the God of your father, hath given you treasure in your sacks: [c]I had your money. And he brought Simeon out unto them.

24 And the man brought the men into Joseph's house, and [q]gave *them* water, and they washed their feet; and he gave their asses provender.

25 And they made ready the present against Joseph came at noon: for they heard that they should eat bread there.

26 ¶ And when Joseph came home, they brought him the present which *was* in their hand into the house, and [r]bowed themselves to him to the earth.

27 And he asked them of *their* [s]welfare,[d] and said, [e]*Is* your father well, the old man [t]of whom ye spake? *Is* he yet alive?

28 And they answered, Thy servant our father *is* in good health, he *is* yet alive. [u]And they bowed down their heads, and made obeisance.

29 And he lifted up his eyes, and

43:9 [i]ch. 44:32 Philem. 18,19
43:11 [j]ch. 32:20 Prov. 18:16 [k]ch. 37:25 Jer. 8:22
43:12 [l]ch. 42:25,35
43:14 [m]Esth. 4:16
43:16 [n]ch. 24:2 & 39:4 & 44:1
43:20 [o]ch. 42:3,10
43:21 [p]ch. 42:27,35
43:24 [q]ch. 18:4 & 24:32
43:26 [r]ch. 37:7,10
43:27 [s]ch. 37:14 [t]ch. 42:11,13
43:28 [u]ch. 37:7,10

[v] Heb. *knowing could we know* [w] Or, *twice by this* [x] Or, *And I, as I have been* [y] Heb. *kill a killing* [z] Heb. *eat* [a] Heb. *roll himself upon us* [b] Heb. *coming down we came down* [c] Heb. *your money came to me* [d] Heb. *peace,* [e] Heb. Is there *peace to your father?*

43:9 LET ME BEAR THE BLAME. Like Reuben (42:37), Judah willingly accepted responsibility for his brother Benjamin. He offered to accept lasting disgrace and blame should Benjamin not come back safely.

43:14 IF I BE BEREAVED. When Israel saw that he could do nothing to change his terrible circumstances, the only thing he could do was place his sons into the hands of God, pray for mercy, and prepare himself for the worst. He was willing to accept God's will even if it meant bereavement and suffering. As things turned out, however, he ended his life rejoicing in God and trusting the One who had guided him all his life.

saw his brother Benjamin, [v]his mother's son, and said, *Is* this your younger brother, [w]of whom ye spake unto me? And he said, God be gracious unto thee, my son.

30 And Joseph made haste; for [x]his bowels did yearn upon his brother: and he sought *where* to weep; and he entered into *his* chamber, and [y]wept there.

31 And he washed his face, and went out, and refrained himself, and said, Set on [z]bread.

32 And they set on for him by himself, and for them by themselves, and for the Egyptians, which did eat with him, by themselves: because the Egyptians might not eat bread with the Hebrews; for that *is* [a]an abomination unto the Egyptians.

33 And they sat before him, the firstborn according to his birthright, and the youngest according to his youth: and the men marvelled one at another.

34 And he took *and sent* messes unto them from before him: but Benjamin's mess was [b]five times so much as any of theirs. And they drank, and [f]were merry with him.

The missing silver cup

44 AND HE commanded [g]the steward of his house, saying, Fill the men's sacks *with* food, as much as they can carry, and put every man's money in his sack's mouth.

2 And put my cup, the silver cup, in the sack's mouth of the youngest, and his corn money. And he did according to the word that Joseph had spoken.

3 As soon as the morning was light, the men were sent away, they and their asses.

4 *And* when they were gone out of the city, *and* not *yet* far off, Joseph said unto his steward, Up, follow after the men; and when thou dost overtake them, say unto them, Wherefore have ye rewarded evil for good?

43:29 [v]ch. 35:17,18 [w]ch. 42:13 **43:30** [x]1 Ki. 3:26 [y]ch. 42:24 **43:31** [z]ver. 25 **43:32** [a]ch. 46:34 Ex. 8:26 **43:34** [b]ch. 45:22

44:8 [c]ch. 43:21 **44:9** [d]ch. 31:32 **44:13** [e]ch. 37:29,34 Num. 14:6 2 Sam. 1:11 **44:14** [f]ch. 37:7 **44:16** [g]ver. 9

5 *Is* not this *it* in which my lord drinketh, and whereby indeed he [h]divineth? ye have done evil in so doing.

6 ¶ And he overtook them, and he spake unto them these same words.

7 And they said unto him, Wherefore saith my lord these words? God forbid that thy servants should do according to this thing:

8 Behold, [c]the money, which we found in our sacks' mouths, we brought again unto thee out of the land of Canaan: how then should we steal out of thy lord's house silver or gold?

9 With whomsoever of thy servants it be found, [d]both let him die, and we also will be my lord's bondmen.

10 And he said, Now also *let* it *be* according unto your words: he with whom it is found shall be my servant; and ye shall be blameless.

11 Then they speedily took down every man his sack to the ground, and opened every man his sack.

12 And he searched, *and* began at the eldest, and left at the youngest: and the cup was found in Benjamin's sack.

13 Then they [e]rent their clothes, and laded every man his ass, and returned to the city.

14 ¶ And Judah and his brethren came to Joseph's house; for he *was* yet there: and they [f]fell before him on the ground.

15 And Joseph said unto them, What deed *is* this that ye have done? wot ye not that such a man as I can certainly [i]divine?

16 And Judah said, What shall we say unto my lord? what shall we speak? or how shall we clear ourselves? God hath found out the iniquity of thy servants: behold, [g]we *are* my lord's servants, both we, and *he* also with whom the cup is found.

[f]Heb. *drank largely* [g]Heb. him *that* was *over his house* [h]Or, *maketh trial?* [i]Or, *make trial?;* see ver. 5

44:5 WHEREBY INDEED HE DIVINETH. Surely Joseph did not practice divination, which was forbidden by God. There are two possible explanations for its being mentioned here. (1) The Hebrew term rendered "he divineth" can also be rendered "be sure to notice." Thus the reading would mean that Joseph would be sure to notice that the cup was gone. (2) It could also be that Joseph was merely adapting to the image that the brothers would have had of him as an Egyptian leader (cf. v. 15).

44:13 RENT THEIR CLOTHES. This was a clear sign of great grief and distress. The brothers could have gone on without Benjamin, but their determination to return and face the consequences with him revealed that their character had indeed changed and that they were truly concerned about their brother and father (cf. vv. 18–34).

44:15 I CAN CERTAINLY DIVINE. See v. 5, note.

17 And he said, [h]God forbid that I should do so: *but* the man in whose hand the cup is found, he shall be my servant; and as for you, get you up in peace unto your father.

18 ¶ Then Judah came near unto him, and said, Oh my lord, let thy servant, I pray thee, speak a word in my lord's ears, and [i]let not thine anger burn against thy servant: for thou *art* even as Pharaoh.

19 My lord asked his servants, saying, Have ye a father, or a brother?

20 And we said unto my lord, We have a father, an old man, and [j]a child of his old age, a little one; and his brother is dead, and he alone is left of his mother, and his father loveth him.

21 And thou saidst unto thy servants, [k]Bring him down unto me, that I may set mine eyes upon him.

22 And we said unto my lord, The lad cannot leave his father: for *if* he should leave his father, *his father* would die.

23 And thou saidst unto thy servants, [l]Except your youngest brother come down with you, ye shall see my face no more.

24 And it came to pass when we came up unto thy servant my father, we told him the words of my lord.

25 And [m]our father said, Go again, *and* buy us a little food.

26 And we said, We cannot go down: if our youngest brother be with us, then will we go down: for we may not see the man's face, except our youngest brother *be* with us.

27 And thy servant my father said unto us, Ye know that [n]my wife bare me two *sons:*

28 And the one went out from me, and I said, [o]Surely he is torn in pieces; and I saw him not since:

29 And if ye [p]take this also from me, and mischief befall him, ye shall bring down my gray hairs with sorrow to the grave.

30 Now therefore when I come to thy servant my father, and the lad *be* not with us; seeing that [q]his life is bound up in the lad's life;

31 It shall come to pass, when he seeth that the lad *is* not *with us,* that he will die: and thy servants shall bring down the gray hairs of thy servant our father with sorrow to the grave.

32 For thy servant became surety for the lad unto my father, saying, [r]If I bring him not unto thee, then I shall bear the blame to my father for ever.

33 Now therefore, I pray thee, [s]let thy servant abide instead of the lad a bondman to my lord; and let the lad go up with his brethren.

34 For how shall I go up to my father, and the lad *be* not with me? lest peradventure I see the evil that shall [j]come on my father.

Joseph reveals his identity

45 THEN JOSEPH could not refrain himself before all them that stood by him; and he cried, Cause every man to go out from me. And there stood no man with him, while Joseph made himself known unto his brethren.

2 And he wept aloud: and the Egyptians and the house of Pharaoh heard.

3 And Joseph said unto his brethren, [t]I *am* Joseph; doth my father yet live? And his brethren could not answer him; for they were [u]troubled[k] at his presence.

4 And Joseph said unto his brethren, Come near to me, I pray you. And they came near. And he said, I *am* Joseph your brother, [v]whom ye sold into Egypt.

5 Now therefore be not grieved, [l]nor angry with yourselves, that ye sold me hither: [w]for God did send me before you to preserve life.

6 For these two years *hath* the famine *been* in the land: and yet *there are* five years, in the which *there shall* neither *be* earing nor harvest.

7 And God sent me before you [m]to

44:17 [h]Prov. 17:15
44:18 [i]ch. 18:30,32 Ex. 32:22
44:20 [j]ch. 37:3
44:21 [k]ch. 42:15,20
44:23 [l]ch. 43:3,5
44:25 [m]ch. 43:2
44:27 [n]ch. 46:19
44:28 [o]ch. 37:33
44:29 [p]ch. 42:36,38
44:30 [q]1 Sam. 18:1
44:32 [r]ch. 43:9
44:33 [s]Ex. 32:32
45:3 [t]Acts 7:13 [u]Job 4:5 & 23:15 Mat. 14:26 Mark 6:50
45:4 [v]ch. 37:28
45:5 [w]ch. 50:20 Ps. 105:16,17

[j] Heb. *find my father* [k] Or, *terrified* [l] Heb. *neither let there be anger in your eyes* [m] Heb. *to put for you a remnant*

44:18–34 JUDAH CAME NEAR UNTO HIM. That Joseph's brothers had experienced a great change of attitude since they sold Joseph into Egypt is seen not only in all the brothers' willingness to suffer as slaves for the sake of Benjamin (vv. 13–16), but especially in Judah's plea for Benjamin (vv. 18–34). They were now ready to bear the blame for their past evil and to pay any price to save Benjamin and prevent overwhelming grief to their father (vv. 16,32–33).

45:5 GOD DID SEND ME. Joseph reveals that many times God overrules the evil actions of humans in order to bring forth His will (cf. 50:20; see article on THE PROVIDENCE OF GOD, p. 80).

preserve you a posterity in the earth,
and to save your lives by a great deliv-
erance.
8 So now *it was* not you *that* sent me
hither, but God: and he hath made me
[x]a father to Pharaoh, and lord of all
his house, and a ruler throughout all
the land of Egypt.
9 Haste ye, and go up to my father,
and say unto him, Thus saith thy son
Joseph, God hath made me lord of all
Egypt: come down unto me, tarry not:
10 And [y]thou shalt dwell in the
land of Goshen, and thou shalt be near
unto me, thou, and thy children, and
thy children's children, and thy flocks,
and thy herds, and all that thou hast:
11 And there will I nourish thee; for
yet *there are* five years of famine; lest
thou, and thy household, and all that
thou hast, come to poverty.
12 And, behold, your eyes see, and
the eyes of my brother Benjamin, that
it is [z]my mouth that speaketh unto
you.
13 And ye shall tell my father of all
my glory in Egypt, and of all that ye
have seen; and ye shall haste and
[a]bring down my father hither.
14 And he fell upon his brother Ben-
jamin's neck, and wept; and Benjamin
wept upon his neck.
15 Moreover he kissed all his breth-
ren, and wept upon them: and after
that his brethren talked with him.
16 ¶ And the fame thereof was
heard in Pharaoh's house, saying, Jo-
seph's brethren are come: and it
[n]pleased Pharaoh well, and his ser-
vants.
17 And Pharaoh said unto Joseph,
Say unto thy brethren, This do ye; lade
your beasts, and go, get you unto the
land of Canaan;
18 And take your father and your
households, and come unto me: and I
will give you the good of the land of
Egypt, and ye shall eat [b]the fat of the
land.

45:8 [x]ch. 41:43 Judg. 17:10
45:10 [y]ch. 47:1
45:12 [z]ch. 42:23
45:13 [a]Acts 7:14
45:18 [b]ch. 27:28 Num. 18:12,29
45:22 [c]ch. 43:34
45:26 [d]Job 29:24 Ps. 126:1 Luke 24:11,41

19 Now thou art commanded, this
do ye; take you wagons out of the land
of Egypt for your little ones, and for
your wives, and bring your father, and
come.
20 Also [o]regard not your stuff; for
the good of all the land of Egypt *is*
yours.
21 And the children of Israel did so:
and Joseph gave them wagons, accord-
ing to the [p]commandment of Pharaoh,
and gave them provision for the way.
22 To all of them he gave each man
changes of raiment; but to Benjamin he
gave three hundred *pieces* of silver, and
[c]five changes of raiment.
23 And to his father he sent after
this *manner;* ten asses [q]laden with the
good things of Egypt, and ten she
asses laden with corn and bread and
meat for his father by the way.
24 So he sent his brethren away,
and they departed: and he said unto
them, See that ye fall not out by the
way.
25 ¶ And they went up out of Egypt,
and came into the land of Canaan unto
Jacob their father,
26 And told him, saying, Joseph *is*
yet alive, and he *is* governor over all
the land of Egypt. [d]And [r]Jacob's
heart fainted, for he believed them not.
27 And they told him all the words
of Joseph, which he had said unto
them: and when he saw the wagons
which Joseph had sent to carry him, the
spirit of Jacob their father revived:
28 And Israel said, *It is* enough; Jo-
seph my son *is* yet alive: I will go and
see him before I die.

Jacob goes to Egypt

46 AND ISRAEL took his journey
with all that he had, and came

[n] Heb. *was good in the eyes of Pharaoh*
[o] Heb. *let not your eye spare* [p] Heb. *mouth*
[q] Heb. *carrying* [r] Heb. *his*

45:7 TO PRESERVE YOU A POSTERITY. God worked through Joseph to preserve the covenant people through whom would come the Christ. It should be noted that even though the Christ would come through Judah's descendant and not Joseph's, God used Joseph to keep the line of Christ alive. Joseph, therefore, was a spiritual ancestor of Christ, something far more important than being a physical ancestor (see Rom. 4:12–16).

45:10 THE LAND OF GOSHEN. Located about forty miles from the present day Cairo, Goshen was situated in the delta of the Nile and was separated from the main centers of Egyptian life. There the Israelites would live in isolation from the Egyptians and develop into a nation.

46:1 AND ISRAEL TOOK HIS JOURNEY. Israel (i.e., Jacob) and his family migrated to Egypt. (1) The resettlement of God's people was the direct consequence of the severe famine that God had brought upon the world (47:13). God literally forced Israel to move to Egypt by His sovereign control (cf. 15:13–14). In that land God's chosen

THE PROVIDENCE OF GOD

Gen. 45:5 "Now therefore be not grieved, nor angry with yourselves, that ye sold me hither: for God did send me before you to preserve life."

After the Lord God created the heavens and the earth (Gen. 1:1), He did not abandon the world to run on its own. Rather, he continues to be involved in the lives of His people and in the care of His creation. God is not like a master clockmaker who fashioned the world, wound it up, and is now letting it slowly unwind on its own; instead, He is the loving Father who cares for what He has made. God's continual care for His creation and His people is called, in doctrinal terms, His providence.

ASPECTS OF PROVIDENCE. There are at least three aspects to God's providence. (1) *Preservation*. By His power God preserves the world that He has created. Nehemiah testifies after exalting God as the Creator of the heavens, the earth, and all things in them, "thou preservest them all" (Neh. 9:6). The confession of David is equally clear: "Thy righteousness *is* like the great mountains; thy judgments *are* a great deep: O LORD, thou preservest man and beast" (Ps. 36:6). This preserving power of God is accomplished through His Son Jesus Christ, as Paul testifies in Col. 1:17: Christ "is before all things, and by him all things consist." The word "consist" (Gk. *sunistēmi) means "to put together, to hold together"; by the power of Christ even the very smallest particles of life are held together.*

(2) *Provision*. Not only does God preserve the world that He created, but He also provides for the needs of His creatures. When God created the world, He created the seasons (Gen. 1:14) and gave food for humans and animals (Gen. 1:29–30). After the flood had destroyed the earth, God renewed this promise of provision with these words: "While the earth remaineth, seedtime and harvest, and cold and heat, and summer and winter, and day and night shall not cease" (Gen. 8:22). Several of the psalms testify to God's goodness in providing for all of His creatures (e.g., Ps. 104; 145). God Himself revealed His creative and caring power to Job (Job 38—41), and Jesus asserted in no uncertain terms that God provides for the birds of the air and the lilies of the field (Mat. 6:26–30; 10:29). His care not only involves the physical needs of humankind, but also the spiritual needs (cf. John 3:16–17). The Bible reveals that God manifests a special love and care for His own people, each of whom He values (e.g., Ps. 91; see Mat. 10:31, note). Paul writes unequivocally to believers in Philippi, "But my God shall supply all your need according to his riches in glory by Christ Jesus" (Phil. 4:19, see note). According to the apostle John, God desires his people "prosper, and be in health" (3 John 2, see note).

(3) *Government*. In addition to God's preservation of and provision for His creation, He also rules the world. Since God is sovereign, the events of history happen under His permissive will and oversight; at times He directly intervenes according to His redemptive purpose (see article on THE WILL OF GOD, p. 1060). Nevertheless, until God consummates history, He has limited His supreme power and rule in this world. Scripture states that Satan is "the god of this world" (2 Cor. 4:4) and exercises considerable control in this present evil age (see 1 John 5:19, note; cf. Luke 13:16; Gal. 1:4; Eph. 6:12; Heb. 2:14). In other words, the world is not now submissive to God's ruling power, but is in rebellion against Him and is enslaved to Satan. Note, however, that this self-limitation on the part of God is only temporary; at the time He has determined by His wisdom, He will destroy Satan and all the hosts of evil (Rev. 19—20).

GOD'S PROVIDENCE AND HUMAN SUFFERING. Biblical revelation shows God's providence to be not an abstract doctrine, but one that concerns everyday living in an evil and fallen world. (1) Everyone experiences suffering at times in his or her life and inevitably asks the question, "Why?" (cf. Job 7:17–21; Ps. 10:1; 22:1; 74:11–12; Jer. 14:8–9,19); such experiences raise the problem of evil and its place in God's plan.

(2) God allows humans to experience the consequences of the sin that entered into the world through the fall of Adam and Eve. Joseph, for example, suffered much because of the jealousy and cruelty of his brothers. He was sold by his brothers into slavery and became a slave of Potiphar in Egypt (Gen. 37; 39). While living a God-fearing life in Egypt, he was unjustly charged with immorality, thrown into prison (Gen. 39), and kept there for well over two years (cf. Gen. 40:1—41:14). Note, however, that God can supersede such deeds so as to work out His will. According to Joseph's testimony, God was working through the sins of his brothers in order to preserve life (Gen. 45:5; 50:20).

(3) Not only do we suffer from the consequences of others' sin, but we also experience the consequences of our own sinful actions. For example, the sin of immorality and adultery often results in the breakdown of one's marriage and family. The sin of unchecked anger against another person can lead to serious injury or even the death of one or both of those involved. The sin of greed may result in a prison sentence for someone who has stolen or embezzled.

(4) Suffering also occurs in the world because Satan, the god of this world, is permitted to do his work by blinding the minds of unbelievers and controlling their lives (2 Cor. 4:4; Eph. 2:1–3). The N.T. is filled with examples of people who experienced suffering because of demons, who tormented them either with mental affliction (e.g., Mark 5:1–14) or with physical ailments (Mat. 9:32–33; 12:22; Mark 9:14–22; Luke 13:11,16; see article on POWER OVER SATAN AND DEMONS, p. 1486).

To say that God allows suffering does not mean that God causes the evil that happens to us in this world, nor that He personally decrees all the tragedies of life. God is never the instigator of evil or ungodliness (Jas. 1:13). Nevertheless, He does at times permit it, direct it, and overrule it in order to bring forth His will, to accomplish His redemptive purpose, and to work things out for the good of those faithful to Him (see Mat. 2:13, note; Rom. 8:28, note; see article on THE SUFFERING OF THE RIGHTEOUS, p. 764).

OUR RELATIONSHIP TO GOD'S PROVIDENCE. In order for us to experience God's providential care in our lives, the Bible reveals that we have certain responsibilities. (1) We must obey God and His revealed will. With Joseph, for example, it is clear that because Joseph honored God by his life of obedience, God honored him by being with him (see Gen. 39:2–3,21,23). Likewise, in order for Jesus Himself to experience God's protective care in the face of the murderous intent of King Herod, Jesus' parents had to obey God and flee to Egypt (see Mat. 2:13, note). Those who fear God and acknowledge Him in all their ways have the promise that God will direct all their steps (Prov. 3:5–7).

(2) In His providence, God directs the affairs of the church and of every one of us as His servants. We must constantly be in tune with God's will for our lives as we serve Him and minister to other people in His name (cf. Acts 18:9–10; 23:11; 26:15–18; 27:22–24).

(3) We must love God and submit to Him by faith in Christ if we want all things to work for our good (see Rom. 8:28, note).

(4) In order to experience God's care in the midst of affliction, we must call out to Him in persistent prayer and faith. Through prayer and trust we experience God's peace (Phil. 4:6–7), we receive strength from the Lord (Eph. 3:16; Phil. 4:13), and we receive God's mercy, grace, and help in time of need (Heb. 4:16; see Phil. 4:6, note). Such prayers of faith may be either on our own behalf or on behalf of others (see Rom. 15:30–32; Col. 4:3, note; see article on INTERCESSION, p. 1268).

to [e]Beer-sheba, and offered sacrifices [f]unto the God of his father Isaac.

2 And God spake unto Israel [g]in the visions of the night, and said, Jacob, Jacob. And he said, Here *am* I.

3 And he said, I *am* God, [h]the God of thy father: fear not to go down into Egypt; for I will there [i]make of thee a great nation:

4 [j]I will go down with thee into Egypt; and I will also surely [k]bring thee up *again:* and [l]Joseph shall put his hand upon thine eyes.

5 And [m]Jacob rose up from Beer-sheba: and the sons of Israel carried Jacob their father, and their little ones, and their wives, in the wagons [n]which Pharaoh had sent to carry him.

6 And they took their cattle, and their goods, which they had gotten in the land of Canaan, and came into Egypt, [o]Jacob, and all his seed with him:

7 His sons, and his sons' sons with him, his daughters, and his sons' daughters, and all his seed brought he with him into Egypt.

8 ¶ And [p]these *are* the names of the children of Israel, which came into Egypt, Jacob and his sons: [q]Reuben, Jacob's firstborn.

9 And the sons of Reuben; Hanoch, and Phallu, and Hezron, and Carmi.

10 ¶ And [r]the sons of Simeon; [s]Jemuel, and Jamin, and Ohad, and [t]Jachin, and [u]Zohar, and Shaul the son of a Canaanitish woman.

11 ¶ And the sons of [s]Levi; [v]Gershon, Kohath, and Merari.

12 ¶ And the sons of [t]Judah; Er, and Onan, and Shelah, and Pharez, and Zerah: but [u]Er and Onan died in the land of Canaan. And [v]the sons of Pharez were Hezron and Hamul.

13 ¶ [w]And the sons of Issachar; Tola, and [w]Phuvah, and Job, and Shimron.

14 ¶ And the sons of Zebulun; Sered, and Elon, and Jahleel.

15 These *be* the sons of Leah, which she bare unto Jacob in Padan-aram, with his daughter Dinah: all the souls of his sons and his daughters *were* thirty and three.

16 ¶ And the sons of Gad; [x]Ziphion, and Haggi, Shuni, and [x]Ezbon, Eri, and [y]Arodi, and Areli.

17 ¶ [y]And the sons of Asher; Jimnah, and Ishuah, and Isui, and Beriah, and Serah their sister: and the sons of Beriah; Heber, and Malchiel.

18 [z]These *are* the sons of Zilpah, [a]whom Laban gave to Leah his daughter, and these she bare unto Jacob, *even* sixteen souls.

19 The sons of Rachel [b]Jacob's wife; Joseph, and Benjamin.

20 ¶ [c]And unto Joseph in the land of Egypt were born Manasseh and Ephraim, which Asenath the daughter of Poti-pherah [z]priest of On bare unto him.

21 ¶ [d]And the sons of Benjamin *were* Belah, and Becher, and Ashbel, Gera, and Naaman, [e]Ehi, and Rosh, [f]Muppim, and [a]Huppim, and Ard.

22 These *are* the sons of Rachel, which were born to Jacob: all the souls *were* fourteen.

23 ¶ [g]And the sons of Dan; [b]Hushim.

24 ¶ [h]And the sons of Naphtali; Jahzeel, and Guni, and Jezer, and Shillem.

25 [i]These *are* the sons of Bilhah, [j]which Laban gave unto Rachel his daughter, and she bare these unto Jacob: all the souls *were* seven.

26 [k]All the souls that came with

46:1 [e]ch. 21:31,33 & 28:10 [f]ch. 26:24,25 & 28:13 & 31:42
46:2 [g]ch. 15:1 Job 33:14,15
46:3 [h]ch. 28:13 [i]ch. 12:2 Deut. 26:5
46:4 [j]ch. 28:15 & 48:21 [k]ch. 15:16 & 50:13,24,25 Ex. 3:8 [l]ch. 50:1
46:5 [m]Acts 7:15 [n]ch. 45:19,21
46:6 [o]Deut. 26:5 Josh. 24:4 Ps. 105:23 Is. 52:4
46:8 [p]Ex. 1:1 [q]Num. 26:5
46:10 [r]Ex. 6:15
46:11 [s]1 Chr. 6:1,16
46:12 [t]1 Chr. 2:3 & 4:21 [u]ch. 38:3,7,10 [v]ch. 38:29
46:13 [w]1 Chr. 7:1
46:16 [x]Num. 26:15 *Zephon*
46:17 [y]1 Chr. 7:30
46:18 [z]ch. 30:10 [a]ch. 29:24
46:19 [b]ch. 44:27
46:20 [c]ch. 41:50
46:21 [d]1 Chr. 7:6 & 8:1 [e]Num. 26:38, *Ahiram* [f]Num. 26:39, Shupham 1 Chr. 7:12, Shuppim
46:23 [g]1 Chr. 7:12
46:24 [h]1 Chr. 7:13
46:25 [i]ch. 30:5,7 [j]ch. 29:29
46:26 [k]Ex. 1:5

s Or, *Nemuel* t Or, *Jarib* u Or, *Zerah;* see 1 Chr. 4:24 v Or, *Gershom* w Or, *Puah, and Jashub* x Or, *Ozni* y Or, *Arod* z Or, *prince* a *Hupham;* see Num. 26:39 b Or, *Shuham;* see Num. 26:42

people would multiply and become a great nation, and from there they would return to Canaan (cf. 50:24). (2) In response to the Egyptians' demand (cf. 43:32; 46:34), the children of Israel lived in isolation in the land of Goshen. There they would remain separated, a people set apart for God, looking for the day of their return to the promised fatherland in Canaan, where they would assume their role in God's redemptive plan (see article on THE CALL OF ABRAHAM, p. 25).

46:3 I *AM* GOD . . . FEAR NOT. God once again promised to be with Jacob and his family, reiterating the promise that his descendants would become a great nation and that they would return to the land of Canaan. We all need God's reassurances of His love, care, and presence as we live upon this earth and experience the difficulties and decisions that are inevitable in this fallen world. If you are sincerely endeavoring to follow the Lord, you have the right to ask God for a reaffirmation of His love for you and His guidance in your life (cf. John 1:12–13).

46:26 THREESCORE AND SIX. The sixty-six persons are those who traveled with Jacob to Egypt. The seventy of v. 27 included Joseph, his two sons, and Jacob. Acts 7:14 gives the number

Jacob into Egypt, which came out of his
[c]loins, besides Jacob's sons' wives,
all the souls *were* threescore and six;
27 And the sons of Joseph, which
were born him in Egypt, *were* two
souls: [l]all the souls of the house of
Jacob, which came into Egypt, *were*
threescore and ten.
28 ¶ And he sent Judah before him
unto Joseph, [m]to direct his face unto
Goshen; and they came [n]into the land
of Goshen.
29 And Joseph made ready his char-
iot, and went up to meet Israel his fa-
ther, to Goshen, and presented himself
unto him; and he [o]fell on his neck, and
wept on his neck a good while.
30 And Israel said unto Joseph,
[p]Now let me die, since I have seen thy
face, because thou *art* yet alive.
31 And Joseph said unto his breth-
ren, and unto his father's house, [q]I
will go up, and show Pharaoh, and say
unto him, My brethren, and my father's
house, which *were* in the land of Ca-
naan, are come unto me;
32 And the men *are* shepherds, for
[d]their trade hath been to feed cattle;
and they have brought their flocks, and
their herds, and all that they have.
33 And it shall come to pass, when
Pharaoh shall call you, and shall say,
[r]What *is* your occupation?
34 That ye shall say, Thy servants'
[s]trade hath been about cattle [t]from
our youth even until now, both we, *and*
also our fathers: that ye may dwell in
the land of Goshen; for every shepherd
is [u]an abomination unto the Egyp-
tians.

47 THEN JOSEPH [v]came and told
Pharaoh, and said, My father
and my brethren, and their flocks, and
their herds, and all that they have, are
come out of the land of Canaan; and,
behold, they *are* in [w]the land of Go-
shen.
2 And he took some of his brethren,
even five men, and [x]presented them
unto Pharaoh.

46:27 [l]Deut. 10:22 See Acts 7:14
46:28 [m]ch. 31:21 [n]ch. 47:1
46:29 [o]ch. 45:14
46:30 [p]Luke 2:29,30
46:31 [q]ch. 47:1
46:33 [r]ch. 47:2,3
46:34 [s]ver. 32 [t]ch. 30:35 & 34:5 & 37:12 [u]ch. 43:32 Ex. 8:26
47:1 [v]ch. 46:31 [w]ch. 45:10 & 46:28
47:2 [x]Acts 7:13
47:3 [y]ch. 46:33 [z]ch. 46:34
47:4 [a]ch. 15:13 Deut. 26:5 [b]ch. 43:1 Acts 7:11 [c]ch. 46:34
47:6 [d]ch. 20:15 [e]ver. 4
47:9 [f]Ps. 39:12 Heb. 11:9,13 [g]Job 14:1 [h]ch. 25:7 & 35:28
47:10 [i]ver. 7
47:11 [j]Ex. 1:11 & 12:37 [k]ver. 6

3 And Pharaoh said unto his breth-
ren, [y]What *is* your occupation? And
they said unto Pharaoh, [z]Thy ser-
vants *are* shepherds, both we, *and* also
our fathers.
4 They said moreover unto Phar-
aoh, [a]For to sojourn in the land are we
come; for thy servants have no pasture
for their flocks; [b]for the famine *is* sore
in the land of Canaan: now therefore,
we pray thee, let thy servants [c]dwell
in the land of Goshen.
5 And Pharaoh spake unto Joseph,
saying, Thy father and thy brethren are
come unto thee:
6 [d]The land of Egypt *is* before thee;
in the best of the land make thy father
and brethren to dwell; [e]in the land of
Goshen let them dwell: and if thou
knowest *any* men of activity among
them, then make them rulers over my
cattle.
7 And Joseph brought in Jacob his
father, and set him before Pharaoh:
and Jacob blessed Pharaoh.
8 And Pharaoh said unto Jacob,
[e]How old *art* thou?
9 And Jacob said unto Pharaoh,
[f]The days of the years of my pilgrim-
age *are* an hundred and thirty years:
[g]few and evil have the days of the
years of my life been, and [h]have not
attained unto the days of the years of
the life of my fathers in the days of
their pilgrimage.
10 And Jacob [i]blessed Pharaoh,
and went out from before Pharaoh.
11 ¶ And Joseph placed his father
and his brethren, and gave them a pos-
session in the land of Egypt, in the best
of the land, in the land of [j]Rameses,
[k]as Pharaoh had commanded.
12 And Joseph nourished his father,
and his brethren, and all his father's
household, with bread, [f] [g]according
to *their* families.

[c] Heb. *thigh;* see ch. 35:11 [d] Heb. *they are men of cattle* [e] Heb. *How many are the days of the years of thy life?* [f] Or, *as a little child is nourished* [g] Heb. *according to the little ones*

of persons as seventy-five, thus including Joseph's grandchildren.

46:34 AN ABOMINATION. The primary occupation of Jacob's family was tending livestock. Traditionally the Egyptians had a strong disdain for shepherds. This animosity helped the Israelites to remain separated from the Egyptians and their ways (cf. 43:2; see also 45:10, note).

47:9 MY PILGRIMAGE. Jacob referred to his life and that of his fathers as a pilgrimage. (1) As a stranger and a pilgrim in the land, he trusted God for possession of the promised land. Thus it was by faith that he lived. Along with Abraham and Isaac, he died without receiving the promises; his ultimate goal was a better country, a heavenly one (see Heb. 11:8–16). (2) All believers are likewise pilgrims and strangers on earth, living by faith and looking for a heavenly "city which hath foundations, whose builder and maker is God" (see Heb. 11:10–13, notes).

Joseph and the famine

13 ¶ And *there was* no bread in all the land; for the famine *was* very sore, [l]so that the land of Egypt and *all* the land of Canaan fainted by reason of the famine.

14 [m]And Joseph gathered up all the money that was found in the land of Egypt, and in the land of Canaan, for the corn which they bought: and Joseph brought the money into Pharaoh's house.

15 And when money failed in the land of Egypt, and in the land of Canaan, all the Egyptians came unto Joseph, and said, Give us bread: for [n]why should we die in thy presence? for the money faileth.

16 And Joseph said, Give your cattle; and I will give you for your cattle, if money fail.

17 And they brought their cattle unto Joseph: and Joseph gave them bread *in exchange* for horses, and for the flocks, and for the cattle of the herds, and for the asses: and he [h]fed them with bread for all their cattle for that year.

18 When that year was ended, they came unto him the second year, and said unto him, We will not hide *it* from my lord, how that our money is spent; my lord also hath our herds of cattle; there is not aught left in the sight of my lord, but our bodies, and our lands:

19 Wherefore shall we die before thine eyes, both we and our land? buy us and our land for bread, and we and our land will be servants unto Pharaoh: and give *us* seed, that we may live, and not die, that the land be not desolate.

20 And Joseph bought all the land of Egypt for Pharaoh; for the Egyptians sold every man his field, because the famine prevailed over them: so the land became Pharaoh's.

21 And as for the people, he removed them to cities from *one* end of the borders of Egypt even to the *other* end thereof.

22 [o]Only the land of the [i]priests bought he not; for the priests had a portion *assigned them* of Pharaoh, and did eat their portion which Pharaoh gave them: wherefore they sold not their lands.

23 Then Joseph said unto the people, Behold, I have bought you this day and your land for Pharaoh: lo, *here is* seed for you, and ye shall sow the land.

24 And it shall come to pass in the increase, that ye shall give the fifth *part* unto Pharaoh, and four parts shall be your own, for seed of the field, and for your food, and for them of your households, and for food for your little ones.

25 And they said, Thou hast saved our lives: [p]let us find grace in the sight of my lord, and we will be Pharaoh's servants.

26 And Joseph made it a law over the land of Egypt unto this day, *that* Pharaoh should have the fifth *part;* [q]except the land of the [j]priests only, *which* became not Pharaoh's.

27 ¶ And Israel [r]dwelt in the land of Egypt, in the country of Goshen; and they had possessions therein, and [s]grew, and multiplied exceedingly.

28 And Jacob lived in the land of Egypt seventeen years: so [k]the whole age of Jacob was an hundred forty and seven years.

29 And the time [t]drew nigh that Israel must die: and he called his son Joseph, and said unto him, If now I have found grace in thy sight, [u]put, I pray thee, thy hand under my thigh, and [v]deal kindly and truly with me; [w]bury me not, I pray thee, in Egypt:

30 But [x]I will lie with my fathers, and thou shalt carry me out of Egypt, and [y]bury me in their buryingplace. And he said, I will do as thou hast said.

31 And he said, Swear unto me. And he sware unto him. And [z]Israel bowed himself upon the bed's head.

Jacob blesses Joseph's sons

48 AND IT came to pass after these things, that *one* told Joseph, Behold, thy father *is* sick: and he took with him his two sons, Manasseh and Ephraim.

2 And *one* told Jacob, and said, Behold,

47:13 [l]ch. 41:30 Acts 7:11 **47:14** [m]ch. 41:56 **47:15** [n]ver. 19 **47:22** [o]Ezra 7:24 **47:25** [p]ch. 33:15 **47:26** [q]ver. 22 **47:27** [r]ver. 11 [s]ch. 46:3 **47:29** [t]See Deut. 31:14 1 Ki. 2:1 [u]ch. 24:2 [v]ch. 24:49 [w]See ch. 50:25 **47:30** [x]2 Sam. 19:37 [y]ch. 49:29 & 50:5,13 **47:31** [z]ch. 48:2 1 Ki. 1:47 Heb. 11:21

[h] Heb. *led them* [i] Or, *princes;* see ch. 41:45 [j] Or, *princes;* see ver. 22 [k] Heb. *the days of the years of his life*

47:30 CARRY ME OUT OF EGYPT. Jacob was about to die without receiving the promise, but by faith in God he looked forward to the day when God would lead the people back to Canaan (see 46:3, note). With this in mind, he requested to be laid to rest in the burial place of his family (cf. Heb. 11:22).

hold, thy son Joseph cometh unto thee: and Israel strengthened himself, and sat upon the bed.

3 And Jacob said unto Joseph, God Almighty appeared unto me at [a]Luz in the land of Canaan, and blessed me,

4 And said unto me, Behold, I will make thee fruitful, and multiply thee, and I will make of thee a multitude of people; and will give this land to thy seed after thee [b]*for* an everlasting possession.

5 ¶ And now thy [c]two sons, Ephraim and Manasseh, which were born unto thee in the land of Egypt before I came unto thee into Egypt, *are* mine; as Reuben and Simeon, they shall be mine.

6 And thy issue, which thou begettest after them, shall be thine, *and* shall be called after the name of their brethren in their inheritance.

7 And as for me, when I came from Padan, [d]Rachel died by me in the land of Canaan in the way, when yet *there was* but a little way to come unto Ephrath: and I buried her there in the way of Ephrath; the same *is* Bethlehem.

8 And Israel beheld Joseph's sons, and said, Who *are* these?

9 And Joseph said unto his father, [e]They *are* my sons, whom God hath given me in this *place.* And he said, Bring them, I pray thee, unto me, and [f]I will bless them.

10 Now [g]the eyes of Israel were [1]dim for age, *so that* he could not see. And he brought them near unto him; and [h]he kissed them, and embraced them.

11 And Israel said unto Joseph, [i]I had not thought to see thy face: and, lo, God hath shown me also thy seed.

12 And Joseph brought them out from between his knees, and he bowed himself with his face to the earth.

13 And Joseph took them both, Ephraim in his right hand toward Israel's left hand, and Manasseh in his left hand toward Israel's right hand, and brought *them* near unto him.

14 And Israel stretched out his right hand, and laid *it* upon Ephraim's head, who *was* the younger, and his left hand upon Manasseh's head, [j]guiding his hands wittingly; for Manasseh *was* the firstborn.

15 ¶ And [k]he blessed Joseph, and said, God, [l]before whom my fathers Abraham and Isaac did walk, the God which fed me all my life long unto this day,

16 The Angel [m]which redeemed me from all evil, bless the lads; and let [n]my name be named on them, and the name of my fathers Abraham and Isaac; and let them [m]grow into a multitude in the midst of the earth.

17 And when Joseph saw that his father [o]laid his right hand upon the head of Ephraim, it [n]displeased him: and he held up his father's hand, to remove it from Ephraim's head unto Manasseh's head.

18 And Joseph said unto his father, Not so, my father: for this *is* the firstborn; put thy right hand upon his head.

19 And his father refused, and said, [p]I know *it,* my son, I know *it:* he also shall become a people, and he also shall be great: but truly [q]his younger brother shall be greater than he, and his seed shall become a [o]multitude of nations.

48:3 [a]ch. 28:13,19 & 35:6,9
48:4 [b]ch. 17:8
48:5 [c]ch. 41:50 & 46:20 Josh. 13:7 & 14:4
48:7 [d]ch. 35:9,16,19
48:9 [e]See ch. 33:5 [f]ch. 27:4
48:10 [g]ch. 27:1 [h]ch. 27:27
48:11 [i]ch. 45:26
48:14 [j]ver. 19
48:15 [k]Heb. 11:21 [l]ch. 17:1
48:16 [m]ch. 28:15 Ps. 34:22 & 121:7 [n]Amos 9:12 Acts 15:17
48:17 [o]ver. 14
48:19 [p]ver. 14 [q]Num. 1:33,35 Deut. 33:17

[1] Heb. *heavy* [m] Heb. *as fishes do increase* [n] *was evil in his eyes* [o] Heb. *fulness*

48:5 THY TWO SONS . . . SHALL BE MINE. Jacob considered Joseph's two sons as his own, thus guaranteeing Joseph a double portion of the inheritance. Ephraim and Manasseh were thus to have equal rights and status with Jacob's other sons, such as Reuben and Simeon. The descendants of Ephraim and Manasseh each became a full tribe.

48:15 THE GOD WHICH FED ME ALL MY LIFE LONG. Jacob left his children with an example of persevering faith in God and a testimony that God had fed him (literally, shepherded him) his entire life, redeeming him from all evil. The book of Hebrews points to Jacob's act of blessing Ephraim and Manasseh as the ultimate proof of his sincere faith in God (Heb. 11:21). The greatest thing a father can pass on to his children is his faith in and commitment to God and His ways. There is no legacy greater than this.

48:19 HIS YOUNGER BROTHER SHALL BE GREATER. It should be noted that numerous times in O.T. history God chose the younger son over the older. He chose Isaac instead of Ishmael (21:12), Jacob instead of Esau (25:23), Joseph instead of Reuben (vv. 21–22; 49:3–4), Ephraim instead of Manasseh (vv. 14–20), Gideon over his brothers (Judg. 6:11–16), and David over his brothers (1 Sam. 16). This emphasizes that what is first among humans is not necessarily first with God. God chooses people on the basis of their sincerity, purity, and love, not their position in the family (see Mat. 19:30, note; 20:26, note; 1 Cor. 1:27–28; Jas. 2:5).

20 And he blessed them that day, saying, [r]In thee shall Israel bless, saying, God make thee as Ephraim and as Manasseh: and he set Ephraim before Manasseh.

21 And Israel said unto Joseph, Behold, I die: but [s]God shall be with you, and bring you again unto the land of your fathers.

22 Moreover [t]I have given to thee one portion above thy brethren, which I took out of the hand [u]of the Amorite with my sword and with my bow.

Jacob blesses his sons

49:1–28Ref — Deut. 33:1–29

49 AND JACOB called unto his sons, and said, Gather yourselves together, that I may [v]tell you *that* which shall befall you [w]in the last days.

2 Gather yourselves together, and hear, ye sons of Jacob; and hearken unto Israel your father.

3 ¶ Reuben, thou *art* [x]my firstborn, my might, and the beginning of my strength, the excellency of dignity, and the excellency of power:

4 Unstable as water, [p]thou shalt not excel; because thou [y]wentest up to thy father's bed; then defiledst thou *it:* [q]he went up to my couch.

5 ¶ [z]Simeon and Levi *are* brethren; [r]instruments of cruelty *are in* their habitations.

6 O my soul, [a]come not thou into their secret; [b]unto their assembly, mine honour, be not thou united: for [c]in their anger they slew a man, and in their selfwill they [s]digged down a wall.

7 Cursed *be* their anger, for *it was* fierce; and their wrath, for it was cruel: I will divide them in Jacob, and scatter them in Israel.

8 ¶ [d]Judah, thou *art he* whom thy brethren shall praise: [e]thy hand *shall be* in the neck of thine enemies; [f]thy father's children shall bow down before thee.

9 Judah *is* [g]a lion's whelp: from the prey, my son, thou art gone up: [h]he stooped down, he couched as a lion, and as an old lion; who shall rouse him up?

10 [i]The sceptre shall not depart from Judah, nor [j]a lawgiver from between his feet, [k]until Shiloh come; [l]and unto him *shall* the gathering of the people *be.*

11 Binding his foal unto the vine, and his ass's colt unto the choice vine; he washed his garments in wine, and his clothes in the blood of grapes:

12 His eyes *shall be* red with wine, and his teeth white with milk.

13 ¶ [m]Zebulun shall dwell at the

[p] Heb. *do not thou excel* [q] Or, *my couch is gone* [r] Or, *their swords* are *weapons of violence* [s] Or, *houghed oxen*

48:20 [r]See Ruth 4:11,12
48:21 [s]ch. 46:4
48:22 [t]Josh. 24:32 John 4:5 [u]ch. 34:28
49:1 [v]Deut. 33:1 Amos 3:7 [w]Deut. 4:30 Is. 39:6 Jer. 23:20 Heb. 1:2
49:3 [x]ch. 29:32
49:4 [y]ch. 35:22 Deut. 27:20
49:5 [z]ch. 29:33,34
49:6 [a]Prov. 1:15,16 [b]Ps. 26:9 Eph. 5:11 [c]ch. 34:26
49:8 [d]Deut. 33:7 [e]Ps. 18:40 [f]1 Chr. 5:2
49:9 [g]Rev. 5:5 [h]Num. 23:24 & 24:9
49:10 [i]Num. 24:17 Jer. 30:21 [j]Ps. 60:7 [k]Is. 11:1 Mat. 21:9 [l]Is. 60:1-5 Luke 2:30-32
49:13 [m]Deut. 33:18,19 Josh. 19:10,11

49:1 JACOB CALLED UNTO HIS SONS. At the close of his life, Jacob gathered together his sons and prophesied about their lives and their future in the God's purpose of redemption. The blessings and the curses of this chapter are conditional on the descendants' relationship with God (see v. 7, note).

49:4 THOU SHALT NOT EXCEL. Reuben was Jacob's firstborn. As such he was entitled to the birthright and the first place of leadership, honor, and power. Instead, his place as leader was taken from him because of his sexual immorality with his father's wife (35:22; Deut. 27:20). In other words, failure in character, manifested by serious sinful actions, may remove one forever from a position of leadership (see article on MORAL QUALIFICATIONS FOR OVERSEERS, p. 1908).

49:7 CURSED *BE* THEIR ANGER. Jacob's curse on Simeon and Levi (vv. 5–7) was of a conditional nature, as were all the blessings and curses of this chapter. Because of the stand for God taken by the Levites (i.e., the family of Levi) at the scene of the golden calf, the curse spoken here was removed and a blessing and honorable place were given them (Ex. 32:26–29; Lev. 25:32–33; Deut. 10:8; 33:8–11). This shows that the curses on a father and his family can be broken and removed by the repentance and faith of his children (Lev. 26:39–42; 2 Chr. 30:7–9; Jer. 31:29–30; Ezek. 18:1–9).

49:10 UNTIL SHILOH COME. The blessing conferred upon Judah (vv. 8–12) indicates that he was given the rights of the firstborn, and hence the blessing promised to Abraham (12:1–3). The essence of this promise was that all nations would be blessed through him by the "seed" of the woman (see 3:15, note; see article on THE CALL OF ABRAHAM, p. 25). (1) Judah was told that his descendants would live in a position of general superiority to his brothers "until Shiloh come" (vv. 8–10). This was partially fulfilled in that the royal line of Israel was the line of King David, a descendant of Judah. (2) "Shiloh" probably means "to whom it belongs" (cf. Ezek. 21:27) and ultimately refers to the coming Messiah, Jesus Christ, who came through the tribe of Judah (Rev. 5:5). Jacob prophesied that all people would be subjected to him (v. 10; Rev. 19:15), and that He would bring great spiritual blessing (vv. 11–12).

49:12 RED WITH WINE. V. 12 should be translated: "His eyes will be darker than wine, his teeth whiter than milk."

haven of the sea; and he *shall be* for an
haven of ships; and his border *shall be*
unto Zidon.
14 ¶ Issachar *is* a strong ass couch-
ing down between two burdens:
15 And he saw that rest *was* good,
and the land that *it was* pleasant; and
bowed [n]his shoulder to bear, and be-
came a servant unto tribute.
16 ¶ [o]Dan shall judge his people,
as one of the tribes of Israel.
17 [p]Dan shall be a serpent by the
way, [t]an adder in the path, that biteth
the horse heels, so that his rider shall
fall backward.
18 [q]I have waited for thy salvation,
O LORD.
19 ¶ [r]Gad, a troop shall overcome
him: but he shall overcome at the last.
20 ¶ [s]Out of Asher his bread *shall*
be fat, and he shall yield royal dainties.
21 ¶ [t]Naphtali *is* a hind let loose:
he giveth goodly words.
22 ¶ Joseph *is* a fruitful bough, *even*
a fruitful bough by a well; *whose*
[u]branches run over the wall:
23 The archers have [u]sorely
grieved him, and shot *at him*, and hated
him:
24 But his [v]bow abode in strength,
and the arms of his hands were made
strong by the hands of [w]the mighty
God of Jacob; ([x]from thence [y]*is* the
shepherd, [z]the stone of Israel:)
25 [a]*Even* by the God of thy father,
who shall help thee; [b]and by the Al-
mighty, [c]who shall bless thee with
blessings of heaven above, blessings of
the deep that lieth under, blessings of
the breasts, and of the womb:
26 The blessings of thy father have
prevailed above the blessings of my
progenitors [d]unto the utmost bound
of the everlasting hills: [e]they shall be
on the head of Joseph, and on the
crown of the head of him that was sep-
arate from his brethren.
27 ¶ Benjamin shall [f]ravin *as* a
wolf: in the morning he shall devour

49:15 [n]1 Sam. 10:9
49:16 [o]Deut. 33:22
49:17 [p]Judg. 18:27
49:18 [q]Ps. 25:5; Is. 25:9
49:19 [r]Deut. 33:20; 1 Chr. 5:18
49:20 [s]Deut. 33:24; Josh. 19:24
49:21 [t]Deut. 33:23
49:23 [u]ch. 37:4,24; Ps. 118:13
49:24 [v]Job 29:20; Ps. 37:15 [w]Ps. 132:2,5 [x]ch. 45:11 & 47:12 [y]Ps. 80:1 [z]Is. 28:16
49:25 [a]ch. 28:13 & 35:3 & 43:23 [b]ch. 17:1 & 35:11 [c]Deut. 33:13
49:26 [d]Deut. 33:15; Hab. 3:6 [e]Deut. 33:16
49:27 [f]Judg. 20:21,25 [g]Num. 23:24; Esth. 8:11; Ezek. 39:10; Zech. 14:1
49:29 [h]ch. 15:15 & 25:8 [i]ch. 47:30; 2 Sam. 19:37 [j]ch. 50:13
49:30 [k]ch. 23:16
49:31 [l]ch. 23:19 & 25:9 [m]ch. 35:29
49:33 [n]ver. 29
50:1 [o]ch. 46:4 [p]2 Ki. 13:14
50:2 [q]ver. 26; 2 Chr. 16:14; Luke 24:1; John 19:39,40
50:3 [r]Num. 20:29; Deut. 34:8
50:4 [s]Esth. 4:2

the prey, [g]and at night he shall divide
the spoil.

The death of Jacob

28 ¶ All these *are* the twelve tribes
of Israel: and this *is it* that their father
spake unto them, and blessed them;
every one according to his blessing he
blessed them.
29 And he charged them, and said
unto them, I [h]am to be gathered unto
my people: [i]bury me with my fathers
[j]in the cave that *is* in the field of
Ephron the Hittite,
30 In the cave that *is* in the field of
Machpelah, which *is* before Mamre, in
the land of Canaan, [k]which Abraham
bought with the field of Ephron the Hit-
tite for a possession of a buryingplace.
31 [l]There they buried Abraham
and Sarah his wife; [m]there they buried
Isaac and Rebekah his wife; and there
I buried Leah.
32 The purchase of the field and of
the cave that *is* therein *was* from the
children of Heth.
33 And when Jacob had made an
end of commanding his sons, he gath-
ered up his feet into the bed, and yield-
ed up the ghost, and [n]was gathered
unto his people.
50 AND JOSEPH [o]fell upon his fa-
ther's face, and [p]wept upon
him, and kissed him.
2 And Joseph commanded his ser-
vants the physicians to [q]embalm his
father: and the physicians embalmed
Israel.
3 And forty days were fulfilled for
him; for so are fulfilled the days of
those which are embalmed: and the
Egyptians [r]mourned[v] for him three-
score and ten days.
4 And when the days of his mourn-
ing were past, Joseph spake unto [s]the

[t] Heb. *an arrow-snake* [u] Heb. *daughters*
[v] Heb. *wept*

50:1 WEPT OVER HIM. Joseph's reaction to his father's death is a model for all believers who experience the death of a Christian loved one. (1) Sincere grief. Joseph wept and entered into a long period of mourning, consisting of seventy days and then several more weeks as he carried Jacob's remains back to Canaan for the burial (vv. 1–4,7–14). It is not abnormal or wrong to grieve weeks or even months over the death of someone very close to us.

(2) Care in preparing for burial (v. 2). Joseph wanted to honor his father's memory in a right and decent way.

(3) Fulfilling last wishes. Joseph honored the promises he made to his father (vv. 5,12–13). Promises made in faith and based on God's will must be carried out after the death of a loved one.

(4) Faithful testimony. Joseph testified to his faith in God's promises by carrying his father back to the promised land of Canaan and laying him in the tomb of Abraham, Isaac, and the others (cf. 1 Thes. 4:13,18; see Phil. 1:21, note).

house of Pharaoh, saying, If now I have found grace in your eyes, speak, I pray you, in the ears of Pharaoh, saying,

5 [t]My father made me swear, saying, Lo, I die: in my grave [u]which I have digged for me in the land of Canaan, there shalt thou bury me. Now therefore let me go up, I pray thee, and bury my father, and I will come again.

6 And Pharaoh said, Go up, and bury thy father, according as he made thee swear.

7 ¶ And Joseph went up to bury his father: and with him went up all the servants of Pharaoh, the elders of his house, and all the elders of the land of Egypt,

8 And all the house of Joseph, and his brethren, and his father's house: only their little ones, and their flocks, and their herds, they left in the land of Goshen.

9 And there went up with him both chariots and horsemen: and it was a very great company.

10 And they came to the threshingfloor of Atad, which *is* beyond Jordan, and there they [v]mourned with a great and very sore lamentation: [w]and he made a mourning for his father seven days.

11 And when the inhabitants of the land, the Canaanites, saw the mourning in the floor of Atad, they said, This *is* a grievous mourning to the Egyptians: wherefore the name of it was called [w]Abel-mizraim, which *is* beyond Jordan.

12 And his sons did unto him according as he commanded them:

13 For [x]his sons carried him into the land of Canaan, and buried him in the cave of the field of Machpelah, which Abraham [y]bought with the field for a possession of a buryingplace of Ephron the Hittite, before Mamre.

14 ¶ And Joseph returned into Egypt, he, and his brethren, and all that went up with him to bury his father, after he had buried his father.

15 ¶ And when Joseph's brethren saw that their father was dead, [z]they said, Joseph will peradventure hate us, and will certainly requite us all the evil which we did unto him.

16 And they [x]sent a messenger unto Joseph, saying, Thy father did command before he died, saying,

17 So shall ye say unto Joseph, Forgive, I pray thee now, the trespass of thy brethren, and their sin; [a]for they did unto thee evil: and now, we pray thee, forgive the trespass of the servants of [b]the God of thy father. And Joseph wept when they spake unto him.

18 And his brethren also went and [c]fell down before his face; and they said, Behold, we *be* thy servants.

19 And Joseph said unto them, [d]Fear not: [e]for *am* I in the place of God?

20 [f]But as for you, ye thought evil against me; *but* [g]God meant it unto good, to bring to pass, as *it is* this day, to save much people alive.

21 Now therefore fear ye not: [h]I will nourish you, and your little ones. And he comforted them, and spake [y]kindly unto them.

Num 6:24-26

The death of Joseph

22 ¶ And Joseph dwelt in Egypt, he, and his father's house: and Joseph lived an hundred and ten years.

23 And Joseph saw Ephraim's children [i]of the third *generation:* [j]the children also of Machir the son of Manasseh [k]were [z]brought up upon Joseph's knees.

24 And Joseph said unto his brethren, I die: and [l]God will surely visit you, and bring you out of this land unto

50:5 [t]ch. 47:29 [u]2 Chr. 16:14 Is. 22:16
50:10 [v]Acts 8:2 [w]1 Sam. 31:13 Job 2:13
50:13 [x]ch. 49:29 Acts 7:16 [y]ch. 23:16
50:15 [z]Job 15:21
50:17 [a]Prov. 28:13 [b]ch. 49:25
50:18 [c]ch. 37:7,10
50:19 [d]ch. 45:5 [e]2 Ki. 5:7
50:20 [f]Ps. 56:5 [g]Acts 3:13-15
50:21 [h]Mat. 5:44
50:23 [i]Job 42:16 [j]Num. 32:39 [k]ch. 30:3
50:24 [l]ch. 15:14 & 46:4 & 48:21 Ex. 3:16,17 Heb. 11:22

[w]i.e. *The mourning of the Egyptians* [x]Heb. *charged* [y]Heb. *to their hearts* [z]Heb. *borne*

50:20 GOD MEANT IT FOR GOOD. See article on THE PROVIDENCE OF GOD, p. 80.

50:25 CARRY UP MY BONES FROM HENCE. Joseph's enduring faith was in God's promise that Canaan would be his people's homeland (13:12–15; 26:3; 28:13). Thus he requested that his bones be taken to the land of promise. Four hundred years later, when the Israelites left Egypt to go to Canaan, they took Joseph's bones with them (Ex. 13:19; Josh. 24:32; cf. Heb. 11:22). Likewise, all believers know that their future lies not in this present world, but in another land, a heavenly country, where they will dwell forever with God and enjoy His eternal presence and blessings. This is His promise to His faithful ones (Heb. 11:8–16; Rev. 21:1–4).

the land [m]which he sware to Abraham,
to Isaac, and to Jacob.
25 And [n]Joseph took an oath of the
children of Israel, saying, God will
surely visit you, and ye shall carry up
my bones from hence.
26 So Joseph died, *being* an hundred
and ten years old: and they embalmed
him, and he was put in a coffin in
Egypt.

50:24 [m]ch. 26:3 & 35:12 & 46:4
50:25 [n]Ex. 13:19 Josh. 24:32 Acts 7:16

EXODUS

Outline

I. Oppression of the Hebrews in Egypt (1:1—11:10)
  A. Burden of the Oppressed (1:1–22)
  B. Preparation of the Deliverer (2:1—4:31)
    1. Moses' Birth and First Forty Years (2:1–15a)
    2. Moses' Exile and Second Forty Years (2:15b-25)
    3. Moses' Call and Return to Egypt (3:1—4:31)
  C. Struggle with the Oppressor (5:1—11:10)
    1. The Request: "Let My People Go" (5:1–3)
    2. The Response: Tyrannical Persecution (5:4–21)
    3. The Reassurance: The Lord Will Manifest His Lordship (5:22—7:13)
    4. The Recourse: The Ten Plagues (7:14—11:10)

II. Deliverance of the Hebrews Out of Egypt (12:1—15:21)
  A. The Passover Deliverance: Redemption by Blood (12:1—13:16)
  B. The Red Sea Deliverance: Redemption by Power (13:17—14:31)
  C. The Songs of Deliverance: Praise to the Redeemer (15:1–21)

III. Education of the Hebrews En Route to Mount Sinai (15:22—18:27)
  A. The Test of Adversity and Providential Care (15:22—17:16)
    1. The First Test: Bitter Waters of Marah (15:22–27)
    2. The Hunger Test: Provision of Quail and Manna (16:1–36)
    3. The Thirst Test: Water at Rephidim (17:1–7)
    4. The Conflict Test: Battle with Amalek (17:8–16)
  B. The Wise Counsel of Jethro (18:1–27)

IV. Covenant with the Hebrews at Mount Sinai (19:1—24:18)
  A. Preparatory Instructions to Moses (19:1—25)
  B. The Ten Commandments: Foundation for Covenant Life (20:1–17)
  C. Ordinances Guarding the Covenant Relationship (20:18—23:19)
  D. Promises Regarding the Promised Land (23:20–33)
  E. Ratification of the Covenant (24:1–18)

V. Worship by the Hebrews Delineated at Mount Sinai (25:1—40:38)
  A. Instructions Concerning the Tabernacle (25:1—27:21)
  B. Instructions Concerning the Priest (28:1—31:18)
  C. The Sin of Idolatry (32:1—34:35)
  D. The Implementation of the Divine Instructions (35:1—40:38)

Author: Moses

Theme: Redemption

Date of Writing: c. 1445–1405 B.C.

Background

Exodus continues the narrative begun in Genesis. The book's title, derived from the Greek word *exodos* (the title used in the Septuagint, i.e., the Greek translation of the O.T.),

means "exit" or "departure." It refers to God's mighty deliverance of Israel from slavery in Egypt and their departure from that land as the people of God.

Two issues related to the background of Exodus have involved major controversy: the date of Israel's exodus from Egypt and the authorship of the book. (1) Two different dates for the exodus have been proposed by scholars. (a) An "early date" (also referred to as the Biblical date) is derived from 1 Ki. 6:1, which states that it occurred 480 years before "the fourth year of Solomon's reign." This dates the exodus c. 1445 B.C. Also, in Judg. 11:26, Jephthah (c. 1100 B.C.) declared that Israel had occupied their land for 300 years, which would date the conquest at approximately 1400 B.C. This chronology for the exodus, conquest, and the period of the judges fits well with the datable history of Israel's first three kings (Saul, David, and Solomon). (b) A "late date" for the exodus (c. 1290) is proposed by liberal critics of the Bible, based on certain assumptions about Egyptian rulers and on a thirteenth century B.C. archaeological dating for the destruction of Canaanite cities during the conquest.

(2) There is also disagreement between conservative and liberal Biblical scholars over the Mosaic authorship of the book of Exodus. (a) Modern interpreters often view the book as a composite work by various editors, completed at a much later time in Israel's history than the time of Moses (called the JEDP theory). (b) However, Jewish tradition from the time of Joshua onward (Josh. 8:31–35), plus the testimony of Jesus (cf. Mark 12:26), early Christianity, and contemporary conservative scholarship, all attribute the book's origin to Moses (see the introduction to Deuteronomy). Furthermore, internal evidence supports Moses' authorship. Numerous details in Exodus indicate that the author was an eyewitness of the recorded events (e.g., 2:12; 9:31–32; 15:27). Also, portions of the book itself testify to Moses' direct involvement in its writing (e.g., 17:14; 24:4; 34:27).

Purpose

Exodus was written to provide an enduring record of the historical and redemptive acts of God whereby Israel was delivered out of Egypt, established as His chosen nation, and given the written revelation concerning God's covenant with her. Also, it was written as a supremely important link in the overall progressive self-revelation of God that culminated in the person of Jesus Christ and in the N.T.

Survey

The book of Exodus begins with Jacob's descendants suffering oppression, slavery, and infanticide in Egypt; the book ends with God's presence, power, and glory manifested (i.e., tabernacling) in the midst of His liberated people in the wilderness. Exodus divides into three major sections. (A) Chs. 1—14 reveal *Israel in Egypt* suffering oppression under a pharaoh who did not know Joseph and God redeeming Israel "with a stretched out arm, and with great judgments" (6:6). Among the monumental events in this part of Israel's history are: (1) Moses' birth, preservation, and preparation (ch. 2); (2) Moses' call at the burning bush (chs. 3—4); (3) the ten plagues (chs. 7—12); (4) the Passover (ch. 12); and (5) the Red Sea crossing (chs. 13—14). Israel's exodus from Egypt is viewed throughout the O.T. as the greatest experience of redemption in the old covenant. (B) Chs. 16—18 describe *Israel in the wilderness* en route to Mount Sinai. God guided His redeemed people by a cloud and pillar of fire and provided manna, quail, and water, while training them to walk by faith and obedience. (C) Chs. 19—40 record *Israel at Mount Sinai* receiving revelation involving (1) the covenant (ch. 19), (2) the Ten Commandments (ch. 20), and (3) the tabernacle and priesthood (chs. 25—31). The book concludes with the completion of the tabernacle and God's glory filling it (ch. 40).

Special Features

Five major features or emphases characterize Exodus. (1) It records the historical circumstances of Israel's birth as a nation. (2) It contains, in the Ten Commandments (ch. 20), God's summary of His moral law and righteous requirements for His people, and thus provides a foundation for Biblical ethics and morals. (3) It is the foremost O.T. book

describing the nature of God's redemptive grace and power in action. In O.T. terms, Exodus describes the supernatural character of God's deliverance of His people from the peril and bondage of sin, Satan, and the world. (4) The entire book is permeated with a majestic revelation of God as (a) glorious in attributes (truthful, merciful, faithful, holy, and omnipotent); (b) Lord over history and powerful kings; (c) Redeemer who enters into covenant with the redeemed; (d) just and righteous as revealed in His moral law and judgments; and (e) worthy of devout worship as the transcendent God who descends to "tabernacle" with His people. (5) Exodus emphasizes the how, what, and why of true worship that should necessarily follow God's redemption of His people.

New Testament Fulfillment

Throughout Exodus there is a foreshadowing of the redemption that is offered under the new covenant. The first Passover, the Red Sea crossing, and the giving of the Law at Mount Sinai are to the old covenant what Jesus' death, resurrection, and the giving of the Holy Spirit at Pentecost are to the new covenant. Types in Exodus which foreshadow Christ and redemption in the N.T. are (1) Moses, (2) the Passover, (3) the Red Sea crossing, (4) manna, (5) the rock and water, (6) the tabernacle, and (7) the high priest. The absolute moral demands of the Ten Commandments are repeated in the N.T. as requirements for new covenant believers.

Reading Exodus

In order to read the entire Old Testament in one year, the book of Exodus should be read in 21 days, according to the following schedule: ☐ 1–2 ☐ 3–5 ☐ 6–7 ☐ 8–9 ☐ 10–12 ☐ 13–14 ☐ 15 ☐ 16–17 ☐ 18–19 ☐ 20–21 ☐ 22–23 ☐ 24–25 ☐ 26–27 ☐ 28 ☐ 29–30 ☐ 31 ☐ 32–33 ☐ 34–35 ☐ 36–37 ☐ 38–39 ☐ 40

NOTES

Israel's growth and bondage

1 NOW [a]THESE *are* the names of
the children of Israel, which came
into Egypt; every man and his house-
hold came with Jacob.
2 Reuben, Simeon, Levi, and Judah,
3 Issachar, Zebulun, and Benjamin,
4 Dan, and Naphtali, Gad, and
Asher.
5 And all the souls that came out of
the [a]loins of Jacob were [b]seventy
souls: for Joseph was in Egypt *already.*
6 And [c]Joseph died, and all his
brethren, and all that generation.
7 ¶ [d]And the children of Israel
were fruitful, and increased abundant-
ly, and multiplied, and waxed exceed-
ing mighty; and the land was filled with
them.
8 Now there arose up a new king
over Egypt, which knew not Joseph.
9 And he said unto his people, Be-
hold, [e]the people of the children of Is-
rael *are* more and mightier than we:
10 [f]Come on, let us [g]deal wisely
with them; lest they multiply, and it
come to pass, that, when there falleth
out any war, they join also unto our en-
emies, and fight against us, and *so* get
them up out of the land.
11 Therefore they did set over them
taskmasters [h]to afflict them with
their [i]burdens. And they built for
Pharaoh treasure cities, Pithom [j]and
Raamses.
12 [b]But the more they afflicted
them, the more they multiplied and
grew. And they were grieved because
of the children of Israel.
13 And the Egyptians made the
children of Israel to serve with rigour:
14 And they [k]made their lives bit-
ter with hard bondage, [l]in mortar,
and in brick, and in all manner of ser-
vice in the field: all their service,
wherein they made them serve, *was*
with rigour.
15 ¶ And the king of Egypt spake to
the Hebrew midwives, of which the
name of the one *was* Shiphrah, and the
name of the other Puah:
16 And he said, When ye do the of-
fice of a midwife to the Hebrew women,
and see *them* upon the stools; if it *be* a
son, then ye shall kill him: but if it *be*
a daughter, then she shall live.
17 But the midwives [m]feared God,
and did not [n]as the king of Egypt com-
manded them, but saved the men chil-
dren alive.
18 And the king of Egypt called for
the midwives, and said unto them, Why
have ye done this thing, and have
saved the men children alive?
19 And [o]the midwives said unto
Pharaoh, Because the Hebrew women
are not as the Egyptian women; for
they *are* lively, and are delivered ere
the midwives come in unto them.
20 [p]Therefore God dealt well with
the midwives: and the people multi-
plied, and waxed very mighty.
21 And it came to pass, because the
midwives feared God, [q]that he made
them houses.
22 And Pharaoh charged all his
people, saying, [r]Every son that is
born ye shall cast into the river, and
every daughter ye shall save alive.

Moses' birth

2 AND THERE went [s]a man of the
house of Levi, and took *to wife* a
daughter of Levi.
2 And the woman conceived, and
bare a son: and [t]when she saw him

1:1 [a]Gen. 46:8 **1:5** [b]Gen. 46:26,27 **1:6** [c]Gen. 50:26 Acts 7:15 **1:7** [d]Gen. 46:3 Deut. 26:5 Ps. 105:24 Acts 7:17 **1:9** [e]Ps. 105:24 **1:10** [f]Ps. 83:3,4 [g]Prov. 16:25 Acts 7:19 **1:11** [h]Gen. 15:13 ch. 3:7 Deut. 26:6 [i]ch. 5:4,5 [j]Gen. 47:11 **1:14** [k]ch. 2:23 & 6:9 Num. 20:15 Acts 7:19,34 [l]Ps. 81:6

1:17 [m]Prov. 16:6 [n]Dan. 3:16,18 Acts 5:29 **1:19** [o]See Josh. 2:4 2 Sam. 17:19,20 **1:20** [p]Prov. 11:18 Eccl. 8:12 Is. 3:10 Heb. 6:10 **1:21** [q]See 1 Sam. 2:35 2 Sam. 7:11,13, 27,29 1 Ki. 11:38 Ps. 127:1 **1:22** [r]Acts 7:19 **2:1** [s]ch. 6:20 Num. 26:59 1 Chr. 23:14 **2:2** [t]Acts 7:20 Heb. 11:23

a Heb. *thigh* b Heb. *And as they afflicted them, so they multiplied*

1:1 THE CHILDREN OF ISRAEL. Israel, the father of the sons listed in vv. 2–6, is also called "Jacob" (see Gen. 32:28, note). His descendants became known as Israelites.

1:7 INCREASED ABUNDANTLY. The Israelites multiplied greatly according to the promises God made to Abraham, Isaac, and Jacob (Gen. 12:2; 17:2,6; 22:17; 48:4; cf. Acts 7:17), growing to such an extent that when they left Egypt they numbered about 600,000 men beside the women and children (12:37). God's prediction of oppression was also fulfilled (cf. v. 11; Gen. 15:13).

1:8 WHICH KNEW NOT JOSEPH. The book of Exodus continues the story of God's dealing with the children of Israel that began in Genesis. (1) The time gap between the death of Joseph (Gen. 50:26) and the beginning of Israel's persecution by the Egyptians (cf. v. 11) was approximately 220 years. (2) If the date of the exodus is set at around 1440 B.C., then the Pharaoh "which knew not Joseph" would probably be Thutmose I (1539–1514 B.C.) (see Acts 7:18). The Pharaoh of the exodus would be Amenhotep II (1447–1421 B.C.). The total time of the Israelites' stay in Egypt was 430 years (Ex. 12:40).

1:11 TASKMASTERS TO AFFLICT THEM. God permitted and used the oppression of Israel in order to separate them from the idolatry and immoral ways of Egypt, and to prepare them for their miraculous deliverance from Egypt and their faith relationship with Him (cf. Josh. 24:14; Ezek. 23:8).

2:2 A SON. The "son" referred to is Moses (cf.

that he *was a* goodly *child*, she hid him three months.

3 And when she could not longer hide him, she took for him an ark of bulrushes, and daubed it with slime and with pitch, and put the child therein; and she laid *it* in the flags by the river's brink.

4 [u]And his sister stood afar off, to wit what would be done to him.

5 ¶ And the [v]daughter of Pharaoh came down to wash *herself* at the river; and her maidens walked along by the river's side; and when she saw the ark among the flags, she sent her maid to fetch it.

6 And when she had opened *it*, she saw the child: and, behold, the babe wept. And she had compassion on him, and said, This *is one* of the Hebrews' children.

7 Then said his sister to Pharaoh's daughter, Shall I go and call to thee a nurse of the Hebrew women, that she may nurse the child for thee?

8 And Pharaoh's daughter said to her, Go. And the maid went and called the child's mother.

9 And Pharaoh's daughter said unto her, Take this child away, and nurse it for me, and I will give *thee* thy wages. And the woman took the child, and nursed it.

10 And the child grew, and she brought him unto Pharaoh's daughter, and he became [w]her son. And she called his name [c]Moses: and she said, Because I drew him out of the water.

Moses flees to Midian

11 ¶ And it came to pass in those days, [x]when Moses was grown, that he went out unto his brethren, and looked on their [y]burdens: and he spied an Egyptian smiting an Hebrew, one of his brethren.

12 And he looked this way and that way, and when he saw that *there was* no man, he [z]slew the Egyptian, and hid him in the sand.

13 And [a]when he went out the second day, behold, two men of the Hebrews strove together: and he said to him that did the wrong, Wherefore smitest thou thy fellow?

14 And he said, [b]Who made thee [d]a prince and a judge over us? intendest thou to kill me, as thou killedst the Egyptian? And Moses feared, and said, Surely this thing is known.

15 Now when Pharaoh heard this thing, he sought to slay Moses. But [c]Moses fled from the face of Pharaoh, and dwelt in the land of Midian: and he sat down by [d]a well.

16 [e]Now the [e]priest of Midian had seven daughters: [f]and they came and drew *water*, and filled the troughs to water their father's flock.

17 And the shepherds came and drove them away: but Moses stood up and helped them, and [g]watered their flock.

18 And when they came to [h]Reuel their father, he said, How *is it that* ye are come so soon today?

19 And they said, An Egyptian delivered us out of the hand of the shepherds, and also drew *water* enough for us, and watered the flock.

20 And he said unto his daughters, And where *is* he? why *is* it *that* ye have left the man? call him, that he may [i]eat bread.

2:4 [u]ch. 15:20 Num. 26:59
2:5 [v]Acts 7:21
2:10 [w]Acts 7:21
2:11 [x]Acts 7:23,24 Heb. 11:24-26
[y]ch. 1:11
2:12 [z]Acts 7:24
2:13 [a]Acts 7:26
2:14 [b]Acts 7:27,28
2:15 [c]Acts 7:29 Heb. 11:27 [d]Gen. 24:11 & 29:2
2:16 [e]ch. 3:1 [f]Gen. 24:11 1 Sam. 9:11
2:17 [g]Gen. 29:10
2:18 [h]Num. 10:29 Called also *Jethro*, or *Jether* ch. 3:1 & 4:18
2:20 [i]Gen. 31:54

[c]i.e. *Drawn out* [d]Heb. *a man, a prince;* see Gen. 13:8 [e]Or, *priest;* see Gen. 41:45

v. 10). His birth, escape from death, and the years of his youth were under the direction of God in order that he might deliver Israel from bondage. All believers need to know that God also works in their lives, using appropriate means to accomplish His will (see Mat. 2:13, note; Rom. 8:28, note).

2:6 HEBREWS. See Gen. 14:13, note.

2:11 MOSES. Moses' ministry in some ways foreshadows the ministry of Jesus Christ. (1) An attempt was made to destroy both Moses and Jesus as infants (1:16; Mat 2:13). (2) Both Moses and Christ ministered as prophet (Deut. 18:15,18; Acts 3:22; 7:37), priest (Ps. 99:6; Heb. 7:24), king (Deut. 33:4–5), and shepherd (Ex. 3:1; John 10:11–14). (3) They both suffered with God's people (Tit. 2:14; Heb. 11:25–26), delivered the people from slavery (Acts 7:35), and brought in a covenant (19:5; 34:10; Heb. 8:5–13).

2:12 HE SLEW THE EGYPTIAN. Moses' willingness to identify with God's people and to defend the Hebrews who were being oppressed demonstrated his faith in God. He rejected the passing pleasures of sin for the honor of suffering for God and with the people of God (cf. Acts 7:23–29; Heb. 11:24–29).

2:15 THE LAND OF MIDIAN. The Midianites, descendants of Abraham by Keturah, lived south and southeast of Canaan in Midian. Moses remained there for forty years (cf. 7:7; Acts 7:23,30), where God prepared him for his future task in this same region — the Sinai Desert. God did important work in his life in the wilderness (see article on THE PROVIDENCE OF GOD, p. 80).

21 And Moses was content to dwell
with the man: and he gave Moses
[j]Zipporah his daughter.
22 And she bare *him* a son, and he
called his name [k]Gershom:[f] for he
said, I have been [l]a stranger in a
strange land.
23 ¶ And it came to pass [m]in pro-
cess of time, that the king of Egypt
died: and the children of Israel
[n]sighed by reason of the bondage, and
they cried, and [o]their cry came up
unto God by reason of the bondage.
24 And God [p]heard their groaning,
and God [q]remembered his [r]covenant
with Abraham, with Isaac, and with Ja-
cob.
25 And God [s]looked upon the chil-
dren of Israel, and God [t]had[g] respect
unto *them*.

Moses and the burning bush

3 NOW MOSES kept the flock of
Jethro his father-in-law, [u]the
priest of Midian: and he led the flock
to the backside of the desert, and came
to [v]the mountain of God, *even* to Ho-
reb.
2 And [w]the angel of the LORD ap-
peared unto him in a flame of fire out
of the midst of a bush: and he looked,
and, behold, the bush burned with fire,
and the bush *was* not consumed.
3 And Moses said, I will now turn
aside, and see this [x]great sight, why
the bush is not burnt.
4 And when the LORD saw that he
turned aside to see, God called [y]unto
him out of the midst of the bush, and
said, Moses, Moses. And he said, Here
am I.
5 And he said, Draw not nigh hither:
[z]put off thy shoes from off thy feet, for
the place whereon thou standest *is*
holy ground.
6 Moreover he said, [a]I *am* the God
of thy father, the God of Abraham, the
God of Isaac, and the God of Jacob. And
Moses hid his face; for [b]he was afraid
to look upon God.
7 ¶ And the LORD said, [c]I have
surely seen the affliction of my people
which *are* in Egypt, and have heard
their cry [d]by reason of their taskmas-
ters; for [e]I know their sorrows;
8 And [f]I am come down to [g]deliv-
er them out of the hand of the Egyp-
tians, and to bring them up out of that
land [h]unto a good land and a large,
unto a land [i]flowing with milk and
honey; unto the place of [j]the Canaan-
ites, and the Hittites, and the Amo-
rites, and the Perizzites, and the Hi-
vites, and the Jebusites.
9 Now therefore, behold, [k]the cry
of the children of Israel is come unto
me: and I have also seen the [l]oppres-
sion wherewith the Egyptians oppress
them.
10 [m]Come now therefore, and I will
send thee unto Pharaoh, that thou

2:21 [j]ch. 18:2 **2:22** [k]ch. 18:3 [l]Acts 7:29 **2:23** [m]Acts 7:30 [n]Deut. 26:7 [o]ch. 3:9 Jas. 5:4 **2:24** [p]ch. 6:5 [q]ch. 6:5 Ps. 105:8,42 [r]Gen. 15:14 **2:25** [s]ch. 4:31 Luke 1:25 [t]ch. 3:7 **3:1** [u]ch. 2:16 [v]ch. 18:5 1 Ki. 19:8 **3:2** [w]Deut. 33:16 Acts 7:30 **3:3** [x]Acts 7:31 **3:4** [y]Deut. 33:16 **3:5** [z]Josh. 5:15 **3:6** [a]Gen. 28:13 ch. 4:5 Mat. 22:32 Acts 7:32 [b]See 1 Ki. 19:13 **3:7** [c]ch. 2:23-25 Ps. 106:44 [d]ch. 1:11 [e]Gen. 18:21 ch. 2:25 **3:8** [f]Gen. 50:24 [g]ch. 6:6,8 [h]Deut. 1:25 & 8:7-9 [i]ver. 17 ch. 13:5 Jer. 11:5 Ezek. 20:6 [j]Gen. 15:21

3:9 [k]ch. 2:23 [l]ch. 1:11,13,14 **3:10** [m]Mic. 6:4

[f] i.e. *A stranger here* [g] Heb. *knew*

2:23 THEIR CRY CAME UP UNTO GOD. After many years of oppression, the people of Israel began to cry unto God for help. When they turned to the Lord, He turned to them (vv. 23–25). Until this time many had been worshiping the gods of Egypt and had probably been calling upon them for help and deliverance (see Josh. 24:14; Ezek. 20:5–10).

3:1 MOSES KEPT THE FLOCK. Mere human education in Pharaoh's court was inadequate to equip Moses for God's work. Solitude with God and forty years of training and hardship tending sheep in the wilderness were also needed to prepare him for his future task of shepherding Israel through the desert (cf. 1 Cor. 2:14).

3:2 THE ANGEL OF THE LORD. The "angel of the LORD" is the Lord Himself (vv. 4–6). God also appeared to Abraham as the "angel of the LORD" (Gen. 22:11; see article on ANGELS AND THE ANGEL OF THE LORD, p. 368).

3:5 HOLY GROUND. God's initial revelation to Moses was of His holiness. Holiness means separation from sin and all evil and commitment to righteousness. Moses, as God's servant, had to remember constantly the fact that the God whom he served was holy—so holy that for a human to look fully upon Him would bring death (v. 6; 19:21; Is. 6:1–7; 1 Tim. 6:16; see article on SANCTIFICATION, p. 1982). God's initial revelation to Abraham was of His great power; here to Moses it was of His holiness. This illustrates the principle of progressive revelation (cf. Ex. 6:1–6; Heb. 1:1–2).

3:7 SEEN THE AFFLICTION OF MY PEOPLE. Just as God was concerned about the misery of His people in Egypt, He is aware of the affliction of all His people. He hears the cry of the afflicted, those who are troubled and oppressed. In such times God's people must cry out to Him that He might mercifully intervene in their behalf. Whether our oppression comes from circumstances, people, Satan, sin, or the world, God's comfort, grace, and help are more than sufficient to meet all our needs (see Rom. 8:32). In God's time He will rescue us (cf. Gen. 15:13).

3:8 MILK AND HONEY. This is a proverbial statement picturing agricultural abundance. The honey included honey from grapes or dates as well as from bees; the juice was boiled down to produce a thick syrup.

mayest bring forth my people the chil-
dren of Israel out of Egypt.
11 ¶ And Moses said unto God,
[n]Who *am* I, that I should go unto Phar-
aoh, and that I should bring forth the
children of Israel out of Egypt?
12 And he said, [o]Certainly I will be
with thee; and this *shall be* a token unto
thee, that I have sent thee: When thou
hast brought forth the people out of
Egypt, ye shall serve God upon this
mountain.
13 And Moses said unto God, Be-
hold, *when* I come unto the children of
Israel, and shall say unto them, The
God of your fathers hath sent me unto
you; and they shall say to me, What *is*
his name? what shall I say unto them?
14 And God said unto Moses, I AM
THAT I AM: and he said, Thus shalt
thou say unto the children of Israel, [p]I
AM hath sent me unto you.
15 And God said moreover unto Mo-
ses, Thus shalt thou say unto the chil-
dren of Israel, The LORD God of your
fathers, the God of Abraham, the God
of Isaac, and the God of Jacob, hath
sent me unto you: this *is* [q]my name for
ever, and this *is* my memorial unto all
generations.
16 Go, and [r]gather the elders of Is-
rael together, and say unto them, The
LORD God of your fathers, the God of
Abraham, of Isaac, and of Jacob, ap-
peared unto me, saying, [s]I have sure-
ly visited you, and *seen* that which is
done to you in Egypt:
17 And I have said, [t]I will bring
you up out of the affliction of Egypt
unto the land of the Canaanites, and
the Hittites, and the Amorites, and the

3:11 [n]See ch. 6:12; 1 Sam. 18:18
3:12 [o]Gen. 31:3; Josh. 1:5; Rom. 8:31
3:14 [p]ch. 6:3; John 8:58; Heb. 13:8
3:15 [q]Ps. 135:13
3:16 [r]ch. 4:29 [s]ch. 2:25; Luke 1:68
3:17 [t]Gen. 15:14,16
3:18 [u]ch. 4:31 [v]ch. 5:1,3 [w]Num. 23:3,4,15,16
3:19 [x]ch. 5:2
3:20 [y]ch. 6:6 & 9:15 [z]Deut. 6:22; Neh. 9:10; Acts 7:36 [a]ch. 12:31
3:21 [b]ch. 11:3 & 12:36; Prov. 16:7
3:22 [c]ch. 11:2 [d]Job 27:17; Prov. 13:22; Ezek. 39:10

Perizzites, and the Hivites, and the Jeb-
usites, unto a land flowing with milk
and honey.
18 And [u]they shall hearken to thy
voice: and [v]thou shalt come, thou and
the elders of Israel, unto the king of
Egypt, and ye shall say unto him, The
LORD God of the Hebrews hath [w]met
with us: and now let us go, we beseech
thee, three days' journey into the wil-
derness, that we may sacrifice to the
LORD our God.
19 ¶ And I am sure that the king of
Egypt [x]will not let you go, [h]no, not
by a mighty hand.
20 And I will [y]stretch out my hand,
and smite Egypt with [z]all my wonders
which I will do in the midst thereof:
and [a]after that he will let you go.
21 And [b]I will give this people fa-
vour in the sight of the Egyptians: and
it shall come to pass, that, when ye go,
ye shall not go empty:
22 [c]But every woman shall borrow
of her neighbour, and of her that so-
journeth in her house, jewels of silver,
and jewels of gold, and raiment: and ye
shall put *them* upon your sons, and
upon your daughters; and [d]ye shall
spoil [i]the Egyptians.

God equips Moses

4 AND MOSES answered and said,
But, behold, they will not believe
me, nor hearken unto my voice: for
they will say, The LORD hath not ap-
peared unto thee.
2 And the LORD said unto him, What

[h] Or, *but by strong hand* [i] Or, *Egypt*

3:12 I WILL BE WITH THEE. See next note for the significance of God's name "I am that I am" as it relates to His presence with His people.

3:14 I AM THAT I AM. The Lord gave Himself the personal name "I am that I am" (from this is derived the Heb. *Yahweh*), a Hebrew phrase that indicates action. God was in effect saying to Moses, "I wish to be known as the God who is present and active." (1) Inherent in the name *Yahweh* is the promise of the living presence of God Himself day by day with His people (cf. v. 12; see Gen. 2:4, note). It expresses His faithful love and care and His desire to redeem His people and live in fellowship with them. This corresponds with the fundamental promise of the covenant, "to be a God unto thee" (see Gen. 17:7, note; Ps. 46). The Lord states that this will be His name forever (v. 15). (2) It is significant that when Jesus Christ was born He was called Immanuel, meaning "God with us" (Mat. 1:23); He also called Himself by the name "I am" (John 8:58).

3:22 BORROW . . . SPOIL THE EGYPTIANS. "Borrow" is the ordinary word meaning "ask" and is so translated eighty-seven times in the KJV. The Israelites had been invited into Goshen and were made slaves unfairly. They deserved back wages, but they were not supposed to take anything by force. God would give them favor so when they asked for silver, gold, and clothing, the Egyptians would give to them abundantly. Thus, instead of sneaking out of Egypt like runaway slaves, they would be able to go out triumphantly, like a victorious army carrying the fruits of victory.

4:2–3 ROD . . . BECAME A SERPENT. Miraculous signs served the purpose of confirming the message and ministry of Moses (vv. 1–9). The manifestation of such signs is also God's intention for His people under the new covenant (see article on SIGNS OF BELIEVERS, p. 1516).

is that in thine hand? And he said, [e]A rod.

3 And he said, Cast it on the ground. And he cast it on the ground, and it became a serpent; and Moses fled from before it.

4 And the LORD said unto Moses, Put forth thine hand, and take it by the tail. And he put forth his hand, and caught it, and it became a rod in his hand:

5 That they may [f]believe that [g]the LORD God of their fathers, the God of Abraham, the God of Isaac, and the God of Jacob, hath appeared unto thee.

6 ¶ And the LORD said furthermore unto him, Put now thine hand into thy bosom. And he put his hand into his bosom: and when he took it out, behold, his hand *was* leprous [h]as snow.

7 And he said, Put thine hand into thy bosom again. And he put his hand into his bosom again; and plucked it out of his bosom, and, behold, [i]it was turned again as his *other* flesh.

8 And it shall come to pass, if they will not believe thee, neither hearken to the voice of the first sign, that they will believe the voice of the latter sign.

9 And it shall come to pass, if they will not believe also these two signs, neither hearken unto thy voice, that thou shalt take of the water of the river, and pour *it* upon the dry *land:* and [j]the water which thou takest out of the river **j**shall become blood upon the dry *land.*

10 ¶ And Moses said unto the LORD, O my Lord, I *am* not **k**eloquent, neither **l**heretofore, nor since thou hast spoken unto thy servant: but [k]I *am* slow of speech, and of a slow tongue.

11 And the LORD said unto him, [l]Who hath made man's mouth? or who maketh the dumb, or deaf, or the seeing, or the blind? have not I the LORD?

12 Now therefore go, and I will be [m]with thy mouth, and teach thee what thou shalt say.

13 And he said, O my Lord, [n]send, I pray thee, by the hand *of him whom* thou **m**wilt send.

14 And the anger of the LORD was kindled against Moses, and he said, *Is* not Aaron the Levite thy brother? I know that he can speak well. And also, behold, [o]he cometh forth to meet thee: and when he seeth thee, he will be glad in his heart.

15 And [p]thou shalt speak unto him, and [q]put words in his mouth: and I will be with thy mouth, and with his mouth, and [r]will teach you what ye shall do.

16 And he shall be thy spokesman unto the people: and he shall be, *even* he shall be to thee instead of a mouth, and [s]thou shalt be to him instead of God.

17 And thou shalt take [t]this rod in thine hand, wherewith thou shalt do signs.

Moses returns to Egypt

18 ¶ And Moses went and returned to **n**Jethro his father-in-law, and said unto him, Let me go, I pray thee, and return unto my brethren which *are* in Egypt, and see whether they be yet alive. And Jethro said to Moses, Go in peace.

19 And the LORD said unto Moses in Midian, Go, return into Egypt: for [u]all the men are dead which sought thy life.

20 And Moses took his wife and his sons, and set them upon an ass, and he returned to the land of Egypt: and Moses took [v]the rod of God in his hand.

21 And the LORD said unto Moses, When thou goest to return into Egypt, see that thou do all those [w]wonders before Pharaoh, which I have put in thine hand: but [x]I will harden his

4:2 [e]ver. 17,20 **4:5** [f]ch. 19:9 [g]ch. 3:15 **4:6** [h]Num. 12:10 2 Ki. 5:27 **4:7** [i]Num. 12:13,14 Deut. 32:39 **4:9** [j]ch. 7:19 **4:10** [k]ch. 6:12 Jer. 1:6 **4:11** [l]Ps. 94:9 **4:12** [m]Is. 50:4 Jer. 1:9 Mat. 10:19 Mark 13:11 Luke 12:11,12 & 21:14,15 **4:13** [n]See Jonah 1:3 **4:14** [o]ver. 27 1 Sam. 10:2,3,5 **4:15** [p]ch. 7:1,2 [q]Num. 23:5,12,16 [r]Deut. 5:31 **4:16** [s]ch. 7:1 **4:17** [t]ver. 2 **4:19** [u]ch. 2:15,23 Mat. 2:20 **4:20** [v]Num. 20:8,9 **4:21** [w]ch. 3:20 [x]ch. 7:3,13 & 9:12,35 Deut. 2:30 Josh. 11:20 Is. 63:17 John 12:40

j Heb. *shall be and shall be* **k** Heb. *a man of words* **l** Heb. *since yesterday, nor since the third day* **m** Or, *shouldest* **n** Heb. *Jether*

4:10 I *AM* NOT ELOQUENT. Moses, in his reluctance to accept God's calling, pointed out his limitation in speaking; God promised to give him help and power (vv. 11–17). When God calls us to a task, He will furnish the means and ability to fulfill that task (cf. 2 Cor. 3:5–6; 4:11–12).

4:11 WHO MAKETH THE . . . BLIND. God has the power to make someone deaf or blind, or to heal the deaf or blind. It does not mean that every person who is mute, deaf, or blind has become so due to the direct desire, decision, and act of God. Such conditions, along with all disease and sickness, are originally the result of Satan's activity and the entrance of sin into the world through Adam (Gen. 3:1–24). They do not necessarily occur because the individual affected has sinned (see John 9:2–3; see article on DIVINE HEALING, p. 1418).

4:21 I WILL HARDEN HIS HEART. See Ex. 7:3, note.

heart, that he shall not let the people go.

22 And thou shalt say unto Pharaoh, Thus saith the LORD, [y]Israel *is* my son, [z]*even* my firstborn:

23 And I say unto thee, Let my son go, that he may serve me: and if thou refuse to let him go, behold, [a]I will slay thy son, *even* thy firstborn.

24 ¶ And it came to pass by the way in the inn, that the LORD [b]met him, and sought to [c]kill him.

25 Then Zipporah took [d]a sharp [o]stone, and cut off the foreskin of her son, and [p]cast *it* at his feet, and said, Surely a bloody husband *art* thou to me.

26 So he let him go: then she said, A bloody husband *thou art*, because of the circumcision.

27 ¶ And the LORD said to Aaron, Go into the wilderness [e]to meet Moses. And he went, and met him in [f]the mount of God, and kissed him.

28 And Moses told [g]Aaron all the words of the LORD who had sent him, and all the [h]signs which he had commanded him.

29 ¶ And Moses and Aaron [i]went and gathered together all the elders of the children of Israel:

30 [j]And Aaron spake all the words which the LORD had spoken unto Moses, and did the signs in the sight of the people.

31 And the people [k]believed: and when they heard that the LORD had [l]visited the children of Israel, and that he [m]had looked upon their affliction, then [n]they bowed their heads and worshipped.

Pharaoh oppresses Israel

5 AND AFTERWARD Moses and Aaron went in, and told Pharaoh, Thus saith the LORD God of Israel, Let my people go, that they may hold [o]a feast unto me in the wilderness.

2 And Pharaoh said, [p]Who *is* the LORD, that I should obey his voice to let Israel go? I know not the LORD, [q]neither will I let Israel go.

3 And they said, [r]The God of the Hebrews hath met with us: let us go, we pray thee, three days' journey into the desert, and sacrifice unto the LORD our God; lest he fall upon us with pestilence, or with the sword.

4 And the king of Egypt said unto them, Wherefore do ye, Moses and Aaron, let the people from their works? get you unto your [s]burdens.

5 And Pharaoh said, Behold, the people of the land now *are* [t]many, and ye make them rest from their burdens.

6 And Pharaoh commanded the same day the [u]taskmasters of the people, and their officers, saying,

7 Ye shall no more give the people straw to make brick, as heretofore: let them go and gather straw for themselves.

8 And the tale of the bricks, which they did make heretofore, ye shall lay upon them; ye shall not diminish *aught* thereof: for they *be* idle; therefore they cry, saying, Let us go *and* sacrifice to our God.

9 [q]Let there more work be laid upon the men, that they may labour therein; and let them not regard vain words.

10 ¶ And the taskmasters of the people went out, and their officers, and they spake to the people, saying, Thus saith Pharaoh, I will not give you straw.

4:22 [y]Hos. 11:1 Rom. 9:4 2 Cor. 6:18 [z]Jer. 31:9 Jas. 1:18
4:23 [a]ch. 11:5 & 12:29
4:24 [b]Num. 22:22 [c]Gen. 17:14
4:25 [d]Josh. 5:2,3
4:27 [e]ver. 14 [f]ch. 3:1
4:28 [g]ver. 15,16 [h]ver. 8,9
4:29 [i]ch. 3:16
4:30 [j]ver. 16
4:31 [k]ver. 8,9 ch. 3:18 [l]ch. 3:16 [m]ch. 2:25 & 3:7 [n]Gen. 24:26 1 Chr. 29:20
5:1 [o]ch. 10:9
5:2 [p]2 Ki. 18:35 Job 21:15 [q]ch. 3:19
5:3 [r]ch. 3:18
5:4 [s]ch. 1:11
5:5 [t]ch. 1:7,9
5:6 [u]ch. 1:11

[o] Or, *knife* [p] Heb. *made it touch* [q] Heb. *Let the work be heavy upon the men*

4:22 ISRAEL ... MY FIRSTBORN. "Firstborn" indicates a special love and relationship with God. God claimed Israel as His son—His firstborn. Later in a narrowing of the sonship theme, God claimed the Davidic dynasty as His son (2 Sam. 7:14; Ps. 2:7), and still later, in a further narrowing, He claimed Jesus as His Son—His firstborn (Luke 1:35; 3:22; Heb. 1:5–13).

4:24 THE LORD . . . SOUGHT TO KILL HIM. Moses had neglected to perform the covenant sign of circumcision in the case of his own son. This was seen as a clear sign of disobedience on the part of Moses and his wife (vv. 24–25; see Gen. 17:11, note). Evidently God afflicted Moses with a potentially fatal illness until he had his son circumcised. This incident demonstrates that God's election of an individual continues only as long as he or she remains obedient (see 2 Pet. 1:10, note).

5:1 TOLD PHARAOH, THUS SAITH THE LORD GOD OF ISRAEL. The narrative of the exodus is basically a conflict between two gods: the Lord and Pharaoh, who in Egyptian religion was believed to be an incarnation of the sun god Re. Pharaoh questioned the power of the God of Israel (v. 2); after all, he had enslaved Israel and therefore had to be more powerful than Israel's God. The ten plagues were the Lord's method of demonstrating to His people that He was more powerful than any or all Egyptian gods; the Nile, the sun, and frogs, for example, were all Egyptian deities.

11 Go ye, get you straw where ye can find it: yet not aught of your work shall be diminished.

12 So the people were scattered abroad throughout all the land of Egypt to gather stubble instead of straw.

13 And the taskmasters hasted *them,* saying, Fulfil your works, [r]*your* daily tasks, as when there was straw.

14 And the officers of the children of Israel, which Pharaoh's taskmasters had set over them, were beaten, *and* demanded, Wherefore have ye not fulfilled your task in making brick both yesterday and today, as heretofore?

15 ¶ Then the officers of the children of Israel came and cried unto Pharaoh, saying, Wherefore dealest thou thus with thy servants?

16 There is no straw given unto thy servants, and they say to us, Make brick: and, behold, thy servants *are* beaten; but the fault *is* in thine own people.

17 But he said, Ye *are* idle, *ye are* idle: therefore ye say, Let us go *and* do sacrifice to the LORD.

18 Go therefore now, *and* work; for there shall no straw be given you, yet shall ye deliver the tale of bricks.

19 And the officers of the children of Israel did see *that* they *were* in evil *case,* after it was said, Ye shall not minish *aught* from your bricks of your daily task.

20 ¶ And they met Moses and Aaron, who stood in the way, as they came forth from Pharaoh:

21 [v]And they said unto them, The LORD look upon you, and judge; because ye have made our savour [s]to be abhorred in the eyes of Pharaoh, and in the eyes of his servants, to put a sword in their hand to slay us.

5:21
[v]ch. 6:9

6:1
[w]ch. 3:19
[x]ch. 12:31,33,39

6:3
[y]Gen. 17:1 & 35:11 & 48:3
[z]ch. 3:14 Ps. 83:18 John 8:58

6:4
[a]Gen. 15:18
[b]Gen. 28:4

6:5
[c]ch. 2:24

6:6
[d]ch. 3:17 Deut. 26:8

God's promise of deliverance

22 And Moses returned unto the LORD, and said, Lord, wherefore hast thou *so* evil entreated this people? why *is* it *that* thou hast sent me?

23 For since I came to Pharaoh to speak in thy name, he hath done evil to this people; [t]neither hast thou delivered thy people at all.

6 THEN THE LORD said unto Moses, Now shalt thou see what I will do to Pharaoh: for [w]with a strong hand shall he let them go, and with a strong hand [x]shall he drive them out of his land.

2 And God spake unto Moses, and said unto him, I *am* [u]the LORD:

3 And I appeared unto Abraham, unto Isaac, and unto Jacob, by *the name of* [y]God Almighty, but by my name [z]JEHOVAH was I not known to them.

4 [a]And I have also established my covenant with them, [b]to give them the land of Canaan, the land of their pilgrimage, wherein they were strangers.

5 And [c]I have also heard the groaning of the children of Israel, whom the Egyptians keep in bondage; and I have remembered my covenant.

6 Wherefore say unto the children of Israel, I *am* the LORD, and [d]I will bring you out from under the burdens

[r] Heb. *a matter of a day in his day* [s] Heb. *to stink;* see Gen. 34:30; 2 Sam. 10:6 [t] Heb. *delivering thou hast not delivered* [u] Or, *JEHOVAH*

5:22 WHY *IS* IT *THAT* THOU HAST SENT ME? Moses either ignored or forgot what God had told him earlier about Pharaoh's responses (3:19–20; 4:21). He was disappointed because his obedience to God was bringing trouble and not immediate success. Often believers under the new covenant forget that God's Word has said that "we must through much tribulation enter into the kingdom of God" (Acts 14:22; cf. John 16:33; 1 Thes. 3:3; 2 Tim. 3:12).

5:23 NEITHER HAST THOU DELIVERED THY PEOPLE. The fulfilling of God's promise of deliverance seemed more unlikely than ever, for the situation was becoming worse rather than better (v. 21). (1) Through these disheartening circumstances, God wanted to teach the people that His deliverance and miraculous power are often preceded by unfavorable conditions and great difficulties that give little reason for hope. (2) Through times of disappointment, the believer must continue to walk by faith in God and His word, trusting God to work out His will in His own time (see Rom. 8:28, note; see article on THE PROVIDENCE OF GOD, p. 80).

6:3 BY MY NAME JEHOVAH WAS I NOT KNOWN TO THEM. The Lord did not make Himself known to Abraham, Isaac, and Jacob by the name "LORD" (Heb. *Yahweh*, see Gen. 2:4, note). (1) This does not mean that the patriarchs were not acquainted with the name, but only that they did not receive the full revelation of the meaning of that name (see 3:14, note). They had indeed used and heard God's name as *Yahweh*, but they had known Him in their experience more as "God Almighty," a name that emphasizes His power to perform or fulfill what He has promised (see Gen. 17:1, note). (2) *Yahweh* is His covenant-keeping name, especially centered on redemption (cf. v. 6). Abraham did not live to see the covenant of Gen. 15 fulfilled, but he did experience God's power.

of the Egyptians, and I will rid you out
of their bondage, and I will [e]redeem
you with a stretched out arm, and with
great judgments:
7 And I will [f]take you to me for a
people, and [g]I will be to you a God:
and ye shall know that I *am* the LORD
your God, which bringeth you out
[h]from under the burdens of the Egyp-
tians.
8 And I will bring you in unto the
land, concerning the which I did
[i]swear[v] to give it to Abraham, to
Isaac, and to Jacob; and I will give it
you for an heritage: I *am* the LORD.
9 ¶ And Moses spake so unto the
children of Israel: [j]but they heark-
ened not unto Moses for [w]anguish of
spirit, and for cruel bondage.
10 And the LORD spake unto Moses,
saying,
11 Go in, speak unto Pharaoh king
of Egypt, that he let the children of Is-
rael go out of his land.
12 And Moses spake before the
LORD, saying, Behold, the children of
Israel have not hearkened unto me;
how then shall Pharaoh hear me,
[k]who *am* of uncircumcised lips?
13 And the LORD spake unto Moses
and unto Aaron, and gave them a
charge unto the children of Israel, and
unto Pharaoh king of Egypt, to bring
the children of Israel out of the land of
Egypt.

The descendants of Israel

14 ¶ These *be* the heads of their fa-
thers' houses: [l]The sons of Reuben
the firstborn of Israel; Hanoch, and
Pallu, Hezron, and Carmi: these *be* the
families of Reuben.

6:6 [e]Deut. 7:8 1 Chr. 17:21
6:7 [f]Deut. 4:20 2 Sam. 7:24 [g]ch. 29:45,46 Rev. 21:7 [h]ch. 5:4,5
6:8 [i]Gen. 15:18 & 26:3
6:9 [j]ch. 5:21
6:12 [k]ver. 30 ch. 4:10 Jer. 1:6
6:14 [l]Gen. 46:9 1 Chr. 5:3
6:15 [m]Gen. 46:10 1 Chr. 4:24
6:16 [n]Gen. 46:11 Num. 3:17
6:17 [o]1 Chr. 6:17
6:18 [p]1 Chr. 6:2,18
6:19 [q]1 Chr. 6:19 & 23:21
6:20 [r]ch. 2:1,2
6:21 [s]1 Chr. 6:37,38
6:22 [t]Lev. 10:4
6:23 [u]Ruth 4:19,20 Mat. 1:4 [v]Lev. 10:1 Num. 3:2 & 26:60
6:24 [w]Num. 26:11

15 [m]And the sons of Simeon; Jemu-
el, and Jamin, and Ohad, and Jachin,
and Zohar, and Shaul the son of a
Canaanitish woman: these *are* the fam-
ilies of Simeon.
16 ¶ And these *are* the names of
[n]the sons of Levi according to their
generations; Gershon, and Kohath,
and Merari: and the years of the life of
Levi *were* an hundred thirty and seven
years.
17 [o]The sons of Gershon; Libni,
and Shimi, according to their families.
18 And [p]the sons of Kohath; Am-
ram, and Izhar, and Hebron, and Uzzi-
el: and the years of the life of Kohath
were an hundred thirty and three years.
19 And [q]the sons of Merari; Maha-
li and Mushi: these *are* the families of
Levi according to their generations.
20 And [r]Amram took him Joche-
bed his father's sister to wife; and she
bare him Aaron and Moses: and the
years of the life of Amram *were* an hun-
dred and thirty and seven years.
21 ¶ And [s]the sons of Izhar; Ko-
rah, and Nepheg, and Zichri.
22 And [t]the sons of Uzziel; Misha-
el, and Elzaphan, and Zithri.
23 And Aaron took him Elisheba,
daughter of [u]Amminadab, sister of
Naashon, to wife; and she bare him
[v]Nadab, and Abihu, Eleazar, and Itha-
mar.
24 And the [w]sons of Korah; Assir,
and Elkanah, and Abiasaph: these *are*
the families of the Korhites.
25 And Eleazar Aaron's son took

[v] Heb. *lift up my hand;* see Gen. 14:22; Deut. 32:40 [w] Heb. *shortness,* or, *straitness*

6:7 I WILL TAKE YOU TO ME FOR A PEOPLE, AND I WILL BE TO YOU A GOD. Vv. 6–7 declare the essential meaning and purpose of the exodus and the making of the covenant at Sinai (19:5): the Lord promised to redeem Israel from bondage (v. 6), adopt them as His people (v. 7), and be their God (v. 7); they in return would promise to do the will of their Redeemer (chs. 19–23).

(1) These verses emphasize that Israel was helplessly held in bondage by a force they could not hope to overcome. Only by the Lord their God could they be freed (vv. 5–6). Because of God's covenant with the patriarchs and His love for His people, He would indeed deliver them (vv. 6–8; Deut. 7:7–8).

(2) God's redemption of Israel from Egypt served as a major basis for the transfer of ownership of Israel to Himself. Israel was God's by creation and election (4:22), and now by redemption.

(3) Historically the redemption of Israel out of Egypt anticipates the greater redemption of the sinful human race through Jesus' death on the cross. All believers are redeemed by Christ from the power of Satan, sin, and the world. They now belong to Him and can trust in His love and promises (see article on BIBLICAL WORDS FOR SALVATION, p. 1726).

6:9 THEY HEARKENED NOT UNTO MOSES. God did not bring Israel out of Egypt because they had great faith, but because of His grace and His faithfulness to His promises (Gen. 17:1–8; 50:24). In the beginning their faith was weak, but through the ten plagues, by which God revealed Himself, His power, and His concern for Israel, He built up their faith until they were able to trust Him in obedience (Ex. 12:28). In other words, God delivered them by grace through faith.

him *one* of the daughters of Putiel to wife; and [x]she bare him Phinehas: these *are* the heads of the fathers of the Levites according to their families.

26 These *are* that Aaron and Moses, to whom the LORD said, Bring out the children of Israel from the land of Egypt according to their [y]armies.

27 These *are* they which spake to Pharaoh king of Egypt, [z]to bring out the children of Israel from Egypt: these *are* that Moses and Aaron.

Aaron to speak for Moses

28 ¶ And it came to pass on the day *when* the LORD spake unto Moses in the land of Egypt,

29 That the LORD spake unto Moses, saying, I *am* the LORD: [a]speak thou unto Pharaoh king of Egypt all that I say unto thee.

30 And Moses said before the LORD, Behold, [b]I *am* of uncircumcised lips, and how shall Pharaoh hearken unto me?

7 AND THE LORD said unto Moses, See, I have made thee [c]a god to Pharaoh: and Aaron thy brother shall be [d]thy prophet.

2 Thou [e]shalt speak all that I command thee: and Aaron thy brother shall speak unto Pharaoh, that he send the children of Israel out of his land.

3 And [f]I will harden Pharaoh's heart, and [g]multiply my [h]signs and my wonders in the land of Egypt.

4 But Pharaoh shall not hearken unto you, [i]that I may lay my hand upon Egypt, and bring forth mine armies, *and* my people the children of Israel, out of the land of Egypt [j]by great judgments.

5 And the Egyptians [k]shall know that I *am* the LORD, when I [l]stretch forth mine hand upon Egypt, and bring out the children of Israel from among them.

6 And Moses and Aaron [m]did as the LORD commanded them, so did they.

7 And Moses *was* [n]fourscore years old, and Aaron fourscore and three years old, when they spake unto Pharaoh.

The rod becomes a serpent

8 ¶ And the LORD spake unto Moses and unto Aaron, saying,

9 When Pharaoh shall speak unto you, saying, [o]Show a miracle for you: then thou shalt say unto Aaron, [p]Take thy rod, and cast *it* before Pharaoh, *and* it shall become a serpent.

10 ¶ And Moses and Aaron went in unto Pharaoh, and they did so [q]as the LORD had commanded: and Aaron cast down his rod before Pharaoh, and before his servants, and it [r]became a serpent.

11 Then Pharaoh also [s]called the wise men and [t]the sorcerers: now the magicians of Egypt, they also [u]did in like manner with their enchantments.

12 For they cast down every man his rod, and they became serpents: but Aaron's rod swallowed up their rods.

Judg. 6:25-32

13 And he hardened Pharaoh's heart, that he hearkened not unto them; as the LORD had said.

The water becomes blood

14 ¶ And the LORD said unto Moses, [v]Pharaoh's heart *is* hardened, he refuseth to let the people go.

15 Get thee unto Pharaoh in the morning; lo, he goeth out unto the water; and thou shalt stand by the river's

6:25 [x]Num. 25:7,11 Josh. 24:33 **6:26** [y]ch. 7:4 & 12:17,51 Num. 33:1 **6:27** [z]ver. 13 ch. 32:7 & 33:1 Ps. 77:20 **6:29** [a]ver. 11 ch. 7:2 **6:30** [b]ver. 12 ch. 4:10 **7:1** [c]ch. 4:16 Jer. 1:10 [d]ch. 4:16 **7:2** [e]ch. 4:15 **7:3** [f]ch. 4:21 [g]ch. 11:9 [h]ch. 4:7 **7:4** [i]ch. 10:1 & 11:9 [j]ch. 6:6 **7:5** [k]ver. 17 ch. 8:22 & 14:4,18 Ps. 9:16 [l]ch. 3:20 **7:6** [m]ver. 2 **7:7** [n]Deut. 29:5 & 31:2 & 34:7 Acts 7:23,30 **7:9** [o]Is. 7:11 John 2:18 & 6:30 [p]ch. 4:2,17 **7:10** [q]ver. 9 [r]ch. 4:3 **7:11** [s]Gen. 41:8 [t]2 Tim. 3:8 [u]ver. 22 ch. 8:7,18 **7:14** [v]ch. 8:15 & 10:1,20,27

7:3 I WILL HARDEN PHARAOH'S HEART. God hardened Pharaoh's heart as punishment because his heart was already hard and opposed to God (cf. 5:2; 7:13–14,22; 8:15,19,32; 9:7). (1) In adding to the hardness of Pharaoh's heart, God was acting on a divine principle that applies to all the unrepentant. When a person persists in rebellion against God and His word, God finally ordains that the heart be hardened (see Rom. 9:18, note). This principle is seen in God giving people up to their sinful desires (see Rom. 1:24, note), and in His sending a delusion on those who refuse to love the truth of His Word (see 2 Thes. 2:10, note). (2) Notice that the judgments of the early plagues softened Pharaoh's heart a little. When God removed each plague, his heart was hardened again, i.e., Pharaoh hardened his own heart whenever God showed mercy (e.g., 8:8–15).

7:12 THEY BECAME SERPENTS. (1) The magicians' rods also turned into serpents, an act accomplished by demonic power. Egypt was fully addicted to magic, occultism, spiritism, and sorcery as their religion. By Aaron's rod swallowing up their rods, however, the God of Israel was demonstrating that His power was greater than the power of the gods of Egypt. (2) In the final days of this age, before the return of Christ, Satan will display miracles through false ministers within the visible church and through the antichrist (cf. 2 Tim. 3:8; see articles on THE GREAT TRIBULATION, p. 1456, and THE AGE OF THE ANTICHRIST, p. 1896). Believers must not assume, therefore, that miraculous occurrences are always evidence that the Lord is working (see Rev. 16:14, note; 19:20, note).

brink against he come; and [w]the rod which was turned to a serpent shalt thou take in thine hand.

16 And thou shalt say unto him, [x]The LORD God of the Hebrews hath sent me unto thee, saying, Let my people go, [y]that they may serve me in the wilderness: and, behold, hitherto thou wouldest not hear.

17 Thus saith the LORD, In this [z]thou shalt know that I *am* the LORD: behold, I will smite with the rod that *is* in mine hand upon the waters which *are* in the river, and [a]they shall be turned [b]to blood.

18 And the fish that *is* in the river shall die, and the river shall stink; and the Egyptians shall [c]loathe to drink of the water of the river.

19 ¶ And the LORD spake unto Moses, Say unto Aaron, Take thy rod, and [d]stretch out thine hand upon the waters of Egypt, upon their streams, upon their rivers, and upon their ponds, and upon all their [x]pools of water, that they may become blood; and *that* there may be blood throughout all the land of Egypt, both in *vessels of* wood, and in *vessels of* stone.

20 And Moses and Aaron did so, as the LORD commanded; and he [e]lifted up the rod, and smote the waters that *were* in the river, in the sight of Pharaoh, and in the sight of his servants; and all the [f]waters that *were* in the river were turned to blood.

21 And the fish that *was* in the river died; and the river stank, and the Egyptians [g]could not drink of the water of the river; and there was blood throughout all the land of Egypt.

22 [h]And the magicians of Egypt did so with their enchantments: and Pharaoh's heart was hardened, neither did he hearken unto them; [i]as the LORD had said.

23 And Pharaoh turned and went into his house, neither did he set his heart to this also.

24 And all the Egyptians digged round about the river for water to drink; for they could not drink of the water of the river.

The plague of frogs

25 And seven days were fulfilled, after that the LORD had smitten the river.

8 AND THE LORD spake unto Moses, Go unto Pharaoh, and say unto him, Thus saith the LORD, Let my people go, [j]that they may serve me.

2 And if thou [k]refuse to let *them* go, behold, I will smite all thy borders with [l]frogs:

3 And the river shall bring forth frogs abundantly, which shall go up and come into thine house, and into [m]thy bedchamber, and upon thy bed, and into the house of thy servants, and upon thy people, and into thine ovens, and into thy [y]kneadingtroughs:

4 And the frogs shall come up both on thee, and upon thy people, and upon all thy servants.

5 ¶ And the LORD spake unto Moses, Say unto Aaron, [n]Stretch forth thine hand with thy rod over the streams, over the rivers, and over the ponds, and cause frogs to come up upon the land of Egypt.

6 And Aaron stretched out his hand over the waters of Egypt; and [o]the frogs came up, and covered the land of Egypt.

7 [p]And the magicians did so with their enchantments, and brought up frogs upon the land of Egypt.

8 ¶ Then Pharaoh called for Moses and Aaron, and said, [q]Entreat the LORD, that he may take away the frogs from me, and from my people; and I

7:15 [w]ver. 10 ch. 4:2,3
7:16 [x]ch. 3:18 [y]ch. 3:12,18 & 5:1,3
7:17 [z]ver. 5 ch. 5:2 [a]ch. 4:9 [b]Rev. 16:4,6
7:18 [c]ver. 24
7:19 [d]ch. 8:5,6,16 & 9:22 & 10:12,21 & 14:21,26
7:20 [e]ch. 17:5 [f]Ps. 78:44 & 105:29
7:21 [g]ver. 18
7:22 [h]ver. 11 [i]ver. 3
8:1 [j]ch. 3:12,18
8:2 [k]ch. 7:14 & 9:2 [l]Rev. 16:13
8:3 [m]Ps. 105:30
8:5 [n]ch. 7:19
8:6 [o]Ps. 78:45 & 105:30
8:7 [p]ch. 7:11
8:8 [q]ch. 9:28 & 10:17

[x] Heb. *gathering of their waters* [y] Or, *dough*

7:20 HE ... SMOTE THE WATERS. The ten miraculous plagues of Egypt (7:20; 8:2,16,21; 9:3, 9,18; 10:4,21; 11:5) had several purposes. (1) They were signs and wonders to show Egypt as well as Israel that the Lord is God above all gods and human beings (v. 5; 9:14–15; 10:2; 15:11), and to exalt God's name "throughout all the earth" (9:16).

(2) They were performed to establish Israel's faith and to convince them of God's power, love, and supremacy. Israel was hereafter to tell of these events to their children in order that they might serve the Lord as God (6:7; 10:2; 12:42).

(3) They demonstrated God's power over the gods of Egypt and all the forces of evil on behalf of His people (12:12; see previous note).

(4) They were judgments of God upon Egypt and her gods in order to compel Pharaoh to let God's people go (8:2,21; 11:1; 12:31–33; cf. Num. 33:4).

8:2 FROGS. In ancient Egypt frogs represented gods and were thus sacred. The Lord, through this plague, was attacking the gods of Egypt in order to show that His power was far superior to all the supernatural powers of Egypt.

will let the people go, that they may do sacrifice unto the LORD.

9 And Moses said unto Pharaoh, [z]Glory over me: [a]when shall I entreat for thee, and for thy servants, and for thy people, [b]to destroy the frogs from thee and thy houses, *that* they may remain in the river only?

10 And he said, [c]Tomorrow. And he said, *Be it* according to thy word: that thou mayest know that [r]*there is* none like unto the LORD our God.

11 And the frogs shall depart from thee, and from thy houses, and from thy servants, and from thy people; they shall remain in the river only.

12 And Moses and Aaron went out from Pharaoh: and Moses [s]cried unto the LORD because of the frogs which he had brought against Pharaoh.

13 And the LORD did according to the word of Moses; and the frogs died out of the houses, out of the villages, and out of the fields.

14 And they gathered them together upon heaps: and the land stank.

15 But when Pharaoh saw that there was [t]respite, [u]he hardened his heart, and hearkened not unto them; as the LORD had said.

The plague of lice

16 ¶ And the LORD said unto Moses, Say unto Aaron, Stretch out thy rod, and smite the dust of the land, that it may become lice throughout all the land of Egypt.

17 And they did so; for Aaron stretched out his hand with his rod, and smote the dust of the earth, and [v]it became lice in man, and in beast; all the dust of the land became lice throughout all the land of Egypt.

18 And [w]the magicians did so with their enchantments to bring forth lice, but they [x]could not: so there were lice upon man, and upon beast.

19 Then the magicians said unto Pharaoh, This *is* [y]the finger of God: and Pharaoh's [z]heart was hardened, and he hearkened not unto them; as the LORD had said.

The swarms of flies

20 ¶ And the LORD said unto Moses, [a]Rise up early in the morning, and stand before Pharaoh; lo, he cometh forth to the water; and say unto him, Thus saith the LORD, [b]Let my people go, that they may serve me.

21 Else, if thou wilt not let my people go, behold, I will send [d]swarms *of flies* upon thee, and upon thy servants, and upon thy people, and into thy houses: and the houses of the Egyptians shall be full of swarms *of flies*, and also the ground whereon they *are*.

22 And [c]I will sever in that day the land of Goshen, in which my people dwell, that no swarms *of flies* shall be there; to the end thou mayest know that I *am* the LORD in the midst of the earth.

23 And I will put [e]a division between my people and thy people: [f]tomorrow shall this sign be.

24 And the LORD did so; and [d]there came a grievous swarm *of flies* into the house of Pharaoh, and *into* his servants' houses, and into all the land of Egypt: the land was [g]corrupted by reason of the swarm *of flies*.

25 ¶ And Pharaoh called for Moses and for Aaron, and said, Go ye, sacrifice to your God in the land.

26 And Moses said, It is not meet so to do; for we shall sacrifice [e]the abomination of the Egyptians to the LORD our God: lo, shall we sacrifice the abomination of the Egyptians before their eyes, and will they not stone us?

27 We will go [f]three days' journey into the wilderness, and sacrifice to the LORD our God, as [g]he shall command us.

28 And Pharaoh said, I will let you go, that ye may sacrifice to the LORD your God in the wilderness; only ye shall not go very far away: [h]entreat for me.

29 And Moses said, Behold, I go out from thee, and I will entreat the LORD that the swarms *of flies* may depart from Pharaoh, from his servants, and from his people, tomorrow: but let not Pharaoh [i]deal deceitfully any more in not letting the people go to sacrifice to the LORD.

8:10 [r]ch. 9:14 Deut. 33:26 2 Sam. 7:22 1 Chr. 17:20 Is. 46:9 Jer. 10:6,7 **8:12** [s]ver. 30 ch. 9:33 & 10:18 & 32:11 Jas. 5:16-18 **8:15** [t]Eccl. 8:11 [u]ch. 7:14 **8:17** [v]Ps. 105:31 **8:18** [w]ch. 7:11 [x]Dan. 5:8 2 Tim. 3:8,9 **8:19** [y]1 Sam. 6:3,9 Ps. 8:3 Mat. 12:28 Luke 11:20 [z]ver. 15 **8:20** [a]ch. 7:15 [b]ver. 1 **8:22** [c]ch. 9:4,6,26 & 10:23 & 11:6,7 & 12:13 **8:24** [d]Ps. 78:45 & 105:31 **8:26** [e]Gen. 43:32 & 46:34 Deut. 7:25,26 & 12:31 **8:27** [f]ch. 3:18 [g]ch. 3:12 **8:28** [h]ver. 8 ch. 9:28 1 Ki. 13:6 **8:29** [i]ver. 15

[z] Or, *Have this honour over me* [a] Or, *against when* [b] Heb. *to cut off* [c] Or, *Against tomorrow* [d] Or, *a mixture of noisome beasts* [e] Heb. *a redemption* [f] Or, *by tomorrow* [g] Or, *destroyed*

8:18–19 THIS *IS* THE FINGER OF GOD. By this saying, the Egyptian magicians were admitting that God's power was far superior to theirs.

30 And Moses went out from Pharaoh, and [j]entreated the LORD.

31 And the LORD did according to the word of Moses; and he removed the swarms *of flies* from Pharaoh, from his servants, and from his people; there remained not one.

32 And Pharaoh [k]hardened his heart at this time also, neither would he let the people go.

The death of Egyptian cattle

9 THEN THE LORD said unto Moses, [l]Go in unto Pharaoh, and tell him, Thus saith the LORD God of the Hebrews, Let my people go, that they may serve me.

2 For if thou [m]refuse to let *them* go, and wilt hold them still,

3 Behold, the [n]hand of the LORD is upon thy cattle which *is* in the field, upon the horses, upon the asses, upon the camels, upon the oxen, and upon the sheep: *there shall be* a very grievous murrain.

4 And [o]the LORD shall sever between the cattle of Israel and the cattle of Egypt: and there shall nothing die of all *that is* the children's of Israel.

5 And the LORD appointed a set time, saying, Tomorrow the LORD shall do this thing in the land.

6 And the LORD did that thing on the morrow, and [p]all the cattle of Egypt died: but of the cattle of the children of Israel died not one.

7 And Pharaoh sent, and, behold, there was not one of the cattle of the Israelites dead. And [q]the heart of Pharaoh was hardened, and he did not let the people go.

The plague of boils and blains

8 ¶ And the LORD said unto Moses and unto Aaron, Take to you handfuls of ashes of the furnace, and let Moses sprinkle it toward the heaven in the sight of Pharaoh.

9 And it shall become small dust in all the land of Egypt, and shall be [r]a boil breaking forth *with* blains upon man, and upon beast, throughout all the land of Egypt.

10 And they took ashes of the furnace, and stood before Pharaoh; and Moses sprinkled it up toward heaven; and it became [s]a boil breaking forth *with* blains upon man, and upon beast.

11 And the [t]magicians could not stand before Moses because of the boils; for the boil was upon the magicians, and upon all the Egyptians.

12 And the LORD hardened the heart of Pharaoh, and he hearkened not unto them; [u]as the LORD had spoken unto Moses.

The plague of hail and fire

13 ¶ And the LORD said unto Moses, [v]Rise up early in the morning, and stand before Pharaoh, and say unto him, Thus saith the LORD God of the Hebrews, Let my people go, that they may serve me.

14 For I will at this time send all my plagues upon thine heart, and upon thy servants, and upon thy people; [w]that thou mayest know that *there is* none like me in all the earth.

15 For now I will [x]stretch out my hand, that I may smite thee and thy people with pestilence; and thou shalt be cut off from the earth.

16 And in very deed for [y]this *cause* have I [h]raised thee up, for to show *in* thee my power; and that my name may be declared throughout all the earth.

17 As yet exaltest thou thyself against my people, that thou wilt not let them go?

18 Behold, tomorrow about this time I will cause it to rain a very grievous hail, such as hath not been in Egypt since the foundation thereof even until now.

19 Send therefore now, *and* gather thy cattle, and all that thou hast in the field; *for upon* every man and beast which shall be found in the field, and shall not be brought home, the hail

8:30 [j]ver. 12
8:32 [k]ver. 15 ch. 4:21
9:1 [l]ch. 8:1
9:2 [m]ch. 8:2
9:3 [n]ch. 7:4
9:4 [o]ch. 8:22
9:6 [p]Ps:78:50
9:7 [q]ch. 7:14 & 8:32
9:9 [r]Rev. 16:2
9:10 [s]Deut. 28:27
9:11 [t]ch. 8:18,19 2 Tim. 3:9
9:12 [u]ch. 4:21
9:13 [v]ch. 8:20
9:14 [w]ch. 8:10
9:15 [x]ch. 3:20
9:16 [y]See ch. 14:17 Prov. 16:4 Rom. 9:17 1 Pet. 2:9

[h] Heb. *made thee stand*

9:3 THY CATTLE. The Egyptians worshiped bulls and other animals. They believed that gods revealed themselves through these animals and were the Egyptians' protectors. Thus, the plague on the livestock was again a direct attack on the polytheism and idolatry of the Egyptians (cf. 20:4–6; 32).

9:6 ALL THE CATTLE OF EGYPT DIED. Livestock that were protected in stables, evidently were not killed (cf. v. 3,19; 11:5; 12:29; 13:15).

9:15–16 FOR THIS *CAUSE* I HAVE RAISED THEE UP. Pharaoh deserved to be cut off when he first said, "Who *is* the LORD, that I should obey his voice" (5:2). Instead of destroying him, however, God permitted him to experience plague after plague so that he would know God has power and that not only he but the entire world would witness God's power.

shall come down upon them, and they
shall die.
20 He that feared the word of the
LORD among the servants of Pharaoh
made his servants and his cattle flee
into the houses:
21 And he that regarded not the
word of the LORD left his servants and
his cattle in the field.
22 ¶ And the LORD said unto Moses,
Stretch forth thine hand toward heav-
en, that there may be [z]hail in all the
land of Egypt, upon man, and upon
beast, and upon every herb of the field,
throughout the land of Egypt.
23 And Moses stretched forth his
rod toward heaven: and [a]the LORD
sent thunder and hail, and the fire ran
along upon the ground; and the LORD
rained hail upon the land of Egypt.
24 So there was hail, and fire min-
gled with the hail, very grievous, such
as there was none like it in all the land
of Egypt since it became a nation.
25 And the hail smote throughout
all the land of Egypt all that *was* in the
field, both man and beast; and the hail
[b]smote every herb of the field, and
brake every tree of the field.
26 [c]Only in the land of Goshen,
where the children of Israel *were,* was
there no hail.
27 ¶ And Pharaoh sent, and called
for Moses and Aaron, and said unto
them, [d]I have sinned this time: [e]the
LORD *is* righteous, and I and my people
are wicked.
28 [f]Entreat the LORD (for *it is*
enough) that there be no *more*
[i]mighty thunderings and hail; and I
will let you go, and ye shall stay no
longer.
29 And Moses said unto him, As
soon as I am gone out of the city, I will
[g]spread abroad my hands unto the
LORD; *and* the thunder shall cease, nei-
ther shall there be any more hail; that
thou mayest know how that the
[h]earth *is* the LORD's.
30 But as for thee and thy servants,
[i]I know that ye will not yet fear the
LORD God.
31 And the flax and the barley was
smitten: [j]for the barley *was* in the ear,
and the flax *was* bolled.
32 But the wheat and the rie were
not smitten: for they *were* [j]not
grown up.
33 And Moses went out of the city
from Pharaoh, and [k]spread abroad his
hands unto the LORD: and the thunders
and hail ceased, and the rain was not
poured upon the earth.
34 And when Pharaoh saw that the
rain and the hail and the thunders were
ceased, he sinned yet more, and hard-
ened his heart, he and his servants.
35 And [l]the heart of Pharaoh was
hardened, neither would he let the chil-
dren of Israel go; as the LORD had spo-
ken [k]by Moses.

The plague of locusts

10 AND THE LORD said unto Mo-
ses, Go in unto Pharaoh: [m]for
I have hardened his heart, and the
heart of his servants, [n]that I might
show these my signs before him:
2 And that [o]thou mayest tell in the
ears of thy son, and of thy son's son,
what things I have wrought in Egypt,
and my signs which I have done among
them; that ye may know how that I *am*
the LORD.
3 And Moses and Aaron came in
unto Pharaoh, and said unto him, Thus
saith the LORD God of the Hebrews,
How long wilt thou refuse to [p]humble
thyself before me? let my people go,
that they may serve me.
4 Else, if thou refuse to let my peo-
ple go, behold, tomorrow will I bring
the [q]locusts into thy coast:
5 And they shall cover the [r]face[l]
of the earth, that one cannot be able to
see the earth: and [s]they shall eat the
residue of that which is escaped, which
remaineth unto you from the hail, and
shall eat every tree which groweth for
you out of the field:
6 And they shall fill thy houses, and
the houses of all thy servants, and the
houses of all the Egyptians; which nei-
ther thy fathers, nor thy fathers' fa-

Num. 10:29

9:22 [z]Rev. 16:21 **9:23** [a]Josh. 10:11 Ps. 18:13 & 78:47 & 105:32 & 148:8 Is. 30:30 Ezek. 38:22 Rev. 8:7 **9:25** [b]Ps. 105:33 **9:26** [c]ch. 8:22 & 9:4,6 & 10:23 & 11:7 & 12:13 Is. 32:18,19 **9:27** [d]ch. 10:16 [e]2 Chr. 12:6 Lam. 1:18 **9:28** [f]ch. 8:8,28 & 10:17 Acts 8:24 **9:29** [g]1 Ki. 8:22,38 Ps. 143:6 Is. 1:15 [h]Ps. 24:1 1 Cor. 10:26,28 **9:30** [i]Is. 26:10 **9:31** [j]Ruth 1:22 & 2:23 **9:33** [k]ver. 29 ch. 8:12 **9:35** [l]ch. 4:21 **10:1** [m]ch. 4:21 & 7:14 [n]ch. 7:4 **10:2** [o]Deut. 4:9 Ps. 44:1 & 71:18 & 78:5 Joel 1:3 **10:3** [p]1 Ki. 21:29 Job 42:6 Jas. 4:10 **10:4** [q]Prov. 30:27 Rev. 9:3 **10:5** [r]ver. 15 [s]ch. 9:32 Joel 1:4 & 2:25

[i] Heb. *voices of God* [j] Heb. *hidden,* or, *dark*
[k] Heb. *by the hand of Moses* [l] Heb. *eye*

10:2 TELL IN THE EARS OF THY SON. God showed great concern that the children in Israel would come to know who He was and would accept Him as their God in faith and obedience. God chose Abraham with the purpose that he should teach his children to keep the way of the Lord (see Gen. 18:19, note). Later He commanded Israel to be diligent in teaching their children the words of the Lord (see Deut. 6:7, note). God knew that if His people failed in this solemn duty, the next generation would turn from Him and His righteous ways.

thers have seen, since the day that they were upon the earth unto this day. And he turned himself, and went out from Pharaoh.

7 And Pharaoh's servants said unto him, How long shall this man be [t]a snare unto us? let the men go, that they may serve the LORD their God: knowest thou not yet that Egypt is destroyed?

8 And Moses and Aaron were brought again unto Pharaoh: and he said unto them, Go, serve the LORD your God: *but* [m]who *are* they that shall go?

9 And Moses said, We will go with our young and with our old, with our sons and with our daughters, with our flocks and with our herds will we go; for [u]we *must hold* a feast unto the LORD.

10 And he said unto them, Let the LORD be so with you, as I will let you go, and your little ones: look *to it;* for evil *is* before you.

11 Not so: go now ye *that are* men, and serve the LORD; for that ye did desire. And they were driven out from Pharaoh's presence.

12 ¶ And the LORD said unto Moses, [v]Stretch out thine hand over the land of Egypt for the locusts, that they may come up upon the land of Egypt, and [w]eat every herb of the land, *even* all that the hail hath left.

13 And Moses stretched forth his rod over the land of Egypt, and the LORD brought an east wind upon the land all that day, and all *that* night; *and* when it was morning, the east wind brought the locusts.

14 And [x]the locusts went up over all the land of Egypt, and rested in all the coasts of Egypt: very grievous *were they;* [y]before them there were no such locusts as they, neither after them shall be such.

15 For they [z]covered the face of the whole earth, so that the land was darkened; and they [a]did eat every herb of the land, and all the fruit of the trees which the hail had left: and there remained not any green thing in the trees, or in the herbs of the field, through all the land of Egypt.

16 ¶ Then Pharaoh [n]called for Moses and Aaron in haste; and he said, [b]I have sinned against the LORD your God, and against you.

17 Now therefore forgive, I pray thee, my sin only this once, and [c]entreat the LORD your God, that he may take away from me this death only.

18 And he [d]went out from Pharaoh, and entreated the LORD.

19 And the LORD turned a mighty strong west wind, which took away the locusts, and [o]cast them [e]into the Red sea; there remained not one locust in all the coasts of Egypt.

20 But the LORD [f]hardened Pharaoh's heart, so that he would not let the children of Israel go.

The plague of darkness

21 ¶ And the LORD said unto Moses, [g]Stretch out thine hand toward heaven, that there may be darkness over the land of Egypt, [p]even darkness *which* may be felt.

22 And Moses stretched forth his hand toward heaven; and there was a [h]thick darkness in all the land of Egypt three days:

23 They saw not one another, neither rose any from his place for three days: [i]but all the children of Israel had light in their dwellings.

24 ¶ And Pharaoh called unto Moses, and [j]said, Go ye, serve the LORD; only let your flocks and your herds be stayed: let your [k]little ones also go with you.

25 And Moses said, Thou must give [q]us also sacrifices and burnt offerings, that we may sacrifice unto the LORD our God.

26 Our cattle also shall go with us; there shall not an hoof be left behind; for thereof must we take to serve the LORD our God; and we know not with what we must serve the LORD, until we come thither.

27 ¶ But the LORD [l]hardened Pharaoh's heart, and he would not let them go.

28 And Pharaoh said unto him, Get thee from me, take heed to thyself, see

10:7 [t]ch. 23:33 Josh. 23:13 1 Sam. 18:21 Eccl. 7:26 1 Cor. 7:35
10:9 [u]ch. 5:1
10:12 [v]ch. 7:19 [w]ver. 4,5
10:14 [x]Ps. 78:46 & 105:34 [y]Joel 2:2
10:15 [z]ver. 5 [a]Ps. 105:35
10:16 [b]ch. 9:27
10:17 [c]ch. 9:28 1 Ki. 13:6
10:18 [d]ch. 8:30
10:19 [e]Joel 2:20
10:20 [f]ch. 4:21 & 11:10
10:21 [g]ch. 9:22
10:22 [h]Ps. 105:28
10:23 [i]ch. 8:22
10:24 [j]ver. 8 [k]ver. 10
10:27 [l]ver. 20 ch. 4:21 &14:4,8

[m] Heb. *who, and who* [n] Heb. *hastened to call* [o] Heb. *fastened* [p] Heb. *that* one *may feel darkness* [q] Heb. *into our hands*

10:9 WE *MUST* HOLD A FEAST. The request to be allowed to make a three-day journey to worship the Lord was sincere. But it was also given without any assurance that the Israelites would return. Pharaoh seemed to have understood this (vv. 11,24).

my face no more; for in *that* day thou
seest my face thou shalt die.
29 And Moses said, Thou hast spo-
ken well, [m]I will see thy face again no
more.

The last plague

11 AND THE LORD said unto Mo-
ses, Yet will I bring one plague
more upon Pharaoh, and upon Egypt;
afterwards he will let you go hence:
[n]when he shall let *you* go, he shall
surely thrust you out hence altogether.
2 Speak now in the ears of the peo-
ple, and let every man borrow of his
neighbour, and every woman of her
neighbour, [o]jewels of silver, and jew-
els of gold.
3 [p]And the LORD gave the people fa-
vour in the sight of the Egyptians.
Moreover the man [q]Moses *was* very
great in the land of Egypt, in the sight
of Pharaoh's servants, and in the sight
of the people.
4 And Moses said, Thus saith the
LORD, [r]About midnight will I go out
into the midst of Egypt:
5 And [s]all the firstborn in the land
of Egypt shall die, from the firstborn of
Pharaoh that sitteth upon his throne,
even unto the firstborn of the maidser-
vant that *is* behind the mill; and all the
firstborn of beasts.
6 [t]And there shall be a great cry
throughout all the land of Egypt, such
as there was none like it, nor shall be
like it any more.
7 [u]But against any of the children
of Israel [v]shall not a dog move his
tongue, against man or beast: that ye
may know how that the LORD doth put
a difference between the Egyptians
and Israel.
8 And [w]all these thy servants shall
come down unto me, and bow down
themselves unto me, saying, Get thee
out, and all the people [r]that follow

10:29 [m]Heb. 11:27
11:1 [n]ch. 12:31,33,39
11:2 [o]ch. 3:22 & 12:35
11:3 [p]ch. 3:21 & 12:36 Ps. 106:46 [q]2 Sam. 7:9 Esth. 9:4
11:4 [r]ch. 12:12,23,29
11:5 [s]ch. 12:12,29 Amos 4:10
11:6 [t]ch. 12:30 Amos 5:17
11:7 [u]ch. 8:22 [v]Josh. 10:21
11:8 [w]ch. 12:33
11:9 [x]ch. 3:19 & 7:4 & 10:1 [y]ch. 7:3
11:10 [z]ch. 10:20,27 Rom. 2:5 & 9:22
12:2 [a]ch. 13:4 Deut. 16:1
12:5 [b]Lev. 22:19-21 Mal. 1:8,14 Heb. 9:14
12:6 [c]Lev. 23:5 Num. 9:3 Deut. 16:1,6

thee: and after that I will go out. And
he went out from Pharaoh in [s]a great
anger.
9 And the LORD said unto Moses,
[x]Pharaoh shall not hearken unto you;
that [y]my wonders may be multiplied
in the land of Egypt.
10 And Moses and Aaron did all
these wonders before Pharaoh: [z]and
the LORD hardened Pharaoh's heart, so
that he would not let the children of
Israel go out of his land.

The Passover

12:14–20pp — Lev. 23:4–8; Num. 28:16–25; Deut. 16:1–8

12 AND THE LORD spake unto Mo-
ses and Aaron in the land of
Egypt, saying,
2 [a]This month *shall be* unto you the
beginning of months: it *shall be* the first
month of the year to you.
3 ¶ Speak ye unto all the congrega-
tion of Israel, saying, In the tenth *day*
of this month they shall take to them
every man a [t]lamb, according to the
house of *their* fathers, a lamb for an
house:
4 And if the household be too little
for the lamb, let him and his neighbour
next unto his house take *it* according
to the number of the souls; every man
according to his eating shall make your
count for the lamb.
5 Your lamb shall be [b]without
blemish, a male [u]of the first year: ye
shall take *it* out from the sheep, or
from the goats:
6 And ye shall keep it up until the
[c]fourteenth day of the same month:
and the whole assembly of the congre-
gation of Israel shall kill it [v]in the
evening.
7 And they shall take of the blood,

[r] Heb. *that is at thy feet;* see Judg. 4:10 & 8:5 [s] Heb. *heat of anger* [t] Or, *kid* [u] Heb. *son of a year* [v] Heb. *between the two evenings*

11:5 FIRSTBORN . . . SHALL DIE. God Himself would bring the final judgment upon the Egyptians; the firstborn son of every family would die. This would be a terrible blow to the Egyptians since the firstborn normally carried on the family's hopes, ambitions, and goals. God's judgment was His just recompense because of their sin and wickedness. Their cruelty to the Hebrews and the drowning of the male babies were in themselves a persecution of God's "firstborn" (4:22). They were reaping what they had sown.

12:2 THE FIRST MONTH OF THE YEAR. Ch. 12 describes the Feast of the Passover (vv. 1–14,21–28) and the Feast of Unleavened Bread (vv. 15–20). These celebrations were based on the historical events of the first Passover at the time of the exodus (chs. 12–14). Because the Passover marked a new beginning for Israel, the month in which it occurred (March-April in our calendar) became "the first month" of a new year for the nation. It was intended to remind the people that their very existence as God's people was the result of their deliverance from Egypt by His mighty redemptive acts.

12:7 THEY SHALL TAKE OF THE BLOOD. The Passover lamb and its blood point to Jesus

and strike *it* on the two side posts and
on the upper door post of the houses,
wherein they shall eat it.
8 And they shall eat the flesh in that
night, roast with fire, and [d]unleav-
ened bread; *and* with bitter *herbs* they
shall eat it.
9 Eat not of it raw, nor sodden at all
with water, but [e]roast *with* fire; his
head with his legs, and with the purte-
nance thereof.
10 [f]And ye shall let nothing of it
remain until the morning; and that
which remaineth of it until the morning
ye shall burn with fire.
11 ¶ And thus shall ye eat it; *with*
your loins girded, your shoes on your
feet, and your staff in your hand; and
ye shall eat it in haste: [g]it *is* the LORD's
passover.
12 For I [h]will pass through the
land of Egypt this night, and will smite
all the firstborn in the land of Egypt,
both man and beast; and [i]against all
the [w]gods of Egypt I will execute judg-
ment: [j]I *am* the LORD.
13 And the blood shall be to you for
a token upon the houses where ye *are*:
and when I see the blood, I will pass
over you, and the plague shall not be
upon you [x]to destroy *you*, when I
smite the land of Egypt.

12:8 [d]ch. 34:25 Deut. 16:3 1 Cor. 5:8
12:9 [e]Deut. 16:7
12:10 [f]ch. 23:18 & 34:25
12:11 [g]Deut. 16:5
12:12 [h]ch. 11:4,5 Amos 5:17 [i]Num. 33:4 [j]ch. 6:2
12:14 [k]ch. 13:9 [l]Lev. 23:4,5 2 Ki. 23:21 [m]ver. 24,43 ch. 13:10
12:15 [n]ch. 13:6,7 & 23:15 Lev. 23:5,6 Deut. 16:3,8 1 Cor. 5:7 [o]Gen. 17:14 Num. 9:13
12:16 [p]Lev. 23:7,8 Num. 28:18,25
12:17 [q]ch. 13:3
12:18 [r]Lev. 23:5 Num. 28:16

14 And this day shall be unto you
[k]for a memorial; and ye shall keep it
a [l]feast to the LORD throughout your
generations; ye shall keep it a feast
[m]by an ordinance for ever.
15 [n]Seven days shall ye eat un-
leavened bread; even the first day ye
shall put away leaven out of your
houses: for whosoever eateth leavened
bread from the first day until the sev-
enth day, [o]that soul shall be cut off
from Israel.
16 And in the first day *there shall be*
[p]an holy convocation, and in the sev-
enth day there shall be an holy convo-
cation to you; no manner of work shall
be done in them, save *that* which every
[y]man must eat, that only may be done
of you.
17 And ye shall observe *the feast of*
unleavened bread; for [q]in this self-
same day have I brought your armies
out of the land of Egypt: therefore shall
ye observe this day in your generations
by an ordinance for ever.
18 ¶ [r]In the first *month*, on the
fourteenth day of the month at even, ye
shall eat unleavened bread, until the

[w] Or, *princes* [x] Heb. *for a destruction*
[y] Heb. *soul*

Christ and His shed blood as "the Lamb of God, which taketh away the sin of the world" (John 1:29,36; cf. Is. 53:7; Acts 8:32–35; 1 Cor. 5:7; Rev. 13:8; see article on THE PASSOVER, p. 110).

12:8 UNLEAVENED BREAD; *AND* WITH BITTER *HERBS*. For the symbolism of the unleavened bread, see article on THE PASSOVER, p. 110. The "bitter *herbs*" would bring to remembrance the bitter time of their slavery in Egypt (cf. Rom. 6:21).

12:11 *WITH* YOUR LOINS GIRDED, YOUR SHOES ON YOUR FEET. This imagery points to the need for decisive and immediate obedience from God's people.

12:14 AN ORDINANCE FOR EVER. The Passover feast was supposed to be an annual festival. Regular participation in the Lord's Supper for the N.T. Christian continues the prophetic significance of the Passover (see 1 Cor. 11:24–25, note; cf. 5:7–8; see article on THE PASSOVER, p. 110).

12:15 THAT SOUL SHALL BE CUT OFF. Willful, deliberate rejection of God's instruction resulted in divine judgment (see also v. 19). The guilty person was removed from the covenant people by death (e.g., 31:14) or expulsion. Likewise, under the new covenant, those of God's people who reject the Lordship of Christ and choose to partake of the leaven of sin are excluded from grace and salvation in Christ (see article on PERSONAL APOSTASY, p. 1946).

12:17 *THE FEAST OF* THE UNLEAVENED BREAD. Vv. 15–20 describe the Feast of Unleavened Bread that Israel was to observe after they entered Canaan. This feast represented the consecration of God's people, based on their redemption from Egypt. In this context "leaven" or yeast, an agent that causes fermentation, symbolized sin, and "unleavened bread" symbolized repentance, repudiation of sin, and consecration to God (see 13:7, note).

(1) All leaven (i.e., worldly corruption and sin) had to be removed from the Israelites' houses. This implied that their lives and homes as believers had to be set apart for God (vv. 15–16) because of what He had done for them (13:8–9). The N.T. establishes a link between this Feast of the Unleavened Bread and believers in Jesus purging out "malice and wickedness" and living in "sincerity and truth" (1 Cor. 5:6–8).

(2) Failure to turn from sin in true faith towards God resulted in divine judgment, i.e., being cut off from God's covenant of promise and salvation (see previous note).

(3) The Passover meal signaled the beginning of the Feast of Unleavened Bread (vv. 6,18), foreshadowing the importance of faith in and obedience to the sacrificial Lamb. Believers committed themselves to repentance from sin and the endeavor to live for God in humble gratitude.

one and twentieth day of the month at even.

19 [s]Seven days shall there be no leaven found in your houses: for whosoever eateth that which is leavened, even that soul shall be cut off from the congregation of Israel, whether he be a stranger, or born in the land.

20 Ye shall eat nothing leavened; in all your habitations shall ye eat unleavened bread.

21 ¶ Then Moses called for all the elders of Israel, and said unto them, [t]Draw out and take you a [z]lamb according to your families, and kill the passover.

22 [u]And ye shall take a bunch of hyssop, and dip *it* in the blood that *is* in the basin, and [v]strike the lintel and the two side posts with the blood that *is* in the basin; and none of you shall go out at the door of his house until the morning.

23 [w]For the LORD will pass through to smite the Egyptians; and when he seeth the blood upon the lintel, and on the two side posts, the LORD will pass over the door, and [x]will not suffer [y]the destroyer to come in unto your houses to smite *you*.

24 And ye shall observe this thing for an ordinance to thee and to thy sons for ever.

25 And it shall come to pass, when ye be come to the land which the LORD will give you, [z]according as he hath promised, that ye shall keep this service.

26 [a]And it shall come to pass, when your children shall say unto you, What mean ye by this service?

27 That ye shall say, [b]It *is* the sacrifice of the LORD's passover, who passed over the houses of the children of Israel in Egypt, when he smote the Egyptians, and delivered our houses. And the people [c]bowed the head and worshipped.

28 And the children of Israel went away, and [d]did as the LORD had commanded Moses and Aaron, so did they.

29 ¶ [e]And it came to pass, that at midnight [f]the LORD smote all the firstborn in the land of Egypt, [g]from the firstborn of Pharaoh that sat on his throne unto the firstborn of the captive that *was* in the [a]dungeon; and all the firstborn of cattle.

30 And Pharaoh rose up in the night, he, and all his servants, and all the Egyptians; and there was a [h]great cry in Egypt; for *there was* not a house where *there was* not one dead.

The exodus begins

31 ¶ And [i]he called for Moses and Aaron by night, and said, Rise up, *and* get you forth from among my people, [j]both ye and the children of Israel; and go, serve the LORD, as ye have said.

32 [k]Also take your flocks and your herds, as ye have said, and be gone; and [l]bless me also.

33 [m]And the Egyptians were urgent upon the people, that they might send them out of the land in haste; for they said, [n]We *be* all dead *men*.

34 And the people took their dough before it was leavened, their [b]kneadingtroughs being bound up in their clothes upon their shoulders.

35 And the children of Israel did according to the word of Moses; and they borrowed of the Egyptians [o]jewels of silver, and jewels of gold, and raiment:

36 [p]And the LORD gave the people favour in the sight of the Egyptians, so that they lent unto them *such things as they required*. And [q]they spoiled the Egyptians.

37 ¶ And [r]the children of Israel journeyed from [s]Rameses to Succoth, about [t]six hundred thousand on foot *that were* men, beside children.

38 And [c]a mixed multitude went up also with them; and flocks, and herds, *even* very much cattle.

39 And they baked unleavened cakes of the dough which they brought forth out of Egypt, for it was not leavened; because [u]they were thrust out of Egypt, and could not tarry, neither

12:19 [s]ch. 23:15 & 34:18
12:21 [t]ver. 3 Num. 9:4 Josh. 5:10 2 Ki. 23:21 Ezra 6:20 Mark 14:12-16
12:22 [u]Heb. 11:28 [v]ver. 7
12:23 [w]ver. 12,13 [x]Ezek. 9:6 Rev. 7:3 [y]2 Sam. 24:16 1 Cor. 10:10 Heb. 11:28
12:25 [z]ch. 3:8,17
12:26 [a]ch. 13:8,14 Deut. 32:7 Josh. 4:6
12:27 [b]ver. 11 [c]ch. 4:31
12:28 [d]Heb. 11:28
12:29 [e]ch. 11:4 [f]Num. 8:17 & 33:4 Ps. 78:51 & 105:36 [g]ch. 4:23 & 11:5
12:30 [h]ch. 11:6 Prov. 21:13 Amos 5:17
12:31 [i]ch. 11:1 Ps. 105:38 [j]ch. 10:9
12:32 [k]ch. 10:26 [l]Gen. 27:34
12:33 [m]ch. 11:8 Ps. 105:38 [n]Gen. 20:3
12:35 [o]ch. 3:22
12:36 [p]ch. 3:21 [q]Gen. 15:14 ch. 3:22 Ps. 105:37
12:37 [r]Num. 33:3,5 [s]Gen. 47:11 [t]Gen. 12:2 Num. 11:21
12:39 [u]ver. 33 ch. 6:1

[z] Or, *kid* [a] Heb. *house of the pit* [b] Or, *dough* [c] Heb. *a great mixture*

12:19 NO LEAVEN FOUND IN YOUR HOUSES. See 13:7, note.

12:26 WHAT MEAN YE BY THIS SERVICE? Parents were expected to use the Passover to teach their children the truth of how God had redeemed them from slavery and sin and made them a special people under His care and rule. Likewise, the Lord's Supper, the N.T. believers' "Passover," is designed to remind us of salvation in Christ and our redemption from sin and satanic bondage (see 1 Cor. 11:24–25, note).

THE PASSOVER

***Ex. 12:11** "And thus shall ye eat it; from your loins girded, your shoes on your feet, and your staff in your hand; and ye shall eat it in haste: it is the LORD's passover."*

HISTORICAL BACKGROUND. Since the time of Israel's departure out of Egypt about 1445 B.C., the Hebrew people (later called Jews) have been celebrating the Passover each year in the spring (generally near the time of Good Friday and Easter).

After more than four hundred years of bondage in Egypt, God determined to deliver the descendants of Abraham, Isaac, and Jacob from slavery. He raised up Moses and commissioned him to be the leader of the exodus (Ex. 3—4). In obedience to God's call, Moses confronted Pharaoh with God's mandate: "Let my people go." To impress upon him the seriousness of this message from the Lord, Moses, by God's power, called down plagues as judgments on the Egyptian nation. During several of these, Pharaoh agreed to let the Israelites go, but then reneged on his decision once the plague was lifted. The time came for the tenth and final plague, the one that would give the Egyptians no other choice than to drive the Israelites out. God sent an angel of death throughout Egypt to destroy "all the firstborn in the land of Egypt, both man and beast" (Ex. 12:12).

Since the Israelites were also living in Egypt, how could they escape the slaying angel? The Lord gave a specific command to His people; to obey it would bring His protection to each Hebrew family and firstborn son. Each family was to take a year-old male lamb without defect and kill it at twilight on the fourteenth day of the month Abib; smaller households could share a single lamb (Ex. 12:4). Some of the blood of the slain lamb was to be sprinkled on the two sides and on the top of the doorframe of their homes. When the angel of death went through the land, he would *pass over* those homes that had the blood sprinkled on them (hence the term *Passover*, from Heb. *pesah*, meaning "to jump past," "to pass by," or "to spare"). Thus by the blood of the slain lamb, the Israelites were spared the judgment of death that came to all the Egyptian firstborn. God commanded the sign of the blood not because He could not otherwise distinguish the Israelites from the Egyptians, but because He wanted to teach His people the importance of obedience and of blood redemption, thus preparing for "the Lamb of God," who centuries later would take away the sin of the world (John 1:29).

On that particular night the Israelites were supposed to be dressed and ready to leave (Ex 12:11). They were commanded to roast, not boil, the lamb, and to prepare unleavened bread (i.e., bread made without yeast) and bitter herbs. As night approached, they would then be ready to eat the food and depart in haste when the Egyptians came and begged them to leave their country. Everything happened as the Lord had spoken (Ex 12:29–36).

THE PASSOVER IN ISRAELITE/JEWISH HISTORY. From that moment in history, God's people celebrated the Passover every spring, in response to His command that the Passover be "an ordinance for ever" (Ex. 12:14). It was, however, a memorial sacrifice. Only the initial sacrifice in Egypt was an effective sacrifice. Before the temple was built, each Passover the Israelites gathered together in households, killed a lamb, removed all leaven from their homes, and ate bitter herbs. More important, they retold the story of the miraculous exodus of their ancestors from the land of Egypt and from slavery to Pharaoh. Thus from generation to generation, the Hebrew people remembered God's redemption and their deliverance from Egypt (see Ex. 12:26, note). Once the temple was built, God commanded that the Passover celebration and the killing of the lamb take place in Jerusalem (cf. Deut. 16:1–6). The O.T. records several times in which an especially significant Passover was celebrated in the holy city (e.g., 2 Ki. 23:21 -23; 2 Chr. 30:1–20; 35:1–19; Ezra 6:19–22).

The Passover was likewise observed by the Jews in N.T. times. The only incident from Jesus' boyhood recorded in the Scriptures occurred when His parents took Him to Jerusalem at twelve years old to celebrate the Passover (Luke 2:41–50). Later in life, Jesus regularly went to Jerusalem for the Passover (e.g., John 2:13). The last supper that Jesus ate with His disciples in Jerusalem, shortly before going to the cross, was a Passover meal (see Mat. 26:1–2,17–29). Jesus Himself was crucified on the Passover, as *the* Passover Lamb (cf. 1 Cor. 5:7) who delivers from sin and death all who believe.

The Jews today still celebrate the Passover, though its nature has changed somewhat. Since there is no longer a temple in Jerusalem where a lamb can be slain in obedience to Deut. 16:1–6, the contemporary Jewish feast (called the *Seder*) is no longer celebrated with a sacrificed lamb. But families still gather together, all yeast is ceremonially removed from Jewish homes, and the story of the exodus from Egypt is retold by the father of the household.

THE PASSOVER AND JESUS CHRIST. For Christians, the Passover contains rich prophetic symbolism that points forward to Jesus Christ. The N.T. explicitly teaches that the Jewish feasts are "a shadow of things to come" (Col. 2:16–17; Heb 10:1), i.e., redemption through the blood of Jesus Christ. Note the following in Ex. 12 that remind us of our Savior and His will for us. (1) The heart and soul of the Passover event was God's saving grace. God brought the Israelites out of Egypt not because they were such a worthy people but because He loved them and because He was faithful to His covenant (see Deut. 7:7–10). Similarly, the salvation we receive from Christ comes to us through the amazing grace of God (see Eph. 2:8–10; Tit. 3:4–5).

(2) The purpose of the blood applied on the door post was to save the firstborn son of each family from death. This blood points to Christ's shedding of His blood on the cross in order to save us from death and from God's wrath against sin (Ex. 12:13,23,27; Heb 9:22).

(3) The Passover lamb was a "sacrifice" (Ex. 12:27) that functioned as a substitute for the firstborn. This sacrifice points to Christ's death as a substitution for the believer's death (see Rom. 3:25, note). Paul explicitly calls Christ our Passover lamb who was sacrificed for us (1 Cor. 5:7).

(4) The male lamb that was marked for death had to be "without blemish" (Ex. 12:5); the lamb prefigures the sinlessness of Christ, the perfect Son of God (cf. John 8:46; Heb. 4:15).

(5) The eating of the lamb represented the identification of the Israelite community with the lamb's death, a death that saved them from physical death. Similarly, taking the Lord's Supper represents our participation in the death of Christ, a death that saves us from spiritual death (1 Cor. 10:16–17; 11:24–26). As in the case of the Passover, only the initial sacrifice, i.e., His death on the cross, was an effective sacrifice. We observe the Lord's Supper as a memorial of Him (i.e., "in remembrance," 1 Cor. 11:24).

(6) The sprinkling of the blood on the door posts was done in obedient faith (Ex. 12:28; cf. Heb. 11:28); this response of faith brought about redemption through the blood (Ex. 12:7,13). Salvation through Christ's blood is obtained only through "the obedience of faith" (Rom 16:26; cf. 1:5).

(7) The Passover lamb was to be eaten along with unleavened bread (Ex. 12:8). Since yeast in the Bible usually represents sin and corruption (see Ex. 13:7, note; Mat. 16:6, note; Mark 8:15, note), this unleavened bread represented the separation of the redeemed Israelites from Egypt, i.e., from the world and from sin (see Ex. 12:15, note). Similarly, God's redeemed people are called to separate themselves from the sinful world and to dedicate themselves to God alone (see articles on SPIRITUAL SEPARATION FOR BELIEVERS, p. 1814, and THE CHRISTIAN'S RELATIONSHIP TO THE WORLD, p. 2004).

had they prepared for themselves any
victual.
40 ¶ Now the sojourning of the chil-
dren of Israel, who dwelt in Egypt, *was*
[v]four hundred and thirty years.
41 And it came to pass at the end of
the four hundred and thirty years, even
the selfsame day it came to pass, that
all [w]the hosts of the LORD went out
from the land of Egypt.
42 It *is* [x]a night[d] to be much ob-
served unto the LORD for bringing them
out from the land of Egypt: this *is* that
night of the LORD to be observed of all
Ex. 14:13-14 the children of Israel in their genera-
tions.

The law of the Passover

43 ¶ And the LORD said unto Moses
and Aaron, This *is* [y]the ordinance of
the passover: There shall no stranger
eat thereof:
44 But every man's servant that is
bought for money, when thou hast
[z]circumcised him, then shall he eat
thereof.
45 [a]A foreigner and an hired ser-
vant shall not eat thereof.
46 In one house shall it be eaten;
thou shalt not carry forth aught of the
flesh abroad out of the house; [b]nei-
ther shall ye break a bone thereof.
47 [c]All the congregation of Israel
shall [e]keep it.
48 And [d]when a stranger shall so-
journ with thee, and will keep the pass-
over to the LORD, let all his males be
circumcised, and then let him come
near and keep it; and he shall be as one
that is born in the land: for no uncir-
cumcised person shall eat thereof.
49 [e]One law shall be to him that is

12:40 [v]Gen. 15:13 Acts 7:6 Gal. 3:17
12:41 [w]ch. 7:4
12:42 [x]See Deut. 16:6
12:43 [y]Num. 9:14
12:44 [z]Gen. 17:12,13
12:45 [a]Lev. 22:10
12:46 [b]Num. 9:12 John 19:33,36
12:47 [c]ver. 6 Num. 9:13
12:48 [d]Num. 9:14
12:49 [e]Num. 9:14 & 15:15,16 Gal. 3:28
12:51 [f]ver. 41 [g]ch. 6:26
13:2 [h]ver. 12,13,15 ch. 22:29,30 Num. 3:13 Deut. 15:19 Luke 2:23
13:3 [i]ch. 12:42 Deut. 16:3 [j]ch. 6:1 [k]ch. 12:8
13:4 [l]ch. 23:15 & 34:18 Deut. 16:1
13:5 [m]ch. 3:8 [n]ch. 6:8 [o]ch. 12:25,26
13:6 [p]ch. 12:15,16

homeborn, and unto the stranger that
sojourneth among you.
50 Thus did all the children of Isra-
el; as the LORD commanded Moses and
Aaron, so did they.
51 [f]And it came to pass the self-
same day, *that* the LORD did bring the
children of Israel out of the land of
Egypt [g]by their armies.

The firstborn set apart

13 AND THE LORD spake unto Mo-
ses, saying,
2 [h]Sanctify unto me all the first-
born, whatsoever openeth the womb
among the children of Israel, *both* of
man and of beast: it *is* mine.
3 ¶ And Moses said unto the people,
[i]Remember this day, in which ye
came out from Egypt, out of the house
of [f]bondage; for [j]by strength of hand
the LORD brought you out from this
place: [k]there shall no leavened bread
be eaten.
4 [l]This day came ye out in the
month Abib.
5 ¶ And it shall be when the LORD
shall [m]bring thee into the land of the
Canaanites, and the Hittites, and the
Amorites, and the Hivites, and the Jeb-
usites, which he [n]sware unto thy fa-
thers to give thee, a land flowing with
milk and honey, [o]that thou shalt keep
this service in this month.
6 [p]Seven days thou shalt eat un-
leavened bread, and in the seventh day
shall be a feast to the LORD.
7 Unleavened bread shall be eaten

[d] Heb. *a night of observations* [e] Heb. *do it*
[f] Heb. *servants*

13:2 SANCTIFY UNTO ME ALL THE FIRSTBORN. Because God had saved the firstborn of all Israel and rescued them from the Egyptians, He now considered them His property. (1) The nation was commanded to acknowledge this by dedicating their firstborn for service to God. Later this obligation was transferred to the Levites as the representatives of the people. However, the people were to "redeem" (or "buy back") such children by paying a price (v. 13; cf. Num. 3:11–13,50–51; 18:16). (2) This act reminded the Israelites that God had redeemed them from slavery and bondage in Egypt and that they belonged to Him. Joseph and Mary presented Jesus as their firstborn in obedience to this law (Luke 2:22–23).

13:7 NEITHER SHALL THERE BE LEAVEN. During the week of the Passover, leaven (Heb. *se'or*, i.e., any yeastlike substance capable of producing fermentation in dough or a liquid) and anything leavened (Heb. *hamets*, i.e., anything that had undergone fermentation or anything with yeast in it) was to be removed from the homes of the Israelites (cf. 12:15,19). In 12:15 and 13:7 *hamets* is translated "leavened bread"; however, the literal meaning of the word is "fermented thing." In other words, nothing with yeast in it was to be seen among them at all. All foods of the Passover were to conform to this divine ordinance concerning leaven or fermentation (see article on THE PASSOVER, p. 110). The principal reason for this prohibition is most likely found in the Biblical teaching that regards fermentation and fermented things as symbolizing corruption, evil, and moral impurity (see Mat. 16:6, note; Mark 8:15, note; 1 Cor. 5:6–8).

(2) Note also that the Law of Moses did not require wine, either fermented or unfermented, to be used during the Passover week. However, for any

seven days; and there shall [q]no leav-
ened bread be seen with thee, neither
shall there be leaven seen with thee in
all thy quarters.
8 ¶ And thou shalt [r]show thy son
in that day, saying, *This is done* be-
cause of that *which* the LORD did unto
me when I came forth out of Egypt.
9 And it shall be for [s]a sign unto
thee upon thine hand, and for a memo-
rial between thine eyes, that the LORD's
law may be in thy mouth: for with a
strong hand hath the LORD brought
thee out of Egypt.
10 [t]Thou shalt therefore keep this
ordinance in his season from year to
year.
11 ¶ And it shall be when the LORD
shall bring thee into the land of the
Canaanites, as he sware unto thee
and to thy fathers, and shall give it
thee,
12 [u]That thou shalt [g]set apart
unto the LORD all that openeth the ma-
trix, and every firstling that cometh of
a beast which thou hast; the males
shall be the LORD's.
13 And [v]every firstling of an ass
thou shalt redeem with a [h]lamb; and
if thou wilt not redeem it, then thou
shalt break his neck: and all the first-
born of man among thy children
[w]shalt thou redeem.
14 ¶ [x]And it shall be when thy son
asketh thee [i]in time to come, saying,
What *is* this? that thou shalt say unto
him, [y]By strength of hand the LORD
brought us out from Egypt, from the
house of bondage:
15 And it came to pass, when Phar-
aoh would hardly let us go, that [z]the
LORD slew all the firstborn in the land
of Egypt, both the firstborn of man, and
the firstborn of beast: therefore I sacri-
fice to the LORD all that openeth the ma-
trix, being males; but all the firstborn
of my children I redeem.
16 And it shall be for [a]a token
upon thine hand, and for frontlets be-
tween thine eyes: for by strength of
hand the LORD brought us forth out of
Egypt.

13:7 [q]ch. 12:19 **13:8** [r]ver. 14 ch. 12:26 **13:9** [s]See ver. 16 Deut. 6:8 Mat. 23:5 **13:10** [t]ch. 12:14,24 **13:12** [u]ver. 2 Lev. 27:26 **13:13** [v]ch. 34:20 Num. 18:15 [w]Num. 3:46,47 & 18:15,16 **13:14** [x]ch. 12:26 Deut. 6:20 Josh. 4:6,21 [y]ver. 3 **13:15** [z]ch. 12:29 **13:16** [a]ver. 9

13:17 [b]ch. 14:11 Num. 14:1-4 [c]Deut. 17:16 **13:18** [d]ch. 14:2 Num. 33:6 **13:19** [e]Gen. 50:25 Josh. 24:32 **13:20** [f]Num. 33:6 **13:21** [g]ch. 14:19,24 Num. 9:15 & 14:14 Deut. 1:33 Neh. 9:12 Ps. 78:14 & 99:7 Is. 4:5 1 Cor. 10:1 **14:2** [h]ch. 13:18 [i]Num. 33:7 [j]Jer. 44:1 **14:3** [k]Ps. 71:11 **14:4** [l]ch. 4:21 & 7:3 [m]ver. 17,18 ch. 9:16 Rom. 9:17,22,23 [n]ch. 7:5

Crossing the Red sea

17 ¶ And it came to pass, when
Pharaoh had let the people go, that
God led them not *through* the way of
the land of the Philistines, although
that *was* near; for God said, Lest perad-
venture the people [b]repent when they
see war, and [c]they return to Egypt:
18 But God [d]led the people about,
through the way of the wilderness of
the Red sea: and the children of Israel
went up [j]harnessed out of the land of
Egypt.
19 And Moses took the bones of Jo-
seph with him: for he had straitly
sworn the children of Israel, saying,
[e]God will surely visit you; and ye shall
carry up my bones away hence with
you.
20 ¶ And [f]they took their journey
from Succoth, and encamped in Etham,
in the edge of the wilderness.
21 And [g]the LORD went before them
by day in a pillar of a cloud, to lead
them the way; and by night in a pillar
of fire, to give them light; to go by day
and night:
22 He took not away the pillar of
the cloud by day, nor the pillar of fire
by night, *from* before the people.

14 AND THE LORD spake unto Mo-
ses, saying,
2 Speak unto the children of Israel,
[h]that they turn and encamp before
[i]Pi-hahiroth, between [j]Migdol and
the sea, over against Baal-zephon: be-
fore it shall ye encamp by the sea.
3 For Pharaoh will say of the chil-
dren of Israel, [k]They *are* entangled in
the land, the wilderness hath shut
them in.
4 And [l]I will harden Pharaoh's
heart, that he shall follow after them;
and I [m]will be honoured upon Phar-
aoh, and upon all his host; [n]that the
Egyptians may know that I *am* the
LORD. And they did so.
5 ¶ And it was told the king of Egypt

[g] Heb. *cause to pass over* [h] Or, *kid* [i] Heb. *tomorrow* [j] Or, *by five in a rank*

wine or food that was used, the Israelites had to conform to this rule of no leaven or fermentation (12:20). Insofar as this event looked forward to the perfect blood sacrifice of Christ (see article on THE PASSOVER, p. 110), it is understandable that there was to be no corruption in that which represented His blood (cf. 34:25; Lev. 2:11; 6:17; 1 Cor. 5:7–8; see Luke 22:18, note; see article on WINE IN NEW TESTAMENT TIMES (1), p. 1538).

13:21 A PILLAR OF A CLOUD. God placed the pillars of cloud and fire as a proof of His presence, love, and care for Israel (cf. 40:38; Num. 9:15–23; 14:14; Deut. 1:33; 1 Cor. 10:1). The cloud and the fire were present with them until they reached the promised land forty years later.

that the people fled: and [o]the heart of
Pharaoh and of his servants was
turned against the people, and they
said, Why have we done this, that we
have let Israel go from serving us?
6 And he made ready his chariot,
and took his people with him:
7 And he took [p]six hundred chosen
chariots, and all the chariots of Egypt,
and captains over every one of them.
8 And the LORD [q]hardened the
heart of Pharaoh king of Egypt, and he
pursued after the children of Israel:
and [r]the children of Israel went out
with an high hand.
9 But the [s]Egyptians pursued after
them, all the horses *and* chariots of
Pharaoh, and his horsemen, and his
army, and overtook them encamping
by the sea, beside Pi-hahiroth, before
Baal-zephon.

14:5 [o]Ps. 105:25
14:7 [p]ch. 15:4
14:8 [q]ver. 4 [r]ch. 6:1 & 13:9 Num. 33:3
14:9 [s]ch. 15:9 Josh. 24:6
14:10 [t]Josh. 24:7 Neh. 9:9 Ps. 34:17
14:11 [u]Ps. 106:7,8
14:12 [v]ch. 5:21
14:13 [w]2 Chr. 20:15,17 Is. 41:10

10 ¶ And when Pharaoh drew nigh,
the children of Israel lifted up their
eyes, and, behold, the Egyptians
marched after them; and they were
sore afraid: and the children of Israel
[t]cried out unto the LORD.
11 [u]And they said unto Moses, Be-
cause *there were* no graves in Egypt,
hast thou taken us away to die in the
wilderness? wherefore hast thou dealt
thus with us, to carry us forth out of
Egypt?
12 [v]*Is* not this the word that we did
tell thee in Egypt, saying, Let us alone,
that we may serve the Egyptians? For
it had been better for us to serve the
Egyptians, than that we should die in
the wilderness.
13 ¶ And Moses said unto the peo-
ple, [w]Fear ye not, stand still, and see
the salvation of the LORD, which he will

THE EXODUS

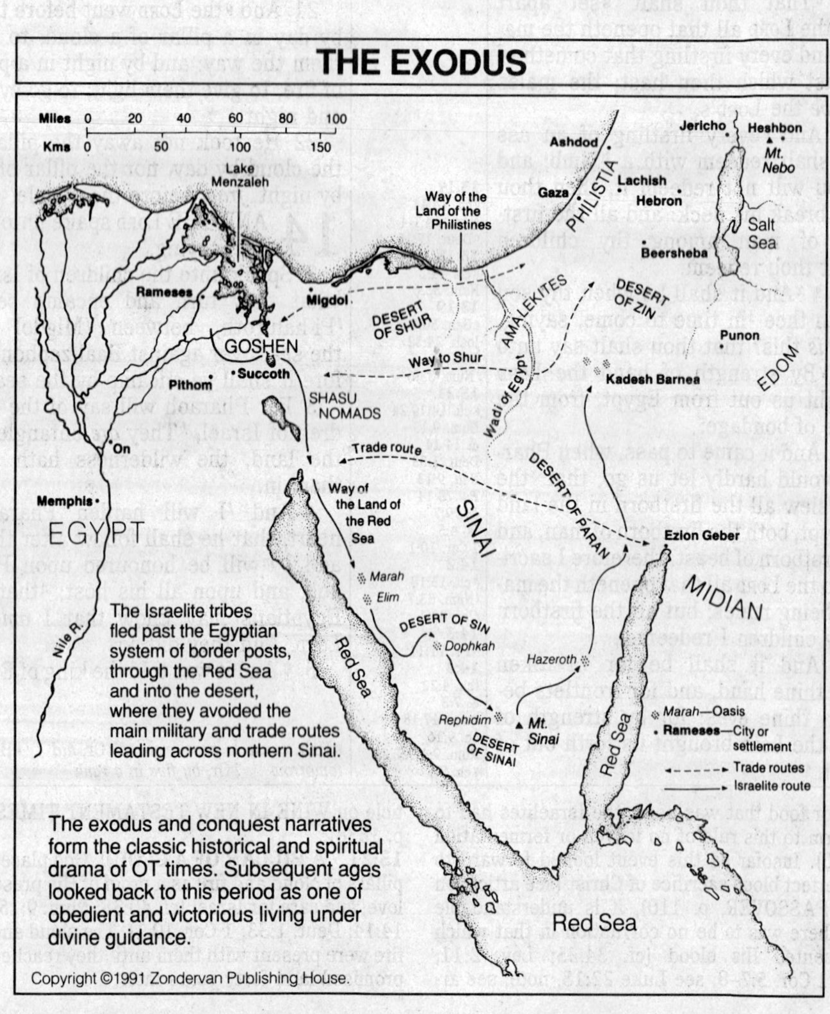

The Israelite tribes fled past the Egyptian system of border posts, through the Red Sea and into the desert, where they avoided the main military and trade routes leading across northern Sinai.

The exodus and conquest narratives form the classic historical and spiritual drama of OT times. Subsequent ages looked back to this period as one of obedient and victorious living under divine guidance.

show to you today: [k]for the Egyptians
whom ye have seen today, ye shall see
them again no more for ever.
14 [x]The LORD shall fight for you,
and ye shall [y]hold your peace.
15 ¶ And the LORD said unto Moses,
Wherefore criest thou unto me? speak
unto the children of Israel, that they go
forward:
16 But [z]lift thou up thy rod, and
stretch out thine hand over the sea,
and divide it: and the children of Israel
shall go on dry *ground* through the
midst of the sea.
17 And I, behold, I will [a]harden the
hearts of the Egyptians, and they shall
follow them: and I will [b]get me honour
upon Pharaoh, and upon all his host,
upon his chariots, and upon his horse-
men.
18 And the Egyptians [c]shall know
that I *am* the LORD, when I have gotten
me honour upon Pharaoh, upon his
chariots, and upon his horsemen.
19 ¶ And the angel of God, [d]which
went before the camp of Israel, re-
moved and went behind them; and the
pillar of the cloud went from before
their face, and stood behind them:
20 And it came between the camp of
the Egyptians and the camp of Israel;
and [e]it was a cloud and darkness *to
them,* but it gave light by night *to these:*
so that the one came not near the other
all the night.
21 And Moses stretched out his
hand over the sea; and the LORD caused
the sea to go *back* by a strong east wind
all that night, and [f]made the sea dry
land, and the waters were [g]divided.
22 And [h]the children of Israel went
into the midst of the sea upon the dry
ground: and the waters *were* [i]a wall
unto them on their right hand, and on
their left.
23 ¶ And the Egyptians pursued,
and went in after them to the midst of
the sea, *even* all Pharaoh's horses, his
chariots, and his horsemen.
24 And it came to pass, that in the
morning watch [j]the LORD looked unto
the host of the Egyptians through the
pillar of fire and of the cloud, and trou-
bled the host of the Egyptians,
25 And took off their chariot
wheels, [1]that they drave them heavi-
ly: so that the Egyptians said, Let us
flee from the face of Israel; for the LORD
[k]fighteth for them against the Egyp-
tians.
26 ¶ And the LORD said unto Moses,
Stretch out thine hand over the sea,
that the waters may come again upon
the Egyptians, upon their chariots, and
upon their horsemen.
27 And Moses stretched forth his
hand over the sea, and the sea [l]re-
turned to his strength when the morn-
ing appeared; and the Egyptians fled
against it; and the LORD [m]overthrew
[n]the[m] Egyptians in the midst of the
sea.
28 And [o]the waters returned, and
[p]covered the chariots, and the horse-
men, *and* all the host of Pharaoh that
came into the sea after them; there re-
mained not so much as one of them.
29 But [q]the children of Israel
walked upon dry *land* in the midst of
the sea; and the waters *were* a wall

14:14 [x]ver. 25 Deut. 1:30 Josh. 10:14,42 2 Chr. 20:29 Is. 31:4 [y]Is. 30:15 **14:16** [z]ver. 21,26 **14:17** [a]ver. 8 [b]ver. 4 **14:18** [c]ver. 4 **14:19** [d]ch. 13:21 Is. 63:9 **14:20** [e]See Is. 8:14 2 Cor. 4:3 **14:21** [f]Ps. 66:6 [g]ch. 15:8 Josh. 3:16 Neh. 9:11 Ps. 74:13 Is. 63:12 **14:22** [h]ch. 15:19 Ps. 66:6 Is. 63:13 1 Cor. 10:1 Heb. 11:29 [i]Hab. 3:10 **14:24** [j]See Ps. 77:17 **14:25** [k]ver. 14 **14:27** [l]Josh. 4:18 [m]ch. 15:1,7 [n]Neh. 9:11 Heb. 11:29 **14:28** [o]Hab. 3:8,13 [p]Ps. 106:11 **14:29** [q]ver. 22 Ps. 78:52,53

[k] Or, *for whereas ye have seen the Egyptians today* [1] Or, *and made them to go heavily* [m] Heb. *shook off*

14:14 THE LORD SHALL FIGHT FOR YOU. God assured the people that He would fight for them, but they had to move forward toward the sea in faith (v. 15). God fights for His people as they walk in faith and obedience to His Word (see 15:3; Neh. 4:20; Ps. 35:1).

14:19–20 THE PILLAR OF THE CLOUD. In the darkness the cloud miraculously protected Israel by moving between the Egyptians and the people. At the same time God's pillar of fire flooded with light the way across the sea so that the Israelites could cross over (cf. v. 24).

14:22 THE MIDST OF THE SEA UPON THE DRY *GROUND*. The Red Sea is literally, "Sea of Reeds" (Heb. *Yam Suph*); it is thought to be the southern end of Lake Menzaleh. The crossing of the Red Sea (13:18–14:31) took place through a direct miraculous act of God (v. 21). Later Bible writers used this event to remind God's people of His power and greatness (Josh. 24:6–7; Ps. 106:7–8; Is. 51:15; Jer. 31:35; Nah. 1:3–4). The deliverance of Israel through the Red Sea confirmed God's promise: "The LORD shall fight for you" (v. 14).

14:22 THE WATERS *WERE* A WALL UNTO THEM. The forming of two great walls of water by a strong wind required a miracle; it was not a mere natural occurrence. The water was piled up on both sides, leaving a path that may have been several miles wide (cf. 15:8; Ps. 74:13).

14:28 THE WATERS RETURNED. When the water returned to normal, it was sufficiently deep to cover the Egyptian chariots and drown their army (cf. 15:4–6). In this way the Lord fought for Israel and defeated the Egyptians, just as He had earlier fought against and defeated the gods of Egypt (the ten plagues).

unto them on their right hand, and on their left.

30 Thus the LORD [r]saved Israel that day out of the hand of the Egyptians; and Israel [s]saw the Egyptians dead upon the sea shore.

31 And Israel saw that great [n]work which the LORD did upon the Egyptians: and the people feared the LORD, and [t]believed the LORD, and his servant Moses.

The song of Moses

15 THEN SANG [u]Moses and the children of Israel this song unto the LORD, and spake, saying, I will sing unto the LORD, for he hath triumphed gloriously: the horse and his rider hath he thrown into the sea.

2 The LORD *is* my strength and [v]song, and he is become my salvation: he *is* my God, and I will prepare him [w]an habitation; my [x]father's God, and I [y]will exalt him.

3 The LORD *is* a man of [z]war: the LORD *is* his [a]name.

4 [b]Pharaoh's chariots and his host hath he cast into the sea: [c]his chosen captains also are drowned in the Red sea.

5 [d]The depths have covered them: [e]they sank into the bottom as a stone.

6 [f]Thy right hand, O LORD, is become glorious in power: thy right hand, O LORD, hath dashed in pieces the enemy.

7 And in the greatness of thine [g]excellency thou hast overthrown them that rose up against thee: thou sentest forth thy wrath, *which* [h]consumed them [i]as stubble.

8 And [j]with the blast of thy nostrils the waters were gathered together, [k]the floods stood upright as an heap, *and* the depths were congealed in the heart of the sea.

9 [l]The enemy said, I will pursue, I will overtake, I will [m]divide the spoil; my lust shall be satisfied upon them; I will draw my sword, my hand shall [o]destroy them.

10 Thou didst [n]blow with thy wind, [o]the sea covered them: they sank as lead in the mighty waters.

11 [p]Who *is* like unto thee, O LORD, among the [p]gods? who *is* like thee, [q]glorious in holiness, fearful *in* praises, [r]doing wonders?

12 Thou stretchedst out thy right hand, the earth swallowed them.

13 Thou in thy mercy hast [s]led forth the people *which* thou hast redeemed: thou hast guided *them* in thy strength unto [t]thy holy habitation.

14 [u]The people shall hear, *and* be afraid: [v]sorrow shall take hold on the inhabitants of Palestina.

15 [w]Then [x]the dukes of Edom shall be amazed; [y]the mighty men of Moab, trembling shall take hold upon them; [z]all the inhabitants of Canaan shall melt away.

16 [a]Fear and dread shall fall upon them; by the greatness of thine arm they shall be *as* still [b]as a stone; till thy people pass over, O LORD, till the people pass over, [c]*which* thou hast purchased.

17 Thou shalt bring them in, and [d]plant them in the mountain of thine inheritance, *in* the place, O LORD, *which* thou hast made for thee to dwell in, *in* the [e]Sanctuary, O LORD, *which* thy hands have established.

18 [f]The LORD shall reign for ever and ever.

19 For the [g]horse of Pharaoh went in with his chariots and with his horsemen into the sea, and [h]the LORD brought again the waters of the sea upon them; but the children of Israel went on dry *land* in the midst of the sea.

20 ¶ And Miriam [i]the prophetess, [j]the sister of Aaron, [k]took a timbrel

[n] Heb. *hand* [o] Or, *repossess* [p] Or, *mighty ones?*

14:30 [r]Ps. 106:8,10 [s]Ps. 59:10
14:31 [t]ch. 4:31 John 2:11
15:1 [u]Ps. 106:12
15:2 [v]Ps. 18:2 Is. 12:2 Hab. 3:18,19 [w]Gen. 28:21,22 [x]ch. 3:15,16 [y]Is. 25:1
15:3 [z]Rev. 19:11 [a]ch. 6:3 Ps. 83:18
15:4 [b]ch. 14:28 [c]ch. 14:7
15:5 [d]ch. 14:28 [e]Neh. 9:11
15:6 [f]Ps. 118:15
15:7 [g]Deut. 33:26 [h]Ps. 59:13 [i]Is. 5:24
15:8 [j]ch. 14:21 [k]Ps. 78:13
15:9 [l]Judg. 5:30 [m]Is. 53:12
15:10 [n]ch. 14:21 [o]ch. 14:28
15:11 [p]1 Ki. 8:23 [q]Is. 6:3 [r]Ps. 77:14
15:13 [s]Ps. 77:15,20 [t]Ps. 78:54
15:14 [u]Josh. 2:9 [v]Ps. 48:6
15:15 [w]Gen. 36:40 [x]Deut. 2:4 [y]Num. 22:3 [z]Josh. 5:1
15:16 [a]Josh. 2:9 [b]1 Sam. 25:37 [c]Ps. 74:2 Jer. 31:11 1 Pet. 2:9
15:17 [d]Ps. 44:2 [e]Ps. 78:54
15:18 [f]Is. 57:15
15:19 [g]ch. 14:23 [h]ch. 14:28
15:20 [i]Judg. 4:4 [j]Num. 26:59 [k]1 Sam. 18:6

14:31 FEARED THE LORD, AND BELIEVED. Seeing God's awful judgment against the Egyptian army, the people "feared the LORD"; and seeing God's miraculous deliverance, they "believed the LORD." When we receive a true revelation of God's majesty and judgment against sin, we will lay hold of Him in faith while growing in the fear of God.

15:1–18 THEN SANG MOSES . . . THIS SONG. This song celebrates God's victory at the Red Sea over Egyptian powers. It is a hymn of praise and thanksgiving to God for His majesty, military might, and faithfulness to His people. The deliverance out of Egypt foreshadows and prophesies the victory of God's people over Satan and the antichrist during the last days; hence one of the songs of the redeemed is called the "song of Moses" (Rev. 15:3).

15:20 PROPHETESS. Miriam is called a "prophetess" because she moved in the Spirit of prophecy and spoke a message from God to the people (see Num. 12:2,6; cf. Judg. 4:4; 2 Ki. 22:14; Is. 8:3; Luke 2:36; see article on THE PROPHET

in her hand; and all the women went out after her [l]with timbrels and with dances.

21 And Miriam [m]answered them, [n]Sing ye to the LORD, for he hath triumphed gloriously; the horse and his rider hath he thrown into the sea.

Deut. 8:10

Bitter waters made sweet

22 So Moses brought Israel from the Red sea, and they went out into the wilderness of [o]Shur; and they went three days in the wilderness, and found no water.

23 ¶ And when they came to [p]Marah, they could not drink of the waters of Marah, for they *were* bitter: therefore the name of it was called [q]Marah.

24 And the people [q]murmured against Moses, saying, What shall we drink?

25 And he cried unto the LORD; and the LORD showed him a tree, [r]*which* when he had cast into the waters, the waters were made sweet: there he [s]made for them a statute and an ordinance, and there [t]he proved them,

26 And said, [u]If thou wilt diligently hearken to the voice of the LORD thy God, and wilt do that which is right in his sight, and wilt give ear to his commandments, and keep all his statutes, I will put none of these [v]diseases upon thee, which I have brought upon the Egyptians: for I *am* the LORD [w]that healeth thee.

Num. 12:10-15

27 ¶ [x]And they came to Elim, where *were* twelve wells of water, and threescore and ten palm trees: and they encamped there by the waters.

15:20 [l]Judg. 11:34 2 Sam. 6:16 Ps. 150:4 **15:21** [m]1 Sam. 18:7 [n]ver. 1 **15:22** [o]Gen. 25:18 **15:23** [p]Num. 33:8 **15:24** [q]ch. 16:2 **15:25** [r]See 2 Ki. 2:21 [s]See Josh. 24:25 [t]Deut. 8:2,16 Judg. 3:1,4 Ps. 66:10 **15:26** [u]Deut. 7:12,15 [v]Deut. 28:27,60 [w]ch. 23:25 Ps. 103:3 **15:27** [x]Num. 33:9

16:1 [y]Num. 33:10,11 [z]Ezek. 30:15 **16:2** [a]1 Cor. 10:10 **16:3** [b]Lam. 4:9 [c]Num. 11:4 **16:4** [d]John 6:31 [e]Deut. 8:2,16 **16:5** [f]See ver. 22 Lev. 25:21 **16:6** [g]See ver. 12,13 & ch. 6:7 Num. 16:28-30 **16:7** [h]See ver. 10 Is. 35:2 & 40:5 John 11:4,40

Quails and manna provided

16 AND THEY [y]took their journey from Elim, and all the congregation of the children of Israel came unto the wilderness of [z]Sin, which *is* between Elim and Sinai, on the fifteenth day of the second month after their departing out of the land of Egypt.

2 And the whole congregation of the children of Israel [a]murmured against Moses and Aaron in the wilderness:

3 And the children of Israel said unto them, [b]Would to God we had died by the hand of the LORD in the land of Egypt, [c]when we sat by the flesh pots, *and* when we did eat bread to the full; for ye have brought us forth into this wilderness, to kill this whole assembly with hunger.

4 ¶ Then said the LORD unto Moses, Behold, I will rain [d]bread from heaven for you; and the people shall go out and gather [r]a certain rate every day, that I may [e]prove them, whether they will walk in my law, or no.

5 And it shall come to pass, that on the sixth day they shall prepare *that* which they bring in; and [f]it shall be twice as much as they gather daily.

6 And Moses and Aaron said unto all the children of Israel, [g]At even, then ye shall know that the LORD hath brought you out from the land of Egypt:

7 And in the morning, then ye shall see [h]the glory of the LORD; for that he heareth your murmurings against the

[q] i.e. *Bitterness* [r] Heb. *the portion of a day in his day*

IN THE OLD TESTAMENT, p. 1002).

15:26 I *AM* THE LORD THAT HEALETH THEE. If the Israelites earnestly heeded and followed God, He would permit none of the diseases or plagues He brought upon the Egyptians to afflict them. This promise reveals that it is God's basic desire to heal His people rather than inflict illness and disease on them (see also 23:25; Deut. 7:15; Ps. 103:3; 107:20; Ezek. 18:23,32; 33:11). For God's promise of healing under the new covenant, see article on DIVINE HEALING, p. 1418.

16:2 MURMURED AGAINST MOSES. The Israelites complained against Moses and God for the third time (cf. 14:10–12; 15:24). In spite of all that God had done for them, they were quick to lose faith in His goodness, His wisdom, and His will for their lives (also see 17:3; Num. 14:2; 16:11,41). Paul warns N.T. believers not to follow Israel's example (1 Cor. 10:10). When serious problems arise, instead of accusing God of neglect and unfaithfulness, we should commit our way to Him and humbly ask for help and guidance in resolving the problem, trusting Him to act on our behalf.

16:4 BREAD FROM HEAVEN. This "bread from heaven" is called "manna" (v. 15). It was a special food miraculously sent from God to feed the people after the exodus from Egypt. It was a white substance that resembled frost, took the form of thin flakes, and tasted like honey (v. 14; Num. 11:9). The supply of manna ceased when Israel entered the promised land and other food became available (Josh. 5:12). It was a type or foreshadowing of Jesus Christ, who as "the true bread from heaven" (John 6:32; cf. Rev. 2:17) gives eternal life (John 6:33,51,58).

16:4 THAT I MAY PROVE THEM. The people were given exact instructions with regard to the bread from heaven. These instructions were to test their willingness to trust and obey God (cf. Deut. 8:2–3). In the same way God sometimes orders the circumstances of our lives so as to test our faith and loyalty to Him.

LORD: and [i]what *are* we, that ye murmur against us?

8 And Moses said, *This shall be,* when the LORD shall give you in the evening flesh to eat, and in the morning bread to the full; for that the LORD heareth your murmurings which ye murmur against him: and what *are* we? your murmurings *are* not against us, but [j]against the LORD.

9 ¶ And Moses spake unto Aaron, Say unto all the congregation of the children of Israel, [k]Come near before the LORD: for he hath heard your murmurings.

10 And it came to pass, as Aaron spake unto the whole congregation of the children of Israel, that they looked toward the wilderness, and, behold, the glory of the LORD [l]appeared in the cloud.

11 ¶ And the LORD spake unto Moses, saying,

12 [m]I have heard the murmurings of the children of Israel: speak unto them, saying, [n]At even ye shall eat flesh, and [o]in the morning ye shall be filled with bread; and ye shall know that I *am* the LORD your God.

13 And it came to pass, that at even [p]the quails came up, and covered the camp: and in the morning [q]the dew lay round about the host.

14 And when the dew that lay was gone up, behold, upon the face of the wilderness *there lay* [r]a small round thing, *as* small as the hoar frost on the ground.

15 And when the children of Israel saw *it,* they said one to another, [s]It *is* manna: for they wist not what it *was.* And Moses said unto them, [s]This *is* the bread which the LORD hath given you to eat.

16 ¶ This *is* the thing which the LORD hath commanded, Gather of it every man according to his eating, [t]an omer [t]for every man, *according to* the number of your [u]persons; take ye every man for *them* which *are* in his tents.

17 And the children of Israel did so, and gathered, some more, some less.

18 And when they did mete *it* with an omer, [u]he that gathered much had nothing over, and he that gathered little had no lack; they gathered every man according to his eating.

19 And Moses said, Let no man leave of it till the morning.

20 Notwithstanding they hearkened not unto Moses; but some of them left of it until the morning, and it bred worms, and stank: and Moses was wroth with them.

21 And they gathered it every morning, every man according to his eating: and when the sun waxed hot, it melted.

22 ¶ And it came to pass, *that* on the sixth day they gathered twice as much bread, two omers for one *man:* and all the rulers of the congregation came and told Moses.

23 And he said unto them, This *is that* which the LORD hath said, Tomorrow *is* [v]the rest of the holy sabbath unto the LORD: bake *that* which ye will bake *today,* and seethe that ye will seethe; and that which remaineth over lay up for you to be kept until the morning.

24 And they laid it up till the morning, as Moses bade: and it did not [w]stink, neither was there any worm therein.

25 And Moses said, Eat that today; for today *is* a sabbath unto the LORD: today ye shall not find it in the field.

26 [x]Six days ye shall gather it; but on the seventh day, *which is* the sabbath, in it there shall be none.

27 ¶ And it came to pass, *that* there went out *some* of the people on the seventh day for to gather, and they found none.

28 And the LORD said unto Moses, How long [y]refuse ye to keep my commandments and my laws?

29 See, for that the LORD hath given you the sabbath, therefore he giveth you on the sixth day the bread of two days; abide ye every man in his place, let no man go out of his place on the seventh day.

30 So the people rested on the seventh day.

31 And the house of Israel called

16:7 [i]Num. 16:11
16:8 [j]See 1 Sam. 8:7 Luke 10:16 Rom. 13:2
16:9 [k]Num. 16:16
16:10 [l]ver. 7 ch. 13:21 Num. 16:19 1 Ki. 8:10,11
16:12 [m]ver. 8 [n]ver. 6 [o]ver. 7
16:13 [p]Num. 11:31 Ps. 78:27,28 & 105:40 [q]Num. 11:9
16:14 [r]Num. 11:7 Deut. 8:3 Neh. 9:15 Ps. 78:24 & 105:40
16:15 [s]John 6:31,49,58 1 Cor. 10:3
16:16 [t]ver. 36
16:18 [u]2 Cor. 8:15
16:23 [v]Gen. 2:3 ch. 20:8 & 31:15 & 35:3 Lev. 23:3
16:24 [w]ver. 20
16:26 [x]ch. 20:9,10
16:28 [y]2 Ki. 17:14 Ps. 78:10,22

[s] Or, *What is this?* or, *It is a portion* [t] Heb. *by the poll,* or, *head* [u] Heb. *souls*

16:21 EVERY MORNING. God gave orders to gather only enough for each day in order to teach the people that their daily existence depended exclusively upon His gift (cf. Mat. 6:11).

16:30 RESTED ON THE SEVENTH DAY. Through His instructions regarding the seventh day (vv. 22–30), God wanted to emphasize that His people were to respond with rest just as He had responded at creation (Gen. 2:1–4). God also knew, from the very beginning, that if His people

the name thereof Manna: and [z]it *was* like coriander seed, white; and the taste of it *was* like wafers *made* with honey.

32 ¶ And Moses said, This *is* the thing which the LORD commandeth, Fill an omer of it to be kept for your generations; that they may see the bread wherewith I have fed you in the wilderness, when I brought you forth from the land of Egypt.

33 And Moses said unto Aaron, [a]Take a pot, and put an omer full of manna therein, and lay it up before the LORD, to be kept for your generations.

34 As the LORD commanded Moses, so Aaron laid it up [b]before the Testimony, to be kept.

35 And the children of Israel did eat manna [c]forty years, [d]until they came to a land inhabited; they did eat manna, until they came unto the borders of the land of Canaan.

36 Now an omer *is* the tenth *part* of an ephah.

The water from the rock

17 AND [e]ALL the congregation of the children of Israel journeyed from the wilderness of Sin, after their journeys, according to the commandment of the LORD, and pitched in Rephidim: and *there was* no water for the people to drink.

2 [f]Wherefore the people did chide with Moses, and said, Give us water that we may drink. And Moses said unto them, Why chide ye with me? wherefore do ye [g]tempt the LORD?

3 And the people thirsted there for water; and the people [h]murmured against Moses, and said, Wherefore *is* this *that* thou hast brought us up out of Egypt, to kill us and our children and our cattle with thirst?

4 And Moses [i]cried unto the LORD, saying, What shall I do unto this people? they be almost ready to [j]stone me.

5 And the LORD said unto Moses, [k]Go on before the people, and take with thee of the elders of Israel; and thy rod, wherewith [l]thou smotest the river, take in thine hand, and go.

6 [m]Behold, I will stand before thee there upon the rock in Horeb; and thou shalt smite the rock, and there shall come water out of it, that the people may drink. And Moses did so in the sight of the elders of Israel.

7 And he called the name of the place [n]Massah,[v] and [w]Meribah, because of the chiding of the children of Israel, and because they tempted the LORD, saying, Is the LORD among us, or not?

The defeat of Amalek

8 ¶ [o]Then came Amalek, and fought with Israel in Rephidim.

9 And Moses said unto [p]Joshua, Choose us out men, and go out, fight with Amalek: tomorrow I will stand on the top of the hill with [q]the rod of God in mine hand.

10 So Joshua did as Moses had said to him, and fought with Amalek: and Moses, Aaron, and Hur went up to the top of the hill.

11 And it came to pass, when Mo-

16:31 [z]Num. 11:7,8
16:33 [a]Heb. 9:4
16:34 [b]ch. 25:16,21 & 40:20 Num. 17:10 Deut. 10:5
16:35 [c]Num. 33:38 John 6:31,49 [d]Josh. 5:12
17:1 [e]Num. 33:12,14
17:2 [f]Num. 20:3 [g]Deut. 6:16 Ps. 78:18,41
17:3 [h]ch. 16:2
17:4 [i]ch. 14:15 [j]John 8:59 & 10:31
17:5 [k]Ezek. 2:6 [l]Num. 20:8
17:6 [m]Num. 20:10,11
17:7 [n]Num. 20:13
17:8 [o]Gen. 36:12 Deut. 25:17
17:9 [p]Called *Jesus* Acts 7:45 [q]ch. 4:20

[v]i.e. *Temptation* [w]i.e. *Chiding,* or, *Strife*

failed to observe the Sabbath, they would deplete both their physical and spiritual strength by continual earthly worries and pursuits; this failure would result in spiritual and godly concerns being relegated to a place of least importance in their lives (see Mat. 12:1, note; Luke 6:2–10, note).

17:6 SMITE THE ROCK. In the N.T., this rock is identified with Jesus Christ, the spring of living water (1 Cor. 10:4). As the rock was smitten, so was Christ smitten by death on the cross (Is. 53:5). As Christ was the source of blessing for Israel, He is the source of blessing and the giver of the Holy Spirit for the church (cf. Ps. 105:41–42; Is. 53:4–5; John 7:37–38; 20:22; Acts 2:1–4).

17:9 JOSHUA. The man chosen to succeed Moses as leader of Israel makes his first appearance here in the Biblical narrative. Joshua means "the LORD saves" or "Yahweh is Savior"; the Greek form of the name is "Jesus" (see Mat. 1:21, note). Appropriately enough, the man who would later conquer Canaan appears first in a military role. God was providentially preparing him for his later wars against the Canaanites.

17:11 MOSES HELD UP HIS HAND. By holding up his hands to the Lord, Moses reveals his dependence on God and his faith in Him. (1) Israel's strength and victory lay only in a continuous drawing near to God in prayer, faith, and obedience. When the prayer of Moses ceased, the flow of divine power to His people ceased (cf. Heb. 7:25, note). (2) This divine principle continues to operate under the new covenant. If we fail to call upon God daily in prayer, then the divine life, protection, blessing, and grace will begin to cease flowing toward us. Our only hope of victory lies in continually drawing near to the throne of grace through Christ, that we might receive the power and grace of God to help us in times of need (Heb. 4:16; 7:25; see Mat. 7:7–8, note).

ses [r]held up his hand, that Israel prevailed: and when he let down his hand, Amalek prevailed.

12 But Moses' hands *were* heavy; and they took a stone, and put *it* under him, and he sat thereon; and Aaron and Hur stayed up his hands, the one on the one side, and the other on the other side; and his hands were steady until the going down of the sun.

13 And Joshua discomfited Amalek and his people with the edge of the sword.

Josh. 3:9-17

14 And the LORD said unto Moses, [s]Write this *for* a memorial in a book, and rehearse *it* in the ears of Joshua: for [t]I will utterly put out the remembrance of Amalek from under heaven.

15 And Moses built an altar, and called the name of it [x]Jehovah-nissi:

16 For he said, [y]Because [z]the LORD hath sworn *that* the LORD *will have* war with Amalek from generation to generation.

The coming of Jethro

18 WHEN [u]JETHRO, the priest of Midian, Moses' father-in-law, heard of all that [v]God had done for Moses, and for Israel his people, *and* that the LORD had brought Israel out of Egypt;

2 Then Jethro, Moses' father-in-law, took Zipporah, Moses' wife, [w]after he had sent her back,

3 And her [x]two sons; of which the [y]name of the one *was* [a]Gershom; for he said, I have been an alien in a strange land:

4 And the name of the other *was* [b]Eliezer; for the God of my father, *said he, was* mine help, and delivered me from the sword of Pharaoh:

5 And Jethro, Moses' father-in-law, came with his sons and his wife unto Moses into the wilderness, where he encamped at [z]the mount of God:

6 And he said unto Moses, I thy father-in-law Jethro am come unto thee, and thy wife, and her two sons with her.

7 ¶ And Moses [a]went out to meet his father-in-law, and did obeisance, and [b]kissed him; and they asked each other of *their* [c]welfare; and they came into the tent.

8 And Moses told his father-in-law all that the LORD had done unto Pharaoh and to the Egyptians for Israel's sake, *and* all the travail that had [d]come upon them by the way, and *how* the LORD [c]delivered them.

9 And Jethro rejoiced for all the goodness which the LORD had done to Israel, whom he had delivered out of the hand of the Egyptians.

10 And Jethro said, [d]Blessed *be* the LORD, who hath delivered you out of the hand of the Egyptians, and out of the hand of Pharaoh, who hath delivered the people from under the hand of the Egyptians.

11 Now I know that the LORD *is* [e]greater than all gods: [f]for in the thing wherein they dealt [g]proudly *he was* above them.

12 And Jethro, Moses' father-in-law, took a burnt offering and sacrifices for God: and Aaron came, and all the elders of Israel, to eat bread with Moses' father-in-law [h]before God.

13 ¶ And it came to pass on the morrow, that Moses sat to judge the people: and the people stood by Moses from the morning unto the evening.

14 And when Moses' father-in-law saw all that he did to the people, he said, What *is* this thing that thou doest to the people? why sittest thou thyself alone, and all the people stand by thee from morning unto even?

15 And Moses said unto his father-in-law, Because [i]the people come unto me to inquire of God:

16 When they have [j]a matter, they come unto me; and I judge between [e]one and another, and I do [k]make

17:11 [r]Jas. 5:16
17:14 [s]ch. 34:27 [t]1 Sam. 15:3,7 & 30:1,17
18:1 [u]ch. 2:16 [v]Ps. 106:2,8
18:2 [w]ch. 4:26
18:3 [x]Acts 7:29 [y]ch. 2:22
18:5 [z]ch. 3:1,12
18:7 [a]Gen. 18:2 [b]Gen. 29:13
18:8 [c]Ps. 81:7
18:10 [d]Gen. 14:20 2 Sam. 18:28
18:11 [e]2 Chr. 2:5 [f]ch. 1:10,16,22 [g]Luke 1:51
18:12 [h]Deut. 12:7
18:15 [i]Lev. 24:12
18:16 [j]ch. 24:14 [k]Lev. 24:15

[x] i.e. *The LORD my banner* [y] Or, *Because the hand* of Amalek is *against the throne of the LORD*, therefore [z] Heb. *the hand upon the throne of the LORD* [a] i.e. *A stranger there* [b] i.e. *My God* is *an help* [c] Heb. *peace* [d] Heb. *found them* [e] Heb. *a man and his fellow*

18:2 JETHRO . . . TOOK ZIPPORAH. Moses may have sent his wife and two sons back to Jethro during the time of his conflict with Pharaoh.

18:11 NOW I KNOW THAT THE LORD *IS* GREATER. The word "know" frequently occurs in the book of Exodus. Moses and the Israelites needed to know who God was and to understand His great power. These manifestations of God's power and deliverance became a witness to Jethro so he could say, "Now I know," and join in the worship of the Lord. These things are recorded so that we too may come to know and worship the true God.

them know the statutes of God, and his laws.

17 And Moses' father-in-law said unto him, The thing that thou doest *is* not good.

18 [f]Thou wilt surely wear away, both thou, and this people that *is* with thee: for this thing *is* too heavy for thee; [l]thou art not able to perform it thyself alone.

19 Hearken now unto my voice, I will give thee counsel, and [m]God shall be with thee: Be thou [n]for the people to God-ward, that thou mayest [o]bring the causes unto God:

20 And thou shalt [p]teach them ordinances and laws, and shalt show them [q]the way wherein they must walk, and [r]the work that they must do.

21 Moreover thou shalt provide out of all the people [s]able men, such as [t]fear God, [u]men of truth, [v]hating covetousness; and place *such* over them, *to be* rulers of thousands, *and* rulers of hundreds, rulers of fifties, and rulers of tens:

22 And let them judge the people [w]at all seasons: [x]and it shall be, *that* every great matter they shall bring unto thee, but every small matter they shall judge: so shall it be easier for thyself, and [y]they shall bear *the burden* with thee.

23 If thou shalt do this thing, and God command thee *so,* then thou shalt be [z]able to endure, and all this people shall also go to [a]their place in peace.

24 So Moses hearkened to the voice of his father-in-law, and did all that he had said.

25 And [b]Moses chose able men out of all Israel, and made them heads over the people, rulers of thousands, rulers of hundreds, rulers of fifties, and rulers of tens.

26 And they [c]judged the people at all seasons: the [d]hard causes they brought unto Moses, but every small matter they judged themselves.

27 ¶ And Moses let his father-in-law depart; and [e]he went his way into his own land.

At mount Sinai

19 IN THE third month, when the children of Israel were gone forth out of the land of Egypt, the same day [f]came they *into* the wilderness of Sinai.

2 For they were departed from [g]Rephidim, and were come *to* the desert of Sinai, and had pitched in the wilderness; and there Israel camped before [h]the mount.

3 And [i]Moses went up unto God, and the LORD [j]called unto him out of the mountain, saying, Thus shalt thou say to the house of Jacob, and tell the children of Israel;

4 [k]Ye have seen what I did unto the Egyptians, and *how* [l]I bare you on eagles' wings, and brought you unto myself.

5 Now [m]therefore, if ye will obey my voice indeed, and keep my cov-

f Heb. *Fading thou wilt fade*

18:18 [l]Num. 11:14,17 **18:19** [m]ch. 3:12 [n]ch. 4:16 [o]Num. 27:5 **18:20** [p]Deut. 5:1 [q]Ps. 143:8 [r]Deut. 1:18 **18:21** [s]ver. 25 2 Chr. 19:5-10 Acts 6:3 [t]2 Sam. 23:3 [u]Ezek. 18:8 [v]Deut. 16:19 **18:22** [w]ver. 26 [x]Lev. 24:11 Deut. 1:17 [y]Num. 11:17 **18:23** [z]ver. 18 [a]ch. 16:29 2 Sam. 19:39 **18:25** [b]Deut. 1:15 **18:26** [c]ver. 22 [d]Job 29:16 **18:27** [e]Num. 10:29,30 **19:1** [f]Num. 33:15 **19:2** [g]ch. 17:1,8 [h]ch. 3:1,12 **19:3** [i]Acts 7:38 [j]ch. 3:4 **19:4** [k]Deut. 29:2 [l]Is. 63:9 **19:5** [m]Deut. 5:2

18:21 PROVIDE ... ABLE MEN. Jethro's counsel that Moses delegate authority to godly men in order to do more efficiently the work of God applies equally today. Several qualifications for leaders of God's people are mentioned in this verse: they must be (1) capable people, (2) people who fear God, (3) people instructed in truth and strongly committed to it, and (4) people who hate dishonest gain and are thus free from covetousness and the love of money.

19:1 THE WILDERNESS OF SINAI. Ch. 19 records the establishment of God's covenant with the people of Israel at Mount Sinai. It is an extension of His covenant with Abraham and his descendants (see Gen. 15:6,18, notes; 17:7, note; 22:18, note). (1) This covenant was based on Israel's prior reconciliation with God and their ongoing fellowship with Him. It defined the conditions by which Israel would remain God's treasured possession, continue in His blessing, and carry out His will for the nation (see Gen. 12:2–3; 26:4).

(2) God intended that Israel be a unique people, chosen and separated unto Him for this purpose. The people were to respond in obedience and gratitude to God by seeking to follow the commandments and by offering the prescribed sacrifices of God's covenant. As a result, they would remain God's special people (cf. Amos 3:2; 9:7)—a kingdom of priests who were holy and pure (see v. 6, note; see article on GOD'S COVENANT WITH THE ISRAELITES, p. 314).

19:4 I BARE YOU ON EAGLES' WINGS. As the mother eagle catches her young on her wings to keep them from crashing while learning to fly, so God was caring for Israel and bringing her not just to Sinai, but to Himself (cf. Deut. 32:11; Is. 43:1–4). This expression demonstrates God's love for Israel and serves as the basis for their obedience and covenant obligation to Him (see next note).

19:5 IF YE WILL OBEY MY VOICE. Israel's continued election as the people of God was conditioned on their obeying Him as their Lord; this is indicated in the "if . . . then" construction of this

enant, then [n]ye shall be a peculiar treasure unto me above all people: for [o]all the earth *is* mine:

6 And ye shall be unto me a [p]kingdom of priests, and an [q]holy nation.
Ex. 20:1-17 These *are* the words which thou shalt speak unto the children of Israel.

7 ¶ And Moses came and called for the elders of the people, and laid before their faces all these words which the LORD commanded him.

8 And [r]all the people answered together, and said, All that the LORD hath spoken we will do. And Moses returned the words of the people unto the LORD.

9 And the LORD said unto Moses, Lo, I come unto thee [s]in a thick cloud, [t]that the people may hear when I speak with thee, and [u]believe thee for ever. And Moses told the words of the people unto the LORD.

10 ¶ And the LORD said unto Moses, Go unto the people, and [v]sanctify them today and tomorrow, and let them [w]wash their clothes,

11 And be ready against the third day: for the third day the LORD [x]will come down in the sight of all the people upon mount Sinai.

12 And thou shalt set bounds unto the people round about, saying, Take heed to yourselves, *that ye* go *not* up into the mount, or touch the border of it: [y]whosoever toucheth the mount shall be surely put to death:

13 There shall not an hand touch it, but he shall surely be stoned, or shot through; whether *it be* beast or man, it shall not live: when the [z]trumpet[g] soundeth long, they shall come up to the mount.

14 ¶ And Moses went down from the mount unto the people, and sanctified the people; and they washed their clothes.

15 And he said unto the people, Be ready against the third day: [a]come not at *your* wives.

16 ¶ And it came to pass on the third day in the morning, that there were [b]thunders and lightnings, and a [c]thick cloud upon the mount, and the [d]voice of the trumpet exceeding loud; so that all the people that *was* in the camp [e]trembled.

17 And [f]Moses brought forth the people out of the camp to meet with God; and they stood at the nether part of the mount.

18 And [g]mount Sinai was altogether on a smoke, because the LORD descended upon it [h]in fire: [i]and the smoke thereof ascended as the smoke of a furnace, and [j]the whole mount quaked greatly.

19 And when the voice of the trumpet sounded long, and waxed louder and louder, [k]Moses spake, and [l]God answered him by a voice.

20 And the LORD came down upon mount Sinai, on the top of the mount: and the LORD called Moses *up* to the top of the mount; and Moses went up.

21 And the LORD said unto Moses, Go down, [h]charge the people, lest

19:5 [n]Deut. 7:6 & 14:2,21 1 Ki. 8:53 Ps. 135:4 [o]ch. 9:29 Deut. 10:14 Job 41:11 Ps. 24:1 **19:6** [p]Deut. 33:2-4 1 Pet. 2:5,9 [q]Deut. 7:6 Is. 62:12 1 Cor. 3:17 **19:8** [r]Deut. 5:27 **19:9** [s]Mat. 17:5 [t]Deut. 4:12,36 John 12:29,30 [u]ch. 14:31 **19:10** [v]Lev. 11:44,45 Heb. 10:22 [w]ver. 14 **19:11** [x]ver. 16,18 ch. 34:5 **19:12** [y]Heb. 12:20 **19:13** [z]ver. 16,19 **19:15** [a]1 Cor. 7:5 **19:16** [b]Heb. 12:18,19 Rev. 8:5 [c]ch. 40:34 2 Chr. 5:14 [d]Rev. 4:1 [e]Heb. 12:21 **19:17** [f]Deut. 4:10 **19:18** [g]Deut. 4:11 & 33:2 Judg. 5:5 Hab. 3:3 [h]ch. 3:2 & 24:17 2 Chr. 7:1-3 [i]Gen. 15:17 Ps. 144:5 Rev. 15:8 [j]Ps. 68:8 Jer. 4:24 Heb. 12:26

19:19 [k]Heb. 12:21 [l]Neh. 9:13 Ps. 81:7

[g] Or, *cornet* [h] Heb. *contest*

verse. And God expected this obedience, so essential in fulfilling His future purposes for them (vv. 5–6), to come from hearts of gratitude responding to His love and care for them, demonstrated especially by their redemption from Egypt (see previous note; see Deut. 6:5). The principle of obedience toward God is equally an essential element in our relationship with Christ under the new covenant (see John 8:31; 14:21; Rom. 4:12; Heb. 3:7–19).

19:5 A PECULIAR TREASURE. Israel was to be God's own treasured possession (cf. Deut. 4:10; Amos 3:2; 9:7). Even though all nations are accountable to God because He is their Creator, Israel was to have a unique relation to God because He was their Redeemer. This purpose for Israel foreshadowed God's purpose for the church (1 Cor. 3:16; Tit. 2:14; 1 Pet. 2:5,9).

19:6 A KINGDOM OF PRIESTS, AND AN HOLY NATION. As part of God's purpose for the Israelites in bringing them out of Egypt, they were to be a "kingdom of priests" (i.e., separated and consecrated for God's service) and a "holy nation." Likewise, believers under the new covenant must be a kingdom of priests (1 Pet. 2:5–9; Rev. 1:6; 5:10; 20:6) and a holy people, i.e., a people separated from the world's ungodly ways and walking in God's righteous ways and holy will (see Acts 9:13, note on the meaning of saint; see article on SANCTIFICATION, p. 1982).

19:16 THUNDERS AND LIGHTNINGS. The awesome manifestations that accompanied God's visitation had several goals: (1) to demonstrate God's holiness, power, and transcendence (v. 9); (2) to instill faith in God and establish the authority of His servant, Moses (v. 9); (3) to establish the fear of God in the hearts of the people so that they might not sin (v. 16; 20:20; cf. Heb. 12:18–21); and (4) to impress upon the people that judgment and death would be the result of willful disobedience to God (vv. 12–25; cf. Heb. 10:26–31).

they break through unto the LORD [m]to
gaze, and many of them perish.
22 And let the priests also, which
come near to the LORD, [n]sanctify
themselves, lest the LORD [o]break forth
upon them.
23 And Moses said unto the LORD,
The people cannot come up to mount
Sinai: for thou chargedst us, saying,
[p]Set bounds about the mount, and
sanctify it.
24 And the LORD said unto him,
Away, get thee down, and thou shalt
come up, thou, and Aaron with thee:
but let not the priests and the people
break through to come up unto the
LORD, lest he break forth upon them.
25 So Moses went down unto the
people, and spake unto them.

19:21 [m]See ch. 3:5; 1 Sam. 6:19
19:22 [n]Lev. 10:3; [o]2 Sam. 6:7,8
19:23 [p]ver. 12
20:1 [q]Deut. 5:22
20:2 [r]Hos. 13:4; [s]ch. 13:3
20:3 [t]Jer. 35:15
20:4 [u]Deut. 27:15
20:5 [v]Is. 44:15,19

The Ten Commandments

20:1–17pp — Deut. 5:6–21

20 AND GOD spake [q]all these
words, saying,
2 [r]I *am* the LORD thy God, which
have brought thee out of the land of
Egypt, [s]out of the house of [i]bond-
age.
3 [t]Thou shalt have no other gods
before me.
4 [u]Thou shalt not make unto thee
any graven image, or any likeness *of
any thing* that *is* in heaven above, or
that *is* in the earth beneath, or that *is*
in the water under the earth:
5 [v]Thou shalt not bow down thy-
self to them, nor serve them: for I the

[i] Heb. *servants*

20:1 AND GOD SPAKE ALL THESE WORDS. For general comments on the place of the Law of God in the O.T., see article on THE OLD TESTAMENT LAW, p. 124.

20:2 THE TEN COMMANDMENTS. The Ten Commandments, recorded here (cf. Deut. 5:6–21), were written by God Himself on two stone tablets and given to Moses and the people of Israel (31:18; 32:16; Deut. 4:13; 10:4). Keeping the commandments provided a way for Israel to respond righteously to God in gratitude for their deliverance out of Egypt; at the same time, such obedience was required in order to remain in the promised land (Deut. 4:1,14; see article on THE OLD TESTAMENT LAW, p. 124).

(1) The Ten Commandments summarize God's moral law for Israel and describe their obligations both to God and others. Christ and the apostles affirm that, as valid expressions of the holy will of God, they remain obligatory for N.T. believers (Mat. 22:37–39; Mark 12:28–34; Luke 10:27; Rom. 13:9; Gal. 5:14; cf. Lev. 19:18; Deut. 6:5; 10:12; 30:6). According to these N.T. passages, the Ten Commandments are summed up by love for God and love for one's neighbor; keeping them is not only a matter of external rules, but also requires action from the heart (see Deut. 6:5, note). Thus the law demands an inner spiritual righteousness that is expressed in outward justice and holiness.

(2) The civil and ceremonial commandments of the O.T. which governed Israel's worship and social life (see article on THE OLD TESTAMENT LAW, p. 124) are no longer binding on the N.T. believer. They were types and shadows of better things to come and have been fulfilled in Jesus Christ (Heb. 10:1; cf. Mat. 7:12; 22:37–40; Rom. 13:8; Gal. 5:14; 6:2). They do, however, contain wisdom and spiritual principles applicable to all generations (see Mat. 5:17, note).

20:3 THOU SHALT HAVE NO OTHER GODS BEFORE ME. This command prohibited the polytheism which characterized all the religions of the ancient Near East. Israel was not to worship or call upon any of the gods of other nations, but was commanded to fear the Lord and serve only Him (cf. Deut. 32:39; Josh. 24:14–15).

When applied to N.T. believers, this commandment means at least three things. (1) The believers' worship must be directed to God alone. There may be no worshiping, praying to, or seeking guidance and help from any "other gods," spirits, or people who have died (cf. Lev. 17:7; Deut. 6:4; 32:17; Ps. 106:37; 1 Cor. 10:19–20). The first commandment is especially directed against the worshiping of spirits (i.e., demons) through spiritism, divination, and other forms of idolatry (cf. Deut. 18:9–22). (2) Believers must be totally consecrated to God. Only God with His revealed will and inspired Word may guide their lives (Mat. 4:4; see article on THE INSPIRATION AND AUTHORITY OF SCRIPTURE, p. 1924). (3) Believers must have as their purpose in life to seek and love God with their whole heart, soul, and might, relying on Him to provide that which is good for their lives (Deut. 6:5; Ps. 119:2; Mat. 6:33; Phil. 3:8; see Mat. 22:37, note; Col. 3:5, note).

20:4 ANY GRAVEN IMAGE. The prohibition against the worship of other gods required that no image be made of them (cf. Deut. 4:19,23–28), nor could anyone make an image of the Lord God Himself. He is too great to be represented by anything made by human hands. As applied to believers in Christ, the second commandment forbids making images of God or creatures for the purpose of worship, prayer, or any sort of spiritual help (cf. Deut. 4:15–16). The principle behind this command applies equally to all three persons of the Trinity. (1) It is impossible for any image or picture of God to truly represent the personal glory and character of God (cf. Is. 40:18). (2) God is so transcendent, so holy and unsearchable, that any image of Him dishonors Him and detracts from His true nature and from what He has revealed about Himself (cf. 32:1–6). (3) The believer's thoughts and concepts of God must not be based on images or pictures of Him, but on God's Word and on His revelation in the person and work of Jesus Christ (cf. John 17:3).

THE OLD TESTAMENT LAW

***Ex. 20:1–2** "And God spake all these words, saying, I am the LORD thy God, which have brought thee out of the land of Egypt, out of the house of bondage."*

Receiving God's law through their leader, Moses, was one of the most important aspects of the Israelites' experience at Mount Sinai. The Mosaic Law (Heb. *torah*, meaning "teaching") can be divided into three categories: (a) the moral law, dealing with God's rules for holy living (Ex. 20:1–17); (b) the civil law, dealing with the legal and social life of Israel as a nation (Ex. 21:1—23:33); and (c) the ceremonial law, dealing with the form and ritual of Israel's worship of the Lord God, including the sacrificial system (Ex. 24:12–31:18). Note the following regarding the nature and function of the O.T. law.

(1) The law was given in connection with the covenant that God made with His people; it set forth the covenant stipulations which they were expected to obey in loyalty to the Lord God to whom they belonged. The Israelites formally accepted these obligations (Ex. 24:1–8; see article on GOD'S COVENANT WITH THE ISRAELITES, p. 314).

(2) Israel's obedience to the law was to be grounded in God's saving mercy and in His deliverance of the people (Ex. 19:4). Note that the law was given to them after they had been saved by the blood of the Passover lamb and redeemed from slavery in Egypt (Ex. 20:2), and while they were living as pilgrims on the earth by God's grace (Ex. 19:4).

(3) The law revealed God's will for His people's behavior (Ex. 19:4–6; 20:1–17; 21:1—24:8) and prescribed blood sacrifices to cover their sin (Lev. 1:5; 16:33). The law was not designed as a way to obtain salvation for the unsaved; the people to whom it was given were already in a saved relationship with God (Ex. 20:2). Rather, through the law they learned how God wanted them to live righteously toward both their Redeemer and their neighbor. Israel was expected to keep the law by God's grace in order to maintain and celebrate their faith relationship with Him (Deut. 28:1–2; 30:15–20).

(4) In both the O.T. and N.T., a committed trust in God and His word (Gen. 15:6) and heartfelt love for Him (Deut. 6:5) formed the foundation for keeping God's commandments. Israel failed exactly at this point, for they often did not make believing in God, loving Him with the whole heart, and desiring to walk in His ways their motive for fulfilling the law. Paul states that Israel did not obtain the righteousness that the law intended because "*they sought it* not by faith" (Rom. 9:32).

(5) The law emphasized the eternal truth that obedience to God from a heart of love (see Gen. 2:9, note; Deut. 6:5, note) would result in a full life and in rich blessings from the Lord (cf. Gen. 2:16, note; Deut. 4:1,40; 5:33; 8:1; Ps. 119:45; Rom. 8:13; 1 John 1:7).

(6) The law expressed the nature and disposition of God, i.e., His love, goodness, justice, and hatred of evil. The Israelite believers were expected to keep God's moral law because they had been created in His image (Lev. 19:2).

(7) Salvation in the O.T. was never based on perfection in keeping all the commandments. Inherent in Israel's relationship with God was the sacrificial system which provided forgiveness for those who transgressed the commandment but who sincerely returned in repentance and faith to God's mercy and provision of blood atonement.

(8) The O.T. law and covenant were not complete, nor were they intended to be permanent. The law acted as a temporary tutor for God's people until Christ came (Gal. 3:22–26). The old covenant has now been replaced by the new covenant, in which God has disclosed fully His plan of salvation through Jesus Christ (Rom. 3:24–26; see Gal. 3:19, note, for more on the nature and function of O.T. law).

(9) The law was given by God and added to the promises "because of transgressions" (Gal. 3:19); i.e., it was designed (a) to regulate conduct, (b) to define what sin was, (c) to show Israel their inherent tendency to violate God's will and do evil, and (d) to awaken their sense of need for God's mercy and redemption (cf. Rom. 3:20; 5:20; 8:2).

LORD thy God *am* [w]a jealous God, [x]vis-
iting the iniquity of the fathers upon
the children unto the third and fourth
generation of them that hate me;
6 And [y]showing mercy unto thou-
sands of them that love me, and keep
my commandments.
7 [z]Thou shalt not take the name of
the LORD thy God in vain; for the LORD
[a]will not hold him guiltless that
taketh his name in vain.
8 [b]Remember the sabbath day, to
keep it holy.
9 [c]Six days shalt thou labour, and
do all thy work:
10 But the [d]seventh day *is* the sab-
bath of the LORD thy God: *in it* thou
shalt not do any work, thou, nor thy
son, nor thy daughter, thy manservant,
nor thy maidservant, nor thy cattle,
[e]nor thy stranger that *is* within thy
gates:
11 For [f]*in* six days the LORD made
heaven and earth, the sea, and all that
in them *is,* and rested the seventh day:
wherefore the LORD blessed the sab-
bath day, and hallowed it.
12 ¶ [g]Honour thy father and thy
mother: that thy days may be long
upon the land which the LORD thy God
giveth thee.
13 [h]Thou shalt not kill.
14 [i]Thou shalt not commit adul-
tery.
15 [j]Thou shalt not steal.

20:5 [w]Deut. 4:24 [x]Num. 14:18,33 1 Ki. 21:29 Ps. 79:8 Jer. 32:18 **20:6** [y]Deut:7:9 Rom. 11:28 **20:7** [z]Mat. 5:33 [a]Mic. 6:11 **20:8** [b]Lev. 26:2 **20:9** [c]Ezek. 20:12 Luke 13:14 **20:10** [d]Gen. 2:2,3 [e]Neh. 13:16-19 **20:11** [f]Gen. 2:2 **20:12** [g]Lev. 19:3 Deut. 5:16 Eph. 6:2

20:13 [h]Rom. 13:9 **20:14** [i]Deut. 5:18 **20:15** [j]Lev. 19:11

20:5 UPON THE CHILDREN. See 34:7, note.

20:7 THE NAME OF THE LORD . . . IN VAIN. Taking God's name "in vain" included making a false promise by it (Lev. 19:12; cf. Mat. 5:33–37), pronouncing it insincerely or thoughtlessly, or cursing and blaspheming (Lev. 24:10–16). God's name must be hallowed, honored, and respected as profoundly sacred, and it may be used only in a holy manner (see Mat. 6:9, note).

20:8 REMEMBER THE SABBATH DAY. The O.T. Sabbath was the seventh day of the week. To keep that day holy meant setting it apart as different from other days by ceasing one's labor in order to rest, serve God, and concentrate on those things which concerned eternity, spiritual life, and God's honor (vv. 9–11; cf. Gen. 2:2–3; Is. 58:13–14). (1) The Israelites were expected to model their conduct after God's work in creation (v. 11; Gen. 2:2–3). (2) The Sabbath was a sign that they belonged to God (31:13). (3) It reminded them of their deliverance from slavery in Egypt (Deut. 5:15; see Mat. 12:1, note).

20:12 HONOUR THY FATHER AND THY MOTHER. This commandment includes all necessary acts of kindness, material support, respect, and obedience to one's parents (Eph. 6:1–3; Col. 3:20). It prohibits unkind words and injurious acts. (1) In 21:15,17, God required the death penalty for any person who hit or cursed father or mother. This shows how much importance God placed on respect for parents (see Eph. 6:1, note). (2) Related to this commandment is the reciprocal duty of the father and mother to love their children and teach them the fear of the Lord and the ways of God (Deut. 4:9; 6:6–7; Eph. 6:4).

20:13 THOU SHALT NOT KILL. The sixth commandment forbids willful murder, i.e., the unauthorized or unlawful taking of life. God prescribed the death penalty for violating this commandment (see Gen. 9:6, note). The N.T. condemns not only murder, but also hate, which prompts one to desire the death of another (1 John 3:15), and any other ungodly action or influence which causes the spiritual death of another (see Mat. 5:22, note; 18:6, note).

20:14 THOU SHALT NOT COMMIT ADULTERY. This seventh commandment prohibiting adultery (cf. Lev. 20:10; Deut. 22:22) encompasses immorality and all sexual sins (Mat. 5:27–32; 1 Cor. 6:13–20). Adultery (i.e., unfaithfulness to one's spouse) is so abominable in God's sight that the Bible everywhere condemns its practice. The Bible teaches the following concerning adultery: (1) It transgresses God's moral law as expressed in the Ten Commandments.

(2) In the O.T. law, it was punishable by death (Lev. 20:10; Deut. 22:22).

(3) It brings permanent and serious consequences (2 Sam. 11:1–17; 12:14; Jer. 23:10–11; 1 Cor. 6:16–18); the one committing adultery will carry reproach for the rest of his or her life (Prov. 6:32–33).

(4) Adultery is an especially heinous sin when committed by leaders of God's people. If and when they commit this sin, it is equivalent to despising God's word and the Lord Himself (2 Sam. 12:9–10). By marital unfaithfulness professed believers disqualify themselves from being chosen for or continuing in church leadership (see article on MORAL QUALIFICATIONS FOR OVERSEERS, p. 1908). Note how in the O.T., adultery filled the land because of the influence of profane prophets and priests (Jer. 23:10–14; 29:23).

(5) Adultery and promiscuous sex among the leaders and members of God's people are normally the result of prior spiritual adultery, i.e., unfaithfulness to God (Hos. 4:13–14; 9:1; see article on PERSONAL APOSTASY, p. 1946).

(6) Adultery begins as a desire in the heart before it is expressed as a physical act. Lust is clearly regarded as sin in the Bible (Job 31:1,7; see Mat. 5:28, note).

(7) Adultery is a sin of such magnitude and consequence that it gives the innocent person the right to end the marriage by divorce (see Mat. 19:9, note; Mark 10:11, note).

(8) Sexual immorality within the church must be disciplined and never tolerated (1 Cor. 5:1–13).

(9) Unrepentant adulterers have no inheritance in the kingdom of God, i.e., they are separated

16 [k]Thou shalt not bear false witness against thy neighbour.

17 [l]Thou shalt not covet thy neighbour's house, [m]thou shalt not covet thy neighbour's wife, nor his manservant, nor his maidservant, nor his ox, nor his ass, nor any thing that *is* thy neighbour's.
Lev. 20:26

18 ¶ And [n]all the people [o]saw the thunderings, and the lightnings, and the noise of the trumpet, and the mountain [p]smoking: and when the people saw *it*, they removed, and stood afar off.

19 And they said unto Moses, [q]Speak thou with us, and we will hear: but [r]let not God speak with us, lest we die.

20 And Moses said unto the people, [s]Fear not: [t]for God is come to prove you, and [u]that his fear may be before your faces, that ye sin not.

Making an altar of earth

21 And the people stood afar off, and Moses drew near unto [v]the thick darkness where God *was*.

22 ¶ And the LORD said unto Moses, Thus thou shalt say unto the children

20:16 [k]ch. 23:1 Deut. 5:20
20:17 [l]Luke 12:15 Eph. 5:3,5 Heb. 13:5 [m]Mat. 5:28
20:18 [n]Heb. 12:18 [o]Rev. 1:10,12 [p]ch. 19:18
20:19 [q]Gal. 3:19 [r]Deut. 5:25
20:20 [s]Is. 41:10,13 [t]Deut. 13:3 [u]Prov. 16:6 Is. 8:13
20:21 [v]ch. 19:16
20:22 [w]Deut. 4:36
20:23 [x]ch. 32:1,2,4
20:24 [y]Lev. 1:2 [z]Deut. 16:6,11 1 Ki. 9:3 2 Chr. 6:6 [a]Gen. 12:2
20:25 [b]Deut. 27:5
21:1 [c]Deut. 4:14
21:2 [d]Jer. 34:14

of Israel, Ye have seen that I have talked with you [w]from heaven.

23 Ye shall not make [x]with me gods of silver, neither shall ye make unto you gods of gold.

24 ¶ An altar of earth thou shalt make unto me, and shalt sacrifice thereon thy burnt offerings, and thy peace offerings, [y]thy sheep, and thine oxen: in all [z]places where I record my name I will come unto thee, and I will [a]bless thee.

25 And [b]if thou wilt make me an altar of stone, thou shalt not [j]build it of hewn stone: for if thou lift up thy tool upon it, thou hast polluted it.

26 Neither shalt thou go up by steps unto mine altar, that thy nakedness be not discovered thereon.

Laws about servants

21:2–6pp — Deut. 15:12–18
21:2–11Ref — Lev. 25:39–55

21 NOW THESE *are* the judgments which thou shalt [c]set before them.

2 [d]If thou buy an Hebrew servant, six years he shall serve: and in the sev-

[j] Heb. *build them with hewing*

from the life and salvation of God (1 Cor. 6:9; Gal. 5:19–21).

(10) Adultery and harlotry are terms used to describe the apostate church and the abominations it produces (Rev. 17:1–5; see Rev. 17:1, note).

20:15 THOU SHALT NOT STEAL. This commandment prohibits stealing money or anything belonging to another. Cheating too is a form of stealing (2 Cor. 8:21). This commandment demands honesty in all our dealings with people.

20:16 NOT BEAR FALSE WITNESS. The ninth commandment protects the name and reputation of other persons. No one is to make false statements about anyone's character or actions. We must speak about all people in a fair and just manner (cf. Lev. 19:16; see John 8:44, note; 2 Cor. 12:20, note). This commandment also applies to lying in general (cf. Lev. 6:2–3; Prov. 14:5; Col. 3:9).

20:17 THOU SHALT NOT COVET. (1) This commandment goes beyond the external sin of word or deed to condemn evil motives and desires. Coveting involves the desire or lust for all that is wrong or belongs to another person. Paul claims that this commandment reveals the depth of human sinfulness (Rom. 7:7–13). (2) This law, as well as the others, exposes the depravity of men and women and calls for them to seek grace and moral power from God (cf. Luke 12:15–21; Rom. 7:24–25; Eph. 5:3). Only by the regenerative power of the Holy Spirit can one live a life pleasing to God (see Rom. 8:2, note).

20:20 FEAR NOT. The sights and sounds at Sinai caused the Israelites to become afraid and to back off to the opposite side of the valley. Moses told them to stop being afraid with this cowardly fear. God was using this display of power in order to inspire in them a godly fear, awe, and reverence that would help to keep them from sinning.

21:1 THESE *ARE* THE JUDGMENTS. This next section (20:22—23:33) contains "the book of the covenant" (24:7), i.e, the laws for the nation of Israel that governed its society and worship. These laws, mostly civil in nature, were applicable only to Israel, her religion, and the conditions and environment existing in that period. However, the principles embodied in these laws—such as reverence for life, justice, and fairness—are eternally valid.

21:2 AN HEBREW SERVANT. Although God did not immediately abolish such evils as slavery or polygamy in Israel, He did regulate them so as to make them more humane (cf. Lev. 25:39–40; Deut. 15:12–18). On the one hand, these practices were not God's ideal. On the other hand, He permitted them for a time because of the hardness of human hearts (cf. Mat. 19:8; see Gen. 29:28, note). Furthermore, God's laws concerning slavery were much more humane than the customs of the nations surrounding them. In the N.T., however, God expressed an even higher standard (see John 13:34, note; Col. 3:22, note).

HEBREW CALENDAR AND SELECTED EVENTS

Sacred Sequence Begins	Hebrew Name	Modern Equivalent	Biblical References	Agriculture	Feasts
1	**Abib; Nisan**	March-April	Ex 12:2; 13:4; 23:15; 34:18; Dt 16:1; Ne 2:1; Est 3:7	Spring (later) rains; barley and flax harvest begins	Passover; Unleavened Bread; Firstfruits
2	**Ziv (Iyyar)***	April-May	1 Ki 6:1,37	Barley havest; dry season begins	
3	**Sivan**	May-June	Est 8:9	Wheat harvest	Pentecost (Weeks)
4	**(Tammuz)***	June-July		Tending vines	
5	**(Ab)***	July-August		Ripening of grapes, figs and olives	
6	**Elul**	August-September	Ne 6:15	Processing grapes, figs and olives	
7	**Ethanim (Tishri)***	September-October	1 Ki 8:2	Autumn (early) rains begin; plowing	Trumpets; Atonement; Tabernacles (Booths)
8	**Bul (Marcheshvan)***	October-November	1 Ki 6:38	Sowing of wheat and barley	
9	**Kislev**	November-December	Ne 1:1, Zec 7:1	Winter rains begin (snow in some areas)	Hanukkah ("Dedication")
10	**Tebeth**	December-January	Est 2:16		
11	**Shebat**	January-February	Zec 1:7		
12	**Adar**	February-March	Ezr 6:15; Est 3:7,13; 8:12; 9:1,15,17,19,21	Almond trees bloom; citrus fruit harvest	Purim
		(Adar Sheni)* **Second Adar**	This intercalary month was added about every three years so the lunar calendar would correspond to the solar year.		

* Names in parentheses are not in the Bible

enth he shall go out free for nothing.

3 If he came in [k]by himself, he shall go out by himself: if he were married, then his wife shall go out with him.

4 If his master have given him a wife, and she have born him sons or daughters; the wife and her children shall be her master's, and he shall go out by himself.

5 [e]And if the servant [l]shall plainly say, I love my master, my wife, and my children; I will not go out free:

6 Then his master shall bring him unto the [f]judges; he shall also bring him to the door, or unto the door post; and his master shall [g]bore his ear through with an awl; and he shall serve him for ever.

7 ¶ And if a man [h]sell his daughter to be a maidservant, she shall not go out as the menservants do.

8 If she [m]please not her master, who hath betrothed her to himself, then shall he let her be redeemed: to sell her unto a strange nation he shall have no power, seeing he hath dealt deceitfully with her.

9 And if he have betrothed her unto his son, he shall deal with her after the manner of daughters.

10 If he take him another *wife;* her food, her raiment, [i]and her duty of marriage, shall he not diminish.

11 And if he do not these three unto her, then shall she go out free without money.

Laws about murder and strife

12 ¶ [j]He that smiteth a man, so that he die, shall be surely put to death.

13 And [k]if a man lie not in wait, but God [l]deliver *him* into his hand; then [m]I will appoint thee a place whither he shall flee.

14 But if a man come [n]presumptuously upon his neighbour, to slay him with guile; [o]thou shalt take him from mine altar, that he may die.

15 ¶ And he that smiteth his father, or his mother, shall be surely put to death.

16 ¶ And [p]he that stealeth a man, and [q]selleth him, or if he be [r]found in his hand, he shall surely be put to death.

17 ¶ And [s]he that [n]curseth his father, or his mother, shall surely be put to death.

18 ¶ And if men strive together, and one smite [o]another with a stone, or with *his* fist, and he die not, but keepeth *his* bed:

19 If he rise again, and walk abroad [t]upon his staff, then shall he that smote *him* be quit: only he shall pay *for* [p]the loss of his time, and shall cause *him* to be thoroughly healed.

20 ¶ And if a man smite his servant, or his maid, with a rod, and he die under his hand; he shall be surely [q]punished.

21 Notwithstanding, if he continue a day or two, he shall not be punished: for he *is* his money.

22 ¶ If men strive, and hurt a woman with child, so that her fruit depart *from her,* and yet no mischief follow: he shall be surely punished, according as the woman's husband will lay upon him; and he shall [u]pay as the judges *determine.*

23 And if *any* mischief follow, then thou shalt give life for life,

21:5 [e]Deut. 15:16,17
21:6 [f]ch. 12:12 [g]Ps. 40:6
21:7 [h]Neh. 5:5
21:10 [i]1 Cor. 7:5
21:12 [j]Gen. 9:6 Mat. 26:52
21:13 [k]Deut. 19:4,5 [l]1 Sam. 24:4,10, 18
[m]Num. 35:11 Deut. 19:3 Josh. 20:2
21:14 [n]Deut. 19:11,12 Heb. 10:26 [o]1 Ki. 2:28-34
21:16 [p]Deut. 24:7 [q]Gen. 37:28 [r]ch. 22:4
21:17 [s]Mark 7:10
21:19 [t]2 Sam. 3:29
21:22 [u]ver. 30 Deut. 22:18,19

[k] Heb. *with his body* [l] Heb. *saying shall say*
[m] Heb. *be evil in the eyes of* [n] Or, *revileth*
[o] Or, *his neighbour* [p] Heb. *his ceasing*
[q] Heb. *avenged*

21:12–17 BE SURELY PUT TO DEATH. These verses list four crimes to which God assigned the death penalty: premeditated murder (vv. 12,14), inflicting physical harm on parents (v. 15), kidnapping (v. 16), and verbal cursing of parents (v. 17). This punishment indicates the importance God put upon proper interpersonal relationships (murder and kidnapping) and proper family relationships (treatment of parents).

21:22–23 SO THAT HER FRUIT DEPART *FROM HER.* In addition to the protection of living persons, God required the protection of unborn children. (1) "Her fruit depart *from her*" refers to giving birth prematurely to a child because of violence done to the pregnant woman. If this happened, the one causing the premature birth had to pay a fine.

(2) If there was serious injury to the mother or the child, then the offending party had to pay according to the law of retaliation. Note that if death resulted to the mother or the child, then the perpetrator was guilty of murder and had to pay with his life (v. 23). In other words, the unborn child is viewed in this passage as a human being; its death is considered murder.

(3) Note that this is the only instance in the law where accidental manslaughter called for the death penalty (cf. Deut. 19:4–10). The principle is clear—God seeks to protect those who are least able to protect themselves (i.e., the unborn).

24 [v]Eye for eye, tooth for tooth, hand for hand, foot for foot,

25 Burning for burning, wound for wound, stripe for stripe.

26 ¶ And if a man smite the eye of his servant, or the eye of his maid, that it perish; he shall let him go free for his eye's sake.

27 And if he smite out his manservant's tooth, or his maidservant's tooth; he shall let him go free for his tooth's sake.

28 ¶ If an ox gore a man or a woman, that they die: then [w]the ox shall be surely stoned, and his flesh shall not be eaten; but the owner of the ox *shall be* quit.

29 But if the ox were wont to push with his horn in time past, and it hath been testified to his owner, and he hath not kept him in, but that he hath killed a man or a woman; the ox shall be stoned, and his owner also shall be put to death.

30 If there be laid on him a sum of money, then he shall give for [x]the ransom of his life whatsoever is laid upon him.

31 Whether he have gored a son, or have gored a daughter, according to this judgment shall it be done unto him.

32 If the ox shall push a manservant or a maidservant; he shall give unto their master [y]thirty shekels of silver, and the [z]ox shall be stoned.

33 ¶ And if a man shall open a pit, or if a man shall dig a pit, and not cover it, and an ox or an ass fall therein;

34 The owner of the pit shall make *it* good, *and* give money unto the owner of them; and the dead *beast* shall be his.

35 ¶ And if one man's ox hurt another's, that he die; then they shall sell the live ox, and divide the money of it; and the dead *ox* also they shall divide.

36 Or if it be known that the ox hath used to push in time past, and his owner hath not kept him in; he shall surely pay ox for ox; and the dead shall be his own.

Laws about property

22 IF A man shall steal an ox, or a [r]sheep, and kill it, or sell it; he shall restore five oxen for an ox, and [a]four sheep for a sheep.

2 ¶ If a thief be found [b]breaking up, and be smitten that he die, *there shall* [c]no blood *be shed* for him.

3 If the sun be risen upon him, *there shall be* blood *shed* for him; *for* he should make full restitution; if he have nothing, then he shall be [d]sold for his theft.

4 If the theft be certainly [e]found in his hand alive, whether it be ox, or ass, or sheep; he shall [f]restore double.

5 ¶ If a man shall cause a field or vineyard to be eaten, and shall put in his beast, and shall feed in another man's field; of the best of his own field, and of the best of his own vineyard, shall he make restitution.

6 ¶ If fire break out, and catch in thorns, so that the stacks of corn, or the standing corn, or the field, be consumed *therewith;* he that kindled the fire shall surely make restitution.

7 ¶ If a man shall deliver unto his neighbour money or stuff to keep, and it be stolen out of the man's house; [g]if the thief be found, let him pay double.

8 If the thief be not found, then the master of the house shall be brought unto the [h]judges, *to see* whether he have put his hand unto his neighbour's goods.

9 For all manner of trespass, *whether it be* for ox, for ass, for sheep, for raiment, *or* for any manner of lost thing, which *another* challengeth to be his, the [i]cause of both parties shall come before the judges; *and* whom the judges shall condemn, he shall pay double unto his neighbour.

10 If a man deliver unto his neighbour an ass, or an ox, or a sheep, or any beast, to keep; and it die, or be hurt, or driven away, no man seeing *it:*

11 *Then* shall an [j]oath of the LORD be between them both, that he hath not put his hand unto his neighbour's goods; and the owner of it shall accept *thereof,* and he shall not make *it* good.

12 And [k]if it be stolen from him, he shall make restitution unto the owner thereof.

13 If it be torn in pieces, *then* let him bring it *for* witness, *and* he shall not make good that which was torn.

14 ¶ And if a man borrow *aught* of his neighbour, and it be hurt, or die, the owner thereof *being* not with it, he shall surely make *it* good.

15 *But* if the owner thereof *be* with it, he shall not make *it* good: if it *be* an hired *thing,* it came for his hire.

21:24 [v]Lev. 24:20 Deut. 19:21 Mat. 5:38
21:28 [w]Gen. 9:5
21:30 [x]ver. 22 Num. 35:31
21:32 [y]See Zech. 11:12, 13 Mat. 26:15 & 27:3,9 [z]ver. 28
22:1 [a]2 Sam. 12:6 See Prov. 6:31 Luke 19:8
22:2 [b]Mat. 24:43 [c]Num. 35:27
22:3 [d]ch. 21:2
22:4 [e]ch. 21:16 [f]See ver. 1,7 Prov. 6:31
22:7 [g]ver. 4
22:8 [h]ch. 21:6 ver. 28
22:9 [i]Deut. 25:1 2 Chr. 19:10
22:11 [j]Heb. 6:16
22:12 [k]Gen. 31:39

[r] Or, *goat*

Laws about personal actions

16 ¶ And [l]if a man entice a maid that is not betrothed, and lie with her, he shall surely endow her to be his wife.

17 If her father utterly refuse to give her unto him, he shall [s]pay money according to the [m]dowry of virgins.

18 ¶ [n]Thou shalt not suffer a witch to live.

19 ¶ [o]Whosoever lieth with a beast shall surely be put to death.

20 ¶ [p]He that sacrificeth unto *any* god, save unto the LORD only, he shall be utterly destroyed.

21 ¶ [q]Thou shalt neither vex a stranger, nor oppress him: for ye were strangers in the land of Egypt.

22 ¶ [r]Ye shall not afflict any widow, or fatherless child.

23 If thou afflict them in any wise, and they [s]cry at all unto me, I will surely [t]hear their cry;

24 And my [u]wrath shall wax hot, and I will kill you with the sword; and [v]your wives shall be widows, and your children fatherless.

25 ¶ [w]If thou lend money to *any of* my people *that is* poor by thee, thou shalt not be to him as an usurer, neither shalt thou lay upon him usury.

26 [x]If thou at all take thy neighbour's raiment to pledge, thou shalt deliver it unto him by that the sun goeth down:

27 For that *is* his covering only, it *is* his raiment for his skin: wherein shall he sleep? and it shall come to pass, when he crieth unto me, that I will hear; for I *am* [y]gracious.

28 ¶ [z]Thou shalt not revile the [a]gods,[t] nor curse the ruler of thy people.

29 ¶ Thou shalt not delay *to offer* [b]the[u] first of thy ripe fruits, and of thy [v]liquors: [c]the firstborn of thy sons shalt thou give unto me.

30 [d]Likewise shalt thou do with thine oxen, *and* with thy sheep: [e]seven days it shall be with his dam; on the eighth day thou shalt give it me.

31 ¶ And ye shall be [f]holy men unto me: [g]neither shall ye eat *any* flesh *that is* torn of beasts in the field; ye shall cast it to the dogs.

23 THOU [h]SHALT not [w]raise a false report: put not thine hand with the wicked to be an [i]unrighteous witness.

2 ¶ [j]Thou shalt not follow a multitude to *do* evil; [k]neither shalt thou [x]speak in a cause to decline after many to wrest *judgment:*

3 ¶ Neither shalt thou countenance a poor man in his cause.

4 ¶ [l]If thou meet thine enemy's ox or his ass going astray, thou shalt surely bring it back to him again.

5 [m]If thou see the ass of him that hateth thee lying under his burden, [y]and wouldest forbear to help him, thou shalt surely help with him.

6 [n]Thou shalt not wrest the judgment of thy poor in his cause.

7 [o]Keep thee far from a false matter; [p]and the innocent and righteous slay thou not: for [q]I will not justify the wicked.

8 ¶ And [r]thou shalt take no gift: for the gift blindeth [z]the wise, and perverteth the words of the righteous.

9 ¶ Also [s]thou shalt not oppress a stranger: for ye know the [a]heart of a stranger, seeing ye were strangers in the land of Egypt.

22:16 [l]Deut. 22:28,29
22:17 [m]Gen. 34:12
22:18 [n]1 Sam. 28:3
22:19 [o]Lev. 18:23
22:20 [p]Deut. 17:2,3,5
22:21 [q]Deut. 10:19
22:22 [r]Jas. 1:27
22:23 [s]Luke 18:7 [t]Ps. 18:6
22:24 [u]Ps. 69:24 [v]Ps. 109:9
22:25 [w]Ps. 15:5
22:26 [x]Deut. 24:6
22:27 [y]ch. 34:6
22:28 [z]Eccl. 10:20 [a]Ps. 82:6
22:29 [b]ch. 23:16 [c]ch. 13:2,12
22:30 [d]Deut. 15:19 [e]Lev. 22:27
22:31 [f]Lev. 19:2 [g]Ezek. 4:14
23:1 [h]Ps. 101:5 [i]Acts 6:11
23:2 [j]Gen. 7:1 [k]Lev. 19:15
23:4 [l]Rom. 12:20
23:5 [m]Deut. 22:4
23:6 [n]Eccl. 5:8
23:7 [o]Eph. 4:25 [p]Mat. 27:4 [q]Rom. 1:18
23:8 [r]Prov. 15:27
23:9 [s]ch. 22:21

[s] Heb. *weigh;* see Gen. 23:16 [t] Or, *judges* [u] Heb. *thy fulness* [v] Heb. *tear* [w] Or, *receive* [x] Heb. *answer* [y] Or, *wilt thou cease to help him?* or, *and wouldest cease to leave* thy business *for him; thou shalt surely leave* it to join *with him* [z] Heb. *the seeing* [a] Heb. *soul*

22:18 A WITCH. A witch was a woman who practiced witchcraft and occultism, e.g., divination, sorcery, contact with the dead (see Acts 19:19, note; Rev. 9:21, note). To seek power, guidance, or knowledge from the supernatural realm of the dead or through demonic activity was, and is, an abomination to God (cf. Lev. 19:31; 20:27; Deut. 18:9–12; 1 Sam. 28:7; Mal. 3:5).

22:22–24 WIDOW . . . CHILD. The regulations in vv. 22–27 reveal that God was deeply concerned about the hardships of the widow, the poor, and the disadvantaged, and was moved with compassion toward them (cf. Deut. 24:6,12–13; Job 22:6; 24:7; Ezek. 18:12,16; see Mark 6:34, note; 8:2, note; Luke 2:36–37, note; 7:13, note; see article on THE CARE OF THE POOR AND NEEDY, p. 1312).

22:25 IF THOU LEND MONEY. God prohibited the charging of "usury" (interest) for loans to the needy to supply their basic needs (cf. Lev. 25:25, 35,39,47). God wanted to prevent the poor from being exploited by the rich. This law did not, however, forbid loaning money for reasonable interest to non-Israelites for commercial purposes (cf. Deut. 23:19–20; Hab. 2:6; Mat. 25:27; Luke 19:23).

The law about the Sabbath

10 And [t]six years thou shalt sow thy land, and shalt gather in the fruits thereof:

11 But the seventh *year* thou shalt let it rest and lie still; that the poor of thy people may eat: and what they leave the beasts of the field shall eat. In like manner thou shalt deal with thy vineyard, *and* with thy [b]oliveyard.

12 [u]Six days thou shalt do thy work, and on the seventh day thou shalt rest: that thine ox and thine ass may rest, and the son of thy handmaid, and the stranger, may be refreshed.

13 And in all *things* that I have said unto you [v]be circumspect: and [w]make no mention of the name of other gods, neither let it be heard out of thy mouth.

Laws about appointed feasts

14 ¶ [x]Three times thou shalt keep a feast unto me in the year.

15 [y]Thou shalt keep the feast of unleavened bread: (thou shalt eat unleavened bread seven days, as I commanded thee, in the time appointed of the month Abib; for in it thou camest out from Egypt: [z]and none shall appear before me empty:)

16 [a]And the feast of harvest, the firstfruits of thy labours, which thou hast sown in the field: and [b]the feast of ingathering, *which is* in the end of the year, when thou hast gathered in thy labours out of the field.

17 [c]Three times in the year all thy males shall appear before the Lord GOD.

18 [d]Thou shalt not offer the blood of my sacrifice with leavened bread; neither shall the fat of my [c]sacrifice remain until the morning.

19 [e]The first of the firstfruits of thy land thou shalt bring into the house of the LORD thy God. [f]Thou shalt not seethe a kid in his mother's milk.

Promise of God's protection

20 ¶ [g]Behold, I send an Angel before thee, to keep thee in the way, and to bring thee into the place which I have prepared.

21 Beware of him, and obey his voice, [h]provoke him not; for he will [i]not pardon your transgressions: for [j]my name *is* in him.

22 But if thou shalt indeed obey his voice, and do all that I speak; then [k]I will be an enemy unto thine enemies, and [d]an adversary unto thine adversaries.

23 [l]For mine Angel shall go before thee, and [m]bring thee in unto the Amorites, and the Hittites, and the Perizzites, and the Canaanites, the Hivites, and the Jebusites: and I will cut them off.

24 Thou shalt not [n]bow down to their gods, nor serve them, [o]nor do after their works: [p]but thou shalt utterly overthrow them, and quite break down their images.

Lev. 11:44-45

25 And ye shall [q]serve the LORD your God, and [r]he shall bless thy bread, and thy water; and [s]I will take sickness away from the midst of thee.

26 ¶ [t]There shall nothing cast their young, nor be barren, in thy land: the number of thy days I will [u]fulfil.

27 I will send [v]my fear before thee,

23:10 [t]Lev. 25:3,4
23:12 [u]Luke 13:14
23:13 [v]1 Tim. 4:16 [w]Num. 32:38
23:14 [x]ch. 34:23
23:15 [y]ch. 12:15 [z]ch. 34:20
23:16 [a]ch. 34:22 [b]Deut. 16:13
23:17 [c]Deut. 16:16
23:18 [d]Deut. 16:4
23:19 [e]Deut. 26:10 [f]Deut. 14:21
23:20 [g]ch. 14:19
23:21 [h]Num. 14:11 Ps. 78:40,56 [i]Deut. 18:19 1 John 5:16 [j]Is. 9:6 Jer. 23:6
23:22 [k]Deut. 30:7 Jer. 30:20
23:23 [l]ver. 20 [m]Josh. 24:8
23:24 [n]ch. 20:5 [o]Deut. 12:30,31 [p]Num. 33:52
23:25 [q]Deut. 6:13 Mat. 4:10 [r]Deut. 28:5 [s]ch. 15:26 Deut. 7:15
23:26 [t]Deut. 7:14 & 28:4 Mal. 3:11 [u]1 Chr. 23:1
23:27 [v]Deut. 2:25

[b] Or, *olive trees* [c] Or, *feast* [d] Or, *I will afflict them that afflict thee*

23:15 FEAST OF UNLEAVENED BREAD. See 12:17, note.

23:16 THE FEAST OF HARVEST. This is also called the "feast of weeks" (34:22) or the "day of Pentecost" (Acts 2:1; 20:16; see Lev. 23:10, note).

23:16 THE FEAST OF INGATHERING. This is also called the "feast of tabernacles" or "booths" (see Lev. 23:34).

23:20 AN ANGEL. This probably was "the angel of the LORD" (see 3:2, note).

23:24 DO AFTER THEIR WORKS. God commanded His people not to adopt the religions nor to conform to the morals of the societies around them. Israel failed to observe fully this requirement and as a result they were not protected by the Lord (vv. 20–23). Under the new covenant, believers who conform to the ways of the world will also forfeit the promises and protection of God (see v. 25). We cannot have the blessings and presence of God and at the same time participate in the sinful ways of the world (see 2 Cor. 6:16–18; see article on SPIRITUAL SEPARATION FOR BELIEVERS, p. 1814).

23:25–26 TAKE SICKNESS AWAY. God connected the removal of sickness from among His people with their wholehearted devotion to Him and their separation from the ungodly influence around them. We should not conclude, however, that the sickness of an individual necessarily indicates he or she has conformed to the wicked ways of society. This passage does suggest that the worldliness of God's people as a whole will cause God to withdraw a portion of His blessing and power from them, thus affecting even the righteous among God's people (cf. 1 Cor. 12:26).

and will [w]destroy all the people to whom thou shalt come, and I will make all thine enemies turn their [e]backs unto thee.

28 And [x]I will send hornets before thee, which shall drive out the Hivite, the Canaanite, and the Hittite, from before thee.

29 [y]I will not drive them out from before thee in one year; lest the land become desolate, and the beast of the field multiply against thee.

30 By little and little I will drive them out from before thee, until thou be increased, and inherit the land.

31 And [z]I will set thy bounds from the Red sea even unto the sea of the Philistines, and from the desert unto the river: for I will [a]deliver the inhabitants of the land into your hand; and thou shalt drive them out before thee.

32 [b]Thou shalt make no covenant with them, nor with their gods.

33 They shall not dwell in thy land, lest they make thee sin against me: for if thou serve their gods, [c]it will surely be a snare unto thee.

The covenant affirmed

24 AND HE said unto Moses, Come up unto the LORD, thou, and Aaron, [d]Nadab, and Abihu, [e]and seventy of the elders of Israel; and worship ye afar off.

2 And Moses alone shall come near the LORD: but they shall not come nigh; neither shall the people go up with him.

3 ¶ And Moses came and told the people all the words of the LORD, and all the judgments: and all the people answered with one voice, and said, [f]All the words which the LORD hath said will we do.

4 And Moses [g]wrote all the words of the LORD, and rose up early in the morning, and builded an altar under the hill, and twelve [h]pillars, according to the twelve tribes of Israel.

5 And he sent young men of the children of Israel, which offered burnt offerings, and sacrificed peace offerings of oxen unto the LORD.

6 And Moses [i]took half of the blood, and put *it* in basins; and half of the blood he sprinkled on the altar.

7 And he [j]took the book of the covenant, and read in the audience of the people: and they said, All that the LORD hath said will we do, and be obedient.

8 And Moses took the blood, and sprinkled *it* on the people, and said, Behold [k]the blood of the covenant, which the LORD hath made with you concerning all these words.

9 ¶ Then went up Moses, and Aaron, Nadab, and Abihu, and seventy of the elders of Israel:

10 And they [l]saw the God of Israel: and *there was* under his feet as it were a paved work of a [m]sapphire stone, and as it were the [n]body of heaven in *his* clearness.

11 And upon the nobles of the children of Israel he [o]laid not his hand: also [p]they saw God, and did [q]eat and drink.

12 ¶ And the LORD said unto Moses, [r]Come up to me into the mount, and be there: and I will give thee [s]tables of stone, and a law, and commandments which I have written; that thou mayest teach them.

23:27 [w]Deut. 7:23
23:28 [x]Josh. 24:12
23:29 [y]Deut. 7:22
23:31 [z]Gen. 15:18 Deut. 11:24 1 Ki. 4:21,24 [a]Josh. 21:44
23:32 [b]ch. 34:12,15
23:33 [c]1 Sam. 18:21 Ps. 106:36
24:1 [d]Lev. 10:1,2 [e]ch. 1:5 Num. 11:16
24:3 [f]ver. 7 ch. 19:8 Deut. 5:27 Gal. 3:19
24:4 [g]Deut. 31:9 [h]Gen. 28:18
24:6 [i]Heb. 9:18
24:7 [j]Heb. 9:19
24:8 [k]1 Pet. 1:2
24:10 [l]John 1:18 1 John 4:12 [m]Ezek. 1:26 Rev. 4:3 [n]Mat. 17:2
24:11 [o]ch. 19:21 [p]Gen. 32:30 Judg. 13:22 [q]1 Cor. 10:18
24:12 [r]ver. 2,15 [s]ch. 32:15

e Heb. *neck*

24:8 THE BLOOD OF THE COVENANT. The covenant was sealed with Israel through the sprinkling of blood, indicating that atoning sacrifices were necessary to maintain their relationship with God. (1) The blood signified cleansing and forgiveness made possible by means of a life sacrificed to God; such sacrifices opened the way to reconciliation with God and the people's obedience to the faith (cf. Rom. 1:5; Heb. 9:19–20).

(2) The ultimate significance of "the blood of the covenant" was realized when Christ shed His blood on the cross and established the new covenant (cf. Mark 14:24; Heb. 9:11–18). His sacrificial death cleanses believers from sin as they seek to walk in the way of holiness (1 John 1:7—2:2).

(3) Obedience and blood (vv. 7–8) must always be joined together to validate God's acceptance of His people and their consecration to Him. Only after the people pledged to obey God through the atoning blood could they participate in the covenant blessings (see article on GOD'S COVENANT WITH THE ISRAELITES, p. 314). In a similar vein, the apostle Peter states that we are "elect . . . unto obedience and sprinkling of the blood of Jesus Christ" (1 Pet. 1:2).

24:11 THEY SAW GOD, AND DID EAT AND DRINK. We are not told in what manner God revealed Himself. We do know that He did not manifest Himself fully, since no human can see God's full glory and live (see 33:18–23). The appearance of God and the accompanying meal signified that after atonement had been made and the people had consecrated themselves to the Lord, then fellowship with Him was possible; this is a N.T. principle as well (cf. Mat. 26:28; Heb. 12:18–24).

13 And Moses rose up, and [t]his minister Joshua: and Moses went up into the mount of God.

14 And he said unto the elders, Tarry ye here for us, until we come again unto you: and, behold, Aaron and Hur *are* with you: if any man have any matters to do, let him come unto them.

15 And Moses went up into the mount, and [u]a cloud covered the mount.

16 And [v]the glory of the LORD abode upon mount Sinai, and the cloud covered it six days: and the seventh day he called unto Moses out of the midst of the cloud.

17 And the sight of the glory of the LORD *was* like [w]devouring fire on the top of the mount in the eyes of the children of Israel.

18 And Moses went into the midst of the cloud, and gat him up into the mount: and [x]Moses was in the mount forty days and forty nights.

Offerings for the tabernacle

25:1–7pp — Ex. 35:4–9

25 AND THE LORD spake unto Moses, saying,

2 Speak unto the children of Israel, that they [f]bring me an [g]offering: [y]of every man that giveth it willingly with his heart ye shall take my offering.

3 And this *is* the offering which ye shall take of them; gold, and silver, and brass,

4 And blue, and purple, and scarlet, and [z]fine[h] linen, and goats' *hair*,

5 And rams' skins dyed red, and badgers' skins, and shittim wood,

6 [a]Oil for the light, [b]spices for anointing oil, and for [c]sweet incense,

7 Onyx stones, and stones to be set in the [d]ephod, and in the [e]breastplate.

8 And let them make me a [f]sanctuary; that [g]I may dwell among them.

9 [h]According to all that I show thee, *after* the pattern of the tabernacle, and the pattern of all the instruments thereof, even so shall ye make *it*.

The ark

25:10–20pp — Ex. 37:1–9

10 ¶ [i]And they shall make an ark *of* shittim wood: two cubits and a half *shall be* the length thereof, and a cubit and a half the breadth thereof, and a cubit and a half the height thereof.

11 And thou shalt overlay it with pure gold, within and without shalt thou overlay it, and shalt make upon it a crown of gold round about.

12 And thou shalt cast four rings of gold for it, and put *them* in the four corners thereof; and two rings *shall be* in

24:13 [t]ch. 32:17
24:15 [u]ch. 19:9; Mat. 17:5
24:16 [v]ch. 16:10
24:17 [w]ch. 3:2; Deut. 4:36; Heb. 12:18,29
24:18 [x]ch. 34:28; Deut. 9:9
25:2 [y]ch. 35:5,21; 1 Chr. 29:3,5,9,14; Ezra 2:68; Neh. 11:2; 2 Cor. 8:12 & 9:7
25:4 [z]Gen. 41:42
25:6 [a]ch. 27:20 [b]ch. 30:23 [c]ch. 30:34
25:7 [d]ch. 28:4,6 [e]ch. 28:15
25:8 [f]ch. 36:1,3,4; Lev. 4:6 & 10:4 & 21:12; Heb. 9:1,2 [g]ch. 29:45; 1 Ki. 6:13; 2 Cor. 6:16; Heb. 3:6; Rev. 21:3
25:9 [h]ver. 40
25:10 [i]ch. 37:1; Deut. 10:3; Heb. 9:4

f Heb. *take for me* **g** Or, *heave offering*
h Or, *silk*

24:16–17 THE GLORY OF THE LORD. The Lord's glory is revealed in a brilliant manifestation of light emanating from God's being (see 40:34, note; cf. 1 Tim. 6:16).

25:9 THE TABERNACLE. In ch. 25, God gives His instruction concerning the tabernacle. The historical, spiritual, and typological significance of the tabernacle must be based on what the Bible says about it. (1) The tabernacle was a "sanctuary" (v. 8), a place set apart for the Lord to dwell among His people and meet with them (v. 22; 29:45–46; Num. 5:3; Ezek. 43:7,9). God's glory was over the tabernacle day and night. When God's glory moved, then Israel had to move. God guided them in this manner while they were in the wilderness (40:36–38; Num. 9:15–16).

(2) It was a "tabernacle of testimony" (38:21), i.e., it contained the Ten Commandments. The Ten Commandments were a constant reminder of God's holiness and His demands for their lives. Our relationship to God can never be separated from our obedience to His law.

(3) It was the place where God provided forgiveness of sins through a blood sacrifice (29:10–14). Thus it pointed toward the ultimate sacrifice of Christ on the cross for the sins of the human race (see Heb. 8:1–2; 9:11–14).

(4) It pointed to heaven, i.e., to a heavenly tabernacle where Christ, our eternal high priest, lives forever to pray for us (Heb. 9:11–12,24–28).

(5) It pointed toward God's final redemption when the new heaven and new earth will come, i.e., "the tabernacle of God *is* with men, and he will dwell with them, and they shall be his people, and God himself shall be with them" (Rev. 21:3).

25:10 ARK. The ark was a chest which contained the Ten Commandments (cf. vv. 16,22), a pot of manna (16:33–34), and Aaron's rod (Num. 17:10; Heb. 9:4). It was covered by a lid called the "mercy seat" (v. 21). Fixed at both ends of the mercy seat were two carved, winged cherubim (see v. 18, note). It was placed in the most holy place of the tabernacle (26:34) and represented the throne of God, before which the high priest stood once a year on the Day of Atonement to sprinkle blood on the mercy seat as an atonement for the unintentional sins of the people during the previous year (see article on THE DAY OF ATONEMENT, p. 188).

the one side of it, and two rings in the other side of it.

13 And thou shalt make staves *of* shittim wood, and overlay them with gold.

14 And thou shalt put the staves into the rings by the sides of the ark, that the ark may be borne with them.

15 [j]The staves shall be in the rings of the ark: they shall not be taken from it.

16 And thou shalt put into the ark [k]the testimony which I shall give thee.

17 And [l]thou shalt make a mercy seat *of* pure gold: two cubits and a half *shall be* the length thereof, and a cubit and a half the breadth thereof.

18 And thou shalt make two cherubims *of* gold, *of* beaten work shalt thou make them, in the two ends of the mercy seat.

19 And make one cherub on the one end, and the other cherub on the other end: *even* [i]of the mercy seat shall ye make the cherubims on the two ends thereof.

20 And [m]the cherubims shall stretch forth *their* wings on high, covering the mercy seat with their wings, and their faces *shall look* one to another; toward the mercy seat shall the faces of the cherubims be.

21 [n]And thou shalt put the mercy seat above upon the ark; and [o]in the ark thou shalt put the testimony that I shall give thee.

22 And [p]there I will meet with thee, and I will commune with thee from above the mercy seat, from [q]between the two cherubims which *are* upon the ark of the testimony, of all *things* which I will give thee in commandment unto the children of Israel.

25:15 [j]1 Ki. 8:8
25:16 [k]ch. 16:34 & 31:18 Deut. 31:26 1 Ki. 8:9 2 Ki. 11:12 Heb. 9:4
25:17 [l]ch. 37:6 Rom. 3:25 Heb. 9:5
25:20 [m]1 Ki. 8:7 1 Chr. 28:18 Heb. 9:5
25:21 [n]ch. 26:34 [o]ver. 16
25:22 [p]ch. 29:42,43 [q]Num. 7:89 1 Sam. 4:4 2 Sam. 6:2 2 Ki. 19:15 Ps. 80:1 Is. 37:16
25:23 [r]ch. 37:10 1 Ki. 7:48 2 Chr. 4:8 Heb. 9:2
25:29 [s]ch. 37:16 Num. 4:7
25:30 [t]Lev. 24:5,6
25:31 [u]ch. 37:17 1 Ki. 7:49 Zech. 4:2 Heb. 9:2 Rev. 1:12

The table

25:23–29pp — Ex. 37:10–16

23 ¶ [r]Thou shalt also make a table *of* shittim wood: two cubits *shall be* the length thereof, and a cubit the breadth thereof, and a cubit and a half the height thereof.

24 And thou shalt overlay it with pure gold, and make thereto a crown of gold round about.

25 And thou shalt make unto it a border of an handbreadth round about, and thou shalt make a golden crown to the border thereof round about.

26 And thou shalt make for it four rings of gold, and put the rings in the four corners that *are* on the four feet thereof.

27 Over against the border shall the rings be for places of the staves to bear the table.

28 And thou shalt make the staves *of* shittim wood, and overlay them with gold, that the table may be borne with them.

29 And thou shalt make [s]the dishes thereof, and spoons thereof, and covers thereof, and bowls thereof, [j]to cover withal: *of* pure gold shalt thou make them.

30 And thou shalt set upon the table [t]showbread before me always.

The candlestick

25:31–39pp — Ex. 37:17–24

31 ¶ [u]And thou shalt make a candlestick *of* pure gold: *of* beaten work shall the candlestick be made: his shaft, and his branches, his bowls, his knobs, and his flowers, shall be of the same.

[i] Or, *of the* matter *of the mercy seat* [j] Or, *to pour out withal*

25:16 THE TESTIMONY. This was the two stone tablets on which were inscribed the Ten Commandments that Moses received on the mountain (31:18).

25:17 MERCY SEAT. The mercy seat was the lid of the ark. On it the high priest sprinkled the shed blood of the sacrificial offering to make atonement for sins. This act was symbolic of God's forgiving mercy (Lev. 16:14–15; 17:11; see Rom. 3:25, note). Thus the mercy seat and the blood foreshadowed the forgiveness available to sinful people through the atoning sacrifice of Christ (Rom. 3:21–25; Heb. 4:14–16; 7:26).

25:18 TWO CHERUBIMS. These were carvings of the angelic beings who hover around God's throne in heaven (cf. Heb. 8:5; Rev. 4:6,8). They symbolized God's presence and kingship among His people on earth (1 Sam. 4:4; 2 Sam. 6:2; 2 Ki. 19:15). Their place upon the ark testified to the truth that God would remain among His people only as long as blood sacrifice was made and the people endeavored to keep God's commandments.

25:30 THE TABLE SHOWBREAD. The bread placed upon the table represented the presence of the Lord that sustained Israel in all of life (cf. Lev. 24:5–9; Is. 63:9). It points to Christ, the bread of life (see 16:4, note; Mat. 26:26–29; 1 Cor. 10:16).

25:31 CANDLESTICK. This was actually a lampstand that held seven oil lamps and furnished light in the tabernacle. The burning lamps represented God's light or presence in the midst of the camp (Jer. 25:10; cf. Rev. 21:22–26).

32 And six branches shall come out of the sides of it; three branches of the candlestick out of the one side, and three branches of the candlestick out of the other side:

33 [v]Three bowls made like unto almonds, *with* a knob and a flower in one branch; and three bowls made like almonds in the other branch, *with* a knob and a flower: so in the six branches that come out of the candlestick.

34 And [w]in the candlestick *shall be* four bowls made like unto almonds, *with* their knobs and their flowers.

35 And *there shall be* a knob under two branches of the same, and a knob under two branches of the same, and a knob under two branches of the same, according to the six branches that proceed out of the candlestick.

36 Their knobs and their branches shall be of the same: all it *shall be* one beaten work *of* pure gold.

37 And thou shalt make the seven lamps thereof: and [x]they shall [k]light the lamps thereof, that they may [y]give light over against [l]it.

38 And the tongs thereof, and the snuffdishes thereof, *shall be of* pure gold.

39 *Of* a talent of pure gold shall he make it, with all these vessels.

40 And [z]look that thou make *them* after their pattern, [m]which was shown thee in the mount.

The tabernacle

26:1–37pp — Ex. 36:8–38

26 MOREOVER [a]THOU shalt make the tabernacle *with* ten curtains *of* fine twined linen, and blue, and purple, and scarlet: *with* cherubims [n]of cunning work shalt thou make them.

2 The length of one curtain *shall be* eight and twenty cubits, and the breadth of one curtain four cubits: and every one of the curtains shall have one measure.

3 The five curtains shall be coupled together one to another; and *other* five curtains *shall be* coupled one to another.

4 And thou shalt make loops of blue upon the edge of the one curtain from the selvedge in the coupling; and likewise shalt thou make in the uttermost edge of *another* curtain, in the coupling of the second.

5 Fifty loops shalt thou make in the one curtain, and fifty loops shalt thou make in the edge of the curtain that *is* in the coupling of the second; that the loops may take hold one of another.

6 And thou shalt make fifty taches of gold, and couple the curtains together with the taches: and it shall be one tabernacle.

7 ¶ And [b]thou shalt make curtains *of* goats' *hair* to be a covering upon the tabernacle: eleven curtains shalt thou make.

8 The length of one curtain *shall be* thirty cubits, and the breadth of one curtain four cubits: and the eleven curtains *shall be all* of one measure.

9 And thou shalt couple five curtains by themselves, and six curtains by themselves, and shalt double the sixth curtain in the forefront of the tabernacle.

10 And thou shalt make fifty loops on the edge of the one curtain *that is* outmost in the coupling, and fifty loops in the edge of the curtain which coupleth the second.

11 And thou shalt make fifty taches of brass, and put the taches into the loops, and couple the [o]tent together, that it may be one.

12 And the remnant that remaineth of the curtains of the tent, the half curtain that remaineth, shall hang over the backside of the tabernacle.

13 And a cubit on the one side, and a cubit on the other side [p]of that which remaineth in the length of the curtains of the tent, it shall hang over the sides of the tabernacle on this side and on that side, to cover it.

14 And [c]thou shalt make a covering for the tent *of* rams' skins dyed red, and a covering above *of* badgers' skins.

15 ¶ And thou shalt make boards

25:33 [v]ch. 37:19
25:34 [w]ch. 37:20-22
25:37 [x]ch. 27:21 & 30:8 Lev. 24:3,4 2 Chr. 13:11 [y]Num. 8:2
25:40 [z]ch. 26:30 Num. 8:4 1 Chr. 28:11,19 Acts 7:44 Heb. 8:5
26:1 [a]ch. 36:8
26:7 [b]ch. 36:14
26:14 [c]ch. 36:19

[k] Or, *cause to ascend* [l] Heb. *the face of it* [m] Heb. *which thou wast caused to see* [n] Heb. *the work of a cunning workman,* or, *embroiderer* [o] Or, *covering* [p] Heb. *in the remainder,* or, *surplusage*

26:1 FINE TWINED LINEN. Exact instructions were given for building the tabernacle. It had to be constructed according to God's pattern because it was His house and He was the designer (cf. 25:9). Salvation and communion with God are possible only on His terms and according to His pattern and revelation (see Mat. 5:17, note; Acts 7:44, note).

THE TABERNACLE

Most Holy Place with the ark of the covenant
10 cubits square (*15 ft. square*)

Curtain

Holy Place, with the golden table
for the bread of the Presence,
golden lampstand, and
altar of incense.
length: 20 cubits (*30 ft.*)
width: 10 cubits (*15 ft.*)

CUBITS 0 5 10 15 20
FEET 0' 10' 20' 30'

W N S E

50 cubits

100 cubits (*150 ft. long*)

10 — 20 cubits

Hugh Claycombe

Basin

Bronze Altar

Entrance 20 cubits
(*30 ft. wide*)

The new religious observances revealed to Moses in the desert centered on rituals connected with the tabernacle and amplified Israel's sense of separateness, purity and oneness under the Lordship of their covenant God.

TABERNACLE FURNISHINGS

The symbolism of God's redemptive covenant was preserved in the tabernacle, making each element an object lesson for the worshiper. Reconstruction of the furnishing is possible because of extremely detailed descriptions and precise measurements recorded in Ex 25–40.

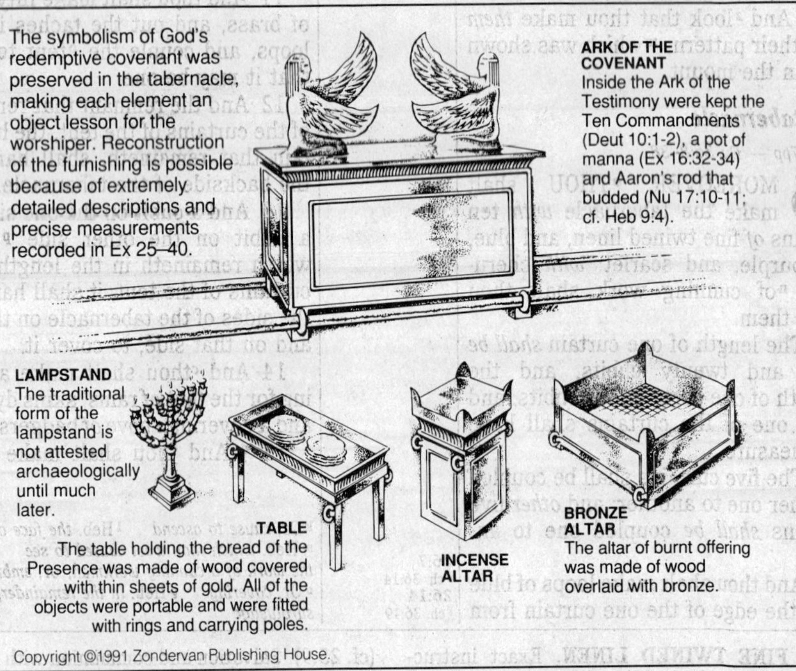

for the tabernacle *of* shittim wood standing up.

16 Ten cubits *shall be* the length of a board, and a cubit and a half *shall be* the breadth of one board.

17 Two [q]tenons *shall there be* in one board, set in order one against another: thus shalt thou make for all the boards of the tabernacle.

18 And thou shalt make the boards for the tabernacle, twenty boards on the south side southward.

19 And thou shalt make forty sockets of silver under the twenty boards; two sockets under one board for his two tenons, and two sockets under another board for his two tenons.

20 And for the second side of the tabernacle on the north side *there shall be* twenty boards:

21 And their forty sockets *of* silver; two sockets under one board, and two sockets under another board.

22 And for the sides of the tabernacle westward thou shalt make six boards.

23 And two boards shalt thou make for the corners of the tabernacle in the two sides.

24 And they shall be [r]coupled together beneath, and they shall be coupled together above the head of it unto one ring: thus shall it be for them both; they shall be for the two corners.

25 And they shall be eight boards, and their sockets *of* silver, sixteen sockets; two sockets under one board, and two sockets under another board.

26 ¶ And thou shalt make bars *of* shittim wood; five for the boards of the one side of the tabernacle,

27 And five bars for the boards of the other side of the tabernacle, and five bars for the boards of the side of the tabernacle, for the two sides westward.

28 And the middle bar in the midst of the boards shall reach from end to end.

29 And thou shalt overlay the boards with gold, and make their rings *of* gold *for* places for the bars: and thou shalt overlay the bars with gold.

30 And thou shalt rear up the tabernacle [d]according to the fashion thereof which was shown thee in the mount.

31 ¶ And [e]thou shalt make a veil *of* blue, and purple, and scarlet, and fine twined linen of cunning work: with cherubims shall it be made:

32 And thou shalt hang it upon four pillars of shittim *wood* overlaid with gold: their hooks *shall be of* gold, upon the four sockets of silver.

33 ¶ And thou shalt hang up the veil under the taches, that thou mayest bring in thither within the veil [f]the ark of the testimony: and the veil shall divide unto you between [g]the holy *place* and the most holy.

34 And [h]thou shalt put the mercy seat upon the ark of the testimony in the most holy *place*.

35 And [i]thou shalt set the table without the veil, and [j]the candlestick over against the table on the side of the tabernacle toward the south: and thou shalt put the table on the north side.

36 And [k]thou shalt make an hanging for the door of the tent, *of* blue, and purple, and scarlet, and fine twined linen, wrought with needlework.

37 And thou shalt make for the hanging [l]five pillars *of* shittim *wood*, and overlay them with gold, *and* their hooks *shall be of* gold: and thou shalt cast five sockets of brass for them.

The altar

27:1–8pp — Ex. 38:1–7

27 AND THOU shalt make [m]an altar *of* shittim wood, five cubits

26:30 [d]ch. 25:9,40 & 27:8 Acts 7:44 Heb. 8:5
26:31 [e]ch. 36:35 Lev. 16:2 2 Chr. 3:14 Mat. 27:51 Heb. 9:3
26:33 [f]ch. 25:16 & 40:21 [g]Lev. 16:2 Heb. 9:2,3
26:34 [h]ch. 25:21 & 40:20 Heb. 9:5
26:35 [i]ch. 40:22 Heb. 9:2 [j]ch. 40:24
26:36 [k]ch. 36:37
26:37 [l]ch. 36:38
27:1 [m]ch. 38:1 Ezek. 43:13

[q] Heb. *hands* [r] Heb. *twinned*

26:33 THE VEIL. The veil or curtain separated the holy place (i.e., the place where the priest prayed and gave thanks on behalf of the people) from the most holy place (i.e., the dwelling place of God). This portrayed the solemn truth that humans could not freely approach God because of their sinful condition. (1) Access to the most holy place was severely restricted. The high priest could enter only one day each year to represent the people, and then only if he brought with him the blood of an atoning sacrifice (cf. 30:10; Lev. 16:12ff; Heb. 9:6–8). The way for all God's people to enter freely into God's presence had not yet been provided (Heb. 9:8).

(2) The only way to have perfect access to God would be by tearing away the veil and removing the existing order of the tabernacle. This Jesus Christ did by shedding His blood on the cross. His body represented the veil that at the time of His death was torn asunder (Mat. 27:51; Col. 1:20–22; Heb. 10:20). Now every believer may "enter into the holiest by the blood of Jesus" (Heb. 10:19).

27:1 AN ALTAR. The altar, later called the "altar of burnt offering" (cf. 30:28; 31:9; Lev. 4:7, 10,18), was used for the sacrifice of animals in order to make atonement (i.e., cover sin and pro-

long, and five cubits broad; the altar shall be foursquare: and the height thereof *shall be* three cubits.

2 And thou shalt make the horns of it upon the four corners thereof: his horns shall be of the same: and [n]thou shalt overlay it with brass.

3 And thou shalt make his pans to receive his ashes, and his shovels, and his basins, and his fleshhooks, and his firepans: all the vessels thereof thou shalt make *of* brass.

4 And thou shalt make for it a grate of network *of* brass; and upon the net shalt thou make four brasen rings in the four corners thereof.

5 And thou shalt put it under the compass of the altar beneath, that the net may be even to the midst of the altar.

6 And thou shalt make staves for the altar, staves *of* shittim wood, and overlay them with brass.

7 And the staves shall be put into the rings, and the staves shall be upon the two sides of the altar, to bear it.

8 Hollow with boards shalt thou make it: [o]as [s]it was shown thee in the mount, so shall they make *it*.

The court of the tabernacle

27:9–19pp — Ex. 38:9–20

9 ¶ And [p]thou shalt make the court of the tabernacle: for the south side southward *there shall be* hangings for the court *of* fine twined linen of an hundred cubits long for one side:

10 And the twenty pillars thereof and their twenty sockets *shall be of* brass; the hooks of the pillars and their fillets *shall be of* silver.

11 And likewise for the north side in length *there shall be* hangings of an hundred *cubits* long, and his twenty pillars and their twenty sockets *of* brass; the hooks of the pillars and their fillets *of* silver.

12 ¶ And *for* the breadth of the court on the west side *shall be* hangings of fifty cubits: their pillars ten, and their sockets ten.

13 And the breadth of the court on the east side eastward *shall be* fifty cubits.

14 The hangings of one side *of the gate shall be* fifteen cubits: their pillars three, and their sockets three.

15 And on the other side *shall be* hangings fifteen *cubits:* their pillars three, and their sockets three.

16 ¶ And for the gate of the court *shall be* an hanging of twenty cubits, *of* blue, and purple, and scarlet, and fine twined linen, wrought with needlework: *and* their pillars *shall be* four, and their sockets four.

17 All the pillars round about the court *shall be* filleted with silver; their hooks *shall be of* silver, and their sockets *of* brass.

18 ¶ The length of the court *shall be* an hundred cubits, and the breadth [t]fifty every where, and the height five cubits *of* fine twined linen, and their sockets *of* brass.

19 All the vessels of the tabernacle in all the service thereof, and all the pins thereof, and all the pins of the court, *shall be of* brass.

Oil for the lamp

27:20–21pp — Lev. 24:1–3

20 ¶ And [q]thou shalt command the children of Israel, that they bring thee pure oil olive beaten for the light, to cause the lamp [u]to burn always.

21 In the tabernacle of the congregation [r]without the veil, which *is* before the testimony, [s]Aaron and his sons shall order it from evening to morning before the LORD: [t]*it shall be* a statute for ever unto their generations on the behalf of the children of Israel.

27:2 [n]See Num. 16:38
27:8 [o]ch. 25:40 & 26:30
27:9 [p]ch. 38:9
27:20 [q]Lev. 24:2
27:21 [r]ch. 26:31,33 [s]ch. 30:8 1 Sam. 3:3 2 Chr. 13:11 [t]ch. 28:43 & 29:9,28 Lev. 3:17 & 16:34 Num. 18:23 & 19:21

[s]Heb. *he showed* [t]Heb. *fifty by fifty*
[u]Heb. *to ascend up*

vide forgiveness, see article on THE DAY OF ATONEMENT, p. 188). The blood of the sacrificial animal was put on the horns of the altar and poured at its base (cf. 29:12; Lev. 4:7,18,25, 30,34). This atoning ritual emphasized that sin deserves death, but that God would accept innocent blood in the place of the sinner (cf. Lev. 16).

27:2 THE HORNS. These were projections at each of the four corners of the altar, symbolizing the power and protection of the sacrifice (cf. 1 Ki. 1:50–51; 2:28; Ps. 18:2).

27:20–21 THE LAMP TO BURN ALWAYS. The burning light symbolized the continual presence of God among the people. The congregation of Israel was to be filled with the light, life, and presence of God. Notice that the lamps would not keep burning without the people's cooperation and obedience.

The priest's garments

28:6–14pp — Ex. 39:2–7

28 AND TAKE thou unto thee
[u]Aaron thy brother, and his
sons with him, from among the chil-
dren of Israel, that he may minister
unto me in the priest's office, *even* Aar-
on, Nadab and Abihu, Eleazar and Itha-
mar, Aaron's sons.
2 And [v]thou shalt make holy gar-
ments for Aaron thy brother for glory
and for beauty.
3 And [w]thou shalt speak unto all
that are wisehearted, [x]whom I have
filled with the spirit of wisdom, that
they may make Aaron's garments to
consecrate him, that he may minister
unto me in the priest's office.
4 And these *are* the garments which
they shall make; [y]a breastplate, and
[z]an ephod, and [a]a robe, and [b]a broi-
dered coat, a mitre, and a girdle: and
they shall make holy garments for Aar-
on thy brother, and his sons, that he
may minister unto me in the priest's
office.
5 And they shall take gold, and
blue, and purple, and scarlet, and fine
linen.
6 ¶ [c]And they shall make the
ephod *of* gold, *of* blue, and *of* purple, *of*
scarlet, and fine twined linen, with
cunning work.
7 It shall have the two shoulder-
pieces thereof joined at the two edges
thereof; and *so* it shall be joined to-
gether.
8 And the ▾curious girdle of the
ephod, which *is* upon it, shall be
of the same, according to the work
thereof; *even of* gold, *of* blue, and
purple, and scarlet, and fine twined
linen.
9 And thou shalt take two onyx
stones, and grave on them the names
of the children of Israel:
10 Six of their names on one stone,
and *the other* six names of the rest on
the other stone, according to their
birth.
11 With the work of an engraver in
stone, *like* the engravings of a signet,
shalt thou engrave the two stones with
the names of the children of Israel:
thou shalt make them to be set in
ouches of gold.
12 And thou shalt put the two
stones upon the shoulders of the ephod
for stones of memorial unto the chil-
dren of Israel: and [d]Aaron shall bear
their names before the LORD upon his
two shoulders [e]for a memorial.
13 ¶ And thou shalt make ouches *of*
gold;
14 And two chains *of* pure gold at
the ends; *of* wreathen work shalt thou
make them, and fasten the wreathen
chains to the ouches.

The priest's breastplate

28:15–28pp — Ex. 39:8–21

15 ¶ And [f]thou shalt make the
breastplate of judgment with cunning
work; after the work of the ephod thou
shalt make it; *of* gold, *of* blue, and *of*
purple, and *of* scarlet, and *of* fine
twined linen, shalt thou make it.
16 Foursquare it shall be *being* dou-
bled; a span *shall be* the length thereof,
and a span *shall be* the breadth thereof.

28:1 [u]Num. 18:7 Heb. 5:1,4 **28:2** [v]ch. 29:5,29 & 31:10 & 39:1,2 Lev. 8:7,30 Num. 20:26,28 **28:3** [w]ch. 31:6 & 36:1 [x]ch. 31:3 & 35:30,31 **28:4** [y]ver. 15 [z]ver. 6 [a]ver. 31 [b]ver. 39 **28:6** [c]ch. 39:2 **28:12** [d]ver. 29 ch. 39:7 [e]See Josh. 4:7 Zech. 6:14 **28:15** [f]ch. 39:8

▾Or, *embroidered*

28:1 AARON . . . PRIEST'S OFFICE. The Lord gave instructions concerning the ministry of Aaron, the high priest, and the duties of the priesthood in general (chs. 28–29). A priest was someone who stood before God as a representative of the people. (1) The priests were to burn incense, supervise the lampstand and the table of the bread of God's Presence, offer sacrifices on the altar, and bless the people. They also judged civil cases (e.g., Num. 5:5–31) and taught the law (cf. Neh. 8:7–8).

(2) The priests acted as intermediaries between the people and God (cf. vv. 12,29–30), mediating the will and covenant of God to the people (Jer. 33:20–26; Mal. 2:4) and mediating the people's sinfulness before God. In fulfilling these tasks, they performed service to God (Heb. 9:6), made atonement for the sin of the people and of themselves (29:33; Heb. 9:7–8), and testified concerning the holiness of God (v. 38; Num. 18:1).

(3) For N.T. believers, Jesus is the priest of God's people. He initiated the new covenant through His death (Heb. 9:15–22) and offered Himself as the perfect sacrifice (Heb. 9:23–28). He sympathizes with our weakness (Heb. 4:15), appears before God on our behalf (Heb. 9:24), brings our salvation to completion (Heb. 10:14), and makes it possible for us to draw near to God the Father (Heb. 4:16; 6:19–20; 7:25; 10:19–22).

28:4 A BREASTPLATE. This was a square on which were placed twelve small precious stones in four horizontal rows of three stones each; on these stones the names of the twelve sons of Israel were engraved (vv. 15–21,29–30).

28:6 EPHOD. The ephod was a loose-fitting, sleeveless garment extending to the knees that was worn like an apron over the priest's robe (vv. 6–20; 39:1–21).

17 [g]And thou shalt [w]set in it settings of stones, *even* four rows of stones: *the first* row *shall be* a [x]sardius, a topaz, and a carbuncle: *this shall be* the first row.

18 And the second row *shall be* an emerald, a sapphire, and a diamond.

19 And the third row a ligure, an agate, and an amethyst.

20 And the fourth row a beryl, and an onyx, and a jasper: they shall be set in gold in their [y]inclosings.

21 And the stones shall be with the names of the children of Israel, twelve, according to their names, *like* the engravings of a signet; every one with his name shall they be according to the twelve tribes.

22 ¶ And thou shalt make upon the breastplate chains at the ends *of* wreathen work *of* pure gold.

23 And thou shalt make upon the breastplate two rings of gold, and shalt put the two rings on the two ends of the breastplate.

24 And thou shalt put the two wreathen *chains* of gold in the two rings *which are* on the ends of the breastplate.

25 And *the other* two ends of the two wreathen *chains* thou shalt fasten in the two ouches, and put *them* on the shoulderpieces of the ephod before it.

26 ¶ And thou shalt make two rings of gold, and thou shalt put them upon the two ends of the breastplate in the border thereof, which *is* in the side of the ephod inward.

27 And two *other* rings of gold thou shalt make, and shalt put them on the two sides of the ephod underneath, toward the forepart thereof, over against the *other* coupling thereof, above the curious girdle of the ephod.

28 And they shall bind the breastplate by the rings thereof unto the rings of the ephod with a lace of blue, that *it* may be above the curious girdle of the ephod, and that the breastplate be not loosed from the ephod.

29 And Aaron shall bear the names of the children of Israel in the breastplate of judgment upon his heart, when he goeth in unto the holy *place,* [h]for a memorial before the LORD continually.

30 ¶ And [i]thou shalt put in the breastplate of judgment the Urim and the Thummim; and they shall be upon Aaron's heart, when he goeth in before the LORD: and Aaron shall bear the judgment of the children of Israel upon his heart before the LORD continually.

The priest's robe

28:31–43pp — Ex. 39:22–31

31 ¶ And [j]thou shalt make the robe of the ephod all *of* blue.

32 And there shall be an hole in the top of it, in the midst thereof: it shall have a binding of woven work round about the hole of it, as it were the hole of an habergeon, that it be not rent.

33 ¶ And *beneath* upon the [z]hem of it thou shalt make pomegranates *of* blue, and *of* purple, and *of* scarlet, round about the hem thereof; and bells of gold between them round about:

34 A golden bell and a pomegranate, a golden bell and a pomegranate, upon the hem of the robe round about.

35 And it shall be upon Aaron to minister: and his sound shall be heard when he goeth in unto the holy *place* before the LORD, and when he cometh out, that he die not.

36 ¶ And [k]thou shalt make a plate *of* pure gold, and grave upon it, *like* the engravings of a signet, HOLINESS TO THE LORD.

37 And thou shalt put it on a blue lace, that it may be upon the mitre; upon the forefront of the mitre it shall be.

38 And it shall be upon Aaron's forehead, that Aaron may [l]bear the iniquity of the holy things, which the children of Israel shall hallow in all their holy gifts; and it shall be always upon his forehead, that they may be [m]accepted before the LORD.

39 ¶ And thou shalt embroider the

28:17 [g]ch. 39:10
28:29 [h]ver. 12
28:30 [i]Lev. 8:8 Num. 27:21 Deut. 33:8 1 Sam. 28:6 Ezra 2:63 Neh. 7:65
28:31 [j]ch. 39:22
28:36 [k]ch. 39:30 Zech. 14:20
28:38 [l]ver. 43 Lev. 10:17 & 22:9 Num. 18:1 Is. 53:11 Ezek. 4:4-6 John 1:29 Heb. 9:28 1 Pet. 2:24 [m]Lev. 1:4 & 22:27 Is. 56:7

[w] Heb. *fill in it fillings of stone* [x] Or, *ruby*
[y] Heb. *fillings* [z] Or, *skirts*

28:29 AARON SHALL BEAR THE NAMES OF THE CHILDREN OF ISRAEL. As high priest, Aaron represented the people before the Lord when he entered the holy place (vv. 12,29). In doing so, he foreshadowed Jesus our High Priest, who entered heaven to appear before His Father as our representative (Heb. 9:24; see article on CHRIST IN THE OLD TESTAMENT, p. 562).

28:30 THE URIM AND THE THUMMIM. Scripture does not explain what is meant by the Urim and Thummim. The literal meaning may be "lights" and "perfections," or "curses" and "perfections." They were probably used for casting lots to receive a "yes" or "no" answer in order to communicate God's will in particular cases (cf. Lev. 8:8; Num. 27:21; Deut. 33:8; 1 Sam. 28:6).

coat of fine linen, and thou shalt make the mitre *of* fine linen, and thou shalt make the girdle *of* needlework.

40 ¶ [n]And for Aaron's sons thou shalt make coats, and thou shalt make for them girdles, and bonnets shalt thou make for them, for glory and for beauty.

41 And thou shalt put them upon Aaron thy brother, and his sons with him; and shalt [o]anoint them, and [p]consecrate[a] them, and sanctify them, that they may minister unto me in the priest's office.

42 And thou shalt make them [q]linen breeches to cover [b]their nakedness; from the loins even unto the thighs they shall [c]reach:

43 And they shall be upon Aaron, and upon his sons, when they come in unto the tabernacle of the congregation, or when they come near [r]unto the altar to minister in the holy *place;* that they [s]bear not iniquity, and die: [t]*it shall be* a statute for ever unto him and his seed after him.

Consecrating the priests

29:1–37pp — Lev. 8:1–36

29 AND THIS *is* the thing that thou shalt do unto them to hallow them, to minister unto me in the priest's office: [u]Take one young bullock, and two rams without blemish,

2 And [v]unleavened bread, and cakes unleavened tempered with oil, and wafers unleavened anointed with oil: *of* wheaten flour shalt thou make them.

3 And thou shalt put them into one basket, and bring them in the basket, with the bullock and the two rams.

4 And Aaron and his sons thou shalt bring unto the door of the tabernacle of the congregation, [w]and shalt wash them with water.

5 [x]And thou shalt take the garments, and put upon Aaron the coat, and the robe of the ephod, and the ephod, and the breastplate, and gird him with [y]the curious girdle of the ephod:

6 [z]And thou shalt put the mitre upon his head, and put the holy crown upon the mitre.

7 Then shalt thou take the anointing [a]oil, and pour *it* upon his head, and anoint him.

8 And [b]thou shalt bring his sons, and put coats upon them.

9 And thou shalt gird them with girdles, Aaron and his sons, and [d]put the bonnets on them: and [c]the priest's office shall be theirs for a perpetual statute: and thou shalt [d]consecrate[e] Aaron and his sons.

10 And thou shalt cause a bullock to be brought before the tabernacle of the congregation: and [e]Aaron and his sons shall put their hands upon the head of the bullock.

11 And thou shalt kill the bullock before the LORD, *by* the door of the tabernacle of the congregation.

12 And thou [f]shalt take of the blood of the bullock, and put *it* upon [g]the horns of the altar with thy finger, and pour all the blood beside the bottom of the altar.

13 And [h]thou shalt take all the fat that covereth the inwards, and [f]the caul *that is* above the liver, and the two kidneys, and the fat that *is* upon them, and burn *them* upon the altar.

14 But [i]the flesh of the bullock, and his skin, and his dung, shalt thou burn with fire without the camp: it *is* a sin offering.

15 ¶ [j]Thou shalt also take one ram; and Aaron and his sons shall [k]put their hands upon the head of the ram.

16 And thou shalt slay the ram, and thou shalt take his blood, and sprinkle *it* round about upon the altar.

17 And thou shalt cut the ram in pieces, and wash the inwards of him, and his legs, and put *them* unto his pieces, and [g]unto his head.

18 And thou shalt burn the whole ram upon the altar: it *is* a burnt offering

28:40 [n]ver. 4 ch. 39:27-29,41 Ezek. 44:17,18
28:41 [o]ch. 29:7 & 30:30 & 40:15 Lev. 10:7 [p]ch. 29:9 Lev. 8 Heb. 7:28
28:42 [q]ch. 39:28 Lev. 6:10 & 16:4 Ezek. 44:18
28:43 [r]ch. 20:26 [s]Lev. 5:1,17 & 20:19,20 & 22:9 Num. 9:13 & 18:22 [t]ch. 27:21 Lev. 17:7
29:1 [u]Lev. 8:2
29:2 [v]Lev. 2:4 & 6:20-22
29:4 [w]ch. 40:12 Lev. 8:6 Heb. 10:22
29:5 [x]ch. 28:2 Lev. 8:7 [y]ch. 28:8
29:6 [z]Lev. 8:9
29:7 [a]ch. 30:25 Lev. 8:12 & 10:7 & 21:10 Num. 35:25
29:8 [b]Lev. 8:13
29:9 [c]Num. 18:7 [d]ch. 28:41 Lev. 8:22 Heb. 7:28
29:10 [e]Lev. 1:4 & 8:14
29:12 [f]Lev. 8:15 [g]ch. 27:2
29:13 [h]Lev. 3:3
29:14 [i]Lev. 4:11,12,21 Heb. 13:11
29:15 [j]Lev. 8:18 [k]Lev. 1:4-9

[a] Heb. *fill their hand* [b] Heb. *flesh of their nakedness* [c] Heb. *be* [d] Heb. *bind* [e] Heb. *fill the hand of* [f] It seemeth by anatomy, and the Hebrew doctors, to be *the midriff* [g] Or, *upon*

29:4 WASH . . . WITH WATER. The ceremonial washing with water symbolized the purity that was to characterize the priests.

29:10 A BULLOCK. When the priests laid their hands on the bull's head, they symbolized identification with the animal and perhaps the transfer of the people's sins to the animal. Thus, the bull became a substitutionary sacrifice that died because of the people's sins (v. 14). This ceremony points to the substitutionary sacrifice of Christ, who became our sin offering (cf. Is. 53:5; Gal. 3:13; Heb. 13:11–13).

unto the LORD: it *is* a [l]sweet savour, an offering made by fire unto the LORD.

19 ¶ [m]And thou shalt take the other ram; and Aaron and his sons shall put their hands upon the head of the ram.

20 Then shalt thou kill the ram, and take of his blood, and put *it* upon the tip of the right ear of Aaron, and upon the tip of the right ear of his sons, and upon the thumb of their right hand, and upon the great toe of their right foot, and sprinkle the blood upon the altar round about.

21 And thou shalt take of the blood that *is* upon the altar, and of [n]the anointing oil, and sprinkle *it* upon Aaron, and upon his garments, and upon his sons, and upon the garments of his sons with him: and [o]he shall be hallowed, and his garments, and his sons, and his sons' garments with him.

22 Also thou shalt take of the ram the fat and the rump, and the fat that covereth the inwards, and the caul *above* the liver, and the two kidneys, and the fat that *is* upon them, and the right shoulder; for it *is* a ram of consecration:

23 [p]And one loaf of bread, and one cake of oiled bread, and one wafer out of the basket of the unleavened bread that *is* before the LORD:

24 And thou shalt put all in the hands of Aaron, and in the hands of his sons; and shalt [q]wave[h] them *for* a wave offering before the LORD.

25 [r]And thou shalt receive them of their hands, and burn *them* upon the altar for a burnt offering, for a sweet savour before the LORD: it *is* an offering made by fire unto the LORD.

26 And thou shalt take [s]the breast of the ram of Aaron's consecration, and wave it *for* a wave offering before the LORD: and [t]it shall be thy part.

27 And thou shalt sanctify [u]the breast of the wave offering, and the shoulder of the heave offering, which is waved, and which is heaved up, of the ram of the consecration, *even* of *that* which *is* for Aaron, and of *that* which is for his sons:

28 And it shall be Aaron's and his sons' [v]by a statute for ever from the children of Israel: for it *is* an heave offering: and [w]it shall be an heave offering from the children of Israel of the sacrifice of their peace offerings, *even* their heave offering unto the LORD.

29:18 [l]Gen. 8:21
29:19 [m]ver. 3 Lev. 8:22
29:21 [n]ch. 30:25,31 [o]ver. 1 Heb. 9:22
29:23 [p]Lev. 8:26
29:24 [q]Lev. 7:30
29:25 [r]Lev. 8:28
29:26 [s]Lev. 8:29 [t]Lev. 7:33
29:27 [u]Lev. 7:31,34 Num. 18:11,18 Deut. 18:3
29:28 [v]Lev. 10:15 [w]Lev. 7:34
29:29 [x]Num. 20:26,28 [y]Num. 18:8
29:30 [z]Num. 20:28 [a]Lev. 8:35 & 9:1,8
29:31 [b]Lev. 8:31
29:32 [c]Mat. 12:4
29:33 [d]Lev. 10:14,15,17 [e]Lev. 22:10
29:34 [f]Lev. 7:18 & 8:32
29:35 [g]Lev. 8:33-35
29:36 [h]Heb. 10:11 [i]ch. 40:10
29:37 [j]ch. 40:10 [k]Mat. 23:19
29:38 [l]Num. 28:3 1 Chr. 16:40 Ezra 3:3 [m]See Dan. 12:11
29:39 [n]Ezek. 46:13-15
29:41 [o]1 Ki. 18:29,36 2 Ki. 16:15 Ezra 9:4,5 Ps. 141:2

29 ¶ And the holy garments of Aaron [x]shall be his sons' after him, [y]to be anointed therein, and to be consecrated in them.

30 *And* [z]that[i] son that is priest in his stead shall put them on [a]seven days, when he cometh into the tabernacle of the congregation to minister in the holy *place*.

31 ¶ And thou shalt take the ram of the consecration, and [b]seethe his flesh in the holy place.

32 And Aaron and his sons shall eat the flesh of the ram, and the [c]bread that *is* in the basket, *by* the door of the tabernacle of the congregation.

33 And [d]they shall eat those things wherewith the atonement was made, to consecrate *and* to sanctify them: [e]but a stranger shall not eat *thereof*, because they *are* holy.

34 And if aught of the flesh of the consecrations, or of the bread, remain unto the morning, then [f]thou shalt burn the remainder with fire: it shall not be eaten, because it *is* holy.

35 And thus shalt thou do unto Aaron, and to his sons, according to all *things* which I have commanded thee: [g]seven days shalt thou consecrate them.

36 And thou shalt [h]offer every day a bullock *for* a sin offering for atonement: and thou shalt cleanse the altar, when thou hast made an atonement for it, [i]and thou shalt anoint it, to sanctify it.

37 Seven days thou shalt make an atonement for the altar, and sanctify it; [j]and it shall be an altar most holy: [k]whatsoever toucheth the altar shall be holy.

38 ¶ Now this *is that* which thou shalt offer upon the altar; [l]two lambs of the first year [m]day by day continually.

39 The one lamb thou shalt offer [n]in the morning; and the other lamb thou shalt offer at even:

40 And with the one lamb a tenth deal of flour mingled with the fourth part of an hin of beaten oil; and the fourth part of an hin of wine *for* a drink offering.

41 And the other lamb thou shalt [o]offer at even, and shalt do thereto according to the meat offering of the morning, and according to the drink of-

[h] Or, *shake to and fro* [i] Heb. he *of his sons*

fering thereof, for a sweet savour, an
offering made by fire unto the LORD.
42 *This shall be* [p]a continual burnt
offering throughout your generations
at the door of the tabernacle of the con-
gregation before the LORD: [q]where I
will meet you, to speak there unto
thee.
43 And there I will meet with the
children of Israel, and [j]*the tabernacle*
[r]shall be sanctified by my glory.
44 And I will sanctify the taberna-
cle of the congregation, and the altar:
I will [s]sanctify also both Aaron and
his sons, to minister to me in the
priest's office.
45 ¶ And [t]I will dwell among the
children of Israel, and will be their
God.
46 And they shall know that [u]I *am*
the LORD their God, that brought them
forth out of the land of Egypt, that I
may dwell among them: I *am* the LORD
their God.

The altar of incense

30:1–5pp — Ex. 37:25–28

30 AND THOU shalt make [v]an al-
tar [w]to burn incense upon: *of*
shittim wood shalt thou make it.
2 A cubit *shall be* the length thereof,
and a cubit the breadth thereof; four-
square shall it be: and two cubits *shall*
be the height thereof: the horns thereof
shall be of the same.
3 And thou shalt overlay it with
pure gold, the [k]top thereof, and the
[l]sides thereof round about, and the
horns thereof; and thou shalt make
unto it a crown of gold round about.
4 And two golden rings shalt thou
make to it under the crown of it, by the
two [m]corners thereof, upon the two
sides of it shalt thou make *it;* and they
shall be for places for the staves to
bear it withal.
5 And thou shalt make the staves *of*
shittim wood, and overlay them with
gold.
6 And thou shalt put it before the
veil that *is* by the ark of the testimony,
before the [x]mercy seat that *is* over the
testimony, where I will meet with thee.
7 And Aaron shall burn thereon
[y]sweet[n] incense every morning:
when [z]he dresseth the lamps, he shall
burn incense upon it.
8 And when Aaron [o]lighteth the
lamps [p]at even, he shall burn incense
upon it, a perpetual incense before the
LORD throughout your generations.
9 Ye shall offer no [a]strange in-
cense thereon, nor burnt sacrifice, nor
meat offering; neither shall ye pour
drink offering thereon.
10 And [b]Aaron shall make an
atonement upon the horns of it once in
a year with the blood of the sin offering
of atonements: once in the year shall
he make atonement upon it throughout
your generations: it *is* most holy unto
the LORD.

The offerings for the tabernacle

11 ¶ And the LORD spake unto Mo-
ses, saying,
12 [c]When thou takest the sum of
the children of Israel after [q]their
number, then shall they give every man
[d]a ransom for his soul unto the LORD,
when thou numberest them; that there
be no [e]plague among them, when *thou*
numberest them.
13 [f]This they shall give, every one
that passeth among them that are
numbered, half a shekel after the shek-
el of the sanctuary: ([g]a shekel *is* twen-
ty gerahs:) [h]an half shekel *shall be* the
offering of the LORD.
14 Every one that passeth among
them that are numbered, from twenty
years old and above, shall give an offer-
ing unto the LORD.
15 The [i]rich shall not [r]give more,
and the poor shall not [s]give less than
half a shekel, when *they* give an offer-
ing unto the LORD, to make an atone-
ment for your souls.
16 And thou shalt take the atone-

29:42 [p]ch. 30:8 [q]ch. 25:22
29:43 [r]1 Ki. 8:11 2 Chr. 5:14 Ezek. 43:5 Hag. 2:7,9
29:44 [s]Lev. 21:15
29:45 [t]Ex. 25:8 Lev. 26:12 Zech. 2:10 John 14:17,23 Rev. 21:3
29:46 [u]ch. 20:2
30:1 [v]ch. 37:25 [w]See ver. 7,8,10 Rev. 8:3
30:6 [x]ch. 25:21,22
30:7 [y]ver. 34 1 Sam. 2:28 1 Chr. 23:13 Luke 1:9 [z]ch. 27:21
30:9 [a]Lev. 10:1
30:10 [b]Lev. 16:18
30:12 [c]2 Sam. 24:2 [d]See Num. 31:50 Mat. 20:28 1 Pet. 1:18,19 [e]2 Sam. 24:15
30:13 [f]Mat. 17:24 [g]Num. 3:47 [h]ch. 38:26
30:15 [i]Prov. 22:2 Eph. 6:9

[j] Or, Israel [k] Heb. *roof* [l] Heb. *walls* [m] Heb. *ribs* [n] Heb. *incense of spices* [o] Or, *setteth up* Heb. *causeth to ascend* [p] Heb. *between the two evens* [q] Heb. *them that are to be numbered* [r] Heb. *multiply* [s] Heb. *diminish*

30:1 BURN INCENSE. The burning incense symbolized the continual worship and prayers of God's people (v. 8; Ps. 141:2; Luke 1:10; Rev. 8:3–4; see Rev. 5:8, note). The altar for burning incense could be desecrated (v. 9), indicating that prayer that was not offered to the glory of God or with hearts committed to holiness was, and is, unacceptable to the Lord (cf. Ps. 66:18–19; Is. 1:15–16).

30:10 ATONEMENT. For comments on atonement and how it points to Jesus Christ and the new covenant, see article on THE DAY OF ATONEMENT, p. 188.

ment money of the children of Israel,
and [j]shalt appoint it for the service of
the tabernacle of the congregation;
that it may be [k]a memorial unto the
children of Israel before the LORD, to
make an atonement for your souls.

The laver, oil and perfume

17 ¶ And the LORD spake unto Mo-
ses, saying,
18 [l]Thou shalt also make a laver
of brass, and his foot *also of* brass, to
wash *withal:* and thou shalt [m]put it be-
tween the tabernacle of the congrega-
tion and the altar, and thou shalt put
water therein.
19 For Aaron and his sons [n]shall
wash their hands and their feet
thereat:
20 When they go into the tabernacle
of the congregation, they shall wash
with water, that they die not; or when
they come near to the altar to minister,
to burn offering made by fire unto the
LORD:
21 So they shall wash their hands
and their feet, that they die not: and
[o]it shall be a statute for ever to them,
even to him and to his seed throughout
their generations.
22 ¶ Moreover the LORD spake unto
Moses, saying,
23 Take thou also unto thee [p]prin-
cipal spices, of pure [q]myrrh five hun-
dred *shekels,* and of sweet cinnamon
half so much, *even* two hundred and fif-
ty *shekels,* and of sweet [r]calamus two
hundred and fifty *shekels,*
24 And of [s]cassia five hundred
shekels, after the shekel of the sanctu-
ary, and of oil olive an [t]hin:
25 And thou shalt make it an oil of
holy ointment, an ointment compound
after the art of the †apothecary: it
shall be [u]an holy anointing oil.
26 [v]And thou shalt anoint the tab-
ernacle of the congregation therewith,
and the ark of the testimony,
27 And the table and all his vessels,
and the candlestick and his vessels,
and the altar of incense,
28 And the altar of burnt offering
with all his vessels, and the laver and
his foot.
29 And thou shalt sanctify them,
that they may be most holy: [w]whatso-
ever toucheth them shall be holy.
30 [x]And thou shalt anoint Aaron
and his sons, and consecrate them,
that *they* may minister unto me in the
priest's office.
31 And thou shalt speak unto the
children of Israel, saying, This shall be
an holy anointing oil unto me through-
out your generations.
32 Upon man's flesh shall it not be
poured, neither shall ye make *any other*
like it, after the composition of it: [y]it
is holy, *and* it shall be holy unto you.
33 [z]Whosoever compoundeth *any*
like it, or whosoever putteth *any* of it
upon a stranger, [a]shall even be cut off
from his people.
34 ¶ And the LORD said unto Moses,
[b]Take unto thee sweet spices, stacte,
and onycha, and galbanum; *these* sweet
spices with pure frankincense: of each
shall there be a like *weight:*
35 And thou shalt make it a per-
fume, a confection [c]after the art of the
apothecary, ‖tempered together, pure
and holy:
36 And thou shalt beat *some* of it
very small, and put of it before the tes-
timony in the tabernacle of the congre-
gation, [d]where I will meet with thee:
[e]it shall be unto you most holy.
37 And *as for* the perfume which
thou shalt make, [f]ye shall not make
to yourselves according to the compo-
sition thereof: it shall be unto thee holy
for the LORD.
38 [g]Whosoever shall make like
unto that, to smell thereto, shall even
be cut off from his people.

The appointment of the workmen

31:2–6pp — Ex. 35:30–35

31 AND THE LORD spake unto Mo-
ses, saying,
2 [h]See, I have called by name Be-
zaleel the [i]son of Uri, the son of Hur,
of the tribe of Judah:
3 And I have [j]filled him with the
spirit of God, in wisdom, and in under-
standing, and in knowledge, and in all
manner of workmanship,

30:16 [j]ch. 38:25 [k]Num. 16:40 **30:18** [l]ch. 38:8 1 Ki. 7:38 [m]ch. 40:30 **30:19** [n]ch. 40:31,32 Ps. 26:6 Is. 52:11 John 13:10 Heb. 10:22 **30:21** [o]ch. 28:43 **30:23** [p]Sol. 4:14 Ezek. 27:22 [q]Ps. 45:8 Prov. 7:17 [r]Sol. 4:14 Jer. 6:20 **30:24** [s]Ps. 45:8 [t]ch. 29:40 **30:25** [u]ch. 37:29 Num. 35:25 Ps. 89:20 & 133:2 **30:26** [v]ch. 40:9 Lev. 8:10 Num. 7:1 **30:29** [w]ch. 29:37 **30:30** [x]ch. 29:7 Lev. 8:12,30 **30:32** [y]ver. 25,37 **30:33** [z]ver. 38 [a]Gen. 17:14 ch. 12:15 Lev. 7:20,21 **30:34** [b]ch. 25:6 & 37:29 **30:35** [c]ver. 25 **30:36** [d]ch. 29:42 Lev. 16:2 [e]ver. 32 ch. 29:37 Lev. 2:3 **30:37** [f]ver. 32 **30:38** [g]ver. 33 **31:2** [h]ch. 35:30 & 36:1 [i]1 Chr. 2:20 **31:3** [j]ch. 35:31 1 Ki. 7:14

† Or, *perfumer* ‖ Heb. *salted*

31:3 FILLED HIM WITH THE SPIRIT OF GOD. The idea of being "filled . . . with the Spirit of God" here means spiritual equipping and enabling for special service to God. It is appropriate under the new covenant to pray that the Spirit will give us both physical skills and spiritual gifts to fulfill the will of God for our lives (see article on SPIRITUAL GIFTS FOR BELIEVERS, p. 1790).

4 To devise cunning works, to work in gold, and in silver, and in brass,

5 And in cutting of stones, to set *them,* and in carving of timber, to work in all manner of workmanship.

6 And I, behold, I have given with him [k]Aholiab, the son of Ahisamach, of the tribe of Dan: and in the hearts of all that are [l]wisehearted I have put wisdom, that they may make all that I have commanded thee;

Num. 27:18

7 [m]The tabernacle of the congregation, and [n]the ark of the testimony, and [o]the mercy seat that *is* thereupon, and all the [v]furniture of the tabernacle,

8 And [p]the table and his furniture, and [q]the pure candlestick with all his furniture, and the altar of incense,

9 And [r]the altar of burnt offering with all his furniture, and [s]the laver and his foot,

10 And [t]the cloths of service, and the holy garments for Aaron the priest, and the garments of his sons, to minister in the priest's office,

11 [u]And the anointing oil, and [v]sweet incense for the holy *place:* according to all that I have commanded thee shall they do.

The Sabbath

12 ¶ And the LORD spake unto Moses, saying,

13 Speak thou also unto the children of Israel, saying, [w]Verily my sabbaths ye shall keep: for it *is* a sign between me and you throughout your generations; that *ye* may know that I *am* the LORD that doth sanctify you.

14 [x]Ye shall keep the sabbath therefore; for it *is* holy unto you: every one that defileth it shall surely be put to death: for [y]whosoever doeth *any* work therein, that soul shall be cut off from among his people.

15 [z]Six days may work be done; but in the [a]seventh *is* the sabbath of rest, [w]holy to the LORD: whosoever doeth *any* work in the sabbath day, he shall surely be put to death.

16 Wherefore the children of Israel shall keep the sabbath, to observe the sabbath throughout their generations, *for* a perpetual covenant.

17 It *is* [b]a sign between me and the children of Israel for ever: for [c]*in* six days the LORD made heaven and earth, and on the seventh day he rested, and was refreshed.

18 ¶ And he gave unto Moses, when he had made an end of communing with him upon mount Sinai, [d]two tables of testimony, tables of stone, written with the finger of God.

The golden calf

32 AND WHEN the people saw that Moses [e]delayed to come down out of the mount, the people gathered themselves together unto Aaron, and said unto him, [f]Up, make us gods, which shall [g]go before us; for *as for* this Moses, the man that brought us up out of the land of Egypt, we wot not what is become of him.

2 And Aaron said unto them, Break off the [h]golden earrings, which *are* in the ears of your wives, of your sons, and of your daughters, and bring *them* unto me.

3 And all the people brake off the golden earrings which *were* in their ears, and brought *them* unto Aaron.

4 [i]And he received *them* at their hand, and fashioned it with a graving tool, after he had made it a molten calf: and they said, These *be* thy gods, O Israel, which brought thee up out of the land of Egypt.

5 And when Aaron saw *it,* he built an altar before it; and Aaron made [j]proclamation, and said, Tomorrow *is* a feast to the LORD.

6 And they rose up early on the morrow, and offered burnt offerings, and brought peace offerings; and the [k]people sat down to eat and to drink, and rose up to play.

7 ¶ And the LORD said unto Moses,

31:6 [k]ch. 35:34 [l]ch. 28:3 & 35:10,35 & 36:1
31:7 [m]ch. 36:8 [n]ch. 37:1 [o]ch. 37:6
31:8 [p]ch. 37:10 [q]ch. 37:17
31:9 [r]ch. 38:1 [s]ch. 38:8
31:10 [t]ch. 39:1,41 Num. 4:5,6
31:11 [u]ch. 30:25,31 [v]ch. 30:34
31:13 [w]Lev. 19:3,30 & 26:2 Ezek. 20:12,20
31:14 [x]ch. 20:8 Deut. 5:12 [y]Num. 15:35
31:15 [z]ch. 20:9 [a]Gen. 2:2
31:17 [b]ver. 13 [c]Gen. 2:2
31:18 [d]ch. 32:15 Deut. 4:13 & 5:22 2 Cor. 3:3
32:1 [e]ch. 24:18 Deut. 9:9 [f]Acts 7:40 [g]ch. 13:21
32:2 [h]Judg. 8:24-27
32:4 [i]ch. 20:23 Deut. 9:16 Judg. 17:3,4 1 Ki. 12:28 Neh. 9:18 Ps. 106:19 Acts 7:41
32:5 [j]Lev. 23:2,4,21,37 2 Ki. 10:20 2 Chr. 30:5
32:6 [k]1 Cor. 10:7

[v] Heb. *vessels* [w] Heb. *holiness*

32:4 A MOLTEN CALF. As a leader, Aaron seriously compromised God's standard in order to please the people he served. He gave in to the godless pressure of the Israelites and violated the second commandment (20:4–5). Only Moses' intercession saved him from God's wrath and from death (Deut. 9:20).

32:6 ROSE UP TO PLAY. The people began to indulge in sensuous dancing and sexual immorality. According to v. 25, they "*were* naked" (literally, "became ungovernable and made themselves naked"). Thus, the sin of the Israelites involved uncovering the nakedness of others for sexual play and pleasure, something strictly forbidden in God's law (Lev. 18:6–30; 20:11,17,19–21; see article on STANDARDS OF SEXUAL MORALITY, p. 1964).

[l]Go, get thee down; for thy people,
which thou broughtest out of the land
of Egypt, [m]have corrupted *themselves:*
8 They have turned aside quickly
out of the way which [n]I commanded
them: they have made them a molten
calf, and have worshipped it, and have
sacrificed thereunto, and said, [o]These
be thy gods, O Israel, which have
brought thee up out of the land of
Egypt.
9 And the LORD said unto Moses, [p]I
have seen this people, and, behold, it *is*
a stiffnecked people:
10 Now therefore [q]let me alone,
that [r]my wrath may wax hot against
them, and that I may consume them:
and [s]I will make of thee a great na-
tion.
11 [t]And Moses besought [x]the
LORD his God, and said, LORD, why doth
thy wrath wax hot against thy people,
which thou hast brought forth out of
the land of Egypt with great power, and
with a mighty hand?
12 [u]Wherefore should the Egyp-
tians speak, and say, For mischief did
he bring them out, to slay them in the
mountains, and to consume them from
the face of the earth? Turn from thy
fierce wrath, and [v]repent of this evil
against thy people.
13 Remember Abraham, Isaac, and
Israel, thy servants, to whom thou
[w]swarest by thine own self, and saidst
unto them, [x]I will multiply your seed
as the stars of heaven, and all this land
that I have spoken of will I give unto
your seed, and they shall inherit *it* for
ever.
14 And the LORD [y]repented of the
evil which he thought to do unto his
people.
15 ¶ And [z]Moses turned, and went
down from the mount, and the two ta-
bles of the testimony *were* in his hand:
the tables *were* written on both their
sides; on the one side and on the other
were they written.
16 And the [a]tables *were* the work
of God, and the writing *was* the writing
of God, graven upon the tables.
17 And when Joshua heard the
noise of the people as they shouted, he
said unto Moses, *There is* a noise of war
in the camp.
18 And he said, *It is* not the voice of
them that shout for mastery, neither *is*
it the voice of *them that* cry for [y]being
overcome: *but* the noise of *them that*
sing do I hear.
19 ¶ And it came to pass, as soon as
he came nigh unto the camp, that [b]he
saw the calf, and the dancing: and Mo-

32:7 [l]Deut. 9:12 Dan. 9:24 [m]Gen. 6:11,12
32:8 [n]ch. 20:3,4,23 [o]1 Ki. 12:28
32:9 [p]2 Chr. 30:8 Is. 48:4 Acts 7:51
32:10 [q]Deut. 9:14,19 [r]ch. 22:24 [s]Num. 14:12
32:11 [t]Deut. 9:18,26-29
32:12 [u]Num. 14:13 [v]ver. 14
32:13 [w]Gen. 22:16 Heb. 6:13 [x]Gen. 12:7 & 13:15 & 15:7,18 & 26:4 & 35:11,12
32:14 [y]2 Sam. 24:16
32:15 [z]Deut. 9:15
32:16 [a]ch. 31:18
32:19 [b]Deut. 9:16,17

[x] Heb. *the face of the LORD* [y] Heb. *weakness*

32:10 CONSUME THEM. Because of the people's apostasy and sin, God declared His intention to destroy them and raise up another nation through Moses.

32:11 MOSES BESOUGHT THE LORD. The intercession of Moses for the people of Israel (vv. 11–14) reveals that God answers the prayers of His faithful servants and allows them to share in His redemptive purposes and decisions. (1) God clearly desired to destroy the rebellious people (v. 10). Yet Moses, acting as a mediator between the Lord and the people, earnestly interceded in order to turn away God's wrath and change His stated intention.

(2) Because of that intense prayer of Moses, the Lord relented (v. 14; see Jas. 5:16, note; see article on INTERCESSION, p. 1268).

(3) The great truth emphasized here is that God makes His servants co-workers with Him (1 Cor. 3:9). He appoints them mediators and intercessors for the lost (Rom. 9:2, note), and in some measure the fate of those perishing is in their hands (see Mat. 9:38, note). Thus, God has ordained that the sincere intercession of a righteous person may move Him to change His temporal will and bring redemption instead of judgment (cf. Ezek. 22:30). Prayer does indeed change things (cf. Ps. 106:44–45; Jer. 18:8; 26:3,13,19; Amos 7:2–6; Jonah 3:10).

(4) God does not disregard the intercession of a faithful servant as long as hope for redemption remains. Intercession will be rejected by God only when sin has reached its limit (cf. Jer. 15:1; Ezek. 14:14,16).

(5) It is an unfathomable mystery that God should be persuaded by the intercession of a fallible human being to alter His announced course of action and turn from wrath to mercy. God is not an implacable deity or a God of inflexible fate, but a personal God who delights to be moved by the love, faith, and prayers of His faithful people (see article on THE PROVIDENCE OF GOD, p. 80).

32:14 REPENTED. The Hebrew word translated "repented" means to change one's mind or purpose, to relent from or to alter a planned course of action previously stated. God does not repent the way a human being must repent, for He is totally free from sin.

32:19 BRAKE THEM BENEATH THE MOUNT. Moses did not shatter the tablets of stone because of uncontrolled passion, but because of a righteous, godly indignation against sin (cf. vv. 10,34–35). Christ too manifested godly anger against sin (John 2:15; 11:33, note). Such anger will be demonstrated by all who have a genuine concern for God's glory and holiness and for human suffering.

ses' anger waxed hot, and he cast the
tables out of his hands, and brake them
beneath the mount.
20 [c]And he took the calf which
they had made, and burnt *it* in the fire,
and ground *it* to powder, and strawed
it upon the water, and made the chil-
dren of Israel drink *of it.*
21 And Moses said unto Aaron,
[d]What did this people unto thee, that
thou hast brought so great a sin upon
them?
22 And Aaron said, Let not the an-
ger of my lord wax hot: [e]thou knowest
the people, that they *are set* on mis-
chief.
23 For they said unto me, Make us
gods, which shall go before us: for *as
for* this Moses, the man that brought us
up out of the land of Egypt, we wot not
what is become of him.
24 And I said unto them, Whoso-
ever hath any gold, let them break *it*
off. So they gave *it* me: then I cast it
into the fire, and there came out this
calf.
25 ¶ And when Moses saw that the
people *were* [f]naked; (for Aaron [g]had
made them naked unto *their* shame
among [z]their enemies:)
26 Then Moses stood in the gate of
the camp, and said, Who *is* on the
LORD's side? *let him come* unto me. And
all the sons of Levi gathered them-
selves together unto him.
27 And he said unto them, Thus
saith the LORD God of Israel, Put every
man his sword by his side, *and* go in
and out from gate to gate throughout
the camp, and [h]slay every man his
brother, and every man his companion,
and every man his neighbour.
28 And the children of Levi did ac-
cording to the word of Moses: and
there fell of the people that day about
three thousand men.
29 [i]For[a] Moses had said, [b]Con-
secrate yourselves today to the LORD,
even every man upon his son, and upon
his brother; that he may bestow upon
you a blessing this day.
30 ¶ And it came to pass on the mor-
row, that Moses said unto the people,
[j]Ye have sinned a great sin: and now
I will go up unto the LORD; [k]peradven-
ture I shall [l]make an atonement for
your sin.
31 And Moses [m]returned unto the
LORD, and said, Oh, this people have
sinned a great sin, and have [n]made
them gods of gold.
32 Yet now, if thou wilt forgive their
sin—; and if not, [o]blot me, I pray
thee, [p]out of thy book which thou hast
written.
33 And the LORD said unto Moses,
[q]Whosoever hath sinned against me,
him will I blot out of my book.
34 Therefore now go, lead the peo-
ple unto *the place* of which I have spo-
ken unto thee: [r]behold, mine Angel
shall go before thee: nevertheless [s]in
the day when I visit I will visit their sin
upon them.
35 And the LORD plagued the peo-
ple, because [t]they made the calf,
which Aaron made.

The renewal of the covenant

33 AND THE LORD said unto Mo-
ses, Depart, *and* go up hence,
thou [u]and the people which thou hast
brought up out of the land of Egypt,
unto the land which I sware unto Abra-
ham, to Isaac, and to Jacob, saying,
[v]Unto thy seed will I give it:
2 [w]And I will send an angel before
thee; [x]and I will drive out the Canaan-
ite, the Amorite, and the Hittite, and
the Perizzite, the Hivite, and the Jebu-
site:

32:20 [c]Deut. 9:21 **32:21** [d]Gen. 26:10 **32:22** [e]ch. 14:11 **32:25** [f]ch. 33:4,5 [g]2 Chr. 28:19 **32:27** [h]Num. 25:5 **32:29** [i]1 Sam. 15:18,22 Prov. 21:3 Zech. 13:3 **32:30** [j]1 Sam. 12:20,23 [k]2 Sam. 16:12 [l]Num. 25:13 **32:31** [m]Deut. 9:18 [n]ch. 20:23 **32:32** [o]Ps. 69:28 Rom. 9:3 [p]Dan. 12:1 Phil. 4:3 Rev. 3:5 & 21:27 **32:33** [q]Lev. 23:30 Ezek. 18:4 **32:34** [r]ch. 33:2,14 [s]Deut. 32:35 Rom. 2:5,6 **32:35** [t]2 Sam. 12:9 **33:1** [u]ch. 32:7 [v]Gen. 12:7 **33:2** [w]ch. 32:34 [x]Josh. 24:11

[z] Heb. *those that rose up against them* [a] Or, *And Moses said, Consecrate yourselves today to the LORD, because every man* hath been *against his son, and against his brother* [b] Heb. *Fill your hands*

32:26 WHO *IS* ON THE LORD'S SIDE. Moses' call for loyalty to God reflects the principle that in the midst of spiritual decline and apostasy, the only path for the faithful is the one marked out by decisive obedience to His law and clear separation from apostasy (see Rev. 18:4, note; cf. Josh. 24:15; 1 Ki. 18:21; see article on PERSONAL APOSTASY, p. 1946).

32:29 A BLESSING. Because the children of Levi remained faithful to the Lord, they turned the curse that had been pronounced upon them (Gen. 49:7) into a blessing (cf. Num. 3). They were appointed to care for the tabernacle and to assist the priests (Num. 1:47–53; 3:5–9,12,41,45; 4:2–3). God's curses and blessings are often conditioned on one's actions and can be reversed by repentance and obedience.

32:32 FORGIVE THEIR SIN. Moses' love for the sinful people (cf. Rom. 9:3) points to the love of a greater mediator, Christ Jesus, who "made intercession for the transgressors" (Is. 53:12; Rom. 8:34; see Mat. 26:39, note; 1 Tim. 2:5, note; Heb. 7:25, note).

3 [y]Unto a land flowing with milk and honey: for I will not go up in the midst of thee; for thou *art* a [z]stiffnecked people: lest [a]I consume thee in the way.

4 ¶ And when the people heard these evil tidings, [b]they mourned: [c]and no man did put on him his ornaments.

5 For the LORD had said unto Moses, Say unto the children of Israel, Ye *are* a stiffnecked people: I will come up [d]into the midst of thee in a moment, and consume thee: therefore now put off thy ornaments from thee, that I may [e]know what to do unto thee.

6 And the children of Israel stripped themselves of their ornaments by the mount Horeb.

7 And Moses took the tabernacle, and pitched it without the camp, afar off from the camp, [f]and called it the Tabernacle of the congregation. And it came to pass, *that* every one which [g]sought the LORD went out unto the tabernacle of the congregation, which *was* without the camp.

8 And it came to pass, when Moses went out unto the tabernacle, *that* all the people rose up, and stood every man [h]*at* his tent door, and looked after Moses, until he was gone into the tabernacle.

9 And it came to pass, as Moses entered into the tabernacle, the cloudy pillar descended, and stood *at* the door of the tabernacle, and *the* LORD [i]*talked with Moses.*

10 And all the people saw the cloudy pillar stand *at* the tabernacle door: and all the people rose up and [j]worshipped, every man *in* his tent door.

11 And [k]the LORD spake unto Moses face to face, as a man speaketh unto his friend. And he turned again into the camp: but [l]his servant Joshua, the son of Nun, a young man, departed not out of the tabernacle.

12 ¶ And Moses said unto the LORD, See, [m]thou sayest unto me, Bring up this people: and thou hast not let me know whom thou wilt send with me. Yet thou hast said, [n]I know thee by name, and thou hast also found grace in my sight.

13 Now therefore, I pray thee, [o]if I have found grace in thy sight, [p]show me now thy way, that I may know thee, that I may find grace in thy sight: and consider that this nation *is* [q]thy people.

14 And he said, [r]My presence

33:3 [y]ch. 3:8 [z]ch. 32:9 [a]Num. 16:21,45
33:4 [b]Num. 14:1,39 [c]Ezra 9:3 Esth. 4:1,4 Ezek. 24:17,23
33:5 [d]See Num. 16:45, 46 [e]Ps. 139:23
33:7 [f]ch. 29:42,43 [g]Deut. 4:29
33:8 [h]Num. 16:27
33:9 [i]ch. 25:22 & 31:18 Ps. 99:7
33:10 [j]ch. 4:31
33:11 [k]Num. 12:8 Deut. 34:10 [l]ch. 24:13
33:12 [m]ch. 32:34 [n]ver. 17 John 10:14,15 2 Tim. 2:19
33:13 [o]ch. 34:9 [p]Ps. 25:4 & 27:11 & 86:11 & 119:33 [q]Deut. 9:26,29
33:14 [r]Is. 63:9

33:3 I WILL NOT GO UP. Because of Israel's sin, God stated that an angel would take His place on the way to the promised land (vv. 1–3). However, Moses, not wanting to accept this decision, once again interceded with God (vv. 12–14), as he had done in the previous chapter. Notice the sequence of events that took place in regard to Israel's sin with the golden calf (32:1–6), Moses' perseverance in prayer, and God's revelation to him. (1) God intended to destroy the people (32:10). Moses' intercession (32:11–13) provided a basis for God to change His course of action and not fulfill His threat to destroy the people (32:14; see 32:11, note). (2) God then decided to allow the people to go into Canaan, but led only by Moses and an angel (32:34). God clearly and sincerely stated that He Himself would not go with them (33:3). (3) After more prayer (33:12–13) the Lord changed His plan, granted Moses' petition, and agreed that His presence would accompany them (vv. 14–17; see article on INTERCESSION, p. 1268).

God's response to Moses' intercession reveals something of His ways (cf. v. 13) with His people. Not every decision of God is absolutely fixed and irrevocable. Rather He is a God who responds to His people (see 32:11, note); at times He changes His declared course of action when His people sincerely call upon Him in prayer and commit themselves to Him and His will. God always remains free to change His declared judgment in order to show love and mercy (cf. Jonah 3).

33:11 HIS FRIEND. God considered Moses as a close friend with whom he could talk face to face. This special relationship was partly due to the fact that Moses was sincerely devoted to God and to His cause, desires, and purposes. Moses was one with the Spirit of God to such an extent that he shared the very feelings of God, suffering when He suffered and grieving when He grieved at sin (cf. 32:19). Every believer should seek to know the ways of God through prayer and to grow into such a profound union with Him and His purposes that he or she is indeed a friend of God.

33:11 JOSHUA . . . DEPARTED NOT OUT OF THE TABERNACLE. Joshua not only faithfully served Moses, God's anointed, but also diligently developed a personal communion with God. From his youth, he learned to tarry long with the Lord. Such devotion prepared him to become Moses' successor.

33:12 MOSES SAID. Through Moses' prayer, God relented, changed His resolve (cf. v. 3), and agreed to go with Moses and the people (v. 14, see v. 3, note).

33:13 SHOW ME NOW THY WAY. All God's children should fervently pray to know His ways, i.e., His heart, purpose, wisdom, holy principles, and even His suffering. In doing so, we come to know God Himself.

shall go *with thee,* and I will give thee [s]rest.

15 And he said unto him, [t]If thy presence go not *with me,* carry us not up hence.

16 For wherein shall it be known here that I and thy people have found grace in thy sight? [u]*is it* not in that thou goest with us? so [v]shall we be separated, I and thy people, from all the people that *are* upon the face of the earth.

Moses beholds God's glory

17 And the LORD said unto Moses, [w]I will do this thing also that thou hast spoken: for [x]thou hast found grace in my sight, and I know thee by name.

18 And he said, I beseech thee, show me [y]thy glory.

19 And he said, I will make all my goodness pass before thee, and I will proclaim the name of the LORD before thee; [z]and will be [a]gracious to whom I will be gracious, and will show mercy on whom I will show mercy.

20 And he said, Thou canst not see my face: for [b]there shall no man see me, and live.

21 And the LORD said, Behold, *there is* a place by me, and thou shalt stand upon a rock:

22 And it shall come to pass, while my glory passeth by, that I will put thee [c]in a cleft of the rock, and will [d]cover thee with my hand while I pass by:

23 And I will take away mine hand, and thou shalt see my back parts: but my face shall [e]not be seen.

The second tables of stone

34 AND THE LORD said unto Moses, [f]Hew thee two tables of stone like unto the first: [g]and I will write upon *these* tables the words that were in the first tables, which thou brakest.

2 And be ready in the morning, and come up in the morning unto mount Sinai, and present thyself there to me [h]in the top of the mount.

3 And no man shall [i]come up with thee, neither let any man be seen throughout all the mount; neither let the flocks nor herds feed before that mount.

4 ¶ And he hewed two tables of stone like unto the first; and Moses rose up early in the morning, and went up unto mount Sinai, as the LORD had commanded him, and took in his hand the two tables of stone.

5 And the LORD descended in the cloud, and stood with him there, and [j]proclaimed the name of the LORD.

6 And the LORD passed by before him, and proclaimed, The LORD, The LORD [k]God, merciful and gracious, longsuffering, and abundant in [l]goodness and [m]truth,

7 [n]Keeping mercy for thousands, [o]forgiving iniquity and transgression and sin, and [p]that will by no means clear *the guilty;* visiting the iniquity of the fathers upon the children, and upon the children's children, unto the third and to the fourth *generation.*

8 And Moses made haste, and [q]bowed his head toward the earth, and worshipped.

9 And he said, If now I have found grace in thy sight, O Lord, [r]let my Lord, I pray thee, go among us; for [s]it *is* a stiffnecked people; and pardon our iniquity and our sin, and take us for [t]thine inheritance.

10 ¶ And he said, Behold, [u]I make a covenant: before all thy people I will [v]do marvels, such as have not been done in all the earth, nor in any nation:

33:14 [s]Josh. 21:44
33:15 [t]ver. 3
33:16 [u]Num. 14:14 [v]ch. 34:10 Deut. 4:7,34
33:17 [w]Jas. 5:16 [x]ver. 12
33:18 [y]1 Tim. 6:16
33:19 [z]Rom. 9:15,16,18 [a]Rom. 4:4,16
33:20 [b]Gen. 32:30
33:22 [c]Is. 2:21 [d]Ps. 91:1,4
33:23 [e]John 1:18
34:1 [f]ch. 32:16,19 [g]ver. 28 Deut. 10:2,4
34:2 [h]ch. 19:20
34:3 [i]ch. 19:12,13,21
34:5 [j]ch. 33:19
34:6 [k]Neh. 9:17 Joel 2:13 [l]Rom. 2:4 [m]Ps. 108:4
34:7 [n]ch. 20:6 [o]Ps. 103:3 & 130:4 Dan. 9:9 Eph. 4:32 1 John 1:9 [p]Josh. 24:19 Job 10:14 Mic. 6:11 Nah. 1:3
34:8 [q]ch. 4:31
34:9 [r]ch. 33:15,16 [s]ch. 33:3 [t]Ps. 33:12 & 94:14
34:10 [u]Deut. 5:2 [v]Deut. 4:32 Ps. 77:14

33:17 FOR THOU HAST FOUND GRACE IN MY SIGHT. Note that God answered Moses' prayer because He respected him, considered him a friend, and was pleased with him. Moses found favor because, even though Aaron and the nation disobeyed God, he remained loyal to the Lord and mediated between the Lord and Israel.

34:6–7 THE LORD ... MERCIFUL AND GRACIOUS. For comments on God's name as "LORD" (i.e., *Yahweh*), see Gen. 2:4, note; Ex. 3:14, note. Here God gives further light on the meaning of that name and on His innermost nature. The Lord is a God whose compassion, kindness, and forgiveness are united with truth, holiness, and justice. The fact that God is gracious and compassionate shows that He will not punish anyone unless and until His longsuffering and love are rejected and despised.

34:7 INIQUITY OF THE FATHERS . . . CHILDREN. Parents should take note that their sins, spiritual neglect, or failure to separate themselves from all the ungodliness of the world can have tragic consequences upon their children. Children suffer for the sins of the parents in the sense that they generally follow their parents along the path of temptation or spiritual compromise, thereby adopting evil habits and attitudes that will lead them away from God and toward destruction.

and all the people among which thou
art shall see the work of the LORD: for
it *is* [w]a terrible thing that I will do with
thee.
11 [x]Observe thou that which I
command thee this day: behold, [y]I
drive out before thee the Amorite, and
the Canaanite, and the Hittite, and the
Perizzite, and the Hivite, and the Jebu-
site.
12 [z]Take heed to thyself, lest thou
make a covenant with the inhabitants
of the land whither thou goest, lest it
be for [a]a snare in the midst of thee:
13 But ye shall [b]destroy their al-
tars, break their [c]images, and [c]cut
down their groves:
14 For thou shalt worship [d]no oth-
er god: for the LORD, whose [e]name *is*
Jealous, *is* a [f]jealous God:
15 [g]Lest thou make a covenant
with the inhabitants of the land, and
they [h]go a-whoring after their gods,
and do sacrifice unto their gods, and
one [i]call thee, and thou [j]eat of his
sacrifice;
16 And thou take of [k]their daugh-
ters unto thy sons, and their daughters
[l]go a-whoring after their gods, and
make thy sons go a-whoring after their
gods.
17 [m]Thou shalt make thee no mol-
ten gods.
18 ¶ The feast of [n]unleavened
bread shalt thou keep. Seven days thou
shalt eat unleavened bread, as I com-
manded thee, in the time of the month
Abib: for in the [o]month Abib thou
camest out from Egypt.
19 [p]All that openeth the matrix *is*
mine; and every firstling among thy
cattle, *whether* ox or sheep, *that is male*.
20 But [q]the firstling of an ass thou
shalt redeem with a [d]lamb: and if thou
redeem *him* not, then shalt thou break
his neck. All the firstborn of thy sons
thou shalt redeem. And none shall ap-
pear before me [r]empty.
21 ¶ [s]Six days thou shalt work, but
on the seventh day thou shalt rest: in
earing time and in harvest thou shalt
rest.
22 ¶ [t]And thou shalt observe the
feast of weeks, of the firstfruits of
wheat harvest, and the feast of ingath-
ering at the [e]year's end.

23 ¶ [u]Thrice in the year shall all
your menchildren appear before the
Lord GOD, the God of Israel.
24 For I will [v]cast out the nations
before thee, and [w]enlarge thy borders:
[x]neither shall any man desire thy
land, when thou shalt go up to appear
before the LORD thy God thrice in the
year.
25 [y]Thou shalt not offer the blood
of my sacrifice with leaven; [z]neither
shall the sacrifice of the feast of the
passover be left unto the morning.
26 [a]The first of the firstfruits of
thy land thou shalt bring unto the
house of the LORD thy God. [b]Thou
shalt not seethe a kid in his mother's
milk.
27 And the LORD said unto Moses,
Write thou [c]these words: for after the
tenor of these words I have made a cov-
enant with thee and with Israel.
28 [d]And he was there with the
LORD forty days and forty nights; he did
neither eat bread, nor drink water. And
[e]he wrote upon the tables the words
of the covenant, the ten [f]command-
ments.

Moses' shining face

29 ¶ And it came to pass, when Mo-
ses came down from mount Sinai with
the [f]two tables of testimony in Moses'
hand, when he came down from the
mount, that Moses wist not that [g]the
skin of his face shone while he talked
with him.
30 And when Aaron and all the chil-
dren of Israel saw Moses, behold, the
skin of his face shone; and they were
afraid to come nigh him.
31 And Moses called unto them;
and Aaron and all the rulers of the con-
gregation returned unto him: and Mo-
ses talked with them.
32 And afterward all the children of
Israel came nigh: [h]and he gave them
in commandment all that the LORD had
spoken with him in mount Sinai.
33 And *till* Moses had done speak-
ing with them, he put [i]a veil on his
face.
34 But [j]when Moses went in be-

34:10 [w]Ps. 145:6
34:11 [x]Deut. 6:25 [y]ch. 33:2
34:12 [z]ch. 23:32 [a]ch. 23:33
34:13 [b]Deut. 12:3 [c]2 Ki. 18:4 2 Chr. 34:3,4
34:14 [d]ch. 20:3,5 [e]See Is. 9:6 & 57:15 [f]ch. 20:5
34:15 [g]ver. 12 [h]Judg. 2:17 [i]Num. 25:2 [j]1 Cor. 8:4,7,10
34:16 [k]Deut. 7:3 1 Ki. 11:2 Ezra 9:2 Neh. 13:25 [l]Num. 25:1,2 1 Ki. 11:4
34:17 [m]ch. 32:8
34:18 [n]ch. 12:15 [o]ch. 13:4
34:19 [p]ch. 22:29
34:20 [q]ch. 13:13 [r]ch. 23:15 Deut. 16:16 1 Sam. 9:7,8 2 Sam. 24:24
34:21 [s]ch. 20:9 Luke 13:14
34:22 [t]ch. 23:16
34:23 [u]ch. 23:14,17
34:24 [v]ch. 33:2 Ps. 78:55 [w]Deut. 12:20 & 19:8 [x]See Gen. 35:5 Acts 18:10
34:25 [y]ch. 23:18 [z]ch. 12:10
34:26 [a]ch. 23:19 [b]ch. 23:19
34:27 [c]Deut. 31:9
34:28 [d]ch. 24:18 [e]ver. 1 ch. 31:18 Deut. 4:13 & 10:2,4
34:29 [f]ch. 32:15 [g]Mat. 17:2 2 Cor. 3:7,13
34:32 [h]ch. 24:3
34:33 [i]2 Cor. 3:13
34:34 [j]2 Cor. 3:16

[c]Heb. *statues* [d]Or, *kid* [e]Heb. *revolution of the year* [f]Heb. *words*

34:28 FORTY DAYS. Moses was sustained supernaturally by God during his forty-day fast in which he did not eat food or drink water. Biblically and physiologically, a fast that includes abstinence from water should be no longer than three days (see Mat. 6:16, note).

fore the LORD to speak with him, he took the veil off, until he came out. And he came out, and spake unto the children of Israel *that* which he was commanded.

35 And the children of Israel saw the face of Moses, that the skin of Moses' face shone: and Moses put the veil upon his face again, until he went in to speak with him.

Sabbath regulations

35:4–9pp — Ex. 25:1–7
35:10–19pp — Ex. 39:32–41

35 AND MOSES gathered all the congregation of the children of Israel together, and said unto them, [k]These *are* the words which the LORD hath commanded, that *ye* should do them.

2 [l]Six days shall work be done, but on the seventh day there shall be to you [g]an holy day, a sabbath of rest to the LORD: whosoever doeth work therein shall be put to death.

3 [m]Ye shall kindle no fire throughout your habitations upon the sabbath day.

4 ¶ And Moses spake unto all the congregation of the children of Israel, saying, [n]This *is* the thing which the LORD commanded, saying,

5 Take ye from among you an offering unto the LORD: [o]whosoever *is* of a willing heart, let him bring it, an offering of the LORD; gold, and silver, and brass,

6 And blue, and purple, and scarlet, and fine linen, and goats' *hair,*

7 And rams' skins dyed red, and badgers' skins, and shittim wood,

8 And oil for the light, [p]and spices for anointing oil, and for the sweet incense,

9 And onyx stones, and stones to be set for the ephod, and for the breastplate.

10 And [q]every wisehearted among you shall come, and make all that the LORD hath commanded;

11 [r]The tabernacle, his tent, and his covering, his taches, and his boards, his bars, his pillars, and his sockets,

12 [s]The ark, and the staves thereof, *with* the mercy seat, and the veil of the covering,

13 The [t]table, and his staves, and all his vessels, [u]and the showbread,

14 [v]The candlestick also for the light, and his furniture, and his lamps, with the oil for the light,

15 [w]And the incense altar, and his staves, [x]and the anointing oil, and [y]the sweet incense, and the hanging for the door at the entering in of the tabernacle,

16 [z]The altar of burnt offering, with his brasen grate, his staves, and all his vessels, the laver and his foot,

17 [a]The hangings of the court, his pillars, and their sockets, and the hanging for the door of the court,

18 The pins of the tabernacle, and the pins of the court, and their cords,

19 [b]The cloths of service, to do service in the holy *place,* the holy garments for Aaron the priest, and the garments of his sons, to minister in the priest's office.

Offerings for the tabernacle

20 ¶ And all the congregation of the children of Israel departed from the presence of Moses.

21 And they came, every one [c]whose heart stirred him up, and every one whom his spirit made willing, *and* they brought the LORD's offering to the work of the tabernacle of the congregation, and for all his service, and for the holy garments.

22 And they came, both men and women, as many as were willing-hearted, *and* brought bracelets, and earrings, and rings, and tablets, all jewels of gold: and every man that offered *offered* an offering of gold unto the LORD.

23 And [d]every man, with whom was found blue, and purple, and scarlet, and fine linen, and goats' *hair,* and red skins of rams, and badgers' skins, brought *them.*

24 Every one that did offer an offering of silver and brass brought the LORD's offering: and every man, with whom was found shittim wood for any work of the service, brought *it.*

35:1 [k]ch. 34:32
35:2 [l]ch. 20:9 Lev. 23:3
35:3 [m]ch. 16:23
35:4 [n]ch. 25:1,2
35:5 [o]ch. 25:2
35:8 [p]ch. 25:6
35:10 [q]ch. 31:6
35:11 [r]ch. 26:1,2
35:12 [s]ch. 25:10
35:13 [t]ch. 25:23 [u]ch. 25:30 Lev. 24:5,6
35:14 [v]ch. 25:31
35:15 [w]ch. 30:1 [x]ch. 30:25 [y]ch. 30:34
35:16 [z]ch. 27:1
35:17 [a]ch. 27:9
35:19 [b]ch. 31:10 & 39:1,41 Num. 4:5,6
35:21 [c]ver. 5,22,26,29 ch. 36:2
35:23 [d]1 Chr. 29:8

[g] Heb. *holiness*

35:1—40:38 WORDS ... COMMANDED. These chapters repeat in general the material of chs. 25—31, except that here the instructions given to Moses for the tabernacle are carried out. This section is included to emphasize how crucial it is that God's people take His instructions with the utmost seriousness and follow them diligently.

25 And all the women that were [e]wisehearted did spin with their hands, and brought that which they had spun, *both* of blue, and of purple, *and* of scarlet, and of fine linen.

26 And all the women whose heart stirred them up in wisdom spun goats' *hair.*

27 And [f]the rulers brought onyx stones, and stones to be set, for the ephod, and for the breastplate;

28 And [g]spice, and oil for the light, and for the anointing oil, and for the sweet incense.

29 The children of Israel brought a [h]willing offering unto the LORD, every man and woman, whose heart made them willing to bring for all manner of work, which the LORD had commanded to be made by the hand of Moses.

The workmen gathered

35:30–35pp — Ex. 31:2–6

30 ¶ And Moses said unto the children of Israel, See, [i]the LORD hath called by name Bezaleel the son of Uri, the son of Hur, of the tribe of Judah;

31 And he hath filled him with the spirit of God, in wisdom, in understanding, and in knowledge, and in all manner of workmanship;

32 And to devise curious works, to work in gold, and in silver, and in brass,

33 And in the cutting of stones, to set *them,* and in carving of wood, to make any manner of cunning work.

34 And he hath put in his heart that he may teach, *both* he, and [j]Aholiab, the son of Ahisamach, of the tribe of Dan.

35 Them hath he [k]filled with wisdom of heart, to work all manner of work, of the engraver, and of the cunning workman, and of the embroiderer, in blue, and in purple, in scarlet, and in fine linen, and of the weaver, *even* of them that do any work, and of those that devise cunning work.

Num. 11:24-29

36 THEN WROUGHT Bezaleel and Aholiab, and every [l]wisehearted man, in whom the LORD put wisdom and understanding to know how to work all manner of work for the service of the [m]sanctuary, according to all that the LORD had commanded.

2 And Moses called Bezaleel and Aholiab, and every wisehearted man, in whose heart the LORD had put wisdom, *even* every one [n]whose heart stirred him up to come unto the work to do it:

3 And they received of Moses all the offering, which the children of Israel [o]had brought for the work of the service of the sanctuary, to make it *withal.* And they brought yet unto him free offerings every morning.

4 And all the wise men, that wrought all the work of the sanctuary, came every man from his work which they made;

5 ¶ And they spake unto Moses, saying, [p]The people bring much more than enough for the service of the work, which the LORD commanded to make.

6 And Moses gave commandment, and they caused it to be proclaimed throughout the camp, saying, Let neither man nor woman make any more work for the offering of the sanctuary. So the people were restrained from bringing.

7 For the stuff they had was sufficient for all the work to make it, and too much.

The work for the tabernacle

36:8–38pp — Ex. 26:1–37

8 ¶ [q]And every wisehearted man among them that wrought the work of the tabernacle made ten curtains *of* fine twined linen, and blue, and purple, and scarlet: *with* cherubims of cunning work made he them.

9 The length of one curtain *was* twenty and eight cubits, and the breadth of one curtain four cubits: the curtains *were* all of one size.

10 And he coupled the five curtains one unto another: and *the other* five curtains he coupled one unto another.

11 And he made loops of blue on the edge of one curtain from the selvedge in the coupling: likewise he made in the uttermost side of *another* curtain, in the coupling of the second.

12 [r]Fifty loops made he in one curtain, and fifty loops made he in the edge of the curtain which *was* in the coupling of the second: the loops held one *curtain* to another.

13 And he made fifty taches of gold, and coupled the curtains one unto another with the taches: so it became one tabernacle.

14 ¶ [s]And he made curtains *of*

35:25 [e]ch. 28:3 & 31:6 & 36:1 **35:27** [f]1 Chr. 29:6 Ezra 2:68 **35:28** [g]ch. 30:23 **35:29** [h]ver. 21 1 Chr. 29:9 **35:30** [i]ch. 31:2 **35:34** [j]ch. 31:6 **35:35** [k]ver. 31 ch. 31:3,6 1 Ki. 7:14 2 Chr. 2:14 Is. 28:26 **36:1** [l]ch. 28:3 & 31:6 & 35:10,35 [m]ch. 25:8 **36:2** [n]ch. 35:21,26 1 Chr. 29:5 **36:3** [o]ch. 35:27 **36:5** [p]2 Cor. 8:2,3 **36:8** [q]ch. 26:1 **36:12** [r]ch. 26:5 **36:14** [s]ch. 26:7

goats' *hair* for the tent over the tabernacle: eleven curtains he made them.
15 The length of one curtain *was* thirty cubits, and four cubits *was* the breadth of one curtain: the eleven curtains *were* of one size.
16 And he coupled five curtains by themselves, and six curtains by themselves.
17 And he made fifty loops upon the uttermost edge of the curtain in the coupling, and fifty loops made he upon the edge of the curtain which coupleth the second.
18 And he made fifty taches *of* brass to couple the tent together, that it might be one.
19 [t]And he made a covering for the tent *of* rams' skins dyed red, and a covering *of* badgers' skins above *that.*
20 ¶ [u]And he made boards for the tabernacle *of* [v]shittim wood, standing up.
21 The length of a board *was* ten cubits, and the breadth of a board one cubit and a half.
22 One board had two tenons, equally distant one from another: thus did he make for all the boards of the tabernacle.
23 And he made boards for the tabernacle; twenty boards for the south side southward:
24 And forty sockets of silver he made under the twenty boards; two sockets under one board for his two tenons, and two sockets under another board for his two tenons.
25 And for the other side of the tabernacle, *which is* toward the north corner, he made twenty boards,
26 And their forty sockets of silver; two sockets under one board, and two sockets under another board.
27 And for the sides of the tabernacle westward he made six boards.
28 And two boards made he for the corners of the tabernacle in the two sides.
29 And they were [h]coupled beneath, and coupled together at the head thereof, to one ring: thus he did to both of them in both the corners.
30 And there were eight boards; and their sockets *were* sixteen sockets of silver, [i]under every board two sockets.
31 ¶ And he made [w]bars of shittim wood; five for the boards of the one side of the tabernacle,

36:19 [t]ch. 26:14
36:20 [u]ch. 26:15 [v]ch. 25:5,10 Num. 15:1 Deut. 10:3 Josh. 2:1
36:31 [w]ch. 26:26
36:35 [x]ch. 26:31
36:37 [y]ch. 26:36
37:1 [z]ch. 25:10
37:6 [a]ch. 25:17

32 And five bars for the boards of the other side of the tabernacle, and five bars for the boards of the tabernacle for the sides westward.
33 And he made the middle bar to shoot through the boards from the one end to the other.
34 And he overlaid the boards with gold, and made their rings *of* gold *to be* places for the bars, and overlaid the bars with gold.
35 ¶ And he made [x]a veil *of* blue, and purple, and scarlet, and fine twined linen: *with* cherubims made he it of cunning work.
36 And he made thereunto four pillars *of* shittim *wood,* and overlaid them with gold: their hooks *were of* gold; and he cast for them four sockets of silver.
37 ¶ And he made an [y]hanging for the tabernacle door *of* blue, and purple, and scarlet, and fine twined linen, [j]of needlework;
38 And the five pillars of it with their hooks: and he overlaid their chapiters and their fillets with gold: but their five sockets *were of* brass.

The construction of the ark

37:1–9pp — Ex. 25:10–20

37 AND BEZALEEL made [z]the ark *of* shittim wood: two cubits and a half *was* the length of it, and a cubit and a half the breadth of it, and a cubit and a half the height of it:
2 And he overlaid it with pure gold within and without, and made a crown of gold to it round about.
3 And he cast for it four rings of gold, *to be set* by the four corners of it; even two rings upon the one side of it, and two rings upon the other side of it.
4 And he made staves *of* shittim wood, and overlaid them with gold.
5 And he put the staves into the rings by the sides of the ark, to bear the ark.
6 ¶ And he made the [a]mercy seat *of* pure gold: two cubits and a half *was* the length thereof, and one cubit and a half the breadth thereof.
7 And he made two cherubims *of* gold, beaten out of one piece made he them, on the two ends of the mercy seat;
8 One cherub [k]on the end on this

[h] Heb. *twinned* [i] Heb. *two sockets, two sockets under one board* [j] Heb. *the work of a needleworker,* or, *embroiderer* [k] Or, *out of*

side, and another cherub [l]on the *other* end on that side: out of the mercy seat made he the cherubims on the two ends thereof.

9 And the cherubims spread out *their* wings on high, *and* covered with their wings over the mercy seat, with their faces one to another; *even* to the mercy seatward were the faces of the cherubims.

The table and the candlestick

37:10–16pp — Ex. 25:23–29
37:17–24pp — Ex. 25:31–39

10 ¶ And he made [b]the table *of* shittim wood: two cubits *was* the length thereof, and a cubit the breadth thereof, and a cubit and a half the height thereof:

11 And he overlaid it with pure gold, and made thereunto a crown of gold round about.

12 Also he made thereunto a border of an handbreadth round about; and made a crown of gold for the border thereof round about.

13 And he cast for it four rings of gold, and put the rings upon the four corners that *were* in the four feet thereof.

14 Over against the border were the rings, the places for the staves to bear the table.

15 And he made the staves *of* shittim wood, and overlaid them with gold, to bear the table.

16 And he made the vessels which *were* upon the table, his [c]dishes, and his spoons, and his bowls, and his covers [m]to cover withal, *of* pure gold.

17 ¶ And he made the [d]candlestick *of* pure gold: *of* beaten work made he the candlestick; his shaft, and his branch, his bowls, his knobs, and his flowers, were of the same:

18 And six branches going out of the sides thereof; three branches of the candlestick out of the one side thereof, and three branches of the candlestick out of the other side thereof:

19 Three bowls made after the fashion of almonds in one branch, a knob and a flower; and three bowls made like almonds in another branch, a knob and a flower: so throughout the six branches going out of the candlestick.

20 And in the candlestick *were* four bowls made like almonds, his knobs, and his flowers:

21 And a knob under two branches of the same, and a knob under two branches of the same, and a knob under two branches of the same, according to the six branches going out of it.

22 Their knobs and their branches were of the same: all of it *was* one beaten work *of* pure gold.

23 And he made his seven lamps, and his snuffers, and his snuffdishes, *of* pure gold.

24 *Of* a talent of pure gold made he it, and all the vessels thereof.

The altar of incense

37:25–28pp — Ex. 30:1–5

25 ¶ [e]And he made the incense altar *of* shittim wood: the length of it *was* a cubit, and the breadth of it a cubit; *it was* foursquare; and two cubits *was* the height of it; the horns thereof were of the same.

26 And he overlaid it with pure gold, *both* the top of it, and the sides thereof round about, and the horns of it: also he made unto it a crown of gold round about.

27 And he made two rings of gold for it under the crown thereof, by the two corners of it, upon the two sides thereof, to be places for the staves to bear it withal.

28 And he made the staves *of* shittim wood, and overlaid them with gold.

29 ¶ And he made [f]the holy anointing oil, and the pure incense of sweet spices, according to the work of the apothecary.

The altar of burnt offering

38:1–7pp — Ex. 27:1–8

38 AND [g]HE made the altar of burnt offering *of* shittim wood: five cubits *was* the length thereof, and five cubits the breadth thereof; *it was* foursquare; and three cubits the height thereof.

2 And he made the horns thereof on the four corners of it; the horns thereof were of the same: and he overlaid it with brass.

3 And he made all the vessels of the altar, the pots, and the shovels, and the basins, *and* the fleshhooks, and the firepans: all the vessels thereof made he *of* brass.

4 And he made for the altar a brasen

37:10 [b]ch. 25:23
37:16 [c]ch. 25:29
37:17 [d]ch. 25:31
37:25 [e]ch. 30:1 & 40:26 1 Ki. 9:25 2 Chr. 29:6,7 Is. 60:6 Heb. 7:25
37:29 [f]ch. 30:23,34 Ps. 133:2 Is. 11:2 & 61:1 1 John 2:20
38:1 [g]ch. 27:1

[l] Or, *out of* [m] Or, *to pour out withal*

grate of network under the compass thereof beneath unto the midst of it.

5 And he cast four rings for the four ends of the grate of brass, *to be* places for the staves.

6 And he made the staves *of* shittim wood, and overlaid them with brass.

7 And he put the staves into the rings on the sides of the altar, to bear it withal; he made the altar hollow with boards.

8 ¶ And he made [h]the laver *of* brass, and the foot of it *of* brass, of the [n]looking glasses of *the women* [o]assembling, which assembled *at* the door of the tabernacle of the congregation.

The court of the tabernacle

38:9–20pp — Ex. 27:9–19

9 ¶ And he made [i]the court: on the south side southward the hangings of the court *were of* fine twined linen, an hundred cubits:

10 Their pillars *were* twenty, and their brasen sockets twenty; the hooks of the pillars and their fillets *were of* silver.

11 And for the north side *the hangings were* an hundred cubits, their pillars *were* twenty, and their sockets of brass twenty; the hooks of the pillars and their fillets *of* silver.

12 And for the west side *were* hangings of fifty cubits, their pillars ten, and their sockets ten; the hooks of the pillars and their fillets *of* silver.

13 And for the east side eastward fifty cubits.

14 The hangings of the one side *of the gate were* fifteen cubits; their pillars three, and their sockets three.

15 And for the other side of the court gate, on this hand and that hand, *were* hangings of fifteen cubits; their pillars three, and their sockets three.

16 All the hangings of the court round about *were* of fine twined linen.

17 And the sockets for the pillars *were of* brass; the hooks of the pillars and their fillets *of* silver; and the overlaying of their chapiters *of* silver; and all the pillars of the court *were* filleted with silver.

18 And the hanging for the gate of the court *was* needlework, *of* blue, and purple, and scarlet, and fine twined linen: and twenty cubits *was* the length, and the height in the breadth *was* five cubits, answerable to the hangings of the court.

19 And their pillars *were* four, and their sockets *of* brass four; their hooks *of* silver, and the overlaying of their chapiters and their fillets *of* silver.

20 And all the [j]pins of the tabernacle, and of the court round about, *were of* brass.

21 ¶ This is the sum of the tabernacle, *even* of [k]the tabernacle of testimony, as it was counted, according to the commandment of Moses, *for* the service of the Levites, [l]by the hand of Ithamar, son to Aaron the priest.

22 And [m]Bezaleel the son of Uri, the son of Hur, of the tribe of Judah, made all that the LORD commanded Moses.

23 And with him *was* Aholiab, son of Ahisamach, of the tribe of Dan, an engraver, and a cunning workman, and an embroiderer in blue, and in purple, and in scarlet, and fine linen.

The valuable metals used

24 All the gold that was occupied for the work in all the work of the holy *place*, even the gold of the offering, was twenty and nine talents, and seven hundred and thirty shekels, after [n]the shekel of the sanctuary.

25 And the silver of them that were numbered of the congregation *was* an hundred talents, and a thousand seven hundred and threescore and fifteen shekels, after the shekel of the sanctuary:

26 [o]A bekah for [p]every man, *that is*, half a shekel, after the shekel of the sanctuary, for every one that went to be numbered, from twenty years old and upward, for [p]six hundred thousand and three thousand and five hundred and fifty *men*.

27 And of the hundred talents of silver were cast [q]the sockets of the sanctuary, and the sockets of the veil; an hundred sockets of the hundred talents, a talent for a socket.

28 And of the thousand seven hundred seventy and five *shekels* he made hooks for the pillars, and overlaid their chapiters, and [r]filleted them.

29 And the brass of the offering *was* seventy talents, and two thousand and four hundred shekels.

38:8 [h]ch. 30:18
38:9 [i]ch. 27:9
38:20 [j]ch. 27:19
38:21 [k]Num. 1:50,53 & 9:15 & 10:11 & 17:7,8 2 Chr. 24:6 Acts 7:44 [l]Num. 4:28,33
38:22 [m]ch. 31:2,6
38:24 [n]ch. 30:13,24 Lev. 5:15 & 27:3,25 Num. 3:47 & 18:16
38:26 [o]ch. 30:13,15 [p]Num. 1:46
38:27 [q]ch. 26:19,21,25, 32
38:28 [r]ch. 27:17

[n] Or, *brasen glasses* [o] Heb. *assembling by troops* as 1 Sam. 2:22 [p] Heb. *a poll*

30 And therewith he made the sockets to the door of the tabernacle of the congregation, and the brasen altar, and the brasen grate for it, and all the vessels of the altar,

31 And the sockets of the court round about, and the sockets of the court gate, and all the pins of the tabernacle, and all the pins of the court round about.

The garments of the priesthood

39:2–7pp — Ex. 28:6–14

39 AND OF [s]the blue, and purple, and scarlet, they made [t]cloths of service, to do service in the holy *place,* and made the holy garments for Aaron; [u]as the LORD commanded Moses.

2 [v]And he made the ephod *of* gold, blue, and purple, and scarlet, and fine twined linen.

3 And they did beat the gold into thin plates, and cut *it into* wires, to work *it* in the blue, and in the purple, and in the scarlet, and in the fine linen, *with* cunning work.

4 They made shoulderpieces for it, to couple *it* together: by the two edges was it coupled together.

5 And the curious girdle of his ephod, that *was* upon it, *was* of the same, according to the work thereof; *of* gold, blue, and purple, and scarlet, and fine twined linen; as the LORD commanded Moses.

6 ¶ [w]And they wrought onyx stones enclosed in ouches of gold, graven, as signets are graven, with the names of the children of Israel.

7 And he put them on the shoulders of the ephod, *that they should be* stones for a [x]memorial to the children of Israel; as the LORD commanded Moses.

The priest's breastplate

39:8–21pp — Ex. 28:15–28

8 ¶ [y]And he made the breastplate *of* cunning work, like the work of the ephod; *of* gold, blue, and purple, and scarlet, and fine twined linen.

9 It was foursquare; they made the breastplate double: a span *was* the length thereof, and a span the breadth thereof, *being* doubled.

10 [z]And they set in it four rows of stones: *the first* row *was* a [q]sardius, a topaz, and a carbuncle: this *was* the first row.

11 And the second row, an emerald, a sapphire, and a diamond.

12 And the third row, a ligure, an agate, and an amethyst.

13 And the fourth row, a beryl, an onyx, and a jasper: *they were* enclosed in ouches of gold in their enclosings.

14 And the stones *were* according to the names of the children of Israel, [a]twelve, according to their names, *like* the engravings of a signet, every one with his name, according to the twelve tribes.

15 And they made upon the breastplate chains at the ends, *of* wreathen work *of* pure gold.

16 And they made two ouches *of* gold, and two gold rings; and put the two rings in the two ends of the breastplate.

17 And they put the [b]two wreathen chains of gold in the two rings on the ends of the breastplate.

18 And the two ends of the two wreathen chains they fastened in the two ouches, and put them on the shoulderpieces of the ephod, before it.

19 And they made two rings of gold, and put *them* on the two ends of the breastplate, upon the border of it, which *was* on the side of the ephod inward.

20 And they made two *other* golden rings, and put them on the two sides of the ephod underneath, toward the forepart of it, over against the *other* coupling thereof, above the curious girdle of the ephod.

21 And they did bind the breastplate by his rings unto the rings of the ephod with a lace of blue, that it might be above the curious girdle of the ephod, and that the breastplate might not be loosed from the ephod; as the LORD commanded Moses.

The robe of the ephod

39:22–31pp — Ex. 28:31–43

22 ¶ [c]And he made the robe of the ephod *of* woven work, all *of* blue.

23 And *there was* an hole in the midst of the robe, as the hole of an ha-

39:1 [s]ch. 35:23 [t]ch. 31:10 & 35:19 [u]ch. 28:4
39:2 [v]ch. 28:6
39:6 [w]ch. 28:9
39:7 [x]ch. 28:12
39:8 [y]ch. 28:15
39:10 [z]ch. 28:17
39:14 [a]Rev. 21:12
39:17 [b]Ex. 28:40
39:22 [c]ch. 28:31

[q] Or, *ruby*

bergeon, *with* a band round about the hole, that it should not rend.

24 And they made upon the hems of the robe pomegranates *of* blue, and purple, and scarlet, *and* twined *linen.*

25 And they made [d]bells *of* pure gold, and put the bells between the pomegranates upon the hem of the robe, round about between the pomegranates;

26 A bell and a pomegranate, a bell and a pomegranate, round about the hem of the robe to minister *in;* as the LORD commanded Moses.

27 ¶ [e]And they made coats *of* fine linen *of* woven work for Aaron, and for his sons,

28 [f]And a mitre *of* fine linen, and goodly bonnets *of* fine linen, and [g]linen breeches *of* fine twined linen,

29 [h]And a girdle *of* fine twined linen, and blue, and purple, and scarlet, *of* needlework; as the LORD commanded Moses.

30 ¶ [i]And they made the plate of the holy crown *of* pure gold, and wrote upon it a writing, *like to* the engravings of a signet, HOLINESS TO THE LORD.

31 And they tied unto it a lace of blue, to fasten *it* on high upon the mitre; as the LORD commanded Moses.

The tabernacle finished

39:32–41pp — Ex. 35:10–19

32 ¶ Thus was all the work of the tabernacle of the tent of the congregation finished: and the children of Israel did [j]according to all that the LORD commanded Moses, so did they.

33 ¶ And they brought the tabernacle unto Moses, the tent, and all his furniture, his taches, his boards, his bars, and his pillars, and his sockets,

34 And the covering of rams' skins dyed red, and the covering of badgers' skins, and the veil of the covering,

35 The ark of the testimony, and the staves thereof, and the mercy seat,

36 The table, *and* all the vessels thereof, and the showbread,

37 The pure candlestick, *with* the lamps thereof, *even with* the lamps to be set in order, and all the vessels thereof, and the oil for light,

38 And the golden altar, and the anointing oil, and [r]the sweet incense, and the hanging for the tabernacle door,

39 The brasen altar, and his grate of brass, his staves, and all his vessels, the laver and his foot,

40 The hangings of the court, his pillars, and his sockets, and the hanging for the court gate, his cords, and his pins, and all the vessels of the service of the tabernacle, for the tent of the congregation,

41 The cloths of service to do service in the holy *place,* and the holy garments for Aaron the priest, and his sons' garments, to minister in the priest's office.

42 According to all that the LORD commanded Moses, so the children of Israel [k]made all the work.

43 And Moses did look upon all the work, and, behold, they had done it as the LORD had commanded, even so had they done it: and Moses [l]blessed them.

Assembling the tabernacle

40 AND THE LORD spake unto Moses, saying,

2 On the first day of the [m]first month shalt thou set up [n]the tabernacle of the tent of the congregation.

3 And [o]thou shalt put therein the ark of the testimony, and cover the ark with the veil.

4 And [p]thou shalt bring in the table, and [q]set in order [s]the things that are to be set in order upon it; [r]and thou shalt bring in the candlestick, and light the lamps thereof.

5 [s]And thou shalt set the altar of gold for the incense before the ark of the testimony, and put the hanging of the door to the tabernacle.

6 And thou shalt set the altar of the burnt offering before the door of the tabernacle of the tent of the congregation.

7 And [t]thou shalt set the laver between the tent of the congregation and the altar, and shalt put water therein.

8 And thou shalt set up the court round about, and hang up the hanging at the court gate.

9 And thou shalt take the anointing oil, and [u]anoint the tabernacle, and all that *is* therein, and shalt hallow it, and

39:25 [d]ch. 28:33 **39:27** [e]ch. 28:39,40 **39:28** [f]ch. 28:4,39 Ezek. 44:18 [g]ch. 28:42 **39:29** [h]ch. 28:39 **39:30** [i]ch. 28:36,37 **39:32** [j]ver. 42,43 ch. 25:40 **39:42** [k]ch. 35:10 **39:43** [l]Lev. 9:22,23 Num. 6:23 Josh. 22:6 2 Sam. 6:18 1 Ki. 8:14 2 Chr. 30:27 **40:2** [m]ch. 12:2 & 13:4 [n]ver. 17 ch. 26:1,30 **40:3** [o]ver. 21 ch. 26:33 Num. 4:5 **40:4** [p]ver. 22 ch. 26:35 [q]ver. 23 ch. 25:30 [r]ver. 24,25 **40:5** [s]ver. 26 **40:7** [t]ver. 30 ch. 30:18 **40:9** [u]ch. 30:26

[r] Heb. *the incense of sweet spices* [s] Heb. *the order thereof*

all the vessels thereof: and it shall be holy.

10 And thou shalt anoint the altar of the burnt offering, and all his vessels, and sanctify the altar: and [v]it shall be an altar [t]most holy.

11 And thou shalt anoint the laver and his foot, and sanctify it.

12 [w]And thou shalt bring Aaron and his sons unto the door of the tabernacle of the congregation, and wash them with water.

13 And thou shalt put upon Aaron the holy garments, [x]and anoint him, and sanctify him; that he may minister unto me in the priest's office.

14 And thou shalt bring his sons, and clothe them with coats:

15 And thou shalt anoint them, as thou didst anoint their father, that they may minister unto me in the priest's office: for their anointing shall surely be [y]an everlasting priesthood throughout their generations.

16 Thus did Moses: according to all that the LORD commanded him, so did he.

17 ¶ And it came to pass in the first month in the second year, on the first *day* of the month, *that* the [z]tabernacle was reared up.

18 And Moses reared up the tabernacle, and fastened his sockets, and set up the boards thereof, and put in the bars thereof, and reared up his pillars.

19 And he spread abroad the tent over the tabernacle, and put the covering of the tent above upon it; as the LORD commanded Moses.

20 ¶ And he took and put [a]the testimony into the ark, and set the staves on the ark, and put the mercy seat above upon the ark:

21 And he brought the ark into the tabernacle, and [b]set up the veil of the covering, and covered the ark of the testimony; as the LORD commanded Moses.

22 ¶ [c]And he put the table in the tent of the congregation, upon the side of the tabernacle northward, without the veil.

40:10 [v]ch. 29:36,37
40:12 [w]Lev. 8:1-13
40:13 [x]ch. 28:41
40:15 [y]Num. 25:13
40:17 [z]ver. 2 Num. 7:1
40:20 [a]ch. 25:16
40:21 [b]ch. 26:33
40:22 [c]ch. 26:35
40:23 [d]ver. 4
40:24 [e]ch. 26:35
40:25 [f]ver. 4 ch. 25:37
40:26 [g]ver. 5 ch. 30:6
40:27 [h]ch. 30:7
40:28 [i]ver. 5 ch. 26:36
40:29 [j]ver. 6 [k]ch. 29:38
40:30 [l]ver. 7 ch. 30:18
40:32 [m]ch. 30:19,20
40:33 [n]ver. 8 ch. 27:9,16
40:34 [o]ch. 29:43 Lev. 16:2 Num. 9:15 1 Ki. 8:10,11 2 Chr. 5:13 & 7:2 Is. 6:4 Hag. 2:7,9 Rev. 15:8
40:35 [p]Lev. 16:2 1 Ki. 8:11 2 Chr. 5:14
40:36 [q]Num. 9:17 & 10:11 Neh. 9:19

23 [d]And he set the bread in order upon it before the LORD; as the LORD had commanded Moses.

24 ¶ [e]And he put the candlestick in the tent of the congregation, over against the table, on the side of the tabernacle southward.

25 And [f]he lighted the lamps before the LORD; as the LORD commanded Moses.

26 ¶ [g]And he put the golden altar in the tent of the congregation before the veil:

27 [h]And he burnt sweet incense thereon; as the LORD commanded Moses.

28 ¶ [i]And he set up the hanging *at* the door of the tabernacle.

29 [j]And he put the altar of burnt offering *by* the door of the tabernacle of the tent of the congregation, and [k]offered upon it the burnt offering and the meat offering; as the LORD commanded Moses.

30 ¶ [l]And he set the laver between the tent of the congregation and the altar, and put water there, to wash *withal.*

31 And Moses and Aaron and his sons washed their hands and their feet thereat:

32 When they went into the tent of the congregation, and when they came near unto the altar, they washed; [m]as the LORD commanded Moses.

33 [n]And he reared up the court round about the tabernacle and the altar, and set up the hanging of the court gate. So Moses finished the work.

The glory of the LORD

34 ¶ [o]Then a cloud covered the tent of the congregation, and the glory of the LORD filled the tabernacle.

35 And Moses [p]was not able to enter into the tent of the congregation, because the cloud abode thereon, and the glory of the LORD filled the tabernacle.

36 [q]And when the cloud was taken up from over the tabernacle, the chil-

[t] Heb. *holiness of holinesses*

40:34 THE GLORY OF THE LORD. The book of Exodus ends with the glory of the Lord filling the tabernacle. (1) This manifestation foreshadows the Lord's dwelling in and among His people through the true church (cf. 1 Cor. 3:16; Eph. 2:18–22). It further foreshadows God's future dwelling among all His faithful saints in the new heaven and new earth (Rev. 21:3).

(2) The "glory of the LORD" is sometimes referred to as the "Shekinah" glory (see article on THE GLORY OF GOD, p. 1186).

dren of Israel [u]went onward in all
their journeys:
37 But [r]if the cloud were not taken
up, then they journeyed not till the day
that it was taken up.
38 For [s]the cloud of the LORD *was*
upon the tabernacle by day, and fire
was on it by night, in the sight of all the
house of Israel, throughout all their
journeys.

40:37 [r]Num. 9:19-22
40:38 [s]ch. 13:21 Num. 9:15

[u] Heb. *journeyed*

LEVITICUS

Outline

I. The Way of Access to God: Atonement (1:1—16:34)
  A. Through Sacrifices (1:1—7:38)
    1. The Burnt Offering (1:1–17)
    2. The Meat Offering (2:1–16)
    3. The Peace Offering (3:1–17)
    4. The Sin Offering for Unintentional Sins (4:1—5:13)
    5. The Guilt Offering (5:14—6:7)
    6. The Continual Burnt Offering and Offerings of Priests (6:8–23)
    7. The Disposition of the Victim in a Sin Offering, Trespass Offering, and Peace Offering (6:24—7:27)
    8. The Wave Offering and Summary of the Offerings (7:28–38)
  B. Through Priestly Intercession (8:1—10:20)
  C. Through Purification Laws (11:1—15:33)
  D. Through the Annual Day of Atonement (16:1–34)
II. The Way of Living Unto God: Holiness (17:1—27:34)
  A. Through Revelation About the Blood (17:1–16)
  B. Through Moral Standards (18:1—22:33)
  C. Through Regular Worship (23:1—24:23)
  D. Through Reparation Laws, Obedience, and Consecration (25:1—27:34)

Author: Moses

Theme: Holiness

Date of Writing: 1445–1405 B.C.

Background

Leviticus is closely related to the book of Exodus. Exodus records how the Israelites were delivered from Egypt, received God's law, and built the tabernacle according to God's pattern; it concludes with the Holy One coming to indwell the newly constructed tabernacle (Ex. 40:34). Leviticus contains God's instruction given to Moses during the two months between the completion of the tabernacle (Ex. 40:17) and Israel's departure from Mount Sinai (Num. 10:11). The title "Leviticus" is derived not from the Hebrew Bible, but from the Greek and Latin versions. This title might lead some to believe that the book concerns only the Levitical priests. However, this is not the case, since much of the book relates to all of Israel.

Leviticus is the third book of Moses. More than fifty times it affirms that its contents are God's direct words and revelation to Moses for Israel, which Moses subsequently preserved in written form. Jesus refers to a passage in Leviticus and attributes it to Moses (Mark 1:44). The apostle Paul refers to a passage in this book by saying, "Moses writes that . . ." (Rom. 10:5). Critics who attribute Leviticus to a much later priestly editor do so by rejecting the integrity of Biblical testimony (see the introduction to Exodus).

Purpose

Leviticus was written to instruct the Israelites and their priestly mediators about their access to God by means of atoning blood and to make clear God's standard of holy living for His chosen people.

Survey

Leviticus preeminently involves two important themes: atonement and holiness. (A) Chs. 1—16 contain God's provision for redemption from sin and from the alienation between God and humankind that has resulted from sin. Variations of the verb "to make atonement" (Heb. *kaphar*) occur some forty-eight times in Leviticus; the noun "atonement" occurs three times. The basic meaning of the verb is "to cover, to make a covering." The O.T. blood sacrifices (chs. 1—7) were temporary blood coverings for sin (cf. Heb. 10:4) until such time as Jesus Christ would die as the perfect sacrifice to "take away the sin of the world" (cf. John 1:29; Rom. 3:25; Heb. 10:11–12). The Levitical priests (chs. 8—10) foreshadow Christ's ministry of mediation, while the annual Day of Atonement (ch. 16) foreshadows the crucifixion.

(B) Chs. 17—27 present a series of practical standards by which God called His people to purity and holy living. God's recurring command is, "Ye shall be holy: for I the LORD your God *am* holy" (e.g., 19:2; 20:7,26). The Hebrew words for "holy" occur over one hundred times, and when applied to humans denote lives of purity and obedience. Holiness is expressed in ceremony (ch. 17) and worship (chs. 23—25), but especially in issues of daily living (chs. 18—22). Leviticus ends with an exhortation by Moses (ch. 26) and instruction concerning certain special vows (ch. 27).

Special Features

Four major features or emphases characterize Leviticus. (1) Revelation as a direct word from God is emphasized more in Leviticus than in any other book of the Bible. No less than thirty-eight times it is explicitly stated that the Lord spoke to Moses. (2) Instruction concerning the sacrificial system and substitutionary atonement is given in minute detail in this book. (3) Ch. 16 is the foremost chapter in the Bible describing the Day of Atonement. (4) Leviticus stresses the theme that the people of Israel were to fulfill their priestly calling through lives of spiritual and moral purity, separation from other nations, and obedience to God.

New Testament Fulfillment

Because of the twofold emphasis on blood atonement and holiness, this book has enduring relevance for believers under the new covenant. The N.T. teaches that the atoning blood of sacrificial animals, prominent in Leviticus, was "a shadow of good things to come" (Heb. 10:1) and pointed to Christ's once-for-all-time sacrifice for sin (Heb. 9:12). The command to be holy can be fully realized through the precious blood of Christ in the new covenant believer, whose calling is to be holy in all areas of life (1 Pet. 1:15). The second great commandment as stated by Jesus was derived from Lev. 19:18, "Thou shalt love thy neighbour as thyself" (Mat. 22:39).

Reading Leviticus

In order to read the entire Old Testament in one year, the book of Leviticus should be read in 14 days, according to the following schedule: ☐ 1–3 ☐ 4–5 ☐ 6–7 ☐ 8 ☐ 9–10 ☐ 11–12 ☐ 13–14 ☐ 15 ☐ 16–18 ☐ 19–21 ☐ 22–23 ☐ 24 ☐ 25 ☐ 26–27

NOTES

The law of burnt offering

1 AND THE LORD [a]called unto Mo-
ses, and spake unto him [b]out of
the tabernacle of the congregation,
saying,
2 Speak unto the children of Israel,
and say unto them, [c]If any man of
you bring an offering unto the LORD,
ye shall bring your offering of the
cattle, *even* of the herd, and of the
flock.
3 If his offering *be* a burnt sacrifice
of the herd, let him offer a male [d]with-
out blemish: he shall offer it of his own
voluntary will at the door of the taber-
nacle of the congregation before the
LORD.
4 [e]And he shall put his hand upon
the head of the burnt offering; and it
shall be [f]accepted for him [g]to make
atonement for him.
5 And he shall kill the [h]bullock be-
fore the LORD: [i]and the priests, Aar-
on's sons, shall bring the blood, [j]and
sprinkle the blood round about upon
the altar that *is by* the door of the tab-
ernacle of the congregation.
6 And he shall flay the burnt offer-
ing, and cut it into his pieces.

1:1 [a]Ex. 19:3 [b]Ex. 40:34
1:2 [c]ch. 22:18,19
1:3 [d]Deut. 15:21 Eph. 5:27 Heb. 9:14 1 Pet. 1:19
1:4 [e]ch. 3:2,8,13 & 4:15 [f]Rom. 12:1 Phil. 4:18 [g]2 Chr. 29:23,24
1:5 [h]Mic. 6:6 [i]2 Chr. 35:11 [j]Heb. 12:24
1:7 [k]Gen. 22:9
1:9 [l]Gen. 8:21 Ezek. 20:28,41 2 Cor. 2:15
1:10 [m]ver. 3
1:11 [n]ver. 5 Ex. 40:22 Ezek. 8:5

7 And the sons of Aaron the priest
shall put fire upon the altar, and [k]lay
the wood in order upon the fire:
8 And the priests, Aaron's sons,
shall lay the parts, the head, and the
fat, in order upon the wood that *is* on
the fire which *is* upon the altar:
9 But his inwards and his legs shall
he wash in water: and the priest shall
burn all on the altar, *to be* a burnt sacri-
fice, an offering made by fire, of a
[l]sweet savour unto the LORD.
10 ¶ And if his offering *be* of the
flocks, *namely,* of the sheep, or of the
goats, for a burnt sacrifice; he shall
bring it a male [m]without blemish.
11 [n]And he shall kill it on the side
of the altar northward before the LORD:
and the priests, Aaron's sons, shall
sprinkle his blood round about upon
the altar.
12 And he shall cut it into his
pieces, with his head and his fat: and
the priest shall lay them in order on the
wood that *is* on the fire which *is* upon
the altar:
13 But he shall wash the inwards
and the legs with water: and the priest
shall bring *it* all, and burn *it* upon the
altar: it *is* a burnt sacrifice, an offering

1:2 BRING AN OFFERING. The term "offering" (Heb. *corban*) is related to the verb which means "to draw near." Hence, an offering was a gift that the Israelite believer brought near to God in order that he himself might approach God and enjoy His fellowship and blessing (cf. Ps. 73:28).

(1) Five offerings are described in chs. 1–7: the burnt offering (1:3–17), the meat, i.e., grain offering (2:1–16), the peace offering (3:1–17), the sin offering (ch. 4), and the guilt offering (5:14—6:7; 7:1–7).

(2) Worshipers presented offerings in order to express thanksgiving and faith, renew fellowship, deepen their dedication to the Lord, or ask for forgiveness. Offerings were in a real sense "enacted" prayers (cf. Ps. 116:17; Hos. 14:2; Heb. 13:15).

(3) In many cases, an offering involved a sacrifice, i.e., an animal's life was taken (see 9:8, note).

(4) These offerings taught Israel that: (a) humans are basically sinful beings whose sins merit death; (b) without the shedding of blood there is no forgiveness (17:11; Heb. 9:22); (c) atonement for sin must be made by substitution (v. 4; 17:11); (d) God's holiness must regulate and direct every area of human life (cf. Lev. 10:3); and (e) God desires to be gracious, to forgive, and to have fellowship with men and women (Ex. 34:6–7).

(5) In order to make the offering acceptable to God, there had to be genuine heartfelt repentance and a sincere commitment to walk in goodness and righteousness (23:27–29; Is. 1:11–17; Mic. 6:6–8).

1:3 BURNT SACRIFICE. The Hebrew term for burnt sacrifice or offering means "that which ascends" to God. The entire offering was burned up, signifying that complete consecration to God was essential to true worship. At the same time, forgiveness of sin was involved (v. 4), emphasizing that before worshipers could devote themselves to God, they had to be cleansed from sin (cf. Mat. 5:23–24). According to the writer of Hebrews, Jesus is the ultimate fulfillment of the burnt offering (Heb. 10:5–10).

1:4 PUT HIS HAND UPON. An Israelite sacrificing an animal leaned on the animal, signfying that he was identifying himself with the animal as it stood in his place. This act presented the idea of substitution (cf. 16:21–22; 24:14). When the animal died, it was as if the person who brought it also died, yet remained alive to serve God. In like manner, Christians entrust themselves to Christ and become one with Him in His death (Rom. 6:3–11; cf. 2 Cor. 5:21; Heb. 9:14). They are thus called upon to live as people risen from the dead and to present themselves as living sacrifices to God (Rom. 12:1; Heb. 13:15).

1:5 KILL THE BULLOCK. See 9:8, note.

1:9 A SWEET SAVOUR UNTO THE LORD. God was well pleased with the person's sacrifice given in obedient faith. Paul applies this expression both to the offering of Christ (Eph. 5:2) and to the good deeds of believers (Phil. 4:18; cf. Heb. 13:16).

made by fire, of a sweet savour unto the LORD.

14 ¶ And if the burnt sacrifice for his offering to the LORD *be* of fowls, then he shall bring his offering of [o]turtledoves, or of young pigeons.

15 And the priest shall bring it unto the altar, and [a]wring off his head, and burn *it* on the altar; and the blood thereof shall be wrung out at the side of the altar:

16 And he shall pluck away his crop with [b]his feathers, and cast it [p]beside the altar on the east part, by the place of the ashes:

17 And he shall cleave it with the wings thereof, *but* [q]shall not divide *it* asunder: and the priest shall burn it upon the altar, upon the wood that *is* upon the fire: [r]it *is* a burnt sacrifice, an offering made by fire, of a sweet savour unto the LORD.

The law of meat offerings

2 AND WHEN any will offer [s]a meat offering unto the LORD, his offering shall be *of* fine flour; and he shall pour oil upon it, and put frankincense thereon:

2 And he shall bring it to Aaron's sons the priests: and he shall take thereout his handful of the flour thereof, and of the oil thereof, with all the frankincense thereof; and the priest shall burn [t]the memorial of it upon the altar, *to be* an offering made by fire, of a sweet savour unto the LORD:

3 And [u]the remnant of the meat offering *shall be* Aaron's and his sons': [v]*it is* a thing most holy of the offerings of the LORD made by fire.

4 ¶ And if thou bring an oblation of a meat offering baked in the oven, *it shall be* unleavened cakes of fine flour mingled with oil, or unleavened wafers [w]anointed with oil.

5 ¶ And if thy oblation *be* a meat offering *baked* [c]in a pan, it shall be *of* fine flour unleavened, mingled with oil.

6 Thou shalt part it in pieces, and pour oil thereon: it *is* a meat offering.

7 ¶ And if thy oblation *be* a meat offering *baked* in the fryingpan, it shall be made *of* fine flour with oil.

8 And thou shalt bring the meat offering that is made of these things unto the LORD: and when it is presented unto the priest, he shall bring it unto the altar.

9 And the priest shall take from the meat offering [x]a memorial thereof, and shall burn *it* upon the altar: *it is* an [y]offering made by fire, of a sweet savour unto the LORD.

10 And [z]that which is left of the meat offering *shall be* Aaron's and his sons': *it is* a thing most holy of the offerings of the LORD made by fire.

11 No meat offering, which ye shall bring unto the LORD, shall be made with [a]leaven: for ye shall burn no leaven, nor any honey, in any offering of the LORD made by fire.

12 ¶ [b]As for the oblation of the firstfruits, ye shall offer them unto the LORD: but they shall not [d]be burnt on the altar for a sweet savour.

13 And every oblation of thy meat offering [c]shalt thou season with salt; neither shalt thou suffer [d]the salt of the covenant of thy God to be lacking from thy meat offering: [e]with all thine offerings thou shalt offer salt.

14 And if thou offer a meat offering of thy firstfruits unto the LORD, [f]thou shalt offer for the meat offering of thy firstfruits green ears of corn dried by the fire, *even* corn beaten out of [g]full ears.

15 And [h]thou shalt put oil upon it, and lay frankincense thereon: it *is* a meat offering.

16 And the priest shall burn [i]the memorial of it, *part* of the beaten corn thereof, and *part* of the oil thereof, with all the frankincense thereof: *it is* an offering made by fire unto the LORD.

The law of peace offerings

3 AND IF his oblation *be* a [j]sacrifice of peace offering, if he offer *it*

1:14 [o]ch. 5:7
1:16 [p]ch. 6:10
1:17 [q]Gen. 15:10 [r]ver. 9,13
2:1 [s]ch. 6:14 & 9:17 Num. 15:4
2:2 [t]ver. 9 ch. 5:12 & 6:15 & 24:7 Is. 66:3 Acts 10:4
2:3 [u]ch. 7:9 & 10:12,13 [v]Ex. 29:37 Num. 18:9
2:4 [w]Ex. 29:2
2:9 [x]ver. 2 ch. 6:15 [y]Ex. 29:18
2:10 [z]ver. 3
2:11 [a]ch. 6:17 See Mat. 16:12 Mark 8:15 Luke 12:1 1 Cor. 5:8 Gal. 5:9
2:12 [b]Ex. 22:29 ch. 23:10,11
2:13 [c]Mark 9:49 Col. 4:6 [d]Num. 18:19 [e]Ezek. 43:24
2:14 [f]ch. 23:10,14 [g]2 Ki. 4:42
2:15 [h]ver. 1
2:16 [i]ver. 2
3:1 [j]ch. 7:11,29 & 22:21

[a] Or, *pinch off the head with the nail* [b] Or, *the filth thereof* [c] Or, *on a flat plate,* or, *slice*
[d] Heb. *ascend*

2:1 A MEAT OFFERING. The meat (or better, grain) offering was a gift presented to God as an act of worship, symbolizing the dedication to God of the fruit of a person's labor. It implied that all human work should be done as unto the Lord and that one's daily food should be received with thanksgiving unto Him (cf. 1 Cor. 10:31; see Col. 3:23, note).

2:11 NO LEAVEN, NOR ANY HONEY. These were forbidden on the altar because they were used to aid fermentation. Fermentation involves change, decomposition, or decay, and often symbolized evil (see Ex. 13:7, note).

3:1 SACRIFICE OF PEACE. The peace offering

of the herd; whether *it be* a male or female, he shall offer it [k]without blemish before the LORD.

2 And [l]he shall lay his hand upon the head of his offering, and kill it *at* the door of the tabernacle of the congregation: and Aaron's sons the priests shall sprinkle the blood upon the altar round about.

3 And he shall offer of the sacrifice of the peace offering an offering made by fire unto the LORD; [m]the [e]fat that covereth the inwards, and all the fat that *is* upon the inwards,

4 And the two kidneys, and the fat that *is* on them, which *is* by the flanks, and the [f]caul above the liver, with the kidneys, it shall he take away.

5 And Aaron's sons [n]shall burn it on the altar upon the burnt sacrifice, which *is* upon the wood that *is* on the fire: *it is* an offering made by fire, of a sweet savour unto the LORD.

6 ¶ And if his offering for a sacrifice of peace offering unto the LORD *be* of the flock; male or female, [o]he shall offer it without blemish.

7 If he offer a lamb for his offering, then shall he offer it before the LORD.

8 And he shall lay his hand upon the head of his offering, and kill it before the tabernacle of the congregation: and Aaron's sons shall sprinkle the blood thereof round about upon the altar.

9 And he shall offer of the sacrifice of the peace offering an offering made by fire unto the LORD; the fat thereof, *and* the whole rump, it shall he take off hard by the backbone; and the fat that covereth the inwards, and all the fat that *is* upon the inwards,

10 And the two kidneys, and the fat that *is* upon them, which *is* by the flanks, and the caul above the liver, with the kidneys, it shall he take away.

11 And the priest shall burn it upon the altar: *it is* [p]the food of the offering made by fire unto the LORD.

12 ¶ And if his offering *be* a goat, then [q]he shall offer it before the LORD.

13 And he shall lay his hand upon the head of it, and kill it before the tabernacle of the congregation: and the sons of Aaron shall sprinkle the blood thereof upon the altar round about.

14 And he shall offer thereof his offering, *even* an offering made by fire unto the LORD; the fat that covereth the inwards, and all the fat that *is* upon the inwards,

15 And the two kidneys, and the fat that *is* upon them, which *is* by the flanks, and the caul above the liver, with the kidneys, it shall he take away.

16 And the priest shall burn them upon the altar: *it is* the food of the offering made by fire for a sweet savour: [r]all the fat *is* the LORD's.

17 *It shall be* a [s]perpetual statute for your generations throughout all your dwellings, that ye eat neither [t]fat nor [u]blood.

The sin offering

4 AND THE LORD spake unto Moses, saying,

2 Speak unto the children of Israel, saying, [v]If a soul shall sin through ignorance against any of the commandments of the LORD *concerning things* which ought not to be done, and shall do against any of them:

3 [w]If the priest that is anointed do

3:1 [k]ch. 1:3
3:2 [l]Ex. 29:10 ch. 1:4,5
3:3 [m]Ex. 29:13,22 ch. 4:8,9
3:5 [n]Ex. 29:13 ch. 6:12
3:6 [o]ver. 1
3:11 [p]See ch. 21:6,8, 17,21,22 & 22:25 Ezek. 44:7 Mal. 1:7,12
3:12 [q]ver. 1,7
3:16 [r]ch. 7:23,25 1 Sam. 2:15 2 Chr. 7:7
3:17 [s]ch. 6:18 & 7:36 & 17:7 & 23:14 [t]ver. 16 compare with Deut. 32:14 Neh. 8:10 [u]Gen. 9:4 ch. 7:23,26 & 17:10,14 Deut. 12:16 1 Sam. 14:33 Ezek. 44:7,15
4:2 [v]ch. 5:15,17 Num. 15:22 1 Sam. 14:27 Ps. 19:12
4:3 [w]ch. 8:12

[e] Or, *suet* [f] Or, *midriff over the liver,* and *over the kidneys*

was brought before God in order to have fellowship with Him, to express thanksgiving (7:12–16; 22:29), or to make a vow (7:16). (1) For the offerer, it involved commitment to the covenant and celebrated peace and reconciliation between God and the worshiper. (2) This offering points forward to the peace and fellowship that believers have with God and other believers on the basis of Christ's death on the cross (cf. Col. 1:20; 1 John 1:3), and to the final communion when we shall all sit down with God in His kingdom (Ps. 22:26; Luke 14:15; Rev. 19:6–10).

3:17 FAT NOR BLOOD. These elements are both vital to life (see 17:11, note). Hence, they are used to represent the life of the sacrificial victim, a life that belonged only to God (cf. v. 16).

4:3 A SIN OFFERING. God required a sin offering in order that those who sinned in ignorance, out of weakness, or without deliberate intention (v. 2) could receive forgiveness. Deliberate, rebellious sins, on the other hand, were to be punished by death (Num. 15:30–31; Heb. 10:28). A trespass offering, similar to the sin offering, was used for those who were guilty of a sin or injury for which full restitution could be made (6:2–6; see 5:15, note), and it was necessary for ritual cleansing (12:6–8; 14:13–17; Num. 6:11).

(1) The sin offering foreshadows the atoning death of Christ and His bearing the punishment of our sins. His death, however, was infinitely more perfect than the O.T. sin offering in that it provided a single atonement for *all* sin (Is. 53; 2 Cor. 5:21; Eph. 1:7; Heb. 9:11–12; see article on THE DAY OF ATONEMENT, p. 188). (2) We as N.T. believers continually need the atoning blood of Christ to cover mistakes, weaknesses, and unintentional fail-

OLD TESTAMENT SACRIFICES

Sacrifice	OT References	Elements	Purpose
BURNT OFFERING	Lev 1; 6:8-13; 8:18-21; 16:24	Bull, ram or male bird (dove or young pigeon for poor); wholly consumed; no defect	Voluntary act of worship; atonement for unintentional sin in general; expression of devotion, commitment and complete surrender to God
GRAIN OFFERING	Lev 2; 6:14-23	Grain, fine flour, olive oil, incense, baked bread (cakes or wafers), salt; no yeast or honey; accompanied burnt offering and fellowship offering (along with drink offering)	Voluntary act of worship; recognition of God's goodness and provisions; devotion to God
FELLOWSHIP OFFERING	Lev 3; 7:11-34	Any animal without defect from herd or flock; variety of breads	Voluntary act of worship; thanksgiving and fellowship (it included a communal meal)
SIN OFFERING	Lev 4:1-5:13; 6:24-30; 8:14-17; 16:3-22	1. Young bull: for high priest and congregation 2. Male goat: for leader 3. Female goat or lamb: for common person 4. Dove or pigeon: for the poor 5. Tenth of an ephah of fine flour: for the very poor	Mandatory atonement for specific unintentional sin; confession of sin; forgiveness of sin; cleansing from defilement
GUILT OFFERING	Lev 5:14-6:7; 7:1-6	Ram or lamb	Mandatory atonement for unintentional sin requiring restitution; cleansing from defilement; make restitution; pay 20% fine

When more than one kind of offering was presented (as in Nu 7:16, 17), the procedure was usually as follows: (1) sin offering or guilt offering, (2) burnt offering, (3) fellowship offering and grain offering (along with a drink offering). This sequence furnishes part of the spiritual significance of the sacrificial system. First, sin had to be dealt with (sin offering or guilt offering). Second, the worshiper committed himself completely to God (burnt offering and grain offering). Third, fellowship or communion between the Lord, the priest and the worshiper (fellowship offering) was established.

sin according to the sin of the people;
then let him bring for his sin, which he
hath sinned, [x]a young bullock without
blemish unto the LORD for a sin offer-
ing.
4 And he shall bring the bullock
[y]unto the door of the tabernacle of the
congregation before the LORD; and
shall lay his hand upon the bullock's
head, and kill the bullock before the
LORD.
5 And the priest that is anointed
[z]shall take of the bullock's blood, and
bring it to the tabernacle of the congre-
gation:
6 And the priest shall dip his finger
in the blood, and sprinkle of the blood
seven times before the LORD, before the
veil of the sanctuary.
7 And the priest shall [a]put *some* of
the blood upon the horns of the altar of
sweet incense before the LORD, which *is*
in the tabernacle of the congregation;
and shall pour [b]all the blood of the
bullock at the bottom of the altar of the
burnt offering, which *is at* the door of
the tabernacle of the congregation.
8 And he shall take off from it all
the fat of the bullock for the sin offer-
ing; the fat that covereth the inwards,
and all the fat that *is* upon the inwards,
9 And the two kidneys, and the fat
that *is* upon them, which *is* by the
flanks, and the caul above the liver,
with the kidneys, it shall he take away,
10 [c]As it was taken off from the
bullock of the sacrifice of peace offer-
ings: and the priest shall burn them
upon the altar of the burnt offering.
11 [d]And the skin of the bullock,
and all his flesh, with his head, and
with his legs, and his inwards, and his
dung,
12 Even the whole bullock shall he
carry forth [g]without the camp unto a
clean place, [e]where the ashes are
poured out, and [f]burn him on the
wood with fire: [h]where the ashes are
poured out shall he be burnt.
13 ¶ And [g]if the whole congrega-
tion of Israel sin through ignorance,
[h]and the thing be hid from the eyes of
the assembly, and they have done
somewhat against any of the command-
ments of the LORD *concerning things*
which should not be done, and are
guilty;
14 When the sin, which they have
sinned against it, is known, then the
congregation shall offer a young bull-
ock for the sin, and bring him before
the tabernacle of the congregation.
15 And the elders of the congrega-
tion [i]shall lay their hands upon the
head of the bullock before the LORD:
and the bullock shall be killed before
the LORD.
16 [j]And the priest that is anointed
shall bring of the bullock's blood to the
tabernacle of the congregation:
17 And the priest shall dip his fin-
ger *in some* of the blood, and sprinkle
it seven times before the LORD, *even* be-
fore the veil.
18 And he shall put *some* of the
blood upon the horns of the altar which
is before the LORD, that *is* in the taber-
nacle of the congregation, and shall
pour out all the blood at the bottom of
the altar of the burnt offering, which *is*
at the door of the tabernacle of the con-
gregation.
19 And he shall take all his fat from
him, and burn *it* upon the altar.
20 And he shall do with the bullock
as he did [k]with the bullock for a sin
offering, so shall he do with this: [l]and
the priest shall make an atonement for
them, and it shall be forgiven them.
21 And he shall carry forth the bull-
ock without the camp, and burn him as
he burned the first bullock: it *is* a sin
offering for the congregation.
22 ¶ When a ruler hath sinned, and
[m]done *somewhat* through ignorance
against any of the commandments of
the LORD his God *concerning things*

4:3 [x]ch. 9:2 **4:4** [y]ch. 1:3,4 **4:5** [z]ch. 16:14 Num. 19:4 **4:7** [a]ch. 8:15 & 9:9 & 16:18 [b]ch. 5:9 **4:10** [c]ch. 3:3-5 **4:11** [d]Ex. 29:14 Num. 19:5 **4:12** [e]ch. 6:11 [f]Heb. 13:11 **4:13** [g]Num. 15:24 Josh. 7:11 [h]ch. 5:2-4,17 **4:15** [i]ch. 1:4 **4:16** [j]ver. 5 Heb. 9:12-14 **4:20** [k]ver. 3 [l]Num. 15:25 **4:22** [m]ver. 2,13

[g]Heb. *to without the camp* [h]Heb. *at the pouring out of the ashes*

ings that flow from the frailty of human nature (Ps. 19:12). Sins coming from a rebellious disposition against God and His word, however, will bring us under judgment and spiritual death unless we confess them and repent of them through renewed faith in Christ's atonement (Heb. 2:3; 10:26,31; 2 Pet. 2:20–21).

4:12 WITHOUT THE CAMP. The burning of the sacrificial animal "without the camp" was to symbolize the complete removal of sin. The N.T. relates this to the suffering of Jesus outside the gate (i.e., outside Jerusalem) in order to sanctify His people through His own blood (cf. John 19:17–18; Heb. 13:10–15). The Christian is also called upon to "go forth therefore unto him without the camp" (i.e., to leave behind the sinful pleasures of this world), in order to seek a heavenly city and to offer up the sacrifice of praise and thanksgiving to God (see Heb. 13:13, note).

which should not be done, and is guilty;

23 Or [n]if his sin, wherein he hath sinned, come to his knowledge; he shall bring his offering, a kid of the goats, a male without blemish:

24 And [o]he shall lay his hand upon the head of the goat, and kill it in the place where they kill the burnt offering before the LORD: it *is* a sin offering.

25 [p]And the priest shall take of the blood of the sin offering with his finger, and put *it* upon the horns of the altar of burnt offering, and shall pour out his blood at the bottom of the altar of burnt offering.

26 And he shall burn all his fat upon the altar, as [q]the fat of the sacrifice of peace offerings: [r]and the priest shall make an atonement for him as concerning his sin, and it shall be forgiven him.

27 ¶ And [s]if [i]any one of the [j]common people sin through ignorance, while he doeth *somewhat against* any of the commandments of the LORD *concerning things* which ought not to be done, and be guilty;

28 Or [t]if his sin, which he hath sinned, come to his knowledge: then he shall bring his offering, a kid of the goats, a female without blemish, for his sin which he hath sinned.

29 [u]And he shall lay his hand upon the head of the sin offering, and slay the sin offering in the place of the burnt offering.

30 And the priest shall take of the blood thereof with his finger, and put *it* upon the horns of the altar of burnt offering, and shall pour out all the blood thereof at the bottom of the altar.

31 And [v]he shall take away all the fat thereof, [w]as the fat is taken away from off the sacrifice of peace offerings; and the priest shall burn *it* upon the altar for a [x]sweet savour unto the LORD; [y]and the priest shall make an atonement for him, and it shall be forgiven him.

32 And if he bring a lamb for a sin offering, [z]he shall bring it a female without blemish.

33 And he shall lay his hand upon the head of the sin offering, and slay it for a sin offering in the place where they kill the burnt offering.

34 And the priest shall take of the blood of the sin offering with his finger, and put *it* upon the horns of the altar of burnt offering, and shall pour out all the blood thereof at the bottom of the altar:

35 And he shall take away all the fat thereof, as the fat of the lamb is taken away from the sacrifice of the peace offerings; and the priest shall burn them upon the altar, [a]according to the offerings made by fire unto the LORD: [b]and the priest shall make an atonement for his sin that he hath committed, and it shall be forgiven him.

5 AND IF a soul sin, [c]and hear the voice of swearing, and *is* a witness, whether he hath seen or known *of it;* if he do not utter *it,* then he shall [d]bear his iniquity.

2 Or [e]if a soul touch any unclean thing, whether *it be* a carcase of an unclean beast, or a carcase of unclean cattle, or the carcase of unclean creeping things, and *if* it be hidden from him; he also shall be unclean, and [f]guilty.

3 Or if he touch [g]the uncleanness of man, whatsoever uncleanness *it be* that a man shall be defiled withal, and it be hid from him; when he knoweth *of it,* then he shall be guilty.

4 Or if a soul swear, pronouncing with *his* lips [h]to do evil, or [i]to do good, whatsoever *it be* that a man shall pronounce with an oath, and it be hid from him; when he knoweth *of it,* then he shall be guilty in one of these.

5 And it shall be, when he shall be guilty in one of these *things,* that he shall [j]confess that he hath sinned in that *thing:*

6 And he shall bring his trespass offering unto the LORD for his sin which he hath sinned, a female from the flock, a lamb or a kid of the goats, for a sin offering; and the priest shall make an atonement for him concerning his sin.

4:23 [n]ver. 14 ch. 5:4
4:24 [o]ver. 4 Is. 53:6
4:25 [p]ver. 30
4:26 [q]ch. 3:5 [r]ver. 20 Num. 15:28
4:27 [s]ver. 2 Num. 15:27
4:28 [t]ver. 23
4:29 [u]ver. 4,24
4:31 [v]ch. 3:14 [w]ch. 3:3 [x]Gen. 8:21 Ex. 29:18 ch. 1:9 Ezra 6:10 [y]ver. 26
4:32 [z]ver. 28
4:35 [a]ch. 3:5 [b]ver. 26,31
5:1 [c]1 Ki. 8:31 Prov. 29:24 Mat. 26:63 [d]ver. 17 ch. 7:18 & 17:16 & 19:8 & 20:17 Num. 9:13
5:2 [e]ch. 11:24,28,31, 39 Num. 19:11,13,16 [f]ver. 17
5:3 [g]ch. 12 & 13 & 15
5:4 [h]See 1 Sam. 25:22 Acts 23:12 [i]See Mark 6:23
5:5 [j]ch. 16:21 & 26:40 Num. 5:7 Ezra 10:11,12

i Heb. *any soul* j Heb. *people of the land*

5:5 HE SHALL CONFESS. To confess sin is to admit to God that we have sinned and that our thoughts, words, and actions were wrong. Confession of sin is required by God for forgiveness (Hos. 5:15; 1 John 1:9) and must always be accompanied by turning away from confessed sin (Prov. 28:13; Dan. 9:3–19; Mark 1:5), praying for forgiveness (Ps. 38:18; 51:1), and humbling oneself under God's judgment (Neh. 9:33). See Luke 15:11–24 for an example of true confession and forgiveness in the story of the prodigal son (cf. Acts 19:18; Jas. 5:16).

7 And [k]if [k]he be not able to bring a lamb, then he shall bring for his trespass, which he hath committed, two [l]turtledoves, or two young pigeons, unto the LORD; one for a sin offering, and the other for a burnt offering.

8 And he shall bring them unto the priest, who shall offer *that* which *is* for the sin offering first, and [m]wring off his head from his neck, but shall not divide *it* asunder:

9 And he shall sprinkle of the blood of the sin offering upon the side of the altar; and [n]the rest of the blood shall be wrung out at the bottom of the altar: it *is* a sin offering.

10 And he shall offer the second *for* a burnt offering, according to the [o]manner:[l] [p]and the priest shall make an atonement for him for his sin which he hath sinned, and it shall be forgiven him.

11 ¶ But if he be not able to bring two turtledoves, or two young pigeons, then he that sinned shall bring for his offering the tenth part of an ephah of fine flour for a sin offering; [q]he shall put no oil upon it, neither shall he put *any* frankincense thereon: for it *is* a sin offering.

12 Then shall he bring it to the priest, and the priest shall take his handful of it, [r]*even* a memorial thereof, and burn *it* on the altar, [s]according to the offerings made by fire unto the LORD: it *is* a sin offering.

13 [t]And the priest shall make an atonement for him as touching his sin that he hath sinned in one of these, and it shall be forgiven him: and [u]*the remnant* shall be the priest's, as a meat offering.

14 ¶ And the LORD spake unto Moses, saying,

15 [v]If a soul commit a trespass, and sin through ignorance, in the holy things of the LORD; then [w]he shall bring for his trespass unto the LORD a ram without blemish out of the flocks, with thy estimation by shekels of silver, after [x]the shekel of the sanctuary, for a trespass offering:

16 And he shall make amends for the harm that he hath done in the holy thing, and [y]shall add the fifth part thereto, and give it unto the priest: [z]and the priest shall make an atonement for him with the ram of the trespass offering, and it shall be forgiven him.

17 ¶ And if a soul sin, and commit any of these things which are forbidden to be done by the commandments of the LORD; [a]though he wist *it* not, yet is he [b]guilty, and shall bear his iniquity.

18 [c]And he shall bring a ram without blemish out of the flock, with thy estimation, for a trespass offering, unto the priest: [d]and the priest shall make an atonement for him concerning his ignorance wherein he erred and wist *it* not, and it shall be forgiven him.

19 It *is* a trespass offering: [e]he hath certainly trespassed against the LORD.

6 AND THE LORD spake unto Moses, saying,

2 If a soul sin, and [f]commit a trespass against the LORD, and [g]lie unto his neighbour in that [h]which was delivered him to keep, or in [m,n]fellowship, or in a thing taken away by violence, or hath [i]deceived his neighbour;

3 Or [j]have found that which was lost, and lieth concerning it, and [k]sweareth falsely; in any of all these that a man doeth, sinning therein:

4 Then it shall be, because he hath sinned, and is guilty, that he shall re-

5:7 [k]ch. 12:8 & 14:21 [l]ch. 1:14
5:8 [m]ch. 1:15
5:9 [n]ch. 4:7,18,30,34
5:10 [o]ch. 1:14 [p]ch. 4:26
5:11 [q]Num. 5:15
5:12 [r]ch. 2:2 [s]ch. 4:35
5:13 [t]ch. 4:26 [u]ch. 2:3
5:15 [v]ch. 22:14 [w]Ezra 10:19 [x]Ex. 30:13 ch. 27:25
5:16 [y]ch. 6:5 & 22:14 & 27:13,15,27,31 Num. 5:7 [z]ch. 4:26
5:17 [a]ver. 15 ch. 4:2,13,22,27 [b]ver. 1,2
5:18 [c]ver. 15 [d]ver. 16
5:19 [e]Ezra 10:2
6:2 [f]Num. 5:6 [g]ch. 19:11 Acts 5:4 Col. 3:9 [h]Ex. 22:7,10 [i]Prov. 24:28 & 26:19
6:3 [j]Deut. 22:1-3 [k]Ex. 22:11 ch. 19:12 Jer. 7:9 Zech. 5:4

[k] Heb. *his hand cannot reach to the sufficiency of a lamb* [l] Or, *ordinance* [m] Or, *in dealing* [n] Heb. *putting of the hand*

5:11 FINE FLOUR FOR A SIN OFFERING. The shedding of blood in the sin offering was important in that it pointed ahead to the death of Jesus and the shedding of His blood on the cross for our sins. But what about those who were so poor that they could not afford a goat or a lamb for an offering? God also wanted them to confess their sins, bring an offering, and seek His forgiveness. Thus He provided that such people could bring turtledoves or young pigeons in the place of goats or lambs. If they were too poor even for that, they could bring a little fine flour and God would accept that as a sin offering (cf. "almost" in Heb. 9:22; see also Heb. 10:1–10). Note that Christ's sacrifice on Calvary is the only sacrifice that can really take away sin (Heb. 10:4,12,14).

5:15 TRESPASS OFFERING. The trespass or guilt offering was required when someone intentionally or unintentionally disregarded the property rights of another person (cf. 5:14—6:7; Josh. 7:1; 22:20). An offering had to be brought along with restitution for the wrong done, plus a twenty percent fine (v. 16; 6:5). This offering was also used when any of the Lord's commandments was unintentionally broken (v. 17).

store that which he took violently away, or the thing which he hath deceitfully gotten, or that which was delivered him to keep, or the lost thing which he found,

5 Or all that about which he hath sworn falsely; he shall even [l]restore it in the principal, and shall add the fifth part more thereto, *and* give it unto him to whom it appertaineth, [o] [p]in the day of his trespass offering.

6 And he shall bring his trespass offering unto the LORD, [m]a ram without blemish out of the flock, with thy estimation, for a trespass offering, unto the priest:

7 [n]And the priest shall make an atonement for him before the LORD: and it shall be forgiven him for any thing of all that he hath done in trespassing therein.

The burnt offering

8 ¶ And the LORD spake unto Moses, saying,

9 Command Aaron and his sons, saying, This *is* the law of the burnt offering: It *is* the burnt offering, [q]because of the burning upon the altar all night unto the morning, and the fire of the altar shall be burning in it.

10 [o]And the priest shall put on his linen garment, and his linen breeches shall he put upon his flesh, and take up the ashes which the fire hath consumed with the burnt offering on the altar, and he shall put them [p]beside the altar.

11 And [q]he shall put off his garments, and put on other garments, and carry forth the ashes without the camp [r]unto a clean place.

12 And the fire upon the altar shall be burning in it; it shall not be put out: and the priest shall burn wood on it every morning, and lay the burnt offering in order upon it; and he shall burn thereon [s]the fat of the peace offerings.

13 The fire shall ever be burning upon the altar; it shall never go out.

The meat offering

14 ¶ [t]And this *is* the law of the meat offering: the sons of Aaron shall offer it before the LORD, before the altar.

15 And he shall take of it his handful, of the flour of the meat offering, and of the oil thereof, and all the frankincense which *is* upon the meat offering, and shall burn *it* upon the altar *for* a sweet savour, *even* the [u]memorial of it, unto the LORD.

16 And [v]the remainder thereof shall Aaron and his sons eat: [w]with unleavened bread shall it be eaten in the holy place; in the court of the tabernacle of the congregation they shall eat it.

17 [x]It shall not be baked with leaven. [y]I have given it *unto them for* their portion of my offerings made by fire; [z]it *is* most holy, as *is* the sin offering, and as the trespass offering.

18 [a]All the males among the children of Aaron shall eat of it. [b]*It shall be* a statute for ever in your generations concerning the offerings of the LORD made by fire: [c]every one that toucheth them shall be holy.

19 ¶ And the LORD spake unto Moses, saying,

20 [d]This *is* the offering of Aaron and of his sons, which they shall offer unto the LORD in the day when he is anointed; the tenth part of an [e]ephah of fine flour for a meat offering perpetual, half of it in the morning, and half thereof at night.

21 In a pan it shall be made with oil; *and when it is* baked, thou shalt bring it in: *and* the baked pieces of the meat offering shalt thou offer *for* a sweet savour unto the LORD.

22 And the priest of his sons [f]that is anointed in his stead shall offer it: *it is* a statute for ever unto the LORD; [g]it shall be wholly burnt.

23 For every meat offering for the priest shall be wholly burnt: it shall not be eaten.

The sin offering

24 ¶ And the LORD spake unto Moses, saying,

25 Speak unto Aaron and to his sons, saying, [h]This *is* the law of the sin offering: [i]In the place where the burnt offering is killed shall the sin offering be killed before the LORD: [j]it *is* most holy.

26 [k]The priest that offereth it for sin shall eat it: [l]in the holy place shall it be eaten, in the court of the tabernacle of the congregation.

6:5 [l]ch. 5:16 Num. 5:7 2 Sam. 12:6
6:6 [m]ch. 5:15
6:7 [n]ch. 4:26
6:10 [o]Ex. 28:39-41,43 ch. 16:4 Ezek. 44:17,18 [p]ch. 1:16
6:11 [q]Ezek. 44:19 [r]ch. 4:12
6:12 [s]ch. 3:3,9,14
6:14 [t]ch. 2:1 Num. 15:4
6:15 [u]ch. 2:2,9
6:16 [v]ch. 2:3 Ezek. 44:29 [w]ver. 26 ch. 10:12,13 Num. 18:10
6:17 [x]ch. 2:11 [y]Num. 18:9,10 [z]ver. 25 Ex. 29:37 ch. 2:3 & 7:1
6:18 [a]ver. 29 Num. 18:10 [b]ch. 3:17 [c]Ex. 29:37 ch. 22:3-7
6:20 [d]Ex. 29:2 [e]Ex. 16:36
6:22 [f]ch. 4:3 [g]Ex. 29:25
6:25 [h]ch. 4:2 [i]ch. 1:3,5,11 [j]ver. 17
6:26 [k]ch. 10:17,18 Num. 18:9,10 Ezek. 44:28,29 [l]ver. 16

[o] Or, *in the day of his being found guilty*
[p] Heb. *in the day of his trespass*
[q] Or, *for the burning*

27 [m]Whatsoever shall touch the flesh thereof shall be holy: and when there is sprinkled of the blood thereof upon any garment, thou shalt wash that whereon it was sprinkled in the holy place.

28 But the earthen vessel wherein it is sodden [n]shall be broken: and if it be sodden in a brasen pot, it shall be both scoured, and rinsed in water.

29 [o]All the males among the priests shall eat thereof: [p]it *is* most holy.

30 [q]And no sin offering, whereof *any* of the blood is brought into the tabernacle of the congregation to reconcile *withal* in the holy *place*, shall be eaten: it shall be burnt in the fire.

The trespass offering

7 LIKEWISE [r]THIS *is* the law of the trespass offering: [s]it *is* most holy.

2 [t]In the place where they kill the burnt offering shall they kill the trespass offering: and the blood thereof shall he sprinkle round about upon the altar.

3 And he shall offer of it [u]all the fat thereof; the rump, and the fat that covereth the inwards.

4 And the two kidneys, and the fat that *is* on them, which *is* by the flanks, and the caul *that is* above the liver, with the kidneys, it shall he take away:

5 And the priest shall burn them upon the altar *for* an offering made by fire unto the LORD: it *is* a trespass offering.

6 [v]Every male among the priests shall eat thereof: it shall be eaten in the holy place: [w]it *is* most holy.

7 As the sin offering *is*, so *is* [x]the trespass offering: *there is* one law for them: the priest that maketh atonement therewith shall have *it*.

8 And the priest that offereth any man's burnt offering, *even* the priest shall have to himself the skin of the burnt offering which he hath offered.

9 And [y]all the meat offering that is baked in the oven, and all that is dressed in the fryingpan, and [r]in the pan, shall be the priest's that offereth it.

10 And every meat offering, mingled with oil, and dry, shall all the sons of Aaron have, one *as much* as another.

The peace offering

11 And [z]this *is* the law of the sacrifice of peace offerings, which he shall offer unto the LORD.

12 If he offer it for a thanksgiving, then he shall offer with the sacrifice of thanksgiving unleavened cakes mingled with oil, and unleavened wafers [a]anointed with oil, and cakes mingled with oil, of fine flour, fried.

13 Besides the cakes, he shall offer *for* his offering [b]leavened bread with the sacrifice of thanksgiving of his peace offerings.

14 And of it he shall offer one out of the whole oblation *for* an heave offering unto the LORD, [c]*and* it shall be the priest's that sprinkleth the blood of the peace offerings.

15 [d]And the flesh of the sacrifice of his peace offerings for thanksgiving shall be eaten the same day that it is offered; he shall not leave any of it until the morning.

16 But [e]if the sacrifice of his offering *be* a vow, or a voluntary offering, it shall be eaten the same day that he offereth his sacrifice: and on the morrow also the remainder of it shall be eaten:

17 But the remainder of the flesh of the sacrifice on the third day shall be burnt with fire.

18 And if *any* of the flesh of the sacrifice of his peace offerings be eaten at all on the third day, it shall not be accepted, neither shall it be [f]imputed unto him that offereth it: it shall be an [g]abomination, and the soul that eateth of it shall bear his iniquity.

19 And the flesh that toucheth any unclean *thing* shall not be eaten; it shall be burnt with fire: and as for the flesh, all that be clean shall eat thereof.

6:27 [m]Ex. 29:37 & 30:29
6:28 [n]ch. 11:33 & 15:12
6:29 [o]ver. 18 Num. 18:10 [p]ver. 25
6:30 [q]ch. 4:7,11,12,18, 21 & 10:18 & 16:27 Heb. 13:11
7:1 [r]ch. 5 & 6:1-7 [s]ch. 6:17,25 & 21:22
7:2 [t]ch. 1:3,5,11 & 4:24,29,33
7:3 [u]Ex. 29:13 ch. 3:4,9,10,14-16 & 4:8,9
7:6 [v]ch. 6:16-18 Num. 18:9,10 [w]ch. 2:3
7:7 [x]ch. 6:25,26 & 14:13
7:9 [y]ch. 2:3,10 Num. 18:9 Ezek. 44:29
7:11 [z]ch. 3:1 & 22:18,21 Ezek. 45:15
7:12 [a]ch. 2:4 Num. 6:15
7:13 [b]Amos 4:5
7:14 [c]Num. 18:8,11,19
7:15 [d]ch. 22:30
7:16 [e]ch. 19:6-8
7:18 [f]Num. 18:27 [g]ch. 11:10,11,41 & 19:7

[r] Or, *on the flat plate*, or, *slice*

7:2 UPON THE ALTAR. In the O.T., ritualized forms of worship were a means of communication between God and His people. They were dramatized prayers expressing the people's repentance and their pleas for forgiveness and reconciliation. They also expressed the Israelites' gratitude and dedication to God. On God's part they were dramatized divine promises, warnings, and teachings which declared God's attitude toward His people and what He expected from them (see 1:2, note).

7:13 LEAVENED BREAD. Leavened bread could be used with the peace offering because it was not placed upon the altar (cf. 2:11, note).

20 But the soul that eateth *of* the flesh of the sacrifice of peace offerings, that *pertain* unto the LORD, [h]having his uncleanness upon him, even that soul [i]shall be cut off from his people.

21 Moreover the soul that shall touch any unclean *thing, as* [j]the uncleanness of man, or *any* [k]unclean beast, or any [l]abominable unclean *thing*, and eat of the flesh of the sacrifice of peace offerings, which *pertain* unto the LORD, even that soul [m]shall be cut off from his people.

Forbidden portions

22 ¶ And the LORD spake unto Moses, saying,

23 Speak unto the children of Israel, saying, [n]Ye shall eat no manner of fat, of ox, or of sheep, or of goat.

24 And the fat of the [o]beast[s] that dieth of itself, and the fat of that which is torn with beasts, may be used in any other use: but ye shall in no wise eat of it.

25 For whosoever eateth the fat of the beast, of which men offer an offering made by fire unto the LORD, even the soul that eateth *it* shall be cut off from his people.

26 [p]Moreover ye shall eat no manner of blood, *whether it be* of fowl or of beast, in any of your dwellings.

27 Whatsoever soul *it be* that eateth any manner of blood, even that soul shall be cut off from his people.

The portion for priests

28 ¶ And the LORD spake unto Moses, saying,

29 Speak unto the children of Israel, saying, [q]He that offereth the sacrifice of his peace offerings unto the LORD shall bring his oblation unto the LORD of the sacrifice of his peace offerings.

30 [r]His own hands shall bring the offerings of the LORD made by fire, the fat with the breast, it shall he bring, that [s]the breast may be waved *for* a wave offering before the LORD.

31 [t]And the priest shall burn the fat upon the altar: [u]but the breast shall be Aaron's and his sons'.

32 And [v]the right shoulder shall ye give unto the priest *for* an heave offering of the sacrifices of your peace offerings.

33 He among the sons of Aaron, that offereth the blood of the peace offerings, and the fat, shall have the right shoulder for *his* part.

34 For [w]the wave breast and the heave shoulder have I taken of the children of Israel from off the sacrifices of their peace offerings, and have given them unto Aaron the priest and unto his sons by a statute for ever from among the children of Israel.

35 ¶ This *is the portion* of the anointing of Aaron, and of the anointing of his sons, out of the offerings of the LORD made by fire, in the day *when* he presented them to minister unto the LORD in the priest's office;

36 Which the LORD commanded to be given them of the children of Israel, [x]in the day that he anointed them, *by* a statute for ever throughout their generations.

37 This *is* the law [y]of the burnt offering, [z]of the meat offering, [a]and of the sin offering, [b]and of the trespass offering, [c]and of the consecrations, and [d]of the sacrifice of the peace offerings;

38 Which the LORD commanded Moses in mount Sinai, in the day that he commanded the children of Israel [e]to offer their oblations unto the LORD, in the wilderness of Sinai.

The anointing of priests

8:1–36pp — Ex. 29:1–37

8 AND THE LORD spake unto Moses, saying,

2 [f]Take Aaron and his sons with

7:20 [h]ch. 15:3; 1 Cor. 11:28; [i]Gen. 17:14
7:21 [j]ch. 12 & 13 & 15; [k]ch. 11:24,28; [l]Ezek. 4:14; [m]ver. 20
7:23 [n]ch. 3:17
7:24 [o]ch. 17:15; Deut. 14:21; Ezek. 4:14 & 44:31
7:26 [p]Gen. 9:4; ch. 3:17 & 17:10-14; Ezek. 33:25; John 6:53; Acts 15:20,29
7:29 [q]ch. 3:1 & 22:21; Ezek. 45:15
7:30 [r]ch. 3:3,4,9,14; [s]Ex. 29:24,27; ch. 8:27 & 9:21; Num. 6:20
7:31 [t]ch. 3:5,11,16; [u]ver. 34
7:32 [v]ver. 34; ch. 9:21; Num. 6:20
7:34 [w]Ex. 29:28; ch. 10:14,15; Num. 18:18,19; Deut. 18:3
7:36 [x]Ex. 40.13,15; ch. 8:12,30
7:37 [y]ch. 6:9; [z]ch. 6:14; [a]ch. 6:25; [b]ver. 1; [c]Ex. 29:1; ch. 6:20; [d]ver. 11
7:38 [e]ch. 1:2
8:2 [f]Ex. 29:1-3

[s] Heb. *carcase*

7:20 UNCLEANNESS . . . CUT OFF. Persons who were ceremonially unclean and yet participated in the sacrifices and offerings were subject to the severe judgment of God. This rule was designed to teach the people how great an abomination it was for a person to claim to be in a covenantal relationship with God, yet deliberately and knowingly to cling to sin. See 1 Cor. 11:27–30, where Paul warns that all who partake of the Lord's Supper in an unworthy manner will receive God's wrath and judgment.

7:30 WAVE OFFERING. The "wave offering" was the priests' portion of the peace offering. It was waved toward the sanctuary as a sign of dedication unto God and then waved toward the offerer or priest, indicating that the Lord was now putting the offering at his or her disposal.

8:2 AARON AND HIS SONS. Ch. 8 describes the ordination of Aaron and his sons to the priesthood. In the O.T. the worshiper who approached

him, and [g]the garments, and [h]the anointing oil, and a bullock for the sin offering, and two rams, and a basket of unleavened bread;

3 And gather thou all the congregation together unto the door of the tabernacle of the congregation.

4 And Moses did as the LORD commanded him; and the assembly was gathered together unto the door of the tabernacle of the congregation.

5 And Moses said unto the congregation, [i]This *is* the thing which the LORD commanded to be done.

6 And Moses brought Aaron and his sons, [j]and washed them with water.

7 [k]And he put upon him the [l]coat, and girded him with the girdle, and clothed him with the robe, and put the ephod upon him, and he girded him with the curious girdle of the ephod, and bound *it* unto him therewith.

8 And he put the breastplate upon him: also he [m]put in the breastplate the Urim and the Thummim.

9 [n]And he put the mitre upon his head; also upon the mitre, *even* upon his forefront, did he put the golden plate, the holy crown; as the LORD [o]commanded Moses.

10 [p]And Moses took the anointing oil, and anointed the tabernacle and all that *was* therein, and sanctified them.

11 And he sprinkled thereof upon the altar seven times, and anointed the altar and all his vessels, both the laver and his foot, to sanctify them.

12 And he [q]poured of the anointing oil upon Aaron's head, and anointed him, to sanctify him.

13 [r]And Moses brought Aaron's sons, and put coats upon them, and girded them with girdles, and [t]put bonnets upon them; as the LORD commanded Moses.

14 [s]And he brought the bullock for the sin offering: and Aaron and his sons [t]laid their hands upon the head of the bullock for the sin offering.

8:2 [g]Ex. 28:2,4 [h]Ex. 30:24,25
8:5 [i]Ex. 29:4
8:6 [j]Ex. 29:4
8:7 [k]Ex. 29:5 [l]Ex. 28:4
8:8 [m]Ex. 28:30
8:9 [n]Ex. 29:6 [o]Ex. 28:37
8:10 [p]Ex. 30:26-29
8:12 [q]Ex. 29:7 & 30:30 ch. 21:10,12 Ps. 133:2
8:13 [r]Ex. 29:8,9
8:14 [s]Ex. 29:10 Ezek. 43:19 [t]ch. 4:4
8:15 [u]Ex. 29:12,36 ch. 4:7 Ezek. 43:20,26 Heb. 9:22
8:16 [v]Ex. 29:13 ch. 4:8
8:17 [w]Ex. 29:14 ch. 4:11,12
8:18 [x]Ex. 29:15
8:21 [y]Ex. 29:18
8:22 [z]Ex. 29:19,31

15 And he slew *it;* [u]and Moses took the blood, and put *it* upon the horns of the altar round about with his finger, and purified the altar, and poured the blood at the bottom of the altar, and sanctified it, to make reconciliation upon it.

16 [v]And he took all the fat that *was* upon the inwards, and the caul *above* the liver, and the two kidneys, and their fat, and Moses burned *it* upon the altar.

17 But the bullock, and his hide, his flesh, and his dung, he burnt with fire without the camp; as the LORD [w]commanded Moses.

18 ¶ [x]And he brought the ram for the burnt offering: and Aaron and his sons laid their hands upon the head of the ram.

19 And he killed *it;* and Moses sprinkled the blood upon the altar round about.

20 And he cut the ram into pieces; and Moses burnt the head, and the pieces, and the fat.

21 And he washed the inwards and the legs in water; and Moses burnt the whole ram upon the altar: it *was* a burnt sacrifice for a sweet savour, *and* an offering made by fire unto the LORD; [y]as the LORD commanded Moses.

22 ¶ And [z]he brought the other ram, the ram of consecration: and Aaron and his sons laid their hands upon the head of the ram.

23 And he slew *it;* and Moses took of the blood of it, and put *it* upon the tip of Aaron's right ear, and upon the thumb of his right hand, and upon the great toe of his right foot.

24 And he brought Aaron's sons, and Moses put of the blood upon the tip of their right ear, and upon the thumbs of their right hands, and upon the great toes of their right feet: and Moses

[t] Heb. *bound*

God needed not only an offering (chs. 1–7), but also the mediation of a priest (cf. 1 Tim. 2:5). The Levitical priesthood described here finds its fulfillment in Jesus Christ, the believer's high priest (Heb. 2:17). (1) A priest was appointed on behalf of people as a mediator between God and humans (Heb. 5:1). His purpose was to help men and women draw near to God and to bring them to forgiveness and salvation (Heb. 7:24–25; 10:14).

(2) The priest brought people near to God by offering gifts and sacrifices for sin, and by teaching the law of God (Deut. 33:8–10; Heb. 5:1; 8:3; 9:7,13).

(3) Under the new covenant the priestly office is no longer needed; the N.T. includes no priestly ministry among the ministry gifts of believers (cf. Eph. 4:11). Jesus Christ is now the high priest of the new covenant (Heb. 9:15–22), replacing the imperfect O.T. priesthood. He is a perfect priest "forever" (cf. 1 Tim. 2:5; Heb. 7:25; 9:23–28; see 2:17, note; see article on THE OLD COVENANT AND THE NEW COVENANT, p. 1954).

sprinkled the blood upon the altar
round about.
25 [a]And he took the fat, and the
rump, and all the fat that *was* upon the
inwards, and the caul *above* the liver,
and the two kidneys, and their fat, and
the right shoulder:
26 [b]And out of the basket of un-
leavened bread, that *was* before the
LORD, he took one unleavened cake,
and a cake of oiled bread, and one wa-
fer, and put *them* on the fat, and upon
the right shoulder:
27 And he put all [c]upon Aaron's
hands, and upon his sons' hands, and
waved them *for* a wave offering before
the LORD.
28 [d]And Moses took them from off
their hands, and burnt *them* on the al-
tar upon the burnt offering: they *were*
consecrations for a sweet savour: it *is*
an offering made by fire unto the LORD.
29 And Moses took the breast, and
waved it *for* a wave offering before the
LORD: *for* of the ram of consecration it
was Moses' [e]part; as the LORD com-
manded Moses.
30 And [f]Moses took of the anoint-
ing oil, and of the blood which *was*
upon the altar, and sprinkled *it* upon
Aaron, *and* upon his garments, and
upon his sons, and upon his sons' gar-
ments with him; and sanctified Aaron,
and his garments, and his sons, and his
sons' garments with him.
31 ¶ And Moses said unto Aaron
and to his sons, [g]Boil the flesh *at* the
door of the tabernacle of the congrega-
tion: and there eat it with the bread
that *is* in the basket of consecrations,
as I commanded, saying, Aaron and his
sons shall eat it.
32 [h]And that which remaineth of
the flesh and of the bread shall ye burn
with fire.
33 And ye shall not go out of the
door of the tabernacle of the congrega-
tion *in* seven days, until the days of
your consecration be at an end: for
[i]seven days shall he consecrate you.

8:25
[a]Ex. 29:22
8:26
[b]Ex. 29:23
8:27
[c]Ex. 29:24
8:28
[d]Ex. 29:25
8:29
[e]Ex. 29:26
8:30
[f]Ex. 29:21 & 30:30 Num. 3:3
8:31
[g]Ex. 29:31,32 1 Sam. 2:13-17
8:32
[h]Ex. 29:34
8:33
[i]Ex. 29:30,35 Ezek. 43:25,26
8:34
[j]Heb. 7:16
8:35
[k]Num. 3:7 & 9:19 Deut. 11:1 1 Ki. 2:3
9:1
[l]Ezek. 43:27
9:2
[m]Ex. 29:1 ch. 4:3 & 8:14
[n]ch. 8:18
9:3
[o]ch. 4:23 Ezra 6:17 & 10:19
9:4
[p]ch. 2:4
[q]ver. 6,23 Ex. 29:43
9:6
[r]ver. 23 Ex. 24:16 2 Chr. 5:13,14
9:7
[s]ch. 4:3 1 Sam. 3:14 Heb. 5:3 & 7:27 & 9:7
[t]ch. 4:16,20 Heb. 5:1

34 [j]As he hath done this day, *so*
the LORD hath commanded to do, to
make an atonement for you.
35 Therefore shall ye abide *at* the
door of the tabernacle of the congrega-
tion day and night seven days, and
[k]keep the charge of the LORD, that ye
die not: for so I am commanded.
36 So Aaron and his sons did all
things which the LORD commanded by
the hand of Moses.

The offerings of Aaron

9 AND [l]IT came to pass on the
eighth day, *that* Moses called Aar-
on and his sons, and the elders of Is-
rael;
2 And he said unto Aaron, [m]Take
thee a young calf for a sin offering,
[n]and a ram for a burnt offering, with-
out blemish, and offer *them* before the
LORD.
3 And unto the children of Israel
thou shalt speak, saying, [o]Take ye a
kid of the goats for a sin offering; and
a calf and a lamb, *both* of the first year,
without blemish, for a burnt offering;
4 Also a bullock and a ram for peace
offerings, to sacrifice before the LORD;
and [p]a meat offering mingled with oil:
for [q]today the LORD will appear unto
you.
5 ¶ And they brought *that* which Mo-
ses commanded before the tabernacle
of the congregation: and all the congre-
gation drew near and stood before the
LORD.
6 And Moses said, This *is* the thing
which the LORD commanded that ye
should do: and [r]the glory of the LORD
shall appear unto you.
7 And Moses said unto Aaron, Go
unto the altar, and [s]offer thy sin offer-
ing, and thy burnt offering, and make
an atonement for thyself, and for the
people: and [t]offer the offering of the
people, and make an atonement for
them; as the LORD commanded.
8 ¶ Aaron therefore went unto the

9:8 SLEW THE CALF. God instituted the animal sacrifice as an ordinance whereby sinners might draw near to Him in repentance and faith and so experience His forgiveness, salvation, and fellowship. (1) The offering of the animal was an object lesson, pointing to the principle of vicarious sacrifice and substitutionary atonement. The life of the innocent animal was offered in the place of the sinful and guilty worshiper (see 1:4, note).

(2) The sacrifice expressed a person's repentance and constituted both a confession of sin and a recognition of the need for cleansing and redemption (16:30–34; see 1:2, note).

(3) When a sacrifice was made in faith and obedience, God was pleased with the act of the worshiper and so imparted to that individual the desired grace and forgiveness (4:3,20; 5:15–16).

(4) The sacrifice provided atonement through a "covering up" of sin (see article on THE DAY OF ATONEMENT, p. 188).

altar, and slew the calf of the sin offering, which *was* for himself.

9 [u]And the sons of Aaron brought the blood unto him: and he dipped his finger in the blood, and [v]put *it* upon the horns of the altar, and poured out the blood at the bottom of the altar:

10 [w]But the fat, and the kidneys, and the caul above the liver of the sin offering, he burnt upon the altar; [x]as the LORD commanded Moses.

11 [y]And the flesh and the hide he burnt with fire without the camp.

12 And he slew the burnt offering; and Aaron's sons presented unto him the blood, [z]which he sprinkled round about upon the altar.

13 [a]And they presented the burnt offering unto him, with the pieces thereof, and the head: and he burnt *them* upon the altar.

14 [b]And he did wash the inwards and the legs, and burnt *them* upon the burnt offering on the altar.

15 ¶ [c]And he brought the people's offering, and took the goat, which *was* the sin offering for the people, and slew it, and offered it for sin, as the first.

16 And he brought the burnt offering, and offered it [d]according to the [u]manner.

17 And he brought [e]the meat offering, and [v]took an handful thereof, and burnt *it* upon the altar, [f]beside the burnt sacrifice of the morning.

18 He slew also the bullock and the ram *for* [g]a sacrifice of peace offerings, which *was* for the people: and Aaron's sons presented unto him the blood, which he sprinkled upon the altar round about,

19 And the fat of the bullock and of the ram, the rump, and that which covereth *the inwards,* and the kidneys, and the caul *above* the liver:

20 And they put the fat upon the breasts, [h]and he burnt the fat upon the altar:

21 And the breasts and the right shoulder Aaron waved [i]*for* a wave offering before the LORD; as Moses commanded.

22 And Aaron lifted up his hand toward the people, and [j]blessed them, and came down from offering of the sin offering, and the burnt offering, and peace offerings.

23 And Moses and Aaron went into the tabernacle of the congregation, and came out, and blessed the people: [k]and the glory of the LORD appeared unto all the people.

24 And [l]there came a fire out from before the LORD, and consumed upon the altar the burnt offering and the fat: *which* when all the people saw, [m]they shouted, and fell on their faces.

The death of Nadab and Abihu

10 AND [n]NADAB and Abihu, the sons of Aaron, [o]took either of them his censer, and put fire therein, and put incense thereon, and offered [p]strange fire before the LORD, which he commanded them not.

2 And there [q]went out fire from the LORD, and devoured them, and they died before the LORD.

9:9 [u]ch. 8:15 [v]See ch. 4:7 Heb. 9:22,23
9:10 [w]ch. 8:16 [x]ch. 4:8
9:11 [y]ch. 4:11 & 8:17
9:12 [z]ch. 1:5 & 8:19
9:13 [a]ch. 8:20
9:14 [b]ch. 8:21
9:15 [c]ver. 3 Is. 53:10 Heb. 2:17 & 5:3
9:16 [d]ch. 1:3,10
9:17 [e]ver. 4 ch. 2:1,2 [f]Ex. 29:38
9:18 [g]ch. 3:1
9:20 [h]ch. 3:5,16
9:21 [i]Ex. 29:24 ch. 7:30-34
9:22 [j]Num. 6:23 Deut. 21:5 Luke 24:50
9:23 [k]ver. 6 Num. 14:10
9:24 [l]Gen. 4:4 Judg. 6:21 1 Ki. 18:38 2 Chr. 7:1 Ps. 20:3 [m]1 Ki. 18:39 2 Chr. 7:3 Ezra 3:11
10:1 [n]Num. 3:3,4 1 Chr. 24:2 [o]ch. 16:12 [p]Ex. 30:9
10:2 [q]Num. 16:35

[u] Or, *ordinance* [v] Heb. *filled his hand out of it*

(5) Note that from the N.T. perspective, the animal sacrifices were imperfect in that they could not bring the worshipers into the state of mature faith and obedience that is now available under the new covenant (Heb. 10:1–4). The ordinance served as a shadow or a preliminary sketch of the "one sacrifice for sins for ever" that was provided when Jesus Christ offered His body once for all (Heb. 10:12).

10:1 STRANGE FIRE. Nadab and Abihu may have put into their censers (i.e., fire pans) coals of fire from an unauthorized source (cf. Ex. 30:7–9). Also the offering of incense on the altar was to be done only by the high priest (Ex. 30:7–9). Some interpreters have suggested that Nadab and Abihu did this under the influence of alcohol (see vv. 9–10).

10:2 FIRE . . . DEVOURED THEM. Nadab and Abihu were killed because, as priests, they defiantly rebelled against God and His law and thus profaned the holy place (v. 3). (1) They had been explicitly forbidden to offer "strange fire" before the Lord (see previous note; cf. Ex. 30:9–10). By their act those who were supposed to teach God's law refused to take His commandments seriously. While professing to be holy ministers of God, they really were serving their own desires and ideas, and there was no fear of God in their lives.

(2) These two men were leaders of God's people. When God's ministers commit blatant sin, it does great damage to God and His redemptive purposes on earth. Their transgressions defile the church and all God's people, and bring dishonor to Him. For this reason the Bible teaches that only those who have demonstrated a Christian life of perseverance in loyalty to God and His word may be appointed as overseers of God's people (see 1 Tim. 3:1–7; see article on MORAL QUALIFICATIONS FOR OVERSEERS, p. 1908).

3 Then Moses said unto Aaron, This *is it* that the LORD spake, saying, I will be sanctified in them [r]that come nigh me, and before all the people I will be [s]glorified. [t]And Aaron held his peace.

4 And Moses called Mishael and Elzaphan, the sons of [u]Uzziel the uncle of Aaron, and said unto them, Come near, carry your brethren from before the sanctuary out of the camp.

5 So they went near, and carried them in their coats out of the camp; as Moses had said.

6 And Moses said unto Aaron, and unto Eleazar and unto Ithamar, his sons, [v]Uncover not your heads, neither rend your clothes; lest ye die, and lest [w]wrath come upon all the people: but let your brethren, the whole house of Israel, bewail the burning which the LORD hath kindled.

7 [x]And ye shall not go out from the door of the tabernacle of the congregation, lest ye die: [y]for the anointing oil of the LORD *is* upon you. And they did according to the word of Moses.

8 ¶ And the LORD spake unto Aaron, saying,

9 [z]Do not drink wine nor strong drink, thou, nor thy sons with thee, when ye go into the tabernacle of the congregation, lest ye die: *it shall be* a statute for ever throughout your generations:

10 And that ye may [a]put difference between holy and unholy, and between unclean and clean;

11 [b]And that ye may teach the children of Israel all the statutes which the LORD hath spoken unto them by the hand of Moses.

12 ¶ And Moses spake unto Aaron, and unto Eleazar and unto Ithamar, his sons that were left, Take [c]the meat offering that remaineth of the offerings of the LORD made by fire, and eat it without leaven beside the altar: for [d]it *is* most holy:

13 And ye shall eat it in the holy place, because it *is* thy due, and thy sons' due, of the sacrifices of the LORD made by fire: for [e]so I am commanded.

14 And [f]the wave breast and heave shoulder shall ye eat in a clean place; thou, and thy sons, and thy daughters with thee: for *they be* thy due, and thy sons' due, *which* are given out of the sacrifices of peace offerings of the children of Israel.

15 [g]The heave shoulder and the wave breast shall they bring with the offerings made by fire of the fat, to wave *it for* a wave offering before the LORD; and it shall be thine, and thy sons' with thee, by a statute for ever; as the LORD hath commanded.

16 ¶ And Moses diligently sought [h]the goat of the sin offering, and, behold, it was burnt: and he was angry with Eleazar and Ithamar, the sons of Aaron *which were* left *alive,* saying,

17 [i]Wherefore have ye not eaten the sin offering in the holy place, seeing it *is* most holy, and *God* hath given it you to bear the iniquity of the congregation, to make atonement for them before the LORD?

18 Behold, [j]the blood of it was not brought in within the holy *place:* ye should indeed have eaten it in the holy *place,* [k]as I commanded.

19 And Aaron said unto Moses, Behold, [l]this day have they offered their sin offering and their burnt offering before the LORD; and such things have befallen me: and *if* I had eaten the sin offering today, [m]should it have been accepted in the sight of the LORD?

20 And when Moses heard *that,* he was content.

Clean and unclean animals

11:1–23pp — Deut. 14:3–20

11 AND THE LORD spake unto Moses and to Aaron, saying unto them,

2 Speak unto the children of Israel, saying, [n]These *are* the beasts which ye shall eat among all the beasts that *are* on the earth.

3 Whatsoever parteth the hoof, and is clovenfooted, *and* cheweth the cud, among the beasts, that shall ye eat.

10:3 [r]Ex. 19:22 Is. 52:11 Ezek. 20:41 [s]Ezek. 28:22 [t]Ps. 39:9
10:4 [u]Ex. 6:18,22 Num. 3:19,30
10:6 [v]ch. 21:10 Num. 6:6,7 [w]Num. 16:22,46 Josh. 7:1 2 Sam. 24:1
10:7 [x]ch. 21:12 [y]ch. 8:30
10:9 [z]Luke 1:15 1 Tim. 3:3 Tit. 1:7
10:10 [a]Ezek. 44:23
10:11 [b]Deut. 24:8 Neh. 8:2,8 Jer. 18:18 Mal. 2:7
10:12 [c]Num. 18:9 [d]ch. 21:22
10:13 [e]ch. 2:3 & 6:16
10:14 [f]Ex. 29:24,26,27 ch. 7:31,34 Num. 18:11
10:15 [g]ch. 7:29,30
10:16 [h]ch. 9:3,15
10:17 [i]ch. 6:26,29
10:18 [j]ch. 6:30 [k]ch. 6:26,30
10:19 [l]ch. 9:8,12 [m]Is. 1:11-15
11:2 [n]Deut. 14:4 Ezek. 4:14 Dan. 1:8 Mat. 15:11 Acts 10:12,14 Rom. 14:14 Heb. 9:10 & 13:9

10:9 DO NOT DRINK WINE. Abstinence from intoxicating wine was required of all priests when performing their religious duties. (1) They were expected to be a holy vessel before God and the people whom they were to teach soberly the way of God (vv. 10–11; see Eph. 5:18, notes). (2) The violation of this ordinance about abstinence was serious enough to incur the penalty of death. The point is clear—God considered any amount of intoxicating drink incompatible with His highest standard of godliness, wise discernment, and sensitivity to the leadership of the Holy Spirit (see Prov. 23:29–35; 1 Tim. 3:3, note; Tit. 2:2, note).

4 Nevertheless these shall ye not eat of them that chew the cud, or of them that divide the hoof: *as* the camel, because he cheweth the cud, but divideth not the hoof; he *is* unclean unto you.

5 And the coney, because he cheweth the cud, but divideth not the hoof; he *is* unclean unto you.

6 And the hare, because he cheweth the cud, but divideth not the hoof; he *is* unclean unto you.

7 And the swine, though he divide the hoof, and be clovenfooted, yet he cheweth not the cud; [o]he *is* unclean to you.

8 Of their flesh shall ye not eat, and their carcase shall ye not touch; [p]they *are* unclean to you.

9 ¶ [q]These shall ye eat of all that *are* in the waters: whatsoever hath fins and scales in the waters, in the seas, and in the rivers, them shall ye eat.

10 And all that have not fins and scales in the seas, and in the rivers, of all that move in the waters, and of any living thing which *is* in the waters, they *shall be* an [r]abomination unto you:

11 They shall be even an abomination unto you; ye shall not eat of their flesh, but ye shall have their carcases in abomination.

12 Whatsoever hath no fins nor scales in the waters, that *shall be* an abomination unto you.

13 ¶ [s]And these *are they which* ye shall have in abomination among the fowls; they shall not be eaten, they *are* an abomination: the eagle, and the ossifrage, and the ospray,

14 And the vulture, and the kite after his kind;

15 Every raven after his kind;

16 And the owl, and the night hawk, and the cuckoo, and the hawk after his kind,

17 And the little owl, and the cormorant, and the great owl,

18 And the swan, and the pelican, and the gier eagle,

19 And the stork, the heron after her kind, and the lapwing, and the bat.

20 All fowls that creep, going upon *all* four, *shall be* an abomination unto you.

21 Yet these may ye eat of every flying creeping thing that goeth upon *all* four, which have legs above their feet, to leap withal upon the earth;

22 *Even* these of them ye may eat; [t]the locust after his kind, and the bald locust after his kind, and the beetle after his kind, and the grasshopper after his kind.

23 But all *other* flying creeping things, which have four feet, *shall be* an abomination unto you.

24 And for these ye shall be unclean: whosoever toucheth the carcase of them shall be unclean until the even.

25 And whosoever beareth *aught* of the carcase of them [u]shall wash his clothes, and be unclean until the even.

26 *The carcases* of every beast which divideth the hoof, and *is* not clovenfooted, nor cheweth the cud, *are* unclean unto you: every one that toucheth them shall be unclean.

27 And whatsoever goeth upon his paws, among all manner of beasts that go on *all* four, those *are* unclean unto you: whoso toucheth their carcase shall be unclean until the even.

28 And he that beareth the carcase of them shall wash his clothes, and be unclean until the even: they *are* unclean unto you.

29 ¶ These also *shall be* unclean unto you among the creeping things that creep upon the earth; the weasel, and [v]the mouse, and the tortoise after his kind,

30 And the ferret, and the chameleon, and the lizard, and the snail, and the mole.

31 These *are* unclean to you among all that creep: whosoever doth touch them, when they be dead, shall be unclean until the even.

32 And upon whatsoever *any* of them, when they are dead, doth fall, it shall be unclean; whether *it be* any vessel of wood, or raiment, or skin, or sack, whatsoever vessel *it be*, wherein *any* work is done, [w]it must be put into water, and it shall be unclean until the even; so it shall be cleansed.

33 And every earthen vessel, whereinto *any* of them falleth, whatsoever *is* in it shall be unclean; and [x]ye shall break it.

34 Of all meat which may be eaten, *that* on which *such* water cometh shall be unclean: and all drink that may be drunk in every *such* vessel shall be unclean.

35 And every *thing* whereupon *any part* of their carcase falleth shall be unclean; *whether it be* oven, or ranges for pots, they shall be broken down: *for*

11:7 [o]Is. 65:4 & 66:3,17
11:8 [p]Is. 52:11 Mark 7:2,15,18 Acts 10:14,15 & 15:29 1 Cor. 8:8 Heb. 9:10
11:9 [q]Deut. 14:9
11:10 [r]ch. 7:18 Deut. 14:3
11:13 [s]Deut. 14:12
11:22 [t]Mat. 3:4 Mark 1:6
11:25 [u]ch. 14:8 & 15:5 Num. 19:10,22 & 31:24 Rev. 7:14
11:29 [v]Is. 66:17
11:32 [w]ch. 15:12
11:33 [x]ch. 6:28 & 15:12 Ps. 2:9 Jer. 48:38 2 Tim. 2:21 Rev. 2:27

they *are* unclean, and shall be unclean unto you.

36 Nevertheless a fountain or pit, [w]*wherein there is* plenty of water, shall be clean: but that which toucheth their carcase shall be unclean.

37 And if *any part* of their carcase fall upon any sowing seed which is to be sown, it *shall be* clean.

38 But if *any* water be put upon the seed, and *any part* of their carcase fall thereon, it *shall be* unclean unto you.

39 And if any beast, of which ye may eat, die; he that toucheth the carcase thereof shall be unclean until the even.

40 And [y]he that eateth of the carcase of it shall wash his clothes, and be unclean until the even: he also that beareth the carcase of it shall wash his clothes, and be unclean until the even.

41 And every creeping thing that creepeth upon the earth *shall be* an abomination; it shall not be eaten.

42 Whatsoever goeth upon the belly, and whatsoever goeth upon *all* four, or whatsoever [x]hath more feet among all creeping things that creep upon the earth, them ye shall not eat; for they *are* an abomination.

43 [z]Ye shall not make your [y]selves abominable with any creeping thing that creepeth, neither shall ye make yourselves unclean with them, that ye should be defiled thereby.

44 For I *am* the LORD your God: ye shall therefore sanctify yourselves, and [a]ye shall be holy; for I *am* holy: neither shall ye defile yourselves with any manner of creeping thing that creepeth upon the earth.

45 [b]For I *am* the LORD that bringeth you up out of the land of Egypt, to be your God: [c]ye shall therefore be holy, for I *am* holy. Lev 18:

46 This *is* the law of the beasts, and of the fowl, and of every living creature that moveth in the waters, and of every creature that creepeth upon the earth:

47 [d]To make a difference between the unclean and the clean, and between the beast that may be eaten and the beast that may not be eaten.

11:40 [y]ch. 17:15 & 22:8 Deut. 14:21 Ezek. 4:14 & 44:31
11:43 [z]ch. 20:25
11:44 [a]Ex. 19:6 ch. 19:2 & 20:7,26 Amos 3:3 Mat. 5:48 1 Thes. 4:7 1 Pet. 1:15,16 Rev. 22:11,14
11:45 [b]Ex. 6:7 & 20:2 Ps. 105:43-45 Hos. 11:1 [c]ver. 44
11:47 [d]ch. 10:10 Ezek. 44:23 Mal. 3:18
12:2 [e]ch. 15:19 Job 14:4 Ps. 51:5 [f]Luke 2:22 [g]ch. 15:19
12:3 [h]Gen. 17:12 Luke 1:59 & 2:21 John 7:22,23 Rom. 3:19 Gal. 5:3

Purification after childbirth

12 AND THE LORD spake unto Moses, saying,

2 Speak unto the children of Israel, saying, If a [e]woman have conceived seed, and born a man child: then [f]she shall be unclean seven days; [g]according to the days of the separation for her infirmity shall she be unclean.

3 And in the [h]eighth day the flesh of his foreskin shall be circumcised.

4 And she shall then continue in the blood of her purifying three and thirty days; she shall touch no hallowed thing, nor come into the sanctuary, until the days of her purifying be fulfilled.

5 But if she bear a maid child, then

[w] Heb. *a gathering together of waters* [x] Heb. *doth multiply feet* [y] Heb. *souls*

11:44 YE SHALL BE HOLY. The instructions concerning clean and unclean (i.e., proper and improper) food (ch. 11) were given apparently for health reasons, but also as standards to help Israel remain a people separated from the ungodly society about them (cf. Deut. 14:1–2). These dietary instructions are no longer binding upon N.T. believers since Christ fulfilled their significance and purpose (cf. Mat. 5:17; 15:1–20; Acts 10:14–15; Col. 2:16; 1 Tim. 4:3). However, the principles embodied in those instructions are still valid today.

(1) Christians today must distinguish themselves from their surrounding society by eating, drinking, and dressing so as to glorify God in their bodies (cf. 1 Cor. 6:20; 10:31), and by rejecting all unholy social customs of unbelievers. They must be "holy in all manner of conversation [behavior]" (1 Pet. 1:15).

(2) The detailed emphasis on ceremonial cleanliness highlighted the necessity of moral separation of God's people in thought and deed from the surrounding world (Ex. 19:6; 2 Cor. 7:1; see article on SPIRITUAL SEPARATION FOR BELIEVERS, p. 1814). All aspects of life must be regulated by the will of God (1 Cor. 10:31).

12:2 BORN A MAN CHILD ... UNCLEAN. Parenthood is God's will for man and woman and can be one of the greatest joys of life (Gen. 1:28; 9:1; Ps. 127:3; 128:3). However, the discharges associated with childbirth had to be treated as unclean (15:16–19; Ex. 19:15; see next note) and symbolized the results of the fall of humankind (see Gen. 3:15, note). (1) Children are now born with a sinful nature (see 1 John 1:8, note). The psalmist's words in Ps. 51:5 apply here: "Behold, I was shapen in iniquity; and in sin did my mother conceive me." (2) Children also face the reality of physical death (Gen. 2:16–17; 5:3) and the possibility of eternal death unless they accept Christ's redemption. Death was never God's intention or perfect will for humans. The uncleanness associated with childbearing expresses the truth that the newborn child needs a Savior. (3) Christian parents, knowing the sinful tendencies with which their children are born, should pray earnestly that they might accept Christ as Lord and be born again, regenerated by the Holy Spirit (see articles on REGENERATION, p. 1597, and PARENTS AND CHILDREN, p. 1880).

she shall be unclean two weeks, as in her separation: and she shall continue in the blood of her purifying threescore and six days.

6 And [i]when the days of her purifying are fulfilled, for a son, or for a daughter, she shall bring a lamb [z]of the first year for a burnt offering, and a young pigeon, or a turtledove, for a sin offering, unto the door of the tabernacle of the congregation, unto the priest:

7 Who shall offer it before the LORD, and make an atonement for her; and she shall be cleansed from the issue of her blood. This *is* the law for her that hath born a male or a female.

8 [j]And if [a]she be not able to bring a lamb, then she shall bring two turtles, or two young pigeons; the one for the burnt offering, and the other for a sin offering: [k]and the priest shall make an atonement for her, and she shall be clean.

Laws about skin plagues

13 AND THE LORD spake unto Moses and Aaron, saying,

2 When a man shall have in the skin of his flesh a [b]rising, [l]a scab, or bright spot, and it be in the skin of his flesh *like* the plague of leprosy; [m]then he shall be brought unto Aaron the priest, or unto one of his sons the priests:

3 And the priest shall look on the plague in the skin of the flesh: and *when* the hair in the plague is turned white, and the plague in sight *be* deeper than the skin of his flesh, it *is* a plague of leprosy: and the priest shall look on him, and pronounce him unclean.

4 If the bright spot *be* white in the skin of his flesh, and in sight *be* not deeper than the skin, and the hair thereof be not turned white; then the priest shall shut up *him that hath* the plague seven days:

5 And the priest shall look on him the seventh day: and, behold, *if* the plague in his sight be at a stay, *and* the plague spread not in the skin; then the priest shall shut him up seven days more:

6 And the priest shall look on him again the seventh day: and, behold, *if* the plague *be* somewhat dark, *and* the plague spread not in the skin, the priest shall pronounce him clean: it *is but* a scab: and he [n]shall wash his clothes, and be clean.

7 But if the scab spread much abroad in the skin, after that he hath been seen of the priest for his cleansing, he shall be seen of the priest again:

8 And *if* the priest see that, behold, the scab spreadeth in the skin, then the priest shall pronounce him unclean: it *is* a leprosy.

9 ¶ When the plague of leprosy is in a man, then he shall be brought unto the priest;

10 [o]And the priest shall see *him:* and, behold, *if* the rising *be* white in the skin, and it have turned the hair white, and *there be* [c]quick raw flesh in the rising;

11 It *is* an old leprosy in the skin of his flesh, and the priest shall pronounce him unclean, and shall not shut him up: for he *is* unclean.

12 And if a leprosy break out abroad in the skin, and the leprosy cover all the skin of *him that hath* the plague from his head even to his foot, wheresoever the priest looketh;

13 Then the priest shall consider: and, behold, *if* the leprosy have covered all his flesh, he shall pronounce *him* clean *that hath* the plague: it is all turned white: he *is* clean.

14 But when raw flesh appeareth in him, he shall be unclean.

15 And the priest shall see the raw flesh, and pronounce him to be unclean: *for* the raw flesh *is* unclean: it *is* a leprosy.

16 Or if the raw flesh turn again, and be changed unto white, he shall come unto the priest;

17 And the priest shall see him:

12:6 [i]Luke 2:22 **12:8** [j]ch. 5:7 Luke 2:24 [k]ch. 4:26 **13:2** [l]Deut. 28:27 Is. 3:17 [m]Deut. 17:8,9 & 24:8 Mal. 2:7 Luke 17:14

13:6 [n]ch. 11:25 & 14:8 **13:10** [o]Num. 12:10,12 2 Ki. 5:27 2 Chr. 26:20

[z] Heb. *a son of his year* [a] Heb. *her hand find not sufficiency of* [b] Or, *swelling* [c] Heb. *the quickening of living flesh*

13:3 PRONOUNCE HIM UNCLEAN. Uncleanness here must be equated with whatever did not accord with God's will and holiness. It could be caused by that which was associated with parenthood (see previous note), sickness (chs. 13—14; Num. 5:2; 12:10–14), or death (Num. 5:2; 31:19; 35:33). All these things deviate from the perfection God intended at creation. In other words, the laws of uncleanness constantly reminded the people of the devastating results of their sin.

and, behold, *if* the plague be turned
into white; then the priest shall pro-
nounce *him* clean *that hath* the plague:
he *is* clean.
18 ¶ The flesh also, in which, *even*
in the skin thereof, was a [p]boil, and is
healed,
19 And in the place of the boil there
be a white rising, or a bright spot,
white, and somewhat reddish, and it be
shown to the priest;
20 And if, when the priest seeth it,
behold, it *be* in sight lower than the
skin, and the hair thereof be turned
white; the priest shall pronounce him
unclean: it *is* a plague of leprosy bro-
ken out of the boil.
21 But if the priest look on it, and,
behold, *there be* no white hairs therein,
and *if* it *be* not lower than the skin, but
be somewhat dark; then the priest
shall shut him up seven days:
22 And if it spread much abroad in
the skin, then the priest shall pro-
nounce him unclean: it *is* a plague.
23 But if the bright spot stay in his
place, *and* spread not, it *is* a burning
boil; and the priest shall pronounce
him clean.
24 ¶ Or if there be *any* flesh, in the
skin whereof *there is* [d]a hot burning,
and the quick *flesh* that burneth have a
white bright spot, somewhat reddish,
or white;
25 Then the priest shall look upon
it: and, behold, *if* the hair in the bright
spot be turned white, and it *be in* sight
deeper than the skin; it *is* a leprosy bro-
ken out of the burning: wherefore the
priest shall pronounce him unclean: it
is the [q]plague of leprosy.
26 But if the priest look on it, and,
behold, *there be* no white hair in the
bright spot, and it *be* no lower than the
other skin, but *be* somewhat dark; then
the priest shall shut him up seven
days:
27 And the priest shall look upon
him the seventh day: *and* if it be spread
much abroad in the skin, then the
priest shall pronounce him unclean: it
is the plague of leprosy.
28 And if the bright spot stay in his
place, *and* spread not in the skin, but
it *be* somewhat dark; it *is* a rising of the
burning, and the priest shall pro-
nounce him clean: for it *is* an inflamma-
tion of the burning.
29 ¶ If a man or woman have a
plague upon the head or the beard;

13:18 [p]Ex. 9:9 & 15:26
13:25 [q]Ex. 4:6,7 Num. 12:10 2 Sam. 3:29 2 Ki. 5:27 Luke 5:12-14
13:30 [r]Deut. 24:8 Mal. 2:7 1 Cor. 12:9 [s]Deut. 28:27 Is. 3:17
13:33 [t]Job 1:20 Rom. 8:13
13:37 [u]ch. 10:10 Jer. 15:19 Ezek. 22:26 & 44:23
13:40 [v]Is. 15:2 Amos 8:10

30 Then the [r]priest shall see the
plague: and, behold, if it *be* in sight
deeper than the skin; *and there be* in it
a yellow thin hair; then the priest shall
pronounce him unclean: it *is* a dry
[s]scall, *even* a leprosy upon the head or
beard.
31 And if the priest look on the
plague of the scall, and, behold, it *be*
not in sight deeper than the skin, and
that there is no black hair in it; then the
priest shall shut up *him that hath* the
plague of the scall seven days:
32 And in the seventh day the priest
shall look on the plague: and, behold,
if the scall spread not, and there be in
it no yellow hair, and the scall *be* not
in sight deeper than the skin;
33 He shall be [t]shaven, but the
scall shall he not shave; and the priest
shall shut up *him that hath* the scall
seven days more:
34 And in the seventh day the priest
shall look on the scall: and, behold, *if*
the scall be not spread in the skin, nor
be in sight deeper than the skin; then
the priest shall pronounce him clean:
and he shall wash his clothes, and be
clean.
35 But if the scall spread much in
the skin after his cleansing;
36 Then the priest shall look on
him: and, behold, if the scall be spread
in the skin, the priest shall not seek for
yellow hair; he *is* unclean.
37 But if the scall be in his sight at
a stay, and *that* there is black hair
grown up therein; the scall is healed,
he *is* clean: and the [u]priest shall pro-
nounce him clean.
38 ¶ If a man also or a woman have
in the skin of their flesh bright spots,
even white bright spots;
39 Then the priest shall look: and,
behold, *if* the bright spots in the skin
of their flesh *be* darkish white; it *is* a
freckled spot *that* groweth in the skin;
he *is* clean.
40 And the man whose [e]hair is
fallen off his head, he *is* [v]bald; *yet is*
he clean.
41 And he that hath his hair fallen
off from the part of his head toward his
face, he *is* forehead bald: *yet is* he
clean.
42 And if there be in the bald head,
or bald forehead, a white reddish sore;

[d] Heb. a *burning of fire* [e] Heb. *head is pilled*

it *is* a leprosy sprung up in his bald head, or his bald forehead.

43 Then the priest shall look upon it: and, behold, *if* the rising of the sore *be* white reddish in his bald head, or in his bald forehead, as the leprosy appeareth in the skin of the flesh;

44 He is a leprous man, he *is* unclean: the priest shall pronounce him utterly unclean; his plague *is* in his head.

45 And the leper in whom the plague *is,* his clothes shall be rent, and his head bare, and he shall [w]put a covering upon his upper lip, and shall cry, [x]Unclean, unclean.

46 All the days wherein the plague *shall be* in him he shall be defiled; he *is* unclean: he shall dwell alone; [y]without the camp *shall* his habitation *be.*

Leprosy in garments

47 ¶ The garment also that the plague of leprosy is in, *whether it be* a woollen garment, or a linen garment;

48 Whether *it be* in the warp, or woof; of linen, or of woollen; whether in a skin, or in any [f]thing made of skin;

49 And if the plague be greenish or reddish in the garment, or in the skin, either in the warp, or in the woof, or in any [g]thing of skin; it *is* a plague of leprosy, and shall be shown unto the priest:

50 And the priest shall look upon the plague, and shut up *it that hath* the plague seven days:

51 And he shall look on the plague on the seventh day: if the plague be spread in the garment, either in the warp, or in the woof, or in a skin, *or* in any work that is made of skin; the plague *is* [z]a fretting leprosy; it *is* unclean.

52 He shall therefore burn that garment, whether warp or woof, in woollen or in linen, or any thing of skin, wherein the plague is: for it *is* a fretting leprosy; it shall be burnt in the fire.

53 And if the priest shall look, and, behold, the plague be not spread in the garment, either in the warp, or in the woof, or in any thing of skin;

54 Then the priest shall command that they wash *the thing* wherein the plague *is,* and he shall shut it up seven days more:

55 And the priest shall look on the plague, after that it is washed: and, behold, *if* the plague have not changed his colour, and the plague be not spread; it *is* unclean; thou shalt burn it in the fire; it *is* fret inward, [h]*whether* it *be* bare within or without.

56 And if the priest look, and, behold, the plague *be* somewhat dark after the washing of it; then he shall rend it out of the garment, or out of the skin, or out of the warp, or out of the woof:

57 And if it appear still in the garment, either in the warp, or in the woof, or in any thing of skin; it *is* a spreading *plague:* thou shalt burn that wherein the plague *is* with fire.

58 And the garment, either warp, or woof, or whatsoever thing of skin *it be,* which thou shalt wash, if the plague be departed from them, then it shall be washed the second time, and shall be clean.

59 This *is* the law of the plague of leprosy in a garment of woollen or linen, either in the warp, or woof, or any thing of skins, to pronounce it clean, or to pronounce it unclean.

The cleansing of lepers

14 AND THE LORD spake unto Moses, saying,

2 This shall be the law of the leper in the day of his cleansing: He [a]shall be brought unto the priest:

3 And the priest shall go forth out of the camp; and the priest shall look, and, behold, *if* the plague of leprosy be healed in the leper;

4 Then shall the priest command to take for him that is to be cleansed two [i]birds alive *and* clean, and [b]cedar wood, and [c]scarlet, and [d]hyssop:

5 And the priest shall command that one of the birds be killed in an earthen vessel over running water:

6 As for the living bird, he shall take it, and the cedar wood, and the scarlet, and the hyssop, and shall dip them and the living bird in the blood of the bird *that was* killed over the running water:

7 And he shall [e]sprinkle upon him that is to be cleansed from the leprosy [f]seven times, and shall pronounce him clean, and shall let the living bird loose [j]into the open field.

8 And he that is to be cleansed

13:45 [w]Ezek. 24:17,22 Mic. 3:7 [x]Lam. 4:15
13:46 [y]Num. 5:2 & 12:14 2 Ki. 7:3 & 15:5 2 Chr. 26:21 Luke 17:12
13:51 [z]ch. 14:44

14:2 [a]Mat. 8:2,4 Mark 1:40,44 Luke 5:12,14 & 17:14
14:4 [b]Num. 19:6 [c]Heb. 9:19 [d]Ps. 51:7
14:7 [e]Num. 19:18,19 Is. 52:15 Heb. 9:13,21 & 12:24 [f]2 Ki. 5:10,14 Ps. 51:2

[f] Heb. *work of* [g] Heb. *vessel,* or, *instrument*
[h] Heb. whether *it* be *bald in the head thereof,* or *in the forehead thereof* [i] Or, *sparrows*
[j] Heb. *upon the face of the field*

[g]shall wash his clothes, and shave off all his hair, [h]and wash himself in water, that he may be clean: and after that he shall come into the camp, and [i]shall tarry abroad out of his tent seven days.

9 But it shall be on the seventh day, that he shall shave all his hair off his head and his beard and his eyebrows, even all his hair he shall shave off: and he shall wash his clothes, also he shall wash his flesh in water, and he shall be clean.

10 And on the eighth day [j]he shall take two he lambs without blemish, and one ewe lamb [k]of the first year without blemish, and three tenth deals of fine flour *for* [k]a meat offering, mingled with oil, and one log of oil.

11 And the priest that maketh *him* clean shall present the man that is to be made clean, and those things, before the LORD, *at* the door of the tabernacle of the congregation:

12 And the priest shall take one he lamb, and [l]offer him for a trespass offering, and the log of oil, and [m]wave them *for* a wave offering before the LORD:

13 And he shall slay the lamb [n]in the place where he shall kill the sin offering and the burnt offering, in the holy place: for [o]as the sin offering *is* the priest's, *so is* the trespass offering: [p]it *is* most holy:

14 And the priest shall take *some* of the blood of the trespass offering, and the priest shall put *it* [q]upon the tip of the right ear of him that is to be cleansed, and upon the thumb of his right hand, and upon the great toe of his right foot:

15 And the priest shall take *some* of the log of oil, and pour *it* into the palm of his own left hand:

16 And the priest shall dip his right finger in the oil that *is* in his left hand, and shall sprinkle of the oil with his finger seven times before the LORD:

17 And of the rest of the oil that *is* in his hand shall the priest put upon the tip of the right ear of him that is to be cleansed, and upon the thumb of his right hand, and upon the great toe of his right foot, upon the blood of the trespass offering:

18 And the remnant of the oil that *is* in the priest's hand he shall pour upon the head of him that is to be cleansed: [r]and the priest shall make an atonement for him before the LORD.

19 And the priest shall offer [s]the sin offering, and make an atonement for him that is to be cleansed from his uncleanness; and afterward he shall kill the burnt offering:

20 And the priest shall offer the burnt offering and the meat offering upon the altar: and the priest shall make an atonement for him, and he shall be clean.

21 And [t]if he *be* poor, and [1]cannot get so much; then he shall take one lamb *for* a trespass offering [m]to be waved, to make an atonement for him, and one tenth deal of fine flour mingled with oil for a meat offering, and a log of oil;

22 [u]And two turtledoves, or two young pigeons, such as he is able to get; and the one shall be a sin offering, and the other a burnt offering.

23 [v]And he shall bring them on the eighth day for his cleansing unto the priest, unto the door of the tabernacle of the congregation, before the LORD.

24 [w]And the priest shall take the lamb of the trespass offering, and the log of oil, and the priest shall wave them *for* a wave offering before the LORD:

25 And he shall kill the lamb of the trespass offering, [x]and the priest shall take *some* of the blood of the trespass offering, and put *it* upon the tip of the right ear of him that is to be cleansed, and upon the thumb of his right hand, and upon the great toe of his right foot:

26 And the priest shall pour of the oil into the palm of his own left hand:

27 And the priest shall sprinkle with his right finger *some* of the oil that *is* in his left hand seven times before the LORD:

28 And the priest shall put of the oil that *is* in his hand upon the tip of the right ear of him that is to be cleansed, and upon the thumb of his right hand, and upon the great toe of his right foot, upon the place of the blood of the trespass offering:

29 And the rest of the oil that *is* in the priest's hand he shall put upon the head of him that is to be cleansed, to make an atonement for him before the LORD.

14:8 [g]ch. 13:6 [h]ch. 11:25 Eph. 5:26 Heb. 10:22 Rev. 1:5,6 [i]Num. 12:15
14:10 [j]Mat. 8:4 Mark 1:44 Luke 5:14 [k]ch. 2:1 Num. 15:4
14:12 [l]ch. 5:2,18 & 6:6,7 [m]Ex. 29:24
14:13 [n]Ex. 29:11 ch. 1:5 & 4:4 [o]ch. 7:7 [p]ch. 2:3 & 7:6 & 21:22
14:14 [q]Ex. 29:20 ch. 8:23
14:18 [r]ch. 4:26 & 5:6
14:19 [s]ch. 5:1,6 & 12:7
14:21 [t]ch. 5:7 & 12:8
14:22 [u]ch. 12:8 & 15:14,15
14:23 [v]ver. 10,11
14:24 [w]ver. 12
14:25 [x]ver. 14,17

[k] Heb. *the daughter of her year* [1] Heb. *his hand reach not* [m] Heb. *for a waving*

30 And he shall offer the one of [y]the turtledoves, or of the young pigeons, such as he can get;

31 *Even* such as he is able to get, the one *for* a sin offering, and the other *for* a burnt offering, with the meat offering: and the priest shall make an atonement for him that is to be cleansed before the LORD.

32 This *is* the law *of him* in whom *is* the plague of leprosy, whose hand is not able to get [z]*that which pertaineth* to his cleansing.

Leprosy in houses

33 ¶ And the LORD spake unto Moses and unto Aaron, saying,

34 [a]When ye be come into the land of Canaan, which I give to you for a possession, and I put the plague of leprosy in a house of the land of your possession;

35 And he that owneth the house shall come and tell the priest, saying, It seemeth to me *there is* as it were [b]a plague in the house:

36 Then the priest shall command that they [n]empty the house, before the priest go *into it* to see the plague, that all that *is* in the house be not made unclean: and afterward the priest shall go in to see the house:

37 And he shall look on the plague, and, behold, *if* the plague *be* in the walls of the house with hollow strakes, greenish or reddish, which in sight *are* lower than the wall;

38 Then the priest shall go out of the house to the door of the house, and shut up the house seven days:

39 And the priest shall come again the seventh day, and shall look: and, behold, *if* the plague be spread in the walls of the house;

40 Then the priest shall command that they take away the stones in which the plague *is,* and they shall cast them into an unclean place without the city:

41 And he shall cause the house to be scraped within round about, and they shall pour out the dust that they scrape off without the city into an unclean place:

42 And they shall take other stones, and put *them* in the place of those stones; and he shall take other mortar, and shall plaster the house.

43 And if the plague come again, and break out in the house, after that he hath taken away the stones, and after he hath scraped the house, and after it is plastered;

44 Then the priest shall come and look, and, behold, *if* the plague be spread in the house, it *is* [c]a fretting leprosy in the house: it *is* unclean.

45 And he shall break down the house, the stones of it, and the timber thereof, and all the mortar of the house; and he shall carry *them* forth out of the city into an unclean place.

46 Moreover he that goeth into the house all the while that it is shut up shall be unclean until the even.

47 And he that lieth in the house shall wash his clothes; and he that eateth in the house shall wash his clothes.

48 And if the priest [o]shall come in, and look *upon it,* and, behold, the plague hath not spread in the house, after the house was plastered: then the priest shall pronounce the house clean, because the plague is healed.

49 And [d]he shall take to cleanse the house two birds, and cedar wood, and scarlet, and hyssop:

50 And he shall kill the one of the birds in an earthen vessel over running water:

51 And he shall take the cedar wood, and the hyssop, and the scarlet, and the living bird, and dip them in the blood of the slain bird, and in the running water, and sprinkle the house seven times:

52 And he shall cleanse the house with the blood of the bird, and with the running water, and with the living bird, and with the cedar wood, and with the hyssop, and with the scarlet:

53 But he shall let go the living bird out of the city into the open fields, and [e]make an atonement for the house: and it shall be clean.

54 This *is* the law for all manner of plague of leprosy, and [f]scall,

55 And for the [g]leprosy of a garment, [h]and of a house,

56 And [i]for a rising, and for a scab, and for a bright spot:

57 To [j]teach [p]when *it is* unclean, and when *it is* clean: this *is* the law of leprosy.

14:30 [y]ver. 22 ch. 15:14,15 **14:32** [z]ver:10 **14:34** [a]Gen. 17:8 Num. 32:22 Deut. 7:1 & 32:49 **14:35** [b]Ps. 91:10 Prov. 3:33 Zech. 5:4

14:44 [c]ch. 13:51 Zech. 5:4 **14:49** [d]ver. 4 **14:53** [e]ver. 20 **14:54** [f]ch. 13:30 **14:55** [g]ch. 13:47 [h]ver. 34 **14:56** [i]ch. 13:2 **14:57** [j]Deut. 24:8 Ezek. 44:23

[n] Or, *prepare* [o] Heb. *in coming in shall come in* [p] Heb. *in the day of the unclean, and in the day of the clean*

Laws about uncleanness

15 AND THE LORD spake unto Moses and to Aaron, saying,

2 Speak unto the children of Israel, and say unto them, [k]When any man hath a [q]running issue out of his flesh, *because of* his issue he *is* unclean.

3 And this shall be his uncleanness in his issue: whether his flesh run with his issue, or his flesh be stopped from his issue, it *is* his uncleanness.

4 Every bed, whereon he lieth that hath the issue, is unclean: and every [r]thing, whereon he sitteth, shall be unclean.

5 And whosoever toucheth his bed shall wash his clothes, [l]and bathe *himself* in water, and be unclean until the even.

6 And he that sitteth on *any* thing whereon he sat that hath the issue shall wash his clothes, and bathe *himself* in water, and be unclean until the even.

7 And he that toucheth the flesh of him that hath the issue shall wash his clothes, and bathe *himself* in water, and be unclean until the even.

8 And if he that hath the issue spit upon him that is clean; then he shall wash his clothes, and bathe *himself* in water, and be unclean until the even.

9 And what saddle soever he rideth upon that hath the issue shall be unclean.

10 And whosoever toucheth any thing that was under him shall be unclean until the even: and he that beareth *any of* those things shall wash his clothes, and bathe *himself* in water, and be unclean until the even.

11 And whomsoever he toucheth that hath the issue, and hath not rinsed his hands in water, he shall wash his clothes, and bathe *himself* in water, and be unclean until the even.

12 And the [m]vessel of earth, that he toucheth which hath the issue, shall be broken: and every vessel of wood shall be rinsed in water.

13 And when he that hath an issue is cleansed of his issue; then [n]he shall number to himself seven days for his cleansing, and wash his clothes, and bathe his flesh in running water, and shall be clean.

14 And on the eighth day he shall take to him [o]two turtledoves, or two young pigeons, and come before the LORD unto the door of the tabernacle of the congregation, and give them unto the priest:

15 And the priest shall offer them, [p]the one *for* a sin offering, and the other *for* a burnt offering; [q]and the priest shall make an atonement for him before the LORD for his issue.

16 And [r]if any man's seed of copulation go out from him, then he shall wash all his flesh in water, and be unclean until the even.

17 And every garment, and every skin, whereon is the seed of copulation, shall be washed with water, and be unclean until the even.

18 The woman also with whom man shall lie *with* seed of copulation, they shall *both* bathe *themselves* in water, and [s]be unclean until the even.

19 ¶ And [t]if a woman have an issue, *and* her issue in her flesh be blood, she shall be [s]put apart seven days: and whosoever toucheth her shall be unclean until the even.

20 And every thing that she lieth upon in her separation shall be unclean: every thing also that she sitteth upon shall be unclean.

21 And whosoever toucheth her bed shall wash his clothes, and bathe *himself* in water, and be unclean until the even.

22 And whosoever toucheth any thing that she sat upon shall wash his clothes, and bathe *himself* in water, and be unclean until the even.

23 And if it *be* on *her* bed, or on any thing whereon she sitteth, when he toucheth it, he shall be unclean until the even.

24 And [u]if any man lie with her at all, and her flowers be upon him, he shall be unclean seven days; and all the bed whereon he lieth shall be unclean.

15:2 [k]ch. 22:4 Num. 5:2 2 Sam. 3:29
15:5 [l]ch. 11:25 & 17:15
15:12 [m]ch. 6:28 & 11:32,33
15:13 [n]ver. 28 ch. 14:8 Num. 19:11,12
15:14 [o]ch. 14:22,23
15:15 [p]ch. 14:30,31 [q]ch. 14:19,31
15:16 [r]ch. 22:4 Deut. 23:10
15:18 [s]Ex. 19:15 1 Sam. 21:4 1 Cor. 6:18
15:19 [t]ch. 12:2
15:24 [u]See ch. 20:18

[q] Or, *running of the reins* [r] Heb. *vessel*
[s] Heb. *in her separation*

15:5 WASH HIS CLOTHES, AND BATHE. Chs. 11 – 15 show God's concern over the physical health and well-being of His people. The ancient people around them did not know anything about hygiene, sanitation, the importance of washing, or the prevention of infectious diseases, nor did they show adequate care for the poor and the sick. The laws of God promoted concern for these things and encouraged the people to treat their lives and their God as holy.

25 And if [v]a woman have an issue of her blood many days out of the time of her separation, or if it run beyond the time of her separation; all the days of the issue of her uncleanness shall be as the days of her separation: she *shall be* unclean.

26 Every bed whereon she lieth all the days of her issue shall be unto her as the bed of her separation: and whatsoever she sitteth upon shall be unclean, as the uncleanness of her separation.

27 And whosoever toucheth those things shall be unclean, and shall wash his clothes, and bathe *himself* in water, and be unclean until the even.

28 But [w]if she be cleansed of her issue, then she shall number to herself seven days, and after that she shall be clean.

29 And on the eighth day she shall take unto her two turtles, or two young pigeons, and bring them unto the priest, to the door of the tabernacle of the congregation.

30 And the priest shall offer the one *for* a sin offering, and the other *for* a burnt offering; and the priest shall make an atonement for her before the LORD for the issue of her uncleanness.

31 Thus shall ye [x]separate the children of Israel from their uncleanness; that they die not in their uncleanness, when they [y]defile my tabernacle that *is* among them.

32 [z]This *is* the law of him that hath an issue, [a]and *of him* whose seed goeth from him, and is defiled therewith;

33 [b]And of her that is sick of her flowers, and of him that hath an issue, of the man, [c]and of the woman, [d]and of him that lieth with her that is unclean.

The day of Atonement

16:2–34pp — Lev. 23:26–32; Num. 29:7–11

16 AND THE LORD spake unto Moses after [e]the death of the two sons of Aaron, when they offered before the LORD, and died;

2 And the LORD said unto Moses, Speak unto Aaron thy brother, that he [f]come not at all times into the holy *place* within the veil before the mercy seat, which *is* upon the ark; that he die not: for [g]I will appear in the cloud upon the mercy seat.

3 Thus shall Aaron [h]come into the holy *place:* [i]with a young bullock for a sin offering, and a ram for a burnt offering.

4 He shall put on [j]the holy linen coat, and he shall have the linen breeches upon his flesh, and shall be girded with a linen girdle, and with the linen mitre shall he be attired: these *are* holy garments; therefore [k]shall he wash his flesh in water, and *so* put them on.

5 And he shall take of [l]the congregation of the children of Israel two kids of the goats for a sin offering, and one ram for a burnt offering.

6 And Aaron shall offer his bullock of the sin offering, which *is* for himself, and [m]make an atonement for himself, and for his house.

7 And he shall take the two goats, and present them before the LORD *at* the door of the tabernacle of the congregation.

8 And Aaron shall cast lots upon the two goats; one lot for the LORD, and the other lot for the [t]scapegoat.

9 And Aaron shall bring the goat upon which the LORD'S lot [u]fell, and offer him *for* a sin offering.

10 But the goat, on which the lot fell to be the scapegoat, shall be presented alive before the LORD, to make [n]an atonement with him, *and* to let him go for a scapegoat into the wilderness.

11 And Aaron shall bring the bullock of the sin offering, which *is* for himself, and shall make an atonement for himself, and for his house, and shall kill the bullock of the sin offering which *is* for himself:

12 And he shall take [o]a censer full of burning coals of fire from off the altar before the LORD, and his hands full of [p]sweet incense beaten small, and bring *it* within the veil:

13 [q]And he shall put the incense upon the fire before the LORD, that the cloud of the incense may cover the

15:25 [v]Mat. 9:20 Mark 5:25 Luke 8:43
15:28 [w]ver. 13-15
15:31 [x]ch. 11:47 Deut. 24:8 Ezek. 44:23 Heb. 12:15 [y]Num. 5:3 & 19:13,20 Ezek. 5:11 & 23:38
15:32 [z]ver. 2 [a]ver. 16
15:33 [b]ver. 19 [c]ver. 25 [d]ver. 24
16:1 [e]ch. 10:1,2
16:2 [f]Ex. 30:10 ch. 23:27 Heb. 9:7 & 10:19 [g]Ex. 25:22 & 40:34 1 Ki. 8:10-12
16:3 [h]Ex. 25:21 [i]ch. 4:3
16:4 [j]Ex. 28:39,42,43 ch. 6:10 Ezek. 44:17,18 [k]Ex. 30:20 ch. 8:6,7
16:5 [l]See ch. 4:14 Num. 29:11 2 Chr. 29:21 Ezra 6:17 Ezek. 45:22,23
16:6 [m]ch. 9:7 Heb. 5:2 & 7:27,28 & 9:7
16:10 [n]1 John 2:2
16:12 [o]ch. 10:1 Num. 16:18,46 Rev. 8:5 [p]Ex. 30:34
16:13 [q]Ex. 30:7,8 Num. 16:7,18,46

[t]Heb. *Azazel* [u]Heb. *went up*

16:1–34 THE DAY OF ATONEMENT. This entire chapter describes the Day of Atonement. For comments on this important Jewish day and how the process of atonement points forward to Jesus Christ and the new covenant, see article on THE DAY OF ATONEMENT, p. 188.

[r]mercy seat that *is* upon the testimony, that he die not:

14 And [s]he shall take of the blood of the bullock, and [t]sprinkle *it* with his finger upon the mercy seat eastward; and before the mercy seat shall he sprinkle of the blood with his finger seven times.

15 ¶ [u]Then shall he kill the goat of the sin offering, that *is* for the people, and bring his blood [v]within the veil, and do with that blood as he did with the blood of the bullock, and sprinkle it upon the mercy seat, and before the mercy seat:

16 And he shall [w]make an atonement for the holy *place,* because of the uncleanness of the children of Israel, and because of their transgressions in all their sins: and so shall he do for the tabernacle of the congregation, that [v]remaineth among them in the midst of their uncleanness.

17 [x]And there shall be no man in the tabernacle of the congregation when he goeth in to make an atonement in the holy *place,* until he come out, and have made an atonement for himself, and for his household, and for all the congregation of Israel.

18 And he shall go out unto the altar that *is* before the LORD, and [y]make an atonement for it; and shall take of the blood of the bullock, and of the blood of the goat, and put *it* upon the horns of the altar round about.

19 And he shall sprinkle of the blood upon it with his finger seven times, and cleanse it, and [z]hallow it from the uncleanness of the children of Israel.

20 ¶ And when he hath made an end of [a]reconciling the holy *place,* and the tabernacle of the congregation, and the altar, he shall bring the live goat:

21 And Aaron shall lay both his hands upon the head of the live goat, and confess over him all the iniquities of the children of Israel, and all their transgressions in all their sins, [b]putting them upon the head of the goat, and shall send *him* away by the hand of [w]a fit man into the wilderness:

22 And the goat shall [c]bear upon him all their iniquities unto a land [x]not inhabited: and he shall let go the goat in the wilderness.

Deut. 26:6-9

23 And Aaron shall come into the tabernacle of the congregation, [d]and shall put off the linen garments, which he put on when he went into the holy *place,* and shall leave them there:

24 And he shall wash his flesh with water in the holy place, and put on his garments, and come forth, [e]and offer his burnt offering, and the burnt offering of the people, and make an atonement for himself, and for the people.

25 And [f]the fat of the sin offering shall he burn upon the altar.

26 And he that let go the goat for the scapegoat shall wash his clothes, [g]and bathe his flesh in water, and afterward come into the camp.

27 [h]And the bullock *for* the sin offering, and the goat *for* the sin offering, whose blood was brought in to make atonement in the holy *place,* shall *one* carry forth without the camp; and they shall burn in the fire their skins, and their flesh, and their dung.

28 And he that burneth them shall wash his clothes, and bathe his flesh in water, and afterward he shall come into the camp.

29 ¶ And *this* shall be a statute for ever unto you: *that* [i]in the seventh month, on the tenth *day* of the month, ye shall afflict your souls, and do no work at all, *whether it be* one of your own country, or a stranger that sojourneth among you:

30 For on that day shall *the priest* make an atonement for you, to [j]cleanse you, *that* ye may be clean from all your sins before the LORD.

31 [k]It *shall be* a sabbath of rest unto you, and ye shall afflict your souls, by a statute for ever.

32 [l]And the priest, whom he shall anoint, and whom he shall [m]consecrate[y] to minister in the priest's office in his father's stead, shall make the atonement, and [n]shall put on the linen clothes, *even* the holy garments:

33 And [o]he shall make an atonement for the holy sanctuary, and he shall make an atonement for the tabernacle of the congregation, and for the altar, and he shall make an atonement for the priests, and for all the people of the congregation.

34 [p]And this shall be an everlasting statute unto you, to make an atonement for the children of Israel for all their sins [q]once a year. And he did as the LORD commanded Moses.

16:13 [r]Ex. 25:21 **16:14** [s]ch. 4:5 Heb. 9:25 & 10:4 [t]ch. 4:6 **16:15** [u]Heb. 2:17 & 5:2 & 9:7,28 [v]ver. 2 Heb. 6:19 & 9:3,7,12 **16:16** [w]See Ex. 29:36 Ezek. 45:18 Heb. 9:22,23 **16:17** [x]See Ex. 34:3 Luke 1:10 **16:18** [y]Ex. 30:10 ch. 4:7,18 Heb. 9:22,23 **16:19** [z]Ezek. 43:20 **16:20** [a]ver. 16 Ezek. 45:20 **16:21** [b]Is. 53:6 **16:22** [c]Is. 53:11,12 John 1:29 Heb. 9:28 1 Pet. 2:24 **16:23** [d]Ezek. 42:14 & 44:19

16:24 [e]ver. 3,5 **16:25** [f]ch. 4:10 **16:26** [g]ch. 15:5 **16:27** [h]ch. 4:12,21 & 6:30 Heb. 13:11 **16:29** [i]Ex. 30:10 ch. 23:27 Num. 29:7 **16:30** [j]Jer. 33:8 Eph. 5:26 Heb. 9:13,14 & 10:1,2 1 John 1:7,9 **16:31** [k]ch. 23:32 **16:32** [l]ch. 4:3,5,16 [m]Ex. 29:29,30 Num. 20:26,28 [n]ver. 4 **16:33** [o]ver. 6,16-18,24 **16:34** [p]ch. 23:31 Num. 29:7 [q]Ex. 30:10 Heb. 9:7,25

[v]Heb. *dwelleth* [w]Heb. *a man of opportunity*
[x]Heb. *of separation* [y]Heb. *fill his hand*

Laws about special sacrifices

17 AND THE LORD spake unto Moses, saying,
2 Speak unto Aaron, and unto his
sons, and unto all the children of Israel, and say unto them; This *is* the thing
which the LORD hath commanded, saying,
3 What man soever *there be* of the
house of Israel, [r]that killeth an ox, or
lamb, or goat, in the camp, or that
killeth *it* out of the camp,
4 [s]And bringeth it not unto the
door of the tabernacle of the congregation, to offer an offering unto the LORD
before the tabernacle of the LORD; blood
shall be [t]imputed unto that man; he
hath shed blood; and that man [u]shall
be cut off from among his people:
5 To the end that the children of Israel may bring their sacrifices, [v]which
they offer in the open field, even that
they may bring them unto the LORD,
unto the door of the tabernacle of the
congregation, unto the priest, and offer
them *for* peace offerings unto the LORD.
6 And the priest [w]shall sprinkle
the blood upon the altar of the LORD *at*
the door of the tabernacle of the congregation, and [x]burn the fat for a
sweet savour unto the LORD.
7 And they shall no more offer their
sacrifices [y]unto devils, after whom
they [z]have gone a-whoring. This shall
be a statute for ever unto them
throughout their generations.
8 ¶ And thou shalt say unto them,
Whatsoever man *there be* of the house
of Israel, or of the strangers which sojourn among you, [a]that offereth a
burnt offering or sacrifice,
9 And bringeth it not unto the door
of the tabernacle of the congregation,
to offer it unto the LORD; even that man
shall be cut off from among his people.
10 ¶ [b]And whatsoever man *there be*
of the house of Israel, or of the strangers that sojourn among you, that
eateth any manner of blood; [c]I will
even set my face against that soul that
eateth blood, and will cut him off from
among his people.
11 For the life of the flesh *is* in the
blood: and I have given it to you upon
the altar [d]to make an atonement for
your souls: for [e]it *is* the blood *that*
maketh an atonement for the soul.
12 Therefore I said unto the children of Israel, No soul of you shall eat
blood, neither shall any stranger that
sojourneth among you eat blood.
13 And whatsoever man *there be* of
the children of Israel, or of the strangers that sojourn among you, [z]which
[f]hunteth and catcheth any beast or
fowl that may be eaten; he shall even
[g]pour out the blood thereof, and
[h]cover it with dust.
14 [i]For *it is* the life of all flesh; the
blood of it *is* for the life thereof: therefore I said unto the children of Israel,
Ye shall eat the blood of no manner of
flesh: for the life of all flesh *is* the blood
thereof: whosoever eateth it shall be
cut off.
15 [j]And every soul that eateth
[a]that which died *of itself*, or that
which was torn *with beasts, whether it be*
one of your own country, or a stranger,
[k]he shall both wash his clothes, [l]and
bathe *himself* in water, and be unclean
until the even: then shall he be clean.
16 But if he wash *them* not, nor
bathe his flesh; then [m]he shall bear his
iniquity.

Unlawful sexual relations

18 AND THE LORD spake unto Moses, saying,
2 Speak unto the children of Israel,

[z] Heb. *that hunteth any hunting* [a] Heb. *a carcase*

17:3 [r]See Deut. 12:5, 15,21 **17:4** [s]Deut. 12:5,6,13, 14 [t]Rom. 5:13 [u]Gen. 17:14 **17:5** [v]Gen. 21:33 & 22:2 & 31:54 Deut. 12:2 **17:6** [w]ch. 3:2 [x]Ex. 29:18 Num. 18:17 **17:7** [y]Deut. 32:17 2 Chr. 11:15 1 Cor. 10:20 [z]Ex. 34:15 Deut. 31:16 Ezek. 23:8 **17:8** [a]ch. 1:2,3 **17:10** [b]Gen. 9:4 Deut. 12:16,23 & 15:23 1 Sam. 14:33 [c]ch. 20:3,5,6 **17:11** [d]Mat. 26:28 Rom. 3:25 Eph. 1:7 Col. 1:14,20 1 Pet. 1:2 1 John 1:7 [e]Heb. 9:22 **17:13** [f]ch. 7:26 [g]Deut. 12:16,24 [h]Ezek. 24:7 **17:14** [i]ver. 11,12 Gen. 9:4 Deut. 12:23 **17:15** [j]Ex. 22:31 Ezek. 4:14 & 44:31 [k]ch. 11:25 [l]ch. 15:5 **17:16** [m]ch. 5:1

17:7 UNTO DEVILS. The word translated "devils" is literally "hairy ones" and probably refers to goat idols. Evidently during the time of Moses, Israel offered sacrifices to desert demons in order to secure their help or their favor. This kind of action represented spiritual unfaithfulness to the Lord God and was strictly forbidden.

17:11 THE LIFE OF THE FLESH *IS* IN THE BLOOD. This passage gives the reason for the shedding of the blood of a sacrificial animal and its meaning for atonement. The blood of the animal was identified with its life (v. 14); thus the blood atoned for human sin at the price of life. In other words, human beings did not have to give their lives for sin because the animal's life was payment in their place (see article on THE DAY OF ATONEMENT, p. 188). This principle of substitutionary atonement by the blood of another helps us understand the importance of the blood of Christ in receiving our salvation under the new covenant. As Jesus Christ shed His blood on the cross, He substituted His life for the sinner's life (Rom. 5:1). Since His life was without sin and perfect before God, His blood is of infinite worth and results in perfect salvation for all who accept and follow Him (cf. Col. 1:14; Heb. 9:13–14; 1 John 1:7; Rev. 7:14).

THE DAY OF ATONEMENT

***Lev. 16:33** "And he shall make an atonement for the holy sanctuary, and he shall make an atonement for the tabernacle of the congregation, and for the altar, and he shall make an atonement for the priests, and for all the people of the congregation."*

THE NEED FOR ATONEMENT. The word "atonement" (Heb. *kippurim*, from *kaphar*, meaning "to cover over") has the idea of covering over sin by making an equivalent payment (i.e., a "ransom"), so that adequate recompense is made for the offense (note the "ransom" principle in Ex. 30:12; Num. 35:31; Ps. 49:7; Is. 43:3).

(1) The need for atonement arose from the fact that Israel's sin (Lev. 16:30), if not atoned for, would subject them to the wrath of God (cf. Rom. 1:18; Col. 3:6; 1 Thes. 2:16). Thus the purpose of the Day of Atonement was to provide a comprehensive sacrifice for all sins that may not have been atoned for in the sacrifices offered throughout the preceding year. Thereby the people would be cleansed from their sins of the past year, avert God's wrath toward them, and maintain God's fellowship with them (Lev. 16:30–34; Heb. 9:7).

(2) Because God desired to save Israel, forgive their sins, and reconcile them to Himself, He furnished a way of salvation by accepting in their place the death of an innocent life (i.e., the animal that was sacrificed). This animal bore their guilt and penalty (Lev. 17:11; cf. Is. 53:4,6,11) and covered over their sins by its shed blood.

THE RITUAL OF THE DAY OF ATONEMENT. Lev. 16 describes the Day of Atonement, the most important holy day of the Jewish year. On this day the high priest, clad in sacred garments, first prepared himself with special cleansings. Then, before making atonement for the sins of the people, he had to offer a bullock for his own sins. Next he took two goats and cast lots: one became the sacrifice, the other became the scapegoat (Lev. 16:8). He killed the first goat, took its blood, entered the holy place behind the veil, and sprinkled the blood on the mercy seat, thus placing the blood between God and the tablets of the law which were under the mercy seat (laws which they had broken but now were covered by the blood); in this way atonement was made for the sins of the entire nation (Lev. 16:15–16). As a final step he took the live goat, laid his hands on its head, confessed over it all the iniquities and transgressions of the Israelites, and sent it away into the wilderness, symbolizing that their sins were being carried out of the camp to disappear in the wilderness (Lev. 16:21–22).

(1) The Day of Atonement was to be a solemn assembly, a day in which the people fasted and humbled themselves before the Lord (Lev. 16:31); this response emphasized the seriousness of sin and the fact that the atoning work of God was effective only for those who had a repentant heart and a persevering faith (cf. Lev. 23:27; Num. 15:30; 29:7).

(2) The Day of Atonement accomplished atonement for all sins and transgressions not atoned for during the previous year (Lev. 16:16,21). It had to be repeated every year in the same manner.

CHRIST AND THE DAY OF ATONEMENT. The Day of Atonement is replete with symbolism that points to the work of our Lord and Savior Jesus Christ. In the N.T., the author of Hebrews emphasizes the new covenant fulfillment of the typology of the Day of Atonement ritual (see Heb. 9:6—10:18; see article on CHRIST IN THE OLD TESTAMENT, p. 562).

(1) The fact that the O.T. sacrificial rituals had to be repeated annually indicates that there was something temporary about them. They pointed ahead to the time when Christ would come to take away permanently all confessed sin (cf. Heb. 9:28; 10:10–18).

(2) The two goats represent the atonement, forgiveness, reconciliation, and cleansing accomplished by Christ. The slain goat represents His substitutionary and sacrificial death for sinners as payment for sins (Rom. 3:24–26; Heb. 9:11–12,24–26). The scapegoat, sent away bearing the sins of the nation, typifies Christ's sacrifice which removes sin and guilt from all those who repent (Ps. 103:12; Is. 53:6,11–12; John 1:29; Heb. 9:26).

(3) The sacrifices on the Day of Atonement provided a "covering over" of sin, *not* a taking away of sin. Christ's blood shed on the cross, however, is God's ultimate atonement for humankind and takes away sin permanently (cf. Heb. 10:4,10–11). Christ as the perfect sacrifice (Heb. 9:26; 10:5–10) paid the full penalty for our sins (Rom. 3:25–26; 6:23; Gal. 3:13; 2 Cor. 5:21) and effected the propitiation that turns away the wrath of God, reconciles us with Him, and renews our fellowship with Him (Rom. 5:6–11; 2 Cor. 5:18–19; 1 Pet. 1:18–19; 1 John 2:2).

(4) The holy place where the high priest entered with the blood to make atonement represents God's throne in heaven; Christ entered this heavenly holy of holies after His death, bearing His own blood to make atonement for the believer before the throne of God (Ex. 30:10; Heb. 9:7–8,11–12,24–28).

(5) The mercy seat on which the high priest sprinkled the blood emphasizes that the forgiveness of sins is possible only by God's grace and mercy, not because of any work that we have done (Eph. 2:8–10).

(6) Since animal sacrifices were a type of Christ's perfect sacrifice and found their fulfillment in Christ's sacrifice of Himself, there is no more need for animal sacrifices after His death on Calvary (Heb. 9:12–18).

and say unto them, [n]I am the LORD your God.

3 [o]After the doings of the land of Egypt, wherein ye dwelt, shall ye not do: and [p]after the doings of the land of Canaan, whither I bring you, shall ye not do: neither shall ye walk in their ordinances.

4 [q]Ye shall do my judgments, and keep mine ordinances, to walk therein: I *am* the LORD your God.

5 Ye shall therefore keep my statutes, and my judgments: [r]which if a man do, he shall live in them: [s]I *am* the LORD.

Deut. 7:1-6

6 ¶ None of you shall approach to any that is [b]near of kin to him, to uncover *their* nakedness: I *am* the LORD.

7 [t]The nakedness of thy father, or the nakedness of thy mother, shalt thou not uncover: she *is* thy mother; thou shalt not uncover her nakedness.

8 [u]The nakedness of thy father's wife shalt thou not uncover: it *is* thy father's nakedness.

9 [v]The nakedness of thy sister, the daughter of thy father, or daughter of thy mother, *whether she be* born at home, or born abroad, *even* their nakedness thou shalt not uncover.

10 The nakedness of thy son's daughter, or of thy daughter's daughter, *even* their nakedness thou shalt not uncover: for theirs *is* thine own nakedness.

11 The nakedness of thy father's wife's daughter, begotten of thy father, she *is* thy sister, thou shalt not uncover her nakedness.

12 [w]Thou shalt not uncover the nakedness of thy father's sister: she *is* thy father's near kinswoman.

13 Thou shalt not uncover the nakedness of thy mother's sister: for she *is* thy mother's near kinswoman.

14 [x]Thou shalt not uncover the nakedness of thy father's brother, thou shalt not approach to his wife: she *is* thine aunt.

15 [y]Thou shalt not uncover the nakedness of thy daughter-in-law: she *is* thy son's wife; thou shalt not uncover her nakedness.

16 [z]Thou shalt not uncover the nakedness of thy brother's wife: it *is* thy brother's nakedness.

17 [a]Thou shalt not uncover the nakedness of a woman and her daughter, neither shalt thou take her son's daughter, or her daughter's daughter, to uncover her nakedness; *for* they *are* her near kinswomen: it *is* wickedness.

18 Neither shalt thou take [c]a wife to her sister, [b]to vex *her,* to uncover her nakedness, beside the other in her life *time.*

19 [c]Also thou shalt not approach unto a woman to uncover her nakedness, as long as she is put apart for her uncleanness.

20 Moreover [d]thou shalt not lie carnally with thy neighbour's wife, to defile thyself with her.

21 And thou shalt not let any of thy seed [e]pass through *the fire* to [f]Molech, neither shalt thou [g]profane the name of thy God: I *am* the LORD.

22 [h]Thou shalt not lie with mankind, as with womankind: it *is* abomination.

23 [i]Neither shalt thou lie with any beast to defile thyself therewith: neither shall any woman stand before a

18:2 [n]Ex. 6:7 Ezek. 20:5,7,19, 20
18:3 [o]Ezek. 20:7 [p]Ex. 23:24
18:4 [q]Ezek. 20:19
18:5 [r]Ezek. 20:11,13, 21 Rom. 10:5 Gal. 3:12 [s]Ex. 6:2,6
18:7 [t]ch. 20:11
18:8 [u]Gen. 49:4 ch. 20:11 1 Cor. 5:1
18:9 [v]ch. 20:17
18:12 [w]ch. 20:19
18:14 [x]ch. 20:20
18:15 [y]Gen. 38:18,26
18:16 [z]See Deut. 25:5
18:17 [a]ch. 20:14
18:18 [b]1 Sam. 1:6,8
18:19 [c]ch. 20:18 Ezek. 18:6 & 22:10
18:20 [d]Ex. 20:14 ch. 20:10 Deut. 5:18 & 22:22 Mat. 5:27 Rom. 2:22 1 Cor. 6:9 Heb. 13:4
18:21 [e]ch. 20:2 2 Ki. 16:3 [f]1 Ki. 11:7,33 Called Acts 7:43, *Moloch* [g]ch. 19:12 & 20:3 Ezek. 36:20
18:22 [h]ch. 20:13 1 Cor. 6:9 1 Tim. 1:10
18:23 [i]Ex. 22:19

[b] Heb. *remainder of his flesh*   [c] Or, one *wife to another*

18:3 NEITHER SHALL YE WALK IN THEIR ORDINANCES. The people of God have always been tempted to accept the practices and standards of morality of the society to which they belong. Therefore, God commands His people to make His word the only standard by which to judge right and wrong. We must never conform to the surrounding society and accept its way of life. God must be the sole source and standard for all human moral and spiritual conduct (see article on SPIRITUAL SEPARATION FOR BELIEVERS, p. 1814).

18:6 UNCOVER *THEIR* NAKEDNESS. This phrase has general sexual connotations but does not necessarily mean consummated sex acts (see vv. 6–17). Any kind of sexual activity involving the uncovering of, exposing of, or looking at the nakedness of a person other than a lawful husband or wife (cf. 20:17) oversteps the boundaries of purity and is a serious sin before God (see article on STANDARDS OF SEXUAL MORALITY, p. 1964).

18:21 PASS THROUGH *THE FIRE.* The Canaanites sacrificed infants to their gods as part of their religious rites. This detestable practice was strictly forbidden by God (cf. 20:2–5; Jer. 32:35). Today the practice of killing unborn children for the sake of convenience or as a form of birth control is an equally detestable sin and an abomination to God.

18:22 IT *IS* ABOMINATION. Sexual activity with a person of the same sex (i.e., sodomy, see Gen. 19:5, note) is said to be an abomination to the Lord. In other words, this act is especially detestable and repugnant to Him (see Rom. 1:27, note).

beast to lie down thereto: it *is* [j]confu-
sion.
24 [k]Defile not ye yourselves in any
of these things: [l]for in all these the
nations are defiled which I cast out be-
fore you:
25 And [m]the land is defiled: there-
fore I do [n]visit the iniquity thereof
upon it, and the land itself vomiteth out
her inhabitants.
26 [o]Ye shall therefore keep my
statutes and my judgments, and shall
not commit *any* of these abominations;
neither any of your own nation, nor any
stranger that sojourneth among you:
27 (For all these abominations have
the men of the land done, which *were*
before you, and the land is defiled;)
28 That [p]the land spew not you out
also, when ye defile it, as it spewed out
the nations that *were* before you.
29 For whosoever shall commit any
of these abominations, even the souls
that commit *them* shall be cut off from
among their people.
30 Therefore shall ye keep mine or-
dinance, [q]that *ye* commit not *any one*
of these abominable customs, which
were committed before you, and that
ye defile not yourselves therein: I *am*
the LORD your God.

Personal conduct

19 AND THE LORD spake unto Mo-
ses, saying,
2 Speak unto all the congregation of
the children of Israel, and say unto
them, [r]Ye shall be holy: for I the LORD
your God *am* holy.
3 ¶ [s]Ye shall fear every man his
mother, and his father, and [t]keep my
sabbaths: I *am* the LORD your God.
4 ¶ [u]Turn ye not unto idols, [v]nor
make to yourselves molten gods: I *am*
the LORD your God.
5 ¶ And [w]if ye offer a sacrifice of
peace offerings unto the LORD, ye shall
offer it at your own will.
6 It shall be eaten the same day ye
offer it, and on the morrow: and if
aught remain until the third day, it
shall be burnt in the fire.
7 And if it be eaten at all on the
third day, it *is* abominable; it shall not
be accepted.
8 Therefore *every one* that eateth it
shall bear his iniquity, because he hath
profaned the hallowed thing of the
LORD: and that soul shall be cut off from
among his people.
9 ¶ And [x]when ye reap the harvest
of your land, thou shalt not wholly reap
the corners of thy field, neither shalt
thou gather the gleanings of thy har-
vest.
10 And thou shalt not glean thy
vineyard, neither shalt thou gather *ev-
ery* grape of thy vineyard; thou shalt
leave them for the poor and stranger:
I *am* the LORD your God.
11 ¶ [y]Ye shall not steal, neither
deal falsely, [z]neither lie one to an-
other.
12 ¶ And ye shall not [a]swear by my
name falsely, [b]neither shalt thou pro-
fane the name of thy God: I *am* the
LORD.
13 ¶ [c]Thou shalt not defraud thy
neighbour, neither rob *him:* [d]the
wages of him that is hired shall not
abide with thee all night until the
morning.
14 ¶ Thou shalt not curse the deaf,
[e]nor put a stumblingblock before the
blind, but shalt fear thy God: I *am* the
LORD.
15 ¶ Ye shall do no unrighteousness
in judgment: thou shalt not respect the
person of the poor, nor honour the per-
son of the mighty: *but* in righteousness
shalt thou judge thy neighbour.
16 ¶ [f]Thou shalt not go up and
down *as* a talebearer among thy peo-
ple: neither shalt thou [g]stand against
the blood of thy neighbour: I *am* the
LORD.
17 ¶ [h]Thou shalt not hate thy
brother in thine heart: [i]thou shalt in
any wise rebuke thy neighbour, [d]and
not suffer sin upon him.
18 ¶ [j]Thou shalt not avenge, nor
bear any grudge against the children of

18:23 [j]ch. 20:12
18:24 [k]Mat. 15:18-20 1 Cor. 3:17 [l]Deut. 18:12
18:25 [m]Num. 35:34 Ezek. 36:17 [n]Is. 26:21 Jer. 5:9
18:26 [o]ver. 5,30
18:28 [p]Jer. 9:19
18:30 [q]ver. 3
19:2 [r]ch. 11:44
19:3 [s]Ex. 20:12 [t]Ex. 20:8
19:4 [u]Ex. 20:4 [v]Ex. 34:17
19:5 [w]ch. 7:16
19:9 [x]Deut. 24:19
19:11 [y]Ex. 20:15 [z]Eph. 4:25
19:12 [a]Ex. 20:7 Deut. 5:11 Mat. 5:33 Jas. 5:12 [b]ch. 18:21
19:13 [c]Mark 10:19 [d]Mal. 3:5
19:14 [e]Deut 27:18
19:16 [f]Ex. 23:1 [g]Ex. 23:1,7 1 Ki. 21:13
19:17 [h]1 John 2:9,11 & 3:15 [i]Mat. 18:15 Eph. 5:11 1 Tim. 5:20
19:18 [j]Rom. 12:17,19

[d] Or, *that thou bear not sin for him*

19:2 YE SHALL BE HOLY. Because God's people must be like Him, He calls them to manifest and express His divine nature by being separate from the ungodly customs and sins of the surrounding nations and by serving Him in love and righteousness (see 11:44, note). This call to holiness was first given to Adam and Eve, who were created in God's image in order to reflect God's character (Gen. 1:26). Every generation of believers should be "followers of God" (Eph. 5:1) and "be holy: for I the LORD your God *am* holy" (cf. Mat. 5:48; Rom. 12:1–2; see articles on SANCTIFICATION, p. 1982, and SPIRITUAL SEPARATION FOR BELIEVERS, p. 1814).

19:18 LOVE THY NEIGHBOUR. "Neighbour" refers to anyone we come into contact with, not

thy people, [k]but thou shalt love thy neighbour as thyself: I *am* the LORD.

19 ¶ Ye shall keep my statutes. Thou shalt not let thy cattle gender with a diverse kind: [l]thou shalt not sow thy field with mingled seed: [m]neither shall a garment mingled of linen and woollen come upon thee.

20 ¶ And whosoever lieth carnally with a woman, that *is* a bondmaid, [e][f]betrothed to an husband, and not at all redeemed, nor freedom given her; [g][h]she shall be scourged; they shall not be put to death, because she was not free.

21 And [n]he shall bring his trespass offering unto the LORD, unto the door of the tabernacle of the congregation, *even* a ram for a trespass offering.

22 And the priest shall make an atonement for him with the ram of the trespass offering before the LORD for his sin which he hath done: and the sin which he hath done shall be forgiven him.

23 ¶ And when ye shall come into the land, and shall have planted all manner of trees for food, then ye shall count the fruit thereof as uncircumcised: three years shall it be as uncircumcised unto you: it shall not be eaten of.

24 But in the fourth year all the fruit thereof shall be [i]holy [o]to praise the LORD *withal.*

25 And in the fifth year shall ye eat of the fruit thereof, that it may yield unto you the increase thereof: I *am* the LORD your God.

26 ¶ [p]Ye shall not eat *any thing* with the blood: [q]neither shall ye use enchantment, nor observe times.

27 [r]Ye shall not round the corners of your heads, neither shalt thou mar the corners of thy beard.

28 Ye shall not [s]make any cuttings in your flesh for the dead, nor print any marks upon you: I *am* the LORD.

29 ¶ [t]Do not [j]prostitute thy daughter, to cause her to be a whore; lest the land fall to whoredom, and the land become full of wickedness.

30 ¶ [u]Ye shall keep my sabbaths, and [v]reverence my sanctuary: I *am* the LORD.

31 ¶ [w]Regard not them that have familiar spirits, neither seek after wizards, to be defiled by them: I *am* the LORD your God.

32 ¶ [x]Thou shalt rise up before the hoary head, and honour the face of the old man, and [y]fear thy God: I *am* the LORD.

33 ¶ And [z]if a stranger sojourn with thee in your land, ye shall not [k]vex him.

34 [a]*But* the stranger that dwelleth with you shall be unto you as one born among you, and [b]thou shalt love him as thyself; for ye were strangers in the land of Egypt: I *am* the LORD your God.

35 ¶ [c]Ye shall do no unrighteousness in judgment, in meteyard, in weight, or in measure.

36 [d]Just balances, just [l]weights, a just ephah, and a just hin, shall ye have: I *am* the LORD your God, which brought you out of the land of Egypt.

37 [e]Therefore shall ye observe all my statutes, and all my judgments, and do them: I *am* the LORD.

19:18 [k]Mat. 5:43
19:19 [l]Deut. 22:9,10 [m]Deut. 22:11
19:21 [n]ch. 5:15
19:24 [o]Deut. 12:17,18 Prov. 3:9
19:26 [p]ch. 17:10 [q]Deut. 18:10,11, 14 1 Sam. 15:23 2 Chr. 33:6 Mal. 3:5
19:27 [r]ch. 21:5 Is. 15:2 Jer. 9:26
19:28 [s]Jer. 16:6
19:29 [t]Deut. 23:17
19:30 [u]ver. 3 ch. 26:2 [v]Eccl. 5:1
19:31 [w]Ex. 22:18 Is. 8:19 Acts 16:16
19:32 [x]1 Tim. 5:1 [y]ver. 14
19:33 [z]Ex. 22:21
19:34 [a]Ex. 12:48 [b]Deut. 10:19
19:35 [c]ver. 15
19:36 [d]Deut. 25:13,15
19:37 [e]ch. 18:4,5 Deut. 4:5,6 & 5:1 & 6:25

[e] Or, *abused by any for man* [f] Heb. *reproached by,* or, [g] Or, *they* [h] Heb. *there shall be a scourging* [i] Heb. *holiness of praises to the LORD* [j] Heb. *profane* [k] Or, *oppress* [l] Heb. *stones*

just someone who lives near us. This commandment regulating Israel's treatment of others was cited by Christ (Mat. 22:39), Paul (Rom. 13:9), and James (Jas. 2:8). Vv. 9–18 describe practical ways for us to show love and care for our neighbors.

19:19 LINEN AND WOOLEN. Some of the laws in Leviticus applied only to Israel under the old covenant (e.g., vv. 19–25), while others are still applicable for those under the new covenant (e.g., vv. 11–18,26,31; see Mat. 5:17, note). Regarding the former, some were given in order to keep the Israelites from participating in the pagan practices of their surrounding cultures. For example, the prohibition regarding the mixing of two kinds of material may have been based on the fact that pagan priests attempted to practice sorcery by mixing different types of fabrics into their garments. The verse as a whole addresses the principle of purity without mixture.

19:31 FAMILIAR SPIRITS ... WIZARDS. This refers to mediums or spiritists who sought to contact the dead for the purpose of obtaining prophetic knowledge. Any who transgress God's commands by turning to spiritists are in reality dealing with Satan and demons (20:6; Deut. 18:10–11).

19:34 LOVE HIM AS THYSELF. Loving one's neighbor includes loving strangers (foreigners, resident aliens) who come to live in one's community. Jesus emphasizes the same thing in the parable of the Good Samaritan (Luke 10:25–37). God Himself loved His people while they were foreigners, and He expects us to do the same. He is the kind of God who wants to bless all the nations of the world (Gen. 12:3; John 3:16).

Punishments for sin

20 AND THE LORD spake unto Moses, saying,

2 [f]Again, thou shalt say to the children of Israel, [g]Whosoever *he be* of the children of Israel, or of the strangers that sojourn in Israel, that giveth *any* of his seed unto Molech; he shall surely be put to death: the people of the land shall stone him with stones.

3 And [h]I will set my face against that man, and will cut him off from among his people; because he hath given of his seed unto Molech, to [i]defile my sanctuary, and [j]to profane my holy name.

4 And if the people of the land do any ways hide their eyes from the man, when he giveth of his seed unto Molech, and [k]kill him not:

5 Then [l]I will set my face against that man, and [m]against his family, and will cut him off, and all that [n]go a-whoring after him, to commit whoredom with Molech, from among their people.

6 ¶ And [o]the soul that turneth after such as have familiar spirits, and after wizards, to go a-whoring after them, I will even set my face against that soul, and will cut him off from among his people.

7 ¶ [p]Sanctify yourselves therefore, and be ye holy: for I *am* the LORD your God.

8 [q]And ye shall keep my statutes, and do them: [r]I *am* the LORD which sanctify you.

9 ¶ [s]For every one that curseth his father or his mother shall be surely put to death: he hath cursed his father or his mother; [t]his blood *shall be* upon him.

10 ¶ And [u]the man that committeth adultery with *another* man's wife, *even he* that committeth adultery with his neighbour's wife, the adulterer and the adulteress shall surely be put to death.

11 [v]And the man that lieth with his father's wife hath uncovered his father's nakedness: both of them shall surely be put to death; their blood *shall be* upon them.

12 [w]And if a man lie with his daughter-in-law, both of them shall surely be put to death: [x]they have wrought confusion; their blood *shall be* upon them.

13 [y]If a man also lie with mankind, as he lieth with a woman, both of them have committed an abomination: they shall surely be put to death; their blood *shall be* upon them.

14 [z]And if a man take a wife and her mother, it *is* wickedness: they shall be burnt with fire, both he and they; that there be no wickedness among you.

15 [a]And if a man lie with a beast, he shall surely be put to death: and ye shall slay the beast.

16 And if a woman approach unto any beast, and lie down thereto, thou shalt kill the woman, and the beast: they shall surely be put to death; their blood *shall be* upon them.

17 [b]And if a man shall take his sister, his father's daughter, or his mother's daughter, and see her nakedness, and she see his nakedness; it *is* a wicked thing; and they shall be cut off in the sight of their people; he hath uncovered his sister's nakedness; he shall bear his iniquity.

18 [c]And if a man shall lie with a woman having her sickness, and shall uncover her nakedness; he hath [m]discovered her fountain, and she hath uncovered the fountain of her blood: and both of them shall be cut off from among their people.

19 [d]And thou shalt not uncover the nakedness of thy mother's sister, nor of thy father's sister: [e]for he uncovereth his near kin: they shall bear their iniquity.

20 [f]And if a man shall lie with his uncle's wife, he hath uncovered his uncle's nakedness: they shall bear their sin; they shall die childless.

21 [g]And if a man shall take his brother's wife, it *is* [n]an unclean thing: he hath uncovered his brother's nakedness; they shall be childless.

22 ¶ Ye shall therefore keep all my [h]statutes, and all my judgments, and do them: that the land, whither I bring you to dwell therein, [i]spew you not out.

23 [j]And ye shall not walk in the manners of the nation, which I cast out before you: for they committed all these things, and [k]therefore I abhorred them.

24 But [l]I have said unto you, Ye shall inherit their land, and I will give

20:2 [f]ch. 18:2 [g]ch. 18:21 2 Ki. 23:10 2 Chr. 33:6 Jer. 7:31
20:3 [h]ch. 17:10 [i]Ezek. 5:11 & 23:38,39 [j]ch. 18:21
20:4 [k]Deut. 17:2,3,5
20:5 [l]ch. 17:10 [m]Ex. 20:5 [n]ch. 17:7
20:6 [o]ch. 19:31
20:7 [p]ch. 19:2
20:8 [q]ch. 19:37 [r]Ex. 31:13
20:9 [s]Ex. 21:17 Deut. 27:16 Prov. 20:20 Mat. 15:4 [t]ver. 11,12,13,16, 27 2 Sam. 1:16
20:10 [u]ch. 18:20 Deut. 22:22
20:11 [v]ch. 18:8 Deut. 27:23
20:12 [w]ch. 18:15 [x]ch. 18:23
20:13 [y]ch. 18:22 Deut. 23:17 Gen. 19:5 Judg. 19:22
20:14 [z]ch. 18:17 Deut. 27:23
20:15 [a]ch. 18:23 Deut. 27:21
20:17 [b]ch. 18:9 Deut. 27:22 Gen. 20:12
20:18 [c]ch. 15:24
20:19 [d]ch. 18:12 [e]ch. 18:6
20:20 [f]ch. 18:14
20:21 [g]ch. 18:16
20:22 [h]ch. 18:26 & 19:37 [i]ch. 18:25
20:23 [j]ch. 18:3,24 [k]ch. 18:27 Deut. 9:5
20:24 [l]Ex. 3:17 & 6:8

[m]Heb. *made naked* [n]Heb. *a separation*

it unto you to possess it, a land that floweth with milk and honey: I *am* the LORD your God, [m]which have separated you from *other* people.

25 [n]Ye shall therefore put difference between clean beasts and unclean, and between unclean fowls and clean: [o]and ye shall not make your souls abominable by beast, or by fowl, or by any manner of living thing that [o]creepeth on the ground, which I have separated from you as unclean.

Deut. 10:12-13

26 And ye shall be holy unto me: [p]for I the LORD *am* holy, and have severed you from *other* people, that ye should be mine.

27 ¶ [q]A man also or woman that hath a familiar spirit, or that is a wizard, shall surely be put to death: they shall stone them with stones: [r]their blood *shall be* upon them.

The sanctity of the priesthood

21 AND THE LORD said unto Moses, Speak unto the priests the sons of Aaron, and say unto them, [s]There shall none be defiled for the dead among his people:

2 But for his kin, that is near unto him, *that is,* for his mother, and for his father, and for his son, and for his daughter, and for his brother,

3 And for his sister a virgin, that is nigh unto him, which hath had no husband; for her may he be defiled.

4 *But* [p]he shall not defile himself, *being* a chief man among his people, to profane himself.

5 [t]They shall not make baldness upon their head, neither shall they shave off the corner of their beard, nor make any cuttings in their flesh.

6 They shall be holy unto their God, and [u]not profane the name of their God: for the offerings of the LORD made by fire, *and* the bread of their God, they do offer: therefore they shall be holy.

7 [v]They shall not take a wife *that is* a whore, or profane; neither shall they take a woman [w]put away from her husband: for he *is* holy unto his God.

8 Thou shalt sanctify him therefore; for he offereth the bread of thy God: he shall be holy unto thee: for I the LORD, which sanctify you, *am* holy.

9 ¶ [x]And the daughter of any priest, if she profane herself by playing the whore, she profaneth her father: she shall be burnt with fire.

10 [y]And *he that is* the high priest among his brethren, upon whose head the anointing oil was poured, and [z]that is consecrated to put on the garments, [a]shall not uncover his head, nor rend his clothes;

11 Neither shall he [b]go in to any dead body, nor defile himself for his father, or for his mother;

12 [c]Neither shall he go out of the sanctuary, nor profane the sanctuary of his God; for [d]the crown of the anointing oil of his God *is* upon him: I *am* the LORD.

13 And [e]he shall take a wife in her virginity.

14 A widow, or a divorced woman, or profane, *or* an harlot, these shall he not take: but he shall take a virgin of his own people to wife.

15 Neither shall he profane his seed among his people: for [f]I the LORD do sanctify him.

16 ¶ And the LORD spake unto Moses, saying,

20:24 [m]ver. 26 Ex. 19:5 & 33:16 Deut. 7:6 & 14:2 1 Ki. 8:53 **20:25** [n]ch. 11:47 Deut. 14:4 [o]ch. 11:43 **20:26** [p]ver. 7 ch. 19:2 1 Pet. 1:16 **20:27** [q]ch. 19:31 [r]ver. 9 **21:1** [s]Ezek. 44:25 **21:5** [t]ch. 19:27 **21:6** [u]ch. 18:21 & 19:12 **21:7** [v]Ezek. 44:22 [w]See Deut. 24:1,2 **21:9** [x]Gen. 38:24 **21:10** [y]Ex. 29:29 ch. 8:12 [z]Ex. 28:2 ch. 16:32 [a]ch. 10:6 **21:11** [b]Num. 19:14 **21:12** [c]ch. 10:7 [d]Ex. 28:36 ch. 8:9,12,30 **21:13** [e]ver. 7 Ezek. 44:22 **21:15** [f]ver. 8

o Or, *moveth* p Or, *being an husband among his people, he shall not defile himself* for his wife; see Ezek. 24:16,17

21:1 THE PRIESTS. Ch. 21 deals with the qualifications and high standards for those who were to serve as ministers of God's people. They were to be examples of godliness both in their ceremonial duties and in their personal character and deeds; consequently, God placed upon them a higher standard than was required for membership in the covenant people of God.

21:6 HOLY UNTO THEIR GOD. Priests were to be separated from all ungodly customs and to live blameless lives that conformed to God's will. Failure to do so would "profane the name of their God" (to "profane" means to desecrate the name of the Lord and to deprive it of its holiness). This principle of holiness is continued in the new covenant, for God desires only those who live holy and righteous lives before God's people to be His chosen overseers (1 Tim. 3:1–7; see 4:12, note).

21:7 NOT TAKE A WIFE . . . A WHORE. Priests were forbidden to marry women who had been immoral or even those who had been divorced; they were to marry only virgins or widows of priests (cf. vv. 13–15; Ezek. 44:22). Through this law God revealed that His spiritual leaders were expected to serve as examples of God's highest ideal for marriage and the family. In the N.T. God requires that a man must serve as a model of faithfulness to his wife and family in order to be chosen for the office of an overseer (see article on MORAL QUALIFICATIONS FOR OVERSEERS, p. 1908).

17 Speak unto Aaron, saying, Whosoever *he be* of thy seed in their generations that hath *any* blemish, let him not [g]approach to offer the [q]bread of his God.

18 For whatsoever man *he be* that hath a blemish, he shall not approach: a blind man, or a lame, or he that hath a flat nose, or any thing [h]superfluous,

19 Or a man that is brokenfooted, or brokenhanded,

20 Or crookbacked, or [r]a dwarf, or that hath a blemish in his eye, or be scurvy, or scabbed, or [i]hath his stones broken;

21 No man that hath a blemish of the seed of Aaron the priest shall come nigh to [j]offer the offerings of the LORD made by fire: he hath a blemish; he shall not come nigh to offer the bread of his God.

22 He shall eat the bread of his God, *both* of the [k]most holy, and of the [l]holy.

23 Only he shall not go in unto the veil, nor come nigh unto the altar, because he hath a blemish; that [m]he profane not my sanctuaries: for I the LORD do sanctify them.

24 And Moses told *it* unto Aaron, and to his sons, and unto all the children of Israel.

22 AND THE LORD spake unto Moses, saying,

2 Speak unto Aaron and to his sons, that they [n]separate themselves from the holy things of the children of Israel, and that they [o]profane not my holy name *in those things* which they [p]hallow unto me: I *am* the LORD.

3 Say unto them, Whosoever *he be* of all your seed among your generations, that goeth unto the holy things, which the children of Israel hallow unto the LORD, [q]having his uncleanness upon him, that soul shall be cut off from my presence: I *am* the LORD.

4 What man soever of the seed of Aaron *is* a leper, or hath [r]a [s]running issue; he shall not eat of the holy things, [s]until he be clean. And [t]whoso toucheth any thing *that is* unclean *by* the dead, or [u]a man whose seed goeth from him;

5 Or [v]whosoever toucheth any creeping thing, whereby he may be made unclean, or [w]a man of whom he may take uncleanness, whatsoever uncleanness he hath;

6 The soul which hath touched any such shall be unclean until even, and shall not eat of the holy things, unless he [x]wash his flesh with water.

7 And when the sun is down, he shall be clean, and shall afterward eat of the holy things; because [y]it *is* his food.

8 [z]That which dieth of itself, or is torn *with beasts*, he shall not eat to defile himself therewith: I *am* the LORD.

9 They shall therefore keep mine ordinance, [a]lest they bear sin for it, and die therefore, if they profane it: I the LORD do sanctify them.

10 [b]There shall no stranger eat *of* the holy thing: a sojourner of the priest, or an hired servant, shall not eat *of* the holy thing.

11 But if the priest buy *any* soul [t]with his money, he shall eat of it, and he that is born in his house: [c]they shall eat of his meat.

12 If the priest's daughter also be *married* unto [u]a stranger, she may not eat of an offering of the holy things.

13 But if the priest's daughter be a widow, or divorced, and have no child, and is [d]returned unto her father's house, [e]as in her youth, she shall eat of her father's meat: but there shall no stranger eat thereof.

14 ¶ [f]And if a man eat *of* the holy thing unwittingly, then he shall put the fifth *part* thereof unto it, and shall give *it* unto the priest with the holy thing.

15 And [g]they shall not profane the

21:17 [g]ch. 10:3 Num. 16:5 **21:18** [h]ch. 22:23 **21:20** [i]Deut. 23:1 **21:21** [j]ver. 6 **21:22** [k]ch. 2:3,10 & 6:17,29 & 7:1 & 24:9 Num. 18:9 [l]ch. 22:10-12 Num. 18:19 **21:23** [m]ver. 12 **22:2** [n]Num. 6:3 [o]ch. 18:21 [p]Ex. 28:38 Num. 18:32 Deut. 15:19 **22:3** [q]ch. 7:20 **22:4** [r]ch. 15:2 [s]ch. 14:2 & 15:13 [t]Num. 19:11 [u]ch. 15:16 **22:5** [v]ch. 11:24 [w]ch. 15:7,19 **22:6** [x]ch. 15:5 **22:7** [y]ch. 21:22 Num. 18:11,13 **22:8** [z]Ex. 22:31 ch. 17:15 Ezek. 44:31 **22:9** [a]Ex. 28:43 **22:10** [b]See 1 Sam. 21:6 **22:11** [c]Num. 8:11,13 **22:13** [d]Gen. 38:11 [e]ch. 10:14 **22:14** [f]ch. 5:15,16 Num. 18:11,19 **22:15** [g]Num. 18:32

[q] Or, *food* [r] Or, *too slender* [s] Heb. *running of the reins* [t] Heb. *with the purchase of his money* [u] Heb. *a man a stranger*

21:17 HATH *ANY* BLEMISH. Physical defects disqualified Aaron's descendants from serving as priests and from presenting offerings on behalf of the people (vv. 17–23). (1) Wholeness of body represented God's purpose that the priests were to serve as examples of the fullness of life as God intended; consequently, they would be most effective in God's service when free from physical imperfections. However, those who were disqualified from serving as ministers of God could yet partake of the bread of God (v. 22), i.e., the full salvation provided by God's covenant. (2) God's requirement for a perfect body in the priesthood prefigured Christ's moral perfection (Heb. 9:13–14) and hints at God's spiritual requirements for N.T. overseers. Any who serve in this capacity must be blameless and above reproach spiritually (see 1 Tim. 3:2, note; see article on MORAL QUALIFICATIONS FOR OVERSEERS, p. 1908).

holy things of the children of Israel, which they offer unto the LORD;

16 Or [v]suffer them [h]to bear the iniquity of trespass, when they eat their holy things: for I the LORD do sanctify them.

Sacrifices of blemished animals

17 ¶ And the LORD spake unto Moses, saying,

18 Speak unto Aaron, and to his sons, and unto all the children of Israel, and say unto them, [i]Whatsoever *he be* of the house of Israel, or of the strangers in Israel, that will offer his oblation for all his vows, and for all his freewill offerings, which they will offer unto the LORD for a burnt offering;

19 [j]*Ye shall offer* at your own will a male without blemish, of the beeves, of the sheep, or of the goats.

20 [k]*But* whatsoever hath a blemish, *that* shall ye not offer: for it shall not be acceptable for you.

21 And [l]whosoever offereth a sacrifice of peace offerings unto the LORD [m]to accomplish *his* vow, or a freewill offering in beeves or [w]sheep, it shall be perfect to be accepted; there shall be no blemish therein.

22 [n]Blind, or broken, or maimed, or having a wen, or scurvy, or scabbed, ye shall not offer these unto the LORD, nor make [o]an offering by fire of them upon the altar unto the LORD.

23 Either a bullock or a [x]lamb that hath any thing [p]superfluous or lacking in his parts, that mayest thou offer *for* a freewill offering; but for a vow it shall not be accepted.

24 Ye shall not offer unto the LORD that which is bruised, or crushed, or broken, or cut; neither shall ye make *any offering thereof* in your land.

25 Neither [q]from a stranger's hand shall ye offer [r]the bread of your God of any of these; because their [s]corruption *is* in them, *and* blemishes *be* in them: they shall not be accepted for you.

26 ¶ And the LORD spake unto Moses, saying,

22:16 [h]ver. 9
22:18 [i]ch. 1:2,3,10
22:19 [j]ch. 1:3
22:20 [k]Deut. 15:21 Mal. 1:8,14 Eph. 5:27 Heb. 9:14 1 Pet. 1:19
22:21 [l]ch. 3:1,6 [m]Num. 15:3,8 Ps. 61:8 & 65:1 Eccl. 5:4,5
22:22 [n]ver. 20 Mal. 1:8 [o]ch. 1:9,13 & 3:3,5
22:23 [p]ch. 21:18
22:25 [q]Num. 15:15,16 [r]ch. 21:6,17 [s]Mal. 1:14
22:27 [t]Ex. 22:30
22:28 [u]Deut. 22:6
22:29 [v]ch. 7:12 Ps. 107:22 & 116:17 Amos 4:5
22:30 [w]ch. 7:15
22:31 [x]ch. 19:37 Num. 15:40 Deut. 4:40
22:32 [y]ch. 18:21 [z]ch. 10:3 Mat. 6:9 Luke 11:2 [a]ch. 20:8
22:33 [b]ch. 19:36 Num. 15:41
23:2 [c]ver. 4,37 [d]Ex. 32:5 2 Ki. 10:20 Ps. 81:3
23:3 [e]Ex. 20:9 & 23:12 & 31:15 ch. 19:3 Deut. 5:13 Luke 13:14
23:4 [f]ver. 37 Ex. 23:14
23:5 [g]Ex. 12:6,14,18 & 13:3,10 Deut. 16:1-8

27 [t]When a bullock, or a sheep, or a goat, is brought forth, then it shall be seven days under the dam; and from the eighth day and thenceforth it shall be accepted for an offering made by fire unto the LORD.

28 And *whether it be* cow or [y]ewe, ye shall not kill it [u]and her young both in one day.

29 And when ye will [v]offer a sacrifice of thanksgiving unto the LORD, offer *it* at your own will.

30 On the same day it shall be eaten up; ye shall leave [w]none of it until the morrow: I *am* the LORD.

31 [x]Therefore shall ye keep my commandments, and do them: I *am* the LORD.

32 [y]Neither shall ye profane my holy name; but [z]I will be hallowed among the children of Israel: I *am* the LORD which [a]hallow you,

33 [b]That brought you out of the land of Egypt, to be your God: I *am* the LORD.

Feasts of the LORD

23:4–8pp — Ex. 12:14–20; Num. 28:16–25; Deut. 16:1–8
23:15–22pp — Num. 28:26–31; Deut. 16:9–12
23:23–25pp — Num. 29:1–6
23:26–32pp — Lev. 16:2–34; Num. 29:7–11
23:33–43pp — Num. 29:12–39; Deut. 16:13–17

23

AND THE LORD spake unto Moses, saying,

2 Speak unto the children of Israel, and say unto them, *Concerning* [c]the feasts of the LORD, which ye shall [d]proclaim *to be* holy convocations, *even* these *are* my feasts.

3 [e]Six days shall work be done: but the seventh day *is* the sabbath of rest, an holy convocation; ye shall do no work *therein:* it *is* the sabbath of the LORD in all your dwellings.

4 ¶ [f]These *are* the feasts of the LORD, *even* holy convocations, which ye shall proclaim in their seasons.

5 [g]In the fourteenth *day* of the first month at even *is* the LORD's passover.

[v] Or, *lade themselves with the iniquity of trespass in their eating* [w] Or, *goats* [x] Or, *kid*
[y] Or, *she goat*

23:2 THE FEASTS OF THE LORD. This chapter presents a list of the "feasts of the LORD," i.e., the sacred days of celebration and worship. These days were symbols of redemption and consecration, demonstrating that Israel and all they possessed belonged to God. There were two cycles of these feasts: a weekly cycle and an annual cycle. All were feasts except for the Day of Atonement, which was the one fast day required by the law. These cycles helped to tie their worship to the events in their daily lives, for they were not to separate worship from life.

23:5 THE LORD'S PASSOVER. See article on THE PASSOVER, p. 110.

OLD TESTAMENT FEASTS

Name	OT References	OT Time	Today	Description	NT References
Sabbath	Ex 20:8-11; 31:12-17; Lev 23:3; Dt 5:12-15	7th day	Same	Day of rest; no work	Mt 12:1-14; Mk 2:23–3:5; Lk 4 4:16-30; 6:1-10; 13:10 -16; 14:1-5; Jn 5:1-15; 9:1-34; Ac 13:14-48; 17:2; 18:4; Heb 4:1-11
Sabbath Year	Ex 23:10-11; Lev 25:1-7	7th year	Same	Year of rest; fallow fields	
Year of Jubilee	Lev 25:8-55; 27:17-24; Nu 36:4	50th year	Same	Cancelled debts; liberation of slaves and endentured servants; land returned to original family owners	
Passover	Ex 12:1-14; Lev 23:5; Nu 9:1-14; 28:16; Dt 16:1-3a, 4b-7	1st month (Abib) 14	Mar-Apr	Slaying and eating a lamb, together with bitter herbs and bread made without yeast, in every household	Mt 26:1-2, 17-29; Mk 14:12-26; Lk 22:7-38; Jn 2:13-25; 11:55-56; Jn 13:1-30; 1Co 5:7
Unleavened Bread	Ex 12:15-20; 13:3-10; 23:15; 34:18; Lev 23:6-8; Nu 28:17-25; Dt 16:3b,4a,8	1st month (Abib) 15-21	Mar-Apr	Eating bread made without yeast; holding several assemblies; making designated offerings	Mt 26:17; Mk 14:1,12; Luke 22:1,7; Ac 12:3; 20:6; 1Co 5:6-8
Firstfruits	Lev 23:9-14	1st month (Abib) 16	Mar-Apr	Presenting a sheaf of the first of the barley harvest as a wave offering; making a burnt offering and a grain offering	Ro 8:23; 1Co 15:20-23
Weeks **(Pentecost)(Harvest)**	Ex 23:16a; 34:22a; Lev 23:15-21; Nu 28:26-31; Dt 16:9-12	3rd month (Sivan) 6	May-June	A festival of joy; mandatory and voluntary offerings, including the firstfruits of the wheat harvest	Ac 2:1-41; 20:16; 1Co 16:8
Trumpets (Later: Rosh Hashanah–New Year's Day)	Lev 23:23-25; Nu 29:1-6	7th month (Tishri) 1	Sept-Oct	An assembly on a day of rest commemorated with trumpet blasts and sacrifices	
Day of Atonement (Yom Kippur)	Lev 16; 23:26-32; Nu 29:7-11	7th month (Tishri) 10	Sept-Oct	A day of rest, fasting and sacrifices of atonement for priests and people and atonement for the tabernacle and altar	Ac 27:9; Ro 3:24-26; Heb 9:1-14, 23-26; 10:19-22
Tabernacles (Booths)(Ingathering)	Ex 23:16b;34:22b; Lev 23:33-36a, 39-43; Nu 29:12-34; Dt 16:13-15; Zec 14:16-19	7th month (Tishri) 15-21	Sept-Oct	A week of celebration for the harvest; living in booths and offering sacrifices	Jn 7:2-37
Sacred Assembly	Lev 23:36b; Nu 29:35-38	7th month (Tishri) 22	Sept-Oct	A day of convocation, rest and offering sacrifices	Jn 7:37-44
Dedication		9th month	Dec	A commemoration of the purification of the temple in Maccabean era (166-164 B.C.)	Jn 10:22-39
Purim	Est 9:18-32	12th month (Adar) 14,15	Feb-Mar	A day of joy and feasting and giving presents	

6 And on the fifteenth day of the same month *is* the feast of unleavened bread unto the LORD: seven days ye must eat unleavened bread.

7 [h]In the first day ye shall have an holy convocation: ye shall do no servile work therein.

8 But ye shall offer an offering made by fire unto the LORD seven days: in the seventh day *is* an holy convocation: ye shall do no servile work *therein.*

9 ¶ And the LORD spake unto Moses, saying,

10 Speak unto the children of Israel, and say unto them, [i]When ye be come into the land which I give unto you, and shall reap the harvest thereof, then ye shall bring a [z] [a]sheaf of [j]the firstfruits of your harvest unto the priest:

11 And he shall [k]wave the sheaf before the LORD, to be accepted for you: on the morrow after the sabbath the priest shall wave it.

12 And ye shall offer that day when ye wave the sheaf an he lamb without blemish of the first year for a burnt offering unto the LORD.

13 [l]And the meat offering thereof *shall be* two tenth deals of fine flour mingled with oil, an offering made by fire unto the LORD *for* a sweet savour: and the drink offering thereof *shall be* of wine, the fourth *part* of an hin.

14 And ye shall eat neither bread, nor parched corn, nor green ears, until the selfsame day that ye have brought an offering unto your God: *it shall be* a statute for ever throughout your generations in all your dwellings.

15 ¶ And [m]ye shall count unto you from the morrow after the sabbath, from the day that ye brought the sheaf of the wave offering; seven sabbaths shall be complete:

16 Even unto the morrow after the seventh sabbath shall ye number [n]fifty days; and ye shall offer [o]a new meat offering unto the LORD.

17 Ye shall bring out of your habitations two wave loaves of two tenth deals: they shall be of fine flour; they shall be baked with leaven; *they are* [p]the firstfruits unto the LORD.

18 And ye shall offer with the bread seven lambs without blemish of the first year, and one young bullock, and two rams: they shall be *for* a burnt offering unto the LORD, with their meat offering, and their drink offerings, *even* an offering made by fire, of sweet savour unto the LORD.

19 Then ye shall sacrifice [q]one kid of the goats for a sin offering, and two lambs of the first year for a sacrifice of [r]peace offerings.

20 And the priest shall wave them with the bread of the firstfruits *for* a wave offering before the LORD, with the two lambs: [s]they shall be holy to the LORD for the priest.

21 And ye shall proclaim on the selfsame day, *that* it may be an holy convocation unto you: ye shall do no servile work *therein: it shall be* a statute for ever in all your dwellings throughout your generations.

22 ¶ And [t]when ye reap the harvest of your land, thou shalt not make clean riddance of the corners of thy field when thou reapest, neither shalt thou gather any gleaning of thy harvest: thou shalt leave them unto the poor, and to the stranger: I *am* the LORD your God.

23 ¶ And the LORD spake unto Moses, saying,

24 Speak unto the children of Israel, saying, In the [u]seventh month, in the first *day* of the month, shall ye have a sabbath, [v]a memorial of blowing of trumpets, an holy convocation.

23:7 [h]Ex. 12:16 Num. 28:18,25
23:10 [i]Ex. 34:26 Deut. 16:9 Josh. 3:15 [j]Rom. 11:16 Jas. 1:18 Rev. 14:4
23:11 [k]Ex. 29:24
23:13 [l]ch. 2:14-16
23:15 [m]Ex. 34:22 ch. 25:8 Deut. 16:9
23:16 [n]Acts 2:1 [o]Num. 28:26
23:17 [p]Ex. 23:16,19 Num. 15:17-21
23:19 [q]ch. 4:23,28 Num. 28:30 [r]ch. 3:1
23:20 [s]Num. 18:12 Deut. 18:4
23:22 [t]ch. 19:9
23:24 [u]Num. 29:1 [v]ch. 25:9

[z] Or, *handful* [a] Heb. *omer*

23:6 FEAST OF UNLEAVENED BREAD. See Ex. 12:17, note.

23:10 THE FIRSTFRUITS. The Feast of Firstfruits (vv. 10–14), acknowledging that the fruit of the ground came from the Lord, occurred in connection with the Feast of Unleavened Bread. The firstfruits were to be consecrated to the Lord. This points to the N.T. believer's dedication of all of life to God. Christians are the firstfruits of Christ's saving work (Jas. 1:18; Rev. 14:4).

23:15 SEVEN SABBATHS. The Feast of Weeks (cf. Deut. 16:10), also called the Feast of Pentecost, occurred at the end of the wheat harvest, fifty days ("Pentecost" means "fiftieth") after the Feast of Firstfruits (v. 16). On this day God's people gave thanks for His abundant gifts of food and for all that sustained them. It was on the day of Pentecost that God poured forth the Holy Spirit upon Christ's disciples (Acts 2:1–4).

23:24 BLOWING OF TRUMPETS. The Feast of Trumpets occurred on the first day of the seventh month, probably as a reminder of and a preparation for the approaching Day of Atonement (cf. vv. 26–32). God wanted Israel to think on spiritual things, especially on their covenant relationship with Him.

25 Ye shall do no servile work *therein:* but ye shall offer an offering made by fire unto the LORD.

26 ¶ And the LORD spake unto Moses, saying,

27 [w]Also on the tenth *day* of this seventh month *there shall be* a day of atonement: it shall be an holy convocation unto you; and ye shall afflict your souls, and offer an offering made by fire unto the LORD.

28 And ye shall do no work in that same day: for it *is* a day of atonement, to make an atonement for you before the LORD your God.

29 For whatsoever soul *it be* that shall not be afflicted in that same day, [x]he shall be cut off from among his people.

30 And whatsoever soul *it be* that doeth any work in that same day, [y]the same soul will I destroy from among his people.

31 Ye shall do no manner of work: *it shall be* a statute for ever throughout your generations in all your dwellings.

32 It *shall be* unto you a sabbath of rest, and ye shall afflict your souls: in the ninth *day* of the month at even, from even unto even, shall ye [b]celebrate your sabbath.

33 ¶ And the LORD spake unto Moses, saying,

34 Speak unto the children of Israel, saying, [z]The fifteenth day of this seventh month *shall be* the feast of tabernacles *for* seven days unto the LORD.

35 On the first day *shall be* an holy convocation: ye shall do no servile work *therein.*

36 Seven days ye shall offer an offering made by fire unto the LORD: [a]on the eighth day shall be an holy convocation unto you; and ye shall offer an offering made by fire unto the LORD: it *is* a [b]solemn[c] assembly; *and* ye shall do no servile work *therein.*

37 [c]These *are* the feasts of the LORD, which ye shall proclaim *to be* holy convocations, to offer an offering made by fire unto the LORD, a burnt offering, and a meat offering, a sacrifice, and drink offerings, every thing upon his day:

38 [d]Beside the sabbaths of the LORD, and beside your gifts, and beside all your vows, and beside all your freewill offerings, which ye give unto the LORD.

39 Also in the fifteenth day of the seventh month, when ye have [e]gathered in the fruit of the land, ye shall keep a feast unto the LORD seven days: on the first day *shall be* a sabbath, and on the eighth day *shall be* a sabbath.

40 And [f]ye shall take you on the first day the [d]boughs of goodly trees, branches of palm trees, and the boughs of thick trees, and willows of the brook; [g]and ye shall rejoice before the LORD your God seven days.

41 [h]And ye shall keep it a feast unto the LORD seven days in the year. *It shall be* a statute for ever in your generations: ye shall celebrate it in the seventh month.

42 [i]Ye shall dwell in booths seven days; all that are Israelites born shall dwell in booths:

43 [j]That your generations may know that I made the children of Israel to dwell in booths, when I brought them out of the land of Egypt: I *am* the LORD your God.

44 And Moses [k]declared unto the children of Israel the feasts of the LORD.

The oil and the showbread

24:1–3pp — Ex. 27:20–21

24 AND THE LORD spake unto Moses, saying,

2 [l]Command the children of Israel, that they bring unto thee pure oil olive beaten for the light, [e]to cause the lamps to burn continually.

3 Without the veil of the testimony, in the tabernacle of the congregation, shall Aaron order it from the evening unto the morning before the LORD continually: *it shall be* a statute for ever in your generations.

23:27 [w]ch. 16:30 Num. 29:7 **23:29** [x]Gen. 17:14 **23:30** [y]ch. 20:3,5,6 **23:34** [z]Ex. 23:16 Num. 29:12 Deut. 16:13 Ezra 3:4 Neh. 8:14 Zech. 14:16 John 7:2 **23:36** [a]Num. 29:35 Neh. 8:18 John 7:37 [b]Deut. 16:8 2 Chr. 7:9 **23:37** [c]ver. 2,4 **23:38** [d]Num. 29:39 **23:39** [e]Ex. 23:16 Deut. 16:13 **23:40** [f]Neh. 8:15 [g]Deut. 16:14,15 **23:41** [h]Num. 29:12 Neh. 8:18 **23:42** [i]Neh. 8:14-16 **23:43** [j]Deut. 31:13 **23:44** [k]ver. 2 **24:2** [l]Ex. 27:20

[b] Heb. *rest* [c] Heb. day of *restraint* [d] Heb. *fruit* [e] Heb. *to cause to ascend*

23:27 DAY OF ATONEMENT. See article on THE DAY OF ATONEMENT, p. 188.

23:34–43 FEAST OF TABERNACLES. The Feast of Tabernacles was so called because during this feast the people left their houses and lived in temporary booths or tents made from tree branches (vv. 40–42). This act reminded the people of the goodness of God to them during their forty years in the wilderness when they had no permanent dwelling place. It was also called the Feast of Ingathering, for it celebrated the conclusion of the harvest of summer fruits and nuts.

24:2 THE LIGHT. See Ex. 27:20–21, note.

4 He shall order the lamps upon [m]the pure candlestick before the LORD continually.

5 ¶ And thou shalt take fine flour, and bake twelve [n]cakes thereof: two tenth deals shall be in one cake.

6 And thou shalt set them in two rows, six on a row, [o]upon the pure table before the LORD.

7 And thou shalt put pure frankincense upon *each* row, that it may be on the bread for a memorial, *even* an offering made by fire unto the LORD.

8 [p]Every sabbath he shall set it in order before the LORD continually, *being taken* from the children of Israel by an everlasting covenant.

9 And [q]it shall be Aaron's and his sons'; [r]and they shall eat it in the holy place: for it *is* most holy unto him of the offerings of the LORD made by fire by a perpetual statute.

Death for blasphemy

10 ¶ And the son of an Israelitish woman, whose father *was* an Egyptian, went out among the children of Israel: and this son of the Israelitish *woman* and a man of Israel strove together in the camp;

11 And the Israelitish woman's son blasphemed the name of *the LORD,* and [s]cursed. And they [t]brought him unto Moses: (and his mother's name *was* Shelomith, the daughter of Dibri, of the tribe of Dan:)

12 And they [u]put him in ward, [v]that[f] the mind of the LORD might be shown them.

13 And the LORD spake unto Moses, saying,

14 Bring forth him that hath cursed without the camp; and let all that heard *him* [w]lay their hands upon his head, and let all the congregation stone him.

15 And thou shalt speak unto the children of Israel, saying, Whosoever curseth his God [x]shall bear his sin.

16 And he that [y]blasphemeth the name of the LORD, he shall surely be put to death, *and* all the congregation shall certainly stone him: as well the stranger, as he that is born in the land, when he blasphemeth the name of *the LORD,* shall be put to death.

17 ¶ [z]And he that [g]killeth any man shall surely be put to death.

18 [a]And he that killeth a beast shall make it good; [h]beast for beast.

19 And if a man cause a blemish in his neighbour; as [b]he hath done, so shall it be done to him;

20 Breach for breach, eye for eye, tooth for tooth: as he hath caused a blemish in a man, so shall it be done to him *again.*

21 [c]And he that killeth a beast, he shall restore it: [d]and he that killeth a man, he shall be put to death.

22 Ye shall have [e]one manner of law, as well for the stranger, as for one of your own country: for I *am* the LORD your God.

23 ¶ And Moses spake to the children of Israel, [f]that they should bring forth him that had cursed out of the camp, and stone him with stones. And the children of Israel did as the LORD commanded Moses.

Sabbath and jubilee years

25:8–38Ref — Deut. 15:1–11
25:39–55Ref — Ex. 21:2–11; Deut. 15:12–18

25 AND THE LORD spake unto Moses in mount Sinai, saying,

2 Speak unto the children of Israel, and say unto them, When ye come into the land which I give you, then shall the land [i]keep [g]a sabbath unto the LORD.

3 Six years thou shalt sow thy field, and six years thou shalt prune thy vineyard, and gather in the fruit thereof;

4 But in the seventh year shall be a sabbath of rest unto the land, a sabbath for the LORD: thou shalt neither sow thy field, nor prune thy vineyard.

5 [h]That which groweth of its own accord of thy harvest thou shalt not reap, neither gather the grapes [j]of thy vine undressed: *for* it is a year of rest unto the land.

6 And the sabbath of the land shall be meat for you; for thee, and for thy servant, and for thy maid, and for thy

24:4 [m]Ex. 31:8 & 39:37
24:5 [n]Ex. 25:30
24:6 [o]1 Ki. 7:48 2 Chr. 4:19 & 13:11 Heb. 9:2
24:8 [p]Num. 4:7 1 Chr. 9:32 2 Chr. 2:4
24:9 [q]1 Sam. 21:6 Mat. 12:4 Mark 2:26 Luke 6:4 [r]Ex. 29:33 ch. 8:31
24:11 [s]Job 1:5,11,22 Is. 8:21 [t]Ex. 18:22,26
24:12 [u]Num. 15:34 [v]Ex. 18:15 Num. 27:5
24:14 [w]Deut. 13:9 & 17:7
24:15 [x]ch. 20:17 Num. 9:13
24:16 [y]1 Ki. 21:10,13 Mat. 12:31 Mark 3:28
24:17 [z]Ex. 21:12 Num. 35:31 Deut. 19:11,12
24:18 [a]ver. 21
24:19 [b]Ex. 21:24 Deut. 19:21 Mat. 5:38 & 7:2
24:21 [c]Ex. 21:33 [d]ver. 17
24:22 [e]Ex. 12:49 ch. 19:34 Num. 15:16
24:23 [f]ver. 14
25:2 [g]Ex. 23:10 See ch. 26:34,35
25:5 [h]2 Ki. 19:29

[f] Heb. *to expound unto them according to the mouth of the LORD* [g] Heb. *smiteth the life of a man* [h] Heb. *life for life* [i] Heb. *rest* [j] Heb. *of thy separation*

24:5 THOU SHALT . . . BAKE TWELVE CAKES. The twelve loaves of the showbread represented the twelve tribes of Israel and the Israelites' realization that they dwelt in the presence of God and were always to be dedicated to Him (cf. Ex. 25:30, note).

hired servant, and for thy stranger that
sojourneth with thee,
7 And for thy cattle, and for the
beast that *are* in thy land, shall all the
increase thereof be meat.
8 ¶ And thou shalt number seven
sabbaths of years unto thee, seven
times seven years; and the space of the
seven sabbaths of years shall be unto
thee forty and nine years.
9 Then shalt thou cause the trum-
pet [k]of the jubilee to sound on the
tenth *day* of the seventh month, [i]in
the day of atonement shall ye make the
trumpet sound throughout all your
land.
10 And ye shall hallow the fiftieth
year, and [j]proclaim liberty through-
out *all* the land unto all the inhabitants
thereof: it shall be a jubilee unto you;
[k]and ye shall return every man unto
his possession, and ye shall return ev-
ery man unto his family.
11 A jubilee shall that fiftieth year
be unto you: [l]ye shall not sow, neither
reap that which groweth of itself in it,
nor gather *the grapes* in it of thy vine
undressed.
12 For it *is* the jubilee; it shall be
holy unto you: [m]ye shall eat the in-
crease thereof out of the field.
13 [n]In the year of this jubilee ye
shall return every man unto his pos-
session.
14 And if thou sell aught unto thy
neighbour, or buyest *aught* of thy
neighbour's hand, ye shall not oppress
one another:
15 [o]According to the number of
years after the jubilee thou shalt buy of
thy neighbour, *and* according unto the
number of years of the fruits he shall
sell unto thee:
16 According to the multitude of
years thou shalt increase the price
thereof, and according to the fewness
of years thou shalt diminish the price
of it: for *according* to the number *of the
years* of the fruits doth he sell unto
thee.
17 [p]Ye shall not therefore oppress

25:9 [i]ch. 23:24,27
25:10 [j]Is. 61:2 & 63:4 Jer. 34:8,15,17 Luke 4:19 [k]ver. 13 Num. 36:4
25:11 [l]ver. 5
25:12 [m]ver. 6,7
25:13 [n]ver. 10 ch. 27:24 Num. 36:4
25:15 [o]ch. 27:18
25:17 [p]ver. 14
[q]ver. 43 ch. 19:14,32
25:18 [r]ch. 19:37 [s]ch. 26:5 Deut. 12:10 Ps. 4:8
25:19 [t]ch. 26:5 Ezek. 34:25
25:20 [u]Mat. 6:25 [v]ver. 4,5
25:21 [w]See Ex. 16:29
25:22 [x]2 Ki. 19:29 [y]Josh. 5:11
25:23 [z]Deut. 32:43 [a]Ps. 39:12
25:25 [b]Ruth 2:20 [c]See Ruth 3:2,9, 12
25:27 [d]ver. 50-52
25:28 [e]ver. 13

one another; [q]but thou shalt fear thy
God: for I *am* the LORD your God.
18 ¶ [r]Wherefore ye shall do my
statutes, and keep my judgments, and
do them; [s]and ye shall dwell in the
land in safety.
19 And the land shall yield her fruit,
and [t]ye shall eat your fill, and dwell
therein in safety.
20 And if ye shall say, [u]What shall
we eat the seventh year? behold, [v]we
shall not sow, nor gather in our in-
crease:
21 Then I will [w]command my bless-
ing upon you in the sixth year, and it
shall bring forth fruit for three years.
22 [x]And ye shall sow the eighth
year, and eat *yet* of [y]old fruit until the
ninth year; until her fruits come in ye
shall eat *of* the old *store.*
23 ¶ The land shall not be sold
[l][m]for ever: for [z]the land *is* mine; for
ye *are* [a]strangers and sojourners
with me.
24 And in all the land of your pos-
session ye shall grant a redemption for
the land.
25 ¶ [b]If thy brother be waxen poor,
and hath sold away *some* of his posses-
sion, and if [c]any of his kin come to
redeem it, then shall he redeem that
which his brother sold.
26 And if the man have none to re-
deem it, and [n]himself be able to re-
deem it;
27 Then [d]let him count the years of
the sale thereof, and restore the over-
plus unto the man to whom he sold it;
that he may return unto his posses-
sion.
28 But if he be not able to restore *it*
to him, then that which is sold shall
remain in the hand of him that hath
bought it until the year of jubilee:
[e]and in the jubilee it shall go out, and
he shall return unto his possession.
29 And if a man sell a dwelling

[k] Heb. *loud of sound* [l] Or, *to be quite cut off* [m] Heb. *for cutting off* [n] Heb. *his hand hath attained and found sufficiency*

25:8–34 A JUBILEE. Three features characterized the Year of Jubilee (a year that came every fifty years). (1) All Israelite slaves were to be freed. (2) All ancestral property that had been sold had to be returned to the original family. (3) The land was to be left untilled. God's purpose in instituting this special year was to guarantee justice and to keep the rich from accumulating wealth and land at the expense of the disadvantaged.

25:23 THE LAND. God told the Israelites that they were not the actual owners of the land, for it belonged to Him; they were simply the stewards of it. In a similar way, the material possessions of N.T. believers belong to the Lord. We have been appointed as stewards who must manage all our possessions justly for God, for ourselves, and for others (cf. Mat. 25:14–27; Luke 16:10–12; 1 Cor. 4:1–7).

house in a walled city, then he may redeem it within a whole year after it is sold; *within* a full year may he redeem it.

30 And if it be not redeemed within the space of a full year, then the house that *is* in the walled city shall be established for ever to him that bought it throughout his generations: it shall not go out in the jubilee.

31 But the houses of the villages which have no wall round about them shall be counted as the fields of the country: [o]they may be redeemed, and they shall go out in the jubilee.

32 Notwithstanding [f]the cities of the Levites, *and* the houses of the cities of their possession, may the Levites redeem at any time.

33 And if [p]a man purchase of the Levites, then the house that was sold, and the city of his possession, shall go out in *the year of* jubilee: for the houses of the cities of the Levites *are* their possession among the children of Israel.

34 But [g]the field of the suburbs of their cities may not be sold; for it *is* their perpetual possession.

35 ¶ And if thy brother be waxen poor, and [q]fallen in decay with thee; then thou shalt [h]relieve[r] him: *yea, though he be* a stranger, or a sojourner; that he may live with thee.

36 [i]Take thou no usury of him, or increase: but [j]fear thy God; that thy brother may live with thee.

37 Thou shalt not give him thy money upon usury, nor lend him thy victuals for increase.

38 [k]I *am* the LORD your God, which brought you forth out of the land of Egypt, to give you the land of Canaan, *and* to be your God.

39 ¶ And [l]if thy brother *that dwelleth* by thee be waxen poor, and be sold unto thee; thou shalt not [s]compel him to serve as a bondservant:

40 *But* as an hired servant, *and* as a sojourner, he shall be with thee, *and* shall serve thee unto the year of jubilee:

41 And *then* shall he depart from thee, *both* he and his children [m]with him, and shall return unto his own family, and [n]unto the possession of his fathers shall he return.

42 For they *are* [o]my servants, which I brought forth out of the land of Egypt: they shall not be sold [t]as bondmen.

43 [p]Thou shalt not rule over him [q]with rigour; but [r]shalt fear thy God.

44 Both thy bondmen, and thy bondmaids, which thou shalt have, *shall be* of the heathen that are round about you; of them shall ye buy bondmen and bondmaids.

45 Moreover of [s]the children of the strangers that do sojourn among you, of them shall ye buy, and of their families that *are* with you, which they begat in your land: and they shall be your possession.

46 And [t]ye shall take them as an inheritance for your children after you, to inherit *them for* a possession; [u]they shall be your bondmen for ever: but over your brethren the children of Israel, ye shall not rule one over another with rigour.

47 ¶ And if a sojourner or stranger [v]wax rich by thee, and [u]thy brother *that dwelleth* by him wax poor, and sell himself unto the stranger *or* sojourner by thee, or to the stock of the stranger's family:

48 After that he is sold he may be redeemed again; one of his brethren may [v]redeem him:

49 Either his uncle, or his uncle's son, may redeem him, or *any* that is nigh of kin unto him of his family may redeem him; or if [w]he be able, he may redeem himself.

50 And he shall reckon with him that bought him from the year that he was sold to him unto the year of jubilee: and the price of his sale shall be according unto the number of years, [x]according to the time of an hired servant shall it be with him.

51 If *there be* yet many years *behind,*

25:32 [f]See Num. 35:2
25:34 [g]See Acts 4:36,37
25:35 [h]Deut. 15:7 Luke 6:35 1 John 3:17
25:36 [i]Ex. 22:25 Deut. 23:19 [j]Neh. 5:9
25:38 [k]ch. 22:32,33
25:39 [l]Ex. 21:2 Deut. 15:12 1 Ki. 9:22
25:41 [m]Ex. 21:3 [n]ver. 28
25:42 [o]ver. 55 Rom. 6:22 1 Cor. 7:23
25:43 [p]Eph. 6:9 [q]Ex. 1:13 [r]Ex. 1:17 Deut. 25:18 Mal. 3:5
25:45 [s]Is. 56:3,6
25:46 [t]Is. 14:2
25:47 [u]ver. 25,35
25:48 [v]Neh. 5:5
25:49 [w]ver. 26
25:50 [x]Job 7:1 Is. 16:14

[o] Heb. *redemption belongeth unto it* [p] Or, one *of the Levites redeem* them [q] Heb. *his hand faileth* [r] Heb. *strengthen* [s] Heb. *serve thyself with him with the service;* see ver. 46 [t] Heb. *with the sale of a bondman* [u] Heb. *ye shall serve yourselves with them;* see ver. 39 [v] Heb. *his hand obtain*

25:36 NO USURY. See Ex. 22:25, note.

25:44 BONDMEN ... OF THE HEATHEN. Slavery was a fact of life in Biblical days. That God allowed Israel to purchase slaves from the pagan nations around them was a blessing for the slaves purchased, for God required His people to treat their slaves with much more dignity than they received in their own country (cf. Ex. 20:10).

according unto them he shall give
again the price of his redemption out of
the money that he was bought for.
52 And if there remain but few
years unto the year of jubilee, then he
shall count with him, *and* according
unto his years shall he give him again
the price of his redemption.
53 *And* as a yearly hired servant
shall he be with him: *and the other* shall
not rule with rigour over him in thy
sight.
54 And if he be not redeemed [w]in
these *years,* then he shall go out in the
year of jubilee, *both* he, and his chil-
dren with him.
55 For unto me the children of Isra-
el *are* servants; they *are* my servants
whom I brought forth out of the land of
Egypt: I *am* the LORD your God.

The blessings for obedience

26 YE SHALL make you [y]no idols
nor graven image, neither rear
you up a [x]standing image, neither
shall ye set up *any* [y] [z]image of stone
in your land, to bow down unto it: for
I *am* the LORD your God.
2 ¶ [z]Ye shall keep my sabbaths,
and reverence my sanctuary: I *am* the
LORD.
3 ¶ [a]If ye walk in my statutes, and
keep my commandments, and do them;
4 [b]Then I will give you rain in due
season, [c]and the land shall yield her
increase, and the trees of the field shall
yield their fruit.
5 And [d]your threshing shall reach
unto the vintage, and the vintage shall
reach unto the sowing time: and [e]ye
shall eat your bread to the full, and
[f]dwell in your land safely.
6 And [g]I will give peace in the
land, and [h]ye shall lie down, and none
shall make *you* afraid: and I will [a]rid
[i]evil beasts out of the land, neither
shall [j]the sword go through your
land.

26:1 [y]Ex. 20:4,5 Deut. 5:8 **26:2** [z]ch. 19:30 **26:3** [a]Deut. 28:1-14 **26:4** [b]Is. 30:23 [c]Ps. 67:6 Zech. 8:12 **26:5** [d]Amos 9:13 [e]ch. 25:19 [f]ch. 25:18 **26:6** [g]Is. 45:7 [h]Ps. 4:8 Hos. 2:18 Zeph. 3:13 [i]2 Ki. 17:25 [j]Ezek. 14:17 **26:8** [k]Deut. 32:30 **26:9** [l]Ex. 2:25 [m]Gen. 17:6,7 Ps. 107:38 **26:10** [n]ch. 25:22 **26:11** [o]Ex. 25:8 Josh. 22:19 Ps. 76:2 Rev. 21:3 **26:12** [p]2 Cor. 6:16 **26:14** [q]Deut. 28:15 Lam. 2:17 Mal. 2:2 **26:16** [r]Deut. 28:22 [s]1 Sam. 2:33 [t]Deut. 28:33,51 Job 31:8 Mic. 6:15 **26:17** [u]ch. 17:10 [v]Deut. 28:25 [w]Ps. 106:41

7 And ye shall chase your enemies,
and they shall fall before you by the
sword.
8 And [k]five of you shall chase an
hundred, and an hundred of you shall
put ten thousand to flight: and your en-
emies shall fall before you by the
sword.
9 For I will [l]have respect unto you,
and [m]make you fruitful, and multiply
you, and establish my covenant with
you.
10 And ye shall eat [n]old store, and
bring forth the old because of the new.
11 [o]And I will set my tabernacle
among you: and my soul shall not ab-
hor you.
12 [p]And I will walk among you,
and will be your God, and ye shall be
my people.
13 I *am* the LORD your God, which
brought you forth out of the land of
Egypt, that ye should not be their bond-
men; and I have broken the bands of
your yoke, and made you go upright.

The punishments for disobedience

14 ¶ [q]But if ye will not hearken
unto me, and will not do all these com-
mandments;
15 And if ye shall despise my stat-
utes, or if your soul abhor my judg-
ments, so that ye will not do all my
commandments, *but* that ye break my
covenant:
16 I also will do this unto you; I will
even appoint [b]over you terror, [r]con-
sumption, and the burning ague, that
shall [s]consume the eyes, and cause
sorrow of heart: and [t]ye shall sow
your seed in vain, for your enemies
shall eat it.
17 And [u]I will set my face against
you, and [v]ye shall be slain before your
enemies: [w]they that hate you shall

[w] Or, *by these* means [x] Or, *pillar* [y] Or, *figured stone* [z] Heb. *a stone of picture* [a] Heb. *cause to cease* [b] Heb. *upon you*

26:14 IF YE WILL NOT HEARKEN UNTO ME. Ch. 26 reveals the pathos, anguish, and heartache of God as He lamented the fact that He might be compelled to punish the people He had redeemed. If they, in utter ingratitude, rejected His love and were unwilling to have Him as their God, He would have no other choice but to bring upon them sorrow and calamity. The Lord's promises and warnings were spoken from the depth of divine love and with the sincere desire that such discipline and judgment would never be necessary for His chosen people (read also Deut. 28—30).

26:17 SET MY FACE AGAINST YOU. The greatest tragedy of sin, rebellion, and disobedience toward God is that He may set His face against us, i.e., withdraw His presence and care, His grace and strength, from us. In its place, we will be exposed to His direct judgment and to all the problems and dangers of life without His protection and guidance. The price of rejecting God and His righteous standards is enormous. To be in His will, in His presence, and in His care are the greatest blessings of life (vv. 3–13).

reign over you; and [x]ye shall flee
when none pursueth you.
18 And if ye will not yet for all this
hearken unto me, then I will punish
you [y]seven times more for your sins.
19 And I will [z]break the pride of
your power; and I [a]will make your
heaven as iron, and your earth as
brass:
20 And your [b]strength shall be
spent in vain: for [c]your land shall not
yield her increase, neither shall the
trees of the land yield their fruits.
21 ¶ And if ye walk [c]contrary unto
me, and will not hearken unto me; I
will bring seven times more plagues
upon you according to your sins.
22 [d]I will also send wild beasts
among you, which shall rob you of your
children, and destroy your cattle, and
make you few in number; and [e]your
high ways shall be desolate.
23 And if ye [f]will not be reformed
by me by these things, but will walk
contrary unto me;
24 [g]Then will I also walk contrary
unto you, and will punish you yet seven
times for your sins.
25 And [h]I will bring a sword upon
you, that shall avenge the quarrel of
my covenant: and when ye are gath-
ered together within your cities, [i]I
will send the pestilence among you;
and ye shall be delivered into the hand
of the enemy.
26 [j]*And* when I have broken the
staff of your bread, ten women shall
bake your bread in one oven, and they
shall deliver *you* your bread again by
weight: and [k]ye shall eat, and not be
satisfied.
27 And if ye will not for all this
hearken unto me, but walk contrary
unto me;
28 Then I will walk contrary unto
you also [l]in fury; and I, even I, will
chastise you seven times for your sins.
29 [m]And ye shall eat the flesh of
your sons, and the flesh of your daugh-
ters shall ye eat.
30 And [n]I will destroy your high
places, and cut down your images, and
cast your carcases upon the carcases
of your idols, and my soul shall abhor
you.
31 And I will make your cities
waste, and [o]bring your sanctuaries
unto desolation, and I will not smell
the savour of your sweet odours.
32 [p]And I will bring the land into
desolation: and your enemies which
dwell therein shall be astonished at it.
33 And [q]I will scatter you among
the heathen, and will draw out a sword
after you: and your land shall be deso-
late, and your cities waste.
34 [r]Then shall the land enjoy her
sabbaths, as long as it lieth desolate,
and ye *be* in your enemies' land; *even*
then shall the land rest, and enjoy her
sabbaths.
35 As long as it lieth desolate it
shall rest; because it did not rest in
your [s]sabbaths, when ye dwelt
upon it.
36 And upon them that are left *alive*
of you [t]I will send a faintness into
their hearts in the lands of their ene-
mies; and [u]the sound of a [d]shaken
leaf shall chase them; and they shall
flee, as fleeing from a sword; and they
shall fall when none pursueth.
37 And [v]they shall fall one upon
another, as it were before a sword,
when none pursueth: and [w]ye shall
have no power to stand before your en-
emies.
38 And ye shall perish among the
heathen, and the land of your enemies
shall eat you up.
39 And they that are left of you
[x]shall pine away in their iniquity in
your enemies' lands; and also in the
iniquities of their fathers shall they
pine away with them.
40 [y]If they shall confess their iniq-
uity, and the iniquity of their fathers,
with their trespass which they tres-
passed against me, and that also they
have walked contrary unto me;
41 And *that* I also have walked con-
trary unto them, and have brought
them into the land of their enemies; if
then their [z]uncircumcised hearts be
[a]humbled, and they then accept of the
punishment of their iniquity:
42 Then will I [b]remember my
covenant with Jacob, and also my
covenant with Isaac, and also my cov-
enant with Abraham will I remember;
and I will [c]remember the land.
43 [d]The land also shall be left of
them, and shall enjoy her sabbaths,
while she lieth desolate without them:
and they shall accept of the punish-
ment of their iniquity: because, even
because they [e]despised my judg-

[c] Or, *at all adventures with me;* see ver. 24
[d] Heb. *driven*

26:17 [x]ver. 36 Ps. 53:5 **26:18** [y]1 Sam. 2:5 **26:19** [z]Is. 25:11 [a]Deut. 28:23 **26:20** [b]Ps. 127:1 [c]Deut. 11:17 **26:22** [d]Deut. 32:24 [e]2 Chr. 15:5 Zech. 7:14 **26:23** [f]Jer. 2:30 Amos 4:6-12 **26:24** [g]Ps. 18:26 **26:25** [h]Ezek. 5:17 [i]Deut. 28:21 **26:26** [j]Ps. 105:16 [k]Mic. 6:14 **26:28** [l]Jer. 21:5 Ezek. 5:13,15 & 8:18 **26:29** [m]Deut. 28:53 **26:30** [n]2 Chr. 34:3 Ezek. 6:3-6,13 **26:31** [o]Ps. 74:7 **26:32** [p]Jer. 9:11

26:33 [q]Deut. 4:27 Ezek. 12:15 & 20:23 & 22:15 Zech. 7:14 **26:34** [r]2 Chr. 36:21 **26:35** [s]ch. 25:2 **26:36** [t]Ezek. 21:7,12,15 [u]ver. 17 Prov. 28:1 **26:37** [v]See Judg. 7:22 1 Sam. 14:15,16 Is. 10:4 [w]Josh. 7:12,13 Judg. 2:14 **26:39** [x]Deut. 28:65 Zech. 10:9 **26:40** [y]Num. 5:7 Neh. 9:2 Luke 15:18 1 John 1:9 **26:41** [z]Acts 7:51 Rom. 2:29 [a]2 Chr. 12:6,7 **26:42** [b]Ex. 2:24 & 6:5 Ezek. 16:60 [c]Ps. 136:23 **26:43** [d]ver. 34,35 [e]ver. 15

ments, and because their soul abhorred my statutes.

44 And yet for all that, when they be in the land of their enemies, [f]I will not cast them away, neither will I abhor them, to destroy them utterly, and to break my covenant with them: for I *am* the LORD their God.

45 But I will [g]for their sakes remember the covenant of their ancestors, [h]whom I brought forth out of the land of Egypt [i]in the sight of the heathen, that I might be their God: I *am* the LORD.

46 [j]These *are* the statutes and judgments and laws, which the LORD made between him and the children of Israel [k]in mount Sinai by the hand of Moses.

Vows and tithes to the LORD

27 AND THE LORD spake unto Moses, saying,

2 Speak unto the children of Israel, and say unto them, [l]When a man shall make a singular vow, the persons *shall be* for the LORD by thy estimation.

3 And thy estimation shall be of the male from twenty years old even unto sixty years old, even thy estimation shall be fifty shekels of silver, [m]after the shekel of the sanctuary.

4 And if it *be* a female, then thy estimation shall be thirty shekels.

5 And if *it be* from five years old even unto twenty years old, then thy estimation shall be of the male twenty shekels, and for the female ten shekels.

6 And if *it be* from a month old even unto five years old, then thy estimation shall be of the male five shekels of silver, and for the female thy estimation *shall be* three shekels of silver.

7 And if *it be* from sixty years old and above; if *it be* a male, then thy estimation shall be fifteen shekels, and for the female ten shekels.

8 But if he be poorer than thy estimation, then he shall present himself before the priest, and the priest shall value him; according to his ability that vowed shall the priest value him.

9 And if *it be* a beast, whereof men bring an offering unto the LORD, all that *any man* giveth of such unto the LORD shall be holy.

10 He shall not alter it, nor change it, a good for a bad, or a bad for a good: and if he shall at all change beast for beast, then it and the exchange thereof shall be holy.

11 And if *it be* any unclean beast, of which they do not offer a sacrifice unto the LORD, then he shall present the beast before the priest:

12 And the priest shall value it, whether it be good or bad: [e]as thou valuest it, *who art* the priest, so shall it be.

13 [n]But if he will at all redeem it, then he shall add a fifth *part* thereof unto thy estimation.

14 ¶ And when a man shall sanctify his house *to be* holy unto the LORD, then the priest shall estimate it, whether it be good or bad: as the priest shall estimate it, so shall it stand.

15 [o]And if he that sanctified it will redeem his house, then he shall add the fifth *part* of the money of thy estimation unto it, and it shall be his.

16 And if a man shall sanctify unto the LORD *some part* of a field of his possession, then thy estimation shall be according to the seed thereof: [f]an homer of barley seed *shall be valued* at fifty shekels of silver.

17 If he sanctify his field from the year of jubilee, according to thy estimation it shall stand.

18 But if he sanctify his field after the jubilee, then the priest shall [p]reckon unto him the money according to the years that remain, even unto the year of the jubilee, and it shall be abated from thy estimation.

19 [q]And if he that sanctified the field will in any wise redeem it, then he shall add the fifth *part* of the money of thy estimation unto it, and it shall be assured to him.

20 And if he will not redeem the field, or if he have sold the field to another man, it shall not be redeemed any more.

21 But the field, [r]when it goeth out in the jubilee, shall be holy unto the

26:44 [f]Deut. 4:31 2 Ki. 13:23 Rom. 11:2
26:45 [g]Rom. 11:28 [h]ch. 22:33 & 25:38 [i]Ps. 98:2 Ezek. 20:9,14,22
26:46 [j]ch. 27:34 Deut. 6:1 & 12:1 John 1:17 [k]ch. 25:1
27:2 [l]Num. 6:2 See Judg. 11:30, 31,39 1 Sam. 1:11,28
27:3 [m]Ex. 30:13
27:13 [n]ver. 15,19
27:15 [o]ver. 13
27:18 [p]ch. 25:15,16
27:19 [q]ver. 13
27:21 [r]ch. 25:10,28,31

[e] Heb. *according to thy estimation, O priest*
[f] Or, the land of *an homer*

27:2 VOW. Ch. 27 deals with things vowed or promised to the Lord, such as persons, animals, houses, and land. A value was placed on them in case the one who made the promise wanted to buy back the gift.

LORD, as a field [s]devoted; [t]the pos-
session thereof shall be the priest's.
22 And if *a man* sanctify unto the
LORD a field which he hath bought,
which *is* not of the fields of [u]his pos-
session;
23 [v]Then the priest shall reckon
unto him the worth of thy estimation,
even unto the year of the jubilee: and he
shall give thine estimation in that day,
as a holy thing unto the LORD.
24 [w]In the year of the jubilee the
field shall return unto him of whom it
was bought, *even* to him to whom the
possession of the land *did belong*.
25 And all thy estimations shall be
according to the shekel of the sanctu-
ary: [x]twenty gerahs shall be the
shekel.
26 ¶ Only the [y]firstling[g] of the
beasts, which should be the LORD's
firstling, no man shall sanctify it;
whether *it be* ox, or sheep: it *is* the
LORD's.
27 And if *it be* of an unclean beast,
then he shall redeem *it* according to
thine estimation, [z]and shall add a
fifth *part* of it thereto: or if it be not
redeemed, then it shall be sold accord-
ing to thy estimation.
28 [a]Notwithstanding no devoted
thing, that a man shall devote unto the
LORD of all that he hath, *both* of man
and beast, and of the field of his pos-
session, shall be sold or redeemed: ev-
ery devoted thing *is* most holy unto the
LORD.
29 [b]None devoted, which shall be
devoted of men, shall be redeemed; *but*
shall surely be put to death.
30 And [c]all the tithe of the land,
whether of the seed of the land, *or* of the
fruit of the tree, *is* the LORD's: *it is* holy
unto the LORD.
31 [d]And if a man will at all redeem
aught of his tithes, he shall add thereto
the fifth *part* thereof.
32 And concerning the tithe of the
herd, or of the flock, *even* of whatso-
ever [e]passeth under the rod, the tenth
shall be holy unto the LORD.
33 He shall not search whether it be
good or bad, [f]neither shall he change
it: and if he change it at all, then both
it and the change thereof shall be holy;
it shall not be redeemed.
34 [g]These *are* the commandments,
which the LORD commanded Moses for
the children of Israel in mount Sinai.

27:21 [s]ver. 28 [t]Num. 18:14 Ezek. 44:29 **27:22** [u]ch. 25:10,25 **27:23** [v]ver. 18 **27:24** [w]ch. 25:28 **27:25** [x]Ex. 30:13 Num. 3:47 & 18:16 Ezek. 45:12 **27:26** [y]Ex. 13:2,12 & 22:30 **27:27** [z]ver. 11,12 **27:28** [a]ver. 21 Josh. 6:17-19 **27:29** [b]Num. 21:2 **27:30** [c]Gen. 28:22 Num. 18:21,24 2 Chr. 31:5,6,12 Neh. 13:12 Mal. 3:8 **27:31** [d]ver. 13 **27:32** [e]Jer. 33:13 Ezek. 20:37 Mic. 7:14 **27:33** [f]ver. 10 **27:34** [g]ch. 26:46

[g] Heb. *firstborn*

27:30 TITHE. A tithe is a tenth of both the produce of the land and the livestock that was given to the Lord. The tithe of Israel was given to support the Levites (Num. 18:28) and priests (Num. 18:26), to assist in sacred meals (Deut. 14:22–27), and to give aid to the poor, the fatherless, and the widows (Deut. 14:28–29; see article on TITHES AND OFFERINGS, p. 1388).

NUMBERS

Outline

I. God Prepares the "Exodus Generation" to Inherit the Land (1:1—10:10)
  A. Preparing to March (1:1—4:49)
    1. Numbering Israel's Fighting Men (1:1–54)
    2. Arranging the Camp (2:1–34)
    3. Organizing the Levites (3:1—4:49)
  B. Sanctifying the People (5:1—10:10)

II. The "Exodus Generation" Forfeits Their Inheritance Through Sin and Unbelief (10:11—25:18)
  A. Murmurings on the Way to Kadesh-barnea (10:11—12:16)
  B. Rebellion and Unbelief at Kadesh-barnea (13:1—14:45)
  C. Sin and Rebellion in the Wilderness (15:1—19:22)
  D. Disobedience on the Way to Moab (20:1—25:18)

III. God Prepares a New Generation to Possess the Land (26:1—36:13)
  A. Numbering the New Generation (26:1–65)
  B. Instructing the People (27:1—30:16)
  C. Defeating the Midianites (31:1–54)
  D. Settling the Transjordan (32:1–42)
  E. Recounting the Journey from Egypt to Moab (33:1–49)
  F. Promise of Victory over Canaan (33:50–56)
  G. Preparing to Enter and Divide the Land (34:1—36:13)

Author: Moses

Theme: Wilderness Wanderings

Date of Writing: c. 1405 B.C.

Background

The book's title, "Numbers," first occurs in the Greek and Latin versions and is derived from the two censuses or "numberings" of Israelite men in the book (chs. 1 and 26). Most of the book, however, describes Israel's experiences while wandering "in the wilderness." Thus this book is known in the Hebrew O.T. as "In the Wilderness" (*bemidbar*).

Chronologically, Numbers is a sequel to the history recorded in the book of Exodus. After approximately one year at Mount Sinai—during which time God established His covenant with Israel, gave Moses the law and the pattern for the tabernacle, and instructed him concerning the contents of Leviticus—the Israelites prepared to continue their journey to the land God had promised them as the descendants of Abraham, Isaac, and Jacob. Shortly before departing from Mount Sinai, however, God directed Moses to number all the Israelite men who were eligible to go to war (1:2–3). Nineteen days afterwards, the nation departed from there on a brief journey to Kadesh-barnea (10:11). Numbers records Israel's serious rebellion at Kadesh and her subsequent thirty-nine years of judgment in the wilderness, until God brought an entirely new generation of Israelites to the plains of Moab, which lay across the Jordan River from Jericho and the promised land.

Authorship has historically been ascribed to Moses (1) by the Jewish and Samaritan Pentateuch, (2) by Jewish tradition, (3) by Jesus and N.T. writers, (4) by ancient Christian writers, (5) by modern conservative scholars, and (6) by internal evidence of the book itself (e.g., 33:1–2). Moses undoubtedly kept a diary during the wilderness wanderings and then put the contents of Numbers in narrative form sometime shortly before his death (c. 1405 B.C.). Moses' practice of referring to himself in the third person was commonplace in ancient writings and does not weaken the credibility of his authorship.

Purpose

Numbers was written to tell why Israel did not enter the promised land immediately after leaving Mount Sinai. It illustrates God's requirement of faith for His people, His chastisements and judgments for rebellion, and how His ongoing purpose was eventually realized.

Survey

The primary message of Numbers is clear: God's people progressed forward only by trusting Him and His promises and by obeying His word. Although passing through the wilderness was necessary for a season, it was not God's original intention that the wilderness test be prolonged so that a whole generation of Israelites live and die there. The short journey from Mount Sinai to Kadesh, however, became a thirty-nine year affliction and judgment because of their unbelief. Throughout most of Numbers the "exodus generation" of Israelites was faithless, rebellious, and ungrateful for God's miracles and provisions. Major murmuring occurred among the people soon after leaving Mount Sinai (ch. 11); Miriam and Aaron spoke against Moses (ch. 12); Israel as a whole rebelled in stubborn unbelief at Kadesh and refused to advance into Canaan (ch. 14); Korah and many Levites rebelled against Moses (ch. 16); pushed to the limits by a rebellious people, Moses finally sinned in angry exasperation (ch. 20); and Israel worshiped Baal (ch. 25). All Israelites who were twenty years old and older at Kadesh (except Joshua and Caleb) perished in the wilderness. A new generation of Israelites was finally brought to the eastern border of the promised land (chs. 26—36).

Special Features

Six major features or emphases characterize Numbers. (1) It is the "Book of Wilderness Wanderings," revealing clearly why Israel did not immediately possess the promised land after leaving Mount Sinai but instead had to wander aimlessly in the wilderness for thirty-nine more years. (2) It is the "Book of Murmurings," recording again and again the murmuring discontent and bitter complaint of the Israelites toward God and His dealings with them. (3) The book illustrates the principle that without faith, it is impossible to please God (cf. Heb. 11:6). Throughout the book one sees that God's people move forward only by trusting Him with unwavering faith, believing His promises, and leaning on Him as their source of life and hope. (4) Numbers profoundly reveals the principle that if one generation fails, God will raise up another one to fulfill His promises and carry out His mission. (5) The census prior to Kadesh-barnea (chs. 1—4) and the census later at the plains of Moab before entering Canaan (ch. 26) reveal that it was not the insufficient size of Israel's army that kept her out of Canaan at Kadesh but the inadequacy of her faith and obedience. (6) It is the "Book of Divine Discipline," demonstrating that God does discipline and exercise judgment toward His own people when they persist in complaint and unbelief (cf. chs. 13—14).

New Testament Fulfillment

Israel's murmurings and unbelief are mentioned as warnings for believers under the new covenant (1 Cor. 10:5–11; Heb. 3:16—4:6). The seriousness of Balaam's sin (chs. 22—24) and Korah's rebellion (ch. 16) are also mentioned (2 Pet. 2:15–16; Jude 11; Rev. 2:14). Jesus refers to the bronze serpent (21:7–9) to illustrate His being lifted up so that those who believe in Him might not perish but have eternal life (John 3:14–16). Also, Christ Jesus

is compared to the wilderness rock from which Israel drank (1 Cor. 10:4) and the heavenly manna which they ate (John 6:31–33).

Reading Numbers

In order to read the entire Old Testament in one year, the book of Numbers should be read in 16 days, according to the following schedule: □ 1–2 □ 3–4 □ 5–6 □ 7–8 □ 9–10 □ 11–13 □ 14–15 □ 16–17 □ 18–19 □ 20–21 □ 22–23 □ 24–26 □ 27–28 □ 29–31 □ 32–33 □ 34–36

NOTES

The census of the people

1 AND THE LORD spake unto Moses [a]in the wilderness of Sinai, [b]in the tabernacle of the congregation, on the first *day* of the second month, in the second year after they were come out of the land of Egypt, saying,

2 [c]Take ye the sum of all the congregation of the children of Israel, after their families, by the house of their fathers, with the number of *their* names, every male by their polls;

3 From twenty years old and upward, all that are able to go forth to war in Israel: thou and Aaron shall number them by their armies.

4 And with you there shall be a man of every tribe; every one head of the house of his fathers.

5 ¶ And these *are* the names of the men that shall stand with you: of *the tribe of* Reuben; Elizur the son of Shedeur.

6 Of Simeon; Shelumiel the son of Zurishaddai.

7 Of Judah; [a]Nahshon the son of Amminadab.

8 Of Issachar; Nethaneel the son of Zuar.

9 Of Zebulun; Eliab the son of Helon.

10 Of the children of Joseph: of Ephraim; Elishama the son of Ammihud: of Manasseh; Gamaliel the son of Pedahzur.

11 Of Benjamin; Abidan the son of Gideoni.

12 Of Dan; Ahiezer the son of Ammishaddai.

13 Of Asher; Pagiel the son of Ocran.

14 Of Gad; Eliasaph the son of [b]Deuel.

15 Of Naphtali; Ahira the son of Enan.

16 [d]These *were* the renowned of the congregation, princes of the tribes of their fathers, [e]heads of thousands in Israel.

17 ¶ And Moses and Aaron took these men which are expressed [f]by *their* names:

18 And they assembled all the congregation together on the first *day* of the second month, and they declared their [g]pedigrees after their families, by the house of their fathers, according to the number of the names, from twenty years old and upward, by their polls.

19 As the LORD commanded Moses, so he numbered them in the wilderness of Sinai.

20 And the [h]children of Reuben, Israel's eldest son, by their generations, after their families, by the house of their fathers, according to the number of the names, by their polls, every male from twenty years old and upward, all that were able to go forth to war;

21 Those that were numbered of them, *even* of the tribe of Reuben, *were* forty and six thousand and five hundred.

22 ¶ Of the [i]children of Simeon, by their generations, after their families, by the house of their fathers, those that were numbered of them, according to the number of the names, by their polls, every male from twenty years old and upward, all that were able to go forth to war;

23 Those that were numbered of them, *even* of the tribe of Simeon, *were* fifty and nine thousand and three hundred.

24 ¶ Of the [j]children of Gad, by their generations, after their families, by the house of their fathers, according to the number of the names, from twenty years old and upward, all that were able to go forth to war;

25 Those that were numbered of them, *even* of the tribe of Gad, *were* forty and five thousand six hundred and fifty.

1:1 [a]Ex. 19:1 ch. 10:11,12 [b]Ex. 25:22
1:2 [c]Ex. 30:12 & 38:26 ch. 26:2,63,64 2 Sam. 24:2 1 Chr. 21:2
1:16 [d]ch. 7:2 1 Chr. 27:16 [e]Ex. 18:21,25
1:17 [f]Is. 43:1
1:18 [g]Ezra 2:59
1:20 [h]ch. 2:10,11 & 32:6,15,21,29
1:22 [i]ch. 2:12,13 & 26:12-14
1:24 [j]ch. 2:14,15 & 26:15-18 & 32:2,29 & 34:14

[a] Called *Naasson* in Mat. 1:4 [b] ch. 2:14 he is called *Reuel*

1:1 THE LORD SPAKE UNTO MOSES. What Moses wrote was by inspiration from God, a fact repeated in the book over and over. It is emphasized in the first verse, the last verse, and at the beginning of many of the chapters of this book.

1:1 WILDERNESS OF SINAI. God's command to Moses came ten and a half months after the people arrived at Mount Sinai (i.e, thirteen months after the exodus). The events recorded in Numbers occurred over a period of approximately thirty-nine years, the total time of Israel's wandering in the desert.

1:2 THE SUM OF ALL THE CONGREGATION. The purpose of the census was to organize Israel into a nation and an army (v. 3). Taking a census emphasized that each individual was important to God's redemptive purposes and that the nation's activity was to be ordered and fully accountable to Him (cf. Phil. 4:3; 2 Tim. 2:19).

26 ¶ Of the [k]children of Judah, by their generations, after their families, by the house of their fathers, according to the number of the names, from twenty years old and upward, all that were able to go forth to war;

27 Those that were numbered of them, *even* of the tribe of Judah, *were* [l]threescore and fourteen thousand and six hundred.

28 ¶ Of the [m]children of Issachar, by their generations, after their families, by the house of their fathers, according to the number of the names, from twenty years old and upward, all that were able to go forth to war;

29 Those that were numbered of them, *even* of the tribe of Issachar, *were* fifty and four thousand and four hundred.

30 ¶ Of the [n]children of Zebulun, by their generations, after their families, by the house of their fathers, according to the number of the names, from twenty years old and upward, all that were able to go forth to war;

31 Those that were numbered of them, *even* of the tribe of Zebulun, *were* fifty and seven thousand and four hundred.

32 ¶ Of the children of Joseph, *namely,* of the [o]children of Ephraim, by their generations, after their families, by the house of their fathers, according to the number of the names, from twenty years old and upward, all that were able to go forth to war;

33 Those that were numbered of them, *even* of the tribe of Ephraim, *were* forty thousand and five hundred.

34 ¶ Of the [p]children of Manasseh, by their generations, after their families, by the house of their fathers, according to the number of the names, from twenty years old and upward, all that were able to go forth to war;

35 Those that were numbered of them, *even* of the tribe of Manasseh, *were* thirty and two thousand and two hundred.

36 ¶ Of the [q]children of Benjamin, by their generations, after their families, by the house of their fathers, according to the number of the names, from twenty years old and upward, all that were able to go forth to war;

37 Those that were numbered of them, *even* of the tribe of Benjamin, *were* thirty and five thousand and four hundred.

38 ¶ Of the [r]children of Dan, by their generations, after their families, by the house of their fathers, according to the number of the names, from twenty years old and upward, all that were able to go forth to war;

39 Those that were numbered of them, *even* of the tribe of Dan, *were* threescore and two thousand and seven hundred.

40 ¶ Of the [s]children of Asher, by their generations, after their families, by the house of their fathers, according to the number of the names, from twenty years old and upward, all that were able to go forth to war;

41 Those that were numbered of them, *even* of the tribe of Asher, *were* forty and one thousand and five hundred.

42 ¶ Of the children of Naphtali, throughout their generations, after their families, by the house of their fathers, according to the number of the names, from twenty years old and upward, all that were able to go forth to war;

43 Those that were numbered of them, *even* of the tribe of Naphtali, *were* fifty and three thousand and four hundred.

44 [t]These *are* those that were numbered, which Moses and Aaron numbered, and the princes of Israel, *being* twelve men: each one was for the house of his fathers.

45 So were all those that were numbered of the children of Israel, by the house of their fathers, from twenty years old and upward, all that were able to go forth to war in Israel;

46 Even all they that were numbered were [u]six hundred thousand and three thousand and five hundred and fifty.

47 ¶ But [v]the Levites after the tribe of their fathers were not numbered among them.

1:26 [k]ch. 2:3,4 & 26:19-22 2 Sam. 24:9
1:27 [l]2 Chr. 17:14
1:28 [m]ch. 2:5,6
1:30 [n]ch. 2:7,8 & 26:26,27
1:32 [o]ch. 2:18,19 & 26:35-37
1:34 [p]ch. 2:20,21 & 26:28-34
1:36 [q]ch. 2:22,23 & 26:38-41
1:38 [r]ch. 2:25,26 & 26:42,43
1:40 [s]ch. 2:27,28 & 26:44-47
1:44 [t]ch. 26:64
1:46 [u]Ex. 38:26 See Ex. 12:37 ch. 2:32 & 26:51
1:47 [v]ch. 2:33 See ch. 3 & 4 & 26:57 1 Chr. 6 & 21:6

1:46 SIX HUNDRED THOUSAND. The census taken at Mount Sinai totaled 603,550 males above the age of twenty, not including the Levites (vv. 45–47). The nation of Israel, therefore, totaled perhaps at least two million people. For this many people to have been sustained in the wilderness would have required a perpetual miracle, a truth that the Word of God clearly stresses (cf. Ex. 16:4–15,31–33; Num. 20:8; Deut. 8:2–4; 29:5; Ps. 78:26–28; 1 Cor. 10:4).

48 For the LORD had spoken unto Moses, saying,

49 [w]Only thou shalt not number the tribe of Levi, neither take the sum of them among the children of Israel:

50 [x]But thou shalt appoint the Levites over the tabernacle of testimony, and over all the vessels thereof, and over all things that *belong* to it: they shall bear the tabernacle, and all the vessels thereof; and they shall minister unto it, [y]and shall encamp round about the tabernacle.

51 [z]And when the tabernacle setteth forward, the Levites shall take it down: and when the tabernacle is to be pitched, the Levites shall set it up: [a]and the stranger that cometh nigh shall be put to death.

52 And the children of Israel shall pitch their tents, [b]every man by his own camp, and every man by his own standard, throughout their hosts.

53 [c]But the Levites shall pitch round about the tabernacle of testimony, that there be no [d]wrath upon the congregation of the children of Israel: and the Levites shall keep the charge of the tabernacle of testimony.

54 And the children of Israel did according to all that the LORD commanded Moses, so did they.

The camps and tribal captains

2 AND THE LORD spake unto Moses and unto Aaron, saying,

2 [e]Every man of the children of Israel shall pitch by his own standard, with the ensign of their father's house: [f]far[c] off about the tabernacle of the congregation shall they pitch.

3 And on the east side toward the rising of the sun shall they of the standard of the camp of Judah pitch throughout their armies: and [g]Nahshon the son of Amminadab *shall be* captain of the children of Judah.

4 And his host, and those that were numbered of them, *were* threescore and fourteen thousand and six hundred.

5 And those that do pitch next unto him *shall be* the tribe of Issachar: and Nethaneel the son of Zuar *shall be* captain of the children of Issachar.

6 And his host, and those that were numbered thereof, *were* fifty and four thousand and four hundred.

7 *Then* the tribe of Zebulun: and Eliab the son of Helon *shall be* captain of the children of Zebulun.

8 And his host, and those that were numbered thereof, *were* fifty and seven thousand and four hundred.

9 All that were numbered in the camp of Judah *were* an hundred thousand and fourscore thousand and six thousand and four hundred, throughout their armies. [h]These shall first set forth.

10 ¶ On the south side *shall be* the standard of the camp of Reuben according to their armies: and the captain of the children of Reuben *shall be* Elizur the son of Shedeur.

11 And his host, and those that were numbered thereof, *were* forty and six thousand and five hundred.

12 And those which pitch by him *shall be* the tribe of Simeon: and the captain of the children of Simeon *shall be* Shelumiel the son of Zurishaddai.

13 And his host, and those that were numbered of them, *were* fifty and nine thousand and three hundred.

14 Then the tribe of Gad: and the captain of the sons of Gad *shall be* Eliasaph the son of [d]Reuel.

15 And his host, and those that were numbered of them, *were* forty and five thousand and six hundred and fifty.

16 All that were numbered in the camp of Reuben *were* an hundred thousand and fifty and one thousand and four hundred and fifty, throughout their armies. [i]And they shall set forth in the second rank.

17 ¶ [j]Then the tabernacle of the congregation shall set forward with the camp of the Levites in the midst of the camp: as they encamp, so shall

1:49 [w]ch. 2:33 & 26:62
1:50 [x]Ex. 38:21 ch. 3:7,8 & 4:15,25-27,33 [y]ch. 3:23,29,35,38
1:51 [z]ch. 10:17,21 [a]ch. 3:10,38 & 18:22
1:52 [b]ch. 2:2,34
1:53 [c]ver. 50 [d]Lev. 10:6 ch. 8:19 & 16:46 & 18:5 1 Sam. 6:19
2:2 [e]ch. 1:52 [f]Josh. 3:4
2:3 [g]ch. 10:14 Ruth 4:20 1 Chr. 2:10 Mat. 1:4
2:9 [h]ch. 10:14
2:16 [i]ch. 10:18
2:17 [j]ch. 10:17,21

[c] Heb. *over against* [d] *Deuel;* see ch. 1:14 & 7:42,47 & 10:20

1:52 EVERY MAN BY HIS OWN STANDARD. The camp of the Israelites was organized with an inner circle of Levites around the tabernacle and an outer circle of the twelve tribes, with three tribes on each side of the tabernacle. The line of march was also organized so that when the cloud lifted they could move quickly, and when the cloud settled, they could find their places in the camp without confusion. The Bible teaches organization, not for organization's sake, but for smooth operation of the work that needs to be done. The tabernacle in the center of the camp symbolized that the life of the nation revolved around the Lord and the worship of Him as their Redeemer.

they set forward, every man in his place by their standards.

18 ¶ On the west side *shall be* the standard of the camp of Ephraim according to their armies: and the captain of the sons of Ephraim *shall be* Elishama the son of Ammihud.

19 And his host, and those that were numbered of them, *were* forty thousand and five hundred.

20 And by him *shall be* the tribe of Manasseh: and the captain of the children of Manasseh *shall be* Gamaliel the son of Pedahzur.

21 And his host, and those that were numbered of them, *were* thirty and two thousand and two hundred.

22 Then the tribe of Benjamin: and the captain of the sons of Benjamin *shall be* Abidan the son of Gideoni.

23 And his host, and those that were numbered of them, *were* thirty and five thousand and four hundred.

24 All that were numbered of the camp of Ephraim *were* an hundred thousand and eight thousand and an hundred, throughout their armies. [k]And they shall go forward in the third rank.

25 ¶ The standard of the camp of Dan *shall be* on the north side by their armies: and the captain of the children of Dan *shall be* Ahiezer the son of Ammishaddai.

26 And his host, and those that were numbered of them, *were* threescore and two thousand and seven hundred.

27 And those that encamp by him *shall be* the tribe of Asher: and the captain of the children of Asher *shall be* Pagiel the son of Ocran.

28 And his host, and those that were numbered of them, *were* forty and one thousand and five hundred.

29 ¶ Then the tribe of [l]Naphtali: and the captain of the children of Naphtali *shall be* Ahira the son of Enan.

30 And his host, and those that were numbered of them, *were* fifty and three thousand and four hundred.

31 All they that were numbered in the camp of Dan *were* an hundred thousand and fifty and seven thousand and six hundred. [m]They shall go hindmost with their standards.

32 ¶ These *are* those which were numbered of the children of Israel by the house of their fathers: [n]all those that were numbered of the camps throughout their hosts *were* six hundred thousand and three thousand and five hundred and fifty.

33 But [o]the Levites were not numbered among the children of Israel; as the LORD commanded Moses.

34 And the children of Israel did according to all that the LORD commanded Moses: [p]so they pitched by their standards, and so they set forward, every one after their families, according to the house of their fathers.

The Levites

3 THESE ALSO *are* the generations of Aaron and Moses in the day *that* the LORD spake with Moses in mount Sinai.

2 And these *are* the names of the sons of Aaron; Nadab the [q]firstborn, and Abihu, Eleazar, and Ithamar.

3 These *are* the names of the sons of Aaron, [r]the priests which were anointed, [e]whom he consecrated to minister in the priest's office.

4 [s]And Nadab and Abihu died before the LORD, when they offered strange fire before the LORD, in the wilderness of Sinai, and they had no children: and Eleazar and Ithamar ministered in the priest's office in the sight of Aaron their father.

5 ¶ And the LORD spake unto Moses, saying,

6 [t]Bring the tribe of Levi near, and present them before Aaron the priest, that they may minister unto him.

7 And they shall keep his charge, and the charge of the whole congregation before the tabernacle of the congregation, to do [u]the service of the tabernacle.

8 And they shall keep all the instru-

[e] Heb. *whose hand he filled*

2:24 [k]ch. 10:22
2:29 [l]Gen. 30:8 & 49:21 2 Ki. 15:29 Rev. 7:6
2:31 [m]ch. 10:25
2:32 [n]Ex. 38:26 ch. 1:46 & 11:21
2:33 [o]ch. 1:47
2:34 [p]ch. 24:2,5,6
3:2 [q]Ex. 6:23
3:3 [r]Ex. 28:41 Lev. 8
3:4 [s]Lev. 10:1 ch. 26:61 1 Chr. 24:2
3:6 [t]ch. 8:6 & 18:2
3:7 [u]See ch. 1:50 & 8:11,15,24,26

3:3 PRIESTS WHICH WERE ANOINTED. The purpose of anointing the priests with oil was to "consecrate" them to the service of God. (1) Likewise, in the N.T., when believers are anointed by the Holy Spirit, they are set apart and empowered for service and witness in God's kingdom (Acts 1:8; 2:4). (2) The Hebrew name "Messiah" and the Greek name "Christ" both mean "the anointed one" (see Mat. 1:1, note). Everything Christ did, He performed under the anointing of the Holy Spirit (see article on JESUS AND THE HOLY SPIRIT, p. 1550).

3:4 OFFERED STRANGE FIRE. See Lev. 10:1–2, notes.

ments of the tabernacle of the congregation, and the charge of the children of Israel, to do the service of the tabernacle.

9 And [v]thou shalt give the Levites unto Aaron and to his sons: they *are* wholly given unto him out of the children of Israel.

10 And thou shalt appoint Aaron and his sons, [w]and they shall wait on their priest's office: [x]and the stranger that cometh nigh shall be put to death.

11 And the LORD spake unto Moses, saying,

12 And I, behold, [y]I have taken the Levites from among the children of Israel instead of all the firstborn that openeth the matrix among the children of Israel: therefore the Levites shall be mine;

13 Because [z]all the firstborn *are* mine; [a]*for* on the day that I smote all the firstborn in the land of Egypt I hallowed unto me all the firstborn in Israel, both man and beast: mine shall they be: I *am* the LORD.

14 ¶ And the LORD spake unto Moses in the wilderness of Sinai, saying,

15 Number the children of Levi after the house of their fathers, by their families: [b]every male from a month old and upward shalt thou number them.

16 And Moses numbered them according to the [f]word of the LORD, as he was commanded.

17 [c]And these were the sons of Levi by their names; Gershon, and Kohath, and Merari.

18 And these *are* the names of the sons of Gershon by their families; [d]Libni, and Shimei.

19 And the sons of Kohath by their families; [e]Amram, and Izehar, Hebron, and Uzziel.

20 [f]And the sons of Merari by their families; Mahli, and Mushi. These *are* the families of the Levites according to the house of their fathers.

21 Of Gershon *was* the family of the Libnites, and the family of the Shimites: these *are* the families of the Gershonites.

22 Those that were numbered of them, according to the number of all the males, from a month old and upward, *even* those that were numbered of them *were* seven thousand and five hundred.

23 [g]The families of the Gershonites shall pitch behind the tabernacle westward.

24 And the chief of the house of the father of the Gershonites *shall be* Eliasaph the son of Lael.

25 And [h]the charge of the sons of Gershon in the tabernacle of the congregation *shall be* [i]the tabernacle, and [j]the tent, [k]the covering thereof, and [l]the hanging for the door of the tabernacle of the congregation,

26 And [m]the hangings of the court, and [n]the curtain for the door of the court, which *is* by the tabernacle, and by the altar round about, and [o]the cords of it for all the service thereof.

27 ¶ [p]And of Kohath *was* the family of the Amramites, and the family of the Izeharites, and the family of the Hebronites, and the family of the Uzzielites: these *are* the families of the Kohathites.

28 In the number of all the males, from a month old and upward, *were* eight thousand and six hundred, keeping the charge of the sanctuary.

29 [q]The families of the sons of Kohath shall pitch on the side of the tabernacle southward.

30 And the chief of the house of the father of the families of the Kohathites *shall be* Elizaphan the son of Uzziel.

31 And [r]their charge *shall be* [s]the ark, and [t]the table, and [u]the candlestick, and [v]the altars, and the vessels of the sanctuary wherewith they minister, and [w]the hanging, and all the service thereof.

32 And Eleazar the son of Aaron the priest *shall be* chief over the chief of the Levites, *and have* the oversight of them that keep the charge of the sanctuary.

33 ¶ Of Merari *was* the family of the Mahlites, and the family of the Mushites: these *are* the families of Merari.

34 And those that were numbered of them, according to the number of all the males, from a month old and upward, *were* six thousand and two hundred.

35 And the chief of the house of the father of the families of Merari *was* Zuriel the son of Abihail: [x]*these* shall pitch on the side of the tabernacle northward.

36 And [y]*under*[g] the custody and charge of the sons of Merari *shall be* the boards of the tabernacle, and the bars

3:9 [v]ch. 8:19 & 18:6
3:10 [w]ch. 18:7 [x]ver. 38 ch. 1:51 & 16:40
3:12 [y]ver. 41 ch. 8:16 & 18:6
3:13 [z]Ex. 13:2 Lev. 27:26 ch. 8:17 Luke 2:23 [a]Ex. 13:12,15 ch. 8:17
3:15 [b]ver. 39 ch. 26:62
3:17 [c]Gen. 46:11 Ex. 6:16 ch. 26:57 1 Chr. 6:1,16 & 23:6
3:18 [d]Ex. 6:17
3:19 [e]Ex. 6:18
3:20 [f]Ex. 6:19
3:23 [g]ch. 1:53
3:25 [h]ch. 4:24-26 [i]Ex. 25:9 [j]Ex. 26:1 [k]Ex. 26:7,14 [l]Ex. 26:36
3:26 [m]Ex. 27:9 [n]Ex. 27:16 [o]Ex. 35:18
3:27 [p]1 Chr. 26:23
3:29 [q]ch. 1:53
3:31 [r]ch. 4:15 [s]Ex. 25:10 [t]Ex. 25:23 [u]Ex. 25:31 [v]Ex. 27:1 & 30:1 [w]Ex. 26:32
3:35 [x]ch. 1:53
3:36 [y]ch. 4:31,32

[f] Heb. *mouth* [g] Heb. *the office of the charge*

thereof, and the pillars thereof, and the sockets thereof, and all the vessels thereof, and all that serveth thereto,

37 And the pillars of the court round about, and their sockets, and their pins, and their cords.

38 ¶ [z]But those that encamp before the tabernacle toward the east, *even* before the tabernacle of the congregation eastward, *shall be* Moses, and Aaron and his sons, [a]keeping the charge of the sanctuary [b]for the charge of the children of Israel; and [c]the stranger that cometh nigh shall be put to death.

39 [d]All that were numbered of the Levites, which Moses and Aaron numbered at the commandment of the LORD, throughout their families, all the males from a month old and upward, *were* twenty and two thousand.

40 ¶ And the LORD said unto Moses, [e]Number all the firstborn of the males of the children of Israel from a month old and upward, and take the number of their names.

41 [f]And thou shalt take the Levites for me (I *am* the LORD) instead of all the firstborn among the children of Israel; and the cattle of the Levites instead of all the firstlings among the cattle of the children of Israel.

42 And Moses numbered, as the LORD commanded him, all the firstborn among the children of Israel.

43 And all the firstborn males by the number of names, from a month old and upward, of those that were numbered of them, were twenty and two thousand two hundred and threescore and thirteen.

44 ¶ And the LORD spake unto Moses, saying,

45 [g]Take the Levites instead of all the firstborn among the children of Israel, and the cattle of the Levites instead of their cattle; and the Levites shall be mine: I *am* the LORD.

46 And for those that are to be [h]redeemed of the two hundred and threescore and thirteen of the firstborn of the children of Israel, [i]which are more than the Levites;

47 Thou shalt even take [j]five shekels apiece by the poll, after the shekel of the sanctuary shalt thou take *them:* ([k]the shekel *is* twenty gerahs:)

48 And thou shalt give the money, wherewith the odd number of them is to be redeemed, unto Aaron and to his sons.

49 And Moses took the redemption money of them that were over and above them that were redeemed by the Levites:

50 Of the firstborn of the children of Israel took he the money; [l]a thousand three hundred and threescore and five *shekels,* after the shekel of the sanctuary:

51 And Moses [m]gave the money of them that were redeemed unto Aaron and to his sons, according to the word of the LORD, as the LORD commanded Moses.

The descendants of Kohath

4 AND THE LORD spake unto Moses and unto Aaron, saying,

2 Take the sum of the sons of Kohath from among the sons of Levi, after their families, by the house of their fathers,

3 [n]From thirty years old and upward even until fifty years old, all that enter into the host, to do the work in the tabernacle of the congregation.

4 [o]This *shall be* the service of the sons of Kohath in the tabernacle of the congregation, *about* [p]the most holy things:

5 ¶ And when the camp setteth forward, Aaron shall come, and his sons, and they shall take down [q]the covering veil, and cover the [r]ark of testimony with it:

6 And shall put thereon the covering of badgers' skins, and shall spread over *it* a cloth wholly of blue, and shall put in [s]the staves thereof.

7 And upon the [t]table of showbread they shall spread a cloth of blue, and put thereon the dishes, and the spoons, and the bowls, and covers to [h]cover withal: and the continual bread shall be thereon:

8 And they shall spread upon them a cloth of scarlet, and cover the same

3:38 [z]ch. 1:53 [a]ch. 18:5 [b]ver. 7,8 [c]ver. 10
3:39 [d]See ch. 26:62
3:40 [e]ver. 15
3:41 [f]ver. 12,45
3:45 [g]ver. 12,41
3:46 [h]Ex. 13:13 ch. 18:15 [i]ver. 39,43
3:47 [j]Lev. 27:6 ch. 18:16 [k]Ex. 30:13
3:50 [l]ver. 46,47
3:51 [m]ver. 48
4:3 [n]See ch. 8:24 1 Chr. 23:3,24,27
4:4 [o]ver. 15 [p]ver. 19
4:5 [q]Ex. 26:31 [r]Ex. 25:10,16
4:6 [s]Ex. 25:13
4:7 [t]Ex. 25:23,29,30

[h] Or, *pour out withal*

3:43 FIRSTBORN. The low number of "firstborn" compared with the approximately 600,000 men of 1:46 is explained by the fact that the "firstborn males" may refer only to those born between the time of the exodus from Egypt (cf. Ex. 13:1–2) and the numbering of the twelve tribes that occurred thirteen months later.

with a covering of badgers' skins, and shall put in the staves thereof.

9 And they shall take a cloth of blue, and cover the [u]candlestick of the light, [v]and his lamps, and his tongs, and his snuffdishes, and all the oil vessels thereof, wherewith they minister unto it:

10 And they shall put it and all the vessels thereof within a covering of badgers' skins, and shall put *it* upon a bar.

11 And upon [w]the golden altar they shall spread a cloth of blue, and cover it with a covering of badgers' skins, and shall put to the staves thereof:

12 And they shall take all the instruments of ministry, wherewith they minister in the sanctuary, and put *them* in a cloth of blue, and cover them with a covering of badgers' skins, and shall put *them* on a bar:

13 And they shall take away the ashes from the altar, and spread a purple cloth thereon:

14 And they shall put upon it all the vessels thereof, wherewith they minister about it, *even* the censers, the fleshhooks, and the shovels, and the [i]basins, all the vessels of the altar; and they shall spread upon it a covering of badgers' skins, and put to the staves of it.

15 And when Aaron and his sons have made an end of covering the sanctuary, and all the vessels of the sanctuary, as the camp is to set forward; after that [x]the sons of Kohath shall come to bear *it:* [y]but they shall not touch *any* holy thing, lest they die. [z]These *things are* the burden of the sons of Kohath in the tabernacle of the congregation.

16 ¶ And to the office of Eleazar the son of Aaron the priest *pertaineth* [a]the oil for the light, and the [b]sweet incense, and [c]the daily meat offering, and the [d]anointing oil, *and* the oversight of all the tabernacle, and of all that therein *is,* in the sanctuary, and in the vessels thereof.

17 ¶ And the LORD spake unto Moses and unto Aaron, saying,

18 Cut ye not off the tribe of the families of the Kohathites from among the Levites:

4:9 [u]Ex. 25:31 [v]Ex. 25:37,38
4:11 [w]Ex. 30:1,3
4:15 [x]ch. 7:9 & 10:21 Deut. 31:9 2 Sam. 6:13 1 Chr. 15:2,15 [y]2 Sam. 6:6,7 1 Chr. 13:9,10 [z]ch. 3:31
4:16 [a]Ex. 25:6 Lev. 24:2 [b]Ex. 30:34 [c]Ex. 29:38 [d]Ex. 30:25
4:19 [e]ver. 4
4:20 [f]See Ex. 19:21 1 Sam. 6:19
4:23 [g]ver. 3
4:25 [h]ch. 3:25,26
4:28 [i]ver. 33

19 But thus do unto them, that they may live, and not die, when they approach unto [e]the most holy things: Aaron and his sons shall go in, and appoint them every one to his service and to his burden:

20 [f]But they shall not go in to see when the holy things are covered, lest they die.

The descendants of Gershon

21 ¶ And the LORD spake unto Moses, saying,

22 Take also the sum of the sons of Gershon, throughout the houses of their fathers, by their families;

23 [g]From thirty years old and upward until fifty years old shalt thou number them; all that enter in [j]to perform the service, to do the work in the tabernacle of the congregation.

24 This *is* the service of the families of the Gershonites, to serve, and for [k]burdens:

25 And [h]they shall bear the curtains of the tabernacle, and the tabernacle of the congregation, his covering, and the covering of the badgers' skins that *is* above upon it, and the hanging for the door of the tabernacle of the congregation,

26 And the hangings of the court, and the hanging for the door of the gate of the court, which *is* by the tabernacle and by the altar round about, and their cords, and all the instruments of their service, and all that is made for them: so shall they serve.

27 At the [l]appointment of Aaron and his sons shall be all the service of the sons of the Gershonites, in all their burdens, and in all their service: and ye shall appoint unto them in charge all their burdens.

28 This *is* the service of the families of the sons of Gershon in the tabernacle of the congregation: and their charge *shall be* [i]under the hand of Ithamar the son of Aaron the priest.

The descendants of Merari

29 ¶ As for the sons of Merari, thou

[i] Or, *bowls* [j] Heb. *to war the warfare* [k] Or, *carriage* [l] Heb. *mouth*

4:20 BUT THEY SHALL NOT GO IN . . . LEST THEY DIE. The holiness of God will either destroy (vv. 14,20; see Lev. 10:2, note) or sanctify (Is. 6:1–7; see Lev. 19:2, note). God was teaching His people that His presence brings blessing if He is obeyed and honored, but judgment if He is treated with irreverence and dishonor (cf. 1 Cor. 11:27–29).

shalt number them after their families, by the house of their fathers;

30 [j]From thirty years old and upward even unto fifty years old shalt thou number them, every one that entereth into the [m]service, to do the work of the tabernacle of the congregation.

31 And [k]this *is* the charge of their burden, according to all their service in the tabernacle of the congregation; [l]the boards of the tabernacle, and the bars thereof, and the pillars thereof, and sockets thereof,

32 And the pillars of the court round about, and their sockets, and their pins, and their cords, with all their instruments, and with all their service: and by name ye shall [m]reckon the instruments of the charge of their burden.

33 This *is* the service of the families of the sons of Merari, according to all their service, in the tabernacle of the congregation, under the hand of Ithamar the son of Aaron the priest.

The results of the census

34 ¶ [n]And Moses and Aaron and the chief of the congregation numbered the sons of the Kohathites after their families, and after the house of their fathers,

35 From thirty [o]years old and upward even unto fifty years old, every one that entereth into the service, for the work in the tabernacle of the congregation:

36 And those that were numbered of them by their families were two thousand seven hundred and fifty.

37 These *were* they that were numbered of the families of the Kohathites, all that might do service in the tabernacle of the congregation, which Moses and Aaron did number according to the commandment of the LORD by the hand of Moses.

38 And those that were numbered of the sons of Gershon, throughout their families, and by the house of their fathers,

39 From thirty years old and upward even unto fifty years old, every one that entereth into the service, for the work in the tabernacle of the congregation,

40 Even those that were numbered of them, throughout their families, by the house of their fathers, were two thousand and six hundred and thirty.

41 [p]These *are* they that were numbered of the families of the sons of Gershon, of all that might do service in the tabernacle of the congregation, whom Moses and Aaron did number according to the commandment of the LORD.

42 ¶ And those that were numbered of the families of the sons of Merari, throughout their families, by the house of their fathers,

43 From thirty years old and upward even unto fifty years old, every one that entereth into the service, for the work in the tabernacle of the congregation,

44 Even those that were numbered of them after their families, were three thousand and two hundred.

45 These *be* those that were numbered of the families of the sons of Merari, whom Moses and Aaron numbered [q]according to the word of the LORD by the hand of Moses.

46 All those that were numbered of the Levites, whom Moses and Aaron and the chief of Israel numbered, after their families, and after the house of their fathers,

47 [r]From thirty years old and upward even unto fifty years old, every one that came to do the service of the ministry, and the service of the burden in the tabernacle of the congregation,

48 Even those that were numbered of them, were eight thousand and five hundred and fourscore.

49 According to the commandment of the LORD they were numbered by the hand of Moses, [s]every one according to his service, and according to his burden: thus were they numbered of him, [t]as the LORD commanded Moses.

Concerning the unclean

5 AND THE LORD spake unto Moses, saying,

2 Command the children of Israel,

4:30 [j]ver. 3
4:31 [k]ch. 3:36,37 [l]Ex. 26:15
4:32 [m]Ex. 38:21
4:34 [n]ver. 2
4:35 [o]ver. 47 ch. 8:24,26 1 Chr. 23:24 Luke 3:23 1 Tim. 3:6
4:41 [p]ver. 22
4:45 [q]ver. 29
4:47 [r]ver. 3,23,30
4:49 [s]ver. 15,24,31 [t]ver. 1,21

[m] Heb. *warfare*

5:2 PUT OUT OF THE CAMP. People with leprosy or discharges, or those who had come into contact with the dead, were ceremonially unclean (see Lev. 12:2; 13:3, notes). Such people were put outside the camp because God would not dwell in the midst of uncleanness (v. 3). The N.T. applies the moral principle contained in this regulation to church members who flagrantly transgress God's

that they put out of the camp every [u]leper, and every one that hath an [v]issue, and whosoever is defiled by the [w]dead:

3 Both male and female shall ye put out, without the camp shall ye put them; that they defile not their camps, [x]in the midst whereof I dwell.

4 And the children of Israel did so, and put them out without the camp: as the LORD spake unto Moses, so did the children of Israel.

Suspected adultery

5 ¶ And the LORD spake unto Moses, saying,

6 Speak unto the children of Israel, [y]When a man or woman shall commit any sin that men commit, to do a trespass against the LORD, and that person be guilty;

7 [z]Then they shall confess their sin which they have done: and he shall recompense his trespass [a]with the principal thereof, and add unto it the fifth *part* thereof, and give *it* unto *him* against whom he hath trespassed.

8 But if the man have no kinsman to recompense the trespass unto, let the trespass be recompensed unto the LORD, *even* to the priest; beside [b]the ram of the atonement, whereby an atonement shall be made for him.

9 And every [c]offering[n] of all the holy things of the children of Israel, which they bring unto the priest, shall be his.

10 And every man's hallowed things shall be his: whatsoever any man giveth the priest, it shall be [d]his.

11 ¶ And the LORD spake unto Moses, saying,

12 Speak unto the children of Israel, and say unto them, If any man's wife go aside, and commit a trespass against him,

13 And a man [e]lie with her carnally, and it be hid from the eyes of her husband, and be kept close, and she be defiled, and *there be* no witness against her, neither she be taken *with the manner;*

14 And the spirit of jealousy come upon him, and he be jealous of his wife, and she be defiled: or if the spirit of jealousy come upon him, and he be jealous of his wife, and she be not defiled:

15 Then shall the man bring his wife unto the priest, and he shall [f]bring her offering for her, the tenth *part* of an ephah of barley meal; he shall pour no oil upon it, nor put frankincense thereon; for it *is* an offering of jealousy, an offering of memorial, [g]bringing iniquity to remembrance.

16 And the priest shall bring her near, and set her before the LORD:

17 And the priest shall take holy water in an earthen vessel; and of the dust that is in the floor of the tabernacle the priest shall take, and put *it* into the water:

18 And the priest shall set the woman before the LORD, and uncover the woman's head, and put the offering of memorial in her hands, which *is* the jealousy offering: and the priest shall have in his hand the bitter water that causeth the curse:

19 And the priest shall charge her by an oath, and say unto the woman, If no man have lain with thee, and if thou hast not gone aside to uncleanness [o][p]*with another* instead of thy husband, be thou free from this bitter water that causeth the curse:

20 But if thou hast gone aside *to another* instead of thy husband, and if thou be defiled, and some man have lain with thee beside thine husband:

21 Then the priest shall [h]charge the woman with an oath of cursing, and the priest shall say unto the woman, [i]The LORD make thee a curse and an oath among thy people, when the LORD doth make thy thigh to [q]rot, and thy belly to swell;

22 And this water that causeth the curse [j]shall go into thy bowels, to make *thy* belly to swell, and *thy* thigh

5:2 [u]Lev. 13:3,46 [v]Lev. 15:2 [w]Lev. 21:1 ch. 9:6,10 & 19:11,13 & 31:19
5:3 [x]Lev. 26:11,12 2 Cor. 6:16
5:6 [y]Lev. 6:2,3
5:7 [z]Lev. 5:5 & 26:40 Josh. 7:19 [a]Lev. 6:5
5:8 [b]Lev. 6:6,7 & 7:7
5:9 [c]Ex. 29:28 Lev. 6:17,18,26 & 7:6,7,9,10,14
5:10 [d]Lev. 10:13
5:13 [e]Lev. 18:20
5:15 [f]Lev. 5:11 [g]1 Ki. 17:18 Ezek. 29:16
5:21 [h]Josh. 6:26 1 Sam. 14:24 Neh. 10:29 [i]Jer. 29:22
5:22 [j]Ps. 109:18

[n] Or, *heave offering* [o] Or, being *in the power of thy husband* [p] Heb. *under thy husband* [q] Heb. *fall*

truth or righteousness; they must be "put out" of the congregation if the body of believers expects to receive the blessing and presence of God (cf. 1 Cor. 5; 2 Cor. 6:14–18; 2 Thes. 3:14; 2 John 10–11; see Mat. 18:15, note).

5:18 WOMAN BEFORE THE LORD. If a husband had reason to suspect that his wife had committed adultery but there was no evidence, the husband could have the wife brought before the Lord in order to determine her guilt or innocence. This protected her from false accusation, as well as provided a means for determining guilt when needed. If she was guilty, she became ill as the result of God's judgment (vv. 21–28).

to rot: [k]And the woman shall say,
Amen, amen.
23 And the priest shall write these
curses in a book, and he shall blot *them*
out with the bitter water:
24 And he shall cause the woman to
drink the bitter water that causeth the
curse: and the water that causeth the
curse shall enter into her, *and become*
bitter.
25 Then the priest shall take the
jealousy offering out of the woman's
hand, and shall [l]wave the offering be-
fore the LORD, and offer it upon the al-
tar:
26 [m]And the priest shall take an
handful of the offering, *even* the memo-
rial thereof, and burn *it* upon the altar,
and afterward shall cause the woman
to drink the water.
27 And when he hath made her to
drink the water, then it shall come to
pass, *that,* if she be defiled, and have
done trespass against her husband,
that the water that causeth the curse
shall enter into her, *and become* bitter,
and her belly shall swell, and her thigh
shall rot: and the woman [n]shall be a
curse among her people.
28 And if the woman be not defiled,
but be clean; then she shall be free, and
shall conceive seed.
29 This *is* the law of jealousies,
when a wife goeth aside *to another* [o]in-
stead of her husband, and is defiled;
30 Or when the spirit of jealousy
cometh upon him, and he be jealous
over his wife, and shall set the woman
before the LORD, and the priest shall ex-
ecute upon her all this law.
31 Then shall the man be guiltless
from iniquity, and this woman [p]shall
bear her iniquity.

5:22 [k]Deut. 27:15
5:25 [l]Lev. 8:27
5:26 [m]Lev. 2:2,9
5:27 [n]ver. 21
5:29 [o]ver. 19
5:31 [p]Lev. 20:17,19,20
6:2 [q]Lev. 27:2 Judg. 13:5 Acts 21:23 Rom. 1:1
6:3 [r]Amos 2:12 Luke 1:15
6:5 [s]Judg. 13:5 & 16:17 1 Sam. 1:11
6:6 [t]Lev. 21:11 ch. 19:11,16
6:7 [u]Lev. 21:1,2,11 ch. 9:6
6:8 [v]2 Cor. 6:17,18

The law of a Nazarite

6 AND THE LORD spake unto Moses,
saying,
2 Speak unto the children of Israel,
and say unto them, When either man or
woman shall [q]separate[r] *themselves*
to vow a vow of a Nazarite, to separate
themselves unto the LORD:
3 [r]He shall separate *himself* from
wine and strong drink, and shall drink
no vinegar of wine, or vinegar of strong
drink, neither shall he drink any liquor
of grapes, nor eat moist grapes, or
dried.
4 All the days of his [s]separation
shall he eat nothing that is made of the
[t]vine tree, from the kernels even to
the husk.
5 All the days of the vow of his sepa-
ration there shall no [s]razor come
upon his head: until the days be ful-
filled, in the which he separateth *him-
self* unto the LORD, he shall be holy, *and*
shall let the locks of the hair of his
head grow.
6 All the days that he separateth
himself unto the LORD [t]he shall come
at no dead body.
7 [u]He shall not make himself un-
clean for his father, or for his mother,
for his brother, or for his sister, when
they die: because the [u]consecration of
his God *is* upon his head.
8 [v]All the days of his separation he
is holy unto the LORD.

[r] Or, *make* themselves *Nazarites* [s] Or, *Nazariteship* [t] Heb. *vine of the wine* [u] Heb. *separation*

6:2 A NAZARITE. The word "Nazarite" (Heb. *nazir*, from *nazar*, "to set apart") designates one who was set apart and dedicated wholly to the Lord. The dedication could be for a specific period of time or for life (Judg. 13:5; 1 Sam. 1:11). (1) The Nazarites were raised up by God Himself in order that through their lifestyle they might demonstrate His highest standard of holiness, sanctity, and commitment in the presence of the people (cf. Amos 2:11–12). (2) The Nazarite vow was totally voluntary. It was designed to teach Israel that total devotion to God must come first from a person's heart and then come to expression in self-denial (vv. 3–4), visible profession (v. 5), and personal purity (vv. 6–8). The complete devotion of a Nazarite serves as an example of what every Christian should seek to be.

6:3 WINE . . . STRONG DRINK. For comments on how the Nazarite was to relate to wine and strong drink, see article on WINE IN THE OLD TESTAMENT, p. 220.

6:3 LIQUOR OF GRAPES. The word translated "liquor" (Heb. *mishrah*) refers to a drink made by steeping the grapes or the remains of pressed grapes in water.

6:5 THE HAIR . . . GROW. The Nazarite was to let his hair grow long as a visible symbol of his separation to the Lord. According to Paul, long hair was normally a dishonor to a man (1 Cor. 11:14); thus for a Nazarite to have long hair may have symbolized his willingness to bear reproach and ridicule for the Lord. The command not to go near a dead person (v. 6) stressed that death was never God's will when He created the human race. Death is the antithesis of life and the consequence of sin; thus a corpse was viewed as unclean (see Lev. 12:2, note; 13:3, note).

WINE IN THE OLD TESTAMENT

Num. 6:3 "He shall separate himself *from wine and strong drink, and shall drink no vinegar of wine, or vinegar of strong drink, neither shall he drink any liquor of grapes, nor eat moist grapes, or dried."*

HEBREW WORDS FOR WINE. In general, there are two Hebrew words translated as "wine" in the Bible. (1) The first and most common word is *yayin*, a generic term used approximately 141 times in the O.T. to indicate various kinds of fermented or unfermented wine (see Neh. 5:18, which speaks of "all sorts of wine [*yayin*]"). (a) On the one hand, *yayin* is applied to all kinds of fermented grape juice (see Gen. 9:20–21; 19:32–33; 1 Sam. 25:36–37; Prov. 23:30–31). The tragic results of using fermented wine are described in various places in the O.T., notably Prov. 23:29–35 (see next section).

(b) On the other hand, *yayin* is also used for the sweet unfermented juice of the grape. It can refer to fresh juice as it is pressed from grapes. Isaiah prophesies, "The treaders shall tread out no wine [*yayin*] in *their* presses" (Is. 16:10); likewise Jeremiah says, "I have caused wine [*yayin*] to fail from the winepresses; none shall tread with shouting" (Jer. 48:33). In fact, Jeremiah even refers to the juice still in the grape as *yayin* (see Jer. 40:10,12). Further evidence that *yayin* at times refers to unfermented juice of the grape is found in Lamentations, where the author describes nursing infants as crying out to their mothers for their normal food of "corn and wine" (Lam. 2:12). The fact that unfermented grape juice can go by the term "wine" is supported by various scholarly studies. *The Jewish Encyclopedia* (1901) states: "Fresh wine before fermentation was called *yayin-mi-gat* [wine of the vat] (Sanh, 70a)." Also, the *Encyclopaedia Judaica* (1971) attests to the fact that the term *yayin* was used to refer to the juice of the grape in several stages, including "the newly pressed wine prior to fermentation." The Babylonian Talmud ascribes to Rabbi Hiyya a statement concerning "wine [*yayin*] from the press" (*Baba Bathra*, 97a). And in *Halakot Gedalot* it is said, "One may press out a cluster of grapes, since the juice of the grape is considered wine [*yayin*] in connection with the laws of the Nazarite" (cited by Louis Ginzberg in *American Jewish Yearbook*, 1923, pp. 408–409). For a discussion of *oinos*, the N.T. Greek equivalent of the Hebrew word *yayin*, see articles on WINE IN NEW TESTAMENT TIMES (1) and (2), p. 1538 and p. 1594.

(2) The other Hebrew word translated "wine" is *tirosh*, a word meaning "new wine" or "harvest wine." *Tirosh* occurs thirty-eight times in the O.T.; it never refers to fermented drink, but always to the unfermented fruit of the vine, such as the juice that is still in the grape cluster (Is. 65:8) or sweet juice from newly harvested grapes (Deut. 11:14; Prov. 3:10; Joel 2:24). Brown, Driver, Briggs (*A Hebrew and English Lexicon of the Old Testament*) states that *tirosh* means "must, fresh or new wine"; *The Jewish Encyclopedia* (1901) states that " '*tirosh*' includes all kinds of sweet juices and must, and does not include fermented wine." *Tirosh* has "a blessing . . . in it" (Is. 65:8); fermented wine, however, is a mocker (Prov. 20:1) and brings drunkenness (see Prov. 23:31, note).

(3) In addition to these two words for wine, there is another Hebrew word that occurs twenty-three times in the O.T. and often in the same context—*shekar*, usually translated as "strong drink" (e.g., Num. 6:3). This translation is unfortunate, since it implies "distilled liquor," a drink that did not exist among the Hebrews in Bible times. Some scholars say *shekar* most often refers to a fermented drink, perhaps made from palm juice, pomegranates, apples, or dates; some interpreters include beer as a "strong drink" (e.g., Holladay, *Lexicon*). *The Jewish Encyclopedia* (1901) suggests that when *yayin* was distinguished from *shekar*, the former was a form of fermented drink diluted with water whereas the latter was undiluted. At times, however, it can refer to a sweet satisfying unfermented juice (Robert P. Teachout, "The Use of 'Wine' in the Old Testament," Th.D.

dissertation, Dallas Theological Seminary, 1979; cf. also Robert Young, *Analytical Concordance to the Bible*, under "strong drink"). *Shekar* is related to *shakar*, a Hebrew verb that means "to drink deeply," not "to become drunk." In most instances, it is best to understand that when *yayin* and *shekar* are used together, they form a single figure of speech referring to intoxicating beverages.

THE OLD TESTAMENT PERSPECTIVE ON FERMENTED WINE. There are various places in the O.T. where the use of *yayin* and *shekar* as fermented beverages is condemned. (1) The Bible first describes the evil effects of intoxicating wine in the story of Noah (Gen. 9:20–27). He planted a vineyard, harvested it, made intoxicating wine from the grapes, and drank from it. Doing so led to drunkenness, immodesty, indiscretion, and the family tragedy of a curse placed on Canaan. At the time of Abraham, intoxicating wine was a factor in the incest that led to the pregnancies of Lot's daughters (Gen. 19:31–38).

(2) Because of the corrupting potential of alcoholic drinks, God commanded all priests of Israel to abstain from all types of wine and strong drink during their time of ministry unto Him. God regarded the violation of this command sufficiently serious to warrant the death penalty for the offending priest (Lev. 10:9–11).

(3) God also revealed His will concerning wine and strong drink by making abstinence a requirement for all who took the Nazarite vow (see next section).

(4) Solomon's God-given wisdom led him to write: "Wine *is* a mocker, strong drink *is* raging: and whosoever is deceived thereby is not wise" (see Prov. 20:1, note). Alcoholic beverages can cause one to mock God's standard of righteousness and to lose self-control with regard to sin and immorality.

(5) Finally, the Scriptures unequivocally state that in order to avoid woe and sorrow and instead to follow God's will, the righteous must not even look upon or desire any fermented wine that can intoxicate and cause addiction (see Prov. 23:29–35, notes).

THE NAZARITES AND WINE. Nazarites were expected to declare that all Israelites should live on as high a level of separation and commitment to God as they themselves did (see Num. 6:2, note). God gave them clear instructions concerning the use of wine. (1) The Nazarite was to abstain from "wine and strong drink" (Num. 6:3; see Deut. 14:26, note); in fact, they were not permitted to partake of any product made from the grape, either in liquid or solid form. Most likely God gave this command as a safeguard against the temptation to use intoxicating drinks and against the possibility of a Nazarite drinking alcoholic wine by mistake (Num. 6:3–4). God did not want a totally devoted person to be exposed to the possibility of intoxication or addiction (cf. Lev. 10:8–11; Prov. 31:4–5). Thus, the highest standard put before God's people concerning alcoholic beverages was total abstinence (Num. 6:3–4).

(2) Drinking alcohol often leads to various other sins (such as sexual immorality or criminal activity). The Nazarites were to eat or drink nothing that came from the vine in order to teach them that they must avoid sin and anything that borders on it, leads to it, or tempts one to commit it.

(3) God's standard for the Nazarites of total abstinence from wine and strong drink was ridiculed and rejected by many of those in Israel during Amos's day. This prophet stated that the ungodly of Israel "gave the Nazarites wine to drink" (see Amos 2:12, note). The prophet Isaiah also declared, "The priest and the prophet have erred through strong drink, they are swallowed up of wine, they are out of the way through strong drink; they err in vision, they stumble *in* judgment. For all tables are full of vomit *and* filthiness" (Is. 28:7–8). This occurred because these leaders refused God's high standard of total abstinence (see Prov. 31:4–5, note).

(4) The essential spirit of Nazaritism—i.e., total consecration to God and His highest standards—is a demand placed upon the believer in Christ (cf. Rom. 12:1; 2 Cor. 6:17; 7:1). Abstinence from anything that might draw one into sin, stimulate a desire for harmful things, open the way to drug or alcohol addiction, or cause a brother to stumble is as necessary for the believer today as it was for the Nazarite in O.T. times (see 1 Thes. 5:6, note; Tit. 2:2, note; see articles on WINE IN NEW TESTAMENT TIMES (1) and (2), p. 1538 and p. 1594).

9 And if any man die very suddenly by him, and he hath defiled the head of his consecration; then he shall [w]shave his head in the day of his cleansing, on the seventh day shall he shave it.

10 And [x]on the eighth day he shall bring two turtles, or two young pigeons, to the priest, to the door of the tabernacle of the congregation:

11 And the priest shall offer the one for a sin offering, and the other for a burnt offering, and make an atonement for him, for that he sinned by the dead, and shall hallow his head that same day.

12 And he shall consecrate unto the LORD the days of his separation, and shall bring a lamb of the first year [y]for a trespass offering: but the days that were before shall [v]be lost, because his separation was defiled.

13 ¶ And this *is* the law of the Nazarite, [z]when the days of his separation are fulfilled: he shall be brought unto the door of the tabernacle of the congregation:

14 And he shall offer his offering unto the LORD, one he lamb of the first year without blemish for a burnt offering, and one ewe lamb of the first year without blemish [a]for a sin offering, and one ram without blemish [b]for peace offerings,

15 And a basket of unleavened bread, [c]cakes of fine flour mingled with oil, and wafers of unleavened bread [d]anointed with oil, and their meat offering, and their [e]drink offerings.

16 And the priest shall bring *them* before the LORD, and shall offer his sin offering, and his burnt offering:

17 And he shall offer the ram *for* a sacrifice of peace offerings unto the LORD, with the basket of unleavened bread: the priest shall offer also his meat offering, and his drink offering.

18 [f]And the Nazarite shall shave the head of his separation *at* the door of the tabernacle of the congregation, and shall take the hair of the head of his separation, and put *it* in the fire which *is* under the sacrifice of the peace offerings.

19 And the priest shall take the [g]sodden shoulder of the ram, and one unleavened cake out of the basket, and one unleavened wafer, and [h]shall put *them* upon the hands of the Nazarite, after *the hair of* his separation is shaven:

20 And the priest shall wave them *for* a wave offering before the LORD: [i]this *is* holy for the priest, with the wave breast and heave shoulder: and after that the Nazarite may drink wine.

21 This *is* the law of the Nazarite who hath vowed, *and of* his offering unto the LORD for his separation, beside *that* that his hand shall get: according to the vow which he vowed, so he must do after the law of his separation.

The Aaronic benediction

22 ¶ And the LORD spake unto Moses, saying,

23 Speak unto Aaron and unto his sons, saying, On this wise [j]ye shall

6:9 [w]Acts 18:18 & 21:24 **6:10** [x]Lev. 5:7 & 14:22 & 15:14,29 **6:12** [y]Lev. 5:6 **6:13** [z]Acts 21:26 **6:14** [a]Lev. 4:2,27,32 [b]Lev. 3:6 **6:15** [c]Lev. 2:4 [d]Ex. 29:2 [e]ch. 15:5,7,10 **6:18** [f]Acts 21:24 **6:19** [g]1 Sam. 2:15 [h]Ex. 29:23,24 **6:20** [i]Ex. 29:27,28 **6:23** [j]Lev. 9:22 Deut. 10:8 & 21:5 Josh. 8:33 1 Chr. 23:13

[v]Heb. *fall*

6:14 OFFER HIS OFFERING. After completing his vow of separation, the Nazarite was to offer the same kind of sacrifices that the high priest offered on the day of his ordination (cf. Lev. 8—9); all those in Israel, men or women (v. 2), who completely dedicated themselves to God were as important in God's sight as the highest minister in the congregation. Greatness in God's kingdom is not based on position and power, but on consecration and commitment (see Luke 22:24–30, note).

6:20 THE NAZARITE MAY DRINK WINE. After the Nazarite terminated his vow, he was permitted to drink wine (Heb. *yayin*; see article on WINE IN THE OLD TESTAMENT, p. 220). God had not yet specifically forbidden the use of fermented *yayin*. Its prohibition applied at this time only to situations involving total consecration to God (vv. 1–4; Lev. 10:9–11). In the process of progressive revelation, God later stated explicitly that *all* His people were to refrain from fermented *yayin* that could intoxicate (see Prov. 23:29–35; see 23:31, note).

6:23 BLESS THE CHILDREN OF ISRAEL. Vv. 22–27 show God's gracious response to His people if they maintained purity in the congregation and expressed the kind of heart-devotion seen in a Nazarite vow (see v. 2, note). "To bless" (Heb. *barak*) conveys the idea that God's presence, activity, and love are brought into a person's life and environment. (1) This blessing was set before God's faithful servants under the conditions He had established (Deut. 11:27).

(2) The priestly blessing consisted of three parts: (a) The imparting of God's blessing and protection from evil forces and all that was adverse to one's welfare in life (v. 24; cf. Ps. 71:1–6). (b) The shining of the Lord's face, i.e., God's favor, goodwill, and grace toward the people (v. 25), is the opposite of His anger (cf. Ps. 27:1; 31:16; Prov. 15:30; 16:14; Is. 57:17). Grace is God's mercy, love, and saving power (see article on FAITH AND GRACE, p. 1738). (c) The Lord's lifting up

bless the children of Israel, saying unto them,

24 The LORD bless thee, and [k]keep thee:

25 The LORD [l]make his face shine upon thee, and [m]be gracious unto thee:

26 [n]The LORD lift up his countenance upon thee, and [o]give thee

Num. 12:3-7 peace.

27 [p]And they shall put my name upon the children of Israel; and [q]I will bless them.

The dedication offerings

7 AND IT came to pass on the day that Moses had fully [r]set up the tabernacle, and had anointed it, and sanctified it, and all the instruments thereof, both the altar and all the vessels thereof, and had anointed them, and sanctified them;

2 That [s]the princes of Israel, heads of the house of their fathers, who *were* the princes of the tribes, [w]and were over them that were numbered, offered:

3 And they brought their offering before the LORD, six covered wagons, and twelve oxen; a wagon for two of the princes, and for each one an ox: and they brought them before the tabernacle.

4 And the LORD spake unto Moses, saying,

5 Take *it* of them, that they may be to do the service of the tabernacle of the congregation; and thou shalt give them unto the Levites, to every man according to his service.

6 And Moses took the wagons and the oxen, and gave them unto the Levites.

7 Two wagons and four oxen [t]he gave unto the sons of Gershon, according to their service:

8 [u]And four wagons and eight oxen he gave unto the sons of Merari, according unto their service, [v]under the hand of Ithamar the son of Aaron the priest.

9 But unto the sons of Kohath he gave none: because [w]the service of the sanctuary belonging unto them [x]*was that* they should bear upon their shoulders.

10 ¶ And the princes offered for [y]dedicating of the altar in the day that it was anointed, even the princes offered their offering before the altar.

11 And the LORD said unto Moses, They shall offer their offering, each prince on his day, for the dedicating of the altar.

12 ¶ And he that offered his offering the first day was [z]Nahshon the son of Amminadab, of the tribe of Judah:

13 And his offering *was* one silver charger, the weight thereof *was* an hundred and thirty *shekels,* one silver bowl of seventy shekels, after [a]the shekel of the sanctuary; both of them *were* full of fine flour mingled with oil for a [b]meat offering:

14 One spoon of ten *shekels* of gold, full of [c]incense:

15 [d]One young bullock, one ram, one lamb [e]of the first year, for a burnt offering:

16 One kid of the goats for a [f]sin offering:

17 And for [g]a sacrifice of peace offerings, two oxen, five rams, five he goats, five lambs of the first year: this *was* the offering of Nahshon the son of Amminadab.

18 ¶ On the second day Nethaneel the son of Zuar, prince of Issachar, did offer:

19 He offered *for* his offering one silver charger, the weight whereof *was* an hundred and thirty *shekels,* one silver bowl of seventy shekels, after the shekel of the sanctuary; both of them full of fine flour mingled with oil for a meat offering:

20 One spoon of gold of ten *shekels,* full of incense:

21 One young bullock, one ram, one lamb of the first year, for a burnt offering:

6:24 [k]Ps. 121:7 John 17:11 **6:25** [l]Ps. 31:16 & 67:1 & 80:3,7,19 & 119:135 Dan. 9:17 [m]Gen. 43:29 Ex. 33:19 Mal. 1:9 **6:26** [n]Ps. 4:6 [o]John 14:27 Phil. 4:7 2 Thes. 3:16 **6:27** [p]Deut. 28:10 2 Chr. 7:14 Is. 43:7 Dan. 9:18,19 [q]ch. 23:20 Ps. 5:12 & 67:7 & 115:12,13 Eph. 1:3 **7:1** [r]Ex. 40:18 Lev. 8:10,11 **7:2** [s]ch. 1:4 **7:7** [t]ch. 4:23 **7:8** [u]ch. 4:33 [v]ch. 4:28,33 **7:9** [w]ch. 4:15 [x]ch. 4:6,8,10,12, 14 2 Sam. 6:13 **7:10** [y]See Deut. 20:5 1 Ki. 8:63 2 Chr. 7:5,9 Ezra 6:16 Neh. 12:27 **7:12** [z]ch. 2:3 **7:13** [a]Ex. 30:13 [b]Lev. 2:1 **7:14** [c]Ex. 30:34 **7:15** [d]Lev. 1:2 [e]Ex. 12:5 **7:16** [f]Lev. 4:23 **7:17** [g]Lev. 3:1

[w]Heb. *who stood*

His countenance upon them (v. 26), i.e., caring for and giving His blessings with heartfelt love (cf. Ps. 4:7–8; 33:18; 34:17). What God gives is "peace" (v. 26). Peace (Heb. *shalom*) means being complete so that nothing is lacking and receiving all that is necessary to make life truly life (cf. Mal. 2:5), including hope for the future (Jer. 29:11). The opposite of "peace" is not only the lack of harmony, but evil in all its forms (cf. Rom. 1:7; 1 Cor. 1:3; 1 Thes. 5:23; see article on THE PEACE OF GOD, p. 1122).

(3) God's blessing upon His people would result in salvation going forth like a lighted torch to all the nations (Ps. 67; 133:3; Ezek. 34:26; see Mat. 28:19, note); Luke 24:50, note.

22 One kid of the goats for a sin offering:
23 And for a sacrifice of peace offerings, two oxen, five rams, five he goats, five lambs of the first year: this *was* the offering of Nethaneel the son of Zuar.
24 ¶ On the third day Eliab the son of Helon, prince of the children of Zebulun, *did offer:*
25 His offering *was* one silver charger, the weight whereof *was* an hundred and thirty *shekels,* one silver bowl of seventy shekels, after the shekel of the sanctuary; both of them full of fine flour mingled with oil for a meat offering:
26 One golden spoon of ten *shekels,* full of incense:
27 One young bullock, one ram, one lamb of the first year, for a burnt offering:
28 One kid of the goats for a sin offering:
29 And for a sacrifice of peace offerings, two oxen, five rams, five he goats, five lambs of the first year: this *was* the offering of Eliab the son of Helon.
30 ¶ On the fourth day [h]Elizur the son of Shedeur, prince of the children of Reuben, *did offer:*
31 His offering *was* one silver charger of the weight of an hundred and thirty *shekels,* one silver bowl of seventy shekels, after the shekel of the sanctuary; both of them full of fine flour mingled with oil for a meat offering:
32 One golden spoon of ten *shekels,* full of incense:
33 One young bullock, one ram, one lamb of the first year, for a burnt offering:
34 One kid of the goats for a sin offering:
35 And for a sacrifice of peace offerings, two oxen, five rams, five he goats, five lambs of the first year: this *was* the offering of Elizur the son of Shedeur.
36 ¶ On the fifth day [i]Shelumiel the son of Zurishaddai, prince of the children of Simeon, *did offer:*
37 His offering *was* one silver charger, the weight whereof *was* an hundred and thirty *shekels,* one silver bowl of seventy shekels, after the shekel of the sanctuary; both of them full of fine flour mingled with oil for a meat offering:
38 One golden spoon of ten *shekels,* full of incense:

7:30 [h]ch. 1:5 & 2:10
7:36 [i]ver. 41 ch. 1:6 & 2:12
7:42 [j]ch. 1:14 & 2:14
7:45 [k]Ps. 40:6
7:48 [l]ch. 1:10 & 2:18
7:50 [m]Deut. 33:10 Ps. 66:15 & 141:2 Ezek. 8:11 Mal. 1:11 Luke 1:10 Rev. 5:8 & 8:3
7:54 [n]ch. 1:10 & 2:20

39 One young bullock, one ram, one lamb of the first year, for a burnt offering:
40 One kid of the goats for a sin offering:
41 And for a sacrifice of peace offerings, two oxen, five rams, five he goats, five lambs of the first year: this *was* the offering of Shelumiel the son of Zurishaddai.
42 ¶ On the sixth day [j]Eliasaph the son of [x]Deuel, prince of the children of Gad, *offered:*
43 His offering *was* one silver charger of the weight of an hundred and thirty *shekels,* a silver bowl of seventy shekels, after the shekel of the sanctuary; both of them full of fine flour mingled with oil for a meat offering:
44 One golden spoon of ten *shekels,* full of incense:
45 One young bullock, one ram, one lamb of the first year, for [k]a burnt offering:
46 One kid of the goats for a sin offering:
47 And for a sacrifice of peace offerings, two oxen, five rams, five he goats, five lambs of the first year: this *was* the offering of Eliasaph the son of Deuel.
48 ¶ On the seventh day [l]Elishama the son of Ammihud, prince of the children of Ephraim, *offered:*
49 His offering *was* one silver charger, the weight whereof *was* an hundred and thirty *shekels,* one silver bowl of seventy shekels, after the shekel of the sanctuary; both of them full of fine flour mingled with oil for a meat offering:
50 One golden spoon of ten *shekels,* full of [m]incense:
51 One young bullock, one ram, one lamb of the first year, for a burnt offering:
52 One kid of the goats for a sin offering:
53 And for a sacrifice of peace offerings, two oxen, five rams, five he goats, five lambs of the first year: this *was* the offering of Elishama the son of Ammihud.
54 ¶ On the eighth day *offered* [n]Gamaliel the son of Pedahzur, prince of the children of Manasseh:
55 His offering *was* one silver charger of the weight of an hundred

[x] Or, *Reuel*

and thirty *shekels,* one silver bowl of seventy shekels, after the shekel of the sanctuary; both of them full of fine flour mingled with oil for a meat offering:

56 One golden spoon of ten *shekels,* full of incense:

57 One young bullock, one ram, one lamb of the first year, for a burnt offering:

58 One kid of the goats for a sin offering:

59 And for a sacrifice of peace offerings, two oxen, five rams, five he goats, five lambs of the first year: this *was* the offering of Gamaliel the son of Pedahzur.

60 ¶ On the ninth day [o]Abidan the son of Gideoni, prince of the children of Benjamin, *offered:*

61 His offering *was* one silver charger, the weight whereof *was* an hundred and thirty *shekels,* one silver bowl of seventy shekels, after the shekel of the sanctuary; both of them full of fine flour mingled with oil for a meat offering:

62 One golden spoon of ten *shekels,* full of incense:

63 One young bullock, one ram, one lamb of the first year, for a burnt offering:

64 One kid of the goats for a sin offering:

65 And for a sacrifice of peace offerings, two oxen, five rams, five he goats, five lambs of the first year: this *was* the offering of Abidan the son of Gideoni.

66 ¶ On the tenth day [p]Ahiezer the son of Ammishaddai, prince of the children of Dan, *offered:*

67 His offering *was* one silver charger, the weight whereof *was* an hundred and thirty *shekels,* one silver bowl of seventy shekels, after the shekel of the sanctuary; both of them full of fine flour mingled with oil for a meat offering:

68 One golden spoon of ten *shekels,* full of incense:

69 One young bullock, one ram, one lamb of the first year, for a burnt offering:

70 One kid of the goats for a sin offering:

71 And for a sacrifice of peace offerings, two oxen, five rams, five he goats, five lambs of the first year: this *was* the offering of Ahiezer the son of Ammishaddai.

7:60 [o]ch. 1:11 & 2:22
7:66 [p]ch. 1:12 & 2:25

7:72 [q]ch. 1:13 & 2:27
7:78 [r]ch. 1:15 & 2:29
7:84 [s]2 Chr. 7:9 [t]Judg. 5:9
7:85 [u]Ex. 30:13,24 & 38:24-26 Lev. 5:15 & 27:3,25 ch. 3:47

72 ¶ On the eleventh day [q]Pagiel the son of Ocran, prince of the children of Asher, *offered:*

73 His offering *was* one silver charger, the weight whereof *was* an hundred and thirty *shekels,* one silver bowl of seventy shekels, after the shekel of the sanctuary; both of them full of fine flour mingled with oil for a meat offering:

74 One golden spoon of ten *shekels,* full of incense:

75 One young bullock, one ram, one lamb of the first year, for a burnt offering:

76 One kid of the goats for a sin offering:

77 And for a sacrifice of peace offerings, two oxen, five rams, five he goats, five lambs of the first year: this *was* the offering of Pagiel the son of Ocran.

78 ¶ On the twelfth day [r]Ahira the son of Enan, prince of the children of Naphtali, *offered:*

79 His offering *was* one silver charger, the weight whereof *was* an hundred and thirty *shekels,* one silver bowl of seventy shekels, after the shekel of the sanctuary; both of them full of fine flour mingled with oil for a meat offering:

80 One golden spoon of ten *shekels,* full of incense:

81 One young bullock, one ram, one lamb of the first year, for a burnt offering:

82 One kid of the goats for a sin offering:

83 And for a sacrifice of peace offerings, two oxen, five rams, five he goats, five lambs of the first year: this *was* the offering of Ahira the son of Enan.

84 This *was* [s]the dedication of the altar, in the day when it was anointed, by [t]the princes of Israel: twelve chargers of silver, twelve silver bowls, twelve spoons of gold:

85 Each charger of silver *weighing* an hundred and thirty *shekels,* each bowl seventy: all the silver vessels *weighed* two thousand and four hundred *shekels,* after the [u]shekel of the sanctuary:

86 The golden spoons *were* twelve, full of incense, *weighing* ten *shekels* apiece, after the shekel of the sanctuary: all the gold of the spoons *was* an hundred and twenty *shekels.*

87 All the oxen for the burnt offering *were* twelve bullocks, the rams

twelve, the lambs of the first year twelve, with their meat offering: and the kids of the goats for sin offering twelve.

88 And all the oxen for the sacrifice of the peace offerings *were* twenty and four bullocks, the rams sixty, the he goats sixty, the lambs of the first year sixty. This *was* the dedication of the altar, after that it was [v]anointed.

89 And when Moses was gone into the tabernacle of the congregation [w]to speak with [y]him, then he heard [x]the voice of one speaking unto him from off the mercy seat that *was* upon the ark of testimony, from between the two cherubims: and he spake unto him.

The candlestick

8 AND THE LORD spake unto Moses, saying,

2 Speak unto Aaron, and say unto him, When thou [y]lightest the lamps, the seven lamps shall give light over against the candlestick.

3 And Aaron did so; he lighted the lamps thereof over against the candlestick, as the LORD commanded Moses.

4 [z]And this work of the candlestick *was of* beaten gold, unto the shaft thereof, unto the flowers thereof, *was* [a]beaten work: [b]according unto the pattern which the LORD had shown Moses, so he made the candlestick.

Purification of the Levites

5 ¶ And the LORD spake unto Moses, saying,

6 Take the Levites from among the children of Israel, and cleanse them.

7 And thus shalt thou do unto them, to cleanse them: Sprinkle [c]water of purifying upon them, and [d]let[z] them shave all their flesh, and let them wash their clothes, and *so* make themselves clean.

8 Then let them take a young bullock with [e]his meat offering, *even* fine flour mingled with oil, and another young bullock shalt thou take for a sin offering.

9 [f]And thou shalt bring the Levites before the tabernacle of the congregation: [g]and thou shalt gather the whole assembly of the children of Israel together:

10 And thou shalt bring the Levites before the LORD: and the children of Israel [h]shall put their hands upon the Levites:

11 And Aaron shall [a]offer the Levites before the LORD *for* an [b]offering of the children of Israel, that [c]they may execute the service of the LORD.

12 [i]And the Levites shall lay their hands upon the heads of the bullocks: and thou shalt offer the one *for* a sin offering, and the other *for* a burnt offering, unto the LORD, to make an atonement for the Levites.

13 And thou shalt set the Levites before Aaron, and before his sons, and offer them *for* an offering unto the LORD.

14 Thus shalt thou separate the Levites from among the children of Israel: and the Levites shall be [j]mine.

15 And after that shall the Levites go in to do the service of the tabernacle of the congregation: and thou shalt cleanse them, and [k]offer them *for* an offering.

16 For they *are* wholly given unto me from among the children of Israel; [l]instead of such as open every womb, *even instead of* the firstborn of all the children of Israel, have I taken them unto me.

17 [m]For all the firstborn of the children of Israel *are* mine, *both* man and beast: on the day that I smote every firstborn in the land of Egypt I sanctified them for myself.

7:88 [v]ver. 1
7:89 [w]Ex. 33:9,11 [x]Ex. 25:22
8:2 [y]Ex. 25:37 & 40:25
8:4 [z]Ex. 25:31 [a]Ex. 25:18 [b]Ex. 25:40
8:7 [c]ch. 19:9,17,18 [d]Lev. 14:8,9
8:8 [e]Lev. 2:1
8:9 [f]See Ex. 29:4 & 40:12 [g]Lev. 8:3
8:10 [h]Lev. 1:4
8:12 [i]Ex. 29:10
8:14 [j]ch. 3:45 & 16:9
8:15 [k]ver. 11,13
8:16 [l]ch. 3:12,45
8:17 [m]Ex. 13:2,12,13,15 ch. 3:13 Luke 2:23

[y] i.e. *God* [z] Heb. *let them cause a razor to pass over* [a] Heb. *wave* [b] Heb. *wave offering* [c] Heb. *they may be to execute*

8:6–26 THE LEVITES. These verses describe the purification and consecration of the Levites, those appointed to help the priests in the ministry of worship (v. 19).

8:11 LEVITES . . . *FOR* AN OFFERING. The same Hebrew word is used here as is translated "wave offering" in Lev. 7:30. The "wave offering" was the priests' portion of the peace offering. It was waved toward the sanctuary as a sign of dedication to God and then waved toward the offerer or priest, indicating that the Lord was putting the offering at his or her disposal. Here the Levites themselves are a wave offering to the Lord. Seeing that the Levites could not be waved literally, the dedication was carried out symbolically.

8:14 SEPARATE THE LEVITES. By their example, the Levites symbolized the godly separation that ought to characterize the entire nation of Israel.

8:17 FIRSTBORN . . . *ARE* MINE. All Israelite firstborn belonged to the Lord (Ex. 13:11–16); however, God allowed the Levites to become substitutes for all the firstborn (3:9,11–13,40–41, 45–51; 8:14–19).

18 And I have taken the Levites for all the firstborn of the children of Israel.

19 And [n]I have given the Levites *as* [d]a gift to Aaron and to his sons from among the children of Israel, to do the service of the children of Israel in the tabernacle of the congregation, and to make an atonement for the children of Israel: [o]that there be no plague among the children of Israel, when the children of Israel come nigh unto the sanctuary.

20 And Moses, and Aaron, and all the congregation of the children of Israel, did to the Levites according unto all that the LORD commanded Moses concerning the Levites, so did the children of Israel unto them.

21 [p]And the Levites were purified, and they washed their clothes; and Aaron offered them *as* an offering before the LORD; and Aaron made an atonement for them to cleanse them.

22 [q]And after that went the Levites in to do their service in the tabernacle of the congregation before Aaron, and before his sons: [r]as the LORD had commanded Moses concerning the Levites, so did they unto them.

23 ¶ And the LORD spake unto Moses, saying,

24 This *is it* that *belongeth* unto the Levites: [s]from twenty and five years old and upward they shall go in to wait upon the service of the tabernacle of the congregation:

25 And from the age of fifty years they shall [e]cease waiting upon the service *thereof*, and shall serve no more:

26 But shall minister with their brethren in the tabernacle of the congregation, [t]to keep the charge, and shall do no service. Thus shalt thou do unto the Levites touching their charge.

The Passover command

9 AND THE LORD spake unto Moses in the wilderness of Sinai, in the first month of the second year after they were come out of the land of Egypt, saying,

2 Let the children of Israel also keep [u]the passover at his appointed season.

3 In the fourteenth day of this month, [f]at even, ye shall keep it in his appointed season: according to all the rites of it, and according to all the ceremonies thereof, shall ye keep it.

4 And Moses spake unto the children of Israel, that they should keep the passover.

5 And [v]they kept the passover on the fourteenth day of the first month at even in the wilderness of Sinai: according to all that the LORD commanded Moses, so did the children of Israel.

6 ¶ And there were certain men, who were [w]defiled by the dead body of a man, that they could not keep the passover on that day: [x]and they came before Moses and before Aaron on that day:

7 And those men said unto him, We *are* defiled by the dead body of a man: wherefore are we kept back, that we may not offer an offering of the LORD in his appointed season among the children of Israel?

8 And Moses said unto them, Stand still, and [y]I will hear what the LORD will command concerning you.

9 ¶ And the LORD spake unto Moses, saying,

10 Speak unto the children of Israel, saying, If any man of you or of your posterity shall be unclean by reason of a dead body, or *be* in a journey afar off, yet he shall keep the passover unto the LORD.

11 [z]The fourteenth day of the second month at even they shall keep it, *and* [a]eat it with unleavened bread and bitter *herbs*.

12 [b]They shall leave none of it unto the morning, [c]nor break any bone of it: [d]according to all the ordinances of the passover they shall keep it.

13 But the man that *is* clean, and is not in a journey, and forbeareth to keep the passover, even the same soul [e]shall be cut off from among his people: because he [f]brought not the offering of the LORD in his appointed season, that man shall [g]bear his sin.

14 And if a stranger shall sojourn among you, and will keep the passover unto the LORD; according to the ordinance of the passover, and according to the manner thereof, so shall he do: [h]ye shall have one ordinance, both for the stranger, and for him that was born in the land.

8:19 [n]ch. 3:9 [o]ch. 1:53 & 16:46 & 18:5 2 Chr. 26:16 **8:21** [p]ver. 7 **8:22** [q]ver. 15 [r]ver. 5 **8:24** [s]See ch. 4:3 1 Chr. 23:3,24,27 **8:26** [t]ch. 1:53 **9:2** [u]Ex. 12:1 Lev. 23:5 ch. 28:16 Deut. 16:1,2

9:5 [v]Josh. 5:10 **9:6** [w]ch. 5:2 & 19:11,16 See John 18:28 [x]Ex. 18:15,19,26 ch. 27:2 **9:8** [y]ch. 27:5 **9:11** [z]2 Chr. 30:2,15 [a]Ex. 12:8 **9:12** [b]Ex. 12:10 [c]Ex. 12:46 John 19:36 [d]Ex. 12:43 **9:13** [e]Gen. 17:14 Ex. 12:15 [f]ver. 7 [g]ch. 5:31 **9:14** [h]Ex. 12:49

[d] Heb. *given* [e] Heb. *return from the warfare of the service* [f] Heb. *between the two evenings*

The cloud of guidance

15 ¶ And [i]on the day that the tabernacle was reared up the cloud covered the tabernacle, *namely,* the tent of the testimony: and [j]at even there was upon the tabernacle as it were the appearance of fire, until the morning.

16 So it was always: the cloud covered it *by day,* and the appearance of fire by night.

17 And when the cloud [k]was taken up from the tabernacle, then after that the children of Israel journeyed: and in the place where the cloud abode, there the children of Israel pitched their tents.

18 At the commandment of the LORD the children of Israel journeyed, and at the commandment of the LORD they pitched: [l]as long as the cloud abode upon the tabernacle they rested in their tents.

19 And when the cloud [g]tarried long upon the tabernacle many days, then the children of Israel [m]kept the charge of the LORD, and journeyed not.

20 And *so* it was, when the cloud was a few days upon the tabernacle; according to the commandment of the LORD they abode in their tents, and according to the commandment of the LORD they journeyed.

21 And *so* it was, when the cloud [h]abode from even unto the morning, and *that* the cloud was taken up in the morning, then they journeyed: whether *it was* by day or by night that the cloud was taken up, they journeyed.

22 Or *whether it were* two days, or a month, or a year, that the cloud tarried upon the tabernacle, remaining thereon, the children of Israel [n]abode in their tents, and journeyed not: but when it was taken up, they journeyed.

23 At the commandment of the LORD they rested in the tents, and at the commandment of the LORD they journeyed: they [o]kept the charge of the LORD, at the commandment of the LORD by the hand of Moses.

The two silver trumpets

10 AND THE LORD spake unto Moses, saying,

2 Make thee two trumpets of silver; of a whole piece shalt thou make them: that thou mayest use them for the [p]calling of the assembly, and for the journeying of the camps.

3 And when [q]they shall blow with them, all the assembly shall assemble themselves to thee at the door of the tabernacle of the congregation.

4 And if they blow *but* with one *trumpet,* then the princes, *which are* [r]heads of the thousands of Israel, shall gather themselves unto thee.

5 When ye blow an alarm, then [s]the camps that lie on the east parts shall go forward.

6 When ye blow an alarm the second time, then the camps that lie [t]on the south side shall take their journey: they shall blow an alarm for their journeys.

7 But when the congregation is to be gathered together, [u]ye shall blow, but ye shall not [v]sound an alarm.

8 [w]And the sons of Aaron, the priests, shall blow with the trumpets; and they shall be to you for an ordinance for ever throughout your generations.

9 And [x]if ye go to war in your land against the enemy that [y]oppresseth you, then ye shall blow an alarm with the trumpets; and ye shall be [z]remem-

9:15 [i]Ex. 40:34 Neh. 9:12,19 Ps. 78:14 [j]Ex. 13:21 & 40:38 **9:17** [k]Ex. 40:36 ch. 10:11,33,34 Ps. 80:1 **9:18** [l]1 Cor. 10:1 **9:19** [m]ch. 1:53 & 3:8 **9:22** [n]Ex. 40:36,37 **9:23** [o]ver. 19 **10:2** [p]Is. 1:13 **10:3** [q]Jer. 4:5 Joel 2:15 **10:4** [r]Ex. 18:21 ch. 1:16 & 7:2 **10:5** [s]ch. 2:3 **10:6** [t]ch. 2:10 **10:7** [u]ver. 3 [v]Joel 2:1 **10:8** [w]ch. 31:6 Josh. 6:4 1 Chr. 15:24 2 Chr. 13:12 **10:9** [x]ch. 31:6 Josh. 6:5 2 Chr. 13:14 [y]Judg. 2:18 & 4:3 & 6:9 & 10:8,12 [z]Gen. 8:1 Ps. 106:4

[g] Heb. *prolonged* [h] Heb. *was*

9:15–23 CLOUD . . . FIRE. The cloud by day and the fire by night served as a sign of divine provision, protection, and guidance for Israel in the wilderness. (1) The Bible emphasizes that the people were to move or stay only as the supernatural sign indicated. However, God's guidance did not eliminate the need for human wisdom and planning, for Moses requested Hobab to give them advice as to the best places to camp in the wilderness (10:29–32).

(2) Obeying God and following His will are thus dependent on both God's supernatural guidance and our own forethought and wisdom based on the principles of His word. It is important that we remain near Him at all times and not separate ourselves from His protection and will.

(3) God's promise to lead His O.T. people still applies to believers. He will guide us by His word and by His Spirit (Rom. 8:4). He will direct the paths of all who acknowledge Him (Prov. 3:6; cf. Ps. 37:23; Acts 5:19–20; 8:26; 13:1–4).

10:9 YE SHALL BE REMEMBERED. God would help His people in war only if He was summoned by the sound of the trumpets (cf. Ex. 28:12, 29; 39:7). In other words, God placed certain conditions on the Israelites for receiving His help. God may not move on our behalf if we refuse to draw near to Him in prayer, crying out for His grace, protection, and presence.

bered before the LORD your God, and ye shall be saved from your enemies.

10 Also [a]in the day of your gladness, and in your solemn days, and in the beginnings of your months, ye shall blow with the trumpets over your burnt offerings, and over the sacrifices of your peace offerings; that they may be to you [b]for a memorial before your God: I *am* the LORD your God.

The departure from Sinai

11 ¶ And it came to pass on the twentieth *day* of the second month, in the second year, that the cloud [c]was taken up from off the tabernacle of the testimony.

12 And the children of Israel took [d]their journeys out of the [e]wilderness of Sinai; and the cloud rested in the [f]wilderness of Paran.

13 And they first took their journey [g]according to the commandment of the LORD by the hand of Moses.

14 ¶ [h]In the first *place* went the standard of the camp of the children of Judah according to their armies: and over his host *was* [i]Nahshon the son of Amminadab.

15 And over the host of the tribe of the children of Issachar *was* Nethaneel the son of Zuar.

16 And over the host of the tribe of the children of Zebulun *was* Eliab the son of Helon.

17 And [j]the tabernacle was taken down; and the sons of Gershon and the sons of Merari set forward, [k]bearing the tabernacle.

18 ¶ And [l]the standard of the camp of Reuben set forward according to their armies: and over his host *was* Elizur the son of Shedeur.

19 And over the host of the tribe of the children of Simeon *was* Shelumiel the son of Zurishaddai.

20 And over the host of the tribe of the children of Gad *was* Eliasaph the son of Deuel.

21 And the Kohathites set forward, bearing the [m]sanctuary: and [i]*the other* did set up the tabernacle against they came.

22 ¶ And [n]the standard of the camp of the children of Ephraim set forward according to their armies: and over his host *was* Elishama the son of Ammihud.

23 And over the host of the tribe of the children of Manasseh *was* Gamaliel the son of Pedahzur.

24 And over the host of the tribe of the children of Benjamin *was* Abidan the son of Gideoni.

25 ¶ And [o]the standard of the camp of the children of Dan set forward, *which was* the rearward of all the camps throughout their hosts: and over his host *was* Ahiezer the son of Ammishaddai.

26 And over the host of the tribe of the children of Asher *was* Pagiel the son of Ocran.

27 And over the host of the tribe of the children of Naphtali *was* Ahira the son of Enan.

28 [p]Thus[j] *were* the journeyings of the children of Israel according to their armies, when they set forward.

29 ¶ And Moses said unto Hobab, the son of [q]Raguel the Midianite, Moses' father-in-law, We are journeying unto the place of which the LORD said, [r]I will give it you: come thou with us, and [s]we will do thee good: for [t]the LORD hath spoken good concerning Israel. Ps. 67

30 And he said unto him, I will not go; but I will depart to mine own land, and to my kindred.

31 And he said, Leave us not, I pray thee; forasmuch as thou knowest how we are to encamp in the wilderness, and thou mayest be to us [u]instead of eyes.

32 And it shall be, if thou go with us, yea, it shall be, that [v]what goodness the LORD shall do unto us, the same will we do unto thee.

33 ¶ And they departed from [w]the mount of the LORD three days' journey: and the ark of the covenant of the LORD [x]went before them in the three days' journey, to search out a resting place for them.

34 And [y]the cloud of the LORD *was*

[i] i.e. *the Gershonites and the Merarites;* see ver. 17; ch. 1:51 [j] Heb. *These*

10:10 [a]ch. 29:1 Lev. 23:24 1 Chr. 15:24 [b]ver. 9 **10:11** [c]ch. 9:17 **10:12** [d]Ex. 40:36 ch. 2:9,16 [e]Ex. 19:1 ch. 1:1 & 9:5 [f]Gen. 21:21 ch. 12:16 & 13:3,26 **10:13** [g]ver. 5,6 **10:14** [h]ch. 2:3,9 [i]ch. 1:7 **10:17** [j]ch. 1:51 [k]ch. 4:24,31 **10:18** [l]ch. 2:16 **10:21** [m]ch. 4:4,15 & 7:9 **10:22** [n]ch. 2:24 **10:25** [o]ch. 2:31 Josh. 6:9 **10:28** [p]ch. 2:34 **10:29** [q]Ex. 2:18 [r]Gen. 12:7 [s]Judg. 1:16 [t]Gen. 32:12 Ex. 3:8 **10:31** [u]Job 29:15 **10:32** [v]Judg. 1:16 **10:33** [w]See Ex. 3:1 [x]Deut. 1:33 Josh. 3:3,4,6 Ezek. 20:6 **10:34** [y]Ex. 13:21 Neh. 9:12,19

10:29 COME THOU WITH US. Moses invited his brother-in-law, a non-Israelite, to come with them and share the good which God had promised to Israel. The door was always open for Gentiles to join Israel, to make the God of Israel their God, and to share in God's promises and blessings. Hobab appears not to have accepted this invitation (but see Judg. 1:16; 4:11); later on Rahab, Ruth, and many other Gentiles found acceptance and blessing with the Lord and His people.

upon them by day, when they went out of the camp.

35 And it came to pass, when the ark set forward, that Moses said, [z]Rise up, LORD, and let thine enemies be scattered; and let them that hate thee flee before thee.

36 And when it rested, he said, Return, O LORD, unto the [k]many thousands of Israel.

The people complain

11 AND [a]*WHEN* the people [l]complained, [m]it displeased the LORD: and the LORD heard *it;* [b]and his anger was kindled; and the [c]fire of the LORD burnt among them, and consumed *them that were* in the uttermost parts of the camp.

2 And the people cried unto Moses; and when Moses [d]prayed unto the LORD, the fire [n]was quenched.

3 And he called the name of the place [o]Taberah: because the fire of the LORD burnt among them.

God sends quail

4 ¶ And the [e]mixed multitude that *was* among them [p]fell a-lusting: and the children of Israel also [q]wept again, and said, [f]Who shall give us flesh to eat?

5 [g]We remember the fish, which we did eat in Egypt freely; the cucumbers, and the melons, and the leeks, and the onions, and the garlic:

6 But now [h]our soul *is* dried away: *there is* nothing at all, beside this manna, *before* our eyes.

7 And [i]the manna *was* as coriander seed, and the [r]colour thereof as the colour of bdellium.

8 *And* the people went about, and gathered *it,* and ground *it* in mills, or beat *it* in a mortar, and baked *it* in pans, and made cakes of it: and [j]the taste of it was as the taste of fresh oil.

9 And [k]when the dew fell upon the camp in the night, the manna fell upon it.

10 ¶ Then Moses heard the people weep throughout their families, every man in the door of his tent: and [l]the anger of the LORD was kindled greatly; Moses also was displeased.

11 [m]And Moses said unto the LORD, Wherefore hast thou afflicted thy servant? and wherefore have I not found favour in thy sight, that thou layest the burden of all this people upon me?

12 Have I conceived all this people? have I begotten them, that thou shouldest say unto me, [n]Carry them in thy bosom, as a [o]nursing father beareth the sucking child, unto the land which thou [p]swarest unto their fathers?

13 [q]Whence should I have flesh to give unto all this people? for they weep unto me, saying, Give us flesh, that we may eat.

14 [r]I am not able to bear all this people alone, because *it is* too heavy for me.

15 And if thou deal thus with me, [s]kill me, I pray thee, out of hand, if I have found favour in thy sight; and let me not [t]see my wretchedness.

16 ¶ And the LORD said unto Moses, Gather unto me [u]seventy men of the elders of Israel, whom thou knowest to be the elders of the people, and [v]officers over them; and bring them unto the tabernacle of the congregation, that they may stand there with thee.

10:35 [z]Ps. 68:1,2 & 132:8
11:1 [a]Deut. 9:22 [b]Ps. 78:21 [c]Lev. 10:2 2 Ki. 1:12
11:2 [d]Jas. 5:16
11:4 [e]As Ex. 12:38 [f]Ps. 78:18 1 Cor. 10:6
11:5 [g]Ex. 16:3
11:6 [h]ch. 21:5
11:7 [i]Ex. 16:14,31
11:8 [j]Ex. 16:31
11:9 [k]Ex. 16:13,14
11:10 [l]Ps. 78:21
11:11 [m]Deut. 1:12
11:12 [n]Is. 40:11 [o]Is. 49:23 1 Thes. 2:7 [p]Gen. 26:3 & 50:24 Ex. 13:5
11:13 [q]Mat. 15:33 Mark 8:4
11:14 [r]Ex. 18:18
11:15 [s]See 1 Ki. 19:4 Jonah 4:3 [t]Rev. 3:17
11:16 [u]See Ex. 24:1,9 [v]Deut. 16:18

[k] Heb. *ten thousand thousands* [l] Or, *were as it were complainers* [m] Heb. *it was evil in the ears of* [n] Heb. *sunk* [o] i.e. *A burning* [p] Heb. *lusted a lust* [q] Heb. *returned and wept* [r] Heb. *eye of it as the eye of*

11:1 THE PEOPLE COMPLAINED. After only three days into their journey (10:33), the people began to murmur and complain because circumstances were not ideal. (1) How quickly they forgot their deliverance from Egyptian slavery and God's mighty acts on their behalf. They would not trust God and commit their lives and future to Him. This brought on them God's anger and judgment. (2) As N.T. believers we must never cease to be grateful for Christ's sacrificial death for us, our deliverance from sin, and God's gracious provision for guidance and blessing in life.

11:4 MIXED MULTITUDE . . . A-LUSTING. These were the non-Israelites who joined the people in the exodus (Ex. 12:38). They influenced Israel to rebel against God and desire the presumed pleasures of Egypt (v. 5).

11:6 MANNA. See Ex. 16:4, note.

11:12 A NURSING FATHER. Moses expected to lead a triumphant army into the promised land. Instead, the people were acting like spiritual babies, and Moses felt it was too much for him to carry them. God then took His Spirit that was on Moses and put it on the seventy elders to help him in the spiritual leadership of the people (vv. 16–17). Thus Moses knew that by the Spirit's power he could face the challenges of any task to which God called him, for he did not have to bear the burdens in his own strength.

17 And I will [w]come down and talk with thee there: and [x]I will take of the spirit which *is* upon thee, and will put *it* upon them; and they shall bear the burden of the people with thee, that thou bear *it* not thyself alone.

18 And say thou unto the people, [y]Sanctify yourselves against tomorrow, and ye shall eat flesh: for ye have wept [z]in the ears of the LORD, saying, Who shall give us flesh to eat? [a]for *it was* well with us in Egypt: therefore the LORD will give you flesh, and ye shall eat.

19 Ye shall not eat one day, nor two days, nor five days, neither ten days, nor twenty days;

20 [b]*But* even a [s]whole month, until it come out at your nostrils, and it be loathsome unto you: because that ye have despised the LORD which *is* among you, and have wept before him, saying, [c]Why came we forth out of Egypt?

21 And Moses said, [d]The people, among whom I *am, are* six hundred thousand footmen; and thou hast said, I will give them flesh, that they may eat a whole month.

22 [e]Shall the flocks and the herds be slain for them, to suffice them? or shall all the fish of the sea be gathered together for them, to suffice them?

23 And the LORD said unto Moses, [f]Is the LORD's hand waxed short? thou shalt see now whether [g]my word shall come to pass unto thee or not.

24 ¶ And Moses went out, and told the people the words of the LORD, and [h]gathered the seventy men of the elders of the people, and set them round about the tabernacle.

25 And the LORD [i]came down in a cloud, and spake unto him, and took of the spirit that *was* upon him, and gave *it* unto the seventy elders: and it came to pass, *that,* [j]when the spirit rested upon them, [k]they prophesied, and did not cease.

26 But there remained two *of the* men in the camp, the name of the one *was* Eldad, and the name of the other Medad: and the spirit rested upon them; and they *were* of them that were written, but [l]went not out unto the tabernacle: and they prophesied in the camp.

27 And there ran a young man, and told Moses, and said, Eldad and Medad do prophesy in the camp.

28 And Joshua the son of Nun, the servant of Moses, *one* of his young men, answered and said, My lord Moses, [m]forbid them.

29 And Moses said unto him, Enviest thou for my sake? [n]would God that all the LORD's people were prophets, *and* that the LORD would put his spirit upon them! Judg. 4:4

30 And Moses gat him into the camp, he and the elders of Israel.

31 ¶ And there went forth a [o]wind from the LORD, and brought quails from the sea, and let *them* fall by the camp, [t]as it were a day's journey on this side, and as it were a day's journey on

11:17 [w]ver. 25 Ex. 19:20 [x]1 Sam. 10:6 2 Ki. 2:15
11:18 [y]Ex. 19:10 [z]Ex. 16:7 [a]ver. 5 Acts 7:39
11:20 [b]Ps. 78:29 & 106:15 [c]ch. 21:5
11:21 [d]Gen. 12:2 Ex. 12:37 ch. 1:46
11:22 [e]See 2 Ki. 7:2
11:23 [f]Is. 50:2 & 59:1 [g]ch. 23:19 Ezek. 12:25
11:24 [h]ver. 16
11:25 [i]ver. 17 ch. 12:5 [j]See. 2 Ki. 2:15 [k]See 1 Sam. 10:5, 6,10 Joel 2:28 Acts 2:17,18 1 Cor. 14:1
11:26 [l]See 1 Sam. 20:26 Jer. 36:5
11:28 [m]See Mark 9:38 Luke 9:49
11:29 [n]1 Cor. 14:5
11:31 [o]Ex. 16:13 Ps. 78:26-28

[s] Heb. *month of days* [t] Heb. *as it were the way of a day*

11:20 BECAUSE THAT YE HAVE DESPISED THE LORD. The people complained bitterly about God's ways with them; they were like spoiled children who cried to have their own way (vv. 1,4–6). God let them have what they wanted, but "sent leanness into their soul" (Ps. 106:15; cf. Ps. 78:29–33; some translations have, "sent a wasting disease among them"). This episode is a solemn warning about insisting on our way and desires, rather than humbly submitting to God's way and being grateful for His provisions. To reject God's ways of dealing with us is tantamount to unbelief and rebellion against Him; this brings His judgment (cf. Ps. 78:17–22).

11:25 WHEN THE SPIRIT RESTED UPON THEM, THEY PROPHESIED. Scripture teaches that prophecy often accompanies the falling of God's Spirit upon His people (cf. 1 Sam. 10:5–6; 2 Chr. 20:14; 24:19–20; Mic. 3:8; Zec. 7:12; Joel 2:28). The record in Acts about the outpouring of the Holy Spirit on the day of Pentecost and afterward indicates that Spirit-filled believers prophesied and spoke in other tongues by the impulse of the Spirit (Acts 2:4; 10:44–47; 19:6; see article on SPIRITUAL GIFTS FOR BELIEVERS, p. 1790).

11:29 WOULD GOD THAT ALL THE LORD'S PEOPLE WERE PROPHETS. When Eldad and Medad kept prophesying in the camp, Joshua wanted Moses to stop them. Moses, however, had learned his lesson. He saw that the normal level of spiritual life desired for all God's people was that they could prophesy when the Spirit of God was upon them. In O.T. times the Holy Spirit only came upon or filled a few to empower them for service or for prophecy. Joel prophesied that a time would come when all God's people would be filled with the Spirit (Joel 2:28–29). This prophecy was fulfilled on the day of Pentecost when the Spirit was poured out on "all flesh" (Acts 2:4,16–17). Believers who have not been baptized in the Holy Spirit are not experiencing what God has promised them and what Jesus waits to give them (Acts 1:8; 2:39; 1 Cor. 14:1–2,5,39).

the other side, round about the camp, and as it were two cubits *high* upon the face of the earth.

32 And the people stood up all that day, and all *that* night, and all the next day, and they gathered the quails: he that gathered least gathered ten [p]homers: and they spread *them* all abroad for themselves round about the camp.

33 And while the [q]flesh *was* yet between their teeth, ere it was chewed, the wrath of the LORD was kindled against the people, and the LORD smote the people with a very great plague.

34 And he called the name of that place [u]Kibroth-hattaavah: because there they buried the people that lusted.

35 [r]*And* the people journeyed from Kibroth-hattaavah unto Hazeroth; and [v]abode at Hazeroth.

Miriam and Aaron

12 AND MIRIAM and Aaron spake against Moses because of the [w]Ethiopian woman whom he had married: for [s]he had [x]married an Ethiopian woman.

2 And they said, Hath the LORD indeed spoken only by Moses? [t]hath he not spoken also by us? And the LORD [u]heard *it.*

3 (Now the man Moses *was* very meek, above all the men which *were* upon the face of the earth.)

4 [v]And the LORD spake suddenly unto Moses, and unto Aaron, and unto Miriam, Come out ye three unto the tabernacle of the congregation. And they three came out.

5 [w]And the LORD came down in the pillar of the cloud, and stood *in* the door of the tabernacle, and called Aaron and Miriam: and they both came forth.

6 And he said, Hear now my words: If there be a prophet among you, *I* the LORD will make myself known unto him [x]in a vision, *and* will speak unto him [y]in a dream.

7 [z]My servant Moses *is* not so, [a]who *is* faithful in all [b]mine house.

8 With him will I speak [c]mouth to mouth, even [d]apparently, and not in dark speeches; and [e]the similitude of the LORD shall he behold: wherefore then [f]were ye not afraid to speak against my servant Moses?

9 And the anger of the LORD was kindled against them; and he departed.

10 And the cloud departed from off the tabernacle; and, [g]behold, Miriam *became* [h]leprous, *white* as snow: and Aaron looked upon Miriam, and, behold, *she was* leprous.

11 And Aaron said unto Moses, Alas, my lord, I beseech thee, [i]lay not the sin upon us, wherein we have done foolishly, and wherein we have sinned.

12 Let her not be [j]as one dead, of whom the flesh is half consumed when he cometh out of his mother's womb.

13 And Moses cried unto the LORD, saying, Heal her now, O God, I beseech thee.

14 ¶ And the LORD said unto Moses, If her father had but spit in her face, should she not be ashamed seven days? let her be [k]shut out from the camp seven days, and after that let her be received in *again.*

15 [l]And Miriam was shut out from the camp seven days: and the people

11:32 [p]Ex. 16:36 Ezek. 45:11
11:33 [q]Ps. 78:30,31
11:35 [r]ch. 33:17
12:1 [s]Ex. 2:21
12:2 [t]Ex. 15:20 Mic. 6:4 [u]Gen. 29:33 ch. 11:1 2 Ki. 19:4 Is. 37:4 Ezek. 35:12,13
12:4 [v]Ps. 76:9
12:5 [w]ch. 11:25 & 16:19
12:6 [x]Gen. 46:2 Job 33:15 Ezek. 1:1 Dan. 8:2 & 10:8,16 Luke 1:11 Acts 10:11,17 & 22:17,18 [y]Gen. 31:10 1 Ki. 3:5 Mat. 1:20
12:7 [z]Ps. 105:26 [a]Heb. 3:2,5 [b]1 Tim. 3:11
12:8 [c]Ex. 33:11 Deut. 34:10 [d]1 Cor. 13:12 [e]Ex. 33:19 [f]2 Pet. 2:10 Jude 8
12:10 [g]Deut. 24:9 [h]2 Ki. 5:27 & 15:5 2 Chr. 26:19,20
12:11 [i]2 Sam. 24:10 Prov. 30:32
12:12 [j]Ps. 88:4
12:14 [k]Lev. 13:46 ch. 5:2,3
12:15 [l]Deut. 24:9 2 Chr. 26:20,21

[u] i.e. *The graves of lust* [v] Heb. *they were in* [w] Or, *Cushite* [x] Heb. *taken*

12:1 ETHIOPIAN WOMAN. Moses' marriage to an Ethiopian woman was neither morally or legally wrong. Miriam and Aaron's complaint was a pretense to cover their jealousy of Moses' authority (v. 2).

12:3 MOSES . . . MEEK. This reference to Moses as the meekest man on earth is probably a parenthetical comment added by Joshua after Moses' death. Moses' meekness lay in his humble trust in God and His Lordship so that he was free of selfishness and ungodly ambitions. When challenged or threatened, Moses depended on God and trusted Him for aid and defense. Scripture assures us that God delights to come to the aid of the humble (Ps. 22:26; 25:9; 147:6; 149:4; Mat. 5:5; 1 Pet. 5:6). Jesus, a prophet like Moses (Acts 7:37), was meek and lowly in heart (Mat. 11:29), and He too trusted God while being persecuted (1 Pet. 2:23).

12:10 MIRIAM *BECAME* LEPROUS. The sin of Miriam and Aaron in questioning the authority of Moses was that they did not fear God or respect God's word through His prophet Moses. Moses was the mediator of the old covenant, just as Jesus is the mediator of the new (cf. Heb. 3:2–6). God spoke directly to Moses (v. 8), and thus Moses' word to the people was the authoritative word of God. Though Miriam and Aaron were leaders in Israel, they had no right to challenge the authority of Moses. Just as God showed them that they were not on the same level as Moses, so believers today have no right to put themselves on the same level as Scripture.

journeyed not till Miriam was brought in *again.*

16 And afterward the people removed from [m]Hazeroth, and pitched in the wilderness of Paran.

Twelve spies sent to Canaan

13 AND THE LORD spake unto Moses, saying,

2 [n]Send thou men, that they may search the land of Canaan, which I give unto the children of Israel: of every tribe of their fathers shall ye send a man, every one a ruler among them.

3 And Moses by the commandment of the LORD sent them [o]from the wilderness of Paran: all those men *were* heads of the children of Israel.

4 And these *were* their names: of the tribe of Reuben, Shammua the son of Zaccur.

5 Of the tribe of Simeon, Shaphat the son of Hori.

6 [p]Of the tribe of Judah, [q]Caleb the son of Jephunneh.

7 Of the tribe of Issachar, Igal the son of Joseph.

8 Of the tribe of Ephraim, [r]Oshea the son of Nun.

9 Of the tribe of Benjamin, Palti the son of Raphu.

10 Of the tribe of Zebulun, Gaddiel the son of Sodi.

11 Of the tribe of Joseph, *namely,* of the tribe of Manasseh, Gaddi the son of Susi.

12 Of the tribe of Dan, Ammiel the son of Gemalli.

13 Of the tribe of Asher, Sethur the son of Michael.

14 Of the tribe of Naphtali, Nahbi the son of Vophsi.

15 Of the tribe of Gad, Geuel the son of Machi.

16 These *are* the names of the men which Moses sent to spy out the land. And Moses called [s]Oshea the son of Nun Jehoshua.

17 ¶ And Moses sent them to spy out the land of Canaan, and said unto them, Get you up this *way* [t]southward, and go up into [u]the mountain:

18 And see the land, what it *is;* and the people that dwelleth therein, whether they *be* strong or weak, few or many;

19 And what the land *is* that they dwell in, whether it *be* good or bad; and what cities *they be* that they dwell in, whether in tents, or in strong holds;

20 And what the land *is,* whether it *be* [v]fat or lean, whether there be wood therein, or not. And [w]be ye of good courage, and bring of the fruit of the land. Now the time *was* the time of the firstripe grapes.

21 ¶ So they went up, and searched the land [x]from the wilderness of Zin unto [y]Rehob, as men come to Hamath.

22 And they ascended by the south, and came unto Hebron; where [z]Ahiman, Sheshai, and Talmai, [a]the children of Anak, *were.* (Now [b]Hebron was built seven years before [c]Zoan in Egypt.)

23 [d]And they came unto the [y]brook of Eshcol, and cut down from thence a branch with one cluster of grapes, and they bare it between two upon a staff; and *they brought* of the pomegranates, and of the figs.

24 The place was called the [y]brook [z]Eshcol, because of the cluster of grapes which the children of Israel cut down from thence.

The spies return

25 And they returned from searching of the land after forty days.

26 ¶ And they went and came to Moses, and to Aaron, and to all the congregation of the children of Israel, [e]unto the wilderness of Paran, to [f]Kadesh; and brought back word unto them, and unto all the congregation, and showed them the fruit of the land.

27 And they told him, and said, We came unto the land whither thou sentest us, and surely it floweth with [g]milk and honey; [h]and this *is* the fruit of it.

28 Nevertheless [i]the people *be* strong that dwell in the land, and the cities *are* walled, *and* very great: and moreover we saw [j]the children of Anak there.

29 [k]The Amalekites dwell in the land of the south: and the Hittites, and the Jebusites, and the Amorites, dwell in the mountains: and the Canaanites dwell by the sea, and by the coast of Jordan.

30 And [l]Caleb stilled the people before Moses, and said, Let us go up at once, and possess it; for we are well able to overcome it.

31 [m]But the men that went up with

12:16 [m]ch. 11:35 & 33:18
13:2 [n]ch. 32:8 Deut. 1:22
13:3 [o]ch. 12:16 & 32:8 Deut. 1:19 & 9:23
13:6 [p]ch. 34:19 1 Chr. 4:15 [q]ver. 30 ch. 14:6,30 Josh. 14:6,7,13,14 Judg. 1:12
13:8 [r]ver. 16
13:16 [s]ver. 8 Ex. 17:9 ch. 14:6
13:17 [t]ver. 21 [u]Judg. 1:9
13:20 [v]Neh. 9:25,35 Ezek. 34:14 [w]Deut. 31:6,7,23
13:21 [x]ch. 34:3 Josh. 15:1 [y]Josh. 19:28
13:22 [z]Josh. 15:13,14 [a]ver. 33 [b]Josh. 21:11 [c]Ps. 78:12 Is. 19:11
13:23 [d]Deut. 1:24,25
13:26 [e]ver. 3 [f]ch. 20:1 Deut. 1:19 Josh. 14:6
13:27 [g]Ex. 3:8 [h]Deut. 1:25
13:28 [i]Deut. 1:28 [j]ver. 33
13:29 [k]Ex. 17:8 Judg. 6:3
13:30 [l]See ch. 14:6,24
13:31 [m]ch. 32:9 Deut. 1:28 Josh. 14:8

y Or, *valley* z i.e. *A cluster of grapes*

him said, We be not able to go up
against the people; for they *are* stron-
ger than we.
32 And they [n]brought up an evil re-
port of the land which they had
searched unto the children of Israel,
saying, The land, through which we
have gone to search it, *is* a land that
eateth up the inhabitants thereof; and
[o]all the people that we saw in it *are*
[a]men of a great stature.
33 And there we saw the giants,
[p]the sons of Anak, *which come* of the
giants: and we were in our own sight
[q]as grasshoppers, and so we were
[r]in their sight.

The rebellion of Israel

14 AND ALL the congregation lift-
ed up their voice, and cried; and
[s]the people wept that night.
2 [t]And all the children of Israel
murmured against Moses and against
Aaron: and the whole congregation
said unto them, Would God that we had
died in the land of Egypt! or [u]would
God we had died in this wilderness!
3 And wherefore hath the LORD
brought us unto this land, to fall by the
sword, that our wives and our children
should be a prey? were it not better for
us to return into Egypt?
4 And they said one to another,
[v]Let us make a captain, and [w]let us
return into Egypt.
5 Then [x]Moses and Aaron fell on
their faces before all the assembly of
the congregation of the children of Is-
rael.
6 ¶ [y]And Joshua the son of Nun,
and Caleb the son of Jephunneh, *which*
were of them that searched the land,
rent their clothes:
7 And they spake unto all the com-
pany of the children of Israel, saying,
[z]The land, which we passed through
to search it, *is* an exceeding good land.
8 If the LORD [a]delight in us, then he
will bring us into this land, and give it
us; [b]a land which floweth with milk
and honey.
9 Only [c]rebel not ye against the
LORD, [d]neither fear ye the people of
the land; for [e]they *are* bread for us:
their [b]defence is departed from them,
[f]and the LORD *is* with us: fear them
not.
10 [g]But all the congregation bade
stone them with stones. And [h]the glo-
ry of the LORD appeared in the taberna-
cle of the congregation before all the
children of Israel.
11 ¶ And the LORD said unto Moses,
How long will this people [i]provoke
me? and how long will it be ere they
[j]believe me, for all the signs which I
have shown among them?
12 I will smite them with the pesti-
lence, and disinherit them, and [k]will
make of thee a greater nation and
mightier than they.
13 ¶ And [l]Moses said unto the
LORD, Then the Egyptians shall hear *it*,
(for thou broughtest up this people in
thy might from among them;)
14 And they will tell *it* to the inhabi-

[a] Heb. *men of statures* [b] Heb. *shadow*

13:32 [n]ch. 14:36,37 [o]Amos 2:9
13:33 [p]Deut. 9:2 [q]Is. 40:22 [r]1 Sam. 17:42
14:1 [s]ch. 11:4
14:2 [t]Ex. 16:2 [u]See ver. 28,29
14:4 [v]Neh. 9:17 [w]See Deut. 17:16 Acts 7:39
14:5 [x]ch. 16:4,22
14:6 [y]ch. 13:6,8
14:7 [z]ch. 13:27
14:8 [a]Deut. 10:15 2 Sam. 15:25,26 1 Ki. 10:9 Ps. 147:11 [b]ch. 13:27
14:9 [c]Deut. 9:7,23,24 [d]Deut. 7:18 [e]ch. 24:8 [f]Gen. 48:21 Deut. 20:1,3,4 & 31:6,8
14:10 [g]Ex. 17:4 [h]Ex. 16:10 Lev. 9:23
14:11 [i]ver. 23 Ps. 95:8 Heb. 3:8 [j]Deut. 9:23 Ps. 78:22,32,42 John 12:37
14:12 [k]Ex. 32:10
14:13 [l]Ex. 32:12 Ezek. 20:9,14

13:32 AN EVIL REPORT. The unbelief of the ten spies had two dimensions to it: (1) God's past faithfulness to His people did not bring these ten men into a loyal relationship with Him, and (2) they did not trust in God and His promises concerning their future (cf. Gen. 15:18; 17:8; Ex. 33:2). Their lack of faith stood in marked contrast to that of Caleb and Joshua (see next note).

14:6 JOSHUA . . . CALEB. Both Joshua and Caleb stood against the majority opinion of the spies (13:25–33). Basing their report on a firm commitment to God and full confidence in His promises to Israel, they refused to accept the overwhelming decision of God's people — even at the risk of their lives (vv. 6–10). This crucial event in Israel's wilderness journey teaches us that we must not assume that the majority opinion, even of the church, is always right. Faithful believers must be willing to stand on God's word even if the majority are against them (see 2 Tim. 1:15, note).

14:11 ERE THEY BELIEVE ME. At the heart of Israel's rebellion was *unbelief* that grew out of their failure to remember God's past faithfulness, to trust Him as their Lord, and to accept Him at His word. To their way of thinking, they could no longer rely on the Lord under all circumstances. (1) To believe in God means to accept all He says as truth and act accordingly, to cast one's life upon His promises, to walk in His ways, and to love Him with all your heart and with all your soul (Deut. 10:12; see article on FAITH AND GRACE, p. 1738). (2) The presence of faith leads us to be accepted by God and counted righteous before Him (see Gen. 15:6, note); the absence of faith condemns us (John 3:36).

14:13 THE EGYPTIANS SHALL HEAR *IT*. Moses is a classic example of a person so dedicated to the Lord that he is more concerned about God's reputation than his own success and honor (see v. 12). When believers gratefully comprehend all that God has done for them through Christ, they too will desire above all to exalt the Lord and His glory (cf. vv. 21–22), and to keep His name from falling into reproach among unbelievers.

tants of this land: [m]*for* they have heard
that thou LORD *art* among this people,
that thou LORD art seen face to face,
and *that* [n]thy cloud standeth over
them, and *that* thou goest before them,
by day time in a pillar of a cloud, and
in a pillar of fire by night.
15 ¶ Now *if* thou shalt kill *all* this
people as one man, then the nations
which have heard the fame of thee will
speak, saying,
16 Because the LORD was not [o]able
to bring this people into the land which
he sware unto them, therefore he hath
slain them in the wilderness.
17 And now, I beseech thee, let the
power of my LORD be great, according
as thou hast spoken, saying,
18 The LORD *is* [p]longsuffering, and
of great mercy, forgiving iniquity and
transgression, and by no means clear-
ing *the guilty,* [q]visiting the iniquity of
the fathers upon the children unto the
third and fourth *generation.*
19 [r]Pardon, I beseech thee, the in-
iquity of this people [s]according unto
the greatness of thy mercy, and [t]as
thou hast forgiven this people, from
Egypt even [c]until now.
20 And the LORD said, I have par-
doned [u]according to thy word:
21 But *as* truly *as* I live, [v]all the
earth shall be filled with the glory of
the LORD.
22 [w]Because all those men which
have seen my glory, and my miracles,
which I did in Egypt and in the wilder-
ness, and have tempted me now
[x]these ten times, and have not heark-
ened to my voice;
23 [y]Surely[d] they shall not see the
land which I sware unto their fathers,

14:14 [m]Ex. 15:14 [n]Ex. 13:21 Neh. 9:12
14:16 [o]Deut. 9:28
14:18 [p]Ex. 34:6,7 [q]Ex. 20:5
14:19 [r]Ex. 34:9 [s]Ps. 106:45 [t]Ps. 78:38
14:20 [u]1 John 5:14-16
14:21 [v]Ps. 72:19
14:22 [w]Deut. 1:35 Heb. 3:17 [x]Gen. 31:7
14:23 [y]ch. 32:11 Ezek. 20:15
14:24 [z]Josh. 14:6,8,9,14 [a]ch. 32:12
14:25 [b]Deut. 1:40
14:27 [c]Ex. 16:28 [d]Ex. 16:12
14:28 [e]ver. 21 Deut. 1:35 Heb. 3:17 [f]See ver. 2
14:29 [g]ch. 1:45 & 26:64
14:30 [h]ver. 38 Deut. 1:36,38
14:31 [i]Deut. 1:39 [j]Ps. 106:24
14:32 [k]1 Cor. 10:5
14:33 [l]ch. 32:13 Ps. 107:40 [m]See Deut. 2:14

neither shall any of them that pro-
voked me see it:
24 But my servant [z]Caleb, because
he had another spirit with him, and
[a]hath followed me fully, him will I
bring into the land whereinto he went;
and his seed shall possess it.
25 (Now the Amalekites and the Ca-
naanites dwelt in the valley.) Tomor-
row turn you, [b]and get you into the
wilderness by the way of the Red sea.
26 ¶ And the LORD spake unto Mo-
ses and unto Aaron, saying,
27 [c]How long *shall I bear with* this
evil congregation, which murmur
against me? [d]I have heard the mur-
murings of the children of Israel, which
they murmur against me.
28 Say unto them, [e]*As truly as* I
live, saith the LORD, [f]as ye have spo-
ken in mine ears, so will I do to you:
29 Your carcases shall fall in this
wilderness; and [g]all that were num-
bered of you, according to your
whole number, from twenty years old
and upward, which have murmured
against me,
30 Doubtless ye shall not come into
the land, *concerning* which I [e]sware to
make you dwell therein, [h]save Caleb
the son of Jephunneh, and Joshua the
son of Nun.
31 [i]But your little ones, which ye
said should be a prey, them will I bring
in, and they shall know the land which
[j]ye have despised.
32 But *as for* you, [k]your carcases,
they shall fall in this wilderness.
33 And your children shall [l]wan-
der[f] in the wilderness [m]forty years,

[c] Or, *hitherto* [d] Heb. *If they see the land*
[e] Heb. *lifted up my hand* [f] Or, *feed*

14:20 I HAVE PARDONED. The granting of pardon or forgiveness does not always mean the end of punishment (see vv. 21–23,27–37; cf. 2 Sam. 7:14).

14:29 YOUR CARCASES SHALL FALL. The N.T. explicitly declares that God intended His judgment on Israel for her disobedience and unbelief to serve as a warning for all believers (1 Cor. 10:11). (1) The Israelites had the good news preached to them (Heb. 4:6), were redeemed by the blood (Ex. 6:6; 12:13), passed through the Red Sea (Ex. 14:22), were bapized (cf. Ex. 14:19,29–30 with 1 Cor. 10:2), partook of spiritual food (1 Cor. 10:3), drank from the spiritual drink, the living water of Christ (Ex. 17:6; 1 Cor. 10:4), and were led by the Holy Spirit (Num. 11:17,25).

(2) In spite of this redemption and experience of God's grace, the people complained against Him (vv. 2,27), hardened their hearts (Heb. 3:8), rebelled against their Lord (vv. 2,9), spurned Him in unbelief (vv. 11,23), refused to listen to His voice (v. 22), ceased to obey His commandments (v. 41), and turned back from following the Lord (v. 43).

(3) Their disobedience brought upon them the wrath of God (1 Cor. 10:5–10; Heb. 3:10,17), death and destruction (vv. 29,35), the failure to enter the land of Canaan (vv. 22–23), and the forfeiture of God's rest (Ps. 95:7–11; Heb. 3:11,18; see article on GOD'S COVENANT WITH THE ISRAELITES, p. 314).

(4) Based on Israel's failure in the wilderness, all believers in Christ are exhorted to "take heed . . . lest there be in any of you an evil heart of unbelief, in departing from the living God" (Heb. 3:12) and in failing to "enter into that rest," i.e., heaven (Heb. 4:11).

and [n]bear your whoredoms, until your carcases be wasted in the wilderness.

34 [o]After the number of the days in which ye searched the land, *even* [p]forty days, each day for a year, shall ye bear your iniquities, *even* forty years, [q]and ye shall know my [g]breach of promise.

35 [r]I the LORD have said, I will surely do it unto all [s]this evil congregation, that are gathered together against me: in this wilderness they shall be consumed, and there they shall die.

36 [t]And the men, which Moses sent to search the land, who returned, and made all the congregation to murmur against him, by bringing up a slander upon the land,

37 Even those men that did bring up the evil report upon the land, [u]died by the plague before the LORD.

38 [v]But Joshua the son of Nun, and Caleb the son of Jephunneh, *which were* of the men that went to search the land, lived *still.*

39 And Moses told these sayings unto all the children of Israel: [w]and the people mourned greatly.

40 ¶ And they rose up early in the morning, and gat them up into the top of the mountain, saying, Lo, [x]we *be here,* and will go up unto the place which the LORD hath promised: for we have sinned.

41 And Moses said, Wherefore now do ye transgress [y]the commandment of the LORD? but it shall not prosper.

42 [z]Go not up, for the LORD *is* not among you; that ye be not smitten before your enemies.

43 For the Amalekites and the Canaanites *are* there before you, and ye shall fall by the sword: [a]because ye are turned away from the LORD, therefore the LORD will not be with you.

44 [b]But they presumed to go up unto the hill top: nevertheless the ark of the covenant of the LORD, and Moses, departed not out of the camp.

45 [c]Then the Amalekites came down, and the Canaanites which dwelt in that hill, and smote them, and discomfited them, *even* unto [d]Hormah.

Offerings required of Israel

15 AND THE LORD spake unto Moses, saying,

2 [e]Speak unto the children of Israel, and say unto them, When ye be come into the land of your habitations, which I give unto you,

3 And [f]will make an offering by fire unto the LORD, a burnt offering, or a sacrifice [g]in [h]performing a vow, or in a freewill offering, or [h]in your solemn feasts, to make a [i]sweet savour unto the LORD, of the herd, or of the flock:

4 Then [j]shall he that offereth his offering unto the LORD bring [k]a meat offering of a tenth deal of flour mingled [l]with the fourth *part* of an hin of oil.

5 [m]And the fourth *part* of an hin of wine for a drink offering shalt thou prepare with the burnt offering or sacrifice, for one lamb.

6 [n]Or for a ram, thou shalt prepare *for* a meat offering two tenth deals of flour mingled with the third *part* of an hin of oil.

7 And for a drink offering thou shalt offer the third *part* of an hin of wine, *for* a sweet savour unto the LORD.

8 And when thou preparest a bullock *for* a burnt offering, or *for* a sacrifice in performing a vow, or [o]peace offerings unto the LORD:

9 Then shall he bring [p]with a bullock a meat offering of three tenth deals of flour mingled with half an hin of oil.

10 And thou shalt bring for a drink offering half an hin of wine, *for* an offering made by fire, of a sweet savour unto the LORD.

11 [q]Thus shall it be done for one bullock, or for one ram, or for a lamb, or a kid.

12 According to the number that ye shall prepare, so shall ye do to every one according to their number.

14:33 [n]Ezek. 23:35 **14:34** [o]ch. 13:25 [p]Ps. 95:10 Ezek. 4:6 [q]See 1 Ki. 8:56 Heb. 4:1 **14:35** [r]ch. 23:19 [s]ver. 27,29 1 Cor. 10:5 **14:36** [t]ch. 13:31,32 **14:37** [u]1 Cor. 10:10 **14:38** [v]Josh. 14:6,10 **14:39** [w]Ex. 33:4 **14:40** [x]Deut. 1:41 **14:41** [y]ver. 25 2 Chr. 24:20 **14:42** [z]Deut. 1:42 **14:43** [a]2 Chr. 15:2 **14:44** [b]Deut. 1:43 **14:45** [c]ver. 43 Deut. 1:44 [d]ch. 21:3 Judg. 1:17 **15:2** [e]ver. 18 Lev. 23:10 Deut. 7:1 **15:3** [f]Lev. 1:2,3 [g]Lev. 7:16 & 22:18,21 [h]Lev. 23:8,12,36 ch. 28:19,27 Deut. 16:10 [i]Gen. 8:21 Ex. 29:18 **15:4** [j]Lev. 2:1 & 6:14 [k]Ex. 29:40 Lev. 23:13 [l]Lev. 14:10 ch. 28:5 **15:5** [m]ch. 28:7,14 **15:6** [n]ch. 28:12,14 **15:8** [o]Lev. 7:11 **15:9** [p]ch. 28:12,14 **15:11** [q]ch. 28

[g] Or, *altering of my purpose* [h] Heb. *separating*

14:43 THE LORD WILL NOT BE WITH YOU. Despite their shallow repentance and momentary expression of trust in the promises of God (v. 40), the Israelites ignored God's warning. They made the fatal mistake of believing they could possess the promised land without obedience, faith, and devoted fellowship with God (vv. 40–44). In their momentary but misguided trust, they were defeated (v. 45). The crucial lesson for all who are in Christ is that the riches of God's covenant cannot be obtained without the obedience of faith (cf. Rom. 1:5). Simply mouthing words of trust by itself is not adequate. This message is emphasized through the Scriptures (e.g., ch. 32; Deut. 1:20–40; Ps. 95:10; 106:24ff; Amos 2:10; 5:25; 1 Cor. 10:1–11; Heb. 3:7—4:13.

13 All that are born of the country shall do these things after this manner, in offering an offering made by fire, of a sweet savour unto the LORD.

14 And if a stranger sojourn with you, or whosoever *be* among you in your generations, and will offer an offering made by fire, of a sweet savour unto the LORD; as ye do, so he shall do.

15 [r]One ordinance *shall be both* for you of the congregation, and also for the stranger that sojourneth *with you,* an ordinance for ever in your generations: as ye *are,* so shall the stranger be before the LORD.

16 One law and one manner shall be for you, and for the stranger that sojourneth with you.

17 ¶ And the LORD spake unto Moses, saying,

18 [s]Speak unto the children of Israel, and say unto them, When ye come into the land whither I bring you,

19 Then it shall be, that, when ye eat of [t]the bread of the land, ye shall offer up an heave offering unto the LORD.

20 [u]Ye shall offer up a cake of the first of your dough *for* an heave offering: as *ye do* [v]the heave offering of the threshingfloor, so shall ye heave it.

21 Of the first of your dough ye shall give unto the LORD an heave offering in your generations.

Offering for unintentional sins

22 ¶ And [w]if ye have erred, and not observed all these commandments, which the LORD hath spoken unto Moses,

23 *Even* all that the LORD hath commanded you by the hand of Moses, from the day that the LORD commanded *Moses,* and henceforward among your generations;

24 Then it shall be, [x]if *aught* be committed by ignorance [i]without the knowledge of the congregation, that all the congregation shall offer one young bullock for a burnt offering, for a sweet savour unto the LORD, [y]with his meat offering, and his drink offering, according to the [j]manner, and [z]one kid of the goats for a sin offering.

15:15 [r]ver. 29 Ex. 12:49 ch. 9:14
15:18 [s]ver. 2 Deut. 26:1
15:19 [t]Josh. 5:11,12
15:20 [u]Deut. 26:2,10 Prov. 3:9,10 [v]Lev. 2:14 & 23:10,16
15:22 [w]Lev. 4:2
15:24 [x]Lev. 4:13 [y]ver. 8-10 [z]See Lev. 4:23
15:25 [a]Lev. 4:20
15:27 [b]Lev. 4:27,28
15:28 [c]Lev. 4:35
15:29 [d]ver. 15
15:30 [e]Deut. 17:12 Ps. 19:13 Heb. 10:26
15:31 [f]2 Sam. 12:9 Prov. 13:13 [g]Lev. 5:1 Ezek. 18:20
15:32 [h]Ex. 31:14,15 & 35:2,3
15:34 [i]Lev. 24:12
15:35 [j]Ex. 31:14,15

25 [a]And the priest shall make an atonement for all the congregation of the children of Israel, and it shall be forgiven them; for it *is* ignorance: and they shall bring their offering, a sacrifice made by fire unto the LORD, and their sin offering before the LORD, for their ignorance:

26 And it shall be forgiven all the congregation of the children of Israel, and the stranger that sojourneth among them; seeing all the people *were* in ignorance.

27 ¶ And [b]if any soul sin through ignorance, then he shall bring a she goat of the first year for a sin offering.

28 [c]And the priest shall make an atonement for the soul that sinneth ignorantly, when he sinneth by ignorance before the LORD, to make an atonement for him; and it shall be forgiven him.

29 [d]Ye shall have one law for him that [k]sinneth through ignorance, *both for* him that is born among the children of Israel, and for the stranger that sojourneth among them.

30 ¶ [e]But the soul that doeth *aught* [l]presumptuously, *whether he be* born in the land, or a stranger, the same reproacheth the LORD; and that soul shall be cut off from among his people.

31 Because he hath [f]despised the word of the LORD, and hath broken his commandment, that soul shall utterly be cut off; [g]his iniquity *shall be* upon him.

Stoning the sabbath breaker

32 ¶ And while the children of Israel were in the wilderness, [h]they found a man that gathered sticks upon the sabbath day.

33 And they that found him gathering sticks brought him unto Moses and Aaron, and unto all the congregation.

34 And they put him [i]in ward, because it was not declared what should be done to him.

35 And the LORD said unto Moses, [j]The man shall be surely put to death:

i Heb. *from the eyes* j Or, *ordinance* k Heb. *doth* l Heb. *with an high hand*

15:31 DESPISED THE WORD. God distinguished between unintentional sins (vv. 22–29) and intentional sins, i.e., those committed willfully in defiance of Him and His word (vv. 30–31). Unintentional sin required atonement (vv. 24–28), though it did not separate one from the chosen people of God. Deliberate sin and defiance, however, separated a person from the people of God and the redemption provided for them (vv. 30–31; see 1 John 3:15).

all the congregation shall [k]stone him
with stones without the camp.
36 And all the congregation
brought him without the camp, and
stoned him with stones, and he died; as
the LORD commanded Moses.

The fringes of remembrance

37 ¶ And the LORD spake unto Mo-
ses, saying,
38 Speak unto the children of Isra-
el, and bid [l]them that they make them
fringes in the borders of their garments
throughout their generations, and that
they put upon the fringe of the borders
a ribband of blue:
39 And it shall be unto you for a
fringe, that ye may look upon it, and
remember all the commandments of
the LORD, and do them; and that ye
[m]seek not after your own heart and
your own eyes, after which ye use [n]to
go a-whoring:
40 That ye may remember, and do
all my commandments, and be [o]holy
unto your God.
41 I *am* the LORD your God, which
brought you out of the land of Egypt, to
be your God: I *am* the LORD your God.

The rebellion of Korah

16 NOW [p]KORAH, the son of Iz-
har, the son of Kohath, the son
of Levi, and Dathan and Abiram, the
sons of Eliab, and On, the son of Pe-
leth, sons of Reuben, took *men:*
2 And they rose up before Moses,
with certain of the children of Israel,
two hundred and fifty princes of the as-
sembly, [q]famous in the congregation,
men of renown:
3 And [r]they gathered themselves
together against Moses and against
Aaron, and said unto them, [m]*Ye take*
too much upon you, seeing [s]all the
congregation *are* holy, every one of
them, [t]and the LORD *is* among them:
wherefore then lift ye up yourselves
above the congregation of the LORD?
4 And when Moses heard *it,* [u]he
fell upon his face:
5 And he spake unto Korah and
unto all his company, saying, Even to-
morrow the LORD will show who *are* his,
and *who is* [v]holy; and will cause *him*
to come near unto him: even *him* whom
he hath [w]chosen will he cause to
[x]come near unto him.
6 This do; Take you censers, Korah,
and all his company;
7 And put fire therein, and put in-
cense in them before the LORD tomor-
row: and it shall be *that* the man whom
the LORD doth choose, he *shall be* holy:
ye take too much upon you, ye sons of
Levi.
8 And Moses said unto Korah, Hear,
I pray you, ye sons of Levi:
9 *Seemeth it but* [y]a small thing unto
you, that the God of Israel hath [z]sepa-
rated you from the congregation of Is-
rael, to bring you near to himself to do
the service of the tabernacle of the
LORD, and to stand before the congrega-
tion to minister unto them?
10 And he hath brought thee near *to*
him, and all thy brethren the sons of
Levi with thee: and seek ye the priest-
hood also?
11 For which cause *both* thou and
all thy company *are* gathered together
against the LORD: [a]and what *is* Aaron,
that ye murmur against him?
12 ¶ And Moses sent to call Dathan
and Abiram, the sons of Eliab: which
said, We will not come up:
13 *Is it* a small thing that thou hast
brought us up out of a land that floweth

[m] Heb. It is *much for you*

15:35 [k]Lev. 24:14 1 Ki. 21:13 Acts 7:58 **15:38** [l]Deut. 22:12 Mat. 23:5 **15:39** [m]See Deut. 29:19 [n]Ps. 73:27 & 106:39 Jas. 4:4 **15:40** [o]Lev. 11:44,45 Rom. 12:1 Col. 1:22 1 Pet. 1:15,16 **16:1** [p]Ex. 6:21 ch. 26:9 & 27:3 Jude 11 **16:2** [q]ch. 26:9 **16:3** [r]Ps. 106:16 [s]Ex. 19:6 [t]Ex. 29:45 ch. 14:14 & 35:34 **16:4** [u]ch. 14:5 & 20:6 **16:5** [v]ver. 3 Lev. 21:6-8,12,15 [w]Ex. 28:1 ch. 17:5 1 Sam. 2:28 [x]Ezek. 40:46 & 44:15,16 **16:9** [y]1 Sam. 18:23 Is. 7:13 [z]ch. 3:41,45 & 8:14 Deut. 10:8 **16:11** [a]Ex. 16:8

16:3 AGAINST MOSES. The story of Korah, Dathan, and Abiram concerns three ambitious Levites maneuvering to get more power and a higher position for themselves as priests (v. 10). They challenged Moses' authority and the commandment that Aaron alone was to be high priest (vv. 3–11). By this action, they were rejecting God and His revealed word regarding who would lead God's people (see 12:10, note). Consequently, they received the just condemnation of God (vv. 31–35), as will all those in the kingdom of God who "love the uppermost rooms at feasts, and the chief seats" (Mat. 23:6).

16:10 SEEK YE THE PRIESTHOOD ALSO? Korah and the men thought they could choose for themselves who would lead the people. But God made it plain that He was in charge. Under the new covenant God still decides the type of people who are to serve as overseers of His church. He has set certain holy standards and qualifications for those who desire to serve (1 Tim. 3:1–12; 4:12–16; Tit. 1:5–9; see article on MORAL QUALIFICATIONS FOR OVERSEERS, p. 1908). When church members set aside God's standards for an overseer, seeking to choose leadership in disregard of His word, they are reflecting the rebellious attitude of Korah and the others who stood with him. Leadership must be based on God's revealed will for His church.

with milk and honey, to kill us in the wilderness, except thou [b]make thyself altogether a prince over us?

14 Moreover thou hast not brought us into [c]a land that floweth with milk and honey, or given us inheritance of fields and vineyards: wilt thou [n]put out the eyes of these men? we will not come up.

15 And Moses was very wroth, and said unto the LORD, [d]Respect not thou their offering: [e]I have not taken one ass from them, neither have I hurt one of them.

16 And Moses said unto Korah, [f]Be thou and all thy company [g]before the LORD, thou, and they, and Aaron, tomorrow:

17 And take every man his censer, and put incense in them, and bring ye before the LORD every man his censer, two hundred and fifty censers; thou also, and Aaron, each *of you* his censer.

18 And they took every man his censer, and put fire in them, and laid incense thereon, and stood in the door of the tabernacle of the congregation with Moses and Aaron.

19 And Korah gathered all the congregation against them unto the door of the tabernacle of the congregation: and [h]the glory of the LORD appeared unto all the congregation.

20 And the LORD spake unto Moses and unto Aaron, saying,

21 [i]Separate yourselves from among this congregation, that I may [j]consume them in a moment.

22 And they [k]fell upon their faces, and said, O God, [l]the God of the spirits of all flesh, shall one man sin, and wilt thou be wroth with all the congregation?

23 ¶ And the LORD spake unto Moses, saying,

24 Speak unto the congregation, saying, Get you up from about the tabernacle of Korah, Dathan, and Abiram.

25 And Moses rose up and went unto Dathan and Abiram; and the elders of Israel followed him.

26 And he spake unto the congregation, saying, [m]Depart, I pray you, from the tents of these wicked men, and touch nothing of theirs, lest ye be consumed in all their sins.

27 So they gat up from the tabernacle of Korah, Dathan, and Abiram, on every side: and Dathan and Abiram came out, and stood in the door of their tents, and their wives, and their sons, and their little children.

28 And Moses said, [n]Hereby ye shall know that the LORD hath sent me to do all these works; for *I have* not *done them* [o]of mine own mind.

29 If these men die [o]the common death of all men, or if they be [p]visited after the visitation of all men; *then* the LORD hath not sent me.

30 But if the LORD [p]make [q]a new thing, and the earth open her mouth, and swallow them up, with all that *appertain* unto them, and they [r]go down quick into the pit; then ye shall understand that these men have provoked the LORD.

31 ¶ [s]And it came to pass, as he had made an end of speaking all these words, that the ground clave asunder that *was* under them:

32 And the earth opened her mouth, and swallowed them up, and their houses, and [t]all the men that *appertained* unto Korah, and all *their* goods.

33 They, and all that *appertained* to them, went down alive into the pit, and the earth closed upon them: and they perished from among the congregation.

34 And all Israel that *were* round about them fled at the cry of them: for they said, Lest the earth swallow us up *also*.

35 And there [u]came out a fire from the LORD, and consumed [v]the two hundred and fifty men that offered incense.

36 ¶ And the LORD spake unto Moses, saying,

37 Speak unto Eleazar the son of Aaron the priest, that he take up the censers out of the burning, and scatter thou the fire yonder; for [w]they are hallowed.

38 The censers of these [x]sinners against their own souls, let them make them broad plates *for* a covering of the altar: for they offered them before the LORD, therefore they are hallowed: [y]and they shall be a sign unto the children of Israel.

16:13 [b]Ex. 2:14 Acts 7:27,35
16:14 [c]Ex. 3:8 Lev. 20:24
16:15 [d]Gen. 4:4,5 [e]1 Sam. 12:3 Acts 20:33
16:16 [f]ver. 6,7 [g]1 Sam. 12:3,7
16:19 [h]ver. 42 Ex. 16:7,10 Lev. 9:6,23 ch. 14:10
16:21 [i]ver. 45 See Gen. 19:17,22 Jer. 51:6 [j]ver. 45 Ex. 32:10 & 33:5
16:22 [k]ver. 45 ch. 14:5 [l]ch. 27:16 Job 12:10 Eccl. 12:7 Heb. 12:9
16:26 [m]Gen. 19:12,14
16:28 [n]Ex. 3:12 John 5:36 [o]ch. 24:13 Ezek. 13:17 John 5:30 & 6:38
16:29 [p]Ex. 20:5 & 32:34 Job 35:15
16:30 [q]Job 31:3 Is. 28:21 [r]ver. 33 Ps. 55:15
16:31 [s]ch. 26:10 & 27:3 Deut. 11:6 Ps. 106:17
16:32 [t]See ver. 17 & ch. 26:11 1 Chr. 6:22,37
16:35 [u]Lev. 10:2 ch. 11:1 Ps. 106:18 [v]ver. 17
16:37 [w]See Lev. 27:28
16:38 [x]Prov. 20:2 Hab. 2:10 [y]ch. 17:10 & 26:10 Ezek. 14:8

n Heb. *bore out* o Heb. *as every man dieth* p Heb. *create a creature*

16:32 AND THEIR HOUSES. The sons of Korah did not die with their father, for they evidently did not participate in his rebellion (see 26:11).

39 And Eleazar the priest took the brasen censers, wherewith they that were burnt had offered; and they were made broad *plates for* a covering of the altar:

40 *To be* a memorial unto the children of Israel, [z]that no stranger, which *is* not of the seed of Aaron, come near to offer incense before the LORD; that he be not as Korah, and as his company: as the LORD said to him by the hand of Moses.

41 ¶ But on the morrow [a]all the congregation of the children of Israel murmured against Moses and against Aaron, saying, Ye have killed the people of the LORD.

42 And it came to pass, when the congregation was gathered against Moses and against Aaron, that they looked toward the tabernacle of the congregation: and, behold, [b]the cloud covered it, and [c]the glory of the LORD appeared.

43 And Moses and Aaron came before the tabernacle of the congregation.

44 ¶ And the LORD spake unto Moses, saying,

45 [d]Get you up from among this congregation, that I may consume them as in a moment. And [e]they fell upon their faces.

46 ¶ And Moses said unto Aaron, Take a censer, and put fire therein from off the altar, and put on incense, and go quickly unto the congregation, and make an atonement for them: [f]for there is wrath gone out from the LORD; the plague is begun.

47 And Aaron took as Moses commanded, and ran into the midst of the congregation; and, behold, the plague was begun among the people: and he put on incense, and made an atonement for the people.

48 And he stood between the dead and the living; and [g]the plague was stayed.

49 Now they that died in the plague were fourteen thousand and seven hundred, beside them that died about the matter of Korah.

50 And Aaron returned unto Moses unto the door of the tabernacle of the congregation: and the plague was stayed.

The budding of Aaron's rod

17 AND THE LORD spake unto Moses, saying,

2 Speak unto the children of Israel, and take of every one of them a rod according to the house of *their* fathers, of all their princes according to the house of their fathers twelve rods: write thou every man's name upon his rod.

3 And thou shalt write Aaron's name upon the rod of Levi: for one rod *shall be* for the head of the house of their fathers.

4 And thou shalt lay them up in the tabernacle of the congregation before the testimony, [h]where I will meet with you.

5 And it shall come to pass, *that* the man's rod, [i]whom I shall choose, shall blossom: and I will make to cease from me the murmurings of the children of Israel, [j]whereby they murmur against you.

6 ¶ And Moses spake unto the children of Israel, and every one of their princes gave him [q]a rod apiece, for each prince one, according to their fathers' houses, *even* twelve rods: and the rod of Aaron *was* among their rods.

7 And Moses laid up the rods before the LORD in [k]the tabernacle of witness.

8 And it came to pass, that on the morrow Moses went into the tabernacle of witness; and, behold, the rod of Aaron for the house of Levi was budded, and brought forth buds, and bloomed blossoms, and yielded almonds.

9 And Moses brought out all the rods from before the LORD unto all the

16:40 [z]ch. 3:10 2 Chr. 26:18
16:41 [a]ch. 14:2 Ps. 106:25
16:42 [b]Ex. 40:34 [c]ver. 19 ch. 20:6
16:45 [d]ver. 21,24 [e]ver. 22 ch. 20:6
16:46 [f]Lev. 10:6 ch. 8:19 & 11:33 1 Chr. 27:24
16:48 [g]ch. 25:8 Ps. 106:30
17:4 [h]Ex. 25:22 & 29:42,43 & 30:36
17:5 [i]ch. 16:5 [j]ch. 16:11
17:7 [k]Ex. 38:21 ch. 18:2 Acts 7:44

[q]Heb. *a rod for one prince, a rod for one prince*

16:41–50 YE HAVE KILLED THE PEOPLE OF THE LORD. When God's judgment fell on Korah and his allies, the Israelites complained against Moses as if he had brought the judgment. The people had been so deceived by the rebels that they thought they were the most spiritual men among them. God's people need discernment to make sure that they do not follow leaders who are not of God (see article on FALSE TEACHERS, p. 1508).

17:3 AARON'S NAME UPON THE ROD OF LEVI. Ch. 17 defends God's choice of the tribe of Levi as ministers and Aaron as high priest. The Lord provided a miracle to demonstrate His choice of leadership (v. 8). Under the new covenant, godly leaders who faithfully proclaim God's word must be recognized and obeyed (Heb. 13:17; cf. Rom. 13:1–4; 1 Tim. 2:1–3).

children of Israel: and they looked, and
took every man his rod.
10 ¶ And the LORD said unto Moses,
Bring [l]Aaron's rod again before the
testimony, to be kept [m]for a token
against the [r]rebels; [n]and thou shalt
quite take away their murmurings
from me, that they die not.
11 And Moses did *so:* as the LORD
commanded him, so did he.
12 And the children of Israel spake
unto Moses, saying, Behold, we die, we
perish, we all perish.
13 [o]Whosoever cometh any thing
near unto the tabernacle of the LORD
shall die: shall we be consumed with
dying?

Duties of priests and Levites

18 AND THE LORD said unto Aaron, [p]Thou and thy sons and
thy father's house with thee shall
[q]bear the iniquity of the sanctuary:
and thou and thy sons with thee shall
bear the iniquity of your priesthood.
2 And thy brethren also of the tribe
of Levi, the tribe of thy father, bring
thou with thee, that they may be
[r]joined unto thee, and [s]minister unto
thee: but [t]thou and thy sons with thee
shall minister before the tabernacle of
witness.
3 And they shall keep thy charge,
and [u]the charge of all the tabernacle:
[v]only they shall not come nigh the
vessels of the sanctuary and the altar,
[w]that neither they, nor ye also, die.
4 And they shall be joined unto
thee, and keep the charge of the tabernacle of the congregation, for all the
service of the tabernacle: [x]and a
stranger shall not come nigh unto you.
5 And ye shall keep [y]the charge of
the sanctuary, and the charge of the
altar: [z]that there be no wrath any
more upon the children of Israel.
6 And I, behold, I have [a]taken your
brethren the Levites from among the
children of Israel: [b]to you *they are* given *as* a gift for the LORD, to do the service of the tabernacle of the congregation.
7 Therefore [c]thou and thy sons

17:10 [l]Heb. 9:4 [m]ch. 16:38 [n]ver. 5 **17:13** [o]ch. 1:51,53 & 18:4,7 **18:1** [p]ch. 17:13 [q]Ex. 28:38 **18:2** [r]See Gen. 29:34 [s]ch. 3:6,7 [t]ch. 3:10 **18:3** [u]ch. 3:25,31,36 [v]ch. 16:40 [w]ch. 4:15 **18:4** [x]ch. 3:10 **18:5** [y]Ex. 27:21 & 30:7 Lev. 24:3 ch. 8:2 [z]ch. 16:46 **18:6** [a]ch. 3:12,45 [b]ch. 3:9 & 8:19 **18:7** [c]ver. 5 ch. 3:10

[d]Heb. 9:3,6 **18:8** [e]Lev. 6:16,18 & 7:6,32 ch. 5:9 [f]Ex. 29:29 & 40:13,15 **18:9** [g]Lev. 2:2,3 & 10:12,13 [h]Lev. 6:25,26 [i]Lev. 7:7 **18:10** [j]Lev. 6:16,26 **18:11** [k]Ex. 29:27,28 [l]Lev. 22:2,3 **18:12** [m]Ex. 23:19 Neh. 10:35,36 [n]Ex. 22:29 **18:13** [o]Ex. 23:19 Lev. 2:14 Deut. 26:2 **18:14** [p]Lev. 27:28 **18:15** [q]Ex. 13:2 Lev. 27:26 ch. 3:13 [r]Ex. 13:13

with thee shall keep your priest's office for every thing of the altar, and
[d]within the veil; and ye shall serve: I
have given your priest's office *unto you*
as a service of gift: and the stranger
that cometh nigh shall be put to death.

Tithes and offerings

8 ¶ And the LORD spake unto Aaron,
Behold, [e]I also have given thee the
charge of mine heave offerings of all
the hallowed things of the children of
Israel; unto thee have I given them
[f]by reason of the anointing, and to thy
sons, by an ordinance for ever.
9 This shall be thine of the most
holy things, *reserved* from the fire: every oblation of theirs, every [g]meat offering of theirs, and every [h]sin offering of theirs, and every [i]trespass
offering of theirs, which they shall render unto me, *shall be* most holy for thee
and for thy sons.
10 [j]In the most holy *place* shalt
thou eat it; every male shall eat it: it
shall be holy unto thee.
11 And this *is* thine; [k]the heave offering of their gift, with all the wave
offerings of the children of Israel: I
have given them unto thee, and to thy
sons and to thy daughters with thee, by
a statute for ever: [l]every one that is
clean in thy house shall eat of it.
12 [m]All the [s]best of the oil, and all
the best of the wine, and of the wheat,
[n]the firstfruits of them which they
shall offer unto the LORD, them have I
given thee.
13 *And* whatsoever is first ripe in
the land, [o]which they shall bring unto
the LORD, shall be thine; every one that
is clean in thine house shall eat *of* it.
14 [p]Every thing devoted in Israel
shall be thine.
15 Every thing that openeth [q]the
matrix in all flesh, which they bring
unto the LORD, *whether it be* of men or
beasts, shall be thine: nevertheless
[r]the firstborn of man shalt thou surely redeem, and the firstling of unclean
beasts shalt thou redeem.
16 And those that are to be re-

[r] Heb. *children of rebellion* [s] Heb. *fat*

18:1 BEAR THE INIQUITY. The priests and Levites were held responsible for any offenses or desecration against the tabernacle of the Lord. They had to take great care to serve God and do what the Lord required (cf. Lev. 10:7).

18:8 GIVEN THEE . . . OFFERINGS. God determined that the priests and Levites were to be supported through the offerings of the people (vv. 8–24). In the same manner those who minister today must be supported by the offerings of those to whom they minister (1 Cor. 9:13–14).

deemed from a month old shalt thou
redeem, [s]according to thine estima-
tion, for the money of five shekels, af-
ter the shekel of the sanctuary,
[t]which *is* twenty gerahs.
17 [u]But the firstling of a cow, or
the firstling of a sheep, or the firstling
of a goat, thou shalt not redeem; they
are holy: [v]thou shalt sprinkle their
blood upon the altar, and shalt burn
their fat *for* an offering made by fire, for
a sweet savour unto the LORD.
18 And the flesh of them shall be
thine, as the [w]wave breast and as the
right shoulder are thine.
19 All the heave offerings of the
holy things, which the children of Isra-
el offer unto the LORD, have I given
thee, and thy sons and thy daughters
with thee, by a statute for ever: [x]it *is*
a covenant of salt for ever before the
LORD unto thee and to thy seed with
thee.
20 ¶ And the LORD spake unto Aar-
on, Thou shalt have no inheritance in
their land, neither shalt thou have any
part among them: [y]I *am* thy part and
thine inheritance among the children
of Israel.
21 And, behold, [z]I have given the
children of Levi all the tenth in Israel
for an inheritance, for their service
which they serve, *even* [a]the service of
the tabernacle of the congregation.
22 [b]Neither must the children of
Israel henceforth come nigh the taber-
nacle of the congregation, [c]lest they
bear sin, [t]and die.
23 [d]But the Levites shall do the
service of the tabernacle of the congre-
gation, and they shall bear their iniqui-
ty: *it shall be* a statute for ever through-
out your generations, that among the
children of Israel they have no inheri-
tance.
24 But the tithes of the children of
Israel, which they offer *as* an heave of-
fering unto the LORD, I have given to
the Levites to inherit: therefore I have
said unto them, Among the children of
Israel they shall have no inheritance.
25 ¶ And the LORD spake unto Mo-
ses, saying,
26 Thus speak unto the Levites,
and say unto them, When ye take of the
children of Israel the tithes which I
have given you from them for your in-
heritance, then ye shall offer up an
heave offering of it for the LORD, *even*
[e]a tenth *part* of the tithe.
27 And *this* your heave offering
shall be reckoned unto you, as though
it were the corn of the threshingfloor,
and as the fulness of the winepress.
28 Thus ye also shall offer an heave
offering unto the LORD of all your
tithes, which ye receive of the children
of Israel; and ye shall give thereof the
LORD's heave offering to Aaron the
priest.
29 Out of all your gifts ye shall offer
every heave offering of the LORD, of all
the [u]best thereof, *even* the hallowed
part thereof out of it.
30 Therefore thou shalt say unto
them, When ye have heaved the best
thereof from it, [f]then it shall be count-
ed unto the Levites as the increase of
the threshingfloor, and as the increase
of the winepress.
31 And ye shall eat it in every place,
ye and your households: for it *is* [g]your
reward for your service in the taberna-
cle of the congregation.
32 And ye shall [h]bear no sin by
reason of it, when ye have heaved from
it the best of it: neither shall ye [i]pol-
lute the holy things of the children of
Israel, lest ye die.

Purification of the unclean

19 AND THE LORD spake unto Mo-
ses and unto Aaron, saying,
2 This *is* the ordinance of the law

18:16 [s]Lev. 27:6 [t]Ex. 30:13
18:17 [u]Deut. 15:19 [v]Lev. 3:2,5
18:18 [w]Ex. 29:26,28
18:19 [x]Lev. 2:13 2 Chr. 13:5
18:20 [y]Deut. 10:9 & 12:12 & 14:27,29 & 18:1,2 Josh. 13:14,33 & 14:3 & 18:7 Ezek. 44:28
18:21 [z]ver. 24,26 Lev. 27:30,32 Neh. 10:37 & 12:44 Heb. 7:5,8,9 [a]ch. 3:7,8
18:22 [b]ch. 1:51 [c]Lev. 22:9
18:23 [d]ch. 3:7
18:26 [e]Neh. 10:38
18:30 [f]ver. 27
18:31 [g]Mat. 10:10 Luke 10:7 1 Cor. 9:13 1 Tim. 5:18
18:32 [h]Lev. 19:8 & 22:16 [i]Lev. 22:2,15

[t]Heb. *to die* [u]Heb. *fat;* see ver. 12

18:19 A COVENANT OF SALT. Salt represents preservation and permanence and highlights the irrevocability of the covenant (cf. Lev. 2:13).

18:20 I *AM* THY ... INHERITANCE. The priests and Levites were to have no earthly inheritance, for God Himself was their portion and inheritance. In principle, this promise extends to all believers in Christ. Our inheritance must not be on this earth, for we are but strangers and pilgrims. We must seek the heavenly things, for God dwells in heaven (Heb. 11:9–16). Our witness is this: "The LORD *is* my portion, saith my soul; therefore will I hope in him" (Lam. 3:24).

19:2 RED HEIFER. The sacrifice of the red heifer provided for the cleansing of anyone who was ritually unclean or defiled and therefore unable to draw near to God in worship (vv. 11,14,16). A red heifer without defect was killed and burned outside the camp (vv. 3–6). The ashes were kept, mixed with water (vv. 9,17), and applied to those who were defiled (vv. 12,18). This purification rite cleansed that person, allowing him or her to approach God once again. The book of Hebrews contrasts the cleansing effect of Christ's blood to that

which the LORD hath commanded, say-
ing, Speak unto the children of Israel,
that they bring thee a red heifer with-
out spot, wherein *is* no blemish, [j]*and*
upon which never came yoke:
3 And ye shall give her unto Eleazar
the priest, that he may bring her
[k]forth without the camp, and *one* shall
slay her before his face:
4 And Eleazar the priest shall take
of her blood with his finger, and
[l]sprinkle of her blood directly before
the tabernacle of the congregation sev-
en times:
5 And *one* shall burn the heifer in
his sight; [m]her skin, and her flesh, and
her blood, with her dung, shall he burn:
6 And the priest shall take [n]cedar
wood, and hyssop, and scarlet, and
cast *it* into the midst of the burning of
the heifer.
7 [o]Then the priest shall wash his
clothes, and he shall bathe his flesh in
water, and afterward he shall come
into the camp, and the priest shall be
unclean until the even.
8 And he that burneth her shall
wash his clothes in water, and bathe
his flesh in water, and shall be unclean
until the even.
9 And a man *that is* clean shall gath-
er up [p]the ashes of the heifer, and lay
them up without the camp in a clean
place, and it shall be kept for the con-
gregation of the children of Israel [q]for
a water of separation: it *is* a purifica-
tion for sin.
10 And he that gathereth the ashes
of the heifer shall wash his clothes,
and be unclean until the even: and it
shall be unto the children of Israel, and
unto the stranger that sojourneth
among them, for a statute for ever.
11 ¶ [r]He that toucheth the dead
body of any [v]man shall be unclean
seven days.
12 [s]He shall purify himself with it
on the third day, and on the seventh
day he shall be clean: but if he purify
not himself the third day, then the sev-
enth day he shall not be clean.
13 Whosoever toucheth the dead
body of any man that is dead, and puri-

19:2 [j]Deut. 21:3
1 Sam. 6:7
19:3 [k]Lev. 4:12,21
& 16:27
Heb. 13:11
19:4 [l]Lev. 4:6
& 16:14,19
Heb. 9:13
19:5 [m]Ex. 29:14
Lev. 4:11,12
19:6 [n]Lev. 14:4,6,49
19:7 [o]Lev. 11:25
& 15:5
19:9 [p]Heb. 9:13
[q]ver. 13,20,21
19:11 [r]ver. 16
Lev. 21:1
ch. 5:2
& 9:6,10
& 31:19
Lam. 4:14
Hag. 2:13
19:12 [s]ch. 31:19
19:13 [t]Lev. 15:31
[u]ver. 9
ch. 8:7
[v]Lev. 7:20
& 22:3
19:15 [w]Lev. 11:32
ch. 31:20
19:16 [x]ver. 11
19:17 [y]ver. 9
19:18 [z]Ps. 51:7
19:19 [a]Lev. 14:9
19:20 [b]ver. 13
19:22 [c]Hag. 2:13

fieth not himself, [t]defileth the taber-
nacle of the LORD; and that soul shall
be cut off from Israel: because [u]the
water of separation was not sprinkled
upon him, he shall be unclean; [v]his
uncleanness *is* yet upon him.
14 This *is* the law, when a man dieth
in a tent: all that come into the tent,
and all that *is* in the tent, shall be un-
clean seven days.
15 And every [w]open vessel, which
hath no covering bound upon it, *is* un-
clean.
16 And [x]whosoever toucheth one
that is slain with a sword in the open
fields, or a dead body, or a bone of a
man, or a grave, shall be unclean seven
days.
17 And for an unclean *person* they
shall take of the [y]ashes[w] of the burnt
heifer of purification for sin, and [x]run-
ning water shall be put thereto in a ves-
sel:
18 And a clean person shall take
[z]hyssop, and dip *it* in the water, and
sprinkle *it* upon the tent, and upon all
the vessels, and upon the persons that
were there, and upon him that touched
a bone, or one slain, or one dead, or a
grave:
19 And the clean *person* shall sprin-
kle upon the unclean on the third day,
and on the seventh day: [a]and on the
seventh day he shall purify himself,
and wash his clothes, and bathe him-
self in water, and shall be clean at
even.
20 But the man that shall be un-
clean, and shall not purify himself, that
soul shall be cut off from among the
congregation, because he hath [b]de-
filed the sanctuary of the LORD: the wa-
ter of separation hath not been sprin-
kled upon him; he *is* unclean.
21 And it shall be a perpetual stat-
ute unto them, that he that sprinkleth
the water of separation shall wash his
clothes; and he that toucheth the water
of separation shall be unclean until
even.
22 And [c]whatsoever the unclean

[v] Heb. *soul of man* [w] Heb. *dust* [x] Heb. *living waters shall be given*

of the ashes of the red heifer (Heb. 9:13–14; see next note).

19:9 A PURIFICATION FOR SIN. Heb. 9:13–14 contrasts the blood of Christ to the ashes of the red heifer. As the Israelites had in the ashes a ready means of purification, so believers in Christ have a ready fountain of the blood of Christ in which, by faith and repentance, they may find cleansing "from all sin" (1 John 1:7). By this cleansing they may draw near to God, receive mercy, and obtain grace to help in time of need (Heb. 4:16; 7:25).

person toucheth shall be unclean; and
[d]the soul that toucheth *it* shall be un-
clean until even.

20 THEN [e]CAME the children of
Israel, *even* the whole congre-
gation, into the desert of Zin in the first
month: and the people abode in Ka-
desh; and [f]Miriam died there, and
was buried there.

Water from the rock

2 [g]And there was no water for the
congregation: [h]and they gathered
themselves together against Moses
and against Aaron.
3 And the people [i]chode with Mo-
ses, and spake, saying, Would God that
we had died [j]when our brethren died
before the LORD!
4 And [k]why have ye brought up the
congregation of the LORD into this wil-
derness, that we and our cattle should
die there?
5 And wherefore have ye made us to
come up out of Egypt, to bring us in
unto this evil place? it *is* no place of
seed, or of figs, or of vines, or of pome-
granates; neither *is* there any water to
drink.
6 And Moses and Aaron went from
the presence of the assembly unto the
door of the tabernacle of the congrega-
tion, and [l]they fell upon their faces:
and [m]the glory of the LORD appeared
unto them.
7 ¶ And the LORD spake unto Moses,
saying,
8 [n]Take the rod, and gather thou
the assembly together, thou, and Aar-
on thy brother, and speak ye unto the
rock before their eyes; and it shall give
forth his water, and [o]thou shalt bring
forth to them water out of the rock: so
thou shalt give the congregation and
their beasts drink.
9 And Moses took the rod [p]from
before the LORD, as he commanded him.
10 And Moses and Aaron gathered
the congregation together before the
rock, and he said unto them, [q]Hear
now, ye rebels; must we fetch you wa-
ter out of this rock?
11 And Moses lifted up his hand,
and with his rod he smote the rock
twice: and [r]the water came out abun-
dantly, and the congregation drank,
and their beasts *also*.
12 ¶ And the LORD spake unto Mo-
ses and Aaron, Because [s]ye believed
me not, to [t]sanctify me in the eyes of
the children of Israel, therefore ye
shall not bring this congregation into
the land which I have given them.
13 [u]This *is* the water of [v]Meri-
bah;[y] because the children of Israel
strove with the LORD, and he was sanc-
tified in them.

Edom refuses Israel passage

14 ¶ [w]And Moses sent messengers
from Kadesh unto the king of Edom,
[x]Thus saith thy brother Israel, Thou
knowest all the travail that hath [z]be-
fallen us:

19:22 [d]Lev. 15:5 **20:1** [e]ch. 33:36 [f]Ex. 15:20 ch. 26:59 **20:2** [g]Ex. 17:1 [h]ch. 16:19,42 **20:3** [i]Ex. 17:2 ch. 14:2 [j]ch. 11:1,33 & 14:37 & 16:32,35,49 **20:4** [k]Ex. 17:3 **20:6** [l]ch. 14:5 & 16:4,22,45 [m]ch. 14:10 **20:8** [n]Ex. 17:5 [o]Neh. 9:15 Is. 43:20 & 48:21 **20:9** [p]ch. 17:10 **20:10** [q]Ps. 106:33 **20:11** [r]Ex. 17:6 Deut. 8:15 1 Cor. 10:4 **20:12** [s]Deut. 1:37 [t]Lev. 10:3 Ezek. 20:41 & 36:23 1 Pet. 3:15 **20:13** [u]Deut. 33:8 Ps. 106:32 [v]Ex. 17:7 **20:14** [w]Judg. 11:16,17 [x]Deut. 2:4 Obad. 10,12

[y]i.e. *Strife* [z]Heb. *found us*

20:1 IN THE FIRST MONTH. The events in this chapter begin in the fortieth year after the exodus from Egypt (see vv. 22–29; 33:38). The people had wandered in the wilderness for thirty-nine years. Most of the first generation had died because of their unbelief without receiving what was promised (see chs. 13—14); soon their children would enter the promised land.

20:8 SPEAK YE UNTO THE ROCK. Moses and Aaron were commanded by God to speak to the rock, not to strike it as had been done at Horeb (Ex. 17:1–7; see next note).

20:12 YE SHALL NOT BRING THIS CONGREGATION INTO THE LAND. Moses was forbidden to lead God's people into Canaan because he had not carefully followed the Lord's command (compare v. 8 with v. 11). Moses was the spiritual leader of God's people, the one through whom God gave the law. His responsibility to obey the word of the Lord was greater because of his greater position and influence (cf. Jas. 3:1). (1) Moses' sin was twofold. First, he spoke rashly as if God's glory and power resided in himself and Aaron (v. 10; cf. Ps. 106:33). Second, he then acted rashly by smiting the rock twice in anger rather than speaking to it as God had instructed (v. 11).

(2) In speaking and acting rashly, Moses showed that he did not believe God (v. 12) and thus "rebelled" against His command (v. 24). At that critical time, Moses lacked faith and obedience, always the correct response to God's revealed word (cf. Deut. 9:23; 1 Sam. 12:15; 1 Ki. 13:21; 2 Ki. 17:14; Ps. 106:33). In addition, Moses failed to treat God as the holy and worthy God, choosing not to fear Him and obey His command.

(3) Through these verses God reminds all ministers of the gospel that their responsibility to obey the word of God is greater because of their position and influence. Just as Moses disqualified himself from leading the people into Canaan, so also ministers today can permanently disqualify themselves from certain areas of leadership by their unfaithfulness to God's commandments (1 Tim. 3:1–7; see article on MORAL QUALIFICATIONS FOR OVERSEERS, p. 1908).

15 [y]How our fathers went down into Egypt, [z]and we have dwelt in Egypt a long time; [a]and the Egyptians vexed us, and our fathers:

16 And [b]when we cried unto the LORD, he heard our voice, and [c]sent an angel, and hath brought us forth out of Egypt: and, behold, we *are* in Kadesh, a city in the uttermost of thy border:

17 [d]Let us pass, I pray thee, through thy country: we will not pass through the fields, or through the vineyards, neither will we drink *of* the water of the wells: we will go by the king's *high* way, we will not turn to the right hand nor to the left, until we have passed thy borders.

18 And Edom said unto him, Thou shalt not pass by me, lest I come out against thee with the sword.

19 And the children of Israel said unto him, We will go by the high way: and if I and my cattle drink of thy water, [e]then I will pay for it: I will only, without *doing* any thing *else,* go through on my feet.

20 And he said, [f]Thou shalt not go through. And Edom came out against him with much people, and with a strong hand.

21 Thus Edom [g]refused to give Israel passage through his border: wherefore Israel [h]turned away from him.

The death of Aaron

22 ¶ And the children of Israel, *even* the whole congregation, journeyed from [i]Kadesh, [j]and came unto mount Hor.

23 And the LORD spake unto Moses and Aaron in mount Hor, by the coast of the land of Edom, saying,

24 Aaron shall be [k]gathered unto his people: for he shall not enter into the land which I have given unto the children of Israel, because [l]ye rebelled against my [a]word at the water of Meribah.

25 [m]Take Aaron and Eleazar his son, and bring them up unto mount Hor:

26 And strip Aaron of his garments, and put them upon Eleazar his son: and Aaron shall be gathered *unto his people,* and shall die there.

27 And Moses did as the LORD commanded: and they went up into mount Hor in the sight of all the congregation.

28 [n]And Moses stripped Aaron of his garments, and put them upon Eleazar his son; and [o]Aaron died there in the top of the mount: and Moses and Eleazar came down from the mount.

29 And when all the congregation saw that Aaron was dead, they mourned for Aaron [p]thirty days, *even* all the house of Israel.

21 AND *WHEN* [q]king Arad the Canaanite, which dwelt in the south, heard tell that Israel came [r]by the way of the spies; then he fought against Israel, and took *some* of them prisoners.

The serpent of brass

2 [s]And Israel vowed a vow unto the LORD, and said, If thou wilt indeed deliver this people into my hand, then [t]I will utterly destroy their cities.

3 And the LORD hearkened to the voice of Israel, and delivered up the Canaanites; and they utterly destroyed them and their cities: and he called the name of the place [b]Hormah.

4 ¶ And [u]they journeyed from mount Hor by the way of the Red sea, to [v]compass the land of Edom: and the soul of the people was much [c d]discouraged because of the way.

5 And the people [w]spake against God, and against Moses, [x]Wherefore have ye brought us up out of Egypt to die in the wilderness? for *there is* no bread, neither *is there any* water; and [y]our soul loatheth this light bread.

6 And [z]the LORD sent [a]fiery serpents among the people, and they bit the people; and much people of Israel died.

7 ¶ [b]Therefore the people came to Moses, and said, We have sinned, for

20:15 [y]Gen. 46:6 Acts 7:15 [z]Ex. 12:40 [a]Ex. 1:11 Deut. 26:6 Acts 7:19 **20:16** [b]Ex. 2:23 & 3:7 [c]Ex. 3:2 & 14:19 **20:17** [d]See ch. 21:22 **20:19** [e]Deut. 2:6 **20:20** [f]Judg. 11:17 **20:21** [g]See Deut. 2:27, 29 [h]Deut. 2:8 Judg. 11:18 **20:22** [i]ch. 33:37 [j]ch. 21:4 **20:24** [k]Gen. 25:8 Deut. 32:50 [l]ver. 12 **20:25** [m]ch. 33:38 Deut. 32:50 **20:28** [n]Ex. 29:29,30 [o]ch. 33:38 Deut. 10:6 **20:29** [p]Deut. 34:8 **21:1** [q]ch. 33:40 Judg. 1:16 [r]ch. 13:21 **21:2** [s]Gen. 28:20 Judg. 11:30 [t]Lev. 26:25 **21:4** [u]ch. 20:22 & 33:41 [v]Judg. 11:18 **21:5** [w]Ps. 78:19 [x]Ex. 17:3 [y]ch. 11:6 **21:6** [z]1 Cor. 10:9 [a]Deut. 8:15 **21:7** [b]Ps. 78:34

[a] Heb. *mouth* [b] i.e. *Utter destruction* [c] Or, *grieved* [d] Heb. *shortened*

21:3 UTTERLY DESTROYED THEM. God, through Israel, completely destroyed the Canaanites in the south. Total destruction was His just action upon those who were irreparably committed to sin, immorality, violence, and unrighteousness. As the Lord of history God has the right to decide when it is best to destroy the wicked to accomplish His redemptive purpose for the human race. In the O.T. God at times used Israel to accomplish His purpose. Under the new covenant He no longer uses believers to destroy the ungodly. At the end of the age, however, God Himself will again render judgment upon all who reject Christ and His way of salvation (Rev. 6—19).

[c]we have spoken against the LORD, and against thee; [d]pray unto the LORD, that he take away the serpents from us. And Moses prayed for the people.

8 And the LORD said unto Moses, Make thee a fiery serpent, and set it upon a pole: and it shall come to pass, that every one that is bitten, when he looketh upon it, shall live.

9 And [e]Moses made a serpent of brass, and put it upon a pole, and it came to pass, that if a serpent had bitten any man, when he beheld the ser-
Deut. 7:15 pent of brass, he lived.

Israel moves on

10 ¶ And the children of Israel set forward, and [f]pitched in Oboth.

11 And they journeyed from Oboth, and [g]pitched at [e]Ije-abarim, in the wilderness which *is* before Moab, toward the sunrising.

12 ¶ [h]From thence they removed, and pitched in the valley of Zared.

13 From thence they removed, and pitched on the other side of Arnon, which *is* in the wilderness that cometh out of the coasts of the Amorites: for [i]Arnon *is* the border of Moab, between Moab and the Amorites.

14 Wherefore it is said in the book of the wars of the LORD, [f]What he did in the Red sea, and in the brooks of Arnon,

15 And at the stream of the brooks that goeth down to the dwelling of Ar, [j]and [g]lieth upon the border of Moab.

16 And from thence *they went* [k]to Beer: that *is* the well whereof the LORD spake unto Moses, Gather the people together, and I will give them water.

17 ¶ [l]Then Israel sang this song, [h]Spring up, O well; [i]sing ye unto it:

18 The princes digged the well, the nobles of the people digged it, by *the direction of* [m]the lawgiver, with their staves. And from the wilderness *they went* to Mattanah:

19 And from Mattanah to Nahaliel: and from Nahaliel to Bamoth:

20 And from Bamoth *in* the valley, that *is* in the [j]country of Moab, to the top of [k]Pisgah, which looketh [n]toward [l]Jeshimon.

Defeat of Sihon and Og

21 ¶ And [o]Israel sent messengers unto Sihon king of the Amorites, saying,

22 [p]Let me pass through thy land: we will not turn into the fields, or into the vineyards; we will not drink *of* the waters of the well: *but* we will go along by the king's *high* way, until we be past thy borders.

23 [q]And Sihon would not suffer Israel to pass through his border: but Sihon gathered all his people together, and went out against Israel into the wilderness: [r]and he came to Jahaz, and fought against Israel.

24 And [s]Israel smote him with the edge of the sword, and possessed his land from Arnon unto Jabbok, even unto the children of Ammon: for the border of the children of Ammon *was* strong.

25 And Israel took all these cities: and Israel dwelt in all the cities of the Amorites, in Heshbon, and in all the [m]villages thereof.

26 For Heshbon *was* the city of Sihon the king of the Amorites, who had fought against the former king of Moab, and taken all his land out of his hand, even unto Arnon.

27 Wherefore they that speak in proverbs say, Come into Heshbon, let the city of Sihon be built and prepared:

28 For there is [t]a fire gone out of Heshbon, a flame from the city of Sihon: it hath consumed [u]Ar of Moab, *and* the lords of the high places of Arnon.

29 Woe to thee, Moab! thou art undone, O people of [v]Chemosh: he hath given his sons that escaped, and his daughters, into captivity unto Sihon king of the Amorites.

30 We have shot at them; Heshbon is perished even [w]unto Dibon, and we

21:7 [c]ver. 5 [d]Ex. 8:8 1 Sam. 12:19 1 Ki. 13:6 Acts 8:24
21:9 [e]2 Ki. 18:4 John 3:14,15
21:10 [f]ch. 33:43
21:11 [g]ch. 33:44
21:12 [h]Deut. 2:13
21:13 [i]ch. 22:36 Judg. 11:18
21:15 [j]Deut. 2:18,29
21:16 [k]Judg. 9:21
21:17 [l]Ex. 15:1 Ps. 105:2 & 106:12
21:18 [m]Is. 33:22
21:20 [n]ch. 23:28
21:21 [o]Deut. 2:26,27 Judg. 11:19
21:22 [p]ch. 20:17
21:23 [q]Deut. 29:7 [r]Deut. 2:32 Judg. 11:20
21:24 [s]Deut. 2:33 Josh. 12:1 Neh. 9:22 Ps. 135:10 & 136:19 Amos 2:9
21:28 [t]Jer. 48:45,46 [u]Deut. 2:9,18 Is. 15:1
21:29 [v]Judg. 11:24 1 Ki. 11:7,33 2 Ki. 23:13 Jer. 48:7,13
21:30 [w]Jer. 48:18,22

[e] Or, *Heaps of Abarim* [f] Or, *Vaheb in Suphah* [g] Heb. *leaneth* [h] Heb. *Ascend* [i] Or, *answer* [j] Heb. *field* [k] Or, *The hill* [l] Or, *The wilderness* [m] Heb. *daughters*

21:9 SERPENT OF BRASS. The life-giving power of the brass serpent anticipates the sacrificial death of Jesus Christ, who was lifted up on the cross in order to bring life to all who look to Him. Concerning this event Jesus Himself said: "As Moses lifted up the serpent in the wilderness, even so must the Son of man be lifted up: that whosoever believeth in him should not perish, but have eternal life" (John 3:14–15). Those today who desire to be delivered from their sin and receive salvation must turn their hearts in believing obedience to the word of God in Christ.

have laid them waste even unto No-
phah, which *reacheth* unto [x]Medeba.
31 ¶ Thus Israel dwelt in the land of
the Amorites.
32 And Moses sent to spy out
[y]Jaazer, and they took the villages
thereof, and drove out the Amorites
that *were* there.
33 ¶ [z]And they turned and went up
by the way of Bashan: and Og the king
of Bashan went out against them, he,
and all his people, to the battle [a]at
Edrei.
34 And the LORD said unto Moses,
[b]Fear him not: for I have delivered
him into thy hand, and all his people,
and his land; and [c]thou shalt do to
him as thou didst unto Sihon king of
the Amorites, which dwelt at Heshbon.
35 [d]So they smote him, and his
sons, and all his people, until there
was none left him alive: and they pos-
sessed his land.

Balak sends for Balaam

22 AND [e]THE children of Israel
set forward, and pitched in the
plains of Moab on this side Jordan *by*
Jericho.
2 ¶ And [f]Balak the son of Zippor
saw all that Israel had done to the Am-
orites.
3 And [g]Moab was sore afraid of the
people, because they *were* many: and
Moab was distressed because of the
children of Israel.
4 And Moab said unto [h]the elders
of Midian, Now shall this company lick
up all *that are* round about us, as the ox
licketh up the grass of the field. And
Balak the son of Zippor *was* king of the
Moabites at that time.
5 [i]He sent messengers therefore
unto Balaam the son of Beor to [j]Pe-
thor, which *is* by the river of the land
of the children of his people, to call
him, saying, Behold, there is a people
come out from Egypt: behold, they cov-
er the [n]face of the earth, and they
abide over against me:
6 Come now therefore, I pray thee,
[k]curse me this people; for they *are* too
mighty for me: peradventure I shall
prevail, *that* we may smite them, and
that I may drive them out of the land:
for I wot that he whom thou blessest *is*
blessed, and he whom thou cursest is
cursed.
7 And the elders of Moab and the
elders of Midian departed with [l]the
rewards of divination in their hand;
and they came unto Balaam, and spake
unto him the words of Balak.
8 And he said unto them, [m]Lodge
here this night, and I will bring you
word again, as the LORD shall speak
unto me: and the princes of Moab
abode with Balaam.
9 [n]And God came unto Balaam,
and said, What men *are* these with
thee?
10 And Balaam said unto God, Ba-
lak the son of Zippor, king of Moab,
hath sent unto me, *saying,*
11 Behold, *there is* a people come
out of Egypt, which covereth the face
of the earth: come now, curse me them;
peradventure [o]I shall be able to over-
come them, and drive them out.
12 And God said unto Balaam, Thou
shalt not go with them; thou shalt
not curse the people: for [o]they *are*
blessed.
13 And Balaam rose up in the morn-
ing, and said unto the princes of Balak,
Get you into your land: for the LORD re-
fuseth to give me leave to go with you.
14 And the princes of Moab rose up,
and they went unto Balak, and said,
Balaam refuseth to come with us.
15 ¶ And Balak sent yet again
princes, more, and more honourable
than they.
16 And they came to Balaam, and
said to him, Thus saith Balak the son
of Zippor, [p]Let nothing, I pray thee,
hinder thee from coming unto me:
17 For I will promote thee unto very
great honour, and I will do whatsoever
thou sayest unto me: [p]come therefore,
I pray thee, curse me this people.

[n] Heb. *eye* [o] Heb. *I shall prevail in fighting against him* [p] Heb. *Be not thou letted from*

21:30 [x]Is. 15:2 **21:32** [y]ch. 32:1 Jer. 48:32 **21:33** [z]Deut. 3:1 & 29:7 [a]Josh. 13:12 **21:34** [b]Deut. 3:2 [c]ver. 24 Ps. 135:10 & 136:20 **21:35** [d]Deut. 3:3 & 29:7 Josh. 13:12 Ps. 135:10 **22:1** [e]ch. 33:48 **22:2** [f]Judg. 11:25 **22:3** [g]Ex. 15:15 **22:4** [h]ch. 31:8 Josh. 13:21 **22:5** [i]Deut. 23:4 Josh. 13:22 & 24:9 Neh. 13:1,2 Mic. 6:5 2 Pet. 2:15 Jude 11 Rev. 2:14 [j]See ch. 23:7 Deut. 23:4 **22:6** [k]ch. 23:7 **22:7** [l]1 Sam. 9:7,8 **22:8** [m]ver. 19 **22:9** [n]ver. 20 Gen. 20:3 **22:12** [o]ch. 23:20 Rom. 11:28 **22:17** [p]ver. 6

22:5 BALAAM. Balaam was not an Israelite but an internationally known priest-diviner. Balak believed that this man could place curses upon others (v. 6) by influencing the will of the gods and spirits through his secret knowledge of sorcery, incantations, and mysterious manipulations (vv. 2–7; cf. 24:1). (1) Balaam may at one time have been a true follower of God (cf. v. 18) who later departed from the faith and became a sorcerer (v. 7; cf. 31:16; Deut. 23:4–5; 2 Pet. 2:15; Jude 11). (2) Like all false prophets, he had no genuine concern for the honor of God or the holiness of His people. Unable to curse God's people, Balaam led them into sin and immorality (25:1–6; 31:16; Rev. 2:14). For this he was killed (31:8; see 25:2, note).

18 And Balaam answered and said unto the servants of Balak, [q]If Balak would give me his house full of silver and gold, [r]I cannot go beyond the word of the LORD my God, to do less or more.

19 Now therefore, I pray you, [s]tarry ye also here this night, that I may know what the LORD will say unto me more.

20 [t]And God came unto Balaam at night, and said unto him, If the men come to call thee, rise up, *and* go with them; but [u]yet the word which I shall say unto thee, that shalt thou do.

Balaam's ass speaks

21 And Balaam rose up in the morning, and saddled his ass, and went with the princes of Moab.

22 ¶ And God's anger was kindled because he went: [v]and the angel of the LORD stood in the way for an adversary against him. Now he was riding upon his ass, and his two servants *were* with him.

23 And [w]the ass saw the angel of the LORD standing in the way, and his sword drawn in his hand: and the ass turned aside out of the way, and went into the field: and Balaam smote the ass, to turn her into the way.

24 But the angel of the LORD stood in a path of the vineyards, a wall *being* on this side, and a wall on that side.

25 And when the ass saw the angel of the LORD, she thrust herself unto the wall, and crushed Balaam's foot against the wall: and he smote her again.

26 And the angel of the LORD went further, and stood in a narrow place, where *was* no way to turn either to the right hand or to the left.

27 And when the ass saw the angel of the LORD, she fell down under Balaam: and Balaam's anger was kindled, and he smote the ass with a staff.

28 And the LORD [x]opened the mouth of the ass, and she said unto Balaam, What have I done unto thee, that thou hast smitten me these three times?

29 And Balaam said unto the ass, Because thou hast mocked me: I would there were a sword in mine hand, [y]for now would I kill thee.

30 [z]And the ass said unto Balaam, *Am* not I thine ass, [q]upon which thou hast ridden [r]ever since *I was* thine unto this day? was I ever wont to do so unto thee? And he said, Nay.

31 Then the LORD [a]opened the eyes of Balaam, and he saw the angel of the LORD standing in the way, and his sword drawn in his hand: and he [b]bowed down his head, and [s]fell flat on his face.

32 And the angel of the LORD said unto him, Wherefore hast thou smitten thine ass these three times? behold, I went out [t]to withstand thee, because *thy* way is [c]perverse before me:

33 And the ass saw me, and turned from me these three times: unless she had turned from me, surely now also I had slain thee, and saved her alive.

34 And Balaam said unto the angel of the LORD, [d]I have sinned; for I knew not that thou stoodest in the way against me: now therefore, if it [u]displease thee, I will get me back again.

35 And the angel of the LORD said unto Balaam, Go with the men: [e]but only the word that I shall speak unto thee, that thou shalt speak. So Balaam went with the princes of Balak.

36 ¶ And when Balak heard that Balaam was come, [f]he went out to meet him unto a city of Moab, [g]which *is* in the border of Arnon, which *is* in the utmost coast.

37 And Balak said unto Balaam, Did I not earnestly send unto thee to call thee? wherefore camest thou not unto me? am I not able indeed [h]to promote thee to honour?

38 And Balaam said unto Balak, Lo,

22:18 [q]ch. 24:13 [r]1 Ki. 22:14 2 Chr. 18:13
22:19 [s]ver. 8
22:20 [t]ver. 9 [u]ver. 35 ch. 23:12,26 & 24:13
22:22 [v]Ex. 4:24
22:23 [w]See 2 Ki. 6:17 Dan. 10:7 Acts 22:9 2 Pet. 2:16 Jude 11
22:28 [x]2 Pet. 2:16
22:29 [y]Prov. 12:10
22:30 [z]2 Pet. 2:16
22:31 [a]See Gen. 21:19 2 Ki. 6:17 Luke 24:16,31 [b]Ex. 34:8
22:32 [c]2 Pet. 2:14,15
22:34 [d]1 Sam. 15:24,30 & 26:21 2 Sam. 12:13 Job 34:31,32
22:35 [e]ver. 20
22:36 [f]Gen. 14:17 [g]ch. 21:13
22:37 [h]ver. 17 ch. 24:11

[q] Heb. *who hast ridden upon me* [r] Or, *ever since thou* wast [s] Or, *bowed himself* [t] Heb. *to be an adversary unto thee* [u] Heb. *be evil in thine eyes*

22:18 THE LORD MY GOD. Balaam's reference to "the LORD my God" may indicate that his worship of many gods included the worship of the God of Israel. Scripture depicts Balaam as a man motivated by money rather than by righteousness (Deut. 23:3–6; 2 Pet. 2:15–16; Jude 11).

22:22 GOD'S ANGER WAS KINDLED. God permitted Balaam to go, but was angry with him because he was still considering Balak's offer. Balaam's spiritual blindness was revealed through the incident of the donkey (vv. 22,32–33).

22:28 OPENED THE MOUTH OF THE ASS. The N.T. states that the donkey spoke with a "man's voice" (2 Pet. 2:16).

I am come unto thee: have I now any
power at all to say any thing? [i]the
word that God putteth in my mouth,
that shall I speak.
39 And Balaam went with Balak,
and they came unto [v]Kirjath-huzoth.
40 And Balak offered oxen and
sheep, and sent to Balaam, and to the
princes that *were* with him.
41 And it came to pass on the mor-
row, that Balak took Balaam, and
brought him up into the [j]high places
of Baal, that thence he might see the
utmost *part* of the people.

Balaam's parables

23 AND BALAAM said unto Ba-
lak, [k]Build me here seven al-
tars, and prepare me here seven oxen
and seven rams.
2 And Balak did as Balaam had spo-
ken; and Balak and Balaam [l]offered
on *every* altar a bullock and a ram.
3 And Balaam said unto Balak,
[m]Stand by thy burnt offering, and I
will go: peradventure the LORD will
come [n]to meet me: and whatsoever he
showeth me I will tell thee. And [w]he
went to an high place.
4 [o]And God met Balaam: and he
said unto him, I have prepared seven
altars, and I have offered upon *every*
altar a bullock and a ram.
5 And the LORD [p]put a word in Ba-
laam's mouth, and said, Return unto
Balak, and thus thou shalt speak.
6 And he returned unto him, and, lo,
he stood by his burnt sacrifice, he, and
all the princes of Moab.
7 And he [q]took up his parable, and
said, Balak the king of Moab hath
brought me from Aram, out of the
mountains of the east, *saying,* [r]Come,
curse me Jacob, and come, [s]defy Is-
rael.
8 [t]How shall I curse, whom God
hath not cursed? or how shall I defy,
whom the LORD hath not defied?
9 For from the top of the rocks I see
him, and from the hills I behold him: lo,
[u]the people shall dwell alone, and
[v]shall not be reckoned among the na-
tions.

22:38 [i]ch. 23:26 & 24:13 1 Ki. 22:14 2 Chr. 18:13
22:41 [j]Deut. 12:2
23:1 [k]ver. 29
23:2 [l]ver. 14,30
23:3 [m]ver. 15 [n]ch. 24:1
23:4 [o]ver. 16
23:5 [p]ver. 16 ch. 22:35 Deut. 18:18 Jer. 1:9
23:7 [q]ver. 18 ch. 24:3,15,23 Job 27:1 & 29:1 Ps. 78:2 [r]ch. 22:6,11,17 [s]1 Sam. 17:10
23:8 [t]Is. 47:12
23:9 [u]Deut. 33:28 [v]Ex. 33:16 Ezra 9:2 Eph. 2:14
23:10 [w]Gen. 13:16 & 22:17 [x]Ps. 116:15
23:11 [y]ch. 22:11
23:12 [z]ch. 22:38
23:14 [a]ver. 1,2
23:16 [b]ver. 5 ch. 22:35
23:18 [c]Judg. 3:20
23:19 [d]1 Sam. 15:29 Mal. 3:6 Jas. 1:17
23:20 [e]Gen. 12:2 & 22:17 ch. 22:12
23:21 [f]Rom. 4:7,8 [g]Ps. 89:15
23:22 [h]ch. 24:8

10 [w]Who can count the dust of Ja-
cob, and the number of the fourth *part*
of Israel? Let [x]me die [x]the death of
the righteous, and let my last end be
like his!
11 And Balak said unto Balaam,
What hast thou done unto me? [y]I took
thee to curse mine enemies, and, be-
hold, thou hast blessed *them* alto-
gether.
12 And he answered and said,
[z]Must I not take heed to speak that
which the LORD hath put in my mouth?
13 And Balak said unto him, Come,
I pray thee, with me unto another
place, from whence thou mayest see
them: thou shalt see but the utmost
part of them, and shalt not see them
all: and curse me them from thence.
14 ¶ And he brought him into the
field of Zophim, to the top of [y]Pisgah,
[a]and built seven altars, and offered a
bullock and a ram on *every* altar.
15 And he said unto Balak, Stand
here by thy burnt offering, while I meet
the LORD yonder.
16 And the LORD met Balaam, and
[b]put a word in his mouth, and said, Go
again unto Balak, and say thus.
17 And when he came to him, be-
hold, he stood by his burnt offering,
and the princes of Moab with him. And
Balak said unto him, What hath the
LORD spoken?
18 And he took up his parable, and
said, [c]Rise up, Balak, and hear;
hearken unto me, thou son of Zippor:
19 [d]God *is* not a man, that he
should lie; neither the son of man, that
he should repent: hath he said, and
shall he not do *it?* or hath he spoken,
and shall he not make it good?
20 Behold, I have received *com-
mandment* to bless: and [e]he hath
blessed: and I cannot reverse it.
21 [f]He hath not beheld iniquity in
Jacob, neither hath he seen perverse-
ness in Israel; the LORD his God *is* with
him, [g]and the shout of a king *is* among
them.
22 [h]God brought them out of

[v] Or, *A city of streets* [w] Or, *he went solitary*
[x] Heb. *my soul,* or, *my life* [y] Or, *The hill*

23:19 NOT A MAN, THAT HE SHOULD LIE . . . REPENT. God is not unreliable, fickle, or changeable, but by His very nature He is faithful and loyal to His promises and commitments. This attribute of God does not exclude the possibility, however, of God changing His mind or plans under certain circumstances. For example, God does sometimes change His plans in regard to judgment as a response to the intercessory prayers of His faithful people (see Ex. 32:11,14, notes) or as a result of the repentance of a wicked people (Jonah 3:1–10; 4:2).

Egypt; he hath as it were [i]the strength of an unicorn.

23 Surely *there is* no enchantment [z]against Jacob, neither *is there* any divination against Israel: according to this time it shall be said of Jacob and of Israel, [j]What hath God wrought!

24 Behold, the people shall rise up [k]as a great lion, and lift up himself as a young lion: [l]he shall not lie down until he eat *of* the prey, and drink the blood of the slain.

25 ¶ And Balak said unto Balaam, Neither curse them at all, nor bless them at all.

26 But Balaam answered and said unto Balak, Told not I thee, saying, [m]All that the LORD speaketh, that I must do?

27 ¶ And Balak said unto Balaam, [n]Come, I pray thee, I will bring thee unto another place; peradventure it will please God that thou mayest curse me them from thence.

28 And Balak brought Balaam unto the top of Peor, that looketh [o]toward Jeshimon.

29 And Balaam said unto Balak, [p]Build me here seven altars, and prepare me here seven bullocks and seven rams.

30 And Balak did as Balaam had said, and offered a bullock and a ram on *every* altar.

24 AND WHEN Balaam saw that it pleased the LORD to bless Israel, he went not, as at [q]other times, [a]to seek for enchantments, but he set his face toward the wilderness.

2 And Balaam lifted up his eyes, and he saw Israel [r]abiding *in his tents* according to their tribes; and [s]the spirit of God came upon him.

3 [t]And he took up his parable, and said, Balaam the son of Beor hath said, and the man [b]whose eyes are open hath said:

4 He hath said, which heard the words of God, which saw the vision of the Almighty, [u]falling *into a trance,* but having his eyes open:

5 How goodly are thy tents, O Jacob, *and* thy tabernacles, O Israel!

6 As the valleys are they spread forth, as gardens by the river's side, [v]as the trees of lign aloes [w]which the LORD hath planted, *and* as cedar trees beside the waters.

7 He shall pour the water out of his buckets, and his seed *shall be* [x]in many waters, and his king shall be higher than [y]Agag, and his [z]kingdom shall be exalted.

8 [a]God brought him forth out of Egypt; he hath as it were the strength of an unicorn: he shall [b]eat up the nations his enemies, and shall [c]break their bones, and [d]pierce *them* through with his arrows.

9 [e]He couched, he lay down as a lion, and as a great lion: who shall stir him up? [f]Blessed *is* he that blesseth thee, and cursed *is* he that curseth thee.

10 ¶ And Balak's anger was kindled against Balaam, and he [g]smote his hands together: and Balak said unto Balaam, [h]I called thee to curse mine enemies, and, behold, thou hast altogether blessed *them* these three times.

11 Therefore now flee thou to thy place: [i]I thought to promote thee unto great honour; but, lo, the LORD hath kept thee back from honour.

12 And Balaam said unto Balak, Spake I not also to thy messengers which thou sentest unto me, saying,

13 [j]If Balak would give me his house full of silver and gold, I cannot go beyond the commandment of the LORD, to do *either* good or bad of mine own mind; *but* what the LORD saith, that will I speak?

14 And now, behold, I go unto my people: come *therefore, and* [k]I will advertise thee what this people shall do to thy people [l]in the latter days.

15 ¶ And he took up his parable, and said, Balaam the son of Beor hath said, and the man whose eyes are open hath said:

16 He hath said, which heard the words of God, and knew the knowledge of the most High, *which* saw the vision of the Almighty, falling *into a trance,* but having his eyes open:

17 [m]I shall see him, but not now: I shall behold him, but not nigh: there

23:22 [i]Deut. 33:17 Job 39:10
23:23 [j]Ps. 31:19 & 44:1
23:24 [k]Gen. 49:9 [l]Gen. 49:27
23:26 [m]ver. 12 ch. 22:38
23:27 [n]ver. 13
23:28 [o]ch. 21:10
23:29 [p]ver. 1
24:1 [q]ch. 23:3,15
24:2 [r]ch. 2:2 [s]ch. 11:25 1 Sam. 10:10 & 19:20,23 2 Chr. 15:1
24:3 [t]ch. 23:7,18
24:4 [u]See 1 Sam. 19:24 Ezek. 1:28
24:6 [v]Ps. 1:3 Jer. 17:8 [w]Ps. 104:16
24:7 [x]Jer. 51:13 Rev. 17:1,15 [y]1 Sam. 15:9 [z]2 Sam. 5:12 1 Chr. 14:2
24:8 [a]ch. 23:22 [b]ch. 14:9 & 23:24 [c]Ps. 2:9 Jer. 50:17 [d]Ps. 45:5
24:9 [e]Gen. 49:9 [f]Gen. 12:3
24:10 [g]Ezek. 21:14,17 [h]ch. 23:11 Neh. 13:2
24:11 [i]ch. 22:17,37
24:13 [j]ch. 22:18
24:14 [k]Mic. 6:5 Rev. 2:14 [l]Gen. 49:1 Dan. 2:28
24:17 [m]Rev. 1:7

[z] Or, *in* [a] Heb. *to the meeting of enchantments*
[b] Heb. *who had his eyes shut,* but now opened

24:2 SPIRIT OF GOD CAME UPON HIM. The Spirit coming upon Balaam here is not synonymous with the filling with the Spirit recorded in the N.T. (Acts 2:1–4). The Spirit came upon him for the purpose of revelation, not for endorsement as a prophet. God, on occasion, uses individuals who are not in a right relationship with Him to accomplish His purpose (cf. John 11:49–52).

shall come [n]a Star out of Jacob,
and [o]a Sceptre shall rise out of Isra-
el, and shall [p]smite[c] the corners of
Moab, and destroy all the children of
Sheth.
18 And [q]Edom shall be a posses-
sion, Seir also shall be a possession for
his enemies; and Israel shall do val-
iantly.
19 [r]Out of Jacob shall come he that
shall have dominion, and shall destroy
him that remaineth of the city.
20 ¶ And when he looked on Ama-
lek, he took up his parable, and said,
Amalek *was* [s]the[d] first of the na-
tions; but his latter end [t]*shall be*[e]
that he perish for ever.
21 And he looked on the Kenites,
and took up his parable, and said,
Strong is thy dwellingplace, and thou
puttest thy nest in a rock.
22 Nevertheless [f]the Kenite shall
be wasted, [g]until Asshur shall carry
thee away captive.
23 And he took up his parable, and
said, Alas, who shall live when God
doeth this!
24 And ships *shall come* from the
coast of [u]Chittim, and shall afflict As-
shur, and shall afflict [v]Eber, and he
also shall perish for ever.
25 And Balaam rose up, and went
and [w]returned to his place: and Balak
also went his way.

Israel's idolatry in Shittim

25 AND ISRAEL abode in
[x]Shittim, and [y]the people be-
gan to commit whoredom with the
daughters of Moab.
2 And [z]they called the people unto
[a]the sacrifices of their gods: and the
people did eat, and [b]bowed down to
their gods.
3 And Israel joined himself unto
Baal-peor: and [c]the anger of the LORD
was kindled against Israel.
4 And the LORD said unto Moses,
[d]Take all the heads of the people, and
hang them up before the LORD against
the sun, [e]that the fierce anger of
the LORD may be turned away from
Israel.
5 And Moses said unto [f]the judges
of Israel, [g]Slay ye every one his men
that were joined unto Baal-peor.
6 ¶ And, behold, one of the children
of Israel came and brought unto his
brethren a Midianitish woman in the
sight of Moses, and in the sight of all
the congregation of the children of Is-
rael, [h]who *were* weeping *before* the
door of the tabernacle of the congrega-
tion.
7 And [i]when Phinehas, [j]the son
of Eleazar, the son of Aaron the priest,
saw *it*, he rose up from among the con-
gregation, and took a javelin in his
hand;
8 And he went after the man of Isra-
el into the tent, and thrust both of them
through, the man of Israel, and the
woman through her belly. So [k]the
plague was stayed from the children of
Israel.
9 And [l]those that died in the
plague were twenty and four thousand.
10 ¶ And the LORD spake unto Mo-
ses, saying,
11 [m]Phinehas, the son of Eleazar,
the son of Aaron the priest, hath
turned my wrath away from the chil-
dren of Israel, while he was zealous
[h]for my sake among them, that I con-

24:17 [n]Mat. 2:2 [o]Gen. 49:10 [p]2 Sam. 8:2
24:18 [q]2 Sam. 8:14
24:19 [r]Gen. 49:10
24:20 [s]Ex. 17:8 [t]Ex. 17:14
24:24 [u]Gen. 10:4 [v]Gen. 10:21,25
24:25 [w]See ch. 31:8
25:1 [x]ch. 33:49 Josh. 2:1 [y]1 Cor. 10:8
25:2 [z]Josh. 22:17 Hos. 9:10 [a]Ex. 34:15 [b]Ex. 20:5
25:3 [c]Ps. 106:29
25:4 [d]Deut. 4:3 [e]ver. 11 Deut. 13:17
25:5 [f]Ex. 18:21 [g]Deut. 13:6,9
25:6 [h]Joel 2:17
25:7 [i]Ps. 106:30 [j]Ex. 6:25
25:8 [k]Ps. 106:30
25:9 [l]Deut. 4:3 1 Cor. 10:8
25:11 [m]Ps. 106:30

[c] Or, *smite through the princes of Moab* [d] Or, *the first of the nations that warred against Israel* [e] Or, shall be *even to destruction* [f] Heb. *Kain* [g] Or, *how long* shall it be ere *Asshur carry thee away captive?* [h] Heb. *with my zeal*

24:17 THERE SHALL COME A STAR. Many commentators see vv. 15–19 as referring to the coming of Christ and His universal reign over all the nations (cf. Gen. 49:10; Ps. 45:6; Mat. 2:2; Rev. 2:28; 19:15; 22:16). Others believe it refers only to King David (cf. 2 Sam. 7:12).

25:2 BOWED DOWN TO THEIR GODS. After Balaam had failed in his attempt to separate the Israelites from the Lord, he counseled the Moabites to try separating the Israelites from their God by enticing them into immorality and the sensual worship of false gods (see 31:16; Rev. 2:14, note). As punishment, he was put to death (31:8; cf. Josh 13:22).

25:4 TAKE ALL THE HEADS OF THE PEOPLE, AND HANG THEM UP. This verse reveals the intensity of God's displeasure with the heads or leaders of His covenant people. They were executed for their outrageous behavior and their failure to be examples of separation from sexual immorality and idolatry.

25:11 ZEALOUS FOR MY SAKE. Phinehas reacted to the moral degeneration and idolatry among God's people in holy anger (vv. 1–8). (1) His exceptional zeal for God's honor (v. 13) was evident in his love of righteousness and hatred of sin, as God Himself shows. His zeal typifies the zeal of Christ for God's holiness (see Heb. 1:9, note). (2) The Lord gave Phinehas the promise of "an everlasting priesthood" (vv. 12–13; cf. 1 Chr. 6:4ff). To be sincerely zealous for the Lord's sake is always rewarded with great blessings from God.

sumed not the children of Israel in [n]my jealousy.

12 Wherefore say, [o]Behold, I give unto him my covenant of peace:

13 And he shall have it, and [p]his seed after him, *even* the covenant of [q]an everlasting priesthood; because he was [r]zealous for his God, and [s]made an atonement for the children of Israel.

14 Now the name of the Israelite that was slain, *even* that was slain with the Midianitish woman, *was* Zimri, the son of Salu, a prince of a [i]chief house among the Simeonites.

15 And the name of the Midianitish woman that was slain *was* Cozbi, the daughter of [t]Zur; he *was* head over a people, *and* of a chief house in Midian.

16 ¶ And the LORD spake unto Moses, saying,

17 [u]Vex the Midianites, and smite them:

18 For they vex you with their [v]wiles, wherewith they have beguiled you in the matter of Peor, and in the matter of Cozbi, the daughter of a prince of Midian, their sister, which was slain in the day of the plague for Peor's sake.

Israel's second census

26 AND IT came to pass after the plague, that the LORD spake unto Moses and unto Eleazar the son of Aaron the priest, saying,

2 [w]Take the sum of all the congregation of the children of Israel, [x]from twenty years old and upward, throughout their fathers' house, all that are able to go to war in Israel.

3 And Moses and Eleazar the priest spake with them [y]in the plains of Moab by Jordan *near* Jericho, saying,

4 *Take the sum of the people,* from twenty years old and upward; as the LORD [z]commanded Moses and the children of Israel, which went forth out of the land of Egypt.

5 ¶ [a]Reuben, the eldest son of Israel: the children of Reuben; Hanoch, *of whom cometh* the family of the Hanochites: of Pallu, the family of the Palluites:

6 Of Hezron, the family of the Hezronites: of Carmi, the family of the Carmites.

7 These *are* the families of the Reubenites: and they that were numbered of them were forty and three thousand and seven hundred and thirty.

8 And the sons of Pallu; Eliab.

9 And the sons of Eliab; Nemuel, and Dathan, and Abiram. This *is that* Dathan and Abiram, *which were* [b]famous in the congregation, who strove against Moses and against Aaron in the company of Korah, when they strove against the LORD:

10 [c]And the earth opened her mouth, and swallowed them up together with Korah, when that company died, what time the fire devoured two hundred and fifty men: [d]and they became a sign.

11 Notwithstanding [e]the children of Korah died not.

12 ¶ The sons of Simeon after their families: of [f]Nemuel, the family of the Nemuelites: of Jamin, the family of the Jaminites: of [g]Jachin, the family of the Jachinites:

13 Of [h]Zerah, the family of the Zarhites: of Shaul, the family of the Shaulites.

14 These *are* the families of the Simeonites, twenty and two thousand and two hundred.

15 ¶ The children of Gad after their families: of [i]Zephon, the family of the Zephonites: of Haggi, the family of the Haggites: of Shuni, the family of the Shunites:

16 Of [j]Ozni, the family of the Oznites: of Eri, the family of the Erites:

17 Of [j]Arod, the family of the Arodites: of Areli, the family of the Arelites.

18 These *are* the families of the children of Gad according to those that were numbered of them, forty thousand and five hundred.

19 ¶ [k]The sons of Judah *were* Er and Onan: and Er and Onan died in the land of Canaan.

20 And [l]the sons of Judah after their families were; of Shelah, the fam-

25:11 [n]Ex. 20:5 Ps. 78:58 Ezek. 16:38 **25:12** [o]Mal. 2:4,5 **25:13** [p]See 1 Chr. 6:4 [q]Ex. 40:15 [r]Acts 22:3 Rom. 10:2 [s]Heb. 2:17 **25:15** [t]ch. 31:8 Josh. 13:21 **25:17** [u]ch. 31:2 **25:18** [v]ch. 31:16 Rev. 2:14 **26:2** [w]Ex. 30:12 & 38:25,26 ch. 1:2 [x]ch. 1:3 **26:3** [y]ver. 63 ch. 22:1 & 31:12 & 33:48 & 35:1 **26:4** [z]ch. 1:1 **26:5** [a]Gen. 46:8 Ex. 6:14 1 Chr. 5:1 **26:9** [b]ch. 16:1,2 **26:10** [c]ch. 16:32,35 [d]ch. 16:38 See 1 Cor. 10:6 2 Pet. 2:6 **26:11** [e]Ex. 6:24 1 Chr. 6:22 **26:12** [f]Gen. 46:10 Ex. 6:15 *Jemuel* [g]1 Chr. 4:24 *Jarib* **26:13** [h]Gen. 46:10 *Zohar* **26:15** [i]Gen. 46:16 *Ziphion* **26:17** [j]Gen. 46:16 *Arodi* **26:19** [k]Gen. 38:2 & 46:12 **26:20** [l]1 Chr. 2:3

[i] Heb. *house of a father* [j] Or, *Ezbon;* see Gen. 46:16

26:2 SUM OF ALL THE CONGREGATION. God ordered a second census (cf. 1:2–3) in order to prepare the nation for their military responsibilities upon entering Canaan (v. 2) and possessing the inheritance of their land (vv. 53–56).

ily of the Shelanites: of Pharez, the
family of the Pharzites: of Zerah, the
family of the Zarhites.
21 And the sons of Pharez were; of
Hezron, the family of the Hezronites: of
Hamul, the family of the Hamulites.
22 These *are* the families of Judah
according to those that were numbered
of them, threescore and sixteen thou-
sand and five hundred.
23 ¶ [m]*Of* the sons of Issachar after
their families: *of* Tola, the family of the
Tolaites: of [k]Pua, the family of the
Punites:
24 Of [l]Jashub, the family of the Ja-
shubites: of Shimron, the family of the
Shimronites.
25 These *are* the families of Issa-
char according to those that were num-
bered of them, threescore and four
thousand and three hundred.
26 ¶ [n]*Of* the sons of Zebulun after
their families: of Sered, the family of
the Sardites: of Elon, the family of the
Elonites: of Jahleel, the family of the
Jahleelites.
27 These *are* the families of the Zeb-
ulunites according to those that were
numbered of them, threescore thou-
sand and five hundred.
28 ¶ [o]The sons of Joseph after
their families *were* Manasseh and
Ephraim.
29 Of the sons of Manasseh: of
[p]Machir, the family of the Machirites:
and Machir begat Gilead: of Gilead
come the family of the Gileadites.
30 These *are* the sons of Gilead: *of*
[q]Jeezer, the family of the Jeezerites: of
Helek, the family of the Helekites:
31 And *of* Asriel, the family of the
Asrielites: and *of* Shechem, the family
of the Shechemites:
32 And *of* Shemida, the family of the
Shemidaites: and *of* Hepher, the family
of the Hepherites.
33 ¶ And [r]Zelophehad the son of
Hepher had no sons, but daughters:
and the names of the daughters of Ze-
lophehad *were* Mahlah, and Noah, Hog-
lah, Milcah, and Tirzah.
34 These *are* the families of Manas-
seh, and those that were numbered of
them, fifty and two thousand and seven
hundred.
35 ¶ These *are* the sons of Ephraim
after their families: of Shuthelah, the
family of the Shuthalhites: of [s]Be-
cher, the family of the Bachrites: of Ta-
han, the family of the Tahanites.

26:23 [m]Gen. 46:13 1 Chr. 7:1
26:26 [n]Gen. 46:14
26:28 [o]Gen. 46:20
26:29 [p]Josh. 17:1 1 Chr. 7:14,15
26:30 [q]Called *Abiezer* Josh. 17:2 Judg. 6:11,24,34
26:33 [r]ch. 27:1 & 36:11
26:35 [s]1 Chr. 7:20 *Bered*
26:38 [t]Gen. 46:21 1 Chr. 7:6 [u]Gen. 46:21 *Ehi* 1 Chr. 8:1 *Aharah*
26:39 [v]Gen. 46:21 *Muppim and Huppim*
26:40 [w]1 Chr. 8:3 *Addar*
26:42 [x]Gen. 46:23
26:44 [y]Gen. 46:17 1 Chr. 7:30
26:48 [z]Gen. 46:24 1 Chr. 7:13
26:49 [a]1 Chr. 7:13 *Shallum*

36 And these *are* the sons of Shu-
thelah: of Eran, the family of the Eran-
ites.
37 These *are* the families of the
sons of Ephraim according to those
that were numbered of them, thirty and
two thousand and five hundred. These
are the sons of Joseph after their fami-
lies.
38 ¶ [t]The sons of Benjamin after
their families: of Bela, the family of the
Belaites: of Ashbel, the family of the
Ashbelites: of [u]Ahiram, the family of
the Ahiramites:
39 Of [v]Shupham, the family of the
Shuphamites: of Hupham, the family of
the Huphamites.
40 And the sons of Bela were [w]Ard
and Naaman: *of Ard,* the family of the
Ardites: *and* of Naaman, the family of
the Naamites.
41 These *are* the sons of Benjamin
after their families: and they that were
numbered of them *were* forty and five
thousand and six hundred.
42 ¶ [x]These *are* the sons of Dan af-
ter their families: of [m]Shuham, the
family of the Shuhamites. These *are*
the families of Dan after their families.
43 All the families of the Shuham-
ites, according to those that were num-
bered of them, *were* threescore and four
thousand and four hundred.
44 ¶ [y]*Of* the children of Asher after
their families: of Jimna, the family of
the Jimnites: of Jesui, the family of the
Jesuites: of Beriah, the family of the
Beriites.
45 Of the sons of Beriah: of Heber,
the family of the Heberites: of Malchi-
el, the family of the Malchielites.
46 And the name of the daughter of
Asher *was* Sarah.
47 These *are* the families of the
sons of Asher according to those that
were numbered of them; *who were* fifty
and three thousand and four hundred.
48 ¶ [z]*Of* the sons of Naphtali after
their families: of Jahzeel, the family of
the Jahzeelites: of Guni, the family of
the Gunites:
49 Of Jezer, the family of the Jezer-
ites: of [a]Shillem, the family of the
Shillemites.
50 These *are* the families of Naphta-
li according to their families: and they
that were numbered of them *were* forty
and five thousand and four hundred.

k Or, *Phuvah* **l** Or, *Job* **m** Or, *Hushim*

51 [b]These *were* the numbered of the children of Israel, six hundred thousand and a thousand seven hundred and thirty.

52 ¶ And the LORD spake unto Moses, saying,

53 [c]Unto these the land shall be divided for an inheritance according to the number of names.

54 [d]To many thou shalt [n]give the more inheritance, and to few thou shalt [o]give the less inheritance: to every one shall his inheritance be given according to those that were numbered of him.

55 Notwithstanding the land shall be [e]divided by lot: according to the names of the tribes of their fathers they shall inherit.

56 According to the lot shall the possession thereof be divided between many and few.

57 ¶ [f]And these *are* they that were numbered of the Levites after their families: of Gershon, the family of the Gershonites: of Kohath, the family of the Kohathites: of Merari, the family of the Merarites.

58 These *are* the families of the Levites: the family of the Libnites, the family of the Hebronites, the family of the Mahlites, the family of the Mushites, the family of the Korathites. And Kohath begat Amram.

59 And the name of Amram's wife *was* [g]Jochebed, the daughter of Levi, whom *her mother* bare to Levi in Egypt: and she bare unto Amram Aaron and Moses, and Miriam their sister.

60 [h]And unto Aaron was born Nadab, and Abihu, Eleazar, and Ithamar.

61 And [i]Nadab and Abihu died, when they offered strange fire before the LORD.

62 [j]And those that were numbered of them were twenty and three thousand, all males from a month old and upward: [k]for they were not numbered among the children of Israel, because there was [l]no inheritance given them among the children of Israel.

63 ¶ These *are* they that were numbered by Moses and Eleazar the priest, who numbered the children of Israel [m]in the plains of Moab by Jordan *near* Jericho.

64 [n]But among these there was not a man of them whom Moses and Aaron the priest numbered, when they numbered the children of Israel in the wilderness of Sinai.

65 For the LORD had said of them, They [o]shall surely die in the wilderness. And there was not left a man of them, [p]save Caleb the son of Jephunneh, and Joshua the son of Nun.

26:51 [b]See ch. 1:46
26:53 [c]Josh. 11:23 & 14:1
26:54 [d]ch. 33:54
26:55 [e]ch. 33:54 & 34:13 Josh. 11:23 & 14:2
26:57 [f]Gen. 46:11 Ex. 6:16-19 1 Chr. 6:1,16
26:59 [g]Ex. 2:1,2 & 6:20
26:60 [h]ch. 3:2
26:61 [i]Lev. 10:1,2 ch. 3:4 1 Chr. 24:2
26:62 [j]See ch. 3:39 [k]ch. 1:49 [l]ch. 18:20,23,24 Deut. 10:9 Josh. 13:14,33
26:63 [m]ver. 3
26:64 [n]ch. 1 Deut. 2:14,15
26:65 [o]ch. 14:28,29 1 Cor. 10:5,6 [p]ch. 14:30
27:1 [q]ch. 26:33 & 36:1,11 Josh. 17:3
27:3 [r]ch. 14:35 & 26:64,65 [s]ch. 16:1,2
27:4 [t]Josh. 17:4
27:5 [u]Ex. 18:15,19
27:7 [v]ch. 36:2

The daughters of Zelophehad

27:1–11pp — Num. 36:1–12

27 THEN CAME the daughters of [q]Zelophehad, the son of Hepher, the son of Gilead, the son of Machir, the son of Manasseh, of the families of Manasseh the son of Joseph: and these *are* the names of his daughters; Mahlah, Noah, and Hoglah, and Milcah, and Tirzah.

2 And they stood before Moses, and before Eleazar the priest, and before the princes and all the congregation, *by* the door of the tabernacle of the congregation, saying,

3 Our father [r]died in the wilderness, and he was not in the company of them that gathered themselves together against the LORD [s]in the company of Korah; but died in his own sin, and had no sons.

4 Why should the name of our father be [p]done away from among his family, because he hath no son? [t]Give unto us *therefore* a possession among the brethren of our father.

5 And Moses [u]brought their cause before the LORD.

6 ¶ And the LORD spake unto Moses, saying,

7 The daughters of Zelophehad speak right: [v]thou shalt surely give them a possession of an inheritance among their father's brethren; and thou shalt cause the inheritance of their father to pass unto them.

8 And thou shalt speak unto the children of Israel, saying, If a man die, and have no son, then ye shall cause

[n] Heb. *multiply his inheritance* [o] Heb. *diminish his inheritance* [p] Heb. *diminished*

27:4 GIVE UNTO US . . . A POSSESSION. Hebrew law had made no provision for the inheritance of the land if a father left no sons. God therefore established the law that the father's daughter could inherit the family's share of land (vv. 3–11). This law shows the place of dignity and honor that women were given in Israel.

his inheritance to pass unto his daughter.

9 And if he have no daughter, then ye shall give his inheritance unto his brethren.

10 And if he have no brethren, then ye shall give his inheritance unto his father's brethren.

11 And if his father have no brethren, then ye shall give his inheritance unto his kinsman that is next to him of his family, and he shall possess it: and it shall be unto the children of Israel [w]a statute of judgment, as the LORD commanded Moses.

Joshua to succeed Moses

12 ¶ And the LORD said unto Moses, [x]Get thee up into this mount Abarim, and see the land which I have given unto the children of Israel.

13 And when thou hast seen it, thou also [y]shalt be gathered unto thy people, as Aaron thy brother was gathered.

14 For ye [z]rebelled against my commandment in the desert of Zin, in the strife of the congregation, to sanctify me at the water before their eyes: that *is* the [a]water of Meribah in Kadesh in the wilderness of Zin.

15 ¶ And Moses spake unto the LORD, saying,

16 Let the LORD, [b]the God of the spirits of all flesh, set a man over the congregation,

17 [c]Which may go out before them, and which may go in before them, and which may lead them out, and which may bring them in; that the congregation of the LORD be not [d]as sheep which have no shepherd.

udg. :9-10

18 ¶ And the LORD said unto Moses, Take thee Joshua the son of Nun, a man [e]in whom *is* the spirit, and [f]lay thine hand upon him;

19 And set him before Eleazar the priest, and before all the congregation; and [g]give him a charge in their sight.

20 And [h]thou shalt put *some* of thine honour upon him, that all the congregation of the children of Israel [i]may be obedient.

21 [j]And he shall stand before Eleazar the priest, who shall ask *counsel* for him [k]after the judgment of Urim before the LORD: [l]at his word shall they go out, and at his word they shall come in, *both* he, and all the children of Israel with him, even all the congregation.

22 And Moses did as the LORD commanded him: and he took Joshua, and set him before Eleazar the priest, and before all the congregation:

23 And he laid his hands upon him, [m]and gave him a charge, as the LORD commanded by the hand of Moses.

The daily burnt offering

28 AND THE LORD spake unto Moses, saying,

2 Command the children of Israel, and say unto them, My offering, *and* [n]my bread for my sacrifices made by fire, *for* [q]a sweet savour unto me, shall ye observe to offer unto me in their due season.

3 And thou shalt say unto them, [o]This *is* the offering made by fire which ye shall offer unto the LORD; two lambs of the first year without spot [r]day by day, *for* a continual burnt offering.

4 The one lamb shalt thou offer in the morning, and the other lamb shalt thou offer [s]at even;

5 And [p]a tenth *part* of an ephah of flour for a [q]meat offering, mingled with the fourth *part* of an [r]hin of beaten oil.

q Heb. *a savour of my rest* r Heb. *in a day*
s Heb. *between the two evenings*

27:11 [w]ch. 35:29
27:12 [x]ch. 33:47 Deut. 3:27 & 32:49
27:13 [y]ch. 20:24,28 & 31:2 Deut. 10:6
27:14 [z]ch. 20:12,24 Deut. 1:37 & 32:51 Ps. 106:32 [a]Ex. 17:7
27:16 [b]ch. 16:22 Heb. 12:9
27:17 [c]Deut. 31:2 1 Sam. 8:20 & 18:13 2 Chr. 1:10 [d]1 Ki. 22:17 Zech. 10:2 Mat. 9:36 Mark 6:34
27:18 [e]Gen. 41:38 Judg. 3:10 1 Sam. 16:13,18 [f]Deut. 34:9
27:19 [g]Deut. 31:7
27:20 [h]See ch. 11:17,28 [i]Josh. 1:16,17
27:21 [j]Judg. 20:18,23,26 1 Sam. 23:9 & 30:7 [k]Ex. 28:30 [l]Josh. 9:14 1 Sam. 22:10,13, 15
27:23 [m]Deut. 3:28 & 31:7
28:2 [n]Lev. 3:11 & 21:6,8 Mal. 1:7,12
28:3 [o]Ex. 29:38
28:5 [p]Ex. 16:36 ch. 15:4 [q]Lev. 2:1 [r]Ex. 29:40

27:18 IN WHOM *IS* THE SPIRIT. "Spirit" here refers to the Holy Spirit. Among Joshua's many qualifications for leadership, his greatest was that he was Spirit-led. As a man who was anointed by the Spirit of the Lord and had proven himself open to being led by Him, he was preeminently qualified to be commissioned (v. 19) and invested with authority (v. 20) for leading the people.

27:21 JUDGMENT OF URIM. See Ex. 28:30, note.

28:3 A CONTINUAL BURNT OFFERING. Chs. 28—29 stress the importance of continual sacrifices and offerings made unto the Lord. They were to be made (1) daily (vv. 3–8), (2) on the weekly Sabbath days (vv. 9–10), (3) at the beginning of each month (vv. 11–15), and (4) on certain days of the sacred year (28:16—29:40). The continual need for drawing near to God with sacrifice emphasized the truth that regular and unceasing communion with God was necessary for His continued presence and blessing. This spiritual principle has not changed. Believers today must draw near to God daily in prayer and worship in order to receive His saving grace and help (Luke 18:1; 1 Thes. 5:17; cf. Heb. 4:16; 7:25).

6 *It is* [s]a continual burnt offering, which was ordained in mount Sinai for a sweet savour, a sacrifice made by fire unto the LORD.

7 And the drink offering thereof *shall be* the fourth *part* of an hin for the one lamb: [t]in the holy *place* shalt thou cause the strong wine to be poured unto the LORD *for* a drink offering.

8 And the other lamb shalt thou offer at even: as the meat offering of the morning, and as the drink offering thereof, thou shalt offer *it,* a sacrifice made by fire, of a sweet savour unto the LORD.

The offering on the Sabbath

9 ¶ And on the sabbath day two lambs of the first year without spot, and two tenth deals of flour *for* a meat offering, mingled with oil, and the drink offering thereof:

10 *This is* [u]the burnt offering of every sabbath, beside the continual burnt offering, and his drink offering.

The offering at the new moon

11 ¶ And [v]in the beginnings of your months ye shall offer a burnt offering unto the LORD; two young bullocks, and one ram, seven lambs of the first year without spot;

12 And [w]three tenth deals of flour *for* a meat offering, mingled with oil, for one bullock; and two tenth deals of flour *for* a meat offering, mingled with oil, for one ram;

13 And a several tenth deal of flour mingled with oil *for* a meat offering unto one lamb; *for* a burnt offering of a sweet savour, a sacrifice made by fire unto the LORD.

14 And their drink offerings shall be half an hin of wine unto a bullock, and the third *part* of an hin unto a ram, and a fourth *part* of an hin unto a lamb: this *is* the burnt offering of every month throughout the months of the year.

15 And [x]one kid of the goats for a sin offering unto the LORD shall be offered, beside the continual burnt offering, and his drink offering.

The feast of unleavened bread

28:16–25pp — Ex. 12:14–20; Lev. 23:4–8; Deut. 16:1–8
28:26–31pp — Lev. 23:15–22; Deut. 16:9–12

16 [y]And in the fourteenth day of the first month *is* the passover of the LORD.

17 [z]And in the fifteenth day of this month *is* the feast: seven days shall unleavened bread be eaten.

18 In the [a]first day *shall be* an holy convocation; ye shall do no manner of servile work *therein:*

19 But ye shall offer a sacrifice made by fire *for* a burnt offering unto the LORD; two young bullocks, and one ram, and seven lambs of the first year: [b]they shall be unto you without blemish:

20 And their meat offering *shall be of* flour mingled with oil: three tenth deals shall ye offer for a bullock, and two tenth deals for a ram;

21 A several tenth deal shalt thou offer for every lamb, throughout the seven lambs:

22 And [c]one goat *for* a sin offering, to make an atonement for you.

23 Ye shall offer these beside the burnt offering in the morning, which *is* for a continual burnt offering.

24 After this manner ye shall offer daily, throughout the seven days, the meat of the sacrifice made by fire, of a sweet savour unto the LORD: it shall be offered beside the continual burnt offering, and his drink offering.

25 And [d]on the seventh day ye shall have an holy convocation; ye shall do no servile work.

26 ¶ Also [e]in the day of the firstfruits, when ye bring a new meat offering unto the LORD, after your weeks *be out,* ye shall have an holy convocation; ye shall do no servile work:

27 But ye shall offer the burnt offering for a sweet savour unto the LORD; [f]two young bullocks, one ram, seven lambs of the first year;

28 And their meat offering of flour mingled with oil, three tenth deals unto one bullock, two tenth deals unto one ram,

29 A several tenth deal unto one lamb, throughout the seven lambs;

30 *And* one kid of the goats, to make an atonement for you.

31 Ye shall offer *them* beside the continual burnt offering, and his meat offering, ([g]they shall be unto you without blemish) and their drink offerings.

28:6 [s]Ex. 29:42 See Amos 5:25
28:7 [t]Ex. 29:42
28:10 [u]Ezek. 46:4
28:11 [v]ch. 10:10 1 Sam. 20:5 1 Chr. 23:31 2 Chr. 2:4 Ezra 3:5 Neh. 10:33 Is. 1:13,14 Ezek. 45:17 & 46:6 Hos. 2:11 Col. 2:16
28:12 [w]ch. 15:4-12
28:15 [x]ver. 22 ch. 15:24
28:16 [y]Ex. 12:6,18 Lev. 23:5 ch. 9:3 Deut. 16:1 Ezek. 45:21
28:17 [z]Lev. 23:6
28:18 [a]Ex. 12:16 Lev. 23:7
28:19 [b]ver. 31 Lev. 22:20 ch. 29:8 Deut. 15:21
28:22 [c]ver. 15
28:25 [d]Ex. 13:6 Lev. 23:8
28:26 [e]Ex. 23:16 & 34:22 Lev. 23:10,15 Deut. 16:10 Acts 2:1
28:27 [f]See Lev. 23:18, 19
28:31 [g]ver. 19

Feast of the trumpets offerings

29:1–6pp — Lev. 23:23–25

29 AND IN the seventh month, on the first *day* of the month, ye shall have an holy convocation; ye shall do no servile work: [h]it is a day of blowing the trumpets unto you.

2 And ye shall offer a burnt offering for a sweet savour unto the LORD; one young bullock, one ram, *and* seven lambs of the first year without blemish:

3 And their meat offering *shall be of* flour mingled with oil, three tenth deals for a bullock, *and* two tenth deals for a ram,

4 And one tenth deal for one lamb, throughout the seven lambs:

5 And one kid of the goats *for* a sin offering, to make an atonement for you:

6 Beside [i]the burnt offering of the month, and his meat offering, and [j]the daily burnt offering, and his meat offering, and their drink offerings, [k]according unto their manner, for a sweet savour, a sacrifice made by fire unto the LORD.

Day of Atonement offerings

29:7–11pp — Lev. 16:2–34; 23:26–32

7 ¶ And [l]ye shall have on the tenth *day* of this seventh month an holy convocation; and ye shall [m]afflict your souls: ye shall not do any work *therein:*

8 But ye shall offer a burnt offering unto the LORD *for* a sweet savour; one young bullock, one ram, *and* seven lambs of the first year; [n]they shall be unto you without blemish:

9 And their meat offering *shall be of* flour mingled with oil, three tenth deals to a bullock, *and* two tenth deals to one ram,

10 A several tenth deal for one lamb, throughout the seven lambs:

11 One kid of the goats *for* a sin offering; beside [o]the sin offering of atonement, and the continual burnt offering, and the meat offering of it, and their drink offerings.

Feast of tabernacles offerings

29:12–39pp — Lev. 23:33–43; Deut. 16:13–17

12 ¶ And [p]on the fifteenth day of the seventh month ye shall have an holy convocation; ye shall do no servile work, and ye shall keep a feast unto the LORD seven days:

13 And [q]ye shall offer a burnt offering, a sacrifice made by fire, of a sweet savour unto the LORD; thirteen young bullocks, two rams, *and* fourteen lambs of the first year; they shall be without blemish:

14 And their meat offering *shall be of* flour mingled with oil, three tenth deals unto every bullock of the thirteen bullocks, two tenth deals to each ram of the two rams,

15 And a several tenth deal to each lamb of the fourteen lambs:

16 And one kid of the goats *for* a sin offering; beside the continual burnt offering, his meat offering, and his drink offering.

17 ¶ And on the second day *ye shall offer* twelve young bullocks, two rams, fourteen lambs of the first year without spot:

18 And their meat offering and their drink offerings for the bullocks, for the rams, and for the lambs, *shall be* according to their number, [r]after the manner:

19 And one kid of the goats *for* a sin offering; beside the continual burnt offering, and the meat offering thereof, and their drink offerings.

20 ¶ And on the third day eleven bullocks, two rams, fourteen lambs of the first year without blemish;

21 And their meat offering and their drink offerings for the bullocks, for the rams, and for the lambs, *shall be* according to their number, [s]after the manner:

22 And one goat *for* a sin offering; beside the continual burnt offering, and his meat offering, and his drink offering.

23 ¶ And on the fourth day ten bullocks, two rams, *and* fourteen lambs of the first year without blemish:

24 Their meat offering and their drink offerings for the bullocks, for the rams, and for the lambs, *shall be* according to their number, after the manner:

25 And one kid of the goats *for* a sin offering; beside the continual burnt offering, his meat offering, and his drink offering.

26 ¶ And on the fifth day nine bullocks, two rams, *and* fourteen lambs of the first year [t]without spot:

27 And their meat offering and their drink offerings for the bullocks, for the rams, and for the lambs, *shall be* ac-

29:1 [h]Lev. 23:24
29:6 [i]ch. 28:11 [j]ch. 28:3 [k]ch. 15:11,12
29:7 [l]Lev. 16:29 & 23:27 [m]Ps. 35:13 Is. 58:5
29:8 [n]ch. 28:19
29:11 [o]Lev. 16:3,5
29:12 [p]Lev. 23:34 Deut. 16:13 Ezek. 45:25
29:13 [q]Ezra 3:4 Dan. 9:24 Heb. 7:18,19 & 8:13 & 10:1-18
29:18 [r]ver. 3,4,9,10 ch. 15:12 & 28:7,14
29:21 [s]ver. 18
29:26 [t]Heb. 7:26 1 Pet. 1:19 Rev. 5:6-14

cording to their number, after the manner:

28 And one goat *for* a sin offering; beside the continual burnt offering, and his meat offering, and his drink offering.

29 ¶ And on the sixth day eight bullocks, two rams, *and* fourteen lambs of the first year without blemish:

30 And their meat offering and their drink offerings for the bullocks, for the rams, and for the lambs, *shall be* according to their number, after the manner:

31 And one goat *for* a sin offering; beside the continual burnt offering, his meat offering, and his drink offering.

32 ¶ And on the seventh day seven bullocks, two rams, *and* fourteen lambs of the first year without blemish:

33 And their meat offering and their drink offerings for the bullocks, for the rams, and for the lambs, *shall be* according to their number, after the manner:

34 And one goat *for* a sin offering; beside the continual burnt offering, his meat offering, and his drink offering.

35 ¶ On the eighth day ye shall have a [u]solemn assembly: ye shall do no servile work *therein:*

36 But ye shall offer a burnt offering, a sacrifice made by fire, of a sweet savour unto the LORD: one bullock, one ram, seven lambs of the first year without blemish:

37 Their meat offering and their drink offerings for the bullock, for the ram, and for the lambs, *shall be* according to their number, after the manner:

38 And one goat *for* a sin offering; beside the continual burnt offering, and his meat offering, and his drink offering.

39 These *things* ye shall [t]do unto the LORD in your [v]set feasts, beside your [w]vows, and your freewill offerings, for your burnt offerings, and for your meat offerings, and for your drink offerings, and for your peace offerings.

40 And Moses told the children of Israel according to all that the LORD commanded Moses.

29:35 [u]Lev. 23:36
29:39 [v]Lev. 23:2 1 Chr. 23:31 2 Chr. 31:3 Ezra 3:5 Neh. 10:33 Is. 1:14 [w]Lev. 7:11,16 & 22:21,23
30:1 [x]ch. 1:4,16 & 7:2
30:2 [y]Lev. 27:2 Deut. 23:21 Judg. 11:30,35 Eccl. 5:4 [z]Lev. 5:4 Mat. 14:9 Acts 23:14 [a]Job 22:27 Ps. 22:25 & 50:14 & 66:13,14 & 116:14,18 Nah. 1:15
30:6 [b]Ps. 56:12
30:8 [c]Gen. 3:16

The laws about vows

30 AND MOSES spake unto [x]the heads of the tribes concerning the children of Israel, saying, This *is* the thing which the LORD hath commanded.

2 [y]If a man vow a vow unto the LORD, or [z]swear an oath to bind his soul with a bond; he shall not [u]break his word, he shall [a]do according to all that proceedeth out of his mouth.

3 If a woman also vow a vow unto the LORD, and bind *herself* by a bond, *being* in her father's house in her youth;

4 And her father hear her vow, and her bond wherewith she hath bound her soul, and her father shall hold his peace at her: then all her vows shall stand, and every bond wherewith she hath bound her soul shall stand.

5 But if her father disallow her in the day that he heareth; not any of her vows, or of her bonds wherewith she hath bound her soul, shall stand: and the LORD shall forgive her, because her father disallowed her.

6 And if she had at all an husband, when [b]she[v] vowed, or uttered aught out of her lips, wherewith she bound her soul;

7 And her husband heard *it,* and held his peace at her in the day that he heard *it:* then her vows shall stand, and her bonds wherewith she bound her soul shall stand.

8 But if her husband [c]disallowed her on the day that he heard *it;* then he shall make her vow which she vowed, and that which she uttered with her lips, wherewith she bound her soul, of none effect: and the LORD shall forgive her.

9 But every vow of a widow, and of her that is divorced, wherewith they have bound their souls, shall stand against her.

10 And if she vowed in her husband's house, or bound her soul by a bond with an oath;

11 And her husband heard *it,* and

[t] Or, *offer* [u] Heb. *profane* [v] Heb. *her vows were upon her*

30:2 VOW A VOW. This chapter makes it clear that God required His people to keep their promises to Him and to others. Through these laws He impressed them with the serious nature of any vows and pledges made, and He emphasized that insincerity, lying, and hypocrisy had no place among God's people. However, special provisions were made concerning rash vows of youth (vv. 3–5) and vows that affected the relationship between husband and wife or father and daughter.

held his peace at her, *and* disallowed her not: then all her vows shall stand, and every bond wherewith she bound her soul shall stand.

12 But if her husband [w]hath utterly made them void on the day he heard *them; then* whatsoever proceeded out of her lips concerning her vows, or concerning the bond of her soul, shall not stand: her husband hath made them void; and the LORD shall forgive her.

13 Every vow, and every binding oath to afflict the soul, her husband may establish it, or her husband may make it void.

14 But if her husband altogether hold his peace at her from day to day; then he establisheth all her vows, or all her bonds, which *are* upon her: he confirmeth them, because he held his peace at her in the day that he heard *them.*

15 But if he shall any ways make them void after that he hath heard *them;* then he shall bear her iniquity.

16 These *are* the statutes, which the LORD commanded Moses, between a man and his wife, between the father and his daughter, *being yet* in her youth in her father's house.

The killing of the Midianites

31 AND THE LORD spake unto Moses, saying,

2 [d]Avenge the children of Israel of the Midianites: afterward shalt thou [e]be gathered unto thy people.

3 And Moses spake unto the people, saying, Arm some of yourselves unto the war, and let them go against the Midianites, and avenge the LORD of Midian.

4 [x]Of every tribe a thousand, throughout all the tribes of Israel, shall ye send to the war.

5 So there were delivered out of the thousands of Israel, a thousand of *every* tribe, twelve thousand armed for war.

6 And Moses sent them to the war, a thousand of *every* tribe, them and Phinehas the son of Eleazar the priest, to the war, with the holy instruments, and [f]the trumpets to blow in his hand.

7 And they warred against the Midianites, as the LORD commanded Moses; and [g]they slew all the [h]males.

8 And they slew the kings of Midian, beside the rest of them that were slain; *namely,* [i]Evi, and Rekem, and Zur, and Hur, and Reba, five kings of Midian: [j]Balaam also the son of Beor they slew with the sword.

9 And the children of Israel took *all* the women of Midian captives, and their little ones, and took the spoil of all their cattle, and all their flocks, and all their goods.

10 And they burnt all their cities wherein they dwelt, and all their goodly castles, with fire.

11 And [k]they took all the spoil, and all the prey, *both* of men and of beasts.

12 And they brought the captives, and the prey, and the spoil, unto Moses, and Eleazar the priest, and unto the congregation of the children of Israel, unto the camp at the plains of Moab, which *are* by Jordan *near* Jericho.

Purification of those who killed

13 ¶ And Moses, and Eleazar the priest, and all the princes of the congregation, went forth to meet them without the camp.

14 And Moses was wroth with the officers of the host, *with* the captains over thousands, and captains over hundreds, which came from the [y]battle.

15 And Moses said unto them, Have ye saved [l]all the women alive?

16 Behold, [m]these caused the children of Israel, through the [n]counsel of Balaam, to commit trespass against the LORD in the matter of Peor, and [o]there was a plague among the congregation of the LORD.

17 Now therefore [p]kill every male among the little ones, and kill every woman that hath known man by lying with [z]him.

18 But all the women children, that have not known a man by lying with him, keep alive for yourselves.

19 And [q]do ye abide without the camp seven days: whosoever hath

31:2 [d]ch. 25:17 [e]ch. 27:13
31:6 [f]ch. 10:9
31:7 [g]Deut. 20:13 Judg. 21:11 1 Sam. 27:9 1 Ki. 11:15,16 [h]See Judg. 6:1,2, 33
31:8 [i]Josh. 13:21 [j]Josh. 13:22
31:11 [k]Deut. 20:14
31:15 [l]See Deut. 20:14 1 Sam. 15:3
31:16 [m]ch. 25:2 [n]ch. 24:14 2 Pet. 2:15 Rev. 2:14 [o]ch. 25:9
31:17 [p]Judg. 21:11
31:19 [q]ch. 5:2

[w] Heb. *making void hath made them void*
[x] Heb. *A thousand of a tribe, a thousand of a tribe*
[y] Heb. *host of war*
[z] Heb. *a male*

31:3 AGAINST THE MIDIANITES. Just as many in Israel had died for their sins (11:1; 14:37; 16:31–34; 25:9; Ex. 32:35; Lev. 10:2), so would the Midianites die for their attempt to corrupt God's people (vv. 7–8; 25:1–9).

killed any person, and [r]whosoever
hath touched any slain, purify *both*
yourselves and your captives on the
third day, and on the seventh day.
20 And purify all *your* raiment, and
all [a]that is made of skins, and all
work of goats' *hair*, and all things made
of wood.
21 ¶ And Eleazar the priest said
unto the men of war which went to the
battle, This *is* the ordinance of the law
which the LORD commanded Moses;
22 Only the gold, and the silver, the
brass, the iron, the tin, and the lead,
23 Every thing that may abide the
fire, ye shall make *it* go through the
fire, and it shall be clean: nevertheless
it shall be purified [s]with the water of
separation: and all that abideth not the
fire ye shall make go through the wa-
ter.
24 [t]And ye shall wash your
clothes on the seventh day, and ye
shall be clean, and afterward ye shall
come into the camp.

The division of the prey

25 ¶ And the LORD spake unto Mo-
ses, saying,
26 Take the sum of the prey [b]that
was taken, *both* of man and of beast,
thou, and Eleazar the priest, and the
chief fathers of the congregation:
27 And [u]divide the prey into two
parts; between them that took the war
upon them, who went out to battle, and
between all the congregation:
28 And levy a tribute unto the LORD
of the men of war which went out to
battle: [v]one soul of five hundred, *both*
of the persons, and of the beeves, and
of the asses, and of the sheep:
29 Take *it* of their half, and give *it*
unto Eleazar the priest, *for* an heave
offering of the LORD.
30 And of the children of Israel's
half, thou shalt take [w]one portion of
fifty, of the persons, of the beeves, of
the asses, and of the [c]flocks, of all
manner of beasts, and give them unto
the Levites, [x]which keep the charge of
the tabernacle of the LORD.
31 And Moses and Eleazar the
priest did as the LORD commanded Mo-
ses.
32 And the booty, *being* the rest of
the prey which the men of war had
caught, was six hundred thousand and
seventy thousand and five thousand
sheep,

31:19 [r]ch. 19:11
31:23 [s]ch. 19:9,17
31:24 [t]Lev. 11:25
31:27 [u]Josh. 22:8 1 Sam. 30:24
31:28 [v]See ver. 30,47 & ch. 18:26
31:30 [w]See ver. 42-47 [x]ch. 3:7,8,25,31, 36 & 18:3,4
31:37 [y]Lev. 25:23 Deut. 10:14 Job 41:11 Ps. 24:1 & 50:12 Prov. 3:9 Luke 20:25 1 Cor. 10:26,28
31:41 [z]See ch. 18:8,19
31:47 [a]ver. 30

33 And threescore and twelve thou-
sand beeves,
34 And threescore and one thou-
sand asses,
35 And thirty and two thousand per-
sons in all, of women that had not
known man by lying with him.
36 And the half, *which was* the por-
tion of them that went out to war, was
in number three hundred thousand and
seven and thirty thousand and five
hundred sheep:
37 And the LORD's [y]tribute of the
sheep was six hundred and threescore
and fifteen.
38 And the beeves *were* thirty and
six thousand; of which the LORD's trib-
ute *was* threescore and twelve.
39 And the asses *were* thirty thou-
sand and five hundred; of which the
LORD's tribute *was* threescore and one.
40 And the persons *were* sixteen
thousand; of which the LORD's tribute
was thirty and two persons.
41 And Moses gave the tribute,
which was the LORD's heave offering,
unto Eleazar the priest, [z]as the LORD
commanded Moses.
42 And of the children of Israel's
half, which Moses divided from the
men that warred,
43 (Now the half *that pertained unto*
the congregation was three hundred
thousand and thirty thousand *and* sev-
en thousand and five hundred sheep,
44 And thirty and six thousand
beeves,
45 And thirty thousand asses and
five hundred,
46 And sixteen thousand persons;)
47 Even [a]of the children of Israel's
half, Moses took one portion of fifty,
both of man and of beast, and gave
them unto the Levites, which kept the
charge of the tabernacle of the LORD; as
the LORD commanded Moses.
48 ¶ And the officers which *were*
over thousands of the host, the cap-
tains of thousands, and captains of
hundreds, came near unto Moses:
49 And they said unto Moses, Thy
servants have taken the sum of the
men of war which *are* under our
[d]charge, and there lacketh not one
man of us.
50 We have therefore brought an
oblation for the LORD, what every man

[a] Heb. *instrument,* or, *vessel of skins* [b] Heb. *of the captivity* [c] Or, *goats* [d] Heb. *hand*

hath [e]gotten, of jewels of gold, chains, and bracelets, rings, earrings, and tablets, [b]to make an atonement for our souls before the LORD.

51 And Moses and Eleazar the priest took the gold of them, *even* all wrought jewels.

52 And all the gold of the [f]offering that they offered up to the LORD, of the captains of thousands, and of the captains of hundreds, was sixteen thousand seven hundred and fifty shekels.

53 (*For* [c]the men of war had taken spoil, every man for himself.)

54 And Moses and Eleazar the priest took the gold of the captains of thousands and of hundreds, and brought it into the tabernacle of the congregation, [d]*for* a memorial for the children of Israel before the LORD.

Tribes to possess Gilead

32 NOW THE children of Reuben and the children of Gad had a very great multitude of cattle: and when they saw the land of [e]Jazer, and the land of Gilead, that, behold, the place *was* a place for cattle;

2 The children of Gad and the children of Reuben came and spake unto Moses, and to Eleazar the priest, and unto the princes of the congregation, saying,

3 Ataroth, and Dibon, and Jazer, and [f]Nimrah, and Heshbon, and Elealeh, and [g]Shebam, and Nebo, and [h]Beon,

4 *Even* the country [i]which the LORD smote before the congregation of Israel, *is* a land for cattle, and thy servants have cattle:

5 Wherefore, said they, if we have found grace in thy sight, let this land be given unto thy servants for a possession, *and* bring us not over Jordan.

6 ¶ And Moses said unto the children of Gad and to the children of Reuben, Shall your brethren go to war, and shall ye sit here?

7 And wherefore [g]discourage ye the heart of the children of Israel from going over into the land which the LORD hath given them?

8 Thus did your fathers, [j]when I sent them from Kadesh-barnea [k]to see the land.

9 For [l]when they went up unto the valley of Eshcol, and saw the land, they discouraged the heart of the children of Israel, that they should not go into the land which the LORD had given them.

10 [m]And the LORD's anger was kindled the same time, and he sware, saying,

11 Surely none of the men that came up out of Egypt, [n]from twenty years old and upward, shall see the land which I sware unto Abraham, unto Isaac, and unto Jacob; because [o]they have not [h]wholly followed me:

12 Save Caleb the son of Jephunneh the Kenezite, and Joshua the son of Nun: [p]for they have wholly followed the LORD.

13 And the LORD's anger was kindled against Israel, and he made them [q]wander in the wilderness forty years, until [r]all the generation, that had done evil in the sight of the LORD, was consumed.

14 And, behold, ye are risen up in your fathers' stead, an increase of sinful men, to augment yet the [s]fierce anger of the LORD toward Israel.

15 For if ye [t]turn away from after him, he will yet again leave them in the wilderness; and ye shall destroy all this people.

16 ¶ And they came near unto him, and said, We will build sheepfolds here for our cattle, and cities for our little ones:

17 But [u]we ourselves will go ready armed before the children of Israel, until we have brought them unto their place: and our little ones shall dwell in the fenced cities because of the inhabitants of the land.

18 [v]We will not return unto our houses, until the children of Israel have inherited every man his inheritance.

19 For we will not inherit with them on yonder side Jordan, or forward; [w]because our inheritance is fallen to us on this side Jordan eastward.

20 ¶ And [x]Moses said unto them, If ye will do this thing, if ye will go armed before the LORD to war,

21 And will go all of you armed over Jordan before the LORD, until he hath driven out his enemies from before him,

22 And [y]the land be subdued before the LORD: then afterward [z]ye shall return, and be guiltless before the LORD, and before Israel; and [a]this land

31:50 [b]Ex. 30:12,16
31:53 [c]Deut. 20:14
31:54 [d]Ex. 30:16
32:1 [e]ch. 21:32 Josh. 13:25 2 Sam. 24:5
32:3 [f]ver. 36 *Beth-nimrah* [g]ver. 38 *Shibmah* [h]ver. 38 *Baal-meon*
32:4 [i]ch. 21:24,34
32:8 [j]ch. 13:3,26 [k]Deut. 1:22
32:9 [l]ch. 13:24,31 Deut. 1:24,28
32:10 [m]ch. 14:11,21 Deut. 1:34
32:11 [n]ch. 14:28,29 Deut. 1:35 [o]ch. 14:24,30
32:12 [p]ch. 14:24 Deut. 1:36 Josh. 14:8,9
32:13 [q]ch. 14:33-35 [r]ch. 26:64,65
32:14 [s]Deut. 1:34
32:15 [t]Deut. 30:17 Josh. 22:16,18 2 Chr. 7:19
32:17 [u]Josh. 4:12,13
32:18 [v]Josh. 22:4
32:19 [w]ver. 33 Josh. 12:1 & 13:8
32:20 [x]Deut. 3:18 Josh. 1:14 & 4:12,13
32:22 [y]Deut. 3:20 Josh. 11:23 & 18:1 [z]Josh. 22:4 [a]Deut. 3:12,15,16,18 Josh. 1:15 & 13:8,32 & 22:4,9

[e] Heb. *found* [f] Heb. *heave offering* [g] Heb. *break* [h] Heb. *fulfilled after me*

shall be your possession before the LORD.

23 But if ye will not do so, behold, ye have sinned against the LORD: and be sure [b]your sin will find you out.

24 [c]Build you cities for your little ones, and folds for your sheep; and do that which hath proceeded out of your mouth.

25 And the children of Gad and the children of Reuben spake unto Moses, saying, Thy servants will do as my lord commandeth.

26 [d]Our little ones, our wives, our flocks, and all our cattle, shall be there in the cities of Gilead:

27 [e]But thy servants will pass over, every man armed for war, before the LORD to battle, as my lord saith.

28 So [f]concerning them Moses commanded Eleazar the priest, and Joshua the son of Nun, and the chief fathers of the tribes of the children of Israel:

29 And Moses said unto them, If the children of Gad and the children of Reuben will pass with you over Jordan, every man armed to battle, before the LORD, and the land shall be subdued before you; then ye shall give them the land of Gilead for a possession:

30 But if they will not pass over with you armed, they shall have possessions among you in the land of Canaan.

31 And the children of Gad and the children of Reuben answered, saying, As the LORD hath said unto thy servants, so will we do.

32 We will pass over armed before the LORD into the land of Canaan, that the possession of our inheritance on this side Jordan *may be* ours.

33 And [g]Moses gave unto them, *even* to the children of Gad, and to the children of Reuben, and unto half the tribe of Manasseh the son of Joseph, [h]the kingdom of Sihon king of the Amorites, and the kingdom of Og king of Bashan, the land, with the cities thereof in the coasts, *even* the cities of the country round about.

34 ¶ And the children of Gad built [i]Dibon, and Ataroth, and [j]Aroer,

32:23 [b]Gen. 4:7 & 44:16 Is. 59:12
32:24 [c]ver. 16,34
32:26 [d]Josh. 1:14
32:27 [e]Josh. 4:12
32:28 [f]Josh. 1:13
32:33 [g]Deut. 3:12-17 & 29:8 Josh. 12:6 & 13:8 & 22:4 [h]ch. 21:24,33,35
32:34 [i]ch. 33:45,46 [j]Deut. 2:36
32:35 [k]ver. 1,3 *Jazer*
32:36 [l]ver. 3 *Nimrah* [m]ver. 24
32:37 [n]ch. 21:27
32:38 [o]Is. 46:1 [p]ch. 22:41 [q]See ver. 3 Ex. 23:13 Josh. 23:7
32:39 [r]Gen. 50:23
32:40 [s]Deut. 3:12,13,15 Josh. 13:31 & 17:1
32:41 [t]Deut. 3:14 Josh. 13:30 1 Chr. 2:21 [u]Judg. 10:4 1 Ki. 4:13
33:3 [v]Ex. 12:37 [w]Ex. 12:2 & 13:4 [x]Ex. 14:8
33:4 [y]Ex. 12:29 [z]Ex. 12:12 & 18:11 Is. 19:1 Rev. 12:8
33:5 [a]Ex. 12:37
33:6 [b]Ex. 13:20

35 And Atroth, Shophan, and [k]Jaazer, and Jogbehah,

36 And [l]Beth-nimrah, and Bethharan, [m]fenced cities: and folds for sheep.

37 And the children of Reuben [n]built Heshbon, and Elealeh, and Kirjathaim,

38 And [o]Nebo and [p]Baal-meon, ([q]their names being changed,) and Shibmah: and [1]gave other names unto the cities which they builded.

39 And the children of [r]Machir the son of Manasseh went to Gilead, and took it, and dispossessed the Amorite which *was* in it.

40 And Moses [s]gave Gilead unto Machir the son of Manasseh; and he dwelt therein.

41 And [t]Jair the son of Manasseh went and took the small towns thereof, and called them [u]Havoth-jair.

42 And Nobah went and took Kenath, and the villages thereof, and called it Nobah, after his own name.

Journey from Egypt to Canaan

33 THESE *ARE* the journeys of the children of Israel, which went forth out of the land of Egypt with their armies under the hand of Moses and Aaron.

2 And Moses wrote their goings out according to their journeys by the commandment of the LORD: and these *are* their journeys according to their goings out.

3 And they [v]departed from Rameses in [w]the first month, on the fifteenth day of the first month; on the morrow after the passover the children of Israel went out [x]with an high hand in the sight of all the Egyptians.

4 For the Egyptians buried all *their* firstborn, [y]which the LORD had smitten among them: [z]upon their gods also the LORD executed judgments.

5 [a]And the children of Israel removed from Rameses, and pitched in Succoth.

6 And they departed from [b]Succoth, and pitched in Etham, which *is* in the edge of the wilderness.

[1]Heb. *they called by names the names of the cities*

32:20 IF YE WILL GO ARMED. Moses would allow the tribes of Reuben and Gad to settle in the land on the east side of Jordan only if they promised to help the other tribes in their conquest of Canaan. It would be considered a great sin if they sought their own selfish interest while others gave of themselves to do battle for the Lord (v. 23).

7 And [c]they removed from Etham, and turned again unto Pi-hahiroth, which *is* before Baal-zephon: and they pitched before Migdol.

8 And they departed from before Pi-hahiroth, and [d]passed through the midst of the sea into the wilderness, and went three days' journey in the wilderness of Etham, and pitched in Marah.

9 And they removed from Marah, and [e]came unto Elim: and in Elim *were* twelve fountains of water, and threescore and ten palm trees; and they pitched there.

10 And they removed from Elim, and encamped by the Red sea.

11 And they removed from the Red sea, and encamped in the [f]wilderness of Sin.

12 And they took their journey out of the wilderness of Sin, and encamped in Dophkah.

13 And they departed from Dophkah, and encamped in Alush.

14 And they removed from Alush, and encamped at [g]Rephidim, where was no water for the people to drink.

15 And they departed from Rephidim, and pitched in the [h]wilderness of Sinai.

16 And they removed from the desert of Sinai, and pitched [i]at [j]Kibroth-hattaavah.

17 And they departed from Kibroth-hattaavah, and [j]encamped at Hazeroth.

18 And they departed from Hazeroth, and pitched in [k]Rithmah.

19 And they departed from Rithmah, and pitched at Rimmon-parez.

20 And they departed from Rimmon-parez, and pitched in Libnah.

21 And they removed from Libnah, and pitched at Rissah.

22 And they journeyed from Rissah, and pitched in Kehelathah.

23 And they went from Kehelathah, and pitched in mount Shapher.

24 And they removed from mount Shapher, and encamped in Haradah.

25 And they removed from Haradah, and pitched in Makheloth.

26 And they removed from Makheloth, and encamped at Tahath.

27 And they departed from Tahath, and pitched at Tarah.

28 And they removed from Tarah, and pitched in Mithcah.

33:7 [c]Ex. 14:2,9
33:8 [d]Ex. 14:22 & 15:22,23
33:9 [e]Ex. 15:27
33:11 [f]Ex. 16:1
33:14 [g]Ex. 17:1 & 19:2
33:15 [h]Ex. 16:1 & 19:1,2
33:16 [i]ch. 11:34
33:17 [j]ch. 11:35
33:18 [k]ch. 12:16
33:30 [l]Deut. 10:6
33:32 [m]See Gen. 36:27 Deut. 10:6 1 Chr. 1:42 [n]Deut. 10:7
33:35 [o]Deut. 2:8 1 Ki. 9:26 & 22:48
33:36 [p]ch. 20:1 & 27:14
33:37 [q]ch. 20:22,23 & 21:4
33:38 [r]ch. 20:25,28 Deut. 10:6 & 32:50
33:40 [s]ch. 21:1
33:41 [t]ch. 21:4
33:43 [u]ch. 21:10
33:44 [v]ch. 21:11 [w]ch. 21:11
33:45 [x]ch. 32:34
33:46 [y]Jer. 48:22 Ezek. 6:14
33:47 [z]ch. 21:20 Deut. 32:49
33:48 [a]ch. 22:1

29 And they went from Mithcah, and pitched in Hashmonah.

30 And they departed from Hashmonah, and [l]encamped at Moseroth.

31 And they departed from Moseroth, and pitched in Bene-jaakan.

32 And they removed from [m]Bene-jaakan, and [n]encamped at Hor-hagidgad.

33 And they went from Hor-hagidgad, and pitched in Jotbathah.

34 And they removed from Jotbathah, and encamped at Ebronah.

35 And they departed from Ebronah, [o]and encamped at Ezion-geber.

36 And they removed from Ezion-geber, and pitched in the [p]wilderness of Zin, which *is* Kadesh.

37 And they removed from [q]Kadesh, and pitched in mount Hor, in the edge of the land of Edom.

38 And [r]Aaron the priest went up into mount Hor at the commandment of the LORD, and died there, in the fortieth year after the children of Israel were come out of the land of Egypt, in the first *day* of the fifth month.

39 And Aaron *was* an hundred and twenty and three years old when he died in mount Hor.

40 And [s]king Arad the Canaanite, which dwelt in the south in the land of Canaan, heard of the coming of the children of Israel.

41 And they departed from mount [t]Hor, and pitched in Zalmonah.

42 And they departed from Zalmonah, and pitched in Punon.

43 And they departed from Punon, and [u]pitched in Oboth.

44 And [v]they departed from Oboth, and pitched in [w]Ije-abarim,[k] in the border of Moab.

45 And they departed from Iim, and pitched [x]in Dibon-gad.

46 And they removed from Dibon-gad, and encamped in Almon-[y]diblathaim.

47 And they removed from Almon-diblathaim, [z]and pitched in the mountains of Abarim, before Nebo.

48 And they departed from the mountains of Abarim, and [a]pitched in the plains of Moab by Jordan *near* Jericho.

49 And they pitched by Jordan, from

[j] i.e. *The graves of lust* [k] Or, *Heaps of Abarim*

Beth-jeshimoth *even* unto [b]Abel-shittim[1] in the plains of Moab.

50 ¶ And the LORD spake unto Moses in the plains of Moab by Jordan *near* Jericho, saying,

51 Speak unto the children of Israel, and say unto them, [c]When ye are passed over Jordan into the land of Canaan;

52 [d]Then ye shall drive out all the inhabitants of the land from before you, and destroy all their pictures, and destroy all their molten images, and quite pluck down all their high places:

53 And ye shall dispossess *the inhabitants of* the land, and dwell therein: for I have given you the land to possess it.

54 And [e]ye shall divide the land by lot for an inheritance among your families: *and* to the more ye shall [m]give the more inheritance, and to the fewer ye shall [n]give the less inheritance: every man's *inheritance* shall be in the place where his lot falleth; according to the tribes of your fathers ye shall inherit.

55 But if ye will not drive out the inhabitants of the land from before you; then it shall come to pass, that those which ye let remain of them *shall be* [f]pricks in your eyes, and thorns in your sides, and shall vex you in the land wherein ye dwell.

56 Moreover it shall come to pass, *that* I shall do unto you, as I thought to do unto them.

The borders of Canaan

34 AND THE LORD spake unto Moses, saying,

2 Command the children of Israel, and say unto them, When ye come into [g]the land of Canaan; (this *is* the land that shall fall unto you for an inheritance, *even* the land of Canaan with the coasts thereof:)

3 Then [h]your south quarter shall be from the wilderness of Zin along by the coast of Edom, and your south border shall be the outmost coast of [i]the salt sea eastward:

4 And your border shall turn from the south [j]to the ascent of Akrabbim, and pass on to Zin: and the going forth thereof shall be from the south [k]to Kadesh-barnea, and shall go on to [l]Hazar-addar, and pass on to Azmon:

5 And the border shall fetch a compass from Azmon [m]unto the river of Egypt, and the goings out of it shall be at the sea.

6 And *as for* the western border, ye shall even have the great sea for a border: this shall be your west border.

7 And this shall be your north border: from the great sea ye shall point out for you [n]mount Hor:

8 From mount Hor ye shall point out *your border* [o]unto the entrance of Hamath; and the goings forth of the border shall be to [p]Zedad:

9 ¶ And the border shall go on to Ziphron, and the goings out of it shall be at [q]Hazar-enan: this shall be your north border.

10 And ye shall point out your east border from Hazar-enan to Shepham:

11 And the coast shall go down from Shepham [r]to Riblah, on the east side of Ain; and the border shall descend, and shall reach unto the [o]side of the sea [s]of Chinnereth eastward:

12 And the border shall go down to Jordan, and the goings out of it shall be at [t]the salt sea: this shall be your land with the coasts thereof round about.

13 And Moses commanded the children of Israel, saying, [u]This *is* the land which ye shall inherit by lot, which the LORD commanded to give unto the nine tribes, and to the half tribe:

14 [v]For the tribe of the children of Reuben according to the house of their fathers, and the tribe of the children of Gad according to the house of their fathers, have received *their inheritance;* and half the tribe of Manasseh have received their inheritance:

15 The two tribes and the half tribe have received their inheritance on this

33:49 [b]ch. 25:1 Josh. 2:1 **33:51** [c]Deut. 7:1,2 & 9:1 Josh. 3:17 **33:52** [d]Ex. 23:24,33 & 34:13 Deut. 7:2,5 & 12:3 Josh. 11:12 Judg. 2:2 **33:54** [e]ch. 26:53-55 **33:55** [f]Josh. 23:13 Judg. 2:3 Ps. 106:34,36 **34:2** [g]Gen. 17:8 Deut. 1:7 Ps. 78:55 Ezek. 47:14 **34:3** [h]Josh. 15:1 See Ezek. 47:13 [i]Gen. 14:3 Josh. 15:2 **34:4** [j]Josh. 15:3 [k]ch. 13:26 & 32:8 [l]See Josh. 15:3,4 **34:5** [m]Gen. 15:18 Josh. 15:4,47 1 Ki. 8:65 Is. 27:12 **34:7** [n]ch. 33:37 **34:8** [o]ch. 13:21 2 Ki. 14:25 [p]Ezek. 47:15 **34:9** [q]Ezek. 47:17 **34:11** [r]2 Ki. 23:33 Jer. 39:5,6 [s]Deut. 3:17 Josh. 11:2 & 19:35 Mat. 14:34 Luke 5:1 **34:12** [t]ver. 3 **34:13** [u]ver. 2 Josh. 14:1,2 **34:14** [v]ch. 32:33 Josh. 14:2

[1] Or, *The plains of Shittim* [m] Heb. *multiply his inheritance* [n] Heb. *diminish his inheritance* [o] Heb. *shoulder*

33:55 IF YE WILL NOT DRIVE OUT. If the Israelites failed to drive out completely the wicked Canaanites and destroy their idolatrous worship centers, then God would cause those Canaanites to be trouble for them and He Himself would judge them. Likewise, if the church of Jesus Christ tolerates sin in its midst, trouble, destruction, and death will come to the church and to the souls of her members. God Himself will allow His people to be trampled under foot by the evil world that they have failed to resist (see Mat. 5:13, note).

side Jordan *near* Jericho eastward, toward the sunrising.

16 And the LORD spake unto Moses, saying,

17 These *are* the names of the men which shall divide the land unto you: [w]Eleazar the priest, and Joshua the son of Nun.

18 And ye shall take one [x]prince of every tribe, to divide the land by inheritance.

19 And the names of the men *are* these: Of the tribe of Judah, Caleb the son of Jephunneh.

20 And of the tribe of the children of Simeon, Shemuel the son of Ammihud.

21 Of the tribe of Benjamin, Elidad the son of Chislon.

22 And the prince of the tribe of the children of Dan, Bukki the son of Jogli.

23 The prince of the children of Joseph, for the tribe of the children of Manasseh, Hanniel the son of Ephod.

24 And the prince of the tribe of the children of Ephraim, Kemuel the son of Shiphtan.

25 And the prince of the tribe of the children of Zebulun, Elizaphan the son of Parnach.

26 And the prince of the tribe of the children of Issachar, Paltiel the son of Azzan.

27 And the prince of the tribe of the children of Asher, Ahihud the son of Shelomi.

28 And the prince of the tribe of the children of Naphtali, Pedahel the son of Ammihud.

29 These *are they* whom the LORD commanded to divide the inheritance unto the children of Israel in the land of Canaan.

Cities for the Levites

35:6–34Ref — Deut. 4:41–43; 19:1–14; Josh. 20:1–9

35 AND THE LORD spake unto Moses in [y]the plains of Moab by Jordan *near* Jericho, saying,

2 [z]Command the children of Israel, that they give unto the Levites of the inheritance of their possession cities to dwell in; and ye shall give *also* unto the Levites [a]suburbs for the cities round about them.

3 And the cities shall they have to dwell in; and the suburbs of them shall be for their cattle, and for their goods, and for all their beasts.

4 And the suburbs of the cities, which ye shall give unto the Levites, *shall reach* from the wall of the city and outward a thousand cubits round about.

5 And ye shall measure from without the city on the east side two thousand cubits, and on the south side two thousand cubits, and on the west side two thousand cubits, and on the north side two thousand cubits; and the city *shall be* in the midst: this shall be to them the suburbs of the cities.

6 And among the cities which ye shall give unto the Levites *there shall be* [b]six cities for refuge, which ye shall appoint for the manslayer, that he may flee thither: and [p]to them ye shall add forty and two cities.

7 *So* all the cities which ye shall give to the Levites *shall be* [c]forty and eight cities: them *shall ye give* with their suburbs.

8 And the cities which ye shall give *shall be* [d]of the possession of the children of Israel: [e]from *them that have* many ye shall give many; but from *them that have* few ye shall give few: every one shall give of his cities unto the Levites according to his inheritance which [q]he inheriteth.

The cities of refuge

9 ¶ And the LORD spake unto Moses, saying,

10 Speak unto the children of Israel, and say unto them, [f]When ye be come over Jordan into the land of Canaan;

11 Then [g]ye shall appoint you cities to be cities of refuge for you; that the slayer may flee thither, which killeth any person [r]at unawares.

12 [h]And they shall be unto you cities for refuge from the avenger; that

34:17 [w]Josh. 14:1 & 19:51 **34:18** [x]ch. 1:4,16 **35:1** [y]See ch. 33:50 **35:2** [z]Josh. 14:3,4 & 21:2 See Ezek. 45:1 & 48:8

[a]See Lev. 25:34 **35:6** [b]ver. 13 Deut. 4:41 Josh. 20:2,7,8 & 21:3,13 **35:7** [c]Josh. 21:41 **35:8** [d]Josh. 21:3 [e]ch. 26:54 **35:10** [f]Deut. 19:2 Josh. 20:2 **35:11** [g]Ex. 21:13 **35:12** [h]Deut. 19:6 Josh. 20:3,5,6

[p] Heb. *above them ye shall give* [q] Heb. *they inherit* [r] Heb. *by error*

35:11 CITIES OF REFUGE. Cities of refuge were established to protect someone who killed a person accidentally. One accused of murder could flee to one of the cities and receive protection until he could receive a fair trial (v. 12). If found guilty of willful murder, he was put to death immediately (vv. 16–21). If he was guilty of only involuntary manslaughter, he was to remain in that city until the death of the high priest; then he could safely return to his home (vv. 22–28).

the manslayer die not, until he stand before the congregation in judgment.

13 And of these cities which ye shall give [i]six cities shall ye have for refuge.

14 [j]Ye shall give three cities on this side Jordan, and three cities shall ye give in the land of Canaan, *which* shall be cities of refuge.

15 These six cities shall be a refuge, *both* for the children of Israel, and [k]for the stranger, and for the sojourner among them: that every one that killeth any person unawares may flee thither.

16 [l]And if he smite him with an instrument of iron, so that he die, he *is* a murderer: the murderer shall surely be put to death.

17 And if he smite him [s]with throwing a stone, wherewith he may die, and he die, he *is* a murderer: the murderer shall surely be put to death.

18 Or *if* he smite him with an hand-weapon of wood, wherewith he may die, and he die, he *is* a murderer: the murderer shall surely be put to death.

19 [m]The revenger of blood himself shall slay the murderer: when he meeteth him, he shall slay him.

20 But [n]if he thrust him of hatred, or hurl at him [o]by laying of wait, that he die;

21 Or in enmity smite him with his hand, that he die: he that smote *him* shall surely be put to death; *for* he *is* a murderer: the revenger of blood shall slay the murderer, when he meeteth him.

22 But if he thrust him suddenly [p]without enmity, or have cast upon him any thing without laying of wait,

23 Or with any stone, wherewith a man may die, seeing *him* not, and cast *it* upon him, that he die, and *was* not his enemy, neither sought his harm:

24 Then [q]the congregation shall judge between the slayer and the revenger of blood according to these judgments:

25 And the congregation shall deliver the slayer out of the hand of the revenger of blood, and the congregation shall restore him to the city of his refuge, whither he was fled: and [r]he shall abide in it unto the death of the high priest, [s]which was anointed with the holy oil.

26 But if the slayer shall at any time come without the border of the city of his refuge, whither he was fled;

27 And the revenger of blood find him without the borders of the city of his refuge, and the revenger of blood kill the slayer; [t]he[t] shall not be guilty of blood:

28 Because he should have remained in the city of his refuge until the death of the high priest: but after the death of the high priest the slayer shall return into the land of his possession.

29 So these *things* shall be for [u]a statute of judgment unto you throughout your generations in all your dwellings.

30 Whoso killeth any person, the murderer shall be put to death by the [v]mouth of witnesses: but one witness shall not testify against any person *to cause him* to die.

31 Moreover ye shall take no satisfaction for the life of a murderer, which *is* [u]guilty of death: but he shall be surely put to death.

32 And ye shall take no satisfaction for him that is fled to the city of his refuge, that he should come again to dwell in the land, until the death of the priest.

33 So ye shall not pollute the land wherein ye *are:* for blood [w]it defileth the land: and [v]the land cannot be cleansed of the blood that is shed therein, but [x]by the blood of him that shed it.

34 [y]Defile not therefore the land which ye shall inhabit, wherein I dwell: for [z]I the LORD dwell among the children of Israel.

35:13 [i]ver. 6 **35:14** [j]Deut. 4:41 Josh. 20:8 **35:15** [k]ch. 15:16 **35:16** [l]Ex. 21:12,14 Lev. 24:17 Deut. 19:11,12 **35:19** [m]ver. 21,24,27 Deut. 19:6,12 Josh. 20:3,5 **35:20** [n]Gen. 4:8 2 Sam. 3:27 & 20:10 1 Ki. 2:31,32 [o]Ex. 21:14 Deut. 19:11 **35:22** [p]Ex. 21:13 **35:24** [q]ver. 12 Josh. 20:6

35:25 [r]Josh. 20:6 [s]Ex. 29:7 Lev. 4:3 & 21:10 **35:27** [t]Ex. 22:2 **35:29** [u]ch. 27:11 **35:30** [v]Deut. 17:6 & 19:15 Mat. 18:16 2 Cor. 13:1 Heb. 10:28 **35:33** [w]Ps. 106:38 Mic. 4:11 [x]Gen. 9:6 **35:34** [y]Lev. 18:25 Deut. 21:23 [z]Ex. 29:45,46

s Heb. *with a stone of the hand* t Heb. *no blood* shall be *to him* u Heb. *faulty to die* v Heb *there can be no expiation for the land*

35:33 NOT POLLUTE THE LAND. To fail to put a murderer to death polluted and defiled the land. "To defile" means that failure to avenge the death of the innocent person would cause God to withdraw His presence, blessing, and help from the land (see Deut. 21:1–9). God's holiness and justice required that no murderer be allowed to go free. Capital punishment in Israel expressed God's holy desire that righteousness and the sanctity of innocent life be maintained among His people as a holy nation (see Gen. 9:6, note).

The marriage of heiresses

36:1–12pp — Num. 27:1–11

36 AND THE chief fathers of the families of the [a]children of Gilead, the son of Machir, the son of Manasseh, of the families of the sons of Joseph, came near, and spake before Moses, and before the princes, the chief fathers of the children of Israel:

2 And they said, [b]The LORD commanded my lord to give the land for an inheritance by lot to the children of Israel: and [c]my lord was commanded by the LORD to give the inheritance of Zelophehad our brother unto his daughters.

3 And if they be married to any of the sons of the *other* tribes of the children of Israel, then shall their inheritance be [d]taken from the inheritance of our fathers, and shall be put to the inheritance of the tribe [w]whereunto they are received: so shall it be taken from the lot of our inheritance.

4 And when [e]the jubilee of the children of Israel shall be, then shall their inheritance be put unto the inheritance of the tribe whereunto they are received: so shall their inheritance be taken away from the inheritance of the tribe of our fathers.

5 And Moses commanded the children of Israel according to the word of the LORD, saying, The tribe of the sons of Joseph [f]hath said well.

6 This *is* the thing which the LORD doth command concerning the daughters of Zelophehad, saying, Let them [x]marry to whom they think best; [g]only to the family of the tribe of their father shall they marry.

7 So shall not the inheritance of the children of Israel remove from tribe to tribe: for every one of the children of Israel shall [h]keep[y] himself to the inheritance of the tribe of his fathers.

8 And [i]every daughter, that possesseth an inheritance in any tribe of the children of Israel, shall be wife unto one of the family of the tribe of her father, that the children of Israel may enjoy every man the inheritance of his fathers.

9 Neither shall the inheritance remove from *one* tribe to another tribe; but every one of the tribes of the children of Israel shall keep himself to his own inheritance.

10 Even as the LORD commanded Moses, so did the daughters of Zelophehad:

11 [j]For Mahlah, Tirzah, and Hoglah, and Milcah, and Noah, the daughters of Zelophehad, were married unto their father's brothers' sons:

12 *And* they were married [z]into the families of the sons of Manasseh the son of Joseph, and their inheritance remained in the tribe of the family of their father.

13 These *are* the commandments and the judgments, [k]which the LORD commanded by the hand of Moses unto the children of Israel [l]in the plains of Moab by Jordan *near* Jericho.

36:1 [a]ch. 26:29
36:2 [b]ch. 26:55 & 33:54 Josh. 17:4 [c]ch. 27:1,7 Josh. 17:3,4
36:3 [d]ch. 27:4 marg.
36:4 [e]Lev. 25:10
36:5 [f]ch. 27:7
36:6 [g]ver. 11,12
36:7 [h]1 Ki. 21:3
36:8 [i]1 Chr. 23:22
36:11 [j]ch. 27:1
36:13 [k]Deut. 33:4 [l]ch. 26:3 & 33:50

[w] Heb. *unto whom they shall be* [x] Heb. *be wives* [y] Heb. *cleave to the* [z] Heb. *to some that were of the families*

DEUTERONOMY

Outline

Introduction (1:1–5)
- I. Moses' First Address: Recounting Israel's Recent History (1:6—4:43)
  - A. Leaving Mount Sinai (1:6–18)
  - B. Unbelief at Kadesh-barnea (1:19–46)
  - C. Wilderness Wanderings (2:1–15)
  - D. Advancing to the Plains of Moab (2:16—3:29)
  - E. Moses' Exhortation to Obedience (4:1–43)
- II. Moses' Second Address: Main Obligations of the Covenant (4:44—26:19)
  - A. The Ten Commandments (4:44—5:33)
  - B. The Shema and Imperatives (6:1–25)
  - C. Practical Commands, Promises, and Warnings (7:1—11:32)
  - D. Commands Concerning Worship (12:1–32)
  - E. Commands Concerning False Prophets (13:1–18)
  - F. Commands Concerning Food, Tithes, and the Sabbatical Year (14:1—15:23)
  - G. Commands Concerning Annual Feasts (16:1–17)
  - H. Commands Concerning Leaders (16:18—18:22)
  - I. Civil and Social Laws (19:1—26:19)
- III. Moses' Third Address: Renewing and Ratifying the Covenant (27:1—30:20)
  - A. Moses Solemnly Charges Israel (27:1–26)
  - B. Promised Blessings for Obedience and Curses for Disobedience (28:1–68)
  - C. Restatement of the Covenant and Pertinent Exhortations (29:1–30:20)
- IV. Final Activities of Moses and His Death (31:1—34:12)
  - A. Moses Charges Israel and Commissions Joshua (31:1–29)
  - B. Song of Moses (31:30—32:47)
  - C. God's Instruction to Moses (32:48–52)
  - D. Moses Blesses the Tribes (33:1–29)
  - E. Death and Burial of Moses, and Final Summary (34:1–12)

Author: Moses

Theme: Covenant Renewal

Date of Writing: c. 1405 B.C.

Background

The title "Deuteronomy" (derived from the Septuagint) means "Second Law." The book consists of Moses' farewell messages in which he reviewed and renewed God's covenant with Israel for the sake of the new generation of Israelites. They had come to the end of their wilderness wandering and were now ready to enter the land of Canaan. For the most part this new generation had no personal recollection of the first Passover, the Red Sea crossing, or the giving of the Law at Mount Sinai. They needed an inspired recounting of God's covenant, law, and faithfulness, as well as a fresh declaration concerning the accompanying blessings for obedience and curses for disobedience. Unlike Numbers, which records the wilderness wanderings of the rebellious "exodus generation" of Israelites over

a span of thirty-nine years, Deuteronomy covers a short span of perhaps one month at one location on the plains of Moab directly east of Jericho and the Jordan River.

Deuteronomy was written by Moses (31:9,24–26; cf. 4:44–46; 29:1) and bequeathed to Israel as a covenant document to be read before all the people in its entirety every seven years (31:10–13). Moses probably completed the book shortly before his death about 1405 B.C. Mosaic authorship of Deuteronomy is attested to (1) by the Jewish and Samaritan Pentateuch, (2) by O.T. writers (e.g., Josh. 1:7; 1 Ki. 2:3; 2 Ki. 14:6; Ezra 3:2; Neh. 1:8–9; Dan. 9:11), (3) by Jesus (Mat. 19:7–9; John 5:45–47) and other N.T. writers (e.g., Acts 3:22–23; Rom. 10:19), (4) by ancient Christian scholars, (5) by modern conservative scholars, and (6) by internal evidence (e.g., similarity in literary structure to secular suzerainty covenant treaties written in the fifteenth century B.C.). The account of Moses' death (ch. 34) was undoubtedly added soon after its occurrence (most likely by Joshua) as a fitting tribute to Moses, the servant of the Lord.

Purpose

Moses' original purpose in addressing Israel's new generation before turning the reins of leadership over to Joshua for the conquest was to exhort and instruct them concerning (1) God's mighty deeds and promises, (2) their own covenant obligations of faith and obedience, and (3) their need to consecrate themselves to fear the Lord, to walk in His ways, and to love and honor Him with all their heart, soul, and strength.

Survey

As a covenant renewal document, Deuteronomy is organized like a suzerainty covenant treaty of that time: (1) preamble (1:1–5); (2) historical prologue (1:6—4:43); (3) main stipulations (4:44—26:19); (4) curses and blessings (27:1—30:20); and (5) arrangements for its continuation (31:1—33:39).

With all the earnestness that he possessed, Moses reviewed and renewed God's covenant with Israel primarily by means of three inspired addresses. (1) Moses' first address reviewed Israel's history and failure since Mount Sinai and summoned the new generation to fear God and obey Him (1:6—4:43). (2) Moses' second address reviewed and applied many covenant laws dealing with issues such as Sabbath observance, worship, the poor, annual festivals, inheritance and property rights, sexual immorality, treatment of servants, and administration of justice (4:44—26:19). (3) Moses' third address prophesied blessings and curses that would fall the Israelites according to their obedience or disobedience (27:1—30:20). The remaining chapters include Moses' appointment of Joshua as his successor and a testimony about Moses' death (31:1—34:12).

Special Features

Four major features or emphases characterize Deuteronomy. (1) It provided the new generation of Israelites (who were soon to enter Canaan) the necessary foundation and motivation for inheriting the promised land by focusing on the nature of God and His covenant with Israel. (2) It is "The Book of the Second Law" in that Moses, Israel's 120-year-old leader, restated and summarized (in sermonic form) the word of the Lord embodied in the four preceding books of the Pentateuch. (3) It is "the Book of Remembrance." A characteristic admonition of Deuteronomy is, "Remember, and forget not." Rather than representing a quest for "new truth," Deuteronomy exhorts Israel to retain and obey the previously revealed truth of God as already given in His absolute and unchanging word. (4) An important keynote of the book is the "faith-plus-obedience" formula. Israel was called to trust God with their whole being and to obey His commandments unswervingly. Faith-plus-obedience would enable them to inherit the promises with God's full blessing. The absence of faith and obedience, on the other hand, would introduce the cycle of failure and judgment.

New Testament Fulfillment

When Jesus was tempted by the devil, He responded by quoting passages from Deuteronomy (Mat. 4:4,7,10, quoting Deut. 8:3; 6:16; 6:13). When Jesus was asked what was the greatest commandment, His reply was from Deuteronomy (Mat. 22:37; cf. Deut. 6:5). The N.T. books quote or allude to Deuteronomy nearly a hundred times. A clear Messianic prophecy (18:15–19) is referred to twice in Acts (3:22–23; 7:37). The spiritual character of Deuteronomy is foundational to N.T. revelation.

Reading Deuteronomy

In order to read the entire Old Testament in one year, the book of Deuteronomy should be read in 14 days, according to the following schedule: □ 1–2 □ 3–4 □ 5–7 □ 8–10 □ 11–12 □ 13–15 □ 16–17 □ 18–21 □ 22–24 □ 25–27 □ 28 □ 29–30 □ 31–32 □ 33–34

NOTES

Moses tells of God's guidance

1 THESE *BE* the words which Moses spake unto all Israel [a]on this side Jordan in the wilderness, in the plain over against [a]the Red *sea,* between Paran, and Tophel, and Laban, and Hazeroth, and Dizahab.

2 (*There are* eleven days' *journey* from Horeb by the way of mount Seir [b]unto Kadesh-barnea.)

3 And it came to pass [c]in the fortieth year, in the eleventh month, on the first *day* of the month, *that* Moses spake unto the children of Israel, according unto all that the LORD had given him in commandment unto them;

4 [d]After he had slain Sihon the king of the Amorites, which dwelt in Heshbon, and Og the king of Bashan, which dwelt at Astaroth [e]in Edrei:

5 On this side Jordan, in the land of Moab, began Moses to declare this law, saying,

6 The LORD our God spake unto us [f]in Horeb, saying, Ye have dwelt long [g]enough in this mount:

7 Turn you, and take your journey, and go to the mount of the Amorites, and unto [b]all *the places* nigh thereunto, in the plain, in the hills, and in the vale, and in the south, and by the sea side, to the land of the Canaanites, and unto Lebanon, unto the great river, the river Euphrates.

8 Behold, I have [c]set the land before you: go in and possess the land which the LORD sware unto your fathers, [h]Abraham, Isaac, and Jacob, to give unto them and to their seed after them.

The choice of leaders

9 ¶ And [i]I spake unto you at that time, saying, I am not able to bear you myself alone:

10 The LORD your God hath multiplied you, and, behold, [j]ye *are* this day as the stars of heaven for multitude.

11 ([k]The LORD God of your fathers make you a thousand times so many more as ye *are,* and bless you, [l]as he hath promised you!)

12 [m]How can I myself alone bear your cumbrance, and your burden, and your strife?

13 [d]Take you wise men, and understanding, and known among your tribes, and I will make them rulers over you.

14 And ye answered me, and said, The thing which thou hast spoken *is* good *for us* to do.

15 So I took [n]the chief of your tribes, wise men, and known, [o]and [e]made them heads over you, captains over thousands, and captains over hundreds, and captains over fifties, and captains over tens, and officers among your tribes.

16 And I charged your judges at that time, saying, Hear *the causes* between your brethren, and [p]judge righteously between *every* man and his [q]brother, and the stranger *that is* with him.

17 [r]Ye shall not [f]respect persons in judgment; *but* ye shall hear the small as well as the great; ye shall not be afraid of the face of man; for [s]the judgment *is* God's: and the cause that is too hard for you, [t]bring *it* unto me, and I will hear it.

18 And I commanded you at that time all the things which ye should do.

The report of the spies

19 ¶ And when we departed from Horeb, [u]we went through all that great and terrible wilderness, which ye saw by the way of the mountain of the Amorites, as the LORD our God commanded us; and [v]we came to Kadesh-barnea.

20 And I said unto you, Ye are come unto the mountain of the Amorites, which the LORD our God doth give unto us.

21 Behold, the LORD thy God hath set the land before thee: go up *and* possess *it,* as the LORD God of thy fathers hath said unto thee; [w]fear not, neither be discouraged.

22 ¶ And ye came near unto me every one of you, and said, We will send

1:1 [a]Josh. 9:1,10
1:2 [b]Num. 13:26; ch. 9:23
1:3 [c]Num. 33:38
1:4 [d]Num. 21:24,33; [e]Num. 21:33; Josh. 13:12
1:6 [f]Ex. 3:1; [g]See Ex. 19:1; Num. 10:11
1:8 [h]Gen. 12:7 & 15:18 & 17:7,8 & 26:4 & 28:13
1:9 [i]Ex. 18:18; Num. 11:14
1:10 [j]Gen. 15:5; ch. 10:22 & 28:62
1:11 [k]2 Sam. 24:3; [l]Gen. 15:5 & 22:17 & 26:4; Ex. 32:13
1:12 [m]1 Ki. 3:8,9
1:15 [n]Ex. 18:25; [o]Ex. 18:25
1:16 [p]ch. 16:18; John 7:24; [q]Lev. 24:22
1:17 [r]Lev. 19:15; ch. 16:19; 1 Sam. 16:7; Prov. 24:23; Jas. 2:1; [s]2 Chr. 19:6; [t]Ex. 18:22,26
1:19 [u]Num. 10:12; ch. 8:15; Jer. 2:6; [v]Num. 13:26
1:21 [w]Josh. 1:9

[a] Or, *Zuph* [b] Heb. *all his neighbours* [c] Heb. *given* [d] Heb. *Give* [e] Heb. *gave* [f] Heb. *acknowledge faces*

1:1 THE WORDS WHICH MOSES SPAKE. The N.T. often refers to the contents of Deuteronomy. Jesus quoted from this book when He was tempted by Satan (Mat. 4:4,7,10; cf. Deut. 8:3; 6:13,16) and as He taught about our relationship with God embodied in "the first and great commandment" (Mat. 22:37–38; cf. Deut. 6:5; 10:12; 30:6; compare Deut. 17:6; 19:15 with Mat. 18:16; John 8:17).

men before us, and they shall search us out the land, and bring us word again by what way we must go up, and into what cities we shall come.

23 And the saying pleased me well: and [x]I took twelve men of you, one of a tribe:

24 And [y]they turned and went up into the mountain, and came unto the valley of Eshcol, and searched it out.

25 And they took of the fruit of the land in their hands, and brought *it* down unto us, and brought us word again, and said, [z]*It is* a good land which the LORD our God doth give us.

The murmuring of Israel

26 [a]Notwithstanding ye would not go up, but rebelled against the commandment of the LORD your God:

27 And ye murmured in your tents, and said, Because the LORD [b]hated us, he hath brought us forth out of the land of Egypt, to deliver us into the hand of the Amorites, to destroy us.

28 Whither shall we go up? our brethren have [c]discouraged[g] our heart, saying, [d]The people *is* greater and taller than we; the cities *are* great and walled up to heaven; and moreover we have seen the sons of the [e]Anakims there.

29 Then I said unto you, Dread not, neither be afraid of them.

30 [f]The LORD your God which goeth before you, he shall fight for you, according to all that he did for you in Egypt before your eyes;

31 And in the wilderness, where thou hast seen how that the LORD thy God [g]bare thee, as a man doth bear his son, in all the way that ye went, until ye came into this place.

32 Yet in this thing [h]ye did not believe the LORD your God,

33 [i]Who went in the way before you, [j]to search you out a place to pitch your tents *in*, in fire by night, to show you by what way ye should go, and in a cloud by day.

34 And the LORD heard the voice of your words, and was wroth, [k]and sware, saying,

35 [l]Surely there shall not one of these men of this evil generation see that good land, which I sware to give unto your fathers,

36 [m]Save Caleb the son of Jephunneh; he shall see it, and to him will I give the land that he hath trodden upon, and to his children, because [n]he hath [h]wholly followed the LORD.

37 [o]Also the LORD was angry with me for your sakes, saying, Thou also shalt not go in thither.

38 [p]*But* Joshua the son of Nun, [q]which standeth before thee, he shall go in thither: [r]encourage him: for he shall cause Israel to inherit it.

39 [s]Moreover your little ones, which [t]ye said should be a prey, and your children, which in that day [u]had no knowledge between good and evil, they shall go in thither, and unto them will I give it, and they shall possess it.

40 [v]But *as for* you, turn you, and take your journey into the wilderness by the way of the Red sea.

41 Then ye answered and said unto me, [w]We have sinned against the LORD, we will go up and fight, according to all that the LORD our God commanded us. And when ye had girded on every man his weapons of war, ye were ready to go up into the hill.

42 And the LORD said unto me, Say unto them, [x]Go not up, neither fight; for I *am* not among you; lest ye be smitten before your enemies.

43 So I spake unto you; and ye would not hear, but rebelled against the commandment of the LORD, and

1:23 [x]Num. 13:3
1:24 [y]Num. 13:22-24
1:25 [z]Num. 13:27
1:26 [a]Num. 14:1-4 Ps. 106:24
1:27 [b]ch. 9:28
1:28 [c]Josh. 2:11 [d]Num. 13:28, 31-33 ch. 9:1,2 [e]Num. 13:28
1:30 [f]Ex. 14:14 Neh. 4:20
1:31 [g]Ex. 19:4 ch. 32:11,12 Is. 46:3,4 & 63:9 Hos. 11:3 See Acts 13:18
1:32 [h]Ps. 106:24 Jude 5
1:33 [i]Ex. 13:21 Ps. 78:14 [j]Num. 10:33 Ezek. 20:6
1:34 [k]ch. 2:14,15
1:35 [l]Num. 14:22 Ps. 95:11
1:36 [m]Num. 14:24 Josh. 14:9 [n]Num. 14:24
1:37 [o]Num. 20:12 & 27:14 ch. 3:26 & 4:21 & 34:4 Ps. 106:32
1:38 [p]Num. 14:30 [q]Ex. 24:13 & 33:11 See 1 Sam. 16:22 [r]Num. 27:18,19 ch. 31:7,23
1:39 [s]Num. 14:31 [t]Num. 14:3 [u]Is. 7:15,16 Rom. 9:11
1:40 [v]Num. 14:25
1:41 [w]Num. 14:40
1:42 [x]Num. 14:42

[g] Heb. *melted* [h] Heb. *fulfilled* to go *after*

1:26 REBELLED AGAINST THE COMMANDMENT. The people of Israel should have entered the promised land thirty-nine years before (vv. 2–3); but because of their disobedience and failure to do the will of God, their entrance was delayed (Num. 14:33–34). Failure to live in God's will and to walk after the Spirit (Rom. 8:12–15; Gal. 5:16) can result in a delay in or even the total loss of God's plan for our lives. We should have a holy fear of being out of the Lord's will and losing His presence, grace, and protection in our lives (see article on THE WILL OF GOD, p. 1060).

1:35 THERE SHALL NOT ONE ... SEE THAT GOOD LAND. All Israelites who refused to enter the promised land (see previous note; see Num 14:4,26–35) were thereafter denied entrance in that land. Disobedience can often be tragic because it may result in an irreversibly lost opportunity as well as in divine judgment.

1:36 WHOLLY FOLLOWED THE LORD. Notice the blessings of God that are reserved for those who "wholly follow the LORD." God "shall fight for you" (v. 30), bear "thee, as a man doth bear his son" (v. 31), go "in the way before you," and "show you by what way ye should go" (v. 33).

[y]went[i] presumptuously up into the
hill.
44 And the Amorites, which dwelt
in that mountain, came out against
you, and chased you, [z]as bees do, and
destroyed you in Seir, *even* unto Hor-
mah.
45 And ye returned and wept before
the LORD; but the LORD would not heark-
en to your voice, nor give ear unto you.
46 [a]So ye abode in Kadesh many
days, according unto the days that ye
abode *there.*

The years in the wilderness

2 THEN WE turned, and took our
journey into the wilderness by the
way of the Red sea, [b]as the LORD
spake unto me: and we compassed
mount Seir many days.
2 And the LORD spake unto me, say-
ing,
3 Ye have compassed this mountain
[c]long enough: turn you northward.
4 And command thou the people,
saying, [d]Ye *are* to pass through the
coast of your brethren the children of
Esau, which dwell in Seir; and they
shall be afraid of you: take ye good
heed unto yourselves therefore:
5 Meddle not with them; for I will
not give you of their land, [j]no, not so
much as a footbreadth; [e]because I
have given mount Seir unto Esau *for* a
possession.
6 Ye shall buy meat of them for
money, that ye may eat; and ye shall
also buy water of them for money, that
ye may drink.
7 For the LORD thy God hath blessed
thee in all the works of thy hand: he
knoweth thy walking through this
great wilderness: [f]these forty years
the LORD thy God *hath been* with thee;
thou hast lacked nothing.
8 [g]And when we passed by from
our brethren the children of Esau,
which dwelt in Seir, through the way of
the plain from [h]Elath, and from Ezion-
geber, we turned and passed by the
way of the wilderness of Moab.
9 And the LORD said unto me, [k]Dis-
tress not the Moabites, neither con-
tend with them in battle: for I will not
give thee of their land *for* a possession;

1:43 [y]Num. 14:44
1:44 [z]Ps. 118:12
1:46 [a]Num. 13:25 & 20:1,22 Judg. 11:17
2:1 [b]Num. 14:25 ch. 1:40
2:3 [c]See ver. 7,14
2:4 [d]Num. 20:14
2:5 [e]Gen. 36:8 Josh. 24:4
2:7 [f]ch. 8:2-4
2:8 [g]Judg. 11:18 [h]1 Ki. 9:26
2:9 [i]Num. 21:28 [j]Gen. 19:36,37
2:10 [k]Gen. 14:5 [l]Num. 13:22,33 ch. 9:2
2:12 [m]ver. 22 Gen. 14:6 & 36:20
2:13 [n]Num. 21:12
2:14 [o]Num. 13:26 [p]Num. 14:33 & 26:64 [q]Num. 14:35 ch. 1:34,35 Ezek. 20:15
2:15 [r]Ps. 78:33 & 106:26
2:19 [s]Gen. 19:38
2:20 [t]Gen. 14:5 *Zuzims*
2:21 [u]See ver. 10

because I have given [i]Ar unto [j]the
children of Lot *for* a possession.
10 [k]The Emims dwelt therein in
times past, a people great, and many,
and tall, as [l]the Anakims;
11 Which also were accounted
giants, as the Anakims; but the Moab-
ites call them Emims.
12 [m]The Horims also dwelt in Seir
beforetime; but the children of Esau
[l]succeeded them, when they had de-
stroyed them from before them, and
dwelt in their [m]stead; as Israel did
unto the land of his possession, which
the LORD gave unto them.
13 Now rise up, *said I,* and get you
over [n]the [n]brook Zered. And we went
over the brook Zered.
14 And the space in which we came
[o]from Kadesh-barnea, until we were
come over the brook Zered, *was* thirty
and eight years; [p]until all the genera-
tion of the men of war were wasted out
from among the host, [q]as the LORD
sware unto them.
15 For indeed the [r]hand of the
LORD was against them, to destroy
them from among the host, until they
were consumed.
16 ¶ So it came to pass, when all the
men of war were consumed and dead
from among the people,
17 That the LORD spake unto me,
saying,
18 Thou art to pass over through
Ar, the coast of Moab, this day:
19 And *when* thou comest nigh over
against the children of Ammon, dis-
tress them not, nor meddle with them:
for I will not give thee of the land of the
children of Ammon *any* possession; be-
cause I have given it unto [s]the chil-
dren of Lot *for* a possession.
20 (That also was accounted a land
of giants: giants dwelt therein in old
time; and the Ammonites call them
[t]Zamzummims;
21 [u]A people great, and many, and
tall, as the Anakims; but the LORD de-
stroyed them before them; and they

i Heb. *ye were presumptuous, and went up*
j Heb. *even to the treading of the sole of the foot*
k Or, *Use no hostility against Moab* l Heb. *inherited them* m Or, *room* n Or, *valley*

2:7 GOD *HATH BEEN* WITH THEE. Although the Israelites had to pay for their sins of rebellion and unbelief (v. 15; 1:26–40), God continued to be with them because they confessed their sin (1:45–46). God will continue to bless and guide those who repent, in spite of their failure and their temporary departure from a life of holiness according to God's law.

succeeded them, and dwelt in their stead:

22 As he did to the children of Esau, [v]which dwelt in Seir, when he destroyed [w]the Horims from before them; and they succeeded them, and dwelt in their stead even unto this day:

23 And [x]the Avims which dwelt in Hazerim, *even* unto Azzah, [y]the Caphtorims, which came forth out of Caphtor, destroyed them, and dwelt in their stead.)

24 ¶ Rise ye up, take your journey, and [z]pass over the river Arnon: behold, I have given into thine hand Sihon the Amorite, king of Heshbon, and his land: [o]begin to possess *it*, and contend with him in battle.

25 [a]This day will I begin to put the dread of thee and the fear of thee upon the nations *that are* under the whole heaven, who shall hear report of thee, and shall tremble, and be in anguish because of thee.

The victory over Sihon

26 ¶ And I sent messengers out of the wilderness of Kedemoth unto Sihon king of Heshbon [b]with words of peace, saying,

27 [c]Let me pass through thy land: I will go along by the high way, I will neither turn unto the right hand nor to the left.

28 Thou shalt sell me meat for money, that I may eat; and give me water for money, that I may drink: [d]only I will pass through on my feet;

29 ([e]As the children of Esau which dwell in Seir, and the Moabites which dwell in Ar, did unto me;) until I shall pass over Jordan into the land which the LORD our God giveth us.

30 [f]But Sihon king of Heshbon would not let us pass by him: for [g]the LORD thy God [h]hardened his spirit, and made his heart obstinate, that he might deliver him into thy hand, as *appeareth* this day.

31 And the LORD said unto me, Behold, I have begun to [i]give Sihon and his land before thee: begin to possess, that thou mayest inherit his land.

32 [j]Then Sihon came out against us, he and all his people, to fight at Jahaz.

33 And [k]the LORD our God delivered him before us; and [l]we smote him, and his sons, and all his people.

34 And we took all his cities at that time, and [m]utterly destroyed [p]the men, and the women, and the little ones, of every city, we left none to remain:

35 Only the cattle we took for a prey unto ourselves, and the spoil of the cities which we took.

36 [n]From Aroer, which *is* by the brink of the river of Arnon, and *from* the city that *is* by the river, even unto Gilead, there was not one city too strong for us: [o]the LORD our God delivered all unto us:

37 Only unto the land of the children of Ammon thou camest not, *nor* unto any place of the river [p]Jabbok, nor unto the cities in the mountains, nor unto [q]whatsoever the LORD our God forbad us.

The victory over Og

3 THEN WE turned, and went up the way to Bashan: and [r]Og the king of Bashan came out against us, he and all his people, to battle [s]at Edrei.

2 And the LORD said unto me, Fear him not: for I will deliver him, and all his people, and his land, into thy hand; and thou shalt do unto him as thou didst unto [t]Sihon king of the Amorites, which dwelt at Heshbon.

3 So the LORD our God delivered into our hands Og also, the king of Bashan, and all his people: [u]and we smote him until none was left to him remaining.

4 And we took all his cities at that time, there was not a city which we took not from them, threescore cities, [v]all the region of Argob, the kingdom of Og in Bashan.

5 All these cities *were* fenced with high walls, gates, and bars; beside unwalled towns a great many.

6 And we utterly destroyed them, as we did unto Sihon king [w]of Heshbon, utterly destroying the men, women, and children, of every city.

7 But all the cattle, and the spoil of

2:22 [v]Gen. 36:8 [w]Gen. 14:6 & 36:20-30
2:23 [x]Josh. 13:3 [y]Gen. 10:14 Amos 9:7
2:24 [z]Num. 21:13 Judg. 11:18
2:25 [a]Ex. 15:14,15
2:26 [b]ch. 20:10
2:27 [c]Num. 21:21,22 Judg. 11:19
2:28 [d]Num. 20:19
2:29 [e]See Num. 20:18 ch. 23:3,4 Judg. 11:17
2:30 [f]Num. 21:23 [g]Josh. 11:20 [h]Ex. 4:21
2:31 [i]ch. 1:8
2:32 [j]Num. 21:23
2:33 [k]ch. 7:2 & 20:16 [l]Num. 21:24 ch. 29:7
2:34 [m]Lev. 27:28 ch. 7:2,26
2:36 [n]ch. 3:12 & 4:48 Josh. 13:9 [o]Ps. 44:3
2:37 [p]Gen. 32:22 Num. 21:24 ch. 3:16 [q]ver. 5,9,19
3:1 [r]Num. 21:33 ch. 29:7 [s]ch. 1:4
3:2 [t]Num. 21:34
3:3 [u]Num. 21:35
3:4 [v]1 Ki. 4:13
3:6 [w]ch. 2:24 Ps. 135:10-12

o Heb. *begin, possess* p Heb. *every city of men, and women, and little ones*

2:30 THE LORD . . . HARDENED HIS SPIRIT. God does not harden anyone's heart arbitrarily (Heb. 3:7–13). He hardened Sihon's heart because he had already set his heart against God and Israel (see Ex. 7:3, note).

the cities, we took for a prey to ourselves.

8 And we took at that time out of the hand of the two kings of the Amorites the land that *was* on this side Jordan, from the river of Arnon unto mount Hermon;

9 (*Which* [x]Hermon the Sidonians call Sirion; and the Amorites call it [y]Shenir;)

10 [z]All the cities of the plain, and all Gilead, and [a]all Bashan, unto Salchah and Edrei, cities of the kingdom of Og in Bashan.

11 [b]For only Og king of Bashan remained of the remnant of [c]giants; behold, his bedstead *was* a bedstead of iron; *is* it not in [d]Rabbath of the children of Ammon? nine cubits *was* the length thereof, and four cubits the breadth of it, after the cubit of a man.

The distribution of the land

12 And this land, *which* we possessed at that time, [e]from Aroer, which *is* by the river Arnon, and half mount Gilead, and [f]the cities thereof, gave I unto the Reubenites and to the Gadites.

13 [g]And the rest of Gilead, and all Bashan, *being* the kingdom of Og, gave I unto the half tribe of Manasseh; all the region of Argob, with all Bashan, which was called the land of giants.

14 [h]Jair the son of Manasseh took all the country of Argob [i]unto the coasts of Geshuri and Maachathi; and [j]called them after his own name, Bashan-havoth-jair, unto this day.

15 [k]And I gave Gilead unto Machir.

16 And unto the Reubenites [l]and unto the Gadites I gave from Gilead even unto the river Arnon half the valley, and the border even unto the river Jabbok, [m]*which is* the border of the children of Ammon;

17 The plain also, and Jordan, and the coast *thereof*, from [n]Chinnereth [o]even unto the sea of the plain, [p]*even* the salt sea, [q]under Ashdoth-pisgah eastward.

18 ¶ And I commanded you at that time, saying, The LORD your God hath given you this land to possess it: [q]ye shall pass over armed before your brethren the children of Israel, all *that are* [r]meet for the war.

19 But your wives, and your little ones, and your cattle, (*for* I know that ye have much cattle,) shall abide in your cities which I have given you;

20 Until the LORD have given rest unto your brethren, as well as unto you, and *until* they also possess the land which the LORD your God hath given them beyond Jordan: and *then* shall ye [r]return every man unto his possession, which I have given you.

21 ¶ And [s]I commanded Joshua at that time, saying, Thine eyes have seen all that the LORD your God hath done unto these two kings: so shall the LORD do unto all the kingdoms whither thou passest.

22 Ye shall not fear them: for [t]the LORD your God he shall fight for you.

Moses forbidden to cross Jordan

23 And [u]I besought the LORD at that time, saying,

24 O Lord GOD, thou hast begun to show thy servant [v]thy greatness, and thy mighty hand: for [w]what God *is there* in heaven or in earth, that can do according to thy works, and according to thy might?

25 I pray thee, let me go over, and see [x]the good land that *is* beyond Jordan, that goodly mountain, and Lebanon.

26 But the LORD [y]was wroth with me for your sakes, and would not hear

3:9 [x]ch. 4:48 [y]1 Chr. 5:23
3:10 [z]ch. 4:49 [a]Josh. 12:5 & 13:11
3:11 [b]Amos 2:9 [c]Gen. 14:5 [d]2 Sam. 12:26 Jer. 49:2 Ezek. 21:20
3:12 [e]ch. 2:36 Josh. 12:2 [f]Num. 32:33 Josh. 12:6 & 13:8
3:13 [g]Josh. 13:29
3:14 [h]1 Chr. 2:22 [i]Josh. 13:13 2 Sam. 3:3 & 10:6 [j]Num. 32:41
3:15 [k]Num. 32:39
3:16 [l]2 Sam. 24:5 [m]Num. 21:24 Josh. 12:2
3:17 [n]Num. 34:11 [o]Num. 34:12 ch. 4:49 Josh. 12:3 [p]Gen. 14:3
3:18 [q]Num. 32:20
3:20 [r]Josh. 22:4
3:21 [s]Num. 27:23
3:22 [t]Ex. 14:14 ch. 1:30 & 20:4
3:23 [u]See 2 Cor. 12:8,9
3:24 [v]ch. 11:2 [w]Ex. 15:11 2 Sam. 7:22 Ps. 71:19 & 86:8 & 89:6,8
3:25 [x]Ex. 3:8 ch. 4:22
3:26 [y]ch. 1:37 & 31:2

[q] Or, *under the springs of Pisgah*, or, *the hill*
[r] Heb. *sons of power*

3:22 THE LORD . . . SHALL FIGHT FOR YOU. The Israelites faced powerful enemies whom they could not defeat in their own strength. Israel's natural tendency was to fear the awful consequences of defeat. Only by looking to God could they gain victory (see vv. 2–3; 1:30; 2:24–25,31,33,36; 20:4). When committed believers face seemingly insurmountable difficulties and overwhelming opposition, God promises to be with them and to give them strength and power to accomplish His will for them (see Mat. 6:30, note; Phil. 4:6–7, notes).

3:25 LET ME GO OVER. Moses had seriously disobeyed God and was told he would not be allowed to enter Canaan (Num. 20:8–12). Yet he pleaded with God to change His mind and allow him to cross the Jordan River and enter into the promised land. God refused (v. 26) in order to teach that sin by a spiritual leader has grave consequences and will incur a stricter judgment (cf. Jas. 3:1); spiritual leaders of God's people can disqualify themselves from certain areas of ministry if they seriously fail to be examples of obedience (cf. Num. 20:12; see 20:8,12, notes).

me: and the LORD said unto me, Let it
suffice thee; speak no more unto me of
this matter.
27 [z]Get thee up into the top of
[s]Pisgah, and lift up thine eyes west-
ward, and northward, and southward,
and eastward, and behold *it* with thine
eyes: for thou shalt not go over this
Jordan.
28 But [a]charge Joshua, and en-
courage him, and strengthen him: for
he shall go over before this people, and
he shall cause them to inherit the land
which thou shalt see.
29 So we abode in [b]the valley over
against Beth-peor.

Moses commands obedience

4 NOW THEREFORE hearken, O Is-
rael, unto [c]the statutes and unto
the judgments, which I teach you, for
to do *them,* that ye may live, and go in
and possess the land which the LORD
God of your fathers giveth you.
2 [d]Ye shall not add unto the word
which I command you, neither shall ye
diminish *aught* from it, that ye may
keep the commandments of the LORD
your God which I command you.
3 Your eyes have seen what the
LORD did because of [e]Baal-peor: for all
the men that followed Baal-peor, the
LORD thy God hath destroyed them
from among you.
4 But ye that did cleave unto the
LORD your God *are* alive every one of
you this day.
5 Behold, I have taught you stat-
utes and judgments, even as the LORD
my God commanded me, that ye should
do so in the land whither ye go to pos-
sess it.
6 Keep therefore and do *them;* for
this *is* [f]your wisdom and your under-
standing in the sight of the nations,
which shall hear all these statutes, and
say, Surely this great nation *is* a wise
and understanding people.
7 For [g]what nation *is there so* great,
who *hath* [h]God *so* nigh unto them, as
the LORD our God *is* in all *things that* we
call upon him *for?*
8 And what nation *is there so* great,
that hath statutes and judgments *so*
righteous as all this law, which I set
before you this day?
9 Only take heed to thyself, and
[i]keep thy soul diligently, lest thou
forget the things which thine eyes have
seen, and lest they depart from thy
heart all the days of thy life: but
[j]teach them thy sons, and thy sons'
sons;
10 *Specially* [k]the day that thou
stoodest before the LORD thy God in Ho-
reb, when the LORD said unto me, Gath-
er me the people together, and I will
make them hear my words, that they
may learn to fear me all the days that
they shall live upon the earth, and *that*
they may teach their children.
11 And ye came near and stood un-
der the mountain; and the [l]mountain
burned with fire unto the [t]midst of
heaven, with darkness, clouds, and
thick darkness.

3:27 [z]Num. 27:12
3:28 [a]Num. 27:18,23 ch. 31:3,7
3:29 [b]ch. 34:6
4:1 [c]Lev. 19:37 ch. 5:1 Ezek. 20:11 Rom. 10:5
4:2 [d]Josh. 1:7
4:3 [e]Josh. 22:17 Ps. 106:28
4:6 [f]Job 28:28 Ps. 19:7 Prov. 1:7
4:7 [g]2 Sam. 7:23 [h]Ps. 46:1 Is. 55:6
4:9 [i]Prov. 4:23 [j]Gen. 18:19 ch. 6:7 & 11:19 Ps. 78:5,6 Eph. 6:4
4:10 [k]Ex. 19:9,16
4:11 [l]Ex. 19:18

[s] Or, *The hill* [t] Heb. *heart*

4:1 DO *THEM*, THAT YE MAY LIVE. Life, blessing, and the possession of Canaan were dependent on Israel's relationship to God (vv. 1,6, 15–26,40). The promises of God are linked, for every succeeding generation, with holding fast to the Lord (v. 4), fearing Him (v. 10), teaching our children the ways of the Lord (vv. 9–10), and seeking Him with all our heart and all our soul (v. 29) in true faith and love (5:29; 6:5; see John 14:21, note; Rom. 1:5, note; Gal. 5:6, note; cf. Hab. 2:4; Amos 5:4).

4:2 YE SHALL NOT ADD . . . DIMINISH. Anything that contradicts, modifies, or changes Scripture must be rejected by those who follow God. His Word, the Bible itself, is our highest authority and the ultimate guide to truth (12:32; Prov. 30:6; Gal. 3:15; Rev. 22:18–19; see article on THE INSPIRATION AND AUTHORITY OF SCRIPTURE, p. 1924).

4:6 KEEP . . . AND DO *THEM*. See Mat. 5:17, note on the O.T. law and the Christian.

4:6 THE NATIONS. One important reason that Israel had for remaining faithful to God's law was to draw other nations to the Lord by demonstrating the wisdom and benefits of following His ways (vv. 5–8). Like Israel, N.T. believers are a chosen race, a royal priesthood, a holy nation, and God's own possession—a people whom God wants to proclaim His excellencies and Lordship (1 Pet. 2:9; Rev. 1:6; 5:10).

4:9 LEST THOU FORGET . . . TEACH THEM THY SONS. We must diligently remember God's past work in our lives and continue to abide in His word lest love for God and spiritual realities diminish from our hearts. Negligence in this area can result in tragic spiritual ruin for our children and grandchildren. A diligent and persevering adherence to God and His laws is necessary in order to pass on a spiritual inheritance to our children.

4:9 SONS AND THY SONS' SONS. See 6:7, note.

4:10 LEARN TO FEAR ME. See article on THE FEAR OF THE LORD, p. 282.

12 [m]And the LORD spake unto you out of the midst of the fire: ye heard the voice of the words, but saw no similitude; [n]only[u] *ye heard* a voice.

13 [o]And he declared unto you his covenant, which he commanded you to perform, *even* [p]ten commandments; and [q]he wrote them upon two tables of stone.

14 ¶ And [r]the LORD commanded me at that time to teach you statutes and judgments, that ye might do them in the land whither ye go over to possess it.

Idolatry forbidden

15 [s]Take ye therefore good heed unto yourselves; for ye saw no manner of [t]similitude on the day *that* the LORD spake unto you in Horeb out of the midst of the fire:

16 Lest ye [u]corrupt *yourselves,* and [v]make you a graven image, the similitude of any figure, [w]the likeness of male or female,

17 The likeness of any beast that *is* on the earth, the likeness of any winged fowl that flieth in the air,

18 The likeness of any thing that creepeth on the ground, the likeness of any fish that *is* in the waters beneath the earth:

19 And lest thou [x]lift up thine eyes unto heaven, and when thou seest the sun, and the moon, and the stars, *even* [y]all the host of heaven, shouldest be driven to [z]worship them, and serve them, which the LORD thy God hath [v]divided unto all nations under the whole heaven.

20 But the LORD hath taken you, and [a]brought you forth out of the iron furnace, *even* out of Egypt, [b]to be unto him a people of inheritance, as *ye are* this day.

4:12 [m]ch. 5:4,22 [n]Ex. 20:22 1 Ki. 19:12
4:13 [o]ch. 9:9,11 [p]Ex. 34:28 [q]Ex. 24:12 & 31:18
4:14 [r]Ex. 21:1 & ch. 22 & ch. 23
4:15 [s]Josh. 23:11 [t]Is. 40:18
4:16 [u]Ex. 32:7 [v]ver. 23 Ex. 20:4,5 ch. 5:8 [w]Rom. 1:23
4:19 [x]ch. 17:3 Job 31:26 [y]2 Ki. 21:3 [z]Rom. 1:25
4:20 [a]1 Ki. 8:51 Jer. 11:4 [b]Ex. 19:5 ch. 9:29
4:21 [c]Num. 20:12 ch. 1:37 & 3:26
4:22 [d]See 2 Pet. 1:13-15 [e]ch. 3:27 [f]ch. 3:25
4:23 [g]ver. 9 [h]ver. 16 Ex. 20:4,5
4:24 [i]Ex. 24:17 ch. 9:3 Is. 33:14 Heb. 12:29 [j]Ex. 20:5 ch. 6:15
4:25 [k]2 Ki. 17:17
4:26 [l]ch. 30:18,19 Is. 1:2 Mic. 6:2
4:27 [m]Lev. 26:33 Neh. 1:8
4:28 [n]ch. 28:64 1 Sam. 26:19 Jer. 16:13 [o]Ps. 115:4,5 & 135:15,16 Is. 44:9 & 46:7

21 Furthermore [c]the LORD was angry with me for your sakes, and sware that I should not go over Jordan, and that I should not go in unto that good land, which the LORD thy God giveth thee *for* an inheritance:

22 But [d]I must die in this land, [e]I must not go over Jordan: but ye shall go over, and possess [f]that good land.

23 Take heed unto yourselves, [g]lest ye forget the covenant of the LORD your God, which he made with you, [h]and make you a graven image, *or* the likeness of any *thing,* which the LORD thy God hath forbidden thee.

24 For [i]the LORD thy God *is* a consuming fire, *even* [j]a jealous God.

25 ¶ When thou shalt beget children, and children's children, and ye shall have remained long in the land, and shall corrupt *yourselves,* and make a graven image, *or* the likeness of any *thing,* and [k]shall do evil in the sight of the LORD thy God, to provoke him to anger:

26 [l]I call heaven and earth to witness against you this day, that ye shall soon utterly perish from off the land whereunto ye go over Jordan to possess it; ye shall not prolong *your* days upon it, but shall utterly be destroyed.

27 And the LORD [m]shall scatter you among the nations, and ye shall be left few in number among the heathen, whither the LORD shall lead you.

28 And [n]there ye shall serve gods, the work of men's hands, wood and stone, [o]which neither see, nor hear, nor eat, nor smell.

29 [p]But if from thence thou shalt

4:29 [p]Lev. 26:39; ch. 30:1-3; 2 Chr. 15:4; Neh. 1:9; Is. 55:6,7

[u]Heb. *save a voice* [v]Or, *imparted*

4:16 A GRAVEN IMAGE. See Ex. 20:4, note.

4:24 GOD *IS* A CONSUMING FIRE. This descriptive phrase refers to God's holy jealousy, anger, and judgment against those who depart from His word and righteous ways into some form of idolatry (v. 23; Heb. 12:25,29; cf. Ezek. 1:13–14,27–28; Dan. 7:9–10; Rev. 1:14–15; 19:11–12).

4:24 JEALOUS GOD. God is a "jealous God" in that He will not tolerate unfaithfulness (i.e., the worship of other gods) on the part of His people (v. 23). This type of jealousy is holy and righteous. Likewise, in the marriage union, there should be a holy jealousy that guards the affection and love of the spouses for each other. Marriage partners must expect exclusive love and loyalty, demanding that each remain completely faithful and true in the marriage relationship.

4:26 HEAVEN AND EARTH TO WITNESS. Moses gives six predictions about Israel's history, in the event that they become disobedient and unfaithful (vv. 25–31): (1) dispersion among the nations (vv. 26–27); (2) suffering in exile (vv. 27–28); (3) reconciliation with God for those who seek Him with all their heart and soul (vv. 29–31); (4) distress and tribulation "in the latter days" (v. 30); (5) a return to God in the latter days (v. 30); and (6) restoration of the covenant with their fathers (v. 31; see also Deut. 29—30; Mat. 23:39, note; Rom. 11:1, note).

seek the LORD thy God, thou shalt find
him, if thou seek him with all thy heart
and with all thy soul.
30 When thou art in tribulation, and
all these things [w]are come upon thee,
[q]*even* in the latter days, if thou [r]turn
to the LORD thy God, and shalt be obedi-
ent unto his voice;
31 (For the LORD thy God *is* [s]a mer-
ciful God;) he will not forsake thee, nei-
ther destroy thee, nor forget the cov-
enant of thy fathers which he sware
unto them.

Israel as a chosen nation

4:41–43Ref — Num. 35:6–34; Deut. 19:1–14; Josh. 20:1–9

32 For [t]ask now of the days that
are past, which were before thee, since
the day that God created man upon
the earth, and *ask* [u]from the one side
of heaven unto the other, whether
there hath been *any such thing* as this
great thing *is,* or hath been heard
like it?
33 [v]Did *ever* people hear the voice
of God speaking out of the midst of the
fire, as thou hast heard, and live?
34 Or hath God assayed to go *and*
take him a nation from the midst of *an-
other* nation, [w]by temptations, [x]by
signs, and by wonders, and by war, and
[y]by a mighty hand, and [z]by a
stretched out arm, [a]and by great ter-
rors, according to all that the LORD your
God did for you in Egypt before your
eyes?
35 Unto thee it was shown, that
thou mightest know that the LORD
he *is* God; [b]*there is* none else beside
him.
36 [c]Out of heaven he made thee to
hear his voice, that he might instruct
thee: and upon earth he showed thee
his great fire; and thou heardest his
words out of the midst of the fire.
37 And because [d]he loved thy fa-
thers, therefore he chose their seed af-
ter them, and [e]brought thee out in his
sight with his mighty power out of
Egypt;
38 [f]To drive out nations from be-
fore thee greater and mightier than
thou *art,* to bring thee in, to give thee
their land *for* an inheritance, as *it is*
this day.
39 Know therefore this day, and
consider *it* in thine heart, that [g]the
LORD he *is* God in heaven above, and
upon the earth beneath: *there is* none
else.
40 [h]Thou shalt keep therefore his
statutes, and his commandments,
which I command thee this day, [i]that
it may go well with thee, and with thy
children after thee, and that thou may-
est prolong *thy* days upon the earth,
which the LORD thy God giveth thee, for
ever.
41 ¶ Then Moses [j]severed three
cities on this side Jordan toward the
sunrising;
42 [k]That the slayer might flee
thither, which should kill his neigh-
bour unawares, and hated him not in
times past; and that fleeing unto one of
these cities he might live:
43 *Namely,* [l]Bezer in the wilder-
ness, in the plain country, of the Reu-
benites; and Ramoth in Gilead, of the
Gadites; and Golan in Bashan, of the
Manassites.
44 ¶ And this *is* the law which Mo-
ses set before the children of Israel:
45 These *are* the testimonies, and
the statutes, and the judgments, which
Moses spake unto the children of
Israel, after they came forth out of
Egypt,
46 On this side Jordan, [m]in the val-
ley over against Beth-peor, in the land
of Sihon king of the Amorites, who
dwelt at Heshbon, whom Moses and
the children of Israel [n]smote, after
they were come forth out of Egypt:
47 And they possessed his land,
and the land [o]of Og king of Bashan,
two kings of the Amorites, which *were*
on this side Jordan toward the sunris-
ing;
48 [p]From Aroer, which *is* by the
bank of the river Arnon, even unto
mount Sion, which *is* [q]Hermon,
49 And all the plain on this side Jor-
dan eastward, even unto the sea of the
plain, under the [r]springs of Pisgah.

4:30 [q]Gen. 49:1 ch. 31:29 Jer. 23:20 Hos. 3:5 [r]Joel 2:12
4:31 [s]2 Chr. 30:9 Neh. 9:31 Ps. 116:5 Jonah 4:2
4:32 [t]Job 8:8 [u]Mat. 24:31
4:33 [v]Ex. 24:11 & 33:20 ch. 5:24,26
4:34 [w]ch. 7:19 [x]Ex. 7:3 [y]Ex. 13:3 [z]Ex. 6:6 [a]ch. 26:8 & 34:12
4:35 [b]ch. 32:39 1 Sam. 2:2 Is. 45:5,18 Mark 12:29
4:36 [c]Ex. 19:9,19 & 20:18,22 & 24:16 Heb. 12:18
4:37 [d]ch. 10:15 [e]Ex. 13:3,9,14
4:38 [f]ch. 7:1 & 9:1,4,5
4:39 [g]Josh. 2:11
4:40 [h]Lev. 22:31 [i]ch. 5:16 & 6:3,18 & 12:25,28 & 22:7 Eph. 6:3
4:41 [j]Num. 35:6
4:42 [k]ch. 19:4
4:43 [l]Josh. 20:8
4:46 [m]ch. 3:29 [n]Num. 21:24 ch. 1:4
4:47 [o]Num. 21:35 ch. 3:3,4
4:48 [p]ch. 2:36 & 3:12 [q]ch. 3:9 Ps. 133:3
4:49 [r]ch. 3:17

[w] Heb. *have found thee*

4:29 WITH ALL THY HEART . . . THY SOUL. To find God and know Him in His fullness, one must seek Him with wholehearted devotion (cf. 6:5; 10:12; 11:13; 13:3; 26:16; 30:6,10; see Phil. 3:8–11, note). Knowing God and experiencing the power, blessing, and righteousness of His kingdom do not come easily; they will happen only to those who diligently seek God (Heb. 11:6) and desire His nearness, the fullness of His Spirit, and His gift of eternal life.

The Ten Commandments

5:6–21pp — Ex. 20:1–17

5 AND MOSES called all Israel, and said unto them, Hear, O Israel, the statutes and judgments which I speak in your ears this day, that ye may learn them, and [x]keep, and do them.

2 [s]The LORD our God made a covenant with us in Horeb.

3 The LORD [t]made not this covenant with our fathers, but with us, *even* us, who *are* all of us here alive this day.

4 [u]The LORD talked with you face to face in the mount out of the midst of the fire,

5 ([v]I stood between the LORD and you at that time, to show you the word of the LORD: for [w]ye were afraid by reason of the fire, and went not up into the mount;) saying,

6 ¶ [x]I *am* the LORD thy God, which brought thee out of the land of Egypt, from the house of [y]bondage.

7 [y]Thou shalt have none other gods before me.

8 [z]Thou shalt not make thee *any* graven image, *or* any likeness *of any thing* that *is* in heaven above, or that *is* in the earth beneath, or that *is* in the waters beneath the earth:

9 Thou shalt not bow down thyself unto them, nor serve them: for I the LORD thy God *am* a jealous God, [a]visiting the iniquity of the fathers upon the children unto the third and fourth *generation* of them that hate me,

10 [b]And showing mercy unto thousands of them that love me and keep my commandments.

11 [c]Thou shalt not take the name of the LORD thy God in vain: for the LORD will not hold *him* guiltless that taketh his name in vain.

12 [d]Keep the sabbath day to sanctify it, as the LORD thy God hath commanded thee.

13 [e]Six days thou shalt labour, and do all thy work:

14 But the seventh day *is* the [f]sabbath of the LORD thy God: *in it* thou shalt not do any work, thou, nor thy son, nor thy daughter, nor thy manservant, nor thy maidservant, nor thine ox, nor thine ass, nor any of thy cattle, nor thy stranger that *is* within thy gates; that thy manservant and thy maidservant may rest as well as thou.

15 [g]And remember that thou wast a servant in the land of Egypt, and *that* the LORD thy God brought thee out thence [h]through a mighty hand and by a stretched out arm: therefore the LORD thy God commanded thee to keep the sabbath day.

16 ¶ [i]Honour thy father and thy mother, as the LORD thy God hath commanded thee; [j]that thy days may be prolonged, and that it may go well with thee, in the land which the LORD thy God giveth thee.

17 [k]Thou shalt not kill.

18 [l]Neither shalt thou commit adultery.

19 [m]Neither shalt thou steal.

20 [n]Neither shalt thou bear false witness against thy neighbour.

21 [o]Neither shalt thou desire thy neighbour's wife, neither shalt thou covet thy neighbour's house, his field, or his manservant, or his maidservant, his ox, or his ass, or any *thing* that *is* thy neighbour's.

22 ¶ These words the LORD spake unto all your assembly in the mount out of the midst of the fire, of the cloud, and of the thick darkness, with a great voice: and he added no more. And [p]he wrote them in two tables of stone, and delivered them unto me.

23 [q]And it came to pass, when ye heard the voice out of the midst of the darkness, (for the mountain did burn with fire,) that ye came near unto me,

5:2 [s]Ex. 19:5 ch. 4:23 **5:3** [t]See Mat. 13:17 Heb. 8:9 **5:4** [u]Ex. 19:9,19 & 20:22 ch. 4:33,36 & 34:10 **5:5** [v]Ex. 20:21 Gal. 3:19 [w]Ex. 19:16 & 20:18 & 24:2 **5:6** [x]Ex. 20:2 **5:7** [y]Ex. 20:3 **5:8** [z]Ex. 20:4 **5:9** [a]Ex. 34:7 **5:10** [b]Jer. 32:18 Dan. 9:4 **5:11** [c]Ex. 20:7 Lev. 19:12 Mat. 5:33 **5:12** [d]Ex. 20:8 **5:13** [e]Ex. 23:12 & 35:2 Ezek. 20:12 **5:14** [f]Gen. 2:2 Ex. 16:29 Heb. 4:4 **5:15** [g]ch. 15:15 & 16:12 & 24:18,22 [h]ch. 4:34,37 **5:16** [i]Ex. 20:12 Lev. 19:3 ch. 27:16 Eph. 6:2,3 Col. 3:20 [j]ch. 4:40 **5:17** [k]Ex. 20:13 Mat. 5:21 **5:18** [l]Ex. 20:14 Luke 18:20 Jas. 2:11 **5:19** [m]Ex. 20:15 Rom. 13:9 **5:20** [n]Ex. 20:16 **5:21** [o]Ex. 20:17 Mic. 2:2 Hab. 2:9 Luke 12:15 Rom. 7:7 **5:22** [p]Ex. 24:12 & 31:18 ch. 4:13 **5:23** [q]Ex. 20:18,19

[x] Heb. *keep to do them* [y] Heb. *servants*

5:2 A COVENANT. Israel's salvation was a divine gift given according to God's covenant agreement that He would adopt Israel as His sons and daughters in order to care for them and bless them, that they might live long in the land God gave them (4:40). In grateful response Israel was to accept God as their Lord to be worshiped, loved, honored, and obeyed in living faith. For a discussion of God's covenant with Israel, see articles on GOD'S COVENANT WITH ABRAHAM, ISAAC, AND JACOB, p. 48, and GOD'S COVENANT WITH THE ISRAELITES, p. 314; for a discussion of the covenant that believers in Christ have committed themselves to, see Luke 22:20, note, and article on THE OLD COVENANT AND THE NEW COVENANT, p. 1954.

5:7–21 TEN COMMANDMENTS. This section repeats the Ten Commandments as originally given in Ex. 20 (see notes on that chapter; see article on THE OLD TESTAMENT LAW, p. 124).

even all the heads of your tribes, and
your elders;
24 And ye said, Behold, the LORD
our God hath shown us his glory and
his greatness, and [r]we have heard his
voice out of the midst of the fire: we
have seen this day that God doth talk
with man, and he [s]liveth.
25 Now therefore why should we
die? for this great fire will consume us:
[t]if we [z]hear the voice of the LORD our
God any more, then we shall die.
26 [u]For who *is there of* all flesh,
that hath heard the voice of the living
God speaking out of the midst of the
fire, as we *have,* and lived?
27 Go thou near, and hear all that
the LORD our God shall say: and
[v]speak thou unto us all that the LORD
our God shall speak unto thee; and we
will hear *it,* and do *it.*
28 And the LORD heard the voice of
your words, when ye spake unto me;
and the LORD said unto me, I have
heard the voice of the words of this
people, which they have spoken unto
thee: [w]they have well said all that they
have spoken.
29 [x]O that there were such an
heart in them, that they would fear me,
and [y]keep all my commandments al-
ways, [z]that it might be well with
them, and with their children for ever!
30 Go say to them, Get you into
your tents again.
31 But as for thee, stand thou here
by me, [a]and I will speak unto thee all
the commandments, and the statutes,
and the judgments, which thou shalt

5:24 [r]Ex. 19:19 [s]ch. 4:33 Judg. 13:22
5:25 [t]ch. 18:16
5:26 [u]ch. 4:33
5:27 [v]Ex. 20:19 Heb. 12:19
5:28 [w]ch. 18:17
5:29 [x]ch. 32:29 Ps. 81:13 Is. 48:18 Mat. 23:37 Luke 19:42 [y]ch. 11:1 [z]ch. 4:40
5:31 [a]Gal. 3:19
5:32 [b]ch. 17:20 & 28:14 Josh. 1:7 Prov. 4:27
5:33 [c]ch. 10:12 Jer. 7:23 [d]ch. 4:40
6:1 [e]ch. 12:1
6:2 [f]ch. 10:12,13 Eccl. 12:13 [g]ch. 4:40 Prov. 3:1,2
6:3 [h]Gen. 22:17 [i]Ex. 3:8
6:4 [j]John 17:3 1 Cor. 8:4,6
6:5 [k]Mat. 22:37 Mark 12:30

teach them, that they may do *them* in
the land which I give them to pos-
sess it.
32 Ye shall observe to do therefore
as the LORD your God hath commanded
you: [b]ye shall not turn aside to the
right hand or to the left.
33 Ye shall walk in [c]all the ways
which the LORD your God hath com-
manded you, that ye may live, [d]and
that it may be well with you, and *that* ye
may prolong *your* days in the land
which ye shall possess.

Love the LORD thy God

6 NOW THESE *are* [e]the command-
ments, the statutes, and the judg-
ments, which the LORD your God com-
manded to teach you, that ye might do
them in the land whither ye [a]go to pos-
sess it:
2 [f]That thou mightest fear the
LORD thy God, to keep all his statutes
and his commandments, which I com-
mand thee, thou, and thy son, and thy
son's son, all the days of thy life; [g]and
that thy days may be prolonged.
3 ¶ Hear therefore, O Israel, and ob-
serve to do *it;* that it may be well with
thee, and that ye may increase mighti-
ly, [h]as the LORD God of thy fathers
hath promised thee, in [i]the land that
floweth with milk and honey.
4 [j]Hear, O Israel: The LORD our
God *is* one LORD:
5 And [k]thou shalt love the LORD thy

[z] Heb. *add to hear* [a] Heb. *pass over*

5:29 O THAT THERE WERE SUCH AN HEART IN THEM. The Biblical history of salvation is nothing other than the tireless attempts of God to draw men and women away from their sin and its destructive consequences, and to Himself.

6:4–9 HEAR, O ISRAEL. This passage is commonly referred to as "the Shema" (from Heb. *shama'*, "to hear"). It was a familiar passage to the Jews in Jesus' time, being recited daily by devout Jews and regularly in the synagogue services. The Shema is the classic declaration of the monotheistic character of God (see next note), followed by a twofold injunction to Israel: (1) to love God with all their heart, soul, and might (vv. 5–6), and (2) to teach diligently their faith to their children (vv. 7–9).

6:4 THE LORD OUR GOD *IS* ONE LORD. This verse—along with vv. 5–9; 11:13–21; Num. 15:37–41—teaches monotheism. This doctrine affirms that God is the one true God, is not a pantheon of different gods, is all-powerful among all the gods and spirits of the world (Ex. 15:11), and must be the sole object of Israel's love and obedience (vv. 4–5). This aspect of "oneness" serves as the basis for prohibiting the worship of other gods (Ex. 20:2). It does not contradict the N.T. revelation of God as a triune being who, though one in essence, is manifested as Father, Son, and Holy Spirit (see Mat. 3:17, note, and Mark 1:11, note, for comments on the triune nature of God).

6:5 LOVE THE LORD THY GOD. God seeks fellowship with His people and gives them this one indispensable command which will attach them to Himself. (1) By responding in love, gratitude, and loyalty to Him for His love (4:37), they will come to know and enjoy Him in a covenant relationship. (2) On this, the "first and great commandment," along with the second commandment to love one's neighbor (cf. Lev. 19:18), depends the whole law and the prophets (Mat. 22:37–40). (3) True obedience to God and His commandments is possible only when it springs from faith in and love for God (cf. 7:9; 10:12; 11:1,13,22; 13:3; 19:9; 30:6,16,20; see Mat. 22:39, note; John 14:15;

God [l]with all thine heart, and with all thy soul, and with all thy might.

6 And [m]these words, which I command thee this day, shall be in thine heart:

7 And [n]thou shalt [b]teach them diligently unto thy children, and shalt talk of them when thou sittest in thine house, and when thou walkest by the way, and when thou liest down, and when thou risest up.

8 [o]And thou shalt bind them for a sign upon thine hand, and they shall be as frontlets between thine eyes.

9 [p]And thou shalt write them upon the posts of thy house, and on thy gates.

10 And it shall be, when the LORD thy God shall have brought thee into the land which he sware unto thy fathers, to Abraham, to Isaac, and to Jacob, to give thee great and goodly cities, [q]which thou buildest not,

11 And houses full of all good *things*, which thou filledst not, and wells digged, which thou diggedst not, vineyards and olive trees, which thou plantedst not; [r]when thou shalt have eaten and be full;

12 *Then* beware lest thou forget the LORD, which brought thee forth out of the land of Egypt, from the house of [c]bondage.

13 Thou shalt [s]fear the LORD thy God, and serve him, and [t]shalt swear by his name.

14 Ye shall not go after other gods, [u]of the gods of the people which *are* round about you;

15 (For [v]the LORD thy God *is* a jealous God among you) [w]lest the anger of the LORD thy God be kindled against thee, and destroy thee from off the face of the earth.

16 ¶ [x]Ye shall not tempt the LORD your God, [y]as ye tempted *him* in Massah.

17 Ye shall [z]diligently keep the commandments of the LORD your God, and his testimonies, and his statutes, which he hath commanded thee.

18 And thou [a]shalt do *that which is* right and good in the sight of the LORD: that it may be well with thee, and that thou mayest go in and possess the good land which the LORD sware unto thy fathers,

19 [b]To cast out all thine enemies from before thee, as the LORD hath spoken.

20 *And* [c]when thy son asketh thee [d]in time to come, saying, What *mean* the testimonies, and the statutes, and the judgments, which the LORD our God hath commanded you?

21 Then thou shalt say unto thy son, We were Pharaoh's bondmen in Egypt; and the LORD brought us out of Egypt [d]with a mighty hand:

22 [e]And the LORD showed signs and wonders, great and [e]sore, upon Egypt, upon Pharaoh, and upon all his household, before our eyes:

23 And he brought us out from thence, that he might bring us in, to give us the land which he sware unto our fathers.

24 And the LORD commanded us to do all these statutes, [f]to fear the LORD our God, [g]for our good always, that

6:5 [l]2 Ki. 23:25
6:6 [m]ch. 11:18 Ps. 119:11,98
6:7 [n]ch. 11:19 Ps. 78:4-6
6:8 [o]Prov. 6:21 & 7:3
6:9 [p]ch. 11:20 Is. 57:8
6:10 [q]Josh. 24:13 Ps. 105:44
6:11 [r]ch. 8:10
6:13 [s]Mat. 4:10 Luke 4:8 [t]Is. 45:23 & 65:16 Jer. 4:2
6:14 [u]ch. 13:7
6:15 [v]Ex. 20:5 ch. 4:24 [w]ch. 7:4 & 11:17
6:16 [x]Mat. 4:7 Luke 4:12 [y]1 Cor. 10:9
6:17 [z]Ps. 119:4
6:18 [a]Ex. 15:26 ch. 12:28 & 13:18
6:19 [b]Num. 33:52,53
6:20 [c]Ex. 13:14
6:21 [d]Ex. 13:3
6:22 [e]Ex. 7 & 8 & 9 & 10
6:24 [f]ver. 2 [g]Job 35:7,8 Jer. 32:39

[b] Heb. *whet*, or, *sharpen* [c] Heb. *bondmen*, or, *servants* [d] Heb. *tomorrow* [e] Heb. *evil*

21:16; 1 John 4:19).

6:6 THESE WORDS . . . IN THINE HEART. It is God's firm desire that His word be in the hearts of His people (cf. Ps. 119:11; Jer. 31:33; see article on THE HEART, p. 932). Paul states explicitly in Colossians, "Let the word of Christ dwell in you richly in all wisdom" (Col. 3:16; cf. 2 Tim. 3:15–17). This can be accomplished only by daily and continually abiding in the Scriptures (Ps. 119:97–100; John 8:31–32). One approach is to read the N.T. through twice every year and the O.T. once (cf. Is. 29:13; see Jas. 1:21, note).

6:7 TEACH THEM DILIGENTLY UNTO THY CHILDREN. One key way to express love for God (v. 5) is to be concerned with the spiritual welfare of our children and to endeavor to bring them into a faithful relationship with God. (1) Godly training of the child should be a foremost concern of parents (cf. Ps. 103:13; see Luke 1:17, note; 2 Tim. 3:3, note; see article on PARENTS AND CHILDREN, p. 1880).

(2) Spiritual instruction must be centered in the home, with both the father and mother taking part. Devotion to the Lord in the home is not an option; rather, it is a direct commandment from the Lord (vv. 7–9; Ex. 20:12; Lev. 20:9; Prov. 1:8; 6:20; cf. 2 Tim. 1:5).

(3) The purpose of parental instruction is to teach the children to fear the Lord, to walk in all His ways, to love and appreciate Him, and to serve Him with all their heart and soul (10:12; Eph. 6:4).

(4) The believer must diligently give his/her children a God-centered education where everything is related to God and His ways (cf. 4:9; 11:19; 32:46; Gen. 18:19; Ex. 10:2; 12:26–27; 13:14–16; Is. 38:19).

THE FEAR OF THE LORD

***Deut. 6:1–2** "Now these* are *the commandments, the statutes, and the judgments, which the LORD your God commanded to teach you, that ye might do* them *in the land whither ye go to possess it: That thou mightest fear the LORD thy God, to keep all his statutes and his commandments, which I command thee, thou, and thy son, and thy son's son, all the days of thy life; and that thy days may be prolonged."*

A frequent command given to God's people in the O.T. is to "fear God" or to "fear the LORD." It is important that we know what this command means for us as believers. Only as we truly fear the Lord will we be delivered from slavery to all abnormal fears.

THE MEANING OF THE FEAR OF THE LORD. The comprehensive command to "fear the LORD" includes a variety of different aspects of the believer's relationship with God. (1) Essential to fearing God is a recognition of His holiness, justice, and righteousness as a counterpart to His love and mercy, i.e., knowing Him and understanding fully who He is (cf. Prov. 2:5). Such fear is based on the acknowledgement that God is a holy God, whose very nature causes Him to judge sin.

(2) To fear the Lord is to regard Him with holy awe and reverence and to honor God as God because of His great glory, holiness, majesty, and power (see Phil. 2:12, note). For example, when the Israelites at Mount Sinai saw God manifest Himself through "thunders and lightnings, and a thick cloud upon the mount, and the voice of the trumpet exceeding loud," they all "trembled" in fear (Ex. 19:16) and begged Moses to speak to them rather than the Lord God Himself (Ex. 20:18–19; Deut. 5:22–27). Again, the psalmist in Ps. 33, in his reflections on God as Creator, states explicitly: "Let all the earth fear the LORD: let all the inhabitants of the world stand in awe of him, For he spake, and it was *done*; he commanded, and it stood fast" (Ps. 33:8–9).

(3) True fear of the Lord causes believers to place their faith and trust in Him alone for salvation. For example, after the Israelites crossed over the Red Sea on dry ground and saw the enormous destruction of the Egyptian army, they "feared the LORD, and believed the LORD" (see Ex. 14:31, note). Similarly, the psalmist calls upon all those who fear the Lord to "trust in the LORD: he *is* their help and their shield" (Ps. 115:11). In other words, the fear of the Lord produces in God's people a confident hope and trust in Him. It is little wonder, then, that such people are saved (Ps. 85:9) and receive His forgiving love and mercy (Luke 1:50; cf. Ps. 103:11; 130:4).

(4) Finally, to fear God involves recognizing that He is a God who is angry about sin and has the power to punish those who transgress His righteous laws, both in time and in eternity (cf. Ps. 76:7–8). When Adam and Eve sinned in the Garden of Eden, they were afraid of the Lord and tried to hide from His presence (Gen. 3:8–10). Moses experienced this aspect of the fear of God when he spent forty days and nights in prayer on behalf of the sinful Israelites: "I was afraid of the anger and hot displeasure, wherewith the LORD was wroth against you to destroy you" (Deut. 9:19). Similarly in the N.T., immediately after acknowledging the coming vengeance and judgment of God, the author of Hebrews wrote: "*It is* a fearful thing to fall into the hands of the living God" (Heb. 10:31).

REASONS FOR THE FEAR OF THE LORD. The reasons for fearing the Lord proceed from the meaning of the fear of the Lord. (1) We should fear Him because of His great power as the Creator of all things and all people (Ps. 33:6–9; 96:4–5; Jonah 1:9). (2) Furthermore, the awesome power that He continues to exercise over the elements of creation and over us is cause for fearing God (Ex. 20:18–20; Eccl. 3:14; Jonah 1:11–16; Mark 4:39–41). (3) When we realize the holiness of our God, i.e., His separation from

sin and constant opposition to it, the normal response of the human spirit is to fear Him (Rev. 15:4). (4) Anyone who sees the brightness of the glory of God cannot help but become afraid (Mat. 17:1–8). (5) The continual blessings we receive from God, especially the forgiveness of our sins (Ps. 130:4), should lead us to fear and love Him (1 Sam. 12:24; Ps. 34:9; 67:7; Jer. 5:24; see article on THE PROVIDENCE OF GOD, p. 80). (6) Beyond all doubt, the fact that God is a God of justice who will judge the entire human race generates the fear of Him (Deut. 17:12–13; Is. 59:18–19; Mal. 3:5; Heb. 10:26–31). It is a solemn and holy truth that God is constantly watching and evaluating our actions, both good and bad, and that we will be held accountable for those actions, both now and in the day of our personal judgment.

PERSONAL IMPLICATIONS ABOUT THE FEAR OF THE LORD. The fear of the Lord is far more than a mere Biblical doctrine; it directly applies to our daily lives in numerous ways. (1) First, if we truly fear the Lord, we will live a life of obedience to His commandments and say "No" to sin. One reason why God inspired fear in the Israelites at Mount Sinai was so that they might learn to turn away from sin and to obey His law (Ex. 20:20). Repeatedly in Moses' final address to the Israelites, he related the fear of the Lord to serving and obeying Him (e.g., Deut. 5:29; 6:2,24; 8:6; 10:12; 13:4; 17:19; 31:12). According to the psalmists, fearing the Lord is equivalent to delighting in His commandments (Ps. 112:1) and keeping His precepts (Ps. 119:63). Solomon taught that "by the fear of the LORD *men* depart from evil" (Prov. 16:6; cf. 8:13). In Ecclesiastes, the whole duty of the human race is summarized in two brief imperatives: "Fear God, and keep his commandments" (Eccl. 12:13). Conversely, anyone who is content to live a life of wickedness does so because "*there is* no fear of God before his eyes" (Ps. 36:1–4).

(2) An important corollary to the previous implication is that believers must teach their children to fear the Lord by training them to abhor sin and keep God's holy commandments (Deut. 4:10; 6:1–2,6–9). The Bible often states that "the fear of the LORD *is* the beginning of wisdom" (Ps. 111:10; Prov. 9:10; cf. Job 28:28; Prov. 1:7). Since a basic goal for our children's education is for them to live according to God's principles of wisdom (Prov. 1:1–6), teaching them to fear the Lord is a critical first step (see article on PARENTS AND CHILDREN, p. 1880).

(3) The fear of the Lord has a sanctifying effect on God's people. Just as there is a sanctifying effect in the truth of God's word (John 17:17), so there is a sanctifying effect in the fear of God. It moves us to hate sin and turn away from evil (Prov. 3:7; 8:13; 16:6). It causes us to be careful and restrained in our speech (Prov. 10:19; Eccl. 5:2,6–7). It protects us from the breakdown of our consciences and of our moral resolve. The fear of the Lord is clean and cleansing (Ps. 19:9), holy and redeeming in its effect.

(4) The holy fear of the Lord motivates God's people to worship Him with their whole being. If we truly fear God, we will worship and glorify Him as Lord of all (Ps. 22:23). David equates the worshiping congregation with "them that fear him" (Ps. 22:25). Likewise, at the end of history when the heavenly angel who proclaims the everlasting gospel calls all on earth to fear God, he immediately adds, "and give glory to him . . . and worship him that made heaven, and earth, and the sea" (Rev. 14:6–7).

(5) God has promised to reward all those who fear Him. "By humility *and* the fear of the LORD *are* riches, and honour, and life" (Prov. 22:4). Other promised rewards include protection from death (Prov. 14:26–27), provisions for our daily needs (Ps. 34:9; 111:5), and a long life (Prov. 10:27). Those who fear the Lord know "that it shall be well with them," regardless of what happens in the world around them (Eccl. 8:12–13).

(6) Finally, the fear of the Lord is accompanied by assurance and comfort for God's people. The N.T. directly links the fear of the Lord with the comfort of the Holy Spirit (Acts 9:31). Those who live without fearing the Lord have no sense of His presence, grace, and protection (see Deut. 1:26, note), while those who fear God and keep His commandments have a deep experience of spiritual security and of the anointing of the Holy Spirit. They can be sure that God will "deliver their soul from death" (Ps. 33:18–19; see articles on DEATH, p. 782, and ASSURANCE OF SALVATION, p. 2010).

[h]he might preserve us alive, as *it is* at this day.

25 And [i]it shall be our righteousness, if we observe to do all these commandments before the LORD our God, as he hath commanded us.

God will defeat the nations

7 WHEN THE [j]LORD thy God shall bring thee into the land whither thou goest to possess it, and hath cast out many nations before thee, [k]the Hittites, and the Girgashites, and the Amorites, and the Canaanites, and the Perizzites, and the Hivites, and the Jebusites, seven nations [l]greater and mightier than thou;

2 And when the LORD thy God shall [m]deliver them before thee; thou shalt smite them, *and* [n]utterly destroy them; [o]thou shalt make no covenant with them, nor show mercy unto them:

3 [p]Neither shalt thou make marriages with them; thy daughter thou shalt not give unto his son, nor his daughter shalt thou take unto thy son.

4 For they will turn away thy son from following me, that they may serve other gods: [q]so will the anger of the LORD be kindled against you, and destroy thee suddenly.

5 But thus shall ye deal with them; ye shall [r]destroy their altars, and break down their [f]images, and cut down their groves, and burn their graven images with fire.

6 [s]For thou *art* an holy people unto the LORD thy God: [t]the LORD thy God hath chosen thee to be a special people unto himself, above all people that *are* upon the face of the earth.

Jos. 23:11-13

7 The LORD did not set his love upon you, nor choose you, because ye were more in number than any people; for ye *were* [u]the fewest of all people:

8 But [v]because the LORD loved you, and because he would keep [w]the oath which he had sworn unto your fathers, [x]hath the LORD brought you out with a mighty hand, and redeemed you out of the house of bondmen, from the hand of Pharaoh king of Egypt.

9 Know therefore that the LORD thy God, he *is* God, [y]the faithful God, [z]which keepeth covenant and mercy with them that love him and keep his commandments to a thousand generations;

10 And [a]repayeth them that hate him to their face, to destroy them: [b]he will not be slack to him that hateth him, he will repay him to his face.

11 Thou shalt therefore keep the commandments, and the statutes, and the judgments, which I command thee this day, to do them.

12 ¶ [c]Wherefore it shall come to pass, [g]if ye hearken to these judgments, and keep, and do them, that the LORD thy God shall keep unto thee [d]the covenant and the mercy which he sware unto thy fathers:

13 And he will [e]love thee, and bless thee, and multiply thee: [f]he will also bless the fruit of thy womb, and the fruit of thy land, thy corn, and thy wine, and thine oil, the increase of thy kine, and the flocks of thy sheep, in the land which he sware unto thy fathers to give thee.

14 Thou shalt be blessed above all people: [g]there shall not be male or female barren among you, or among your cattle.

15 And the LORD will take away from thee all sickness, and will put none of the [h]evil diseases of Egypt, which thou knowest, upon thee; but will lay them upon all *them* that hate thee.

Deut 32:3

16 And [i]thou shalt consume all the people which the LORD thy God shall deliver thee; [j]thine eye shall have no pity upon them: neither shalt thou serve their gods; for that *will be* [k]a snare unto thee.

17 If thou shalt say in thine heart,

6:24 [h]ch. 4:1 Ps. 41:2 **6:25** [i]Lev. 18:5 Rom. 10:3,5 **7:1** [j]ch. 31:3 [k]Ex. 33:2 [l]ch. 4:38 **7:2** [m]ch. 23:14 [n]Josh. 6:17 & 8:24 & 9:24 [o]Josh. 2:14 Judg. 1:24 & 2:2 **7:3** [p]1 Ki. 11:2 Ezra 9:2 **7:4** [q]ch. 6:15 **7:5** [r]Ex. 23:24 & 34:13 ch. 12:2,3 **7:6** [s]Ps. 50:5 Jer. 2:3 [t]Ex. 19:5 Amos 3:2 1 Pet. 2:9 **7:7** [u]ch. 10:22 **7:8** [v]ch. 10:15 [w]Luke 1:55,72,73 [x]Ex. 13:3,14 **7:9** [y]1 Cor. 1:9 2 Cor. 1:18 2 Thes. 3:3 2 Tim. 2:13 Heb. 11:11 [z]Neh. 1:5 Dan. 9:4 **7:10** [a]Is. 59:18 [b]ch. 32:35 **7:12** [c]ch. 28:1 [d]Ps. 105:8,9 **7:13** [e]John 14:21 [f]ch. 28:4 **7:14** [g]Ex. 23:26 **7:15** [h]Ex. 15:26 ch. 28:27,60 **7:16** [i]ver. 2 [j]ch. 19:13,21 [k]Judg. 8:27

f Heb. *statues*, or, *pillars* g Heb. *because*

7:3 NEITHER . . . MAKE MARRIAGES. Any intimate or close association with people of the world will eventually destroy the separateness and holiness of God's people. Such matters as intermarriage of God's people with unbelievers or close friendship with unbelievers may turn believers away from following God (v. 4; see article on SPIRITUAL SEPARATION FOR BELIEVERS, p. 1814).

7:9 MERCY WITH THEM THAT LOVE HIM. God's choosing of Israel was motivated by His love for them (vv. 7–8). Moreover, God promised to faithfully keep His covenant and show mercy to generation after generation of "them that love him and keep his commandments" (cf. 6:4–9). Not only was God's love contingent upon this response of love and obedience, but also their prosperity (vv. 13–14), good health (v. 15), and military success (v. 16).

7:15 TAKE AWAY . . . ALL SICKNESS. See Ex. 23:25–26, note.

These nations *are* more than I; how can
I [l]dispossess them?
18 [m]Thou shalt not be afraid of
them: *but* shalt well [n]remember what
the LORD thy God did unto Pharaoh, and
unto all Egypt;
19 [o]The great temptations which
thine eyes saw, and the signs, and the
wonders, and the mighty hand, and the
stretched out arm, whereby the LORD
thy God brought thee out: so shall the
LORD thy God do unto all the people of
whom thou art afraid.
20 [p]Moreover the LORD thy God
will send the hornet among them, until
they that are left, and hide themselves
from thee, be destroyed.
21 Thou shalt not be affrighted at
them: for the LORD thy God *is* [q]among
you, [r]a mighty God and terrible.
22 [s]And the LORD thy God will
[h]put out those nations before thee by
little and little: thou mayest not con-
sume them at once, lest the beasts of
the field increase upon thee.
23 But the LORD thy God shall deliv-
er them [i]unto thee, and shall destroy
them with a mighty destruction, until
they be destroyed.
24 And [t]he shall deliver their
kings into thine hand, and thou shalt
destroy their name [u]from under heav-
en: [v]there shall no man be able to
stand before thee, until thou have de-
stroyed them.
25 The graven images of their gods
[w]shall ye burn with fire: thou [x]shalt
not desire the silver or gold *that is* on
them, nor take *it* unto thee, lest thou
be [y]snared therein: for it *is* [z]an abom-
ination to the LORD thy God.

7:17 [l]Num. 33:53
7:18 [m]ch. 31:6 [n]Ps. 105:5
7:19 [o]ch. 4:34 & 29:3
7:20 [p]Josh. 24:12
7:21 [q]Num. 16:3 Josh. 3:10 [r]Neh. 9:32
7:22 [s]Ex. 23:29,30
7:24 [t]Josh. 10:24,25,42 [u]Ex. 17:14 [v]Josh. 23:9
7:25 [w]Ex. 32:20 1 Chr. 14:12 [x]Josh. 7:1,21 [y]Judg. 8:27 Zeph. 1:3 [z]ch. 17:1
7:26 [a]Lev. 27:28 Josh. 6:17 & 7:1
8:1 [b]ch. 4:1 & 5:32,33 & 6:1-3
8:2 [c]ch. 1:3 & 2:7 Amos 2:10 [d]Ex. 16:4 ch. 13:3 [e]John 2:25
8:3 [f]Ex. 16:2,3 [g]Ex. 16:12,14,35 [h]Mat. 4:4 Luke 4:4
8:4 [i]ch. 29:5 Neh. 9:21
8:5 [j]2 Sam. 7:14 Ps. 89:32 Prov. 3:12 Heb. 12:5,6 Rev. 3:19
8:6 [k]ch. 5:33

26 Neither shalt thou bring an
abomination into thine house, lest thou
be a cursed thing like it: *but* thou shalt
utterly detest it, and thou shalt utterly
abhor it; [a]for it *is* a cursed thing.

God's mercies in the wilderness

8 ALL THE commandments which I
command thee this day [b]shall ye
observe to do, that ye may live, and
multiply, and go in and possess the
land which the LORD sware unto your
fathers.
2 And thou shalt remember all the
way which the LORD thy God [c]led thee
these forty years in the wilderness, to
humble thee, *and* [d]to prove thee, [e]to
know what *was* in thine heart, whether
thou wouldest keep his command-
ments, or no.
3 And he humbled thee, and [f]suf-
fered thee to hunger, and [g]fed thee
with manna, which thou knewest not,
neither did thy fathers know; that he
might make thee know that man doth
[h]not live by bread only, but by every
word that proceedeth out of the mouth
of the LORD doth man live.
4 [i]Thy raiment waxed not old upon
thee, neither did thy foot swell, these
forty years.
5 [j]Thou shalt also consider in
thine heart, that, as a man chasteneth
his son, *so* the LORD thy God chasteneth
thee.
6 Therefore thou shalt keep the
commandments of the LORD thy God,
[k]to walk in his ways, and to fear him.
7 For the LORD thy God bringeth

[h] Heb. *pluck off* [i] Heb. *before thy face*

7:26 BRING AN ABOMINATION INTO THINE HOUSE. The "abomination" refers to the gold and silver on the idols of the Canaanites (v. 25); anything connected to idolatry had to be destroyed. This admonition to the Israelites to remove whatever was detestable from their houses has application today. Anything that promotes sin and immorality and is contrary to God's holy nature must not be allowed into our homes (cf. Ezek. 5:7,9). Therefore, believers must be extremely careful that they do not allow the influence of immoral lifestyles of the ungodly to penetrate their homes through people or through the entertainment media (cf. 12:29–31; 18:12–13; Prov. 6:16–19). Rather than permitting evil, sin, and ungodliness to be brought into our homes, we must instead "utterly detest it, and . . . abhor it," for to tolerate and enjoy evil within our homes is to fall under the curse of God (cf. 23:14; see Rom. 1:32, note).

8:3 MAN DOTH NOT LIVE BY BREAD ONLY. The Lord brought testings and troubles to His people in the wilderness in order to teach them that one's life does not consist merely in the physical, but rather that one's well-being (both physically and spiritually) depends on one's relationship to God and obedience to His word. The Lord Jesus quoted this passage in the hour of His temptation (Mat. 4:4; cf. Gen. 3:4, note). At times the Lord may permit difficulties in our lives as a form of fatherly discipline in order to train us to depend on Him more firmly and to receive His word more willingly (vv. 4–5; cf. Heb. 12:3–13).

8:7 A LAND OF BROOKS OF WATER. At the time of Israel's entrance into Canaan it was a land with brooks, streams, springs of water, and deep pools. Israel's scarcity of water in the time of Elijah was a judgment of God (1 Ki. 17:1—18:46). Even today God may use drought to humble His people and to bring judgment on sinners (vv.

thee into a good land, [l]a land of brooks of water, of fountains and depths that spring out of valleys and hills;

8 A land of wheat, and barley, and vines, and fig trees, and pomegranates; a land [j]of oil olive, and honey;

9 A land wherein thou shalt eat bread without scarceness, thou shalt not lack any *thing* in it; a land [m]whose stones *are* iron, and out of whose hills thou mayest dig brass.

10 [n]When thou hast eaten and art full, then thou shalt bless the LORD thy God for the good land which he hath given thee.

Judg. 5:1-2

Warning against pride

11 Beware that thou forget not the LORD thy God, in not keeping his commandments, and his judgments, and his statutes, which I command thee this day:

12 [o]Lest *when* thou hast eaten and art full, and hast built goodly houses, and dwelt *therein;*

13 And *when* thy herds and thy flocks multiply, and thy silver and thy gold is multiplied, and all that thou hast is multiplied;

14 [p]Then thine heart be lifted up, and thou [q]forget the LORD thy God, which brought thee forth out of the land of Egypt, from the house of bondage;

15 Who [r]led thee through that great and terrible wilderness, [s]*wherein were* fiery serpents, and scorpions, and drought, where *there was* no water; [t]who brought thee forth water out of the rock of flint;

16 Who fed thee in the wilderness with [u]manna, which thy fathers knew not, that he might humble thee, and that he might prove thee, [v]to do thee good at thy latter end;

17 [w]And thou say in thine heart, My power and the might of *mine* hand hath gotten me this wealth.

18 But thou shalt remember the LORD thy God: [x]for *it is* he that giveth thee power to get wealth, [y]that he may establish his covenant which he sware unto thy fathers, as *it is* this day.

19 And it shall be, if thou do at all forget the LORD thy God, and walk after other gods, and serve them, and worship them, [z]I testify against you this day that ye shall surely perish.

20 As the nations which the LORD destroyeth before your face, [a]so shall ye perish; because ye would not be obedient unto the voice of the LORD your God.

9 HEAR, O Israel: Thou *art* to [b]pass over Jordan this day, to go in to possess nations [c]greater and mightier than thyself, cities great and [d]fenced up to heaven,

2 A people great and tall, [e]the children of the Anakims, whom thou knowest, and *of whom* thou hast heard *say*, Who can stand before the children of Anak!

3 Understand therefore this day, that the LORD thy God *is* he which [f]goeth over before thee; *as* a [g]consuming fire [h]he shall destroy them, and he shall bring them down before thy face: [i]so shalt thou drive them out, and destroy them quickly, as the LORD hath said unto thee.

4 [j]Speak not thou in thine heart, after that the LORD thy God hath cast them out from before thee, saying, For my righteousness the LORD hath brought me in to possess this land: but

j Heb. *of olive tree of oil*

8:7 [l]ch. 11:10-12
8:9 [m]ch. 33:25
8:10 [n]ch. 6:11,12
8:12 [o]ch. 28:47 & 32:15 Hos. 13:6
8:14 [p]1 Cor. 4:7 [q]Ps. 106:21
8:15 [r]Is. 63:12-14 Jer. 2:6 [s]Num. 21:6 Hos. 13:5 [t]Num. 20:11
8:16 [u]Ex. 16:15 [v]Jer. 24:5,6 Heb. 12:11
8:17 [w]ch. 9:4
8:18 [x]Prov. 10:22 Hos. 2:8 [y]ch. 7:8,12
8:19 [z]ch. 4:26 & 30:18
8:20 [a]Dan. 9:11,12
9:1 [b]ch. 11:31 Josh. 3:16 & 4:19 [c]ch. 4:38 & 11:23 [d]ch. 1:28
9:2 [e]Num. 13:22,28, 32,33
9:3 [f]ch. 31:3 Josh. 3:11 [g]ch. 4:24 Heb. 12:29 [h]ch. 7:23 [i]Ex. 23:31 ch. 7:24
9:4 [j]ch. 8:17 Rom. 11:6,20 1 Cor. 4:4,7

19–20; see 11:17).

8:12–14 *WHEN* THOU HAST EATEN AND ART FULL . . . THOU FORGOT THE LORD THY GOD. In times of prosperity and abundance people are inclined to become satisfied with life on earth as it is and to find their enjoyment in material blessings. Prosperity brings the temptation to forget God and His commandments, to no longer seek spiritual blessings, and to fail to grieve over the sin and evil in the world (see article on RICHES AND POVERTY, p. 1568).

8:18 POWER TO GET WEALTH. This verse affirms that God at times blessed Israel as a sign or confirmation that He was fulfilling His covenant with Abraham and his descendants. Unfortunately, many times in the world wealth is gained by means that are contrary to godly principles and practices (see article on RICHES AND POVERTY, p. 1568); such wealth should not be seen as one of God's blessings.

9:4 FOR THE WICKEDNESS OF THESE NATIONS. The nations of Canaan were destroyed by God because of their extreme wickedness; their depravity was so terrible and widespread that God determined that they had to be completely removed like a dreaded cancer. Thus Israel's conquest and extermination of the Canaanites were capital punishment on a national level. Likewise, virtually uncontrolled wickedness had existed in Noah's day (see Gen. 6:1–7) and will characterize the world at the end of time (Mat. 24:37–39; 2 Tim. 3:1–5; Rev. 9:20–21; 19:11–21).

[k]for the wickedness of these nations the LORD doth drive them out from before thee.

5 [l]Not for thy righteousness, or for the uprightness of thine heart, dost thou go to possess their land: but for the wickedness of these nations the LORD thy God doth drive them out from before thee, and that he may perform [m]the word which the LORD sware unto thy fathers, Abraham, Isaac, and Jacob.

The golden calf

6 Understand therefore, that the LORD thy God giveth thee not this good land to possess it for thy righteousness; for thou *art* [n]a stiffnecked people.

7 ¶ Remember, *and* forget not, how thou provokedst the LORD thy God to wrath in the wilderness: [o]from the day that thou didst depart out of the land of Egypt, until ye came unto this place, ye have been rebellious against the LORD.

8 Also [p]in Horeb ye provoked the LORD to wrath, so that the LORD was angry with you to have destroyed you.

9 [q]When I was gone up into the mount to receive the tables of stone, *even* the tables of the covenant which the LORD made with you, then [r]I abode in the mount forty days and forty nights, I neither did eat bread nor drink water:

10 [s]And the LORD delivered unto me two tables of stone written with the finger of God; and on them *was written* according to all the words, which the LORD spake with you in the mount out of the midst of the fire [t]in the day of the assembly.

11 And it came to pass at the end of forty days and forty nights, *that* the LORD gave me the two tables of stone, *even* the tables of the covenant.

12 And the LORD said unto me, [u]Arise, get thee down quickly from hence; for thy people which thou hast brought forth out of Egypt have corrupted *themselves;* they are [v]quickly turned aside out of the way which I commanded them; they have made them a molten image.

13 Furthermore [w]the LORD spake unto me, saying, I have seen this people, and, behold, [x]it *is* a stiffnecked people:

14 [y]Let me alone, that I may destroy them, and [z]blot out their name from under heaven: [a]and I will make of thee a nation mightier and greater than they.

15 [b]So I turned and came down from the mount, and [c]the mount burned with fire: and the two tables of the covenant *were* in my two hands.

16 And [d]I looked, and, behold, ye had sinned against the LORD your God, *and* had made you a molten calf: ye had turned aside quickly out of the way which the LORD had commanded you.

17 And I took the two tables, and cast them out of my two hands, and brake them before your eyes.

18 And I [e]fell down before the LORD, as at the first, forty days and forty nights: I did neither eat bread, nor drink water, because of all your sins which ye sinned, in doing wickedly in the sight of the LORD, to provoke him to anger.

19 [f]For I was afraid of the anger and hot displeasure, wherewith the LORD was wroth against you to destroy you. [g]But the LORD hearkened unto me at that time also.

20 And the LORD was very angry with Aaron to have destroyed him: and I prayed for Aaron also the same time.

21 And [h]I took your sin, the calf which ye had made, and burnt it with fire, and stamped it, *and* ground *it* very small, *even* until it was as small as dust: and I cast the dust thereof into the brook that descended out of the mount.

22 And at [i]Taberah, and at [j]Massah, and at [k]Kibroth-hattaavah, ye provoked the LORD to wrath.

23 Likewise [l]when the LORD sent you from Kadesh-barnea, saying, Go up and possess the land which I have giv-

9:4 [k]Gen. 15:16 Lev. 18:24 ch. 18:12
9:5 [l]Tit. 3:5 [m]Gen. 12:7 & 13:15 & 15:7 & 17:8 & 26:4
9:6 [n]ver. 13 Ex. 32:9 & 33:3 & 34:9
9:7 [o]Ex. 14:11 & 16:2 & 17:2 Num. 11:4 & 20:2 & 25:2 ch. 31:27
9:8 [p]Ex. 32:4 Ps. 106:19
9:9 [q]Ex. 24:12,15 [r]Ex. 24:18 & 34:28
9:10 [s]Ex. 31:18 [t]Ex. 19:17 & 20:1 ch. 4:10 & 10:4
9:12 [u]Ex. 32:7 [v]ch. 31:29 Judg. 2:17
9:13 [w]Ex. 32:9 [x]ver. 6 ch. 10:16 & 31:27 2 Ki. 17:14
9:14 [y]Ex. 32:10 [z]ch. 29:20 [a]Num. 14:12
9:15 [b]Ex. 32:15 [c]Ex. 19:18 ch. 4:11 & 5:23
9:16 [d]Ex. 32:19
9:18 [e]Ex. 34:28
9:19 [f]Ex. 32:10,11 [g]Ex. 32:14 & 33:17 ch. 10:10 Ps. 106:23
9:21 [h]Ex. 32:20 Is. 31:7
9:22 [i]Num. 11:1,3,5 [j]Ex. 17:7 [k]Num. 11:4,34
9:23 [l]Num. 13:3 & 14:1

9:5 NOT FOR THY RIGHTEOUSNESS. Israel's possession of the land was not a reward for their own past faithfulness. Rather, it was given as God's gracious gift based on His love and mercy. However, Moses warned the people that continued possession of the land would be contingent upon their perseverance in faith and in obedience to God; if Israel became wicked like the Canaanites, they too would be dispossessed of the land (30:15–20). In other words, God's love and mercy in giving them the land were not unconditional; if they turned away from the Lord and forgot His word, they too would perish (8:11,14,19–20; cf. 11:22–28).

en you; then ye rebelled against the commandment of the LORD your God, and [m]ye believed him not, nor hearkened to his voice.

24 [n]Ye have been rebellious against the LORD from the day that I knew you.

25 [o]Thus I fell down before the LORD forty days and forty nights, as I fell down *at the first;* because the LORD had said he would destroy you.

26 [p]I prayed therefore unto the LORD, and said, O Lord GOD, destroy not thy people and thine inheritance, which thou hast redeemed through thy greatness, which thou hast brought forth out of Egypt with a mighty hand.

27 Remember thy servants, Abraham, Isaac, and Jacob; look not unto the stubbornness of this people, nor to their wickedness, nor to their sin:

28 Lest [q]the land whence thou broughtest us out say, [r]Because the LORD was not able to bring them into the land which he promised them, and because he hated them, he hath brought them out to slay them in the wilderness.

29 [s]Yet they *are* thy people and thine inheritance, which thou broughtest out by thy mighty power and by thy stretched out arm.

The second tables of stone

10 AT THAT time the LORD said unto me, [t]Hew thee two tables of stone like unto the first, and come up unto me into the mount, and [u]make thee an ark of wood.

2 And I will write on the tables the words that were in the first tables which thou brakest, and [v]thou shalt put them in the ark.

3 And I made an ark of [w]shittim wood, and [x]hewed two tables of stone like unto the first, and went up into the mount, having the two tables in mine hand.

4 And he wrote on the tables, according to the first writing, the ten [k]commandments, [y]which the LORD spake unto you in the mount out of the midst of the fire in the day of the assembly: and the LORD gave them unto me.

5 And I turned myself and [z]came down from the mount, and [a]put the tables in the ark which I had made; [b]and there they be, as the LORD commanded me.

6 ¶ And the children of Israel took their journey from Beeroth [c]of the children of Jaakan to [d]Mosera: [e]there Aaron died, and there he was buried; and Eleazar his son ministered in the priest's office in his stead.

7 [f]From thence they journeyed unto Gudgodah; and from Gudgodah to Jotbath, a land of rivers of waters.

8 ¶ At that time [g]the LORD separated the tribe of Levi, [h]to bear the ark of the covenant of the LORD, [i]to stand before the LORD to minister unto him, and [j]to bless in his name, unto this day.

9 [k]Wherefore Levi hath no part nor inheritance with his brethren; the LORD *is* his inheritance, according as the LORD thy God promised him.

10 And [l]I stayed in the mount, according to the [l]first time, forty days and forty nights; and [m]the LORD hearkened unto me at that time also, *and* the LORD would not destroy thee.

11 [n]And the LORD said unto me, Arise, [m]take *thy* journey before the people, that they may go in and possess the land, which I sware unto their fathers to give unto them.

God's great requirement

12 ¶ And now, Israel, [o]what doth the LORD thy God require of thee, but

[k] Heb. *words* [l] Or, *former days* [m] Heb. *go in journey*

9:23 [m]Ps. 106:24,25 **9:24** [n]ch. 31:27 **9:25** [o]ver. 18 **9:26** [p]Ex. 32:11 **9:28** [q]Ex. 6:6-8; 1 Sam. 14:25 [r]Ex. 32:12; Num. 14:16 **9:29** [s]ch. 4:20; 1 Ki. 8:51; Neh. 1:10 **10:1** [t]Ex. 34:1,2 [u]Ex. 25:10 **10:2** [v]Ex. 25:16,21 **10:3** [w]Ex. 25:5,10 [x]Ex. 34:4 **10:4** [y]Ex. 20:1 **10:5** [z]Ex. 34:29 [a]Ex. 40:20 [b]1 Ki. 8:9 **10:6** [c]Num. 33:31 [d]Num. 33:30 [e]Num. 20:28 & 33:38 **10:7** [f]Num. 33:32,33 **10:8** [g]Num. 3:6 [h]Num. 4:15 [i]ch. 18:5 [j]Num. 6:23; ch. 21:5 **10:9** [k]ch. 18:1,2; Ezek. 44:28 **10:10** [l]Ex. 34:28; ch. 9:18,25 [m]Ex. 32:14,33,34 & 33:17; ch. 9:19 **10:11** [n]Ex. 33:1 **10:12** [o]Mic. 6:8

10:4 TEN COMMANDMENTS. See Ex. 20, notes.

10:12 LOVE HIM ... WITH ALL THY HEART. Repeatedly God emphasized to Israel the necessity of love which comes from "the heart" (see 4:29, note; 6:5, note; see article on THE HEART, p. 932). (1) God did not want His people to substitute heartfelt love for Him with mere outward religious forms, such as keeping commandments, offering sacrifices, etc. It was necessary that they always obey God from a heart that sincerely loved and honored Him. For N.T. believers, faith and love from the heart are also essential to our relationship with God (see John 21:15, note; Col. 3:4, note). (2) It is indeed possible to read the Scriptures, pray, attend church, and partake of the Lord's Supper without a heartfelt devotion to God Himself; this is what is meant by legalism (see Mark 7:6, note). Outward obedience and correct religious practices have validity and significance only as they are based on knowing Jesus Christ through sincere faith in and love for Him, because of who He is and what He has done for us.

[p]to fear the LORD thy God, [q]to walk in all his ways, and [r]to love him, and to serve the LORD thy God with all thy heart and with all thy soul,

13 To keep the commandments of the LORD, and his statutes, which I command thee this day [s]for thy good?

eut. 1:26-8

14 Behold, [t]the heaven and the heaven of heavens *is* the LORD's thy God, [u]the earth *also*, with all that therein *is*.

15 [v]Only the LORD had a delight in thy fathers to love them, and he chose their seed after them, *even* you above all people, as *it is* this day.

16 Circumcise therefore [w]the foreskin of your heart, and be no more [x]stiffnecked.

17 For the LORD your God *is* [y]God of gods, and [z]Lord of lords, a great God, [a]a mighty, and a terrible, which [b]regardeth not persons, nor taketh reward:

18 [c]He doth execute the judgment of the fatherless and widow, and loveth the stranger, in giving him food and raiment.

19 [d]Love ye therefore the stranger: for ye were strangers in the land of Egypt.

20 [e]Thou shalt fear the LORD thy God; him shalt thou serve, and to him shalt thou [f]cleave, [g]and swear by his name.

21 [h]He *is* thy praise, and he *is* thy God, [i]that hath done for thee these great and terrible things, which thine eyes have seen.

22 Thy fathers went down into Egypt [j]with threescore and ten persons; and now the LORD thy God hath made thee [k]as the stars of heaven for multitude.

Love and obey God

11 THEREFORE THOU shalt [l]love the LORD thy God, and [m]keep his charge, and his statutes, and his judgments, and his commandments, always.

2 And know ye this day: for *I speak* not with your children which have not known, and which have not seen [n]the chastisement of the LORD your God, [o]his greatness, his mighty hand, and his stretched out arm,

3 [p]And his miracles, and his acts, which he did in the midst of Egypt unto Pharaoh the king of Egypt, and unto all his land;

4 And what he did unto the army of Egypt, unto their horses, and to their chariots; [q]how he made the water of the Red sea to overflow them as they pursued after you, and *how* the LORD hath destroyed them unto this day;

5 And what he did unto you in the wilderness, until ye came into this place;

6 And [r]what he did unto Dathan and Abiram, the sons of Eliab, the son of Reuben: how the earth opened her mouth, and swallowed them up, and their households, and their tents, and all the [n]substance that [o]*was* in their possession, in the midst of all Israel:

7 But [s]your eyes have seen all the great acts of the LORD which he did.

8 Therefore shall ye keep all the commandments which I command you this day, that ye may [t]be strong, and go in and possess the land, whither ye go to possess it;

9 And [u]that ye may prolong *your* days in the land, [v]which the LORD sware unto your fathers to give unto them and to their seed, [w]a land that floweth with milk and honey.

10 ¶ For the land, whither thou goest in to possess it, *is* not as the land of Egypt, from whence ye came out, where thou sowedst thy seed, and wateredst *it* with thy foot, as a garden of herbs:

11 [x]But the land, whither ye go to possess it, *is* a land of hills and valleys, *and* drinketh water of the rain of heaven:

12 A land which the LORD thy God [p]careth for: [y]the eyes of the LORD thy God *are* always upon it, from the beginning of the year even unto the end of the year.

13 ¶ And it shall come to pass, if ye shall hearken [z]diligently unto my commandments which I command you this day, [a]to love the LORD your God, and to serve him with all your heart and with all your soul,

14 That [b]I will give *you* the rain of your land in his due season, [c]the first rain and the latter rain, that thou mayest gather in thy corn, and thy wine, and thine oil.

15 [d]And I will [q]send grass in thy

10:12 [p]ch. 6:13 [q]ch. 5:33 [r]ch. 6:5 Mat. 22:37 **10:13** [s]ch. 6:24 **10:14** [t]1 Ki. 8:27 [u]Ex. 19:5 **10:15** [v]ch. 4:37 **10:16** [w]ch. 30:6 Jer. 4:4 Rom. 2:28,29 Col. 2:11 [x]ch. 9:6,13 **10:17** [y]Dan. 2:47 [z]Rev. 19:16 [a]ch. 7:21 [b]Acts 10:34 Rom. 2:11 Eph. 6:9 1 Pet. 1:17 **10:18** [c]Ps. 68:5 **10:19** [d]Lev. 19:33,34 **10:20** [e]Mat. 4:10 [f]ch. 11:22 [g]Ps. 63:11 **10:21** [h]Ex. 15:2 Jer. 17:14 [i]Ps. 106:21,22 **10:22** [j]Gen. 46:27 Acts 7:14 [k]Gen. 15:5 **11:1** [l]ch. 10:12 [m]Zech. 3:7 **11:2** [n]ch. 8:5 [o]ch. 5:24 **11:3** [p]Ps. 78:12 & 135:9 **11:4** [q]Ps. 106:11 **11:6** [r]Num. 16:1,31 **11:7** [s]ch. 5:3 & 7:19 **11:8** [t]Josh. 1:6,7 **11:9** [u]ch. 4:40 Prov. 10:27 [v]ch. 9:5 [w]Ex. 3:8 **11:11** [x]ch. 8:7 **11:12** [y]1 Ki. 9:3 **11:13** [z]ver. 22 ch. 6:17 [a]ch. 10:12 **11:14** [b]Lev. 26:4 ch. 28:12 [c]Joel 2:23 Jas. 5:7 **11:15** [d]Ps. 104:14

[n] Or, *living substance which followed them*
[o] Heb. *was at their feet* [p] Heb. *seeketh*
[q] Heb. *give*

fields for thy cattle, that thou mayest [e]eat and be full.

16 Take heed to yourselves, [f]that your heart be not deceived, and ye turn aside, and [g]serve other gods, and worship them;

17 And *then* [h]the LORD's wrath be kindled against you, and he [i]shut up the heaven, that there be no rain, and that the land yield not her fruit; and *lest* [j]ye perish quickly from off the good land which the LORD giveth you.

18 ¶ Therefore [k]shall ye lay up these my words in your heart and in your soul, and [l]bind them for a sign upon your hand, that they may be as frontlets between your eyes.

19 [m]And ye shall teach them your children, speaking of them when thou sittest in thine house, and when thou walkest by the way, when thou liest down, and when thou risest up.

20 [n]And thou shalt write them upon the door posts of thine house, and upon thy gates:

21 That [o]your days may be multiplied, and the days of your children, in the land which the LORD sware unto your fathers to give them, [p]as the days of heaven upon the earth.

22 ¶ For if [q]ye shall diligently keep all these commandments which I command you, to do them, to love the LORD your God, to walk in all his ways, and [r]to cleave unto him;

23 Then will the LORD [s]drive out all these nations from before you, and ye shall [t]possess greater nations and mightier than yourselves.

24 [u]Every place whereon the soles of your feet shall tread shall be yours: [v]from the wilderness and Lebanon, from the river, the river Euphrates, even unto the uttermost sea shall your coast be.

25 [w]There shall no man be able to

11:15 [e]ch. 6:11; Joel 2:19
11:16 [f]ch. 29:18; Job 31:27; [g]ch. 8:19
11:17 [h]ch. 6:15; [i]1 Ki. 8:35; 2 Chr. 6:26; [j]ch. 4:26 & 8:19,20; Josh. 23:13,15,16
11:18 [k]ch. 6:6 & 32:46; [l]ch. 6:8
11:19 [m]ch. 4:9,10 & 6:7
11:20 [n]ch. 6:9
11:21 [o]ch. 4:40; Prov. 3:2 & 4:10; [p]Ps. 72:5 & 89:29
11:22 [q]ver. 13; ch. 6:17; [r]ch. 10:20 & 30:20
11:23 [s]ch. 4:38; [t]ch. 9:1
11:24 [u]Josh. 1:3 & 14:9; [v]Gen. 15:18; Ex. 23:31; Num. 34:3
11:25 [w]ch. 7:24; [x]ch. 2:25; [y]Ex. 23:27
11:26 [z]ch. 30:1,15,19
11:27 [a]ch. 28:2
11:28 [b]ch. 28:15
11:29 [c]ch. 27:12,13; Josh. 8:33
11:30 [d]Gen. 12:6; Judg. 7:1
11:31 [e]ch. 9:1; Josh. 1:11
11:32 [f]ch. 5:32 & 12:32
12:1 [g]ch. 6:1; [h]ch. 4:10; 1 Ki. 8:40

stand before you: *for* the LORD your God shall [x]lay the fear of you and the dread of you upon all the land that ye shall tread upon, [y]as he hath said unto you.

26 ¶ [z]Behold, I set before you this day a blessing and a curse;

27 [a]A blessing, if ye obey the commandments of the LORD your God, which I command you this day:

28 And a [b]curse, if ye will not obey the commandments of the LORD your God, but turn aside out of the way which I command you this day, to go after other gods, which ye have not known.

Josh 1:7-

29 And it shall come to pass, when the LORD thy God hath brought thee in unto the land whither thou goest to possess it, that thou shalt put [c]the blessing upon mount Gerizim, and the curse upon mount Ebal.

30 *Are* they not on the other side Jordan, by the way where the sun goeth down, in the land of the Canaanites, which dwell in the champaign over against Gilgal, [d]beside the plains of Moreh?

31 [e]For ye shall pass over Jordan to go in to possess the land which the LORD your God giveth you, and ye shall possess it, and dwell therein.

32 And ye shall observe [f]to do all the statutes and judgments which I set before you this day.

Sacrifice at one altar only

12 THESE [g]*ARE* the statutes and judgments, which ye shall observe to do in the land, which the LORD God of thy fathers giveth thee to possess it, [h]all the days that ye live upon the earth.

2 [i]Ye shall utterly destroy all the

12:2 [i]Ex. 34:13; ch. 7:5

11:19 TEACH THEM YOUR CHILDREN. See 6:7, note.

11:26 A BLESSING AND A CURSE. God set before His people the choice of receiving a blessing or a curse. If they obeyed God's word and remained separated from the sin and evil of the surrounding nations, then God's blessing would come upon them and overtake them (see 28:1–14). On the other hand, if they conformed to the ways of the ungodly, God's curse would come upon them and overtake them (see 28:15–68). (1) Unfortunately, for the most part Israel did not take God's warning seriously. All too often they adopted the ways of the unbelievers and thus fell under His curse. (2) God places the same choice (i.e., "a blessing and a curse") before N.T. believers. If we abhor sin, follow Christ, and seek to serve Him continually, then His blessing and power will be ours. If we depart from God and His righteous ways, we will lose God's presence, help, and covenant protection.

12:2 DESTROY ALL THE PLACES. The Israelites were ordered to destroy all the places of worship of the pagan nations and to worship God only at the divinely appointed place and in the manner He commanded (vv. 2–15). To leave the altars of pagan worship in place would tempt the Israelites into beginning pagan worship practices.

places, wherein the nations which ye shall [r]possess served their gods, [j]upon the high mountains, and upon the hills, and under every green tree:

3 And [k]ye shall [s]overthrow their altars, and break their pillars, and burn their groves with fire; and ye shall hew down the graven images of their gods, and destroy the names of them out of that place.

4 [l]Ye shall not do so unto the LORD your God.

5 But unto the place which the LORD your God shall [m]choose out of all your tribes to put his name there, *even* unto his habitation shall ye seek, and thither thou shalt come:

6 And [n]thither ye shall bring your burnt offerings, and your sacrifices, and your [o]tithes, and heave offerings of your hand, and your vows, and your freewill offerings, and the firstlings of your herds and of your flocks:

7 And [p]there ye shall eat before the LORD your God, and [q]ye shall rejoice in all that ye put your hand unto, ye and your households, wherein the LORD thy God hath blessed thee.

8 Ye shall not do after all *the things* that we do here this day, [r]every man whatsoever *is* right in his own eyes.

9 For ye are not as yet come to the rest and to the inheritance, which the LORD your God giveth you.

10 But *when* [s]ye go over Jordan, and dwell in the land which the LORD your God giveth you to inherit, and *when* he giveth you rest from all your enemies round about, so that ye dwell in safety;

11 Then there shall be [t]a place which the LORD your God shall choose to cause his name to dwell there; thither shall ye bring all that I command you; your burnt offerings, and your sacrifices, your tithes, and the heave offering of your hand, and all [t]your choice vows which ye vow unto the LORD:

12 And [u]ye shall rejoice before the LORD your God, ye, and your sons, and your daughters, and your menservants, and your maidservants, and the

12:2 [j]2 Ki. 16:4 & 17:10,11 Jer. 3:6
12:3 [k]Num. 33:52 Judg. 2:2
12:4 [l]ver. 31
12:5 [m]ver. 11 ch. 26:2 Josh. 9:27 1 Ki. 8:29 2 Chr. 7:12
12:6 [n]Lev. 17:3,4 [o]ver. 17 ch. 14:22,23 & 15:19,20
12:7 [p]ch. 14:26 [q]ver. 12,18 Lev. 23:40 ch. 16:11,14,15
12:8 [r]Judg. 17:6 & 21:25
12:10 [s]ch. 11:31
12:11 [t]ver. 5,14,18,21, 26 & ch. 14:23 & 15:20 & 16:2 Josh. 18:1 1 Ki. 8:29
12:12 [u]ver. 7 [v]ch. 10:9 & 14:29
12:13 [w]Lev. 17:4
12:14 [x]ver. 11
12:15 [y]ver. 21 [z]ver. 22 [a]ch. 14:5 & 15:22
12:16 [b]Gen. 9:4 Lev. 7:26 & 17:10 ch. 15:23 & ver. 23
12:18 [c]ver. 11,12 ch. 14:23
12:19 [d]ch. 14:27
12:20 [e]Gen. 15:18 & 28:14 Ex. 34:24 ch. 11:24 & 19:8

Levite that *is* within your gates; forasmuch as [v]he hath no part nor inheritance with you.

13 [w]Take heed to thyself that thou offer not thy burnt offerings in every place that thou seest:

14 [x]But in the place which the LORD shall choose in one of thy tribes, there thou shalt offer thy burnt offerings, and there thou shalt do all that I command thee.

15 Notwithstanding [y]thou mayest kill and eat flesh in all thy gates, whatsoever thy soul lusteth after, according to the blessing of the LORD thy God which he hath given thee: [z]the unclean and the clean may eat thereof, [a]as of the roebuck, and as of the hart.

16 [b]Only ye shall not eat the blood; ye shall pour it upon the earth as water.

17 ¶ Thou mayest not eat within thy gates the tithe of thy corn, or of thy wine, or of thy oil, or the firstlings of thy herds or of thy flock, nor any of thy vows which thou vowest, nor thy freewill offerings, or heave offering of thine hand:

18 [c]But thou must eat them before the LORD thy God in the place which the LORD thy God shall choose, thou, and thy son, and thy daughter, and thy manservant, and thy maidservant, and the Levite that *is* within thy gates: and thou shalt rejoice before the LORD thy God in all that thou puttest thine hands unto.

19 [d]Take heed to thyself that thou forsake not the Levite [u]as long as thou livest upon the earth.

20 ¶ When the LORD thy God shall enlarge thy border, [e]as he hath promised thee, and thou shalt say, I will eat flesh, because thy soul longeth to eat flesh; thou mayest eat flesh, whatsoever thy soul lusteth after.

21 If the place which the LORD thy God hath chosen to put his name there be too far from thee, then thou shalt kill of thy herd and of thy flock, which

[r] Or, *inherit* [s] Heb. *break down* [t] Heb. *the choice of your vows* [u] Heb. *all thy days*

12:5 THE PLACE . . . GOD SHALL CHOOSE. The Israelites were not only to worship the Lord in their homes, but also at a particular place chosen by God Himself (eventually the temple in Jerusalem). Believers still need a common place where they can meet with other believers to call upon God in faith and worship. It must be a place where God has "put his name" (v. 5), i.e., a place where His word is truly believed, His Spirit is present, and holiness is characteristic of the people's lives (cf. 1 Cor. 1:2).

the LORD hath given thee, as I have
commanded thee, and thou shalt eat in
thy gates whatsoever thy soul lusteth
after.
22 [f]Even as the roebuck and the
hart is eaten, so thou shalt eat them:
the unclean and the clean shall eat *of*
them alike.
23 [g]Only [v]be sure that thou eat
not the blood: [h]for the blood *is* the life;
and thou mayest not eat the life with
the flesh.
24 Thou shalt not eat it; thou shalt
pour it upon the earth as water.
25 Thou shalt not eat it; [i]that it
may go well with thee, and with thy
children after thee, [j]when thou shalt
do *that which is* right in the sight of the
LORD.
26 Only thy [k]holy things which
thou hast, and [l]thy vows, thou shalt
take, and go unto the place which the
LORD shall choose:
27 And [m]thou shalt offer thy burnt
offerings, the flesh and the blood, upon
the altar of the LORD thy God: and the
blood of thy sacrifices shall be poured
out upon the altar of the LORD thy God,
and thou shalt eat the flesh.
28 Observe and hear all these
words which I command thee, [n]that it
may go well with thee, and with thy
children after thee for ever, when thou
doest *that which is* good and right in the
sight of the LORD thy God.
29 ¶ When [o]the LORD thy God shall
cut off the nations from before thee,
whither thou goest to possess them,
and thou [w]succeedest them, and
dwellest in their land;
30 Take heed to thyself that thou be
not snared [x]by following them, after
that they be destroyed from before
thee; and that thou inquire not after
their gods, saying, How did these na-
tions serve their gods? even so will I do
likewise.
31 [p]Thou shalt not do so unto the
LORD thy God: for every [y]abomination
to the LORD, which he hateth, have they
done unto their gods; for [q]even their
sons and their daughters they have
burnt in the fire to their gods.
32 What thing soever I command
you, observe to do it: [r]thou shalt not
add thereto, nor diminish from it.

Warning against idolatry

13 IF THERE arise among you a
prophet, or a [s]dreamer of
dreams, [t]and giveth thee a sign or a
wonder,
2 And [u]the sign or the wonder
come to pass, whereof he spake unto
thee, saying, Let us go after other
gods, which thou hast not known, and
let us serve them;
3 Thou shalt not hearken unto the
words of that prophet, or that dreamer
of dreams: for the LORD your God
[v]proveth you, to know whether ye
love the LORD your God with all your
heart and with all your soul.
4 Ye shall [w]walk after the LORD
your God, and fear him, and keep his
commandments, and obey his voice,
and ye shall serve him, and [x]cleave
unto him.
5 And [y]that prophet, or that
dreamer of dreams, shall be put to
death; because he hath [z]spoken to

12:22 [f]ver. 15
12:23 [g]ver. 16 [h]Gen. 9:4 Lev. 17:11,14
12:25 [i]ch. 4:40 Is. 3:10 [j]Ex. 15:26 ch. 13:18 1 Ki. 11:38
12:26 [k]Num. 5:9,10 [l]1 Sam. 1:21,22, 24
12:27 [m]Lev. 1:5,9,13 & 17:11
12:28 [n]ver. 25
12:29 [o]Ex. 23:23 ch. 19:1 Josh. 23:4
12:31 [p]Lev. 18:3,26,30 [q]ch. 18:10 Jer. 32:35 Ezek. 23:37
12:32 [r]ch. 4:2 Josh. 1:7 Rev. 22:18
13:1 [s]Zech. 10:2 [t]Mat. 24:24 2 Thes. 2:9
13:2 [u]See ch. 18:22 Mat. 7:22
13:3 [v]ch. 8:2 See Mat. 24:24 2 Thes. 2:11
13:4 [w]2 Ki. 23:3 2 Chr. 34:31 [x]ch. 30:20
13:5 [y]Jer. 14:15 Zech. 13:3

[v] Heb. *be strong* [w] Heb. *inheritest,* or, *possessest them* [x] Heb. *after them* [y] Heb. *abomination of the* [z] Heb. *spoken revolt against the LORD*

13:3 NOT HEARKEN UNTO ... THAT PROPHET. Fundamental to the believers' relationship to the Lord is their faithfulness to God and His revealed word (8:3). Vv. 1–5 teach that the temptation to compromise our allegiance to God will come at times from those who appear to be spiritual. Several implications follow for our lives as believers. (1) God will at times test the sincerity of our love and commitment to Him and His word (cf. 8:2).

(2) God sometimes tests us by allowing to arise among His people those who claim to speak for God and who provide "a sign or a wonder" (vv. 1–2). Such individuals may speak under great anointing, prophesy the future correctly, and perform miracles, signs, and wonders. At the same time, however, they may preach a gospel that is contrary to Biblical revelation, adding to God's Word or taking away from it (cf. 4:2; 12:32). If we follow these false leaders, we will be led away from absolute loyalty to Him and His inspired Word (v. 5).

(3) The N.T. also warns that false prophets and false teachers will greatly distort the gospel of Christ in the last days of this age. Believers must resolve to remain faithful to God's written revelation as found in the Bible. The validity of an individual's ministry and teaching must not be evaluated solely on his gift of preaching, powers of prophecy, performance of miracles, or numbers of conversions. Such criteria will become increasingly undependable as the end-time approaches. The standard for truth must always be the infallible Word of God (see articles on FALSE TEACHERS, p. 1508, and THE INSPIRATION AND AUTHORITY OF SCRIPTURE, p. 1924).

turn *you* away from the LORD your God,
which brought you out of the land of
Egypt, and redeemed you out of the
house of bondage, to thrust thee out of
the way which the LORD thy God com-
manded thee to walk in. [z]So shalt
thou put the evil away from the midst
of thee.
6 ¶ [a]If thy brother, the son of thy
mother, or thy son, or thy daughter, or
[b]the wife of thy bosom, or thy friend,
[c]which *is* as thine own soul, entice
thee secretly, saying, Let us go and
serve other gods, which thou hast not
known, thou, nor thy fathers;
7 *Namely,* of the gods of the people
which *are* round about you, nigh unto
thee, or far off from thee, from the *one*
end of the earth even unto the *other* end
of the earth;
8 Thou shalt [d]not consent unto
him, nor hearken unto him; neither
shall thine eye pity him, neither shalt
thou spare, neither shalt thou conceal
him:
9 But [e]thou shalt surely kill him;
[f]thine hand shall be first upon him to
put him to death, and afterwards the
hand of all the people.
10 And thou shalt stone him with
stones, that he die; because he hath
sought to thrust thee away from the
LORD thy God, which brought thee out
of the land of Egypt, from the house of
[a]bondage.
11 And [g]all Israel shall hear, and
fear, and shall do no more any such
wickedness as this is among you.
12 ¶ [h]If thou shalt hear *say* in one
of thy cities, which the LORD thy God
hath given thee to dwell there, saying,
13 *Certain* men, [b]the children of
Belial, [i]are gone out from among you,
and have [j]withdrawn the inhabitants
of their city, saying, [k]Let us go and
serve other gods, which ye have not
known;
14 Then shalt thou inquire, and
make search, and ask diligently; and,
behold, *if it be* truth, *and* the thing cer-
tain, *that* such abomination is wrought
among you;
15 Thou shalt surely smite the in-
habitants of that city with the edge of
the sword, [l]destroying it utterly, and
all that *is* therein, and the cattle there-
of, with the edge of the sword.
16 And thou shalt gather all the
spoil of it into the midst of the street
thereof, and shalt [m]burn with fire the
city, and all the spoil thereof every
whit, for the LORD thy God: and it shall
be [n]an heap for ever; it shall not be
built again.
17 And [o]there shall cleave nought
of the [c]cursed thing to thine hand:
that the LORD may [p]turn from the
fierceness of his anger, and show thee
mercy, and have compassion upon
thee, and multiply thee, [q]as he hath
sworn unto thy fathers;
18 When thou shalt hearken to the
voice of the LORD thy God, [r]to keep all
his commandments which I command
thee this day, to do *that which is* right
in the eyes of the LORD thy God.
14 YE *ARE* [s]the children of the
LORD your God: [t]ye shall not
cut yourselves, nor make any baldness
between your eyes for the dead.
2 [u]For thou *art* an holy people unto
the LORD thy God, and the LORD hath
chosen thee to be a peculiar people
unto himself, above all the nations that
are upon the earth.

Clean and unclean animals

14:3–20pp — Lev. 11:1–23

3 ¶ [v]Thou shalt not eat any abomi-
nable thing.
4 [w]These *are* the beasts which ye
shall eat: the ox, the sheep, and the
goat,
5 The hart, and the roebuck, and
the fallow deer, and the wild goat,
and the [d,e]pygarg, and the wild ox, and
the chamois.
6 And every beast that parteth the
hoof, and cleaveth the cleft into two
claws, *and* cheweth the cud among the
beasts, that ye shall eat.
7 Nevertheless these ye shall not
eat of them that chew the cud, or of
them that divide the cloven hoof; *as* the
camel, and the hare, and the coney: for
they chew the cud, but divide not the
hoof; *therefore* they *are* unclean unto
you.
8 And the swine, because it divideth
the hoof, yet cheweth not the cud, it *is*
unclean unto you: ye shall not eat of
their flesh, [x]nor touch their dead car-
case.
9 ¶ [y]These ye shall eat of all that
are in the waters: all that have fins and
scales shall ye eat:
10 And whatsoever hath not fins

13:5 [z]ch. 17:7 1 Cor. 5:13 **13:6** [a]ch. 17:2 [b]See Gen. 16:5 ch. 28:54 Prov. 5:20 [c]1 Sam. 18:1,3 & 20:17 **13:8** [d]Prov. 1:10 **13:9** [e]ch. 17:5 [f]ch. 17:7 Acts 7:58 **13:11** [g]ch. 19:20 **13:12** [h]Judg. 20:1,2 **13:13** [i]1 John 2:19 Jude 19 [j]2 Ki. 17:21 [k]ver. 2,6 **13:15** [l]Lev. 27:28 Josh. 6:17,21 **13:16** [m]Josh. 6:24 [n]Josh. 8:28 Jer. 49:2 **13:17** [o]Josh. 6:18 [p]Josh. 7:26 [q]Gen. 22:17 & 26:4,24 & 28:14 **13:18** [r]ch. 12:25,28,32 **14:1** [s]Rom. 8:16 & 9:8,26 Gal. 3:26 [t]Lev. 19:28 & 21:5 Jer. 16:6 & 41:5 & 47:5 1 Thes. 4:13 **14:2** [u]Lev. 20:26 ch. 7:6 & 26:18,19 **14:3** [v]Ezek. 4:14 Acts 10:13,14 **14:4** [w]Lev. 11:2 **14:8** [x]Lev. 11:26,27 **14:9** [y]Lev. 11:9

[a] Heb. *bondmen* [b] Or, *naughty men* [c] Or, *devoted* [d] Or, *bison* [e] Heb. *dishon*

and scales ye may not eat; it *is* unclean
unto you.
11 ¶ *Of* all clean birds ye shall eat.
12 [z]But these *are they* of which ye
shall not eat: the eagle, and the ossi-
frage, and the ospray,
13 And the glede, and the kite, and
the vulture after his kind,
14 And every raven after his kind,
15 And the owl, and the night hawk,
and the cuckoo, and the hawk after his
kind,
16 The little owl, and the great owl,
and the swan,
17 And the pelican, and the gier ea-
gle, and the cormorant,
18 And the stork, and the heron af-
ter her kind, and the lapwing, and the
bat.
19 And [a]every creeping thing that
flieth *is* unclean unto you: [b]they shall
not be eaten.
20 *But of* all clean fowls ye may eat.
21 ¶ [c]Ye shall not eat *of* any thing
that dieth of itself: thou shalt give it
unto the stranger that *is* in thy gates,
that he may eat it; or thou mayest sell
it unto an alien: [d]for thou *art* an holy
people unto the LORD thy God. [e]Thou
shalt not seethe a kid in his mother's
milk.

Laws about tithes

22 [f]Thou shalt truly tithe all the
increase of thy seed, that the field
bringeth forth year by year.
23 [g]And thou shalt eat before the
LORD thy God, in the place which he
shall choose to place his name there,
the tithe of thy corn, of thy wine, and
of thine oil, and [h]the firstlings of thy
herds and of thy flocks; that thou may-
est learn to fear the LORD thy God al-
ways.
24 And if the way be too long for
thee, so that thou art not able to carry
it; *or* [i]if the place be too far from thee,
which the LORD thy God shall choose to
set his name there, when the LORD thy
God hath blessed thee:
25 Then shalt thou turn *it* into mon-
ey, and bind up the money in thine
hand, and shalt go unto the place
which the LORD thy God shall choose:
26 And thou shalt bestow that mon-
ey for whatsoever thy soul lusteth af-
ter, for oxen, or for sheep, or for wine,
or for strong drink, or for whatsoever
thy soul [f]desireth: [j]and thou shalt
eat there before the LORD thy God, and
thou shalt rejoice, thou, and thine
household,
27 And [k]the Levite that *is* within
thy gates; thou shalt not forsake him;
for [l]he hath no part nor inheritance
with thee.
28 ¶ [m]At the end of three years
thou shalt bring forth all the tithe of
thine increase the same year, and shalt
lay *it* up within thy gates:
29 [n]And the Levite, (because [o]he
hath no part nor inheritance with

14:12 [z]Lev. 11:13
14:19 [a]Lev. 11:20 [b]See Lev. 11:21
14:21 [c]Lev. 17:15 & 22:8 Ezek. 4:14 [d]ver. 2 [e]Ex. 23:19 & 34:26
14:22 [f]Lev. 27:30 ch. 12:6,17 Neh. 10:37
14:23 [g]ch. 12:5-7,17,18 [h]ch. 15:19,20
14:24 [i]ch. 12:21
14:26 [j]ch. 12:7,18 & 26:11
14:27 [k]ch. 12:12,18,19 [l]Num. 18:20 ch. 18:1,2
14:28 [m]ch. 26:12 Amos 4:4
14:29 [n]ch. 26:12 [o]ver. 27 ch. 12:12

[f]Heb. *asketh of thee*

14:26 STRONG DRINK ... THOU, AND THINE HOUSEHOLD. This verse applies to special occasions for worship and thanksgiving to God by the entire household, including men, women, youth, and little children. Because of this, it is highly unreasonable to suggest that God is here instructing His people and their families to consume intoxicating and addictive types of "wine" (*yayin*) and "strong drink" (*shekar*; see article on WINE IN THE OLD TESTAMENT, p. 220, for the usual meaning of these two words). An alternative translation for *shekar* is "sweet drink," which is the preferred meaning here. Any attempt to arrive at a correct interpretation of this verse must take into account the following observations.

(1) The purpose of the worship service was "that thou mayest learn to fear the LORD thy God always" (v. 23). In order to worship God properly and to learn to fear Him, we need to be totally sober (see Eph. 5:18, note; 1 Thes. 5:6, note; see article on THE FEAR OF THE LORD, p. 282). Note that God requires total abstinence from intoxicating beverages in order to distinguish between the holy and the profane, to teach rightly His commandments (Lev. 10:9), and to insure we do not forget God's law and do wrong (see Prov. 31:4–5, notes).

(2) The Levite priests were to be present at the worship service (vv. 27–29). God commanded these priests not to drink from intoxicating types of "wine nor strong drink" (on penalty of death) during the time of their priestly ministry unto Him (Lev. 10:9). It would be totally contrary to God's holy character to commend the free use of intoxicants by the worshipers while in the company of the priests.

(3) The nature of the festival was a harvest feast, during which time fresh harvest products would be used. This suggests that new fresh juice is in view here (see v. 23).

(4) Also the modern discovery of the terrible deformative consequences of alcohol on unborn children must be considered before alleging that an all-knowing God blessed, sanctioned, or commanded Israelite fathers, mothers, and small children to "rejoice" before Him while consuming intoxicating and addictive beverages (see Prov. 23:31, note; see article on WINE IN NEW TESTAMENT TIMES (2), p. 1594).

thee,) and the stranger, and the fatherless, and the widow, which *are* within thy gates, shall come, and shall eat and be satisfied; that [p]the LORD thy God may bless thee in all the work of thine hand which thou doest.

The sabbath years of release

15:1–11Ref — Lev. 25:8–38

15 AT THE end of [q]*every* seven years thou shalt make a release.

2 And this *is* the manner of the release: Every [g]creditor that lendeth *aught* unto his neighbour shall release *it;* he shall not exact *it* of his neighbour, or of his brother; because it is called the LORD's release.

3 [r]Of a foreigner thou mayest exact *it again:* but *that* which is thine with thy brother thine hand shall release;

4 [h]Save when there shall be no poor among you; [s]for the LORD shall greatly bless thee in the land which the LORD thy God giveth thee *for* an inheritance to possess it:

5 Only [t]if thou carefully hearken unto the voice of the LORD thy God, to observe to do all these commandments which I command thee this day.

6 For the LORD thy God blesseth thee, as he promised thee: and [u]thou shalt lend unto many nations, but thou shalt not borrow; and [v]thou shalt reign over many nations, but they shall not reign over thee.

7 ¶ If there be among you a poor man of one of thy brethren within any of thy gates in thy land which the LORD thy God giveth thee, [w]thou shalt not harden thine heart, nor shut thine hand from thy poor brother:

8 [x]But thou shalt open thine hand wide unto him, and shalt surely lend him sufficient for his need, *in that* which he wanteth.

9 Beware that there be not a [i]thought in thy [j]wicked heart, saying, The seventh year, the year of release, is at hand; and thine [y]eye be evil against thy poor brother, and thou givest him nought; and [z]he cry unto the LORD against thee, and [a]it be sin unto thee.

10 Thou shalt surely give him, and [b]thine heart shall not be grieved when thou givest unto him: because that [c]for this thing the LORD thy God shall bless thee in all thy works, and in all that thou puttest thine hand unto.

11 For [d]the poor shall never cease out of the land: therefore I command thee, saying, Thou shalt open thine hand wide unto thy brother, to thy poor, and to thy needy, in thy land.

Hebrew slaves to be freed

15:12–18pp — Ex. 21:2–6
15:12–18Ref — Lev. 25:38–55

12 ¶ *And* [e]if thy brother, an Hebrew man, or an Hebrew woman, be sold unto thee, and serve thee six years; then in the seventh year thou shalt let him go free from thee.

13 And when thou sendest him out free from thee, thou shalt not let him go away empty:

14 Thou shalt furnish him liberally out of thy flock, and out of thy floor, and out of thy winepress: *of that* wherewith the LORD thy God hath [f]blessed thee thou shalt give unto him.

15 And [g]thou shalt remember that thou wast a bondman in the land of Egypt, and the LORD thy God redeemed thee: therefore I command thee this thing today.

16 And it shall be, [h]if he say unto thee, I will not go away from thee; because he loveth thee and thine house, because he is well with thee;

17 Then thou shalt take an awl, and thrust *it* through his ear unto the door,

14:29 [p]ch. 15:10 See Mal. 3:10
15:1 [q]Ex. 21:2 & 23:10,11 Lev. 25:2,4 ch. 31:10 Jer. 34:14
15:3 [r]See ch. 23:20
15:4 [s]ch. 28:8
15:5 [t]ch. 28:1
15:6 [u]ch. 28:12,44 [v]ch. 28:13 Prov. 22:7
15:7 [w]1 John 3:17
15:8 [x]Lev. 25:35 Mat. 5:42 Luke 6:34,35
15:9 [y]ch. 28:54,56 Mat. 20:15 [z]ch. 24:15 [a]Mat. 25:41,42
15:10 [b]2 Cor. 9:5,7 [c]ch. 14:29 & 24:19
15:11 [d]Mat. 26:11 Mark 14:7 John 12:8
15:12 [e]Ex. 21:2 Lev. 25:39 Jer. 34:14
15:14 [f]Prov. 10:22
15:15 [g]ch. 5:15 & 16:12
15:16 [h]Ex. 21:5,6

[g] Heb. *master of the lending of his hand* [h] Or, *To the end that there be no poor among you* [i] Heb. *word* [j] Heb. *Belial*

15:7–11 A POOR MAN. Obedience to God's law was expected to grow out of a sincere desire to obey God and to help those in need (cf. 24:19–21; Lev. 19:10). (1) God cares about our attitude and desire to help the poor and the unfortunate. We must use our material possessions to help those who have real needs (see article on THE CARE OF THE POOR AND NEEDY, p. 1312). The spirit of greed and selfishness that ignores the needs of others deprives us of God's blessing (vv. 9–10). (2) The N.T. emphasizes the need for pity, sympathy, and kindness toward those who have suffered setbacks or experienced unfortunate circumstances that brought them into poverty or want (Mat. 25:31–36; Gal. 6:2,10).

15:13 NOT . . . GO AWAY EMPTY. The Israelites were not allowed to send their slaves away without adequate provision (cf. v. 12). Love for others (cf. Lev. 19:18) demanded that sufficient food and supplies be given to them so that they could get by until they began to earn a living. Similarly, the principle of love and justice under the new covenant requires that we treat our employees with compassion, fairness, and justice.

and he shall be thy servant for ever.
And also unto thy maidservant thou
shalt do likewise.
18 It shall not seem hard unto thee,
when thou sendest him away free from
thee; for he hath been worth [i]a double
hired servant *to thee,* in serving thee
six years: and the LORD thy God shall
bless thee in all that thou doest.

Offering the firstlings

19 ¶ [j]All the firstling males that
come of thy herd and of thy flock thou
shalt sanctify unto the LORD thy God:
thou shalt do no work with the firstling
of thy bullock, nor shear the firstling of
thy sheep.
20 [k]Thou shalt eat *it* before the
LORD thy God year by year in the place
which the LORD shall choose, thou and
thy household.
21 [l]And if there be *any* blemish
therein, *as if it be* lame, or blind, *or have*
any ill blemish, thou shalt not sacrifice
it unto the LORD thy God.
22 Thou shalt eat it within thy
gates: [m]the unclean and the clean *per-
son shall eat it* alike, as the roebuck,
and as the hart.
23 [n]Only thou shalt not eat the
blood thereof; thou shalt pour it upon
the ground as water.

The Passover

*16:1–8pp — Ex. 12:14–20; Lev. 23:4–8;
Num. 28:16–25*

16 OBSERVE THE [o]month of
Abib, and keep the passover
unto the LORD thy God: for [p]in the
month of Abib the LORD thy God
brought thee forth out of Egypt [q]by
night.
2 Thou shalt therefore sacrifice the
passover unto the LORD thy God, of the
flock and [r]the herd, in the [s]place
which the LORD shall choose to place
his name there.
3 [t]Thou shalt eat no leavened
bread with it; seven days shalt thou eat
unleavened bread therewith, *even* the
bread of affliction; for thou camest
forth out of the land of Egypt in haste:
that thou mayest remember the day
when thou camest forth out of the land
of Egypt all the days of thy life.
4 [u]And there shall be no leavened
bread seen with thee in all thy coast
seven days; [v]neither shall there *any
thing* of the flesh, which thou sac-
rificedst the first day at even, remain
all night until the morning.
5 Thou mayest not [k]sacrifice the
passover within any of thy gates,
which the LORD thy God giveth thee:
6 But at the place which the LORD
thy God shall choose to place his name
in, there thou shalt sacrifice the pass-
over [w]at even, at the going down of the
sun, at the season that thou camest
forth out of Egypt.
7 And thou shalt [x]roast and eat *it*
[y]in the place which the LORD thy God
shall choose: and thou shalt turn in the
morning, and go unto thy tents.
8 Six days thou shalt eat unleav-
ened bread: and [z]on the seventh day
shall be a [l]solemn assembly to the
LORD thy God: thou shalt do no work
therein.

Feasts of weeks and tabernacles

16:9–12pp — Lev. 23:15–22; Num. 28:26–31

9 ¶ [a]Seven weeks shalt thou num-
ber unto thee: begin to number the sev-
en weeks from *such time as* thou begin-
nest *to put* the sickle to the corn.
10 And thou shalt keep the feast of
weeks unto the LORD thy God with [m]a
tribute of a freewill offering of thine
hand, which thou shalt give *unto the
LORD thy God,* [b]according as the LORD
thy God hath blessed thee:
11 And [c]thou shalt rejoice before
the LORD thy God, thou, and thy son,
and thy daughter, and thy manservant,
and thy maidservant, and the Levite
that *is* within thy gates, and the strang-
er, and the fatherless, and the widow,
that *are* among you, in the place which
the LORD thy God hath chosen to place
his name there.

16:13–17pp — Lev. 23:33–43; Num. 29:12–39

12 [d]And thou shalt remember that
thou wast a bondman in Egypt: and
thou shalt observe and do these stat-
utes.
13 ¶ [e]Thou shalt observe the feast
of tabernacles seven days, after that

15:18 [i]See Is. 16:14 & 21:16
15:19 [j]Ex. 13:2 & 34:19 Lev. 27:26 Num. 3:13
15:20 [k]ch. 12:5-7,17 & 14:23 & 16:11,14
15:21 [l]Lev. 22:20
15:22 [m]ch. 12:15,22
15:23 [n]ch. 12:16,23
16:1 [o]Ex. 12:2 [p]Ex. 13:4 [q]Ex. 12:29,42
16:2 [r]Num. 28:19 [s]ch. 12:5,26
16:3 [t]Ex. 12:15,19,39 & 13:3,6,7 & 34:18
16:4 [u]Ex. 13:7 [v]Ex. 12:10 & 34:25
16:6 [w]Ex. 12:6
16:7 [x]Ex. 12:8,9 2 Chr. 35:13 [y]2 Ki. 23:23 John 2:13 & 11:55
16:8 [z]Ex. 12:16 & 13:6 Lev. 23:8
16:9 [a]Ex. 23:16 & 34:22 Lev. 23:15 Acts 2:1
16:10 [b]1 Cor. 16:2
16:11 [c]ver. 14 ch. 12:7,12
16:12 [d]ch. 15:15
16:13 [e]Ex. 23:16 Lev. 23:34 Num. 29:12

[k] Or, *kill* [l] Heb. *restraint;* see Lev. 23:36 [m] Or, *sufficiency*

16:1 PASSOVER. See article on THE PASSOVER, p. 110.

16:10 FEAST OF WEEKS. For comments on the various holy days and feasts of Israel, see Lev. 23, notes.

thou hast gathered in thy [n]corn and thy wine:

14 And [f]thou shalt rejoice in thy feast, thou, and thy son, and thy daughter, and thy manservant, and thy maidservant, and the Levite, the stranger, and the fatherless, and the widow, that *are* within thy gates.

15 [g]Seven days shalt thou keep a solemn feast unto the LORD thy God in the place which the LORD shall choose: because the LORD thy God shall bless thee in all thine increase, and in all the works of thine hands, therefore thou shalt surely rejoice.

16 ¶ [h]Three times in a year shall all thy males appear before the LORD thy God in the place which he shall choose; in the feast of unleavened bread, and in the feast of weeks, and in the feast of tabernacles: and [i]they shall not appear before the LORD empty:

17 Every man *shall give* [o]as he is able, [j]according to the blessing of the LORD thy God which he hath given thee.

Appointment of judges and officers

18 ¶ [k]Judges and officers shalt thou make thee in all thy gates, which the LORD thy God giveth thee, throughout thy tribes: and they shall judge the people with just judgment.

19 [l]Thou shalt not wrest judgment; [m]thou shalt not respect persons, [n]neither take a gift: for a gift doth blind the eyes of the wise, and pervert the [p]words of the righteous.

20 [q]That which is altogether just shalt thou follow, that thou mayest [o]live, and inherit the land which the LORD thy God giveth thee.

21 ¶ [p]Thou shalt not plant thee a grove of any trees near unto the altar of the LORD thy God, which thou shalt make thee.

22 [q]Neither shalt thou set thee up *any* [r]image; which the LORD thy God hateth.

17 THOU [r]SHALT not sacrifice unto the LORD thy God *any* bullock, or [s]sheep, wherein is blemish, *or* any evilfavouredness: for that *is* an abomination unto the LORD thy God.

16:14 [f]Neh. 8:9
16:15 [g]Lev. 23:39
16:16 [h]Ex. 23:14 & 34:23 [i]Ex. 23:15 & 34:20
16:17 [j]ver. 10
16:18 [k]ch. 1:16 1 Chr. 23:4 2 Chr. 19:5
16:19 [l]Ex. 23:2,6 Lev. 19:15 [m]ch. 1:17 [n]Ex. 23:8 Eccl. 7:7
16:20 [o]Ezek. 18:5
16:21 [p]Ex. 34:13 1 Ki. 14:15 & 16:33 2 Ki. 17:16 & 21:3 2 Chr. 33:3
16:22 [q]Lev. 26:1
17:1 [r]ch. 15:21 Mal. 1:8,13
17:2 [s]ch. 13:6 [t]Josh. 7:11 & 23:16 Judg. 2:20 2 Ki. 18:12 Hos. 8:1
17:3 [u]ch. 4:19 Job 31:26 [v]Jer. 7:22,23 & 19:5 & 32:35
17:4 [w]ch. 13:12,14
17:5 [x]Lev. 24:14 ch. 13:10 Josh. 7:25
17:6 [y]Num. 35:30 ch. 19:15 Mat. 18:16 John 8:17 2 Cor. 13:1 1 Tim. 5:19 Heb. 10:28
17:7 [z]ch. 13:9 Acts 7:58 [a]ch. 13:5 & 19:19
17:8 [b]2 Chr. 19:10 Hag. 2:11 Mal. 2:7 [c]Ex. 21:13,20,22, 28 [d]ch. 12:5 & 19:17
17:9 [e]Jer. 18:18 [f]ch. 19:17 [g]Ezek. 44:24

The administration of justice

2 ¶ [s]If there be found among you, within any of thy gates which the LORD thy God giveth thee, man or woman, that hath wrought wickedness in the sight of the LORD thy God, [t]in transgressing his covenant,

3 And hath gone and served other gods, and worshipped them, either [u]the sun, or moon, or any of the host of heaven, [v]which I have not commanded;

4 [w]And it be told thee, and thou hast heard *of it,* and inquired diligently, and, behold, *it be* true, *and* the thing certain, *that* such abomination is wrought in Israel:

5 Then shalt thou bring forth that man or that woman, which have committed that wicked thing, unto thy gates, *even* that man or that woman, and [x]shalt stone them with stones, till they die.

6 [y]At the mouth of two witnesses, or three witnesses, shall he that is worthy of death be put to death; *but* at the mouth of one witness he shall not be put to death.

7 [z]The hands of the witnesses shall be first upon him to put him to death, and afterward the hands of all the people. So [a]thou shalt put the evil away from among you.

8 ¶ [b]If there arise a matter too hard for thee in judgment, [c]between blood and blood, between plea and plea, and between stroke and stroke, *being* matters of controversy within thy gates: then shalt thou arise, [d]and get thee up into the place which the LORD thy God shall choose;

9 And [e]thou shalt come unto the priests the Levites, and [f]unto the judge that shall be in those days, and inquire; [g]and they shall show thee the sentence of judgment:

10 And thou shalt do according to the sentence, which they of that place which the LORD shall choose shall show thee; and thou shalt observe to do according to all that they inform thee:

[n] Heb. *floor, and thy winepress* [o] Heb. *according to the gift of his hand* [p] Or, *matters* [q] Heb. *Justice, justice* [r] Or, *statue,* or, *pillar* [s] Or, *goat*

17:7 PUT THE EVIL AWAY. The Israelites were commanded to keep themselves pure by removing from their midst those who lived ungodly lives and transgressed the covenant. The N.T. also requires that congregations discipline sinning members and expel those who continue to live in sin and immorality (see Mat. 18:15–17; 1 Cor. 5:1–13; cf. 2 Cor. 2:6–7).

11 According to the sentence of the law which they shall teach thee, and according to the judgment which they shall tell thee, thou shalt do: thou shalt not decline from the sentence which they shall show thee, *to* the right hand, nor *to* the left.

12 And [h]the man that will do presumptuously, [t]and will not hearken unto the priest [i]that standeth to minister there before the LORD thy God, or unto the judge, even that man shall die: and [j]thou shalt put away the evil from Israel.

13 [k]And all the people shall hear, and fear, and do no more presumptuously.

The choice of a king

14 ¶ When thou art come unto the land which the LORD thy God giveth thee, and shalt possess it, and shalt dwell therein, and shalt say, [l]I will set a king over me, like as all the nations that *are* about me;

15 Thou shalt in any wise set *him* king over thee, [m]whom the LORD thy God shall choose: *one* [n]from among thy brethren shalt thou set king over thee: thou mayest not set a stranger over thee, which *is* not thy brother.

16 But he shall not multiply [o]horses to himself, nor cause the people [p]to return to Egypt, to the end that he should multiply horses: forasmuch as [q]the LORD hath said unto you, [r]Ye shall henceforth return no more that way.

17 Neither shall he multiply wives to himself, that [s]his heart turn not away: neither shall he greatly multiply to himself silver and gold.

18 [t]And it shall be, when he sitteth upon the throne of his kingdom, that he shall write him a copy of this law in a book out of [u]*that which is* before the priests the Levites:

19 And [v]it shall be with him, and he shall read therein all the days of his life: that he may learn to fear the LORD his God, to keep all the words of this law and these statutes, to do them:

20 That his heart be not lifted up above his brethren, and that he [w]turn not aside from the commandment, *to* the right hand, or *to* the left: to the end that he may prolong *his* days in his kingdom, he, and his children, in the midst of Israel.

The portion for the priests

18 THE PRIESTS the Levites, *and* all the tribe of Levi, [x]shall have no part nor inheritance with Israel: they [y]shall eat the offerings of the LORD made by fire, and his inheritance.

2 Therefore shall they have no inheritance among their brethren: the LORD *is* their inheritance, as he hath said unto them.

3 ¶ And this shall be the priest's due from the people, from them that offer a sacrifice, whether *it be* ox or sheep; and [z]they shall give unto the priest the shoulder, and the two cheeks, and the maw.

4 [a]The firstfruit *also* of thy corn, of thy wine, and of thine oil, and the first of the fleece of thy sheep, shalt thou give him.

5 For [b]the LORD thy God hath chosen him out of all thy tribes, [c]to stand to minister in the name of the LORD, him and his sons for ever.

6 ¶ And if a Levite come from any of thy gates out of all Israel, where he [d]sojourned, and come with all the desire of his mind [e]unto the place which the LORD shall choose;

7 Then he shall minister in the name of the LORD his God, [f]as all his brethren the Levites *do*, which stand there before the LORD.

8 They shall have like [g]portions to eat, beside [u]that which cometh of the sale of his patrimony.

Forbidden pagan practices

9 ¶ When thou art come into the land which the LORD thy God giveth thee, [h]thou shalt not learn to do after the abominations of those nations.

10 There shall not be found among you *any one* that maketh his son or his

17:12 [h]Num. 15:30 [i]ch. 18:5,7 [j]ch. 13:5
17:13 [k]ch. 13:11 & 19:20
17:14 [l]1 Sam. 8:5,19,20
17:15 [m]1 Sam. 10:24 1 Chr. 22:10 [n]Jer. 30:21
17:16 [o]1 Ki. 4:26 & 10:26,28 [p]Is. 31:1 Ezek. 17:15 [q]Ex. 13:17 Num. 14:3 [r]ch. 28:68 Jer. 42:15 Hos. 11:5
17:17 [s]See 1 Ki. 11:3,4
17:18 [t]2 Ki. 11:12 [u]ch. 31:9 2 Ki. 22:8
17:19 [v]Ps. 119:97,98
17:20 [w]ch. 5:32 1 Ki. 15:5
18:1 [x]Num. 18:20 & 26:62 ch. 10:9 [y]Num. 18:8 1 Cor. 9:13
18:3 [z]Lev. 7:30-34
18:4 [a]Ex. 22:29 Num. 18:12
18:5 [b]Ex. 28:1 Num. 3:10 [c]ch. 10:8
18:6 [d]Num. 35:2 [e]ch. 12:5
18:7 [f]2 Chr. 31:2
18:8 [g]2 Chr. 31:4 Neh. 12:44
18:9 [h]Lev. 18:26,27,30 ch. 12:29

[t] Heb. *not to hearken* [u] Heb. *his sales by the fathers*

18:9–11 ABOMINATIONS OF THOSE NATIONS. These verses contain a list of occult magic practices, common in the religions of Canaan, that were an abomination to God and forbidden by Him. Those among God's people in the O.T. who practiced such things were to be put to death (Lev. 20:27). Likewise, the N.T. declares that those who practice such things will not enter the kingdom of God (Gal. 5:20–21; Rev. 22:15).

18:10 PASS THROUGH THE FIRE. Moses reminds the Israelites not to emulate the Canaanite practice of child sacrifices to pagan gods, per-

daughter [i]to pass through the fire,
[j]*or* that useth divination, *or* an ob-
server of times, or an enchanter, or a
witch,
11 [k]Or a charmer, or a consulter
with familiar spirits, or a wizard, or a
[l]necromancer.
12 For all that do these things *are*
an abomination unto the LORD: and
[m]because of these abominations the
LORD thy God doth drive them out from
before thee.
13 Thou shalt be [n]perfect[v] with
the LORD thy God.
14 For these nations, which thou
shalt [w]possess, hearkened unto ob-
servers of times, and unto diviners: but
as for thee, the LORD thy God hath not
suffered thee so *to do.*

The promise of a prophet

15 ¶ [o]The LORD thy God will raise
up unto thee a Prophet from the midst
of thee, of thy brethren, like unto me;
unto him ye shall hearken;
16 According to all that thou desi-
redst of the LORD thy God in Horeb [p]in
the day of the assembly, saying, [q]Let
me not hear again the voice of the LORD
my God, neither let me see this great
fire any more, that I die not.
17 And the LORD said unto me,
[r]They have well *spoken that* which
they have spoken.
18 [s]I will raise them up a Prophet
from among their brethren, like unto
thee, and [t]will put my words in his
mouth; [u]and he shall speak unto them
all that I shall command him.
19 [v]And it shall come to pass, *that*
whosoever will not hearken unto my
words which he shall speak in my
name, I will require *it* of him.
20 But [w]the prophet, which shall
presume to speak a word in my name,
which I have not commanded him to
speak, or [x]that shall speak in the
name of other gods, even that prophet
shall die.
21 And if thou say in thine heart,
How shall we know the word which the
LORD hath not spoken?
22 [y]When a prophet speaketh in
the name of the LORD, [z]if the thing fol-
low not, nor come to pass, that *is* the
thing which the LORD hath not spoken,
but the prophet hath spoken it [a]pre-
sumptuously: thou shalt not be afraid
of him.

Cities of refuge for murderers

19:1–14Ref — Num. 35:6–34; Deut. 4:41–43; Josh. 20:1–9

19 WHEN THE LORD thy God
[b]hath cut off the nations,
whose land the LORD thy God giveth
thee, and thou [x]succeedest them, and
dwellest in their cities, and in their
houses;
2 [c]Thou shalt separate three cities
for thee in the midst of thy land, which
the LORD thy God giveth thee to pos-
sess it.
3 Thou shalt prepare thee a way,
and divide the coasts of thy land, which
the LORD thy God giveth thee to inherit,
into three parts, that every slayer may
flee thither.
4 ¶ And [d]this *is* the case of the
slayer, which shall flee thither, that he
may live: Whoso killeth his neighbour
ignorantly, whom he hated not [y]in
time past;
5 As when a man goeth into the
wood with his neighbour to hew wood,
and his hand fetcheth a stroke with the
axe to cut down the tree, and the
[z]head slippeth from the [a]helve, and
[b]lighteth upon his neighbour, that he

18:10 [i]Lev. 18:21 ch. 12:31 [j]Lev. 20:27 Is. 8:19 **18:11** [k]Lev. 20:27 [l]1 Sam. 28:7 **18:12** [m]Lev. 18:24 ch. 9:4 **18:13** [n]Gen. 17:1 **18:15** [o]John 1:45 Acts 3:22 **18:16** [p]ch. 9:10 [q]Ex. 20:19 Heb. 12:19 **18:17** [r]ch. 5:28 **18:18** [s]John 1:45 Acts 3:22 [t]Is. 51:16 John 17:8 [u]John 4:25 & 8:28 & 12:49,50 **18:19** [v]Acts 3:23 **18:20** [w]Jer. 14:14,15 [x]ch. 13:1,2 Jer. 2:8 **18:22** [y]Jer. 28:9 [z]See ch. 13:2 [a]ver. 20 **19:1** [b]ch. 12:29 **19:2** [c]Ex. 21:13 Num. 35:10,14 Josh. 20:2 **19:4** [d]Num. 35:15 ch. 4:42

[v]Or, *upright,* or, *sincere* [w]Or, *inherit* [x]Heb. *inheritest,* or, *possessest* [y]Heb. *from yesterday the third day* [z]Heb. *iron* [a]Heb. *wood* [b]Heb. *findeth*

formed in order to attempt to influence the course of future events (cf. Lev. 20:2–5).

18:10 DIVINATION ... OBSERVER OF TIMES. Those who used divination sought to predict future events or uncover secrets by the aid of evil spirits or by some human means (cf. Rev. 9:21, note). In contrast, God's way for us to gain truth is to listen to faithful prophets who declare His word (vv. 14–22).

18:11 CHARMER ... NECROMANCER. This list includes mediums, spiritists, or anyone who calls up the dead or consults with the world of spirits (i.e., demons) in order to discover secrets, predict the future, or gain power. Communication with the dead is actually a communication with demons (cf. 1 Sam. 28:8–14; 2 Ki. 21:6; Is. 8:19).

18:15 A PROPHET ... LIKE UNTO ME. The ultimate prophet like Moses (vv. 15,18) was Jesus Christ, the Messiah (see Acts 3:22, note). Like Moses, this Prophet was to be an Israelite and would speak God's word (vv. 18–19). The Jews of Jesus' time were expecting the coming of this great Prophet (John 1:21,45; 4:19,29; 6:14; Acts 3:22–26; 7:37).

die; he shall flee unto one of those cities, and live:

6 [e]Lest the avenger of the blood pursue the slayer, while his heart is hot, and overtake him, because the way is long, and [c]slay him; whereas he *was* not worthy of death, inasmuch as he hated him not [d]in time past.

7 Wherefore I command thee, saying, Thou shalt separate three cities for thee.

8 And if the LORD thy God [f]enlarge thy coast, as he hath sworn unto thy fathers, and give thee all the land which he promised to give unto thy fathers;

9 If thou shalt keep all these commandments to do them, which I command thee this day, to love the LORD thy God, and to walk ever in his ways; [g]then shalt thou add three cities more for thee, beside these three:

10 That innocent blood be not shed in thy land, which the LORD thy God giveth thee *for* an inheritance, and *so* blood be upon thee.

11 ¶ But [h]if any man hate his neighbour, and lie in wait for him, and rise up against him, and smite him [e]mortally that he die, and fleeth into one of these cities:

12 Then the elders of his city shall send and fetch him thence, and deliver him into the hand of the avenger of blood, that he may die.

13 [i]Thine eye shall not pity him, [j]but thou shalt put away *the guilt of* innocent blood from Israel, that it may go well with thee.

14 ¶ [k]Thou shalt not remove thy neighbour's landmark, which they of old time have set in thine inheritance, which thou shalt inherit in the land that the LORD thy God giveth thee to possess it.

Laws about witnesses

15 ¶ [l]One witness shall not rise up against a man for any iniquity, or for any sin, in any sin that he sinneth: at the mouth of two witnesses, or at the mouth of three witnesses, shall the matter be established.

16 ¶ If a false witness [m]rise up against any man to testify against him [f]*that which is* wrong;

17 Then both the men, between whom the controversy *is,* shall stand before the LORD, [n]before the priests and the judges, which shall be in those days;

18 And the judges shall make diligent inquisition: and, behold, *if* the witness *be* a false witness, *and* hath testified falsely against his brother;

19 [o]Then shall ye do unto him, as he had thought to have done unto his brother: so [p]shalt thou put the evil away from among you.

20 [q]And those which remain shall hear, and fear, and shall henceforth commit no more any such evil among you.

21 [r]And thine eye shall not pity; *but* [s]life *shall go* for life, eye for eye, tooth for tooth, hand for hand, foot for foot.

Laws about military service

20 WHEN THOU goest out to battle against thine enemies, and seest [t]horses, and chariots, *and* a people more than thou, be not afraid of them: for the LORD thy God *is* [u]with thee, which brought thee up out of the land of Egypt.

2 And it shall be, when ye are come nigh unto the battle, that the priest shall approach and speak unto the people,

3 And shall say unto them, Hear, O Israel, ye approach this day unto battle against your enemies: let not your hearts [g]faint, fear not, and do not [h]tremble, neither be ye terrified because of them;

4 For the LORD your God *is* he that goeth with you, [v]to fight for you against your enemies, to save you.

5 ¶ And the officers shall speak unto the people, saying, What man *is there* that hath built a new house, and hath not [w]dedicated it? let him go and return to his house, lest he die in the battle, and another man dedicate it.

19:6 [e]Num. 35:12 **19:8** [f]Gen. 15:18 ch. 12:20 **19:9** [g]Josh. 20:7 **19:11** [h]Num. 35:16,24 ch. 27:24 Prov. 28:17 **19:13** [i]ch. 13:8 [j]Num. 35:33,34 1 Ki. 2:31 **19:14** [k]ch. 27:17 Prov. 22:28 Hos. 5:10 **19:15** [l]Num. 35:30 ch. 17:6 Mat. 18:16 John 8:17 2 Cor. 13:1 1 Tim. 5:19 Heb. 10:28 **19:16** [m]Ps. 27:12 & 35:11 **19:17** [n]ch. 17:9 & 21:5 **19:19** [o]Prov. 19:5 Dan. 6:24 [p]ch. 13:5 & 17:7 & 21:21 & 22:21 **19:20** [q]ch. 17:13 & 21:21 **19:21** [r]ver. 13 [s]Ex. 21:23,24 Lev. 24:20 Mat. 5:38 **20:1** [t]See Ps. 20:7 Is. 31:1 [u]Num. 23:21 ch. 31:6,8 2 Chr. 13:12 & 32:7,8 **20:4** [v]ch. 1:30 & 3:22 Josh. 23:10 **20:5** [w]See Neh. 12:27

c Heb. *smite him in life* d Heb. *from yesterday the third day* e Heb. *in life* f Or, *falling away* g Heb. *be tender* h Heb. *make haste*

19:21 EYE SHALL NOT PITY. The principle stated here is that punishment of crime should be commensurate with the offense, but not excessive (see Ex. 21:23–25; Lev. 24:17–20). Leniency toward those who harm the innocent and unprotected encourages evil and violence in the land (v. 19). The N.T. does not abrogate this principle for governing society (cf. Rom. 13:1–4), but does forbid the law of retaliation in personal relationships (cf. Mat. 5:38–41).

6 And what man *is he* that hath planted a vineyard, and hath not *yet* [x]eaten of it? let him *also* go and return unto his house, lest he die in the battle, and another man eat of it.

7 [y]And what man *is there* that hath betrothed a wife, and hath not taken her? let him go and return unto his house, lest he die in the battle, and another man take her.

8 And the officers shall speak further unto the people, and they shall say, [z]What man *is there that is* fearful and fainthearted? let him go and return unto his house, lest his brethren's heart [i]faint as well as his heart.

9 And it shall be, when the officers have made an end of speaking unto the people, that they shall make captains of the armies [j]to lead the people.

10 ¶ When thou comest nigh unto a city to fight against it, [a]then proclaim peace unto it.

11 And it shall be, if it make thee answer of peace, and open unto thee, then it shall be, *that* all the people *that is* found therein shall be tributaries unto thee, and they shall serve thee.

12 And if it will make no peace with thee, but will make war against thee, then thou shalt besiege it:

13 And when the LORD thy God hath delivered it into thine hands, [b]thou shalt smite every male thereof with the edge of the sword:

14 But the women, and the little ones, and [c]the cattle, and all that is in the city, *even* all the spoil thereof, shalt thou [k]take unto thyself; and [d]thou shalt eat the spoil of thine enemies, which the LORD thy God hath given thee.

15 Thus shalt thou do unto all the cities *which are* very far off from thee, which *are* not of the cities of these nations.

16 But [e]of the cities of these people, which the LORD thy God doth give thee *for* an inheritance, thou shalt save alive nothing that breatheth:

17 But thou shalt utterly destroy them; *namely*, the Hittites, and the Amorites, the Canaanites, and the Perizzites, the Hivites, and the Jebusites; as the LORD thy God hath commanded thee:

18 That [f]they teach you not to do after all their abominations, which they have done unto their gods; so should ye [g]sin against the LORD your God.

19 ¶ When thou shalt besiege a city a long time, in making war against it to take it, thou shalt not destroy the trees thereof by forcing an axe against them: for thou mayest eat of them, and thou shalt not cut them down ([l]for the tree of the field *is* man's *life*) [m]to employ *them* in the siege:

20 Only the trees which thou knowest that they *be* not trees for meat, thou shalt destroy and cut them down; and thou shalt build bulwarks against the city that maketh war with thee, until [n]it be subdued.

Laws about unsolved murders

21 IF *ONE* be found slain in the land which the LORD thy God giveth thee to possess it, lying in the field, *and* it be not known who hath slain him:

2 Then thy elders and thy judges shall come forth, and they shall measure unto the cities which *are* round about him that is slain:

3 And it shall be, *that* the city *which is* next unto the slain man, even the elders of that city shall take an heifer, which hath not been wrought with, *and* which hath not drawn in the yoke;

4 And the elders of that city shall bring down the heifer unto a rough valley, which is neither eared nor sown, and shall strike off the heifer's neck there in the valley:

5 And the priests the sons of Levi shall come near; for [h]them the LORD thy God hath chosen to minister unto him, and to bless in the name of the LORD; and [i]by their [o]word shall every controversy and every stroke be *tried:*

6 And all the elders of that city, *that are* next unto the slain *man,* [j]shall wash their hands over the heifer that is beheaded in the valley:

7 And they shall answer and say, Our hands have not shed this blood, neither have our eyes seen *it.*

8 Be merciful, O LORD, unto thy people Israel, whom thou hast redeemed, [k]and lay not innocent blood [p]unto thy people of Israel's charge. And the blood shall be forgiven them.

20:6 [x]See Lev. 19:23, 24 ch. 28:30 **20:7** [y]ch. 24:5 **20:8** [z]Judg. 7:3 **20:10** [a]2 Sam. 20:18,20 **20:13** [b]Num. 31:7 **20:14** [c]Josh. 8:2 [d]Josh. 22:8 **20:16** [e]Num. 21:2,3,35 & 33:52 ch. 7:1,2 Josh. 11:14 **20:18** [f]ch. 7:4 & 12:30,31 & 18:9

[g]Ex. 23:33 **21:5** [h]ch. 10:8 1 Chr. 23:13 [i]ch. 17:8,9 **21:6** [j]See Ps. 19:12 & 26:6 Mat. 27:24 **21:8** [k]Jonah 1:14

[i] Heb. *melt* [j] Heb. to be *in the head of the people* [k] Heb. *spoil* [l] Or, *for, O man, the tree of the field* is *to be employed in the siege* [m] Heb. *to go from before thee* [n] Heb. *it come down* [o] Heb. *mouth* [p] Heb. *in the midst*

9 So [l]shalt thou put away the *guilt of* innocent blood from among you, when thou shalt do *that which is* right in the sight of the LORD.

Laws about captive wives

10 ¶ When thou goest forth to war against thine enemies, and the LORD thy God hath delivered them into thine hands, and thou hast taken them captive,

11 And seest among the captives a beautiful woman, and hast a desire unto her, that thou wouldest have her to thy wife;

12 Then thou shalt bring her home to thine house; and she shall shave her head, and [q] [r]pare her nails;

13 And she shall put the raiment of her captivity from off her, and shall remain in thine house, and [m]bewail her father and her mother a full month: and after that thou shalt go in unto her, and be her husband, and she shall be thy wife.

14 And it shall be, if thou have no delight in her, then thou shalt let her go whither she will; but thou shalt not sell her at all for money, thou shalt not make merchandise of her, because thou hast [n]humbled her.

Laws concerning sons

15 ¶ If a man have two wives, one beloved, [o]and another hated, and they have born him children, *both* the beloved and the hated; and *if* the firstborn son be hers that was hated:

16 Then it shall be, [p]when he maketh his sons to inherit *that* which he hath, *that* he may not make the son of the beloved firstborn before the son of the hated, *which is indeed* the firstborn:

17 But he shall acknowledge the son of the hated *for* the firstborn, [q]by giving him a double portion of all [s]that he hath: for he *is* [r]the beginning of his strength; [s]the right of the firstborn *is* his.

18 ¶ If a man have a stubborn and rebellious son, which will not obey the voice of his father, or the voice of his mother, and *that,* when they have chastened him, will not hearken unto them:

19 Then shall his father and his mother lay hold on him, and bring him out unto the elders of his city, and unto the gate of his place;

20 And they shall say unto the elders of his city, This our son *is* stubborn and rebellious, he will not obey our voice; *he is* a glutton, and a drunkard.

21 And all the men of his city shall stone him with stones, that he die: [t]so shalt thou put evil away from among you; [u]and all Israel shall hear, and fear.

Miscellaneous laws

22 ¶ And if a man have committed a sin [v]worthy of death, and he be to be put to death, and thou hang him on a tree:

23 [w]His body shall not remain all night upon the tree, but thou shalt in any wise bury him that day; (for [x]he that is hanged *is* [y]accursed[t] of God;) that [z]thy land be not defiled, which the LORD thy God giveth thee *for* an inheritance.

22

THOU [a]SHALT not see thy brother's ox or his sheep go astray, and hide thyself from them: thou shalt in any case bring them again unto thy brother.

2 And if thy brother *be* not nigh unto thee, or if thou know him not, then thou shalt bring it unto thine own house, and it shall be with thee until thy brother seek after it, and thou shalt restore it to him again.

3 In like manner shalt thou do with his ass; and so shalt thou do with his raiment; and with all lost thing of thy brother's, which he hath lost, and thou hast found, shalt thou do likewise: thou mayest not hide thyself.

21:9 [l]ch. 19:13 **21:13** [m]See Ps. 45:10 **21:14** [n]Gen. 34:2 ch. 22:29 Judg. 19:24 **21:15** [o]Gen. 29:33 **21:16** [p]1 Chr. 5:2 & 26:10 2 Chr. 11:19,22 **21:17** [q]See 1 Chr. 5:1 [r]Gen. 49:3 [s]Gen. 25:31,33

21:21 [t]ch. 13:5 & 19:19,20 & 22:21,24 [u]ch. 13:11 **21:22** [v]ch. 19:6 & 22:26 Acts 23:29 & 25:11,25 & 26:31 **21:23** [w]Josh. 8:29 & 10:26,27 John 19:31 [x]Gal. 3:13 [y]Num. 25:4 2 Sam. 21:6 [z]Lev. 18:25 Num. 35:34 **22:1** [a]Ex. 23:4

[q] Or, *suffer to grow* [r] Heb. *make,* or, *dress*
[s] Heb. *that is found with him* [t] Heb. *the curse of God*

21:10 THINE ENEMIES. The "enemies" referred to here are those *outside* of Canaan (cf. 20:15). God's people had earlier been instructed not to marry Canaanite people (7:1,3–4). The instructions given in vv. 10–14 protected the dignity of women captives by forbidding their mistreatment.

21:15 TWO WIVES. Having more than one wife (polygamy) typically produces strained relationships, or favoritism and preferential treatment inevitably enter such marital arrangements (cf. Gen. 29:30; see Gen. 2:24, note; 4:19, note). Polygamy did exist in the patriarchal age; though God did not approve of multiple wives, He did give guidelines to regulate the already existing practice (see Gen. 29:28, note).

MAJOR ETHICAL CONCERNS IN THE COVENANT

1. PERSONHOOD
Everyone's person is to be secure (Ex 20:13; Dt 5:17; Ex 21:16-21, 26-31; Lev 19:14; Dt 24:7; 27:18).

2. FALSE ACCUSATION
Everyone is to be secure against slander and false accusation (Ex 20:16; Dt 5:20; Ex 23:1-3; Lev 19:16; Dt 19:15-21).

3. WOMAN
No woman is to be taken advantage of within her subordinate status in society (Ex 21:7-11, 20, 26-32; 22:16-17; Dt. 21:10-14; 22:13-30; 24:1-5).

4. PUNISHMENT
Punishment for wrongdoing shall not be excessive so that the culprit is dehumanized (Dt 25:1-5).

5. DIGNITY
Every Israelite's dignity and right to be God's freedman and servant are to be honored and safeguarded (Ex 21:2, 5-6; Lev 25; Dt 15:12-18).

6. INHERITANCE
Every Israelite's inheritance in the promised land is to be secure (Lev 25; Nu 27:5-7; 36:1-9; Dt 25:5-10).

7. PROPERTY
Everyone's property is to be secure (Ex 20:15; Dt 5:19; Ex 21:33-36; 22:1-15; 23:4-5; Lev 19:35-36; Dt 22: 1-4; 25:13-15).

8. FRUIT OF LABOR
Everyone is to receive the fruit of his labors (Lev 19:13; Dt 24:14; 25:4).

9. FRUIT OF THE GROUND
Everyone is to share the fruit of the ground (Ex 23:10-11; Lev 19:9-10; 23:22; 25:3-55; Dt. 14:28-29; 24:19-21).

10. REST ON SABBATH
Everyone, down to the humblest servant and the resident alien, is to share in the weekly rest of God's Sabbath (Ex 20:8-11; Dt 5:12-15; Ex 23:12).

11. MARRIAGE
The marriage relationship is to be kept inviolate (Ex 20:14; Dt 5:18; see also Lev 18:6-23; 20:10-21; Dt 22:13-30).

12. EXPLOITATION
No one, however disabled, impoverished or powerless, is to be oppressed or exploited (Ex 22:21-27; Lev 19:14, 33-34; 25:35-36; Dt 23:19; 24:6, 12-15, 17; 27:18).

13. FAIR TRIAL
Everyone is to have free access to the courts and is to be afforded a fair trial (Ex 23:6,8; Lev 19:15; Dt 1:17; 10:17-18; 16:18-20; 17:8-13; 19:15-21).

14. SOCIAL ORDER
Every person's God-given place in the social order is to be honored (Ex 20:12; Dt 5:16; Ex 21:15, 17; 22:28; Lev 19:3, 32; 20:9; Dt 17:8-13; 21:15-21; 27:16).

15. LAW
No one shall be above the law, not even the king (Dt 17:18-20).

16. ANIMALS
Concern for the welfare of other creatures is to be extended to the animal world (Ex 23:5, 11; Lev 25:7, Dt 22:4, 6-7; 25:4).

4 ¶ [b]Thou shalt not see thy brother's ass or his ox fall down by the way, and hide thyself from them: thou shalt surely help him to lift *them* up again.

5 ¶ The woman shall not wear that which pertaineth unto a man, neither shall a man put on a woman's garment: for all that do so *are* abomination unto the LORD thy God.

6 ¶ If a bird's nest chance to be before thee in the way in any tree, or on the ground, *whether they be* young ones, or eggs, and the dam sitting upon the young, or upon the eggs, [c]thou shalt not take the dam with the young:

7 *But* thou shalt in any wise let the dam go, and take the young to thee; [d]that it may be well with thee, and *that* thou mayest prolong *thy* days.

8 ¶ When thou buildest a new house, then thou shalt make a battlement for thy roof, that thou bring not blood upon thine house, if any man fall from thence.

9 ¶ [e]Thou shalt not sow thy vineyard with divers seeds: lest the [u]fruit of thy seed which thou hast sown, and the fruit of thy vineyard, be defiled.

10 ¶ [f]Thou shalt not plow with an ox and an ass together.

11 ¶ [g]Thou shalt not wear a garment of divers sorts, *as* of woollen and linen together.

12 ¶ Thou shalt make thee [h]fringes upon the four [v]quarters of thy vesture, wherewith thou coverest *thyself.*

Laws about sexual conduct

13 ¶ If any man take a wife, and go in unto her, and hate her,

14 And give occasions of speech against her, and bring up an evil name upon her, and say, I took this woman, and when I came to her, I found her not a maid:

15 Then shall the father of the damsel, and her mother, take and bring forth *the tokens of* the damsel's virginity unto the elders of the city in the gate:

16 And the damsel's father shall say unto the elders, I gave my daughter unto this man to wife, and he hateth her;

17 And, lo, he hath given occasions of speech *against her,* saying, I found not thy daughter a maid; and yet these *are the tokens of* my daughter's virginity. And they shall spread the cloth before the elders of the city.

18 And the elders of that city shall take that man and chastise him;

19 And they shall amerce him in an hundred *shekels* of silver, and give *them* unto the father of the damsel, because he hath brought up an evil name upon a virgin of Israel: and she shall be his wife; he may not put her away all his days.

20 But if this thing be true, *and the tokens of* virginity be not found for the damsel:

21 Then they shall bring out the damsel to the door of her father's house, and the men of her city shall stone her with stones that she die: because she hath [i]wrought folly in Israel, to play the whore in her father's house: [j]so shalt thou put evil away from among you.

22 ¶ [k]If a man be found lying with a woman married to an husband, then they shall both of them die, *both* the man that lay with the woman, and the woman: so shalt thou put away evil from Israel.

23 ¶ If a damsel *that is* a virgin be [l]betrothed unto an husband, and a man find her in the city, and lie with her;

24 Then ye shall bring them both out unto the gate of that city, and ye shall stone them with stones that they die; the damsel, because she cried not, *being* in the city; and the man, because he hath [m]humbled his neighbour's wife: [n]so thou shalt put away evil from among you.

25 ¶ But if a man find a betrothed damsel in the field, and the man [o]force[w] her, and lie with her: then the man only that lay with her shall die:

26 But unto the damsel thou shalt

22:4 [b]Ex. 23:5
22:6 [c]Lev. 22:28
22:7 [d]ch. 4:40
22:9 [e]Lev. 19:19
22:10 [f]See 2 Cor. 6:14-16
22:11 [g]Lev. 19:19
22:12 [h]Num. 15:38
22:21 [i]Gen. 34:7 Judg. 20:6,10 2 Sam. 13:12,13 [j]ch. 13:5
22:22 [k]Lev. 20:10 John 8:5 Num. 5:22-27
22:23 [l]Mat. 1:18,19
22:24 [m]ch. 21:14 [n]ver. 21,22 1 Cor. 5:2,13
22:25 [o]2 Sam. 13:14

[u] Heb. *fulness of thy seed* [v] Heb. *wings*
[w] Or, *take strong hold of her*

22:17 MY DAUGHTER'S VIRGINITY. It was important that an Israelite girl remain pure and chaste and be a virgin at marriage. Much of the responsibility for this fell upon the parents (v. 15). Likewise, Christian parents have the same responsibility to make every effort to protect their daughters (and their sons) against premarital sexual activities. They must teach them God's principle of purity and guide them into godly and chaste convictions with regard to sexual matters (see article on STANDARDS OF SEXUAL MORALITY, p. 1964).

do nothing; *there is* in the damsel no sin *worthy* of death: for as when a man riseth against his neighbour, and slayeth him, even so *is* this matter:

27 For he found her in the field, *and* the betrothed damsel cried, and *there was* none to save her.

28 ¶ [p]If a man find a damsel *that is* a virgin, which is not betrothed, and lay hold on her, and lie with her, and they be found;

29 Then the man that lay with her shall give unto the damsel's father fifty *shekels* of silver, and she shall be his wife; [q]because he hath humbled her, he may not put her away all his days.

30 ¶ [r]A man shall not take his father's wife, nor [s]discover his father's skirt.

Persons to be excluded

23 HE THAT is wounded in the stones, or hath his privy member cut off, shall not enter into the congregation of the LORD.

2 A bastard shall not enter into the congregation of the LORD; even to his tenth generation shall he not enter into the congregation of the LORD.

3 [t]An Ammonite or Moabite shall not enter into the congregation of the LORD; even to their tenth generation shall they not enter into the congregation of the LORD for ever:

4 [u]Because they met you not with bread and with water in the way, when ye came forth out of Egypt; and [v]because they hired against thee Balaam the son of Beor of Pethor of Mesopotamia, to curse thee.

5 Nevertheless the LORD thy God would not hearken unto Balaam; but the LORD thy God turned the curse into a blessing unto thee, because the LORD thy God loved thee.

6 [w]Thou shalt not seek their peace nor their [x]prosperity all thy days for ever.

7 ¶ Thou shalt not abhor an Edomite; [x]for he *is* thy brother: thou shalt not abhor an Egyptian; because [y]thou wast a stranger in his land.

8 The children that are begotten of them shall enter into the congregation of the LORD in their third generation.

Camp sanitation in wartime

9 ¶ When the host goeth forth against thine enemies, then keep thee from every wicked thing.

10 ¶ [z]If there be among you any man, that is not clean by reason of uncleanness that chanceth him by night, then shall he go abroad out of the camp, he shall not come within the camp:

11 But it shall be, when evening [y]cometh on, [a]he shall wash *himself* with water: and when the sun is down, he shall come into the camp *again*.

12 ¶ Thou shalt have a place also without the camp, whither thou shalt go forth abroad:

13 And thou shalt have a paddle upon thy weapon; and it shall be, when thou [z]wilt ease thyself abroad, thou shalt dig therewith, and shalt turn back and cover that which cometh from thee:

14 For the LORD thy God [b]walketh in the midst of thy camp, to deliver thee, and to give up thine enemies before thee; therefore shall thy camp be holy: that he see no [a]unclean thing in thee, and turn away from thee.

Various laws

15 ¶ [c]Thou shalt not deliver unto his master the servant which is escaped from his master unto thee:

16 He shall dwell with thee, *even* among you, in that place which he shall choose in one of thy gates, where it [b]liketh him best: [d]thou shalt not oppress him.

17 ¶ There shall be no [c]whore [e]of the daughters of Israel, nor [f]a sodomite of the sons of Israel.

18 Thou shalt not bring the hire of a whore, or the price of a dog, into the house of the LORD thy God for any vow: for even both these *are* abomination unto the LORD thy God.

19 ¶ [g]Thou shalt not lend upon usury to thy brother; usury of money,

22:28 [p]Ex. 22:16,17 **22:29** [q]ver. 24 **22:30** [r]Lev. 18:8 & 20:11 ch. 27:20 1 Cor. 5:1 [s]See Ruth 3:9 Ezek. 16:8 **23:3** [t]Neh. 13:1,2 **23:4** [u]See ch. 2:29 [v]Num. 22:5,6 **23:6** [w]Ezra 9:12 **23:7** [x]Gen. 25:24-26 Obad. 10,12 [y]Ex. 22:21 & 23:9 Lev. 19:34 ch. 10:19

23:10 [z]Lev. 15:16 **23:11** [a]Lev. 15:5 **23:14** [b]Lev. 26:12 **23:15** [c]1 Sam. 30:15 **23:16** [d]Ex. 22:21 **23:17** [e]Lev. 19:29 See Prov. 2:16 [f]Gen. 19:5 2 Ki. 23:7 **23:19** [g]Ex. 22:25 Lev. 25:36,37

[x] Heb. *good* [y] Heb. *turneth toward* [z] Heb. *sittest down* [a] Heb. *nakedness of anything* [b] Heb. *is good for him* [c] Or, *sodomitess*

23:1 NOT ENTER INTO THE CONGREGATION. This should be understood to mean that the individual was excluded only from active participation in corporate worship. The individual could still enjoy fellowship with God and participate in the blessings He provided for all those who had faith in Him (cf. Is. 56:3–5).

23:4 BALAAM. See Num. 22:4–24:25 and notes.

23:19 USURY. See Ex. 22:25, note.

usury of victuals, usury of any thing
that is lent upon usury:
20 [h]Unto a stranger thou mayest
lend upon usury; but unto thy brother
thou shalt not lend upon usury: [i]that
the LORD thy God may bless thee in all
that thou settest thine hand to in the
land whither thou goest to possess it.
21 ¶ [j]When thou shalt vow a vow
unto the LORD thy God, thou shalt not
slack to pay it: for the LORD thy God will
surely require it of thee; and it would
be sin in thee.
22 But if thou shalt forbear to vow,
it shall be no sin in thee.
23 [k]That which is gone out of thy
lips thou shalt keep and perform; *even*
a freewill offering, according as thou
hast vowed unto the LORD thy God,
which thou hast promised with thy
mouth.
24 ¶ When thou comest into thy
neighbour's vineyard, then thou may-
est eat grapes thy fill at thine own plea-
sure; but thou shalt not put *any* in thy
vessel.
25 When thou comest into the
standing corn of thy neighbour, [l]then
thou mayest pluck the ears with thine
hand; but thou shalt not move a sickle
unto thy neighbour's standing corn.

24 WHEN A [m]man hath taken a
wife, and married her, and it
come to pass that she find no favour in
his eyes, because he hath found
[d]some uncleanness in her: then let
him write her a bill of [e]divorcement,
and give *it* in her hand, and send her
out of his house.
2 And when she is departed out of
his house, she may go and be another
man's *wife*.
3 And *if* the latter husband hate her,
and write her a bill of divorcement, and
giveth *it* in her hand, and sendeth her
out of his house; or if the latter hus-
band die, which took her *to be* his wife;
4 [n]Her former husband, which sent
her away, may not take her again to be
his wife, after that she is defiled; for
that *is* abomination before the LORD:
and thou shalt not cause the land to
sin, which the LORD thy God giveth thee
for an inheritance.
5 ¶ [o]When a man hath taken a new
wife, he shall not go out to war, [f]nei-
ther shall he be charged with any busi-
ness: *but* he shall be free at home one
year, and shall [p]cheer up his wife
which he hath taken.
6 ¶ No man shall take the nether or
the upper millstone to pledge: for he
taketh *a man's* life to pledge.
7 ¶ [q]If a man be found stealing any
of his brethren of the children of Israel,
and maketh merchandise of him, or
selleth him; then that thief shall die;
[r]and thou shalt put evil away from
among you.
8 ¶ Take heed in [s]the plague of lep-
rosy, that thou observe diligently, and
do according to all that the priests the
Levites shall teach you: as I command-
ed them, *so* ye shall observe to do.
9 [t]Remember what the LORD thy
God did [u]unto Miriam by the way, af-
ter that ye were come forth out of
Egypt.
10 ¶ When thou dost [g]lend thy
brother any thing, thou shalt not go
into his house to fetch his pledge.
11 Thou shalt stand abroad, and the
man to whom thou dost lend shall
bring out the pledge abroad unto thee.
12 And if the man *be* poor, thou
shalt not sleep with his pledge:
13 [v]In any case thou shalt deliver
him the pledge again when the sun
goeth down, that he may sleep in his
own raiment, and [w]bless thee: and [x]it
shall be righteousness unto thee be-
fore the LORD thy God.
14 ¶ Thou shalt not [y]oppress an

23:20 [h]See Lev. 19:34 ch. 15:3 [i]ch. 15:10
23:21 [j]Num. 30:2 Eccl. 5:4,5
23:23 [k]Num. 30:2 Ps. 66:13,14
23:25 [l]Mat. 12:1 Mark 2:23 Luke 6:1
24:1 [m]Mat. 5:31 & 19:7 Mark 10:4
24:4 [n]Jer. 3:1
24:5 [o]ch. 20:7 [p]Prov. 5:18
24:7 [q]Ex. 21:16 [r]ch. 19:19
24:8 [s]Lev. 13:2 & 14:2
24:9 [t]See Luke 17:32 1 Cor. 10:6 [u]Num. 12:10
24:13 [v]Ex. 22:26 [w]Job 29:11 2 Cor. 9:13 2 Tim. 1:18 [x]Dan. 4:27
24:14 [y]Mal. 3:5

[d] Heb. *matter of nakedness* [e] Heb. *cutting off*
[f] Heb. *not any thing shall pass upon him*
[g] Heb. *lend the loan of any thing to*

23:21 VOW. See Num. 30:1, note.

24:1 A BILL OF DIVORCEMENT. Divorce is the result of human sin (cf. Mat. 19:8). The instructions in vv. 1–4 were guidelines given by God to regulate divorce in ancient Israel. Note the following concerning these verses: (1) The term "uncleanness" probably refers to disgraceful or immoral conduct that is less serious than adultery. It cannot refer to adultery since the penalty for adultery was death, not divorce (cf. 22:13–22).

(2) The "bill of divorcement" was a legal document given to the woman in order to break the marriage covenant, protect her, and release her from all obligation to her former husband.

(3) After receiving the certificate of divorce, the woman was free to remarry. However, she was never to return to her former husband if her second marriage was terminated (vv. 2–4).

(4) When divorce happens, it is a tragedy (cf. Mal. 2:16; see Gen. 2:24, note), but it is not a sin if based on Biblical grounds (see Mat. 19:9, note; 1 Cor. 7:15, note). God Himself divorced Israel because of her unfaithfulness and spiritual adultery (Is. 50:1; Jer. 3:1,6–8).

hired servant *that is* poor and needy,
whether he be of thy brethren, or of thy
strangers that *are* in thy land within
thy gates:
15 At his day [z]thou shalt give *him*
his hire, neither shall the sun go down
upon it; for he *is* poor, and [h]setteth his
heart upon it: [a]lest he cry against thee
unto the LORD, and it be sin unto thee.
16 [b]The fathers shall not be put to
death for the children, neither shall the
children be put to death for the fathers:
every man shall be put to death for his
own sin.
17 ¶ [c]Thou shalt not pervert the
judgment of the stranger, *nor* of the fa-
therless; [d]nor take a widow's raiment
to pledge:
18 But [e]thou shalt remember that
thou wast a bondman in Egypt, and the
LORD thy God redeemed thee thence:
therefore I command thee to do this
thing.
19 ¶ [f]When thou cuttest down
thine harvest in thy field, and hast for-
got a sheaf in the field, thou shalt not
go again to fetch it: it shall be for the
stranger, for the fatherless, and for the
widow: that the LORD thy God may
[g]bless thee in all the work of thine
hands.
20 When thou beatest thine olive
tree, [i]thou shalt not go over the
boughs again: it shall be for the strang-
er, for the fatherless, and for the
widow.
21 When thou gatherest the grapes
of thy vineyard, thou shalt not glean *it*
[j]afterward: it shall be for the strang-
er, for the fatherless, and for the
widow.
22 And [h]thou shalt remember that
thou wast a bondman in the land of
Egypt: therefore I command thee to do
this thing.

25

25 IF THERE be a [i]controversy
between men, and they come
unto judgment, that *the judges* may
judge them; then they [j]shall justify
the righteous, and condemn the
wicked.
2 And it shall be, if the wicked man
be [k]worthy to be beaten, that the
judge shall cause him to lie down,
[l]and to be beaten before his face, ac-
cording to his fault, by a certain num-
ber.
3 [m]Forty stripes he may give him,
and not exceed: lest, *if* he should ex-
ceed, and beat him above these with
many stripes, then thy brother should
[n]seem vile unto thee.
4 ¶ [o]Thou shalt not muzzle the ox
when he [k]treadeth out *the corn.*
5 ¶ [p]If brethren dwell together,
and one of them die, and have no child,
the wife of the dead shall not marry
without unto a stranger: her [q]hus-
band's[1] brother shall go in unto her,
and take her to him to wife, and per-
form the duty of an husband's brother
unto her.
6 And it shall be, *that* the firstborn
which she beareth [r]shall succeed in
the name of his brother *which is* dead,
that [s]his name be not put out of Is-
rael.
7 And if the man like not to take his
[m]brother's wife, then let his brother's
wife go up to the [t]gate unto the el-
ders, and say, My husband's brother
refuseth to raise up unto his brother a
name in Israel, he will not perform the
duty of my husband's brother.
8 Then the elders of his city shall
call him, and speak unto him: and *if* he
stand *to it*, and say, [u]I like not to take
her;
9 Then shall his brother's wife
come unto him in the presence of the
elders, and [v]loose his shoe from off
his foot, and spit in his face, and shall

24:15 [z]Lev. 19:13 Jer. 22:13 Jas. 5:4 [a]Jas. 5:4 **24:16** [b]Jer. 31:29 Ezek. 18:20 **24:17** [c]Prov. 22:22 Jer. 5:28 Ezek. 22:29 Zech. 7:10 [d]Ex. 22:26 **24:18** [e]ver. 22 ch. 16:12 **24:19** [f]Lev. 19:9 & 23:22 [g]Ps. 41:1 Prov. 19:17 **24:22** [h]ver. 18 **25:1** [i]ch. 19:17 Ezek. 44:24 [j]See Prov. 17:15 **25:2** [k]Luke 12:48 [l]Mat. 10:17 **25:3** [m]2 Cor. 11:24 [n]Job 18:3 **25:4** [o]Prov. 12:10 1 Tim. 5:18 **25:5** [p]Mat. 22:24 Luke 20:28 [q]Gen. 38:8 Ruth 1:12,13 & 3:9 **25:6** [r]Gen. 38:9 [s]Ruth 4:10 **25:7** [t]Ruth 4:1,2 **25:8** [u]Ruth 4:6 **25:9** [v]Ruth 4:7

[h] Heb. *lifteth his soul unto it* [i] Heb. *thou shalt not bough it after thee* [j] Heb. *after thee* [k] Heb. *thresheth* [1] Or, *next kinsman* [m] Or, *next kinsman's wife*

24:14 POOR AND NEEDY. God often warned Israel not to take advantage of the poor, but to treat them with compassion and respect. Believers who fail to treat the poor and needy fairly will bring God's condemnation upon themselves (v. 15; cf. Jas. 5:1–6; see article on THE CARE OF THE POOR AND NEEDY, p. 1312).

24:17 STRANGER ... FATHERLESS ... WIDOW. God is especially concerned for the refugee, orphan, and the widow (Ex. 22:21–22; 23:9). To help those who are disadvantaged greatly pleases God (see Luke 7:13, note; Heb. 13:2; Jas. 1:27).

25:4 NOT MUZZLE THE OX. This command provided that working animals be given sufficient feed to maintain strength and health. They were to be treated humanely and rewarded for their labor. Even more, people deserve fair treatment for their labor. The N.T. applies this principle to ministers of the gospel (see 1 Cor. 9:9–11; 1 Tim. 5:17–18). Those who labor in the ministry or for Christian institutions should be paid reasonable and fair wages.

answer and say, So shall it be done unto that man that will not [w]build up his brother's house.

10 And his name shall be called in Israel, The house of him that hath his shoe loosed.

11 ¶ When men strive together one with another, and the wife of the one draweth near for to deliver her husband out of the hand of him that smiteth him, and putteth forth her hand, and taketh him by the secrets:

12 Then thou shalt cut off her hand, [x]thine eye shall not pity *her.*

13 ¶ [y]Thou shalt not have in thy bag [n]divers weights, a great and a small.

14 Thou shalt not have in thine house [o]divers measures, a great and a small.

15 *But* thou shalt have a perfect and just weight, a perfect and just measure shalt thou have: [z]that thy days may be lengthened in the land which the LORD thy God giveth thee.

16 For [a]all that do such things, *and* all that do unrighteously, *are* an abomination unto the LORD thy God.

17 ¶ [b]Remember what Amalek did unto thee by the way, when ye were come forth out of Egypt;

18 How he met thee by the way, and smote the hindmost of thee, *even* all *that were* feeble behind thee, when thou *wast* faint and weary; and he [c]feared not God.

19 Therefore it shall be, [d]when the LORD thy God hath given thee rest from all thine enemies round about, in the land which the LORD thy God giveth thee *for* an inheritance to possess it, *that* thou shalt [e]blot out the remembrance of Amalek from under heaven; thou shalt not forget *it.*

Firstfruits and tithes

26 AND IT shall be, when thou *art* come in unto the land which the LORD thy God giveth thee *for* an inheritance, and possessest it, and dwellest therein;

2 [f]That thou shalt take of the first of all the fruit of the earth, which thou shalt bring of thy land that the LORD thy God giveth thee, and shalt put *it* in a basket, and shalt [g]go unto the place which the LORD thy God shall choose to place his name there.

3 And thou shalt go unto the priest that shall be in those days, and say unto him, I profess this day unto the LORD thy God, that I am come unto the country which the LORD sware unto our fathers for to give us.

4 And the priest shall take the basket out of thine hand, and set it down before the altar of the LORD thy God.

5 And thou shalt speak and say before the LORD thy God, [h]A Syrian [i]ready to perish *was* my father, and [j]he went down into Egypt, and sojourned there with a [k]few, and became there a nation, great, mighty, and populous:

6 And [l]the Egyptians evil entreated us, and afflicted us, and laid upon us hard bondage:

7 And [m]when we cried unto the LORD God of our fathers, the LORD heard our voice, and looked on our affliction, and our labour, and our oppression:

8 And [n]the LORD brought us forth out of Egypt with a mighty hand, and with an outstretched arm, and [o]with great terribleness, and with signs, and with wonders:

9 And he hath brought us into this place, and hath given us this land, *even* [p]a land that floweth with milk and honey. 1 S 2:1-

10 And now, behold, I have brought the firstfruits of the land, which thou, O LORD, hast given me. And thou shalt set it before the LORD thy God, and worship before the LORD thy God:

11 And [q]thou shalt rejoice in every good *thing* which the LORD thy God hath given unto thee, and unto thine house,

25:9 [w]Ruth 4:11
25:12 [x]ch. 19:13
25:13 [y]Lev. 19:35,36 Prov. 11:1 Ezek. 45:10 Mic. 6:11
25:15 [z]Ex. 20:12
25:16 [a]Prov. 11:1 1 Thes. 4:6
25:17 [b]Ex. 17:8
25:18 [c]Ps. 36:1 Prov. 16:6 Rom. 3:18
25:19 [d]1 Sam. 15:3 [e]Ex. 17:14
26:2 [f]Ex. 23:19 & 34:26 Num. 18:13 ch. 16:10 Prov. 3:9 [g]ch. 12:5
26:5 [h]Hos. 12:12 [i]Gen. 43:1,2 & 45:7,11 [j]Gen. 46:1,6 Acts 7:15 [k]Gen. 46:27 ch. 10:22
26:6 [l]Ex. 1:11,14
26:7 [m]Ex. 2:23-25 & 3:9 & 4:31
26:8 [n]Ex. 12:37,51 & 13:3,14,16 ch. 5:15 [o]ch. 4:34
26:9 [p]Ex. 3:8
26:11 [q]ch. 12:7,12,18 & 16:11

[n] Heb. *a stone and a stone*
[o] Heb. *an ephah and an ephah*

26:8 THE LORD BROUGHT US FORTH. Israel was expected to remember always that her existence and redemption came about because of what God had done for her. (1) She was to confess this truth publicly (vv. 3–9) and respond to God with offerings, thanksgiving, joy, goodness toward others, and obedience to His commandment (vv. 12–15). (2) We, as believers in Christ, likewise owe our lives and salvation to the mercy of God through Christ. We have been redeemed and purchased by His death and have become His own possession (Eph. 1:14; 1 Pet. 1:18–19; 2:9–10). Henceforth, we must live in gratitude as living sacrifices unto our Lord, not being conformed to this world, but being transformed by the Holy Spirit that we may do His will (Rom. 12:1–2; see Eph. 2:9, note).

thou, and the Levite, and the stranger
that *is* among you.
12 ¶ When thou hast made an end of
tithing all the [r]tithes of thine increase
the third year, *which is* [s]the year of
tithing, and hast given *it* unto the Le-
vite, the stranger, the fatherless, and
the widow, that they may eat within
thy gates, and be filled;
13 Then thou shalt say before the
LORD thy God, I have brought away the
hallowed things out of *mine* house, and
also have given them unto the Levite,
and unto the stranger, to the father-
less, and to the widow, according to all
thy commandments which thou hast
commanded me: I have not trans-
gressed thy commandments, [t]neither
have I forgotten *them:*
14 [u]I have not eaten thereof in my
mourning, neither have I taken away
aught thereof for *any* unclean *use,* nor
given *aught* thereof for the dead: *but* I
have hearkened to the voice of the LORD
my God, *and* have done according to all
that thou hast commanded me.
15 [v]Look down from thy holy habi-
tation, from heaven, and bless thy peo-
ple Israel, and the land which thou
hast given us, as thou swarest unto our
fathers, a land that floweth with milk
and honey.
16 ¶ This day the LORD thy God hath
commanded thee to do these statutes
and judgments: thou shalt therefore
keep and do them with all thine heart,
and with all thy soul.
17 Thou hast [w]avouched the LORD
this day to be thy God, and to walk in
his ways, and to keep his statutes, and
his commandments, and his judg-
ments, and to hearken unto his voice:
18 And [x]the LORD hath avouched
thee this day to be his peculiar people,
as he hath promised thee, and that *thou*
shouldest keep all his commandments;
19 And to make thee [y]high above
all nations which he hath made, in
praise, and in name, and in honour; and
that thou mayest be [z]an holy people
unto the LORD thy God, as he hath spo-
ken.

The altar at mount Ebal

27 AND MOSES with the elders of
Israel commanded the people,
saying, Keep all the commandments
which I command you this day.
2 And it shall be on the day [a]when
ye shall pass over Jordan unto the land
which the LORD thy God giveth thee,
that [b]thou shalt set thee up great
stones, and plaster them with plaster:
3 And thou shalt write upon them
all the words of this law, when thou art
passed over, that thou mayest go in
unto the land which the LORD thy God
giveth thee, a land that floweth with
milk and honey; as the LORD God of thy
fathers hath promised thee.
4 Therefore it shall be when ye be
gone over Jordan, *that* ye shall set up
these stones, which I command you
this day, [c]in mount Ebal, and thou
shalt plaster them with plaster.
5 And there shalt thou build an al-
tar unto the LORD thy God, an altar of
stones: [d]thou shalt not lift up *any* iron
tool upon them.
6 Thou shalt build the altar of the
LORD thy God of whole stones: and thou
shalt offer burnt offerings thereon unto
the LORD thy God:
7 And thou shalt offer peace offer-
ings, and shalt eat there, and rejoice
before the LORD thy God.
8 And thou shalt write upon the
stones all the words of this law very
plainly.
9 ¶ And Moses and the priests the
Levites spake unto all Israel, saying,
Take heed, and hearken, O Israel;
[e]this day thou art become the people
of the LORD thy God.
10 Thou shalt therefore obey the
voice of the LORD thy God, and do his
commandments and his statutes,
which I command thee this day.
11 ¶ And Moses charged the people
the same day, saying,
12 These shall stand [f]upon mount
Gerizim to bless the people, when ye
are come over Jordan; Simeon, and
Levi, and Judah, and Issachar, and Jo-
seph, and Benjamin:
13 And [g]these shall stand upon
mount Ebal [p]to curse; Reuben, Gad,
and Asher, and Zebulun, Dan, and
Naphtali.
14 ¶ And [h]the Levites shall speak,
and say unto all the men of Israel with
a loud voice,
15 [i]Cursed *be* the man that
maketh *any* graven or molten image,
an abomination unto the LORD, the
work of the hands of the craftsman,
and putteth *it* in *a* secret *place.* [j]And

26:12 [r]Lev. 27:30 Num. 18:24 [s]ch. 14:28,29
26:13 [t]Ps. 119:141,153, 176
26:14 [u]Lev. 7:20 & 21:1,11 Hos. 9:4
26:15 [v]Is. 63:15 Zech. 2:13
26:17 [w]Ex. 20:19
26:18 [x]Ex. 6:7 & 19:5 ch. 7:6 & 14:2 & 28:9
26:19 [y]ch. 4:7,8 & 28:1 [z]Ex. 19:6 ch. 7:6 & 28:9 1 Pet. 2:9
27:2 [a]Josh. 4:1 [b]Josh. 8:32
27:4 [c]ch. 11:29 Josh. 8:30,31
27:5 [d]Ex. 20:25 Josh. 8:31
27:9 [e]ch. 26:18
27:12 [f]ch. 11:29 Josh. 8:33 Judg. 9:7
27:13 [g]ch. 11:29 Josh. 8:33
27:14 [h]ch. 33:10 Josh. 8:33 Dan. 9:11
27:15 [i]Ex. 20:4,23 & 34:17 Lev. 19:4 & 26:1 ch. 4:16,23 & 5:8 Is. 44:9 Hos. 13:2 [j]See Num. 5:22 Jer. 11:5 1 Cor. 14:16

[p] Heb. *for a cursing*

all the people shall answer and say, Amen.

16 [k]Cursed *be* he that setteth light by his father or his mother. And all the people shall say, Amen.

17 [l]Cursed *be* he that removeth his neighbour's landmark. And all the people shall say, Amen.

18 [m]Cursed *be* he that maketh the blind to wander out of the way. And all the people shall say, Amen.

19 [n]Cursed *be* he that perverteth the judgment of the stranger, fatherless, and widow. And all the people shall say, Amen.

20 [o]Cursed *be* he that lieth with his father's wife; because he uncovereth his father's skirt. And all the people shall say, Amen.

21 [p]Cursed *be* he that lieth with any manner of beast. And all the people shall say, Amen.

22 [q]Cursed *be* he that lieth with his sister, the daughter of his father, or the daughter of his mother. And all the people shall say, Amen.

23 [r]Cursed *be* he that lieth with his mother-in-law. And all the people shall say, Amen.

24 [s]Cursed *be* he that smiteth his neighbour secretly. And all the people shall say, Amen.

25 [t]Cursed *be* he that taketh reward to slay an innocent person. And all the people shall say, Amen.

26 [u]Cursed *be* he that confirmeth not *all* the words of this law to do them. And all the people shall say, Amen.

The blessings of obedience

28 AND IT shall come to pass, [v]if thou shalt hearken diligently unto the voice of the LORD thy God, to observe *and* to do all his commandments which I command thee this day, that the LORD thy God [w]will set thee on high above all nations of the earth:

2 And all these blessings shall come on thee, and [x]overtake thee, if thou shalt hearken unto the voice of the LORD thy God.

3 [y]Blessed *shalt* thou *be* in the city, and blessed *shalt* thou *be* [z]in the field.

4 Blessed *shall be* [a]the fruit of thy body, and the fruit of thy ground, and the fruit of thy cattle, the increase of thy kine, and the flocks of thy sheep.

5 Blessed *shall be* thy basket and thy [q]store.

6 [b]Blessed *shalt* thou *be* when thou comest in, and blessed *shalt* thou *be* when thou goest out.

7 The LORD [c]shall cause thine enemies that rise up against thee to be smitten before thy face: they shall come out against thee one way, and flee before thee seven ways.

8 The LORD shall [d]command the blessing upon thee in thy [r]storehouses, and in all that thou [e]settest thine hand unto; and he shall bless thee in the land which the LORD thy God giveth thee.

9 [f]The LORD shall establish thee an holy people unto himself, as he hath sworn unto thee, if thou shalt keep the commandments of the LORD thy God, and walk in his ways.

10 And all people of the earth shall see that thou art [g]called by the name of the LORD; and they shall be [h]afraid of thee.

11 And [i]the LORD shall make thee plenteous [s]in goods, in the fruit of thy [t]body, and in the fruit of thy cattle, and in the fruit of thy ground, in the land which the LORD sware unto thy fathers to give thee.

12 The LORD shall open unto thee his good treasure, the heaven [j]to give the rain unto thy land in his season, and [k]to bless all the work of thine hand: and [l]thou shalt lend unto many nations, and thou shalt not borrow.

13 And the LORD shall make thee [m]the head, and not the tail; and thou shalt be above only, and thou shalt not be beneath; if that thou hearken unto the commandments of the LORD thy God, which I command thee this day, to observe and to do *them:*

14 [n]And thou shalt not go aside from any of the words which I command thee this day, *to* the right hand, or *to* the left, to go after other gods to serve them.

27:16 [k]Ex. 20:12 & 21:17 Lev. 19:3 ch. 21:18
27:17 [l]ch. 19:14 Prov. 22:28
27:18 [m]Lev. 19:14
27:19 [n]Ex. 22:21,22 ch. 10:18 & 24:17 Mal. 3:5
27:20 [o]Lev. 18:8 ch. 22:30
27:21 [p]Lev. 18:23
27:22 [q]Lev. 18:9
27:23 [r]Lev. 18:17
27:24 [s]Ex. 20:13 Lev. 24:17 Num. 35:31
27:25 [t]Ex. 23:7,8 ch. 10:17 Ezek. 22:12
27:26 [u]Jer. 11:3 Gal. 3:10
28:1 [v]Ex. 15:26 Lev. 26:3 Is. 55:2 [w]ch. 26:19
28:2 [x]Zech. 1:6
28:3 [y]Ps. 128:1,4 [z]Gen. 39:5
28:4 [a]Gen. 22:17 & 49:25 ch. 7:13 Prov. 10:22
28:6 [b]Ps. 121:8
28:7 [c]Lev. 26:7,8 2 Sam. 22:38,39, 41
28:8 [d]Lev. 25:21 [e]ch. 15:10
28:9 [f]Ex. 19:5,6 ch. 7:6 & 26:18,19
28:10 [g]Num. 6:27 2 Chr. 7:14 Is. 63:19 Dan. 9:18,19 [h]ch. 11:25
28:11 [i]ch. 30:9 Prov. 10:22
28:12 [j]Lev. 26:4 ch. 11:14 [k]ch. 14:29 [l]ch. 15:6
28:13 [m]Is. 9:14,15
28:14 [n]ch. 5:32

[q] Or, *dough,* or, *kneading-trough* [r] Or, *barns*
[s] Or, *for good* [t] Heb. *belly*

27:15 PUTTETH *IT* IN *A* SECRET *PLACE*. Many of the sins listed here were done in secret (vv. 15,24). Israel thereby acknowledged that a person was accountable to God even when he or she was alone. All our actions and thoughts occur in the sight and presence of God (see Ps. 139).

28:3 BLESSED *SHALT* THOU *BE*. See Luke 24:50, note.

The curses of disobedience

15 ¶ But it shall come to pass, [o]if thou wilt not hearken unto the voice of the LORD thy God, to observe to do all his commandments and his statutes which I command thee this day; that all these curses shall come upon thee, and overtake thee:

16 Cursed *shalt* thou *be* in the city, and cursed *shalt* thou *be* in the field.

17 Cursed *shall be* thy basket and thy store.

18 Cursed *shall be* the fruit of thy body, and the fruit of thy land, the increase of thy kine, and the flocks of thy sheep.

19 Cursed *shalt* thou *be* when thou comest in, and cursed *shalt* thou *be* when thou goest out.

20 The LORD shall send upon thee [p]cursing, [q]vexation, and [r]rebuke, in all that thou settest thine hand unto [u]for to do, until thou be destroyed, and until thou perish quickly; because of the wickedness of thy doings, whereby thou hast forsaken me.

21 The LORD shall make [s]the pestilence cleave unto thee, until he have consumed thee from off the land, whither thou goest to possess it.

22 [t]The LORD shall smite thee with a consumption, and with a fever, and with an inflammation, and with an extreme burning, and with the [v]sword, and with [u]blasting, and with mildew; and they shall pursue thee until thou perish.

23 And [v]thy heaven that *is* over thy head shall be brass, and the earth that *is* under thee *shall be* iron.

24 The LORD shall make the rain of thy land powder and dust: from heaven shall it come down upon thee, until thou be destroyed.

25 [w]The LORD shall cause thee to be smitten before thine enemies: thou shalt go out one way against them, and flee seven ways before them: and [x]shalt be [w]removed into all the kingdoms of the earth.

26 And [y]thy carcase shall be meat unto all fowls of the air, and unto the beasts of the earth, and no man shall fray *them* away.

27 The LORD will smite thee with [z]the botch of Egypt, and with [a]the emerods, and with the scab, and with the itch, whereof thou canst not be healed.

28 The LORD shall smite thee with madness, and blindness, and [b]astonishment of heart:

29 And thou shalt [c]grope at noonday, as the blind gropeth in darkness, and thou shalt not prosper in thy ways: and thou shalt be only oppressed and spoiled evermore, and no man shall save *thee*.

30 [d]Thou shalt betroth a wife, and another man shall lie with her: [e]thou shalt build an house, and thou shalt not dwell therein: [f]thou shalt plant a vineyard, and shalt not gather the grapes thereof.

31 Thine ox *shall be* slain before thine eyes, and thou shalt not eat thereof: thine ass *shall be* violently taken away from before thy face, and [x]shall not be restored to thee: thy sheep *shall be* given unto thine enemies, and thou shalt have none to rescue *them*.

32 Thy sons and thy daughters *shall be* given unto another people, and thine eyes shall look, and [g]fail *with longing* for them all the day long: and *there shall be* no might in thine hand.

33 [h]The fruit of thy land, and all thy labours, shall a nation which thou knowest not eat up; and thou shalt be only oppressed and crushed always:

34 So that thou shalt be mad for the sight of thine eyes which thou shalt see.

35 The LORD shall smite thee in the knees, and in the legs, with a sore botch that cannot be healed, from the sole of thy foot unto the top of thy head.

36 The LORD shall [i]bring thee, and thy king which thou shalt set over thee, unto a nation which neither thou nor thy fathers have known; and [j]there shalt thou serve other gods, wood and stone.

37 And thou shalt become [k]an astonishment, a proverb, [l]and a byword, among all nations whither the LORD shall lead thee.

28:15 [o]Lev. 26:14 Lam. 2:17 Dan. 9:11 Mal. 2:2
28:20 [p]Mal. 2:2 [q]1 Sam. 14:20 Zech. 14:13 [r]Is. 30:17 & 51:20 & 66:15
28:21 [s]Lev. 26:25
28:22 [t]Lev. 26:16 [u]Amos 4:9
28:23 [v]Lev. 26:19
28:25 [w]ch. 32:30 Is. 30:17 [x]Jer. 15:4 & 24:9 Ezek. 23:46
28:26 [y]1 Sam. 17:44,46 Jer. 7:33 & 16:4
28:27 [z]Ex. 15:26 [a]1 Sam. 5:6
28:28 [b]Jer. 4:9
28:29 [c]Job 5:14 Is. 59:10
28:30 [d]Job 31:10 Jer. 8:10 [e]Job 31:8 Jer. 12:13 Amos 5:11 Mic. 6:15 Zeph. 1:13 [f]ch. 20:6
28:32 [g]Ps. 119:82
28:33 [h]Lev. 26:16 Jer. 5:17
28:36 [i]2 Ki. 17:4,6 & 24:12,14 2 Chr. 33:11 [j]ch. 4:28 Jer. 16:13
28:37 [k]Jer. 24:9 Zech. 8:13 [l]Ps. 44:14

[u]Heb. *which thou wouldest do* [v]Or, *drought* [w]Heb. *for a removing* [x]Heb. *shall not return to thee*

28:15 IT SHALL COME TO PASS. Moses prophesied the consequences of turning away from God: chastisement, destruction, great sorrow, captivity, and dispersion among the nations (vv. 15–68).

38 [m]Thou shalt carry much seed out into the field, and shalt gather *but* little in; for [n]the locust shall consume it.

39 Thou shalt plant vineyards, and dress *them,* but shalt neither drink *of* the wine, nor gather *the grapes;* for the worms shall eat them.

40 Thou shalt have olive trees throughout all thy coasts, but thou shalt not anoint *thyself* with the oil; for thine olive shall cast *his fruit.*

41 Thou shalt beget sons and daughters, but [y]thou shalt not enjoy them; for [o]they shall go into captivity.

42 All thy trees and fruit of thy land shall the locust [z]consume.

43 The stranger that *is* within thee shall get up above thee very high; and thou shalt come down very low.

44 [p]He shall lend to thee, and thou shalt not lend to him: [q]he shall be the head, and thou shalt be the tail.

45 Moreover [r]all these curses shall come upon thee, and shall pursue thee, and overtake thee, till thou be destroyed; because thou hearkenedst not unto the voice of the LORD thy God, to keep his commandments and his statutes which he commanded thee:

46 And they shall be upon thee [s]for a sign and for a wonder, and upon thy seed for ever.

47 [t]Because thou servedst not the LORD thy God with joyfulness, and with gladness of heart, [u]for the abundance of all *things;*

48 Therefore shalt thou serve thine enemies which the LORD shall send against thee, in hunger, and in thirst, and in nakedness, and in want of all *things:* and he [v]shall put a yoke of iron upon thy neck, until he have destroyed thee.

49 [w]The LORD shall bring a nation against thee from far, from the end of the earth, [x]*as swift* as the eagle flieth; a nation whose tongue thou shalt not [a]understand;

50 A nation [y]of[b] fierce countenance, [z]which shall not regard the person of the old, nor show favour to the young:

51 And he shall [a]eat the fruit of thy cattle, and the fruit of thy land, until thou be destroyed: which *also* shall not leave thee *either* corn, wine, or oil, *or* the increase of thy kine, or flocks of thy sheep, until he have destroyed thee.

52 And he shall [b]besiege thee in all thy gates, until thy high and fenced walls come down, wherein thou trustedst, throughout all thy land: and he shall besiege thee in all thy gates throughout all thy land, which the LORD thy God hath given thee.

53 And [c]thou shalt eat the fruit of thine own [c]body, the flesh of thy sons and of thy daughters, which the LORD thy God hath given thee, in the siege, and in the straitness, wherewith thine enemies shall distress thee:

54 *So that* the man *that is* tender among you, and very delicate, [d]his eye shall be evil toward his brother, and toward [e]the wife of his bosom, and toward the remnant of his children which he shall leave:

55 So that he will not give to any of them of the flesh of his children whom he shall eat: because he hath nothing left him in the siege, and in the straitness, wherewith thine enemies shall distress thee in all thy gates.

56 The tender and delicate woman among you, which would not adventure to set the sole of her foot upon the ground for delicateness and tenderness, [f]her eye shall be evil toward the husband of her bosom, and toward her son, and toward her daughter,

57 And toward her [d]young one that cometh out [g]from between her feet, and toward her children which she shall bear: for she shall eat them for want of all *things* secretly in the siege and straitness, wherewith thine enemy shall distress thee in thy gates.

58 If thou wilt not observe to do all the words of this law that are written in this book, that thou mayest fear [h]this glorious and fearful name, THE LORD THY GOD;

59 Then the LORD will make thy plagues [i]wonderful, and the plagues of thy seed, *even* great plagues, and of

28:38 [m]Mic. 6:15 Hag. 1:6 [n]Joel 1:4 **28:41** [o]Lam. 1:5 **28:44** [p]ver. 12 [q]ver. 13 **28:45** [r]ver. 15 **28:46** [s]Is. 8:18 Ezek. 14:8 **28:47** [t]Neh. 9:35-37 [u]ch. 32:15 **28:48** [v]Jer. 28:14 **28:49** [w]Jer. 5:15 & 6:22,23 Luke 19:43 [x]Jer. 48:40 & 49:22 Lam. 4:19 Hos. 8:1 **28:50** [y]Prov. 7:13 Eccl. 8:1 Dan. 8:23 [z]2 Chr. 36:17 Is. 47:6 **28:51** [a]ver. 33 Is. 1:7 **28:52** [b]2 Ki. 25:1,2,4 **28:53** [c]Lev. 26:29 2 Ki. 6:28,29 Jer. 19:9 Lam. 2:20 & 4:10 **28:54** [d]ch. 15:9 [e]ch. 13:6 **28:56** [f]ver. 54 **28:57** [g]Gen. 49:10 **28:58** [h]Ex. 6:3 **28:59** [i]Dan. 9:12

y Heb. *they shall not be thine* z Or, *possess* a Heb. *hear* b Heb. *strong of face* c Heb. *belly* d Heb. *afterbirth*

28:49–57 A NATION AGAINST THEE. These verses describe an invasion of the land of Canaan which could apply both to the Babylonian invasion (described in Hab. 1:6,8 as an eagle; cf. 2 Ki. 25:1–21; Jer. 39:1–10; 52:28–30) and to the siege by the Romans in A.D. 70 (see Luke 21:20, note).

long continuance, and sore sicknesses,
and of long continuance.
60 Moreover he will bring upon thee
all [j]the diseases of Egypt, which thou
wast afraid of; and they shall cleave
unto thee.
61 Also every sickness, and every
plague, which *is* not written in the book
of this law, them will the LORD [e]bring
upon thee, until thou be destroyed.
62 And ye [k]shall be left few in
number, whereas ye were [l]as the
stars of heaven for multitude; because
thou wouldest not obey the voice of the
LORD thy God.
63 And it shall come to pass, *that* as
the LORD [m]rejoiced over you to do you
good, and to multiply you; so the LORD
[n]will rejoice over you to destroy you,
and to bring you to nought; and ye shall
be plucked from off the land whither
thou goest to possess it.
64 And the LORD [o]shall scatter
thee among all people, from the one
end of the earth even unto the other;
and [p]there thou shalt serve other
gods, which neither thou nor thy fa-
thers have known, *even* wood and
stone.
65 And [q]among these nations
shalt thou find no ease, neither shall
the sole of thy foot have rest: [r]but the
LORD shall give thee there a trembling
heart, and failing of eyes, and [s]sorrow
of mind:
66 And thy life shall hang in doubt
before thee; and thou shalt fear day
and night, and shalt have none assur-
ance of thy life:
67 [t]In the morning thou shalt say,
Would God it were even! and at even
thou shalt say, Would God it were
morning! for the fear of thine heart
wherewith thou shalt fear, and [u]for
the sight of thine eyes which thou shalt
see.
68 And the LORD [v]shall bring thee
into Egypt again with ships, by the way
whereof I spake unto thee, [w]Thou
shalt see it no more again: and there ye
shall be sold unto your enemies for
bondmen and bondwomen, and no man
shall buy *you*.

28:60 [j]ch. 7:15
28:62 [k]ch. 4:27 [l]ch. 10:22 Neh. 9:23
28:63 [m]ch. 30:9 Jer. 32:41 [n]Prov. 1:26 Is. 1:24
28:64 [o]Lev. 26:33 ch. 4:27,28 Neh. 1:8 Jer. 16:13 [p]ver. 36
28:65 [q]Amos 9:4 [r]Lev. 26:36 [s]Lev. 26:16
28:67 [t]Job 7:4 [u]ver. 34
28:68 [v]Jer. 43:7 Hos. 8:13 & 9:3 [w]ch. 17:16
29:1 [x]ch. 5:2,3
29:2 [y]Ex. 19:4
29:3 [z]ch. 4:34 & 7:19
29:4 [a]See Is. 6:9,10 & 63:17 John 8:43 Acts 28:26,27 Eph. 4:18
29:5 [b]ch. 1:3 & 8:2 [c]ch. 8:4
29:6 [d]Ex. 16:12 ch. 8:3
29:7 [e]Num. 21:23,24, 33 ch. 2:32
29:8 [f]Num. 32:33 ch. 3:12,13
29:9 [g]ch. 4:6 1 Ki. 2:3 [h]Josh. 1:7
29:11 [i]See Josh. 9:21, 23,27
29:12 [j]Neh. 10:29

Keep the covenant

29 THESE *ARE* the words of the
covenant, which the LORD com-
manded Moses to make with the chil-
dren of Israel in the land of Moab, be-
side [x]the covenant which he made
with them in Horeb.
2 ¶ And Moses called unto all Isra-
el, and said unto them, [y]Ye have seen
all that the LORD did before your eyes
in the land of Egypt unto Pharaoh, and
unto all his servants, and unto all his
land;
3 [z]The great temptations which
thine eyes have seen, the signs, and
those great miracles:
4 Yet [a]the LORD hath not given you
an heart to perceive, and eyes to see,
and ears to hear, unto this day.
5 [b]And I have led you forty years in
the wilderness: [c]your clothes are not
waxen old upon you, and thy shoe is
not waxen old upon thy foot.
6 [d]Ye have not eaten bread, nei-
ther have ye drunk wine or strong
drink: that ye might know that I *am* the
LORD your God.
7 And when ye came unto this
place, [e]Sihon the king of Heshbon,
and Og the king of Bashan, came out
against us unto battle, and we smote
them:
8 And we took their land, and
[f]gave it for an inheritance unto the
Reubenites, and to the Gadites, and to
the half tribe of Manasseh.
9 [g]Keep therefore the words of this
covenant, and do them, that ye may
[h]prosper in all that ye do.
10 ¶ Ye stand this day all of you be-
fore the LORD your God; your captains
of your tribes, your elders, and your of-
ficers, *with* all the men of Israel,
11 Your little ones, your wives, and
thy stranger that *is* in thy camp, from
[i]the hewer of thy wood unto the draw-
er of thy water:
12 That thou shouldest [f]enter into
covenant with the LORD thy God, and
[j]into his oath, which the LORD thy God
maketh with thee this day:

[e] Heb. *cause to ascend* [f] Heb. *pass*

28:64 SCATTER THEE AMONG ALL PEOPLE. The scattering of Israel occurred several times throughout their history—when they were taken captive by the Assyrians (722–721 B.C.; see 2 Ki. 17:6), the Babylonians (586 B.C.; see 2 Ki. 25:21), the Greeks (to Alexandria in Egypt, 3rd century B.C.), and the Romans (A.D. 70; see Luke 21:20–24; see also Deut. 30:3, note on Israel's restoration).

29:1 THE WORDS OF THE COVENANT. See article on GOD'S COVENANT WITH THE ISRAELITES, p. 314.

GOD'S COVENANT WITH THE ISRAELITES

***Deut. 29:1** "These* are *the words of the covenant, which the* L*ORD* *commanded Moses to make with the children of Israel in the land of Moab, beside the covenant which he made with them in Horeb."*

THE COVENANT AT MOUNT SINAI (HOREB). God had made a covenant with Abraham and renewed it with Isaac and Jacob (see article on GOD'S COVENANT WITH THE ABRAHAM, ISAAC, AND JACOB, p. 48). His covenant with the Israelites, made at the foot of Mount Sinai (see Ex. 19:1, note), encompasses the two basic principles discussed in the above-mentioned article: God alone establishes the promises and obligations of His covenant, and humans are expected to accept them in obedient faith. The main difference between this covenant and the earlier one is that God outlined its promises and responsibilities before ratification (Ex. 24:1–8).

(1) God's promises in this covenant were essentially the same as those made to Abraham (see Ex. 19:1, note). He promised (a) to give the Israelites the land of Canaan after redeeming them from bondage in Egypt (Ex. 6:3–6; 19:4; 23:20,23), and (b) to be their God and to adopt them as His people (Ex. 6:7; 19:6; see Deut. 5:2, note). God's ultimate goal was to bring the Savior into the world through the covenant people.

(2) Before God would fulfill all these promises, He required the Israelites to commit themselves to keep His laws spoken to them while they were stationed at Mount Sinai. After God revealed the Ten Commandments and many other laws of the covenant (see article on THE OLD TESTAMENT LAW, p. 124), the Israelites vowed with one voice, "All the words which the LORD hath said will we do" (Ex. 24:3). Without this solemn promise to accept the requirements of God's law, the covenant between them and the Lord God would not have been confirmed (cf. Ex. 24:8, note).

(3) This agreement to follow the law of God remained a condition of the covenant. Only by persevering in obedience to the commandments of the Lord and by offering the prescribed sacrifices of His covenant would Israel continue as God's treasured possession and keep on receiving His blessings. In other words, Israel's continued election as the people of God was conditioned on obeying Him as their Lord (see Ex. 19:5, note).

(4) God also stipulated clearly what would happen if His people failed to keep the obligations of the covenant. The penalty for disobedience was removal from the covenant people, either by banishment or death (see Ex. 31:14–15). This penalty repeats God's warning at the time of the exodus, namely, that those who did not follow His instructions for the Passover would be cut off from the people (Ex. 12:15,19; see 12:15, note). These were not idle threats. At Kadesh, for example, when the Israelites rebelled against the Lord in unbelief and refused to enter Canaan because they feared the inhabitants, God became angry with them and caused them to wander in the wilderness for the next thirty-nine years; there all Israelites over age twenty died (excluding Caleb and Joshua, see Num. 13:26—14:39; 14:29, note). Their disobedience and unbelief caused them to forfeit living in the land of God's promised rest (cf. Ps. 95:7–11; Heb. 3:9–11,18).

(5) The obedience which God expected from His people was not perfection but a sincere and earnest obedience. Inherent in the covenant was a recognition that at times, because of the weakness of human nature, they would fail (see Deut. 30:20, note). In order to remove the guilt of sin and to reconcile the people to Himself, God provided the sacrificial system in general and the annual Day of Atonement in particular (see article on THE DAY OF ATONEMENT, p. 188). The people could confess their sins, offer various sacrifices, and so become reconciled to their Lord. However, God would judge severely willful disobedience, rebellion, and apostasy.

(6) Through His covenant with the Israelites, God intended that people in other nations, by observing Israel's faithfulness to God and the accompanying blessings, would want to draw near to the Lord and become a part of the community of faith (see Deut. 4:6, note). Eventually, through the promised Redeemer, the nations of the world would be invited to accept these promises too. Thus, the covenant had a missionary emphasis.

THE COVENANT RENEWED ON THE PLAINS OF MOAB. After the rebellious and unfaithful generation of Israelites had died during their thirty-nine years of wandering in the wilderness, God called a whole new generation of Israelites and prepared them to enter the promised land by renewing the covenant with Him. To conquer the land of Canaan successfully would require their commitment to this covenant and the assurance that the Lord God would be with them.

(1) This renewal of the covenant is the main focus of the book of Deuteronomy (see introduction to Deuteronomy). After an opening preamble (Deut. 1:1–5), Deuteronomy summarizes the history of God's dealings with His people since leaving Sinai (Deut. 1:6—4:43), recites the main stipulations of the covenant (Deut. 4:44—26:19), reminds the Israelites of the curses and blessings of the covenant (Deut. 27:1—30:20), and closes with the arrangements for its continuation (Deut. 31:1—33:29). Though not specifically mentioned in the book, we may assume that the nation of Israel with one voice agreed with a hearty "Amen" to stipulations of the covenant, even as the previous generation had done at Mount Sinai (cf. Ex. 24:1–8; Deut. 27).

(2) The basic format of this covenant remained the same as the covenant at Mount Sinai. A recurring theme throughout Deuteronomy is that if the people of God obeyed all the words of the covenant, God would bless them; if they did not, God would curse and punish them instead (see especially Deut. 27—30). The only way in which they and their descendants could remain forever in the land of Canaan was by keeping the covenant through loving the Lord (see Deut. 6:5, note) and obeying God's law (Deut. 30:15–20).

(3) Moses instructed the people to refresh their memories periodically concerning the covenant. Every seven years, at the Feast of Tabernacles, all the Israelites were to gather together in the place God would choose; there they would be reminded of their covenant by listening to the reading of the Law of Moses and by promising to obey what they had heard (Deut. 31:9–13).

(4) The O.T. records several notable examples of this procedure of covenant remembrance and renewal. After the land had been conquered and shortly before Joshua died, he called all the people together for this purpose (Josh. 24). The people's response was clear and unmistakable: "The LORD our God will we serve, and his voice will we obey" (Josh. 24:24). Thereupon "Joshua made a covenant with the people" (Josh. 24:25). Similarly, Jehoiada led a covenant-renewal ceremony at the crowning of Joash (2 Ki. 11:17), as did Josiah (2 Ki. 23:1–3), Hezekiah (cf. 2 Chr. 29:10), and Ezra (Neh. 8:1—10:39).

(5) The call to covenant remembrance and renewal is relevant today. The N.T. is God's covenant with us. We remember His covenant with us as we read and study His revelation to us with its promises and stipulations, as we hear it proclaimed in the preaching of God's word, and most specifically, as we partake of the Lord's Supper (see 1 Cor. 11:17–34). Through the Lord's Supper we also renew our commitment to love the Lord and to serve Him with our whole heart (see 1 Cor. 11:20, note).

13 That he may [k]establish thee today for a people unto himself, and *that* he may be unto thee a God, [l]as he hath said unto thee, and [m]as he hath sworn unto thy fathers, to Abraham, to Isaac, and to Jacob.

14 Neither with you only [n]do I make this covenant and this oath;

15 But with *him* that standeth here with us this day before the LORD our God, [o]and also with *him* that *is* not here with us this day:

16 (For ye know how we have dwelt in the land of Egypt; and how we came through the nations which ye passed by;

17 And ye have seen their abominations, and their [g]idols, wood and stone, silver and gold, which *were* among them:)

18 Lest there should be among you man, or woman, or family, or tribe, [p]whose heart turneth away this day from the LORD our God, to go *and* serve the gods of these nations; [q]lest there should be among you a root that beareth [h] [i]gall and wormwood;

19 And it come to pass, when he heareth the words of this curse, that he bless himself in his heart, saying, I shall have peace, though I walk [r]in the [s]imagination[j] of mine heart, [t]to add [k]drunkenness to thirst:

20 [u]The LORD will not spare him, but then [v]the anger of the LORD and [w]his jealousy shall smoke against that man, and all the curses that are written in this book shall lie upon him, and the LORD [x]shall blot out his name from under heaven.

21 And the LORD [y]shall separate him unto evil out of all the tribes of Israel, according to all the curses of the covenant that [l]are written in this book of the law:

22 So that the generation to come of your children that shall rise up after you, and the stranger that shall come from a far land, shall say, when they see the plagues of that land, and the sicknesses [m]which the LORD hath laid upon it;

23 *And that* the whole land thereof *is* brimstone, [z]and salt, *and* burning, *that* it is not sown, nor beareth, nor any grass groweth therein, [a]like the overthrow of Sodom, and Gomorrah, Admah, and Zeboim, which the LORD overthrew in his anger, and in his wrath:

24 Even all nations shall say, [b]Wherefore hath the LORD done thus unto this land? what *meaneth* the heat of this great anger?

25 Then men shall say, Because they have forsaken the covenant of the LORD God of their fathers, which he made with them when he brought them forth out of the land of Egypt:

26 For they went and served other gods, and worshipped them, gods whom they knew not, and [n]*whom* he had not [o]given unto them:

27 And the anger of the LORD was kindled against this land, [c]to bring upon it all the curses that are written in this book:

28 And the LORD [d]rooted them out of their land in anger, and in wrath, and

29:13 [k]ch. 28:9 [l]Ex. 6:7 [m]Gen. 17:7
29:14 [n]Jer. 31:31
29:15 [o]Acts 2:39 1 Cor. 7:14
29:18 [p]ch. 11:16 [q]Acts 8:23 Heb. 12:15
29:19 [r]Num. 15:39 Eccl. 11:9 [s]Jer. 3:17 & 7:24 [t]Is. 30:1
29:20 [u]Ezek. 14:7 [v]Ps. 74:1 [w]Ps. 79:5 Ezek. 23:25 [x]ch. 9:14
29:21 [y]Mat. 24:51
29:23 [z]Jer. 17:6 Zeph. 2:9 [a]Gen. 19:24 Jer. 20:16
29:24 [b]1 Ki. 9:8,9 Jer. 22:8,9
29:27 [c]Dan. 9:11,13,14
29:28 [d]1 Ki. 14:15 Ps. 52:5 Prov. 2:22

[g] Heb. *dungy gods* [h] Or, *a poisonful herb* [i] Heb. *rosh* [j] Or, *stubbornness* [k] Heb. *the drunken to the thirsty* [l] Heb. *is written* [m] Heb. *wherewith the LORD hath made it sick* [n] Or, who *had not given to them* any portion [o] Heb. *divided*

29:18–21 WHOSE HEART TURNETH AWAY . . . FROM THE LORD. These verses concern an *individual* among God's elect people who turned away from the Lord. (1) The promises of life and blessing were made to Israel as a whole, i.e., as a corporate body or nation (cf. 28:1; 30:15–20). An individual within God's chosen people participated in the promised blessings only as he or she entered into a faith relationship with God and persevered in that relationship (see article on ELECTION AND PREDESTINATION, p. 1846).

(2) Eternal life and temporal blessing could be forfeited by any individual in Israel who turned his or her heart away from God (v. 18).

(3) For those in Israel who belonged to God, and then turned away from Him (v. 18) and persisted in their own way (v. 19), there remained no longer any opportunity for forgiveness of sin. They could expect only the wrath of God and the blotting out of their names from under heaven (v. 20; see article on PERSONAL APOSTASY, p. 1946).

29:19 I SHALL HAVE PEACE, THOUGH I WALK IN THE IMAGINATION OF MINE HEART. Among God's chosen people would be those who walked in their own sinful way, yet claimed to "have peace." Similarly, the N.T. speaks about those within the church who profess to have peace, salvation, and eternal life, yet do not endeavor to follow God's will (see 1 John 2:4, note; Rev. 2:14, note). God says that their profession of salvation is not valid and compares them to a root that spreads defilement and death like a poison throughout the congregation (cf. Heb. 12:15). Terrible judgment will come upon those individuals (see previous note).

in great indignation, and cast them into another land, as *it is* this day.

29 The secret *things belong* unto the LORD our God: but those *things which are* revealed *belong* unto us and to our children for ever, that *we* may do all the words of this law.

The rewards of repentance

30 AND [e]IT shall come to pass, when [f]all these things are come upon thee, the blessing and the curse, which I have set before thee, and [g]thou shalt call *them* to mind among all the nations, whither the LORD thy God hath driven thee,

2 And shalt [h]return unto the LORD thy God, and shalt obey his voice according to all that I command thee this day, thou and thy children, with all thine heart, and with all thy soul;

3 [i]That then the LORD thy God will turn thy captivity, and have compassion upon thee, and will return and [j]gather thee from all the nations, whither the LORD thy God hath scattered thee.

4 [k]If *any* of thine be driven out unto the outmost *parts* of heaven, from thence will the LORD thy God gather thee, and from thence will he fetch thee:

5 And the LORD thy God will bring thee into the land which thy fathers possessed, and thou shalt possess it; and he will do thee good, and multiply thee above thy fathers.

6 And [l]the LORD thy God will circumcise thine heart, and the heart of thy seed, to love the LORD thy God with all thine heart, and with all thy soul, that thou mayest live.

7 And the LORD thy God will put all these curses upon thine enemies, and on them that hate thee, which persecuted thee.

8 And thou shalt return and obey the voice of the LORD, and do all his commandments which I command thee this day.

9 [m]And the LORD thy God will make thee plenteous in every work of thine hand, in the fruit of thy body, and in the fruit of thy cattle, and in the fruit of thy land, for good: for the LORD will again [n]rejoice over thee for good, as he rejoiced over thy fathers:

10 If thou shalt hearken unto the voice of the LORD thy God, to keep his commandments and his statutes which are written in this book of the law, *and* if thou turn unto the LORD thy God with all thine heart, and with all thy soul.

Closing advice

11 ¶ For this commandment which I command thee this day, [o]it *is* not hidden from thee, neither *is* it far off.

12 [p]It *is* not in heaven, that thou shouldest say, Who shall go up for us to heaven, and bring it unto us, that we may hear it, and do it?

13 Neither *is* it beyond the sea, that thou shouldest say, Who shall go over the sea for us, and bring it unto us, that we may hear it, and do it?

14 But the word *is* very nigh unto thee, in thy mouth, and in thy heart, that thou mayest do it.

15 ¶ See, [q]I have set before thee this day life and good, and death and evil;

16 In that I command thee this day to love the LORD thy God, to walk in his ways, and to keep his commandments and his statutes and his judgments,

30:1 [e]Lev. 26:40 [f]ch. 28 [g]ch. 4:29,30 1 Ki. 8:47
30:2 [h]Neh. 1:9 Is. 55:7 Lam. 3:40 Joel 2:12
30:3 [i]Ps. 106:45 & 126:1,4 Jer. 29:14 Lam. 3:22,32 [j]Ps. 147:2 Jer. 32:37 Ezek. 34:13 & 36:24
30:4 [k]ch. 28:64 Neh. 1:9
30:6 [l]ch. 10:16 Jer. 32:39 Ezek. 11:19 & 36:26
30:9 [m]ch. 28:11 [n]ch. 28:63 Jer. 32:41
30:11 [o]Is. 45:19
30:12 [p]Rom. 10:6
30:15 [q]ver. 1,19 ch. 11:26

30:3 GATHER THEE FROM ALL THE NATIONS. Moses prophesied a restoration of Israel that would involve their repentance and return to God (v. 2), a deliverance from captivity (vv. 3–4), a regathering to the Lord (v. 5), spiritual renewal (v. 6), and blessing (vv. 7–10). The final restoration of Israel includes: (1) a universal restoration of the "remnant" of Israel (vv. 3–5; Is. 10:21–23; 11:11–12; Jer. 30:24; 31:1,8,10; Ezek. 39:25,28);

(2) a repentance and a turning to the Messiah (vv. 2,8,10; Is. 11:10,12; Jer. 23:5–8; Ezek. 37:21–25; Hos. 5:15; 6:1–3; Rom. 11:25–27; see Mat. 23:39, note; see article on ISRAEL IN GOD'S PLAN OF SALVATION, p. 1748);

(3) spiritual renewal (vv. 3–6; Jer. 32:37–41; Ezek. 11:17–20);

(4) blessing for Israel (Jer. 31:8,10,12–13,28; Ezek. 28:25–26; Amos 9:11–15);

(5) Israel's ministering for God to the nations (Is. 49:5–6; 55:3–5; 60:1–5; 61:5–6);

(6) judgment on Israel (Ezek. 20:34–38; Mal. 3:2–5; 4:1) and of the nations (Jer. 25:29–33; Dan. 2:44–45; Joel 3:1–2,12–14; see Mat. 25:32, note; see article on THE GREAT TRIBULATION, p. 1456);

(7) great blessing upon all those who survive the judgments of Christ after the great tribulation (Is. 19:22–24; 49:5; Mic. 4:1–4; Zech. 2:10–12; Rev. 20:1–4; see Mat. 25:32, note);

(8) Israel's permanent possession of the land in peace, safety, and security (Jer. 32:37–41);

(9) restoration in the latter days (Hos. 3:4–5);

(10) Christ and the church reigning over Israel and the nations (see Rev. 20:4, note).

that thou mayest live and multiply: and the LORD thy God shall bless thee in the land whither thou goest to possess it.

17 But if thine heart turn away, so that thou wilt not hear, but shalt be drawn away, and worship other gods, and serve them;

18 [r]I denounce unto you this day, that ye shall surely perish, *and that* ye shall not prolong *your* days upon the land, whither thou passest over Jordan to go to possess it.

19 [s]I call heaven and earth to record this day against you, *that* [t]I have set before you life and death, blessing and cursing: therefore choose life, that both thou and thy seed may live:

20 That thou mayest love the LORD thy God, *and* that thou mayest obey his voice, and that thou mayest cleave unto him: for he *is* thy [u]life, and the length of thy days: that thou mayest dwell in the land which the LORD sware unto thy fathers, to Abraham, to Isaac, and to Jacob, to give them.

The appointment of Joshua

31 AND MOSES went and spake these words unto all Israel.

2 And he said unto them, I [v]*am* an hundred and twenty years old this day; I can no more [w]go out and come in: also the LORD hath said unto me, [x]Thou shalt not go over this Jordan.

3 The LORD thy God, [y]he will go over before thee, *and* he will destroy these nations from before thee, and thou shalt possess them: *and* Joshua, he shall go over before thee, [z]as the LORD hath said.

4 [a]And the LORD shall do unto them [b]as he did to Sihon and to Og, kings of the Amorites, and unto the land of them, whom he destroyed.

5 And [c]the LORD shall give them up before your face, that ye may do unto them according unto all the commandments which I have commanded you.

6 [d]Be strong and of a good courage, [e]fear not, nor be afraid of them: for the LORD thy God, [f]he *it is* that doth go with thee; [g]he will not fail thee, nor forsake thee.

7 ¶ And Moses called unto Joshua, and said unto him in the sight of all Israel, [h]Be strong and of a good courage: for thou must go with this people unto the land which the LORD hath sworn unto their fathers to give them; and thou shalt cause them to inherit it.

8 And the LORD, [i]he *it is* that doth go before thee; [j]he will be with thee, he will not fail thee, neither forsake thee: fear not, neither be dismayed.

Provision for teaching the law

9 ¶ And Moses wrote this law, [k]and delivered it unto the priests the sons of Levi, [l]which bare the ark of the covenant of the LORD, and unto all the elders of Israel.

10 And Moses commanded them, saying, At the end of *every* seven years, in the solemnity of the [m]year of release, [n]in the feast of tabernacles,

11 When all Israel is come to [o]appear before the LORD thy God in the place which he shall choose, [p]thou shalt read this law before all Israel in their hearing.

12 [q]Gather the people together, men, and women, and children, and thy stranger that *is* within thy gates, that they may hear, and that they may learn, and fear the LORD your God, and

30:18 [r]ch. 4:26 & 8:19
30:19 [s]ch. 4:26 & 31:28 [t]ver. 15
30:20 [u]Ps. 27:1 & 66:9 John 11:25
31:2 [v]Ex. 7:7 ch. 34:7 [w]Num. 27:17 1 Ki. 3:7 [x]Num. 20:12 & 27:13 ch. 3:27
31:3 [y]ch. 9:3 [z]Num. 27:21 ch. 3:28
31:4 [a]ch. 3:21 [b]Num. 21:24,33
31:5 [c]ch. 7:2
31:6 [d]Josh. 10:25 1 Chr. 22:13 [e]ch. 1:29 & 7:18 [f]ch. 20:4 [g]Josh. 1:5 Heb. 13:5
31:7 [h]ver. 23 ch. 1:38 & 3:28 Josh. 1:6
31:8 [i]Ex. 13:21 & 33:14 ch. 9:3 [j]Josh. 1:5,9 1 Chr. 28:20
31:9 [k]ver. 25 ch. 17:18 [l]Num. 4:15 Josh. 3:3 1 Chr. 15:12,15
31:10 [m]ch. 15:1 [n]Lev. 23:34
31:11 [o]ch. 16:16 [p]Josh. 8:34,35 2 Ki. 23:2 Neh. 8:1-3
31:12 [q]ch. 4:10

30:20 LOVE THE LORD THY GOD. The Israelites were commanded to maintain their relationship with God by loving Him and obeying His voice (see 6:5, note). To express that obedience, however, they had to recognize their inability to fulfill the law by bringing sacrifices of atonement for their shortcomings (see Lev. 1:2, note; see article on THE DAY OF ATONEMENT, p. 188). Life and salvation were never promised as a reward for perfect obedience. The law assumed the imperfection of faith and obedience on the part of God's people and thus provided the sacrificial system which atoned for sin. Israel's ultimate hope rested in the mercy and grace of God.

31:8 HE WILL NOT FAIL THEE. The N.T. applies this promise to all those who sincerely receive Christ as Lord and Savior (Heb. 13:5). (1) Believers are assured that if they love God above all else and depend on Him rather than material security, the Lord will never desert or forsake them, but will be their helper (cf. 1 Ki. 8:57; Jas. 1:5; see Mat. 6:30,33, notes). (2) Because of this promise, we must "be strong and of a good courage" (v. 6), persevering in trials, resisting temptations, trusting in the Lord, and fully obeying Him.

31:9 MOSES WROTE THIS LAW. The commands of God were delivered to the people by Moses in written form. These commands included not just the words of Deuteronomy but the entire Pentateuch (i.e., the first five books of the Bible). They were the Word of God in written form, the Holy Scriptures inspired, preserved, and formed in Biblical history (cf. vv. 24–26; Ex. 24:4,7; Num. 33:2; Mat. 8:4; John 5:46; 7:19; see article on THE INSPIRATION AND AUTHORITY OF SCRIPTURE, p. 1924).

observe to do all the words of this law:
13 And *that* their children, [r]which
have not known *any thing,* [s]may hear,
and learn to fear the LORD your God, as
long as ye live in the land whither ye
go over Jordan to possess it.

The LORD appears to Moses

14 ¶ And the LORD said unto Moses,
[t]Behold, thy days approach that thou
must die: call Joshua, and present
yourselves in the tabernacle of the con-
gregation, that [u]I may give him a
charge. And Moses and Joshua went,
and presented themselves in the taber-
nacle of the congregation.
15 And [v]the LORD appeared in the
tabernacle in a pillar of a cloud: and
the pillar of the cloud stood over the
door of the tabernacle.
16 ¶ And the LORD said unto Moses,
Behold, thou shalt [p]sleep with thy fa-
thers; and this people will [w]rise up,
and [x]go a-whoring after the gods of
the strangers of the land, whither they
go *to be* among them, and will [y]for-
sake me, and [z]break my covenant
which I have made with them.
17 Then my anger shall be kindled
against them in that day, and [a]I will
forsake them, and I will [b]hide my face
from them, and they shall be devoured,
and many evils and troubles shall
[q]befall them; so that they will say in
that day, [c]Are not these evils come
upon us, because our God *is* [d]not
among us?
18 And [e]I will surely hide my face
in that day for all the evils which they
shall have wrought, in that they are
turned unto other gods.
19 Now therefore write ye this song
for you, and teach it the children of Is-
rael: put it in their mouths, that this
song may be [f]a witness for me against
the children of Israel.
20 For when I shall have brought
them into the land which I sware unto
their fathers, that floweth with milk
and honey; and they shall have eaten
and filled themselves, [g]and waxen fat;
[h]then will they turn unto other gods,
and serve them, and provoke me, and
break my covenant.
21 And it shall come to pass,
[i]when many evils and troubles are be-
fallen them, that this song shall testify
[r]against them as a witness; for it
shall not be forgotten out of the
mouths of their seed: for [j]I know their
imagination [k]which they [s]go about,
even now, before I have brought them
into the land which I sware.
22 ¶ Moses therefore wrote this
song the same day, and taught it the
children of Israel.
23 [l]And he gave Joshua the son of
Nun a charge, and said, [m]Be strong
and of a good courage: for thou shalt
bring the children of Israel into the
land which I sware unto them: and I
will be with thee.
24 ¶ And it came to pass, when Mo-
ses had made an end of writing the
words of this law in a book, until they
were finished,
25 That Moses commanded the Le-
vites, which bare the ark of the cov-
enant of the LORD, saying,
26 Take this book of the law, [n]and
put it in the side of the ark of the cov-
enant of the LORD your God, that it may
be there [o]for a witness against thee.
27 [p]For I know thy rebellion, and
thy [q]stiff neck: behold, while I am yet
alive with you this day, ye have been
rebellious against the LORD; and how
much more after my death?
28 ¶ Gather unto me all the elders
of your tribes, and your officers, that I
may speak these words in their ears,
[r]and call heaven and earth to record
against them.
29 For I know that after my death
ye will utterly [s]corrupt *yourselves,* and
turn aside from the way which I have
commanded you; and [t]evil will befall
you [u]in the latter days; because ye
will do evil in the sight of the LORD, to
provoke him to anger through the work
of your hands.

The song of Moses

30 And Moses spake in the ears of
all the congregation of Israel the words
of this song, until they were ended.

31:13 [r]ch. 11:2 [s]Ps. 78:6,7
31:14 [t]Num. 27:13 ch. 34:5 [u]Num. 27:19
31:15 [v]Ex. 33:9
31:16 [w]Ex. 32:6 [x]Ex:34:15 Judg. 2:17 [y]ch. 32:15 Judg. 2:12 & 10:6,13 [z]Judg. 2:20
31:17 [a]2 Chr. 15:2 [b]ch. 32:20 Is. 8:17 & 64:7 Ezek. 39:23 [c]Judg. 6:13 [d]Num. 14:42
31:18 [e]ver. 17
31:19 [f]ver. 26
31:20 [g]ch. 32:15 Neh. 9:25 Hos. 13:6 [h]ver. 16
31:21 [i]ver. 17 [j]Hos. 5:3 & 13:5,6 [k]Amos 5:25,26
31:23 [l]ver. 14 [m]ver. 7 Josh. 1:6
31:26 [n]See 2 Ki. 22:8 [o]ver. 19
31:27 [p]ch. 9:24 & 32:20 [q]Ex. 32:9 ch. 9:6
31:28 [r]ch. 30:19 & 32:1
31:29 [s]ch. 32:5 Judg. 2:19 Hos. 9:9 [t]ch. 28:15 [u]Gen. 49:1 ch. 4:30

[p] Heb. *lie down* [q] Heb. *find them* [r] Heb. *before* [s] Heb. *do*

31:16 WILL FORSAKE ME. The Lord knew Israel's history and their basic disposition toward unfaithfulness (see v. 21). Thus God prophetically revealed to Moses their future apostasy and His corresponding judgments (vv. 16–18). This prophecy was to be preserved in the form of a song as God's warning to later generations (v. 19; ch. 32).

31:30 THIS SONG. Moses' song (ch. 32) was designed to impress upon the Israelites that their whole existence was a result of God's faithfulness

32 GIVE [v]EAR, O ye heavens,
and I will speak; and hear, O
earth, the words of my mouth.
2 [w]My doctrine shall drop as the
rain, my speech shall distil as the dew,
[x]as the small rain upon the tender
herb, and as the showers upon the
grass:
3 Because I will publish the name of
the LORD: [y]ascribe ye greatness unto
our God.
4 *He is* [z]the Rock, [a]his work *is*
perfect: for all his ways *are* judgment:
[b]a God of truth and [c]without iniquity,
just and right *is* he.
5 [d]They[t] have corrupted them-
selves, [u]their spot *is* not *the spot* of his
children: *they are* a [e]perverse and
crooked generation.
6 Do ye thus [f]requite the LORD, O
foolish people and unwise? *is* not he
[g]thy father *that* hath [h]bought thee?
hath he not [i]made thee, and estab-
lished thee?
7 ¶ Remember the days of old, con-
sider the years of [v]many generations:
[j]ask thy father, and he will show
thee; thy elders, and they will tell thee.
8 When the Most High [k]divided to
the nations their inheritance, when he
[l]separated the sons of Adam, he set
the bounds of the people according to
the number of the children of Israel.
9 For [m]the LORD's portion *is* his peo-
ple; Jacob *is* the [w]lot of his inheri-
tance.
10 He found him [n]in a desert land,
and in the waste howling wilderness;
he [x]led him about, he instructed him,
he [o]kept him as the apple of his eye.
11 [p]As an eagle stirreth up her
nest, fluttereth over her young,
spreadeth abroad her wings, taketh
them, beareth them on her wings:
12 *So* the LORD alone did lead him,
and *there was* no strange god with him.

32:1 [v]Is. 1:2
32:2 [w]1 Cor. 3:6 [x]Ps. 72:6
32:3 [y]1 Chr. 29:11
32:4 [z]Ps. 18:2 [a]2 Sam. 22:31 [b]Jer. 10:10 [c]Job 34:10
32:5 [d]ch. 31:29 [e]Phil. 2:15
32:6 [f]Ps. 116:12 [g]Is. 63:16 [h]Ps. 74:2 [i]ver. 15
32:7 [j]Ex. 13:14
32:8 [k]Zech. 9:2 [l]Gen. 11:8
32:9 [m]Ex. 19:5
32:10 [n]Jer. 2:6 [o]Ps. 17:8
32:11 [p]Is. 31:5

32:13 [q]Is. 58:14
32:14 [r]Ps. 81:16 [s]Gen. 49:11
32:15 [t]ch. 31:20 [u]Is. 1:4 [v]Is. 51:13 [w]Ps. 95:1
32:16 [x]1 Cor. 10:22
32:17 [y]Rev. 9:20
32:18 [z]Is. 17:10 [a]Jer. 2:32
32:20 [b]Mat. 17:17
32:21 [c]Ps. 78:58 [d]Ps. 31:6 [e]Rom. 10:19

13 [q]He made him ride on the high
places of the earth, that he might eat
the increase of the fields; and he made
him to suck honey out of the rock, and
oil out of the flinty rock;
14 Butter of kine, and milk of
sheep, with fat of lambs, and rams of
the breed of Bashan, and goats, [r]with
the fat of kidneys of wheat; and thou
didst drink the pure [s]blood of the
grape.
15 ¶ But Jeshurun waxed fat, and
kicked: [t]thou art waxen fat, thou art
grown thick, thou art covered *with fat-
ness;* then he [u]forsook God *which*
[v]made him, and lightly esteemed the
[w]Rock of his salvation.
16 [x]They provoked him to jealousy
with strange *gods,* with abominations
provoked they him to anger.
17 [y]They sacrificed unto devils,
[y]not to God; to gods whom they knew
not, to new *gods that* came newly up,
whom your fathers feared not.
18 [z]Of the Rock *that* begat thee
thou art unmindful, and hast [a]forgot-
ten God that formed thee.
19 And when the LORD saw *it,* he
[z]abhorred *them,* because of the pro-
voking of his sons, and of his daugh-
ters.
20 And he said, I will hide my face
from them, I will see what their end
shall be: for they *are* a very froward gen-
eration, [b]children in whom *is* no faith.
21 [c]They have moved me to jealou-
sy with *that which is* not God; they have
provoked me to anger [d]with their
vanities: and [e]I will move them to
jealousy with *those which are* not a peo-

[t] Heb. *He hath corrupted to himself* [u] Or, that they are *not his children,* that is *their blot* [v] Heb. *generation and generation* [w] Heb. *cord* [x] Or, *compassed him about* [y] Or, which were *not God;* see ver. 21 [z] Or, *despised*

and mercy. The Lord alone guided and sustained them (cf. 32:9–13). Israel's response, on the other hand, was in large measure that of wickedness and folly (32:5–6). The song concluded by warning Israel that future infidelity, rebellion, and apostasy would bring God's severe judgments on the nation (see previous note).

32:15 WAXED FAT. Prosperity was a major factor in Israel's forgetting God and embracing idolatry (cf. 8:7–20). History has repeatedly shown that in times of ease and plenty, God's people are most prone to forget God and to stop seeking His face. During adverse circumstances, however, God's people are more likely to approach God earnestly and ask for His help (cf. the book of Judges).

32:17 DEVILS. Behind the false gods and religions of this world are the spiritual powers of devils or demons (Ps. 106:37; 1 Cor. 10:20; see article on THE NATURE OF IDOLATRY, p. 428). Demons may act through their followers even to the point of performing miracles (Ex. 7:11,22; 2 Thes. 2:9–10; Rev. 13:13; 19:20). The N.T. recognizes the existence of such evil spirits and urges believers to battle against them through the power and authority of Christ (Eph. 6:12; see article on POWER OVER SATAN AND DEMONS, p. 1486).

ple; I will provoke them to anger with a foolish nation.

22 For [f]a fire is kindled in mine anger, and [a]shall burn unto the lowest hell, and [b]shall consume the earth with her increase, and set on fire the foundations of the mountains.

23 I will [g]heap mischiefs upon them; [h]I will spend mine arrows upon them.

24 *They shall be* burnt with hunger, and devoured with [c]burning heat, and with bitter destruction: I will also send the teeth of beasts upon them, with the poison of serpents of the dust.

25 The sword without, and terror [d]within, shall [e]destroy both the young man and the virgin, the suckling *also* with the man of gray hairs.

26 I said, I would scatter them into corners, I would make the remembrance of them to cease from among men:

27 Were it not that I feared the wrath of the enemy, lest their adversaries should behave themselves strangely, *and* lest they should say, [f]Our hand *is* high, and the LORD hath not done all this.

28 For they *are* a nation void of counsel, neither *is there any* understanding in them.

29 [i]O that they were wise, *that* they understood this, *that* they would consider their latter end!

30 How should one chase a thousand, and two put ten thousand to flight, except their Rock [j]had sold them, and the LORD had shut them up?

31 For their rock *is* not as our Rock, [k]even our enemies themselves *being* judges.

32 For [l]their vine [g]*is* of the vine of Sodom, and of the fields of Gomorrah: their grapes *are* grapes of gall, their clusters *are* bitter:

33 Their wine *is* [m]the poison of dragons, and the cruel [n]venom of asps.

34 *Is* not this [o]laid up in store with me, *and* sealed up among my treasures?

35 [p]To me *belongeth* vengeance, and recompence; their foot shall slide in *due* time: for [q]the day of their calamity *is* at hand, and the things that shall come upon them make haste.

36 [r]For the LORD shall judge his people, [s]and repent himself for his servants, when he seeth that *their* [h]power is gone, and [t]*there is* none shut up, or left.

37 And he shall say, [u]Where *are* their gods, *their* rock in whom they trusted,

38 Which did eat the fat of their sacrifices, *and* drank the wine of their drink offerings? let them rise up and help you, *and* be [i]your protection.

39 See now that [v]I, *even* I, *am* he, and [w]*there is* no god with me: [x]I kill, and I make alive; I wound, and I heal: neither *is there any* that can deliver out of my hand. 1 Ki. 13:6

40 For I lift up my hand to heaven, and say, I live for ever.

41 [y]If I whet my glittering sword, and mine hand take hold on judgment; I will render vengeance to mine enemies, and will reward them that hate me.

42 I will make mine arrows [z]drunk with blood, and my sword shall devour flesh; *and that* with the blood of the slain and of the captives, from the beginning of [a]revengers upon the enemy.

43 [b]Rejoice,[j] O ye nations, *with* his people: for he will [c]avenge the blood of his servants, and will render vengeance to his adversaries, and [d]will be merciful unto his land, *and* to his people.

44 ¶ And Moses came and spake all the words of this song in the ears of the people, he, and [k]Hoshea the son of Nun.

45 And Moses made an end of speaking all these words to all Israel:

46 And he said unto them, [e]Set your hearts unto all the words which I testify among you this day, which ye shall command your children to observe to do, all the words of this law.

47 For it *is* not a vain thing for you; [f]because it *is* your life: and through this thing ye shall prolong *your* days in the land, whither ye go over Jordan to possess it.

Moses to die on mount Nebo

48 [g]And the LORD spake unto Moses that selfsame day, saying,

32:22 [f]Lam. 4:11 **32:23** [g]Is. 26:15 [h]Ps. 7:12,13 **32:29** [i]Luke 19:42 **32:30** [j]Ps. 44:12 **32:31** [k]1 Sam. 4:8 Jer. 40:3 **32:32** [l]Is. 1:10 **32:33** [m]Ps. 58:4 [n]Rom. 3:13 **32:34** [o]Jer. 2:22 Rom. 2:5 **32:35** [p]Heb. 10:30 [q]2 Pet. 2:3 **32:36** [r]Ps. 135:14 [s]Jer. 31:20 Joel 2:14

[t]2 Ki. 14:26 **32:37** [u]Judg. 10:14 Jer. 2:28 **32:39** [v]Ps. 102:27 [w]Is. 45:5,18,22 [x]1 Sam. 2:6 Hos. 6:1 **32:41** [y]Is. 66:16 **32:42** [z]Jer. 46:10 [a]Jer. 30:14 Lam. 2:5 **32:43** [b]Rom. 15:10 [c]Rev. 19:2 [d]Ps. 85:1 **32:46** [e]Ezek. 40:4 **32:47** [f]Prov. 3:2 Rom. 10:5 **32:48** [g]Num. 27:12,13

[a] Or, *hath burned* [b] Or, *hath consumed* [c] Heb. *burning coals* [d] Heb. *from the chambers* [e] Heb. *bereave* [f] Or, *Our high hand, and not the LORD, hath done all this* [g] Or, is worse *than the vine of Sodom* [h] Heb. *hand* [i] Heb. *an hiding for you* [j] Or, *Praise his people, ye nations:* or, *Sing ye* [k] Or, *Joshua*

49 Get thee up into this [h]mountain
Abarim, *unto* mount Nebo, which *is* in
the land of Moab, that *is* over against
Jericho; and behold the land of Canaan,
which I give unto the children of Israel
for a possession:
50 And die in the mount whither
thou goest up, and be gathered unto
thy people; as [i]Aaron thy brother died
in mount Hor, and was gathered unto
his people:
51 Because [j]ye trespassed against
me among the children of Israel at the
waters of [1]Meribah-Kadesh, in the
wilderness of Zin; because ye [k]sancti-
fied me not in the midst of the children
of Israel.
52 [l]Yet thou shalt see the land be-
fore *thee;* but thou shalt not go thither
unto the land which I give the children
of Israel.

Moses blesses the tribes

33:1–29Ref — Gen. 49:1–28

33 AND THIS *is* [m]the blessing,
wherewith Moses [n]the man of
God blessed the children of Israel be-
fore his death.
2 And he said, [o]The LORD came
from Sinai, and rose up from Seir unto
them; he shined forth from mount Pa-
ran, and he came with [p]ten thousands
of saints: from his right hand *went* [m]a
fiery law for them.
3 Yea, [q]he loved the people; [r]all
his saints *are* in thy hand: and they
[s]sat down at thy feet; *every one* shall
[t]receive of thy words.
4 [u]Moses commanded us a law,
[v]*even* the inheritance of the congrega-
tion of Jacob.
5 And he was [w]king in [x]Jeshurun,
when the heads of the people *and* the
tribes of Israel were gathered together.
6 ¶ Let Reuben live, and not die;
and let *not* his men be few.
7 ¶ And this *is the blessing* of Judah:
and he said, Hear, LORD, the voice of
Judah, and bring him unto his people:
[y]let his hands be sufficient for him;
and be thou [z]an help *to him* from his
enemies.
8 ¶ And of Levi he said, [a]*Let* thy
Thummim and thy Urim *be* with thy
holy one, [b]whom thou didst prove at
Massah, *and with* whom thou didst
strive at the waters of Meribah;
9 Who said unto his father and to
his mother, I have not [c]seen him;
[d]neither did he acknowledge his
brethren, nor knew his own children:
for [e]they have observed thy word, and
kept thy covenant.
10 [f]They[n] shall teach Jacob thy
judgments, and Israel thy law: [o]they
shall put incense [p]before thee, [g]and
whole burnt sacrifice upon thine altar.
11 Bless, LORD, his substance, and
[h]accept the work of his hands: smite
through the loins of them that rise
against him, and of them that hate him,
that they rise not again.
12 ¶ *And* of Benjamin he said, The
beloved of the LORD shall dwell in safe-
ty by him; *and the LORD* shall cover him
all the day long, and he shall dwell be-
tween his shoulders.
13 ¶ And of Joseph he said,
[i]Blessed of the LORD *be* his land, for
the precious things of heaven, for [j]the
dew, and for the deep that coucheth be-
neath,
14 And for the precious fruits
brought forth by the sun, and for the
precious things [q]put forth by the
[r]moon,
15 And for the chief things of [k]the
ancient mountains, and for the pre-
cious things [l]of the lasting hills,
16 And for the precious things of
the earth and fulness thereof, and *for*
the good will of [m]him that dwelt in the
bush: let *the blessing* [n]come upon the
head of Joseph, and upon the top of
the head of him *that was* separated
from his brethren.
17 His glory *is like* the [o]firstling of

32:49 [h]ch. 34:1 **32:50** [i]Num. 20:25,28 **32:51** [j]Num. 20:11-13 [k]See Lev. 10:3 **32:52** [l]Num. 27:12 **33:1** [m]Gen. 49:28 [n]Ps. 90,title **33:2** [o]Hab. 3:3 [p]Dan. 7:10 Rev. 5:11 **33:3** [q]Ps. 47:4 Hos. 11:1 [r]1 Sam. 2:9 [s]Luke 10:39 [t]Prov. 2:1 **33:4** [u]John 1:17 [v]Ps. 119:111 **33:5** [w]See Gen. 36:31 [x]ch. 32:15 **33:7** [y]Gen. 49:8 [z]Ps. 146:5 **33:8** [a]Ex. 28:30 [b]ch. 8:2,3,16 Ps. 81:7 **33:9** [c]Gen. 29:32 [d]Ex. 32:26,27,28 [e]Mal. 2:5,6 **33:10** [f]Lev. 10:11 Mal. 2:7 [g]Lev. 1:9 Ps. 51:19 **33:11** [h]2 Sam. 24:23 Ezek. 20:40 **33:13** [i]Gen. 49:25 [j]Gen. 27:28 **33:15** [k]Gen. 49:26 [l]Hab. 3:6 **33:16** [m]Ex. 3:2,4 [n]Gen. 49:26 **33:17** [o]1 Chr. 5:1

[1] Or, *Strife at Kadesh* [m] Heb. *a fire of law* [n] Or, *Let them teach* [o] Or, *let them put incense* [p] Heb. *at thy nose* [q] Heb. *thrust forth* [r] Heb. *moons*

33:5 JESHURUN. This is a name for Israel meaning "the upright one, the law-keeper, the one upholding justice" (cf. v. 26; 32:15).

33:9 NEITHER ... ACKNOWLEDGE HIS BRETHREN. After Israel's sin with the golden calf (see Ex. 32), the Levites stood with God even against their nearest relatives. They held fast to the covenant and chastened those who participated in the worship of the golden calf. God rewarded them for their zeal for His cause by appointing them as guardians of the law (v. 10) and as those who would offer sacrifices (v. 10). Our love for and dedication to God and His word must always be first in our lives and take priority over friends, family, or church (Mat. 10:37–38; Luke 14:26).

his bullock, and his horns *are like* [p]the horns of [s]unicorns: with them [q]he shall push the people together to the ends of the earth: and [r]they *are* the ten thousands of Ephraim, and they *are* the thousands of Manasseh.

18 ¶ And of Zebulun he said, [s]Rejoice, Zebulun, in thy going out; and, Issachar, in thy tents.

19 They shall [t]call the people unto the mountain; there [u]they shall offer sacrifices of righteousness: for they shall suck *of* the abundance of the seas, and *of* treasures hid in the sand.

20 ¶ And of Gad he said, Blessed *be* he that [v]enlargeth Gad: he dwelleth as a lion, and teareth the arm with the crown of the head.

21 And [w]he provided the first part for himself, because there, *in* a portion of the lawgiver, *was he* [t]seated; and [x]he came with the heads of the people, he executed the justice of the LORD, and his judgments with Israel.

22 ¶ And of Dan he said, Dan *is* a lion's whelp: [y]he shall leap from Bashan.

23 ¶ And of Naphtali he said, O Naphtali, [z]satisfied with favour, and full with the blessing of the LORD: [a]possess thou the west and the south.

24 ¶ And of Asher he said, [b]*Let* Asher *be* blessed with children; let him be acceptable to his brethren, and let him [c]dip his foot in oil.

25 [u]Thy shoes *shall be* [d]iron and brass; and as thy days, *so shall* thy strength *be.*

26 ¶ *There is* [e]none like unto the God of [f]Jeshurun, [g]*who* rideth upon the heaven in thy help, and in his excellency on the sky.

27 The eternal God *is thy* [h]refuge, and underneath *are* the everlasting arms: and [i]he shall thrust out the enemy from before thee; and shall say, Destroy *them.*

28 [j]Israel then shall dwell in safety alone: [k]the fountain of Jacob *shall be* upon a land of corn and wine; also his [l]heavens shall drop down dew.

33:17 [p]Num. 23:22 [q]Ps. 44:5 [r]Gen. 48:19
33:18 [s]Gen. 49:13
33:19 [t]Is. 2:3 [u]Ps. 4:5
33:20 [v]1 Chr. 12:8
33:21 [w]Num. 32:16,17 [x]Josh. 4:12
33:22 [y]Josh. 19:47
33:23 [z]Gen. 49:21 [a]See Josh. 19:32
33:24 [b]Gen. 49:20 [c]Job 29:6
33:25 [d]ch. 8:9
33:26 [e]Ex. 15:11 [f]ch. 32:15 [g]Ps. 68:4
33:27 [h]Ps. 90:1 [i]ch. 9:3-5
33:28 [j]Jer. 23:6 [k]ch. 8:7,8 [l]Gen. 27:28
33:29 [m]Ps. 144:15 [n]2 Sam. 7:23 [o]Ps. 115:9 [p]Ps. 18:44 [q]ch. 32:13
34:1 [r]Num. 27:12 [s]ch. 3:27 [t]Gen. 14:14
34:2 [u]ch. 11:24
34:3 [v]2 Chr. 28:15
34:4 [w]Gen. 12:7 [x]ch. 3:27
34:5 [y]ch. 32:50
34:6 [z]See Jude 9
34:7 [a]ch. 31:2 [b]Gen 27:1
34:8 [c]See Gen. 50:3,10 Num. 20:29
34:9 [d]Is. 11:2 Dan. 6:3 [e]Num. 27:18,23

29 [m]Happy *art* thou, O Israel: [n]who *is* like unto thee, O people saved by the LORD, [o]the shield of thy help, and who *is* the sword of thy excellency! and thine enemies [p]shall[v] be found liars unto thee; and [q]thou shalt tread upon their high places.

The death of Moses

34 AND MOSES went up from the plains of Moab [r]unto the mountain of Nebo, to the top of [w]Pisgah, that *is* over against Jericho. And the LORD [s]showed him all the land of Gilead, [t]unto Dan,

2 And all Naphtali, and the land of Ephraim, and Manasseh, and all the land of Judah, [u]unto the utmost sea,

3 And the south, and the plain of the valley of Jericho, [v]the city of palm trees, unto Zoar.

4 And the LORD said unto him, [w]This *is* the land which I sware unto Abraham, unto Isaac, and unto Jacob, saying, I will give it unto thy seed: [x]I have caused thee to see *it* with thine eyes, but thou shalt not go over thither.

5 ¶ [y]So Moses the servant of the LORD died there in the land of Moab, according to the word of the LORD.

6 And he buried him in a valley in the land of Moab, over against Bethpeor: but [z]no man knoweth of his sepulchre unto this day.

7 ¶ [a]And Moses *was* an hundred and twenty years old when he died: [b]his eye was not dim, nor his [x]natural force [y]abated.

8 ¶ And the children of Israel wept for Moses in the plains of Moab [c]thirty days: so the days of weeping *and* mourning for Moses were ended.

9 ¶ And Joshua the son of Nun was full of the [d]spirit of wisdom; for [e]Moses had laid his hands upon him: and the children of Israel hearkened unto

[s] Heb. *an unicorn* [t] Heb. *ceiled* [u] Or, Under *thy shoes* shall be *iron* [v] Or, *shall be subdued* [w] Or, *The hill* [x] Heb. *moisture* [y] Heb. *fled*

34:1 MOSES WENT UP. Those who have lived their lives in fellowship with God do not fear death. Because of their trust in God, they can even anticipate death with peace and joy (cf. Luke 2:29; Phil. 1:23). Like Moses, they have been given only a glimpse of the promised land (vv. 1–4); only after death do they inherit the "city which hath foundations, whose builder and maker *is* God" (Heb. 11:10; see Phil. 1:21, note).

34:5 MOSES THE SERVANT OF THE LORD DIED. This record of Moses' death was probably written by Joshua soon after the great leader's death (v. 9). Moses was not allowed to enter the land before his death (v. 4). However, many years later Moses did enter the land when he appeared on the Mount of Transfiguration and spoke with Jesus (Mat. 17:3).

him, and did as the LORD commanded
Moses.
10 ¶ And there [f]arose not a proph-
et since in Israel like unto Moses,
[g]whom the LORD knew face to face,
11 In all [h]the signs and the won-
ders, which the LORD sent him to do in
the land of Egypt to Pharaoh, and to all
his servants, and to all his land,
12 And in all that mighty hand, and
in all the great terror which Moses
showed in the sight of all Israel.

34:10 [f]ch. 18:15 [g]Ex. 33:11 ch. 5:4
34:11 [h]ch. 7:19

34:10 AROSE NOT A PROPHET ... LIKE UNTO MOSES. Moses' great distinctions were his intimate fellowship with God and his understanding of the nature and person of God. The foremost desire of all believers should be to know God and experience His close fellowship. It is their greatest privilege and right as God's children (John 1:12; 17:3; Rom. 8:14–15; Gal. 4:6). No person in Christ, possessing an inner life of devotion and an outer life of godliness, will be denied the presence and grace of God. The fellowship of God—the Father, the Son, and the Holy Spirit—is the believer's greatest promise and reward (John 14:15–21,23,26; Rev. 3:20).

JOSHUA

Outline

I. Preparing for Entry and Entering Canaan (1:1—5:15)
 A. Joshua Is Commissioned by God (1:1–9)
 B. Preparations for Crossing the Jordan (1:10—3:13)
 C. Crossing the Jordan River (3:14—4:25)
 D. Circumcision, Passover, and Encounter at Gilgal (5:1–15)
II. Conquering the Promised Land (6:1—13:7)
 A. Conquests in Central Canaan (6:1—8:35)
  1. Victory at Jericho (6:1–27)
  2. Defeat at Ai because of Achan's Sin (7:1–26)
  3. Victory at Ai (8:1–29)
  4. Worship and Covenant Renewal at Shechem (8:30–35)
 B. Conquests in Southern Canaan (9:1—10:43)
  1. Treaty with the Gibeonites (9:1–27)
  2. Destruction of the Amorite Coalition (10:1–43)
 C. Conquests in Northern Canaan (11:1–15)
 D. Summary of the Conquered Territories (11:16—12:24)
 E. Summary of the Unconquered Territories (13:1–7)
III. Dividing the Inheritance (13:8—22:34)
 A. Tribes East of the Jordan (13:8–33)
 B. Tribes West of the Jordan (14:1—19:51)
 C. Special Allotments (20:1—21:45)
  1. Six Cities of Refuge (20:1–9)
  2. Cities of the Levites (21:1–45)
 D. Return of the Eastern Tribes (22:1–34)
IV. Joshua's Farewell Messages (23:1—24:28)
 A. Addresses Israel's Rulers (23:1–16)
 B. Addresses All Israel; Covenant Renewal at Shechem (24:1–28)
Conclusion (24:29–33)
 A. Death and Burial of Joshua (24:29–31)
 B. Burial of Joseph's Bones (24:32)
 C. Death and Burial of Eleazer (24:33)

Author: Joshua

Theme: Conquering Canaan

Date of Writing: 14th century B.C.

Background

The book of Joshua is a continuation of the history of the Pentateuch. It records Israel's crossing the Jordan River into Canaan after the death of Moses, as well as the conquest and settlement of Canaan by the twelve tribes under Joshua's leadership. The Biblical date for Israel's invasion of Canaan is about 1405 B.C. The book covers the next 25–30 years

of Israel's history, telling how God "gave unto Israel all the land which he sware to give unto their fathers" (21:43).

Appropriately, the book is named after its principal character who predominates as God's leader throughout the book. Joshua's personal history prepared him well as leader for the conquest. Living near the end of Israel's oppression in Egypt, Joshua witnessed God's ten plague judgments, the first Passover, the miraculous Red Sea crossing, and the supernatural signs (and judgments) during Israel's wilderness journeys. He served Moses as military leader in the battle against the Amalekites soon after leaving Egypt (Ex. 17:8–16), and he alone accompanied Moses up Mount Sinai when God gave Israel the Ten Commandments (Ex. 24:12–18). As Moses' assistant, Joshua demonstrated an intense devotion and heart for God by often tarrying long in the presence of the Lord (Ex. 33:11). He was a man who treasured God's holy presence. He must have learned much from Moses, his trusted counselor and guide, about the ways of God and the difficulties of leading the people. At Kadesh-barnea Joshua served Moses as one of the twelve spies that scouted the land of Canaan; along with Caleb, Joshua vigorously resisted the majority report of unbelief (Num. 14). Many years before replacing Moses as Israel's leader, Joshua demonstrated himself to be a man of faith, vision, courage, loyalty, resolute obedience, prayer, and dedication to God and His word. By the time he was chosen to replace Moses, he was a man "in whom *is* the spirit" (Num. 27:18; cf. Deut. 34:9).

Authorship of the book is credited to Joshua by Jewish tradition (the Talmud). The act of writing is mentioned twice in the book in connection with Joshua (18:9; 24:26). Internal evidence strongly indicates that the author was an eyewitness of the conquest (cf. "us" in 5:6; note that Rahab was still alive when the author wrote, 6:25). The parts of the book added after the death of Joshua—e.g., 15:13–17 (cf. Judg. 1:9–13); 24:29–33—were perhaps written by one of the "elders that overlived Joshua" (24:31). Joshua died about 1375 B.C. at the age of 110 (24:29).

Purpose

Joshua was written as a record of God's faithfulness in fulfilling His covenant promises to Israel concerning the land of Canaan (23:14; cf. Gen. 12:6–7). The conquest victories are presented as God's acts of redemption for Israel and His acts of judgment upon a decadent Canaanite culture (see Deut. 9:4). Violence in the book must be viewed from this perspective. Archaeology confirms that gross immorality and cruelty characterized the Canaanite people whom Israel replaced in the land.

Survey

Joshua begins where Deuteronomy ends. Israel was still encamped on the plains of Moab (Deut. 34:1), directly east of Jericho and the Jordan River. The book divides into three sections. (1) Section one (1:1—5:15) describes Joshua's commissioning by God as Moses' successor and Israel's preparation for entering Canaan (1:1—3:13), their crossing the Jordan (3:14—4:24), and their first covenant activities in the land (ch. 5). God promised Joshua: "every place that the sole of your foot shall tread upon, that I have given unto you" (1:3).

(2) Section two (6:1—13:7) describes how Israel marched in obedience against well-armed city-states with fortified walls. God gave His people decisive victories in central (chs. 6–8), southern (chs. 9–10), and northern (chs. 11–12) Canaan, whereby Israel gained control of the hill country (south to north) and the Negev. The highly unusual manner in which Jericho was conquered clearly demonstrated to Israel who the Captain of their salvation was (ch. 6). Israel's defeat at Ai reveals the book's honesty and the serious obedience that God required of Israel (ch. 7).

(3) Section three (13:8—22:34) records the distribution of the land by Joshua to the twelve tribes, the inheritance of Caleb, the six cities of refuge, and the forty-eight Levite cities among the tribes. The book concludes with two farewell messages by Joshua (23:1—24:28) and an epitaph to Joshua and Eleazer (24:29–33).

Special Features

Seven major features or emphases characterize this book. (1) It is the first of the O.T. historical books to describe Israel's history as a nation in Palestine. (2) It provides considerable insight into the remarkable life of Joshua as God's choice for completing Moses' work; his task was to establish Israel as the covenant people in the land of promise. (3) The book records numerous divine miracles on Israel's behalf, the two most dramatic being the fall of Jericho (ch. 6) and the prolongation of the daylight hours at the battle of Gibeon (ch. 10). (4) It is the foremost O.T. book describing the concept of "holy war" as a specific and limited mission prescribed by God within the larger context of salvation history. (5) The book emphasizes three grand truths about God's relationship to His covenant people: (a) His faithfulness, (b) His holiness, and (c) His salvation. (6) The book highlights the importance of keeping alive the heritage of God's saving acts on behalf of His people and of perpetuating that heritage from one generation to the next. (7) The book's lengthy account of Achan's transgression and subsequent punishment (ch. 7), along with other admonitions, warnings, and punishments, emphasizes the importance of the fear of the Lord in the hearts of God's people.

New Testament Fulfillment

Joshua's name (Heb. *Yehoshua* or *Yeshua*) is the Hebrew equivalent of the name "Jesus" in the N.T. (see 1:1, note). In his role of leading Israel into the promised land, Joshua is an O.T. type or foreshadowing of Jesus, whose role is to bring "many sons into glory" (Heb. 2:10; 4:1–13; cf. 2 Cor. 2:14). Also, as the first Joshua wielded the sword of God's terrible judgment in conquest, so the second Joshua will wield it in conquest over the nations at the end of history (Rev. 19:11–16).

Reading Joshua

In order to read the entire Old Testament in one year, the book of Joshua should be read in 9 days, according to the following schedule: ☐ 1–2 ☐ 3–4 ☐ 5–6 ☐ 7–9 ☐ 10–12 ☐ 13–15 ☐ 16–19 ☐ 20–22 ☐ 23–24

NOTES

The LORD instructs Joshua

1 NOW AFTER the death of Moses
the servant of the LORD it came to
pass, that the LORD spake unto Joshua
the son of Nun, Moses' [a]minister, say-
ing,
2 [b]Moses my servant is dead; now
therefore arise, go over this Jordan,
thou, and all this people, unto the land
which I do give to them, *even* to the
children of Israel.
3 [c]Every place that the sole of your
foot shall tread upon, that have I given
unto you, as I said unto Moses.
4 [d]From the wilderness and this
Lebanon even unto the great river, the
river Euphrates, all the land of the Hit-
tites, and unto the great sea toward the
going down of the sun, shall be your
coast.
5 [e]There shall not any man be able
to stand before thee all the days of thy
life: [f]as I was with Moses, *so* [g]I will
be with thee: [h]I will not fail thee, nor
forsake thee.
6 [i]Be strong and of a good cour-
age: for [a]unto this people shalt thou
divide for an inheritance the land,
which I sware unto their fathers to give
them.
7 Only be thou strong and very cou-
rageous, that thou mayest observe to
do according to all the law, [j]which
Moses my servant commanded thee:
[k]turn not from it *to* the right hand or
to the left, that thou mayest [b]prosper
whithersoever thou goest.
8 [l]This book of the law shall not
depart out of thy mouth; but [m]thou

1:1 [a]Ex. 24:13 Deut. 1:38
1:2 [b]Deut. 34:5
1:3 [c]Deut. 11:24
1:4 [d]Gen. 15:18 Ex. 23:31 Num. 34:3-12
1:5 [e]Deut. 7:24 [f]Ex. 3:12 [g]Deut. 31:8,23 ch. 3:7 & 6:27 Is. 43:2,5 [h]Deut. 31:6,8
1:6 [i]Deut. 31:7,23
1:7 [j]Num. 27:23 Deut. 31:7 ch. 11:15 [k]Deut. 5:32 & 28:14
1:8 [l]Deut. 17:18,19 [m]Ps. 1:2

[a] Or, *thou shalt cause this people to inherit the land* [b] Or, *do wisely*

1:1 JOSHUA THE SON OF NUN. Joshua had been an intimate and faithful assistant of Moses during the forty years of wilderness wandering (Ex. 17:8–13; 24:13; 32:17–19; Num. 13:8,16). As one filled with the Spirit, he had been commissioned as Moses' successor (Num. 27:18–23; Deut. 34:9). God was now calling him to lead His people into the land of promise (see Gen. 12:6–7; 15:18–21). The name Joshua means "the LORD saves" (or "the LORD is salvation"). The Greek form for this name is "Jesus" (see Mat. 1:21, note). Joshua is a type (or representative) of Jesus Christ in that he led God's people into the promised land and to victory over their enemies (Heb. 4:1,6–8; see article on CHRIST IN THE OLD TESTAMENT, p. 562). The conquest of Canaan (Palestine) began about 1405 B.C.; Joshua's leadership of Israel covered about twenty-five years.

1:2 GO OVER THIS JORDAN . . . UNTO THE LAND. Like the experiences of Israel in the wilderness, their entrance into and conquest of Canaan can be called an "example" that was "written for our admonition" (cf. 1 Cor. 10:11). (1) The promised land and its conquest by the people of God typifies not heaven, but believers' present spiritual inheritance and salvation in Christ.

(2) Although believers already possess salvation and in one sense are in the "heavenly places in Christ" (Eph. 1:3), they must yet fight the fight of faith to ensure their possession of final salvation and eternal rest (1 Tim. 1:18–20; 4:16; 6:12). As with the taking of Canaan, the possession of salvation and eternal life involves spiritual warfare and conquest (Eph. 6:10–20).

(3) For Joshua and the Israelites, the possession of the promised land was realized and maintained by faith in God, expressed in obedience to His word and in warfare against God's enemies (vv. 7–9; cf. Deut. 28). For the believer under the new covenant, the possession of salvation and God's blessings are likewise maintained by a present living faith in Christ (see article on FAITH AND GRACE, p. 1738) that is expressed in obedience to His word (see John 3:36, note) and in spiritual warfare against sin, the flesh, and Satan (Gal. 5:16–21; see Eph. 6:11, note). Thus, possession of the land (i.e., the Lord's inheritance) may be forfeited, as Joshua warns (23:16). The hope of final possession of God's ultimate rest lies in faith in God's promises (v. 6), in His power (3:14–17), and in His personal presence (vv. 5,9).

1:5 I WILL BE WITH THEE. God's foundational promise to Joshua—"I will be with thee: I will not fail thee, nor forsake thee"—is likewise God's commitment to all believers in the struggles of their faith (Mat. 28:20; Heb. 13:5–6; cf. Deut. 31:6; see Ex. 3:14, note). God's abiding presence with us is now a reality through His Son (Mat. 1:23) and the gift of the Holy Spirit (Luke 24:49).

1:7 OBSERVE . . . ALL THE LAW. In order to possess the promised land, Joshua and the Israelites had to commit themselves to obeying God's written Word (see next note). The Word of God written in the "book" (i.e., Scripture, v. 8) was to be their central authority as opposed to all human ideas, tradition, or religions. This principle is applicable to believers under both the old and new covenants.

1:8 THIS BOOK OF THE LAW. This phrase refers to the first five books of the Bible, which record God's words, commands, and revelation to Moses (cf. Deut. 31:9–12,24–26). Joshua was to be faithful to God's word by talking about it (cf. Deut. 6:7), meditating on it (cf. Ps. 1:2; 119:97), and obeying it fully (cf. Ezra 7:10; Jas. 1:22–25).

1:8 MEDITATE THEREIN DAY AND NIGHT. "Meditate" (Heb. *hagah*) means to read quietly or to talk to yourself as you think. It involves reflecting upon God's words and ways and applying them to every area of your life (Ps. 1:2; 63:6; 77:12; 143:5).

1:8 PROSPEROUS . . . GOOD SUCCESS. Those who know and follow God's word and law will be prosperous and successful in that they pos-

shalt meditate therein day and night, that thou mayest observe to do according to all that is written therein: for then thou shalt make thy way prosperous, and then thou shalt [c]have good success.

osh. 2:5

9 [n]Have not I commanded thee? Be strong and of a good courage; [o]be not afraid, neither be thou dismayed: for the LORD thy God *is* with thee whithersoever thou goest.

10 ¶ Then Joshua commanded the officers of the people, saying,

11 Pass through the host, and command the people, saying, Prepare you victuals; for [p]within three days ye shall pass over this Jordan, to go in to possess the land, which the LORD your God giveth you to possess it.

12 ¶ And to the Reubenites, and to the Gadites, and to half the tribe of Manasseh, spake Joshua, saying,

13 Remember [q]the word which Moses the servant of the LORD commanded you, saying, The LORD your God hath given you rest, and hath given you this land.

14 Your wives, your little ones, and your cattle, shall remain in the land which Moses gave you on this side Jordan; but ye shall pass before your brethren [d]armed, all the mighty men of valour, and help them;

15 Until the LORD have given your brethren rest, as *he hath given* you, and they also have possessed the land which the LORD your God giveth them: [r]then ye shall return unto the land of your possession, and enjoy it, which Moses the LORD's servant gave you on this side Jordan toward the sunrising.

16 ¶ And they answered Joshua, saying, All that thou commandest us we will do, and whithersoever thou sendest us, we will go.

17 According as we hearkened unto Moses in all things, so will we hearken unto thee: only the LORD thy God [s]be with thee, as he was with Moses.

18 Whosoever *he be* that doth rebel against thy commandment, and will not hearken unto thy words in all that thou commandest him, he shall be put to death: only be strong and of a good courage.

Two spies sent to Jericho

2 AND JOSHUA the son of Nun [e]sent [t]out of Shittim two men to spy secretly, saying, Go view the land, even Jericho. And they went, and [u]came into an harlot's house, named [v]Rahab, and [f]lodged there.

2 And [w]it was told the king of Jericho, saying, Behold, there came men in hither tonight of the children of Israel to search out the country.

3 And the king of Jericho sent unto Rahab, saying, Bring forth the men that are come to thee, which are entered into thine house: for they be come to search out all the country.

4 [x]And the woman took the two men, and hid them, and said thus, There came men unto me, but I wist not whence they *were*:

5 And it came to pass *about the time*

1:9 [n]Deut. 31:7,8,23 [o]Ps. 27:1 Jer. 1:8
1:11 [p]Deut. 9:1 & 11:31
1:13 [q]Num. 32:20-28 ch. 22:2-4
1:15 [r]ch. 22:4
1:17 [s]1 Sam. 20:13 1 Ki. 1:37
2:1 [t]Num. 25:1 [u]Heb. 11:31 Jas. 2:25 [v]Mat. 1:5
2:2 [w]ver. 22
2:4 [x]See 2 Sam. 17:19,20

[c] Or, *do wisely* [d] Heb. *marshalled by five* as Ex. 13:18 [e] Or, *had sent* [f] Heb. *lay*

sess the wisdom to live righteously and to achieve God's goal for their lives (Ps. 14:2; 119:99; Prov. 1:3; 10:5). The requirements for prosperity and success are: (1) be strong, courageous, and diligent (vv. 6–7); (2) make God's Word your authoritative guide for all beliefs and actions (v. 7); (3) study and meditate daily on God's Word (v. 8); and (4) determine to seek earnestly the presence of God throughout our lives (vv. 5,9). This message to Joshua provides us with a set of general principles for successful living. However, we must be careful never to conclude that God is bound to furnish material prosperity to everyone who follows these conditions. Such general principles are not absolute guarantees, for they are subject to God's higher choices for each of us; sometimes He permits us to undergo suffering and adversity (see 1 John 2, note).

2:1 HARLOT'S HOUSE. Rahab's house (perhaps an inn) would have been a good place for strangers to enter and gain information without undue alarm or suspicion.

2:1 RAHAB. Rahab was a sinful woman from a pagan background who recognized the God of Israel as the true God of heaven and earth (vv. 10–11). She abandoned Canaan's gods, in faith joined with Israel and its God (Heb. 11:31; Jas. 2:25), and eventually became an ancestor of the Messiah (Mat. 1:5–6). The salvation of Rahab illustrates that even while God is in the process of judgment, any person who "feareth him, and worketh righteousness, is accepted with him" (Acts 10:35).

2:5 WHITHER THE MEN WENT I WOT [KNOW] NOT. Rahab's lie does not justify lying in special circumstances by N.T. believers (cf. Ex. 20:16; Deut. 5:20). At this time, Rahab was not a member of the covenant community and was not bound to the moral laws of the covenant. Her lying never receives approval in Scripture, only her faith and works (Heb. 11:31; Jas. 2:25). God in no way needed to rely on deception to fulfill His covenant promises or to protect the spies (1:5–6).

of shutting of the gate, when it was
dark, that the men went out: whither
the men went I wot not: pursue after
them quickly; for ye shall overtake
them.
6 But [y]she had brought them up to
the roof of the house, and hid them
with the stalks of flax, which she had
laid in order upon the roof.
7 And the men pursued after them
the way to Jordan unto the fords: and
as soon as they which pursued after
them were gone out, they shut the
gate.
8 ¶ And before they were laid down,
she came up unto them upon the roof;
9 And she said unto the men, I
know that the LORD hath given you the
land, and that [z]your terror is fallen
upon us, and that all the inhabitants of
the land [g]faint because of you.
10 For we have heard how the LORD
[a]dried up the water of the Red sea for
you, when ye came out of Egypt; and
[b]what ye did unto the two kings of the
Amorites, that *were* on the other side
Jordan, Sihon and Og, whom ye utterly
destroyed.
11 And as soon as we had [c]heard
these things, [d]our hearts did melt, nei-
ther [h]did there remain any more cour-
age in any man, because of you: for
[e]the LORD your God, he *is* God in heav-
en above, and in earth beneath.
12 Now therefore, I pray you,
[f]swear unto me by the LORD, since I
have shown you kindness, that ye will
also show kindness unto [g]my father's
house, and [h]give me a true token:
13 And *that* ye will save alive my fa-
ther, and my mother, and my brethren,
and my sisters, and all that they have,
and deliver our lives from death.
14 And the men answered her, Our
life [i]for yours, if ye utter not this our
business. And it shall be, when the
LORD hath given us the land, that [i]we
will deal kindly and truly with thee.
15 Then she [j]let them down by a
cord through the window: for her
house *was* upon the town wall, and she
dwelt upon the wall.
16 And she said unto them, Get you
to the mountain, lest the pursuers

2:6 [y]See Ex. 1:17 2 Sam. 17:19
2:9 [z]Gen. 35:5 Ex. 23:27 Deut. 2:25 & 11:25
2:10 [a]Ex. 14:21 ch. 4:23 [b]Num. 21:24,34, 35
2:11 [c]Ex. 15:14,15 [d]ch. 5:1 & 7:5 Is. 13:7 [e]Deut. 4:39
2:12 [f]See 1 Sam. 20:14,15,17 [g]See 1 Tim. 5:8 [h]ver. 18
2:14 [i]Judg. 1:24 Mat. 5:7
2:15 [j]Acts 9:25
2:17 [k]Ex. 20:7
2:18 [l]ver. 12 [m]ch. 6:23
2:19 [n]1 Ki. 2:32 Mat. 27:25
2:24 [o]Ex. 23:31 ch. 6:2 & 21:44
3:1 [p]ch. 2:1
3:2 [q]ch. 1:10,11

meet you; and hide yourselves there
three days, until the pursuers be re-
turned: and afterward may ye go your
way.
17 And the men said unto her, We
will be [k]blameless of this thine oath
which thou hast made us swear.
18 [l]Behold, *when* we come into the
land, thou shalt bind this line of scarlet
thread in the window which thou didst
let us down by: [m]and thou shalt
[j]bring thy father, and thy mother, and
thy brethren, and all thy father's
household, home unto thee.
19 And it shall be, *that* whosoever
shall go out of the doors of thy house
into the street, his blood *shall be* upon
his head, and we *will be* guiltless: and
whosoever shall be with thee in the
house, [n]his blood *shall be* on our head,
if *any* hand be upon him.
20 And if thou utter this our busi-
ness, then we will be quit of thine oath
which thou hast made us to swear.
21 And she said, According unto
your words, so *be* it. And she sent them
away, and they departed: and she
bound the scarlet line in the window.
22 And they went, and came unto
the mountain, and abode there three
days, until the pursuers were returned:
and the pursuers sought *them* through-
out all the way, but found *them* not.
23 ¶ So the two men returned, and
descended from the mountain, and
passed over, and came to Joshua the
son of Nun, and told him all *things* that
befell them:
24 And they said unto Joshua, Truly
[o]the LORD hath delivered into our
hands all the land; for even all the in-
habitants of the country do [g]faint be-
cause of us.

Israel crosses the Jordan

3 AND JOSHUA rose early in the
morning; and they removed [p]from
Shittim, and came to Jordan, he and all
the children of Israel, and lodged there
before they passed over.
2 And it came to pass [q]after three

[g] Heb. *melt* [h] Heb. *rose up* [i] Heb. *instead of you to die* [j] Heb. *gather*

2:18 SCARLET LINE. The scarlet cord parallels the Passover lamb. Just as the blood of the lamb was put on the houses of the Israelites in order to protect them from the judgment of God (Ex. 12:21–23), so the scarlet cord hanging from Rahab's home brought safety and deliverance for her household. For this reason, some see the scarlet cord as a type of the blood of Christ, similar to the blood of the Passover lamb (see article on THE PASSOVER, p. 110).

days, that the officers went through the host;

3 And they commanded the people, saying, [r]When ye see the ark of the covenant of the LORD your God, [s]and the priests the Levites bearing it, then ye shall remove from your place, and go after it.

4 [t]Yet there shall be a space between you and it, about two thousand cubits by measure: come not near unto it, that ye may know the way by which ye must go: for ye have not passed *this* way [k]heretofore.

5 And Joshua said unto the people, [u]Sanctify yourselves: for tomorrow the LORD will do wonders among you.

6 And Joshua spake unto the priests, saying, [v]Take up the ark of the covenant, and pass over before the people. And they took up the ark of the covenant, and went before the people.

7 ¶ And the LORD said unto Joshua, This day will I begin to [w]magnify thee in the sight of all Israel, that they may know that, [x]as I was with Moses, *so* I will be with thee.

8 And thou shalt command [y]the priests that bear the ark of the covenant, saying, When ye are come to the brink of the water of Jordan, [z]ye shall stand still in Jordan.

9 ¶ And Joshua said unto the children of Israel, Come hither, and hear the words of the LORD your God.

10 And Joshua said, Hereby ye shall know that [a]the living God *is* among you, and *that* he will without fail [b]drive out from before you the Canaanites, and the Hittites, and the Hivites, and the Perizzites, and the Girgashites, and the Amorites, and the Jebusites.

11 Behold, the ark of the covenant of [c]the Lord of all the earth passeth over before you into Jordan.

3:3 [r]See Num. 10:33 [s]Deut. 31:9,25
3:4 [t]Ex. 19:12
3:5 [u]Ex. 19:10,14,15 Lev. 20:7 Num. 11:18 ch. 7:13 1 Sam. 16:5 Joel 2:16
3:6 [v]Num. 4:15
3:7 [w]ch. 4:14 1 Chr. 29:25 2 Chr. 1:1 [x]ch. 1:5
3:8 [y]ver. 3 [z]ver. 17
3:10 [a]Deut. 5:26 1 Sam. 17:26 2 Ki. 19:4 Hos. 1:10 Mat. 16:16 1 Thes. 1:9 [b]Ex. 33:2 Deut. 7:1 Ps. 44:2
3:11 [c]ver. 13 Mic. 4:13 Zech. 4:14 & 6:5
3:12 [d]ch. 4:2
3:13 [e]ver. 15,16 [f]ver. 11 [g]Ps. 78:13 & 114:3
3:14 [h]Acts 7:45
3:15 [i]ver. 13 [j]1 Chr. 12:15 Jer. 12:5 & 49:19 [k]ch. 4:18 & 5:10,12
3:16 [l]1 Ki. 4:12 & 7:46 [m]Deut. 3:17 [n]Gen. 14:3 Num. 34:3
3:17 [o]See Ex. 14:29
4:1 [p]Deut. 27:2 ch. 3:17
4:2 [q]ch. 3:12

12 Now therefore [d]take you twelve men out of the tribes of Israel, out of every tribe a man.

13 And it shall come to pass, [e]as soon as the soles of the feet of the priests that bear the ark of the LORD, [f]the Lord of all the earth, shall rest in the waters of Jordan, *that* the waters of Jordan shall be cut off *from* the waters that come down from above; and they [g]shall stand upon an heap.

14 ¶ And it came to pass, when the people removed from their tents, to pass over Jordan, and the priests bearing the [h]ark of the covenant before the people;

15 And as they that bare the ark were come unto Jordan, and [i]the feet of the priests that bare the ark were dipped in the brim of the water, (for [j]Jordan overfloweth all his banks [k]all the time of harvest,)

16 That the waters which came down from above stood *and* rose up upon an heap very far from the city Adam, that *is* beside [l]Zaretan: and those that came down [m]toward the sea of the plain, *even* [n]the salt sea, failed, *and* were cut off: and the people passed over right against Jericho.

17 And the priests that bare the ark of the covenant of the LORD stood firm on dry ground in the midst of Jordan, [o]and all the Israelites passed over on dry ground, until all the people were passed clean over Jordan. Judg. 7:9-23

4 AND IT came to pass, when all the people were clean passed [p]over Jordan, that the LORD spake unto Joshua, saying,

2 [q]Take you twelve men out of the people, out of every tribe a man,

3 And command ye them, saying, Take you hence out of the midst of Jor-

[k] Heb. *since yesterday, and the third day*

3:3 ARK OF THE COVENANT. God was more than invisibly present among His people, for the "ark of the covenant" stood as a symbol of His presence in their midst (Ex. 25:22; cf. Num. 10:35). As they were now led into the possession of the promised land, the Lord also openly manifested Himself in miracles (vv. 5,14–17; 4:18).

3:5 SANCTIFY YOURSELVES. The act of purification (cf. Ex. 19:10,14–15) points to the principle that God will not act powerfully on behalf of His people if they are not inwardly clean and aligned with His will. Before we ask God to perform signs and wonders in our midst, we must first make sure our hearts are pure and our desires guided by His Holy Spirit (see Acts 2:38, note; 3:26, note).

3:13 THE WATERS ... SHALL STAND UPON AN HEAP. God divided the waters at the Jordan just as He had divided the waters at the Red Sea (Ex. 14). This miracle provided clear evidence that the living God was among His people. By this experiential demonstration of His power, God strengthened the faith of His people so that they might face the challenges of possessing the promised land. Without such power, they could not have taken walled cities or advanced forward in spite of the giants of opposition to conquer the new land.

dan, out of the place where [r]the priests' feet stood firm, twelve stones, and ye shall carry them over with you, and leave them in [s]the lodging place, where ye shall lodge this night.

4 Then Joshua called the twelve men, whom he had prepared of the children of Israel, out of every tribe a man:

5 And Joshua said unto them, Pass over before the ark of the LORD your God into the midst of Jordan, and take you up every man of you a stone upon his shoulder, according unto the number of the tribes of the children of Israel:

6 That this may be a sign among you, *that* [t]when your children ask *their fathers* [1]in time to come, saying, What *mean* ye by these stones?

7 Then ye shall answer them, That [u]the waters of Jordan were cut off before the ark of the covenant of the LORD; when it passed over Jordan, the waters of Jordan were cut off: and these stones shall be for [v]a memorial unto the children of Israel for ever.

8 And the children of Israel did so as Joshua commanded, and took up twelve stones out of the midst of Jordan, as the LORD spake unto Joshua, according to the number of the tribes of the children of Israel, and carried them over with them unto the place where they lodged, and laid them down there.

9 And Joshua set up twelve stones in the midst of Jordan, in the place where the feet of the priests which bare the ark of the covenant stood: and they are there unto this day.

10 ¶ For the priests which bare the ark stood in the midst of Jordan, until every thing was finished that the LORD commanded Joshua to speak unto the people, according to all that Moses commanded Joshua: and the people hasted and passed over.

11 And it came to pass, when all the people were clean passed over, that the ark of the LORD passed over, and the priests, in the presence of the people.

12 And [w]the children of Reuben, and the children of Gad, and half the tribe of Manasseh, passed over armed before the children of Israel, as Moses spake unto them:

13 About forty thousand [m]prepared for war passed over before the LORD unto battle, to the plains of Jericho.

14 ¶ On that day the LORD [x]magnified Joshua in the sight of all Israel; and they feared him, as they feared Moses, all the days of his life.

15 And the LORD spake unto Joshua, saying,

16 Command the priests that bear [y]the ark of the testimony, that they come up out of Jordan.

17 Joshua therefore commanded the priests, saying, Come ye up out of Jordan.

18 And it came to pass, when the priests that bare the ark of the covenant of the LORD were come up out of the midst of Jordan, *and* the soles of the priests' feet were [n]lifted up unto the dry land, that the waters of Jordan returned unto their place, [z]and [o]flowed over all his banks, as *they did* before.

19 ¶ And the people came up out of Jordan on the tenth *day* of the first month, and encamped [a]in Gilgal, in the east border of Jericho.

20 And [b]those twelve stones, which they took out of Jordan, did Joshua pitch in Gilgal.

21 And he spake unto the children of Israel, saying, [c]When your children shall ask their fathers [1]in time to come, saying, What *mean* these stones?

22 Then ye shall let your children know, saying, [d]Israel came over this Jordan on dry land.

23 For the LORD your God dried up the waters of Jordan from before you, until ye were passed over, as the LORD your God did to the Red sea, [e]which

4:3 [r]ch. 3:13 [s]ver. 19,20 **4:6** [t]Ex. 12:26 & 13:14 Deut. 6:20 **4:7** [u]ch. 3:13,16 [v]Ex. 12:14 Num. 16:40 **4:12** [w]Num. 32:20,27, 28 **4:14** [x]ch. 3:7 **4:16** [y]Ex. 25:16,22 **4:18** [z]ch. 3:15 **4:19** [a]ch. 5:9 **4:20** [b]ver. 3 **4:21** [c]ver. 6 **4:22** [d]ch. 3:17 **4:23** [e]Ex. 14:21

[1]Heb. *tomorrow* [m]Or, *ready armed* [n]Heb. *plucked up* [o]Heb. *went*

4:6 YOUR CHILDREN. God desired that His people always be concerned about the faith of their children (see Deut. 6:7, note). The stones of remembrance set up on the bank of the Jordan provided an occasion for parents to teach their children about God's power and faithfulness. Through such teaching these children would come to "fear the LORD your God for ever" (v. 24; see article on THE FEAR OF THE LORD, p. 282.

4:21 WHAT *MEAN* THESE STONES? A monument of stones was frequently used to remind future generations about God's salvation and His grace toward His people. Believers today can still choose certain things or places as memorials to commemorate the good things God has done for them. These memorials should aid in instructing our children to look to God for guidance and help throughout their lives on earth.

he dried up from before us, until we were gone over:

24 [f]That all the people of the earth might know the hand of the LORD, that it *is* [g]mighty: that ye might [h]fear the LORD your God [p]for ever.

5 AND IT came to pass, when all the kings of the Amorites, which *were* on the side of Jordan westward, and all the kings of the Canaanites, [i]which *were* by the sea, [j]heard that the LORD had dried up the waters of the Jordan from before the children of Israel, until we were passed over, that their heart melted, [k]neither was there spirit in them any more, because of the children of Israel.

Circumcising of the nation

2 ¶ At that time the LORD said unto Joshua, Make thee [l]sharp[q] knives, and circumcise again the children of Israel the second time.

3 And Joshua made him sharp knives, and circumcised the children of Israel at [r]the hill of the foreskins.

4 And this *is* the cause why Joshua did circumcise: [m]All the people that came out of Egypt, *that were* males, *even* all the men of war, died in the wilderness by the way, after they came out of Egypt.

5 Now all the people that came out were circumcised: but all the people *that were* born in the wilderness by the way as they came forth out of Egypt, *them* they had not circumcised.

6 For the children of Israel walked [n]forty years in the wilderness, till all the people *that were* men of war, which came out of Egypt, were consumed, because they obeyed not the voice of the LORD: unto whom the LORD sware that [o]he would not show them the land, which the LORD sware unto their fathers that he would give us, [p]a land that floweth with milk and honey.

7 And [q]their children, *whom* he raised up in their stead, them Joshua circumcised: for they were uncircumcised, because they had not circumcised them by the way.

8 And it came to pass, [s]when they had done circumcising all the people, that they abode in their places in the camp, [r]till they were whole.

9 And the LORD said unto Joshua, This day have I rolled away [s]the reproach of Egypt from off you. Wherefore the name of the place is called [t]Gilgal[t] unto this day.

10 ¶ And the children of Israel encamped in Gilgal, and kept the passover [u]on the fourteenth day of the month at even in the plains of Jericho.

11 And they did eat of the old corn of the land on the morrow after the passover, unleavened cakes, and parched *corn* in the selfsame day.

12 ¶ And [v]the manna ceased on the morrow after they had eaten of the old corn of the land; neither had the children of Israel manna any more; but they did eat of the fruit of the land of Canaan that year.

The fall of Jericho

13 ¶ And it came to pass, when Joshua was by Jericho, that he lifted up his eyes and looked, and, behold, there stood [w]a man over against him [x]with his sword drawn in his hand: and Joshua went unto him, and said unto him, *Art* thou for us, or for our adversaries?

14 And he said, Nay; but *as* [u]captain of the host of the LORD am I now come. And Joshua [y]fell on his face to the earth, and did worship, and said unto him, What saith my lord unto his servant?

15 And the captain of the LORD's host said unto Joshua, [z]Loose thy shoe from off thy foot; for the place

4:24 [f]1 Ki. 8:42,43 2 Ki. 19:19 [g]Ex. 15:16 1 Chr. 29:12 [h]Ex. 14:31 Deut. 6:2 Jer. 10:7
5:1 [i]Num. 13:29 [j]Ex. 15:14,15 [k]1 Ki. 10:5
5:2 [l]Ex. 4:25
5:4 [m]Num. 14:29 & 26:64,65 Deut. 2:16
5:6 [n]Num. 14:33 Deut. 1:3 [o]Num. 14:23 Heb. 3:11 [p]Ex. 3:8
5:7 [q]Num. 14:31 Deut. 1:39
5:8 [r]See Gen. 34:25
5:9 [s]Gen. 34:14 [t]ch. 4:19
5:10 [u]Ex. 12:6 Num. 9:5
5:12 [v]Ex. 16:35
5:13 [w]Gen. 18:2 & 32:24 Ex. 23:23 Zech. 1:8 Acts 1:10 [x]Num. 22:23
5:14 [y]Gen. 17:3
5:15 [z]Ex. 3:5 Acts 7:33

[p] Heb. *all days* [q] Or, *knives of flints* [r] Or, *Gibeah-haaraloth* [s] Heb. *when the people had made an end to be circumcised* [t] i.e. *Rolling* [u] Or, *prince;* see Dan. 10:13,21

5:2 CIRCUMCISE AGAIN THE CHILDREN OF ISRAEL. Under the old covenant circumcision marked every male as a child of Abraham and a servant of the Lord God. Circumcision qualified them to partake of the blessings of the covenant (see Gen. 17:11, note). It was, moreover, a sign of their obedience to the covenant. Even though God's people had invaded the promised land, the spiritual preparation of circumcision and the Passover was needed before they could begin the actual conquest.

5:14 CAPTAIN OF THE HOST OF THE LORD. Here Joshua is made aware of the unseen presence of God and His heavenly army prepared to do battle alongside His faithful people (cf. Acts 12:5–11; 18:9–10; 23:11; 27:23). Joshua's experience teaches us as believers that we are not alone in our struggles on this earth. There are spiritual forces fighting on our behalf as well as against us (see Heb. 1:14). We have the Holy Spirit, who remains constantly at our side as our helper and defender (John 14:16–23).

whereon thou standest *is* holy. And Joshua did so.

6

NOW JERICHO [v]was straitly shut up because of the children of Israel: none went out, and none came in.

2 And the LORD said unto Joshua, See, [a]I have given into thine hand Jericho, and the [b]king thereof, *and* the mighty men of valour.

3 And ye shall compass the city, all *ye* men of war, *and* go round about the city once. Thus shalt thou do six days.

4 And seven priests shall bear before the ark seven [c]trumpets of rams' horns: and the seventh day ye shall compass the city seven times, and [d]the priests shall blow with the trumpets.

5 And it shall come to pass, that when they make a long *blast* with the ram's horn, *and* when ye hear the sound of the trumpet, all the people shall shout with a great shout; and the wall of the city shall fall down [w]flat, and the people shall ascend up every man straight before him.

6 ¶ And Joshua the son of Nun called the priests, and said unto them, Take up the ark of the covenant, and let seven priests bear seven trumpets of rams' horns before the ark of the LORD.

7 And he said unto the people, Pass on, and compass the city, and let him that is armed pass on before the ark of the LORD.

8 ¶ And it came to pass, when Joshua had spoken unto the people, that the seven priests bearing the seven trumpets of rams' horns passed on before the LORD, and blew with the trumpets: and the ark of the covenant of the LORD followed them.

9 ¶ And the armed men went before the priests that blew with the trumpets, [e]and the [x]rearward came after the ark, *the priests* going on, and blowing with the trumpets.

10 And Joshua had commanded the people, saying, Ye shall not shout, nor [y]make any noise with your voice, neither shall *any* word proceed out of your mouth, until the day I bid you shout; then shall ye shout.

11 So the ark of the LORD compassed the city, going about *it* once: and they came into the camp, and lodged in the camp.

12 ¶ And Joshua rose early in the morning, [f]and the priests took up the ark of the LORD.

13 And seven priests bearing seven trumpets of rams' horns before the ark of the LORD went on continually, and blew with the trumpets: and the armed men went before them; but the rearward came after the ark of the LORD, *the priests* going on, and blowing with the trumpets.

14 And the second day they compassed the city once, and returned into the camp: so they did six days.

15 And it came to pass on the seventh day, that they rose early about the dawning of the day, and compassed the city after the same manner seven times: only on that day they compassed the city seven times.

16 And it came to pass at the seventh time, when the priests blew with the trumpets, Joshua said unto the people, Shout; for the LORD hath given you the city.

17 ¶ And the city shall be [z]accursed, *even* it, and all that *are* therein, to the LORD: only Rahab the harlot shall live, she and all that *are* with her in the house, because [g]she hid the messengers that we sent.

18 And ye, [h]in any wise keep *yourselves* from the accursed thing, lest ye make *yourselves* accursed, when ye

6:2 [a]ch. 2:9,24 & 8:1 [b]Deut. 7:24 **6:4** [c]See Judg. 7:16, 22 [d]Num. 10:8 **6:9** [e]Num. 10:25 **6:12** [f]Deut. 31:25 **6:17** [g]ch. 2:4 **6:18** [h]Deut. 7:26 & 13:17 ch. 7:1,11,12

[v] Heb. *did shut up, and was shut up* [w] Heb. *under it* [x] Heb. *gathering* host [y] Heb. *make your voice to be heard* [z] Or, *devoted;* see Lev. 27:28

6:1 JERICHO. The city of Jericho covered about eight acres. It was a fortress city not just for its residents, but also for the inhabitants of the nearby countryside. The walls may have been as much as thirty feet high and twenty feet thick. Jericho was considered to be invincible, being protected by the gods of the Canaanites. The capture of Jericho was the key to Joshua's whole war strategy, for it would demonstrate that Israel's God was superior to the Canaanite gods; hence the defeat of the Canaanites was certain.

6:17 THE CITY SHALL BE ACCURSED. To be accursed (Heb. *herem*) means "to destroy or devote." The object or person was devoted to God either for judgment or for His service. All the people of Jericho were sentenced to utter destruction (Deut. 13:16). The principle of *herem* teaches that God, the Creator, may justly destroy those who are given over to evil and unrighteousness (cf. Jer. 18:6–7; 45:4; Mat. 10:28; Luke 13:3; see article on THE DESTRUCTION OF THE CANAANITES, p. 336). Note also that Jericho was the firstfruits of the conquest; other cities were not treated the same way as Jericho.

take of the accursed thing, and make
the camp of Israel a curse, [i]and trou-
ble it.
19 But all the silver, and gold, and
vessels of brass and iron, *are* [a]conse-
crated unto the LORD: they shall come
into the treasury of the LORD.
20 So the people shouted when *the
priests* blew with the trumpets: and it
came to pass, when the people heard
the sound of the trumpet, and the peo-
ple shouted with a great shout, that
[j]the wall fell down [b]flat, so that the
people went up into the city, every man
straight before him, and they took the
city.
21 And they [k]utterly destroyed all
that *was* in the city, both man and wom-
an, young and old, and ox, and sheep,
and ass, with the edge of the sword.
22 But Joshua had said unto the two
men that had spied out the country, Go
into the harlot's house, and bring out
thence the woman, and all that she
hath, [l]as ye sware unto her.
23 And the young men that were
spies went in, and brought out Rahab,
[m]and her father, and her mother, and
her brethren, and all that she had; and
they brought out all her [c]kindred, and
left them without the camp of Israel.
24 And they burnt the city with fire,
and all that *was* therein: [n]only the sil-
ver, and the gold, and the vessels of
brass and of iron, they put into the
treasury of the house of the LORD.
25 And Joshua saved Rahab the
harlot alive, and her father's house-
hold, and all that she had; and [o]she
dwelleth in Israel *even* unto this day;
because she hid the messengers,
which Joshua sent to spy out Jericho.

6:18 [i]ch. 7:25 1 Ki. 18:17,18 Jonah 1:12
6:20 [j]ver. 5 Heb. 11:30
6:21 [k]Deut. 7:2
6:22 [l]ch. 2:14 Heb. 11:31
6:23 [m]ch. 2:13
6:24 [n]ver. 19
6:25 [o]See Mat. 1:5
6:26 [p]1 Ki. 16:34
6:27 [q]ch. 1:5 [r]ch. 9:1,3
7:1 [s]ch. 22:20
7:4 [t]Lev. 26:17 Deut. 28:25

26 ¶ And Joshua adjured *them* at
that time, saying, [p]Cursed *be* the man
before the LORD, that riseth up and
buildeth this city Jericho: he shall lay
the foundation thereof in his firstborn,
and in his youngest *son* shall he set up
the gates of it.
27 [q]So the LORD was with Joshua;
and [r]his fame was *noised* throughout
all the country.

Achan's sin

7 BUT THE children of Israel com-
mitted a trespass in the accursed
thing: for [s]Achan, [d] the son of Carmi,
the son of [e]Zabdi, the son of Zerah, of
the tribe of Judah, took of the accursed
thing: and the anger of the LORD was
kindled against the children of Israel.
2 And Joshua sent men from Jericho
to Ai, which *is* beside Beth-aven, on the
east side of Beth-el, and spake unto
them, saying, Go up and view the coun-
try. And the men went up and
viewed Ai.
3 And they returned to Joshua, and
said unto him, Let not all the people go
up; but let [f]about two or three thou-
sand man go up and smite Ai; *and*
make not all the people to labour
thither; for they *are but* few.
4 So there went up thither of the
people about three thousand men:
[t]and they fled before the men of Ai.
5 And the men of Ai smote of them
about thirty and six men: for they
chased them *from* before the gate *even*

[a] Heb. *holiness* [b] Heb. *under it* [c] Heb. *families* [d] 1 Chr. 2:7, *Achar* [e] Or, *Zimri;* see 1 Chr. 2:6 [f] Heb. *about* 2000 *men, or about* 3000 *men*

6:20 THE WALL FELL DOWN FLAT. The walls collapsed by a direct act of God. The city was taken because of Israel's obedience to God's word and faith in His miraculous power (Heb. 11:30; 1 John 5:4). Since the city was not rebuilt for several hundred years, very little of the remains of this level of the destroyed city have been found. Most of what was left weathered away.

6:21 THEY UTTERLY DESTROYED ALL. For comments on how the mass destruction of the Canaanites is consistent with God's love and righteousness, see article on THE DESTRUCTION OF THE CANAANITES, p. 336.

7:1–26 ACHAN ... THE ANGER OF THE LORD. The sin of Achan, its consequence within Israel, and the severe penalty upon Achan and his family reveal several principles of judgment when God's people flagrantly sin. (1) When there is serious sin or the toleration of serious sin among God's people, the blessing of God is either diminished, hindered, or lost altogether. God will not bless a people who refuse to remove sin from their midst (vv. 1,11–13,20–21,25; cf. 1 Cor. 5:1–13).

(2) Open sin within the congregation of God's people exposes its members to the destructive influence of the enemy from without (e.g., Satan and the world; vv. 4–13).

(3) If such sin is tolerated and not corrected, it will result in eventual judgment (v. 13). If, however, the sin is exposed, confessed, and removed, then God's blessing, presence, and grace return (vv. 22–26; 8:1,18–19; cf. Acts 4:31—5:11).

(4) Sin among the people of God, therefore, must be regarded with the utmost seriousness. Purity must be guarded and obedience demanded. Otherwise, the spiritual development of a congregation will either be stunted or cease altogether (cf. Rev. 3:1–3,14–18).

THE DESTRUCTION OF THE CANAANITES

Josh. 6:21 "And they utterly destroyed all that was *in the city, both man and woman, young and old, and ox, and sheep, and ass, with the edge of the sword."*

(1) Before the nation of Israel entered into the promised land, God had given strict instructions as to what they should do to the people there—they were to be completely destroyed. "But of the cities of these people, which the LORD thy God doth give thee *for* an inheritance, thou shalt save alive nothing that breatheth: But thou shalt utterly destroy them; *namely*, the Hittites, and the Amorites, the Canaanites, and the Perizzites, the Hivites, and the Jebusites; as the LORD thy God hath commanded thee" (Deut. 20:16–17; cf. Num. 33:51–53).

(2) The Lord repeated this command after the Israelites crossed over the Jordan into Canaan. On several occasions the author of Joshua states that Israel's destruction of the cities and the Canaanites was at the Lord's command (Josh. 6:2; 8:1–2; 10:8). Believers under the new covenant have often wondered how this order of mass destruction of human beings is consistent with the revelation of God's love, righteousness, and hatred of evil elsewhere in the Bible.

(3) The destruction of Jericho is an account of the righteous judgment of God upon a desperately wicked people whose measure of sin was now full (Gen. 15:16; Deut. 9:4–5). In other words, God annihilated the people of that city and other inhabitants of Canaan because they had given themselves over fully to moral depravity. Archaeology reveals that the people of Canaan were involved in all kinds of idolatry, cult prostitution, violence, burning of children as sacrifices to their gods, and spiritism (cf. Deut. 12:31; 18:9–13; see Josh. 23:12, note).

(4) The complete destruction of the Canaanites was necessary to safeguard Israel from the overwhelming influence of Canaanite idolatry and sin. God knew that if the wicked nations had been allowed to continue, they would "teach you . . . to do after all their abominations, which they have done unto their gods; so should ye sin against the LORD your God" (Deut. 20:18). This verse expresses the continuing Biblical principle that God's people must keep themselves separate from their surrounding evil society (Deut. 7:2–4; 12:1–4; see articles on SPIRITUAL SEPARATION FOR BELIEVERS, p. 1814, and THE CHRISTIAN'S RELATIONSHIP TO THE WORLD, p. 2004).

(5) The destruction of Canaanite cities and people demonstrates a basic principle of God's judgment: when a people's iniquity is full and overflows, God's mercy gives way to judgment (cf. Josh. 11:20). God had earlier applied this same principle at the time of the flood (Gen. 6:5,11–12) and at the destruction of the wicked cities of Sodom and Gomorrah (Gen. 18:20–33; 19:24–25).

(6) The subsequent history of the nation of Israel confirms the importance of this principle and of God's command that all the heathen nations be destroyed. The Israelites in fact disobeyed the command of the Lord and did not utterly drive out all of the people living in Canaan. As a result, they began to follow after their abominations and serve their idol gods (see Judg. 1:28, note; 2:2,17, notes). The book of Judges is the story of what the Lord did in response to this apostasy.

(7) Finally, the destruction of that generation of Canaanites is a type and foreshadowing of the final judgment of God upon the unrighteous at the end of the age. God's second and true Joshua, i.e., Jesus Christ, will return in righteousness with the armies of heaven to judge and to wage war against all the ungodly (Rev. 19:11–21). All who have rejected His offer of grace and salvation and who have continued in sin will perish as did the Canaanites. God will overthrow every worldly power and establish His righteous kingdom upon earth (Rev. 18:20–21; 20:4–10; 21:1–4).

unto Shebarim, and smote them [g]in
the going down: wherefore [u]the
hearts of the people melted, and be-
came as water.
6 ¶ And Joshua [v]rent his clothes,
and fell to the earth upon his face be-
fore the ark of the LORD until the even-
tide, he and the elders of Israel, and
[w]put dust upon their heads.
7 And Joshua said, Alas, O Lord
GOD, [x]wherefore hast thou at all
brought this people over Jordan, to de-
liver us into the hand of the Amorites,
to destroy us? would to God we had
been content, and dwelt on the other
side Jordan!
8 O Lord, what shall I say, when Is-
rael turneth their [h]backs before their
enemies!
9 For the Canaanites and all the in-
habitants of the land shall hear *of it*,
and shall environ us round, and [y]cut
off our name from the earth: and
[z]what wilt thou do unto thy great
name?
10 ¶ And the LORD said unto Joshua,
Get thee up; wherefore [i]liest thou
thus upon thy face?
11 [a]Israel hath sinned, and they
have also transgressed my covenant
which I commanded them: [b]for they
have even taken of the accursed thing,
and have also stolen, and [c]dissembled
also, and they have put *it* even among
their own stuff.
12 [d]Therefore the children of Isra-
el could not stand before their ene-
mies, *but* turned *their* backs before
their enemies, because [e]they were ac-
cursed: neither will I be with you any
more, except ye destroy the accursed
from among you.
13 Up, [f]sanctify the people, and
say, [g]Sanctify yourselves against to-
morrow: for thus saith the LORD God of
Israel, *There is* an accursed thing in the
midst of thee, O Israel: thou canst not
stand before thine enemies, until ye
take away the accursed thing from
among you.
14 In the morning therefore ye shall
be brought according to your tribes:
and it shall be, *that* the tribe which
[h]the LORD taketh shall come according
to the families *thereof;* and the family
which the LORD shall take shall come
by households; and the household
which the LORD shall take shall come
man by man.
15 [i]And it shall be, *that* he that is
taken with the accursed thing shall be
burnt with fire, he and all that he hath:
because he hath [j]transgressed the
covenant of the LORD, and because he
[k]hath wrought [j]folly in Israel.
16 ¶ So Joshua rose up early in the
morning, and brought Israel by their
tribes; and the tribe of Judah was
taken:
17 And he brought the family of Ju-
dah; and he took the family of the Zar-
hites: and he brought the family of the
Zarhites man by man; and Zabdi was
taken:
18 And he brought his household
man by man; and Achan, the son of
Carmi, the son of Zabdi, the son of Ze-
rah, of the tribe of Judah, [l]was taken.
19 And Joshua said unto Achan, My
son, [m]give, I pray thee, glory to the
LORD God of Israel, [n]and make confes-
sion unto him; and [o]tell me now what
thou hast done; hide *it* not from me.
20 And Achan answered Joshua,
and said, Indeed I have sinned against
the LORD God of Israel, and thus and
thus have I done:
21 When I saw among the spoils a
goodly Babylonish garment, and two
hundred shekels of silver, and a
[k]wedge of gold of fifty shekels weight,
then I coveted them, and took them;
and, behold, they *are* hid in the earth in
the midst of my tent, and the silver un-
der it.
22 ¶ So Joshua sent messengers,
and they ran unto the tent; and, behold,
it was hid in his tent, and the silver un-
der it.
23 And they took them out of the
midst of the tent, and brought them
unto Joshua, and unto all the children

7:5 [u]ch. 2:9,11 Lev. 26:36
7:6 [v]Gen. 37:29,34 [w]1 Sam. 4:12 2 Sam. 1:2 & 13:19 Neh. 9:1 Job 2:12
7:7 [x]Ex. 17:3 Num. 21:5
7:9 [y]Deut. 32:26 [z]See Ex. 32:12 Num. 14:13
7:11 [a]ver. 1 [b]ch. 6:17,18 [c]See Acts 5:1,2
7:12 [d]See Num. 14:45 Judg. 2:14 [e]Deut. 7:26 ch. 6:18 Hag. 2:13,14
7:13 [f]Ex. 19:10 [g]ch. 3:5
7:14 [h]Prov. 16:33
7:15 [i]See 1 Sam. 14:38,39 [j]ver. 11 [k]Gen. 34:7 Judg. 20:6
7:18 [l]1 Sam. 14:42
7:19 [m]See 1 Sam. 6:5 Jer. 13:16 John 9:24 [n]Num. 5:6,7 2 Chr. 30:22 Ezra 10:10,11 Dan. 9:4 [o]1 Sam. 14:43

[g] Or, *in Morad* [h] Heb. *necks* [i] Heb. *fallest* [j] Or, *wickedness* [k] Heb. *tongue*

7:12 NOT STAND BEFORE THEIR ENEMIES. The truth of this verse applies not only to God's people corporately, but also to individual members. Persistent and unrepentant sin in a person's life will cut him or her off from the grace of God. Such individuals no longer live under the help and protection of God and will not be able to stand against the enemies of their souls who attack and seek to destroy them. Slavery to sin, tragedy, and spiritual death will result unless sin is removed (v. 13).

of Israel, and [l]laid them out before the LORD.

24 And Joshua, and all Israel with him, took Achan the son of Zerah, and the silver, and the garment, and the wedge of gold, and his sons, and his daughters, and his oxen, and his asses, and his sheep, and his tent, and all that he had: and they brought them unto [p]the valley of Achor.

25 And Joshua said, [q]Why hast thou troubled us? the LORD shall trouble thee this day. [r]And all Israel stoned him with stones, and burned them with fire, after they had stoned them with stones.

26 And they [s]raised over him a great heap of stones unto this day. So [t]the LORD turned from the fierceness of his anger. Wherefore the name of that place was called, [u]The valley of [m]Achor, unto this day.

The destruction of Ai

8 AND THE LORD said unto Joshua, [v]Fear not, neither be thou dismayed: take all the people of war with thee, and arise, go up to Ai: see, [w]I have given into thy hand the king of Ai, and his people, and his city, and his land:

2 And thou shalt do to Ai and her king as thou didst unto [x]Jericho and her king: only [y]the spoil thereof, and the cattle thereof, shall ye take for a prey unto yourselves: lay thee an ambush for the city behind it.

3 ¶ So Joshua arose, and all the people of war, to go up against Ai: and Joshua chose out thirty thousand mighty men of valour, and sent them away by night.

4 And he commanded them, saying, Behold, [z]ye shall lie in wait against the city, *even* behind the city: go not very far from the city, but be ye all ready:

5 And I, and all the people that *are* with me, will approach unto the city: and it shall come to pass, when they come out against us, as at the first, that [a]we will flee before them,

6 (For they will come out after us) till we have [n]drawn them from the city; for they will say, They flee before us, as at the first: therefore we will flee before them.

7 Then ye shall rise up from the ambush, and seize upon the city: for the LORD your God will deliver it into your hand.

8 And it shall be, when ye have taken the city, *that* ye shall set the city on fire: according to the commandment of the LORD shall ye do. [b]See, I have commanded you.

9 ¶ Joshua therefore sent them forth: and they went to lie in ambush, and abode between Beth-el and Ai, on the west side of Ai: but Joshua lodged that night among the people.

10 And Joshua rose up early in the morning, and numbered the people, and went up, he and the elders of Israel, before the people to Ai.

11 [c]And all the people, *even the people* of war that *were* with him, went up, and drew nigh, and came before the city, and pitched on the north side of Ai: now *there was* a valley between them and Ai.

12 And he took about five thousand men, and set them to lie in ambush between Beth-el and Ai, on the west side [o]of the city.

13 And when they had set the people, *even* all the host that *was* on the north of the city, and their liers in wait on the west of the city, Joshua went that night into the midst of the valley.

14 ¶ And it came to pass, when the king of Ai saw *it*, that they hasted and rose up early, and the men of the city went out against Israel to battle, he and all his people, at a time appointed, before the plain; but he [d]wist not that

7:24 [p]ver. 26 ch. 15:7
7:25 [q]ch. 6:18 1 Chr. 2:7 Gal. 5:12 [r]Deut. 17:5
7:26 [s]ch. 8:29 2 Sam. 18:17 Lam. 3:53 [t]Deut. 13:17 2 Sam. 21:14 [u]ver. 24
8:1 [v]Deut. 1:21 & 7:18 & 31:8 ch. 1:9 [w]ch. 6:2
8:2 [x]ch. 6:21 [y]Deut. 20:14
8:4 [z]Judg. 20:29
8:5 [a]Judg. 20:32
8:8 [b]2 Sam. 13:28
8:11 [c]ver. 5
8:14 [d]Judg. 20:34 Eccl. 9:12

[l]Heb. *poured* [m]i.e. *Trouble* [n]Heb. *pulled* [o]Or, *of Ai*

7:24 TOOK ACHAN . . . HIS SONS. God punished the family of Achan because the narrative clearly implies that they knew about his sin and probably condoned it. Note that Deut. 24:16 prohibits the punishment of the children for the sins of their fathers. As a close-knit unit, all members of the family had the mutual responsibility to encourage, warn, and exhort one another so that all would remain committed to God and His word. Having evidently failed in this regard, they suffered the same consequences as Achan.

7:25 STONED HIM WITH STONES. The eternal destiny of Achan and his family cannot be easily determined. The O.T. emphasizes physical death as punishment for sin, but it is not clear with regard to the eternal and ultimate judgment of individuals.

there were liers in ambush against him
behind the city.
15 And Joshua and all Israel
[e]made as if they were beaten before
them, and fled by the way of the wilder-
ness.
16 And all the people that *were* in Ai
were called together to pursue after
them: and they pursued after Joshua,
and were drawn away from the city.
17 And there was not a man left in
Ai or Beth-el, that went not out after
Israel: and they left the city open, and
pursued after Israel.
18 And the LORD said unto Joshua,
Stretch out the spear that *is* in thy
hand toward Ai; for I will give it into
thine hand. And Joshua stretched out
the spear that *he had* in his hand to-
ward the city.
19 And the ambush arose quickly
out of their place, and they ran as soon
as he had stretched out his hand: and
they entered into the city, and took it,
and hasted and set the city on fire.
20 And when the men of Ai looked
behind them, they saw, and, behold,
the smoke of the city ascended up to
heaven, and they had no [p]power to
flee this way or that way: and the peo-
ple that fled to the wilderness turned
back upon the pursuers.
21 And when Joshua and all Israel
saw that the ambush had taken the
city, and that the smoke of the city as-
cended, then they turned again, and
slew the men of Ai.
22 And the other issued out of the
city against them; so they were in the
midst of Israel, some on this side, and
some on that side: and they smote
them, so that they [f]let none of them
remain or escape.
23 And the king of Ai they took
alive, and brought him to Joshua.
24 And it came to pass, when Israel
had made an end of slaying all the in-
habitants of Ai in the field, in the wil-
derness wherein they chased them,
and when they were all fallen on the
edge of the sword, until they were con-
sumed, that all the Israelites returned
unto Ai, and smote it with the edge of
the sword.
25 And *so* it was, *that* all that fell
that day, both of men and women, *were*
twelve thousand, *even* all the men
of Ai.
26 For Joshua drew not his hand
back, wherewith he stretched out the
spear, until he had utterly destroyed
all the inhabitants of Ai.
27 [g]Only the cattle and the spoil of
that city Israel took for a prey unto
themselves, according unto the word
of the LORD which he [h]commanded
Joshua.
28 And Joshua burnt Ai, and made
it [i]an heap for ever, *even* a desolation
unto this day.
29 [j]And the king of Ai he hanged
on a tree until eventide: [k]and as soon
as the sun was down, Joshua com-
manded that they should take his car-
case down from the tree, and cast it at
the entering of the gate of the city, and
[l]raise thereon a great heap of stones,
that remaineth unto this day.

An altar built in mount Ebal

30 ¶ Then Joshua built an altar unto
the LORD God of Israel [m]in mount Ebal,
31 As Moses the servant of the LORD
commanded the children of Israel, as it
is written in the [n]book of the law of
Moses, an altar of whole stones, over
which no man hath lift up *any* iron: and
[o]they offered thereon burnt offerings
unto the LORD, and sacrificed peace of-
ferings.
32 ¶ And [p]he wrote there upon the
stones a copy of the law of Moses,
which he wrote in the presence of the
children of Israel.

8:15 [e]Judg. 20:36
8:22 [f]Lev. 7:29; Deut. 7:2; Job 20:5; Luke 17:26-30; 1 Thes. 5:3
8:27 [g]Num. 31:22,26 [h]ver. 2
8:28 [i]Deut. 13:16
8:29 [j]ch. 10:26 [k]Deut. 21:22,23; ch. 10:27 [l]ch. 7:26 & 10:27
8:30 [m]Deut. 27:4,5
8:31 [n]Ex. 20:25; Deut. 27:5,6 [o]Ex. 20:24
8:32 [p]Deut. 27:2,8

p Heb. *hand*

8:30 JOSHUA BUILT AN ALTAR. This episode of building an altar at Mount Ebal and reading the law (v. 34) reveals four principles for understanding the book of Joshua. (1) The right to possess the promised land was dependent upon the proclamation of, and loyalty to, the covenant of God (Deut. 30:15–18).

(2) Israel's access to God was always by faith through sacrifice and blood atonement (vv. 30–31).

(3) The continuance of the blessings of God was dependent upon their holding fast to Him with heartfelt faith and love (Deut. 28—29; 30:11–20; see Josh. 7:1–26, note). Life, blessing, peace, and salvation in Canaan were not unconditional. Faith in God's promises as embodied in the altar, blood atonement, and the commandments was essential in maintaining a covenant relationship with God (Deut. 29:18–21).

(4) The written Word of God was the ultimate authority for His people and the basis upon which they experienced either His blessing or curse (vv. 31–32,34; 1:8; cf. Deut. 27—30; Mat. 7:24–27).

33 And all Israel, and their elders, and officers, and their judges, stood on this side the ark and on that side before the priests the Levites, [q]which bare the ark of the covenant of the LORD, as well [r]the stranger, as he that was born among them; half of them over against mount Gerizim, and half of them over against mount Ebal; [s]as Moses the servant of the LORD had commanded before, that they should bless the people of Israel.

34 And afterward [t]he read all the words of the law, [u]the blessings and cursings, according to all that is written in the book of the law.

35 There was not a word of all that Moses commanded, which Joshua read not before all the congregation of Israel, [v]with the women, and the little ones, and [w]the strangers that ¶were conversant among them.

The trickery of the Gibeonites

9 AND IT came to pass, when all the kings which *were* on this side Jordan, in the hills, and in the valleys, and in all the coasts of [x]the great sea over against Lebanon, [y]the Hittite, and the Amorite, the Canaanite, the Perizzite, the Hivite, and the Jebusite, heard *thereof;*

2 That they [z]gathered themselves together, to fight with Joshua and with Israel, with one ʳaccord.

3 ¶ And when the inhabitants of [a]Gibeon [b]heard what Joshua had done unto Jericho and to Ai,

4 They did work wilily, and went and made as if they had been ambassadors, and took old sacks upon their asses, and wine bottles, old, and rent, and bound up;

5 And old shoes and clouted upon their feet, and old garments upon them; and all the bread of their provision was dry *and* mouldy.

6 And they went to Joshua [c]unto the camp at Gilgal, and said unto him, and to the men of Israel, We be come from a far country: now therefore make ye a league with us.

7 And the men of Israel said unto the [d]Hivites, Peradventure ye dwell among us; and [e]how shall we make a league with you?

8 And they said unto Joshua, [f]We *are* thy servants. And Joshua said unto them, Who *are* ye? and from whence come ye?

9 And they said unto him, [g]From a very far country thy servants are come because of the name of the LORD thy God: for we have [h]heard the fame of him, and all that he did in Egypt,

10 And [i]all that he did to the two kings of the Amorites, that *were* beyond Jordan, to Sihon king of Heshbon, and to Og king of Bashan, which *was* at Ashtaroth.

11 Wherefore our elders and all the inhabitants of our country spake to us, saying, Take victuals ˢwith you for the journey, and go to meet them, and say unto them, We *are* your servants: therefore now make ye a league with us.

12 This our bread we took hot *for* our provision out of our houses on the day we came forth to go unto you; but now, behold, it is dry, and it is mouldy:

13 And these bottles of wine, which we filled, *were* new; and, behold, they be rent: and these our garments and our shoes are become old by reason of the very long journey.

14 And ᵗthe men took of their victuals, [j]and asked not *counsel* at the mouth of the LORD.

15 And Joshua [k]made peace with them, and made a league with them, to let them live: and the princes of the congregation sware unto them.

16 ¶ And it came to pass at the end of three days after they had made a league with them, that they heard that they *were* their neighbours, and *that* they dwelt among them.

17 And the children of Israel journeyed, and came unto their cities on the third day. Now their cities *were* [l]Gibeon, and Chephirah, and Beeroth, and Kirjath-jearim.

8:33 [q]Deut. 31:9,25 [r]Deut. 31:12 [s]Deut. 11:29 & 27:12
8:34 [t]Deut. 31:11 Neh. 8:3 [u]Deut. 28:2,15,45 & 29:20,21 & 30:19
8:35 [v]Deut. 31:12 [w]ver. 33
9:1 [x]Num. 34:6 [y]Ex. 3:17 & 23:23
9:2 [z]Ps. 83:3,5
9:3 [a]ch. 10:2 2 Sam. 21:1,2 [b]ch. 6:27
9:6 [c]ch. 5:10
9:7 [d]ch. 11:19 [e]Ex. 23:32 Deut. 7:2 Judg. 2:2
9:8 [f]Deut. 20:11
9:9 [g]Deut. 20:15 [h]Ex. 15:14 Josh. 2:10
9:10 [i]Num. 21:24,33
9:14 [j]Num. 27:21
9:15 [k]ch. 11:19 2 Sam. 21:2
9:17 [l]ch. 18:25,26,28 Ezra 2:25

¶ Heb. *walked* ʳ Heb. *mouth* ˢ Heb. *in your hand* ᵗ Or, *they received the men by reason of their victuals*

9:14 ASKED NOT *COUNSEL* . . . OF THE LORD. Joshua and the leaders of Israel failed to pray and seek God's will with regard to the Gibeonites. They presumptuously entered into a covenant with them which they could not break (v. 18). This ill-advised decision brought the ungodly Canaanites within Israel's midst (an action forbidden in Deut. 7). In all the decisions of life we should seek God's will and pray for His wisdom and guidance, thereby enabling us to avoid sorrows and tragedies.

18 And the children of Israel smote them not, [m]because the princes of the congregation had sworn unto them by the LORD God of Israel. And all the congregation murmured against the princes.

19 But all the princes said unto all the congregation, We have sworn unto them by the LORD God of Israel: now therefore we may not touch them.

20 This we will do to them; we will even let them live, lest [n]wrath be upon us, because of the oath which we sware unto them.

21 And the princes said unto them, Let them live; but let them be [o]hewers of wood and drawers of water unto all the congregation; as the princes had [p]promised them.

22 ¶ And Joshua called for them, and he spake unto them, saying, Wherefore have ye beguiled us, saying, [q]We *are* very far from you; when [r]ye dwell among us?

23 Now therefore ye *are* [s]cursed, and there shall [u]none of you be freed from being bondmen, and hewers of wood and drawers of water for the house of my God.

24 And they answered Joshua, and said, Because it was certainly told thy servants, how that the LORD thy God [t]commanded his servant Moses to give you all the land, and to destroy all the inhabitants of the land from before you, therefore [u]we were sore afraid of our lives because of you, and have done this thing.

25 And now, behold, we *are* [v]in thine hand: as it seemeth good and right unto thee to do unto us, do.

26 And so did he unto them, and delivered them out of the hand of the children of Israel, that they slew them not.

27 And Joshua [v]made them that day [w]hewers of wood and drawers of water for the congregation, and for the altar of the LORD, even unto this day, [x]in the place which he should choose.

The sun stands still

10 NOW IT came to pass, when Adoni-zedec king of Jerusalem had heard how Joshua had taken Ai, and had utterly destroyed it; [y]as he had done to Jericho and her king, so he had done to [z]Ai and her king; and [a]how the inhabitants of Gibeon had made peace with Israel, and were among them;

2 That they [b]feared greatly, because Gibeon *was* a great city, as one of the [w]royal cities, and because it *was* greater than Ai, and all the men thereof *were* mighty.

3 Wherefore Adoni-zedec king of Jerusalem sent unto Hoham king of Hebron, and unto Piram king of Jarmuth, and unto Japhia king of Lachish, and unto Debir king of Eglon, saying,

4 Come up unto me, and help me, that we may smite Gibeon: [c]for it hath made peace with Joshua and with the children of Israel.

5 Therefore the five kings of the Amorites, the king of Jerusalem, the king of Hebron, the king of Jarmuth, the king of Lachish, the king of Eglon, [d]gathered themselves together, and went up, they and all their hosts, and encamped before Gibeon, and made war against it.

6 ¶ And the men of Gibeon sent unto Joshua [e]to the camp to Gilgal, saying, Slack not thy hand from thy servants; come up to us quickly, and save us, and help us: for all the kings of the Amorites that dwell in the mountains are gathered together against us.

7 So Joshua ascended from Gilgal, he, and [f]all the people of war with him, and all the mighty men of valour.

8 ¶ And the LORD said unto Joshua, [g]Fear them not: for I have delivered them into thine hand; [h]there shall not a man of them stand before thee.

9 Joshua therefore came unto them suddenly, *and* went up from Gilgal all night.

10 And the LORD [i]discomfited them before Israel, and slew them with a great slaughter at Gibeon, and chased them along the way that goeth up [j]to Beth-horon, and smote them to [k]Azekah, and unto Makkedah.

11 And it came to pass, as they fled from before Israel, *and* were in the go-

[u]Heb. *not be cut off from you* [v]Heb. *gave,* or, *delivered to be* [w]Heb. *cities of the kingdom*

9:18 [m]Ps. 15:4 Eccl. 5:2 **9:20** [n]See 2 Sam. 21:1, 2,6 Ezek. 17:13,15, 18,19 Zech. 5:3,4 Mal. 3:5 **9:21** [o]Deut. 29:11 [p]ver. 15 **9:22** [q]ver. 6,9 [r]ver. 16 **9:23** [s]Gen. 9:25 **9:24** [t]Ex. 23:32 Deut. 7:1,2 [u]Ex. 15:14 **9:25** [v]Gen. 16:6 **9:27** [w]ver. 21,23 [x]Deut. 12:5 **10:1** [y]ch. 6:21 [z]ch. 8:22,26,28 [a]ch. 9:15 **10:2** [b]Ex. 15:14-16 Deut. 11:25 **10:4** [c]ver. 1 ch. 9:15 **10:5** [d]ch. 9:2 **10:6** [e]ch. 5:10 & 9:6 **10:7** [f]ch. 8:1 **10:8** [g]ch. 11:6 Judg. 4:14 [h]ch. 1:5 **10:10** [i]Judg. 4:15 1 Sam. 7:10,12 Is. 28:21 [j]ch. 16:3,5 [k]ch. 15:35

10:8 FEAR THEM NOT. Even though Israel had made a mistake in entering into a covenant with the Gibeonites (see previous note), God helped His people defend them (cf. 9:18–20). Often failures that cause us to miss the perfect will of God are used by Him as occasions to demonstrate His faithfulness and love to us.

ing down to Beth-horon, [l]that the
LORD cast down great stones from
heaven upon them unto Azekah, and
they died: *they were* more which died
with hailstones than *they* whom the
children of Israel slew with the sword.
12 ¶ Then spake Joshua to the LORD
in the day when the LORD delivered up
the Amorites before the children of Is-
rael, and he said in the sight of Israel,
[m]Sun, [x]stand thou still upon Gibeon;
and thou, Moon, in the valley of [n]Aja-
lon.
13 And the sun stood still, and the
moon stayed, until the people had
avenged themselves upon their ene-
mies. [o]*Is* not this written in the book
of [y]Jasher? So the sun stood still in
the midst of heaven, and hasted not to
go down about a whole day.
14 And there was [p]no day like that
before it or after it, that the LORD
hearkened unto the voice of a man: for
[q]the LORD fought for Israel.
15 ¶ [r]And Joshua returned, and all
Israel with him, unto the camp to Gil-
gal.
16 But these five kings fled, and hid
themselves in a cave at Makkedah.
17 And it was told Joshua, saying,
The five kings are found hid in a cave
at Makkedah.
18 And Joshua said, Roll great
stones upon the mouth of the cave, and
set men by it for to keep them:
19 And stay ye not, *but* pursue after
your enemies, and [z]smite the hind-
most of them; suffer them not to enter
into their cities: for the LORD your God
hath delivered them into your hand.
20 And it came to pass, when Josh-
ua and the children of Israel had made
an end of slaying them with a very
great slaughter, till they were con-
sumed, that the rest *which* remained of
them entered into fenced cities.
21 And all the people returned to
the camp to Joshua at Makkedah in
peace: [s]none moved his tongue
against any of the children of Israel.
22 Then said Joshua, Open the
mouth of the cave, and bring out those
five kings unto me out of the cave.
23 And they did so, and brought
forth those five kings unto him out of
the cave, the king of Jerusalem, the
king of Hebron, the king of Jarmuth,
the king of Lachish, *and* the king of Eg-
lon.
24 And it came to pass, when they
brought out those kings unto Joshua,
that Joshua called for all the men of
Israel, and said unto the captains of
the men of war which went with him,
Come near, [t]put your feet upon the
necks of these kings. And they came
near, and put their feet upon the necks
of them.
25 And Joshua said unto them,
[u]Fear not, nor be dismayed, be strong
and of good courage: for [v]thus shall
the LORD do to all your enemies against
whom ye fight.
26 And afterward Joshua smote
them, and slew them, and hanged them
on five trees: and they [w]were hanging
upon the trees until the evening.
27 And it came to pass at the time
of the going down of the sun, *that* Josh-
ua commanded, and they [x]took them
down off the trees, and cast them into
the cave wherein they had been hid,
and laid great stones in the cave's
mouth, *which remain* until this very
day.

Conquest of the south

28 ¶ And that day Joshua took Mak-
kedah, and smote it with the edge of
the sword, and the king thereof he ut-
terly destroyed, them, and all the souls
that *were* therein; he let none remain:
and he did to the king of Makkedah
[y]as he did unto the king of Jericho.
29 Then Joshua passed from Mak-

10:11 [l]Is. 30:30 Rev. 16:21 **10:12** [m]Is. 28:21 Hab. 3:11 [n]Judg. 12:12 **10:13** [o]2 Sam. 1:18 **10:14** [p]See Is. 38:8 [q]ver. 42 Deut. 1:30 ch. 23:3 **10:15** [r]ver. 43 **10:21** [s]Ex. 11:7

10:24 [t]Ps. 107:40 Is. 26:5,6 Mal. 4:3 **10:25** [u]Deut. 31:6,8 ch. 1:9 [v]Deut. 3:21 & 7:19 **10:26** [w]ch. 8:29 **10:27** [x]Deut. 21:23 ch. 8:29 **10:28** [y]ch. 6:21

[x] Heb. *be silent* [y] Or, *The upright?* [z] Heb. *cut off the tail*

10:12 SPAKE JOSHUA TO THE LORD. Joshua prayed for a miracle and God answered his prayer. Believers should not hesitate to pray for the Lord to work in extraordinary ways on their behalf. God's people live in a hostile and evil world and are faced with such challenges and difficulties that miracles are sometimes needed to fulfill His plan and purpose in their lives.

10:13 THE SUN STOOD STILL. The precise method God used in prolonging the daylight is not given. God could have slowed the earth's rotation, tilted the earth on its axis as in the north where the sun does not set, or caused a refraction of the sun's rays. Whatever God chose to do, the prolongation of that day was an extraordinary answer to prayer (vv. 12–14). The God who created the world and the heavenly bodies with their functions can also suspend their natural movements for His own purposes (cf. Is. 38:7–8).

kedah, and all Israel with him, unto Libnah, and fought against Libnah:

30 And the LORD delivered it also, and the king thereof, into the hand of Israel; and he smote it with the edge of the sword, and all the souls that *were* therein; he let none remain in it; but did unto the king thereof as he did unto the king of Jericho.

31 ¶ And Joshua passed from Libnah, and all Israel with him, unto Lachish, and encamped against it, and fought against it:

32 And the LORD delivered Lachish into the hand of Israel, which took it on the second day, and smote it with the edge of the sword, and all the souls that *were* therein, according to all that he had done to Libnah.

33 ¶ Then Horam king of [z]Gezer came up to help Lachish; and Joshua smote him and his people, until he had left him none remaining.

34 ¶ And from Lachish Joshua passed unto Eglon, and all Israel with him; and they encamped against it, and fought against it:

35 And they took it on that day, and smote it with the edge of the sword, and all the souls that *were* therein he utterly destroyed that day, according to all that he had done to Lachish.

36 And Joshua went up from Eglon, and all Israel with him, unto [a]Hebron; and they fought against it:

37 And they took it, and smote it with the edge of the sword, and the king thereof, and all the cities thereof, and all the souls that *were* therein; he left none remaining, according to all that he had done to Eglon; but destroyed it utterly, and all the souls that *were* therein.

38 ¶ And Joshua returned, and all Israel with him, to [b]Debir; and fought against it:

39 And he took it, and the king thereof, and all the cities thereof; and they smote them with the edge of the sword, and utterly destroyed all the souls that *were* therein; he left none remaining: as he had done to Hebron, so he did to Debir, and to the king thereof; as he had done also to Libnah, and to her king.

40 ¶ So Joshua smote all the country of the hills, and of the south, and of the vale, and of the springs, and all their kings: he left none remaining, but utterly destroyed all that breathed, as the LORD God of Israel [c]commanded.

41 And Joshua smote them from Kadesh-barnea even unto [d]Gaza, [e]and all the country of Goshen, even unto Gibeon.

42 And all these kings and their land did Joshua take at one time, [f]because the LORD God of Israel fought for Israel.

43 And Joshua returned, and all Israel with him, unto the camp to Gilgal.

Conquest of the north

11 AND IT came to pass, when Jabin king of Hazor had heard *those things*, that he [g]sent to Jobab king of Madon, and to the king [h]of Shimron, and to the king of Achshaph,

2 And to the kings that *were* on the north of the mountains, and of the plains south of [i]Chinneroth, and in the valley, and in the borders [j]of Dor on the west,

3 *And to* the Canaanite on the east and on the west, and *to* the Amorite, and the Hittite, and the Perizzite, and the Jebusite in the mountains, [k]and *to* the Hivite under [l]Hermon [m]in the land of Mizpeh.

4 And they went out, they and all their hosts with them, much people, [n]even as the sand that *is* upon the sea shore in multitude, with horses and chariots very many.

5 And when all these kings were [a]met together, they came and pitched together at the waters of Merom, to fight against Israel.

6 ¶ And the LORD said unto Joshua, [o]Be not afraid because of them: for tomorrow about this time will I deliver them up all slain before Israel: thou shalt [p]hough their horses, and burn their chariots with fire.

7 So Joshua came, and all the people of war with him, against them by the waters of Merom suddenly; and they fell upon them.

8 And the LORD delivered them into the hand of Israel, who smote them, and chased them unto [b]great Zidon, and unto [q]Misrephoth-maim,[c,d] and unto the valley of Mizpeh eastward; and they smote them, until they left them none remaining.

9 And Joshua did unto them as the

10:33 [z]ch. 16:3,10 1 Ki. 9:16,17 1 Chr. 20:4
10:36 [a]See ch. 14:13 & 15:13 Judg. 1:10
10:38 [b]See ch. 15:15 Judg. 1:11
10:40 [c]Deut. 20:16,17
10:41 [d]Gen. 10:19 [e]ch. 11:16
10:42 [f]ver. 14
11:1 [g]ch. 10:3 [h]ch. 19:15
11:2 [i]Num. 34:11 [j]ch. 17:11 Judg. 1:27 1 Ki. 4:11
11:3 [k]Judg. 3:3 [l]ch. 13:11 [m]Gen. 31:49
11:4 [n]Gen. 22:17 & 32:12 Judg. 7:12 1 Sam. 13:5
11:6 [o]ch. 10:8 [p]2 Sam. 8:4
11:8 [q]ch. 13:6

[a] Heb. *assembled by appointment* [b] Or, *Zidon-rabbah* [c] Or, *Salt pits* [d] Heb. *Burnings*

LORD bade him: he houghed their
horses, and burnt their chariots with
fire.

10 ¶ And Joshua at that time turned
back, and took Hazor, and smote the
king thereof with the sword: for Hazor
beforetime was the head of all those
kingdoms.

11 And they smote all the souls that
were therein with the edge of the
sword, utterly destroying *them:* there
was not [e]any left to breathe: and he
burnt Hazor with fire.

12 And all the cities of those kings,
and all the kings of them, did Joshua
take, and smote them with the edge of
the sword, *and* he utterly destroyed
them, [r]as Moses the servant of the
LORD commanded.

13 But *as for* the cities that stood
still [f]in their strength, Israel burned
none of them, save Hazor only; *that* did
Joshua burn.

14 And all the spoil of these cities,
and the cattle, the children of Israel
took for a prey unto themselves; but
every man they smote with the edge of
the sword, until they had destroyed
them, neither left they any to breathe.

15 ¶ [s]As the LORD commanded Mo-
ses his servant, so [t]did Moses com-
mand Joshua, and [u]so did Joshua;
[g]he left nothing undone of all that the
LORD commanded Moses.

16 So Joshua took all that land,
[v]the hills, and all the south country,
[w]and all the land of Goshen, and the
valley, and the plain, and the mountain
of Israel, and the valley of the same;

17 [x]*Even* from [h]the mount Halak,
that goeth up to Seir, even unto Baal-
gad in the valley of Lebanon under
mount Hermon: and [y]all their kings
he took, and smote them, and slew
them.

18 Joshua made war a long time
with all those kings.

19 There was not a city that made
peace with the children of Israel, save
[z]the Hivites the inhabitants of Gibe-
on: all *other* they took in battle.

20 For [a]it was of the LORD to hard-
en their hearts, that they should come
against Israel in battle, that he might
destroy them utterly, *and* that they
might have no favour, but that he
might destroy them, [b]as the LORD
commanded Moses.

21 ¶ And at that time came Joshua,
and cut off [c]the Anakims from the
mountains, from Hebron, from Debir,
from Anab, and from all the mountains
of Judah, and from all the mountains of
Israel: Joshua destroyed them utterly
with their cities.

22 There was none of the Anakims
left in the land of the children of Israel:
only in Gaza, in [d]Gath, [e]and in Ash-
dod, there remained.

23 So Joshua took the whole land,
[f]according to all that the LORD said
unto Moses; and Joshua gave it for an
inheritance unto Israel [g]according to
their divisions by their tribes. [h]And
the land rested from war.

Defeated kings

12 NOW THESE *are* the kings of
the land, which the children of
Israel smote, and possessed their land
on the other side Jordan toward the ris-
ing of the sun, [i]from the river Arnon
[j]unto mount Hermon, and all the
plain on the east:

2 [k]Sihon king of the Amorites, who
dwelt in Heshbon, *and* ruled from Aro-
er, which *is* upon the bank of the river
Arnon, and from the middle of the riv-
er, and from half Gilead, even unto the
river Jabbok, *which is* the border of the
children of Ammon;

3 And [l]from the plain to the sea of
Chinneroth on the east, and unto the
sea of the plain, *even* the salt sea on the
east, [m]the way to Beth-jeshimoth; and

11:12 [r]Num. 33:52
11:15 [s]Ex. 34:11,12 [t]Deut. 31:7,8 [u]ch. 1:7
11:16 [v]ch. 12:8 [w]ch. 10:41
11:17 [x]ch. 12:7 [y]Deut. 7:24 ch. 12:7
11:19 [z]ch. 9:3,7
11:20 [a]Deut. 2:30 Judg. 14:4 1 Sam. 2:25 [b]Deut. 20:16,17
11:21 [c]Num. 13:22,33 Deut. 1:28 ch. 15:13,14
11:22 [d]1 Sam. 17:4 [e]ch. 15:46
11:23 [f]Num. 34:2 [g]Num. 26:53 ch. 14 & 15 [h]ver. 18 ch. 14:15 & 21:44 & 22:4 & 23:1
12:1 [i]Num. 21:24 [j]Deut. 3:8,9
12:2 [k]Num. 21:24
12:3 [l]Deut. 3:17 [m]ch. 13:20

[e] Heb. *any breath* [f] Heb. *on their heap*
[g] Heb. *he removed nothing* [h] Or, *the smooth mountain*

11:18 JOSHUA MADE WAR A LONG TIME. The conquest of Canaan was an extended series of campaigns lasting about five years. This can be deduced from the age of Caleb, for five years had elapsed from the beginning of the conquest until he was given Hebron (see 14:6–13; Deut. 2:14).

11:20 LORD ... HARDEN THEIR HEARTS. Because the wickedness of the Canaanites was so terrible, God decided they must be destroyed (see article on THE DESTRUCTION OF THE CANAANITES, p. 336). To accomplish this he hardened their hearts so that they resolved stubbornly to make war against Israel. There may come a time when a person or nation becomes so wicked that mercy is withdrawn and judgment is inevitable (cf. Heb. 10:26–31).

11:23 JOSHUA TOOK THE WHOLE LAND. This verse summarizes the book of Joshua; ch. 12 follows with a brief review of the conquests of Moses and Joshua.

CONQUEST OF CANAAN

When the Israelite tribes approached Canaan after four decades of desert existence, they first had to subdue the tribes in Transjordanian region, under Moses' leadership.

The military strategy of Joshua was brilliant in its simplicity. It had four goals: first, to cross the Jordan and gain a foothold in Canaan by seizing Jericho and its strategic plains, fords and roads; second, to capture the high ground around Bethel, Gibeon and Upper Beth Horon in order to dominate the hill country north and south of the ridge; third, to attack and neutralize lowland towns like Lachish; and finally, to break the power of the mighty urban coalition of northern towns led by Hazor. All of this took place about 1400 B.C.

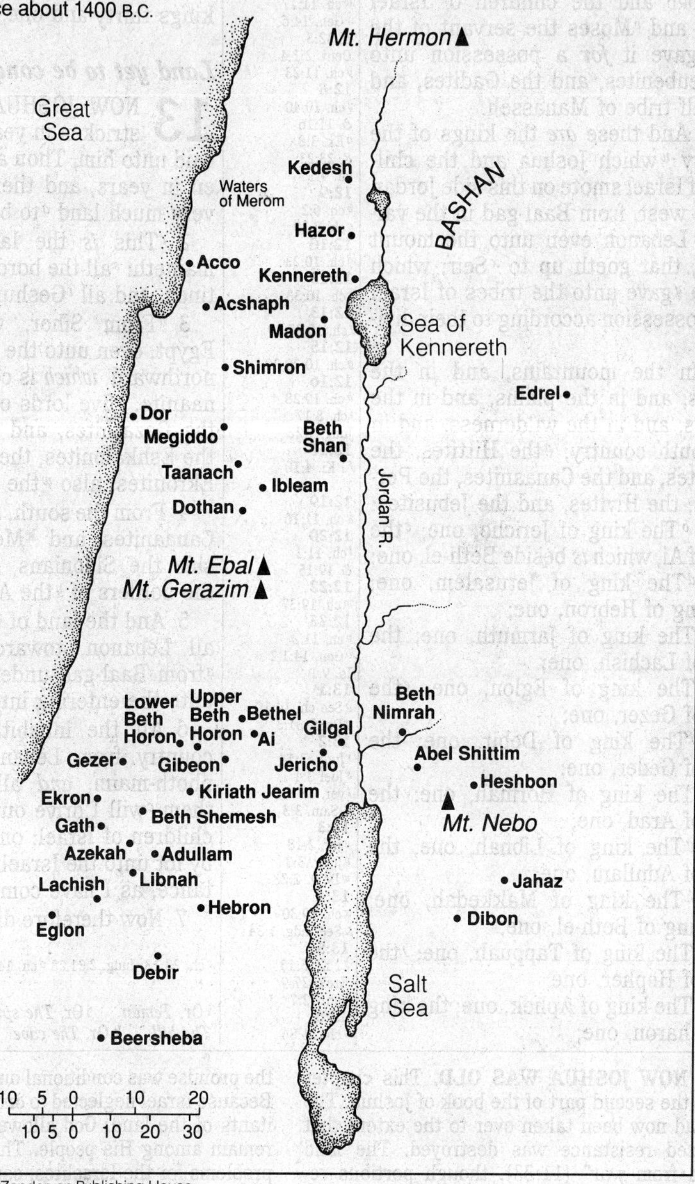

from [i]the south, under [n]Ashdoth-
pisgah:[j]
4 ¶ And [o]the coast of Og king of
Bashan, *which was* of [p]the remnant of
the giants, [q]that dwelt at Ashtaroth
and at Edrei,
5 And reigned in [r]mount Hermon,
[s]and in Salcah, and in all Bashan,
[t]unto the border of the Geshurites
and the Maachathites, and half Gilead,
the border of Sihon king of Heshbon.
6 [u]Them did Moses the servant of
the LORD and the children of Israel
smite: and [v]Moses the servant of the
LORD gave it *for* a possession unto
the Reubenites, and the Gadites, and
the half tribe of Manasseh.
7 ¶ And these *are* the kings of the
country [w]which Joshua and the chil-
dren of Israel smote on this side Jordan
on the west, from Baal-gad in the val-
ley of Lebanon even unto the mount
Halak, that goeth up to [x]Seir; which
Joshua [y]gave unto the tribes of Israel
for a possession according to their divi-
sions;
8 [z]In the mountains, and in the
valleys, and in the plains, and in the
springs, and in the wilderness, and in
the south country; [a]the Hittites, the
Amorites, and the Canaanites, the Per-
izzites, the Hivites, and the Jebusites:
9 ¶ [b]The king of Jericho, one; [c]the
king of Ai, which *is* beside Beth-el, one;
10 [d]The king of Jerusalem, one;
the king of Hebron, one;
11 The king of Jarmuth, one; the
king of Lachish, one;
12 The king of Eglon, one; [e]the
king of Gezer, one;
13 [f]The king of Debir, one; the
king of Geder, one;
14 The king of Hormah, one; the
king of Arad, one;
15 [g]The king of Libnah, one; the
king of Adullam, one;
16 [h]The king of Makkedah, one;
[i]the king of Beth-el, one;
17 The king of Tappuah, one; [j]the
king of Hepher, one;
18 The king of Aphek, one; the king
of Lasharon, one;

12:3 [n]Deut. 3:17 & 4:49
12:4 [o]Num. 21:33 Deut. 3:4,10 [p]Deut. 3:11 ch. 13:12 [q]Deut. 1:4
12:5 [r]Deut. 3:8 [s]Deut. 3:10 ch. 13:11 [t]Deut. 3:14
12:6 [u]Num. 21:24,35 [v]Num. 32:29,33 ch. 13:8
12:7 [w]ch. 11:17 [x]Gen. 14:6 & 32:3 Deut. 2:1,4 [y]ch. 11:23
12:8 [z]ch. 10:40 & 11:16 [a]Ex. 3:8 & 23:23 ch. 9:1
12:9 [b]ch. 6:2 [c]ch. 8:29
12:10 [d]ch. 10:23
12:12 [e]ch. 10:33
12:13 [f]ch. 10:38,39
12:15 [g]ch. 10:29,30
12:16 [h]ch. 10:28 [i]ch. 8:17 Judg. 1:22
12:17 [j]1 Ki. 4:10
12:19 [k]ch. 11:10
12:20 [l]ch. 11:1 & 19:15
12:22 [m]ch. 19:37
12:23 [n]ch. 11:2 [o]Gen. 14:1,2 Is. 9:1
13:1 [p]See ch. 14:10 [q]Deut. 31:3
13:2 [r]Judg. 3:1 [s]Joel 3:4 [t]ver. 13 2 Sam. 3:3
13:3 [u]Jer. 2:18 [v]Judg. 3:3 [w]Deut. 2:23
13:4 [x]ch. 19:30 [y]See Judg. 1:34
13:5 [z]1 Ki. 5:18 Ezek. 27:9 [a]ch. 12:7
13:6 [b]ch. 11:8

19 The king of Madon, one; [k]the
king of Hazor, one;
20 The king of [l]Shimron-meron,
one; the king of Achshaph, one;
21 The king of Taanach, one; the
king of Megiddo, one;
22 [m]The king of Kedesh, one; the
king of Jokneam of Carmel, one;
23 The king of Dor in the [n]coast of
Dor, one; the king of [o]the nations of
Gilgal, one;
24 The king of Tirzah, one: all the
kings thirty and one.

Land yet to be conquered

13 NOW JOSHUA [p]was old *and*
stricken in years; and the LORD
said unto him, Thou art old *and* strick-
en in years, and there remaineth yet
very much land [q]to be possessed.
2 [r]This *is* the land that yet re-
maineth: [s]all the borders of the Philis-
tines, and all [t]Geshuri,
3 [u]From Sihor, which *is* before
Egypt, even unto the borders of Ekron
northward, *which* is counted to the Ca-
naanite: [v]five lords of the Philistines;
the Gazathites, and the Ashdothites,
the Eshkalonites, the Gittites, and the
Ekronites; also [w]the Avites:
4 From the south, all the land of the
Canaanites, and [k]Mearah that *is* be-
side the Sidonians, [x]unto Aphek, to
the borders of [y]the Amorites:
5 And the land of [z]the Giblites, and
all Lebanon, toward the sunrising,
[a]from Baal-gad under mount Hermon
unto the entering into Hamath.
6 All the inhabitants of the hill
country from Lebanon unto [b]Misre-
photh-maim, *and* all the Sidonians,
them [c]will I drive out from before the
children of Israel: only [d]divide thou it
by lot unto the Israelites for an inheri-
tance, as I have commanded thee.
7 Now therefore divide this land for

[c]ch. 23:13; Judg. 2:21,23 [d]ch. 14:1,2

i Or, *Teman* j Or, *The springs of Pisgah,* or, *The hill* k Or, *The cave*

13:1 NOW JOSHUA WAS OLD. This chapter begins the second part of the book of Joshua. The land had now been taken over to the extent that organized resistance was destroyed. The land "rested from war" (11:23), though portions remained to be conquered (vv. 2–6).

13:6 THEM WILL I DRIVE OUT. God promised to drive out the Canaanites before Israel, yet the promise was conditional on Israel's obedience. Because Israel neglected to drive out all the inhabitants of the land, God allowed some of them to remain among His people. This led to numerous problems for the Israelites, especially that of falling into idolatry. God is not bound to His promises if we are not faithful to their conditions.

13:7 DIVIDE THIS LAND FOR AN INHERI-

an inheritance unto the nine tribes, and the half tribe of Manasseh,

Land east of the Jordan

8 With whom the Reubenites and the Gadites have received their inheritance, [e]which Moses gave them, beyond Jordan eastward, *even* as Moses the servant of the LORD gave them;

9 From Aroer, that *is* upon the bank of the river Arnon, and the city that *is* in the midst of the river, [f]and all the plain of Medeba unto Dibon;

10 And [g]all the cities of Sihon king of the Amorites, which reigned in Heshbon, unto the border of the children of Ammon;

11 [h]And Gilead, and the border of the Geshurites and Maachathites, and all mount Hermon, and all Bashan unto Salcah;

12 All the kingdom of Og in Bashan, which reigned in Ashtaroth and in Edrei, who remained of [i]the remnant of the giants: [j]for these did Moses smite, and cast them out.

13 Nevertheless the children of Israel expelled [k]not the Geshurites, nor the Maachathites: but the Geshurites and the Maachathites dwell among the Israelites until this day.

14 [l]Only unto the tribe of Levi he gave none inheritance; the sacrifices of the LORD God of Israel made by fire *are* their inheritance, [m]as he said unto them.

15 ¶ And Moses gave unto the tribe of the children of Reuben *inheritance* according to their families.

16 And their coast was [n]from Aroer, that *is* on the bank of the river Arnon, [o]and the city that *is* in the midst of the river, [p]and all the plain by Medeba;

17 Heshbon, and all her cities that *are* in the plain; Dibon, and [q]Bamoth-baal,[1] and Beth-baal-meon,

18 [r]And Jahaza, and Kedemoth, and Mephaath,

19 [s]And Kirjathaim, and [t]Sibmah, and Zareth-shahar in the mount of the valley,

20 And Beth-peor, and [u]Ashdoth-pisgah,[m] and Beth-jeshimoth,

21 [v]And all the cities of the plain, and all the kingdom of Sihon king of the Amorites, which reigned in Heshbon, [w]whom Moses smote [x]with the princes of Midian, Evi, and Rekem, and Zur, and Hur, and Reba, *which were* dukes of Sihon, dwelling in the country.

22 ¶ [y]Balaam also the son of Beor, the [n]soothsayer, did the children of Israel slay with the sword among them that were slain by them.

23 And the border of the children of Reuben was Jordan, and the border *thereof.* This *was* the inheritance of the children of Reuben after their families, the cities and the villages thereof.

24 And Moses gave *inheritance* unto the tribe of Gad, *even* unto the children of Gad according to their families.

25 [z]And their coast was Jazer, and all the cities of Gilead, [a]and half the land of the children of Ammon, unto Aroer that *is* before [b]Rabbah;

26 And from Heshbon unto Ramath-mizpeh, and Betonim; and from Mahanaim unto the border of Debir;

27 And in the valley, [c]Beth-aram, and Beth-nimrah, [d]and Succoth, and Zaphon, the rest of the kingdom of Sihon king of Heshbon, Jordan and *his* border, *even* unto the edge [e]of the sea of Chinnereth on the other side Jordan eastward.

28 This *is* the inheritance of the children of Gad after their families, the cities, and their villages.

29 ¶ And Moses gave *inheritance* unto the half tribe of Manasseh: and *this* was *the possession* of the half tribe of the children of Manasseh by their families.

30 And their coast was from Mahanaim, all Bashan, all the kingdom of Og king of Bashan, and [f]all the towns of Jair, which *are* in Bashan, threescore cities:

31 And half Gilead, and [g]Ashtaroth, and Edrei, cities of the kingdom of Og in Bashan, *were pertaining* unto the children of Machir the son of Manasseh, *even* to the one half of the [h]children of Machir by their families.

32 These *are the countries* which Moses did distribute for inheritance in the

13:8 [e]Num. 32:33 Deut. 3:12,13 ch. 22:4
13:9 [f]ver. 16 Num. 21:30
13:10 [g]Num. 21:24,25
13:11 [h]ch. 12:5
13:12 [i]Deut. 3:11 ch. 12:4 [j]Num. 21:24,35
13:13 [k]ver. 11
13:14 [l]Num. 18:20,23,24 ch. 14:3,4 [m]ver. 33
13:16 [n]ch. 12:2 [o]Num. 21:28 [p]ver. 9 Num. 21:30
13:17 [q]Num. 32:38
13:18 [r]Num. 21:23
13:19 [s]Num. 32:37 [t]Num. 32:38
13:20 [u]Deut. 3:17 ch. 12:3
13:21 [v]Deut. 3:10 [w]Num. 21:24 [x]Num. 31:8
13:22 [y]Num. 22:5 & 31:8
13:25 [z]Num. 32:35 [a]Compare Num. 21:26,28,29 with Deut. 2:19 & Judg. 11:13,15 [b]2 Sam. 11:1 & 12:26
13:27 [c]Num. 32:36 [d]Gen. 33:17 1 Ki. 7:46 [e]Num. 34:11
13:30 [f]Num. 32:41 1 Chr. 2:23
13:31 [g]ch. 12:4 [h]Num. 32:39,40

[1] Or, *The high places of Baal, and house of Baal-meon* [m] Or, *Springs of Pisgah,* or, *The hill* [n] Or, *diviner*

TANCE. The dividing of the land among the twelve tribes is described in chs. 13—22 and was a deep spiritual experience for the Israelites. It fulfilled God's promise concerning the land and inspired hope for a greater fulfillment of the peace they now enjoyed (cf. Ps. 16:6).

plains of Moab, on the other side Jordan, by Jericho, eastward.

33 [i]But unto the tribe of Levi Moses gave not *any* inheritance: the LORD God of Israel *was* their inheritance, [j]as he said unto them.

Land west of the Jordan

14 AND THESE *are the countries* which the children of Israel inherited in the land of Canaan, [k]which Eleazar the priest, and Joshua the son of Nun, and the heads of the fathers of the tribes of the children of Israel, distributed for inheritance to them.

2 [l]By lot *was* their inheritance, as the LORD commanded by the hand of Moses, for the nine tribes, and *for* the half tribe.

3 [m]For Moses had given the inheritance of two tribes and an half tribe on the other side Jordan: but unto the Levites he gave none inheritance among them.

4 For [n]the children of Joseph were two tribes, Manasseh and Ephraim: therefore they gave no part unto the Levites in the land, save cities to dwell *in*, with their suburbs for their cattle and for their substance.

5 [o]As the LORD commanded Moses, so the children of Israel did, and they divided the land.

6 ¶ Then the children of Judah came unto Joshua in Gilgal: and Caleb the son of Jephunneh the [p]Kenezite said unto him, Thou knowest [q]the thing that the LORD said unto Moses the man of God concerning me and thee [r]in Kadesh-barnea.

7 Forty years old *was* I when Moses the servant of the LORD [s]sent me from Kadesh-barnea to espy out the land; and I brought him word again as *it was* in mine heart.

8 Nevertheless [t]my brethren that went up with me made the heart of the people melt: but I wholly [u]followed the LORD my God.

9 And Moses sware on that day, saying, [v]Surely the land [w]whereon thy feet have trodden shall be thine inheritance, and thy children's for ever, because thou hast wholly followed the LORD my God.

10 And now, behold, the LORD hath kept me alive, [x]as he said, these forty and five years, even since the LORD spake this word unto Moses, while *the children of* Israel [o]wandered in the wilderness: and now, lo, I *am* this day fourscore and five years old.

11 [y]As yet I *am as* strong this day as *I was* in the day that Moses sent me: as my strength *was* then, even so *is* my strength now, for war, both [z]to go out, and to come in.

12 Now therefore give me this mountain, whereof the LORD spake in that day; for thou heardest in that day how [a]the Anakims *were* there, and *that* the cities *were* great *and* fenced: [b]if so be the LORD *will be* with me, then [c]I shall be able to drive them out, as the LORD said.

13 And Joshua [d]blessed him, [e]and gave unto Caleb the son of Jephunneh Hebron for an inheritance.

14 [f]Hebron therefore became the inheritance of Caleb the son of Jephunneh the Kenezite unto this day, because that he [g]wholly followed the LORD God of Israel.

15 And [h]the name of Hebron before *was* Kirjath-arba; *which Arba was* a great man among the Anakims. [i]And the land had rest from war.

The borders of Judah

15:15–19pp — Judg. 1:11–15

15 *THIS* THEN was the lot of the tribe of the children of Judah by their families; [j]*even* to the border of Edom the [k]wilderness of Zin southward *was* the uttermost part of the south coast.

2 And their south border was from the shore of the salt sea, from the [p]bay that looketh southward:

3 And it went out to the south side [l]to [q]Maaleh-acrabbim, and passed

[o] Heb. *walked* [p] Heb. *tongue* [q] Or, *The going up to Acrabbim*

13:33 [i]ver. 14 ch. 18:7 [j]Num. 18:20 Deut. 10:9 & 18:1,2
14:1 [k]Num. 34:17,18
14:2 [l]Num. 26:55 & 33:54 & 34:13
14:3 [m]ch. 13:8,32,33
14:4 [n]Gen. 48:5 1 Chr. 5:1,2
14:5 [o]Num. 35:2 ch. 21:2
14:6 [p]Num. 32:12 & ch. 15:17 [q]Num. 14:24,30 [r]Num. 13:26
14:7 [s]Num. 13:6 & 14:6
14:8 [t]Num. 13:31,32 [u]Num. 14:24 Deut. 1:36
14:9 [v]Num. 14:23,24 [w]See Num. 13:22
14:10 [x]Num. 14:30
14:11 [y]See Deut. 34:7 [z]Deut. 31:2
14:12 [a]Num. 13:28,33 [b]Rom. 8:31 [c]ch. 15:14 Judg. 1:20
14:13 [d]ch. 22:6 [e]ch. 10:37 & 15:13
14:14 [f]ch. 21:12 [g]ver. 8,9
14:15 [h]Gen. 23:2 ch. 15:13 [i]ch. 11:23
15:1 [j]Num. 34:3 [k]Num. 33:36
15:3 [l]Num. 34:4

14:14 CALEB . . . FOLLOWED THE LORD. Caleb remained faithful to God and received fully his promised inheritance (vv. 9–14). His life illustrates the believer's faithfulness and acceptance of the promise of the Father under the new covenant—i.e., the Holy Spirit (Acts 1:4–5). After repentance and acceptance of God's new covenant terms, believers must go on to receive whatever spiritual gifts God wishes to bestow (cf. Rom. 12:6–8; 1 Cor. 12:4–31), and to manifest the fruit of the Spirit (cf. Gal. 5:22–25) and wisdom (cf. Acts 6:3; 1 Cor. 2:6–16; Eph. 1:17; Jas. 3:13–18). All of these are the inheritance of those filled with the Spirit and power (cf. Acts 1:4–8; 2:4).

along to Zin, and ascended up on the
south side unto Kadesh-barnea, and
passed along to Hezron, and went up to
Adar, and fetched a compass to Kar-
kaa:
4 *From thence* it passed [m]toward
Azmon, and went out unto the river of
Egypt; and the goings out of that coast
were at the sea: this shall be your
south coast.
5 And the east border *was* the salt
sea, *even* unto the end of Jordan. And
their border in the north quarter *was*
from the bay of the sea at the uttermost
part of Jordan:
6 And the border went up to [n]Beth-
hoglah, and passed along by the north
by Beth-arabah; and the border went
up [o]to the stone of Bohan the son of
Reuben:
7 And the border went up toward
Debir from [p]the valley of Achor, and
so northward, looking toward Gilgal,
that *is* before the going up to Adum-
mim, which *is* on the south side of the
river: and the border passed toward
the waters of En-shemesh, and the go-
ings out thereof were at [q]En-rogel:
8 And the border went up [r]by the
valley of the son of Hinnom unto the
south side of the [s]Jebusite; the same
is Jerusalem: and the border went up to
the top of the mountain that *lieth* be-
fore the valley of Hinnom westward,
which *is* at the end [t]of the valley of
the giants northward:
9 And the border was drawn from
the top of the hill unto [u]the fountain
of the water of Nephtoah, and went out
to the cities of mount Ephron; and the
border was drawn [v]to Baalah, which
is [w]Kirjath-jearim:
10 And the border compassed from
Baalah westward unto mount Seir, and
passed along unto the side of mount
Jearim, which *is* Chesalon, on the north
side, and went down to Beth-shemesh,
and passed on to [x]Timnah:
11 And the border went out unto the
side of [y]Ekron northward: and the
border was drawn to Shicron, and
passed along to mount Baalah, and
went out unto Jabneel; and the goings
out of the border were at the sea.
12 And the west border *was* [z]to the
great sea, and the coast *thereof.* This *is*
the coast of the children of Judah round
about according to their families.
13 ¶ [a]And unto Caleb the son of Je-
phunneh he gave a part among the chil-
dren of Judah, according to the com-
mandment of the LORD to Joshua, *even*
[b]the[r] city of Arba the father of Anak,
which *city is* Hebron.
14 And Caleb drove thence [c]the
three sons of Anak, [d]Sheshai, and
Ahiman, and Talmai, the children of
Anak.
15 And [e]he went up thence to the
inhabitants of Debir: and the name of
Debir before *was* Kirjath-sepher.
16 ¶ [f]And Caleb said, He that
smiteth Kirjath-sepher, and taketh it,
to him will I give Achsah my daughter
to wife.
17 And [g]Othniel the [h]son of Ke-
naz, the brother of Caleb, took it: and
he gave him Achsah his daughter to
wife.
18 [i]And it came to pass, as she
came *unto him,* that she moved him to
ask of her father a field: and [j]she
lighted off *her* ass; and Caleb said unto
her, What wouldest thou?
19 Who answered, Give me a
[k]blessing; for thou hast given me a
south land; give me also springs of wa-
ter. And he gave her the upper springs,
and the nether springs.
20 This *is* the inheritance of the
tribe of the children of Judah according
to their families.
21 And the uttermost cities of the
tribe of the children of Judah toward
the coast of Edom southward were
Kabzeel, and Eder, and Jagur,
22 And Kinah, and Dimonah, and
Adadah,
23 And Kedesh, and Hazor, and Ith-
nan,
24 Ziph, and Telem, and Bealoth,
25 And Hazor, Hadattah, and Keri-
oth, *and* Hezron, which *is* Hazor,
26 Amam, and Shema, and Mola-
dah,
27 And Hazar-gaddah, and Hesh-
mon, and Beth-palet,
28 And Hazar-shual, and Beer-she-
ba, and Bizjothjah,
29 Baalah, and Iim, and Azem,
30 And Eltolad, and Chesil, and
Hormah,
31 And [l]Ziklag, and Madmannah,
and Sansannah,
32 And Lebaoth, and Shilhim, and
Ain, and Rimmon: all the cities *are*
twenty and nine, with their villages:

15:4 [m]Num. 34:5
15:6 [n]ch. 18:19 [o]ch. 18:17
15:7 [p]ch. 7:26 [q]2 Sam. 17:17 1 Ki. 1:9
15:8 [r]ch. 18:16 2 Ki. 23:10 Jer. 19:2,6 [s]ch. 18:28 Judg. 1:21 & 19:10 [t]ch. 18:16
15:9 [u]ch. 18:15 [v]1 Chr. 13:6 [w]Judg. 18:12
15:10 [x]Gen. 38:13 Judg. 14:1
15:11 [y]ch. 19:43
15:12 [z]ver. 47 Num. 34:6,7
15:13 [a]ch. 14:13 [b]ch. 14:15
15:14 [c]Judg. 1:11,20 [d]Num. 13:22
15:15 [e]ch. 10:38 Judg. 1:11
15:16 [f]Judg. 1:12
15:17 [g]Judg. 1:13 & 3:9 [h]Num. 32:12 ch. 14:6
15:18 [i]Judg. 1:14 [j]See Gen. 24:64 1 Sam. 25:23
15:19 [k]Gen. 33:11
15:31 [l]1 Sam. 27:6

[r] Or, *Kirjath-arba*

33 *And* in the valley, [m]Eshtaol, and
Zoreah, and Ashnah,
34 And Zanoah, and En-gannim,
Tappuah, and Enam,
35 Jarmuth, and Adullam, Socoh,
and Azekah,
36 And Sharaim, and Adithaim, and
Gederah, [s]and Gederothaim; fourteen
cities with their villages:
37 Zenan, and Hadashah, and Mig-
dal-gad,
38 And Dilean, and Mizpeh, [n]and
Joktheel,
39 Lachish, and Bozkath, and Eg-
lon,
40 And Cabbon, and Lahmam, and
Kithlish,
41 And Gederoth, Beth-dagon, and
Naamah, and Makkedah; sixteen cities
with their villages:
42 Libnah, and Ether, and Ashan,
43 And Jiphtah, and Ashnah, and
Nezib,
44 And Keilah, and Achzib, and Ma-
reshah; nine cities with their villages:
45 Ekron, with her towns and her
villages:
46 From Ekron even unto the sea,
all that *lay* [t]near Ashdod, with their
villages:
47 Ashdod with her towns and her
villages, Gaza with her towns and her
villages, unto [o]the river of Egypt, and
[p]the great sea, and the border *thereof:*
48 ¶ And in the mountains, Shamir,
and Jattir, and Socoh,
49 And Dannah, and Kirjath-san-
nah, which *is* Debir,
50 And Anab, and Eshtemoh, and
Anim,
51 [q]And Goshen, and Holon, and
Giloh; eleven cities with their villages:
52 Arab, and Dumah, and Eshean,
53 And [u]Janum, and Beth-tappu-
ah, and Aphekah,
54 And Humtah, and [r]Kirjath-
arba, which *is* Hebron, and Zior; nine
cities with their villages:
55 Maon, Carmel, and Ziph, and Jut-
tah,
56 And Jezreel, and Jokdeam, and
Zanoah,
57 Cain, Gibeah, and Timnah; ten
cities with their villages:
58 Halhul, Beth-zur, and Gedor,

15:33 [m]Num. 13:23
15:38 [n]2 Ki. 14:7
15:47 [o]ver. 4 [p]Num. 34:6
15:51 [q]ch. 10:41 & 11:16
15:54 [r]ver. 13 ch. 14:15
15:60 [s]ch. 18:14
15:63 [t]See Judg. 1:8,21 2 Sam. 5:6 [u]Judg. 1:21
16:2 [v]ch. 18:13 Judg. 1:26
16:3 [w]ch. 18:13 2 Chr. 8:5 [x]1 Ki. 9:15 1 Chr. 7:28
16:4 [y]ch. 17:14
16:5 [z]ch. 18:13 [a]2 Chr. 8:5
16:6 [b]ch. 17:7
16:7 [c]1 Chr. 7:28
16:8 [d]ch. 17:9

59 And Maarath, and Beth-anoth,
and Eltekon; six cities with their vil-
lages:
60 [s]Kirjath-baal, which *is* Kirjath-
jearim, and Rabbah; two cities with
their villages:
61 In the wilderness, Beth-arabah,
Middin, and Secacah,
62 And Nibshan, and the city of
Salt, and En-gedi; six cities with their
villages.
63 ¶ As for the Jebusites the inhabi-
tants of Jerusalem, [t]the children of Ju-
dah could not drive them out: [u]but the
Jebusites dwell with the children of Ju-
dah at Jerusalem unto this day.

Ephraim and Manasseh

16 AND THE lot of the children of
Joseph [v]fell from Jordan by
Jericho, unto the water of Jericho on
the east, to the wilderness that goeth
up from Jericho throughout mount
Beth-el,
2 And goeth out from Beth-el to
[v]Luz, and passeth along unto the bor-
ders of Archi to Ataroth,
3 And goeth down westward to the
coast of Japhleti, [w]unto the coast of
Beth-horon the nether, and to [x]Gezer:
and the goings out thereof are at the
sea.
4 [y]So the children of Joseph, Ma-
nasseh and Ephraim, took their inheri-
tance.
5 ¶ And the border of the children of
Ephraim according to their families
was *thus:* even the border of their in-
heritance on the east side was [z]Ata-
roth-addar, [a]unto Beth-horon the up-
per;
6 And the border went out toward
the sea to [b]Michmethah on the north
side; and the border went about east-
ward unto Taanath-shiloh, and passed
by it on the east to Janohah;
7 And it went down from Janohah to
Ataroth, [c]and to Naarath, and came to
Jericho, and went out at Jordan.
8 The border went out from Tappu-
ah westward unto the [d]river Kanah;
and the goings out thereof were at the
sea. This *is* the inheritance of the tribe

[s] Or, *or* [t] Heb. *by the place of* [u] Or, *Janus*
[v] Heb. *went forth*

16:1 CHILDREN OF JOSEPH. Joseph, the eleventh son of Jacob, did not have a tribe named after him because his inheritance was given to his two sons, Ephraim and Manasseh (Gen. 48:14–22). As a result, Joseph received a double portion of the land in that Ephraim and Manasseh constituted two separate, complete tribes.

of the children of Ephraim by their families.

9 And [e]the separate cities for the children of Ephraim *were* among the inheritance of the children of Manasseh, all the cities with their villages.

10 [f]And they drave not out the Canaanites that dwelt in Gezer: but the Canaanites dwell among the Ephraimites unto this day, and serve under tribute.

17 THERE WAS also a lot for the tribe of Manasseh; for he *was* the [g]firstborn of Joseph; *to wit,* for [h]Machir the firstborn of Manasseh, the father of Gilead: because he was a man of war, therefore he had [i]Gilead and Bashan.

2 There was also *a lot* for [j]the rest of the children of Manasseh by their families; [k]for the children of [w]Abiezer, and for the children of Helek, [l]and for the children of Asriel, and for the children of Shechem, [m]and for the children of Hepher, and for the children of Shemida: these *were* the male children of Manasseh the son of Joseph by their families.

3 ¶ But [n]Zelophehad, the son of Hepher, the son of Gilead, the son of Machir, the son of Manasseh, had no sons, but daughters: and these *are* the names of his daughters, Mahlah, and Noah, Hoglah, Milcah, and Tirzah.

4 And they came near before [o]Eleazar the priest, and before Joshua the son of Nun, and before the princes, saying, [p]The LORD commanded Moses to give us an inheritance among our brethren. Therefore according to the commandment of the LORD he gave them an inheritance among the brethren of their father.

5 And there fell ten portions to Manasseh, beside the land of Gilead and Bashan, which *were* on the other side Jordan;

6 Because the daughters of Manasseh had an inheritance among his sons: and the rest of Manasseh's sons had the land of Gilead.

7 ¶ And the coast of Manasseh was from Asher to [q]Michmethah, that *lieth* before Shechem; and the border went along on the right hand unto the inhabitants of En-tappuah.

8 *Now* Manasseh had the land of Tappuah: but [r]Tappuah on the border of Manasseh *belonged* to the children of Ephraim;

9 And the coast descended unto the [x]river Kanah, southward of the river: [s]these cities of Ephraim *are* among the cities of Manasseh: the coast of Manasseh also *was* on the north side of the river, and the outgoings of it were at the sea:

10 Southward *it was* Ephraim's, and northward *it was* Manasseh's, and the sea is his border; and they met together in Asher on the north, and in Issachar on the east.

11 [t]And Manasseh had in Issachar and in Asher [u]Beth-shean and her towns, and Ibleam and her towns, and the inhabitants of Dor and her towns, and the inhabitants of En-dor and her towns, and the inhabitants of Taanach and her towns, and the inhabitants of Megiddo and her towns, *even* three countries.

12 Yet [v]the children of Manasseh could not drive out *the inhabitants of* those cities; but the Canaanites would dwell in that land.

13 Yet it came to pass, when the children of Israel were waxen strong, that they put the Canaanites to [w]tribute; but did not utterly drive them out.

14 [x]And the children of Joseph spake unto Joshua, saying, Why hast thou given me *but* [y]one lot and one portion to inherit, seeing I *am* [z]a great people, forasmuch as the LORD hath blessed me hitherto?

15 And Joshua answered them, If

16:9 [e]ch. 17:9
16:10 [f]Judg. 1:29 See 1 Ki. 9:16
17:1 [g]Gen. 41:51 & 46:20 & 48:18 [h]Gen. 50:23 [i]Deut. 3:15
17:2 [j]Num. 26:29-32 [k]1 Chr. 7:18 [l]Num. 26:31 [m]Num. 26:32
17:3 [n]Num. 26:33 & 27:1 & 36:2
17:4 [o]ch. 14:1 [p]Num. 27:6,7
17:7 [q]ch. 16:6
17:8 [r]ch. 16:8
17:9 [s]ch. 16:9
17:11 [t]1 Chr. 7:29 [u]1 Sam. 31:10 1 Ki. 4:12
17:12 [v]Judg. 1:27,28
17:13 [w]ch. 16:10
17:14 [x]ch. 16:4 [y]Gen. 48:22 [z]Gen. 48:19 Num. 26:34,37

[w]Num. 26:30 in *Jeezer* [x]Or, *brook of reeds*

17:4 ACCORDING TO THE COMMANDMENT OF THE LORD. This verse makes it clear that the people regarded the Pentateuch as the word of God to be obeyed in every detail. The written Word of God, revealed by Him to Moses, constituted the standard of authority for all God's people, including Eleazar the priest and Joshua (v. 4).

17:13 DID NOT UTTERLY DRIVE THEM OUT. Israel failed to possess the land fully and to completely drive out the Canaanites for two reasons. (1) They wanted the profit and affluence gained from the forced labor and tribute of the Canaanites. Compromising the will of God for ease and money sowed the seeds for later widespread apostasy (cf. Judg. 1:21,27–29; 2:11–13). (2) Some of the Canaanites, with their "iron chariots" (vv. 16–18; Judg. 1:19), had armaments superior to those of the Israelites, which they could not overcome in their own strength. They were beginning to lose their confidence in the power of their God to overcome their enemies (cf. Ps. 20:6–8).

thou *be* a great people, *then* get thee up to the wood *country,* and cut down for thyself there in the land of the Perizzites, and of the [y]giants, if mount Ephraim be too narrow for thee.

16 And the children of Joseph said, The hill is not enough for us: and all the Canaanites that dwell in the land of the valley have [a]chariots of iron, *both they* who *are* of Beth-shean and her towns, and *they* who *are* [b]of the valley of Jezreel.

17 And Joshua spake unto the house of Joseph, *even* to Ephraim and to Manasseh, saying, Thou *art* a great people, and hast great power: thou shalt not have one lot *only:*

18 But the mountain shall be thine; for it *is* a wood, and thou shalt cut it down: and the outgoings of it shall be thine: for thou shalt drive out the Canaanites, [c]though they have iron chariots, *and* though they *be* strong.

Assigning the inherited land

18 AND THE whole congregation of the children of Israel assembled together [d]at Shiloh, and [e]set up the tabernacle of the congregation there. And the land was subdued before them.

2 And there remained among the children of Israel seven tribes, which had not yet received their inheritance.

3 And Joshua said unto the children of Israel, [f]How long *are* ye slack to go to possess the land, which the LORD God of your fathers hath given you?

4 Give out from among you three men for *each* tribe: and I will send them, and they shall rise, and go through the land, and describe it according to the inheritance of them; and they shall come *again* to me.

5 And they shall divide it into seven parts: [g]Judah shall abide in their coast on the south, and [h]the house of Joseph shall abide in their coasts on the north.

6 Ye shall therefore describe the land *into* seven parts, and bring *the description* hither to me, [i]that I may cast lots for you here before the LORD our God.

7 [j]But the Levites have no part among you; for the priesthood of the LORD *is* their inheritance: [k]and Gad, and Reuben, and half the tribe of Manasseh, have received their inheritance beyond Jordan on the east, which Moses the servant of the LORD gave them.

8 ¶ And the men arose, and went away: and Joshua charged them that went to describe the land, saying, Go and walk through the land, and describe it, and come again to me, that I may here cast lots for you before the LORD in Shiloh.

9 And the men went and passed through the land, and described it by cities into seven parts in a book, and came *again* to Joshua to the host at Shiloh.

10 ¶ And Joshua cast lots for them in Shiloh before the LORD: and there Joshua divided the land unto the children of Israel according to their divisions.

The land of Benjamin

11 ¶ And the lot of the tribe of the children of Benjamin came up according to their families: and the coast of their lot came forth between the children of Judah and the children of Joseph.

12 [l]And their border on the north side was from Jordan; and the border went up to the side of Jericho on the north side, and went up through the mountains westward; and the goings out thereof were at the wilderness of Beth-aven.

13 And the border went over from thence toward Luz, to the side of Luz, [m]which *is* Beth-el, southward; and the border descended to Ataroth-adar, near the hill that *lieth* on the south side [n]of the nether Beth-horon.

14 And the border was drawn *thence,* and compassed the corner of the sea southward, from the hill that *lieth* before Beth-horon southward; and the goings out thereof were at [o]Kir-

17:16 [a]Judg. 1:19 & 4:3 [b]ch. 19:18 1 Ki. 4:12
17:18 [c]Deut. 20:1
18:1 [d]ch. 19:51 & 21:2 & 22:9 Jer. 7:12 [e]Judg. 18:31 1 Sam. 1:3,24 & 4:3,4
18:3 [f]Judg. 18:9
18:5 [g]ch. 15:1 [h]ch. 16:1,4
18:6 [i]ver. 10 ch. 14:2
18:7 [j]ch. 13:33 [k]ch. 13:8
18:12 [l]See ch. 16:1
18:13 [m]Gen. 28:19 Judg. 1:23 [n]ch. 16:3
18:14 [o]See ch. 15:9

[y] Or, *Rephaims;* see Gen. 14:5 & 15:20

18:1 SET UP THE TABERNACLE. Israel moved its center of worship from Gilgal to Shiloh. There they set up the tabernacle, the place in which the Ark of the Covenant was kept and where God manifested His presence among the people in a special way (cf. Ex. 25:8; 27:21; 34:26). The tabernacle remained at Shiloh throughout the time of the judges (i.e., about 300 years), until such time as it was captured by the Philistines during the time of Samuel (1 Sam. 4:3—5:1).

jath-baal, which *is* Kirjath-jearim, a
city of the children of Judah: this *was*
the west quarter.
15 And the south quarter *was* from
the end of Kirjath-jearim, and the
border went out on the west, and
went out to [p]the well of waters of
Nephtoah:
16 And the border came down to the
end of the mountain that *lieth* before
[q]the valley of the son of Hinnom, *and*
which *is* in the valley of the giants
on the north, and descended to the
valley of Hinnom, to the side of Jeb-
usion the south, and descended to
[r]En-rogel,
17 And was drawn from the north,
and went forth to En-shemesh, and
went forth toward Geliloth, which *is*
over against the going up of Adummim,
and descended to [s]the stone of Bohan
the son of Reuben,
18 And passed along toward the
side over against [t]Arabah[z] north-
ward, and went down unto Arabah:
19 And the border passed along to
the side of Beth-hoglah northward:
and the outgoings of the border were
at the north [a]bay of the salt sea at
the south end of Jordan: this *was* the
south coast.
20 And Jordan was the border of it
on the east side. This *was* the inheri-
tance of the children of Benjamin, by
the coasts thereof round about, accord-
ing to their families.
21 Now the cities of the tribe of the
children of Benjamin according to their
families were Jericho, and Beth-hog-
lah, and the valley of Keziz,
22 And Beth-arabah, and Zemara-
im, and Beth-el,
23 And Avim, and Parah, and Oph-
rah,
24 And Chephar-haammonai, and
Ophni, and Gaba; twelve cities with
their villages:
25 Gibeon, and Ramah, and Bee-
roth,
26 And Mizpeh, and Chephirah, and
Mozah,
27 And Rekem, and Irpeel, and Tar-
alah,
28 And Zelah, Eleph, and [u]Jebusi,
which *is* Jerusalem, Gibeath, *and* Kir-
jath; fourteen cities with their villages.
This *is* the inheritance of the children
of Benjamin according to their fami-
lies.

18:15 [p]ch. 15:9
18:16 [q]ch. 15:8 [r]ch. 15:7
18:17 [s]ch. 15:6
18:18 [t]ch. 15:6
18:28 [u]ch. 15:8

19:1 [v]ver. 9
19:2 [w]1 Chr. 4:28
19:9 [x]ver. 1
19:11 [y]Gen. 49:13 [z]ch. 12:22

The land of Simeon

19:2–10pp — 1 Chr. 4:28–33

19 AND THE second lot came
forth to Simeon, *even* for the
tribe of the children of Simeon accord-
ing to their families: [v]and their inheri-
tance was within the inheritance of the
children of Judah.
2 And [w]they had in their inheri-
tance Beer-sheba, or Sheba, and Mola-
dah,
3 And Hazar-shual, and Balah, and
Azem,
4 And Eltolad, and Bethul, and Hor-
mah,
5 And Ziklag, and Beth-marcaboth,
and Hazar-susah,
6 And Beth-lebaoth, and Sharuhen;
thirteen cities and their villages:
7 Ain, Remmon, and Ether, and
Ashan; four cities and their villages:
8 And all the villages that *were*
round about these cities to Baalath-
beer, Ramath of the south. This *is* the
inheritance of the tribe of the children
of Simeon according to their families.
9 Out of the portion of the children
of Judah *was* the inheritance of the chil-
dren of Simeon: for the part of the chil-
dren of Judah was too much for them:
[x]therefore the children of Simeon had
their inheritance within the inheri-
tance of them.

The land of Zebulun

10 ¶ And the third lot came up for
the children of Zebulun according to
their families: and the border of their
inheritance was unto Sarid:
11 [y]And their border went up to-
ward the sea, and Maralah, and
reached to Dabbasheth, and reached to
the river that *is* [z]before Jokneam;
12 And turned from Sarid eastward
toward the sunrising unto the border of
Chisloth-tabor, and then goeth out to
Daberath, and goeth up to Japhia,
13 And from thence passeth on
along on the east to Gittah-hepher, to
Ittah-kazin, and goeth out to Remmon-
[b]methoar to Neah;
14 And the border compasseth it on
the north side to Hannathon: and the
outgoings thereof are in the valley of
Jiphthah-el:
15 And Kattath, and Nahallal, and

[z] Or, *The plain* [a] Heb. *tongue* [b] Or, *which is drawn*

Shimron, and Idalah, and Bethlehem: twelve cities with their villages.

16 This *is* the inheritance of the children of Zebulun according to their families, these cities with their villages.

The land of Issachar

17 ¶ *And* the fourth lot came out to Issachar, for the children of Issachar according to their families.

18 And their border was toward Jezreel, and Chesulloth, and Shunem,

19 And Haphraim, and Shion, and Anaharath,

20 And Rabbith, and Kishion, and Abez,

21 And Remeth, and En-gannim, and En-haddah, and Beth-pazzez;

22 And the coast reacheth to Tabor, and Shahazimah, and Beth-shemesh; and the outgoings of their border were at Jordan: sixteen cities with their villages.

23 This *is* the inheritance of the tribe of the children of Issachar according to their families, the cities and their villages.

The land of Asher

24 ¶ And the fifth lot came out for the tribe of the children of Asher according to their families.

25 And their border was Helkath, and Hali, and Beten, and Achshaph,

26 And Alammelech, and Amad, and Misheal; and reacheth to Carmel westward, and to Shihor-libnath;

27 And turneth toward the sunrising to Beth-dagon, and reacheth to Zebulun, and to the valley of Jiphthah-el toward the north side of Beth-emek, and Neiel, and goeth out to Cabul on the left hand,

28 And Hebron, and Rehob, and Hammon, and Kanah, [a]*even* unto great Zidon;

29 And *then* the coast turneth to Ramah, and to the strong city [b]Tyre; and the coast turneth to Hosah; and the outgoings thereof are at the sea from the coast to [c]Achzib:

30 Ummah also, and Aphek, and Rehob: twenty and two cities with their villages.

31 This *is* the inheritance of the tribe of the children of Asher according to their families, these cities with their villages.

19:28 [a]ch. 11:8 Judg. 1:31
19:29 [b]2 Sam. 5:11 [c]Judg. 1:31

The land of Naphtali

32 ¶ The sixth lot came out to the children of Naphtali, *even* for the children of Naphtali according to their families.

33 And their coast was from Heleph, from Allon to Zaanannim, and Adami, Nekeb, and Jabneel, unto Lakum; and the outgoings thereof were at Jordan:

34 And *then* [d]the coast turneth westward to Aznoth-tabor, and goeth out from thence to Hukkok, and reacheth to Zebulun on the south side, and reacheth to Asher on the west side, and to Judah upon Jordan toward the sunrising.

35 And the fenced cities *are* Ziddim, Zer, and Hammath, Rakkath, and [e]Chinnereth,

36 And Adamah, and Ramah, and Hazor,

37 And Kedesh, and Edrei, and En-hazor,

38 And Iron, and Migdal-el, Horem, and Beth-anath, and Beth-shemesh; nineteen cities with their villages.

39 This *is* the inheritance of the tribe of the children of Naphtali according to their families, the cities and their villages.

The land of Dan

40 ¶ *And* the seventh lot came out for the tribe of the children of Dan according to their families.

41 And the coast of their inheritance was Zorah, and Eshtaol, and Ir-shemesh,

42 And [f]Shaalabbin, and Ajalon, and Jethlah,

43 And Elon, and Thimnathah, and Ekron,

44 And Eltekeh, and Gibbethon, and Baalath,

45 And Jehud, and Bene-berak, and Gath-rimmon,

46 And Me-jarkon, and Rakkon, with the border [c]before [d]Japho.

47 And [g]the coast of the children of Dan went out *too little* for them: therefore the children of Dan went up to fight against Leshem, and took it, and smote it with the edge of the sword, and possessed it, and dwelt therein, and called Leshem, [h]Dan, after the name of Dan their father.

19:34 [d]Deut. 33:23
19:35 [e]Deut. 3:17 ch. 11:2 & 12:3 Mark 6:53 Luke 5:1
19:42 [f]Judg. 1:35
19:47 [g]See Judg. 18 [h]Judg. 18:29

[c] Or, *over against* [d] Or, *Joppa;* see Acts 9:36

48 This *is* the inheritance of the tribe of the children of Dan according to their families, these cities with their villages.

49 ¶ When they had made an end of dividing the land for inheritance by their coasts, the children of Israel gave an inheritance to Joshua the son of Nun among them:

50 According to the word of the LORD they gave him the city which he asked, *even* [i]Timnath-[j]serah in mount Ephraim: and he built the city, and dwelt therein.

51 [k]These *are* the inheritances, which Eleazar the priest, and Joshua the son of Nun, and the heads of the fathers of the tribes of the children of Israel, divided for an inheritance by lot [l]in Shiloh before the LORD, at the door of the tabernacle of the congregation. So they made an end of dividing the country.

The six cities of refuge

20:1–9Ref — Num. 35:9–34; Deut. 4:41–43; 19:1–14

20 THE LORD also spake unto Joshua, saying,

2 Speak to the children of Israel, saying, [m]Appoint out for you cities of refuge, whereof I spake unto you by the hand of Moses:

3 That the slayer that killeth *any* person unawares *and* unwittingly may flee thither: and they shall be your refuge from the avenger of blood.

4 And when he that doth flee unto one of those cities shall stand at the entering of the gate of the city, and shall declare his cause in the ears of the elders of that city, they shall take him into the city unto them, and give him a place, that he may dwell among them.

5 [n]And if the avenger of blood pursue after him, then they shall not deliver the slayer up into his hand; because he smote his neighbour unwittingly, and hated him not beforetime.

6 And he shall dwell in that city, [o]until he stand before the congregation for judgment, *and* until the death of the high priest that shall be in those days: then shall the slayer return, and come unto his own city, and unto his own house, unto the city from whence he fled.

19:50 [i]ch. 24:30 [j]1 Chr. 7:24 **19:51** [k]Num. 34:17 ch. 14:1 [l]ch. 18:1,10 **20:2** [m]Ex. 21:13 Num. 35:6,11,14 Deut. 19:2,9 **20:5** [n]Num. 35:12 **20:6** [o]Num. 35:12,25

20:7 [p]ch. 21:32 1 Chr. 6:76 [q]ch. 21:21 2 Chr. 10:1 [r]ch. 14:15 & 21:11,13 [s]Luke 1:39 **20:8** [t]Deut. 4:43 ch. 21:36 1 Chr. 6:78 [u]ch. 21:38 1 Ki. 22:3 [v]ch. 21:27 **20:9** [w]Num. 35:15 [x]ver. 6 **21:1** [y]ch. 14:1 & 17:4 **21:2** [z]ch. 18:1 [a]Num. 35:2 **21:4** [b]ver. 8,19 [c]See ch. 24:33 **21:5** [d]ver. 20 **21:6** [e]ver. 27

7 ¶ And they [e]appointed [p]Kedesh in Galilee in mount Naphtali, and [q]Shechem in mount Ephraim, and [r]Kirjath-arba, which *is* Hebron, in [s]the mountain of Judah.

8 And on the other side Jordan by Jericho eastward, they assigned [t]Bezer in the wilderness upon the plain out of the tribe of Reuben, and [u]Ramoth in Gilead out of the tribe of Gad, and [v]Golan in Bashan out of the tribe of Manasseh.

9 [w]These were the cities appointed for all the children of Israel, and for the stranger that sojourneth among them, that whosoever killeth *any* person at unawares might flee thither, and not die by the hand of the avenger of blood, [x]until he stood before the congregation.

Cities for the Levites

21:4–39pp — 1 Chr. 6:54–80

21 THEN CAME near the heads of the fathers of the Levites unto [y]Eleazar the priest, and unto Joshua the son of Nun, and unto the heads of the fathers of the tribes of the children of Israel;

2 And they spake unto them at [z]Shiloh in the land of Canaan, saying, [a]The LORD commanded by the hand of Moses to give us cities to dwell in, with the suburbs thereof for our cattle.

3 And the children of Israel gave unto the Levites out of their inheritance, at the commandment of the LORD, these cities and their suburbs.

4 And the lot came out for the families of the Kohathites: and [b]the children of Aaron the priest, *which were* of the Levites, [c]had by lot out of the tribe of Judah, and out of the tribe of Simeon, and out of the tribe of Benjamin, thirteen cities.

5 And [d]the rest of the children of Kohath *had* by lot out of the families of the tribe of Ephraim, and out of the tribe of Dan, and out of the half tribe of Manasseh, ten cities.

6 And [e]the children of Gershon *had* by lot out of the families of the tribe of Issachar, and out of the tribe of Asher, and out of the tribe of Naphtali, and out of the half tribe of Manasseh in Bashan, thirteen cities.

e Heb. *sanctified*

7 [f]The children of Merari by their families *had* out of the tribe of Reuben, and out of the tribe of Gad, and out of the tribe of Zebulun, twelve cities.

8 [g]And the children of Israel gave by lot unto the Levites these cities with their suburbs, [h]as the LORD commanded by the hand of Moses.

9 ¶ And they gave out of the tribe of the children of Judah, and out of the tribe of the children of Simeon, these cities which are *here* [f]mentioned by name,

10 Which the children of Aaron, *being* of the families of the Kohathites, *who were* of the children of Levi, had: for their's was the first lot.

11 [i]And they gave them [g]the city of Arba the father of [j]Anak, which *city is* Hebron, [k]in the hill *country* of Judah, with the suburbs thereof round about it.

12 But [l]the fields of the city, and the villages thereof, gave they to Caleb the son of Jephunneh for his possession.

13 ¶ Thus [m]they gave to the children of Aaron the priest [n]Hebron with her suburbs, *to be* a city of refuge for the slayer; [o]and Libnah with her suburbs,

14 And [p]Jattir with her suburbs, [q]and Eshtemoa with her suburbs,

15 And [r]Holon with her suburbs, [s]and Debir with her suburbs,

16 And [t]Ain with her suburbs, [u]and Juttah with her suburbs, *and* [v]Beth-shemesh with her suburbs; nine cities out of those two tribes.

17 And out of the tribe of Benjamin, [w]Gibeon with her suburbs, [x]Geba with her suburbs,

18 Anathoth with her suburbs, and [y]Almon with her suburbs; four cities.

19 All the cities of the children of Aaron, the priests, *were* thirteen cities with their suburbs.

20 ¶ [z]And the families of the children of Kohath, the Levites which remained of the children of Kohath, even they had the cities of their lot out of the tribe of Ephraim.

21 For they gave them [a]Shechem with her suburbs in mount Ephraim, *to be* a city of refuge for the slayer; and Gezer with her suburbs,

22 And Kibzaim with her suburbs, and Beth-horon with her suburbs; four cities.

23 And out of the tribe of Dan, Eltekeh with her suburbs, Gibbethon with her suburbs,

24 Aijalon with her suburbs, Gathrimmon with her suburbs; four cities.

25 And out of the half tribe of Manasseh, Tanach with her suburbs, and Gath-rimmon with her suburbs; two cities.

26 All the cities *were* ten with their suburbs for the families of the children of Kohath that remained.

27 ¶ [b]And unto the children of Gershon, of the families of the Levites, out of the *other* half tribe of Manasseh *they gave* [c]Golan in Bashan with her suburbs, *to be* a city of refuge for the slayer; and Beesh-terah with her suburbs; two cities.

28 And out of the tribe of Issachar, Kishon with her suburbs, Dabareh with her suburbs,

29 Jarmuth with her suburbs, Engannim with her suburbs; four cities.

30 And out of the tribe of Asher, Mishal with her suburbs, Abdon with her suburbs,

31 Helkath with her suburbs, and Rehob with her suburbs; four cities.

32 And out of the tribe of Naphtali, [d]Kedesh in Galilee with her suburbs, *to be* a city of refuge for the slayer; and Hammoth-dor with her suburbs, and Kartan with her suburbs; three cities.

33 All the cities of the Gershonites according to their families *were* thirteen cities with their suburbs.

34 ¶ [e]And unto the families of the children of Merari, the rest of the Levites, out of the tribe of Zebulun, Jokneam with her suburbs, and Kartah with her suburbs,

35 Dimnah with her suburbs, Nahalal with her suburbs; four cities.

36 And out of the tribe of Reuben, [f]Bezer with her suburbs, and Jahazah with her suburbs,

37 Kedemoth with her suburbs, and Mephaath with her suburbs; four cities.

38 And out of the tribe of Gad, [g]Ramoth in Gilead with her suburbs, *to be* a city of refuge for the slayer; and Mahanaim with her suburbs,

39 Heshbon with her suburbs, Jazer with her suburbs; four cities in all.

40 So all the cities for the children of Merari by their families, which were remaining of the families of the Le-

21:7 [f]ver. 34
21:8 [g]ver. 3 [h]Num. 35:2
21:11 [i]1 Chr. 6:55 [j]ch. 15:13,14 [k]ch. 20:7 Luke 1:39
21:12 [l]ch. 14:14 1 Chr. 6:56
21:13 [m]1 Chr. 6:57 [n]ch. 15:54 & 20:7 [o]ch. 15:42
21:14 [p]ch. 15:48 [q]ch. 15:50
21:15 [r]1 Chr. 6:58 *Hilen* ch. 15:51 [s]ch. 15:49
21:16 [t]1 Chr. 6:59 *Ashan* ch. 15:42 [u]ch. 15:55 [v]ch. 15:10
21:17 [w]ch. 18:25 [x]ch. 18:24 *Gaba*
21:18 [y]1 Chr. 6:60 *Alemeth*
21:20 [z]ver. 5 1 Chr. 6:66
21:21 [a]ch. 20:7
21:27 [b]ver. 6 1 Chr. 6:71 [c]ch. 20:8
21:32 [d]ch. 20:7
21:34 [e]ver. 7 See 1 Chr. 6:77
21:36 [f]ch. 20:8
21:38 [g]ch. 20:8

f Heb. *called* g Or, *Kirjath-arba;* see Gen. 23:2

vites, were *by* their lot twelve cities.

41 [h]All the cities of the Levites within the possession of the children of Israel *were* forty and eight cities with their suburbs.

42 These cities were every one with their suburbs round about them: thus *were* all these cities.

43 ¶ And the LORD gave unto Israel [i]all the land which he sware to give unto their fathers; and they possessed it, and dwelt therein.

44 [j]And the LORD gave them rest round about, according to all that he sware unto their fathers: and [k]there stood not a man of all their enemies before them; the LORD delivered all their enemies into their hand.

45 [l]There failed not aught of any good thing which the LORD had spoken unto the house of Israel; all came to pass.

Eastern tribes return home

22 THEN JOSHUA called the Reubenites, and the Gadites, and the half tribe of Manasseh,

2 And said unto them, Ye have kept [m]all that Moses the servant of the LORD commanded you, [n]and have obeyed my voice in all that I commanded you:

3 Ye have not left your brethren these many days unto this day, but have kept the charge of the commandment of the LORD your God.

4 And now the LORD your God hath given rest unto your brethren, as he promised them: therefore now return ye, and get you unto your tents, *and* unto the land of your possession, [o]which Moses the servant of the LORD gave you on the other side Jordan.

5 But [p]take diligent heed to do the commandment and the law, which Moses the servant of the LORD charged you, [q]to love the LORD your God, and to walk in all his ways, and to keep his commandments, and to cleave unto him, and to serve him with all your heart and with all your soul. 1 Sam. 12:14-15

6 So Joshua [r]blessed them, and sent them away: and they went unto their tents.

7 ¶ Now to the *one* half of the tribe of Manasseh Moses had given *possession* in Bashan: [s]but unto the *other* half thereof gave Joshua among their brethren on this side Jordan westward. And when Joshua sent them away also unto their tents, then he blessed them,

8 And he spake unto them, saying, Return with much riches unto your tents, and with very much cattle, with silver, and with gold, and with brass, and with iron, and with very much raiment: [t]divide the spoil of your enemies with your brethren.

9 ¶ And the children of Reuben and the children of Gad and the half tribe of Manasseh returned, and departed from the children of Israel out of Shiloh, which *is* in the land of Canaan, to go unto [u]the country of Gilead, to the land of their possession, whereof they were possessed, according to the word of the LORD by the hand of Moses.

10 ¶ And when they came unto the borders of Jordan, that *are* in the land of Canaan, the children of Reuben and the children of Gad and the half tribe of Manasseh built there an altar by Jordan, a great altar to see to.

11 ¶ And the children of Israel [v]heard say, Behold, the children of Reuben and the children of Gad and the half tribe of Manasseh have built an altar over against the land of Canaan, in the borders of Jordan, at the passage of the children of Israel.

12 And when the children of Israel heard *of it*, [w]the whole congregation of

21:41 [h]Num. 35:7
21:43 [i]Gen. 13:15 & 15:18 & 26:3 & 28:4,13
21:44 [j]ch. 11:23 & 22:4 [k]Deut. 7:24
21:45 [l]ch. 23:14
22:2 [m]Num. 32:20 Deut. 3:18 [n]ch. 1:16,17
22:4 [o]Num. 32:33
22:5 [p]Deut. 6:6,17 & 11:22 Jer. 12:16 [q]Deut. 10:12
22:6 [r]Gen. 47:7 Ex. 39:43 ch. 14:13 2 Sam. 6:18 Luke 24:50
22:7 [s]ch. 17:5
22:8 [t]Num. 31:27 1 Sam. 30:24
22:9 [u]Num. 32:1,26,29
22:11 [v]Deut. 13:12 Judg. 20:12
22:12 [w]Judg. 20:1

21:45 FAILED NOT AUGHT . . . WHICH THE LORD HAD SPOKEN. Vv. 43–45 emphasize God's faithfulness in keeping His word to the forefathers (Gen. 24:7; 26:3; 50:24), for He had given the promised land to the descendants of Abraham. (1) Note that the book of Joshua presents the conquest of Canaan as both complete (10:40–42; 11:23; 12:7–24) and incomplete (13:2–6; 14:12; 17:12–18; 23:5). God was faithful in fulfilling His promise to the Israelites. Yet they had to do their part in faithfully obeying the covenant, or they would fail to possess the land completely (1:6–9; 23:6–14).

(2) Likewise under the new covenant, God will faithfully fulfill all His promises to us as believers; yet we have to do our part in faithful obedience if we are to possess fully God's promises and kingdom (Luke 12:31). If receiving God's promises falls short, the failure lies with us, not with our Lord. It is God's desire to give His people the kingdom (cf. Luke 12:32).

22:12 ISRAEL . . . TO WAR AGAINST THEM. The children of Israel were ready to go to war against some of their brothers because they believed they had built an altar in rebellion against the Lord God (vv. 10–11). Note the following elements: (1) Joshua and the Israelites felt that God's holiness and truth were being abandoned (vv. 12,-

the children of Israel gathered themselves together at Shiloh, to go up to war against them.

13 And the children of Israel [x]sent unto the children of Reuben, and to the children of Gad, and to the half tribe of Manasseh, into the land of Gilead, [y]Phinehas the son of Eleazar the priest,

14 And with him ten princes, of each **[h]**chief house a prince throughout all the tribes of Israel; and [z]each one *was* an head of the house of their fathers among the thousands of Israel.

15 ¶ And they came unto the children of Reuben, and to the children of Gad, and to the half tribe of Manasseh, unto the land of Gilead, and they spake with them, saying,

16 Thus saith the whole congregation of the LORD, What trespass *is* this that ye have committed against the God of Israel, to turn away this day from following the LORD, in that ye have builded you an altar, [a]that ye might rebel this day against the LORD?

17 *Is* the iniquity [b]of Peor too little for us, from which we are not cleansed until this day, although there was a plague in the congregation of the LORD,

18 But that ye must turn away this day from following the LORD? and it will be, *seeing* ye rebel today against the LORD, that tomorrow [c]he will be wroth with the whole congregation of Israel.

19 Notwithstanding, if the land of your possession *be* unclean, *then* pass ye over unto the land of the possession of the LORD, [d]wherein the LORD's tabernacle dwelleth, and take possession among us: but rebel not against the LORD, nor rebel against us, in building you an altar beside the altar of the LORD our God.

20 [e]Did not Achan the son of Zerah commit a trespass in the accursed thing, and wrath fell on all the congregation of Israel? and that man perished not alone in his iniquity.

21 ¶ Then the children of Reuben and the children of Gad and the half tribe of Manasseh answered, and said unto the heads of the thousands of Israel,

22 The LORD [f]God of gods, the LORD God of gods, he [g]knoweth, and Israel he shall know; if *it be* in rebellion, or if in transgression against the LORD, (save us not this day,)

23 That we have built us an altar to turn from following the LORD, or if to offer thereon burnt offering or meat offering, or if to offer peace offerings thereon, let the LORD himself [h]require *it;*

24 And if we have not *rather* done it for fear of *this* thing, saying, **[i]**In time to come your children might speak unto our children, saying, What have ye to do with the LORD God of Israel?

25 For the LORD hath made Jordan a border between us and you, ye children of Reuben and children of Gad; ye have no part in the LORD: so shall your children make our children cease from fearing the LORD.

26 Therefore we said, Let us now prepare to build us an altar, not for burnt offering, nor for sacrifice:

27 But *that* it *may be* [i]a witness between us, and you, and our generations after us, that we might [j]do the service of the LORD before him with our burnt offerings, and with our sacrifices, and with our peace offerings; that your children may not say to our children in time to come, Ye have no part in the LORD.

28 Therefore said we, that it shall be, when they should *so* say to us or to our generations in time to come, that we may say *again,* Behold the pattern of the altar of the LORD, which our fathers made, not for burnt offerings, nor for sacrifices; but it *is* a witness between us and you.

29 God forbid that we should rebel against the LORD, and turn this day from following the LORD, [k]to build an altar for burnt offerings, for meat offerings, or for sacrifices, beside the altar

22:13 [x]Deut. 13:14 Judg. 20:12 [y]Ex. 6:25 Num. 25:7,11-13
22:14 [z]Num. 1:4
22:16 [a]See Lev. 17:8,9 Deut. 12:13,14
22:17 [b]Num. 25:3,4 Deut. 4:3
22:18 [c]Num. 16:22
22:19 [d]ch. 18:1
22:20 [e]ch. 7:1,5
22:22 [f]Deut. 10:17 [g]Job 10:7 & 23:10 Jer. 12:3 2 Cor. 11:11,31
22:23 [h]Deut. 18:19 1 Sam. 20:16
22:27 [i]ver. 34 Gen. 31:48 ch. 24:27 [j]Deut. 12:5
22:29 [k]Deut. 12:13,14

h Heb. *house of the father* **i** Heb. *Tomorrow*

16,18; cf. Lev. 17:8–9; Deut. 13:12–15). They were willing to fight their own people in order to defend the truth and purity of God (cf. Eph. 4:15).

(2) To demonstrate their love for their fellow Israelites, Joshua and the children of Israel first sent a delegation to attempt to resolve the problem and achieve reconciliation (vv. 13–20).

(3) Understanding and reconciliation were achieved without war (vv. 21–34), and both faithfulness to God and love for others were upheld.

(4) Truth and love continue under the new covenant. Believers must stand for God's truth and holiness without compromise, while at the same time acting in love toward those they must oppose (see Eph. 4:15, note).

of the LORD our God that *is* before his
tabernacle.
30 ¶ And when Phinehas the priest,
and the princes of the congregation
and heads of the thousands of Israel
which *were* with him, heard the words
that the children of Reuben and the
children of Gad and the children of Ma-
nasseh spake, [j]it pleased them.
31 And Phinehas the son of Eleazar
the priest said unto the children of
Reuben, and to the children of Gad,
and to the children of Manasseh, This
day we perceive that the LORD *is*
[l]among us, because ye have not com-
mitted this trespass against the LORD:
[k]now ye have delivered the children of
Israel out of the hand of the LORD.
32 ¶ And Phinehas the son of Elea-
zar the priest, and the princes, re-
turned from the children of Reuben,
and from the children of Gad, out of the
land of Gilead, unto the land of Canaan,
to the children of Israel, and brought
them word again.
33 And the thing pleased the chil-
dren of Israel; and the children of Isra-
el [m]blessed God, and did not intend to
go up against them in battle, to destroy
the land wherein the children of Reu-
ben and Gad dwelt.
34 And the children of Reuben and
the children of Gad called the altar
[n]*Ed:*[l] for it *shall be* a witness be-
tween us that the LORD *is* God.

Joshua's address to Israel

23 AND IT came to pass a long
time after that the LORD [o]had
given rest unto Israel from all their en-
emies round about, that Joshua
[p]waxed old *and* [m]stricken in age.
2 And Joshua [q]called for all Israel,
and for their elders, and for their
heads, and for their judges, and for
their officers, and said unto them, I am
old *and* stricken in age:
3 And ye have seen all that the LORD
your God hath done unto all these na-
tions because of you; for the [r]LORD
your God *is* he that hath fought for you.
4 Behold, [s]I have divided unto you
by lot these nations that remain, to be
an inheritance for your tribes, from Jor-
dan, with all the nations that I have cut
off, even unto the great sea [n]west-
ward.
5 And the LORD your God, [t]he shall
expel them from before you, and drive
them from out of your sight; and ye
shall possess their land, [u]as the LORD
your God hath promised unto you.
6 [v]Be ye therefore very coura-
geous to keep and to do all that is writ-
ten in the book of the law of Moses,
[w]that ye turn not aside therefrom *to*
the right hand or *to* the left;
7 That ye [x]come not among these
nations, these that remain among you;
neither [y]make mention of the name of
their gods, nor cause to swear *by them*,
neither serve them, nor bow your-
selves unto them:
8 [o]But [z]cleave unto the LORD your
God, as ye have done unto this day.
9 [a]For[p] the LORD hath driven out
from before you great nations and
strong: but *as for* you, [b]no man hath
been able to stand before you unto this
day.
10 [c]One man of you shall chase a
thousand: for the LORD your God, he *it*
is that fighteth for you, [d]as he hath
promised you.
11 [e]Take good heed therefore unto
[q]yourselves, that ye love the LORD
your God.
12 Else if ye do in any wise [f]go

22:31 [l]Lev. 26:11,12 2 Chr. 15:2
22:33 [m]1 Chr. 29:20 Neh. 8:6 Dan. 2:19 Luke 2:28
22:34 [n]ch. 24:27
23:1 [o]ch. 21:44 & 22:4 [p]ch. 13:1
23:2 [q]Deut. 31:28 ch. 24:1 1 Chr. 28:1
23:3 [r]Ex. 14:14 ch:10:14,42
23:4 [s]ch. 13:2,6 & 18:10
23:5 [t]Ex. 23:30 & 33:2 & 34:11 Deut. 11:23 ch. 13:6 [u]Num. 33:53
23:6 [v]ch. 1:7 [w]Deut. 5:32 & 28:14
23:7 [x]Ex. 23:33 Deut. 7:2,3 Prov. 4:14 Eph. 5:11 [y]Ex. 23:13 Jer. 5:7 Zeph. 1:5 See Num. 32:38
23:8 [z]Deut. 10:20 ch. 22:5
23:9 [a]Deut. 11:23 [b]ch. 1:5
23:10 [c]Lev. 26:8 Deut. 32:30 [d]Ex. 14:14 Deut. 3:22
23:11 [e]ch. 22:5
23:12 [f]2 Pet. 2:20,21

[j] Heb. *it was good in their eyes* [k] Heb. *then*
[l] i.e. A witness [m] Heb. *come into days*
[n] Heb. *at the sunset* [o] Or, *For if ye will cleave*
[p] Or, *Then the* LORD *will drive* [q] Heb. *your souls*

22:34 A WITNESS . . . THE LORD *IS* GOD. The altar erected on the east side of the Jordan was to function as a witness and a memorial to future generations that those tribes were bound to remain faithful to the Lord and to serve only Him. Visible ties of faith passed on between generations, such as a special Bible, a gift, a photo, a memorial, or a family tradition, can similarly remind Christians and their children of their commitment to God.

23:11 LOVE THE LORD. Joshua exhorted Israel to cleave to the Lord and love Him diligently, just as He had loved them (cf. Deut. 7:7,13; 11:1; 19:9). Love for and gratitude to God provided the inner motivation for them to obey His word (v. 6) and to remain separate from the ungodly ways of the nations (vv. 7,12). N.T. believers are called to the same kind of love and commitment (cf. Mat. 22:37; Mark 12:30; John 14:15; Gal. 5:6; 1 John 4:19).

23:12 CLEAVE UNTO . . . THESE NATIONS. With Baal as one of the principal male deities, the religion of the Canaanites was most degrading. (1) Their religion promoted both female and male cult prostitution, and their worship consisted in immoral orgies and sexual acts. Their prophets and

back, and cleave unto the remnant of these nations, *even* these that remain among you, and shall [g]make marriages with them, and go in unto them, and they to you:

13 Know for a certainty that [h]the LORD your God will no more drive out *any of* these nations from before you; [i]but they shall be snares and traps unto you, and scourges in your sides, and thorns in your eyes, until ye perish from off this good land which the LORD
1 Ki. 19:18 your God hath given you.

14 And, behold, this day [j]I *am* going the way of all the earth: and ye know in all your hearts and in all your souls, that [k]not one thing hath failed of all the good things which the LORD your God spake concerning you; all are come to pass unto you, *and* not one thing hath failed thereof.

15 [l]Therefore it shall come to pass, *that* as all good things are come upon you, which the LORD your God promised you; so shall the LORD bring upon you [m]all evil things, until he have destroyed you from off this good land which the LORD your God hath given you.

16 When ye have transgressed the covenant of the LORD your God, which he commanded you, and have gone and served other gods, and bowed yourselves to them; then shall the anger of the LORD be kindled against you, and ye shall perish quickly from off the good land which he hath given unto you.

Israel renews the covenant

24 AND JOSHUA gathered all the tribes of Israel to [n]Shechem, and [o]called for the elders of Israel, and for their heads, and for their judges, and for their officers; and they [p]presented themselves before God.

2 And Joshua said unto all the people, Thus saith the LORD God of Israel, [q]Your fathers dwelt on the other side of the flood in old time, *even* Terah, the father of Abraham, and the father of Nachor: and [r]they served other gods.

3 And [s]I took your father Abraham from the other side of the flood, and led him throughout all the land of Canaan, and multiplied his seed, and [t]gave him Isaac.

4 And I gave unto Isaac [u]Jacob and Esau: and I gave unto [v]Esau mount Seir, to possess it; [w]but Jacob and his children went down into Egypt.

5 [x]I sent Moses also and Aaron, and [y]I plagued Egypt, according to that which I did among them: and afterward I brought you out.

6 And I [z]brought your fathers out of Egypt: and [a]ye came unto the sea; [b]and the Egyptians pursued after your fathers with chariots and horsemen unto the Red sea.

7 And when they cried unto the LORD, [c]he put darkness between you and the Egyptians, [d]and brought the sea upon them, and covered them; and [e]your eyes have seen what I have done in Egypt: and ye dwelt in the wilderness [f]a long season.

8 And I brought you into the land of the Amorites, which dwelt on the other side Jordan; [g]and they fought with you: and I gave them into your hand, that ye might possess their land; and I destroyed them from before you.

9 Then [h]Balak the son of Zippor, king of Moab, arose and warred against Israel, and [i]sent and called Balaam the son of Beor to curse you:

23:12 [g]Deut. 7:3
23:13 [h]Judg. 2:3 [i]Ex. 23:33 1 Ki. 11:4
23:14 [j]1 Ki. 2:2 [k]Luke 21:33
23:15 [l]Deut. 28:63 [m]Deut. 28:15,16
24:1 [n]Gen. 35:4 [o]ch. 23:2
[p]1 Sam. 10:19
24:2 [q]Gen. 11:26,31 [r]ver. 14
24:3 [s]Gen. 12:1 Acts 7:2,3 [t]Ps. 127:3
24:4 [u]Gen. 25:24-26 [v]Gen. 36:8 Deut. 2:5 [w]Gen. 46:1,6
24:5 [x]Ex. 3:10 [y]Ex. 7 & 8 & 9 & 10
24:6 [z]Ex. 12:37,51 [a]Ex. 14:2 [b]Ex. 14:9
24:7 [c]Ex. 14:20 [d]Ex. 14:27,28 [e]Deut. 4:34 [f]ch. 5:6
24:8 [g]Num. 21:21,33 Deut. 2:32
24:9 [h]Judg. 11:25 [i]Num. 22:5

---

priests were the official murderers of little children, sacrificing newborn babies in their temples (see article on THE DESTRUCTION OF THE CANAANITES, p. 336). (2) God knew that if His people associated with the Canaanites, they too would adopt those shameful ways. The call of God for the separation of His people from the ungodly world remains the same in the N.T. (see article on THE CHRISTIAN'S RELATIONSHIP TO THE WORLD, p. 2004).

23:13 KNOW FOR A CERTAINTY. The promises of God were not unconditional for the Israelites. Love for God expressed in obedience to His commandments, faith in His provision, and separation from the ungodly were the conditions for God's blessings, fellowship, and strength (vv. 3–13). God Himself provided the grace necessary for maintaining the covenant fellowship between Himself and the people.

24:1 JOSHUA GATHERED ALL THE TRIBES. At the end of his life, Joshua called all the people together one final time to lead them in a ceremony of covenant renewal in which they committed themselves to serve the Lord in faithfulness and loyal devotion. He did not focus on himself as their leader; rather, he drew attention to God's past goodness to and care of Israel (vv. 2–13) and repeatedly admonished them to remain loyal to the Lord (vv. 14–28). Genuine leaders of God's people must share Joshua's concern for God's honor. They must exhort the people to love the Lord, serve Him only, and remain separated from the world.

10 [j]But I would not hearken unto
Balaam; [k]therefore he blessed you
still: so I delivered you out of his hand.
11 And [l]ye went over Jordan, and
came unto Jericho: and [m]the men of
Jericho fought against you, the Amo-
rites, and the Perizzites, and the Ca-
naanites, and the Hittites, and the Gir-
gashites, the Hivites, and the
Jebusites; and I delivered them into
your hand.
12 And [n]I sent the hornet before
you, which drave them out from before
you, *even* the two kings of the Amo-
rites; *but* [o]not with thy sword, nor
with thy bow.
13 And I have given you a land for
which ye did not labour, and [p]cities
which ye built not, and ye dwell in
them; of the vineyards and oliveyards
which ye planted not do ye eat.
14 ¶ [q]Now therefore fear the LORD,
and serve him in [r]sincerity and in
truth: and [s]put away the gods which
your fathers served on the other side of
the flood, and [t]in Egypt; and serve ye
the LORD.
15 And if it seem evil unto you to
serve the LORD, [u]choose you this day
whom ye will serve; whether [v]the
gods which your fathers served that
were on the other side of the flood, or
[w]the gods of the Amorites, in whose
land ye dwell: [x]but as for me and my
house, we will serve the LORD.
16 And the people answered and
said, God forbid that we should forsake
the LORD, to serve other gods;
17 For the LORD our God, he *it is* that
brought us up and our fathers out of
the land of Egypt, from the house of

24:10 [j]Deut. 23:5 [k]Num. 23:11,20
24:11 [l]ch. 3:14,17 [m]ch. 6:1 & 10:1
24:12 [n]Ex. 23:28 Deut. 7:20 [o]Ps. 44:3,6
24:13 [p]Deut. 6:10,11
24:14 [q]Deut. 10:12 1 Sam. 12:24 [r]Gen. 17:1 & 20:5 Deut. 18:13 2 Cor. 1:12 [s]ver. 2,23 Ezek. 20:18 [t]Ezek. 20:7,8 & 23:3
24:15 [u]Ruth 1:15 1 Ki. 18:21 [v]ver. 2 [w]Ex. 23:24,32,33 [x]Gen. 18:19
24:19 [y]Mat. 6:24 [z]1 Sam. 6:20 [a]Ex. 20:5 [b]Ex. 23:21
24:20 [c]1 Chr. 28:9 Ezra 8:22 Is. 1:28 Jer. 17:13 [d]ch. 23:15 Is. 63:10 Acts 7:42
24:22 [e]Ps. 119:173
24:23 [f]ver. 14 Gen. 35:2
24:25 [g]Ex. 15:25 2 Ki. 11:17 [h]ver. 1
24:26 [i]Deut. 31:24 [j]Judg. 9:6 [k]Gen. 28:18 ch. 4:3

bondage, and which did those great
signs in our sight, and preserved us in
all the way wherein we went, and
among all the people through whom we
passed:
18 And the LORD drave out from be-
fore us all the people, even the Amo-
rites which dwelt in the land: *therefore*
will we also serve the LORD; for he *is*
our God.
19 And Joshua said unto the people,
[y]Ye cannot serve the LORD: for he *is* an
[z]holy God; he *is* [a]a jealous God; [b]he
will not forgive your transgressions
nor your sins.
20 [c]If ye forsake the LORD, and
serve strange gods, [d]then he will turn
and do you hurt, and consume you, af-
ter that he hath done you good.
21 And the people said unto Joshua,
Nay; but we will serve the LORD.
22 And Joshua said unto the people,
Ye *are* witnesses against yourselves
that [e]ye have chosen you the LORD, to
serve him. And they said, *We are* wit-
nesses.
23 Now therefore [f]put away, *said*
he, the strange gods which *are* among
you, and incline your heart unto the
LORD God of Israel.
24 And the people said unto Joshua,
The LORD our God will we serve, and his
voice will we obey.
25 So Joshua [g]made a covenant
with the people that day, and set them
a statute and an ordinance [h]in She-
chem.
26 ¶ And Joshua [i]wrote these
words in the book of the law of God,
and took [j]a great stone, and [k]set it

24:15 AS FOR ME AND MY HOUSE, WE WILL SERVE THE LORD. Inherent in the salvation provided by God is the issue of personal choice. Each believer must continually choose whom he or she will serve. As with Joshua and the Israelites, serving the Lord is not merely a one-time choice (cf. 1:16–18; Deut. 30:19–20); we must choose time after time to persevere in the faith and to obey the Lord God. The renewal of right choices by the believer involves the fear of the Lord, loyalty to the truth, obedience from a sincere heart, and the renunciation of sin with its associated pleasures (vv. 14–16). Failure to choose to serve and love the Lord will eventually result in judgment and destruction (v. 20; 23:11–13).

24:16 GOD FORBID THAT WE SHOULD FORSAKE THE LORD. The people's promise to serve only the Lord was kept, but only as long as Joshua and the elders with him lived. Not long after Joshua's death the people forsook the Lord and began serving other gods (Judg. 2:11–19).

24:25 JOSHUA MADE A COVENANT WITH THE PEOPLE. The renewal of the covenant between the Lord and Israel involved a twofold commitment: (1) God committed Himself to care for His people, and (2) the Israelites committed themselves to serve the Lord God alone. It was a permanent and binding contract between Israel and God. Under the new covenant established by the death of Christ, believers have also made a commitment to follow Christ in repentance, faith, and obedience. He in return has committed Himself to be our Lord and Savior, and to lead us to a heavenly home with the Father. As with Israel in the O.T., God first came to us in mercy and grace and established the terms of the new covenant. We, like Israel of old, must live under the terms of the covenant (see article on THE OLD COVENANT AND THE NEW COVENANT, p. 1954).

up there [l]under an oak, that *was* by the sanctuary of the LORD.

27 And Joshua said unto all the people, Behold, this stone shall be [m]a witness unto us; for [n]it hath heard all the words of the LORD which he spake unto us: it shall be therefore a witness unto you, lest ye deny your God.

28 So [o]Joshua let the people depart, every man unto his inheritance.

The death of Joshua

24:29–31pp — Judg. 2:6–9

29 ¶ [p]And it came to pass after these things, that Joshua the son of Nun, the servant of the LORD, died, *being* an hundred and ten years old.

30 And they buried him in the border of his inheritance in [q]Timnath-serah, which *is* in mount Ephraim, on the north side of the hill of Gaash.

31 And [r]Israel served the LORD all the days of Joshua, and all the days of the elders that [r]overlived Joshua, and which had [s]known all the works of the LORD, that he had done for Israel.

32 ¶ And the [t]bones of Joseph, which the children of Israel brought up out of Egypt, buried they in Shechem, in a parcel of ground [u]which Jacob bought of the sons of Hamor the father of Shechem for an hundred [s]pieces of silver: and it became the inheritance of the children of Joseph.

33 And Eleazar the son of Aaron died; and they buried him in a hill *that pertained to* [v]Phinehas his son, which was given him in mount Ephraim.

24:26 [l]Gen. 35:4
24:27 [m]See Gen. 31:48, 52 [n]Deut. 32:1
24:28 [o]Judg. 2:6
24:29 [p]Judg. 2:8
24:30 [q]ch. 19:50
24:31 [r]Judg. 2:7 [s]Deut. 11:2
24:32 [t]Gen. 50:25 Ex. 13:19 [u]Gen. 33:19
24:33 [v]Ex. 6:25 Judg. 20:28

[r] Heb. *prolonged* their *days after Joshua* [s] Or, *lambs*

JUDGES

Outline

I. Israel's Disobedience and Apostasy Introduced (1:1—3:6)
  A. Israel Fails to Purge the Land (1:1—2:5)
  B. Israel Experiences a Downward Spiral (2:6—3:6)
II. History of Israel's Foreign Oppression and Delivering Judges (3:7—16:31)
  A. Mesopotamian Oppression / Othniel's Deliverance (3:7–11)
  B. Moabite Oppression / Ehud's Deliverance (3:12–30)
  C. Philistine Oppression / Shamgar's Deliverance (3:31)
  D. Canaanite Oppression / Deborah-Barak's Deliverance (4:1—5:31)
  E. Midianite Oppression / Gideon's Deliverance (6:1—8:35)
  F. Hard Times Under Abimelech, Tola, and Jair (9:1—10:5)
  G. Ammonite Oppression / Jephthah's Deliverance (10:6—12:7)
  H. Minor Judges—Ibzan, Elon, and Abdon (12:8–15)
  I. Philistine Oppression / Samson's Life (13:1—16:31)
    1. Samson's Birth and Calling (13:1–25)
    2. Samson's Marriage to an Unbeliever (14:1–20)
    3. Samson's Exploits (15:1–20)
    4. Samson's Downfall and Restoration (16:1–31)
III. Illustrations of Israel's Spiritual, Moral, and Social Chaos (17:1—21:25)
  A. Idolatry (17:1—18:31)
    1. An Example of Personal Idolatry (17:1–13)
    2. An Example of Tribal Idolatry (18:1–31)
  B. Immorality (19:1–30)
    1. An Example of Personal Immorality (19:1–9)
    2. An Example of Tribal Immorality (19:10–30)
  C. Tribal Strife (20:1—21:25)

Author: Anonymous

Theme: Apostasy and Deliverance

Date of Writing: c. 1050–1000 B.C.

Background

The book of Judges is the main historical link between Joshua and the time of Israel's kings. The period of the judges dates from about 1375 to 1050 B.C., during which time Israel was a confederacy of tribes. The book derives its name from the individuals whom God raised up periodically to lead and deliver the Israelites after they had backslidden and fallen under the oppression of foreign neighbors. The judges (thirteen are mentioned in this book) came from different tribes and functioned as military leaders and civil magistrates. Many remained tribal in their sphere of influence, while some served the whole territory of Israel. Samuel, generally regarded as the last of the judges and the first of the prophets, is not included in this book.

The authorship of Judges is uncertain. The book itself indicates the following time frame for its composition: (1) its writing occurred after the removal of the ark from Shiloh at the

time of Eli and Samuel (18:31; 20:27; cf. 1 Sam. 4:3–11); (2) the author's frequent reference to the time of the judges by stating that "in those days *there was* no king in Israel" (17:6; 18:1; 19:1; 21:25), suggests that Israel's monarchy already existed when the book was written; (3) Jerusalem had not yet been taken from the Jebusites (1:21; cf. 2 Sam. 5:7). These three clues indicate the book was completed sometime after the beginning of King Saul's reign (c. 1050 B.C.) but before King David captured Jerusalem (c. 1000 B.C.). The Jewish Talmud associates the origin of the book with Samuel, which is a real possibility.

This much is certain: the book records and evaluates the period of the judges from the perspective of the covenant (e.g., 2:1–5). Moses had prophesied that oppression from foreign nations would come upon the Israelites as one of God's curses if they departed from the covenant (Deut. 28:25,33,48). The book of Judges underscores the historical reality of that prophecy.

Purpose

Historically, Judges provides the main record of Israel's history in the promised land from the death of Joshua to the time of Samuel. Theologically, it reveals the spiritual and moral decline of the tribes after settling in the promised land, showing clearly the adverse consequences that always occurred when Israel forgot her covenant with the Lord and went instead in the direction of idolatry and immorality.

Survey

Judges divides into three basic sections. (1) Section one (1:1—3:6) records Israel's failure to thoroughly complete the conquest and describes her downward direction after the death of Joshua. (2) Section two (3:7—16:31) comprises the main body of the book. It records six examples of Israel's recurring experience during the time of the judges involving cycles of apostasy, foreign oppression, servitude, crying out to God in distress, and God delivering the Israelites through leaders anointed by His Spirit. Among the thirteen judges (all are included in this section of the book), the best known are Deborah and Barak (as a team), Gideon, Jephthah, and Samson (cf. Heb. 11:32). (3) Section three (17:1—21:25) closes with vivid stories from the time of the judges that illustrate the depth of moral and social corruption that resulted from Israel's spiritual apostasy. The book reminds us that the only lesson we as humans learn consistently from history is that we do not learn from history.

Special Features

Six major features or emphases characterize the book of Judges. (1) It records events in Israel's turbulent history between the conquest of Palestine and the beginning of the monarchy. (2) It underscores three simple but profound truths: (a) to be God's people means that God must be King and Lord of His people; (b) sin is always destructive to God's people; and (c) when God's people humble themselves, pray, and turn from their wicked ways, He will hear from heaven and heal their land (cf. 2 Chr. 7:14). (3) It emphasizes that whenever Israel lost sight of her identity as the covenant people under God's kingship, the nation plunged into repeated cycles of spiritual, moral, and social chaos with "every man [doing] *that which was* right in his own eyes" (21:25; cf. 17:6). (4) It reveals several oft-repeated patterns that occur in the history of God's people under both covenants: (a) unless God's people give Him their whole hearts in loving obedience and diligent spiritual vigilance, their hearts become hardened and unresponsive to God, leading to backsliding and eventual apostasy; (b) God is longsuffering, and whenever His people cry out in repentance, He is merciful to restore them by raising up Spirit-endowed and empowered individuals to deliver them from the oppressive judgment of sin; and (c) the very anointed leaders whom God uses to deliver His people often become corrupt themselves because of a fundamental deficiency in humility, character, or righteousness. (5) The six major cycles in the book involving apostasy, oppression, distress, and deliverance all begin in the same way: "the children of Israel did evil in the sight of the LORD" (e.g., 2:11; 3:7). (6) The book reveals that God used foreign nations more evil than His own people in order to judge the

latter for their sins and to bring about their repentance and revival. Only this intervention of God kept Israel from completely being absorbed by the paganism all around her.

New Testament Fulfillment

The book of Judges reveals an enduring divine principle: when God uses a person greatly in His service, "the Spirit of the LORD [comes] upon him" (3:10; cf. 6:34; 11:29; 14:6,19; 15:14). At the outset of Jesus' ministry, the Spirit descended upon Him at His baptism (Mat. 3:16; Luke 3:21–22a). Before ascending to His Father, Jesus instructed His disciples to wait for the promise of the Spirit (Acts 1:4–5); the reason given was that they would receive power when the Holy Spirit came upon them (Acts 1:8; cf. 4:33). Under both covenants, God's way of overthrowing the enemy and advancing His kingdom is by the energy, strength, and power of the Holy Spirit working through yielded and obedient human vessels.

Reading Judges

In order to read the entire Old Testament in one year, the book of Judges should be read in 10 days, according to the following schedule: ☐ 1–2 ☐ 3–4 ☐ 5–6 ☐ 7–8 ☐ 9 ☐ 10–11 ☐ 12–13 ☐ 14–16 ☐ 17–18 ☐ 19–21

NOTES

Fighting the Canaanites

1:11–15pp — Josh. 15:15–19

1 NOW AFTER the death of Joshua it came to pass, that the children of Israel [a]asked the LORD, saying, Who shall go up for us against the Canaanites first, to fight against them?

2 And the LORD said, [b]Judah shall go up: behold, I have delivered the land into his hand.

3 And Judah said unto Simeon his brother, Come up with me into my lot, that we may fight against the Canaanites; and [c]I likewise will go with thee into thy lot. So Simeon went with him.

4 And Judah went up; and the LORD delivered the Canaanites and the Perizzites into their hand: and they slew of them in [d]Bezek ten thousand men.

5 And they found Adoni-bezek in Bezek: and they fought against him, and they slew the Canaanites and the Perizzites.

6 But Adoni-bezek fled; and they pursued after him, and caught him, and cut off his thumbs and his great toes.

7 And Adoni-bezek said, Threescore and ten kings, having [a]their thumbs and their great toes cut off, [b]gathered *their meat* under my table: [e]as I have done, so God hath requited me. And they brought him to Jerusalem, and there he died.

8 Now [f]the children of Judah had fought against Jerusalem, and had taken it, and smitten it with the edge of the sword, and set the city on fire.

9 ¶ [g]And afterward the children of Judah went down to fight against the Canaanites, that dwelt in the mountain, and in the south, and in the [c]valley.

10 And Judah went against the Canaanites that dwelt in Hebron: (now the name of Hebron before *was* [h]Kirjath-arba:) and they slew Sheshai, and Ahiman, and Talmai.

11 [i]And from thence he went against the inhabitants of Debir: and the name of Debir before *was* Kirjath-sepher:

12 [j]And Caleb said, He that smiteth Kirjath-sepher, and taketh it, to him will I give Achsah my daughter to wife.

13 And Othniel the son of Kenaz, [k]Caleb's younger brother, took it: and he gave him Achsah his daughter to wife.

14 [l]And it came to pass, when she came *to him*, that she moved him to ask of her father a field: and she lighted from off *her* ass; and Caleb said unto her, What wilt thou?

15 And she said unto him, [m]Give me a blessing: for thou hast given me a south land; give me also springs of water. And Caleb gave her the upper springs and the nether springs.

16 ¶ [n]And the children of the Kenite, Moses' father-in-law, went up out [o]of the city of palm trees with the children of Judah into the wilderness of Judah, which *lieth* in the south of [p]Arad; [q]and they went and dwelt among the people.

17 [r]And Judah went with Simeon his brother, and they slew the Canaanites that inhabited Zephath, and utterly destroyed it. And the name of the city was called [s]Hormah.

18 Also Judah took [t]Gaza with the coast thereof, and Askelon with the coast thereof, and Ekron with the coast thereof.

19 And [u]the LORD was with Judah; and [d]he drave out *the inhabitants of* the mountain; but could not drive out the inhabitants of the valley, because they had [v]chariots of iron.

20 [w]And they gave Hebron unto Caleb, as Moses said: and he expelled thence the three sons of Anak.

21 [x]And the children of Benjamin did not drive out the Jebusites that inhabited Jerusalem; but the Jebusites dwell with the children of Benjamin in Jerusalem unto this day.

22 ¶ And the house of Joseph, they

1:1 [a]Num. 27:21 ch. 20:18 **1:2** [b]Gen. 49:8 **1:3** [c]ver. 17 **1:4** [d]1 Sam. 11:8 **1:7** [e]Lev. 24:19 1 Sam. 15:33 Jas. 2:13 **1:8** [f]See Josh. 15:63 **1:9** [g]Josh. 10:36 & 11:21 & 15:13 **1:10** [h]Josh. 14:15 & 15:13,14 **1:11** [i]Josh. 15:15 **1:12** [j]Josh. 15:16,17 **1:13** [k]ch. 3:9 **1:14** [l]Josh. 15:18,19 **1:15** [m]Gen. 33:11 **1:16** [n]ch. 4:11,17 1 Sam. 15:6 1 Chr. 2:55 [o]Deut. 34:3 [p]Num. 21:1 [q]1 Sam. 15:6 **1:17** [r]ver. 3 [s]Num. 21:3 Josh. 19:4 **1:18** [t]Josh. 11:22 **1:19** [u]ver. 2 2 Ki. 18:7 [v]Josh. 17:16,18 **1:20** [w]Num. 14:24 Deut. 1:36 Josh. 14:9,13,14 & 15:13,14 **1:21** [x]See Josh. 15:63 & 18:28

[a] Heb. *the thumbs of their hands and of their feet* [b] Or, *gleaned* [c] Or, *low country* [d] Or, *he possessed the mountain*

1:1 AFTER THE DEATH OF JOSHUA. The events recorded in the book of Judges extend from about 1375 B.C. to 1050 B.C. when Saul was anointed king. Thirteen judges are generally associated with the book. They are Othniel (3:7–11), Ehud (3:12–30), Shamgar (3:31), Deborah and Barak (4:1—5:31), Gideon (6:1—8:35), Tola (10:1–2), Jair (10:3–5), Jephthah (10:6—12:7), Ibzan (12:8–10), Elon (12:11–12), Abdon (12:13–15), and Samson (13:1—16:31). Their leadership was primarily regional rather than over all the tribes. The ministry of some of the judges overlap (cf. Judg. 3:30—4:1).

1:6 CUT OFF HIS THUMBS. This was done in order to disable the king and thus prevent him from ever again entering into military battle.

also went up against Beth-el: [y]and the
LORD *was* with them.
23 And the house of Joseph [z]sent
to descry Beth-el. (Now the name of the
city before *was* [a]Luz.)
24 And the spies saw a man come
forth out of the city, and they said unto
him, Show us, we pray thee, the en-
trance into the city, and [b]we will show
thee mercy.
25 And when he showed them the
entrance into the city, they smote the
city with the edge of the sword; but
they let go the man and all his family.
26 And the man went into the land
of the Hittites, and built a city, and
called the name thereof Luz: which *is*
the name thereof unto this day.
27 ¶ [c]Neither did Manasseh drive
out *the inhabitants of* Beth-shean and
her towns, nor Taanach and her towns,
nor the inhabitants of Dor and her
towns, nor the inhabitants of Ibleam
and her towns, nor the inhabitants of
Megiddo and her towns: but the Ca-
naanites would dwell in that land.
28 And it came to pass, when Israel
was strong, that they put the Canaan-
ites to tribute, and did not utterly drive
them out.
29 ¶ [d]Neither did Ephraim drive
out the Canaanites that dwelt in Gezer;
but the Canaanites dwelt in Gezer
among them.
30 ¶ Neither did Zebulun drive out
the inhabitants of Kitron, nor the [e]in-
habitants of Nahalol; but the Canaan-
ites dwelt among them, and became
tributaries.
31 ¶ [f]Neither did Asher drive out
the inhabitants of Accho, nor the in-
habitants of Zidon, nor of Ahlab, nor of
Achzib, nor of Helbah, nor of Aphik,
nor of Rehob:
32 But the Asherites [g]dwelt
among the Canaanites, the inhabitants

1:22 [y]ver. 19
1:23 [z]Josh. 2:1 & 7:2 ch. 18:2 [a]Gen. 28:19
1:24 [b]Josh. 2:12,14
1:27 [c]Josh. 17:11-13
1:29 [d]Josh. 16:10 1 Ki. 9:16
1:30 [e]Josh. 19:15
1:31 [f]Josh. 19:24-30
1:32 [g]Ps. 106:34,35
1:33 [h]Josh. 19:38 [i]ver. 32 [j]ver. 30
1:35 [k]Josh. 19:42
1:36 [l]Num. 34:4 Josh. 15:3
2:1 [m]ver. 5 [n]Gen. 17:7
2:2 [o]Deut. 7:2 [p]Deut. 12:3 [q]Ps. 106:34
2:3 [r]Josh. 23:13 [s]ch. 3:6 [t]Ex. 23:33 Deut. 7:16 Ps. 106:36

of the land: for they did not drive them
out.
33 ¶ [h]Neither did Naphtali drive
out the inhabitants of Beth-shemesh,
nor the inhabitants of Beth-anath; but
he [i]dwelt among the Canaanites, the
inhabitants of the land: nevertheless
the inhabitants of Beth-shemesh and of
Beth-anath [j]became tributaries unto
them.
34 And the Amorites forced the
children of Dan into the mountain: for
they would not suffer them to come
down to the valley:
35 But the Amorites would dwell in
mount Heres [k]in Aijalon, and in Sha-
albim: yet the hand of the house of Jo-
seph [e]prevailed, so that they became
tributaries.
36 And the coast of the Amorites
was [l]from [f]the going up to Akrab-
bim, from the rock, and upward.

Israel's disobedience

2:6–9pp — Josh. 24:29–31

2 AND AN [g]angel of the LORD came
up from Gilgal [m]to Bochim, and
said, I made you to go up out of Egypt,
and have brought you unto the land
which I sware unto your fathers; and
[n]I said, I will never break my cov-
enant with you.
2 And [o]ye shall make no league
with the inhabitants of this land; [p]ye
shall throw down their altars: [q]but ye
have not obeyed my voice: why have ye
done this?
3 Wherefore I also said, I will not
drive them out from before you; but
they shall be [r]*as thorns* in your sides,
and [s]their gods shall be a [t]snare
unto you.
4 And it came to pass, when the an-
gel of the LORD spake these words unto

e Heb. *was heavy* f Or, *Maaleh-akrabbim* g Or, *messenger*

1:28 DID NOT UTTERLY DRIVE THEM OUT. Joshua had destroyed many of the Canaanites; yet after his death a considerable number remained within the land (vv. 1,28–30,32–33,35). God had commanded Israel to drive out the Canaanites completely because of their corrupt and sensual form of religion (Deut. 7:2–4; see article on THE DESTRUCTION OF THE CANAANITES, p. 336). Israel's ultimate failure to do this caused them to compromise with the Canaanites and brought ruin and defeat to the people of God.

2:1 ANGEL OF THE LORD. The angel of the Lord rebuked Israel for her failure to drive out the Canaanites (note; Ex. 3:2, note; see article on ANGELS AND THE ANGEL OF THE LORD, p. 368).

2:2 NO LEAGUE WITH THE INHABITANTS. God's refusal to help the Israelites completely drive out the enemy was largely due to their failure to be a separated and holy people who abhorred the evil ways of the pagan people around them (cf. Deut. 7:2,5,16; 12:3; 30:16).

2:3 WHEREFORE . . . I WILL NOT DRIVE THEM OUT. Our failure to seek God earnestly and to follow His righteous ways will cause Him to withdraw His help, power, and protection from our lives.

ANGELS AND THE ANGEL OF THE LORD

Judg. 2:1 "And an angel of the LORD came up from Gilgal to Bochim, and said, I made you to go up out of Egypt, and have brought you unto the land which I sware unto your fathers; and I said, I will never break my covenant with you."

The Bible mentions angels frequently; this article provides an overview of the Scriptural teaching about angels.

ANGELS. The word "angel" (Heb. *malak*; Gk. *angelos*) means "messenger." Angels are God's heavenly messengers or servants (Heb. 1:13–14), created by God before the earth began (Job 38:4–7; Ps. 148:2,5; Col. 1:16). (1) The Bible speaks of good and evil angels, though it stresses that all angels were originally created good and holy (Gen. 1:31). Having the freedom of choice, numerous angels joined in Satan's rebellion (Ezek. 28:12–17; 2 Pet. 2:4; Jude 6; Rev. 12:9; see Mat. 4:10, note) and turned from their original state of grace as servants of God, thereby forfeiting their heavenly role. Undoubtedly, the demons of the N.T. must be identified with these fallen angels (Mat. 25:41; see Jude 6, note; see article on POWER OVER SATAN AND DEMONS, p. 1486).

(2) The Bible speaks of a vast host of good angels (1 Ki. 22:19; Ps. 68:17; 148:2; Dan. 7:9–10; Rev. 5:11), though the names of only two of them are recorded in Scripture: Michael (Dan. 12:1; Jude 9; Rev. 12:7) and Gabriel (Dan. 9:21; Luke 1:19,26). Apparently they are divided into different ranks: Michael is called an archangel (lit. "leading angel," Jude 9; cf. 1 Thes. 4:16); there are seraphim (Is. 6:2), cherubim (Ezek. 10:1–3), angels with authority and dominion (Eph. 3:10; Col. 1:16), and the myriads of angelic ministering spirits (Heb. 1:13–14; Rev. 5:11).

(3) As spiritual beings, good angels praise God (Heb. 1:6; Rev. 5:11; 7:11), do His will (Num. 22:22; Ps. 103:20), behold His face (Mat. 18:10), are subject to Christ (1 Pet. 3:22), are superior to humans (Heb. 2:6–7), and inhabit heavenly spheres (Mark 13:32; Gal. 1:8). They do not marry (Mat. 22:30), will never die (Luke 20:34–36), and must not be worshiped (Col. 2:18; Rev. 19:9–10). They can appear in human form (usually as young men without wings, cf. Gen. 18:2,16 with 19:1; Heb. 13:2).

(4) Angels perform numerous activities on earth at the command of God. They had a distinct role in revealing the law of God to Moses (Acts 7:38; cf. Gal. 3:19; Heb. 2:2). Their duties are primarily related to their part in the redemptive mission of Christ (see Mat. 1:20–24; 2:13; 28:2; Luke 1—2; Acts 1:10; Rev. 14:6–7). They rejoice over one sinner who repents (Luke 15:10), serve on behalf of God's people (Dan. 3:25; 6:22; Mat. 18:10; Heb. 1:14), observe the life of the Christian congregation (1 Cor. 11:10; Eph. 3:10; 1 Tim. 5:21), bring messages from God (Zech. 1:14–17; Acts 10:1–8; 27:23–24), bring answers to prayer (Dan. 9:21–23; Acts 10:4), sometimes help interpret prophetic dreams and visions (Dan. 7:15–16), strengthen God's people in trials (Mat. 4:11; Luke 22:43), protect saints who fear God and hate evil (Ps. 34:7; 91:11; Dan. 6:22; Acts 12:7–10), punish those who are God's enemies (2 Ki. 19:35; Acts 12:23; Rev. 14:17—16:21), war against the demonic (Rev. 12:7–9), and bring the saved to heaven (Luke 16:22).

(5) During the end-time events, the war between Michael with the good angels and Satan with his demonic host will intensify (Rev. 12:7–9). Angels will come with Christ when He returns (Mat. 24:30–31) and will be present at the judgment of the entire human race (Luke 12:8–9).

THE ANGEL OF THE LORD. Special mention must be made of "the angel of the LORD" (sometimes, "the angel of God"), a unique angel who appears in both O.T. and N.T. (1) The first such appearance was to Hagar in the desert (Gen. 16:7); other appearances involved such people as Abraham (Gen. 22:11,15), Jacob (Gen. 31:11–13), Moses (Ex.

3:2), all the Israelites during the exodus (Ex. 14:19) and later at Bochim (Judg. 2:1,4), Balaam (Num. 22:22–36), Joshua (Josh. 5:13–15, where the "captain of the host of the LORD" is most likely the angel of the Lord), Gideon (Judg. 6:11), David (1 Chr. 21:16), Elijah (2 Ki. 1:3–4), Daniel (Dan. 6:22), and Joseph (Mat. 1:20; 2:13).

(2) The angel of the Lord had several tasks similar to those of angels in general. Sometimes he simply brought messages from the Lord to His people (Gen. 22:15–18; 31:11–13; Mat. 1:20). At other times, God sent His angel to provide for the needs of His people (1 Ki. 19:5–7), to protect them from harm (Ex. 14:19; 23:20; Dan. 6:22), and on occasion to destroy their enemies (Ex. 23:23; 2 Ki. 19:34–35; cf. Is. 63:9). When God's people themselves rebelled and sinned greatly, His angel could be used to destroy them (2 Sam. 24:16–17).

(3) The identity of the angel of the Lord has been debated, particularly because of the way he often addressed people. Note the following: (a) In Judg. 2:1, the angel of the Lord says, "*I* made you to go up out of Egypt, and have brought you unto the land which *I* sware unto your fathers; and *I* said, *I* will never break my covenant with you" (italics added). When compared with other passages in Scripture describing the same event, these actions were the actions of the Lord, the covenant God of the Israelites. He was the one who swore to Abraham, Isaac, and Jacob to give their descendants the land of Canaan (Gen. 13:14–17; 17:8; 26:2–4; 28:13); He swore that this covenant would be everlasting (Gen. 17:7); He brought the Israelites up out of Egypt (Ex. 20:1–2); and He brought them into the promised land (Josh. 1:1–2). (b) When the angel of the Lord appeared before Joshua, Joshua fell down and worshiped Him (Josh. 5:14). Such a response has led many to believe that this angel was a visible manifestation of the Lord God Himself; otherwise, the angel would have instructed Joshua not to worship Him (cf. Rev. 19:10; 22:8–9). (c) Even more explicitly, the angel of the Lord who appeared to Moses in the burning bush said in no uncertain terms: "I *am* the God of thy father, the God of Abraham, the God of Isaac, and the God of Jacob" (Ex. 3:6; see Gen. 16:7, note; Ex. 3:2, note).

(4) Because the angel of the Lord is so closely identified with the Lord Himself, and because he appeared in human form, some consider him to be an appearance of the eternal Christ, the second person of the Holy Trinity, prior to his incarnation and virgin birth.

all the children of Israel, that the people lifted up their voice, and wept.

5 And they called the name of that place [h]Bochim: and they sacrificed there unto the LORD.

6 ¶ And when [u]Joshua had let the people go, the children of Israel went every man unto his inheritance to possess the land.

7 [v]And the people served the LORD all the days of Joshua, and all the days of the elders that [i]outlived Joshua, who had seen all the great works of the LORD, that he did for Israel.

8 And [w]Joshua the son of Nun, the servant of the LORD, died, *being* an hundred and ten years old.

9 [x]And they buried him in the border of his inheritance in [y]Timnath-heres, in the mount of Ephraim, on the north side of the hill Gaash.

10 And also all that generation were gathered unto their fathers: and there arose another generation after them, which [z]knew not the LORD, nor yet the works which he had done for Israel.

11 ¶ And the children of Israel did evil in the sight of the LORD, and served Baalim:

12 And they [a]forsook the LORD God of their fathers, which brought them out of the land of Egypt, and followed [b]other gods, of the gods of the people that *were* round about them, and [c]bowed themselves unto them, and provoked the LORD to anger.

13 And they forsook the LORD, [d]and served Baal and Ashtaroth.

14 ¶ [e]And the anger of the LORD was hot against Israel, and he [f]delivered them into the hands of spoilers that spoiled them, and [g]he sold them into the hands of their enemies round about, so that they [h]could not any longer stand before their enemies.

15 Whithersoever they went out, the hand of the LORD was against them for evil, as the LORD had said, and [i]as the LORD had sworn unto them: and they were greatly distressed.

The LORD raises up judges

16 ¶ Nevertheless [j]the LORD raised up judges, which [j]delivered them out of the hand of those that spoiled them.

17 And yet they would not hearken

2:6 [u]Josh. 22:6
2:7 [v]Josh. 24:31
2:8 [w]Josh. 24:29
2:9 [x]Josh. 24:30 [y]Josh. 19:50 & 24:30 *Timnath-serah*
2:10 [z]Ex. 5:2 1 Sam. 2:12 1 Chr. 28:9 Gal. 4:8 Tit. 1:16
2:12 [a]Deut. 31:16 [b]Deut. 6:14 [c]Ex. 20:5
2:13 [d]ch. 10:6 Ps. 106:36
2:14 [e]ch. 3:8 Ps. 106:40-42 [f]2 Ki. 17:20 [g]ch. 3:8 Is. 50:1 [h]Lev. 26:37 Josh. 7:12,13
2:15 [i]Lev. 26 Deut. 28
2:16 [j]ch. 3:9,10,15

[h] i.e. *Weepers* [i] Heb. *prolonged days after Joshua* [j] Heb. *saved*

2:10 THERE AROSE ANOTHER GENERATION . . . WHICH KNEW NOT THE LORD. The cyclical pattern of spiritual decline and renewal began with the passing of the generation that had taken the promised land and the emergence of a new generation of Israelites. The pattern reflected in the book of Judges revolves around the following process: (1) the new generation drifts away from the righteous commitment of their fathers and departs from a personal relationship with the Lord (v. 10); (2) this leads to their conformity to the lifestyles and values of the surrounding culture and results in general apostasy (vv. 11–13); (3) the judgment of God comes to Israel in the form of oppression and bondage from one of their enemies (vv. 14–15); (4) the Israelites subsequently cry out to God from their distress and repent of their backsliding (vv. 15,18); (5) God raises up a Spirit-empowered leader who serves as a deliverer to free the Israelites from their bondage and to restore them to God (vv. 16,18).

2:13 BAAL AND ASHTAROTH. "Baal," the chief god worshiped by the Canaanites, was the god of fertility, rain, and vegetation. Baal worship involved cult prostitution and child sacrifice. Israel's compromise with Baalism was repeatedly condemned by the prophets (1 Ki. 17—18; 22:17–27; 2 Ki. 1; 13; 17; Jer. 10:12–16; 14:22; Hos. 2:8, 16–17). "Ashtaroth," the goddess of war and fertility and female consort of Baal, was depicted by figurines or statues.

2:16 THE LORD RAISED UP JUDGES. The judges served as military and tribal leaders in a time when Israel was undergoing spiritual, social, and moral decline. God raised them up to deliver His people from their enemies after they repented and returned to God. The judges possessed outstanding qualities of leadership and accomplished great feats through God's help and power (v. 18; 6:11–16; 13:24–25; 14:6).

2:17 TURNED QUICKLY OUT OF THE WAY WHICH THEIR FATHERS WALKED. The key to understanding the fundamental nature of Israel's spiritual decline is found in vv. 10–17. (1) During the time of the judges the new generation of Israelites departed from the ways and teachings of their fathers. They forsook their covenant relationship with God (v. 10) and turned to evil (v. 11–13). They began to question the standards and laws of the founding generation (v. 17).

(2) They turned aside from seriously obeying God's word (vv. 2,17) and lived instead according to their own desires (cf. 17:6; 21:25).

(3) The Israelites failed to separate themselves completely from the evil culture of the Canaanites (vv. 11–13; 1:28). Instead, they preferred the materialistic benefits and immoral pleasures of the Canaanites (vv. 12–13; 1:27–28,30,33; see article on THE NATURE OF IDOLATRY, p. 428). They intermarried with the Canaanites (3:5–6) and began to worship Baal and Ashtaroth (v. 13). Thus, the inevitable syncretism of the two cultures and lifestyles took place.

(4) This history illustrates that the natural di-

unto their judges, but they [k]went a-
whoring after other gods, and bowed
themselves unto them: they turned
quickly out of the way which their fa-
thers walked in, obeying the command-
ments of the LORD; *but* they did not so.
18 And when the LORD raised them
up judges, then [l]The LORD was with
the judge, and delivered them out of
the hand of their enemies all the days
of the judge: [m]for it repented the LORD
because of their groanings by reason of
them that oppressed them and vexed
them.
19 And it came to pass, [n]when the
judge was dead, *that* they returned, and
[k]corrupted *themselves* more than their
fathers, in following other gods to
serve them, and to bow down unto
them; [1]they ceased not from their
own doings, nor from their stubborn
way.
20 ¶ [o]And the anger of the LORD
was hot against Israel; and he said, Be-
cause that this people hath [p]trans-
gressed my covenant which I com-
manded their fathers, and have not
hearkened unto my voice;
21 [q]I also will not henceforth drive
out any from before them of the nations
which Joshua left when he died:
22 [r]That through them I may
[s]prove Israel, whether they will keep
the way of the LORD to walk therein, as
their fathers did keep *it*, or not.
23 Therefore the LORD [m]left those
nations, without driving them out hast-
ily; neither delivered he them into the
hand of Joshua.

3

NOW THESE *are* [t]the nations
which the LORD left, to prove Israel
by them, *even* as many *of Israel* as had
not known all the wars of Canaan;
2 Only that the generations of the
children of Israel might know, to teach
them war, at the least such as before
knew nothing thereof;
3 *Namely,* [u]five lords of the Philis-
tines, and all the Canaanites, and the
Sidonians, and the Hivites that dwelt
in mount Lebanon, from mount Baal-
hermon unto the entering in of Ha-
math.
4 [v]And they were to prove Israel
by them, to know whether they would
hearken unto the commandments of
the LORD, which he commanded their
fathers by the hand of Moses.
5 ¶ [w]And the children of Israel
dwelt among the Canaanites, Hittites,
and Amorites, and Perizzites, and Hi-
vites, and Jebusites:
6 And [x]they took their daughters

2:17 [k]Ex. 34:15 Lev. 17:7 **2:18** [l]Josh. 1:5 [m]Gen. 6:6 Ps. 106:44 **2:19** [n]ch. 3:12 **2:20** [o]ver. 14 [p]Josh. 23:16 **2:21** [q]Josh. 23:13 **2:22** [r]ch. 3:1,4 [s]Deut. 8:2,16 **3:1** [t]ch. 2:21,22 **3:3** [u]Josh. 13:3 **3:4** [v]ch. 2:22 **3:5** [w]Ps. 106:35 **3:6** [x]Ex. 34:16 Deut. 7:3

[k] Or, *were corrupt* [1] Heb. *they let nothing fall of their* [m] Or, *suffered*

rection of human nature since the fall is downward; the spiritual vitality of an individual or group of believers will diminish unless spiritual renewal periodically occurs by God's grace through repentance, prayer, and recommitment (cf. 2 Chr. 7:14; Is. 57:15; Mat. 5:6; Jude 20).

2:19 CORRUPTED THEMSELVES MORE THAN THEIR FATHERS. This verse reveals a progressive deterioration in Israel. Each successive generation is characterized by greater apostasy and spiritual corruption. Similarly, second- and third-generation believers under the new covenant should ask themselves if they are as committed and devoted to God as was the generation that preceded them. Or are they conforming more and more to the ways of their society, while rejecting the original standards of their fathers?

2:19 THEY CEASED NOT . . . FROM THEIR STUBBORN WAY. The serious failure of many of God's chosen people to remain faithful to Him and His word is a recurring theme throughout Biblical history. (1) The O.T. reveals God's people repeatedly turning from His love, righteousness, forgiveness, and revelation. Examples of this are the rejection of God's will by Adam (Gen. 3:1–7), Adam's descendants (Gen. 6:1–7), Noah's descendants (Gen. 11:1–9), and the children of Israel (Ex. 32; book of Judges; 1 and 2 Kings; Acts 7:34–53).

(2) Likewise in the N.T., Christ and the apostles reveal that toward the end of the age many within the church will depart from true faith in Christ and His revelation in the Bible (Mat. 24:10–12,24; 2 Tim. 1:15; 4:1–4; Rev. 2—3).

(3) However, Scripture emphasizes that a righteous remnant will remain faithful to God and His revelation during times of spiritual decline. Among the many Biblical examples of faithful men and women are Enoch (Gen. 5:21–24); Noah (Gen. 6:9–12); Abraham (Gen. 12–24; 18:19); Joseph (Gen. 37–50); Moses (Ex. 33:11–14; Deut. 34); Joshua and Caleb (Num. 14:1–10); Ruth (Ruth 2:12); Samuel (1 Sam. 2:26; 3:19); Elijah (1 Ki. 18:20–22; 19:9–18; Rom. 11:2–5); the prophets (Acts 7:52); John the Baptist (Luke 1:15–17); Simeon and Anna (Luke 2:25–38); the disciples (Acts 5:27–42); Paul (2 Tim. 4:6–8); the overcomers of Rev. 2—3; and the blameless of Rev. 14:1–5,12, who constitute a great multitude from every nation that have washed their robes and made them white in the blood of the Lamb (cf. Rev. 7:9–17).

3:6 THEY TOOK THEIR DAUGHTERS. Israel's syncretism of Canaanite culture through intermarriage nearly destroyed their identity as a distinct people of God. Such intermarriage had been forbidden by Israel's covenant with the Lord (Ex. 34:15–16; Deut. 7:3–4; Josh. 23:12–13). The

to be their wives, and gave their daughters to their sons, and served their gods.

Othniel

7 [y]And the children of Israel did evil in the sight of the LORD, and forgat the LORD their God, [z]and served Baalim and [a]the groves.

8 ¶ Therefore the anger of the LORD was hot against Israel, and he [b]sold them into the hand of [c]Chushan-rishathaim king of [n]Mesopotamia: and the children of Israel served Chushan-rishathaim eight years.

9 And when the children of Israel [d]cried unto the LORD, the LORD [e]raised up a [o]deliverer to the children of Israel, who delivered them, *even* [f]Othniel the son of Kenaz, Caleb's younger brother.

10 And [g]the spirit of the LORD [p]came upon him, and he judged Israel, and went out to war: and the LORD delivered Chushan-rishathaim king of [q]Mesopotamia into his hand; and his hand prevailed against Chushan-rishathaim.

Judg. 6:34

11 And the land had rest forty years. And Othniel the son of Kenaz died.

Ehud

12 ¶ [h]And the children of Israel did evil again in the sight of the LORD: and the LORD strengthened [i]Eglon the king of Moab against Israel, because they had done evil in the sight of the LORD.

13 And he gathered unto him the children of Ammon and [j]Amalek, and went and smote Israel, and possessed [k]the city of palm trees.

14 So the children of Israel [l]served Eglon the king of Moab eighteen years.

15 But when the children of Israel [m]cried unto the LORD, the LORD raised them up a deliverer, Ehud the son of Gera, [r]a Benjamite, a man [n]lefthanded: and by him the children of Israel sent a present unto Eglon the king of Moab.

16 But Ehud made him a dagger which had two edges, of a cubit length; and he did gird it under his raiment upon his right thigh.

17 And he brought the present unto Eglon king of Moab: and Eglon *was* a very fat man.

18 And when he had made an end to offer the present, he sent away the people that bare the present.

19 But he himself turned again [o]from the [s]quarries that *were* by Gilgal, and said, I have a secret errand unto thee, O king: who said, Keep silence. And all that stood by him went out from him.

20 And Ehud came unto him; and he was sitting in [p]a summer parlour, which he had for himself alone. And Ehud said, I have a message from God unto thee. And he arose out of *his* seat.

21 And Ehud put forth his left hand,

3:7 [y]ch. 2:11 [z]ch. 2:13 [a]Ex. 34:13 Deut. 16:21 ch. 6:25
3:8 [b]ch. 2:14 [c]Hab. 3:7
3:9 [d]ver. 15 ch. 4:3 & 6:7 &10:10 Ps. 22:5 & 106:44 [e]ch. 2:16 [f]ch. 1:13
3:10 [g]Num. 27:18 ch. 6:34 & 11:29 & 13:25 & 14:6,19 1 Sam. 11:6 2 Chr. 15:1
3:12 [h]ch. 2:19 [i]1 Sam. 12:9
3:13 [j]ch. 5:14 [k]ch. 1:16
3:14 [l]Deut. 28:48
3:15 [m]ver. 9 Ps. 78:34 [n]ch. 20:16
3:19 [o]Josh. 4:20
3:20 [p]Amos 3:15

[n] Heb. *Aram-naharaim* [o] Heb. *saviour* [p] Heb. *was* [q] Heb. *Aram* [r] Or, *the son of Jemini* [s] Or, *graven images*

book of Judges demonstrates the disastrous effects of Israel's compromise.

3:7 ISRAEL DID EVIL. The book of Judges records that Israel went through six major cycles of apostasy, bondage, calling out to God, God's deliverance, and then falling away again (see 2:10, note). There are several basic truths revealed in these historical events: (1) The natural direction of God's people even after revival and restoration is spiritual decline again. Only a fervent faith, sincere gratitude, a persistent attempt to seek God's face, and a constant rejection of the ungodly ways of pagan society will enable God's people to maintain their first love, vision, and purity.

(2) The history of salvation reveals a people reluctant to learn from and profit by the spiritual decline and tragic consequences of previous generations of believers.

(3) Rebellion and unbelief are not insignificant. They are an affront to a righteous God and as such will be visited by His judgment. When the people of God lower or compromise their God-given standards, they will lose God's promised blessings and fatherly presence.

(4) God is a merciful God, ready to respond to the cries of repentance by His people. He always makes possible a new beginning by grace through faith in Him (see article on CHRIST'S MESSAGE TO THE SEVEN CHURCHES, p. 2036).

3:10 THE SPIRIT OF THE LORD CAME UPON HIM. The judges of Israel were supernaturally empowered by God's Spirit (cf. Gideon, 6:34; Jephthah, 11:29; Samson, 13:25; 14:6,19; 15:14); i.e., they were charismatic leaders. Through this spiritual enabling, they received the power and wisdom needed to perform extraordinary works for God and Israel (see 10:7, note).

3:21 EHUD . . . TOOK THE DAGGER. Ehud's action was not murder, but an act of war under the direct command of God (v. 15). Under the new covenant, the holy war of Israel as a theocracy has been replaced by spiritual warfare against Satan and his demonic forces (see Rom. 8:13, note; Eph. 6:11, note).

and took the dagger from his right
thigh, and thrust it into his belly:
22 And the haft also went in after
the blade; and the fat closed upon the
blade, so that he could not draw the
dagger out of his belly; and [t]the dirt
came out.
23 Then Ehud went forth through
the porch, and shut the doors of the
parlour upon him, and locked them.
24 When he was gone out, his ser-
vants came; and when they saw that,
behold, the doors of the parlour *were*
locked, they said, Surely he [q]cov-
ereth[u] his feet in his summer cham-
ber.
25 And they tarried till they were
ashamed: and, behold, he opened not
the doors of the parlour; therefore they
took a key, and opened *them:* and, be-
hold, their lord *was* fallen down dead
on the earth.
26 And Ehud escaped while they
tarried, and passed beyond the quar-
ries, and escaped unto Seirath.
27 And it came to pass, when he
was come, that [r]he blew a trumpet in
the [s]mountain of Ephraim, and the
children of Israel went down with him
from the mount, and he before them.
28 And he said unto them, Follow
after me: for [t]the LORD hath delivered
your enemies the Moabites into your
hand. And they went down after him,
and took [u]the fords of Jordan toward
Moab, and suffered not a man to pass
over.
29 And they slew of Moab at that
time about ten thousand men, all
[v]lusty, and all men of valour; and
there escaped not a man.
30 So Moab was subdued that day
under the hand of Israel. And [v]the
land had rest fourscore years.
31 ¶ And after him was [w]Shamgar
the son of Anath, which slew of the
Philistines six hundred men [x]with an
ox goad: [y]and he also delivered [z]Is-
rael.

Deborah

4 AND [a]THE children of Israel
again did evil in the sight of the
LORD, when Ehud was dead.
2 And the LORD [b]sold them into the
hand of Jabin king of Canaan, that
reigned in [c]Hazor; the captain of
whose host *was* [d]Sisera, which dwelt
in [e]Harosheth of the Gentiles.
3 And the children of Israel cried
unto the LORD: for he had nine hundred
[f]chariots of iron; and twenty years
[g]he mightily oppressed the children of
Israel.
4 ¶ And Deborah, a prophetess, the
wife of Lapidoth, she judged Israel at
that time. 1 Sam. 10:5-11
5 [h]And she dwelt under the palm
tree of Deborah between Ramah and
Beth-el in mount Ephraim: and the
children of Israel came up to her for
judgment.
6 And she sent and called [i]Barak
the son of Abinoam out [j]of Kedesh-
naphtali, and said unto him, Hath not
the LORD God of Israel commanded,
saying, Go and draw toward mount Ta-
bor, and take with thee ten thousand
men of the children of Naphtali and of
the children of Zebulun?
7 And [k]I will draw unto thee to the
[l]river Kishon Sisera, the captain of Ja-
bin's army, with his chariots and his
multitude; and I will deliver him into
thine hand.
8 And Barak said unto her, If thou
wilt go with me, then I will go: but if
thou wilt not go with me, *then* I will
not go.
9 And she said, I will surely go with
thee: notwithstanding the journey that
thou takest shall not be for thine hon-
our; for the LORD shall [m]sell Sisera into
the hand of a woman. And Deborah
arose, and went with Barak to Kedesh.
10 ¶ And Barak called [n]Zebulun
and Naphtali to Kedesh; and he went
up with ten thousand men [o]at his feet:
and Deborah went up with him.
11 Now Heber [p]the Kenite, *which*
was of the children of [q]Hobab the fa-
ther-in-law of Moses, had severed him-
self from the Kenites, and pitched his
tent unto the plain of Zaanaim, [r]which
is by Kedesh.
12 And they showed Sisera that
Barak the son of Abinoam was gone up
to mount Tabor.

3:24 [q]1 Sam. 24:3 **3:27** [r]ch. 5:14 & 6:34 1 Sam. 13:3 [s]Josh. 17:15 **3:28** [t]ch. 7:9,15 1 Sam. 17:47 [u]Josh. 2:7 ch. 12:5 **3:30** [v]ver. 11 **3:31** [w]ch. 5:6,8 1 Sam. 13:19,22 It seems to concern only the country next to the Philistines [x]1 Sam. 17:47,50 [y]ch. 2:16 [z]So part is called Israel, ch. 4:1,3 & 10:7,17 & 11:4 1 Sam. 4:1 **4:1** [a]ch. 2:19 **4:2** [b]ch. 2:14 [c]Josh. 11:1,10 & 19:36 [d]1 Sam. 12:9 Ps. 83:9 It seems to concern only North Israel [e]ver. 13,16 **4:3** [f]ch. 1:19 [g]ch. 5:8 Ps. 106:42 **4:5** [h]Gen. 35:8 **4:6** [i]Heb. 11:32 [j]Josh. 19:37 **4:7** [k]Ex. 14:4 [l]ch. 5:21 1 Ki. 18:40 Ps. 83:9,10 **4:9** [m]ch. 2:14 **4:10** [n]ch. 5:18 [o]See Ex. 11:8 1 Ki. 20:10 **4:11** [p]ch. 1:16 [q]Num. 10:29 [r]ver:6

[t]Or, *it came out at the fundament* [u]Or, *doeth his easement* [v]Heb. *fat*

4:4 DEBORAH. Deborah was a prophetess; she had the prophetic gifts which enabled her to hear messages from God and to communicate His will to the people (vv. 6–7; see article on THE PROPHET IN THE OLD TESTAMENT, p. 1002). Deborah's close relationship with God gave her great influence among her people (v. 8).

13 And Sisera [w]gathered together all his chariots, *even* nine hundred chariots of iron, and all the people that *were* with him, from Harosheth of the Gentiles unto the river of Kishon.

14 And Deborah said unto Barak, Up; for this *is* the day in which the LORD hath delivered Sisera into thine hand: [s]is not the LORD gone out before thee? So Barak went down from mount Tabor, and ten thousand men after him.

15 And [t]the LORD discomfited Sisera, and all *his* chariots, and all *his* host, with the edge of the sword before Barak; so that Sisera lighted down off *his* chariot, and fled away on his feet.

16 But Barak pursued after the chariots, and after the host, unto Harosheth of the Gentiles: and all the host of Sisera fell upon the edge of the sword; *and* there was not [x]a man left.

17 Howbeit Sisera fled away on his feet to the tent of Jael the wife of Heber the Kenite: for *there was* peace between Jabin the king of Hazor and the house of Heber the Kenite.

18 ¶ And Jael went out to meet Sisera, and said unto him, Turn in, my lord, turn in to me; fear not. And when he had turned in unto her into the tent, she covered him with a [y]mantle.

19 And he said unto her, Give me, I pray thee, a little water to drink; for I am thirsty. And she opened [u]a bottle of milk, and gave him drink, and covered him.

20 Again he said unto her, Stand in the door of the tent, and it shall be, when any man doth come and inquire of thee, and say, Is there any man here? that thou shalt say, No.

21 Then Jael Heber's wife [v]took a nail of the tent, and [z]took an hammer in her hand, and went softly unto him, and smote the nail into his temples, and fastened it into the ground: for he was fast asleep and weary. So he died.

22 And, behold, as Barak pursued Sisera, Jael came out to meet him, and said unto him, Come, and I will show thee the man whom thou seekest. And when he came into her *tent,* behold, Sisera lay dead, and the nail *was* in his temples.

23 So God subdued on that day Jabin the king of Canaan before the children of Israel.

24 And the hand of the children of Israel [a]prospered, and prevailed against Jabin the king of Canaan, until they had destroyed Jabin king of Canaan.

The song of Deborah

5 THEN [w]SANG Deborah and Barak the son of Abinoam on that day, saying,

2 Praise ye the LORD for the [x]avenging of Israel, [y]when the people willingly offered themselves. 2 Sa 22:4 50

3 [z]Hear, O ye kings; give ear, O ye princes; I, *even* I, will sing unto the LORD; I will sing *praise* to the LORD God of Israel.

4 LORD, [a]when thou wentest out of Seir, when thou marchedst out of the field of Edom, [b]the earth trembled, and the heavens dropped, the clouds also dropped water.

5 [c]The mountains [b]melted from before the LORD, *even* [d]that Sinai from before the LORD God of Israel.

6 In the days of Shamgar the son of Anath, in the days of Jael, [e]the highways were unoccupied, and the [c]travellers walked through [d]byways.

7 *The inhabitants of* the villages ceased, they ceased in Israel, until that I Deborah arose, that I arose [f]a mother in Israel.

8 They [g]chose new gods; then *was* war in the gates: [h]was there a shield

4:14 [s]Deut. 9:3; 2 Sam. 5:24; Ps. 68:7; Is. 52:12
4:15 [t]Ps. 83:9,10; See Josh. 10:10
4:19 [u]ch. 5:25
4:21 [v]ch. 5:26
5:1 [w]See Ex. 15:1
5:2 [x]Ps. 18:47; [y]2 Chr. 17:16
5:3 [z]Deut. 32:1,3
5:4 [a]Deut. 33:2; [b]Ps. 68:8
5:5 [c]Ps. 97:5; [d]Ex. 19:18
5:6 [e]Is. 33:8
5:7 [f]Is. 49:23
5:8 [g]Deut. 32:16; [h]1 Sam. 13:19,22

[w] Heb. *gathered by cry,* or, *proclamation*
[x] Heb. *unto one* [y] Or, *rug,* or, *blanket*
[z] Heb. *put* [a] Heb. *going went and was hard*
[b] Heb. *flowed* [c] Heb. *walkers of paths*
[d] Heb. *crooked ways*

4:14 IS NOT THE LORD GONE OUT BEFORE THEE? It is essential that God goes before us to prepare the way. Unless He does so and guides us along the way, our endeavors will fail. Consequently, we should earnestly seek to be open to God's continual leading in our lives (cf. Ex. 33:15).

5:1 SANG DEBORAH AND BARAK. The song of Deborah and Barak is a song of praise to God (v. 3) for His mercy and righteous deeds on behalf of Israel (v. 11). Throughout the O.T. heartfelt singing to the Lord by the saints was an important part of expressing their gratitude to God for His redeeming power (cf. Ex. 15; 1 Chr. 15–16; 2 Chr. 20:22; the Psalms; see article on PRAISE, p. 816). N.T. believers are also told to offer praise to God for His love toward them. Praise, considered by God as a holy sacrifice to Him (Heb. 13:15), often takes the form of song (Heb. 2:12; Jas. 5:13; Rev. 15:3). Spiritual songs of praise (cf. Eph. 5:19; Col. 3:16) can be sung with the mind (i.e., using understood language) or with the spirit (i.e., using the language of the Spirit; see 1 Cor. 14:15).

or spear seen among forty thousand in Israel?

9 My heart *is* toward the governors of Israel, that offered themselves willingly among the people. Bless ye the LORD.

10 [i]Speak,[e] ye [j]that ride on white asses, [k]ye that sit in judgment, and walk by the way.

11 *They that are delivered* from the noise of archers in the places of drawing water, there shall they rehearse the [l]righteous[f] acts of the LORD, *even* the righteous acts *toward the inhabitants* of his villages in Israel: then shall the people of the LORD go down to the gates.

12 [m]Awake, awake, Deborah: awake, awake, utter a song: arise, Barak, and [n]lead thy captivity captive, thou son of Abinoam.

13 Then he made him that remaineth [o]have dominion over the nobles among the people: the LORD made me have dominion over the mighty.

14 Out of Ephraim *was there* a root of them against Amalek; after thee, Benjamin, among thy people; out of Machir came down governors, and out of Zebulun they that [g]handle the pen of the writer.

15 And the princes of Issachar *were* with Deborah; even Issachar, and also Barak: he was sent on [h]foot into the valley. [i]For the divisions of Reuben *there were* great [j]thoughts of heart.

16 Why abodest thou among the sheepfolds, to hear the bleatings of the flocks? [k]For the divisions of Reuben *there were* great searchings of heart.

17 [p]Gilead abode beyond Jordan: and why did Dan remain in ships? [q]Asher continued on the sea [l]shore, and abode in his [m]breaches.

18 [r]Zebulun and Naphtali *were* a people *that* [n]jeoparded their lives unto the death in the high places of the field.

19 The kings came *and* fought, then fought the kings of Canaan in Taanach by the waters of Megiddo; [s]they took no gain of money.

20 [t]They fought from heaven; [u]the stars in their [o]courses fought against Sisera.

21 [v]The river of Kishon swept them away, that ancient river, the river Kishon. O my soul, thou hast trodden down strength.

22 Then were the horsehoofs broken by the means of the [p]pransings, the pransings of their mighty ones.

23 Curse ye Meroz, said the angel of the LORD, curse ye bitterly the inhabitants thereof; [w]because they came not to the help [x]of the LORD, to the help of the LORD against the mighty.

24 Blessed above women shall [y]Jael the wife of Heber the Kenite be, [z]blessed shall she be above women in the tent.

25 [a]He asked water, *and* she gave *him* milk; she brought forth butter in a lordly dish.

26 She put her hand to the nail, and her right hand to the workmen's hammer; and [q]with the hammer she smote Sisera, she smote off his head, when she had pierced and stricken through his temples.

27 [r]At her feet he bowed, he fell, he lay down: at her feet he bowed, he fell: where he bowed, there he fell down [s]dead.

28 The mother of Sisera looked out at a window, and cried through the lattice, Why is his chariot *so* long in coming? why tarry the wheels of his chariot?

29 Her wise ladies answered her, yea, she returned [t]answer to herself,

30 [b]Have they not sped? have they *not* divided the prey; [u]to every man a damsel *or* two; to Sisera a prey of divers colours, a prey of divers colours of needlework, of divers colours of needlework on both sides, *meet* for the necks of *them that take* the spoil?

31 [c]So let all thine enemies perish, O LORD: but *let* them that love him *be* [d]as the sun [e]when he goeth forth in his might. And the land had rest forty years.

Gideon

6 AND [f]THE children of Israel did evil in the sight of the LORD: and the LORD delivered them into the hand [g]of Midian seven years.

2 And the hand of Midian [v]prevailed against Israel: *and* because of

5:10 [i]Ps. 145:5 [j]ch. 10:4 [k]Ps. 107:32
5:11 [l]Ps. 145:7
5:12 [m]Ps. 57:8 [n]Ps. 68:18
5:13 [o]Ps. 49:14
5:17 [p]See Josh. 13:25, 31 [q]Josh. 19:29
5:18 [r]ch. 4:10
5:19 [s]Ps. 44:12
5:20 [t]Ps. 77:17,18 [u]ch. 4:15
5:21 [v]ch. 4:7
5:23 [w]Neh. 3:5 [x]1 Sam. 18:17
5:24 [y]ch. 4:17 [z]Luke 1:28
5:25 [a]ch. 4:19
5:30 [b]Ex. 15:9
5:31 [c]Ps. 83:9,10 [d]2 Sam. 23:4 [e]Ps. 19:4,5
6:1 [f]ch. 2:19 [g]Hab. 3:7

[e] Or, *Meditate* [f] Heb. *righteousnesses of the LORD* [g] Heb. *draw with the pen* [h] Heb. *his feet* [i] Or, *In the divisions* [j] Heb. *impressions* [k] Or, *In* [l] Or, *port* [m] Or, *creeks* [n] Heb. *exposed to reproach* [o] Heb. *paths* [p] Or, *tramplings*, or, *plungings* [q] Heb. *she hammered* [r] Heb. *Between* [s] Heb. *destroyed* [t] Heb. *her words* [u] Heb. *to the head of a man* [v] Heb. *was strong*

the Midianites the children of Israel
made them [h]the dens which *are* in the
mountains, and caves, and strong
holds.
3 And *so* it was, when Israel had
sown, that the Midianites came up, and
[i]the Amalekites, [j]and the children
of the east, even they came up against
them;
4 And they encamped against them,
and [k]destroyed the increase of the
earth, till thou come unto Gaza, and
left no sustenance for Israel, neither
[w]sheep, nor ox, nor ass.
5 For they came up with their cattle
and their tents, and they came [l]as
grasshoppers for multitude; *for* both
they and their camels were without
number: and they entered into the land
to destroy it.
6 And Israel was greatly impover-
ished because of the Midianites; and
the children of Israel [m]cried unto the
LORD.
7 ¶ And it came to pass, when the
children of Israel cried unto the LORD
because of the Midianites,
8 That the LORD sent [x]a prophet
unto the children of Israel, which said
unto them, Thus saith the LORD God of
Israel, I brought you up from Egypt,
and brought you forth out of the house
of bondage;
9 And I delivered you out of the
hand of the Egyptians, and out of the
hand of all that oppressed you, and
[n]drave them out from before you, and
gave you their land;

6:2 [h]1 Sam. 13:6 Heb. 11:38
6:3 [i]ch. 3:13 [j]Gen. 29:1 ch. 7:12 1 Ki. 4:30 Job 1:3
6:4 [k]Lev. 26:16 Deut. 28:30 Mic. 6:15
6:5 [l]ch. 7:12
6:6 [m]Hos. 5:15
6:9 [n]Ps. 44:2,3
6:10 [o]2 Ki. 17:35,37,38 Jer. 10:2
6:11 [p]Josh. 17:2 [q]Heb. 11:32 called *Gedeon*
6:12 [r]ch. 13:3 Luke 1:11,28 [s]Josh. 1:5
6:13 [t]Is. 59:1 [u]Ps. 44:1 [v]2 Chr. 15:2
6:14 [w]1 Sam. 12:11 [x]Josh. 1:9
6:15 [y]See 1 Sam. 9:21
6:16 [z]Ex. 3:12

10 And I said unto you, I *am* the
LORD your God; [o]fear not the gods of
the Amorites, in whose land ye dwell:
but ye have not obeyed my voice.
11 ¶ And there came an angel of the
LORD, and sat under an oak which *was*
in Ophrah, that *pertained* unto Joash
[p]the Abi-ezrite: and his son [q]Gideon
threshed wheat by the winepress, [y]to
hide *it* from the Midianites.
12 And the [r]angel of the LORD ap-
peared unto him, and said unto him,
The LORD *is* [s]with thee, thou mighty
man of valour.
13 And Gideon said unto him, Oh
my Lord, if the LORD be with us, why
then is all this befallen us? and
[t]where *be* all his miracles [u]which our
fathers told us of, saying, Did not the
LORD bring us up from Egypt? but now
the LORD hath [v]forsaken us, and deliv-
ered us into the hands of the Midian-
ites.
14 And the LORD looked upon him,
and said, [w]Go in this thy might, and
thou shalt save Israel from the hand of
the Midianites: [x]have not I sent thee?
15 And he said unto him, Oh my
Lord, wherewith shall I save Israel?
behold, [y]my family *is* poor in Manas-
seh, and I *am* the least in my father's
house.
16 And the LORD said unto him,
[z]Surely I will be with thee, and thou
shalt smite the Midianites as one man.

[w] Or, *goat* [x] Heb. *a man a prophet* [y] Heb. *to cause* it *to flee*

6:1 ISRAEL DID EVIL. Once more God's people reverted to a syncretistic religion that conformed to the ways of the Canaanites. As a result, for seven years God permitted the Midianites, assisted by the Amalekites and tribes from the east, to invade and oppress Israel (6:3). They were forced to hide in caves and conceal their grain and produce (vv. 2–5); they called on God only when the situation became unbearable (v. 6).

6:6 ISRAEL . . . CRIED UNTO THE LORD. Israel turned to God as a last resort and only because of their oppression. (1) The fundamental problem with the Israelites was that their faith in God was founded, not on love for and gratitude to the Lord God, but on self-centered desires and ambitions. They sought God only in times of crisis when they felt they needed Him. (2) Believers under the new covenant also need to examine their type of faith. As believers, do we follow the Lord because we truly love and appreciate Him for who He is and what He has done? Or do we serve Him primarily for what we can receive from Him? If our faith and devotion to God are genuine, we will follow the Lord even if it means trouble, suffering, persecution, and loss (see article on FAITH AND GRACE, p. 1738).

6:13 WHERE *BE* ALL HIS MIRACLES. Gideon's question should also be asked by N.T. believers. If God's miraculous power is lacking among us, we need to seek His kingdom and righteousness until God's mighty acts are again manifested in our midst (see articles on SIGNS OF BELIEVERS, p. 1516, THE KINGDOM OF GOD, p. 1428, and DIVINE HEALING, p. 1418).

6:14 THE LORD LOOKED UPON HIM. Evidently the "LORD" (v. 14) and "the angel of the LORD" (v. 12) are identical. Theologians refer to this appearance as a theophany, i.e., a manifestation of God in physical form (cf. v. 22; see Gen. 12:7, note; see article on ANGELS AND THE ANGEL OF THE LORD, p. 368).

6:16 I WILL BE WITH THEE. All those who, like Gideon, earnestly seek to serve God can depend on the active presence of God with them. This promise is made to N.T. believers by Jesus Christ Himself (Mat. 28:19–20).

17 And he said unto him, If now I have found grace in thy sight, then [a]show me a sign that thou talkest with me.

18 [b]Depart not hence, I pray thee, until I come unto thee, and bring forth my [z]present, and set *it* before thee. And he said, I will tarry until thou come again.

19 ¶ [c]And Gideon went in, and made ready [a]a kid, and unleavened cakes of an ephah of flour: the flesh he put in a basket, and he put the broth in a pot, and brought *it* out unto him under the oak, and presented *it.*

20 And the angel of God said unto him, Take the flesh and the unleavened cakes, and [d]lay *them* upon this rock, and [e]pour out the broth. And he did so.

21 ¶ Then the angel of the LORD put forth the end of the staff that *was* in his hand, and touched the flesh and the unleavened cakes; and [f]there rose up fire out of the rock, and consumed the flesh and the unleavened cakes. Then the angel of the LORD departed out of his sight.

22 And when Gideon [g]perceived that he *was* an angel of the LORD, Gideon said, Alas, O Lord GOD! [h]for because I have seen an angel of the LORD face to face.

23 And the LORD said unto him, [i]Peace *be* unto thee; fear not: thou shalt not die.

24 Then Gideon built an altar there unto the LORD, and called it [b]Jehovah-shalom: unto this day it *is* yet [j]in Ophrah of the Abi-ezrites.

25 ¶ And it came to pass the same night, that the LORD said unto him, Take thy father's young bullock, [c]even the second bullock of seven years old, and throw down the altar of Baal that thy father hath, and [k]cut down the grove that *is* by it:

26 And build an altar unto the LORD thy God upon the top of this [d]rock, [e]in the ordered place, and take the second bullock, and offer a burnt sacrifice with the wood of the grove which thou shalt cut down.

27 Then Gideon took ten men of his servants, and did as the LORD had said unto him: and *so* it was, because he feared his father's household, and the men of the city, that he could not do *it* by day, that he did *it* by night.

28 ¶ And when the men of the city arose early in the morning, behold, the altar of Baal was cast down, and the grove was cut down that *was* by it, and the second bullock was offered upon the altar *that was* built.

29 And they said one to another, Who hath done this thing? And when they inquired and asked, they said, Gideon the son of Joash hath done this thing.

30 Then the men of the city said unto Joash, Bring out thy son, that he may die: because he hath cast down the altar of Baal, and because he hath cut down the grove that *was* by it.

31 And Joash said unto all that stood against him, Will ye plead for Baal? will ye save him? he that will plead for him, let him be put to death whilst *it is yet* morning: if he *be* a god, let him plead for himself, because *one* hath cast down his altar.

32 Therefore on that day he called him [l]Jerubbaal,[f] saying, Let Baal plead against him, because he hath thrown down his altar. Judg. 16:23-30

33 ¶ Then all [m]the Midianites and the Amalekites and the children of the east were gathered together, and went over, and pitched in [n]the valley of Jezreel.

34 But [o]the spirit of the LORD [g]came upon Gideon, and he [p]blew a trumpet; and Abiezer [h]was gathered after him. Judg. 11:29

35 And he sent messengers throughout all Manasseh; who also was gathered after him: and he sent messengers unto Asher, and unto Zebulun, and unto Naphtali; and they came up to meet them.

36 ¶ And Gideon said unto God, If

6:17 [a]ver. 36,37 2 Ki. 20:8 Ps. 86:17 Is. 7:11
6:18 [b]Gen. 18:3,5
6:19 [c]Gen. 18:6-8
6:20 [d]ch. 13:19 [e]See 1 Ki. 18:33, 34
6:21 [f]Lev. 9:24
6:22 [g]ch. 13:21 [h]Gen. 16:13 Ex. 33:20 ch. 13:22
6:23 [i]Dan. 10:19
6:24 [j]ch. 8:32
6:25 [k]Ex. 34:13 Deut. 7:5
6:32 [l]1 Sam. 12:11 2 Sam. 11:21 *Jerubbesheth;* i.e. *Let the shameful* thing *plead:* See Jer. 11:13 Hos. 9:10
6:33 [m]ver. 3 [n]Josh. 17:16
6:34 [o]ch. 3:10 1 Chr. 12:18 2 Chr. 24:20 [p]Num. 10:3 ch. 3:27

[z] Or, *meat offering* [a] Heb. *a kid of the goats* [b] i.e. *The LORD* send *peace* [c] Or, *and* [d] Heb. *strong place* [e] Or, *in an orderly manner* [f] i.e. *Let Baal plead* [g] Heb. *clothed* [h] Heb. *was called after him*

6:34 SPIRIT OF THE LORD CAME UPON GIDEON. The verb "came upon" literally means "to clothe with." God's Spirit clothed Himself with Gideon in order to equip him to serve God's people, and Gideon went forth in the power of the Spirit (cf. 1 Chr. 12:18; 2 Chr. 24:20; Luke 24:49). The experience of having the Spirit come upon and live in a person is promised to all those who believe in Jesus Christ (see Acts 2:4,38–39; see article on BAPTISM IN THE HOLY SPIRIT, p. 1652).

thou wilt save Israel by mine hand, as thou hast said,

37 [q]Behold, I will put a fleece of wool in the floor; *and* if the dew be on the fleece only, and *it be* dry upon all the earth *beside,* then shall I know that thou wilt save Israel by mine hand, as thou hast said.

38 And it was so: for he rose up early on the morrow, and thrust the fleece together, and wringed the dew out of the fleece, a bowl full of water.

39 And Gideon said unto God, [r]Let not thine anger be hot against me, and I will speak but this once: let me prove, I pray thee, but this once with the fleece; let it now be dry only upon the fleece, and upon all the ground let there be dew.

40 And God did so that night: for it was dry upon the fleece only, and there was dew on all the ground.

The defeat of the Midianites

7 THEN [s]JERUBBAAL, who *is* Gideon, and all the people that *were* with him, rose up early, and pitched beside the well of Harod: so that the host of the Midianites were on the north side of them, by the hill of Moreh, in the valley.

2 And the LORD said unto Gideon, The people that *are* with thee *are* too many for me to give the Midianites into their hands, lest Israel [t]vaunt themselves against me, saying, Mine own hand hath saved me.

3 Now therefore go to, proclaim in the ears of the people, saying, [u]Whosoever *is* fearful and afraid, let him return and depart early from mount Gilead. And there returned of the people twenty and two thousand; and there remained ten thousand.

4 And the LORD said unto Gideon, The people *are* yet *too* many; bring them down unto the water, and I will try them for thee there: and it shall be, *that* of whom I say unto thee, This shall go with thee, the same shall go with thee; and of whomsoever I say unto thee, This shall not go with thee, the same shall not go.

5 So he brought down the people unto the water: and the LORD said unto Gideon, Every one that lappeth of the water with his tongue, as a dog lappeth, him shalt thou set by himself; likewise every one that boweth down upon his knees to drink.

6 And the number of them that lapped, *putting* their hand to their mouth, were three hundred men: but all the rest of the people bowed down upon their knees to drink water.

7 And the LORD said unto Gideon, [v]By the three hundred men that lapped will I save you, and deliver the Midianites into thine hand: and let all the *other* people go every man unto his place.

8 So the people took victuals in their hand, and their trumpets: and he sent all *the rest of* Israel every man unto his tent, and retained those three hundred men: and the host of Midian was beneath him in the valley.

9 ¶ And it came to pass the same [w]night, that the LORD said unto him, Arise, get thee down unto the host; for I have delivered it into thine hand.

10 But if thou fear to go down, go thou with Phurah thy servant down to the host:

11 And thou shalt [x]hear what they

6:37 [q]See Ex. 4:3-7
6:39 [r]Gen. 18:32
7:1 [s]ch. 6:32
7:2 [t]Deut. 8:17; 1 Cor. 1:29
7:3 [u]Deut. 20:8
7:7 [v]1 Sam. 14:6
7:9 [w]Gen. 46:2,3
7:11 [x]ver. 13-15; See Gen. 24:14; 1 Sam:14:9,10

6:37 A FLEECE OF WOOL. Gideon put out a fleece in order to strengthen his faith and bolster his confidence that God had indeed called him to deliver Israel (v. 36). Gideon's request for reassurance was accompanied by an attitude of faith, humility, and obedience. (1) The God who understands human nature (cf. Ps. 103:14) responded with love and grace. All God's faithful children have the right to ask God to strengthen their faith (cf. Gen. 17:17–20; Ex. 3:2; 4:1–9; Mark 9:24). (2) Even those who are filled with the Spirit may experience fear or uncertainty in difficult circumstances. In such times, God desires to encourage us and strengthen our faith (vv. 38–40).

7:2 THE PEOPLE . . . *ARE* TOO MANY. The command to reduce the army from 32,000 to 300 (vv. 2–7) illustrates four Biblical truths. (1) Only God's presence and activity can ensure victory for His people. God is able to work mightily through a small number of dedicated people. It is "not by might, nor by power, but by my spirit, saith the LORD" (Zech. 4:6). (2) Spiritual dedication, not great numbers, is of primary importance to God (cf. Rev. 3:4–5). (3) Our ultimate resource and strength to meet all of life's challenges can be found in God alone (Phil. 4:13). (4) Pride in "our" accomplishment inevitably becomes a hindrance to receiving fully God's power and help (Prov. 8:13).

7:11 THINE HANDS BE STRENGTHENED. God encouraged Gideon in order to alleviate his fear and strengthen his faith (cf. v. 10). Believers, committed to the will of God and faithfully serving Him, will at times need the encouragement of God. When those times come, we should pray that God will inspire us through His Spirit with faith, hope, and courage (see 2 Cor. 1:4–11; Phil. 4:6–7).

say; and afterward shall thine hands be strengthened to go down unto the host. Then went he down with Phurah his servant unto the outside of the [i]armed men that *were* in the host.

12 And the Midianites and the Amalekites and [y]all the children of the east lay along in the valley like grasshoppers for multitude; and their camels *were* without number, as the sand by the sea side for multitude.

13 And when Gideon was come, behold, *there was* a man that told a dream unto his fellow, and said, Behold, I dreamed a dream, and, lo, a cake of barley bread tumbled into the host of Midian, and came unto a tent, and smote it that it fell, and overturned it, that the tent lay along.

14 And his fellow answered and said, This *is* nothing else save the sword of Gideon the son of Joash, a man of Israel: *for* into his hand hath God delivered Midian, and all the host.

15 ¶ And it was *so,* when Gideon heard the telling of the dream, and [j]the interpretation thereof, that he worshipped, and returned into the host of Israel, and said, Arise; for the LORD hath delivered into your hand the host of Midian.

16 And he divided the three hundred men *into* three companies, and he put [k]a trumpet in every man's hand, with empty pitchers, and [l]lamps within the pitchers.

17 And he said unto them, Look on me, and do likewise: and, behold, when I come to the outside of the camp, it shall be *that,* as I do, so shall ye do.

18 When I blow with a trumpet, I and all that *are* with me, then blow ye the trumpets also on every side of all the camp, and say, *The sword* of the LORD, and of Gideon.

19 ¶ So Gideon, and the hundred men that *were* with him, came unto the outside of the camp in the beginning of the middle watch; and they had but newly set the watch: and they blew the trumpets, and brake the pitchers that *were* in their hands.

20 And the three companies blew the trumpets, and brake the pitchers, and held the lamps in their left hands, and the trumpets in their right hands to blow *withal:* and they cried, The sword of the LORD, and of Gideon.

21 And they [z]stood every man in his place round about the camp: [a]and all the host ran, and cried, and fled.

22 And the three hundred [b]blew the trumpets, and [c]the LORD set [d]every man's sword against his fellow, even throughout all the host: and the host fled to Beth-shittah [m]in Zererath, *and* to the [n]border of Abel-meholah, unto Tabbath.

23 And the men of Israel gathered themselves together out of Naphtali, and out of Asher, and out of all Manasseh, and pursued after the Midianites. 1 Sam. 17:38-51

24 ¶ And Gideon sent messengers throughout all [e]mount Ephraim, saying, Come down against the Midianites, and take before them the waters unto Beth-barah and Jordan. Then all the men of Ephraim gathered themselves together, and [f]took the waters unto [g]Beth-barah and Jordan.

25 And they took [h]two princes of the Midianites, Oreb and Zeeb; and they slew Oreb upon [i]the rock Oreb, and Zeeb they slew at the winepress of Zeeb, and pursued Midian, and brought the heads of Oreb and Zeeb to Gideon on the [j]other side Jordan.

8 AND [k]THE men of Ephraim said unto him, [o]Why hast thou served us thus, that thou calledst us not, when thou wentest to fight with the Midianites? And they did chide with him [p]sharply.

2 And he said unto them, What have I done now in comparison of you? *Is* not the gleaning of the grapes of Ephraim better than the vintage of Abiezer?

3 [l]God hath delivered into your hands the princes of Midian, Oreb and Zeeb: and what was I able to do in comparison of you? Then their [m]anger[q] was abated toward him, when he had said that.

4 ¶ And Gideon came to Jordan, *and* passed over, he, and the three hundred men that *were* with him, faint, yet pursuing *them.*

5 And he said unto the men of [n]Succoth, Give, I pray you, loaves of bread unto the people that follow me; for they *be* faint, and I am pursuing af-

7:12 [y]ch. 6:5,33 & 8:10
7:21 [z]Ex. 14:13,14 2 Chr. 20:17 [a]2 Ki. 7:7
7:22 [b]Josh. 6:4,16,20 See 2 Cor. 4:7 [c]Ps. 83:9 Is. 9:4 [d]1 Sam. 14:20 2 Chr. 20:23
7:24 [e]ch:3:27 [f]ch. 3:28 [g]John 1:28
7:25 [h]ch. 8:3 Ps. 83:11 [i]Is. 10:26 [j]ch. 8:4
8:1 [k]See ch. 12:1 2 Sam. 19:41
8:3 [l]ch. 7:24,25 Phil. 2:3 [m]Prov. 15:1
8:5 [n]Gen. 33:17 Ps. 60:6

[i] Or, *ranks by five* [j] Heb. *the breaking thereof*
[k] Heb. *trumpets in the hand of all of them*
[l] Or, *firebrands,* or, *torches* [m] Or, *toward*
[n] Heb. *lip* [o] Heb. *What thing* is *this thou hast done unto us* [p] Heb. *strongly* [q] Heb. *spirit*

ter Zebah and Zalmunna, kings of Midian.

6 ¶ And the princes of Succoth said, [o]*Are* the hands of Zebah and Zalmunna now in thine hand, that [p]we should give bread unto thine army?

7 And Gideon said, Therefore when the LORD hath delivered Zebah and Zalmunna into mine hand, [q]then I will [r]tear your flesh with the thorns of the wilderness and with briers.

8 ¶ And he went up thence [r]to Penuel, and spake unto them likewise: and the men of Penuel answered him as the men of Succoth had answered *him.*

9 And he spake also unto the men of Penuel, saying, When I [s]come again in peace, [t]I will break down this tower.

10 ¶ Now Zebah and Zalmunna *were* in Karkor, and their hosts with them, about fifteen thousand *men,* all that were left of [u]all the hosts of the children of the east: for there fell [v]an hundred and twenty thousand men that drew sword.

11 ¶ And Gideon went up by the way of them that dwelt in tents on the east of [w]Nobah and Jogbehah, and smote the host: for the host was [x]secure.

12 And when Zebah and Zalmunna fled, he pursued after them, and [y]took the two kings of Midian, Zebah and Zalmunna, and [s]discomfited all the host.

13 ¶ And Gideon the son of Joash returned from battle before the sun *was up,*

14 And caught a young man of the men of Succoth, and inquired of him: and he [t]described unto him the princes of Succoth, and the elders thereof, *even* threescore and seventeen men.

15 And he came unto the men of Succoth, and said, Behold Zebah and Zalmunna, with whom ye did [z]upbraid me, saying, *Are* the hands of Zebah and Zalmunna now in thine hand, that we should give bread unto thy men *that are* weary?

8:6 [o]See 1 Ki. 20:11 [p]See 1 Sam. 25:11
8:7 [q]ver. 16
8:8 [r]Gen. 32:30 1 Ki. 12:25
8:9 [s]1 Ki. 22:27 [t]ver. 17
8:10 [u]ch. 7:12 [v]ch. 20:2,15,17,25 2 Ki. 3:26
8:11 [w]Num. 32:35,42 [x]ch. 18:27 1 Thes. 5:3
8:12 [y]Ps. 83:11
8:15 [z]ver. 6

8:16 [a]ver. 7
8:17 [b]ver. 9 [c]1 Ki. 12:25
8:18 [d]ch. 4:6 Ps. 89:12
8:21 [e]Ps. 83:11
8:23 [f]1 Sam. 8:7 & 10:19 & 12:12
8:24 [g]Gen. 25:13 & 37:25,28

16 [a]And he took the elders of the city, and thorns of the wilderness and briers, and with them he [u]taught the men of Succoth.

17 [b]And he beat down the tower of [c]Penuel, and slew the men of the city.

18 ¶ Then said he unto Zebah and Zalmunna, What manner of men *were they* whom ye slew at [d]Tabor? And they answered, As thou *art,* so *were* they; each one [v]resembled the children of a king.

19 And he said, they *were* my brethren, *even* the sons of my mother: *as* the LORD liveth, if ye had saved them alive, I would not slay you.

20 And he said unto Jether his firstborn, Up, *and* slay them. But the youth drew not his sword: for he feared, because he *was* yet a youth.

21 Then Zebah and Zalmunna said, Rise thou, and fall upon us: for as the man *is, so is* his strength. And Gideon arose, and [e]slew Zebah and Zalmunna, and took away the [w]ornaments that *were* on their camels' necks.

Gideon refuses the kingship

22 ¶ Then the men of Israel said unto Gideon, Rule thou over us, both thou, and thy son, and thy son's son also: for thou hast delivered us from the hand of Midian.

23 And Gideon said unto them, I will not rule over you, neither shall my son rule over you: [f]the LORD shall rule over you.

24 ¶ And Gideon said unto them, I would desire a request of you, that ye would give me every man the earrings of his prey. (For they had golden earrings, [g]because they *were* Ishmaelites.)

25 And they answered, We will willingly give *them.* And they spread a garment, and did cast therein every man the earrings of his prey.

[r] Heb. *thresh* [s] Heb. *terrified* [t] Heb. *writ* [u] Heb. *made to know* [v] Heb. *according to the form* [w] Or, *ornaments like the moon*

8:6 GIVE BREAD UNTO THINE ARMY? By refusing to help Gideon's army, the Israelites of Succoth and Penuel (v. 8) were allying themselves with Israel's enemy, a decision for which they were punished (vv. 15–17). Likewise, N.T. believers are required to take a definite stand for Christ and righteousness; otherwise, they are viewed in reality as being against Him (Mat. 12:30).

8:16–17 HE TOOK THE ELDERS . . . AND SLEW THE MEN. The punishment inflicted by Gideon on the Israelites of Succoth and Penuel was severe but justifiable. To be a member of God's people while refusing to stand by those fighting God's battle is a terrible offense in the Lord's eyes (see previous note).

26 And the weight of the golden earrings that he requested was a thousand and seven hundred *shekels* of gold; beside ornaments, and [x]collars, and purple raiment that *was* on the kings of Midian, and beside the chains that *were* about their camels' necks.

27 And Gideon [h]made an ephod thereof, and put it in his city, *even* [i]in Ophrah: and all Israel [j]went thither a-whoring after it: which thing became [k]a snare unto Gideon, and to his house.

28 ¶ Thus was Midian subdued before the children of Israel, so that they lifted up their heads no more. [l]And the country was in quietness forty years in the days of Gideon.

Gideon's death

29 ¶ And Jerubbaal the son of Joash went and dwelt in his own house.

30 And Gideon had [m]threescore and ten sons [y]of his body begotten: for he had many wives.

31 [n]And his concubine that *was* in Shechem, she also bare him a son, whose name he [z]called Abimelech.

32 ¶ And Gideon the son of Joash died [o]in a good old age, and was buried in the sepulchre of Joash his father, [p]in Ophrah of the Abi-ezrites.

33 And it came to pass, [q]as soon as Gideon was dead, that the children of Israel turned again, and [r]went a-whoring after Baalim, [s]and made Baal-berith their god.

34 And the children of Israel [t]remembered not the LORD their God, who had delivered them out of the hands of all their enemies on every side:

35 [u]Neither showed they kindness to the house of Jerubbaal, *namely*, Gideon, according to all the goodness which he had shown unto Israel.

8:27 [h]ch. 17:5 [i]ch. 6:24 [j]Ps. 106:39 [k]Deut. 7:16
8:28 [l]ch. 5:31
8:30 [m]ch. 9:2,5
8:31 [n]ch. 9:1
8:32 [o]Gen. 25:8 Job 5:26 [p]ver. 27 ch. 6:24
8:33 [q]ch. 2:19 [r]ch. 2:17 [s]ch. 9:4,46
8:34 [t]Ps. 78:11,42 & 106:13,21
8:35 [u]ch. 9:16-18 Eccl. 9:14

9:1 [v]ch. 8:31
9:2 [w]ch. 8:30 [x]Gen. 29:14
9:3 [y]Gen. 29:15
9:4 [z]ch. 8:33 [a]ch. 11:3 2 Chr. 13:7 Acts 17:5
9:5 [b]ch. 6:24 [c]2 Ki. 11:1,2
9:7 [d]Deut. 11:29 & 27:12 Josh. 8:33 John 4:20

Abimelech

9 AND ABIMELECH the son of Jerubbaal went to Shechem unto [v]his mother's brethren, and communed with them, and with all the family of the house of his mother's father, saying,

2 Speak, I pray you, in the ears of all the men of Shechem, [a]Whether *is* better for you, either that all the sons of Jerubbaal, *which are* [w]threescore and ten persons, reign over you, or that one reign over you? remember also that I *am* [x]your bone and your flesh.

3 And his mother's brethren spake of him in the ears of all the men of Shechem all these words: and their hearts inclined [b]to follow Abimelech; for they said, He *is* our [y]brother.

4 And they gave him threescore and ten *pieces* of silver out of the house of [z]Baal-berith, wherewith Abimelech hired [a]vain and light persons, which followed him.

5 And he went unto his father's house [b]at Ophrah, and [c]slew his brethren the sons of Jerubbaal, *being* threescore and ten persons, upon one stone: notwithstanding yet Jotham the youngest son of Jerubbaal was left; for he hid himself.

6 And all the men of Shechem gathered together, and all the house of Millo, and went, and made Abimelech king, [c]by the plain of the pillar that *was* in Shechem.

7 ¶ And when they told *it* to Jotham, he went and stood in the top of [d]mount Gerizim, and lifted up his voice, and cried, and said unto them, Hearken unto me, ye men of Shechem, that God may hearken unto you.

[x] Or, *sweet jewels* [y] Heb. *going out of his thigh* [z] Heb. *set* [a] Heb. *What* is *good? whether* [b] Heb. *after* [c] Or, *by the oak of the pillar;* see Josh. 24:26

8:27 GIDEON MADE AN EPHOD. This "ephod" was probably a copy of the outer garment used by the high priest when serving God (Ex. 28:6, note). Gideon probably made it with good intentions, as a memorial to Israel's success in the work of God. However, the ephod was unauthorized by God and became an object of veneration, glorifying Gideon and Israel's achievement. This idolatrous act brought spiritual disaster to the nation and to Gideon's household. We can learn from this tragic mistake of Gideon's that: (1) To exalt and glorify churches, institutions, or human leaders who possess special charisma will result in spiritual corruption and death. (2) When planning to do something for God, we must pray for wisdom to foresee potential consequences which may eventually do great damage to the kingdom of God.

9:4–5 ABIMELECH . . . SLEW HIS BRETHREN. This great tragedy in Gideon's family was the result of Gideon's polygamy (8:30–31). His concubine in Shechem gave birth to Abimelech, who later killed seventy of his brothers. Gideon had leadership ability on the battlefield, but not in the home. God, on the other hand, places a great importance on the family. Under the new covenant He commands that no one be appointed as an overseer of God's people who cannot manage himself or his household well (1 Tim. 3:1–5).

8 [e]The trees went forth *on a time* to anoint a king over them; and they said unto the olive tree, [f]Reign thou over us.

9 But the olive tree said unto them, Should I leave my fatness, [g]wherewith by me they honour God and man, and [d]go to be promoted over the trees?

10 And the trees said to the fig tree, Come thou, *and* reign over us.

11 But the fig tree said unto them, Should I forsake my sweetness, and my good fruit, and go to be promoted over the trees?

12 Then said the trees unto the vine, Come thou, *and* reign over us.

13 And the vine said unto them, Should I leave my wine, [h]which cheereth God and man, and go to be promoted over the trees?

14 Then said all the trees unto the [e]bramble, Come thou, *and* reign over us.

15 And the bramble said unto the trees, If in truth ye anoint me king over you, *then* come *and* put your trust in my [i]shadow: and if not, [j]let fire come out of the bramble, and devour the [k]cedars of Lebanon.

16 Now therefore, if ye have done truly and sincerely, in that ye have made Abimelech king, and if ye have dealt well with Jerubbaal and his house, and have done unto him [l]according to the deserving of his hands;

17 (For my father fought for you, and [f]adventured his life far, and delivered you out of the hand of Midian:

18 [m]And ye are risen up against my father's house this day, and have slain his sons, threescore and ten persons, upon one stone, and have made Abimelech, the son of his maidservant, king over the men of Shechem, because he *is* your brother;)

19 If ye then have dealt truly and sincerely with Jerubbaal and with his house this day, *then* [n]rejoice ye in Abimelech, and let him also rejoice in you:

20 But if not, [o]let fire come out from Abimelech, and devour the men of Shechem, and the house of Millo; and let fire come out from the men of Shechem, and from the house of Millo, and devour Abimelech.

21 And Jotham ran away, and fled, and went to [p]Beer, and dwelt there, for fear of Abimelech his brother.

22 ¶ When Abimelech had reigned three years over Israel,

23 Then [q]God sent an evil spirit between Abimelech and the men of Shechem; and the men of Shechem [r]dealt treacherously with Abimelech:

24 [s]That the cruelty *done* to the threescore and ten sons of Jerubbaal might come, and their blood be laid upon Abimelech their brother, which slew them; and upon the men of Shechem, which [g]aided him in the killing of his brethren.

25 And the men of Shechem set liers in wait for him in the top of the mountains, and they robbed all that came along that way by them: and it was told Abimelech.

26 And Gaal the son of Ebed came with his brethren, and went over to Shechem: and the men of Shechem put their confidence in him.

27 And they went out into the fields, and gathered their vineyards, and trode *the grapes*, and made merry, and went into [t]the house of their god, and did eat and drink, and cursed Abimelech.

28 And Gaal the son of Ebed said, [u]Who *is* Abimelech, and who *is* Shechem, that we should serve him? *is* not *he* the son of Jerubbaal? and Zebul his officer? serve the men of [v]Hamor the father of Shechem: for why should we serve him?

29 And [w]would to God this people were under my hand! then would I remove Abimelech. And he said to Abimelech, Increase thine army, and come out.

30 ¶ And when Zebul the ruler of the city heard the words of Gaal the son of Ebed, his anger was [h]kindled.

31 And he sent messengers unto

9:8 [e]See 2 Ki. 14:9 [f]ch. 8:22,23
9:9 [g]Ps. 104:15
9:13 [h]Ps. 104:15
9:15 [i]Is. 30:2 Dan. 4:12 Hos. 14:7 [j]ver. 20 Num. 21:28 Ezek. 19:14 [k]2 Ki. 14:9 Is. 2:13 & 37:24 Ezek. 31:3
9:16 [l]ch. 8:35
9:18 [m]ver. 5,6
9:19 [n]Is. 8:6 Phil. 3:3
9:20 [o]ver. 15,56,57
9:21 [p]2 Sam. 20:14
9:23 [q]1 Sam. 16:14 & 18:9,10 See 1 Ki. 22:22 2 Chr. 18:22 Is. 19:14 [r]Is. 33:1
9:24 [s]1 Ki. 2:32 Esth. 9:25 Mat. 23:35,36
9:27 [t]ver. 4
9:28 [u]1 Sam. 25:10 1 Ki. 12:16 [v]Gen. 34:2,6
9:29 [w]2 Sam. 15:4

[d] Heb. *go up and down for other trees* [e] Or, *thistle* [f] Heb. *cast his life* [g] Heb. *strengthened his hands to kill* [h] Or, *hot*

9:13 WINE. The Hebrew word used here for wine is *tirosh*, meaning "new wine." *Tirosh* typically refers to fresh, pure juice of the grape, the produce of the vine (see Is. 65:8, note; see article on WINE IN THE OLD TESTAMENT, p. 220).

9:23 GOD SENT AN EVIL SPIRIT. God used demonic spirits to punish Abimelech and the men of Shechem for the murder of Gideon's sons. The evil spirit caused strife and mistrust (see 1 Sam. 16:14,23, notes).

Abimelech [i]privily, saying, Behold, Gaal the son of Ebed and his brethren be come to Shechem; and, behold, they fortify the city against thee.

32 Now therefore up by night, thou and the people that *is* with thee, and lie in wait in the field:

33 And it shall be, *that* in the morning, as soon as the sun is up, thou shalt rise early, and set upon the city: and, behold, *when* he and the people that *is* with him come out against thee, then mayest thou do to them [j]as thou shalt find occasion.

34 ¶ And Abimelech rose up, and all the people that *were* with him, by night, and they laid wait against Shechem in four companies.

35 And Gaal the son of Ebed went out, and stood in the entering of the gate of the city: and Abimelech rose up, and the people that *were* with him, from lying in wait.

36 And when Gaal saw the people, he said to Zebul, Behold, there come people down from the top of the mountains. And Zebul said unto him, Thou seest the shadow of the mountains as *if they were* men.

37 And Gaal spake again and said, See there come people down by the [k]middle of the land, and another company come along by the plain of Meonenim.

38 Then said Zebul unto him, Where *is* now thy mouth, wherewith thou [x]saidst, Who *is* Abimelech, that we should serve him? *is* not this the people that thou hast despised? go out, I pray now, and fight with them.

39 And Gaal went out before the men of Shechem, and fought with Abimelech.

40 And Abimelech chased him, and he fled before him, and many were overthrown *and* wounded, *even* unto the entering of the gate.

41 And Abimelech dwelt at Arumah: and Zebul thrust out Gaal and his brethren, that they should not dwell in Shechem.

42 And it came to pass on the morrow, that the people went out into the field; and they told Abimelech.

43 And he took the people, and divided them into three companies, and laid wait in the field, and looked, and, behold, the people *were* come forth out of the city; and he rose up against them, and smote them.

44 And Abimelech, and the company that *was* with him, rushed forward, and stood in the entering of the gate of the city: and the two *other* companies ran upon all *the people* that *were* in the fields, and slew them.

45 And Abimelech fought against the city all that day; and [y]he took the city, and slew the people that *was* therein, and [z]beat down the city, and sowed it with salt.

46 ¶ And when all the men of the tower of Shechem heard *that,* they entered into an hold of the house [a]of the god Berith.

47 And it was told Abimelech, that all the men of the tower of Shechem were gathered together.

48 And Abimelech gat him up to mount [b]Zalmon, he and all the people that *were* with him; and Abimelech took an axe in his hand, and cut down a bough from the trees, and took it, and laid *it* on his shoulder, and said unto the people that *were* with him, What ye have seen [l]me do, make haste, *and* do as I *have done.*

49 And all the people likewise cut down every man his bough, and followed Abimelech, and put *them* to the hold, and set the hold on fire upon them; so that all the men of the tower of Shechem died also, about a thousand men and women.

50 ¶ Then went Abimelech to Thebez, and encamped against Thebez, and took it.

51 But there was a strong tower within the city, and thither fled all the men and women, and all they of the city, and shut *it* to them, and gat them up to the top of the tower.

52 And Abimelech came unto the tower, and fought against it, and went hard unto the door of the tower to burn it with fire.

53 And a certain woman [c]cast a piece of a millstone upon Abimelech's head, and all to brake his skull.

54 Then [d]he called hastily unto the young man his armourbearer, and said unto him, Draw thy sword, and slay me, that men say not of me, A woman slew him. And his young man thrust him through, and he died.

55 And when the men of Israel saw

9:38 [x]ver. 28,29
9:45 [y]ver. 20
[z]Deut. 29:23
1 Ki. 12:25
2 Ki. 3:25
9:46 [a]ch. 8:33
9:48 [b]Ps. 68:14
9:53 [c]2 Sam. 11:21
9:54 [d]1 Sam. 31:4

i Heb. *craftily,* or, *to Tormah* j Heb. *as thine hand shall find* k Heb. *navel* l Heb. *I have done*

that Abimelech was dead, they departed every man unto his place.

56 ¶ [e]Thus God rendered the wickedness of Abimelech, which he did unto his father, in slaying his seventy brethren:

57 And all the evil of the men of Shechem did God render upon their heads: and upon them came [f]the curse of Jotham the son of Jerubbaal.

Israel cries for deliverance

10 AND AFTER Abimelech there [g]arose to [m] [n]defend Israel Tola the son of Puah, the son of Dodo, a man of Issachar; and he dwelt in Shamir in mount Ephraim.

2 And he judged Israel twenty and three years, and died, and was buried in Shamir.

3 ¶ And after him arose Jair, a Gileadite, and judged Israel twenty and two years.

4 And he had thirty sons that [h]rode on thirty ass colts, and they had thirty cities, [i]which are called [j]Havoth-jair[o] unto this day, which *are* in the land of Gilead.

5 And Jair died, and was buried in Camon.

6 ¶ And [k]the children of Israel did evil again in the sight of the LORD, and [l]served Baalim, and Ashtaroth, and [m]the gods of Syria, and the gods of [n]Zidon, and the gods of Moab, and the gods of the children of Ammon, and the gods of the Philistines, and forsook the LORD, and served not him.

7 And the anger of the LORD was hot against Israel, and he [o]sold them into the hands of the Philistines, and into the hands of the children of Ammon.

8 And that year they vexed and [p]oppressed the children of Israel: eighteen years, all the children of Israel that *were* on the other side Jordan in the land of the Amorites, which *is* in Gilead.

9 Moreover the children of Ammon passed over Jordan to fight also against Judah, and against Benjamin, and against the house of Ephraim; so that Israel was sore distressed.

10 ¶ [p]And the children of Israel cried unto the LORD, saying, We have sinned against thee, both because we have forsaken our God, and also served Baalim.

11 And the LORD said unto the children of Israel, *Did* not *I deliver you* [q]from the Egyptians, and [r]from the Amorites, [s]from the children of Ammon, [t]and from the Philistines?

12 [u]The Zidonians also, [v]and the Amalekites, and the Maonites, [w]did oppress you; and ye cried to me, and I delivered you out of their hand.

13 [x]Yet ye have forsaken me, and served other gods: wherefore I will deliver you no more.

14 Go and [y]cry unto the gods which ye have chosen; let them deliver you in the time of your tribulation.

15 ¶ And the children of Israel said unto the LORD, We have sinned: [z]do thou unto us whatsoever [q]seemeth good unto thee; deliver us only, we pray thee, this day.

16 [a]And they put away the [r]strange gods from among them, and

9:56 [e]ver. 24 Job 31:3 Prov. 5:22
9:57 [f]ver. 20
10:1 [g]ch. 2:16
10:4 [h]ch. 5:10 & 12:14 [i]Deut. 3:14 [j]Num. 32:41
10:6 [k]ch. 2:11 & 3:7 & 4:1 & 6:1 & 13:1 [l]ch. 2:13 [m]ch. 2:12 [n]1 Ki. 11:33 Ps. 106:36
10:7 [o]ch. 2:14 1 Sam. 12:9
10:10 [p]1 Sam. 12:10
10:11 [q]Ex. 14:30 [r]Num. 21:21,24, 25 [s]ch. 3:12,13 [t]ch. 3:31
10:12 [u]ch. 5:19 [v]ch. 6:3 [w]Ps. 106:42,43
10:13 [x]Jer. 2:13
10:14 [y]Deut. 32:37,38
10:15 [z]1 Sam. 3:18 2 Sam. 15:26
10:16 [a]2 Chr. 7:14 & 15:8 Jer. 18:7,8

[m] Or, *deliver* [n] Heb. *save* [o] Or, *The villages of Jair* [p] Heb. *crushed* [q] Heb. *is good in thine eyes* [r] Heb. *gods of strangers*

10:6 ISRAEL DID EVIL AGAIN. Once again the Israelites forsook the Lord and served other gods (see article on THE NATURE OF IDOLATRY, p. 428). (1) In the Canaanite religion a person could be devoted to religion and at the same time indulge in cult prostitution. In seeking fertility from the gods, the adherents of those religions found that religion and sinful sexual pleasures were compatible.

(2) In a similar vein, some who profess to be Christians teach that salvation is compatible with sexual looseness. They allege that since salvation is by grace, grace automatically blots out any and all sins. Thus sexual immorality, drunkenness, robbery, homosexuality, cruelty, and the like need not be forsaken in order to have salvation in Christ.

(3) Such a doctrine is a perversion of God's redemption for His people and must be rejected by all who are loyal to God and His word (see Mat. 7:21, note; 1 John 2:4, note; Rev. 21:8, note; see article on STANDARDS OF SEXUAL MORALITY, p. 1964).

10:7 THE ANGER OF THE LORD WAS HOT. Anger at sin and wickedness is an inherent attribute of God (see article on THE ATTRIBUTES OF GOD, p. 912). It is an expression of His goodness and love for righteousness. When believers express anger against sin, cruelty, evil, or injustice, it is not wrong, for such individuals share in the divine nature and participate in His love of righteousness and hatred of evil (see Mark 3:5; Rom. 1:18, note; Heb. 1:9, note).

10:16 HIS SOUL WAS GRIEVED FOR THE MISERY OF ISRAEL. Although the Israelites justly deserved the affliction and suffering they were undergoing, God was still deeply moved by their misery. (1) Their suffering and plight grieved

served the LORD: and [b]his soul [s]was grieved for the misery of Israel.

17 Then the children of Ammon were [t]gathered together, and encamped in Gilead. And the children of Israel assembled themselves together, and encamped in [c]Mizpeh.

18 And the people *and* princes of Gilead said one to another, What man *is he* that will begin to fight against the children of Ammon? he shall [d]be head over all the inhabitants of Gilead.

Jephthah

11 NOW [e]JEPHTHAH the Gileadite was [f]a mighty man of valour, and he *was* the son of [u]an harlot: and Gilead begat Jephthah.

2 And Gilead's wife bare him sons; and his wife's sons grew up, and they thrust out Jephthah, and said unto him, Thou shalt not inherit in our father's house; for thou *art* the son of a strange woman.

3 Then Jephthah fled [v]from his brethren, and dwelt in the land of Tob: and there were gathered [g]vain men to Jephthah, and went out with him.

4 ¶ And it came to pass [w]in process of time, that the children of Ammon made war against Israel.

5 And it was so, that when the children of Ammon made war against Israel, the elders of Gilead went to fetch Jephthah out of the land of Tob:

6 And they said unto Jephthah, Come, and be our captain, that we may fight with the children of Ammon.

7 And Jephthah said unto the elders of Gilead, [h]Did not ye hate me, and expel me out of my father's house? and why are ye come unto me now when ye are in distress?

8 [i]And the elders of Gilead said unto Jephthah, Therefore we [j]turn again to thee now, that thou mayest go with us, and fight against the children of Ammon, and be [k]our head over all the inhabitants of Gilead.

9 And Jephthah said unto the elders of Gilead, If ye bring me home again to fight against the children of Ammon, and the LORD deliver them before me, shall I be your head?

10 And the elders of Gilead said unto Jephthah, [l]The LORD [x]be witness between us, if we do not so according to thy words.

11 Then Jephthah went with the elders of Gilead, and the people made him [m]head and captain over them: and Jephthah uttered all his words [n]before the LORD in Mizpeh.

12 ¶ And Jephthah sent messengers unto the king of the children of Ammon, saying, What hast thou to do with me, that thou art come against me to fight in my land?

13 And the king of the children of Ammon answered unto the messengers of Jephthah, [o]Because Israel took away my land, when they came up out of Egypt, from Arnon even unto [p]Jabbok, and unto Jordan: now therefore restore those *lands* again peaceably.

14 And Jephthah sent messengers again unto the king of the children of Ammon:

15 And said unto him, Thus saith Jephthah, [q]Israel took not away the land of Moab, nor the land of the children of Ammon:

16 But when Israel came up from Egypt, and walked through the wilderness unto the Red sea, and [r]came to Kadesh;

17 Then [s]Israel sent messengers unto the king of Edom, saying, Let me, I pray thee, pass through thy land: [t]but the king of Edom would not hearken *thereto.* And in like manner they sent unto the king of Moab: but he would not *consent:* and Israel [u]abode in Kadesh.

18 Then they went along through the wilderness, and [v]compassed the land of Edom, and the land of Moab, and [w]came by the east side of the land

10:16 [b]Ps. 106:44,45 Is. 63:9
10:17 [c]Gen. 31:49 ch. 11:11,29
10:18 [d]ch. 11:8,11
11:1 [e]Heb. 11:32 called *Jephthae* [f]ch. 6:12 2 Ki. 5:1
11:3 [g]ch. 9:4 1 Sam. 22:2
11:7 [h]Gen. 26:27
11:8 [i]ch. 10:18 [j]Luke 17:4 [k]ch. 10:18
11:10 [l]Jer. 42:5
11:11 [m]ver. 8 [n]ch. 10:17 & 20:1 1 Sam. 10:17 & 11:15
11:13 [o]Num. 21:24-26 [p]Gen. 32:22
11:15 [q]Deut. 2:9,19
11:16 [r]Num. 13:26 & 20:1 Deut. 1:46
11:17 [s]Num. 20:14 [t]Num. 20:18,21 [u]Num. 20:1
11:18 [v]Num. 21:4 Deut. 2:1-8 [w]Num. 21:11

[s] Heb. *was shortened* [t] Heb. *cried together* [u] Heb. *a woman an harlot* [v] Heb. *from the face* [w] Heb. *after days* [x] Heb. *be the hearer between us*

His heart, just as the miseries of a child grieve and hurt a loving father. In a sense, God was heartbroken by their trouble (cf. Ezek. 6:9) and was moved by compassion to be merciful toward them (cf. Hos. 11:7–9).

(2) God's tender mercies are open to all who have sinned, who are suffering grievous consequences, and who repent and seek forgiveness. In such situations we can depend on God to be touched by our misery and suffering, to have pity on us, and to restore us to a place of fellowship and blessing.

(3) God's compassion for a lost world moved Him to send His Son to reconcile sinners unto Himself (John 3:16).

of Moab, [x]and pitched on the other
side of Arnon, but came not within the
border of Moab: for Arnon *was* the bor-
der of Moab.
19 And [y]Israel sent messengers
unto Sihon king of the Amorites, the
king of Heshbon; and Israel said unto
him, [z]Let us pass, we pray thee,
through thy land into my place.
20 [a]But Sihon trusted not Israel to
pass through his coast: but Sihon gath-
ered all his people together, and
pitched in Jahaz, and fought against Is-
rael.
21 And the LORD God of Israel deliv-
ered Sihon and all his people into the
hand of Israel, and they [b]smote them:
so Israel possessed all the land of the
Amorites, the inhabitants of that coun-
try.
22 And they possessed [c]all the
coasts of the Amorites, from Arnon
even unto Jabbok, and from the wilder-
ness even unto Jordan.
23 So now the LORD God of Israel
hath dispossessed the Amorites from
before his people Israel, and shouldest
thou possess it?
24 Wilt not thou possess that which
[d]Chemosh thy god giveth thee to pos-
sess? So whomsoever [e]the LORD our
God shall drive out from before us,
them will we possess.
25 And now *art* thou any thing bet-
ter than [f]Balak the son of Zippor,
king of Moab? did he ever strive
against Israel, or did he ever fight
against them,
26 While Israel dwelt in [g]Heshbon
and her towns, and in [h]Aroer and her
towns, and in all the cities that *be*
along by the coasts of Arnon, three
hundred years? why therefore did ye
not recover *them* within that time?
27 Wherefore I have not sinned
against thee, but thou doest me wrong
to war against me: the LORD [i]the
Judge [j]be judge this day between the
children of Israel and the children of
Ammon.
28 Howbeit the king of the children
of Ammon hearkened not unto the
words of Jephthah which he sent him.
29 ¶ Then [k]the spirit of the LORD
came upon [y]Jephthah, and he passed
over Gilead, and Manasseh, and
passed over Mizpeh of Gilead, and from
Mizpeh of Gilead he passed over *unto*
the children of Ammon.
30 And Jephthah [l]vowed a vow
unto the LORD, and said, If thou shalt
without fail deliver the children of Am-
mon into mine hands,
31 Then it shall be, that [z]whatso-
ever cometh forth of the doors of my
house to meet me, when I return in
peace from the children of Ammon,
[m]shall surely be the LORD's, [n]and[a] I
will offer it up for a burnt offering.
32 ¶ So Jephthah passed over unto
the children of Ammon to fight against
them; and the LORD delivered them into
his hands.
33 And he smote them from Aroer,
even till thou come to [o]Minnith, *even*
twenty cities, and unto [b]the plain of
the vineyards, with a very great
slaughter. Thus the children of Ammon
were subdued before the children of Is-
rael.
34 ¶ And Jephthah came to [p]Miz-
peh unto his house, and, behold, [q]his
daughter came out to meet him with
timbrels and with dances: and she *was*
his only child; [c,d]beside her he had
neither son nor daughter.
35 And it came to pass, when he
saw her, that he [r]rent his clothes, and
said, Alas, my daughter! thou hast
brought me very low, and thou art one
of them that trouble me: for I [s]have
opened my mouth unto the LORD, and
[t]I cannot go back.
36 And she said unto him, My fa-
ther, *if* thou hast opened thy mouth
unto the LORD, [u]do to me according to
that which hath proceeded out of thy
mouth; forasmuch as [v]the LORD hath
taken vengeance for thee of thine ene-
mies, *even* of the children of Ammon.
37 And she said unto her father, Let
this thing be done for me: let me alone
two months, that I may [e]go up and
down upon the mountains, and bewail
my virginity, I and my fellows.
38 And he said, Go. And he sent her
away *for* two months: and she went
with her companions, and bewailed her
virginity upon the mountains.

11:18 [x]Num. 21:13 & 22:36
11:19 [y]Num. 21:21 Deut. 2:26 [z]Num. 21:22 Deut. 2:27
11:20 [a]Num. 21:23 Deut. 2:32
11:21 [b]Num. 21:24,25 Deut. 2:33,34
11:22 [c]Deut. 2:36
11:24 [d]Num. 21:29 1 Ki. 11:7 Jer. 48:7 [e]Deut. 9:4,5 & 18:12 Josh. 3:10
11:25 [f]Num. 22:2 See Josh. 24:9
11:26 [g]Num. 21:25 [h]Deut. 2:36
11:27 [i]Gen. 18:25 [j]Gen. 16:5 & 31:53 1 Sam. 24:12,15
11:29 [k]ch. 3:10
11:30 [l]Gen. 28:20
11:31 [m]See 1 Sam. 1:11, 28 [n]Ps. 66:13
11:33 [o]Ezek. 27:17
11:34 [p]ver. 11 ch. 10:17 [q]Ex. 15:20 Ps. 68:25 Jer. 31:4
11:35 [r]Gen. 37:29,34 [s]Eccl. 5:2 [t]Num. 30:2
11:36 [u]Num. 30:2 [v]2 Sam. 18:19,31

[y] Jephthah seems to have been Judge only of Northeast *Israel* [z] Heb. *that which cometh forth, which shall come forth* [a] Or, *or I will offer it* [b] Or, *Abel* [c] Or, *he had not of his own either son or daughter* [d] Heb. *of himself* [e] Heb. *go and go down*

11:29 SPIRIT OF THE LORD. See 3:10, note.

39 And it came to pass at the end of two months, that she returned unto her father, who [w]did with her *according* to his vow which he had vowed: and she knew no man. And it was a [f]custom in Israel,

40 *That* the daughters of Israel went [g]yearly [h]to lament the daughter of Jephthah the Gileadite four days in a year.

Jephthah and Ephraim

12 AND [x]THE men of Ephraim [i]gathered themselves together, and went northward, and said unto Jephthah, Wherefore passedst thou over to fight against the children of Ammon, and didst not call us to go with thee? we will burn thine house upon thee with fire.

2 And Jephthah said unto them, I and my people were at great strife with the children of Ammon; and when I called you, ye delivered me not out of their hands.

3 And when I saw that ye delivered *me* not, I [y]put my life in my hands, and passed over against the children of Ammon, and the LORD delivered them into my hand: wherefore then are ye come up unto me this day, to fight against me?

4 Then Jephthah gathered together all the men of Gilead, and fought with Ephraim: and the men of Gilead smote Ephraim, because they said, Ye Gileadites [z]*are* fugitives of Ephraim among the Ephraimites, *and* among the Manassites.

5 And the Gileadites took the [a]passages of Jordan before the Ephraimites: and it was *so,* that when those Ephraimites which were escaped said, Let me go over; that the men of Gilead said unto him, *Art* thou an Ephraimite? If he said, Nay;

6 Then said they unto him, Say now [j]Shibboleth: and he said Sibboleth: for he could not frame to pronounce *it* right. Then they took him, and slew him at the passages of Jordan: and there fell at that time of the Ephraimites forty and two thousand.

7 And Jephthah judged Israel six years. Then died Jephthah the Gileadite, and was buried in *one of* the cities of Gilead.

Ibzan, Elon and Abdon

8 ¶ And after him [k]Ibzan of Bethlehem judged Israel.

9 And he had thirty sons, and thirty daughters, *whom* he sent abroad, and took in thirty daughters from abroad for his sons. And he judged Israel seven years.

10 Then died Ibzan, and was buried at Bethlehem.

11 ¶ And after him [l]Elon, a Zebulonite, judged Israel; and he judged Israel ten years.

12 And Elon the Zebulonite died, and was buried in Aijalon in the country of Zebulun.

13 ¶ And after him [m]Abdon the son of Hillel, a Pirathonite, judged Israel.

14 And he had forty sons and thirty [n]nephews, that [b]rode on threescore and ten ass colts: and he judged Israel eight years.

15 And Abdon the son of Hillel the Pirathonite died, and was buried in Pirathon in the land of Ephraim, [c]in the mount of the Amalekites.

13 AND THE children of Israel [d]did[o] evil again in the sight of the LORD; [p]and the LORD delivered them [e]into the hand of the Philistines forty years.

11:39 [w]ver. 31; 1 Sam. 1:22,24
12:1 [x]See ch. 8:1
12:3 [y]1 Sam. 19:5; Ps. 119:109
12:4 [z]See 1 Sam. 25:10
12:5 [a]Josh. 22:11; ch. 3:28
12:14 [b]ch. 5:10 & 10:4
12:15 [c]ch. 3:13,27 & 5:14
13:1 [d]ch. 2:11 & 3:7 & 4:1 & 6:1 & 10:6; [e]1 Sam. 12:9

[f] Or, *ordinance* [g] Heb. *from year to year* [h] Or, *to talk with* [i] Heb. *were called* [j] Which signifieth *a stream,* or, *flood* [k] He seems to have been only a civil Judge to do justice in Northeast *Israel* [l] A civil Judge in Northeast *Israel* [m] A civil Judge also in Northeast *Israel* [n] Heb. *sons' sons* [o] Heb. *added to commit* [p] This seems a partial captivity

11:39 VOW . . . SHE KNEW NO MAN. It seems apparent that Jephthah did not physically sacrifice his daughter's life (vv. 30–31), for at least two reasons. (1) He would have been acquainted with God's law sternly forbidding human sacrifice and would know that God considered such action an intolerable abomination (Lev. 18:21; 20:2–5; Deut. 12:31; 18:10–12). (2) The emphasis that "she knew no man" (i.e., did not marry) implies that she was presented to God as a living sacrifice, to devote her entire life to service and chastity at the national sanctuary (cf. Ex. 38:8; 1 Sam. 2:22).

13:1 THE PHILISTINES. A great movement of Philistines migrated to the south coast of Canaan about 1200 B.C., possibly from Crete (Jer. 47:4; Amos 9:7, where Caphtor means Crete). They became the principal enemy of the Hebrews during the years 1200–1000 B.C. (i.e., until the time of David). Because of their ability to make iron weapons, they possessed a military advantage over Israel (1 Sam. 13:19–22). The word "Palestine" is derived from the term "Philistine."

The birth of Samson

2 ¶ And there was a certain man of
[f]Zorah, of the family of the Danites,
whose name *was* Manoah; and his wife
was barren, and bare not.
3 And the [g]angel of the LORD ap-
peared unto the woman, and said unto
her, Behold now, thou *art* barren, and
bearest not: but thou shalt conceive,
and bear a son.
4 Now therefore beware, I pray
thee, and [h]drink not wine nor strong
drink, and eat not any unclean *thing:*
5 For, lo, thou shalt conceive, and
bear a son; and no [i]razor shall come
on his head: for the child shall be [j]a
Nazarite unto God from the womb: and
he shall [k]begin to deliver Israel out of
the hand of the Philistines.
6 ¶ Then the woman came and told
her husband, saying, [l]A man of God
came unto me, and his [m]countenance
was like the countenance of an angel of
God, very terrible: but I [n]asked him
not whence he *was,* neither told he me
his name:
7 But he said unto me, Behold, thou
shalt conceive, and bear a son; and
now drink no wine nor strong drink,
neither eat any unclean *thing:* for the
child shall be a Nazarite to God from
the womb to the day of his death.
8 ¶ Then Manoah entreated the
LORD, and said, O my Lord, let the man
of God which thou didst send come
again unto us, and teach us what we
shall do unto the child that shall be
born.
9 And God hearkened to the voice of
Manoah, and the angel of God came
again unto the woman as she sat in the
field: but Manoah her husband *was* not
with her.
10 And the woman made haste, and
ran, and showed her husband, and said
unto him, Behold, the man hath ap-
peared unto me, that came unto me the
other day.
11 And Manoah arose, and went af-
ter his wife, and came to the man, and
said unto him, *Art* thou the man that
spakest unto the woman? And he said,
I *am.*
12 And Manoah said, Now let thy
words come to pass. [q]How shall we
order the child, and [r] [s]*how* shall we
do unto him?
13 And the angel of the LORD said
unto Manoah, Of all that I said unto the
woman let her beware.
14 She may not eat of any *thing* that
cometh of the vine, [o]neither let her
drink wine or strong drink, nor eat any
unclean *thing:* all that I commanded
her let her observe.
15 ¶ And Manoah said unto the an-
gel of the LORD, I pray thee, [p]let us
detain thee, until we shall have made
ready a kid [t]for thee.
16 And the angel of the LORD said
unto Manoah, Though thou detain me,
I will not eat of thy bread: and if thou
wilt offer a burnt offering, thou must
offer it unto the LORD. For Manoah
knew not that he *was* an angel of the
LORD.
17 And Manoah said unto the angel
of the LORD, What *is* thy name, that
when thy sayings come to pass we may
do thee honour?
18 And the angel of the LORD said
unto him, [q]Why askest thou thus after
my name, seeing it *is* secret?
19 So Manoah took a kid with a
meat offering, [r]and offered *it* upon a
rock unto the LORD: and *the angel* did
wondrously; and Manoah and his wife
looked on.
20 For it came to pass, when the
flame went up toward heaven from off
the altar, that the angel of the LORD as-
cended in the flame of the altar. And

13:2 [f]Josh. 19:41 **13:3** [g]ch. 6:12 Luke 1:11,13,28, 31 **13:4** [h]ver. 14 Num. 6:2,3 Luke 1:15 **13:5** [i]Num. 6:5 1 Sam. 1:11 [j]Num. 6:2 [k]See 1 Sam. 7:13 2 Sam. 8:1 1 Chr. 18:1 **13:6** [l]Deut. 33:1 1 Sam. 2:27 & 9:6 [m]Mat. 28:3 Luke 9:29 Acts 6:15 [n]ver. 17,18

13:14 [o]ver. 4 **13:15** [p]Gen. 18:5 ch. 6:18 **13:18** [q]Gen. 32:29 **13:19** [r]ch. 6:19,20

[q] Heb. *What shall be the manner of the* [r] Or, what *shall he do?* [s] Heb. what shall be *his work?* [t] Heb. *before thee*

13:4 DRINK NOT WINE NOR STRONG DRINK. Whereas Samson's mother was instructed to be careful not to drink wine or any fermented drink during the time of her conception and pregnancy for spiritual reasons (vv. 4–5), modern medical science advises the same for physical reasons. Leading authorities on human birth defects warn that women drinking even moderate amounts of alcohol during conception or pregnancy stand a greater chance of experiencing miscarriages or causing incurable birth defects in their babies (see article on WINE IN NEW TESTAMENT TIMES (2), p. 1594).

13:5 THE CHILD SHALL BE A NAZARITE. God intended Samson to be a Nazarite and live according to God's highest standards for His people (for an explanation of the Nazarite vow, see Num. 6:2, note; see article on WINE IN THE OLD TESTAMENT, p. 220).

13:7 WINE NOR STRONG DRINK. See article on WINE IN THE OLD TESTAMENT, p. 220.

Manoah and his wife looked on *it,* and [s]fell on their faces to the ground.

21 But the angel of the LORD did no more appear to Manoah and to his wife. [t]Then Manoah knew that he *was* an angel of the LORD.

22 And Manoah said unto his wife, [u]We shall surely die, because we have seen God.

23 But his wife said unto him, If the LORD were pleased to kill us, he would not have received a burnt offering and a meat offering at our hands, neither would he have shown us all these *things,* nor would as at this time have told us *such things* as these.

24 ¶ And the woman bare a son, and called his name [v]Samson: and [w]the child grew, and the LORD blessed him.

25 [x]And the spirit of the LORD began to move him at times in [u]the camp of Dan [y]between Zorah and Eshtaol.

The marriage of Samson

14 AND SAMSON went down [z]to Timnath, and [a]saw a woman in Timnath of the daughters of the Philistines.

2 And he came up, and told his father and his mother, and said, I have seen a woman in Timnath of the daughters of the Philistines: now therefore [b]get her for me to wife.

3 Then his father and his mother said unto him, *Is there* never a woman among the daughters of [c]thy brethren, or among all my people, that thou goest to take a wife of the [d]uncircumcised Philistines? And Samson said unto his father, Get her for me; for [v]she pleaseth me well.

4 But his father and his mother knew not that it *was* [e]of the LORD, that he sought an occasion against the Philistines: for at that time [f]the Philistines had dominion over Israel.

5 ¶ Then went Samson down, and his father and his mother, to Timnath, and came to the vineyards of Timnath: and, behold, a young lion roared [w]against him.

6 And [g]the spirit of the LORD came mightily upon him, and he rent him as he would have rent a kid, and *he had* nothing in his hand: but he told not his father or his mother what he had done.

7 And he went down, and talked with the woman; and she pleased Samson well.

8 ¶ And after a time he returned to take her, and he turned aside to see the carcase of the lion: and, behold, *there was* a swarm of bees and honey in the carcase of the lion.

9 And he took thereof in his hands, and went on eating, and came to his father and mother, and he gave them, and they did eat: but he told not them that he had taken the honey out of the carcase of the lion.

10 ¶ So his father went down unto the woman: and Samson made there a feast; for so used the young men to do.

11 And it came to pass, when they saw him, that they brought thirty companions to be with him.

12 ¶ And Samson said unto them, I will now [h]put forth a riddle unto you: if ye can certainly declare it me [i]within the seven days of the feast, and find

13:20 [s]Lev. 9:24 1 Chr. 21:16 Ezek. 1:28 Mat. 17:6
13:21 [t]ch. 6:22
13:22 [u]Gen. 32:30 Ex. 33:20 Deut. 5:26 ch. 6:22
13:24 [v]Heb. 11:32 [w]1 Sam. 3:19 Luke 1:80 & 2:52
13:25 [x]ch. 3:10 1 Sam. 11:6 Mat. 4:1 [y]Josh. 15:33 ch. 18:11
14:1 [z]Gen. 38:13 Josh. 15:10 [a]Gen. 34:2
14:2 [b]Gen. 21:21 & 34:4
14:3 [c]Gen. 24:3,4 [d]Gen. 34:14 Ex. 34:16 Deut. 7:3
14:4 [e]Josh. 11:20 1 Ki. 12:15 2 Ki. 6:33 2 Chr. 10:15 & 22:7 & 25:20 [f]ch. 13:1 Deut. 28:48
14:6 [g]ch. 3:10 & 13:25 1 Sam. 11:6
14:12 [h]1 Ki. 10:1 Ezek. 17:2 Luke 14:7 [i]Gen. 29:27

[u] Heb. *Mahaneh-dan* as ch. 18:12 [v] Heb. *she is right in mine eyes* [w] Heb. *in meeting him*

14:3 A WIFE OF THE UNCIRCUMCISED. Although the Lord had blessed Samson and empowered him with the Spirit (13:24–25; 14:6,19; 15:14), he made fatal errors that led to spiritual failure and physical death. Among these are the following: (1) He did not anchor his life in the word of God. He showed a lack of concern and respect for God's commandments, specifically ignoring God's law concerning mixed marriages (Ex. 34:16; Deut. 7:3; cf. Gen. 24:3–4; 26:34–35).

(2) He disregarded his parents' God-given instruction and rejected his godly heritage in order to fulfill his own desires (13:5,8,14,24–25).

(3) Unlike Moses, who chose to endure adversity with God's people rather than enjoy the passing pleasure of sin (Heb. 11:25), Samson chose to express his human emotions and desires in ways that did not please God (14:3; 16:1,4; see 15:7, note).

(4) He misused God's gifts and empowerment for personal gain and advantage.

14:4 IT *WAS* OF THE LORD. This statement does not mean that God initiated Samson's intention to marry an unbeliever. Samson was motivated by his own desire to seek marital companionship outside of God's people (cf. Jas. 1:13–14). However, God did use the sin of Samson as an occasion to accomplish His purpose against the Philistines (v. 4; cf. Gen. 50:20).

14:6 THE SPIRIT OF THE LORD. Samson's great physical strength was not his own, but resulted from the Spirit coming upon him (v. 19; 15:14; 16:28–30). Under the new covenant, the Holy Spirit also comes upon believers, though not to make us physically strong; rather, the Holy Spirit empowers us to live and witness for Christ (see article on BAPTISM IN THE HOLY SPIRIT, p. 1652).

it out, then I will give you thirty [x]sheets and thirty [j]change of garments:

13 But if ye cannot declare *it* me, then shall ye give me thirty sheets and thirty change of garments. And they said unto him, Put forth thy riddle, that we may hear it.

14 And he said unto them, Out of the eater came forth meat, and out of the strong came forth sweetness. And they could not in three days expound the riddle.

15 And it came to pass on the seventh day, that they said unto Samson's wife, [k]Entice thy husband, that he may declare unto us the riddle, [l]lest we burn thee and thy father's house with fire: have ye called us [y]to take that we have? *is it* not *so?*

16 And Samson's wife wept before him, and said, [m]Thou dost but hate me, and lovest me not: thou hast put forth a riddle unto the children of my people, and hast not told *it* me. And he said unto her, Behold, I have not told *it* my father nor my mother, and shall I tell *it* thee?

17 And she wept before him [z]the seven days, while their feast lasted: and it came to pass on the seventh day, that he told her, because she lay sore upon him: and she told the riddle to the children of her people.

18 And the men of the city said unto him on the seventh day before the sun went down, What *is* sweeter than honey? and what *is* stronger than a lion? And he said unto them, If ye had not plowed with my heifer, ye had not found out my riddle.

19 ¶ And [n]the spirit of the LORD came upon him, and he went down to Ashkelon, and slew thirty men of them, and took their [a]spoil, and gave change of garments unto them which expounded the riddle. And his anger was kindled, and he went up to his father's house.

20 But Samson's wife [o]was *given* to his companion, whom he had used as [p]his friend.

The revenge of Samson

15 BUT IT came to pass within a while after, in the time of wheat harvest, that Samson visited his wife with a kid; and he said, I will go in to my wife into the chamber. But her father would not suffer him to go in.

2 And her father said, I verily thought that thou hadst utterly [q]hated her; therefore I gave her to thy companion: *is* not her younger sister fairer than she? [b]take her, I pray thee, instead of her.

3 ¶ And Samson said concerning them, [c]Now shall I be more blameless than the Philistines, though I do them a displeasure.

4 And Samson went and caught three hundred foxes, and took [d]firebrands, and turned tail to tail, and put a firebrand in the midst between two tails.

5 And when he had set the brands on fire, he let *them* go into the standing corn of the Philistines, and burnt up both the shocks, and also the standing corn, with the vineyards *and* olives.

6 ¶ Then the Philistines said, Who hath done this? And they answered, Samson, the son-in-law of the Timnite, because he had taken his wife, and given her to his companion. [r]And the Philistines came up, and burnt her and her father with fire.

7 ¶ And Samson said unto them, Though ye have done this, yet will I be avenged of you, and after that I will cease.

8 And he smote them hip and thigh with a great slaughter: and he went down and dwelt in the top of the rock Etam.

9 ¶ Then the Philistines went up, and pitched in Judah, and spread themselves [s]in Lehi.

10 And the men of Judah said, Why are ye come up against us? And they answered, To bind Samson are we come up, to do to him as he hath done to us.

11 Then three thousand men of Judah [e]went to the top of the rock Etam, and said to Samson, Knowest thou not

14:12 [j]Gen. 45:22 2 Ki. 5:22
14:15 [k]ch. 16:5 [l]ch. 15:6
14:16 [m]ch. 16:15
14:19 [n]ch. 3:10 & 13:25
14:20 [o]ch. 15:2 [p]John 3:29
15:2 [q]ch. 14:20
15:6 [r]ch. 14:15
15:9 [s]ver. 19

[x] Or, *shirts* [y] Heb. *to possess us,* or, *to impoverish us?* [z] Or, the rest of *the seven days* [a] Or, *apparel* [b] Heb. *let her be thine* [c] Or, *Now shall I be blameless from the Philistines, though* [d] Or, *torches* [e] Heb. *went down*

15:7 AVENGED OF YOU. Samson's fight with the Philistines was primarily motivated by personal anger and revenge, rather than concern for God's deliverance of the Hebrew people. This selfishness and lack of commitment to God eventually led to his ruin (16:1,20–21).

that the Philistines *are* [t]rulers over us? what *is* this *that* thou hast done unto us? And he said unto them, As they did unto me, so have I done unto them.

12 And they said unto him, We are come down to bind thee, that we may deliver thee into the hand of the Philistines. And Samson said unto them, Swear unto me, that ye will not fall upon me yourselves.

13 And they spake unto him, saying, No; but we will bind thee fast, and deliver thee into their hand: but surely we will not kill thee. And they bound him with two new cords, and brought him up from the rock.

14 ¶ *And* when he came unto Lehi, the Philistines shouted against him: and [u]the spirit of the LORD came mightily upon him, and the cords that *were* upon his arms became as flax that was burnt with fire, and his bands [f]loosed from off his hands.

15 And he found a [g]new jawbone of an ass, and put forth his hand, and took it, and [v]slew a thousand men therewith.

Sam. 1:6-7

16 And Samson said, With the jawbone of an ass, [h]heaps upon heaps, with the jaw of an ass have I slain a thousand men.

17 And it came to pass, when he had made an end of speaking, that he cast away the jawbone out of his hand, and called that place [i]Ramath-lehi.

18 ¶ And he was sore athirst, and called on the LORD, and said, [w]Thou hast given this great deliverance into the hand of thy servant: and now shall I die for thirst, and fall into the hand of the uncircumcised?

19 But God clave an hollow place that *was* in [j]the jaw, and there came water thereout; and when he had drunk, [x]his spirit came again, and he revived: wherefore he called the name thereof [k]En-hakkore, which *is* in Lehi unto this day.

15:11 [t]ch. 14:4
15:14 [u]ch. 3:10 & 14:6
15:15 [v]Lev. 26:8 Josh. 23:10 ch. 3:31
15:18 [w]Ps. 3:7
15:19 [x]Gen. 45:27 Is. 40:29

15:20 [y]ch. 13:1
16:2 [z]1 Sam. 23:26 Acts 9:24
16:5 [a]ch. 14:15

20 [l]And he judged Israel [y]in the days of the Philistines twenty years.

Samson and Delilah

16 THEN WENT Samson to Gaza, and saw there [m]an harlot, and went in unto her.

2 *And it was told* the Gazites, saying, Samson is come hither. And they [z]compassed *him* in, and laid wait for him all night in the gate of the city, and were [n]quiet all the night, saying, In the morning, when it is day, we shall kill him.

3 And Samson lay till midnight, and arose at midnight, and took the doors of the gate of the city, and the two posts, and went away with them, [o]bar and all, and put *them* upon his shoulders, and carried them up to the top of an hill that *is* before Hebron.

4 ¶ And it came to pass afterward, that he loved a woman [p]in the valley of Sorek, whose name *was* Delilah.

5 And the lords of the Philistines came up unto her, and said unto her, [a]Entice him, and see wherein his great strength *lieth,* and by what *means* we may prevail against him, that we may bind him to [q]afflict him: and we will give thee every one of us eleven hundred *pieces* of silver.

6 ¶ And Delilah said to Samson, Tell me, I pray thee, wherein thy great strength *lieth,* and wherewith thou mightest be bound to afflict thee.

7 And Samson said unto her, If they bind me with seven [r][g]green withs that were never dried, then shall I be weak, and be as [s]another man.

[f]Heb. *were melted* [g]Heb. *moist* [h]Heb. *an heap, two heaps* [i]i.e. *The lifting up of the jawbone,* or, *casting away of the jawbone* [j]Or, *Lehi* [k]i.e. *The well of him that called,* or, *cried* [l]He seems to have judged Southwest Israel during twenty years of their servitude of the Philistines [m]Heb. *a woman an harlot* [n]Heb. *silent* [o]Heb. *with the bar* [p]Or, *by the brook* [q]Or, *humble* [r]Or, *new cords* [s]Heb. *one*

15:14 THE SPIRIT OF THE LORD CAME MIGHTILY UPON HIM. An empowerment from the Spirit in the O.T. does not mean that God endorsed that person's way of life (cf. Num. 24:2). Indeed, there were many objectionable aspects to Samson's lifestyle.

15:20 JUDGED ISRAEL ... TWENTY YEARS. During the twenty years Samson was judge of Israel, he never succeeded in delivering the people from the oppression of the Philistines. His record consisted only of sporadic exploits against that heathen nation. What might God have accomplished through Samson if he had been faithful to his calling and genuinely dedicated to God's purpose for his life as the chosen deliverer of Israel?

16:1 AN HARLOT. Samson's problem of insatiable lust eventually led to his downfall (cf. vv. 4,19–21). He was more concerned with satisfying his sexual passion than with pleasing his holy God (vv. 1–3).

8 Then the lords of the Philistines brought up to her seven green withs which had not been dried, and she bound him with them.

9 Now *there were* men lying in wait, abiding with her in the chamber. And she said unto him, The Philistines *be* upon thee, Samson. And he brake the withs, as a thread of tow is broken when it [t]toucheth the fire. So his strength was not known.

10 And Delilah said unto Samson, Behold, thou hast mocked me, and told me lies: now tell me, I pray thee, wherewith thou mightest be bound.

11 And he said unto her, If they bind me fast with new ropes [u]that never were occupied, then shall I be weak, and be as another man.

12 Delilah therefore took new ropes, and bound him therewith, and said unto him, The Philistines *be* upon thee, Samson. And *there were* liers in wait abiding in the chamber. And he brake them from off his arms like a thread.

13 And Delilah said unto Samson, Hitherto thou hast mocked me, and told me lies: tell me wherewith thou mightest be bound. And he said unto her, If thou weavest the seven locks of my head with the web.

14 And she fastened *it* with the pin, and said unto him, The Philistines *be* upon thee, Samson. And he awaked out of his sleep, and went away with the pin of the beam, and with the web.

15 ¶ And she said unto him, [b]How canst thou say, I love thee, when thine heart *is* not with me? thou hast mocked me these three times, and hast not told me wherein thy great strength *lieth*.

16 And it came to pass, when she pressed him daily with her words, and urged him, *so* that his soul was [v]vexed unto death;

17 That he [c]told her all his heart, and said unto her, [d]There hath not come a razor upon mine head; for I *have been* a Nazarite unto God from my mother's womb: if I be shaven, then my strength will go from me, and I shall become weak, and be like any *other* man.

18 And when Delilah saw that he had told her all his heart, she sent and called for the lords of the Philistines, saying, Come up this once, for he hath shown me all his heart. Then the lords of the Philistines came up unto her, and brought money in their hand.

19 [e]And she made him sleep upon her knees; and she called for a man, and she caused him to shave off the seven locks of his head; and she began to afflict him, and his strength went from him.

20 And she said, The Philistines *be* upon thee, Samson. And he awoke out of his sleep, and said, I will go out as at other times before, and shake myself. And he wist not that the LORD [f]was departed from him.

21 ¶ But the Philistines took him, and [w]put out his eyes, and brought him down to Gaza, and bound him with fetters of brass; and he did grind in the prison house.

22 Howbeit the hair of his head began to grow again [x]after he was shaven.

Samson's revenge and death

23 Then the lords of the Philistines gathered them together for to offer a great sacrifice unto Dagon their god, and to rejoice: for they said, Our god hath delivered Samson our enemy into our hand.

24 And when the people saw him, they [g]praised their god: for they said, Our god hath delivered into our hands our enemy, and the destroyer of our country, [y]which slew many of us.

25 And it came to pass, when their hearts were [h]merry, that they said, Call for Samson, that he may make us

16:15 [b]ch. 14:16 **16:17** [c]Mic. 7:5 [d]Num. 6:5 ch. 13:5

16:19 [e]Prov. 7:26,27 **16:20** [f]Num. 14:9,42,43 Josh. 7:12 1 Sam. 16:14 & 18:12 & 28:15,16 2 Chr. 15:2 **16:24** [g]Dan. 5:4 **16:25** [h]ch. 9:27

[t] Heb. *smelleth* [u] Heb. *wherewith work hath not been done* [v] Heb. *shortened* [w] Heb. *bored out* [x] Or, *as when he was shaven* [y] Heb. *and who multiplied our slain*

16:19 HIS STRENGTH WENT FROM HIM. Samson entered into compromise with Delilah by continuing to disregard God's instruction to remain separate from the wicked nations in Canaan (Deut. 7:1–4). He failed to realize that compromise with idol worshipers and immoral people opens up one's life to the power of Satan, to delusion, and to utter defeat (vv. 19–21).

16:20 THE LORD WAS DEPARTED FROM HIM. Samson is an example of those believers who think that God will remain with them even while they continue in sinful and immoral conduct. The Lord departed from this judge because of his continued disobedience (cf. 1 Cor. 9:27; Heb. 3:6–19). This passage strongly warns that it is possible for the Lord to depart from a persistently sinful person without him or her realizing it.

sport. And they called for Samson out
of the prison house; and he made
[z]them sport: and they set him be-
tween the pillars.
26 And Samson said unto the lad
that held him by the hand, Suffer me
that I may feel the pillars whereupon
the house standeth, that I may lean
upon them.
27 Now the house was full of men
and women; and all the lords of the
Philistines *were* there; and *there were*
upon the [i]roof about three thousand
men and women, that beheld while
Samson made sport.
28 And Samson called unto the
LORD, and said, O Lord GOD, [j]remem-
ber me, I pray thee, and strengthen me,
I pray thee, only this once, O God, that
I may be at once avenged of the Philis-
tines for my two eyes.
29 And Samson took hold of the two
middle pillars upon which the house
stood, and [a]on which it was borne up,
of the one with his right hand, and of
the other with his left.
30 And Samson said, Let [b]me die
with the Philistines. And he bowed
himself with *all his* might; and the
house fell upon the lords, and upon all
the people that *were* therein. So the
dead which he slew at his death were
more than *they* which he slew in his
life.
31 Then his brethren and all the
house of his father came down, and
took him, and brought *him* up, and
[k]buried him between Zorah and Esh-
taol in the buryingplace of Manoah his
father. And he judged Israel twenty
years.

Micah's idols and priest

17 AND THERE was a man of
mount Ephraim, whose name
was Micah.
2 And he said unto his mother, The
eleven hundred *shekels* of silver that
were taken from thee, about which
thou cursedst, and spakest of also in
mine ears, behold, the silver *is* with
me; I took it. And his mother said,
[l]Blessed *be thou* of the LORD, my son.
3 And when he had restored the
eleven hundred *shekels* of silver to his
mother, his mother said, I had wholly
dedicated the silver unto the LORD from
my hand for my son, to [m]make a grav-
en image and a molten image: now
therefore I will restore it unto thee.
4 Yet he restored the money unto
his mother; and his mother [n]took two
hundred *shekels* of silver, and gave
them to the founder, who made thereof
a graven image and a molten image:
and they were in the house of Micah.
5 And the man Micah had an house
of gods, and made an [o]ephod, and
[p]teraphim, and [q]consecrated[c] one
of his sons, who became his priest.
6 [r]In those days *there was* no king

16:27 [i]Deut. 22:8
16:28 [j]Jer. 15:15
16:31 [k]ch. 13:25
17:2 [l]Gen. 14:19
17:3 [m]See Ex. 20:4,23 Lev. 19:4
17:4 [n]Is. 46:6
17:5 [o]ch. 8:27 [p]Gen. 31:19,30 Hos. 3:4 [q]Ex. 29:9
17:6 [r]ch. 18:1 & 19:1 & 21:25

[z] Heb. *before them* [a] Or, *he leaned on them*
[b] Heb. *my soul* [c] Heb. *filled the hand*

16:28 SAMSON CALLED UNTO THE LORD. Samson, now with a repentant spirit and a renewed faith in God, called upon the Lord, and his prayer was answered. This demonstration of Samson's faith resulted in his inclusion among the heroes of faith (see Heb. 11:32).

17:1 MICAH. The chronological history of the book of Judges ends with ch. 16. Beginning with the episode of Micah, the book's final section (17:1—21:25) illustrates the low moral standards, the debased religious practices, and the chaotic social order of Israel during the period of the judges. These illustrations demonstrate that if God's word and sound moral principles are disregarded, both individuals and society as a whole will be destroyed (cf. Prov. 14:34; 21:7). Twice the writer observes that "every man did *that which was* right in his own eyes" (17:6; 21:25; cf. Prov. 14:12). God's way was rejected, resulting in despair, disorder, and death.

17:5 AN HOUSE OF GODS. Because Micah did not submit to the authority of God's inspired, written revelation through Moses, he deceived himself and did what was right in his own eyes (v. 6; cf. Deut. 11:18–25; Josh. 1:5–8). He deceived himself into believing that he could receive God's blessing (v. 13) and at the same time break the clear commandments of Scripture. His sin involved stealing (v. 2), worshiping idols (vv. 3–5), disobeying the commands of God (v. 6), and appointing his own son as priest (vv. 5–13; Num. 16:17; Deut. 21:5; cf. 2 Tim. 4:3). Proper discernment and sound moral judgment were lost in Israel when the nation departed from God's covenant.

17:6 EVERY MAN DID *THAT WHICH WAS* RIGHT IN HIS OWN EYES. People who do what is right in their own eyes inevitably do what is evil in the eyes of God (cf. 2:11; 4:1; 6:1; 10:6). This lawless attitude is as prevalent in our day as it was in the days of Micah. People want to do their own thing and resent being told what they can or cannot do—even by God and His Word. Those who disregard God's absolute standards in favor of human subjective wishes will end in chaos spiritually, morally, and socially. True believers, on the other hand, will gladly submit to God's standards and values as revealed in His written Word.

in Israel, [s]but every man did *that which was* right in his own eyes.

7 ¶ And there was a young man out of [t]Bethlehem-judah of the family of Judah, who *was* a Levite, and he sojourned there.

8 And the man departed out of the city from Bethlehem-judah to sojourn where he could find *a place:* and he came to mount Ephraim to the house of Micah, [d]as he journeyed.

9 And Micah said unto him, Whence comest thou? And he said unto him, I *am* a Levite of Bethlehem-judah, and I go to sojourn where I may find *a place.*

10 And Micah said unto him, Dwell with me, [u]and be unto me a [v]father and a priest, and I will give thee ten *shekels* of silver by the year, and [e] [f]a suit of apparel, and thy victuals. So the Levite went in.

11 And the Levite was content to dwell with the man; and the young man was unto him as one of his sons.

12 And Micah [w]consecrated the Levite; and the young man [x]became his priest, and was in the house of Micah.

13 Then said Micah, Now know I that the LORD will do me good, seeing I have a Levite to *my* priest.

Danites overtake Laish

18 IN [y]THOSE days *there was* no king in Israel: and in those days [z]the tribe of the Danites sought them an inheritance to dwell in; for unto that day *all their* inheritance had not fallen unto them among the tribes of Israel.

2 And the children of Dan sent of their family five men from their coasts, [g]men of valour, from [a]Zorah, and from Eshtaol, [b]to spy out the land, and to search it; and they said unto them, Go, search the land: who when they came to mount Ephraim, to the [c]house of Micah, they lodged there.

3 When they *were* by the house of Micah, they knew the voice of the young man the Levite: and they turned in thither, and said unto him, Who brought thee hither? and what makest thou in this *place?* and what hast thou here?

4 And he said unto them, Thus and thus dealeth Micah with me, and hath [d]hired me, and I am his priest.

5 And they said unto him, [e]Ask counsel, we pray thee, [f]of God, that we may know whether our way which we go shall be prosperous.

6 And the priest said unto them, [g]Go in peace: before the LORD *is* your way wherein ye go.

7 ¶ Then the five men departed, and came to [h]Laish, and saw the people that *were* therein, [i]how they dwelt careless, after the manner of the Zidonians, quiet and secure; and *there was* no [h]magistrate in the land, that might put *them* to shame in *any* thing; and they *were* far from the Zidonians, and had no business with *any* man.

8 And they came unto their brethren to [j]Zorah and Eshtaol: and their brethren said unto them, What *say* ye?

9 And they said, [k]Arise, that we may go up against them: for we have seen the land, and, behold, it *is* very good: and *are* ye [l]still? be not slothful to go, *and* to enter to possess the land.

10 When ye go, ye shall come unto a people [m]secure, and to a large land: for God hath given it into your hands; [n]a place where *there is* no want of any thing that *is* in the earth.

11 ¶ And there went from thence of the family of the Danites, out of Zorah and out of Eshtaol, six hundred men [i]appointed with weapons of war.

12 And they went up, and pitched in [o]Kirjath-jearim, in Judah: wherefore they called that place [p]Mahaneh-dan unto this day: behold, *it is* behind Kirjath-jearim.

13 And they passed thence unto mount Ephraim, and came unto [q]the house of Micah.

14 ¶ [r]Then answered the five men that went to spy out the country of Laish, and said unto their brethren, Do ye know that [s]there is in these houses an ephod, and teraphim, and a graven image, and a molten image? now therefore consider what ye have to do.

15 And they turned thitherward, and came to the house of the young man the Levite, *even* unto the house of Micah, and [j]saluted him.

16 And the [t]six hundred men appointed with their weapons of war, which *were* of the children of Dan, stood by the entering of the gate.

17 And [u]the five men that went to

17:6 [s]Deut. 12:8 **17:7** [t]See Josh. 19:15 ch. 19:1 Ruth 1:1,2 Mic. 5:2 Mat. 2:1,5,6 **17:10** [u]ch. 18:19 [v]Gen. 45:8 Job 29:16 **17:12** [w]ver. 5 [x]ch. 18:30 **18:1** [y]ch. 17:6 & 21:25 [z]Josh. 19:47 **18:2** [a]ch. 13:25 [b]Num. 13:17 Josh. 2:1 [c]ch. 17:1 **18:4** [d]ch. 17:10 **18:5** [e]1 Ki. 22:5 Is. 30:1 Hos. 4:12 [f]See ch. 17:5 & ver. 14

18:6 [g]1 Ki. 22:6 **18:7** [h]Josh. 19:47 called *Leshem* [i]ver. 27,28 **18:8** [j]ver. 2 **18:9** [k]Num. 13:30 Josh. 2:23,24 [l]1 Ki. 22:3 **18:10** [m]ver. 7,27 [n]Deut. 8:9 **18:12** [o]Josh. 15:60 [p]ch. 13:25 **18:13** [q]ver. 2 **18:14** [r]1 Sam. 14:28 [s]ch. 17:5 **18:16** [t]ver. 11 **18:17** [u]ver. 2,14

[d] Heb. *in making his way* [e] Or, *a double suit* [f] Heb. *an order of garments* [g] Heb. *sons* [h] Heb. *possessor,* or, *heir of restraint* [i] Heb. *girded* [j] Heb. *asked him of peace*

spy out the land went up, *and* came in
thither, *and* took [v]the graven image,
and the ephod, and the teraphim, and
the molten image: and the priest stood
in the entering of the gate with the six
hundred men *that were* appointed with
weapons of war.
18 And these went into Micah's
house, and fetched the carved image,
the ephod, and the teraphim, and the
molten image. Then said the priest
unto them, What do ye?
19 And they said unto him, Hold thy
peace, [w]lay thine hand upon thy
mouth, and go with us, [x]and be to us
a father and a priest: *is it* better for
thee to be a priest unto the house of
one man, or that thou be a priest unto
a tribe and a family in Israel?
20 And the priest's heart was glad,
and he took the ephod, and the tera-
phim, and the graven image, and went
in the midst of the people.
21 So they turned and departed,
and put the little ones and the cattle
and the carriage before them.
22 ¶ *And* when they were a good
way from the house of Micah, the men
that *were* in the houses near to Micah's
house were gathered together, and
overtook the children of Dan.
23 And they cried unto the children
of Dan. And they turned their faces,
and said unto Micah, What aileth thee,
[k]that thou comest with such a com-
pany?
24 And he said, Ye have taken away
my gods which I made, and the priest,
and ye are gone away: and what have
I more? and what *is* this *that* ye say
unto me, What aileth thee?
25 And the children of Dan said
unto him, Let not thy voice be heard
among us, lest [l]angry fellows run
upon thee, and thou lose thy life, with
the lives of thy household.
26 And the children of Dan went
their way: and when Micah saw that
they *were* too strong for him, he turned
and went back unto his house.
27 And they took *the things* which
Micah had made, and the priest which
he had, and came unto Laish, unto a
people *that were* at quiet and secure:
[y]and they smote them with the edge
of the sword, and burnt the city with
fire.
28 And *there was* no deliverer, be-
cause it *was* [z]far from Zidon, and they
had no business with *any* man; and it
was in the valley that *lieth* [a]by Beth-
rehob. And they built a city, and dwelt
therein.
29 And [b]they called the name of
the city [c]Dan, after the name of Dan
their father, who was born unto Israel:
howbeit the name of the city *was* Laish
at the first.
30 ¶ And the children of Dan set up
the graven image: and Jonathan, the
son of Gershom, the son of Manasseh,
he and his sons were priests to the
tribe of Dan [d]until the day of the cap-
tivity of the land.
31 And they set them up Micah's
graven image, which he made, [e]all the
time that the house of God was in Shi-
loh.

The Levite and his concubine

19 AND IT came to pass in those
days, [f]when *there was* no king
in Israel, that there was a certain Le-
vite sojourning on the side of mount
Ephraim, who took to him [m]a concu-
bine out of [g]Bethlehem-judah.
2 And his concubine played the
whore against him, and went away
from him unto her father's house to
Bethlehem-judah, and was there
[n] [o]four whole months.
3 And her husband arose, and went

18:17 [v]ch. 17:4,5 **18:19** [w]Job 21:5 & 29:9 & 40:4 Mic. 7:16 [x]ch. 17:10

18:27 [y]Josh. 19:47 **18:28** [z]ver. 7 [a]Num. 13:21 2 Sam. 10:6 **18:29** [b]Josh. 19:47 [c]Gen. 14:14 ch. 20:1 1 Ki. 12:29,30 & 15:20 **18:30** [d]ch. 13:1 1 Sam. 4:2,3,10, 11 **18:31** [e]Josh. 18:1 ch. 19:18 & 21:12 **19:1** [f]ch. 17:6 & 18:1 & 21:25 [g]ch. 17:7

[k]Heb. *that thou art gathered together?* [l]Heb. *bitter of soul* [m]Heb. *a woman a concubine,* or, *a wife a concubine* [n]Or, *a year and four months* [o]Heb. *days four months*

18:20 THE PRIEST'S HEART WAS GLAD. The prominence given to the priest in chs. 17—18 emphasizes that not only the people, but also the sacred ministry had become corrupt. This priest was willing to serve as priest of other gods solely for money and position (17:12).

19:1 IN THOSE DAYS. The events recorded in ch. 19 reveal how depraved and immoral some in Israel had become after they turned from God. (1) Some Israelites (i.e., the sons of Benjamin) became homosexuals, rapists, and murderers (vv. 22–30). (2) A Levite (i.e., minister of God's word) submitted his wife to rape and death in order to save himself (vv. 1,22,25–30). Hence, both laity and ministers alike fall into the depths of depravity when God and His word are forsaken (cf. Hos. 9:9; 10:9).

19:1 CONCUBINE. In the Bible a concubine was a woman lawfully united in marriage to a man, but in a position inferior to that of a regular wife. Nowhere does the O.T. sanction this polygamous practice (Ex. 21:7–11; Deut. 21:10–14; see Gen. 29:28, note).

after her, to speak [p]friendly unto her, *and* to bring her again, having his servant with him, and a couple of asses: and she brought him into her father's house: and when the father of the damsel saw him, he rejoiced to meet him.

4 And his father-in-law, the damsel's father, retained him; and he abode with him three days: so they did eat and drink, and lodged there.

5 ¶ And it came to pass on the fourth day, when they arose early in the morning, that he rose up to depart: and the damsel's father said unto his son-in-law, [h]Comfort[q] thine heart with a morsel of bread, and afterward go your way.

6 And they sat down, and did eat and drink both of them together: for the damsel's father had said unto the man, Be content, I pray thee, and tarry all night, and let thine heart be merry.

7 And when the man rose up to depart, his father-in-law urged him: therefore he lodged there again.

8 And he arose early in the morning on the fifth day to depart: and the damsel's father said, Comfort thine heart, I pray thee. And they tarried [r]until afternoon, and they did eat both of them.

9 And when the man rose up to depart, he, and his concubine, and his servant, his father-in-law, the damsel's father, said unto him, Behold, now the day [s]draweth toward evening, I pray you tarry all night: behold, [t]the day groweth to an end, lodge here, that thine heart may be merry; and tomorrow get you early on your way, that thou mayest go [u]home.

10 But the man would not tarry that night, but he rose up and departed, and came [v]over against [i]Jebus, which *is* Jerusalem; and *there were* with him two asses saddled, his concubine also *was* with him.

11 *And* when they *were* by Jebus, the day was far spent; and the servant said unto his master, Come, I pray thee, and let us turn in into this city [j]of the Jebusites, and lodge in it.

12 And his master said unto him, We will not turn aside hither into the city of a stranger, that *is* not of the children of Israel; we will pass over [k]to Gibeah.

13 And he said unto his servant, Come, and let us draw near to one of these places to lodge all night, in Gibeah, or in [l]Ramah.

14 And they passed on and went their way; and the sun went down upon them *when they were* by Gibeah, which *belongeth* to Benjamin.

15 And they turned aside thither, to go in *and* to lodge in Gibeah: and when he went in, he sat him down in a street of the city: for *there was* no man that [m]took them into his house to lodging.

16 ¶ And, behold, there came an old man from [n]his work out of the field at even, which *was* also of mount Ephraim; and he sojourned in Gibeah: but the men of the place *were* Benjamites.

17 And when he had lifted up his eyes, he saw a wayfaring man in the street of the city: and the old man said, Whither goest thou? and whence comest thou?

18 And he said unto him, We *are* passing from Bethlehem-judah toward the side of mount Ephraim; from thence *am* I: and I went to Bethlehem-judah, but I *am* *now* going to [o]the house of the LORD; and there *is* no man that receiveth me to house.

19 Yet there is both straw and provender for our asses; and there is bread and wine also for me, and for thy handmaid, and for the young man *which is* with thy servants: *there is* no want of any thing.

20 And the old man said, [p]Peace *be* with thee; howsoever *let* all thy wants *lie* upon me; [q]only lodge not in the street.

21 [r]So he brought him into his house, and gave provender unto the asses: [s]and they washed their feet, and did eat and drink.

22 ¶ *Now* as they were making their

19:5 [h]Gen. 18:5
19:10 [i]Josh. 18:28
19:11 [j]Josh. 15:8,63
19:12 [k]Josh. 18:28
19:13 [l]Josh. 18:25
19:15 [m]Mat. 25:43
19:16 [n]Ps. 104:23
19:18 [o]Josh. 18:1 ch. 18:31 & 20:18 1 Sam. 1:3,7
19:20 [p]Gen 43:23 ch. 6:23 [q]Gen. 19:2
19:21 [r]Gen. 24:32 & 43:24 [s]Gen. 18:4 John 13:5

[p]Heb. *to her heart* [q]Heb. *Strengthen* [r]Heb. *till the day declined* [s]Heb. *is weak* [t]Heb. it is *the pitching* time *of the day* [u]Heb. *to thy tent* [v]Heb. *to over against*

19:22 BRING FORTH THE MAN. One of the greatest examples of corruption and depravity occurred at Gibeah, when those who were once God's people gave themselves over to the lust of homosexuality and rape (cf. Hos. 9:9; 10:9). They had become like the Sodomites (Gen. 19:1–11). Scripture views sodomy and lesbianism as one of the end results of God's rejection of a perverse person or people (see Rom. 1:27, note). If not repented of, homosexuality will lead to "a reprobate mind" (Rom. 1:28) and may produce the kind of brutality described here (19:25).

hearts merry, behold, [t]the men of the city, certain [u]sons of Belial, beset the house round about, *and* beat at the door, and spake to the master of the house, the old man, saying, [v]Bring forth the man that came into thine house, that we may know him.

23 And [w]the man, the master of the house, went out unto them, and said unto them, Nay, my brethren, *nay,* I pray you, do not *so* wickedly; seeing that this man is come into mine house, [x]do not this folly.

24 [y]Behold, *here is* my daughter a maiden, and his concubine; them I will bring out now, and [z]humble ye them, and do with them what seemeth good unto you: but unto this man do not [w]so vile a thing.

25 But the men would not hearken to him: so the man took his concubine, and brought her forth unto them; and they [a]knew her, and abused her all the night until the morning: and when the day began to spring, they let her go.

26 Then came the woman in the dawning of the day, and fell down at the door of the man's house where her lord *was,* till it was light.

27 And her lord rose up in the morning, and opened the doors of the house, and went out to go his way: and, behold, the woman his concubine was fallen down *at* the door of the house, and her hands *were* upon the threshold.

28 And he said unto her, Up, and let us be going. But [b]none answered. Then the man took her *up* upon an ass, and the man rose up, and gat him unto his place.

29 ¶ And when he was come into his house, he took a knife, and laid hold on his concubine, and [c]divided her, *together* with her bones, into twelve pieces, and sent her into all the coasts of Israel.

30 And it was so, that all that saw it said, There was no such deed done nor seen from the day that the children of Israel came up out of the land of Egypt unto this day: consider of it, [d]take advice, and speak *your minds.*

19:22 [t]Gen. 19:4 ch. 20:5 Hos. 9:9 & 10:9 [u]Deut. 13:13 [v]Gen 19:5 Rom. 1:26,27 **19:23** [w]Gen. 19:6,7 [x]2 Sam. 13:12 **19:24** [y]Gen. 19:8 [z]Gen. 34:2 Deut. 21:14 **19:25** [a]Gen. 4:1 **19:28** [b]ch. 20:5 **19:29** [c]ch. 20:6 See 1 Sam. 11:7 **19:30** [d]ch. 20:7

20:1 [e]ver. 11 Josh. 22:12 ch. 21:5 1 Sam. 11:7 [f]ch. 18:29 1 Sam. 3:20 2 Sam. 3:10 & 24:2 [g]Judg. 10:17 & 11:11 1 Sam. 7:5 & 10:17 **20:2** [h]ch. 8:10 **20:4** [i]ch. 19:15 **20:5** [j]ch. 19:22 [k]ch. 19:25,26 **20:6** [l]ch. 19:29 [m]Josh. 7:15 **20:7** [n]ch. 19:30

The rout of Benjamin

20 THEN [e]ALL the children of Israel went out, and the congregation was gathered together as one man, from [f]Dan even to Beer-sheba, with the land of Gilead, unto the LORD [g]in Mizpeh.

2 And the chief of all the people, *even* of all the tribes of Israel, presented themselves in the assembly of the people of God, four hundred thousand footmen [h]that drew sword.

3 (Now the children of Benjamin heard that the children of Israel were gone up to Mizpeh.) Then said the children of Israel, Tell *us,* how was this wickedness?

4 And [x]the Levite, the husband of the woman that was slain, answered and said, [i]I came into Gibeah that *belongeth* to Benjamin, I and my concubine, to lodge.

5 [j]And the men of Gibeah rose against me, and beset the house round about upon me by night, *and* thought to have slain me: [k]and my concubine have they [y]forced, that she is dead.

6 And [l]I took my concubine, and cut her in pieces, and sent her throughout all the country of the inheritance of Israel: for they [m]have committed lewdness and folly in Israel.

7 Behold, ye *are* all children of Israel; [n]give here your advice and counsel.

8 ¶ And all the people arose as one man, saying, We will not any *of us* go to his tent, neither will we any *of us* turn into his house.

9 But now this *shall be* the thing which we will do to Gibeah; *we will go up* by lot against it;

10 And we will take ten men of an hundred throughout all the tribes of Israel, and an hundred of a thousand, and a thousand out of ten thousand, to fetch victual for the people, that they may do, when they come to Gibeah of Benjamin, according to all the folly that they have wrought in Israel.

11 So all the men of Israel were

[w]Heb. *the matter of this folly* [x]Heb. *the man the Levite* [y]Heb. *humbled*

20:1 THE CHILDREN OF ISRAEL WENT OUT. Because the tribes of Israel had failed to enforce God's law or promote righteousness, the result was the horrible sin described in ch. 19 and the refusal of the Benjamites to punish the evildoers (vv. 12–14). Israel as a whole departed from sincere obedience to God's word and the tribe of Benjamin entered into complete apostasy. Civil war broke out, many thousands were killed, and the tribe of Benjamin was almost annihilated.

gathered against the city, [z]knit together as one man.

12 ¶ [o]And the tribes of Israel sent men through all the tribe of Benjamin, saying, What wickedness *is* this that is done among you?

13 Now therefore deliver *us* the men, [p]the children of Belial, which *are* in Gibeah, that we may put them to death, and [q]put away evil from Israel. But the children of Benjamin would not hearken to the voice of their brethren the children of Israel:

14 But the children of Benjamin gathered themselves together out of the cities unto Gibeah, to go out to battle against the children of Israel.

15 And the children of Benjamin were numbered at that time out of the cities twenty and six thousand men that drew sword, beside the inhabitants of Gibeah, which were numbered seven hundred chosen men.

16 Among all this people *there were* seven hundred chosen men [r]lefthanded; every one could sling stones at an hair *breadth,* and not miss.

17 And the men of Israel, beside Benjamin, were numbered four hundred thousand men that drew sword: all these *were* men of war.

18 ¶ And the children of Israel arose, and [s]went up to the house of God, and [t]asked counsel of God, and said, Which of us shall go up first to the battle against the children of Benjamin? And the LORD said, Judah *shall go up* first.

19 And the children of Israel rose up in the morning, and encamped against Gibeah.

20 And the men of Israel went out to battle against Benjamin; and the men of Israel put themselves in array to fight against them at Gibeah.

21 And [u]the children of Benjamin came forth out of Gibeah, and destroyed down to the ground of the Israelites that day twenty and two thousand men.

20:12 [o]Deut. 13:14 Josh. 22:13,16
20:13 [p]Deut. 13:13 ch. 19:22 [q]Deut. 17:12
20:16 [r]ch. 3:15 1 Chr. 12:2
20:18 [s]ver. 23,26 [t]Num. 27:21 ch. 1:1
20:21 [u]Gen. 49:27

20:23 [v]ver. 26,27
20:25 [w]ver. 21
20:26 [x]ver. 18
20:27 [y]Josh. 18:1 1 Sam. 4:3,4
20:28 [z]Josh. 24:33 [a]Deut. 10:8 & 18:5
20:29 [b]See Josh. 8:4

22 And the people the men of Israel encouraged themselves, and set their battle again in array in the place where they put themselves in array the first day.

23 ([v]And the children of Israel went up and wept before the LORD until even, and asked counsel of the LORD, saying, Shall I go up again to battle against the children of Benjamin my brother? And the LORD said, Go up against him.)

24 And the children of Israel came near against the children of Benjamin the second day.

25 And [w]Benjamin went forth against them out of Gibeah the second day, and destroyed down to the ground of the children of Israel again eighteen thousand men; all these drew the sword.

26 ¶ Then all the children of Israel, and all the people, [x]went up, and came unto the house of God, and wept, and sat there before the LORD, and fasted that day until even, and offered burnt offerings and peace offerings before the LORD.

27 And the children of Israel inquired of the LORD, (for [y]the ark of the covenant of God *was* there in those days,

28 [z]And Phinehas, the son of Eleazar, the son of Aaron, [a]stood before it in those days,) saying, Shall I yet again go out to battle against the children of Benjamin my brother, or shall I cease? And the LORD said, Go up; for tomorrow I will deliver them into thine hand.

29 And Israel [b]set liers in wait round about Gibeah.

30 And the children of Israel went up against the children of Benjamin on the third day, and put themselves in array against Gibeah, as at other times.

31 And the children of Benjamin

z Heb. *fellows*

20:13 BENJAMIN WOULD NOT HEARKEN. The tribe of Benjamin sympathized more with the evil individuals in their midst than with the innocent victim who had undergone such cruelty (19:25). (1) By refusing to punish these evil members of their group, the entire tribe demonstrated (a) that they did not value justice, and (b) that they had lost all moral sensitivity and loyalty to God's law. Because of this, God punished the whole tribe of Benjamin (cf. vv. 18,35,48).

(2) A parallel to this situation exists today under the new covenant when churches refuse to discipline or expel sinning members. The toleration of sin and immorality (i.e., an attitude that does not want to apply Biblical discipline) indicates the loss of moral sensitivity and loyalty to God and His Word by the congregation itself. God's judgment upon such a congregation is certain (see Mat. 13:30, note; 18:15, note; 1 Cor. 5:1, notes).

went out against the people, *and* were drawn away from the city; and they began [a]to smite of the people, *and* kill, as at other times, in the highways, of which one goeth up to [b]the house of God, and the other to Gibeah in the field, about thirty men of Israel.

32 And the children of Benjamin said, They *are* smitten down before us, as at the first. But the children of Israel said, Let us flee, and draw them from the city unto the highways.

33 And all the men of Israel rose up out of their place, and put themselves in array at Baal-tamar: and the liers in wait of Israel came forth out of their places, *even* out of the meadows of Gibeah.

34 And there came against Gibeah ten thousand chosen men out of all Israel, and the battle was sore: [c]but they knew not that evil *was* near them.

35 And the LORD smote Benjamin before Israel: and the children of Israel destroyed of the Benjamites that day twenty and five thousand and an hundred men: all these drew the sword.

36 So the children of Benjamin saw that they were smitten: [d]for the men of Israel gave place to the Benjamites, because they trusted unto the liers in wait which they had set beside Gibeah.

37 [e]And the liers in wait hasted, and rushed upon Gibeah; and the liers in wait [c]drew *themselves* along, and smote all the city with the edge of the sword.

38 Now there was an appointed [d]sign between the men of Israel [e]and the liers in wait, that they should make a great [f]flame with smoke rise up out of the city.

39 And when the men of Israel retired in the battle, Benjamin began [g]to smite *and* kill of the men of Israel about thirty persons: for they said, Surely they are smitten down before us, as *in* the first battle.

40 But when the flame began to arise up out of the city with a pillar of smoke, the Benjamites [f]looked behind them, and, behold, [h]the flame of the city ascended up to heaven.

41 And when the men of Israel turned again, the men of Benjamin were amazed: for they saw that evil [i]was come upon them.

42 Therefore they turned *their backs* before the men of Israel unto the way of the wilderness; but the battle overtook them; and them which *came* out of the cities they destroyed in the midst of them.

43 *Thus* they inclosed the Benjamites round about, *and* chased them, *and* trode them down [j]with ease [k]over against Gibeah toward the sunrising.

44 And there fell of Benjamin eighteen thousand men; all these *were* men of valour.

45 And they turned and fled toward the wilderness unto the rock of [g]Rimmon: and they gleaned of them in the highways five thousand men; and pursued hard after them unto Gidom, and slew two thousand men of them.

46 So that all which fell that day of Benjamin were twenty and five thousand men that drew the sword; all these *were* men of valour.

47 [h]But six hundred men turned and fled to the wilderness unto the rock Rimmon, and abode in the rock Rimmon four months.

48 And the men of Israel turned again upon the children of Benjamin, and smote them with the edge of the sword, as well the men of *every* city, as the beast, and all that [l]came to hand: also they set on fire all the cities that [m]they came to.

Wives for the Benjaminites

21 NOW [i]THE men of Israel had sworn in Mizpeh, saying, There shall not any of us give his daughter unto Benjamin to wife.

2 And the people came [j]to the house of God, and abode there till even before God, and lifted up their voices, and wept sore;

3 And said, O LORD God of Israel, why is this come to pass in Israel, that there should be today one tribe lacking in Israel?

4 And it came to pass on the morrow, that the people rose early, and

20:34 [c]Josh. 8:14 Is. 47:11
20:36 [d]Josh. 8:15
20:37 [e]Josh. 8:19
20:40 [f]Josh. 8:20
20:45 [g]Josh. 15:32
20:47 [h]ch. 21:13
21:1 [i]ch. 20:1
21:2 [j]ch. 20:18,26

[a] Heb. *to smite of the people wounded as at* [b] Or, *Beth-el* [c] Or, *made a long* sound with the trumpet [d] Or, *time* [e] Heb. *with* [f] Heb. *elevation* [g] Heb. *to smite the wounded* [h] Heb. *the whole consumption* [i] Heb. *touched them* [j] Or, from *Menuchah* [k] Heb. *unto over against* [l] Heb. *was found* [m] Heb. *were found*

[k]built there an altar, and offered burnt offerings and peace offerings.

5 And the children of Israel said, Who *is there* among all the tribes of Israel that came not up with the congregation unto the LORD? [l]For they had made a great oath concerning him that came not up to the LORD to Mizpeh, saying, He shall surely be put to death.

6 And the children of Israel repented them for Benjamin their brother, and said, There is one tribe cut off from Israel this day.

7 How shall we do for wives for them that remain, seeing we have sworn by the LORD that we will not give them of our daughters to wives?

8 ¶ And they said, What one *is there* of the tribes of Israel that came not up to Mizpeh to the LORD? And, behold, there came none to the camp from [m]Jabesh-gilead to the assembly.

9 For the people were numbered, and, behold, *there were* none of the inhabitants of Jabesh-gilead there.

10 And the congregation sent thither twelve thousand men of the valiantest, and commanded them, saying, [n]Go and smite the inhabitants of Jabesh-gilead with the edge of the sword, with the women and the children.

11 And this *is* the thing that ye shall do, [o]Ye shall utterly destroy every male, and every woman that [n]hath lain by man.

12 And they found among the inhabitants of Jabesh-gilead four hundred [o]young virgins, that had known no man by lying with any male: and they brought them unto the camp to [p]Shiloh, which *is* in the land of Canaan.

13 And the whole congregation sent *some* [p]to speak to the children of Benjamin [q]that *were* in the rock Rimmon, and to [r]call[q] peaceably unto them.

14 And Benjamin came again at that time; and they gave them wives which they had saved alive of the women of Jabesh-gilead: and yet so they sufficed them not.

21:4 [k]2 Sam. 24:25
21:5 [l]ch. 5:23
21:8 [m]1 Sam 11:1 & 31:11
21:10 [n]ver. 5 ch. 5:23 1 Sam. 11:7
21:11 [o]Num. 31:17
21:12 [p]Josh. 18:1
21:13 [q]ch. 20:47 [r]Deut. 20:10

15 And the people [s]repented them for Benjamin, because that the LORD had made a breach in the tribes of Israel.

16 ¶ Then the elders of the congregation said, How shall we do for wives for them that remain, seeing the women are destroyed out of Benjamin?

17 And they said, *There must be* an inheritance for them that be escaped of Benjamin, that a tribe be not destroyed out of Israel.

18 Howbeit we may not give them wives of our daughters: [t]for the children of Israel have sworn, saying, Cursed *be* he that giveth a wife to Benjamin.

19 Then they said, Behold, *there is* a feast of the LORD in Shiloh [r]yearly *in a place* which *is* on the north side of Beth-el, [s]on the east side [t]of the highway that goeth up from Beth-el to Shechem, and on the south of Lebonah.

20 Therefore they commanded the children of Benjamin, saying, Go and lie in wait in the vineyards;

21 And see, and, behold, if the daughters of Shiloh come out [u]to dance in dances, then come ye out of the vineyards, and catch you every man his wife of the daughters of Shiloh, and go to the land of Benjamin.

22 And it shall be, when their fathers or their brethren come unto us to complain, that we will say unto them, [u]Be favourable unto them for our sakes: because we reserved not to each man his wife in the war: for ye did not give unto them at this time, *that* ye should be guilty.

23 And the children of Benjamin did so, and took *them* wives, according to their number, of them that danced, whom they caught: and they went and returned unto their inheritance, and

21:15 [s]ver. 6
21:18 [t]ver. 1 ch. 11:35
21:21 [u]See Ex. 15:20 ch. 11:34 1 Sam. 18:6

[n] Heb. *knoweth the lying* with *man* [o] Heb. *young women virgins* [p] Heb. *and spake and called* [q] Or, *proclaim peace* [r] Heb. *from year to year* [s] Or, *toward the sunrising* [t] Or, *on* [u] Or, *Gratify us in them*

21:7 FOR THEM THAT REMAIN. Only 600 Benjamites survived the war (see 20:47).

21:10 SMITE THE INHABITANTS OF JABESH-GILEAD. Most of the Israelites in Jabesh-gilead were killed because they refused to join with Israel in the war against the Benjamites. Their sin was seen in not standing with God and His people against the heinous sin committed by some of their brethren (19:22–25).

[v]repaired the cities, and dwelt in
them.
24 And the children of Israel de-
parted thence at that time, every man
to his tribe and to his family, and they
went out from thence every man to his
inheritance.
25 [w]In those days *there was* no king
in Israel: [x]every man did *that which*
was right in his own eyes.

21:23 [v]See ch. 20:48
21:25 [w]ch. 17:6 & 18:1
21:25 [x]Deut. 12:8 ch. 17:6

21:25 EVERY MAN DID *THAT WHICH WAS* RIGHT IN HIS OWN EYES. The book of Judges ends by emphasizing that during the time of the judges, the Israelites ignored God's standards for them and did what was right in their own judgment. But as Proverbs points out, human thoughts and opinions are a poor judgment of what is right (Prov. 14:12; 16:25). To make our opinions rather than God's Word the guide for our lives is nothing less than rebellion against Him. Nehemiah writes concerning this: "They were disobedient, and rebelled against thee, and cast thy law behind their backs.... Nevertheless for thy great mercies' sake thou didst not utterly consume them, nor forsake them; for thou *art* a gracious and merciful God" (Neh. 9:26,31).

RUTH

Outline

I. Naomi's Adversity (1:1–5)
II. Naomi and Ruth (1:6–22)
  A. Naomi's Decision to Leave Moab (1:6–13)
  B. Ruth's Steadfast Love (1:14–18)
  C. Naomi and Ruth Go to Bethlehem (1:19–22)
III. Ruth Meets Boaz in the Harvest Field (2:1–23)
  A. God's Providence in Ruth's Decision (2:1–3)
  B. God's Provision through Ruth's Decision (2:4–16)
  C. Ruth Shares with Naomi (2:17–23)
IV. Ruth and Boaz at the Threshing Floor (3:1–18)
  A. Naomi's Instruction about Boaz (3:1–5)
  B. Ruth's Kinsman-Redeemer Request to Boaz (3:6–9)
  C. Boaz's Response to Ruth (3:10–18)
V. Boaz Marries Ruth (4:1–13)
  A. The Kinsman-Redeemer Agreement (4:1–12)
  B. Marriage and a Son (4:13)
VI. Naomi's Fulfillment (4:14–17)
VII. Genealogy: Perez to David (4:18–22)

Author: Anonymous

Theme: Redeeming Love

Date of Writing: 10th century B.C.

Background

Historically, the book of Ruth describes events in the life of an Israelite family during the time of the judges (1:1; c. 1375–1050 B.C.). Geographically, the setting for the first eighteen verses is the land of Moab (east of the Dead Sea). The remainder of the book is located in or near Bethlehem of Judah. Liturgically, the book of Ruth became one of the five scrolls of the third part of the Hebrew Bible, the *Hagiographa* ("Holy Writings"), each one of which was read publicly at one of the annual Jewish feasts. Since the central drama of Ruth occurred at harvest time, the book was customarily read at the Harvest Feast (Pentecost).

Inasmuch as the book traces Ruth's descendants no further than King David (4:21–22), it was most likely written during David's reign. The book's author is nowhere identified in Scripture, though Jewish tradition (e.g., the Talmud) attributes authorship to Samuel.

Purpose

Ruth was written to describe how through self-giving love and the righteous fulfillment of God's law a virtuous and devout young Moabite woman became the great-grandmother of Israel's King David. The book was also written to preserve an admirable story from the time of the judges about a godly family whose faithfulness in hardship stood in sharp contrast to the general spiritual and moral decline in Israel at that time (see the introduction to Judges).

Survey

This story of redeeming love opens with Elimelech leaving Judah and relocating his family in Moab because of famine (1:1–2). Adversity continued to follow Elimelech as he and his two sons died in Moab (1:3–5), leaving their wives widows. Four main episodes then follow. (1) Naomi (Elimelech's widow) and her devout Moabite daughter-in-law, Ruth, returned to Bethlehem in Judah (1:6–22). (2) In God's providence Ruth met Boaz, a wealthy kinsman of Elimelech (ch. 2). (3) Prompted by Naomi, Ruth conveyed to Boaz her interest in the possibility of marriage according to the kinsman-redeemer law (ch. 3). (4) As a kinsman-redeemer, Boaz bought Naomi's property and married Ruth, and they bore a son named Obed—the grandfather of David (ch. 4). Whereas the book opens with bleak adversity, it concludes with glorious fulfillment—for Naomi, Ruth, Boaz, and Israel.

Special Features

Six major features or emphases characterize the book of Ruth. (1) It is one of two books in the Bible named after a woman (the other one being Esther). (2) Written against the dark backdrop of Israel's unfaithfulness and apostasy during the period of the judges, this book describes the joys and sorrows of a godly family at Bethlehem during those chaotic times. (3) It illustrates that God's plan of redemption included Gentiles who, during O.T. times, were grafted into the commonwealth of Israel upon repentance and faith in the Lord. (4) Redemption is a central theme throughout the book, with the kinsman-redeemer role of Boaz being one of the clearest O.T. illustrations or types of the mediatorial ministry of Jesus Christ. (5) The most recognized verse in the book is Ruth's words to Naomi while still in Moab: "whither thou goest, I will go; and where thou lodgest, I will lodge: thy people *shall be* my people, and thy God my God" (1:16). (6) It gives a realistic portrait of life with its struggles and tragedies, yet describes how the faith and faithfulness of godly people enabled God to turn tragedy into triumph and defeat into redemption.

New Testament Fulfillment

Four N.T. truths are illustrated in the book. (1) Human adversity becomes God's opportunity for advancing His great redemptive purposes (cf. Phil. 1:12). (2) Ruth's inclusion in redemption demonstrates that participation in God's kingdom is not by physical descent, but by conforming one's life to God's will through the "obedience of faith" (Rom. 16:26; cf. Rom. 1:5). (3) Ruth's place in the ancestry of David and Jesus (see Mat. 1:5) signifies that people of all nations will be represented in the kingdom of the great "Son of David" (Rev. 5:9; 7:9). (4) Boaz as the kinsman-redeemer is a type of the great Redeemer, Jesus Christ (Mat. 20:28; see Ruth 4:10, note).

Reading Ruth

In order to read the entire Old Testament in one year, the book of Ruth should be read in 1 day: ☐ Ruth

NOTES

Naomi and Ruth

1 NOW IT came to pass in the days when [a]the judges [a]ruled, that there was [b]a famine in the land. And a certain man of [c]Bethlehem-judah went to sojourn in the country of Moab, he, and his wife, and his two sons.

2 And the name of the man *was* Elimelech, and the name of his wife Naomi, and the name of his two sons Mahlon and Chilion, [d]Ephrathites of Bethlehem-judah. And they came [e]into the country of Moab, and [b]continued there.

3 And Elimelech Naomi's husband died; and she was left, and her two sons.

4 And they took them wives of the women of Moab; the name of the one *was* Orpah, and the name of the other Ruth: and they dwelled there about ten years.

5 And Mahlon and Chilion died also both of them; and the woman was left of her two sons and her husband.

6 ¶ Then she arose with her daughters-in-law, that she might return from the country of Moab: for she had heard in the country of Moab how that the LORD had [f]visited his people in [g]giving them bread.

7 Wherefore she went forth out of the place where she was, and her two daughters-in-law with her; and they went on the way to return unto the land of Judah.

8 And Naomi said unto her two daughters-in-law, [h]Go, return each to her mother's house: [i]the LORD deal kindly with you, as ye have dealt with [j]the dead, and with me.

9 The LORD grant you that ye may find [k]rest, each *of you* in the house of her husband. Then she kissed them; and they lifted up their voice, and wept.

10 And they said unto her, Surely we will return with thee unto thy people.

11 And Naomi said, Turn again, my daughters: why will ye go with me? *are* there yet *any more* sons in my womb, [l]that they may be your husbands?

12 Turn again, my daughters, go *your way;* for I am too old to have an husband. If I should say, I have hope, [c]*if* I should have an husband also tonight, and should also bear sons;

13 Would ye [d]tarry for them till they were grown? would ye stay for them from having husbands? nay, my daughters; for [e]it grieveth me much for your sakes that [m]the hand of the LORD is gone out against me.

14 And they lifted up their voice, and wept again: and Orpah kissed her mother-in-law; but Ruth [n]clave unto her.

15 And she said, Behold, thy sister-in-law is gone back unto her people, and unto [o]her gods: [p]return thou after thy sister-in-law.

1:1 [a]Judg. 2:16 [b]Gen. 12:10 & 26:1 2 Ki. 8:1 [c]Judg. 17:8
1:2 [d]Gen. 35:19 [e]Judg. 3:30
1:6 [f]Ex. 4:31 Luke 1:68 [g]Mat. 6:11
1:8 [h]See Josh. 24:15 [i]2 Tim. 1:16-18 [j]ver. 5 ch. 2:20
1:9 [k]ch. 3:1.
1:11 [l]Gen. 38:11 Deut. 25:5
1:13 [m]Judg. 2:15 Job 19:21
1:14 [n]Prov. 17:17 & 18:24
1:15 [o]Judg. 11:24 [p]See Josh. 24:15, 19 2 Ki. 2:2 Luke 24:28

[a] Heb. *judged* [b] Heb. *were* [c] Or, if *I were with an husband* [d] Heb. *hope* [e] Heb. *I have much bitterness*

1:1 WHEN THE JUDGES RULED. The story of Ruth takes place during the time of the judges. It reveals that during the pathetic moral and spiritual apostasy of that time (cf. Judg. 17:6, note; 21:25, note), there was a godly remnant who continued to love and honor God. The book emphasizes that God is active in the lives of those who remain faithful to Him and His word (see 2:12, note).

1:3 NAOMI'S HUSBAND DIED. Naomi, although a faithful follower of the Lord, experienced great adversity. (1) She and her family suffered the effects of famine and were displaced from their home (v. 1). Furthermore, she lost her husband (v. 3) and her two sons. It appears that the Lord had forsaken her and even turned against her (cf. vv. 13,21). (2) However, the story shows that God continued to be concerned for her, working through others to help her in her time of need. Like Naomi, believers may be faithful and loyal to Christ, yet experience great adversity in their lives. This does not mean that God has forsaken them or is punishing them. Scripture repeatedly emphasizes that God lovingly continues to cause all things to work for our good in times of trouble (see Rom. 8:28,36, notes).

1:12 MY DAUGHTERS, GO *YOUR WAY.* Although it would likely mean loneliness for Naomi, she urged her two daughters-in-law to remain in their own homeland. She believed that they would have no opportunity for remarriage and happiness with her. The book emphasizes the selfless devotion and love that existed between Naomi and Ruth and teaches us that true piety always includes loving care and personal sacrifice for members of our own families (see Eph. 5:21—6:4, notes).

1:13 THE HAND OF THE LORD IS GONE OUT AGAINST ME. Naomi believed that her adversity demonstrated that she no longer had God's favor, but that He was against her (vv. 13,20–21). This personal viewpoint turned out to be erroneous (2:20; 4:14–15). We must not consider all adversity and hardship to be the result of God's actions or displeasure with us, for Satan and ordinary human experiences will at times inflict difficulties and hardships on us irrespective of our dedication to the Lord (see Luke 13:11, note).

16 And Ruth said, [q]Entreat[f] me
not to leave thee, *or* to return from fol-
lowing after thee: for whither thou go-
est, I will go; and where thou lodgest,
I will lodge: [r]thy people *shall be* my
people, and thy God my God:
17 Where thou diest, will I die, and
there will I be buried: [s]the LORD do so
to me, and more also, *if aught* but death
part thee and me.
18 [t]When she saw that she [g]was
stedfastly minded to go with her, then
she left speaking unto her.
19 ¶ So they two went until they
came to Bethlehem. And it came to
pass, when they were come to Bethle-
hem, that [u]all the city was moved
about them, and they said, [v]*Is* this Na-
omi?
20 And she said unto them, Call me
not [h]Naomi, call me [i]Mara: for the
Almighty hath dealt very bitterly
with me.
21 I went out full, [w]and the LORD
hath brought me home again empty:
why *then* call ye me Naomi, seeing the
LORD hath testified against me, and the
Almighty hath afflicted me?
22 So Naomi returned, and Ruth the
Moabitess, her daughter-in-law, with
her, which returned out of the country
of Moab: and they came to Bethlehem
[x]in the beginning of barley harvest.

Boaz speaks with Ruth

2 AND NAOMI had a [y]kinsman of
her husband's, a mighty man of
wealth, of the family of Elimelech; and
his name *was* [z]Boaz.[j]
2 And Ruth the Moabitess said unto
Naomi, Let me now go to the field, and
[a]glean ears of corn after *him* in whose
sight I shall find grace. And she said
unto her, Go, my daughter.
3 And she went, and came, and
gleaned in the field after the reapers:
and her [k]hap was to light on a part of
the field *belonging* unto Boaz, who *was*
of the kindred of Elimelech.
4 ¶ And, behold, Boaz came from
Bethlehem, and said unto the reapers,
[b]The LORD *be* with you. And they an-
swered him, The LORD bless thee.
5 Then said Boaz unto his servant
that was set over the reapers, Whose
damsel *is* this?
6 And the servant that was set over
the reapers answered and said, It *is* the
Moabitish damsel [c]that came back
with Naomi out of the country of Moab:
7 And she said, I pray you, let me
glean and gather after the reapers
among the sheaves: so she came, and
hath continued even from the morning
until now, that she tarried a little in the
house.
8 Then said Boaz unto Ruth, Hear-
est thou not, my daughter? Go not to
glean in another field, neither go from
hence, but abide here fast by my maid-
ens:
9 *Let* thine eyes *be* on the field that
they do reap, and go thou after them:
have I not charged the young men that
they shall not touch thee? and when
thou art athirst, go unto the vessels,
and drink of *that* which the young men
have drawn.
10 Then she [d]fell on her face, and
bowed herself to the ground, and said
unto him, Why have I found grace in
thine eyes, that thou shouldest take
knowledge of me, seeing I *am* a
stranger?
11 And Boaz answered and said
unto her, It hath fully been shown me,
[e]all that thou hast done unto thy
mother-in-law since the death of thine
husband: and *how* thou hast left thy fa-
ther and thy mother, and the land of
thy nativity, and art come unto a peo-
ple which thou knewest not heretofore.
12 [f]The LORD recompense thy
work, and a full reward be given thee

1:16 [q]2 Ki. 2:2,4,6 [r]ch. 2:11,12
1:17 [s]1 Sam. 3:17 & 25:22 2 Sam. 19:13 2 Ki. 6:31
1:18 [t]Acts 21:14
1:19 [u]Mat. 21:10 [v]See Is. 23:7 Lam. 2:15
1:21 [w]Job 1:21
1:22 [x]Ex. 9:31,32 ch. 2:23 2 Sam. 21:9
2:1 [y]ch. 3:2,12 [z]ch. 4:21
2:2 [a]Lev. 19:9 Deut. 24:19
2:4 [b]Luke 1:28 2 Thes. 3:16
2:6 [c]ch. 1:22
2:10 [d]1 Sam. 25:23
2:11 [e]ch. 1:14,16,17
2:12 [f]1 Sam. 24:19

[f] Or, *Be not against me* [g] Heb. *strengthened herself* [h] i.e. *Pleasant* [i] i.e. *Bitter* [j] Called *Booz* in Mat. 1:5 [k] Heb. *hap happened*

1:16 THY GOD MY GOD. Naomi had evidently imparted to Ruth her faith in the Lord God by example and teaching (cf. Deut. 11:18–19). Ruth's faith in God caused her to remain faithful in her love for Naomi. Ruth illustrates the divine principle that "he that loseth his life for my sake shall find it" (Mat. 10:39; cf. Ruth 4:13–17).

2:2 GLEAN EARS OF CORN. In the law of Moses, God had commanded Israel to permit the poor and needy to gather the grain left in the fields after harvest (Lev. 19:9; 23:22; Deut. 24:19). God wants those who have enough to share with those in need (cf. 2 Cor. 8:13–15; see article on THE CARE OF THE POOR AND NEEDY, p. 1312).

2:4 BOAZ. Boaz's prayerful greetings and his care for Ruth and Naomi (vv. 8–12) show him to be a righteous believer in the Lord.

2:12 THE LORD . . . UNDER WHOSE WINGS THOU ART COME TO TRUST. This is the key verse in the book of Ruth. Even in the midst of great apostasy during the period of the judges, God watched over those who sought Him in sin-

of the LORD God of Israel, [g]under whose wings thou art come to trust.

13 Then she said, [h]Let[1] me find favour in thy sight, my lord; for that thou hast comforted me, and for that thou hast spoken [m]friendly unto thine handmaid, [i]though I be not like unto one of thine handmaidens.

14 And Boaz said unto her, At mealtime come thou hither, and eat of the bread, and dip thy morsel in the vinegar. And she sat beside the reapers: and he reached her parched *corn,* and she did eat, and [j]was sufficed, and left.

15 And when she was risen up to glean, Boaz commanded his young men, saying, Let her glean even among the sheaves, and [n]reproach her not:

16 And let fall also *some* of the handfuls of purpose for her, and leave *them,* that she may glean *them,* and rebuke her not.

17 So she gleaned in the field until even, and beat out that she had gleaned: and it was about an ephah of barley.

18 ¶ And she took *it* up, and went into the city: and her mother-in-law saw what she had gleaned: and she brought forth, and gave to her [k]that she had reserved after she was sufficed.

19 And her mother-in-law said unto her, Where hast thou gleaned today? and where wroughtest thou? blessed be he that did [l]take knowledge of thee. And she showed her mother-in-law with whom she had wrought, and said, The man's name with whom I wrought today *is* Boaz.

20 And Naomi said unto her daughter-in-law, [m]Blessed *be* he of the LORD, who [n]hath not left off his kindness to the living and to the dead. And Naomi said unto her, The man *is* near of kin unto us, [o]one[o] of our next kinsmen.

21 And Ruth the Moabitess said, He said unto me also, Thou shalt keep fast by my young men, until they have ended all my harvest.

22 And Naomi said unto Ruth her daughter-in-law, *It is* good, my daughter, that thou go out with his maidens, that they [p]meet thee not in any other field.

23 So she kept fast by the maidens of Boaz to glean unto the end of barley harvest and of wheat harvest; and dwelt with her mother-in-law.

Ruth visits Boaz

3 THEN NAOMI her mother-in-law said unto her, My daughter, [p]shall I not seek [q]rest for thee, that it may be well with thee?

2 And now *is* not Boaz of our kindred, [r]with whose maidens thou wast? Behold, he winnoweth barley tonight in the threshingfloor.

3 Wash thyself therefore, [s]and anoint thee, and put thy raiment upon thee, and get thee down to the floor: *but* make not thyself known unto the man, until he shall have done eating and drinking.

4 And it shall be, when he lieth down, that thou shalt mark the place where he shall lie, and thou shalt go in, and [q]uncover his feet, and lay thee down; and he will tell thee what thou shalt do.

5 And she said unto her, All that thou sayest unto me I will do.

6 ¶ And she went down unto the

2:12 [g]ch. 1:16 Ps. 17:8
2:13 [h]Gen. 33:15 1 Sam. 1:18 [i]1 Sam. 25:41
2:14 [j]ver. 18
2:18 [k]ver. 14
2:19 [l]ver. 10 Ps. 41:1
2:20 [m]ch. 3:10 2 Sam. 2:5 Job 29:13 [n]Prov. 17:17 [o]ch. 3:9 & 4:6
3:1 [p]1 Cor. 7:36 1 Tim. 5:8 [q]ch. 1:9
3:2 [r]ch. 2:8
3:3 [s]2 Sam. 14:2

[1] Or, *I find favour* [m] Heb. *to the heart* [n] Heb. *shame her not* [o] Or, *one that hath right to redeem* [p] Or, *fall upon thee* [q] Or, *lift up the clothes that are on his feet*

cere trust and committed faith (cf. Ps. 17:8; 36:7; 63:7). The story of Ruth is about God's providence and provision in the lives of all those who trust in Him and follow His ways. As Abraham responded to the Lord's call in faith, so Ruth's trust in the Lord caused her to leave her country and kindred in order to follow His redemptive purpose (cf. Gen. 12:1–4).

2:20 THE LORD, WHO HATH NOT LEFT OFF HIS KINDNESS. Naomi began to understand that God had not forsaken her and that His love and kindness toward her were indeed continuing. Her attitude changed from her earlier perception that God had turned against her (see 1:13, note).

2:20 ONE OF OUR NEXT KINSMEN. Boaz, as a close relative of Naomi and Ruth, was required by the law of Moses to provide for the needs of his relatives (cf. Lev. 25:25–28,47–49; Deut. 25:5–10). Boaz fulfilled this obligation by marrying Ruth and purchasing the land of her former husband's father (cf. 2:20—4:14).

3:4 UNCOVER HIS FEET, AND LAY THEE DOWN. Ruth's lying down at Boaz's feet must be viewed in the light of the customs of that day. It was done discreetly and without sexual connotations. As Boaz remained at the threshing floor during the night to protect his crop, Ruth went there and by her action conveyed to Boaz her desire for him to marry her as her deceased husband's next of kin (i.e., as the kinsman-redeemer, see vv. 6–9).

floor, and did according to all that her mother-in-law bade her.

7 And when Boaz had eaten and drunk, and [t]his heart was merry, he went to lie down at the end of the heap of corn: and she came softly, and uncovered his feet, and laid her down.

8 ¶ And it came to pass at midnight, that the man was afraid, and [r]turned himself: and, behold, a woman lay at his feet.

9 And he said, Who *art* thou? And she answered, I *am* Ruth thine handmaid: [u]spread therefore thy skirt over thine handmaid; for thou *art* [v]a[s] near kinsman.

10 And he said, [w]Blessed *be* thou of the LORD, my daughter: *for* thou hast shown more kindness in the latter end than [x]at the beginning, inasmuch as thou followedst not young men, whether poor or rich.

11 And now, my daughter, fear not; I will do to thee all that thou requirest: for all the [t]city of my people doth know that thou *art* [y]a virtuous woman.

Sam. :1-7

12 And now it is true that I *am thy* [z]near kinsman: howbeit [a]there is a kinsman nearer than I.

13 Tarry this night, and it shall be in the morning, *that* if he will [b]perform unto thee the part of a kinsman, well; let him do the kinsman's part: but if he will not do the part of a kinsman to thee, then will I do the part of a kinsman to thee, [c]*as* the LORD liveth: lie down until the morning.

14 ¶ And she lay at his feet until the morning: and she rose up before one could know another. And he said, [d]Let it not be known that a woman came into the floor.

15 Also he said, Bring the [u]veil that *thou hast* upon thee, and hold it. And when she held it, he measured six *measures* of barley, and laid *it* on her: and she went into the city.

16 And when she came to her mother-in-law, she said, Who *art* thou, my daughter? And she told her all that the man had done to her.

17 And she said, These six *measures* of barley gave he me; for he said to me, Go not empty unto thy mother-in-law.

3:7 [t]Judg. 19:6,9,22 2 Sam. 13:28 Esth. 1:10
3:9 [u]Ezek. 16:8 [v]ver. 12 ch. 2:20
3:10 [w]ch. 2:20 [x]ch. 1:8
3:11 [y]Prov. 12:4
3:12 [z]ver. 9 [a]ch. 4:1
3:13 [b]Deut. 25:5 ch. 4:5 Mat. 22:24 [c]Judg. 8:19 Jer. 4:2
3:14 [d]Rom. 12:17 & 14:16 1 Cor. 10:32 2 Cor. 8:21 1 Thes. 5:22
3:18 [e]Ps. 37:3,5
4:1 [f]ch. 3:12
4:2 [g]1 Ki. 21:8 Prov. 31:23
4:4 [h]Jer. 32:7,8 [i]Gen. 23:18 [j]Lev. 25:25
4:5 [k]Gen. 38:8 Deut. 25:5,6 ch. 3:13 Mat. 22:24
4:6 [l]ch. 3:12,13
4:7 [m]Deut. 25:7,9

18 Then said she, [e]Sit still, my daughter, until thou know how the matter will fall: for the man will not be in rest, until he have finished the thing this day.

Boaz and Ruth marry

4 THEN WENT Boaz up to the gate, and sat him down there: and, behold, [f]the kinsman of whom Boaz spake came by; unto whom he said, Ho, such a one! turn aside, sit down here. And he turned aside, and sat down.

2 And he took ten men of [g]the elders of the city, and said, Sit ye down here. And they sat down.

3 And he said unto the kinsman, Naomi, that is come again out of the country of Moab, selleth a parcel of land, which *was* our brother Elimelech's:

4 And [v]I thought to advertise thee, saying, [h]Buy *it* [i]before the inhabitants, and before the elders of my people. If thou wilt redeem *it*, redeem *it*: but if thou wilt not redeem *it, then* tell me, that I may know: [j]for *there is* none to redeem *it* beside thee; and I *am* after thee. And he said, I will redeem *it*.

5 Then said Boaz, What day thou buyest the field of the hand of Naomi, thou must buy *it* also of Ruth the Moabitess, the wife of the dead, [k]to raise up the name of the dead upon his inheritance.

6 ¶ [l]And the kinsman said, I cannot redeem *it* for myself, lest I mar mine own inheritance: redeem thou my right to thyself; for I cannot redeem *it*.

7 [m]Now this *was the manner* in former time in Israel concerning redeeming and concerning changing, for to confirm all things; a man plucked off his shoe, and gave *it* to his neighbour: and this *was* a testimony in Israel.

8 Therefore the kinsman said unto Boaz, Buy *it* for thee. So he drew off his shoe.

9 ¶ And Boaz said unto the elders, and *unto* all the people, Ye *are* witnesses this day, that I have bought all that *was* Elimelech's, and all that *was*

[r] Or, *took hold on* [s] Or, *one that hath right to redeem* [t] Heb. *gate* [u] Or, *sheet,* or *apron* [v] Heb. *I said I will reveal* in *thine ear*

3:9 THY SKIRT OVER THINE HANDMAID. By this gesture, Ruth was asking Boaz to take her for his wife (see also Ezek. 16:8). The covering symbolizes protection, care, and support.

3:12 A KINSMAN NEARER THAN I. The nearest relative had the first right to marry Ruth and also inherit the family land. Only if he refused was Boaz free to marry Ruth (see 4:1–6).

Chilion's and Mahlon's, of the hand of Naomi.

10 Moreover Ruth the Moabitess, the wife of Mahlon, have I purchased to be my wife, to raise up the name of the dead upon his inheritance, [n]that the name of the dead be not cut off from among his brethren, and from the gate of his place: ye *are* witnesses this day.

11 And all the people that *were* in the gate, and the elders, said, *We are* witnesses. [o]The LORD make the woman that is come into thine house like Rachel and like Leah, which two did [p]build the house of Israel: and [w]do thou worthily in [q]Ephratah, and [x]be famous in Bethlehem:

12 And let thy house be like the house of Pharez, [r]whom Tamar bare unto Judah, of [s]the seed which the LORD shall give thee of this young woman.

Obed is born: the Davidic line

4:18–22pp — 1 Chr. 2:5–15; Mat. 1:3–6; Luke 3:31–33

13 ¶ So Boaz [t]took Ruth, and she was his wife: and when he went in unto her, [u]the LORD gave her conception, and she bare a son.

14 And [v]the women said unto Naomi, Blessed *be* the LORD, which hath not [y]left thee this day without a [z]kinsman, that his name may be famous in Israel.

15 And he shall be unto thee a restorer of *thy* life, and [a]a nourisher of [b]thine old age: for thy daughter-in-law, which loveth thee, which is [w]better to thee than seven sons, hath borne him.

16 And Naomi took the child, and laid it in her bosom, and became nurse unto it.

17 [x]And the women her neighbours gave it a name, saying, There is a son born to Naomi; and they called his name Obed: he *is* the father of Jesse, the father of David.

18 ¶ Now these *are* the generations of Pharez: [y]Pharez begat Hezron,

19 And Hezron begat Ram, and Ram begat Amminadab,

20 And Amminadab begat [z]Nahshon, and Nahshon begat [a]Salmon,[c]

21 And Salmon begat Boaz, and Boaz begat Obed,

22 And Obed begat Jesse, and Jesse begat [b]David.

4:10 [n]Deut. 25:6 **4:11** [o]Ps. 127:3 & 128:3 [p]Deut. 25:9 [q]Gen. 35:16 **4:12** [r]1 Chr. 2:4 Mat. 1:3 [s]1 Sam. 2:20 **4:13** [t]ch. 3:11 [u]Gen. 29:31 **4:14** [v]Luke 1:58 **4:15** [w]1 Sam. 1:8 **4:17** [x]Luke 1:58 **4:18** [y]1 Chr. 2:4 **4:20** [z]Num. 1:7 [a]Mat. 1:4 **4:22** [b]1 Chr. 2:15 Mat. 1:6

[w] Or, *get thee riches,* or, *power* [x] Heb. *proclaim* thy name [y] Heb. *caused to cease unto thee* [z] Or, *redeemer* [a] Heb. *to nourish* [b] Heb. *thy gray hairs* [c] Or, *Salmah*

4:10 RUTH . . . HAVE I PURCHASED TO BE MY WIFE. Boaz became a redeemer in two ways. (1) He married Ruth and preserved the name of Elimelech, Naomi's deceased husband. The first-born son of Boaz and Ruth was considered a son of Elimelech's line (vv. 5,10). (2) Boaz redeemed (i.e., bought) the family land that Naomi had sold and restored it to Elimelech's line (vv. 3,7–10).

Boaz is an O.T. type of Jesus Christ, who likewise redeems the believer in two ways. (1) He has purchased us by His own blood and thereby keeps our lives and names from perishing in sin (John 3:16; 1 Pet. 1:18–19). (2) He includes us as the redeemed in His eternal inheritance in the new heaven and earth (Mat. 5:5; Rev. 21:1–7).

4:14 THE LORD . . . HAS NOT LEFT THEE. Although Naomi had experienced great sorrow and adversity in her life, she had maintained her faith in God. Because of her persevering faith, God so ordered events that her life ended in goodness and blessing. She could testify at the end of her life that "the Lord is very pitiful [i.e., full of pity and compassion], and of tender mercy" (Jas. 5:11).

4:17 A SON BORN . . . THE FATHER OF DAVID. God honored the decision of a virtuous young woman who forsook her pagan homeland in order to remain loyal to her mother-in-law and to the God of Israel (1:16), by allowing her to become a part of the earthly family through whom Christ came into the world (cf. Mat. 1:5).

1 SAMUEL

Outline

I. Samuel: Prophetic Leader of Israel (1:1—8:22)
 A. Birth of a Prophetic Leader (1:1—2:11)
  1. Hannah's Sorrow and Supplication (1:1–18)
  2. Hannah's Prophetic Son (1:19–28)
  3. Hannah's Prophetic Song (2:1–11)
 B. Corruption of the Old Leadership (2:12–36)
 C. Transition from Eli to Samuel (3:1—6:21)
  1. Samuel's Prophetic Calling (3:1–21)
  2. Judgment of Eli's House and Ministry (4:1–22)
  3. The Ark Taken and Restored (5:1—6:21)
 D. Revival Under the Leadership of Samuel (7:1–17)
 E. Israel Demands a King (8:1–22)
  1. Israel Rejects Samuel's Sons as Leaders (8:1–5)
  2. Israel Rejects God as King (8:6–22)

II. Saul: First King of Israel (9:1—15:35)
 A. Transition from Samuel to Saul (9:1—12:25)
  1. Selection of Saul (9:1–27)
  2. Samuel Anoints Saul (10:1–27)
  3. Saul's Victory over the Ammonites (11:1–11)
  4. Samuel Renews the Kingdom at Gilgal (11:12–15)
  5. Samuel's Farewell Address (12:1–25)
 B. The Early Kingship of Saul (13:1—15:35)
  1. Saul's Wars and Foolishness (13:1—14:52)
  2. Saul's Disobedience and Rejection (15:1–35)

III. David: An Anointed Man in Waiting (16:1—31:13)
 A. Samuel Anoints David (16:1–13)
 B. God Takes His Spirit from Saul (16:14–23)
 C. David in Contest with Goliath (17:1–58)
 D. David in the Court of Saul (18:1—19:17)
  1. David and Jonathan (18:1–4)
  2. David Serves Saul (18:5–16)
  3. David Marries Michal (18:17–28)
  4. Saul Fears David and Seeks His Life (18:29—19:17)
 E. David in Exile (19:18—31:13)
  1. David with Samuel (19:18–24)
  2. David Protected by Jonathan (20:1–42)
  3. David Aided by Ahimelech the Priest (21:1–9)
  4. David at Gath (21:10–15)
  5. A Band of Strong Men Rally Around David (22:1—26:25)
  6. David's Refuge in Philistia (27:1—30:31)
  7. The Death of Saul (31:1–13)

Author: Anonymous

Theme: Theocratic Kingship

Date of Writing: Late 10th century B.C.

Background

1 and 2 Samuel are one book in the Hebrew O.T. They are named after the prophet Samuel, who was held in high esteem as a strong spiritual leader of Israel and the one whom God used to set in order the theocratic monarchy. 1 Samuel covers nearly one century of Israel's history—from Samuel's birth to Saul's death (c. 1105–1010 B.C.)—and forms the main historical link between the time of the judges and the first of Israel's kings. Whereas 2 Samuel deals solely with King David, 1 Samuel covers three major transitions in national leadership: from Eli to Samuel, from Samuel to Saul, and from Saul to David.

The issue of authorship involves 1 and 2 Samuel as a single literary unit. Since part of 1 Samuel and all of 2 Samuel were written after Samuel's death, Samuel served only as one contributing author (cf. 1 Sam. 10:25). The final composition was written by an inspired prophetic historian who used several sources, including the records of Samuel (cf. 2 Sam. 1:18; 1 Chr. 27:24; 29:29). The identity of this inspired historian is unknown to us. The book was completed probably soon after 930 B.C., since 1 Samuel seems to assume the division of the kingdom (1 Sam. 27:6) and 2 Samuel ends with the last days of David.

Purpose

1 Samuel describes the crucial turning point in Israel's history from rule by the judges to rule by a king. The book sets forth the tension between the people's expectation of a king (a despotic ruler "like all the nations," 8:5) and God's pattern of a theocracy, in which He was their King. The book shows clearly that Saul's disobedience to God and his violation of the theocratic requirements of his office led God to reject and replace him as king.

Survey

The content of 1 Samuel focuses on three key national leaders: Samuel, Saul, and David. (1) Samuel was the last of the judges and the first to occupy the prophetic office (though he was not the first prophet, cf. Deut. 34:10; Judg. 4:4). As a man of great piety and prophetic gifts, Samuel (a) wisely directed Israel in a revival of true worship (ch. 7), (b) laid the foundation that gave the prophets their due place in Israel (19:20; cf. Acts 3:24; 13:20; Heb. 11:32), and (c) clearly established the monarchy as a theocratic kingship (15:1,12,28; 16:1). Samuel's importance as spiritual leader of God's people during a period of great change in Israel's history is second only to that of Moses at the time of the exodus.

(2) Saul became Israel's first king because of the people's demand for a human king "like all the nations" (8:5,20). Saul quickly demonstrated that he was spiritually unfit to fill the theocratic office; thus he was later rejected by God (chs. 13; 15).

(3) David, God's next choice to be His representative as king, was anointed by Samuel (ch. 16). David refused to usurp Saul's throne by force or subversion, and left his own promotion in God's hands. Chs. 19—30 largely describe David's flight from an insanely jealous Saul, and the patience with which David waited for God to act in his own time. The book concludes with the tragic death of Saul (ch. 31).

Special Features

Six major features or emphases characterize 1 Samuel. (1) It sets forth clearly God's holy standards for the kingship of Israel. Israel's kings were to be leaders who submitted to God as the true King of Israel, obeyed His law, and allowed themselves to be guided and corrected by His revelation through the prophets. (2) It records the foundational beginning of prominence for the prophetic office in Israel as a spiritual equal to the priesthood. The book contains the first O.T. references to a "company of prophets" (10:5; 19:18–24). (3) It stresses the importance and power of prayer (1:10–28; 2:1–10; 7:5–10; 8:5–6; 9:15; 12:19–

23), God's word (1:23; 9:27; 15:1,10,23), and the Spirit of prophecy (2:27–36; 3:20; 10:6,10; 19:20–24: 28:6). (4) It contains rich biographical information about and insights into the lives of three key leaders of Israel—Samuel (chs. 1—7), Saul (chs. 8—31), and David (chs. 16—31). (5) It is replete with well-known Bible stories, such as God speaking to young Samuel (ch. 3), David and Goliath (ch. 17), David and Jonathan (chs. 18—20), Saul's jealousy and fear of David (chs. 18—30), and Saul and the witch of Endor (ch. 28). (6) It is the source of some oft-quoted words: "Ichabod"—meaning "no glory," for "the glory is departed" (4:21); "Eben-ezer"—meaning "stone of help," for "hitherto hath the LORD helped us"(7:12); and "let the king live" (10:24), paraphrased in the KJV as "God save the king." Also, it is the first O.T. book to use the phrase "LORD of hosts" (e.g., 1:3).

New Testament Fulfillment

1 Samuel records two prophetic types of Jesus' ministry as prophet, priest, and king. (1) Samuel—God's main prophetic and priestly representative to Israel—foreshadowed the ministry of Jesus as God's foremost prophetic and priestly representative to Israel. (2) David—born in Bethlehem, a shepherd and God's anointed king who served the purposes of God for his own generation (Acts 13:36)—became the primary O.T. type and forerunner of Israel's Messianic king. The N.T. speaks of Jesus Christ as "the Son of David" (e.g., Mat. 1:1; 9:27; 21:9), "the seed of David according to the flesh" (Rom. 1:3), and "the root and the offspring of David" (Rev. 22:16).

Reading 1 Samuel

In order to read the entire Old Testament in one year, the book of 1 Samuel should be read in 11 days, according to the following schedule: □ 1–2 □ 3–7 □ 8–10 □ 11–13 □ 14–15 □ 16–17 □ 18–19 □ 20–22 □ 23–25 □ 26–28 □ 29–31

NOTES

Samuel's birth

1 NOW THERE was a certain man
of Ramathaim-zophim, of mount
Ephraim, and his name *was* [a]Elkanah,
the son of Jeroham, the son of Elihu,
the son of Tohu, the son of Zuph, [b]an
Ephrathite:
2 And he had two wives; the name
of the one *was* Hannah, and the name
of the other Peninnah: and Peninnah
had children, but Hannah had no chil-
dren.
3 And this man went up out of his
city [c]yearly[a] [d]to worship and to sac-
rifice unto the LORD of hosts in [e]Shi-
loh. And the two sons of Eli, Hophni
and Phinehas, the priests of the LORD,
were there.
4 ¶ And when the time was that El-
kanah [f]offered, he gave to Peninnah
his wife, and to all her sons and her
daughters, portions:
5 But unto Hannah he gave [b]a wor-
thy portion; for he loved Hannah: [g]but
the LORD had shut up her womb.
6 And her adversary also [h]pro-
voked[c] her sore, for to make her fret,
because the LORD had shut up her
womb.
7 And *as* he did so year by year,
[d] [e]when she went up to the house of
the LORD, so she provoked her; there-
fore she wept, and did not eat.
8 Then said Elkanah her husband to
her, Hannah, why weepest thou? and
why eatest thou not? and why is thy
heart grieved? *am* not I [i]better to thee
than ten sons?
9 ¶ So Hannah rose up after they
had eaten in Shiloh, and after they had
drunk. Now Eli the priest sat upon a
seat by a post of [j]the temple of the
LORD.
10 [k]And she *was* [f]in bitterness of
soul, and prayed unto the LORD, and
wept sore.
11 And she [l]vowed a vow, and
said, O LORD of hosts, if thou wilt in-
deed [m]look on the affliction of thine
handmaid, and [n]remember me, and
not forget thine handmaid, but wilt
give unto thine handmaid [g]a man
child, then I will give him unto the LORD
all the days of his life, and [o]there shall
no razor come upon his head.
12 And it came to pass, as she
[h]continued praying before the LORD,
that Eli marked her mouth.
13 Now Hannah, she spake in her
heart; only her lips moved, but her
voice was not heard: therefore Eli
thought she had been drunken.
14 And Eli said unto her, How long
wilt thou be drunken? put away thy
wine from thee.
15 And Hannah answered and said,
No, my lord, I *am* a woman [i]of a sor-
rowful spirit: I have drunk neither wine
nor strong drink, but have [p]poured
out my soul before the LORD.
16 Count not thine handmaid for a
daughter of [q]Belial: for out of the
abundance of my [j]complaint and grief
have I spoken hitherto.
17 Then Eli answered and said,
[r]Go in peace: and [s]the God of Israel
grant *thee* thy petition that thou hast
asked of him.
18 And she said, [t]Let thine hand-
maid find grace in thy sight. So the
woman [u]went her way, and did eat,
and her countenance was no more *sad.*
19 ¶ And they rose up in the morn-
ing early, and worshipped before the
LORD, and returned, and came to their
house to Ramah: and Elkanah [v]knew
Hannah his wife; and [w]the LORD re-
membered her.
20 Wherefore it came to pass,
[k]when the time was come about after

1:1 [a]1 Chr. 6:27,34 [b]Ruth 1:2
1:3 [c]Ex. 23:14 Luke 2:41 [d]Deut. 12:5 [e]Josh. 18:1
1:4 [f]Deut. 12:17
1:5 [g]Gen. 30:2
1:6 [h]Job 24:21
1:8 [i]Ruth 4:15
1:9 [j]ch. 3:3
1:10 [k]Job 7:11
1:11 [l]Gen. 28:20 [m]Ps. 25:18 [n]Gen. 8:1 [o]Num. 6:5
1:15 [p]Ps. 62:8
1:16 [q]Deut. 13:13
1:17 [r]Judg. 18:6 Mark 5:34 [s]Ps. 20:4,5
1:18 [t]Ruth 2:13 [u]Eccl. 9:7
1:19 [v]Gen. 4:1 [w]Gen. 30:22

[a] Heb. *from year to year* [b] Or, *a double portion* [c] Heb. *angered her* [d] Or, *from the time that she* [e] Heb. *from her going up* [f] Heb. *bitter of soul* [g] Heb. *seed of men* [h] Heb. *multiplied to pray* [i] Heb. *hard of spirit* [j] Or, *meditation* [k] Heb. *in revolution of days*

1:5 THE LORD HAD SHUT HER WOMB. Hannah's barrenness is ascribed directly to the activity of God. He had withheld children from her to prepare her for the birth of her son Samuel. In the same way, God at times may cause us to experience disappointments or lead us into situations in which we feel inadequate or inferior in order to continue working out His will in our lives. We should do as Hannah did—take our situations and hurts directly to the Lord and wait upon Him (cf. vv. 10–19; see Rom. 8:28, note).

1:11 I WILL GIVE HIM UNTO THE LORD. Hannah showed her devotion to the Lord by her willingness to dedicate her son to the work of the Lord. Christian parents today may likewise express their commitment to God and His kingdom by giving their sons and daughters to the ministry or to the work of missions in other lands. Those parents who continue to support, encourage, and pray for their children will find great favor with God.

1:11 NO RAZOR . . . HEAD. Uncut hair was a sign of the Nazarite vow (see Num. 6:5,14, notes).

1:20 SHE BARE A SON . . . SAMUEL. Al-

Hannah had conceived, that she bare a son, and called his name [1]Samuel, *saying,* Because I have asked him of the LORD.

Samuel dedicated

21 And the man Elkanah, and all his house, [x]went up to offer unto the LORD the yearly sacrifice, and his vow.

22 But Hannah went not up; for she said unto her husband, *I will not go up* until the child be weaned, and *then* I will [y]bring him, that he may appear before the LORD, and there [z]abide [a]for ever.

23 And [b]Elkanah her husband said unto her, Do what seemeth thee good; tarry until thou have weaned him; [c]only the LORD establish his word. So the woman abode, and gave her son suck until she weaned him.

24 ¶ And when she had weaned him, she [d]took him up with her, with three bullocks, and one ephah of flour, and a bottle of wine, and brought him unto [e]the house of the LORD in Shiloh: and the child *was* young.

25 And they slew a bullock, and [f]brought the child to Eli.

26 And she said, Oh my lord, [g]*as* thy soul liveth, my lord, I *am* the woman that stood by thee here, praying unto the LORD.

27 [h]For this child I prayed; and the LORD hath given me my petition which I asked of him:

28 Therefore also I have [m]lent him to the LORD; as long as he liveth [n]he shall be lent to the LORD. And he [i]worshipped the LORD there.

1:21 [x]ver. 3
1:22 [y]Luke 2:22 [z]ver. 11:28 [a]Ex. 21:6
1:23 [b]Num. 30:7 [c]2 Sam. 7:25
1:24 [d]Deut. 12:5,6,11 [e]Josh. 18:1
1:25 [f]Luke 2:22
1:26 [g]2 Ki. 2:2,4,6
1:27 [h]Mat. 7:7
1:28 [i]Gen. 24:26,52

Hannah's song of praise

2 AND HANNAH [j]prayed, and said, [k]My heart rejoiceth in the LORD, [l]mine horn is exalted in the LORD: my mouth is enlarged over mine enemies; because I [m]rejoice in thy salvation.

2 [n]*There is* none holy as the LORD: for *there is* [o]none beside thee: neither *is there* any rock like our God. Ps. 13:5-6

3 Talk no more so exceeding proudly; [p]let *not* [o]arrogancy come out of your mouth: for the LORD *is* a God of knowledge, and by him actions are weighed.

4 [q]The bows of the mighty men *are* broken, and they that stumbled are girded with strength.

5 *They that were* full have hired out themselves for bread; and *they that were* hungry ceased: so that [r]the barren hath born seven; and [s]she that hath many children is waxed feeble.

6 [t]The LORD killeth, and maketh alive: he bringeth down to the grave, and bringeth up.

7 The LORD [u]maketh poor, and maketh rich: [v]he bringeth low, and lifteth up.

8 [w]He raiseth up the poor out of the dust, *and* lifteth up the beggar from the dunghill, [x]to set *them* among princes, and to make them inherit the throne of glory: for [y]the pillars of the earth *are* the LORD's, and he hath set the world upon them.

9 [z]He will keep the feet of his saints, and the wicked shall be silent in darkness; for by strength shall no man prevail.

2:1 [j]Phil. 4:6 [k]See Luke 1:46 [l]Ps. 92:10 [m]Ps. 9:14
2:2 [n]Ex. 15:11 [o]Deut. 4:35
2:3 [p]Ps. 94:4 Jude 15
2:4 [q]Ps. 37:15
2:5 [r]Ps. 113:9 [s]Is. 54:1
2:6 [t]Job 5:18 Hos. 6:1
2:7 [u]Job 1:21 [v]Ps. 75:7
2:8 [w]Luke 1:52 [x]Job 36:7 [y]Job 38:4-6
2:9 [z]Ps. 91:11

[1] i.e. *Asked of God* [m] Or, *returned him, whom I have obtained by petition, to the LORD* [n] Or, *he whom I have obtained by petition shall be returned* [o] Heb. *hard*

though this book deals largely with the transition in Israel's history from the period of the judges to the establishment of the kingship, the first eight chapters concentrate on the birth, early life, and prophetic leadership of Samuel, the last judge. This prophet of God preceded the institution of the king in Israel, who stood under the word and Spirit of God as represented by Samuel (11:14—12:25). Throughout the Bible, the prophet as God's representative to Israel took precedence over the kingship and all other offices (cf. Mal. 4:5–6; Luke 7:24–28).

1:28 HE SHALL BE LENT TO THE LORD. Hannah should be lifted up as an example of godly motherhood. From the time she first desired to have a child, she prayerfully and purposefully presented her child before the Lord (vv. 10–28). She regarded her child as a gracious gift from God and expressed her intention to fulfill her vow by dedicating the child unto the Lord (vv. 11,24–28; see article on PARENTS AND CHILDREN, p. 1880).

2:1 HANNAH PRAYED. Hannah's prophetic song celebrates God's providential care of those who remain faithful to Him (v. 9; cf. Mary's song in Luke 1:46–55). She rejoiced also in His salvation, for He is holy, and He alone is God (v. 2). All followers of the Lord Jesus should trust in the Lord's ways with them. Anything that He allows to come into our lives should be brought to Him in prayer, with full confidence that not only can nothing separate us from His love, but also He will ultimately bring good out of whatever happens to us (Rom. 8:31–39).

10 The adversaries of the LORD shall be [a]broken to pieces; [b]out of heaven shall he thunder upon them: [c]the LORD shall judge the ends of the earth; and he shall give strength unto his king, and [d]exalt the horn of his anointed.

11 And Elkanah went to Ramah to his house. [e]And the child did minister unto the LORD before Eli the priest.

The sons of Eli

1 Chr. 16:7-43

12 ¶ Now the sons of Eli *were* [p]sons of Belial; [f]they knew not the LORD.

13 And the priests' custom with the people *was, that,* when any man offered sacrifice, the priest's servant came, while the flesh was in seething, with a fleshhook of three teeth in his hand;

14 And he struck *it* into the pan, or kettle, or caldron, or pot; all that the fleshhook brought up the priest took for himself. So they did in Shiloh unto all the Israelites that came thither.

15 Also before they [g]burnt the fat, the priest's servant came, and said to the man that sacrificed, Give flesh to roast for the priest; for he will not have sodden flesh of thee, but raw.

16 And *if* any man said unto him, Let them not fail to burn the fat [q]presently, and *then* take *as much* as thy soul desireth; then he would answer him, *Nay;* but thou shalt give *it me* now: and if not, I will take *it* by force.

17 Wherefore the sin of the young men was very great [h]before the LORD: for men [i]abhorred the offering of the LORD.

18 ¶ [j]But Samuel ministered before the LORD, *being* a child, [k]girded with a linen ephod.

19 Moreover his mother made him a little coat, and brought *it* to him from year to year, when she [l]came up with her husband to offer the yearly sacrifice.

20 ¶ And Eli [m]blessed Elkanah and his wife, and said, The LORD give thee seed of this woman for the [r]loan which is [n]lent to the LORD. And they went unto their own home.

21 And the LORD [o]visited Hannah, so that she conceived, and bare three sons and two daughters. And the child Samuel [p]grew before the LORD.

22 ¶ Now Eli was very old, and heard all that his sons did unto all Israel; and how they lay with [q]the women that [s]assembled *at* the door of the tabernacle of the congregation.

23 And he said unto them, Why do ye such things? for [t]I hear of your evil dealings by all this people.

24 Nay, my sons; for *it is* no good report that I hear: ye make the LORD's people [u]to transgress.

25 If one man sin against another, the judge shall judge him: but if a man [r]sin against the LORD, who shall entreat for him? Notwithstanding they hearkened not unto the voice of their father, [s]because the LORD would slay them.

26 And the child Samuel [t]grew on, and was [u]in favour both with the LORD, and also with men.

The prophecy of doom to Eli

27 ¶ [v]And there came a man of God unto Eli, and said unto him, Thus saith the LORD, [w]Did I plainly appear unto the house of thy father, when they were in Egypt in Pharaoh's house?

28 And did I [x]choose him out of all the tribes of Israel *to be* my priest, to

[p] Deut. 13:13 [q] Heb. *as on the day* [r] Or, *petition which she asked* [s] Heb. *assembled by troops* [t] Or, *I hear evil words of you* [u] Or, *to cry out*

2:10 [a]Ps. 2:9 [b]Ps. 18:13 [c]Ps. 96:13 [d]Ps. 89:24
2:11 [e]ver. 18 ch. 3:1
2:12 [f]Judg. 2:10 Rom. 1:28
2:15 [g]Lev. 3:3,4,5,16
2:17 [h]Gen. 6:11 [i]Mal. 2:8
2:18 [j]ver. 11 [k]Ex. 28:4
2:19 [l]ch. 1:3
2:20 [m]Gen. 14:19 [n]ch. 1:28
2:21 [o]Gen. 21:1 [p]ver. 26 Judg. 13:24
2:22 [q]Ex. 38:8
2:25 [r]Num. 15:30 [s]Josh. 11:20
2:26 [t]ver. 21 [u]Prov. 3:4
2:27 [v]1 Ki. 13:1 [w]Ex. 4:14,27
2:28 [x]Ex. 28:1,4 Num. 16:5

2:12 SONS OF BELIAL. "Belial," a Hebrew word meaning worthlessness, also suggests wickedness. This means the sons of Eli were wicked men, corrupt ministers in God's house who used their position as an opportunity for greedy gain and for sexual immorality (vv. 13–17,22; cf. Phil. 3:17–18). Their father Eli, the high priest, refused to discipline them or to disqualify them from the priesthood (see v. 29, note).

2:23 I HEAR OF YOUR EVIL DEALINGS. Eli protested the evil actions of his sons, yet he failed to remove them from their ministerial office (cf. Num. 15:30–31). Eli's failure was regarded as equivalent to despising God (i.e., God's holy nature and His standard for the priesthood, v. 30). God's Word declares that no immoral minister may serve as a leader of God's people; such persons must be removed from their positions of leadership (see article on MORAL QUALIFICATIONS FOR OVERSEERS, p. 1908).

2:25 THE LORD WOULD SLAY THEM. Eli's sons had hardened their hearts and were sinning openly and without shame (cf. Num. 15:30–31). Therefore Eli's instruction had no moral effect on them. For them the day of salvation had passed, and they were already appointed by God to condemnation and death (cf. Rom. 1:21–32; Heb. 3; 10:26–31). They would die as a result of their own willful disobedience and failure to repent.

offer upon mine altar, to burn incense,
to wear an ephod before me? and [y]did
I give unto the house of thy father all
the offerings made by fire of the chil-
dren of Israel?
29 Wherefore [z]kick ye at my sacri-
fice and at mine offering, which I have
commanded *in my* [a]habitation; and ho-
nourest thy sons above me, to make
yourselves fat with the chiefest of all
the offerings of Israel my people?
30 Wherefore the LORD God of Israel
saith, [b]I said indeed *that* thy house,
and the house of thy father, should
walk before me for ever: but now the
LORD saith, [c]Be it far from me; for
them that honour me [d]I will honour,
and [e]they that despise me shall be
lightly esteemed.
31 Behold, [f]the days come, that I
will cut off thine arm, and the arm of
thy father's house, that there shall not
be an old man in thine house.
32 And thou shalt see [v]an enemy
in my habitation, in all *the wealth* which
God shall give Israel: and there shall
not be [g]an old man in thine house for
ever.
33 And the man of thine, *whom* I
shall not cut off from mine altar, *shall
be* to consume thine eyes, and to grieve
thine heart: and all the increase of
thine house shall die [w]in the flower of
their age.
34 And this *shall be* [h]a sign unto
thee, that shall come upon thy two
sons, on Hophni and Phinehas; [i]in
one day they shall die both of them.
35 And [j]I will raise me up a faith-
ful priest, *that* shall do according to
that which *is* in mine heart and in my
mind: and [k]I will build him a sure
house; and he shall walk before [l]mine
anointed for ever.
36 [m]And it shall come to pass, *that*
every one that is left in thine house
shall come *and* crouch to him for a
piece of silver and a morsel of bread,
and shall say, [x]Put me, I pray thee,
into [y]one of the priests' offices, that
I may eat a piece of bread.

The LORD calls Samuel

3 AND [n]THE child Samuel minis-
tered unto the LORD before Eli. And
[o]the word of the LORD was precious in
those days; *there was* no open vision.
2 And it came to pass at that time,
when Eli *was* laid down in his place,
and his eyes began to wax dim, *that* he
could not see;
3 And ere [p]the lamp of God went
out [q]in the temple of the LORD, where
the ark of God *was,* and Samuel was
laid down *to sleep;*
4 That the LORD called Samuel: and
he answered, Here *am* I.
5 And he ran unto Eli, and said,
Here *am* I; for thou calledst me. And he
said, I called not; lie down again. And
he went and lay down.
6 And the LORD called yet again,
Samuel. And Samuel arose and went to

2:28 [y]Lev. 2:3,10 & 6:16 & 7:7,8,34,35 Num. 5:9
2:29 [z]Deut. 32:15 [a]Deut. 12:5
2:30 [b]Ex. 29:9 [c]Jer. 18:9,10 [d]Ps. 91:14 [e]Mal. 2:9
2:31 [f]1 Ki. 2:27 See ch. 4:11,18,20 & 14:3 & 22:18
2:32 [g]Zech. 8:4
2:34 [h]1 Ki. 13:3 [i]ch. 4:11
2:35 [j]1 Ki. 2:35 Ezek. 44:15 [k]2 Sam. 7:11,27 1 Ki. 11:38 [l]Ps. 18:50
2:36 [m]1 Ki. 2:27
3:1 [n]ch. 2:11 [o]Ps. 74:9 Amos. 8:11
3:3 [p]Ex. 27:20 [q]ch. 1:9

[v] Or, *the affliction of the tabernacle, for all the wealth which God would have given Israel* [w] Heb. *men* [x] Heb. *Join* [y] Or, *somewhat about the priesthood*

2:29 HONOUREST THY SONS ABOVE ME. Eli failed utterly to provide spiritual leadership for his family and thus for Israel. (1) As a father he was unable to train his sons in the way of righteousness. When they seduced the women serving at the door of the tabernacle (v. 22), Eli demonstrated neither the will nor the spiritual authority necessary to remove them from the ministry (3:13; cf. Deut. 21:18–21).

(2) Eli's failure as a father and a minister of the Lord resulted in the following: (a) God's judgment on Eli, his sons, and his family (vv. 30–36; 4:17–18); (b) a decline in respect for the office of the priesthood (v. 17); (c) the general spiritual decline of God's people (v. 22–24); and (d) the departure of the glory of the Lord from Israel (4:21).

(3) The entire Bible emphasizes the necessity of godliness and the true fear of God as His standard for those who would lead God's people (cf. 1 Tim. 3:1–10).

2:31 I WILL CUT OFF THINE ARM. Eli and his descendants were removed from their priestly service forever. Their unfaithfulness and immorality had permanently disqualified them from being spiritual leaders and godly examples for Israel (cf. vv. 30–34; 3:13–14).

2:35 FAITHFUL PRIEST. This refers initially to Samuel, who served as priest, judge (7:6, 15–17), and prophet (3:20–21). From an early age he was trained by the high priest Eli for his sacred duties (vv. 1–11; 1:24–28), and he eventually succeeded Eli as high priest. He was consistently faithful to God throughout his life. In this way he points forward to the perfect priest, Jesus the Messiah (the Anointed One; cf. Ps. 110; Heb. 5:6). (1) Above all, a priest was called to be faithful, i.e., to adhere firmly to what is in God's heart and Word; that implies steadfast allegiance, devotion, fidelity, and an unwillingness to be turned aside from God and His ways. (2) The N.T. teaches that only those who have clearly demonstrated faithfulness to God are to be spiritual leaders of God's people (cf. Mat. 24:45; 25:21; 1 Tim. 3:1–13; 4:16; 2 Tim. 2:2).

Eli, and said, Here *am* I; for thou didst call me. And he answered, I called not, my son; lie down again.

7 [z]Now Samuel [r]did not yet know the LORD, neither was the word of the LORD yet revealed unto him.

8 And the LORD called Samuel again the third time. And he arose and went to Eli, and said, Here *am* I; for thou didst call me. And Eli perceived that the LORD had called the child.

9 Therefore Eli said unto Samuel, Go, lie down: and it shall be, if he call thee, that thou shalt say, Speak, LORD; for thy servant heareth. So Samuel went and lay down in his place.

10 And the LORD came, and stood, and called as at other times, Samuel, Samuel. Then Samuel answered, Speak; for thy servant heareth.

11 ¶ And the LORD said to Samuel, Behold, I will do a thing in Israel, [s]at which both the ears of every one that heareth it shall tingle.

12 In that day I will perform against Eli [t]all *things* which I have spoken concerning his house: [a]when I begin, I will also make an end.

13 [u]For[b] I have told him that I will [v]judge his house for ever for the iniquity which he knoweth; because [w]his sons made themselves [c]vile, and he [x]restrained[d] them not.

14 And therefore I have sworn unto the house of Eli, that the iniquity of Eli's house [y]shall not be purged with sacrifice nor offering for ever.

15 ¶ And Samuel lay until the morning, and opened the doors of the house of the LORD. And Samuel feared to show Eli the vision.

16 Then Eli called Samuel, and said, Samuel, my son. And he answered, Here *am* I.

17 And he said, What *is* the thing that *the* LORD hath said unto thee? I pray thee hide *it* not from me: [z]God do so to thee, and [e]more also, if thou hide *any* [f]thing from me of all the things that he said unto thee.

18 And Samuel told him [g]every whit, and hid nothing from him. And he said, [a]It *is* the LORD: let him do what seemeth him good.

19 ¶ And Samuel [b]grew, and [c]the LORD was with him, [d]and did let none of his words fall to the ground.

20 And all Israel [e]from Dan even to Beer-sheba knew that Samuel *was* [h]established *to be* a prophet of the LORD.

21 And the LORD appeared again in Shiloh: for the LORD revealed himself to Samuel in Shiloh by [f]the word of the LORD.

Israel defeated by the Philistines

4 AND THE word of Samuel [i][j]came to all Israel. Now Israel went out against the Philistines to battle, and pitched beside [g]Eben-ezer: and the Philistines pitched in Aphek.

2 And the Philistines put themselves in array against Israel: and when [k]they joined battle, Israel was smitten before the Philistines: and

3:7 [r]See Acts 19:2
3:11 [s]2 Ki. 21:12
3:12 [t]ch. 2:30-36
3:13 [u]ch. 2:29-31 [v]Ezek. 7:3 & 18:30 [w]ch. 2:12,17,22 [x]ch. 2:23,25
3:14 [y]Num. 15:30,31
3:17 [z]Ruth 1:17
3:18 [a]Job 1:21 Is. 39:8
3:19 [b]ch. 2:21 [c]Gen. 39:2,21,23 [d]ch. 9:6
3:20 [e]Judg. 20:1
3:21 [f]ver. 1,4
4:1 [g]ch. 7:12

[z] Or, *Thus did Samuel before he knew the LORD, and before the word of the LORD was revealed unto him* [a] Heb. *beginning and ending* [b] Or, *And I will tell him* [c] Or, *accursed* [d] Heb. *frowned not upon them* [e] Heb. *so add* [f] Or, *word* [g] Heb. *all the things,* or, *words* [h] Or, *faithful* [i] Or, *came to pass* [j] Heb. *was* [k] Heb. *the battle was spread*

3:13 JUDGE HIS HOUSE FOREVER. Although Eli personally could be forgiven for his failure in the ministry, God would not restore him or his descendants to their position as priests. No calling to be a minister or overseer can be considered irrevocable (see Rom. 11:29, note).

3:20 A PROPHET OF THE LORD. Samuel is one of the first persons to occupy the prophetic office, though he was not the first person with a prophetic gift (cf. Abraham, Gen. 20:7; Moses, Deut. 18:15,18; Deborah, Judg. 4:4). (1) Because of the corruption of the priesthood and spiritual decline among God's people, God called Samuel to proclaim His word to the people (vv. 19–21), to provide an example of faithfulness to His will (2:35), to call them to repentance and renewal (7:3), and to act as a mediator between God and the people (7:8–9).

(2) Around Samuel gathered other prophets, called "the company of the prophets" (19:20; 2 Ki. 2:3,5; 4:38). The school of the prophets at Ramah was under the leadership of Samuel (cf. 19:20–22). Through him these prophets were edified, nurtured, and instructed concerning God's will for Israel. The aim of such a school or association of prophets was to bring about spiritual renewal and the recovery of God's covenant purpose for Israel. Anyone could come and learn God's ways from them.

4:2 ISRAEL WAS SMITTEN. Israel suffered defeat because the priesthood had become corrupt and the people were living in disobedience to God's commandments. They took the ark of the covenant into battle, thinking that it would assure them victory (see next note); instead, they should have repented of and corrected their sinful ways if they wanted God's blessing.

they slew of [l]the army in the field about four thousand men.

3 ¶ And when the people were come into the camp, the elders of Israel said, Wherefore hath the LORD smitten us today before the Philistines? Let us [m]fetch the ark of the covenant of the LORD out of Shiloh unto us, that, when it cometh among us, it may save us out of the hand of our enemies.

4 So the people sent to Shiloh, that they might bring from thence the ark of the covenant of the LORD of hosts, [h]which dwelleth *between* [i]the cherubims: and the two sons of Eli, Hophni and Phinehas, *were* there with the ark of the covenant of God.

5 And when the ark of the covenant of the LORD came into the camp, all Israel shouted with a great shout, so that the earth rang again.

6 And when the Philistines heard the noise of the shout, they said, What *meaneth* the noise of this great shout in the camp of the Hebrews? And they understood that the ark of the LORD was come into the camp.

7 And the Philistines were afraid, for they said, God is come into the camp. And they said, Woe unto us! for there hath not been such a thing [n]heretofore.

8 Woe unto us! who shall deliver us out of the hand of these mighty Gods? these *are* the Gods that smote the Egyptians with all the plagues in the wilderness.

9 [j]Be strong, and quit yourselves like men, O ye Philistines, that ye be not servants unto the Hebrews, [k]as they have been to you: [o]quit yourselves like men, and fight.

10 ¶ And the Philistines fought, and [l]Israel was smitten, and they fled every man into his tent: and there was a very great slaughter; for there fell of Israel thirty thousand footmen.

11 And [m]the ark of God was taken; and [n]the two sons of Eli, Hophni and Phinehas, [p]were slain.

4:4 [h]2 Sam. 6:2 [i]Num. 7:89
4:9 [j]1 Cor. 16:13 [k]Judg. 13:1
4:10 [l]ver. 2 Lev. 26:17 Deut. 28:25
4:11 [m]ch. 2:32 Ps. 78:61 [n]ch. 2:34 Ps. 78:64
4:12 [o]2 Sam. 1:2 [p]Josh. 7:6 2 Sam. 13:19 & 15:32 Neh. 9:1 Job 2:12
4:13 [q]ch. 1:9
4:15 [r]ch. 3:2
4:16 [s]2 Sam. 1:4
4:20 [t]Gen. 35:17

The death of Eli

12 ¶ And there ran a man of Benjamin out of the army, and [o]came to Shiloh the same day with his clothes rent, and [p]with earth upon his head.

13 And when he came, lo, Eli sat upon [q]a seat by the wayside watching: for his heart trembled for the ark of God. And when the man came into the city, and told *it,* all the city cried out.

14 And when Eli heard the noise of the crying, he said, What *meaneth* the noise of this tumult? And the man came in hastily, and told Eli.

15 Now Eli was ninety and eight years old; and [r]his eyes [q]were dim, that he could not see.

16 And the man said unto Eli, I *am* he that came out of the army, and I fled today out of the army. And he said, [s]What [r]is there done, my son?

17 And the messenger answered and said, Israel is fled before the Philistines, and there hath been also a great slaughter among the people, and thy two sons also, Hophni and Phinehas, are dead, and the ark of God is taken.

18 And it came to pass, when he made mention of the ark of God, that he fell from off the seat backward by the side of the gate, and his neck brake, and he died: for he was an old man, and heavy. [s]And he had judged Israel forty years.

19 ¶ And his daughter-in-law, Phinehas' wife, was with child, *near* [t]to be delivered: and when she heard the tidings that the ark of God was taken, and that her father-in-law and her husband were dead, she bowed herself and travailed; for her pains [u]came upon her.

20 And about the time of her death [t]the women that stood by her said

[l] Heb. *the array* [m] Heb. *take unto us* [n] Heb. *yesterday,* or, *the third day* [o] Heb. *be men* [p] Heb. *died* [q] Heb. *stood* [r] Heb. *is the thing* [s] He seems to have been a Judge to do justice only, and that in Southwest *Israel* [t] Or, *to cry out* [u] Heb. *were turned*

4:3 FETCH THE ARK OF THE COVENANT. The ark represented God's presence in Israel (cf. Ex. 25:10–22; Num. 10:33–36). The people thought that the ark would unconditionally guarantee God's favor and power. They failed to understand that a symbol of spiritual things does not itself assure one of the reality to which it points. God remained with His people only as long as they sought to maintain their covenant relationship to Him. Likewise, under the new covenant, submitting to water baptism or partaking of the Lord's Supper will be of no spiritual benefit unless one truly submits to the Lord and His righteous ways (cf. 1 Cor. 11:27–30).

4:17 HOPHNI AND PHINEHAS ARE DEAD. The deaths of Hophni and Phinehas and the capture of the ark emphasize that God will judge those who accept immoral spiritual leaders with personal disaster and with the departure of His glory.

unto her, Fear not; for thou hast borne a son. But she answered not, [v]neither did she regard *it.*

21 And she named the child [u]I-chabod,[w] saying, [v]The glory is departed from Israel: because the ark of God was taken, and because of her father-in-law and her husband.

22 And she said, The glory is departed from Israel: for the ark of God is taken.

The Philistines move the ark

5 AND THE Philistines took the ark of God, and brought it [w]from Eben-ezer unto Ashdod.

2 When the Philistines took the ark of God, they brought it into the house of [x]Dagon, and set it by Dagon.

3 ¶ And when they of Ashdod arose early on the morrow, behold, Dagon *was* [y]fallen upon his face to the earth before the ark of the LORD. And they took Dagon, and [z]set him in his place again.

4 And when they arose early on the morrow morning, behold, Dagon *was* fallen upon his face to the ground before the ark of the LORD; and [a]the head of Dagon and both the palms of his hands *were* cut off upon the threshold; only [x]*the stump of* Dagon was left to him.

5 Therefore neither the priests of Dagon, nor any that come into Dagon's house, [b]tread on the threshold of Dagon in Ashdod unto this day.

6 But [c]the hand of the LORD was heavy upon them of Ashdod, and he [d]destroyed them, and smote them with [e]emerods, *even* Ashdod and the coasts thereof.

7 And when the men of Ashdod saw that *it was* so, they said, The ark of the God of Israel shall not abide with us: for his hand is sore upon us, and upon Dagon our god.

8 They sent therefore and gathered all the lords of the Philistines unto them, and said, What shall we do with the ark of the God of Israel? And they answered, Let the ark of the God of Israel be carried about unto Gath. And they carried the ark of the God of Israel about *thither.*

4:21 [u]ch. 14:3 [v]Ps. 26:8 & 78:61
5:1 [w]ch. 4:1 & 7:12
5:2 [x]Judg. 16:23
5:3 [y]Is. 19:1 & 46:1,2 [z]Is. 46:7
5:4 [a]Jer. 50:2 Ezek. 6:4,6 Mic. 1:7
5:5 [b]Zeph. 1:9
5:6 [c]ver. 7,11 Ex. 9:3 Ps. 32:4 Acts 13:11 [d]ch. 6:5 [e]Deut. 28:27 Ps. 78:66
5:9 [f]Deut. 2:15 ch. 7:13 & 12:15 [g]ver. 11 [h]ver. 6 Ps. 78:66
5:11 [i]ver. 6,9
6:2 [j]Gen. 41:8 Ex. 7:11 Dan. 2:2 & 5:7 Mat. 2:4
6:3 [k]Ex. 23:15 Deut. 16:16 [l]Lev. 5:15,16 [m]ver. 9
6:4 [n]See ver. 17,18 Josh. 13:3 Judg. 3:3
6:5 [o]ch. 5:6 [p]Josh. 7:19 Is. 42:12 Mal. 2:2 John 9:24

9 And it was *so,* that, after they had carried it about, [f]the hand of the LORD was against the city [g]with a very great destruction: and [h]he smote the men of the city, both small and great, and they had emerods in their secret parts.

10 ¶ Therefore they sent the ark of God to Ekron. And it came to pass, as the ark of God came to Ekron, that the Ekronites cried out, saying, They have brought about the ark of the God of Israel to [y]us, to slay us and our people.

11 So they sent and gathered together all the lords of the Philistines, and said, Send away the ark of the God of Israel, and let it go again to his own place, that it slay [z]us not, and our people: for there was a deadly destruction throughout all the city; [i]the hand of God was very heavy there.

12 And the men that died not were smitten with the emerods: and the cry of the city went up to heaven.

The ark returned to Israel

6 AND THE ark of the LORD was in the country of the Philistines seven months.

2 And the Philistines [j]called for the priests and the diviners, saying, What shall we do to the ark of the LORD? tell us wherewith we shall send it to his place.

3 And they said, If ye send away the ark of the God of Israel, send it not [k]empty; but in any wise return him [l]a trespass offering: then ye shall be healed, and it shall [m]be known to you why his hand is not removed from you.

4 Then said they, What *shall be* the trespass offering which we shall return to him? They answered, Five golden emerods, and five golden mice, [n]*according to* the number of the lords of the Philistines: for one plague *was* on [a]you all, and on your lords.

5 Wherefore ye shall make images of your emerods, and images of your mice that [o]mar the land; and ye shall [p]give glory unto the God of Israel:

[v] Heb. *set not her heart* [w] i.e. *Where is the glory?* or, There is *no glory* [x] Or, *the fishy part* [y] Heb. *me, to slay me and my* [z] Heb. *me not, and my* [a] Heb. *them*

4:21 ICHABOD. This name means "no glory." The glory of Israel was God and His manifested presence on earth among His people (see Ex. 24:16, note). Phinehas's widow was rightly concerned about the departure of God's presence (vv. 19–22), just as new covenant believers must be concerned if the Spirit's presence, power, holiness, and gifts are absent from us.

peradventure he will [q]lighten his hand from off you, and from off [r]your gods, and from off your land.

6 Wherefore then do ye harden your hearts, [s]as the Egyptians and Pharaoh hardened their hearts? when he had wrought [b]wonderfully among them, [t]did they not let [c]the people go, and they departed?

7 Now therefore make [u]a new cart, and take two milch kine, [v]on which there hath come no yoke, and tie the kine to the cart, and bring their calves home from them:

8 And take the ark of the LORD, and lay it upon the cart; and put [w]the jewels of gold, which ye return him *for* a trespass offering, in a coffer by the side thereof; and send it away, that it may go.

9 And see, if it goeth up by the way of his own coast to [x]Beth-shemesh, *then* [d]he hath done us this great evil: but if not, then [y]we shall know that *it is* not his hand *that* smote us; it *was* a chance *that* happened to us.

10 ¶ And the men did so; and took two milch kine, and tied them to the cart, and shut up their calves at home:

11 And they laid the ark of the LORD upon the cart, and the coffer with the mice of gold and the images of their emerods.

12 And the kine took the straight way to the way of Beth-shemesh, *and* went along the highway, lowing as they went, and turned not aside *to* the right hand or *to* the left; and the lords of the Philistines went after them unto the border of Beth-shemesh.

13 And *they of* Beth-shemesh *were* reaping their wheat harvest in the valley: and they lifted up their eyes, and saw the ark, and rejoiced to see *it*.

14 And the cart came into the field of Joshua, a Beth-shemite, and stood there, where *there was* a great stone: and they clave the wood of the cart, and offered the kine a burnt offering unto the LORD.

15 And the Levites took down the ark of the LORD, and the coffer that *was* with it, wherein the jewels of gold *were*, and put *them* on the great stone: and the men of Beth-shemesh offered burnt offerings and sacrificed sacrifices the same day unto the LORD.

16 And when [z]the five lords of the Philistines had seen *it*, they returned to Ekron the same day.

17 [a]And these *are* the golden emerods which the Philistines returned *for* a trespass offering unto the LORD; for Ashdod one, for Gaza one, for Askelon one, for Gath one, for Ekron one;

18 And the golden mice, *according to* the number of all the cities of the Philistines *belonging* to the five lords, *both* of fenced cities, and of country villages, even unto the [e]great *stone of* Abel, whereon they set down the ark of the LORD: *which stone remaineth* unto this day in the field of Joshua, the Beth-shemite.

19 ¶ And [b]he smote the men of Beth-shemesh, because they had looked into the ark of the LORD, even he smote of the people fifty thousand and threescore and ten men: and the people lamented, because the LORD had smitten *many* of the people with a great slaughter.

20 And the men of Beth-shemesh said, [c]Who is able to stand before this holy LORD God? and to whom shall he go up from us?

21 ¶ And they sent messengers to the inhabitants of [d]Kirjath-jearim, saying, The Philistines have brought again the ark of the LORD; come ye down, *and* fetch it up to you.

7 AND THE men of [e]Kirjath-jearim came, and fetched up the ark of the LORD, and brought it into the house of [f]Abinadab in the hill, and sanctified Eleazar his son to keep the ark of the LORD.

2 And it came to pass, while the ark abode in Kirjath-jearim, that the time

6:5 [q]See ch. 5:6,11 Ps. 39:10 [r]ch. 5:3,4,7
6:6 [s]Ex. 7:13 & 8:15 & 14:17 [t]Ex. 12:31
6:7 [u]2 Sam. 6:3 [v]Num. 19:2
6:8 [w]ver. 4,5
6:9 [x]Josh. 15:10 [y]ver. 3
6:16 [z]Josh. 13:3
6:17 [a]ver. 4
6:19 [b]See Ex. 19:21 2 Sam. 6:7
6:20 [c]2 Sam. 6:9 Mal. 3:2
6:21 [d]Josh. 18:14 1 Chr. 13:5,6
7:1 [e]ch. 6:21 Ps. 132:6 [f]2 Sam. 6:4

[b]Or, *reproachfully* [c]Heb. *them* [d]Or, *it*
[e]Or, *great stone*

6:12 TO THE WAY OF BETH-SHEMESH. God caused the cows to take the ark back to Israel. Beth-shemesh was a town across the border within the territory of Judah (cf. Josh. 21:16).

6:19 SMOTE THE MEN OF BETH-SHEMESH. Many of the people of Beth-shemesh disregarded the commandment of the Lord not to look at or touch the holy objects of the sanctuary (Num. 4:15,20). By examining the ark of the Lord, they demonstrated a total absence of the fear of the Lord and of reverence for what is holy. Honor, respect, and a reverent fear should characterize God's people in their relationship to their holy God. The numbers 50,000 and 70 probably mean that 70 of the people of Beth-shemesh died, bringing the total of all who died (including the Philistines) to a round number of 50,000.

was long; for it was twenty years: and
all the house of Israel lamented after
the LORD.

Philistines defeated at Mizpah

3 ¶ And Samuel spake unto all the
house of Israel, saying, If ye do [g]re-
turn unto the LORD with all your hearts,
then [h]put away the strange gods and
[i]Ashtaroth from among you, and
[j]prepare your hearts unto the LORD,
and [k]serve him only: and he will deliv-
er you out of the hand of the Philis-
tines.
4 Then the children of Israel did put
away [l]Baalim and Ashtaroth, and
served the LORD only.
5 And Samuel said, [m]Gather all Is-
rael to Mizpeh, and I will pray for you
unto the LORD.
6 And they gathered together to
Mizpeh, [n]and drew water, and poured
it out before the LORD, and [o]fasted on
that day, and said there, [p]We have
sinned against the LORD. And Samuel
judged the children of Israel in Mizpeh.
7 And when the Philistines heard
that the children of Israel were gath-
ered together to Mizpeh, the lords of
the Philistines went up against Israel.
And when the children of Israel heard
it, they were afraid of the Philistines.
8 And the children of Israel said to
Samuel, [q]Cease[f] not to cry unto the
LORD our God for us, that he will save
us out of the hand of the Philistines.
9 ¶ And Samuel took a sucking
lamb, and offered *it for* a burnt offering
wholly unto the LORD: and [r]Samuel
cried unto the LORD for Israel; and the
LORD [g]heard him.
10 And as Samuel was offering up
the burnt offering, the Philistines drew
near to battle against Israel: [s]but the
LORD thundered with a great thunder
on that day upon the Philistines, and

7:3 [g]Deut. 30:2-10 Is. 55:7 Hos. 6:1 Joel 2:12 [h]Gen. 35:2 Josh. 24:14 [i]Judg. 2:13 [j]2 Chr. 30:19 Job 11:13 [k]Deut. 6:13 & 10:20 Luke 4:8
7:4 [l]Judg. 2:11
7:5 [m]Judg. 20:1
7:6 [n]2 Sam. 14:14 [o]Neh. 9:1,2 Dan. 9:3-5 Joel 2:12 [p]Judg. 10:10 Ps. 106:6
7:8 [q]Is. 37:4
7:9 [r]Ps. 99:6 Jer. 15:1
7:10 [s]Josh. 10:10 Judg. 4:15 & 5:20 ch. 2:10 2 Sam. 22:14,15
7:12 [t]Gen. 28:18 Josh. 4:9 [u]ch. 4:1
7:13 [v]Judg. 13:1 [w]ch. 13:5
7:15 [x]ch. 12:11 Judg. 2:16
7:17 [y]ch. 8:4 [z]Judg. 21:4
8:1 [a]Deut. 16:18 2 Chr. 19:5 [b]Judg. 10.1 & 12:14 compared with Judg. 5:10
8:3 [c]Jer. 22:15-17 [d]Ex. 18:21 1 Tim. 3:3 & 6:10

discomfited them; and they were smit-
ten before Israel.
11 And the men of Israel went out
of Mizpeh, and pursued the Philistines,
and smote them, until *they came* under
Beth-car.
12 Then Samuel [t]took a stone, and
set *it* between Mizpeh and Shen, and
called the name of it [u]Eben-ezer,[h]
saying, Hitherto hath the LORD
helped us.
13 ¶ [v]So the Philistines were sub-
dued, and they [w]came no more into the
coast of Israel: and the hand of the
LORD was against the Philistines all
the days of Samuel.
14 And the cities which the Philis-
tines had taken from Israel were re-
stored to Israel, from Ekron even unto
Gath; and the coasts thereof did Israel
deliver out of the hands of the Philis-
tines. And there was peace between Is-
rael and the Amorites.
15 And Samuel [x]judged Israel all
the days of his life.
16 And he went from year to year
[i]in circuit to Beth-el, and Gilgal, and
Mizpeh, and judged Israel in all those
places.
17 And [y]his return *was* to Ramah;
for there *was* his house; and there he
judged Israel; and there he [z]built an
altar unto the LORD.

Israel demands a king

8 AND IT came to pass, when Sam-
uel was old, that he [a]made his
[b]sons judges over Israel.
2 Now the name of his firstborn was
[j]Joel; and the name of his second,
Abiah: *they were* judges in Beer-sheba.
3 And his sons [c]walked not in his
ways, but turned aside [d]after lucre,

[f] Heb. *Be not silent from us from crying* [g] Or, *answered* [h] i.e. *The stone of help* [i] Heb. *and he circuited* [j] *Vashni* in 1 Chr. 6:28

7:3 IF YE DO RETURN UNTO THE LORD . . . HE WILL DELIVER YOU. Samuel emphasized the Biblical principle that if God's people hope to receive His protection and deliverance, they must first turn to Him with all their hearts and put away all forms of idolatry and compromise (cf. Rom. 12:1–2). All those who sincerely desire to please God may expect His care, blessing, and deliverance (cf. Ex. 23:22; Deut. 20:1–4; Josh. 1:5–9).

7:8 CEASE NOT TO CRY UNTO THE LORD. Throughout our lives, victory over spiritual adversaries is dependent on unceasing prayer to God. Prayer brings God into every aspect of our lives: our work, plans, family, problems, and successes (see Luke 18:1,7, notes). To fail to pray opens us up to Satan's attack and our defeat. Samuel's response to the people's request was to offer a lamb as a burnt offering, signifying renewed dedication to the Lord, and to pray to the Lord on their behalf (v. 9).

8:1–3 HIS SONS. Samuel made his sons judges in the southern part of Israel, but they did not follow their father's good example (v. 3). This was their choice, however, and the Bible does not blame Samuel the way it does Eli (2:29). Evidently Samuel had not allowed them to function as priests. Their behavior shows that children of godly parents must still make their own choices.

and [e]took bribes, and perverted judgment.

4 Then all the elders of Israel gathered themselves together, and came to Samuel unto Ramah,

5 And said unto him, Behold, thou art old, and thy sons walk not in thy ways: now [f]make us a king to judge us like all the nations.

6 ¶ But the thing [k]displeased Samuel, when they said, Give us a king to judge us. And Samuel prayed unto the LORD.

7 And the LORD said unto Samuel, Hearken unto the voice of the people in all that they say unto thee: for [g]they have not rejected thee, but [h]they have rejected me, that I should not reign over them.

8 According to all the works which they have done since the day that I brought them up out of Egypt even unto this day, wherewith they have forsaken me, and served other gods, so do they also unto thee.

9 Now therefore [l]hearken unto their voice: [m]howbeit yet protest solemnly unto them, and [i]show them the manner of the king that shall reign over them.

10 ¶ And Samuel told all the words of the LORD unto the people that asked of him a king.

11 And he said, [j]This will be the manner of the king that shall reign over you: [k]He will take your sons, and appoint *them* for himself, for his chariots, and *to be* his horsemen; and *some* shall run before his chariots.

12 And he will appoint him captains over thousands, and captains over fifties; and *will set them* to ear his ground, and to reap his harvest, and to make his instruments of war, and instruments of his chariots.

13 And he will take your daughters *to be* confectionaries, and *to be* cooks, and *to be* bakers.

14 And [l]he will take your fields, and your vineyards, and your oliveyards, *even* the best *of them,* and give *them* to his servants.

15 And he will take the tenth of your seed, and of your vineyards, and give to his [n]officers, and to his servants.

16 And he will take your menservants, and your maidservants, and your goodliest young men, and your asses, and put *them* to his work.

17 He will take the tenth of your sheep: and ye shall be his servants.

18 And ye shall cry out in that day because of your king which ye shall have chosen you; and the LORD [m]will not hear you in that day.

19 ¶ Nevertheless the people [n]refused to obey the voice of Samuel; and they said, Nay; but we will have a king over us;

20 That we also may be [o]like all the nations; and that our king may judge us, and go out before us, and fight our battles.

21 And Samuel heard all the words

8:3 [e]Deut. 16:19 Ps. 15:5
8:5 [f]ver. 19,20 Deut. 17:14 Hos. 13:10 Acts 13:21
8:7 [g]See Ex. 16:8 [h]ch. 10:19 & 12:17,19 Hos. 13:10,11
8:9 [i]ver. 11
8:11 [j]See Deut. 17:16 ch. 10:25 [k]ch. 14:52
8:14 [l]1 Ki. 21:7 See Ezek. 46:18
8:18 [m]Is. 1:15 Mic. 3:4
8:19 [n]Jer. 44:16
8:20 [o]ver. 5

[k] Heb. *was evil in the eyes of Samuel* [l] Or, *obey* [m] Or, *notwithstanding when thou hast solemnly protested against them, then thou shalt show* [n] Heb. *eunuchs;* see Gen. 37:36

8:5 MAKE US A KING. Kingship was part of the promises in God's covenant with Abraham (Gen. 17:6); and in Jacob's blessing of his sons, he assigned the kingship to the tribe of Judah (Gen. 49:10). Moses foretold of the day when Israel would no longer be content with the direct rule of God (Deut. 17:14–15; 28:36). That prophecy came to pass here through Israel's demand for a human king. God saw their request as a rejection of Himself as King of Israel (v. 7) and as a demonstration of their eagerness to compromise their role as God's special people. (1) The people asked for a human king so that "we also may be like all the nations; and that our king may judge us, and go out before us, and fight our battles" (v. 20). They mistakenly believed the reason for their troubles and defeats was inadequate government, when in reality it was their sin. Hence, they conformed to the ways of the pagan societies around them rather than trusting in God.

(2) Although this was not the time God had chosen for them to have a king, and although their motivation was wrong, the Lord gave them what they asked for. Afterward, He purposed to guide His people in spite of the flawed government of Israel's monarchy (12:14–15,19–25). This points to God's love and patience with human weakness.

8:7 THEY HAVE REJECTED ME. Until this time Israel's government had been a theocracy, i.e., God Himself ruled Israel as their King. He ruled through direct guidance, through special revelation and the written Word, and through chosen and anointed leaders. When Israel requested a monarchial government, her kings took office by virtue of hereditary succession rather than by God's direct choice. This resulted in the reigns of evil and immoral kings and thereby impaired God's Lordship over His people. At the end of history, God will again resume direct reign over His people through Jesus Christ, and "of his kingdom there shall be no end" (Luke 1:33; cf. 1 Tim. 1:17; Rev. 20:4–6; 21:1–8).

of the people, and he rehearsed them in the ears of the LORD.

22 And the LORD said to Samuel, [p]Hearken unto their voice, and make them a king. And Samuel said unto the men of Israel, Go ye every man unto his city.

Saul anointed by Samuel

9 NOW THERE was a man of Benjamin, whose name *was* [q]Kish, the son of Abiel, the son of Zeror, the son of Bechorath, the son of Aphiah, [o]a Benjamite, a mighty man of [p]power.

2 And he had a son, whose name *was* Saul, a choice young man, and a goodly: and *there was* not among the children of Israel a goodlier person than he: [r]from his shoulders and upward *he was* higher than any of the people.

3 And the asses of Kish Saul's father were lost. And Kish said to Saul his son, Take now one of the servants with thee, and arise, go seek the asses.

4 And he passed through mount Ephraim, and passed through the land of [s]Shalisha, but they found *them* not: then they passed through the land of Shalim, and *there they were* not: and he passed through the land of the Benjamites, but they found *them* not.

5 *And* when they were come to the land of Zuph, Saul said to his servant that *was* with him, Come, and let us return; lest my father leave *caring* for the asses, and take thought for us.

6 And he said unto him, Behold now, *there is* in this city [t]a man of God, and *he is* an honourable man; [u]all that he saith cometh surely to pass: now let us go thither; peradventure he can show us our way that we should go.

7 Then said Saul to his servant, But, behold, *if* we go, [v]what shall we bring the man? for the bread [q]is spent in our vessels, and *there is* not a present to bring to the man of God: what [r]have we?

8 And the servant answered Saul again, and said, Behold, [s]I have here at hand the fourth part of a shekel of silver: *that* will I give to the man of God, to tell us our way.

9 (Beforetime in Israel, when a man [w]went to inquire of God, thus he spake, Come, and let us go to the seer: for *he that is* now *called* a Prophet was beforetime called [x]a Seer.)

10 Then said Saul to his servant, [t]Well said; come, let us go. So they went unto the city where the man of God *was*.

11 ¶ *And* as they went up [u]the hill to the city, [y]they found young maidens going out to draw water, and said unto them, Is the seer here?

12 And they answered them, and said, He is; behold, *he is* before you: make haste now, for he came today to the city; for [z]*there is* a [v]sacrifice of the people today [a]in the high place:

13 As soon as ye be come into the city, ye shall straightway find him, before he go up to the high place to eat: for the people will not eat until he come, because he doth bless the sacrifice; *and* afterwards they eat that be bidden. Now therefore get you up; for about [w]this time ye shall find him.

14 And they went up into the city:

8:22 [p]ver. 7 Hos. 13:11 **9:1** [q]ch. 14:51 1 Chr. 8:33 & 9:39 **9:2** [r]ch. 10:23 **9:4** [s]2 Ki. 4:42 **9:6** [t]Deut. 33:1 1 Ki. 13:1 [u]ch. 3:19 **9:7** [v]See Judg. 6:18 & 13:17 1 Ki. 14:3 2 Ki. 4:42 & 8:8 **9:9** [w]Gen. 25:22 [x]2 Sam. 24:11 2 Ki. 17:13 1 Chr. 26:28 & 29:29 2 Chr. 16:7,10 Is. 30:10 Amos 7:12 **9:11** [y]Gen. 24:11 **9:12** [z]Gen. 31:54 ch. 16:2 [a]1 Ki. 3:2

[o] Or, *the son of a man of Jemini* [p] Or, *substance* [q] Heb. *is gone out of* [r] Heb. *is with us* [s] Heb. *there is found in my hand* [t] Heb. *Thy word* is *good* [u] Heb. *in the ascent of the city* [v] Or, *feast* [w] Heb. *today*

8:22 MAKE [APPOINT] THEM A KING. Although it was not God's will to give Israel a king at this time, He nevertheless did so. This is an example of history proceeding according to God's permissive will rather than His perfect will (see 1 Tim. 2:4, note; see article on THE WILL OF GOD, p. 1060). God permitted the appointment of a king and monarchial government in spite of its eventual trouble and disaster (vv. 10–18) for the following reasons: (1) To show the need for God's perfect kingdom and thus to foreshadow Jesus Christ as King of kings (Mat. 2:2; 21:5; 1 Tim. 1:17; 6:15; Rev. 19:16); (2) To teach His people that no type of government on earth will resolve their problems or guarantee peace and safety as long as sinful people exist. Only in the new heaven and new earth will righteousness reign and complete peace and happiness be the lot of all people (Rev. 21—22).

9:9 SEER. A seer (Heb. *ro'eh*, "one who sees") was a person with a special God-given ability to see in the spiritual realm or foresee future events (cf. v. 19; 2 Sam. 24:11; 2 Chr. 29:25; 35:15). Often God revealed present or future events to the prophet through dreams and visions (cf. Num. 12:6); thus when the gift of prophecy was rare, it was reported that there was "no open vision" (3:1). Later in Israel's history the seer came to be less prominent than the prophet, whose primary task was to speak to God's covenant people about what he saw or heard from God concerning their loyalty to God (see article on THE PROPHET IN THE OLD TESTAMENT, p. 1002).

and when they were come into the city,
behold, Samuel came out against
them, for to go up to the high place.
15 ¶ [b]Now the LORD had told Sam-
uel in his ear a day before Saul came,
saying,
16 Tomorrow about this time I will
send thee a man out of the land of Ben-
jamin, [c]and thou shalt anoint him *to*
be captain over my people Israel, that
he may save my people out of the hand
of the Philistines: for I have [d]looked
upon my people, because their cry is
come unto me.
17 And when Samuel saw Saul, the
LORD said unto him, [e]Behold the man
whom I spake to thee of! this same
shall [x]reign over my people.
18 Then Saul drew near to Samuel
in the gate, and said, Tell me, I pray
thee, where the seer's house *is*.
19 And Samuel answered Saul, and
said, I *am* the seer: go up before me
unto the high place; for ye shall eat
with me today, and tomorrow I will let
thee go, and will tell thee all that *is* in
thine heart.
20 And as for [f]thine asses that
were lost [y]three days ago, set not thy
mind on them; for they are found. And
on whom [g]*is* all the desire of Israel?
Is it not on thee, and on all thy father's
house?
21 And Saul answered and said,
[h]*Am* not I a Benjamite, of the [i]small-
est of the tribes of Israel? and [j]my
family the least of all the families of
the tribe of Benjamin? wherefore then
speakest thou [z]so to me?
22 And Samuel took Saul and his
servant, and brought them into the par-
lour, and made them sit in the chiefest
place among them that were bidden,
which *were* about thirty persons.
23 And Samuel said unto the cook,
Bring the portion which I gave thee, of
which I said unto thee, Set it by thee.
24 And the cook took up [k]the
shoulder, and *that* which *was* upon it,
and set *it* before Saul. And *Samuel* said,
Behold that which is [a]left! set *it* be-
fore thee, *and* eat: for unto this time
hath it been kept for thee since I said,
I have invited the people. So Saul did
eat with Samuel that day.
25 ¶ And when they were come
down from the high place into the city,
Samuel communed with Saul upon
[l]the top of the house.
26 And they arose early: and it
came to pass about the spring of the
day, that Samuel called Saul to the top
of the house, saying, Up, that I may
send thee away. And Saul arose, and
they went out both of them, he and
Samuel, abroad.
27 *And* as they were going down to
the end of the city, Samuel said to Saul,
Bid the servant pass on before us, (and
he passed on,) but stand thou still [b]a
while, that I may show thee the word
of God.

10 THEN [m]SAMUEL took a vial of
oil, and poured *it* upon his head,
[n]and kissed him, and said, *Is it* not
because [o]the LORD hath anointed thee
to be captain over [p]his inheritance?
2 When thou art departed from me
today, then thou shalt find two men by
[q]Rachel's sepulchre in the border of
Benjamin [r]at Zelzah; and they will
say unto thee, The asses which thou
wentest to seek are found: and, lo, thy
father hath left [c]the care of the asses,
and sorroweth for you, saying, What
shall I do for my son?
3 Then shalt thou go on forward
from thence, and thou shalt come to
the plain of Tabor, and there shall meet
thee three men going up [s]to God to
Beth-el, one carrying three kids, and
another carrying three loaves of bread,
and another carrying a bottle of wine:
4 And they will [d]salute thee, and
give thee two *loaves* of bread; which
thou shalt receive of their hands.
5 After that thou shalt come to the

9:15 [b]ch. 15:1 Acts 13:21 **9:16** [c]ch. 10:1 [d]Ex. 2:25 & 3:7,9 **9:17** [e]ch. 16:12 Hos. 13:11 **9:20** [f]ver. 3 [g]ch. 8:5,19 & 12:13 **9:21** [h]ch. 15:17 [i]Judg. 20:46-48 [j]See Judg. 6:15 **9:24** [k]Lev. 7:32,33 Ezek. 24:4 **9:25** [l]Deut. 22:8 2 Sam. 11:2 Acts 10:9 **10:1** [m]ch. 9:16 & 16:13 2 Ki. 9:3,6 [n]Ps. 2:12 [o]Acts 13:21 [p]Deut. 32:9 **10:2** [q]Gen. 35:19,20 [r]Josh. 18:28 **10:3** [s]Gen. 28:22 & 35:1,3,7

[x] Heb. *restrain in* [y] Heb. *today three days* [z] Heb. *according to this word?* [a] Or, *reserved* [b] Heb. *today* [c] Heb. *the business* [d] Heb. *ask thee of peace* as Judg. 18:15

10:1 THE LORD HATH ANOINTED THEE. The purpose of Saul's anointing was (1) to dedicate him to God for the special task to which he was called, and (2) to impart to him enabling grace and gifts for his God-appointed task. "The LORD's anointed" became a common term for Israel's king (cf. 12:3; Lam. 4:20). God's ultimate anointed king is Jesus, the Messiah (Heb. *mashiah*, "the Anointed One"), whom He anointed with the Holy Spirit (John 1:32–33). Subsequently, all Jesus' followers must be anointed with the same Holy Spirit (2 Cor. 1:21; 1 John 2:20) as new covenant priests and kings (cf. 1 Pet. 2:5,9).

10:5 THEY SHALL PROPHESY. This prophesying (vv. 6,10–11,13) most likely involved praise to God through both prophetic utterance and songs inspired by the Holy Spirit (cf. Num. 11:25).

hill of God, [t]where *is* the garrison of the Philistines: and it shall come to pass, when thou art come thither to the city, that thou shalt meet a company of prophets coming down [u]from the high place with a psaltery, and a tabret, and a pipe, and a harp, before them; [v]and they shall prophesy:

6 And [w]the spirit of the LORD will come upon thee, and [x]thou shalt prophesy with them, and shalt be turned into another man.

7 And [e]let it be, when these [y]signs are come unto thee, [z]*that*[f] thou do as occasion serve thee; for [a]God *is* with thee.

8 And thou shalt go down before me [b]to Gilgal; and, behold, I will come down unto thee, to offer burnt offerings, *and* to sacrifice sacrifices of peace offerings: [c]seven days shalt thou tarry, till I come to thee, and show thee what thou shalt do.

Saul becomes king of Israel

9 ¶ And it was *so,* that when he had turned his [g]back to go from Samuel, God [h]gave him another heart: and all those signs came to pass that day.

10 And [d]when they came thither to the hill, behold, [e]a company of prophets met him; and the spirit of God came upon him, and he prophesied among them.

11 And it came to pass, when all that knew him beforetime saw that, behold, he prophesied among the prophets, then the people said [i]one to another, What *is* this *that* is come unto the son of Kish? [f]*Is* Saul also among the prophets?

12 And one [j]of the same place answered and said, But [g]who *is* their father? Therefore it became a proverb, *Is* Saul also among the prophets?

13 And when he had made an end of prophesying, he came to the high place.

14 ¶ And Saul's uncle said unto him and to his servant, Whither went ye? And he said, To seek the asses: and when we saw that *they were* no where, we came to Samuel.

15 And Saul's uncle said, Tell me, I pray thee, what Samuel said unto you.

16 And Saul said unto his uncle, He told us plainly that the asses were found. But of the matter of the kingdom, whereof Samuel spake, he told him not.

17 ¶ And Samuel called the people together [h]unto the LORD [i]to Mizpeh;

18 And said unto the children of Israel, [j]Thus saith the LORD God of Israel, I brought up Israel out of Egypt, and delivered you out of the hand of the Egyptians, and out of the hand of all kingdoms, *and* of them that oppressed you:

19 [k]And ye have this day rejected your God, who himself saved you out of all your adversities and your tribulations; and ye have said unto him, *Nay,* but set a king over us. Now therefore present yourselves before the LORD by your tribes, and by your thousands.

20 And when Samuel had [l]caused all the tribes of Israel to come near, the tribe of Benjamin was taken.

21 When he had caused the tribe of Benjamin to come near by their families, the family of Matri was taken, and Saul the son of Kish was taken: and when they sought him, he could not be found.

22 Therefore they [m]inquired of the LORD further, if the man should yet come thither. And the LORD answered, Behold, he hath hid himself among the stuff.

23 And they ran and fetched him thence: and when he stood among the people, [n]he was higher than any of the people from his shoulders and upward.

24 And Samuel said to all the people, See ye him [o]whom the LORD hath

10:5 [t]ch. 13:3 [u]ch. 9:12 [v]Ex. 15:20,21 2 Ki. 3:15 1 Cor. 14:1
10:6 [w]Num. 11:25 ch. 16:13 [x]ver. 10 ch. 19:23,24
10:7 [y]Ex. 4:8 Luke 2:12 [z]Judg. 9:33 [a]Judg. 6:12
10:8 [b]ch. 11:14,15 [c]ch. 13:8
10:10 [d]ver. 5 [e]ch. 19:20
10:11 [f]Mat. 13:54,55 John 7:15 Acts 4:13
10:12 [g]Is. 54:13 John 6:45
10:17 [h]Judg. 11.11 & 20:1 [i]ch. 7:5,6
10:18 [j]Judg. 6:8,9
10:19 [k]ch. 8:7,19 & 12:12.
10:20 [l]Acts 1:24,26
10:22 [m]ch. 23:2,4,10,11
10:23 [n]ch. 9:2
10:24 [o]2 Sam. 21:6

[e] Heb. *it shall come to pass, that when these signs* [f] Heb. *do for thee as thine hand shall find* [g] Heb. *shoulder* [h] Heb. *turned* [i] Heb. *a man to his neighbour* [j] Heb. *from thence*

10:6 TURNED INTO ANOTHER MAN. God changed the inner disposition of Saul through his anointing by the Holy Spirit (cf. v. 9). This change was not unconditional or permanent, but something that could be maintained only by obedience to God. He later refused to obey God, whereupon the Spirit left him (13:13–14; 15:11; 16:14).

10:9 GOD GAVE HIM ANOTHER HEART. Saul possessed many God-given endowments to help him serve God and Israel in a righteous manner. He had a changed heart, an empowering by the Holy Spirit (v. 6), a strong body (v. 23), a humble attitude (9:21), and the guidance and prayers of Samuel (12:23–25). Note especially the gift of prophecy (vv. 10–13), which was a sign that he had been anointed to kingship. Nevertheless, by his waywardness Saul soon failed to remain faithful to God and His word (13:13–14).

chosen, that *there is* none like him among all the people? And all the people shouted, and said, [p]God[k] save the king.

25 Then Samuel told the people [q]the manner of the kingdom, and wrote *it* in a book, and laid *it* up before the LORD. And Samuel sent all the people away, every man to his house.

26 ¶ And Saul also went home [r]to Gibeah; and there went with him a band of men, whose hearts God had touched.

27 [s]But the [t]children of Belial said, How shall this man save us? And they despised him, [u]and brought him no presents. But [l]he held his peace.

The Ammonites defeated

11 THEN [v]NAHASH the Ammonite came up, and encamped against [w]Jabesh-gilead: and all the men of Jabesh said unto Nahash, [x]Make a covenant with us, and we will serve thee.

2 And Nahash the Ammonite answered them, On this *condition* will I make *a covenant* with you, that I may thrust out all your right eyes, and lay it *for* [y]a reproach upon all Israel.

3 And the elders of Jabesh said unto him, [m]Give us seven days' respite, that we may send messengers unto all the coasts of Israel: and then, if *there be* no man to save us, we will come out to thee.

4 ¶ Then came the messengers [z]to Gibeah of Saul, and told the tidings in the ears of the people: and [a]all the people lifted up their voices, and wept.

5 And, behold, Saul came after the herd out of the field; and Saul said, What *aileth* the people that they weep? And they told him the tidings of the men of Jabesh.

6 [b]And the spirit of God came upon Saul when he heard those tidings, and his anger was kindled greatly.

7 And he took a yoke of oxen, and [c]hewed them in pieces, and sent *them* throughout all the coasts of Israel by the hands of messengers, saying, [d]Whosoever cometh not forth after Saul and after Samuel, so shall it be done unto his oxen. And the fear of the LORD fell on the people, and they came out [n]with one consent. 1 Sam. 16:13

8 And when he numbered them in [e]Bezek, the children [f]of Israel were three hundred thousand, and the men of Judah thirty thousand.

9 And they said unto the messengers that came, Thus shall ye say unto the men of Jabesh-gilead, Tomorrow, by *that time* the sun be hot, ye shall have [o]help. And the messengers came and showed *it* to the men of Jabesh; and they were glad.

10 Therefore the men of Jabesh said, Tomorrow [g]we will come out unto you, and ye shall do with us all that seemeth good unto you.

11 And it was *so* on the morrow, that [h]Saul put the people [i]in three companies; and they came into the midst of the host in the morning watch, and slew the Ammonites until the heat of the day: and it came to pass, that they which remained were scattered, so that two of them were not left together.

12 ¶ And the people said unto Samuel, [j]Who *is* he that said, Shall Saul reign over us? [k]bring the men, that we may put them to death.

13 And Saul said, [l]There shall not a man be put to death this day: for today [m]the LORD hath wrought salvation in Israel.

14 Then said Samuel to the people, Come, and let us go [n]to Gilgal, and renew the kingdom there.

15 And all the people went to Gilgal; and there they made Saul king [o]before the LORD in Gilgal; and [p]there

10:24 [p]1 Ki. 1:25,39 **10:25** [q]ch. 8:11 **10:26** [r]Judg. 20:14 ch. 11:4 **10:27** [s]ch. 11:12 [t]Deut. 13:13 [u]2 Sam. 8:2 1 Ki. 4:21 Mat. 2:11 **11:1** [v]ch. 12:12 [w]Judg. 21:8 [x]Gen. 26:28 1 Ki. 20:34 **11:2** [y]Gen. 34:14 ch. 17:26 **11:4** [z]ch. 10:26 & 15:34 2 Sam. 21:6 [a]Judg. 2:4 **11:6** [b]Judg. 3:10 & 6:34 ch. 10:10 **11:7** [c]Judg. 19:29 [d]Judg. 21:5,8,10 **11:8** [e]Judg. 1:5 [f]2 Sam. 24:9 **11:10** [g]ver. 3 **11:11** [h]See ch. 31:11 [i]Judg. 7:16 **11:12** [j]ch. 10:27 [k]See Luke 19:27 **11:13** [l]2 Sam. 19:22 [m]Ex. 14:13,30 ch. 19:5 **11:14** [n]ch. 10:8 **11:15** [o]ch. 10:17 [p]ch. 10:8

[k] Heb. *Let the king live* [l] Or, *he was as though he had been deaf* [m] Heb. *Forbear us* [n] Heb. *as one man* [o] Or, *deliverance*

10:25 THE MANNER OF THE KINGDOM. Israel's king was to be distinctly different from the kings of other nations. Rather than being an absolute monarch, he was to be a theocratic king, one who was subject to God as the ultimate Ruler of the people (see Deut. 17:14–20 for duties and regulations for kings).

11:6 THE SPIRIT OF GOD CAME UPON SAUL . . . HIS ANGER WAS KINDLED. The promise of the empowering of the Spirit spoken by Samuel at Saul's anointing as king (10:6) was fulfilled here. Note that Saul, as king, gave the same type of military leadership against Israel's enemies as the judges did (cf. Judg. 14:6, where this phrase is used of Samson). One dimension of the Holy Spirit's work in the believer is genuine anger at sin and at the mistreatment of others. Jesus Himself expressed such anger at sin and evil on several occasions (see Luke 19:45, note; John 11:33, note).

they sacrificed sacrifices of peace offerings before the LORD; and there Saul and all the men of Israel rejoiced greatly.

Samuel addresses the people

12 AND SAMUEL said unto all Israel, Behold, I have hearkened unto [q]your voice in all that ye said unto me, and [r]have made a king over you.

2 And now, behold, the king [s]walketh before you: [t]and I am old and grayheaded; and, behold, my sons *are* with you: and I have walked before you from my childhood unto this day.

3 Behold, here I *am:* witness against me before the LORD, and before [u]his anointed: [v]whose ox have I taken? or whose ass have I taken? or whom have I defrauded? whom have I oppressed? or of whose hand have I received *any* [p]bribe [q]to [w]blind mine eyes therewith? and I will restore it you.

4 And they said, Thou hast not defrauded us, nor oppressed us, neither hast thou taken aught of any man's hand.

5 And he said unto them, The LORD *is* witness against you, and his anointed *is* witness this day, [x]that ye have not found aught [y]in my hand. And they answered, *He is* witness.

6 ¶ And Samuel said unto the people, [z]*It is* the LORD that [r]advanced Moses and Aaron, and that brought your fathers up out of the land of Egypt.

7 Now therefore stand still, that I may [a]reason with you before the LORD of all the [b]righteous[s] acts of the LORD, which he did [t]to you and to your fathers.

8 [c]When Jacob was come into Egypt, and your fathers [d]cried unto the LORD, then the LORD [e]sent Moses and Aaron, which brought forth your fathers out of Egypt, and made them dwell in this place.

9 And when they [f]forgat the LORD their God, [g]he sold them into the hand of Sisera, captain of the host of Hazor, and into the hand of [h]the Philistines, and into the hand of the king [i]of Moab, and they fought against them.

10 And they cried unto the LORD, and said, [j]We have sinned, because we have forsaken the LORD, [k]and have served Baalim and Ashtaroth: but now [l]deliver us out of the hand of our enemies, and we will serve thee.

11 And the LORD sent [m]Jerubbaal, and Bedan, and [n]Jephthah, and [o]Samuel, and delivered you out of the hand of your enemies on every side, and ye dwelled safe.

12 And when ye saw that [p]Nahash the king of the children of Ammon came against you, [q]ye said unto me, Nay; but a king shall reign over us: when [r]the LORD your God *was* your king.

13 Now therefore [s]behold the king [t]whom ye have chosen, *and* whom ye have desired! and, behold, [u]the LORD hath set a king over you.

14 If ye will [v]fear the LORD, and serve him, and obey his voice, and not rebel against the [u]commandment of the LORD, then shall both ye and also the king that reigneth over you [v]continue following the LORD your God:

15 But if ye will [w]not obey the voice of the LORD, but rebel against the commandment of the LORD, then shall the hand of the LORD be against you, [x]as *it was* against your fathers. 1 Sa 15:2. 23

16 ¶ Now therefore [y]stand and see this great thing, which the LORD will do before your eyes.

17 *Is it* not [z]wheat harvest today? [a]I will call unto the LORD, and he shall send thunder and rain; that ye may perceive and see that [b]your wickedness *is* great, which ye have done in the sight of the LORD, in asking you a king.

18 So Samuel called unto the LORD; and the LORD sent thunder and rain that

12:1 [q]ch. 8:5,19,20 [r]ch. 10:24 **12:2** [s]Num. 27:17 ch. 8:20 [t]ch. 8:1,5 **12:3** [u]ch. 24:6 2 Sam. 1:14,16 [v]Num. 16:15 Acts 20:33 1 Thes. 2:5 [w]Deut. 16:19 **12:5** [x]John 18:38 Acts 23:9 [y]Ex. 22:4 **12:6** [z]Mic. 6:4 **12:7** [a]Is. 1:18 Mic. 6:2,3 [b]Judg. 5:11 **12:8** [c]Gen. 46:5,6 [d]Ex. 2:23 [e]Ex. 3:10 **12:9** [f]Judg. 3:7 [g]Judg. 4:2 [h]Judg. 10:7 [i]Judg. 3:12 **12:10** [j]Judg. 10:10 [k]Judg. 2:13 [l]Judg. 10:15,16 **12:11** [m]Judg. 6:14,32 [n]Judg. 11:1 [o]ch. 7:13 **12:12** [p]ch. 11:1 [q]ch. 8:5,19 [r]Judg. 8:23 ch. 8:7 **12:13** [s]ch. 10:24 [t]ch. 8:5 [u]Hos. 13:11 **12:14** [v]Josh. 24:14 **12:15** [w]Lev. 26:14 Deut. 28:15 Josh. 24:20 [x]ver. 9 **12:16** [y]Ex. 14:13 **12:17** [z]Prov. 26:1 [a]Josh. 10:12 ch. 7:9,10 Jas. 5:16-18 [b]ch. 8:7

[p] Heb. *ransom* [q] Or, *that I should hide mine eyes at him* [r] Or, *made* [s] Heb. *righteousnesses,* or, *benefits* [t] Heb. *with* [u] Heb. *mouth* [v] Heb. *be after*

12:7–18 THAT I MAY REASON WITH YOU. Samuel manifested the true prophet's heart by pleading with the people to remain faithful to God and His commandments. Samuel himself remained faithful to God and His purpose throughout his life and never deviated from his original personal integrity, mission, or message (vv. 3–5; 2:35).

12:14 FEAR THE LORD, AND . . . OBEY HIS VOICE. Samuel made it clear that God's blessing and the welfare of the nation are conditioned not upon having a king, but upon their response of reverence for and service to God with a full obedience to His covenant word (vv. 24–25).

day: and [c]all the people greatly feared
the LORD and Samuel.
19 And all the people said unto
Samuel, [d]Pray for thy servants unto
the LORD thy God, that we die not: for
we have added unto all our sins *this*
evil, to ask us a king.
20 ¶ And Samuel said unto the peo-
ple, Fear not: ye have done all this
wickedness: yet turn not aside from
following the LORD, but serve the LORD
with all your heart;
21 And [e]turn ye not aside: [f]for
then should ye go after vain *things,*
which cannot profit nor deliver; for
they *are* vain.
22 For [g]the LORD will not forsake
his people [h]for his great name's sake:
because [i]it hath pleased the LORD to
make you his people.
23 Moreover as for me, God forbid
that I should sin against the LORD
[j]in[w] ceasing to pray for you: but [k]I
will teach you the [l]good and the right
way:
24 [m]Only fear the LORD, and serve
him in truth with all your heart: for
[n]consider [x]how [o]great *things* he
hath done for you.
25 But if ye shall still do wickedly,
[p]ye shall be consumed, [q]both ye and
your king.

Samuel rebukes Saul

13 SAUL [y]REIGNED one year;
and when he had reigned two
years over Israel,
2 Saul chose him three thousand
men of Israel; *whereof* two thousand
were with Saul in Michmash and in
mount Beth-el, and a thousand were
with Jonathan in [r]Gibeah of Benja-
min: and the rest of the people he sent
every man to his tent.
3 And Jonathan smote [s]the garri-
son of the Philistines that *was* in
[z]Geba, and the Philistines heard *of it.*
And Saul blew the trumpet throughout
all the land, saying, Let the Hebrews
hear.
4 And all Israel heard say *that* Saul
had smitten a garrison of the Philis-
tines, and *that* Israel also [a]was had in
abomination with the Philistines. And
the people were called together after
Saul to Gilgal.
5 ¶ And the Philistines gathered
themselves together to fight with Isra-
el, thirty thousand chariots, and six
thousand horsemen, and people as
the sand which *is* on the sea shore in
multitude: and they came up, and
pitched in Michmash, eastward from
Beth-aven.
6 When the men of Israel saw that
they were in a strait, (for the people
were distressed,) then the people [t]did
hide themselves in caves, and in thick-
ets, and in rocks, and in high places,
and in pits.
7 And *some of* the Hebrews went
over Jordan to the land of Gad and Gile-
ad. As for Saul, he *was* yet in Gilgal,

12:18 [c]Ex. 14:31 Ezra 10:9
12:19 [d]Ex. 9:28 & 10:17 Jas. 5:15 1 John 5:16
12:21 [e]Deut. 11:16 [f]Jer. 16:19 Hab. 2:18 1 Cor. 8:4
12:22 [g]1 Ki. 6:13 [h]Josh. 7:9 Jer. 14:21 [i]Deut. 7:7,8
12:23 [j]Acts 12:5 Rom. 1:9 Col. 1:9 2 Tim. 1:3 [k]Ps. 34:11 Prov. 4:11 [l]1 Ki. 8:36 2 Chr. 6:27 Jer. 6:16
12:24 [m]Eccl. 12:13 [n]Is. 5:12 [o]Deut. 10:21
12:25 [p]Josh. 24:20 [q]Deut. 28:36
13:2 [r]ch. 10:26
13:3 [s]ch. 10:5
13:6 [t]Judg. 6:2

[w]Heb. *from ceasing* [x]Or, *what a great* thing
[y]Heb. *the son of one year in his reigning*
[z]Or, *The hill* [a]Heb. *did stink;* see Gen. 34:30; Ex. 5:21

12:21 *GO* AFTER VAIN *THINGS*. Samuel warned the Israelites not to follow after useless and powerless idol gods; only the Lord God could give them the help they needed in any time of crisis. For more about idolatry, see article on THE NATURE OF IDOLATRY, p. 428.

12:22 THE LORD WILL NOT FORSAKE HIS PEOPLE. God continued to work with Israel even though they had made a wrong choice and departed from His perfect will for them. In His mercy and patience, God will often keep on helping us even when we make wrong choices and enter a path that is not wholly His will for our lives. When we stray, we must seek forgiveness and resume obeying and serving God with our whole heart (v. 24). If we do so, God will bless us in our present situation. However, if we persist in going our own way, we will bring destruction upon ourselves (v. 25).

12:23 GOD FORBID THAT I SHOULD SIN AGAINST THE LORD IN CEASING TO PRAY. Samuel was a man of prayer. (1) He was born in answer to his mother's prayer (1:10–20); he prayed for God's people and through prayer saw Israel delivered from their enemy (7:5–14); he prayed when Israel rejected God (8:6); he prayed continually for God's people to fear the Lord and serve Him in truth (12:23–24). (2) Ps. 99:6 states that he was "among them that call upon [God's] name." Jer. 15:1 indicates that as an intercessor, Samuel had the same stature before God as Moses. (3) Samuel so understood the nature, power, and significance of intercessory prayer that he considered it a sin to cease to intercede (see article on INTERCESSION, p. 1268).

12:24 ONLY FEAR THE LORD ... SERVE HIM. Although King Saul now became ruler of Israel, Samuel as a prophet of God continued to call both the king and the people to walk in God's way (v. 23). Representing God and His word, the prophet stood apart from Saul and all future kings of Israel as God's voice (3:20; 15:1; Ex. 7:1–2). Israel's kings were to remain subject to the authority, teaching, and rebuke of God through His prophets (cf. 13:13–14; 15:17–23; 2 Sam. 12:1–15).

THE NATURE OF IDOLATRY

***1 Sam. 12:20–21** "And Samuel said unto the people, Fear not: ye have done all this wickedness: yet turn not aside from following the* LORD*, but serve the* LORD *with all your heart; and turn ye not aside: for* then should ye go *after vain* things, *which cannot profit nor deliver; for they* are *vain."*

Idolatry is a sin that recurs throughout the history of God's people. The first recorded instance was in the family of Jacob (Israel); note that just before he arrived in Bethel, Jacob commanded that their images be put away (Gen. 35:1–4). The first story recorded in the Bible in which Israel as a whole engaged in idolatry was the worship of the golden calf while Moses was on Mount Sinai (Ex. 32:1–6). During the time of the judges God's people frequently turned to idols. Though there is no evidence of idolatry during the time of Saul or David, the latter years of King Solomon set in motion a consistent pattern of idolatry in Israel (1 Ki. 11:1–8). In the history of the divided kingdom, all of the kings of the northern kingdom of Israel were idolatrous, as were many of the kings of the southern kingdom of Judah. Only after the exile did the idolatrous worship of other gods cease among the Jews.

ATTRACTIVENESS OF IDOLATRY. Why was idolatry so attractive to the Israelites? Several factors were involved. (1) The Israelites were surrounded by heathen nations who believed that the worship of several gods was superior to the worship of a single God. In other words, more was better. God's people were influenced by these nations and constantly imitated them instead of obeying God's command to keep themselves holy and separate from them.

(2) The gods of the other nations did not require the kind of obedience that the Lord God of Israel demanded. For example, many of the pagan religions included sexual immorality with temple prostitutes as part of their religious rituals. This practice undoubtedly appealed to many within Israel. God, on the other hand, required His people to obey His high moral standards as defined in His law in order to maintain a saving relationship with Him. They had to resist consistently the tendency toward immorality and other sinful practices condoned or blessed by the pagan religions.

(3) Because of the demonic character of idols (see next section), idolatry at times produced genuine and demonstrable results for those who worshiped idols. The demonic powers behind the idols were able, though on a limited basis, to impart temporary material and physical benefits. Fertility gods promised the birth of children, weather gods (sun, moon, rain, etc.) promised the appropriate conditions for abundant crops; and warrior gods promised protection from enemies and victory in battle. Such promised benefits were attractive to the Israelites, and for this reason many were willing to serve these idols.

ESSENTIAL CHARACTER OF IDOLATRY. We cannot understand idolatry's attractiveness unless we understand its true nature. (1) The Bible makes it plain that an idol in and of itself is nothing (Jer. 2:11; 16:20). An idol is a mere piece of wood or stone, carved out by human hands, that has no power of its own. Samuel calls idols vain or useless things (1 Sam. 12:21), and Paul states explicitly: "we know that an idol *is* nothing in the world" (1 Cor. 8:4; cf. 10:19–20). For this reason the psalmists (e.g., Ps. 115:4–8; 135:15–18) and prophets (e.g., 1 Ki. 18:27; Is. 44:9–20; 46:1–7; Jer. 10:3–5) frequently mocked idols.

(2) However, behind all idols are demons, spiritual beings controlled by the devil. Both Moses (see Deut. 32:17, note) and the psalmist (Ps. 106:36–37) equate false gods with devils. Note too what Paul says in his letter to the Corinthians about eating meat sacrificed to idols: "the things which the Gentiles sacrifice, they sacrifice to devils, and

not to God" (1 Cor. 10:20). In other words, the power behind idolatry is the power and activity of devils (demons), and demons do indeed have great power in this world. Christians know, of course, that the power of Jesus Christ is greater than that of demons (see article on POWER OVER SATAN AND DEMONS, p. 1486). Nevertheless, Satan as "the god of this world" (2 Cor. 4:4) exercises tremendous power in this present evil age (see 1 John 5:19, note; cf. Luke 13:16; Gal. 1:4; Eph. 6:12; Heb. 2:14). He has the power to produce lying signs and false wonders (2 Thes. 2:9; Rev. 13:2–8,13; 16:13–14; 19:20) and to bestow physical and material benefits on people. Undoubtedly, this power sometimes contributes to the prosperity of the wicked (cf. Ps. 10:2–6; 37:16,35; 49:6; 73:3–12).

(3) The relationship between idolatry and demons is seen more clearly when we realize how intricately pagan religious practices are linked with spiritism, sorcery, divination, enchantment, witchcraft, necromancy, and the like (cf. 2 Ki. 21:3–6; Is. 8:19; see Deut. 18:9–11, notes; Rev. 9:21, note). According to Scripture, all of these occult practices involve paying homage to demons. For example, when the witch at Endor was asked by Saul to bring up Samuel from the dead, she saw a god "ascending out of the earth," which proved to represent Samuel (1 Sam. 28:8–14); she had expected a demon to come out of the underworld (See 1 Sam. 28:12, note).

(4) The N.T. calls covetousness a form of idolatry (Col. 3:5). The connection is obvious: because demons are able to give material benefits, people who are not satisfied with what they have but are greedy for more will not hesitate to give their allegiance to the principles and desires of those spiritual beings who can get them what they want. Though such people may not worship gods made out of wood and stone, they do in reality worship the demons that stand behind greed and covetousness; hence, they are idolaters. Thus Jesus' statement that we "cannot serve God and mammon" (Mat. 6:24) is essentially the same as Paul's admonition that believers may "not drink the cup of the Lord, and the cup of devils" (1 Cor. 10:21).

GOD'S RESPONSE TO IDOLATRY. God will not tolerate any form of idolatry. (1) He frequently warned against it in the O.T. (a) In the Ten Commandments, the first two take a direct stand against the worship of any other god than the Lord God of Israel (see Ex. 20:3–4, notes). (b) This type of instruction was repeated elsewhere by God (e.g., Ex. 23:13,24; 34:14–17; Deut. 4:23–24; 6:14; Josh. 23:7; Judg. 6:10; 2 Ki. 17:35,37–38). (c) Linked with the command not to serve other gods was a command to destroy all the idols and to break down the images of the heathen nations in the land of Canaan (Ex. 23:24; 34:13; Deut. 7:4–5; 12:2–3).

(2) The history of the Israelites was all too often the history of idol worship. God became very angry with His people for failing to destroy all of the idols in the promised land and for adopting the worship of false gods instead. The Lord punished them by allowing their enemies to gain control over them. (a) The book of Judges presents an ever-recurring cycle: the Israelites began to serve the idol gods of the nations that they failed to drive out; God allowed their enemies to gain power over them; God's people cried out to the Lord; the Lord heard and sent a judge to deliver them. (b) The idolatry of the northern kingdom went on unhindered for nearly two centuries. Finally, God's patience ran out, and He allowed the Assyrians to destroy Israel's capital and to scatter the ten tribes (2 Ki. 17:6–18). (c) The southern kingdom of Judah did have a number of God-fearing kings, such as Hezekiah and Josiah; but because of wicked kings like Manasseh, idolatry became entrenched in the nation of Judah (2 Ki. 21:1–9). As a result God said through the prophets that He would allow Jerusalem to be destroyed (2 Ki. 21:10–16). In spite of these warnings, idolatry continued (see, e.g., Is. 48:4–5; Jer. 2:4–30; 16:18–21; Ezek. 8), until God finally fulfilled His prophecy through King Nebuchadnezzar of Babylon, who captured Jerusalem, burned the temple, and sacked the city (2 Ki. 25).

(3) The N.T. also warns all believers against idolatry. (a) Idolatry manifests itself in various forms today. It explicitly appears in the false world religions, as well as in sorcery, satanism, and other forms of the occult. It is found wherever men and women

give themselves over to greed and materialism, rather than trusting in God alone. Finally, it occurs within the church when people believe that they can serve God and experience His salvation and blessings, and at one and the same time participate in the immoral and wicked practices of the world. (b) Consequently, the N.T. admonishes us not to be covetous, greedy, or immoral (Col. 3:5; cf. Mat. 6:19–24; Rom. 7:7; Heb. 13:5–6; see article on RICHES AND POVERTY, p. 1568), but rather to flee from all forms of idolatry (1 Cor. 10:14; 1 John 5:21). God backs up his warnings with the statement that those who engage in any form of idolatry will not inherit His kingdom (1 Cor. 6:9–10; Gal. 5:20–21; Rev. 22:15).

and all the people [b]followed him trembling.

8 ¶ [u]And he tarried seven days, according to the set time that Samuel *had appointed:* but Samuel came not to Gilgal; and the people were scattered from him.

9 And Saul said, Bring hither a burnt offering to me, and peace offerings. And he offered the burnt offering.

10 And it came to pass, that as soon as he had made an end of offering the burnt offering, behold, Samuel came; and Saul went out to meet him, that he might [c]salute him.

11 ¶ And Samuel said, What hast thou done? And Saul said, Because I saw that the people were scattered from me, and *that* thou camest not within the days appointed, and *that* the Philistines gathered themselves together at Michmash;

12 Therefore said I, The Philistines will come down now upon me to Gilgal, and I have not [d]made supplication unto the LORD: I forced myself therefore, and offered a burnt offering.

13 And Samuel said to Saul, [v]Thou hast done foolishly: [w]thou hast not kept the commandment of the LORD thy God, which he commanded thee: for now would the LORD have established thy kingdom upon Israel for ever.

14 [x]But now thy kingdom shall not continue: [y]the LORD hath sought him a man after his own heart, and the LORD hath commanded him *to be* captain over his people, because thou hast not kept *that* which the LORD commanded thee.

Saul's small army

15 And Samuel arose, and gat him up from Gilgal unto Gibeah of Benjamin. And Saul numbered the people *that were* [e]present with him, [z]about six hundred men.

16 And Saul, and Jonathan his son, and the people *that were* present with them, abode in [f]Gibeah of Benjamin: but the Philistines encamped in Michmash.

17 ¶ And the spoilers came out of the camp of the Philistines in three companies: one company turned unto the way *that leadeth to* [a]Ophrah, unto the land of Shual:

18 And another company turned the way *to* [b]Beth-horon: and another company turned *to* the way of the border that looketh to the valley of [c]Zeboim toward the wilderness.

19 ¶ Now [d]there was no smith found throughout all the land of Israel: for the Philistines said, Lest the Hebrews make *them* swords or spears:

20 But all the Israelites went down to the Philistines, to sharpen every man his share, and his coulter, and his axe, and his mattock.

21 Yet they had [g]a file for the mattocks, and for the coulters, and for the forks, and for the axes, and [h]to sharpen the goads.

22 So it came to pass in the day of battle, that [e]there was neither sword nor spear found in the hand of any of the people that *were* with Saul and Jonathan: but with Saul and with Jonathan his son was there found.

23 [f]And the [i]garrison of the Phi-

13:8 [u]ch. 10:8
13:13 [v]2 Chr. 16:9 [w]ch. 15:11
13:14 [x]ch. 15:28 [y]Ps. 89:20 Acts 13:22
13:15 [z]ch. 14:2
13:17 [a]Josh. 18:23
13:18 [b]Josh. 16:3 & 18:13,14 [c]Neh. 11:34 Gen. 14:2
13:19 [d]See 2 Ki. 24:14 Jer. 24:1
13:22 [e]See Judg. 5:8
13:23 [f]ch. 14:1,4

[b] Heb. *trembled after him* [c] Heb. *bless him* [d] Heb. *entreated the face* [e] Heb. *found* [f] Heb. *Geba; see ver. 3* [g] Heb. *a file with mouths* [h] Heb. *to set* [i] Or, *standing camp*

13:13 THOU HAST NOT KEPT THE COMMANDMENT OF THE LORD. The Lord had specifically commanded Saul to wait in Gilgal for the arrival of Samuel who would offer sacrifices and provide instruction (10:8). God tested Saul's obedience by the providential delay of Samuel beyond the agreed-upon seven days. In desperation (v. 8) and presumption (v. 9), Saul himself proceeded to offer a sacrifice contrary to God's word. Because Saul failed to keep the commandment of the Lord, Samuel told him that God would take the kingdom away from him (vv. 13–14). Though Saul retained the kingship for the rest of his life, his son Jonathan would not succeed him to the throne.

13:14 A MAN AFTER HIS OWN HEART. David is this man. (1) David was a man after God's heart in the following ways: (a) he believed in God from his youth (17:34,37); (b) he diligently and continually sought the face and counsel of God in childlike dependence (23:2,4; 30:8; 2 Sam. 2:1; 5:19,23); (c) he worshiped God with his whole being and directed all of Israel to do the same (1 Chr. 15—16); (d) he humbly recognized that God was the real King of Israel and that he was only God's representative (2 Sam. 5:12); and (e) in his public conduct he largely obeyed the Lord and carried out His will (cf. Acts 13:22).

(2) In his later life, however, on several occasions David caused deep grief to God and ceased to be a man after God's own heart. He despised God and His word by committing the sins of adultery and murder (2 Sam. 12:7–14), and by numbering Israel against God's will (1 Chr. 21:1–17).

listines went out to the passage of Michmash.

Jonathan attacks the Philistines

14 NOW [j]IT came to pass upon a day, that Jonathan the son of Saul said unto the young man that bare his armour, Come, and let us go over to the Philistines' garrison, that *is* on the other side. But he told not his father.

2 And Saul tarried in the uttermost part of Gibeah under a pomegranate tree which *is* in Migron: and the people that *were* with him *were* [g]about six hundred men;

3 And [h]Ahiah, the son of Ahitub, [i]Ichabod's brother, the son of Phinehas, the son of Eli, the LORD's priest in Shiloh, [j]wearing an ephod. And the people knew not that Jonathan was gone.

4 ¶ And between the passages, by which Jonathan sought to go over [k]unto the Philistines' garrison, *there was* a sharp rock on the one side, and a sharp rock on the other side: and the name of the one *was* Bozez, and the name of the other Seneh.

5 The [k]forefront of the one *was* situate northward over against Michmash, and the other southward over against Gibeah.

6 And Jonathan said to the young man that bare his armour, Come, and let us go over unto the garrison of these uncircumcised: it may be that the LORD will work for us: for *there is* no restraint to the LORD [l]to save by many or by few.

7 And his armourbearer said unto him, Do all that *is* in thine heart: turn thee; behold, I *am* with thee according to thy heart.

8 Then said Jonathan, Behold, we will pass over unto *these* men, and we will discover ourselves unto them.

9 If they say thus unto us, [l]Tarry until we come to you; then we will stand still in our place, and will not go up unto them.

10 But if they say thus, Come up unto us; then we will go up: for the LORD hath delivered them into our hand: and [m]this *shall be* a sign unto us.

11 And both of them discovered themselves unto the garrison of the Philistines: and the Philistines said, Behold, the Hebrews come forth out of the holes where they had hid themselves.

12 And the men of the garrison answered Jonathan and his armourbearer, and said, Come up to us, and we will show you a thing. And Jonathan said unto his armourbearer, Come up after me: for the LORD hath delivered them into the hand of Israel.

13 And Jonathan climbed up upon his hands and upon his feet, and his armourbearer after him: and they fell before Jonathan; and his armourbearer slew after him.

14 And that first slaughter, which Jonathan and his armourbearer made, was about twenty men, within as it were [m]an half acre of land, *which* a yoke *of oxen might plow.*

15 And [n]there was trembling in the host, in the field, and among all the people: the garrison, and [o]the spoilers, they also trembled, and the earth quaked: so it was [p]a[n] very great trembling.

The Philistines flee

16 And the watchmen of Saul in Gibeah of Benjamin looked; and, behold, the multitude melted away, and they [q]went on beating down *one another.*

17 Then said Saul unto the people that *were* with him, Number now, and see who is gone from us. And when they had numbered, behold, Jonathan and his armourbearer *were* not *there.*

18 And Saul said unto Ahiah, Bring hither the ark of God. For the ark of God was at that time with the children of Israel.

14:2 [g]ch. 13:15
14:3 [h]ch. 22:9,11,20 called *Ahimelech* [i]ch. 4:21 [j]ch. 2:28
14:4 [k]ch. 13:23
14:6 [l]Judg. 7:4,7 2 Chr. 14:11
14:10 [m]See Gen. 24:14 Judg. 7:11
14:15 [n]2 Ki. 7:7 Job 18:11 [o]ch. 13:17 [p]Gen. 35:5
14:16 [q]ver. 20

[j] Or, *there was a day* [k] Heb. *tooth* [l] Heb. *Be still* [m] Or, *half a furrow of an acre of land* [n] Heb. *a trembling of God*

14:1 THE PHILISTINES. This chapter emphasizes that Israel defeated the Philistines only because God acted on their behalf. Israel was discouraged, outnumbered, and inadequately armed (13:19–22). They had no reasonable hope for victory, yet they won the battle because "the LORD saved Israel that day" (v. 23). When circumstances seem to be against us and our resources inadequate, as children of God we have the right to call upon God to help us in our time of need (see Heb. 4:16, note). He has promised to be "a very present help in trouble" (Ps. 46:1) and to supply grace for all our needs (2 Cor. 12:9).

19 ¶ And it came to pass, while Saul [r]talked unto the priest, that the [o]noise that *was* in the host of the Philistines went on and increased: and Saul said unto the priest, Withdraw thine hand.

20 And Saul and all the people that *were* with him [p]assembled themselves, and they came to the battle: and, behold, [s]every man's sword was against his fellow, *and there was* a very great discomfiture.

21 Moreover the Hebrews *that* were with the Philistines before that time, which went up with them into the camp *from the country* round about, even they also *turned* to be with the Israelites that *were* with Saul and Jonathan.

22 Likewise all the men of Israel which [t]had hid themselves in mount Ephraim, *when* they heard that the Philistines fled, even they also followed hard after them in the battle.

23 [u]So the LORD saved Israel that day: and the battle passed over [v]unto Beth-aven.

Jonathan breaks Saul's oath

24 ¶ And the men of Israel were distressed that day: for Saul had [w]adjured the people, saying, Cursed *be* the man that eateth *any* food until evening, that I may be avenged on mine enemies. So none of the people tasted *any* food.

25 [x]And all *they of* the land came to a wood; and there was [y]honey upon the ground.

26 And when the people were come into the wood, behold, the honey dropped; but no man put his hand to his mouth: for the people feared the oath.

27 But Jonathan heard not when his father charged the people with the oath: wherefore he put forth the end of the rod that *was* in his hand, and dipped it in an honeycomb, and put his hand to his mouth; and his eyes were enlightened.

28 Then answered one of the people, and said, Thy father straitly charged the people with an oath, saying, Cursed *be* the man that eateth *any* food this day. And the people were [q]faint.

29 Then said Jonathan, My father hath troubled the land: see, I pray you, how mine eyes have been enlightened, because I tasted a little of this honey.

30 How much more, if haply the people had eaten freely today of the spoil of their enemies which they found? for had there not been now a much greater slaughter among the Philistines?

31 And they smote the Philistines that day from Michmash to Aijalon: and the people were very faint.

32 And the people flew upon the spoil, and took sheep, and oxen, and calves, and slew *them* on the ground: and the people did eat *them* [z]with the blood.

33 ¶ Then they told Saul, saying, Behold, the people sin against the LORD, in that they eat with the blood. And he said, Ye have [r]transgressed: roll a great stone unto me this day.

34 And Saul said, Disperse yourselves among the people, and say unto them, Bring me hither every man his ox, and every man his sheep, and slay *them* here, and eat; and sin not against the LORD in eating with the blood. And all the people brought every man his ox [s]with him that night, and slew *them* there.

35 And Saul [a]built an altar unto the LORD: [t]the same was the first altar that he built unto the LORD.

36 ¶ And Saul said, Let us go down after the Philistines by night, and spoil them until the morning light, and let us not leave a man of them. And they said, Do whatsoever seemeth good unto thee. Then said the priest, Let us draw near hither unto God.

37 And Saul asked counsel of God, Shall I go down after the Philistines? wilt thou deliver them into the hand of Israel? But [b]he answered him not that day.

38 And Saul said, [c]Draw ye near hither, all the [d]chief of the people: and know and see wherein this sin hath been this day.

39 For, [e]*as* the LORD liveth, which saveth Israel, though it be in Jonathan my son, he shall surely die. But *there was* not a man among all the people *that* answered him.

40 Then said he unto all Israel, Be ye on one side, and I and Jonathan my son will be on the other side. And the

14:19 [r]Num. 27:21
14:20 [s]Judg. 7:22; 2 Chr. 20:23
14:22 [t]ch. 13:6
14:23 [u]Ex. 14:30; Hos. 1:7; [v]ch. 13:5
14:24 [w]Josh. 6:26
14:25 [x]Deut. 9:28; Mat. 3:5; [y]Ex. 3:8; Num. 13:27; Mat:3:4
14:32 [z]Lev. 3:17 & 7:26 & 17:10 & 19:26; Deut. 12:16,23,24
14:35 [a]ch. 7:17
14:37 [b]ch. 28:6
14:38 [c]Josh. 7:14; ch. 10:19; [d]Judg. 20:2
14:39 [e]2 Sam. 12:5

[o] Or, *tumult* [p] Heb. *were cried together* [q] Or, *weary* [r] Or, *dealt treacherously* [s] Heb. *in his hand* [t] Heb. *that altar he began to build unto the LORD*

people said unto Saul, Do what seemeth good unto thee.

41 Therefore Saul said unto the LORD God of Israel, [f]Give[u] a perfect *lot.* [g]And Saul and Jonathan were taken: but the people [v]escaped.

42 And Saul said, Cast *lots* between me and Jonathan my son. And Jonathan was taken.

43 Then Saul said to Jonathan, [h]Tell me what thou hast done. And Jonathan told him, and said, [i]I did but taste a little honey with the end of the rod that *was* in mine hand, *and,* lo, I must die.

44 And Saul answered, [j]God do so and more also: [k]for thou shalt surely die, Jonathan.

45 And the people said unto Saul, Shall Jonathan die, who hath wrought this great salvation in Israel? God forbid: [l]*as* the LORD liveth, there shall not one hair of his head fall to the ground; for he hath wrought with God this day. So the people rescued Jonathan, that he died not.

46 Then Saul went up from following the Philistines: and the Philistines went to their own place.

Saul wars against other nations

47 ¶ So Saul took the kingdom over Israel, and fought against all his enemies on every side, against Moab, and against the children of [m]Ammon, and against Edom, and against the kings of [n]Zobah, and against the Philistines: and whithersoever he turned himself, he vexed *them.*

48 And he [w]gathered an host, and [o]smote the Amalekites, and delivered Israel out of the hands of them that spoiled them.

49 Now [p]the sons of Saul were Jonathan, and Ishui, and Melch-ishua: and the names of his two daughters *were these;* the name of the firstborn Merab, and the name of the younger Michal:

50 And the name of Saul's wife *was* Ahinoam, the daughter of Ahimaaz: and the name of the captain of his host *was* [x]Abner, the son of Ner, Saul's uncle.

51 [q]And Kish *was* the father of Saul; and Ner the father of Abner *was* the son of Abiel.

52 And there was sore war against the Philistines all the days of Saul: and when Saul saw any strong man, or any valiant man, [r]he took him unto him.

Saul rejected as king

15 SAMUEL ALSO said unto Saul, [s]The LORD sent me to anoint thee *to be* king over his people, over Israel: now therefore hearken thou unto the voice of the words of the LORD.

2 Thus saith the LORD of hosts, I remember *that* which Amalek did to Israel, [t]how he laid *wait* for him in the way, when he came up from Egypt.

3 Now go and smite Amalek, and [u]utterly destroy all that they have, and spare them not; but slay both man and woman, infant and suckling, ox and sheep, camel and ass.

4 And Saul gathered the people together, and numbered them in Telaim, two hundred thousand footmen, and ten thousand men of Judah.

5 And Saul came to a city of Amalek, and [y]laid wait in the valley.

6 ¶ And Saul said unto [v]the Kenites, [w]Go, depart, get you down from among the Amalekites, lest I destroy you with them: for [x]ye showed kindness to all the children of Israel, when they came up out of Egypt. So the Kenites departed from among the Amalekites.

7 [y]And Saul smote the Amalekites from [z]Havilah *until* thou comest to [a]Shur, that *is* over against Egypt.

14:41 [f]Prov. 16:33 Acts. 1:24 [g]Josh. 7:16 ch. 10:20,21
14:43 [h]Josh. 7:19 [i]ver. 27
14:44 [j]Ruth 1:17 [k]ver. 39
14:45 [l]2 Sam. 14:11 1 Ki. 1:52 Luke 21:18
14:47 [m]ch. 11:11 [n]2 Sam. 10:6
14:48 [o]ch. 15:3,7
14:49 [p]ch. 31:2 1 Chr. 8:33
14:51 [q]ch. 9:1
14:52 [r]ch. 8:11
15:1 [s]ch. 9:16
15:2 [t]Ex. 17:8,14 Num. 24:20 Deut. 25:17-19
15:3 [u]Lev. 27:28,29 Josh. 6:17,21
15:6 [v]Num. 24:21 Judg. 1:16 & 4:11 [w]Gen. 18:25 & 19:12,14 Rev. 18:4 [x]Ex. 18:10,19 Num. 10:29,32
15:7 [y]ch. 14:48 [z]Gen. 2:11 & 25:18 [a]Gen. 16:7

[u] Or, *Show the innocent* [v] Heb. *went forth* [w] Or, *wrought mightily* [x] Heb. *Abiner* [y] Or, *fought*

15:2 I REMEMBER *THAT* WHICH AMALEK DID. The Amalekites (i.e., descendants of Amalek) had been the first to oppose God and the nation of Israel in the wilderness (Ex. 17:8–13). They represented all evil power and opposition to God, His people, and His truth. It was Saul's responsibility to destroy the Amalekites and their evil ways completely (v. 3). Under the cloak of religious zeal, he refused to obey fully the command of God regarding the Amalekites and was subsequently rejected by God as king (vv. 18–23).

15:3 SLAY . . . INFANT AND SUCKLING. The extent of the wickedness, cruelty, and continued rebellion of the Amalekites was so great that the removal of innocent children from earth was an act of mercy. Note that because of the extreme wickedness of humankind in Noah's day, God in sorrow and grief had decided to destroy everyone, including children and infants (Gen. 6:5–7). Here also God decided that the Amalekites had to be utterly blotted out. It was better that the children of the Amalekites die in infancy than live under the corrupt and wicked influence of their parents.

8 And [b]he took Agag the king of
the Amalekites alive, and [c]utterly de-
stroyed all the people with the edge of
the sword.
9 But Saul and the people [d]spared
Agag, and the best of the sheep, and of
the oxen, and [z]of the fatlings, and the
lambs, and all *that was* good, and would
not utterly destroy them: but every
thing *that was* vile and refuse, that they
destroyed utterly.
10 ¶ Then came the word of the
LORD unto Samuel, saying,
11 [e]It repenteth me that I have set
up Saul *to be* king: for he is [f]turned
back from following me, [g]and hath not
performed my commandments. And it
[h]grieved Samuel; and he cried unto
the LORD all night.
12 And when Samuel rose early to
meet Saul in the morning, it was told
Samuel, saying, Saul came to [i]Car-
mel, and, behold, he set him up a place,
and is gone about, and passed on, and
gone down to Gilgal.
13 And Samuel came to Saul: and
Saul said unto him, [j]Blessed *be* thou
of the LORD: I have performed the com-
mandment of the LORD.
14 And Samuel said, What *meaneth*
then this bleating of the sheep in mine
ears, and the lowing of the oxen which
I hear?
15 And Saul said, They have
brought them from the Amalekites:
[k]for the people spared the best of the
sheep and of the oxen, to sacrifice unto
the LORD thy God; and the rest we have
utterly destroyed.

15:8 [b]See 1 Ki. 20:34, 35 [c]See ch. 30:1 **15:9** [d]ver. 3,15 **15:11** [e]ver. 35 Gen. 6:6,7 2 Sam. 24:16 [f]Josh. 22:16 1 Ki. 9:6 [g]ver. 3,9 ch. 13:13 [h]ver. 35 ch. 16:1 **15:12** [i]Josh. 15:55 **15:13** [j]Gen. 14:19 Judg. 17:2 Ruth 3:10 **15:15** [k]ver. 9,21 Gen. 3:12 Prov. 28:13

15:17 [l]ch. 9:21 **15:20** [m]ver. 13 **15:21** [n]ver. 15 **15:22** [o]Is. 1:11-13,16,17 Jer. 7:22,23 Mic. 6:6-8 Heb. 10:6-9 [p]Eccl. 5:1 Hos. 6:6 Mat. 5:24 & 9:13 & 12:7 Mark 12:33

16 Then Samuel said unto Saul,
Stay, and I will tell thee what the LORD
hath said to me this night. And he said
unto him, Say on.
17 And Samuel said, [l]When thou
wast little in thine own sight, *wast* thou
not *made* the head of the tribes of Isra-
el, and the LORD anointed thee king
over Israel?
18 And the LORD sent thee on a jour-
ney, and said, Go and utterly destroy
the sinners the Amalekites, and fight
against them until [a]they be con-
sumed.
19 Wherefore then didst thou not
obey the voice of the LORD, but didst fly
upon the spoil, and didst evil in the
sight of the LORD?
20 And Saul said unto Samuel, Yea,
[m]I have obeyed the voice of the LORD,
and have gone the way which the LORD
sent me, and have brought Agag the
king of Amalek, and have utterly de-
stroyed the Amalekites.
21 [n]But the people took of the
spoil, sheep and oxen, the chief of the
things which should have been utterly
destroyed, to sacrifice unto the LORD
thy God in Gilgal.
22 And Samuel said, [o]Hath the 
LORD *as great* delight in burnt offerings
and sacrifices, as in obeying the voice
of the LORD? Behold, [p]to obey *is* better
than sacrifice, *and* to hearken than the
fat of rams.
23 For rebellion *is as* the sin of

[z] Or, *of the second sort* [a] Heb. *they consume them*

15:9 BUT SAUL . . . WOULD NOT UTTERLY DESTROY THEM. Saul rebelled against and disobeyed God and His clear instructions (vv. 2–3,18–19) because he was not committed to the will of God with all his heart. He felt God's word was good but not so sacred that it must be followed in every detail. His rejection of the word of the Lord (vv. 22–23) is all the more significant because he had already been confronted for his disobedience (13:13).

15:22 TO OBEY *IS* BETTER THAN SACRIFICE. Obeying God's word from the heart is better than any outward form of worship, service to God, or personal sacrifice. Saul's sin was placing his own conception of what was right above Biblical revelation; this sin will likewise be the focal point of the final apostasy predicted for the period just before Jesus returns to the earth (Mat. 24:11,24; 2 Thes. 2:9–12; 2 Tim. 4:3–4; cf. 2 Pet. 2). Worship, prayer, praise, spiritual gifts, and service to God are worthless in His sight if not accompanied by explicit obedience to Him and His righteous standards (cf. Is. 58:2; 59:2; 1 Cor. 13).

15:23 REBELLION . . . WITCHCRAFT. The sin of "witchcraft" is seeking to manipulate events, people, or the future by the spirits of the departed dead (cf. Lev. 19:26; Deut. 18:9–12). Rebellion against God's word is similar to this sin in that both involve a rejection of God's Lordship and an attempt to determine the outcome of things in a manner other than God's way. Furthermore, both sins take the transgressor out from under God's protection and put him under the destructive power of Satan and evil spirits (cf. 16:14; 18:10; 19:9).

15:23 REJECTED THEE FROM *BEING* KING. (1) Saul's disqualification from being king and the consequent rejection of his dynasty did not mean that God had forever rejected Saul personally. Although Saul's position as king would never again be restored, he could still receive forgiveness and enjoy a saving relationship with God by sincerely repenting and serving the Lord (vv. 24–25,31).

(2) This same principle operates under the new covenant. A spiritual leader may fail morally and

[b]witchcraft, and stubbornness *is as*
iniquity and idolatry. Because thou
hast rejected the word of the LORD, [q]he
1 Ki. 2:2-4 hath also rejected thee from *being* king.
24 ¶ [r]And Saul said unto Samuel,
I have sinned: for I have transgressed
the commandment of the LORD, and thy
words: because I [s]feared the people,
and obeyed their voice.
25 Now therefore, I pray thee, par-
don my sin, and turn again with me,
that I may worship the LORD.
26 And Samuel said unto Saul, I
will not return with thee: [t]for thou
hast rejected the word of the LORD, and
the LORD hath rejected thee from being
king over Israel.
27 And as Samuel turned about to
go away, [u]he laid hold upon the skirt
of his mantle, and it rent.
28 And Samuel said unto him,
[v]The LORD hath rent the kingdom of
Israel from thee this day, and hath giv-
en it to a neighbour of thine, *that is* bet-
ter than thou.
29 And also the [c]Strength of Israel
[w]will not lie nor repent: for he *is* not
a man, that he should repent.
30 Then he said, I have sinned: *yet*
[x]honour me now, I pray thee, before
the elders of my people, and before Is-
rael, and turn again with me, that I
may worship the LORD thy God.
31 So Samuel turned again after
Saul; and Saul worshipped the LORD.
32 ¶ Then said Samuel, Bring ye
hither to me Agag the king of the Ama-
lekites. And Agag came unto him deli-
cately. And Agag said, Surely the bit-
terness of death is past.
33 And Samuel said, [y]As thy
sword hath made women childless, so
shall thy mother be childless among
women. And Samuel hewed Agag in
pieces before the LORD in Gilgal.
34 ¶ Then Samuel went to Ramah;
and Saul went up to his house to [z]Gib-
eah of Saul.
35 And [a]Samuel came no more to
see Saul until the day of his death: nev-
ertheless Samuel [b]mourned for Saul:

15:23 [q]ch. 13:14
15:24 [r]See 2 Sam. 12:13 [s]Ex. 23:2 Is. 51:12,13
15:26 [t]ch. 2:30
15:27 [u]See 1 Ki. 11:30
15:28 [v]ch. 28:17,18 1 Ki. 11:31
15:29 [w]Num. 23:19 Ezek. 24:14 2 Tim. 2:13 Tit. 1:2
15:30 [x]John 5:44 & 12:43
15:33 [y]Ex. 17:11 Num. 14:45 See Judg. 1:7
15:34 [z]ch. 11:4
15:35 [a]See ch. 19:24 [b]ver. 11 ch. 16:1
[c]ver. 11
16:1 [d]ch. 15:35 [e]ch. 15:23 [f]ch. 9:16 2 Ki. 9:1 [g]Ps. 78:70 Acts 13:22
16:2 [h]ch. 9:12 & 20:29
16:3 [i]Ex. 4:15 [j]ch. 9:16
16:4 [k]ch. 21:1 [l]1 Ki. 2:13 2 Ki. 9:22
16:5 [m]Ex. 19:10
16:6 [n]ch. 17:13 Called *Elihu* 1 Chr. 27:18 [o]1 Ki. 12:26
16:7 [p]Ps. 147:10 [q]Is. 55:8 [r]2 Cor. 10:7 [s]1 Ki. 8:39
16:8 [t]ch. 17:13

and the LORD [c]repented that he had
made Saul king over Israel.

David chosen to be king

16 AND THE LORD said unto Sam-
uel, [d]How long wilt thou
mourn for Saul, seeing [e]I have reject-
ed him from reigning over Israel? [f]fill
thine horn with oil, and go, I will send
thee to Jesse the Bethlehemite: for [g]I
have provided me a king among his
sons.
2 And Samuel said, How can I go?
if Saul hear *it*, he will kill me. And the
LORD said, Take an heifer [d]with thee,
and say, [h]I am come to sacrifice to the
LORD.
3 And call Jesse to the sacrifice, and
[i]I will show thee what thou shalt do:
and [j]thou shalt anoint unto me *him*
whom I name unto thee.
4 And Samuel did that which the
LORD spake, and came to Bethlehem.
And the elders of the town [k]trembled
at his [e]coming, and said, [l]Comest
thou peaceably?
5 And he said, Peaceably: I am
come to sacrifice unto the LORD:
[m]sanctify yourselves, and come with
me to the sacrifice. And he sanctified
Jesse and his sons, and called them to
the sacrifice.
6 ¶ And it came to pass, when they
were come, that he looked on [n]Eliab,
and [o]said, Surely the LORD's anointed
is before him.
7 But the LORD said unto Samuel,
Look not on [p]his countenance, or on
the height of his stature; because I
have refused him: [q]for *the LORD seeth*
not as man seeth; for man [r]looketh on
the [f]outward appearance, but the
LORD looketh on the [s]heart.
8 Then Jesse called [t]Abinadab,
and made him pass before Samuel. And
he said, Neither hath the LORD chosen
this.

[b] Heb. *divination* [c] Or, *Eternity*, or, *Victory* [d] Heb. *in thine hand* [e] Heb. *meeting* [f] Heb. *eyes*

thus be rejected permanently by God from his spiritual office, yet be open to full forgiveness, salvation, and fellowship with God (see article on MORAL QUALIFICATIONS FOR OVERSEERS, p. 1908).

15:35 THE LORD REPENTED. "Repented" (Heb. *naham*) expresses God's deep emotion and sorrow at Saul's rebellion. God's grief included regret that He had made Saul king over Israel. However, note that God does not repent in the way people do, for when we repent, we must change our fundamental attitude toward God and toward sin.

9 Then Jesse made [u]Shammah[g] to pass by. And he said, Neither hath the LORD chosen this.

10 Again, Jesse made seven of his sons to pass before Samuel. And Samuel said unto Jesse, The LORD hath not chosen these.

11 And Samuel said unto Jesse, Are here all *thy* children? And he said, [v]There remaineth yet the youngest, and, behold, he keepeth the sheep. And Samuel said unto Jesse, [w]Send and fetch him: for we will not sit [h]down till he come hither.

12 And he sent, and brought him in. Now he *was* [x]ruddy, *and* withal [i]of a beautiful countenance, and goodly to look to. [y]And the LORD said, Arise, anoint him: for this *is* he.

13 Then Samuel took the horn of oil, and [z]anointed him in the midst of his brethren: and [a]the spirit of the LORD came upon David from that day forward. So Samuel rose up, and went to Ramah.

Chr. 2:18

David plays the harp

14 ¶ [b]But the spirit of the LORD departed from Saul, and [c]an evil spirit from the LORD [j]troubled him.

15 And Saul's servants said unto him, Behold now, an evil spirit from God troubleth thee.

16 Let our lord now command thy servants, *which are* [d]before thee, to seek out a man, *who is* a cunning player on an harp: and it shall come to pass, when the evil spirit from God is upon thee, that he shall [e]play with his hand, and thou shalt be well.

17 And Saul said unto his servants, Provide me now a man that can play well, and bring *him* to me.

18 Then answered one of the servants, and said, Behold, I have seen a son of Jesse the Bethlehemite, *that is* cunning in playing, and [f]a mighty valiant man, and a man of war, and prudent in [k]matters, and a comely person, and [g]the LORD *is* with him.

16:9 [u]ch. 17:13 **16:11** [v]ch. 17:12 [w]2 Sam. 7:8 **16:12** [x]ch. 17:42 [y]See ch. 9:17 **16:13** [z]ch. 10:1 [a]Num. 27:18 Judg. 11:29 & 13:25 ch. 10:6,10 **16:14** [b]Judg. 16:20 [c]Judg. 9:23 **16:16** [d]ver. 21,22 Gen. 41:46 [e]ver. 23 2 Ki. 3:15 **16:18** [f]ch. 17:32,34-36 [g]ch. 3:19 & 18:12,14

16:19 [h]ver. 11 ch. 17:15 **16:20** [i]ch. 10:27 & 17:18 **16:21** [j]Gen. 41:46 **16:23** [k]ver. 14,16 **17:1** [l]Josh. 15:35 **17:4** [m]2 Sam. 21:19 [n]Josh. 11:22

19 ¶ Wherefore Saul sent messengers unto Jesse, and said, Send me David thy son, [h]which *is* with the sheep.

20 And Jesse [i]took an ass *laden* with bread, and a bottle of wine, and a kid, and sent *them* by David his son unto Saul.

21 And David came to Saul, and [j]stood before him: and he loved him greatly; and he became his armourbearer.

22 And Saul sent to Jesse, saying, Let David, I pray thee, stand before me; for he hath found favour in my sight.

23 And it came to pass, when [k]the *evil* spirit from God was upon Saul, that David took an harp, and played with his hand: so Saul was refreshed, and was well, and the evil spirit departed from him.

1 Ki 18:21-39

David and Goliath

17 NOW THE Philistines gathered together their armies to battle, and were gathered together at [l]Shochoh, which *belongeth* to Judah, and pitched between Shochoh and Azekah, in [l]Ephes-dammim.

2 And Saul and the men of Israel were gathered together, and pitched by the valley of Elah, and [m]set the battle in array against the Philistines.

3 And the Philistines stood on a mountain on the one side, and Israel stood on a mountain on the other side: and *there was* a valley between them.

4 ¶ And there went out a champion out of the camp of the Philistines, named [m]Goliath, of [n]Gath, whose height *was* six cubits and a span.

5 And *he had* an helmet of brass upon his head, and he *was* [n]armed with a coat of mail; and the weight of

[g] *Shimeah* in 2 Sam. 13:3; *Shimma* in 1 Chr. 2:13 [h] Heb. *round* [i] Heb. *fair of eyes* [j] Or, *terrified* [k] Or, *speech* [l] Or, *The coast of Dammim,* called *Pas-dammim* in 1 Chr. 11:13 [m] Heb. *ranged the battle* [n] Heb. *clothed*

16:12 ARISE, ANOINT HIM. Already at an early age David developed a heart and desire for God as his spiritual Shepherd (see Ps. 23). David's earnest heart for God (v. 7) was the primary reason God chose him as Israel's next king.

16:14 THE SPIRIT OF THE LORD DEPARTED FROM SAUL. Because Saul had rebelled against the will of God, he was given over to demonic influence (see 15:23). Evil spirits operate under the permissive will of our sovereign God and at times under His direct will (Judg. 9:23; 1 Ki. 22:19–23; see also Luke 11:26, note; 22:3; Rom. 1:21–32; 2 Thes. 2:8–12; see article on THE WILL OF GOD, p. 1060).

16:23 EVIL SPIRIT DEPARTED. Apparently the Holy Spirit was active in David's music so that Saul received temporary relief from the demonic oppression which had come as God's judgment on Saul.

the coat *was* five thousand shekels of brass.

6 And *he had* greaves of brass upon his legs, and a [o]target of brass between his shoulders.

7 And the staff of his spear *was* like a weaver's beam; and his spear's head *weighed* six hundred shekels of iron: and one bearing a shield went before him.

8 And he stood and cried unto the armies of Israel, and said unto them, Why are ye come out to set *your* battle in array? *am* not I a Philistine, and ye [o]servants to Saul? choose you a man for you, and let him come down to me.

9 If he be able to fight with me, and to kill me, then will we be your servants: but if I prevail against him, and kill him, then shall ye be our servants, and [p]serve us.

10 And the Philistine said, I [q]defy the armies of Israel this day; give me a man, that we may fight together.

11 When Saul and all Israel heard those words of the Philistine, they were dismayed, and greatly afraid.

12 ¶ Now David *was* [r]the son of that [s]Ephrathite of Bethlehem-judah, whose name *was* Jesse; and he had [t]eight sons: and the man went among men *for* an old man in the days of Saul.

13 And the three eldest sons of Jesse went *and* followed Saul to the battle: and the [u]names of his three sons that went to the battle *were* Eliab the firstborn, and next unto him Abinadab, and the third Shammah.

14 And David *was* the youngest: and the three eldest followed Saul.

15 But David went and returned from Saul [v]to feed his father's sheep at Bethlehem.

16 And the Philistine drew near morning and evening, and presented himself forty days.

17 And Jesse said unto David his son, Take now for thy brethren an ephah of this parched *corn,* and these ten loaves, and run to the camp to thy brethren;

18 And carry these ten [p]cheeses unto the [q]captain of *their* thousand, and [w]look how thy brethren fare, and take their pledge.

19 Now Saul, and they, and all the men of Israel, *were* in the valley of Elah, fighting with the Philistines.

20 ¶ And David rose up early in the morning, and left the sheep with a keeper, and took, and went, as Jesse had commanded him; and he came to the [x]trench,[r] as the host was going forth to the [s]fight, and shouted for the battle.

21 For Israel and the Philistines had put the battle in array, army against army.

22 And David left [t]his carriage in the hand of the keeper of the carriage, and ran into the army, and came and saluted his brethren.

23 And as he talked with them, behold, there came up the champion, the Philistine of Gath, Goliath by name, out of the armies of the Philistines, and spake [y]according to the same words: and David heard *them.*

24 And all the men of Israel, when they saw the man, fled [u]from him, and were sore afraid.

25 And the men of Israel said, Have ye seen this man that is come up? surely to defy Israel is he come up: and it shall be, *that* the man who killeth him, the king will enrich him with great riches, and [z]will give him his daughter, and make his father's house free in Israel.

26 And David spake to the men that stood by him, saying, What shall be done to the man that killeth this Philistine, and taketh away [a]the reproach from Israel? for who *is* this [b]uncircumcised Philistine, that he should [c]defy the armies of [d]the living God?

27 And the people answered him after this manner, saying, [e]So shall it be done to the man that killeth him.

28 ¶ And Eliab his eldest brother heard when he spake unto the men; and Eliab's [f]anger was kindled against David, and he said, Why camest thou down hither? and with whom hast thou left those few sheep in the wilderness? I know thy pride, and the naughtiness of thine heart; for thou art come down that thou mightest see the battle.

29 And David said, What have I now done? [g]*Is there* not a cause?

30 ¶ And he turned from him toward another, and [h]spake after the same [v]manner: and the people answered him again after the former manner.

17:8 [o]ch. 8:17
17:9 [p]ch. 11:1
17:10 [q]ver. 26; 2 Sam. 21:21
17:12 [r]ver. 58; Ruth 4:22; ch. 16:1,18; [s]Gen. 35:19; [t]ch. 16:10,11; See 1 Chr. 2:13-15
17:13 [u]ch. 16:6,8,9
17:15 [v]ch. 16:19
17:18 [w]Gen. 37:14
17:20 [x]ch. 26:5
17:23 [y]ver. 8
17:25 [z]Josh. 15:16
17:26 [a]ch. 11:2; [b]ch. 14:6; [c]ver. 10; [d]Deut. 5:26
17:27 [e]ver. 25
17:28 [f]Gen. 37:4,8,11; Mat. 10:36
17:29 [g]ver. 17
17:30 [h]ver. 26,27

[o] Or, *gorget* [p] Heb. *cheeses of milk* [q] Heb. *captain of a thousand* [r] Or, *place of the carriage* [s] Or, *battle array,* or, *place of fight* [t] Heb. *the vessels from upon him* [u] Heb. *from his face* [v] Heb. *word*

31 And when the words were heard which David spake, they rehearsed *them* before Saul: and he [w]sent for him.

32 ¶ And David said to Saul, [i]Let no man's heart fail because of him; [j]thy servant will go and fight with this Philistine.

33 And Saul said to David, [k]Thou art not able to go against this Philistine to fight with him: for thou *art but* a youth, and he a man of war from his youth.

34 And David said unto Saul, Thy servant kept his father's sheep, and there came a lion, and a bear, and took a [x]lamb out of the flock:

35 And I went out after him, and smote him, and delivered *it* out of his mouth: and when he arose against me, I caught *him* by his beard, and smote him, and slew him.

36 Thy servant slew both the lion and the bear: and this uncircumcised Philistine shall be as one of them, seeing he hath defied the armies of the living God.

37 David said moreover, [l]The LORD that delivered me out of the paw of the lion, and out of the paw of the bear, he will deliver me out of the hand of this Philistine. And Saul said unto David, Go, and [m]the LORD be with thee.

38 ¶ And Saul [y]armed David with his armour, and he put an helmet of brass upon his head; also he armed him with a coat of mail.

39 And David girded his sword upon his armour, and he assayed to go; for he had not proved *it*. And David said unto Saul, I cannot go with these; for I have not proved *them*. And David put them off him.

40 And he took his staff in his hand, and chose him five smooth stones out of the [z]brook, and put them in a shepherd's [a]bag which he had, even in a scrip; and his sling *was* in his hand: and he drew near to the Philistine.

41 And the Philistine came on and drew near unto David; and the man that bare the shield *went* before him.

42 And when the Philistine looked about, and saw David, he [n]disdained him: for he was *but* a youth, and [o]ruddy, and of a fair countenance.

43 And the Philistine said unto David, [p]*Am* I a dog, that thou comest to me with staves? And the Philistine cursed David by his gods.

44 And the Philistine [q]said to David, Come to me, and I will give thy flesh unto the fowls of the air, and to the beasts of the field.

45 Then said David to the Philistine, Thou comest to me with a sword, and with a spear, and with a shield: [r]but I come to thee in the name of the LORD of hosts, the God of the armies of Israel, whom thou hast [s]defied.

46 This day will the LORD [b]deliver thee into mine hand; and I will smite thee, and take thine head from thee; and I will give [t]the carcases of the host of the Philistines this day unto the fowls of the air, and to the wild beasts of the earth; [u]that all the earth may know that there is a God in Israel.

47 And all this assembly shall know that the LORD [v]saveth not with sword and spear: for [w]the battle *is* the LORD's, and he will give you into our hands.

48 And it came to pass, when the Philistine arose, and came and drew nigh to meet David, that David hasted, and ran toward the army to meet the Philistine.

49 And David put his hand in his bag, and took thence a stone, and slang *it*, and smote the Philistine in his forehead, that the stone sunk into his forehead; and he fell upon his face to the earth.

50 So [x]David prevailed over the

17:32 [i]Deut. 20:1,3 [j]ch. 16:18
17:33 [k]See Num. 13:31 Deut. 9:2
17:37 [l]2 Cor. 1:10 2 Tim. 4:17,18 [m]ch. 20:13 1 Chr. 22:11,16
17:42 [n]1 Cor. 1:27,28 [o]ch. 16:12
17:43 [p]ch. 24:14 2 Sam. 3:8 & 9:8 & 16:9 2 Ki. 8:13
17:44 [q]1 Ki. 20:10,11
17:45 [r]2 Sam. 22:33,35 2 Cor. 10:4 Heb. 11:33,34 [s]ver. 10
17:46 [t]Deut. 28:26 [u]Josh. 4:24 1 Ki. 8:43 & 18:36 2 Ki. 19:19 Is. 52:10
17:47 [v]Hos. 1:7 Zech. 4:6 [w]2 Chr. 20:15
17:50 [x]ch. 21:9 See Judg. 3:31 & 15:15 2 Sam. 23:21

[w] Heb. *took him* [x] Or, *kid* [y] Heb. *clothed David with his clothes* [z] Or, *valley* [a] Heb. *vessel* [b] Heb. *shut thee up*

17:50 DAVID PREVAILED OVER THE PHILISTINE. David's victory over Goliath came as a result of his faith in God that had already been tested and proven in his life. We can identify five specific factors that led to his triumph: (1) David had a heart for God (16:7) that caused him to seek the Lord and His face continually (cf. 1 Chr. 16:10–11).

(2) David had a zealous and deep concern for the honor and reputation of the Lord God of Israel (vv. 26,36,46). He recognized that Goliath was defying not just the armies of Israel, but the Lord God Himself.

(3) David's confidence in the Lord's power had been strengthened by his memory of previous times when he had prayed for and experienced God's deliverance (vv. 34–37; cf. Ps. 29:3–4).

(4) David trusted not in himself but in God to achieve the victory over Goliath and the Philistines (vv. 37,45–47; cf. Ps. 33:16–17; 44:6–7; Hos. 1:7).

(5) The Spirit of the Lord came mightily upon

Philistine with a sling and with a stone, and smote the Philistine, and slew him; but *there was* no sword in the hand of David.

51 Therefore David ran, and stood upon the Philistine, and took his sword, and drew it out of the sheath thereof, and slew him, and cut off his head therewith. And when the Philistines saw their champion was dead, [y]they fled.

1 Ki. 18:41-46

52 And the men of Israel and of Judah arose, and shouted, and pursued the Philistines, until thou come to the valley, and to the gates of Ekron. And the wounded of the Philistines fell down by the way to [z]Shaaraim, even unto Gath, and unto Ekron.

53 And the children of Israel returned from chasing after the Philistines, and they spoiled their tents.

54 And David took the head of the Philistine, and brought it to Jerusalem; but he put his armour in his tent.

55 ¶ And when Saul saw David go forth against the Philistine, he said unto Abner, the captain of the host, Abner, [a]whose son *is* this youth? And Abner said, *As* thy soul liveth, O king, I cannot tell.

56 And the king said, Inquire thou whose son the stripling *is*.

57 And as David returned from the slaughter of the Philistine, Abner took him, and brought him before Saul [b]with the head of the Philistine in his hand.

58 And Saul said to him, Whose son *art* thou, *thou* young man? And David answered, [c]*I am* the son of thy servant Jesse the Bethlehemite.

Saul's hatred of David

18 AND IT came to pass, when he had made an end of speaking unto Saul, that [d]the soul of Jonathan was knit with the soul of David, [e]and Jonathan loved him as his own soul.

2 And Saul took him that day, [f]and would let him go no more home to his father's house.

3 Then Jonathan and David made a covenant, because he loved him as his own soul.

4 And Jonathan stripped himself of the robe that *was* upon him, and gave it to David, and his garments, even to his sword, and to his bow, and to his girdle.

5 ¶ And David went out whithersoever Saul sent him, *and* [c]behaved himself wisely: and Saul set him over the men of war, and he was accepted in the sight of all the people, and also in the sight of Saul's servants.

6 And it came to pass as they came, when David was returned from the slaughter of the [d]Philistine, that [g]the women came out of all cities of Israel, singing and dancing, to meet king Saul, with tabrets, with joy, and with [e]instruments of music.

7 And the women [h]answered *one another* as they played, and said, [i]Saul hath slain his thousands, and David his ten thousands.

8 And Saul was very wroth, and the saying [j]displeased[f] him; and he said, They have ascribed unto David ten thousands, and to me they have ascribed *but* thousands: and *what* can he have more but [k]the kingdom?

9 And Saul eyed David from that day and forward.

10 ¶ And it came to pass on the morrow, that [l]the evil spirit from God came upon Saul, [m]and he prophesied in the midst of the house: and David played with his hand, as at other times: [n]and *there was* a javelin in Saul's hand.

11 And Saul [o]cast the javelin; for he said, I will smite David even to the wall *with it*. And David avoided out of his presence twice.

12 ¶ And Saul was [p]afraid of David, because [q]the LORD was with him, and was [r]departed from Saul.

13 Therefore Saul removed him from him, and made him his captain

17:51 [y]Heb. 11:34
17:52 [z]Josh. 15:36
17:55 [a]See ch. 16:21,22
17:57 [b]ver. 54
17:58 [c]ver. 12
18:1 [d]Gen. 44:30 [e]ch. 19:2 & 20:17 2 Sam. 1:26 Deut. 13:6
18:2 [f]ch. 17:15
18:6 [g]Ex. 15:20 Judg. 11:34
18:7 [h]Ex. 15:21 [i]ch. 21:11 & 29:5
18:8 [j]Eccl. 4:4 [k]ch. 15:28
18:10 [l]ch. 16:14 [m]ch. 19:24 1 Ki. 18:29 Acts 16:16 [n]ch. 19:9
18:11 [o]ch. 19:10 & 20:33
18:12 [p]ver. 15,29 [q]ch. 16:13,18 [r]ch. 16:14 & 28:15

[c] Or, *prospered;* see ver. 14,15,30 [d] Or, *Philistines* [e] Heb. *threestringed instruments* [f] Heb. *was evil in his eyes*

Him (16:13; cf. Zech. 4:6).

Whenever God's children face seemingly insurmountable problems and situations, those giants can be overcome if we exercise faith like David and depend upon the power of the Holy Spirit (see Eph. 3:20–21; Phil. 4:13).

18:10 THE EVIL SPIRIT FROM GOD CAME UPON SAUL, AND HE PROPHESIED. We must not understand this text to mean that God directly sent a demonic spirit into Saul, but that God permitted an evil spirit to enter him (see 16:14, note; see article on THE WILL OF GOD, p. 1060). The Hebrew word for "prophesy" can refer to either true or false prophecy. Saul was not prophesying here by God's Spirit; rather, his prophecy was probably demonic utterances and ravings.

over a thousand; and [s]he went out and came in before the people.

14 And David [g]behaved himself wisely in all his ways; and [t]the LORD *was* with him.

15 Wherefore when Saul saw that he behaved himself very wisely, he was afraid of him.

16 But [u]all Israel and Judah loved David, because he went out and came in before them.

17 ¶ And Saul said to David, Behold my elder daughter Merab, [v]her will I give thee to wife: only be thou [h]valiant for me, and fight [w]the LORD's battles. For Saul said, [x]Let not mine hand be upon him, but let the hand of the Philistines be upon him.

18 And David said unto Saul, [y]Who *am* I? and what *is* my life, *or* my father's family in Israel, that I should be son-in-law to the king?

19 But it came to pass at the time when Merab Saul's daughter should have been given to David, that she was given unto [z]Adriel the [a]Meholathite to wife.

20 [b]And Michal Saul's daughter loved David: and they told Saul, and the thing [i]pleased him.

21 And Saul said, I will give him her, that she may be a snare to him, and that [c]the hand of the Philistines may be against him. Wherefore Saul said to David, Thou shalt [d]this day be my son-in-law in *the one of* the twain.

22 ¶ And Saul commanded his servants, *saying,* Commune with David secretly, and say, Behold, the king hath delight in thee, and all his servants love thee: now therefore be the king's son-in-law.

23 And Saul's servants spake those words in the ears of David. And David said, Seemeth it to you *a* light *thing* to be a king's son-in-law, seeing that I *am* a poor man, and lightly esteemed?

24 And the servants of Saul told him, saying, [j]On this manner spake David.

25 And Saul said, Thus shall ye say to David, The king desireth not any [e]dowry, but an hundred foreskins of the Philistines, to be [f]avenged of the king's enemies. But Saul [g]thought to make David fall by the hand of the Philistines.

26 And when his servants told David these words, it pleased David well to be the king's son-in-law: and [h]the days were not [k]expired.

27 Wherefore David arose and went, he and [i]his men, and slew of the Philistines two hundred men; and [j]David brought their foreskins, and they gave them in full tale to the king, that he might be the king's son-in-law. And Saul gave him Michal his daughter to wife.

28 ¶ And Saul saw and knew that the LORD *was* with David, and *that* Michal Saul's daughter loved him.

29 And Saul was yet the more afraid of David; and Saul became David's enemy continually.

30 Then the princes of the Philistines [k]went forth: and it came to pass, after they went forth, *that* David [l]behaved himself more wisely than all the servants of Saul; so that his name was much [l]set by.

Saul tries to kill David

19 AND SAUL spake to Jonathan his son, and to all his servants, that they should kill David.

2 But Jonathan Saul's son [m]delighted much in David: and Jonathan told David, saying, Saul my father seeketh to kill thee: now therefore, I pray thee, take heed to thyself until the morning, and abide in a secret *place,* and hide thyself:

3 And I will go out and stand beside my father in the field where thou *art,* and I will commune with my father of thee; and what I see, that I will tell thee.

4 ¶ And Jonathan [n]spake good of David unto Saul his father, and said unto him, Let not the king [o]sin against his servant, against David; because he hath not sinned against thee, and because his works *have been* to thee-ward very good:

5 For he did put his [p]life in his hand, and [q]slew the Philistine, and [r]the LORD wrought a great salvation for all Israel: thou sawest *it,* and didst rejoice: [s]wherefore then wilt thou [t]sin against innocent blood, to slay David without a cause?

6 And Saul hearkened unto the voice of Jonathan: and Saul sware,

18:13 [s]ver. 16 Num. 27:17 2 Sam. 5:2 **18:14** [t]Gen. 39:2,3,23 Josh. 6:27 **18:16** [u]ver. 5 **18:17** [v]ch. 17:25 [w]Num. 32:20,27, 29 ch. 25:28 [x]ver. 21,25 2 Sam. 12:9 **18:18** [y]See ver. 23 ch. 9:21 2 Sam. 7:18 **18:19** [z]2 Sam. 21:8 [a]Judg. 7:22 **18:20** [b]ver. 28 **18:21** [c]ver. 17 [d]See ver. 26 **18:25** [e]Gen. 34:12 Ex. 22:17 [f]ch. 14:24 [g]ver. 17

18:26 [h]See ver. 21 **18:27** [i]ver. 13 [j]2 Sam. 3:14 **18:30** [k]2 Sam. 11:1 [l]ver. 5 **19:2** [m]ch. 18:1 **19:4** [n]Prov. 31:8,9 [o]Gen. 42:22 Prov. 17:13 **19:5** [p]Judg. 9:17 [q]ch. 17:49,50 [r]1 Sam. 11:13 1 Chr. 11:14 [s]ch. 20:32 [t]Mat. 27:4

[g] Or, *prospered;* see ver. 5 [h] Heb. *a son of valour* [i] Heb. *was right in his eyes* [j] Heb. *According to these words* [k] Heb. *fulfilled* [l] Heb. *precious*

As the LORD liveth, he shall not be
slain.
7 And Jonathan called David, and
Jonathan showed him all those things.
And Jonathan brought David to Saul,
and he was in his presence, [u]as [m]in
times past.
8 ¶ And there was war again: and
David went out, and fought with the
Philistines, and slew them with a great
slaughter; and they fled from [n]him.
9 And [v]the evil spirit from the LORD
was upon Saul, as he sat in his house
with his javelin in his hand: and David
played with *his* hand.
10 And Saul sought to smite David
even to the wall with the javelin; but he
slipped away out of Saul's presence,
and he smote the javelin into the wall:
and David fled, and escaped that night.
11 [w]Saul also sent messengers
unto David's house, to watch him, and
to slay him in the morning: and Michal
David's wife told him, saying, If thou
save not thy life tonight, tomorrow
thou shalt be slain.
12 ¶ So Michal [x]let David down
through a window: and he went, and
fled, and escaped.
13 And Michal took an [y]image,[o]
and laid *it* in the bed, and put a pillow
of goats' *hair* for his bolster, and cov-
ered *it* with a cloth.
14 And when Saul sent messengers
to take David, she said, He *is* sick.
15 And Saul sent the messengers
again to see David, saying, Bring him
up to me in the bed, that I may slay
him.
16 And when the messengers were
come in, behold, *there was* an image in
the bed, with a pillow of goats' *hair* for
his bolster.
17 And Saul said unto Michal, Why

19:7 [u]ch. 16:21 & 18:2,13
19:9 [v]ch. 16:14 & 18:10,11
19:11 [w]Ps. 59,title
19:12 [x]See Josh. 2:15 Acts 9:24,25
19:13 [y]Gen. 31:19
19:17 [z]2 Sam. 2:22
19:20 [a]See John 7:32,45 [b]ch. 10:5,6 1 Cor. 14:3,24,25 [c]Num. 11:25 Joel 2:28
19:23 [d]ch. 10:10
19:24 [e]Is. 20:2 [f]Mic. 1:8 See 2 Sam. 6:14, 20 [g]ch. 10:11

hast thou deceived me so, and sent
away mine enemy, that he is escaped?
And Michal answered Saul, He said
unto me, Let me go; [z]why should I kill
thee?
18 ¶ So David fled, and escaped,
and came to Samuel to Ramah, and
told him all that Saul had done to him.
And he and Samuel went and dwelt in
Naioth.
19 And it was told Saul, saying, Be-
hold, David *is* at Naioth in Ramah.
20 And [a]Saul sent messengers to
take David: [b]and when they saw the
company of the prophets prophesying,
and Samuel standing *as* appointed over
them, the spirit of God was upon the
messengers of Saul, and they also
[c]prophesied.
21 And when it was told Saul, he
sent other messengers, and they
prophesied likewise. And Saul sent
messengers again the third time, and
they prophesied also.
22 Then went he also to Ramah,
and came to a great well that *is* in Se-
chu: and he asked and said, Where *are*
Samuel and David? And *one* said, Be-
hold, *they be* at Naioth in Ramah.
23 And he went thither to Naioth in
Ramah: and [d]the spirit of God was
upon him also, and he went on, and
prophesied, until he came to Naioth in
Ramah.
24 [e]And he stripped off his clothes
also, and prophesied before Samuel in
like manner, and [p]lay down [f]naked
all that day and all that night. Where-
fore they say, [g]*Is* Saul also among the
prophets?

[m] Heb. *yesterday third day* [n] Heb. *his face*
[o] Heb. *teraphim* [p] Heb. *fell;* see Num. 24:4

19:20 THE COMPANY OF THE PROPHETS. Samuel had founded a "school of the prophets." An association of prophets is also referred to in the time of Elijah and Elisha (cf. 1 Ki. 20:35; 2 Ki. 6:1–7). Such schools were organized in order to encourage those who were prophetically gifted to develop righteous and devout lives through spiritual training, so that their ministry might check apostasy and encourage righteous obedience to God's word. Of special note is the strong influence and prominence that these schools gave to the Holy Spirit (cf. 10:5–6).

19:21 THEY PROPHESIED. Vv. 18–24 reveal that the Spirit of God may come upon individuals for judgment or for blessing. (1) Saul had sent "messengers" to arrest David. To hinder their mission the Spirit of God overpowered them with His presence and influence. Saul himself was later overcome by the Spirit and humiliated by being laid out in a trance all day and all night. (2) This passage makes clear that the Holy Spirit's coming upon an individual for prophecy or any other charismatic manifestation does not always mean that the person is in a right relation with God. Saul was in rebellion against God, yet slain by the Spirit (cf. Mat. 7:22–23).

19:24 LAY DOWN NAKED. The word "naked" in the Bible does not always mean complete nudity. The expression may refer to a person divested of his armor or without his outer garment (John 21:7; cf. Is. 20:2; Mic. 1:8).

David and Jonathan

20 AND DAVID fled from Naioth in Ramah, and came and said before Jonathan, What have I done? what *is* mine iniquity? and what *is* my sin before thy father, that he seeketh my life?

2 And he said unto him, God forbid; thou shalt not die: behold, my father will do nothing either great or small, but that he will show it me: and why should my father hide this thing from me? it *is* not *so.*

3 And David sware moreover, and said, Thy father certainly knoweth that I have found grace in thine eyes; and he saith, Let not Jonathan know this, lest he be grieved: but truly *as* the LORD liveth, and *as* thy soul liveth, *there is* but a step between me and death.

4 Then said Jonathan unto David, [q]Whatsoever thy soul [r]desireth, I will even do *it* for thee.

5 And David said unto Jonathan, Behold, tomorrow *is* the [h]new moon, and I should not fail to sit with the king at meat: but let me go, that I may [i]hide myself in the field unto the third *day* at even.

6 If thy father at all miss me, then say, David earnestly asked *leave* of me that he might run [j]to Bethlehem his city: for *there is* a yearly [k]sacrifice[s] there for all the family.

7 [l]If he say thus, *It is* well; thy servant shall have peace: but if he be very wroth, *then* be sure that [m]evil is determined by him.

8 Therefore thou shalt [n]deal kindly with thy servant; for [o]thou hast brought thy servant into a covenant of the LORD with thee: notwithstanding, [p]if there be in me iniquity, slay me thyself; for why shouldest thou bring me to thy father?

9 And Jonathan said, Far be it from thee: for if I knew certainly that evil were determined by my father to come upon thee, then would not I tell it thee?

10 Then said David to Jonathan, Who shall tell me? or what *if* thy father answer thee roughly?

11 ¶ And Jonathan said unto David, Come, and let us go out into the field. And they went out both of them into the field.

12 And Jonathan said unto David, O LORD God of Israel, when I have [t]sounded my father about tomorrow any time, *or* the third *day,* and, behold, *if there be* good toward David, and I then send not unto thee, and [u]show it thee;

13 [q]The LORD do so and much more to Jonathan: but if it please my father *to do* thee evil, then I will show it thee, and send thee away, that thou mayest go in peace: and [r]the LORD be with thee, as he hath been with my father.

14 And thou shalt not only while yet I live show me the kindness of the LORD, that I die not:

15 But *also* [s]thou shalt not cut off thy kindness from my house for ever: no, not when the LORD hath cut off the enemies of David every one from the face of the earth.

16 So Jonathan [v]made *a covenant* with the house of David, *saying,* [t]Let the LORD even require *it* at the hand of David's enemies.

17 And Jonathan caused David to swear again, [w]because he loved him: [u]for he loved him as he loved his own soul.

18 Then Jonathan said to David, [v]Tomorrow *is* the new moon: and thou shalt be missed, because thy seat will be [x]empty.

19 And *when* thou hast stayed three days, *then* thou shalt go down [y][z]quickly, and come to [w]the place where thou didst hide thyself [a]when the business was *in hand,* and shalt remain by the stone [b]Ezel.

20 And I will shoot three arrows on the side *thereof,* as though I shot at a mark.

21 And, behold, I will send a lad, *saying,* Go, find out the arrows. If I expressly say unto the lad, Behold, the arrows *are* on this side of thee, take them; then come thou: for *there is* peace to thee, and [c]no hurt; [x]*as* the LORD liveth.

22 But if I say thus unto the young man, Behold, the arrows *are* beyond thee; go thy way: for the LORD hath sent thee away.

23 And *as touching* [y]the matter which thou and I have spoken of, be-

20:5 [h]Num. 10:10 & 28:11 [i]ch. 19:2
20:6 [j]ch:16:4 [k]ch. 9:12
20:7 [l]See Deut. 1:23 2 Sam. 17:4 [m]ch. 25:17 Esth. 7:7
20:8 [n]Josh. 2:14 [o]ver. 16 ch. 18:3 & 23:18 [p]2 Sam. 14:32
20:13 [q]Ruth 1:17 [r]Josh. 1:5 ch. 17:37 1 Chr. 22:11,16
20:15 [s]2 Sam. 9:1,3,7 & 21:7
20:16 [t]ch. 25:22 See ch. 31:2 2 Sam. 4:7 & 21:8
20:17 [u]ch. 18:1
20:18 [v]ver. 5
20:19 [w]ch. 19:2
20:21 [x]Jer. 4:2
20:23 [y]ver. 14,15 See ver. 42

[q] Or, *Say what* is *thy mind, and I will do*
[r] Heb. *speaketh,* or, *thinketh* [s] Or, *feast*
[t] Heb. *searched* [u] Heb. *uncover thine ear*
[v] Heb. *cut* [w] Or, *by his love toward him*
[x] Heb. *missed* [y] Or, *diligently* [z] Heb. *greatly* [a] Heb. *in the day of the business*
[b] Or, *that showeth the way* [c] Heb. *not any thing*

hold, the LORD *be* between thee and me for ever.

24 ¶ So David hid himself in the field: and when the new moon was come, the king sat him down to eat meat.

25 And the king sat upon his seat, as at other times, *even* upon a seat by the wall: and Jonathan arose, and Abner sat by Saul's side, and David's place was empty.

26 Nevertheless Saul spake not any thing that day: for he thought, Something hath befallen him, he *is* [z]not clean; surely he *is* not clean.

27 And it came to pass on the morrow, *which was* the second *day* of the month, that David's place was empty: and Saul said unto Jonathan his son, Wherefore cometh not the son of Jesse to meat, neither yesterday, nor today?

28 And Jonathan [a]answered Saul, David earnestly asked *leave* of me *to go* to Bethlehem:

29 And he said, Let me go, I pray thee; for our family hath a sacrifice in the city; and my brother, he hath commanded me *to be there:* and now, if I have found favour in thine eyes, let me get away, I pray thee, and see my brethren. Therefore he cometh not unto the king's table.

30 Then Saul's anger was kindled against Jonathan, and he said unto him, [d] [e]Thou son of the perverse rebellious *woman,* do not I know that thou hast chosen the son of Jesse to thine own confusion, and unto the confusion of thy mother's nakedness?

31 For as long as the son of Jesse liveth upon the ground, thou shalt not be established, nor thy kingdom. Wherefore now send and fetch him unto me, for he [f]shall surely die.

32 And Jonathan answered Saul his father, and said unto him, [b]Wherefore shall he be slain? what hath he done?

33 And Saul [c]cast a javelin at him to smite him: [d]whereby Jonathan knew that it was determined of his father to slay David.

34 So Jonathan arose from the table in fierce anger, and did eat no meat the second day of the month: for he was grieved for David, because his father had done him shame.

35 ¶ And it came to pass in the morning, that Jonathan went out into the field at the time appointed with David, and a little lad with him.

36 And he said unto his lad, Run, find out now the arrows which I shoot. *And* as the lad ran, he shot an arrow [g]beyond him.

37 And when the lad was come to the place of the arrow which Jonathan had shot, Jonathan cried after the lad, and said, *Is* not the arrow beyond thee?

38 And Jonathan cried after the lad, Make speed, haste, stay not. And Jonathan's lad gathered up the arrows, and came to his master.

39 But the lad knew not any thing: only Jonathan and David knew the matter.

40 And Jonathan gave his [h]artillery unto [i]his lad, and said unto him, Go, carry *them* to the city.

41 ¶ *And* as soon as the lad was gone, David arose out of *a place* toward the south, and fell on his face to the ground, and bowed himself three times: and they kissed one another, and wept one with another, until David exceeded.

42 And Jonathan said to David, [e]Go in peace, [j]forasmuch as we have sworn both of us in the name of the LORD, saying, The LORD be between me and thee, and between my seed and thy seed for ever. And he arose and departed: and Jonathan went into the city.

David visits Ahimelech

21 THEN CAME David to Nob to [f]Ahimelech the priest: and Ahimelech was [g]afraid at the meeting of David, and said unto him, Why *art* thou alone, and no man with thee?

2 And David said unto Ahimelech the priest, The king hath commanded me a business, and hath said unto me, Let no man know any thing of the busi-

20:26 [z]Lev. 7:21 & 15:5
20:28 [a]ver. 6
20:32 [b]ch. 19:5 Mat. 27:23 Luke 23:22
20:33 [c]ch. 18:11 [d]ver. 7
20:42 [e]ch. 1:17
21:1 [f]ch. 14:3 called *Ahiah* Called also *Abiathar* Mark 2:26 [g]ch. 16:4

[d] Or, *Thou perverse rebel* [e] Heb. *Son of perverse rebellion* [f] Heb. is *the son of death* [g] Heb. *to pass over him* [h] Heb. *instruments* [i] Heb. *that* was *his* [j] Or, the LORD be witness of that *which;* see ver. 23

21:1 THEN CAME DAVID TO NOB. Chs. 21—22 record David's flight from Saul and his failure to trust God completely. In an attempt to save his life, David lied (vv. 2), sought refuge among the ungodly Philistines (vv. 10–15), and indirectly caused the death of the priests and many others (22:11–23; cf. Ps. 52). By resorting to deception, David failed to commit his life unconditionally to the Lord and His protection.

ness whereabout I send thee, and what I have commanded thee: and I have appointed *my* servants to such and such a place.

3 Now therefore what is under thine hand? give *me* five *loaves of* bread in mine hand, or what there is [k]present.

4 And the priest answered David, and said, *There is* no common bread under mine hand, but there is [h]hallowed bread; [i]if the young men have kept themselves at least from women.

5 And David answered the priest, and said unto him, Of a truth women *have been* kept from us about these three days, since I came out, and the [j]vessels of the young men are holy, and *the bread is* in a manner common, [l]yea, though it were sanctified this day [k]in the vessel.

6 So the priest [l]gave him hallowed *bread:* for there was no bread there but the showbread, [m]that was taken from before the LORD, to put hot bread in the day when it was taken away.

7 Now a certain man of the servants of Saul *was* there that day, detained before the LORD; and his name *was* [n]Doeg, an Edomite, the chiefest of the herdmen that *belonged* to Saul.

David escapes to Gath

8 ¶ And David said unto Ahimelech, And is there not here under thine hand spear or sword? for I have neither brought my sword nor my weapons with me, because the king's business required haste.

9 And the priest said, The sword of Goliath the Philistine, whom thou slewest in [o]the valley of Elah, [p]behold, it *is here* wrapped in a cloth behind the ephod: if thou wilt take that, take *it:* for *there is* no other save that here. And David said, *There is* none like that; give it me.

10 ¶ And David arose, and fled that day for fear of Saul, and went to [m]Achish the king of Gath.

11 And [q]the servants of Achish said unto him, *Is* not this David the king of the land? did they not sing one to another of him in dances, saying, [r]Saul hath slain his thousands, and David his ten thousands?

12 And David [s]laid up these words in his heart, and was sore afraid of Achish the king of Gath.

13 And [t]he changed his behaviour before them, and feigned himself mad in their hands, and [n]scrabbled on the doors of the gate, and let his spittle fall down upon his beard.

14 Then said Achish unto his servants, Lo, ye see the man [o]is mad: wherefore *then* have ye brought him to me?

15 Have I need of mad men, that ye have brought this *fellow* to play the mad man in my presence? shall this *fellow* come into my house?

David's flight continues

22 DAVID THEREFORE departed thence, and [u]escaped [v]to the cave Adullam: and when his brethren and all his father's house heard *it,* they went down thither to him.

2 [w]And every one *that was* in distress, and every one that [p]*was* in debt, and every one *that was* [q]discontented, gathered themselves unto him; and he became a captain over them: and there were with him about four hundred men.

3 ¶ And David went thence to Mizpeh of Moab: and he said unto the king of Moab, Let my father and my mother, I pray thee, come forth, *and be* with you, till I know what God will do for me.

4 And he brought them before the king of Moab: and they dwelt with him all the while that David was in the hold.

5 ¶ And the prophet [x]Gad said unto David, Abide not in the hold; depart, and get thee into the land of Judah. Then David departed, and came into the forest of Hareth.

6 ¶ When Saul heard that David was discovered, and the men that *were* with him, (now Saul abode in Gibeah under a [r]tree in Ramah, having his spear in his hand, and all his servants *were* standing about him;)

7 Then Saul said unto his servants that stood about him, Hear now, ye Benjamites; will the son of Jesse [y]give every one of you fields and vineyards, *and* make you all captains of thousands, and captains of hundreds;

8 That all of you have conspired against me, and *there is* none that showeth me that [z]my son hath made

21:4 [h]Ex. 25:30 Lev. 24:5 Mat. 12:4 [i]Ex. 19:15 Zech. 7:3
21:5 [j]1 Thes. 4:4 [k]Lev. 8:26
21:6 [l]Mat. 12:3,4 Mark 2:25,26 Luke 6:3,4 [m]Lev. 24:8,9
21:7 [n]ch. 22:9 Ps. 52,title
21:9 [o]ch. 17:2,50 [p]See ch. 31:10
21:11 [q]Ps. 56,title [r]ch. 18:7 & 29:5
21:12 [s]Luke 2:19
21:13 [t]Ps. 34,title
22:1 [u]Ps. 57,title & 142,title [v]2 Sam. 23:13
22:2 [w]Judg. 11:3
22:5 [x]2 Sam. 24:11 1 Chr. 21:9 2 Chr. 29:25
22:7 [y]ch. 8:14
22:8 [z]ch. 18:3 & 20:30

[k] Heb. *found* [l] Or, *especially when this day there is* other *sanctified in the vessel* [m] Or, *Abimelech;* see Ps. 34, title [n] Or, *made marks* [o] Or, *playeth the mad man* [p] Heb. *had a creditor* [q] Heb. *bitter of soul* [r] Or, *grove in a high place*

a league with the son of Jesse, and *there is* none of you that is sorry for me, or showeth unto me that my son hath stirred up my servant against me, to lie in wait, as at this day?

9 ¶ Then answered [a]Doeg the Edomite, which was set over the servants of Saul, and said, I saw the son of Jesse coming to Nob, to [b]Ahimelech the son of [c]Ahitub.

10 [d]And he inquired of the LORD for him, and [e]gave him victuals, and gave him the sword of Goliath the Philistine.

Saul has Ahimelech killed

11 Then the king sent to call Ahimelech the priest, the son of Ahitub, and all his father's house, the priests that *were* in Nob: and they came all of them to the king.

12 And Saul said, Hear now, thou son of Ahitub. And he answered, [s]Here I *am,* my lord.

13 And Saul said unto him, Why have ye conspired against me, thou and the son of Jesse, in that thou hast given him bread, and a sword, and hast inquired of God for him, that he should rise against me, to lie in wait, as at this day?

14 Then Ahimelech answered the king, and said, And who *is so* faithful among all thy servants as David, which is the king's son-in-law, and goeth at thy bidding, and is honourable in thine house?

15 Did I then begin to inquire of God for him? be it far from me: let not the king impute *any* thing unto his servant, *nor* to all the house of my father: for thy servant knew nothing of all this, [t]less or more.

16 And the king said, Thou shalt surely die, Ahimelech, thou, and all thy father's house.

17 ¶ And the king said unto the [u] [v]footmen that stood about him, Turn, and slay the priests of the LORD; because their hand also *is* with David, and because they knew when he fled, and did not show it to me. But the servants of the king [f]would not put forth their hand to fall upon the priests of the LORD.

22:9 [a]ch. 21:7 Ps. 52,title & ver. 1-3 [b]ch. 21:1 [c]ch. 14:3
22:10 [d]Num. 27:21 [e]ch. 21:6,9
22:17 [f]See Ex. 1:17
22:18 [g]See ch. 2:31
22:19 [h]ver. 9,11
22:20 [i]ch. 23:6 [j]ch. 2:33
22:23 [k]1 Ki. 2:26
23:1 [l]Josh. 15:44
23:2 [m]ver. 4,6,9 ch. 30:8 2 Sam. 5:19,23

18 And the king said to Doeg, Turn thou, and fall upon the priests. And Doeg the Edomite turned, and he fell upon the priests, and [g]slew on that day fourscore and five persons that did wear a linen ephod.

19 [h]And Nob, the city of the priests, smote he with the edge of the sword, both men and women, children and sucklings, and oxen, and asses, and sheep, with the edge of the sword.

20 ¶ [i]And one of the sons of Ahimelech the son of Ahitub, named Abiathar, [j]escaped, and fled after David.

21 And Abiathar showed David that Saul had slain the LORD's priests.

22 And David said unto Abiathar, I knew *it* that day, when Doeg the Edomite *was* there, that he would surely tell Saul: I have occasioned *the death* of all the persons of thy father's house.

23 Abide thou with me, fear not: [k]for he that seeketh my life seeketh thy life: but with me thou *shalt be* in safeguard.

David at Keilah

23 THEN THEY told David, saying, Behold, the Philistines fight against [l]Keilah, and they rob the threshingfloors.

2 Therefore David [m]inquired of the LORD, saying, Shall I go and smite these Philistines? And the LORD said unto David, Go, and smite the Philistines, and save Keilah.

3 And David's men said unto him, Behold, we be afraid here in Judah: how much more then if we come to Keilah against the armies of the Philistines?

4 Then David inquired of the LORD yet again. And the LORD answered him and said, Arise, go down to Keilah; for I will deliver the Philistines into thine hand.

5 So David and his men went to Keilah, and fought with the Philistines, and brought away their cattle, and smote them with a great slaughter. So David saved the inhabitants of Keilah.

6 And it came to pass, when Abia-

[s]Heb. *Behold me* [t]Heb. *little or great*
[u]Or, *guard* [v]Heb. *runners*

22:18 SLEW ... FOURSCORE AND FIVE PERSONS. God allowed Doeg to kill eighty-five of God's ministers, plus other innocent men, women, and children. In a fallen world, the innocent sometimes suffer unjustly. God's people should not be alarmed when they suffer at the hands of evil people. In this life we will experience tribulation (Acts 14:22), but in the life to come abundant blessing that far exceeds our present suffering and agonies (Rom. 8:18–39).

thar the son of Ahimelech [n]fled to David to Keilah, *that* he came down *with* an ephod in his hand.

7 ¶ And it was told Saul that David was come to Keilah. And Saul said, God hath delivered him into mine hand; for he is shut in, by entering into a town that hath gates and bars.

8 And Saul called all the people together to war, to go down to Keilah, to besiege David and his men.

9 ¶ And David knew that Saul secretly practised mischief against him; and [o]he said to Abiathar the priest, Bring hither the ephod.

10 Then said David, O LORD God of Israel, thy servant hath certainly heard that Saul seeketh to come to Keilah, [p]to destroy the city for my sake.

11 Will the men of Keilah deliver me up into his hand? will Saul come down, as thy servant hath heard? O LORD God of Israel, I beseech thee, tell thy servant. And the LORD said, He will come down.

12 Then said David, Will the men of Keilah [w]deliver me and my men into the hand of Saul? And the LORD said, They will deliver *thee* up.

13 ¶ Then David and his men, [q]*which were* about six hundred, arose and departed out of Keilah, and went whithersoever they could go. And it was told Saul that David was escaped from Keilah; and he forbare to go forth.

14 And David abode in the wilderness in strong holds, and remained in [r]a mountain in the wilderness of [s]Ziph. And Saul [t]sought him every day, but God delivered him not into his hand.

Saul pursues David

15 And David saw that Saul was come out to seek his life: and David *was* in the wilderness of Ziph in a wood.

16 ¶ And Jonathan Saul's son arose, and went to David into the wood, and strengthened his hand in God.

17 And he said unto him, Fear not: for the hand of Saul my father shall not find thee; and thou shalt be king over Israel, and I shall be next unto thee; and [u]that also Saul my father knoweth.

18 And they two [v]made a covenant before the LORD: and David abode in the wood, and Jonathan went to his house.

19 ¶ Then [w]came up the Ziphites to Saul to Gibeah, saying, Doth not David hide himself with us in strong holds in the wood, in the hill of Hachilah, which *is* [x]on the south of [y]Jeshimon?

20 Now therefore, O king, come down according to all the desire of thy soul to come down; and [x]our part *shall be* to deliver him into the king's hand.

21 And Saul said, Blessed *be* ye of the LORD; for ye have compassion on me.

22 Go, I pray you, prepare yet, and know and see his place where his [z]haunt is, *and* who hath seen him there: for it is told me *that* he dealeth very subtly.

23 See therefore, and take knowledge of all the lurking places where he hideth himself, and come ye again to me with the certainty, and I will go with you: and it shall come to pass, if he be in the land, that I will search him out throughout all the thousands of Judah.

24 And they arose, and went to Ziph before Saul: but David and his men *were* in the wilderness [y]of Maon, in the plain on the south of Jeshimon.

25 Saul also and his men went to seek *him.* And they told David: wherefore he came down [a]into a rock, and abode in the wilderness of Maon. And when Saul heard *that,* he pursued after David in the wilderness of Maon.

26 And Saul went on this side of the mountain, and David and his men on that side of the mountain: [z]and David made haste to get away for fear of Saul; for Saul and his men [a]compassed David and his men round about to take them.

27 ¶ [b]But there came a messenger unto Saul, saying, Haste thee, and come; for the Philistines have [b]invaded the land.

28 Wherefore Saul returned from pursuing after David, and went against the Philistines: therefore they called that place [c]Sela-hammahlekoth.

29 ¶ And David went up from thence, and dwelt in strong holds at [c]En-gedi.

David spares Saul

24 AND IT came to pass, [d]when Saul was returned from [d]fol-

23:6 [n]ch. 22:20 **23:9** [o]Num. 27:21 ch. 30:7 **23:10** [p]ch. 22:19 **23:13** [q]ch. 22:2 & 25:13 **23:14** [r]Ps. 11:1 [s]Josh. 15:55 [t]Ps. 54:3,4 **23:17** [u]ch. 24:20 **23:18** [v]ch. 18:3 & 20:16,42 2 Sam. 21:7 **23:19** [w]See ch. 26:1 Ps. 54,title **23:20** [x]Ps. 54:3 **23:24** [y]Josh. 15:55 ch. 25:2 **23:26** [z]Ps. 31:22 [a]Ps. 17:9 **23:27** [b]See 2 Ki. 19:9 **23:29** [c]2 Chr. 20:2 **24:1** [d]ch. 23:28

[w] Heb. *shut up* [x] Heb. *on the right hand* [y] Or, *The wilderness?* [z] Heb. *foot shall be* [a] Or, *from the rock* [b] Heb. *spread themselves upon* [c] i.e. *The rock of divisions* [d] Heb. *after*

lowing the Philistines, that it was told
him, saying, Behold, David *is* in the wil-
derness of En-gedi.
2 Then Saul took three thousand
chosen men out of all Israel, and
[e]went to seek David and his men upon
the rocks of the wild goats.
3 And he came to the sheepcotes by
the way, where *was* a cave; and [f]Saul
went in to [g]cover his feet: and [h]David
and his men remained in the sides of
the cave.
4 [i]And the men of David said unto
him, Behold the day of which the LORD
said unto thee, Behold, I will deliver
thine enemy into thine hand, that thou
mayest do to him as it shall seem good
unto thee. Then David arose, and cut
off the skirt of [e]Saul's robe privily.
5 And it came to pass afterward,
that [j]David's heart smote him, be-
cause he had cut off Saul's skirt.
6 And he said unto his men, [k]The
LORD forbid that I should do this thing
unto my master, the LORD's anointed, to
stretch forth mine hand against him,
seeing he *is* the anointed of the LORD.
7 So David [l]stayed[f] his servants
with these words, and suffered them
not to rise against Saul. But Saul rose
up out of the cave, and went on *his* way.
8 David also arose afterward, and
went out of the cave, and cried after
Saul, saying, My lord the king. And
when Saul looked behind him, David
stooped with his face to the earth, and
bowed himself.
9 ¶ And David said to Saul,
[m]Wherefore hearest thou men's
words, saying, Behold, David seeketh
thy hurt?
10 Behold, this day thine eyes have
seen how that the LORD had delivered
thee today into mine hand in the cave:
and *some* bade *me* kill thee: but *mine eye*
spared thee; and I said, I will not put
forth mine hand against my lord; for he
is the LORD's anointed.
11 Moreover, my father, see, yea,
see the skirt of thy robe in my hand: for
in that I cut off the skirt of thy robe,
and killed thee not, know thou and see
that *there is* [n]neither evil nor trans-
gression in mine hand, and I have not
sinned against thee; yet thou [o]huntest
my soul to take it.
12 [p]The LORD judge between me
and thee, and the LORD avenge me of
thee: but mine hand shall not be upon
thee.
13 As saith the proverb of the an-
cients, Wickedness proceedeth from
the wicked: but mine hand shall not be
upon thee.
14 After whom is the king of Israel
come out? after whom dost thou pur-
sue? [q]after a dead dog, after [r]a flea.
15 [s]The LORD therefore be judge,
and judge between me and thee, and
[t]see, and [u]plead my cause, and [g]de-
liver me out of thine hand.
16 ¶ And it came to pass, when Da-
vid had made an end of speaking these
words unto Saul, that Saul said, [v]*Is*
this thy voice, my son David? And Saul
lifted up his voice, and wept.
17 [w]And he said to David, Thou *art*
[x]more righteous than I: for [y]thou
hast rewarded me good, whereas I
have rewarded thee evil.
18 And thou hast shown this day
how that thou hast dealt well with me:
forasmuch as when [z]the LORD had
[a]delivered me into thine hand, thou
killedst me not.
19 For if a man find his enemy, will
he let him go well away? wherefore the
LORD reward thee good for that thou
hast done unto me this day.
20 And now, behold, [b]I know well
that thou shalt surely be king, and that
the kingdom of Israel shall be estab
lished in thine hand.
21 [c]Swear now therefore unto me
by the LORD, [d]that thou wilt not cut off
my seed after me, and that thou wilt
not destroy my name out of my father's
house.
22 And David sware unto Saul. And
Saul went home; but David and his
men gat them up unto [e]the hold.

24:2 [e]Ps. 38:12 **24:3** [f]ver. 10 [g]Judg. 3:24 [h]Ps. 57,title & 142,title **24:4** [i]ch. 26:8 **24:5** [j]2 Sam. 24:10 **24:6** [k]ch. 26:11 **24:7** [l]Ps. 7:4 Mat. 5:44 Rom. 12:17,19 **24:9** [m]Ps. 141:6 Prov. 16:28 & 17:9 **24:11** [n]Ps. 7:3 & 35:7 [o]ch. 26:20 **24:12** [p]Gen. 16:5 Judg. 11:27 ch. 26:10 Job. 5:8 **24:14** [q]ch. 17:43 2 Sam. 9:8 [r]ch. 26:20 **24:15** [s]ver. 12 [t]2 Chr. 24:22 [u]Ps. 35:1 & 43:1 Mic. 7:9 **24:16** [v]ch. 26:17 **24:17** [w]ch. 26:21 [x]Gen. 38:26 [y]Mat. 5:44 **24:18** [z]ch. 26:23 [a]ch. 23:12 & 26:8 **24:20** [b]ch. 23:17 **24:21** [c]Gen. 21:23 [d]2 Sam. 21:6,8 **24:22** [e]ch. 23:29

[e] Heb. *the robe which* was *Saul's* [f] Heb. *cut off* [g] Heb. *judge*

24:6 THE LORD'S ANOINTED. This phrase refers only to Saul in his appointed role as king of Israel; it does not mean that he was presently anointed by the Holy Spirit. David had received no direction from God to remove Saul from the throne through assassination. (1) Vv. 6–10 provide no basis for the failure to discipline or to oppose church leaders and overseers who fail morally or who depart from the teachings of God's Word (see 1 Tim. 3:1–13; 5:19–20; Tit. 1:5–9). Such leaders must be removed from their positions. (2) Furthermore, church leaders may not use these verses to claim that they are not accountable for their conduct to other leaders and to the body of Christ.

David, Nabal and Abigail

25 AND [f]SAMUEL died; and all the Israelites were gathered together, and [g]lamented him, and buried him in his house at Ramah. And David arose, and went down [h]to the wilderness of Paran.

2 And *there was* a man [i]in Maon, whose [h]possessions *were* in [j]Carmel; and the man *was* very great, and he had three thousand sheep, and a thousand goats: and he was shearing his sheep in Carmel.

3 Now the name of the man *was* Nabal; and the name of his wife Abigail: and *she was* a woman of good understanding, and of a beautiful countenance: but the man *was* churlish and evil in his doings; and he *was* of the house of Caleb.

4 ¶ And David heard in the wilderness that Nabal did [k]shear his sheep.

5 And David sent out ten young men, and David said unto the young men, Get you up to Carmel, and go to Nabal, and greet him in my name:

6 And thus shall ye say to him that liveth *in prosperity,* [l]Peace *be* both to thee, and peace *be* to thine house, and peace *be* unto all that thou hast.

7 And now I have heard that thou hast shearers: now thy shepherds which were with us, we [i]hurt them not, [m]neither was there aught missing unto them, all the while they were in Carmel.

8 Ask thy young men, and they will show thee. Wherefore let the young men find favour in thine eyes: for we come in [n]a good day: give, I pray thee, whatsoever cometh to thine hand unto thy servants, and to thy son David.

9 And when David's young men came, they spake to Nabal according to all those words in the name of David, and [j]ceased.

10 ¶ And Nabal answered David's servants, and said, [o]Who *is* David? and who *is* the son of Jesse? there be many servants now a days that break away every man from his master.

11 [p]Shall I then take my bread, and my water, and my [k]flesh that I have killed for my shearers, and give *it* unto men, whom I know not whence they *be?*

12 So David's young men turned their way, and went again, and came and told him all those sayings.

13 And David said unto his men, Gird ye on every man his sword. And they girded on every man his sword; and David also girded on his sword: and there went up after David about four hundred men; and two hundred [q]abode by the stuff.

14 ¶ But one of the young men told Abigail, Nabal's wife, saying, Behold, David sent messengers out of the wilderness to salute our master; and he [l]railed on them.

15 But the men *were* very good unto us, and [r]we were not [i]hurt, neither missed we any thing, as long as we were conversant with them, when we were in the fields:

16 They were [s]a wall unto us both by night and day, all the while we were with them keeping the sheep.

17 Now therefore know and consider what thou wilt do; for [t]evil is determined against our master, and against all his household: for he *is such* a son of [u]Belial, that *a man* cannot speak to him.

18 ¶ Then Abigail made haste, and [v]took two hundred loaves, and two bottles of wine, and five sheep ready dressed, and five measures of parched *corn,* and an hundred [m]clusters of raisins, and two hundred cakes of figs, and laid *them* on asses.

19 And she said unto her servants, [w]Go on before me; behold, I come after you. But she told not her husband Nabal.

20 And it was *so, as* she rode on the ass, that she came down by the covert of the hill, and, behold, David and his men came down against her; and she met them.

25:1 [f]ch. 28:3 [g]Num. 20:29 Deut. 34:8 [h]Gen. 21:21 Ps. 120:5
25:2 [i]ch. 23:24 [j]Josh. 15:55
25:4 [k]Gen. 38:13 2 Sam. 13:23
25:6 [l]1 Chr. 12:18 Luke 10:5
25:7 [m]ver. 15,21
25:8 [n]Neh. 8:10 Esth. 9:19
25:10 [o]Judg. 9:28
25:11 [p]Judg. 8:6
25:13 [q]ch. 30:24
25:15 [r]ver. 7
25:16 [s]Ex. 14:22 Job 1:10
25:17 [t]ch. 20:7 [u]Deut. 13:13 Judg. 19:22
25:18 [v]Gen. 32:13 Prov. 18:16 & 21:14
25:19 [w]Gen. 32:16,20

[h] Or, *business* [i] Heb. *shamed* [j] Heb. *rested* [k] Heb. *slaughter* [l] Heb. *flew upon them* [m] Or, *lumps*

25:1 SAMUEL DIED. The death of Samuel brought to an end the life of one of God's most faithful servants. (1) He was zealous for God and did more than any other person of his day to follow that which was in the heart of God (2:35; 12:7–25; 15:10–11,35). He provides a high example of integrity, honesty, faithfulness, and moral blamelessness (12:1–5). (2) He left behind him a reputation that ranks him among the greatest of God's people in the O.T. God Himself spoke of him in the same breath as Moses (Jer. 15:1). Samuel and other righteous prophets, not the kings, represent the highest moral and spiritual leadership under the old covenant.

21 Now David had said, Surely in
vain have I kept all that this *fellow* hath
in the wilderness, so that nothing was
missed of all that *pertained* unto him:
and he hath [x]requited me evil for
good.
22 [y]So and more also do God unto
the enemies of David, if I [z]leave of all
that *pertain* to him by the morning light
[a]any that pisseth against the wall.
23 And when Abigail saw David,
she hasted, and [b]lighted off the ass,
and fell before David on her face, and
bowed herself to the ground,
24 And fell at his feet, and said,
Upon me, my lord, *upon* me *let this* iniq-
uity *be:* and let thine handmaid, I pray
thee, speak in thine [n]audience, and
hear the words of thine handmaid.
25 Let not my lord, I pray thee,
[o]regard this man of Belial, *even* Nabal:
for as his name *is,* so *is* he; [p]Nabal *is*
his name, and folly *is* with him: but I
thine handmaid saw not the young men
of my lord, whom thou didst send.
26 Now therefore, my lord, [c]*as* the
LORD liveth, and *as* thy soul liveth, see-
ing the LORD hath [d]withholden thee
from coming to *shed* blood, and from
[e]avenging[q] thyself with thine own
hand, now [f]let thine enemies, and
they that seek evil to my lord, be as
Nabal.
27 And now [g]this [r]blessing which
thine handmaid hath brought unto my
lord, let it even be given unto the young
men that follow my lord.
28 I pray thee, forgive the trespass
of thine handmaid: for [h]the LORD will
certainly make my lord a sure house;
because my lord [i]fighteth the battles
of the LORD, and [j]evil hath not been
found in thee *all* thy days.
29 Yet a man is risen to pursue
thee, and to seek thy soul: but the soul
of my lord shall be bound in the bundle
of life with the LORD thy God; and the
souls of thine enemies, them shall he
[k]sling out, [s]*as out* of the middle of a
sling.
30 And it shall come to pass, when
the LORD shall have done to my lord ac-
cording to all the good that he hath
spoken concerning thee, and shall
have appointed thee ruler over Israel;
31 That this shall be [t]no grief unto
thee, nor offence of heart unto my lord,
either that thou hast shed blood cause-
less, or that my lord hath avenged him-
self: but when the LORD shall have dealt
well with my lord, then remember thine
handmaid.
32 ¶ And David said to Abigail,
[l]Blessed *be* the LORD God of Israel,
which sent thee this day to meet me:
33 And blessed *be* thy advice, and
blessed *be* thou, which hast [m]kept me
this day from coming to *shed* blood, and
from avenging myself with mine own
hand.
34 For in very deed, *as* the LORD God
of Israel liveth, which hath [n]kept me
back from hurting thee, except thou
hadst hasted and come to meet me,
surely there had [o]not been left unto
Nabal by the morning light any that
pisseth against the wall.
35 So David received of her hand
that which she had brought him, and
said unto her, [p]Go up in peace to thine
house; see, I have hearkened to thy
voice, and have [q]accepted thy person.
36 ¶ And Abigail came to Nabal;
and, behold, [r]he held a feast in his
house, like the feast of a king; and Na-
bal's heart *was* merry within him, for
he *was* very drunken: wherefore she
told him nothing, less or more, until
the morning light.
37 But it came to pass in the morn-
ing, when the wine was gone out of Na-
bal, and his wife had told him these
things, that his heart died within him,
and he became *as* a stone.
38 And it came to pass about ten
days *after,* that the LORD smote Nabal,
that he died.
39 ¶ And when David heard that Na-
bal was dead, he said, [s]Blessed *be* the
LORD, that hath [t]pleaded the cause of
my reproach from the hand of Nabal,
and hath [u]kept his servant from evil:
for the LORD hath [v]returned the wick-
edness of Nabal upon his own head.

25:21 [x]Ps. 109:5 **25:22** [y]Ruth 1:17 ch. 3:17 & 20:13,16 [z]ver. 34 [a]1 Ki. 14:10 & 21:21 2 Ki. 9:8 **25:23** [b]Josh. 15:18 Judg. 1:14 **25:26** [c]2 Ki. 2:2 [d]ver. 33 Gen. 20:6 [e]Rom. 12:19 [f]2 Sam. 18:32 **25:27** [g]Gen. 33:11 ch. 30:26 2 Ki. 5:15 **25:28** [h]2 Sam. 7:11,27 1 Ki. 9:5 1 Chr. 17:10,25 [i]ch. 18:17 [j]ch. 24:11 **25:29** [k]Jer. 10:18 **25:32** [l]Gen. 24:27 Ex. 18:10 Luke 1:68 **25:33** [m]ver. 26 **25:34** [n]ver. 26 [o]ver. 22 **25:35** [p]ch. 20:42 2 Sam. 15:9 2 Ki. 5:19 Luke 7:50 & 8:48 [q]Gen. 19:21 **25:36** [r]2 Sam. 13:23 **25:39** [s]ver. 32 [t]Prov. 22:23 [u]ver. 26,34 [v]1 Ki. 2:44

[n] Heb. *ears* [o] Heb. *lay it to his heart* [p] i.e. *Fool* [q] Heb. *saving thyself* [r] Or, *present*
[s] Heb. *in the midst of the bought of a sling*
[t] Heb. *no staggering,* or, *stumbling*

25:32 GOD . . . SENT THEE. God sent Abigail to prevent David from doing a great injustice to all of Nabal's men (v. 34). David recognized how wrong he had been in planning to exercise such extreme vengeance against them. At times God sends others to us with godly advice that opens our eyes and protects us from doing wrong. When others counsel us, we must judge our plans by God's Word and the direction of the Spirit in our hearts (see Rom. 8:14, note).

And David sent and communed with
Abigail, to take her to him to wife.
40 And when the servants of David
were come to Abigail to Carmel, they
spake unto her, saying, David sent us
unto thee, to take thee to him to wife.
41 And she arose, and bowed her-
self on *her* face to the earth, and said,
Behold, *let* thine handmaid *be* a servant
to wash the feet of the servants of my
lord.
42 And Abigail hasted, and arose,
and rode upon an ass, with five dam-
sels of hers that went after her; and
she went after the messengers of Da-
vid, and became his wife.
43 David also took Ahinoam [w]of
Jezreel; [x]and they were also both of
them his wives.
44 ¶ But Saul had given [y]Michal
his daughter, David's wife, to [u]Phalti
the son of Laish, which *was* of [z]Gal-
lim.

David spares Saul again

26 AND THE Ziphites came unto
Saul to Gibeah, saying, [a]Doth
not David hide himself in the hill of Ha-
chilah, *which is* before Jeshimon?
2 Then Saul arose, and went down
to the wilderness of Ziph, having three
thousand chosen men of Israel with
him, to seek David in the wilderness of
Ziph.
3 And Saul pitched in the hill of Ha-
chilah, which *is* before Jeshimon, by
the way. But David abode in the wilder-
ness, and he saw that Saul came after
him into the wilderness.
4 David therefore sent out spies,
and understood that Saul was come in
very deed.
5 ¶ And David arose, and came to
the place where Saul had pitched: and
David beheld the place where Saul lay,
and [b]Abner the son of Ner, the captain
of his host: and Saul lay in the
[c]trench,[v] and the people pitched
round about him.
6 Then answered David and said to
Ahimelech the Hittite, and to Abishai
[d]the son of Zeruiah, brother to Joab,
saying, Who will [e]go down with me to
Saul to the camp? And Abishai said, I
will go down with thee.

25:43 [w]Josh. 15:56 [x]ch. 27:3 & 30:5
25:44 [y]2 Sam. 3:14 [z]Is. 10:30
26:1 [a]ch. 23:19 Ps. 54,title
26:5 [b]ch. 14:50 & 17:55 [c]ch. 17:20
26:6 [d]1 Chr. 2:16 [e]Judg. 7:10,11

7 So David and Abishai came to the
people by night: and, behold, Saul lay
sleeping within the trench, and his
spear stuck in the ground at his bol-
ster: but Abner and the people lay
round about him.
8 Then said Abishai to David, God
hath [f]delivered thine enemy into
thine hand this day: now therefore let
me smite him, I pray thee, with the
spear even to the earth at once, and I
will not *smite* him the second time.
9 And David said to Abishai, De-
stroy him not: [g]for who can stretch
forth his hand against the LORD's
anointed, and be guiltless?
10 David said furthermore, *As* the
LORD liveth, [h]the LORD shall smite him;
or [i]his day shall come to die; or he
shall [j]descend into battle, and perish.
11 [k]The LORD forbid that I should
stretch forth mine hand against the
LORD's anointed: but, I pray thee, take
thou now the spear that *is* at his bol-
ster, and the cruse of water, and let
us go.
12 So David took the spear and the
cruse of water from Saul's bolster; and
they gat them away, and no man saw
it, nor knew *it,* neither awaked: for they
were all asleep; because [l]a deep sleep
from the LORD was fallen upon them.
13 ¶ Then David went over to the
other side, and stood on the top of an
hill afar off; a great space *being* be-
tween them:
14 And David cried to the people,
and to Abner the son of Ner, saying,
Answerest thou not, Abner? Then Ab-
ner answered and said, Who *art* thou
that criest to the king?
15 And David said to Abner, *Art* not
thou a *valiant* man? and who *is* like to
thee in Israel? wherefore then hast
thou not kept thy lord the king? for
there came one of the people in to de-
stroy the king thy lord.
16 This thing *is* not good that thou
hast done. *As* the LORD liveth, ye *are*
[m]worthy to die, because ye have not
kept your master, the LORD's anointed.
And now see where the king's spear *is,*

26:8 [f]ch. 24:18
26:9 [g]ch. 24:6,7 2 Sam. 1:16
26:10 [h]ch. 25:38 Luke 18:7 Rom. 12:19 [i]See Gen. 47:29 Deut. 31:14 Job 7:1 & 14:5 [j]ch. 31:6
26:11 [k]ch. 24:6,12
26:12 [l]Gen. 2:21 & 15:12
26:16 [m]2 Sam. 12:5

[u]*Phaltiel* in 2 Sam. 3:15 [v]Or, *midst of his carriages*

26:9 THE LORD'S ANOINTED. David refused to kill Saul because he had been assured that God Himself would remove Saul and that David would become king at God's appointed time (see v. 10; 13:13–14; 15:23; 16:12–13). David and Saul's unique situation must not be deemed grounds for permitting spiritual leaders in the church to continue in sin or evil (see 24:6, note).

and the cruse of water that *was* at his
bolster.
17 And Saul knew David's voice,
and said, [n]*Is* this thy voice, my son
David? And David said, *It is* my voice,
my lord, O king.
18 And he said, [o]Wherefore doth
my lord thus pursue after his servant?
for what have I done? or what evil *is* in
mine hand?
19 Now therefore, I pray thee, let
my lord the king hear the words of his
servant. If the LORD have [p]stirred thee
up against me, let him [w]accept an of-
fering: but if *they be* the children of
men, cursed *be* they before the LORD;
[q]for they have driven me out this day
from [x]abiding in the [r]inheritance of
the LORD, saying, Go, serve other gods.
20 Now therefore, let not my blood
fall to the earth before the face of the
LORD: for the king of Israel is come out
to seek [s]a flea, as when one doth hunt
a partridge in the mountains.
21 ¶ Then said Saul, [t]I have
sinned: return, my son David: for I will
no more do thee harm, because my soul
was [u]precious in thine eyes this day:
behold, I have played the fool, and have
erred exceedingly.
22 And David answered and said,
Behold the king's spear! and let one of
the young men come over and fetch it.
23 [v]The LORD render to every man
his righteousness and his faithfulness:
for the LORD delivered thee into *my*
hand today, but I would not stretch
forth mine hand against the LORD's
anointed.
24 And, behold, as thy life was
much set by this day in mine eyes, so
let my life be much set by in the eyes
of the LORD, and let him deliver me out
of all tribulation.
25 Then Saul said to David, Blessed
be thou, my son David: thou shalt both
do great *things,* and also shalt still
[w]prevail. So David went on his way,
and Saul returned to his place.

David lives with the Philistines

27 AND DAVID said in his heart, I
shall now [y]perish one day by
the hand of Saul: *there is* nothing better
for me than that I should speedily es-
cape into the land of the Philistines;
and Saul shall despair of me, to seek
me any more in any coast of Israel: so
shall I escape out of his hand.
2 And David arose, [x]and he passed
over with the six hundred men that
were with him [y]unto Achish, the son of
Maoch, king of Gath.
3 And David dwelt with Achish at
Gath, he and his men, every man with
his household, *even* David [z]with his
two wives, Ahinoam the Jezreelitess,
and Abigail the Carmelitess, Nabal's
wife.
4 And it was told Saul that David
was fled to Gath: and he sought no
more again for him.
5 ¶ And David said unto Achish, If
I have now found grace in thine eyes,
let them give me a place in some town
in the country, that I may dwell there:
for why should thy servant dwell in the
royal city with thee?
6 Then Achish gave him Ziklag that
day: wherefore [a]Ziklag pertaineth
unto the kings of Judah unto this
day.
7 And [z]the time that David dwelt
in the country of the Philistines was
[b]a full year and four months.
8 ¶ And David and his men went up,
and invaded [c]the Geshurites, [d]and
the [a]Gezrites, and the [e]Amalekites:
for those *nations were* of old the inhabi-
tants of the land, [f]as thou goest to
Shur, even unto the land of Egypt.
9 And David smote the land, and
left neither man nor woman alive, and
took away the sheep, and the oxen,
and the asses, and the camels, and
the apparel, and returned, and came
to Achish.
10 And Achish said, [b]Whither
have ye made a road today? And David
said, Against the south of Judah, and
against the south of [g]the Jerahmeel-

26:17 [n]ch. 24:16
26:18 [o]ch. 24:9,11
26:19 [p]2 Sam. 16:11 & 24:1 [q]Deut. 4:28 [r]2 Sam. 14:16 & 20:19
26:20 [s]ch. 24:14
26:21 [t]ch. 15:24 & 24:17 [u]ch. 18:30
26:23 [v]Ps. 7:8 & 18:20
26:25 [w]Gen. 32:28

27:2 [x]ch. 25:13 [y]ch. 21:10
27:3 [z]ch. 25:43
27:6 [a]See Josh. 15:31 & 19:5
27:7 [b]ch. 29:3
27:8 [c]Josh. 13:2 [d]Josh. 16:10 Judg. 1:29 [e]Ex. 17:16 See ch. 15:7,8 [f]Gen. 25:18
27:10 [g]See 1 Chr. 2:9,25

[w] Heb. *smell;* see Gen. 8:21; Lev. 26:31
[x] Heb. *cleaving* [y] Heb. *be consumed* [z] Heb. *the number of days* [a] Or, *Gerzites* [b] Or, *Did you not make a road*

27:1 THE LAND OF THE PHILISTINES. Fearing Saul's instability, David here failed to trust in God; this chapter records his consequent unethical behavior. He took refuge among the enemies of God (v. 1), acted in an inhuman manner without the approval of God (vv. 8–11), and resorted to deception (vv. 10–12). The inspired writer of this account tells us about David's actions without approving them. Events recorded in Scripture do not necessarily mean that they are sanctioned by God. Read 1 Chronicles 22:8 for God's evaluation of David's career as a warrior.

ites, and against the south of [h]the Kenites.

11 And David saved neither man nor woman alive, to bring *tidings* to Gath, saying, Lest they should tell on us, saying, So did David, and so *will be* his manner all the while he dwelleth in the country of the Philistines.

12 And Achish believed David, saying, He hath made his people Israel [c]utterly to abhor him; therefore he shall be my servant for ever.

28 AND [i]IT came to pass in those days, that the Philistines gathered their armies together for warfare, to fight with Israel. And Achish said unto David, Know thou assuredly, that thou shalt go out with me to battle, thou and thy men.

2 And David said to Achish, Surely thou shalt know what thy servant can do. And Achish said to David, Therefore will I make thee keeper of mine head for ever.

Saul and the woman at Endor

3 ¶ Now [j]Samuel was dead, and all Israel had lamented him, and buried him in [k]Ramah, even in his own city. And Saul had put away [l]those that had familiar spirits, and the wizards, out of the land.

4 And the Philistines gathered themselves together, and came and pitched in [m]Shunem: and Saul gathered all Israel together, and they pitched in [n]Giboa.

5 And when Saul saw the host of the Philistines, he was [o]afraid, and his heart greatly trembled.

6 And when Saul inquired of the LORD, [p]the LORD answered him not, neither by [q]dreams, nor [r]by Urim, nor by prophets.

7 ¶ Then said Saul unto his servants, Seek me a woman that hath a familiar spirit, that I may go to her, and inquire of her. And his servants said to him, Behold, *there is* a woman that hath a familiar spirit at En-dor.

8 And Saul disguised himself, and put on other raiment, and he went, and two men with him, and they came to the woman by night: and [s]he said, I pray thee, divine unto me by the familiar spirit, and bring me *him* up, whom I shall name unto thee.

9 And the woman said unto him, Behold, thou knowest what Saul hath done, how he hath [t]cut off those that have familiar spirits, and the wizards, out of the land: wherefore then layest thou a snare for my life, to cause me to die?

10 And Saul sware to her by the LORD, saying, *As* the LORD liveth, there shall no punishment happen to thee for this thing.

11 Then said the woman, Whom shall I bring up unto thee? And he said, Bring me up Samuel.

12 And when the woman saw Samuel, she cried with a loud voice: and the woman spake to Saul, saying, Why hast thou deceived me? for thou *art* Saul.

13 And the king said unto her, Be not afraid: for what sawest thou? And the woman said unto Saul, I saw [u]gods ascending out of the earth.

14 And he said unto her, [d]What form *is* he of? And she said, An old man cometh up; and he *is* covered with [v]a mantle. And Saul perceived that it *was* Samuel, and he stooped with *his* face to the ground, and bowed himself.

15 ¶ And Samuel said to Saul, Why hast thou disquieted me, to bring me up? And Saul answered, [w]I am sore distressed; for the Philistines make

27:10 [h]Judg. 1:16 **28:1** [i]ch. 29:1 **28:3** [j]ch. 5:1 [k]See ch 1:19 [l]ver. 9 Ex. 22:18 Lev. 19:31 & 20:2 Deut. 18:10,11 **28:4** [m]Josh. 118 2 Ki. 4:8 [n]ch. 31:1 **28:5** [o]Job 18:11 **28:6** [p]ch. 14:37 Prov. 1:28 Lam. 2:9 [q]Num. 12:6 [r]Ex. 28:30 Num. 27:21 Deut. 33:8 **28:8** [s]Deut. 18:11 1 Chr. 10:13 Is. 8:19 **28:9** [t]ver. 3 **28:13** [u]Ex. 22:28 **28:14** [v]ch. 15:27 2 Ki. 2:8,13 **28:15** [w]Prov. 5:11-13 & 14:14

[c] Heb. *to stink* [d] Heb. *What is his form?*

28:6 THE LORD ANSWERED HIM NOT. Saul sought a prophetic word from God in the midst of his trouble, but received none. In despair he then turned to divination or a medium (vv. 7–25). Persisting in ungodly ways instead of following the leading of the Spirit cuts us off from God's help. Calling upon Him will be useless unless we turn from our ungodly ways (see Mat. 3:2, note).

28:12 THE WOMAN SAW SAMUEL. God sent the spirit of Samuel to appear to Saul. Note the following facts: (1) Spiritism is sternly condemned in Scripture (Deut. 18:9–12; cf. Ex. 22:18; Lev. 19:26,31). Mediums do not really contact the dead, but usually communicate with deceiving spirits. This story gives no justification for attempting to make contact with the dead.

(2) The woman was amazed and terrified when Samuel actually appeared. This implies that she was expecting not Samuel but a demonic spirit. Clearly Samuel's appearance was not the result of her witchcraft.

(3) The appearance of the prophet was brought about by an extraordinary act of God Himself, in order to deliver God's final message of defeat and death to the king.

war against me, and [x]God is departed from me, and [y]answereth me no more, neither [e]by prophets, nor by dreams: therefore I have called thee, that thou mayest make known unto me what I shall do.

16 Then said Samuel, Wherefore then dost thou ask of me, seeing the LORD is departed from thee, and is become thine enemy?

17 And the LORD hath done [f]to him, [z]as he spake by [g]me: for the LORD hath rent the kingdom out of thine hand, and given it to thy neighbour, *even* to David:

18 [a]Because thou obeyedst not the voice of the LORD, nor executedst his fierce wrath upon Amalek, therefore hath the LORD done this thing unto thee this day.

19 Moreover the LORD will also deliver Israel with thee into the hand of the Philistines: and tomorrow *shalt* thou and thy sons *be* with me: the LORD also shall deliver the host of Israel into the hand of the Philistines.

20 Then Saul [h]fell straightway all along on the earth, and was sore afraid, because of the words of Samuel: and there was no strength in him; for he had eaten no bread all the day, nor all the night.

21 ¶ And the woman came unto Saul, and saw that he was sore troubled, and said unto him, Behold, thine handmaid hath obeyed thy voice, and I have [b]put my life in my hand, and have hearkened unto thy words which thou spakest unto me.

22 Now therefore, I pray thee, hearken thou also unto the voice of thine handmaid, and let me set a morsel of bread before thee; and eat, that thou mayest have strength, when thou goest on thy way.

23 But he refused, and said, I will not eat. But his servants, together with the woman, compelled him; and he hearkened unto their voice. So he arose from the earth, and sat upon the bed.

24 And the woman had a fat calf in the house; and she hasted, and killed it, and took flour, and kneaded *it*, and did bake unleavened bread thereof:

25 And she brought *it* before Saul, and before his servants; and they did eat. Then they rose up, and went away that night.

28:15 [x]ch. 18:12 [y]ver. 6 **28:17** [z]ch. 15:28 **28:18** [a]ch. 15:9 1 Ki. 20:42 1 Chr. 10:13 Jer. 48:10 **28:21** [b]Judg. 12:3 ch. 19:5 Job 13:14

29:1 [c]ch. 28:1 [d]ch. 4:1 **29:2** [e]ch. 28:1,2 **29:3** [f]See ch. 27:7 [g]Dan. 6:5 **29:4** [h]1 Chr. 12:19 [i]As ch. 14:21 **29:5** [j]ch. 18:7 & 21:11 **29:6** [k]2 Sam. 3:25 2 Ki. 19:27 [l]ver. 3

The Philistines dismiss David

29 NOW [c]THE Philistines gathered together all their armies [d]to Aphek: and the Israelites pitched by a fountain which *is* in Jezreel.

2 And the lords of the Philistines passed on by hundreds, and by thousands: but David and his men passed on in the rearward [e]with Achish.

3 Then said the princes of the Philistines, What *do* these Hebrews *here?* And Achish said unto the princes of the Philistines, *Is* not this David, the servant of Saul the king of Israel, which hath been with me [f]these days, or these years, and I have [g]found no fault in him since he fell *unto me* unto this day?

4 And the princes of the Philistines were wroth with him; and the princes of the Philistines said unto him, [h]Make this fellow return, that he may go again to his place which thou hast appointed him, and let him not go down with us to battle, lest [i]in the battle he be an adversary to us: for wherewith should he reconcile himself unto his master? *should it* not *be* with the heads of these men?

5 *Is* not this David, of whom they sang one to another in dances, saying, [j]Saul slew his thousands, and David his ten thousands?

6 ¶ Then Achish called David, and said unto him, Surely, *as* the LORD liveth, thou hast been upright, and [k]thy going out and thy coming in with me in the host *is* good in my sight: for [l]I have not found evil in thee since the day of thy coming unto me unto this day: nevertheless [i]the lords favour thee not.

7 Wherefore now return, and go in peace, that thou [j]displease not the lords of the Philistines.

8 ¶ And David said unto Achish, But what have I done? and what hast thou found in thy servant so long as I have been [k]with thee unto this day, that I may not go fight against the enemies of my lord the king?

9 And Achish answered and said to David, I know that thou *art* good in my

[e] Heb. *by the hand of prophets* [f] Or, *for himself* [g] Heb. *mine hand* [h] Heb. *made haste, and fell with the fulness of his stature*
[i] Heb. *thou art not good in the eyes of the lords*
[j] Heb. *do not evil in the eyes of the lords*
[k] Heb. *before thee*

sight, [m]as an angel of God: notwithstanding [n]the princes of the Philistines have said, He shall not go up with us to the battle.

10 Wherefore now rise up early in the morning with thy master's servants that are come with thee: and as soon as ye be up early in the morning, and have light, depart.

11 So David and his men rose up early to depart in the morning, to return into the land of the Philistines. [o]And the Philistines went up to Jezreel.

David smites the Amalekites

30 AND IT came to pass, when David and his men were come to Ziklag on the third day, that the [p]Amalekites had invaded the south, and Ziklag, and smitten Ziklag, and burned it with fire;

2 And had taken the women captives, that *were* therein: they slew not any, either great or small, but carried *them* away, and went on their way.

3 ¶ So David and his men came to the city, and, behold, *it was* burned with fire; and their wives, and their sons, and their daughters, were taken captives.

4 Then David and the people that *were* with him lifted up their voice and wept, until they had no more power to weep.

5 And David's [q]two wives were taken captives, Ahinoam the Jezreelitess, and Abigail the wife of Nabal the Carmelite.

6 And David was greatly distressed; [r]for the people spake of stoning him, because the soul of all the people was [1]grieved, every man for his sons and for his daughters: but [s]David encouraged himself in the LORD his God.

7 [t]And David said to Abiathar the priest, Ahimelech's son, I pray thee, bring me hither the ephod. And Abiathar brought thither the ephod to David.

8 [u]And David inquired at the LORD, saying, Shall I pursue after this troop? shall I overtake them? And he answered him, Pursue: for thou shalt surely overtake *them*, and without fail recover *all*.

9 So David went, he and the six hundred men that *were* with him, and came to the brook Besor, where those that were left behind stayed.

10 But David pursued, he and four hundred men: [v]for two hundred abode behind, which were so faint that they could not go over the brook Besor.

11 ¶ And they found an Egyptian in the field, and brought him to David, and gave him bread, and he did eat; and they made him drink water;

12 And they gave him a piece of [w]a cake of figs, and two clusters of raisins: and [x]when he had eaten, his spirit came again to him: for he had eaten no bread, nor drunk *any* water, three days and three nights.

13 And David said unto him, To whom *belongest* thou? and whence *art* thou? And he said, I *am* a young man of Egypt, servant to an Amalekite; and my master left me, because three days agone I fell sick.

14 We made an invasion *upon* the south of [y]the Cherethites, and upon *the coast* which *belongeth* to Judah, and upon the south of [z]Caleb; and we burned Ziklag with fire.

15 And David said to him, Canst thou bring me down to this company? And he said, Swear unto me by God, that thou wilt neither kill me, nor deliver me into the hands of my master, and I will bring thee down to this company.

16 ¶ And when he had brought him down, behold, *they were* spread abroad upon all the earth, [a]eating and drinking, and dancing, because of all the great spoil that they had taken out of the land of the Philistines, and out of the land of Judah.

17 And David smote them from the twilight even unto the evening of [m]the next day: and there escaped not a man of them, save four hundred young men, which rode upon camels, and fled.

18 And David recovered all that the Amalekites had carried away: and David rescued his two wives.

19 And there was nothing lacking to them, neither small nor great, neither sons nor daughters, neither spoil,

29:9 [m]2 Sam. 14:17,20 & 19:27 [n]ver. 4
29:11 [o]2 Sam. 4:4
30:1 [p]See ch. 15:7 & 27:8
30:5 [q]ch. 25:42,43 2 Sam. 2:2
30:6 [r]Ex. 17:4 [s]Ps. 42:5 & 56:3,4,11 Hab. 3:17,18
30:7 [t]ch. 23:6,9
30:8 [u]ch. 23:2,4
30:10 [v]ver. 21
30:12 [w]ch. 25:18 2 Ki. 20:7 [x]Judg. 15:19 ch. 14:27
30:14 [y]ver. 16 2 Sam. 8:18 1 Ki. 1:38,44 Ezek. 25:16 Zeph. 2:5 [z]Josh. 14:13 & 15:13
30:16 [a]1 Thes. 5:3

1 Heb. *bitter* m Heb. *their morrow*

30:7 EPHOD. The ephod was a sacred garment worn by the high priest. It was adorned with precious stones that enabled a person to learn God's will in certain situations, similar to how the Urim and Thummim were used (cf. Ex. 28:30, note).

nor any *thing* that they had taken to them: [b]David recovered all.

20 And David took all the flocks and the herds, *which* they drave before those *other* cattle, and said, This *is* David's spoil.

21 ¶ And David came to the [c]two hundred men, which were so faint that they could not follow David, whom they had made also to abide at the brook Besor: and they went forth to meet David, and to meet the people that *were* with him: and when David came near to the people, he [n]saluted them.

22 Then answered all the wicked men and *men* [d]of Belial, of [o]those that went with David, and said, Because they went not with us, we will not give them *aught* of the spoil that we have recovered, save to every man his wife and his children, that they may lead *them* away, and depart.

23 Then said David, Ye shall not do so, my brethren, with that which the LORD hath given us, who hath preserved us, and delivered the company that came against us into our hand.

24 For who will hearken unto you in this matter? but [e]as his part *is* that goeth down to the battle, so *shall* his part *be* that tarrieth by the stuff: they shall part alike.

25 And it was *so* from that day [p]forward, that he made it a statute and an ordinance for Israel unto this day.

26 ¶ And when David came to Ziklag, he sent of the spoil unto the elders of Judah, *even* to his friends, saying, Behold a [q]present for you of the spoil of the enemies of the LORD;

27 To *them* which *were* in Beth-el, and to *them* which *were* in [f]south Ramoth, and to *them* which *were* in [g]Jattir,

28 And to *them* which *were* in [h]Aroer, and to *them* which *were* in Siphmoth, and to *them* which *were* in [i]Eshtemoa,

29 And to *them* which *were* in Rachal, and to *them* which *were* in the cities of [j]the Jerahmeelites, and to *them* which *were* in the cities of the [k]Kenites,

30 And to *them* which *were* in [l]Hormah, and to *them* which *were* in Chorashan, and to *them* which *were* in Athach,

31 And to *them* which *were* in [m]Hebron, and to all the places where David himself and his men were wont to haunt.

The death of Saul

31:1–13pp — 2 Sam. 1:4–12; 1 Chr. 10:1–12

31 NOW [n]THE Philistines fought against Israel: and the men of Israel fled from before the Philistines, and fell down [r]slain in mount [o]Gilboa.

2 And the Philistines followed hard upon Saul and upon his sons; and the Philistines slew [p]Jonathan, and Abinadab, and Melchi-shua, Saul's sons.

3 And [q]the battle went sore against Saul, and the [s]archers [t]hit him; and he was sore wounded of the archers.

4 [r]Then said Saul unto his armourbearer, Draw thy sword, and thrust me through therewith; lest [s]these uncircumcised come and thrust me through, and [u]abuse me. But his armourbearer would not; [t]for he was sore afraid. Therefore Saul took a sword, and [u]fell upon it.

5 And when his armourbearer saw that Saul was dead, he fell likewise upon his sword, and died with him.

6 So Saul died, and his three sons, and his armourbearer, and all his men, that same day together.

7 ¶ And when the men of Israel that *were* on the other side of the valley, and *they* that *were* on the other side Jordan, saw that the men of Israel fled, and that Saul and his sons were dead, they forsook the cities, and fled; and the Philistines came and dwelt in them.

8 And it came to pass on the mor-

30:19 [b]ver. 8 **30:21** [c]ver. 10 **30:22** [d]Deut. 13:13 Judg. 19:22 **30:24** [e]See Num. 31:27 Josh. 22:8 **30:27** [f]Josh. 19:8 [g]Josh. 15:48 **30:28** [h]Josh. 13:16 [i]Josh. 15:50 **30:29** [j]ch. 27:10 [k]Judg. 1:16 **30:30** [l]Judg. 1:17 **30:31** [m]Josh. 14:13 2 Sam. 2:1 **31:1** [n]1 Chr. 10:1-12 [o]ch. 28:4 **31:2** [p]ch. 14:49 **31:3** [q]See 2 Sam. 1:6 **31:4** [r]See Judg. 9:54 [s]ch. 14:6 [t]2 Sam. 1:14 [u]ch. 14:6

[n] Or, *asked them how they did* [o] Heb. *men* [p] Heb. *and forward* [q] Heb. *blessing* [r] Or, *wounded* [s] Heb. *shooters, men with bows* [t] Heb. *found him* [u] Or, *mock me*

30:24 SO *SHALL* HIS PART. David determined that those who remained at home to care faithfully for the belongings of those who went to war were to have an equal share in the spoils of battle. This principle may be applied to the sending of foreign missionaries into other lands to preach the gospel. Those who remain home and faithfully support and pray for those who go, will share equally in the heavenly rewards and in the approval of God (see Mat. 10:41, note).

row, when the Philistines came to strip
the slain, that they found Saul and his
three sons fallen in mount Gilboa.
9 And they cut off his head, and
stripped off his armour, and sent into
the land of the Philistines round about,
to [v]publish *it in* the house of their
idols, and among the people.
10 [w]And they put his armour in the
house of [x]Ashtaroth: and [y]they fastened his body to the wall of [z]Beth-shan.
11 ¶ [a]And when the inhabitants of
Jabesh-gilead heard [▾]of that which
the Philistines had done to Saul;
12 [b]All the valiant men arose, and
went all night, and took the body of
Saul and the bodies of his sons from
the wall of Beth-shan, and came to Jabesh, and [c]burnt them there.
13 And they took their bones, and
[d]buried *them* under a tree at Jabesh,
[e]and fasted seven days.

31:9 [v]2 Sam. 1:20
31:10 [w]ch. 21:9 [x]Judg. 2:13 [y]2 Sam. 21:12 [z]Josh. 17:11 Judg. 1:27
31:11 [a]ch. 11:3,9,11
31:12 [b]See ch. 11:1-11 2 Sam. 2:4-7 [c]2 Chr. 16:14 Jer. 34:5 Amos 6:10
31:13 [d]2 Sam. 21:12-14 [e]Gen. 50:10

▾ Or, *concerning him*

2 SAMUEL

Outline

- I. David's Remarkable Success as King (1:1—10:19)
  - A. David's Political Success (1:1—5:25)
    1. David Laments the Death of Saul and Jonathan (1:1–27)
    2. David's Years as King Over Judah (2:1—4:12)
    3. David Enthroned King Over all Israel (5:1–5)
    4. David Conquers Jerusalem and Establishes It as the Political Center (5:6–10)
    5. David Extends the Kingdom (5:11–25)
  - B. David's Spiritual Success (6:1—7:29)
    1. David Establishes Jerusalem as the Religious Center (6:1–23)
    2. David Wishes to Build God a House (7:1–3)
    3. God's Covenant with David (7:4–17)
    4. David's Response (7:18–29)
  - C. David's Military Success (8:1—10:19)
    1. David's Victories Over Philistia, Moab, Zobah, Syria, Edom (8:1–12)
    2. David's Righteous Rule in Jerusalem (8:13—9:13)
    3. David's Victory Over Ammon (10:1–19)
- II. David's Shameful Transgression as King (11:1—12:14)
  - A. David's Adultery with Bathsheba (11:1–5)
  - B. David's Murder of Uriah and Cover-up (11:6–27)
  - C. David's Guilt and Judgment Pronounced by the Prophet Nathan (12:1–14)
- III. David's Years of Reaping Sin's Consequences (12:15—20:26)
  - A. Judgment on David's Household: Immorality and Death (12:15—15:6)
    1. Death of His Son of Adultery (12:15–25)
    2. Joab's Loyalty (12:26–31)
    3. Amnon Rapes Tamar, a Half-sister (13:1–20)
    4. Absalom Kills Amnon in Revenge (13:21–36)
    5. Absalom's Flight, Return, and Deceit (13:37—15:6)
  - B. Judgment on David's Kingdom: Insurrection and Murder (15:7—20:26)
    1. Absalom's Insurrection (15:7–12)
    2. David Flees Jerusalem in Disgrace (15:13—16:14)
    3. Absalom Rules in Jerusalem (16:15—17:29)
    4. Absalom Overthrown and Murdered (18:1–32)
    5. David's Lament and Joab's Rebuke (18:33—19:8)
    6. David Restored as King (19:9–43)
    7. Sheba's Insurrection and Murder (20:1–26)
- IV. The Last Years of David as King (21:1—24:25)
  - A. A Three-year Famine (21:1–14)
  - B. War with the Philistines (21:15–22)
  - C. David's Psalm of Praise (22:1–51)
  - D. David's Last Words (23:1–7)
  - E. David's Mighty Men (23:8–39)
  - F. David's Census and God's Plague (24:1–17)
  - G. David's Intercession and God's Mercy (24:18–25)

Author: Anonymous

Theme: David's Reign

Date of Writing: Late 10th century B.C.

Background

Since 1 and 2 Samuel were originally a single book in the Hebrew O.T., the background of 2 Samuel is discussed more fully at the beginning of 1 Samuel (see the introduction to 1 Samuel). It may be noted here that whereas the events in 1 Samuel (extending from the birth of Samuel to the death of Saul) cover almost a century of time (c. 1105–1010 B.C.), 2 Samuel records only the reign of David, a period of forty years (c. 1010–970 B.C.).

Purpose

2 Samuel continues the prophetic history of the theocratic character of Israel's monarchy. It profoundly illustrates from David's kingship and personal life the terms of the covenant for Israel as set forth by Moses in Deuteronomy: covenant obedience results in God's blessings; disregard for God's law results in curses and judgment (see Deut. 27—30).

Survey

The full record of David's life extends from 1 Sam. 16:1 to 1 Ki. 2:11. 2 Samuel begins with Saul's death and David's anonting at Hebron as king over Judah for seven and one-half years (chs. 1—4). The rest of the book focuses on David's next thirty-three years as king over all Israel at Jerusalem (chs. 5—24). The watershed of the book and David's life is his adultery with Bathsheba and murder of Uriah (ch. 11). Before this dark chapter, David represented many of the ideals of a theocratic king. Under the favor, wisdom, and anointing of God, David (1) captured Jerusalem from the Jebusites and made it his capital (ch. 5), (2) brought back the ark of the covenant to Jerusalem amidst great rejoicing and celebration (ch. 6), and (3) subdued Israel's enemies, beginning with the Philistines (ch. 8—10). "David . . . grew great, and the LORD God of hosts *was* with him" (5:10). His strong leadership attracted "mighty men" and inspired intense loyalty. David understood that God had established him as king over Israel, and he openly acknowledged God's rule over himself and the nation. God prophetically promised that a descendant of David would sit on his throne, one who would perfectly fulfill the role of theocratic king (7:12–17; cf. Isa.9:6–7; 11:1–5; Jer. 23:5–6; 33:14–16).

However, after David's tragic sins of adultery and murder, moral disintegration and rebellion plagued his family (chs. 12—17) and the entire nation (chs. 18—20). Great national blessing was changed to national judgment. Although David sincerely repented and experienced the mercy of God's forgiveness (12:13; cf. Ps. 51), the consequences of his transgression continued to the end of his life and even afterwards (cf. 12:7–12). Nevertheless, God did not reject David as king as He had rejected Saul (cf. 1 Sam. 15:23). Indeed David's heart for God (see his psalms) and his abhorrence of all idolatry made him the example by which all subsequent kings of Israel were measured (cf. 2 Ki. 18:3; 22:2). 2 Samuel ends with David purchasing the threshing floor of Araunah, which became the future site of the temple (24:18–25).

Special Features

Five major features or emphases characterize 2 Samuel. (1) It records key events in the forty-year reign of King David, including his capture of Jerusalem from the Jebusites and his formation of it into the political and religious center of Israel. His life falls exactly midway between Abraham and Jesus Christ. (2) The book's pivotal center (ch. 11) records David's tragic sins involving Bathsheba and her husband Uriah. The prophetic historian of this book emphasizes that though David's adultery and murder were done secretly, the sin was judged openly by God at every level of David's life—personal, family, and national. (3) It reveals an important and enduring principle of leadership in God's kingdom: the greater

God's favor and anointing on a leader's life, the greater will be God's judgment if that leader violates God's trust by committing moral or ethical transgression. Though David is commended in Scripture as a man after God's own heart, God's favor changed to judgment and God's blessings to curses after he sinned, just as Moses had warned Israel (cf. Deut. 28). (4) The chapters describing the ongoing rippling effects of David's transgression on his family and the entire nation (chs. 12—21) reveal how intricately the well-being of an entire people is tied to the spiritual and moral condition of their leader. (5) It highlights the enduring moral lesson that success and prosperity often lead to moral flabbiness, which in turn leads to moral failure. David's exemplary life and reign were tragically marred by adultery and murder at the pinnacle of his success and power as king.

New Testament Fulfillment

David's rule as king in chs. 1—10 is a type of the Messianic King. His establishment of Jerusalem as the holy city, God's gift to him of the Davidic covenant, and his reception of the prophetic promise of an everlasting kingdom all point ahead to the final "Son of David," Jesus Christ, and to His present and future kingdom as revealed in the N.T. (cf. Is. 9:7; Mat. 21:9; 22:45; Luke 1:32–33). For further insight into the N.T. application related to David, see the introduction to 1 Samuel.

Reading 2 Samuel

In order to read the entire Old Testament in one year, the book of 2 Samuel should be read in 10 days, according to the following schedule: ☐ 1–3 ☐ 4–6 ☐ 7–8 ☐ 9–11 ☐ 12–14 ☐ 15–17 ☐ 18–19 ☐ 20–21 ☐ 22 ☐ 23–24

NOTES

The news of Saul's death

1:4–12pp — 1 Sam. 31:1–13; 1 Chr. 10:1–12

1 NOW IT came to pass after the
death of Saul, when David was re-
turned from [a]the slaughter of the Am-
alekites, and David had abode two
days in Ziklag;
2 It came even to pass on the third
day, that, behold, [b]a man came out of
the camp from Saul [c]with his clothes
rent, and earth upon his head: and *so*
it was, when he came to David, that he
fell to the earth, and did obeisance.
3 And David said unto him, From
whence comest thou? And he said unto
him, Out of the camp of Israel am I es-
caped.
4 And David said unto him, How
went the matter? I pray thee, tell me.
And he answered, That the people are
fled from the battle, and many of the
people also are fallen and dead; and
Saul and Jonathan his son are dead
also.
5 And David said unto the young
man that told him, How knowest thou
that Saul and Jonathan his son be
dead?
6 And the young man that told him
said, As I happened by chance upon
[d]mount Gilboa, behold, [e]Saul leaned
upon his spear; and, lo, the chariots
and horsemen followed hard after him.
7 And when he looked behind him,
he saw me, and called unto me. And I
answered, [a]Here *am* I.
8 And he said unto me, Who *art*
thou? And I answered him, I *am* an Am-
alekite.
9 He said unto me again, Stand, I
pray thee, upon me, and slay me: for
[b]anguish is come upon me, because
my life *is* yet whole in me.
10 So I stood upon him, and [f]slew
him, because I was sure that he could
not live after that he was fallen: and I
took the crown that *was* upon his head,
and the bracelet that *was* on his arm,
and have brought them hither unto my
lord.
11 Then David took hold on his
clothes, and [g]rent them; and likewise
all the men that *were* with him:
12 And they mourned, and wept,
and fasted until even, for Saul, and for
Jonathan his son, and for the people of
the LORD, and for the house of Israel;
because they were fallen by the sword.
13 ¶ And David said unto the young
man that told him, Whence *art* thou?
And he answered, I *am* the son of a
stranger, an Amalekite.
14 And David said unto him, [h]How
wast thou not [i]afraid to [j]stretch
forth thine hand to destroy the LORD's
anointed?
15 And [k]David called one of the
young men, and said, Go near, *and* fall
upon him. And he smote him that he
died.
16 And David said unto him, [l]Thy
blood *be* upon thy head; for [m]thy
mouth hath testified against thee, say-
ing, I have slain the LORD's anointed.

David's lament

17 ¶ And David lamented with this
lamentation over Saul and over Jona-
than his son:
18 ([n]Also he bade them teach the
children of Judah *the use of* the bow:
behold, *it is* written [o]in the book [c]of
Jasher.)
19 The beauty of Israel is slain
upon thy high places: [p]how are the
mighty fallen!
20 [q]Tell *it* not in Gath, publish *it*
not in the streets of Askelon; lest [r]the
daughters of the Philistines rejoice,
lest the daughters of [s]the uncircum-
cised triumph.
21 Ye [t]mountains of Gilboa, [u]*let
there be* no dew, neither *let there be* rain,
upon you, nor fields of offerings: for
there the shield of the mighty is vilely
cast away, the shield of Saul, *as though
he had* not *been* [v]anointed with oil.
22 From the blood of the slain, from
the fat of the mighty, [w]the bow of Jona-
than turned not back, and the sword of
Saul returned not empty.
23 Saul and Jonathan *were* lovely
and [d]pleasant in their lives, and in
their death they were not divided: they
were swifter than eagles, they were
[x]stronger than lions.
24 Ye daughters of Israel, weep

1:1 [a]1 Sam. 30:17,26 **1:2** [b]ch. 4:10 [c]1 Sam. 4:12 **1:6** [d]1 Sam. 31:1 [e]See 1 Sam. 31:2-4 **1:10** [f]Judg. 9:54 **1:11** [g]ch. 3:31 & 13:31 **1:14** [h]Num. 12:8 [i]1 Sam. 31:4 [j]1 Sam. 24:6 & 26:9 Ps. 105:15 **1:15** [k]ch. 4:10,12 **1:16** [l]1 Sam. 26:9 1 Ki. 2:32,33,37 [m]ver. 10 Luke 19:22 **1:18** [n]1 Sam. 31:3 [o]Josh. 10:13 **1:19** [p]ver. 27 **1:20** [q]1 Sam. 31:9 Mic. 1:10 See Judg. 16:23 [r]See Ex. 15:20 Judg. 11:34 1 Sam. 18:6 [s]1 Sam. 31:4 **1:21** [t]1 Sam. 31:1 [u]Judg. 5:23 Job 3:3,4 Jer. 20:14 [v]1 Sam. 10:1 **1:22** [w]1 Sam. 18:4 **1:23** [x]Judg. 14:18

[a] Heb. *Behold me* [b] Or, *my coat of mail,* or, *my embroidered coat hindereth me, that my* [c] Or, *of the upright* [d] Or, *sweet*

1:10 I . . . SLEW HIM. The Amalekite lied about the manner of Saul's death (see the true account in 1 Sam. 31:3–6). He was seeking honor and favor from David, but instead his fabricated story resulted in his death (v. 15).

over Saul, who clothed you in scarlet, with *other* delights, who put on ornaments of gold upon your apparel.

25 How are the mighty fallen in the midst of the battle! O Jonathan, *thou wast* slain in thine high places.

26 I am distressed for thee, my brother Jonathan: very pleasant hast thou been unto me: [y]thy love to me was wonderful, passing the love of women.

27 [z]How are the mighty fallen, and the weapons of war perished!

David anointed king of Judah

2 AND IT came to pass after this, that David [a]inquired of the LORD, saying, Shall I go up into any of the cities of Judah? And the LORD said unto him, Go up. And David said, Whither shall I go up? And he said, Unto [b]Hebron.

2 So David went up thither, and his [c]two wives also, Ahinoam the Jezreelitess, and Abigail Nabal's wife the Carmelite.

3 And [d]his men that *were* with him did David bring up, every man with his household: and they dwelt in the cities of Hebron.

4 [e]And the men of Judah came, and there they anointed David king over the house of Judah. And they told David, saying, *That* [f]the men of Jabesh-gilead *were they* that buried Saul.

5 ¶ And David sent messengers unto the men of Jabesh-gilead, and said unto them, [g]Blessed *be* ye of the LORD, that ye have shown this kindness unto your lord, *even* unto Saul, and have buried him.

6 And now [h]the LORD show kindness and truth unto you: and I also will requite you this kindness, because ye have done this thing.

7 Therefore now let your hands be strengthened, and [e]be ye valiant: for your master Saul is dead, and also the house of Judah have anointed me king over them.

War between Israel and Judah

3:2–5pp — 1 Chr. 3:1–4

8 ¶ But [i]Abner the son of Ner, captain of [f]Saul's host, took [g]Ish-bosheth the son of Saul, and brought him over to Mahanaim;

9 And made him king over Gilead, and over the Ashurites, and over Jezreel, and over Ephraim, and over Benjamin, and over all Israel.

10 Ish-bosheth Saul's son *was* forty years old when he began to reign over Israel, and reigned two years. But the house of Judah followed David.

11 And [j]the [h]time that David was king in Hebron over the house of Judah was seven years and six months.

12 ¶ And Abner the son of Ner, and the servants of Ish-bosheth the son of Saul, went out from Mahanaim to [k]Gibeon.

13 And Joab the son of Zeruiah, and the servants of David, went out, and met [i]together by [l]the pool of Gibeon: and they sat down, the one on the one side of the pool, and the other on the other side of the pool.

14 And Abner said to Joab, Let the young men now arise, and play before us. And Joab said, Let them arise.

15 Then there arose and went over by number twelve of Benjamin, which *pertained* to Ish-bosheth the son of Saul, and twelve of the servants of David.

16 And they caught every one his fellow by the head, and *thrust* his sword in his fellow's side; so they fell down together: wherefore that place was called [j]Helkath-hazzurim, which *is* in Gibeon.

1:26 [y]1 Sam. 18:1,3 & 19:2 & 20:17,41 & 23:16
1:27 [z]ver. 19
2:1 [a]Judg. 1:1 1 Sam. 23:2,4,9 & 30:7,8 [b]ver. 11 1 Sam. 30:31 ch. 5:1,3 1 Ki. 2:11
2:2 [c]1 Sam. 30:5
2:3 [d]1 Sam. 27:2,3 & 30:1 1 Chr. 12:1
2:4 [e]ver. 11 ch. 5:5 [f]1 Sam. 31:11,13
2:5 [g]Ruth 2:20 & 3:10
2:6 [h]2 Tim. 1:16,18
2:8 [i]1 Sam. 14:50
2:11 [j]ch. 5:5 1 Ki. 2:11
2:12 [k]Josh. 18:25
2:13 [l]Jer. 41:12

[e] Heb. *be ye the sons of valour* [f] Heb. *the host which* was *Saul's* [g] Or, *Esh-baal*; see 1 Chr. 8:33 & 9:39 [h] Heb. *number of days* [i] Heb. *them together* [j] i.e. *The field of strong men*

1:26 THY LOVE TO ME. David spoke of Jonathan's extraordinary friendship in terms of their devotion, commitment, and oneness of purpose. Jonathan had accepted the Lord's choice of David as the next king without jealousy or bitterness (1 Sam. 20:13–16).

2:4 ANOINTED DAVID KING OVER . . . JUDAH. Chs. 2—4 describe the placing of David as king over Judah and his civil war with Ish-bosheth, Saul's son and successor as the king of the remaining tribes of Israel (vv. 8–11). Seven and a half years later David became king over the entire nation (5:1–5). Possibly Ps. 18 represents David's celebration of his complete deliverance from his enemies at this time (cf. 1 Sam. 30:1–31, which describes another victory of David immediately preceding Saul's death and David's ascension to the throne). David did not rush to take control of the entire nation. He sought the Lord (v. 1) and was willing to be king over one tribe until the Lord opened the door for him to be king over all Israel.

17 And there was a very sore battle that day; and Abner was beaten, and the men of Israel, before the servants of David.

18 ¶ And there were [m]three sons of Zeruiah there, Joab, and Abishai, and Asahel: and Asahel *was* [n]as light [k]of foot [o]as[l] a wild roe.

19 And Asahel pursued after Abner; and in going he turned not to the right hand nor to the left [m]from following Abner.

20 Then Abner looked behind him, and said, *Art* thou Asahel? And he answered, I *am*.

21 And Abner said to him, Turn thee aside to thy right hand or to thy left, and lay thee hold on one of the young men, and take thee his [p]armour.[n] But Asahel would not turn aside from following of him.

22 And Abner said again to Asahel, Turn thee aside from following me: wherefore should I smite thee to the ground? how then should I hold up my face to Joab thy brother?

23 Howbeit he refused to turn aside: wherefore Abner with the hinder end of the spear smote him [q]under the fifth *rib*, that the spear came out behind him; and he fell down there, and died in the same place: and it came to pass, *that* as many as came to the place where Asahel fell down and died stood still.

24 Joab also and Abishai pursued after Abner: and the sun went down when they were come to the hill of Ammah, that *lieth* before Giah by the way of the wilderness of Gibeon.

25 ¶ And the children of Benjamin gathered themselves together after Abner, and became one troop, and stood on the top of an hill.

26 Then Abner called to Joab, and said, Shall the sword devour for ever? knowest thou not that it will be bitterness in the latter end? how long shall it be then, ere thou bid the people return from following their brethren?

27 And Joab said, *As* God liveth, unless [r]thou hadst spoken, surely then [o]in the morning the people had [p]gone up every one from following his brother.

28 So Joab blew a trumpet, and all the people stood still, and pursued after Israel no more, neither fought they any more.

29 And Abner and his men walked all that night through the plain, and passed over Jordan, and went through all Bithron, and they came to Mahanaim.

30 And Joab returned from following Abner: and when he had gathered all the people together, there lacked of David's servants nineteen men and Asahel.

31 But the servants of David had smitten of Benjamin, and of Abner's men, *so that* three hundred and threescore men died.

32 ¶ And they took up Asahel, and buried him in the sepulchre of his father, which *was in* Bethlehem. And Joab and his men went all night, and they came to Hebron at break of day.

3 NOW THERE was long war between the house of Saul and the house of David: but David waxed stronger and stronger, and the house of Saul waxed weaker and weaker.

2 ¶ And [s]unto David were sons born in Hebron: and his firstborn was Amnon, [t]of Ahinoam the Jezreelitess;

3 And his second, [q]Chileab, of Abigail the wife of Nabal the Carmelite; and the third, Absalom the son of Maacah the daughter of Talmai king [u]of Geshur;

4 And the fourth, [v]Adonijah the son of Haggith; and the fifth, Shephatiah the son of Abital;

5 And the sixth, Ithream, by Eglah David's wife. These were born to David in Hebron.

6 ¶ And it came to pass, while there was war between the house of Saul and the house of David, that Abner made himself strong for the house of Saul.

7 And Saul had a concubine, whose name *was* [w]Rizpah, the daughter of Aiah: and *Ish-bosheth* said to Abner, Wherefore hast thou [x]gone in unto my father's concubine?

8 Then was Abner very wroth for the words of Ish-bosheth, and said, *Am* I [y]a dog's head, which against Judah do show kindness this day unto the house of Saul thy father, to his brethren, and to his friends, and have not delivered thee into the hand of David, that thou chargest me today with a fault concerning this woman?

2:18 [m]1 Chr. 2:16 [n]1 Chr. 12:8 [o]Ps. 18:33
2:21 [p]Judg. 14:19
2:23 [q]ch. 3:27 & 4:6 & 20:10
2:27 [r]ver. 14 Prov. 17:14
3:2 [s]1 Chr. 3:1-4 [t]1 Sam. 25:43
3:3 [u]1 Sam. 27:8 ch. 13:37
3:4 [v]1 Ki. 1:5
3:7 [w]ch. 21:8,10 [x]ch. 16:21
3:8 [y]Deut. 23:18 1 Sam. 24:14 ch. 9:8 & 16:9

k Heb. *of his feet* l Heb. *as one of the roes that is in the field* m Heb. *from after Abner* n Or, *spoil* o Heb. *from the morning* p Or, *gone away* q Or, *Daniel* in 1 Chr. 3:1

9 [z]So do God to Abner, and more
also, except, [a]as the LORD hath sworn
to David, even so I do to him;
10 To translate the kingdom from
the house of Saul, and to set up the
throne of David over Israel and over
Judah, [b]from Dan even to Beer-sheba.
11 And he could not answer Abner
a word again, because he feared him.
12 ¶ And Abner sent messengers to
David on his behalf, saying, Whose *is*
the land? saying *also*, Make thy league
with me, and, behold, my hand *shall be*
with thee, to bring about all Israel unto
thee.
13 ¶ And he said, Well; I will make
a league with thee: but one thing I re-
quire of thee, [r]that is, [c]Thou shalt
not see my face, except thou first bring
[d]Michal Saul's daughter, when thou
comest to see my face.
14 And David sent messengers to
Ish-bosheth Saul's son, saying, Deliver
me my wife Michal, which I espoused to
me [e]for an hundred foreskins of the
Philistines.
15 And Ish-bosheth sent, and took
her from *her* husband, *even* from
[f]Phaltiel the son of Laish.
16 And her husband went with her
[s]along weeping behind her to [g]Bahu-
rim. Then said Abner unto him, Go, re-
turn. And he returned.

Abner visits David

17 ¶ And Abner had communication
with the elders of Israel, saying, Ye
sought for David [t]in times past *to be*
king over you:
18 Now then do *it*: [h]for the LORD
hath spoken of David, saying, By the
hand of my servant David I will save
my people Israel out of the hand of the
Philistines, and out of the hand of all
their enemies.
19 And Abner also spake in the ears
of [i]Benjamin: and Abner went also to
speak in the ears of David in Hebron all
that seemed good to Israel, and that
seemed good to the whole house of
Benjamin.
20 So Abner came to David to He-
bron, and twenty men with him. And
David made Abner and the men that
were with him a feast.
21 And Abner said unto David, I will
arise and go, and [j]will gather all Isra-
el unto my lord the king, that they may
make a league with thee, and that thou
mayest [k]reign over all that thine heart
desireth. And David sent Abner away;
and he went in peace.
22 ¶ And, behold, the servants of
David and Joab came from *pursuing* a
troop, and brought in a great spoil with
them: but Abner *was* not with David in
Hebron; for he had sent him away, and
he was gone in peace.
23 When Joab and all the host that
was with him were come, they told
Joab, saying, Abner the son of Ner
came to the king, and he hath sent him
away, and he is gone in peace.
24 Then Joab came to the king, and
said, What hast thou done? behold, Ab-
ner came unto thee; why *is* it *that* thou
hast sent him away, and he is quite
gone?
25 Thou knowest Abner the son of
Ner, that he came to deceive thee, and
to know [l]thy going out and thy com-
ing in, and to know all that thou doest.

Joab kills Abner

26 And when Joab was come out
from David, he sent messengers after
Abner, which brought him again from
the well of Sirah: but David knew *it*
not.
27 And when Abner was returned to
Hebron, Joab [m]took him aside in the
gate to speak with him [u]quietly, and
smote him there [n]under the fifth *rib*,
that he died, for the blood of [o]Asahel
his brother.
28 ¶ And afterward when David
heard *it*, he said, I and my kingdom
are guiltless before the LORD for ever
from the [v]blood of Abner the son of
Ner:
29 [p]Let it rest on the head of Joab,
and on all his father's house; and let
there not [w]fail from the house of Joab
one [q]that hath an issue, or that is a
leper, or that leaneth on a staff, or that
falleth on the sword, or that lacketh
bread.
30 So Joab and Abishai his brother
slew Abner, because he had slain their
brother [r]Asahel at Gibeon in the bat-
tle.
31 ¶ And David said to Joab, and to
all the people that *were* with him,
[s]Rend your clothes, and [t]gird you
with sackcloth, and mourn before Ab-

3:9 [z]Ruth 1:17; 1 Ki. 19:2; [a]1 Sam. 15:28 & 16:1,12 & 28:17; 1 Chr. 12:23
3:10 [b]Judg. 20:1; ch. 17:11; 1 Ki. 4:25
3:13 [c]Gen. 43:3; [d]1 Sam. 18:20
3:14 [e]1 Sam. 18:25,27
3:15 [f]1 Sam. 25:44, *Phalti*
3:16 [g]ch. 19:16
3:18 [h]ver. 9
3:19 [i]1 Chr. 12:29
3:21 [j]ver. 10,12; [k]1 Ki. 11:37
3:25 [l]1 Sam. 29:6; Is. 37:28
3:27 [m]1 Ki. 2:5; ch. 20:9,10; [n]ch. 4:6; [o]ch. 2:23
3:29 [p]1 Ki. 2:32,33; [q]Lev. 15:2
3:30 [r]ch. 2:23
3:31 [s]Josh. 7:6; ch. 1:2,11; [t]Gen. 37:34

[r] Heb. *saying* [s] Heb. *going and weeping* [t] Heb. *both yesterday and the third day* [u] Or, *peaceably* [v] Heb. *bloods* [w] Heb. *be cut off*

ner. And king David *himself* followed the [x]bier.

32 And they buried Abner in Hebron: and the king lifted up his voice, and wept at the grave of Abner; and all the people wept.

33 And the king lamented over Abner, and said, Died Abner as a [u]fool dieth?

34 Thy hands *were* not bound, nor thy feet put into fetters: as a man falleth before [y]wicked men, *so* fellest thou. And all the people wept again over him.

35 And when all the people came [v]to cause David to eat meat while it was yet day, David sware, saying, [w]So do God to me, and more also, if I taste bread, or aught else, [x]till the sun be down.

36 And all the people took notice *of it,* and it [z]pleased them: as whatsoever the king did pleased all the people.

37 For all the people and all Israel understood that day that it was not of the king to slay Abner the son of Ner.

38 And the king said unto his servants, Know ye not that there is a prince and a great man fallen this day in Israel?

39 And I *am* this day [a]weak, though anointed king; and these men the sons of Zeruiah [y]*be* too hard for me: [z]the LORD shall reward the doer of evil according to his wickedness.

The murder of Ish-bosheth

4 AND WHEN Saul's son heard that Abner was dead in Hebron, [a]his hands were feeble, and all the Israelites were [b]troubled.

2 And Saul's son had two men *that were* captains of bands: the name of the one *was* Baanah, and the name of the [b]other Rechab, the sons of Rimmon a Beerothite, of the children of Benjamin: (for [c]Beeroth also was reckoned to Benjamin:

3 And the Beerothites fled to [d]Gittaim, and were sojourners there until this day.)

4 And [e]Jonathan, Saul's son, had a son *that was* lame of *his* feet. He was five years old when the tidings came of Saul and Jonathan [f]out of Jezreel, and his nurse took him up, and fled: and it came to pass, as she made haste to flee, that he fell, and became lame. And his name *was* [c]Mephibosheth.

5 And the sons of Rimmon the Beerothite, Rechab and Baanah, went, and came about the heat of the day to the house of Ish-bosheth, who lay on a bed at noon.

6 And they came thither into the midst of the house, *as though* they would have fetched wheat; and they smote him [g]under the fifth *rib:* and Rechab and Baanah his brother escaped.

7 For when they came into the house, he lay on his bed in his bedchamber, and they smote him, and slew him, and beheaded him, and took his head, and gat them away through the plain all night.

8 And they brought the head of Ish-bosheth unto David to Hebron, and said to the king, Behold the head of Ish-bosheth the son of Saul thine enemy, [h]which sought thy life; and the LORD hath avenged my lord the king this day of Saul, and of his seed.

9 ¶ And David answered Rechab and Baanah his brother, the sons of Rimmon the Beerothite, and said unto them, *As* the LORD liveth, [i]who hath redeemed my soul out of all adversity,

10 When [j]one told me, saying, Behold, Saul is dead, [d]thinking to have brought good tidings, I took hold of him, and slew him in Ziklag, [e]who *thought* that I would have given him a reward for his tidings:

11 How much more, when wicked men have slain a righteous person in his own house upon his bed? shall I not therefore now [k]require his blood of your hand, and take you away from the earth?

12 And David [l]commanded his young men, and they slew them, and cut off their hands and their feet, and hanged *them* up over the pool in Hebron. But they took the head of Ish-bosheth

3:33 [u]ch. 13:12,13
3:35 [v]ch. 12:17 Jer. 16:7 [w]Ruth 1:17 [x]ch. 1:12
3:39 [y]ch. 19:7 [z]See ch. 19:13 1 Ki. 2:5,6,33,34 2 Tim. 4:14
4:1 [a]Ezra 4:4 Is. 13:7 [b]Mat. 2:3
4:2 [c]Josh. 18:25
4:3 [d]Neh. 11:33
4:4 [e]ch. 9:3 [f]1 Sam. 29:1,11
4:6 [g]ch. 2:23
4:8 [h]1 Sam. 19:2,10, 11
4:9 [i]Gen. 48:16 1 Ki. 1:29
4:10 [j]ch. 1:2,4,15
4:11 [k]Gen. 9:5,6
4:12 [l]ch. 1:15

[x] Heb. *bed* [y] Heb. *children of iniquity* [z] Heb. *was good in their eyes* [a] Heb. *tender* [b] Heb. *second* [c] Or, *Merib-baal;* see 1 Chr. 8:34 & 9:40 [d] Heb. *he was in his own eyes as a bringer* [e] Or, *which was the reward I gave him for his tidings*

4:12 THEY SLEW THEM. David's ascent to the throne was a bloody one, involving civil war between the tribes and much political maneuvering—all of which illustrates why God's perfect will for Israel was not a human king (1 Sam. 8:5–7,19–22).

sheth, and buried *it* in the [m]sepulchre
of Abner in Hebron.

David made king of Israel

5:1–3pp — 1 Chr. 11:1–3

5 THEN [n]CAME all the tribes of Is-
rael to David unto Hebron, and
spake, saying, Behold, [o]we *are* thy
bone and thy flesh.
2 Also in time past, when Saul was
king over us, [p]thou wast he that led-
dest out and broughtest in Israel: and
the LORD said to thee, [q]Thou shalt feed
my people Israel, and thou shalt be a
captain over Israel.
3 [r]So all the elders of Israel came
to the king to Hebron; [s]and king Da-
vid made a league with them in Hebron
[t]before the LORD: and they anointed
David king over Israel.
4 ¶ David *was* thirty years old when
he began to reign, [u]*and* he reigned for-
ty years.
5 In Hebron he reigned over Judah
[v]seven years and six months: and in
Jerusalem he reigned thirty and three
years over all Israel and Judah.

The capture of Jerusalem

5:6–10pp — 1 Chr. 11:4–9
5:11–16pp — 1 Chr. 3:5–9; 14:1–7

6 ¶ And the king and his men went
[w]to Jerusalem unto [x]the Jebusites,
the inhabitants of the land: which
spake unto David, saying, Except thou
take away the blind and the lame, thou
shalt not come in hither: [f]thinking,
David cannot come in hither.
7 Nevertheless David took the
strong hold of Zion: [y]the same *is* the
city of David.
8 And David said on that day, Who-
soever getteth up to the gutter, and
smiteth the Jebusites, and the lame
and the blind, *that are* hated of David's
soul, [z]*he shall be chief and captain.*
[g]Wherefore they said, The blind and
the lame shall not come into the house.
9 So David dwelt in the fort, and
called it [a]the city of David. And David
built round about from Millo and in-
ward.
10 And David [h]went on, and grew
great, and the LORD God of hosts *was*
with him.
11 ¶ And [b]Hiram king of Tyre sent
messengers to David, and cedar trees,
and carpenters, and [i]masons: and
they built David an house.
12 And David perceived that the
LORD had established him king over Is-
rael, and that he had exalted his king-
dom for his people Israel's sake.
13 ¶ And [c]David took *him* more
concubines and wives out of Jerusa-
lem, after he was come from Hebron:
and there were yet sons and daughters
born to David.
14 And [d]these *be* the names of
those that were born unto him in Jeru-
salem; [j]Shammuah, and Shobab, and
Nathan, and Solomon,
15 Ibhar also, and [k]Elishua, and
Nepheg, and Japhia,
16 And Elishama, and [l]Eliada, and
Eliphalet.

The Philistines defeated

5:17–25pp — 1 Chr. 14:8–17

17 ¶ [e]But when the Philistines
heard that they had anointed David
king over Israel, all the Philistines
came up to seek David; and David
heard *of it*, [f]and went down to the
hold.
18 The Philistines also came and

4:12 [m]ch. 3:32
5:1 [n]1 Chr. 11:1 [o]Gen. 29:14
5:2 [p]1 Sam. 18:13 [q]1 Sam. 16:1
5:3 [r]1 Chr. 11:3 [s]2 Ki. 11:17 [t]Judg. 11:11; 1 Sam. 23:18
5:4 [u]1 Chr. 26:31 & 29:27
5:5 [v]ch. 2:11; 1 Chr. 3:4
5:6 [w]Judg. 1:21 [x]Josh. 15:63; Judg. 1:8 & 19:11,12
5:7 [y]1 Ki. 2:10 & 8:1
5:8 [z]1 Chr. 11:6-9
5:9 [a]ver. 7
5:11 [b]1 Ki. 5:2
5:13 [c]Deut. 17:17; 1 Chr. 3:9
5:14 [d]1 Chr. 3:5
5:17 [e]1 Chr. 11:16 [f]ch. 23:14

[f] Or, *saying, David shall not* [g] Or, *Because they had said, even the blind and the lame, He shall not come into the house* [h] Heb. *went going and growing* [i] Heb. *hewers of the stone of the wall* [j] Or, *Shimea;* see 1 Chr. 3:5 [k] Or, *Elishama;* see 1 Chr. 3:6 [l] Or, *Beeliada;* see 1 Chr. 14:7

5:6 JERUSALEM. David captured Jerusalem and made it the capital of Israel. Spiritually, it eventually became the most important city on earth as the center of God's redemptive action for the human race. It was in Jerusalem that Christ was crucified and rose from the dead, and that the Holy Spirit was poured out upon the assembled followers of Jesus. The Bible calls it the city of God (Ps. 46:4; 48:1; 87:3; Heb. 12:22; Rev. 3:12; see article on THE CITY OF JERUSALEM, p. 622).

5:13 DAVID TOOK *HIM* MORE CONCUBINES AND WIVES. This verse reveals David's most serious character weakness—his strong desire for women (cf. 3:1–5; 5:13). (1) David's failure to resist and subdue his sensual desires led him to violate God's command in Deut. 17:15–17 (which forbad Israel's kings to multiply wives for themselves), to act cruelly toward Michal and her husband (3:14–16), to commit adultery with Bathsheba (11:1–5), and to have Uriah her husband murdered (11:6–27). (2) David's lust for women was the source of great sin, sorrow, and suffering for his family (12:9–14; chs. 13—18). After David's sin with Bathsheba, God sent judgment and calamity upon David for the rest of his life (12:10).

spread themselves in [g]the valley of Rephaim.

19 And David [h]inquired of the LORD, saying, Shall I go up to the Philistines? wilt thou deliver them into mine hand? And the LORD said unto David, Go up: for I will doubtless deliver the Philistines into thine hand.

20 And David came to [i]Baal-perazim, and David smote them there, and said, The LORD hath broken forth upon mine enemies before me, as the breach of waters. Therefore he called the name of that place [m]Baal-perazim.

21 And there they left their images, and David and his men [j]burned[n] them.

22 ¶ [k]And the Philistines came up yet again, and spread themselves in the valley of Rephaim.

23 And when [l]David inquired of the LORD, he said, Thou shalt not go up; *but* fetch a compass behind them, and come upon them over against the mulberry trees.

24 And let it be, when thou [m]hearest the sound of a going in the tops of the mulberry trees, that then thou shalt bestir thyself: for then [n]shall the LORD go out before thee, to smite the host of the Philistines.

25 And David did so, as the LORD had commanded him; and smote the Philistines from [o]Geba until thou come to [p]Gazer.

Bringing the ark to Jerusalem

6:1–11pp — 1 Chr. 13:1–14
6:12–19pp — 1 Chr. 15:25–16:3

6 AGAIN, DAVID gathered together all *the* chosen *men* of Israel, thirty thousand.

2 And [q]David arose, and went with all the people that *were* with him from [o]Baale of Judah, to bring up from thence the ark of God, [p]whose name is called by the name of the LORD of hosts [r]that dwelleth *between* the cherubims.

3 And they [q]set the ark of God upon a new cart, and brought it out of the house of Abinadab that *was* in [r]Gibeah: and Uzzah and Ahio, the sons of Abinadab, drave the new cart.

4 And they brought it out of [s]the house of Abinadab which *was* at Gibeah, [s]accompanying the ark of God: and Ahio went before the ark.

5 And David and all the house of Israel played before the LORD on all manner of *instruments made of* fir wood, even on harps, and on psalteries, and on timbrels, and on cornets, and on cymbals.

6 ¶ And when they came to [t]Nachon's threshingfloor, Uzzah put forth *his hand* to the ark of God, and took hold of it; for the oxen [t]shook *it*.

7 And the anger of the LORD was kindled against Uzzah; and [u]God smote him there for *his* [u]error; and there he died by the ark of God.

8 And David was displeased, because the LORD had [v]made a breach upon Uzzah: and he called the name of the place [w]Perez-uzzah to this day.

9 And [v]David was afraid of the LORD that day, and said, How shall the ark of the LORD come to me?

10 So David would not remove the ark of the LORD unto him into the city of David: but David carried it aside into the house of Obed-edom [w]the Gittite.

11 [x]And the ark of the LORD contin-

5:18 [g]Josh. 15:8 Is. 17:5
5:19 [h]1 Sam. 23:2,4
5:20 [i]Is. 28:21
5:21 [j]Deut. 7:5,25
5:22 [k]1 Chr. 14:13
5:23 [l]ver. 19
5:24 [m]2 Ki. 7:6 [n]Judg. 4:14
5:25 [o]1 Chr. 14:16 *Gibeon* [p]Josh. 16:10
6:2 [q]1 Chr. 13:5,6 [r]1 Sam. 4:4 Ps. 80:1
6:4 [s]1 Sam. 7:1
6:6 [t]1 Chr. 13:9 he is called *Chidon*
6:7 [u]1 Sam. 6:19
6:9 [v]Ps. 119:120
6:10 [w]1 Chr. 13:13
6:11 [x]1 Chr. 13:14

[m] i.e. *The plain of breaches* [n] Or, *took them away* [o] Or, *Baalah* i.e. *Kirjath-jearim;* see Josh. 15:9 [p] Or, *at which the name, even the name of the LORD of hosts, was called upon* [q] Heb. *made to ride* [r] Or, *The hill* [s] Heb. *with* [t] Or, *stumbled* [u] Or, *rashness* [v] Heb. *broken* [w] i.e. *The breach of Uzzah*

5:19 DAVID INQUIRED OF THE LORD. One of David's greatest strengths was his conviction that God's help and direction were absolutely essential for success in battle. Thus he made it a regular practice to inquire of the Lord. Fulfilling God's purpose for our lives will likewise depend on our seeking God's guidance through prayer and on our being led by the Holy Spirit who dwells within us (cf. Rom. 8:1–17).

6:7 THE ANGER OF THE LORD. God struck down Uzzah because David and the high priest had not assigned the Levites to carry or handle the ark in accordance with the command of God (Num. 1:47–52). (1) God had ordered that no one was to touch the ark, the symbol of His presence and majesty (Num. 4:15; cf. 1 Chr. 15:13–15). Uzzah's action grew out of his ignorance of God's command or his lack of the fear of the Lord (cf. 1 Chr. 15:2).

(2) Uzzah is an example of the inherent dangers in having a zeal for God without knowledge of God's word and ways. David's plan to bring back the ark to Jerusalem, and Uzzah's desire to steady it when it teetered on the cart, demonstrated a zeal for God's kingdom, yet at the same time led to a careless attitude toward the standards of God's sacred word. Ignorance is no excuse. God's inspired revelation expresses His will regarding all of life and must be followed by those who claim Him as their Lord (cf. Lev. 10:1–3; Josh. 7; Acts 5:1–11).

ued in the house of Obed-edom the Git-
tite three months: and the LORD
[y]blessed Obed-edom, and all his
household.
12 ¶ And it was told king David,
saying, The LORD hath blessed the
house of Obed-edom, and all that *per-*
taineth unto him, because of the ark of
God. [z]So David went and brought up
the ark of God from the house of Obed-
edom into the city of David with glad-
ness.
13 And it was *so*, that when [a]they
that bare the ark of the LORD had gone
six paces, he sacrificed [b]oxen and fat-
lings.
14 And David [c]danced before the
LORD with all *his* might; and David *was*
girded [d]with a linen ephod.
15 [e]So David and all the house of
Israel brought up the ark of the LORD
with shouting, and with the sound of
the trumpet.
16 And as the ark of the LORD came
into the city of David, Michal Saul's
daughter looked through a window,
and saw king David leaping and danc-
ing before the LORD; and she despised
him in her heart.
17 ¶ And [f]they brought in the ark
of the LORD, and set it in [g]his place, in
the midst of the tabernacle that David
had [x]pitched for it: and David [h]of-
fered burnt offerings and peace offer-
ings before the LORD.
18 And as soon as David had made
an end of offering burnt offerings and
peace offerings, [i]he blessed the peo-
ple in the name of the LORD of hosts.
19 [j]And he dealt among all the
people, *even* among the whole multi-
tude of Israel, as well to the women as
men, to every one a cake of bread, and
a good piece *of flesh,* and a flagon *of*
wine. So all the people departed every
one to his house.
20 ¶ [k]Then David returned to bless
his household. And Michal the daugh-
ter of Saul came out to meet David, and
said, How glorious was the king of Is-
rael today, who [l]uncovered himself
today in the eyes of the handmaids of
his servants, as one of the [m]vain fel-
lows [y]shamelessly uncovereth him-
self!
21 And David said unto Michal, *It*
was before the LORD, [n]which chose me
before thy father, and before all his
house, to appoint me ruler over the
people of the LORD, over Israel: there-
fore will I play before the LORD.
22 And I will yet be more vile than
thus, and will be base in mine own
sight: and [z]of the maidservants which
thou hast spoken of, of them shall I be
had in honour.
23 Therefore Michal the daughter
of Saul had no child [o]unto the day of
her death.

Nathan's prophecy

7:1–17pp — 1 Chr. 17:1–15

7 AND IT came to pass, [p]when the
king sat in his house, and the LORD
had given him rest round about from all
his enemies;
2 That the king said unto Nathan
the prophet, See now, I dwell in [q]an
house of cedar, [r]but the ark of God
dwelleth within [s]curtains.
3 And Nathan said to the king, Go,
do all that *is* in thine heart; for the LORD
is with thee.
4 ¶ And it came to pass that night,
that the word of the LORD came unto
Nathan, saying,
5 Go and tell [a]my servant David,
Thus saith the LORD, [t]Shalt thou build
me an house for me to dwell in?
6 Whereas I have not dwelt in *any*
house [u]since the time that I brought
up the children of Israel out of Egypt,
even to this day, but have walked in [v]a
tent and in a tabernacle.
7 In all *the places* wherein I have
[w]walked with all the children of Israel

6:11 [y]Gen. 39:5
6:12 [z]1 Chr. 15:25
6:13 [a]Num. 4:15 Josh. 3:3 1 Chr. 15:2,15 [b]See 1 Ki. 8:5
6:14 [c]Ps. 30:11 [d]1 Sam. 2:18
6:15 [e]1 Chr. 15:28
6:17 [f]1 Chr. 16:1 [g]1 Chr. 15:1 Ps. 132:8 [h]1 Ki. 8:5,62,63
6:18 [i]1 Ki. 8:55
6:19 [j]1 Chr. 16:3
6:20 [k]Ps. 30,title [l]ver. 14,16 [m]Judg. 9:4
6:21 [n]1 Sam. 13:14
6:23 [o]See 1 Sam. 15:35 Is. 22:14
7:1 [p]1 Chr. 17:1
7:2 [q]ch. 5:11 [r]See Acts 7:46 [s]Ex. 26:1
7:5 [t]1 Ki. 5:3 & 8:19 1 Chr. 22:8
7:6 [u]1 Ki. 8:16 [v]Ex. 40:18,19,34
7:7 [w]Lev. 26:11 Deut. 23:14

[x]Heb. *stretched* [y]Or, *openly* [z]Or, *of the handmaids* of my servants [a]Heb. *to my servant, to David*

6:12 ARK . . . INTO THE CITY OF DAVID. David brought the ark to Jerusalem (cf. 5:6–7) and transformed that city into the worship center and capital of Israel. This time he followed the instructions of the Lord and had Levites carry the ark (1 Chr. 15:12). Two of David's greatest achievements as king centered around "the city of David": (1) his formation of Israel into a strong unified nation with its capital being the well-fortified city of Jerusalem, and (2) the establishment in that location of the worship of the Lord as Israel's greatest priority (cf. 7:1–29; 1 Chr. 15:1—17:27).

6:20 UNCOVERED HIMSELF. Michal felt that David had behaved in an unbecoming manner for the king of Israel (cf. v. 16). "Uncovered himself" means that David had laid aside his royal clothing and appeared in a simple tunic such as slaves wore.

spake I a word with [b]any of the tribes
of Israel, whom I commanded [x]to feed
my people Israel, saying, Why build ye
not me an house of cedar?
8 Now therefore so shalt thou say
unto my servant David, Thus saith the
LORD of hosts, [y]I took thee from the
sheepcote, [c]from following the sheep,
to be ruler over my people, over Israel:
9 And [z]I was with thee whitherso-
ever thou wentest, [a]and have cut off
all thine enemies [d]out of thy sight,
and have made thee a great name, like
unto the name of the great *men* that *are*
in the earth.
10 Moreover I will appoint a place
for my people Israel, and will [b]plant
them, that they may dwell in a place of
their own, and move no more; [c]neither
shall the children of wickedness afflict
them any more, as beforetime,
11 And as [d]since the time that I
commanded judges *to be* over my peo-
ple Israel, and have caused thee to rest
from all thine enemies. Also the LORD
telleth thee [e]that he will make thee an
house.
12 ¶ And [f]when thy days be ful-
filled, and thou [g]shalt sleep with thy
fathers, [h]I will set up thy seed after
thee, which shall proceed out of thy
bowels, and I will establish his king-
dom.
13 [i]He shall build an house for my
name, and I will [j]stablish the throne
of his kingdom for ever.
14 [k]I will be his father, and he
shall be my son. [l]If he commit iniqui-
ty, I will chasten him with the rod of
men, and with the stripes of the chil-
dren of men:
15 But my mercy shall not depart
away from him, [m]as I took *it* from
Saul, whom I put away before thee.
16 And [n]thine house and thy king-
dom shall be established for ever be-
fore thee: thy throne shall be estab-
lished for ever.
17 According to all these words,

7:7 [x]Mat. 2:6; Acts 20:28
7:8 [y]1 Sam. 16:11,12
7:9 [z]1 Sam. 18:14; ch. 5:10; [a]1 Sam. 31:6
7:10 [b]Ps. 44:2 & 80:8; Jer. 24:6; [c]Ps. 89:22
7:11 [d]Judg. 2:14; 1 Sam. 12:9; [e]ver. 27; Ex. 1:21
7:12 [f]1 Ki. 2:1; [g]Deut. 31:16; [h]Ps. 132:11
7:13 [i]1 Ki. 5:5 & 8:19; [j]ver. 16
7:14 [k]Heb. 1:5; [l]Ps. 89:30
7:15 [m]1 Sam. 15:23,28 & 16:14
7:16 [n]ver. 13; John 12:34
7:18 [o]Gen. 32:10
7:19 [p]Is. 55:8
7:20 [q]Ps. 139:1
7:22 [r]1 Chr. 16:25; 2 Chr. 2:5; Jer. 10:6; [s]Deut. 3:24 & 4:35 & 32:39
7:23 [t]Ps. 147:20; [u]Deut. 9:26
7:24 [v]Deut. 26:18; [w]Ps. 48:14

and according to all this vision, so did
Nathan speak unto David.

David's prayer

7:18–29pp — 1 Chr. 17:16–27

18 ¶ Then went king David in, and
sat before the LORD, and he said, [o]Who
am I, O Lord GOD? and what *is* my
house, that thou hast brought me hith-
erto?
19 And this was yet a small thing in
thy sight, O Lord GOD; but thou hast
spoken also of thy servant's house for
a great while to come. [p]And *is* this the
[e]manner of man, O Lord GOD?
20 And what can David say more
unto thee? for thou, Lord GOD, [q]know-
est thy servant.
21 For thy word's sake, and accord-
ing to thine own heart, hast thou done
all these great things, to make thy ser-
vant know *them*.
22 Wherefore [r]thou art great,
O LORD God: for [s]*there is* none like
thee, neither *is there any* God beside
thee, according to all that we have
heard with our ears.
23 And [t]what one nation in the
earth *is* like thy people, *even* like Isra-
el, whom God went to redeem for a peo-
ple to himself, and to make him a
name, and to do for you great things
and terrible, for thy land, before [u]thy
people, which thou redeemedst to thee
from Egypt, *from* the nations and their
gods?
24 For [v]thou hast confirmed to
thyself thy people Israel *to be* a people
unto thee for ever: [w]and thou, LORD,
art become their God.
25 And now, O LORD God, the word
that thou hast spoken concerning thy
servant, and concerning his house, es-
tablish *it* for ever, and do as thou hast
said.
26 And let thy name be magnified

[b] Or, *any of the judges;* see 1 Chr. 17:6
[c] Heb. *from after* [d] Heb. *from thy face*
[e] Heb. *law*

7:12 I WILL ESTABLISH HIS KINGDOM. Using the voice of the prophet Nathan, God established His covenant with David. For more on this, see article on GOD'S COVENANT WITH DAVID, p. 470.

7:16 THY KINGDOM SHALL BE ESTABLISHED FOR EVER. God's covenant with David was fulfilled ultimately in Jesus Christ (see article on GOD'S COVENANT WITH DAVID, p. 470).

7:18 WHO *AM* I . . . THAT THOU HAST BROUGHT ME HITHERTO? The Lord did not give David His covenant promise because of David's merit, righteousness, or good deeds; rather, it was established out of His mercy and grace—for the sake of His word (v. 21), the glory of His name (v. 26), the destiny of His people Israel (5:12), and ultimately the salvation of all nations (Is. 11:1, 10). David accepted God's promise in humility and faith.

GOD'S COVENANT WITH DAVID

2 Sam. 7:16 "And thine house and thy kingdom shall be established for ever before thee: thy throne shall be established for ever."

THE NATURE OF THE COVENANT WITH DAVID. (1) Though the word "covenant" does not actually occur in 2 Sam. 7, it is clear that God was establishing a covenant with David. In Ps. 89:3–4, for example, God says: "I have made a covenant with my chosen, I have sworn unto David my servant, Thy seed will I establish for ever, and build up thy throne to all generations" (see also Ps. 89:34–36). This promise that the throne of God's people would be established forever by David's seed is precisely the promise that God made with David in 2 Sam. 7 (note especially v. 16). Furthermore, later in 2 Samuel, David himself makes a reference to the "everlasting covenant" that God made with him (2 Sam. 23:5), undoubtedly referring back to 2 Sam. 7.

(2) The same two principles at work in other covenants in the O.T. are also evident here: God alone established the promises and obligation of His covenant, and human beings were expected to accept them in obedient faith (see articles on GOD'S COVENANT WITH ABRAHAM, ISAAC, AND JACOB, p. 48, and GOD'S COVENANT WITH THE ISRAELITES, p. 314). (a) In this covenant arrangement with David, God made an immediate promise that He would establish the kingdom of David's son, Solomon, who would build a house for the Lord, i.e., the temple (2 Sam. 7:11–13). (b) At the same time, God's promise that David's house or dynasty would endure forever over the Israelites was conditioned on the faithful obedience of David and his descendants. In other words, this covenant was eternal only in the sense that God intended to keep always a son of David on the throne in Jerusalem, provided the rulers of Judah remained faithful and obedient to Him.

(3) For the next four centuries, the line of David remained unbroken on the throne of Judah. But when the kings of Judah, particularly Manasseh and those who reigned after King Josiah, continually rebelled against God by worshiping idols and disobeying His law, God finally did remove them from occupying the throne. He allowed King Nebuchadnezzar of Babylon to invade the land of Judah, lay siege to the city of Jerusalem, and eventually destroy the city with its temple (see 2 Ki. 25; 2 Chr. 36). God's people were now, for the first time since their sojourn in Egypt, under the control of foreign rulers.

JESUS CHRIST AND THIS COVENANT. There was one aspect to God's covenant with David, however, that was unconditional—that the kingdom of David would *ultimately* be established forever. (1) The apex of God's promise was that from the Davidic family line would come a descendant who would be the Messianic and eternal King. This King would be ruler over the faithful of Israel and of all the nations (cf. Is. 9:6–7; 11:1,10; Mic. 5:2,4). He would come forth from the city of Bethlehem (Mic. 5:2,4), and His rule would extend to the ends of the earth (Zech. 9:10). He would be called "THE LORD OUR RIGHTEOUSNESS" (Jer. 23:5–6) and would bring salvation from sin (Zech. 13:1). The fulfillment of the Davidic promise began with the birth of Jesus Christ, which was announced by the angel Gabriel to Mary, a devout daughter from the family of David (Luke 1:30–33; cf. Acts 2:29–35).

(2) This promise was an extension of the covenant given in Gen. 3:15, which predicted the defeat of Satan through an offspring of Eve (see Gen. 3:15, note); it was a continuation of the covenant given to Abraham and his descendants (see article on GOD'S COVENANT WITH ABRAHAM, ISAAC, AND JACOB, p. 48).

(3) The fulfillment of this promise involved the resurrection of Christ from the dead and His exaltation to the right hand of God in heaven (Acts 2:29–33), from where he now rules as King of kings and Lord of lords. Christ's first task as exalted Lord was the outpouring of the Holy Spirit upon His people (Acts 1:8; 2:4,33).

(4) The kingly rule of Christ is characterized by a call to all people to turn from sin and the perverse world, to accept Christ as Lord and Savior, and to receive the Holy Spirit (Acts 2:32–40).

(5) The eternal kingship of Christ includes (a) His present rulership over the kingdom of God and His headship over the church, (b) His future millennial rule over the nations (Rev. 2:26–27; 20:4), and (c) His everlasting kingdom in the new heaven and the new earth (Rev. 21—22).

for ever, saying, The LORD of hosts *is* the God over Israel: and let the house of thy servant David be established before thee.

27 For thou, O LORD of hosts, God of Israel, hast revealed to thy servant, saying, I will build thee an house: therefore hath thy servant found in his heart to pray this prayer unto thee.

28 And now, O Lord GOD, thou *art* that God, and [x]thy words be true, and thou hast promised this goodness unto thy servant:

29 Therefore now [f]let it please thee to bless the house of thy servant, that it may continue for ever before thee: for thou, O Lord GOD, hast spoken *it:* and with thy blessing let the house of thy servant be blessed [y]for ever.

David's military victories

8:1–14pp — 1 Chr. 18:1–13
8:15–18pp — 1 Chr. 18:14–17

8 AND AFTER this it came to pass, that David smote the Philistines, and subdued them: and David took [g]Metheg-ammah out of the hand of the Philistines.

2 And [z]he smote Moab, and measured them with a line, casting them down to the ground; even with two lines measured he to put to death, and with one full line to keep alive. And *so* the Moabites became David's servants, *and* [a]brought gifts.

3 ¶ David smote also [h]Hadadezer, the son of Rehob, king of [b]Zobah, as he went to recover [c]his border at the river Euphrates.

4 And David took [i]from him a thousand [j]*chariots,* and seven hundred horsemen, and twenty thousand footmen: and David [d]houghed all the chariot *horses,* but reserved of them *for* an hundred chariots.

5 [e]And when the Syrians of Damascus came to succour Hadadezer king of Zobah, David slew of the Syrians two and twenty thousand men.

6 Then David put garrisons in Syria of Damascus: and the Syrians became servants to David, *and* brought gifts. [f]And the LORD preserved David whithersoever he went.

7 And David took [g]the shields of gold that were on the servants of Hadadezer, and brought them to Jerusalem.

8 And from [k]Betah, and from [l]Berothai, cities of Hadadezer, king David took exceeding much brass.

9 ¶ When [m]Toi king of Hamath heard that David had smitten all the host of Hadadezer,

10 Then Toi sent [h]Joram his son unto king David, to [n]salute him, and to bless him, because he had fought against Hadadezer, and smitten him: for Hadadezer [o]had wars with Toi. And *Joram* [p]brought with him vessels of silver, and vessels of gold, and vessels of brass:

11 Which also king David [i]did dedicate unto the LORD, with the silver and gold that he had dedicated of all nations which he subdued;

12 Of Syria, and of Moab, and of the children of Ammon, and of the Philistines, and of Amalek, and of the spoil of Hadadezer, son of Rehob, king of Zobah.

13 And David gat *him* a name when he returned from [q]smiting of the Syrians in [j]the valley of salt, [k]*being*[r] eighteen thousand *men.*

14 ¶ And he put garrisons in Edom; throughout all Edom put he garrisons, and [l]all they of Edom became David's servants. And the LORD preserved David whithersoever he went.

15 And David reigned over all Israel; and David executed judgment and justice unto all his people.

16 [m]And Joab the son of Zeruiah *was* over the host; and [n]Jehoshaphat the son of Ahilud *was* [s]recorder;

17 And [o]Zadok the son of Ahitub, and Ahimelech the son of Abiathar, *were* the priests; and Seraiah *was* the [t]scribe;

18 [p]And Benaiah the son of Jehoiada *was over* both the [q]Cherethites and the Pelethites; and David's sons were [u]chief rulers.

David and Mephibosheth

9 AND DAVID said, Is there yet any that is left of the house of Saul, that I may [r]show him kindness for Jonathan's sake?

7:28 [x] John 17:17
7:29 [y] ch. 22:51
8:2 [z] Num. 24:17 [a] See 1 Sam. 10:27
8:3 [b] ch. 10:6 Ps. 60,title [c] See Gen. 15:18
8:4 [d] Josh. 11:6,9
8:5 [e] 1 Ki. 11:23
8:6 [f] ver. 14 ch. 7:9
8:7 [g] See 1 Ki. 10:16
8:10 [h] 1 Chr. 18:10, *Hadoram*
8:11 [i] 1 Ki. 7:51
8:13 [j] 2 Ki. 14:7 [k] See 1 Chr. 18:12 Ps. 60,title
8:14 [l] Gen. 27:29,37,40 Num. 24:18
8:16 [m] ch. 19:13 & 20:23 1 Chr. 11:6 [n] 1 Ki. 4:3
8:17 [o] 1 Chr. 24:3
8:18 [p] 1 Chr. 18:17 [q] 1 Sam. 30:14
9:1 [r] 1 Sam. 18:3 Prov. 27:10

[f] Heb. *be thou pleased and bless* [g] Or, *The bridle of Ammah* [h] Or, *Hadarezer;* see 1 Chr. 18:3 [i] Or, *of his* [j] As 1 Chr. 18:4 [k] Or, *Tibhath* [l] Or, *Chun;* see 1 Chr. 18:8 [m] *Tou;* see 1 Chr. 18:9 [n] Heb. *ask him of peace* [o] Heb. *was a man of wars with* [p] Heb. *in his hand were* [q] Heb. *his smiting* [r] Or, slaying [s] Or, *remembrancer,* or, *writer of chronicles* [t] Or, *secretary* [u] Or, *princes*

2 And *there was* of the house of Saul a servant whose name *was* [s]Ziba. And when they had called him unto, David the king said unto him, *Art* thou Ziba? And he said, Thy servant *is he.*

3 And the king said, *Is* there not yet any of the house of Saul, that I may show [t]the kindness of God unto him? And Ziba said unto the king, Jonathan hath yet a son, *which is* [u]lame on *his* feet.

4 And the king said unto him, Where *is* he? And Ziba said unto the king, Behold, he *is* in the house of [v]Machir, the son of Ammiel, in Lo-debar.

5 ¶ Then king David sent, and fetched him out of the house of Machir, the son of Ammiel, from Lo-debar.

6 Now when [v]Mephibosheth, the son of Jonathan, the son of Saul, was come unto David, he fell on his face, and did reverence. And David said, Mephibosheth. And he answered, Behold thy servant!

7 ¶ And David said unto him, Fear not: for I will surely show thee kindness for Jonathan thy father's sake, and will restore thee all the land of Saul thy father; and thou shalt eat bread at my table continually.

8 And he bowed himself, and said, What *is* thy servant, that thou shouldest look upon such [w]a dead dog as I *am?*

9 ¶ Then the king called to Ziba, Saul's servant, and said unto him, [x]I have given unto thy master's son all that pertained to Saul and to all his house.

10 Thou therefore, and thy sons, and thy servants, shall till the land for him, and thou shalt bring in *the fruits,* that thy master's son may have food to eat: but Mephibosheth thy master's son [y]shall eat bread always at my table. Now Ziba had [z]fifteen sons and twenty servants.

11 Then said Ziba unto the king, According to all that my lord the king hath commanded his servant, so shall thy servant do. As for Mephibosheth, *said the king,* he shall eat at my table, as one of the king's sons.

12 And Mephibosheth had a young son, [a]whose name *was* Micha. And all that dwelt in the house of Ziba *were* servants unto Mephibosheth.

13 So Mephibosheth dwelt in Jerusalem: [b]for he did eat continually at the king's table; and [c]was lame on both his feet.

9:2 [s]ch. 16:1 & 19:17,29
9:3 [t]1 Sam. 20:14 [u]ch. 4:4
9:4 [v]ch. 17:27
9:8 [w]ch. 16:9
9:9 [x]ch. 16:4 & 19:29
9:10 [y]ver. 7,11,13 ch. 19:28 [z]ch. 19:17
9:12 [a]1 Chr. 8:34
9:13 [b]ver. 7,10 2 Ki. 25:29 [c]ver. 3
10:1 [d]1 Chr. 19:1
10:4 [e]Is. 20:4 & 47:2
10:6 [f]Gen. 34:30 Ex. 5:21 1 Sam. 13:4 [g]ch. 8:3,5 [h]Judg. 11:3,5

Victory over the Ammonites

10:1–19pp — 1 Chr. 19:1–19

10 AND IT came to pass after this, that the [d]king of the children of Ammon died, and Hanun his son reigned in his stead.

2 Then said David, I will show kindness unto Hanun the son of Nahash, as his father showed kindness unto me. And David sent to comfort him by the hand of his servants for his father. And David's servants came into the land of the children of Ammon.

3 And the princes of the children of Ammon said unto Hanun their lord, [w]Thinkest thou that David doth honour thy father, that he hath sent comforters unto thee? hath not David *rather* sent his servants unto thee, to search the city, and to spy it out, and to overthrow it?

4 Wherefore Hanun took David's servants, and shaved off the one half of their beards, and cut off their garments in the middle, [e]*even* to their buttocks, and sent them away.

5 When they told *it* unto David, he sent to meet them, because the men were greatly ashamed: and the king said, Tarry at Jericho until your beards be grown, and *then* return.

6 ¶ And when the children of Ammon saw that they [f]stank before David, the children of Ammon sent and hired [g]the Syrians of Beth-rehob, and the Syrians of Zoba, twenty thousand footmen, and of king Maacah a thousand men, and of [h]Ish-tob[x] twelve thousand men.

7 And when David heard of *it,* he

[v]Called *Merib-baal* in 1 Chr. 8:34 [w]Heb. *In thine eyes doth David* [x]Or, *The men of Tob*

9:1 SHOW HIM KINDNESS FOR JONATHAN'S SAKE. Ch. 9 records how David kept his promise to his close friend, Jonathan. David had made a covenant with Jonathan years before to show kindness to his family always (1 Sam. 20:11–23). Mephibosheth was a son of Jonathan (vv. 3,6; cf. 4:4). This is the first of two acts of kindness reported of David (cf. 10:1–5). David's remarkable kindness stands in sharp contrast to the two acts of wickedness (adultery and murder) which immediately follow (11:1–27).

sent Joab, and all the host of [i]the
mighty men.
8 And the children of Ammon came
out, and put the battle in array at the
entering in of the gate: and [j]the Syri-
ans of Zoba, and of Rehob, and Ish-tob,
and Maacah, *were* by themselves in the
field.
9 When Joab saw that the front of
the battle was against him before and
behind, he chose of all the choice *men*
of Israel, and put *them* in array against
the Syrians:
10 And the rest of the people he de-
livered into the hand of Abishai his
brother, that he might put *them* in array
against the children of Ammon.
11 And he said, If the Syrians be too
strong for me, then thou shalt help me:
but if the children of Ammon be too
strong for thee, then I will come and
help thee.
12 [k]Be of good courage, and let us
[l]play the men for our people, and for
the cities of our God: and [m]the LORD do
that which seemeth him good.
13 And Joab drew nigh, and the peo-
ple that *were* with him, unto the battle
against the Syrians: and they fled be-
fore him.
14 And when the children of Am-
mon saw that the Syrians were fled,
then fled they also before Abishai, and
entered into the city. So Joab returned
from the children of Ammon, and came
to Jerusalem.
15 ¶ And when the Syrians saw that
they were smitten before Israel, they
gathered themselves together.

10:7 [i]ch. 23:8 **10:8** [j]ver. 6 **10:12** [k]Deut. 31:6 [l]1 Sam. 4:9 1 Cor. 16:13 [m]1 Sam. 3:18 **10:18** [n]1 Chr. 19:18 *footmen* **10:19** [o]ch. 8:6 **11:1** [p]1 Chr. 20:1 **11:2** [q]Deut. 22:8

16 And Hadarezer sent, and
brought out the Syrians that *were* be-
yond [y]the river: and they came to He-
lam; and [z]Shobach the captain of the
host of Hadarezer *went* before them.
17 And when it was told David, he
gathered all Israel together, and
passed over Jordan, and came to He-
lam. And the Syrians set themselves in
array against David, and fought with
him.
18 And the Syrians fled before Isra-
el; and David slew *the men of* seven
hundred chariots of the Syrians, and
forty thousand [n]horsemen, and smote
Shobach the captain of their host, who
died there.
19 And when all the kings *that were*
servants to Hadarezer saw that they
were smitten before Israel, they made
peace with Israel, and [o]served them.
So the Syrians feared to help the chil-
dren of Ammon any more.

David's sin against Uriah

11 AND IT came to pass, [a]after
the year was expired, at the
time when kings go forth *to battle,* that
[p]David sent Joab, and his servants
with him, and all Israel; and they de-
stroyed the children of Ammon, and be-
sieged Rabbah. But David tarried still
at Jerusalem.
2 ¶ And it came to pass in an even-
ingtide, that David arose from off his
bed, [q]and walked upon the roof of the

[y] i.e. *Euphrates* [z] Or, *Shophach;* see 1 Chr. 19:16 [a] Heb. *at the return of the year*

11:1 DAVID TARRIED STILL AT JERUSALEM. Ch. 11 records David's tragic sin and fall. Instead of leading his army into battle as he had done before, David stayed behind in Jerusalem. He had developed a softness that soon led to his spiritual and moral collapse. His life of ease and luxury as king bred self-confidence and self-indulgence. At about this time he ceased to be a man after God's own heart (see 1 Sam. 13:14). David's fall from grace (cf. Gal. 5:4) stands as a warning to all believers: "let him that thinketh he standeth take heed lest he fall" (1 Cor. 10:12).

11:2 HE SAW A WOMAN. Chs. 11 — 24 record David's serious spiritual failures and God's subsequent judgment upon him for the rest of his life. (1) This account of David's sins and the consequent tragedies in his personal and family life serves as a serious example and warning for the N.T. believer, not just for Israel. Concerning similar events at the time of the exodus, the Holy Spirit through the apostle Paul emphasized, "These things happened unto them for examples: and they were written for our admonition, upon whom the ends of the world are come" (1 Cor. 10:11). Thus we should take every precaution not to desire evil things, act immorally, or try the Lord (cf. 1 Cor. 10:6–9).

(2) David's experience demonstrates how far a person may fall when he or she turns away from God and the guidance of the Holy Spirit. When God first called David to be king, he was a man after God's own heart (1 Sam. 13:14; Acts 13:22); in striking down Uriah and taking his wife, however, David was despising God and His word (12:9–10; cf. 1 Cor. 10:12).

(3) Although David repented of his sins and received God's forgiveness, God did not eliminate their consequences. Likewise, a believer may commit terrible sins and then through godly sorrow and sincere repentance receive God's grace and forgiveness. Nevertheless, the restoration of one's relationship with God does not mean that he or she will escape temporal punishment or be delivered from the consequences of specific

king's house: and from the roof he
[r]saw a woman washing herself; and
the woman *was* very beautiful to look
upon.
3 And David sent and inquired after
the woman. And *one* said, *Is* not this
[b]Bath-sheba, the daughter of [c]Eli-
am, the wife [s]of Uriah the Hittite?
4 And David sent messengers, and
took her; and she came in unto him,
and [t]he lay with her; [d]for she was
[u]purified from her uncleanness: and
she returned unto her house.
5 And the woman conceived, and
sent and told David, and said, I *am* with
child.
6 ¶ And David sent to Joab, *saying,*
Send me Uriah the Hittite. And Joab
sent Uriah to David.
7 And when Uriah was come unto
him, David demanded *of him* [e]how
Joab did, and how the people did, and
how the war prospered.
8 And David said to Uriah, Go down
to thy house, and [v]wash thy feet. And
Uriah departed out of the king's house,
and there [f]followed him a mess *of*
meat from the king.
9 But Uriah slept at the door of the
king's house with all the servants of
his lord, and went not down to his
house.
10 And when they had told David,
saying, Uriah went not down unto his
house, David said unto Uriah, Camest
thou not from *thy* journey? why *then*
didst thou not go down unto thine
house?
11 And Uriah said unto David,
[w]The ark, and Israel, and Judah, abide
in tents; and [x]my lord Joab, and the
servants of my lord, are encamped in
the open fields; shall I then go into
mine house, to eat and to drink, and to
lie with my wife? *as* thou livest, and *as*
thy soul liveth, I will not do this thing.
12 And David said to Uriah, Tarry
here today also, and tomorrow I will let
thee depart. So Uriah abode in Jerusa-
lem that day, and the morrow.
13 And when David had called him,
he did eat and drink before him; and he
made him [y]drunk: and at even he
went out to lie on his bed [z]with the
servants of his lord, but went not down
to his house.
14 ¶ And it came to pass in the
morning, that David [a]wrote a letter to
Joab, and sent *it* by the hand of Uriah.
15 And he wrote in the letter, say-
ing, Set ye Uriah in the forefront of the
[g]hottest battle, and retire ye [h]from
him, that he may [b]be smitten, and die.
16 And it came to pass, when Joab
observed the city, that he assigned Uri-
ah unto a place where he knew that
valiant men *were.*
17 And the men of the city went out,
and fought with Joab: and there fell
some of the people of the servants of
David; and Uriah the Hittite died also.
18 ¶ Then Joab sent and told David
all the things concerning the war;
19 And charged the messenger,
saying, When thou hast made an end of
telling the matters of the war unto the
king,
20 And if so be that the king's wrath
arise, and he say unto thee, Wherefore

11:2 [r]Gen. 34:2 Job 31:1 Mat. 5:28 **11:3** [s]ch. 23:39 **11:4** [t]Ps. 51,title Jas. 1:14 [u]Lev. 15:19,28 & 18:19 **11:8** [v]Gen. 18:4 & 19:2 **11:11** [w]ch. 7:2,6 [x]ch. 20:6 **11:13** [y]Gen. 19:33,35 [z]ver. 9 **11:14** [a]See 1 Ki. 21:8,9 **11:15** [b]ch. 12:9

[b] Or, *Bath-shuah;* see 1 Chr. 3:5 [c] Or, *Ammiel* [d] Or, *and when she had purified herself, &c., she returned* [e] Heb. *of the peace of* [f] Heb. *went out after him* [g] Heb. *strong* [h] Heb. *from after him*

sins (vv. 10–11,14).

(4) God did not condone or excuse David's sins under the pretense that David was only human, that his sins were merely weaknesses or human failures, or that he as king could understandably resort to evil and cruelty. David did not have to do what he did. Even in the imperfect redemption of the old covenant, people such as the prophet Samuel manifested a persevering loyalty to and faith in God through the grace available to them (cf. 1 Sam. 12:1–5,23; see 1 Sam. 25:1 note). The writer of this book clearly condemns rather than excuses David's great transgressions.

(5) The correct response to sin is to repent in all sincerity, to come to God that we might receive forgiveness, grace, and mercy (Ps. 51; Heb. 4:16; 7:25), and to be willing to accept God's punishment for our sin without bitterness or rebellion. David both recognized and admitted his terrible sins, turned his heart back to God, and accepted God's rebuke in humility (12:9–13,20; 16:5–12; 24:10–25; Ps. 51).

11:11 THE ARK, AND ISRAEL. Uriah proved to be a better man than David. His actions were based on his commitment to God and his comradeship with those fighting the Lord's battle. He paid for his dedication with his life.

11:14–15 DAVID WROTE A LETTER ... THAT HE MAY BE SMITTEN, AND DIE. Instead of confessing his sin, David decided to have Uriah murdered and then to take his wife. The words that the apostle John applied to Cain and all other murderers (1 John 3:12–15) apply also to David at this time: "whosoever hateth his brother is a murderer: and ye know that no murderer hath eternal life abiding in him" (1 John 3:15). He could be restored only through sincere and heartfelt repentance before God (see ch. 12; Ps. 51).

approached ye so nigh unto the city when ye did fight? knew ye not that they would shoot from the wall?

21 Who smote [c]Abimelech the son of [d]Jerubbesheth? did not a woman cast a piece of a millstone upon him from the wall, that he died in Thebez? why went ye nigh the wall? then say thou, Thy servant Uriah the Hittite is dead also.

22 ¶ So the messenger went, and came and showed David all that Joab had sent him for.

23 And the messenger said unto David, Surely the men prevailed against us, and came out unto us into the field, and we were upon them even unto the entering of the gate.

24 And the shooters shot from off the wall upon thy servants; and *some* of the king's servants be dead, and thy servant Uriah the Hittite is dead also.

25 Then David said unto the messenger, Thus shalt thou say unto Joab, Let not this thing [i]displease thee, for the sword devoureth [j]one as well as another: make thy battle more strong against the city, and overthrow it: and encourage thou him.

26 ¶ And when the wife of Uriah heard that Uriah her husband was dead, she mourned for her husband.

27 And when the mourning was past, David sent and fetched her to his house, and she [e]became his wife, and bare him a son. But the thing that David had done [k]displeased the LORD.

David repents

11:1; 12:29–31pp — 1 Chr. 20:1–3

12 AND THE LORD sent Nathan unto David. And [f]he came unto him, and [g]said unto him, There were two men in one city; the one rich, and the other poor.

2 The rich *man* had exceeding many flocks and herds:

3 But the poor *man* had nothing, save one little ewe lamb, which he had bought and nourished up: and it grew up together with him, and with his children; it did eat of his own [l]meat, and drank of his own cup, and lay in his bosom, and was unto him as a daughter.

4 And there came a traveller unto the rich man, and he spared to take of his own flock and of his own herd, to dress for the wayfaring man that was come unto him; but took the poor man's lamb, and dressed it for the man that was come to him.

5 And David's anger was greatly kindled against the man; and he said to Nathan, *As* the LORD liveth, the man that hath done this *thing* [h]shall[m] surely die:

6 And he shall restore the lamb [i]fourfold, because he did this thing, and because he had no pity.

7 ¶ And Nathan said to David, Thou *art* the man. Thus saith the LORD God of Israel, I [j]anointed thee king over Israel, and I delivered thee out of the hand of Saul;

8 And I gave thee thy master's house, and thy master's wives into thy bosom, and gave thee the house of Israel and of Judah; and if *that had been* too little, I would moreover have given unto thee such and such things.

9 [k]Wherefore hast thou [l]despised the commandment of the LORD, to do evil in his sight? [m]thou hast killed Uriah the Hittite with the sword, and hast taken his wife *to be* thy wife, and hast

11:21 [c]Judg. 9:53 [d]Judg. 6:32 *Jerubbaal*
11:27 [e]ch. 12:9
12:1 [f]Ps. 51,title [g]See ch. 14:5 1 Ki. 20:35-41 Is. 5:3
12:5 [h]1 Sam. 26:16
12:6 [i]Ex. 22:1 Luke 19:8
12:7 [j]1 Sam. 16:13
12:9 [k]See 1 Sam. 15:19 [l]Num. 15:31 [m]ch. 11:15-17,27

i Heb. *be evil in thine eyes* **j** Heb. *so and such* **k** Heb. *was evil in the eyes of* **l** Heb. *morsel* **m** Or, is *worthy to die,* or, is *a son of death*

11:27 THE THING ... DISPLEASED THE LORD. David's sins of adultery, cold-blooded murder, and subsequent cover-up were an exceptional evil in God's sight. He became guilty of breaking the sixth, seventh, eighth, ninth, and tenth commandments (Ex. 20:13–17). His sins were made greater because he was a shepherd over God's people (5:2) and the one who was responsible to administer justice and righteousness in Israel (8:15).

12:9 HAST THOU DESPISED THE COMMANDMENT OF THE LORD. The prophet Nathan declared that David, in committing adultery, murder, and deceit, was guilty of despising "the commandment of the LORD" and despising God Himself (v. 10). "Despise" (Heb. *bazah*) means to treat contemptuously, to scorn, to make of little account. Thus by his actions, David was declaring God to be of little account, unworthy of love and devotion.

(1) Likewise in the church today, ministers of God who commit adultery reflect their estimate of God and His holy Word. They treat the gospel and the blood of Christ contemptuously, as if they are petty and unworthy of fidelity.

(2) The Scriptures state that any professed believer who enters into an adulterous relationship disqualify himself from the office of an overseer (1 Tim. 3:2; see article on MORAL QUALIFICATIONS FOR OVERSEERS, p. 1908).

slain him with the sword of the children of Ammon.

10 Now therefore [n]the sword shall never depart from thine house; because thou hast despised me, and hast taken the wife of Uriah the Hittite to be thy wife.

11 Thus saith the LORD, Behold, I will raise up evil against thee out of thine own house, and I will [o]take thy wives before thine eyes, and give *them* unto thy neighbour, and he shall lie with thy wives in the sight of this sun.

12 For thou didst *it* secretly: [p]but I will do this thing before all Israel, and before the sun.

13 [q]And David said unto Nathan, [r]I have sinned against the LORD. And Nathan said unto David, The LORD also hath [s]put away thy sin; thou shalt not die.

14 Howbeit, because by this deed thou hast given great occasion to the enemies of the LORD [t]to blaspheme, the child also *that is* born unto thee shall surely die.

15 ¶ And Nathan departed unto his house. And the LORD struck the child that Uriah's wife bare unto David, and it was very sick.

16 David therefore besought God for the child; and David [n]fasted, and went in, and [u]lay all night upon the earth.

17 And the elders of his house arose, *and went* to him, to raise him up from the earth: but he would not, neither did he eat bread with them.

18 And it came to pass on the seventh day, that the child died. And the servants of David feared to tell him that the child was dead: for they said, Behold, while the child was yet alive, we spake unto him, and he would not hearken unto our voice: how will he then [o]vex himself, if we tell him that the child is dead?

19 But when David saw that his servants whispered, David perceived that the child was dead: therefore David said unto his servants, Is the child dead? And they said, He is dead.

20 Then David arose from the earth, and washed, and anointed *himself,* and changed his apparel, and came into the house of the LORD, and [v]worshipped: then he came to his own house; and when he required, they set bread before him, and he did eat.

21 Then said his servants unto him, What thing *is* this that thou hast done? thou didst fast and weep for the child, *while it was* alive; but when the child was dead, thou didst rise and eat bread.

22 And he said, While the child was yet alive, I fasted and wept: [w]for I

12:10 [n]Amos 7:9
12:11 [o]Deut. 28:30 ch. 16:22
12:12 [p]ch. 16:22
12:13 [q]See 1 Sam. 15:24 [r]ch. 24:10 Job 7:20 Prov. 28:13 [s]ch. 24:10 Job 7:21 Mic. 7:18 Zech. 3:4
12:14 [t]Is. 52:5 Ezek. 36:20,23 Rom. 2:24
12:16 [u]ch. 13:31
12:20 [v]Job 1:20
12:22 [w]See Is. 38:1,5 Jonah 3:9

[n] Heb. *fasted a fast* [o] Heb. *do hurt*

12:10 THE SWORD SHALL NEVER DEPART FROM THINE HOUSE. Because David had despised God and killed Uriah in order to take Uriah's wife for himself, God pronounced judgment on David and his family that would be fulfilled in violence, strife, and murder (i.e., the sword) for the rest of his life (approximately twenty-five years). The Scriptures record at least four events as a result of this curse: the death of the child (v. 14), the murder of Amnon by Absalom (13:29), the killing of Absalom when he turned against his father (18:9–17), and the execution of Adonijah (1 Ki. 2:24–25).

12:11–12 THUS SAITH THE LORD ... I WILL. David's dreadful punishment as prophesied by Nathan was not merely the natural consequences of his sin, nor was God passively permitting things to happen to David; rather, it was the result of God's direct actions. Three times God used the term "I will": "*I will* raise up evil against thee"; "*I will* take thy wives before thine eyes"; "*I will* do this thing before all Israel." He would experience atrocities at the hands of his own children, such as the raping of David's daughter Tamar by Amnon (13:7–14; see 13:1, note) and the violation of David's wives by Absalom (16:22).

12:12 BEFORE ALL ISRAEL. The prescribed punishment in Israel for adultery and murder was death (Lev. 20:10; 24:17). However, God remitted the punishment in this instance, not so much because of David's repentance, but because He had to vindicate Himself and His righteousness publicly before all Israel and the nations. For the rest of David's life he was an example of the righteous judgment of God upon a spiritual leader who had sinned greatly.

12:13 THE LORD ALSO HATH PUT AWAY THY SIN. David's sin was forgiven by God in that the death penalty and eternal punishment were remitted (cf. 1 John 3:15). Thus, David was restored to salvation and fellowship with God (cf. Ps. 51). In spite of this, his reputation was forever blemished and the effects of his sin continued throughout the remainder of his life and family history. David's experience after he was forgiven and restored is a sober lesson for those who treat sin casually as something that God simply forgives and forgets.

12:15 NATHAN DEPARTED UNTO HIS HOUSE. David admitted his sin to Nathan (v. 13). Shortly thereafter, David repented before God and accepted His judgment (see Ps. 51 for David's prayer of confession and repentance).

said, Who can tell *whether* GOD will be gracious to me, that the child may live?

23 But now he is dead, wherefore should I fast? can I bring him back again? I shall go to him, but [x]he shall not return to me.

24 ¶ And David comforted Bathsheba his wife, and went in unto her, and lay with her: and [y]she bare a son, and [z]he called his name Solomon: and the LORD loved him.

25 And he sent by the hand of Nathan the prophet; and he called his name [p]Jedidiah, because of the LORD.

Victory over the Ammonites

26 ¶ And [a]Joab fought against [b]Rabbah of the children of Ammon, and took the royal city.

27 And Joab sent messengers to David, and said, I have fought against Rabbah, and have taken the city of waters.

28 Now therefore gather the rest of the people together, and encamp against the city, and take it: lest I take the city, and [q]it be called after my name.

29 And David gathered all the people together, and went to Rabbah, and fought against it, and took it.

30 [c]And he took their king's crown from off his head, the weight whereof *was* a talent of gold with the precious stones: and it was *set* on David's head. And he brought forth the spoil of the city [r]in great abundance.

31 And he brought forth the people that *were* therein, and put *them* under saws, and under harrows of iron, and under axes of iron, and made them pass through the brickkiln: and thus did he unto all the cities of the children of Ammon. So David and all the people returned unto Jerusalem.

12:23 [x]Job 7:8-10
12:24 [y]Mat. 1:6 [z]1 Chr. 22:9
12:26 [a]1 Chr. 20:1 [b]Deut. 3:11
12:30 [c]1 Chr. 20:2
13:1 [d]ch. 3:2,3 [e]1 Chr. 3:9
13:3 [f]See 1 Sam. 16:9
13:6 [g]Gen. 18:6

Amnon defiles Tamar

13 AND IT came to pass after this, [d]that Absalom the son of David had a fair sister, whose name *was* [e]Tamar; and Amnon the son of David loved her.

2 And Amnon was so vexed, that he fell sick for his sister Tamar; for she *was* a virgin; and [s]Amnon thought it hard for him to do any thing to her.

3 But Amnon had a friend, whose name *was* Jonadab, [f]the son of Shimeah David's brother: and Jonadab *was* a very subtle man.

4 And he said unto him, Why *art* thou, *being* the king's son, [t]lean [u]from day to day? wilt thou not tell me? And Amnon said unto him, I love Tamar, my brother Absalom's sister.

5 And Jonadab said unto him, Lay thee down on thy bed, and make thyself sick: and when thy father cometh to see thee, say unto him, I pray thee, let my sister Tamar come, and give me meat, and dress the meat in my sight, that I may see *it*, and eat *it* at her hand.

6 ¶ So Amnon lay down, and made himself sick: and when the king was come to see him, Amnon said unto the king, I pray thee, let Tamar my sister come, and [g]make me a couple of cakes in my sight, that I may eat at her hand.

7 Then David sent home to Tamar, saying, Go now to thy brother Amnon's house, and dress him meat.

8 So Tamar went to her brother Amnon's house; and he was laid down. And she took [v]flour, and kneaded *it*, and made cakes in his sight, and did bake the cakes.

[p] i.e. *Beloved of the LORD* [q] Heb. *my name be called upon it* [r] Heb. *very great* [s] Heb. *it was marvellous,* or, *hidden in the eyes of Amnon* [t] Heb. *thin* [u] Heb. *morning by morning* [v] Or, *paste*

12:24 BATHSHEBA HIS WIFE. Did David benefit from his sins of lust and murder? He engineered the death of Bathsheba's husband and then possessed the woman he desired. Perhaps the severity of God's punishment of David for the next twenty-five years was due partly to the fact that David had not faced the reality that he had no legal or moral right to take and keep Uriah's wife: (1) God had commanded that kings were not to multiply wives (Deut. 17:17); and (2) he had disobeyed several of the Ten Commandments in this episode (see 11:27, note). For this God declared, "the sword shall never depart from thine house; because thou . . . hast taken the wife of Uriah the Hittite to be thy wife" (v. 10).

13:1 TAMAR . . . AMNON. The series of narratives in chs. 13—22 are mainly accounts of the fulfillment of God's purpose to raise up evil against David. (1) Ch. 13 records the first result of David's sins of lust, adultery, and murder (cf. Gal. 6:7). Incest and murder broke out within his own home, as David's lust was first reproduced in his son Amnon. (2) Since David destroyed the happiness of Uriah's house, God destroyed the happiness of David's house. Many times, God lays upon the transgressor great suffering and sorrow so that he and others might fear God and turn away from sin (cf. Num. 14:20–36).

9 And she took a pan, and poured *them* out before him; but he refused to eat. And Amnon said, [h]Have out all men from me. And they went out every man from him.

10 And Amnon said unto Tamar, Bring the meat into the chamber, that I may eat of thine hand. And Tamar took the cakes which she had made, and brought *them* into the chamber to Amnon her brother.

11 And when she had brought *them* unto him to eat, he [i]took hold of her, and said unto her, Come lie with me, my sister.

12 And she answered him, Nay, my brother, do not [j]force[w] me; for [k]no[x] such thing ought to be done in Israel: do not thou this [l]folly.

13 And I, whither shall I cause my shame to go? and as for thee, thou shalt be as one of the fools in Israel. Now therefore, I pray thee, speak unto the king; [m]for he will not withhold me from thee.

14 Howbeit he would not hearken unto her voice: but, being stronger than she, [n]forced her, and lay with her.

15 ¶ Then Amnon hated her [y]exceedingly; so that the hatred wherewith he hated her *was* greater than the love wherewith he had loved her. And Amnon said unto her, Arise, be gone.

16 And she said unto him, *There is* no cause: this evil in sending me away *is* greater than the other that thou didst unto me. But he would not hearken unto her.

17 Then he called his servant that ministered unto him, and said, Put now this *woman* out from me, and bolt the door after her.

18 And *she had* [o]a garment of divers colours upon her: for with such robes were the king's daughters *that were* virgins apparelled. Then his servant brought her out, and bolted the door after her.

13:9 [h]Gen. 45:1
13:11 [i]Gen. 39:12
13:12 [j]Gen. 34:2 [k]Lev. 18:9,11 & 20:17 [l]Gen. 34:7 Judg. 19:23 & 20:6
13:13 [m]See Lev. 18:9,11
13:14 [n]Deut. 22:25 See ch. 12:11
13:18 [o]Gen. 37:3 Judg. 5:30
13:19 [p]Josh. 7:6 ch. 1:2 Job 2:12 [q]Jer. 2:37
13:22 [r]Gen. 24:50 & 31:24 [s]Lev. 19:17,18
13:23 [t]See Gen. 38:12, 13 1 Sam. 25:4,36
13:28 [u]Judg. 19:6,9,22 Ruth 3:7 1 Sam. 25:36 Esth. 1:10

19 ¶ And Tamar put [p]ashes on her head, and rent her garment of divers colours that *was* on her, and [q]laid her hand on her head, and went on crying.

20 And Absalom her brother said unto her, Hath [z]Amnon thy brother been with thee? but hold now thy peace, my sister: he *is* thy brother; [a]regard not this thing. So Tamar remained [b]desolate in her brother Absalom's house.

21 ¶ But when king David heard of all these things, he was very wroth.

22 And Absalom spake unto his brother Amnon [r]neither good nor bad: for Absalom [s]hated Amnon, because he had forced his sister Tamar.

Absalom kills Amnon

23 ¶ And it came to pass after two full years, that Absalom [t]had sheepshearers in Baal-hazor, which *is* beside Ephraim: and Absalom invited all the king's sons.

24 And Absalom came to the king, and said, Behold now, thy servant hath sheepshearers; let the king, I beseech thee, and his servants go with thy servant.

25 And the king said to Absalom, Nay, my son, let us not all now go, lest we be chargeable unto thee. And he pressed him: howbeit he would not go, but blessed him.

26 Then said Absalom, If not, I pray thee, let my brother Amnon go with us. And the king said unto him, Why should he go with thee?

27 But Absalom pressed him, that he let Amnon and all the king's sons go with him.

28 ¶ Now Absalom had commanded his servants, saying, Mark ye now when Amnon's [u]heart is merry with wine, and when I say unto you, Smite

[w] Heb. *humble me* [x] Heb. *it ought not so to be done* [y] Heb. *with great hatred greatly* [z] Heb. *Aminon* [a] Heb. *set not thine heart* [b] Heb. *and desolate*

13:21 DAVID . . . WAS VERY WROTH. David was very angry at the rape of his daughter by his firstborn son (1 Chr. 3:1). Yet, he could not bring himself to rebuke and punish Amnon as he should have (see Lev. 20:17). (1) David's own sexual immorality with Bathsheba weakened and undermined his ability to discipline his sons and manage his own household. Since David was not above reproach himself (see Prov. 6:32–33), he lacked the authority and moral courage to rebuke his son. His own poor example destroyed his moral influence with those under his care. (2) Under the new covenant, leaders in the church must be examples of holiness so that when they rebuke sin, they need not fear reproach and thereby compromise God's standards as revealed in His Word (1 Tim. 3:1–13).

13:28 SMITE AMNON; THEN KILL HIM. God permitted Absalom's vengeance to punish Amnon's crime against Tamar. At times God uses human sin to achieve His purposes, punishing one wrongdoer through the sin of another.

Amnon; then kill him, fear not: [c]have
not I commanded you? be courageous,
and be [d]valiant.
29 And the servants of Absalom did
unto Amnon as Absalom had com-
manded. Then all the king's sons
arose, and every man [e]gat him up
upon his mule, and fled.
30 ¶ And it came to pass, while they
were in the way, that tidings came to
David, saying, Absalom hath slain all
the king's sons, and there is not one of
them left.
31 Then the king arose, and [v]tare
his garments, and [w]lay on the earth;
and all his servants stood by with their
clothes rent.
32 And [x]Jonadab, the son of Shim-
eah David's brother, answered and
said, Let not my lord suppose *that* they
have slain all the young men the king's
sons; for Amnon only is dead: for by
the [f]appointment of Absalom this
hath been [g]determined from the day
that he forced his sister Tamar.
33 Now therefore [y]let not my lord
the king take the thing to his heart, to
think that all the king's sons are dead:
for Amnon only is dead.

Absalom flees to Geshur

34 [z]But Absalom fled. And the
young man that kept the watch lifted
up his eyes, and looked, and, behold,
there came much people by the way of
the hill side behind him.
35 And Jonadab said unto the king,
Behold, the king's sons come: [h]as thy
servant said, so it is.
36 And it came to pass, as soon as
he had made an end of speaking, that,
behold, the king's sons came, and lift-
ed up their voice and wept: and the
king also and all his servants wept
[i]very sore.
37 ¶ But Absalom fled, and went to
[a]Talmai, the son of [j]Ammihud, king
of Geshur. And *David* mourned for his
son every day.
38 So Absalom fled, and went to
[b]Geshur, and was there three years.
39 And *the soul of* king David
[k]longed to go forth unto Absalom: for
he was [c]comforted concerning Am-
non, seeing he was dead.

Absalom's return

14 NOW JOAB the son of Zeruiah
perceived that the king's heart
was [d]toward Absalom.
2 And Joab sent to [e]Tekoah, and
fetched thence a wise woman, and said
unto her, I pray thee, feign thyself to be
a mourner, [f]and put on now mourning
apparel, and anoint not thyself with oil,
but be as a woman that had a long time
mourned for the dead:
3 And come to the king, and speak
on this manner unto him. So Joab [g]put
the words in her mouth.
4 ¶ And when the woman of Tekoah
spake to the king, she [h]fell on her face
to the ground, and did obeisance, and
said, [i]Help,[l] O king.
5 And the king said unto her, What
aileth thee? And she answered, [j]I *am*
indeed a widow woman, and mine hus-
band is dead.
6 And thy handmaid had two sons,
and they two strove together in the
field, and *there was* [m]none to part
them, but the one smote the other, and
slew him.
7 And, behold, the whole family is
risen against thine handmaid, and they
said, Deliver him that smote his broth-
er, that we may kill him, for the life of
his brother whom he slew; and we will
destroy the heir also: and so they shall
quench my coal which is left, and shall
not leave to my husband *neither* name
nor remainder [n]upon the earth.
8 And the king said unto the wom-
an, Go to thine house, and I will give
charge concerning thee.

13:31 [v]ch. 1:11 [w]ch. 12:16
13:32 [x]ver. 3
13:33 [y]ch. 19:19
13:34 [z]ver. 38
13:37 [a]ch. 3:3
13:38 [b]ch. 14:23,32 & 15:8
13:39 [c]Gen. 38:12
14:1 [d]ch. 13:39
14:2 [e]2 Chr. 11:6 [f]See Ruth 3:3
14:3 [g]ver. 19 Ex. 4:15
14:4 [h]1 Sam. 20:41 ch. 1:2 [i]See 2 Ki. 6:26,28
14:5 [j]See ch. 12:1

c Or, *will you not, since I have commanded you?* **d** Heb. *sons of valour* **e** Heb. *rode* **f** Heb. *mouth* **g** Or, *settled* **h** Heb. *according to the word of thy servant* **i** Heb. *with a great weeping greatly* **j** Or, *Ammihur* **k** Or, *was consumed* **l** Heb. *Save* **m** Heb. *no deliverer between them* **n** Heb. *upon the face of the earth*

13:36 THE KING . . . WEPT. After Absalom killed Amnon, David was grief-stricken. The agony of David as a result of God's chastisement has no parallel in Biblical history. God permitted sin and Satan to inflict great suffering upon him. Though David was forgiven by God and did not suffer eternal punishment for his sin (see12:13, note), nevertheless the temporal consequences, both natural and divine, continued unabated until his death. The actions of Absalom and Amnon were only the beginning of the evil that God raised up against David (12:11) because he had despised God and His Word by cruelly killing Uriah in order to conceal his sin with Bathsheba (12:9–10).

9 And the woman of Tekoah said
unto the king, My lord, O king, [k]the
iniquity *be* on me, and on my father's
house: [l]and the king and his throne *be*
guiltless.
10 And the king said, Whosoever
saith *aught* unto thee, bring him to me,
and he shall not touch thee any more.
11 Then said she, I pray thee, let
the king remember the LORD thy God,
[o]that thou wouldest not suffer [m]the
revengers of blood to destroy any
more, lest they destroy my son. And he
said, [n]*As* the LORD liveth, there shall
not one hair of thy son fall to the earth.
12 Then the woman said, Let thine
handmaid, I pray thee, speak *one* word
unto my lord the king. And he said,
Say on.
13 And the woman said, Wherefore
then hast thou thought such a thing
against [o]the people of God? for the
king doth speak this thing as one
which is faulty, in that the king doth
not fetch home again [p]his banished.
14 For we [q]must needs die, and *are*
as water spilt on the ground, which
cannot be gathered up again; [p]neither
doth God respect *any* person: yet doth
he [r]devise means, that his banished
be not expelled from him.
15 Now therefore that I am come to
speak of this thing unto my lord the
king, *it is* because the people have
made me afraid: and thy handmaid
said, I will now speak unto the king; it
may be that the king will perform the
request of his handmaid.
16 For the king will hear, to deliver
his handmaid out of the hand of the
man *that would* destroy me and my son
together out of the inheritance of God.
17 Then thine handmaid said, The
word of my lord the king shall now be
[q]comfortable: for [s]as an angel of
God, so *is* my lord the king [r]to discern
good and bad: therefore the LORD thy
God will be with thee.
18 Then the king answered and said
unto the woman, Hide not from me, I
pray thee, the thing that I shall ask
thee. And the woman said, Let my lord
the king now speak.
19 And the king said, *Is not* the
hand of Joab with thee in all this? And
the woman answered and said, *As* thy
soul liveth, my lord the king, none can
turn to the right hand or to the left
from aught that my lord the king hath
spoken: for thy servant Joab, he bade
me, and [t]he put all these words in the
mouth of thine handmaid:
20 To fetch about this form of
speech hath thy servant Joab done this
thing: and my lord *is* wise, [u]according
to the wisdom of an angel of God, to
know all *things* that *are* in the earth.
21 ¶ And the king said unto Joab,
Behold now, I have done this thing: go
therefore, bring the young man Absa-
lom again.
22 And Joab fell to the ground on
his face, and bowed himself, and
[s]thanked the king: and Joab said, To-
day thy servant knoweth that I have
found grace in thy sight, my lord,
O king, in that the king hath fulfilled
the request of [t]his servant.
23 So Joab arose [v]and went to Ge-
shur, and brought Absalom to Jerusa-
lem.
24 And the king said, Let him turn
to his own house, and let him [w]not see
my face. So Absalom returned to his
own house, and saw not the king's
face.
25 ¶ [u]But in all Israel there was
none to be so much praised as Absalom
for his beauty: [x]from the sole of his
foot even to the crown of his head there
was no blemish in him.
26 And when he polled his head,
(for it was at every year's end that he
polled *it:* because *the hair* was heavy on
him, therefore he polled it:) he weighed
the hair of his head at two hundred
shekels after the king's weight.
27 And [y]unto Absalom there were
born three sons, and one daughter,
whose name *was* Tamar: she was a
woman of a fair countenance.
28 ¶ So Absalom dwelt two full
years in Jerusalem, [z]and saw not the
king's face.
29 Therefore Absalom sent for Joab,
to have sent him to the king; but he
would not come to him: and when he
sent again the second time, he would
not come.
30 Therefore he said unto his ser-
vants, See, Joab's field is [v]near mine,
and he hath barley there; go and set it

14:9 [k]Gen. 27:13 1 Sam. 25:24 Mat. 27:25 [l]ch. 3:28,29 1 Ki. 2:33
14:11 [m]Num. 35:19 [n]1 Sam. 14:45 Acts 27:34
14:13 [o]Judg. 20:2 [p]ch. 13:37,38
14:14 [q]Job 34:15 Heb. 9:27 [r]Num. 35:15,25, 28
14:17 [s]ver. 20 ch. 19:27
14:19 [t]ver. 3
14:20 [u]ver. 17 ch. 19:27
14:23 [v]ch. 13:37
14:24 [w]Gen. 43:3 ch. 3:13
14:25 [x]Is. 1:6
14:27 [y]See ch. 18:18
14:28 [z]ver. 24

[o] Heb. *that the revenger of blood do not multiply to destroy* [p] Or, *because God hath not taken away his life, he hath also devised means* [q] Heb. *for rest* [r] Heb. *to hear* [s] Heb. *blessed* [t] Or, *thy* [u] Heb. *And as Absalom there was not a beautiful man in all Israel to praise greatly* [v] Heb. *near my place*

on fire. And Absalom's servants set the field on fire.

31 Then Joab arose, and came to Absalom unto *his* house, and said unto him, Wherefore have thy servants set my field on fire?

32 And Absalom answered Joab, Behold, I sent unto thee, saying, Come hither, that I may send thee to the king, to say, Wherefore am I come from Geshur? *it had been* good for me *to have been* there still: now therefore let me see the king's face; and if there be *any* iniquity in me, let him kill me.

33 So Joab came to the king, and told him: and when he had called for Absalom, he came to the king, and bowed himself on his face to the ground before the king: and the king [a]kissed Absalom.

Absalom's revolt against David

15 AND [b]IT came to pass after this, that Absalom [c]prepared him chariots and horses, and fifty men to run before him.

2 And Absalom rose up early, and stood beside the way of the gate: and it was *so,* that when any man that had a controversy [w]came to the king for judgment, then Absalom called unto him, and said, Of what city *art* thou? And he said, Thy servant *is* of one of the tribes of Israel.

3 And Absalom said unto him, See, thy matters *are* good and right; but [x]*there is* no man *deputed* of the king to hear thee.

4 Absalom said moreover, [d]Oh that I were made judge in the land, that every man which hath any suit or cause might come unto me, and I would do him justice!

5 And it was *so,* that when any man came nigh *to him* to do him obeisance, he put forth his hand, and took him, and kissed him.

6 And on this manner did Absalom to all Israel that came to the king for judgment: [e]so Absalom stole the hearts of the men of Israel.

7 ¶ And it came to pass [f]after forty years, that Absalom said unto the king, I pray thee, let me go and pay my vow, which I have vowed unto the LORD, in Hebron.

8 [g]For thy servant [h]vowed a vow [i]while I abode at Geshur in Syria, saying, If the LORD shall bring me again indeed to Jerusalem, then I will serve the LORD.

9 And the king said unto him, Go in peace. So he arose, and went to Hebron.

10 ¶ But Absalom sent spies throughout all the tribes of Israel, saying, As soon as ye hear the sound of the trumpet, then ye shall say, Absalom reigneth in Hebron.

11 And with Absalom went two hundred men out of Jerusalem, *that were* [j]called; and they went [k]in their simplicity, and they knew not any thing.

12 And Absalom sent for Ahithophel the Gilonite, [l]David's counsellor, from his city, *even* from [m]Giloh, while he offered sacrifices. And the conspiracy was strong; for the people [n]increased continually with Absalom.

David and his household flee

13 ¶ And there came a messenger to David, saying, [o]The hearts of the men of Israel are after Absalom.

14 And David said unto all his servants that *were* with him at Jerusalem, Arise, and let us [p]flee; for we shall not *else* escape from Absalom: make speed to depart, lest he overtake us suddenly, and [y]bring evil upon us, and smite the city with the edge of the sword.

15 And the king's servants said unto the king, Behold, thy servants *are ready to do* whatsoever my lord the king shall [z]appoint.

16 And [q]the king went forth, and all his household [a]after him. And the

14:33 [a]Gen. 33:4 & 45:15 Luke 15:20
15:1 [b]ch. 12:11 [c]1 Ki. 1:5
15:4 [d]Judg. 9:29
15:6 [e]Rom. 16:18
15:7 [f]1 Sam. 16:1
15:8 [g]1 Sam. 16:2 [h]Gen. 28:20,21 [i]ch. 13:38
15:11 [j]1 Sam. 9:13 & 16:3,5 [k]Gen. 20:5
15:12 [l]Ps. 41:9 & 55:12-14 [m]Josh. 15:51 [n]Ps. 3:1
15:13 [o]ver. 6 Judg. 9:3
15:14 [p]ch. 19:9 Ps. 3,title
15:16 [q]Ps. 3,title

[w]Heb. *to come* [x]Or, *none will hear thee from the king* downward [y]Heb. *thrust* [z]Heb. *choose* [a]Heb. *at his feet*

15:6 ABSALOM STOLE THE HEARTS . . . OF ISRAEL. Absalom conspired for four years to steal the throne from his father, and the people increasingly turned against David (vv. 1–15). Absalom's success reveals that David, because of his sin and consequent failure to manage his own house, had lost much of the people's respect. His ability to lead, once based on a persevering faithfulness to his God, was now eroded because of his sin and severely marred reputation.

15:14 ARISE, AND LET US FLEE. David was forced to flee from his own son, who now sought to kill him and gain the throne. David left Jerusalem "and wept as he went" (v. 30). David likely remembered his sin and recognized that this was part of God's retribution (cf. 12:9–12; 16:10–11). David, now a humiliated fugitive, humbly accepted God's dealing with him (vv. 25–26; cf. 16:9–13).

king left [r]ten women, *which were* concubines, to keep the house.

17 And the king went forth, and all the people after him, and tarried in a place that was far off.

18 And all his servants passed on beside him; [s]and all the Cherethites, and all the Pelethites, and all the Gittites, six hundred men which came after him from Gath, passed on before the king.

19 ¶ Then said the king to [t]Ittai the Gittite, Wherefore goest thou also with us? return to thy place, and abide with the king: for thou *art* a stranger, and also an exile.

20 Whereas thou camest *but* yesterday, should I this day [b]make thee go up and down with us? seeing I go [u]whither I may, return thou, and take back thy brethren: mercy and truth *be* with thee.

21 And Ittai answered the king, and said, [v]*As* the LORD liveth, and *as* my lord the king liveth, surely in what place my lord the king shall be, whether in death or life, even there also will thy servant be.

22 And David said to Ittai, Go and pass over. And Ittai the Gittite passed over, and all his men, and all the little ones that *were* with him.

23 And all the country wept with a loud voice, and all the people passed over: the king also himself passed over the brook [c]Kidron, and all the people passed over, toward the way of the [w]wilderness.

24 ¶ And lo Zadok also, and all the Levites *were* with him, bearing the ark of the covenant of God: and they set down the ark of God; and Abiathar went up, until all the people had done passing out of the city.

25 And the king said unto Zadok, Carry back the ark of God into the city: if I shall find favour in the eyes of the LORD, he [x]will bring me again, and show me *both* it, and his habitation:

26 But if he thus say, I have no [y]delight in thee; behold, *here am* I, [z]let him do to me as seemeth good unto him.

27 The king said also unto Zadok the priest, *Art not* thou a [a]seer? return into the city in peace, and [b]your two sons with you, Ahimaaz thy son, and Jonathan the son of Abiathar.

28 See, [c]I will tarry in the plain of the wilderness, until there come word from you to certify me.

29 Zadok therefore and Abiathar carried the ark of God again to Jerusalem: and they tarried there.

30 ¶ And David went up by the ascent of *mount* Olivet, [d]and wept as he went up, and [d]had his head covered, and he went [e]barefoot: and all the people that *was* with him [f]covered every man his head, and they went up, [g]weeping as they went up.

31 ¶ And *one* told David, saying, [h]Ahithophel *is* among the conspirators with Absalom. And David said, O LORD, I pray thee, [i]turn the counsel of Ahithophel into foolishness.

32 ¶ And it came to pass, that *when* David was come to the top *of the mount*, where he worshipped God, behold, Hushai the [j]Archite came to meet him [k]with his coat rent, and earth upon his head:

33 Unto whom David said, If thou passest on with me, then thou shalt be [l]a burden unto me:

34 But if thou return to the city, and say unto Absalom, [m]I will be thy servant, O king; *as* I *have been* thy father's servant hitherto, so *will* I now also *be* thy servant: then mayest thou for me defeat the counsel of Ahithophel.

35 And *hast thou* not there with thee Zadok and Abiathar the priests? therefore it shall be, *that* what thing soever thou shalt hear out of the king's house, [n]thou shalt tell *it* to Zadok and Abiathar the priests.

36 Behold, *they have* there [o]with them their two sons, Ahimaaz Zadok's *son*, and Jonathan Abiathar's *son;* and by them ye shall send unto me every thing that ye can hear.

37 So Hushai [p]David's friend came into the city, [q]and Absalom came into Jerusalem.

Ziba's lie

16 AND [r]WHEN David was a little past the top *of the hill*, behold, [s]Ziba the servant of Mephibosheth met him, with a couple of asses saddled, and upon them two hundred *loaves* of bread, and an hundred bunches of raisins, and an hundred of summer fruits, and a bottle of wine.

15:16 [r]ch. 16:21,22
15:18 [s]ch. 8:18
15:19 [t]ch. 18:2
15:20 [u]1 Sam. 23:13
15:21 [v]Ruth 1:16,17
15:23 [w]ch. 16:2
15:25 [x]Ps. 43:3
15:26 [y]Num. 14:8 ch. 22:20 1 Ki. 10:9 2 Chr. 9:8 Is. 62:4 [z]1 Sam. 3:18
15:27 [a]1 Sam. 9:9 [b]See ch. 17:17
15:28 [c]ch. 17:16
15:30 [d]ch. 19:4 Esth. 6:12 [e]Is. 20:2,4 [f]Jer. 14:3,4 [g]Ps. 126:6
15:31 [h]Ps. 3:1,2 & 55:12 [i]ch. 16:23 & 17:14,23
15:32 [j]Josh. 16:2 [k]ch. 1:2
15:33 [l]ch. 19:35
15:34 [m]ch. 16:19
15:35 [n]ch. 17:15,16
15:36 [o]ver. 27
15:37 [p]ch. 16:16 1 Chr. 27:33 [q]ch. 16:15
16:1 [r]ch. 15:30,32 [s]ch. 9:2

[b]Heb. *make thee wander in going* [c]Called *Cedron* in John 18:1 [d]Heb. *going up, and weeping*

2 And the king said unto Ziba, What meanest thou by these? And Ziba said, The asses *be* for the king's household to ride on; and the bread and summer fruit for the young men to eat; and the wine, [t]that such as be faint in the wilderness may drink.

3 And the king said, And where *is* thy master's son? [u]And Ziba said unto the king, Behold, he abideth at Jerusalem: for he said, Today shall the house of Israel restore me the kingdom of my father.

4 Then said the king to Ziba, Behold, thine *are* all that *pertained* unto Mephibosheth. And Ziba said, [e]I humbly beseech thee *that* I may find grace in thy sight, my lord, O king.

Shimei curses David

5 ¶ And when king David came to Bahurim, behold, thence came out a man of the family of the house of Saul, whose name *was* [v]Shimei, the son of Gera: [f]he came forth, and cursed still as he came.

6 And he cast stones at David, and at all the servants of king David: and all the people and all the mighty men *were* on his right hand and on his left.

7 And thus said Shimei when he cursed, Come out, come out, thou [g]bloody man, and thou [w]man of Belial:

8 The LORD hath [x]returned upon thee all [y]the blood of the house of Saul, in whose stead thou hast reigned; and the LORD hath delivered the kingdom into the hand of Absalom thy son: and, [h]behold, thou *art taken* in thy mischief, because thou *art* a bloody man.

9 ¶ Then said Abishai the son of Zeruiah unto the king, Why should this [z]dead dog [a]curse my lord the king? let me go over, I pray thee, and take off his head.

10 And the king said, [b]What have I to do with you, ye sons of Zeruiah? so let him curse, because [c]the LORD hath said unto him, Curse David. [d]Who shall then say, Wherefore hast thou done so?

11 And David said to Abishai, and to all his servants, Behold, [e]my son, which [f]came forth of my bowels, seeketh my life: how much more now *may this* Benjamite *do it?* let him alone, and let him curse; for the LORD hath bidden him.

12 It may be that the LORD will look on mine [i]affliction, and that the LORD will [g]requite me good for his cursing this day.

13 And as David and his men went by the way, Shimei went along on the hill's side over against him, and cursed as he went, and threw stones at him, and [j]cast dust.

14 And the king, and all the people that *were* with him, came weary, and refreshed themselves there.

The advice of Ahithophel

15 ¶ And [h]Absalom, and all the people the men of Israel, came to Jerusalem, and Ahithophel with him.

16 And it came to pass, when Hushai the Archite, [i]David's friend, was come unto Absalom, that Hushai said unto Absalom, [k]God save the king, God save the king.

17 And Absalom said to Hushai, *Is* this thy kindness to thy friend? [j]why wentest thou not with thy friend?

18 And Hushai said unto Absalom, Nay; but whom the LORD, and this people, and all the men of Israel, choose, his will I be, and with him will I abide.

19 And again, [k]whom should I serve? *should I* not *serve* in the presence of his son? as I have served in thy father's presence, so will I be in thy presence.

20 ¶ Then said Absalom to Ahithophel, Give counsel among you what we shall do.

21 And Ahithophel said unto Absalom, Go in unto thy father's [l]concubines, which he hath left to keep the house; and all Israel shall hear that thou [m]art abhorred of thy father: then shall [n]the hands of all that *are* with thee be strong.

22 So they spread Absalom a tent upon the top of the house; and Absa-

16:2 [t]ch. 15:23 & 17:29
16:3 [u]ch. 19:27
16:5 [v]ch. 19:16 1 Ki. 2:8,44
16:7 [w]Deut. 13:13
16:8 [x]Judg. 9:24,56,57 1 Ki. 2:32,33 [y]See ch. 1:16 & 3:28,29 & 4:11,12
16:9 [z]1 Sam. 24:14 ch. 9:8 [a]Ex. 22:28
16:10 [b]ch. 19:22 1 Pet. 2:23 [c]See 2 Ki. 18:25 Lam. 3:38 [d]Rom. 9:20
16:11 [e]ch. 12:11 [f]Gen. 15:4
16:12 [g]Rom. 8:28
16:15 [h]ch. 15:37
16:16 [i]ch. 15:37
16:17 [j]ch. 19:25 Prov. 17:17
16:19 [k]ch. 15:34
16:21 [l]ch. 15:16 & 20:3 [m]Gen. 34:30 1 Sam. 13:4 [n]ch. 2:7 Zech. 8:13

[e] Heb. *I do obeisance* [f] Or, *he still came forth and cursed* [g] Heb. *man of blood* [h] Heb. *behold thee in thy evil* [i] Or, *tears* [j] Heb. *dusted* him *with dust* [k] Heb. *Let the king live*

16:3 HE ABIDETH AT JERUSALEM. For more on this allegation about Mephibosheth, see 19:24–30.

16:22 HIS FATHER'S CONCUBINES. In open defiance of his father, Absalom committed adultery with David's own wives. Scripture states that the evil deed of Absalom took place "upon the top of the house" and "in the sight of all Israel." This

lom went in unto his father's concu-
bines [o]in the sight of all Israel.
23 And the counsel of Ahithophel,
which he counselled in those days, *was*
as if a man had inquired at the [l]oracle
of God: so *was* all the counsel of Ahith-
ophel [p]both with David and with Ab-
salom.

17 MOREOVER AHITHOPHEL
said unto Absalom, Let me now
choose out twelve thousand men, and
I will arise and pursue after David this
night:
2 And I will come upon him while he
is [q]weary and weak handed, and will
make him afraid: and all the people
that *are* with him shall flee; and I will
[r]smite the king only:
3 And I will bring back all the peo-
ple unto thee: the man whom thou
seekest *is* as if all returned: *so* all the
people shall be in peace.
4 And the saying [s]pleased[m] Absa-
lom well, and all the elders of Israel.

The advice of Hushai

5 Then said Absalom, Call now Hu-
shai the Archite also, and let us hear
likewise [n]what he saith.
6 And when Hushai was come to
Absalom, Absalom spake unto him,
saying, Ahithophel hath spoken after
this manner: shall we do *after* his
[o]saying? if not; speak thou.
7 And Hushai said unto Absalom,
The counsel that Ahithophel hath
[p]given *is* not good at this time.
8 For, said Hushai, thou knowest
thy father and his men, that they *be*
mighty men, and they *be* [q]chafed in
their minds, as [t]a bear robbed of her
whelps in the field: and thy father *is* a
man of war, and will not lodge with the
people.
9 Behold, he is hid now in some pit,
or in some *other* place: and it will come
to pass, when some of them be [r]over-
thrown at the first, that whosoever
heareth it will say, There is a slaughter
among the people that follow Absalom.
10 And he also *that is* valiant,
whose heart *is* as the heart of a lion,
shall utterly [u]melt: for all Israel
knoweth that thy father *is* a mighty
man, and *they* which *be* with him *are*
valiant men.
11 Therefore I counsel that all Isra-
el be generally gathered unto thee,
[v]from Dan even to Beer-sheba, [w]as
the sand that *is* by the sea for multi-
tude; and [s]that thou go to battle in
thine own person.
12 So shall we come upon him in
some place where he shall be found,
and we will light upon him as the dew
falleth on the ground: and of him and
of all the men that *are* with him there
shall not be left so much as one.
13 Moreover, if he be gotten into a
city, then shall all Israel bring ropes to
that city, and we will draw it into the
river, until there be not one small stone
found there.
14 And Absalom and all the men of
Israel said, The counsel of Hushai the
Archite *is* better than the counsel of
Ahithophel. For [x]the LORD had [t]ap-
pointed to defeat the good counsel of
Ahithophel, to the intent that the LORD
might bring evil upon Absalom.
15 ¶ [y]Then said Hushai unto Za-
dok and to Abiathar the priests, Thus
and thus did Ahithophel counsel Absa-
lom and the elders of Israel; and thus
and thus have I counselled.
16 Now therefore send quickly, and
tell David, saying, Lodge not this night
[z]in the plains of the wilderness, but
speedily pass over; lest the king be
swallowed up, and all the people that
are with him.
17 [a]Now Jonathan and Ahimaaz
[b]stayed by [c]En-rogel; for they might
not be seen to come into the city: and
a wench went and told them; and they
went and told king David.
18 Nevertheless a lad saw them,
and told Absalom: but they went both
of them away quickly, and came to a
man's house [d]in Bahurim, which had
a well in his court; whither they went
down.
19 And [e]the woman took and

16:22 [o]ch. 12:11,12
16:23 [p]ch. 15:12
17:2 [q]See Deut. 25:18 ch:16:14 [r]Zech. 13:7
17:4 [s]1 Sam. 18:20
17:8 [t]Hos. 13:8
17:10 [u]Josh. 2:11
17:11 [v]Judg. 20:1 [w]Gen. 22:17
17:14 [x]ch. 15:31,34
17:15 [y]ch. 15:35
17:16 [z]ch. 15:28
17:17 [a]ch. 15:27,36 [b]Josh. 2:4 [c]Josh. 15:7 & 18:16
17:18 [d]ch. 16:5
17:19 [e]See Josh. 2:6

[l]Heb. *word* [m]Heb. *was right in the eyes of* [n]Heb. *what* is *in his mouth* [o]Heb. *word?* [p]Heb. *counselled* [q]Heb. *bitter of soul* [r]Heb. *fallen* [s]Heb. *that thy face,* or, *presence go* [t]Heb. *commanded*

was in fulfillment of God's judgment: "Behold, I will raise up evil against thee out of thine own house, and I will even take thy wives before thine eyes, and give *them* unto thy neighbour and he shall lie with thy wives in the sight of the sun. . . . I will do this thing before all Israel" (12:11–12). For a son to violate his father's wives was the greatest insult to a father. David had sinned grievously and suffered for it here.

spread a covering over the well's
mouth, and spread ground corn there-
on; and the thing was not known.
20 And when Absalom's servants
came to the woman to the house, they
said, Where *is* Ahimaaz and Jonathan?
And [f]the woman said unto them, They
be gone over the brook of water. And
when they had sought and could not
find *them,* they returned to Jerusalem.
21 And it came to pass, after they
were departed, that they came up out
of the well, and went and told king Da-
vid, and said unto David, [g]Arise, and
pass quickly over the water: for thus
hath Ahithophel counselled against
you.
22 Then David arose, and all the
people that *were* with him, and they
passed over Jordan: by the morning
light there lacked not one of them that
was not gone over Jordan.
23 ¶ And when Ahithophel saw that
his counsel was not [u]followed, he sad-
dled *his* ass, and arose, and gat him
home to his house, to [h]his city, and
[i]put[v] his household in order, and
[j]hanged himself, and died, and was
buried in the sepulchre of his father.
24 Then David came to [k]Mahana-
im. And Absalom passed over Jordan,
he and all the men of Israel with
him.
25 ¶ And Absalom made Amasa
captain of the host instead of Joab:
which Amasa *was* a man's son, whose
name *was* [w]Ithra an Israelite, that
went in to [l]Abigail[x] the daughter of
[y]Nahash, sister to Zeruiah Joab's
mother.
26 So Israel and Absalom pitched in
the land of Gilead.
27 ¶ And it came to pass, when Da-
vid was come to Mahanaim, that
[m]Shobi the son of Nahash of Rabbah of
the children of Ammon, and [n]Machir
the son of Ammiel of Lo-debar, and
[o]Barzillai the Gileadite of Rogelim,
28 Brought beds, and [z]basins, and
earthen vessels, and wheat, and bar-
ley, and flour, and parched *corn,* and
beans, and lentiles, and parched
pulse,
29 And honey, and butter, and
sheep, and cheese of kine, for David,
and for the people that *were* with him,
to eat: for they said, The people *is* hun-
gry, and weary, and thirsty, [p]in the
wilderness.

17:20 [f]See Ex. 1:19 Josh. 2:4,5
17:21 [g]ver. 15,16
17:23 [h]ch. 15:12 [i]2 Ki. 20:1 [j]Mat. 27:5
17:24 [k]Gen. 32:2 Josh. 13:26 ch. 2:8
17:25 [l]1 Chr. 2:16,17
17:27 [m]See ch. 10:1 & 12:29 [n]ch. 9:4 [o]ch. 19:31,32 1 Ki. 2:7
17:29 [p]ch. 16:2

Absalom killed by Joab

18 AND DAVID numbered the peo-
ple that *were* with him, and set
captains of thousands and captains of
hundreds over them.
2 And David sent forth a third part
of the people under the hand of Joab,
and a third part under the hand of
Abishai the son of Zeruiah, Joab's
brother, [q]and a third part under the
hand of Ittai the Gittite. And the king
said unto the people, I will surely go
forth with you myself also.
3 [r]But the people answered, Thou
shalt not go forth: for if we flee away,
they will not [a]care for us; neither if
half of us die, will they care for us: but
now *thou art* [b]worth ten thousand of
us: therefore now *it is* better that thou
[c]succour us out of the city.
4 And the king said unto them,
What seemeth you best I will do. And
the king stood by the gate side, and all
the people came out by hundreds and
by thousands.
5 And the king commanded Joab
and Abishai and Ittai, saying, *Deal*
gently for my sake with the young man,
even with Absalom. [s]And all the peo-
ple heard when the king gave all the
captains charge concerning Absalom.
6 ¶ So the people went out into the
field against Israel: and the battle was
in the [t]wood of Ephraim;
7 Where the people of Israel were
slain before the servants of David, and
there was there a great slaughter that
day of twenty thousand *men.*
8 For the battle was there scattered
over the face of all the country: and the
wood [d]devoured more people that day
than the sword devoured.
9 ¶ And Absalom met the servants
of David. And Absalom rode upon a
mule, and the mule went under the
thick boughs of a great oak, and his
head caught hold of the oak, and he
was taken up between the heaven and
the earth; and the mule that *was* under
him went away.
10 And a certain man saw *it,* and
told Joab, and said, Behold, I saw Ab-
salom hanged in an oak.

18:2 [q]ch. 15:19
18:3 [r]ch. 21:17
18:5 [s]ver. 12
18:6 [t]Josh. 17:15,18

[u]Heb. *done* [v]Heb. *gave charge concerning his house* [w]Or, *Jether an Ishmaelite* [x]Heb. *Abigal* [y]Or, *Jesse;* see 1 Chr. 2:13,16 [z]Or, *cups* [a]Heb. *set their heart on us* [b]Heb. *as ten thousand of us* [c]Heb. *be to succour* [d]Heb. *multiplied to devour*

11 And Joab said unto the man that told him, And, behold, thou sawest *him,* and why didst thou not smite him there to the ground? and I would have given thee ten *shekels* of silver, and a girdle.

12 And the man said unto Joab, Though I should [e]receive a thousand *shekels* of silver in mine hand, *yet* would I not put forth mine hand against the king's son: [u]for in our hearing the king charged thee and Abishai and Ittai, saying, [f]Beware that none *touch* the young man Absalom.

13 Otherwise I should have wrought falsehood against mine own life: for there is no matter hid from the king, and thou thyself wouldest have set thyself against *me.*

14 Then said Joab, I may not tarry thus [g]with thee. And he took three darts in his hand, and thrust them through the heart of Absalom, while he *was* yet alive in the [h]midst of the oak.

15 And ten young men that bare Joab's armour compassed about and smote Absalom, and slew him.

16 And Joab blew the trumpet, and the people returned from pursuing after Israel: for Joab held back the people.

17 And they took Absalom, and cast him into a great pit in the wood, and [v]laid a very great heap of stones upon him: and all Israel fled every one to his tent.

18 ¶ Now Absalom in his lifetime had taken and reared up for himself a pillar, which *is* in [w]the king's dale: for he said, [x]I have no son to keep my name in remembrance: and he called the pillar after his own name: and it is called unto this day, Absalom's place.

David told of Absalom's death

19 ¶ Then said Ahimaaz the son of Zadok, Let me now run, and bear the king tidings, how that the LORD hath [i]avenged him of his enemies.

20 And Joab said unto him, Thou shalt not [j]bear tidings this day, but thou shalt bear tidings another day: but this day thou shalt bear no tidings, because the king's son is dead.

21 Then said Joab to Cushi, Go tell the king what thou hast seen. And Cushi bowed himself unto Joab, and ran.

22 Then said Ahimaaz the son of Zadok yet again to Joab, But [k]howsoever, let me, I pray thee, also run after Cushi. And Joab said, Wherefore wilt thou run, my son, seeing that thou hast no tidings [l]ready?

23 But howsoever, *said he,* let me run. And he said unto him, Run. Then Ahimaaz ran by the way of the plain, and overran Cushi.

24 And David sat between the two gates: and [y]the watchman went up to the roof over the gate unto the wall, and lifted up his eyes, and looked, and behold a man running alone.

25 And the watchman cried, and told the king. And the king said, If he *be* alone, *there is* tidings in his mouth. And he came apace, and drew near.

26 And the watchman saw another man running: and the watchman called unto the porter, and said, Behold *another* man running alone. And the king said, He also bringeth tidings.

27 And the watchman said, [m]Me thinketh the running of the foremost is like the running of Ahimaaz the son of Zadok. And the king said, He *is* a good man, and cometh with good tidings.

28 And Ahimaaz called, and said unto the king, [n] [o]All is well. And he fell down to the earth upon his face before the king, and said, Blessed *be* the LORD thy God, which hath [p]delivered up the men that lifted up their hand against my lord the king.

29 And the king said, [q]Is the young man Absalom safe? And Ahimaaz answered, When Joab sent the king's servant, and *me* thy servant, I saw a great tumult, but I knew not what *it was.*

30 And the king said *unto him,* Turn aside, *and* stand here. And he turned aside, and stood still.

31 And, behold, Cushi came; and Cushi said, [r]Tidings, my lord the king: for the LORD hath avenged thee this day of all them that rose up against thee.

32 And the king said unto Cushi, *Is* the young man Absalom safe? And Cushi answered, The enemies of my lord the king, and all that rise against thee

18:12 [u]ver. 5
18:17 [v]Josh. 7:26
18:18 [w]Gen. 14:17 [x]See ch. 14:27
18:24 [y]2 Ki. 9:17

[e] Heb. *weigh upon mine hand* [f] Heb. *Beware whosoever* ye be *of* [g] Heb. *before thee* [h] Heb. *heart* [i] Heb. *judged him from the hand* [j] Heb. *be a man of tidings* [k] Heb. *be what may* [l] Or, *convenient* [m] Heb. *I see the running* [n] Or, *Peace* be to thee [o] Heb. *Peace* [p] Heb. *shut up* [q] Heb. Is there *peace?* [r] Heb. *Tidings is brought*

to do *thee* hurt, be as *that* young
man *is.*
33 ¶ And the king was much moved,
and went up to the chamber over the
gate, and wept: and as he went, thus he
said, [z]O my son Absalom, my son, my
son Absalom! would God I had died for
thee, O Absalom, my son, my son!
19 AND IT was told Joab, Behold,
the king weepeth and mourneth
for Absalom.
2 And the [s]victory that day was
turned into mourning unto all the peo-
ple: for the people heard say that day
how the king was grieved for his son.
3 And the people gat them by
stealth that day [a]into the city, as peo-
ple being ashamed steal away when
they flee in battle.
4 But the king [b]covered his face,
and the king cried with a loud voice,
[c]O my son Absalom, O Absalom, my
son, my son!
5 And Joab came into the house to
the king, and said, Thou hast shamed
this day the faces of all thy servants,
which this day have saved thy life, and
the lives of thy sons and of thy daugh-
ters, and the lives of thy wives, and the
lives of thy concubines;
6 [t]In that thou lovest thine ene-
mies, and hatest thy friends. For thou
hast declared this day, [u]that thou re-
gardest neither princes nor servants:
for this day I perceive, that if Absalom
had lived, and all we had died this day,
then it had pleased thee well.
7 Now therefore arise, go forth, and
speak [v]comfortably unto thy ser-
vants: for I swear by the LORD, if thou
go not forth, there will not tarry one
with thee this night: and that will be
worse unto thee than all the evil that
befell thee from thy youth until now.
8 Then the king arose, and sat in
the gate. And they told unto all the
people, saying, Behold, the king doth
sit in the gate. And all the people came
before the king: for Israel had fled ev-
ery man to his tent.

David's return to Jerusalem

9 ¶ And all the people were at strife
throughout all the tribes of Israel, say-
ing, The king saved us out of the hand
of our enemies, and he delivered us out
of the hand of the Philistines; and now
he is [d]fled out of the land for Absalom.
10 And Absalom, whom we anoint-
ed over us, is dead in battle. Now there-
fore why [w]speak ye not a word of
bringing the king back?
11 ¶ And king David sent to Zadok
and to Abiathar the priests, saying,
Speak unto the elders of Judah, saying,
Why are ye the last to bring the king
back to his house? seeing the speech of
all Israel is come to the king, *even* to
his house.
12 Ye *are* my brethren, ye *are* [e]my
bones and my flesh: wherefore then are
ye the last to bring back the king?
13 [f]And say ye to Amasa, *Art* thou
not of my bone, and of my flesh? [g]God
do so to me, and more also, if thou be
not captain of the host before me con-
tinually in the room of Joab.
14 And he bowed the heart of all the
men of Judah, [h]even as *the heart of* one
man; so that they sent *this word* unto
the king, Return thou, and all thy ser-
vants.
15 So the king returned, and came
to Jordan. And Judah came to [i]Gilgal,
to go to meet the king, to conduct the
king over Jordan.
16 ¶ And [j]Shimei the son of Gera,
a Benjamite, which *was* of Bahurim,
hasted and came down with the men of
Judah to meet king David.
17 And *there were* a thousand men of
Benjamin with him, and [k]Ziba the ser-
vant of the house of Saul, and his fif-
teen sons and his twenty servants with
him; and they went over Jordan before
the king.
18 And there went over a ferry boat
to carry over the king's household, and
to do [x]what he thought good. And
Shimei the son of Gera fell down before
the king, as he was come over Jordan;
19 And said unto the king, [l]Let not
my lord impute iniquity unto me, nei-
ther do thou remember [m]that which
thy servant did perversely the day that
my lord the king went out of Jerusalem,
that the king should [n]take it to his
heart.
20 For thy servant doth know that I

18:33 [z]ch. 19:4
19:3 [a]ver. 32
19:4 [b]ch. 15:30 [c]ch. 18:33
19:9 [d]ch. 15:14
19:12 [e]ch. 5:1
19:13 [f]ch. 17:25 [g]Ruth 1:17
19:14 [h]Judg. 20:1
19:15 [i]Josh. 5:9
19:16 [j]ch. 16:5 1 Ki. 2:8
19:17 [k]ch. 9:2,10 & 16:1,2
19:19 [l]1 Sam. 22:15 [m]ch. 16:5,6 [n]ch. 13:33

[s] Heb. *salvation,* or, *deliverance* [t] Heb. *By loving* [u] Heb. *that princes* or, *servants* are *not to thee* [v] Heb. *to the heart of thy servants* [w] Heb. are *ye silent?* [x] Heb. *the good in his eyes*

18:33 ABSALOM! WOULD GOD I HAD DIED FOR THEE. David's unremitting grief was more than that of a father for his son; it was grief for a son slain in the very act of rebellion and sin.

have sinned: therefore, behold, I am come the first this day of all [o]the house of Joseph to go down to meet my lord the king.

21 But Abishai the son of Zeruiah answered and said, Shall not Shimei be put to death for this, because he [p]cursed the LORD's anointed?

22 And David said, [q]What have I to do with you, ye sons of Zeruiah, that ye should this day be adversaries unto me? [r]shall there any man be put to death this day in Israel? for do not I know that I *am* this day king over Israel?

23 Therefore [s]the king said unto Shimei, Thou shalt not die. And the king sware unto him.

24 ¶ And [t]Mephibosheth the son of Saul came down to meet the king, and had neither dressed his feet, nor trimmed his beard, nor washed his clothes, from the day the king departed until the day he came *again* in peace.

25 And it came to pass, when he was come to Jerusalem to meet the king, that the king said unto him, [u]Wherefore wentest not thou with me, Mephibosheth?

26 And he answered, My lord, O king, my servant deceived me: for thy servant said, I will saddle me an ass, that I may ride thereon, and go to the king; because thy servant *is* lame.

27 And [v]he hath slandered thy servant unto my lord the king; [w]but my lord the king *is* as an angel of God: do therefore *what is* good in thine eyes.

28 For all *of* my father's house were but [y]dead men before my lord the king: [x]yet didst thou set thy servant among them that did eat at thine own table. What right therefore have I yet to cry any more unto the king?

29 And the king said unto him, Why speakest thou any more of thy matters? I have said, Thou and Ziba divide the land.

30 And Mephibosheth said unto the king, Yea, let him take all, forasmuch as my lord the king is come again in peace unto his own house.

31 ¶ And [y]Barzillai the Gileadite came down from Rogelim, and went over Jordan with the king, to conduct him over Jordan.

32 Now Barzillai was a very aged man, *even* fourscore years old: and [z]he had provided the king of sustenance while he lay at Mahanaim; for he *was* a very great man.

33 And the king said unto Barzillai, Come thou over with me, and I will feed thee with me in Jerusalem.

34 And Barzillai said unto the king, [z]How long have I to live, that I should go up with the king unto Jerusalem?

35 I *am* this day [a]fourscore years old: *and* can I discern between good and evil? can thy servant taste what I eat or what I drink? can I hear any more the voice of singing men and singing women? wherefore then should thy servant be yet a burden unto my lord the king?

36 Thy servant will go a little way over Jordan with the king: and why should the king recompense it me with such a reward?

37 Let thy servant, I pray thee, turn back again, that I may die in mine own city, *and be buried* by the grave of my father and of my mother. But behold thy servant [b]Chimham; let him go over with my lord the king; and do to him what shall seem good unto thee.

38 And the king answered, Chimham shall go over with me, and I will do to him that which shall seem good unto thee: and whatsoever thou shalt [a]require of me, *that* will I do for thee.

39 And all the people went over Jordan. And when the king was come over, the king [c]kissed Barzillai, and blessed him; and he returned unto his own place.

40 Then the king went on to Gilgal, and [b]Chimham went on with him: and all the people of Judah conducted the king, and also half the people of Israel.

41 ¶ And, behold, all the men of Israel came to the king, and said unto the king, Why have our brethren the men of Judah stolen thee away, and [d]have brought the king, and his household, and all David's men with him, over Jordan?

42 And all the men of Judah answered the men of Israel, Because the king *is* [e]near of kin to us: wherefore then be ye angry for this matter? have we eaten at all of the king's *cost?* or hath he given us any gift?

43 And the men of Israel answered the men of Judah, and said, We have

19:20 [o]See ch. 16:5
19:21 [p]Ex. 22:28 1 Sam. 26:9
19:22 [q]ch. 16:10 [r]1 Sam. 11:13
19:23 [s]1 Ki. 2:8,9,37,46
19:24 [t]ch. 9:6
19:25 [u]ch. 16:17
19:27 [v]ch. 16:3 [w]ch. 14:17,20
19:28 [x]ch. 9:7,10,13
19:31 [y]1 Ki. 2:7
19:32 [z]ch. 17:27
19:35 [a]Ps. 90:10
19:37 [b]1 Ki. 2:7 Jer. 41:17
19:39 [c]Gen. 31:55
19:41 [d]ver. 15
19:42 [e]ver. 12

[y] Heb. *men of death* [z] Heb. *How many days are the years of my life?* [a] Heb. *choose*
[b] Heb. *Chimhan*

ten parts in the king, and we have also more *right* in David than ye: why then did ye [c]despise us, that our advice should not be first had in bringing back our king? And [f]the words of the men of Judah were fiercer than the words of the men of Israel.

Sheba leads Israel to revolt

20 AND THERE happened to be there a man of Belial, whose name *was* Sheba, the son of Bichri, a Benjamite: and he blew a trumpet, and said, [g]We have no part in David, neither have we inheritance in the son of Jesse: [h]every man to his tents, O Israel.

2 So every man of Israel went up from after David, *and* followed Sheba the son of Bichri: but the men of Judah clave unto their king, from Jordan even to Jerusalem.

3 ¶ And David came to his house at Jerusalem; and the king took the ten women *his* [i]concubines, whom he had left to keep the house, and put them in [d]ward, and fed them, but went not in unto them. So they were [e]shut up unto the day of their death, [f]living in widowhood.

4 ¶ Then said the king to Amasa, [j]Assemble[g] me the men of Judah within three days, and be thou here present.

5 So Amasa went to assemble *the men of* Judah: but he tarried longer than the set time which he had appointed him.

6 And David said to Abishai, Now shall Sheba the son of Bichri do us more harm than *did* Absalom: take thou [k]thy lord's servants, and pursue after him, lest he get him fenced cities, and [h]escape us.

7 And there went out after him Joab's men, and the [l]Cherethites, and the Pelethites, and all the mighty men: and they went out of Jerusalem, to pursue after Sheba the son of Bichri.

8 When they *were* at the great stone which *is* in Gibeon, Amasa went before them. And Joab's garment that he had put on was girded unto him, and upon it a girdle *with* a sword fastened upon his loins in the sheath thereof; and as he went forth it fell out.

9 And Joab said to Amasa, *Art* thou in health, my brother? [m]And Joab took Amasa by the beard with the right hand to kiss him.

19:43 [f]See Judg. 8:1 & 12:1
20:1 [g]ch. 19:43 [h]1 Ki. 12:16 2 Chr. 10:16
20:3 [i]ch. 15:16 & 16:21,22
20:4 [j]ch. 19:13
20:6 [k]ch. 11:11 1 Ki. 1:33
20:7 [l]ch. 8:18 1 Ki. 1:38
20:9 [m]Mat. 26:49 Luke 22:47

10 But Amasa took no heed to the sword that *was* in Joab's hand: so [n]he smote him therewith [o]in the fifth *rib*, and shed out his bowels to the ground, and [i]struck him not again; and he died. So Joab and Abishai his brother pursued after Sheba the son of Bichri.

11 And one of Joab's men stood by him, and said, He that favoureth Joab, and he that *is* for David, *let him go* after Joab.

12 And Amasa wallowed in blood in the midst of the highway. And when the man saw that all the people stood still, he removed Amasa out of the highway into the field, and cast a cloth upon him, when he saw that every one that came by him stood still.

13 When he was removed out of the highway, all the people went on after Joab, to pursue after Sheba the son of Bichri.

14 ¶ And he went through all the tribes of Israel unto [p]Abel, and to Beth-maachah, and all the Berites: and they were gathered together, and went also after him.

15 And they came and besieged him in Abel of Beth-maachah, and they [q]cast up a bank against the city, and [j]it stood in the trench: and all the people that *were* with Joab [k]battered the wall, to throw it down.

16 ¶ Then cried a wise woman out of the city, Hear, hear; say, I pray you, unto Joab, Come near hither, that I may speak with thee.

17 And when he was come near unto her, the woman said, *Art* thou Joab? And he answered, I *am he.* Then she said unto him, Hear the words of thine handmaid. And he answered, I do hear.

18 Then she spake, saying, [l]They were wont to speak in old time, saying, They shall surely ask *counsel* at Abel: and so they ended *the matter.*

19 I *am one of them that are* peaceable *and* faithful in Israel: thou seekest to destroy a city and a mother in Israel: why wilt thou swallow up [r]the inheritance of the LORD?

20:10 [n]1 Ki. 2:5 [o]ch. 2:23
20:14 [p]2 Ki. 15:29 2 Chr. 16:4
20:15 [q]2 Ki. 19:32
20:19 [r]1 Sam. 26:19 ch. 21:3

[c] Heb. *set us at light* [d] Heb. *an house of ward* [e] Heb. *bound* [f] Heb. *in widowhood of life* [g] Heb. *Call* [h] Heb. *deliver himself from our eyes* [i] Heb. *doubled not his stroke* [j] Or, *it stood against the outmost wall* [k] Heb. *marred to throw down* [l] Or, *They plainly spake in the beginning, saying, Surely they will ask of Abel, and so make an end*

20 And Joab answered and said, Far be it, far be it from me, that I should swallow up or destroy.

21 The matter *is* not so: but a man of mount Ephraim, Sheba the son of Bichri [m]by name, hath lifted up his hand against the king, *even* against David: deliver him only, and I will depart from the city. And the woman said unto Joab, Behold, his head shall be thrown to thee over the wall.

22 Then the woman went unto all the people [s]in her wisdom. And they cut off the head of Sheba the son of Bichri, and cast *it* out to Joab. And he blew a trumpet, and they [n]retired from the city, every man to his tent. And Joab returned to Jerusalem unto the king.

23 ¶ Now [t]Joab *was* over all the host of Israel: and Benaiah the son of Jehoiada *was* over the Cherethites and over the Pelethites:

24 And Adoram *was* [u]over the tribute: and [v]Jehoshaphat the son of Ahilud *was* [o]recorder:

25 And Sheva *was* scribe: and [w]Zadok and Abiathar *were* the priests:

26 [x]And Ira also the Jairite was [y]a [p] chief ruler about David.

David repays the Gibeonites

21 THEN THERE was a famine in the days of David three years, year after year; and David [q]inquired of the LORD. And the LORD answered, *It is* for Saul, and for *his* bloody house, because he slew the Gibeonites.

2 And the king called the Gibeonites, and said unto them; (now the Gibeonites *were* not of the children of Israel, but [z]of the remnant of the Amorites; and the children of Israel had sworn unto them: and Saul sought to slay them in his zeal to the children of Israel and Judah.)

3 Wherefore David said unto the Gibeonites, What shall I do for you? and wherewith shall I make the atonement, that ye may bless [a]the inheritance of the LORD?

4 And the Gibeonites said unto him, [r]We will have no silver nor gold of Saul, nor of his house; neither for us shalt thou kill any man in Israel. And he said, What ye shall say, *that* will I do for you.

5 And they answered the king, The man that consumed us, and that [s]devised against us *that* we should be destroyed from remaining in any of the coasts of Israel,

6 Let seven men of his sons be delivered unto us, and we will hang them up unto the LORD [b]in Gibeah of Saul, [c]*whom* [t] the LORD did choose. And the king said, I will give *them.*

7 But the king spared Mephibosheth, the son of Jonathan the son of Saul, because of [d]the LORD's oath that *was* between them, between David and Jonathan the son of Saul.

8 But the king took the two sons of [e]Rizpah the daughter of Aiah, whom she bare unto Saul, Armoni and Mephibosheth; and the five sons of [u]Michal the daughter of Saul, whom she [v]brought up for Adriel the son of Barzillai the Meholathite:

9 And he delivered them into the hands of the Gibeonites, and they hanged them in the hill [f]before the LORD: and they fell *all* seven together, and were put to death in the days of harvest, in the first *days,* in the beginning of barley harvest.

10 ¶ And [g]Rizpah the daughter of Aiah took sackcloth, and spread it for her upon the rock, [h]from the beginning of harvest until water dropped upon them out of heaven, and suffered neither the birds of the air to rest on them by day, nor the beasts of the field by night.

11 And it was told David what Riz-

20:22 [s]Eccl. 9:14,15 **20:23** [t]ch. 8:16,18 **20:24** [u]1 Ki. 4:6 [v]ch. 8:16 1 Ki. 4:3 **20:25** [w]ch. 8:17 1 Ki. 4:4 **20:26** [x]ch. 23:38 [y]Gen. 41:45 Ex. 2:16 ch. 8:18 **21:2** [z]Josh. 9:3,15-17 **21:3** [a]ch. 20:19 **21:6** [b]1 Sam. 10:26 [c]1 Sam. 10:24 **21:7** [d]1 Sam. 18:3 & 20:8,15 **21:8** [e]ch. 3:7 **21:9** [f]ch. 6:17 **21:10** [g]ver. 8 ch. 3:7 [h]See Deut. 21:23

[m] Heb. *by his name* [n] Heb. *were scattered* [o] Or, *remembrancer* [p] Or, *a prince* [q] Heb. *sought the face* [r] Or, It is *not silver nor gold that we have to do with Saul or his house, neither* pertains it *to us to kill* [s] Or, *cut us off* [t] Or, *chosen of the LORD* [u] Or, *Michal's sister* [v] Heb. *bare to Adriel;* see 1 Sam. 18:19

21:1 THERE WAS A FAMINE. Chs. 21—24 contain supplementary accounts of events related to David's reign. They are not presented in chronological order; rather, they comprise an appendix to 1 and 2 Samuel. Several of the events occurred early in David's reign.

21:1 BECAUSE HE SLEW THE GIBEONITES. Joshua and Israel had made a league with the Gibeonites that they would not be killed along with the other Canaanites (Josh. 9:15–21). Evidently Saul had broken this vow (v. 2). To break a vow was a serious transgression against God's law (Num. 30:1–2). The term "*his* bloody house" implies that Saul's sons had participated in killing the Gibeonites (v. 8; see next note).

pah the daughter of Aiah, the concu-
bine of Saul, had done.
12 ¶ And David went and took the
bones of Saul and the bones of Jona-
than his son from the men of [i]Jabesh-
gilead, which had stolen them from the
street of Beth-shan, where the Philis-
tines had hanged them, when the Phi-
listines had slain Saul in Gilboa:
13 And he brought up from thence
the bones of Saul and the bones of Jon-
athan his son; and they gathered the
bones of them that were hanged.
14 And the bones of Saul and Jona-
than his son buried they in the country
of Benjamin in [j]Zelah, in the sepul-
chre of Kish his father: and they per-
formed all that the king commanded.
And after that [k]God was entreated for
the land.

Victories over the Philistines

21:15–22pp — 1 Chr. 20:4–8

15 ¶ Moreover the Philistines had
yet war again with Israel; and David
went down, and his servants with him,
and fought against the Philistines: and
David waxed faint.
16 And Ishbi-benob, which *was* of
the sons of [w]the giant, the weight of
whose [x]spear *weighed* three hundred
shekels of brass in weight, he being
girded with a new *sword,* thought to
have slain David.
17 But Abishai the son of Zeruiah
succoured him, and smote the Philis-
tine, and killed him. Then the men of
David sware unto him, saying, [l]Thou
shalt go no more out with us to battle,
that thou quench not the [m]light[y] of
Israel.
18 [n]And it came to pass after this,
that there was again a battle with the
Philistines at Gob: then [o]Sibbechai
the Hushathite slew [z]Saph, which
was of the sons of [w]the giant.
19 And there was again a battle in
Gob with the Philistines, where Elha-
nan the son of [a]Jaare-oregim, a Beth-
lehemite, slew [p]*the brother of* Goliath
the Gittite, the staff of whose spear
was like a weaver's beam.
20 And [q]there was yet a battle in
Gath, where was a man of *great* stat-
ure, that had on every hand six fingers,
and on every foot six toes, four and
twenty in number; and he also was
born to [w]the giant.
21 And when he [b]defied Israel,
Jonathan the son of [r]Shimeah the
brother of David slew him.
22 [s]These four were born to the
giant in Gath, and fell by the hand of
David, and by the hand of his servants.

David's psalm of praise

22:1–51pp — Ps. 18:1–50

22 AND DAVID [t]spake unto the
LORD the words of this song in
the day *that* the LORD had [u]delivered
him out of the hand of all his enemies,
and out of the hand of Saul:
2 And he said, [v]The LORD *is* my
rock, and my fortress, and my deliv-
erer;
3 The God of my rock; [w]in him will
I trust: *he is* my [x]shield, and the
[y]horn of my salvation, my high [z]tow-
er, and my [a]refuge, my saviour; thou
savest me from violence.
4 I will call on the LORD, *who is* wor-
thy to be praised: so shall I be saved
from mine enemies.
5 When the [c]waves of death com-
passed me, the floods of [d]ungodly
men made me afraid;
6 The [b]sorrows[e] of hell com-
passed me about; the snares of death
prevented me;
7 In my distress [c]I called upon the
LORD, and cried to my God: and he did
[d]hear my voice out of his temple, and
my cry *did enter* into his ears.
8 Then [e]the earth shook and trem-
bled; [f]the foundations of heaven
moved and shook, because he was
wroth.
9 There went up a smoke [f]out of
his nostrils, and [g]fire out of his mouth
devoured: coals were kindled by it.
10 He [h]bowed the heavens also,
and came down; and [i]darkness *was*
under his feet.
11 And he rode upon a cherub, and

21:12 [i]1 Sam. 31:11-13
21:14 [j]Josh. 18:28 [k]See Josh. 7:26 ch. 24:25
21:17 [l]ch. 18:3 [m]1 Ki. 11:36
21:18 [n]1 Chr. 20:4 [o]1 Chr. 11:29
21:19 [p]See 1 Chr. 20:5
21:20 [q]1 Chr. 20:6
21:21 [r]1 Sam. 16:9, *Shammah*
21:22 [s]1 Chr. 20:8
22:1 [t]Ex. 15:1 Judg. 5:1 [u]Ps. 18,title, & 34:19
22:2 [v]Deut. 32:4
22:3 [w]Heb. 2:13 [x]Gen. 15:1 [y]Luke 1:69 [z]Prov. 18:10 [a]Ps. 9:9 Jer. 16:19
22:6 [b]Ps. 116:3
22:7 [c]Ps. 116:4 [d]Ex. 3:7
22:8 [e]Ps. 77:18 [f]Job 26:11
22:9 [g]Ps. 97:3
22:10 [h]Is. 64:1 [i]Ex. 20:21

[w] Or, *Rapha* [x] Heb. *the staff,* or, *the head* [y] Heb. *candle,* or, *lamp* [z] Or, *Sippai* [a] Or, *Jair* [b] Or, *reproached* [c] Or, *pangs* [d] Heb. *Belial* [e] Or, *cords* [f] Heb. *by*

21:14 GOD WAS INTREATED. After the deaths of these seven men (vv. 8–9), God once again resumed answering the prayers of His people (cf. Josh. 7—8). This text also indicates that these seven men had been implicated in the killing of the Gibeonites; in cases where the children were not involved in the sins of their father, they were not to be punished (see Deut. 24:16; 2 Ki. 14:6; Ezek. 18:1–4,14–17).

did fly: and he was seen [j]upon the
wings of the wind.
12 And he made [k]darkness pavil-
ions round about him, [g]dark waters,
and thick clouds of the skies.
13 Through the brightness before
him were [l]coals of fire kindled.
14 The LORD [m]thundered from
heaven, and the most High uttered his
voice.
15 And he sent out [n]arrows, and
scattered them; lightning, and discom-
fited them.
16 And the channels of the sea ap-
peared, the foundations of the world
were discovered, at the [o]rebuking of
the LORD, at the blast of the breath of
his nostrils.
17 [p]He sent from above, he took
me; he drew me out of [h]many waters;
18 [q]He delivered me from my
strong enemy, *and* from them that hat-
ed me: for they were too strong for me.
19 They prevented me in the day of
my calamity: but the LORD was my stay.
20 [r]He brought me forth also into
a large place: he delivered me, because
he [s]delighted in me.
21 [t]The LORD rewarded me accord-
ing to my righteousness: according to
the [u]cleanness of my hands hath he
recompensed me.
22 For I have [v]kept the ways of the
LORD, and have not wickedly departed
from my God.
23 For all his [w]judgments *were* be-
fore me: and *as for* his statutes, I did
not depart from them.
24 I was also [x]upright [i]before
him, and have kept myself from mine
iniquity.
25 Therefore [y]the LORD hath rec-
ompensed me according to my righ-
teousness; according to my cleanness
[j]in his eyesight.
26 With [z]the merciful thou wilt
show thyself merciful, *and* with the up-
right man thou wilt show thyself up-
right.
27 With the pure thou wilt show
thyself pure; and [a]with the froward
thou wilt [k]show thyself unsavoury.
28 And the [b]afflicted people thou
wilt save: but thine eyes *are* upon [c]the
haughty, *that* thou mayest bring *them*
down.
29 For thou *art* my [l]lamp, O LORD:
and the LORD will lighten my darkness.
30 For by thee I have [m]run through
a troop: by my God have I leaped over
a wall.
31 *As for* God, [d]his way *is* perfect;
[e]the word of the LORD *is* [n]tried: he *is*
a buckler to all them that trust in him.
32 For [f]who *is* God, save the LORD?
and who *is* a rock, save our God?
33 God *is* my [g]strength *and* power:
and he [h]maketh[o] my way [i]perfect.
34 He [p]maketh my feet [j]like
hinds' *feet:* and [k]setteth me upon my
high places.
35 [l]He teacheth my hands [q]to
war; so that a bow of steel is broken by
mine arms.
36 Thou hast also given me the
shield of thy salvation: and thy gentle-
ness hath [r]made me great.
37 Thou hast [m]enlarged my steps
under me; so that my [s]feet did not
slip.
38 I have pursued mine enemies,
and destroyed them; and turned not
again until I had consumed them.
39 And I have consumed them, and
wounded them, that they could not
arise: yea, they are fallen [n]under my
feet.
40 For thou hast [o]girded me with
strength to battle: [p]them that rose up
against me hast thou [t]subdued un-
der me.
41 Thou hast also given me the
[q]necks of mine enemies, that I might
destroy them that hate me.
42 They looked, but *there was* none
to save; *even* [r]unto the LORD, but he
answered them not.
43 Then did I beat them as small
[s]as the dust of the earth, I did stamp
them [t]as the mire of the street, *and*
did spread them abroad.

22:11 [j]Ps. 104:3
22:12 [k]Ps. 97:2
22:13 [l]ver. 9
22:14 [m]1 Sam. 2:10
22:15 [n]Ps. 7:13
22:16 [o]Ex. 15:8
22:17 [p]Ps. 144:7
22:18 [q]ver. 1
22:20 [r]Ps. 31:8 [s]ch. 15:26
22:21 [t]Ps. 7:8 [u]Ps. 24:4
22:22 [v]Ps. 119:3
22:23 [w]Deut. 7:12
22:24 [x]Job 1:1
22:25 [y]ver. 21
22:26 [z]Mat. 5:7
22:27 [a]Lev. 26:23
22:28 [b]Ps. 72:12 [c]Job 40:11
22:31 [d]Dan. 4:37 [e]Ps. 12:6
22:32 [f]Is. 45:5,6
22:33 [g]Ps. 27:1 Is. 12:2 [h]Heb. 13:21 [i]Ps. 101:2,6
22:34 [j]ch. 2:18 [k]Is. 33:16
22:35 [l]Ps. 144:1
22:37 [m]Prov. 4:12
22:39 [n]Mal. 4:3
22:40 [o]Ps. 18:32 [p]Ps. 44:5
22:41 [q]Gen. 49:8
22:42 [r]Prov. 1:28
22:43 [s]Ps. 18:42 [t]Is. 10:6

[g]Heb. *binding of waters* [h]Or, *great* [i]Heb. *to him* [j]Heb. *before his eyes* [k]Or, *wrestle* [l]Or, *candle* [m]Or, *broken a troop* [n]Or, *refined* [o]Heb. *riddeth,* or, *looseth* [p]Heb. *equalleth* [q]Heb. *for the war* [r]Heb. *multiplied me* [s]Heb. *ankles* [t]Heb. *caused to bow*

22:22 I HAVE KEPT THE WAYS OF THE LORD. David was not maintaining that he had never sinned or that he was perfect. He was expressing his desire to please the Lord with a heart that had been, up to this point, habitually turned toward Him in faith. The psalm was probably composed shortly after God delivered him from Saul (2:4; 1 Sam. 31:6) and before he fell into his sins of murder and adultery (11:1 — 12:15).

44 [u]Thou also hast delivered me
from the strivings of my people, thou
hast kept me *to be* [v]head of the hea-
then: [w]a people *which* I knew not shall
serve me.
45 [u]Strangers shall [v]submit
themselves unto me: as soon as they
hear, they shall be obedient unto me.
46 Strangers shall fade away, and
they shall be afraid [x]out of their close
places.
47 The LORD liveth; and blessed *be*
my rock; and exalted be the God of the
[y]rock of my salvation.
48 It *is* God that [z]avengeth[w] me,
and that [a]bringeth down the people
under me,
49 And that bringeth me forth from
mine enemies: thou also hast lifted me
up on high above them that rose up
against me: thou hast delivered me
from the [b]violent man.
50 Therefore I will give thanks unto
1 Chr. 16:7-43 thee, O LORD, among [c]the heathen,
and I will sing praises unto thy name.
51 [d]*He is* the tower of salvation for
his king: and showeth mercy to his
[e]anointed, unto David, and [f]to his
seed for evermore.

David's last words

23 NOW THESE *be* the last words
of David. David the son of Jesse
said, [g]and the man *who was* raised up
on high, [h]the anointed of the God of
Jacob, and the sweet psalmist of Israel,
said,
2 [i]The spirit of the LORD spake by
Neh. 9:30 me, and his word *was* in my tongue.
3 The God of Israel said, [j]the Rock
of Israel spake to me, [x]He that ruleth
over men *must be* just, ruling [k]in the
fear of God.
4 And *he shall be* as the light of the
morning, *when* the sun riseth, *even* a
morning without clouds; *as* the tender
grass *springing* out of the earth by clear
shining after rain.
5 Although my house *be* not so with
God; [l]yet he hath made with me an
everlasting covenant, ordered in all
things, and sure: for *this is* all my salva-
tion, and all *my* desire, although he
make *it* not to grow.
6 ¶ But *the sons* of Belial *shall be* all
of them as thorns thrust away, because
they cannot be taken with hands:
7 But the man *that* shall touch them
must be [y]fenced with iron and the
staff of a spear; and they shall be utter-

22:44 [u]ch. 3:1 [v]Deut. 28:13 [w]Is. 55:5
22:46 [x]Mic. 7:17
22:47 [y]Ps. 89:26
22:48 [z]1 Sam. 25:39 [a]Ps. 144:2
22:49 [b]Ps. 140:1
22:50 [c]Rom. 15:9
22:51 [d]Ps. 144:10 [e]Ps. 89:20 [f]Ps. 89:29
23:1 [g]Ps. 78:70 [h]1 Sam. 16:12,13 Ps. 89:20
23:2 [i]2 Pet. 1:21
23:3 [j]Deut. 32:4 [k]Ex. 18:21
23:5 [l]Ps. 89:29
23:9 [m]1 Chr. 11:12
23:11 [n]1 Chr. 11:27 [o]See 1 Chr. 11:13, 14
23:13 [p]1 Chr. 11:15 [q]1 Sam. 22:1 [r]ch. 5:18
23:14 [s]1 Sam. 22:4,5

ly burned with fire in the *same* place.

David's mighty men

23:8–39pp — 1 Chr. 11:10–41

8 ¶ These *be* the names of the
mighty men whom David had: [z]The
Tachmonite that sat in the seat, chief
among the captains; the same *was*
Adino the Eznite: [a]*he lift up his spear*
against eight hundred, [b]whom he
slew at one time.
9 And after him *was* [m]Eleazar the
son of Dodo the Ahohite, *one* of the
three mighty men with David, when
they defied the Philistines *that* were
there gathered together to battle, and
the men of Israel were gone away:
10 He arose, and smote the Philis-
tines until his hand was weary, and his
hand clave unto the sword: and the
LORD wrought a great victory that day;
and the people returned after him only
to spoil.
11 And after him *was* [n]Shammah
the son of Agee the Hararite. [o]And the
Philistines were gathered together
[c]into a troop, where was a piece of
ground full of lentiles: and the people
fled from the Philistines.
12 But he stood in the midst of the
ground, and defended it, and slew the
Philistines: and the LORD wrought a
great victory.
13 And [p]three[d] of the thirty chief
went down, and came to David in the
harvest time unto [q]the cave of Adul-
lam: and the troop of the Philistines
pitched in [r]the valley of Rephaim.
14 And David *was* then in [s]an hold,
and the garrison of the Philistines *was*
then *in* Bethlehem.
15 And David longed, and said, Oh
that one would give me drink of the wa-
ter of the well of Bethlehem, which *is*
by the gate!
16 And the three mighty men brake
through the host of the Philistines, and
drew water out of the well of Bethle-
hem, that *was* by the gate, and took *it,*
and brought *it* to David: nevertheless
he would not drink thereof, but poured
it out unto the LORD.
17 And he said, Be it far from me,

[u] Heb. *Sons of the stranger* [v] Or, *yield feigned obedience* [w] Heb. *giveth avengement for me* [x] Or, *Be thou ruler* [y] Heb. *filled* [z] Or, *Josheb-bassebet the Tachmonite, head of the three* [a] See 1 Chr. 11:11 [b] Heb. *slain* [c] Or, *for foraging* [d] Or, *the three captains over the thirty*

O LORD, that I should do this: *is not this* [t]the blood of the men that went in jeopardy of their lives? therefore he would not drink it. These things did these three mighty men.

18 And [u]Abishai, the brother of Joab, the son of Zeruiah, was chief among three. And he lifted up his spear against three hundred, [e]*and* slew *them,* and had the name among three.

19 Was he not most honourable of three? therefore he was their captain: howbeit he attained not unto the *first* three.

20 And Benaiah the son of Jehoiada, the son of a valiant man, of [v]Kabzeel, [f]who had done many acts, [w]he slew two [g]lionlike men of Moab: he went down also and slew a lion in the midst of a pit in time of snow:

21 And he slew an Egyptian, [x]a[h] goodly man: and the Egyptian had a spear in his hand; but he went down to him with a staff, and plucked the spear out of the Egyptian's hand, and slew him with his own spear.

22 These *things* did Benaiah the son of Jehoiada, and had the name among three mighty men.

23 He was [i]more honourable than the thirty, but he attained not to the *first* three. And David set him [y]over his [j]guard.

24 [z]Asahel the brother of Joab *was* one of the thirty; Elhanan the son of Dodo of Bethlehem,

25 [a]Shammah the Harodite, Elika the Harodite,

26 Helez the Paltite, Ira the son of Ikkesh the Tekoite,

27 Abiezer the Anethothite, Mebunnai the Hushathite,

28 Zalmon the Ahohite, Maharai the Netophathite,

29 Heleb the son of Baanah, a Netophathite, Ittai the son of Ribai out of Gibeah of the children of Benjamin,

23:17 [t]Lev. 17:10
23:18 [u]1 Chr. 11:20
23:20 [v]Josh. 15:21 [w]Ex. 15:15
23:21 [x]1 Chr. 11:23
23:23 [y]ch. 8:18 & 20:23
23:24 [z]ch. 2:18
23:25 [a]See 1 Chr. 11:27
23:30 [b]Judg. 2:9
23:38 [c]ch. 20:26
23:39 [d]ch. 11:3,6
24:1 [e]ch. 20:1 [f]1 Chr. 27:23,24
24:2 [g]Judg. 20:1 [h]Jer. 17:5

30 Benaiah the Pirathonite, Hiddai of the [k]brooks of [b]Gaash,

31 Abi-albon the Arbathite, Azmaveth the Barhumite,

32 Eliahba the Shaalbonite, of the sons of Jashen, Jonathan,

33 Shammah the Hararite, Ahiam the son of Sharar the Hararite,

34 Eliphelet the son of Ahasbai, the son of the Maachathite, Eliam the son of Ahithophel the Gilonite,

35 Hezrai the Carmelite, Paarai the Arbite,

36 Igal the son of Nathan of Zobah, Bani the Gadite,

37 Zelek the Ammonite, Nahari the Beerothite, armourbearer to Joab the son of Zeruiah,

38 [c]Ira an Ithrite, Gareb an Ithrite,

39 [d]Uriah the Hittite: thirty and seven in all.

The census of Israel and Judah

24:1–17pp — 1 Chr. 21:1–17

24 AND [e]AGAIN the anger of the LORD was kindled against Israel, and he moved David against them to say, [f]Go, number Israel and Judah.

2 For the king said to Joab the captain of the host, which *was* with him, [l]Go now through all the tribes of Israel, [g]from Dan even to Beer-sheba, and number ye the people, that [h]I may know the number of the people.

3 And Joab said unto the king, Now the LORD thy God add unto the people, how many soever they be, an hundredfold, and that the eyes of my lord the king may see *it:* but why doth my lord the king delight in this thing?

4 Notwithstanding the king's word prevailed against Joab, and against the captains of the host. And Joab and the

[e] Heb. *slain* [f] Heb. *great of acts* [g] Heb. *lions of God* [h] Heb. *a man of countenance,* or, *sight:* called [i] Or, *honourable among the thirty* [j] Or, *council* [k] Or, *valleys* [l] Or, *Compass*

24:1 GO, NUMBER ISRAEL AND JUDAH. Note the following concerning David's sin in numbering the people: (1) Here it is stated that God incited David to number Israel, whereas 1 Chr. 21:1 says that "Satan provoked David to number Israel." God at times will use Satan to achieve His divine purposes by permitting him to test God's people (cf. Job 1:12; 2:6; Mat. 4:1–11; 1 Pet. 4:19; 5:8). God evidently allowed Satan to tempt David because of his pride and lack of trust in God. David's will was involved in the sin (vv. 3–4; 1 Chr. 21:3–4), for he could have resisted Satan.

(2) The mention of "the anger of the LORD . . . against Israel" presupposes that Israel had committed a grave offense against God. God's anger is stirred only when people sin, and the people evidently had done something to merit this punishment (although the nature of their sin is not mentioned).

(3) The nature of David's sin was probably pride, expressed (a) in his leadership of a powerful and numerous people, and (b) in his self-exaltation and boasting of his great accomplishments and strength. David was glorying in human ability and great numbers rather than in the power and righteousness of God.

captains of the host went out from the
presence of the king, to number the
people of Israel.

5 ¶ And they passed over Jordan,
and pitched in [i]Aroer, on the right
side of the city that *lieth* in the midst
of the [m]river of Gad, and toward [j]Jazer:

6 Then they came to Gilead, and to
the [n]land of Tahtim-hodshi; and they
came to [k]Dan-jaan, and about to [l]Zidon,

7 And came to the strong hold of
Tyre, and to all the cities of the Hivites,
and of the Canaanites: and they went
out to the south of Judah, *even* to Beer-sheba.

8 So when they had gone through
all the land, they came to Jerusalem at
the end of nine months and twenty
days.

9 And Joab gave up the sum of the
number of the people unto the king:
[m]and there were in Israel eight hundred
thousand valiant men that drew
the sword; and the men of Judah *were*
five hundred thousand men.

10 ¶ And [n]David's heart smote him
after that he had numbered the people.
And David said unto the LORD, [o]I have
sinned greatly in that I have done: and
now, I beseech thee, O LORD, take away
the iniquity of thy servant; for I have
[p]done very foolishly.

11 For when David was up in the
morning, the word of the LORD came
unto the prophet [q]Gad, David's
[r]seer, saying,

12 Go and say unto David, Thus
saith the LORD, I offer thee three *things*;
choose thee one of them, that I may *do
it* unto thee.

13 So Gad came to David, and told
him, and said unto him, Shall [s]seven
years of famine come unto thee in thy
land? or wilt thou flee three months before
thine enemies, while they pursue
thee? or that there be three days' pestilence
in thy land? now advise, and see
what answer I shall return to him that
sent me.

14 And David said unto Gad, I am in
a great strait: let us fall now into the
hand of the LORD; [t]for his mercies *are*
[o]great: and [u]let me not fall into the
hand of man.

15 ¶ So [v]the LORD sent a pestilence
upon Israel from the morning even to
the time appointed: and there died of
the people from Dan even to Beer-sheba
seventy thousand men.

16 [w]And when the angel stretched
out his hand upon Jerusalem to destroy
it, [x]the LORD repented him of the evil,
and said to the angel that destroyed
the people, It is enough: stay now thine
hand. And the angel of the LORD was by
the threshingplace of [y]Araunah the
Jebusite.

17 And David spake unto the LORD
when he saw the angel that smote the
people, and said, Lo, [z]I have sinned,
and I have done wickedly: but these
sheep, what have they done? let thine
hand, I pray thee, be against me, and
against my father's house.

David builds an altar

24:18–25pp — 1 Chr. 21:18–26

18 ¶ And Gad came that day to David,
and said unto him, [a]Go up, rear an
altar unto the LORD in the threshingfloor
of [p]Araunah the Jebusite.

19 And David, according to the saying
of Gad, went up as the LORD commanded.

20 And Araunah looked, and saw
the king and his servants coming on
toward him: and Araunah went out,
and bowed himself before the king on
his face upon the ground.

21 And Araunah said, Wherefore is
my lord the king come to his servant?
[b]And David said, To buy the threshingfloor
of thee, to build an altar
unto the LORD, that [c]the plague may
be stayed from the people.

22 And Araunah said unto David,
Let my lord the king take and offer up
what *seemeth* good unto him: [d]behold,
here be oxen for burnt sacrifice, and
threshing instruments and *other* instruments
of the oxen for wood.

23 All these *things* did Araunah, *as*
a king, give unto the king. And Arau-

24:5 [i]Deut. 2:36 Josh. 13:9,16 [j]Num. 32:1,3
24:6 [k]Josh. 19:47 Judg. 18:29 [l]Josh. 19:28 Judg. 18:28
24:9 [m]See 1 Chr. 21:5
24:10 [n]1 Sam. 24:5 [o]ch. 12:13 [p]1 Sam. 13:13
24:11 [q]1 Sam. 22:5 [r]1 Sam. 9:9 1 Chr. 29:29
24:13 [s]See 1 Chr. 21:12
24:14 [t]Ps. 103:8,13,14 & 119:156 [u]See Is. 47:6 Zech. 1:15
24:15 [v]1 Chr. 21:14 & 27:24
24:16 [w]Ex. 12:23 [x]Gen. 6:6 1 Sam. 15:11 Joel 2:13,14 [y]1 Chr. 21:15, *Ornan:* See ver. 18 2 Chr. 3:1
24:17 [z]1 Chr. 21:17
24:18 [a]1 Chr. 21:18
24:21 [b]See Gen. 23:8-16 [c]Num. 16:48,50
24:22 [d]1 Ki. 19:21

[m] Or, *valley* [n] Or, *nether land newly inhabited* [o] Or, *many* [p] Heb. *Araniah*

24:17 LET THINE HAND ... BE AGAINST ME. David knew that because he was the leader of Israel, his sin was greater than the sin of the people. In concern for them, he was ready to accept all the punishment. One of David's greatest character traits was his willingness to accept humbly God's punishment for his misdeeds (cf. 15:26; 16:10–12).

nah said unto the king, The LORD thy
God [e]accept thee.
24 And the king said unto Araunah,
Nay; but I will surely buy *it* of thee at
a price: neither will I offer burnt offer-
ings unto the LORD my God of that
which doth cost me nothing. So [f]Da-
vid bought the threshingfloor and the
oxen for fifty shekels of silver.
25 And David built there an altar
unto the LORD, and offered burnt offer-
ings and peace offerings. [g]So the LORD
was entreated for the land, and [h]the
plague was stayed from Israel.

24:23 [e]Ezek. 20:40,41
24:24 [f]See 1 Chr. 21:24, 25
24:25 [g]ch. 21:14 [h]ver. 21

24:24 THAT WHICH DOTH COST ME NOTHING. David's words express the truth that the true value to God of our gifts, service, and life is measured primarily by the sacrifice involved. Self-denial and the willingness to suffer because of righteousness are principles of Christ's kingdom (Mat. 5:10–12; Mark 8:34; 10:21–27). Christianity that costs nothing is worth nothing (cf. Is. 1:11; Mal 1:8).

1 KINGS

Outline

I. The Reign of Solomon (1:1—11:43)
  A. Solomon Succeeds David as King (1:1—2:11)
  B. Solomon Solidifies His Position as King (2:12–46)
  C. Solomon's Wisdom and Administration (3:1—4:34)
  D. Solomon's Success and Fame (5:1—10:29)
    1. Preparations for the Temple (5:1–18)
    2. Construction of the Temple (6:1–38)
    3. Construction of Solomon's Palace (7:1–12)
    4. Furnishings of the Temple (7:13–51)
    5. Dedication of the Temple (8:1–66)
    6. Ratification of the Davidic Covenant (9:1–9)
    7. Solomon's Activities and Fame (9:10—10:29)
  E. Solomon's Downfall and Death (11:1–43)
    1. Solomon's Flagrant Polygamy and Idolatry (11:1–8)
    2. The Judgment of Division Foretold by God (11:9–13)
    3. God Raises Adversaries Against Solomon (11:14–28)
    4. The Prophecy of Ahijah (11:29–40)
    5. The Death of Solomon (11:41–43)

II. The Division of the Kingdom: Israel and Judah (12:1—22:53)
  A. The Judgment of Division Occurs (12:1–24)
  B. Reign of Jeroboam (Israel) (12:25—14:20)
  C. Reign of Rehoboam (Judah) (14:21–31)
  D. Reign of Abijam (Judah) (15:1–8)
  E. Reign of Asa (Judah) (15:9–24)
  F. Reign of Nadab (Israel) (15:25–31)
  G. Reign of Baasha (Israel) (15:32—16:7)
  H. Reign of Elah (Israel) (16:8–14)
  I. Reign of Zimri (Israel) (16:15–20)
  J. Reign of Omri (Israel) (16:21–28)
  K. Reign of Ahab (Israel) (16:29—22:40)
    1. The Beginning of Ahab's Reign (16:29–34)
    2. Ahab and the Prophet Elijah (17:1—19:21)
    3. Ahab's Battles with Syria (20:1–43)
    4. Ahab and Naboth's Vineyard (21:1–29)
    5. Ahab's Fatal Battle with Syria (22:1–40)
  L. Reign of Jehoshaphat (Judah) (22:41–50)
  M. Reign of Ahaziah (Israel) (22:51–53)

Author: Anonymous

Theme: Kings of Israel and Judah

Date of Writing: c. 560–550 B.C.

Background

1 and 2 Kings follow immediately upon the history recorded in 1 and 2 Samuel. Together these four books selectively cover the entire history of the kings of Israel and Judah (c. 1050–586 B.C.). 1 and 2 Kings chronologically cover four centuries of that history—from the time of King Solomon (970 B.C.) to the time of the Babylonian exile (586 B.C.). 1 Kings alone covers about 120 years—Solomon's reign of forty years (970–930 B.C.) and approximately the first eighty years after the kingdom was divided (c. 930–852 B.C.).

1 and 2 Kings were originally a single volume in the Hebrew O.T. Therefore, the issue of authorship relates to them as one book. The last recorded event (2 Ki. 25:27) is the release of King Jehoiachin from prison in Babylon (c. 560 B.C.) Thus 1 and 2 Kings in their completed form likely date from the decade 560–550 B.C. Although the author is undesignated, it is clear that he was an inspired prophetic historian who interpreted the reign of all the kings of Israel and Judah in the light of God's covenant with the Hebrew people. It is also clear that he used various written sources by name: (1) "the book of the acts of Solomon" (11:41), (2) "the book of the chronicles of the kings of Israel" (e.g., 14:19), (3) "the book of the chronicles of the kings of Judah" (e.g., 14:29). These sources were probably written records kept by prophets rather than the official court annals. It is also probable that the author consulted other prophetic sources such as those mentioned in 1 Chr. 29:29. For an overview of the kings of Israel and Judah, see the chart on KINGS OF ISRAEL AND JUDAH, p. 599.

Purpose

1 and 2 Kings were written to provide the Hebrew people in the Babylonian exile with a prophetic interpretation of their history so that they would understand why the nation split in 930 B.C., why the northern kingdom of Israel fell in 722 B.C., and why the Davidic kingdom and Jerusalem fell in 586 B.C. The author emphasizes that the division and collapse of Israel and Judah were the direct and inevitable consequence of idolatry and unrighteousness on the part of the kings and the nation as a whole. In view of this fact, the author evaluates the success or failure of each king according to his faithfulness or unfaithfulness to God and the covenant. No matter what success a king had politically or economically, he was judged a failure if he did not uphold the covenant. This prophetic understanding was presented so that the captives might forever turn away from idolatry, turn to God, and follow His commandments in future generations.

Survey

1 Kings divides into two major parts. (1) Part One describes the reign of King Solomon (chs. 1—11). The opening chapters describe the circumstances under which he became king (chs. 1—2) and his request for wisdom by which to rule the nation (ch. 3). The next seven chapters describe Solomon's rise to world prominence and Israel's zenith in prosperity, peace, power, and glory—all during the first twenty years of Solomon's reign. During this time Solomon built and dedicated the temple in Jerusalem (chs. 6; 8). Ch. 11 describes Solomon's second twenty years—years of indulgence, flagrant polygamy, idolatry, and erosion of the nation's foundations. By the time of Solomon's death, the seeds had been sown for the kingdom's division and decline.

(2) Part Two describes the split of the kingdom under Solomon's son, Rehoboam, and the next eighty years of the political and spiritual decline of both kingdoms under their separate succession of kings (chs. 12—22). The major personalities in this half of the book are kings Rehoboam in the southern kingdom and Jeroboam in the northern kingdom, King Ahab and his wicked wife Jezebel (north), and the prophet Elijah (north).

Special Features

Four major features or emphases characterize 1 Kings. (1) It presents the prophets as God's representatives and spokesmen to the kings of Israel and Judah—e.g., Ahijah

(11:29–40; 14:5–18), Shemaiah (12:22–24), Micaiah (22:8–28), and especially Elijah (chs. 17—19). (2) It emphasizes prophecy and its fulfillment in the history of the kings. Numerous times a recorded prophecy is stated as having been fulfilled (e.g., 2 Sam. 7:13 and 1 Ki 8:20; 11:29–39 and 12:15; ch. 13 and 2 Ki. 23:16–18). (3) It contains many well-known Bible stories—e.g., the wisdom of Solomon (chs. 3—4), the dedication of the temple (ch. 8), the visit of the queen of Sheba to Jerusalem (ch. 10), and the ministry of Elijah, especially his showdown with Baalism on Mount Carmel (ch. 18). (4) It includes vast amounts of chronological data about the kings of Israel and Judah that is sometimes difficult to synchronize. However, most problems are satisfactorily resolved by recognizing the probability of overlapping reigns, co-regencies of sons with their fathers, and different ways to calculate the beginning of a king's reign.

New Testament Fulfillment

The N.T. records that Jesus declared to His generation that the significance of His life and kingdom surpassed the wisdom, authority, glory, and splendor of Solomon and his reign: "behold, a greater than Solomon *is* here" (Mat. 12:42). Moreover, the glory of God that filled Solomon's temple at its dedication came to tabernacle among the human race in Jesus, the only begotten Son of the Father (John 1:14).

Reading 1 Kings

In order to read the entire Old Testament in one year, the book of 1 Kings should be read in 11 days, according to the following schedule: ☐ 1 ☐ 2–3 ☐ 4–6 ☐ 7–8 ☐ 9 ☐ 10–11 ☐ 12–14 ☐ 15–17 ☐ 18–19 ☐ 20–21 ☐ 22

NOTES

Adonijah seeks to be king

1 NOW KING David was old *and* [a]stricken in years; and they covered him with clothes, but he gat no heat.

2 Wherefore his servants said unto him, [b]Let there be sought for my lord the king [c]a young virgin: and let her stand before the king, and let her [d]cherish him, and let her lie in thy bosom, that my lord the king may get heat.

3 So they sought for a fair damsel throughout all the coasts of Israel, and found Abishag a [a]Shunammite, and brought her to the king.

4 And the damsel *was* very fair, and cherished the king, and ministered to him: but the king knew her not.

5 ¶ Then [b]Adonijah the son of Haggith exalted himself, saying, I will [e]be king: and he prepared him chariots and horsemen, and fifty men to run before him.

6 And his father had not displeased him [f]at any time in saying, Why hast thou done so? and he also *was a* very goodly *man;* [c]and *his mother* bare him after Absalom.

7 And [g]he conferred with Joab the son of Zeruiah, and with [d]Abiathar the priest: and [e]they [h]following Adonijah helped *him.*

8 But Zadok the priest, and Benaiah the son of Jehoiada, and Nathan the prophet, and [f]Shimei, and Rei, and [g]the mighty men which *belonged* to David, were not with Adonijah.

9 And Adonijah slew sheep and oxen and fat cattle by the stone of Zoheleth, which *is* by [i]En-rogel, and called all his brethren the king's sons, and all the men of Judah the king's servants:

10 But Nathan the prophet, and Benaiah, and the mighty men, and Solomon his brother, he called not.

11 ¶ Wherefore Nathan spake unto Bath-sheba the mother of Solomon, saying, Hast thou not heard that Adonijah the son of [h]Haggith doth reign, and David our lord knoweth *it* not?

12 Now therefore come, let me, I pray thee, give thee counsel, that thou mayest save thine own life, and the life of thy son Solomon.

13 Go and get thee in unto king David, and say unto him, Didst not thou, my lord, O king, swear unto thine handmaid, saying, [i]Assuredly Solomon thy son shall reign after me, and he shall sit upon my throne? why then doth Adonijah reign?

14 Behold, while thou yet talkest there with the king, I also will come in after thee, and [j]confirm thy words.

15 ¶ And Bath-sheba went in unto the king into the chamber: and the king was very old; and Abishag the Shunammite ministered unto the king.

16 And Bath-sheba bowed, and did obeisance unto the king. And the king said, [k]What wouldest thou?

17 And she said unto him, My lord, [j]thou swarest by the LORD thy God unto thine handmaid, *saying,* Assuredly Solomon thy son shall reign after me, and he shall sit upon my throne.

18 And now, behold, Adonijah reigneth; and now, my lord the king, thou knowest *it* not:

19 [k]And he hath slain oxen and fat cattle and sheep in abundance, and hath called all the sons of the king, and Abiathar the priest, and Joab the captain of the host: but Solomon thy servant hath he not called.

1:3 [a]Josh. 19:18
1:5 [b]2 Sam. 3:4
1:6 [c]2 Sam. 3:3; 1 Chr. 3:2
1:7 [d]2 Sam. 20:25; [e]ch. 2:22,28
1:8 [f]ch. 4:18; [g]2 Sam. 23:8
1:11 [h]2 Sam. 3:4
1:13 [i]1 Chr. 22:9
1:17 [j]ver. 13,30
1:19 [k]ver. 7-9,25

[a] Heb. *entered into days* [b] Heb. *Let them seek* [c] Heb. *a damsel, a virgin* [d] Heb. *be a cherisher unto him* [e] Heb. *reign* [f] Heb. *from his days* [g] Heb. *his words were with Joab* [h] Heb. *helped after Adonijah* [i] Or, *The well Rogel* [j] Heb. *fill up* [k] Heb. *What to thee?*

1:6 HIS FATHER HAD NOT DISPLEASED HIM. Adonijah, David's fourth son, rebelled against his father by proclaiming himself king of Israel, even though God and David had designated Solomon as the next king (vv. 5,17,30; 2:15). (1) Until his death David had trouble with his sons. In spite of his record as a good ruler, he failed greatly as a father, neglecting or refusing to teach, guide, and "displease" (i.e., discipline) his sons properly as prescribed in Deut. 6:1–9. As a result, David's life was full of grief and sorrow. His first son, Amnon, raped his half-sister Tamar and was subsequently killed by his half-brother, Absalom (2 Sam. 13:1–33). David's third son, Absalom, rebelled against and attempted to kill his father (2 Sam. 15 — 18). Now his fourth son was rebelling and was later executed by Solomon (2:23–25).

(2) Because David failed to follow God's will regarding his family, he experienced one sorrow after another throughout his life. There is no fruit of discipleship more important in our lives than endeavoring with all our hearts to remain faithful to our spouse and children and to lead them into a life of godliness through teaching and example (see article on PARENTS AND CHILDREN, p. 1880).

20 And thou, my lord, O king, the eyes of all Israel *are* upon thee, that thou shouldest tell them who shall sit on the throne of my lord the king after him.

21 Otherwise it shall come to pass, when my lord the king shall [l]sleep with his fathers, that I and my son Solomon shall be counted [1]offenders.

22 ¶ And, lo, while she yet talked with the king, Nathan the prophet also came in.

23 And they told the king, saying, Behold Nathan the prophet. And when he was come in before the king, he bowed himself before the king with his face to the ground.

24 And Nathan said, My lord, O king, hast thou said, Adonijah shall reign after me, and he shall sit upon my throne?

25 [m]For he is gone down this day, and hath slain oxen and fat cattle and sheep in abundance, and hath called all the king's sons, and the captains of the host, and Abiathar the priest; and, behold, they eat and drink before him, and say, [n]God[m] save king Adonijah.

26 But me, *even* me thy servant, and Zadok the priest, and Benaiah the son of Jehoiada, and thy servant Solomon, hath he not called.

27 Is this thing done by my lord the king, and thou hast not showed *it* unto thy servant, who should sit on the throne of my lord the king after him?

Solomon anointed king

1:28–53pp — 1 Chr. 29:21–25

28 ¶ Then king David answered and said, Call me Bath-sheba. And she came [n]into the king's presence, and stood before the king.

29 And the king sware, and said, [o]*As* the LORD liveth, that hath redeemed my soul out of all distress,

30 [p]Even as I sware unto thee by the LORD God of Israel, saying, Assuredly Solomon thy son shall reign after me, and he shall sit upon my throne in my stead; even so will I certainly do this day.

31 Then Bath-sheba bowed with *her* face to the earth, and did reverence to the king, and said, [q]Let my lord king David live for ever.

32 ¶ And king David said, Call me Zadok the priest, and Nathan the prophet, and Benaiah the son of Jehoiada. And they came before the king.

33 The king also said unto them, [r]Take with you the servants of your lord, and cause Solomon my son to ride upon [o]mine own mule, and bring him down to [s]Gihon:

34 And let Zadok the priest and Nathan the prophet [t]anoint him there king over Israel: and [u]blow ye with the trumpet, and say, God save king Solomon.

35 Then ye shall come up after him, that he may come and sit upon my throne; for he shall be king in my stead: and I have appointed him to be ruler over Israel and over Judah.

36 And Benaiah the son of Jehoiada answered the king, and said, Amen: the LORD God of my lord the king say so *too*.

37 [v]As the LORD hath been with my lord the king, even so be he with Solomon, and [w]make his throne greater than the throne of my lord king David.

38 So Zadok the priest, and Nathan the prophet, [x]and Benaiah the son of Jehoiada, and the Cherethites, and the Pelethites, went down, and caused Solomon to ride upon king David's mule, and brought him to Gihon.

39 And Zadok the priest took an horn of [y]oil out of the tabernacle, and [z]anointed Solomon. And they blew the trumpet; [a]and all the people said, God save king Solomon.

40 And all the people came up after him, and the people piped with [p]pipes, and rejoiced with great joy, so that the earth rent with the sound of them.

41 ¶ And Adonijah and all the guests that *were* with him heard *it* as they had made an end of eating. And when Joab heard the sound of the trumpet, he said, Wherefore *is this* noise of the city being in an uproar?

42 And while he yet spake, behold, Jonathan the son of Abiathar the priest came: and Adonijah said unto him, Come in; for [b]thou *art* a valiant man, and bringest good tidings.

43 And Jonathan answered and said to Adonijah, Verily our lord king David hath made Solomon king.

44 And the king hath sent with him Zadok the priest, and Nathan the

1:21 [l]Deut. 31:16 ch. 2:10
1:25 [m]ver. 19 [n]1 Sam. 10:24
1:29 [o]2 Sam. 4:9
1:30 [p]ver. 17
1:31 [q]Neh. 2:3 Dan 2:4
1:33 [r]2 Sam. 20:6 [s]2 Chr. 32:30
1:34 [t]1 Sam. 10:1 & 16:3,12 2 Sam. 2:4 & 5:3 ch. 19:16 2 Ki. 9:3 & 11:12 [u]2 Sam. 15:10 2 Ki 9:13 & 11:14
1:37 [v]Josh. 1:5,17 1 Sam. 20:13 [w]ver. 47
1:38 [x]2 Sam. 8:18 & 23:20-23
1:39 [y]Ex. 30:23,25,32 Ps. 89:20 [z]1 Chr. 29:22 [a]1 Sam. 10:24
1:42 [b]2 Sam. 18:27

[1] Heb. *sinners* [m] Heb. *Let king Adonijah live* [n] Heb. *before the king* [o] Heb. *which* belongeth *to me* [p] Or, *flutes*

prophet, and Benaiah the son of Jehoiada, and the Cherethites, and the Pelethites, and they have caused him to ride upon the king's mule:

45 And Zadok the priest and Nathan the prophet have anointed him king in Gihon: and they are come up from thence rejoicing, so that the city rang again. This *is* the noise that ye have heard.

46 And also Solomon [c]sitteth on the throne of the kingdom.

47 And moreover the king's servants came to bless our lord king David, saying, [d]God make the name of Solomon better than thy name, and make his throne greater than thy throne. [e]And the king bowed himself upon the bed.

48 And also thus said the king, Blessed *be* the LORD God of Israel, which hath [f]given *one* to sit on my throne this day, mine eyes even seeing *it*.

49 And all the guests that *were* with Adonijah were afraid, and rose up, and went every man his way.

50 ¶ And Adonijah feared because of Solomon, and arose, and went, and [g]caught hold on the horns of the altar.

51 And it was told Solomon, saying, Behold, Adonijah feareth king Solomon: for, lo, he hath caught hold on the horns of the altar, saying, Let king Solomon swear unto me today that he will not slay his servant with the sword.

52 And Solomon said, If he will show himself a worthy man, [h]there shall not an hair of him fall to the earth: but if wickedness shall be found in him, he shall die.

53 So king Solomon sent, and they brought him down from the altar. And he came and bowed himself to king Solomon: and Solomon said unto him, Go to thine house.

1:46 [c]1 Chr. 29:23
1:47 [d]ver. 37 [e]Gen. 47:31
1:48 [f]ch. 3:6 Ps. 132:11,12
1:50 [g]ch. 2:28
1:52 [h]1 Sam. 14:45 2 Sam. 14:11

David's last words and death

2:10–12pp — 1 Chr. 29:26–28

2 NOW [i]THE days of David drew nigh that he should die; and he charged Solomon his son, saying,

2 [j]I go the way of all the earth: [k]be thou strong therefore, and show thyself a man;

3 And keep the charge of the LORD thy God, to walk in his ways, to keep his statutes, and his commandments, and his judgments, and his testimonies, as it is written in the law of Moses, that thou mayest [l]prosper[q] in all that thou doest, and whithersoever thou turnest thyself:

4 That the LORD may [m]continue his word which he spake concerning me, saying, [n]If thy children take heed to their way, to [o]walk before me in truth with all their heart and with all their soul, [p]there shall not [r]fail thee (said he) a man on the throne of Israel. 1 Ki. 9:3-8

5 Moreover thou knowest also what Joab the son of Zeruiah [q]did to me, *and* what he did to the two captains of the hosts of Israel, unto [r]Abner the son of Ner, and unto [s]Amasa the son of Jether, whom he slew, and [s]shed the blood of war in peace, and put the blood of war upon his girdle that *was* about his loins, and in his shoes that *were* on his feet.

6 Do therefore [t]according to thy wisdom, and let not his hoar head go down to the grave in peace.

7 But show kindness unto the sons of [u]Barzillai the Gileadite, and let them be of those that [v]eat at thy table: for so [w]they came to me when I fled because of Absalom thy brother.

8 And, behold, *thou hast* with thee [x]Shimei the son of Gera, a Benjamite of Bahurim, which cursed me with a [t]grievous curse in the day when I

2:1 [i]Gen. 47:29 Deut. 31:14
2:2 [j]Josh. 23:14 [k]Deut. 17:19,20
2:3 [l]Deut. 29:9 Josh. 1:7 1 Chr. 22:12,13
2:4 [m]2 Sam. 7:25 [n]Ps. 132:12 [o]2 Ki. 20:3 [p]2 Sam. 7:12,13 ch. 8:25
2:5 [q]2 Sam. 3:39 & 18:5,12,14 [r]2 Sam. 3:27 [s]2 Sam. 20:10
2:6 [t]ver. 9 Prov. 20:26
2:7 [u]2 Sam. 19:31,38 [v]2 Sam. 9:7,10 & 19:28 [w]2 Sam. 17:27
2:8 [x]2 Sam. 16:5

[q] Or, *do wisely* [r] Heb. *be cut off from thee from the throne* [s] Heb. *put* [t] Heb. *strong*

1:50 THE HORNS OF THE ALTAR. The horns of the altar were symbolic of God's mercy, forgiveness, and protection. Adonijah fled to the altar, believing that Solomon would not kill him in such a sacred place (cf. Ex. 21:13–14).

2:4 IF THY CHILDREN TAKE HEED. David had learned through painful experience and discipline that success and God's blessing depended on remaining in the ways and truth of God. Thus, David was deeply concerned that Solomon live a life of obedience and faithfulness to God. Yet Solomon and his sons ultimately failed to heed David's admonition and turned from God and His covenant (cf. 2 Chr. 7:17–22); the result was God's judgment on Solomon (11:1–13), the division of the kingdom (12:1–33), and the eventual destruction of both the northern and southern kingdoms. The ultimate fulfillment of God's promises to David was realized only in Jesus Christ (Acts 15:16–18).

2:5 JOAB . . . DID TO THE TWO CAPTAINS. David instructed Solomon to begin his reign by exercising justice on Joab, who was worthy of death for murdering Abner and Amasa (2 Sam. 3:27; 20:9–10; cf. Mat. 26:52).

went to Mahanaim: but [y]he came down to meet me at Jordan, and [z]I sware to him by the LORD, saying, I will not put thee to death with the sword.

9 Now therefore [a]hold him not guiltless: for thou *art* a wise man, and knowest what thou oughtest to do unto him; but his hoar head [b]bring thou down to the grave with blood.

10 So [c]David slept with his fathers, and was buried in [d]the city of David.

11 And the days that David [e]reigned over Israel *were* forty years: seven years reigned he in Hebron, and thirty and three years reigned he in Jerusalem.

12 ¶ [f]Then sat Solomon upon the throne of David his father; and his kingdom was established greatly.

13 ¶ And Adonijah the son of Haggith came to Bath-sheba the mother of Solomon. And she said, [g]Comest thou peaceably? And he said, Peaceably.

14 He said moreover, I have somewhat to say unto thee. And she said, Say on.

15 And he said, Thou knowest that the kingdom was mine, and *that* all Israel set their faces on me, that I should reign: howbeit the kingdom is turned about, and is become my brother's: for [h]it was his from the LORD.

16 And now I ask one petition of thee, [u]deny me not. And she said unto him, Say on.

17 And he said, Speak, I pray thee, unto Solomon the king, (for he will not say thee nay,) that he give me [i]Abishag the Shunammite to wife.

18 And Bath-sheba said, Well; I will speak for thee unto the king.

19 ¶ Bath-sheba therefore went unto king Solomon, to speak unto him for Adonijah. And the king rose up to meet her, and [j]bowed himself unto her, and sat down on his throne, and caused a seat to be set for the king's mother; [k]and she sat on his right hand.

20 Then she said, I desire one small petition of thee; *I pray thee,* say me not nay. And the king said unto her, Ask on, my mother: for I will not say thee nay.

21 And she said, Let Abishag the Shunammite be given to Adonijah thy brother to wife.

22 And king Solomon answered and said unto his mother, And why dost thou ask Abishag the Shunammite for Adonijah? ask for him the kingdom also; for he *is* mine elder brother; even for him, and for [l]Abiathar the priest, and for Joab the son of Zeruiah.

23 Then king Solomon sware by the LORD, saying, [m]God do so to me, and more also, if Adonijah have not spoken this word against his own life.

24 Now therefore, *as* the LORD liveth, which hath established me, and set me on the throne of David my father, and who hath made me an house, as he [n]promised, Adonijah shall be put to death this day.

25 And king Solomon sent by the hand of Benaiah the son of Jehoiada; and he fell upon him that he died.

26 ¶ And unto Abiathar the priest said the king, Get thee to [o]Anathoth, unto thine own fields; for thou *art* [v]worthy of death: but I will not at this time put thee to death, [p]because thou barest the ark of the Lord GOD before David my father, and because [q]thou hast been afflicted in all wherein my father was afflicted.

27 So Solomon thrust out Abiathar from being priest unto the LORD; that he might [r]fulfil the word of the LORD, which he spake concerning the house of Eli in Shiloh.

28 ¶ Then tidings came to Joab: for Joab [s]had turned after Adonijah,

[u] Heb. *turn not away my face* [v] Heb. *a man of death*

2:8 [y]2 Sam. 19:18 [z]2 Sam. 19:23
2:9 [a]Ex. 20:7 Job 9:28 [b]Gen. 42:38 & 44:31
2:10 [c]ch. 1:21 Acts 2:29 & 13:36 [d]2 Sam. 5:7
2:11 [e]2 Sam. 5:4 1 Chr. 29:26,27
2:12 [f]1 Chr. 29:23 2 Chr. 1:1
2:13 [g]1 Sam. 16:4,5
2:15 [h]1 Chr. 22:9,10 & 28:5-7 Dan. 2:21
2:17 [i]ch. 1:3,4
2:19 [j]Ex. 20:12 [k]See Ps. 45:9
2:22 [l]ch. 1:7
2:23 [m]Ruth 1:17
2:24 [n]2 Sam. 7:11,13 1 Chr. 22:10
2:26 [o]Josh. 21:18 [p]1 Sam. 23:6 2 Sam. 15:24,29 [q]1 Sam. 22:20,23 2 Sam. 15:24
2:27 [r]1 Sam. 2:31-35
2:28 [s]ch. 1:7

2:9 BRING THOU DOWN . . . WITH BLOOD. How sad that David's final recorded instruction to Solomon was to do an evil that he himself had sworn he would not do (cf. v. 8). David was thus breaking his word to Shimei (see 2 Sam. 19:23). This unforgiving severity must not be justified as pleasing to and blameless before God, but neither should it be judged entirely by N.T. standards (cf. Acts 17:30).

2:27 FULFILL THE WORD OF THE LORD. Nearly 120 years before this, a man of God had given a prophetic word to Eli the high priest concerning God's judgment on his house (cf. 1 Sam. 2:27–36). Part of his prophecy was fulfilled quickly (1 Sam. 4:10–22); part of it covered a long period of time. Abiathar's removal from the priesthood was part of the fulfillment of God's word to Eli. God never forgets. He always watches to see that His word is fulfilled (Jer. 1:12), though it sometimes encompasses a long span of time, even decades and generations. God's word will be fully realized.

though he turned not after Absalom. And Joab fled unto the tabernacle of the LORD, and [t]caught hold on the horns of the altar.

29 And it was told king Solomon that Joab was fled unto the tabernacle of the LORD; and, behold, *he is* by the altar. Then Solomon sent Benaiah the son of Jehoiada, saying, Go, fall upon him.

30 And Benaiah came to the tabernacle of the LORD, and said unto him, Thus saith the king, Come forth. And he said, Nay; but I will die here. And Benaiah brought the king word again, saying, Thus said Joab, and thus he answered me.

31 And the king said unto him, [u]Do as he hath said, and fall upon him, and bury him; [v]that thou mayest take away the innocent blood, which Joab shed, from me, and from the house of my father.

32 And the LORD [w]shall return his blood upon his own head, who fell upon two men more righteous [x]and better than he, and slew them with the sword, my father David not knowing *thereof, to wit,* [y]Abner the son of Ner, captain of the host of Israel, and [z]Amasa the son of Jether, captain of the host of Judah.

33 Their blood shall therefore return upon the head of Joab, and [a]upon the head of his seed for ever: [b]but upon David, and upon his seed, and upon his house, and upon his throne, shall there be peace for ever from the LORD.

34 So Benaiah the son of Jehoiada went up, and fell upon him, and slew him: and he was buried in his own house in the wilderness.

35 ¶ And the king put Benaiah the son of Jehoiada in his room over the host: and [c]Zadok the priest did the king put in the room of [d]Abiathar.

36 ¶ And the king sent and called for [e]Shimei, and said unto him, Build thee an house in Jerusalem, and dwell there, and go not forth thence any whither.

37 For it shall be, *that* on the day thou goest out, and passest over [f]the brook Kidron, thou shalt know for certain that thou shalt surely die: [g]thy blood shall be upon thine own head.

38 And Shimei said unto the king, The saying *is* good: as my lord the king hath said, so will thy servant do. And Shimei dwelt in Jerusalem many days.

39 And it came to pass at the end of three years, that two of the servants of Shimei ran away unto [h]Achish son of Maachah king of Gath. And they told Shimei, saying, Behold, thy servants *be* in Gath.

40 And Shimei arose, and saddled his ass, and went to Gath to Achish to seek his servants: and Shimei went, and brought his servants from Gath.

41 And it was told Solomon that Shimei had gone from Jerusalem to Gath, and was come again.

42 And the king sent and called for Shimei, and said unto him, Did I not make thee to swear by the LORD, and protested unto thee, saying, Know for a certain, on the day thou goest out, and walkest abroad any whither, that thou shalt surely die? and thou saidst unto me, The word *that* I have heard *is* good.

43 Why then hast thou not kept the oath of the LORD, and the commandment that I have charged thee with?

44 The king said moreover to Shimei, Thou knowest [i]all the wickedness which thine heart is privy to, that thou didst to David my father: therefore the LORD shall [j]return thy wickedness upon thine own head;

45 And king Solomon *shall be* blessed, and [k]the throne of David shall be established before the LORD for ever.

46 So the king commanded Benaiah the son of Jehoiada; which went out, and fell upon him, that he died. And the [l]kingdom was established in the hand of Solomon.

Prayer for wisdom granted

3:4–15pp — 2 Chr. 1:2–13

3 AND [m]SOLOMON made affinity with Pharaoh king of Egypt, and took Pharaoh's daughter, and brought her into the [n]city of David, until he had made an end of building his [o]own house, and [p]the house of the LORD, and [q]the wall of Jerusalem round about.

2 [r]Only the people sacrificed in

2:28 [t]ch. 1:50 **2:31** [u]Ex. 21:14 [v]Num. 35:33 Deut. 19:13 & 21:8,9 **2:32** [w]Judg. 9:24,57 [x]2 Chr. 21:13 [y]2 Sam. 3:27 [z]2 Sam. 20:10 **2:33** [a]2 Sam. 3:29 [b]Prov. 25:5 **2:35** [c]Num. 25:11-13 1 Sam. 2:35 See 1 Chr. 6:53 & 24:3 [d]ver. 27 **2:36** [e]ver. 8 2 Sam. 16:5 **2:37** [f]2 Sam. 15:23 [g]Lev. 20:9 Josh. 2:19 2 Sam. 1:16 **2:39** [h]1 Sam. 27:2 **2:44** [i]2 Sam. 16:5 [j]Ezek. 17:19 **2:45** [k]Prov. 25:5 **2:46** [l]ver. 12 2 Chr. 1:1 **3:1** [m]ch. 7:8 & 9:24 [n]2 Sam. 5:7 [o]ch. 7:1 [p]ch. 6 [q]ch. 9:15,19 **3:2** [r]Lev. 17:3-5 Deut. 12:2,4,5 ch. 22:43

3:2 SACRIFICED IN HIGH PLACES. Before the temple was built in Jerusalem as the central place of sacrifice, Israel offered sacrifices to God on hill tops or other elevated places, sometimes at the former sites of Canaanite pagan worship. Offering sacrifices at these places was forbidden by

high places, because there was no
house built unto the name of the LORD,
until those days.
3 And Solomon [s]loved the LORD,
[t]walking in the statutes of David his
father: only he sacrificed and burnt in-
cense in high places.
4 And [u]the king went to Gibeon to
sacrifice there; [v]for that *was* the great
high place: a thousand burnt offerings
did Solomon offer upon that altar.
5 ¶ [w]In Gibeon the LORD appeared
to Solomon [x]in a dream by night: and
God said, Ask what I shall give thee.
6 [y]And Solomon said, Thou hast
shown unto thy servant David my fa-
ther great [w]mercy, according as he
[z]walked before thee in truth, and in
righteousness, and in uprightness of
heart with thee; and thou hast kept for
him this great kindness, that thou
[a]hast given him a son to sit on his
throne, as *it is* this day.
7 And now, O LORD my God, thou
hast made thy servant king instead of
David my father: and I *am but* a little
child: I know not *how* [b]to go out or
come in.
8 And thy servant *is* in the midst of
thy people which thou [c]hast chosen, a
great people, [d]that cannot be num-
bered nor counted for multitude.
9 [e]Give therefore thy servant an
[x]understanding heart [f]to judge thy
people, that I may [g]discern between
good and bad: for who is able to judge
this thy so great a people?
10 And the speech pleased the

3:3 [s]Deut. 6:5 & 30:16,20 Rom. 8:28 1 Cor. 8:3 [t]ver. 6,14
3:4 [u]2 Chr. 1:3 [v]1 Chr. 16:39 2 Chr. 1:3
3:5 [w]ch. 9:2 2 Chr. 1:7 [x]Num. 12:6 Mat. 1:20
3:6 [y]2 Chr. 1:8 [z]ch. 2:4 & 9:4 2 Ki. 20:3
[a]ch. 1:48
3:7 [b]Num. 27:17
3:8 [c]Deut. 7:6 [d]Gen. 13:16 & 15:5
3:9 [e]2 Chr. 1:10 Prov. 2:3-9 Jas. 1:5 [f]Ps. 72:1,2 [g]Heb. 5:14

[w]Or, *bounty* [x]Heb. *hearing*

O.T. law, for all the Canaanite high places were to be destroyed (Lev. 17:3–5; Deut. 7:5; 12:3). Altars for worship and sacrifice were to be built at only divinely designated places (Ex. 20:24; Deut. 12:5, 8,13–14).

3:9 GIVE THEREFORE THY SERVANT AN UNDERSTANDING HEART. Solomon began his reign in faith in and love for the Lord (v. 3). He prayed for wisdom and a discerning heart (vv. 5–9); God was pleased with his request (v. 10) and granted his prayer (vv. 11–14). However, God's gift of wisdom did not guarantee that Solomon would always persist in godliness. For this reason God emphasized that long life would be his "if thou wilt walk in my ways" (v. 14). Solomon's unfaithfulness later in life prevented the full realization of God's will for his life (11:1–8).

3:10 PLEASED THE LORD. God is pleased

SOLOMON'S JERUSALEM

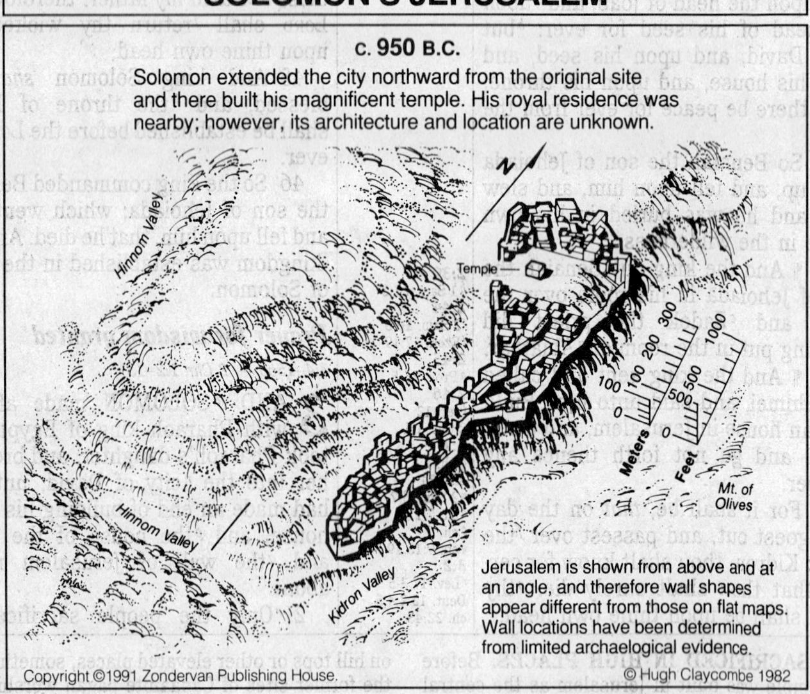

Lord, that Solomon had asked this thing.

11 And God said unto him, Because thou hast asked this thing, and hast [h]not asked for thyself [y]long life; neither hast asked riches for thyself, nor hast asked the life of thine enemies; but hast asked for thyself understanding [z]to discern judgment;

12 [i]Behold, I have done according to thy words: [j]lo, I have given thee a wise and an understanding heart; so that there was none like thee before thee, neither after thee shall any arise like unto thee.

13 And I have also [k]given thee that which thou hast not asked, both [l]riches, and honour: so that there [a]shall not be any among the kings like unto thee all thy days.

14 And if thou wilt walk in my ways, to keep my statutes and my commandments, [m]as thy father David did walk, then I will [n]lengthen thy days.

15 And Solomon [o]awoke; and, behold, *it was* a dream. And he came to Jerusalem, and stood before the ark of the covenant of the LORD, and offered up burnt offerings, and offered peace offerings, and [p]made a feast to all his servants.

Solomon's wise decision

16 ¶ Then came there two women, *that were* harlots, unto the king, and [q]stood before him.

17 And the one woman said, O my lord, I and this woman dwell in one house; and I was delivered of a child with her in the house.

18 And it came to pass the third day after that I was delivered, that this woman was delivered also: and we *were* together; *there was* no stranger with us in the house, save we two in the house.

19 And this woman's child died in the night; because she overlaid it.

20 And she arose at midnight, and took my son from beside me, while thine handmaid slept, and laid it in her bosom, and laid her dead child in my bosom.

21 And when I rose in the morning to give my child suck, behold, it was dead: but when I had considered it in the morning, behold, it was not my son, which I did bear.

22 And the other woman said, Nay; but the living *is* my son, and the dead *is* thy son. And this said, No; but the dead *is* thy son, and the living *is* my son. Thus they spake before the king.

23 Then said the king, The one saith, This *is* my son that liveth, and thy son *is* the dead: and the other saith, Nay; but thy son *is* the dead, and my son *is* the living.

24 And the king said, Bring me a sword. And they brought a sword before the king.

25 And the king said, Divide the living child in two, and give half to the one, and half to the other.

26 Then spake the woman whose the living child *was* unto the king, for [r]her bowels [b]yearned upon her son, and she said, O my lord, give her the living child, and in no wise slay it. But the other said, Let it be neither mine nor thine, *but* divide *it*.

27 Then the king answered and said, Give her the living child, and in no wise slay it: she *is* the mother thereof.

28 And all Israel heard of the judgment which the king had judged; and they feared the king: for they saw that the [s]wisdom of God *was* [c]in him, to do judgment.

Appointment of court officials

4 SO KING Solomon was king over all Israel.

2 And these *were* the princes which he had; Azariah the son of Zadok [d]the priest,

3 Elihoreph and Ahiah, the sons of Shisha, [e]scribes; [t]Jehoshaphat the son of Ahilud, the [f]recorder.

4 And [u]Benaiah the son of Jehoiada *was* over the host: and Zadok and [v]Abiathar *were* the priests:

5 And Azariah the son of Nathan *was* over [w]the officers: and Zabud the son of Nathan *was* [x]principal officer, *and* [y]the king's friend:

6 And Ahishar *was* over the house-

3:11 [h]Jas. 4:3
3:12 [i]1 John 5:14,15 [j]ch. 4:29-31 Eccl. 1:16
3:13 [k]Mat. 6:33 Eph. 3:20 [l]ch. 4:21,24
3:14 [m]ch. 15:5 [n]Ps. 91:16 Prov. 3:2
3:15 [o]Gen. 41:7 [p]Gen. 40:20 ch. 8:65 Esth. 1:3 Dan. 5:1 Mark 6:21
3:16 [q]Num. 27:2
3:26 [r]Gen. 43:30 Is. 49:15 Jer. 31:20 Hos. 11:8
3:28 [s]ver. 9,11,12
4:3 [t]2 Sam. 8:16 & 20:24
4:4 [u]ch. 2:35 [v]See ch. 2:27
4:5 [w]ver. 7 [x]2 Sam. 8:18 & 20:26 [y]2 Sam. 15:37 & 16:16 1 Chr. 27:33

[y] Heb. *many days* [z] Heb. *to hear* [a] Or, *hath not been* [b] Heb. *were hot* [c] Heb. *in the midst of him* [d] Or, *the chief officer* [e] Or, *secretaries* [f] Or, *remembrancer*

---

when believers sincerely seek and pray for godly wisdom and a discerning heart. "If any of you lack wisdom, let him ask of God, that giveth to all *men* liberally, and upbraideth not; and it shall be given him" (Jas. 1:5; cf. Prov. 2:2–6; 3:15; Luke 12:31; Eph. 5:17; Jas. 3:17).

hold: and [z]Adoniram the son of Abda *was* over the [g]tribute.

7 ¶ And Solomon had twelve officers over all Israel, which provided victuals for the king and his household: each man his month in a year made provision.

8 And these *are* their names: [h]The son of Hur, in mount Ephraim:

9 [i]The son of Dekar, in Makaz, and in Shaalbim, and Beth-shemesh, and Elon-beth-hanan:

10 [j]The son of Hesed, in Aruboth; to him *pertained* Sochoh, and all the land of Hepher:

11 [k]The son of Abinadab, in all the region of Dor; which had Taphath the daughter of Solomon to wife:

12 Baana the son of Ahilud; *to him pertained* Taanach and Megiddo, and all Beth-shean, which *is* by Zartanah beneath Jezreel, from Beth-shean to Abel-meholah, *even* unto *the place that is* beyond Jokneam:

13 [l]The son of Geber, in Ramoth-gilead; to him *pertained* [a]the towns of Jair the son of Manasseh, which *are* in Gilead; to him *also pertained* [b]the region of Argob, which *is* in Bashan, threescore great cities with walls and brasen bars:

14 Ahinadab the son of Iddo *had* [m]Mahanaim:

15 Ahimaaz *was* in Naphtali; he also took Basmath the daughter of Solomon to wife:

16 Baanah the son of Hushai *was* in Asher and in Aloth:

17 Jehoshaphat the son of Paruah, in Issachar:

18 Shimei the son of Elah, in Benjamin:

19 Geber the son of Uri *was* in the country of Gilead, *in* [c]the country of Sihon king of the Amorites, and of Og king of Bashan; and *he was* the only officer which *was* in the land.

20 ¶ Judah and Israel *were* many, [d]as the sand which *is* by the sea in multitude, [e]eating and drinking, and making merry.

21 And [f]Solomon reigned over all kingdoms from [g]the river unto the land of the Philistines, and unto the border of Egypt: [h]they brought presents, and served Solomon all the days of his life.

The household provisions

22 ¶ And Solomon's [n]provision for one day was thirty [o]measures of fine flour, and threescore measures of meal,

23 Ten fat oxen, and twenty oxen out of the pastures, and an hundred sheep, beside harts, and roebucks, and fallowdeer, and fatted fowl.

24 For he had dominion over all *the region* on this side the river, from Tiphsah even to Azzah, over [i]all the kings on this side the river: and [j]he had peace on all sides round about him.

25 And Judah and Israel [k]dwelt [p]safely, [l]every man under his vine and under his fig tree, [m]from Dan even to Beer-sheba, all the days of Solomon.

26 ¶ And [n]Solomon had forty thousand stalls of [o]horses for his chariots, and twelve thousand horsemen.

27 And [p]those officers provided victual for king Solomon, and for all that came unto king Solomon's table, every man in his month: they lacked nothing.

28 Barley also and straw for the horses and [q]dromedaries brought they unto the place where *the officers* were, every man according to his charge.

Solomon's great wisdom

29 ¶ And [q]God gave Solomon wisdom and understanding exceeding

4:6 [z]ch. 5:14
4:13 [a]Num. 32:41 [b]Deut. 3:4
4:19 [c]Deut. 3:8
4:20 [d]Gen. 22:17 ch. 3:8 Prov. 14:28 [e]Ps. 72:3,7 Mic. 4:4
4:21 [f]2 Chr. 9:26 Ps. 72:8 [g]Gen. 15:18 Josh. 1:4 [h]Ps. 68:29 & 72:10,11
4:24 [i]Ps. 72:11 [j]1 Chr. 22:9
4:25 [k]See Jer. 23:6 [l]Mic. 4:4 Zech. 3:10 [m]Judg. 20:1
4:26 [n]ch. 10:26 2 Chr. 1:14 [o]See Deut. 17:16
4:27 [p]ver. 7
4:29 [q]ch. 3:12

[g] Or, *levy* [h] Or, *Ben-hur* [i] Or, *Ben-dekar* [j] Or, *Ben-hesed* [k] Or, *Ben-abin-adab* [l] Or, *Ben-geber* [m] Or, *to Mahanaim* [n] Heb. *bread* [o] Heb. *cors* [p] Heb. *confidently* [q] Or, *mules,* or, *swift beasts*

4:24 PEACE ON ALL SIDES. During Solomon's rule, Israel as a nation reached its pinnacle of power, peace, and prosperity (vv. 20–28). Politically and materially Solomon's reign was a success; spiritually, however, Solomon's slide into idolatry would leave his reign judged to be a failure (11:1–8).

4:29–34 GOD GAVE SOLOMON WISDOM. Solomon's wisdom involved a breadth of understanding and discernment concerning life and his responsibilities as king (cf. 3:9). He wrote 3,000 proverbs (v. 32), many of which have been preserved in the book of Proverbs. (1) How could Solomon, who was given such godly wisdom, eventually turn from the Lord to serve other gods? Clearly, to have wisdom and to follow wisdom are two different issues. Solomon's greatest failure was that he did not apply his own spiritual wisdom to every area of his life. Though he was the wisest man of his time, he did not live as wisely as some of God's faithful people.

(2) Solomon was brought to spiritual ruin pri-

much, and largeness of heart, even as
the sand that *is* on the sea shore.
30 And Solomon's wisdom excelled
the wisdom of all the children [r]of the
east country, and all [s]the wisdom of
Egypt.
31 For he was [t]wiser than all men;
[u]than Ethan the Ezrahite, [v]and He-
man, and Chalcol, and Darda, the sons
of Mahol: and his fame was in all na-
tions round about.
32 And [w]he spake three thousand
proverbs: and his [x]songs were a thou-
sand and five.
33 And he spake of trees, from the
cedar tree that *is* in Lebanon even unto
the hyssop that springeth out of the
wall: he spake also of beasts, and of
fowl, and of creeping things, and of
fishes.
34 And [y]there came of all people to
hear the wisdom of Solomon, from all
kings of the earth, which had heard of
his wisdom.

Preparing to build the temple

5:1–16pp — 2 Chr. 2:1–18

5 AND [z]HIRAM king of Tyre sent
his servants unto Solomon; for he
had heard that they had anointed him
king in the room of his father: [a]for Hi-
ram was ever a lover of David.
2 And [b]Solomon sent to Hiram,
saying,
3 Thou knowest how that David my
father could not build an house unto
the name of the LORD his God [c]for the
wars which were about him on every
side, until the LORD put them under the
soles of his feet.
4 But now the LORD my God hath
given me [d]rest on every side, *so that*
there is neither adversary nor evil oc-
current.
5 [e]And, behold, I [r]purpose to
build an house unto the name of the
LORD my God, [f]as the LORD spake unto
David my father, saying, Thy son,
whom I will set upon thy throne in thy
room, he shall build an house unto my
name.
6 Now therefore command thou that
they hew me [g]cedar trees out of Leba-
non; and my servants shall be with thy
servants: and unto thee will I give hire
for thy servants according to all that
thou shalt [r]appoint: for thou knowest
that *there is* not among us any that can
skill to hew timber like unto the Sido-
nians.
7 ¶ And it came to pass, when Hi-
ram heard the words of Solomon, that
he rejoiced greatly, and said, Blessed
be the LORD this day, which hath given
unto David a wise son over this great
people.
8 And Hiram sent to Solomon, say-
ing, I have [s]considered the things
which thou sentest to me for: *and* I
will do all thy desire concerning tim-
ber of cedar, and concerning timber
of fir.
9 My servants shall bring *them*
down from Lebanon unto the sea: and
I will convey them by sea in floats unto
the place that thou shalt [t]appoint me,
and will cause them to be discharged
there, and thou shalt receive *them:* and
thou shalt accomplish my desire, [h]in
giving food for my household.
10 So Hiram gave Solomon cedar
trees and fir trees *according to* all his
desire.
11 [i]And Solomon gave Hiram
twenty thousand [u]measures of wheat
for food to his household, and twenty
measures of pure oil: thus gave Solo-
mon to Hiram year by year.
12 And the LORD gave Solomon wis-
dom, [j]as he promised him: and there
was peace between Hiram and Solo-
mon; and they two made a league to-
gether.
13 ¶ And king Solomon raised a

4:30 [r]Gen. 25:6 [s]See Acts 7:22
4:31 [t]ch. 3:12 [u]1 Chr. 15:19 Ps. 89,title [v]See 1 Chr. 2:6 & 6:33 & 15:19 Ps. 88,title
4:32 [w]Prov. 1:1 Eccl. 12:9 [x]Sol. 1:1
4:34 [y]ch. 10:1 2 Chr. 9:1,23
5:1 [z]ver. 10,18 2 Chr. 2:3 *Huram* [a]2 Sam. 5:11 1 Chr. 14:1 Amos 1:9
5:2 [b]2 Chr. 2:3
5:3 [c]1 Chr. 22:8 & 28:3
5:4 [d]ch. 4:24 1 Chr. 22:9
5:5 [e]2 Chr. 2:4 [f]2 Sam. 7:13 1 Chr. 17:12
5:6 [g]2 Chr. 2:8,10
5:9 [h]See Ezra 3:7 Ezek. 27:17 Acts 12:20
5:11 [i]See 2 Chr. 2:10
5:12 [j]ch. 3:12

[r]Heb. *say* [s]Heb. *heard* [t]Heb. *send* [u]Heb. *cors*

marily because he married so many foreign women (11:1–8). Two factors were involved: (a) He did this to form political and military alliances, and in so doing failed to trust that the Lord would keep his kingdom secure from foreign threats. (b) He undoubtedly found it difficult to resist the lusts of the flesh in his desire for women, also a character flaw of his father David.

5:5 I PURPOSE TO BUILD A HOUSE . . . OF THE LORD. Chs. 5–8 record the steps taken by Solomon to build the temple where God would continuously manifest His presence and glory. The temple was a dwelling place for God and a place for the people to gather to worship Him (cf. 8:15–21; 2 Sam. 7:12–13). It was built in Jerusalem on Mount Moriah (2 Chr. 3:1; cf. Gen. 22:2) and took seven years to complete (6:38; see 6:2, note). God gave David the plans for the temple by revelation of the Holy Spirit (1 Chr. 28:12), and David provided many of the resources before he died.

[v]levy out of all Israel; and the levy was thirty thousand men.

14 And he sent them to Lebanon, ten thousand a month by courses: a month they were in Lebanon, *and* two months at home: and [k]Adoniram *was* over the levy.

15 [l]And Solomon had threescore and ten thousand that bare burdens, and fourscore thousand hewers in the mountains;

16 Beside the chief of Solomon's officers which *were* over the work, three thousand and three hundred, which ruled over the people that wrought in the work.

17 And the king commanded, and they brought great stones, costly stones, *and* [m]hewed stones, to lay the foundation of the house.

18 And Solomon's builders and Hiram's builders did hew *them,* and the [w]stonesquarers: so they prepared timber and stones to build the house.

The description of the temple

6:1–29pp — 2 Chr. 3:1–14

6 AND [n]IT came to pass in the four hundred and eightieth year after the children of Israel were come out of the land of Egypt, in the fourth year of Solomon's reign over Israel, in the month Zif, which *is* the second month, that [o]he [x]began to build the house of the LORD.

2 And [p]the house which king Solomon built for the LORD, the length thereof *was* threescore cubits, and the breadth thereof twenty *cubits,* and the height thereof thirty cubits.

3 And the porch before the temple of the house, twenty cubits *was* the length thereof, according to the breadth of the house; *and* ten cubits *was* the breadth thereof before the house.

4 And for the house he made [q]windows[y] of narrow lights.

5 ¶ And [z]against the wall of the house he built [r]chambers[a] round about, *against* the walls of the house round about, *both* of the temple [s]and of the oracle: and he made [b]chambers round about:

6 The nethermost chamber *was* five cubits broad, and the middle *was* six cubits broad, and the third *was* seven cubits broad: for without *in the wall* of the house he made [c]narrowed rests round about, that *the beams* should not be fastened in the walls of the house.

7 And [t]the house, when it was in building, was built of stone made ready before it was brought thither: so that there was neither hammer nor axe *nor* any tool of iron heard in the house, while it was in building.

8 The door for the middle chamber *was* in the right [d]side of the house: and they went up with winding stairs into the middle *chamber,* and out of the middle into the third.

9 [u]So he built the house, and finished it; and covered the house [e]with beams and boards of cedar.

10 And *then* he built chambers against all the house, five cubits high: and they rested on the house with timber of cedar.

11 ¶ And the word of the LORD came to Solomon, saying,

12 *Concerning* this house which thou art in building, [v]if thou wilt walk in my statutes, and execute my judgments, and keep all my commandments to walk in them; then will I per-

5:14 [k]ch. 4:6 **5:15** [l]ch. 9:21 2 Chr. 2:18 **5:17** [m]1 Chr. 22:2 **6:1** [n]2 Chr. 3:1,2 [o]Acts 7:47 **6:2** [p]See Ezek. 41:1 **6:4** [q]See Ezek. 40:16 **6:5** [r]See Ezek. 41:6 [s]ver. 16,19-21,31 **6:7** [t]See Deut. 27:5,6 **6:9** [u]ver. 14,38 **6:12** [v]ch. 2:4 & 9:4

[v]Heb. *tribute* of men [w]Or, *Giblites* as Ezek. 27:9 [x]Heb. *built* [y]Or, *windows broad within, and narrow without:* or, *skewed and closed* [z]Or, *upon,* or, *joining to* [a]Heb. *floors* [b]Heb. *ribs* [c]Heb. *narrowings,* or, *rebatements* [d]Heb. *shoulder* [e]Or, *the vault-beams and the ceilings with cedar*

6:1 FOUR HUNDRED AND EIGHTIETH YEAR AFTER. This verse is crucial in establishing the date for the exodus of Israel out of Egypt. Solomon began to build the house of the Lord about 966 B.C. This date has been determined by integrating Biblical data with Assyrian chronological records. The exodus occurred 480 years before that date; this would place that event at about 1446 B.C. (cf. Acts 13:19–20).

6:2 THE HOUSE . . . FOR THE LORD. The temple, housing the ark of the covenant (see Ex. 25:16), symbolized God's presence and character among His people. The temple communicated the truth that God desired to dwell in the midst of His people (Lev. 26:12; cf. John 14:21–23). It was a visible sign and pledge of His covenant relationship with the people (Ex. 29:45–46), and it was built that God's name might dwell there (5:5; 8:16; 9:3). The name of God is "holy" (Lev. 20:3; 1 Chr. 16:10,35; Ezek. 39:7). Thus, God wanted to be known and worshiped by Israel as the Holy One and the Sanctifier of His people (Ex. 29:43–46; Ezek. 37:26–28). For more detail, see article on THE TEMPLE, p. 654.

6:12 IF THOU WILT WALK IN MY STATUTES. The books of 1 and 2 Kings record the tragic history of the persistent failure of God's people to meet this condition (cf. 2:3–4; 3:14).

form my word with thee, [w]which I spake unto David thy father:

13 And I [x]will dwell among the children of Israel, and will not [y]forsake my people Israel.

14 So Solomon built the house, and finished it.

15 And he built the walls of the house within with boards of cedar, [f]both the floor of the house, and the walls of the ceiling: *and* he covered *them* on the inside with wood, and covered the floor of the house with planks of fir.

16 And he built twenty cubits on the sides of the house, both the floor and the walls with boards of cedar: he even built *them* for it within, *even* for the oracle, *even* for the [z]most holy *place*.

17 And the house, that *is*, the temple before it, was forty cubits *long*.

18 And the cedar of the house within *was* carved with [g]knobs and [h]open flowers: all *was* cedar; there was no stone seen.

19 And the oracle he prepared in the house within, to set there the ark of the covenant of the LORD.

20 And the oracle in the forepart *was* twenty cubits in length, and twenty cubits in breadth, and twenty cubits in the height thereof: and he overlaid it with [i]pure gold; and *so* covered the altar *which was of* cedar.

21 So Solomon overlaid the house within with pure gold: and he made a partition by the chains of gold before the oracle; and he overlaid it with gold.

22 And the whole house he overlaid with gold, until he had finished all the house: also [a]the whole altar that *was* by the oracle he overlaid with gold.

23 ¶ And within the oracle [b]he made two cherubims *of* [j] [k]olive tree, *each* ten cubits high.

24 And five cubits *was* the one wing of the cherub, and five cubits the other wing of the cherub: from the uttermost part of the one wing unto the uttermost part of the other *were* ten cubits.

25 And the other cherub *was* ten cubits: both the cherubims *were* of one measure and one size.

26 The height of the one cherub *was* ten cubits, and so *was it* of the other cherub.

27 And he set the cherubims within the inner house: and [c]they[l] stretched forth the wings of the cherubims, so that the wing of the one touched the *one* wall, and the wing of the other cherub touched the other wall; and their wings touched one another in the midst of the house.

28 And he overlaid the cherubims with gold.

29 And he carved all the walls of the house round about with carved figures of cherubims and palm trees and [h]open flowers, within and without.

30 And the floor of the house he overlaid with gold, within and without.

31 ¶ And for the entering of the oracle he made doors *of* olive tree: the lintel *and* side posts *were* [m]a fifth part *of the wall*.

32 The [n]two doors also *were of* olive tree; and he carved upon them carvings of cherubims and palm trees and [h]open flowers, and overlaid *them* with gold, and spread gold upon the cherubims, and upon the palm trees.

33 So also made he for the door of the temple posts *of* olive tree, [o]a fourth part *of the wall*.

34 And the two doors *were of* fir tree: the [d]two leaves of the one door *were* folding, and the two leaves of the other door *were* folding.

35 And he carved *thereon* cherubims and palm trees and open flowers: and covered *them* with gold fitted upon the carved work.

36 ¶ And he built the inner court with three rows of hewed stone, and a row of cedar beams.

37 ¶ [e]In the fourth year was the foundation of the house of the LORD laid, in the month Zif:

38 And in the eleventh year, in the month Bul, which *is* the eighth month, was the house finished [p]throughout all the parts thereof, and according to all the fashion of it. So was he [f]seven years in building it.

The palace buildings

7 BUT SOLOMON was building his own house [g]thirteen years, and he finished all his house.

2 ¶ He built also the house of the forest of Lebanon; the length thereof

6:12 [w]2 Sam. 7:13 1 Chr. 22:10
6:13 [x]Ex. 25:8 2 Cor. 6:16 Rev. 21:3 [y]Deut. 31:6
6:16 [z]Ex. 26:33 Lev. 16:2 ch. 8:6 2 Chr. 3:8 Ezek. 45:3
6:22 [a]Ex. 30:1,3,6
6:23 [b]Ex. 37:7-9 2 Chr. 3:10-12
6:27 [c]Ex. 25:20 & 37:9 2 Chr. 5:8
6:34 [d]Ezek. 41:23-25
6:37 [e]ver. 1
6:38 [f]Compare ver. 1
7:1 [g]ch. 9:10 2 Chr. 8:1

[f] Or, *from the floor of the house unto the walls*
[g] Or, *goards* [h] Heb. *openings of flowers*
[i] Heb. *shut up* [j] Or, *oily* [k] Heb. *trees of oil*
[l] Or, *the cherubims stretched forth their wings*
[m] Or, *fivesquare* [n] Or, *leaves of the doors*
[o] Or, *foursquare* [p] Or, *with all the appurtenances thereof, and with all the ordinances thereof*

SOLOMON'S TEMPLE

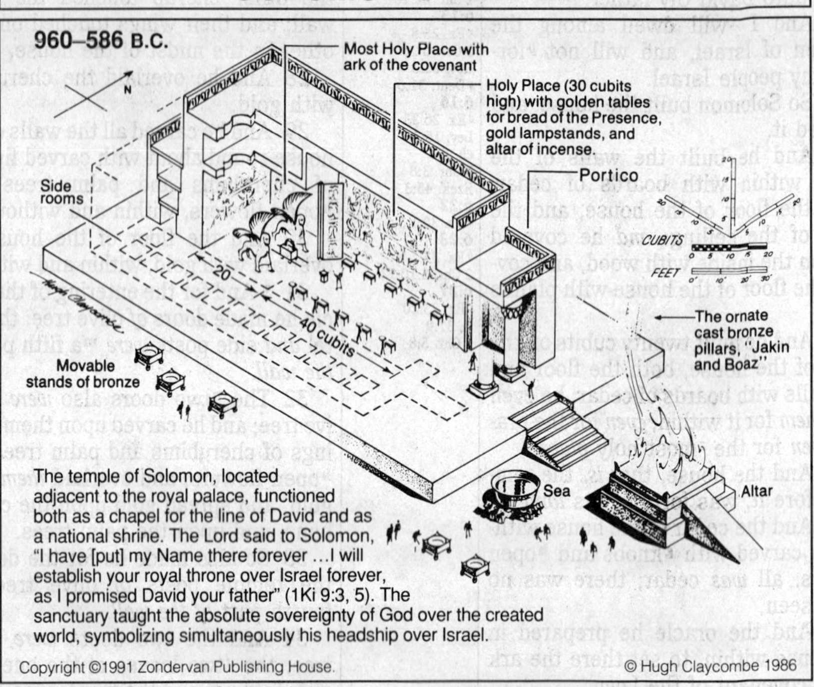

The temple of Solomon, located adjacent to the royal palace, functioned both as a chapel for the line of David and as a national shrine. The Lord said to Solomon, "I have [put] my Name there forever …I will establish your royal throne over Israel forever, as I promised David your father" (1Ki 9:3, 5). The sanctuary taught the absolute sovereignty of God over the created world, symbolizing simultaneously his headship over Israel.

TEMPLE FURNISHINGS

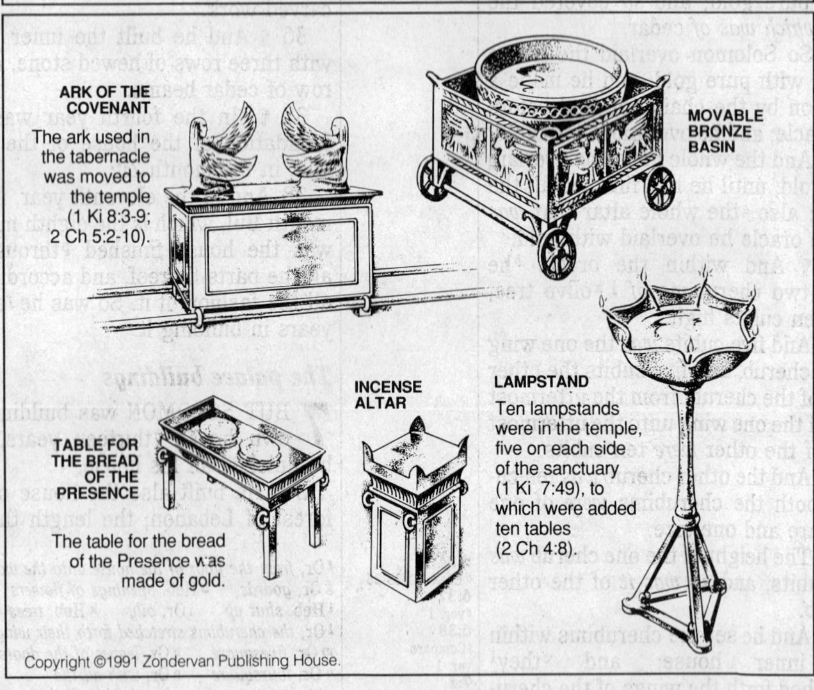

ARK OF THE COVENANT The ark used in the tabernacle was moved to the temple (1 Ki 8:3-9; 2 Ch 5:2-10).

LAMPSTAND Ten lampstands were in the temple, five on each side of the sanctuary (1 Ki 7:49), to which were added ten tables (2 Ch 4:8).

TABLE FOR THE BREAD OF THE PRESENCE The table for the bread of the Presence was made of gold.

was an hundred cubits, and the breadth thereof fifty cubits, and the height thereof thirty cubits, upon four rows of cedar pillars, with cedar beams upon the pillars.

3 And *it was* covered with cedar above upon the [q]beams, that *lay* on forty-five pillars, fifteen *in* a row.

4 And *there were* windows *in* three rows, and [r]light *was* against light *in* three ranks.

5 And all the [s]doors and posts *were* square, with the windows: and light *was* against light *in* three ranks.

6 ¶ And he made a porch of pillars; the length thereof *was* fifty cubits, and the breadth thereof thirty cubits: and the porch *was* [t]before them: and the *other* pillars and the thick beam *were* [t]before them.

7 ¶ Then he made a porch for the throne where he might judge, *even* the porch of judgment: and *it was* covered with cedar [u]from one side of the floor to the other.

8 ¶ And his house where he dwelt *had* another court within the porch, *which* was of the like work. Solomon made also an house for Pharaoh's daughter, [h]whom he had taken *to wife,* like unto this porch.

9 All these *were of* costly stones, according to the measures of hewed stones, sawed with saws, within and without, even from the foundation unto the coping, and *so* on the outside toward the great court.

10 And the foundation *was of* costly stones, even great stones, stones of ten cubits, and stones of eight cubits.

11 And above *were* costly stones, after the measures of hewed stones, and cedars.

12 And the great court round about *was* with three rows of hewed stones, and a row of cedar beams, both for the inner court of the house of the LORD, [i]and for the porch of the house.

The temple furnishings

7:23–26pp — 2 Chr. 4:2–5
7:38–51pp — 2 Chr. 4:6,10–5:1

13 ¶ And king Solomon sent and fetched [j]Hiram out of Tyre.

14 [k]He *was* [v]a widow's son of the tribe of Naphtali, and [l]his father *was* a man of Tyre, a worker in brass: and [m]he was filled with wisdom, and understanding, and cunning to work all works in brass. And he came to king Solomon, and wrought all his work.

15 For he [w]cast [n]two pillars of brass, of eighteen cubits high apiece: and a line of twelve cubits did compass either of them about.

16 And he made two chapiters *of* molten brass, to set upon the tops of the pillars: the height of the one chapiter *was* five cubits, and the height of the other chapiter *was* five cubits:

17 *And* nets of checker work, and wreaths of chain work, for the chapiters which *were* upon the top of the pillars; seven for the one chapiter, and seven for the other chapiter.

18 And he made the pillars, and two rows round about upon the one network, to cover the chapiters that *were* upon the top, with pomegranates: and so did he for the other chapiter.

19 And the chapiters that *were* upon the top of the pillars *were* of lily work in the porch, four cubits.

20 And the chapiters upon the two pillars *had pomegranates* also above, over against the belly which *was* by the network: and the pomegranates *were* [o]two hundred in rows round about upon the other chapiter.

21 [p]And he set up the pillars in the porch of the temple: and he set up the right pillar, and called the name thereof [x]Jachin: and he set up the left pillar, and called the name thereof [y]Boaz.

22 And upon the top of the pillars *was* lily work: so was the work of the pillars finished.

23 ¶ And he made [q]a molten sea, ten cubits [z]from the one brim to the other: *it was* round all about, and his height *was* five cubits: and a line of thirty cubits did compass it round about.

24 And under the brim of it round about *there were* knobs compassing it, ten in a cubit, [r]compassing the sea round about: the knobs *were* cast in two rows, when it was cast.

25 It stood upon [s]twelve oxen, three looking toward the north, and three looking toward the west, and

7:8 [h]ch. 3:1; 2 Chr. 8:11
7:12 [i]John 10:23; Acts 3:11
7:13 [j]2 Chr. 4:11; *Huram:* See ver. 40
7:14 [k]2 Chr. 2:14; [l]2 Chr. 4:16; [m]Ex. 31:3 & 36:1
7:15 [n]2 Ki. 25:17; 2 Chr. 3:15 & 4:12; Jer. 52:21
7:20 [o]See 2 Chr. 3:16 & 4:13; Jer. 52:23
7:21 [p]2 Chr. 3:17
7:23 [q]2 Ki. 25:13; 2 Chr. 4:2; Jer. 52:17
7:24 [r]2 Chr. 4:3
7:25 [s]2 Chr. 4:4,5; Jer. 52:20

[q] Heb. *ribs* [r] Heb. *sight against sight* [s] Or, *spaces and pillars were square in prospect* [t] Or, *according to them* [u] Heb. *from floor to floor* [v] Heb. *the son of a widow woman* [w] Heb. *fashioned* [x] i.e. *He shall establish* [y] i.e. *In it is strength* [z] Heb. *from his brim to his brim*

three looking toward the south, and three looking toward the east: and the sea *was set* above upon them, and all their hinder parts *were* inward.

26 And it *was* an handbreadth thick, and the brim thereof was wrought like the brim of a cup, with flowers of lilies: it contained [t]two thousand baths.

27 ¶ And he made ten bases of brass; four cubits *was* the length of one base, and four cubits the breadth thereof, and three cubits the height of it.

28 And the work of the bases *was* on this *manner:* they had borders, and the borders *were* between the ledges:

29 And on the borders that *were* between the ledges *were* [u]lions, oxen, and cherubims: and upon the ledges *there was* a base above: and beneath the lions and oxen *were* certain additions made of thin work.

30 And every base had four brasen wheels, and plates of brass: and the four corners thereof had undersetters: under the laver *were* undersetters molten, at the side of every addition.

31 And the mouth of it within the chapiter and above *was* a cubit: but the mouth thereof *was* round *after* the work of the base, a cubit and an half: and also upon the mouth of it *were* gravings with their borders, foursquare, not round.

32 And under the borders *were* four wheels; and the axletrees of the wheels *were* [a]*joined* to the base: and the height of a wheel *was* a cubit and half a cubit.

33 And the work of the wheels *was* like the work of a chariot wheel: their axletrees, and their naves, and their felloes, and their spokes, *were* all molten.

34 And *there were* four undersetters to the four corners of one base: *and* the undersetters *were* of the very base itself.

35 And in the top of the base *was there* a round compass of half a cubit high: and on the top of the base the ledges thereof and the borders thereof *were* of the same.

36 For on the plates of the ledges thereof, and on the borders thereof, he graved cherubims, lions, and palm trees, according to the [b]proportion of every one, and additions round about.

37 After this *manner* he made the ten bases: all of them had one casting, one measure, *and* one size.

38 ¶ Then [v]made he ten lavers of brass: one laver contained forty baths: *and* every laver was four cubits: *and* upon every one of the ten bases one laver.

39 And he put five bases on the right [c]side of the house, and five on the left side of the house: and he set the sea on the right side of the house eastward over against the south.

40 ¶ And [d]Hiram made the lavers, and the shovels, and the basins. So Hiram made an end of doing all the work that he made king Solomon for the house of the LORD:

41 The two pillars, and the *two* bowls of the chapiters that *were* on the top of the two pillars; and the two [w]networks, to cover the two bowls of the chapiters which *were* upon the top of the pillars;

42 And four hundred pomegranates for the two networks, *even* two rows of pomegranates for one network, to cover the two bowls of the chapiters that *were* [e]upon the pillars;

43 And the ten bases, and ten lavers on the bases;

44 And one sea, and twelve oxen under the sea;

45 [x]And the pots, and the shovels, and the basins: and all these vessels, which Hiram made to king Solomon for the house of the LORD, *were of* [f]bright brass.

46 [y]In the plain of Jordan did the king cast them, [g]in the clay ground between [z]Succoth and [a]Zarthan.

47 And Solomon left all the vessels *unweighed,* [h]because they were exceeding many: neither was the weight of the brass [b]found[i] out.

48 And Solomon made all the vessels that *pertained* unto the house of the LORD: [c]the altar of gold, and [d]the table of gold, whereupon [e]the showbread *was,*

49 And the candlesticks of pure gold, five on the right *side,* and five on the left, before the oracle, with the flowers, and the lamps, and the tongs *of* gold,

50 And the bowls, and the snuffers, and the basins, and the spoons, and the

7:26 [t]See 2 Chr. 4:5 **7:29** [u]Gen. 3:24 ch. 6:27 Ps. 18:10 Ezek. 1:10 & 41:18,19 Rev. 4:6-8

7:38 [v]2 Chr. 4:6 **7:41** [w]ver. 17,18 **7:45** [x]Ex. 27:3 2 Chr. 4:16 **7:46** [y]2 Chr. 4:17 [z]Gen. 33:17 [a]Josh. 3:16 **7:47** [b]1 Chr. 22:14 **7:48** [c]Ex. 37:25 [d]Ex. 37:10 [e]Lev. 24:5-8

[a] Heb. *in the base* [b] Heb. *nakedness* [c] Heb. *shoulder* [d] Heb. *Hirom;* see ver. 13 [e] Heb. *upon the face of the pillars* [f] Heb. *made bright,* or, *scoured* [g] Heb. *in the thickness of the ground* [h] Heb. *for the exceeding multitude* [i] Heb. *searched*

[j]censers *of* pure gold; and the hinges
of gold, *both* for the doors of the inner
house, the most holy *place, and* for the
doors of the house, *to wit,* of the tem-
ple.
51 So was ended all the work that
king Solomon made for the house of
the LORD. And Solomon brought in the
[k]things [f]which David his father had
dedicated; *even* the silver, and the gold,
and the vessels, did he put among the
treasures of the house of the LORD.

The ark brought to the temple

8:1–21pp — 2 Chr. 5:2–6:11

8 THEN [g]SOLOMON assembled the
elders of Israel, and all the heads
of the tribes, the [l]chief of the fathers
of the children of Israel, unto king Sol-
omon in Jerusalem, [h]that they might
bring up the ark of the covenant of the
LORD [i]out of the city of David, which
is Zion.
2 And all the men of Israel assem-
bled themselves unto king Solomon at
the [j]feast in the month Ethanim,
which *is* the seventh month.
3 And all the elders of Israel came,
[k]and the priests took up the ark.
4 And they brought up the ark of the
LORD, [l]and the tabernacle of the con-
gregation, and all the holy vessels that
were in the tabernacle, even those did
the priests and the Levites bring up.
5 And king Solomon, and all the
congregation of Israel, that were as-
sembled unto him, *were* with him be-
fore the ark, [m]sacrificing sheep and
oxen, that could not be told nor num-
bered for multitude.
6 And the priests [n]brought in the
ark of the covenant of the LORD unto
[o]his place, into the oracle of the
house, to the most holy *place, even*
[p]under the wings of the cherubims.
7 For the cherubims spread forth
their two wings over the place of the
ark, and the cherubims covered the ark
and the staves thereof above.
8 And they [q]drew out the staves,
that the [m]ends of the staves were seen
out in the [n]holy *place* before the ora-
cle, and they were not seen without:
and there they are unto this day.
9 [r]*There was* nothing in the ark
[s]save the two tables of stone, which
Moses [t]put there at Horeb, [u]when[o]
the LORD made *a covenant* with the chil-
dren of Israel, when they came out of
the land of Egypt.
10 And it came to pass, when the
priests were come out of the holy *place,*
that the cloud [v]filled the house of the
LORD,
11 So that the priests could not
stand to minister because of the cloud:
for the glory of the LORD had filled the
house of the LORD.
12 ¶ [w]Then spake Solomon, The
LORD said that he would dwell [x]in the
thick darkness.
13 [y]I have surely built thee an

7:51 [f]2 Sam. 8:11 **8:1** [g]2 Chr. 5:2 [h]2 Sam. 6:17 [i]2 Sam. 5:7 & 6:12,16 **8:2** [j]Lev. 23:34 2 Chr. 7:8 **8:3** [k]Num. 4:15 **8:4** [l]2 Chr. 1:3 **8:5** [m]2 Sam. 6:13 **8:6** [n]2 Sam. 6:17 [o]Ex. 26:33,34 ch. 6:19 [p]ch. 6:27 **8:8** [q]Ex. 25:14 **8:9** [r]Ex. 25:21 Deut. 10:2 [s]Deut. 10:5 Heb. 9:4 [t]Ex. 40:20 [u]Ex. 34:27,28 **8:10** [v]Ex. 40:34 **8:12** [w]2 Chr. 6:1 [x]Ps. 18:11 **8:13** [y]2 Sam. 7:13

[j] Heb. *ash pans* [k] Heb. *holy things of David* [l] Heb. *princes* [m] Heb. *heads* [n] Or, *ark* as 2 Chr. 5:9 [o] Or, *where*

8:1 ARK OF THE COVENANT. The ark of the covenant was the only article of furniture in the Most Holy Place. It was a rectangular chest 3 and 3/4 feet long by 2 and 1/4 feet wide by 2 and 1/4 feet high, made of acacia wood and overlaid with pure gold inside and out. The ark originally contained three reminders of God's kingship over Israel: (1) the stone tablets on which the Ten Commandments were engraved (cf. Ex. 25:16,21; 40:20; see Ex. 25:10, note); (2) a golden jar full of manna, which God had provided daily for Israel during her years in the wilderness; and (3) Aaron's almond rod that supernaturally budded. However, by Solomon's time the ark contained only the two tablets of stone (2 Chr. 5:10). On the lid of the ark was the "mercy seat," on which the blood of sacrifices was sprinkled once a year by the high priest on the Day of Atonement. Two gold cherubs carved as one piece, facing each other with their wings spread forward, hovered over the mercy seat in an arch. At the center of the mercy seat the presence of God was symbolized by a brilliant supernatural light called the *Shekinah* (see article on THE GLORY OF GOD, p. 1186).

8:4 THE TABERNACLE. The tabernacle was the tent-like structure that had provided a portable place of worship for the Israelites as they had moved about in the wilderness. After they had settled in their homeland, David expressed a desire to build a permanent house of worship for the Lord (see 2 Sam. 7:1–13; see article on THE TEMPLE, p. 654).

8:11 THE GLORY OF THE LORD. The glory of the Lord filled the temple after the ark of the covenant was brought into it (vv. 5–11). Where God's word is dwelling and is obeyed, there His glory abides (see Ex. 40:34, note; cf. John 15:7–11; 17:17–22; see article on THE GLORY OF GOD, p. 1186).

8:13 AN HOUSE TO DWELL IN. The fact that God lived in the temple did not mean that He dwelt in no other place, for God is everywhere (cf. v. 27). What it did mean was that God's presence and power would be manifested in a special way in the temple. In the same manner, Christ's presence with His people is manifested in a special way

house to dwell in, [z]a settled place for
thee to abide in for ever.
14 And the king turned his face
about, and [a]blessed all the congrega-
tion of Israel: (and all the congregation
of Israel stood;)
15 And he said, [b]Blessed *be* the
LORD God of Israel, which [c]spake with
his mouth unto David my father, and
hath with his hand fulfilled *it*, saying,
16 Since the day that I brought
forth my people Israel out of Egypt, I
chose no city out of all the tribes of
Israel to build an house, that [d]my
name might be therein; but I chose
[e]David to be over my people Israel.
17 And [f]it was in the heart of Da-
vid my father to build an house for the
name of the LORD God of Israel.
18 [g]And the LORD said unto David
my father, Whereas it was in thine
heart to build an house unto my name,
thou didst well that it was in thine
heart.
19 Nevertheless [h]thou shalt not
build the house; but thy son that shall
come forth out of thy loins, he shall
build the house unto my name.
20 And the LORD hath performed his
word that he spake, and I am risen up
in the room of David my father, and sit
on the throne of Israel, [i]as the LORD
promised, and have built an house for
the name of the LORD God of Israel.
21 And I have set there a place for
the ark, wherein *is* [j]the covenant of
the LORD, which he made with our fa-
thers, when he brought them out of the
land of Egypt.

Solomon's prayer of dedication

8:22–53pp — 2 Chr. 6:12–40

22 ¶ And Solomon stood before
[k]the altar of the LORD in the presence
of all the congregation of Israel, and
[l]spread forth his hands toward
heaven:
23 And he said, LORD God of Israel,
[m]*there is* no God like thee, in heaven
above, or on earth beneath, [n]who
keepest covenant and mercy with thy
servants that [o]walk before thee with
all their heart:
24 Who hast kept with thy servant
David my father that thou promisedst
him: thou spakest also with thy mouth,

8:13 [z]Ps. 132:14
8:14 [a]2 Sam. 6:18
8:15 [b]Luke 1:68 [c]2 Sam. 7:5,25
8:16 [d]ver. 29 [e]1 Sam. 16:1 2 Sam. 7:8 1 Chr. 28:4
8:17 [f]2 Sam. 7:2
8:18 [g]2 Chr. 6:8,9
8:19 [h]2 Sam. 7:5,12,13
8:20 [i]1 Chr. 28:5,6
8:21 [j]ver. 9 Deut. 31:26
8:22 [k]2 Chr. 6:12 [l]Ex. 9:33 Ezra 9:5
8:23 [m]Ex. 15:11 2 Sam. 7:22 [n]Deut. 7:9 Neh. 1:5 Dan. 9:4 [o]Gen. 17:1 ch. 3:6 2 Ki. 20:3
8:25 [p]2 Sam. 7:12,16 ch. 2:4
8:26 [q]2 Sam. 7:25
8:27 [r]2 Chr. 2:6 Is. 66:1 Jer. 23:24 Acts 7:49 & 17:24 [s]2 Cor. 12:2
8:29 [t]Deut. 12:11 [u]Dan. 6:10
8:30 [v]Neh. 1:6
8:31 [w]Lev. 5:1 [x]Ex. 22:11
8:32 [y]Deut. 25:1
8:33 [z]Lev. 26:17 Deut. 28:25 [a]Lev. 26:39

and hast fulfilled *it* with thine hand, as
it is this day.
25 Therefore now, LORD God of Isra-
el, keep with thy servant David my fa-
ther that thou promisedst him, saying,
[p]There[p] shall not fail thee a man in
my sight to sit on the throne of Israel;
[q]so that thy children take heed to
their way, that they walk before me as
thou hast walked before me.
26 [q]And now, O God of Israel, let
thy word, I pray thee, be verified,
which thou spakest unto thy servant
David my father.
27 But [r]will God indeed dwell on
the earth? behold, the heaven and
[s]heaven of heavens cannot contain
thee; how much less this house that I
have builded?
28 Yet have thou respect unto the
prayer of thy servant, and to his suppli-
cation, O LORD my God, to hearken
unto the cry and to the prayer, which
thy servant prayeth before thee today:
29 That thine eyes may be open to-
ward this house night and day, *even* to-
ward the place of which thou hast said,
[t]My name shall be there: that thou
mayest hearken unto the prayer which
thy servant shall make [u]toward[r] this
place.
30 [v]And hearken thou to the sup-
plication of thy servant, and of thy peo-
ple Israel, when they shall pray [r]to-
ward this place: and hear thou in
heaven thy dwellingplace: and when
thou hearest, forgive.
31 ¶ If any man trespass against his
neighbour, [w]and[s] [x]an oath be laid
upon him to cause him to swear, and
the oath come before thine altar in this
house:
32 Then hear thou in heaven, and
do, and judge thy servants, [y]con-
demning the wicked, to bring his way
upon his head; and justifying the righ-
teous, to give him according to his
righteousness.
33 ¶ [z]When thy people Israel be
smitten down before the enemy, be-
cause they have sinned against thee,
and [a]shall turn again to thee, and con-
fess thy name, and pray, and make

p Heb. *There shall not be cut off unto thee a man from my sight* q Heb. *only if* r Or, *in this place* s Heb. *and he require an oath of him*

---

when they gather together in His name (Mat. 18:20).

8:29 MY NAME. The name of God represents His presence, character, and glory.

supplication unto thee [t]in this house:

34 Then hear thou in heaven, and forgive the sin of thy people Israel, and bring them again unto the land which thou gavest unto their fathers.

35 ¶ [b]When heaven is shut up, and there is no rain, because they have sinned against thee; if they pray toward this place, and confess thy name, and turn from their sin, when thou afflictest them:

36 Then hear thou in heaven, and forgive the sin of thy servants, and of thy people Israel, that thou [c]teach them [d]the good way wherein they should walk, and give rain upon thy land, which thou hast given to thy people for an inheritance.

37 ¶ [e]If there be in the land famine, if there be pestilence, blasting, mildew, locust, *or* if there be caterpillar; if their enemy besiege them in the land of their [u]cities; whatsoever plague, whatsoever sickness *there be;*

38 What prayer and supplication soever be *made* by any man, *or* by all thy people Israel, which shall know every man the plague of his own heart, and spread forth his hands toward this house:

39 Then hear thou in heaven thy dwellingplace, and forgive, and do, and give to every man according to his ways, whose heart thou knowest; (for thou, *even* thou only, [f]knowest the hearts of all the children of men;)

40 [g]That they may fear thee all the days that they live in the land which thou gavest unto our fathers.

41 Moreover concerning a stranger, that *is* not of thy people Israel, but cometh out of a far country for thy name's sake;

42 (For they shall hear of thy great name, and of thy [h]strong hand, and of thy stretched out arm;) when he shall come and pray toward this house;

43 Hear thou in heaven thy dwellingplace, and do according to all that the stranger calleth to thee for: [i]that all people of the earth may know thy name, to [j]fear thee, as *do* thy people Israel; and that they may know that [v]this house, which I have builded, is called by thy name.

44 ¶ If thy people go out to battle against their enemy, whithersoever thou shalt send them, and shall pray unto the LORD [w]toward the city which thou hast chosen, and *toward* the house that I have built for thy name:

45 Then hear thou in heaven their prayer and their supplication, and maintain their [x]cause.

46 If they sin against thee, ([k]for *there is* no man that sinneth not,) and thou be angry with them, and deliver them to the enemy, so that they carry them away captives [l]unto the land of the enemy, far or near;

47 [m]*Yet* if they shall [y]bethink themselves in the land whither they were carried captives, and repent, and make supplication unto thee in the land of them that carried them captives, [n]saying, We have sinned, and have done perversely, we have committed wickedness;

48 And *so* [o]return unto thee with all their heart, and with all their soul, in the land of their enemies, which led them away captive, and [p]pray unto thee toward their land, which thou gavest unto their fathers, the city which thou hast chosen, and the house which I have built for thy name:

49 Then hear thou their prayer and their supplication in heaven thy dwellingplace, and maintain their [x]cause,

50 And forgive thy people that have sinned against thee, and all their transgressions wherein they have transgressed against thee, and [q]give them compassion before them who carried them captive, that they may have compassion on them:

51 For [r]they *be* thy people, and thine inheritance, which thou brought-

8:35 [b]Lev. 26:19 Deut. 28:23
8:36 [c]Ps. 25:4 & 27:11 & 94:12 [d]1 Sam. 12:23
8:37 [e]Lev. 26:16,25,26
8:39 [f]1 Sam. 16:7 1 Chr. 28:9 Ps. 11:4 Jer. 17:10 Acts 1:24
8:40 [g]Ps. 130:4
8:42 [h]Deut. 3:24
8:43 [i]1 Sam. 17:46 2 Ki. 19:19 [j]Ps. 102:15
8:46 [k]2 Chr. 6:36 Eccl. 7:20 Jas. 3:2 1 John 1:8,10 [l]Lev. 26:34,44 Deut. 28:36,64
8:47 [m]Lev. 26:40 [n]Neh. 1:6 Ps. 106:6 Dan. 9:5
8:48 [o]Jer. 29:12-14 [p]Dan. 6:10
8:50 [q]Ezra 7:6 Ps. 106:46
8:51 [r]Deut. 9:29 Neh. 1:10

[t] Or, *toward* [u] Or, *jurisdiction* [v] Heb. *thy name is called upon this house* [w] Heb. *the way of the city* [x] Or, *right* [y] Heb. *bring back to their heart*

8:39 FORGIVE . . . AND GIVE TO EVERY MAN ACCORDING TO HIS WAYS. Solomon understood that God would forgive His people if they turned from their sin and sincerely repented in regret and sorrow (vv. 35–36). He also acknowledged that God might have to discipline them, in order that "they may fear thee all the days that they live in the land" (v. 40).

8:46 *THERE IS* NO MAN THAT SINNETH NOT. Solomon's words are not an attempt to justify his or Israel's sins; rather, he was expressing the truth that since sin is universally present, turning away from God is always a possibility for His people (vv. 46–50; cf. Rom. 3:23; 1 John 1:10). If apostasy does occur, deliverance is also possible if they repent and return to God (vv. 46–51).

est forth out of Egypt, [s]from the midst of the furnace of iron:

52 That thine eyes may be open unto the supplication of thy servant, and unto the supplication of thy people Israel, to hearken unto them in all that they call for unto thee.

53 For thou didst separate them from among all the people of the earth, *to be* thine inheritance, [t]as thou spakest by the hand of Moses thy servant, when thou broughtest our fathers out of Egypt, O Lord GOD.

54 And it was *so,* that when Solomon had made an end of praying all this prayer and supplication unto the LORD, he arose from before the altar of the LORD, from kneeling on his knees with his hands spread up to heaven.

55 And he stood, [u]and blessed all the congregation of Israel with a loud voice, saying,

56 Blessed *be* the LORD, that hath given rest unto his people Israel, according to all that he promised: [v]there hath not [z]failed one word of all his good promise, which he promised by the hand of Moses his servant.

57 The LORD our God be with us, as he was with our fathers: [w]let him not leave us, nor forsake us:

58 That he may [x]incline our hearts unto him, to walk in all his ways, and to keep his commandments, and his statutes, and his judgments, which he commanded our fathers.

59 And let these my words, wherewith I have made supplication before the LORD, be nigh unto the LORD our God day and night, that he maintain the cause of his servant, and the cause of his people Israel [a]at all times, as the matter shall require:

60 [y]That all the people of the earth may know that [z]the LORD *is* God, *and that there is* none else.

61 Let your [a]heart therefore be perfect with the LORD our God, to walk in his statutes, and to keep his commandments, as at this day.

8:51 [s]Deut. 4:20 Jer. 11:4
8:53 [t]Ex. 19:5 Deut. 9:26,29
8:55 [u]2 Sam. 6:18
8:56 [v]Deut. 12:10 Josh. 21:45 & 23:14
8:57 [w]Deut. 31:6 Josh. 1:5
8:58 [x]Ps. 119:36
8:60 [y]Josh. 4:24 1 Sam. 17:46 [z]Deut. 4:35,39
8:61 [a]ch. 11:4 & 15:3,14 2 Ki. 20:3
8:62 [b]2 Chr. 7:4
8:64 [c]2 Chr. 7:7 [d]2 Chr. 4:1
8:65 [e]ver. 2 Lev. 23:34 [f]Num. 34:8 Josh. 13:5 Judg. 3:3 2 Ki. 14:25 [g]Gen. 15:18 Num. 34:5 [h]2 Chr. 7:8
8:66 [i]2 Chr. 7:9
9:1 [j]2 Chr. 7:11 [k]ch. 7:1 [l]2 Chr. 8:6
9:2 [m]ch. 3:5
9:3 [n]2 Ki. 20:5 Ps. 10:17

The offering and feast

8:62–66pp — 2 Chr. 7:1–10

62 ¶ And [b]the king, and all Israel with him, offered sacrifice before the LORD.

63 And Solomon offered a sacrifice of peace offerings, which he offered unto the LORD, two and twenty thousand oxen, and an hundred and twenty thousand sheep. So the king and all the children of Israel dedicated the house of the LORD.

64 [c]The same day did the king hallow the middle of the court that *was* before the house of the LORD: for there he offered burnt offerings, and meat offerings, and the fat of the peace offerings: because [d]the brasen altar that *was* before the LORD *was* too little to receive the burnt offerings, and meat offerings, and the fat of the peace offerings.

65 And at that time Solomon held [e]a feast, and all Israel with him, a great congregation, from [f]the entering in of Hamath unto [g]the river of Egypt, before the LORD our God, [h]seven days and seven days, *even* fourteen days.

66 [i]On the eighth day he sent the people away: and they [b]blessed the king, and went unto their tents joyful and glad of heart for all the goodness that the LORD had done for David his servant, and for Israel his people.

The covenant with Solomon

9:1–9pp — 2 Chr. 7:11–22

9 AND [j]IT came to pass, when Solomon had finished the building of the house of the LORD, [k]and the king's house, and [l]all Solomon's desire which he was pleased to do,

2 That the LORD appeared to Solomon the second time, [m]as he had appeared unto him at Gibeon.

3 And the LORD said unto him, [n]I

[z] Heb. *fallen* [a] Heb. *the thing of a day in his day* [b] Or, *thanked*

8:57 THE LORD OUR GOD BE WITH US. Solomon's prayer is an ideal model for what we should desire in our walk with the Lord. He asked: (1) for the Lord's protecting presence and help (v. 57), (2) for God to confirm His word by fulfilling His good promises (vv. 26,56), (3) for a work of divine grace in their hearts to keep God's word and to love His righteous ways (v. 58), (4) for God to answer daily prayers and to supply daily needs (v. 59), (5) for an increased understanding of God's great and awesome nature (v. 60), and (6) for a heart totally devoted to God and His will (v. 61).

9:3 THE LORD SAID UNTO HIM. God's response to Solomon's prayer affirmed that He had heard and answered. However, God added that He would establish Solomon's house and the kingdom of Israel only if he and the people would remain faithful and not turn away from His command-

have heard thy prayer and thy supplication, that thou hast made before me: I have hallowed this house, which thou hast built, [o]to put my name there for ever; [p]and mine eyes and mine heart shall be there perpetually.

4 And if thou wilt [q]walk before me, [r]as David thy father walked, in integrity of heart, and in uprightness, to do according to all that I have commanded thee, *and* wilt keep my statutes and my judgments:

5 Then I will establish the throne of thy kingdom upon Israel for ever, [s]as I promised to David thy father, saying, There shall not fail thee a man upon the throne of Israel.

6 [t]*But* if ye shall at all turn from following me, ye or your children, and will not keep my commandments *and* my statutes which I have set before you, but go and serve other gods, and worship them:

7 [u]Then will I cut off Israel out of the land which I have given them; and this house, which I have hallowed [v]for my name, will I cast out of my sight; [w]and Israel shall be a proverb and a byword among all people:

8 And [x]at this house, *which* is high, every one that passeth by it shall be astonished, and shall hiss; and they shall say, [y]Why hath the LORD done thus unto this land, and to this house?

1 Chr. 28:6-9

9 And they shall answer, Because they forsook the LORD their God, who brought forth their fathers out of the land of Egypt, and have taken hold upon other gods, and have worshipped them, and served them: therefore hath the LORD brought upon them all this evil.

Solomon's accomplishments

9:10–28pp — 2 Chr. 8:1–18

10 ¶ And [z]it came to pass at the end of twenty years, when Solomon had built the two houses, the house of the LORD, and the king's house,

11 [a](*Now* Hiram the king of Tyre had furnished Solomon with cedar trees and fir trees, and with gold, according to all his desire,) that then king Solomon gave Hiram twenty cities in the land of Galilee.

12 And Hiram came out from Tyre to see the cities which Solomon had given him; and they [c]pleased him not.

13 And he said, What cities *are* these which thou hast given me, my brother? [b]And he called them the land of [d]Cabul unto this day.

14 And Hiram sent to the king sixscore talents of gold.

15 ¶ And this *is* the reason of [c]the levy which king Solomon raised; for to build the house of the LORD, and his own house, and [d]Millo, and the wall of Jerusalem, and [e]Hazor, and [f]Megiddo, and [g]Gezer.

16 *For* Pharaoh king of Egypt had gone up, and taken Gezer, and burnt it with fire, [h]and slain the Canaanites that dwelt in the city, and given it *for* a present unto his daughter, Solomon's wife.

17 And Solomon built Gezer, and [i]Beth-horon the nether,

18 And [j]Baalath, and Tadmor in the wilderness, in the land,

19 And all the cities of store that Solomon had, and cities for [k]his chariots, and cities for his horsemen, and [e]that which Solomon [l]desired to build in Jerusalem, and in Lebanon, and in all the land of his dominion.

20 [m]*And* all the people *that were* left of the Amorites, Hittites, Perizzites, Hivites, and Jebusites, which *were* not of the children of Israel,

21 Their children [n]that were left after them in the land, [o]whom the children of Israel also were not able utterly to destroy, [p]upon those did Solomon levy a tribute of [q]bondservice unto this day.

22 But of the children of Israel did Solomon [r]make no bondmen: but they *were* men of war, and his servants, and

9:3 [o]ch. 8:29 [p]Deut. 11:12
9:4 [q]Gen. 17:1 [r]ch. 15:5
9:5 [s]2 Sam. 7:12,16 ch. 2:4 1 Chr. 22:10
9:6 [t]2 Sam. 7:14 2 Chr. 7:19,20
9:7 [u]2 Ki. 17:23 & 25:21 [v]Jer. 7:14 [w]Deut. 28:37
9:8 [x]2 Chr. 7:21 [y]Deut. 29:24-26 Jer. 22:8,9
9:10 [z]ch. 6:37,38 & 7:1 2 Chr. 8:1
9:11 [a]2 Chr. 8:2
9:13 [b]Josh. 19:27
9:15 [c]ch. 5:13 [d]ver. 24 2 Sam. 5:9 [e]Josh. 19:36 [f]Josh. 17:11 [g]Josh. 16:10
9:16 [h]Josh. 16:10
9:17 [i]Josh. 16:3 2 Chr. 8:5
9:18 [j]Josh. 19:44 2 Chr. 8:4,6
9:19 [k]ch. 4:26 [l]ver. 1
9:20 [m]2 Chr. 8:7
9:21 [n]Judg. 3:1 [o]Josh. 15:63 & 17:12 [p]Judg. 1:28 [q]Ezra 2:55,58 Neh. 7:57
9:22 [r]Lev. 25:39

[c]Heb. *were not right in his eyes* [d]i.e. *Displeasing*, or, *Dirty* [e]Heb. *the desire of Solomon which he desired*

ments (vv. 4–9). All of Scripture expresses this principle: God's promises are fulfilled only when we seek to follow Him and His ways (see John 14:13–21; 15:7).

9:7 THIS HOUSE . . . WILL I CAST OUT OF MY SIGHT. God said he would no longer manifest His presence, power, and glory in the temple if the people failed to follow His ways sincerely (vv. 6–9). This warning applies under the new covenant as well. If a church fails to obey the words of Christ and the teachings of the N.T. apostles, turning instead to false doctrine and the ungodly ways of the world, then God's Spirit and power will be withdrawn from it, and God will remove it from His kingdom (see Rev. 2:5, note).

his princes, and his captains, and rulers of his chariots, and his horsemen.

23 These *were* the chief of the officers that *were* over Solomon's work, [s]five hundred and fifty, which bare rule over the people that wrought in the work.

24 ¶ But [t]Pharaoh's daughter came up out of the city of David unto [u]her house which *Solomon* had built for her: [v]then did he build Millo.

25 ¶ [w]And three times in a year did Solomon offer burnt offerings and peace offerings upon the altar which he built unto the LORD, and he burnt incense [f]upon the altar that *was* before the LORD. So he finished the house.

26 ¶ And [x]king Solomon made a navy of ships in [y]Ezion-geber, which *is* beside Eloth, on the [g]shore of the Red sea, in the land of Edom.

27 [z]And Hiram sent in the navy his servants, shipmen that had knowledge of the sea, with the servants of Solomon.

28 And they came to [a]Ophir, and fetched from thence gold, four hundred and twenty talents, and brought *it* to king Solomon.

The visit of the Queen of Sheba

10:1–13pp — 2 Chr. 9:1–12

10 AND WHEN the [b]queen of Sheba heard of the fame of Solomon concerning the name of the LORD, she came [c]to prove him with hard questions.

2 And she came to Jerusalem with a very great train, with camels that bare spices, and very much gold, and precious stones: and when she was come to Solomon, she communed with him of all that was in her heart.

3 And Solomon told her all her [h]questions: there was not *any* thing hid from the king, which he told her not.

4 And when the queen of Sheba had seen all Solomon's wisdom, and the house that he had built,

5 And the meat of his table, and the sitting of his servants, and the [i]attendance of his ministers, and their apparel, and his [j]cupbearers, [d]and his ascent by which he went up unto the house of the LORD; there was no more spirit in her.

6 And she said to the king, It was a true [e]report that I heard in mine own land of thy [f]acts and of thy wisdom.

7 Howbeit I believed not the words, until I came, and mine eyes had seen *it:* and, behold, the half was not told me: [k]thy wisdom and prosperity exceedeth the fame which I heard.

8 [g]Happy *are* thy men, happy *are* these thy servants, which stand continually before thee, *and* that hear thy wisdom.

9 [h]Blessed be the LORD thy God, which delighted in thee, to set thee on the throne of Israel: because the LORD loved Israel for ever, therefore made he thee king, [i]to do judgment and justice.

10 And she [j]gave the king an hundred and twenty talents of gold, and of spices very great store, and precious stones: there came no more such abundance of spices as these which the queen of Sheba gave to king Solomon.

11 [k]And the navy also of Hiram, that brought gold from Ophir, brought in from Ophir great plenty of [l]almug[l] trees, and precious stones.

12 [m]And the king made of the almug trees [m] [n]pillars for the house of the LORD, and for the king's house, harps also and psalteries for singers: there came no such [n]almug trees, nor were seen unto this day.

13 And king Solomon gave unto the queen of Sheba all her desire, whatsoever she asked, beside *that* which Solomon gave her [o]of his royal bounty. So she turned and went to her own country, she and her servants.

The splendor of Solomon

10:14–29pp — 2 Chr. 1:14–17; 9:13–28

14 ¶ Now the weight of gold that came to Solomon in one year was six hundred threescore and six talents of gold,

15 Beside *that he had* of the merchantmen, and of the traffic of the spice merchants, and [o]of all the kings of Arabia, and of the [p]governors of the country.

16 ¶ And king Solomon made two hundred targets *of* beaten gold: six hundred *shekels* of gold went to one target.

9:23 [s]See 2 Chr. 8:10
9:24 [t]ch. 3:1; 2 Chr. 8:11; [u]ch. 7:8; [v]2 Sam. 5:9; ch. 11:27; 2 Chr. 32:5
9:25 [w]2 Chr. 8:12,13,16
9:26 [x]2 Chr. 8:17,18; [y]Num. 33:35; Deut. 2:8; ch. 22:48
9:27 [z]ch. 10:11
9:28 [a]Job 22:24
10:1 [b]2 Chr. 9:1; Mat. 12:42; Luke 11:31; [c]See Judg. 14:12; Prov. 1:6
10:5 [d]1 Chr. 26:16
10:6 [e]Heb. *word*; [f]Or, *sayings*
10:8 [g]Prov. 8:34
10:9 [h]ch. 5:7; [i]2 Sam. 8:15; Ps. 72:2; Prov. 8:15
10:10 [j]Ps. 72:10,15
10:11 [k]ch. 9:27; [l]2 Chr. 2:8 & 9:10,11
10:12 [m]2 Chr. 9:11; [n]2 Chr. 9:10
10:15 [o]2 Chr. 9:24; Ps. 72:10

f Heb. *upon it* **g** Heb. *lip* **h** Heb. *words*
i Heb. *standing* **j** Or, *butlers* **k** Heb. *thou hast added wisdom and goodness to the fame*
l Or, *algum trees* **m** Or, *rails* **n** Heb. *a prop*
o Heb. *according to the hand of king Solomon*
p Or, *captains*

17 And *he made* [p]three hundred
shields *of* beaten gold; three pound of
gold went to one shield: and the king
put them in the [q]house of the forest of
Lebanon.
18 ¶ [r]Moreover the king made a
great throne of ivory, and overlaid it
with the best gold.
19 The throne had six steps, and
the top of the throne *was* round [q]be-
hind: and *there were* [r]stays on either
side on the place of the seat, and two
lions stood beside the stays.
20 And twelve lions stood there on
the one side and on the other upon the
six steps: there was not [s]the like
made in any kingdom.
21 ¶ [s]And all king Solomon's
drinking vessels *were of* gold, and all
the vessels of the house of the forest of
Lebanon *were of* pure gold; [t]none *were*
of silver: it was nothing accounted of in
the days of Solomon.
22 For the king had at sea a navy of
[t]Tharshish with the navy of Hiram:
once in three years came the navy of
Tharshish, bringing gold, and silver,
[u]ivory, and apes, and peacocks.
23 So [u]king Solomon exceeded all
the kings of the earth for riches and for
wisdom.
24 ¶ And all the earth [v]sought to
Solomon, to hear his wisdom, which
God had put in his heart.
25 And they brought every man his
present, vessels of silver, and vessels
of gold, and garments, and armour, and
spices, horses, and mules, a rate year
by year.
26 ¶ [v]And Solomon [w]gathered to-
gether chariots and horsemen: and he
had a thousand and four hundred char-
iots, and twelve thousand horsemen,
whom he bestowed in the cities for
chariots, and with the king at Jerusa-
lem.
27 [x]And the king [w]made silver *to*
be in Jerusalem as stones, and cedars
made he *to be* as the sycamore trees
that *are* in the vale, for abundance.
28 ¶ [y]And[x] Solomon had horses
brought out of Egypt, and linen yarn:
the king's merchants received the lin-
en yarn at a price.
29 And a chariot came up and went
out of Egypt for six hundred *shekels* of
silver, and an horse for an hundred and
fifty: [z]and so for all the kings of the
Hittites, and for the kings of Syria, did
they bring *them* out [y]by their means.

10:17 [p]ch. 14:26 [q]ch. 7:2
10:18 [r]2 Chr. 9:17
10:21 [s]2 Chr. 9:20
10:22 [t]Gen. 10:4 2 Chr. 20:36
10:23 [u]ch. 3:12,13 & 4:30
10:26 [v]ch. 4:26 2 Chr. 1:14 & 9:25 [w]Deut. 17:16
10:27 [x]2 Chr. 1:15-17
10:28 [y]Deut. 17:16 2 Chr. 1:16 & 9:28
10:29 [z]Josh. 1:4 2 Ki. 7:6
11:1 [a]Neh. 13:26 [b]Deut. 17:17
11:2 [c]Ex. 34:16 Deut. 7:3,4

Solomon takes foreign wives

11 BUT [a]KING Solomon loved
[b]many strange women, [z]to-
gether with the daughter of Pharaoh,
women of the Moabites, Ammonites,
Edomites, Zidonians, *and* Hittites;
2 Of the nations *concerning* which
the LORD said unto the children of Isra-
el, [c]Ye shall not go in to them, neither
shall they come in unto you: *for* surely
they will turn away your heart after
their gods: Solomon clave unto these
in love.
3 And he had seven hundred wives,
princesses, and three hundred concu-

[q] Heb. *on the hinder part thereof* [r] Heb. *hands* [s] Heb. *so* [t] Or, there was *no silver* in them [u] Or, *elephants' teeth* [v] Heb. *sought the face of* [w] Heb. *gave* [x] Heb. *And the going forth of the horses which* was *Solomon's* [y] Heb. *by their hand* [z] Or, *beside*

11:1 KING SOLOMON LOVED MANY STRANGE WOMEN. Ch. 11 describes Solomon's spiritual decline and its results. (1) Solomon began as a man who loved the Lord, walked in His statutes, and built His temple (3:3; 6:1). He experienced God's love, grace, and salvation; he was given special spiritual understanding (3:10–14; 2 Sam. 12:24) and wrote Holy Scripture under the inspiration of the Holy Spirit (see 4:29–34, note).

(2) Nevertheless, Solomon became hardened by the deceitfulness of sin and turned away from the Lord to other gods; he provoked the Lord to anger and was consequently punished by God (vv. 1–13; cf. Deut. 29:14–21; 30:15–20; Heb. 3:12–14).

(3) Solomon's fatal error was to seek power, success, wealth, and sensual pleasure through compromise with and tolerance of idolatry and sin. Solomon sought (a) unholy alliances with heathen nations (Tyre, 9:10–14; Egypt, 3:1; 10:28–29; other nations, 9:25—10:13), (b) many foreign wives and concubines to seal these alliances (vv. 1–8; see next note; Gen. 29:28, note), (c) and more and more wealth and glory (10:14–19; cf. 1 Tim. 6:9).

(4) Read Deut. 17:14–20 for God's commands for kings about allying with foreigners, procuring horses from Egypt, multiplying wives, and ever seeking more gold. The Bible nowhere states that Solomon ever repented of his sins (see v. 43, note).

11:2 OF THE NATIONS . . . YE SHALL NOT GO IN TO THEM. Solomon's possession of many wives not only ignored God's commandment to kings not to multiply wives (cf. Deut. 17:17), but also transgressed God's prohibition against marrying pagan wives from the Canaanites (Ex. 34:12–16; Josh. 23:12–13). Solomon clearly failed to meditate carefully on the law of God that "he may learn to fear the LORD his God, to keep all the words of this law" (Deut. 17:19).

bines: and his wives turned away his
heart.
4 For it came to pass, when Solo-
mon was old, [d]*that* his wives turned
away his heart after other gods: and
his [e]heart was not perfect with the
LORD his God, [f]as *was* the heart of Da-
vid his father.
5 For Solomon went after [g]Ashto-
reth the goddess of the Zidonians, and
after [a]Milcom the abomination of the
Ammonites.
6 And Solomon did evil in the sight
of the LORD, and [b]went not fully after
the LORD, as *did* David his father.
7 [h]Then did Solomon build an high
place for [i]Chemosh, the abomination
of Moab, in [j]the hill that *is* before Je-
rusalem, and for Molech, the abomina-
tion of the children of Ammon.
8 And likewise did he for all his
strange wives, which burnt incense
and sacrificed unto their gods.
9 ¶ And the LORD was angry with
Solomon, because his heart was turned
from the LORD God of Israel, [k]which
had appeared unto him twice,
10 And [l]had commanded him con-
cerning this thing, that he should not
go after other gods: but he kept not
that which the LORD commanded.
11 Wherefore the LORD said unto
Solomon, Forasmuch as this [c]is done
of thee, and thou hast not kept my cov-
enant and my statutes, which I have
commanded thee, [m]I will surely rend
the kingdom from thee, and will give it
to thy servant.
12 Notwithstanding in thy days I
will not do it for David thy father's

11:4 [d]Deut. 17:17 Neh. 13:26 [e]ch. 8:61 [f]ch. 9:4
11:5 [g]ver. 33 Judg. 2:13 2 Ki. 23:13
11:7 [h]Num. 33:52 [i]Num. 21:29 Judg. 11:24 [j]2 Ki. 23:13
11:9 [k]ch. 3:5 & 9:2
11:10 [l]ch. 6:12 & 9:6
11:11 [m]ver. 31 ch. 12:15,16
11:13 [n]2 Sam. 7:15 [o]ch. 12:20 [p]Deut. 12:11
11:14 [q]1 Chr. 5:26
11:15 [r]2 Sam. 8:14 1 Chr. 18:12 [s]Num. 24:19 Deut. 20:13

sake: *but* I will rend it out of the hand
of thy son.
13 [n]Howbeit I will not rend away
all the kingdom; *but* will give [o]one
tribe to thy son for David my servant's
sake, and for Jerusalem's sake [p]which
I have chosen.

Solomon's adversaries

14 ¶ And the LORD [q]stirred up an
adversary unto Solomon, Hadad the
Edomite: he *was* of the king's seed in
Edom.
15 [r]For it came to pass, when Da-
vid was in Edom, and Joab the captain
of the host was gone up to bury the
slain, [s]after he had smitten every
male in Edom;
16 (For six months did Joab remain
there with all Israel, until he had cut
off every male in Edom:)
17 That Hadad fled, he and certain
Edomites of his father's servants with
him, to go into Egypt; Hadad *being* yet
a little child.
18 And they arose out of Midian,
and came to Paran: and they took men
with them out of Paran, and they came
to Egypt, unto Pharaoh king of Egypt;
which gave him an house, and appoint-
ed him victuals, and gave him land.
19 And Hadad found great favour in
the sight of Pharaoh, so that he gave
him to wife the sister of his own wife,
the sister of Tahpenes the queen.
20 And the sister of Tahpenes bare

[a] Called *Molech* in ver. 7 [b] Heb. *fulfilled not after* [c] Heb. *is with thee*

11:4 PERFECT . . . AS *WAS* THE HEART OF DAVID. David's heart was "perfect," not in the sense that he never failed God miserably, but that he never entered into idolatry and the worship of other gods. In his adultery with Bathsheba and his attempted coverup, David grievously sinned to the point of despising God and His word (2 Sam. 12:9–10). Yet, he never worshiped or depended on other gods, as did many of the kings of Israel (cf. 15:5).

11:5–7 SOLOMON WENT AFTER ASHTORETH . . . MILCOM. Solomon first tolerated the false gods of his wives, then turned his own heart to them (vv. 2–9). (1) In addition to his worship of the Lord, Solomon added the worship of the Sidonian goddess Ashtoreth (involving immoral rituals and the worship of the stars), the Moabite god Milcom or Molech (involving child sacrifice, cf. Lev. 18:21; 20:1–5), and the Ammonite god Chemosh (a sun-god). No longer could Solomon say that the covenant Lord was the only true God (cf. Deut. 6:4).

(2) Solomon's apostasy shows that mere knowledge of God and His word is not an adequate defense against sin and apostasy. Sin comes from the heart and can be resisted only so long as one's heart is turned in faith and love toward God (Deut. 6:4–9; cf. 1 Ki. 3:9, note). Solomon, a preacher who warned others, fell into such blatant sin that he directly sanctioned spiritism, encouraged immorality and cruelty, defiled Israel, and dishonored the one true God.

11:11 REND THE KINGDOM FROM THEE. God's judgment on Solomon resulted in the division of Israel into two kingdoms, only one of which was ruled by Solomon's successors (vv. 9–13,31)—the tribe of Judah (including Simeon, cf. Josh. 19:1), given to his son Rehoboam to preserve the Messianic line (vv. 13,32). The ten tribes were soon to be given to Jeroboam (vv. 31–36).

him Genubath his son, whom Tahpenes
weaned in Pharaoh's house: and Genu-
bath was in Pharaoh's household
among the sons of Pharaoh.
21 [t]And when Hadad heard in
Egypt that David slept with his fathers,
and that Joab the captain of the host
was dead, Hadad said to Pharaoh,
[d]Let me depart, that I may go to mine
own country.
22 Then Pharaoh said unto him,
But what hast thou lacked with me,
that, behold, thou seekest to go to
thine own country? And he answered,
[e]Nothing: howbeit let me go in any
wise.
23 ¶ And God stirred him up *another*
adversary, Rezon the son of Eliadah,
which fled from his lord [u]Hadadezer
king of Zobah:
24 And he gathered men unto him,
and became captain over a band,
[v]when David slew them *of Zobah:* and
they went to Damascus, and dwelt
therein, and reigned in Damascus.
25 And he was an adversary to Isra-
el all the days of Solomon, beside the
mischief that Hadad *did:* and he ab-
horred Israel, and reigned over Syria.

Jeroboam's rebellion

26 ¶ And [w]Jeroboam the son of Ne-
bat, an Ephrathite of Zereda, Solo-
mon's servant, whose mother's name
was Zeruah, a widow woman, even he
[x]lifted up *his* hand against the king.
27 And this *was* the cause that he
lifted up *his* hand against the king:
[y]Solomon built Millo, *and* [f]repaired
the breaches of the city of David his
father.
28 And the man Jeroboam *was* a
mighty man of valour: and Solomon
seeing the young man that he [g]was
industrious, he made him ruler over all
the [h]charge of the house of Joseph.
29 And it came to pass at that time
when Jeroboam went out of Jerusalem,
that the prophet [z]Ahijah the Shilonite
found him in the way; and he had clad
himself with a new garment; and they
two *were* alone in the field:
30 And Ahijah caught the new gar-
ment that *was* on him, and [a]rent it *in*
twelve pieces:
31 And he said to Jeroboam, Take
thee ten pieces: for [b]thus saith the
LORD, the God of Israel, Behold, I will
rend the kingdom out of the hand of
Solomon, and will give ten tribes to
thee:
32 (But he shall have one tribe for
my servant David's sake, and for Jeru-
salem's sake, the city which I have
chosen out of all the tribes of Israel:)
33 [c]Because that they have for-
saken me, and have worshipped Ashto-
reth the goddess of the Zidonians, Che-
mosh the god of the Moabites, and
Milcom the god of the children of Am-
mon, and have not walked in my ways,
to do *that which is* right in mine eyes,
and *to keep* my statutes and my judg-
ments, as *did* David his father.
34 Howbeit I will not take the whole
kingdom out of his hand: but I will
make him prince all the days of his life
for David my servant's sake, whom I
chose, because he kept my command-
ments and my statutes:
35 But [d]I will take the kingdom
out of his son's hand, and will give it
unto thee, *even* ten tribes.
36 And unto his son will I give one
tribe, that [e]David my servant may
have a [i]light always before me in Je-
rusalem, the city which I have chosen
me to put my name there.
37 And I will take thee, and thou
shalt reign according to all that thy
soul desireth, and shalt be king over
Israel.
38 And it shall be, if thou wilt
hearken unto all that I command thee,
and wilt walk in my ways, and do *that
is* right in my sight, to keep my statutes
and my commandments, as David my
servant did; that [f]I will be with thee,
and [g]build thee a sure house, as I built
for David, and will give Israel unto
thee.
39 And I will for this afflict the seed
of David, but not for ever.
40 Solomon sought therefore to kill
Jeroboam. And Jeroboam arose, and
fled into Egypt, unto Shishak king of
Egypt, and was in Egypt until the death
of Solomon.

The death of Solomon

11:41–43pp — 2 Chr. 9:29–31

41 ¶ And [h]the rest of the [j]acts of
Solomon, and all that he did, and his
wisdom, *are* they not written in the
book of the acts of Solomon?

11:21 [t]ch. 2:10,34
11:23 [u]2 Sam. 8:3
11:24 [v]2 Sam. 8:3 & 10:8,18
11:26 [w]ch. 12:2 2 Chr. 13:6 [x]2 Sam. 20:21
11:27 [y]ch. 9:24
11:29 [z]ch. 14:2
11:30 [a]See 1 Sam. 15:27 & 24:5
11:31 [b]ver. 11,13
11:33 [c]ver. 5-7
11:35 [d]ch. 12:16,17
11:36 [e]ch. 15:4 2 Ki. 8:19
11:38 [f]Josh. 1:5 [g]2 Sam. 7:11,27
11:41 [h]2 Chr. 9:29

[d] Heb. *Send me away* [e] Heb. *Not* [f] Heb. *closed* [g] Heb. *did work* [h] Heb. *burden*
[i] Heb. *lamp,* or, *candle* [j] Or, *words,* or, *things*

42 [i]And the [k]time that Solomon reigned in Jerusalem over all Israel *was* forty years.

43 [j]And Solomon slept with his fathers, and was buried in the city of David his father: and [k]Rehoboam his son reigned in his stead.

Rehoboam, king of Israel

12:1–24pp — 2 Chr. 10:1–11:4

12 AND [l]REHOBOAM went to Shechem: for all Israel were come to Shechem to make him king.

2 And it came to pass, when [m]Jeroboam the son of Nebat, who was yet in [n]Egypt, heard *of it,* (for he was fled from the presence of king Solomon, and Jeroboam dwelt in Egypt;)

3 That they sent and called him. And Jeroboam and all the congregation of Israel came, and spake unto Rehoboam, saying,

4 Thy father made our [o]yoke grievous: now therefore make thou the grievous service of thy father, and his heavy yoke which he put upon us, lighter, and we will serve thee.

5 And he said unto them, Depart yet *for* three days, then come again to me. And the people departed.

6 ¶ And king Rehoboam consulted with the old men, that stood before Solomon his father while he yet lived, and said, How do ye advise that I may answer this people?

7 And they spake unto him, saying, [p]If thou wilt be a servant unto this people this day, and wilt serve them, and answer them, and speak good words to them, then they will be thy servants for ever.

8 But he forsook the counsel of the old men, which they had given him, and consulted with the young men that were grown up with him, *and* which stood before him:

9 And he said unto them, What counsel give ye that we may answer this people, who have spoken to me, saying, Make the yoke which thy father did put upon us lighter?

10 And the young men that were grown up with him spake unto him, saying, Thus shalt thou speak unto this people that spake unto thee, saying, Thy father made our yoke heavy, but make thou *it* lighter unto us; thus shalt thou say unto them, My little *finger* shall be thicker than my father's loins.

11 And now whereas my father did lade you with a heavy yoke, I will add to your yoke: my father hath chastised you with whips, but I will chastise you with scorpions.

12 ¶ So Jeroboam and all the people came to Rehoboam the third day, as the king had appointed, saying, Come to me again the third day.

13 And the king answered the people [l]roughly, and forsook the old men's counsel that they gave him;

14 And spake to them after the counsel of the young men, saying, My father made your yoke heavy, and I will add to your yoke: my father *also* chastised you with whips, but I will chastise you with scorpions.

15 Wherefore the king hearkened not unto the people; for [q]the cause was from the LORD, that he might perform his saying, which the LORD [r]spake by Ahijah the Shilonite unto Jeroboam the son of Nebat.

16 ¶ So when all Israel saw that the king hearkened not unto them, the people answered the king, saying, [s]What portion have we in David? neither *have we* inheritance in the son of Jesse: to your tents, O Israel: now see to thine own house, David. So Israel departed unto their tents.

17 But [t]*as for* the children of Israel which dwelt in the cities of Judah, Rehoboam reigned over them.

18 Then king Rehoboam [u]sent Adoram, who *was* over the tribute; and all Israel stoned him with stones, that he died. Therefore king Rehoboam [m]made speed to get him up to his chariot, to flee to Jerusalem.

19 So [v]Israel [n]rebelled against the house of David unto this day.

11:42 [i]2 Chr. 9:30
11:43 [j]2 Chr. 9:31 [k]Mat. 1.7 called *Roboam*
12:1 [l]2 Chr. 10:1
12:2 [m]ch. 11:26 [n]ch. 11:40
12:4 [o]1 Sam. 8:11-18 ch. 4:7
12:7 [p]2 Chr. 10:7 Prov. 15:1
12:15 [q]ver. 24 Judg. 14:4 2 Chr. 10:15 & 22:7 & 25:20 [r]ch. 11:11,31
12:16 [s]2 Sam. 20:1
12:17 [t]ch. 11:13,36
12:18 [u]ch. 4:6 & 5:14
12:19 [v]2 Ki. 17:21

[k]Heb. *days* [l]Heb. *hardly* [m]Heb. *strengthened himself* [n]Or, *fell away*

11:43 AND SOLOMON SLEPT. The same chapter that mentions Solomon's apostasy speaks of his death, without any indication that he repented and returned to God. The Chronicler records David's warning to Solomon: "but if thou forsake [God], he will cast thee off for ever" (1 Chr. 28:19). The Scriptural truth revealed here is that Solomon, who was once in grace, did not remain in that grace. The Word of God warns us here: if a king who had experienced such great gifts, ministry, and graces could fall, then let all who stand take heed lest they fall (1 Cor. 10:12).

20 And it came to pass, when all Is-
rael heard that Jeroboam was come
again, that they sent and called him
unto the congregation, and made him
king over all Israel: there was none
that followed the house of David, but
the tribe of Judah [w]only.
21 ¶ And when [x]Rehoboam was
come to Jerusalem, he assembled all
the house of Judah, with the tribe of
Benjamin, an hundred and fourscore
thousand chosen men, which were
warriors, to fight against the house of
Israel, to bring the kingdom again to
Rehoboam the son of Solomon.
22 But [y]the word of God came unto
Shemaiah the man of God, saying,
23 Speak unto Rehoboam, the son
of Solomon, king of Judah, and unto all
the house of Judah and Benjamin, and
to the remnant of the people, saying,
24 Thus saith the LORD, Ye shall not
go up, nor fight against your brethren
the children of Israel: return every man
to his house; [z]for this thing is from
me. They hearkened therefore to the
word of the LORD, and returned to de-
part, according to the word of the LORD.

12:20 [w]ch. 11:13,32
12:21 [x]2 Chr. 11:1
12:22 [y]2 Chr. 11:2
12:24 [z]ver. 15
12:25 [a]See Judg. 9:45 [b]Judg. 8:17
12:27 [c]Deut. 12:5,6
12:28 [d]2 Ki. 10:29 & 17:16 [e]Ex. 32:4,8
12:29 [f]Gen. 28:19 Hos. 4:15 [g]Judg. 18:29
12:30 [h]ch. 13:34 2 Ki. 17:21
12:31 [i]ch. 13:32 [j]Num. 3:10 ch. 13:33 2 Ki. 17:32 2 Chr. 11:14,15

Two golden calves

25 ¶ Then Jeroboam [a]built She-
chem in mount Ephraim, and dwelt
therein; and went out from thence, and
built [b]Penuel.
26 And Jeroboam said in his heart,
Now shall the kingdom return to the
house of David:
27 If this people [c]go up to do sacri-
fice in the house of the LORD at Jerusa-
lem, then shall the heart of this people
turn again unto their lord, *even* unto
Rehoboam king of Judah, and they
shall kill me, and go again to Rehobo-
am king of Judah.
28 Whereupon the king took coun-
sel, and [d]made two calves *of* gold, and
said unto them, It is too much for you
to go up to Jerusalem: [e]behold thy
gods, O Israel, which brought thee up
out of the land of Egypt.
29 And he set the one in [f]Beth-el,
and the other put he in [g]Dan.
30 And this thing became [h]a sin:
for the people went *to worship* before
the one, *even* unto Dan.
31 And he made an [i]house of high
places, [j]and made priests of the low-

12:20 JEROBOAM . . . KING OVER ALL ISRAEL. At the death of Solomon (11:43), the Hebrew nation split into two kingdoms. (1) The northern kingdom, called Israel, was first ruled by Jeroboam. The southern kingdom, called Judah, was first ruled by Rehoboam, Solomon's son (v. 17). The division continued until the ten northern tribes were taken into captivity by Assyria in 722 B.C. The southern kingdom was carried into captivity in 586 B.C. by the Babylonians. The history of the two kingdoms is recorded in 1 Ki. 12—22; 2 Ki. 1—25; and 2 Chr. 10—36.

(2) The story of Israel and Judah reveals their persistence in breaking God's covenant. The Bible indicates that all the kings of the northern kingdom did evil in the eyes of the Lord (e.g., 16:25,30; 22:52; 2 Ki. 3:3; 10:29); the majority of the kings of Judah departed from the covenant. Only a few of the kings of Judah, notably Hezekiah (2 Ki. 18:1—20:21) and Josiah (2 Ki. 22:1—23:29), "did *that which was* right in the sight of the LORD" (2 Ki. 18:3; 22:2).

12:24 FOR THIS THING IS FROM ME. It was the Lord who brought about the division of His people. The existence of two nations was designed by Him (1) as a punishment for their idolatry, and (2) as a means for preserving a faithful remnant through Judah (11:13). Though Israel as a whole departed from God, a remnant in Judah remained faithful to the covenant, and through them God was able to fulfill His promises and redemptive purpose.

12:28 TWO CALVES *OF* GOLD . . . BEHOLD THY GODS. Jeroboam of the northern kingdom established a counterfeit religious system by offering the people the worship of their gods through idols (vv. 27–30; cf. Ex. 20:3–4), after the pattern of the golden calf made by Aaron (Ex. 32:8). He appointed priests "which were not of the sons of Levi" (v. 31), hence ordaining men to the ministry who were not qualified according to God's law (see next note).

Jeroboam's establishment of a false religious system produced two results: (1) Most people who remained in the northern kingdom accepted Baal worship along with its immoral practice of cult prostitution. (2) The majority of the godly remnant who desired to remain loyal to God and His law suffered greatly as they "left their . . . possession" and moved to the southern kingdom in order to worship the Lord according to His original revelation and commandments (2 Chr. 11:13–14). "Out of all the tribes of Israel such as set their hearts to seek the LORD God of Israel came to Jerusalem, to sacrifice unto the LORD God of their fathers" (2 Chr. 11:16; cf. 15:9).

12:31 MADE PRIESTS . . . WHICH WERE NOT OF THE SONS OF LEVI. Jeroboam appointed priests who were not qualified according to God's standards in Num. 3:6–9; 8:5–20. Under the new covenant the Levitical priesthood no longer exists, but God has still established certain essential qualifications for those who would be ordained for pastoral or church leadership. These spiritual and moral qualifications are listed in 1 Tim. 3:1–7 and Tit. 1:5–9 (see article on MORAL QUALIFICATIONS FOR OVERSEERS, p. 1908).

THE DIVIDED KINGDOM

930–586 B.C.

After the reign of Solomon, the kingdom was divided into ten northern tribes (Israel) and two southern tribes (Judah and part of Benjamin).

Sidon
SIDONIANS
Tyre
Dan
Hazor
ARAM-DAMASCUS
Damascus
GESHUR
Sea of Kinnereth
Ashtaroth
Yarmuk R.
Megiddo
Jezreel
Ramoth Gilead
ISRAEL
Tirzah
Samaria
Shechem
Jabbok R.
Great Sea
Jordan R.
Aphek
Peniel
Joppa
AMMON
Gibbethon
Bethel
Rabbah
Gezer
Jerusalem
Lachish
Gaza
Hebron
Dibon
PHILISTINES
Salt Sea
Rapha
Arad
Arnon R.
Beersheba
MOAB
JUDAH
Kir Hareseth
Zered R.
Tamar
Bozrah
Kadesh Barnea
EDOM
Teman
EGYPT
Elath
Eastern arm of the Red Sea

Miles 10 5 0 10 20
Kms 10 5 0 10 20 30

Original borders c. 930 B.C.

Borders of Israel and Judah under Jeroboam II and Uzziah

The Aramean wars were fierce and destructive contests between the kingdom of Damascus and Israel during the greater part of the ninth century. These so-called Aramean-Ephraimitic wars ended with the conquests of Jeroboam II and an era of great prosperity for Israel.

The campaigns of Tiglath-Pileser III of Assyria were enormously destructive, following a celebrated pattern of siege warfare. By 732 B.C. the northern kingdom was tributary to the Assyrians.

The final capture and destruction of Samaria took place in 722/721B.C. after a long siege.

The Benjamite frontier was an issue that brought Judah and Israel into conflict early in their history. After a struggle between Asa and Baasha, the border was finally fixed south of Bethel in the territory of Benjamin.

est of the people, which were not of the sons of Levi.

32 And Jeroboam ordained a feast in the eighth month, on the fifteenth day of the month, like unto [k]the feast that *is* in Judah, and he [o]offered upon the altar. So did he in Beth-el, [p]sacrificing unto the calves that he had made: [l]and he placed in Beth-el the priests of the high places which he had made.

33 So he [o]offered upon the altar which he had made in Beth-el the fifteenth day of the eighth month, *even* in the month which he had [m]devised of his own heart; and ordained a feast unto the children of Israel: and he offered upon the altar, [q]and [n]burnt incense.

The man of God from Judah

13 AND, BEHOLD, there [o]came a man of God out of Judah by the word of the LORD unto Beth-el: [p]and Jeroboam stood by the altar [r]to burn incense.

2 And he cried against the altar in the word of the LORD, and said, O altar, altar, thus saith the LORD; Behold, a child shall be born unto the house of David, [q]Josiah by name; and upon thee shall he offer the priests of the high places that burn incense upon thee, and men's bones shall be burnt upon thee.

3 And he gave [r]a sign the same day, saying, This *is* the sign which the LORD hath spoken; Behold, the altar shall be rent, and the ashes that *are* upon it shall be poured out.

4 And it came to pass, when king Jeroboam heard the saying of the man of God, which had cried against the altar in Beth-el, that he put forth his hand from the altar, saying, Lay hold on him. And his hand, which he put forth against him, dried up, so that he could not pull it in again to him.

5 The altar also was rent, and the ashes poured out from the altar, according to the sign which the man of God had given by the word of the LORD.

6 And the king answered and said unto the man of God, [s]Entreat now the face of the LORD thy God, and pray for me, that my hand may be restored me again. And the man of God besought [s]the LORD, and the king's hand was restored him again, and became as *it was* before. 1 Ki. 17:17-24

7 And the king said unto the man of God, Come home with me, and refresh thyself, and [t]I will give thee a reward.

8 And the man of God said unto the king, [u]If thou wilt give me half thine house, I will not go in with thee, neither will I eat bread nor drink water in this place:

9 For so was it charged me by the word of the LORD, saying, [v]Eat no bread, nor drink water, nor turn again by the same way that thou camest.

10 So he went another way, and returned not by the way that he came to Beth-el.

11 ¶ Now there dwelt an old prophet in Beth-el; and his [t]sons came and told him all the works that the man of God had done that day in Beth-el: the words which he had spoken unto the king, them they told also to their father.

12 And their father said unto them, What way went he? For his sons had seen what way the man of God went, which came from Judah.

13 And he said unto his sons, Saddle me the ass. So they saddled him the ass; and he rode thereon,

14 And went after the man of God, and found him sitting under an oak: and he said unto him, *Art* thou the man of God that camest from Judah? And he said, I *am*.

15 Then he said unto him, Come home with me, and eat bread.

16 And he said, [w]I may not return with thee, nor go in with thee: neither will I eat bread nor drink water with thee in this place:

17 For [u]it was said to me [x]by the word of the LORD, Thou shalt eat no bread nor drink water there, nor turn again to go by the way that thou camest.

18 He said unto him, I *am* a prophet

12:32 [k]Lev. 23:33,34 Num. 29:12 ch. 8:2,5 [l]Amos 7:13
12:33 [m]Num. 15:39 [n]ch. 13:1
13:1 [o]2 Ki. 23:17 [p]ch. 12:32,33
13:2 [q]2 Ki. 23:15,16
13:3 [r]Is. 7:14 John 2:18 1 Cor. 1:22
13:6 [s]Ex. 8:8 & 9:28 & 10:17 Num. 21:7 Acts 8:24 Jas. 5:16
13:7 [t]1 Sam. 9:7 2 Ki. 5:15
13:8 [u]Num. 22:18 & 24:13
13:9 [v]1 Cor. 5:11
13:16 [w]ver. 8:9
13:17 [x]ch. 20:35 1 Thes. 4:15

[o] Or, *went up to the altar* [p] Or, *to sacrifice* [q] Heb. *to burn incense* [r] Or, *to offer* [s] Heb. *the face of the LORD* [t] Heb. *son* [u] Heb. *a word* was

13:2 JOSIAH. This prophecy was made 300 years before Josiah was born. For the fulfillment of the prophecy, see 2 Ki. 23:15–20.

13:9 THE WORD OF THE LORD. The prophet as God's spokesman was under the highest obligation to follow the entire word of the Lord. This particular prophet later failed to obey God's instruction and paid with his life (vv. 11–24).

also as thou *art;* and an angel spake
unto me by the word of the LORD, say-
ing, Bring him back with thee into
thine house, that he may eat bread and
drink water. *But* he lied unto him.
19 So he went back with him, and
did eat bread in his house, and drank
water.
20 ¶ And it came to pass, as they
sat at the table, that the word of the
LORD came unto the prophet that
brought him back:
21 And he cried unto the man of
God that came from Judah, saying,
Thus saith the LORD, Forasmuch as
thou hast disobeyed the mouth of the
LORD, and hast not kept the command-
ment which the LORD thy God com-
manded thee,
22 But camest back, and hast eaten
bread and drunk water in the place, of
the which *the* LORD did say to thee, Eat
no bread, and drink no water; thy car-
case shall not come unto the sepulchre
of thy fathers.
23 ¶ And it came to pass, after he
had eaten bread, and after he had
drunk, that he saddled for him the ass,
to wit, for the prophet whom he had
brought back.
24 And when he was gone, [y]a lion
met him by the way, and slew him: and
his carcase was cast in the way, and
the ass stood by it, the lion also stood
by the carcase.
25 And, behold, men passed by, and
saw the carcase cast in the way, and
the lion standing by the carcase:
and they came and told *it* in the city
where the old prophet dwelt.
26 And when the prophet that
brought him back from the way heard
thereof, he said, It *is* the man of God,
who was disobedient unto the word of
the LORD: therefore the LORD hath deliv-
ered him unto the lion, which hath
[v]torn him, and slain him, according to
the word of the LORD, which he spake
unto him.
27 And he spake to his sons, say-
ing, Saddle me the ass. And they sad-
dled *him.*
28 And he went and found his car-
case cast in the way, and the ass and
the lion standing by the carcase: the
lion had not eaten the carcase, nor
[v]torn the ass.
29 And the prophet took up the car-
case of the man of God, and laid it upon
the ass, and brought it back: and the
old prophet came to the city, to mourn
and to bury him.
30 And he laid his carcase in his
own grave; and they mourned over
him, *saying,* [z]Alas, my brother!
31 And it came to pass, after he had
buried him, that he spake to his sons,
saying, When I am dead, then bury me
in the sepulchre wherein the man of
God *is* buried; [a]lay my bones beside
his bones:
32 [b]For the saying which he cried
by the word of the LORD against the al-
tar in Beth-el, and against all the
houses of the high places which *are* in
the cities of [c]Samaria, shall surely
come to pass.
33 ¶ [d]After this thing Jeroboam re-
turned not from his evil way, but
[w]made again of the lowest of the peo-
ple priests of the high places: whoso-
ever would, he [e]consecrated[x] him,
and he became *one* of the priests of the
high places.
34 [f]And this thing became sin
unto the house of Jeroboam, even [g]to
cut *it* off, and to destroy *it* from off the
face of the earth.

13:24 [y]ch. 20:36
13:30 [z]Jer. 22:18
13:31 [a]2 Ki. 23:17,18
13:32 [b]ver. 2 2 Ki. 23:16,19 [c]See ch. 16:24
13:33 [d]ch. 12:31,32 2 Chr. 11:15 & 13:9 [e]Judg. 17:12
13:34 [f]ch. 12:30 [g]ch. 14:10

[v]Heb. *broken* [w]Heb. *returned and made*
[x]Heb. *filled his hand*

13:21–22 THOU HAST DISOBEYED THE MOUTH OF THE LORD. The story of the unnamed disobedient prophet was recorded as an example and warning to believers today (cf. 1 Cor. 10:1–13). (1) The Scriptures stand as the believer's highest obligation in all things pertaining to God's will for his or her life. The words and teachings of recognized ministers of God or even angels must never be accepted if they contradict the instructions and standards of written revelation found in the original and fundamental testimony of Christ and the apostles (1 Cor. 14:29; Gal. 1:8–9; see 1 John 4:1, note).

(2) Disobedience to what God has commanded brings punishment, regardless of past faithfulness and service (vv. 20–25).

(3) The most perilous position of any believer is to maintain a careless attitude toward the Word of God. The greatest cause of failure among God's people is not taking God's Word as a matter of life and death (see Gen. 3:4, note).

(4) God demands the greatest measure of faithfulness to His commands from those who are called to proclaim His word (cf. 1 Tim. 3:1–11; Tit. 1:5–9; Jas. 3:1). They must be examples to the people of God.

13:24 A LION . . . SLEW HIM. It must not be assumed that the prophet received eternal punishment after he died. His disobedience is in the same category as that of Moses (see Num. 20:12, note).

The prophecy against Jeroboam

14 AT THAT time Abijah the son
of Jeroboam fell sick.
2 And Jeroboam said to his wife,
Arise, I pray thee, and disguise thyself,
that thou be not known to be the wife
of Jeroboam; and get thee to Shiloh: behold,
there *is* Ahijah the prophet,
which told me that [h]*I should be* king
over this people.
3 [i]And take [y]with thee ten
loaves, and [z]cracknels, and a [a]cruse
of honey, and go to him: he shall tell
thee what shall become of the child.
4 And Jeroboam's wife did so, and
arose, [j]and went to Shiloh, and came
to the house of Ahijah. But Ahijah
could not see; for his eyes [b]were set
by reason of his age.
5 ¶ And the LORD said unto Ahijah,
Behold, the wife of Jeroboam cometh to
ask a thing of thee for her son; for he
is sick: thus and thus shalt thou say
unto her: for it shall be, when she cometh
in, that she shall feign herself *to be*
another *woman*.
6 And it was *so*, when Ahijah heard
the sound of her feet, as she came in
at the door, that he said, Come in, thou
wife of Jeroboam; why feignest thou
thyself *to be* another? for I *am* sent to
thee *with* [c]heavy *tidings*.
7 Go, tell Jeroboam, Thus saith the
LORD God of Israel, [k]Forasmuch as I
exalted thee from among the people,
and made thee prince over my people
Israel,
8 And [l]rent the kingdom away
from the house of David, and gave it
thee: and *yet* thou hast not been as my
servant David, [m]who kept my commandments,
and who followed me with
all his heart, to do *that* only *which was*
right in mine eyes;
9 But hast done evil above all that
were before thee: [n]for thou hast gone
and made thee other gods, and molten
images, to provoke me to anger, and
[o]hast cast me behind thy back:
10 Therefore, behold, [p]I will bring
evil upon the house of Jeroboam, and
[q]will cut off from Jeroboam him that
pisseth against the wall, [r]*and* him
that is shut up and left in Israel, and
will take away the remnant of the
house of Jeroboam, as a man taketh
away dung, till it be all gone.
11 [s]Him that dieth of Jeroboam in
the city shall the dogs eat; and him
that dieth in the field shall the fowls of
the air eat: for the LORD hath spoken *it*.
12 Arise thou therefore, get thee to
thine own house: *and* [t]when thy feet
enter into the city, the child shall die.
13 And all Israel shall mourn for
him, and bury him: for he only of Jeroboam
shall come to the grave, because
in him [u]there is found *some* good thing
toward the LORD God of Israel in the
house of Jeroboam.
14 [v]Moreover the LORD shall raise
him up a king over Israel, who shall cut
off the house of Jeroboam that day: but
what? even now.
15 For the LORD shall smite Israel,
as a reed is shaken in the water, and
he shall [w]root up Israel out of this
[x]good land, which he gave to their fathers,
and shall scatter them [y]beyond
the river, [z]because they have made
their groves, provoking the LORD to anger.
16 And he shall give Israel up because
of the sins of Jeroboam, [a]who
did sin, and who made Israel to sin.
17 ¶ And Jeroboam's wife arose,
and departed, and came to [b]Tirzah:
and [c]when she came to the threshold
of the door, the child died;
18 And they buried him; and all Israel
mourned for him, [d]according to
the word of the LORD, which he spake
by the hand of his servant Ahijah the
prophet.
19 And the rest of the acts of Jeroboam,
how he [e]warred, and how he
reigned, behold, they *are* written in the
book of the chronicles of the kings of
Israel.
20 And the days which Jeroboam
reigned *were* two and twenty years: and
he [d]slept with his fathers, and Nadab
his son reigned in his stead.

Rehoboam, king of Judah

14:21,25–31pp — 2 Chr. 12:9–16

21 ¶ And Rehoboam the son of Solo-

14:2 [h]ch. 11:31 **14:3** [i]See 1 Sam. 9:7,8 **14:4** [j]ch. 11:29 **14:7** [k]See 2 Sam. 12:7,8 **14:8** [l]ch. 11:31 [m]ch. 11:33,38 & 15:5 **14:9** [n]ch. 12:28 2 Chr. 11:15 [o]Neh. 9:26 Ps. 50:17 **14:10** [p]ch. 15:29 [q]ch. 21:21 2 Ki. 9:8 [r]Deut. 32:36 2 Ki. 14:26 **14:11** [s]ch. 16:4 & 21:24 **14:12** [t]ver. 17 **14:13** [u]2 Chr. 12:12 & 19:3 **14:14** [v]ch. 15:27-29 **14:15** [w]2 Ki. 17:6 Ps. 52:5 [x]Josh. 23:15,16 [y]2 Ki. 15:29 [z]Ex. 34:13 Deut. 12:3 **14:16** [a]ch. 12:30 & 13:34 & 15:30,34 & 16:2 **14:17** [b]ch. 16:6,8 [c]ver. 12 **14:18** [d]ver. 13 **14:19** [e]2 Chr. 13:2

[y] Heb. *in thine hand* [z] Or, *cakes* [a] Or, *bottle*
[b] Heb. *stood for his hoariness* [c] Heb. *hard*
[d] Heb. *lay down*

14:15 SHALL SCATTER THEM BEYOND THE RIVER. Ahijah prophesied the captivity of Israel; in 722 B.C. Israel was defeated and thousands were carried away across the river Euphrates by the Assyrians (cf. 2 Ki. 15:29; 17:6,18).

mon reigned in Judah. [f]Rehoboam *was* forty and one years old when he began to reign, and he reigned seventeen years in Jerusalem, the city [g]which the LORD did choose out of all the tribes of Israel, to put his name there. [h]And his mother's name *was* Naamah an Ammonitess.

22 [i]And Judah did evil in the sight of the LORD, and they [j]provoked him to jealousy with their sins which they had committed, above all that their fathers had done.

23 For they also built them [k]high places, and [e]images, [l]and groves, on every high hill, and [m]under every green tree.

24 [n]And there were also sodomites in the land: *and* they did according to all the abominations of the nations which the LORD cast out before the children of Israel.

25 ¶ [o]And it came to pass in the fifth year of king Rehoboam, *that* Shishak king of Egypt came up against Jerusalem:

26 [p]And he took away the treasures of the house of the LORD, and the treasures of the king's house; he even took away all: and he took away all the shields of gold [q]which Solomon had made.

27 And king Rehoboam made in their stead brasen shields, and committed *them* unto the hands of the chief of the [f]guard, which kept the door of the king's house.

28 And it was *so,* when the king went into the house of the LORD, that the guard bare them, and brought them back into the guard chamber.

29 ¶ [r]Now the rest of the acts of Rehoboam, and all that he did, *are* they not written in the book of the chronicles of the kings of Judah?

30 And there was [s]war between Rehoboam and Jeroboam all *their* days.

31 [t]And Rehoboam slept with his fathers, and was buried with his fathers in the city of David. [u]And his mother's name *was* Naamah an Ammonitess. And [v]Abijam his son reigned in his stead.

14:21 [f]2 Chr. 12:13 [g]ch. 11:36 [h]ver. 31.
14:22 [i]2 Chr. 12:1 [j]Deut. 32:21
14:23 [k]Deut. 12:2 Ezek. 16:24,25 [l]2 Ki. 17:9,10 [m]Is. 57:5
14:24 [n]Deut. 23:17 ch. 15:12 2 Ki. 23:7
14:25 [o]ch. 11:40 2 Chr. 12:2
14:26 [p]2 Chr. 12:9-11 [q]ch. 10:17
14:29 [r]2 Chr. 12:15
14:30 [s]ch. 12:24 & 15:6 2 Chr. 12:15
14:31 [t]2 Chr. 12:16 [u]ver. 21 [v]2 Chr. 12:16 *Abijah* Mat. 1:7 *Abia*
15:1 [w]2 Chr. 13:1
15:2 [x]2 Chr. 11:20-22 [y]2 Chr. 13:2 *Michaiah the daughter of Uriel* [z]2 Chr. 11:21 *Absalom*
15:3 [a]ch. 11:4 Ps. 119:80
15:4 [b]ch. 11:32,36 2 Chr. 21:7 [c]ch. 11:36
15:5 [d]ch. 14:8 [e]2 Sam. 11:4,15 & 12:9
15:6 [f]ch. 14:30
15:7 [g]2 Chr. 13:2,3,22

Abijam, king of Judah

15:1–2,6–8pp — 2 Chr. 13:1–2,22–14:1

15 NOW [w]IN the eighteenth year of king Jeroboam the son of Nebat reigned Abijam over Judah.

2 Three years reigned he in Jerusalem. [x]And his mother's name *was* [y]Maachah, the daughter of [z]Abishalom.

3 And he walked in all the sins of his father, which he had done before him: and [a]his heart was not perfect with the LORD his God, as the heart of David his father.

4 Nevertheless [b]for David's sake did the LORD his God give him a [c]lamp[g] in Jerusalem, to set up his son after him, and to establish Jerusalem:

5 Because David [d]did *that which was* right in the eyes of the LORD, and turned not aside from any *thing* that he commanded him all the days of his life, [e]save only in the matter of Uriah the Hittite.

6 [f]And there was war between Rehoboam and Jeroboam all the days of his life.

7 [g]Now the rest of the acts of Abijam, and all that he did, *are* they not written in the book of the chronicles of

[e] Or, *standing images,* or, *statues* [f] Heb. *runners* [g] Or, *candle*

14:22 JUDAH DID EVIL. The tribe of Judah, ruled by Rehoboam (v. 21), did little better than the ten tribes of Israel. They also forsook the Lord and gave themselves over to terrible sin (see next note; cf. 2 Chr. 11—12).

14:24 SODOMITES. The apostasy of Judah led to the depraved sin of homosexuality and male prostitution (cf. Rom. 1:25–28). God's people accepted "the abominations of the nations" and were thus conquered by the ungodly nations (vv. 25–26). Christ reemphasized this principle of judgment for believers who conform to the world (see Mat. 5:13, note).

14:26 TOOK AWAY THE TREASURES OF THE HOUSE OF GOD. God permitted Shishak, the king of Egypt, to invade the temple and to carry away its treasures. The temple, where God had manifested His glory during Solomon's early rule (8:11), became a scene of disgrace just five years after the death of Solomon, as God's own people had cast aside His righteous ways.

15:3 HEART WAS NOT PERFECT. This phrase typically refers to one who was an idolater. David's heart is said to be perfect because he never turned to other gods; to have a perfect heart does not imply moral perfection (cf. v. 5; see 11:44, note).

15:4 A LAMP. "Lamp" as used here means that God had determined never to extinguish the Davidic line and covenant. The lamp eventually became "the light of the world" in the person of Jesus Christ (John 8:12; cf. Luke 2:4).

the kings of Judah? And there was war
between Abijam and Jeroboam.
8 [h]And Abijam slept with his fa-
thers; and they buried him in the city
of David: and Asa his son reigned in his
stead.

Asa, king of Judah

15:9–22pp — 2 Chr. 14:2–3; 15:16–16:6
15:23–24pp — 2 Chr. 16:11–17:1

9 ¶ And in the twentieth year of Jer-
oboam king of Israel reigned Asa over
Judah.
10 And forty and one years reigned
he in Jerusalem. And his [h]mother's
name *was* Maachah, the daughter of
Abishalom.
11 [i]And Asa did *that which was*
right in the eyes of the LORD, as *did* Da-
vid his father.
12 [j]And he took away the sodom-
ites out of the land, and removed all
the idols that his fathers had made.
13 And also [k]Maachah his mother,
even her he removed from *being* queen,
because she had made an idol in a
grove; and Asa [i]destroyed her idol,
and [l]burnt *it* by the brook Kidron.
14 [m]But the high places were not
removed: nevertheless Asa's [n]heart
was perfect with the LORD all his days.
15 And he brought in the [j]things
which his father had dedicated, and the
things which himself had dedicated,
into the house of the LORD, silver, and
gold, and vessels.
16 ¶ And there was war between
Asa and Baasha king of Israel all their
days.
17 And [o]Baasha king of Israel
went up against Judah, and built [p]Ra-
mah, [q]that he might not suffer any to
go out or come in to Asa king of Judah.
18 Then Asa took all the silver and
the gold *that were* left in the treasures
of the house of the LORD, and the trea-
sures of the king's house, and deliv-
ered them into the hand of his ser-
vants: and king Asa sent them to
[r]Ben-hadad, the son of Tabrimon, the
son of Hezion, king of Syria, that dwelt
at [s]Damascus, saying,

15:8 [h]2 Chr. 14:1
15:11 [i]2 Chr. 14:2
15:12 [j]ch. 14:24 & 22:46
15:13 [k]2 Chr. 15:16 [l]Ex. 32:20
15:14 [m]ch. 22:43 2 Chr. 15:17,18 [n]See ver. 3
15:17 [o]2 Chr. 16:1 [p]Josh. 18:25 [q]See ch. 12:27
15:18 [r]2 Chr. 16:2 [s]ch. 11:23,24
15:20 [t]2 Ki. 15:29 [u]Judg. 18:29 [v]2 Sam. 20:14
15:22 [w]2 Chr. 16:6 [x]Josh. 21:17 [y]Josh. 18:26
15:23 [z]2 Chr. 16:12
15:24 [a]2 Chr. 17:1 [b]Mat. 1:8 called *Josaphat*
15:26 [c]ch. 12:30 & 14:16
15:27 [d]ch. 14:14 [e]Josh. 19:44

19 *There is* a league between me and
thee, *and* between my father and thy
father: behold, I have sent unto thee a
present of silver and gold; come and
break thy league with Baasha king of
Israel, that he may [k]depart from me.
20 So Ben-hadad hearkened unto
king Asa, and sent the captains of the
hosts which he had against the cities of
Israel, and smote [t]Ijon, and [u]Dan,
and [v]Abel-beth-maachah, and all Cin-
neroth, with all the land of Naphtali.
21 And it came to pass, when Baa-
sha heard *thereof,* that he left off build-
ing of Ramah, and dwelt in Tirzah.
22 [w]Then king Asa made a procla-
mation throughout all Judah; none *was*
[l]exempted: and they took away the
stones of Ramah, and the timber there-
of, wherewith Baasha had builded; and
king Asa built with them [x]Geba of
Benjamin, and [y]Mizpah.
23 The rest of all the acts of Asa,
and all his might, and all that he did,
and the cities which he built, *are* they
not written in the book of the chroni-
cles of the kings of Judah? Neverthe-
less [z]in the time of his old age he was
diseased in his feet.
24 And Asa slept with his fathers,
and was buried with his fathers in the
city of David his father: [a]and [b]Je-
hoshaphat his son reigned in his stead.

Nadab, king of Israel

25 ¶ And Nadab the son of Jeroboam
[m]began to reign over Israel in the sec-
ond year of Asa king of Judah, and
reigned over Israel two years.
26 And he did evil in the sight of the
LORD, and walked in the way of his fa-
ther, and in [c]his sin wherewith he
made Israel to sin.
27 ¶ [d]And Baasha the son of Ahi-
jah, of the house of Issachar, conspired
against him; and Baasha smote him at
[e]Gibbethon, which *belonged* to the

[h] i.e. *grandmother's;* see ver. 2 [i] Heb. *cut off* [j] Heb. *holy* [k] Heb. *go up* [l] Heb. *free* [m] Heb. *reigned*

15:9 ASA. Asa was a good king whose reign was characterized by faithfulness to God. However, he failed to trust God fully in his later years (see 2 Chr. 16). His reign was significant because he led the people to renounce their ungodly ways and turn away from the wicked practices of the Canaanites. True revival always includes turning away from practices that offend God and violate His word (see 2 Chr. 14—16 for more about Asa's reign).

15:24 JEHOSHAPHAT. Jehoshaphat was a good king who endeavored to teach the people God's word and who sought to remain faithful to the Lord (for details concerning his reign, see 22:41–50; 2 Chr. 17:1—21:1).

Philistines; for Nadab and all Israel laid siege to Gibbethon.

28 Even in the third year of Asa king of Judah did Baasha slay him, and reigned in his stead.

29 And it came to pass, when he reigned, *that* he smote all the house of Jeroboam; he left not to Jeroboam any that breathed, until he had destroyed him, according unto [f]the saying of the LORD, which he spake by his servant Ahijah the Shilonite:

30 [g]Because of the sins of Jeroboam which he sinned, and which he made Israel sin, by his provocation wherewith he provoked the LORD God of Israel to anger.

31 ¶ Now the rest of the acts of Nadab, and all that he did, *are* they not written in the book of the chronicles of the kings of Israel?

32 [h]And there was war between Asa and Baasha king of Israel all their days.

Baasha, king of Israel

33 In the third year of Asa king of Judah began Baasha the son of Ahijah to reign over all Israel in Tirzah, twenty and four years.

34 And he did evil in the sight of the LORD, and walked in [i]the way of Jeroboam, and in his sin wherewith he made Israel to sin.

16 THEN THE word of the LORD came to [j]Jehu the son of Hanani against Baasha, saying,

2 [k]Forasmuch as I exalted thee out of the dust, and made thee prince over my people Israel; and [l]thou hast walked in the way of Jeroboam, and hast made my people Israel to sin, to provoke me to anger with their sins;

3 Behold, I will [m]take away the posterity of Baasha, and the posterity of his house; and will make thy house like [n]the house of Jeroboam the son of Nebat.

4 [o]Him that dieth of Baasha in the city shall the dogs eat; and him that dieth of his in the fields shall the fowls of the air eat.

5 Now the rest of the acts of Baasha, and what he did, and his might, [p]*are* they not written in the book of the chronicles of the kings of Israel?

6 So Baasha slept with his fathers, and was buried in [q]Tirzah: and Elah his son reigned in his stead.

7 And also by the hand of the prophet [r]Jehu the son of Hanani came the word of the LORD against Baasha, and against his house, even for all the evil that he did in the sight of the LORD, in provoking him to anger with the work of his hands, in being like the house of Jeroboam; and because [s]he killed him.

Elah, king of Israel

8 ¶ In the twenty and sixth year of Asa king of Judah began Elah the son of Baasha to reign over Israel in Tirzah, two years.

9 [t]And his servant Zimri, captain of half *his* chariots, conspired against him, as he was in Tirzah, drinking himself drunk in the house of Arza [n]steward of *his* house in Tirzah.

10 And Zimri went in and smote him, and killed him, in the twenty and seventh year of Asa king of Judah, and reigned in his stead.

11 ¶ And it came to pass, when he began to reign, as soon as he sat on his throne, *that* he slew all the house of Baasha: he left him [u]not one that pisseth against a wall, [o]neither of his kinsfolks, nor of his friends.

12 Thus did Zimri destroy all the house of Baasha, [v]according to the word of the LORD, which he spake against Baasha [w]by[p] Jehu the prophet,

13 For all the sins of Baasha, and the sins of Elah his son, by which they sinned, and by which they made Israel to sin, in provoking the LORD God of Israel to anger [x]with their vanities.

14 Now the rest of the acts of Elah, and all that he did, *are* they not written in the book of the chronicles of the kings of Israel?

Zimri, king of Israel

15 ¶ In the twenty and seventh year of Asa king of Judah did Zimri reign

15:29 [f]ch. 14:10,14
15:30 [g]ch. 14:9,16
15:32 [h]ver. 16
15:34 [i]ch. 12:28,29 & 13:33 & 14:16
16:1 [j]ver. 7 2 Chr. 19:2 & 20:34
16:2 [k]ch. 14:7 [l]ch. 15:34
16:3 [m]ver. 11 [n]ch. 14:10 & 15:29
16:4 [o]ch. 14:11
16:5 [p]2 Chr. 16:1
16:6 [q]ch. 14:17 & 15:21
16:7 [r]ver. 1 [s]ch. 15:27,29 See Hos. 1:4
16:9 [t]2 Ki. 9:31
16:11 [u]1 Sam. 25:22
16:12 [v]ver. 3 [w]ver. 1
16:13 [x]Deut. 32:21 1 Sam. 12:21 Is. 41:29 Jonah 2:8 1 Cor. 8:4 & 10:19

[n] Heb. *which was over* [o] Or, *both his kingsmen and his friends* [p] Heb. *by the hand of*

16:7 THE PROPHET JEHU. When God's leaders and people forsook His law and adopted the ungodly ways of the Canaanites, God sent them prophets to proclaim His truth and righteousness. Such prophets are needed today as well (see articles on THE PROPHET IN THE OLD TESTAMENT, p. 1002, and THE MINISTRY GIFTS OF THE CHURCH, p. 1852).

seven days in Tirzah. And the people *were* encamped [y]against Gibbethon, which *belonged* to the Philistines.

16 And the people *that were* encamped heard say, Zimri hath conspired, and hath also slain the king: wherefore all Israel made Omri, the captain of the host, king over Israel that day in the camp.

17 And Omri went up from Gibbethon, and all Israel with him, and they besieged Tirzah.

18 And it came to pass, when Zimri saw that the city was taken, that he went into the palace of the king's house, and burnt the king's house over him with fire, and died,

19 For his sins which he sinned in doing evil in the sight of the LORD, [z]in walking in the way of Jeroboam, and in his sin which he did, to make Israel to sin.

20 Now the rest of the acts of Zimri, and his treason that he wrought, *are* they not written in the book of the chronicles of the kings of Israel?

Omri, king of Israel

21 ¶ Then were the people of Israel divided into two parts: half of the people followed Tibni the son of Ginath, to make him king; and half followed Omri.

22 But the people that followed Omri prevailed against the people that followed Tibni the son of Ginath: so Tibni died, and Omri reigned.

23 ¶ In the thirty and first year of Asa king of Judah began Omri to reign over Israel, twelve years: six years reigned he in Tirzah.

24 And he bought the hill Samaria of Shemer for two talents of silver, and built on the hill, and called the name of the city which he built, after the name of Shemer, owner of the hill, [a]Samaria.[q]

25 ¶ But [b]Omri wrought evil in the eyes of the LORD, and did worse than all that *were* before him.

26 For he [c]walked in all the way of Jeroboam the son of Nebat, and in his sin wherewith he made Israel to sin, to provoke the LORD God of Israel to anger with their [d]vanities.

27 Now the rest of the acts of Omri which he did, and his might that he showed, *are* they not written in the book of the chronicles of the kings of Israel?

28 So Omri slept with his fathers, and was buried in Samaria: and Ahab his son reigned in his stead.

Ahab, king of Israel

29 ¶ And in the thirty and eighth year of Asa king of Judah began Ahab the son of Omri to reign over Israel: and Ahab the son of Omri reigned over Israel in Samaria twenty and two years.

30 And Ahab the son of Omri did evil in the sight of the LORD above all that *were* before him.

31 And it came to pass, [r]as if it had been a light thing for him to walk in the sins of Jeroboam the son of Nebat, [e]that he took to wife Jezebel the daughter of Ethbaal king of the [f]Zidonians, [g]and went and served Baal, and worshipped him.

32 And he reared up an altar for Baal in [h]the house of Baal, which he had built in Samaria.

33 [i]And Ahab made a grove; and Ahab [j]did more to provoke the LORD God of Israel to anger than all the kings of Israel that were before him.

34 ¶ In his days did Hiel the Bethelite build Jericho: he laid the foundation thereof in Abiram his firstborn, and set up the gates thereof in his youngest *son* Segub, [k]according to the word of the LORD, which he spake by Joshua the son of Nun.

Elijah fed by ravens

17 AND [s]ELIJAH the Tishbite, *who was* of the inhabitants of Gilead, said unto Ahab, [l]*As* the LORD

[q] Heb. *Shomeron* [r] Heb. *was it a light thing*
[s] Heb. *Elijahu;* in Luke 1:17 & 4:25, he is called *Elias*

16:15 [y]ch. 15:27
16:19 [z]ch. 12:28 & 15:26,34
16:24 [a]See ch. 13:32 2 Ki. 17:24 John 4:4
16:25 [b]Mic. 6:16
16:26 [c]ver. 19 [d]ver. 13
16:31 [e]Deut. 7:3 [f]Judg. 18:7 [g]ch. 21:25,26 2 Ki. 10:18 & 17:16
16:32 [h]2 Ki. 10:21,26,27
16:33 [i]2 Ki. 13:6 & 17:10 & 21:3 Jer. 17:2 [j]ver. 30 ch. 21:25
16:34 [k]Josh. 6:26
17:1 [l]2 Ki. 3:14

16:30 AHAB. Sin and evil became progressively worse in Israel during the reign of King Ahab. Outright rebellion and hardness of heart against God's commandments prevailed. The worship of Baal increased. In the face of such apostasy, God sent the mighty prophet Elijah to Israel to oppose the corrupt religious system and to proclaim God's purpose for His kingdom (17:1).

16:31 BAAL. See Josh. 23:12, note; Judg. 2:13, note.

17:1 ELIJAH. Elijah was a prophet in the northern kingdom during the reigns of Ahab and his son Ahaziah. The name Elijah, meaning "The LORD is my God," represents the unshakable conviction of Elijah's life (18:21,39). The principal narratives about his life are found in 1 Ki. 17—19;

God of Israel liveth, [m]before whom I stand, [n]there shall not be dew nor rain [o]these years, but according to my word.

2 And the word of the LORD came unto him, saying,

3 Get thee hence, and turn thee eastward, and hide thyself by the brook Cherith, that *is* before Jordan.

4 And it shall be, *that* thou shalt drink of the brook; and I have commanded the ravens to feed thee there.

5 So he went and did according unto the word of the LORD: for he went and dwelt by the brook Cherith, that *is* before Jordan.

6 And the ravens brought him bread and flesh in the morning, and bread and flesh in the evening; and he drank of the brook.

7 And it came to pass [t]after a while, that the brook dried up, because there had been no rain in the land.

Elijah raises the widow's son

8 ¶ And the word of the LORD came unto him, saying,

9 Arise, get thee to [p]Zarephath, which *belongeth* to Zidon, and dwell there: behold, I have commanded a widow woman there to sustain thee.

10 So he arose and went to Zarephath. And when he came to the gate of the city, behold, the widow woman *was* there gathering of sticks: and he called to her, and said, Fetch me, I pray thee, a little water in a vessel, that I may drink.

11 And as she was going to fetch *it,* he called to her, and said, Bring me, I pray thee, a morsel of bread in thine hand.

12 And she said, *As* the LORD thy God liveth, I have not a cake, but an handful of meal in a barrel, and a little oil in a cruse: and, behold, I *am* gathering two sticks, that I may go in and dress it for me and my son, that we may eat it, and die.

13 And Elijah said unto her, Fear not; go *and* do as thou hast said: but make me thereof a little cake first, and bring *it* unto me, and after make for thee and for thy son.

14 For thus saith the LORD God of Israel, The barrel of meal shall not waste, neither shall the cruse of oil fail, until the day *that* the LORD [u]sendeth rain upon the earth.

15 And she went and did according to the saying of Elijah: and she, and he,

17:1
[m] Deut. 10:8
[n] Jas. 5:17
[o] Luke 4:25
17:9
[p] Obad. 20
Luke 4:26
called *Sarepta*

[t] Heb. *at the end of days* [u] Heb. *giveth*

21:17–29; 2 Ki. 1—2.

(1) Elijah's life centered around the conflict between the worship of the Lord and the worship of Baal. His mission was to awaken the Israelites to their apostasy and to call them back to loyalty to the God of Israel (18:21,36–37). Thus, Elijah was a restorer and a reformer who sought to reestablish the covenant.

(2) The O.T. ends with the prophecy that Elijah would appear again before "the coming of the great and dreadful day of the LORD" (Mal. 4:5); this prophecy was partially fulfilled in the appearance of John the Baptist (Mat. 11:7–14; Luke 1:17) and may have a future fulfillment before the return of Christ (cf. Mat. 17:11; Rev. 11:3–6; see Rev. 11:3, note).

(3) Elijah's unwavering devotion to God and His covenant makes him forever both an example of faith, courage, and loyalty to God in the face of intense opposition and persecution, and an example of faithful persistence in opposing false religion and false prophets.

17:1 THERE SHALL NOT BE DEW NOR RAIN. As God's messenger, Elijah spoke a word of judgment from the Lord against disobedient Israel. God would withhold the rain for three and a half years (cf. Deut. 11:13–17). This word of judgment also mocked Baal, for the worshipers of Baal believed he controlled rain and was responsible for abundant crops. The N.T. states that this drought in Israel came as the result of Elijah's earnest prayers (Jas. 5:17).

17:4 I HAVE COMMANDED THE RAVENS TO FEED THEE. God sustained Elijah at the brook Cherith because he had stood with God against the apostasy of the people (vv. 3–7; cf. Ps. 25:10). As Elijah had borne the burden of God, the Lord would now bear his burden (cf. Ps. 68:19–20).

17:7 THE BROOK DRIED UP. When the brook dried up, God directed Elijah to go to a pagan territory inhabited by Baal worshipers, and there God provided for Elijah through a poor widow (v. 9). The experience further strengthened Elijah's confidence in God's providence. Sometimes adversity occurs even though we are in God's will; through such experiences He may help us in a different and greater way than we had expected.

17:15 SHE . . . AND HER HOUSE, DID EAT *MANY* DAYS. The needs and misery of a poor widow were not insignificant to God. He sent Elijah to strengthen her faith and give material blessings at a time when she felt all was lost (v. 12). The widow's faith in God and His word through the prophet Elijah led her to exchange the certain for the uncertain, the seen for the unseen (vv. 10–16; cf. Heb. 11:27). The believing widow not only received from God's prophet a material blessing, but also a spiritual blessing.

and her house, did eat [v]*many* days.
16 *And* the barrel of meal wasted
not, neither did the cruse of oil fail, ac-
cording to the word of the LORD, which
he spake [w]by Elijah.
17 ¶ And it came to pass after these
things, *that* the son of the woman, the
mistress of the house, fell sick; and his
sickness was so sore, that there was
no breath left in him.
18 And she said unto Elijah, [q]What
have I to do with thee, O thou man of
God? art thou come unto me to call my
sin to remembrance, and to slay my
son?
19 And he said unto her, Give me
thy son. And he took him out of her
bosom, and carried him up into a loft,
where he abode, and laid him upon his
own bed.
20 And he cried unto the LORD, and
said, O LORD my God, hast thou also
brought evil upon the widow with
whom I sojourn, by slaying her son?
21 [r]And he [x]stretched himself
upon the child three times, and cried
unto the LORD, and said, O LORD my
God, I pray thee, let this child's soul
come [y]into him again.
22 And the LORD heard the voice of
Elijah; and the soul of the child came
into him again, and he [s]revived.
23 And Elijah took the child, and
brought him down out of the chamber
into the house, and delivered him unto
his mother: and Elijah said, See, thy
son liveth.
24 ¶ And the woman said to Elijah,
Now by this [t]I know that thou *art* a
man of God, *and* that the word of the
LORD in thy mouth *is* truth.

Ki.
:9-14

Elijah and
18 … came to pass *after*
[u]many days, that the word of
the LORD came to Elijah in the third
year, saying, Go, show thyself unto
Ahab; and [v]I will send rain upon the
earth.
2 And Elijah went to show himself
unto Ahab. And *there was* a sore famine
in Samaria.
3 And Ahab called [z]Obadiah,
which *was* [a]the governor of *his* house.
(Now Obadiah feared the LORD greatly:
4 For it was *so*, when [b]Jezebel cut
off the prophets of the LORD, that Oba-
diah took an hundred prophets, and hid
them by fifty in a cave, and fed them
with bread and water.)
5 And Ahab said unto Obadiah, Go
into the land, unto all fountains of wa-
ter, and unto all brooks: peradventure
we may find grass to save the horses
and mules alive, [c]that we lose not all
the beasts.
6 So they divided the land between
them to pass throughout it: Ahab went
one way by himself, and Obadiah went
another way by himself.
7 ¶ And as Obadiah was in the way,
behold, Elijah met him: and he knew
him, and fell on his face, and said, *Art*
thou that my lord Elijah?
8 And he answered him, I *am*: go,
tell thy lord, Behold, Elijah *is here*.
9 And he said, What have I sinned,
that thou wouldest deliver thy servant
into the hand of Ahab, to slay me?
10 *As* the LORD thy God liveth, there
is no nation or kingdom, whither my
lord hath not sent to seek thee: and
when they said, *He is* not *there;* he took
an oath of the kingdom and nation, that
they found thee not.
11 And now thou sayest, Go, tell thy
lord, Behold, Elijah *is here*.
12 And it shall come to pass, *as*
soon as I am gone from thee, that [w]the
spirit of the LORD shall carry thee
whither I know not; and *so* when I
come and tell Ahab, and he cannot find
thee, he shall slay me: but I thy servant
fear the LORD from my youth.

17:18 [q]See Luke 5:8
17:21 [r]2 Ki. 4:34,35
17:22 [s]Heb. 11:35
17:24 [t]John 3:2 & 16:30
18:1 [u]Luke 4:25 Jas. 5:17 [v]Deut. 28:12
18:12 [w]2 Ki. 2:16 Ezek. 3:12,14 Mat. 4:1 Acts 8:39

[v]Or, *a full year* [w]Heb. *by the hand of* [x]Heb. *measured* [y]Heb. *into his inward parts* [z]Heb. *Obadiahu* [a]Heb. *over his house* [b]Heb. *Izebel* [c]Heb. *that we cut not off ourselves from the beasts*

17:17 THE SON . . . NO BREATH LEFT IN HIM. We confront here one of the perplexing mysteries of life. At the very time God was miraculously providing flour and oil, trouble and sorrow occurred. Sometimes sickness or even greater tragedy may come to those who are doing God's will and who are actively involved in the work of His kingdom.

17:22 THE LORD HEARD THE VOICE OF ELIJAH. God restored the boy to life in answer to Elijah's prayer. This is the first instance recorded in the Bible of someone being raised from the dead (cf. 2 Ki. 4:34; Acts 20:10). The three miracles listed in ch. 17 strikingly manifested the glory and love of God. They demonstrated to Elijah and the woman that in the midst of tragic circumstances, God's power and love are active on behalf of those who love Him and are called according to His purpose (see Rom. 8:28, note).

13 Was it not told my lord what I did
when Jezebel slew the prophets of the
LORD, how I hid an hundred men of the
LORD's prophets by fifty in a cave, and
fed them with bread and water?
14 And now thou sayest, Go, tell thy
lord, Behold, Elijah *is here:* and he shall
slay me.
15 And Elijah said, *As* the LORD of
hosts liveth, before whom I stand, I
will surely show myself unto him to-
day.
16 So Obadiah went to meet Ahab,
and told him: and Ahab went to meet
Elijah.

Elijah on mount Carmel

17 ¶ And it came to pass, when
Ahab saw Elijah, that Ahab said unto
him, [x]*Art* thou he that [y]troubleth Is-
rael?
18 And he answered, I have not
troubled Israel; but thou, and thy fa-
ther's house, [z]in that ye have forsak-
en the commandments of the LORD, and
thou hast followed Baalim.
19 Now therefore send, *and* gather
to me all Israel unto mount [a]Carmel,
and the prophets of Baal four hundred
and fifty, [b]and the prophets of the
groves four hundred, which eat at Jeze-
bel's table.
20 So Ahab sent unto all the chil-
dren of Israel, and [c]gathered the
prophets together unto mount Carmel.
21 And Elijah came unto all the peo-
ple, and said, [d]How long halt ye be-
tween two [d]opinions? if the LORD *be*
God, follow him: but if Baal, [e]*then* fol-
low him. And the people answered him
not a word.
22 Then said Eliajah unto the peo-
ple, [f]I, *even* I only, remain a prophet
of the LORD; [g]but Baal's prophets *are*
four hundred and fifty men.
23 Let them therefore give us two
bullocks; and let them choose one bull-
ock for themselves, and cut it in
pieces, and lay *it* on wood, and put no
fire *under:* and I will dress the other
bullock, and lay *it* on wood, and put no
fire *under:*
24 And call ye on the name of your
gods, and I will call on the name of the
LORD: and the God that [h]answereth by
fire, let him be God. And all the people
answered and said, [e]It is well spoken.
25 And Elijah said unto the proph-
ets of Baal, Choose you one bullock for
yourselves, and dress *it* first; for ye *are*
many; and call on the name of your
gods, but put no fire *under.*
26 And they took the bullock which
was given them, and they dressed *it,*
and called on the name of Baal from
morning even until noon, saying, O
Baal, [f]hear us. But *there was* [i]no
voice, nor any that [g]answered. And
they [h]leaped upon the altar which
was made.
27 And it came to pass at noon, that
Elijah mocked them, and said, Cry
[i]aloud: for he *is* a god; either [j]he is
talking, or he [k]is pursuing, or he is in
a journey, *or* peradventure he sleepeth,
and must be awaked.
28 And they cried aloud, and [j]cut
themselves after their manner with
knives and lancets, till [l]the blood
gushed out upon them.
29 And it came to pass, when mid-

18:17 [x]ch. 21:20 [y]Josh. 7:25 Acts 16:20 **18:18** [z]2 Chr. 15:2 **18:19** [a]Josh. 19:26 [b]ch. 16:33 **18:20** [c]ch. 22:6 **18:21** [d]2 Ki. 17:41 Mat. 6:24 [e]See Josh. 24:15 **18:22** [f]ch. 19:10,14 [g]ver. 19 **18:24** [h]ver. 38 1 Chr. 21:26 **18:26** [i]Ps. 115:5 [illegible]10:5 **18:28** [j]Lev. 19:28 Deut. 14:1

[d] Or, *thoughts?* [e] Heb. *The word* is *good* [f] Or, *answer* [g] Or, *heard* [h] Or, *leaped up* [illegible] *at the altar* [i] Heb. *with a great* [illegible] *pursuit* [l] Heb. [illegible] [k] Heb. *hath a*

18:18 YE HAVE FORSAKEN THE COMMANDMENTS OF THE LORD. Elijah's courageous confrontation with Ahab and with unrighteousness in Israel made him a model prophet of Israel and the most qualified person to be a prototype of the forerunner for the Lord Jesus Christ (cf. Mal. 4:5–6; Luke 1:17). (1) He was a true "man of God" (17:24), one who spoke not as a people-pleaser but as a faithful bondservant of God (cf. Gal. 1:10; 1 Thes. 2:4; see Luke 1:17, note).

(2) As Elijah was called to defend the true God of Israel, all ministers of the new covenant are called to defend the gospel of Christ against distortion, compromise, and corruption (see Phil. 1:17, note; Jude 3, note).

18:21 IF THE LORD *BE* GOD, FOLLOW HIM. Elijah challenged the people to make a definitive choice between following God or following (cf. Ezek. 20:31,39). Israel believed they could worship both deities at the same time. They were guilty of a divided heart (cf. Deut. 6:4–5) that tried to serve two masters. Christ Himself warned against this fatal attitude (Mat. 6:24; cf. Deut. 30:19; Josh. 24:14–15; see article on SPIRITUAL SEPARATION FOR BELIEVERS, p. 1814).

18:27 ELIJAH MOCKED THEM. Elijah's mockery of the prophets of Baal reveals his fierce indignation at the immoral and cruel idolatry that Israel had embraced; his sarcasm and his uncompromising attitude expressed his unwavering loyalty to the God whom he loved and served. Compare Elijah's reaction with Jesus' anger and intolerance at the defiling of the temple (see Luke 19:45, note).

day was past, [k]and they prophesied until the *time* of the [m]offering of the *evening* sacrifice, that *there was* [l]neither voice, nor any to answer, nor any [n]that regarded.

30 And Elijah said unto all the people, Come near unto me. And all the people came near unto him. [m]And he repaired the altar of the LORD *that was* broken down.

31 And Elijah took twelve stones, according to the number of the tribes of the sons of Jacob, unto whom the word of the LORD came, saying, [n]Israel shall be thy name:

32 And with the stones he built an altar [o]in the name of the LORD: and he made a trench about the altar, as great as would contain two measures of seed.

33 And he [p]put the wood in order, and cut the bullock in pieces, and laid *him* on the wood, and said, Fill four barrels with water, and [q]pour *it* on the burnt sacrifice, and on the wood.

34 And he said, Do *it* the second time. And they did *it* the second time. And he said, Do *it* the third time. And they did *it* the third time.

35 And the water [o]ran round about the altar; and he filled [r]the trench also with water.

18:29 [k]1 Cor. 11:4,5 [l]ver. 26
18:30 [m]ch. 19:10
18:31 [n]Gen. 32:28 2 Ki. 17:34
18:32 [o]Col. 3:17
18:33 [p]Lev. 1:6-8 [q]See Judg. 6:20
18:35 [r]ver. 32,38
18:36 [s]Ex. 3:6 [t]ch. 8:43 2 Ki. 19:19 [u]Num. 16:28
18:38 [v]Lev. 9:24 Judg. 6:21 1 Chr. 21:26 2 Chr. 7:1
18:39 [w]ver. 24
18:40 [x]2 Ki. 10:25 [y]Deut. 13:5 & 18:20

36 And it came to pass at *the time of* the offering of the *evening* sacrifice, that Elijah the prophet came near, and said, LORD [s]God of Abraham, Isaac, and of Israel, [t]let it be known this day that thou *art* God in Israel, and *that* I *am* thy servant, and *that* [u]I have done all these things at thy word.

37 Hear me, O LORD, hear me, that this people may know that thou *art* the LORD God, and *that* thou hast turned their heart back again.

38 Then [v]the fire of the LORD fell, and consumed the burnt sacrifice, and the wood, and the stones, and the dust, and licked up the water that *was* in the trench.

39 And when all the people saw *it*, they fell on their faces: and they said, [w]The LORD, he *is* the God; the LORD, he *is* the God. Job 1:6-22

40 And Elijah said unto them, [x]Take[p] the prophets of Baal; let not one of them escape. And they took them: and Elijah brought them down to the brook Kishon, and [y]slew them there.

41 ¶ And Elijah said unto Ahab, Get

[m] Heb. *ascending* [n] Heb. *attention* [o] Heb. *went* [p] Or, *Apprehend*

18:36 ELIJAH ... SAID, LORD, GOD OF ABRAHAM. Elijah's courage and faith have virtually no parallel in the entire history of redemption. His challenge to the king (vv. 16–19), rebuke of all Israel (vv. 21–24), and confrontation with the 450 priests of Baal (vv. 22,27) were undertaken with only the weapons of prayer and faith in God. His confidence in God is indicated by the brevity (41 words in Hebrew) and simplicity of his prayer (vv. 36–37; see article on EFFECTIVE PRAYING, p. 540).

18:37 THOU HAST TURNED THEIR HEART BACK AGAIN. The purpose of Elijah's confrontation with the prophets of Baal and then his prayer was to reveal the grace of God to His people. He wanted to turn their hearts back to God (v. 37). Similarly, John the Baptist, the "Elijah" of the N.T. (see 17:1, note), had as his goal to turn the hearts of many back to God in preparation for the coming of Christ.

18:38 THE FIRE OF THE LORD FELL. The Lord miraculously provided fire to consume the sacrifice (cf. 1 Chr. 21:26; 2 Chr. 7:1). The miracle vindicated Elijah as God's prophet and proved that Israel's Lord alone was the living God whom they were to serve. In a similar way, believers should pray for and expect the manifestation of God in their midst through the Holy Spirit (see 1 Cor. 12:4–11; 14:1–40).

18:40 SLEW THEM THERE. Note the following about the slaying of the prophets of Baal: (1) Their death sentence was just, for it was done in obedience to the law of Moses (Deut. 13:6–9; 17:2–5). The N.T. has no such commandment; violent action against false teachers is prohibited (Mat. 5:44), though God does command rejection of and separation from them (Mat. 24:23–24; 2 Cor. 6:14–18; Gal. 1:6–9; 2 John 7–11; Jude 3–4; see article on FALSE TEACHERS, p. 1508).

(2) Elijah's action against the false prophets of Baal represented God's wrath against those who were trying to destroy the faith and spiritual heritage of His chosen people, and expressed Elijah's own love for and loyalty to his Lord. Thus, his spirit and heart were in harmony with God; his moral and spiritual sensitivity was outraged at the tragic defection of Israel from their covenant God, the One who had loved and redeemed them.

(3) Elijah's destruction of the false prophets also manifested a deep concern for the people of Israel themselves who were being spiritually destroyed by false religion. Jesus had this same attitude (Mat. 23; see also Luke 19:27), as did Paul the apostle (Gal. 1:6–9; see Gal. 1:9, note). Furthermore, note that God's wrath will be poured out on all stubborn and unrepentant people at "the day of wrath and revelation of the righteous judgment of God" (Rom. 2:5; cf. 11:22; Rev. 19:11–21; 20:7–10).

thee up, eat and drink; for *there is* [q]a
sound of abundance of rain.
42 So Ahab went up to eat and to
drink. And Elijah went up to the top of
Carmel; [z]and he cast himself down
upon the earth, and put his face be-
tween his knees,
43 And said to his servant, Go up
now, look toward the sea. And he
went up, and looked, and said, *There is*
nothing. And he said, Go again seven
times.
44 And it came to pass at the sev-
enth time, that he said, Behold, there
ariseth a little cloud out of the sea, like
a man's hand. And he said, Go up, say
unto Ahab, [r]Prepare *thy chariot,* and
get thee down, that the rain stop thee
not.
45 And it came to pass in the mean
while, that the heaven was black with
clouds and wind, and there was a great
rain. And Ahab rode, and went to Jez-
reel.
46 And the hand of the LORD was on
Elijah; and he [a]girded up his loins,
and ran before Ahab [s]to the entrance
of Jezreel.

18:42 [z]Jas. 5:17,18
18:46 [a]2 Ki. 4:29 & 9:1
19:1 [b]ch. 18:40
19:2 [c]Ruth 1:17 ch. 20:10 2 Ki. 6:31

Elijah flees from Jezebel

19 AND AHAB told Jezebel all that
Elijah had done, and withal
how he had [b]slain all the prophets
with the sword.
2 Then Jezebel sent a messenger
unto Elijah, saying, [c]So let the gods
do *to me,* and more also, if I make not
thy life as the life of one of them by
tomorrow about this time.
3 And when he saw *that,* he arose,
and went for his life, and came to Beer-
sheba, which *belongeth* to Judah, and
left his servant there.
4 ¶ But he himself went a day's
journey into the wilderness, and came

[q] Or, *a sound of a noise of rain* [r] Heb. *Tie,* or, *Bind* [s] Heb. *till thou come to Jezreel*

18:42 ELIJAH . . . PUT HIS FACE BETWEEN HIS KNEES. The N.T. cites Elijah's faith and persistent prayer as an example and encouragement to all God's faithful people with regard to the power of prayer (Jas. 5:18; see article on EFFECTIVE PRAYING, p. 540). Elijah's prayer was (1) the prayer of a righteous man (Jas. 5:16; cf. Ps. 66:18), (2) the prayer of a man with a human nature like ours (Jas. 5:17), (3) an earnest and persistent prayer of faith (vv. 18:42–44; Jas. 5:17; cf. Mat. 21:21–22; Mark 9:23; Luke 18:1; Eph. 6:18; Heb. 11:6), and (4) a prayer that accomplished much (v. 45; Jas. 5:16–17).

18:43 GO AGAIN SEVEN TIMES. The number seven in Scripture symbolizes something that is full and complete. In this chapter Elijah engaged in a complete intercession with three aspects: (1) he interceded to restore the altar and honor of God in the land (vv. 21,24,30–39); (2) he interceded by engaging in spiritual warfare against the false religion and cult of Baalism and Asherah (vv. 19,27, 40); and (3) he interceded with God by intense and persistent prayer for the outpouring of rain (vv. 41–46).

Insofar as the O.T. compares the outpouring of the Spirit with the outpouring of rain (e.g., Hos. 6:1–3; Joel 2:23–29), Elijah's confrontation with Baalism illustrates the three main kinds of intercession that must characterize the prayers of God's people: (1) intercession for the restoration of God's honor and glory and for a revival among God's people; (2) intercession involving spiritual warfare against demonic strongholds; and (3) intercession for spiritual drought to be broken by the outpouring of God's Spirit and by a spiritual awakening (see article on INTERCESSION, p. 1268).

19:3 HE AROSE, AND WENT FOR HIS LIFE. Elijah's expression of faith and the supernatural victories in ch. 18 were followed by fear, a flight for his life, and discouragement—all results of Jezebel's intention to destroy his life (v. 2). (1) Since Elijah had received no word from the Lord to remain in Jezreel, to have stayed would have been to risk his life unnecessarily (cf. 18:1). His destiny was Mount Horeb (i.e., Mount Sinai).

(2) Elijah's forced departure for Judah and the wilderness serves as an example of those who "for righteousness' sake" (see Mat. 5:10, note) have been ill-treated and forced to wander in deserts, mountains, caves, and holes in the ground (Heb. 11:37–38). Like Elijah there are prophets who have had to leave their churches, preachers their pulpits, professors their classrooms, and lay people their work because they stood against sin, spoke according to God's Word, and followed the path of righteousness for His name's sake. Great is their reward in heaven (Mat. 5:10–12).

19:4 TAKE AWAY MY LIFE. Elijah—overcome by exhaustion, discouragement, and grief—prayed that God would deliver him from the heavy prophetic burden and let him depart to his heavenly rest. (1) Elijah's feelings were not unlike that of (a) the apostle Paul, when he spoke of "having a desire to depart, and to be with Christ" (Phil. 1:23), or (b) the heroes of faith, who "desire[d] a better *country*, that is, an heavenly" (Heb. 11:16; see also Moses in Num. 11:15).

(2) The following are some of the reasons why Elijah was profoundly discouraged. (a) Apparent failure: he had expected the conversion of all Israel and possibly even Jezebel, yet he now had to flee for his life instead. The hope, labor, and struggle of his whole life appeared to be ending in failure (vv. 1–4). (b) Loneliness: he felt that he stood alone in the conflict for God's truth and righteousness (v. 10; cf. Paul, 2 Tim. 4:16). (c) Physical exhaustion after a long and strenuous journey (vv. 3–4; 18:46).

and sat down under a juniper tree: and
he [d]requested [t]for himself that he
might die; and said, It is enough; now,
O LORD, take away my life; for I *am* not
better than my fathers.
5 And as he lay and slept under a
juniper tree, behold, then an angel
touched him, and said unto him, Arise
and eat.
6 And he looked, and, behold, *there*
was a cake baked on the coals, and a
cruse of water at his [u]head. And he
did eat and drink, and laid him down
again.
7 And the angel of the LORD came
again the second time, and touched
him, and said, Arise *and* eat; because
the journey *is* too great for thee.
8 And he arose, and did eat and
drink, and went in the strength of that
meat [e]forty days and forty nights unto
[f]Horeb the mount of God.

Elijah in the mountain cave

9 ¶ And he came thither unto a
cave, and lodged there; and, behold,
the word of the LORD *came* to him, and
he said unto him, What doest thou
here, Elijah?
10 And he said, [g]I have been very
[h]jealous for the LORD God of hosts: for
the children of Israel have forsaken thy
covenant, thrown down thine altars,
and [i]slain thy prophets with the
sword; and [j]I, *even* I only, am left; and
they seek my life, to take it away.
11 And he said, Go forth, and stand
[k]upon the mount before the LORD.
And, behold, the LORD passed by, and
[l]a great and strong wind rent the
mountains, and brake in pieces the
rocks before the LORD; *but* the LORD *was*
not in the wind: and after the wind an
earthquake; *but* the LORD *was* not in the
earthquake:
12 And after the earthquake a fire;
but the LORD *was* not in the fire: and
after the fire a still small voice.
13 And it was *so*, when Elijah heard
it, that [m]he wrapped his face in his
mantle, and went out, and stood in the
entering in of the cave. [n]And, behold,
there came a voice unto him, and said,
What doest thou here, Elijah?
14 [o]And he said, I have been very
jealous for the LORD God of hosts: be-
cause the children of Israel have for-
saken thy covenant, thrown down
thine altars, and slain thy prophets
with the sword; and I, *even* I only, am
left; and they seek my life, to take it
away.
15 And the LORD said unto him, Go,
return on thy way to the wilderness of
Damascus: [p]and when thou comest,
anoint Hazael *to be* king over Syria:
16 And [q]Jehu the son of Nimshi

19:4 [d]Num. 11:15 Jonah 4:3,8 **19:8** [e]Ex. 34:28 Deut. 9:9,18 Mat. 4:2 [f]Ex. 3:1 **19:10** [g]Rom. 11:3 [h]Num. 25:11,13 Ps. 69:9 [i]ch. 18:4 [j]ch. 18:22 Rom. 11:3 **19:11** [k]Ex. 24:12 [l]Ezek. 1:4 & 37:7 **19:13** [m]Ex. 3:6 Is. 6:2 [n]ver. 9 **19:14** [o]ver. 10 **19:15** [p]2 Ki. 8:12,13 **19:16** [q]2 Ki. 9:1-3

[t]Heb. *for his life* [u]Heb. *bolster*

19:5 AN ANGEL TOUCHED HIM. God dealt with the discouraged Elijah in an understanding and caring manner (cf. Heb. 4:14–15). (1) He allowed Elijah to sleep (vv. 5–6). (2) He nourished him with food (vv. 5–7). (3) He visited him with an awe-inspiring revelation of His power and presence (vv. 11–13). (4) He provided additional revelation and direction (vv. 15–18). (5) He gave him a faithful companion with a kindred spirit (vv. 16, 19–21). In other words, when God's children are discouraged in the place where God has put them, they can through Christ ask God to give strength, grace, and encouragement, and to make them adequate for their situation (see Heb. 2:18; 3:6; 7:25).

19:8 FORTY DAYS AND FORTY NIGHTS. Some take this fast, along with the experience of Moses (Ex. 34:28) and Christ (Mat. 4:2), as examples of long fasts. However, these individuals did not fast in the ordinary sense. Moses, in the presence of God in the cloud, was supernaturally sustained. Elijah was given two supernatural meals that kept giving him strength for forty days (vv. 6–8). Jesus was led by the Spirit into the wilderness and did not become hungry until after the forty days (see Mat. 4:2, note; 6:16, note).

19:11–12 THE LORD PASSED BY. To encourage Elijah and strengthen his faith, God visited him on Mount Horeb (i.e., Mount Sinai, the mountain of revelation). This visitation was accompanied by a great wind, earthquake, and fire, but the Lord was in none of those events. Instead, the revelation of God came in the form of "a still small voice." Elijah learned that God's work proceeds and advances "not by might, nor by power, but by my spirit, saith the LORD of hosts" (cf. Zech. 4:6). God had in fact not deserted His prophet or His faithful people. By His Spirit and eternal word, He would bring redemption, righteousness, and eternal salvation.

19:16 ELISHA . . . SHALT THOU ANOINT *TO BE* PROPHET. God directed Elijah to anoint Elisha to be his successor. Note that not only were priests and kings anointed to their respective offices, but prophets as well. Elisha was to (1) minister to Elijah, (2) help Hazael (king of Syria) and Jehu (king of Israel) defeat the enemies of God (vv. 16–17), and (3) proclaim the word of God to the faithful remnant (v. 18). Elijah and Elisha's ministries covered a span of 75 years (875–800 B.C., during the reigns of Ahab, Ahaziah, Joram, Jehu, Jehoahaz, and Joash). Elisha was a faithful servant to the older prophet and was known as the one "which poured water on the hands of Elijah" (2 Ki. 3:11).

EFFECTIVE PRAYING

***1 Ki. 18:42b-45** "And Elijah went up to the top of Carmel; and he cast himself down upon the earth, and put his face between his knees, And said to his servant, Go up now, look toward the sea. And he went up, and looked, and said,* There is *nothing. And he said, Go again seven times. And it came to pass at the seventh time, that he said, Behold, there ariseth a little cloud out of the sea, like a man's hand. And he said, Go up, say unto Ahab, Prepare* thy chariot, *and get thee down, that the rain stop thee not. And it came to pass in the mean while, that the heaven was black with clouds and wind, and there was a great rain. And Ahab rode, and went to Jezreel."*

Prayer refers to the multifaceted communication of believers with the Lord God. In addition to such words as "prayer" and "praying," this activity is described as calling upon God (Ps. 17:6), calling upon the name of the LORD (Gen. 4:26), crying unto the LORD (Ps. 3:4), lifting up one's soul unto God (Ps. 25:1), seeking the LORD (Is. 55:6), coming boldly unto the throne of grace (Heb. 4:16), and drawing near to God (Heb. 10:22).

REASONS FOR PRAYER. The Bible provides some clear reasons why believers ought to pray. (1) First and foremost, believers are commanded by God to pray. The command to pray comes from the lips of psalmists (1 Chr. 16:11; Ps. 105:4), prophets (Is. 55:6; Amos 5:4,6), apostles (Eph. 6:17–18; Col. 4:2; 1 Thes. 5:17), and the Lord Jesus Himself (Mat. 26:41; Luke 18:1; John 16:24). God desires our fellowship; by prayer we maintain our relationship with Him.

(2) Prayer is the necessary link to receiving God's blessings and power, and the fulfillment of His promises. Numerous Bible passages illustrate this principle. Jesus, for example, promised that His followers would receive the Holy Spirit if they persisted in asking, seeking, and knocking at the door of their heavenly Father (Luke 11:5–13). Thus, after Jesus' ascension, His followers continually devoted themselves to prayer in the upper room (Acts 1:14) until with power (cf. Acts 1:8) the Holy Spirit was poured out on the day of Pentecost (Acts 2:1–4). When the apostles gathered together after their arrest and release by the Jewish authorities, they prayed earnestly for the Holy Spirit to give them boldness and influence when speaking His word. "And when they had prayed, the place was shaken where they were assembled together; and they were all filled with the Holy Ghost, and they spake the word of God with boldness" (Acts 4:31). The apostle Paul frequently requested prayers on his behalf, knowing that his work would not be successful unless Christians were praying for him (e.g., Rom. 15:30–32; 2 Cor. 1:11; Eph. 6:18–20; Phil. 1:19; Col. 4:3–4; see article on INTERCESSION, p. 1268). James states explicitly that physical healing can come to the believer in response to "the prayer of faith" (Jas. 5:14–15).

(3) In His plan of salvation for humankind, God has ordained that believers be co-workers with Him in the redemptive process. In some respects God has limited Himself to the holy, believing, persevering prayers of His people. There are many things that will not be accomplished in God's kingdom without the intercessory prayers of believers (see Ex. 33:11, note). For example, God desires to send forth workers into the gospel harvest; Christ teaches that this will only be accomplished to God's full purpose through the prayers of His people: "Pray ye therefore the Lord of the harvest, that he will send forth labourers into his harvest" (Mat. 9:38). In other words, God's power to accomplish many of His purposes is released only through the earnest and effectual prayers of His people

on behalf of the progress of His kingdom. If we fail to pray, we may actually be hindering the accomplishment of God's redemptive purpose, both for ourselves as individuals and for the church as a body.

REQUIREMENTS OF EFFECTIVE PRAYING. Several conditions must be met for our prayers to be effective. (1) Our prayers will not be answered unless we have a sincere, true faith. Jesus states explicitly: "What things soever ye desire, when ye pray, believe that ye receive *them*, and ye shall have *them*" (Mark 11:24). To the father of a demon-possessed boy, He spoke these words: "all things *are* possible to him that believeth" (Mark 9:23). The author of Hebrews exhorts us to draw near to God "with a true heart in full assurance of faith" (Heb. 10:22), and James encourages us to ask of God "in faith, nothing wavering" (Jas. 1:6; cf. 5:15).

(2) Prayer must also be made in Jesus' name. Jesus Himself expressed this principle when He said: "And whatsoever ye shall ask in my name, that will I do, that the Father may be glorified in the Son. If ye shall ask any thing in my name, I will do *it*" (John 14:13–14). Our prayers should be made in harmony with the person, character, and will of our Lord (see John 14:13, note).

(3) Prayer can only be effective if it is made according to the perfect will of God: "And this is the confidence that we have in him, that, if we ask any thing according to his will, he heareth us" (1 John 5:14; see article on THE WILL OF GOD, p. 1060). One of the petitions in Jesus' model prayer, the Lord's Prayer, confirms this: "Thy will be done in earth, as *it is* in heaven" (Mat. 6:10; cf. Luke 11:2; note Jesus' own prayer in Gethsemane, Mat. 26:42). In many instances we know God's will because He has revealed it to us in the Scriptures. We can be sure that any prayer that is truly based upon the promises of God in His Word will indeed be effective. Elijah was certain that the Lord God of Israel would answer his prayer with fire and later with rain because the prophetic word of the Lord had come to him (1 Ki. 18:1), and he was fully confident that none of the heathen gods was greater than or even as powerful as the Lord God of Israel (1 Ki. 18:21–24). At other times God's will becomes clear only as we earnestly seek to determine what it is. Then once we know His will about any given issue, we can pray with confidence and faith that God will answer (see 1 John 5:14, note).

(4) Not only must we pray according to God's will, but we must be *in* God's will if we expect Him to hear and answer us. God will give us the things we ask for only if we seek first His kingdom and His righteousness (see Mat. 6:33, note). The apostle John unequivocally states: "And whatsoever we ask, we receive of him, because we keep his commandments, and do those things that are pleasing in his sight" (1 John 3:22, see note). Obeying God's commandments, loving Him, and pleasing Him are indispensable conditions for receiving answers to prayer. When James wrote that the prayers of the righteous are effectual, he meant both a person who has been made righteous by faith in Christ and one who is living a righteous, God-fearing, and obedient life—such as the prophet Elijah (Jas. 5:16–18; cf. Ps. 34:13–14). Already in the O.T. this same point is stressed. God made clear that Moses' prayers on behalf of the Israelites were effective because of his obedient relationship with the Lord and his loyalty to Him (see Ex. 33:17, note). Conversely, the psalmist claims that if we cherish sin in our lives, "the Lord will not hear" our prayers (Ps. 66:18; see Jas. 4:3, note). This sort of attitude was the main reason why the Lord turned his ear away from the prayers of the idolatrous and wicked Israelites (Is. 1:15). But if God's people repent of their sins and turn from their wicked ways, the Lord promises to again turn His ear toward them, forgive their sins, and heal their land (2 Chr. 7:14; cf. 6:36–39; Luke 18:14). Note that the prayer of the high priest for the forgiveness of the sins of the Israelites on the Day of Atonement would not be heard until his own sinful condition had been cleansed (see Ex. 26:33, note; see article on THE DAY OF ATONEMENT, p. 188).

(5) Finally, for prayer to be effective we must be persistent. This is the main point of the parable of the persistent widow (see Luke 18:1–7; see 18:1, note). Jesus' instruction to "ask . . . seek . . . knock" (Mat. 7:7–8) teaches perseverance in prayer (see Mat. 7:7–8, note). The apostle Paul also admonishes us to be steadfast in prayer (Col. 4:2,

note; 1 Thes. 5:17, note). Likewise, the O.T saints recognized this principle. For example, only as long as Moses persevered in prayer with his hands lifted toward God were the Israelites successful in their battle against the Amalekites (see Ex.17:11, note). After Elijah received the prophetic word that rain was coming, he still persisted in prayer until the rain came (1 Ki. 18:41–45). On a previous occasion, this great prophet had persistently and earnestly prayed for God to give life back to the dead son of the widow of Zarephath until the Lord answered his prayer (1 Ki. 17:17–23).

SCRIPTURAL ELEMENTS AND METHODS OF EFFECTIVE PRAYING. (1) What elements constitute effective prayer? (a) To pray effectively, we must praise and adore God (Ps. 150; Acts 2:47; Rom. 15:11; see article on PRAISE, p. 816). (b) Closely related and equally important is thanksgiving to God (see Ps. 100:4; Mat. 11:25–26; Phil. 4:6). (c) Sincere confession of known sins is essential to the prayer of faith (Jas. 5:15–16; cf. Ps. 51; Luke 18:13; 1 John 1:9). (d) God also instructs us to petition Him according to our needs; as James writes, we do not receive the things we want because we do not ask, or we ask with wrong motives (Jas. 4:2–3; cf. Ps. 27:7–12; Mat. 7:7–11; Phil. 4:6). (e) And we must pray fervently for others (Num. 14:13–19; Ps. 122:6–9; Luke 22:31–32; 23:34; see article on INTERCESSION, p. 1268).

(2) How ought we to pray? Jesus emphasizes the sincerity of our heart, for we are not heard simply for our empty words (Mat. 6:7). We can pray silently (1 Sam. 1:13) or we can pray out loud (Neh. 9:4; Ezek. 11:13). We can pray in our own words or using the words of the Scriptures. We can pray with the mind or we can pray with the Spirit (i.e., in tongues, 1 Cor. 14:14–18). We can even pray by groaning, i.e., not using any human words (Rom. 8:26), knowing that the Spirit will bring those inaudible requests to the Lord. Yet another method of praying is singing to the Lord (Ps. 92:1–2; Eph. 5:19–20; Col. 3:16). Earnest prayer to the Lord will at times be accompanied with fasting (Ezra 8:21; Neh. 1:4; Dan. 9:3–4; Mark 9:29; Luke 2:37; Acts 14:23; see Mat. 6:16, note).

(3) What posture is appropriate for prayer? The Bible records praying while standing (1 Ki. 8:22; Neh. 9:4–5), sitting (1 Chr. 17:16; Luke 10:13), kneeling (Ezr. 9:5; Dan. 6:10; Acts 20:36), lying on a bed (Ps. 63:6), bowing down to the ground (Ex. 34:8; Ps. 95:6), lying upon the ground (2 Sam. 12:16; Mat. 26:39), and lifting up hands to heaven (Ps. 28:2; Is. 1:15; 1 Tim. 2:8).

EXAMPLES OF EFFECTIVE PRAYING. The Bible is filled with examples of prayers that were powerful and effective. (1) Moses had numerous intercessory prayers that God answered, even when He had told Moses that He would follow a different course of action (see article on INTERCESSION, p. 1268). (2) A repentant Samson prayed for one more opportunity to fulfill his life's task of defeating the Philistines; God answered this prayer by giving him strength to pull down the pillars of the building in which they were celebrating the power of their gods (Judg. 16:21–30). (3) The prophet Elijah had at least four powerful prayers answered, all of which brought glory to the God of Israel (see 1 Ki. 17—18; cf. Jas. 5:17–18). (4) King Hezekiah became sick and was told by Isaiah that he would die (2 Ki. 20:1; Is. 38:1). Feeling his life and work were incomplete, Hezekiah turned his face to the wall and prayed intensely for God to give him more time. God sent Isaiah back to Hezekiah, assuring him of healing and fifteen more years of life (2 Ki. 20:2–6; Is. 38:2–6). (5) Daniel undoubtedly prayed to the Lord in the den of lions, asking for deliverance from their mouths, and the Lord granted his request (Dan. 6:10,16–22). (6) The early Christians prayed earnestly for Peter's release from prison, and God sent an angel to free him (Acts 12:3–11; cf. 12:5, note). Such examples should fill us with holy desire and faith to pray effectively according to the principles outlined in the Scriptures.

shalt thou anoint *to be* king over Israel: and [r]Elisha the son of Shaphat of Abel-meholah shalt thou anoint *to be* prophet in thy room.

17 And [s]it shall come to pass, *that* him that escapeth the sword of Hazael shall Jehu slay: and him that escapeth from the sword of Jehu [t]shall Elisha slay.

18 [u]Yet [v]I have left *me* seven thousand in Israel, all the knees which have not bowed unto Baal, [v]and every mouth which hath not kissed him.

Elijah and Elisha

19 ¶ So he departed thence, and found Elisha the son of Shaphat, who *was* plowing *with* twelve yoke *of oxen* before him, and he with the twelfth: and Elijah passed by him, and cast his mantle upon him.

20 And he left the oxen, and ran after Elijah, and said, [w]Let me, I pray thee, kiss my father and my mother, and *then* I will follow thee. And he said unto him, [w]Go back again: for what have I done to thee?

21 And he returned back from him, and took a yoke of oxen, and slew them, and [x]boiled their flesh with the instruments of the oxen, and gave unto the people, and they did eat. Then he arose, and went after Elijah, and ministered unto him.

Ahab defeats Ben-hadad

20 AND BEN-HADAD the king of Syria gathered all his host together: and *there were* thirty and two kings with him, and horses, and chariots: and he went up and besieged Samaria, and warred against it.

2 And he sent messengers to Ahab king of Israel into the city, and said unto him, Thus saith Ben-hadad,

3 Thy silver and thy gold *is* mine; thy wives also and thy children, *even* the goodliest, *are* mine.

4 And the king of Israel answered and said, My lord, O king, according to thy saying, I *am* thine, and all that I have.

5 And the messengers came again, and said, Thus speaketh Ben-hadad, saying, Although I have sent unto thee, saying, Thou shalt deliver me thy silver, and thy gold, and thy wives, and thy children;

6 Yet I will send my servants unto thee tomorrow about this time, and they shall search thine house, and the houses of thy servants; and it shall be, *that* whatsoever is [x]pleasant in thine eyes, they shall put *it* in their hand, and take *it* away.

7 Then the king of Israel called all the elders of the land, and said, Mark, I pray you, and see how this *man* seeketh mischief: for he sent unto me for my wives, and for my children, and for my silver, and for my gold; and [y]I denied him not.

8 And all the elders and all the people said unto him, Hearken not *unto him*, nor consent.

9 Wherefore he said unto the messengers of Ben-hadad, Tell my lord the king, All that thou didst send for to thy servant at the first I will do: but this thing I may not do. And the messengers departed, and brought him word again.

10 And Ben-hadad sent unto him, and said, [y]The gods do so unto me, and more also, if the dust of Samaria shall suffice for handfuls for all the people that [z]follow me.

11 And the king of Israel answered and said, Tell *him*, Let not him that girdeth on *his harness* boast himself as he that putteth it off.

12 And it came to pass, when *Ben-hadad* heard this [a]message, as he *was* [z]drinking, he and the kings in the [b]pavilions, that he said unto his ser-

19:16 [r]Luke 4:27 called *Eliseus* **19:17** [s]2 Ki. 8:12 & 9:14 & 10:6 & 13:3 [t]See Hos. 6:5 **19:18** [u]Rom. 11:4 [v]See Hos. 13:2 **19:20** [w]Mat. 8:21,22 Luke 9:61,62 **19:21** [x]2 Sam. 24:22 **20:10** [y]ch. 19:2 **20:12** [z]ver. 16

[v] Or, *I will leave* [w] Heb. *Go return* [x] Heb. *desirable* [y] Heb. *I kept not back from him* [z] Heb. are *at my feet* [a] Heb. *word* [b] Or, *tents*

19:18 SEVEN THOUSAND IN ISRAEL. The 7,000 in Israel who did not bow their knees to Baal are joined by the suffering faithful of all generations who overcome apostasy, compromise, and worldliness among God's people, and who persevere in love, faith, and obedience to God and His Word. They are those who refuse to be caught up by the evil ways of the world, who have washed their robes and made them white in the blood of the Lamb (Rev. 7:14), who are persecuted for righteousness' sake (Mat. 5:10), and who steadfastly remain in the narrow way (Mat. 7:14; see articles on SPIRITUAL SEPARATION FOR BELIEVERS, p. 1814, and THE CHRISTIAN'S RELATIONSHIP TO THE WORLD, p. 2004). Throughout Scripture it is the faithful and overcoming remnant that is known by the Lord (2 Tim. 2:19). God promises to keep them by His power through faith (1 Pet. 1:5), and the Lamb will lead them home (Rev. 7:17).

vants, [c]Set *yourselves in array.* And
they set *themselves in array* against the
city.
13 ¶ And, behold, there [d]came a
prophet unto Ahab king of Israel, say-
ing, Thus saith the LORD, Hast thou
seen all this great multitude? behold,
[a]I will deliver it into thine hand this
day; and thou shalt know that I *am* the
LORD.
14 And Ahab said, By whom? And
he said, Thus saith the LORD, *Even* by
the [e]young men of the princes of the
provinces. Then he said, Who shall
[f]order the battle? And he answered,
Thou.
15 Then he numbered the young
men of the princes of the provinces,
and they were two hundred and thirty
two: and after them he numbered all
the people, *even* all the children of Isra-
el, *being* seven thousand.
16 And they went out at noon. But
Ben-hadad *was* [b]drinking himself
drunk in the pavilions, he and the
kings, the thirty and two kings that
helped him.
17 And the young men of the
princes of the provinces went out first;

20:13 [a]ver. 28

20:16 [b]ver. 12 ch. 16:9

[c] Or, *Place the engines And they placed* engines [d] Heb. *approached* [e] Or, *servants* [f] Heb. *bind,* or, *tie*

20:13 I WILL DELIVER IT INTO THINE HAND. In spite of the unfaithfulness of Ahab and the people of Israel, God showed them mercy and delivered Samaria from the Syrian army (v. 20). A year later God gave Israel a great victory over Syria east of the Jordan River near the city of Aphek (vv. 22–29). Ahab, however, refused to submit to and worship the true God of Israel.

THE LIVES OF ELIJAH AND ELISHA

and Ben-hadad sent out, and they told
him, saying, There are men come out of
Samaria.
18 And he said, Whether they be
come out for peace, take them alive; or
whether they be come out for war, take
them alive.
19 So these young men of the
princes of the provinces came out of
the city, and the army which followed
them.
20 And they slew every one his
man: and the Syrians fled; and Israel
pursued them: and Ben-hadad the king
of Syria escaped on an horse with the
horsemen.
21 And the king of Israel went out,
and smote the horses and chariots, and
slew the Syrians with a great slaugh-
ter.
22 ¶ And the prophet came to the
king of Israel, and said unto him, Go,
strengthen thyself, and mark, and see
what thou doest: [c]for at the return of
the year the king of Syria will come up
against thee.
23 And the servants of the king of
Syria said unto him, Their gods *are*
gods of the hills; therefore they were
stronger than we; but let us fight
against them in the plain, and surely
we shall be stronger than they.
24 And do this thing, Take the
kings away, every man out of his place,
and put captains in their rooms:
25 And number thee an army, like
the army [g]that thou hast lost, horse
for horse, and chariot for chariot: and
we will fight against them in the plain,
and surely we shall be stronger than
they. And he hearkened unto their
voice, and did so.
26 And it came to pass at the return
of the year, that Ben-hadad numbered
the Syrians, and went up to [d]Aphek,
[h]to fight against Israel.
27 And the children of Israel were
numbered, and [i]were all present, and
went against them: and the children of
Israel pitched before them like two lit-
tle flocks of kids; but the Syrians filled
the country.
28 ¶ And there came a man of God,
and spake unto the king of Israel, and
said, Thus saith the LORD, Because the
Syrians have said, The LORD *is* God of
the hills, but he *is* not God of the val-
leys, therefore [e]will I deliver all this
great multitude into thine hand, and ye
shall know that I *am* the LORD.
29 And they pitched one over
against the other seven days. And *so* it
was, that in the seventh day the battle
was joined: and the children of Israel
slew of the Syrians an hundred thou-
sand footmen in one day.
30 But the rest fled to Aphek, into
the city; and *there* a wall fell upon twen-
ty and seven thousand of the men *that
were* left. And Ben-hadad fled, and
came into the city, [j] [k]into an inner
chamber.
31 ¶ And his servants said unto
him, Behold now, we have heard that
the kings of the house of Israel *are*
merciful kings: let us, I pray thee,
[f]put sackcloth on our loins, and ropes
upon our heads, and go out to the king
of Israel: peradventure he will save thy
life.
32 So they girded sackcloth on their
loins, and *put* ropes on their heads, and
came to the king of Israel, and said,
Thy servant Ben-hadad saith, I pray
thee, let me live. And he said, *Is* he yet
alive? he *is* my brother.
33 Now the men did diligently ob-
serve whether *any thing would come*
from him, and did hastily catch *it:* and
they said, Thy brother Ben-hadad.
Then he said, Go ye, bring him. Then
Ben-hadad came forth to him; and he
caused him to come up into the chariot.
34 And *Ben-hadad* said unto him,
[g]The cities, which my father took
from thy father, I will restore; and thou
shalt make streets for thee in Damas-
cus, as my father made in Samaria.
Then *said Ahab,* I will send thee away
with this covenant. So he made a cov-
enant with him, and sent him away.

Ahab judged

35 ¶ And a certain man of [h]the

20:22 [c]2 Sam. 11:1
20:26 [d]Josh. 13:4
20:28 [e]ver. 13
20:31 [f]Gen. 37:34
20:34 [g]ch. 15:20
20:35 [h]2 Ki. 2:3,5,7,15

[g] Heb. *that was fallen* [h] Heb. *to the war with Israel* [i] Or, *were victualled* [j] Or, *from chamber to chamber* [k] Heb. *into a chamber within a chamber*

20:35 SONS OF THE PROPHETS. These were students of the prophets who in some sense were discipled by older and more renowned prophets like Elisha (cf. 2 Ki. 2:3,5,7,15; 4:1,38; 5:22; 6:1; 9:1). They stood in close association with the master prophet, opposed the worship of Baal, and promoted obedience and faithfulness to the Lord God. They were known for prophesying by the power of the Spirit.

sons of the prophets said unto his
neighbour [i]in the word of the LORD,
Smite me, I pray thee. And the man re-
fused to smite him.
36 Then said he unto him, Because
thou hast not obeyed the voice of the
LORD, behold, as soon as thou art de-
parted from me, a lion shall slay thee.
And as soon as he was departed from
him, [j]a lion found him, and slew him.
37 Then he found another man, and
said, Smite me, I pray thee. And the
man smote him, [1]so that in smiting he
wounded *him.*
38 So the prophet departed, and
waited for the king by the way, and dis-
guised himself with ashes upon his
face.
39 And [k]as the king passed by, he
cried unto the king: and he said, Thy
servant went out into the midst of the
battle; and, behold, a man turned
aside, and brought a man unto me, and
said, Keep this man: if by any means he
be missing, then [l]shall thy life be for
his life, or else thou shalt [m]pay a tal-
ent of silver.
40 And as thy servant was busy
here and there, [n]he was gone. And the
king of Israel said unto him, So *shall*
thy judgment *be;* thyself hast decided
it.
41 And he hasted, and took the
ashes away from his face; and the king
of Israel discerned him that he *was* of
the prophets.
42 And he said unto him, Thus saith
the LORD, [m]Because thou hast let go
out of *thy* hand a man whom I appoint-
ed to utter destruction, therefore thy
life shall go for his life, and thy people
for his people.
43 And the king of Israel [n]went to
his house heavy and displeased, and
came to Samaria.

Naboth's vineyard

21 AND IT came to pass after
these things, *that* Naboth the
Jezreelite had a vineyard, which *was* in
Jezreel, hard by the palace of Ahab
king of Samaria.
2 And Ahab spake unto Naboth,
saying, Give me thy [o]vineyard, that I
may have it for a garden of herbs, be-
cause it *is* near unto my house: and I
will give thee for it a better vineyard
than it; *or,* if it [o]seem good to thee, I
will give thee the worth of it in money.
3 And Naboth said to Ahab, The
LORD forbid it me, [p]that I should give
the inheritance of my fathers unto
thee.
4 And Ahab came into his house
heavy and displeased because of the
word which Naboth the Jezreelite had
spoken to him: for he had said, I will
not give thee the inheritance of my fa-
thers. And he laid him down upon his
bed, and turned away his face, and
would eat no bread.
5 ¶ But Jezebel his wife came to
him, and said unto him, Why is thy spir-
it so sad, that thou eatest no bread?
6 And he said unto her, Because I
spake unto Naboth the Jezreelite, and
said unto him, Give me thy vineyard for
money; or else, if it please thee, I will
give thee *another* vineyard for it: and he
answered, I will not give thee my vine-
yard.
7 And Jezebel his wife said unto
him, Dost thou now govern the king-
dom of Israel? arise, *and* eat bread, and
let thine heart be merry: I will give thee
the vineyard of Naboth the Jezreelite.
8 So she wrote letters in Ahab's
name, and sealed *them* with his seal,
and sent the letters unto the elders and
to the nobles that *were* in his city,
dwelling with Naboth.
9 And she wrote in the letters, say-
ing, Proclaim a fast, and set Naboth
[p]on high among the people:
10 And set two men, sons of Belial,
before him, to bear witness against
him, saying, Thou didst [q]blaspheme
God and the king. And *then* carry him
out, and [r]stone him, that he may die.
11 And the men of his city, *even* the
elders and the nobles who were the in-
habitants in his city, did as Jezebel had
sent unto them, *and* as it *was* written
in the letters which she had sent unto
them.
12 [s]They proclaimed a fast, and
set Naboth on high among the people.
13 And there came in two men, chil-
dren of Belial, and sat before him: and
the men of Belial witnessed against
him, *even* against Naboth, in the pres-
ence of the people, saying, Naboth did
blaspheme God and the king. [t]Then
they carried him forth out of the city,
and stoned him with stones, that he
died.

20:35 [i]ch. 13:17,18
20:36 [j]ch. 13:24
20:39 [k]See 2 Sam. 12:1 [l]2 Ki. 10:24
20:42 [m]ch. 22:31-37
20:43 [n]ch. 21:4
21:2 [o]1 Sam. 8:14
21:3 [p]Lev. 25:23 Num. 36:7 Ezek. 46:18
21:10 [q]Ex. 22:28 Lev. 24:15,16 Acts 6:11 [r]Lev. 24:14
21:12 [s]Is. 58:4
21:13 [t]See 2 Ki. 9:26

[1]Heb. *smiting and wounding* [m]Heb. *weigh* [n]Heb. *he was not* [o]Heb. *be good in thine eyes* [p]Heb. *in the top of the people*

14 Then they sent to Jezebel, saying, Naboth is stoned, and is dead.

15 ¶ And it came to pass, when Jezebel heard that Naboth was stoned, and was dead, that Jezebel said to Ahab, Arise, take possession of the vineyard of Naboth the Jezreelite, which he refused to give thee for money: for Naboth is not alive, but dead.

16 And it came to pass, when Ahab heard that Naboth was dead, that Ahab rose up to go down to the vineyard of Naboth the Jezreelite, to take possession of it.

17 ¶ [u]And the word of the LORD came to Elijah the Tishbite, saying,

18 Arise, go down to meet Ahab king of Israel, [v]which *is* in Samaria: behold, *he is* in the vineyard of Naboth, whither he is gone down to possess it.

19 And thou shalt speak unto him, saying, Thus saith the LORD, Hast thou killed, and also taken possession? And thou shalt speak unto him, saying, Thus saith the LORD, [w]In the place where dogs licked the blood of Naboth shall dogs lick thy blood, even thine.

20 And Ahab said to Elijah, [x]Hast thou found me, O mine enemy? And he answered, I have found *thee:* because [y]thou hast sold thyself to work evil in the sight of the LORD.

21 Behold, [z]I will bring evil upon thee, and will take away thy posterity, and will cut off from Ahab [a]him that pisseth against the wall, and [b]him that is shut up and left in Israel,

22 And will make thine house like the house of [c]Jeroboam the son of Nebat, and like the house of [d]Baasha the son of Ahijah, for the provocation wherewith thou hast provoked *me* to anger, and made Israel to sin.

23 And [e]of Jezebel also spake the LORD, saying, The dogs shall eat Jezebel by the [q]wall of Jezreel.

24 [f]Him that dieth of Ahab in the city the dogs shall eat; and him that dieth in the field shall the fowls of the air eat.

25 ¶ But [g]there was none like unto Ahab, which did sell himself to work wickedness in the sight of the LORD, [h]whom Jezebel his wife [r]stirred up.

26 And he did very abominably in following idols, according to all *things* [i]as did the Amorites, whom the LORD cast out before the children of Israel.

27 And it came to pass, when Ahab heard those words, that he rent his clothes, and [j]put sackcloth upon his flesh, and fasted, and lay in sackcloth, and went softly.

28 And the word of the LORD came to Elijah the Tishbite, saying,

29 Seest thou how Ahab humbleth himself before me? because he humbleth himself before me, I will not bring the evil in his days: *but* [k]in his son's days will I bring the evil upon his house.

Micaiah's prophecy

22:1–28pp — 2 Chr. 18:1–27

22 AND THEY continued three years without war between Syria and Israel.

2 And it came to pass in the third year, that [l]Jehoshaphat the king of Judah came down to the king of Israel.

3 And the king of Israel said unto his servants, Know ye that [m]Ramoth in Gilead *is* ours, and we *be* [s]still, *and* take it not out of the hand of the king of Syria?

4 And he said unto Jehoshaphat,

21:17 [u]Ps. 9:12 **21:18** [v]ch. 13:32; 2 Chr. 22:9 **21:19** [w]ch. 22:38 **21:20** [x]ch. 18:17 [y]2 Ki. 17:17; Rom. 7:14 **21:21** [z]ch. 14:10; 2 Ki. 9:8 [a]1 Sam. 25:22 [b]ch. 14:10 **21:22** [c]ch. 15:29 [d]ch. 16:3,11 **21:23** [e]2 Ki. 9:36 **21:24** [f]ch. 14:11 & 16:4 **21:25** [g]ch. 16:30 [h]ch. 16:31 **21:26** [i]Gen. 15:16; 2 Ki. 21:11 **21:27** [j]Gen. 37:34 **21:29** [k]2 Ki. 9:25 **22:2** [l]2 Chr. 18:2 **22:3** [m]Deut. 4:43

[q] Or, *ditch* [r] Or, *incited* [s] Heb. *silent from taking it*

21:17 THE WORD OF THE LORD CAME TO ELIJAH. God hates injustice within the community of His people. For the death of the innocent Naboth, Elijah prophesied that Ahab and Jezebel would suffer (vv. 17–29). God's principle of retribution and justice continues under the new covenant. For example, Paul states that "he that doeth wrong [to another person] shall receive for the wrong which he hath done: and there is no respect of persons" (see Col. 3:25, note). God's people must treat one another with righteousness, justice, and lovingkindness (Mic. 6:8; Col. 4:1; cf. Gal. 6:7).

21:19 SHALL DOGS LICK THY BLOOD. This prophecy was fulfilled when Ahab was killed in battle and the dogs licked up the blood washed from his chariot (22:35,38). Ahab's sons also died violent deaths: Ahaziah was killed by a fall (2 Ki. 1:2,17); Jehoram was killed by Jehu and his body was cast into Naboth's plot of ground (2 Ki. 9:22–26). Ahab's wife, Jezebel, also died a violent death (see 2 Ki. 9:30–37).

21:25 JEZEBEL. The goal of this wicked wife of Ahab was to uproot the worship of the Lord and to substitute the Baal of Tyre as the chief god of Israel; she failed to do so. Instead, her name has become synonymous with wickedness, witchcraft, treachery, and spiritual seduction. John uses the name Jezebel for a false prophetess within the church of Thyatira, who was leading God's people into immorality and worldliness (see Rev. 2:20, note).

Wilt thou go with me to battle to Ra-
moth-gilead? And Jehoshaphat said to
the king of Israel, [n]I *am* as thou *art*,
my people as thy people, my horses as
thy horses.
5 And Jehoshaphat said unto the
king of Israel, Inquire, I pray thee, at
the word of the LORD today.
6 Then the king of Israel [o]gathered
the prophets together, about four hun-
dred men, and said unto them, Shall I
go against Ramoth-gilead to battle, or
shall I forbear? And they said, Go up;
for the Lord shall deliver *it* into the
hand of the king.
7 And [p]Jehoshaphat said, *Is there*
not here a prophet of the LORD besides,
that we might inquire of him?
8 And the king of Israel said unto
Jehoshaphat, *There is* yet one man, Mi-
caiah the son of Imlah, by whom we
may inquire of the LORD: but I hate him;
for he doth not prophesy good concern-
ing me, but evil. And Jehoshaphat said,
Let not the king say so.
9 Then the king of Israel called an
[t]officer, and said, Hasten *hither* Mica-
iah the son of Imlah.
10 And the king of Israel and Je-
hoshaphat the king of Judah sat each
on his throne, having put on their
robes, in a [u]void place in the entrance
of the gate of Samaria; and all the
prophets prophesied before them.
11 And Zedekiah the son of Chenaa-
nah made him horns of iron: and he
said, Thus saith the LORD, With these
shalt thou push the Syrians, until thou
have consumed them.
12 And all the prophets prophesied
so, saying, Go up to Ramoth-gilead,
and prosper: for the LORD shall deliver
it into the king's hand.
13 And the messenger that was
gone to call Micaiah spake unto him,
saying, Behold now, the words of the
prophets *declare* good unto the king
with one mouth: let thy word, I pray
thee, be like the word of one of them,
and speak *that which is* good.
14 And Micaiah said, *As* the LORD
liveth, [q]what the LORD saith unto me,
that will I speak.
15 ¶ So he came to the king. And
the king said unto him, Micaiah, shall
we go against Ramoth-gilead to battle,
or shall we forbear? And he answered
him, Go, and prosper: for the LORD shall
deliver *it* into the hand of the king.
16 And the king said unto him, How
many times shall I adjure thee that
thou tell me nothing but *that which is*
true in the name of the LORD?
17 And he said, I saw all Israel
[r]scattered upon the hills, as sheep
that have not a shepherd: and the LORD
said, These have no master: let them
return every man to his house in peace.
18 And the king of Israel said unto
Jehoshaphat, Did I not tell thee that he
would prophesy no good concerning
me, but evil?
19 And he said, Hear thou therefore
the word of the LORD: [s]I saw the LORD
sitting on his throne, [t]and all the host
of heaven standing by him on his right
hand and on his left.
20 And the LORD said, Who shall
[v]persuade Ahab, that he may go up
and fall at Ramoth-gilead? And one
said on this manner, and another said
on that manner.
21 And there came forth a spirit,
and stood before the LORD, and said, I
will persuade him.
22 And the LORD said unto him,
Wherewith? And he said, I will go
forth, and I will be a lying spirit in the
mouth of all his prophets. And he said,
[u]Thou shalt persuade *him*, and prevail
also: go forth, and do so.
23 [v]Now therefore, behold, the

22:4 [n]2 Ki. 3:7
22:6 [o]ch. 18:19
22:7 [p]2 Ki. 3:11
22:14 [q]Num. 22:38
22:17 [r]Mat. 9:36
22:19 [s]Is. 6:1 Dan. 7:9 [t]Job 1:6 & 2:1 Dan. 7:10 Zech. 1:10 Mat. 18:10 Heb. 1:7,14
22:22 [u]Judg. 9:23 Job 12:16 Ezek. 14:9 2 Thes. 2:11
22:23 [v]Ezek. 14:9

[t] Or, *eunuch* [u] Heb. *floor* [v] Or, *deceive*

22:6 FOUR HUNDRED MEN. These four hundred prophets of Ahab (see vv. 22–23) were not true prophets of the Lord, but religionists who prophesied what the king wanted to hear (cf. v. 8; see article on THE PROPHET IN THE OLD TESTAMENT, p. 1002).

22:15 GO, AND PROSPER. Micaiah mimicked the prediction of the false prophets in such a way that Ahab knew he was not serious (cf. v. 16). Micaiah then proceeded to make known the true prophetic vision he had received (v. 17). The meaning was clear: Ahab would die and Israel would retreat home.

22:23 A LYING SPIRIT. The lying spirit can be understood as one of Satan's agents, i.e., an evil spirit sent by God in order to condemn Ahab and the false prophets in their sin. Their hearts were hardened against the truth to such an extent that God finally gave them over to a lie as the due penalty for their sin (cf. Rom. 1:21–27). This same kind of judging will take place in the last days of this age, when God will send "a strong delusion" (2 Thes. 2:11) upon all who "received not the love of the truth . . . but had pleasure in unrighteousness" (2 Thes. 2:10,12). The deception will come from the "working of Satan . . . that they all might

LORD hath put a lying spirit in the mouth of all these thy prophets, and the LORD hath spoken evil concerning thee.

24 But Zedekiah the son of Chenaanah went near, and smote Micaiah on the cheek, and said, [w]Which way went the spirit of the LORD from me to speak unto thee?

25 And Micaiah said, Behold, thou shalt see in that day, when thou shalt go [w]into [x]an inner chamber to hide thyself.

26 And the king of Israel said, Take Micaiah, and carry him back unto Amon the governor of the city, and to Joash the king's son;

27 And say, Thus saith the king, Put this *fellow* in the prison, and feed him with bread of affliction and with water of affliction, until I come in peace.

28 And Micaiah said, If thou return at all in peace, [x]the LORD hath not spoken by me. And he said, Hearken, O people, every one of you.

Ahab's defeat and death

22:29–36pp — 2 Chr. 18:28–34

29 So the king of Israel and Jehoshaphat the king of Judah went up to Ramoth-gilead.

30 And the king of Israel said unto Jehoshaphat, [y]I will disguise myself, and enter into the battle; but put thou on thy robes. And the king of Israel [y]disguised himself, and went into the battle.

31 But the king of Syria commanded his thirty and two captains that had rule over his chariots, saying, Fight neither with small nor great, save only with the king of Israel.

32 And it came to pass, when the captains of the chariots saw Jehoshaphat, that they said, Surely it *is* the king of Israel. And they turned aside to fight against him: and Jehoshaphat [z]cried out.

33 And it came to pass, when the captains of the chariots perceived that it *was* not the king of Israel, that they turned back from pursuing him.

34 And a *certain* man drew a bow at a venture, and smote the king of Israel between the [z]joints of the harness: wherefore he said unto the driver of his chariot, Turn thine hand, and carry me out of the host; for I am [a]wounded.

35 And the battle [b]increased that day: and the king was stayed up in his chariot against the Syrians, and died at even: and the blood ran out of the wound into the [c]midst of the chariot.

36 And there went a proclamation throughout the host about the going down of the sun, saying, Every man to his city, and every man to his own country.

37 ¶ So the king died, and [d]was brought to Samaria; and they buried the king in Samaria.

38 And *one* washed the chariot in the pool of Samaria; and the dogs licked up his blood; and they washed his armour; according [a]unto the word of the LORD which he spake.

39 Now the rest of the acts of Ahab, and all that he did, and [b]the ivory house which he made, and all the cities that he built, *are* they not written in the book of the chronicles of the kings of Israel?

40 So Ahab slept with his fathers; and Ahaziah his son reigned in his stead.

Jehoshaphat, king of Judah

22:41–50pp — 2 Chr. 20:31–21:1

41 ¶ And [c]Jehoshaphat the son of Asa began to reign over Judah in the fourth year of Ahab king of Israel.

42 Jehoshaphat *was* thirty and five years old when he began to reign; and he reigned twenty and five years in Jerusalem. And his mother's name *was* Azubah the daughter of Shilhi.

43 And [d]he walked in all the ways of Asa his father; he turned not aside from it, doing *that which was* right in the eyes of the LORD: nevertheless [e]the high places were not taken away; *for* the people offered and burnt incense yet in the high places.

44 And [f]Jehoshaphat made peace with the king of Israel.

45 Now the rest of the acts of Je-

22:24 [w]2 Chr. 18:23
22:28 [x]Num. 16:29 Deut. 18:20-22
22:30 [y]2 Chr. 35:22
22:32 [z]2 Chr. 18:31 Prov. 13:20
22:38 [a]ch. 21:19
22:39 [b]Amos 3:15
22:41 [c]2 Chr. 20:31
22:43 [d]2 Chr. 17:3 [e]ch. 14:23 & 15:14 2 Ki. 12:3
22:44 [f]2 Chr. 19:2 2 Cor. 6:14

[w] Or, *from chamber to chamber* [x] Heb. *a chamber in a chamber* [y] Or, *when he was to disguise himself, and enter into the battle* [z] Heb. *joints and the breastplate* [a] Heb. *made sick* [b] Heb. *ascended* [c] Heb. *bosom* [d] Heb. *came*

be damned who believed not the truth" (2 Thes. 2:9,12; see 2 Thes. 2:10–12, notes).

22:41 JEHOSHAPHAT. For more on the reign of Jehoshaphat, see 15:24, note.

hoshaphat, and his might that he
showed, and how he warred, *are* they
not written in the book of the chronicles of the kings of Judah?
46 [g]And the remnant of the sodomites, which remained in the days of his
father Asa, he took out of the land.
47 [h]*There was* then no king in
Edom: a deputy *was* king.
48 [i]Jehoshaphat [j]made[e] ships
of Tharshish to go to Ophir for gold:
[k]but they went not; for the ships were
broken at [l]Ezion-geber.
49 Then said Ahaziah the son of
Ahab unto Jehoshaphat, Let my servants go with thy servants in the ships.
But Jehoshaphat would not.
50 ¶ And [m]Jehoshaphat slept with
his fathers, and was buried with his fathers in the city of David his father:
and Jehoram his son reigned in his stead.

22:46 [g]ch. 14:24 & 15:12
22:47 [h]Gen. 25:23 2 Sam. 8:14 2 Ki. 3:9 & 8:20
22:48 [i]2 Chr. 20:35 [j]ch. 10:22 [k]2 Chr. 20:37 [l]ch. 9:26
22:50 [m]2 Chr. 21:1
22:51 [n]ver. 40
22:52 [o]ch. 15:26
22:53 [p]Judg. 2:11 ch. 16:31

Ahaziah, king of Israel

51 ¶ [n]Ahaziah the son of Ahab began to reign over Israel in Samaria the
seventeenth year of Jehoshaphat king
of Judah, and reigned two years over
Israel.
52 And he did evil in the sight of the
LORD, and [o]walked in the way of his
father, and in the way of his mother,
and in the way of Jeroboam the son of
Nebat, who made Israel to sin:
53 For [p]he served Baal, and worshipped him, and provoked to anger
the LORD God of Israel, according to all
that his father had done.

[e] Or, had *ten ships*

2 KINGS

Outline

I. The Divided Kingdom: Israel and Judah (1:1—17:41)
  A. Reign of Ahaziah Continued (Israel) (1:1–18; cf. 1 Ki. 22:51–53)
  B. Reign of Jehoram (Israel) (2:1—8:15)
    1. Prophetic Transition from Elijah to Elisha (2:1–25)
    2. Evaluation of Jehoram (3:1–3)
    3. Jehoram Defeats Moab (3:4–27)
    4. Elisha's Miraculous Ministry (4:1—8:15)
  C. Reign of Jehoram (Judah) (8:16–24)
  D. Reign of Ahaziah (Judah) (8:25–29)
  E. Reign of Jehu (Israel) (9:1—10:36)
    1. Jehu Anointed by Elisha (9:1–10)
    2. Jehu's Bloody Purge of Israel (9:11—10:36)
  F. Reign of Athaliah (Judah) (11:1–16)
  G. Reign of Joash (Judah) (11:17—12:21)
  H. Reign of Jehoahaz (Israel) (13:1–9)
  I. Reign of Jehoash (Israel) (13:10–25)
  J. Reign of Amaziah (Judah) (14:1–22)
  K. Reign of Jeroboam II (Israel) (14:23–29)
  L. Reign of Azariah (Judah) (15:1–7)
  M. Reign of Zechariah (Israel) (15:8–12)
  N. Reign of Shallum (Israel) (15:13–15)
  O. Reign of Menahem (Israel) (15:16–22)
  P. Reign of Pekahiah (Israel) 15:23–26)
  Q. Reign of Pekah (Israel) (15:27–31)
  R. Reign of Jotham (Judah) (15:32–38)
  S. Reign of Ahaz (Judah) (16:1–20)
  T. Reign of Hoshea (Israel) (17:1–41)
    1. Evaluation and Imprisonment of Hoshea (17:1–4)
    2. Final Collapse of Israel (17:5–23)
    3. Israel's Captivity and Resettlement of the Land (17:24–41)

II. The Single Kingdom: Judah After Israel's Collapse (18:1—25:21)
  A. Reign of Hezekiah (18:1—20:21)
    1. Revival and Reform (18:1–8)
    2. Review of Israel's Fall and God's Deliverance of Judah from Two Assyrian Invasions (18:9—19:37)
    3. Hezekiah's Illness and Healing (20:1–11)
    4. Hezekiah's Foolishness and Death (20:12–21)
  B. Reign of Manasseh (21:1–18)
  C. Reign of Amon (21:19–26)
  D. Reign of Josiah (22:1—23:30)
    1. Revival and Reform (22:1—23:25)
    2. God's Wrath Delayed but not Averted and Josiah's Death (23:26–30)
  E. Reign of Jehoahaz (23:31–33)
  F. Reign of Jehoiakim (23:34—24:7)

G. Reign of Jehoiachin (24:8–16)
H. Reign of Zedekiah (24:17—25:21)
1. Fall of Jerusalem (25:1–7)
2. Destruction of the Temple and City Walls (25:8–10,13–17)
3. Final Deportation of the People to Babylon (25:11–21)
III. Postlude (25:22–30)

Author: Anonymous

Theme: Kings of Israel and Judah

Date of Writing: c. 560–550 B.C.

Background

Since 1 and 2 Kings are one continuous history, important background information for 2 Kings is contained in the introduction to 1 Kings. 2 Kings resumes tracing the decline of Israel and Judah, beginning at about 852 B.C. It records the two great national calamities that brought about the dissolution of the kingdoms of Israel and Judah: (1) the destruction of Israel's capital, Samaria, and that nation's deportation to Assyria in 722 B.C.; and (2) the destruction of Jerusalem and Judah's deportation to Babylon in 586 B.C. 2 Kings covers the last 130 years of Judah's 345-year history. The greater instability of Israel (i.e., the northern ten tribes) is evidenced by its constant change of kings (nineteen) and dynasties (nine) in 210 years, compared with Judah's twenty kings and one dynasty (briefly interrupted) over 345 years.

Many O.T. writing prophets ministered during the time recorded in 2 Kings. They reminded, warned, and exhorted the kings concerning their responsibilities to God as His theocratic representatives. Amos and Hosea prophesied in Israel, while Joel, Isaiah, Micah, Nahum, Habakkuk, Zephaniah, and Jeremiah prophesied in Judah. The books by these prophets provide important historical and theological revelation not contained in 2 Kings concerning the spiritual and moral decline of both nations.

Purpose

2 Kings has the same purpose as 1 Kings (see the introduction to 1 Kings). In brief the original purpose was to provide the Hebrew people, especially the exiles in Babylon, with a prophetic interpretation and understanding of their history during the divided monarchy, in order that they might not repeat the sins of their forefathers.

Survey

The history of 2 Kings divides into two major eras: (1) the history of both kingdoms before the fall of Israel (the ten tribes) in 722 B.C. (chs. 1—17), and (2) the history of Judah after the collapse of Israel until her own fall in 586 B.C. (chs. 18—25). On the one hand, Israel had an unbroken succession of kings who "wrought evil in the sight of the LORD" (e.g., 3:2). 2 Kings records that in the midst of Israel's terrible apostasy, God raised up mighty prophets such as Elijah and Elisha to call the nation and her leaders back to God and His covenant (chs. 1—9).

Judah, on the other hand, did at times have a reprieve from evil kings in godly rulers like Hezekiah (chs. 18—21) and Josiah (chs. 22—23), who sought to turn the heart of the nation back to God. Nevertheless, such kings were unable to alter permanently the prevailing tide of idolatry, immorality, and violence. After Josiah's death (ch. 23), Judah's slide to destruction was rapid, culminating in Nebuchadnezzar's sack of Jerusalem in 586 B.C. (ch. 25).

Special Features

Five major features or emphases characterize 2 Kings. (1) It emphasizes (as did 1 Kings) the importance of the prophets and their revelation as God's primary means for getting His

message through to the kings and people of Israel and Judah—e.g., Elijah and Elisha (chs. 1—13), Jonah (14:25), Isaiah (19:1–7,20–34), and Huldah (22:14–20). (2) It highlights the miraculous ministry of Elisha throughout much of the first half of the book (chs. 2—13). (3) It gives only two kings in all of Israel and Judah unqualified approval as being faithful to God and the people: Hezekiah (18:1—20:21) and Josiah (22:1—23:29). (4) It reveals that unrighteous leaders will eventually lead a people to ruin and illustrates the enduring principle that "righteousness exalteth a nation: but sin *is* a reproach to any people" (Prov. 14:34). (5) It contains many well-known Bible stories, such as Elijah going to heaven in a whirlwind (ch. 2), Elisha raising the Shunamite's son from the dead (ch. 4), the healing of Naaman (ch. 5), the floating of an axe-head in water (ch. 6), the violent death of Jezebel as prophesied by Elijah (ch. 9), the great revivals under Hezekiah (ch. 18) and Josiah (ch. 23), and Hezekiah's serious sickness and healing (ch. 20).

New Testament Fulfillment

2 Kings makes clear that the sin and unfaithfulness of Judah's kings (i.e., David's descendants) resulted in the destruction of Jerusalem and the Davidic kingdom. However, the N.T. makes equally clear that God in His faithfulness fulfilled His covenant promise to David through Jesus Christ, "the son of David" (Mat. 1:1; 9:27–31; 21:9), whose reign and kingdom will have no end (Luke 1:32–33; cf. Is. 9:7).

Reading 2 Kings

In order to read the entire Old Testament in one year, the book of 2 Kings should be read in 10 days, according to the following schedule: ☐ 1–3 ☐ 4–5 ☐ 6–7 ☐ 8–9 ☐ 10–12 ☐ 13–15 ☐ 16–17 ☐ 18–19 ☐ 20–22 ☐ 23–25

NOTES

Elijah's prophecy to Ahaziah

1 THEN MOAB [a]rebelled against
Israel [b]after the death of Ahab.
2 And Ahaziah fell down through a
lattice in his upper chamber that *was* in
Samaria, and was sick: and he sent
messengers, and said unto them, Go,
inquire of Baal-zebub the god of [c]Ek-
ron whether I shall recover of this dis-
ease.
3 But the angel of the LORD said to
Elijah the Tishbite, Arise, go up to
meet the messengers of the king of Sa-
maria, and say unto them, *Is it* not be-
cause *there is* not a God in Israel, *that*
ye go to inquire of Baal-zebub the god
of Ekron?
4 Now therefore thus saith the LORD,
[a]Thou shalt not come down from that
bed on which thou art gone up, but
shalt surely die. And Elijah departed.
5 ¶ And when the messengers
turned back unto him, he said unto
them, Why are ye now turned back?
6 And they said unto him, There
came a man up to meet us, and said
unto us, Go, turn again unto the king
that sent you, and say unto him, Thus
saith the LORD, *Is it* not because *there is*
not a God in Israel, *that* thou sendest
to inquire of Baal-zebub the god of Ek-
ron? therefore thou shalt not come
down from that bed on which thou art
gone up, but shalt surely die.
7 And he said unto them, [b]What
manner of man *was he* which came up
to meet you, and told you these words?
8 And they answered him, *He was*
[d]an hairy man, and girt with a girdle
of leather about his loins. And he said,
It *is* Elijah the Tishbite.
9 Then the king sent unto him a
captain of fifty with his fifty. And he
went up to him: and, behold, he sat on
the top of an hill. And he spake unto
him, Thou man of God, the king hath
said, Come down.
10 And Elijah answered and said to
the captain of fifty, If I *be* a man of God,
then [e]let fire come down from heaven,
and consume thee and thy fifty. And

1:1 [a]2 Sam. 8:2 [b]ch. 3:5
1:2 [c]1 Sam. 5:10
1:8 [d]See Zech. 13:4 Mat. 3:4
1:10 [e]Luke 9:54
1:13 [f]1 Sam. 26:21 Ps. 72:14

there came down fire from heaven, and
consumed him and his fifty.
11 Again also he sent unto him an-
other captain of fifty with his fifty. And
he answered and said unto him, O man
of God, thus hath the king said, Come
down quickly.
12 And Elijah answered and said
unto them, If I *be* a man of God, let fire
come down from heaven, and consume
thee and thy fifty. And the fire of God
came down from heaven, and con-
sumed him and his fifty.
13 ¶ And he sent again a captain of
the third fifty with his fifty. And the
third captain of fifty went up, and came
and [c]fell on his knees before Elijah,
and besought him, and said unto him,
O man of God, I pray thee, let my life,
and the life of these fifty thy servants,
[f]be precious in thy sight.
14 Behold, there came fire down
from heaven, and burnt up the two cap-
tains of the former fifties with their fif-
ties: therefore let my life now be pre-
cious in thy sight.
15 And the angel of the LORD said
unto Elijah, Go down with him: be not
afraid of him. And he arose, and went
down with him unto the king.
16 And he said unto him, Thus saith
the LORD, Forasmuch as thou hast sent
messengers to inquire of Baal-zebub
the god of Ekron, *is it* not because *there*
is no God in Israel to inquire of his
word? therefore thou shalt not come
down off that bed on which thou art
gone up, but shalt surely die.
17 ¶ So he died according to the
word of the LORD which Elijah had spo-
ken. And [d]Jehoram reigned in his
stead in the second year of Jehoram the
son of Jehoshaphat king of Judah; be-
cause he had no son.
18 Now the rest of the acts of Ahazi-
ah which he did, *are* they not written in

[a] Heb. *The bed whither thou art gone up, thou shall not come down from it* [b] Heb. *What* was *the manner of the man?* [c] Heb. *bowed*
[d] The second year that *Jehoram* was *Prorex,* and the eighteenth of *Jehoshaphat;* see ch. 3:1

1:8 AN HAIRY MAN. The description of Elijah as a "hairy man" may refer to his cloak. A shaggy mantle of sheepskin, goatskin, or camel's hair was a mark of the prophetic office from Elijah on, including John the Baptist (cf. Zech. 13:4; Mat. 3:4; Heb. 11:37). Elijah's leather girdle or wide belt was what the poor normally wore. The prophet's dress was a sign of contempt for the materialistic display of the wealthy upper class (cf. Is. 20:2; Mat. 11:7–8).

1:10 THERE CAME DOWN FIRE FROM HEAVEN. The king and his soldiers, in rebellion against God and His word, sought to arrest Elijah. The fire came directly by God's hand (v. 12) as a judgment against Ahaziah, who had stubbornly persisted in opposing God and the prophet.

the book of the chronicles of the kings of Israel?

Elijah taken up to heaven

2 AND IT came to pass, when the LORD would [g]take up Elijah into heaven by a whirlwind, that Elijah went with [h]Elisha from Gilgal.

2 And Elijah said unto Elisha, [i]Tarry here, I pray thee; for the LORD hath sent me to Beth-el. And Elisha said *unto him, As* the LORD liveth, and [j]*as* thy soul liveth, I will not leave thee. So they went down to Beth-el.

3 And [k]the sons of the prophets that *were* at Beth-el came forth to Elisha, and said unto him, Knowest thou that the LORD will take away thy master from thy head today? And he said, Yea, I know *it;* hold ye your peace.

4 And Elijah said unto him, Elisha, tarry here, I pray thee; for the LORD hath sent me to Jericho. And he said, *As* the LORD liveth, and *as* thy soul liveth, I will not leave thee. So they came to Jericho.

5 And the sons of the prophets that *were* at Jericho came to Elisha, and said unto him, Knowest thou that the LORD will take away thy master from thy head today? And he answered, Yea, I know *it;* hold ye your peace.

6 And Elijah said unto him, Tarry, I pray thee, here; for the LORD hath sent me to Jordan. And he said, *As* the LORD liveth, and *as* thy soul liveth, I will not leave thee. And they two went on.

7 And fifty men of the sons of the prophets went, and stood [e]to view afar off: and they two stood by Jordan.

8 And Elijah took his mantle, and wrapped *it* together, and smote the waters, and [l]they were divided hither and thither, so that they two went over on dry ground.

9 ¶ And it came to pass, when they were gone over, that Elijah said unto Elisha, Ask what I shall do for thee, before I be taken away from thee. And Elisha said, I pray thee, let a double portion of thy spirit be upon me.

10 And he said, [f]Thou hast asked a hard thing: *nevertheless,* if thou see me *when I am* taken from thee, it shall be so unto thee; but if not, it shall not be *so.*

11 And it came to pass, as they still went on, and talked, that, behold, *there appeared* [m]a chariot of fire, and horses of fire, and parted them both asunder; and Elijah went up by a whirlwind into heaven.

12 ¶ And Elisha saw *it,* and he cried, [n]My father, my father, the chariot of Israel, and the horsemen thereof. And he saw him no more: and he took hold of his own clothes, and rent them in two pieces.

Beginning of Elisha's ministry

13 He took up also the mantle of Elijah that fell from him, and went back, and stood by the [g]bank of Jordan;

14 And he took the mantle of Elijah that fell from him, and smote the waters, and said, Where *is* the LORD God of Elijah? and when he also had smitten the waters, [o]they parted hither and thither: and Elisha went over.

15 And when the sons of the prophets which *were* [p]to view at Jericho saw him, they said, The spirit of Elijah doth rest on Elisha. And they came to meet

2:1 [g]Gen. 5:24 [h]1 Ki. 19:21
2:2 [i]See Ruth 1:15,16 [j]ver. 4,6 1 Sam. 1:26 ch. 4:30
2:3 [k]ver. 5,7,15 1 Ki. 20:35 ch. 4:1,38 & 9:1
2:8 [l]ver. 14 Ex. 14:21 Josh. 3:16
2:11 [m]ch. 6:17 Ps. 104:4
2:12 [n]ch. 13:14
2:14 [o]ver. 8
2:15 [p]ver. 7

[e] Heb. *in sight,* or, *over against* [f] Heb. *Thou hast done hard in asking* [g] Heb. *lip*

2:3 SONS OF THE PROPHETS. The sons of the prophets (see 1 Ki. 20:35, note) appear to have been located primarily in three areas—Gilgal, Bethel, and Jericho (see 2:3,5,15; 4:38). God evidently sent Elijah to these communities in order to encourage them one last time and to announce that Elisha would be their new leader (cf. vv. 1,15).

2:9 A DOUBLE PORTION OF THY SPIRIT. The term "double portion" does not necesasrily mean twice the spiritual power of Elijah; rather, it refers to a father-son relationship, where the first-born son received twice the inheritance the other sons received (Deut. 21:17). Elisha was asking his spiritual father to give him an abundant measure of his prophetic spirit in order that he might carry on Elijah's mission. God granted Elisha's request, knowing that the young prophet was willing to remain faithful to Him in the face of the spiritual, moral, and doctrinal apostasy all around him.

2:11–12 A CHARIOT OF FIRE, AND HORSES OF FIRE. Elijah was taken to heaven, as was Enoch (Gen. 5:24), without experiencing death. (1) The miraculous transporting of Elijah to heaven was God's emphatic seal of approval on the prophet's work, spirit, and ministry. Elijah had been totally united to the word of God throughout his ministry. To the very last he had lived for God's honor, stood against the sin and idolatry of an apostate people, and encouraged the faithful remnant in Israel. He was given a dramatic escort to heaven in triumph. (2) The translation of Elijah and Enoch is like the future catching away of God's faithful people at the return of Christ (1 Thes. 4:16–17).

him, and bowed themselves to the ground before him.

16 ¶ And they said unto him, Behold now, there be with thy servants fifty [h]strong men; let them go, we pray thee, and seek thy master: [q]lest peradventure the spirit of the LORD hath taken him up, and cast him upon [i]some mountain, or into some valley. And he said, Ye shall not send.

17 And when they urged him till he was ashamed, he said, Send. They sent therefore fifty men; and they sought three days, but found him not.

18 And when they came again to him, (for he tarried at Jericho,) he said unto them, Did I not say unto you, Go not?

19 ¶ And the men of the city said unto Elisha, Behold, I pray thee, the situation of this city *is* pleasant, as my lord seeth: but the water *is* naught, and the ground [j]barren.

20 And he said, Bring me a new cruse, and put salt therein. And they brought *it* to him.

21 And he went forth unto the spring of the waters, and [r]cast the salt in there, and said, Thus saith the LORD, I have healed these waters; there shall not be from thence any more death or barren *land.*

22 So the waters were healed unto this day, according to the saying of Elisha which he spake.

23 ¶ And he went up from thence unto Beth-el: and as he was going up by the way, there came forth little children out of the city, and mocked him, and said unto him, Go up, thou bald head; go up, thou bald head.

24 And he turned back, and looked on them, and cursed them in the name of the LORD. And there came forth two she bears out of the wood, and tare forty and two children of them.

2:16 [q]See 1 Ki. 18:12 Ezek. 8:3 Acts 8:39 ch. 1:17
2:21 [r]See Ex. 15:25 ch. 4:41 & 6:6 John 9:6
3:2 [s]1 Ki. 16:31,32
3:3 [t]1 Ki. 12:28,31,32
3:4 [u]See Is. 16:1
3:5 [v]ch. 1:1
3:7 [w]1 Ki. 22:4

25 And he went from thence to mount Carmel, and from thence he returned to Samaria.

Jehoram's siege against Moab

3 NOW JEHORAM the son of Ahab began to reign over Israel in Samaria the eighteenth year of Jehoshaphat king of Judah, and reigned twelve years.

2 And he wrought evil in the sight of the LORD; but not like his father, and like his mother: for he put away the [k]image of Baal [s]that his father had made.

3 Nevertheless he cleaved unto [t]the sins of Jeroboam the son of Nebat, which made Israel to sin; he departed not therefrom.

4 ¶ And Mesha king of Moab was a sheepmaster, and rendered unto the king of Israel an hundred thousand [u]lambs, and an hundred thousand rams, with the wool.

5 But it came to pass, when [v]Ahab was dead, that the king of Moab rebelled against the king of Israel.

6 ¶ And king Jehoram went out of Samaria the same time, and numbered all Israel.

7 And he went and sent to Jehoshaphat the king of Judah, saying, The king of Moab hath rebelled against me: wilt thou go with me against Moab to battle? And he said, I will go up: [w]I *am* as thou *art,* my people as thy people, *and* my horses as thy horses.

8 And he said, Which way shall we go up? And he answered, The way through the wilderness of Edom.

9 So the king of Israel went, and the king of Judah, and the king of Edom:

[h] Heb. *sons of strength* [i] Heb. *one of the mountains* [j] Heb. *causing to miscarry* [k] Heb. *statue*

2:23 MOCKED HIM. Some suppose the boys who mocked Elisha were a gang organized to oppose his ministry. Though the Hebrew word *na'ar* is used as a general word for "boy" and is often applied to older youths when used alone (cf. Gen. 22:5; 41:12), the Hebrew here is *na'arim qatanim* ("little boys"). Older youths would undoubtedly have been out in the fields. But as happens even today, this outsider coming into a village attracted a group of small boys. These children may have heard their parents mock the news that Elijah had gone up to heaven, possibly saying, "If Elisha says that, then let him show us how it is done. Let him go up, the old baldhead." The mockery against the prophet demonstrated disdain for the Lord Himself (cf. Ezek. 16:8; Acts 5:4).

2:24 CURSED THEM IN THE NAME OF THE LORD. To avenge the honor of the Lord, Elisha pronounced upon them the divine judgment expressed in the covenant law of blessing and cursing (Lev. 26:21–22; Deut. 30:19). God Himself judged the depraved children by sending the two bears (cf. Gal. 6:7). The judgment at Bethel was a warning to Israel that God's covenant curses awaited them if they persisted in rebellion agaimst God (cf. Deut. 30:15–20). Note that the bears injured the children, but apparently did not kill them.

and they fetched a compass of seven days' journey: and there was no water for the host, and for the cattle [l]that followed them.

10 And the king of Israel said, Alas! that the LORD hath called these three kings together, to deliver them into the hand of Moab!

11 But [x]Jehoshaphat said, *Is there* not here a prophet of the LORD, that we may inquire of the LORD by him? And one of the king of Israel's servants answered and said, Here *is* Elisha the son of Shaphat, which poured water on the hands of Elijah.

12 And Jehoshaphat said, The word of the LORD is with him. So the king of Israel and Jehoshaphat and the king of Edom [y]went down to him.

13 And Elisha said unto the king of Israel, [z]What have I to do with thee? [a]get thee to [b]the prophets of thy father, and to the prophets of thy mother. And the king of Israel said unto him, Nay: for the LORD hath called these three kings together, to deliver them into the hand of Moab.

14 And Elisha said, [c]*As* the LORD of hosts liveth, before whom I stand, surely, were it not that I regard the presence of Jehoshaphat the king of Judah, I would not look toward thee, nor see thee.

15 But now bring me [d]a minstrel. And it came to pass, when the minstrel played, that [e]the hand of the LORD came upon him.

16 And he said, Thus saith the LORD, [f]Make this valley full of ditches.

17 For thus saith the LORD, Ye shall not see wind, neither shall ye see rain; yet that valley shall be filled with water, that ye may drink, both ye, and your cattle, and your beasts.

18 And this is *but* a light thing in the sight of the LORD: he will deliver the Moabites also into your hand.

19 And ye shall smite every fenced city, and every choice city, and shall fell every good tree, and stop all wells of water, and [m]mar every good piece of land with stones.

20 And it came to pass in the morning, when [g]the meat offering was offered, that, behold, there came water by the way of Edom, and the country was filled with water.

21 ¶ And when all the Moabites heard that the kings were come up to fight against them, they [n]gathered all that were able to [o]put on armour, and upward, and stood in the border.

22 And they rose up early in the morning, and the sun shone upon the water, and the Moabites saw the water on the other side *as* red as blood:

23 And they said, This *is* blood: the kings are surely [p]slain, and they have smitten one another: now therefore, Moab, to the spoil.

24 And when they came to the camp of Israel, the Israelites rose up and smote the Moabites, so that they fled before them: but [q]they went forward smiting the Moabites, even in *their* country.

25 And they beat down the cities, and on every good piece of land cast every man his stone, and filled it; and they stopped all the wells of water, and felled all the good trees: [r]only in [h]Kir-haraseth left they the stones thereof; howbeit the slingers went about *it*, and smote it.

26 ¶ And when the king of Moab saw that the battle was too sore for him, he took with him seven hundred men that drew swords, to break through *even* unto the king of Edom: but they could not.

27 Then [i]he took his eldest son

3:11 [x]1 Ki. 22:7
3:12 [y]ch. 2:25
3:13 [z]Ezek. 14:3 [a]Judg. 10:14 Ruth 1:15 [b]1 Ki. 18:19
3:14 [c]1 Ki. 17:1 ch. 5:16
3:15 [d]See 1 Sam. 10:5 [e]Ezek. 1:3 & 3:14,22 & 8:1
3:16 [f]ch. 4:3
3:20 [g]Ex. 29:39,40
3:25 [h]Is. 16:7,11
3:27 [i]Amos 2:1

[l]Heb. *at their feet* [m]Heb. *grieve* [n]Heb. *were cried together* [o]Heb. *gird himself with a girdle* [p]Heb. *destroyed* [q]Or, *they smote in it even smiting* [r]Heb. *until he left the stones thereof in Kir-haraseth*

3:15 THE MINSTREL PLAYED. The music of the harp helped seal off all outside distraction and the unbelief around Elisha, bringing him into a frame of mind and spirit so as to receive the Lord's revelation.

3:27 ELDEST SON . . . OFFERED HIM *FOR* A BURNT OFFERING. The king of Moab put his eldest son to death as an offering to the god Chemosh (see 1 Ki. 11:7), in an effort to persuade the supposed deity to help his army in battle. This human sacrifice was in reality a sacrifice unto Satan and demons (see article on THE NATURE OF IDOLATRY, p. 428). "The things which the Gentiles sacrifice, they sacrifice to devils" (1 Cor. 10:20). Archaeologists have discovered a Moabite stone which confirms that the king of Moab really did carry out this wicked deed.

3:27 THERE WAS GREAT INDIGNATION AGAINST ISRAEL. The armies of Israel withdrew in a hasty retreat. The wrath of the Moabite army that came against them was presumably the result of the human sacrifice offered to the demonic power behind Chemosh (see previous note). It appears that power is unleashed in the spiritual

that should have reigned in his stead, and offered him *for* a burnt offering upon the wall. And there was great indignation against Israel: [j]and they departed from him, and returned to *their own* land.

The widow's pot of oil

4 NOW THERE cried a certain woman of the wives of [k]the sons of the prophets unto Elisha, saying, Thy servant my husband is dead; and thou knowest that thy servant did fear the LORD: and the creditor is come [l]to take unto him my two sons to be bondmen.

2 And Elisha said unto her, What shall I do for thee? tell me, what hast thou in the house? And she said, Thine handmaid hath not any thing in the house, save a pot of oil.

3 Then he said, Go, borrow thee vessels abroad of all thy neighbours, *even* empty vessels; [m]borrow[s] not a few.

4 And when thou art come in, thou shalt shut the door upon thee and upon thy sons, and shalt pour out into all those vessels, and thou shalt set aside that which is full.

5 So she went from him, and shut the door upon her and upon her sons, who brought *the vessels* to her; and she poured out.

6 And it came to pass, when the vessels were full, that she said unto her son, Bring me yet a vessel. And he said unto her, *There is* not a vessel more. And the oil stayed.

7 Then she came and told the man of God. And he said, Go, sell the oil, and pay thy [t]debt, and live thou and thy children of the rest.

3:27 [j]ch. 8:20
4:1 [k]1 Ki. 20:35 [l]See Lev. 25:39 Mat. 18:25
4:3 [m]See ch. 3:16
4:8 [n]Josh. 19:18
4:16 [o]Gen. 18:10,14

The Shunammite's son

8 ¶ And [u]it fell on a day, that Elisha passed to [n]Shunem, where *was* a great woman; and she [v]constrained him to eat bread. And *so* it was, *that* as oft as he passed by, he turned in thither to eat bread.

9 And she said unto her husband, Behold now, I perceive that this *is* an holy man of God, which passeth by us continually.

10 Let us make a little chamber, I pray thee, on the wall; and let us set for him there a bed, and a table, and a stool, and a candlestick: and it shall be, when he cometh to us, that he shall turn in thither.

11 And it fell on a day, that he came thither, and he turned into the chamber, and lay there.

12 And he said to Gehazi his servant, Call this Shunammite. And when he had called her, she stood before him.

13 And he said unto him, Say now unto her, Behold, thou hast been careful for us with all this care; what *is* to be done for thee? wouldest thou be spoken for to the king, or to the captain of the host? And she answered, I dwell among mine own people.

14 And he said, What then *is* to be done for her? And Gehazi answered, Verily she hath no child, and her husband is old.

15 And he said, Call her. And when he had called her, she stood in the door.

16 And he said, [o]About this [w]season, according to the time of life, thou

[s] Or, *scant not* [t] Or, *creditor* [u] Heb. *there was a day* [v] Heb. *laid hold on him* [w] Heb. *set time*

---

realm by blood sacrifices—both for incomparably great good, as through Christ's blood, and for abominable evil, as in the sacrifice here. It could well be that blood sacrifices offered to demonic powers release them to do battle more effectively against the spiritual forces of the Lord (cf. Eph. 6:12).

4:1 A CERTAIN WOMAN . . . OF THE SONS OF THE PROPHETS. The miraculous acts of Elisha recorded in ch. 4 present spiritual truths in dramatic action. The narrative of the widow and her two children reveals that God cares for His faithful who are in need and distress. The widow and her children represent God's forsaken and oppressed people. In both the O.T. and N.T., compassion for and care of the needy are signs of genuine faith in God and true piety (Ex. 22:22–24; Deut. 10:18; 14:29; Job 29:12; Jas. 1:27; see article on THE CARE OF THE POOR AND NEEDY, p. 1312).

4:8 SHUNEM, WHERE *WAS* A GREAT WOMAN. The narrative of this wealthy Shunammite woman contains three key episodes. (1) God blessed the faithful woman by giving her a son (vv. 8–17). (2) God caused her to be severely tested by permitting the son to be taken from her (vv. 18–21). (3) God restored her son's life as she held firmly to God's word of promise (vv. 22–37). Many times God allows His faithful ones to pass through inexplicable trials and afflictions (cf. Heb. 11:17–40; Job 1—2), but then later they experience His love, grace, and compassion as they hold fast to Him in faith (cf. Ps. 25:10; Rom. 8:28; Heb. 11:6).

shalt embrace a son. And she said,
Nay, my lord, *thou* man of God, [p]do not
lie unto thine handmaid.
17 And the woman conceived, and
bare a son at that season that Elisha
had said unto her, according to the
time of life.
18 ¶ And when the child was grown,
it fell on a day, that he went out to his
father to the reapers.
19 And he said unto his father, My
head, my head. And he said to a lad,
Carry him to his mother.
20 And when he had taken him, and
brought him to his mother, he sat on
her knees till noon, and *then* died.
21 And she went up, and laid him on
the bed of the man of God, and shut *the*
door upon him, and went out.
22 And she called unto her hus-
band, and said, Send me, I pray thee,
one of the young men, and one of the
asses, that I may run to the man of
God, and come again.
23 And he said, Wherefore wilt thou
go to him today? *it is* neither new
moon, nor sabbath. And she said, *It*
shall be [x]well.
24 Then she saddled an ass, and
said to her servant, Drive, and go for-
ward; [y]slack not *thy* riding for me, ex-
cept I bid thee.
25 So she went and came unto the
man of God [q]to mount Carmel. And it
came to pass, when the man of God
saw her afar off, that he said to Gehazi
his servant, Behold, *yonder is* that Shu-
nammite:
26 Run now, I pray thee, to meet
her, and say unto her, *Is it* well with
thee? *is it* well with thy husband? *is it*
well with the child? And she answered,
It is well.
27 And when she came to the man
of God to the hill, she caught [r]him[z]
by the feet: but Gehazi came near to
thrust her away. And the man of God
said, Let her alone; for her soul *is*
[s]vexed[a] within her: and the LORD
hath hid *it* from me, and hath not
told me.
28 Then she said, Did I desire a son
of my lord? [t]did I not say, Do not de-
ceive me?
29 Then he said to Gehazi, [u]Gird
up thy loins, and take my staff in thine
hand, and go thy way: if thou meet any
man, [v]salute him not; and if any sa-
lute thee, answer him not again: and
[w]lay my staff upon the face of the
child.
30 And the mother of the child said,
[x]*As* the LORD liveth, and *as* thy soul
liveth, I will not leave thee. And he
arose, and followed her.
31 And Gehazi passed on before
them, and laid the staff upon the face
of the child; but *there was* neither voice,
nor [b]hearing. Wherefore he went
again to meet him, and told him, say-
ing, The child is [y]not awaked.
32 And when Elisha was come into
the house, behold, the child was dead,
and laid upon his bed.
33 He [z]went in therefore, and shut
the door upon them twain, [a]and
prayed unto the LORD.
34 And he went up, and lay upon the
child, and put his mouth upon his
mouth, and his eyes upon his eyes, and
his hands upon his hands: and [b]he
stretched himself upon the child; and
the flesh of the child waxed warm.
35 Then he returned, and walked in
the house [c]to and fro; and went up,
and [c]stretched himself upon him: and
[d]the child sneezed seven times, and
the child opened his eyes.
36 And he called Gehazi, and said,
Call this Shunammite. So he called her.
And when she was come in unto him,
he said, Take up thy son.
37 Then she went in, and fell at his
feet, and bowed herself to the ground,
and [e]took up her son, and went out. 2 Ki. 19:19-36

4:16 [p]ver. 28 **4:25** [q]ch. 2:25 **4:27** [r]Mat. 28:9 [s]1 Sam. 1:10 **4:28** [t]ver. 16 **4:29** [u]1 Ki. 18:46 ch. 9:1 [v]Luke 10:4 [w]See Ex. 7:19 & 14:16 ch. 2:8,14 Acts 19:12 **4:30** [x]ch. 2:2 **4:31** [y]John 11:11 **4:33** [z]ver. 4 Mat. 6:6 [a]1 Ki. 17:20 **4:34** [b]1 Ki. 17:21 Acts 20:10 **4:35** [c]1 Ki. 17:21 [d]ch. 8:1,5 **4:37** [e]1 Ki. 17:23 Heb. 11:35

[x] Heb. *peace* [y] Heb. *restrain not for me to ride* [z] Heb. *by his feet* [a] Heb. *bitter* [b] Heb. *attention* [c] Heb. *once hither, and once thither*

4:21 MAN OF GOD. Elisha was especially known by people from all walks of life as "the man of God" (e.g., 4:9,16,22,25,27,40; 5:8; 6:6,9–10; 7:18; 8:4,8,11). The highest tribute that can be paid to any minister is that he is a "man of God." The following are five characteristics of this man of God. (1) He maintained intimate and persevering communion with God. He knew God and was known by Him. (2) He was a holy man, fully set apart from the religious and moral compromise of his day and dedicated to the Lord God of Israel. (3) He empathized with God over the sins of the covenant people and opposed the tide of idolatry and apostasy in Israel. (4) The Spirit of the Lord was upon him, enabling him to speak with spiritual authority as God's representative and to proclaim the word of the Lord faithfully. (5) As a prophet of enormous stature and gifts, his ministry was affirmed by God with mighty miracles and signs.

Poisonous food made harmless

38 ¶ And Elisha came again to
[f]Gilgal: and *there was* a [g]dearth in
the land; and the sons of the prophets
were [h]sitting before him: and he said
unto his servant, Set on the great pot,
and seethe pottage for the sons of the
prophets.

39 And one went out into the field to
gather herbs, and found a wild vine,
and gathered thereof wild gourds his
lap full, and came and shred *them* into
the pot of pottage: for they knew *them*
not.

40 So they poured out for the men
to eat. And it came to pass, as they
were eating of the pottage, that they
cried out, and said, O *thou* man of God,
there is [i]death in the pot. And they
could not eat *thereof.*

41 But he said, Then bring meal.
And [j]he cast *it* into the pot; and he
said, Pour out for the people, that they
may eat. And there was no [d]harm in
the pot.

The feeding of the hundred men

42 ¶ And there came a man from
[k]Baal-shalisha, [l]and brought the
man of God bread of the firstfruits,
twenty loaves of barley, and full ears of
corn [e]in the husk thereof. And he
said, Give unto the people, that they
may eat.

43 And his servitor said, [m]What,
should I set this before an hundred
men? He said again, Give the people,
that they may eat: for thus saith the
LORD, [n]They shall eat, and shall leave
thereof.

44 So he set *it* before them, and they
did eat, [o]and left *thereof,* according to
the word of the LORD.

4:38 [f]ch. 2:1 [g]ch. 8:1 [h]ch. 2:3 Luke 10:39 Acts 22:3
4:40 [i]Ex. 10:17
4:41 [j]See Ex. 15:25 ch. 2:21 & 5:10 John 9:6
4:42 [k]1 Sam. 9:4 [l]1 Sam. 9:7 1 Cor. 9:11 Gal. 6:6
4:43 [m]Luke 9:13 John 6:9 [n]Luke 9:17 John 6:11
4:44 [o]Mat. 14:20 & 15:37 John 6:13

The cure of Naaman the leper

5 NOW [p]NAAMAN, captain of the
host of the king of Syria, was [q]a
great man [f]with his master, and
[g] [h]honourable, because by him the
LORD had given [i]deliverance unto Syr-
ia: he was also a mighty man in valour,
but he was a leper.

2 And the Syrians had gone out by
companies, and had brought away cap-
tive out of the land of Israel a little
maid; and she [j]waited on Naaman's
wife.

3 And she said unto her mistress,
Would God my lord *were* [f]with the
prophet that *is* in Samaria! for he
would [k]recover him of his leprosy.

4 And *one* went in, and told his lord,
saying, Thus and thus said the maid
that *is* of the land of Israel.

5 And the king of Syria said, Go to,
go, and I will send a letter unto the
king of Israel. And he departed, and
[r]took [l]with him ten talents of silver,
and six thousand *pieces* of gold, and ten
changes of raiment.

6 And he brought the letter to the
king of Israel, saying, Now when this
letter is come unto thee, behold, I have
therewith sent Naaman my servant to
thee, that thou mayest recover him of
his leprosy.

7 And it came to pass, when the
king of Israel had read the letter, that
he rent his clothes, and said, *Am* I
[s]God, to kill and to make alive, that
this man doth send unto me to recover
a man of his leprosy? wherefore con-
sider, I pray you, and see how he seek-
eth a quarrel against me.

5:1 [p]Luke 4:27 [q]Ex. 11:3
5:5 [r]1 Sam. 9:8 ch. 8:8,9
5:7 [s]Gen. 30:2 Deut. 32:39 1 Sam. 2:6

[d] Heb. *evil thing* [e] Or, *in his scrip,* or, *garment* [f] Heb. *before* [g] Or, *gracious* [h] Heb. *lifted up,* or, *accepted in countenance* [i] Or, *victory* [j] Heb. *was before* [k] Heb. *gather in* [l] Heb. *in his hand*

4:38–44 DEARTH IN THE LAND. These two narratives concerning the needs of the "sons of the prophets" illustrate the truth that "the eye of the LORD *is* upon them that fear him, upon them that hope in his mercy; to deliver their soul from death, and to keep them alive in famine" (Ps. 33:18–19). The remnant who remain faithful to God's Word are under the special care of the Lord (cf. Mark 16:18).

4:39 TO GATHER HERBS. Unlike the affluent lifestyle of the wealthy, the lifestyle of the "sons of the prophets" (see 1 Ki. 20:35, note) was simple, involving faithful service and self-denial (cf. 2 Cor. 4:7–12; 6:4–10).

4:42 BROUGHT THE MAN OF GOD . . . THE FIRSTFRUITS. Evidently, the man from Baal-shalisha refused to give his offering to the corrupt priests and Levites (1 Ki. 12:28–31). Instead, being a godly man, he brought his offering to true prophets of the Lord, those who were faithful to His word and covenant obligations.

5:1 NAAMAN. The story of Naaman demonstrates the providence of God (vv. 1–14), His saving power and grace (vv. 15–19), and His judgment upon sin (vv. 20–27). Prominent in the narrative is the truth that God's grace and salvation were not confined to Israel, but that He desired to have compassion on the non-Israelites and lead them to know the one true God (see Luke 4:18–19,25–27).

8 ¶ And it was *so,* when Elisha the man of God had heard that the king of Israel had rent his clothes, that he sent to the king, saying, Wherefore hast thou rent thy clothes? let him come now to me, and he shall know that there is a prophet in Israel.

9 So Naaman came with his horses and with his chariot, and stood at the door of the house of Elisha.

10 And Elisha sent a messenger unto him, saying, Go and [t]wash in Jordan seven times, and thy flesh shall come again to thee, and thou shalt be clean.

11 But Naaman was wroth, and went away, and said, Behold, [m, n]I thought, He will surely come out to me, and stand, and call on the name of the LORD his God, and [o]strike his hand over the place, and recover the leper.

12 *Are* not [p]Abana and Pharpar, rivers of Damascus, better than all the waters of Israel? may I not wash in them, and be clean? So he turned and went away in a rage.

13 And his servants came near, and spake unto him, and said, My father, *if* the prophet had bid thee *do some* great thing, wouldest thou not have done *it?* how much rather then, when he saith to thee, Wash, and be clean?

14 Then went he down, and dipped himself seven times in Jordan, according to the saying of the man of God: and [u]his flesh came again like unto the flesh of a little child, and [v]he was clean. 2 Ki. 20:1-7

15 ¶ And he returned to the man of God, he and all his company, and came, and stood before him: and he said, Behold, now I know that *there is* [w]no God in all the earth, but in Israel: now therefore, I pray thee, take [x]a blessing of thy servant.

16 But he said, [y]*As* the LORD liveth, before whom I stand, [z]I will receive none. And he urged him to take *it;* but he refused.

17 And Naaman said, Shall there not then, I pray thee, be given to thy servant two mules' burden of earth? for thy servant will henceforth offer neither burnt offering nor sacrifice unto other gods, but unto the LORD.

18 In this thing the LORD pardon thy servant, *that* when my master goeth into the house of Rimmon to worship there, and [a]he leaneth on my hand, and I bow myself in the house of Rimmon: when I bow down myself in the house of Rimmon, the LORD pardon thy servant in this thing.

19 And he said unto him, Go in peace. So he departed from him a little way.

20 ¶ But Gehazi, the servant of Elisha the man of God, said, Behold, my master hath spared Naaman this Syri-

5:10 [t]See ch. 4:41 John 9:7
5:14 [u]Job 33:25
[v]Luke 4:27
5:15 [w]Dan 2:47 & 3:29 & 6:26,27 [x]Gen. 33:11
5:16 [y]ch. 3:14 [z]Gen. 14:23 See Mat. 10:8 Acts 8:18,20
5:18 [a]ch. 7:2,17

[m]Heb. *I said* [n]Or, *I said with myself, He will surely come out* [o]Heb. *move up and down* [p]Or, *Amana*

5:10 WASH IN JORDAN. Elisha instructed Naaman to wash himself in the muddy waters of the Jordan River as a simple demonstration of humility and obedience. Furthermore, by doing so, Naaman would find it impossible to ascribe the cure to humans or to natural means. Both the Israelites and Syrians knew that the Jordan could not heal leprosy. Naaman needed to know that his healing came miraculously by the grace and power of God through the word of His prophet.

5:13–14 WASH, AND BE CLEAN. This passage, along with many others in the O.T., is prophetic of Jesus Christ, God's promised Messiah. For an analysis of this subject, see article on CHRIST IN THE OLD TESTAMENT, p. 562.

5:15 *THERE IS* NO GOD IN ALL THE EARTH, BUT IN ISRAEL. It is amazing that Naaman, though a foreigner, was miraculously delivered from leprosy and converted to the true God, while many lepers in Israel remained unclean. Christ Himself mentioned Naaman (Luke 4:27) in order to emphasize that when God's people disobey Him and His word, He will take His kingdom from them and raise up others to experience His salvation, righteousness, and kingdom power (cf. Mat. 8:10–13; 23:37–39).

5:16 I WILL RECEIVE NONE. God does not offer His services for a price only to those who can afford it. Thus Elisha felt it would be inappropriate for him to profit from what God had done through him (cf. Mat. 10:8; 2 Cor. 2:17). Naaman's healing was a merciful act of God, which no amount of money could repay. He was now under an obligation of lifetime devotion to God (v. 17).

5:20 I WILL . . . TAKE SOMEWHAT OF HIM. Gehazi, the servant of Elisha, had a covetous heart and therefore sought to corrupt God's gracious act for the sake of material prosperity. His transgressions included betraying Elisha, lying to Naaman and Elisha, and dishonoring the name of God. The N.T. likewise refers to people who preach the word of God for selfish gain (2 Cor. 2:17). Unfortunately, there are ministers who seek to enrich themselves and accumulate great material abundance by proclaiming the shed blood of Christ, offering salvation to the lost, healing the sick, or counseling those in distress. They are using the word of God and making merchandise of God's mercy; they turn the "riches of Christ" (Eph. 3:8) into "the treasures in Egypt" (Heb. 11:26).

CHRIST IN THE OLD TESTAMENT

***2 Ki. 5:14** "Then went he down, and dipped himself seven times in the Jordan, according to the saying of the man of God: and his flesh came again like unto the flesh of a little child, and he was clean."*

One of the fundamental N.T. teachings is that Jesus Christ (the Messiah) is the fulfillment of the O.T. The writer to the Hebrews suggests that Christ is the heir of all that God had spoken through the prophets (Heb. 1:1–2). Jesus himself asserted that He had come to fulfill the law and the prophets (Mat. 5:17). After His glorious resurrection, He demonstrated to His followers from Moses, the prophets, and the psalms (i.e., from the three main divisions of the Hebrew O.T.) that God had long ago predicted everything that had happened to Him (Luke 24:25–27,44–46). To better understand the O.T.'s prophecies about Jesus Christ, we must say something about *typology*.

PRINCIPLES OF TYPOLOGY. A careful study of the O.T. reveals elements (called *types*, from Gk. *tupos*) that are fulfilled in the coming of the Messiah (who is the *antitype*); in other words, there is a correspondence between persons, events, or things in the O.T. and Jesus Christ in the N.T. Note two basic principles with respect to this pattern of prophecy and fulfillment: (1) In seeing how an O.T. passage points forward to Christ, we must always begin by looking at the passage as revealing an event within God's history of redemption; i.e., we must first examine an O.T. passage as a historical event and then see how it points forward to the coming of Jesus Christ as the promised Messiah.

(2) We must recognize that the Messianic fulfillment of an O.T. passage is often on a higher spiritual plane than the O.T. event. In fact, the O.T. people involved in the story may not themselves have seen that what they were experiencing was prophetic of the coming Son of God. For example, David probably did not realize when he wrote Ps. 22 that his suffering was prophetic of the suffering of Christ on the cross. Nor did the weeping exiles going past Rachel's tomb in Ramah (Jer. 31:15) know that some day their tears would be fulfilled in the death of all male babies two years old and under in Bethlehem (Mat. 2:18). Often we are able to see an O.T. passage as prophetic of our Lord only in the light of N.T. revelation.

CATEGORIES OF PROPHETIC TYPES. We can identify at least four different patterns in which the O.T. points forward to and is prophetic of the coming of Christ in the N.T. (1) *Specific O.T. texts quoted in the N.T.* Certain passages of the O.T. are obviously prophetic of Christ because they are quoted as such in the N.T. For example, Matthew cites Is. 7:14 to prove that the O.T. prophesied the virgin birth of Christ (Mat. 1:23) and Mic. 5:2 to prove that Jesus was to be born in Bethlehem (Mat. 2:6). Mark reminds his readers (Mark 1:2–3) that the coming of John the Baptist as the forerunner of Christ was prophesied both by Isaiah (Is. 40:3) and Malachi (Mal. 3:1). Zechariah foretold Jesus' triumphal entry into Jerusalem on Palm Sunday (Zec. 9:9; cf. Mat. 21:1–5; John 12:14–15). David's experience expressed in Ps. 22:18 anticipates the soldiers at the cross dividing up Jesus' clothing (John 19:23–24), and his statement in Ps 16:8–11 is interpreted as a clear prediction of the resurrection of Jesus (Acts 2:25–32; 13:35–37). The writer of the letter to the Hebrews asserts that Melchizedek (cf. Gen. 14:18–20; Ps. 110:4) is a type of Christ, our eternal high priest. There are many other examples that could be cited.

(2) *Allusions by N.T. writers to O.T. passages.* Another pattern whereby Christ can be found in the O.T are those N.T. passages that, without actually quoting a specific text, refer to O.T. persons, events, or things as prophetic of Christ. For example, in the very first prophetic text in the Bible (Gen. 3:15), God promises to send the seed of the woman to destroy the seed of the serpent. Surely Paul had this passage in mind when he says

that Christ was born of a woman to redeem those who are under the power of the law (Gal. 4:4–5; cf. Rom. 16:20), as did the apostle John when he maintains that the Son of God came to "destroy the works of the devil" (1 John 3:8). John the Baptist's reference to Jesus as the Lamb of God who takes away the sin of the world (John 1:29,36) points back to Lev. 16 and Is. 53:7, and Paul's reference to Jesus as "our passover" (1 Cor. 5:7) shows that the killing of the passover lamb prophesied of Christ's death for us (Ex. 12:1–14). Jesus himself said that Moses lifting up the serpent in the wilderness (Num. 21:4–9) was prophetic of Him hanging on a cross. And when John says that Jesus, the Word of God, was involved in the creation of all things (John 1:1–3), we cannot help but think of Ps. 33:6: "By the word of the LORD were the heavens made" (cf. Heb. 1:3,10–12). These are only a few of the many N.T. allusions to O.T. passages concerning Christ.

(3) *O.T. person, events, or things that relate especially to redemption.* Israel's exodus from Egypt, which is viewed throughout the O.T. as the greatest redemptive event under the old covenant, foreshadows Christ and the redemption which He brings under the new covenant. Some types in the book of Exodus that foreshadow Christ and His redemption are Moses, the Passover, the Red Sea crossing, manna, the water from the rock, the tabernacle and its furnishings, and the high priest.

(4) *Patterns in O.T. events that foreshadow the way God deals with us in Christ.* Many of the stories in the O.T. manifest a pattern of God's dealings with his people that is brought to fulfillment in Jesus Christ. Note the following examples: (a) Abraham had to wait patiently nearly twenty-five years for God to open the womb of Sarah and give them Isaac. Nothing he did could hurry along the birth of that son of God's promise. This pattern is fulfilled in the N.T., as God sent forth His own Son as Savior of the world, in the fullness of time (Gal. 4:4); nothing humans did could hurry it along. Our salvation comes only by God's initiative (cf. John 3:16), not by human effort. (b) Before the Israelites were redeemed out of Egypt by God's gracious power, they had to cry out in desperation to their God to be freed from their enemies (Ex. 2:23–24; 3:7). This is prophetic of God's redemptive plan in Christ for us. Before we can expect deliverance by God's grace from our sins and spiritual enemies, we must cry out in repentance before him and ask for his saving grace (cf. Acts 2:37–38; 16:29–33; 17:30–31). All those who call upon the name of the Lord shall be saved. (c) When Naaman the Syrian sought healing from the God of Israel for his leprosy, he was told to wash seven times in the Jordan River. Though this made him angry initially, he had to humble himself and submit to the Jordan washing in order to be healed (2 Ki. 5:1–14). This passage foreshadows Jesus and the new covenant—both that God's saving grace reaches beyond the limits of the nation of Israel (cf. Luke 4:27; Acts 22:21; Rom. 15:8–12), and that in order to receive salvation, we must forsake our pride, humble ourselves before God (cf. Jas. 4:10; 1 Pet. 5:6), and seek to be washed in the blood of Jesus, God's provision for our cleansing (cf. Acts 22:16; 1 Cor. 6:11; Tit. 3:5; 1 John 1:7,9; Rev. 1:5).

In summary, the O.T. is indeed a book of stories of godly people in the past who serve as our models and examples (cf. 1 Cor. 10:1–13; Heb. 11; Jas. 5:16–18). But it is much more than that; it is "our schoolmaster *to bring us* unto Christ, that we might be justified by faith" (Gal. 3:24).

an, in not receiving at his hands that
which he brought: but, *as* the LORD
liveth, I will run after him, and take
somewhat of him.
21 So Gehazi followed after Naa-
man. And when Naaman saw *him* run-
ning after him, he lighted down from
the chariot to meet him, and said, [q]*Is*
all well?
22 And he said, All *is* well. My mas-
ter hath sent me, saying, Behold, even
now there be come to me from mount
Ephraim two young men of the sons of
the prophets: give them, I pray thee, a
talent of silver, and two changes of
garments.
23 And Naaman said, Be content,
take two talents. And he urged him,
and bound two talents of silver in two
bags, with two changes of garments,
and laid *them* upon two of his servants;
and they bare *them* before him.
24 And when he came to the [r]tow-
er, he took *them* from their hand, and
bestowed *them* in the house: and he let
the men go, and they departed.
25 But he went in, and stood before
his master. And Elisha said unto him,
Whence *comest thou,* Gehazi? And he
said, Thy servant went [s]no whither.
26 And he said unto him, Went not
mine heart *with thee,* when the man
turned again from his chariot to meet
thee? *Is it* a time to receive money, and
to receive garments, and oliveyards,
and vineyards, and sheep, and oxen,
and menservants, and maidservants?
27 The leprosy therefore of Naaman
[b]shall cleave unto thee, and unto thy
seed for ever. And he went out from his
presence [c]a leper *as white* as snow.

Recovery of the lost axe head

6 AND [d]THE sons of the prophets
said unto Elisha, Behold now, the
place where we dwell with thee is too
strait for us.
2 Let us go, we pray thee, unto Jor-
dan, and take thence every man a
beam, and let us make us a place there,
where we may dwell. And he answered,
Go ye.
3 And one said, Be content, I pray
thee, and go with thy servants. And he
answered, I will go.
4 So he went with them. And when
they came to Jordan, they cut down
wood.
5 But as one was felling a beam, the
[t]axe head fell into the water: and he
cried, and said, Alas, master! for it was
borrowed.
6 And the man of God said, Where
fell it? And he showed him the place.
And [e]he cut down a stick, and cast *it*
in thither; and the iron did swim.
7 Therefore said he, Take *it* up to
thee. And he put out his hand, and
took it.

Elisha strikes the Syrians blind

8 ¶ Then the king of Syria warred
against Israel, and took counsel with
his servants, saying, In such and such
a place *shall be* my [u]camp.
9 And the man of God sent unto the
king of Israel, saying, Beware that
thou pass not such a place; for thither
the Syrians are come down.
10 And the king of Israel sent to the
place which the man of God told him
and warned him of, and saved himself
there, not once nor twice.
11 Therefore the heart of the king
of Syria was sore troubled for this
thing; and he called his servants, and
said unto them, Will ye not show me
which of us *is* for the king of Israel?
12 And one of his servants said,
[v]None, my lord, O king: but Elisha,
the prophet that *is* in Israel, telleth the
king of Israel the words that thou
speakest in thy bedchamber.
13 ¶ And he said, Go and spy where
he *is,* that I may send and fetch him.
And it was told him, saying, Behold, *he*
is in [f]Dothan.
14 Therefore sent he thither horses,
and chariots, and a [w]great host: and
they came by night, and compassed the
city about.
15 And when the [x]servant of the

5:27 [b]1 Tim. 6:10 [c]Ex. 4:6 Num. 12:10 ch. 15:5
6:1 [d]ch. 4:38
6:6 [e]ch. 2:21
6:13 [f]Gen. 37:17

[q] Heb. Is there *peace?* [r] Or, *secret place*
[s] Heb. *not hither or thither* [t] Heb. *iron*
[u] Or, *encamping* [v] Heb. *No* [w] Heb. *heavy*
[x] Or, *minister*

6:5 THE AXE HEAD. The story of the lost axe head illustrates God's interest and care in what might appear to be an insignificant matter. An iron axe head in those days was a very expensive tool, and this poor man felt keenly his responsibility for the borrowed tool. The miracle served (1) to communicate God's heart of compassion for the man in his predicament, (2) to demonstrate the power of God at work through the prophet and thus to further confirm his authority and ministry, and (3) to increase the faith of the younger prophets with Elisha (cf. vv. 1–7).

man of God was risen early, and gone forth, behold, an host compassed the city both with horses and chariots. And his servant said unto him, Alas, my master! how shall we do?

16 And he answered, Fear not: for [g]they that *be* with us *are* more than they that *be* with them.

17 And Elisha prayed, and said, LORD, I pray thee, open his eyes, that he may see. And the LORD opened the eyes of the young man; and he saw: and, behold, the mountain *was* full of [h]horses and chariots of fire round about Elisha.

18 And when they came down to him, Elisha prayed unto the LORD, and said, Smite this people, I pray thee, with blindness. And [i]he smote them with blindness according to the word of Elisha.

19 ¶ And Elisha said unto them, This *is* not the way, neither *is* this the city: [y]follow me, and I will bring you to the man whom ye seek. But he led them to Samaria.

20 And it came to pass, when they were come into Samaria, that Elisha said, LORD, open the eyes of these *men*, that they may see. And the LORD opened their eyes, and they saw; and, behold, *they were* in the midst of Samaria.

21 And the king of Israel said unto Elisha, when he saw them, My father, shall I smite *them?* shall I smite *them?*

22 And he answered, Thou shalt not smite *them:* wouldest thou smite those whom thou hast taken captive with thy sword and with thy bow? [j]set bread and water before them, that they may eat and drink, and go to their master.

6:16 [g]2 Chr. 32:7 Ps. 55:18 Rom. 8:31
6:17 [h]ch. 2:11 Ps. 34:7 & 68:17 Zech. 1:8 & 6:1-7
6:18 [i]Gen. 19:11
6:22 [j]Rom. 12:20
6:23 [k]ver. 8,9 ch. 5:2
6:29 [l]Lev. 26:29 Deut. 28:53,57
6:30 [m]1 Ki. 21:27

23 And he prepared great provision for them: and when they had eaten and drunk, he sent them away, and they went to their master. So [k]the bands of Syria came no more into the land of Israel.

Famine in Samaria

24 ¶ And it came to pass after this, that Ben-hadad king of Syria gathered all his host, and went up, and besieged Samaria.

25 And there was a great famine in Samaria: and, behold, they besieged it, until an ass's head was *sold* for fourscore *pieces* of silver, and the fourth part of a cab of dove's dung for five *pieces* of silver.

26 And as the king of Israel was passing by upon the wall, there cried a woman unto him, saying, Help, my lord, O king.

27 And he said, [z]If the LORD do not help thee, whence shall I help thee? out of the barnfloor, or out of the winepress?

28 And the king said unto her, What aileth thee? And she answered, This woman said unto me, Give thy son, that we may eat him today, and we will eat my son tomorrow.

29 So [l]we boiled my son, and did eat him: and I said unto her on the [a]next day, Give thy son, that we may eat him: and she hath hid her son.

30 ¶ And it came to pass, when the king heard the words of the woman, that he [m]rent his clothes; and he

[y] Heb. *come ye after me* [z] Or, *Let not the LORD save thee* [a] Heb. *other*

6:16–17 THEY THAT *BE* WITH US *ARE* MORE THAN THEY THAT *BE* WITH THEM. An unseen spiritual realm exists, consisting of a host of ministering angels who are active in the lives of God's people (Gen. 32:2; Is. 63:9). Several principles may be derived from this event. (1) Not only is God for His people (Rom. 8:31), but also armies of His angels stand by, ready to defend the believer and God's kingdom (v. 17; Ps. 34:7; see article on ANGELS AND THE ANGEL OF THE LORD, p. 368).

(2) All Bible-believing Christians should continually pray that God would deliver them from spiritual blindness and open the eyes of their hearts to see more clearly the spiritual reality of God's kingdom (cf. Luke 24:31; Eph. 1:18–21) and its heavenly hosts (cf. Heb. 1:14).

(3) God's ministering spirits are not far off, but are very close (Gen. 32:1–2), observing the actions and faith of God's children and working on their behalf (Acts 7:55–60; 1 Cor. 4:9; Eph. 3:10; 1 Tim. 5:21).

(4) The real battle in God's kingdom is not against flesh and blood. It is a spiritual battle "against the rulers of the darkness of this world, against spiritual wickedness in the high *places*" (Eph. 6:12; cf. Rev. 12:7–9; see Eph. 6:11, note).

(5) There is a cause and effect relationship in spiritual battles; the outcome of spiritual battles is determined in part by the faith and prayers of the saints (vv. 16–20; Eph. 6:18–19; see Mat. 9:38, note).

6:28 THY SON, THAT WE MAY EAT HIM. Because Israel had lost the faith and departed from a covenant trust in God, His people committed horrible deeds against their own children during a time of severe famine. A major result of casting aside God and His word is the loss of family love and affection (cf. Deut. 28:15,53–57).

passed by upon the wall, and the people looked, and, behold, *he had* sackcloth within upon his flesh.

31 Then he said, [n]God do so and more also to me, if the head of Elisha the son of Shaphat shall stand on him this day.

The prophecy of Elisha

32 But Elisha sat in his house, and [o]the elders sat with him; and *the king* sent a man from before him: but ere the messenger came to him, he said to the elders, [p]See ye how this son of [q]a murderer hath sent to take away mine head? look, when the messenger cometh, shut the door, and hold him fast at the door: *is* not the sound of his master's feet behind him?

33 And while he yet talked with them, behold, the messenger came down unto him: and he said, Behold, this evil *is* of the LORD; [r]what should I wait for the LORD any longer?

7 THEN ELISHA said, Hear ye the word of the LORD; Thus saith the LORD, [s]Tomorrow about this time *shall* a measure of fine flour *be sold* for a shekel, and two measures of barley for a shekel, in the gate of Samaria.

2 [t]Then [u]a[b] lord on whose hand the king leaned answered the man of God, and said, Behold, [v]*if* the LORD would make windows in heaven, might this thing be? And he said, Behold, thou shalt see *it* with thine eyes, but shalt not eat thereof.

3 ¶ And there were four leprous men [w]at the entering in of the gate: and they said one to another, Why sit we here until we die?

4 If we say, We will enter into the city, then the famine *is* in the city, and we shall die there: and if we sit still here, we die also. Now therefore come, and let us fall unto the host of the Syrians: if they save us alive, we shall live; and if they kill us, we shall but die.

5 And they rose up in the twilight, to go unto the camp of the Syrians: and when they were come to the uttermost part of the camp of Syria, behold, *there was* no man there.

6 For the Lord had made the host of the Syrians [x]to hear a noise of chariots, and a noise of horses, *even* the noise of a great host: and they said one to another, Lo, the king of Israel hath hired against us [y]the kings of the Hittites, and the kings of the Egyptians, to come upon us.

7 Wherefore they [z]arose and fled in the twilight, and left their tents, and their horses, and their asses, even the camp as it *was,* and fled for their life.

8 And when these lepers came to the uttermost part of the camp, they went into one tent, and did eat and drink, and carried thence silver, and gold, and raiment, and went and hid *it;* and came again, and entered into another tent, and carried thence *also,* and went and hid *it.*

9 Then they said one to another, We do not well: this day *is* a day of good tidings, and we hold our peace: if we tarry till the morning light, [c]some mischief will come upon us: now therefore come, that we may go and tell the king's household.

10 So they came and called unto the porter of the city: and they told them, saying, We came to the camp of the Syrians, and, behold, *there was* no man there, neither voice of man, but horses tied, and asses tied, and the tents as they *were.*

11 And he called the porters; and they told *it* to the king's house within.

12 ¶ And the king arose in the night, and said unto his servants, I will now show you what the Syrians have done to us. They know that we *be* hungry; therefore are they gone out of the camp to hide themselves in the field, saying, When they come out of the city, we shall catch them alive, and get into the city.

13 And one of his servants answered and said, Let *some* take, I pray thee, five of the horses that remain, which are left [d]in the city, (behold, they *are* as all the multitude of Israel that are left in it: behold, *I say,* they *are* even as all the multitude of the Israelites that are consumed:) and let us send and see.

14 They took therefore two chariot horses; and the king sent after the host of the Syrians, saying, Go and see.

15 And they went after them unto

6:31 [n]Ruth 1:17 1 Ki. 19:2
6:32 [o]Ezek. 8:1 & 20:1 [p]Luke 13:32 [q]1 Ki. 18:4
6:33 [r]Job 2:9
7:1 [s]ver. 18,19
7:2 [t]ver. 17,19,20 [u]ch. 5:18 [v]Mal. 3:10
7:3 [w]Lev. 13:46
7:6 [x]2 Sam. 5:24 ch. 19:7 Job 15:21 [y]1 Ki. 10:29
7:7 [z]Ps. 48:4-6 Prov. 28:1

[b] Heb. *a lord which* belonged *to the king leaning upon his hand* [c] Heb. *we shall find punishment* [d] Heb. *in it*

7:1 A MEASURE OF FINE FLOUR . . . FOR A SHEKEL. Elisha prophesied that the shortage of food would soon end and that food prices would drop to a normal level (cf. v. 16).

Jordan: and, lo, all the way *was* full of garments and vessels, which the Syrians had cast away in their haste. And the messengers returned, and told the king.

16 And the people went out, and spoiled the tents of the Syrians. So a measure of fine flour was *sold* for a shekel, and two measures of barley for a shekel, [a]according to the word of the LORD.

17 ¶ And the king appointed the lord on whose hand he leaned to have the charge of the gate: and the people trode upon him in the gate, and he died, [b]as the man of God had said, who spake when the king came down to him.

18 And it came to pass as the man of God had spoken to the king, saying, [c]Two measures of barley for a shekel, and a measure of fine flour for a shekel, shall be tomorrow about this time in the gate of Samaria:

19 And that lord answered the man of God, and said, Now, behold, *if* the LORD should make windows in heaven, might such a thing be? And he said, Behold, thou shalt see it with thine eyes, but shalt not eat thereof.

20 And so it fell out unto him: for the people trode upon him in the gate, and he died.

The Shunammite comes home

8 THEN SPAKE Elisha unto the woman, [d]whose son he had restored to life, saying, Arise, and go thou and thine household, and sojourn wheresoever thou canst sojourn: for the LORD [e]hath called for a famine; and it shall also come upon the land seven years.

2 And the woman arose, and did after the saying of the man of God: and she went with her household, and sojourned in the land of the Philistines seven years.

3 And it came to pass at the seven years' end, that the woman returned out of the land of the Philistines: and she went forth to cry unto the king for her house and for her land.

4 And the king talked with [f]Gehazi the servant of the man of God, saying, Tell me, I pray thee, all the great things that Elisha hath done.

5 And it came to pass, as he was telling the king how he had [g]restored a dead body to life, that, behold, the woman, whose son he had restored to life, cried to the king for her house and for her land. And Gehazi said, My lord, O king, this *is* the woman, and this *is* her son, whom Elisha restored to life.

6 And when the king asked the woman, she told him. So the king appointed unto her a certain [e]officer, saying, Restore all that *was* hers, and all the fruits of the field since the day that she left the land, even until now.

Hazael anointed king of Syria

7 ¶ And Elisha came to Damascus; and Ben-hadad the king of Syria was sick; and it was told him, saying, The man of God is come hither.

8 And the king said unto [h]Hazael, [i]Take a present in thine hand, and go, meet the man of God, and [j]inquire of the LORD by him, saying, Shall I recover of this disease?

9 So Hazael went to meet him, and took a present [f]with him, even of every good thing of Damascus, forty camels' burden, and came and stood before him, and said, Thy son Ben-hadad king of Syria hath sent me to thee, saying, Shall I recover of this disease?

10 And Elisha said unto him, Go, say unto him, Thou mayest certainly recover: howbeit the LORD hath shown me that [k]he shall surely die.

11 And he settled his countenance

7:16 [a]ver. 1 **7:17** [b]ver. 2 **7:18** [c]ver. 1 **8:1** [d]ch. 4:35 [e]Ps. 105:16 Hag. 1:11 **8:4** [f]ch. 5:27 **8:5** [g]ch. 4:35 **8:8** [h]1 Ki. 19:15 [i]1 Sam. 9:7 1 Ki. 14:3 ch. 5:5 [j]ch. 1:2 **8:10** [k]ver. 15

[e] Or, *eunuch* [f] Heb. *in his hand*

7:16 ACCORDING TO THE WORD OF THE LORD. Through the event recorded in this chapter, the Israelites understood that "the word of the LORD" was indeed true, that in mercy God had saved the apostate nation from calamity in order that they might repent and return to Him, and that unbelief and failure to follow God's word would result in further judgment (vv. 2,17–20).

8:1 THE LORD HATH CALLED FOR A FAMINE. God sent a famine upon Israel as a punishment for their apostasy (cf. Deut. 11:16–17; 28:38–40). The author does not say when it occurred, though it was evidently before the judgment upon Gehazi (v. 5; 5:27) and after the raising of the Shunammite's son (v. 1; 4:32–37). This is probably the same famine as the one mentioned in 4:38.

8:2 THE WOMAN AROSE. Because the woman demonstrated a sincere faith and remained faithful to God's prophet in a time of general apostasy (4:8–37), the Lord guided and helped her in her time of need (cf. Mat. 10:41; Rev. 3:10).

8:11–12 THE MAN OF GOD WEPT. In a vision from the Spirit of revelation, Elisha saw that Haza-

[g]stedfastly, until he was ashamed: and the man of God [l]wept.

12 And Hazael said, Why weepeth my lord? And he answered, Because I know [m]the evil that thou wilt do unto the children of Israel: their strong holds wilt thou set on fire, and their young men wilt thou slay with the sword, and [n]wilt dash their children, and rip up their women with child.

13 And Hazael said, But what, [o]*is* thy servant a dog, that he should do this great thing? And Elisha answered, [p]The LORD hath shown me that thou *shalt be* king over Syria.

14 So he departed from Elisha, and came to his master; who said to him, What said Elisha to thee? And he answered, He told me *that* thou shouldest surely recover.

15 And it came to pass on the morrow, that he took a thick cloth, and dipped *it* in water, and spread *it* on his face, so that he died: and Hazael reigned in his stead.

Jehoram, king of Judah

8:16–24pp — 2 Chr. 21:5–10,20

16 ¶ And in the fifth year of Joram the son of Ahab king of Israel, Jehoshaphat *being* then king of Judah, [q]Jehoram the son of Jehoshaphat king of Judah [h]began to reign.

17 [r]Thirty and two years old was he when he began to reign; and he reigned eight years in Jerusalem.

18 And he walked in the way of the kings of Israel, as did the house of Ahab: for [s]the daughter of Ahab was his wife: and he did evil in the sight of the LORD.

19 Yet the LORD would not destroy Judah for David his servant's sake, [t]as he promised him to give him always a [i]light, *and* to his children.

20 ¶ In his days [u]Edom revolted from under the hand of Judah, [v]and made a king over themselves.

21 So Joram went over to Zair, and all the chariots with him: and he rose by night, and smote the Edomites which compassed him about, and the captains of the chariots: and the people fled into their tents.

22 [j]Yet Edom revolted from under the hand of Judah unto this day. [w]Then Libnah revolted at the same time.

23 And the rest of the acts of Joram, and all that he did, *are* they not written in the book of the chronicles of the kings of Judah?

24 And Joram slept with his fathers, and was buried with his fathers in the city of David: and [x]Ahaziah[k] his son reigned in his stead.

Ahaziah, king of Judah

8:25–29pp — 2 Chr. 22:1–6

25 ¶ In the twelfth year of Joram the son of Ahab king of Israel did Ahaziah the son of Jehoram king of Judah begin to reign.

26 [y]Two and twenty years old *was* Ahaziah when he began to reign; and he reigned one year in Jerusalem. And his mother's name *was* Athaliah, the [l]daughter of Omri king of Israel.

27 [z]And he walked in the way of the house of Ahab, and did evil in the sight of the LORD, as *did* the house of Ahab: for he *was* the son-in-law of the house of Ahab.

28 ¶ And he went [a]with Joram the son of Ahab to the war against Hazael king of Syria in Ramoth-gilead; and the Syrians wounded Joram.

29 And [b]king Joram went back to be healed in Jezreel of the wounds [m]which the Syrians had given him at [n]Ramah, when he fought against Hazael king of Syria. [c]And Ahaziah the son of Jehoram king of Judah went down to see Joram the son of Ahab in Jezreel, because he was [o]sick.

8:11 [l]Luke 19:41
8:12 [m]ch. 10:32 & 12:17 &13:3,7 Amos 1:3 [n]ch. 15:16 Hos. 13:16 Amos 1:13
8:13 [o]1 Sam. 17:43 [p]1 Ki. 19:15
8:16 [q]2 Chr. 21:3
8:17 [r]2 Chr. 21:5
8:18 [s]ver. 26
8:19 [t]2 Sam. 7:13 1 Ki. 11:36 & 15:4 2 Chr. 21:7
8:20 [u]Gen. 27:40 ch. 3:27 2 Chr. 21:8-10 [v]1 Ki. 22:47
8:22 [w]2 Chr. 21:10
8:24 [x]2 Chr. 22:1
8:26 [y]See 2 Chr. 22:2
8:27 [z]2 Chr. 22:3,4
8:28 [a]2 Chr. 22:5
8:29 [b]ch. 9:15 [c]ch. 9:16 2 Chr. 22:6,7

[g]Heb. *and set it* [h]Heb. *reigned.* Began to reign in consort with his father [i]Heb. *candle,* or, *lamp* [j]And see fulfilled in Gen. 27:40 [k]Called *Azariah* in 2 Chr. 22:6 and *Jehoahaz* in 2 Chr. 21:17 & 25:23 [l]Or, *granddaughter;* see ver. 18 [m]Heb. *wherewith the Syrians had wounded* [n]Called *Ramoth* in ver. 28 [o]Heb. *wounded*

el would become king of Syria and perpetrate terrible evil against Israel (vv. 12–13). Elisha wept because of what was coming upon Israel as a result of their apostasy. As a true man of God, he felt a deep sorrow both for God who had been abandoned by His own people and for those people who now had to suffer severe judgment for their sins. In like manner Jesus wept over Jerusalem (Luke 19:41) and Paul over the church (Acts 20:28–31). The words of Elisha do not endorse the future cruelty of Hazael, but only describe the terrible practices of depraved humans in times of war (cf. Is. 13:15; Hos. 10:14).

Jehu anointed king of Israel

9 AND ELISHA the prophet called one of the [d]children of the prophets, and said unto him, [e]Gird up thy loins, and take this box of oil in thine hand, [f]and go to Ramoth-gilead:

2 And when thou comest thither, look out there Jehu the son of Jehoshaphat the son of Nimshi, and go in, and make him arise up from among [g]his brethren, and carry him to an [p]inner chamber;

3 Then [h]take the box of oil, and pour *it* on his head, and say, Thus saith the LORD, I have anointed thee king over Israel. Then open the door, and flee, and tarry not.

4 ¶ So the young man, *even* the young man the prophet, went to Ramoth-gilead.

5 And when he came, behold, the captains of the host *were* sitting; and he said, I have an errand to thee, O captain. And Jehu said, Unto which of all us? And he said, To thee, O captain.

6 And he arose, and went into the house; and he poured the oil on his head, and said unto him, [i]Thus saith the LORD God of Israel, I have anointed thee king over the people of the LORD, *even* over Israel.

7 And thou shalt smite the house of Ahab thy master, that I may avenge the blood of my servants the prophets, and the blood of all the servants of the LORD, [j]at the hand of Jezebel.

8 For the whole house of Ahab shall perish: and [k]I will cut off from Ahab [l]him that pisseth against the wall, and [m]him that is shut up and left in Israel:

9 And I will make the house of Ahab like the house of [n]Jeroboam the son of Nebat, and like the house of [o]Baasha the son of Ahijah:

10 [p]And the dogs shall eat Jezebel in the portion of Jezreel, and *there shall be* none to bury *her*. And he opened the door, and fled.

11 ¶ Then Jehu came forth to the servants of his lord: and *one* said unto him, *Is* all well? wherefore came [q]this mad *fellow* to thee? And he said unto them, Ye know the man, and his communication.

12 And they said, *It is* false; tell us now. And he said, Thus and thus spake he to me, saying, Thus saith the LORD, I have anointed thee king over Israel.

13 Then they hasted, and [r]took every man his garment, and put *it* under him on the top of the stairs, and blew with trumpets, saying, Jehu [q]is king.

Jehu kills Joram and Ahaziah

9:21–29pp — 2 Chr. 22:7–9

14 So Jehu the son of Jehoshaphat the son of Nimshi conspired against Joram. (Now Joram had kept Ramoth-gilead, he and all Israel, because of Hazael king of Syria.

15 But [s]king [r]Joram was returned to be healed in Jezreel of the wounds which the Syrians [s]had given him, when he fought with Hazael king of Syria.) And Jehu said, If it be your minds, *then* [t]let none go forth *nor* escape out of the city to go to tell *it* in Jezreel.

16 So Jehu rode in a chariot, and went to Jezreel; for Joram lay there. [t]And Ahaziah king of Judah was come down to see Joram.

17 And there stood a watchman on the tower in Jezreel, and he spied the company of Jehu as he came, and said, I see a company. And Joram said, Take an horseman, and send to meet them, and let him say, *Is it* peace?

18 So there went one on horseback to meet him, and said, Thus saith the king, *Is it* peace? And Jehu said, What hast thou to do with peace? turn thee behind me. And the watchman told, saying, The messenger came to them, but he cometh not again.

9:1 [d]1 Ki. 20:35 [e]ch. 4:29 Jer. 1:17 [f]ch. 8:28,29
9:2 [g]ver. 5,11
9:3 [h]1 Ki. 19:16
9:6 [i]1 Ki. 19:16 2 Chr. 22:7
9:7 [j]1 Ki. 18:4 & 21:15
9:8 [k]1 Ki. 14:10 & 21:21 [l]1 Sam. 25:22 [m]Deut. 32:36
9:9 [n]1 Ki. 14:10 & 15:29 & 21:22 [o]1 Ki. 16:3,11
9:10 [p]ver. 35,36 1 Ki. 21:23
9:11 [q]Jer. 29:26 John 10:20 Acts 26:24 1 Cor. 4:10
9:13 [r]Mat. 21:7
9:15 [s]ch. 8:29
9:16 [t]ch. 8:29

[p] Heb. *chamber in a chamber* [q] Heb. *reigneth* [r] Heb. *Jehoram* [s] Heb. *smote* [t] Heb. *let no escaper go*

9:7 SMITE THE HOUSE OF AHAB. Years earlier Elijah had foretold the complete destruction of the descendants of Ahab (1 Ki. 21:19–24).

9:8 THE WHOLE HOUSE OF AHAB SHALL PERISH. God caused the fall of the house of Ahab because it had remained stubborn and unrepentant in its idolatry and apostasy, corrupting the entire nation of Israel (cf. Rom. 2:5–6). God's righteous judgment on Ahab's house (ch. 10), Ahab's son Joram (vv. 22–26; see 1 Ki. 21:19), and Ahab's wife Jezebel (vv. 30–37) shows that God will surely judge all who lead His people into unrighteousness. Scripture teaches plainly that God will reward every person according to his or her deeds (Rom. 2:6; cf. 2 Tim. 4:14), and that there will be "tribulation and anguish, upon every soul of man that doeth evil" (Rom. 2:9).

19 Then he sent out a second on horseback, which came to them, and said, Thus saith the king, *Is it* peace? And Jehu answered, What hast thou to do with peace? turn thee behind me.

20 And the watchman told, saying, He came even unto them, and cometh not again: and the [u]driving *is* like the driving of Jehu the son of Nimshi; for he driveth [v]furiously.

21 And Joram said, [w]Make ready. And his chariot was made ready. And [u]Joram king of Israel and Ahaziah king of Judah went out, each in his chariot, and they went out against Jehu, and [x]met him in the portion of Naboth the Jezreelite.

22 And it came to pass, when Joram saw Jehu, that he said, *Is it* peace, Jehu? And he answered, What peace, so long as the whoredoms of thy mother Jezebel and her witchcrafts *are so* many?

23 And Joram turned his hands, and fled, and said to Ahaziah, *There is* treachery, O Ahaziah.

24 And Jehu [y]drew a bow with his full strength, and smote Jehoram between his arms, and the arrow went out at his heart, and he [z]sunk down in his chariot.

25 Then said *Jehu* to Bidkar his captain, Take up, *and* cast him in the portion of the field of Naboth the Jezreelite: for remember how that, when I and thou rode together after Ahab his father, [v]the LORD laid this burden upon him;

26 Surely I have seen yesterday the [a]blood of Naboth, and the blood of his sons, saith the LORD; and I will requite thee in this [b]plat, saith the LORD. Now therefore take *and* cast him into the plat *of ground,* according to the word of the LORD.

27 ¶ But when Ahaziah the king of Judah saw *this,* he fled by the way of the garden house. And Jehu followed after him, and said, Smite him also in the chariot. *And they did so* at the going up to Gur, which *is* by Ibleam. And he fled to [w]Megiddo, and died there.

9:21 [u]2 Chr. 22:7
9:25 [v]1 Ki. 21:29
9:27 [w]In the kingdom of *Samaria* 2 Chr. 22:9

28 And his servants carried him in a chariot to Jerusalem, and buried him in his sepulchre with his fathers in the city of David.

29 And in the eleventh year of Joram the son of Ahab began Ahaziah to reign over Judah.

The death of Jezebel

30 ¶ And when Jehu was come to Jezreel, Jezebel heard *of it;* [x]and she [c]painted her face, and tired her head, and looked out at a window.

31 And as Jehu entered in at the gate, she said, [y]*Had* Zimri peace, who slew his master?

32 And he lifted up his face to the window, and said, Who *is* on my side? who? And there looked out to him two *or* three [d]eunuchs.

33 And he said, Throw her down. So they threw her down: and *some* of her blood was sprinkled on the wall, and on the horses: and he trode her under foot.

34 And when he was come in, he did eat and drink, and said, Go, see now this cursed *woman,* and bury her: for [z]she *is* a king's daughter.

35 And they went to bury her: but they found no more of her than the skull, and the feet, and the palms of *her* hands.

36 Wherefore they came again, and told him. And he said, This *is* the word of the LORD, which he spake [e]by his servant Elijah the Tishbite, saying, [a]In the portion of Jezreel shall dogs eat the flesh of Jezebel:

37 And the carcase of Jezebel shall be [b]as dung upon the face of the field in the portion of Jezreel; *so* that they shall not say, This *is* Jezebel.

Ahab's kin destroyed

10 AND AHAB had seventy sons in Samaria. And Jehu wrote let-

9:30 [x]Ezek. 23:40
9:31 [y]1 Ki. 16:9-20
9:34 [z]1 Ki. 16:31
9:36 [a]1 Ki. 21:23
9:37 [b]Ps. 83:10

[u] Or, *marching* [v] Heb. *in madness* [w] Heb. *Bind* [x] Heb. *found* [y] Heb. *filled his hand with a bow* [z] Heb. *bowed* [a] Heb. *bloods* [b] Or, *portion* [c] Heb. *put her eyes in painting* [d] Or, *chamberlains* [e] Heb. *by the hand of*

9:25 CAST HIM IN . . . THE FIELD OF NABOTH. Ahab and Jezebel, the parents of King Joram, had ruthlessly defrauded Naboth in order to steal his field (1 Ki. 21:1–24). Now the dead body of their son was cast into that very field. The sins of parents may bear fruit in their children years after the parents' death.

10:1 JEHU WROTE LETTERS. Jehu challenged the officials of Samaria to select a king from the sons of Ahab and then face the consequences of conflict with himself (vv. 1–4). The rulers, however, became terrified by this psychological warfare and swore allegiance to Jehu. They then obeyed the order of Jehu to kill Ahab's descendants (vv. 5–8).

ters, and sent to Samaria, unto the rul-
ers of Jezreel, to the elders, and to
[f]them that brought up Ahab's *chil-
dren,* saying,
2 Now as soon as this letter cometh
to you, seeing your master's sons *are*
with you, and *there are* with you chari-
ots and horses, a fenced city also, and
armour;
3 Look even out the best and meet-
est of your master's sons, and set *him*
on his father's throne, and fight for
your master's house.
4 But they were exceedingly afraid,
and said, Behold, two kings stood not
before him: how then shall we stand?
5 And he that *was* over the house,
and he that *was* over the city, the el-
ders also, and the bringers up *of the
children,* sent to Jehu, saying, *We are*
thy servants, and will do all that thou
shalt bid us; we will not make any
king: do thou *that which is* good in thine
eyes.
6 Then he wrote a letter the second
time to them, saying, If ye *be* [g]mine,
and *if* ye will hearken unto my voice,
take ye the heads of the men your mas-
ter's sons, and come to me to Jezreel by
tomorrow this time. Now the king's
sons, *being* seventy persons, *were* with
the great men of the city, which
brought them up.
7 And it came to pass, when the let-
ter came to them, that they took the
king's sons, and [c]slew seventy per-
sons, and put their heads in baskets,
and sent him *them* to Jezreel.
8 ¶ And there came a messenger,
and told him, saying, They have
brought the heads of the king's sons.
And he said, Lay ye them in two heaps
at the entering in of the gate until the
morning.
9 And it came to pass in the morn-
ing, that he went out, and stood, and
said to all the people, Ye *be* righteous:
behold, [d]I conspired against my mas-
ter, and slew him: but who slew all
these?
10 Know now that there shall [e]fall
unto the earth nothing of the word of
the LORD, which the LORD spake con-
cerning the house of Ahab: for the LORD
hath done *that* which he spake [f]by[h]
his servant Elijah.
11 So Jehu slew all that remained of
the house of Ahab in Jezreel, and all his
great men, and his [i]kinsfolks, and his
priests, until he left him none remain-
ing.
12 ¶ And he arose and departed,
and came to Samaria. *And* as he *was* at
the [j]shearing house in the way,
13 [g]Jehu [k]met with the brethren
of Ahaziah king of Judah, and said,
Who *are* ye? And they answered, We *are*
the brethren of Ahaziah; and we go
down [l]to salute the children of the
king and the children of the queen.
14 And he said, Take them alive.
And they took them alive, and slew
them at the pit of the shearing house,
even two and forty men: neither left he
any of them.
15 ¶ And when he was departed
thence, He [k]lighted on [h]Jehonadab
the son of [i]Rechab *coming* to meet
him: and he [m]saluted him, and said to
him, Is thine heart right, as my heart
is with thy heart? And Jehonadab an-
swered, It is. If it be, [j]give *me* thine
hand. And he gave *him* his hand; and he
took him up to him into the chariot.
16 And he said, Come with me, and
see my [k]zeal for the LORD. So they
made him ride in his chariot.
17 And when he came to Samaria,
[l]he slew all that remained unto Ahab
in Samaria, till he had destroyed him,
according to the saying of the LORD,
[m]which he spake to Elijah.

Massacre of Baal worshippers

18 ¶ And Jehu gathered all the peo-
ple together, and said unto them,
[n]Ahab served Baal a little; *but* Jehu
shall serve him much.
19 Now therefore call unto me all
the [o]prophets of Baal, all his ser-
vants, and all his priests; let none be
wanting: for I have a great sacrifice *to
do* to Baal; whosoever shall be want-
ing, he shall not live. But Jehu did *it* in
subtlety, to the intent that he might de-
stroy the worshippers of Baal.
20 And Jehu said, [n]Proclaim a sol-
emn assembly for Baal. And they pro-
claimed *it.*
21 And Jehu sent through all Israel:
and all the worshippers of Baal came,
so that there was not a man left that
came not. And they came into the

10:7 [c]1 Ki. 21:21
10:9 [d]ch. 9:14,24
10:10 [e]1 Sam. 3:19; Jer. 44:28 [f]1 Ki. 21:19,21,29
10:13 [g]ch. 8:29; 2 Chr. 22:8
10:15 [h]Jer. 35:6 [i]1 Chr. 2:55 [j]Ezra 10:19
10:16 [k]1 Ki. 19:10
10:17 [l]ch. 9:8; 2 Chr. 22:8 [m]1 Ki. 21:21
10:18 [n]1 Ki. 16:31,32
10:19 [o]1 Ki. 22:6

[f] Heb. *nourishers* [g] Heb. *for me* [h] Heb. *by the hand of* [i] Or, *acquaintance* [j] Heb. *house of shepherds binding* sheep [k] Heb. *found* [l] Heb. *to the peace of* [m] Heb. *blessed* [n] Heb. *Sanctify*

[p]house of Baal; and the house of Baal
was [o]full from one end to another.
22 And he said unto him that *was*
over the vestry, Bring forth vestments
for all the worshippers of Baal. And he
brought them forth vestments.
23 And Jehu went, and Jehonadab
the son of Rechab, into the house of
Baal, and said unto the worshippers of
Baal, Search, and look that there be
here with you none of the servants of
the LORD, but the worshippers of Baal
only.
24 And when they went in to offer
sacrifices and burnt offerings, Jehu ap-
pointed fourscore men without, and
said, *If* any of the men whom I have
brought into your hands escape, *he that*
letteth him go, [q]his life *shall be* for the
life of him.
25 And it came to pass, as soon as
he had made an end of offering the
burnt offering, that Jehu said to the
guard and to the captains, Go in, *and*
slay them; let none come forth. And
they smote them with [p]the edge of the
sword; and the guard and the captains
cast *them* out, and went to the city of
the house of Baal.
26 And they brought forth the [r]im-
ages[q] out of the house of Baal, and
burned them.
27 And they brake down the image
of Baal, and brake down the house of
Baal, [s]and made it a draught house
unto this day.
28 Thus Jehu destroyed Baal out of
Israel.
29 ¶ Howbeit *from* the sins of Jero-
boam the son of Nebat, who made Isra-
el to sin, Jehu departed not from after
them, *to wit,* [t]the golden calves that

10:21 [p]1 Ki. 16:32
10:24 [q]1 Ki. 20:39
10:26 [r]1 Ki. 14:23
10:27 [s]Ezra 6:11 Dan. 2:5 & 3:29
10:29 [t]1 Ki. 12:28,29
10:30 [u]See ver. 35 ch. 13:1,10 & 14:23 & 15:8,12
10:31 [v]1 Ki. 14:16
10:32 [w]ch. 8:12
10:33 [x]Amos 1:3
11:1 [y]2 Chr. 22:10 [z]ch. 8:26

were in Beth-el, and that *were* in Dan.
30 And the LORD said unto Jehu, Be-
cause thou hast done well in executing
that which is right in mine eyes, *and*
hast done unto the house of Ahab ac-
cording to all that *was* in mine heart,
[u]thy children of the fourth *generation*
shall sit on the throne of Israel.
31 But Jehu [r]took no heed to walk
in the law of the LORD God of Israel with
all his heart: for he departed not from
[v]the sins of Jeroboam, which made Is-
rael to sin.
32 ¶ In those days the LORD began
[s]to cut Israel short: and [w]Hazael
smote them in all the coasts of Israel;
33 From Jordan [t]eastward, all the
land of Gilead, the Gadites, and the
Reubenites, and the Manassites, from
Aroer, which *is* by the river Arnon,
[u]even [x]Gilead and Bashan.
34 Now the rest of the acts of Jehu,
and all that he did, and all his might,
are they not written in the book of the
chronicles of the kings of Israel?
35 And Jehu slept with his fathers:
and they buried him in Samaria. And
Jehoahaz his son reigned in his stead.
36 And [v]the time that Jehu reigned
over Israel in Samaria *was* twenty and
eight years.

Jehoash, king of Judah

11:1–21pp — 2 Chr. 22:10–23:21

11 AND WHEN [y]Athaliah [z]the
mother of Ahaziah saw that her

[o] Or, so *full,* that they stood *mouth to mouth* [p] Heb. *the mouth* [q] Heb. *statues* [r] Heb. *observed not* [s] Heb. *to cut off the ends* [t] Heb. *toward the rising of the sun* [u] Or, *even to Gilead and Bashan* [v] Heb. *the days* were

10:28 JEHU DESTROYED BAAL. Jehu had been chosen by God to destroy the idolatrous dynasty of Ahab (cf. v. 30; 9:6–10). Inherent in that call was the commission to eradicate Baalism, an unspeakably vile and cruel religion associated with fornication, drunkenness, and human sacrifice (vv. 18–28; see Judg. 2:13, note). The complete destruction of the house of Ahab and the religion of Baal was an act of mercy for the Israelites. Had both continued, Israel would have quickly become spiritually and morally ripe for judgment and destruction.

10:31 TOOK NO HEED TO WALK IN THE LAW OF THE LORD. Jehu, though zealous for God, did not serve Him with all his heart. He permitted the worship of the golden calves for political reasons (v. 29) and took little interest in God's law. Hence, the spiritual reformation that God had intended for Israel was hindered because of a leadership failure involving personal ambition and love of power. Great revivals and reformations die when self-seeking interest takes priority over God's purpose. Because Jehu served God out of motives tainted by carnal self-interest rather than out of sincere concern for truth and righteousness, God later punished his house (cf. Hos. 1:4).

11:1 ATHALIAH ... DESTROYED THE SEED ROYAL. Athaliah, the only non-Davidic ruler in Judah's history, was queen during a six-year reign of terror. This daughter of wicked Ahab and Jezebel had married Joram, the son of Judah's King Jehoshaphat. When King Ahaziah (see 9:27), the only son of Joram and Athaliah, was killed in Jehu's purge of Ahab's house during a visit in the north, the treacherous Athaliah mounted Judah's throne and attempted to purge it of David's descendants, including all her own grandsons. However Jehosheba, the wife of the high priest Je-

son was dead, she arose and destroyed all the [w]seed royal.

2 But [x]Jehosheba, the daughter of king Joram, sister of Ahaziah, took [y]Joash the son of Ahaziah, and stole him from among the king's sons *which were* slain; and they hid him, *even* him and his nurse, in the bedchamber from Athaliah, so that he was not slain.

3 And he was with her hid in the house of the LORD six years. And Athaliah did reign over the land.

4 ¶ And [a]the seventh year Jehoiada sent and fetched the rulers over hundreds, with the captains and the guard, and brought them to him into the house of the LORD, and made a covenant with them, and took an oath of them in the house of the LORD, and showed them the king's son.

5 And he commanded them, saying, This *is* the thing that ye shall do; A third part of you that enter in [b]on the sabbath shall even be keepers of the watch of the king's house;

6 And a third part *shall be* at the gate of Sur; and a third part at the gate behind the guard: so shall ye keep the watch of the house, [z]that it be not broken down.

7 And two [a] [b]parts of all you that go forth on the sabbath, even they shall keep the watch of the house of the LORD about the king.

8 And ye shall compass the king round about, every man with his weapons in his hand: and he that cometh within the ranges, let him be slain: and be ye with the king as he goeth out and as he cometh in.

9 [c]And the captains over the hundreds did according to all *things* that Jehoiada the priest commanded: and they took every man his men that were to come in on the sabbath, with them that should go out on the sabbath, and came to Jehoiada the priest.

10 And to the captains over hundreds did the priest give king David's spears and shields, [d]that *were* in the temple of the LORD.

11 And the guard stood, every man with his weapons in his hand, round about the king, from the right [c]corner of the temple to the left corner of the temple, *along* by the altar and the temple.

12 And he brought forth the king's son, and put the crown upon him, and *gave him* the testimony; and they made him king, and anointed him; and they clapped their hands, and said, [e]God [d]save the king.

13 ¶ [f]And when Athaliah heard the noise of the guard *and* of the people, she came to the people into the temple of the LORD.

14 And when she looked, behold, the king stood by [g]a pillar, as the manner *was*, and the princes and the trumpeters by the king, and all the people of the land rejoiced, and blew with trumpets: and Athaliah rent her clothes, and cried, Treason, Treason.

15 But Jehoiada the priest commanded the captains of the hundreds, the officers of the host, and said unto them, Have her forth without the ranges: and him that followeth her kill with the sword. For the priest had said, Let her not be slain in the house of the LORD.

16 And they laid hands on her; and she went by the way by the which the horses came into the king's house: and there was she slain.

17 ¶ [h]And Jehoiada made a covenant between the LORD and the king and the people, that they should be the LORD's people; [i]between the king also and the people.

18 And all the people of the land went into the [j]house of Baal, and brake it down; his altars and his images [k]brake they in pieces thoroughly, and slew Mattan the priest of Baal before the altars. And [l]the priest ap-

11:4 [a]2 Chr. 23:1 **11:5** [b]1 Chr. 9:25 **11:9** [c]2 Chr. 23:8 **11:10** [d]2 Sam. 8:7

11:12 [e]1 Sam. 10:24 **11:13** [f]2 Chr. 23:12 **11:14** [g]ch. 23:3 2 Chr. 34:31 **11:17** [h]2 Chr. 23:16 [i]2 Sam. 5:3 **11:18** [j]ch. 10:26 [k]Deut. 12:3 2 Chr. 23:17 [l]2 Chr. 23:18

[w]Heb. *seed of the kingdom* [x]*Jehoshabeath* in 2 Chr. 22:11 [y]Or, *Jehoash* [z]Or, *from breaking up* [a]Or, *companies* [b]Heb. *hands* [c]Heb. *shoulder* [d]Heb. *Let the king live*

hoiada, hid the infant son of Ahaziah named Joash and thereby preserved the Davidic line, from which the Messiah would be born (vv. 2–3; 2 Sam. 7:11, 16; 1 Ki. 8:25; cf. Mat. 1:8–9).

11:4 JEHOIADA. Jehoiada, the husband of Jehosheba, was the high priest of the Lord during the rule of Athaliah in the southern kingdom (v. 2; cf. 2 Chr. 22:11). He instigated Athaliah's overthrow (cf. 2 Chr. 23), set Joash on the throne, and guided him in devotion and loyalty to the Lord (v. 12; 2 Chr. 23:11). What Jehoiada did preserved the Messianic line. He effectively directed the young king Joash in renewing the covenant between the Lord and His people and in destroying the religion of Baal (vv. 17–18).

pointed [e]officers over the house of the
LORD.
19 And he took the rulers over hun-
dreds, and the captains, and the guard,
and all the people of the land; and they
brought down the king from the house
of the LORD, and came by the way of the
gate of the guard to the king's house.
And he sat on the throne of the kings.
20 And all the people of the land re-
joiced, and the city was in quiet: and
they slew Athaliah with the sword *be-*
side the king's house.
21 [m]Seven years old *was* Jehoash
when he began to reign.

12:1–21pp — 2 Chr. 24:1–14; 24:23–27

12 IN THE seventh year of Jehu
[n]Jehoash began to reign; and
forty years reigned he in Jerusalem.
And his mother's name *was* Zibiah of
Beer-sheba.
2 And Jehoash did *that which was*
right in the sight of the LORD all his
days wherein Jehoiada the priest in-
structed him.
3 But [o]the high places were not
taken away: the people still sacrificed
and burnt incense in the high places.

Jehoash repairs the temple

4 ¶ And Jehoash said to the priests,
[p]All the money of the [f] [g]dedicated
things that is brought into the house of
the LORD, *even* [q]the money of every one
that passeth *the account,* [h]the money
that every man is set at, *and* all the
money that [r]cometh[i] into any man's
heart to bring into the house of the
LORD,
5 Let the priests take *it* to them, ev-
ery man of his acquaintance: and let
them repair the breaches of the house,
wheresoever any breach shall be
found.
6 But it was *so, that* [j]in the three
and twentieth year of king Jehoash
[s]the priests had not repaired the
breaches of the house.
7 [t]Then king Jehoash called for Je-
hoiada the priest, and the *other* priests,
and said unto them, Why repair ye not
the breaches of the house? now there-
fore receive no *more* money of your ac-
quaintance, but deliver it for the
breaches of the house.
8 And the priests consented to re-
ceive no *more* money of the people, nei-
ther to repair the breaches of the
house.
9 But Jehoiada the priest took [u]a
chest, and bored a hole in the lid of it,
and set it beside the altar, on the right
side as one cometh into the house of
the LORD: and the priests that kept the
[k]door put therein all the money *that*
was brought into the house of the LORD.
10 And it was *so,* when they saw
that *there was* much money in the
chest, that the king's [l]scribe and the
high priest came up, and they [m]put up
in bags, and told the money that was
found in the house of the LORD.
11 And they gave the money, being
told, into the hands of them that did
the work, that had the oversight of the
house of the LORD: and they [n]laid it
out to the carpenters and builders, that
wrought upon the house of the LORD,
12 And to masons, and hewers of
stone, and to buy timber and hewed
stone to repair the breaches of the
house of the LORD, and for all that
[o]was laid out for the house to repair
it.
13 Howbeit [v]there were not made
for the house of the LORD bowls of sil-
ver, snuffers, basins, trumpets, any
vessels of gold, or vessels of silver, of
the money *that was* brought into the
house of the LORD:
14 But they gave that to the work-
men, and repaired therewith the house
of the LORD.
15 Moreover [w]they reckoned not
with the men, into whose hand they de-
livered the money to be bestowed on
workmen: for they dealt faithfully.
16 [x]The trespass money and sin

11:21 [m]2 Chr. 24:1
12:1 [n]2 Chr. 24:1
12:3 [o]1 Ki. 15:14 & 22:43 ch. 14:4
12:4 [p]ch. 22:4 [q]Ex. 30:13 [r]Ex. 35:5 1 Chr. 29:9
12:6 [s]2 Chr. 24:5
12:7 [t]2 Chr. 24:6
12:9 [u]2 Chr. 24:8
12:13 [v]See 2 Chr. 24:14
12:15 [w]ch. 22:7
12:16 [x]Lev. 5:15,18

[e] Heb. *offices* [f] Or, *holy things* [g] Heb. *holinesses* [h] Heb. *the money of the souls of his estimation* [i] Heb. *ascendeth upon the heart of a man* [j] Heb. *in the twentieth year and third year* [k] Heb. *threshold* [l] Or, *secretary* [m] Heb. *bound up* [n] Heb. *brought it forth* [o] Heb. *went forth*

12:2 JEHOASH. As long as Jehoiada the high priest was his counselor, Jehoash (Joash) served the Lord. However, after Jehoiada's death, Jehoash forsook the Lord and began to serve idols (2 Chr. 24:17–18). He multiplied his sin by murdering Zechariah, the son of Jehoiada, who had condemned him for forsaking the Lord (2 Chr. 24:20–22). In just recompense, Jehoash was killed by his own servants for this murder (v. 20; 2 Chr. 24:25; see next note). Jehoash began well as king but ended in spiritual ruin (cf. Mat. 24:13; Gal. 3:3; Rev. 2:10).

money was not brought into the house
of the LORD: [y]it was the priests'.
17 ¶ Then [z]Hazael king of Syria
went up, and fought against Gath, and
took it: and [a]Hazael set his face to go
up to Jerusalem.
18 And Jehoash king of Judah
[b]took all the hallowed things that Je-
hoshaphat, and Jehoram, and Ahaziah,
his fathers, kings of Judah, had dedi-
cated, and his own hallowed things,
and all the gold *that was* found in the
treasures of the house of the LORD, and
in the king's house, and sent *it* to Haza-
el king of Syria: and he [p]went away
from Jerusalem.
19 ¶ And the rest of the acts of Jo-
ash, and all that he did, *are* they not
written in the book of the chronicles of
the kings of Judah?
20 And [c]his servants arose, and
made a conspiracy, and slew Joash in
the [q]house of Millo, which goeth
down to Silla.
21 For [d]Jozachar the son of Shime-
ath, and Jehozabad the son of [r]Sho-
mer, his servants, smote him, and he
died; and they buried him with his fa-
thers in the city of David: and [e]Amazi-
ah his son reigned in his stead.

Jehoahaz, king of Israel

13 IN [s]THE three and twentieth
year of Joash the son of Ahazi-
ah king of Judah Jehoahaz the son of
Jehu began to reign over Israel in Sa-
maria, *and reigned* seventeen years.
2 And he did *that which was* evil in
the sight of the LORD, and [t]followed
the sins of Jeroboam the son of Nebat,
which made Israel to sin; he departed
not therefrom.
3 ¶ And [f]the anger of the LORD was
kindled against Israel, and he deliv-
ered them into the hand of [g]Hazael
king of Syria, and into the hand of Ben-
hadad the son of Hazael, all *their* days.
4 And Jehoahaz [h]besought the
LORD, and the LORD hearkened unto
him: for [i]he saw the oppression of Is-
rael, because the king of Syria op-
pressed them.
5 ([j]And the LORD gave Israel a sav-
iour, so that they went out from under
the hand of the Syrians: and the chil-
dren of Israel dwelt in their tents, [u]as
beforetime.
6 Nevertheless they departed not
from the sins of the house of Jeroboam,
who made Israel sin, *but* [v]walked
therein: [k]and there [w]remained the
grove also in Samaria.)
7 Neither did he leave of the people
to Jehoahaz but fifty horsemen, and ten
chariots, and ten thousand footmen;
for the king of Syria had destroyed
them, [l]and had made them like the
dust by threshing.
8 ¶ Now the rest of the acts of Jeho-
ahaz, and all that he did, and his might,
are they not written in the book of the
chronicles of the kings of Israel?
9 And Jehoahaz slept with his fa-
thers; and they buried him in Samaria:
and [x]Joash his son reigned [y]in his
stead.

Jehoash, king of Israel

10 ¶ In the thirty and seventh year
of Joash king of Judah began [z]Jehoash
the son of Jehoahaz to reign over Israel
in Samaria, *and reigned* sixteen years.
11 And he did *that which was* evil in
the sight of the LORD; he departed not
from all the sins of Jeroboam the son of
Nebat, who made Israel sin: *but* he
walked therein.
12 [m]And the rest of the acts of Jo-
ash, and [n]all that he did, and [o]his
might wherewith he fought against
Amaziah king of Judah, *are* they not
written in the book of the chronicles of
the kings of Israel?
13 And Joash slept with his fathers;
and Jeroboam sat upon his throne: and
Joash was buried in Samaria with the
kings of Israel.

The death of Elisha

14 ¶ Now Elisha was fallen sick of
his sickness whereof he died. And Jo-

12:16 [y]Lev. 7:7 Num. 18:9
12:17 [z]ch. 8:12 [a]See 2 Chr. 24:23
12:18 [b]1 Ki. 15:18 ch. 18:15,16
12:20 [c]ch. 14:5 2 Chr. 24:25
12:21 [d]2 Chr. 24:26 *Zabad* [e]2 Chr. 24:27
13:3 [f]Judg. 2:14 [g]ch. 8:12
13:4 [h]Ps. 78:34 [i]Ex. 3:7 ch. 14:26
13:5 [j]See ver. 25 ch. 14:25,27
13:6 [k]1 Ki. 16:33
13:7 [l]Amos 1:3
13:12 [m]ch. 14:15 [n]See ver. 14 & 25 [o]ch. 14:9 2 Chr. 25:17

[p]Heb. *went up* [q]Or, *Beth-millo* [r]Or, *Shimrith* [s]Heb. *the twentieth year and third year* [t]Heb. *walked after* [u]Heb. *as yesterday, and third day* [v]Heb. *he walked* [w]Heb. *stood* [x]*Jehoash* in ver. 10 [y]Alone [z]In consort with his father; see ch. 14:1

12:20 SLEW JOASH. The conspiracy against Joash occurred because he had rejected the Lord, begun to worship other gods, and killed the high priest, Zechariah (2 Chr. 24:17–22,25).

13:14 ELISHA WAS FALLEN SICK. Elisha, through whom God had performed many wonderful miracles, eventually succumbed to a fatal illness. Reality dictates that great people of faith die, and ironically death sometimes comes through sickness even to those who have themselves had a healing ministry. Among the consequences of the fall of Adam and Eve are sickness and death; no

ash the king of Israel came down unto
him, and wept over his face, and said,
O my father, my father, [p]the chariot
of Israel, and the horsemen thereof.
15 And Elisha said unto him, Take
bow and arrows. And he took unto him
bow and arrows.
16 And he said to the king of Israel,
[a]Put thine hand upon the bow. And he
put his hand *upon it:* and Elisha put his
hands upon the king's hands.
17 And he said, Open the window
eastward. And he opened *it.* Then Eli-
sha said, Shoot. And he shot. And he
said, The arrow of the LORD's deliver-
ance, and the arrow of deliverance
from Syria: for thou shalt smite the
Syrians in [q]Aphek, till thou have con-
sumed *them.*
18 And he said, Take the arrows.
And he took *them.* And he said unto the
king of Israel, Smite upon the ground.
And he smote thrice, and stayed.
19 And the man of God was wroth
with him, and said, Thou shouldest
have smitten five or six times; then
hadst thou smitten Syria till thou hadst
consumed *it:* [r]whereas now thou shalt
smite Syria *but* thrice.
20 ¶ And Elisha died, and they bur-
ied him. And the bands of the Moabites
invaded the land at the coming in of the
year.
21 And it came to pass, as they
were burying a man, that, behold, they
spied a band *of men;* and they cast the
man into the sepulchre of Elisha: and
when the man [b]was let down, and
touched the bones of Elisha, he re-
vived, and stood up on his feet.
22 ¶ But [s]Hazael king of Syria op-
pressed Israel all the days of Jehoahaz.
23 And the LORD was gracious unto
them, and had compassion on them,
and [t]had respect unto them, [u]be-
cause of his covenant with Abraham,
Isaac, and Jacob, and would not de-
stroy them, neither cast he them from
his [c]presence as yet.
24 So Hazael king of Syria died; and
Ben-hadad his son reigned in his stead.
25 And Jehoash the son of Jehoahaz
[d]took again out of the hand of Ben-ha-
dad the son of Hazael the cities, which
he had taken out of the hand of Jehoa-
haz his father by war. [v]Three times
did Joash beat him, and recovered the
cities of Israel.

13:14 [p]ch. 2:12
13:17 [q]1 Ki. 20:26
13:19 [r]ver. 25
13:22 [s]ch. 8:12
13:23 [t]Ex. 2:24,25 [u]Ex. 32:13
13:25 [v]ver. 18,19
14:1 [w]ch. 13:10 [x]2 Chr. 25:1
14:4 [y]ch. 12:3

Amaziah, king of Judah

14:1–7pp — 2 Chr. 25:1–4,11–12
14:8–22pp — 2 Chr. 25:17–26:2

14 IN [w]THE second year of Joash
son of Jehoahaz king of Israel
reigned [x]Amaziah the son of Joash
king of Judah.
2 He was twenty and five years old
when he began to reign, and reigned
twenty and nine years in Jerusalem.
And his mother's name *was* Jehoaddan
of Jerusalem.
3 And he did *that which was* right in
the sight of the LORD, yet not like David
his father: he did according to all
things as Joash his father did.
4 [y]Howbeit the high places were
not taken away: as yet the people did
sacrifice and burnt incense on the high
places.

[a] Heb. *Make thine hand to ride* [b] Heb. *went down* [c] Heb. *face* [d] Heb. *returned and took*

one is exempt from them.

13:14 THE CHARIOT OF ISRAEL, AND THE HORSEMEN THEREOF. King Joash recognized Elisha's God as the real defender of Israel (cf. 2:12). Joash knew beyond a doubt that with the death of Elisha, the strength and protection of Israel would be gone. In any age when there is no prophetic word to God's people, spiritual death and apostasy are sure to occur (cf. Jer. 21—22; see article on THE MINISTRY GIFTS OF THE CHURCH, p. 1852).

13:17–18 EASTWARD . . . THE ARROW. The shooting of the arrow toward the east (i.e., the area held by Syria, 10:32–33) was a symbolic action predicting that Israel was going to overthrow the oppression of Syria. It was a pledge that God would keep Israel safe. By striking the ground with arrows only three times, King Jehoash demonstrated that he lacked the zeal, commitment, and faith necessary for the Lord to fulfill His promise. Consequently, he would not completely defeat the Syrians (v. 19).

13:21 TOUCHED THE BONES OF ELISHA, HE REVIVED. Elisha died and was buried, but even in the grave God manifested His power as a testimony to Elisha's character as a life-giving prophet (cf. 4:32–37; 1 Ki. 17:17–24). This miracle suggests that the influence of a godly person does not necessarily cease at death but can yet be a source of spiritual life for others (cf. John 12:24; 2 Cor. 4:11–12).

14:1 AMAZIAH. This king began well, but later fell into idolatry (2 Chr. 25:14), for he did not have "a perfect heart" (2 Chr. 25:2); i.e., he had not firmly resolved to do God's will at any cost. Essential to perseverance in the faith is an unwavering intention to remain faithful to God and His commandments until the end of our time on this earth, regardless of what may happen to us (Phil. 3:8–16).

5 ¶ And it came to pass, as soon as the kingdom was confirmed in his hand, that he slew his servants [z]which had slain the king his father.

6 But the children of the murderers he slew not: according unto that which is written in the book of the law of Moses, wherein the LORD commanded, saying, [a]The fathers shall not be put to death for the children, nor the children be put to death for the fathers; but every man shall be put to death for his own sin.

7 [b]He slew of Edom in [c]the valley of salt ten thousand, and took [e]Selah by war, [d]and called the name of it Joktheel unto this day.

8 ¶ [e]Then Amaziah sent messengers to Jehoash, the son of Jehoahaz son of Jehu, king of Israel, saying, Come, let us look one another in the face.

9 And Jehoash the king of Israel sent to Amaziah king of Judah, saying, [f]The thistle that *was* in Lebanon sent to the [g]cedar that *was* in Lebanon, saying, Give thy daughter to my son to wife: and there passed by a wild beast that *was* in Lebanon, and trode down the thistle.

10 Thou hast indeed smitten Edom, and [h]thine heart hath lifted thee up: glory *of this,* and tarry [f]at home: for why shouldest thou meddle to *thy* hurt, that thou shouldest fall, *even* thou, and Judah with thee?

11 But Amaziah would not hear. Therefore Jehoash king of Israel went up; and he and Amaziah king of Judah looked one another in the face at [i]Beth-shemesh, which *belongeth* to Judah.

12 And Judah [g]was put to the worse before Israel; and they fled every man to their tents.

13 And Jehoash king of Israel took Amaziah king of Judah, the son of Jehoash the son of Ahaziah, at Beth-shemesh, and came to Jerusalem, and brake down the wall of Jerusalem from [j]the gate of Ephraim unto [k]the corner gate, four hundred cubits.

14 And he took all [l]the gold and silver, and all the vessels that were found in the house of the LORD, and in the treasures of the king's house, and hostages, and returned to Samaria.

15 ¶ [m]Now the rest of the acts of Jehoash which he did, and his might, and how he fought with Amaziah king of Judah, *are* they not written in the book of the chronicles of the kings of Israel?

16 And Jehoash slept with his fathers, and was buried in Samaria with the kings of Israel; and Jeroboam his son reigned in his stead.

17 ¶ [n]And Amaziah the son of Joash king of Judah lived after the death of Jehoash son of Jehoahaz king of Israel fifteen years.

18 And the rest of the acts of Amaziah, *are* they not written in the book of the chronicles of the kings of Judah?

19 Now [o]they made a conspiracy against him in Jerusalem: and he fled to [p]Lachish; but they sent after him to Lachish, and slew him there.

20 And they brought him on horses: and he was buried at Jerusalem with his fathers in the city of David.

21 ¶ And all the people of Judah took [q]Azariah, which *was* sixteen years old, and made him king instead of his father Amaziah.

22 He built [r]Elath, and restored it to Judah, after that the king slept with his fathers.

Jeroboam II, king of Israel

23 ¶ In the fifteenth year of Amaziah the son of Joash king of Judah Jeroboam the son of Joash king of Israel began to reign in Samaria, *and reigned* forty and one years.

24 And he did *that which was* evil in the sight of the LORD: he departed not from all the sins of Jeroboam the son of Nebat, who made Israel to sin.

25 He restored the coast of Israel [s]from the entering of Hamath unto

14:5 [z]ch. 12:20
14:6 [a]Deut. 24:16 Ezek. 18:4,20
14:7 [b]2 Chr. 25:11 [c]2 Sam. 8:13 Ps. 60,title [d]Josh. 15:38
14:8 [e]2 Chr. 25:17,18
14:9 [f]See Judg. 9:8 [g]1 Ki. 4:33
14:10 [h]Deut. 8:14 2 Chr. 32:25 Ezek. 28:2,5,17 Hab. 2:4
14:11 [i]Josh. 19:38 & 21:16
14:13 [j]Neh. 8:16 & 12:39 [k]Jer. 31:38 Zech. 14:10
14:14 [l]1 Ki. 7:51
14:15 [m]ch. 13:12
14:17 [n]2 Chr. 25:25
14:19 [o]2 Chr. 25:27 [p]Josh. 10:31
14:21 [q]ch. 15:13 & 2 Chr. 26:1, he is called *Uzziah*
14:22 [r]ch. 16:6 2 Chr. 26:2
14:25 [s]Num. 13:21 & 34:8

[e] Or, *The rock was smitten* [f] Heb. *at thy house* [g] Heb.

14:25 HE RESTORED THE COAST OF ISRAEL. Israel regained land and the people attained great material prosperity during the reign of Jeroboam II (cf. Amos 6:4–6; Hos. 12:8). However, the prophets Amos and Hosea, who ministered to Israel during his reign, saw clearly the rotten foundations on which Israel's prosperity was built and foretold Israel's approaching doom in no uncertain terms. In reality, the prosperity that occurred during the reign of Jeroboam II contributed to the spiritual complacency, moral degeneracy, social injustice, and religious apostasy that brought Israel's downfall about twenty-eight years later (see v. 26, note).

14:25 JONAH. Jonah, the son of Amittai, is the well-known prophet who was swallowed by a great

[t]the sea of the plain, according to the word of the LORD God of Israel, which he spake by the hand of his servant [u]Jonah, the son of Amittai, the prophet, which *was* of [v]Gath-hepher.

26 For the LORD [w]saw the affliction of Israel, *that it was* very bitter: for [x]*there was* not any shut up, nor any left, nor any helper for Israel.

27 [y]And the LORD said not that he would blot out the name of Israel from under heaven: but he saved them by the hand of Jeroboam the son of Joash.

28 ¶ Now the rest of the acts of Jeroboam, and all that he did, and his might, how he warred, and how he recovered Damascus, and Hamath, [z]*which belonged* to Judah, for Israel, *are* they not written in the book of the chronicles of the kings of Israel?

29 And Jeroboam slept with his fathers, *even* with the kings of Israel; and [a]Zachariah his son reigned in his stead.

Azariah, king of Judah

15:1–7pp — 2 Chr. 26:3–4,21–23

15 IN THE twenty and seventh year of Jeroboam king of Israel [b]began [c]Azariah son of Amaziah king of Judah to reign.

2 Sixteen years old was he when he began to reign, and he reigned two and fifty years in Jerusalem. And his mother's name *was* Jecholiah of Jerusalem.

3 And he did *that which was* right in the sight of the LORD, according to all that his father Amaziah had done;

4 [d]Save that the high places were not removed: the people sacrificed and burnt incense still on the high places.

5 ¶ And the LORD [e]smote the king, so that he was a leper unto the day of his death, and [f]dwelt in a several house. And Jotham the king's son *was* over the house, judging the people of the land.

6 And the rest of the acts of Azariah, and all that he did, *are* they not written in the book of the chronicles of the kings of Judah?

7 So Azariah slept with his fathers; and [g]they buried him with his fathers in the city of David: and Jotham his son reigned in his stead.

Zechariah, king of Israel

8 ¶ In the thirty and eighth year of Azariah king of Judah did Zachariah the son of Jeroboam reign over Israel in Samaria six months.

9 And he did *that which was* evil in the sight of the LORD, as his fathers had done: he departed not from the sins of Jeroboam the son of Nebat, who made Israel to sin.

10 And Shallum the son of Jabesh conspired against him, and [h]smote him before the people, and slew him, and reigned in his stead.

11 And the rest of the acts of Zachariah, behold, they *are* written in the book of the chronicles of the kings of Israel.

12 This *was* [i]the word of the LORD which he spake unto Jehu, saying, Thy sons shall sit on the throne of Israel unto the fourth *generation.* And so it came to pass.

Shallum, king of Israel

13 ¶ Shallum the son of Jabesh began to reign in the nine and thirtieth

14:25 [t]Deut. 3:17 [u]Jonah 1:1 Mat. 12:39,40, called *Jonas* [v]Josh. 19:13
14:26 [w]ch. 13:4 [x]Deut. 32:36
14:27 [y]ch. 13:5
14:28 [z]2 Sam. 8:6 1 Ki. 11:24 2 Chr. 8:3
14:29 [a]After an interregnum of 11 years ch. 15:8
15:1 [b]ch. 14:21 2 Chr. 26:1,3,4 [c]Called *Uzziah* ver. 13,30 2 Chr. 26:1
15:4 [d]ver. 35 ch. 12:3 & 14:4
15:5 [e]2 Chr. 26:19-21 [f]Lev. 13:46
15:7 [g]2 Chr. 26:23
15:10 [h]As prophesied, Amos 7:9
15:12 [i]ch. 10:30

---

fish and who brought God's message of repentance to the Assyrians (Jonah 1:1,17; 3:1–10). He lived and prophesied during the reign of Jeroboam II and was a contemporary of Hosea and Amos.

14:26 THE LORD SAW THE AFFLICTION OF ISRAEL. In compassion for His people, God used Jeroboam to help Israel (vv. 26–27). (1) However, God's goodness did not lead them to repentance. The time of Israel's prosperity was also a time of corruption spiritually, morally, and socially. Both Amos and Hosea (see v. 25, note) spoke of a people deeply depraved. Luxury, debauchery, immorality, injustice, violence, and deceit of all kinds were the normal way of life (Amos 2:6–8; 3:9; 5:11–13; 6:4–7). About this period of Israel's history, Hosea wrote: "*There is* no truth, nor mercy, nor knowledge of God in the land. By swearing, and lying, and killing, and stealing, and committing adultery, they break out, and blood toucheth blood" (Hos. 4:1–2).

(2) This was an agonizing time for both God and His prophets (Hos. 1:1–2; 3:1–5; 11:1–12). The prophets spoke, but Israel would not hear. Therefore, the Lord caused Israel to be "carried away out of their own land to Assyria" (17:23).

15:1 AZARIAH. Azariah, also called Uzziah (2 Chr. 26), was king of Judah for fifty-two years (v. 2). The very year that he died, God commissioned the prophet Isaiah as a messenger to Judah and Israel (Is. 6; see 2 Chr. 26 for more details about Azariah's life).

15:5 THE LORD SMOTE THE KING. Azariah was struck with leprosy because (1) he disobeyed God by assuming the function of the priesthood, and (2) in pride he refused to repent of his presumptuous sin (see 2 Chr. 26:16–21).

year of [j]Uzziah king of Judah; and he reigned [h]a full month in Samaria.

14 For Menahem the son of Gadi went up from [k]Tirzah, and came to Samaria, and smote Shallum the son of Jabesh in Samaria, and slew him, and reigned in his stead.

15 And the rest of the acts of Shallum, and his conspiracy which he made, behold, they *are* written in the book of the chronicles of the kings of Israel.

16 ¶ Then Menahem smote [l]Tiphsah, and all that *were* therein, and the coasts thereof from Tirzah: because they opened not *to him,* therefore he smote *it; and* all [m]the women therein that were with child he ripped up.

Menahem, king of Israel

17 In the nine and thirtieth year of Azariah king of Judah began Menahem the son of Gadi to reign over Israel, *and reigned* ten years in Samaria.

18 And he did *that which was* evil in the sight of the LORD: he departed not all his days from the sins of Jeroboam the son of Nebat, who made Israel to sin.

19 *And* [n]Pul the king of Assyria came against the land: and Menahem gave Pul a thousand talents of silver, that his hand might be with him to [o]confirm the kingdom in his hand.

20 And Menahem [i]exacted the money of Israel, *even* of all the mighty men of wealth, of each man fifty shekels of silver, to give to the king of Assyria. So the king of Assyria turned back, and stayed not there in the land.

21 ¶ And the rest of the acts of Menahem, and all that he did, *are* they not written in the book of the chronicles of the kings of Israel?

22 And Menahem slept with his fathers; and Pekahiah his son reigned in his stead.

Pekahiah, king of Israel

23 ¶ In the fiftieth year of Azariah king of Judah Pekahiah the son of Menahem began to reign over Israel in Samaria, *and reigned* two years.

24 And he did *that which was* evil in the sight of the LORD: he departed not from the sins of Jeroboam the son of Nebat, who made Israel to sin.

25 But Pekah the son of Remaliah, a captain of his, conspired against him, and smote him in Samaria, in the palace of the king's house, with Argob and Arieh, and with him fifty men of the Gileadites: and he killed him, and reigned in his room.

26 And the rest of the acts of Pekahiah, and all that he did, behold, they *are* written in the book of the chronicles of the kings of Israel.

Pekah, king of Israel

27 ¶ In the two and fiftieth year of Azariah king of Judah [p]Pekah the son of Remaliah began to reign over Israel in Samaria, *and reigned* twenty years.

28 And he did *that which was* evil in the sight of the LORD: he departed not from the sins of Jeroboam the son of Nebat, who made Israel to sin.

29 In the days of Pekah king of Israel [q]came Tiglath-pileser king of Assyria, and took [r]Ijon, and Abel-beth-maachah, and Janoah, and Kedesh, and Hazor, and Gilead, and Galilee, all the land of Naphtali, and carried them captive to Assyria.

30 And Hoshea the son of Elah made a conspiracy against Pekah the son of Remaliah, and smote him, and slew him, and [s]reigned in his stead, [t]in the twentieth year of Jotham the son of Uzziah.

31 And the rest of the acts of Pekah, and all that he did, behold, they *are* written in the book of the chronicles of the kings of Israel.

15:13 [j]Mat. 1:8,9 called *Ozias* and ver. 1 *Azariah*
15:14 [k]1 Ki. 14:17
15:16 [l]1 Ki. 4:24 [m]ch. 8:12
15:19 [n]1 Chr. 5:26 Is. 66:19 Hos. 8:9 [o]ch. 14:5
15:27 [p]Is. 7:1
15:29 [q]1 Chr. 5:26 Is. 9:1 [r]1 Ki. 15:20
15:30 [s]After an anarchy for some years ch. 17:1 Hos. 10:3,7,15 [t]in the fourth year of Ahaz, in the twentieth year after Jotham had begun to reign: *Ush*

[h] Heb. *a month of days* [i] Heb. *caused to come forth*

15:16 WOMEN . . . HE RIPPED UP. Some of the kings of Israel committed the most barbarous atrocities (see Is. 13:18; Hos. 10:14; 13:16; Amos 1:13). Furthermore, God had predicted that Israel's kings would lead God's people into apostasy (see 1 Sam. 8:7; 10:19). By now, Israel had become so evil that her doom and destruction were imminent (see next note).

15:29 CARRIED THEM CAPTIVE TO ASSYRIA. This invasion by Tiglath-pileser III of Assyria (733 B.C.) represented the first stage of Israel's captivity in exile. Those living in the northern and eastern sections of Israel were carried away from their homeland into Mesopotamia (cf. 16:5–9; 2 Chr. 28:16–21; Is. 7:1–17). This beginning of the end for the northern kingdom came as a result of God's judgment for their continued sin. Samaria, the capital of the northern kingdom, was captured eleven years later (17:6).

Jotham, king of Judah

15:33–38pp — 2 Chr. 27:1–4,7–9

32 ¶ In the second year of Pekah the son of Remaliah king of Israel began [u]Jotham the son of Uzziah king of Judah to reign.

33 Five and twenty years old was he when he began to reign, and he reigned sixteen years in Jerusalem. And his mother's name *was* Jerusha, the daughter of Zadok.

34 And he did *that which was* right in the sight of the LORD: he did [v]according to all that his father Uzziah had done.

35 ¶ [w]Howbeit the high places were not removed: the people sacrificed and burned incense still in the high places. [x]He built the higher gate of the house of the LORD.

36 ¶ Now the rest of the acts of Jotham, and all that he did, *are* they not written in the book of the chronicles of the kings of Judah?

37 In those days the LORD began to send against Judah [y]Rezin the king of Syria, and [z]Pekah the son of Remaliah.

38 And Jotham slept with his fathers, and was buried with his fathers in the city of David his father: and Ahaz his son reigned in his stead.

Ahaz, king of Judah

16:1–20pp — 2 Chr. 28:1–27

16 IN THE seventeenth year of Pekah the son of Remaliah [a]Ahaz the son of Jotham king of Judah began to reign.

2 Twenty years old *was* Ahaz when he began to reign, and reigned sixteen years in Jerusalem, and did not *that which was* right in the sight of the LORD his God, like David his father.

3 But he walked in the way of the kings of Israel, yea, [b]and made his son to pass through the fire, according to the [c]abominations of the heathen, whom the LORD cast out from before the children of Israel.

4 And he sacrificed and burnt incense in the high places, and [d]on the hills, and under every green tree.

5 ¶ [e]Then Rezin king of Syria and Pekah son of Remaliah king of Israel came up to Jerusalem to war: and they besieged Ahaz, but could not overcome *him*.

6 At that time Rezin king of Syria [f]recovered Elath to Syria, and drave the Jews from [j]Elath: and the Syrians came to Elath, and dwelt there unto this day.

7 So Ahaz sent messengers [g]to [k]Tiglath-pileser king of Assyria, saying, I *am* thy servant and thy son: come up, and save me out of the hand of the king of Syria, and out of the hand of the king of Israel, which rise up against me.

8 And Ahaz [h]took the silver and gold that was found in the house of the LORD, and in the treasures of the king's house, and sent *it for* a present to the king of Assyria.

9 And the king of Assyria hearkened unto him: for the king of Assyria went up against [l]Damascus, and [i]took it, and carried *the people of* it captive to Kir, and slew Rezin.

10 ¶ And king Ahaz went to Damascus to meet Tiglath-pileser king of Assyria, and saw an altar that *was* at Damascus: and king Ahaz sent to Urijah the priest the fashion of the altar, and the pattern of it, according to all the workmanship thereof.

11 And Urijah the priest built an altar according to all that king Ahaz had sent from Damascus: so Urijah the priest made *it* against king Ahaz came from Damascus.

12 And when the king was come from Damascus, the king saw the altar: and [j]the king approached to the altar, and offered thereon.

13 And he burnt his burnt offering and his meat offering, and poured his drink offering, and sprinkled the blood

15:32 [u]2 Chr. 27:1
15:34 [v]ver. 3
15:35 [w]ver. 4 [x]2 Chr. 27:3
15:37 [y]ch. 16:5 Is. 7:1 [z]ver. 27
16:1 [a]2 Chr. 28:1
16:3 [b]Lev. 18:21 2 Chr. 28:3 Ps. 106:37,38 [c]Deut. 12:31
16:4 [d]Deut. 12:2 1 Ki. 14:23
16:5 [e]Is. 7:1,4
16:6 [f]ch. 14:22
16:7 [g]ch. 15:29
16:8 [h]ch. 12:18 See 2 Chr. 28:21
16:9 [i]Foretold Amos 1:5
16:12 [j]2 Chr. 26:16,19

[j] Heb. *Eloth* [k] Heb. *Tilgath-pileser;* 1 Chr. 5:26 & 2 Chr. 28:20 have *Tilgath-pilneser*
[l] Heb. *Dammesek*

16:3 MADE HIS SON TO PASS THROUGH THE FIRE. Under the reign of Ahaz, Judah entered into a dark time of spiritual chaos and corruption. Apostasy reached such depths that the king himself performed the pagan religious practice of sacrificing children by fire to pagan gods (cf. Lev. 18:21; 2 Chr. 28:3; Jer. 19:5).

16:9 ASSYRIA WENT UP AGAINST DAMASCUS. See the prophecy of Amos concerning the Assyrian capture of Damascus (Amos 1:3–5; cf. Is. 8:4; 17:1).

of [m]his peace offerings, upon the altar.

14 And he brought also [k]the brasen altar, which *was* before the LORD, from the forefront of the house, from between the altar and the house of the LORD, and put it on the north side of the altar.

15 And king Ahaz commanded Urijah the priest, saying, Upon the great altar burn [l]the morning burnt offering, and the evening meat offering, and the king's burnt sacrifice, and his meat offering, with the burnt offering of all the people of the land, and their meat offering, and their drink offerings; and sprinkle upon it all the blood of the burnt offering, and all the blood of the sacrifice: and the brasen altar shall be for me to inquire *by*.

16 Thus did Urijah the priest, according to all that king Ahaz commanded.

17 ¶ [m]And king Ahaz cut off [n]the borders of the bases, and removed the laver from off them; and took down [o]the sea from off the brasen oxen that *were* under it, and put it upon a pavement of stones.

18 And the covert for the sabbath that they had built in the house, and the king's entry without, turned he from the house of the LORD for the king of Assyria.

19 ¶ Now the rest of the acts of Ahaz which he did, *are* they not written in the book of the chronicles of the kings of Judah?

20 And Ahaz slept with his fathers, and [p]was buried with his fathers in the city of David: and Hezekiah his son reigned in his stead.

16:14 [k]2 Chr. 4:1
16:15 [l]Ex. 29:39-41
16:17 [m]2 Chr. 28:24 [n]1 Ki. 7:27,28 [o]1 Ki. 7:23,25
16:20 [p]2 Chr. 28:27
17:1 [q]After an interregnum ch. 15:30
17:3 [r]ch. 18:9
17:5 [s]ch. 18:9
17:6 [t]ch. 18:10,11 Hos. 13:16 Foretold [u]Lev. 26:32,33 Deut. 28:36,64 & 29:27,28 [v]1 Chr. 5:26
17:8 [w]Lev. 18:3 Deut. 18:9 ch. 16:3

Samaria captured by Assyria

17:3–7pp — 2 Ki. 18:9–12

17 IN THE twelfth year of Ahaz king of Judah began [q]Hoshea the son of Elah to reign in Samaria over Israel nine years.

2 And he did *that which was* evil in the sight of the LORD, but not as the kings of Israel that were before him.

3 ¶ Against him came up [r]Shalmaneser king of Assyria; and Hoshea became his servant, and gave him [n]presents.

4 And the king of Assyria found conspiracy in Hoshea: for he had sent messengers to So king of Egypt, and brought no present to the king of Assyria, as *he had done* year by year: therefore the king of Assyria shut him up, and bound him in prison.

5 ¶ Then [s]the king of Assyria came up throughout all the land, and went up to Samaria, and besieged it three years.

6 ¶ [t]In the ninth year of Hoshea the king of Assyria took Samaria, and [u]carried Israel away into Assyria, [v]and placed them in Halah and in Habor *by* the river of Gozan, and in the cities of the Medes.

The sins of Israel and Judah

7 For *so* it was, that the children of Israel had sinned against the LORD their God, which had brought them up out of the land of Egypt, from under the hand of Pharaoh king of Egypt, and had feared other gods,

8 And [w]walked in the statutes of

[m] Heb. *which* were *his* [n] Or, *tribute*

17:6 CARRIED ISRAEL AWAY INTO ASSYRIA. In 722 B.C., after 210 years of idolatry, spiritual rebellion, and moral corruption, God decreed the ultimate fall and exile of the nation of Israel (i.e., the ten tribes of the northern kingdom). The relentless progress of evil among God's people had reached a point of no return. Their measure of iniquity was full. God's only recourse was a judgment that dissolved the nation; only a believing and faithful remnant was left to experience the fulfillment of God's promises (cf. Rom. 9:27).

17:7 SINNED AGAINST THE LORD THEIR GOD. In vv. 7–41 the Holy Spirit gives the theological and moral reasons why God brought about the downfall of His redeemed covenant people and removed them from his sight (v. 18). (1) They forgot God's love and grace, manifested in their redemption from Egypt (v. 7). (2) They served the gods of the pagan societies around them, thinking that they would find success, well-being, and guidance (vv. 7,12,17; cf. Col. 3:5, note). (3) They adopted the customs and lifestyles of the ungodly world (vv. 8–11,15–17). (4) They rejected God's prophets and their message of righteousness (vv. 13–15; cf. Acts 7:51). (5) They openly rebelled against God's written revelation and covenant (vv. 13–16). (6) They gave themselves over to spiritism and all kinds of immorality (vv. 9,15–17).

This message warns all God's people under the new covenant (see 1 Cor. 10:1–12). God will remove from His kingdom all those (both individuals and churches) who fail to abide faithfully in His Word and love. The results of abandoning God are judgment, ruin, suffering, and ultimate rejection (cf. Rev. 2:5; 3:15–16).

17:8 WALKED IN THE STATUTES OF THE HEATHEN. Israel all too eagerly accepted the lifestyle and standards of those who were not

the heathen, whom the LORD cast out from before the children of Israel, and of the kings of Israel, which they had made.

9 And the children of Israel did secretly *those* things that *were* not right against the LORD their God, and they built them high places in all their cities, [x]from the tower of the watchmen to the fenced city.

10 [y]And they set them up [o]images and [z]groves [a]in every high hill, and under every green tree:

11 And there they burnt incense in all the high places, as *did* the heathen whom the LORD carried away before them; and wrought wicked things to provoke the LORD to anger:

12 For they served idols, [b]whereof the LORD had said unto them, [c]Ye shall not do this thing.

13 Yet the LORD testified against Israel, and against Judah, [p]by all the prophets, *and by* all [d]the seers, saying, [e]Turn ye from your evil ways, and keep my commandments *and* my statutes, according to all the law which I commanded your fathers, and which I sent to you by my servants the prophets.

14 Notwithstanding they would not hear, but [f]hardened their necks, like to the neck of their fathers, that did not believe in the LORD their God.

15 And they rejected his statutes, [g]and his covenant that he made with their fathers, and his testimonies which he testified against them; and they followed [h]vanity, and [i]became vain, and went after the heathen that *were* round about them, *concerning* whom the LORD had charged them, that they should [j]not do like them.

16 And they left all the commandments of the LORD their God, and [k]made them molten images, *even* two calves, [l]and made a grove, and worshipped all the host of heaven, [m]and served Baal.

17 [n]And they caused their sons and their daughters to pass through the fire, and [o]used divination and enchantments, and [p]sold themselves to do evil in the sight of the LORD, to provoke him to anger.

18 Therefore the LORD was very angry with Israel, and removed them out of his sight: there was none left [q]but the tribe of Judah only.

19 Also [r]Judah kept not the commandments of the LORD their God, but walked in the statutes of Israel which they made.

20 And the LORD rejected all the seed of Israel, and afflicted them, and [s]delivered them into the hand of spoilers, until he had cast them out of his sight.

21 For [t]he rent Israel from the house of David; and [u]they made Jeroboam the son of Nebat king: and Jeroboam drave Israel from following the LORD, and made them sin a great sin.

22 For the children of Israel walked in all the sins of Jeroboam which he did; they departed not from them;

23 Until the LORD removed Israel out of his sight, [v]as he had said by all

17:9 [x]ch. 18:8 **17:10** [y]1 Ki. 14:23 Is. 57:5 [z]Ex. 34:13 Deut. 16:21 Mic. 5:14 [a]Deut. 12:2 ch. 16:4 **17:12** [b]Ex. 20:3,4 Lev. 26:1 Deut. 5:7,8 [c]Deut. 4:19 **17:13** [d]1 Sam. 9:9 [e]Jer. 18:11 & 25:5 & 35:15 **17:14** [f]Deut. 31:27 Prov. 29:1 **17:15** [g]Deut. 29:25 [h]Deut. 32:21 1 Ki. 16:13 1 Cor. 8:4 [i]Ps. 115:8 Rom. 1:21 [j]Deut. 12:30,31 **17:16** [k]Ex. 32:8 1 Ki. 12:28 [l]1 Ki. 14:15 [m]1 Ki. 16:31 & 22:53 ch. 11:18 **17:17** [n]Lev. 18:21 ch. 16:3 Ezek. 23:37 [o]Deut. 18:10 [p]1 Ki. 21:20 **17:18** [q]1 Ki. 11:13,32 **17:19** [r]Jer. 3:8 **17:20** [s]ch. 13:3 & 15:29 **17:21** [t]1 Ki. 11:11,31 [u]1 Ki. 12:20,28 **17:23** [v]1 Ki. 14:16

o Heb. *statues* p Heb. *by the hand of all*

God's people. Although separation from the nations was one of God's fundamental requirements for Israel (Lev. 18:3,30; Deut. 12:29–31; 18:9–14), the people adopted heathen customs from those surrounding nations instead (see article on SPIRITUAL SEPARATION FOR BELIEVERS, p. 1814). Conforming to the world's way of living is one of the great perils that God's people face in every generation and culture (see Rom. 12:2).

17:13 THE PROPHETS. Israel rejected God's prophets, those who spoke against sin and called for repentance and obedience to the Lord's word and statutes (e.g. Judg. 6:8–10; 1 Ki. 13:1–3; 14:6–16; cf. Acts 7:51–53). They rejected the ministries of Elijah, Elisha, Amos, Hosea, and other prophets. The refusal to hear and obey God's word, along with the spurning of the prophetic message against sin and evil, are unmistakable signs of apostasy (see 2 Tim. 4:3–4, note).

17:16 WORSHIPPED ALL THE HOST OF HEAVEN. The Israelites worshiped astral deities and other gods because they believed such gods would provide a better life, i.e., greater prosperity, fertility, health, pleasure, well-being, and security (see Judg. 2:13, note). For this reason Paul calls "greed" idolatry (see Col. 3:5, note); Jesus Himself states that pursuing prosperity and wealth as one's goal in life is incompatible with serving God (Mat. 6:24; cf. Eph. 5:5).

17:18 THE TRIBE OF JUDAH. The southern kingdom consisted of the tribe of Judah, elements of the tribes of Benjamin and Simeon, and some from the ten tribes in Israel who had migrated to the southern kingdom to worship God at Jerusalem (see 2 Chr. 19:4; 30:1,10–11,25–26; 34:5–7; 35:17–18). Thus, the nation of Judah became the people through whom God's covenant with the Hebrew people was maintained. Note that descendants from tribes of Israel were present in Palestine in N.T. times (Acts 26:7; cf. Luke 2:36; Phil. 3:5).

EXILE OF NORTHERN KINGDOM

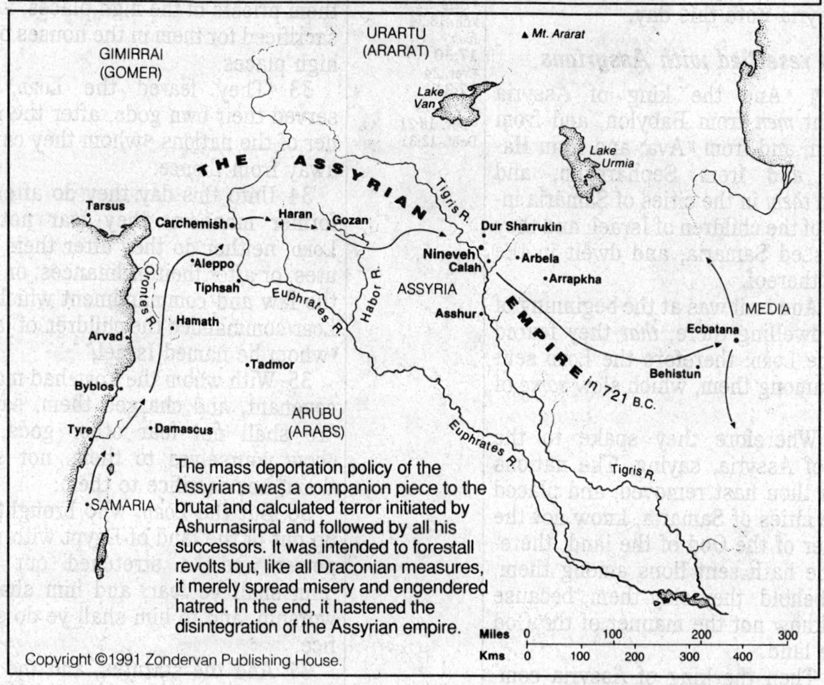

The mass deportation policy of the Assyrians was a companion piece to the brutal and calculated terror initiated by Ashurnasirpal and followed by all his successors. It was intended to forestall revolts but, like all Draconian measures, it merely spread misery and engendered hatred. In the end, it hastened the disintegration of the Assyrian empire.

EXILE OF THE SOUTHERN KINGDOM

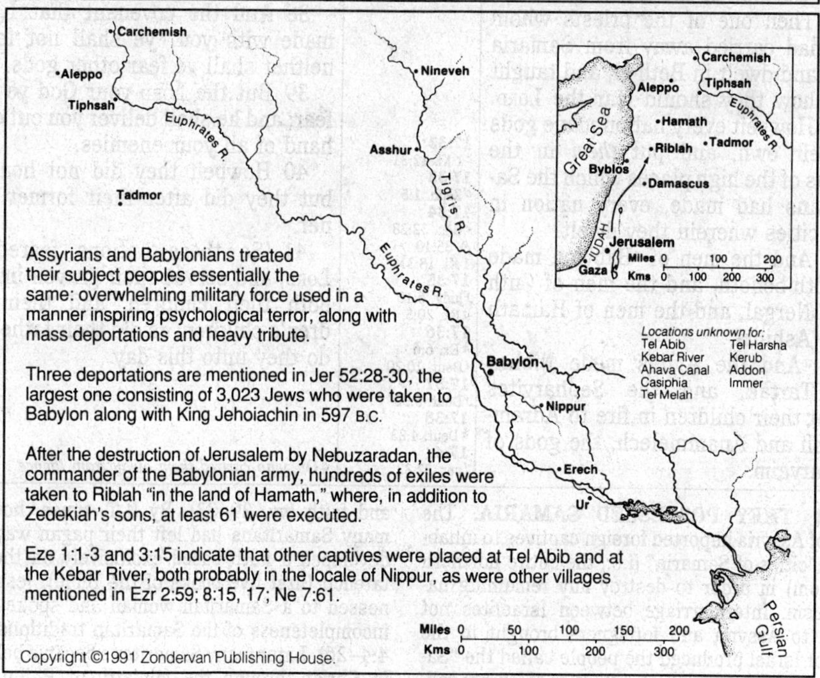

Assyrians and Babylonians treated their subject peoples essentially the same: overwhelming military force used in a manner inspiring psychological terror, along with mass deportations and heavy tribute.

Three deportations are mentioned in Jer 52:28-30, the largest one consisting of 3,023 Jews who were taken to Babylon along with King Jehoiachin in 597 B.C.

After the destruction of Jerusalem by Nebuzaradan, the commander of the Babylonian army, hundreds of exiles were taken to Riblah "in the land of Hamath," where, in addition to Zedekiah's sons, at least 61 were executed.

Eze 1:1-3 and 3:15 indicate that other captives were placed at Tel Abib and at the Kebar River, both probably in the locale of Nippur, as were other villages mentioned in Ezr 2:59; 8:15, 17; Ne 7:61.

his servants the prophets. [w]So was Israel carried away out of their own land to Assyria unto this day.

Israel resettled with Assyrians

24 ¶ [x]And the king of Assyria brought *men* from Babylon, and from Cuthah, and from [y]Ava, and from Hamath, and from Sepharvaim, and placed *them* in the cities of Samaria instead of the children of Israel: and they possessed Samaria, and dwelt in the cities thereof.

25 And *so* it was at the beginning of their dwelling there, *that* they feared not the LORD: therefore the LORD sent lions among them, which slew *some* of them.

26 Wherefore they spake to the king of Assyria, saying, The nations which thou hast removed, and placed in the cities of Samaria, know not the manner of the God of the land: therefore he hath sent lions among them, and, behold, they slay them, because they know not the manner of the God of the land.

27 Then the king of Assyria commanded, saying, Carry thither one of the priests whom ye brought from thence; and let them go and dwell there, and let him teach them the manner of the God of the land.

28 Then one of the priests whom they had carried away from Samaria came and dwelt in Beth-el, and taught them how they should fear the LORD.

29 Howbeit every nation made gods of their own, and put *them* in the houses of the high places which the Samaritans had made, every nation in their cities wherein they dwelt.

30 And the men of [z]Babylon made Succoth-benoth, and the men of Cuth made Nergal, and the men of Hamath made Ashima,

31 [a]And the Avites made Nibhaz and Tartak, and the Sepharvites [b]burnt their children in fire to Adrammelech and Anammelech, the gods of Sepharvaim.

32 So they feared the LORD, [c]and made unto themselves of the lowest of them priests of the high places, which sacrificed for them in the houses of the high places.

33 [d]They feared the LORD, and served their own gods, after the manner of the nations ¶whom they carried away from thence.

34 Unto this day they do after the former manners: they fear not the LORD, neither do they after their statutes, or after their ordinances, or after the law and commandment which the LORD commanded the children of Jacob, [e]whom he named Israel;

35 With whom the LORD had made a covenant, and charged them, saying, [f]Ye shall not fear other gods, nor [g]bow yourselves to them, nor serve them, nor sacrifice to them:

36 But the LORD, who brought you up out of the land of Egypt with great power and [h]a stretched out arm, [i]him shall ye fear, and him shall ye worship, and to him shall ye do sacrifice.

37 And the statutes, and the ordinances, and the law, and the commandment, which he wrote for you, [j]ye shall observe to do for evermore; and ye shall not fear other gods.

38 And the covenant that I have made with you [k]ye shall not forget; neither shall ye fear other gods.

39 But the LORD your God ye shall fear; and he shall deliver you out of the hand of all your enemies.

40 Howbeit they did not hearken, but they did after their former manner.

41 [l]So these nations feared the LORD, and served their graven images, both their children, and their children's children: as did their fathers, so do they unto this day.

17:23 [w]ver. 6
17:24 [x]Ezra 4:2,10 [y]ch. 18:34 *Ivah*
17:30 [z]ver. 24
17:31 [a]Ezra 4:9 [b]Lev. 18:21 Deut. 12:31
17:32 [c]1 Ki. 12:31
17:33 [d]Zeph. 1:5
17:34 [e]Gen. 32:28 & 35:10 1 Ki. 18:31
17:35 [f]Judg. 6:10 [g]Ex. 20:5
17:36 [h]Ex. 6:6 [i]Deut. 10:20
17:37 [j]Deut. 5:32
17:38 [k]Deut. 4:23
17:41 [l]ver. 32,33

¶ Or, *who carried them away from thence*

17:24 THEY POSSESSED SAMARIA. The king of Assyria imported foreign captives to inhabit the "cities of Samaria" (i.e., the entire northern kingdom) in order to destroy any remaining nationalism. Intermarriage between Israelites not taken to Assyria and foreigners brought to the land of Israel produced the people called the "Samaritans." The result was a mixture of foreign religious and cultural traditions with Hebrew customs and faith (vv. 29–33). By N.T. times, however, many Samaritans had left their pagan ways and developed a faith based exclusively on the Pentateuch (first five books of the Bible). Jesus witnessed to a Samaritan woman and spoke of the incompleteness of the Samaritan traditions (John 4:4–26). Later many Samaritans became believers in Christ through the ministry of Philip (Acts 8:5–25).

Hezekiah, king of Judah

18:2–4pp — 2 Chr. 29:1–2; 31:1
18:5–7pp — 2 Chr. 31:20–21
18:9–12pp — 2 Ki. 17:3–7

18 NOW IT came to pass in the
third year of Hoshea son of
Elah king of Israel, *that* [m]Hezekiah the
son of Ahaz king of Judah began to
reign.
2 Twenty and five years old was he
when he began to reign; and he reigned
twenty and nine years in Jerusalem.
His mother's name also *was* [n]Abi, the
daughter of Zachariah.
3 And he did *that which was* right in
the sight of the LORD, according to all
that David his father did.
4 ¶ [o]He removed the high places,
and brake the [r]images, and cut down
the groves, and brake in pieces the
[p]brasen serpent that Moses had
made: for unto those days the children
of Israel did burn incense to it: and he
called it [s]Nehushtan.
5 He [q]trusted in the LORD God of
Israel; [r]so that after him was none
like him among all the kings of Judah,
nor *any* that were before him.
6 For he [s]clave to the LORD, *and* de-
parted not [t]from following him, but
kept his commandments, which the
LORD commanded Moses.
7 And the LORD [t]was with him; *and*
he [u]prospered whithersoever he went
forth: and he [v]rebelled against the
king of Assyria, and served him not.
8 [w]He smote the Philistines, *even*
unto [u]Gaza, and the borders thereof,
[x]from the tower of the watchmen to
the fenced city.
9 ¶ And [y]it came to pass in the
fourth year of king Hezekiah, which
was the seventh year of Hoshea son of
Elah king of Israel, *that* Shalmaneser
king of Assyria came up against Sa-
maria, and besieged it.
10 And at the end of three years
they took it: *even* in the sixth year of
Hezekiah, that *is* [z]the ninth year of
Hoshea king of Israel, Samaria was
taken.
11 [a]And the king of Assyria did
carry away Israel unto Assyria, and
put them [b]in Halah and in Habor *by*
the river of Gozan, and in the cities of
the Medes:
12 Because they obeyed not the
voice of the LORD their God, but trans-
gressed his covenant, *and* all that Mo-
ses the servant of the LORD command-
ed, and would not hear *them,* nor do
them.
13 ¶ Now [c]in the fourteenth year of
king Hezekiah did [v]Sennacherib king
of Assyria come up against all the
fenced cities of Judah, and took them.
14 And Hezekiah king of Judah sent
to the king of Assyria to Lachish, say-
ing, I have offended; return from me:
that which thou puttest on me will I
bear. And the king of Assyria appoint-
ed unto Hezekiah king of Judah three
hundred talents of silver and thirty tal-
ents of gold.
15 And Hezekiah [d]gave *him* all the
silver that was found in the house of
the LORD, and in the treasures of the
king's house.
16 At that time did Hezekiah cut off
the gold from the doors of the temple of
the LORD, and *from* the pillars which
Hezekiah king of Judah had overlaid,
and gave [w]it to the king of Assyria.

18:1 [m]2 Chr. 28:27 & 29:1 He is called *Ezekias* Mat. 1:9
18:2 [n]2 Chr. 29:1 *Abijah*
18:4 [o]2 Chr. 31:1 [p]Num. 21:9
18:5 [q]ch. 19:10 Job 13:15 Ps. 13:5 [r]ch. 23:25
18:6 [s]Deut. 10:20 Josh. 23:8
18:7 [t]2 Chr. 15:2 [u]1 Sam. 18:5,14 Ps. 60:12 [v]ch. 16:7
18:8 [w]1 Chr. 4:41 Is. 14:29 [x]ch. 17:9
18:9 [y]ch. 17:3
18:10 [z]ch. 17:6
18:11 [a]ch. 17:6 [b]1 Chr. 5:26
18:13 [c]2 Chr. 32:1 Is. 36:1
18:15 [d]ch. 16:8

[r] Heb. *statues* [s] i.e. *A piece of brass* [t] Heb. *from after him* [u] Heb. *Azzah* [v] Heb. *Sanherib* [w] Heb. *them*

18:5 HE TRUSTED IN THE LORD. After telling of the fall of Samaria and the northern kingdom, the author resumes the history of Judah (the southern kingdom), beginning with the reign of the good king Hezekiah. He was considered to be one of the greatest kings Judah ever had, because of his trust in and reliance upon God. Hezekiah trusted deeply in the Lord, kept His commandments (vv. 3–6), and exhorted the people to turn from sin and return to God (2 Chr. 30:6–9). At the beginning of his reign he repaired and cleansed the house of the Lord, restored the priests and Levites to their ministry, and reinstated the celebration of the Passover feast (2 Chr. 29:3; 30:5). He vigorously sought to destroy all idolatrous altars and high places in Judah (v. 4). See chs. 19—20; 2 Chr. 29—32 and Is. 36—39 for additional information on Hezekiah's reign.

18:7 REBELLED AGAINST THE KING OF ASSYRIA. At this time in Judah's history, the southern kingdom also fell under Assyrian dominance, being required to pay an annual tribute. Hezekiah identified with an international conspiracy against Assyria and refused to pay any more money. The result of this attempt at independence is recorded in 18:13—19:37.

18:13 CITIES OF JUDAH . . . TOOK THEM. In 701 B.C. the Assyrian king Sennacherib responded to Judah's rebellion by capturing many of its important cities. His personal records indicate that he took forty-six walled cities. Hezekiah, seeing no hope in further resistance, apologetically submitted to Sennacherib and depleted Judah's treasury in order to pay Assyria's assessment (vv. 14–16).

The Assyrian threats

18:13, 17–37pp — Is. 36:1–22
18:17–35pp — 2 Chr. 32:9–19

17 ¶ And the king of Assyria sent
Tartan and Rabsaris and Rab-shakeh
from Lachish to king Hezekiah with a
[x]great host against Jerusalem. And
they went up and came to Jerusalem.
And when they were come up, they
came and stood by the conduit of the
upper pool, [e]which *is* in the highway
of the fuller's field.
18 And when they had called to the
king, there came out to them Eliakim
the son of Hilkiah, which *was* over the
household, and Shebna the [y]scribe,
and Joah the son of Asaph the recorder.
19 And Rab-shakeh said unto them,
Speak ye now to Hezekiah, Thus saith
the great king, the king of Assyria,
[f]What confidence *is* this wherein thou
trustest?
20 Thou [z]sayest, (but *they are but*
[a]vain words,) [b]*I have* counsel and
strength for the war. Now on whom
dost thou trust, that thou rebellest
against me?
21 [g]Now, behold, thou [c]trustest
upon the staff of this bruised reed, *even*
upon Egypt, on which if a man lean, it
will go into his hand, and pierce it: so
is Pharaoh king of Egypt unto all that
trust on him.
22 But if ye say unto me, We trust
in the LORD our God: *is* not that he,
[h]whose high places and whose altars
Hezekiah hath taken away, and hath
said to Judah and Jerusalem, Ye shall
worship before this altar in Jerusalem?
23 Now therefore, I pray thee, give
[d]pledges to my lord the king of Assyr-
ia, and I will deliver thee two thousand
horses, if thou be able on thy part to set
riders upon them.
24 How then wilt thou turn away
the face of one captain of the least of
my master's servants, and put thy
trust on Egypt for chariots and for
horsemen?
25 Am I now come up without the
LORD against this place to destroy it?
The LORD said to me, Go up against this
land, and destroy it.
26 Then said Eliakim the son of Hil-
kiah, and Shebna, and Joah, unto Rab-
shakeh, Speak, I pray thee, to thy ser-
vants in the Syrian language; for we
understand *it:* and talk not with us in
the Jews' language in the ears of the
people that *are* on the wall.
27 But Rab-shakeh said unto them,
Hath my master sent me to thy master,
and to thee, to speak these words? *hath
he* not *sent me* to the men which sit on
the wall, that they may eat their own
dung, and drink [e]their own piss with
you?
28 Then Rab-shakeh stood and
cried with a loud voice in the Jews' lan-
guage, and spake, saying, Hear the
word of the great king, the king of As-
syria:
29 Thus saith the king, [i]Let not
Hezekiah deceive you: for he shall not
be able to deliver you out of his hand:
30 Neither let Hezekiah make you
trust in the LORD, saying, The LORD will
surely deliver us, and this city shall not
be delivered into the hand of the king
of Assyria.
31 Hearken not to Hezekiah: for
thus saith the king of Assyria,
[f][g]Make *an agreement* with me by a
present, and come out to me, and *then*
eat ye every man of his own vine, and
every one of his fig tree, and drink ye
every one the waters of his [h]cistern:
32 Until I come and take you away
to a land like your own land, [j]a land
of corn and wine, a land of bread and
vineyards, a land of oil olive and of hon-
ey, that ye may live, and not die: and
hearken not unto Hezekiah, when he
[i]persuadeth you, saying, The LORD
will deliver us.
33 [k]Hath any of the gods of the na-
tions delivered at all his land out of the
hand of the king of Assyria?
34 [l]Where *are* the gods of Hamath,
and of Arpad? where *are* the gods of
Sepharvaim, Hena, and [m]Ivah? have

18:17 [e]Is. 7:3
18:19 [f]2 Chr. 32:10
18:21 [g]Ezek. 29:6,7
18:22 [h]ver. 4; 2 Chr. 31:1 & 32:12
18:29 [i]2 Chr. 32:15
18:32 [j]Deut. 8:7,8
18:33 [k]ch. 19:12; 2 Chr. 32:14; Is. 10:10,11
18:34 [l]ch. 19:13; [m]ch. 17:24 *Ava*

[x] Heb. *heavy* [y] Or, *secretary* [z] Or, *talkest* [a] Heb. *word of the lips* [b] Or, *But counsel and strength* are *for the war* [c] Heb. *trustest thee* [d] Or, *hostages* [e] Heb. *the water of their feet* [f] Or, *Seek my favour* [g] Heb. *Make with me a blessing* [h] Or, *pit* [i] Or, *deceiveth*

18:30 NEITHER LET HEZEKIAH MAKE YOU TRUST IN THE LORD. For some unspecified reason, King Sennacherib of Assyria again invaded Judah with a large army and besieged Jerusalem (v. 17). The Assyrian generals sought to intimidate Hezekiah and all of Jerusalem by defiantly belittling the Lord God and mocking the people's trust in Him. This blasphemy against God resulted in an angelic intervention by God, whereby 185,000 of Sennacherib's army were slain and Judah was delivered (19:6–37; 2 Chr. 32:21–22; Is. 37:14–20,33–38).

they delivered Samaria out of mine
hand?
35 Who *are* they among all the gods
of the countries, that have delivered
their country out of mine hand, [n]that
the LORD should deliver Jerusalem out
of mine hand?
36 But the people held their peace,
and answered him not a word: for the
king's commandment was, saying, Answer him not.
37 Then came Eliakim the son of
Hilkiah, which *was* over the household,
and Shebna the scribe, and Joah the
son of Asaph the recorder, to Hezekiah
[o]with *their* clothes rent, and told him
the words of Rab-shakeh.

Hezekiah sends to Isaiah

19:1–13pp — Is. 37:1–13

19 AND [p]IT came to pass, when
king Hezekiah heard *it,* that he
rent his clothes, and covered himself
with sackcloth, and went into the
house of the LORD.
2 And he sent Eliakim, which *was*
over the household, and Shebna the
scribe, and the elders of the priests,
covered with sackcloth, to [q]Isaiah the
prophet the son of Amoz.
3 And they said unto him, Thus
saith Hezekiah, This day *is* a day of
trouble, and of rebuke, and [j]blasphemy: for the children are come to the
birth, and *there is* not strength to bring
forth.
4 [r]It may be the LORD thy God will
hear all the words of Rab-shakeh,
[s]whom the king of Assyria his master
hath sent to reproach the living God;
and will [t]reprove the words which the
LORD thy God hath heard: wherefore lift
up *thy* prayer for the remnant that are
[k]left.
5 So the servants of king Hezekiah
came to Isaiah.
6 ¶ [u]And Isaiah said unto them,
Thus shall ye say to your master, Thus
saith the LORD, Be not afraid of the
words which thou hast heard, with
which the [v]servants of the king of Assyria have blasphemed me.
7 Behold, I will send [w]a blast upon
him, and he shall hear a rumour, and
shall return to his own land; and I will
cause him to fall by the sword in his
own land.
8 ¶ So Rab-shakeh returned, and
found the king of Assyria warring
against Libnah: for he had heard that
he was departed [x]from Lachish.
9 And [y]when he heard say of Tirhakah king of Ethiopia, Behold, he is
come out to fight against thee: he sent
messengers again unto Hezekiah, saying,
10 Thus shall ye speak to Hezekiah
king of Judah, saying, Let not thy God
[z]in whom thou trustest deceive thee,
saying, Jerusalem shall not be delivered into the hand of the king of Assyria.
11 Behold, thou hast heard what
the kings of Assyria have done to all
lands, by destroying them utterly: and
shalt thou be delivered?
12 [a]Have the gods of the nations
delivered them which my fathers have
destroyed; *as* Gozan, and Haran, and
Rezeph, and the children of [b]Eden
which *were* in Thelasar?
13 [c]Where *is* the king of Hamath,
and the king of Arpad, and the king of
the city of Sepharvaim, of Hena, and
Ivah?

Hezekiah's prayer

19:14–19pp — Is. 37:14–20

14 ¶ [d]And Hezekiah received the
letter of the hand of the messengers,
and read it: and Hezekiah went up into
the house of the LORD, and spread it
before the LORD.
15 And Hezekiah prayed before the
LORD, and said, O LORD God of Israel,
[e]which dwellest *between* the cherubims, [f]thou art the God, *even* thou

18:35 [n]Dan. 3:15 **18:37** [o]Is. 33:7 **19:1** [p]Is. 37:1 **19:2** [q]Luke 3:4 called *Esaias* **19:4** [r]2 Sam. 16:12 [s]ch. 18:35 [t]Ps. 50:21 **19:6** [u]Is. 37:6 [v]ch. 18:17 **19:7** [w]ver. 35-37 Jer. 51:1 **19:8** [x]ch. 18:14 **19:9** [y]See 1 Sam. 23:27 **19:10** [z]ch. 18:5 **19:12** [a]ch. 18:33,34 [b]Ezek. 27:23 **19:13** [c]ch. 18:34 **19:14** [d]Is. 37:14 **19:15** [e]Ps. 80:1 [f]Is. 44:6

[j] Or, *provocation* [k] Heb. *found*

19:1 HEZEKIAH ... WENT INTO THE HOUSE OF THE LORD. Hezekiah had great confidence in God (18:5). Faced with the threat of the Assyrians (18:17–37) and horrified at the mockery of the Lord (18:30–35), he turned to God and entreated Isaiah to pray for Jerusalem and God's remnant people (vv. 2–4).

19:15 HEZEKIAH PRAYED. Hezekiah took the defiant letter which demanded Jerusalem's surrender, spread it out before the Lord, and prayed earnestly to Him. When troubles come into our lives and circumstances seem out of control, we must do just as Hezekiah did—draw near to God in fervent and trusting prayer. God has promised to deliver His people from the hands of their enemies and permit nothing to happen that is out of His will (Mat. 6:25–34). By clinging to God in trust and faith, we will have His peace to guard our hearts and minds (Phil. 4:6–7).

alone, of all the kingdoms of the earth; thou hast made heaven and earth.

16 LORD, [g]bow down thine ear, and hear: [h]open, LORD, thine eyes, and see: and hear the words of Sennacherib, [i]which hath sent him to reproach the living God.

17 Of a truth, LORD, the kings of Assyria have destroyed the nations and their lands,

18 And have [1]cast their gods into the fire: for they *were* no gods, but [j]the work of men's hands, wood and stone: therefore they have destroyed them.

19 Now therefore, O LORD our God, I beseech thee, save thou us out of his hand, [k]that all the kingdoms of the earth may know that thou *art* the LORD God, *even* thou only.

The divine deliverance

19:20–37pp — Is. 37:21–38
19:35–37pp — 2 Chr. 32:20–21

20 ¶ Then Isaiah the son of Amoz sent to Hezekiah, saying, Thus saith the LORD God of Israel, [l]*That* which thou hast prayed to me against Sennacherib king of Assyria [m]I have heard.

21 This *is* the word that the LORD hath spoken concerning him; The virgin [n]the daughter of Zion hath despised thee, *and* laughed thee to scorn; the daughter of Jerusalem [o]hath shaken her head at thee.

22 Whom hast thou reproached and blasphemed? and against whom hast thou exalted *thy* voice, and lifted up thine eyes on high? *even* against [p]the Holy *One* of Israel.

23 [q]By[m] thy messengers thou hast reproached the Lord, and hast said, [r]With the multitude of my chariots I am come up to the height of the mountains, to the sides of Lebanon, and will cut down [n]the tall cedar trees thereof, *and* the choice fir trees thereof: and I will enter into the lodgings of his borders, *and into* [o]the forest of his Carmel.

24 I have digged and drunk strange waters, and with the sole of my feet have I dried up all the rivers of [p]besieged places.

25 [q]Hast thou not heard long ago *how* [s]I have done it, *and* of ancient times that I have formed it? now have I brought it to pass, that [t]thou shouldest be to lay waste fenced cities *into* ruinous heaps.

26 Therefore their inhabitants were [r]of small power, they were dismayed and confounded; they were *as* the grass of the field, and *as* the green herb, *as* [u]the grass on the housetops, and *as* *corn* blasted before it be grown up.

27 But [v]I know thy [s]abode, and thy going out, and thy coming in, and thy rage against me.

28 Because thy rage against me and thy tumult is come up into mine ears, therefore [w]I will put my hook in thy nose, and my bridle in thy lips, and I will turn thee back [x]by the way by which thou camest.

29 And this *shall be* a sign unto thee, Ye shall eat this year such things as grow of themselves, and in the second year that which springeth of the same; and in the third year sow ye, and reap, and plant vineyards, and eat the fruits thereof.

30 [y]And [t]the remnant that is escaped of the house of Judah shall yet again take root downward, and bear fruit upward.

31 For out of Jerusalem shall go forth a remnant, and [u]they that escape out of mount Zion: [z]the zeal of the LORD *of hosts* shall do this.

32 Therefore thus saith the LORD concerning the king of Assyria, He shall not come into this city, nor shoot an arrow there, nor come before it with shield, nor cast a bank against it.

33 By the way that he came, by the

19:16 [g]Ps. 31:2 [h]2 Chr. 6:40 [i]ver. 4
19:18 [j]Jer. 10:3
19:19 [k]Ps. 83:18
19:20 [l]Is. 37:21 [m]Ps. 65:2
19:21 [n]Lam. 2:13 [o]Ps. 22:7,8
19:22 [p]Jer. 51:5
19:23 [q]ch. 18:17 [r]Ps. 20:7
19:25 [s]Is. 45:7 [t]Is. 10:5
19:26 [u]Ps. 129:6
19:27 [v]Ps. 139:1
19:28 [w]Ezek. 29:4 [x]ver. 33,36
19:30 [y]2 Chr. 32:22
19:31 [z]Is. 9:7

[1] Heb. *given* [m] Heb. *By the hand of* [n] Heb. *the tallness* [o] Or, *the forest* and *his fruitful field;* see Is. 10:18 [p] Or, *fenced* [q] Or, *Hast thou not heard* how *I have made it long ago, and formed it of ancient times? should I now bring it to be laid waste,* and *fenced cities* to be *ruinous heaps?* [r] Heb. *short of hand* [s] Or, *sitting* [t] Heb. *the escaping of the house of Judah that remaineth* [u] Heb. *the escaping*

19:19 THAT ALL ... MAY KNOW THAT THOU *ART* THE LORD GOD. Hezekiah's prayer for the glory of God and the vindication of His ways and purposes in history manifests the highest desire of all who love the Lord. Moses (Ex. 32:12; Num. 14:13–16; Deut. 9:26–29) and David (Ps. 59:13; 83:18) also exhibited this desire in their prayers. We as believers must be so identified with God that our main concern is to uphold His reputation and honor (cf. John 17:4–6). Our chief prayer should be, "Hallowed be thy name" (Mat. 6:9).

same shall he return, and shall not come into this city, saith the LORD.

34 For [a]I will defend this city, to save it, for mine own sake, and [b]for my servant David's sake.

35 ¶ And [c]it came to pass that night, that the angel of the LORD went out, and smote in the camp of the Assyrians an hundred fourscore and five thousand: and when they arose early in the morning, behold, they *were* all dead corpses.

36 So Sennacherib king of Assyria departed, and went and returned, and dwelt at [d]Nineveh.

37 And it came to pass, as he was worshipping in the house of Nisroch his god, that [e]Adrammelech and Sharezer his sons [f]smote him with the sword: and they escaped into the land of [v]Armenia. And [g]Esar-haddon his son reigned in his stead.

The sickness of Hezekiah

20:1–11pp — 2 Chr. 32:24–26; Is. 38:1–8

20 IN [h]THOSE days was Hezekiah sick unto death. And the prophet Isaiah the son of Amoz came to him, and said unto him, Thus saith the LORD, [w]Set thine house in order; for thou shalt die, and not live.

2 Then he turned his face to the wall, and prayed unto the LORD, saying,

3 I beseech thee, O LORD, [i]remember now how I have walked before thee in truth and with a perfect heart, and have done *that which is* good in thy sight. And Hezekiah wept [x]sore.

4 And it came to pass, afore Isaiah was gone out into the middle [y]court, that the word of the LORD came to him, saying,

5 Turn again, and tell Hezekiah [j]the captain of my people, Thus saith the LORD, the God of David thy father, [k]I have heard thy prayer, I have seen [l]thy tears: behold, I will heal thee: on the third day thou shalt go up unto the house of the LORD.

6 And I will add unto thy days fifteen years; and I will deliver thee and this city out of the hand of the king of Assyria; and [m]I will defend this city for mine own sake, and for my servant David's sake.

7 And [n]Isaiah said, Take a lump of figs. And they took and laid *it* on the boil, and he recovered. 2 Chr. 7:14

8 ¶ And Hezekiah said unto Isaiah, [o]What *shall be* the sign that the LORD will heal me, and that I shall go up into the house of the LORD the third day?

9 And Isaiah said, [p]This sign shalt thou have of the LORD, that the LORD will do the thing that he hath spoken: shall the shadow go forward ten degrees, or go back ten degrees?

10 And Hezekiah answered, It is a light thing for the shadow to go down ten degrees: nay, but let the shadow return backward ten degrees.

11 And Isaiah the prophet cried unto the LORD: and [q]he brought the shadow ten degrees backward, by which it had gone down in the [z]dial of Ahaz.

Hezekiah's foolishness

20:12–19pp — Is. 39:1–8
20:20–21pp — 2 Chr. 32:32–33

12 ¶ [r]At that time [a]Berodach-baladan, the son of Baladan, king of Babylon, sent letters and a present unto Hezekiah: for he had heard that Hezekiah had been sick.

13 And [s]Hezekiah hearkened unto them, and showed them all the house of his [b]precious things, the silver, and the gold, and the spices, and the precious ointment, and *all* the house of his [c] [d]armour, and all that was found in his treasures: there was nothing in his house, nor in all his dominion, that Hezekiah showed them not.

14 ¶ Then came Isaiah the prophet unto king Hezekiah, and said unto him,

19:34 [a]ch. 20:6 [b]1 Ki. 11:12
19:35 [c]Is. 37:36
19:36 [d]Gen. 10:11
19:37 [e]2 Chr. 32:21 [f]ver. 7 [g]Ezra 4:2
20:1 [h]Is. 38:1
20:3 [i]Neh. 13:22
20:5 [j]1 Sam. 9:16 & 10:1 [k]ch. 19:20 Ps. 65:2 [l]Ps. 39:12 & 56:8
20:6 [m]ch. 19:34
20:7 [n]Is. 38:21
20:8 [o]See Judg. 6:17, 37,39 Is. 7:11,14 & 38:22
20:9 [p]See Is. 38:7,8
20:11 [q]See Is. 38:8
20:12 [r]Is. 39:1
20:13 [s]2 Chr. 32:27,31

[v]Heb. *Ararat* [w]Heb. *Give charge concerning thine house* [x]Heb. *with a great weeping* [y]Or, *city* [z]Heb. *degrees* [a]Or, *Merodach-baladan* [b]Or, *spicery* [c]Or, *jewels* [d]Heb. *vessels*

19:35 THE ANGEL OF THE LORD. This miraculous deliverance of Judah from the Assyrians is one of the great redemptive moments in O.T. history, recorded no less than three times in Scripture (vv. 35–36; 2 Chr. 32:21–22: Is. 37:36). The most powerful political kingdom on earth stood against the little nation of Judah. When defeat looked inevitable, God intervened and delivered His people. In mercy God manifested His willingness to renew the covenant and to be Judah's God and Protector if the people would place their trust in Him.

20:1 FOR THOU SHALT DIE. See Is. 38:1, note.

20:5 I HAVE HEARD THY PRAYER ... I WILL HEAL THEE. See Is. 38:5, note.

20:11 BROUGHT THE SHADOW TEN DEGREES BACKWARD. See Is. 38:8, note.

What said these men? and from
whence came they unto thee? And Hez-
ekiah said, They are come from a far
country, *even* from Babylon.
15 And he said, What have they
seen in thine house? And Hezekiah an-
swered, [t]All *the things* that *are* in mine
house have they seen: there is nothing
among my treasures that I have not
showed them.
16 And Isaiah said unto Hezekiah,
Hear the word of the LORD.
17 Behold, the days come, that all
that *is* in thine house, and that which
thy fathers have laid up in store unto
this day, [u]shall be carried into Bab-
ylon: nothing shall be left, saith the
LORD.
18 And of thy sons that shall issue
from thee, which thou shalt beget,
[v]shall they take away; and they shall
be eunuchs in the palace of the king of
Babylon.
19 Then said Hezekiah unto Isaiah,
[w]Good *is* the word of the LORD which
thou hast spoken. And he said, [e]*Is it*
not *good,* if peace and truth be in my
days?
20 ¶ [x]And the rest of the acts of
Hezekiah, and all his might, and how
he [y]made a pool, and a conduit, and
[z]brought water into the city, *are* they
not written in the book of the chroni-
cles of the kings of Judah?
21 And [a]Hezekiah slept with his
fathers: and Manasseh his son reigned
in his stead.

Manasseh, king of Judah

21:1–10pp — 2 Chr. 33:1–10
21:17–18pp — 2 Chr. 33:18–20

21 MANASSEH [b]*WAS* twelve
years old when he began to
reign, and reigned fifty and five years
in Jerusalem. And his mother's name
was Hephzibah.
2 And he did *that which was* evil in
the sight of the LORD, [c]after the abomi-
nations of the heathen, whom the LORD
cast out before the children of Israel.
3 For he built up again the high
places [d]which Hezekiah his father
had destroyed; and he reared up altars
for Baal, and made a grove, [e]as did
Ahab king of Israel; and [f]worshipped
all the host of heaven, and served
them.
4 And [g]he built altars in the house
of the LORD, of which the LORD said, [h]In
Jerusalem will I put my name.
5 And he built altars for all the host
of heaven in the two courts of the
house of the LORD.
6 [i]And he made his son pass
through the fire, and observed [j]times,
and used enchantments, and dealt with
familiar spirits and wizards: he
wrought much wickedness in the sight
of the LORD, to provoke *him* to anger.
7 And he set a graven image of the
grove that he had made in the house,
of which the LORD said to David, and to
Solomon his son, [k]In this house, and
in Jerusalem, which I have chosen out
of all tribes of Israel, will I put my
name for ever:
8 [l]Neither will I make the feet of
Israel move any more out of the land
which I gave their fathers; only if they
will observe to do according to all that
I have commanded them, and accord-
ing to all the law that my servant Mo-
ses commanded them.
9 But they hearkened not: and Ma-
nasseh [m]seduced them to do more evil
than did the nations whom the LORD de-
stroyed before the children of Israel.
10 ¶ And the LORD spake by his ser-
vants the prophets, saying,
11 [n]Because Manasseh king of Ju-

20:15 [t]ver. 13 **20:17** [u]ch. 24:13 & 25:13 Jer. 27:21 & 52:17 **20:18** [v]ch. 24:12 2 Chr. 33:11 **20:19** [w]1 Sam. 3:18 Job 1:21 Ps. 39:9 **20:20** [x]2 Chr. 32:32 [y]Neh. 3:16 [z]2 Chr. 32:30 **20:21** [a]2 Chr. 32:33 **21:1** [b]2 Chr. 33:1 **21:2** [c]ch. 16:3 **21:3** [d]ch. 18:4 [e]1 Ki. 16:32 [f]Deut. 4:19 & 17:3 ch. 17:16 **21:4** [g]Jer. 32:34 [h]2 Sam. 7:13 1 Ki. 8:29 & 9:3 **21:6** [i]Lev. 18:21 & 20:2 ch. 16:3 & 17:17 [j]Lev. 19:26,31 Deut. 18:10,11 ch. 17:17 **21:7** [k]2 Sam. 7:13 1 Ki. 8:29 & 9:3 ch. 23:27 Jer. 32:34 **21:8** [l]2 Sam. 7:10 **21:9** [m]Prov. 29:12 **21:11** [n]ch. 23:26,27 & 24:3,4 Jer. 15:4

[e] Or, *Shall there not be peace and truth*

20:17 CARRIED INTO BABYLON. Isaiah's prediction of Judah's exile into Babylon was fulfilled about 115 years later when Nebuchadnezzar, king of Babylon, destroyed Jerusalem, stripped the land and temple of all their riches, and took the people of Judah away as captives to his nation (cf. 24:10–13; 2 Chr. 33:11; Dan. 1:1–3).

21:9 MANASSEH SEDUCED THEM TO DO MORE EVIL. During his long reign of fifty-five years, Manasseh plunged Judah into her darkest era of idolatry. This wicked king had nothing but contempt for the God of his father, Hezekiah. He led God's people into greater evil than the pagan nations that Joshua had destroyed. Why did God allow Manasseh to influence Judah to do such great wickedness? The answer is: God does not always remove ungodly leaders from their positions of influence. He holds His people responsible for requiring their leaders to align themselves with His Word. He expects them to reject as false any leader who is not faithful to the teachings of His Word. In this way, God tests His people's loyalty to Him, to His revelation, and to His godly standards (see Deut. 13:3, note).

21:10 THE PROPHETS. Isaiah was probably still prophesying in Manasseh's time. Among other things, a prophet was to be a voice for righteousness when God's people were conforming to the

dah hath done these abominations, [o]*and* hath done wickedly above all that the Amorites did, which *were* before him, and [p]hath made Judah also to sin with his idols:

12 Therefore thus saith the LORD God of Israel, Behold, I *am* bringing *such* evil upon Jerusalem and Judah, that whosoever heareth of it, both [q]his ears shall tingle.

13 And I will stretch over Jerusalem [r]the line of Samaria, and the plummet of the house of Ahab: and I will wipe Jerusalem as *a man* wipeth a dish, [f]wiping *it,* and turning *it* upside down.

14 And I will forsake the remnant of mine inheritance, and deliver them into the hand of their enemies; and they shall become a prey and a spoil to all their enemies;

15 Because they have done *that which was* evil in my sight, and have provoked me to anger, since the day their fathers came forth out of Egypt, even unto this day.

16 [s]Moreover Manasseh shed innocent blood very much, till he had filled Jerusalem [g]from one end to another; beside his sin wherewith he made Judah to sin, in doing *that which was* evil in the sight of the LORD.

17 ¶ Now [t]the rest of the acts of Manasseh, and all that he did, and his sin that he sinned, *are* they not written in the book of the chronicles of the kings of Judah?

18 And [u]Manasseh slept with his fathers, and was buried in the garden of his own house, in the garden of Uzza: and Amon his son reigned in his stead.

Amon, king of Judah

21:19–24pp — 2 Chr. 33:21–25

19 ¶ [v]Amon *was* twenty and two years old when he began to reign, and he reigned two years in Jerusalem. And his mother's name *was* Meshullemeth, the daughter of Haruz of Jotbah.

20 And he did *that which was* evil in the sight of the LORD, [w]as his father Manasseh did.

21 And he walked in all the way that his father walked in, and served the idols that his father served, and worshipped them:

22 And he [x]forsook the LORD God of his fathers, and walked not in the way of the LORD.

23 ¶ [y]And the servants of Amon conspired against him, and slew the king in his own house.

24 And the people of the land slew all them that had conspired against king Amon; and the people of the land made Josiah his son king in his stead.

25 Now the rest of the acts of Amon which he did, *are* they not written in the book of the chronicles of the kings of Judah?

26 And he was buried in his sepulchre in the garden of Uzza: and [z]Josiah his son reigned in his stead.

The book of the law found

22:1–20pp — 2 Chr. 34:1–2,8–28

22 JOSIAH [a]*WAS* eight years old when he began to reign, and he reigned thirty and one years in Jerusalem. And his mother's name *was* Jedidah, the daughter of Adaiah of [b]Boscath.

2 And he did *that which was* right in the sight of the LORD, and walked in all the way of David his father, and [c]turned not aside to the right hand or to the left.

21:11 [o]1 Ki. 21:26 [p]ver. 9
21:12 [q]1 Sam. 3:11 Jer. 19:3
21:13 [r]See Is. 34:11 Lam. 2:8 Amos 7:7,8
21:16 [s]ch. 24:4
21:17 [t]2 Chr. 33:11-19
21:18 [u]2 Chr. 33:20
21:19 [v]2 Chr. 33:21-23
21:20 [w]ver. 2
21:22 [x]1 Ki. 11:33
21:23 [y]2 Chr. 33:24,25
21:26 [z]Mat. 1:10 called *Josias*
22:1 [a]2 Chr. 34:1 [b]Josh. 15:39
22:2 [c]Deut. 5:32

[f]Heb. *he wipeth and turneth* it *upon the face thereof* [g]Heb. *from mouth to mouth*

---

ways of the world (see article on THE PROPHET IN THE OLD TESTAMENT, p. 1002).

21:14 I WILL FORSAKE THE REMNANT OF MINE INHERITANCE. Judah was the focus of redemptive history at this time, forming what was left of God's elect people. Like the northern kingdom, however, a large number of them, by worshiping false gods, cast aside the salvation that God had prepared for them. Only those who persevere in genuine faith are assured of remaining a part of God's elect people (see article on ELECTION AND PREDESTINATION, p. 1846).

21:17 THE REST OF THE ACTS OF MANASSEH. See 2 Chr. 33:1–19 for a record of other events, including Manasseh's repentance at the end of his life.

22:1 JOSIAH. Josiah was the last of the righteous kings of Judah. At an early age (sixteen years old) he began earnestly to seek the Lord (2 Chr. 34:3), and four years later he began to purge Judah of false worship (2 Chr. 34:3–4). As the temple was being repaired, Hilkiah found the Book of the Law written by Moses (2 Chr. 34:15). This discovery brought a renewed commitment to God's Word, and a measure of spiritual reform was accomplished throughout the land (23:1–30). The prophets Jeremiah and Habakkuk aided Josiah in his attempt to bring the people back to God; for the spiritual condition of the people of Josiah's time, see Jer. 1—12; Hab. 1:2–4).

3 ¶ [d]And it came to pass in the
eighteenth year of king Josiah, *that* the
king sent Shaphan the son of Azaliah,
the son of Meshullam, the scribe, to
the house of the LORD, saying,
4 Go up to Hilkiah the high priest,
that he may sum the silver which is
[e]brought into the house of the LORD,
which [f]the keepers of the [h]door have
gathered of the people:
5 And let them [g]deliver it into the
hand of the doers of the work, that
have the oversight of the house of the
LORD: and let them give it to the doers
of the work which *is* in the house of the
LORD, to repair the breaches of the
house,
6 Unto carpenters, and builders,
and masons, and to buy timber and
hewn stone to repair the house.
7 Howbeit [h]there was no reckon-
ing made with them of the money that
was delivered into their hand, because
they dealt faithfully.
8 ¶ And Hilkiah the high priest said
unto Shaphan the scribe, [i]I have
found the book of the law in the house
of the LORD. And Hilkiah gave the book
to Shaphan, and he read it.
9 And Shaphan the scribe came to
the king, and brought the king word
again, and said, Thy servants have
[i]gathered the money that was found
in the house, and have delivered it into
the hand of them that do the work, that
have the oversight of the house of the
LORD.
10 And Shaphan the scribe showed
the king, saying, Hilkiah the priest
hath delivered me a book. And Sha-
phan read it before the king.
11 And it came to pass, when the
king had heard the words of the book
of the law, that he rent his clothes.

22:3 [d]2 Chr. 34:8
22:4 [e]ch. 12:4 [f]ch. 12:9
22:5 [g]ch. 12:11,12,14
22:7 [h]ch. 12:15
22:8 [i]Deut. 31:24 2 Chr. 34:14
22:12 [j]*Abdon* 2 Chr. 34:20
22:13 [k]Deut. 29:27
22:14 [l]*Tikvath* 2 Chr. 34:22
22:16 [m]Deut. 29:27 Dan. 9:11-14
22:17 [n]Deut. 29:25-27
22:18 [o]2 Chr. 34:26

12 And the king commanded Hilki-
ah the priest, and Ahikam the son of
Shaphan, and [j]Achbor the son of
[j]Michaiah, and Shaphan the scribe,
and Asahiah a servant of the king's,
saying,
13 Go ye, inquire of the LORD for me,
and for the people, and for all Judah,
concerning the words of this book that
is found: for great *is* [k]the wrath of the
LORD that is kindled against us, be-
cause our fathers have not hearkened
unto the words of this book, to do ac-
cording unto all that which is written
concerning us.
14 So Hilkiah the priest, and Ahi-
kam, and Achbor, and Shaphan, and
Asahiah, went unto Huldah the proph-
etess, the wife of Shallum the son of
[l]Tikvah, the son of [k]Harhas, keeper
of the [l]wardrobe; (now she dwelt in
Jerusalem [m]in the college;) and they
communed with her.
15 ¶ And she said unto them, Thus
saith the LORD God of Israel, Tell the
man that sent you to me,
16 Thus saith the LORD, Behold, [m]I
will bring evil upon this place, and
upon the inhabitants thereof, *even* all
the words of the book which the king
of Judah hath read:
17 [n]Because they have forsaken
me, and have burned incense unto oth-
er gods, that they might provoke me to
anger with all the works of their hands;
therefore my wrath shall be kindled
against this place, and shall not be
quenched.
18 But to [o]the king of Judah which
sent you to inquire of the LORD, thus
shall ye say to him, Thus saith the LORD

[h] Heb. *threshold* [i] Heb. *melted* [j] Or, *Micah* [k] Or, *Hasrah* [l] Heb. *garments* [m] Or, *in the second part*

22:3 EIGHTEENTH YEAR OF KING JOSIAH. Josiah's dedication to God reveals that a young person (Josiah was twenty-six years old at this time) can have a zeal for the Lord and His cause equal to or greater than that of many older adults.

22:8 THE BOOK OF THE LAW. The "book of the law" found by Hilkiah had been "given by Moses" (2 Chr. 34:14); it was most likely a copy of the entire Pentateuch, the first five books of the Bible (cf. 23:25; Deut. 31:24–26). This discovery bears witness to God's guiding and controlling hand, which had watched over His inspired Word and protected it from destruction by idolators and apostates. Indeed, the inspired written Word of God is indestructible (Is. 40:8).

22:13 GO YE, INQUIRE OF THE LORD. Josiah desired to know whether the sins of Judah had reached such a point that divine judgment was inevitable. (1) Through Huldah the prophetess, God said that His people would someday surely be delivered into the hands of their enemies (vv. 14–17). In other words, when God's people persist in sin, there comes a time when His judgment can no longer be averted. (2) For far too many years, God's people had "mocked the messengers of God, and despised his words, and misused his prophets, until the wrath of the LORD arose against his people, till *there was* no remedy" (2 Chr. 36:16). Josiah's revival merely delayed the approaching destruction of Judah, but could not avert it (vv. 18–20; 23:24–27).

God of Israel, *As touching* the words
which thou hast heard;
19 Because thine [p]heart was ten-
der, and thou hast [q]humbled thyself
before the LORD, when thou heardest
what I spake against this place, and
against the inhabitants thereof, that
they should become [r]a desolation and
[s]a curse, and hast rent thy clothes,
and wept before me; I also have heard
thee, saith the LORD.
20 Behold therefore, I will gather
thee unto thy fathers, and thou [t]shalt
be gathered into thy grave in peace;
and thine eyes shall not see all the evil
which I will bring upon this place. And
they brought the king word again.

The renewal of the covenant

23:1–3pp — 2 Chr. 34:29–32
23:4–20Ref — 2 Chr. 34:3–7,33
23:21–23pp — 2 Chr. 35:1,18–19
23:28–30pp — 2 Chr. 35:20–36:1

23 AND [u]THE king sent, and they
gathered unto him all the el-
ders of Judah and of Jerusalem.
2 And the king went up into the
house of the LORD, and all the men of
Judah and all the inhabitants of Jerusa-
lem with him, and the priests, and the
prophets, and all the people, [n]both
small and great: and he read in their
ears all the words of the book of the
covenant [v]which was found in the
house of the LORD.
3 ¶ And the king [w]stood by a pillar,
and made a covenant before the LORD,
to walk after the LORD, and to keep his
commandments and his testimonies
and his statutes with all *their* heart and
all *their* soul, to perform the words of
this covenant that were written in this
book. And all the people stood to the
covenant.
4 And the king commanded Hilkiah
the high priest, and the priests of the
second order, and the keepers of the
door, to bring forth out of the temple of
the LORD all the vessels that were made
for Baal, and for [x]the grove, and for all
the host of heaven: and he burned them
without Jerusalem in the fields of Kid-
ron, and carried the ashes of them unto
Beth-el.
5 And he [o]put down the [p]idola-
trous priests, whom the kings of Judah
had ordained to burn incense in the
high places in the cities of Judah, and
in the places round about Jerusalem;
them also that burned incense unto
Baal, to the sun, and to the moon, and
to the [q]planets, and to [y]all the hosts
of heaven.
6 And he brought out the [z]grove
from the house of the LORD, without Je-
rusalem, unto the brook Kidron, and
burned it at the brook Kidron, and
stamped *it* small to powder, and cast
the powder thereof upon [a]the graves
of the children of the people.
7 And he brake down the houses
[b]of the sodomites, that *were* by the
house of the LORD, [c]where the women
wove [r]hangings for the grove.
8 And he brought all the priests out
of the cities of Judah, and defiled the
high places where the priests had
burned incense, from [d]Geba to Beer-
sheba, and brake down the high places
of the gates that *were* in the entering in
of the gate of Joshua the governor of
the city, which *were* on a man's left
hand at the gate of the city.
9 [e]Nevertheless the priests of the
high places came not up to the altar of
the LORD in Jerusalem, [f]but they did
eat of the unleavened bread among
their brethren.
10 And he defiled [g]Topheth, which
is in [h]the valley of the children of Hin-
nom, [i]that no man might make his

22:19 [p]Ps. 51:17 Is. 57:15 [q]1 Ki. 21:29 [r]Lev. 26:31,32 [s]Jer. 26:6 & 44:22 **22:20** [t]Ps. 37:37 Is. 57:1,2 **23:1** [u]2 Chr. 34:29,30 **23:2** [v]ch. 22:8 **23:3** [w]ch. 11:14,17 **23:4** [x]ch. 21:3,7 **23:5** [y]ch. 21:3 **23:6** [z]ch. 21:7 [a]2 Chr. 34:4 **23:7** [b]1 Ki. 14:24 & 15:12 [c]Ezek. 16:16 **23:8** [d]1 Ki. 15:22 **23:9** [e]See Ezek. 44:10-14 [f]1 Sam. 2:36 **23:10** [g]Is. 30:33 Jer. 7:31 & 19:6,11-13 [h]Josh. 15:8 [i]Lev. 18:21 Deut. 18:10 Ezek. 23:37,39

[n] Heb. *from small even unto great* [o] Heb. *caused to cease* [p] Heb. *Chemarim* [q] Or, *twelve signs,* or, *constellations* [r] Heb. *houses*

22:19 HEART WAS TENDER . . . HUMBLED. Josiah pleased God because he humbled himself before the Lord. Humbling oneself before God is a primary condition for becoming renewed and receiving God's grace. It involves: (1) believing that God's judgments toward us are right and just, in accordance with what we deserve (v. 13); (2) knowing that we, without His grace, are captives to sin and evil, and that we are dependent upon Him for all good (cf. Prov. 3:7; Rom. 12:3; 1 Cor. 1:4); (3) having a contrite heart before God because of our spiritually poor condition (Ps. 51:17; cf. Lev. 26:40–41; Num. 12:3; 2 Chr. 12:5–6; Prov. 22:4); (4) fearing God's Word with deep sincerity (v. 11; 2 Chr. 34:18–19).

23:4 HE BURNED THEM. Josiah's reforms follow the Scriptural principle that repentance for specific sins is essential to true revival. Whenever genuine repentance occurs, specific sins will be identified, false believers expelled, worldly practices forsaken, and godly standards restored. Any talk of the need for revival and repentance in the churches without specifying what must be changed indicates that the commitment to a real change in people's hearts and lifestyles is lacking.

son or his daughter to pass through the fire to Molech.

11 And he took away the horses that the kings of Judah had given to the sun, at the entering in of the house of the LORD, by the chamber of Nathan-melech the [s]chamberlain, which *was* in the suburbs, and burned the chariots of the sun with fire.

12 And the altars that *were* [j]on the top of the upper chamber of Ahaz, which the kings of Judah had made, and the altars which [k]Manasseh had made in the two courts of the house of the LORD, did the king beat down, and [t]brake *them* down from thence, and cast the dust of them into the brook Kidron.

13 And the high places that *were* before Jerusalem, which *were* on the right hand of [u]the mount of corruption, which [l]Solomon the king of Israel had builded for Ashtoreth the abomination of the Zidonians, and for Chemosh the abomination of the Moabites, and for Milcom the abomination of the children of Ammon, did the king defile.

14 And he [m]brake in pieces the [v]images, and cut down the groves, and filled their places with the bones of men.

15 ¶ Moreover the altar that *was* at Beth-el, *and* the high place [n]which Jeroboam the son of Nebat, who made Israel to sin, had made, both that altar and the high place he brake down, and burned the high place, *and* stamped *it* small to powder, and burned the grove.

16 And as Josiah turned himself, he spied the sepulchres that *were* there in the mount, and sent, and took the bones out of the sepulchres, and burned *them* upon the altar, and polluted it, according to the [o]word of the LORD which the man of God proclaimed, who proclaimed these words.

17 Then he said, What title *is* that that I see? And the men of the city told him, *It is* [p]the sepulchre of the man of God, which came from Judah, and proclaimed these things that thou hast done against the altar of Beth-el.

18 And he said, Let him alone; let no man move his bones. So they let his bones [w]alone, with the bones of [q]the prophet that came out of Samaria.

19 And all the houses also of the high places that *were* [r]in the cities of Samaria, which the kings of Israel had made to provoke *the* LORD to anger, Josiah took away, and did to them according to all the acts that he had done in Beth-el.

20 And [s]he [t]slew[x] all the priests of the high places that *were* there upon the altars, and [u]burned men's bones upon them, and returned to Jerusalem.

21 ¶ And the king commanded all the people, saying, [v]Keep the passover unto the LORD your God, [w]as *it is* written in the book of this covenant.

22 Surely [x]there was not holden such a passover from the days of the judges that judged Israel, nor in all the days of the kings of Israel, nor of the kings of Judah;

23 But in the eighteenth year of king Josiah, *wherein* this passover was holden to the LORD in Jerusalem.

24 ¶ Moreover the *workers with* familiar spirits, and the wizards, and the [y]images,[y] and the idols, and all the abominations that were spied in the land of Judah and in Jerusalem, did Josiah put away, that he might perform the words of [z]the law which were written in the book that Hilkiah the priest found in the house of the LORD.

25 [a]And like unto him was there no king before him, that turned to the LORD with all his heart, and with all his soul, and with all his might, according to all the law of Moses; neither after him arose there *any* like him.

26 ¶ Notwithstanding the LORD turned not from the fierceness of his

23:12 [j]See Jer. 19:13 Zeph. 1:5 [k]ch. 21:5
23:13 [l]1 Ki. 11:7
23:14 [m]Ex. 23:24 Deut. 7:5,25
23:15 [n]1 Ki. 12:28,33
23:16 [o]1 Ki. 13:2
23:17 [p]1 Ki. 13:1,30
23:18 [q]1 Ki. 13:31
23:19 [r]See 2 Chr. 34:6, 7
23:20 [s]1 Ki. 13:2 [t]Ex. 22:20 1 Ki. 18:40 ch. 11:18 [u]2 Chr. 34:5
23:21 [v]2 Chr. 35:1 [w]Ex. 12:3 Lev. 23:5 Num. 9:2 Deut. 16:2
23:22 [x]2 Chr. 35:18,19
23:24 [y]Gen. 31:19 [z]Lev. 19:31 & 20:27 Deut. 18:11
23:25 [a]ch. 18:5

[s]Or, *eunuch*, or, *officer* [t]Or, *ran from thence* [u]i.e. the mount of Olives [v]Heb. *statues* [w]Heb. *to escape* [x]Or, *sacrificed* [y]Or, *teraphim*

23:25 THERE WAS NO KING BEFORE HIM. Josiah is described here as the most faithful and dedicated of all the kings who had reigned over God's people, including David himself (see 2 Sam. 12:7–15). In terms of personal commitment and faithfulness to God's word, Josiah was the greatest (cf. 18:5; Deut. 6:5; Jer. 22:15–16).

23:26 THE LORD TURNED NOT FROM ... HIS GREAT WRATH. In spite of the moral leadership of Josiah and his spiritual revival and reforms, Judah had declined so far as a nation that deep and lasting national change was no longer possible. Judgment against Judah was only postponed (see Jer. 11; 13:27), for both the people and the priests were evil at heart. Thus, after the death of Josiah, spiritual and moral degeneration occurred rapidly, and God was obliged to destroy the kingdom only twenty-two years later.

great wrath, wherewith his anger was
kindled against Judah, [b]because of all
the [z]provocations that Manasseh had
provoked him withal.
27 And the LORD said, I will remove
Judah also out of my sight, as [c]I have
removed Israel, and will cast off this
city Jerusalem which I have chosen,
and the house of which I said, [d]My
name shall be there.
28 Now the rest of the acts of Josi-
ah, and all that he did, *are* they not
written in the book of the chronicles of
the kings of Judah?
29 ¶ [e]In his days Pharaoh-nechoh
king of Egypt went up against the king
of Assyria to the river Euphrates: and
king Josiah went against him; and he
slew him at [f]Megiddo, when he [g]had
seen him.
30 [h]And his servants carried him
in a chariot dead from Megiddo, and
brought him to Jerusalem, and buried
him in his own sepulchre. And [i]the
people of the land took Jehoahaz the
son of Josiah, and anointed him, and
made him king in his father's stead.

Jehoahaz, king of Judah

23:31–34pp — 2 Chr. 36:2–4

31 ¶ [a]Jehoahaz *was* twenty and
three years old when he began to reign;
and he reigned three months in Jerusa-
lem. And his mother's name *was* [j]Ha-
mutal, the daughter of Jeremiah of Lib-
nah.
32 And he did *that which was* evil in
the sight of the LORD, according to all
that his fathers had done.
33 And Pharaoh-nechoh put him in
bands [k]at Riblah in the land of Ha-
math, [b]that he might not reign in Jeru-
salem; and [l]put[c] the land to a tribute
of an hundred talents of silver, and a
talent of gold.
34 And [m]Pharaoh-nechoh made
Eliakim the son of Josiah king in the
room of Josiah his father, and [n]turned
his name to [o]Johoiakim, and took Je-
hoahaz away: [p]and he came to Egypt,
and died there.
35 And Jehoiakim gave [q]the silver
and the gold to Pharaoh; but he taxed
the land to give the money according to
the commandment of Pharaoh: he ex-
acted the silver and the gold of the peo-
ple of the land, of every one according
to his taxation, to give *it* unto Pharaoh-
nechoh.

Jehoiakim, king of Judah

23:36–24:6pp — 2 Chr. 36:5–8

36 ¶ [r]Jehoiakim *was* twenty and
five years old when he began to reign;
and he reigned eleven years in Jerusa-
lem. And his mother's name was Zebu-
dah, the daughter of Pedaiah of Ru-
mah.
37 And he did *that which was* evil in
the sight of the LORD, according to all
that his fathers had done.

24

IN [s]HIS days Nebuchadnezzar
king of Babylon came up, and
Jehoiakim became his servant three
years: then he turned and rebelled
against him.
2 [t]And the LORD sent against him
bands of the Chaldees, and bands of
the Syrians, and bands of the Moab-

23:26 [b]ch. 21:11,12 & 24:3,4 Jer. 15:4 **23:27** [c]ch. 17:18,20 & 18:11 & 21:13 [d]1 Ki. 8:29 & 9:3 ch. 21:4,7 **23:29** [e]2 Chr. 35:20 [f]Zech. 12:11 [g]ch. 14:8 **23:30** [h]2 Chr. 35:24 [i]2 Chr. 36:1 **23:31** [j]ch. 24:18 **23:33** [k]ch. 25:6 Jer. 52:27 [l]2 Chr. 36:3 **23:34** [m]2 Chr. 36:4 [n]ch. 24:17 Dan. 1:7 [o]Mat. 1:11 called *Jakim* [p]Jer. 22:11 Ezek. 19:3 **23:35** [q]ver. 33 **23:36** [r]2 Chr. 36:5 **24:1** [s]2 Chr. 36:6 Jer. 25:1,9 Dan. 1:1 **24:2** [t]Jer. 25:9 & 32:28 Ezek. 19:8

[z] Heb. *angers* [a] Called *Shallum* in 1 Chr. 3:15; Jer. 22:11 [b] Or, *because he reigned* [c] Heb. *set a mulct upon the land*

24:1 NEBUCHADNEZZAR KING OF BABYLON. Nebuchadnezzar, the powerful king of the Neo-Babylonian empire, reigned from 605–562 B.C. In 605 he invaded Palestine and took back to Babylon certain hostages from Jerusalem. This began the seventy-year captivity of Judah predicted by Jeremiah (Jer. 25:11–12). Jeremiah, Ezekiel, and Daniel prophesied during Nebuchadnezzar's time. The destruction and captivity of Judah by Nebuchadnezzar occurred in three phases.

(1) In 605 B.C. King Jehoiakim was conquered; along with temple treasures and royal personnel (including Daniel and his three Hebrew friends, Dan. 1:1–7), the king was bound in chains and taken to Babylon (vv. 1–7; 2 Chr. 36:6–7).

(2) In 597 B.C., Jerusalem was again invaded, this time resulting in King Jehoiachin, the rest of the temple treasures, and 10,000 men being carried away to Babylon (vv. 14–16), among whom was the prophet Ezekiel.

(3) In 586 B.C., the Babylonians invaded Jerusalem for the final time; this time they destroyed the city and its temple. King Zedekiah with all but some of the poorest people were deported to Babylon (25:1–12; Jer. 52:29).

24:1 BABYLON. Babylon, also called the Neo-Babylonian Empire, broke the supremacy of Assyria and dominated the world from 605–539 B.C. The Babylonian Empire lasted about seventy years, the same seventy years of Judah's captivity. Babylon was in turn conquered by King Cyrus of Persia (539 B.C.), who allowed the Jews to return to their homeland (2 Chr. 36:22–23; Ezra 1:1–4).

24:2 ACCORDING TO THE WORD OF THE LORD. The captivity of the southern kingdom by Babylon had been predicted 150 years before it occurred (Is. 6:11–12; 39:6). Jeremiah foretold that it would last seventy years (Jer. 25:11–12).

ites, and bands of the children of Am-
mon, and sent them against Judah to
destroy it, [u]according to the word of
the LORD, which he spake [d]by his ser-
vants the prophets.
3 Surely at the commandment of
the LORD came *this* upon Judah, to re-
move *them* out of his sight, [v]for the
sins of Manasseh, according to all that
he did;
4 [w]And also for the innocent blood
that he shed: for he filled Jerusalem
with innocent blood; which the LORD
would not pardon.
5 ¶ Now the rest of the acts of Jehoi-
akim, and all that he did, *are* they not
written in the book of the chronicles of
the kings of Judah?
6 [x]So Jehoiakim slept with his fa-
thers: and Jehoiachin his son reigned
in his stead.
7 And [y]the king of Egypt came not
again any more out of his land: for
[z]the king of Babylon had taken from
the river of Egypt unto the river Eu-
phrates all that pertained to the king of
Egypt.

Jehoiachin, king of Judah

24:8–17pp — 2 Chr. 36:9–10

8 ¶ [a]Jehoiachin[e] *was* eighteen
years old when he began to reign, and
he reigned in Jerusalem three months.
And his mother's name *was* Nehushta,
the daughter of Elnathan of Jerusalem.
9 And he did *that which was* evil in
the sight of the LORD, according to all
that his father had done.
10 ¶ [b]At that time the servants of
Nebuchadnezzar king of Babylon came
up against Jerusalem, and the city
[f]was besieged.
11 And Nebuchadnezzar king of
Babylon came against the city, and his
servants did besiege it.
12 [c]And Jehoiachin the king of Ju-
dah went out to the king of Babylon,
he, and his mother, and his servants,
and his princes, and his [g]officers:
[d]and the king of Babylon [e]took him
[f]in the eighth year of his reign.
13 [g]And he carried out thence all
the treasures of the house of the LORD,
and the treasures of the king's house,
and [h]cut in pieces all the vessels of
gold which Solomon king of Israel had
made in the temple of the LORD, [i]as
the LORD had said.
14 And [j]he carried away all Jeru-
salem, and all the princes, and all the
mighty men of valour, [k]*even* ten thou-
sand captives, and [l]all the craftsmen
and smiths: none remained, save [m]the
poorest sort of the people of the land.
15 And [n]he carried away Jehoia-
chin to Babylon, and the king's mother,
and the king's wives, and his [g]offi-
cers, and the mighty of the land, *those*
carried he into captivity from Jerusa-
lem to Babylon.
16 And [o]all the men of might, *even*
seven thousand, and craftsmen and
smiths a thousand, all *that were* strong
and apt for war, even them the king of
Babylon brought captive to Babylon.
17 ¶ And [p]the king of Babylon
made Mattaniah [q]his father's brother
king in his stead, and [r]changed his
name to Zedekiah.

Zedekiah, king of Judah

24:18–20pp — 2 Chr. 36:11–16; Jer. 52:1–3

18 [s]Zedekiah *was* twenty and one
years old when he began to reign, and
he reigned eleven years in Jerusalem.
And his mother's name *was* [t]Hamu-
tal, the daughter of Jeremiah of Libnah.
19 [u]And he did *that which was* evil
in the sight of the LORD, according to all
that Jehoiakim had done.
20 For through the anger of the
LORD it came to pass in Jerusalem and

24:2 [u]ch. 20:17 & 21:12-14 & 23:27
24:3 [v]ch. 21:2,11 & 23:26
24:4 [w]ch. 21:16
24:6 [x]See 2 Chr. 36:6,8 Jer. 22:18 & 36:30
24:7 [y]Jer. 37:5,7 [z]Jer. 46:2
24:8 [a]2 Chr. 36:9
24:10 [b]Dan. 1:1
24:12 [c]Jer. 24:1 & 29:1,2 Ezek. 17:12 [d]*Nebuchadnezzar's eighth year* Jer. 25:1 [e]ch. 25:27 [f]Jer. 52:28
24:13 [g]ch. 20:17 Is. 39:6 [h]Dan. 5:2,3 [i]Jer. 20:5
24:14 [j]Jer. 24:1 [k]Jer. 52:28 [l]1 Sam. 13:19,22 [m]ch. 25:12
24:15 [n]2 Chr. 36:10 Esth. 2:6 Jer. 22:24
24:16 [o]Jer. 52:28
24:17 [p]Jer. 37:1 [q]1 Chr. 3:15 2 Chr. 36:10 [r]2 Chr. 36:4
24:18 [s]2 Chr. 36:11 Jer. 52:1 [t]ch. 23:31
24:19 [u]2 Chr. 36:12

[d]Heb. *by the hand of* [e]Called *Jeconiah* in 1 Chr. 3:16; Jer. 24:1 and *Coniah* in Jer. 22:24 [f]Heb. *came into siege* [g]Or, *eunuchs*

24:3 TO REMOVE *THEM* OUT OF HIS SIGHT. The fall of Judah was God's judgment upon an obstinate and unrepentant people who followed the terrible sins of Manasseh. (1) Apostasy had reached its limit. The priests and prophets uttered lies (Jer. 5:31; 6:13). Love of dishonest gain, cheating (Jer. 6:13), immorality and prostitution (Jer. 5:8–9), injustice and violence (Jer. 6:7), falsehood (Jer. 8:9–10), and infidelity (Jer. 9:2–3) characterized the lifestyles of the people. (2) The severe judgment of God upon His O.T. people serves as a warning to believers today. If God did not spare the natural branches, neither will He spare those who have been grafted in if they conform to the world and a lifestyle of sin (see Rom. 11:18–25).

24:20 ZEDEKIAH REBELLED AGAINST THE KING OF BABYLON. Zedekiah rebelled partly because false prophets had declared a positive message that God would destroy Babylon and not Judah. Jeremiah's message, though unpopular, proclaimed the opposite—that God would bring His rebellious people under the rule of Babylon. It was Jeremiah's message that came to pass,

Judah, until he had cast them out from his presence, [v]that Zedekiah rebelled against the king of Babylon.

Jerusalem destroyed

25:1–12pp — Jer. 39:1–10
25:1–21pp — 2 Chr. 36:17–20; Jer. 52:4–27
25:22–26pp — Jer. 40:7–9; 41:1–3, 16–18

25 AND IT came to pass [w]in the ninth year of his reign, in the tenth month, in the tenth *day* of the month, *that* Nebuchadnezzar king of Babylon came, he, and all his host, against Jerusalem, and pitched against it; and they built forts against it round about.

2 And the city was besieged unto the eleventh year of king Zedekiah.

3 And on the ninth *day* of the [x]*fourth* month the famine prevailed in the city, and there was no bread for the people of the land.

4 ¶ And [y]the city was broken up, and all the men of war *fled* by night by the way of the gate between two walls, which *is* by the king's garden: (now the Chaldees *were* against the city round about:) and [z]*the king* went the way toward the plain.

5 And the army of the Chaldees pursued after the king, and overtook him in the plains of Jericho: and all his army were scattered from him.

6 So they took the king, and brought him up to the king of Babylon [a]to Riblah; and they [h]gave judgment upon him.

7 And they slew the sons of Zedekiah before his eyes, and [b]put[i] out the eyes of Zedekiah, and bound him with fetters of brass, and carried him to Babylon.

8 ¶ And in the fifth month, [c]on the seventh *day* of the month, which *is* [d]the nineteenth year of king Nebuchadnezzar king of Babylon, [e]came Nebuzar-adan, [j]captain of the guard, a servant of the king of Babylon, unto Jerusalem:

9 [f]And he burnt the house of the LORD, [g]and the king's house, and all the houses of Jerusalem, and every great *man's* house burnt he with fire.

10 And all the army of the Chaldees, that *were with* the captain of the guard, [h]brake down the walls of Jerusalem round about.

11 [i]Now the rest of the people *that were* left in the city, and the [k]fugitives that fell away to the king of Babylon, with the remnant of the multitude, did Nebuzar-adan the captain of the guard carry away.

12 But the captain of the guard [j]left of the poor of the land *to be* vinedressers and husbandmen.

13 And [k]the [l]pillars of brass that *were* in the house of the LORD, and [m]the bases, and [n]the brasen sea that *was* in the house of the LORD, did the Chaldees break in pieces, and carried the brass of them to Babylon.

14 And [o]the pots, and the shovels, and the snuffers, and the spoons, and all the vessels of brass wherewith they ministered, took they away.

15 And the firepans, and the bowls, *and* such things as *were* of gold, *in* gold, and of silver, *in* silver, the captain of the guard took away.

16 The two pillars, [l]one sea, and the bases which Solomon had made for the house of the LORD; [p]the brass of all these vessels was without weight.

17 [q]The height of the one pillar *was* eighteen cubits, and the chapiter upon it *was* brass: and the height of the chapiter three cubits; and the wreathen work, and pomegranates upon the chapiter round about, all of brass: and like unto these had the second pillar with wreathen work.

24:20 [v]2 Chr. 36:13 Ezek. 17:15
25:1 [w]2 Chr. 36:17 Jer. 34:2 Ezek. 24:1
25:3 [x]Jer. 39:2
25:4 [y]Jer. 39:2 [z]Jer. 39:4-7 Ezek. 12:12
25:6 [a]ch. 23:33 Jer. 52:9
25:7 [b]Jer. 39:7
25:8 [c]Jer. 52:12 [d]ch. 24:12 [e]Jer. 39:9
25:9 [f]2 Chr. 36:19 [g]Jer. 39:8 Amos 2:5
25:10 [h]Neh. 1:3 Jer. 52:14
25:11 [i]Jer. 39:9
25:12 [j]ch. 24:14
25:13 [k]Jer. 27:19 & 52:17 [l]1 Ki. 7:15 [m]1 Ki. 7:27 [n]1 Ki. 7:23
25:14 [o]Ex. 27:3 1 Ki. 7:45
25:16 [p]1 Ki. 7:47
25:17 [q]1 Ki. 7:15 Jer. 52:21

h Heb. *spake judgment with him* **i** Heb. *made blind* **j** Or, *chief marshal* **k** Heb. *fallen away* **l** Heb. *the one sea*

---

demonstrating that he was a true prophet of the Lord (cf. Deut. 18:21–22; see article on THE PROPHET IN THE OLD TESTAMENT, p. 1002).

25:1 BUILT FORTS AGAINST IT. The siege against Jerusalem began in 588 B.C. and lasted eighteen months (vv. 1–3). Its calamities are described in Lam. 2:20–21; 4:3–20; 5:2–15; Ezek. 5:10. One-third of the people died of hunger and plague, while another one-third died by the sword (Ezek. 5:12; see also Jer. 38:17–19; 39:1; 52:4; Ezek. 24:1–2).

25:7 SLEW THE SONS OF ZEDEKIAH. Zedekiah, the youngest son of Josiah, reigned for eleven years. He departed from the faith of his righteous father and often persecuted the prophet Jeremiah. Zedekiah could have avoided the tragedies that overtook him if he had listened to Jeremiah (see Jer. 38:14–28). Likewise, if a church and its people do not listen to a godly pastor, the church runs the risk of finding itself destroyed and her children captivated by the evil of the world.

18 ¶ [r]And the captain of the guard took [s]Seraiah the chief priest, and [t]Zephaniah the second priest, and the three keepers of the [m]door:

19 And out of the city he took an [n]officer that was set over the men of war, and [u]five men of them that [o]were in the king's presence, which were found in the city, and the [p]principal scribe of the host, which mustered the people of the land, and threescore men of the people of the land *that were* found in the city:

20 And Nebuzar-adan captain of the guard took these, and brought them to the king of Babylon to Riblah:

21 And the king of Babylon smote them, and slew them at Riblah in the land of Hamath. [v]So Judah was carried away out of their land.

22 ¶ [w]And *as for* the people that remained in the land of Judah, whom Nebuchadnezzar king of Babylon had left, even over them he made Gedaliah the son of Ahikam, the son of Shaphan, ruler.

23 And when all the [x]captains of the armies, they and their men, heard that the king of Babylon had made Gedaliah governor, there came to Gedaliah to Mizpah, even Ishmael the son of Nethaniah, and Johanan the son of Careah, and Seraiah the son of Tanhumeth the Netophathite, and Jaazaniah the son of a Maachathite, they and their men.

24 And Gedaliah sware to them, and to their men, and said unto them, Fear not to be the servants of the Chaldees: dwell in the land, and serve the king of Babylon; and it shall be well with you.

25 But [y]it came to pass in the seventh month, that Ishmael the son of Nethaniah, the son of Elishama, of the seed [q]royal, came, and ten men with him, and smote Gedaliah, that he died, and the Jews and the Chaldees that were with him at Mizpah.

26 And all the people, both small and great, and the captains of the armies, arose, [z]and came to Egypt: for they were afraid of the Chaldees.

25:18 [r]Jer. 52:24 [s]1 Chr. 6:14 Ezra 7:1 [t]Jer. 21:1
25:19 [u]Jer. 52:25
25:21 [v]Lev. 26:33 Deut. 28:36,64 ch. 23:27
25:22 [w]Jer. 40:5
25:23 [x]Jer. 40:7-9
25:25 [y]Jer. 41:1,2
25:26 [z]Jer. 43:4,7
25:27 [a]Jer. 52:31 [b]See Gen. 40:13, 20
25:29 [c]2 Sam. 9:7

Jehoiachin in captivity

25:27–30pp — Jer. 52:31–34

27 ¶ [a]And it came to pass in the seven and thirtieth year of the captivity of Jehoiachin king of Judah, in the twelfth month, on the seven and twentieth *day* of the month, *that* Evil-merodach king of Babylon in the year that he began to reign [b]did lift up the head of Jehoiachin king of Judah out of prison;

28 And he spake [r]kindly to him, and set his throne above the throne of the kings that *were* with him in Babylon;

29 And changed his prison garments: and he did [c]eat bread continually before him all the days of his life.

30 And his allowance *was* a continual allowance given him of the king, a daily rate for every day, all the days of his life.

[m] Heb. *threshold* [n] Or, *eunuch* [o] Heb. *saw the king's face* [p] Or, *scribe of the captain of the host* [q] Heb. *of the kingdom* [r] Heb. *good things with him*

25:21 SO JUDAH WAS CARRIED AWAY. When Judah was led away into captivity, the earthly political kingdom of David ended. But in spite of the destruction of the nation, the promise concerning David's descendants remained (see 2 Sam. 7:14–16; see article on GOD'S COVENANT WITH DAVID, p. 470). God continued preparing for the coming of David's Son, the Christ, whose kingdom would have no end (Luke 1:33). Through David's Messianic descendant, God would eventually form "a chosen generation, a royal priesthood, an holy nation, a peculiar people" (1 Pet. 2:9).

KINGS OF ISRAEL AND JUDAH

This chart depicts the reigns of the kings of Israel and Judah from Jeroboam of Israel and Rehoboam of Judah until the fall of Jerusalem. As best can be determined, the dates reflect the official reign of each king and not any years of his co-regency with another king. The center column is divided into increments of twenty years; the outside columns give the passages in 1 and 2 Kings and 2 Chronicles where the reign of each king is described. By using this chart, you can see at a glance both the length of each reign and the kings in Israel and Judah who were contemporaries. The final column depicts when the major prophets lived and ministered.

PASSAGES	KINGS OF ISRAEL	DATE B.C	KINGS OF JUDAH	PASSAGES I Kings	PASSAGES 2 Chron.	PROPHETS
I Kings						
12:25–14:20	JEROBOAM I	930	REHOBOAM	12:1-24; 14:21-31	10:1–12:16	
			ABIJAH	15:1-8	13:1-14:1	
15:25-31	NADAB	910	ASA	15:9-24	14:2–16:14	
15:32–16:7	BAASHA					
		890				
16:8-14	ELAH					
16:15-22	ZIMRI, TIBNI/OMRI					
16:23-28	OMRI					
16:29–22:40	AHAB					Elijah
		870	JEHOSHAPHAT	22:41-50	17:1–21:3	
2 Kings						
1:1-18	AHAZIAH					
3:1–8:15	JORAM					Elisha
		850				

KINGS OF ISRAEL AND JUDAH

PASSAGES	KINGS OF ISRAEL	DATE B.C	KINGS OF JUDAH	PASSAGES		PROPHETS
2 Kings		850		2 Kings	2 Chron.	Elisha (cont.)
			JEHORAM	8:16-24	21:4-20	
9:30 –10:36	JEHU		AHAZIAH	8:25-29	22:1-9	
			ATHALIAH	11:1-21	22:10 –23:21	
			JOASH	12:1-21	24:1-27	
		830				
13:1-9	JEHOAHAZ					
		810				
13:10-25	JEHOASH					
			AMAZIAH	14:1-22	25:1-28	
		790				
14:23-29	JEROBOAM II					Jonah
			AZARIAH (UZZIAH)	15:1-7	26:1-23	
		770				Amos
						Hosea
15:8-15	ZECHARIAH, SHALLUM					
15:16-22	MENAHEM	750				

KINGS OF ISRAEL AND JUDAH

PASSAGES	KINGS OF ISRAEL	DATE B.C	KINGS OF JUDAH	PASSAGES		PROPHETS
2 Kings				2 Kings	2 Chron.	
		750				Hosea (cont.)
15:23-26	PEKAHIAH					Isaiah
15:27-31	PEKAH		JOTHAM	15:32-38	27:1-8	Micah
17:1-6	HOSHEA	730	AHAZ	16:1-20	28:1-27	
	FALL OF SAMARIA	722				
			HEZEKIAH	18:1 –20:21	29:1 –32:33	
		710				
		690				
			MANASSEH	21:1-18	33:1-20	
		670				
		650				

KINGS OF ISRAEL AND JUDAH

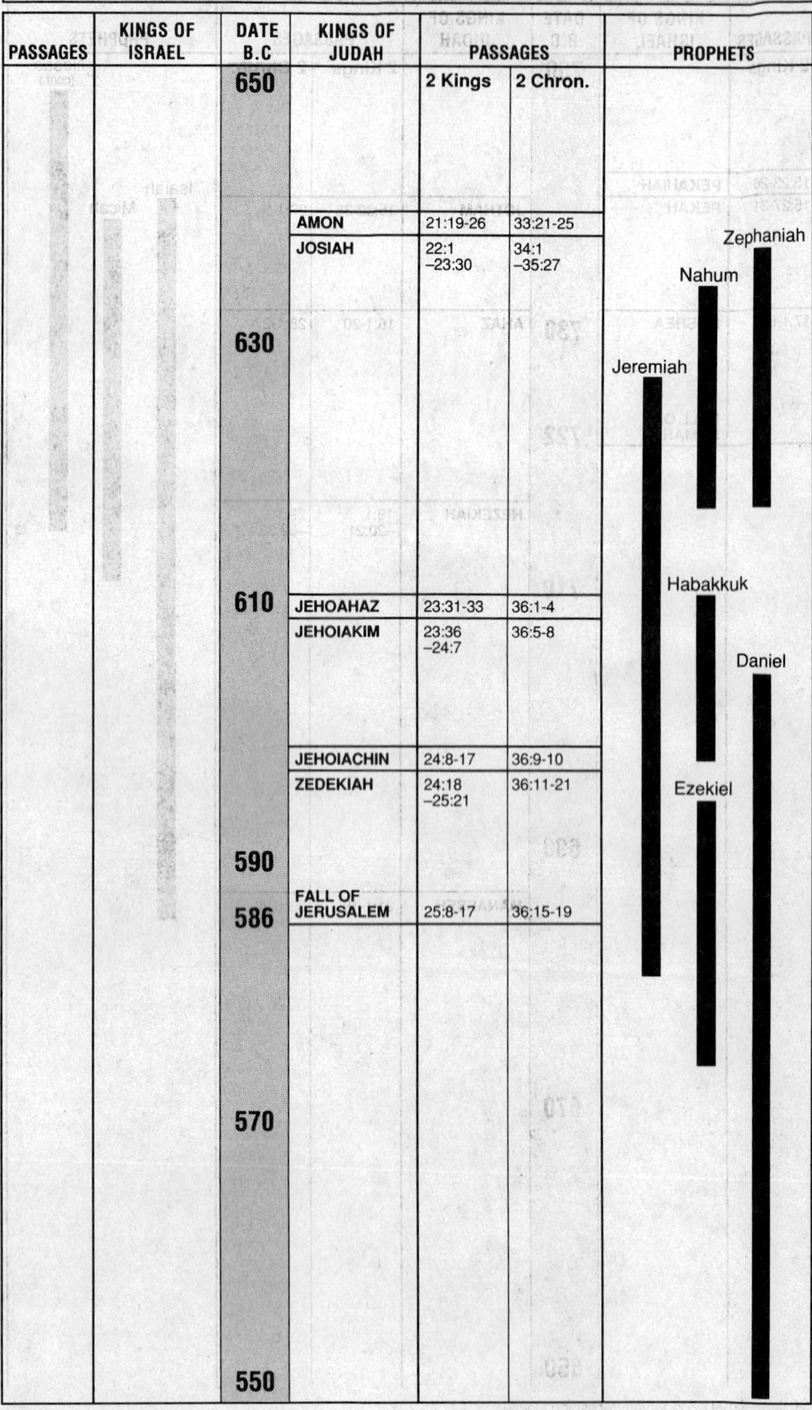

PASSAGES	KINGS OF ISRAEL	DATE B.C	KINGS OF JUDAH	PASSAGES 2 Kings	PASSAGES 2 Chron.	PROPHETS
		650				
			AMON	21:19-26	33:21-25	Zephaniah, Nahum
			JOSIAH	22:1 –23:30	34:1 –35:27	
		630				Jeremiah
		610	JEHOAHAZ	23:31-33	36:1-4	Habakkuk
			JEHOIAKIM	23:36 –24:7	36:5-8	Daniel
			JEHOIACHIN	24:8-17	36:9-10	
			ZEDEKIAH	24:18 –25:21	36:11-21	Ezekiel
		590				
		586	FALL OF JERUSALEM	25:8-17	36:15-19	
		570				
		550				

1 CHRONICLES

Outline

I. Genealogies: Adam to Post-Exilic Restoration (1:1—9:44)
   - A. Adam to Abraham (1:1–27)
   - B. Abraham to Jacob (1:28–54)
   - C. Jacob to David (2:1–55)
   - D. David to the Babylonian Exile (3:1–24)
   - E. Genealogies of the Twelve Tribes (4:1—8:40)
   - F. Genealogies of the Remnant (9:1–34)
     1. The Tribes Who Returned (9:1–39)
     2. The Priests Who Returned (9:10–13)
     3. The Levites Who Returned (9:14–34)
   - G. Genealogy of Saul (9:35–44)

II. David: The Enduring Significance of His Reign (10:1—29:30)
   - A. The Death of Saul and His Sons (10:1–14)
   - B. The Capture of Jerusalem and David's Mighty Men (11:1—12:40)
   - C. Returning the Ark, Restoring Worship, and Establishing the Kingdom (13:1—16:43)
   - D. The Davidic Covenant (17:1–27)
   - E. David's Military Victories (18:1—20:8)
   - F. David's Sinful Census (21:1–30)
   - G. David Thoroughly Prepares for Building the Temple (22:1–19)
   - H. David Organizes the Levites for Temple Ministry (23:1—26:32)
   - I. David's Administrative Organization (27:1–34)
   - J. David's Final Preparation for Succession and the Temple (28:1—29:20)
   - K. Solomon Made King and David's Death (29:21–30)

Author: Ezra (?)

Theme: Israel's "Redemptive" History

Date of Writing: 450–420 B.C.

Background

The history recorded in 1 and 2 Chronicles is pre-exilic; the origin and perspective of the books, however, are post-exilic, written in the second half of the fifth century B.C., sometime after Ezra and a second large company of Jewish exiles from Babylon and Persia had returned to Palestine (457 B.C.). The invasions and destruction of Jerusalem by King Nebuchadnezzar (605–586 B.C.), along with the subsequent 70 + years of Babylonian captivity, had crushed many of the Jews' hopes and ideals as the covenant people. Therefore, the exiles who returned to rebuild Jerusalem and the temple needed a spiritual foundation laid, i.e., a sense of identity with their past redemptive history and an understanding concerning the character of their present faith and future hope as the covenant people. 1 and 2 Chronicles were written to address this need among the returned exiles.

The books of Chronicles, Ezra, and Nehemiah were all written for the Jews who had returned to Palestine from exile, and they closely resemble one another in style, language,

perspective, and purpose. Scholars commonly believe that these were all the work of one author or compiler, who, according to the Talmud and most ancient Jewish and Christian scholars, was Ezra, the priest and scribe. Since 1 and 2 Chronicles were written from a priestly perspective and probably in Ezra's lifetime, and since the closing verses of 2 Chronicles (36:22–23) are repeated in Ezra 1:1–3, the talmudic tradition that Ezra was "the Chronicler" is substantiated.

The author consulted numerous written sources when writing Chronicles, including certain O.T. books and noncanonical records of kings and prophets (see 1 Chr. 29:29; 2 Chr. 9:29; 12:15; 20:34; 32:32). According to the apocryphal book 2 Maccabees (2:13–15), Nehemiah during his governorship established a library in Jerusalem, in which he placed numerous records of the kings and the prophets. As a spiritual leader, Ezra was given access to all available documents to use in compiling the Chronicles. This tradition is ancient and may accurately reflect what means by which the Holy Spirit guided and inspired the composition of these two books.

Purpose

The Chronicles were written to reconnect the returned Jewish exiles with their ancestry and redemptive history. In doing so, it underscored three issues: (1) the importance for the Jews to preserve their racial and spiritual heritage; (2) the importance of the law, the temple, and the priesthood in their ongoing relationship with God, far more important than their allegiance to an earthly king; and (3) Israel's ultimate hope in God's promise of a Messianic descendant of David to sit on the throne forever (1 Chr. 17:14).

Survey

Although the origin and perspective of 1 and 2 Chronicles is post-exilic, they contain an overview of O.T. history from Adam to the decree of Cyrus (c. 538 B.C.), when the Jews were permitted to return to their homeland from exile in Babylon and Persia. 1 Chronicles is organized around two major topics: Israel's genealogical history (chs. 1—9) and the reign of King David (chs. 10—29).

(1) Chs. 1—9 trace Israel's unique redemptive history from Adam to Abraham to David to the Babylonian exile. The tribe of Judah is placed first among Jacob's twelve sons because the house of David, the temple, and the Messiah all came from Judah. The genealogies reveal how God chose and preserved a remnant for Himself from the beginning of human history to the post-exilic present. The priestly perspective of this book is evident in the special attention given to the families of the priests and Levites.

(2) Chs. 10—29 are devoted to the reign of David. David's mighty men (chs. 11—12) and his great victories (chs. 14; 18—20) are commended. Also, the Levites, priests, and musicians in his administration are highlighted (chs. 23—26). The author placed emphasis on David recovering the ark of the covenant and establishing Jerusalem as Israel's center of worship (chs. 13—16; 22; 28—29). 1 Chronicles differs from 2 Samuel in its omission of the prophetic revelation of David's dark sins of adultery and murder and the subsequent trail of tragic consequences. In its place, 1 Chronicles inserts what 2 Samuel omits: David's diligent and detailed provisions for building the temple and establishing the worship of the Lord God. Under the Holy Spirit's leading, its omissions and additions were designed to meet the needs of God's people in the post-exilic community.

Special Features

Five major features or emphases characterize 1 Chronicles. (1) It covers roughly the same scope of history as does 1 and 2 Samuel. (2) Its genealogies (chs. 1—9) are the longest and most comprehensive genealogical records in the Bible. Since 1 and 2 Chronicles were located last in the original Hebrew arrangement of O.T. books, these genealogies were conveniently located so as to provide inspiration and content for the genealogies of the Messiah at the beginning of the N.T. (3) It vividly describes the unprecedented revival and restoration of all forms of worship when David brought the ark of the covenant to Jerusalem (chs. 15—16). (4) It emphasizes God's covenant with David (ch. 17) as central to Israel's

hope for the promised Messiah. (5) Its selective history reflects the priestly perspective of the inspired author concerning the reestablishment of the temple, the law, and the priesthood in the post-exilic Jerusalem community.

New Testament Fulfillment

The genealogical record from Adam to the Babylonian exile, including the Davidic kings and their descendants (chs. 3—4), provides the necessary data for the N.T. genealogies of Jesus the Messiah in Matthew (1:1–17) and of Jesus the Son of God in Luke (3:23–28). The portrait of David in 1 Chronicles, seated on the throne of the Lord and ruling over His kingdom (17:14), foreshadows the coming of the Messianic "Son of David," Jesus Christ.

Historical Reliability of Chronicles

Careless critics have viewed Chronicles as invented or distorted history, generally less reliable than what is recorded in Samuel and Kings. It is true that Chronicles is a highly selective history; it is not true, however, that it is invented or unreliable. It is true that Chronicles stresses the bright side of Jewish history; it is not true that it denies her failures (e.g., 1 Chr. 21). When omitting history recorded in Samuel and Kings, the Chronicler presupposes a knowledge of these books by his readers. Both the prophetic judgments of Samuel and Kings and the priestly hopes of Chronicles are true and necessary. Many of the historical statements found only in 1 Chronicles have been authenticated as reliable by archaeological discoveries; none has been proven untenable. Also, careful scholarship has provided legitimate explanations concerning the superficial problem of large figures in Chronicles. Chronicles stands as an important and reliable part of the whole of God's inspired record of the old covenant.

Reading 1 Chronicles

In order to read the entire Old Testament in one year, the book of 1 Chronicles should be read in 11 days, according to the following schedule: ☐ 1–2 ☐ 3–4 ☐ 5–6 ☐ 7–8 ☐ 9–10 ☐ 11–13 ☐ 14–16 ☐ 17–19 ☐ 20–22 ☐ 23–25 ☐ 26–29

NOTES

Descendants of the patriarchs

1:5–7pp — Gen. 10:2–5
1:8–16pp — Gen. 10:6–20
1:17–23pp — Gen. 10:21–31; 11:10–27
1:29–31pp — Gen. 25:12–16
1:32–33pp — Gen. 36:10–14
1:35–37pp — Gen. 36:10–14
1:38–42pp — Gen. 36:20–28

1 ADAM, [a]SHETH, Enosh,
2 Kenan, Mahalaleel, Jered,
3 Henoch, Methuselah, Lamech,
4 Noah, Shem, Ham, and Japheth.
5 ¶ [b]The sons of Japheth; Gomer,
and Magog, and Madai, and Javan, and
Tubal, and Meshech, and Tiras.
6 And the sons of Gomer; Ash-
chenaz, and [a]Riphath, and Togarmah.
7 And the sons of Javan; Elishah,
and Tarshish, Kittim, and [b]Dodanim.
8 ¶ [c]The sons of Ham; Cush, and
Mizraim, Put, and Canaan.
9 And the sons of Cush; Seba, and
Havilah, and Sabta, and Raamah, and
Sabtecha. And the sons of Raamah;
Sheba, and Dedan.
10 And Cush [d]begat Nimrod: he be-
gan to be mighty upon the earth.
11 And Mizraim begat Ludim, and
Anamim, and Lehabim, and Naph-
tuhim,
12 And Pathrusim, and Casluhim,
(of whom came the Philistines,) and
[e]Caphthorim.
13 And [f]Canaan begat Zidon his
firstborn, and Heth,
14 The Jebusite also, and the Amo-
rite, and the Girgashite,
15 And the Hivite, and the Arkite,
and the Sinite,
16 And the Arvadite, and the Zema-
rite, and the Hamathite.
17 ¶ The sons of [g]Shem; Elam, and
Asshur, and Arphaxad, and Lud, and
Aram, and Uz, and Hul, and Gether,
and [c]Meshech.

1:1 [a]Gen. 4:25,26 & 5:3,9
1:5 [b]Gen. 10:2
1:8 [c]Gen. 10:6
1:10 [d]Gen. 10:8,13
1:12 [e]Deut. 2:23
1:13 [f]Gen. 10:15
1:17 [g]Gen. 10:22 & 11:10
1:19 [h]Gen. 10:25
1:20 [i]Gen. 10:26
1:24 [j]Gen. 11:10 Luke 3:36
1:25 [k]Gen. 11:15
1:27 [l]Gen. 17:5
1:28 [m]Gen. 21:2 [n]Gen. 16:11,15
1:29 [o]Gen. 25:13-16
1:32 [p]Gen. 25:1
1:34 [q]Gen. 21:2 [r]Gen. 25:25,26

18 And Arphaxad begat Shelah, and
Shelah begat Eber.
19 And unto Eber were born two
sons: the name of the one *was* [h]Pe-
leg;[d] because in his days the earth
was divided: and his brother's name
was Joktan.
20 And [i]Joktan begat Almodad,
and Sheleph, and Hazarmaveth, and Je-
rah,
21 Hadoram also, and Uzal, and
Diklah,
22 And Ebal, and Abimael, and
Sheba,
23 And Ophir, and Havilah, and Jo-
bab. All these *were* the sons of Joktan.
24 ¶ [j]Shem, Arphaxad, Shelah,
25 [k]Eber, Peleg, Reu,
26 Serug, Nahor, Terah,
27 [l]Abram; the same *is* Abraham.
28 The sons of Abraham; [m]Isaac,
and [n]Ishmael.
29 ¶ These *are* their generations:
The [o]firstborn of Ishmael, Nebaioth;
then Kedar, and Adbeel, and Mibsam,
30 Mishma, and Dumah, Massa,
[e]Hadad, and Tema,
31 Jetur, Naphish, and Kedemah.
These are the sons of Ishmael.
32 ¶ Now [p]the sons of Keturah,
Abraham's concubine: she bare Zim-
ran, and Jokshan, and Medan, and Mid-
ian, and Ishbak, and Shuah. And the
sons of Jokshan; Sheba, and Dedan.
33 And the sons of Midian; Ephah,
and Epher, and Henoch, and Abida,
and Eldaah. All these *are* the sons of
Keturah.
34 And [q]Abraham begat Isaac.
[r]The sons of Isaac; Esau and Israel.

[a] Or, *Diphath,* as it is in some copies [b] Or, *Rodanim,* according to some copies [c] Or, *Mash;* see Gen. 10:23 [d] i.e. *Division* [e] Or, *Hadar;* see Gen. 25:15

1:1 THE GENEALOGIES. The inclusion of genealogies in this book serves several purposes. (1) Like all of 1 Chr., the genealogies served to reconnect the returned exiles with their ancestry and redemptive past, thus enabling them to recover a sense of their roots and heritage.

(2) The genealogies revealed how God chose and preserved a remnant for Himself from the beginning of human history to the post-exilic present.

(3) The genealogies' immediate objective was to help the families of Israel resettle the land according to previous family ownership (cf. Lev. 25) and to mark clearly the tribe of Levi from which the priests were to come.

(4) Their ultimate objective was to trace the descendants of the family line through which God would bring salvation to the world. God had chosen Abraham (v. 27), and from Abraham another family, Israel (v. 34), and from the family of Israel (2:1), the tribe of Judah, from which came the Davidic line (3:1). From the family of David, God promised that a Messianic Son would come, who would bring redemption from Satan and sin (see Gen. 3:15, note; see articles on GOD'S COVENANT WITH ABRAHAM, ISAAC, AND JACOB, p. 48, and GOD'S COVENANT WITH DAVID, p. 470).

1:1–4 ADAM, SETH, ENOSH. These names are taken from Gen. 5:1–32 and show that the Chronicler believed the first chapters of Genesis to be reliable history and not legend.

35 ¶ The sons of [s]Esau; Eliphaz,
Reuel, and Jeush, and Jaalam, and Ko-
rah.
36 The sons of Eliphaz; Teman, and
Omar, [f]Zephi, and Gatam, Kenaz, and
Timna, and Amalek.
37 The sons of Reuel; Nahath, Ze-
rah, Shammah, and Mizzah.
38 And [t]the sons of Seir; Lotan,
and Shobal, and Zibeon, and Anah, and
Dishon, and Ezar, and Dishan.
39 And the sons of Lotan; Hori, and
[g]Homam: and Timna *was* Lotan's sis-
ter.
40 The sons of Shobal; [h]Alian, and
Manahath, and Ebal, [i]Shephi, and
Onam. And the sons of Zibeon; Aiah,
and Anah.
41 The sons of Anah; [u]Dishon. And
the sons of Dishon; [j]Amram, and
Eshban, and Ithran, and Cheran.
42 The sons of Ezer; Bilhan, and
Zavan, *and* [k]Jakan. The sons of Di-
shan; Uz, and Aran.

The kings of Edom

1:43–54pp — Gen. 36:31–43

43 ¶ Now these *are* the [v]kings that
reigned in the land of Edom before *any*
king reigned over the children of Isra-
el; Bela the son of Beor: and the name
of his city *was* Dinhabah.
44 And when Bela was dead, Jobab
the son of Zerah of Bozrah reigned in
his stead.
45 And when Jobab was dead, Hu-
sham of the land of the Temanites
reigned in his stead.
46 And when Husham was dead,
Hadad the son of Bedad, which smote
Midian in the field of Moab, reigned in
his stead: and the name of his city *was*
Avith.
47 And when Hadad was dead,
Samlah of Masrekah reigned in his
stead.
48 [w]And when Samlah was dead,
Shaul of Rehoboth by the river reigned
in his stead.
49 And when Shaul was dead, Baal-
hanan the son of Achbor reigned in his
stead.
50 And when Baal-hanan was dead,
[l]Hadad reigned in his stead: and the
name of his city *was* [m]Pai; and his
wife's name *was* Mehetabel, the daugh-
ter of Matred, the daughter of Meza-
hab.
51 ¶ Hadad died also. And the
[x]dukes of Edom were; duke Timnah,
duke [n]Aliah, duke Jetheth,
52 Duke Aholibamah, duke Elah,
duke Pinon,
53 Duke Kenaz, duke Teman, duke
Mibzar,
54 Duke Magdiel, duke Iram. These
are the dukes of Edom.

From Israel to David

2:1–2pp — Gen. 35:23–26
2:5–15pp — Ruth 4:18–22; Mat. 1:3–6

2 THESE *ARE* the sons of [o]Israel;
[y]Reuben, Simeon, Levi, and Ju-
dah, Issachar, and Zebulun,
2 Dan, Joseph, and Benjamin, Naph-
tali, Gad, and Asher.
3 ¶ The sons of [z]Judah; Er, and
Onan, and Shelah: *which* three were
born unto him of the daughter of
[a]Shua the Canaanitess. And [b]Er, the
firstborn of Judah, was evil in the sight
of the LORD; and he slew him.
4 And [c]Tamar his daughter-in-law
bare him Pharez and Zerah. All the
sons of Judah *were* five.
5 The sons of [d]Pharez; Hezron,
and Hamul.
6 And the sons of Zerah; [p]Zimri,
[e]and Ethan, and Heman, and Calcol,
and [q]Dara: five of them in all.
7 And the sons of [f]Carmi; [r]Achar,
the troubler of Israel, who trans-
gressed in the thing [g]accursed.

1:35 [s]Gen. 36:9,10 **1:38** [t]Gen. 36:20 **1:41** [u]Gen. 36:25 **1:43** [v]Gen. 36:31 **1:48** [w]Gen. 36:37

1:51 [x]Gen. 36:40 **2:1** [y]Gen. 29:32 & 30:5 & 35:18,22 & 46:8 **2:3** [z]Gen. 38:3 & 46:12 Num. 26:19 [a]Gen. 38:2 [b]Gen. 38:7 **2:4** [c]Gen. 38:29,30 **2:5** [d]Gen. 46:12 Ruth 4:18 **2:6** [e]1 Ki. 4:31 **2:7** [f]See ch. 4:1 [g]Josh. 6:18 & 7:1

[f] Or, *Zepho;* see Gen. 36:11 [g] Or, *Heman;* see Gen. 36:22 [h] Or, *Alvan;* see Gen. 36:23 [i] Or, *Shepho;* see Gen. 36:23 [j] Or, *Hemdan;* see Gen. 36:26 [k] Or, *Akan;* see Gen. 36:27 [l] Or, *Hadar;* see Gen. 36:39 [m] Or, *Pau;* see Gen. 36:39 [n] Or, *Alvah* [o] Or, *Jacob* [p] Or, *Zabdi;* see Josh. 7:1 [q] Or, *Darda* [r] Or, *Achan*

2:1 THE SONS OF ISRAEL. In ch. 1 the author of Chronicles lists descendants from Adam (v. 1) to Abraham (v. 27) to Israel (v. 34). Through the sons of Israel (i.e., Jacob) came the chosen people, through whom God had determined to bless "all families of the earth" (Gen. 12:3). In chs. 2—8 the author traces the genealogy of Israel's twelve sons. The genealogy of Judah is placed first among the tribes (v. 3) since the main stream of redemptive history flowed through it, and particularly through David and his descendants (cf. 3:1; 2 Sam. 23:5), to the Messiah.

2:5 THE SONS OF. The genealogies are selective, choosing only certain descendants. The phrase "the son of" can also mean "the descendant of." Thus some sons or generations may be omitted.

8 And the sons of Ethan; Azariah.

9 The sons also of Hezron, that were born unto him; Jerahmeel, and [s]Ram, and [t]Chelubai.

10 And Ram [h]begat Amminadab; and Amminadab begat Nahshon, [i]prince of the children of Judah;

11 And Nahshon begat [u]Salma, and Salma begat Boaz,

12 And Boaz begat Obed, and Obed begat Jesse.

13 ¶ [j]And Jesse begat his firstborn Eliab, and Abinadab the second, and [v]Shimma the third,

14 Nethaneel the fourth, Raddai the fifth,

15 Ozem the sixth, David the seventh:

16 Whose sisters *were* Zeruiah, and Abigail. [k]And the sons of Zeruiah; Abishai, and Joab, and Asahel, three.

17 And [l]Abigail bare Amasa: and the father of Amasa *was* [w]Jether the Ishmaelite.

18 ¶ And Caleb the son of Hezron begat *children* of Azubah *his* wife, and of Jerioth: her sons *are* these; Jesher, and Shobab, and Ardon.

19 And when Azubah was dead, Caleb took unto him [m]Ephrath, which bare him Hur.

20 And Hur begat Uri, and Uri begat [n]Bezaleel.

21 ¶ And afterward Hezron went in to the daughter of [o]Machir the father of Gilead, whom he [x]married when he *was* threescore years old; and she bare him Segub.

22 And Segub begat Jair, who had three and twenty cities in the land of Gilead.

23 [p]And he took Geshur, and Aram, with the towns of Jair, from them, with Kenath, and the towns thereof, *even* threescore cities. All these *belonged to* the sons of Machir the father of Gilead.

24 And after that Hezron was dead in Caleb-ephratah, then Abiah Hezron's wife bare him [q]Ashur the father of Tekoa.

25 ¶ And the sons of Jerahmeel the firstborn of Hezron were, Ram the firstborn, and Bunah, and Oren, and Ozem, *and* Ahijah.

26 Jerahmeel had also another wife, whose name *was* Atarah; she *was* the mother of Onam.

27 And the sons of Ram the firstborn of Jerahmeel were, Maaz, and Jamin, and Eker.

28 And the sons of Onam were, Shammai, and Jada. And the sons of Shammai; Nadab, and Abishur.

29 And the name of the wife of Abishur *was* Abihail, and she bare him Ahban, and Molid.

30 And the sons of Nadab; Seled, and Appaim: but Seled died without children.

31 And the sons of Appaim; Ishi. And the sons of Ishi; Sheshan. And [r]the children of Sheshan; Ahlai.

32 And the sons of Jada the brother of Shammai; Jether, and Jonathan: and Jether died without children.

33 And the sons of Jonathan; Peleth, and Zaza. These were the sons of Jerahmeel.

34 ¶ Now Sheshan had no sons, but daughters. And Sheshan had a servant, an Egyptian, whose name *was* Jarha.

35 And Sheshan gave his daughter to Jarha his servant to wife; and she bare him Attai.

36 And Attai begat Nathan, and Nathan begat [s]Zabad,

37 And Zabad begat Ephlal, and Ephlal begat Obed,

38 And Obed begat Jehu, and Jehu begat Azariah,

39 And Azariah begat Helez, and Helez begat Eleasah,

40 And Eleasah begat Sisamai, and Sisamai begat Shallum,

41 And Shallum begat Jekamiah, and Jekamiah begat Elishama.

42 ¶ Now the sons of Caleb the brother of Jerahmeel *were*, Mesha his firstborn, which *was* the father of Ziph; and the sons of Mareshah the father of Hebron.

43 And the sons of Hebron; Korah, and Tappuah, and Rekem, and Shema.

44 And Shema begat Raham, the father of Jorkoam: and Rekem begat Shammai.

45 And the son of Shammai *was* Maon: and Maon *was* the father of Beth-zur.

46 And Ephah, Caleb's concubine, bare Haran, and Moza, and Gazez: and Haran begat Gazez.

2:10 [h]Ruth 4:19,20 Mat. 1:4 [i]Num. 1:7 & 2:3
2:13 [j]1 Sam. 16:6
2:16 [k]2 Sam. 2:18
2:17 [l]2 Sam. 17:25
2:19 [m]ver. 50
2:20 [n]Ex. 31:2
2:21 [o]Num. 27:1
2:23 [p]Num. 32:41 Deut. 3:14 Josh. 13:30
2:24 [q]ch. 4:5
2:31 [r]See ver. 34,35
2:36 [s]ch. 11:41

[s] Or, *Aram;* see Mat. 1:3,4 [t] Or, *Caleb;* see ver. 18,42 [u] Or, *Salmon;* see Ruth 4:21; Mat. 1:4 [v] Or, *Shammah;* see 1 Sam. 16:9 [w] Or, *Ithra an Israelite;* see 2 Sam. 17:25 [x] Heb. *took*

47 And the sons of Jahdai; Regem, and Jotham, and Gesham, and Pelet, and Ephah, and Shaaph.

48 Maachah, Caleb's concubine, bare Sheber, and Tirhanah.

49 She bare also Shaaph the father of Madmannah, Sheva the father of Machbenah, and the father of Gibea: and the daughter of Caleb *was* [t]Achsah.

50 ¶ These were the sons of Caleb the son of Hur, the firstborn of [y]Ephratah; Shobal the father of Kirjath-jearim,

51 Salma the father of Bethlehem, Hareph the father of Beth-gader.

52 And Shobal the father of Kirjath-jearim had sons; [z]Haroeh, *and* [a]half of the Manahethites.

53 And the families of Kirjath-jearim; the Ithrites, and the Puhites, and the Shumathites, and the Mishraites; of them came the Zareathites, and the Eshtaulites.

54 The sons of Salma; Bethlehem, and the Netophathites, [b]Ataroth, the house of Joab, and half of the Manahethites, the Zorites.

55 And the families of the scribes which dwelt at Jabez; the Tirathites, the Shimeathites, *and* Suchathites. These *are* the [u]Kenites that came of Hemath, the father of the house of [v]Rechab.

The family of David

3:1–4pp — 2 Sam. 3:2–5
3:5–8pp — 2 Sam. 5:14–16; 1 Chr. 14:4–7

3 NOW THESE were the sons of David, which were born unto him in Hebron; the firstborn [w]Amnon, of Ahinoam the [x]Jezreelitess; the second [c]Daniel, of Abigail the Carmelitess:

2 The third, Absalom the son of Maachah the daughter of Talmai king of Geshur: the fourth, Adonijah the son of Haggith:

3 The fifth, Shephatiah of Abital: the sixth, Ithream by [y]Eglah his wife.

4 *These* six were born unto him in Hebron; and [z]there he reigned seven years and six months: and [a]in Jerusalem he reigned thirty and three years.

5 [b]And these were born unto him in Jerusalem; [d]Shimea, and Shobab, and Nathan, and [c]Solomon, four, of [e]Bath-shua the daughter of [f]Ammiel:

6 Ibhar also, and [g]Elishama, and Eliphelet,

7 And Nogah, and Nepheg, and Japhia,

8 And Elishama, and [h]Eliada, and Eliphelet, [d]nine.

9 *These were* all the sons of David, beside the sons of the concubines, and [e]Tamar their sister.

The family of Solomon

10 ¶ And Solomon's son *was* [f]Rehoboam, [i]Abia his son, Asa his son, Jehoshaphat his son,

11 Joram his son, [j]Ahaziah his son, Joash his son,

12 Amaziah his son, [k]Azariah his son, Jotham his son,

13 Ahaz his son, Hezekiah his son, Manasseh his son,

14 Amon his son, Josiah his son.

15 And the sons of Josiah *were,* the firstborn [l]Johanan, the second [m]Jehoiakim, the third [n]Zedekiah, the fourth Shallum.

16 And the sons of [g]Jehoiakim: [o]Jeconiah his son, Zedekiah [h]his son.

17 ¶ And the sons of Jeconiah; Assir, [p]Salathiel [i]his son,

18 Malchiram also, and Pedaiah, and Shenazar, Jecamiah, Hoshama, and Nedabiah.

19 And the sons of Pedaiah *were,* Zerubbabel, and Shimei: and the sons of Zerubbabel; Meshullam, and Hananiah, and Shelomith their sister:

20 And Hashubah, and Ohel, and

2:49 [t]Josh. 15:17
2:55 [u]Judg. 1:16 [v]Jer. 35:2
3:1 [w]2 Sam. 3:2 [x]Josh. 15:56
3:3 [y]2 Sam. 3:5
3:4 [z]2 Sam. 2:11 [a]2 Sam. 5:5
3:5 [b]ch. 14:4 [c]2 Sam. 12:24
3:8 [d]See 2 Sam. 5:14-16
3:9 [e]2 Sam. 13:1
3:10 [f]1 Ki. 11:43
3:16 [g]Mat. 1:11 [h]2 Ki. 24:17 being his uncle
3:17 [i]Mat. 1:12

[y] Or, *Ephrath;* see ver. 19 [z] Or, *Reaiah;* see ch. 4:2 [a] Or, *half of the Menuchites,* or, *Hatsiham-menuchoth* [b] Or, *Atarites,* or, *crowns of the house of Joab* [c] Or, *Chileab;* see 2 Sam. 3:3 [d] Or, *Shammua;* see 2 Sam. 5:14 [e] Or, *Bath-sheba;* see 2 Sam. 11:3 [f] Or, *Eliam;* see 2 Sam. 11:3 [g] Or, *Elishua;* see 2 Sam. 5:15 [h] Or, *Beeliada;* see ch. 14:7 [i] Called *Abijam* in 1 Ki. 15:1 [j] Called *Azariah* in 2 Chr. 22:6; *Jehoahaz* in 2 Chr. 21:17 [k] Called *Uzziah* in 2 Ki. 15:30 [l] Called *Jehoahaz* in 2 Ki. 23:30 [m] Called *Eliakim* in 2 Ki. 23:34 [n] Called *Mattaniah* in 2 Ki. 24:17 [o] Called *Jehoiachin* in 2 Ki. 24:6; *Coniah* in Jer. 22:24 [p] Heb. *Shealtiel*

3:1 SONS OF DAVID. The author gives special attention to the descendants of David. It was from the family of David that God had promised to bring the Messianic king to rule God's people (see 2 Sam. 7:12–17). The author wants to show that although the kingdom of David had been destroyed, the descendants of David lived on. Thus God could and would fulfill His promises.

Berechiah, and Hasadiah, Jushab-hesed, five.

21 And the sons of Hananiah; Pelatiah, and Jesaiah: the sons of Rephaiah, the sons of Arnan, the sons of Obadiah, the sons of Shechaniah.

22 And the sons of Shechaniah; Shemaiah: and the sons of Shemaiah; [j]Hattush, and Igeal, and Bariah, and Neariah, and Shaphat, six.

23 And the sons of Neariah; Elioenai, and [q]Hezekiah, and Azrikam, three.

24 And the sons of Elioenai *were*, Hodaiah, and Eliashib, and Pelaiah, and Akkub, and Johanan, and Dalaiah, and Anani, seven.

The family of Judah

4 THE SONS of Judah; [k]Pharez, Hezron, and [r]Carmi, and Hur, and Shobal.

2 And [s]Reaiah the son of Shobal begat Jahath; and Jahath begat Ahumai, and Lahad. These *are* the families of the Zorathites.

3 And these *were of* the father of Etam; Jezreel, and Ishma, and Idbash: and the name of their sister *was* Hazelelponi:

4 And Penuel the father of Gedor, and Ezer the father of Hushah. These *are* the sons of [l]Hur, the firstborn of Ephratah, the father of Bethlehem.

5 ¶ And [m]Ashur the father of Tekoa had two wives, Helah and Naarah.

6 And Naarah bare him Ahuzam, and Hepher, and Temeni, and Haahashtari. These *were* the sons of Naarah.

7 And the sons of Helah *were*, Zereth, and Jezoar, and Ethnan.

8 And Coz begat Anub, and Zobebah, and the families of Aharhel the son of Harum.

9 ¶ And Jabez was [n]more honourable than his brethren: and his mother called his name [t]Jabez, saying, Because I bare him with sorrow.

10 And Jabez called on the God of Israel, saying, [u]Oh that thou wouldest bless me indeed, and enlarge my coast, and that thine hand might be with me, and that thou wouldest [v]keep *me* from evil, that it may not grieve me! And God granted him that which he requested.

11 ¶ And Chelub the brother of Shuah begat Mehir, which *was* the father of Eshton.

12 And Eshton begat Beth-rapha, and Paseah, and Tehinnah the father of [w]Ir-nahash. These *are* the men of Rechah.

13 And the sons of Kenaz; [o]Othniel, and Seraiah: and the sons of Othniel; [x]Hathath.

14 And Meonothai begat Ophrah: and Seraiah begat Joab, the father of [p]the [y]valley of [z]Charashim; for they were craftsmen.

15 And the sons of Caleb the son of Jephunneh; Iru, Elah, and Naam: and the sons of Elah, [a]even Kenaz.

16 And the sons of Jehaleleel; Ziph, and Ziphah, Tiria, and Asareel.

17 And the sons of Ezra *were*, Jether, and Mered, and Epher, and Jalon: and she bare Miriam, and Shammai, and Ishbah the father of Eshtemoa.

18 And his wife [b]Jehudijah bare Jered the father of Gedor, and Heber the father of Socho, and Jekuthiel the father of Zanoah. And these *are* the sons of Bithiah the daughter of Pharaoh, which Mered took.

19 And the sons of *his* wife [c]Hodiah the sister of Naham, the father of Keilah the Garmite, and Eshtemoa the Maachathite.

20 And the sons of Shimon *were*, Amnon, and Rinnah, Ben-hanan, and Tilon. And the sons of Ishi *were*, Zoheth, and Ben-zoheth.

21 ¶ The sons of Shelah [q]the son of

3:22 [j]Ezra 8:2
4:1 [k]Gen. 46:12
4:4 [l]ch. 2:50
4:5 [m]ch. 2:24
4:9 [n]Gen. 34:19
4:13 [o]Josh. 15:17
4:14 [p]Neh. 11:35
4:21 [q]Gen. 38:1,5

[q]Heb. *Hiskijahu* [r]Called *Chelubai* in ch. 2:9; *Caleb* in ch. 2:18 [s]Or, *Haroeh;* see ch. 2:52 [t]i.e. *sorrowful* [u]Heb. *If thou wilt* [v]Heb. *do* me [w]Or, *the city of Nahash* [x]Or, *Hathath* and *Meonothai,* who *begat* [y]Or, inhabitants *of the valley* [z]i.e. *Craftsmen* [a]Or, *Uknaz* [b]Or, *the Jewess* [c]Or, *Jehudijah,* mentioned before

4:10 JABEZ CALLED ON THE GOD OF ISRAEL. The righteous example of Jabez stresses the truth that God blesses those who faithfully call upon Him. Note that Jabez was "more honourable than his brethren" (v. 9). Jabez demonstrates that God's divine blessing and protection do not come automatically, but occur as the result of our commitment to Him and His cause on earth, and as a result of our prayers (see Mat. 6:13; see article on EFFECTIVE PRAYING, p. 540). The Chronicler's point of view is well expressed in 2 Chr. 20:20, "Believe in the LORD your God, so shall ye be established." Jabez's prayer is a model for all believers.

4:10 KEEP *ME* FROM EVIL. See Mat. 6:13, note.

Judah *were,* Er the father of Lecah, and
Laadah the father of Mareshah, and
the families of the house of them that
wrought fine linen, of the house of Ash-
bea,
22 And Jokim, and the men of
Chozeba, and Joash, and Saraph, who
had the dominion in Moab, and Jashu-
bi-lehem. And *these are* ancient things.
23 These *were* the potters, and
those that dwelt among plants and
hedges: there they dwelt with the king
for his work.

The family of Simeon

4:28–33pp — Josh. 19:2–10

24 ¶ The sons of Simeon *were,*
[d]Nemuel, and Jamin, [e]Jarib, Zerah,
and Shaul:
25 Shallum his son, Mibsam his
son, Mishma his son.
26 And the sons of Mishma; Ham-
uel his son, Zacchur his son, Shimei his
son.
27 And Shimei had sixteen sons and
six daughters; but his brethren had not
many children, neither did all their
family multiply, [f]like to the children
of Judah.
28 And they dwelt at [r]Beer-sheba,
and Moladah, and Hazar-shual,
29 And at [g]Bilhah, and at Ezem,
and at [h]Tolad,
30 And at Bethuel, and at Hormah,
and at Ziklag,
31 And at Beth-marcaboth, and
[i]Hazar-susim, and at Beth-birei, and
at Shaaraim. These *were* their cities
unto the reign of David.
32 And their villages *were,* [j]Etam,
and Ain, Rimmon, and Tochen, and
Ashan, five cities:
33 And all their villages that *were*
round about the same cities, unto
[k]Baal. These *were* their habitations,
and [l]their genealogy.
34 And Meshobab, and Jamlech,
and Joshah the son of Amaziah,
35 And Joel, and Jehu the son of
Josibiah, the son of Seraiah, the son of
Asiel,
36 And Elioenai, and Jaakobah, and
Jeshohaiah, and Asaiah, and Adiel, and
Jesimiel, and Benaiah,
37 And Ziza the son of Shiphi, the
son of Allon, the son of Jedaiah, the son
of Shimri, the son of Shemaiah;
38 These [m]mentioned by *their*
names *were* princes in their families:

4:28 [r]Josh. 19:2
4:41 [s]2 Ki. 18:8
4:43 [t]See 1 Sam. 15:8 & 30:17 & 2 Sam. 8:12
5:1 [u]Gen. 29:32 & 49:3 [v]Gen. 35:22 & 49:4 [w]Gen. 48:15,22
5:2 [x]Gen. 49:8,10 Ps. 60:7 & 108:8 [y]Mic. 5:2 Mat. 2:6
5:3 [z]Gen. 46:9 Ex. 6:14 Num. 26:5
5:7 [a]See ver. 17

and the house of their fathers in-
creased greatly.
39 ¶ And they went to the entrance
of Gedor, *even* unto the east side of the
valley, to seek pasture for their flocks.
40 And they found fat pasture and
good, and the land *was* wide, and quiet,
and peaceable; for *they* of Ham had
dwelt there of old.
41 And these written by name came
in the days of Hezekiah king of Judah,
and [s]smote their tents, and the habi-
tations that were found there, and de-
stroyed them utterly unto this day, and
dwelt in their rooms: because *there was*
pasture there for their flocks.
42 And *some* of them, *even* of the
sons of Simeon, five hundred men,
went to mount Seir, having for their
captains Pelatiah, and Neariah, and
Rephaiah, and Uzziel, the sons of Ishi.
43 And they smote [t]the rest of the
Amalekites that were escaped, and
dwelt there unto this day.

The family of Reuben

5 NOW THE sons of Reuben the
firstborn of Israel, (for [u]he *was*
the firstborn; but, forasmuch as he
[v]defiled his father's bed, [w]his birth-
right was given unto the sons of Joseph
the son of Israel: and the genealogy is
not to be reckoned after the birthright.
2 For [x]Judah prevailed above his
brethren, and of him *came* the [y]chief
[n]ruler; but the birthright *was* Jo-
seph's:)
3 The sons, *I say,* of [z]Reuben the
firstborn of Israel *were,* Hanoch, and
Pallu, Hezron, and Carmi.
4 The sons of Joel; Shemaiah his
son, Gog his son, Shimei his son,
5 Micah his son, Reaia his son, Baal
his son,
6 Beerah his son, whom [o]Tilgath-
pilneser king of Assyria carried away
captive: he *was* prince of the Reuben-
ites.
7 And his brethren by their families,
[a]when the genealogy of their genera-

[d] Or, *Jemeul;* see Gen. 46:10; Ex. 6:15; Num. 26:12 [e] Or, *Jachin, Zohar* [f] Heb. *unto* [g] Or, *Balah;* see Josh. 19:3 [h] Or, *Eltolad;* see Josh. 19:4 [i] Or, *Hazar-susah;* see Josh. 19:5 [j] Or, *Ether;* see Josh. 19:7 [k] Or, *Baalath-beer;* see Josh. 19:8 [l] Or, *as they divided themselves by nations among them* [m] Heb. *coming* [n] Or, *prince* [o] Or, *Tiglath-pileser;* see 2 Ki. 15:29 & 16:7

tions was reckoned, *were* the chief, Jeiel, and Zechariah,

8 And Bela the son of Azaz, the son of [p]Shema, the son of Joel, who dwelt in [b]Aroer, even unto Nebo and Baalmeon:

9 And eastward he inhabited unto the entering in of the wilderness from the river Euphrates: because their cattle were multiplied [c]in the land of Gilead.

10 And in the days of Saul they made war [d]with the Hagarites, who fell by their hand: and they dwelt in their tents [q]throughout all the east *land* of Gilead.

The family of Gad

11 ¶ And the children of Gad dwelt over against them, in the land of [e]Bashan unto Salcah:

12 Joel the chief, and Shapham the next, and Jaanai, and Shaphat in Bashan.

13 And their brethren of the house of their fathers *were,* Michael, and Meshullam, and Sheba, and Jorai, and Jachan, and Zia, and Heber, seven.

14 These *are* the children of Abihail the son of Huri, the son of Jaroah, the son of Gilead, the son of Michael, the son of Jeshishai, the son of Jahdo, the son of Buz;

15 Ahi the son of Abdiel, the son of Guni, chief of the house of their fathers.

16 And they dwelt in Gilead in Bashan, and in her towns, and in all the suburbs of [f]Sharon, upon [r]their borders.

17 All these were reckoned by genealogies in the days of [g]Jotham king of Judah, and in the days of [h]Jeroboam king of Israel.

18 ¶ The sons of Reuben, and the Gadites, and half the tribe of Manasseh, [s]of valiant men, men able to bear buckler and sword, and to shoot with bow, and skilful in war, *were* four and forty thousand seven hundred and threescore, that went out to the war.

19 And they made war with the Hagarites, with [i]Jetur, and Nephish, and Nodab.

5:8 [b]Josh. 13:15,16
5:9 [c]Josh. 22:9
5:10 [d]Gen. 25:12
5:11 [e]Josh. 13:11,24
5:16 [f]ch. 27:29
5:17 [g]2 Ki. 15:5,32 [h]2 Ki. 14:16,28
5:19 [i]Gen. 25:15 ch. 1:31
5:20 [j]See ver. 22 [k]Ps. 22:4,5
5:22 [l]2 Ki. 15:29 & 17:6
5:25 [m]2 Ki. 17:7
5:26 [n]2 Ki. 15:19 [o]2 Ki. 15:29 [p]2 Ki. 17:6 & 18:11
6:1 [q]Gen. 46:11 Ex. 6:16 Num. 26:57 ch. 23:6
6:2 [r]See ver. 22

20 And [j]they were helped against them, and the Hagarites were delivered into their hand, and all that *were* with them: for they cried to God in the battle, and he was entreated of them; because they [k]put their trust in him.

21 And they [t]took away their cattle; of their camels fifty thousand, and of sheep two hundred and fifty thousand, and of asses two thousand, and of [u]men an hundred thousand.

22 For there fell down many slain, because the war *was* of God. And they dwelt in their steads until [l]the captivity.

The half tribe of Manasseh

23 ¶ And the children of the half tribe of Manasseh dwelt in the land: they increased from Bashan unto Baalhermon and Senir, and unto mount Hermon.

24 And these *were* the heads of the house of their fathers, even Epher, and Ishi, and Eliel, and Azriel, and Jeremiah, and Hodaviah, and Jahdiel, mighty men of valour, [v]famous men, *and* heads of the house of their fathers.

25 ¶ And they transgressed against the God of their fathers, and went [m]a whoring after the gods of the people of the land, whom God destroyed before them.

26 And the God of Israel stirred up the spirit of [n]Pul king of Assyria, and the spirit of [o]Tilgath-pilneser king of Assyria, and he carried them away, even the Reubenites, and the Gadites, and the half tribe of Manasseh, and brought them unto [p]Halah, and Habor, and Hara, and to the river Gozan, unto this day.

The family of Levi

6:54–80pp — Josh. 21:4–39

6 THE SONS of Levi; [q]Gershon,[w] Kohath, and Merari.

2 And the sons of Kohath; Amram, [r]Izhar, and Hebron, and Uzziel.

[p] Or, *Shemaiah;* see ver. 4 [q] Heb. *upon all the face of the east* [r] Heb. *their goings forth* [s] Heb. *sons of valour* [t] Heb. *led captive* [u] Heb. *souls of men* [v] Heb. *men of names* [w] Or, *Gershom;* see ver. 16

5:25–26 THEY TRANSGRESSED AGAINST . . . GOD. Throughout Chronicles, the writer underscores the truth that disobedience and sin bring judgment and calamity, whereas obedience and faithfulness bring peace and blessing (see 2 Chr. 7:14; 15:2–7; 19:2; 21:12–15; 24:20; 28:9; 34:24–25). This spiritual principle, which holds true in the N.T., should motivate us to fear the Lord and to obey the leadership of the Holy Spirit (see Rom. 2:6–10; 8:5–17; 1 Cor. 10:1–13).

3 And the children of Amram; Aaron, and Moses, and Miriam. The sons also of Aaron; [s]Nadab, and Abihu, Eleazar, and Ithamar.

4 ¶ Eleazar begat Phinehas, Phinehas begat Abishua,

5 And Abishua begat Bukki, and Bukki begat Uzzi,

6 And Uzzi begat Zerahiah, and Zerahiah begat Meraioth,

7 Meraioth begat Amariah, and Amariah begat Ahitub,

8 And [t]Ahitub begat Zadok, and [u]Zadok begat Ahimaaz,

9 And Ahimaaz begat Azariah, and Azariah begat Johanan,

10 And Johanan begat Azariah, (he *it is* [v]that executed the priest's office [x]in the [w]temple that Solomon built in Jerusalem:)

11 And [x]Azariah begat Amariah, and Amariah begat Ahitub,

12 And Ahitub begat Zadok, and Zadok begat [y]Shallum,

13 And Shallum begat Hilkiah, and Hilkiah begat Azariah,

14 And Azariah begat [y]Seraiah, and Seraiah begat Jehozadak,

15 And Jehozadak went *into captivity*, [z]when the LORD carried away Judah and Jerusalem by the hand of Nebuchadnezzar.

16 ¶ The sons of Levi; [a]Gershom,[z] Kohath, and Merari.

17 And these *be* the names of the sons of Gershom; Libni, and Shimei.

18 And the sons of Kohath *were*, Amram, and Izhar, and Hebron, and Uzziel.

19 The sons of Merari; Mahli, and Mushi. And these *are* the families of the Levites according to their fathers.

20 Of Gershom; Libni his son, Jahath his son, [b]Zimmah his son,

21 [a]Joah his son, [b]Iddo his son, Zerah his son, [c]Jeaterai his son.

22 The sons of Kohath; [d]Amminadab his son, Korah his son, Assir his son,

23 Elkanah his son, and Ebiasaph his son, and Assir his son,

24 Tahath his son, [e]Uriel his son, Uzziah his son, and Shaul his son.

25 And the sons of Elkanah; [c]Amasai, and Ahimoth.

26 *As for* Elkanah: the sons of Elkanah; [f]Zophai his son, and [d]Nahath his son,

27 [e]Eliab his son, Jeroham his son, Elkanah his son.

28 And the sons of Samuel; the firstborn [g]Vashni, and Abiah.

29 The sons of Merari; Mahli, Libni his son, Shimei his son, Uzza his son,

30 Shimea his son, Haggiah his son, Asaiah his son.

31 And these *are they* whom David set over the service of song in the house of the LORD, after that the [f]ark had rest.

32 And they ministered before the dwellingplace of the tabernacle of the congregation with singing, until Solomon had built the house of the LORD in Jerusalem: and *then* they waited on their office according to their order.

33 And these *are* they that [h]waited with their children. Of the sons of the Kohathites: Heman a singer, the son of Joel, the son of Shemuel,

34 The son of Elkanah, the son of Jeroham, the son of Eliel, the son of [i]Toah,

35 The son of [j]Zuph, the son of Elkanah, the son of Mahath, the son of Amasai,

36 The son of Elkanah, the son of Joel, the son of Azariah, the son of Zephaniah,

37 The son of Tahath, the son of Assir, the son of [g]Ebiasaph, the son of Korah,

38 The son of Izhar, the son of Kohath, the son of Levi, the son of Israel.

39 And his brother Asaph, who

6:3 [s]Lev. 10:1 **6:8** [t]2 Sam. 8:17 [u]2 Sam. 15:27 **6:10** [v]See 2 Chr. 26:17, 18 [w]1 Ki. 6 2 Chr. 3 **6:11** [x]See Ezra 7:3 **6:14** [y]Neh. 11:11 **6:15** [z]2 Ki. 25:18 **6:16** [a]Ex. 6:16 **6:20** [b]ver. 42 **6:25** [c]See ver. 35,36 **6:26** [d]ver. 34 *Toah* **6:27** [e]ver. 34 *Eliel* **6:31** [f]ch. 16:1 **6:37** [g]Ex. 6:24

[x]Heb. *in the house* [y]Or, *Meshullam;* see ch. 9:11 [z]Or, *Gershon;* see ver. 1 [a]Or, *Ethan;* see ver. 42 [b]Or, *Adaiah;* see ver. 41 [c]Or, *Ethni;* see ver. 41 [d]Or, *Izhar;* see ver. 2,18 [e]Or, *Zephaniah, Azariah, Joel;* see ver. 36 [f]Or, *Zuph;* see ver. 35; 1 Sam. 1:1 [g]Called also *Joel* in ver. 33; 1 Sam. 8:2 [h]Heb. *stood* [i]Or, *Nahath;* see ver. 26 [j]Or, *Zophai*

6:1 THE SONS OF LEVI. Ch. 6 gives the descendants of Levi, the line of the high priests, down to the captivity, and lists the Levitical cities. The sons of Levi had been chosen by God for spiritual service in the tabernacle (Num. 3—4) and in the temple (1 Chr. 23—26). In effect, this chapter points to the importance of true worship according to the instruction of God.

6:32 MINISTERED . . . WITH SINGING. Worshiping God in song is a form of ministry to Him (cf. Eph. 5:18–20) and something with which He is well pleased. Through singing we may present ourselves to Him in faith and love (see Eph. 5:19, note).

stood on his right hand, *even* Asaph the son of Berachiah, the son of Shimea,

40 The son of Michael, the son of Baaseiah, the son of Malchiah,

41 The son of [h]Ethni, the son of Zerah, the son of Adaiah,

42 The son of Ethan, the son of Zimmah, the son of Shimei,

43 The son of Jahath, the son of Gershom, the son of Levi.

44 And their brethren the sons of Merari *stood* on the left hand: [k]Ethan the son of [l]Kishi, the son of Abdi, the son of Malluch,

45 The son of Hashabiah, the son of Amaziah, the son of Hilkiah,

46 The son of Amzi, the son of Bani, the son of Shamer,

47 The son of Mahli, the son of Mushi, the son of Merari, the son of Levi.

48 Their brethren also the Levites *were* appointed unto all manner of service of the tabernacle of the house of God.

The family of Aaron

49 ¶ But Aaron and his sons offered [i]upon the altar of the burnt offering, and [j]on the altar of incense, *and were appointed* for all the work of the *place* most holy, and to make an atonement for Israel, according to all that Moses the servant of God had commanded.

50 And these *are* the sons of Aaron; Eleazar his son, Phinehas his son, Abishua his son,

51 Bukki his son, Uzzi his son, Zerahiah his son,

52 Meraioth his son, Amariah his son, Ahitub his son,

53 Zadok his son, Ahimaaz his son.

54 ¶ [k]Now these *are* their dwelling places throughout their castles in their coasts, of the sons of Aaron, of the families of the Kohathites: for theirs was the lot.

55 [l]And they gave them Hebron in the land of Judah, and the suburbs thereof round about it.

56 [m]But the fields of the city, and the villages thereof, they gave to Caleb the son of Jephunneh.

57 And [n]to the sons of Aaron they gave the cities of Judah, *namely,* Hebron, *the city* of refuge, and Libnah with her suburbs, and Jattir, and Eshtemoa, with their suburbs,

58 And [m]Hilen with her suburbs, Debir with her suburbs,

59 And [n]Ashan with her suburbs, and Beth-shemesh with her suburbs:

60 And out of the tribe of Benjamin; Geba with her suburbs, and [o]Alemeth with her suburbs, and Anathoth with her suburbs. All their cities throughout their families *were* thirteen cities.

61 And unto the sons of Kohath, [o]*which were* left of the family of that tribe, *were cities given* out of the half tribe, *namely, out of* the half *tribe* of Manasseh, [p]by lot, ten cities.

62 And to the sons of Gershom throughout their families out of the tribe of Issachar, and out of the tribe of Asher, and out of the tribe of Naphtali, and out of the tribe of Manasseh in Bashan, thirteen cities.

63 Unto the sons of Merari *were given* by lot, throughout their families, out of the tribe of Reuben, and out of the tribe of Gad, and out of the tribe of Zebulun, [q]twelve cities.

64 And the children of Israel gave to the Levites *these* cities with their suburbs.

65 And they gave by lot out of the tribe of the children of Judah, and out of the tribe of the children of Simeon, and out of the tribe of the children of Benjamin, these cities, which are called by *their* names.

66 And [r]*the residue* of the families of the sons of Kohath had cities of their coasts out of the tribe of Ephraim.

67 [s]And they gave unto them, *of* the cities of refuge, Shechem in mount Ephraim with her suburbs; *they gave* also Gezer with her suburbs,

68 And [t]Jokmeam with her suburbs, and Beth-horon with her suburbs,

69 And Aijalon with her suburbs, and Gath-rimmon with her suburbs:

70 And out of the half tribe of Manasseh; Aner with her suburbs, and Bileam with her suburbs, for the family of the remnant of the sons of Kohath.

71 Unto the sons of Gershom *were given* out of the family of the half tribe of Manasseh, Golan in Bashan with her suburbs, and [u]Ashtaroth with her suburbs:

72 And out of the tribe of Issachar; [v]Kedesh with her suburbs, Daberath with her suburbs,

6:41 [h]See ver. 21
6:49 [i]Lev. 1:9 [j]Ex. 30:7
6:54 [k]Josh. 21
6:55 [l]Josh. 21:11,12
6:56 [m]Josh. 14:13 & 15:13
6:57 [n]Josh. 21:13
6:61 [o]ver. 66 [p]Josh. 21:5
6:63 [q]Josh. 21:7,34
6:66 [r]ver. 61
6:67 [s]Josh. 21:21
6:68 [t]See Josh. 21:22-35 where many of these cities have other names
6:71 [u]Josh. 21:27 *Beeshterah*
6:72 [v]Josh. 21:28 *Kishon*

[k] Called *Jeduthun* in ch. 9:16 & 25:1,3,6
[l] Or, *Kushaiah;* see ch. 15:17 [m] Or, *Holon;* see Josh. 21:15 [n] Or, *Ain;* see Josh. 21:16
[o] Or, *Almon;* see Josh. 21:18

73 And Ramoth with her suburbs, and Anem with her suburbs:

74 And out of the tribe of Asher; Mashal with her suburbs, and Abdon with her suburbs,

75 And Hukok with her suburbs, and Rehob with her suburbs:

76 And out of the tribe of Naphtali; Kedesh in Galilee with her suburbs, and Hammon with her suburbs, and Kirjathaim with her suburbs.

77 Unto the rest of the children of Merari *were given* out of the tribe of Zebulun, Rimmon with her suburbs, Tabor with her suburbs:

78 And on the other side Jordan by Jericho, on the east side of Jordan, *were given them* out of the tribe of Reuben, Bezer in the wilderness with her suburbs, and Jahzah with her suburbs,

79 Kedemoth also with her suburbs, and Mephaath with her suburbs:

80 And out of the tribe of Gad; Ramoth in Gilead with her suburbs, and Mahanaim with her suburbs,

81 And Heshbon with her suburbs, and Jazer with her suburbs.

The family of Issachar

7 NOW THE sons of Issachar *were,* [w]Tola, and [p]Puah, Jashub, and Shimrom, four.

2 And the sons of Tola; Uzzi, and Rephaiah, and Jeriel, and Jahmai, and Jibsam, and Shemuel, heads of their father's house, *to wit,* of Tola: *they were* valiant men of might in their generations; [x]whose number *was* in the days of David two and twenty thousand and six hundred.

3 And the sons of Uzzi; Izrahiah: and the sons of Izrahiah; Michael and Obadiah, and Joel, Ishiah, five: all of them chief men.

4 And with them, by their generations, after the house of their fathers, *were* bands of soldiers for war, six and thirty thousand *men:* for they had many wives and sons.

5 And their brethren among all the families of Issachar *were* valiant men of might, reckoned in all by their genealogies fourscore and seven thousand.

The family of Benjamin

6 ¶ *The sons* of [y]Benjamin: Bela, and Becher, and Jediael, three.

7 And the sons of Bela; Ezbon, and Uzzi, and Uzziel, and Jerimoth, and Iri, five; heads of the house of *their* fathers, mighty men of valour; and were reckoned by their genealogies twenty and two thousand and thirty and four.

8 And the sons of Becher; Zemira, and Joash, and Eliezer, and Elioenai, and Omri, and Jerimoth, and Abiah, and Anathoth, and Alameth. All these *are* the sons of Becher.

9 And the number of them, after their genealogy by their generations, heads of the house of their fathers, mighty men of valour, *was* twenty thousand and two hundred.

10 The sons also of Jediael; Bilhan: and the sons of Bilhan; Jeush, and Benjamin, and Ehud, and Chenaanah, and Zethan, and Tharshish, and Ahishahar.

11 All these the sons of Jediael, by the heads of their fathers, mighty men of valour, *were* seventeen thousand and two hundred *soldiers,* fit to go out for war *and* battle.

12 [z]Shuppim also, and Huppim, the children of [q]Ir, *and* Hushim, the sons of [r]Aher.

The family of Naphtali

13 ¶ The sons of Naphtali; Jahziel, and Guni, and Jezer, and [a]Shallum, the sons of Bilhah.

14 ¶ The sons of Manasseh; Ashriel, whom she bare: (*but* his concubine the Aramitess bare Machir the father of Gilead:

15 And Machir took to wife *the sister* of Huppim and Shuppim, whose sister's name *was* Maachah;) and the name of the second *was* Zelophehad: and Zelophehad had daughters.

16 And Maachah the wife of Machir bare a son, and she called his name Peresh; and the name of his brother *was* Sheresh; and his sons *were* Ulam and Rakem.

17 And the sons of Ulam; [b]Bedan. These *were* the sons of Gilead, the son of Machir, the son of Manasseh.

18 And his sister Hammoleketh bare Ishod, and [c]Abiezer, and Mahalah.

19 And the sons of Shemidah were, Ahian, and Shechem, and Likhi, and Aniam.

The family of Ephraim

20 ¶ And [d]the sons of Ephraim; Shuthelah, and Bered his son, and Ta-

7:1 [w]Gen. 46:13 Num. 26:23
7:2 [x]2 Sam. 24:1,2 ch. 27:1
7:6 [y]Gen. 46:21 Num. 26:38 ch. 8:1
7:12 [z]Num. 26:39 *Shupham* and *Hupham*
7:13 [a]Gen. 46:24 *Shillem*
7:17 [b]1 Sam. 12:11
7:18 [c]Num. 26:30 *Jeezer*
7:20 [d]Num. 26:35

[p] *Phuvah, Job* [q] Or, *Iri;* see ver. 7 [r] Or, *Ahiram;* see Num. 26:38

hath his son, and Eladah his son, and Tahath his son,

21 ¶ And Zabad his son, and Shuthelah his son, and Ezer, and Elead, whom the men of Gath *that were* born in *that* land slew, because they came down to take away their cattle.

22 And Ephraim their father mourned many days, and his brethren came to comfort him.

23 ¶ And when he went in to his wife, she conceived, and bare a son, and he called his name Beriah, because it went evil with his house.

24 (And his daughter *was* Sherah, who built Beth-horon the nether, and the upper, and Uzzen-sherah.)

25 And Rephah *was* his son, also Resheph, and Telah his son, and Tahan his son,

26 Laadan his son, Ammihud his son, Elishama his son,

27 [s]Non his son, Jehoshuah his son.

28 ¶ And their possessions and habitations *were,* Beth-el and the towns thereof, and eastward [e]Naaran, and westward Gezer, with the [t]towns thereof; Shechem also and the towns thereof, unto Gaza and the towns thereof:

29 And by the borders of the children of [f]Manasseh, Beth-shean and her towns, Taanach and her towns, [g]Megiddo and her towns, Dor and her towns. In these dwelt the children of Joseph the son of Israel.

The family of Asher

30 ¶ [h]The sons of Asher; Imnah, and Isuah, and Ishuai, and Beriah, and Serah their sister.

31 And the sons of Beriah; Heber, and Malchiel, who *is* the father of Birzavith.

32 And Heber begat Japhlet, and [i]Shomer, and Hotham, and Shua their sister.

33 And the sons of Japhlet; Pasach, and Bimhal, and Ashvath. These *are* the children of Japhlet.

34 And the sons of [j]Shamer; Ahi, and Rohgah, Jehubbah, and Aram.

35 And the sons of his brother Helem; Zophah, and Imna, and Shelesh, and Amal.

36 The sons of Zophah; Suah, and Harnepher, and Shual, and Beri, and Imrah,

37 Bezer, and Hod, and Shamma, and Shilshah, and Ithran, and Beera.

38 And the sons of Jether; Jephunneh, and Pispah, and Ara.

39 And the sons of Ulla; Arah, and Haniel, and Rezia.

40 All these *were* the children of Asher, heads of *their* father's house, choice *and* mighty men of valour, chief of the princes. And the number throughout the genealogy of them that were apt to the war *and* to battle *was* twenty and six thousand men.

The family of Benjamin

8:28–38pp — 1 Chr. 9:34–44

8 NOW BENJAMIN begat [k]Bela his firstborn, Ashbel the second, and Aharah the third,

2 Nohah the fourth, and Rapha the fifth.

3 And the sons of Bela were, [u]Addar, and Gera, and Abihud,

4 And Abishua, and Naaman, and Ahoah,

5 And Gera, and [v]Shephuphan, and Huram.

6 And these *are* the sons of Ehud: these are the heads of the fathers of the inhabitants of Geba, and they removed them to [l]Manahath:

7 And Naaman, and Ahiah, and Gera, he removed them, and begat Uzza, and Ahihud.

8 And Shaharaim begat *children* in the country of Moab, after he had sent them away; Hushim and Baara *were* his wives.

9 And he begat of Hodesh his wife, Jobab, and Zibia, and Mesha, and Malcham,

10 And Jeuz, and Shachia, and Mirma. These *were* his sons, heads of the fathers.

11 And of Hushim he begat Abitub, and Elpaal.

12 The sons of Elpaal; Eber, and Misham, and Shamed, who built Ono, and Lod, with the towns thereof:

13 Beriah also, and [m]Shema, who *were* heads of the fathers of the inhabitants of Aijalon, who drove away the inhabitants of Gath:

14 And Ahio, Shashak, and Jeremoth,

15 And Zebadiah, and Arad, and Ader,

7:28 [e]Josh. 16:7 *Naarath*
7:29 [f]Josh. 17:7 [g]Josh. 17:11
7:30 [h]Gen. 46:17 Num. 26:44
7:32 [i]ver. 34 *Shamer*
7:34 [j]ver. 32 *Shomer*
8:1 [k]Gen. 46:21 Num. 26:38 ch. 7:6
8:6 [l]ch. 2:52
8:13 [m]ver. 21

[s] Or, *Nun;* see Num. 13:8,16 [t] Heb. *daughters* [u] Or, *Ard;* see Gen. 46:21 [v] Or, *Shupham;* see Num. 26:39; see ch. 7:12

16 And Michael, and Ispah, and Joha, the sons of Beriah;
17 And Zebadiah, and Meshullam, and Hezeki, and Heber,
18 Ishmerai also, and Jezliah, and Jobab, the sons of Elpaal;
19 And Jakim, and Zichri, and Zabdi,
20 And Elienai, and Zilthai, and Eliel,
21 And Adaiah, and Beraiah, and Shimrath, the sons of [w]Shimhi;
22 And Ishpan, and Heber, and Eliel,
23 And Abdon, and Zichri, and Hanan,
24 And Hananiah, and Elam, and Antothijah,
25 And Iphedeiah, and Penuel, the sons of Shashak;
26 And Shamsherai, and Shehariah, and Athaliah,
27 And Jaresiah, and Eliah, and Zichri, the sons of Jeroham.
28 These *were* heads of the fathers, by their generations, chief *men*. These dwelt in Jerusalem.
29 And at Gibeon dwelt the [x]father of Gibeon; whose [n]wife's name *was* Maachah:
30 And his firstborn son Abdon, and Zur, and Kish, and Baal, and Nadab,
31 And Gedor, and Ahio, and [y]Zacher.
32 And Mikloth begat [z]Shimeah. And these also dwelt with their brethren in Jerusalem, over against them.
33 ¶ And [o]Ner begat Kish, and Kish begat Saul, and Saul begat Jonathan, and Malchi-shua, and [p]Abinadab, and [a]Esh-baal.
34 And the son of Jonathan *was* [b]Merib-baal; and Merib-baal begat [q]Micah.
35 And the sons of Micah *were*, Pithon, and Melech, and [c]Tarea, and Ahaz.
36 And Ahaz begat [r]Jehoadah; and Jehoadah begat Alemeth, and Azmaveth, and Zimri; and Zimri begat Moza,
37 And Moza begat Binea: [s]Rapha *was* his son, Eleasah his son, Azel his son:
38 And Azel had six sons, whose names *are* these, Azrikam, Bocheru, and Ishmael, and Sheariah, and Obadiah, and Hanan. All these *were* the sons of Azel.
39 And the sons of Eshek his brother *were*, Ulam his firstborn, Jehush the second, and Eliphelet the third.
40 And the sons of Ulam were mighty men of valour, archers, and had many sons, and sons' sons, an hundred and fifty. All these *are* of the sons of Benjamin.

8:29 [n]ch. 9:35 **8:33** [o]1 Sam. 14:51 [p]1 Sam. 14:49 *Ishui* **8:34** [q]2 Sam. 9:12 **8:36** [r]*Jarah* ch. 9:42 **8:37** [s]ch. 9:43 *Rephaiah*

Inhabitants in Jerusalem

9:1–17pp — Neh. 11:3–19

9 SO [t]ALL Israel were reckoned by genealogies; and, behold, they *were* written in the book of the kings of Israel and Judah, *who* were carried away to Babylon for their transgression.
2 ¶ [u]Now the first inhabitants that *dwelt* in their possessions in their cities *were*, the Israelites, the priests, Levites, and [v]the Nethinims.
3 And in [w]Jerusalem dwelt of the children of Judah, and of the children of Benjamin, and of the children of Ephraim, and Manasseh;
4 Uthai the son of Ammihud, the son of Omri, the son of Imri, the son of Bani, of the children of Pharez the son of Judah.
5 And of the Shilonites; Asaiah the firstborn, and his sons.
6 And of the sons of Zerah; Jeuel, and their brethren, six hundred and ninety.
7 And of the sons of Benjamin; Sallu the son of Meshullam, the son of Hodaviah, the son of Hasenuah,
8 And Ibneiah the son of Jeroham, and Elah the son of Uzzi, the son of Michri, and Meshullam the son of Shephathiah, the son of Reuel, the son of Ibnijah;
9 And their brethren, according to their generations, nine hundred and fif-

9:1 [t]Ezra 2:59 **9:2** [u]Ezra 2:70 Neh. 7:73 [v]Josh. 9:27 Ezra 2:43 & 8:20 **9:3** [w]Neh. 11:1

[w]Or, *Shema;* see ver. 13 [x]Called *Jehiel* in ch. 9:35 [y]Or, *Zechariah;* see ch. 9:37 [z]Or, *Shimeam;* see ch. 9:38 [a]Or, *Ishbosheth;* see 2 Sam. 2:8 [b]Or, *Mephibosheth;* see 2 Sam. 4:4 & 9:6,10 [c]Or, *Tahrea;* see ch. 9:41

9:1 SO ALL ISRAEL. Ch. 9 is concerned with the community of God's people (i.e., "all Israel") after their return from exile in Babylon, emphasizing their continuity with Israel before the exile (cf. Neh. 9). This first verse gives the reason for their captivity, while the rest of the chapter deals with the priests, the Levites, and the temple servants (v. 2) whom God appointed to restore the true order of worship that had been lost during the captivity.

ty and six. All these men *were* chief of
the fathers in the house of their fa-
thers.
10 ¶ [x]And of the priests; Jedaiah,
and Jehoiarib, and Jachin,
11 And [d]Azariah the son of Hilki-
ah, the son of Meshullam, the son of
Zadok, the son of Meraioth, the son of
Ahitub, the ruler of the house of God;
12 And Adaiah the son of Jeroham,
the son of Pashur, the son of Mal-
chijah, and Maasiai the son of Adiel,
the son of Jahzerah, the son of Meshul-
lam, the son of Meshillemith, the son
of Immer;
13 And their brethren, heads of the
house of their fathers, a thousand and
seven hundred and threescore; [e]very
able men for the work of the service of
the house of God.
14 And of the Levites; Shemaiah
the son of Hasshub, the son of Azri-
kam, the son of Hashabiah, of the sons
of Merari;
15 And Bakbakkar, Heresh, and
Galal, and Mattaniah the son of Micah,
the son of Zichri, the son of Asaph;
16 And Obadiah the son of Shema-
iah, the son of Galal, the son of Jedu-
thun, and Berechiah the son of Asa, the
son of Elkanah, that dwelt in the vil-
lages of the Netophathites.
17 And the porters *were,* Shallum,
and Akkub, and Talmon, and Ahiman,
and their brethren: Shallum *was* the
chief;
18 Who hitherto *waited* in the king's
gate eastward: they *were* porters in the
companies of the children of Levi.
19 And Shallum the son of Kore, the
son of Ebiasaph, the son of Korah, and
his brethren, of the house of his father,
the Korahites, *were* over the work
of the service, keepers of the [f]gates
of the tabernacle: and their fathers,
being over the host of the LORD, *were*
keepers of the entry.
20 And [y]Phinehas the son of Elea-
zar was the ruler over them in time
past, *and* the LORD *was* with him.
21 *And* Zechariah the son of Me-
shelemiah *was* porter of the door of the
tabernacle of the congregation.
22 All these *which were* chosen to be
porters in the gates *were* two hundred
and twelve. These were reckoned by
their genealogy in their villages, whom
[z]David and Samuel [a]the seer [g]did
ordain in their [h]set office.
23 So they and their children *had*
the oversight of the gates of the house
of the LORD, *namely,* the house of the
tabernacle, by wards.
24 In four quarters were the por-
ters, toward the east, west, north, and
south.
25 And their brethren, *which were* in
their villages, *were* to come [b]after sev-
en days from time to time with them.
26 For these Levites, the four chief
porters, were in *their* [h]set office, and
were over the [i]chambers and treasur-
ies of the house of God.
27 ¶ And they lodged round about
the house of God, because the charge
was upon them, and the opening there-
of every morning *pertained* to them.
28 And *certain* of them had the
charge of the ministering vessels, that
they should [j]bring them in and out by
tale.
29 *Some* of them also *were* appoint-
ed to oversee the vessels, and all the
[k]instruments of the sanctuary, and
the fine flour, and the wine, and the oil,
and the frankincense, and the spices.
30 And *some* of the sons of the
priests made [c]the ointment of the
spices.
31 And Mattithiah, *one* of the Le-
vites, who *was* the firstborn of Shallum
the Korahite, had the [h]set office
[d]over the things that were made [l]in
the pans.
32 And *other* of their brethren, of
the sons of the Kohathites, [e]*were* over
the [m]showbread, to prepare *it* every
sabbath.
33 And these *are* [f]the singers,
chief of the fathers of the Levites, *who
remaining* in the chambers *were* free:
for [n]they were employed in *that* work
day and night.
34 These chief fathers of the Le-
vites *were* chief throughout their gener-
ations; these dwelt at Jerusalem.

The family of Saul

9:34–44pp — 1 Chr. 8:28–38

35 ¶ And in Gibeon dwelt the father
of Gibeon, Jehiel, whose wife's name
was [g]Maachah:
36 And his firstborn son Abdon,

9:10 [x]Neh. 11:10
9:20 [y]Num. 31:6
9:22 [z]ch. 26:1,2 [a]1 Sam. 9:9
9:25 [b]2 Ki. 11:5
9:30 [c]Ex. 30:23
9:31 [d]Lev. 2:5 & 6:21
9:32 [e]Lev. 24:8
9:33 [f]ch. 6:31 & 25:1
9:35 [g]ch. 8:29

[d] Or, *Seraiah;* see Neh. 11:11 [e] Heb. *mighty men of valour* [f] Heb. *thresholds* [g] Heb. *founded* [h] Or, *trust* [i] Or, *storehouses* [j] Heb. *bring them in by tale, and carry them out by tale* [k] Or, *vessels* [l] Or, *on flat plates,* or, *slices* [m] Heb. *bread of ordering* [n] Heb. *upon them*

then Zur, and Kish, and Baal, and Ner, and Nadab,

37 And Gedor, and Ahio, and Zechariah, and Mikloth.

38 And Mikloth begat Shimeam. And they also dwelt with their brethren at Jerusalem, over against their brethren.

39 [h]And Ner begat Kish; and Kish begat Saul; and Saul begat Jonathan, and Malchi-shua, and Abinadab, and Esh-baal.

40 And the son of Jonathan *was* Merib-baal: and Merib-baal begat Micah.

41 And the sons of Micah *were*, Pithon, and Melech, and Tahrea, [i]*and Ahaz.*

42 And Ahaz begat Jarah; and Jarah begat Alemeth, and Azmaveth, and Zimri; and Zimri begat Moza;

43 And Moza begat Binea; and Rephaiah his son, Eleasah his son, Azel his son.

44 And Azel had six sons, whose names *are* these, Azrikam, Bocheru, and Ishmael, and Sheariah, and Obadiah, and Hanan: these *were* the sons of Azel.

Saul killed on mount Gilboa

10:1–12pp — 1 Sam. 31:1–13; 2 Sam. 1:4–12

10 NOW [j]THE Philistines fought against Israel; and the men of Israel fled from before the Philistines, and fell down [o]slain in mount Gilboa.

2 And the Philistines followed hard after Saul, and after his sons; and the Philistines slew Jonathan, and [p]Abinadab, and Malchi-shua, the sons of Saul.

3 And the battle went sore against Saul, and the [q]archers [r]hit him, and he was wounded of the archers.

4 Then said Saul to his armourbearer, Draw thy sword, and thrust me through therewith; lest these uncircumcised come and [s]abuse me. But his armourbearer would not; for he was sore afraid. So Saul took a sword, and fell upon it.

5 And when his armourbearer saw that Saul was dead, he fell likewise on the sword, and died.

6 So Saul died, and his three sons, and all his house died together.

7 And when all the men of Israel that *were* in the valley saw that they fled, and that Saul and his sons were dead, then they forsook their cities, and fled: and the Philistines came and dwelt in them.

8 ¶ And it came to pass on the morrow, when the Philistines came to strip the slain, that they found Saul and his sons fallen in mount Gilboa.

9 And when they had stripped him, they took his head, and his armour, and sent into the land of the Philistines round about, to carry tidings unto their idols, and to the people.

10 [k]And they put his armour in the house of their gods, and fastened his head in the temple of Dagon.

11 ¶ And when all Jabesh-gilead heard all that the Philistines had done to Saul.

12 They arose, all the valiant men, and took away the body of Saul, and the bodies of his sons, and brought them to Jabesh, and buried their bones under the oak in Jabesh, and fasted seven days.

13 ¶ So Saul died for his transgression which he [t]committed against the LORD, [l]*even* against the word of the LORD, which he kept not, and also for asking *counsel* of *one that had* a familiar spirit, [m]to inquire *of it;*

14 And inquired not of the LORD: therefore he slew him, and [n]turned the kingdom unto David the son of [u]Jesse.

David, king of all Israel

11:1–3pp — 2 Sam. 5:1–3
11:4–9pp — 2 Sam. 5:6–10

11 THEN [o]ALL Israel gathered themselves to David unto He-

9:39 [h]ch. 8:33 **9:41** [i]ch. 8:35 **10:1** [j]1 Sam. 31:1,2 **10:10** [k]1 Sam. 31:10 **10:13** [l]1 Sam. 13:13 & 15:23 [m]1 Sam. 28:7 **10:14** [n]1 Sam. 15:28 2 Sam. 3:9,10 & 5:3 **11:1** [o]2 Sam. 5:1

[o] Or, *wounded* [p] Or, *Ishui;* see 1 Sam. 14:49 [q] Heb. *shooters with bows* [r] Heb. *found him* [s] Or, *mock me* [t] Heb. *transgressed* [u] Heb. *Isai*

10:1 THE PHILISTINES FOUGHT AGAINST ISRAEL. With ch. 10 the writer begins a historical summary of Israel's past, starting with the monarchical era. In this chapter, he states the reason for the rejection of Saul and the transfer of the kingdom to David (vv. 13–14). The remaining events in this book deal with the history of David and the enduring significance of his reign.

10:13 SAUL DIED FOR HIS TRANSGRESSION. See 1 Sam. 15:23, note on Saul's rejection by God; 1 Sam. 28:12, note on Saul's encounter with the witch of Endor.

11:1 DAVID. Ch. 11 begins the story of David; 2 Sam. 2—5 tells more fully just how David be-

bron, saying, Behold, we *are* thy bone and thy flesh.

2 And moreover [v]in time past, even when Saul was king, thou *wast* he that leddest out and broughtest in Israel: and the LORD thy God said unto thee, Thou shalt [p]feed[w] my people Israel, and thou shalt be ruler over my people Israel.

3 Therefore came all the elders of Israel to the king to Hebron; and David made a covenant with them in Hebron before the LORD; and [q]they anointed David king over Israel, according to the word of the LORD [x]by [r]Samuel.

4 ¶ And David and all Israel [s]went to Jerusalem, which *is* Jebus; [t]where the Jebusites *were,* the inhabitants of the land.

5 And the inhabitants of Jebus said to David, Thou shalt not come hither. Nevertheless David took the castle of Zion, which *is* the city of David.

6 And David said, Whosoever smiteth the Jebusites first shall be [y]chief and captain. So Joab the son of Zeruiah went first up, and was chief.

7 And David dwelt in the castle; therefore they called [z]it the city of David.

8 And he built the city round about, even from Millo round about: and Joab [a]repaired the rest of the city.

9 So David [b]waxed greater and greater: for the LORD of hosts *was* with him.

David's mighty men

11:10–41pp — 2 Sam. 23:8–39

10 ¶ [u]These also *are* the chief of the mighty men whom David had, who [c]strengthened themselves with him in his kingdom, *and* with all Israel, to make him king, according to [v]the word of the LORD concerning Israel.

11 And this *is* the number of the mighty men whom David had; Jashobeam, [d]an Hachmonite, the chief of the captains: he lifted up his spear against three hundred slain *by him* at one time.

12 And after him *was* Eleazar the son of Dodo, the Ahohite, who *was one* of the three mighties.

13 He was with David at [e]Pas-dammim, and there the Philistines were gathered together to battle, where was a parcel of ground full of barley; and the people fled from before the Philistines.

14 And they [f]set themselves in the midst of *that* parcel, and delivered it, and slew the Philistines; and the LORD saved *them* by a great [w]deliverance.

15 ¶ Now [g]three of the thirty captains [x]went down to the rock to David, into the cave of Adullam; and the host of the Philistines encamped [y]in the valley of Rephaim.

16 And David *was* then in the hold, and the Philistines' garrison *was* then at Bethlehem.

17 And David longed, and said, Oh that one would give me drink of the water of the well of Bethlehem, that *is* at the gate!

18 And the three brake through the host of the Philistines, and drew water out of the well of Bethlehem, that *was* by the gate, and took *it,* and brought *it* to David: but David would not drink *of* it, but poured it out to the LORD,

19 And said, My God forbid it me, that I should do this thing: shall I drink

11:2 [p]Ps. 78:71
11:3 [q]2 Sam. 5:3 [r]1 Sam. 16:1,12, 13
11:4 [s]2 Sam. 5:6 [t]Judg. 1:21 & 19:10
11:10 [u]2 Sam. 23:8 [v]1 Sam. 16:1,12
11:14 [w]Judg. 1:21 & 19:10
11:15 [x]2 Sam. 23:13 [y]ch. 14:9

[v] Heb. *both yesterday and the third day* [w] Or, *rule* [x] Heb. *by the hand of* [y] Heb. *head* [z] i.e. *Zion;* see 2 Sam. 5:7 [a] Heb. *revived* [b] Heb. *went in going and increasing* [c] Or, *held strongly with him* [d] Or, *son of Hachmoni* [e] Or, *Ephes-dammim;* see 1 Sam. 17:1 [f] Or, *stood* [g] Or, *three captains over the thirty*

came king over Judah and then over all Israel. (1) A comparison with the parallel accounts of David in 2 Sam. makes it apparent that the writer of Chronicles omits most of the difficulties David experienced, along with his personal moral failures and shame (2 Sam. 1—4; 11—21). These omissions coincide with the writer's twofold purpose: (a) to emphasize those historical events that were important to God's purpose in salvation history, and (b) to encourage the disheartened post-exilic community that was resettling in its homeland. (2) This same purpose is reflected in the author's focus on Solomon's building of the temple and his omission of Solomon's apostasy and idolatry as described in 1 Ki. 11.

11:1 ALL ISRAEL GATHERED THEMSELVES TO DAVID. The first seven years of David's reign as king at Hebron over two tribes are assumed but not described. The narrative begins with David becoming king over all Israel.

11:5 THE CASTLE OF ZION. Zion was one of the hills on which Jerusalem stood. It was formerly the site of a Jebusite fortress that David had captured (2 Sam. 5:6–9; see article on THE CITY OF JERUSALEM, p. 622). The hill became sacred when David brought the ark of the covenant to Zion. Later the name Zion was applied to the city of Jerusalem (2 Ki. 19:21; Ps. 48; Is. 1:8), the congregation of Israel, (Is. 33:14; 34:8), and heaven itself (Heb. 12:22; cf. Rev. 14:1).

the blood of these men [h]that have put
their lives in jeopardy? for with *the*
jeopardy of their lives they brought it.
Therefore he would not drink it. These
things did these three mightiest.

20 ¶ [z]And Abishai the brother of
Joab, he was chief of the three: for lift-
ing up his spear against three hundred,
he slew *them,* and had a name among
the three.

21 [a]Of the three, he was more hon-
ourable than the two; for he was their
captain: howbeit he attained not to the
first three.

22 Benaiah the son of Jehoiada, the
son of a valiant man of Kabzeel, [i]who
had done many acts; [b]he slew two
lionlike men of Moab: also he went
down and slew a lion in a pit in a snowy
day.

23 And he slew an Egyptian, [j]a
man of *great* stature, five cubits high;
and in the Egyptian's hand *was* a spear
like a weaver's beam; and he went
down to him with a staff, and plucked
the spear out of the Egyptian's hand,
and slew him with his own spear.

24 These *things* did Benaiah the son
of Jehoiada, and had the name among
the three mighties.

25 Behold, he was honourable
among the thirty, but attained not to
the *first* three: and David set him over
his guard.

26 ¶ Also the valiant men of the ar-
mies *were,* [c]Asahel the brother of
Joab, Elhanan the son of Dodo of Beth-
lehem,

27 [k]Shammoth the [l]Harorite, He-
lez the [m]Pelonite,

28 Ira the son of Ikkesh the Teko-
ite, Abiezer the Antothite,

29 [n]Sibbecai the Hushathite,
[o]Ilai the Ahohite,

30 Maharai the Netophathite, [p]He-
led the son of Baanah the Netopha-
thite,

31 Ithai the son of Ribai of Gibeah,
that pertained to the children of Benja-
min, Benaiah the Pirathonite,

32 [q]Hurai of the brooks of Gaash,
[r]Abiel the Arbathite,

33 Azmaveth the Baharumite, Eli-
ahba the Shaalbonite,

11:20
[z]2 Sam. 23:18
11:21
[a]2 Sam. 23:19
11:22
[b]2 Sam. 23:20
11:26
[c]2 Sam. 23:24

34 The sons of [s]Hashem the Gizo-
nite, Jonathan the son of Shage the Ha-
rarite,

35 Ahiam the son of [t]Sacar the
Hararite, [u]Eliphal the son of [v]Ur,

36 Hepher the Mecherathite, Ahijah
the Pelonite,

37 [w]Hezro the Carmelite, [x]Naarai
the son of Ezbai,

38 Joel the brother of Nathan, Mib-
har [y]the son of Haggeri,

39 Zelek the Ammonite, Naharai
the Berothite, the armourbearer of
Joab the son of Zeruiah,

40 Ira the Ithrite, Gareb the Ithrite,

41 Uriah the Hittite, Zabad the son
of Ahlai,

42 Adina the son of Shiza the Reu-
benite, a captain of the Reubenites,
and thirty with him,

43 Hanan the son of Maachah, and
Joshaphat the Mithnite,

44 Uzzia the Ashterathite, Shama
and Jehiel the sons of Hothan the Aro-
erite,

45 Jediael the [z]son of Shimri, and
Joha his brother, the Tizite,

46 Eliel the Mahavite, and Jeribai,
and Joshaviah, the sons of Elnaam, and
Ithmah the Moabite,

47 Eliel, and Obed, and Jasiel the
Mesobaite.

David's supporters

12 NOW [d]THESE *are* they that
came to David to [e]Ziklag,
[a]while he yet kept himself close be-
cause of Saul the son of Kish: and they
were among the mighty men, helpers of
the war.

2 *They were* armed with bows, and
could use both the right hand and [f]the
left in *hurling* stones and *shooting* ar-
rows out of a bow, *even* of Saul's breth-
ren of Benjamin.

12:1
[d]1 Sam. 27:2
[e]1 Sam. 27:6
12:2
[f]Judg. 20:16

[h] Heb. *with their lives?* [i] Heb. *great of deeds*
[j] Heb. *a man of measure* [k] Or, *Shammah*
[l] Or, *Harodite;* see 2 Sam. 23:25 [m] Or,
Paltite; see 2 Sam. 23:26 [n] Or, *Mebunnai*
[o] Or, *Zalmon* [p] Or, *Heleb* [q] Or, *Hiddai*
[r] Or, *Abi-albon* [s] Or, *Jashen;* see 2 Sam.
23:32,33 [t] Or, *Sharar* [u] Or, *Eliphelet*
[v] Or, *Ahasbai* [w] Or, *Hezrai* [x] Or, *Paarai the*
Arbite [y] Or, *the Haggerite* [z] Or, *Shimrite*
[a] Heb. being *yet shut up*

11:41 URIAH THE HITTITE. Uriah is listed as one of the mighty men who faithfully gave David strong support (v. 10). Yet David took this warrior's wife for himself and had Uriah murdered (see 2 Sam. 11). David's sin was considered so terrible that he lived under God's punishment for the rest of his life. This sin is alluded to in the first chapter of the N.T. (Mat. 1:6; see 2 Sam. 12, notes on David's sin).

THE CITY OF JERUSALEM

1 Chr. 11:7–8 ***"And David dwelt in the castle; therefore they called it the city of David. And he built the city round about, even from Millo round about: and Joab repaired the rest of the city."***

HISTORY OF THE CITY OF JERUSALEM. The first reference to the city of Jerusalem is probably Gen. 14:18, where Melchizedek is listed as the king of Salem (i.e., Jerusalem; see Gen. 14:18, note). When the Israelites were ready to cross over the Jordan to enter the promised land, the city then was called "the Jebusite [city]" (Jos. 15:8) or "Jebus" (1 Chr. 11:4). It was never captured during Joshua's conquest of the land of Canaan, and remained in the hands of the Canaanites until David became king. David's army stormed Jebus and took possession of it, and David made it his capital city (2 Sam. 5:5–7; 1 Chr. 11:4–7). Jerusalem served as the political capital of Israel during the united kingdom and later of the southern kingdom of Judah. Solomon, David's successor, built the temple to the Lord God in Jerusalem (1 Ki. 5—8; 2 Chr. 2—5; see article on THE TEMPLE, p. 654), so that the city also became the religious center for the worship of the covenant Lord.

Because of Israel's sin, in 586 B.C. Nebuchadnezzar of Babylon beseiged the city and eventually destroyed it with its temple (2 Ki. 25:1–11; 2 Chr. 36:17–19). It remained a pile of rubble until the Jews returned in 536 B.C. from Persia to rebuild both the temple and the city (Ezra 3:8–13; 5:1—6:15; Neh. 3—4). By N.T times, Jerusalem had once again become the center of Jewish political and religious life. In A.D. 70, however, after frequent rebellion by the Jews against the Roman authorities, the city and its temple were once again destroyed.

When David made Jerusalem his capital city, it began taking on various other names in keeping with its character—names such as: "Zion" (2 Sam. 5:7), "the city of David" (1 Ki. 2:10), "the holy city" (Neh. 11:1), "the city of God" (Ps. 46:4), "the city of the great King" (Ps. 48:2), "the city of righteousness, the faithful city" (Is. 1:26), "the city of the LORD" (Is. 60:14), "The LORD *is* there" (Ezek. 48:35), and "a city of truth" (Zec. 8:3). Some of these names are prophetic names for the future city of Jerusalem.

THE MEANING OF JERUSALEM FOR THE ISRAELITES. The city of Jerusalem had special meaning for God's people in the O.T. (1) When God reviewed His law with the Israelites on the border of Canaan, He prophesied through Moses that at some point in the future He would choose a place in which "to put his name" (Deut. 12:5,11,21; 14:23–24). This place was to be the city of Jerusalem (1 Ki. 11:13; 14:21) where the temple of the living God was erected; thus it received the names of "the holy city," "the city of God," and "the city of the LORD." Three times a year all the Israelite males were expected to journey to Jerusalem, to "appear before the LORD thy God in the place which he shall choose; in the feast of unleavened bread, and in the feast of weeks, and in the feast of tabernacles" (Deut. 16:16; cf. 16:2,6,11,15).

(2) Jerusalem was the city where God revealed His word to His people (Is. 2:3); that is, it was "the valley of vision" (Is. 22:1). Furthermore, it was the place where God ruled over His people Israel (Ps. 99:1–2; cf. 48:1–3,12–14). Thus when the Israelites prayed, they were instructed to pray "toward the city" (1 Ki. 8:44; cf. Dan. 6:10). The mountains that surrounded Jerusalem symbolized the Lord surrounding His people in His eternal steadfastness (Ps. 125:1–2). In essence, therefore, Jerusalem was a symbol of all that God wanted for His people. Whenever God's people were in Jerusalem, they were to remember the ruling power of God, His holiness, His faithfulness to His people, and His eternal commitment to be their God.

(3) When, therefore, the people of God destroyed their relationship with Him by their constant idolatry and refusal to obey His commandments (see article on THE NATURE OF IDOLATRY, p. 428), the Lord allowed the nation of Babylon to destroy Jerusalem,

along with the temple. By allowing this long-standing symbol of His constant presence among them to be destroyed, God was signifying that He Himself was withdrawing from His people. Note that God's promise of an "eternal covenant" with His people was always conditional upon their obedience to His revealed will (see article on GOD'S COVENANT WITH THE ISRAELITES, p. 314). Thus, God was warning His people then and now that they must remain faithful to Him and be obedient to His law if they want to continue to receive His blessings and promises.

THE MEANING OF JERUSALEM FOR THE CHRISTIAN CHURCH. The city of Jerusalem was also important for the Christian church. (1) Jerusalem was the birthplace of Christianity. It was there that Jesus Christ was crucified and arose from the dead. It was likewise in Jerusalem that the exalted Christ poured out the Holy Spirit on His disciples at Pentecost (Acts 2). From that city the gospel message of Jesus Christ spread "unto the uttermost part of the earth" (Acts 1:8; cf. Luke 24:47). The church in Jerusalem was the mother church of all churches and the home church of the apostles (Acts 1:12–26; 8:1). When controversy broke out over whether Gentiles who believed in Jesus had to be circumcised, Jerusalem was the city where the first major church council convened to decide this issue (Acts 15:1–31; Gal. 2:1–10).

(2) N.T. writers accepted much of the O.T. significance of Jerusalem, but changed its application from the earthly city to a heavenly city. In other words, to them Jerusalem as the holy city was no longer here on earth but in heaven where God dwells and Christ rules at His right hand; from there He sends His blessings and from there Jesus will return. Paul speaks about the "Jerusalem which is above," who is the mother of us all (Gal. 4:26). The author to the Hebrews indicates that in coming to Jesus Christ for salvation, believers have come not to an earthly mountain, but "unto mount Zion, and unto the city of the living God, the heavenly Jerusalem" (Heb. 12:22). And instead of preparing a city on earth for believers, God is busy preparing the new Jerusalem, which will some day come "down from God out of heaven, prepared as a bride adorned for her husband" (Rev. 21:2; cf. 3:12). On that great day, God's covenant promises will be fully realized: "Behold, the tabernacle of God *is* with men, and he will dwell with them, and they shall be his people, and God himself shall be with them, and be their God" (Rev. 21:3). God and the Lamb will reign for ever and ever on their throne in this holy city (Rev. 22:3).

(3) Does the earthly city of Jerusalem still have a future role in the millennial kingdom of God? Is. 65:18 begins with a strong adversative: there will be new heavens and a new earth (Is. 65:17), *but* the present Jerusalem will also have its fulfillment; the remainder of Is. 65 goes on to deal with millennial conditions. Many believe that when Christ returns to establish His millennial rule (Rev. 20:1–6), He will set up His throne in the city of Jerusalem. After the great white throne judgment (Rev. 20:11–15), the heavenly Jerusalem will descend to the new earth and become the headquarters of God's eternal kingdom (see Rev. 21:2, note).

3 The chief *was* Ahiezer, then Joash, the sons of [b]Shemaah the Gibeathite; and Jeziel, and Pelet, the sons of Azmaveth; and Berachah, and Jehu the Antothite,

4 And Ismaiah the Gibeonite, a mighty man among the thirty, and over the thirty; and Jeremiah, and Jahaziel, and Johanan, and Josabad the Gederathite,

5 Eluzai, and Jerimoth, and Bealiah, and Shemariah, and Shephatiah the Haruphite,

6 Elkanah, and Jesiah, and Azareel, and Joezer, and Jashobeam, the Korhites,

7 And Joelah, and Zebadiah, the sons of Jeroham of Gedor.

8 And of the Gadites there separated themselves unto David into the hold to the wilderness men of might, *and* men [c]of war *fit* for the battle, that could handle shield and buckler, whose faces *were like* the faces of lions, and *were* [g]as[d] swift as the roes upon the mountains;

9 Ezer the first, Obadiah the second, Eliab the third,

10 Mishmannah the fourth, Jeremiah the fifth,

11 Attai the sixth, Eliel the seventh,

12 Johanan the eighth, Elzabad the ninth,

13 Jeremiah the tenth, Machbanai the eleventh.

14 These *were* of the sons of Gad, captains of the host: [e]one of the least *was* over an hundred, and the greatest over a thousand.

15 These *are* they that went over Jordan in the first month, when it had [f]overflown all his [h]banks; and they put to flight all *them* of the valleys, *both* toward the east, and toward the west.

16 And there came of the children of Benjamin and Judah to the hold unto David.

17 And David went out [g]to meet them, and answered and said unto them, If ye be come peaceably unto me to help me, mine heart shall [h]be knit unto you: but if *ye be come* to betray me to mine enemies, seeing *there is* no [i]wrong in mine hands, the God of our fathers look *thereon,* and rebuke *it.*

18 Then [i]the[j] spirit came upon [j]Amasai, *who was* chief of the captains, *and he said,* Thine *are we,* David, and on thy side, thou son of Jesse: peace, peace *be* unto thee, and peace *be* to thine helpers; for thy God helpeth thee. Then David received them, and made them captains of the band.

19 And there fell *some* of Manasseh to David, [k]when he came with the Philistines against Saul to battle: but they helped them not: for the lords of the Philistines upon advisement sent him away, saying, [l]He will fall to his master Saul [k]to *the jeopardy of* our heads.

20 As he went to Ziklag, there fell to him of Manasseh, Adnah, and Jozabad, and Jediael, and Michael, and Jozabad, and Elihu, and Zilthai, captains of the thousands that *were* of Manasseh.

21 And they helped David [l]against [m]the band *of the rovers:* for they *were* all mighty men of valour, and were captains in the host.

22 For at *that* time day by day there came to David to help him, until *it was* a great host, like the host of God.

The number of David's men

23 ¶ And these *are* the numbers of the [m] [n]bands *that were* ready armed to the war, *and* [n]came to David to Hebron, to [o]turn the kingdom of Saul to him, [p]according to the word of the LORD.

24 The children of Judah that bare shield and spear *were* six thousand and eight hundred, ready [o]armed to the war.

25 Of the children of Simeon, mighty men of valour for the war, seven thousand and one hundred.

12:8 [g] 2 Sam. 2:18
12:15 [h] Josh. 3:15
12:18 [i] Judg. 6:34 [j] 2 Sam. 17:25
12:19 [k] 1 Sam. 29:2 [l] 1 Sam. 29:4
12:21 [m] 1 Sam. 30:1,9,10
12:23 [n] 2 Sam. 2:3 [o] ch. 10:14 [p] 1 Sam. 16:1

[b] Or, *Hasmaah* [c] Heb. *of the host* [d] Heb. *as the roes upon the mountains to make haste* [e] Or, *one that was least* could resist *an hundred, and the greatest a thousand* [f] Heb. *filled over* [g] Heb. *before them* [h] Heb. *be one* [i] Or, *violence* [j] Heb. *the spirit clothed Amasai* [k] Heb. *on our heads* [l] Or, *with a band* [m] Or, *captains,* or, *men* [n] Heb. *heads* [o] Or, *prepared*

12:18 THE SPIRIT CAME UPON AMASAI. Under the old covenant the Holy Spirit equipped certain persons with power and ability to do tasks to which God had called them (e.g., see Ex. 31:1–5; Judg. 3:10; 6:34; 11:29; 13:25; 1 Sam. 10:10; 11:6; 16:13). In Amasai's case it was the gift of prophetic inspiration. Under the new covenant, Jesus promised that *all* His followers would "receive power, after that the Holy Ghost is come upon [them]" (Acts 1:8; cf. 2:4; see article on BAPTISM IN THE HOLY SPIRIT, p. 1652).

26 Of the children of Levi four thousand and six hundred.

27 And Jehoiada *was* the leader of the Aaronites, and with him *were* three thousand and seven hundred;

28 And [q]Zadok, a young man mighty of valour, and of his father's house twenty and two captains.

29 And of the children of Benjamin, the [p]kindred of Saul, three thousand: for hitherto [r]the[q] greatest part of them had kept the ward of the house of Saul.

30 And of the children of Ephraim twenty thousand and eight hundred, mighty men of valour, [r]famous throughout the house of their fathers.

31 And of the half tribe of Manasseh eighteen thousand, which were expressed by name, to come and make David king.

32 And of the children of Issachar, [s]*which were men* that had understanding of the times, to know what Israel ought to do; the heads of them *were* two hundred; and all their brethren *were* at their commandment.

33 Of Zebulun, such as went forth to battle, [s]expert in war, with all instruments of war, fifty thousand, which could [t]keep rank: *they were* [t]not[u] of double heart.

34 And of Naphtali a thousand captains, and with them with shield and spear thirty and seven thousand.

35 And of the Danites expert in war twenty and eight thousand and six hundred.

36 And of Asher, such as went forth to battle, [v]expert in war, forty thousand.

37 And on the other side of Jordan, of the Reubenites, and the Gadites, and of the half tribe of Manasseh, with all manner of instruments of war for the battle, an hundred and twenty thousand.

38 All these men of war, that could keep rank, came with a perfect heart to Hebron, to make David king over all Israel: and all the rest also of Israel *were* of one heart to make David king.

39 And there they were with David three days, eating and drinking: for their brethren had prepared for them.

40 Moreover they that were nigh them, *even* unto Issachar and Zebulun and Naphtali, brought bread on asses, and on camels, and on mules, and on oxen, *and* [w]meat, meal, cakes of figs, and bunches of raisins, and wine, and oil, and oxen, and sheep abundantly: for *there was* joy in Israel.

12:28 [q]2 Sam. 8:17
12:29 [r]2 Sam. 2:8,9
12:32 [s]Esth. 1:13
12:33 [t]Ps. 12:2

The ark taken to Obed-edom

13:1–14pp — 2 Sam. 6:1–11

13 AND DAVID consulted with the captains of thousands and hundreds, *and* with every leader.

2 And David said unto all the congregation of Israel, If *it seem* good unto you, and *that it be* of the LORD our God, [x]let us send abroad unto our brethren every where, *that are* [u]left in all the land of Israel, and with them *also* to the priests and Levites *which are* [y]in their cities *and* suburbs, that they may gather themselves unto us:

3 And let us [z]bring again the ark of

13:2 [u]1 Sam. 31:1 Is. 37:4

[p] Heb. *brethren* [q] Heb. *a multitude of them* [r] Heb. *men of names* [s] Or, *rangers of battle,* or, *ranged in battle* [t] Or, *set the battle in array* [u] Heb. *without a heart and a heart* [v] Or, *keeping their rank* [w] Or, *victual of meal* [x] Heb. *let us break forth* and *send* [y] Heb. *in the cities of their suburbs* [z] Heb. *bring about*

12:32 UNDERSTANDING OF THE TIMES. According to God's sovereign wisdom, He has a season and a time for all His purposes and for the fulfillment of His promises (cf. Eccl. 3:1). We see this in the realm of nature, and also in His kingdom, where there are appointed times (Ps. 102:13) and seasons of change (Is. 43:18–19) that are crucially important in the ongoing redemptive purpose of God.

(1) Scripture reveals again and again how God's people are often blind to what God is doing or about to do. Israel as a whole was blind and ignorant when God in the fullness of time sent forth His Son to be their Messiah. Likewise, too often the church does not know or discern when God is bringing to fulfillment some aspect of His purpose.

(2) The sons of Issachar are given special mention in Scripture because they, from among Israel's twelve tribes, understood the times and discerned what God was doing in bringing David to the throne as His anointed. Discernment of God's times and seasons is necessary in order to cooperate with God in purposeful action and to embrace or sustain a God-given vision during times of change.

13:3 LET US BRING AGAIN THE ARK OF OUR GOD TO US. The ark had been captured and held by the Philistines for seven months (1 Sam. 4:11; 6:1; see 1 Sam. 4:3,21, notes). It was then returned to Israel and kept at Kirjath-jearim, ten miles from Jerusalem (1 Sam. 7:2). Throughout the reign of Saul it had been neglected and had remained in obscurity.

our God to us: [v]for we inquired not at it in the days of Saul.

4 And all the congregation said that they would do so: for the thing was right in the eyes of all the people.

5 So [w]David gathered all Israel together, from [x]Shihor of Egypt even unto the entering of Hemath, to bring the ark of God [y]from Kirjath-jearim.

6 And David went up, and all Israel, to [z]Baalah, *that is,* to Kirjath-jearim, which *belonged* to Judah, to bring up thence the ark of God the LORD, [a]that dwelleth *between* the cherubims, whose name is called *on it.*

7 And they [a]carried the ark of God [b]in a new cart [c]out of the house of Abinadab: and Uzza and Ahio drave the cart.

8 [d]And David and all Israel played before God with all *their* might, and with [b]singing, and with harps, and with psalteries, and with timbrels, and with cymbals, and with trumpets.

9 ¶ And when they came unto the threshingfloor of [c]Chidon, Uzza put forth his hand to hold the ark; for the oxen [d]stumbled.

10 And the anger of the LORD was kindled against Uzza, and he smote him, [e]because he put his hand to the ark: and there he [f]died before God.

11 And David was displeased, because the LORD had made a breach upon Uzza: wherefore that place is called [e]Perez-uzza to this day.

12 And David was afraid of God that day, saying, How shall I bring the ark of God *home* to me?

13 So David [f]brought not the ark *home* to himself to the city of David, but carried it aside into the house of Obed-edom the Gittite.

14 [g]And the ark of God remained with the family of Obed-edom in his house three months. And the LORD blessed [h]the house of Obed-edom, and all that he had.

David defeats the Philistines

14:1–7pp — 2 Sam. 5:11–16; 1 Chr. 3:5–8
14:8–17pp — 2 Sam. 5:17–25

14 NOW [i]HIRAM king of Tyre sent messengers to David, and timber of cedars, with masons and carpenters, to build him an house.

2 And David perceived that the LORD had confirmed him king over Israel, for his kingdom was lifted up on high, because of his people Israel.

3 ¶ And David took [g]more wives at Jerusalem: and David begat more sons and daughters.

4 Now [j]these *are* the names of *his* children which he had in Jerusalem; Shammua, and Shobab, Nathan, and Solomon,

5 And Ibhar, and Elishua, and Elpalet,

6 And Nogah, and Nepheg, and Japhia,

7 And Elishama, and [h]Beeliada, and Eliphalet.

8 ¶ And when the Philistines heard that [k]David was anointed king over all Israel, all the Philistines went up to seek David. And David heard *of it,* and went out against them.

9 And the Philistines came and spread themselves [l]in the valley of Rephaim.

10 And David inquired of God, saying, Shall I go up against the Philistines? and wilt thou deliver them into mine hand? And the LORD said unto

13:3 [v]1 Sam. 7:1,2
13:5 [w]1 Sam. 7:5 [x]Josh. 13:3 [y]1 Sam. 6:21 & 7:1
13:6 [z]Josh. 15:9,60 [a]1 Sam. 4:4 2 Sam. 6:2
13:7 [b]See Num. 4:15 [c]1 Sam. 7:1
13:8 [d]2 Sam. 6:5
13:10 [e]Num. 4:15 ch. 15:13,15 [f]Lev. 10:2
13:14 [g]2 Sam. 6:11 [h]As Gen. 30:27 ch. 26:5
14:1 [i]2 Sam. 5:11
14:4 [j]ch. 3:5
14:8 [k]2 Sam. 5:17
14:9 [l]ch. 11:15

[a] Heb. *made the ark to ride* [b] Heb. *songs* [c] Called *Nachon* in 2 Sam. 6:6 [d] Heb. *shook* it [e] i.e. *The breach of Uzza* [f] Heb. *removed* [g] Heb. *yet* [h] Or, *Eliada;* see 2 Sam. 5:16

13:10 THE ANGER OF THE LORD WAS KINDLED AGAINST UZZA. Uzza was destroyed because of his action contrary to God's command (see also 2 Sam. 6:1–8; cf. 1 Chr. 15:2,13,15; see Ex. 25:12–15; Num. 4:15, where God had given specific instruction for handling the ark). This story teaches that the worship of and service unto God must be according to His revelation and word (see 2 Sam. 6:7, note).

13:14 THE LORD BLESSED THE HOUSE OF OBED-EDOM. The Lord blessed this family because Obed-edom undoubtedly received the ark with reverence and in obedience to God. What brought death to one man brought blessing to another.

14:2 BECAUSE OF HIS PEOPLE ISRAEL. David's kingdom was highly exalted, not for his own sake, but for the sake of all God's people. David was to establish Israel's position in the world in order that they might serve God in righteousness and truth (see 2 Sam. 7:18, note). Under the new covenant, God also may exalt a person, not for that person's own sake, but in order that God's people might be built up morally and spiritually.

14:3 DAVID TOOK MORE WIVES. For commentary on David taking many wives, see 2 Sam. 5:13, note. This glaring personal fault in David brought terrible tragedy upon himself and his household (see 2 Sam. 12:13, note; 13:1, note).

him, Go up; for I will deliver them into thine hand.

11 So they came up to Baal-perazim; and David smote them there. Then David said, God hath broken in upon mine enemies by mine hand like the breaking forth of waters: therefore they called the name of that place [i]Baal-perazim.

12 And when they had left their gods there, David gave a commandment, and they were burned with fire.

13 [m]And the Philistines yet again spread themselves abroad in the valley.

14 Therefore David inquired again of God; and God said unto him, Go not up after them; turn away from them, [n]and come upon them over against the mulberry trees.

15 And it shall be, when thou shalt hear a sound of going in the tops of the mulberry trees, *that* then thou shalt go out to battle: for God is gone forth before thee to smite the host of the Philistines.

16 David therefore did as God commanded him: and they smote the host of the Philistines from [o]Gibeon even to Gazer.

17 And [p]the fame of David went out into all lands; and the LORD [q]brought the fear of him upon all nations.

The ark brought to Jerusalem

15:25–16:3pp — 2 Sam. 6:12–19

15 AND *DAVID* made him houses in the city of David, and prepared a place for the ark of God, [r]and pitched for it a tent.

2 Then David said, [j]None ought to carry the [s]ark of God but the Levites: for them hath the LORD chosen to carry the ark of God, and to minister unto him for ever.

3 And David [t]gathered all Israel together to Jerusalem, to bring up the ark of the LORD unto his place, which he had prepared for it.

4 And David assembled the children of Aaron, and the Levites:

5 Of the sons of Kohath; Uriel the chief, and his [k]brethren an hundred and twenty:

6 Of the sons of Merari; Asaiah the chief, and his brethren two hundred and twenty:

7 Of the sons of Gershom; Joel the chief, and his brethren an hundred and thirty:

8 Of the sons of [u]Elizaphan; Shemaiah the chief, and his brethren two hundred:

9 Of the sons of [v]Hebron; Eliel the chief, and his brethren fourscore:

10 Of the sons of Uzziel; Amminadab the chief, and his brethren an hundred and twelve.

11 And David called for Zadok and Abiathar the priests, and for the Levites, for Uriel, Asaiah, and Joel, Shemaiah, and Eliel, and Amminadab,

12 And said unto them, Ye *are* the chief of the fathers of the Levites: Sanctify yourselves, *both* ye and your brethren, that ye may bring up the ark of the LORD God of Israel unto *the place that* I have prepared for it.

13 For [w]because ye *did it* not at the first, [x]the LORD our God made a breach upon us, for that we sought him not after the due order.

14:13 [m]2 Sam. 5:22
14:14 [n]2 Sam. 5:23
14:16 [o]2 Sam. 5:25 *Geba*
14:17 [p]Josh. 6:27 2 Chr. 26:8 [q]Deut. 2:25 & 11:25
15:1 [r]ch. 16:1
15:2 [s]Num. 4:2,15 Deut. 10:8 & 31:9
15:3 [t]1 Ki. 8:1 ch. 13:5
15:8 [u]Ex. 6:22
15:9 [v]Ex. 6:18
15:13 [w]2 Sam. 6:3 ch. 13:7 [x]ch. 13:10,11

[i] i.e. *A place of breaches* [j] Heb. It is *not to carry the ark of God, but for the Levites* [k] Or, *kinsmen*

14:14 DAVID INQUIRED AGAIN OF GOD. David did not assume that because it had been God's will to go up against the Philistines before (v. 10), it was also true on this occasion. David's example teaches believers that we will not succeed in life if we do not consistently seek the Lord's will, guidance, and help. Calling upon God for His special grace and presence is an ongoing need for our lives. If we neglect to turn continually to God for His help, we will find ourselves facing life's troubles and demands alone, without the presence of the Holy Spirit (see 2 Sam. 5:19, note).

15:1 *DAVID* . . . PREPARED A PLACE FOR THE ARK. The ark of God contained the two tablets of the law, a jar of manna, and Aaron's rod (see Ex. 25:10–22; Deut. 10:2–5). It represented the instruction, provision, power, and mercy of God found in faithful obedience to Him and His covenant (see Ps. 132:8; Heb. 9). David's placing the ark in Jerusalem was representative of his desire to return the nation to its original and fundamental purpose for existence, i.e., to keep God and His Word central (see Ex. 25:10, note).

15:12 SANCTIFY YOURSELVES. To do the work of the Lord, believers must sanctify or consecrate themselves, i.e., separate themselves from all that offends God and present themselves to Him as instruments of righteousness (cf. Rom. 6:17–22; 12:1–2; see article on SPIRITUAL SEPARATION FOR BELIEVERS, p. 1814). As a holy God, He requires that His servants be holy and consecrated.

15:13 WE SOUGHT HIM NOT. See 13:10, note.

14 So the priests and the Levites sanctified themselves to bring up the ark of the LORD God of Israel.

15 And the children of the Levites bare the ark of God upon their shoulders with the staves thereon, as [y]Moses commanded according to the word of the LORD.

16 And David spake to the chief of the Levites to appoint their brethren *to be* the singers with instruments of music, psalteries and harps and cymbals, sounding, by lifting up the voice with joy.

17 So the Levites appointed [z]Heman the son of Joel; and of his brethren, [a]Asaph the son of Berechiah; and of the sons of Merari their brethren, [b]Ethan the son of Kushaiah;

18 And with them their brethren of the second *degree,* Zechariah, Ben, and Jaaziel, and Shemiramoth, and Jehiel, and Unni, Eliab, and Benaiah, and Maaseiah, and Mattithiah, and Elipheleh, and Mikneiah, and Obed-edom, and Jeiel, the porters.

19 So the singers, Heman, Asaph, and Ethan, *were appointed* to sound with cymbals of brass;

20 And Zechariah, and [1]Aziel, and Shemiramoth, and Jehiel, and Unni, and Eliab, and Maaseiah, and Benaiah, with psalteries [c]on Alamoth;

21 And Mattithiah, and Elipheleh, and Mikneiah, and Obed-edom, and Jeiel, and Azaziah, with harps [d]on the Sheminith to excel.

22 And Chenaniah, chief of the Levites, [m]*was* for [n]song: he instructed about the song, because he *was* skilful.

23 And Berechiah and Elkanah *were* doorkeepers for the ark.

24 And Shebaniah, and Jehoshaphat, and Nethaneel, and Amasai, and Zechariah, and Benaiah, and Eliezer, the priests, [e]did blow with the trumpets before the ark of God: and Obed-edom and Jehiah *were* doorkeepers for the ark.

25 ¶ So [f]David, and the elders of Israel, and the captains over thousands, went to bring up the ark of the covenant of the LORD out of the house of Obed-edom with joy.

26 And it came to pass, when God helped the Levites that bare the ark of the covenant of the LORD, that they offered seven bullocks and seven rams.

27 And David *was* clothed with a robe of fine linen, and all the Levites that bare the ark, and the singers, and Chenaniah the master of the [o]song with the singers: David also *had* upon him an ephod of linen.

28 [g]Thus all Israel brought up the ark of the covenant of the LORD with shouting, and with sound of the cornet, and with trumpets, and with cymbals, making a noise with psalteries and harps.

29 ¶ And it came to pass, [h]*as* the ark of the covenant of the LORD came to the city of David, that Michal the daughter of Saul looking out at a window saw king David dancing and playing: and she despised him in her heart.

16 SO [i]THEY brought the ark of God, and set it in the midst of the tent that David had pitched for it: and they offered burnt sacrifices and peace offerings before God.

2 And when David had made an end of offering the burnt offerings and the peace offerings, he blessed the people in the name of the LORD.

3 And he dealt to every one of Israel, both man and woman, to every one a loaf of bread, and a good piece of flesh, and a flagon *of wine.*

4 ¶ And he appointed *certain* of the Levites to minister before the ark of the LORD, and to [j]record, and to thank and praise the LORD God of Israel:

5 Asaph the chief, and next to him Zechariah, Jeiel, and Shemiramoth, and Jehiel, and Mattithiah, and Eliab, and Benaiah, and Obed-edom: and Jeiel [p]with psalteries and with harps; but Asaph made a sound with cymbals;

6 Benaiah also and Jahaziel the priests with trumpets continually before the ark of the covenant of God.

David's psalm of gratitude

16:8–22pp — Ps. 105:1–15
16:23–33pp — Ps. 96:1–13
16:34–36pp — Ps. 106:1,47–48

7 ¶ Then on that day David deliv-

15:15 [y]Ex. 25:14 Num. 4:15 & 7:9 **15:17** [z]ch. 6:33 [a]ch. 6:39 [b]ch. 6:44 **15:20** [c]Ps. 46,title **15:21** [d]Ps. 6,title **15:24** [e]Num. 10:8 Ps. 81:3 **15:25** [f]2 Sam. 6:12,13 1 Ki. 8:1 **15:28** [g]ch. 13:8 **15:29** [h]2 Sam. 6:16 **16:1** [i]2 Sam. 6:17-19 **16:4** [j]Ps. 38 & 70,title

[1] Or, *Jaaziel;* see ver. 18 [m] Or, was *for the carriage: he instructed about the carriage* [n] Heb. *lifting up* [o] Or, *carriage* [p] Heb. *with instruments of psalteries and harps*

16:7 *THIS PSALM* TO THANK THE LORD. This psalm is a composite of Ps. 105:1–15; 96:1–13; 106:1,47–48. The manner in which David celebrated God's mercy and great deeds for Israel consisted largely of praise and thanksgiving. Under the new covenant all believers are

ered [k]first *this psalm* to thank the LORD
into the hand of Asaph and his brethren.
8 [l]Give thanks unto the LORD, call
upon his name, make known his deeds
among the people.
9 Sing unto him, sing psalms unto
him, talk ye of all his wondrous works.
10 Glory ye in his holy name: let the
heart of them rejoice that seek the
LORD.
11 Seek the LORD and his strength,
seek his face continually.
12 Remember his marvellous works
that he hath done, his wonders, and the
judgments of his mouth;
13 O ye seed of Israel his servant,
ye children of Jacob, his chosen ones.
14 He *is* the LORD our God; his judgments
are in all the earth.
15 Be ye mindful always of his covenant;
the word *which* he commanded
to a thousand generations;
16 *Even of the* [m]*covenant* which he
made with Abraham, and of his oath
unto Isaac;
17 And hath confirmed the same to
Jacob for a law, *and* to Israel *for* an
everlasting covenant,
18 Saying, Unto thee will I give the
land of Canaan, [q]the lot of your inheritance;
19 When ye were but [r]few, [n]even
a few, and strangers in it.
20 And *when* they went from nation
to nation, and from *one* kingdom to another
people;
21 He suffered no man to do them
wrong: yea, he [o]reproved kings for
their sakes,
22 *Saying,* [p]Touch not mine
anointed, and do my prophets no harm.
23 [q]Sing unto the LORD, all the
earth; show forth from day to day his
salvation.
24 Declare his glory among the heathen;
his marvellous works among all
nations.
25 For great *is* the LORD, and greatly
to be praised: he also *is* to be feared
above all gods.
26 For all the gods [r]of the people
are idols: but the LORD made the heavens.
27 Glory and honour *are* in his presence;
strength and gladness *are* in his
place.
28 Give unto the LORD, ye kindreds
of the people, give unto the LORD glory
and strength.
29 Give unto the LORD the glory *due*
unto his name: bring an offering, and
come before him: worship the LORD in
the beauty of holiness.
30 Fear before him, all the earth:
the world also shall be stable, that it be
not moved.
31 Let the heavens be glad, and let
the earth rejoice: and let *men* say
among the nations, The LORD reigneth.
32 Let the sea roar, and the fulness
thereof: let the fields rejoice, and all
that *is* therein.
33 Then shall the trees of the wood
sing out at the presence of the LORD,
because he cometh to judge the earth.
34 [s]O give thanks unto the LORD;
for *he is* good; for his mercy *endureth* for
ever.
35 [t]And say ye, Save us, O God of
our salvation, and gather us together,
and deliver us from the heathen, that
we may give thanks to thy holy name,
and glory in thy praise.
36 [u]Blessed *be* the LORD God of Israel
for ever and ever. And all [v]the
people said, Amen, and praised the
LORD.
37 ¶ So he left there before the ark
of the covenant of the LORD Asaph and
his brethren, to minister before the ark

16:7 [k]See 2 Sam. 23:1
16:8 [l]Ps. 105:1-15
16:16 [m]Gen. 17:2 & 26:3 & 28:13 & 35:11
16:19 [n]Gen. 34:30
16:21 [o]Gen. 12:17 & 20:3 Ex. 7:15-18
16:22 [p]Ps. 105:15
16:23 [q]Ps. 96:1
16:26 [r]Lev. 19:4
16:34 [s]Ps. 106:1 & 107:1 & 118:1 & 136:1
16:35 [t]Ps. 106:47,48
16:36 [u]1 Ki. 8:15 [v]Deut. 27:15

[q]Heb. *the cord* [r]Heb. *men of number*

priests unto God (1 Pet. 2:5,9) and as such should offer the spiritual ministry of praise and thanksgiving to God. "By [Christ] therefore let us offer the sacrifice of praise to God continually, that is, the fruit of *our* lips giving thanks to his name" (Heb. 13:15). The believer's praise and worship must be both in word and in deed (see v. 29, note) and are acceptable to God only as long as he or she is committed to His Word and not conformed to the world (Rom. 12:1–2).

16:10 LET THE HEART OF THEM REJOICE. Our happiness, security, and freedom from anxiety are dependent on our gratitude to God and our perseverance in seeking His face daily (vv. 8–11). Those who continually call out to the Lord with thanksgiving can have confidence that He will walk by their side and be a present help throughout all of life (Ps. 46:1; see Phil. 4:6–7, notes).

16:29 WORSHIP THE LORD IN THE BEAUTY OF HOLINESS. Genuine worship must be done in "holiness" (cf. 2 Chr. 20:21). God accepts spiritual and jubilant worship (15:28) only as long as it is accompanied by an inward disposition of reverence and purity, an earnest desire to be near Him, and the fervent commitment to resist all that offends His holy nature (see v. 7, note).

continually, as every day's work required:

38 And Obed-edom with their brethren, threescore and eight; Obed-edom also the son of Jeduthun and Hosah *to be* porters:

39 And Zadok the priest, and his brethren the priests, [w]before the tabernacle of the LORD [x]in the high place that *was* at Gibeon,

40 To offer burnt offerings unto the LORD upon the altar of the burnt offering continually [y]morning[s] and evening, and *to do* according to all that is written in the law of the LORD, which he commanded Israel;

41 And with them Heman and Jeduthun, and the rest that were chosen, who were expressed by name, to give thanks to the LORD, [z]because his mercy *endureth* for ever;

42 And with them Heman and Jeduthun with trumpets and cymbals for those that should make a sound, and with musical instruments of God. And the sons of Jeduthun *were* [t]porters.

43 [a]And all the people departed every man to his house: and David re-
1 Chr. 29:20 turned to bless his house.

Nathan's warning to David

17:1–15pp — 2 Sam. 7:1–17

17 NOW [b]IT came to pass, as David sat in his house, that David said to Nathan the prophet, Lo, I dwell in an house of cedars, but the ark of the covenant of the LORD *remaineth* under curtains.

2 Then Nathan said unto David, Do all that *is* in thine heart; for God *is* with thee.

3 ¶ And it came to pass the same night, that the word of God came to Nathan, saying,

4 Go and tell David my servant, Thus saith the LORD, Thou shalt not build me an house to dwell in:

5 For I have not dwelt in an house since the day that I brought up Israel unto this day; but [u]have gone from tent to tent, and from *one* tabernacle *to another.*

6 Wheresoever I have walked with all Israel, spake I a word to any of the judges of Israel, whom I commanded to feed my people, saying, Why have ye not built me an house of cedars?

16:39 [w]ch. 21:29 2 Chr. 1:3 [x]1 Ki. 3:4
16:40 [y]Ex. 29:38 Num. 28:3
16:41 [z]ver. 34 2 Chr. 5:13 & 7:3 Ezra 3:11 Jer. 33:11
16:43 [a]2 Sam. 6:19,20
17:1 [b]2 Sam. 7:1
17:13 [c]2 Sam. 7:14,15
17:14 [d]Luke 1:33
17:16 [e]2 Sam. 7:18

7 Now therefore thus shalt thou say unto my servant David, Thus saith the LORD of hosts, I took thee from the sheepcote, *even* [v]from following the sheep, that thou shouldest be ruler over my people Israel:

8 And I have been with thee whithersoever thou hast walked, and have cut off all thine enemies from before thee, and have made thee a name like the name of the great men that *are* in the earth.

9 Also I will ordain a place for my people Israel, and will plant them, and they shall dwell in their place, and shall be moved no more; neither shall the children of wickedness waste them any more, as at the beginning,

10 And since the time that I commanded judges *to be* over my people Israel. Moreover I will subdue all thine enemies. Furthermore I tell thee that the LORD will build thee an house.

11 ¶ And it shall come to pass, when thy days be expired that thou must go *to be* with thy fathers, that I will raise up thy seed after thee, which shall be of thy sons; and I will establish his kingdom.

12 He shall build me an house, and I will establish his throne for ever.

13 [c]I will be his father, and he shall be my son: and I will not take my mercy away from him, as I took *it* from *him* that was before thee:

14 But [d]I will settle him in mine house and in my kingdom for ever: and his throne shall be established for evermore.

15 According to all these words, and according to all this vision, so did Nathan speak unto David.

David's prayer

17:16–27pp — 2 Sam. 7:18–29

16 ¶ [e]And David the king came and sat before the LORD, and said, Who *am* I, O LORD God, and what *is* mine house, that thou hast brought me hitherto?

17 And *yet* this was a small thing in thine eyes, O God; for thou hast *also* spoken of thy servant's house for a

[s] Heb. *in the morning, and in the evening*
[t] Heb. *for the gate* [u] Heb. *have been* [v] Heb. *from after*

17:1–27 GOD'S COVENANT WITH DAVID. Ch. 17 is almost identical with 2 Sam. 7:1–29; see article on GOD'S COVENANT WITH DAVID, p. 470, for the various aspects of this covenant.

great while to come, and hast regarded
me according to the estate of a man of
high degree, O LORD God.
18 What can David *speak* more to
thee for the honour of thy servant? for
thou knowest thy servant.
19 O LORD, for thy servant's sake,
and according to thine own heart, hast
thou done all this greatness, in making
known all *these* [w]great things.
20 O LORD, *there is* none like thee,
neither *is there any* God beside thee, according to all that we have heard with
our ears.
21 And what one nation in the earth
is like thy people Israel, whom God
went to redeem *to be* his own people, to
make thee a name of greatness and terribleness, by driving out nations from
before thy people, whom thou hast redeemed out of Egypt?
22 For thy people Israel didst thou
make thine own people for ever; and
thou, LORD, becamest their God.
23 Therefore now, LORD, let the
thing that thou hast spoken concerning thy servant and concerning his
house be established for ever, and do
as thou hast said.
24 Let it even be established, that
thy name may be magnified for ever,
saying, The LORD of hosts *is* the God of
Israel, *even* a God to Israel: and *let* the
house of David thy servant *be* established before thee.
25 For thou, O my God, [x]hast told
thy servant that thou wilt build him an
house: therefore thy servant hath
found *in his heart* to pray before thee.
26 And now, LORD, thou art God,
and hast promised this goodness unto
thy servant:
27 Now therefore [y]let it please
thee to bless the house of thy servant,
that it may be before thee for ever: for
thou blessest, O LORD, and *it shall be*
blessed for ever.

David's victories

18:1–13pp — 2 Sam. 8:1–14
18:14–17pp — 2 Sam. 8:15–18

18 NOW AFTER this [f]it came to
pass, that David smote the Philistines, and subdued them, and took
Gath and her towns out of the hand of
the Philistines.
2 And he smote Moab; and the Moabites became David's servants, *and*
brought gifts.
3 ¶ And David smote [z]Hadarezer
king of Zobah unto Hamath, as he went
to stablish his dominion by the river
Euphrates.
4 And David took from him a thousand chariots, and [g]seven thousand
horsemen, and twenty thousand footmen: David also houghed all the chariot *horses*, but reserved of them an hundred chariots.
5 And when the Syrians of [a]Damascus came to help Hadarezer king of
Zobah, David slew of the Syrians two
and twenty thousand men.
6 Then David put *garrisons* in Syriadamascus; and the Syrians became David's servants, *and* brought gifts. Thus
the LORD preserved David whithersoever he went.
7 And David took the shields of gold
that were on the servants of Hadarezer, and brought them to Jerusalem.
8 Likewise from [b]Tibhath, and
from Chun, cities of Hadarezer,
brought David very much brass, wherewith [h]Solomon made the brasen sea,
and the pillars, and the vessels of
brass.
9 ¶ Now when [c]Tou king of Hamath heard how David had smitten all
the host of Hadarezer king of Zobah;
10 He sent [d]Hadoram his son to
king David, [e]to inquire of his welfare,
and [f]to congratulate him, because he
had fought against Hadarezer, and
smitten him; (for Hadarezer [g]had war
with Tou;) and *with him* all manner of
vessels of gold and silver and brass.
11 ¶ Them also king David dedicated unto the LORD, with the silver and
the gold that he brought from all *these*
nations; from Edom, and from Moab,
and from the children of Ammon, and
from the Philistines, and from Amalek.

18:1 [f] 2 Sam. 8:1
18:4 [g] 2 Sam. 8:4 *seven hundred*
18:8 [h] 1 Ki. 7:15,23; 2 Chr. 4:12,15,16

[w] Heb. *greatnesses* [x] Heb. *hast revealed the ear of thy servant* [y] Or, *it hath pleased thee* [z] Or, *Hadadezer;* see 2 Sam. 8:3 [a] Heb. *Darmesek* [b] Called *Betah* and *Berothai* in 2 Sam. 8:8 [c] Or, *Toi;* see 2 Sam. 8:9 [d] Or, *Joram;* see 2 Sam. 8:10 [e] Or, *to salute* [f] Heb. *to bless* [g] Heb. *was the man of wars*

18:6 THE LORD PRESERVED DAVID WHITHERSOEVER HE WENT. God desires to help, protect, and give victory to His faithful people. As we search for strength from the Lord and seek His face continually (16:11), a channel of blessing is opened to our lives whereby God helps us in trouble, gives us freedom from Satan's power, and leads us by His Spirit.

12 Moreover [h]Abishai the son of Zeruiah slew of the Edomites in the valley of salt [i]eighteen thousand.

13 ¶ [j]And he put garrisons in Edom; and all the Edomites became David's servants. Thus the LORD preserved David whithersoever he went.

14 ¶ So David reigned over all Israel, and executed judgment and justice among all his people.

15 And Joab the son of Zeruiah *was* over the host; and Jehoshaphat the son of Ahilud, [i]recorder.

16 And Zadok the son of Ahitub, and [j]Abimelech the son of Abiathar, *were* the priests; and [k]Shavsha was scribe;

17 [k]And Benaiah the son of Jehoiada *was* over the Cherethites and the Pelethites; and the sons of David *were* chief [l]about the king.

18:12 [i]2 Sam. 8:13
18:13 [j]2 Sam. 8:14
18:17 [k]2 Sam. 8:18
19:1 [l]2 Sam. 10:1

David and the Ammonites

19:1–19pp — 2 Sam. 10:1–19

19 NOW [l]IT came to pass after this, that Nahash the king of the children of Ammon died, and his son reigned in his stead.

2 And David said, I will show kindness unto Hanun the son of Nahash, because his father showed kindness to me. And David sent messengers to comfort him concerning his father. So the servants of David came into the land of the children of Ammon to Hanun, to comfort him.

3 But the princes of the children of Ammon said to Hanun, [m]Thinkest thou that David doth honour thy father, that he hath sent comforters unto thee? are not his servants come unto thee for to search, and to overthrow, and to spy out the land?

4 Wherefore Hanun took David's servants, and shaved them, and cut off their garments in the midst hard by their buttocks, and sent them away.

5 Then there went *certain,* and told David how the men were served. And he sent to meet them: for the men were greatly ashamed. And the king said, Tarry at Jericho until your beards be grown, and *then* return.

6 ¶ And when the children of Ammon saw that they had made themselves [n]odious to David, Hanun and the children of Ammon sent a thousand talents of silver to hire them chariots and horsemen out of Mesopotamia, and out of Syria-maachah, [m]and out of Zobah.

19:6 [m]ch. 18:5,9

7 So they hired thirty and two thousand chariots, and the king of Maachah and his people; who came and pitched before Medeba. And the children of Ammon gathered themselves together from their cities, and came to battle.

8 And when David heard *of it,* he sent Joab, and all the host of the mighty men.

9 And the children of Ammon came out, and put the battle in array before the gate of the city: and the kings that were come *were* by themselves in the field.

10 Now when Joab saw that [o]the battle was set against him before and behind, he chose out of all the [p]choice of Israel, and put *them* in array against the Syrians.

11 And the rest of the people he delivered unto the hand of [h]Abishai his brother, and they set *themselves* in array against the children of Ammon.

12 And he said, If the Syrians be too strong for me, then thou shalt help me: but if the children of Ammon be too strong for thee, then I will help thee.

13 Be of good courage, and let us behave ourselves valiantly for our people, and for the cities of our God: and let the LORD do *that which is* good in his sight.

14 So Joab and the people that *were* with him drew nigh before the Syrians unto the battle; and they fled before him.

15 And when the children of Ammon saw that the Syrians were fled, they likewise fled before Abishai his brother, and entered into the city. Then Joab came to Jerusalem.

16 ¶ And when the Syrians saw that they were put to the worse before Israel, they sent messengers, and drew forth the Syrians that *were* beyond the [q]river: and [r]Shophach the captain of the host of Hadarezer *went* before them.

17 And it was told David; and he gathered all Israel, and passed over

[h] Heb. *Abshai* [i] Or, *remembrancer* [j] Called *Ahimelech* in 2 Sam. 8:17 [k] Called *Seraiah* in 2 Sam. 8:17 and *Shisha* in 1 Ki. 4:3 [l] Heb. *at the hand of the king* [m] Heb. *In thine eyes doth David* [n] Heb. *to stink* [o] Heb. *the face of the battle was* [p] Or, *young men* [q] i.e. *Euphrates* [r] Or, *Shobach;* see 2 Sam. 10:16

Jordan, and came upon them, and set *the battle* in array against them. So when David had put the battle in array against the Syrians, they fought with him.

18 But the Syrians fled before Israel; and David slew of the Syrians seven thousand *men which fought in* chariots, and forty thousand footmen, and killed Shophach the captain of the host.

19 And when the servants of Hadarezer saw that they were put to the worse before Israel, they made peace with David, and became his servants: neither would the Syrians help the children of Ammon any more.

War with the Philistines

20:1–3pp — 2 Sam. 11:1; 12:29–31
2:4–8pp — 2 Sam. 21:15–22

20 AND [n]IT came to pass, that [s]after the year was expired, at the time that kings go out *to battle,* Joab led forth the power of the army, and wasted the country of the children of Ammon, and came and besieged Rabbah. But David tarried at Jerusalem. And [o]Joab smote Rabbah, and destroyed it.

2 And David [p]took the crown of their king from off his head, and found it [t]to weigh a talent of gold, and *there were* precious stones in it; and it was set upon David's head: and he brought also exceeding much spoil out of the city.

3 And he brought out the people that *were* in it, and cut *them* with saws, and with harrows of iron, and with axes. Even so dealt David with all the cities of the children of Ammon. And David and all the people returned to Jerusalem.

4 ¶ And it came to pass after this, [q]that there [u][v]arose war at [w]Gezer with the Philistines; at which time [r]Sibbechai the Hushathite slew [x]Sippai, *that was* of the children of [y]the giant: and they were subdued.

5 And there was war again with the Philistines; and Elhanan the son of [z]Jair slew Lahmi the brother of Goliath the Gittite, whose spear staff *was* like a weaver's beam.

6 And yet again [s]there was war at Gath, where was [a]a man of *great* stature, whose fingers and toes *were* four and twenty, six *on each hand,* and six *on each foot:* and he also was [b]the son of the giant.

7 But when he [c]defied Israel, Jonathan the son of [d]Shimea David's brother slew him.

8 These were born unto the giant in Gath; and they fell by the hand of David, and by the hand of his servants.

David's census

21:1–26pp — 2 Sam. 24:1–25

21 AND [t]SATAN stood up against Israel, and provoked David to number Israel.

2 And David said to Joab and to the rulers of the people, Go, number Israel from Beer-sheba even to Dan; [u]and bring the number of them to me, that I may know *it.*

3 And Joab answered, The LORD make his people an hundred times so many more as they *be:* but, my lord the king, *are* they not all my lord's servants? why then doth my lord require this thing? why will he be a cause of trespass to Israel?

4 Nevertheless the king's word pre-

20:1 [n]2 Sam. 11:1 [o]2 Sam. 12:26
20:2 [p]2 Sam. 12:30,31
20:4 [q]2 Sam. 21:18 [r]ch. 11:29
20:6 [s]2 Sam. 21:20
21:1 [t]2 Sam. 24:1
21:2 [u]ch. 27:23

[s]Heb. *at the return of the year* [t]Heb. *the weight of* [u]Or, *continued* [v]Heb. *stood* [w]Or, *Gob* [x]Or, *Saph;* see 2 Sam. 21:18 [y]Or, *Rapha* [z]Called *Jaareoregim* in 2 Sam. 21:19 [a]Heb. *a man of measure* [b]Heb. *born to the giant,* or, *Rapha* [c]Or, *reproached* [d]Called *Shammah* in 1 Sam. 16:9

20:3 CUT *THEM* WITH SAWS. The Hebrew word for "cut" can mean "to rule or put into subjection" (see parallel passage in 2 Sam. 12:31). This word may indicate that David subjected the Ammonites to hard tasks and labor involving saws, harrows, and axes.

21:1 SATAN ... PROVOKED DAVID TO NUMBER ISRAEL. God allowed Satan to tempt David after David had accomplished much and achieved great victories (see 2 Sam. 24:1, note). From Satan's temptation of David the following truths should be noted: (1) "Satan" means "adversary" (see Job 1:6); he actively opposes the believer's endeavor to conform to God's will and righteous standards (see Eph. 6:11–12; 1 Pet. 5:8; Rev. 12:17).

(2) Satan often directs his activity toward the human mind, mostly by way of deception (see Gen. 3:1–7,13; 2 Cor. 4:4; Eph. 2:2; 1 Tim. 4:1). He deceived David into thinking that God would endorse this census of the nation.

(3) Satan loves to lead believers into the sins of pride and self-exaltation (see Gen. 3:5; see 1 Chr. 21:8, note). Note that it was after David's great victories and accomplishments (chs. 14—21) that Satan was able to gain this foothold in the king's life (vv. 7–8; see 1 Tim. 3:6).

vailed against Joab. Wherefore Joab departed, and went throughout all Israel, and came to Jerusalem.

5 ¶ And Joab gave the sum of the number of the people unto David. And all *they of* Israel were a thousand thousand and an hundred thousand men that drew sword: and Judah *was* four hundred threescore and ten thousand men that drew sword.

6 [v]But Levi and Benjamin counted he not among them: for the king's word was abominable to Joab.

7 [e]And God was displeased with this thing; therefore he smote Israel.

8 And David said unto God, [w]I have sinned greatly, because I have done this thing: [x]but now, I beseech thee, do away the iniquity of thy servant; for I have done very foolishly.

9 ¶ And the LORD spake unto Gad, David's [y]seer, saying,

10 Go and tell David, saying, Thus saith the LORD, I [f]offer thee three *things:* choose thee one of them, that I may do *it* unto thee.

11 So Gad came to David, and said unto him, Thus saith the LORD, [g]Choose thee

12 [z]Either three years' famine; or three months to be destroyed before thy foes, while that the sword of thine enemies overtaketh *thee;* or else three days the sword of the LORD, even the pestilence, in the land, and the angel of the LORD destroying throughout all the coasts of Israel. Now therefore advise thyself what word I shall bring again to him that sent me.

13 And David said unto Gad, I am in a great strait: let me fall now into the hand of the LORD; for very [h]great *are* his mercies: but let me not fall into the hand of man.

14 ¶ So the LORD sent pestilence upon Israel: and there fell of Israel seventy thousand men.

15 And God sent an [a]angel unto Jerusalem to destroy it: and as he was destroying, the LORD beheld, and [b]he repented him of the evil, and said to the angel that destroyed, It is enough, stay now thine hand. And the angel of the LORD stood by the threshingfloor of [i]Ornan the Jebusite.

16 And David lifted up his eyes, and [c]saw the angel of the LORD stand between the earth and the heaven, having a drawn sword in his hand stretched out over Jerusalem. Then David and the elders *of Israel, who were* clothed in sackcloth, fell upon their faces.

17 And David said unto God, *Is it* not I *that* commanded the people to be numbered? even I it is that have sinned and done evil indeed; but *as for* these sheep, what have they done? let thine hand, I pray thee, O LORD my God, be on me, and on my father's house; but not on thy people, that they should be plagued.

18 ¶ Then the [d]angel of the LORD commanded Gad to say to David, that David should go up, and set up an altar unto the LORD in the threshingfloor of Ornan the Jebusite.

21:6 [v]ch. 27:24
21:8 [w]2 Sam. 24:10 [x]2 Sam. 12:13
21:9 [y]See 1 Sam. 9:9
21:12 [z]2 Sam. 24:13
21:15 [a]2 Sam. 24:16 [b]See Gen. 6:6
21:16 [c]2 Chr. 3:1
21:18 [d]2 Chr. 3:1

[e] Heb. *And it was evil in the eyes of the LORD concerning this thing* [f] Heb. *stretch out* [g] Heb. *Take to thee* [h] Or, *many* [i] Or, *Araunah;* see 2 Sam. 24:18

21:7 GOD . . . SMOTE ISRAEL. It is likely that the people of Israel were in sympathy with David's sinful desire to number the people. Joab himself knew that numbering the people was a great sin that would bring guilt upon all Israel (v. 3). Presumably, therefore, a majority of the people were guilty of favoring the numbering of Israel. Through their spirit of national pride, they participated in David's sin and became subject to judgment (see next note).

21:8 I HAVE SINNED GREATLY. David sinned by taking personal pride in God's using him for great purposes within the kingdom of Israel. By numbering the people, he was attempting to exalt himself and Israel and to rely on their national strength. Such boasting inevitably leads to a spirit of self-trust and superiority and to a life no longer lived in faith and humility. David should have remembered that all the victories of Israel had been accomplished by God's help. Similarly, believers should never boast in their own "greatness" within God's kingdom but in their own weaknesses, "that the power of Christ may rest upon [them]" (2 Cor. 12:9).

21:14 THE LORD SENT A PESTILENCE. David confessed his sin, sincerely repented, and was forgiven (v. 8). Yet God carried out the temporal punishment upon him and the people. The fact that sin often receives divine punishment even after confession and forgiveness is a recurring Biblical principle (see 2 Sam. 11:2, note; 12:13, note). By causing His disobedient children to endure the temporal consequences of sin, God honors His own law, upholds His own authority, purifies His people, and shows Himself a righteous Ruler.

21:15 IT IS ENOUGH, STAY NOW THINE HAND. The Lord is a God who can have feelings of pity even for those who deserve punishment. Because of His love, mercy, and compassion, God may shorten or even cancel a punishment He has intended to carry out (cf. Jonah 3).

19 And David went up at the saying of Gad, which he spake in the name of the LORD.

20 [j]And Ornan turned back, and saw the angel; and his four sons with him hid themselves. Now Ornan was threshing wheat.

21 And as David came to Ornan, Ornan looked and saw David, and went out of the threshingfloor, and bowed himself to David with *his* face to the ground.

22 Then David said to Ornan, [k]Grant me the place of *this* threshingfloor, that I may build an altar therein unto the LORD: thou shalt grant it me for the full price: that the plague may be stayed from the people.

23 And Ornan said unto David, Take *it* to thee, and let my lord the king do *that which is* good in his eyes: lo, I give *thee* the oxen *also* for burnt offerings, and the threshing instruments for wood, and the wheat for the meat offering; I give it all.

24 And king David said to Ornan, Nay; but I will verily buy it for the full price: for I will not take *that* which *is* thine for the LORD, nor offer burnt offerings without cost.

25 So [e]David gave to Ornan for the place six hundred shekels of gold by weight.

26 And David built there an altar unto the LORD, and offered burnt offerings and peace offerings, and called upon the LORD; and [f]he answered him from heaven by fire upon the altar of burnt offering.

27 And the LORD commanded the angel; and he put up his sword again into the sheath thereof.

28 ¶ At that time when David saw that the LORD had answered him in the threshingfloor of Ornan the Jebusite, then he sacrificed there.

29 [g]For the tabernacle of the LORD, which Moses made in the wilderness, and the altar of the burnt offering, *were* at that season in the high place at [h]Gibeon.

30 But David could not go before it to inquire of God: for he was afraid because of the sword of the angel of the LORD.

21:25 [e]2 Sam. 24:24
21:26 [f]Lev. 9:24 2 Chr. 3:1 & 7:1
21:29 [g]ch. 16:39 [h]1 Ki. 3:4 ch. 16:39 2 Chr. 1:3

22:1 [i]Deut. 12:5 2 Sam. 24:18 ch. 21:18,19,26,28 2 Chr. 3:1
22:2 [j]1 Ki. 9:21
22:3 [k]ver. 14 1 Ki. 7:47
22:4 [l]1 Ki. 5:6
22:5 [m]ch. 29:1
22:7 [n]2 Sam. 7:2 1 Ki. 8:17 ch. 17:1 & 28:2 [o]Deut. 12:5,11
22:8 [p]1 Ki. 5:3
22:9 [q]ch. 28:5 [r]1 Ki. 4:25 & 5:4
22:10 [s]2 Sam. 7:13 1 Ki. 5:5 ch. 17:12,13 & 28:6 [t]Heb. 1:5
22:11 [u]ver. 16

22 THEN DAVID said, [i]This *is* the house of the LORD God, and this *is* the altar of the burnt offering for Israel.

Preparing to build the temple

2 And David commanded to gather together [j]the strangers that *were* in the land of Israel; and he set masons to hew wrought stones to build the house of God.

3 And David prepared iron in abundance for the nails for the doors of the gates, and for the joinings; and brass in abundance [k]without weight;

4 Also cedar trees in abundance: for the [l]Zidonians and they of Tyre brought much cedar wood to David.

5 And David said, [m]Solomon my son *is* young and tender, and the house *that is* to be builded for the LORD *must be* exceeding magnifical, of fame and of glory throughout all countries: I will *therefore* now make preparation for it. So David prepared abundantly before his death.

6 ¶ Then he called for Solomon his son, and charged him to build an house for the LORD God of Israel.

7 And David said to Solomon, My son, as for me, [n]it was in my mind to build an house [o]unto the name of the LORD my God:

8 But the word of the LORD came to me, saying, [p]Thou hast shed blood abundantly, and hast made great wars: thou shalt not build an house unto my name, because thou hast shed much blood upon the earth in my sight.

9 [q]Behold, a son shall be born to thee, who shall be a man of rest; and I will give him [r]rest from all his enemies round about: for his name shall be [l]Solomon, and I will give peace and quietness unto Israel in his days.

10 [s]He shall build an house for my name; and [t]he shall be my son, and I *will be* his father; and I will establish the throne of his kingdom over Israel for ever.

11 Now, my son, [u]the LORD be with thee; and prosper thou, and build the

[j] Or, *When Ornan turned back and saw the angel, then he and his four sons with him hid themselves* [k] Heb. *Give* [l] i.e. *Peaceable*

21:24 BURNT OFFERINGS WITHOUT COST. See 2 Sam. 24:24, note.

22:11 NOW, MY SON. Although David was not allowed to build the temple (vv. 7–8), he faithfully dedicated himself to preparing for its construction. His concern was not only for the temple but for his son Solomon, who would oversee the project. Above all, he instructed his son to be careful to

house of the LORD thy God, as he hath said of thee.

12 Only the LORD [v]give thee wisdom and understanding, and give thee charge concerning Israel, that thou mayest keep the law of the LORD thy God.

13 [w]Then shalt thou prosper, if thou takest heed to fulfil the statutes and judgments which the LORD charged Moses with concerning Israel: [x]be strong, and of good courage; dread not, nor be dismayed.

14 Now, behold, [m]in my trouble I have prepared for the house of the LORD an hundred thousand talents of gold, and a thousand thousand talents of silver; and of brass and iron [y]without weight; for it is in abundance: timber also and stone have I prepared; and thou mayest add thereto.

15 Moreover *there are* workmen with thee in abundance, hewers and [n]workers of stone and timber, and all manner of cunning men for every manner of work.

16 Of the gold, the silver, and the brass, and the iron, *there is* no number. Arise *therefore,* and be doing, and [z]the LORD be with thee.

17 ¶ David also commanded all the princes of Israel to help Solomon his son, *saying,*

18 *Is* not the LORD your God with you? [a]and hath he *not* given you rest on every side? for he hath given the inhabitants of the land into mine hand; and the land is subdued before the LORD, and before his people.

19 Now set your heart and your soul to seek the LORD your God; arise therefore, and build ye the sanctuary of the LORD God, to [b]bring the ark of the covenant of the LORD, and the holy vessels of God, into the house that is to be built [c]to the name of the LORD.

Priests and Levites assembled

23 SO WHEN David was old and full of days, he made [d]Solomon his son king over Israel.

2 ¶ And he gathered together all the princes of Israel, with the priests and the Levites.

3 Now the Levites were numbered from the age of [e]thirty years and upward: and their number by their polls, man by man, was thirty and eight thousand.

4 Of which, twenty and four thousand *were* [o]to set forward the work of the house of the LORD; and six thousand *were* [f]officers and judges:

5 Moreover four thousand *were* porters; and four thousand praised the LORD with the instruments [g]which I made, *said David,* to praise *therewith.*

6 And [h]David divided them into [p]courses among the sons of Levi, *namely,* Gershon, Kohath, and Merari.

7 ¶ Of the [i]Gershonites *were,* [q]Laadan, and Shimei.

8 The sons of Laadan; the chief *was* Jehiel, and Zetham, and Joel, three.

9 The sons of Shimei; Shelomith, and Haziel, and Haran, three. These *were* the chief of the fathers of Laadan.

10 And the sons of Shimei *were,* Jahath, [r]Zina, and Jeush, and Beriah. These four *were* the sons of Shimei.

11 And Jahath was the chief, and Zizah the second: but Jeush and Beriah [s]had not many sons; therefore they were in one reckoning, according to *their* father's house.

12 ¶ [j]The sons of Kohath; Amram, Izhar, Hebron, and Uzziel, four.

13 The sons of [k]Amram; Aaron and Moses: and [l]Aaron was separated, that he should sanctify the most holy things, he and his sons for ever, [m]to burn incense before the LORD, [n]to minister unto him, and [o]to bless in his name for ever.

14 Now *concerning* Moses the man of God, [p]his sons were named of the tribe of Levi.

15 [q]The sons of Moses *were,* Gershom, and Eliezer.

22:12 [v]1 Ki. 3:9,12 **22:13** [w]Josh. 1:7,8 ch. 28:7 [x]Deut. 31:7,8 Josh. 1:6,7,9 ch. 28:20 **22:14** [y]As ver. 3 **22:16** [z]ver. 11 **22:18** [a]Deut. 12:10 Josh. 22:4 2 Sam. 7:1 ch. 23:25 **22:19** [b]2 Chr. 5:7 [c]1 Ki. 5:3 **23:1** [d]1 Ki. 1:33 **23:3** [e]Num. 4:3 **23:4** [f]Deut. 16:18 2 Chr. 19:8 **23:5** [g]2 Chr. 29:25,26 **23:6** [h]Ex. 6:16 Num. 26:57 2 Chr. 8:14 **23:7** [i]ch. 26:21 **23:12** [j]Ex. 6:18 **23:13** [k]Ex. 6:20 [l]Ex. 28:1 Heb. 5:4 [m]Ex. 30:7 1 Sam. 2:28 [n]Deut. 21:5 [o]Num. 6:23 **23:14** [p]ch. 26:23 **23:15** [q]Ex. 18:3,4

[m] Or, *in my poverty* [n] i.e. *masons and carpenters* [o] Or, *to oversee* [p] Heb. *divisions* [q] Or, *Libni;* see ch. 6:17 [r] Or, *Zizah* [s] Heb. *did not multiply sons*

observe God's word and seek the Lord with all his heart and soul (vv. 11–13,19; see John 17:1, note on the way parents ought to pray for their children).

23:2 HE GATHERED TOGETHER ALL THE PRINCES OF ISRAEL. David manifested kingly leadership at its best when he arranged for the proper conducting of divine worship. Among other things, he specified the work of the Levites (vv. 4–5); in doing so, he established a foundation for his leadership and strengthened the religious and political structure of the nation.

16 Of the sons of Gershom, [r]Shebuel[t] *was* the chief.

17 And the sons of Eliezer *were,* [s]Rehabiah [u]the chief. And Eliezer had none other sons; but the sons of Rehabiah [v]were very many.

18 Of the sons of Izhar; [w]Shelomith the chief.

19 [t]Of the sons of Hebron; Jeriah the first, Amariah the second, Jahaziel the third, and Jekameam the fourth.

20 Of the sons of Uzziel; Michah the first, and Jesiah the second.

21 ¶ [u]The sons of Merari; Mahli, and Mushi. The sons of Mahli; Eleazar, and [v]Kish.

22 And Eleazar died, and [w]had no sons, but daughters: and their [x]brethren the sons of Kish [x]took them.

23 [y]The sons of Mushi; Mahli, and Eder, and Jeremoth, three.

The duties of the Levites

24 ¶ These *were* the sons of [z]Levi after the house of their fathers; *even* the chief of the fathers, as they were counted by number of names by their polls, that did the work for the service of the house of the LORD, from the age of [a]twenty years and upward.

25 For David said, The LORD God of Israel [b]hath given rest unto his people, [y]that they may dwell in Jerusalem for ever:

26 And also unto the Levites; they shall no *more* [c]carry the tabernacle, nor any vessels of it for the service thereof.

27 For by the last words of David the Levites *were* [z]numbered from twenty years old and above:

28 Because [d]their[a] office *was* to wait on the sons of Aaron for the service of the house of the LORD, in the courts, and in the chambers, and in the purifying of all holy things, and the work of the service of the house of God;

29 Both for [e]the showbread, and for [f]the fine flour for meat offering, and for [g]the unleavened cakes, and for [h]*that which is baked in* the [b]pan, and for that which is fried, and for all manner of [i]measure and size;

30 And to stand every morning to thank and praise the LORD, and likewise at even;

31 And to offer all burnt sacrifices unto the LORD [j]in the sabbaths, in the new moons, and on the [k]set feasts, by number, according to the order commanded unto them, continually before the LORD:

32 And that they should [l]keep the charge of the tabernacle of the congregation, and the charge of the holy *place,* and [m]the charge of the sons of Aaron their brethren, in the service of the house of the LORD.

The division of the priests

24 NOW *THESE are* the divisions of the sons of Aaron. [n]The sons of Aaron; Nadab, and Abihu, Eleazar, and Ithamar.

2 But [o]Nadab and Abihu died before their father, and had no children: therefore Eleazar and Ithamar executed the priest's office.

3 And David distributed them, both Zadok of the sons of Eleazar, and Ahimelech of the sons of Ithamar, according to their offices in their service.

4 And there were more chief men found of the sons of Eleazar than of the sons of Ithamar; and *thus* were they divided. Among the sons of Eleazar *there were* sixteen chief men of the house of *their* fathers, and eight among the sons of Ithamar according to the house of their fathers.

5 Thus were they divided by lot, one sort with another; for the governors of the sanctuary, and governors *of the house* of God, were of the sons of Eleazar, and of the sons of Ithamar.

6 And Shemaiah the son of Nethaneel the scribe, *one* of the Levites, wrote

23:16 [r]ch. 26:24
23:17 [s]ch. 26:25
23:19 [t]ch. 24:23
23:21 [u]ch. 24:26 [v]ch. 24:29
23:22 [w]ch. 24:28 [x]Num. 36:6
23:23 [y]ch. 24:30
23:24 [z]Num. 10:17,21 [a]Num. 1:3 Ezra 3:8
23:25 [b]ch. 22:18
23:26 [c]Num. 4:5
23:28 [d]Neh. 11:24
23:29 [e]Ex. 25:30 [f]Lev. 6:20 [g]Lev. 2:4 [h]Lev. 2:5,7 [i]Lev. 19:35
23:31 [j]Num. 10:10 [k]Lev. 23:4
23:32 [l]Num. 1:53 [m]Num. 3:6-9
24:1 [n]Lev. 10:1,6 Num. 26:60
24:2 [o]Num. 3:4 & 26:61

[t] Or, *Shubael;* see ch. 24:20 [u] Or, *the first* [v] Heb. *were highly multiplied* [w] Or, *Shelomoth;* see ch. 24:22 [x] Or, *kinsmen* [y] Or, *and he dwelleth in Jerusalem* [z] Heb. *number* [a] Heb. *their station* was *at the hand of the sons of Aaron* [b] Or, *flat plate*

24:1 THE DIVISIONS OF THE SONS OF AARON. Ch. 24 deals with the organization of the priests. Their duty consisted in offering sacrifices by which the people might approach God to receive forgiveness and offer obedience to His will. That task ceased with the coming of Christ and the establishment of the new covenant through His blood (see Heb. 3:1; 4:14–16; 7:23–25; 8:1–13; see article on THE OLD COVENANT AND THE NEW COVENANT, p. 1954). Ironically, in N.T. times the priests had so departed from the truth of God's word that they were the ones who instigated the crucifixion of Christ (Mat. 27:1,6,20). Today all believers are to be priests unto the Lord (see 1 Pet. 2:5, note).

them before the king, and the princes,
and Zadok the priest, and Ahimelech
the son of Abiathar, and *before* the chief
of the fathers of the priests and Le-
vites: one [c]principal household being
taken for Eleazar, and *one* taken for
Ithamar.
7 Now the first lot came forth to Je-
hoiarib, the second to Jedaiah,
8 The third to Harim, the fourth to
Seorim,
9 The fifth to Malchijah, the sixth to
Mijamin,
10 The seventh to Hakkoz, the
eighth to [p]Abijah,
11 The ninth to Jeshuah, the tenth
to Shecaniah,
12 The eleventh to Eliashib, the
twelfth to Jakim,
13 The thirteenth to Huppah, the
fourteenth to Jeshebeab,
14 The fifteenth to Bilgah, the six-
teenth to Immer,
15 The seventeenth to Hezir, the
eighteenth to Aphses,
16 The nineteenth to Pethahiah, the
twentieth to Jehezekel,
17 The one and twentieth to Jachin,
the two and twentieth to Gamul,
18 The three and twentieth to Dela-
iah, the four and twentieth to Maaziah.
19 These *were* the orderings of them
in their service [q]to come into the
house of the LORD, according to their
manner, under Aaron their father, as
the LORD God of Israel had commanded
him.
20 ¶ And the rest of the sons of Levi
were these: Of the sons of Amram;
[r]Shubael: of the sons of Shubael; Jeh-
deiah.
21 Concerning [s]Rehabiah: of the
sons of Rehabiah, the first *was* Isshiah.
22 Of the Izharites; [t]Shelomoth: of
the sons of Shelomoth; Jahath.
23 And the sons *of* [u]*Hebron;* Jeriah
the first, Amariah the second, Jahaziel
the third, Jekameam the fourth.
24 *Of* the sons of Uzziel; Michah: of
the sons of Michah; Shamir.
25 The brother of Michah *was* Isshi-
ah: of the sons of Isshiah; Zechariah.
26 [v]The sons of Merari *were* Mahli
and Mushi: the sons of Jaaziah; Beno.
27 ¶ The sons of Merari by Jaaziah;
Beno, and Shoham, and Zaccur, and
Ibri.
28 Of Mahli *came* Eleazar, [w]who
had no sons.
29 Concerning Kish: the son of Kish
was Jerahmeel.
30 [x]The sons also of Mushi; Mahli,
and Eder, and Jerimoth. These *were* the
sons of the Levites after the house of
their fathers.
31 These likewise cast lots over
against their brethren the sons of Aar-
on in the presence of David the king,
and Zadok, and Ahimelech, and the
chief of the fathers of the priests and
Levites, even the principal fathers over
against their younger brethren.

The arrangements for music

25 MOREOVER DAVID and the
captains of the host separated
to the service of the sons of [y]Asaph,
and of Heman, and of Jeduthun, who
should prophesy with harps, with psal-
teries, and with cymbals: and the num-
ber of the workmen according to their
service was:
2 Of the sons of Asaph; Zaccur, and
Joseph, and Nethaniah, and [d]Asare-
lah, the sons of Asaph under the hands
of Asaph, which prophesied [z]accord-
ing[e] to the order of the king.
3 Of Jeduthun: the sons of Jeduthun;
Gedaliah, and [f]Zeri, and Jeshaiah,
Hashabiah, and Mattithiah, [g]six, un-
der the hands of their father Jeduthun,
who prophesied with a harp, to give
thanks and to praise the LORD.
4 Of Heman: the sons of Heman;
Bukkiah, Mattaniah, [h]Uzziel, [i]She-
buel, and Jerimoth, Hananiah, Hanani,
Eliathah, Giddalti, and Romamti-ezer,
Joshbekashah, Mallothi, Hothir, *and*
Mahazioth:
5 All these *were* the sons of Heman
the king's seer in the [j]words of God,

24:10 [p]Neh. 12:4,17 Luke 1:5 **24:19** [q]ch. 9:25 **24:20** [r]ch. 23:16 *Shebuel* **24:21** [s]ch. 23:17 **24:22** [t]ch. 23:18 *Shelomith* **24:23** [u]ch. 23:19 & 26:31 **24:26** [v]Ex. 6:19 ch. 23:21 **24:28** [w]ch. 23:22 **24:30** [x]ch. 23:23 **25:1** [y]ch. 6:33,39,44 **25:2** [z]ver. 6

[c] Heb. *house of the father* [d] Otherwise called *Jesharelah;* see ver. 14 [e] Heb. *by the hands of the king* [f] Or, *Izri;* see ver. 11 [g] With Shimei mentioned; see ver. 17 [h] Or, *Azareel;* see ver. 18 [i] Or, *Shubael;* see ver. 20 [j] Or, *matters*

25:1 PROPHESY WITH HARPS. The usual meaning of "to prophesy" is to use one's voice for the service and glory of God under divine impulse. Here it is used to signify singing and playing music to the praise of God, most likely under the direct influence of the Holy Spirit. Under the new covenant, prophesying came to be a predominant manifestation of the Holy Spirit among those who believe in Christ and who are filled with the Spirit (see Acts 2:17, note; see article on SPIRITUAL GIFTS FOR BELIEVERS, p. 1790).

to lift up the horn. And God gave to
Heman fourteen sons and three daughters.
6 All these *were* under the hands of
their father for song *in* the house of the
LORD, with cymbals, psalteries, and
harps, for the service of the house of
God, [a]according[k] to the king's order
to Asaph, Jeduthun, and Heman.
7 So the number of them, with their
brethren that were instructed in the
songs of the LORD, *even* all that were
cunning, was two hundred fourscore
and eight.
8 ¶ And they cast lots, ward against
ward, as well the small as the great,
[b]the teacher as the scholar.
9 Now the first lot came forth for
Asaph to Joseph: the second to Gedaliah, who with his brethren and sons
were twelve:
10 The third to Zaccur, *he,* his sons,
and his brethren, *were* twelve:
11 The fourth to Izri, *he,* his sons,
and his brethren, *were* twelve:
12 The fifth to Nethaniah, *he,* his
sons, and his brethren, *were* twelve:
13 The sixth to Bukkiah, *he,* his
sons, and his brethren, *were* twelve:
14 The seventh to Jesharelah, *he,*
his sons, and his brethren, *were* twelve:
15 The eighth to Jeshaiah, *he,* his
sons, and his brethren, *were* twelve:
16 The ninth to Mattaniah, *he,* his
sons, and his brethren, *were* twelve:
17 The tenth to Shimei, *he,* his sons,
and his brethren, *were* twelve:
18 The eleventh to Azareel, *he,* his
sons, and his brethren, *were* twelve:
19 The twelfth to Hashabiah, *he,* his
sons, and his brethren, *were* twelve:
20 The thirteenth to Shubael, *he,*
his sons, and his brethren, *were* twelve:
21 The fourteenth to Mattithiah, *he,*
his sons, and his brethren, *were* twelve:
22 The fifteenth to Jeremoth, *he,* his
sons, and his brethren, *were* twelve:
23 The sixteenth to Hananiah, *he,*
his sons, and his brethren, *were* twelve:
24 The seventeenth to Joshbekashah, *he,* his sons, and his brethren,
were twelve:
25 The eighteenth to Hanani, *he,* his
sons, and his brethren, *were* twelve:
26 The nineteenth to Mallothi, *he,*
his sons, and his brethren, *were* twelve:
27 The twentieth to Eliathah, *he,*
his sons, and his brethren, *were* twelve:
28 The one and twentieth to Hothir,
he, his sons, and his brethren, *were*
twelve:
29 The two and twentieth to Giddalti, *he,* his sons, and his brethren, *were*
twelve:
30 The three and twentieth to Mahazioth, *he,* his sons, and his brethren,
were twelve:
31 The four and twentieth to Romamti-ezer, *he,* his sons, and his brethren, *were* twelve.

25:6 [a]ver. 2
25:8 [b]2 Chr. 23:13
26:10 [c]ch. 16:38

The arrangements for porters

26 CONCERNING THE divisions
of the porters: Of the Korhites
was [l]Meshelemiah the son of Kore, of
the sons of [m]Asaph.
2 And the sons of Meshelemiah
were, Zechariah the firstborn, Jediael
the second, Zebadiah the third, Jathniel the fourth,
3 Elam the fifth, Jehohanan the
sixth, Elioenai the seventh.
4 Moreover the sons of Obed-edom
were, Shemaiah the firstborn, Jehozabad the second, Joah the third, and Sacar the fourth, and Nethaneel the fifth,
5 Ammiel the sixth, Issachar the
seventh, Peulthai the eighth: for God
blessed [n]him.
6 Also unto Shemaiah his son were
sons born, that ruled throughout the
house of their father: for they *were*
mighty men of valour.
7 The sons of Shemaiah; Othni, and
Rephael, and Obed, Elzabad, whose
brethren *were* strong men, Elihu, and
Semachiah.
8 All these of the sons of Obed-edom: they and their sons and their
brethren, able men for strength for the
service, *were* threescore and two of
Obed-edom.
9 And Meshelemiah had sons and
brethren, strong men, eighteen.
10 Also [c]Hosah, of the children of
Merari, had sons; Simri the chief, (for
though he was not the firstborn, yet his
father made him the chief;)
11 Hilkiah the second, Tebaliah the

[k] Heb. *by the hands of the king* [l] Or, *Shelemiah;* see ver. 14 [m] Or, *Ebiasaph;* see ch. 6:37 & 9:19 [n] i.e. Obed-edom as ch. 13:14

25:7 THE SONGS OF THE LORD. Singing was primarily a medium to praise God and to glorify His name (see Eph. 5:19, note).

third, Zechariah the fourth: all the sons and brethren of Hosah *were* thirteen.

12 Among these *were* the divisions of the porters, *even* among the chief men, *having* wards one against another, to minister in the house of the LORD.

13 ¶ And they cast lots, [o]as well the small as the great, according to the house of their fathers, for every gate.

14 And the lot eastward fell to [p]Shelemiah. Then for Zechariah his son, a wise counsellor, they cast lots; and his lot came out northward.

15 To Obed-edom southward; and to his sons the house of [q]Asuppim.

16 To Shuppim and Hosah *the lot came forth* westward, with the gate Shallecheth, by the causeway of the going [d]up, ward against ward.

17 Eastward *were* six Levites, northward four a day, southward four a day, and toward Asuppim two *and* two.

18 At Parbar westward, four at the causeway, *and* two at Parbar.

19 These *are* the divisions of the porters among the sons of Kore, and among the sons of Merari.

The arrangements for treasures

20 ¶ And of the Levites, Ahijah *was* [e]over the treasures of the house of God, and over the treasures of the [r]dedicated things.

21 *As concerning* the sons of [s]Laadan; the sons of the Gershonite Laadan, chief fathers, *even* of Laadan the Gershonite, *were* [t]Jehieli.

22 The sons of Jehieli; Zetham, and Joel his brother, *which were* over the treasures of the house of the LORD.

23 Of the Amramites, *and* the Izharites, the Hebronites, *and* the Uzzielites:

24 And [f]Shebuel the son of Gershom, the son of Moses, *was* ruler of the treasures.

25 And his brethren by Eliezer; Rehabiah his son, and Jeshaiah his son, and Joram his son, and Zichri his son, and [g]Shelomith his son.

26 Which Shelomith and his brethren *were* over all the treasures of the dedicated things, which David the king, and the chief fathers, the captains over thousands and hundreds, and the captains of the host, had dedicated.

27 [u]Out of the spoils won in battles did they dedicate to maintain the house of the LORD.

28 And all that Samuel [h]the seer, and Saul the son of Kish, and Abner the son of Ner, and Joab the son of Zeruiah, had dedicated; *and* whosoever had dedicated *any thing, it was* under the hand of Shelomith, and of his brethren.

The officers and judges

29 ¶ Of the Izharites, Chenaniah and his sons *were* for the outward business over Israel, for [i]officers and judges.

30 *And* of the Hebronites, Hashabiah and his brethren, men of valour, a thousand and seven hundred, *were* [v]officers among them of Israel on this side Jordan westward in all the business of the LORD, and in the service of the king.

31 Among the Hebronites *was* [j]Jerijah the chief, *even* among the Hebronites, according to the generations of his fathers. In the fortieth year of the reign of David they were sought for, and there were found among them mighty men of valour [k]at Jazer of Gilead.

32 And his brethren, men of valour, *were* two thousand and seven hundred chief fathers, whom king David made rulers over the Reubenites, the Gadites, and the half tribe of Manasseh, for every matter pertaining to God, and [l]affairs[w] of the king.

Military and civil officials

27 NOW THE children of Israel after their number, *to wit,* the chief fathers and captains of thousands and hundreds, and their officers that served the king in any matter of the courses, which came in and went out month by month throughout all the months of the year, of every course *were* twenty and four thousand.

2 Over the first course for the first month *was* [m]Jashobeam the son of Zabdiel: and in his course *were* twenty and four thousand.

3 Of the children of Perez *was* the chief of all the captains of the host for the first month.

4 And over the course of the second

26:16 [d]1 Ki. 10:5 2 Chr. 9:4
26:20 [e]ch. 28:12 Mal. 3:10
26:24 [f]ch. 23:16
26:25 [g]ch. 23:18
26:28 [h]1 Sam. 9:9
26:29 [i]ch. 23:4
26:31 [j]ch. 23:19 [k]See Josh. 21:39
26:32 [l]2 Chr. 19:11
27:2 [m]2 Sam. 23:8 ch. 11:11

[o] Or, *as well for the small as for the great* [p] Called *Meshelemiah* in ver. 1 [q] Heb. *Gatherings* [r] Heb. *holy things* [s] Or, *Libni;* see ch. 6:17 [t] Or, *Jehiel;* see ch. 23:8 & 29:8 [u] Heb. *Out of the battles and spoils* [v] Heb. *over the charge* [w] Heb. *thing*

month *was* [x]Dodai an Ahohite, and of his course *was* Mikloth also the ruler: in his course likewise *were* twenty and four thousand.

5 The third captain of the host for the third month *was* Benaiah the son of Jehoiada, a [y]chief priest: and in his course *were* twenty and four thousand.

6 This *is that* Benaiah, *who was* [n]mighty *among* the thirty, and above the thirty: and in his course *was* Ammizabad his son.

7 The fourth *captain* for the fourth month *was* [o]Asahel the brother of Joab, and Zebadiah his son after him: and in his course *were* twenty and four thousand.

8 The fifth captain for the fifth month *was* Shamhuth the Izrahite: and in his course *were* twenty and four thousand.

9 The sixth *captain* for the sixth month *was* [p]Ira the son of Ikkesh the Tekoite: and in his course *were* twenty and four thousand.

10 The seventh *captain* for the seventh month *was* [q]Helez the Pelonite, of the children of Ephraim: and in his course *were* twenty and four thousand.

11 The eighth *captain* for the eighth month *was* [r]Sibbecai the Hushathite, of the Zarhites: and in his course *were* twenty and four thousand.

12 The ninth *captain* for the ninth month *was* [s]Abiezer the Anetothite, of the Benjamites: and in his course *were* twenty and four thousand.

13 The tenth *captain* for the tenth month *was* [t]Maharai the Netophathite, of the Zarhites: and in his course *were* twenty and four thousand.

14 The eleventh *captain* for the eleventh month *was* [u]Benaiah the Pirathonite, of the children of Ephraim: and in his course *were* twenty and four thousand.

15 The twelfth *captain* for the twelfth month *was* [z]Heldai the Netophathite, of Othniel: and in his course *were* twenty and four thousand.

16 ¶ Furthermore over the tribes of Israel: the ruler of the Reubenites *was* Eliezer the son of Zichri: of the Simeonites, Shephatiah the son of Maachah:

17 Of the Levites, [v]Hashabiah the son of Kemuel: of the Aaronites, Zadok:

18 Of Judah, [w]Elihu, *one* of the brethren of David: of Issachar, Omri the son of Michael:

19 Of Zebulun, Ishmaiah the son of Obadiah: of Naphtali, Jerimoth the son of Azriel:

20 Of the children of Ephraim, Hoshea the son of Azaziah: of the half tribe of Manasseh, Joel the son of Pedaiah:

21 Of the half *tribe* of Manasseh in Gilead, Iddo the son of Zechariah: of Benjamin, Jaasiel the son of Abner:

22 Of Dan, Azareel the son of Jeroham. These *were* the princes of the tribes of Israel.

23 ¶ But David took not the number of them from twenty years old and under: because [x]the LORD had said he would increase Israel like to the stars of the heavens.

24 Joab the son of Zeruiah began to number, but he finished not, because [y]there fell wrath for it against Israel; neither [a]was the number put in the account of the chronicles of king David.

25 ¶ And over the king's treasures *was* Azmaveth the son of Adiel: and over the storehouses in the fields, in the cities, and in the villages, and in the castles, *was* Jehonathan the son of Uzziah:

26 And over them that did the work of the field for tillage of the ground *was* Ezri the son of Chelub:

27 And over the vineyards *was* Shimei the Ramathite: [b]over the increase of the vineyards for the wine cellars *was* Zabdi the Shiphmite:

28 And over the olive trees and the sycamore trees that *were* in the low plains *was* Baal-hanan the Gederite: and over the cellars of oil *was* Joash:

29 And over the herds that fed in Sharon *was* Shitrai the Sharonite: and over the herds *that were* in the valleys *was* Shaphat the son of Adlai:

30 Over the camels also *was* Obil the Ishmaelite: and over the asses *was* Jehdeiah the Meronothite:

31 And over the flocks *was* Jaziz the Hagerite. All these *were* the rulers of the substance which *was* king David's.

32 Also Jonathan David's uncle was a counsellor, a wise man, and a [c]scribe: and Jehiel the [d]son of Hachmoni *was* with the king's sons:

27:6 [n] 2 Sam. 23:20,22, 23 ch. 11:22
27:7 [o] 2 Sam. 23:24 ch. 11:26
27:9 [p] ch. 11:28
27:10 [q] ch. 11:27
27:11 [r] 2 Sam. 21:18
27:12 [s] ch. 11:28
27:13 [t] 2 Sam. 23:28 ch. 11:30
27:14 [u] ch. 11:31
27:17 [v] ch. 26:30
27:18 [w] 1 Sam. 16:6 *Eliab*
27:23 [x] Gen. 15:5
27:24 [y] 2 Sam. 24:15 ch 21:7

[x] Or, *Dodo;* see 2 Sam. 23:9 [y] Or, *principal officer;* see 1 Ki. 4:5 [z] Or, *Heled;* see ch. 11:30 [a] Heb. *ascended* [b] Heb. *over that which was of the vineyards* [c] Or, *secretary* [d] Or, *Hachmonite*

33 And [z]Ahithophel *was* the king's counsellor: and [a]Hushai the Archite *was* the king's companion:
34 And after Ahithophel *was* Jehoiada the son of Benaiah, and [b]Abiathar: and the general of the king's army *was* [c]Joab.

David's instructions to Solomon

28 AND DAVID assembled all the princes of Israel, [d]the princes of the tribes, and [e]the captains of the companies that ministered to the king by course, and the captains over the thousands, and captains over the hundreds, and [f]the stewards over all the substance and [e]possession of the king, [f]and of his sons, with the [g]officers, and with [g]the mighty men, and with all the valiant men, unto Jerusalem.
2 Then David the king stood up upon his feet, and said, Hear me, my brethren, and my people: *As for me,* [h]I *had* in mine heart to build an house of rest for the ark of the covenant of the LORD, and for [i]the footstool of our God, and had made ready for the building:
3 But God said unto me, [j]Thou shalt not build an house for my name, because thou *hast been* a man of war, and hast shed [h]blood.
4 Howbeit the LORD God of Israel [k]chose me before all the house of my father to be king over Israel for ever: for he hath chosen [l]Judah *to be* the ruler; and of the house of Judah, [m]the house of my father; and [n]among the sons of my father he liked me to make *me* king over all Israel:
5 [o]And of all my sons, (for the LORD hath given me many sons,) [p]he hath chosen Solomon my son to sit upon the throne of the kingdom of the LORD over Israel.
6 And he said unto me, [q]Solomon thy son, he shall build my house and my courts: for I have chosen him *to be* my son, and I will be his father.
7 Moreover I will establish his kingdom for ever, [r]if he be [i]constant to do my commandments and my judgments, as at this day.
8 Now therefore in the sight of all Israel the congregation of the LORD, and in the audience of our God, keep and seek for all the commandments of the LORD your God: that ye may possess this good land, and leave *it* for an inheritance for your children after you for ever.
9 ¶ And thou, Solomon my son, [s]know thou the God of thy father, and serve him [t]with a perfect heart and with a willing mind: for [u]the LORD searcheth all hearts, and understandeth all the imaginations of the thoughts: [v]if thou seek him, he will be found of thee; but if thou forsake him, he will cast thee off for ever. 2 Chr 13:4-12
10 Take heed now; [w]for the LORD hath chosen thee to build an house for the sanctuary: be strong, and do *it.*
11 ¶ Then David gave to Solomon his son [x]the pattern of the porch, and of the houses thereof, and of the treasuries thereof, and of the upper chambers thereof, and of the inner parlours thereof, and of the place of the mercy seat,
12 And the pattern [j]of all that he had by the spirit, of the courts of the house of the LORD, and of all the chambers round about, [y]of the treasuries of the house of God, and of the treasuries of the dedicated things:
13 Also for the courses of the priests and the Levites, and for all the work of the service of the house of the LORD, and for all the vessels of service in the house of the LORD.
14 *He gave* of gold by weight for *things* of gold, for all instruments of all manner of service; *silver also* for all instruments of silver by weight, for all instruments of every kind of service:
15 Even the weight for the candle-

27:33 [z]2 Sam. 15:12 [a]2 Sam. 15:37 & 16:16
27:34 [b]1 Ki. 1:7 [c]ch. 11:6
28:1 [d]ch. 27:16 [e]ch. 27:1,2 [f]ch. 27:25 [g]ch. 11:10
28:2 [h]2 Sam. 7:2 [i]Ps. 99:5 & 132:7
28:3 [j]2 Sam. 7:5,13 1 Ki. 5:3 ch. 17:4 & 22:8
28:4 [k]1 Sam. 16:7-13 [l]Gen. 49:8 ch. 5:2 [m]1 Sam. 16:1 [n]1 Sam. 16:12,13
28:5 [o]ch. 3:1 & 23:1 [p]ch. 22:9
28:6 [q]2 Sam. 7:13,14 ch. 22:9,10 2 Chr. 1:9
28:7 [r]ch. 22:13
28:9 [s]Jer. 9:24 Hos. 4:1 John 17:3 [t]2 Ki. 20:3 [u]1 Sam. 16:7 1 Ki. 8:39 ch. 29:17 Jer. 11:20 & 17:10 & 20:12 Rev. 2:23 [v]2 Chr. 15:2
28:10 [w]ver. 6
28:11 [x]ver. 19 See Ex. 25:40
28:12 [y]ch. 26:20

[e] Or, *cattle* [f] Or, *and his sons* [g] Or, *eunuchs* [h] Heb. *bloods* [i] Heb. *strong* [j] Heb. *of all that was with him*

28:8 KEEP AND SEEK . . . THE COMMANDMENTS. The condition for establishing Solomon's kingdom was a life of obedience and faithfulness to God. Solomon heeded his father's advice in the beginning, but later departed from God (see 1 Ki. 2:4; 11:1, notes).

28:9 KNOW . . . GOD. David's charge to Solomon was that he should know God, serve Him, and seek Him "with a perfect heart and with a willing mind." (1) To know God means to have practical knowledge of His person and ways and to abide in close fellowship with Him and His word (see John 17:3, note; cf. 15:4, note). (2) To seek God means to desire His grace, kingdom power, and righteousness to such an extent that we continually pray for His active presence in our lives and earnestly seek to obey His will (see Mat. 5:6, note on hungering and thirsting for righteousness).

sticks of gold, and for their lamps of gold, by weight for every candlestick, and for the lamps thereof: and for the candlesticks of silver by weight, *both* for the candlestick, and *also* for the lamps thereof, according to the use of every candlestick.

16 And by weight *he gave* gold for the tables of showbread, for every table; and *likewise* silver for the tables of silver:

17 Also pure gold for the fleshhooks, and the bowls, and the cups: and for the golden basins *he gave gold* by weight for every basin; and *likewise silver* by weight for every basin of silver:

18 And for the altar of incense refined gold by weight; and gold for the pattern of the chariot of the [z]cherubims, that spread out *their wings,* and covered the ark of the covenant of the LORD.

19 All *this, said David,* [a]the LORD made me understand in writing by *his* hand upon me, *even* all the works of this pattern.

20 And David said to Solomon his son, [b]Be strong and of good courage, and do *it:* fear not, nor be dismayed: for the LORD God, *even* my God, *will be* with thee; [c]he will not fail thee, nor forsake thee, until thou hast finished all the work for the service of the house of the LORD.

21 And, behold, [d]the courses of the priests and the Levites, *even they shall be with thee* for all the service of the house of God: and *there shall be* with thee for all manner of workmanship [e]every willing skilful man, for any manner of service: also the princes and all the people *will be* wholly at thy commandment.

David invites the people to give

29 FURTHERMORE DAVID the king said unto all the congregation, Solomon my son, whom alone God hath chosen, *is yet* [f]young and tender, and the work *is* great: for the palace *is* not for man, but for the LORD God.

2 Now I have prepared with all my might for the house of my God the gold for *things to be made* of gold, and the silver for *things* of silver, and the brass for *things* of brass, the iron for *things* of iron, and wood for *things* of wood; [g]onyx stones, and *stones* to be set, glistering stones, and of divers colours, and all manner of precious stones, and marble stones in abundance.

3 Moreover, because I have set my affection to the house of my God, I have of mine own proper good, of gold and silver, *which* I have given to the house of my God, over and above all that I have prepared for the holy house,

4 *Even* three thousand talents of gold, of the gold of [h]Ophir, and seven thousand talents of refined silver, to overlay the walls of the houses *withal:*

5 The gold for *things* of gold, and the silver for *things* of silver, and for all manner of work *to be made* by the hands of artificers. And who *then* is willing [k]to consecrate his service this day unto the LORD?

6 ¶ Then [i]the chief of the fathers and princes of the tribes of Israel, and the captains of thousands and of hundreds, with [j]the rulers of the king's work, offered willingly,

7 And gave for the service of the house of God of gold five thousand talents and ten thousand drams, and of silver ten thousand talents, and of brass eighteen thousand talents, and one hundred thousand talents of iron.

8 And they with whom *precious* stones were found gave *them* to the treasure of the house of the LORD, by the hand of [k]Jehiel the Gershonite.

9 Then the people rejoiced, for that they offered willingly, because with perfect heart they [l]offered willingly to the LORD: and David the king also rejoiced with great joy.

David's prayer

10 ¶ Wherefore David blessed the

28:18 [z]Ex. 25:18-22 1 Sam. 4:4 1 Ki. 6:23 **28:19** [a]ver. 11,12 See Ex. 25,40 **28:20** [b]Deut. 31:7,8 Josh. 1:6,7,9 ch. 22:13 [c]Josh. 1:5 **28:21** [d]ch. 24 & 25 & 26 [e]Ex. 35:25,26 **29:1** [f]1 Ki. 3:7 ch. 22:5 Prov. 4:3 **29:2** [g]See Is. 54:11,12 Rev. 21:18 **29:4** [h]1 Ki. 9:28 **29:6** [i]ch. 27:1 [j]ch. 27:25 **29:8** [k]ch. 26:21 **29:9** [l]2 Cor. 9:7

[k] Heb. *to fill his hand*

29:5 CONSECRATE HIS SERVICE THIS DAY UNTO THE LORD. Ch. 29 illustrates the right attitude in giving to God's kingdom work. We must have: (1) a delight and commitment to God's kingdom (vv. 3,17); (2) a willingness to consecrate ourselves as well as our possessions to God (vv. 5–6); (3) joy arising out of a wholehearted giving (v. 9); (4) an acknowledgment that what we have justly gained has come from God (v. 12); (5) humility and thanksgiving for the privilege of having a part in God's eternal purposes (vv. 13–15); (6) motives for giving that come out of a sincere heart and a righteous life (v. 17); (7) prayer that God might continue to direct our hearts to a steadfast faithfulness to Him and His cause on earth (v. 18; see also 2 Cor. 9).

LORD before all the congregation: and David said, Blessed *be* thou, LORD God of Israel our father, for ever and ever.

11 [m]Thine, O LORD, *is* the greatness, and the power, and the glory, and the victory, and the majesty: for all *that is* in the heaven and in the earth *is thine;* thine *is* the kingdom, O LORD, and thou art exalted as head above all.

12 [n]Both riches and honour *come* of thee, and thou reignest over all; and in thine hand *is* power and might; and in thine hand *it is* to make great, and to give strength unto all.

13 Now therefore, our God, we thank thee, and praise thy glorious name.

14 But who *am* I, and what *is* my people, that we should [1]be able to offer so willingly after this sort? for all things *come* of thee, and [m]of thine own have we given thee.

15 For [o]we *are* strangers before thee, and sojourners, as *were* all our fathers: [p]our days on the earth *are* as a shadow, and *there is* none [n]abiding.

16 O LORD our God, all this store that we have prepared to build thee an house for thine holy name *cometh* of thine hand, and *is* all thine own.

17 I know also, my God, that thou [q]triest the heart, and [r]hast pleasure in uprightness. As for me, in the uprightness of mine heart I have willingly offered all these things: and now have I seen with joy thy people, which are [o]present here, to offer willingly unto thee.

18 O LORD God of Abraham, Isaac, and of Israel, our fathers, keep this for ever in the imagination of the thoughts of the heart of thy people, and [p]prepare their heart unto thee:

19 And [s]give unto Solomon my son a perfect heart, to keep thy commandments, thy testimonies, and thy statutes, and to do all *these things,* and to build the palace, *for* the which [t]I have made provision.

Ezra 3:10-13

20 ¶ And David said to all the congregation, Now bless the LORD your God. And all the congregation blessed the LORD God of their fathers, and bowed down their heads, and worshipped the LORD, and the king.

29:11 [m]Mat. 6:13 1 Tim. 1:17 Rev. 5:13
29:12 [n]Rom. 11:36
29:15 [o]Ps. 39:12 Heb. 11:13 1 Pet. 2:11 [p]Job 14:2 Ps. 90:9
29:17 [q]1 Sam. 16:7 ch. 28:9 [r]Prov. 11:20
29:19 [s]Ps. 72:1 [t]ver. 2 ch. 22:14
29:22 [u]1 Ki. 1:35,39
29:24 [v]2 Chr. 30:8 Eccl. 8:2 Ezek. 17:18
29:25 [w]1 Ki. 3:13 2 Chr. 1:12 Eccl. 2:9
29:27 [x]2 Sam. 5:4 1 Ki. 2:11 [y]2 Sam. 5:5
29:28 [z]Gen. 25:8 [a]ch. 23:1
29:30 [b]Dan. 2:21

21 And they sacrificed sacrifices unto the LORD, and offered burnt offerings unto the LORD, on the morrow after that day, *even* a thousand bullocks, a thousand rams, *and* a thousand lambs, with their drink offerings, and sacrifices in abundance for all Israel:

Solomon made king

29:21–25pp — 1 Ki. 1:28–53

22 And did eat and drink before the LORD on that day with great gladness. And they made Solomon the son of David king the second time, and [u]anointed *him* unto the LORD *to be* the chief governor, and Zadok *to be* priest.

23 Then Solomon sat on the throne of the LORD as king instead of David his father, and prospered; and all Israel obeyed him.

24 And all the princes, and the mighty men, and all the sons likewise of king David, [v]submitted themselves unto Solomon the king.

25 And the LORD magnified Solomon exceedingly in the sight of all Israel, and [w]bestowed upon him *such* royal majesty as had not been on any king before him in Israel.

The death of David

29:26–28pp — 1 Ki. 2:10–12

26 ¶ Thus David the son of Jesse reigned over all Israel.

27 [x]And the time that he reigned over Israel *was* forty years; [y]seven years reigned he in Hebron, and thirty and three *years* reigned he in Jerusalem.

28 And he [z]died in a good old age, [a]full of days, riches, and honour: and Solomon his son reigned in his stead.

29 Now the acts of David the king, first and last, behold, they *are* written in the [q]book[r] of Samuel the seer, and in the book of Nathan the prophet, and in the book of Gad the seer,

30 With all his reign and his might, [b]and the times that went over him, and over Israel, and over all the kingdoms of the countries.

[1]Heb. *retain,* or, *obtain strength* [m]Heb. *of thine hand* [n]Heb. *expectation* [o]Or, *found* [p]Or, *stablish* [q]Or, *history* [r]Heb. *words*

29:20 BLESS THE LORD YOUR GOD. To "bless the LORD" is to adore, worship, and praise Him (Ps. 103:1–2). When believers bless God, they recall God's goodness, righteousness, and glory, and then respond in praise and adoration.

2 CHRONICLES

Outline

I. Solomon: Significant Contributions of His Reign (1:1–9:31)
   A. The Establishment of Solomon's Leadership (1:1–17)
   B. The Building of the Temple (2:1—5:1)
   C. The Dedication of the Temple (5:2—7:22)
      1. Installing the Ark (5:2–14)
      2. Solomon's Dedicatory Address (6:1–11)
      3. Solomon's Dedicatory Prayer and God's Glory (6:12—7:3)
      4. Dedicatory Sacrifices and Feasts (7:4–11)
      5. God's Promise and Warning (7:12–22)
   D. The Fame of Solomon (8:1—9:28)
      1. The Accomplishments, Possessions, and Policies (8:1–18)
      2. Queen of Sheba's Praise (9:1–12)
      3. Solomon's Wealth (9:13–28)
   E. The Death of Solomon (9:29–31)

II. Judah's Kings From Rehoboam to the Exile (10:1—36:23)
   A. Schism and the Reign of Rehoboam (10:1—12:16)
   B. The Reigns of Abijah and Asa (13:1—16:14)
   C. Jehoshaphat's Reign (17:1—20:37)
   D. The Reigns of Jehoram, Ahaziah, and Athaliah (21:1—23:15)
   E. Joash's Reign (23:16—24:27)
   F. The Reigns of Amaziah, Uzziah, and Jotham (25:1—27:9)
   G. Ahaz's Reign (28:1–27)
   H. Hezekiah's Reign and Reforms (29:1—32:33)
   I. The Reigns of Manasseh and Amon (33:1–25)
   J. Josiah's Reign and Reforms (34:1—35:27)
   K. Josiah's Successors and the Exile (36:1–21)
   L. Cyrus's Decree (36:22–23)

Author: Ezra (?)

Theme: True Worship, Revival and Reform

Date of Writing: 450–420 B.C.

Background

Since 1 and 2 Chronicles were originally a single book in the Hebrew O.T., the background to 2 Chronicles is discussed more fully in the introduction to 1 Chronicles. 2 Chronicles covers the same period of history as 1 and 2 Kings—namely, the reign of Solomon (971–931 B.C.) and the divided kingdom (930–586 B.C.). Unlike 1 and 2 Kings, which traces the history of both halves of the divided kingdom, 2 Chronicles focuses only on the destiny of Judah. The Chronicler views the southern kingdom of Judah as the main stream of Israel's "redemptive history," since (1) the temple in Jerusalem remained the center for the true worship of God, (2) her kings were the descendants of David, and (3) Judah was the dominant tribe among the returning Jews who rebuilt Jerusalem and the temple. 2 Chron-

icles was written from the priestly perspective of the latter half of the 5th century B.C. when the temple, the priesthood, and the Davidic covenant were again central in importance.

Purpose

Like 1 Chronicles, 2 Chronicles was written to the returned remnant of Jews who faced the urgent need of recovering their spiritual heritage. Rather than emphasizing the dark side of Israel's past, it emphasizes revival, reform, and the recovery of faith for the "beaten-down" exiles, who sought a future and redemptive hope in the promised land.

Survey

The history of 2 Chronicles divides into two major sections. (1) Chs. 1—9 are devoted to Solomon's reign, which became Israel's golden age of peace, power, prosperity, and prestige. Nevertheless, in keeping with the overall purpose of Chronicles, a full two-thirds of these nine chapters focus on the building and dedication of the temple as the center of true Israelite worship of God (chs. 2—7).

(2) Chs. 10—36 are a highly selective account of the kings of Judah after the death of Solomon and the division of the kingdom. In the midst of Judah's spiritual decline and apostasy, 2 Chronicles features certain praiseworthy kings: Asa (chs. 14—15), Jehoshaphat (ch. 17; 19—20), Joash (ch. 24), Hezekiah (chs. 29—32), and Josiah (chs. 34—35), each of whom initiated and led times of spiritual revival and reform. A full seventy percent of chs. 10—36 focuses on those kings responsible for revival and reform, while only thirty percent focuses on the evil kings responsible for the corruption and collapse of the kingdom. The book ends with Cyrus, the king of Persia, permitting the Jewish exiles to return and rebuild their temple in Jerusalem (36:22–23).

Special Features

Four major features or emphases characterize 2 Chronicles. (1) Its scope of history corresponds essentially to the time frame covered in 1 and 2 Kings. (2) Its focus on the temple in Jerusalem most likely accounts for Chronicles being placed in the nonprophetic division of the Hebrew O.T., thus separating it from Samuel and Kings, which are located in the prophetic division. (3) It features five national revivals including: (a) the most extended O.T. account of a spiritual revival under Hezekiah (chs. 29—32) and (b) the dramatic revival under Josiah, when "the book of the law" was found and read publicly, resulting in a renewal of the covenant and the Passover celebration (chs. 34—35). (4) The book's key exhortation is, "Seek the LORD." The author stresses again and again the importance of seeking the Lord diligently with all one's heart (e.g., 1:6–13; 6:14; 7:14; 12:14; 15:1–2,12–15; 16:9,12; 17:4; 19:3; 20:3–4,20; 31:21; 32:20–22; 34:26–28).

New Testament Fulfillment

Though the Davidic kingdom was destroyed, the Davidic line remained and found its fulfillment in Jesus Christ (see the genealogies of Mat. 1:1–17 and Luke 3:23–38). Also the Jerusalem temple has prophetic significance related to Jesus, who declared: "I say unto you, That in this place is *one* greater than the temple" (Mat. 12:6). Jesus also compared His body to the temple: "Destroy this temple, and in three days I will raise it up" (John 2:19). Finally, in the new Jerusalem, God and the Lamb replace the temple: "And I saw no temple therein: for the Lord God Almighty and the Lamb are the temple of it" (Rev. 21:22).

Reading 2 Chronicles

In order to read the entire Old Testament in one year, the book of 2 Chronicles should be read in 12 days, according to the following schedule: ☐ 1–4 ☐ 5–7 ☐ 8–11 ☐ 12–15 ☐ 16–19 ☐ 20–22 ☐ 23–25 ☐ 26–28 ☐ 29–30 ☐ 31–32 ☐ 33–34 ☐ 35–36

NOTES

Solomon asks for wisdom

1:2–13pp — 1 Ki. 3:4–15
1:14–17pp — 1 Ki. 10:26–29; 2 Chr. 9:25–28

1 AND [a]SOLOMON the son of David was strengthened in his kingdom, and [b]the LORD his God *was* with him, and [c]magnified him exceedingly.

2 Then Solomon spake unto all Israel, to [d]the captains of thousands and of hundreds, and to the judges, and to every governor in all Israel, the chief of the fathers.

3 So Solomon, and all the congregation with him, went to the high place that *was* at [e]Gibeon; for there was the tabernacle of the congregation of God, which Moses the servant of the LORD had made in the wilderness.

4 [f]But the ark of God had David brought up from Kirjath-jearim to *the place which* David had prepared for it: for he had pitched a tent for it at Jerusalem.

5 Moreover [g]the brasen altar, that [h]Bezaleel the son of Uri, the son of Hur, had made, [a]he put before the tabernacle of the LORD: and Solomon and the congregation sought unto it.

6 And Solomon went up thither to the brasen altar before the LORD, which *was* at the tabernacle of the congregation, and [i]offered a thousand burnt offerings upon it.

7 ¶ [j]In that night did God appear unto Solomon, and said unto him, Ask what I shall give thee.

8 And Solomon said unto God, Thou hast shown great mercy unto David my father, and hast made me [k]to reign in his stead.

9 Now, O LORD God, let thy promise unto David my father be established: [l]for thou hast made me king over a people [b]like the dust of the earth in multitude.

10 [m]Give me now wisdom and knowledge, that I may [n]go out and come in before this people: for who can judge this thy people, *that is so* great?

11 [o]And God said to Solomon, Because this was in thine heart, and thou hast not asked riches, wealth, or honour, nor the life of thine enemies, neither yet hast asked long life; but hast asked wisdom and knowledge for thyself, that thou mayest judge my people, over whom I have made thee king:

12 Wisdom and knowledge *is* granted unto thee; and I will give thee riches, and wealth, and honour, such as [p]none of the kings have had that *have been* before thee, neither shall there any after thee have the like.

13 ¶ Then Solomon came *from his journey* to the high place that *was* at Gibeon to Jerusalem, from before the tabernacle of the congregation, and reigned over Israel.

14 [q]And Solomon gathered chariots and horsemen: and he had a thousand and four hundred chariots, and twelve thousand horsemen, which he placed in the chariot cities, and with the king at Jerusalem.

15 [r]And the king [c]made silver and gold at Jerusalem *as plenteous* as stones, and cedar trees made he as the sycamore trees that *are* in the vale for abundance.

16 [s]And [d]Solomon had horses brought out of Egypt, and linen yarn: the king's merchants received the linen yarn at a price.

17 And they fetched up, and

1:1 [a]1 Ki. 2:46 [b]Gen. 39:2 [c]1 Chr. 29:25
1:2 [d]1 Chr. 27:1
1:3 [e]1 Ki. 3:4 1 Chr. 16:39 & 21:29
1:4 [f]2 Sam. 6:2,17 1 Chr. 15:1
1:5 [g]Ex. 27:1,2 & 38:1,2 [h]Ex. 31:2
1:6 [i]1 Ki. 3:4
1:7 [j]1 Ki. 3:5
1:8 [k]1 Chr. 28:5
1:9 [l]1 Ki. 3:7,8
1:10 [m]1 Ki. 3:9 [n]Num. 27:17 Deut. 31:2
1:11 [o]1 Ki. 3:11-13
1:12 [p]1 Chr. 29:25 ch. 9:22 Eccl. 2:9
1:14 [q]1 Ki. 4:26 & 10:26 ch. 9:25
1:15 [r]1 Ki. 10:27 ch. 9:27 Job 22:24
1:16 [s]1 Ki. 10:28 ch. 9:28

[a] Or, was *there* [b] Heb. *much as the dust of the earth* [c] Heb. *gave* [d] Heb. *the going forth of the horses which* was *Solomon's*

1:7 ASK WHAT I SHALL GIVE THEE. God, who gives good gifts to His children (cf. Mat. 7:7–11), offered to give Solomon whatever he asked for. We too may ask for good things from the Lord, for He desires to give us the necessary provisions for life (Mat. 6:25–34), the presence of the Holy Spirit (Luke 11:9–13), and grace, mercy, and full salvation to aid us in all matters of life (Heb. 4:16; 7:25).

1:10 GIVE ME NOW WISDOM. Wisdom, i.e., a wise and discerning heart that sees and evaluates everything from the point of view of God and His Word, is one of the greatest treasures in life (Prov. 3:13–15). God desires to give every believer this wisdom. It comes to us through prayer (v. 7; Jas. 1:5), the enlightenment of the Holy Spirit (Rom. 8:5–15; Gal. 5:16–25; Eph. 5:17–18), and the diligent search of Scripture to learn God's ways (Ps. 25:4; 119:2–3; Acts 17:11).

1:12 WISDOM AND KNOWLEDGE *IS* GRANTED UNTO THEE. Solomon was granted wisdom and knowledge, yet this did not guarantee that he would persevere in faithfulness to God. For this reason God told him to be careful to walk in His ways and to keep His commandments (see 1 Ki. 3:14). Possessing wisdom or exceptional knowledge of God's Word does not guarantee that a person will live for God according to that wisdom and follow His ways. Later in life Solomon departed from God and failed to do what he knew was right. He was consequently rejected by God (see 1 Ki. 3:9–10; 4:29–34; 11:1, notes).

brought forth out of Egypt a chariot for six hundred *shekels* of silver, and an horse for an hundred and fifty: and so brought they out *horses* for all the kings of the Hittites, and for the kings of Syria, [e]by their means.

Preparing to build the temple

2:1–18pp — 1 Ki. 5:1–16

2 AND SOLOMON [t]determined to build an house for the name of the LORD, and an house for his kingdom.

2 And [u]Solomon told out threescore and ten thousand men to bear burdens, and fourscore thousand to hew in the mountain, and three thousand and six hundred to oversee them.

3 ¶ And Solomon sent to [f]Huram the king of Tyre, saying, [v]As thou didst deal with David my father, and didst send him cedars to build him an house to dwell therein, *even so deal with me.*

4 Behold, [w]I build an house to the name of the LORD my God, to dedicate *it* to him, *and* [x]to burn before him [g]sweet incense, and for [y]the continual showbread, and for [z]the burnt offerings morning and evening, on the sabbaths, and on the new moons, and on the solemn feasts of the LORD our God. This *is an ordinance* for ever to Israel.

5 And the house which I build *is* great: for [a]great *is* our God above all gods.

6 [b]But who [h]is able to build him an house, seeing the heaven and heaven of heavens cannot contain him? who *am* I then, that I should build him an house, save only to burn sacrifice before him?

7 Send me now therefore a man cunning to work in gold, and in silver, and in brass, and in iron, and in purple, and crimson, and blue, and that can skill [i]to grave with the cunning men that *are* with me in Judah and in Jerusalem, [c]whom David my father did provide.

8 [d]Send me also cedar trees, fir trees, and [j]algum trees, out of Lebanon: for I know that thy servants can skill to cut timber in Lebanon; and, behold, my servants *shall be* with thy servants,

9 Even to prepare me timber in abundance: for the house which I am about to build *shall be* [k]wonderful great.

10 [e]And, behold, I will give to thy servants, the hewers that cut timber, twenty thousand measures of beaten wheat, and twenty thousand measures of barley, and twenty thousand baths of wine, and twenty thousand baths of oil.

11 ¶ Then Huram the king of Tyre answered in writing, which he sent to Solomon, [f]Because the LORD hath loved his people, he hath made thee king over them.

12 Huram said moreover, [g]Blessed *be* the LORD God of Israel, [h]that made heaven and earth, who hath given to David the king a wise son, [l]endued with prudence and understanding, that might build an house for the LORD, and an house for his kingdom.

13 And now I have sent a cunning man, endued with understanding, of Huram my father's,

14 [i]The son of a woman of the daughters of Dan, and his father *was* a man of Tyre, skilful to work in gold, and in silver, in brass, in iron, in stone, and in timber, in purple, in blue, and in fine linen, and in crimson; also to grave any manner of graving, and to find out every device which shall be put to him, with thy cunning men, and with the cunning men of my lord David thy father.

15 Now therefore the wheat, and the barley, the oil, and the wine, which [j]my lord hath spoken of, let him send unto his servants:

16 [k]And we will cut wood out of Lebanon, [m]as much as thou shalt need: and we will bring it to thee in floats by sea to [n]Joppa; and thou shalt carry it up to Jerusalem.

17 ¶ [l]And Solomon numbered all

2:1 [t]1 Ki. 5:5 **2:2** [u]ver. 18; 1 Ki. 5:15 **2:3** [v]1 Chr. 14:1 **2:4** [w]ver. 1 [x]Ex. 30:7 [y]Ex. 25:30; Lev. 24:8 [z]Num. 28:3,9,11 **2:5** [a]Ps. 135:5 **2:6** [b]1 Ki. 8:27; Is. 66:1 **2:7** [c]1 Chr. 22:15 **2:8** [d]1 Ki. 5:6 **2:10** [e]1 Ki. 5:11 **2:11** [f]1 Ki. 10:9; ch. 9:8 **2:12** [g]1 Ki. 5:7 [h]Gen. 1 & 2; Acts 4:24 & 14:15; Rev. 10:6 **2:14** [i]1 Ki. 7:13 **2:15** [j]ver. 10 **2:16** [k]1 Ki. 5:8,9 **2:17** [l]As ver. 2; 1 Ki. 5:13; ch. 8:7,8

[e] Heb. *by their hand* [f] Or, *Hiram* [g] Heb. *incense of spices* [h] Heb. *hath retained,* or, *obtained strength* [i] Heb. *to grave gravings* [j] Or, *almuggim;* see 1 Ki. 10:11 [k] Heb. *great and wonderful* [l] Heb. *knowing prudence and understanding* [m] Heb. *according to all thy need* [n] Heb. *Japho;* see Josh. 19:46; Acts 9:36

2:1 AN HOUSE FOR . . . THE LORD. Solomon inherited from his father David the desire "to build an house for the name of the LORD." Solomon was the one to carry out his father's intentions. The foremost inheritance that any father can bequeath his son is the holy desire to see God's house and kingdom established in purity, truth, and righteousness.

[o]the strangers that *were* in the land of
Israel, after the numbering wherewith
[m]David his father had numbered them;
and they were found an hundred and
fifty thousand and three thousand and
six hundred.
18 And he set [n]threescore and ten
thousand of them *to be* bearers of bur-
dens, and fourscore thousand *to be*
hewers in the mountain, and three
thousand and six hundred overseers to
set the people awork.

Building the temple

3:1–14pp — 1 Ki. 6:1–29

3 THEN [o]SOLOMON began to build
the house of the LORD at [p]Jerusa-
lem in mount Moriah, [p]where *the* LORD
appeared unto David his father, in the
place that David had prepared in the
threshingfloor of [q]Ornan[q] the Jebu-
site.
2 And he began to build in the sec-
ond *day* of the second month, in the
fourth year of his reign.
3 ¶ Now these *are the things* [r]*where-
in* Solomon was [r]instructed for the
building of the house of God. The
length by cubits after the first measure
was threescore cubits, and the breadth
twenty cubits.
4 And the [s]porch that *was* in the
front *of the house,* the length *of it was*
according to the breadth of the house,
twenty cubits, and the height *was* an
hundred and twenty: and he overlaid it
within with pure gold.
5 And [t]the greater house he ceiled
with fir tree, which he overlaid with
fine gold, and set thereon palm trees
and chains.

2:17 [m]1 Chr. 22:2
2:18 [n]As it is ver. 2
3:1 [o]1 Ki. 6:1 [p]Gen. 22:2 [q]1 Chr. 21:18 & 22:1
3:3 [r]1 Ki. 6:2
3:4 [s]1 Ki. 6:3
3:5 [t]1 Ki. 6:15
3:10 [u]1 Ki. 6:23

6 And he [s]garnished the house
with precious stones for beauty: and
the gold *was* gold of Parvaim.
7 He overlaid also the house, the
beams, the posts, and the walls there-
of, and the doors thereof, with gold;
and graved cherubims on the walls.
8 And he made the most holy house,
the length whereof *was* according to
the breadth of the house, twenty cu-
bits, and the breadth thereof twenty
cubits: and he overlaid it with fine gold,
amounting to six hundred talents.
9 And the weight of the nails *was*
fifty shekels of gold. And he overlaid
the upper chambers with gold.
10 [u]And in the most holy house he
made two cherubims [t]of image work,
and overlaid them with gold.
11 ¶ And the wings of the cheru-
bims *were* twenty cubits long: one wing
of the one cherub was five cubits, reach-
ing to the wall of the house: and the
other wing *was likewise* five cubits,
reaching to the wing of the other
cherub.
12 And *one* wing of the other cherub
was five cubits, reaching to the wall of
the house: and the other wing *was* five
cubits *also,* joining to the wing of the
other cherub.
13 The wings of these cherubims
spread themselves forth twenty cubits:
and they stood on their feet, and their
faces *were* [u]inward.

[o] Heb. *the men the strangers* [p] Or, *which was seen of David his father* [q] Or, *Araunah;* see 2 Sam. 24:18 [r] Heb. *founded* [s] Heb. *covered* [t] Or, (as some think) *of moveable work* [u] Or, *toward the house*

3:1 SOLOMON BEGAN TO BUILD THE HOUSE OF THE LORD. A comparison of the temple of Solomon and the temple of Christ (i.e., the church) reveals the following: (1) The temple of Solomon was built by David's son (2:1); the church by David's descendant, the Lord Jesus Christ (Heb. 3:3–6).

(2) The temple of Solomon was built from gold, silver, and precious stone (1 Chr. 29:3–8); the church is built with the redeemed lives of those purchased at the cost of the precious blood of Christ (1 Pet. 1:18–19; 2:5).

(3) The temple of Solomon stood on Mount Moriah (3:1); the church stands on the rock of Jesus' divine person and sacrificial death (Mat. 16:18; Eph. 2:20).

(4) The temple of Solomon had earthly mediating priests (1 Chr. 24); the church has a heavenly high priest to whom all believers may draw near for eternal salvation (Heb. 2:17; 7:25).

(5) The temple of Solomon was made beautiful by gold and decorations (1 Chr. 22:5); the church becomes beautiful by the purity and power of the Holy Spirit within the believer's life (Acts 1:8; 2:4; Gal. 5:22; cf. 1 Pet. 3:3–4).

(6) The temple of Solomon provided a place for God's special dwelling among His people; the church is the special dwelling of the Holy Spirit upon earth (1 Cor. 3:16; 6:19).

(7) The temple of Solomon was earthly and temporal (2 Ki. 25:8–9); the temple of Christ is heavenly and everlasting (Rev. 21—22).

(8) The church, therefore, is the heir and successor of the tabernacle/temple as the visible dwelling place of God on earth (see article on THE TEMPLE, p. 654).

3:1 THRESHINGFLOOR OF ORNAN. For more details about this site for the temple and the circumstances under which it was obtained, see 1 Chr. 21:16–30.

14 ¶ And he made the [v]veil *of* blue,
and purple, and crimson, and fine lin-
en, and [v]wrought cherubims thereon.
15 Also he made before the house
[w]two pillars of thirty and five cubits
[w]high, and the chapiter that *was* on
the top of each of them *was* five cubits.
16 And he made chains, *as* in the
oracle, and put *them* on the heads of
the pillars; and made [x]an hundred
pomegranates, and put *them* on the
chains.
17 And he [y]reared up the pillars
before the temple, one on the right
hand, and the other on the left; and
called the name of that on the right
hand [x]Jachin, and the name of that on
the left [y]Boaz.

The furnishings of the temple

4:2–6,10–5:1pp — 1 Ki. 7:23–26,38–51

4 MOREOVER HE made [z]an altar
of brass, twenty cubits the length
thereof, and twenty cubits the breadth
thereof, and ten cubits the height
thereof.
2 ¶ [a]Also he made a molten sea of
ten cubits [z]from brim to brim, round
in compass, and five cubits the height
thereof; and a line of thirty cubits did
compass it round about.
3 [b]And under it *was* the similitude
of oxen, which did compass it round
about: ten in a cubit, compassing the
sea round about. Two rows of oxen
were cast, when it was cast.
4 It stood upon twelve oxen, three
looking toward the north, and three
looking toward the west, and
three looking toward the south, and
three looking toward the east:
and the sea *was set* above upon them,
and all their hinder parts *were* inward.
5 And the thickness of it *was* an
handbreadth, and the brim of it like the
work of the brim of a cup, [a]with flow-
ers of lilies; *and* it received and held
[c]three thousand baths.
6 ¶ He made also [d]ten lavers, and
put five on the right hand, and five on
the left, to wash in them: [b]such things
as they offered for the burnt offering
they washed in them; but the sea *was*
for the priests to wash in.
7 [e]And he made ten candlesticks
of gold [f]according to their form, and
set *them* in the temple, five on the right
hand, and five on the left.
8 [g]He made also ten tables, and
placed *them* in the temple, five on the
right side, and five on the left. And he
made an hundred [c]basins of gold.
9 ¶ Furthermore [h]he made the
court of the priests, and the great
court, and doors for the court, and
overlaid the doors of them with brass.
10 And [i]he set the sea on the right
side of the east end, over against the
south.
11 And [j]Huram made the pots,
and the shovels, and the [c]basins. And
Huram [d]finished the work that he was
to make for king Solomon for the house
of God;
12 *To wit,* the two pillars, and [k]the
pommels, and the chapiters *which were*
on the top of the two pillars, and the
two wreaths to cover the two pommels
of the chapiters which *were* on the top
of the pillars;
13 And [l]four hundred pomegran-
ates on the two wreaths; two rows of
pomegranates on each wreath, to cover
the two pommels of the chapiters
which *were* [e]upon the pillars.
14 He made also [m]bases, and [f]la-
vers made he upon the bases;
15 One sea, and twelve oxen un-
der it.
16 The pots also, and the shovels,
and the fleshhooks, and all their in-
struments, did [n]Huram his father
make to king Solomon for the house of
the LORD of [g]bright brass.
17 [o]In the plain of Jordan did the
king cast them, in the [h]clay ground
between Succoth and Zeredathah.
18 [p]Thus Solomon made all these
vessels in great abundance: for the
weight of the brass could not be found
out.
19 ¶ And [q]Solomon made all the
vessels that *were for* the house of God,
the golden altar also, and the tables
whereon [r]the showbread *was set;*
20 Moreover the candlesticks with
their lamps, that they should burn [s]af-
ter the manner before the oracle, of
pure gold;
21 And [t]the flowers, and the

3:14 [v]Ex. 26:31 Mat. 27:51 Heb. 9:3
3:15 [w]1 Ki. 7:15 Jer. 52:21
3:16 [x]1 Ki. 7:20
3:17 [y]1 Ki. 7:21
4:1 [z]Ex. 27:1,2 2 Ki. 16:14 Ezek. 43:13,16
4:2 [a]1 Ki. 7:23
4:3 [b]1 Ki. 7:24-26
4:5 [c]See 1 Ki. 7:26
4:6 [d]1 Ki. 7:38
4:7 [e]1 Ki. 7:49 [f]Ex. 25:31 1 Chr. 28:12,19
4:8 [g]1 Ki. 7:48
4:9 [h]1 Ki. 6:36
4:10 [i]1 Ki. 7:39
4:11 [j]See 1 Ki. 7:40
4:12 [k]1 Ki. 7:41
4:13 [l]See 1 Ki. 7:20
4:14 [m]1 Ki. 7:27,43
4:16 [n]1 Ki. 7:14,45
4:17 [o]1 Ki. 7:46
4:18 [p]1 Ki. 7:47
4:19 [q]1 Ki. 7:48-50 [r]Ex. 25:30
4:20 [s]Ex. 27:20,21
4:21 [t]Ex. 25:31

[v]Heb. *caused to ascend* [w]Heb. *long* [x]i.e. *He shall establish* [y]i.e. *In it* is *strength*
[z]Heb. *from his brim to his brim* [a]Or, *like a lilyflower* [b]Heb. *the work of burnt offering*
[c]Or, *bowls* [d]Heb. *finished to make* [e]Heb. *upon the face* [f]Or, *caldrons* [g]Heb. *made bright,* or, *scoured* [h]Heb. *thicknesses of the ground*

lamps, and the tongs, *made he of* gold, *and* that [i]perfect gold;

22 And the snuffers, and the [j]basins, and the spoons, and the censers, *of* pure gold: and the entry of the house, the inner doors thereof for the most holy *place,* and the doors of the house of the temple, *were of* gold.

5 THUS [u]ALL the work that Solomon made for the house of the LORD was finished: and Solomon brought in *all* the things that David his father had dedicated; and the silver, and the gold, and all the instruments, put he among the treasures of the house of God.

Bringing the ark to the temple

5:2–6:11pp — 1 Ki. 8:1–21

2 ¶ [v]Then Solomon assembled the elders of Israel, and all the heads of the tribes, the chief of the fathers of the children of Israel, unto Jerusalem, to bring up the ark of the covenant of the LORD [w]out of the city of David, which *is* Zion.

3 [x]Wherefore all the men of Israel assembled themselves unto the king [y]in the feast which *was* in the seventh month.

4 And all the elders of Israel came; and the Levites took up the ark.

5 And they brought up the ark, and the tabernacle of the congregation, and all the holy vessels that *were* in the tabernacle, these did the priests *and* the Levites bring up.

6 Also king Solomon, and all the congregation of Israel that were assembled unto him before the ark, sacrificed sheep and oxen, which could not be told nor numbered for multitude.

7 And the priests brought in the ark of the covenant of the LORD unto his place, to the oracle of the house, into the most holy *place, even* under the wings of the cherubims:

8 For the cherubims spread forth *their* wings over the place of the ark, and the cherubims covered the ark and the staves thereof above.

9 And they drew out the staves *of the ark,* that the ends of the staves were seen from the ark before the oracle; but they were not seen without. And there it is unto this day.

10 *There was* nothing in the ark save the two tables which Moses [z]put *therein* at Horeb, [k]when the LORD made *a covenant* with the children of Israel, when they came out of Egypt.

11 ¶ And it came to pass, when the priests were come out of the holy *place:* (for all the priests *that were* [l]present were sanctified, *and* did not *then* wait by course:

12 [a]Also the Levites *which were* the singers, all of them of Asaph, of Heman, of Jeduthun, with their sons and their brethren, *being* arrayed in white linen, having cymbals and psalteries and harps, stood at the east end of the altar, [b]and with them an hundred and twenty priests sounding with trumpets:)

13 It came even to pass, as the trumpeters and singers *were* as one, to make one sound to be heard in praising and thanking the LORD; and when they lifted up *their* voice with the trumpets and cymbals and instruments of music, and praised the LORD, *saying,* [c]For *he is* good; for his mercy *endureth* for ever: that *then* the house was filled with a cloud, *even* the house of the LORD;

14 So that the priests could not stand to minister by reason of the cloud: [d]for the glory of the LORD had filled the house of God.

6 THEN [e]SAID Solomon, The LORD hath said that he would dwell in the [f]thick darkness.

2 But I have built an house of habitation for thee, and a place for thy dwelling for ever.

3 And the king turned his face, and blessed the whole congregation of Israel: and all the congregation of Israel stood.

4 And he said, Blessed *be* the LORD God of Israel, who hath with his hands fulfilled *that* which he spake with his mouth to my father David, saying,

5 Since the day that I brought forth my people out of the land of Egypt I chose no city among all the tribes of

5:1 [u]1 Ki. 7:51
5:2 [v]1 Ki. 8:1 [w]2 Sam. 6:12
5:3 [x]1 Ki. 8:2 [y]See ch. 7:8-10
5:10 [z]Deut. 10:2,5 ch. 6:11
5:12 [a]1 Chr. 25:1 [b]1 Chr. 15:24
5:13 [c]Ps. 136 See 1 Chr. 16:34, 41
5:14 [d]Ex. 40:35 ch. 7:2
6:1 [e]1 Ki. 8:12 [f]Lev. 16:2

[i] Heb. *perfections of gold* [j] Or, *bowls* [k] Or, *where* [l] Heb. *found*

5:1 THE HOUSE OF THE LORD. The O.T. dedicates much attention to the temple because of its crucial importance in maintaining the true faith of Israel and their communion with God. See Ex. 25:9, note on the significance of the tabernacle and its typological interpretations for the new covenant; also see article on THE TEMPLE, p. 654.

5:14 THE GLORY OF THE LORD. See Ex. 40:34, note; 1 Ki. 8:11, note; see article on THE GLORY OF GOD, p. 1186.

Israel to build an house in, that my
name might be there; neither chose I
any man to be a ruler over my people
Israel:
6 [g]But I have chosen Jerusalem,
that my name might be there; and
[h]have chosen David to be over my peo-
ple Israel.
7 Now [i]it was in the heart of David
my father to build an house for the
name of the LORD God of Israel.
8 But the LORD said to David my fa-
ther, Forasmuch as it was in thine
heart to build an house for my name,
thou didst well in that it was in thine
heart:
9 Notwithstanding thou shalt not
build the house; but thy son which
shall come forth out of thy loins, he
shall build the house for my name.
10 The LORD therefore hath per-
formed his word that he hath spoken:
for I am risen up in the room of David
my father, and am set on the throne of
Israel, as the LORD promised, and have
built the house for the name of the LORD
God of Israel.
11 And in it have I put the ark,
[j]wherein *is* the covenant of the LORD,
that he made with the children of Is-
rael.

Solomon's prayer of dedication

6:12–40pp — 1 Ki. 8:22–53
6:41–42pp — Ps. 132:8–10

12 ¶ [k]And he stood before the altar
of the LORD in the presence of all the
congregation of Israel, and spread
forth his hands:
13 For Solomon had made a brasen
scaffold, of five cubits [m]long, and five
cubits broad, and three cubits high,
and had set it in the midst of the court:
and upon it he stood, and kneeled
down upon his knees before all the con-
gregation of Israel, and spread forth
his hands toward heaven,
14 And said, O LORD God of Israel,
[l]*there is* no God like thee in the heav-
en, nor in the earth; which keepest cov-
enant, and *showest* mercy unto thy ser-
vants, that walk before thee with all
their hearts:
15 [m]Thou which hast kept with thy
servant David my father that which
thou hast promised him; and spakest
with thy mouth, and hast fulfilled *it*
with thine hand, as *it is* this day.
16 Now therefore, O LORD God of Is-
rael, keep with thy servant David my
father that which thou hast promised
him, saying, [n]There[n] shall not fail
thee a man in my sight to sit upon the
throne of Israel; [o]yet so that thy chil-
dren take heed to their way to walk in
my law, as thou hast walked be-
fore me.
17 Now then, O LORD God of Israel,
let thy word be verified, which thou
hast spoken unto thy servant David.
18 But will God in very deed dwell
with men on the earth? [p]behold, heav-
en and the heaven of heavens cannot
contain thee; how much less this house
which I have built!
19 Have respect therefore to the
prayer of thy servant, and to his suppli-
cation, O LORD my God, to hearken
unto the cry and the prayer which thy
servant prayeth before thee:
20 That thine eyes may be open
upon this house day and night, upon
the place whereof thou hast said that
thou wouldest put thy name there; to
hearken unto the prayer which thy ser-
vant prayeth [o]toward this place.
21 Hearken therefore unto the sup-
plications of thy servant, and of thy
people Israel, which they shall [p]make
toward this place: hear thou from thy
dwelling place, *even* from heaven; and
when thou hearest, forgive.
22 ¶ If a man sin against his neigh-
bour, [q]and an oath be laid upon him
to make him swear, and the oath come
before thine altar in this house;
23 Then hear thou from heaven, and
do, and judge thy servants, by requit-
ing the wicked, by recompensing his

6:6 [g]ch. 12:13 [h]1 Chr. 28:4
6:7 [i]2 Sam. 7:2 1 Chr. 17:1 & 28:2
6:11 [j]ch. 5:10
6:12 [k]1 Ki. 8:22
6:14 [l]Ex. 15:11 Deut. 4:39 & 7:9
6:15 [m]1 Chr. 22:9
6:16 [n]2 Sam. 7:12,16 1 Ki. 2:4 & 6:12 ch. 7:18 [o]Ps. 132:12
6:18 [p]ch. 2:6 Is. 66:1 Acts 7:49

[m] Heb. *the length thereof* [n] Heb. *There shall not a man be cut off* [o] Or, *in this place* [p] Heb. *pray* [q] Heb. *and he require an oath of him*

6:10 THE HOUSE FOR THE NAME OF THE LORD. The Bible often refers to temples in relation to salvation history; the dwelling places of God mentioned are: the tabernacle, Solomon's temple, Ezekiel's temple, Zerubbabel's temple, Herod's temple, Christ's body, the church, the individual believer's physical body, and the New Jerusalem (Rev. 21:22). For more details, see article on THE TEMPLE, p. 654.

6:11 THE ARK. See 1 Ki. 8:1, note.

6:18 HEAVENS CANNOT CONTAIN THEE. See 1 Ki. 8:13, note.

6:21 FORGIVE. See 1 Ki. 8:39, note.

THE TEMPLE

2 Chr. 5:1 "Thus all the work that Solomon made for the house of the LORD was finished: and Solomon brought in all the things that David his father had dedicated; and the silver, and the gold, and all the instruments, put he among the treasures of the house of God."

HISTORY OF THE TEMPLE. (1) The forerunner to the temple was the tabernacle, the tent which God instructed the Israelites to build while they were stationed in the wilderness at Mount Sinai (Ex. 25—27; 30; 36—38; 39:32—40:33). After entering the promised land of Canaan, they retained this mobile sanctuary until the time of King Solomon. During the early years of his reign, he commissioned thousands of people to take part in the construction of the temple of the Lord (see 1 Ki. 5:13–18). In the fourth year of his reign the foundations were laid; seven years later the temple was completed (1 Ki. 6:37–38). The worship of the Lord, especially the sacrifices offered to Him, now had an established place in the city of Jerusalem (see article on THE CITY OF JERUSALEM, p. 622).

(2) During the time of the monarchy, the temple underwent several cycles of defilement and restoration. It was ransacked by Shishak of Egypt during the reign of King Rehoboam (2 Chr. 12:9), and was refurbished by King Asa (2 Chr. 15:8,18). After another period of idolatry and spiritual decline, King Joash repaired the house of the Lord (2 Chr. 24:4–14). Later King Ahaz took some of the temple furnishings, sent them to the king of Assyria as a means of political appeasement, and shut the doors of the temple (2 Chr. 28:21,24). His son Hezekiah once again opened, repaired, and cleansed the temple (2 Chr. 29:1–19), only to have it defiled again by his son Manasseh (2 Chr. 33:1–7). Manasseh's grandson Josiah was the last king of Judah to repair the temple (2 Chr. 34:1,8–13). Idolatry continued among his successors, and God finally allowed King Nebuchadnezzar of Babylon in 586 B.C. to destroy the temple completely (2 Ki. 25:13–17; 2 Chr. 36:18–19).

(3) Fifty years later, King Cyrus allowed the Jews to return from Babylon to Palestine and to rebuild the temple (Ezra 1:1–4). Zerubbabel led the reconstruction effort (Ezra 3:8), though not without opposition from the other people living in that land (Ezra 4:1–4). After a delay of a decade or so, the people were permitted to resume the project (Ezra 4:24—5:2), and it was completed and dedicated in 516 B.C. (Ezra 6:14–18). At the outset of the N.T. era, King Herod spent much time and money repairing and beautifying the second temple (John 2:20); this was the temple that Jesus cleansed on two occasions (see Mat. 21:12–13; John 2:13–21). In A.D. 70, however, after frequent rebellion by the Jews against the Roman authorities, the temple, along with the entire city of Jerusalem, was once again destroyed and made uninhabitable.

THE MEANING OF THE TEMPLE FOR THE ISRAELITES. In many ways the temple had the same significance among the Israelites as did the city of Jerusalem (see article on THE CITY OF JERUSALEM, p. 622). (1) It symbolized the presence and protection of the Lord God among His people (cf. Ex. 25:8; 29:43–46). When the temple was dedicated, God came down from heaven, filled it with His glory (2 Chr. 7:1–2; cf. Ex. 40:34–38), and promised to put His name there (2 Chr. 6:20,33). Thus when God's people wanted to pray to the Lord, they could do so facing the temple (2 Chr. 6:24,26,29,32), and God would hear them "out of his temple" (Ps. 18:6).

(2) The temple also represented God's redemption of His people. There were two important functions that took place there: the daily sacrifices for sin on the bronze altar and the Day of Atonement, when the high priest went into the Most Holy Place to

sprinkle blood on the mercy seat of the ark to atone for the sins of the people (cf. Lev. 16; 1 Ki. 8:6–9). Through these temple rituals, the Israelites were reminded of the costly nature of their redemption and reconciliation with God.

(3) At no time in the history of God's people did God have more than one physical dwelling place or temple. This demonstrated the fact that there is only one God—the Lord, the covenant God of the Israelites.

(4) However, the temple gave no absolute guarantees of God's presence. It symbolized God's presence only insofar as the people rejected all other gods and obeyed God's holy law. Micah, for example, criticized the leaders of God's people for their violence and materialism, while at the same time feeling secure that no evil would befall them as long as they had the symbol of the Lord's presence among them (Mic. 3:9–11). He prophesied that God would teach them a lesson by destroying Jerusalem with its temple. Later Jeremiah took the idolatrous nation of Judah to task for taking comfort in their constant repetition of the words, "The temple of the LORD, The temple of the LORD, The temple of the LORD" (Jer. 7:2–4,8–12). Because of their godless lifestyle, God would destroy the symbol of His presence—the temple (Jer. 7:14–15); He even told Jeremiah that it was useless for him to pray for the nation of Judah, for the Lord would not hear (Jer. 7:16). Their only hope was to amend their ways (Jer. 7:5–7).

THE MEANING OF THE TEMPLE FOR THE CHRISTIAN CHURCH. The role of the temple in the N.T. must be understood against the background of what the temple symbolized in the O.T. (1) Jesus Himself, like the O.T. prophets, criticized the misuse of the temple. His first (John 2:13–17) and last great public acts (Mat. 21:12–13) were to cleanse the temple of those who were destroying its true spiritual purpose (see Luke 19:45, note). He went on to predict the day when the temple would be completely destroyed (Mat. 24:1–2; Mark 13:1–2; Luke 21:5–6).

(2) The early church in Jerusalem frequently entered the temple at the hour of prayer (Acts 2:46; 3:1; 5:21,42). They did this out of custom, however, knowing full well that it was not the only place where one could pray to the Lord (see Acts 4:23–31). Stephen, and later Paul, witnessed that the living God could not be confined to a temple made by human hands (Acts 7:48–50; 17:24).

(3) The focus of worship for Christians shifted from the temple to Jesus Christ Himself. He, not the temple, now represents God's presence among His people. He is the Word of God made flesh (John 1:14), and in Him all the fullness of God dwells (Col. 2:9). In fact, Jesus goes so far as to call Himself the temple (John 2:19–22); by His sacrifice on the cross He fulfilled all of the sacrifices that took place in the temple (cf. Heb. 9:1—10:18). Note also that in His conversation with the Samaritan woman, Jesus stated that worship would soon take place not in a specific building but "in spirit and in truth," i.e., wherever people genuinely believed the truth of God's Word and received God's Spirit through Christ (see John 4:23, note).

(4) Since Jesus Christ embodied the meaning of the temple, and since the church is His body (Rom. 12:5; 1 Cor. 12:12–27; Eph. 1:22–23; Col. 1:18), the church was designated as "the temple of God," being indwelt by Christ and His Spirit (1 Cor. 3:16; 2 Cor. 6:16; cf. Eph. 2:21–22). Through His Spirit, Christ lives in His church and requires His body to be holy. Just as in the O.T. where God would not tolerate any defilement of His temple, so He promises to destroy anyone who defiles His church (1 Cor. 3:16–17; see 3:17, note, for examples of ways in which people corrupt and defile the church).

(5) Not only is the Holy Spirit living in the church, but also in the individual believer as His temple (1 Cor. 6:19). For that reason Paul warns strongly against any defilement of the human body by immorality or impurity (see 1 Cor. 6:18–19, notes).

(6) Finally, note that there is no need for a temple in the new Jerusalem (Rev. 21:22). The reason for this is clear: since the temple was only a symbol of God's presence among His people and not the full reality, no temple is necessary when God and the Lamb are truly living among them: "the Lord God Almighty and the Lamb are the temple of it" (Rev. 21:22).

way upon his own head; and by justifying the righteous, by giving him according to his righteousness.

24 ¶ And if thy people Israel [r]be put to the worse before the enemy, because they have sinned against thee; and shall return and confess thy name, and pray and make supplication before thee [s]in this house;

25 Then hear thou from the heavens, and forgive the sin of thy people Israel, and bring them again unto the land which thou gavest to them and to their fathers.

26 ¶ When the [q]heaven is shut up, and there is no rain, because they have sinned against thee; *yet* if they pray toward this place, and confess thy name, and turn from their sin, when thou dost afflict them;

27 Then hear thou from heaven, and forgive the sin of thy servants, and of thy people Israel, when thou hast taught them the good way, wherein they should walk; and send rain upon thy land, which thou hast given unto thy people for an inheritance.

28 ¶ If there [r]be dearth in the land, if there be pestilence, if there be blasting, or mildew, locusts, or caterpillars; if their enemies besiege them [t]in the cities of their land; whatsoever sore or whatsoever sickness *there be:*

29 *Then* what prayer *or* what supplication soever shall be made of any man, or of all thy people Israel, when every one shall know his own sore and his own grief, and shall spread forth his hands [u]in this house:

30 Then hear thou from heaven thy dwellingplace, and forgive, and render unto every man according unto all his ways, whose heart thou knowest; (for thou only [s]knowest the hearts of the children of men:)

31 That they may fear thee, to walk in thy ways, [v]so long as they live [w]in the land which thou gavest unto our fathers.

32 ¶ Moreover concerning the stranger, [t]which is not of thy people Israel, but is come from a far country for thy great name's sake, and thy mighty hand, and thy stretched out arm; if they come and pray in this house;

33 Then hear thou from the heavens, *even* from thy dwellingplace, and do according to all that the stranger calleth to thee for; that all people of the earth may know thy name, and fear thee, as *doth* thy people Israel, and may know that [x]this house which I have built is called by thy name.

34 If thy people go out to war against their enemies by the way that thou shalt send them, and they pray unto thee toward this city which thou hast chosen, and the house which I have built for thy name;

35 Then hear thou from the heavens their prayer and their supplication, and maintain their [y]cause.

36 If they sin against thee, (for *there is* [u]no man which sinneth not,) and thou be angry with them, and deliver them over before *their* enemies, and [z]they carry them away captives unto a land far off or near;

37 Yet *if* they [a]bethink themselves in the land whither they are carried captive, and turn and pray unto thee in the land of their captivity, saying, We have sinned, we have done amiss, and have dealt wickedly;

38 If they return to thee with all their heart and with all their soul in the land of their captivity, whither they have carried them captives, and pray toward their land, which thou gavest unto their fathers, and *toward* the city which thou hast chosen, and toward the house which I have built for thy name:

39 Then hear thou from the heavens, *even* from thy dwellingplace, their prayer and their supplications, and maintain their [y]cause, and forgive thy people which have sinned against thee.

40 Now, my God, let, I beseech thee, thine eyes be open, and *let* thine ears *be* attent [b]unto the prayer *that is made* in this place.

41 Now [v]therefore arise, O LORD God, into thy [w]resting place, thou, and the ark of thy strength: let thy priests, O LORD God, be clothed with salvation, and let thy saints [x]rejoice in goodness.

42 O LORD God, turn not away the face of thine anointed: [y]remember the mercies of David thy servant.

6:26 [q]1 Ki. 17:1
6:28 [r]ch. 20:9
6:30 [s]1 Chr. 28:9
6:32 [t]John 12:20 Acts 8:27
6:36 [u]Prov. 20:9 Eccl. 7:20 Jas. 3:2 1 John 1:8
6:41 [v]Ps. 132:8-10,16 [w]1 Chr. 28:2 [x]Neh. 9:25
6:42 [y]Ps. 132:1 Is. 55:3

[r] Or, *be smitten* [s] Or, *toward* [t] Heb. *in the land of their gates* [u] Or, *toward this house* [v] Heb. *all the days which* [w] Heb. *upon the face of the land* [x] Heb. *thy name is called upon this house* [y] Or, *right* [z] Heb. *they that take them captives carry them away* [a] Heb. *bring back to their heart* [b] Heb. *to the prayer of this place*

Dedicating the house of God

7:1–10pp — 1 Ki. 8:62–66

7 NOW [z]WHEN Solomon had made an end of praying, the [a]fire came down from heaven, and consumed the burnt offering and the sacrifices; and [b]the glory of the LORD filled the house.

2 [c]And the priests could not enter into the house of the LORD, because the glory of the LORD had filled the LORD's house.

3 And when all the children of Israel saw how the fire came down, and the glory of the LORD upon the house, they bowed themselves with their faces to the ground upon the pavement, and worshipped, and praised the LORD, [d]*saying,* For *he is* good; [e]for his mercy *endureth* for ever.

4 ¶ [f]Then the king and all the people offered sacrifices before the LORD.

5 And king Solomon offered a sacrifice of twenty and two thousand oxen, and an hundred and twenty thousand sheep: so the king and all the people dedicated the house of God.

6 [g]And the priests waited on their offices: the Levites also with instruments of music of the LORD, which David the king had made to praise the LORD, because his mercy *endureth* for ever, when David praised [c]by their ministry; and [h]the priests sounded trumpets before them, and all Israel stood.

7 Moreover [i]Solomon hallowed the middle of the court that *was* before the house of the LORD: for there he offered burnt offerings, and the fat of the peace offerings, because the brasen altar which Solomon had made was not able to receive the burnt offerings, and the meat offerings, and the fat.

8 ¶ [j]Also at the same time Solomon kept the feast seven days, and all Israel with him, a very great congregation, from the entering in of Hamath unto [k]the river of Egypt.

9 And in the eighth day they made [d]a solemn assembly: for they kept the dedication of the altar seven days, and the feast seven days.

10 And [l]on the three and twentieth day of the seventh month he sent the people away into their tents, glad and merry in heart for the goodness that the LORD had shown unto David, and to Solomon, and to Israel his people.

The LORD's promise to Solomon

7:11–22pp — 1 Ki. 9:1–9

11 Thus [m]Solomon finished the house of the LORD, and the king's house: and all that came into Solomon's heart to make in the house of the LORD, and in his own house, he prosperously effected.

12 ¶ And the LORD appeared to Solomon by night, and said unto him, I have heard thy prayer, [n]and have chosen this place to myself for an house of sacrifice.

13 [o]If I shut up heaven that there be no rain, or if I command the locusts to devour the land, or if I send pestilence among my people;

14 If my people, [e]which are called

7:1 [z]1 Ki. 8:54 [a]Lev. 9:24 Judg. 6:21 1 Ki. 18:38 1 Chr. 21:26 [b]1 Ki. 8:10,11
7:2 [c]ch. 5:14
7:3 [d]ch. 5:13 Ps. 136:1 [e]1 Chr. 16:41 ch. 20:21
7:4 [f]1 Ki. 8:62,63
7:6 [g]1 Chr. 15:16 [h]ch. 5:12
7:7 [i]1 Ki. 8:64
7:8 [j]1 Ki. 8:65 [k]Josh. 13:3
7:10 [l]1 Ki. 8:66
7:11 [m]1 Ki. 9:1
7:12 [n]Deut. 12:5
7:13 [o]ch. 6:26,28

c Heb. *by their hand* d Heb. *a restraint*
e Heb. *upon whom my name is called*

7:1 THE GLORY OF THE LORD. The "glory of the LORD" refers to a visible manifestation of God's presence and splendor (see article on THE GLORY OF GOD, p. 1186).

7:12 THE LORD APPEARED TO SOLOMON. See 1 Ki. 9:3, note.

7:14 IF MY PEOPLE . . . HUMBLE . . . PRAY . . . SEEK . . . TURN. God's judgment of His people during times of moral decline, spiritual apathy, and worldly compromise is drought, barrenness, pestilence, and affliction (v. 13). God's promise (see next note), although originally given to Israel, applies equally to His people of any generation who, after experiencing His judgment, meet the following four conditions for the revival of spiritual life and the restoration of God's holy purpose and blessing for His people (cf. Acts 3:19):

(1) "Humble themselves." God's people must recognize their failures, manifest sorrow for their sin, and renew their commitment to do God's will. Humbling oneself before God and His Word means recognizing one's spiritual poverty (11:16; 15:12–13,15; 34:15–19; Ps. 51:17; Mat. 5:3).

(2) "Pray." God's people must cry out to Him in desperation for mercy, and must completely depend upon Him and trust Him for His intervention. The prayer must be earnest and sustained until God answers from heaven (cf. Luke 11:1–13; 18:1–8; Jas. 5:17–18).

(3) "Seek my face." God's people must diligently turn to God with the whole heart and long for His presence—and not just try to escape from adversity (11:16; 19:3; 1 Chr. 16:11; 22:19; Is. 55:6–7).

(4) "Turn from their wicked ways." God's people must genuinely repent by turning from specific sins and all forms of idolatry, renounce conformity to the world, and draw near to God for mercy, forgiveness, and cleansing (29:6–11; 2 Ki. 17:13; Jer. 25:5; Zech. 1:4; Heb. 4:16).

7:14 THEN I WILL HEAR . . . FORGIVE . . .

by my name, shall [p]humble them-
selves, and pray, and seek my face, and
turn from their wicked ways; [q]then
will I hear from heaven, and will
2 Chr. 30:18-20 forgive their sin, and will heal their
land.
15 Now [r]mine eyes shall be open,
and mine ears attent [f]unto the prayer
that is made in this place.
16 For now have [s]I chosen and
sanctified this house, that my name
may be there for ever: and mine eyes
and mine heart shall be there perpetu-
ally.
17 [t]And as for thee, if thou wilt
walk before me, as David thy father
walked, and do according to all that
I have commanded thee, and shalt
observe my statutes and my judg-
ments;
18 Then will I stablish the throne of
thy kingdom, according as I have cov-
enanted with David thy father, saying,
[u]There[g] shall not fail thee a man *to
be* ruler in Israel.
19 [v]But if ye turn away, and for-
sake my statutes and my command-
ments, which I have set before you,
and shall go and serve other gods, and
worship them;
20 Then will I pluck them up by the
roots out of my land which I have given
them; and this house, which I have
sanctified for my name, will I cast out
of my sight, and will make it *to be* a
proverb and a byword among all na-
tions.
21 And this house, which is high,
shall be an astonishment to every one
that passeth by it; so that he shall say,
[w]Why hath the LORD done thus unto
this land, and unto this house?
22 And it shall be answered, Be-
cause they forsook the LORD God of
their fathers, which brought them forth
out of the land of Egypt, and laid hold
on other gods, and worshipped them,
and served them: therefore hath he
brought all this evil upon them.

7:14 [p]Jas. 4:10 [q]ch. 6:27,30
7:15 [r]ch. 6:40
7:16 [s]1 Ki. 9:3 ch. 6:6
7:17 [t]1 Ki. 9:4
7:18 [u]ch. 6:16
7:19 [v]Lev. 26:14,33 Deut. 28:15,36,37
7:21 [w]Deut. 29:24

Solomon's other achievements

8:1–18pp — 1 Ki. 9:10–28

8 AND [x]IT came to pass at the end
of twenty years, wherein Solomon
had built the house of the LORD, and his
own house,
2 That the cities which Huram had
restored to Solomon, Solomon built
them, and caused the children of Israel
to dwell there.
3 And Solomon went to Hamath-zo-
bah, and prevailed against it.
4 [y]And he built Tadmor in the wil-
derness, and all the store cities, which
he built in Hamath.
5 Also he built Beth-horon the up-
per, and Beth-horon the nether, fenced
cities, with walls, gates, and bars;
6 And Baalath, and all the store cit-
ies that Solomon had, and all the chari-
ot cities, and the cities of the horse-
men, and [h]all that Solomon desired to
build in Jerusalem, and in Lebanon,
and throughout all the land of his do-
minion.
7 ¶ [z]*As for* all the people *that were*
left of the Hittites, and the Amorites,
and the Perizzites, and the Hivites,
and the Jebusites, which *were* not of
Israel,
8 *But* of their children, who were
left after them in the land, whom the
children of Israel consumed not, them
did Solomon make to pay tribute until
this day.
9 But of the children of Israel did
Solomon make no servants for his
work; but they *were* men of war, and
chief of his captains, and captains of
his chariots and horsemen.

8:1 [x]1 Ki. 9:10
8:4 [y]1 Ki. 9:17
8:7 [z]1 Ki. 9:20

[f]Heb. *to the prayer of this place* [g]Heb. *There shall not be cut off to thee* [h]Heb. *all the desire of Solomon which he desired to build*

HEAL. When God's four conditions for revival and restoration are met (see previous note), then God's threefold promise of revival will be fulfilled. (1) God will turn His anger away from His people, listen to their desperate cry, and be attentive to their prayer (v. 15). In other words, the first evidence of revival is that God begins to hear and answer prayer from heaven (vv. 14–15) and to show compassion to His people (cf. Ps. 85:4–7; 102:1–2,13; Jer. 33:3; Joel 2:12–13,18–19; see article on FAITH AND GRACE, p. 1738).

(2) God will forgive His people, cleanse them from their sins, and restore His favor, presence, peace, truth, righteousness, and power among them (cf. Ps. 85:9–13; Jer. 33:7–8; Hos. 10:12; Joel 2:25; 2 Cor. 6:14–18).

(3) God will heal His people and their land by again pouring out rain (i.e., physical favor and blessing) and the Holy Spirit (i.e., spiritual awakening among the covenant people and among the spiritually lost, cf. Ps. 51:12–13; Hos. 5:14—6:3,11; Joel 2:28–32).

7:20 THIS HOUSE . . . WILL I CAST OUT OF MY SIGHT. See 1 Ki. 9:7, note.

10 And these *were* the chief of king Solomon's officers, *even* [a]two hundred and fifty, that bare rule over the people.

11 ¶ And Solomon [b]brought up the daughter of Pharaoh out of the city of David unto the house that he had built for her: for he said, My wife shall not dwell in the house of David king of Israel, because *the places are* [i]holy, whereunto the ark of the LORD hath come.

12 ¶ Then Solomon offered burnt offerings unto the LORD on the altar of the LORD, which he had built before the porch,

13 Even after a certain rate [c]every day, offering according to the commandment of Moses, on the sabbaths, and on the new moons, and on the solemn feasts, [d]three times in the year, *even* in the feast of unleavened bread, and in the feast of weeks, and in the feast of tabernacles.

14 ¶ And he appointed, according to the order of David his father, the [e]courses of the priests to their service, and [f]the Levites to their charges, to praise and minister before the priests, as the duty of every day required: the [g]porters also by their courses at every gate: for [j]so had David the man of God commanded.

15 And they departed not from the commandment of the king unto the priests and Levites concerning any matter, or concerning the treasures.

16 Now all the work of Solomon was prepared unto the day of the foundation of the house of the LORD, and until it was finished. *So* the house of the LORD was perfected.

17 ¶ Then went Solomon to [h]Ezion-geber, and to [k]Eloth, at the sea side in the land of Edom.

18 [i]And Huram sent him by the hands of his servants ships, and servants that had knowledge of the sea; and they went with the servants of Solomon to Ophir, and took thence four hundred and fifty talents of gold, and brought *them* to king Solomon.

8:10
[a]See 1 Ki. 9:23
8:11
[b]1 Ki. 3:1 & 7:8 & 9:24
8:13
[c]Ex. 29:38 Num. 28:3,9,11,26 & 29:1
[d]Ex. 23:14 Deut. 16:16
8:14
[e]1 Chr. 24:3
[f]1 Chr. 25:1
[g]1 Chr. 9:17 & 26:1
8:17
[h]1 Ki. 9:26
8:18
[i]1 Ki. 9:27 ch. 9:10,13

9:1
[j]1 Ki. 10:1 Mat. 12:42 Luke 11:31

The visit of the queen of Sheba

9:1–12pp — 1 Ki. 10:1–13

9 AND [j]WHEN the queen of Sheba heard of the fame of Solomon, she came to prove Solomon with hard questions at Jerusalem, with a very great company, and camels that bare spices, and gold in abundance, and precious stones: and when she was come to Solomon, she communed with him of all that was in her heart.

2 And Solomon told her all her questions: and there was nothing hid from Solomon which he told her not.

3 And when the queen of Sheba had seen the wisdom of Solomon, and the house that he had built,

4 And the meat of his table, and the sitting of his servants, and the attendance of his ministers, and their apparel; his [l]cupbearers also, and their apparel; and his ascent by which he went up into the house of the LORD; there was no more spirit in her.

5 And she said to the king, *It was* a true [m]report which I heard in mine own land of thine [n]acts, and of thy wisdom:

6 Howbeit I believed not their words, until I came, and mine eyes had seen *it:* and, behold, the one half of the greatness of thy wisdom was not told me: *for* thou exceedest the fame that I heard.

7 Happy *are* thy men, and happy *are* these thy servants, which stand continually before thee, and hear thy wisdom.

8 Blessed be the LORD thy God, which delighted in thee to set thee on his throne, *to be* king for the LORD thy God: because thy God loved Israel, to establish them for ever, therefore made he thee king over them, to do judgment and justice.

9 And she gave the king an hundred and twenty talents of gold, and of spices great abundance, and precious stones: neither was there any such

[i] Heb. *holiness* [j] Heb. *so was the commandment of David the man of God* [k] Or, *Elath;* see Deut. 2:8; 2 Ki. 14:22 [l] Or, *butlers* [m] Heb. *word* [n] Or, *sayings*

8:11 THE DAUGHTER OF PHARAOH. Solomon's marriage to Pharaoh's daughter was contrary to God's law (see Deut. 17:17; Ex. 34:16). Though Solomon was dedicated to building the temple and keeping many of God's statutes, this marriage shows that he failed to submit every area of his life to God's rule. Failure to resist his strongest temptation eventually resulted in his ruin. Thus he left a vital area of his life open to Satan (see 1 Ki. 4:29–34, note; 11:1, note). Satan needs only one uncommitted or unresolved area of the believer's life to gain a foothold and lead him or her away from God.

spice as the queen of Sheba gave king Solomon.

10 And the servants also of Huram, and the servants of Solomon, [k]which brought gold from Ophir, brought [l]algum trees and precious stones.

11 And the king made *of* the algum trees [o] [p]terraces to the house of the LORD, and to the king's palace, and harps and psalteries for singers: and there were none such seen before in the land of Judah.

12 And king Solomon gave to the queen of Sheba all her desire, whatsoever she asked, beside *that* which she had brought unto the king. So she turned, and went away to her own land, she and her servants.

Solomon's wealth and wisdom

9:13–28pp — 1 Ki. 10:14–29; 2 Chr. 1:14–17

13 ¶ Now the weight of gold that came to Solomon in one year was six hundred and threescore and six talents of gold;

14 Beside *that which* chapmen and merchants brought. And all the kings of Arabia and [q]governors of the country brought gold and silver to Solomon.

15 ¶ And king Solomon made two hundred targets *of* beaten gold: six hundred *shekels* of beaten gold went to one target.

16 And three hundred shields *made he of* beaten gold: three hundred *shekels* of gold went to one shield. And the king put them in the house of the forest of Lebanon.

17 Moreover the king made a great throne of ivory, and overlaid it with pure gold.

18 And *there were* six steps to the throne, with a footstool of gold, *which were* fastened to the throne, and [r]stays on each side of the sitting place, and two lions standing by the stays:

19 And twelve lions stood there on the one side and on the other upon the six steps. There was not the like made in any kingdom.

20 ¶ And all the drinking vessels of king Solomon *were of* gold, and all the vessels of the house of the forest of Lebanon *were of* [s]pure gold: [t]none *were of* silver; it was *not* any thing accounted of in the days of Solomon.

21 For the king's ships went to Tarshish with the servants of Huram: every three years once came the ships of Tarshish bringing gold, and silver, [u]ivory, and apes, and peacocks.

22 And king Solomon passed all the kings of the earth in riches and wisdom.

23 ¶ And all the kings of the earth sought the presence of Solomon, to hear his wisdom, that God had put in his heart.

24 And they brought every man his present, vessels of silver, and vessels of gold, and raiment, harness, and spices, horses, and mules, a rate year by year.

25 ¶ And Solomon [m]had four thousand stalls for horses and chariots, and twelve thousand horsemen; whom he bestowed in the chariot cities, and with the king at Jerusalem.

26 ¶ [n]And he reigned over all the kings [o]from the [v]river even unto the land of the Philistines, and to the border of Egypt.

27 [p]And the king [w]made silver in Jerusalem as stones, and cedar trees made he as the sycamore trees that *are* in the low plains in abundance.

28 [q]And they brought unto Solomon horses out of Egypt, and out of all lands.

Solomon's death and successor

9:29–31pp — 1 Ki. 11:41–43

29 ¶ [r]Now the rest of the acts of Solomon, first and last, *are* they not written in the [x]book of Nathan the prophet, and in the prophecy of [s]Ahijah the Shilonite, and in the visions of [t]Iddo the seer against Jeroboam the son of Nebat?

30 [u]And Solomon reigned in Jerusalem over all Israel forty years.

31 And Solomon slept with his fathers, and he was buried in the city of

9:10 [k]ch. 8:18 [l]1 Ki. 10:11 *almug trees*
9:25 [m]1 Ki. 4:26 & 10:26 ch. 1:14
9:26 [n]1 Ki. 4:21 [o]Gen. 15:18 Ps. 72:8
9:27 [p]1 Ki. 10:27 ch. 1:15
9:28 [q]1 Ki. 10:28 ch. 1:16
9:29 [r]1 Ki. 11:41 [s]1 Ki. 11:29 [t]ch. 12:15 & 13:22
9:30 [u]1 Ki. 11:42,43

[o] Or, *stairs* [p] Heb. *highways* [q] Or, *captains* [r] Heb. *hands* [s] Heb. *shut up* [t] Or, there was *no silver* in them [u] Or, *elephants' teeth* [v] i.e. *Euphrates* [w] Heb. *gave* [x] Heb. *words*

9:29 THE REST OF THE ACTS OF SOLOMON. The author of Chronicles refers to the rest of the acts of Solomon that are more fully recorded in 1 Ki. 11. In Solomon's later years he declined spiritually and departed from God. In the end, Solomon was not only a backslider, but he also set the stage for Israel's division and decline which happened almost immediately after his death. For his tragic spiritual state at the end, see 1 Ki. 11, notes.

David his father: and Rehoboam his son reigned in his stead.

10:1 [v]1 Ki. 12:1
10:2 [w]1 Ki. 11:40

Rehoboam's harsh rule

10:1–11:4pp — 1 Ki. 12:1–24

10 AND [v]REHOBOAM went to Shechem: for to Shechem were all Israel come to make him king.
2 And it came to pass, when Jeroboam the son of Nebat, who *was* in Egypt, [w]whither he had fled from the presence of Solomon the king, heard *it,* that Jeroboam returned out of Egypt.
3 And they sent and called him. So Jeroboam and all Israel came and spake to Rehoboam, saying,
4 Thy father made our yoke grievous: now therefore ease thou somewhat the grievous servitude of thy father, and his heavy yoke that he put upon us, and we will serve thee.
5 And he said unto them, Come again unto me after three days. And the people departed.
6 ¶ And king Rehoboam took counsel with the old men that had stood before Solomon his father while he yet lived, saying, What counsel give ye *me* to return answer to this people?
7 And they spake unto him, saying, If thou be kind to this people, and please them, and speak good words to them, they will be thy servants for ever.
8 But he forsook the counsel which the old men gave him, and took counsel with the young men that were brought up with him, that stood before him.
9 And he said unto them, What advice give ye that we may return answer to this people, which have spoken to me, saying, Ease somewhat the yoke that thy father did put upon us?
10 And the young men that were brought up with him spake unto him, saying, Thus shalt thou answer the people that spake unto thee, saying, Thy father made our yoke heavy, but make thou *it* somewhat lighter for us; thus shalt thou say unto them, My little *finger* shall be thicker than my father's loins.
11 For whereas my father [y]put a heavy yoke upon you, I will put more to your yoke: my father chastised you with whips, but I *will chastise you* with scorpions.
12 So Jeroboam and all the people came to Rehoboam on the third day, as the king bade, saying, Come again to me on the third day.
13 And the king answered them roughly; and king Rehoboam forsook the counsel of the old men,
14 And answered them after the advice of the young men, saying, My father made your yoke heavy, but I will add thereto: my father chastised you with whips, but I *will chastise you* with scorpions.
15 So the king hearkened not unto the people: [x]for the cause was of God, that the LORD might perform his word, which he spake by the [y]hand of Ahijah the Shilonite to Jeroboam the son of Nebat.
16 ¶ And when all Israel *saw* that the king would not hearken unto them, the people answered the king, saying, What portion have we in David? and *we have* none inheritance in the son of Jesse: every man to your tents, O Israel: *and* now, David, see to thine own house. So all Israel went to their tents.
17 But *as for* the children of Israel that dwelt in the cities of Judah, Rehoboam reigned over them.
18 Then king Rehoboam sent Hadoram that *was* over the tribute; and the children of Israel stoned him with stones, that he died. But king Rehoboam [z]made speed to get him up to *his* chariot, to flee to Jerusalem.
19 [z]And Israel rebelled against the house of David unto this day.

10:15 [x]1 Sam. 2:25; 1 Ki. 12:15,24 [y]1 Ki. 11:29
10:19 [z]1 Ki. 12:19
11:1 [a]1 Ki. 12:21

Rehoboam builds strongholds

11 AND [a]WHEN Rehoboam was come to Jerusalem, he gathered of the house of Judah and Benjamin an

[y] Heb. *laded* [z] Heb. *strengthened himself*

10:1 THE DIVIDING OF THE KINGDOM. This chapter marks the point when the nation of Israel was torn apart into two kingdoms (vv. 15–19; see 1 Ki. 12:20,24, notes). The northern kingdom was called Israel, the southern kingdom Judah. The main stream of Hebrew history is viewed at all times in 2 Chr. as being the southern kingdom of Judah. The writer says little of the history of the northern kingdom, focusing attention on the southern kingdom for three reasons: (1) The people of Judah constituted the majority of the post-exilic remnant who returned to Palestine and for whom Chronicles was originally written; (2) Judah remained the center of the worship of the Lord God; and (3) Judah's kings were the descendants of David and thus part of the covenant promise.

hundred and fourscore thousand chosen *men,* which were warriors, to fight against Israel, that he might bring the kingdom again to Rehoboam.

2 But the word of the LORD came [b]to Shemaiah the man of God, saying,

3 Speak unto Rehoboam the son of Solomon, king of Judah, and to all Israel in Judah and Benjamin, saying,

4 Thus saith the LORD, Ye shall not go up, nor fight against your brethren: return every man to his house: for this thing is done of me. And they obeyed the words of the LORD, and returned from going against Jeroboam.

5 ¶ And Rehoboam dwelt in Jerusalem, and built cities for defence in Judah.

6 He built even Bethlehem, and Etam, and Tekoa,

7 And Beth-zur, and Shoco, and Adullam,

8 And Gath, and Mareshah, and Ziph,

9 And Adoraim, and Lachish, and Azekah,

10 And Zorah, and Aijalon, and Hebron, which *are* in Judah and in Benjamin fenced cities.

11 And he fortified the strong holds, and put captains in them, and store of victual, and of oil and wine.

12 And in every several city *he put* shields and spears, and made them exceeding strong, having Judah and Benjamin on his side.

13 ¶ And the priests and the Levites that *were* in all Israel [a]resorted to him out of all their coasts.

14 For the Levites left [c]their suburbs and their possession, and came to Judah and Jerusalem: for [d]Jeroboam and his sons had cast them off from executing the priest's office unto the LORD:

15 [e]And he ordained him priests for the high places, and for [f]the devils, and for [g]the calves which he had made.

16 [h]And after them out of all the tribes of Israel such as set their hearts to seek the LORD God of Israel came to Jerusalem, to sacrifice unto the LORD God of their fathers.

17 So they [i]strengthened the kingdom of Judah, and made Rehoboam the son of Solomon strong, three years: for three years they walked in the way of David and Solomon.

Rehoboam's many wives

18 ¶ And Rehoboam took him Mahalath the daughter of Jerimoth the son of David to wife, *and* Abihail the daughter of Eliab the son of Jesse;

19 Which bare him children; Jeush, and Shamariah, and Zaham.

20 And after her he took [j]Maachah the daughter of Absalom; which bare him Abijah, and Attai, and Ziza, and Shelomith.

21 And Rehoboam loved Maachah the daughter of Absalom above all his wives and his concubines: (for he took eighteen wives, and threescore concubines; and begat twenty and eight sons, and threescore daughters.)

22 And Rehoboam [k]made Abijah the son of Maachah the chief, *to be* ruler among his brethren: for *he thought* to make him king.

23 And he dealt wisely, and dispersed of all his children throughout all the countries of Judah and Benjamin, unto every fenced city: and he

11:2 [b]ch. 12:15
11:14 [c]Num. 35:2 [d]ch. 13:9
11:15 [e]1 Ki. 12:31 & 13:33 & 14:9 Hos. 13:2 [f]Lev. 17:7 1 Cor. 10:20 [g]1 Ki. 12:28
11:16 [h]See ch. 15:9 & 30:11,18
11:17 [i]ch. 12:1
11:20 [j]1 Ki. 15:2 She is called Michaiah the daughter of Uriel ch. 13:2
11:22 [k]See Deut. 21:15-17

[a] Heb. *presented themselves to him*

11:4 THIS THING IS DONE OF ME. It was God who divided Israel in an effort to keep Judah loyal to Him and to separate Judah from the growing spiritual corruption in the other tribes. Sometimes God Himself causes division in order to preserve and protect His revealed truth, His righteous standards, and those godly people who want to remain faithful to Him (see 1 Ki. 12:24, note; Mat. 10:34, note; Eph. 4:3,5,13,15, notes).

11:14–15 JEROBOAM . . . ORDAINED HIM PRIESTS . . . FOR THE DEVILS. See 1 Ki. 12:28, note.

11:16 SUCH AS SET THEIR HEARTS TO SEEK THE LORD. Jeroboam and the northern kingdom abandoned the worship of the Lord as revealed in His Word and covenant and replaced it with idolatry (see 1 Ki. 12:28, note). (1) For this reason all those who wanted to remain true to God left their homes, separated themselves from the northern kingdom, and joined the kingdom of Judah (vv. 14,17). The challenge to remain true to God in the midst of apostasy or moral decline has frequently faced God's people throughout the history of redemption (see Rev. 2:7, note).

(2) Loyalty and commitment to God and His Word may sometimes require separating oneself from one's church and joining or forming another one that is devoted to God's original and fundamental revelation in Christ (see Mat. 21:43, note on Jesus taking the kingdom from the faithless and giving it to those who respond to the gospel; Eph. 4:13, note; see article on SPIRITUAL SEPARATION FOR BELIEVERS, p. 1814).

gave them victual in abundance. And he desired [b]many wives.

Egyptians raid Jerusalem

12:9–16pp — 1 Ki. 14:21, 25–31

12 AND [l]IT came to pass, when Rehoboam had established the kingdom, and had strengthened himself, [m]he forsook the law of the LORD, and all Israel with him.

2 [n]And it came to pass, *that* in the fifth year of king Rehoboam Shishak king of Egypt came up against Jerusalem, because they had transgressed against the LORD,

3 With twelve hundred chariots, and threescore thousand horsemen: and the people *were* without number that came with him out of Egypt; [o]the Lubims, the Sukkiims, and the Ethiopians.

4 And he took the fenced cities which *pertained* to Judah, and came to Jerusalem.

5 ¶ Then came [p]Shemaiah the prophet to Rehoboam, and *to* the princes of Judah, that were gathered together to Jerusalem because of Shishak, and said unto them, Thus saith the LORD, Ye have forsaken me, and therefore have I also left you in the hand of Shishak.

6 Whereupon the princes of Israel and the king [q]humbled themselves; and they said, [r]The LORD *is* righteous.

7 And when the LORD saw that they humbled themselves, [s]the word of the LORD came to Shemaiah, saying, They have humbled themselves; *therefore* I will not destroy them, but I will grant them [c]some deliverance; and my wrath shall not be poured out upon Jerusalem by the hand of Shishak.

8 Nevertheless [t]they shall be his servants; that they may know [u]my service, and the service of the kingdoms of the countries.

9 [v]So Shishak king of Egypt came up against Jerusalem, and took away the treasures of the house of the LORD, and the treasures of the king's house; he took all: he carried away also the shields of gold which Solomon had [w]made.

10 Instead of which king Rehoboam made shields of brass, and committed *them* [x]to the hands of the chief of the guard, that kept the entrance of the king's house.

11 And when the king entered into the house of the LORD, the guard came and fetched them, and brought them again into the guard chamber.

12 And when he humbled himself, the wrath of the LORD turned from him, that he would not destroy *him* altogether: [y]and [d] also in Judah things went well.

13 ¶ So king Rehoboam strengthened himself in Jerusalem, and reigned: for [z]Rehoboam *was* one and forty years old when he began to reign, and he reigned seventeen years in Jerusalem, [a]the city which the LORD had chosen out of all the tribes of Israel, to put his name there. And his mother's name *was* Naamah an Ammonitess.

14 And he did evil, because he

12:1 [l]ch. 11:17 [m]1 Ki. 14:22-24
12:2 [n]1 Ki. 14:24,25
12:3 [o]ch. 16:8
12:5 [p]ch. 11:2
12:6 [q]Jas. 4:10 [r]Ex. 9:27
12:7 [s]1 Ki. 21:28,29
12:8 [t]See Is. 26:13 [u]Deut. 28:47,48
12:9 [v]1 Ki. 14:25,26 [w]1 Ki. 10:16,17 ch. 9:15,16
12:10 [x]1 Ki. 14:27
12:12 [y]Gen. 18:24 & 1 Ki. 14:13 ch. 19:3
12:13 [z]1 Ki. 14:21 [a]ch. 6:6

[b] Heb. *a multitude of wives* [c] Or, *a little while*
[d] Or, *and yet in Judah there were good things*

12:1 ALL ISRAEL. Here the Chronicler uses the term "all Israel" for the southern kingdom (i.e., Judah) alone (cf. v. 4). At other times "all Israel" refers to the northern kingdom (10:16) or to both kingdoms (9:30). Consequently, its meaning must be determined from the context.

12:5 YE HAVE FORSAKEN ME, AND THEREFORE. The writer of Chronicles often emphasizes that God's blessings follow obedience (11:17) while punishment follows disobedience (12:1–6). When King Rehoboam became unfaithful, God ceased to protect him from his enemies (v. 5). We cannot expect God to protect us from harm, the dangers of life, or Satan's attacks if we are unfaithful to Him and His will. God's protecting power comes to us only through a living faith in Christ (see Rom. 8:28; note; 1 Pet. 1:5, note). "The LORD *is* with you, while ye be with him" (15:2).

12:7 THEY HAVE HUMBLED THEMSELVES. If we have sinned and are being punished for it, we should humble ourselves before God and confess that His judgments are righteous (v. 6; cf. 7:14, note). The Lord will forgive our trespasses and restore us to His grace and favor, and He may even reduce the chastisement we must bear.

12:14 HE DID EVIL, BECAUSE HE PREPARED NOT HIS HEART. There is a direct connection between diligently seeking God and His strength and resisting evil. In order to persevere in the faith, we must firmly resolve to seek God's face in earnest prayer; by doing so, we will be able to resist sin, despise the world, obey God's Word, and follow the leading of the Holy Spirit until the day we go to be with God. On the other hand, without this determined purpose in our hearts, we will soon forsake God and His salvation, and conform to the ungodly ways of society.

[e]prepared not his heart to seek the LORD.

15 Now the acts of Rehoboam, first and last, *are* they not written in the [f]book of Shemaiah the prophet, [b]and of Iddo the seer concerning genealogies? [c]And *there were* wars between Rehoboam and Jeroboam continually.

16 And Rehoboam slept with his fathers, and was buried in the city of David: and [d]Abijah his son reigned in his stead.

Abijah, king of Judah

13:1–2,22–14:1pp — 1 Ki. 15:1–2,6–8

13 NOW [e]IN the eighteenth year of king Jeroboam began Abijah to reign over Judah.

2 He reigned three years in Jerusalem. His mother's name also *was* [f]Michaiah the daughter of Uriel of Gibeah. And there was war between Abijah and Jeroboam.

3 And Abijah [g]set the battle in array with an army of valiant men of war, *even* four hundred thousand chosen men: Jeroboam also set the battle in array against him with eight hundred thousand chosen men, *being* mighty men of valour.

4 ¶ And Abijah stood up upon mount [g]Zemaraim, which *is* in mount Ephraim, and said, Hear me, thou Jeroboam, and all Israel;

5 Ought ye not to know that the LORD God of Israel [h]gave the kingdom over Israel to David for ever, *even* to him and to his sons [i]by a covenant of salt?

6 Yet Jeroboam the son of Nebat, the servant of Solomon the son of David, is risen up, and hath [j]rebelled against his lord.

7 And there are gathered unto him [k]vain men, the children of Belial, and have strengthened themselves against Rehoboam the son of Solomon, when Rehoboam was young and tenderhearted, and could not withstand them.

8 And now ye think to withstand the kingdom of the LORD in the hand of the sons of David; and ye *be* a great multitude, and *there are* with you golden calves, which Jeroboam [l]made you for gods.

9 [m]Have ye not cast out the priests of the LORD, the sons of Aaron, and the Levites, and have made you priests after the manner of the nations of *other* lands? [n]so that whosoever cometh [o]to[h] consecrate himself with a young bullock and seven rams, *the same* may be a priest of *them that are* no gods.

10 But as for us, the LORD *is* our God, and we have not forsaken him; and the priests, which minister unto the LORD, *are* the sons of Aaron, and the Levites *wait* upon *their* business:

11 [p]And they burn unto the LORD every morning and every evening burnt sacrifices and sweet incense: the [q]showbread also *set they in order* upon the pure table; and the candlestick of gold with the lamps thereof, [r]to burn every evening: for we keep the charge of the LORD our God; but ye have forsaken him.

12 And, behold, God himself *is* with us for *our* captain, [s]and his priests with sounding trumpets to cry alarm against you. O children of Israel, fight ye not against the LORD God of your fathers; for ye shall not prosper. Ezra 7:10

13 ¶ But Jeroboam caused an ambushment to come about behind them: so they were before Judah, and the ambushment *was* behind them.

14 And when Judah looked back, behold, the battle *was* before and behind: and they cried unto the LORD, and the priests sounded with the trumpets.

15 Then the men of Judah gave a shout: and as the men of Judah shouted, it came to pass, that God [t]smote Jeroboam and all Israel before Abijah and Judah.

16 And the children of Israel fled before Judah: and God delivered them into their hand.

17 And Abijah and his people slew them with a great slaughter: so there

12:15 [b]ch. 9:29 & 13:22 [c]1 Ki. 14:30 **12:16** [d]1 Ki. 14:31 *Abijam* **13:1** [e]1 Ki. 15:1 **13:2** [f]See ch. 11:20 **13:4** [g]Josh. 18:22 **13:5** [h]2 Sam. 7:12,13,16 [i]Num. 18:19 **13:6** [j]1 Ki. 11:26 & 12:20 **13:7** [k]Judg. 9:4 **13:8** [l]1 Ki. 12:28 & 14:9 Hos. 8:6 **13:9** [m]ch. 11:14,15 [n]Ex. 29:35 [o]Ex. 29:1 Lev. 8:2 **13:11** [p]ch. 2:4 [q]Lev. 24:6 [r]Ex. 27:20,21 Lev. 24:2,3 **13:12** [s]Num. 10:8 **13:15** [t]ch. 14:12

[e] Or, *fixed* [f] Heb. *words* [g] Heb. *bound together* [h] Heb. *to fill his hand*

13:1 BEGAN ABIJAH TO REIGN OVER JUDAH. Chronicles records the victory of Abijah as coming because he and Judah relied on God (see v. 18). The author of Kings does not record the incident, however, and states that Abijah "walked in all the sins of his father" (1 Ki. 15:3). The difference in emphasis between Chronicles and Kings is due to each author's purpose in writing. The writer of Kings was interested in evaluating the overall picture of each king's reign. The Chronicler wanted to emphasize the exceptional moments of faith and obedience in order to show Israel that God would help and deliver them if they trusted and obeyed God.

fell down slain of Israel five hundred thousand chosen men.

18 Thus the children of Israel were brought under at that time, and the children of Judah prevailed, [u]because they relied upon the LORD God of their fathers.

19 And Abijah pursued after Jeroboam, and took cities from him, Beth-el with the towns thereof, and Jeshanah with the towns thereof, and [v]Ephrain with the towns thereof.

20 Neither did Jeroboam recover strength again in the days of Abijah: and the LORD [w]struck him, and [x]he died.

21 ¶ But Abijah waxed mighty, and married fourteen wives, and begat twenty and two sons, and sixteen daughters.

22 And the rest of the acts of Abijah, and his ways, and his sayings, *are* written in the [i]story of the prophet [y]Iddo.

Asa, king of Judah

14:2–3pp — 1 Ki. 15:11–12

14 SO ABIJAH slept with his fathers, and they buried him in the city of David: and [z]Asa his son reigned in his stead. In his days the land was quiet ten years.

2 And Asa did *that which was* good and right in the eyes of the LORD his God:

3 For he took away the altars of the strange *gods,* and [a]the high places, and [b]brake down the [j]images, [c]and cut down the groves:

4 And commanded Judah to seek the LORD God of their fathers, and to do the law and the commandment.

5 Also he took away out of all the cities of Judah the high places and the [k]images: and the kingdom was quiet before him.

6 ¶ And he built fenced cities in Judah: for the land had rest, and he had no war in those years; because the LORD had given him rest.

7 Therefore he said unto Judah, Let us build these cities, and make about *them* walls, and towers, gates, and bars, *while* the land *is* yet before us; because we have sought the LORD our God, we have sought *him,* and he hath given us rest on every side. So they built and prospered.

8 And Asa had an army *of men* that bare targets and spears, out of Judah three hundred thousand; and out of Benjamin, that bare shields and drew bows, two hundred and fourscore thousand: all these *were* mighty men of valour.

9 ¶ [d]And there came out against them Zerah the Ethiopian with an host of a thousand thousand, and three hundred chariots; and came unto [e]Mareshah.

10 Then Asa went out against him, and they set the battle in array in the valley of Zephathah at Mareshah.

11 And Asa [f]cried unto the LORD his God, and said, LORD, *it is* [g]nothing with thee to help, whether with many, or with them that have no power: help us, O LORD our God; for we rest on thee, and [h]in thy name we go against this multitude. O LORD, thou *art* our God; let not [l]man prevail against thee.

12 So the LORD [i]smote the Ethiopians before Asa, and before Judah; and the Ethiopians fled.

13 And Asa and the people that *were* with him pursued them unto [j]Gerar: and the Ethiopians were overthrown, that they could not recover them-

13:18 [u]1 Chr. 5:20 Ps. 22:5 **13:19** [v]Josh. 15:9 **13:20** [w]1 Sam. 25:38 [x]1 Ki. 14:20 **13:22** [y]ch. 12:15 **14:1** [z]1 Ki. 15:8 **14:3** [a]See 1 Ki. 15:14 ch. 15:17 [b]Ex. 34:13 [c]1 Ki. 11:7 **14:9** [d]ch. 16:8 [e]Josh. 15:44 **14:11** [f]Ex. 14:10 ch. 13:14 Ps. 22:5 [g]1 Sam. 14:6 [h]1 Sam. 17:45 Prov. 18:10 **14:12** [i]ch. 13:15 **14:13** [j]Gen. 10:19 & 20:1

[i] Or, *commentary* [j] Heb. *statues* [k] Heb. *sun images* [l] Or, *mortal man*

14:2 ASA DID *THAT WHICH WAS* GOOD. During the reigns of Rehoboam (ch. 12) and Abijah (ch. 13; 1 Ki. 15:1–8), the true worship of God in Judah declined while idolatry increased; various places for idolatrous worship were erected (1 Ki. 14:21–24; 15:3). When Asa became king, he set out to purge idolatry and to urge Judah to seek God and obey His commandments (vv. 3–5).

14:4 SEEK THE LORD. Essential to any reformation or revival among God's people is seeking the Lord (see 7:14, note). The writer of Chronicles uses the verb "to seek [the LORD]" eight times in chs. 14—16 (14:4,7; 15:2,4,12–13,15; 16:12) and thirty times altogether. It means to desire and pursue earnestly the Lord's presence, fellowship, kingdom, and holiness (1 Chr. 16:11). Seeking the Lord involves: (1) turning to the Lord with the whole heart and in fervent prayer (Is. 55:6; Jer. 29:12–13); (2) hungering and thirsting for righteousness and God's presence (15:2; Ps. 24:3–6; Is. 51:1; cf. Mat. 5:8; John 4:14; see Mat. 5:6, note); (3) committing yourself firmly to do God's will and abandoning all actions that offend God (vv. 2–7; 7:14); (4) believing in and relying on God as your ultimate help (Heb. 13:6), confident that He "is a rewarder of them that diligently seek him" (Heb. 11:6; 2 Chr. 14:11; see next note).

selves; for they were [m]destroyed be-
fore the LORD, and before his host; and
they carried away very much spoil.
14 And they smote all the cities
round about Gerar; for [k]the fear of the
LORD came upon them: and they spoiled
all the cities; for there was exceeding
much spoil in them.
15 They smote also the tents of cat-
tle, and carried away sheep and camels
in abundance, and returned to Jerusa-
lem.

Asa's reform movement

15:16–19pp — 1 Ki. 15:13–16

15 AND [l]THE spirit of God came
upon Azariah the son of Oded:
2 And he went out [n]to meet Asa,
and said unto him, Hear ye me, Asa,
and all Judah and Benjamin; [m]The
LORD *is* with you, while ye be with him;
and [n]if ye seek him, he will be found
of you; but [o]if ye forsake him, he will
forsake you.
3 Now [p]for a long season Israel
hath been without the true God, and
without [q]a teaching priest, and with-
out law.
4 But [r]when they in their trouble
did turn unto the LORD God of Israel,
and sought him, he was found of them.
5 And in those times *there was* no
peace to him that went out, nor to him
that came in, but great vexations *were*
upon all the inhabitants of the coun-
tries.
6 [s]And nation was [o]destroyed of
nation, and city of city: for God did vex
them with all adversity.
7 Be ye strong therefore, and let not
your hands be weak: for your work
shall be rewarded.
8 And when Asa heard these words,
and the prophecy of Oded the prophet,
he took courage, and put away the
[p]abominable idols out of all the land
of Judah and Benjamin, and out of the

14:14 [k]Gen. 35:5 ch. 17:10
15:1 [l]Num. 24:2 Judg. 3:10 ch. 20:14
15:2 [m]Jas. 4:8 [n]ver. 4,15 1 Chr. 28:9 ch. 33:12,13 Jer. 29:13 Mat. 7:7 [o]ch. 24:20
15:3 [p]Hos. 3:4 [q]Lev. 10:11
15:4 [r]Deut. 4:29
15:6 [s]Mat. 24:7
15:8 [t]ch. 13:19
15:9 [u]ch. 11:16
15:11 [v]ch. 14:15 [w]ch. 14:13
15:12 [x]2 Ki. 23:3 ch. 34:31 Neh. 10:29
15:13 [y]Ex. 22:20 [z]Deut. 13:5,9,15
15:15 [a]ver. 2
15:16 [b]1 Ki. 15:13
15:17 [c]ch. 14:3,5 1 Ki. 15:14

cities [t]which he had taken from
mount Ephraim, and renewed the altar
of the LORD, that *was* before the porch
of the LORD.
9 And he gathered all Judah and
Benjamin, and [u]the strangers with
them out of Ephraim and Manasseh,
and out of Simeon: for they fell to him
out of Israel in abundance, when they
saw that the LORD his God *was* with
him.
10 So they gathered themselves to-
gether at Jerusalem in the third month,
in the fifteenth year of the reign of Asa.
11 [v]And they offered unto the LORD
[q]the same time, of [w]the spoil *which*
they had brought, seven hundred oxen
and seven thousand sheep.
12 And they [x]entered into a cov-
enant to seek the LORD God of their fa-
thers with all their heart and with all
their soul;
13 [y]That whosoever would not
seek the LORD God of Israel [z]should be
put to death, whether small or great,
whether man or woman.
14 And they sware unto the LORD
with a loud voice, and with shouting,
and with trumpets, and with cornets.
15 And all Judah rejoiced at the
oath: for they had sworn with all their
heart, and [a]sought him with their
whole desire; and he was found of
them: and the LORD gave them rest
round about.
16 ¶ And also *concerning* [b]Maa-
chah the [r]mother of Asa the king, he
removed her from *being* queen, because
she had made an [s]idol in a grove: and
Asa cut down her idol, and stamped *it*,
and burnt *it* at the brook Kidron.
17 But [c]the high places were not
taken away out of Israel: nevertheless

[m] Heb. *broken beaten in pieces* [n] Heb. *before Asa* [o] Heb. [p] Heb. *abominations* [q] Heb. *in that day* [r] i.e. *grandmother;* see 1 Ki. 15:2,10 [s] Heb. *horror*

15:2 IF YE SEEK HIM. Seeking the Lord faithfully (see previous note) has wonderful results. (1) Those who seek the Lord will experience the peace of God (14:6–7); this means not just the absence of conflict, but the experience of forgiveness, a clear conscience (Acts 24:16; 1 Tim. 3:9), and a sense of well-being arising from a right relationship with God (cf. Is. 26:3; Acts 10:36; Rom. 5:1; Gal. 5:22; see Rom. 8:1, note; see article on THE PEACE OF GOD, p. 1122).

(2) Those who seek the Lord will receive mercy, grace, and "help in time of need" (see Heb. 4:16, note; cf. 2 Chr. 14:11–15).

(3) Those who seek the Lord will experience the presence of God (vv. 1–4). God promises that those who earnestly seek Him will "find him." Under the new covenant the presence of God through the Holy Spirit brings strength and comfort to believers, leading them into truth, righteousness, and power (see John 14:16–26; 15:26–27; Acts 2:4; Rom. 8:5–16; Gal. 4:6).

(4) Those who seek the Lord will be able to stand firm against their enemies (14:9–15; 16:7–8). Believers will have great strength to wage effective warfare against Satan and his spiritual forces (cf. Eph. 6:10–18; see Mat. 4:10, note).

the heart of Asa was perfect all his
days.
18 ¶ And he brought into the house
of God the things that his father had
dedicated, and that he himself had ded-
icated, silver, and gold, and vessels.
19 And there was no *more* war unto
the five and thirtieth year of the reign
of Asa.

The end of Asa's reign

16:1–6pp — 1 Ki. 15:17–22
16:11–17:1pp — 1 Ki. 15:23–24

16 IN THE six and thirtieth year of
the reign of Asa [d]Baasha king
of Israel came up against Judah, and
built Ramah, [e]to the intent that he
might let none go out or come in to Asa
king of Judah.
2 Then Asa brought out silver and
gold out of the treasures of the house
of the LORD and of the king's house, and
sent to Ben-hadad king of Syria, that
dwelt at [t]Damascus, saying,
3 *There is* a league between me and
thee, as *there was* between my father
and thy father: behold, I have sent thee
silver and gold; go, break thy league
with Baasha king of Israel, that he may
depart from me.
4 And Ben-hadad hearkened unto
king Asa, and sent the captains of
[u]his armies against the cities of Isra-
el; and they smote Ijon, and Dan, and
Abel-maim, and all the store cities of
Naphtali.
5 And it came to pass, when Baasha
heard *it,* that he left off building of Ra-
mah, and let his work cease.
6 Then Asa the king took all Judah;
and they carried away the stones of Ra-
mah, and the timber thereof, where-
with Baasha was building; and he built
therewith Geba and Mizpah.
7 ¶ And at that time [f]Hanani the
seer came to Asa king of Judah, and
said unto him, [g]Because thou hast re-
lied on the king of Syria, and not relied
on the LORD thy God, therefore is the
host of the king of Syria escaped out of
thine hand.
8 Were not [h]the Ethiopians and
[i]the Lubims [v]a huge host, with very
many chariots and horsemen? yet, be-
cause thou didst rely on the LORD, he
delivered them into thine hand.
9 [j]For the eyes of the LORD run to
and fro throughout the whole earth,
[w]to show himself strong in the behalf
of *them* whose heart *is* perfect toward
him. Herein [k]thou hast done foolishly:
therefore from henceforth [l]thou shalt
have wars.
10 Then Asa was wroth with the
seer, and [m]put him in a prison house;
for *he was* in a rage with him because
of this *thing.* And Asa [x]oppressed
some of the people the same time.
11 ¶ [n]And, behold, the acts of Asa,
first and last, lo, they *are* written in the
book of the kings of Judah and Israel.
12 And Asa in the thirty and ninth
year of his reign was diseased in his
feet, until his disease *was* exceeding
great: yet in his disease he [o]sought
not to the LORD, but to the physicians.

16:1 [d]1 Ki. 15:17 [e]ch. 15:9
16:7 [f]1 Ki. 16:1 ch. 19:2 [g]Is. 31:1 Jer. 17:5
16:8 [h]ch. 14:9 [i]ch. 12:3
16:9 [j]Job 34:21 Prov. 5:21 & 15:3 Jer. 16:17 & 32:19 Zech. 4:10 [k]1 Sam. 13:13 [l]1 Ki. 15:32
16:10 [m]ch. 18:26 Jer. 20:2 Mat. 14:3
16:11 [n]1 Ki. 15:23
16:12 [o]Jer. 17:5

[t]Heb. *Darmesek* [u]Heb. *which were his* [v]Heb. *in abundance* [w]Or, *strongly to hold with* them [x]Heb. *crushed*

15:17 THE HEART OF ASA WAS PERFECT ALL HIS DAY. Asa's "perfect" commitment to the Lord is seen in his rejection of idolatry, not necessarily in his conduct in all matters (see next note).

16:7 BECAUSE THOU HAST ... NOT RELIED ON THE LORD THY GOD. Asa failed to persevere in seeking God during his later years. He is an example to all believers that it is indeed possible to fall away from faithfulness to God even after participating in a great spiritual reformation. Three evidences of his spiritual decline are given in this chapter. (1) He stopped relying on the Lord and trusted instead in human resources (vv. 7–9). (2) He rejected and persecuted the prophet of God (v. 10). An unmistakable sign of spiritual decline is the spurning of God's prophets who bring God's word of rebuke and correction (vv. 7–10; see Luke 6:23, note). (3) When physically afflicted, rather than first seeking God for discernment and deliverance, he exclusively sought the help of his physicians, who perhaps used incantations and the medical remedies of the occult (v. 12).

16:9 THE EYES OF THE LORD RUN TO AND FRO. God so values those who are devoted to Him that He searches throughout the earth to mark all who love Him faithfully and identify themselves with His cause (Ezek. 9:3–6). God does this to support and help such people in whatever dangers (see Ex. 14:15–20; 2 Ki. 19:35), affliction (Gen. 37:34; Ex. 2:23–25), or trials (Gen. 22:1–14) they face.

16:9 *THEM* WHOSE HEART *IS* PERFECT TOWARD HIM. God distinguishes between those among His people whose hearts are completely His and those whose hearts are divided between Him and the world. This truth is also seen in Christ's evaluation of the seven churches in Rev. 2—3, where He contrasts the faithful overcomers with the lukewarm members of His churches (Rev. 3:15,21; see article on CHRIST'S MESSAGE TO THE SEVEN CHURCHES, p. 2036).

13 ¶ [p]And Asa slept with his fathers, and died in the one and fortieth year of his reign.

14 And they buried him in his own sepulchres, which he had [y]made for himself in the city of David, and laid him in the bed which was filled [q]with sweet odours and divers kinds *of spices* prepared by the apothecaries' art: and they made [r]a very great burning for him.

Jehoshaphat, king of Judah

17 AND [s]JEHOSHAPHAT his son reigned in his stead, and strengthened himself against Israel.

2 And he placed forces in all the fenced cities of Judah, and set garrisons in the land of Judah, and in the cities of Ephraim, [t]which Asa his father had taken.

3 And the LORD was with Jehoshaphat, because he walked in the first ways [z]of his father David, and sought not unto Baalim;

4 But sought to the *LORD* God of his father, and walked in his commandments, and not after [u]the doings of Israel.

5 Therefore the LORD stablished the kingdom in his hand; and all Judah [v]brought[a] to Jehoshaphat presents; [w]and he had riches and honour in abundance.

6 And his heart [b]was lifted up in the ways of the LORD: moreover [x]he took away the high places and groves out of Judah.

7 ¶ Also in the third year of his reign he sent to his princes, *even* to Ben-hail, and to Obadiah, and to Zechariah, and to Nethaneel, and to Michaiah, [y]to teach in the cities of Judah.

8 And with them *he sent* Levites, *even* Shemaiah, and Nethaniah, and Zebadiah, and Asahel, and Shemiramoth, and Jehonathan, and Adonijah, and Tobijah, and Tob-adonijah, Levites; and with them Elishama and Jehoram, priests.

9 [z]And they taught in Judah, and *had* the book of the law of the LORD with them, and went about throughout all the cities of Judah, and taught the people.

10 ¶ And [a]the fear of the LORD [c]fell upon all the kingdoms of the lands that *were* round about Judah, so that they made no war against Jehoshaphat.

11 Also *some* of the Philistines [b]brought Jehoshaphat presents, and tribute silver; and the Arabians brought him flocks, seven thousand and seven hundred rams, and seven thousand and seven hundred he goats.

12 ¶ And Jehoshaphat waxed great exceedingly; and he built in Judah [d]castles, and cities of store.

13 And he had much business in the cities of Judah: and the men of war, mighty men of valour, *were* in Jerusalem.

14 And these *are* the numbers of them according to the house of their fathers: Of Judah, the captains of thousands; Adnah the chief, and with him mighty men of valour three hundred thousand.

15 And [e]next to him *was* Jehohanan the captain, and with him two hundred and fourscore thousand.

16 And next him *was* Amasiah the son of Zichri, [c]who willingly offered himself unto the LORD; and with him two hundred thousand mighty men of valour.

17 And of Benjamin; Eliada a mighty man of valour, and with him armed men with bow and shield two hundred thousand.

18 And next him *was* Jehozabad, and with him an hundred and fourscore thousand ready prepared for the war.

19 These waited on the king, beside [d]*those* whom the king put in the fenced cities throughout all Judah.

The prophecy against Ahab

18:1–27pp — 1 Ki. 22:1–28

18 NOW JEHOSHAPHAT [e]had riches and honour in abundance, and [f]joined affinity with Ahab.

16:13 [p]1 Ki. 15:24
16:14 [q]Gen. 50:2; Mark 16:1; John 19:39,40; [r]ch. 21:19; Jer. 34:5
17:1 [s]1 Ki. 15:24
17:2 [t]ch. 15:8
17:4 [u]1 Ki. 12:28
17:5 [v]1 Sam. 10:27; 1 Ki. 10:25; [w]1 Ki. 10:27; ch. 18:1
17:6 [x]1 Ki. 22:43; ch. 15:17 & 19:3 & 20:33
17:7 [y]ch. 15:3
17:9 [z]ch. 35:3; Neh. 8:7
17:10 [a]Gen. 35:5
17:11 [b]2 Sam. 8:2
17:16 [c]Judg. 5:2,9
17:19 [d]ver. 2
18:1 [e]ch. 17:5; [f]2 Ki. 8:18

[y] Heb. *digged* [z] Or, *of his father,* and *of David* [a] Heb. *gave* [b] i.e. *was encouraged* [c] Heb. *was* [d] Or, *palaces* [e] Heb. *at his hand*

17:9 THEY TAUGHT . . . THE BOOK OF THE LAW. A spiritual revival will soon die if it is not based solidly upon the Word of God and an earnest commitment to follow its teachings. This is as true under the new covenant as it was under the old. Any spiritual movement not firmly based on the original and fundamental revelation of Christ and the apostles is doomed to failure, or prone to emotionalism or humanism (see 34:30, note; Eph. 2:20, note).

2 [g]And [f]after *certain* years he went down to Ahab to Samaria. And Ahab killed sheep and oxen for him in abundance, and for the people that *he had* with him, and persuaded him to go up *with him* to Ramoth-gilead.

3 And Ahab king of Israel said unto Jehoshaphat king of Judah, Wilt thou go with me to Ramoth-gilead? And he answered him, I *am* as thou *art*, and my people as thy people; and *we will be* with thee in the war.

4 ¶ And Jehoshaphat said unto the king of Israel, [h]Inquire, I pray thee, at the word of the LORD today.

5 Therefore the king of Israel gathered together of prophets four hundred men, and said unto them, Shall we go to Ramoth-gilead to battle, or shall I forbear? And they said, Go up; for God will deliver *it* into the king's hand.

6 But Jehoshaphat said, *Is there* not here a prophet of the LORD [g]besides, that we might inquire of him?

7 And the king of Israel said unto Jehoshaphat, *There is* yet one man, by whom we may inquire of the LORD: but I hate him; for he never prophesied good unto me, but always evil: the same *is* Micaiah the son of Imla. And Jehoshaphat said, Let not the king say so.

8 And the king of Israel called for one *of his* [h]officers, and said, [i]Fetch quickly Micaiah the son of Imla.

9 And the king of Israel and Jehoshaphat king of Judah sat either of them on his throne, clothed in *their* robes, and they sat in a [j]void place at the entering in of the gate of Samaria; and all the prophets prophesied before them.

10 And Zedekiah the son of Chenaanah had made him horns of iron, and said, Thus saith the LORD, With these thou shalt push Syria until [k]they be consumed.

11 And all the prophets prophesied so, saying, Go up to Ramoth-gilead, and prosper: for the LORD shall deliver *it* into the hand of the king.

12 And the messenger that went to call Micaiah spake to him, saying, Behold, the words of the prophets *declare* good to the king [l]with one assent; let thy word therefore, I pray thee, be like one of theirs, and speak thou good.

13 And Micaiah said, *As* the LORD liveth, [i]even what my God saith, that will I speak.

14 And when he was come to the king, the king said unto him, Micaiah, shall we go to Ramoth-gilead to battle, or shall I forbear? And he said, Go ye up, and prosper, and they shall be delivered into your hand.

15 And the king said to him, How many times shall I adjure thee that thou say nothing but the truth to me in the name of the LORD?

16 Then he said, I did see all Israel scattered upon the mountains, as sheep that have no shepherd: and the LORD said, These have no master; let them return *therefore* every man to his house in peace.

17 And the king of Israel said to Jehoshaphat, Did I not tell thee *that* he would not prophesy good unto me, [m]but evil?

18 Again he said, Therefore hear the word of the LORD; I saw the LORD sitting upon his throne, and all the host of heaven standing on his right hand and *on* his left.

19 And the LORD said, Who shall entice Ahab king of Israel, that he may go up and fall at Ramoth-gilead? And one spake saying after this manner, and another saying after that manner.

20 Then there came out a [j]spirit, and stood before the LORD, and said, I will entice him. And the LORD said unto him, Wherewith?

21 And he said, I will go out, and be a lying spirit in the mouth of all his prophets. And *the LORD* said, Thou shalt entice *him*, and thou shalt also prevail: go out, and do *even* so.

22 Now therefore, behold, [k]the LORD hath put a lying spirit in the mouth of these thy prophets, and the LORD hath spoken evil against thee.

23 Then Zedekiah the son of Chenaanah came near, and [l]smote Micaiah upon the cheek, and said, Which way went the spirit of the LORD from me to speak unto thee?

24 And Micaiah said, Behold, thou shalt see on that day when thou shalt

18:2 [g]1 Ki. 22:2
18:4 [h]1 Sam. 23:2,4,9 2 Sam. 2:1
18:13 [i]Num. 22:18,20,35 & 23:12,26 & 24:13 1 Ki. 22:14
18:20 [j]Job 1:6
18:22 [k]Job 12:16 Is. 19:14 Ezek. 14:9
18:23 [l]Jer. 20:2 Mark 14:65 Acts 23:2

[f] Heb. *at the end of years* [g] Heb. *yet*, or, *more* [h] Or, *eunuchs* [i] Heb. *Hasten* [j] Or, *floor* [k] Heb. thou *consume them* [l] Heb. *with one mouth* [m] Or, *but for evil?*

18:14 GO YE UP. See 1 Ki. 22:15, note. **18:22 A LYING SPIRIT.** See 1 Ki. 22:23, note.

go [n]into [o]an inner chamber to hide thyself.

25 Then the king of Israel said, Take ye Micaiah, and carry him back to Amon the governor of the city, and to Joash the king's son;

26 And say, Thus saith the king, [m]Put this *fellow* in the prison, and feed him with bread of affliction and with water of affliction, until I return in peace.

27 And Micaiah said, If thou certainly return in peace, *then* hath not the LORD spoken by me. And he said, Hearken, all ye people.

The defeat and death of Ahab

18:28–34pp — 1 Ki. 22:29–36

28 So the king of Israel and Jehoshaphat the king of Judah went up to Ramoth-gilead.

29 And the king of Israel said unto Jehoshaphat, I will disguise myself, and will go to the battle; but put thou on thy robes. So the king of Israel disguised himself; and they went to the battle.

30 Now the king of Syria had commanded the captains of the chariots that *were* with him, saying, Fight ye not with small or great, save only with the king of Israel.

31 And it came to pass, when the captains of the chariots saw Jehoshaphat, that they said, It *is* the king of Israel. Therefore they compassed about him to fight: but Jehoshaphat cried out, and the LORD helped him; and God moved them *to depart* from him.

32 For it came to pass, that, when the captains of the chariots perceived that it was not the king of Israel, they turned back again [p]from pursuing him.

33 And a *certain* man drew a bow [q]at a venture, and smote the king of Israel [r]between the joints of the harness: therefore he said to his chariot man, Turn thine hand, that thou mayest carry me out of the host; for I am [s]wounded.

34 And the battle increased that day: howbeit the king of Israel stayed *himself* up in *his* chariot against the Syrians until the even: and about the time of the sun going down he died.

Reforms by Jehoshaphat

19 AND JEHOSHAPHAT the king of Judah returned to his house in peace to Jerusalem.

2 And Jehu the son of Hanani [n]the seer went out to meet him, and said to king Jehoshaphat, Shouldest thou help the ungodly, and [o]love them that hate the LORD? therefore *is* [p]wrath upon thee from before the LORD.

3 Nevertheless there are [q]good things found in thee, in that thou hast taken away the groves out of the land, and hast [r]prepared thine heart to seek God.

4 And Jehoshaphat dwelt at Jerusalem: and [t]he went out again through the people from Beer-sheba to mount Ephraim, and brought them back unto the LORD God of their fathers.

5 ¶ And he set judges in the land throughout all the fenced cities of Judah, city by city,

6 And said to the judges, Take heed what ye do: for [s]ye judge not for man, but for the LORD, [t]who *is* with you [u]in the judgment.

7 Wherefore now let the fear of the LORD be upon you; take heed and do *it:* for [u]*there is* no iniquity with the LORD our God, nor [v]respect of persons, nor taking of gifts.

8 ¶ Moreover in Jerusalem did Jehoshaphat [w]set of the Levites, and *of* the priests, and of the chief of the fathers of Israel, for the judgment of the LORD, and for controversies, when they returned to Jerusalem.

9 And he charged them, saying, Thus shall ye do [x]in the fear of the LORD, faithfully, and with a perfect heart.

10 [y]And what cause soever shall come to you of your brethren that dwell in their cities, between blood and blood, between law and command-

18:26 [m]ch. 16:10
19:2 [n]1 Sam. 9:9 [o]Ps. 139:21 [p]ch. 32:25
19:3 [q]ch. 17:4,6 [r]ch. 30:19 Ezra 7:10
19:6 [s]Deut. 1:17 [t]Ps. 82:1 Eccl. 5:8
19:7 [u]Deut. 32:4 Rom. 9:14 [v]Deut. 10:17 Job 34:19 Acts 10:34 Rom. 2:11 Gal. 2:6 Eph. 6:9 Col. 3:25
19:8 [w]Deut. 16:18 ch. 17:8
19:9 [x]2 Sam. 23:3
19:10 [y]Deut. 17:8

[n] Or, *from chamber to chamber* [o] Heb. *a chamber in a chamber* [p] Heb. *from after him* [q] Heb. *in his simplicity* [r] Heb. *between the joints and between the breastplate* [s] Heb. *made sick* [t] Heb. *he returned and went out* [u] Heb. *in the matter of judgment*

19:2 SHOULDEST THOU HELP THE UNGODLY. Jehoshaphat is rebuked for associating with Ahab and helping this enemy of God (cf. ch. 18). Believers should not associate with the ungodly if in that relationship the cause of unrighteousness is advanced, our commitment to God is jeopardized, or the truth of God's Word is compromised.

ment, statutes and judgments, ye shall
even warn them that they trespass not
against the LORD, and so [z]wrath come
upon [a]you, and upon your brethren:
this do, and ye shall not trespass.
11 And, behold, Amariah the chief
priest *is* over you [b]in all matters of the
LORD; and Zebadiah the son of Ishmael,
the ruler of the house of Judah, for all
the king's matters: also the Levites
shall be officers before you. [v]Deal cou-
rageously, and the LORD shall be [c]with
the good.

Moab and Ammon defeated

20 IT CAME to pass after this
also, *that* the children of Moab,
and the children of Ammon, and with
them *other* beside the Ammonites,
came against Jehoshaphat to battle.
2 Then there came some that told
Jehoshaphat, saying, There cometh a
great multitude against thee from be-
yond the sea on this side Syria; and,
behold, they *be* [d]in Hazazon-tamar,
which *is* [e]En-gedi.
3 And Jehoshaphat feared, and set
[w]himself to [f]seek the LORD, and
[g]proclaimed a fast throughout all Ju-
dah.
4 And Judah gathered themselves
together, to ask *help* of the LORD: even
out of all the cities of Judah they came
to seek the LORD.
5 ¶ And Jehoshaphat stood in the
congregation of Judah and Jerusalem,
in the house of the LORD, before the new
court,
6 And said, O LORD God of our fa-
thers, *art* not thou [h]God in heaven?
and [i]rulest *not* thou over all the king-
doms of the heathen? and [j]in thine
hand *is there not* power and might, so
that none is able to withstand thee?
7 *Art* not thou [k]our God, [x]*who*
[l]didst drive out the inhabitants of this
land before thy people Israel, and gav-
est it to the seed of Abraham [m]thy
friend for ever?
8 And they dwelt therein, and have
built thee a sanctuary therein for thy
name, saying,
9 [n]If, *when* evil cometh upon us, *as*
the sword, judgment, or pestilence, or
famine, we stand before this house,
and in thy presence, (for thy [o]name *is*
in this house,) and cry unto thee in our
affliction, then thou wilt hear and help.
10 And now, behold, the children of
Ammon and Moab and mount Seir,
whom thou [p]wouldest not let Israel
invade, when they came out of the land
of Egypt, but [q]they turned from them,
and destroyed them not;
11 Behold, *I say, how* they reward
us, [r]to come to cast us out of thy pos-
session, which thou hast given us to
inherit.
12 O our God, wilt thou not [s]judge
them? for we have no might against
this great company that cometh
against us; neither know we what to
do: but [t]our eyes *are* upon thee.
13 And all Judah stood before the
LORD, with their little ones, their wives,
and their children.
14 ¶ Then upon Jahaziel the son of
Zechariah, the son of Benaiah, the son
of Jeiel, the son of Mattaniah, a Levite
of the sons of Asaph, [u]came the spir-
it of the LORD in the midst of the con-
gregation;
15 And he said, Hearken ye, all Ju-
dah, and ye inhabitants of Jerusalem,
and thou king Jehoshaphat, Thus saith
the LORD unto you, [v]Be not afraid nor

19:10 [z]Num. 16:46 [a]Ezek. 3:18
19:11 [b]1 Chr. 26:30 [c]ch. 15:2
20:2 [d]Gen. 14:7 [e]Josh. 15:62
20:3 [f]ch. 19:3 [g]Ezra 8:21 Jer. 36:9 Jonah 3:5
20:6 [h]Deut. 4:39 Josh. 2:11 1 Ki. 8:23 Mat. 6:9 [i]Ps. 47:2,8 Dan. 4:17 [j]1 Chr. 29:12 Ps. 62:11 Mat. 6:13
20:7 [k]Gen. 17:7 Ex. 6:7 [l]Ps. 44:2 [m]Is. 41:8 Jas. 2:23
20:9 [n]1 Ki. 8:33,37 ch. 6:28-30 [o]ch. 6:20
20:10 [p]Deut. 2:4,9,19 [q]Num. 20:21
20:11 [r]Ps. 83:12
20:12 [s]1 Sam. 3:13 [t]Ps. 25:15 & 121:1,2 & 123:1,2 & 141:8
20:14 [u]Num. 11:25,26 & 24:2 ch. 15:1
20:15 [v]Ex. 14:13,14 Deut. 1:29,30 & 31:6,8 ch. 32:7

v Heb. *Take courage and do* w Heb. *his face*
x Heb. *thou*

20:3 JEHOSHAPHAT FEARED. Faced with the greatest crisis of his life (vv. 1–2), Jehoshaphat met a seemingly impossible circumstance in an exemplary manner. He began to seek the Lord through fasting (v. 3), gathered together others to pray and fast (v. 4), confessed his helplessness (v. 12), obeyed the Holy Spirit (vv. 14–18), put his trust in the Lord and His word (v. 20), and gave thanks to the Lord (vv. 21–22).

20:3 PROCLAIMED A FAST. Seeking the Lord (see 15:2, note) can be intensified through fasting. Fasting should regularly accompany prayer and the believer's desire that God's will be done (see Ezra 8:23; Neh. 9:1–2; Dan. 9:3; see Mat. 4:2; 6:16, notes).

20:6 O LORD GOD OF OUR FATHERS. Jehoshaphat based his prayer and his confidence in God on five principal truths. (1) God has power over all people and situations (vv. 6–7); (2) God has been faithful to His people in the past and present (vv. 7–9); (3) God's people are helpless without Him (v. 12); (4) God's promises are a sure foundation for faith (vv. 14–17,20); and (5) God's active presence among His people means deliverance and victory (v. 17).

20:15 THE BATTLE *IS* NOT YOURS, BUT GOD'S. Here the strength and power of faith are demonstrated by praising God in song in the face of the battle (vv. 18–19). Similarly, Paul exhorts believers to "be strong in the Lord, and in the power of his might" as they fight against the powers and spiritual forces of Satan (Eph. 6:10).

dismayed by reason of this great multitude; for the battle *is* not yours, but God's.

16 Tomorrow go ye down against them: behold, they come up by the [y]cliff of Ziz; and ye shall find them at the end of the [z]brook, before the wilderness of Jeruel.

17 [w]Ye shall not *need* to fight in this *battle:* set yourselves, stand ye *still,* and see the salvation of the LORD with you, O Judah and Jerusalem: fear not, nor be dismayed; tomorrow go out against them: [x]for the LORD *will be* with you.

18 And Jehoshaphat [y]bowed his head with *his* face to the ground: and all Judah and the inhabitants of Jerusalem fell before the LORD, worshipping the LORD.

19 And the Levites, of the children of the Kohathites, and of the children of the Korhites, stood up to praise the LORD God of Israel with a loud voice on high.

20 ¶ And they rose early in the morning, and went forth into the wilderness of Tekoa: and as they went forth, Jehoshaphat stood and said, Hear me, O Judah, and ye inhabitants of Jerusalem; [z]Believe in the LORD your God, so shall ye be established; believe his prophets, so shall ye prosper.

21 And when he had consulted with the people, he appointed singers unto the LORD, [a]and [a]that should praise the beauty of holiness, as they went out before the army, and to say, [b]Praise the LORD; [c]for his mercy *endureth* for ever.

22 ¶ [b]And when they began [c]to sing and to praise, [d]the LORD set ambushments against the children of Ammon, Moab, and mount Seir, which were come against Judah; and [d]they were smitten.

23 For the children of Ammon and Moab stood up against the inhabitants of mount Seir, utterly to slay and destroy *them:* and when they had made an end of the inhabitants of Seir, every one helped [e]to destroy another.

24 And when Judah came toward the watchtower in the wilderness, they looked unto the multitude, and, behold, they *were* dead bodies fallen to the earth, and [f]none escaped.

25 And when Jehoshaphat and his people came to take away the spoil of them, they found among them in abundance both riches with the dead bodies, and precious jewels, which they stripped off for themselves, more than they could carry away: and they were three days in gathering of the spoil, it was so much.

26 ¶ And on the fourth day they assembled themselves in the valley of [g]Berachah; for there they blessed the LORD: therefore the name of the same place was called, The valley of Berachah, unto this day.

27 Then they returned, every man of Judah and Jerusalem, and Jehoshaphat in the [h]forefront of them, to go again to Jerusalem with joy; for the LORD had [e]made them to rejoice over their enemies.

28 And they came to Jerusalem with psalteries and harps and trumpets unto the house of the LORD.

29 And [f]the fear of God was on all the kingdoms of *those* countries, when they had heard that the LORD fought against the enemies of Israel.

30 So the realm of Jehoshaphat was quiet: for his [g]God gave him rest round about.

The death of Jehoshaphat

20:31–21:1pp — 1 Ki. 22:41–50

31 ¶ [h]And Jehoshaphat reigned over Judah: *he was* thirty and five years old when he began to reign, and he reigned twenty and five years in Jerusalem. And his mother's name *was* Azubah the daughter of Shilhi.

32 And he walked in the way of Asa his father, and departed not from it, doing *that which was* right in the sight of the LORD.

33 Howbeit [i]the high places were not taken away: for as yet the people

20:17 [w]Ex. 14:13,14 [x]Num. 14:9 ch. 15:2 & 32:8 **20:18** [y]Ex. 4:31 **20:20** [z]Is. 7:9 **20:21** [a]1 Chr. 16:29 [b]1 Chr. 16:34 Ps 136:1 [c]1 Chr. 16:41 ch. 5:13 **20:22** [d]Judg. 7:22 1 Sam. 14:20 **20:27** [e]Neh. 12:43 **20:29** [f]ch:17:10 **20:30** [g]ch. 15:15 Job 34:29 **20:31** [h]1 Ki. 22:41 **20:33** [i]See ch. 17:6

[y] Heb. *ascent* [z] Or, *valley* [a] Heb. *praisers* [b] Heb. *And in the time that they* [c] Heb. *in singing and praise* [d] Or, *they smote one another* [e] Heb. *for the destruction* [f] Heb. there was *not an escaping* [g] i.e. *Blessing* [h] Heb. *head*

2 Ch 32:2 23

20:33 HIGH PLACES. These were elevated areas where idolatrous worship took place. God wanted His people to destroy these places completely, lest they be led into such worship (Num. 33:52). The attraction that God's people had for these places indicated that they lacked a steadfast and total commitment to the Lord God.

had not [j]prepared their hearts unto the God of their fathers.

34 Now the rest of the acts of Jehoshaphat, first and last, behold, they *are* written in the [i]book of Jehu the son of Hanani, [k]who [j]*is* mentioned in the book of the kings of Israel.

35 ¶ And after this [l]did Jehoshaphat king of Judah join himself with Ahaziah king of Israel, who did very wickedly:

36 [k]And he joined himself with him to make ships to go to Tarshish: and they made the ships in Ezion-geber.

37 Then Eliezer the son of Dodavah of Mareshah prophesied against Jehoshaphat, saying, Because thou hast joined thyself with Ahaziah, the LORD hath broken thy works. [m]And the ships were broken, that they were not able to go [n]to Tarshish.

Jehoram, king of Judah

21:5–10,20pp — 2 Ki. 8:16–24

21 NOW [o]JEHOSHAPHAT slept with his fathers, and was buried with his fathers in the city of David. And Jehoram his son [l]reigned in his stead.

2 And he had brethren the sons of Jehoshaphat, Azariah, and Jehiel, and Zechariah, and Azariah, and Michael, and Shephatiah: all these *were* the sons of Jehoshaphat king of Israel.

3 And their father gave them great gifts of silver, and of gold, and of precious things, with fenced cities in Judah: but the kingdom gave he to [m]Jehoram; because he *was* the firstborn.

4 Now when Jehoram was risen up to the kingdom of his father, he strengthened himself, and slew all his brethren with the sword, and *divers* also of the princes of Israel.

5 ¶ [p]Jehoram *was* thirty and two years old when he began to reign, and he reigned eight years in Jerusalem.

6 And he walked in the way of the kings of Israel, like as did the house of Ahab: for he had the daughter of [q]Ahab to wife: and he wrought *that which was* evil in the eyes of the LORD.

7 Howbeit the LORD would not destroy the house of David, because of the covenant that he had made with David, and as he promised to give a [n]light to him and to his [r]sons for ever.

20:33 [j]ch. 12:14 & 19:3
20:34 [k]1 Ki. 16:1,7
20:35 [l]1 Ki. 22:48,49
20:37 [m]1 Ki. 22:48 [n]ch. 9:21
21:1 [o]1 Ki. 22:50
21:5 [p]In consort 2 Ki. 8:17
21:6 [q]ch. 22:2
21:7 [r]2 Sam. 7:12,13 1 Ki. 11:36 2 Ki. 8:19 Ps. 132:11
21:8 [s]2 Ki. 8:20
21:11 [t]Lev. 20:5
21:13 [u]ver. 11 [v]Ex. 34:15 Deut. 31:16 [w]1 Ki. 16:31-33 2 Ki. 9:22 [x]ver. 4
21:15 [y]ver. 18,19
21:17 [z]ch. 24:7

8 ¶ [s]In his days the Edomites revolted from under the [o]dominion of Judah, and made themselves a king.

9 Then Jehoram went forth with his princes, and all his chariots with him: and he rose up by night, and smote the Edomites which compassed him in, and the captains of the chariots.

10 So the Edomites revolted from under the hand of Judah unto this day. The same time *also* did Libnah revolt from under his hand; because he had forsaken the LORD God of his fathers.

11 Moreover he made high places in the mountains of Judah, and caused the inhabitants of Jerusalem to [t]commit fornication, and compelled Judah *thereto.*

12 ¶ And there came a writing to him from Elijah the prophet, saying, Thus saith the LORD God of David thy father, Because thou hast not walked in the ways of Jehoshaphat thy father, nor in the ways of Asa king of Judah,

13 But hast walked in the way of the kings of Israel, and hast [u]made Judah and the inhabitants of Jerusalem to [v]go a-whoring, like to the [w]whoredoms of the house of Ahab, and also hast [x]slain thy brethren of thy father's house, *which were* better than thyself:

14 Behold, with [p]a great plague will the LORD smite thy people, and thy children, and thy wives, and all thy goods:

15 And thou *shalt have* great sickness by [y]disease of thy bowels, until thy bowels fall out by reason of the sickness day by day.

16 ¶ Moreover the LORD stirred up against Jehoram the spirit of the Philistines, and of the Arabians, that *were* near the Ethiopians:

17 And they came up into Judah, and brake into it, and [q]carried away all the substance that was found in the king's house, and [z]his sons also, and his wives; so that there was never a son left him, save [r]Jehoahaz, the youngest of his sons.

18 ¶ And after all this the LORD

[i] Heb. *words* [j] Heb. *was made to ascend*
[k] At first Jehoshaphat was unwilling; see 1 Ki. 22:49 [l] Alone [m] Jehoram made partner of the kingdom with his father; see 2 Ki. 8:16
[n] Heb. *lamp,* or, *candle* [o] Heb. *hand* [p] Heb. *a great stroke* [q] Heb. *carried captive;* see ch. 22:1 [r] Or, *Ahaziah* in ch. 22:1, or, *Azariah* in ch. 22:6

smote him [a]in his bowels with an in-
curable disease.
19 And it came to pass, that in pro-
cess of time, after the end of two years,
his bowels fell out by reason of his
sickness: so he died of sore diseases.
And his people made no burning for
him, like [b]the burning of his fathers.
20 Thirty and two years old was he
when he began to reign, and he reigned
in Jerusalem eight years, and departed
without being desired. Howbeit they
buried him in the city of David, but not
in the sepulchres of the kings.

Ahaziah, king of Judah

22:1–6pp — 2 Ki. 8:25–29
22:7–9pp — 2 Ki. 9:21–29

22 AND THE inhabitants of Jeru-
salem made [c]Ahaziah his
youngest son king in his stead: for the
band of men that came with the Arabi-
ans to the camp had slain all the [d]el-
dest. So Ahaziah the son of Jehoram
king of Judah reigned.
2 [e]Forty and two years old *was*
Ahaziah when he began to reign, and
he reigned one year in Jerusalem. His
mother's name also *was* [f]Athaliah the
daughter of Omri.
3 He also walked in the ways of the
house of Ahab: for his mother was his
counsellor to do wickedly.
4 Wherefore he did evil in the sight
of the LORD like the house of Ahab: for
they were his counsellors after the
death of his father to his destruction.
5 ¶ He walked also after their coun-
sel, and [g]went with Jehoram the son
of Ahab king of Israel to war against
Hazael king of Syria at Ramoth-gilead:
and the Syrians smote Joram.
6 [h]And he returned to be healed in
Jezreel because of the wounds [s]which
were given him at Ramah, when he
fought with Hazael king of Syria. And
[t]Azariah the son of Jehoram king of
Judah went down to see Jehoram the
son of Ahab at Jezreel, because he was
sick.
7 And the [u]destruction of Ahaziah
[i]was of God by coming to Joram: for
when he was come, he [j]went out with
Jehoram against Jehu the son of Nim-
shi, [k]whom the LORD had anointed to
cut off the house of Ahab.
8 And it came to pass, that, when
Jehu was [l]executing judgment upon
the house of Ahab, and [m]found the
princes of Judah, and the sons of the
brethren of Ahaziah, that ministered to
Ahaziah, he slew them.
9 [n]And he sought Ahaziah: and
they caught him, (for he was hid in Sa-
maria,) and brought him to Jehu: and
when they had slain him, they buried
him: Because, said they, he *is* the son
of Jehoshaphat, who [o]sought the LORD
with all his heart. So the house of Aha-
ziah had no power to keep still the
kingdom.

The murder of the royal family

22:10–23:21pp — 2 Ki. 11:1–21

10 ¶ [p]But when Athaliah the moth-
er of Ahaziah saw that her son was
dead, she arose and destroyed all the
seed royal of the house of Judah.
11 But [q]Jehoshabeath, the daugh-
ter of the king, took Joash the son of
Ahaziah, and stole him from among the
king's sons that were slain, and put
him and his nurse in a bedchamber. So
Jehoshabeath, the daughter of king Je-
horam, the wife of Jehoiada the priest,
(for she was the sister of Ahaziah,) hid
him from Athaliah, so that she slew
him not.
12 And he was with them hid in the
house of God six years: and Athaliah
reigned over the land.
23 AND [r]IN the seventh year Je-
hoiada strengthened himself,
and took the captains of hundreds, Az-
ariah the son of Jeroham, and Ishmael
the son of Jehohanan, and Azariah the
son of Obed, and Maaseiah the son of
Adaiah, and Elishaphat the son of Zich-
ri, into covenant with him.
2 And they went about in Judah, and
gathered the Levites out of all the cit-
ies of Judah, and the chief of the fa-
thers of Israel, and they came to Jeru-
salem.
3 And all the congregation made a
covenant with the king in the house of
God. And he said unto them, Behold,

21:18 [a]ver. 15 **21:19** [b]ch. 16:14 **22:1** [c]ver. 6 ch. 21:17 [d]ch. 21:17 **22:2** [e]2 Ki. 8:26 [f]ch. 21:6 **22:5** [g]2 Ki. 8:28 **22:6** [h]2 Ki. 9:15 **22:7** [i]Judg. 14:4 1 Ki. 12:15 ch. 10:15 [j]2 Ki. 9:21 [k]2 Ki. 9:6,7 **22:8** [l]2 Ki. 10:10,11 [m]2 Ki. 10:13,14 **22:9** [n]2 Ki. 9:27 at *Megiddo* in the kingdom of *Samaria* [o]ch. 17:4 **22:10** [p]2 Ki. 11:1 **22:11** [q]2 Ki. 11:2 *Jehosheba* **23:1** [r]2 Ki. 11:4

[s] Heb. *wherewith they wounded him*
[t] Otherwise called *Ahaziah* in ver. 1 and *Jehoahaz* in ch. 21:17
[u] Heb. *treading down*

22:7 JEHU ... WHOM THE LORD HAD ANOINTED. See 2 Ki. 9:8; 10:28, notes.

22:10 ATHALIAH. See 2 Ki. 11:1, note.

23:1 JEHOIADA. See 2 Ki. 11:4, note on Jehoiada's overthrow of Athaliah (23:10–15) and the placing of Joash on the throne.

the king's son shall reign, as the LORD hath [s]said of the sons of David.

4 This *is* the thing that ye shall do; A third part of you [t]entering on the sabbath, of the priests and of the Levites, *shall be* porters of the [v]doors;

5 And a third part *shall be* at the king's house; and a third part at the gate of the foundation: and all the people *shall be* in the courts of the house of the LORD.

6 But let none come into the house of the LORD, save the priests, and [u]they that minister of the Levites; they shall go in, for they *are* holy: but all the people shall keep the watch of the LORD.

7 And the Levites shall compass the king round about, every man with his weapons in his hand; and whosoever *else* cometh into the house, he shall be put to death: but be ye with the king when he cometh in, and when he goeth out.

8 So the Levites and all Judah did according to all things that Jehoiada the priest had commanded, and took every man his men that were to come in on the sabbath, with them that were to go *out* on the sabbath: for Jehoiada the priest dismissed not [v]the courses.

9 Moreover Jehoiada the priest delivered to the captains of hundreds spears, and bucklers, and shields, that *had been* king David's, which *were* in the house of God.

10 And he set all the people, every man having his weapon in his hand, from the right [w]side of the [x]temple to the left side of the temple, along by the altar and the temple, by the king round about.

11 Then they brought out the king's son, and put upon him the crown, and [w]*gave him* the testimony, and made him king. And Jehoiada and his sons anointed him, and said, [y]God save the king.

12 ¶ Now when Athaliah heard the noise of the people running and praising the king, she came to the people into the house of the LORD:

13 And she looked, and, behold, the king stood at his pillar at the entering in, and the princes and the trumpets by the king: and all the people of the land rejoiced, and sounded with trumpets, also the singers with instruments of music, and [x]such as taught to sing praise. Then Athaliah rent her clothes, and said, [z]Treason, Treason.

14 Then Jehoiada the priest brought out the captains of hundreds that were set over the host, and said unto them, Have her forth of the ranges: and whoso followeth her, let him be slain with the sword. For the priest said, Slay her not in the house of the LORD.

15 So they laid hands on her; and when she was come to the entering [y]of the horse gate by the king's house, they slew her there.

16 ¶ And Jehoiada made a covenant between him, and between all the people, and between the king, that they should be the LORD's people.

17 Then all the people went to the house of Baal, and brake it down, and brake his altars and his images in pieces, and [z]slew Mattan the priest of Baal before the altars.

18 Also Jehoiada appointed the offices of the house of the LORD by the hand of the priests the Levites, whom David had [a]distributed in the house of the LORD, to offer the burnt offerings of the LORD, as *it is* written in the [b]law of Moses, with rejoicing and with singing, *as it was ordained* [c]by[a] David.

19 And he set the [d]porters at the gates of the house of the LORD, that none *which was* unclean in any thing should enter in.

20 [e]And he took the captains of hundreds, and the nobles, and the governors of the people, and all the people of the land, and brought down the king from the house of the LORD: and they came through the high gate into the king's house, and set the king upon the throne of the kingdom.

21 And all the people of the land rejoiced: and the city was quiet, after that they had slain Athaliah with the sword.

Joash restores the temple

24:1–14pp — 2 Ki. 12:1–16
24:23–27pp — 2 Ki. 12:17–21

24 JOASH [f]*WAS* seven years old when he began to reign, and he reigned forty years in Jerusalem. His mother's name also *was* Zibiah of Beer-sheba.

2 And Joash [g]did *that which was*

23:3 [s]2 Sam. 7:12; 1 Ki. 2:4 & 9:5; ch. 6:16 & 7:18 & 21:7
23:4 [t]1 Chr. 9:25
23:6 [u]1 Chr. 23:28,29
23:8 [v]See 1 Chr. 24 & 25
23:11 [w]Deut. 17:18
23:13 [x]1 Chr. 25:8
23:15 [y]Neh. 3:28
23:17 [z]Deut. 13:9
23:18 [a]1 Chr. 23:6,30,31 & 24:1; [b]Num. 28:2; [c]1 Chr. 25:2,6
23:19 [d]1 Chr. 26:1
23:20 [e]2 Ki. 11:19
24:1 [f]2 Ki. 11:21 & 12:1
24:2 [g]See ch. 26:5

[v]Heb. *thresholds* [w]Heb. *shoulder* [x]Heb. *house* [y]Heb. *Let the king live* [z]Heb. *Conspiracy* [a]Heb. *by the hands of David*

right in the sight of the LORD all the
days of Jehoiada the priest.
3 And Jehoiada took for him two
wives; and he begat sons and daugh-
ters.
4 ¶ And it came to pass after this,
that Joash was minded [b]to repair the
house of the LORD.
5 And he gathered together the
priest and the Levites, and said to
them, Go out unto the cities of Judah,
and [h]gather of all Israel money to re-
pair the house of your God from year to
year, and see that ye hasten the mat-
ter. Howbeit the Levites hastened *it*
not.
6 [i]And the king called for Jehoiada
the chief, and said unto him, Why hast
thou not required of the Levites to
bring in out of Judah and out of Jerusa-
lem the collection, *according to the com-
mandment* of [j]Moses the servant of
the LORD, and of the congregation of Is-
rael, for the [k]tabernacle of witness?
7 For [l]the sons of Athaliah, that
wicked woman, had broken up the
house of God; and also all the [m]dedi-
cated things of the house of the LORD
did they bestow upon Baalim.
8 And at the king's commandment
[n]they made a chest, and set it without
at the gate of the house of the LORD.
9 And they made [c]a proclamation
through Judah and Jerusalem, to bring
in to the LORD [o]the collection *that* Mo-
ses the servant of God *laid* upon Israel
in the wilderness.
10 And all the princes and all the
people rejoiced, and brought in, and
cast into the chest, until they had made
an end.
11 Now it came to pass, that at what
time the chest was brought unto the
king's office by the hand of the Levites,
and [p]when they saw that *there was*
much money, the king's scribe and the
high priest's officer came and emptied
the chest, and took it, and carried it to
his place again. Thus they did day by
day, and gathered money in abun-
dance.
12 And the king and Jehoiada gave
it to such as did the work of the service
of the house of the LORD, and hired ma-
sons and carpenters to repair the
house of the LORD, and also such as
wrought iron and brass to mend the
house of the LORD.
13 So the workmen wrought, and
[d]the work was perfected by them, and
they set the house of God in his state,
and strengthened it.
14 And when they had finished *it*,
they brought the rest of the money be-
fore the king and Jehoiada, [q]whereof
were made vessels for the house of the
LORD, *even* vessels to minister, and [e]to
offer *withal*, and spoons, and vessels of
gold and silver. And they offered burnt
offerings in the house of the LORD con-
tinually all the days of Jehoiada.
15 ¶ But Jehoiada waxed old, and
was full of days when he died; an hun-
dred and thirty years old *was he* when
he died.
16 And they buried him in the city of
David among the kings, because he
had done good in Israel, both toward
God, and toward his house.
17 Now after the death of Jehoiada
came the princes of Judah, and made
obeisance to the king. Then the king
hearkened unto them.
18 And they left the house of the
LORD God of their fathers, and served
[r]groves and idols: and [s]wrath came
upon Judah and Jerusalem for this their
trespass.
19 Yet he [t]sent prophets to them,
to bring them again unto the LORD; and

24:5 [h]2 Ki. 12:4
24:6 [i]2 Ki. 12:7 [j]Ex. 30:12-14,16 [k]Num. 1:50 Acts 7:44
24:7 [l]ch. 21:17 [m]2 Ki. 12:4
24:8 [n]2 Ki. 12:9
24:9 [o]ver. 6
24:11 [p]2 Ki. 12:10
24:14 [q]See 2 Ki. 12:13
24:18 [r]1 Ki. 14:23 [s]Judg. 5:8 ch. 19:2 & 28:13 & 29:8 & 32:25
24:19 [t]ch. 36:15 Jer. 7:25,26 & 25:4

[b] Heb. *to renew* [c] Heb. *a voice* [d] Heb. *the healing went up upon the work* [e] Or, *pestils*

24:14 OFFERED BURNT OFFERINGS. Offerings to God were first made after the sin of Adam and Eve (Gen. 4:3–4). Thereafter various types of offerings were established so that God's people might understand the seriousness of sin and the significance of worshiping God (see Lev. 1:2, note). In addition to the burnt offerings mentioned here (cf. Lev. 1:3–17), God required sin offerings (Lev. 4:3–21), trespass offerings (Lev. 5:6–19), and peace offerings (Lev. 3:1–17). The important element in making an offering to God was a sincere heart that brought before Him the best that one possessed (see Lev. 22:21). In the book of Malachi God rebuked the people because they were offering sick or blemished animals (Mal. 1:6–14).

24:17 AFTER THE DEATH OF JEHOIADA. See 2 Ki. 12:2, note.

24:19 HE SENT PROPHETS TO THEM ... BUT THEY WOULD NOT GIVE EAR. Under the old covenant, God sent prophets to exhort His people to be faithful to their God and to live according to the stipulations of the covenant. Under the new covenant, prophets and their messages remain essential to the life of the church. To ignore or reject God's true prophets will result in spiritual death for the church (see article on THE MINISTRY GIFTS OF THE CHURCH, p. 1852).

they testified against them: but they would not give ear.

20 And the spirit of God [u]came[f] upon Zechariah the son of Jehoiada the priest, which stood above the people, and said unto them, Thus saith God, [v]Why transgress ye the commandments of the LORD, that ye cannot prosper? [w]because ye have forsaken the LORD, he hath also forsaken you.

21 And they conspired against him, and [x]stoned him with stones at the commandment of the king in the court of the house of the LORD.

22 Thus Joash the king remembered not the kindness which Jehoiada his father had done to him, but slew his son. And when he died, he said, The LORD look upon *it,* and require *it.*

The defeat and death of Joash

23 ¶ And it came to pass [g]at the end of the year, *that* [y]the host of Syria came up against him: and they came to Judah and Jerusalem, and destroyed all the princes of the people from among the people, and sent all the spoil of them unto the king of [h]Damascus.

24 For the army of the Syrians [z]came with a small company of men, and the LORD [a]delivered a very great host into their hand, because they had forsaken the LORD God of their fathers. So they [b]executed judgment against Joash.

25 And when they were departed from him, (for they left him in great diseases,) [c]his own servants conspired against him for the blood of the [d]sons of Jehoiada the priest, and slew him on his bed, and he died: and they buried him in the city of David, but they buried him not in the sepulchres of the kings.

26 And these are they that conspired against him; [i]Zabad the son of Shimeath an Ammonitess, and Jehozabad the son of [j]Shimrith a Moabitess.

27 ¶ Now *concerning* his sons, and the greatness of [e]the burdens *laid* upon him, and the [k]repairing of the house of God, behold, they *are* written in the [l]story of the book of the kings. [f]And Amaziah his son reigned in his stead.

Amaziah, king of Judah

25:1–4pp — 2 Ki. 14:1–6
25:11–12pp — 2 Ki. 14:7
25:17–28pp — 2 Ki. 14:8–20

25 AMAZIAH [g]*WAS* twenty and five years old *when* he began to reign, and he reigned twenty and nine years in Jerusalem. And his mother's name *was* Jehoaddan of Jerusalem.

2 And he did *that which was* right in the sight of the LORD, [h]but not with a perfect heart.

3 ¶ [i]Now it came to pass, when the kingdom was [m]established to him, that he slew his servants that had killed the king his father.

4 But he slew not their children, but *did* as *it is* written in the law in the book of Moses, where the LORD commanded, saying, [j]The fathers shall not die for the children, neither shall the children die for the fathers, but every man shall die for his own sin.

5 ¶ Moreover Amaziah gathered Judah together, and made them captains over thousands, and captains over hundreds, according to the houses of *their* fathers, throughout all Judah and Benjamin: and he numbered them [k]from twenty years old and above, and found them three hundred thousand choice *men, able* to go forth to war, that could handle spear and shield.

24:20 [u]Judg. 6:34 [v]Num. 14:41 [w]ch. 15:2 **24:21** [x]Mat. 23:35 Acts 7:58,59 **24:23** [y]2 Ki. 12:17 **24:24** [z]Lev. 26:8 Deut. 32:30 Is. 30:17 [a]Lev. 26:25 Deut. 28:25 [b]ch. 22:8 Is. 10:5 **24:25** [c]2 Ki. 12:20 [d]ver. 21 **24:27** [e]2 Ki. 12:18 [f]2 Ki. 12:21 **25:1** [g]2 Ki. 14:1 **25:2** [h]ver. 14 See 2 Ki. 14:4 **25:3** [i]2 Ki. 14:5 **25:4** [j]Deut. 24:16 2 Ki. 14:6 Jer. 31:30 Ezek. 18:20 **25:5** [k]Num. 1:3

[f] Heb. *clothed* [g] Heb. *in the revolution of the year* [h] Heb. *Darmesek* [i] Or, *Jozachar;* see 2 Ki. 12:21 [j] Or, *Shomer* [k] Heb. *founding* [l] Or, *commentary* [m] Heb. *confirmed upon him*

24:20 THE SPIRIT OF GOD CAME UPON ZECHARIAH. The Holy Spirit came upon (lit. "clothed") Zechariah, and he exposed and reproved the sin of Joash and the officials of Judah. The work of conviction concerning sin is a primary function of the Holy Spirit (John 16:8). Often through using a godly spokesman such as Zechariah, the Spirit uncovers guilt in order to lead people to repentance.

24:21 THEY ... STONED HIM WITH STONES. Zechariah was the first recorded prophet in Judah to suffer martyrdom. He died because he remained loyal to God's truth and righteous ways and testified against the apostasy of the king and the people. Jesus referred to this martyrdom and God's planned vengeance on the generation of that time (Mat. 23:35; Luke 11:51). He called Zechariah's blood "righteous" because the prophet stood with God when the majority had forsaken God's ways. The prophet was killed "between the altar and the temple" (Luke 11:51), i.e., the most sacred part of the court of the priests. Israel's rejection of the words of God's prophets ultimately resulted in their own destruction and rejection by God (see 36:16).

25:2 BUT NOT WITH A PERFECT HEART. See 2 Ki. 14:1, note.

6 He hired also an hundred thousand mighty men of valour out of Israel for an hundred talents of silver.

7 But there came a man of God to him, saying, O king, let not the army of Israel go with thee; for the LORD *is* not with Israel, *to wit, with* all the children of Ephraim.

8 But if thou wilt go, do *it,* be strong for the battle: God shall make thee fall before the enemy: for God hath [l]power to help, and to cast down.

9 And Amaziah said to the man of God, But what shall we do for the hundred talents which I have given to the [n]army of Israel? And the man of God answered, [m]The LORD is able to give thee much more than this.

10 Then Amaziah separated them, *to wit,* the army that was come to him out of Ephraim, to go [o]home again: wherefore their anger was greatly kindled against Judah, and they returned home [p]in great anger.

11 ¶ And Amaziah strengthened himself, and led forth his people, and went to [n]the valley of salt, and smote of the children of Seir ten thousand.

12 And *other* ten thousand *left* alive did the children of Judah carry away captive, and brought them unto the top of the rock, and cast them down from the top of the rock, that they all were broken in pieces.

13 ¶ But [q]the soldiers of the army which Amaziah sent back, that they should not go with him to battle, fell upon the cities of Judah, from Samaria even unto Beth-horon, and smote three thousand of them, and took much spoil.

14 ¶ Now it came to pass, after that Amaziah was come from the slaughter of the Edomites, that [o]he brought the gods of the children of Seir, and set them up *to be* [p]his gods, and bowed down himself before them, and burned incense unto them.

15 Wherefore the anger of the LORD was kindled against Amaziah, and he sent unto him a prophet, which said unto him, Why hast thou sought after [q]the gods of the people, which [r]could not deliver their own people out of thine hand?

16 And it came to pass, as he talked with him, that *the king* said unto him, Art thou made of the king's counsel? forbear; why shouldest thou be smitten? Then the prophet forbare, and said, I know that God hath [s]determined[r] to destroy thee, because thou hast done this, and hast not hearkened unto my counsel.

17 ¶ Then [t]Amaziah king of Judah took advice, and sent to Joash, the son of Jehoahaz, the son of Jehu, king of Israel, saying, Come, let us see one another in the face.

18 And Joash king of Israel sent to Amaziah king of Judah, saying, The [s]thistle that *was* in Lebanon sent to the cedar that *was* in Lebanon, saying, Give thy daughter to my son to wife: and there passed by [t]a wild beast that *was* in Lebanon, and trode down the thistle.

19 Thou sayest, Lo, thou hast smitten the Edomites; and thine heart lifteth thee up to boast: abide now at home; why shouldest thou meddle to *thine* hurt, that thou shouldest fall, *even* thou, and Judah with thee?

20 But Amaziah would not hear; for [u]it *came* of God, that he might deliver them into the hand *of their enemies,* because they [v]sought after the gods of Edom.

21 So Joash the king of Israel went up; and they saw one another in the face, *both* he and Amaziah king of Judah, at Beth-shemesh, which *belongeth* to Judah.

22 And Judah was [u]put to the worse before Israel, and they fled every man to his tent.

23 And Joash the king of Israel took Amaziah king of Judah, the son of Joash, the son of [w]Jehoahaz, at Beth-shemesh, and brought him to Jerusalem, and brake down the wall of Jerusalem from the gate of Ephraim to

25:8 [l]ch. 20:6
25:9 [m]Prov. 10:22
25:11 [n]2 Ki. 14:7
25:14 [o]See ch. 28:23 [p]Ex. 20:3,5
25:15 [q]Ps. 96:5 [r]ver:11
25:16 [s]1 Sam. 2:25
25:17 [t]2 Ki. 14:8,9
25:20 [u]1 Ki. 12:15 ch. 22:7 [v]ver. 14
25:23 [w]See ch. 21:17 & 22:1,6

[n] Heb. *band* [o] Heb. *to their place* [p] Heb. *in heat of anger* [q] Heb. *the sons of the band* [r] Heb. *counselled* [s] Or, *furze bush,* or, *thorn* [t] Heb. *a beast of the field* [u] Heb. *smitten*

25:7 LET NOT THE ARMY OF ISRAEL GO WITH THEE. The writer of Chronicles emphasizes God's condemnation of alliances that demonstrated Judah's failure to trust in God (cf. 16:2–9; 22:5; Ezra 4:3). An alliance with those whom God opposes (i.e., the enemies of God) could result in God causing defeat for His people (vv. 7–8). This truth was often reiterated by God's prophets (see Is. 57:13; Jer. 17:5–8; 39:18).

[v]the corner gate, four hundred cubits.
24 And *he took* all the gold and the
silver, and all the vessels that were
found in the house of God with Obed-
edom, and the treasures of the king's
house, the hostages also, and returned
to Samaria.
25 ¶ [x]And Amaziah the son of Jo-
ash king of Judah lived after the death
of Joash son of Jehoahaz king of Israel
fifteen years.
26 Now the rest of the acts of Ama-
ziah, first and last, behold, *are* they not
written in the book of the kings of Ju-
dah and Israel?
27 ¶ Now after the time that Amazi-
ah did turn away [w]from following the
LORD they [x]made a conspiracy against
him in Jerusalem; and he fled to La-
chish: but they sent to Lachish after
him, and slew him there.
28 And they brought him upon
horses, and buried him with his fathers
in the city of [y]Judah.

Uzziah, king of Judah

26:1–4pp — 2 Ki. 14:21–22; 15:1–3
26:21–23pp — 2 Ki. 15:5–7

26 THEN ALL the people of Judah
took [y]Uzziah,[z] who *was* six-
teen years old, and made him king in
the room of his father Amaziah.
2 He built Eloth, and restored it to
Judah, after that the king slept with his
fathers.
3 Sixteen years old *was* Uzziah
when he began to reign, and he reigned
fifty and two years in Jerusalem. His
mother's name also *was* Jecoliah of Je-
rusalem.
4 And he did *that which was* right in
the sight of the LORD, according to all
that his father Amaziah did.
5 And [z]he sought God in the days
of Zechariah, who [a]had understand-
ing [a]in the visions of God: and as long
as he sought the LORD, God made him
to prosper.
6 And he went forth and [b]warred
against the Philistines, and brake
down the wall of Gath, and the wall of
Jabneh, and the wall of Ashdod, and
built cities [b]about Ashdod, and
among the Philistines.
7 And God helped him against [c]the
Philistines, and against the Arabians
that dwelt in Gur-baal, and the Mehu-
nims.
8 And the Ammonites [d]gave gifts
to Uzziah: and his name [c]spread
abroad *even* to the entering in of Egypt;
for he strengthened *himself* exceed-
ingly.
9 Moreover Uzziah built towers in
Jerusalem at the [e]corner gate, and at
the valley gate, and at the turning *of
the wall,* and [d]fortified them.
10 Also he built towers in the
desert, and [e]digged many wells: for
he had much cattle, both in the low
country, and in the plains: husband-
men *also,* and vine dressers in the
mountains, and in [f]Carmel: for he
loved [g]husbandry.
11 Moreover Uzziah had an host of
fighting men, that went out to war by
bands, according to the number of their
account by the hand of Jeiel the scribe
and Maaseiah the ruler, under the
hand of Hananiah, *one* of the king's
captains.
12 The whole number of the chief of
the fathers of the mighty men of valour
were two thousand and six hundred.
13 And under their hand *was* [h]an
army, three hundred thousand and sev-
en thousand and five hundred, that
made war with mighty power, to help
the king against the enemy.
14 And Uzziah prepared for them
throughout all the host shields, and
spears, and helmets, and habergeons,
and bows, and [i]slings *to cast* stones.
15 And he made in Jerusalem en-
gines, invented by cunning men, to be
on the towers and upon the bulwarks,
to shoot arrows and great stones with-

25:25 [x]2 Ki. 14:17 **26:1** [y]2 Ki. 14:21,22 & 15:1 **26:5** [z]See ch. 24:2 [a]Gen. 41:15 Dan. 1:17 & 10:1 **26:6** [b]Is. 14:29 **26:7** [c]ch. 21:16 **26:8** [d]2 Sam. 8:2 ch. 17:11 **26:9** [e]2 Ki. 14:13 Neh. 3:13,19,32 Zech. 14:10

[v]Heb. *the gate of it that looketh* [w]Heb. *from after* [x]Heb. *conspired a conspiracy* [y]i.e. *The city of David* [z]Or, *Azariah* [a]Heb. *in the seeing of God* [b]Or, *in* the country *of Ashdod* [c]Heb. *went* [d]Or, *repaired* [e]Or, *cut out many cisterns* [f]Or, *Fruitful fields* [g]Heb. *ground* [h]Heb. *the power of an army* [i]Heb. *stones of slings*

26:1 UZZIAH. Uzziah's reign is divided into two parts: the years he sought the Lord and the years he was unfaithful to the Lord. The Bible emphasizes that seeking God results in blessing and help, whereas failure to seek God results in spiritual decline and judgment (see vv. 5–7 and 16–20; see 15:2, note).

26:5 AS LONG AS HE SOUGHT THE LORD. As long as Uzziah continued to seek the Lord and follow His righteous ways, he was given grace, strength, and help to rule as king of Judah (see 14:4, note).

al. And his name [j]spread far abroad; for he was marvellously helped, till he was strong.

16 ¶ But [f]when he was strong, his heart was [g]lifted up to *his* destruction: for he transgressed against the LORD his God, and [h]went into the temple of the LORD to burn incense upon the altar of incense.

17 And [i]Azariah the priest went in after him, and with him fourscore priests of the LORD, *that were* valiant men:

18 And they withstood Uzziah the king, and said unto him, *It* [j]*appertaineth* not unto thee, Uzziah, to burn incense unto the LORD, but to the [k]priests the sons of Aaron, that are consecrated to burn incense: go out of the sanctuary; for thou hast trespassed; neither *shall it be* for thine honour from the LORD God.

19 Then Uzziah was wroth, and *had* a censer in his hand to burn incense: and while he was wroth with the priests, [l]the leprosy even rose up in his forehead before the priests in the house of the LORD, from beside the incense altar.

20 And Azariah the chief priest, and all the priests, looked upon him, and, behold, he *was* leprous in his forehead, and they thrust him out from thence; yea, himself [m]hasted also to go out, because the LORD had smitten him.

21 [n]And Uzziah the king was a leper unto the day of his death, and dwelt in a [o]several[k] house, *being* a leper; for he was cut off from the house of the LORD: and Jotham his son *was* over the king's house, judging the people of the land.

22 ¶ Now the rest of the acts of Uzziah, first and last, did [p]Isaiah the prophet, the son of Amoz, write.

23 [q]So Uzziah slept with his fathers, and they buried him with his fathers in the field of the burial which *belonged* to the kings; for they said, He *is* a leper: and Jotham his son reigned in his stead.

Jotham, king of Judah

27:1–4,7–9pp — 2 Ki. 15:33–38

27 JOTHAM [r]*WAS* twenty and five years old when he began to reign, and he reigned sixteen years in Jerusalem. His mother's name also *was* Jerushah, the daughter of Zadok.

2 And he did *that which was* right in the sight of the LORD, according to all that his father Uzziah did: howbeit he entered not into the temple of the LORD. And [s]the people did yet corruptly.

3 He built the high gate of the house of the LORD, and on the wall of [l]Ophel he built much.

4 Moreover he built cities in the mountains of Judah, and in the forests he built castles and towers.

5 ¶ He fought also with the king of the Ammonites, and prevailed against them. And the children of Ammon gave him the same year an hundred talents of silver, and ten thousand measures of wheat, and ten thousand of barley. [m]So much did the children of Ammon pay unto him, both the second year, and the third.

6 So Jotham became mighty, because he [n]prepared his ways before the LORD his God.

7 ¶ Now the rest of the acts of Jotham, and all his wars, and his ways, lo, they *are* written in the book of the kings of Israel and Judah.

8 He was five and twenty years old when he began to reign, and reigned sixteen years in Jerusalem.

9 ¶ [t]And Jotham slept with his fathers, and they buried him in the city of David: and Ahaz his son reigned in his stead.

Ahaz, king of Judah

28:1–27pp — 2 Ki. 16:1–20

28 AHAZ [u]*WAS* twenty years old when he began to reign, and he reigned sixteen years in Jerusalem: but he did not *that which was* right in the sight of the LORD, like David his father:

2 For he walked in the ways of the kings of Israel, and made also [v]molten images for [w]Baalim.

3 Moreover he [o]burnt incense in [x]the valley of the son of Hinnom, and burnt [y]his children in the fire, after the abominations of the heathen whom

26:16 [f]Deut. 32:15 [g]Deut. 8:14 ch. 25:19 [h]2 Ki. 16:12,13 **26:17** [i]1 Chr. 6:10 **26:18** [j]Num. 16:40 & 18:7 [k]Ex. 30:7,8 **26:19** [l]Num. 12:10 2 Ki. 5:27 **26:20** [m]As Esth. 6:12 **26:21** [n]2 Ki. 15:5 [o]Lev. 13:46 Num. 5:2 **26:22** [p]Is. 1:1 **26:23** [q]2 Ki. 15:7 Is. 6:1 **27:1** [r]2 Ki. 15:32 **27:2** [s]2 Ki. 15:35 **27:9** [t]2 Ki. 15:38 **28:1** [u]2 Ki. 16:2 **28:2** [v]Ex. 34:17 Lev. 19:4 [w]Judg. 2:11 **28:3** [x]2 Ki. 23:10 [y]Lev. 18:21 2 Ki. 16:3 ch. 33:6

[j] Heb. *went forth* [k] Heb. *free* [l] Or, *The tower;* see ch. 33:14; Neh. 3:26 [m] Heb. *This* [n] Or, *established* [o] Or, *offered sacrifice*

26:16 WHEN HE WAS STRONG, HIS HEART WAS LIFTED UP. Uzziah failed to realize that all he had accomplished had been with the help of God (vv. 5,7) and others (vv. 8,11–13); the result was pride, and it led him into the sins of presumption and unfaithfulness (see Phil. 2:3, note).

the LORD had cast out before the children of Israel.

4 He sacrificed also and burnt incense in the high places, and on the hills, and under every green tree.

5 Wherefore [z]the LORD his God delivered him into the hand of the king of Syria; and they [a]smote him, and carried away a great multitude of them captives, and brought *them* to [p]Damascus. And he was also delivered into the hand of the king of Israel, who smote him with a great slaughter.

6 ¶ For [b]Pekah the son of Remaliah slew in Judah an hundred and twenty thousand in one day, *which were* all [q]valiant men; because they had forsaken the LORD God of their fathers.

7 And Zichri, a mighty man of Ephraim, slew Maaseiah the king's son, and Azrikam the governor of the house, and Elkanah *that was* [r]next to the king.

8 And the children of Israel carried away captive of their [c]brethren two hundred thousand, women, sons, and daughters, and took also away much spoil from them, and brought the spoil to Samaria.

9 But a prophet of the LORD was there, whose name *was* Oded: and he went out before the host that came to Samaria, and said unto them, Behold, [d]because the LORD God of your fathers was wroth with Judah, he hath delivered them into your hand, and ye have slain them in a rage *that* [e]reacheth up unto heaven.

10 And now ye purpose to keep under the children of Judah and Jerusalem for [f]bondmen and bondwomen unto you: *but are there* not with you, even with you, sins against the LORD your God?

11 Now hear me therefore, and deliver the captives again, which ye have taken captive of your brethren: [g]for the fierce wrath of the LORD *is* upon you.

28:5 [z]Is. 7:1 [a]2 Ki. 16:5,6
28:6 [b]2 Ki. 15:27
28:8 [c]ch. 11:4
28:9 [d]Is. 10:5 & 47:6 Ezek. 25:12,15 & 26:2 Obad. 10 Zech. 1:15 [e]Ezra 9:6 Rev. 18:5
28:10 [f]Lev. 25:39,42,43, 46
28:11 [g]Jas. 2:13

28:15 [h]ver. 12 [i]2 Ki. 6:22 Luke 6:27 Rom. 12:20 [j]Deut. 34:3 Judg. 1:16
28:16 [k]2 Ki. 16:7
28:18 [l]Ezek. 16:27,57
28:19 [m]ch. 21:2

12 Then certain of the heads of the children of Ephraim, Azariah the son of Johanan, Berechiah the son of Meshillemoth, and Jehizkiah the son of Shallum, and Amasa the son of Hadlai, stood up against them that came from the war,

13 And said unto them, Ye shall not bring in the captives hither: for whereas we have offended against the LORD *already,* ye intend to add *more* to our sins and to our trespass: for our trespass is great, and *there is* fierce wrath against Israel.

14 So the armed men left the captives and the spoil before the princes and all the congregation.

15 And the men [h]which were expressed by name rose up, and took the captives, and with the spoil clothed all that were naked among them, and arrayed them, and shod them, and [i]gave them to eat and to drink, and anointed them, and carried all the feeble of them upon asses, and brought them to Jericho, [j]the city of palm trees, to their brethren: then they returned to Samaria.

16 ¶ [k]At that time did king Ahaz send unto the kings of Assyria to help him.

17 For again the Edomites had come and smitten Judah, and carried away [s]captives.

18 [l]The Philistines also had invaded the cities of the low country, and of the south of Judah, and had taken Beth-shemesh, and Ajalon, and Gederoth, and Shocho with the villages thereof, and Timnah with the villages thereof, Gimzo also and the villages thereof: and they dwelt there.

19 For the LORD brought Judah low because of Ahaz king of [m]Israel; for he

[p]Heb. *Darmesek* [q]Heb. *sons of valour* [r]Heb. *the second to the king* [s]Heb. *a captivity*

28:3 BURNT HIS CHILDREN IN THE FIRE. King Ahaz was so given over to idolatry and occult practices that he destroyed his own sons in fire as a sacrifice to heathen gods (see Lev. 20:1–5; Jer. 7:31–32; see 2 Ki. 16:3, note). Children today can also be ruthlessly destroyed – physically through the sins of abortion and child abuse, and spiritually by parents who fail to teach them godly ways based on Scripture (see Deut. 6:7, note) or to separate and protect them from the ungodliness of the world (see article on THE CHRISTIAN'S RELATIONSHIP TO THE WORLD, p. 2004).

28:19 HE MADE JUDAH NAKED. The word translated "naked" is also used to describe Israel's sin before the golden calf (Ex. 32:25). The verb means "to become ungovernable," "to make naked," or "to cast off restraint"; it describes the lifestyle of the ungodly, who cast off moral restraint in order to indulge in sins involving unchastity and nakedness (see Ex. 32:6, note; 1 Thes. 4:3–7, note; see article on STANDARDS OF SEXUAL MORALITY, p. 1964).

[n]made Judah naked, and transgressed sore against the LORD.

20 And [o]Tilgath-pilneser king of Assyria came unto him, and distressed him, but strengthened him not.

21 For Ahaz took away a portion *out* of the house of the LORD, and *out* of the house of the king, and of the princes, and gave *it* unto the king of Assyria: but he helped him not.

22 ¶ And in the time of his distress did he trespass yet more against the LORD: this *is that* king Ahaz.

23 For [p]he sacrificed unto the gods of [t]Damascus, which smote him: and he said, Because the gods of the kings of Syria help them, *therefore* will I sacrifice to them, that [q]they may help me. But they were the ruin of him, and of all Israel.

24 And Ahaz gathered together the vessels of the house of God, and cut in pieces the vessels of the house of God, [r]and shut up the doors of the house of the LORD, and he made him altars in every corner of Jerusalem.

25 And in every several city of Judah he made high places [u]to burn incense unto other gods, and provoked to anger the LORD God of his fathers.

26 ¶ [s]Now the rest of his acts and of all his ways, first and last, behold, they *are* written in the book of the kings of Judah and Israel.

27 And Ahaz slept with his fathers, and they buried him in the city, *even* in Jerusalem: but they brought him not into the sepulchres of the kings of Israel: and Hezekiah his son reigned in his stead.

Hezekiah cleanses the temple

29:1–2pp — 2 Ki. 18:2–3

29 HEZEKIAH [t]BEGAN to reign *when he was* five and twenty years old, and he reigned nine and twenty years in Jerusalem. And his mother's name *was* Abijah, the daughter [u]of Zechariah.

2 And he did *that which was* right in the sight of the LORD, according to all that David his father had done.

3 ¶ He in the first year of his reign, in the first month, [v]opened the doors of the house of the LORD, and repaired them.

4 And he brought in the priests and the Levites, and gathered them together into the east street,

5 And said unto them, Hear me, ye Levites, [w]sanctify now yourselves, and sanctify the house of the LORD God of your fathers, and carry forth the filthiness out of the holy *place*.

6 For our fathers have trespassed, and done *that which was* evil in the eyes of the LORD our God, and have forsaken him, and have [x]turned away their faces from the habitation of the LORD, and [v]turned *their* backs.

7 [y]Also they have shut up the doors of the porch, and put out the lamps, and have not burned incense nor offered burnt offerings in the holy *place* unto the God of Israel.

8 Wherefore the [z]wrath of the LORD was upon Judah and Jerusalem, and he hath delivered them to [a]trouble,[w] to astonishment, and to [b]hissing, as ye see with your eyes.

9 For, lo, [c]our fathers have fallen by the sword, and our sons and our daughters and our wives *are* in captivity for this.

10 Now *it is* in mine heart to make [d]a covenant with the LORD God of Israel, that his fierce wrath may turn away from us.

28:19 [n]Ex. 32:25
28:20 [o]2 Ki. 15:29 & 16:7-9
28:23 [p]See ch. 25:14 [q]Jer. 44:17,18
28:24 [r]See ch. 29:3,7
28:26 [s]2 Ki. 16:19,20
29:1 [t]2 Ki. 18:1
[u]ch. 26:5
29:3 [v]ver. 7 See ch. 28:24
29:5 [w]1 Chr. 15:12 ch. 35:6
29:6 [x]Jer. 2:27 Ezek. 8:16
29:7 [y]ch. 28:24
29:8 [z]ch. 24:18 [a]Deut. 28:25 [b]1 Ki. 9:8 Jer. 18:16 & 19:8 & 25:9,18 & 29:18
29:9 [c]ch. 28:5,6,8,17
29:10 [d]ch. 15:12

[t] Heb. *Darmesek* [u] Or, *to offer* [v] Heb. *given the neck* [w] Heb. *commotion*

29:1 HEZEKIAH. See 2 Ki. 18:5, note.

29:5 SANCTIFY NOW YOURSELVES ... CARRY FORTH THE FILTHINESS. In order for God's people to experience revival and renewal, four things are indispensable. (1) Confession of specific sins. We must recognize those areas of our lives where we have departed from God's will and word and must confess these specific sins before God (vv. 6–7; see Ps. 51:3; cf. Mat. 5:24).

(2) Cleansing the house of the Lord (vv. 5,18). The church is God's house under the new covenant (2 Cor. 6:16; Eph. 2:21–22; 1 Tim. 3:15). Whatever in the church's doctrine, worship, and lifestyle that clearly offends the will of God as revealed in Scripture must be removed. Likewise, the individual believer, as the temple of the Holy Spirit (1 Cor. 6:19), must be cleansed from all unrighteousness (see 1 John 1:9, note; see articles on THE TEMPLE, p. 654, and SANCTIFICATION, p. 1982).

(3) Renewal of the covenant (vv. 10–11). We must renew our dedication to God, His kingdom, and His righteous cause on earth, and we must express a sincere desire to turn from the evil of the world and to resist sin.

(4) Proclaim a blood sacrifice for atonement (vv. 20–24). We must appropriate by faith the blood atonement of Jesus Christ, who suffered on the cross to save and sanctify His people (see Heb. 9:11–14; see 1 Cor. 10:16, note).

11 My sons, [x]be not now negligent: for the LORD hath [e]chosen you to stand before him, to serve him, and that ye should minister unto him, and [y]burn incense.

12 ¶ Then the Levites arose, Mahath the son of Amasai, and Joel the son of Azariah, of the sons of the Kohathites: and of the sons of Merari, Kish the son of Abdi, and Azariah the son of Jehalelel: and of the Gershonites; Joah the son of Zimmah, and Eden the son of Joah:

13 And of the sons of Elizaphan; Shimri, and Jeiel: and of the sons of Asaph; Zechariah, and Mattaniah:

14 And of the sons of Heman; Jehiel, and Shimei: and of the sons of Jeduthun; Shemaiah, and Uzziel.

15 And they gathered their brethren, and [f]sanctified themselves, and came, according to the commandment of the king, [g]by[z] the words of the LORD, [h]to cleanse the house of the LORD.

16 And the priests went into the inner part of the house of the LORD, to cleanse *it,* and brought out all the uncleanness that they found in the temple of the LORD into the court of the house of the LORD. And the Levites took *it,* to carry *it* out abroad into the brook Kidron.

17 Now they began on the first *day* of the first month to sanctify, and on the eighth day of the month came they to the porch of the LORD: so they sanctified the house of the LORD in eight days; and in the sixteenth day of the first month they made an end.

18 Then they went in to Hezekiah the king, and said, We have cleansed all the house of the LORD, and the altar of burnt offering, with all the vessels thereof, and the showbread table, with all the vessels thereof.

19 Moreover all the vessels, which king Ahaz in his reign did [i]cast away in his transgression, have we prepared and sanctified, and, behold, they *are* before the altar of the LORD.

20 ¶ Then Hezekiah the king rose early, and gathered the rulers of the city, and went up to the house of the LORD.

21 And they brought seven bullocks, and seven rams, and seven lambs, and seven he goats, for a [j]sin offering for the kingdom, and for the sanctuary, and for Judah. And he commanded the priests the sons of Aaron to offer *them* on the altar of the LORD.

22 So they killed the bullocks, and the priests received the blood, and [k]sprinkled *it* on the altar: likewise, when they had killed the rams, they sprinkled the blood upon the altar: they killed also the lambs, and they sprinkled the blood upon the altar.

23 And they brought [a]forth the he goats *for* the sin offering before the king and the congregation; and they laid their [l]hands upon them:

24 And the priests killed them, and they made reconciliation with their blood upon the altar, [m]to make an atonement for all Israel: for the king commanded *that* the burnt offering and the sin offering *should be made* for all Israel.

25 [n]And he set the Levites in the house of the LORD with cymbals, with psalteries, and with harps, [o]according to the commandment of David, and of [p]Gad the king's seer, and Nathan the prophet: [q]for *so was* the commandment [b]of the LORD [c]by his prophets.

26 And the Levites stood with the instruments [r]of David, and the priests with [s]the trumpets.

27 And Hezekiah commanded to offer the burnt offering upon the altar. And [d]when the burnt offering began, [t]the song of the LORD began *also* with the trumpets, and with the [e]instruments *ordained* by David king of Israel.

28 And all the congregation worshipped, and the [f]singers sang, and the trumpeters sounded: *and* all *this continued* until the burnt offering was finished.

29 And when they had made an end of offering, [u]the king and all that were [g]present with him bowed themselves, and worshipped.

30 Moreover Hezekiah the king and the princes commanded the Levites to sing praise unto the LORD with the words of David, and of Asaph the seer. And they sang praises with gladness, and they bowed their heads and worshipped.

31 Then Hezekiah answered and said, Now ye have [v]consecrated[h]

29:11 [e]Num. 3:6 & 8:14 & 18:2,6
29:15 [f]ver. 5 [g]ch. 30:12 [h]1 Chr. 23:28
29:19 [i]ch. 28:24
29:21 [j]Lev. 4:3,14
29:22 [k]Lev. 8:14,15,19, 24 Heb. 9:21
29:23 [l]Lev. 4:15,24
29:24 [m]Lev. 14:20
29:25 [n]1 Chr. 16:4 & 25:6 [o]1 Chr. 23:5 & 25:1 ch. 8:14 [p]2 Sam. 24:11 [q]ch. 30:12
29:26 [r]1 Chr. 23:5 Amos 6:5 [s]Num. 10:8,10 1 Chr. 15:24 & 16:6
29:27 [t]ch. 23:18
29:29 [u]ch. 20:18
29:31 [v]ch. 13:9

[x] Or, *be not now deceived* [y] Or, *offer sacrifice* [z] Or, *in the business of the LORD* [a] Heb. *near* [b] Heb. *by the hand of the LORD* [c] Heb. *by the hand of* [d] Heb. *in the time* [e] Heb. *hands of instruments* [f] Heb. *song* [g] Heb. *found* [h] Or, *filled your hand*

yourselves unto the LORD, come near and bring sacrifices and [w]thank offerings into the house of the LORD. And the congregation brought in sacrifices and thank offerings; and as many as were of a free heart burnt offerings.

32 And the number of the burnt offerings, which the congregation brought, was threescore and ten bullocks, an hundred rams, *and* two hundred lambs: all these *were* for a burnt offering to the LORD.

33 And the consecrated things *were* six hundred oxen and three thousand sheep.

34 But the priests were too few, so that they could not flay all the burnt offerings: wherefore [x]their brethren the Levites [i]did help them, till the work was ended, and until the *other* priests had sanctified themselves: [y]for the Levites *were* more [z]upright in heart to sanctify themselves than the priests.

35 And also the burnt offerings *were* in abundance, with [a]the fat of the peace offerings, and [b]the drink offerings for *every* burnt offering. So the service of the house of the LORD was set in order.

36 And Hezekiah rejoiced, and all the people, that God had prepared the people: for the thing was *done* suddenly.

The observance of the Passover

30 AND HEZEKIAH sent to all Israel and Judah, and wrote letters also to Ephraim and Manasseh, that they should come to the house of the LORD at Jerusalem, to keep the passover unto the LORD God of Israel.

2 For the king had taken counsel, and his princes, and all the congregation in Jerusalem, to keep the passover in the second [c]month.

3 For they could not keep it [d]at that time, [e]because the priests had not sanctified themselves sufficiently, neither had the people gathered themselves together to Jerusalem.

4 And the thing [j]pleased the king and all the congregation.

5 So they established a decree to make proclamation throughout all Israel, from Beer-sheba even to Dan, that they should come to keep the passover unto the LORD God of Israel at Jerusalem: for they had not done *it* of a long *time in such sort* as it was written.

6 So the posts went with the letters [k]from the king and his princes throughout all Israel and Judah, and according to the commandment of the king, saying, Ye children of Israel, [f]turn again unto the LORD God of Abraham, Isaac, and Israel, and he will return to the remnant of you, that are escaped out of the hand of [g]the kings of Assyria.

7 And be not ye [h]like your fathers, and like your brethren, which trespassed against the LORD God of their fathers, *who* therefore [i]gave them up to desolation, as ye see.

8 Now [l]be ye not [j]stiffnecked, as your fathers *were, but* [k]yield[m] yourselves unto the LORD, and enter into his sanctuary, which he hath sanctified for ever: and serve the LORD your God,

29:31 [w]Lev. 7:12 **29:34** [x]ch. 35:11 [y]ch. 30:3 [z]Ps. 7:10 **29:35** [a]Lev. 3:16 [b]Num. 15:5,7,10

30:2 [c]Num. 9:10,11 **30:3** [d]Ex. 12:6,18 [e]ch. 29:34 **30:6** [f]Jer. 4:1 Joel 2:13 [g]2 Ki. 15:19 **30:7** [h]Ezek. 20:18 [i]ch. 29:8 **30:8** [j]Deut. 10:16 [k]1 Chr. 29:24 Ezra 10:19

i Heb. *strengthened them* j Heb. *was right in the eyes of the king* k Heb. *from the hand* l Heb. *harden not your necks* m Heb. *give the hand*

30:6 TURN AGAIN UNTO THE LORD GOD. Turning from sinful ways to God is an essential prerequisite of revival (cf. Zech. 1:4). The verb "turn" occurs four times in vv. 6–9, implying that God's people were in a backslidden state, attached more to the ways of the world than to God's ways. The message of repentance found here is applicable to all churches that have left their first love, accepted unbiblical doctrine, and compromised with the world (see article on CHRIST'S MESSAGE TO THE SEVEN CHURCHES, p. 2036).

30:8 YIELD YOURSELVES UNTO THE LORD. Hezekiah emphasizes four truths concerning genuine repentance. (1) God's people must turn to Him with the desire to forsake sin and confess Him as Lord if they want to experience His favor (vv. 6–8). God will not return and bless His people while they take pleasure in sin (Hos. 5:4, 15).

(2) God's people must turn to Him with the sincere intention of obeying His commands. Unless God's people forsake the world's sinful ways and pursue purity of heart and obedience to His word, God will bring calamity and destruction upon them and their families (see v. 7; Mat. 5:13, note).

(3) God's people must turn to Him in submission, worship, and service if they hope to escape His burning anger toward sin. The words "yield yourselves unto the LORD" are literally "to give the hand to the LORD." The hand is given as a pledge of absolute loyalty and fidelity to God and His righteous ways (cf. 2 Ki. 10:15; Ezra 10:19; Ezek. 17:18).

(4) God's people must turn to Him in persevering prayer if they are to experience again His grace and compassion (vv. 9,18–20,27; see 14:4, note).

[l]that the fierceness of his wrath may turn away from you.

9 For if ye turn again unto the LORD, your brethren and your children *shall find* [m]compassion before them that lead them captive, so that they shall come again into this land: for the LORD your God *is* [n]gracious and merciful, and will not turn away *his* face from you, if ye [o]return unto him.

10 So the posts passed from city to city through the country of Ephraim and Manasseh even unto Zebulun: but [p]they laughed them to scorn, and mocked them.

11 Nevertheless [q]divers of Asher and Manasseh and of Zebulun humbled themselves, and came to Jerusalem.

12 Also in Judah [r]the hand of God was to give them one heart to do the commandment of the king and of the princes, [s]by the word of the LORD.

13 ¶ And there assembled at Jerusalem much people to keep the feast of unleavened bread in the second month, a very great congregation.

14 And they arose and took away the [t]altars that *were* in Jerusalem, and all the altars for incense took they away, and cast *them* into the brook Kidron.

15 Then they killed the passover on the fourteenth *day* of the second month: and the priests and the Levites were [u]ashamed, and sanctified themselves, and brought in the burnt offerings into the house of the LORD.

16 And they stood in [n]their place after their manner, according to the law of Moses the man of God: the priests sprinkled the blood, *which they received* of the hand of the Levites.

17 For *there were* many in the congregation that were not sanctified: [v]therefore the Levites had the charge of the killing of the passovers for every one *that was* not clean, to sanctify *them* unto the LORD.

18 For a multitude of the people, *even* [w]many of Ephraim, and Manasseh, Issachar, and Zebulun, had not cleansed themselves, [x]yet did they eat the passover otherwise than it was written. But Hezekiah prayed for them, saying, The good LORD pardon every one

19 *That* [y]prepareth his heart to seek God, the LORD God of his fathers, though *he be* not *cleansed* according to the purification of the sanctuary.

20 And the LORD hearkened to Hezekiah, and healed the people. Ps. 6:1-3

21 And the children of Israel that were [o]present at Jerusalem kept [z]the feast of unleavened bread seven days with great gladness: and the Levites and the priests praised the LORD day by day, *singing* with [p]loud instruments unto the LORD.

22 And Hezekiah spake [a]comfortably[q] unto all the Levites [b]that taught the good knowledge of the LORD: and they did eat throughout the feast seven days, offering peace offerings, and [c]making confession to the LORD God of their fathers.

23 And the whole assembly took counsel to keep [d]other seven days: and they kept *other* seven days with gladness.

24 For Hezekiah king of Judah [e]did[r] give to the congregation a thousand bullocks and seven thousand sheep; and the princes gave to the congregation a thousand bullocks and ten thousand sheep: and a great number of priests [f]sanctified themselves.

25 And all the congregation of Judah, with the priests and the Levites, and all the congregation [g]that came out of Israel, and the strangers that came out of the land of Israel, and that dwelt in Judah, rejoiced.

26 So there was great joy in Jerusalem: for since the time of Solomon the son of David king of Israel *there was* not the like in Jerusalem.

27 ¶ Then the priests the Levites arose and [h]blessed the people: and their voice was heard, and their prayer came *up* to [i]his[s] holy dwellingplace, *even* unto heaven.

31 NOW WHEN all this was finished, all Israel that were [o]present went out to the cities of Judah, and [j]brake the [k]images[t] in pieces, and cut down the groves, and threw down the high places and the altars out of all Judah and Benjamin, in Ephraim also and Manasseh, [u]until they had utterly destroyed them all. Then all the children of Israel returned, every man to his possession, into their own cities.

30:8 [l]ch. 29:10 **30:9** [m]Ps. 106:46 [n]Ex. 34:6 [o]Is. 55:7 **30:10** [p]ch. 36:16 **30:11** [q]ver. 18,21 ch. 11:16 **30:12** [r]Phil. 2:13 [s]ch. 29:25 **30:14** [t]ch. 28:24 **30:15** [u]ch. 29:34 **30:17** [v]ch. 29:34 **30:18** [w]ver. 1,11 [x]Ex. 12:43 **30:19** [y]ch. 19:3

30:21 [z]Ex. 12:15 & 13:6 **30:22** [a]Is. 40:2 [b]Deut. 33:10 ch. 17:9 & 35:3 [c]Ezra 10:11 **30:23** [d]See 1 Ki. 8:65 **30:24** [e]ch. 35:7,8 [f]ch. 29:34 **30:25** [g]ver. 11,18 **30:27** [h]Num. 6:23 [i]Ps. 68:5 **31:1** [j]2 Ki. 18:4 [k]ch. 30:14

[n] Heb. *their standing* [o] Heb. *found* [p] Heb. *instruments of strength* [q] Heb. *to the heart of all* [r] Heb. *lifted up*, or, *offered* [s] Heb. *the habitation of his holiness* [t] Heb. *statues* [u] Heb. *until to make an end*

Hezekiah's reforms

31:20–21pp — 2 Ki. 18:5–7

2 ¶ And Hezekiah appointed [l]the courses of the priests and the Levites after their courses, every man according to his service, the priests and Levites [m]for burnt offerings and for peace offerings, to minister, and to give thanks, and to praise in the gates of the tents of the LORD.

3 *He appointed* also the king's portion of his substance for the burnt offerings, *to wit,* for the morning and evening burnt offerings, and the burnt offerings for the sabbaths, and for the new moons, and for the set feasts, as *it is* written in [n]the law of the LORD.

4 Moreover he commanded the people that dwelt in Jerusalem to give the [o]portion of the priests and the Levites, that they might be encouraged in [p]the law of the LORD.

5 ¶ And as soon as the commandment [v]came abroad, the children of Israel brought in abundance [q]the firstfruits of corn, wine, and oil, and [w]honey, and of all the increase of the field; and the tithe of all *things* brought they in abundantly.

6 And *concerning* the children of Israel and Judah, that dwelt in the cities of Judah, they also brought in the tithe of oxen and sheep, and the [r]tithe of holy things which were consecrated unto the LORD their God, and laid *them* [x]by heaps.

7 In the third month they began to lay the foundation of the heaps, and finished *them* in the seventh month.

8 And when Hezekiah and the princes came and saw the heaps, they blessed the LORD, and his people Israel.

9 Then Hezekiah questioned with the priests and the Levites concerning the heaps.

10 And Azariah the chief priest of the house of Zadok answered him, and said, [s]Since *the people* began to bring the offerings into the house of the LORD, we have had enough to eat, and have left plenty: for the LORD hath blessed his people; and that which is left *is* this great store.

11 ¶ Then Hezekiah commanded to prepare [y]chambers in the house of the LORD; and they prepared *them,*

12 And brought in the offerings and the tithes and the dedicated *things* faithfully: [t]over which Cononiah the Levite *was* ruler, and Shimei his brother *was* the next.

13 And Jehiel, and Azaziah, and Nahath, and Asahel, and Jerimoth, and Jozabad, and Eliel, and Ismachiah, and Mahath, and Benaiah, *were* overseers [z]under the hand of Cononiah and Shimei his brother, at the commandment of Hezekiah the king, and Azariah the ruler of the house of God.

14 And Kore the son of Imnah the Levite, the porter toward the east, *was* over the freewill offerings of God, to distribute the oblations of the LORD, and the most holy things.

15 And [a]next him *were* Eden, and Miniamin, and Jeshua, and Shemaiah, Amariah, and Shecaniah, in [u]the cities of the priests, in *their* set office, to give to their brethren by courses, as well to the great as to the small:

16 Beside their genealogy of males, from three years old and upward, *even* unto every one that entereth into the house of the LORD, his daily portion for their service in their charges according to their courses;

17 Both to the genealogy of the priests by the house of their fathers, and the Levites [v]from twenty years old and upward, in their charges by their courses;

18 And to the genealogy of all their

31:2 [l]1 Chr. 23:6 & 24:1 [m]1 Chr. 23:30,31
31:3 [n]Num. 28 & 29
31:4 [o]Num. 18:8 Neh. 13:10 [p]Mal. 2:7
31:5 [q]Ex. 22:29 Neh. 13:12
31:6 [r]Lev. 27:30 Deut. 14:28
31:10 [s]Mal. 3:10
31:12 [t]Neh. 13:13
31:15 [u]Josh. 21:9
31:17 [v]1 Chr. 23:24,27

[v]Heb. *brake forth* [w]Or, *dates* [x]Heb. *heaps, heaps* [y]Or, *storehouses* [z]Heb. *at the hand* [a]Heb. *at his hand*

31:4 THAT THEY MIGHT BE ENCOURAGED IN THE LAW. Hezekiah commanded the people to give the firstfruits and a tithe of all their produce to the priests and Levites (see Ex. 23:19; Lev. 27:30–33; Num. 18:12,20–24; Deut. 26), thus enabling the priests to devote themselves more fully to God and the ministry of His Word (see article on TITHES AND OFFERINGS, p. 1388). Likewise, under the new covenant, spiritual leaders called by God must be paid from the tithes and offerings of God's people in order that they might "give [themselves] continually to prayer, and to the ministry of the word" (Acts 6:4; see Gal. 6:6–10, note).

31:10 THE LORD HATH BLESSED HIS PEOPLE. As a condition for experiencing the blessing of God, we must be both willing and committed to give of our means for God's work and ministry, locally and abroad (cf. 1 Cor. 9:14; Phil. 4:15–18). Unwillingness to do so is a sign that our love for God and His cause is less than complete. God wants us to serve Him, not money (cf. Mat. 6:24; see 2 Cor. 8—9, notes).

little ones, their wives, and their sons,
and their daughters, through all the
congregation: for in their [b]set office
they sanctified themselves in holiness:
19 Also of the sons of Aaron the
priests, *which were* in [w]the fields of the
suburbs of their cities, in every several
city, the men that were [x]expressed by
name, to give portions to all the males
among the priests, and to all that were
reckoned by genealogies among the
Levites.
20 ¶ And thus did Hezekiah
throughout all Judah, and [y]wrought
that which was good and right and truth
before the LORD his God.
21 And in every work that he began
in the service of the house of God, and
in the law, and in the commandments,
to seek his God, he did *it* with all his
heart, and prospered.

The defeat of Sennacherib

32:9–19pp — 2 Ki. 18:17–35; Is. 36:2–20
32:20–21pp — 2 Ki. 19:35–37; Is. 37:36–38

32 AFTER [z]THESE things, and
the establishment thereof, Sen-
nacherib king of Assyria came, and en-
tered into Judah, and encamped
against the fenced cities, and thought
[c]to win them for himself.
2 And when Hezekiah saw that Sen-
nacherib was come, and that [d]he was
purposed to fight against Jerusalem,
3 He took counsel with his princes
and his mighty men to stop the waters
of the fountains which *were* without the
city: and they did help him.
4 So there was gathered much peo-
ple together, who stopped all the foun-
tains, and the brook that [e]ran through
the midst of the land, saying, Why
should the kings of Assyria come, and
find much water?
5 Also [a]he strengthened himself,
[b]and built up all the wall that was bro-
ken, and raised *it* up to the towers, and
another wall without, and repaired
[c]Millo *in* the city of David, and made
[f]darts and shields in abundance.
6 And he set captains of war over
the people, and gathered them togeth-
er to him in the street of the gate of the
city, and [d]spake[g] comfortably to
them, saying,
7 [e]Be strong and courageous, [f]be
not afraid nor dismayed for the king of
Assyria, nor for all the multitude that
is with him: for [g]*there be* more with us
than with him:
8 With him *is* an [h]arm of flesh; but
[i]with us *is* the LORD our God to help
us, and to fight our battles. And the
people [h]rested themselves upon the
words of Hezekiah king of Judah.
9 ¶ [j]After this did Sennacherib
king of Assyria send his servants to Je-
rusalem, (but he *himself laid siege*
against Lachish, and all his [i]power
with him,) unto Hezekiah king of Ju-
dah, and unto all Judah that *were* at Je-
rusalem, saying,
10 [k]Thus saith Sennacherib king
of Assyria, Whereon do ye trust, that
ye abide [j]in the siege in Jerusalem?
11 Doth not Hezekiah persuade you
to give over yourselves to die by famine
and by thirst, saying, [l]The LORD our
God shall deliver us out of the hand of
the king of Assyria?
12 [m]Hath not the same Hezekiah
taken away his high places and his al-
tars, and commanded Judah and Jeru-
salem, saying, Ye shall worship before
one altar, and burn incense upon it?
13 Know ye not what I and my fa-
thers have done unto all the people of
other lands? [n]were the gods of the na-
tions of those lands any ways able to
deliver their lands out of mine hand?
14 Who *was there* among all the
gods of those nations that my fathers
utterly destroyed, that could deliver
his people out of mine hand, that your

31:19 [w]Lev. 25:34 Num. 35:2 [x]ver. 12-15
31:20 [y]2 Ki. 20:3
32:1 [z]2 Ki. 18:13 Is. 36:1
32:5 [a]Is. 22:9,10 [b]ch. 25:23 [c]2 Sam. 5:9 1 Ki. 9:24
32:6 [d]ch. 30:22 Is. 40:2
32:7 [e]Deut. 31:6 [f]ch. 20:15 [g]2 Ki. 6:16
32:8 [h]Jer. 17:5 1 John 4:4 [i]ch. 13:12 Rom. 8:31
32:9 [j]2 Ki. 18:17
32:10 [k]2 Ki. 18:19
32:11 [l]2 Ki. 18:30
32:12 [m]2 Ki. 18:22
32:13 [n]2 Ki. 18:33-35

[b] Or, *trust* [c] Heb. *to break them up* [d] Heb. *his face* was *to war* [e] Heb. *overflowed* [f] Or, *swords,* or, *weapons* [g] Heb. *spake to their heart* [h] Heb. *leaned* [i] Heb. *dominion* [j] Or, *in the strong hold*

32:1 AFTER THESE THINGS. The Chronicler notes that it was after Hezekiah's acts of faithfulness that Sennacherib invaded Judah (see also 2 Ki. 18—19; Is. 36). Trouble and testing sometimes come to a believer who has been completely faithful and obedient to God. However, the assurance of faith is this: the One who is with us is so great that He can overcome all that the enemy can throw against us (v. 7; cf. 1 John 4:4).

32:7 BE NOT AFRAID. Hezekiah's words of faith may have been inspired by the experience and words of the prophet Elisha (2 Ki. 6:16). Hezekiah's exhortation not to be afraid, together with his promise that "with us *is* the LORD our God to help us, and to fight our battles" (v. 8), is applicable to all who follow the Lord with love, a sincere faith, and a pure heart. According to Isaiah, "sinners in Zion are afraid" (Is. 33:14), but "he that walketh righteously . . . shall dwell on high" (Is. 33:15–16).

God should be able to deliver you out of mine hand?

15 Now therefore [o]let not Hezekiah deceive you, nor persuade you on this manner, neither yet believe him: for no god of any nation or kingdom was able to deliver his people out of mine hand, and out of the hand of my fathers: how much less shall your God deliver you out of mine hand?

16 And his servants spake yet *more* against the LORD God, and against his servant Hezekiah.

17 [p]He wrote also letters to rail on the LORD God of Israel, and to speak against him, saying, [q]As the gods of the nations of *other* lands have not delivered their people out of mine hand, so shall not the God of Hezekiah deliver his people out of mine hand.

18 [r]Then they cried with a loud voice in the Jews' speech unto the people of Jerusalem that *were* on the wall, to affright them, and to trouble them; that they might take the city.

19 And they spake against the God of Jerusalem, as against the gods of the people of the earth, *which were* [s]the work of the hands of man.

20 [t]And for this *cause* Hezekiah the king, and [u]the prophet Isaiah the son of Amoz, prayed and cried to heaven.

21 ¶ [v]And the LORD sent an angel, which cut off all the mighty men of valour, and the leaders and captains in the camp of the king of Assyria. So he returned with shame of face to his own land. And when he was come into the house of his god, they that came forth of his own bowels [k]slew him there with the sword.

22 Thus the LORD saved Hezekiah and the inhabitants of Jerusalem from the hand of Sennacherib the king of Assyria, and from the hand of all *other,* and guided them on every side.

32:15 [o]2 Ki. 18:29
32:17 [p]2 Ki. 19:9 [q]2 Ki. 19:12
32:18 [r]2 Ki. 18:28
32:19 [s]2 Ki. 19:18
32:20 [t]2 Ki. 19:15 [u]2 Ki. 19:2,4
32:21 [v]2 Ki. 19:35

32:23 [w]ch. 17:5 [x]ch. 1:1
32:24 [y]2 Ki. 20:1 Is. 38:1
32:25 [z]Ps. 116:12 [a]ch. 26:16 Hab. 2:4 [b]ch. 24:18
32:26 [c]Jer. 26:18 [d]2 Ki. 20:19
32:29 [e]1 Chr. 29:12
32:30 [f]Is. 22:9,11

23 And many brought gifts unto the LORD to Jerusalem, and [w]presents[1] to Hezekiah king of Judah: so that he was [x]magnified in the sight of all nations from thenceforth.

Hezekiah's sickness and death

32:24–33pp — 2 Ki. 20:1–21; Is. 37:21–38; 38:1–8

24 ¶ [y]In those days Hezekiah was sick to the death, and prayed unto the LORD: and he spake unto him, and he [m]gave him a sign.

25 But Hezekiah [z]rendered not again according to the benefit *done* unto him; for [a]his heart was lifted up: [b]therefore there was wrath upon him, and upon Judah and Jerusalem.

26 [c]Notwithstanding Hezekiah humbled himself for [n]the pride of his heart, *both* he and the inhabitants of Jerusalem, so that the wrath of the LORD came not upon them [d]in the days of Hezekiah.

27 ¶ And Hezekiah had exceeding much riches and honour: and he made himself treasuries for silver, and for gold, and for precious stones, and for spices, and for shields, and for all manner of [o]pleasant jewels;

28 Storehouses also for the increase of corn, and wine, and oil; and stalls for all manner of beasts, and cotes for flocks.

29 Moreover he provided him cities, and possessions of flocks and herds in abundance: for [e]God had given him substance very much.

30 [f]This same Hezekiah also stopped the upper watercourse of Gihon, and brought it straight down to the west side of the city of David. And Hezekiah prospered in all his works.

31 ¶ Howbeit in *the business of* the

[k]Heb. *made him fall* [1]Heb. *precious things* [m]Or, *wrought a miracle for him* [n]Heb. *the lifting up* [o]Heb. *instruments of desire*

32:19 THEY SPAKE AGAINST THE GOD OF JERUSALEM. See 2 Ki. 18:30, note.

32:20 HEZEKIAH . . . ISAIAH . . . PRAYED. See 2 Ki. 19:1–34 and Is. 37:1–35 for the prayer of Hezekiah (see 2 Ki. 19:15,19, notes).

32:21 THE LORD SENT AN ANGEL. See 2 Ki. 19:35, note.

32:24 HEZEKIAH WAS SICK. For a more complete narrative of Hezekiah's sickness and healing and the miraculous sign that accompanied his healing, see 2 Ki. 20:1–11 (cf. Is. 38:1–8; see 38:1,5 notes).

32:31 TO TRY HIM. The story of Hezekiah's dealings with the ambassadors from Babylon is told in 2 Ki. 20:12–19 and Is. 39. God sometimes withdraws evidences of His nearness and favor in order to test the hearts and steadfast trust of His choicest servants. God may also test the genuineness of the devotion of believers in order to train them in humility and prepare them for larger tasks or greater responsibilities. (1) Some of the ways that God tests or tries His people are by (a) prolonged adverse circumstances, as with Joseph in Egypt (Gen. 39—40), (b) physical and emotional affliction, as with Job (Job 1—2), (c) delayed fulfillment of promises from God, as with Abraham

[p]ambassadors of the princes of Babylon, who [g]sent unto him to inquire of the wonder that was *done* in the land, God left him, to [h]try him, that he might know all *that was* in his heart.

32 ¶ Now the rest of the acts of Hezekiah, and his [q]goodness, behold, they *are* written in [i]the vision of Isaiah the prophet, the son of Amoz, *and* in the [j]book of the kings of Judah and Israel.

33 [k]And Hezekiah slept with his fathers, and they buried him in the [r]chiefest of the sepulchres of the sons of David: and all Judah and the inhabitants of Jerusalem did him [l]honour at his death. And Manasseh his son reigned in his stead.

Manasseh, king of Judah

33:1–10pp — 2 Ki. 21:1–10
33:18–20pp — 2 Ki. 21:17–18

33 MANASSEH [m]*WAS* twelve years old when he began to reign, and he reigned fifty and five years in Jerusalem:

2 But did *that which was* evil in the sight of the LORD, like unto the [n]abominations of the heathen, whom the LORD had cast out before the children of Israel.

3 ¶ For [s]he built again the high places which Hezekiah his father had [o]broken down, and he reared up altars for Baalim, and [p]made groves, and worshipped [q]all the host of heaven, and served them.

4 Also he built altars in the house of the LORD, whereof the LORD had said, [r]In Jerusalem shall my name be for ever.

5 And he built altars for all the host of heaven [s]in the two courts of the house of the LORD.

6 [t]And he caused his children to pass through the fire in the valley of the son of Hinnom: also he observed times, and used enchantments, and used witchcraft, and [u]dealt with a familiar spirit, and with wizards: he wrought much evil in the sight of the LORD, to provoke him to anger.

7 And [v]he set a carved image, the idol which he had made, in the house of God, of which God had said to David and to Solomon his son, In this house, and in Jerusalem, which I have chosen before all the tribes of Israel, will I put my name for ever:

8 [w]Neither will I any more remove the foot of Israel from out of the land which I have appointed for your fathers; so that they will take heed to do all that I have commanded them, according to the whole law and the statutes and the ordinances by the hand of Moses.

9 So Manasseh made Judah and the inhabitants of Jerusalem to err, *and* to do worse than the heathen, whom the LORD had destroyed before the children of Israel.

10 And the LORD spake to Manasseh, and to his people: but they would not hearken.

11 ¶ [x]Wherefore the LORD brought upon them the captains of the host [t]of the king of Assyria, which took Manasseh among the thorns, and [y]bound him with [u]fetters, and carried him to Babylon.

12 And when he was in affliction, he besought the LORD his God, and [z]humbled himself greatly before the God of his fathers,

13 And prayed unto him: and he was [a]entreated of him, and heard his

32:31 [g]2 Ki. 20:12 Is. 39:1 [h]Deut. 8:2 **32:32** [i]Is. 36 & 37 & 38 & 39 [j]2 Ki. 18 & 19 & 20 **32:33** [k]2 Ki. 20:21 [l]Prov. 10:7 **33:1** [m]2 Ki. 21:1 **33:2** [n]Deut. 18:9 2 Chr. 28:3 **33:3** [o]2 Ki. 18:4 ch. 30:14 & 31:1 [p]Deut. 16:21 [q]Deut. 17:3 **33:4** [r]Deut. 12:11 1 Ki. 8:29 & 9:3 ch. 6:6 & 7:16 **33:5** [s]ch. 4:9 **33:6** [t]Lev. 18:21 Deut. 18:10 2 Ki. 23:10 ch. 28:3 Ezek. 23:37,39 [u]2 Ki. 21:6 **33:7** [v]2 Ki. 21:7 **33:8** [w]2 Sam. 7:10 **33:11** [x]Deut. 28:36 [y]Job 36:8 Ps. 107:10,11 **33:12** [z]1 Pet. 5:6 **33:13** [a]1 Chr. 5:20 Ezra 8:23

[p] Heb. *interpreters* [q] Heb. *kindnesses* [r] Or, *highest* [s] Heb. *he returned and built* [t] Heb. *which* were *the king's* [u] Or, *chains*

---

and Sarah (Gen. 15—21) and Joseph's dreams (Gen. 37; 42:6; cf. Ps. 105:17–19), (d) a difficult obedience test, as with Abraham and Isaac (Gen. 22) or King Saul (1 Sam. 15), and (e) seasons of spiritual dryness or darkness that come to most of God's people at some point in life.

(2) Learning to trust God and remaining faithful in the midst of trying experiences produce the full-grown fruit of steadfast faith, proven character, mature obedience, and approval by God (cf. 2 Cor. 12:7–10). In the midst of his fiery trial, Job declared: "[God] knoweth the way that I take: *when* he hath tried me, I shall come forth as gold" (Job 23:10; cf. Zech. 13:9). To be tried by God is not necessarily a sign of His disfavor or judgment, but may in fact be a sign of His greater purpose for the one whose heart He tests.

33:13 PRAYED UNTO HIM. Manasseh departed from the God of his father, Hezekiah, and became more evil than any other king in Judah's history. However, in a time of crisis and great distress (vv. 11–12), this king genuinely repented and cried out to God (vv. 12–13). God's forgiveness of Manasseh after his deep repentance and humility dramatically illustrates the truth that even the most wicked sinners can find grace whenever they sincerely humble themselves and call out to God. Unfortunately, as the writer of 2 Kings emphasizes, Manasseh's long and ungodly rule had led many into sin and ruin (2 Ki. 21:9–15). His repen-

supplication, and brought him again to Jerusalem into his kingdom. Then Manasseh [b]knew that the LORD he *was* God.

14 Now after this he built a wall without the city of David, on the west side of [c]Gihon, in the valley, even to the entering in at the fish gate, and compassed [d]about [v]Ophel, and raised it up a very great height, and put captains of war in all the fenced cities of Judah.

15 And he took away [e]the strange gods, and the idol out of the house of the LORD, and all the altars that he had built in the mount of the house of the LORD, and in Jerusalem, and cast *them* out of the city.

16 And he repaired the altar of the LORD, and sacrificed thereon peace offerings and [f]thank offerings, and commanded Judah to serve the LORD God of Israel.

17 [g]Nevertheless the people did sacrifice still in the high places, *yet* unto the LORD their God only.

18 ¶ Now the rest of the acts of Manasseh, and his prayer unto his God, and the words of [h]the seers that spake to him in the name of the LORD God of Israel, behold, they *are written* in the book of the kings of Israel.

19 His prayer also, and *how God* was entreated of him, and all his sins, and his trespass, and the places wherein he built high places, and set up groves and graven images, before he was humbled: behold, they *are* written among the sayings of [w]the seers.

20 ¶ [i]So Manasseh slept with his fathers, and they buried him in his own house: and Amon his son reigned in his stead.

Amon, king of Judah

33:21–25pp — 2 Ki. 21:19–24

21 ¶ [j]Amon *was* two and twenty years old when he began to reign, and reigned two years in Jerusalem.

22 But he did *that which was* evil in the sight of the LORD, as did Manasseh his father: for Amon sacrificed unto all the carved images which Manasseh his father had made, and served them;

23 And humbled not himself before the LORD, [k]as Manasseh his father had humbled himself; but Amon [x]trespassed more and more.

24 [l]And his servants conspired against him, and slew him in his own house.

25 ¶ But the people of the land slew all them that had conspired against king Amon; and the people of the land made Josiah his son king in his stead.

Josiah repairs the temple

34:1–2pp — 2 Ki. 22:1–2
34:3–7Ref — 2 Ki. 23:4–20
34:8–13pp — 2 Ki. 22:3–7

34 JOSIAH [m]*WAS* eight years old when he began to reign, and he reigned in Jerusalem one and thirty years.

2 And he did *that which was* right in the sight of the LORD, and walked in the ways of David his father, and declined *neither* to the right hand, nor to the left.

3 ¶ For in the eighth year of his reign, while he was yet young, he began to [n]seek after the God of David his father: and in the twelfth year he began [o]to purge Judah and Jerusalem [p]from the high places, and the groves, and the carved images, and the molten images.

4 [q]And they brake down the altars of Baalim in his presence; and the [y]images, that *were* on high above them, he cut down; and the groves, and the carved images, and the molten images, he brake in pieces, and made dust *of them*, [r]and strewed *it* upon the [z]graves of them that had sacrificed unto them.

5 And he [s]burnt the bones of the priests upon their altars, and cleansed Judah and Jerusalem.

6 And *so did he* in the cities of Manasseh, and Ephraim, and Simeon, even unto Naphtali, with their [a]mattocks round about.

7 And when he had broken down the altars and the groves, and had [t]beaten the graven images [b]into powder, and cut down all the idols throughout all the land of Israel, he returned to Jerusalem.

8 ¶ Now [u]in the eighteenth year of

33:13 [b]Ps. 9:16 Dan. 4:25
33:14 [c]1 Ki. 1:33 [d]ch. 27:3
33:15 [e]ver. 3,5,7
33:16 [f]Lev. 7:12
33:17 [g]ch. 32:12
33:18 [h]1 Sam. 9:9
33:20 [i]2 Ki. 21:18
33:21 [j]2 Ki. 21:19
33:23 [k]ver. 12
33:24 [l]2 Ki. 21:23,24
34:1 [m]2 Ki. 22:1
34:3 [n]ch. 15:2 [o]1 Ki. 13:2 [p]ch. 33:17,22
34:4 [q]Lev. 26:30 2 Ki. 23:4 [r]2 Ki. 23:6
34:5 [s]1 Ki. 13:2
34:7 [t]Deut. 9:21
34:8 [u]2 Ki. 22:3

[v] Or, *The tower* [w] Or, *Hosai* [x] Heb. *multiplied trespass* [y] Or, *sun images* [z] Heb. *face of the graves* [a] Or, *mauls* [b] Heb. *to make powder*

tance and restoration did not stop the ongoing rippling consequences of his previous influence for evil (cf. 2 Ki. 24:3–4; see 23:26, note).

34:1 JOSIAH. See 2 Ki. 22:1, note.

his reign, when he had purged the land, and the house, he sent Shaphan the son of Azaliah, and Maaseiah the governor of the city, and Joah the son of Joahaz the recorder, to repair the house of the LORD his God.

9 And when they came to Hilkiah the high priest, they delivered [v]the money that was brought into the house of God, which the Levites that kept the doors had gathered of the hand of Manasseh and Ephraim, and of all the remnant of Israel, and of all Judah and Benjamin; and they returned to Jerusalem.

10 And they put *it* in the hand of the workmen that had the oversight of the house of the LORD, and they gave it to the workmen that wrought in the house of the LORD, to repair and amend the house:

11 Even to the artificers and builders gave they *it*, to buy hewn stone, and timber for couplings, and [c]to floor the houses which the kings of Judah had destroyed.

12 And the men did the work faithfully: and the overseers of them *were* Jahath and Obadiah, the Levites, of the sons of Merari; and Zechariah and Meshullam, of the sons of the Kohathites, to set *it* forward; and *other of* the Levites, all that could skill of instruments of music.

13 Also *they were* over the bearers of burdens, and *were* overseers of all that wrought the work in any manner of service: [w]and of the Levites *there were* scribes, and officers, and porters.

Discovery of the book of the law

34:14–28pp — 2 Ki. 22:8–20
34:29–32pp — 2 Ki. 23:1–3

14 ¶ And when they brought out the money that was brought into the house of the LORD, Hilkiah the priest [x]found a book of the law of the LORD *given* [d]by Moses.

15 And Hilkiah answered and said to Shaphan the scribe, I have found the book of the law in the house of the LORD. And Hilkiah delivered the book to Shaphan.

16 And Shaphan carried the book to the king, and brought the king word back again, saying, All that was committed [e]to thy servants, they do *it*.

17 And they have [f]gathered together the money that was found in the house of the LORD, and have delivered it into the hand of the overseers, and to the hand of the workmen.

18 Then Shaphan the scribe told the king, saying, Hilkiah the priest hath given me a book. And Shaphan read [g]it before the king.

19 And it came to pass, when the king had heard the words of the law, that he rent his clothes.

20 And the king commanded Hilkiah, and Ahikam the son of Shaphan, and [h]Abdon the son of Micah, and Shaphan the scribe, and Asaiah a servant of the king's, saying,

21 Go, inquire of the LORD for me, and for them that are left in Israel and in Judah, concerning the words of the book that is found: for great *is* the wrath of the LORD that is poured out upon us, because our fathers have not kept the word of the LORD, to do after all that is written in this book.

22 And Hilkiah, and *they* that the king *had appointed*, went to Huldah the prophetess, the wife of Shallum the son of [y]Tikvath, the son of [i]Hasrah, keeper of the [j]wardrobe; (now she dwelt in Jerusalem [k]in the college:) and they spake to her to that *effect*.

23 ¶ And she answered them, Thus saith the LORD God of Israel, Tell ye the man that sent you to me,

24 Thus saith the LORD, Behold, I will bring evil upon this place, and upon the inhabitants thereof, *even* all the curses that are written in the book which they have read before the king of Judah:

25 Because they have forsaken me, and have burned incense unto other gods, that they might provoke me to anger with all the works of their hands; therefore my wrath shall be poured out upon this place, and shall not be quenched.

26 And as for the king of Judah, who

34:9 [v]See 2 Ki. 12:4
34:13 [w]1 Chr. 23:4,5
34:14 [x]2 Ki. 22:8
34:22 [y]2 Ki. 22:14

[c] Or, *to rafter* [d] Heb. *by the hand of* [e] Heb. *to the hand of* [f] Heb. *poured out*, or, *melted* [g] Heb. *in it* [h] Or, *Achbor;* see 2 Ki. 22:12 [i] Or, *Harhas* [j] Heb. *garments* [k] Or, *in the school*, or, *in the second part*

34:14 FOUND A BOOK OF THE LAW. See 2 Ki. 22:8, note.

34:24 I WILL BRING EVIL UPON THIS PLACE. The sins of the people had reached such a point that God's destructive judgment upon them was inevitable (see 2 Ki. 22:13, note).

sent you to inquire of the LORD, so shall ye say unto him, Thus saith the LORD God of Israel *concerning* the words which thou hast heard;

27 Because thine heart was tender, and thou didst humble thyself before God, when thou heardest his words against this place, and against the inhabitants thereof, and humbledst thyself before me, and didst rend thy clothes, and weep before me; I have even heard *thee* also, saith the LORD.

28 Behold, I will gather thee to thy fathers, and thou shalt be gathered to thy grave in peace, neither shall thine eyes see all the evil that I will bring upon this place, and upon the inhabitants of the same. So they brought the king word again.

29 ¶ [z]Then the king sent and gathered together all the elders of Judah and Jerusalem.

30 And the king went up into the house of the LORD, and all the men of Judah, and the inhabitants of Jerusalem, and the priests, and the Levites, and all the people, [1]great and small: and he read in their ears all the words of the book of the covenant that was found in the house of the LORD.

31 And the king stood in [a]his place, and made a covenant before the LORD, to walk after the LORD, and to keep his commandments, and his testimonies, and his statutes, with all his heart, and with all his soul, to perform the words of the covenant which are written in this book.

32 And he caused all that were [m]present in Jerusalem and Benjamin to stand *to it.* And the inhabitants of Jerusalem did according to the covenant of God, the God of their fathers.

33 And Josiah took away all the [b]abominations out of all the countries that *pertained* to the children of Israel, and made all that were present in Israel to serve, *even* to serve the LORD their God. [c]*And* all his days they departed not [n]from following the LORD, the God of their fathers.

34:29 [z]2 Ki. 23:1
34:31 [a]2 Ki. 11:14 & 23:3 ch. 6:13
34:33 [b]1 Ki. 11:5 [c]Jer. 3:10

Observance of the Passover

35:1,18–19pp — 2 Ki. 23:21–23

35 MOREOVER [d]JOSIAH kept a passover unto the LORD in Jerusalem: and they killed the passover on the [e]fourteenth *day* of the first month.

2 And he set the priests in their [f]charges, and [g]encouraged them to the service of the house of the LORD,

3 And said unto the Levites [h]that taught all Israel, which were holy unto the LORD, [i]Put the holy ark [j]in the house which Solomon the son of David king of Israel did build; [o]*it shall* not *be* a burden upon *your* shoulders: serve now the LORD your God, and his people Israel,

4 And prepare *yourselves* [k]by the houses of your fathers, after your courses, according to the [l]writing of David king of Israel, and according to the [m]writing of Solomon his son.

5 And [n]stand in the holy *place* according to the divisions of [p]the families of the fathers of your brethren [q]the people, and *after* the division of the families of the Levites.

6 So kill the passover, and [o]sanctify yourselves, and prepare your brethren, that *they* may do according to the word of the LORD by the hand of Moses.

7 And Josiah [p]gave[r] to the people, of the flock, lambs and kids, all for the passover offerings, for all that were present, to the number of thirty thousand, and three thousand bullocks: these *were* of the king's substance.

8 And his princes [r]gave willingly unto the people, to the priests, and to the Levites: Hilkiah and Zechariah and

35:1 [d]2 Ki. 23:21,22 [e]Ex. 12:6 Ezra 6:19
35:2 [f]ch. 23:18 Ezra 6:18 [g]ch. 29:5,11
35:3 [h]Deut. 33:10 [i]See ch. 34:14 [j]ch. 5:7
35:4 [k]1 Chr. 9:10 [l]1 Chr. 23 & 24 & 25 & 26 [m]ch. 8:14
35:5 [n]Ps. 134:1
35:6 [o]ch. 29:5,15
35:7 [p]ch. 30:24

[1] Heb. *from great even to small* [m] Heb. *found* [n] Heb. *from after* [o] 1 Chr. 23:26 [p] Heb. *the house of the fathers* [q] Heb. *the sons of the people* [r] Heb. *offered*

34:27 DIDST HUMBLE THYSELF BEFORE GOD. See 7:14, note; 2 Ki. 22:19, note.

34:30 HE READ . . . ALL THE WORDS OF THE BOOK. Every spiritual revival recorded in the O.T. came from a renewed proclamation of and commitment to the word of God. (1) Josiah read the "words of the book of the covenant" before the people, and they returned to the Lord (vv. 30–33). (2) Earlier, Jehoshaphat and the Levites "taught in Judah, and *had* the book of the law of the LORD with them" (17:9). (3) Later, Ezra read from God's law for six hours a day for seven days (Neh. 8:3,18) and explained it in such a way that the people could "understand the reading" (Neh. 8:8). All genuine lasting revivals are accompanied by restoring the Word of God to its appointed place of authority and honor. One sure evidence that revival is beginning among God's people is a great desire to hear, search out, and obey the Word of the Lord (see Acts 2:42).

35:1 JOSIAH KEPT A PASSOVER. See article on THE PASSOVER, p. 110.

Jehiel, rulers of the house of God, gave unto the priests for the passover offerings two thousand and six hundred *small cattle,* and three hundred oxen.

9 Conaniah also, and Shemaiah and Nethaneel, his brethren, and Hashabiah and Jeiel and Jozabad, chief of the Levites, [s]gave unto the Levites for passover offerings five thousand *small cattle,* and five hundred oxen.

10 So the service was prepared, and the priests [q]stood in their place, and the Levites in their courses, according to the king's commandment.

11 And they killed the passover, and the priests [r]sprinkled *the blood* from their hands, and the Levites [s]flayed *them.*

12 And they removed the burnt offerings, that they might give according to the divisions of the families of the people, to offer unto the LORD, as *it is* written [t]in the book of Moses. And so *did they* with the oxen.

13 And they [u]roasted the passover with fire according to the ordinance: but the *other* holy *offerings* [v]sod they in pots, and in caldrons, and in pans, and [t]divided *them* speedily among all the people.

14 And afterward they made ready for themselves, and for the priests: because the priests the sons of Aaron *were busied* in offering of burnt offerings and the fat until night; therefore the Levites prepared for themselves, and for the priests the sons of Aaron.

15 And the singers the sons of Asaph *were* in their [u]place, according to the [w]commandment of David, and Asaph, and Heman, and Jeduthun the king's seer; and the porters [x]*waited* at every gate; they might not depart from their service; for their brethren the Levites prepared for them.

16 So all the service of the LORD was prepared the same day, to keep the passover, and to offer burnt offerings upon the altar of the LORD, according to the commandment of king Josiah.

17 And the children of Israel that were [v]present kept the passover at that time, and the feast of [y]unleavened bread seven days.

35:10 [q]Ezra 6:18
35:11 [r]ch. 29:22 [s]See ch. 29:34
35:12 [t]Lev. 3:3
35:13 [u]Ex. 12:8,9 Deut. 16:7 [v]1 Sam. 2:13-15
35:15 [w]1 Chr. 25:1 [x]1 Chr. 9:17,18 & 26:14
35:17 [y]Ex. 12:15 & 13:6 ch. 30:21
35:18 [z]2 Ki. 23:22,23
35:20 [a]2 Ki. 23:29
35:23 [b]1 Ki. 22:34
35:24 [c]2 Ki. 23:30 [d]Zech. 12:11
35:25 [e]Lam. 4:20 [f]See Mat. 9:23 [g]Jer. 22:20

18 And [z]there was no passover like to that kept in Israel from the days of Samuel the prophet; neither did all the kings of Israel keep such a passover as Josiah kept, and the priests, and the Levites, and all Judah and Israel that were present, and the inhabitants of Jerusalem.

19 In the eighteenth year of the reign of Josiah was this passover kept.

The death of Josiah

35:20–36:1pp — 2 Ki. 23:28–30

20 ¶ [a]After all this, when Josiah had prepared the [w]temple, Necho king of Egypt came up to fight against Carchemish by Euphrates: and Josiah went out against him.

21 But he sent ambassadors to him, saying, What have I to do with thee, thou king of Judah? *I come* not against thee this day, but against [x]the house wherewith I have war: for God commanded me to make haste: forbear thee from *meddling with* God, who *is* with me, that he destroy thee not.

22 Nevertheless Josiah would not turn his face from him, but disguised himself, that he might fight with him, and hearkened not unto the words of Necho from the mouth of God, and came to fight in the valley of Megiddo.

23 And the archers shot at king Josiah; and the king said to his servants, Have me away; for I am sore [b]wounded.[y]

24 [c]His servants therefore took him out of that chariot, and put him in the second chariot that he had; and they brought him to Jerusalem, and he died, and was buried [z]in *one of* the sepulchres of his fathers. And [d]all Judah and Jerusalem mourned for Josiah.

25 ¶ And Jeremiah [e]lamented for Josiah: and [f]all the singing men and the singing women spake of Josiah in their lamentations to this day, [g]and made them an ordinance in Israel: and, behold, they *are* written in the lamentations.

[s] Heb. *offered* [t] Heb. *made them run*
[u] Heb. *station* [v] Heb. *found* [w] Heb. *house*
[x] Heb. *the house of my war* [y] Heb. *made sick*
[z] Or, *among the sepulchres*

35:22 JOSIAH . . . HEARKENED NOT UNTO THE WORDS OF NECHO FROM THE MOUTH OF GOD. Necho's military campaign against the emerging Babylonian world power was from the Lord God. Josiah, although a righteous man, failed to understand the will of God in this matter and attempted to hinder Necho's army. Josiah's failure to seek out God's will and purpose cost him his life.

26 Now the rest of the acts of Josiah, and his [a]goodness, according to *that which was* written in the law of the LORD,

27 And his deeds, first and last, behold, they *are* written in the book of the kings of Israel and Judah.

From Josiah to the captivity

36:2–4pp — 2 Ki. 23:31–34
36:5–8pp — 2 Ki. 23:36–24:6
36:9–10pp — 2 Ki. 24:8–17
36:11–16pp — 2 Ki. 24:18–20; Jer. 52:1–3

36 THEN [h]THE people of the land took Jehoahaz the son of Josiah, and made him king in his father's stead in Jerusalem.

2 Jehoahaz *was* twenty and three years old when he began to reign, and he reigned three months in Jerusalem.

3 And the king of Egypt [b]put him down at Jerusalem, and [c]condemned the land in an hundred talents of silver and a talent of gold.

4 And the king of Egypt made Eliakim his brother king over Judah and Jerusalem, and turned his name to Jehoiakim. And Necho took Jehoahaz his brother, and carried him to Egypt.

5 ¶ [i]Jehoiakim *was* twenty and five years old when he began to reign, and he reigned eleven years in Jerusalem: and he did *that which was* evil in the sight of the LORD his God.

6 [j]Against him came up Nebuchadnezzar king of Babylon, and bound him in [d]fetters, to [k]carry him to Babylon.

7 [l]Nebuchadnezzar also carried of the vessels of the house of the LORD to Babylon, and put them in his temple at Babylon.

8 Now the rest of the acts of Jehoiakim, and his abominations which he did, and that which was found in him, behold, they *are* written in the book of the kings of Israel and Judah: and [e]Jehoiachin his son reigned in his stead.

9 ¶ [m]Jehoiachin *was* eight years old when he began to reign, and he reigned three months and ten days in Jerusalem: and he did *that which was* evil in the sight of the LORD.

10 And [f]when the year was expired, [n]king Nebuchadnezzar sent, and brought him to Babylon, [o]with the [g]goodly vessels of the house of the LORD, and made [p]Zedekiah [q]his[h] brother king over Judah and Jerusalem.

11 ¶ [r]Zedekiah *was* one and twenty years old when he began to reign, and reigned eleven years in Jerusalem.

12 And he did *that which was* evil in the sight of the LORD his God, *and* humbled not himself before Jeremiah the prophet *speaking* from the mouth of the LORD.

13 And he also rebelled against king Nebuchadnezzar, who had made him swear by God: but he [s]stiffened his neck, and hardened his heart from turning unto the LORD God of Israel.

14 ¶ Moreover all the chief of the priests, and the people, transgressed very much after all the abominations of the heathen; and polluted the house of the LORD which he had hallowed in Jerusalem.

15 [t]And the LORD God of their fathers sent to them [i]by his messengers, rising up [j]betimes, and sending; because he had compassion on his people, and on his dwelling place:

16 But [u]they mocked the messen-

36:1 [h]2 Ki. 23:30
36:5 [i]2 Ki. 23:36,37
36:6 [j]2 Ki. 24:1 Foretold, Hab. 1:6 [k]Jer. 36:30
36:7 [l]2 Ki. 24:13 Dan. 1:1,2
36:9 [m]2 Ki. 24:8
36:10 [n]2 Ki. 24:10-17 [o]Dan. 1:1,2 [p]Jer. 37:1 [q]2 Ki. 24:17
36:11 [r]2 Ki. 24:18 Jer. 52:1
36:13 [s]2 Ki. 17:14
36:15 [t]Jer. 25:3,4
36:16 [u]Jer. 5:12

[a] Heb. *kindnesses* [b] Heb. *removed him* [c] Heb. *mulcted* [d] Or, *chains* [e] Called *Jeconiah* in 1 Chr. 3:16, or, *Coniah* in Jer. 22:24 [f] Heb. *at the return of the year* [g] Heb. *vessels of desire* [h] Or, *Mattaniah, his father's brother* [i] Heb. *by the hand of his messengers* [j] i.e. *continually and carefully*

36:6 AGAINST HIM CAME UP NEBUCHADNEZZAR. See 2 Ki. 24:1, note on the three phases of the destruction and captivity of Judah by Nebuchadnezzar.

36:14 TRANSGRESSED ... AFTER ALL THE ABOMINATIONS OF THE HEATHEN. The most prevailing sin of God's people throughout redemptive history has been their failure to remain separate from the unrighteous people and society around them. Instead of despising the immoral customs and lifestyles of the ungodly, all too often the people of God are attracted to and conform to the culture in which they live. By doing so they show themselves unfaithful to God and thereby pollute the house of the Lord (see 2 Ki. 24:3, note). The sad consequence is the destruction of God's people and their families because of their conformity to the ungodly ways of the world (vv. 5–21; see Rom. 12:2, note; see also article on THE CHRISTIAN'S RELATIONSHIP TO THE WORLD, p. 2004).

36:15 BECAUSE HE HAD COMPASSION. God's messengers who expose and condemn His people when they conform to the world (see previous note) are motivated by the compassion of God. They preach their messages with the intense hope that none might perish. The superficial "compassion" of those messengers who bring a word that allows God's people to keep compromising with the surrounding society is, like the messengers themselves, not from God (see 2 Tim. 4:3–4).

36:16 THEY MOCKED THE MESSENGERS

gers of God, and [v]despised his words,
and [w]misused his prophets, until the
[x]wrath of the LORD arose against his
people, till *there was* no [k]remedy.

Defeat and exile to Babylon

36:17–20pp — 2 Ki. 25:1–21; Jer. 52:4–27
36:22–23pp — Ezra 1:1–3

17 [y]Therefore he brought upon
them the king of the Chaldees, who
[z]slew their young men with the sword
in the house of their sanctuary, and
had no compassion upon young man or
maiden, old man, or him that stooped
for age: he gave *them* all into his hand.
18 [a]And all the vessels of the
house of God, great and small, and the
treasures of the house of the LORD, and
the treasures of the king, and of his
princes; all *these* he brought to Babylon.
19 [b]And they burnt the house of
God, and brake down the wall of Jerusalem, and burnt all the palaces thereof with fire, and destroyed all the goodly vessels thereof.
20 And [c]them[1] that had escaped
from the sword carried he away to Babylon; [d]where they were servants to
him and his sons until the reign of the
kingdom of Persia:
21 To fulfil the word of the LORD by
the mouth of [e]Jeremiah, until the land
[f]had enjoyed her sabbaths: *for* as long
as she lay desolate [g]she kept sabbath,
to fulfil threescore and ten years.

Cyrus promises end of captivity

22 ¶ [h]Now in the first year of Cyrus
king of Persia, that the word of the
LORD *spoken* by the mouth of [i]Jeremiah might be accomplished, the LORD
stirred up the spirit of [j]Cyrus king of
Persia, that he made a proclamation
throughout all his kingdom, and *put it*
also in writing, saying,
23 [k]Thus saith Cyrus king of Persia, All the kingdoms of the earth hath
the LORD God of heaven given me; and
he hath charged me to build him an
house in Jerusalem, which *is* in Judah.
Who *is there* among you of all his people? The LORD his God *be* with him, and
let him go up.

36:16 [v]Prov. 1:25 [w]Jer. 38:6 Mat. 23:34 [x]Ps. 79:5
36:17 [y]Deut. 28:49 2 Ki. 25:1 Ezra 9:7 [z]Ps. 74:20
36:18 [a]2 Ki. 25:13
36:19 [b]2 Ki. 25:9 Ps. 79:1,7
36:20 [c]2 Ki. 25:11 [d]Jer. 27:7
36:21 [e]Jer. 26:6,7 [f]Lev. 26:34 Dan. 9:2 [g]Lev. 25:4,5
36:22 [h]Ezra 1:1 [i]Jer. 29:10 [j]Is. 44:28
36:23 [k]Ezra 1:2,3

[k] Heb. *healing* [1] Heb. *the remainder from the sword*

OF GOD. The messengers sent to call God's people to repentance included Isaiah, Jeremiah, and Ezekiel (cf. Jer. 25:3–7; 35:12–15). Scoffing at God's messengers is the same as "despising [God's] words" (v. 16). Anyone who scorns the prophets who expose sin, guilt, and apostasy is rejecting God Himself (see Acts 9:4). Continual rejection of God's prophets resulted in the Israelites hardening their hearts until there was no longer any remedy (see article on THE PROPHET IN THE OLD TESTAMENT, p. 1002).

36:21 *FOR* AS LONG AS SHE LAY DESOLATE SHE KEPT SABBATH. According to God's commandment given at Mount Sinai, every seventh year the land was to lie fallow (Lev. 25:1–7). Israel and Judah had failed to observe these sabbatical years; therefore, through the exile of seventy years, God would enforce the sabbaths (see Jer. 25:11–12; 29:10).

36:22–23 THE LORD STIRRED UP THE SPIRIT OF CYRUS. The writer ends this book by emphasizing that in spite of the sin and apostasy of Judah, God was still at work in fulfilling His promises to the faithful remnant of His people. God would move even the mightiest rulers of the world in order to accomplish His purpose and fulfill His word (cf. Ezra 1:1–3; Jer. 25:11–14; 27:22; 29:10; 33:7–10).

EZRA

Outline

I. The First Return of Exiles to Jerusalem (1:1—6:22)
   A. The Decree and Provision of Cyrus (1:1–11)
   B. List of the Returning Exiles (2:1–70)
   C. Restoration of the Temple Begins (3:1–13)
      1. Sacrifices Reinstituted (3:1–6)
      2. Construction of the Temple Started (3:7–13)
   D. Construction of the Temple Ceases Because of Opposition (4:1–24)
   E. Construction of the Temple Resumes and Is Completed (5:1—6:18)
      1. Encouragement from the Prophets (5:1–2)
      2. Protest from the Governor Tattenai (5:3–17)
      3. Darius Affirms the Temple's Construction (6:1–12)
      4. Temple Completed and Dedicated (6:13–18)
   F. Celebration of the Passover (6:19–22)

II. The Second Return of Exiles to Jerusalem Led by Ezra (7:1—10:44)
   A. The Mission of Ezra Authorized by Artaxerxes (7:1–28)
   B. The Journey of Ezra and Those Who Accompanied Him (8:1–36)
   C. The Reforms of Ezra in Jerusalem (9:1—10:44)
      1. Condemnation of Intermarriage with Pagans (9:1–4)
      2. Ezra's Confession and Intercessory Prayer for the People (9:5–15)
      3. Public Repentance and Reform (10:1–44)

Author: Ezra

Theme: Restoration of a Remnant

Date of Writing: 450–420 B.C.

Background

The book of Ezra is part of a continuous history of the Jews written after their exile, consisting of 1 and 2 Chronicles, Ezra, and Nehemiah. In the Hebrew O.T., Ezra and Nehemiah were originally a single book, as were 1 and 2 Chronicles. Bible scholars commonly believe that the history presented in all these books was primarily the inspired work of one post-exilic author. Although the author is nowhere designated in the Bible, almost all ancient Jewish and Christian sources, as well as many modern scholars, believe that this author was Ezra, the priest and scribe. For more details about Ezra's role as author, see the introduction to 1 Chronicles.

According to tradition, Ezra was the one who collected all the O.T. books together as a unit, originated the form of worship used in the synagogue, and founded the Great Synagogue in Jerusalem where the canon of O.T. Scriptures was eventually settled. Ezra was a godly leader with an uncompromising loyalty to and passionate love for God's Word. His written history in the Chronicles and in Ezra and Nehemiah emphasizes the themes of hope, revival, reform, and restoration for God's people. The entire history was written during the second half of the fifth century B.C.

The book of Ezra records how God fulfilled His prophetic promise made through Jeremiah (Jer. 29:10–14) to restore the Jewish people after seventy years of exile by bringing them back to their own land (1:1). Judah's collapse as a nation and their deportation to Babylon had occurred in three distinct stages. In stage one (605 B.C.), Judah's young nobility, including Daniel, were taken exile; in stage two (597 B.C.), there were 11,000 more exiles, including Ezekiel; and in stage three (586 B.C.), the rest of Judah, except for Jeremiah and the poorest of the people, were carried off. Likewise, the restoration of the exilic remnant, in fulfillment of Jeremiah's prophecy, took place in three stages. In stage 1 (538 B.C.), 50,000 exiles returned, led by Zerubbabel and Joshua (cf. Ezra 2); in stage 2 (457 B.C.), over 1,700 men (plus women and children, totaling 5,000–10,000 Jews) were led back by Ezra (cf. 8:1–14, 18–21); and in stage 3 (444 B.C.), Nehemiah led another group back (cf. Neh. 2:1–10). Note that the first company of Jewish exiles in 538 B.C. returned to Jerusalem approximately seventy years after the first deportation of Jews to exile.

About two years after the Babylonian empire was defeated and replaced by the Persian empire (539 B.C.), the Jewish restoration to their homeland began. The book of Ezra records the first and second stages of the restoration, involving three Persian kings (Cyrus, Darius, and Artaxerxes) and five prominent spiritual leaders: (1) Zerubbabel, who led the first exiles in reestablishing Jerusalem and rebuilding the temple; (2) Joshua, a godly high priest who assisted Zerubbabel; (3) Haggai and (4) Zechariah, two prophets of God who exhorted the people to finish rebuilding the temple; and (5) Ezra, who led the second company of exiles back to Jerusalem and whom God used to restore the people spiritually and morally. If Ezra is the author of this book, as seems likely, he compiled his history under the inspiration of the Holy Spirit by consulting a variety of official letters and documents (e.g., 1:2–4; 4:11–22; 5:7–17; 6:1–12), genealogies (e.g., 2:1–70), and personal memoirs (e.g., 7:27—9:15). The book was written in Hebrew except for 4:8—6:18 and 7:12–26, which were written in Aramaic, the official language of the exiles.

Purpose

This book was written to show God's providence and faithfulness in restoring a Jewish remnant from exile in Babylon (1) by moving the hearts of three different Persian kings to assist God's people in returning to their homeland, resettling Jerusalem, and rebuilding the temple; and (2) by providing godly and capable leaders to lead the returning remnant in a revival of worship, commitment to God's word, and repentance for unfaithfulness to God.

Survey

The ten chapters of Ezra divide naturally into two main sections: (1) Section one (chs. 1—6) records the first return of Jewish exiles to Jerusalem and their rebuilding of the temple; (2) Section two (chs.7—10) describes the second return under Ezra and the spiritual reformation that followed.

(1) Section one begins where 2 Chronicles ends—with the Jewish captivity and the decree of Cyrus, King of Persia (538 B.C.), that permitted the Jews to return to their homeland (1:1–11). Ch. 2 lists those who participated in this first return. Significantly, only about 50,000 Jewish exiles from among one million or more were in the first group to return (1:5; 2:64–65). In ch. 3, Zerubbabel (a descendant of David) and Joshua (the high priest) rallied the people to start rebuilding the destroyed temple. Shrewd enemies of Judah used political means to stop that project for some time (ch. 4), but eventually the work was resumed and the temple was completed in 516 B.C. (chs. 5—6).

(2) A gap of about sixty years occurs between chs. 6 and 7, during which time Esther reigned as queen in Persia with king Ahasuerus (i.e., Xerxes I). Esther became queen about 478 B.C. (see the introduction to Esther). Chs. 7—8 record events about twenty years later when a smaller number of exiles returned from Persia to Jerusalem under Ezra's leadership. Whereas the first returning exiles accomplished the task of rebuilding God's house, Ezra set about to restore God's Law in the hearts of the people (cf. Neh. 8:1–8). Ezra found widespread spiritual and moral backsliding among the men in Judah, evident in their having intermarried with pagan women. In deep grief, Ezra confessed their sin to God and inter-

ceded on their behalf (ch. 9) The book ends with Ezra leading the men in public repentance and severing the marriage ties with their pagan wives (ch. 10).

Special Features

Four major features or emphases characterize the book of Ezra. (1) Ezra-Nehemiah is the only historical record in the Bible of the post-exilic restoration of the Jews in Palestine. (2) A remarkable feature of this book is that its two main divisions (chs. 1—6; chs. 7—10) have a historical gap between them of about sixty years. The whole book covers about eighty years. (3) Ezra demonstrates clearly how God watches over His word to perform it (cf. Jer. 1:12; 29:10); God turned the hearts of Persian kings like channels of water in order to restore His people to their homeland (1:1; 7:11–28; cf. Prov. 21:1). (4) Ezra's treatment of unbelieving pagan women whom the Jewish men (including priests) had married in violation of God's commandments profoundly illustrates how God (a) requires His people to be separated from the pagan world, and (b) sometimes uses radical surgery in order to deal with dangerous and cancerous compromise among His people. Ezra's action strongly reminded the covenant people of their primary calling to be a "kingdom of priests" and a "holy nation" (Ex. 19:6), not just another mixed national entity.

New Testament Fulfillment

The return of a Jewish remnant to their homeland and the rebuilding of the temple reveal that God always longs to restore His wayward people. His ways include not only judgment for apostasy, but also restoration and hope for the believing remnant, through whom God directs the stream of redemption on its ultimate course. This principle is seen in the N.T., where a believing remnant of Jews accepted Jesus as their Messianic Lord, while the main stream of redemption was rechanneled from unbelieving Jews to Gentiles in the early church.

Reading Ezra

In order to read the entire Old Testament in one year, the book of Ezra should be read in 4 days, according to the following schedule: ☐ 1–3 ☐ 4–6 ☐ 7–8 ☐ 9–10

NOTES

The proclamation of Cyrus

1:1–3pp — 2 Chr. 36:22–23

1 NOW IN the first year of Cyrus
king of Persia, that the word of the
LORD [a]by the mouth of Jeremiah might
be fulfilled, the LORD stirred up the
spirit of Cyrus king of Persia, [b]that he
[a]made a proclamation throughout all
his kingdom, and *put it* also in writing,
saying,
2 Thus saith Cyrus king of Persia,
The LORD God of heaven hath given me
all the kingdoms of the earth; and he
hath [c]charged me to build him an
house at Jerusalem, which *is* in Judah.
3 Who *is there* among you of all his
people? his God be with him, and let
him go up to Jerusalem, which *is* in Ju-
dah, and build the house of the LORD
God of Israel, ([d]he *is* the God,) which
is in Jerusalem.
4 And whosoever remaineth in any
place where he sojourneth, let the men
of his place [b]help him with silver, and
with gold, and with goods, and with
beasts, beside the freewill offering for
the house of God that *is* in Jerusalem.
5 ¶ Then rose up the chief of the fa-
thers of Judah and Benjamin, and the
priests, and the Levites, with all *them*
whose spirit [e]God had raised, to go up
to build the house of the LORD which *is*
in Jerusalem.
6 And all they that *were* about them
[c]strengthened their hands with ves-
sels of silver, with gold, with goods,
and with beasts, and with precious
things, beside all *that* was willingly of-
fered.
7 ¶ [f]Also Cyrus the king brought
forth the vessels of the house of the
LORD, [g]which Nebuchadnezzar had
brought forth out of Jerusalem, and
had put them in the house of his gods;
8 Even those did Cyrus king of Per-
sia bring forth by the hand of Mithre-
dath the treasurer, and numbered
them unto [h]Sheshbazzar, the prince of
Judah.
9 And this *is* the number of them:
thirty chargers of gold, a thousand
chargers of silver, nine and twenty
knives,
10 Thirty basins of gold, silver ba-
sins of a second *sort* four hundred and
ten, *and* other vessels a thousand.
11 All the vessels of gold and of sil-
ver *were* five thousand and four hun-
dred. All *these* did Sheshbazzar bring
up with *them of* [d]the captivity that
were brought up from Babylon unto Je-
rusalem.

The people who returned

2:1–70pp — Neh. 7:6–73

2 NOW [i]THESE *are* the children of
the province that went up out of

1:1 [a]2 Chr. 36:22,23 [b]ch. 5:13,14 **1:2** [c]Is. 44:28 & 45:1,13 **1:3** [d]Dan. 6:26 **1:5** [e]Phil. 2:13 **1:7** [f]ch. 5:14 & 6:5 [g]2 Ki. 24:13 2 Chr. 36:7 **1:8** [h]See ch. 5:14 **2:1** [i]Neh. 7:6

[a] Heb. *(caused a voice to pass)* [b] Heb. *lift him up* [c] i.e. *helped them* [d] Heb. *the transportation*

1:1 THAT THE WORD OF THE LORD BY . . . JEREMIAH. Jeremiah had predicted that the Jews would remain in captivity in the land of Babylon for seventy years before returning to Judah (Jer. 25:11–12; 29:10). The seventy-year captivity can be calculated from the first captivity in 605 B.C., the third year of Jehoiakim (2 Ki. 24:1; Dan. 1:1), to 538 B.C. (approximately seventy years later), when the people began to return to their homeland (see 2:1, note).

1:1 THE LORD STIRRED UP THE SPIRIT OF CYRUS. The Lord God directs the stream of redemption throughout history to its appointed end. In doing so He sometimes chooses to humble mighty rulers (e.g., Nebuchadnezzar, Dan. 4), send destructive judgment on rulers (e.g., Pharaoh during the exodus, Ex. 14; Belshazzar in Babylon, Dan. 5), or exalt an international leader (e.g., King Cyrus of Persia, v. 2), in order to fulfill His word and accomplish His purposes. By stirring the spirit of Cyrus to be benevolent toward conquered and exiled peoples, God enabled His word of promise through Jeremiah to be fulfilled on time. Proverbs declares that a king's heart is like rivers of water in the hand of God, which God turns wherever He wishes in order to assure the ongoing course of redemption and the ultimate conclusion of history (Prov. 21:1).

1:2 CYRUS KING OF PERSIA. About 160 years before the appearance of Cyrus, Isaiah had foretold of a ruler named Cyrus who would permit the return of the Jews to their homeland in order to rebuild Jerusalem and the temple (Is. 44:26–28; 45:1,13; see also Is. 41:2; 45:4–5).

1:5 WHOSE SPIRIT GOD HAD RAISED. Through the Holy Spirit, God stirred the hearts of some of His faithful people to return to their land (cf. Phil. 2:13, note). About 50,000 responded to the Lord's call to participate in this first pilgrimage to Palestine. Note that others remained behind in exile (vv. 4,6); their purpose was to encourage and support those who were returning to the land of Judah.

1:8 SHESHBAZZAR. Sheshbazzar, the first governor to be appointed over the returning exiles (cf. 5:14,16), may have been another name for Zerubbabel (cf. 2:2; 3:2,8; 4:3).

2:1 WENT UP OUT OF THE CAPTIVITY. The book of Ezra describes two of the three waves of exiled Israelites who returned to Judah. (1) The first return occurred in 538 B.C. under the leadership of Zerubbabel (v. 2; 3:8; cf. Hag. 1:1,14; Zech.

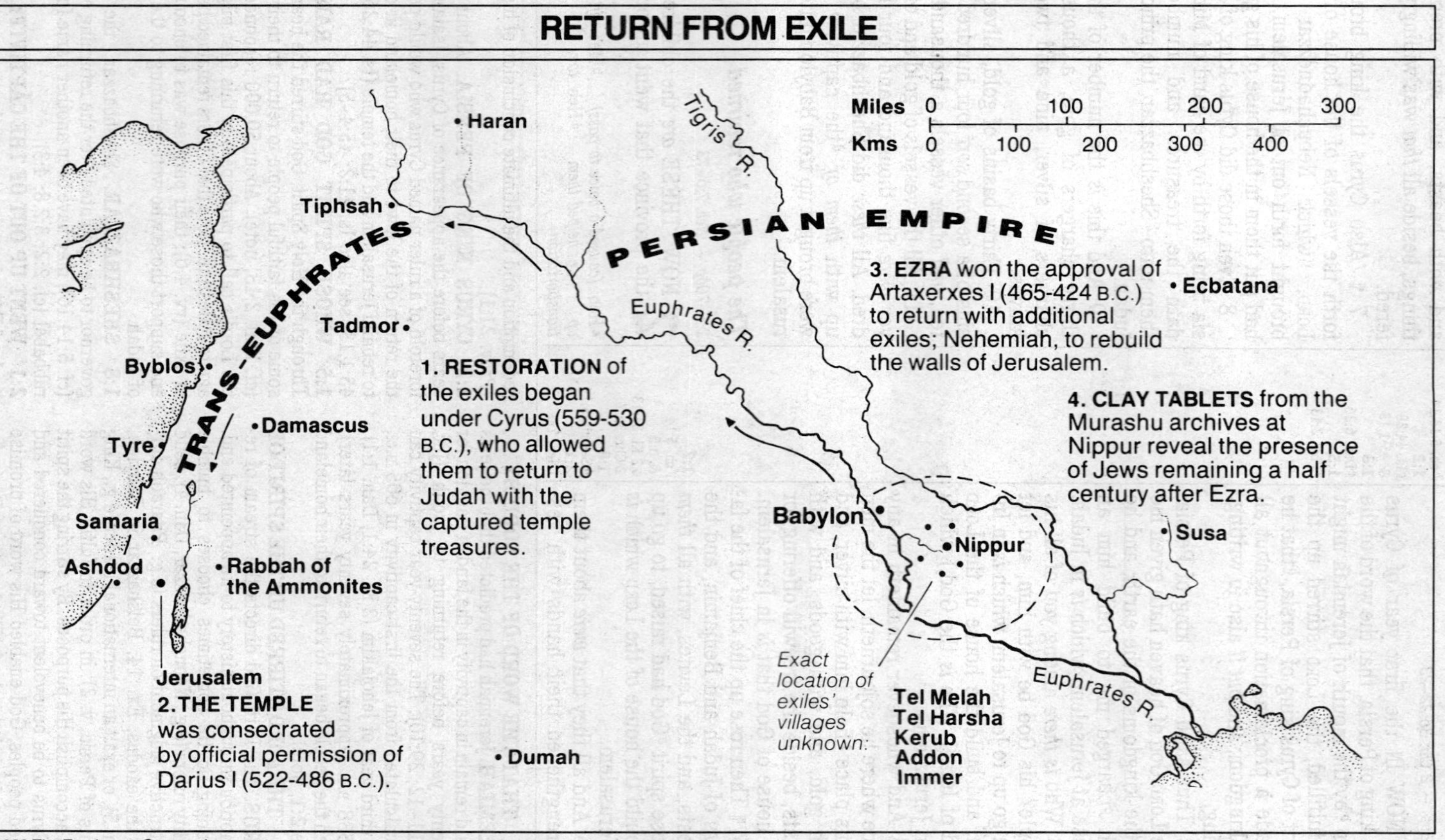
RETURN FROM EXILE
Miles 0 100 200 300
Kms 0 100 200 300 400
Haran
Tigris R.
Tiphsah
PERSIAN EMPIRE
TRANS-EUPHRATES
3. EZRA won the approval of Artaxerxes I (465-424 B.C.) to return with additional exiles; Nehemiah, to rebuild the walls of Jerusalem.
Ecbatana
Euphrates R.
Tadmor
Byblos
1. RESTORATION of the exiles began under Cyrus (559-530 B.C.), who allowed them to return to Judah with the captured temple treasures.
4. CLAY TABLETS from the Murashu archives at Nippur reveal the presence of Jews remaining a half century after Ezra.
Damascus
Tyre
Samaria
Babylon
Nippur
Susa
Ashdod
Rabbah of the Ammonites
Jerusalem
2. THE TEMPLE was consecrated by official permission of Darius I (522-486 B.C.).
Exact location of exiles' villages unknown:
Tel Melah
Tel Harsha
Kerub
Addon
Immer
Euphrates R.
Dumah

the captivity, of those which had been
carried away, [j]whom Nebuchadnez-
zar the king of Babylon had carried
away unto Babylon, and came again
unto Jerusalem and Judah, every one
unto his city;
2 Which came with Zerubbabel:
Jeshua, Nehemiah, [e]Seraiah, [f]Reela-
iah, Mordecai, Bilshan, [g]Mizpar, Big-
vai, [h]Rehum, Baanah. The number of
the men of the people of Israel:
3 The children of Parosh, two thou-
sand an hundred seventy and two.
4 The children of Shephatiah, three
hundred seventy and two.
5 The children of Arah, [k]seven
hundred seventy and five.
6 The children of [l]Pahath-moab, of
the children of Jeshua *and* Joab, two
thousand eight hundred and twelve.
7 The children of Elam, a thousand
two hundred fifty and four.
8 The children of Zattu, nine hun-
dred forty and five.
9 The children of Zaccai, seven
hundred and threescore.
10 The children of [i]Bani, six hun-
dred forty and two.
11 The children of Bebai, six hun-
dred twenty and three.
12 The children of Azgad, a thou-
sand two hundred twenty and two.
13 The children of Adonikam, six
hundred sixty and six.
14 The children of Bigvai, two thou-
sand fifty and six.
15 The children of Adin, four hun-
dred fifty and four.
16 The children of Ater of Hezeki-
ah, ninety and eight.
17 The children of Bezai, three hun-
dred twenty and three.
18 The children of [j]Jorah, an hun-
dred and twelve.
19 The children of Hashum, two
hundred twenty and three.
20 The children of [k]Gibbar, ninety
and five.
21 The children of Bethlehem, an
hundred twenty and three.
22 The men of Netophah, fifty and
six.

2:1 [j]2 Ki. 24:14-16 & 25:11 2 Chr. 36:20
2:5 [k]See Neh. 7:10
2:6 [l]Neh. 7:11
2:31 [m]See ver. 7
2:36 [n]1 Chr. 24:7
2:37 [o]1 Chr. 24:14
2:38 [p]1 Chr. 9:12
2:39 [q]1 Chr. 24:8

23 The men of Anathoth, an hun-
dred twenty and eight.
24 The children of [l]Azmaveth, for-
ty and two.
25 The children of Kirjath-arim,
Chephirah, and Beeroth, seven hun-
dred and forty and three.
26 The children of Ramah and
Gaba, six hundred twenty and one.
27 The men of Michmas, an hun-
dred twenty and two.
28 The men of Beth-el and Ai, two
hundred twenty and three.
29 The children of Nebo, fifty and
two.
30 The children of Magbish, an hun-
dred fifty and six.
31 The children of the other
[m]Elam, a thousand two hundred fifty
and four.
32 The children of Harim, three
hundred and twenty.
33 The children of Lod, [m]Hadid,
and Ono, seven hundred twenty and
five.
34 The children of Jericho, three
hundred forty and five.
35 The children of Senaah, three
thousand and six hundred and thirty.
36 ¶ The priests: the children of
[n]Jedaiah, of the house of Jeshua, nine
hundred seventy and three.
37 The children of [o]Immer, a thou-
sand fifty and two.
38 The children of [p]Pashur, a
thousand two hundred forty and seven.
39 The children of [q]Harim, a thou-
sand and seventeen.
40 ¶ The Levites: the children of
Jeshua and Kadmiel, of the children of
[n]Hodaviah, seventy and four.
41 ¶ The singers: the children of
Asaph, an hundred twenty and eight.
42 ¶ The children of the porters: the
children of Shallum, the children of

[e] Or, *Azariah;* see Neh. 7:7 [f] Or, *Raamiah* [g] Or, *Mispereth* [h] Or, *Nehum* [i] Or, *Binnui;* see Neh. 7:15 [j] Or, *Hariph;* see Neh. 7:24 [k] Or, *Gibeon;* see Neh. 7:25 [l] Or, *Beth-azmaveth;* see Neh. 7:28 [m] Or, *Harid,* as it is in some copies [n] Or, *Judah;* see ch. 3:9; called also *Hodevah* in Neh. 7:43

4:9). Approximately 50,000 people returned (vv. 64–65) and rebuilt the temple, completing it in 516 B.C. (see 6:15, note). The prophets Haggai and Zechariah ministered there during this time (5:1–2).

(2) The second return occurred in 457 B.C. under the leadership of Ezra (chs. 7—10). As leader, Ezra focused on furthering the spiritual life of the people and encouraging their obedience to the law of God (7:10; 10:1–6).

(3) The third return took place in 444 B.C. under the leadership of Nehemiah, who went to Jerusalem to rebuild the wall of the city (Neh. 2:17). The prophet Malachi probably ministered in Judah during the latter days of Ezra and Nehemiah.

Ater, the children of Talmon, the children of Akkub, the children of Hatita, the children of Shobai, *in* all an hundred thirty and nine.

43 ¶ [r]The Nethinims: the children of Ziha, the children of Hasupha, the children of Tabbaoth,

44 The children of Keros, the children of [o]Siaha, the children of Padon,

45 The children of Lebanah, the children of Hagabah, the children of Akkub,

46 The children of Hagab, the children of [p]Shalmai, the children of Hanan,

47 The children of Giddel, the children of Gahar, the children of Reaiah,

48 The children of Rezin, the children of Nekoda, the children of Gazzam,

49 The children of Uzza, the children of Paseah, the children of Besai,

50 the children of Asnah, the children of Mehunim, the children of [q]Nephusim,

51 The children of Bakbuk, the children of Hakupha, the children of Harhur,

52 The children of [r]Bazluth, the children of Mehida, the children of Harsha,

53 The children of Barkos, the children of Sisera, the children of Thamah,

54 The children of Neziah, the children of Hatipha.

55 ¶ The children of [s]Solomon's servants: the children of Sotai, the children of Sophereth, the children of [s]Peruda,

56 The children of Jaalah, the children of Darkon, the children of Giddel,

57 The children of Shephatiah, the children of Hattil, the children of Pochereth of Zebaim, the children of [t]Ami.

58 All the [t]Nethinims, and the children of [u]Solomon's servants, *were* three hundred ninety and two.

59 And these *were* they which went up from Tel-melah, Tel-harsa, Cherub, [u]Addan, *and* Immer: but they could not show their father's house, and their [v]seed, whether they *were* of Israel:

60 The children of Delaiah, the children of Tobiah, the children of Nekoda, six hundred fifty and two.

61 ¶ And of the children of the priests: the children of Habaiah, the children of Koz, the children of Barzillai; which took a wife of the daughters of [v]Barzillai the Gileadite, and was called after their name:

62 These sought their register *among* those that were reckoned by genealogy, but they were not found: [w]therefore [w]were they, as polluted, put from the priesthood.

63 And the [x]Tirshatha said unto them, that they [x]should not eat of the most holy things, till there stood up a priest with [y]Urim and with Thummim.

64 ¶ [z]The whole congregation together *was* forty and two thousand three hundred *and* threescore,

65 Beside their servants and their maids, of whom *there were* seven thousand three hundred thirty and seven: and *there were* among them two hundred singing men and singing women.

66 Their horses *were* seven hundred thirty and six; their mules, two hundred forty and five;

67 Their camels, four hundred thirty and five; *their* asses, six thousand seven hundred and twenty.

68 ¶ [a]And *some* of the chief of the fathers, when they came to the house of the LORD which *is* at Jerusalem, offered freely for the house of God to set it up in his place:

69 They gave after their ability unto the [b]treasure of the work threescore and one thousand drams of gold, and five thousand pound of silver, and one hundred priests' garments.

70 [c]So the priests, and the Levites, and *some* of the people, and the singers, and the porters, and the Nethi-

2:43 [r]1 Chr. 9:2 **2:55** [s]1 Ki. 9:21 **2:58** [t]Josh. 9:21,27 1 Chr. 9:2 [u]1 Ki. 9:21

2:61 [v]2 Sam. 17:27 **2:62** [w]Num. 3:10 **2:63** [x]Lev. 22:2,10,15,16 [y]Ex. 28:30 Num. 27:21 **2:64** [z]Neh. 7:66 **2:68** [a]Neh. 7:70 **2:69** [b]1 Chr. 26:20 **2:70** [c]ch. 6:16,17 Neh. 7:73

[o] Or, *Sia* [p] Or, *Shamlai* [q] Or, *Nephishesim* [r] Or, *Bazlith;* see Neh. 7:54 [s] Or, *Perida;* see Neh. 7:57 [t] Or, *Amon;* see Neh. 7:59 [u] Or, *Addon;* see Neh. 7:61 [v] Or, *pedigree* [w] Heb. *they were polluted from the priesthood* [x] Or, *governor;* see Neh. 8:9

2:64 FORTY AND TWO THOUSAND. The total sum of the numbers given in vv. 3–63 falls about 11,000 short of the 42,360 mentioned here. The additional 11,000 may refer to exiles from tribes other than Judah (cf. v. 70; 6:17; 8:35), women and children, and the unregistered priests (vv. 61–62). Certain numerical differences in Nehemiah's list (7:6–73) may be due to scribal errors in the transmission of numbers.

2:70 ALL ISRAEL. This phrase suggests that people from all twelve tribes were represented in the remnant that returned (see 6:17; 8:35).

nims, dwelt in their cities, and all Israel in their cities.

The altar rebuilt

3 AND WHEN the seventh month was come, and the children of Israel *were* in the cities, the people gathered themselves together as one man to Jerusalem.

2 Then stood up [y]Jeshua the son of Jozadak, and his brethren the priests, and [z]Zerubbabel the son of [d]Shealtiel, and his brethren, and builded the altar of the God of Israel, to offer burnt offerings thereon, as *it is* [e]written in the law of Moses the man of God.

3 And they set the altar upon his bases; for fear *was* upon them because of the people of those countries: and they offered burnt offerings thereon unto the LORD, *even* [f]burnt offerings morning and evening.

4 [g]They kept also the feast of tabernacles, [h]as *it is* written, and [i]*offered* the daily burnt offerings by number, according to the custom, [a]as the duty of every day required;

5 And afterward *offered* the [j]continual burnt offering, both of the new moons, and of all the set feasts of the LORD that were consecrated, and of every one that willingly offered a freewill offering unto the LORD.

6 From the first day of the seventh month began they to offer burnt offerings unto the LORD. But [b]the foundation of the temple of the LORD was not *yet* laid.

7 They gave money also unto the masons, and to the [c]carpenters; and [k]meat, and drink, and oil, unto them of Zidon, and to them of Tyre, to bring cedar trees from Lebanon to the sea of [l]Joppa, [m]according to the grant that they had of Cyrus king of Persia.

Rebuilding of the temple begun

8 ¶ Now in the second year of their coming unto the house of God at Jerusalem, in the second month, began Zerubbabel the son of Shealtiel, and Jeshua the son of Jozadak, and the remnant of their brethren the priests and the Levites, and all they that were come out of the captivity unto Jerusalem; [n]and appointed the Levites, from twenty years old and upward, to set forward the work of the house of the LORD.

9 Then stood [o]Jeshua *with* his sons and his brethren, Kadmiel and his sons, the sons of [d]Judah, [e]together, to set forward the workmen in the house of God: the sons of Henadad, *with* their sons and their brethren the Levites.

10 And when the builders laid the foundation of the temple of the LORD, [p]they set the priests in their apparel with trumpets, and the Levites the sons of Asaph with cymbals, to praise the LORD, after the [q]ordinance of David king of Israel.

11 [r]And they sang together by

3:2 [d]Mat. 1:12 & Luke 3:27 called *Salathiel* [e]Deut. 12:5
3:3 [f]Num. 28:3
3:4 [g]Neh. 8:14 Zech. 14:16 [h]Ex. 23:16 [i]Num. 29:12
3:5 [j]Ex. 29:38 Num. 28:3,11,19, 26
3:7 [k]1 Ki. 5:6,9 2 Chr. 2:10 Acts 12:20 [l]2 Chr. 2:16 Acts 9:36 [m]ch. 6:3
3:8 [n]1 Chr. 23:24,27
3:9 [o]ch. 2:40
3:10 [p]1 Chr. 16:5 [q]1 Chr. 6:31 & 16:4 & 25:1
3:11 [r]Ex. 15:21 2 Chr. 7:3 Neh. 12:24

[y] Or, *Joshua;* see Hag. 1:1 & 2:2; Zech. 3:1
[z] Called *Zorobabel* in Mat. 1:12; Luke 3:27
[a] Heb. *the matter of the day in his day* [b] Heb. *the temple of the LORD was not yet founded*
[c] Or, *workmen* [d] Or, *Hodaviah;* see ch. 2:40
[e] Heb. *as one*

3:2 BUILDED THE ALTAR OF THE GOD OF ISRAEL. The first priority of the returned exiles was to build an altar unto the Lord. The altar was the center of Jewish worship, for on it sacrifices and blood atonement for sin were offered to God (see Ex. 27:1, note). (1) The people were motivated to build the altar, at least in part, because of the danger from "the people of those countries" (v. 3). They knew that God would protect them from harm only as they drew near to Him in faith and obedience (see Ex. 19:5; 29:43; cf. Heb. 4:16). (2) They also understood the basic purpose of their existence. They were to offer sacrifices unto God as "a kingdom of priests, and an holy nation" (Ex. 19:6). Only by fulfilling this spiritual calling could they become what God intended them to be. Likewise, believers in Christ are to be "a royal priesthood, an holy nation, a peculiar people; that ye should show forth the praises of him who hath called you out of darkness into his marvellous light" (1 Pet. 2:9), and to "offer up spiritual sacrifices, acceptable to God by Jesus Christ" (1 Pet. 2:5; see Heb. 13:10). In other words, the church as the people of God in N.T. times is the heir of and successor to Israel.

3:4 FEAST OF TABERNACLES. See Lev. 23:34–43, note.

3:8 THE HOUSE OF THE LORD. The people's highest priority upon returning to Jerusalem was to rebuild the temple and so to reinstate the faithful worship of the Lord. Their years in captivity had taught them that God would not be their protector and helper unless they put Him first in their lives. Likewise, we cannot expect the Lord's help or blessing if our lives and desires are not in accord with His kingdom and righteous cause (Mat. 6:33, note).

3:11 SANG TOGETHER . . . IN PRAISING AND GIVING THANKS. The people sang songs of praise to the Lord when they saw the foundation of the temple laid because it represented God's answer to their prayers and His goodness to them.

course in praising and giving thanks
unto the LORD; [s]because *he is* good,
[t]for his mercy *endureth* for ever to-
ward Israel. And all the people shouted
with a great shout, when they praised
the LORD, because the foundation of the
house of the LORD was laid.
12 But many of the priests and Le-
vites and chief of the fathers, *who were*
ancient men, that had seen the first
house, when the foundation of this
house was laid before their eyes, wept
with a loud voice; and many shouted
aloud for joy:
13 So that the people could not dis-
cern the noise of the shout of joy from
the noise of the weeping of the people:
for the people shouted with a loud
Ps. 9:1-2 shout, and the noise was heard afar off.

Adversaries of Judah

4 NOW WHEN [u]the adversaries of
Judah and Benjamin heard that
[f]the children of the captivity builded
the temple unto the LORD God of Israel;
2 Then they came to Zerubbabel,
and to the chief of the fathers, and said
unto them, Let us build with you: for
we seek your God, as ye *do;* and we do
sacrifice unto him since [v]the days of
Esar-haddon king of Assur, which
brought us up hither.
3 But Zerubbabel, and Jeshua, and
the rest of the chief of the fathers of
Israel, said unto them, [w]Ye have noth-
ing to do with us to build an house unto
our God; but we ourselves together will
build unto the LORD God of Israel, as
[x]king Cyrus the king of Persia hath
commanded us.
4 Then [y]the people of the land
weakened the hands of the people of
Judah, and troubled them in building,
5 And hired counsellors against
them, to frustrate their purpose, all the
days of Cyrus king of Persia, even until
the reign of Darius king of Persia. Neh. 2:18-20
6 And in the reign of [g]Ahasuerus,

3:11 [s]1 Chr. 16:34 Ps. 136:1 [t]1 Chr. 16:41 Jer. 33:11
4:1 [u]See ver. 7-9
4:2 [v]ver. 10 2 Ki. 17:24,32,33 & 19:37
4:3 [w]Neh. 2:20 [x]ch. 1:1-3
4:4 [y]ch. 3:3

[f]Heb. *the sons of the transportation* [g]Heb. *Ahashverosh*

Biblical praise exalts God and His work and is an element of worship in which all the people are to participate (see article on PRAISE, p. 816).

3:12 MANY . . . WEPT WITH A LOUD VOICE, AND MANY SHOUTED ALOUD FOR JOY. Although God's law encouraged worship in an orderly manner, it did not limit worship to a set form or pattern. Some of those who had seen the glory of Solomon's temple burst into tears, undoubtedly relieved that the shame of its destruction was now gone. Others broke into shouts of joy. Our worship of the Lord should always be flexible enough to allow for a variety of spontaneous expressions. God made us all different. We should expect variety when His people yield to the Holy Spirit.

4:1 THE ADVERSARIES OF JUDAH. Believers will always undergo a measure of opposition from the ungodly (2 Cor. 11:13–15; Eph. 6:12; 2 Tim. 3:12). The righteous, who proclaim the truth and rely on God alone, must respond to these threats by constant prayer and sincere faith (see Eph. 6:11, note).

4:2 LET US BUILD WITH YOU. The enemies of God (probably Samaritans, see 2 Ki. 17:24,34) attempted to infiltrate the Jews and disrupt the building of the temple by a pretense of unity and by an offer to join together to advance God's work. (1) The enemies of Judah (v. 1) claimed to worship and sacrifice to the Lord God as did the Jews. However, they retained their own gods as well and did not accept the written Word of God as the fundamental authority for His people (see 2 Ki. 17:24, note). This deceptive offer of help was a sinister plot to undermine the faith and commitment of the restored remnant.

(2) Scripture warns that Satan will seek to distort God's message and bring spiritual ruin to God's holy remnant through offers of cooperation from false believers who are not loyal to the inspired revelation of God's Word (see Mat. 24:24; Acts 20:27–31; 2 Cor. 11:13–15; Rev. 2—3).

(3) Unity among those who worship the Lord is an important Biblical teaching, but such unity must be based on sincere faith, obedient righteousness, and loyalty to God's revealed truth (see Eph. 4:3–13, notes).

4:3 YE HAVE NOTHING TO DO WITH US. Zerubbabel and Jeshua refused to enter into fellowship with "the people of the land" (v. 4), for they lived by the Biblical principle of separation from idolatry and from compromise with the world (see article on SPIRITUAL SEPARATION FOR BELIEVERS, p. 1814). This refusal to accept a pluralistic religion led to opposition and persecution for God's faithful people (vv. 4–24; see 2 Tim. 3:12, note). The adversaries discouraged the people through intimidation, threats, and misrepresention of their intentions (vv. 4–6).

4:5 UNTIL THE REIGN OF DARIUS KING OF PERSIA. This reference to the reign of Darius is repeated in v. 24. This kind of repetition is a way used in the O.T. to show that v. 24 continues where v. 5 left off. The material between these two verses is a parenthesis which completes the account of Samaritan persecution down to Ezra's own day. Then the author comes back to the account of the rebuilding of the temple. Note that vv. 7–23 talk about the city being rebuilt, not the temple. Evidently Ezra had received a decree to rebuild the city, and the Samaritans wanted it revoked.

4:6 IN THE REIGN OF AHASUERUS . . . WROTE THEY *UNTO HIM* AN ACCUSATION. Ahasuerus is the Latinized form of the Hebrew *'ahashwerosh*. Ancient inscriptions show the

in the beginning of his reign, wrote they *unto him* an accusation against the inhabitants of Judah and Jerusalem.

The letter to Artaxerxes

7 ¶ And in the days of Artaxerxes wrote [h]Bishlam, Mithredath, Tabeel, and the rest of their [i]companions, unto Artaxerxes king of Persia; and the writing of the letter *was* written in the Syrian tongue, and interpreted in the Syrian tongue.

8 Rehum the chancellor and Shimshai the [j]scribe wrote a letter against Jerusalem to Artaxerxes the king in this sort:

9 Then *wrote* Rehum the chancellor, and Shimshai the scribe, and the rest of their [k]companions; [z]the Dinaites, the Apharsathchites, the Tarpelites, the Apharsites, the Archevites, the Babylonians, the Susanchites, the Dehavites, *and* the Elamites,

10 [a]And the rest of the nations whom the great and noble Asnapper brought over, and set in the cities of Samaria, and the rest *that are* on this side the river, [b]and [l]at such a time.

11 ¶ This *is* the copy of the letter that they sent unto him, *even* unto Artaxerxes the king; Thy servants the men on this side the river, and at such a time.

12 Be it known unto the king, that the Jews which came up from thee to us are come unto Jerusalem, building the rebellious and the bad city, and have [m]set up the walls *thereof,* and [n]joined the foundations.

13 Be it known now unto the king, that, if this city be builded, and the walls set up *again, then* will they not [o]pay [c]toll, tribute, and custom, and *so* thou shalt endamage the [p]revenue of the kings.

14 Now because [q]we have maintenance from *the king's* palace, and it was not meet for us to see the king's dishonour, therefore have we sent and certified the king;

4:9
[z]2 Ki. 17:30,31
4:10
[a]ver. 1
[b]ver. 11,17 & ch 7:12
4:13
[c]ch. 7:24

4:20
[d]1 Ki. 4:21 Ps. 72:8
[e]Gen. 15:18 Josh. 1:4

15 That search may be made in the book of the records of thy fathers: so shalt thou find in the book of the records, and know that this city *is* a rebellious city, and hurtful unto kings and provinces, and that they have [r]moved sedition [s]within the same of old time: for which cause was this city destroyed.

16 We certify the king that, if this city be builded *again,* and the walls thereof set up, by this means thou shalt have no portion on this side the river.

17 ¶ *Then* sent the king an answer unto Rehum the chancellor, and *to* Shimshai the scribe, and *to* the rest of their [k]companions that dwell in Samaria, and *unto* the rest beyond the river, Peace, and at such a time.

18 The letter which ye sent unto us hath been plainly read before me.

19 And [t]I commanded, and search hath been made, and it is found that this city of old time hath [u]made insurrection against kings, and *that* rebellion and sedition have been made therein.

20 There have been mighty kings also over Jerusalem, which have [d]ruled over all *countries* [e]beyond the river; and toll, tribute, and custom, was paid unto them.

21 [v]Give ye now commandment to cause these men to cease, and that this city be not builded, until *another* commandment shall be given from me.

22 Take heed now that ye fail not to do this: why should damage grow to the hurt of the kings?

23 ¶ Now when the copy of king Artaxerxes' letter *was* read before Rehum, and Shimshai the scribe, and

[h] Or, *in peace* [i] Heb. *societies* [j] Or, *secretary* [k] Chald. *societies* [l] Chald. *Cheeneth* [m] Or, *finished* [n] Chald. *sewed together* [o] Chald. *give* [p] Or, *strength* [q] Chald. *we are salted with the salt of the palace* [r] Chald. *made* [s] Chald. *in the midst thereof* [t] Chald. *by me a decree is set* [u] Chald. *lifted up itself* [v] Chald. *Make a decree*

Greeks called him Xerxes. He reigned over the Persian empire from 485 to 465 B.C. The events of the book of Esther took place during this period.

4:11 THIS *IS* THE COPY OF THE LETTER THAT THEY SENT UNTO . . . ARTAXERXES. Ezra does not give any details of the accusation made by Judah's enemies to King Xerxes (v. 6), but a copy of the letter was sent in Ezra's own day to the next king, Artaxerxes (who reigned from 465 to 424 B.C.). Unfortunately, the letter contained some truth—Jerusalem had rebelled against the Babylonians more than once.

4:23 MADE THEM CEASE BY FORCE AND POWER. Neh. 1:3 gives more details of what the opponents of the Jews did to impede any progress on the city walls. This verse concludes the account of Samaritan persecution (see v. 5, note).

their companions, they went up in haste to Jerusalem unto the Jews, and made them to cease [w]by force and power.

24 Then ceased the work of the house of God which *is* at Jerusalem. So it ceased unto the second year of the reign of Darius king of Persia.

Zerubbabel begins to build again

5 THEN THE prophets, [f]Haggai the prophet, and [g]Zechariah the son of Iddo, prophesied unto the Jews that *were* in Judah and Jerusalem in the name of the God of Israel, *even* unto them.

2 Then rose up [h]Zerubbabel the son of Shealtiel, and Jeshua the son of Jozadak, and began to build the house of God which *is* at Jerusalem: and with them *were* the prophets of God helping them.

3 ¶ At the same time came to them [i]Tatnai, governor on this side the river, and Shethar-boznai, and their companions, and said thus unto them, [j]Who hath commanded you to build this house, and to make up this wall?

4 [k]Then said we unto them after this manner, What are the names of the men [x]that make this building?

5 But [l]the eye of their God was upon the elders of the Jews, that they could not cause them to cease, till the matter came to Darius: and then they returned [m]answer by letter concerning this *matter*.

6 ¶ The copy of the letter that Tatnai, governor on this side the river, and Shethar-boznai, [n]and his companions the Apharsachites, which *were* on this side the river, sent unto Darius the king:

7 They sent a letter unto him, [y]wherein was written thus; Unto Darius the king, all peace.

8 Be it known unto the king, that we went into the province of Judea, to the house of the great God, which is builded with [z]great stones, and timber is laid in the walls, and this work goeth fast on, and prospereth in their hands.

9 Then asked we those elders, *and* said unto them thus, [o]Who commanded you to build this house, and to make up these walls?

10 We asked their names also, to certify thee, that we might write the

5:1 [f]Hag. 1:1 [g]Zech. 1:1
5:2 [h]ch. 3:2
5:3 [i]ver. 6 ch. 6:6 [j]ver. 9
5:4 [k]ver. 10
5:5 [l]See ch. 7:6,28 Ps. 33:18 [m]ch. 6:6
5:6 [n]ch. 4:9
5:9 [o]ver. 3,4

[w] Chald. *by arm and power* [x] Chald. *that build this building?* [y] Chald. *in the midst whereof* [z] Chald. *stones of rolling*

4:24 THEN CEASED THE WORK OF THE HOUSE OF GOD. Work on the temple ceased soon after it began in 538 B.C. and did not resume until eighteen years later, in 520 B.C.

5:1 THE PROPHETS . . . PROPHESIED UNTO THE JEWS. Work on the temple was renewed and accomplished because of the prophetic ministries of Haggai and Zechariah (see Hag. 1:9–11). Their prophecies included (1) direct command (Hag. 1:8), (2) warning and rebuke (Hag. 1:9–11), (3) exhortation (Hag. 2:4), and (4) encouragement through the promise of future blessings (Hag. 2:6–9, note; Zech. 8:3, note). The word of God through Jeremiah had set in motion the beginning of the rebuilding of the temple (1:1); likewise, the word of the Lord through Haggai and Zechariah was now inspiring its completion (6:14).

5:2 THE PROPHETS OF GOD HELPING THEM. The rebuilding of the temple was undertaken through the godly leadership of Zerubbabel and Jeshua. However, Ezra notes two additional contributing factors in the successful restoration of God's house. (1) The ministry and revelation of the prophets Haggai and Zechariah were influential in seeing the project through to completion in spite of many obstacles and setbacks (see previous note). God's work always requires the participation of God's prophets to realize His holy purpose for any given generation.

(2) Another key element in the successful restoration of God's house was the dedication of the elders and the people (vv. 5,8; cf. 7:23). Instead of being apathetic or taking the challenge casually, they pursued the task with great diligence, and God prospered the work of their hands. God's kingdom always advances through the words and actions of committed leaders and people who, by working together, give themselves fully to God's purpose for their generation.

5:3 WHO HATH COMMANDED YOU TO BUILD THIS HOUSE? The people had obeyed the word of the Lord that came through His prophets (v. 1). They committed themselves to work for the glory of God (v. 2), and God was with them in a special way (v. 5). Yet the enemy came and opposed the work (v. 3). In every spiritual advance we can expect our efforts to be opposed and tested by Satan and the enemies of Christ. God's people must respond to such opposition by continually praying to God, trusting Him, and pressing forward until the work is done (see Eph. 6:11, note).

5:5 THE EYE OF THEIR GOD WAS UPON THE ELDERS. Those who commit their lives to God's cause and work are special objects of His watchful care. If you are striving to exalt our Lord's kingdom and His righteousness, He will never withdraw His eyes from you (Job 36:7; cf. Mat. 6:33). This promise belongs to you: "The eyes of the LORD *are* upon the righteous" (Ps. 34:15).

names of the men that *were* the chief of them.

11 And thus they returned us answer, saying, We are the servants of the God of heaven and earth, and build the house that was builded these many years ago, which a great king of Israel builded [p]and set up.

12 But [q]after that our fathers had provoked the God of heaven unto wrath, he gave them into the hand of [r]Nebuchadnezzar the king of Babylon, the Chaldean, who destroyed this house, and carried the people away into Babylon.

13 But in the first year of [s]Cyrus the king of Babylon *the same* king Cyrus made a decree to build this house of God.

14 And [t]the vessels also of gold and silver of the house of God, which Nebuchadnezzar took out of the temple that *was* in Jerusalem, and brought them into the temple of Babylon, those did Cyrus the king take out of the temple of Babylon, and they were delivered unto *one,* [u]whose name *was* Sheshbazzar, whom he had made [a]governor;

15 And said unto him, Take these vessels, go, carry them into the temple that *is* in Jerusalem, and let the house of God be builded in his place.

16 Then came the same Sheshbazzar, *and* [v]laid the foundation of the house of God which *is* in Jerusalem: and since that time even until now hath it been in building, and [w]*yet* it is not finished.

17 Now therefore, if *it seem* good to the king, [x]let there be search made in the king's treasure house, which *is* there at Babylon, whether it be *so,* that a decree was made of Cyrus the king to build this house of God at Jerusalem, and let the king send his pleasure to us concerning this matter.

Darius' search and reply

6 THEN DARIUS the king made a decree, [y]and search was made in the house of the [b]rolls, where the treasures were [c]laid up in Babylon.

2 And there was found at [d]Achmetha, in the palace that *is* in the province of the Medes, a roll, and therein *was* a record thus written:

3 In the first year of Cyrus the king *the same* Cyrus the king made a decree *concerning* the house of God at Jerusalem, Let the house be builded, the place where they offered sacrifices, and let the foundations thereof be strongly laid; the height thereof threescore cubits, *and* the breadth thereof threescore cubits;

4 [z]*With* three rows of great stones, and a row of new timber: and let the expenses be given out of the king's house:

5 And also let [a]the golden and silver vessels of the house of God, which Nebuchadnezzar took forth out of the temple which *is* at Jerusalem, and brought unto Babylon, be restored, and [e]brought again unto the temple which *is* at Jerusalem, *every one* to his place, and place *them* in the house of God.

6 [b]Now *therefore,* Tatnai, governor beyond the river, Shethar-boznai, and [f]your companions the Apharsachites, which *are* beyond the river, be ye far from thence:

7 Let the work of this house of God alone; let the governor of the Jews and the elders of the Jews build this house of God in his place.

8 Moreover [g]I make a decree what ye shall do to the elders of these Jews for the building of this house of God: that of the king's goods, *even* of the tribute beyond the river, forthwith expenses be given unto these men, that they be not [h]hindered.

9 And that which they have need of, both young bullocks, and rams, and lambs, for the burnt offerings of the God of heaven, wheat, salt, wine, and oil, according to the appointment of the priests which *are* at Jerusalem, let it be given them day by day without fail:

10 [c]That they may offer sacrifices [i]of sweet savours unto the God of heaven, and pray for the life of the king, and of his sons.

11 Also I have made a decree, that whosoever shall alter this word, let timber be pulled down from his house, and being set up, [j]let him be hanged

5:11 [p]1 Ki. 6:1
5:12 [q]2 Chr. 36:16,17 [r]2 Ki. 24:2 & 25:8,9,11
5:13 [s]ch. 1:1
5:14 [t]ch. 1:7,8 & 6:5 [u]Hag. 1:14 & 2:2,21
5:16 [v]ch. 3:8,10 [w]ch. 6:15
5:17 [x]ch. 6:1,2
6:1 [y]ch. 5:17
6:4 [z]1 Ki. 6:36
6:5 [a]ch. 1:7,8 & 5:14
6:6 [b]ch. 5:3
6:10 [c]ch. 7:23

[a] Or, *deputy* [b] Chald. *books* [c] Chald. *made to descend* [d] Or, *Ecbatana,* or, *in a coffer* [e] Chald. *go* [f] Chald. *their societies* [g] Chald. *by me a decree is made* [h] Chald. *made to cease* [i] Chald. *of rest* [j] Chald. *let him be destroyed*

5:16 SHESHBAZZAR. See 1:8, note.

thereon; [d]and let his house be made a
dunghill for this.
12 And the God that hath caused
his [e]name to dwell there destroy all
kings and people, that shall put to their
hand to alter *and* to destroy this house
of God which *is* at Jerusalem. I Darius
have made a decree; let it be done with
speed.

The temple rebuilt and dedicated

13 ¶ Then Tatnai, governor on this
side the river, Shethar-boznai, and
their companions, according to that
which Darius the king had sent, so
they did speedily.
14 [f]And the elders of the Jews
builded, and they prospered through
the prophesying of Haggai the prophet
and Zechariah the son of Iddo. And
they builded, and finished *it,* according
to the commandment of the God of Is-
rael, and according to the [k]command-
ment of [g]Cyrus, and [h]Darius, and
[i]Artaxerxes king of Persia.
15 And this house was finished on
the third day of the month Adar, which
was in the sixth year of the reign of
Darius the king.
16 ¶ And the children of Israel, the
priests, and the Levites, and the rest of
[l]the children of the captivity, kept
[j]the dedication of this house of God
with joy,
17 And [k]offered at the dedication
of this house of God an hundred bull-
ocks, two hundred rams, four hundred
lambs; and for a sin offering for all Is-
rael, twelve he goats, according to the
number of the tribes of Israel.
18 And they set the priests in their
[l]divisions, and the Levites in their
[m]courses, for the service of God,
which *is* at Jerusalem; [n]as[m] it is writ-
ten in the book of Moses.
19 And the children of the captivity
kept the passover [o]upon the four-
teenth *day* of the first month.
20 For the priests and the Levites
were [p]purified together, all of them
were pure, and [q]killed the passover for
all the children of the captivity, and for
their brethren the priests, and for
themselves.
21 And the children of Israel, which
were come again out of captivity, and
all such as had separated themselves
unto them from the [r]filthiness of the
heathen of the land, to seek the LORD
God of Israel, did eat,
22 And kept the [s]feast of unleav-
ened bread seven days with joy: for the
LORD had made them joyful, and
[t]turned the heart [u]of the king of As-
syria unto them, to strengthen their
hands in the work of the house of God,
the God of Israel.

Ezra's genealogy and career

7 NOW AFTER these things, in the
reign of [v]Artaxerxes king of Per-
sia, Ezra [w]the son of Seraiah, the son
of Azariah, the son of Hilkiah,
2 The son of Shallum, the son of Za-
dok, the son of Ahitub,
3 The son of Amariah, the son of Az-
ariah, the son of Meraioth,
4 The son of Zerahiah, the son of
Uzzi, the son of Bukki,
5 The son of Abishua, the son of
Phinehas, the son of Eleazar, the son
of Aaron the chief priest:
6 This Ezra went up from Babylon;

6:11 [d]Dan. 2:5 & 3:29
6:12 [e]1 Ki. 9:3
6:14 [f]ch. 5:1,2 [g]ver. 3 ch. 1:1 & 5:13 [h]ch. 4:24 [i]ch. 7:1
6:16 [j]1 Ki. 8:63 2 Chr. 7:5
6:17 [k]ch. 8:35
6:18 [l]1 Chr. 24:1 [m]1 Chr. 23:6
[n]Num. 3:6 & 8:9
6:19 [o]Ex. 12:6
6:20 [p]2 Chr. 30:15 [q]2 Chr. 35:11
6:21 [r]ch. 9:11
6:22 [s]Ex. 12:15 & 13:6 2 Chr. 30:21 & 35:17 [t]Prov. 21:1 [u]2 Ki. 23:29 2 Chr. 33:11 ch. 1:1
7:1 [v]Neh. 2:1 [w]1 Chr. 6:14

[k] Chald. *decree* [l] Chald. *the sons of the transportation* [m] Chald. *according to the writing*

6:15 THE HOUSE WAS FINISHED. The temple was completed in 516 B.C., twenty-one years after the laying of its foundation (3:10). The ark of the covenant, containing the two tables of the law, was not in the new temple, having apparently been destroyed at some unknown time earlier in Judah's history.

7:1 EZRA. A gap of about sixty years occurs between chs. 6 and 7, during which time the events recorded in the book of Esther transpired in Persia. Chs. 7—8 record the second return of exiles from Persia to Jerusalem under Ezra's leadership (about 457 B.C.). Chs. 9—10 describe the spiritual reforms that Ezra instituted in Jerusalem.

7:6 THE HAND OF THE LORD HIS GOD UPON HIM. Three times this chapter says that the hand of the Lord was upon Ezra (vv. 6,9,28; cf. 8:18,22,31). Three reasons are given in v. 10: Ezra had set his heart (1) to study God's Word, (2) to practice it, and (3) to teach it to others (see next note). Loyalty to God and His Word will always be accompanied by the Lord's blessing and help. This principle is affirmed in such N.T. passages as Mat. 5:6; John 14:21; 15:7–10; Acts 10:1–4; 2 Cor. 6:16–18; Heb. 11:6; Jas. 1:21–25; Rev. 3:7–10. In 8:22 Ezra adds another occasion in which the Lord's hand is on His people, namely, that God's favor comes to those who seek Him with their whole heart. Any people who earnestly seek God and who genuinely manifest loyalty to Him and His Word will experience the favorable hand of the Lord upon them.

and he *was* [x]a ready scribe in the law of Moses, which the LORD God of Israel had given: and the king granted him all his request, [y]according to the hand of the LORD his God upon him.

7 [z]And there went up *some* of the children of Israel, and of the priests, and [a]the Levites, and the singers, and the porters, and [b]the Nethinims, unto Jerusalem, in the seventh year of Artaxerxes the king.

8 And he came to Jerusalem in the fifth month, which *was* in the seventh year of the king.

9 For upon the first *day* of the first month [n]began he to go up from Babylon, and on the first *day* of the fifth month came he to Jerusalem, [c]according to the good hand of his God upon him.

10 For Ezra had prepared his heart to [d]seek the law of the LORD, and to do *it*, and to [e]teach in Israel statutes and judgments. (Neh. 10:28-29)

Ezra's letter from Artaxerxes

11 ¶ Now this *is* the copy of the letter that the king Artaxerxes gave unto Ezra the priest, the scribe, *even* a scribe of the words of the commandments of the LORD, and of his statutes to Israel.

12 Artaxerxes, [f]king of kings, [o]unto Ezra the priest, a scribe of the law of the God of heaven, perfect *peace,* [g]and at such a time.

13 I make a decree, that all they of the people of Israel, and *of* his priests and Levites, in my realm, which are minded of their own freewill to go up to Jerusalem, go with thee.

14 Forasmuch as thou art sent [p]of the king, and of his [h]seven counsellors, to inquire concerning Judah and Jerusalem, according to the law of thy God which *is* in thine hand;

15 And to carry the silver and gold, which the king and his counsellors have freely offered unto the God of Israel, [i]whose habitation *is* in Jerusalem,

16 [j]And all the silver and gold that thou canst find in all the province of Babylon, with the freewill offering of the people, and of the priests, [k]offering willingly for the house of their God which *is* in Jerusalem:

17 That thou mayest buy speedily with this money bullocks, rams, lambs, with their [l]meat offerings and their drink offerings, and [m]offer them upon the altar of the house of your God which *is* in Jerusalem.

18 And whatsoever shall seem good to thee, and to thy brethren, to do with the rest of the silver and the gold, that do after the will of your God.

19 The vessels also that are given thee for the service of the house of thy God, *those* deliver thou before the God of Jerusalem.

20 And whatsoever more shall be needful for the house of thy God, which thou shalt have occasion to bestow, bestow *it* out of the king's treasure house.

21 And I, *even* I Artaxerxes the king, do make a decree to all the treasurers which *are* beyond the river, that whatsoever Ezra the priest, the scribe of the law of the God of heaven, shall require of you, it be done speedily,

22 Unto an hundred talents of silver, and to an hundred [q]measures of wheat, and to an hundred baths of wine, and to an hundred baths of oil, and salt without prescribing *how much.*

23 [r]Whatsoever is commanded by the God of heaven, let it be diligently done for the house of the God of heaven: for why should there be wrath

7:6 [x]ver. 11,12 [y]ch. 8:22
7:7 [z]ch. 8:1 [a]See ch. 8:15 [b]ch. 2:43 & 8:20
7:9 [c]Neh. 2:8,18
7:10 [d]Ps. 119:45 [e]ver. 6,25 Deut. 33:10 Neh. 8:1-8 Mal. 2:7
7:12 [f]Ezek. 26:7 Dan. 2:37 [g]ch. 4:10
7:14 [h]Esth. 1:14
7:15 [i]2 Chr. 6:2 Ps. 135:21
7:16 [j]ch. 8:25 [k]1 Chr. 29:6,9
7:17 [l]Num. 15:4-13 [m]Deut. 12:5,11

[n] Heb. was *the foundation of the going up*
[o] Or, *to Ezra the priest, a perfect scribe of the law of the God of heaven,* peace,
[p] Chald. *from before the king*
[q] Chald. *cors*
[r] Heb. *Whatsoever* is *of the decree*

7:10 PREPARED HIS HEART TO SEEK THE LAW . . . TO DO *IT* . . . TO TEACH. Ezra is a model for all who would dedicate themselves as people anointed by God to studying, obeying, and teaching His Word (cf. vv. 6,9). (1) Ezra believed that the law was given through Moses by God Himself and that it was therefore the ultimate authority for all God's people (v. 6; cf. Neh. 8:14).

(2) Ezra purposed in his heart to study (literally "seek") God's Word. He sought to know God's ways and thoughts in all things pertaining to life, the world, and God's purposes among His people. Thus the wisdom of God was in him (v. 25).

(3) Ezra purposed in his heart to obey God's commandments and righteous standards. What he taught, he lived (cf. Acts 1:1; 1 Cor. 9:27; 1 Tim. 4:12,16).

(4) Ezra purposed in his heart to teach God's Word in order to preserve truth, righteousness, and purity among God's people (see 10:10–11; Neh. 8:2–18; see 1 Tim. 1:5, note; see article on BIBLE TRAINING FOR CHRISTIANS, p. 1920).

against the realm of the king and his sons?

24 Also we certify you, that touching any of the priests and Levites, singers, porters, Nethinims, or ministers of this house of God, it shall not be lawful to impose toll, tribute, or custom, upon them.

25 And thou, Ezra, after the wisdom of thy God, that *is* in thine hand, [n]set magistrates and judges, which may judge all the people that *are* beyond the river, all such as know the laws of thy God; and [o]teach ye them that know *them* not.

26 And whosoever will not do the law of thy God, and the law of the king, let judgment be executed speedily upon him, whether *it be* unto death, or [s]to banishment, or to confiscation of goods, or to imprisonment.

27 ¶ [p]Blessed *be* the LORD God of our fathers, [q]which hath put *such a thing* as this in the king's heart, to beautify the house of the LORD which *is* in Jerusalem:

28 And [r]hath extended mercy unto me before the king, and his counsellors, and before all the king's mighty princes. And I was strengthened as [s]the hand of the LORD my God *was* upon me, and I gathered together out of Israel chief men to go up with me.

People returning with Ezra

8 THESE *ARE* now the chief of their fathers, and *this is* the genealogy of them that went up with me from Babylon, in the reign of Artaxerxes the king.

2 Of the sons of Phinehas; Gershom: of the sons of Ithamar; Daniel: of the sons of David; [t]Hattush.

3 Of the sons of Shechaniah, of the sons of [u]Pharosh; Zechariah: and with him were reckoned by genealogy of the males an hundred and fifty.

4 Of the sons of Pahath-moab; Elihoenai the son of Zerahiah, and with him two hundred males.

5 Of the sons of Shechaniah; the son of Jahaziel, and with him three hundred males.

6 Of the sons also of Adin; Ebed the son of Jonathan, and with him fifty males.

7 And of the sons of Elam; Jeshaiah the son of Athaliah, and with him seventy males.

8 And of the sons of Shephatiah; Zebadiah the son of Michael, and with him fourscore males.

9 Of the sons of Joab; Obadiah the son of Jehiel, and with him two hundred and eighteen males.

10 And of the sons of Shelomith; the son of Josiphiah, and with him an hundred and threescore males.

11 And of the sons of Bebai; Zechariah the son of Bebai, and with him twenty and eight males.

12 And of the sons of Azgad; Johanan [t]the son of Hakkatan, and with him an hundred and ten males.

13 And of the last sons of Adonikam, whose names *are* these, Eliphelet, Jeiel, and Shemaiah, and with them threescore males.

14 Of the sons also of Bigvai; Uthai, and [u]Zabbud, and with them seventy males.

The return to Jerusalem

15 ¶ And I gathered them together to the river that runneth to Ahava; and there [v]abode we in tents three days: and I viewed the people, and the priests, and found there none of the [v]sons of Levi.

16 Then sent I for Eliezer, for Ariel, for Shemaiah, and for Elnathan, and for Jarib, and for Elnathan, and for Nathan, and for Zechariah, and for Meshullam, chief men; also for Joiarib, and for Elnathan, men of understanding.

17 And I sent them with commandment unto Iddo the chief at the place Casiphia, and [w]I told them what they should say unto Iddo, *and* to his brethren the Nethinims, at the place Casiphia, that they should bring unto us ministers for the house of our God.

18 And by the good hand of our God upon us they [w]brought us a man of understanding, of the sons of Mahli, the son of Levi, the son of Israel; and Sherebiah, with his sons and his brethren, eighteen;

19 And Hashabiah, and with him Jeshaiah of the sons of Merari, his brethren and their sons, twenty;

20 [x]Also of the Nethinims, whom David and the princes had appointed for the service of the Levites, two hun-

7:25 [n]Ex. 18:21,22 Deut. 16:18 [o]ver. 10 2 Chr. 17:7 Mal. 2:7 Mat. 23:2,3 **7:27** [p]1 Chr. 29:10 [q]ch. 6:22 **7:28** [r]ch. 9:9 [s]ver. 6,9 See ch. 5:5 & 8:18 **8:2** [t]1 Chr. 3:22 **8:3** [u]ch. 2:3 **8:15** [v]See ch. 7:7 **8:18** [w]Neh. 8:7 & 9:4,5 **8:20** [x]See ch. 2:43

[s] Chald. *to rooting out* [t] Or, *the youngest son* [u] Or, *Zaccur*, as some read [v] Or, *pitched* [w] Heb. *I put words in their mouth*

dred and twenty Nethinims: all of them were expressed by name.

21 ¶ Then I [y]proclaimed a fast there, at the river of Ahava, that we might [z]afflict ourselves before our God, to seek of him a [a]right way for us, and for our little ones, and for all our substance.

22 For [b]I was ashamed to require of the king a band of soldiers and horsemen to help us against the enemy in the way: because we had spoken unto the king, saying, [c]The hand of our God *is* upon all them for [d]good that seek him; but his power and his wrath *is* [e]against all them that [f]forsake him.

23 So we fasted and besought our God for this: and he was [g]entreated of us.

24 ¶ Then I separated twelve of the chief of the priests, Sherebiah, Hashabiah, and ten of their brethren with them,

25 And weighed unto them [h]the silver, and the gold, and the vessels, *even* the offering of the house of our God, which the king, and his counsellors, and his lords, and all Israel *there* present, had offered:

26 I even weighed unto their hand six hundred and fifty talents of silver, and silver vessels an hundred talents, *and* of gold an hundred talents;

27 Also twenty basins of gold, of a thousand drams; and two vessels of [x]fine copper, [y]precious as gold.

28 And I said unto them, Ye *are* [i]holy unto the LORD; the vessels *are* [j]holy also; and the silver and the gold *are* a freewill offering unto the LORD God of your fathers.

29 Watch ye, and keep *them,* until ye weigh *them* before the chief of the priests and the Levites, and chief of the fathers of Israel, at Jerusalem, in the chambers of the house of the LORD.

30 So took the priests and the Levites the weight of the silver, and the gold, and the vessels, to bring *them* to Jerusalem unto the house of our God.

31 ¶ Then we departed from the river of Ahava on the twelfth *day* of the first month, to go unto Jerusalem: and [k]the hand of our God was upon us, and he delivered us from the hand of the enemy, and of such as lay in wait by the way.

32 And we [l]came to Jerusalem, and abode there three days.

33 ¶ Now on the fourth day was the silver and the gold and the vessels [m]weighed in the house of our God by the hand of Meremoth the son of Uriah the priest; and with him *was* Eleazar the son of Phinehas; and with them *was* Jozabad the son of Jeshua, and Noadiah the son of Binnui, Levites;

34 By number *and* by weight of every one: and all the weight was written at that time.

35 *Also* the children of those that had been carried away, which were come out of the captivity, [n]offered burnt offerings unto the God of Israel, twelve bullocks for all Israel, ninety and six rams, seventy and seven lambs, twelve he goats *for* a sin offering: all *this was* a burnt offering unto the LORD.

36 ¶ And they delivered the king's [o]commissions unto the king's lieutenants, and to the governors on this side the river: and they furthered the people, and the house of God.

8:21 [y]2 Chr. 20:3 [z]Lev. 16:29 & 23:29 Is. 58:3,5 [a]Ps. 5:8
8:22 [b]1 Cor. 9:15 [c]ch. 7:6,9,28 [d]Ps. 33:18,19 & 34:15,22 Rom. 8:28 [e]Ps. 34:16 [f]2 Chr. 15:2
8:23 [g]1 Chr. 5:20 2 Chr. 33:13 Is. 19:22
8:25 [h]ch. 7:15,16
8:28 [i]Lev. 21:6-8 Deut. 33:8 [j]Lev. 22:2,3 Num. 4:4,15,19,20
8:31 [k]ch. 7:6,9,28
8:32 [l]Neh. 2:11
8:33 [m]ver. 26,30
8:35 [n]ch. 6:17
8:36 [o]ch. 7:21

[x] Heb. *yellow,* or, *shining brass* [y] Heb. *desirable*

8:21 I PROCLAIMED A FAST. Fasting entails abstaining from food for a limited period of time (see Mat. 6:16, note). God's O.T. people fasted in order to express humility, self-denial, and submission to God, and to seek His grace, help, protection, and favor (vv. 21,31). Fasting occurred when they (1) were oppressed by great cares (2 Sam. 12:16–23; 1 Ki. 21:20–27; Ps. 35:13; 69:10); (2) were worshiping God on the Day of Atonement (cf. Lev. 16:29–31; 23:26–32); (3) wanted to show repentance and remorse (1 Ki. 21:27–29; Neh. 9:1–2; Joel 2:12–13; Jonah 3:4–10); (4) were faced with danger (2 Chr. 20:3; Ezra 8:21–23), sickness (2 Sam. 12:15–16), and death (1 Sam. 31:13); (5) were preparing for ministry (Ex. 34:28; Deut. 9:9–18); and (6) were seeking God for revival and restoration (Dan. 9:3–19).

8:21 SEEK OF HIM A RIGHT WAY FOR US. It is always appropriate to pray to God for His care and protection when setting out upon a journey. God's help should not be taken for granted, for His guidance and protection are mediated to us through our prayers. And when we arrive safely at our destination (v. 32), we should never forget to give Him thanks.

8:23 WE FASTED AND BESOUGHT OUR GOD. God looks favorably on a people who humbly and earnestly fast and seek Him about a matter (cf. Neh. 1:4). Just as God responded favorably to Ezra's request, so He will honor all who with sincere hearts seek Him in prayer and fasting (see v. 21, note).

Ezra's prayer

9 NOW WHEN these things were done, the princes came to me, saying, The people of Israel, and the priests, and the Levites, have not [p]separated themselves from the people of the lands, [q]*doing* according to their abominations, *even* of the Canaanites, the Hittites, the Perizzites, the Jebusites, the Ammonites, the Moabites, the Egyptians, and the Amorites.

2 For they have [r]taken of their daughters for themselves, and for their sons: so that the [s]holy seed have [t]mingled themselves with the people of *those* lands: yea, the hand of the princes and rulers hath been chief in this trespass.

3 And when I heard this thing, [u]I rent my garment and my mantle, and plucked off the hair of my head and of my beard, and sat down [v]astonied.

4 Then were assembled unto me every one that [w]trembled at the words of the God of Israel, because of the transgression of those that had been carried away; and I sat astonied until the [x]evening sacrifice.

5 ¶ And at the evening sacrifice I arose up from my [z]heaviness; and having rent my garment and my mantle, I fell upon my knees, and [y]spread out my hands unto the LORD my God,

6 And said, O my God, I am [z]ashamed and blush to lift up my face to thee, my God: for [a]our iniquities are increased over *our* head, and our [a]trespass is [b]grown up unto the heavens.

7 Since the days of our fathers *have* [c]we *been* in a great trespass unto this day; and for our iniquities [d]have we, our kings, *and* our priests, been delivered into the hand of the kings of the lands, to the sword, to captivity, and to a spoil, and to [e]confusion of face, as *it is* this day.

9:1 [p]ch. 6:21 Neh. 9:2 [q]Deut. 12:30,31
9:2 [r]Ex. 34:16 Deut. 7:3 [s]Ex. 22:31 Deut. 7:6 [t]2 Cor. 6:14
9:3 [u]Job 1:20 [v]Ps. 143:4
9:4 [w]ch. 10:3
[x]Ex. 29:39
9:5 [y]Ex. 9:29
9:6 [z]Dan. 9:7,8 [a]Ps. 38:4 [b]2 Chr. 28:9 Rev. 18:5
9:7 [c]Ps. 106:6 Dan. 9:5,6 [d]Deut. 28:36 Neh. 9:30 [e]Dan. 9:7,8

[z] Or, *affliction* [a] Or, *guiltiness*

9:1 THE PEOPLE OF ISRAEL . . . HAVE NOT SEPARATED THEMSELVES FROM THE PEOPLE OF THE LANDS. The past failure of the Jews to separate themselves from the sinful societies around them had led them into idolatry and immorality, and it eventually caused their captivity and exile (2 Chr. 36:14–21). Now, after God had brought a small remnant back to the land (vv. 8–9), the Jews were once again transgressing God's fundamental precept of separation from the lifestyle of the ungodly.

9:2 TAKEN OF THEIR DAUGHTERS FOR THEMSELVES. When Ezra arrived in Jerusalem, he discovered that many of the people, including priests, Levites, and rulers, had married women who worshiped other gods and practiced the heathen abominations and impurities (vv. 1–2,11). Intermarriage with the ungodly was expressly forbidden in the Law of Moses (Ex. 34:11–16; Deut. 7:1–4; cf. Ps. 106:35). The N.T. likewise forbids God's new covenant people in Christ to marry unbelievers (1 Cor. 7:39; cf. 2 Cor. 6:14).

9:2 THE HOLY SEED. Israel's high calling was to be a holy race (cf. Ex. 19:6; Is. 6:13; Mal. 2:15). (1) They were to be a people for God's own possession, reflecting His person and holiness while separating themselves from the immoral ways of those who did not belong to Him (Deut. 7:1–11). (2) N.T. believers are also called to be separated from the world (2 Cor. 6:14–18). Those who confess Jesus as their Lord must be "a holy nation" (1 Pet. 2:9–12), consecrated to doing the will and work of the Father. This implies that a Spirit-filled believer will live a righteous and separated life in fellowship with God (1 Cor. 6:11), living in a way that differs from this evil generation (Acts 2:40; see article on SPIRITUAL SEPARATION FOR BELIEVERS, p. 1814); he or she will always look to fulfill God's will as a true son or daughter of God (Rom. 8:13–16).

9:3 AND WHEN I HEARD THIS THING. Ezra's response of grief and his prayer are a classic example of the concern and distress that all true ministers of God should have when they see God's people conforming to ungodly customs. (1) Ezra was appalled, ashamed, and deeply saddened because of the guilt of the people (vv. 3–6; see 1 Sam. 15:35; Jer. 9; 2 Cor. 11:29).

(2) Ezra possessed a deep sense of the glory, righteousness, and love of God that the people had spurned (vv. 4,8–10). He could not accept what the people were doing (vv. 3,5; 10:1; see also the prayers of Nehemiah in Neh. 9 and Daniel in Dan. 9).

(3) Ezra prayed to God in humility and with tears (vv. 3,5; 10:1).

(4) Ezra linked himself with those for whom he prayed, by referring to "our iniquities" and "our trespasses" (vv. 6–15). He felt the national shame and guilt more deeply than any of them (cf. Is. 53:12).

(5) Ezra comprehended that God's grace and lovingkindness, shown toward the returned remnant in reviving their hope and vision for the future, raising up God's house from ruins, and giving them a wall of protection, were now being jeopardized by the people's disobedience to God's word (vv. 8–15).

(6) Ezra was acutely conscious of God's mercy and grace and thus hoped to see forgiveness and restoration for the people (vv. 8–9,12–14).

(7) Finally, Ezra's remorse attracted others who trembled at "the words of the God of Israel" (v. 4) and understood the disastrous consequences of sin for the people and their families (vv. 7,13–15).

8 And now for a [b]little space grace hath been *shown* from the LORD our God, to leave us a remnant to escape, and to give us [f]a[c] nail in his holy place, that our God may [g]lighten our eyes, and give us a little reviving in our bondage.

9 [h]For we *were* bondmen; [i]yet our God hath not forsaken us in our bondage, but [j]hath extended mercy unto us in the sight of the kings of Persia, to give us a reviving, to set up the house of our God, and [d]to repair the desolations thereof, and to give us [k]a wall in Judah and in Jerusalem.

10 And now, O our God, what shall we say after this? for we have forsaken thy commandments,

11 Which thou hast commanded [e]by thy servants the prophets, saying, The land, unto which ye go to possess it, is an unclean land with the filthiness of the people of the lands, with their abominations, which have filled it [l]from[f] one end to another with their uncleanness.

12 Now therefore [m]give not your daughters unto their sons, neither take their daughters unto your sons, [n]nor seek their peace or their wealth for ever: that ye may be strong, and eat the good of the land, and [o]leave *it* for an inheritance to your children for ever.

13 And after all that is come upon us for our evil deeds, and for our great trespass, seeing that thou our God [p]hast[g] punished us less than our iniquities *deserve*, and hast given us *such* deliverance as this;

14 Should we [q]again break thy commandments, and [r]join in affinity with the people of these abominations? wouldest not thou be [s]angry with us till thou hadst consumed *us*, so that *there should be* no remnant nor escaping?

15 O LORD God of Israel, [t]thou *art* righteous: for we remain yet escaped, as *it is* this day: behold, we *are* [u]before thee [v]in our trespasses: for we cannot stand before thee because of this.

The people's confession

10 NOW [w]WHEN Ezra had prayed, and when he had confessed, weeping and casting himself down [x]before the house of God, there assembled unto him out of Israel a very great congregation of men and women and children: for the people [h]wept very sore.

2 And Shechaniah the son of Jehiel, *one* of the sons of Elam, answered and said unto Ezra, We have [y]trespassed against our God, and have taken strange wives of the people of the land: yet now there is hope in Israel concerning this thing.

3 Now therefore let us make [z]a covenant with our God [i]to put away all the wives, and such as are born of them, according to the counsel of my lord, and of those that [a]tremble at [b]the commandment of our God; and let it be done according to the law.

4 Arise; for *this* matter *belongeth* unto thee: we also *will be* with thee: [c]be of good courage, and do *it*.

5 Then arose Ezra, and made the chief priests, the Levites, and all Israel, [d]to swear that they should do according to this word. And they sware.

6 ¶ Then Ezra rose up from before the house of God, and went into the chamber of Johanan the son of Eliashib: and *when* he came thither, he

9:8 [f]Is. 22:23 [g]Ps. 34:5
9:9 [h]Neh. 9:36 [i]Ps. 136:23 [j]ch. 7:28 [k]Is. 5:2
9:11 [l]2 Ki. 21:16
9:12 [m]Ex. 23:32 Deut. 7:3 [n]Deut. 23:6 [o]Prov. 20:7
9:13 [p]Ps. 103:10
9:14 [q]John 5:14 2 Pet. 2:20 [r]Neh. 13:23 [s]Deut. 9:8
9:15 [t]Neh. 9:33 Dan. 9:14 [u]Rom. 3:19 [v]1 Cor. 15:17
10:1 [w]Dan. 9:20 [x]2 Chr. 20:9
10:2 [y]Neh. 13:27
10:3 [z]2 Chr. 34:31 [a]ch. 9:4 [b]Deut. 7:2,3
10:4 [c]1 Chr. 28:10
10:5 [d]Neh. 5:12

[b]Heb. *moment* [c]Or, *a pin:* i.e. *a constant and sure abode* [d]Heb. *to set up* [e]Heb. *by the hand of thy servants* [f]Heb. *from mouth to mouth* [g]Heb. *hast withheld beneath our iniquities* [h]Heb. *wept a great weeping* [i]Heb. *to bring forth*

10:3 PUT AWAY ALL THE WIVES. Ezra required divorce for several reasons. (1) Marrying heathen women had constituted an act of unfaithfulness to God and His word (vv. 10; 10:2; see 9:2, note). True repentance required separation to rectify the evil.

(2) Divorcing heathen wives was necessary to maintain Israel's purpose as a holy nation separated unto God (see 9:2, note).

(3) The divorce was necessary to prevent the people from adopting the idolatry and immoral ways of the nations. Moses stated, "neither shalt thou make marriages with them . . . for they will turn away thy son away from following me" (Deut. 7:3–4). Divorce in this instance was radical surgery required in order to stop the rippling consequences of compromise that would inevitably lead another generation into apostasy and subject them to the severe judgment of God.

10:4 BE OF GOOD COURAGE AND DO *IT*. Courage and decisive action in a leader are necessary in order to oppose worldly trends among God's people, to issue an earnest call to sinners to turn away from sin and back to God, and to encourage obedience to His word. Ezra demonstrated these qualities when he required the Jews to separate themselves "from the people of the land, and from the strange [foreign] wives" (v. 11).

[e]did eat no bread, nor drink water: for
he mourned because of the transgres-
sion of them that had been carried
away.
7 And they made proclamation
throughout Judah and Jerusalem unto
all the children of the captivity, that
they should gather themselves togeth-
er unto Jerusalem;
8 And that whosoever would not
come within three days, according to
the counsel of the princes and the el-
ders, all his substance should be [j]for-
feited, and himself separated from the
congregation of those that had been
carried away.
9 ¶ Then all the men of Judah and
Benjamin gathered themselves togeth-
er unto Jerusalem within three days. It
was the ninth month, on the twentieth
day of the month; and [f]all the people
sat in the street of the house of God,
trembling because of *this* matter, and
for [k]the great rain.
10 And Ezra the priest stood up,
and said unto them, Ye have trans-
gressed, and [l]have taken strange
wives, to increase the trespass of Is-
rael.
11 Now therefore [g]make confes-
sion unto the LORD God of your fathers,
and do his pleasure: and [h]separate
yourselves from the people of the land,
and from the strange wives.
12 Then all the congregation an-
swered and said with a loud voice, As
thou hast said, so must we do.
13 But the people *are* many, and *it*
is a time of much rain, and we are not
able to stand without, neither *is this* a
work of one day or two: for [m]we are
many that have transgressed in this
thing.
14 Let now our rulers of all the con-
gregation stand, and let all them which
have taken strange wives in our cities
come at appointed times, and with
them the elders of every city, and the
judges thereof, until [i]the fierce wrath
of our God [n]for this matter be turned
from us.
15 ¶ Only Jonathan the son of Asa-
hel and Jahaziah the son of Tikvah
[o]were employed about this *matter:*
and Meshullam and Shabbethai the Le-
vite helped them.
16 And the children of the captivity
did so. And Ezra the priest, *with* cer-
tain chief of the fathers, after the
house of their fathers, and all of them
by *their* names, were separated, and sat
down in the first day of the tenth month
to examine the matter.
17 And they made an end with all
the men that had taken strange wives
by the first day of the first month.

Priests with foreign wives

18 ¶ And among the sons of the
priests there were found that had tak-
en strange wives: *namely,* of the sons
of Jeshua the son of Jozadak, and his
brethren; Maaseiah, and Eliezer, and
Jarib, and Gedaliah.
19 And they [j]gave their hands that
they would put away their wives; and
being [k]guilty, *they offered* a ram of the
flock for their trespass.
20 And of the sons of Immer; Hana-
ni, and Zebadiah.
21 And of the sons of Harim; Maa-
seiah, and Elijah, and Shemaiah, and
Jehiel, and Uzziah.
22 And of the sons of Pashur; Elioe-
nai, Maaseiah, Ishmael, Nethaneel,
Jozabad, and Elasah.
23 Also of the Levites; Jozabad, and
Shimei, and Kelaiah, (the same *is* Keli-
ta,) Pethahiah, Judah, and Eliezer.
24 Of the singers also; Eliashib: and
of the porters; Shallum, and Telem,
and Uri.
25 Moreover of Israel: of the sons of
Parosh; Ramiah, and Jeziah, and Mal-
chiah, and Miamin, and Eleazar, and
Malchijah, and Benaiah.
26 And of the sons of Elam; Matta-

10:6 [e]Deut. 9:18 **10:9** [f]See 1 Sam. 12:18 **10:11** [g]Josh. 7:19 Prov. 28:13 [h]ver. 3 **10:14** [i]2 Chr. 30:8 **10:19** [j]2 Ki. 10:15 1 Chr. 29:24 2 Chr. 30:8 [k]Lev. 6:4,6

[j]Heb. *devoted* [k]Heb. *the showers* [l]Heb. *have caused to dwell,* or, *have brought back* [m]Or, *we have greatly offended in this thing* [n]Or, *till this matter be* dispatched [o]Heb. *stood*

10:11 DO HIS PLEASURE: AND SEPARATE YOURSELVES. The actions of Ezra and the Israelite community at this stage of history should not be considered a standard for those under the new covenant. Concerning marriage and divorce for N.T. believers, the Scriptures teach the following: (1) The believer must not enter into marriage with an unbeliever (1 Cor. 7:39; cf. 2 Cor. 6:14).

(2) If a person becomes a believer after marriage and the spouse remains an unbeliever, the believing spouse must not seek divorce if the unbelieving partner wishes the marriage relationship to continue (1 Cor. 7:12; see 7:14, note).

(3) Divorce is allowed in situations of immorality or abandonment (see Mat. 19:9, note; 1 Cor. 7:11,15, notes).

niah, Zechariah, and Jehiel, and Abdi, and Jeremoth, and Eliah.
27 And of the sons of Zattu; Elioenai, Eliashib, Mattaniah, and Jeremoth, and Zabad, and Aziza.
28 Of the sons also of Bebai; Jehohanan, Hananiah, Zabbai, *and* Athlai.
29 And of the sons of Bani; Meshullam, Malluch, and Adaiah, Jashub, and Sheal, and Ramoth.
30 And of the sons of Pahath-moab; Adna, and Chelal, Benaiah, Maaseiah, Mattaniah, Bezaleel, and Binnui, and Manasseh.
31 And *of* the sons of Harim; Eliezer, Ishijah, Malchiah, Shemaiah, Shimeon,
32 Benjamin, Malluch, *and* Shemariah.
33 Of the sons of Hashum; Mattenai, Mattathah, Zabad, Eliphelet, Jeremai, Manasseh, *and* Shimei.
34 Of the sons of Bani; Maadai, Amram, and Uel,
35 Benaiah, Bedeiah, Chelluh,
36 Vaniah, Meremoth, Eliashib,
37 Mattaniah, Mattenai, and Jaasau,
38 And Bani, and Binnui, Shimei,
39 And Shelemiah, and Nathan, and Adaiah,
40 [p]Machnadebai, Shashai, Sharai,
41 Azareel, and Shelemiah, Shemariah,
42 Shallum, Amariah, *and* Joseph.
43 Of the sons of Nebo; Jeiel, Mattithiah, Zabad, Zebina, Jadau, and Joel, Benaiah.
44 All these had taken strange wives: and *some* of them had wives by whom they had children.

[p] Or, *Mabnadebai*, according to some copies

10:44 WIVES ... CHILDREN. The foreign wives and their children were most likely sent back to their own families among their people.

NEHEMIAH

Outline

I. Rebuilding the Wall of Jerusalem: Led by Nehemiah (1:1—7:73)
  A. Nehemiah's Intercession for Jerusalem (1:1—2:8)
    1. The Burden of His Intercession (1:1–4)
    2. The Content of His Intercession with God (1:5–11)
    3. The Outcome of His Intercession with King Artaxerxes (2:1–8)
  B. Nehemiah Goes to Jerusalem as Governor (2:9–20)
  C. Nehemiah Leads in Reconstructing the Walls (3:1—7:4)
    1. The Builders (3:1–32)
    2. The Opposition (4:1—6:14)
      a. Ridicule (4:1–6)
      b. Conspiracy (4:7–23)
      c. Extortion (5:1–19)
      d. Compromise (6:1–4)
      e. Slander (6:5–9)
      f. Treachery (6:10–14)
    3. The Accomplishment (6:15—7:4)
  D. Nehemiah Registers the Remnant (7:5–73)
II. Reviving the People of Jerusalem: Led by Ezra (8:1—10:39)
  A. Public Declaration of God's Word and Commemoration of the Feast of Tabernacles (8:1–18)
  B. Fasting, Recollection of Past Sins, and Public Confession of Those Sins (9:1–37)
  C. Making a Covenant of Obedience (9:38—10:39)
III. Reforming the Nation: Led by Nehemiah (11:1—13:31)
  A. Redistribution of the Remnant (11:1—12:26)
  B. Dedication of the Walls (12:27–47)
  C. Reforms During Nehemiah's Second Administration (13:1–31)

Author: Ezra and Nehemiah (?)

Theme: Rebuilding the Wall of Jerusalem

Date of Writing: c. 430–420 B.C.

Background

The book of Nehemiah concludes O.T. history, when the Jewish exiles were permitted to return to their homeland from captivity in Babylon and Persia. Together with Ezra (with which it forms a single book in the Hebrew O.T.; see the introduction to Ezra), it records the history of the three returns of exiles to Jerusalem. Ezra covers events associated with the first two returns (538 B.C.; 457 B.C.), and Nehemiah records events during the third return (444 B.C.). Whereas the focus in Ezra is on rebuilding the temple, in Nehemiah it is on rebuilding the wall of Jerusalem. Both books emphasize the importance of spiritual recovery and commitment to God and His Word.

Nehemiah, a contemporary of Ezra, was serving as a cupbearer to Artaxerxes I (king of Persia), when he received news that the exiles who returned to Judah from Babylon and Persia were in reproach and the wall of Jerusalem was still in shambles. After interceding over Jerusalem's plight, Nehemiah was providentially authorized by King Artaxerxes to go to Jerusalem to serve as governor and rebuild the city walls. As an inspired leader, he rallied his countrymen to rebuild the wall completely in only fifty-two days in spite of determined opposition. He served as governor for twelve years; after a brief return to Persia, he served a second term as governor of Judah (cf. 2:1; 13:6–7a).

Ezra the priest assisted Nehemiah in promoting spiritual revival and reform among the returned remnant. Possibly Nehemiah helped Ezra in writing this book. The historicity of the book of Nehemiah is confirmed by ancient documents discovered in 1903 called the Elephantine Papyri, which mention Sanballat (2:19), Johanan (12:23), and the replacement of Nehemiah as governor about 410 B.C.

Purpose

This book was written (1) to complete the recording of the post-exilic history begun in the book of Ezra, and (2) to show what God did on behalf of the remnant through the godly leadership of Nehemiah and Ezra during the third stage of the post-exilic restoration.

Survey

Chs. 1—7 record Nehemiah's role as governor and as leader in rebuilding the wall of Jerusalem. Ch. 1 reveals the spiritual depth of Nehemiah as a man of prayer. While serving the king of Persia, he received news about the sorry plight of Jerusalem and began to intercede earnestly with God to intervene on behalf of the city and its inhabitants. Ch. 2 describes how God used Artaxerxes to commission Nehemiah to be governor of Jerusalem and Nehemiah's arrival at Jerusalem. Chs. 3:1—7:1 reveal the bold, wise, and decisive leadership of Nehemiah in rallying Jerusalem to rebuild its broken-down walls in only fifty-two days, in spite of serious opposition from inside and outside the city.

The second half of the book describes (1) the spiritual restoration that occurred among the people of Jerusalem, led by Ezra the priest (chs. 8—10), and (2) certain national issues addressed by Nehemiah (chs. 11—13). Central to the spiritual restoration was the public reading of God's law, repentance for sin, and a new resolve by the remnant to remember and keep their covenant with God. The last chapter records certain reforms that Nehemiah initiated during his second term as governor (ch. 13).

Special Features

Five major features or emphases characterize the book of Nehemiah. (1) It records the last events of Jewish O.T. history before the intertestamental period. (2) It provides historical background for Malachi, the last book of the O.T., since Nehemiah and Malachi were contemporaries. (3) Nehemiah is a superb Biblical model of a godly leader in government: a man of wisdom, principle, courage, impeccable integrity, unwavering faith, compassion for the oppressed, and great gifts in leadership and organization. Throughout his years as governor, Nehemiah remained righteous, humble, free of greed, self-sacrificing, and uncorrupted by his prominence or power. (4) Nehemiah is one of the foremost O.T. examples of a praying leader (cf. also Daniel). No less than eleven times he is described as addressing God in prayer or intercession (e.g. 1:4–11; 2:4; 4:4,9; 5:19; 6:9,14; 13:14,22,29,31). He was a man who accomplished seemingly impossible tasks because of his complete dependence on God. (5)The book graphically illustrates that prayer, sacrifice, hard work, and tenacity go together in realizing a God-given vision.

New Testament Fulfillment

This book records the completion of all the basic steps in restoration in post-exilic Judaism necessary for the coming of Christ at the outset of the N.T. era: Jerusalem and the temple were rebuilt, the law was restored, the covenant was renewed, and the Davidic lineage was intact. Externally, everything was in place for the coming of the Messiah (cf. Dan. 9:25).

The era depicted in Nehemiah concludes with the prophetic hope that the Lord would soon come to His temple (cf. Mal. 3:1). The N.T. opens with the fulfillment of this post-exilic expectation and hope.

Reading Nehemiah

In order to read the entire Old Testament in one year, the book of Nehemiah should be read in 5 days, according to the following schedule: □ 1–3 □ 4–6 □ 7–8 □ 9–10 □ 11–13

NOTES

CHRONOLOGY: EZRA-NEHEMIAH

Dates below are given according to a Nisan-to-Nisan Jewish calendar (see chart on Hebrew Calendar). Roman numerals represent months; Arabic numerals represent days.

540 B.C. · 530 · 520 · 510 · 500 · 490 · 480 · 470 · 460 · 450 · 440 · 430 B.C.

YEAR	MONTH	DAY	EVENT	REFERENCE
539 B.C.	Oct.	12	Capture of Babylon	Da 5:30
538 **537**	Mar. to Mar.	24 11	Cyrus's first year	Ezr 1:1-4
537(?)			Return under Sheshbazzar	Ezr 1:11
537	VII		Building of altar	Ezr 3:1
536	II		Work on temple begun	Ezr 3:8
536-530			Opposition during Cyrus's reign	Ezr 4:1-5
530-520			Work on temple ceased	Ezr 4:24
520	VI =Sept.	24 21	Work on temple renewed under Darius	Ezr 5:2; Hag 1:14
516	XII =Mar.	3 12	Temple completed	Ezr 6:15
458	I =Apr.	1 8	Ezra departs from Babylon	Ezr 7:6-9
	V =Aug.	1 4	Ezra arrives in Jerusalem	Ezr 7:8-9
	IX =Dec.	20 19	People assemble	Ezr 10:9
	X =Dec.	1 29	Committee begins investigation	Ezr 10:16
457	I =Mar.	1 27	Committee ends investigation	Ezr 10:17
445 **444**	Apr. to Apr.	13 2	20th year of Artaxerxes I	Ne 1:1
445	I =Mar.-Apr.		Nehemiah approaches king	Ne 2:1
	Aug.(?)		Nehemiah arrives in Jerusalem	Ne 2:11
	VI =Oct.	25 2	Completion of wall	Ne 6:15
	VII =Oct. to Nov.	8 5	Public assembly	Ne 7:73-8:1
	VII =Oct.	15-22 22-28	Feast of Tabernacles	Ne 8:14
	VII =Oct.	24 30	Fast	Ne 9:1
433 **432**	Apr. to Apr.	1 19	32nd year of Artaxerxes; Nehemiah's recall and return	Ne 5:14; 13:6

Nehemiah's prayer for Israel

1 THE WORDS of [a]Nehemiah the
son of Hachaliah. And it came to
pass in the month Chisleu, in the twen-
tieth year, as I was in Shushan the pal-
ace,
2 That Hanani, one of my brethren,
came, he and *certain* men of Judah; and
I asked them concerning the Jews that
had escaped, which were left of the
captivity, and concerning Jerusalem.
3 And they said unto me, The rem-
nant that are left of the captivity there
in the province *are* in great affliction
and reproach: [b]the wall of Jerusalem
also [c]*is* broken down, and the gates
thereof are burned with fire.
4 ¶ And it came to pass, when I
heard these words, that I sat down and
wept, and mourned *certain* days, and
fasted, and prayed before the God of
heaven,
5 And said, I beseech thee,
[d]O LORD God of heaven, the great and
terrible God, [e]that keepeth covenant
and mercy for them that love him and
observe his commandments:
6 Let thine ear now be attentive,
and [f]thine eyes open, that thou may-
est hear the prayer of thy servant,
which I pray before thee now, day and
night, for the children of Israel thy ser-
vants, and [g]confess the sins of the
children of Israel, which we have
sinned against thee: both I and my fa-
ther's house have sinned.
7 [h]We have dealt very corruptly
against thee, and have [i]not kept the
commandments, nor the statutes, nor
the judgments, which thou command-
est thy servant Moses.
8 Remember, I beseech thee, the
word that thou commandedst thy ser-
vant Moses, saying, [j]*If* ye transgress,
I will scatter you abroad among the na-
tions:
9 [k]But *if* ye turn unto me, and keep
my commandments, and do them;
[l]though there were of you cast out
unto the uttermost part of the heaven,
yet will I gather them from thence, and
will bring them unto the place that I
have chosen to set my name there.
10 [m]Now these *are* thy servants
and thy people, whom thou hast re-
deemed by thy great power, and by thy
strong hand.
11 O Lord, I beseech thee, [n]let
now thine ear be attentive to the prayer
of thy servant, and to the prayer of thy
servants, who [o]desire to fear thy
name: and prosper, I pray thee, thy ser-
vant this day, and grant him mercy in
the sight of this man. For I was the
king's [p]cupbearer.

Nehemiah's request

2 AND IT came to pass in the month
Nisan, in the twentieth year of
[q]Artaxerxes the king, *that* wine *was*
before him: and [r]I took up the wine,
and gave *it* unto the king. Now I had
not been *beforetime* sad in his presence.
2 Wherefore the king said unto me,
Why *is* thy countenance sad, seeing
thou *art* not sick? this *is* nothing *else*
but [s]sorrow of heart. Then I was very
sore afraid,
3 And said unto the king, [t]Let the
king live for ever: why should not my
countenance be sad, when [u]the city,
the place of my fathers' sepulchres,
lieth waste, and the gates thereof are
consumed with fire?
4 Then the king said unto me, For

1:1 [a]ch. 10:1 **1:3** [b]ch. 2:17 [c]2 Ki. 25:10 **1:5** [d]Dan. 9:4 [e]Ex. 20:6 **1:6** [f]1 Ki. 8:28,29 2 Chr. 6:40 Dan. 9:1 7,18 [g]Dan. 9:20 **1:7** [h]Ps. 106:6 Dan. 9:5 [i]Deut. 28:15 **1:8** [j]Lev. 26:33 Deut. 4:25-27 & 28:64 **1:9** [k]Lev. 26:39 Deut. 4:29-31 & 30:2 [l]Deut. 30:4 **1:10** [m]Deut. 9:29 Dan. 9:15 **1:11** [n]ver. 6 [o]Is. 26:8 Heb. 13:18 [p]ch. 2:1 **2:1** [q]Ezra 7:1 [r]ch. 1:11 **2:2** [s]Prov. 15:13 **2:3** [t]1Ki. 1:31 Dan. 2:4 & 5:10 & 6:6,21 [u]ch. 1:3

1:1 NEHEMIAH. Nehemiah left Persia for Jerusalem in 444 B.C. to be governor of Judah. This was thirteen years after Ezra had arrived there. Nehemiah came with a commission from the king of Persia to rebuild the wall of Jerusalem and fortify the city (2:7–8). In spite of much opposition, Nehemiah completed the wall in fifty-two days (6:15). He was a man of ability, courage, perseverance, and prayer (see 2:4, note), who also cooperated with Ezra in bringing spiritual renewal to the people (ch. 8).

1:4 WEPT . . . FASTED . . . PRAYED. Nehemiah was deeply burdened for his people and for God's work in Judah. For four months (cf. v. 1 with 2:1) he poured out his heart to God in fasting and prayer with many tears because of the trouble afflicting God's people in Jerusalem and Judah (cf. Acts 20:31). His prayer included confession of sin (vv. 6–7), reminders to God of His own word (v. 8; cf. Lev. 26:40–45; Deut. 30:1–6), concern for God's glory and purposes (vv. 5–8), and continual intercession for the children of Israel (v. 6).

1:11 GRANT HIM MERCY IN THE SIGHT OF THIS MAN. "This man" was Artaxerxes, king of Persia (2:1). Nehemiah prayed that God would grant him favor with the king on behalf of the Jews. When we desire to obtain anything from other people, we should first present our concerns to God. He can then move the hearts and minds of influential leaders to do His will (see Esth. 4:16; Prov. 21:1).

2:4 SO I PRAYED. Nehemiah's first impulse always was to pray. Before answering the king's question, he breathed a prayer to God for help and wisdom—just one of the many times in the book where Nehemiah spontaneously called upon God

what dost thou make request? So I
prayed to the God of heaven.
5 And I said unto the king, If it
please the king, and if thy servant have
found favour in thy sight, that thou
wouldest send me unto Judah, unto the
city of my fathers' sepulchres, that I
may build it.
6 And the king said unto me, (the
[a]queen also sitting by him,) For how
long shall thy journey be? and when
wilt thou return? So it pleased the king
to send me; and I set him [v]a time.
7 Moreover I said unto the king, If
it please the king, let letters be given
me to the governors beyond the river,
that they may convey me over till I
come into Judah;
8 And a letter unto Asaph the keep-
er of the king's forest, that he may give
me timber to make beams for the gates
of the palace which *appertained* [w]to the
house, and for the wall of the city, and
for the house that I shall enter into.
And the king granted me, [x]according
to the good hand of my God upon me.

Nehemiah's inspection of the walls

9 ¶ Then I came to the governors
beyond the river, and gave them the
king's letters. Now the king had sent
captains of the army and horsemen
with me.
10 When Sanballat the Horonite,
and Tobiah the servant, the Ammonite,
heard *of it,* it grieved them exceedingly
that there was come a man to seek the
welfare of the children of Israel.
11 So I [y]came to Jerusalem, and
was there three days.

2:6 [v]ch. 5:14 & 13:6
2:8 [w]ch. 3:7 [x]ver. 18 Ezra 5:5 & 7:6,9,28
2:11 [y]Ezra 8:32
2:13 [z]2 Chr. 26:9 ch. 3:13 [a]ver. 17 & ch. 1:3
2:14 [b]ch. 3:15
2:15 [c]2 Sam. 15:23 Jer. 31:40
2:17 [d]ch. 1:3 Ps. 44:13 & 79:4 Jer. 24:9 Ezek. 5:14,15 & 22:4
2:18 [e]ver. 8 [f]2 Sam. 2:7

12 ¶ And I arose in the night, I and
some few men with me; neither told I
any man what my God had put in my
heart to do at Jerusalem: neither *was*
there any beast with me, save the beast
that I rode upon.
13 And I went out by night [z]by the
gate of the valley, even before the drag-
on well, and to the dung port, and
viewed the walls of Jerusalem, which
were [a]broken down, and the gates
thereof were consumed with fire.
14 Then I went on to the [b]gate of
the fountain, and to the king's pool: but
there was no place for the beast *that was*
under me to pass.
15 Then went I up in the night by
the [c]brook, and viewed the wall, and
turned back, and entered by the gate of
the valley, and *so* returned.
16 And the rulers knew not whither
I went, or what I did; neither had I as
yet told *it* to the Jews, nor to the
priests, nor to the nobles, nor to
the rulers, nor to the rest that did
the work.
17 ¶ Then said I unto them, Ye see
the distress that we *are* in, how Jerusa-
lem *lieth* waste, and the gates thereof
are burned with fire: come, and let us
build up the wall of Jerusalem, that we
be no more [d]a reproach.
18 Then I told them of [e]the hand of
my God which was good upon me; as
also the king's words that he had spo-
ken unto me. And they said, Let us rise
up and build. So they [f]strengthened
their hands for *this* good *work.*
19 But when Sanballat the Horo-

[a] Heb. *wife*

(cf. 4:4–5,9; 5:19; 6:9,14; 13:14,22,29,31). (1) In this case, Nehemiah stood before the king and had time only to cry out to God from his heart. In emergencies we do not have time for long prayers. Nehemiah's brief prayer touched God because it had been preceded by four months of praying and fasting. It pays to be "on praying ground."

(2) The habit of praying frequently throughout the day will make way for a greater flow of God's grace, help, and wisdom into our lives. To forget our dependence upon God and the need for His presence with us throughout the day will limit the working of the Holy Spirit in our lives (see Eph. 6:18; 1 Thes. 5:17).

2:8 THE GOOD HAND OF MY GOD UPON ME. The hand of the Lord upon Nehemiah meant at least five things to him. (1) He was sharing in God's purposes (ch. 1). (2) God was actively guiding him (v. 12). (3) God was granting him His favor and help (v. 18; cf. Heb. 4:16). (4) God was with him, enabling him to prosper and succeed in the work of God (v. 20; cf. Luke 24:50, note). (5) He felt renewed courage and faith in God (4:14,20).

2:12 NEITHER TOLD I *ANY* MAN WHAT MY GOD HAD PUT IN MY HEART TO DO. Though Nehemiah arrived as governor with the full authority of the Persian Empire behind him, he did nothing for three days and told no one his God-given plans. We can be sure he was waiting on God, not rushing ahead by trusting in his own strength (see Is. 40:29–31). Then he made a cautious, careful survey of the damage done to the walls by the Samaritans (see Ezra 4:23–24, notes), while at the same time undoubtedly counting the cost (cf. Luke 14:28–30). Most important, instead of criticizing the people for their problems and sorrows, he wanted to see these problems from their own viewpoint. Thus he said nothing until he could understand the situation from their perspective and feel what they felt.

nite, and Tobiah the servant, the Ammonite, and Geshem the Arabian, heard *it,* they laughed us to scorn, and despised us, and said, What *is* this thing that ye do? [g]will ye rebel against the king?

20 Then answered I them, and said unto them, The God of heaven, he will prosper us; therefore we his servants will arise and build: [h]but ye have no portion, nor right, nor memorial, in Jerusalem.

The rebuilding begun

3 THEN [i]ELIASHIB the high priest rose up with his brethren the priests, [j]and they builded the sheep gate; they sanctified it, and set up the doors of it; [k]even unto the tower of Meah they sanctified it, unto the tower of [l]Hananeel.

2 And [b]next unto him builded [m]the men of Jericho. And next to them builded Zaccur the son of Imri.

3 [n]But the fish gate did the sons of Hassenaah build, who *also* laid the beams thereof, and [o]set up the doors thereof, the locks thereof, and the bars thereof.

4 And next unto them repaired Meremoth the son of Urijah, the son of Koz. And next unto them repaired Meshullam the son of Berechiah, the son of Meshezabeel. And next unto them repaired Zadok the son of Baana.

5 And next unto them the Tekoites repaired; but their nobles put not their necks to [p]the work of their Lord.

6 Moreover [q]the old gate repaired Jehoiada the son of Paseah, and Meshullam the son of Besodeiah; they laid the beams thereof, and set up the doors thereof, and the locks thereof, and the bars thereof.

7 And next unto them repaired Melatiah the Gibeonite, and Jadon the Meronothite, the men of Gibeon, and of Mizpah, unto the [r]throne of the governor on this side the river.

8 Next unto him repaired Uzziel the son of Harhaiah, of the goldsmiths. Next unto him also repaired Hananiah the son of *one of* the apothecaries, and they [c]fortified Jerusalem unto the [s]broad wall.

9 And next unto them repaired Rephaiah the son of Hur, the ruler of the half part of Jerusalem.

10 And next unto them repaired Jedaiah the son of Harumaph, even over against his house. And next unto him repaired Hattush the son of Hashabniah.

11 Malchijah the son of Harim, and Hashub the son of Pahath-moab, repaired the [d]other piece, [t]and the tower of the furnaces.

12 And next unto him repaired Shallum the son of Halohesh, the ruler of the half part of Jerusalem, he and his daughters.

13 [u]The valley gate repaired Hanun, and the inhabitants of Zanoah; they built it, and set up the doors thereof, the locks thereof, and the bars thereof, and a thousand cubits on the wall unto [v]the dung gate.

14 But the dung gate repaired Malchiah the son of Rechab, the ruler of part of Beth-haccerem; he built it, and set up the doors thereof, the locks thereof, and the bars thereof.

15 But [w]the gate of the fountain repaired Shallun the son of Col-hozeh, the ruler of part of Mizpah; he built it, and covered it, and set up the doors thereof, the locks thereof, and the bars thereof, and the wall of the pool of [x]Si-

2:19 [g]ch. 6:6 **2:20** [h]Ezra 4:3 **3:1** [i]ch. 12:10 [j]John 5:2 [k]ch. 12:39 [l]Jer. 31:38 Zech. 14:10 **3:2** [m]Ezra 2:34 **3:3** [n]2 Chr. 33:14 ch. 12:39 Zeph. 1:10 [o]See ch. 6:1 & 7:1 **3:5** [p]Judg. 5:23 **3:6** [q]ch. 12:39 **3:7** [r]ch. 2:8 **3:8** [s]ch. 12:38 **3:11** [t]ch. 12:38 **3:13** [u]ch. 2:13 [v]ch:2:13 **3:15** [w]ch. 2:14 [x]John 9:7

[b] Heb. *at his hand* [c] Or, *left Jerusalem unto the broad wall* [d] Heb. *second measure*

2:19 THEY LAUGHED US TO SCORN. Ridicule and scorn often become the lot of faithful children of God who day in and day out sincerely try to live a righteous life among those who do not know God. The world frequently despises the moral standards of Christians and mocks their devotion to Christ. Our confidence and reply should be the same as Nehemiah's—the God of heaven will help us and in the end vindicate the righteous (v. 20; see Rev. 2:7, note; 21:1–7, notes).

2:20 HE WILL PROSPER US. In all matters related to His kingdom, success begins with God. Nehemiah began rebuilding the walls of the city because he knew it was God's will; therefore he was fully confident that God would give him success in doing so. In all God's work, our Lord desires His people to be co-laborers with Him (cf. Phil. 2:12–13). Ch. 4 adds three factors of success that involve effort on our part: (1) "the people had a mind to work" (4:6); (2) the people were prayerful and watchful as they did the work (4:9); and (3) the people demonstrated courage, determination, and faith when confronting opposition from the enemy (4:14). When Jerusalem's wall was finished in fifty-two days, even the Jews' enemies had to acknowledge that this work was accomplished with the help of God (6:15–16). God always does His part when His people do their part in persevering faith.

loah by the king's garden, and unto the stairs that go down from the city of David.

16 After him repaired Nehemiah the son of Azbuk, the ruler of the half part of Beth-zur, unto *the place* over against the sepulchres of David, and to the [y]pool that was made, and unto the house of the mighty.

17 After him repaired the Levites, Rehum the son of Bani. Next unto him repaired Hashabiah, the ruler of the half part of Keilah, in his part.

18 After him repaired their brethren, Bavai the son of Henadad, the ruler of the half part of Keilah.

19 And next to him repaired Ezer the son of Jeshua, the ruler of Mizpah, another piece over against the going up to the armoury at the [z]turning *of the wall.*

20 After him Baruch the son of [e]Zabbai earnestly repaired the other piece, from the turning *of the wall* unto the door of the house of Eliashib the high priest.

21 After him repaired Meremoth the son of Urijah the son of Koz another piece, from the door of the house of Eliashib even to the end of the house of Eliashib.

22 And after him repaired the priests, the men of the plain.

23 After him repaired Benjamin and Hashub over against their house. After him repaired Azariah the son of Maaseiah the son of Ananiah by his house.

24 After him repaired Binnui the son of Henadad another piece, from the house of Azariah unto [a]the turning *of the wall,* even unto the corner.

25 Palal the son of Uzai, over against the turning *of the wall,* and the tower which lieth out from the king's high house, that *was* by the [b]court of the prison. After him Pedaiah the son of Parosh.

26 Moreover [c]the Nethinims [f]dwelt in [d]Ophel,[g] unto *the place* over against [e]the water gate toward the east, and the tower that lieth out.

27 After them the Tekoites repaired another piece, over against the great tower that lieth out, even unto the wall of Ophel.

28 From above the [f]horse gate repaired the priests, every one over against his house.

29 After them repaired Zadok the son of Immer over against his house. After him repaired also Shemaiah the son of Shechaniah, the keeper of the east gate.

30 After him repaired Hananiah the son of Shelemiah, and Hanun the sixth son of Zalaph, another piece. After him repaired Meshullam the son of Berechiah over against his chamber.

31 After him repaired Malchiah the goldsmith's son unto the place of the Nethinims, and of the merchants, over against the gate Miphkad, and to the [h]going up of the corner.

32 And between the going up of the corner unto the sheep gate repaired the goldsmiths and the merchants.

Defence against a conspiracy

4 BUT IT came to pass, [g]that when Sanballat heard that we builded the wall, he was wroth, and took great indignation, and mocked the Jews.

2 And he spake before his brethren and the army of Samaria, and said, What do these feeble Jews? will they [i]fortify themselves? will they sacrifice? will they make an end in a day? will they revive the stones out of the heaps of the rubbish which are burned?

3 Now [h]Tobiah the Ammonite *was* by him, and he said, Even that which they build, if a fox go up, he shall even break down their stone wall.

4 [i]Hear, O our God; for we are

3:16 [y]2 Ki. 20:20 Is. 22:11
3:19 [z]2 Chr. 26:9
3:24 [a]ver. 19
3:25 [b]Jer. 32:2 & 33:1 & 37:21
3:26 [c]Ezra 2:43 ch. 11:21 [d]2 Chr. 27:3 [e]ch. 8:1,3 & 12:37
3:28 [f]2 Ki. 11:16 2 Chr. 23:15 Jer. 31:40
4:1 [g]ch. 2:10,19
4:3 [h]ch. 2:10,19
4:4 [i]Ps. 123:3,4

[e] Or, *Zaccai* [f] Or, which *dwelt in Ophel,* repaired *unto* [g] Or, *The tower* [h] Or, *corner chambers* [i] Heb. *leave to themselves*

4:1 SANBALLAT ... MOCKED THE JEWS. The enemies of the small remnant of Jews opposed the rebuilding of the wall of Jerusalem. Nehemiah and the people encountered ridicule (vv. 1–6), the threat of force (vv. 7–9), discouragement (v. 10), and fear (vv. 11–13). This chapter reveals how opposition to the work of God can be overcome. (1) The ridicule was overcome by prayer and determination (vv. 4–6). (2) The threat of force was overcome by prayer and prudent security (vv. 7–9; see Mark 14:38; Eph. 6:18). (3) The discouragement and fear were overcome by the faith of godly leaders, their encouragement, and their preparation to resist the enemy (vv. 12–18; see Eph. 6:11, note).

4:4 TURN THEIR REPROACH UPON THEIR OWN HEAD. Nehemiah's prayer against the enemy was motivated by his faith in God and his love for God's work and people (cf. Jer. 18:23; Rev. 6:10). It is always right to pray that God will oppose His enemies or turn back the hearts of those who are trying to destroy His work or harm His children.

[i]despised: and [j]turn their reproach upon their own head, and give them for a prey in the land of captivity:

5 And [k]cover not their iniquity, and let not their sin be blotted out from before thee: for they have provoked *thee* to anger before the builders.

6 So built we the wall; and all the wall was joined together unto the half thereof: for the people had a mind to work.

7 ¶ But it came to pass, *that* [l]when Sanballat, and Tobiah, and the Arabians, and the Ammonites, and the Ashdodites, heard that the walls of Jerusalem [k]were made up, *and* that the breaches began to be stopped, then they were very wroth,

8 And [m]conspired all of them together to come *and* to fight against Jerusalem, and [l]to hinder it.

9 Nevertheless [n]we made our prayer unto our God, and set a watch against them day and night, because of them.

10 And Judah said, The strength of the bearers of burdens is decayed, and *there is* much rubbish; so that we are not able to build the wall.

11 And our adversaries said, They shall not know, neither see, till we come in the midst among them, and slay them, and cause the work to cease.

12 And it came to pass, that when the Jews which dwelt by them came, they said unto us ten times, [m]From all places whence ye shall return unto us *they will be upon you.*

13 ¶ Therefore set I [n]in the lower places behind the wall, *and* on the higher places, I even set the people after their families with their swords, their spears, and their bows.

14 And I looked, and rose up, and said unto the nobles, and to the rulers, and to the rest of the people, [o]Be not ye afraid of them: remember the Lord, *which is* [p]great and terrible, and [q]fight for your brethren, your sons, and your daughters, your wives, and your houses.

15 And it came to pass, when our enemies heard that it was known unto us, [r]and God had brought their counsel to nought, that we returned all of us to the wall, every one unto his work.

16 And it came to pass from that time forth, *that* the half of my servants wrought in the work, and the other half of them held both the spears, the shields, and the bows, and the habergeons; and the rulers *were* behind all the house of Judah.

17 They which builded on the wall, and they that bare burdens, with those that laded, *every one* with one of his hands wrought in the work, and with the other *hand* held a weapon.

18 For the builders, every one had his sword girded [o]by his side, and *so* builded. And he that sounded the trumpet *was* by me.

19 ¶ And I said unto the nobles, and to the rulers, and to the rest of the people, The work *is* great and large, and we are separated upon the wall, one far from another.

20 In what place *therefore* ye hear the sound of the trumpet, resort ye thither unto us: [s]our God shall fight for us.

21 So we laboured in the work: and half of them held the spears from the rising of the morning till the stars appeared.

22 Likewise at the same time said I unto the people, Let every one with his servant lodge within Jerusalem, that in the night they may be a guard to us, and labour on the day.

23 So neither I, nor my brethren, nor my servants, nor the men of the guard which followed me, none of us put off our clothes, [p]*saving that* every one put them off for washing.

Poverty and famine

5 AND THERE was a great [t]cry of the people and of their wives against their [u]brethren the Jews.

4:4 [j]Ps. 79:12 Prov. 3:34 **4:5** [k]Ps. 69:27,28 & 109:14,15 Jer. 18:23 **4:7** [l]ver. 1 **4:8** [m]Ps. 83:3-5 **4:9** [n]Ps. 50:15 **4:14** [o]Num. 14:9 Deut. 1:29 [p]Deut. 10:17 [q]2 Sam. 10:12 **4:15** [r]Job 5:12 **4:20** [s]Ex. 14:14,25 Deut. 1:30 & 3:22 & 20:4 Josh. 23:10 **5:1** [t]Is. 5:7 [u]Lev. 25:35-37 Deut. 15:7

[i]Heb. *despite* [k]Heb. *ascended* [l]Heb. *to make an error to it* [m]Or, *That from all places ye must return to us* [n]Heb. *from the lower parts of the place* [o]Heb. *on his loins* [p]Or, *every one* went *with his weapon for water*

4:20 OUR GOD SHALL FIGHT FOR US. When our work for God is genuinely undertaken in faith and humility, in order to bring God glory and to advance His kingdom, using the weapons of the Spirit (see 2 Cor. 10:4, note), we can be assured that no matter how great the difficulties, God will fight for us.

5:1 A GREAT CRY OF THE PEOPLE. Ch. 5 concerns unjust economic inequities among the Jewish people. (1) The rich, i.e., the nobles and rulers (v. 7), were oppressing the poor by making them mortgage their property and borrow money

2 For there were that said, We, our sons, and our daughters, *are* many: therefore we take up corn *for them*, that we may eat, and live.

3 *Some* also there were that said, We have mortgaged our lands, vineyards, and houses, that we might buy corn, because of the dearth.

4 There were also that said, We have borrowed money for the king's tribute, *and that upon* our lands and vineyards.

5 Yet now [v]our flesh *is* as the flesh of our brethren, our children as their children: and, lo, we [w]bring into bondage our sons and our daughters to be servants, and *some* of our daughters are brought unto bondage *already:* neither *is it* in our power *to redeem them;* for other men have our lands and vineyards.

6 ¶ And I was very angry when I heard their cry and these words.

7 Then [q]I consulted with myself, and I rebuked the nobles, and the rulers, and said unto them, [x]Ye exact usury, every one of his brother. And I set a great assembly against them.

8 And I said unto them, We after our ability have [y]redeemed our brethren the Jews, which were sold unto the heathen; and will ye even sell your brethren? or shall they be sold unto us? Then held they their peace, and found nothing *to answer.*

9 Also I said, It *is* not good that ye do: ought ye not to walk [z]in the fear of our God [a]because of the reproach of the heathen our enemies?

10 I likewise, *and* my brethren, and my servants, might exact of them money and corn: I pray you, let us leave off this usury.

11 Restore, I pray you, to them, even this day, their lands, their vineyards, their oliveyards, and their houses, also the hundredth *part* of the money, and of the corn, the wine, and the oil, that ye exact of them.

12 Then said they, We will restore *them,* and will require nothing of them; so will we do as thou sayest. Then I called the priests, [b]and took an oath of them, that they should do according to this promise.

13 Also [c]I shook my lap, and said, So God shake out every man from his house, and from his labour, that performeth not this promise, even thus be he shaken out, and [r]emptied. And all the congregation said, Amen, and praised the LORD. [d]And the people did according to this promise.

14 ¶ Moreover from the time that I was appointed to be their governor in the land of Judah, from the twentieth year [e]even unto the two and thirtieth year of Artaxerxes the king, *that is,* twelve years, I and my brethren have not [f]eaten the bread of the governor.

15 But the former governors that *had been* before me were chargeable unto the people, and had taken of them bread and wine, beside forty shekels of silver; yea, even their servants bare rule over the people: but [g]so did not I, because of the [h]fear of God.

16 Yea, also I continued in the work of this wall, neither bought we any land: and all my servants *were* gathered thither unto the work.

17 Moreover *there were* [i]at my table an hundred and fifty of the Jews and rulers, beside those that came unto us from among the heathen that *are* about us.

18 Now *that* [j]which was prepared *for me* daily *was* one ox *and* six choice

5:5 [v]Is. 58:7 [w]Ex. 21:7 Lev. 25:39 **5:7** [x]Ex. 22:25 Lev. 25:36 Ezek. 22:12 **5:8** [y]Lev. 25:48 **5:9** [z]Lev. 25:36 [a]2 Sam. 12:14 Rom. 2:24 1 Pet. 2:12 **5:12** [b]Ezra 10:5 Jer. 34:8,9 **5:13** [c]Mat. 10:14 Acts 13:51 & 18:6 [d]2 Ki. 23:3 **5:14** [e]ch. 13:6 [f]1 Cor. 9:4,15 **5:15** [g]2 Cor. 11:9 & 12:13 [h]ver. 9 **5:17** [i]2 Sam. 9:7 1 Ki. 18:19 **5:18** [j]1 Ki. 4:22

[q]Heb. *my heart consulted in me* [r]Heb. *empty,* or, *void*

in order to buy food. In some instances the poor were being forced to give their children as slaves to keep from starving (vv. 1–5). In anger, Nehemiah fought against this injustice (v. 6) and brought the offenders to repentance and correction (vv. 12–13). (2) The sin of covetousness, which leads people to take advantage of others in times of trouble, reveals the deep depravity of human nature. God will judge such injustices perpetrated among people (cf. Prov. 28:27; see Col. 3:25, note; see article on THE CARE OF THE POOR AND NEEDY, p. 1312).

5:6 I WAS VERY ANGRY. Nehemiah's anger at injustice and evil was a godly anger. The absence of such anger indicates an indifference to the suffering of the innocent and needy (see Luke 19:45, note).

5:15 THE FEAR OF GOD. Because Nehemiah feared God, he did not use his authority to take advantage of the people, as some other leaders before him had done. Fear of God makes us aware of our accountability to Him and motivates us to turn away from even subtle practices, such as manipulating or defrauding His people.

5:18 ALL SORTS OF WINE. In O.T. times there were "all sorts of wine"—new, old, pure, and mixed wines—some fresh from the grape, some boiled and condensed, some sweet and thick like honey, some mixed with water, and some mixed with drugs. Of these wines, some were fermented,

sheep; also fowls were prepared for me, and once in ten days store of all sorts of wine: yet for all this [k]required not I the bread of the governor, because the bondage was heavy upon this people.

19 [l]Think upon me, my God, for good, *according* to all that I have done for this people.

False rumours about Nehemiah

6 NOW IT came to pass, [m]when Sanballat, and Tobiah, and [s]Geshem the Arabian, and the rest of our enemies, heard that I had builded the wall, and *that* there was no breach left therein; ([n]though at that time I had not set up the doors upon the gates;)

2 That Sanballat and Geshem [o]sent unto me, saying, Come, let us meet together in *some one of* the villages in the plain of [p]Ono. But they [q]thought to do me mischief.

3 And I sent messengers unto them, saying, I *am* doing a great work, so that I cannot come down: why should the work cease, whilst I leave it, and come down to you?

4 Yet they sent unto me four times after this sort; and I answered them after the same manner.

5 Then sent Sanballat his servant unto me in like manner the fifth time with an open letter in his hand;

6 Wherein *was* written, It is reported among the heathen, and [t]Gashmu saith *it*, [r]*that* thou and the Jews think to rebel: for which cause thou buildest the wall, that thou mayest be their king, according to these words.

7 And thou hast also appointed prophets to preach of thee at Jerusalem, saying, *There is* a king in Judah: and now shall it be reported to the king according to these words. Come now therefore, and let us take counsel together.

8 Then I sent unto him, saying, There are no such things done as thou sayest, but thou feignest them out of thine own heart.

9 For they all made us afraid, saying, Their hands shall be weakened from the work, that it be not done. Now therefore, *O God,* strengthen my hands.

10 Afterward I came unto the house of Shemaiah the son of Delaiah the son of Mehetabeel, who *was* shut up; and he said, Let us meet together in the house of God, within the temple, and let us shut the doors of the temple: for they will come to slay thee; yea, in the night will they come to slay thee.

11 And I said, Should such a man as I flee? and who *is there,* that, *being* as I *am,* would go into the temple to save his life? I will not go in.

12 And, lo, I perceived that God had not sent him; but that [s]he pronounced this prophecy against me: for Tobiah and Sanballat had hired him.

13 Therefore *was* he hired, that I should be afraid, and do so, and sin, and *that* they might have *matter* for an evil report, that they might reproach me.

14 [t]My God, think thou upon Tobiah and Sanballat according to these their works, and on the [u]prophetess Noadiah, and the rest of the prophets, that would have put me in fear.

5:18 [k]ver. 14,15
5:19 [l]ch. 13:22
6:1 [m]ch. 2:10,19 [n]ch. 3:1,3
6:2 [o]Prov. 26:24,25 [p]1 Chr. 8:12 ch. 11:35 [q]Ps. 37:12,32
6:6 [r]ch. 2:19
6:12 [s]Ezek. 13:22
6:14 [t]ch. 13:29 [u]Ezek. 13:17

[s] Or, *Gashmu;* see ver. 6 [t] Or, *Geshem;* see ver. 1

others were not (see Prov. 23:30, note; see also articles on WINE IN THE OLD TESTAMENT, p. 220, and WINE IN NEW TESTAMENT TIMES (1) and (2), p. 1538 and p. 1594).

6:3 I *AM* DOING A GREAT WORK. God's people must have a vision of the greatness of the work to which He calls them. Even though our task or contribution as individuals may seem small and inconsequential, corporately as God's people we are "doing a great work." Nehemiah was resolute in his objective of rebuilding the wall; he would not be distracted by friend or foe until the work was completed. Great vision coupled with unwavering faith achieves the realization of God's purpose for our lives and our generation.

6:12 I PERCEIVED THAT GOD HAD NOT SENT HIM. All who claim to be messengers of God must be tested as to whether they are really from God. Some will claim to be believers and proclaim that they are undertaking a ministry ordained by God, yet in reality they are only seeking glory and prosperity for themselves. God's people need discernment to judge the personal character and loyalty to God and His standards of all those who present themselves as spokespersons for God (see article on FALSE TEACHERS, p. 1508).

6:14 THE PROPHETS, THAT WOULD HAVE PUT ME IN FEAR. Nehemiah suffered from false brethren who, although claiming to labor for the honor of God, were in reality in league with God's enemies. This betrayal of God and His kingdom by false brethren is one of the heaviest griefs that true servants of God sometimes have to bear (see Acts 20:28–31; 2 Cor. 11:26).

Building of the walls finished

15 ¶ So the wall was finished in the twenty and fifth *day* of *the month* Elul, in fifty and two days.

16 And it came to pass, that [v]when all our enemies heard *thereof,* and all the heathen that *were* about us saw *these things,* they were much cast down in their own eyes: for [w]they perceived that this work was wrought of our God.

Esth. 4:14–5:2

17 ¶ Moreover in those days the nobles of Judah [u]sent many letters unto Tobiah, and *the letters* of Tobiah came unto them.

18 For *there were* many in Judah sworn unto him, because he *was* the son-in-law of Shechaniah the son of Arah; and his son Johanan had taken the daughter of Meshullam the son of Berechiah.

19 Also they reported his good deeds before me, and uttered my [v]words to him. *And* Tobiah sent letters to put me in fear.

7 NOW IT came to pass, when the wall was built, and I had [x]set up the doors, and the porters and the singers and the Levites were appointed,

2 That I gave my brother Hanani, and Hananiah the ruler [y]of the palace, charge over Jerusalem: for he *was* a faithful man, and [z]feared God above many.

3 And I said unto them, Let not the gates of Jerusalem be opened until the sun be hot; and while they stand by, let them shut the doors, and bar *them:* and appoint watches of the inhabitants of Jerusalem, every one in his watch, and every one *to be* over against his house.

4 Now the city *was* [w]large and great: but the people *were* few therein, and the houses *were* not builded.

List of those who returned

7:6–73pp — Ezra 2:1–70

5 ¶ And my God put into mine heart to gather together the nobles, and the rulers, and the people, that they might be reckoned by genealogy. And I found a register of the genealogy of them which came up at the first, and found written therein,

6 [a]These *are* the children of the province, that went up out of the captivity, of those that had been carried away, whom Nebuchadnezzar the king of Babylon had carried away, and came again to Jerusalem and to Judah, every one unto his city;

7 Who came with Zerubbabel, Jeshua, Nehemiah, [x]Azariah, Raamiah, Nahamani, Mordecai, Bilshan, Mispereth, Bigvai, Nehum, Baanah. The number, *I say,* of the men of the people of Israel *was this;*

8 The children of Parosh, two thousand an hundred seventy and two.

9 The children of Shephatiah, three hundred seventy and two.

10 The children of Arah, six hundred fifty and two.

11 The children of Pahath-moab, of the children of Jeshua and Joab, two thousand and eight hundred *and* eighteen.

12 The children of Elam, a thousand two hundred fifty and four.

13 The children of Zattu, eight hundred forty and five.

14 The children of Zaccai, seven hundred and threescore.

15 The children of [y]Binnui, six hundred forty and eight.

16 The children of Bebai, six hundred twenty and eight.

17 The children of Azgad, two thousand three hundred twenty and two.

18 The children of Adonikam, six hundred threescore and seven.

19 The children of Bigvai, two thousand threescore and seven.

20 The children of Adin, six hundred fifty and five.

6:16 [v]ch. 2:10 & 4:1,7 & 6:1 [w]Ps. 126:2 **7:1** [x]ch. 6:1 **7:2** [y]ch. 2:8 [z]Ex. 18:21 **7:6** [a]Ezra 2:1

[u]Heb. *multiplied their letters passing to Tobiah* [v]Or, *matters* [w]Heb. *broad in spaces* [x]Or, *Seraiah;* see Ezra 2:2 [y]Or, *Bani*

6:15 THE WALL WAS FINISHED. The wall was completed (1) because God was with His people (2:20; 4:15,20); (2) because they had a courageous, dedicated, and persevering leader, Nehemiah, who depended fully on God as his protection and source of strength (vv. 3,9; 5:14–19); and (3) because the people had a mind to work (4:6) and followed their leader in giving themselves fully and courageously to the task.

7:2 HE *WAS* A FAITHFUL MAN, AND FEARED GOD. The Scriptural principle in selecting leaders and overseers for God's work is to appoint those who have persevered in faithfulness to God and His word, and who have demonstrated a godly fear of sin and its consequences (see articles on MORAL QUALIFICATIONS FOR OVERSEERS, p. 1908, and BIBLE TRAINING FOR CHRISTIANS, p. 1920).

21 The children of Ater of Hezekiah, ninety and eight.

22 The children of Hashum, three hundred twenty and eight.

23 The children of Bezai, three hundred twenty and four.

24 The children of [z]Hariph, an hundred and twelve.

25 The children of [a]Gibeon, ninety and five.

26 The men of Bethlehem and Netophah, an hundred fourscore and eight.

27 The men of Anathoth, an hundred twenty and eight.

28 The men of [b]Beth-azmaveth, forty and two.

29 The men of [c]Kirjath-jearim, Chephirah, and Beeroth, seven hundred forty and three.

30 The men of Ramah and Gaba, six hundred twenty and one.

31 The men of Michmas, an hundred and twenty and two.

32 The men of Beth-el and Ai, an hundred twenty and three.

33 The men of the other Nebo, fifty and two.

34 The children of the other [b]Elam, a thousand two hundred fifty and four.

35 The children of Harim, three hundred and twenty.

36 The children of Jericho, three hundred forty and five.

37 The children of Lod, Hadid, and Ono, seven hundred twenty and one.

38 The children of Senaah, three thousand nine hundred and thirty.

39 ¶ The priests: the children of [c]Jedaiah, of the house of Jeshua, nine hundred seventy and three.

40 The children of [d]Immer, a thousand fifty and two.

41 The children of [e]Pashur, a thousand two hundred forty and seven.

42 The children of [f]Harim, a thousand and seventeen.

43 ¶ The Levites: the children of Jeshua, of Kadmiel, *and* of the children of [d]Hodevah, seventy and four.

44 ¶ The singers: the children of Asaph, an hundred forty and eight.

45 ¶ The porters: the children of Shallum, the children of Ater, the children of Talmon, the children of Akkub, the children of Hatita, the children of Shobai, an hundred thirty and eight.

46 ¶ The Nethinims: the children of Ziha, the children of Hashupha, the children of Tabbaoth,

47 The children of Keros, the children of [e]Sia, the children of Padon,

48 The children of Lebana, the children of Hagaba, the children of [f]Shalmai,

49 The children of Hanan, the children of Giddel, the children of Gahar,

50 The children of Reaiah, the children of Rezin, the children of Nekoda,

51 The children of Gazzam, the children of Uzza, the children of Phaseah,

52 The children of Besai, the children of Meunim, the children of [g]Nephishesim,

53 The children of Bakbuk, the children of Hakupha, the children of Harhur,

54 The children of [h]Bazlith, the children of Mehida, the children of Harsha,

55 The children of Barkos, the children of Sisera, the children of Tamah,

56 The children of Neziah, the children of Hatipha.

57 ¶ The children of Solomon's servants: the children of Sotai, the children of Sophereth, the children of [i]Perida,

58 The children of Jaala, the children of Darkon, the children of Giddel,

59 The children of Shephatiah, the children of Hattil, the children of Pochereth of Zebaim, the children of [j]Amon.

60 All the Nethinims, and the children of Solomon's servants, *were* three hundred ninety and two.

61 [g]And these *were* they which went up *also* from Tel-melah, Tel-haresha, Cherub, [k]Addon, and Immer: but they could not show their father's house, nor their [l]seed, whether they *were* of Israel.

62 The children of Delaiah, the children of Tobiah, the children of Nekoda, six hundred forty and two.

63 ¶ And of the priests: the children of Habaiah, the children of Koz, the children of Barzillai, which took *one* of the daughters of Barzillai the Gileadite to wife, and was called after their name.

64 These sought their register *among* those that were reckoned by ge-

7:34 [b]See ver. 12
7:39 [c]1 Chr. 24:7
7:40 [d]1 Chr. 24:14
7:41 [e]See 1 Chr. 9:12 & 24:9
7:42 [f]1 Chr. 24:8
7:61 [g]Ezra 2:59

[z] Or, *Jora* [a] Or, *Gibbar* [b] Or, *Azmaveth* [c] Or, *Kirjath-arim* [d] Or, *Hodaviah;* see Ezra 2:40; or, *Judah;* see Ezra 3:9 [e] Or, *Siaha* [f] Or, *Shamlai* [g] Or, *Nephusim* [h] Or, *Bazluth* [i] Or, *Peruda* [j] Or, *Ami* [k] Or, *Addan* [l] Or, *pedigree*

nealogy, but it was not found: therefore were they, as polluted, put from the priesthood.

65 And [m]the Tirshatha said unto them, that they should not eat of the most holy things, till there stood *up* a priest with Urim and Thummim.

66 ¶ The whole congregation together *was* forty and two thousand three hundred and threescore,

67 Beside their manservants and their maidservants, of whom *there were* seven thousand three hundred thirty and seven: and they had two hundred forty and five singing men and singing women.

68 Their horses, seven hundred thirty and six: their mules, two hundred forty and five:

69 *Their* camels, four hundred thirty and five: six thousand seven hundred and twenty asses.

70 ¶ And [n]some of the chief of the fathers gave unto the work. [h]The Tirshatha gave to the treasure a thousand drams of gold, fifty basins, five hundred and thirty priests' garments.

71 And *some* of the chief of the fathers gave to the treasure of the work [i]twenty thousand drams of gold, and two thousand and two hundred pound of silver.

72 And *that* which the rest of the people gave *was* twenty thousand drams of gold, and two thousand pound of silver, and threescore and seven priests' garments.

73 So the priests, and the Levites, and the porters, and the singers, and *some* of the people, and the Nethinims, and all Israel, dwelt in their cities; [j]and when the seventh month came, the children of Israel *were* in their cities.

7:70 [h]ch. 8:9
7:71 [i]Ezra 2:69
7:73 [j]Ezra 3:1
8:1 [k]Ezra 3:1 [l]ch. 3:26 [m]Ezra 7:6
8:2 [n]Deut. 31:11,12 [o]Lev. 23:24
8:5 [p]Judg. 3:20
8:6 [q]1 Cor. 14:16 [r]Lam. 3:41 1 Tim. 2:8 [s]Ex. 4:31 & 12:27 2 Chr. 20:18

The law read and explained

8 AND ALL [k]the people gathered themselves together as one man into the street that *was* [l]before the water gate; and they spake unto Ezra the [m]scribe to bring the book of the law of Moses, which the LORD had commanded to Israel.

2 And Ezra the priest brought [n]the law before the congregation both of men and women, and all [o]that could hear with understanding, [o]upon the first day of the seventh month.

3 And he read therein before the street that *was* before the water gate [p]from the morning until midday, before the men and the women, and those that could understand; and the ears of all the people *were attentive* unto the book of the law.

4 And Ezra the scribe stood upon a [q]pulpit of wood, which they had made for the purpose; and beside him stood Mattithiah, and Shema, and Anaiah, and Urijah, and Hilkiah, and Maaseiah, on his right hand; and on his left hand, Pedaiah, and Mishael, and Malchiah, and Hashum, and Hashbadana, Zechariah, *and* Meshullam.

5 And Ezra opened the book in the [r]sight of all the people; (for he was above all the people;) and when he opened it, all the people [p]stood up:

6 And Ezra blessed the LORD, the great God. And all the people [q]answered, Amen, Amen, with [r]lifting up their hands: and they [s]bowed their heads, and worshipped the LORD with *their* faces to the ground.

7 Also Jeshua, and Bani, and Sherebiah, Jamin, Akkub, Shabbethai, Hodi-

[m] Or, *the governor;* see ch. 8:9 [n] Heb. *part* [o] Heb. *that understood in hearing* [p] Heb. *from the light* [q] Heb. *tower of wood* [r] Heb. *eyes*

8:1 THE PEOPLE GATHERED THEMSELVES TOGETHER. Chs. 8—10 describe one of the greatest revivals in O.T. times and illustrate several fundamental principles for spiritual renewal and revival. Renewal and revival come only from God; they are mediated through God's Word (vv. 1–8), prayer (v. 6), confession (ch. 9), a broken and contrite heart (v. 9), a turning from the sinful ways and behavior of contemporary society (9:2), and a renewed commitment to walk in God's will and to make God's Word the rule for grateful living (10:29).

8:3 *ATTENTIVE* UNTO THE BOOK OF THE LAW. The revival was initiated by a sincere return to God's Word and a diligent effort to understand its meaning (v. 8). For seven days, six hours each day, Ezra read from the book of the law (vv. 3,18). One of the foremost evidences of true revival among God's people is a deep hunger to hear and to read God's Word.

8:6 THEY BOWED THEIR HEADS, AND WORSHIPPED THE LORD. This chapter of the Bible describes one of the greatest worship services of all time. God desires the adoration of His people and calls them to worship Him regularly (cf. Ps. 29:2; 96:9; see article on WORSHIP, p. 730).

8:7 UNDERSTAND THE LAW. Ezra and the Levites demonstrate what should happen whenever God's Word is proclaimed to His people. Many of the returned exiles no longer understood Hebrew, for their language was now Aramaic. Thus

jah, Maaseiah, Kelita, Azariah, Jozabad, Hanan, Pelaiah, and the Levites, [t]caused the people to understand the law: and the people *stood* in their place.

8 So they read in the book in the law of God distinctly, and gave the sense, and caused *them* to understand the reading.

9 ¶ [u]And Nehemiah, which *is* [s]the Tirshatha, and Ezra the priest the scribe, and the Levites that taught the people, said unto all the people, [v]This day *is* holy unto the LORD your God; [w]mourn not, nor weep. For all the people wept, when they heard the words of the law.

10 Then he said unto them, Go your way, eat the fat, and drink the sweet, [x]and send portions unto them for whom nothing is prepared: for *this* day *is* holy unto our Lord: neither be ye sorry; for the joy of the LORD is your strength.

11 So the Levites stilled all the people, saying, Hold your peace, for the day *is* holy; neither be ye grieved.

12 And all the people went their way to eat, and to drink, and to [y]send portions, and to make great mirth, because they had [z]understood the words that were declared unto them.

13 ¶ And on the second day were gathered together the chief of the fathers of all the people, the priests, and the Levites, unto Ezra the scribe, even [t]to understand the words of the law.

14 And they found written in the law which the LORD had commanded [u]by Moses, that the children of Israel should dwell in [a]booths in the feast of the seventh month:

15 And [b]that they should publish and proclaim in all their cities, and [c]in Jerusalem, saying, Go forth unto the mount, and [d]fetch olive branches, and pine branches, and myrtle branches, and palm branches, and branches of thick trees, to make booths, as *it is* written.

16 ¶ So the people went forth, and brought *them,* and made themselves booths, every one upon the [e]roof of his house, and in their courts, and in the courts of the house of God, and in the street of the [f]water gate, [g]and in the street of the gate of Ephraim.

17 And all the congregation of them that were come again out of the captivity made booths, and sat under the booths: for since the days of Jeshua the son of Nun unto that day had not the children of Israel done so. And there was very [h]great gladness.

18 Also [i]day by day, from the first day unto the last day, he read in the book of the law of God. And they kept the feast seven days; and on the eighth day *was* [v]a solemn assembly, [j]according unto the manner.

8:7 [t]Lev. 10:11 Deut. 33:10 2 Chr. 17:7 Mal. 2:7
8:9 [u]Ezra 2:63 ch. 7:65 & 10:1 [v]Lev. 23:24 Num. 29:1 [w]Deut. 16:14 Eccl. 3:4
8:10 [x]Esth. 9:19 Rev. 11:10
8:12 [y]ver. 10 [z]ver. 7,8
8:14 [a]Lev. 23:34,42 Deut. 16:13
8:15 [b]Lev. 23:4 [c]Deut. 16:16 [d]Lev. 23:40
8:16 [e]Deut. 22:8 [f]ch. 12:37 [g]2 Ki. 14:13 ch. 12:39
8:17 [h]2 Chr. 30:21
8:18 [i]Deut. 31:10 [j]Lev. 23:36 Num. 29:35

[s] Or, *the governor* [t] Or, *that they might instruct in the words of the law* [u] Heb. *by the hand of* [v] Heb. *a restraint*

when the Hebrew Scriptures were read, a group of dedicated men translated it into Aramaic and explained its meaning in a manner that the people could understand and apply to their lives; as a result, the people rejoiced "because they had understood the words that were declared unto them" (v. 12). Revelation, repentance, revival, and rejoicing are all potentially present and waiting to be released by the Holy Spirit through anointed messengers who proclaim God's Word with clarity, power, and conviction.

8:9 ALL THE PEOPLE WEPT, WHEN THEY HEARD THE WORDS OF THE LAW. When the people heard and understood the Word of God, they felt a deep conviction of sin and guilt. (1) The passages of the law that brought a clear revelation of their spiritual condition may have been Lev. 26 and Deut. 28. These chapters speak of God's blessing or judgment, depending on the people's obedience or disobedience to His Word. (2) In revivals, weeping, when accompanied with profound repentance (cf. ch. 9), is a sign of the work of the Holy Spirit (see John 16:8, note). Turning from sin in sorrow brings the forgiveness of God and the joy of salvation (see v. 10, note; Mat. 5:4).

8:10 EAT THE FAT, AND DRINK THE SWEET. The Jews highly prized foods prepared with much fat and drinks that were sweet. Much of the ancient wines were boiled and condensed until they were very sweet and thick like honey or jellies. They had to be greatly diluted before they could be drunk (see 5:18, note).

8:10 THE JOY OF THE LORD IS YOUR STRENGTH. The declaration of God's Word, accompanied by a sincere desire to follow its instruction, will result in a true, heartfelt joy. This "joy of the LORD" is based on reconciliation with God and the presence of the Spirit in our lives. It is maintained by the assurance that we have been forgiven in Christ and restored to fellowship with God, and that we now live in harmony with His will (vv. 10–13; cf. Luke 7:50). Such joy acts (1) as a fortress to guard us from the troubles and temptations of each day (cf. Ps. 119:165; Gal. 5:22; Phil. 4:4), and (2) as the power and motivation to persevere in faith until the end.

WORSHIP

***Neh. 8:5–6** "And Ezra opened the book in the sight of all the people; (for he was above all the people;) and when he opened it, all the people stood up: And Ezra blessed the* LORD*, the great God. And all the people answered, Amen, Amen, with lifting up their hands: and they bowed their heads, and worshipped the* LORD *with their faces* **to the ground."**

The English word "worship" is derived from an Old English word "worthship"; in other words, worship constitutes those actions and attitudes that revere and honor the worthiness of the great God of heaven and earth. Thus, worship is God-centered, not man-centered. In Christian worship we draw near to God in gratitude for what He has done for us in Christ and through the Holy Spirit. It requires a faith commitment to Him and an acknowledgement that He is our God and Lord.

BRIEF HISTORY OF THE WORSHIP OF THE TRUE GOD. Human beings have worshiped God from the beginning of history. Adam and Eve had fellowship regularly with God in the Garden of Eden (cf. Gen. 3:8). Cain and Abel both brought offerings (Heb. *minchah*, "gift, tribute," translated "meat offering" in Lev. 2:1) unto the Lord (Gen. 4:3–4); the descendants of Seth called "upon the name of the LORD" (Gen. 4:26). Noah built an altar to the Lord for a burnt offering after the flood (Gen. 8:20). Abraham dotted the landscape of the promised land with altars for burnt offerings to the Lord (Gen. 12:7–8; 13:4,18; 22:9) and talked intimately with Him (Gen. 18:23–33; 22:11–18).

Not until after the exodus, when the tabernacle was built at Mount Sinai, however, did *public* worship become formalized. Thereafter, regular sacrifices were performed daily and especially on the Sabbath, and God established several annual religious feasts as occasions for Israelite public worship (Ex. 23:14–17; Lev. 1—7; 16; 23:4–44; Deut. 12; 16). This worship later became centralized around the temple in Jerusalem (cf. David's plans as recorded in 1 Chr. 22—26). When the temple was destroyed in 586 B.C., the Jews built synagogues as places of instruction and worship while they were in exile and wherever they settled. These buildings continued to be used for worship even after the building of the second temple under the leadership of Zerubbabel (Ezra 3—6). There were synagogues in Palestine and all over the Roman world during N.T. times (e.g., Luke 4:16; John 6:59; Acts 6:9; 13:14; 14:1; 17:1,10; 18:4; 19:8; 22:19).

Worship in the early church took place both in the Jerusalem temple and in private homes (Acts 2:46–47). Outside of Jerusalem, Christians worshiped, as long as they were permitted, in the synagogues; when that was no longer allowed, they met elsewhere for worship—usually in private homes (cf. Acts 18:7; Rom. 16:5; Col. 4:15; Philem. 2), though sometimes in public halls (Acts 19:9–10).

EXPRESSIONS OF CHRISTIAN WORSHIP. (1) Two key principles govern Christian worship. (a) True worship takes place in spirit and in truth (see John 4:23, note), i.e., worship must take place according to God's revelation of Himself in the Son (cf. John 14:6). Likewise, it involves the human spirit and not just the mind, as well as the manifestations of the Holy Spirit (1 Cor. 12:7–12). (b) The practice of Christian worship must correspond to the N.T. pattern for the church (see Acts 7:44, note). Believers today ought to desire, seek, and expect as the norm for the church all elements found in the worship experience of the N.T. (cf. the hermeneutical principle discussed in the introduction to Acts).

(2) The key feature of O.T. worship was the sacrificial system (see Num. 28—29). Since the sacrifice of Jesus Christ on the cross fulfilled this system, there is no longer any need for the shedding of blood as part of Christian worship (see Heb. 9:1—10:18). Through the sacrament of the Lord's Supper, the N.T. church continually commemorated

this once-for-all sacrifice of Christ (1 Cor. 11:23–26). Also, the church is exhorted to offer "the sacrifice of praise to God continually, that is, the fruit of *our* lips giving thanks to his name" (Heb. 13:15), and to present our bodies as "a living sacrifice, holy, acceptable unto God" (see Rom. 12:1, note).

(3) Praising God is essential to Christian worship. It was a key element in Israel's worship of God (e.g., Ps. 100:4; 106:1; 111:1; 113:1; 117), as well as in early church worship (Acts 2:46–47; 16:25; Rom. 15:10–11; Heb. 2:12; see article on PRAISE, p. 816).

(4) One crucial way to praise God is by singing psalms, hymns, and spiritual songs. The O.T. abounds with exhortations to sing unto the Lord (e.g., 1 Chr. 16:23; Ps. 95:1; 96:1–2; 98:1,5–6; 100:1–2). At the time of the birth of Jesus, the entire heavenly host burst forth into a song of praise (Luke 2:13–14), and the N.T. church was a singing community (1 Cor. 14:15; Eph. 5:19; Col. 3:16; Jas. 5:13). The songs of N.T. Christians were sung either with the mind (i.e., with a known human language) or with the Spirit (i.e., in tongues; see 1 Cor. 14:15, note). Under no circumstances did they view singing as a form of entertainment.

(5) Another important element in worship is seeking God's face in prayer. The O.T. saints constantly communicated with God through prayer (e.g., Gen. 20:17; Num. 11:2; 1 Sam. 8:6; 2 Sam. 7:27; Dan. 9:3–19; cf. Jas. 5:17–18). The apostles prayed continually after Jesus' ascension into heaven (Acts 1:14), and prayer became a regular part of corporate Christian worship (Acts 2:42; 20:36; 1 Thes. 5:17; see article on EFFECTIVE PRAYING, p. 540). These prayers could be on their own behalf (e.g., Acts 4:24–30), or they could be intercessory prayers on behalf of others (e.g., Rom. 15:30–32; Eph. 6:18). At all times Christian prayer must be accompanied by thanksgiving to God (Eph. 5:20; Phil. 4:6; Col. 3:15,17; 1 Thes. 5:18). As with singing, praying could be done with known human languages or in tongues (1 Cor. 14:13–15).

(6) Confession of sin was clearly an important part of O.T. worship. God had established the Day of Atonement for the Israelites as a time for national confession of sin (Lev. 16; see article on THE DAY OF ATONEMENT, p. 188). In his prayer at the dedication of the temple, Solomon acknowledged the importance of confession of sin (1 Ki. 8:30–39). When Ezra and Nehemiah realized how far God's people had departed from His law, they led the entire nation of Judah in an intense public prayer of confession (Neh. 9). So too, in the Lord's Prayer, Jesus teaches believers to ask for the forgiveness of our sins (Mat. 6:12). James instructs believers to confess their sins to one another (Jas 5:16); through such confession we receive assurance of God's gracious pardon (1 John 1:9).

(7) Worship must also include the public reading of Scripture and its true proclamation. In O.T. times God had arranged that every seven years, at the Feast of Tabernacles, all the Israelites were to gather together for a public reading of the Law of Moses (Deut. 31:9–13); the clearest example of this element of O.T. worship came during the time of Ezra and Nehemiah (see Neh. 8:1–12). The reading of Scripture became a regular part of the synagogue worship on the Sabbath (see Luke 4:16–19; Acts 13:15). Similarly, when N.T. believers gathered for worship, they also heard the Word of God (1 Tim. 4:13; cf. Col. 4:16; 1 Thes. 5:27) along with teaching, preaching, and exhortation based on it (1 Tim. 4:13; 2 Tim. 4:2; cf. Acts 19:8–10; 20:7).

(8) Whenever God's O.T. people came together into the courts of the Lord, they were instructed to bring tithes and offerings (Ps. 96:8; Mal. 3:10). Similarly, Paul wrote to the Christians in Corinth concerning the collection for the church in Jerusalem: "Upon the first *day* of the week, let every one of you lay by him in store, as *God* hath prospered him" (1 Cor 16:2). The true worship of God must therefore provide the opportunity to present our tithes and offerings to the Lord.

(9) One unique element in the N.T. worshiping community was the role of the Holy Spirit and His manifestations. Among His manifestations in the body of Christ were the word of wisdom, the word of knowledge, special expressions of faith, gifts of healing, working of miracles, prophecy, distinguishing of spirits, speaking in tongues, and the interpretation of tongues (1 Cor. 12:7–10). The charismatic nature of early Christian

worship is further described in Paul's instructions: "When ye come together, every one of you hath a psalm . . . doctrine . . . tongue . . . revelation . . . interpretation" (1 Cor. 14:26). In his correspondence with the Corinthians, Paul provided principles by which to regulate that aspect of their worship (see 1 Cor. 14:1–33, notes). The overriding principle was that any exercise of the gifts of the Holy Spirit during worship had to strengthen and help the whole congregation (1 Cor. 12:7; 14:26; see article on SPIRITUAL GIFTS FOR BELIEVERS, p. 1790).

(10) The other unique element in N.T. worship was the celebration of the sacraments—baptism and the Lord's Supper. The Lord's Supper (or the "breaking of bread," see Acts 2:42) appears to have been observed daily among the believers right after Pentecost (Acts 2:46–47), and later at least weekly (Acts 20:7,11). Baptism, as commanded by Christ (Mat. 28:19–20), occurred as often as there were conversions and people were added to the church (Acts 2:41; 8:12; 9:18; 10:48; 16:30–33; 19:1–5).

GOD'S BLESSINGS FOR TRUE WORSHIPERS. When true worship takes place, God has many blessings in store for His people. He promises: (1) to be in their midst (Mat. 18:20) and to sit down and have intimate communion with them (Rev. 3:20); (2) to overshadow His people with His glory (cf. Ex. 40:35; 2 Chr. 7:1; 1 Pet. 4:14); (3) to bless His people with an abundance of blessings (Ezek. 34:26), especially with peace (Ps. 29:11; see article on THE PEACE OF GOD, p. 1122); (4) to impart an abundance of joy (Ps. 122:1; John 15:11); (5) to answer the prayers of those who pray to Him in sincere faith (Mark 11:24; Jas. 5:15; see article on EFFECTIVE PRAYING, p. 540); (6) to freshly fill His people with His Holy Spirit and with boldness (Acts 4:31); (7) to send manifestations of the Holy Spirit among His people (1 Cor. 12:7–13); (8) to guide His people into all truth through the Holy Spirit (John 15:26; 16:13); (9) to sanctify His people by His Word and Spirit (John 17:17–19); (10) to comfort, encourage, and edify His people (Is. 40:1; 1 Cor. 14:26; 2 Cor. 1:3–4; 1 Thes. 5:11); (11) to convict His people of sin, righteousness, and judgment by the Holy Spirit (see John 16:8, note); and (12) to save sinners who become convicted of sin at a worship service (1 Cor. 14:22–25).

HINDRANCES TO TRUE WORSHIP. Just because those who claim to be God's people have gathered together for worship is no guarantee that true worship is taking place or that God is accepting their praise and listening to their prayers. (1) If the worship of God is mere form and lip service and the hearts of God's people are far from Him, then God does not accept their worship. Christ severely castigated the Pharisees for their hypocrisy—legalistically following law of God, while their hearts were far from him (Mat. 15:7–9; 23:23–28; Mark 7:5–7). Note the similar criticism that He leveled against the church at Ephesus, which continued to worship the Lord but no longer really loved him supremely (Rev. 2:1–5). Paul warns believers that those who partake of the Lord's Supper without departing from sin and recognizing the body of Christ in believing brothers and sisters (cf. 1 Cor. 10:16), bring damnation to themselves (1 Cor. 11:28–30; see v. 27, note). Thus, we can expect God to draw near to us and accept our worship only if our hearts are in a right relationship with Him (Jas. 4:8; cf. Ps. 24:3–4).

(2) Another hindrance to true worship is a lifestyle of compromise, sin, and immorality. God refused to accept the sacrifices of King Saul because he disobeyed His command (1 Sam. 15:1–23). Isaiah castigates the people of God as a "sinful nation, a people laden with iniquity, a seed of evildoers" (Is. 1:4); at the same time, however, they were offering sacrifices and celebrating their holy days. Thus the Lord declared through Isaiah: "Your new moons and your appointed feasts my soul hateth: they are a trouble unto me; I am weary to bear *them*. And when ye spread forth your hands, I will hide mine eyes from you: yea, when ye make many prayers, I will not hear: your hands are full of blood" (Is. 1:14–15). Likewise in the N.T. church, Jesus urged the worshipers in Sardis to be watchful, because "I have not found thy works perfect before God" (Rev. 3:2). Similarly, James indicates that God will not hear the selfish prayers of those who have not separated themselves from the world (Jas. 4:1–5; see article on EFFECTIVE PRAYING, p. 540). God's people can expect Him to draw near and accept their worship only if they have clean hands and a pure heart (Ps. 24:3–4; Jas. 4:8).

Ezra's prayer

9 NOW IN the twenty and fourth day
of [k]this month the children of Is-
rael were assembled with fasting, and
with sackclothes, [l]and earth upon
them.
2 And [m]the seed of Israel separat-
ed themselves from all [w]strangers,
and stood and confessed their sins, and
the iniquities of their fathers.
3 And they stood up in their place,
and [n]read in the book of the law of the
LORD their God *one* fourth part of the
day; and *another* fourth part they con-
fessed, and worshipped the LORD their
God.
4 ¶ Then stood up upon the [x]stairs,
of the Levites, Jeshua, and Bani, Kad-
miel, Shebaniah, Bunni, Sherebiah,
Bani, *and* Chenani, and cried with a
loud voice unto the LORD their God.
5 Then the Levites, Jeshua, and
Kadmiel, Bani, Hashabniah, Sherebi-
ah, Hodijah, Shebaniah, *and* Pethahi-
ah, said, Stand up *and* bless the LORD
your God for ever and ever: and blessed
be [o]thy glorious name, which is exalt-
ed above all blessing and praise.
6 [p]Thou, *even* thou, *art* LORD alone;
[q]thou hast made heaven, [r]the heav-
en of heavens, with [s]all their host, the
earth, and all *things* that *are* therein,
the seas, and all that *is* therein, and
thou [t]preservest them all; and the
host of heaven worshippeth thee.
7 Thou *art* the LORD the God, who
didst choose [u]Abram, and broughtest
him forth out of Ur of the Chaldees, and
gavest him the name of [v]Abraham;
8 And foundest his heart [w]faithful
before thee, and madest a [x]covenant
with him to give the land of the Ca-
naanites, the Hittites, the Amorites,
and the Perizzites, and the Jebusites,
and the Girgashites, to give *it, I say,* to
his seed, and [y]hast performed thy
words; for thou *art* righteous:

9:1 [k]ch. 8:2 [l]Josh. 7:6 1 Sam. 4:12 2 Sam. 1:2 Job 2:12
9:2 [m]Ezra 10:11 ch. 13:3,30
9:3 [n]ch. 8:7,8
9:5 [o]1 Chr. 29:13
9:6 [p]2 Ki. 19:15,19 Ps. 86:10 Is. 37:16,20 [q]Gen. 1:1 Ex. 20:11 Rev. 14:7 [r]Deut. 10:14 1 Ki. 8:27 [s]Gen. 2:1 [t]Ps. 36:6
9:7 [u]Gen. 11:31 [v]Gen. 17:5
9:8 [w]Gen. 15:6 [x]Gen. 15:18 [y]Josh. 23:14
9:9 [z]Ex. 2:25 [a]Ex. 14:10
9:10 [b]Ex. 7-10,12,14 [c]Ex. 18:11 [d]Jer. 32:20
9:11 [e]Ex. 14:21 Ps. 78:13 [f]Ex. 15:5
9:12 [g]Ex. 13:21
9:13 [h]Ex. 20:1 [i]Rom. 7:12
9:14 [j]Gen. 2:3 Ex. 20:8
9:15 [k]Ex. 16:14 John 6:31 [l]Ex. 17:6 [m]Deut. 1:8 [n]Num. 14:30
9:16 [o]Ps. 106:6 [p]Deut. 31:27
9:17 [q]Ps. 78:11

9 [z]And didst see the affliction of
our fathers in Egypt, and [a]heardest
their cry by the Red sea;
10 And [b]showedst signs and won-
ders upon Pharaoh, and on all his ser-
vants, and on all the people of his land:
for thou knewest that they [c]dealt
proudly against them. So didst thou
[d]get thee a name, as *it is* this day.
11 [e]And thou didst divide the sea
before them, so that they went through
the midst of the sea on the dry land;
and their persecutors thou threwest
into the deeps, [f]as a stone into the
mighty waters.
12 Moreover thou [g]leddest them in
the day by a cloudy pillar; and in the
night by a pillar of fire, to give them
light in the way wherein they
should go.
13 [h]Thou camest down also upon
mount Sinai, and spakest with them
from heaven, and gavest them [i]right
judgments, and [y]true laws, good stat-
utes and commandments:
14 And madest known unto them
thy [j]holy sabbath, and commandedst
them precepts, statutes, and laws, by
the hand of Moses thy servant:
15 And [k]gavest them bread from
heaven for their hunger, and
[l]broughtest forth water for them out
of the rock for their thirst, and promis-
edst them that they should [m]go in to
possess the land [n]which[z] thou hadst
sworn to give them.
16 [o]But they and our fathers dealt
proudly, and [p]hardened their necks,
and hearkened not to thy command-
ments,
17 And refused to obey, [q]neither
were mindful of thy wonders that thou
didst among them; but hardened their
necks, and in their rebellion appointed

[w]Heb. *strange children* [x]Or, *scaffold*
[y]Heb. *laws of truth* [z]Heb. *which thou hadst lift up thine hand to give them*

9:2 SEPARATED THEMSELVES ... CONFESSED THEIR SINS. The actions recorded in this chapter show that the people's repentance was deep and sustained. They continued to seek God by fasting, humbling themselves before Him, confessing their spiritual poverty, and separating themselves from that which offended Him (vv. 1–3).

9:6–37 THOU *ART* LORD. The primary themes of this outstanding prayer are God's gracious endeavor to provide redemption and salvation for Israel and Israel's ungrateful response to that divine love throughout their history. These are recurring themes in the O.T. (see Dan. 9:3–19; Amos 2:9–12; Mic. 6:1–8; cf. Luke 13:34).

9:17 GRACIOUS AND MERCIFUL. The Lord is a gracious and compassionate God; therefore, He is ready to accept again those who have forsaken Him and sinned against His laws whenever they repent. Moreover, He is patient and longsuffering with the faults and shortcomings of His children, as long as their expressed desire is to follow Him fully and to gain complete victory over sin, Satan, and the world (see article on SANCTIFICATION, p. 1982).

[r]a captain to return to their bondage: but thou *art* [a]a God ready to pardon, [s]gracious and merciful, slow to anger, and of great kindness, and forsookest them not.

18 Yea, [t]when they had made them a molten calf, and said, This *is* thy God that brought thee up out of Egypt, and had wrought great provocations;

19 Yet thou in thy [u]manifold mercies forsookest them not in the wilderness: the [v]pillar of the cloud departed not from them by day, to lead them in the way; neither the pillar of fire by night, to show them light, and the way wherein they should go.

20 Thou gavest also thy [w]good spirit to instruct them, and withheldest not thy [x]manna from their mouth, and gavest them [y]water for their thirst.

21 Yea, [z]forty years didst thou sustain them in the wilderness, *so that* they lacked nothing; their [a]clothes waxed not old, and their feet swelled not.

22 Moreover thou gavest them kingdoms and nations, and didst divide them into corners: so they possessed the land of [b]Sihon, and the land of the king of Heshbon, and the land of Og king of Bashan.

23 [c]Their children also multipliedst thou as the stars of heaven, and broughtest them into the land, concerning which thou hadst promised to their fathers, that they should go in to possess *it*.

24 So [d]the children went in and possessed the land, and [e]thou subduedst before them the inhabitants of the land, the Canaanites, and gavest them into their hands, with their kings, and the people of the land, that they might do with them [b]as they would.

25 And they took strong cities, and a [f]fat land, and possessed [g]houses full of all goods, [c]wells digged, vineyards, and oliveyards, and [d]fruit trees in abundance: so they did eat, and were filled, and [h]became fat, and delighted themselves in thy great [i]goodness.

26 Nevertheless they [j]were disobedient, and rebelled against thee, and [k]cast thy law behind their backs, and slew thy [l]prophets which testified against them to turn them to thee, and they wrought great provocations.

27 [m]Therefore thou deliveredst them into the hand of their enemies, who vexed them: and in the time of their trouble, when they cried unto thee, thou [n]heardest *them* from heaven; and according to thy manifold mercies [o]thou gavest them saviours, who saved them out of the hand of their enemies.

28 But after they had rest, [p]they[e] did evil again before thee: therefore leftest thou them in the hand of their enemies, so that they had the dominion over them: yet when they returned, and cried unto thee, thou heardest *them* from heaven; and [q]many times didst thou deliver them according to thy mercies;

29 And testifiedst against them, that thou mightest bring them again unto thy law: yet they dealt proudly, and hearkened not unto thy commandments, but sinned against thy judgments, ([r]which if a man do, he shall live in them;) and [s]withdrew[f] the shoulder, and hardened their neck, and would not hear.

30 Yet many years didst thou [g]forbear them, and testifiedst [t]against them by thy spirit [u]in[h] thy prophets: yet would they not give ear: [v]therefore gavest thou them into the hand of the people of the lands.

Is. 61:1-

31 Nevertheless for thy great mercies' sake [w]thou didst not utterly consume them, nor forsake them; for thou *art* a gracious and merciful God.

32 Now therefore, our God, the great, the [x]mighty, and the terrible God, who keepest covenant and mercy, let not all the [i]trouble seem little before thee, [j]that hath come upon us, on our kings, on our princes, and on our

9:17 [r]Num. 14:4 [s]Joel 2:13
9:18 [t]Ex. 32:4
9:19 [u]Ps. 106:45 [v]1 Cor. 10:1
9:20 [w]Num. 11:17 Is. 63:11 [x]Ex. 16:15 Josh. 5:12 [y]Ex. 17:6
9:21 [z]Deut. 2:7 [a]Deut. 8:4 & 29:5
9:22 [b]Num. 21:21
9:23 [c]Gen. 22:17
9:24 [d]Josh. 1:2 [e]Ps. 44:2,3
9:25 [f]Num. 13:27 [g]Deut. 6:11 [h]Deut. 32:15 [i]Hos. 3:5
9:26 [j]Judg. 2:11 [k]1 Ki. 14:9 Ps. 50:17 [l]1 Ki. 18:4
9:27 [m]Judg. 2:14 Ps. 106:41 [n]Ps. 106:44 [o]Judg. 2:18
9:28 [p]Judg. 3:11 [q]Ps. 106:43
9:29 [r]Lev. 18:5 Rom. 10:5 Gal. 3:12 [s]Zech. 7:11
9:30 [t]2 Ki. 17:13 2 Chr. 36:15 Jer. 7:25 [u]Acts 7:51 1 Pet. 1:11 2 Pet. 1:21 [v]Is. 5:5
9:31 [w]Jer. 4:27
9:32 [x]Ex. 34:6,7

[a] Heb. *a God of pardons* [b] Heb. *according to their will* [c] Or, *cisterns* [d] Heb. *tree of food* [e] Heb. *they returned to do evil* [f] Heb. *they gave a withdrawing shoulder* [g] Heb. *protract over them* [h] Heb. *in the hand of thy prophets* [i] Heb. *weariness* [j] Heb. *that hath found us*

9:20 GAVEST ALSO THY GOOD SPIRIT TO INSTRUCT THEM. The Holy Spirit is our leader into God's truth and righteous ways (see John 14:17, note; 16:13, note; Rom. 8:5–14, note).

9:30 TESTIFIEDST AGAINST THEM BY THY SPIRIT IN THY PROPHETS. A principal work of the Holy Spirit in the O.T. was to rebuke God's people and expose their sin through His faithful prophets. Under the new covenant, the Spirit continues to convict people of sin (see John 16:8,13, notes; see article on THE MINISTRY GIFTS OF THE CHURCH, p. 1852).

priests, and on our prophets, and on
our fathers, and on all thy people,
[y]since the time of the kings of Assyria
unto this day.
33 Howbeit [z]thou *art* just in all
that is brought upon us; for thou hast
done right, but [a]we have done wick-
edly:
34 Neither have our kings, our
princes, our priests, nor our fathers,
kept thy law, nor hearkened unto thy
commandments and thy testimonies,
wherewith thou didst testify against
them.
35 For they have [b]not served thee
in their kingdom, and in thy great
goodness that thou gavest them, and in
the large and fat land which thou gav-
est before them, neither turned they
from their wicked works.
36 Behold, [c]we *are* servants this
day, and *for* the land that thou gavest
unto our fathers to eat the fruit thereof
and the good thereof, behold, we *are*
servants in it:
37 And [d]it yieldeth much increase
unto the kings whom thou hast set
over us because of our sins: also they
have [e]dominion over our bodies, and
over our cattle, at their pleasure, and
we *are* in great distress.

The covenant signed

38 And because of all this we
[f]make a sure *covenant,* and write *it;*
and our princes, Levites, *and* priests,
[k]seal *unto it.*

10 NOW [1]THOSE that sealed
were, Nehemiah, [m]the Tirsha-
tha, [g]the son of Hachaliah, and Zid-
kijah,
2 [h]Seraiah, Azariah, Jeremiah,
3 Pashur, Amariah, Malchijah,
4 Hattush, Shebaniah, Malluch,
5 Harim, Meremoth, Obadiah,
6 Daniel, Ginnethon, Baruch,
7 Meshullam, Abijah, Mijamin,
8 Maaziah, Bilgai, Shemaiah: these
were the priests.
9 And the Levites: both Jeshua the
son of Azaniah, Binnui of the sons of
Henadad, Kadmiel;
10 And their brethren, Shebaniah,
Hodijah, Kelita, Pelaiah, Hanan,
11 Micha, Rehob, Hashabiah,
12 Zaccur, Sherebiah, Shebaniah,
13 Hodijah, Bani, Beninu.
14 The chief of the people; [i]Pa-
rosh, Pahath-moab, Elam, Zatthu,
Bani,
15 Bunni, Azgad, Bebai,
16 Adonijah, Bigvai, Adin,
17 Ater, Hizkijah, Azzur,
18 Hodijah, Hashum, Bezai,
19 Hariph, Anathoth, Nebai,
20 Magpiash, Meshullam, Hezir,
21 Meshezabeel, Zadok, Jaddua,
22 Pelatiah, Hanan, Anaiah,
23 Hoshea, Hananiah, Hashub,
24 Hallohesh, Pileha, Shobek,
25 Rehum, Hashabnah, Maaseiah,
26 And Ahijah, Hanan, Anan,
27 Malluch, Harim, Baanah.
28 ¶ [j]And the rest of the people,
the priests, the Levites, the porters,
the singers, the Nethinims, [k]and all
they that had separated themselves
from the people of the lands unto the
law of God, their wives, their sons, and
their daughters, every one having
knowledge, and having understanding;
29 They clave to their brethren,
their nobles, [l]and entered into a
curse, and into an oath, [m]to walk in
God's law, which was given [n]by Mo-
ses the servant of God, and to observe
and do all the commandments of the
LORD our Lord, and his judgments and
his statutes;
30 And that we would not give
[n]our daughters unto the people of the
land, nor take their daughters for our
sons:
31 [o]And *if* the people of the land
bring ware or any victuals on the sab-
bath day to sell, *that* we would not buy
it of them on the sabbath, or on the
holy day: and *that* we would leave the
[p]seventh year, and the [q]exaction of
[o]every debt.
32 Also we made ordinances for us,
to charge ourselves yearly with the
third part of a shekel for the service of
the house of our God;
33 For [r]the showbread, and for the

9:32 [y]2 Ki. 17:3 **9:33** [z]Ps. 119:137 Dan. 9:14 [a]Ps. 106:6 Dan. 9:5,6,8 **9:35** [b]Deut. 28:47 **9:36** [c]Deut. 28:48 Ezra 9:9 **9:37** [d]Deut. 28:33,51 [e]Deut. 28:48 **9:38** [f]2 Ki. 23:3 2 Chr. 29:10 Ezra 10:3 **10:1** [g]ch. 1:1 **10:2** [h]ch. 12:1-21

10:14 [i]Ezra 2:3 ch. 7:8 **10:28** [j]Ezra 2:36-43 [k]Ezra 9:1 ch. 13:3 **10:29** [l]Deut. 29:12 Ps. 119:106 [m]2 Ki. 23:3 2 Chr. 34:31 **10:30** [n]Ex. 34:16 Deut. 7:3 Ezra 9:12 **10:31** [o]Ex. 20:10 Lev. 23:3 Deut. 5:12 [p]Ex. 23:10 Lev. 25:4 [q]Deut. 15:1 ch. 5:12 **10:33** [r]Lev. 24:5 2 Chr. 2:4

[k] Heb. are *at the sealing,* or, *sealed* [1] Heb. *at the sealings* [m] Or, *the governor* [n] Heb. *by the hand of* [o] Heb. *every hand*

10:29 ENTERED INTO . . . AN OATH. The revival led by Ezra (chs. 8 – 10) resulted in a firm commitment to obey the will of God. This was manifested in the people dedicating themselves: (1) to serve the Lord in faithfulness to His commandments (v. 29); (2) to keep themselves unspotted and separate from the world (vv. 30–31; cf. Jas. 1:27); and (3) to support the work of God with their time, money, and possessions (vv. 32–39).

[s]continual meat offering, and for the continual burnt offering, of the sabbaths, of the new moons, for the set feasts, and for the holy *things,* and for the sin offerings to make an atonement for Israel, and *for* all the work of the house of our God.

34 And we cast the lots among the priests, the Levites, and the people, [t]for the wood offering, to bring *it* into the house of our God, after the houses of our fathers, at times appointed year by year, to burn upon the altar of the LORD our God, [u]as *it is* written in the law:

35 And [v]to bring the firstfruits of our ground, and the firstfruits of all fruit of all trees, year by year, unto the house of the LORD:

36 Also the firstborn of our sons, and of our cattle, as *it is* written [w]in the law, and the firstlings of our herds and of our flocks, to bring to the house of our God, unto the priests that minister in the house of our God:

37 [x]And *that* we should bring the firstfruits of our dough, and our offerings, and the fruit of all manner of trees, of wine and of oil, unto the priests, to the chambers of the house of our God; and [y]the tithes of our ground unto the Levites, that the same Levites might have the tithes in all the cities of our tillage.

38 And the priest the son of Aaron shall be with the Levites, [z]when the Levites take tithes: and the Levites shall bring up the tithe of the tithes unto the house of our God, to [a]the chambers, into the treasure house.

39 For the children of Israel and the children of Levi [b]shall bring the offering of the corn, of the new wine, and the oil, unto the chambers, where *are* the vessels of the sanctuary, and the priests that minister, and the porters, and the singers: [c]and we will not forsake the house of our God.

Job 1:1-5

The repeopling of Jerusalem

11:3–19pp — 1 Chr. 9:1–17

11 AND THE rulers of the people dwelt at Jerusalem: the rest of the people also cast lots, to bring one of ten to dwell in Jerusalem [d]the holy city, and nine parts *to dwell* in *other* cities.

2 And the people blessed all the men, that [e]willingly offered themselves to dwell at Jerusalem.

3 ¶ [f]Now these *are* the chief of the province that dwelt in Jerusalem: but in the cities of Judah dwelt every one in his possession in their cities, *to wit,* Israel, the priests, and the Levites, and [g]the Nethinims, and [h]the children of Solomon's servants.

4 And [i]at Jerusalem dwelt *certain* of the children of Judah, and of the children of Benjamin. Of the children of Judah; Athaiah the son of Uzziah, the son of Zechariah, the son of Amariah, the son of Shephatiah, the son of Mahalaleel, of the children of [j]Perez;

5 And Maaseiah the son of Baruch, the son of Col-hozeh, the son of Hazaiah, the son of Adaiah, the son of Joiarib, the son of Zechariah, the son of Shiloni.

6 All the sons of Perez that dwelt at Jerusalem *were* four hundred threescore and eight valiant men.

7 And these *are* the sons of Benjamin; Sallu the son of Meshullam, the son of Joed, the son of Pedaiah, the son of Kolaiah, the son of Maaseiah, the son of Ithiel, the son of Jesaiah.

8 And after him Gabbai, Sallai, nine hundred twenty and eight.

9 And Joel the son of Zichri *was* their overseer: and Judah the son of Senuah *was* second over the city.

10 [k]Of the priests: Jedaiah the son of Joiarib, Jachin.

11 Seraiah the son of Hilkiah, the son of Meshullam, the son of Zadok, the son of Meraioth, the son of Ahitub, *was* the ruler of the house of God.

12 And their brethren that did the work of the house *were* eight hundred twenty and two: and Adaiah the son of Jeroham, the son of Pelaliah, the son of Amzi, the son of Zechariah, the son of Pashur, the son of Malchiah,

13 And his brethren, chief of the fathers, two hundred forty and two: and Amashai the son of Azareel, the son of Ahasai, the son of Meshillemoth, the son of Immer.

14 And their brethren, mighty men of valour, an hundred twenty and eight: and their overseer *was* Zabdiel, [p]the son of *one of* the great men.

15 Also of the Levites: Shemaiah the son of Hashub, the son of Azrikam, the son of Hashabiah, the son of Bunni;

10:33 [s]See Num. 28 & 29
10:34 [t]ch. 13:31 Is. 40:16 [u]Lev. 6:12
10:35 [v]Ex. 23:19 Lev. 19:23 Num. 18:12
10:36 [w]Ex. 13:2,12,13 Lev. 27:26,27 Num. 18:15,16
10:37 [x]Lev. 23:17 Num. 15:19 & 18:12 Deut. 18:4 & 26:2 [y]Lev. 27:30 Num. 18:21
10:38 [z]Num. 18:26 [a]1 Chr. 9:26 2 Chr. 31:11
10:39 [b]Deut. 12:6,11 2 Chr. 31:12 ch. 13:12 [c]ch. 13:10,11
11:1 [d]ver. 18 Mat. 4:5 & 27:53
11:2 [e]Judg. 5:9
11:3 [f]1 Chr. 9:2,3 [g]Ezra 2:43 [h]Ezra 2:55
11:4 [i]1 Chr. 9:3 [j]Gen. 38:29 *Pharez*
11:10 [k]1 Chr. 9:10

[p]Or, *the son of Haggedolim*

16 And Shabbethai and Jozabad, of the chief of the Levites, [q]*had* the oversight of [l]the outward business of the house of God.

17 And Mattaniah the son of Micha, the son of Zabdi, the son of Asaph, *was* the principal to begin the thanksgiving in prayer: and Bakbukiah the second among his brethren, and Abda the son of Shammua, the son of Galal, the son of Jeduthun.

18 All the Levites in [m]the holy city *were* two hundred fourscore and four.

19 Moreover the porters, Akkub, Talmon, and their brethren that kept [r]the gates, *were* an hundred seventy and two.

20 ¶ And the residue of Israel, of the priests, *and* the Levites, *were* in all the cities of Judah, every one in his inheritance.

21 [n]But the Nethinims dwelt in [s]Ophel: and Ziha and Gispa *were* over the Nethinims.

22 The overseer also of the Levites at Jerusalem *was* Uzzi the son of Bani, the son of Hashabiah, the son of Mattaniah, the son of Micha. Of the sons of Asaph, the singers *were* over the business of the house of God.

23 For [o]*it was* the king's commandment concerning them, that [t]a certain portion should be for the singers, due for every day.

24 And Pethahiah the son of Meshezabeel, of the children of [p]Zerah the son of Judah, *was* [q]at the king's hand in all matters concerning the people.

The villages outside Jerusalem

25 And for the villages, with their fields, *some* of the children of Judah dwelt at [r]Kirjath-arba, and *in* the villages thereof, and at Dibon, and *in* the villages thereof, and at Jekabzeel, and *in* the villages thereof,

26 And at Jeshua, and at Moladah, and at Beth-phelet,

27 And at Hazar-shual, and at Beersheba, and *in* the villages thereof,

28 And at Ziklag, and at Mekonah, and in the villages thereof,

29 And at En-rimmon, and at Zareah, and at Jarmuth,

30 Zanoah, Adullam, and *in* their villages, at Lachish, and the fields thereof, at Azekah, and *in* the villages thereof. And they dwelt from Beer-sheba unto the valley of Hinnom.

31 The children also of Benjamin [u]from Geba *dwelt* [v]at Michmash, and Aija, and Beth-el, and *in* their villages,

32 *And* at Anathoth, Nob, Ananiah,

33 Hazor, Ramah, Gittaim,

34 Hadid, Zeboim, Neballat,

35 Lod, and Ono, [s]the valley of craftsmen.

36 And of the Levites *were* divisions *in* Judah, *and* in Benjamin.

Priests and Levites

12 NOW THESE *are* the [t]priests and the Levites that went up with Zerubbabel the son of Shealtiel, and Jeshua: [u]Seraiah, Jeremiah, Ezra,

2 Amariah, [w]Malluch, Hattush,

3 [x]Shechaniah, [y]Rehum, [z]Meremoth,

4 Iddo, [a]Ginnetho, [v]Abijah,

5 [b]Miamin, [c]Maadiah, Bilgah,

6 Shemaiah, and Joiarib, Jedaiah,

7 [d]Sallu, Amok, Hilkiah, Jedaiah. These *were* the chief of the priests and of their brethren in the days of [w]Jeshua.

8 Moreover the Levites: Jeshua, Binnui, Kadmiel, Sherebiah, Judah, *and* Mattaniah, [x]*which was* over [e]the thanksgiving, he and his brethren.

9 Also Bakbukiah and Unni, their brethren, *were* over against them in the watches.

10 ¶ And Jeshua begat Joiakim, Joiakim also begat Eliashib, and Eliashib begat Joiada,

11 And Joiada begat Jonathan, and Jonathan begat Jaddua.

12 And in the days of Joiakim were priests, the chief of the fathers: of Seraiah, Meraiah; of Jeremiah, Hananiah;

13 Of Ezra, Meshullam; of Amariah, Jehohanan;

14 Of Melicu, Jonathan; of Shebaniah, Joseph;

15 Of Harim, Adna; of Meraioth, Helkai;

16 Of Iddo, Zechariah; of Ginnethon, Meshullam;

17 Of Abijah, Zichri; of Miniamin, of Moadiah, Piltai;

11:16 [l] 1 Chr. 26:29
11:18 [m] ver. 1
11:21 [n] See ch. 3:26
11:23 [o] See Ezra 6:8,9 & 7:20
11:24 [p] Gen. 38:30 *Zarah* [q] 1 Chr. 18:17 & 23:28
11:25 [r] Josh. 14:15
11:35 [s] 1 Chr. 4:14
12:1 [t] Ezra 2:1,2 [u] See ch. 10:2-8
12:4 [v] Luke 1:5
12:7 [w] Ezra 3:2 Hag. 1:1 Zech. 3:1
12:8 [x] ch. 11:17

[q] Heb. were *over* [r] Heb. *at the gates* [s] Or, *The tower* [t] Or, *a sure ordinance* [u] Or, *of Geba* [v] Or, *to Michmash* [w] Or, *Melicu;* see ver. 14 [x] Or, *Shebaniah;* see ver. 14 [y] Or, *Harim;* see ver. 15 [z] Or, *Meraioth;* see ver. 15 [a] Or, *Ginnethon;* see ver. 16 [b] Or, *Miniamin;* see ver. 17 [c] Or, *Moadiah;* see ver. 17 [d] Or, *Sallai;* see ver. 20 [e] i.e. *the psalms of thanksgiving*

18 Of Bilgah, Shammua; of Shemaiah, Jehonathan;

19 And of Joiarib, Mattenai; of Jedaiah, Uzzi;

20 Of Sallai, Kallai; of Amok, Eber;

21 Of Hilkiah, Hashabiah; of Jedaiah, Nethaneel.

22 ¶ The Levites in the days of Eliashib, Joiada, and Johanan, and Jaddua, *were* recorded chief of the fathers: also the priests, to the reign of Darius the Persian.

23 The sons of Levi, the chief of the fathers, *were* written in the book of the [y]chronicles, even until the days of Johanan the son of Eliashib.

24 And the chief of the Levites: Hashabiah, Sherebiah, and Jeshua the son of Kadmiel, with their brethren over against them, to praise *and* to give thanks, [z]according to the commandment of David the man of God, [a]ward over against ward.

25 Mattaniah, and Bakbukiah, Obadiah, Meshullam, Talmon, Akkub, *were* porters keeping the ward at the [f]thresholds of the gates.

26 These *were* in the days of Joiakim the son of Jeshua, the son of Jozadak, and in the days of Nehemiah [b]the governor, and of Ezra the priest, [c]the scribe.

Dedication of the city walls

27 ¶ And at [d]the dedication of the wall of Jerusalem they sought the Levites out of all their places, to bring them to Jerusalem, to keep the dedication with gladness, [e]both with thanksgivings, and with singing, *with* cymbals, psalteries, and with harps.

28 And the sons of the singers gathered themselves together, both out of the plain country round about Jerusalem, and from the villages of Netophathi;

29 Also from the house of Gilgal, and out of the fields of Geba and Azmaveth: for the singers had builded them villages round about Jerusalem.

30 And the priests and the Levites purified themselves, and purified the people, and the gates, and the wall.

31 Then I brought up the princes of Judah upon the wall, and appointed two great *companies of them that gave* thanks, *whereof* [f]*one* went on the right hand upon the wall [g]toward the dung gate:

32 And after them went Hoshaiah, and half of the princes of Judah,

33 And Azariah, Ezra, and Meshullam,

34 Judah, and Benjamin, and Shemaiah, and Jeremiah,

35 And *certain* of the priests' sons [h]with trumpets; *namely,* Zechariah the son of Jonathan, the son of Shemaiah, the son of Mattaniah, the son of Michaiah, the son of Zaccur, the son of Asaph:

36 And his brethren, Shemaiah, and Azarael, Milalai, Gilalai, Maai, Nethaneel, and Judah, Hanani, with [i]the musical instruments of David the man of God, and Ezra the scribe before them.

37 [j]And at the fountain gate, which was over against them, they went up by [k]the stairs of the city of David, at the going up of the wall, above the house of David, even unto [l]the water gate eastward.

38 [m]And the other *company of them that gave* thanks went over against *them,* and I after them, and the half of the people upon the wall, from beyond [n]the tower of the furnaces even unto [o]the broad wall;

39 [p]And from above the gate of Ephraim, and above [q]the old gate, and above [r]the fish gate, [s]and the tower of Hananeel, and the tower of Meah, even unto [t]the sheep gate: and they stood still in [u]the prison gate.

40 So stood the two *companies of them that gave* thanks in the house of God, and I, and the half of the rulers with me:

41 And the priests; Eliakim, Maaseiah, Miniamin, Michaiah, Elioenai, Zechariah, *and* Hananiah, with trumpets;

42 And Maaseiah, and Shemaiah, and Eleazar, and Uzzi, and Jehohanan, and Malchijah, and Elam, and Ezer. And the singers [g]sang loud, with Jezrahiah *their* overseer.

43 Also that day they offered great sacrifices, and rejoiced: for God had made them rejoice with great joy: the wives also and the children rejoiced: so that the joy of Jerusalem was heard even afar off.

44 ¶ [v]And at that time were some appointed over the chambers for the treasures, for the offerings, for the

12:23 [y]1 Chr. 9:14
12:24 [z]1 Chr. 23 & 25 & 26 [a]Ezra 3:11
12:26 [b]ch. 8:9 [c]Ezra 7:6,11
12:27 [d]Deut. 20:5 Ps. 30,title [e]1 Chr. 25:6 2 Chr. 5:13 & 7:6
12:31 [f]See ver. 38 [g]ch. 2:13 & 3:13
12:35 [h]Num. 10:2,8
12:36 [i]1 Chr. 23:5
12:37 [j]ch. 2:14 & 3:15 [k]ch. 3:15 [l]ch. 3:26 & 8:1,3,16
12:38 [m]See ver. 31 [n]ch. 3:11 [o]ch. 3:8
12:39 [p]2 Ki. 14:13 ch. 8:16 [q]ch. 3:6 [r]ch. 3:3 [s]ch. 3:1 [t]ch. 3:32 [u]Jer. 32:2
12:44 [v]2 Chr. 31:11,12 ch. 13:5,12,13

f Or, *treasuries,* or, *assemblies* g Heb. *made* their voice *to be heard*

firstfruits, and for the tithes, to gather
into them out of the fields of the cities
the portions [h]of the law for the priests
and Levites: [i]for Judah rejoiced for
the priests and for the Levites [j]that
waited.
45 And both the singers and the
porters kept the ward of their God, and
the ward of the purification, [w]accord-
ing to the commandment of David, *and*
of Solomon his son.
46 For in the days of David [x]and
Asaph of old *there were* chief of the
singers, and songs of praise and
thanksgiving unto God.
47 And all Israel in the days of Ze-
rubbabel, and in the days of Nehemiah,
gave the portions of the singers and
the porters, every day his portion:
[y]and they [k]sanctified *holy things*
unto the Levites; [z]and the Levites
sanctified *them* unto the children of
Aaron.

Nehemiah's reforms

13 ON THAT day [a]they[l] read in
the book of Moses in the [m]au-
dience of the people; and therein was
found written, [b]that the Ammonite
and the Moabite should not come into
the congregation of God for ever;
2 Because they met not the children
of Israel with bread and with water, but
[c]hired Balaam against them, that he
should curse them: [d]howbeit our God
turned the curse into a blessing.
3 Now it came to pass, when they
had heard the law, [e]that they separat-
ed from Israel all the mixed multitude.
4 ¶ And before this, Eliashib the
priest, [f]having[n] the oversight of the
chamber of the house of our God, *was*
allied unto Tobiah:
5 And he had prepared for him a
great chamber, [g]where aforetime they
laid the meat offerings, the frankin-
cense, and the vessels, and the tithes
of the corn, the new wine, and the oil,
[h]which[o] was commanded *to be given*
to the Levites, and the singers, and the
porters; and the offerings of the
priests.
6 But in all this *time* was not I at
Jerusalem: [i]for in the two and thirti-
eth year of Artaxerxes king of Babylon
came I unto the king, and [p]after cer-
tain days [q]obtained I leave of the
king:
7 And I came to Jerusalem, and un-
derstood of the evil that Eliashib did
for Tobiah, in [j]preparing him a cham-
ber in the courts of the house of God.
8 And it grieved me sore: therefore
I cast forth all the household stuff of
Tobiah out of the chamber.
9 Then I commanded, and they
[k]cleansed the chambers: and thither
brought I again the vessels of the
house of God, with the meat offering
and the frankincense.
10 ¶ And I perceived that the por-
tions of the Levites had [l]not been giv-
en *them:* for the Levites and the sing-
ers, that did the work, were fled every
one to [m]his field.
11 Then [n]contended I with the rul-

12:45 [w]1 Chr. 25 & 26 **12:46** [x]1 Chr. 25:1 **12:47** [y]Num. 18:21,24 [z]Num. 18:26 **13:1** [a]Deut. 31:11,12 2 Ki. 23:2 ch. 8:3,8 & 9:3 Is. 34:16 [b]Deut. 23:3,4 **13:2** [c]Num. 22:5 Josh. 24:9,10 [d]Num. 23:11 & 24:10 Deut. 23:5 **13:3** [e]ch. 9:2 & 10:28 **13:4** [f]ch. 12:44 **13:5** [g]ch. 12:44 [h]Num. 18:21,24 **13:6** [i]ch. 5:14 **13:7** [j]ver. 1,5 **13:9** [k]2 Chr. 29:5 **13:10** [l]Mal. 3:8 [m]Num. 35:2 **13:11** [n]ver. 17,25

[h] i.e. *appointed by the law* [i] Heb. *for the joy of Judah* [j] Heb. *that stood* [k] i.e. *set apart* [l] Heb. *there was read* [m] Heb. *ears* [n] Heb. *being set over* [o] Heb. *the commandment of the Levites* [p] Heb. *at the end of days* [q] Or, *I earnestly requested*

13:3 THEY SEPARATED FROM ISRAEL ALL THE MIXED MULTITUDE. Pagan foreigners were excluded from Israel in order to erect a barrier between God's people and the wicked practices of unbelievers. (1) The key to understanding why God desired this is found in the inherent tendency of His people to conform to the ways, pleasures, and lifestyles of the world. (2) An essential requirement for God's people who would be holy is, therefore, to remain separate from the ways, values, and ungodly customs of our society, and to stand against the prevailing and popular expressions of the spirit of this world. Failure to do so will result in the loss of God's presence and all the good He has determined for us (see Rom. 12:2, note; see article on SPIRITUAL SEPARATION FOR BELIEVERS, p. 1814).

13:7 I CAME TO JERUSALEM. Nehemiah had returned to Persia and was away from Jerusalem for some time (vv. 6–7). When he returned, he discovered that the Jews in Jerusalem had become lax in their moral and spiritual commitment to God. Ch. 13 records a number of these spiritual failures.

13:7 THE EVIL ELIASHIB DID FOR TOBIAH. Tobiah the Ammonite, along with Sanballat, the governor of Samaria, had earlier mocked the Jews' efforts at rebuilding the wall of Jerusalem (2:10,19). Now, however, he had married into a priestly family closely related to Eliashib the high priest, In response, Eliashib himself remodeled and decorated a large room in the temple area as an apartment for Tobiah. When Nehemiah saw this desecration, he burned with righteous indignation and tossed out Tobiah's belongings and the luxurious furnishings Eliashib had put there for him. Nehemiah was hurt because this desecration of God's house was an affront to God's holiness. Modern churches that give space to activities that do not promote God's kingdom might well take note.

ers, and said, [o]Why is the house of
God forsaken? And I gathered them to-
gether, and set them in their [r]place.
12 [p]Then brought all Judah the
tithe of the corn and the new wine and
the oil unto the [s]treasuries.
13 [q]And I made treasurers over
the treasuries, Shelemiah the priest,
and Zadok the scribe, and of the Le-
vites, Pedaiah: and [t]next to them *was*
Hanan the son of Zaccur, the son of
Mattaniah: for they were counted
[r]faithful, and [u]their office *was* to dis-
tribute unto their brethren.
14 [s]Remember me, O my God,
concerning this, and wipe not out my
[v]good deeds that I have done for the
house of my God, and for the [w]offices
thereof.
15 ¶ In those days saw I in Judah
some treading wine presses [t]on the
sabbath, and bringing in sheaves, and
lading asses; as also wine, grapes, and
figs, and all *manner of* burdens,
[u]which they brought into Jerusalem
on the sabbath day: and I testified
against them in the day wherein they
sold victuals.
16 There dwelt men of Tyre also
therein, which brought fish, and all
manner of ware, and sold on the sab-
bath unto the children of Judah, and in
Jerusalem.
17 Then I contended with the no-
bles of Judah, and said unto them,
What evil thing *is* this that ye do, and
profane the sabbath day?
18 [v]Did not your fathers thus, and
did not our God bring all this evil upon
us, and upon this city? yet ye bring
more wrath upon Israel by profaning
the sabbath.

13:11 [o]ch. 10:39
13:12 [p]ch. 10:38
13:13 [q]2 Chr. 31:12 ch. 12:44 [r]1 Cor. 4:2
13:14 [s]ch. 5:19
13:15 [t]Ex. 20:10 [u]ch. 10:31 Jer. 17:21
13:18 [v]Jer. 17:21
13:19 [w]Lev. 23:32 [x]Jer. 17:21
13:22 [y]ch. 12:30
13:23 [z]Ezra 9:2
13:25 [a]Prov. 28:4

19 And it came to pass, that when
the gates of Jerusalem [w]began to be
dark before the sabbath, I commanded
that the gates should be shut, and
charged that they should not be opened
till after the sabbath: [x]and *some* of my
servants set I at the gates, *that* there
should no burden be brought in on the
sabbath day.
20 So the merchants and sellers of
all kind of ware lodged without Jerusa-
lem once or twice.
21 Then I testified against them,
and said unto them, Why lodge ye
[x]about the wall? if ye do *so* again, I
will lay hands on you. From that time
forth came they no *more* on the sab-
bath.
22 And I commanded the Levites
that [y]they should cleanse themselves,
and *that* they should come *and* keep the
gates, to sanctify the sabbath day. Re-
member me, O my God, *concerning* this
also, and spare me according to the
[y]greatness of thy mercy.
23 ¶ In those days also saw I Jews
that [z]had[z] married wives of Ashdod,
of Ammon, *and* of Moab:
24 And their children spake half in
the speech of Ashdod, and [a]could not
speak in the Jews' language, but ac-
cording to the language [b]of each peo-
ple.
25 And I [a]contended with them,
and [c]cursed them, and smote certain

[r] Heb. *standing* [s] Or, *storehouses* [t] Heb. *at their hand* [u] Heb. it was *upon them* [v] Heb. *kindnesses* [w] Or, *observations* [x] Heb. *before the wall?* [y] Or, *multitude* [z] Heb. *had made to dwell* with them [a] Heb. *they discerned not to speak* [b] Heb. *of people and people* [c] Or, *reviled them*

13:12 THEN BROUGHT ALL JUDAH THE TITHE. Nehemiah restored full worship in the temple, along with the ministries of the Levites and singers; as a result, the people were able to bring their tithes to the very room that Eliashib had given to Tobiah. People are much more willing to tithe when they see the worship of God bringing blessing. God also raised up Malachi about this time; his exhortation emphasized God's blessing for faithful tithers (Mal. 3:10). Tithing has always been primarily a matter of blessing rather than law (see article on TITHES AND OFFERINGS, p. 1388). Even before God gave His law at Mount Sinai, Abraham was so blessed by Melchizedek that he gave a tithe of all he had (Gen. 14:19–20). The Spirit-filled believer loves to give and to share, just as the early believers did (Acts 2:44–45; 4:34–37; 11:28–30).

13:17 PROFANE THE SABBATH DAY. God's people were allowing their business interests and their desire for the things of the world to destroy obedience to God's command to make the Sabbath a day of rest. N.T. believers must constantly beware of the temptation to allow the pursuit of riches and success to usurp their desire to honor and worship God as He commands. We must "seek . . . first the kingdom of God, and his righteousness" (Mat. 6:33; see 12:1, note).

13:25 I CONTENDED WITH THEM. There are times when leaders, if they are genuinely people of God, must have a holy anger toward unrighteousness and take drastic steps to correct an evil situation. Gentleness and meekness in the face of open and blatant disregard of God's will within the church are in reality weakness and compromise. Nehemiah's correction shows a zeal for God that

of them, and plucked off their hair, and
made them [b]swear by God, *saying,* Ye
shall not give your daughters unto
their sons, nor take their daughters
unto your sons, or for yourselves.
26 [c]Did not Solomon king of Israel
sin by these things? yet among many
nations was there no king like him,
[d]who was beloved of his God, and God
made him king over all Israel: [e]never-
theless even him did outlandish wom-
en cause to sin.
27 Shall we then hearken unto you
to do all this great evil, to [f]transgress
against our God in marrying strange
wives?
28 And *one* of the sons [g]of Joiada,

13:25
[b]Ezra 10:5
ch. 10:29
13:26
[c]1 Ki. 11:1
[d]2 Sam. 12:24
[e]1 Ki. 11:4
13:27
[f]Ezra 10:2
13:28
[g]ch. 12:10,22
13:29
[h]ch. 6:14
[i]Mal. 2:4,11,12
13:30
[j]ch. 10:30
[k]ch. 12:1
13:31
[l]ch. 10:34
[m]ver. 14,22

the son of Eliashib the high priest, *was*
son-in-law to Sanballat the Horonite:
therefore I chased him from me.
29 [h]Remember them, O my God,
[d]because they have defiled the priest-
hood, and [i]the covenant of the priest-
hood, and of the Levites.
30 [j]Thus cleansed I them from all
strangers, and [k]appointed the wards
of the priests and the Levites, every
one in his business;
31 And for [l]the wood offering, at
times appointed, and for the firstfruits.
[m]Remember me, O my God, for good.

[d] Heb. *for the defilings*

is similar to Christ's when He used a whip to drive the money changers from the temple in Jerusalem (cf. Mat. 21:12–13; John 2:13–16; see Luke 19:45, note).

ESTHER

Outline

I. God's Providence in the Placement of a Queen (1:1—2:18)
  A. Vashti Deposed as Queen of Persia (1:1–22)
    1. The Feast of Ahasuerus (1:1–9)
    2. The Refusal of Vashti (1:10–12)
    3. The Removal of the Old Queen (1:13–22)
  B. Esther Selected as Queen of Persia (2:1–18)
    1. The Search of Ahasuerus (2:1–4)
    2. The Agreement of Esther (2:5–11)
    3. The Selection of the New Queen (2:12–18)
II. God's Providence Amidst a Plot Against Mordecai and the Jews (2:19—4:17)
  A. Mordecai Saves the King's Life (2:19–23)
  B. Haman's Pride and Treacherous Plot (3:1–15)
  C. Mordecai Persuades Esther to Intercede with the King (4:1–17)
III. God's Providence in Delivering His People (5:1—9:32)
  A. Esther's First Banquet: An Initial Request (5:1–8)
  B. Haman's Plot Develops (5:9–14)
  C. Providence in the King's Sleepless Night (6:1–14)
  D. Esther's Second Banquet: Haman's Plot Exposed (7:1–10)
  E. The King's Decree and the Jews' Victory (8:1—9:16)
  F. The Feast of Purim Instituted (9:17–32)
IV. God's Providence in Mordecai's Promotion (10:1–3)

Author: Anonymous

Theme: God's Providential Care

Date of Writing: 460–400 B.C.

Background

After the Babylonian empire was captured, defeated, and replaced by the Persians in 539 B.C., the center of government for the Jewish exiles transferred to Persia. The capital city of Susa is the setting for the story of Esther, during the reign of King Ahasuerus (his Hebrew name)—also called Xerxes I (his Greek name) or Khshayarsha (his Persian name)—who ruled from 486–465 B.C. The book covers the years 483–473 B.C. of Ahasuerus' reign (1:3; 3:7), with most events occuring in 473 B.C. Esther became queen of Persia in 478 B.C. (2:16).

Chronologically, the Esther episode in Persia falls between Ezra 6 and 7, i.e., between the first return of Jewish exiles from Babylon and Persia to Jerusalem in 538 B.C. under Zerubbabel (Ezra 1—6) and the second return led by Ezra in 457 B.C. (Ezra 7—10; see the introduction to Ezra). Though Esther is placed after Nehemiah in our O.T., its events actually occurred thirty years before Nehemiah's return to Jerusalem (444 B.C.) to rebuild the wall (see the introduction to Nehemiah). Whereas the post-exilic books of Ezra and Nehemiah address issues involving the Jewish remnant that returned to Jerusalem, Esther records a development of crucial importance among the Jews who remained in Persia.

The significance of Queen Esther is seen not only in her saving her people from destruction, but also in securing their safety and respect in a foreign land (cf. 8:17; 10:3); this providential act made possible Nehemiah's service in the king's court several decades later and his being selected to rebuild the wall of Jerusalem. If Esther and the Jews (including Nehemiah) had perished in Persia, the distressed remnant in Jerusalem may never have rebuilt their city. The outcome of post-exilic Jewish history would surely have been drastically different.

Though the author of Esther is unknown, it is evident from the book itself that he was personally acquainted with Persian customs, the palace of Susa, and details about King Ahasuerus, indicating that the author likely lived in Persia during the period described in the book. Furthermore, the author's Jewish sympathies and knowledge of Jewish customs suggest he was a Jew. Most likely the author was a younger contemporary of Mordecai, with the latter providing much of the book's firsthand information. The book was put in its present form after the lifetime of Mordecai himself (cf. 10:1–3). Its historical and linguistic details do not support a date later than 400 B.C. The apocryphal "Additions to the Book of Esther" originated a considerable time later than canonical Esther.

Purpose

The book has a twofold purpose. (1) It was written to show how the Jewish people were protected and delivered from impending annihilation by God's intervention through Queen Esther. Though God's name is not specifically mentioned, there is evidence of His providence throughout the book. (2) It was written also to provide a record of and historical background to the Jewish Feast of Purim (3:6–7; 9:26–28) and thereby to keep alive for generations to come the memory of this great deliverance of the Jewish people in Persia (cf. the Passover feast and the Israelites' great deliverance from Egypt). The book also outlines the obligation for the annual commemoration of Purim (9:24,28–32).

Survey

Esther provides a character study of five main persons involved in the story: (1) the Persian king, Ahasuerus; (2) his prime minister, Haman; (3) Vashti, the queen who preceded Esther; (4) Esther, the beautiful Jewish maiden who became queen; and (5) Mordecai, the righteous cousin of Esther who adopted her as his daughter and raised her as a youth. Esther, of course, is the heroine of the story; Haman is the villain; and Mordecai is the hero who, as the primary object of Haman's contempt, is vindicated and exalted in the end. The key figure behind the events of the book is Mordecai, for he influenced and gave righteous counsel to Queen Esther.

God's providence is everywhere present in the book. It is first seen in the selection of a Jewish virgin named Hadassah (Heb.)—Ester (Persian) or Esther (Gk.)—to be queen of Persia at a crucial hour in Jewish history (chs. 1—2; 4:4). God's providence is again evident when Mordecai, the cousin of Esther who had raised her as his daughter (2:7), overheard an assassination plot against the king, exposed it, saved the king's life, and had his deed recorded in the king's chronicles (2:19–34), a fact the king providentially discovered in a timely fashion during a sleepless night (6:1–14).

Haman's hatred for Mordecai was extended to all Jews. He conceived a hideous plot and deceptively persuaded Ahasuerus to issue a decree to annihilate all Jews on the 13th of the month Adar (3:13). Mordecai prevailed upon Esther to intercede with the king on behalf of the Jews. After a three-day fast by all the Jews, Esther risked her life in approaching the king's throne uninvited (ch. 4), received the king's favor (5:1–4), and exposed Haman's plot. Subsequently, the king hung Haman on the gallows which Haman had prepared for Mordecai (7:1–10). A second decree by the king enabled the Jews to triumph over their enemies (8:1—9:16); this triumph became an occasion of great celebration and the beginning of the annual Feast of Purim (9:17–32). The book concludes with a note about the fame of Mordecai (10:1–3).

Special Features

Five special features or emphases characterize the book of Esther. (1) It is one of two books in the Bible named after a woman, the other being Ruth. (2) The book begins and ends with a feast, and it records a total of ten feasts or banquets around which much of the book's drama unfolds. (3) Esther is the last of the five scrolls in the third part of the Hebrew Bible, the *Hagiographa* ("Holy Writings"), each of which is read publicly at one of the great Jewish festivals. This one is read at the Feast of Purim on Adar 14–15, celebrating the great deliverance of the Jewish people in Persia under Queen Esther. (4) Though the book mentions a three-day fast, there are no explicit references to God, worship, or prayer (a feature which has led some critics unwisely to question its spiritual value). (5) Though God's name appears nowhere in Esther, His providence is everywhere evident (e.g., 2:7,17,22; 4:14; 4:16–5:2; 6:1,3–10; 9:1). No other book in the Bible illustrates as powerfully God's providence in preserving the Jewish people in spite of the demonic hatred of their enemies.

New Testament Fulfillment

There is no reference or allusion to this book anywhere in the N.T. However, Haman's hatred for the Jews and his plot to kill and annihilate all Jews in the Persian empire (ch. 3; 7:4) is an O.T. type of the N.T. antichrist, who will seek to destroy all Jews and Christians alike at the end of history (see the book of Revelation).

Reading Esther

In order to read the entire Old Testament in one year, the book of Esther should be read in 3 days, according to the following schedule: ☐ 1–4 ☐ 5–7 ☐ 8–10

NOTES

The removal of queen Vashti

1 NOW IT came to pass in the days
of [a]Ahasuerus, (this *is* Ahasuerus
which reigned, [b]from India even unto
Ethiopia, [c]*over* an hundred and seven
and twenty provinces:)
2 *That* in those days, when the king
Ahasuerus [d]sat on the throne of his
kingdom, which *was* in [e]Shushan the
palace,
3 In the third year of his reign, he
[f]made a feast unto all his princes and
his servants; the power of Persia and
Media, the nobles and princes of the
provinces, *being* before him:
4 When he showed the riches of his
glorious kingdom and the honour of his
excellent majesty many days, *even* an
hundred and fourscore days.
5 And when these days were ex-
pired, the king made a feast unto all
the people that were [a]present in Shu-
shan the palace, both unto great and
small, seven days, in the court of the
garden of the king's palace;
6 *Where were* white, green, and
[b]blue, *hangings,* fastened with cords
of fine linen and purple to silver rings
and pillars of marble: [g]the beds *were
of* gold and silver, upon a pavement
[c]of red, and blue, and white, and
black, marble.
7 And they gave *them* drink in ves-
sels of gold, (the vessels being diverse
one from another,) and [d]royal wine in
abundance, [e]according to the state of
the king.
8 And the drinking *was* according to
the law; none did compel: for so the
king had appointed to all the officers of
his house, that they should do accord-
ing to every man's pleasure.
9 Also Vashti the queen made a
feast for the women *in* the royal house
which *belonged* to king Ahasuerus.
10 ¶ On the seventh day, when the
heart of the king was merry with wine,
he commanded Mehuman, Biztha,
[h]Harbona, Bigtha, and Abagtha, Ze-
thar, and Carcas, the seven [f]cham-
berlains that served in the presence of
Ahasuerus the king,
11 To bring Vashti the queen before
the king with the crown royal, to show
the people and the princes her beauty:
for she *was* [g]fair to look on.
12 But the queen Vashti refused to
come at the king's commandment [h]by
his chamberlains: therefore was the
king very wroth, and his anger burned
in him.
13 ¶ Then the king said to the
[i]wise men, [j]which knew the times,
(for so *was* the king's manner toward
all that knew law and judgment:
14 And the next unto him *was* Car-
shena, Shethar, Admatha, Tarshish,
Meres, Marsena, *and* Memucan, the
[k]seven princes of Persia and Media,
[l]which saw the king's face, *and* which
sat the first in the kingdom;)
15 [i]What shall we do unto the
queen Vashti according to law, be-
cause she hath not performed the com-
mandment of the king Ahasuerus by
the chamberlains?
16 And Memucan answered before
the king and the princes, Vashti the
queen hath not done wrong to the king
only, but also to all the princes, and to
all the people that *are* in all the prov-
inces of the king Ahasuerus.
17 For *this* deed of the queen shall
come abroad unto all women, so that
they shall [m]despise their husbands in
their eyes, when it shall be reported,
The king Ahasuerus commanded Vash-
ti the queen to be brought in before
him, but she came not.
18 *Likewise* shall the ladies of Per-
sia and Media say this day unto all the
king's princes, which have heard of the
deed of the queen. Thus *shall there arise*
too much contempt and wrath.

1:1 [a]Ezra 4:6; Dan. 9:1 [b]ch. 8:9 [c]Dan. 6:1
1:2 [d]1 Ki. 1:46 [e]Neh. 1:1
1:3 [f]Gen. 40:20; ch. 2:18
1:6 [g]ch. 7:8; Amos 2:8 & 6:4
1:10 [h]ch. 7:9
1:13 [i]Jer. 10:7; Dan. 2:12; Mat. 2:1 [j]1 Chr. 12:32
1:14 [k]Ezra 7:14 [l]2 Ki. 25:19
1:17 [m]Eph. 5:33

[a] Heb. *found* [b] Or, *violet* [c] Or, *of porphyre, and marble, and alabaster, and stone of blue colour* [d] Heb. *wine of the kingdom* [e] Heb. *according to the hand of the king* [f] Or, *eunuchs* [g] Heb. *good of countenance* [h] Heb. *which* was *by the hand of* his *eunuchs* [i] Heb. *What to do*

1:1 IN THE DAYS OF AHASUERUS. The Ahasuerus of this book is more commonly known by his Greek name, Xerxes. He ruled as king over Persia from 486 to 465 B.C. Important dates for the book of Esther are: (1) the captivity of the Jews by Nebuchadnezzar in 586 B.C. (2 Ki. 25); (2) the authorized return of the Jews from captivity in 538 B.C. (Ezra 1); (3) Esther's reign as queen of Persia, beginning in 479 B.C. (2:16–17); (4) Ezra's authorized trip from Babylon to Jerusalem in 458 B.C. (Ezra 7). Thus the events of Esther happened approximately twenty-one years before Ezra led a second group of exiles to Jerusalem.

1:13 KNEW THE TIMES. Sometimes the worldly wise are more in touch with the times than are the supposedly wise leaders among believers. For a discussion on understanding the times, see 1 Chr. 12:32, note.

19 [j]If it please the king, let there
go a royal commandment [k]from him,
and let it be written among the laws of
the Persians and the Medes, [n]that[l]
it be not altered, That Vashti come no
more before king Ahasuerus; and let
the king give her royal estate [m]unto
another that is better than she.
20 And when the king's decree
which he shall make shall be published
throughout all his empire, (for it is
great,) all the wives shall [o]give to
their husbands honour, both to great
and small.
21 And the saying [n]pleased the
king and the princes; and the king did
according to the word of Memucan:
22 For he sent letters into all the
king's provinces, [p]into every province
according to the writing thereof, and to
every people after their language, that
every man should [q]bear rule in his
own house, and [o]that *it* should be pub-
lished according to the language of ev-
ery people.

Esther chosen to be queen

2 AFTER THESE things, when the
wrath of king Ahasuerus was ap-
peased, he remembered Vashti, and
what she had done, and [r]what was de-
creed against her.
2 Then said the king's servants that
ministered unto him, Let there be fair
young virgins sought for the king:
3 And let the king appoint officers
in all the provinces of his kingdom,
that they may gather together all the
fair young virgins unto Shushan the
palace, to the house of the women,
[p]unto the custody of [q]Hege the
king's chamberlain, keeper of the
women; and let their things for purifi-
cation be given *them:*
4 And let the maiden which
pleaseth the king be queen instead of
Vashti. And the thing pleased the king;
and he did so.
5 ¶ *Now* in Shushan the palace
there was a certain Jew, whose name
was Mordecai, the son of Jair, the son
of Shimei, the son of Kish, a Benjamite;
6 [s]Who had been carried away
from Jerusalem with the captivity
which had been carried away with
[r]Jeconiah king of Judah, whom Nebu-
chadnezzar the king of Babylon had
carried away.
7 And he [s]brought up Hadassah,
that *is,* Esther, [t]his uncle's daughter:
for she had neither father nor mother,
and the maid *was* [t]fair and beautiful;
whom Mordecai, when her father and
mother were dead, took for his own
daughter.
8 ¶ So it came to pass, when the
king's commandment and his decree
was heard, and when many maidens
were [u]gathered together unto Shu-
shan the palace, to the custody of Heg-
ai, that Esther was brought also unto
the king's house, to the custody of
Hegai, keeper of the women.
9 And the maiden pleased him, and
she obtained kindness of him; and he
speedily gave her her [v]things for puri-
fication, with [u]such things as be-
longed to her, and seven maidens,
which were meet to be given her, out of
the king's house: and [v]he preferred
her and her maids unto the best *place*
of the house of the women.
10 [w]Esther had not shown her peo-

1:19 [n]ch. 8:8 Dan. 6:8
1:20 [o]Eph. 5:33 Col. 3:18 1 Pet. 3:1
1:22 [p]ch. 8:9 [q]Eph. 5:22-24 1 Tim. 2:12
2:1 [r]ch. 1:19,20
2:6 [s]2 Ki. 24:14,15 2 Chr. 36:10,20 Jer. 24:1
2:7 [t]ver. 15
2:8 [u]ver. 3
2:9 [v]ver. 3,12
2:10 [w]ver. 20

[j] Heb. *If it be good with the king* [k] Heb. *from before him* [l] Heb. *that it pass not away* [m] Heb. *unto her companion* [n] Heb. *was good in the eyes of the king* [o] Heb. *that one should publish* it *according to the language of his people* [p] Heb. *unto the hand* [q] Or, *Hegai;* see ver. 8 [r] Or, *Jehoiachin;* see 2 Ki. 24:6 [s] Heb. *nourished* [t] Heb. *fair of form, and good of countenance* [u] Heb. *her portions* [v] Heb. *he changed her*

2:4 LET THE MAIDEN ... BE QUEEN INSTEAD OF VASHTI. The book of Esther, although it contains no explicit mention of God, shows His continuing providence over the Jewish people. He directs, overrules, and uses the actions of men and women to accomplish His purposes and to preserve His chosen people (see article on THE PROVIDENCE OF GOD, p. 80). The book displays God's foresight and providence in the following ways: (1) Because "Vashti refused to come" to the king's party (1:12), Esther, a Jewish maiden, was chosen queen (vv. 5–18); (2) Mordecai, also a Jew and a close relative of Esther, uncovered a plot to kill the king (vv. 21–23); (3) the king gave Esther special favor (5:2,8); (4) the king discovered that Mordecai had saved his life (6:1–2; cf. 2:21–23); (5) the king desired to honor Mordecai at the exact moment that Haman entered (6:1–11); (6) the king helped Esther and the Jewish people who were about to be destroyed (chs. 7–8); (7) Mordecai became very influential with the king (ch. 9:4; 10:2–3).

2:6 CARRIED AWAY . . . WITH THE CAPTIVITY. It was Kish (v. 5), Mordecai's great-grandfather, not Mordecai himself, who was taken from Jerusalem and exiled along with King Jeconiah in 597 B.C.

ple nor her kindred: for Mordecai had
charged her that she should not show
it.
11 And Mordecai walked every day
before the court of the women's house,
[w]to know how Esther did, and what
should become of her.
12 ¶ Now when every maid's turn
was come to go in to king Ahasuerus,
after that she had been twelve months,
according to the manner of the women,
(for so were the days of their purifica-
tions accomplished, *to wit,* six months
with oil of myrrh, and six months with
sweet odours, and with *other* things for
the purifying of the women;)
13 Then thus came *every* maiden
unto the king; whatsoever she desired
was given her to go with her out of the
house of the women unto the king's
house.
14 In the evening she went, and on
the morrow she returned into the sec-
ond house of the women, to the custo-
dy of Shaashgaz, the king's chamber-
lain, which kept the concubines: she
came in unto the king no more, except
the king delighted in her, and that she
were called by name.
15 ¶ Now when the turn of Esther,
[x]the daughter of Abihail the uncle of
Mordecai, who had taken her for his
daughter, was come to go in unto the
king, she required nothing but what
Hegai the king's chamberlain, the
keeper of the women, appointed. And
Esther obtained favour in the sight of
all them that looked upon her.
16 So Esther was taken unto king
Ahasuerus into his house royal in the
tenth month, which *is* the month Te-
beth, in the seventh year of his reign.
17 And the king loved Esther above
all the women, and she obtained grace
and [x]favour [y]in his sight more than
all the virgins; so that he set the royal
crown upon her head, and made her
queen instead of Vashti.
18 Then the king [y]made a great
feast unto all his princes and his ser-
vants, *even* Esther's feast; and he made
a [z]release to the provinces, and gave
gifts, according to the state of the king.

The plot to kill Ahasuerus fails

19 And when the virgins were gath-
ered together the second time, then
Mordecai sat [z]in the king's gate.
20 [a]Esther had not *yet* shown her
kindred nor her people; as Mordecai
had charged her: for Esther did the
commandment of Mordecai, like as
when she was brought up with him.
21 ¶ In those days, while Mordecai
sat in the king's gate, two of the king's
chamberlains, [a]Bigthan and Teresh,
of those which kept [b]the door, were
wroth, and sought to lay hand on the
king Ahasuerus.
22 And the thing was known to
Mordecai, [b]who told *it* unto Esther the
queen; and Esther certified the king
thereof in Mordecai's name.
23 And when inquisition was made
of the matter, it was found out; there-
fore they were both hanged on a tree:
and it was written in [c]the book of the
chronicles before the king.

Haman's plot against the Jews

3 AFTER THESE things did king
Ahasuerus promote Haman the
son of Hammedatha the [d]Agagite, and
advanced him, and set his seat above
all the princes that *were* with him.
2 And all the king's servants, that
were [e]in the king's gate, bowed, and
reverenced Haman: for the king had so
commanded concerning him. But Mor-

2:15 [x]ver. 7
2:18 [y]ch. 1:3
2:19 [z]ver. 21; ch. 3:2
2:20 [a]ver. 10
2:22 [b]ch. 6:2
2:23 [c]ch. 6:1
3:1 [d]Num. 24:7; 1 Sam. 15:8
3:2 [e]ch. 2:19

[w] Heb. *to know the peace* [x] Or, *kindness* [y] Heb. *before him* [z] Heb. *rest* [a] Or, *Bigthana;* see ch. 6:2 [b] Heb. *the threshold*

2:17 MADE HER QUEEN. That the Persian king appointed Esther as queen illustrates how God can turn the hearts of sinful people in order to serve His purposes (cf. Prov. 21:1; see Ezra 1:1, note). Esther was now in a position to help her people when the need arose about five years later. God used the free decisions of those involved to protect His people (4:14).

2:20 AS MORDECAI HAD CHARGED HER. Although Esther had been chosen and crowned queen of the great Persian empire (2:17), she was not puffed up with pride and self-importance because of her newly attained status and power. She did not despise her lowly cousin's advice, nor did she disdain her racial or spiritual heritage; rather, she manifested a true spirit of meekness, humility, and submissiveness after becoming queen, even as she had done before.

3:2 MORDECAI BOWED NOT. Mordecai refused to bow before Haman because of his loyalty to God (v. 4). Evidently the homage paid to Haman by the king's servants and others was either undeserved or bordered on conduct reserved by the Jews only for the worship of God. Thus Mordecai would not consent to bow down or prostrate himself before Haman. Daniel's three companions manifested the same conviction (Dan. 3:1–12).

decai [f]bowed not, nor did *him* reverence.

3 Then the king's servants, which *were* in the king's gate, said unto Mordecai, Why transgressest thou the [g]king's commandment?

4 Now it came to pass, when they spake daily unto him, and he hearkened not unto them, that they told Haman, to see whether Mordecai's matters would stand: for he had told them that he *was* a Jew.

5 And when Haman saw that Mordecai [h]bowed not, nor did him reverence, then was Haman [i]full of wrath.

6 And he thought scorn to lay hands on Mordecai alone; for they had shown him the people of Mordecai: wherefore Haman [j]sought to destroy all the Jews that *were* throughout the whole kingdom of Ahasuerus, *even* the people of Mordecai.

7 ¶ In the first month, that *is,* the month Nisan, in the twelfth year of king Ahasuerus, [k]they cast Pur, that *is,* the lot, before Haman from day to day, and from month to month, *to* the twelfth *month,* that *is,* the month Adar.

8 ¶ And Haman said unto king Ahasuerus, There is a certain people scattered abroad and dispersed among the people in all the provinces of thy kingdom; and [l]their laws *are* diverse from all people; neither keep they the king's laws: therefore it *is* not [c]for the king's profit to suffer them.

9 If it please the king, let it be written [d]that they may be destroyed: and I will [e]pay ten thousand talents of silver to the hands of those that have the charge of the business, to bring *it* into the king's treasuries.

10 And the king [m]took [n]his ring from his hand, and gave it unto Haman the son of Hammedatha the Agagite, the Jews' [f]enemy.

11 And the king said unto Haman, The silver *is* given to thee, the people also, to do with them as it seemeth good to thee.

12 [o]Then were the king's [g]scribes called on the thirteenth day of the first month, and there was written according to all that Haman had commanded unto the king's lieutenants, and to the governors that *were* over every province, and to the rulers of every people of every province [p]according to the writing thereof, and *to* every people after their language; [q]in the name of king Ahasuerus was it written, and sealed with the king's ring.

13 And the letters were [r]sent by posts into all the king's provinces, to destroy, to kill, and to cause to perish, all Jews, both young and old, little children and women, [s]in one day, *even* upon the thirteenth *day* of the twelfth month, which *is* the month Adar, and [t]*to take* the spoil of them for a prey.

14 [u]The copy of the writing for a commandment to be given in every province was published unto all peo-

3:2 [f]ver. 5 Ps. 15:4 **3:3** [g]ver. 2 **3:5** [h]ver. 2 ch. 5:9 [i]Dan. 3:19 **3:6** [j]Ps. 83:4 **3:7** [k]ch. 9:24 **3:8** [l]Ezra 4:13 Acts 16:20 **3:10** [m]Gen. 41:42 [n]ch. 8:2,8 **3:12** [o]ch. 8:9 [p]ch. 1:22 [q]1 Ki. 21:8 ch. 8:8,10 **3:13** [r]ch. 8:10 [s]ch. 8:12 [t]ch. 8:11 **3:14** [u]ch. 8:13,14

[c] Heb. *meet,* or, *equal* [d] Heb. *to destroy them*
[e] Heb. *weigh* [f] Or, *oppressor;* see ch. 7:6
[g] Or, *secretaries*

3:4 HE *WAS* A JEW. Those around Mordecai wanted to know why he did not bow down. He gave them only one answer: he was a Jew. (1) God sent the Jews into captivity to purge them of their idolatry. We see from Ezra and Nehemiah that the Jews who went back to Jerusalem had learned their lesson and wanted a worship free from idolatry; the book of Esther shows that the Jews who did not go back had also learned their lesson. By this time it meant something to be a Jew, and Jews refused to bow down to any human or idol. (2) It should mean something to us to be a Christian. Like Mordecai, we must also take a firm and open stand for Christ and the righteous standards of His Word in the midst of the pressures of a worldly society.

3:6 HAMAN SOUGHT TO DESTROY ALL THE JEWS. Haman, the prime minister of Persia, is the first political figure in the Bible to devise a sinister plan for exterminating all the Jews within his political sphere. This plot of genocide against the Jewish race has its parallel in Antiochus Epiphanes's plot in the second century B.C. (see Dan. 11:28, note), in Hitler's plot in twentieth-century Europe, and in the antichrist at the end of history, who will seek to destroy all Jews and Christians (Rev. 13:15–18).

3:7 THEY CAST PUR. "Pur" is something similar to dice. Haman used it to determine the "lucky day" on which to destroy the Jews. Nearly one year intervened between the throwing of the lot and the execution of the plan. This gave Mordecai and Esther, under the providence of God, time to counter Haman's evil plot.

3:8 THEIR LAWS *ARE* DIVERSE FROM ALL PEOPLE. One of God's purposes in giving the law to Israel was to make them different from all other people. Haman recognized something different in the Jews and hated them for it. Under the new covenant, God still wills that His people be separate and different from the world, a holy people for His own possession (cf. 1 Pet. 2:9). Likewise today, the world will hate God's people because they are different, holy, and righteous (cf. John 15:18–25).

ple, that they should be ready against that day.

15 The posts went out, being hastened by the king's commandment, and the decree was given in Shushan the palace. And the king and Haman sat down to drink; but [v]the city Shushan was perplexed.

4 WHEN MORDECAI perceived all that was done, Mordecai [w]rent his clothes, and put on sackcloth [x]with ashes, and went out into the midst of the city, and [y]cried with a loud and a bitter cry;

2 And came even before the king's gate: for none *might* enter into the king's gate clothed with sackcloth.

3 And in every province, whithersoever the king's commandment and his decree came, *there was* great mourning among the Jews, and fasting, and weeping, and wailing; and [h]many lay in sackcloth and ashes.

Mordecai asks Esther for help

4 ¶ So Esther's maids and her [i]chamberlains came and told *it* her. Then was the queen exceedingly grieved; and she sent raiment to clothe Mordecai, and to take away his sackcloth from him: but he received *it* not.

5 Then called Esther for Hatach, *one* of the king's chamberlains, [j]whom he had appointed to attend upon her, and gave him a commandment to Mordecai, to know what it *was*, and why it *was*.

6 So Hatach went forth to Mordecai unto the street of the city, which *was* before the king's gate.

7 And Mordecai told him of all that had happened unto him, and of [z]the sum of the money that Haman had promised to pay to the king's treasuries for the Jews, to destroy them.

3:15 [v]See ch. 8:15 Prov. 29:2
4:1 [w]2 Sam. 1:11 [x]Josh. 7:6 Ezek. 27:30 [y]Gen. 27:34
4:7 [z]ch. 3:9

8 Also he gave him [a]the copy of the writing of the decree that was given at Shushan to destroy them, to show *it* unto Esther, and to declare *it* unto her, and to charge her that she should go in unto the king, to make supplication unto him, and to make request before him for her people.

9 And Hatach came and told Esther the words of Mordecai.

10 ¶ Again Esther spake unto Hatach, and gave him commandment unto Mordecai;

11 All the king's servants, and the people of the king's provinces, do know, that whosoever, whether man or woman, shall come unto the king into [b]the inner court, who is not called, [c]*there is* one law of his to put *him* to death, except such [d]to whom the king shall hold out the golden sceptre, that he may live: but I have not been called to come in unto the king these thirty days.

12 And they told to Mordecai Esther's words.

13 Then Mordecai commanded to answer Esther, Think not with thyself that thou shalt escape in the king's house, more than all the Jews.

14 For if thou altogether holdest thy peace at this time, *then* shall there enlargement and deliverance arise to the Jews from another place; but thou and thy father's house shall be destroyed: and who knoweth whether thou art come to the kingdom for *such* a time as this?

15 ¶ Then Esther bade *them* return Mordecai *this answer,*

16 Go, gather together all the Jews that are [k]present in Shushan, and fast

4:8 [a]ch. 3:14,15
4:11 [b]ch. 5:1 [c]Dan. 2:9 [d]ch. 5:2 & 8:4

[h]Heb. *sackcloth and ashes were laid under many*
[i]Heb. *eunuchs* [j]Heb. *whom he had set before her* [k]Heb. *found*

4:14 IF THOU ALTOGETHER HOLDEST THY PEACE. Mordecai believed that it was God's purpose to use Esther to deliver Israel and that she had become queen for this very reason. However, Mordecai knew that Esther could fall short of that purpose if she did not do her part in God's redemptive plan. If she refused to help the Jews, she too would "be destroyed" (v. 14). God's sovereign purposes usually include human responsibility (cf. Mat. 26:24; see Ex. 33:3, note; Phil. 2:12, note).

4:14 THOU ART COME TO THE KINGDOM FOR *SUCH* A TIME AS THIS? This passage reveals the basic meaning of the book: God is involved in the events of the world in order to save His people from its evil and to accomplish His redemptive purposes on their behalf. All believers must remember that God is working in what happens around us, in order to deliver us from this present evil world and to bring us to be with Him forever (Rom. 8:29–39; Gal. 1:4; Jude 24).

4:16 IF I PERISH, I PERISH. Esther was willing to give her life in an attempt to save her people. She would do what was right and leave the consequences with God. God will not honor those who remain silent in order to protect their place or position, but He will honor those who, for the sake of God and His word, speak the truth in the face of great loss (see John 16:1–4). Mordecai and Esther were willing to die, if need be, in this fight against

ye for me, and neither eat nor drink [e]three days, night or day: I also and my maidens will fast likewise; and so will I go in unto the king, which *is* not according to the law: [f]and if I perish, I perish.

17 So Mordecai [1]went his way, and did according to all that Esther had commanded him.

Esther's intervention

5 NOW IT came to pass [g]on the third day, that Esther put on *her* royal *apparel,* and stood in [h]the inner court of the king's house, over against the king's house: and the king sat upon his royal throne in the royal house, over against the gate of the house.

2 And it was so, when the king saw Esther the queen standing in the court, *that* [i]she obtained favour in his sight: and [j]the king held out to Esther the golden sceptre that *was* in his hand. So Esther drew near, and touched the top of the sceptre. (Job 13:15)

3 Then said the king unto her, What wilt thou, queen Esther? and what *is* thy request? [k]it shall be even given thee to the half of the kingdom.

4 And Esther answered, If *it seem* good unto the king, let the king and Haman come this day unto the banquet that I have prepared for him.

5 Then the king said, Cause Haman to make haste, that he may do as Esther hath said. So the king and Haman came to the banquet that Esther had prepared.

6 ¶ [l]And the king said unto Esther at the banquet of wine, [m]What *is* thy petition? and it shall be granted thee: and what *is* thy request? even to the half of the kingdom it shall be performed.

7 Then answered Esther, and said, My petition and my request *is:*

8 If I have found favour in the sight of the king, and if it please the king to grant my petition, and [m]to perform my request, let the king and Haman come to the banquet that I shall prepare for them, and I will do tomorrow as the king hath said.

Haman has gallows made

9 ¶ Then went Haman forth that day joyful and with a glad heart: but when Haman saw Mordecai in the king's gate, [n]that he stood not up, nor moved for him, he was full of indignation against Mordecai.

10 Nevertheless Haman [o]refrained himself: and when he came home, he sent and [n]called for his friends, and Zeresh his wife.

11 And Haman told them of the glory of his riches, and [p]the multitude of his children, and all *the things* wherein the king had promoted him, and how he had advanced him above the princes and servants of the king.

12 Haman said moreover, Yea, Esther the queen did let no man come in with the king unto the banquet that she had prepared but myself; and tomorrow am I invited unto her also with the king.

13 Yet all this availeth me nothing, so long as I see Mordecai the Jew sitting at the king's gate.

14 ¶ Then said Zeresh his wife and all his friends unto him, Let a [q]gallows[o] be made of fifty cubits high, and tomorrow [r]speak thou unto the king that Mordecai may be hanged thereon: then go thou in merrily with the king unto the banquet. And the thing pleased Haman; and he caused [s]the gallows to be made.

Mordecai honoured

6 ON THAT night [p]could not the king sleep, and he commanded to bring [t]the book of records of the

4:16 [e]See ch. 5:1 [f]See Gen. 43:14
5:1 [g]See ch. 4:16 [h]See ch. 4:11 & 6:4
5:2 [i]Prov. 21:1 [j]ch. 4:11 & 8:4
5:3 [k]Mark 6:23
5:6 [l]ch. 7:2 [m]ch. 9:12
5:9 [n]ch. 3:5
5:10 [o]2 Sam. 13:22
5:11 [p]ch. 9:7
5:14 [q]ch. 7:9 [r]ch. 6:4 [s]ch. 7:10
6:1 [t]ch. 2:23

[1]Heb. *passed* [m]Heb *to do* [n]Heb. *caused to come* [o]Heb. *tree* [p]Heb. *the king's sleep fled away*

the powers of evil. They are examples of loyal obedience to godly convictions (see Luke 1:17, note on the character and firm convictions of John the Baptist).

5:13 ALL THIS AVAILETH NOTHING. Although Haman had riches, glory, power, and status, he was an unsatisfied and discontented man. Mordecai, on the other hand, had strength of character, godly convictions, and assurance in his God. Haman knew in his heart that Mordecai was the better man and thus hated him for it. In God's sight greatness is never found in riches, power, or position, but in faithfulness, commitment to Him, and pursuit of His righteous goals on earth (see Luke 22:24–30, note).

6:1 BRING THE BOOK. The providential workings of God are clearly evident in ch. 6. He used the sleeplessness of the king to bring about the exaltation of Mordecai by his enemy (vv. 2–11). Day and night God watches over those who are faithful (see 1 Sam. 2:8; Ps. 121; Acts 5:17–19; 18:9–10; Rev. 3:8–9).

chronicles; and they were read before
the king.
2 And it was found written, that
Mordecai had told of [q]Bigthana and
Teresh, two of the king's chamber-
lains, the keepers of the [r]door, who
sought to lay hand on the king Ahasue-
rus.
3 And the king said, What honour
and dignity hath been done to Morde-
cai for this? Then said the king's ser-
vants that ministered unto him, There
is nothing done for him.
4 ¶ And the king said, Who *is* in the
court? Now Haman was come into
[u]the outward court of the king's
house, [v]to speak unto the king to
hang Mordecai on the gallows that he
had prepared for him.
5 And the king's servants said unto
him, Behold, Haman standeth in the
court. And the king said, Let him
come in.
6 So Haman came in. And the king
said unto him, What shall be done unto
the man [s]whom the king delighteth to
honour? Now Haman thought in his
heart, To whom would the king delight
to do honour more than to myself?
7 And Haman answered the king,
For the man [s]whom the king de-
lighteth to honour,
8 [t]Let the royal apparel be
brought [u]which the king *useth* to
wear, and [w]the horse that the king
rideth upon, and the crown royal which
is set upon his head:
9 And let this apparel and horse be
delivered to the hand of one of the
king's most noble princes, that they
may array the man *withal* whom the
king delighteth to honour, and [v]bring
him on horseback through the street of
the city, [x]and proclaim before him,
Thus shall it be done to the man whom
the king delighteth to honour.
10 Then the king said to Haman,
Make haste, *and* take the apparel and
the horse, as thou hast said, and do
even so to Mordecai the Jew, that
sitteth at the king's gate: [w]let nothing
fail of all that thou hast spoken.
11 Then took Haman the apparel
and the horse, and arrayed Mordecai,
and brought him on horseback through
the street of the city, and proclaimed
before him, Thus shall it be done unto
the man whom the king delighteth to
honour.
12 ¶ And Mordecai came again to
the king's gate. But Haman [y]hasted to
his house mourning, [z]and having his
head covered.
13 And Haman told Zeresh his wife
and all his friends every *thing* that had
befallen him. Then said his wise men
and Zeresh his wife unto him, If Morde-
cai *be* of the seed of the Jews, before
whom thou hast begun to fall, thou
shalt not prevail against him, but shalt
surely fall before him.
14 And while they *were* yet talking
with him, came the king's chamber-
lains, and hasted to bring Haman unto
[a]the banquet that Esther had pre-
pared.

The downfall of Haman

7 SO THE king and Haman came
[x]to banquet with Esther the
queen.
2 And the king said again unto Es-
ther on the second day [b]at the ban-
quet of wine, What *is* thy petition,
queen Esther? and it shall be granted
thee: and what *is* thy request? and it
shall be performed, *even* to the half of
the kingdom.
3 Then Esther the queen answered
and said, If I have found favour in thy
sight, O king, and if it please the king,
let my life be given me at my petition,
and my people at my request:
4 For we are [c]sold, I and my peo-
ple, [y]to be destroyed, to be slain, and
to perish. But if we had been sold for
bondmen and bondwomen, I had held
my tongue, although the enemy could
not countervail the king's damage.
5 ¶ Then the king Ahasuerus an-
swered and said unto Esther the
queen, Who is he, and where is he,
[z]that durst presume in his heart to
do so?
6 And Esther said, [a]The adversary
and enemy *is* this wicked Haman. Then
Haman was afraid [b]before the king
and the queen.
7 ¶ And the king arising from the
banquet of wine in his wrath *went* into
the palace garden: and Haman stood

6:4 [u]See ch. 5:1 [v]ch. 5:14 **6:8** [w]1 Ki. 1:33 **6:9** [x]Gen. 41:43 **6:12** [y]2 Chr. 26:20 [z]2 Sam. 15:30 Jer. 14:3,4 **6:14** [a]ch. 5:8 **7:2** [b]ch. 5:6 **7:4** [c]ch. 3:9

[q] Or, *Bigthan;* see ch. 2:21 [r] Heb. *threshold* [s] Heb. *in whose honour the king delighteth* [t] Heb. *Let them bring the royal apparel* [u] Heb. *wherewith the king clotheth* himself [v] Heb. *cause him to ride* [w] Heb. *suffer not a whit to fall* [x] Heb. *to drink* [y] Heb. *that they should destroy, and kill, and cause to perish* [z] Heb. *whose heart hath filled him* [a] Heb. *The man adversary* [b] Or, *at the presence of*

up to make request for his life to Es-
ther the queen; for he saw that there
was evil determined against him by the
king.
8 Then the king returned out of the
palace garden into the place of the ban-
quet of wine; and Haman was fallen
upon [d]the bed whereon Esther *was.*
Then said the king, Will he force the
queen also [c]before me in the house?
As the word went out of the king's
mouth, they [e]covered Haman's face.
9 And [f]Harbonah, one of the cham-
berlains, said before the king, Behold
also, [g]the [d]gallows fifty cubits high,
which Haman had made for Mordecai,
who had spoken good for the king,
standeth in the house of Haman. Then
the king said, Hang him thereon.
10 So [h]they hanged Haman on the
gallows that he had prepared for Mor-
decai. Then was the king's wrath paci-
fied.

The decree is revoked

8 ON THAT day did the king
Ahasuerus give the house of Ha-
man the Jew's enemy unto Esther the
queen. And Mordecai came before the
king; for Esther had told [i]what he *was*
unto her.
2 And the king took off [j]his ring,
which he had taken from Haman, and
gave it unto Mordecai. And Esther set
Mordecai over the house of Haman.
3 ¶ And Esther spake yet again be-
fore the king, and fell down at his feet,
[e]and besought him with tears to put
away the mischief of Haman the Agag-
ite, and his device that he had devised
against the Jews.
4 Then [k]the king held out the gold-
en sceptre toward Esther. So Esther
arose, and stood before the king,
5 And said, If it please the king, and
if I have found favour in his sight, and
the thing *seem* right before the king,
and I *be* pleasing in his eyes, let it be
written to reverse [f]the letters devised
by Haman the son of Hammedatha the
Agagite, [g]which he wrote to destroy
the Jews which *are* in all the king's
provinces:
6 For how can I [h]endure to see
[l]the evil that shall come unto my peo-
ple? or how can I endure to see the de-
struction of my kindred?
7 ¶ Then the king Ahasuerus said
unto Esther the queen and to Mordecai
the Jew, Behold, [m]I have given Esther
the house of Haman, and him they have
hanged upon the gallows, because he
laid his hand upon the Jews.
8 Write ye also for the Jews, as it
liketh you, in the king's name, and seal
it with the king's ring: for the writing
which is written in the king's name,
and sealed with the king's ring, [n]may
no man reverse.
9 [o]Then were the king's scribes
called at that time in the third month,
that *is,* the month Sivan, on the three
and twentieth *day* thereof; and it was
written according to all that Mordecai
commanded unto the Jews, and to the
lieutenants, and the deputies and rul-
ers of the provinces which *are* [p]from
India unto Ethiopia, an hundred twenty
and seven provinces, unto every prov-
ince [q]according to the writing thereof,
and unto every people after their lan-
guage, and to the Jews according to
their writing, and according to their
language.
10 [r]And he wrote in the king
Ahasuerus' name, and sealed *it* with
the king's ring, and sent letters by
posts on horseback, *and* riders on
mules, camels, *and* young dromedar-
ies:
11 Wherein the king granted the
Jews which *were* in every city to gather
themselves together, and to stand for
their life, to destroy, to slay, and to
cause to perish, all the power of the
people and province that would assault
them, *both* little ones and women, and
[s]*to take* the spoil of them for a prey,

7:8 [d]ch. 1:6 [e]Job 9:24 **7:9** [f]ch. 1:10 [g]ch. 5:14 Ps. 7:16 Prov. 11:5,6 **7:10** [h]Ps. 37:35,36 Dan. 6:24 **8:1** [i]ch. 2:7 **8:2** [j]ch. 3:10 **8:4** [k]ch. 4:11 & 5:2

8:6 [l]Neh. 2:3 ch. 7:4 **8:7** [m]ver. 1 Prov. 13:22 **8:8** [n]See ch. 1:19 Dan. 6:8,12,15 **8:9** [o]ch. 3:12 [p]ch. 1:1 [q]ch. 1:22 & 3:12 **8:10** [r]1 Ki. 21:8 ch. 3:12,13 **8:11** [s]See ch. 9:10,15, 16

[c] Heb. *with me* [d] Heb. *tree* [e] Heb. *and she wept, and besought him* [f] Heb. *the device* [g] Or, *who wrote* [h] Heb. *be able that I may see*

8:3 BESOUGHT HIM . . . TO PUT AWAY THE MISCHIEF. Although Haman was hanged as a result of God's just intervention (7:10), the king's edict to destroy the Jews was still in effect. Even the king himself could not reverse the official decree (v. 8). However, in response to Esther's request, a second decree was written that gave the Jews the right to fight back and defend themselves on the day formerly decreed for their destruction (vv. 9–17). God typically does not save His people apart from their faithful participation, yet He is constantly with them working out their deliverance; i.e., Israel's deliverance was the result of the combined activity of both God and faithful believers (see Phil. 2:12–13).

12 [t]Upon one day in all the prov-
inces of king Ahasuerus, *namely,* upon
the thirteenth *day* of the twelfth
month, which *is* the month Adar.
13 [u]The copy of the writing for a
commandment to be given in every
province *was* [i]published unto all peo-
ple, and that the Jews should be ready
against that day to avenge themselves
on their enemies.
14 *So* the posts that rode upon
mules *and* camels went out, being has-
tened and pressed on by the king's
commandment. And the decree was
given at Shushan the palace.
15 ¶ And Mordecai went out from
the presence of the king in royal appar-
el of [j]blue and white, and with a great
crown of gold, and with a garment of
fine linen and purple: and [v]the city of
Shushan rejoiced and was glad.
16 The Jews had [w]light, and glad-
ness, and joy, and honour.
17 And in every province, and in ev-
ery city, whithersoever the king's com-
mandment and his decree came, the
Jews had joy and gladness, a feast
[x]and a good day. And many of the peo-
ple of the land [y]became Jews; for
[z]the fear of the Jews fell upon them.

The victory of the Jews

9 NOW [a]IN the twelfth month, that
is, the month Adar, on the thir-
teenth day of the same, [b]when the
king's commandment and his decree
drew near to be put in execution, in the
day that the enemies of the Jews hoped
to have power over them, (though it
was turned to the contrary, that the
Jews [c]had rule over them that hated
them;)
2 The Jews [d]gathered themselves
together in their cities throughout all
the provinces of the king Ahasuerus, to
lay hand on such as [e]sought their
hurt: and no man could withstand
them; for [f]the fear of them fell upon
all people.
3 And all the rulers of the prov-
inces, and the lieutenants, and the
deputies, and [k]officers of the king,
helped the Jews; because the fear of
Mordecai fell upon them.
4 For Mordecai *was* great in the
king's house, and his fame went out
throughout all the provinces: for this
man Mordecai [g]waxed greater and
greater.
5 Thus the Jews smote all their ene-
mies with the stroke of the sword, and
slaughter, and destruction, and did
[l]what they would unto those that hat-
ed them.
6 And in Shushan the palace the
Jews slew and destroyed five hundred
men.
7 And Parshandatha, and Dalphon,
and Aspatha,
8 And Poratha, and Adalia, and
Aridatha,
9 And Parmashta, and Arisai, and
Aridai, and Vajezatha,
10 [h]The ten sons of Haman the
sons of Hammedatha, the enemy of the
Jews, slew they; [i]but on the spoil laid
they not their hand.
11 On that day the number of those
that were slain in Shushan the palace
[m]was brought before the king.
12 ¶ And the king said unto Esther
the queen, The Jews have slain and de-
stroyed five hundred men in Shushan
the palace, and the ten sons of Haman;
what have they done in the rest of the
king's provinces? now [j]what *is* thy pe-
tition? and it shall be granted thee: or
what *is* thy request further? and it shall
be done.
13 Then said Esther, If it please the
king, let it be granted to the Jews
which *are* in Shushan to do tomorrow
also [k]according unto this day's de-
cree, and [n]let Haman's ten sons [l]be
hanged upon the gallows.
14 And the king commanded it so to
be done: and the decree was given at
Shushan; and they hanged Haman's
ten sons.

8:12 [t]ch. 3:13 & 9:1 **8:13** [u]ch. 3:14,15 **8:15** [v]See ch. 3:15 Prov. 29:2 **8:16** [w]Ps. 97:11 **8:17** [x]1 Sam. 25:8 [y]Ps. 18:43 [z]Gen. 35:5 Ex. 15:16 Deut. 2:25 & 11:25 ch. 9:2 **9:1** [a]ch. 8:12 [b]ch. 3:13 [c]2 Sam. 22:41 **9:2** [d]ver. 16 & ch. 8:11 [e]Ps. 71:13,24 [f]ch. 8:17 **9:4** [g]2 Sam. 3:1 1 Chr. 11:9 Prov. 4:18 **9:10** [h]ch. 5:11 Job 18:19 & 27:13-15 Ps. 21:10 [i]See ch. 8:11 **9:12** [j]ch. 5:6 & 7:2 **9:13** [k]ch. 8:11 [l]2 Sam. 21:6,9

[i] Heb. *revealed* [j] Or, *violet* [k] Heb. *those which did the business that* belonged *to the king* [l] Heb. *according to their will* [m] Heb. *came* [n] Heb. *let men hang*

8:17 THE FEAR OF THE JEWS FELL UPON THEM. Not only did God enable the Jews to defend themselves (see previous note), but God also caused the people of the land to fear the Jews (cf. 9:2; Neh. 6:16). In other words, God's people actually gained in stature through the wicked plot of Haman.

9:5 SMOTE ALL THEIR ENEMIES. The destruction of the Jews' enemies on the thirteenth day of Adar was an act of self-defense; the Jews had been placed in a circumstance of having to fight for their very lives. They resisted those who wanted to exterminate them, yet they showed restraint by not plundering their enemies (vv. 10, 15–16).

15 For the Jews that *were* in Shushan [m]gathered themselves together on the fourteenth day also of the month Adar, and slew three hundred men at Shushan; [n]but on the prey they laid not their hand.

16 But the other Jews that *were* in the king's provinces [o]gathered themselves together, and stood for their lives, and had rest from their enemies, and slew of their foes seventy and five thousand, [p]but they laid not their hands on the prey,

17 On the thirteenth day of the month Adar; and on the fourteenth day [o]of the same rested they, and made it a day of feasting and gladness.

The feast of Purim instituted

18 But the Jews that *were* at Shushan assembled together [q]on the thirteenth *day* thereof, and on the fourteenth thereof; and on the fifteenth *day* of the same they rested, and made it a day of feasting and gladness.

19 Therefore the Jews of the villages, that dwelt in the unwalled towns, made the fourteenth day of the month Adar [r]*a day of* gladness and feasting, [s]and a good day, and of [t]sending portions one to another.

20 ¶ And Mordecai wrote these things, and sent letters unto all the Jews that *were* in all the provinces of the king Ahasuerus, *both* nigh and far,

21 To stablish *this* among them, that they should keep the fourteenth day of the month Adar, and the fifteenth day of the same, yearly,

22 As the days wherein the Jews rested from their enemies, and the month which was turned unto them from sorrow to joy, and from mourning into a good day: that they should make them days of feasting and joy, and of [u]sending portions one to another, and gifts to the poor.

23 And the Jews undertook to do as they had begun, and as Mordecai had written unto them;

24 Because Haman the son of Hammedatha, the Agagite, the enemy of all the Jews, [v]had devised against the Jews to destroy them, and had cast Pur, that *is,* the lot, to [p]consume them, and to destroy them;

25 But [w]when[q] *Esther* came before the king, he commanded by letters that his wicked device, which he devised against the Jews, should [x]return upon his own head, and that he and his sons should be hanged on the gallows.

26 Wherefore they called these days Purim after the name of [r]Pur. Therefore for all the words of [y]this letter, and *of that* which they had seen concerning this matter, and which had come unto them,

27 The Jews ordained, and took upon them, and upon their seed, and upon all such as [z]joined themselves unto them, so as it should not [s]fail, that they would keep these two days according to their writing, and according to their *appointed* time every year;

28 And *that* these days *should be* remembered and kept throughout every generation, every family, every province, and every city; and *that* these days of Purim should not [s]fail from among the Jews, nor the memorial of them [t]perish from their seed.

29 Then Esther the queen, [a]the daughter of Abihail, and Mordecai the Jew, wrote with [u]all authority, to confirm this [b]second letter of Purim.

30 And he sent the letters unto all the Jews, to [c]the hundred twenty and seven provinces of the kingdom of Ahasuerus, *with* words of peace and truth,

31 To confirm these days of Purim in their times *appointed,* according as Mordecai the Jew and Esther the queen had enjoined them, and as they had decreed [v]for themselves and for their seed, the matters of [d]the fastings and their cry.

32 And the decree of Esther con-

9:15 [m]ver. 2 & ch. 8:11 [n]ver. 10
9:16 [o]ver. 2 & ch. 8:11 [p]See ch. 8:11
9:18 [q]ver. 11,15
9:19 [r]Deut. 16:11,14 [s]ch. 8:17 [t]ver. 22 Neh. 8:10,12
9:22 [u]ver. 19 & Neh. 8:10
9:24 [v]ch. 3:6,7
9:25 [w]ver. 13,14 ch. 7:5 & 8:3 [x]ch. 7:10 Ps. 7:16
9:26 [y]ver. 20
9:27 [z]ch. 8:17 Is. 56:3,6 Zech. 2:11
9:29 [a]ch. 2:15 [b]See ch. 8:10 & ver. 20
9:30 [c]ch. 1:1
9:31 [d]ch. 4:3,16

[o]Heb. *in it* [p]Heb. *crush* [q]Heb. *when she came* [r]i.e. *Lot* [s]Heb. *pass* [t]Heb. *be ended* [u]Heb. *all strength* [v]Heb. *for their souls*

9:26 PURIM. Mordecai established the Feast of Purim (cf. vv. 20–23), a two-day festival celebrating God's deliverance of His people from Haman's sinister plot of Jewish genocide. (1) The feast was called "Purim," recalling that Haman used the "Pur" or lot to determine the day the Jews were to be destroyed (see 3:7, note). (2) The Feast of Purim reminds us that God can overrule the laws of chance. God's people should never see themselves as victims of fate or chance. God has a wonderful plan for each of our lives, a plan that fits in with His great plan of redemption. But we must take our stand, as did Mordecai and Esther.

firmed these matters of Purim; and it
was written in the book.

The greatness of Mordecai

10 AND THE king Ahasuerus laid
a tribute upon the land, and
upon [e]the isles of the sea.

2 And all the acts of his power and
of his might, and the declaration of the
greatness of Mordecai, [f]whereunto
the king [w]advanced him, *are* they not
written in the book of the chronicles of
the kings of Media and Persia?

3 For Mordecai the Jew *was* [g]next
unto king Ahasuerus, and great among
the Jews, and accepted of the multi-
tude of his brethren, [h]seeking the
wealth of his people, and speaking
peace to all his seed.

10:1 [e]Gen. 10:5 Ps. 72:10 Is. 24:15
10:2 [f]ch. 8:15 & 9:4
10:3 [g]Gen. 41:40 2 Chr. 28:7 [h]Neh. 2:10 Ps. 122:8,9

[w] Heb. *made him great*

JOB

Outline

I. Prose Prologue: The Crisis (1:1—2:13)
   A. Job an Upright, God-Fearing Man (1:1–5)
   B. Conversation Between the Lord and Satan, and Job's Subsequent Calamities (1:6—2:10)
   C. The Visit of Job's Three Friends (2:11–13)
II. The Dialogues Between Job and His Friends: A Search for Intellectual Answers (3:1—31:40)
   A. First Cycle of Dialogue: The Righteousness of God (3:1—14:22)
      1. Job Laments the Day of His Birth (3:1–26)
      2. Eliphaz's Reply (4:1—5:27)
      3. Job's Rejoinder (6:1—7:21)
      4. Bildad's Reply (8:1–22)
      5. Job's Rejoinder (9:1—10:22)
      6. Zophar's Reply (11:1–20)
      7. Job's Rejoinder (12:1—14:22)
   B. Second Cycle of Dialogue: The Fate of Wicked Man (15:1—21:34)
      1. Eliphaz's Response (15:1–35)
      2. Job's Rejoinder (16:1—17:16)
      3. Bildad's Response (18:1–21)
      4. Job's Rejoinder (19:1–29)
      5. Zophar's Response (20:1–29)
      6. Job's Rejoinder (21:1–34)
   C. Third Cycle of Dialogue: The Sinfulness of Job (22:1—31:40)
      1. Eliphaz's Answer (22:1–30)
      2. Job's Rejoinder (23:1—24:25)
      3. Bildad's Answer (25:1–6)
      4. Job's Rejoinder (26:1–14)
      5. Job's Final Summary of His Basic Position (27:1—31:40)
III. The Speeches of Elihu: The Beginning of Insight (32:1—37:24)
   A. Introduction of Elihu (32:1–6a)
   B. First Speech: God's Instruction to Humans through Affliction (32:6b—33:33)
   C. Second Speech: God's Justice and Job's Presumption (34:1–37)
   D. Third Speech: Uprightness Is Not Without Profit (35:1–16)
   E. Fourth Speech: God's Majestic Greatness and Job's Ignorance (36:1—37:24)
IV. The Lord Answers Job: Firsthand Revelation (38:1—42:6)
   A. God Speaks to Job's Ignorance (38:1—40:2)
   B. Job's Humility (40:3–5)
   C. God Challenges Job's Criticism about His Righteous Rule in the World (40:6—41:34)
   D. Job Confesses His Inadequate Knowledge of God's Ways (42:1–6)
V. Prose Epilogue: The Crisis Ends (42:7–17)
   A. Job Prays for His Three Friends (42:7–9)
   B. Job's Double Portion (42:10–17)

Author: Anonymous

Theme: Why Do the Righteous Suffer?

Date of Writing: Uncertain

Background

Job is classified as one of the wisdom and poetic books of the O.T.: "wisdom" because it deals profoundly with important universal questions of humankind; "poetic" because almost the entire book is in poetic form. Its poetry, however, is based on a real, historical person (see Ezek. 14:14,20) and a real, historical event (see Jas. 5:11). The book's setting is "the land of Uz" (1:1), which later became the territory of Edom located southeast of the Dead Sea or in northern Arabia (cf. Lam. 4:21). Thus the historical background of Job is Arabic rather than Hebrew.

There are two important dates to consider in relation to Job: (1) the date for Job himself and the events described in the book, and (2) the date for the inspired writing of the book. Certain facts indicate that Job himself lived about the time of Abraham (2000 B.C.) or before. The most significant facts are: (1) his having lived 140 years after the events in the book (42:16), suggesting a life span close to 200 years (Abraham lived 175 years); (2) his wealth being measured in terms of livestock (1:3; 42:12); (3) his service as priest for his family, like Abraham, Isaac, and Jacob (1:5); (4) the patriarchal family-clan being the basic social unit, as in Abraham's day (1:4–5,13); (5) the raids by the Sabeans (1:15) and Chaldeans (1:17), which fit the Abrahamic era; (6) the frequent use (thirty-one times) of the common patriarchal name for God, *Shaddai* ("the Almighty"); and (7) the absence of any reference to Israelite history or Mosaic law, suggesting a pre-Mosaic era (before 1500 B.C.).

Three main views exist concerning when the book itself was written. It may have been composed (1) during the patriarchal age (c. 2000 B.C.), shortly after the events occurred and perhaps by Job himself; (2) during the days of Solomon or soon after (c. 950–900 B.C.), since the book's literary form and style are similar to the wisdom literature of that period; or (3) during the time of the exile (c. 586–538 B.C.), when God's people were wrestling theologically with the meaning of their calamity. The unknown author, if other than Job himself, must have had detailed oral and/or written sources from the time of Job which he used under divine prompting and inspiration to write the book as we now have it. Certain parts of the book had to be given by direct revelation from God (e.g. 1:6—2:10).

Purpose

The book of Job wrestles with the age-old question, "If God is just and loving, why does He permit a truly righteous man like Job (1:1,8) to suffer intensely?" In struggling with this issue, the author reveals the following truths. (1) As an opponent of God, Satan received permission to test the genuineness of the faith of a righteous man by afflicting him; but God's grace triumphed over suffering because Job by faith remained steadfast and immovable, even when there appeared to be no physical or temporal benefit in his staying committed to God. (2) God is moved by considerations too vast for the human mind to fully comprehend (37:5); since we do not see with the breadth and vision of the Almighty, we need God's gracious self-disclosure. (3) The real foundation of faith lies not in God's blessings, personal circumstances, or intellectual answers, but in a revelation of God Himself. (4) God sometimes permits Satan to test the righteous with adversity in order to purify their faith and lives, just as gold is refined by the fire (23:10; cf. 1 Pet. 1:6–7); such testing results in an increased measure of spiritual integrity and humility in His people (42:1–10). (5) Though God's dealings at times may seem dark and cruel (as Job himself thought), in the end God is seen to be full of compassion and mercy (42:7–17; cf. Jas. 5:11).

Survey

There are five distinct divisions in the structure of the book of Job: (1) the prologue (chs. 1—2), which describes Job's calamity and the cause behind it; (2) three cycles of dialogue between Job and his three friends, in which they search for intellectual answers to Job's

affliction (chs. 3—31); (3) four monologues by Elihu, a man younger than Job and his three friends, which contain some glimmer of insight into the meaning (though not the cause) of Job's affliction (chs. 32—37); (4) God Himself, who speaks to Job's ignorance and complaint and listens to Job's response to His revelation (38:1—42:6); (5) the epilogue (42:7–17), which records Job's restoration. Job is written entirely in poetic form, except for three passages: (a) the prologue, (b) 32:1–6a, and (c) the epilogue.

Job is presented in ch. 1 as a righteous and God-fearing man (1:1,8) and the greatest of all men of the east (1:3). His circumstances were suddenly reversed by a series of great calamities which destroyed his possessions, children, and health (1:13–22; 2:7–10). Job was completely baffled, not realizing he was deeply involved in a conflict between God and Satan (1:6–12; 2:1–6). Job's three friends—Eliphaz, Bildad, and Zophar—came to comfort Job but instead ended up debating with him about why his misfortunes had occurred. They insisted that since God is just, Job's suffering must represent punishment for hidden sins and that his only recourse was repentance. Job rejected their ready-made answers, affirmed his innocence, and confessed his inability to understand (chs. 3—31). Elihu offered another perspective, namely, that Job's suffering involved God's redemptive purpose of further purifying Job (chs. 32—37).

In the end everyone was silenced, including Job, as God Himself spoke to Job concerning His wisdom and power as the Creator. Job acknowledged his ignorance and insignificance with a repentant and humble heart (chs. 38—41). When Job repented of contending with the Almighty (40:1–4, 8; 42:5–6) and prayed for his friends who had cut him deeply (42:8,10), he was delivered from his fiery trial and restored twofold (42:10). Also Job was vindicated when God stated that Job had spoken of God "*the thing that is* right" (42:7). Job's latter days were blessed more than his life before his affliction (42:12–17). Though God never provided Job with a philosophical understanding of why he suffered, the reader receives this important perspective from the prologue.

Special Features

Seven major features or emphases characterize the book of Job. (1) Job, a native of northern Arabia, was a righteous and God-fearing non-Israelite, living perhaps before the covenant family of Israel even existed (1:1). (2) This book is the most profound one ever written dealing with the mystery of suffering. As dramatic poetry, the book's drama contains stirring pathos and rousing intellectual dialogue. (3) It discloses an important dynamic that operates in every fiery trial of the saints: while Satan attempts to destroy the faith of the saints, God is at work to prove and deepen it. Job's steadfastness in naked faith enabled God's purpose to prevail over Satan's hope (cf. Jas. 5:11). (4) It makes an invaluable contribution to the total Biblical revelation on such key subjects as God, humankind, creation, Satan, sin, righteousness, suffering, justice, repentance, and faith. (5) A large portion of the book records the faulty theological evaluation of Job's suffering by his friends. Perhaps that wrong way of thinking is so frequently repeated in this book because it is a common error among God's people that needs correction. (6) Satan's role as "adversary" of the righteous is demonstrated in Job more than in any other O.T. book. Of the nineteen O.T. references to Satan by name, fourteen of these occur in Job. (7) Job dramatically demonstrates the Biblical principle that believers are transformed by revelation, not information (42:5–6).

New Testament Fulfillment

The Redeemer whom Job confesses (19:25–27), the Mediator for whom he longs (9:32–33), and the answers to his deepest questions and needs all find their fulfillment in Jesus Christ. Jesus identified fully with human suffering (cf. Heb. 4:15–16; 5:8) as God's appointed Redeemer, mediator, wisdom, healer, light, and life. The Spirit of prophecy concerning the coming of Christ is most clearly expressed in 19:25–27. Explicit mention of Job occurs twice in the N.T.: (1) as a quotation (5:13 in 1 Cor. 3:19), and (2) as a reference to Job's steadfastness in affliction and the merciful outcome of God's dealings with him (Jas. 5:11). Job illustrates vividly the N.T. truth that when believers experience persecution or some

other fiery trial of suffering, they must remain steadfast in faith and keep entrusting themselves to Him who judges righteously, just as did Jesus Himself when He suffered (cf. 1 Pet. 2:23). Job 1:6—2:10 remains the best illustration of our adversary as described in 1 Pet. 5:8–9.

Reading Job

In order to read the entire Old Testament in one year, the book of Job should be read in 13 days, according to the following schedule: ☐ 1–2 ☐ 3–5 ☐ 6–8 ☐ 9–11 ☐ 12–14 ☐ 15–18 ☐ 19–21 ☐ 22–24 ☐ 25–28 ☐ 29–31 ☐ 32–35 ☐ 36–39 ☐ 40–42

NOTES

Job and his background

1 THERE WAS a man [a]in the land of Uz, whose name *was* [b]Job; and that man was [c]perfect and upright, and one that [d]feared God, and eschewed evil.

2 And there were born unto him seven sons and three daughters.

3 His [a]substance also was seven thousand sheep, and three thousand camels, and five hundred yoke of oxen, and five hundred she asses, and a very great [b]household; so that this man was the greatest of all the [c]men of the east.

4 And his sons went and feasted *in their* houses, every one his day; and sent and called for their three sisters to eat and to drink with them.

5 And it was so, when the days of *their* feasting were gone about, that Job sent and sanctified them, and rose up early in the morning, [e]and offered burnt offerings *according* to the number of them all: for Job said, It may be that my sons have sinned, and [f]cursed God in their hearts. Thus did Job [d]continually.

1:1 [a]1 Chr. 1:17 [b]Ezek. 14:14 Jas. 5:11 [c]Gen. 17:1 [d]Prov. 16:6 **1:5** [e]ch. 42:8 [f]1 Ki. 21:10 **1:6** [g]ch. 2:1 **1:7** [h]1 Pet. 5:8

Job 23:1… 12

Satan permitted to tempt Job

6 ¶ Now [g]there was a day when the sons of God came to present themselves before the LORD, and [e]Satan came also [f]among them.

7 And the LORD said unto Satan, Whence comest thou? Then Satan answered the LORD, and said, From [h]going to and fro in the earth, and from walking up and down in it.

8 And the LORD said unto Satan, [g]Hast thou considered my servant Job, that *there is* none like him in the earth, a perfect and an upright man, one that feareth God, and escheweth evil?

9 Then Satan answered the LORD,

[a] Or, *cattle* [b] Or, *husbandry* [c] Heb. *sons of the east* [d] Heb. *all the days* [e] Heb. *the Adversary* [f] Heb. *in the midst of them* [g] Heb. *Hast thou set thy heart on*

1:1 JOB. It appears that Job lived in the age of the patriarchs (Abraham, Isaac, and Jacob, approximately 2100–1800 B.C.). Most scholars believe the land of Uz was located southeast of Palestine and the Dead Sea or in northern Arabia (see the introduction to Job). Others believe the land of Uz was located northeast of the Sea of Galilee, toward Damascus.

1:1 PERFECT AND UPRIGHT . . . FEARED GOD . . . ESCHEWED EVIL. (1) Fearing God and turning away from evil are the foundation for Job's blamelessness and uprightness (cf. Prov. 1:7). "Perfect" refers to Job's moral integrity and wholehearted commitment to God; "upright" denotes rightness in word, thought, and action. (2) This declaration concerning Job's righteousness is restated by God Himself in v. 8 and 2:3, clearly affirming that God through His grace can redeem fallen humans so as to make them genuinely good, righteous, and victorious over sin. This statement shames and exposes as error evangelical teachings today that maintain that (a) no believer in Christ, even with the now fully available help of the Holy Spirit, can ever expect to be blameless and upright in this life; and (b) believers must expect to sin every day in word, thought, and deed with no hope of overcoming the flesh in this life.

1:5 MY SONS. As a godly parent, Job was deeply concerned for the spiritual welfare of his children. He watched their conduct and lifestyle, praying to God that they would be kept from evil and would experience God's blessing and salvation. Job exemplifies a father whose heart is turned toward his children by devoting the time and attention necessary to keep them from a life of sin (see Luke 1:17, note; see article on PARENTS AND CHILDREN, p. 1880).

1:6–7 SATAN. Prior to the death and resurrection of Christ, Satan had occasional access to the presence of God, whereby he could question the sincerity and righteousness of a believer (see 1:6–12; 2:1–6; 38:7; Rev. 12:10). However, nowhere in the Bible does it say Satan has direct access to God under the new covenant (see Mat. 4:10, note), though he still aims his accusations at believers. We may overcome these accusations by the blood of Christ, a good conscience, and the Word of God (cf. Mat. 4:3–11; Jas. 4:7; Rev. 12:11). We can be further encouraged by the fact that we have an advocate with the Father, even Jesus Christ (1 John 2:1), who is at His right hand interceding for us (Heb. 7:25).

1:8 HAST THOU CONSIDERED MY SERVANT JOB. Here the book introduces the struggle between God and His great adversary, Satan. God challenged Satan to observe in Job the triumph of divine grace and redemption. In the life of this faithful servant, God demonstrated that His plan to redeem the human race from sin and evil can be achieved.

1:9 DOTH JOB FEAR GOD FOR NOUGHT? Satan reacted to God's claim that Job was a godly man by assaulting both Job and God. (1) Satan questioned Job's motives and therefore the reality of Job's righteousness by insisting that Job's love for God was really self-serving, and that he worshiped God only because it profited him. Satan implied that Job's love for God was not genuine.

(2) Satan further implied that God was naive and had deceived Himself, having obtained Job's devotion by blessing and bribery (vv. 10–11). Satan concluded that God had thereby failed in His attempt to reconcile the human race to Himself. If God were to cease giving Job protection, wealth,

and said, Doth Job fear God for nought?

10 [i]Hast not thou made an hedge about him, and about his house, and about all that he hath on every side? [j]thou hast blessed the work of his hands, and his [h]substance is increased in the land.

11 [k]But put forth thine hand now, and touch all that he hath, [i]and he will [l]curse thee to thy face.

12 And the LORD said unto Satan, Behold, all that he hath *is* in thy [m]power;[j] only upon himself put not forth thine hand. So Satan went forth from the presence of the LORD.

13 ¶ And there was a day [n]when his sons and his daughters *were* eating and drinking wine in their eldest brother's house:

14 And there came a messenger unto Job, and said, The oxen were plowing, and the asses feeding beside them:

15 And the Sabeans fell *upon them*, and took them away; yea, they have slain the servants with the edge of the sword; and I only am escaped alone to tell thee.

16 While he *was* yet speaking, there came also another, and said, [k]The fire of God is fallen from heaven, and hath burned up the sheep, and the servants, and consumed them; and I only am escaped alone to tell thee.

17 While he *was* yet speaking, there came also another, and said, The Chaldeans made out three bands, and [l]fell upon the camels, and have carried them away, yea, and slain the servants with the edge of the sword; and I only am escaped alone to tell thee.

18 While he *was* yet speaking, there came also another, and said, [o]Thy sons and thy daughters *were* eating and drinking wine in their eldest brother's house:

19 And, behold, there came a great wind [m]from the wilderness, and smote the four corners of the house, and it fell upon the young men, and they are dead; and I only am escaped alone to tell thee.

20 Then Job arose, [p]and rent his [n]mantle, and shaved his head, and [q]fell down upon the ground, and worshipped,

21 And said, [r]Naked came I out of my mother's womb, and naked shall I return thither: the LORD [s]gave, and the LORD hath [t]taken away; [u]blessed be the name of the LORD.

22 [v]In all this Job sinned not, nor [o]charged God foolishly. Ps. 91:1-13

1:10 [i]Ps. 34:7 Is. 5:2 [j]Ps. 128:1,2 Prov. 10:22
1:11 [k]ch. 2:5 & 19:21 [l]Is. 8:21 Mal. 3:13,14
1:12 [m]Gen. 16:6
1:13 [n]Eccl. 9:12
1:18 [o]ver. 4,13
1:20 [p]Gen. 37:29 Ezra 9:3 [q]1 Pet. 5:6
1:21 [r]Ps. 49:17 Eccl. 5:15 1 Tim. 6:7 [s]Eccl. 5:19 Jas. 1:17 [t]Gen. 31:16 [u]Eph. 5:20 1 Thes. 5:18
1:22 [v]ch. 2:10

[h] Or, *cattle* [i] Heb. *if he curse thee not to thy face* [j] Heb. *hand* [k] Or, *A great fire* [l] Heb. *rushed* [m] Heb. *from aside* [n] Or, *robe* [o] Or, *attributed folly to God*

health, and happiness, Satan maintained that Job would "curse thee to thy face" (v. 11).

1:10 AN HEDGE ABOUT HIM. Because Satan comes to steal, kill, and destroy (cf. John 10:10), God places a hedge of protection around His people to shield them from Satan's attacks. (1) The "hedge" is like a spiritual "wall of fire" surrounding God's faithful so that Satan cannot harm them. "For I, saith the LORD, will be unto her [Jerusalem] a wall of fire round about" (Zech. 2:5). (2) All believers who are faithfully endeavoring to love God and follow the leading of the Holy Spirit have a right to ask and expect God to place this wall of protection around them and their families.

1:11 TOUCH ALL THAT HE HATH, AND HE WILL CURSE THEE TO THY FACE. In vv. 6–12 the primary questions of the book are proposed. Is it possible for God's people to love and serve Him because of who He is and not just for His gifts? Can the righteous maintain their faith in and love for God in the midst of unexplainable tragedy and undeserved suffering?

1:12 ONLY UPON HIMSELF PUT NOT FORTH THINE HAND. God gave Satan the authority to destroy Job's property and family; however, He limited Satan as to what he could do, for he was not given the power of death over Job. Satan brought both violent weather and violent people against Job (vv. 13–19).

1:16 THE FIRE OF GOD. The "fire of God" is probably a term for lightning (see Num. 11:1; 1 Ki. 18:38).

1:20 FELL DOWN ... AND WORSHIPPED. Job reacted to the disasters that happened to him with intense grief, but also with a humility that submitted to God and continued to worship Him in the midst of extreme adversity (v. 21; 2:10). (1) Job's later reaction to continued calamity involved doubt, anger, and a sense of isolation from God (7:11). Yet even in this time of darkness and wavering faith, he did not turn against God but openly expressed his protest and feelings to Him. (2) The book of Job shows how faithful believers should face the calamities of life. Though we may experience severe sufferings and unexplainable affliction, we should pray for grace to accept what God allows to come upon us and to ask for revelation and understanding concerning its meaning. God will deal with our chaotic feelings and complaints if they are directed toward Him—not in rebellion, but in sincere trust in Him as a loving God. (3) The book reveals that God accepted Job's questionings (chs. 38—41) and in the end praised him for speaking "*the thing that is* right" (42:7).

Satan's second request of God

2 AGAIN [w]THERE was a day when the sons of God came to present themselves before the LORD, and Satan came also among them to present himself before the LORD.

2 And the LORD said unto Satan, From whence comest thou? And [x]Satan answered the LORD, and said, From going to and fro in the earth, and from walking up and down in it.

3 And the LORD said unto Satan, Hast thou considered my servant Job, that *there is* none like him in the earth, [y]a perfect and an upright man, one that feareth God, and escheweth evil? and still he [z]holdeth fast his integrity, although thou movedst me against him, [a]to[p] destroy him without cause.

4 And Satan answered the LORD, and said, Skin for skin, yea, all that a man hath will he give for his life.

5 [b]But put forth thine hand now, and touch his [c]bone and his flesh, and he will curse thee to thy face.

6 [d]And the LORD said unto Satan, Behold, he *is* in thine hand; [q]but save his life.

7 ¶ So went Satan forth from the presence of the LORD, and smote Job with sore boils [e]from the sole of his foot unto his crown.

8 And he took him a potsherd to scrape himself withal; [f]and he sat down among the ashes.

9 ¶ Then said his wife unto him, Dost thou still retain thine integrity? curse God, and die.

10 But he said unto her, Thou speakest as one of the foolish women speaketh. What? [g]shall we receive good at the hand of God, and shall we not receive evil? [h]In all this did not Job [i]sin with his lips.

The friends of Job

11 ¶ Now when Job's three friends heard of all this evil that was come upon him, they came every one from his own place; Eliphaz the [j]Temanite, and Bildad the [k]Shuhite, and Zophar

2:1 [w]ch. 1:6
2:2 [x]ch. 1:7
2:3 [y]ch. 1:1,8 [z]ch. 27:5,6 [a]ch. 9:17
2:5 [b]ch. 1:11 [c]ch. 19:20
2:6 [d]ch. 1:12
2:7 [e]Is. 1:6
2:8 [f]2 Sam. 13:19 ch. 42:6 Ezek. 27:30 Mat. 11:21
2:10 [g]ch. 1:21 Heb. 12:6 Jas. 5:10,11 [h]ch. 1:22 [i]Ps. 39:1
2:11 [j]Gen. 36:11 Jer. 49:7 [k]Gen. 25:2

[p] Heb. *to swallow him up* [q] Or, *only*

2:3 TO DESTROY HIM WITHOUT CAUSE. Job, the innocent sufferer, foreshadows both Jesus Christ and all righteous believers under the new covenant. (1) As the O.T. ideal of the suffering righteous person, Job is a type of Christ—the perfect Righteous Man—who suffered even though He was innocent (see article on CHRIST IN THE OLD TESTAMENT, p. 562). The sinless Christ suffered in His body the consequences of evil and was "smitten of God" (Is. 53:4; 1 Pet. 2:24; 4:1).

(2) Furthermore, Job exemplifies the patient endurance in adversity that is required of the child of God in Christ (Jas. 5:11; cf. also Heb. 11, where many of the heroes of faith suffered and died without receiving deliverance). As Job suffered innocently because of his loyalty to God and His righteousness, all faithful believers will likewise suffer in some measure. The N.T. states that "all that will live godly in Christ Jesus shall suffer persecution" (2 Tim. 3:12)—a suffering seen as entering into "the fellowship of [Christ's] sufferings" (Phil. 3:10; cf. Col. 1:24). Innocent sufferers are thus companions of God (cf. 1 Pet. 4:1; 5:10; see 2:21, note; 4:13, note; see article on THE SUFFERING OF THE RIGHTEOUS, p. 764).

2:6 HE IS IN THINE HAND. God allowed Satan to inflict further pain upon Job because neither Job's full commitment to God could be proven nor God's endeavor to redeem him from sin demonstrated effectively without undeserved suffering. (1) The testing of the faith of a righteous person through such suffering has great significance, because God's honor is at stake in the greatest spiritual struggle of all times, i.e., the conflict between God and Satan. (2) The apostle Peter, writing from a N.T. perspective, states: "ye are in heaviness through manifold temptations [trials]: that the trial of your faith, being much more precious than of gold that perisheth, though it be tried with fire, might be found unto praise and honour and glory at the appearing of Jesus Christ" (1 Pet. 1:6–7).

2:9 CURSE GOD, AND DIE. This advice from Job's wife expresses the heart of Job's test of faith. Throughout the book, his deep anguish caused by the seemingly unjust adversity from God tempted him both to abandon his moral resolve to remain loyal to God and to stop trusting the Lord as a compassionate and merciful God (cf. Jas. 5:11).

2:10 SHALL WE NOT RECEIVE EVIL? True believers must prepare themselves both to be tested by God with adversity and to receive good from His hand. Trusting in God does not mean that He will always exempt us from trouble, nor does faithfulness to God guarantee prosperity and success (see 2:3, note; 1 John 2, note). When adversity comes, the believer who is not conscious of any sin or rebellion against God must commit his or her soul to God. Faith in God as one's loving Lord in the midst of trials and oppression expresses the ultimate triumph of faith (1 Pet. 1:3–9).

2:11 JOB'S THREE FRIENDS. After hearing of Job's adversity, three of his friends came to comfort and sympathize with him. The book of Job records their dialogues with the sufferer. Their perspective represented a popular but incomplete theology, for they believed that only good things happen to the godly, while adversity always indicates sin in one's life. They sincerely tried to help Job by urging him to admit to some grave sin. In the end God rebuked them for their error (42:7).

the Naamathite: for they had made an appointment together to come [l]to mourn with him and to comfort him.

12 And when they lifted up their eyes afar off, and knew him not, they lifted up their voice, and wept; and they rent every one his mantle, and [m]sprinkled dust upon their heads toward heaven.

13 So they sat down with him upon the ground [n]seven days and seven nights, and none spake a word unto him: for they saw that *his* grief was very great.

The speech of Job

3 AFTER THIS opened Job his mouth, and cursed his day.

2 And Job [r]spake, and said,

3 [o]Let the day perish wherein I was born, and the night *in which* it was said, There is a man child conceived.

4 Let that day be darkness; let not God regard it from above, neither let the light shine upon it.

5 Let darkness and [p]the shadow of death [s]stain it; let a cloud dwell upon it; let the blackness of the day terrify it.

6 *As for* that night, let darkness seize upon it; [t]let it not be joined unto the days of the year, let it not come into the number of the months.

7 Lo, let that night be solitary, let no joyful voice come therein.

8 Let them curse it that curse the day, [q]who are ready to raise up [u]their mourning.

9 Let the stars of the twilight thereof be dark; let it look for light, but *have* none; neither let it see [v]the dawning of the day:

10 Because it shut not up the doors of my *mother's* womb, nor hid sorrow from mine eyes.

11 [r]Why died I not from the womb? *why* did I *not* give up the ghost when I came out of the belly?

12 [s]Why did the knees prevent me? or why the breasts that I should suck?

13 For now should I have lain still and been quiet, I should have slept: then had I been at rest,

14 With kings and counsellors of the earth, which [t]built desolate places for themselves;

15 Or with princes that had gold, who filled their houses with silver:

16 Or [u]as an hidden untimely birth I had not been; as infants *which* never saw light.

17 There the wicked cease *from* troubling; and there the [w]weary be at rest.

18 *There* the prisoners rest together; [v]they hear not the voice of the oppressor.

19 The small and great are there; and the servant *is* free from his master.

20 [w]Wherefore is light given to him that is in misery, and life unto the [x]bitter *in* soul;

21 Which [y]long[x] for death, but it *cometh* not; and dig for it more than [z]for hid treasures;

22 Which rejoice exceedingly, *and* are glad, when they can find the grave?

23 *Why is light given* to a man whose way is hid, [a]and whom God hath hedged in?

24 For my sighing cometh [y]before I eat, and my roarings are poured out like the waters.

25 For [z]the thing which I greatly feared is come upon me, and that

2:11 [l]ch. 42:11; Rom. 12:15 **2:12** [m]Neh. 9:1; Lam. 2:10; Ezek. 27:30 **2:13** [n]Gen. 50:10 **3:3** [o]Jer. 20:14 **3:5** [p]ch. 10:21; Jer. 13:16; Amos 5:8 **3:8** [q]Jer. 9:17 **3:11** [r]ch. 10:18 **3:12** [s]Gen. 30:3 **3:14** [t]ch. 15:28 **3:16** [u]Ps. 58:8 **3:18** [v]ch. 39:7 **3:20** [w]Jer. 20:18; [x]2 Ki. 4:27 **3:21** [y]Rev. 9:6; [z]Prov. 2:4 **3:23** [a]Lam. 3:7

[r] Heb. *answered* [s] Or, *challenge it* [t] Or, *let it not rejoice among the days* [u] Or, *a leviathan* [v] Heb. *the eyelids of the morning;* see ch. 41:18 [w] Heb. *wearied in strength* [x] Heb. *wait* [y] Heb. *before my meat* [z] Heb. *I feared a fear, and it came upon me*

3:1 JOB . . . CURSED HIS DAY. Job was bereaved, humiliated, and in pain. His greatest hurt was that God seemed to have left him. (1) In his speech (vv. 2–26) Job told God exactly how he felt. He began by cursing his birth and miserable existence, but note that in all this Job did not curse God. His cry was an expression of pain and despair, not a cry of defiance against God. (2) It is always best for believers to express their doubts and their honest emotions to the Lord in prayer. To go to God with our misery and heartache in order to find Him and evoke His pity is never wrong. Jesus Christ Himself asked God the question, "My God, my God, why hast thou forsaken me?" (Mat. 27:46; cf. also Jer. 20:14–18; Lam. 3:1–18).

3:13 THEN HAD I BEEN AT REST. Job conceived of the grave as a place of rest. He did not see it as extinction, but as a place of continuing personal existence (vv. 13–19; see Ps. 16:10, note on Sheol).

3:25 THE THING WHICH I GREATLY FEARED. Job's greatest desire in life had been for the presence and favor of God; now the thing he dreaded most had happened. God seemed to have forsaken him and he had no idea why. But Job did not curse God; he still prayed to Him for mercy and relief (6:8–9).

THE SUFFERING OF THE RIGHTEOUS

***Job 2:7–8** "So went Satan forth from the presence of the LORD, and smote Job with sore boils from the sole of his foot unto his crown. And he took him a potsherd to scrape himself withal; and he sat down among the ashes."*

Faithfulness to God does not guarantee believers freedom from trouble, pain, and suffering in their lives (see Acts 28:16, note). In fact, Jesus taught that we are to expect it (John 16:1–4,33; see 2 Tim. 3:12, note). The Bible provides numerous examples of godly people who experienced a significant amount of suffering for a variety of reasons—e.g., Joseph, David, Job, Jeremiah, and Paul.

REASONS BELIEVERS SUFFER. There are various reasons why believers suffer. (1) Believers experience suffering as an ongoing consequence of the fall of Adam and Eve. When sin entered the world, pain, sorrow, conflict, and eventual death invaded the lives of all human beings (Gen. 3:16–19). Paul affirms this: "Wherefore, as by one man sin entered into the world, and death by sin; and so death passed upon all men, for that all have sinned" (Rom. 5:12; see note). In fact, the entire created universe groans under the effects of sin and yearns for the time of the new heaven and earth (Rom. 8:20–23; 2 Pet. 3:10–13). Response: we must always cast ourselves on God's grace, strength, and comfort (cf. 1 Cor. 10:13).

(2) Some believers suffer for the same reason that unbelievers do, i.e., as a consequence of their own actions (see article on THE PROVIDENCE OF GOD, p. 80). The principle that "whatsoever a man soweth, that shall he also reap" (Gal. 6:7) applies in a general sense to everyone. If we drive our cars recklessly, we may get into serious accidents. If we are undisciplined in our eating habits, we are likely to have serious health problems. God may use such suffering as a means of disciplining us so that we may achieve "the peaceable fruit of righteousness" (Heb. 12:3–11; see 12:5, note). Response: we must always act in wisdom and in accord with God's Word, and we must avoid whatever will remove us from God's protective care.

(3) Believers also suffer, at least in their inner selves, because they live in a sinful and corrupt world. All around us are the effects of sin; we experience distress and anguish as we see the power that evil holds over so many lives (see Ezek. 9:4; Acts 17:16; 2 Pet. 2:8, note). Response: we must pray to God that He will demonstrate His victory over the power of sin.

(4) Believers suffer at the hands of the devil. (a) Scripture makes it clear that Satan, as "the god of this world" (2 Cor. 4:4), controls this present evil age (see 1 John 5:19, note; cf. Gal. 1:4; Heb. 2:14). He has been given power to afflict us in a variety of ways (cf. 1 Pet. 5:8–9). The story of Job centers around an upright, God-fearing man whom God permitted to be tormented by Satan with unspeakable sufferings (see especially Job 1—2). Jesus testified that one of the women he healed had been bound by Satan for eighteen years (cf. Luke 13:11,16). Paul recognized that his thorn in the flesh was "the messenger of Satan to buffet me" (2 Cor. 12:7). As we engage in spiritual warfare against "the rulers of the darkness of this world" (Eph. 6:12), we will inevitably suffer adversity. In order to deal with such assaults, God has given us spiritual armor (Eph. 6:10–18; see 6:11, note) and spiritual weapons (2 Cor. 10:3–6). Response: we must put on the whole armor of God and pray (Eph. 6:10–18), resolving to persevere faithfully in His strength.

(b) Satan and his followers delight to persecute believers. Those who love the Lord Jesus and follow His principles of truth and righteousness will be persecuted for their faith. In fact, such suffering for righteousness sake may be an indication of our genuine devotion to Christ (see Mat. 5:10, note; 1 Pet. 4:12, note). Response: since all true

believers are called to suffer persecution and reproach for righteousness' sake, we must remain steadfast and immovable, and keep on trusting Him who judges righteously (Mat. 5:10–11; 1 Cor. 15:58; 1 Pet. 2:23).

(5) More positively, another reason why believers suffer is that "we have the mind of Christ" (see 1 Cor. 2:16, note). To be a Christian means to be in Christ, to be one with Him; as a result we share in His sufferings (see 1 Pet. 2:21, note). For example, just as Christ wept in agony over the wicked city of Jerusalem and their refusal to repent and accept salvation (see Luke 19:41, note), so we are to weep over the sinfulness and lostness of humanity. Included in Paul's list of sufferings for Christ's sake (2 Cor. 11:23–32; see 11:23, note) was his daily concern for the churches that he had founded: "Who is weak, and I am not weak? who is offended, and I burn not?" (2 Cor. 11:29). Such mental anguish over those whom we love in Christ should be a natural part of our lives: "weep with them that weep" (Rom. 12:15). In fact, sharing in Christ's sufferings is a prerequisite for being glorified with Christ (Rom. 8:17). Response: we must thank God that just as the sufferings of Christ are ours, so also is His comfort (2 Cor. 1:5).

(6) God Himself may use suffering in our lives as a catalyst to spiritual growth or change. (a) He often uses suffering to call His straying people to repent of their sins and renew their faith and trust in Him (see the book of Judges). Response: we must confess known sin and examine our lives to see if there is anything that displeases the Holy Spirit. (b) God sometimes uses suffering to test our faith, to see whether we will remain faithful to Him. To test Job's faith was the reason He allowed Satan to afflict him (see Job 1:6–12; 2:1–6): would Job remain committed to the Lord, or would he curse God to His face? James calls the various trials we face "the trying of your faith" (Jas. 1:3; see 1:2, note); through them our faith in Christ becomes more mature (see Deut. 8:3, note; 1 Pet. 1:7, note). Response: we must realize that the genuineness of our faith will result in "praise and honour and glory at the appearing of Jesus Christ" (1 Pet. 1:7). (c) God uses suffering not only to strengthen our faith, but also to help us to grow in Christian character and righteousness. According to both Paul and James, God wants us to learn patience through suffering (Rom. 5:3–5; Jas. 1:3). In suffering we learn to depend less on ourselves and more on God and His grace (see Rom. 5:3, note; 2 Cor. 12:9, note). Response: we must be attuned to what God may want us to learn from our suffering. (d) God may also send us pain and affliction so that we might be better able to comfort and encourage other sufferers (see 2 Cor. 1:4, note). Thus the effectiveness of our ministry deepens and increases (2 Cor. 4:7–12; see 4:11–12, note). Response: we must use our experience of pain to encourage and strengthen other believers.

(7) Finally, God can and does use the suffering of the righteous to further the cause of His kingdom and His plan of redemption. For example, all the injustices that Joseph experienced at the hands of his brothers and the Egyptians were part of God's plan "to preserve you a posterity in the earth, and to save your lives by a great deliverance" (Gen. 45:7; see article on THE PROVIDENCE OF GOD, p. 80). The prime example of this principle is the suffering of Christ, "the Holy One and the Just" (Acts 3:14), who experienced persecution, agony, and death so that God's plan of salvation might be fully realized. This does not excuse the wickedness of those who crucified Him (Acts 2:23), but it does indicate how God can use the suffering of the righteous at the hands of sinful people for His own purposes and to His own glory.

GOD'S RELATIONSHIP TO THE SUFFERING OF BELIEVERS. (1) The first thing to remember is this: God is involved in our sufferings. Even though Satan is the god of this world, he is able to afflict our lives only by the permissive will of God (cf. Job 1—2; see articles on THE PROVIDENCE OF GOD, p. 80, and THE WILL OF GOD, p. 1060). God has promised in His Word that He will not allow us to be tried above what we are able to bear (1 Cor. 10:13).

(2) God has also promised to bring good out of all the sufferings and persecution of those who love Him and obey His commandments (see Rom. 8:28, note). Joseph recognized this truth in his own life of suffering (see Gen. 50:20), and the author of Hebrews

shows how God uses the painful parts of our lives for our growth and benefit (see Heb. 12:5, note).

(3) In addition, God has promised to stand by us in our pain, to walk with us "through the valley of the shadow of death" (Ps. 23:4; cf. Is. 43:2). He does so by His Holy Spirit, who comforts us in all our trouble (see 2 Cor. 1:4, note). To each one of His children He sends sufficient grace so that they can bear the trials of life (1 Cor. 10:13; see 2 Cor. 12:9, note).

(4) Finally, do not forget that the Lord Jesus shares your pain. When we pray to Him, we have a sympathetic high priest who Himself experienced the various dimensions of our trials and sufferings (Heb. 4:15). He has indeed "borne our griefs, and carried our sorrows" (Is. 53:4); there is healing for our own sufferings through the sufferings that He bore on our behalf (Is. 53:5).

VICTORY OVER PERSONAL SUFFERING. Now we must address an important issue: when experiencing trials and affliction, what steps can we take to cope with such suffering so as to be victorious over it? (1) First, consider the various reasons why human beings suffer (see section 1, above) and how those reasons apply to you. If you can identify a specific reason, then follow the appropriate response.

(2) Believe that God cares deeply for you, regardless of how severe your circumstances are (see Rom. 8:36, note; 2 Cor. 1:8–10, note; Jas. 5:11, note; 1 Pet. 5:7, note). Suffering should never lead you to deny God's love for you or to reject Him as your Lord and Savior.

(3) Turn to God in earnest prayer and seek His face. Wait upon Him until He delivers you from your affliction (see Ps. 27:8–14; 40:1–3; 130).

(4) Expect God to give you the grace that is necessary to bear your affliction until deliverance comes (1 Cor. 10:13; 2 Cor. 12:7–10). Always remember that "we are more than conquerors through him that loved us" (Rom. 8:37; cf. John 16:33). The Christian faith lies not in the removal of weakness and suffering, but in the manifestation of divine power through human weakness (see 2 Cor. 4:7, note).

(5) Read the Word of God, especially those psalms that give comfort in times of affliction (e.g., Ps. 11; 16; 23; 27; 40; 46; 61; 91; 121; 125; 138).

(6) Seek revelation and discernment from God regarding your particular situation—through prayer, the Scriptures, the enlightenment of the Holy Spirit, or the counsel of a godly and mature believer.

(7) If your suffering is physical in nature, follow the steps as outlined in the article on DIVINE HEALING, p. 1418.

(8) During the time of your suffering, remember the prediction of Christ that you will suffer trouble and affliction in your life as a believer (John 16:33). Look forward with eager anticipation to that time when "God shall wipe away all tears from their eyes; and there shall be no more death, neither sorrow, nor crying, neither shall there be any more pain" (Rev. 21:4).

which I was afraid of is come unto me.
26 I was not in safety, neither had
I rest, neither was I quiet; yet trouble
came.

The speech of Eliphaz

4 THEN ELIPHAZ the Temanite an-
swered and said,
2 *If* we assay [a]to commune with
thee, wilt thou be grieved? but [b]who
can withhold himself from speaking?
3 Behold, thou hast instructed
many, and thou [b]hast strengthened
the weak hands.
4 Thy words have upholden him
that was falling, and thou [c]hast
strengthened [d]the[c] feeble knees.
5 But now it is come upon thee, and
thou faintest; it toucheth thee, and
thou art troubled.
6 *Is* not *this* [e]thy fear, [f]thy confi-
dence, thy hope, and the uprightness of
thy ways?
7 Remember, I pray thee, [g]who
ever perished, being innocent? or
where were the righteous cut off?
8 Even as I have seen, [h]they that
plow iniquity, and sow wickedness,
reap the same.
9 By the blast of God they perish,
and [d]by the breath of his nostrils are
they consumed.
10 The roaring of the lion, and the
voice of the fierce lion, and [i]the teeth
of the young lions, are broken.
11 [j]The old lion perisheth for lack
of prey, and the stout lion's whelps are
scattered abroad.
12 Now a thing was [e]secretly
brought to me, and mine ear received
a little thereof.
13 [k]In thoughts from the visions of
the night, when deep sleep falleth on
men,
14 Fear [f]came upon me, and
[l]trembling, which made [g]all my
bones to shake.
15 Then a spirit passed before my
face; the hair of my flesh stood up:
16 It stood still, but I could not dis-
cern the form thereof: an image *was* be-
fore mine eyes, [h]*there was* silence, and
I heard a voice, *saying,*
17 Shall mortal man be more just
than God? shall a man be more pure
than his maker?
18 Behold, he [m]put no trust in his
servants; [i]and his angels he charged
with folly:
19 How much less *in* them that
dwell in houses of clay, whose founda-
tion *is* in the dust, *which* are crushed
before the moth?
20 [n]They are [j]destroyed from
morning to evening: they perish for
ever without any regarding *it.*
21 Doth not their excellency *which*
is in them go away? they die, even with-
out wisdom.

5 CALL NOW, if there be any that
will answer thee; and to which of
the saints wilt thou [k]turn?
2 For wrath killeth the foolish man,
and [l]envy slayeth the silly one.
3 [o]I have seen the foolish taking

4:3 [b]Is. 35:3
4:4 [c]Is. 35:3 [d]Heb. 12:12
4:6 [e]ch. 1:1 [f]Prov. 3:26
4:7 [g]Ps. 37:25
4:8 [h]Prov. 22:8
4:10 [i]Ps. 58:6
4:11 [j]Ps. 34:10
4:13 [k]ch. 33:15
4:14 [l]Hab. 3:16
4:18 [m]ch. 15:15
4:20 [n]Ps. 90:5,6
5:3 [o]Jer. 12:2,3

[a] Heb. *a word* [b] Heb. *who can refrain from words?* [c] Heb. *the bowing knees* [d] i.e. *by his anger* as Is. 30:33 [e] Heb. *by stealth* [f] Heb. *met me* [g] Heb. *the multitude of my bones* [h] Or, *I heard a still voice* [i] Or, *nor in his angels,* in whom *he put light* [j] Heb. *beaten in pieces* [k] Or, *look?* [l] Or, *indignation*

4:1 ELIPHAZ ... ANSWERED AND SAID. Ch. 4 begins the first of three major cycles of the dialogues of Job with Eliphaz, Bildad, and Zophar. When reading these dialogues, note the following: (1) Although the words of Job's three friends are recorded in Scripture, everything they said is not necessarily true. The Holy Spirit recorded their words, but did not inspire them. At the end of the book, God Himself stated that much of what they said was not right (42:7–8).

(2) Some of their statements are indeed true and are restated in the N.T. (e.g., part of what Eliphaz says in 5:13 is found in 1 Cor. 3:19).

(3) The basic theology and viewpoint of these counselors were defective. They believed (a) that the truly righteous will always prosper while sinners always suffer, and (b) conversely, that poverty and suffering always imply sinfulness, while prosperity and success imply righteousness. God later revealed that this attitude was in error and that their viewpoint was "folly" (42:7–9).

4:7 WHERE WERE THE RIGHTEOUS CUT OFF? The theology that the righteous will not perish and the wicked will be punished is true from an eternal viewpoint (see Gal. 6:7; Heb. 10:13). Ultimately, justice will be done. However, here on earth, so often just retribution does not occur and the innocent do suffer. Failure to recognize this truth was a fundamental error in the thinking of Eliphaz (e.g., Mat. 23:35; Luke 13:4–5; John 9:1–3; 1 Pet. 2:19–20).

4:13 VISIONS OF THE NIGHT. It is not said that Eliphaz's visions were from God. In fact, they were not from God, for they described Him as unconcerned about humankind (vv. 17–21). It is wrong to build theology on dreams and visions that cannot be supported by God's written revelation.

root: but suddenly I cursed his habitation.

4 His children are far from safety, and they are crushed in the gate, neither *is there* any to deliver *them.*

5 Whose harvest the hungry eateth up, and taketh it even out of the thorns, and the robber swalloweth up their substance.

6 Although [m]affliction cometh not forth of the dust, neither doth trouble spring out of the ground;

7 Yet man is born unto [n]trouble, as [o]the sparks fly upward.

8 I would seek unto God, and unto God would I commit my cause:

9 Which doeth great things [p]and unsearchable; marvellous things [q]without number:

10 Who giveth rain upon the earth, and sendeth waters upon the [r]fields:

11 [p]To set up on high those that be low; that those which mourn may be exalted to safety.

12 [q]He disappointeth the devices of the crafty, so that their hands [s]cannot perform *their* enterprise.

13 He taketh the wise in their own craftiness: and the counsel of the froward is carried headlong.

14 They [t]meet with darkness in the daytime, and grope in the noonday as in the night.

15 But [r]he saveth the poor from the sword, from their mouth, and from the hand of the mighty.

16 [s]So the poor hath hope, and iniquity stoppeth her mouth.

17 [t]Behold, happy *is* the man whom God correcteth: therefore despise not thou the chastening of the Almighty:

18 [u]For he maketh sore, and bindeth up: he woundeth, and his hands make whole.

19 [v]He shall deliver thee in six troubles: yea, in seven [w]there shall no evil touch thee.

5:11 [p]Ps. 113:7
5:12 [q]Neh. 4:15
5:15 [r]Ps. 35:10
5:16 [s]1 Sam. 2:8
5:17 [t]Ps. 94:12
5:18 [u]1 Sam. 2:6
5:19 [v]Ps. 34:19 [w]Ps. 91:10
5:20 [x]Ps. 33:19
5:21 [y]Ps. 31:20
5:22 [z]Is. 11:9
5:23 [a]Ps. 91:12
5:25 [b]Ps. 112:2 [c]Ps. 72:16
5:26 [d]Prov. 10:27
5:27 [e]Ps. 111:2
6:4 [f]Ps. 38:2 [g]Ps. 88:15

20 [x]In famine he shall redeem thee from death: and in war [u]from the power of the sword.

21 [y]Thou shalt be hid [v]from the scourge of the tongue: neither shalt thou be afraid of destruction when it cometh.

22 At destruction and famine thou shalt laugh: [z]neither shalt thou be afraid of the beasts of the earth.

23 [a]For thou shalt be in league with the stones of the field: and the beasts of the field shall be at peace with thee.

24 And thou shalt know [w]that thy tabernacle *shall be* in peace; and thou shalt visit thy habitation, and shalt not [x]sin.

25 Thou shalt know also that [b]thy seed *shall be* [y]great, and thine offspring [c]as the grass of the earth.

26 [d]Thou shalt come to *thy* grave in a full age, like as a shock of corn [z]cometh in in his season.

27 Lo this, we have [e]searched it, so it *is;* hear it, and know thou *it* [a]for thy good.

Job's reply

6 BUT JOB answered and said,

2 Oh that my grief were thoroughly weighed, and my calamity [b]laid in the balances together!

3 For now it would be heavier than the sand of the sea: therefore [c]my words are swallowed up.

4 [f]For the arrows of the Almighty *are* within me, the poison whereof drinketh up my spirit: [g]the terrors of

[m] Or, *iniquity* [n] Or, *labour* [o] Heb. *the sons of the burning coal lift up to fly* [p] Heb. *and* there is *no search* [q] Heb. *till* there be *no number* [r] Heb. *outplaces* [s] Or, *cannot perform any thing* [t] Or, *run into* [u] Heb. *from the hands* [v] Or, *when the tongue scourgeth* [w] Or, *that peace is thy tabernacle* [x] Or, *err* [y] Or, *much* [z] Heb. *ascendeth* [a] Heb. *for thyself* [b] Heb. *lifted up* [c] i.e. *I want words to express my grief*

5:17–27 THE MAN WHOM GOD CORRECTETH. To Eliphaz, if God reproves a person and he or she responds rightly, then God will deliver that individual from all adversity and trouble. (1) This mistaken idea is contradicted by the author of Hebrews, who declares that some of the greatest O.T. heroes of faith were persecuted, tempted, destitute, afflicted, ill-treated, and even put to death. These righteous people never received total deliverance in this life (Heb. 11:36–39). (2) The Bible nowhere teaches that God will eliminate from our lives all trouble and suffering. Godly people are not always rescued in this life.

6:4 THE ARROWS OF THE ALMIGHTY *ARE* WITHIN ME. Job recognized that his suffering ultimately came from God, or at least with His knowledge and permission. His greatest anguish was this: God seemed to be against him and he did not know why. When you experience hardship while sincerely endeavoring to please God, you must not give in to the thought that God has ceased to be concerned for you. You may not know why God is allowing such things to happen, but

God do set themselves in array against me.

5 Doth the wild ass bray [d]when he hath grass? or loweth the ox over his fodder?

6 Can that which is unsavoury be eaten without salt? or is there *any* taste in the white of an egg?

7 The things *that* my soul refused to touch *are* as my sorrowful meat.

8 Oh that I might have my request; and that God would grant *me* [e]the thing that I long for!

9 Even that it would please God to destroy me; that he would let loose his hand, and cut me off!

10 Then should I yet have comfort; yea, I would harden myself in sorrow: let him not spare; for [h]I have not concealed the words of [i]the Holy One.

11 What *is* my strength, that I should hope? and what *is* mine end, that I should prolong my life?

12 *Is* my strength the strength of stones? or *is* my flesh [f]of brass?

13 *Is* not my help in me? and is wisdom driven quite from me?

14 [j]To[g] him that is afflicted pity *should be shown* from his friend; but he forsaketh the fear of the Almighty.

15 [k]My brethren have dealt deceitfully as a brook, *and* [l]as the stream of brooks they pass away;

16 Which are blackish by reason of the ice, *and* wherein the snow is hid:

17 What time they wax warm, [h]they vanish: [i]when it is hot, they are [j]consumed out of their place.

18 The paths of their way are turned aside; they go to nothing, and perish.

19 The troops of [m]Tema looked, the companies of [n]Sheba waited for them.

20 They were [o]confounded because they had hoped; they came thither, and were ashamed.

21 [k]For now [p]ye are [l]nothing; ye see *my* casting down, and [q]are afraid.

22 Did I say, Bring unto me? or, Give a reward for me of your substance?

23 Or, Deliver me from the enemy's hand? or, Redeem me from the hand of the mighty?

24 Teach me, and I will hold my tongue: and cause me to understand wherein I have erred.

25 How forcible are right words! but what doth your arguing reprove?

26 Do ye imagine to reprove words, and the speeches of one that is desperate, *which are* as wind?

27 Yea, [m]ye overwhelm the fatherless, and ye [r]dig *a pit* for your friend.

28 Now therefore be content, look upon me; for *it is* [n]evident unto you if I lie.

29 [s]Return, I pray you, let it not be iniquity; yea, return again, my righteousness *is* [o]in it.

30 Is there iniquity in my tongue? cannot [p]my taste discern perverse things?

7 *IS THERE* not [t]an[q] appointed time to man upon earth? *are not* his days also like the days of an hireling?

2 As a servant [r]earnestly desireth the shadow, and as an hireling looketh for *the reward of* his work:

3 So am I made to possess [u]months of vanity, and wearisome nights are appointed to me.

4 [v]When I lie down, I say, When shall I arise, and [s]the night be gone? and I am full of tossings to and fro unto the dawning of the day.

5 My flesh is [w]clothed with worms and clods of dust; my skin is broken, and become loathsome.

6 [x]My days are swifter than a

6:10 [h]Acts 20:20 [i]Lev. 19:2 Is. 57:15
6:14 [j]Prov. 17:17
6:15 [k]Ps. 38:11 [l]Jer. 15:18
6:19 [m]Gen. 25:15 [n]Ps. 72:10
6:20 [o]Jer. 14:3
6:21 [p]ch. 13:4 [q]Ps. 38:11
6:27 [r]Ps. 57:6
6:29 [s]ch. 17:10
7:1 [t]ch. 14:5
7:3 [u]ch. 29:2
7:4 [v]Deut. 28:67
7:5 [w]Is. 14:11
7:6 [x]ch. 9:25

[d] Heb. *at grass* [e] Heb. *my expectation* [f] Heb. *brasen?* [g] Heb. *To him that melteth* [h] Heb. *they are cut off* [i] Heb. *in the heat thereof* [j] Heb. *extinguished* [k] Or, *For now ye are like to them* Heb. *to it* [l] Heb. *not* [m] Heb. *ye cause to fall upon* [n] Heb. *before your face* [o] i.e. *in this matter* [p] Heb. *my palate* [q] Or, a *warfare* [r] Heb. *gapeth after* [s] Heb. *the evening be measured?*

you can know (as did Job) that in the end God Himself will strengthen and establish you, bringing you forth victorious (cf. Rom. 8:35–39; Jas. 5:11; 1 Pet. 5:10).

6:10 I HAVE NOT CONCEALED THE WORDS OF THE HOLY ONE. In all his suffering, Job's consolation was that he did not turn from his Lord, nor did he "conceal" (i.e., deny) God's words. Unaware of any conscious or inadvertent sins, he affirmed his innocence throughout the book (see 16:17; 27:6), convinced that he had always sought to honor and obey God. Therefore he could rejoice, even in his pain.

7:1 JOB ADDRESSES GOD. Job turned from his friends, who did not seem to understand, and prayed instead to his Lord. Job's greatest concern throughout all his discourses was with God. Even when he spoke about God in the third person, he was always conscious of His presence. Job's heart never turned from the God he loved.

weaver's shuttle, and are spent without hope.

7 O remember that [y]my life *is* wind: mine eye [t]shall no more [u]see good.

8 [z]The eye of him that hath seen me shall see me no *more:* thine eyes *are* upon me, and [v]I *am* not.

9 *As* the cloud is consumed and vanisheth away: so [a]he that goeth down to the grave shall come up no *more.*

10 He shall return no more to his house, [b]neither shall his place know him any more.

11 Therefore I will [c]not refrain my mouth; I will speak in the anguish of my spirit; I will [d]complain in the bitterness of my soul.

12 *Am* I a sea, or a whale, that thou settest a watch over me?

13 [e]When I say, My bed shall comfort me, my couch shall ease my complaint;

14 Then thou scarest me with dreams, and terrifiest me through visions:

15 So that my soul chooseth strangling, *and* death rather [w]than my life.

16 [f]I loathe *it;* I would not live always: [g]let me alone; for [h]my days *are* vanity.

17 [i]What *is* man, that thou shouldest magnify him? and that thou shouldest set thine heart upon him?

18 And *that* thou shouldest visit him every morning, *and* try him every moment?

19 How long wilt thou not depart from me, nor let me alone till I swallow down my spittle?

20 I have sinned; what shall I do unto thee, [j]O thou preserver of men? why [k]hast thou set me as a mark against thee, so that I am a burden to myself?

21 And why dost thou not pardon my transgression, and take away mine iniquity? for now shall I sleep in the dust; and thou shalt seek me in the morning, but I *shall* not *be.*

The speech of Bildad

8 THEN ANSWERED Bildad the Shuhite, and said,

2 How long wilt thou speak these *things?* and *how long shall* the words of thy mouth *be like* a strong wind?

3 [l]Doth God pervert judgment? or doth the Almighty pervert justice?

4 If [m]thy children have sinned against him, and he have cast them away [x]for their transgression;

5 [n]If thou wouldest seek unto God betimes, and make thy supplication to the Almighty;

6 If thou *wert* pure and upright;

7:7 [y]Ps. 78:39
7:8 [z]ch. 20:9
7:9 [a]2 Sam. 12:23
7:10 [b]ch. 8:18
7:11 [c]Ps. 39:1,9 [d]1 Sam. 1:10
7:13 [e]ch. 9:27
7:16 [f]ch. 10:1 [g]ch. 14:6 [h]Ps. 62:9
7:17 [i]Ps. 8:4
7:20 [j]Ps. 36:6 [k]Ps. 21:12 Lam. 3:12
8:3 [l]Gen. 18:25
8:4 [m]ch. 1:5,18
8:5 [n]ch. 11:13

[t]Heb. *shall not return* [u]*to see,* i.e. *to enjoy* [v]i.e. *I can live no longer* [w]Heb. *than my bones* [x]Heb. *in the hand of their transgression*

7:11 THE ANGUISH OF MY SPIRIT. Job often spoke of the anguish and bitterness of his spirit and soul (cf. 10:1; 27:2). He had become a man who suffered deeply in every aspect of life. (1) Physically he had lost wealth, children, and health (1:13–19; 2:7–8). (2) Socially he was alienated from his friends and family (2:7–8; 19:13–19). He was scorned by the public (16:10; 30:1–10) and betrayed by his closest friends (6:14–23). (3) Spiritually he felt forsaken by God, believing that the Lord had turned against him (vv. 17–19; 6:4). (4) Afflicted in every possible way, Job underwent a wide range of emotions: anxiety (vv. 4,13–14), uncertainty (9:20), rejection and betrayal (10:3; 12:4), fear (6:4; 9:28), loneliness (19:13–19), and despair that led to a desire for death (ch. 3).

7:16 LET ME ALONE. Job spoke honestly to God about his feelings of unfairness, rejection, and doubt. He even wished that God would leave him alone (vv. 16–19), though at other times he yearned for God to speak with him (14:15; 23:3,5). The faithful who are undergoing severe trials and suffering should express their feelings openly to God in prayer. Speaking from the heart to God about our anguish and bitterness in an attitude of submission is not wrong. Hannah poured out her soul before the Lord because of great concern and provocation (1 Sam. 1:13–16). Jesus Himself offered up "prayers and supplications with strong crying and tears" (Heb. 5:7), and at His death experienced the indescribable darkness of separation from God (Mat. 27:46).

7:20 I HAVE SINNED. Job considered the possibility that his counselors were right, that God had loosed His anger toward him because of some unknown transgression. What Job did not know was that God was indeed watching, not in displeasure, but in compassion and admiration. Though tempted to the limit, Job consistently refused to curse God (cf. 2:9), and thus the redemptive power of God was exalted. In due time, when the test was finished, God revealed His approval publicly (42:8).

8:6 IF THOU *WERT* PURE AND UPRIGHT. The argument of Bildad was essentially the same as Eliphaz's. If Job were really upright, he would be vindicated by God. Job was not vindicated by God; therefore, he must be wicked. Bildad based his argument on his belief that because God was just, He would not bring trouble upon a righteous individual (vv. 3–4,20). Bildad's error was exposed later by God Himself (42:7–8)—and ulti-

surely now he would awake for thee, and make the habitation of thy righteousness prosperous.

7 Though thy beginning was small, yet thy latter end should greatly increase.

8 [o]For inquire, I pray thee, of the former age, and prepare thyself to the search of their fathers:

9 (For [p]we *are but of* yesterday, and know [y]nothing, because our days upon earth *are* a shadow:)

10 Shall not they teach thee, *and* tell thee, and utter words out of their heart?

11 Can the rush grow up without mire? can the flag grow without water?

12 [q]Whilst it *is* yet in his greenness, *and* not cut down, it withereth before any *other* herb.

13 So *are* the paths of all that forget God; and the [r]hypocrite's hope shall perish:

14 Whose hope shall be cut off, and whose trust *shall be* [s]a[z] spider's web.

15 [t]He shall lean upon his house, but it shall not stand: he shall hold it fast, but it shall not endure.

16 He *is* green before the sun, and his branch shooteth forth in his garden.

17 His roots are wrapped about the heap, *and* seeth the place of stones.

18 [u]If he destroy him from his place, then *it* shall deny him, *saying,* I have not seen thee.

19 Behold, this *is* the joy of his way, and [v]out of the earth shall others grow.

20 Behold, God will not cast away a perfect *man,* neither will he [a]help the evil doers:

21 Till he fill thy mouth with laughing, and thy lips with [b]rejoicing.

22 They that hate thee shall be [w]clothed with shame; and the dwellingplace of the wicked [c]shall come to nought.

8:8 [o]Deut. 4:32
8:9 [p]Gen. 47:9 1 Chr. 29:15 ch. 7:6
8:12 [q]Ps. 129:6 Jer. 17:6
8:13 [r]ch. 11:20 Prov. 10:28
8:14 [s]Is. 59:5,6
8:15 [t]ch. 27:18
8:18 [u]ch. 7:10 Ps. 37:36
8:19 [v]Ps. 113:7
8:22 [w]Ps. 35:26 & 109:29

Job's reply

9 THEN JOB answered and said,
2 I know *it is* so of a truth: but how should [x]man be just [d]with God?

3 If he will contend with him, he cannot answer him one of a thousand.

4 [y]*He is* wise in heart, and mighty in strength: who hath hardened *himself* against him, and hath prospered?

5 Which removeth the mountains, and they know not: which overturneth them in his anger.

6 Which [z]shaketh the earth out of her place, and [a]the pillars thereof tremble.

7 Which commandeth the sun, and it riseth not; and sealeth up the stars.

8 [b]Which alone spreadeth out the heavens, and treadeth upon the [e]waves of the sea.

9 [c]Which maketh [f]Arcturus, Orion, and Pleiades, and the chambers of the south.

10 [d]Which doeth great things past finding out; yea, and wonders without number.

11 [e]Lo, he goeth by me, and I see *him* not: he passeth on also, but I perceive him not.

12 [f]Behold, he taketh away, [g]who[g] can hinder him? who will say unto him, What doest thou?

13 *If* God will not withdraw his anger, [h]the [h]proud helpers do stoop under him.

14 How much less shall I answer him, *and* choose out my words *to reason* with him?

15 [i]Whom, though I were righteous, *yet* would I not answer, *but* I would make supplication to my judge.

16 If I had called, and he had answered me; *yet* would I not believe that he had hearkened unto my voice.

9:2 [x]Ps. 143:2 Rom. 3:20
9:4 [y]ch. 36:5
9:6 [z]Is. 2:19,21 Hag. 2:6 Heb. 12:26 [a]ch. 26:11
9:8 [b]Gen. 1:6 Ps. 104:2,3
9:9 [c]Gen. 1:16 Amos 5:8
9:10 [d]Ps. 71:15
9:11 [e]ch. 23:8,9
9:12 [f]Is. 45:9 Jer. 18:6 Rom. 9:20 [g]ch. 11:10
9:13 [h]ch. 26:12
9:15 [i]ch. 10:15

[y] Heb. *not* [z] Heb. *a spider's house* [a] Heb. *take the ungodly by the hand* [b] Heb. *shouting for joy* [c] Heb. *shall not be* [d] Or, *before God?* [e] Heb. *heights* [f] Heb. *Ash, Cesil, and Cimah* [g] Heb. *who can turn him away?* [h] Heb. *helpers of pride,* or, *strength*

mately in the crucifixion of Christ, when God delivered His own Son over to suffering and death (Mat. 27:31–50).

9:2 HOW SHOULD MAN BE JUST WITH GOD? In ch. 9 Job acknowledged that he could not be perfectly righteous before God. He understood that by nature he was inclined toward self and sin and that he was not faultless in God's sight (cf. 7:21). Yet, with all his heart and soul he had resisted evil and turned from it (1:1,8; 2:3). He was confident he had not sinned greatly and thus did not deserve such suffering (6:24; 7:20). Thus Job complained that God had punished him without cause (vv. 16–20). Yet his faith still held firm, for he persisted in calling on God (see 10:2,8–12; cf. Jas. 5:11). He did not curse God as Satan predicted he would (1:11; 2:5), although he did speak words he would later regret (vv. 17,20,22–23,30–31; 42:3–6).

17 For he breaketh me with a tempest, and multiplieth my wounds [j]without cause.

18 He will not suffer me to take my breath, but filleth me with bitterness.

19 If *I speak* of strength, lo, *he is* strong: and if of judgment, who shall set me a time *to plead?*

20 If I justify myself, mine own mouth shall condemn me: *if I say,* I *am* perfect, it shall also prove me perverse.

21 *Though* I *were* perfect, *yet* would I not know my soul: I would despise my life.

22 This *is* one *thing,* therefore I said *it,* [k]He destroyeth the perfect and the wicked.

23 If the scourge slay suddenly, he will laugh at the trial of the innocent.

24 The earth is given into the hand of the wicked: he covereth the faces of the judges thereof; if not, where, *and* who *is* he?

25 Now [l]my days are swifter than a post: they flee away, they see no good.

26 They are passed away as the [i][j]swift ships: [m]as the eagle *that* hasteth to the prey.

27 [n]If I say, I will forget my complaint, I will leave off my heaviness, and comfort *myself:*

28 [o]I am afraid of all my sorrows, I know that thou [p]wilt not hold me innocent.

29 *If* I be wicked, why then labour I in vain?

30 [q]If I wash myself with snow water, and make my hands never so clean;

31 Yet shalt thou plunge me in the ditch, and mine own clothes shall [k]abhor me.

32 For [r]*he is* not a man, as I *am, that* I should answer him, *and* we should come together in judgment.

33 [s]Neither is there [l]any [m]daysman betwixt us, *that* might lay his hand upon us both.

34 [t]Let him take his rod away from me, and let not his fear terrify me:

35 *Then* would I speak, and not fear him; [n]but *it is* not so with me.

10 MY [u]SOUL is [o]weary of my life; I will leave my complaint upon myself; [v]I will speak in the bitterness of my soul.

2 I will say unto God, Do not condemn me; show me wherefore thou contendest with me.

3 *Is it* good unto thee that thou shouldest oppress, that thou shouldest despise [p]the work of thine hands, and shine upon the counsel of the wicked?

4 Hast thou eyes of flesh? or [w]seest thou as man seeth?

5 *Are* thy days as the days of man? *are* thy years as man's days,

6 That thou inquirest after mine iniquity, and searchest after my sin?

7 [q]Thou knowest that I am not wicked; and *there is* none that can deliver out of thine hand.

8 [x]Thine hands [r]have made me and fashioned me together round about; yet thou dost destroy me.

9 Remember, I beseech thee, that [y]thou hast made me as the clay; and wilt thou bring me into dust again?

9:17 [j]ch. 2:3
9:22 [k]Eccl. 9:2,3 Ezek. 21:3
9:25 [l]ch. 7:6,7
9:26 [m]Hab. 1:8
9:27 [n]ch. 7:13
9:28 [o]Ps. 119:120 [p]Ex. 20:7
9:30 [q]Jer. 2:22
9:32 [r]Eccl. 6:10 Is. 45:9 Rom. 9:20
9:33 [s]1 Sam. 2:25
9:34 [t]ch. 13:20 Ps. 39:10
10:1 [u]1 Ki. 19:4 Jonah 4:3 [v]ch. 7:11
10:4 [w]1 Sam. 16:7
10:8 [x]Ps. 119:73
10:9 [y]Gen. 2:7 Is. 64:8

[i]Heb. *ships of desire* [j]Or, *ships of Fbeh* [k]Or, *make me to be abhorred* [l]Heb. *one that should argue* [m]Or, *umpire* [n]Heb. *but I* am *not so with myself* [o]Or, *cut off while I live* [p]Heb. *the labour of thine hands* [q]Heb. It is *upon thy knowledge* [r]Heb. *took pains about me*

9:17 MULTIPLIETH WOUNDS WITHOUT CAUSE. The most difficult thing for Job to accept was God's continuing silence in the midst of a painful situation that seemed to have no purpose. God will sometimes allow us to pass through a dark time of trial when He Himself remains silent and seemingly far away. Yet even in the midst of the darkness of God's silence, He has a plan for our lives, and we must continue to trust Him.

9:33 NEITHER IS THERE ANY DAYSMAN BETWIXT US. Job saw the need for a mediator who could lay one hand on him and the other hand on God and bring them together. Jesus Christ became such a Mediator, for by His death and resurrection He restores us to fellowship with God (1 Tim. 2:5; Heb. 9:15).

10:1 I WILL SPEAK IN THE BITTERNESS OF MY SOUL. In ch. 10 Job continued pouring out to God his bitterness and feelings of being treated unfairly. But even though Job felt God had withdrawn His love from him, he still maintained a trust in God's justice and continued to wrestle with God for a solution to his dilemma.

10:2 SHOW ME WHEREFORE THOU CONTENDEST WITH ME. In none of the prayers of Job did he pray for healing of his body. Job's greatest concern was the "why" of his suffering and of God's apparent abandonment of His servant; to know this was more important to Job than his actual adversity. Being accepted by God as one of His own, even in adversity, was the most critical thing in his life.

10 [z]Hast thou not poured me out
as milk, and curdled me like cheese?
11 Thou hast clothed me with skin
and flesh, and hast [s]fenced me with
bones and sinews.
12 Thou hast granted me life and fa-
vour, and thy visitation hath preserved
my spirit.
13 And these *things* hast thou hid in
thine heart: I know that this *is* with
thee.
14 If I sin, then [a]thou markest me,
and thou wilt not acquit me from mine
iniquity.
15 If I be wicked, [b]woe unto me;
[c]and *if* I be righteous, *yet* will I not
lift up my head. *I am* full of con-
fusion; therefore [d]see thou mine af-
fliction;
16 For it increaseth. [e]Thou hunt-
est me as a fierce lion: and again thou
showest thyself marvellous upon me.
17 Thou renewest [f]thy[t] wit-
nesses against me, and increasest
thine indignation upon me; changes
and war *are* against me.
18 [g]Wherefore then hast thou
brought me forth out of the womb? Oh
that I had given up the ghost, and no
eye had seen me!
19 I should have been as though I
had not been; I should have been car-
ried from the womb to the grave.
20 [h]*Are* not my days few? cease
then, and [i]let me alone, that I may
take comfort a little,
21 Before I go *whence* I shall not re-
turn, [j]*even* to the land of darkness
[k]and the shadow of death;
22 A land of darkness, as darkness
itself; and of the shadow of death, with-
out any order, and *where* the light *is* as
darkness.

10:10 [z]Ps. 139:14-16
10:14 [a]Ps. 139:1
10:15 [b]Is. 3:11 [c]ch. 9:12,15 [d]Ps. 25:18
10:16 [e]Is. 38:13 Lam. 3:10
10:17 [f]Ruth 1:21
10:18 [g]ch. 3:11
10:20 [h]Ps. 39:5 [i]ch. 7:16,19
10:21 [j]Ps. 88:12 [k]Ps. 23:4

11:4 [l]ch. 6:30
11:6 [m]Ezra 9:13
11:7 [n]Eccl. 3:11
11:10 [o]ch. 9:12 Rev. 3:7
11:11 [p]Ps. 10:14
11:12 [q]Rom. 1:22
11:13 [r]1 Sam. 7:3 [s]Ps. 88:9

The speech of Zophar

11 THEN ANSWERED Zophar the
Naamathite, and said,
2 Should not the multitude of words
be answered? and should [u]a man full
of talk be justified?
3 Should thy [v]lies make men hold
their peace? and when thou mockest,
shall no man make thee ashamed?
4 For [l]thou hast said, My doctrine
is pure, and I am clean in thine eyes.
5 But oh that God would speak, and
open his lips against thee;
6 And that he would show thee the
secrets of wisdom, that *they are* double
to that which is! Know therefore that
[m]God exacteth of thee *less* than thine
iniquity *deserveth*.
7 [n]Canst thou by searching find
out God? canst thou find out the Al-
mighty unto perfection?
8 *It is* [w]as high as heaven; what
canst thou do? deeper than hell; what
canst thou know?
9 The measure thereof *is* longer
than the earth, and broader than the
sea.
10 [o]If he [x]cut off, and shut up, or
gather together, then [y]who can hin-
der him?
11 For [p]he knoweth vain men: he
seeth wickedness also; will he not then
consider *it?*
12 For [q]vain[z] man would be wise,
though man be born *like* a wild ass's
colt.
13 If thou [r]prepare thine heart,
and [s]stretch out thine hands toward
him;

[s]Heb. *hedged* [t]i.e. *thy plagues* [u]Heb. *a man of lips* [v]Or, *devices* [w]Heb. *the heights of heaven* [x]Or, *make a change* [y]Heb. *who can turn him away?* [z]Heb. *empty*

10:16 THOU HUNTEST ME AS A FIERCE LION. Because Job was experiencing severe affliction, he felt God was against him. The N.T. provides a more complete revelation about hardship, with the result that the believer can even glory in suffering. (1) Paul wrote to the Corinthians, "We were pressed out of measure, above strength, insomuch that we despaired even of life" (2 Cor. 1:8). Yet in his affliction the apostle blessed God because His presence and Spirit were with him to comfort him (2 Cor. 1:3–4,22). The foremost glory of Paul's suffering, however, was that in some way he was sharing "the sufferings of Christ" (2 Cor. 1:5; cf. 4:10; Phil. 3:10; Col. 1:24; 1 Pet. 4:13).

(2) All the great saints of God have experienced the Scriptural truth that being one with God and His kingdom and being committed to His ways and standards do not necessarily entail deliverance *from* earthly suffering, but deliverance *for* earthly suffering with Christ (see Heb. 13:12–13; Jas. 5:10–11; 1 Pet. 2:21; 4:1).

11:1 ZOPHAR. Zophar harshly accused Job of self-righteousness (vv. 4–6) and stubbornness (vv. 13–20), telling him that he deserved to suffer even more than he had (v. 6). He maintained that if Job would turn from sin, his sufferings would immediately cease, and security, prosperity, and happiness would return (vv. 13–19). Zophar's speech contained serious theological error. The Bible nowhere guarantees a life "clearer than the noonday" (v. 17) for the faithful believer. Rather "we must through much tribulation enter into the kingdom of God" (Acts 14:22).

14 If iniquity *be* in thine hand, put it far away, and [t]let not wickedness dwell in thy tabernacles.

15 [u]For then shalt thou lift up thy face without spot; yea, thou shalt be stedfast, and shalt not fear:

16 Because thou shalt [v]forget *thy* misery, *and* remember *it* as waters *that* pass away:

17 And *thine* age [w]shall[a] be clearer than the noonday; thou shalt shine forth, thou shalt be as the morning.

18 And thou shalt be secure, because there is hope; yea, thou shalt dig *about thee, and* [x]thou shalt take thy rest in safety.

19 Also thou shalt lie down, and none shall make *thee* afraid; yea, many shall [b]make suit unto thee.

20 But [y]the eyes of the wicked shall fail, and [c]they shall not escape, and [z]their hope *shall be as* [d]the giving up of the ghost.

Job's reply

12 AND JOB answered and said,

2 No doubt but ye *are* the people, and wisdom shall die with you.

3 But I have [e]understanding as well as you; [f]I *am* not inferior to you: yea, [g]who knoweth not such things as these?

4 [a]I am *as* one mocked of his neighbour, who [b]calleth upon God, and he answereth him: the just upright *man is* laughed to scorn.

5 [c]He that is ready to slip with *his* feet *is as* a lamp despised in the thought of him that is at ease.

6 [d]The tabernacles of robbers prosper, and they that provoke God are secure; into whose hand God bringeth *abundantly*.

7 But ask now the beasts, and they shall teach thee; and the fowls of the air, and they shall tell thee:

8 Or speak to the earth, and it shall teach thee: and the fishes of the sea shall declare unto thee.

9 Who knoweth not in all these that the hand of the LORD hath wrought this?

10 In whose hand *is* the [h]soul of every living thing, and the breath of [i]all mankind.

11 Doth not the ear try words? and the [e]mouth[j] taste his meat?

12 With the ancient *is* wisdom; and in length of days understanding.

13 [k]With him *is* wisdom and strength, he hath counsel and understanding.

14 Behold, he breaketh down, and it cannot be built again: he shutteth [l]up a man, and there can be no opening.

15 Behold, he [f]withholdeth the waters, and they dry up: also he [g]sendeth them out, and they overturn the earth.

16 With him *is* strength and wisdom: the deceived and the deceiver *are* his.

17 He leadeth counsellors away spoiled, and maketh the judges fools.

18 He looseth the bond of kings, and girdeth their loins with a girdle.

11:14 [t]Ps. 101:3 **11:15** [u]ch. 22:26 Ps. 119:6 1 John 3:21 **11:16** [v]Is. 65:16 **11:17** [w]Ps. 37:6 Prov. 4:18 Is. 58:8,10 **11:18** [x]Lev. 26:5,6 Ps. 3:5 Prov. 3:24 **11:20** [y]Lev. 26:16 Deut. 28:65 [z]ch. 18:14 Prov. 11:7 **12:4** [a]ch. 21:3 [b]Ps. 91:15 **12:5** [c]Prov. 14:2 **12:6** [d]Jer. 12:1 Mal. 3:15 **12:11** [e]ch. 6:30 **12:15** [f]1 Ki. 8:35 [g]Gen. 7:11

[a] Heb. *shall arise above the noonday* [b] Heb. *entreat thy face* [c] Heb. *flight shall perish from them* [d] Or, *a puff of breath* [e] Heb. *an heart* [f] Heb. *I fall not lower than you* [g] Heb. *with whom are not such as these?* [h] Or, *life* [i] Heb. *all flesh of man* [j] Heb. *palate* [k] i.e. *With God* [l] Heb. *upon*

12:5 DESPISED IN THE THOUGHT OF HIM THAT IS AT EASE. Job condemned the way prosperous people often think. In contempt they look down on the poor and needy and justify their lack of sympathy by assuming that the unfortunate have brought adversity on themselves. At the same time the prosperous are "at ease" with their own lifestyle because they believe God has rewarded them for their faith and righteousness. Both assumptions are erroneous, for there are numerous exceptions among those who are citizens of the kingdom of God.

12:13 WITH HIM *IS* WISDOM. We must believe that God is wise and powerful and that His ways with us are the best and the surest means of attaining our highest good (cf. 9:4; 36:5; Is. 40:26, 28; Dan. 2:20; Rom. 16:25,27; see Rom. 8:28, note). (1) The believer must never think that God has promised a trouble-free life (cf. Ps. 34:19). God may send both joy and sorrow in order to detach our love from the things of this world and attach it to Himself.

(2) God directs events in a committed believer's life for the purpose of personal sanctification and the fulfilling of his or her service in the kingdom of God (cf. Jacob in Gen. 28—35; Joseph in Gen. 37:28, see note; see article on THE PROVIDENCE OF GOD, p. 80).

(3) In this life believers can never completely discern the ultimate purpose of everything that happens to them, nor will it always be perfectly clear how God is causing all things to work together for good (Eccl. 3:11; 7:13; 11:5; Rom. 8:28). During those times when we cannot fully understand God's method of dealing with us, we should commit ourselves to our heavenly Father, just as Christ did on the day of His crucifixion (cf. Mat. 27:46; Luke 23:46).

19 He leadeth princes away spoiled, and overthroweth the mighty.

20 [h]He removeth away [m]the speech of the trusty, and taketh away the understanding of the aged.

21 [i]He poureth contempt upon princes, and [n]weakeneth the strength of the mighty.

22 He discovereth deep things out of darkness, and bringeth out to light the shadow of death.

23 [j]He increaseth the nations, and destroyeth them: he enlargeth the nations, and [o]straiteneth them *again*.

24 He taketh away the heart of the chief of the people of the earth, and [k]causeth them to wander in a wilderness *where there is* no way.

25 [l]They grope in the dark without light, and he maketh them to [m]stagger[p] like *a* drunken *man*.

13 LO, MINE eye hath seen all *this,* mine ear hath heard and understood it.

2 [n]What ye know, *the same* do I know also: I *am* not inferior unto you.

3 [o]Surely I would speak to the Almighty, and I desire to reason with God.

4 But ye *are* forgers of lies, [p]ye *are* all physicians of no value.

5 O that ye would altogether hold your peace! and [q]it should be your wisdom.

6 Hear now my reasoning, and hearken to the pleadings of my lips.

7 [r]Will ye speak wickedly for God? and talk deceitfully for him?

8 Will ye accept his person? will ye contend for God?

9 Is it good that he should search you out? or as one man mocketh another, do ye *so* mock him?

10 He will surely reprove you, if ye do secretly accept persons.

11 Shall not his excellency make you afraid? and his dread fall upon you?

12 Your remembrances *are* like unto ashes, your bodies to bodies of clay.

13 [q]Hold your peace, let me alone, that I may speak, and let come on me what *will.*

14 Wherefore [s]do I take my flesh in my teeth, and put my life in mine hand?

15 [t]Though he slay me, yet will I trust in him: [u]but I will [r]maintain mine own ways before him. Ps. 46

16 He also *shall be* my salvation: for an hypocrite shall not come before him.

17 Hear diligently my speech, and my declaration with your ears.

18 Behold now, I have ordered *my* cause; I know that I shall be justified.

19 [v]Who *is* he *that* will plead with me? for now, if I hold my tongue, I shall give up the ghost.

20 [w]Only do not two *things* unto me: then will I not hide myself from thee.

21 [x]Withdraw thine hand far from me: and let not thy dread make me afraid.

22 Then call thou, and I will answer: or let me speak, and answer thou me.

23 How many *are* mine iniquities and sins? make me to know my transgression and my sin.

24 [y]Wherefore hidest thou thy face, and [z]holdest me for thine enemy?

25 [a]Wilt thou break a leaf driven to and fro? and wilt thou pursue the dry stubble?

26 For thou writest bitter things against me, and [b]makest me to possess the iniquities of my youth.

27 [c]Thou puttest my feet also in the stocks, and [s]lookest narrowly unto all my paths; thou settest a print upon the [t]heels of my feet.

28 And he, as a rotten thing, consumeth, as a garment that is motheaten.

12:20 [h]ch. 32:9
12:21 [i]Ps. 107:40 Dan. 2:21
12:23 [j]Ps. 107:38 Is. 9:3
12:24 [k]Ps. 107:4
12:25 [l]ch. 5:14 [m]Ps. 107:27
13:2 [n]ch. 12:3
13:3 [o]ch. 23:3
13:4 [p]ch. 6:21
13:5 [q]Prov. 17:28
13:7 [r]ch. 36:4
13:14 [s]ch. 18:4
13:15 [t]Ps. 23:4 Prov. 14:32 [u]ch. 27:5
13:19 [v]Is. 50:8
13:20 [w]ch. 9:34
13:21 [x]Ps. 39:10
13:24 [y]Deut. 32:20 Is. 8:17 [z]Deut. 32:42 ch. 16:9 Lam. 2:5
13:25 [a]Is. 42:3
13:26 [b]ch. 20:11 Ps. 25:7
13:27 [c]ch. 33:11

[m] Heb. *the lip of the faithful* [n] Or, *looseth the girdle of the strong* [o] Heb. *leadeth in* [p] Heb. *wander* [q] Heb. *Be silent from me* [r] Heb. *prove,* or, *argue* [s] Heb. *observest* [t] Heb. *roots*

13:15 THOUGH HE SLAY ME, YET WILL I TRUST IN HIM. Here is one of the most astounding declarations of faith in God's goodness ever uttered. Whatever God allowed to happen to Job, whatever burden He laid upon him, even though He should "slay" him, Job believed ultimately that God would not fail him. Paul expressed this same confidence in God's love for His faithful people (Rom. 8). Although the Lord may take away comfort after comfort, though health may be destroyed, and though waves of trouble may come upon us, through the grace of Jesus Christ and power of His saving death, we can trust God with unwavering faith, convinced that He is right, just, and good (see Rom. 8:37–39).

14 MAN *THAT is* born of a woman *is* [u]of few days, and [d]full of trouble.

2 [e]He cometh forth like a flower, and is cut down: he fleeth also as a shadow, and continueth not.

3 And [f]dost thou open thine eyes upon such an one, and [g]bringest me into judgment with thee?

4 [v]Who [h]can bring a clean *thing* out of an unclean? not one.

5 [i]Seeing his days *are* determined, the number of his months *are* with thee, thou hast appointed his bounds that he cannot pass;

6 [j]Turn from him, that he may [w]rest, till he shall accomplish, [k]as an hireling, his day.

7 For there is hope of a tree, if it be cut down, that it will sprout again, and that the tender branch thereof will not cease.

8 Though the root thereof wax old in the earth, and the stock thereof die in the ground;

9 *Yet* through the scent of water it will bud, and bring forth boughs like a plant.

10 But man dieth, and [x]wasteth away: yea, man giveth up the ghost, and where *is* he?

11 *As* the waters fail from the sea, and the flood decayeth and drieth up:

12 So man lieth down, and riseth not: [l]till the heavens *be* no more, they shall not awake, nor be raised out of their sleep.

13 O that thou wouldest hide me in the grave, that thou wouldest keep me secret, until thy wrath be past, that thou wouldest appoint me a set time, and remember me!

14 If a man die, shall he live *again?* all the days of my appointed time [m]will I wait, till my change come.

14:1 [d]Eccl. 2:23
14:2 [e]ch. 8:9 Ps. 90:5,6
14:3 [f]Ps. 144:3 [g]Ps. 143:2
14:4 [h]Ps. 51:2,5,10 John 3:6 Rom. 5:12 Eph. 2:3
14:5 [i]ch. 7:1
14:6 [j]ch. 7:16,19 Ps. 39:13 [k]ch. 7:1
14:12 [l]Is. 51:6 Acts 3:21 Rom. 8:20 2 Pet. 3:7 Rev. 20:11 & 21:1
14:14 [m]ch. 13:15
14:15 [n]ch. 13:22
14:16 [o]ch. 10:6,14 Prov. 5:21 Jer. 32:19
14:17 [p]Deut. 32:34 Hos. 13:12
14:21 [q]Eccl. 9:5 Is. 63:16

15 [n]Thou shalt call, and I will answer thee: thou wilt have a desire to the work of thine hands.

16 [o]For now thou numberest my steps: dost thou not watch over my sin?

17 [p]My transgression *is* sealed up in a bag, and thou sewest up mine iniquity.

18 And surely the mountain falling [y]cometh to nought, and the rock is removed out of his place.

19 The waters wear the stones: thou [z]washest away the things which grow *out* of the dust of the earth; and thou destroyest the hope of man.

20 Thou prevailest for ever against him, and he passeth: thou changest his countenance, and sendest him away.

21 His sons come to honour, and [q]he knoweth *it* not; and they are brought low, but he perceiveth *it* not of them.

22 But his flesh upon him shall have pain, and his soul within him shall mourn.

Eliphaz responds

15 THEN ANSWERED Eliphaz the Temanite, and said,

2 Should a wise man utter [a]vain knowledge, and fill his belly with the east wind?

3 Should he reason with unprofitable talk? or with speeches wherewith he can do no good?

4 Yea, [b]thou castest off fear, and restrainest [c]prayer before God.

5 For thy mouth [d]uttereth thine in-

[u] Heb. *short of days* [v] Heb. *Who will give* [w] Heb. *cease* [x] Heb. *is weakened,* or, *cut off* [y] Heb. *fadeth* [z] Heb. *overflowest* [a] Heb. *knowledge of wind* [b] Heb. *thou makest void* [c] Or, *speech* [d] Heb. *teacheth*

14:1 FULL OF TROUBLE. For the believer, a life that is "full of trouble" may be the result of persecution, injustice, poverty, ill health, or Satan's opposition to their fight of faith (see article on THE SUFFERING OF THE RIGHTEOUS, p. 764). God wants all believers who are suffering and are oppressed on this earth to know that a day of resurrection (see next note) and victory is coming, when they will be with God forever (see Rev. 21:1,4, notes). At that time they will experience firsthand that "the sufferings of this present time *are* not worthy *to be compared* with the glory which shall be revealed in us" (see Rom. 8:18, note).

14:14 IF A MAN DIE, SHALL HE LIVE *AGAIN*. Job believed that after he died and entered Sheol (v. 13), God would call him out again (v. 15; cf. 1 Cor. 15:20; 1 Thes. 4:16–17); in other words, Job expressed hope in a personal resurrection (see 19:25–26, notes). The basis for this hope-filled expectation was God's fervent love for His people, i.e., "thou wilt have a desire to the work of thine hands" (v. 15). For a brief moment, Job reached out to God with a towering expression of faith.

15:1 THERE ANSWERED ELIPHAZ. In chs. 15—21 the four participants continued their dispute, developing what they had said before, only with more tenacity. Job steadfastly clung to God, while at the same time maintaining his innocence and insisting on the unfairness of his calamity (e.g., 16:19–21).

iquity, and thou choosest the tongue of the crafty.

6 [r]Thine own mouth condemneth thee, and not I: yea, thine own lips testify against thee.

7 *Art* thou the first man *that* was born? [s]or wast thou made before the hills?

8 [t]Hast thou heard the secret of God? and dost thou restrain wisdom to thyself?

9 [u]What knowest thou, that we know not? *what* understandest thou, which *is* not in us?

10 [v]With us *are* both the grayheaded and very aged men, much elder than thy father.

11 *Are* the consolations of God small with thee? is there any secret thing with thee?

12 Why doth thine heart carry thee away? and what do thy eyes wink at,

13 That thou turnest thy spirit against God, and lettest *such* words go out of thy mouth?

14 [w]What *is* man, that he should be clean? and *he which is* born of a woman, that he should be righteous?

15 [x]Behold, he putteth no trust in his saints; yea, the heavens are not clean in his sight.

16 [y]How much more abominable and filthy *is* man, [z]which drinketh iniquity like water?

17 I will show thee, hear me; and that *which* I have seen I will declare;

18 Which wise men have told [a]from their fathers, and have not hid *it:*

19 Unto whom alone the earth was given, and [b]no stranger passed among them.

20 The wicked man travaileth with pain all *his* days, [c]and the number of years is hidden to the oppressor.

21 [e]A dreadful sound *is* in his ears: [d]in prosperity the destroyer shall come upon him.

22 He believeth not that he shall return out of darkness, and he is waited for of the sword.

23 He [e]wandereth abroad for bread, *saying,* Where *is it?* he knoweth that [f]the day of darkness is ready at his hand.

24 Trouble and anguish shall make him afraid; they shall prevail against him, as a king ready to the battle.

25 For he stretcheth out his hand against God, and strengtheneth himself against the Almighty.

26 He runneth upon him, *even* on *his* neck, upon the thick bosses of his bucklers:

27 [g]Because he covereth his face with his fatness, and maketh collops of fat on *his* flanks.

28 And he dwelleth in desolate cities, *and* in houses which no man inhabiteth, which are ready to become heaps.

29 He shall not be rich, neither shall his substance continue, neither shall he prolong the perfection thereof upon the earth.

30 He shall not depart out of darkness; the flame shall dry up his branches, and by the breath of his mouth shall he go away.

31 Let not him that is deceived [h]trust in vanity: for vanity shall be his recompence.

32 It shall be [f]accomplished [i]before his time, and his branch shall not be green.

33 He shall shake off his unripe grape as the vine, and shall cast off his flower as the olive.

34 For the congregation of hypocrites *shall be* desolate, and fire shall consume the tabernacles of bribery.

35 [j]They conceive mischief, and bring forth [g]vanity, and their belly prepareth deceit.

Job answers

16 THEN JOB answered and said,
2 I have heard many such things: [k]miserable[h] comforters *are* ye all.

3 Shall [i]vain words have an end? or what emboldeneth thee that thou answerest?

4 I also could speak as ye *do:* if your soul were in my soul's stead, I could heap up words against you, and [l]shake mine head at you.

5 *But* I would strengthen you with my mouth, and the moving of my lips should assuage *your grief.*

6 Though I speak, my grief is not assuaged: and *though* I forbear, [j]what am I eased?

7 But now he hath made me weary: thou hast made desolate all my company.

15:6 [r]Luke 19:22 **15:7** [s]Ps. 90:2 Prov. 8:25 **15:8** [t]Rom. 11:34 1 Cor. 2:11 **15:9** [u]ch. 13:2 **15:10** [v]ch. 32:6,7 **15:14** [w]ch. 14:4 Prov. 20:9 Eccl. 7:20 1 John 1:8,10 **15:15** [x]ch. 4:18 & 25:5 **15:16** [y]ch. 4:19 Ps. 14:3 & 53:3 [z]ch. 34:7 Prov. 19:28 **15:18** [a]ch. 8:8 **15:19** [b]Joel 3:17 **15:20** [c]Ps. 90:12 **15:21** [d]1 Thes. 5:3 **15:23** [e]Ps. 59:15 & 109:10 [f]ch. 18:12 **15:27** [g]Ps. 17:10 **15:31** [h]Is. 59:4 **15:32** [i]ch. 22:16 Ps. 55:23 **15:35** [j]Ps. 7:14 Is. 59:4 Hos. 10:13 **16:2** [k]ch. 13:4 **16:4** [l]Ps. 22:7 & 109:25 Lam. 2:15

e Heb. *A sound of fears* f Or, *cut off* g Or, *iniquity* h Or, *troublesome* i Heb. *words of wind* j Heb. *what goeth from me?*

8 And thou hast filled me with wrin-
kles, *which* is a witness *against me:* and
my leanness rising up in me beareth
witness to my face.
9 [m]He teareth *me* in his wrath, who
hateth me: he gnasheth upon me with
his teeth; [n]mine enemy sharpeneth
his eyes upon me.
10 They have [o]gaped upon me with
their mouth; [p]they have smitten me
upon the cheek reproachfully; they
have gathered themselves together
against me.
11 God [q]hath[k] delivered me to the
ungodly, and turned me over into the
hands of the wicked.
12 I was at ease, but he hath broken
me asunder: he hath also taken *me* by
my neck, and shaken me to pieces, and
[r]set me up for his mark.
13 His archers compass me round
about, he cleaveth my reins asunder,
and doth not spare; he poureth out my
gall upon the ground.
14 He breaketh me with breach
upon breach, he runneth upon me like
a giant.
15 I have sewed sackcloth upon my
skin, and [s]defiled my horn in the dust.
16 My face is foul with weeping,
and on my eyelids *is* the shadow of
death;
17 Not for *any* injustice in mine
hands: also my prayer *is* pure.
18 O earth, cover not thou my
blood, and [t]let my cry have no place.
19 Also now, behold, [u]my witness
is in heaven, and my record *is* [l]on
high.
20 My friends [m]scorn me: *but* mine
eye poureth out *tears* unto God.
21 [v]O that one might plead for a
man with God, as a man *pleadeth* for his
[n]neighbour!
22 When [o]a few years are come,
then I shall [w]go the way *whence* I shall
not return.

17

MY [p]BREATH is corrupt, my
days are extinct, [x]the graves
are ready for me.
2 *Are there* not mockers with me?
and doth not mine eye [q]continue in
their [y]provocation?
3 Lay down now, put me in a surety
with thee; who *is* he *that* [z]will strike
hands with me?
4 For thou hast hid their heart from
understanding: therefore shalt thou
not exalt *them.*
5 He that speaketh flattery to *his*
friends, even the eyes of his children
shall fail.
6 He hath made me also [a]a byword
of the people; and [r]aforetime I was as
a tabret.
7 [b]Mine eye also is dim by reason
of sorrow, and all [s]my members *are* as
a shadow.
8 Upright *men* shall be astonied at
this, and the innocent shall stir up him-
self against the hypocrite.
9 The righteous also shall hold on
his way, and he that hath [c]clean
hands [t]shall be stronger and stron-
ger.
10 But as for you all, [d]do ye return,
and come now: for I cannot find *one*
wise *man* among you.
11 [e]My days are past, my purposes
are broken off, *even* [u]the thoughts of
my heart.
12 They change the night into day:
the light *is* [v]short because of dark-
ness.

16:9 [m]ch. 10:16,17 [n]ch. 13:24
16:10 [o]Ps. 22:13 [p]Lam. 3:30 Mic. 5:1
16:11 [q]ch. 1:15,17
16:12 [r]ch. 7:20
16:15 [s]ch. 30:19 Ps. 7:5
16:18 [t]ch. 27:9 Ps. 66:18
16:19 [u]Rom. 1:9
16:21 [v]ch. 31:35 Eccl. 6:10 Is. 45:9 Rom. 9:20
16:22 [w]Eccl. 12:5
17:1 [x]Ps. 88:3,4
17:2 [y]1 Sam. 1:6
17:3 [z]Prov. 17:18
17:6 [a]ch. 30:9
17:7 [b]Ps. 6:7 & 31:9
17:9 [c]Ps. 24:4
17:10 [d]ch. 6:29
17:11 [e]ch. 7:6

[k]Heb. *hath shut me up* [l]Heb. *in the high places* [m]Heb. are *my scorners* [n]Or, *friend* [o]Heb. *years of number* [p]Or, *spirit is spent* [q]Heb. *lodge* [r]Or, *before them* [s]Or, *my thoughts* [t]Heb. *shall add strength* [u]Heb. *the possessions* [v]Heb. *near*

16:9 HE TEARETH *ME* IN HIS WRATH. Job's terrible suffering made him feel that God was a cruel tyrant rather than a merciful Lord. His conviction that he had lived justly and purely (v. 17) caused him to question God's justice (cf. 19:6). Yet, Job also held firmly to his belief that God was indeed just; therefore, if only he could enter into direct contact with God (cf. 13:13–27; 23:1–7) or find someone to plead his case (see 9:33, note), God as his witness would testify to his innocence (vv. 19–21; see next note).

16:19 MY WITNESS *IS* IN HEAVEN. In faith Job rose above his doubts about God's goodness, for he declared that God Himself would testify as a witness of his innocence. He longed for God to plead his cause in the heavenly court of justice. The desire for a mediator to speak with God in our defense became a reality in Jesus Christ, through whom God "reconciled us to himself" (2 Cor. 5:18); "we have an advocate with the Father, Jesus Christ the righteous" (1 John 2:1).

17:1 MY BREATH IS CORRUPT. As a broken man, Job firmly believed he would die soon. He saw himself as a man deserted by God and as the object of his companions' scorn. Job could do nothing but persevere in his conviction about the rightness of his cause (v. 9), maintaining confidence in God's justice, all appearances to the contrary (16:19–22).

13 If I wait, the grave *is* mine house:
I have made my bed in the darkness.
14 I have [w]said to corruption, Thou
art my father: to the worm, *Thou art* my
mother, and my sister.
15 And where *is* now my hope? as
for my hope, who shall see it?
16 They shall go down [f]to the bars
of the pit, when *our* [g]rest together *is*
in the dust.

Bildad reproves Job

18 THEN ANSWERED Bildad the
Shuhite, and said,
2 How long *will it be ere* ye make an
end of words? mark, and afterwards we
will speak.
3 Wherefore are we counted [h]as
beasts, *and* reputed vile in your sight?
4 [i]He teareth [x]himself in his an-
ger: shall the earth be forsaken for
thee? and shall the rock be removed
out of his place?
5 Yea, [j]the light of the wicked
shall be put out, and the spark of his
fire shall not shine.
6 The light shall be dark in his tab-
ernacle, [k]and his [y]candle shall be
put out with him.
7 The steps of his strength shall be
straitened, and [l]his own counsel shall
cast him down.
8 For [m]he is cast into a net by his
own feet, and he walketh upon a snare.
9 The gin shall take *him* by the heel,
and [n]the robber shall prevail against
him.
10 The snare *is* [z]laid for him in the
ground, and a trap for him in the way.
11 [o]Terrors shall make him afraid
on every side, and shall [a]drive him to
his feet.
12 His strength shall be hungerbit-
ten, and [p]destruction *shall be* ready at
his side.
13 It shall devour the [b]strength of
his skin: *even* the firstborn of death
shall devour his strength.
14 [q]His confidence shall be rooted
out of his tabernacle, and it shall bring
him to the king of terrors.
15 It shall dwell in his tabernacle,
because *it is* none of his: brimstone
shall be scattered upon his habitation.
16 [r]His roots shall be dried up be-
neath, and above shall his branch be
cut off.
17 [s]His remembrance shall perish
from the earth, and he shall have no
name in the street.
18 [c]He shall be driven from light
into darkness, and chased out of the
world.
19 [t]He shall neither have son nor
nephew among his people, nor any re-
maining in his dwellings.
20 They that come after *him* shall
be astonied at his day, as they that
[d]went before [e]were affrighted.
21 Surely such *are* the dwellings of
the wicked, and this *is* the place *of him*
that [u]knoweth not God.

Job's response

19 THEN JOB answered and said,
2 How long will ye vex my soul,
and break me in pieces with words?
3 These ten times have ye re-
proached me: ye are not ashamed *that*
ye [f]make yourselves strange to me.
4 And be it indeed *that* I have erred,
mine error remaineth with myself.
5 If indeed ye will [v]magnify *your-*
selves against me, and plead against
me my reproach:
6 Know now that God hath over-
thrown me, and hath compassed me
with his net.
7 Behold, I cry out of [g]wrong, but
I am not heard: I cry aloud, but *there is*
no judgment.
8 He hath fenced up my way that I
cannot pass, and he hath set darkness
in my paths.
9 He hath stripped me of my glory,
and taken the crown *from* my head.
10 He hath destroyed me on every
side, and I am gone: and mine hope
hath he removed like a tree.
11 He hath also kindled his wrath

17:16 [f]Jonah 2:6 [g]ch. 3:17-19
18:3 [h]Ps. 73:22
18:4 [i]ch. 13:14
18:5 [j]Prov. 13:9
18:6 [k]ch. 21:17 Ps. 18:28
18:7 [l]ch. 5:13
18:8 [m]ch. 22:10 Ps. 9:15 & 35:8
18:9 [n]ch. 5:5
18:11 [o]ch. 20:25 Jer. 6:25 & 20:3,4
18:12 [p]ch. 15:23
18:14 [q]ch. 11:20 Ps. 112:10 Prov. 10:28
18:16 [r]ch. 29:19 Is. 5:24 Amos 2:9 Mal. 4:1
18:17 [s]Ps. 34:16 & 109:13 Prov. 2:22 & 10:7
18:19 [t]Is. 14:22 Jer. 22:30
18:21 [u]Jer. 9:3 1 Thes. 4:5
19:5 [v]Ps. 38:16

[w] Heb. *cried,* or, *called* [x] Heb. *his soul*
[y] Or, *lamp* [z] Heb. *hidden* [a] Heb. *scatter him*
[b] Heb. *bars* [c] Heb. *They shall drive him*
[d] Or, *lived with him* [e] Heb. *laid hold on horror*
[f] Or, *harden yourselves against me* [g] Or, *violence*

19:11 AS *ONE OF* HIS ENEMIES. Job was now under the serious misconception that God directly caused his suffering (cf. vv. 8–13). (1) He believed that God had become his enemy who delighted in bringing torment and agony upon his soul. Job was not aware that Satan was the cause of his unrelenting calamity. Although God was permitting Satan to bring harm to Job, it was nevertheless Satan who inflicted the cruel suffering. (2) Believers should be careful not to blame God for what He only permits. In this world many evil things occur; God takes no pleasure in witnessing

against me, and [w]he counteth me unto him as *one of* his enemies.

12 His troops come together, and raise up their way against me, and encamp round about my tabernacle.

13 He hath put my brethren far from me, and mine acquaintance are verily estranged from me.

14 My kinsfolk have failed, and my familiar friends have forgotten me.

15 They that dwell in mine house, and my maids, count me for a stranger: I am an alien in their sight.

16 I called my servant, and he gave *me* no answer; I entreated him with my mouth.

17 My breath is strange to my wife, though I entreated for the children's *sake* of [h]mine own body.

18 Yea, [x]young[i] children despised me; I arose, and they spake against me.

19 [y]All [j]my inward friends abhorred me: and they whom I loved are turned against me.

20 [z]My bone cleaveth to my skin [k]and to my flesh, and I am escaped with the skin of my teeth.

21 Have pity upon me, have pity upon me, O ye my friends; for the hand of God hath touched me.

22 Why do ye [a]persecute me as God, and are not satisfied with my flesh?

23 [l]Oh that my words were now written! oh that they were printed in a book!

24 That they were graven with an iron pen and lead in the rock for ever!

25 For I know *that* my redeemer liveth, and *that* he shall stand at the latter *day* upon the earth:

26 [m]And *though* after my skin *worms* destroy this *body,* yet [b]in my flesh shall I see God:

27 Whom I shall see for myself, and mine eyes shall behold, and not [n]another; [o]*though* my reins be consumed [p]within me.

28 But ye should say, Why persecute we him, [q]seeing the root of the matter is found in me?

29 Be ye afraid of the sword: for wrath *bringeth* the punishments of the sword, that ye may know *there is* a judgment.

19:11 [w]ch. 13:24
19:18 [x]2 Ki. 2:23
19:19 [y]Ps. 55:13
19:20 [z]Ps. 102:5
19:22 [a]Ps. 69:26
19:26 [b]Ps. 17:15 1 Cor. 13:12

Zophar's speech

20 THEN ANSWERED Zophar the Naamathite, and said,

2 Therefore do my thoughts cause me to answer, and for *this* [r]I make haste.

[h]Heb. *my belly* [i]Or, *the wicked* [j]Heb. *the men of my secret* [k]Or, *as* [l]Heb. *Who will give* [m]Or, *After I shall awake, though this* body *be destroyed, yet out of my flesh shall I see God* [n]Heb. *a stranger* [o]Or, *my reins within me are consumed with earnest desire* [for that day [p]Heb. *in my bosom* [q]Or, *and* what *root of matter is found in me?* [r]Heb. *my haste* is *in me*

them. Tragedies happen among His children, which He permits with regret and pity (see 1 Tim. 2:4, note; see article on THE WILL OF GOD, p. 1060).

19:25 I KNOW *THAT* MY REDEEMER LIVETH. In the midst of his suffering and despair, Job clung with great faith to God, believing the Lord would vindicate him in the end (cf. 13:15; 14:14–15). Job viewed God as his "redeemer" or helper. In Bible times a "redeemer" was a relative who with great affection came to protect, defend, help in times of trouble (see Lev. 25:25; Deut. 25:5–10; Ruth 1—4; see also Gen. 48:16; Ex. 6:6; Is. 43:1; Hos. 13:14), and vindicate a suffering kinsman.

19:25 HE SHALL STAND AT THE LATTER *DAY* UPON THE EARTH. By the inspiration of the Holy Spirit, Job's testimony pointed toward Jesus Christ the Redeemer, who would come to save His people from sin and condemnation (Rom. 3:24; Gal. 3:13; 4:5; Eph. 1:7; Tit. 2:14), free them from the fear of death (Heb. 2:14–15; Rom. 8:23), give them eternal life (John 3:16; Rom. 6:23), deliver them from the wrath to come (1 Thes. 1:10), and publicly vindicate them (cf. Rev. 19:11–21; 20:1–6). Here Job was predicting the visible manifestation of this divine Redeemer.

19:26 IN MY FLESH SHALL I SEE GOD. Job prophetically expressed the conviction that after his body had decayed in the grave, he would physically be raised to life and behold his Redeemer-God in a resurrected body. This section contains in seed form God's revelation about the future coming of Christ at the end of time, the resurrection from the dead, and the final vindication of all God's faithful (see previous note; cf. Ps. 16:10; 49:15; Is. 26:19; Dan. 12:2; Hos. 13:14; see article on DEATH, p. 782).

19:27 WHOM I SHALL SEE FOR MYSELF. Job's longing to see his Redeemer-God far outweighed all other desires expressed in this book (see 23:3, note). Job yearned for the day when he could see the Lord's face in full redemption. Likewise, N.T. believers long for the coming of their Savior (1 Cor. 1:7; 2 Tim. 4:8) and the day of consummation, when "the tabernacle of God *is* with men, and he will dwell with them, and they shall be his people, and God himself shall be with them," and "they shall see his face" (Rev. 21:3; 22:4).

3 I have heard the check of my reproach, and the spirit of my understanding causeth me to answer.

4 Knowest thou *not* this of old, since man was placed upon earth,

5 [c]That the triumphing of the wicked *is* [s]short, and the joy of the hypocrite *but* for a moment?

6 [d]Though his excellency mount up to the heavens, and his head reach unto the [t]clouds;

7 *Yet* he shall perish for ever like his own dung: they which have seen him shall say, Where *is* he?

8 He shall fly away [e]as a dream, and shall not be found: yea, he shall be chased away as a vision of the night.

9 The eye also *which* saw him shall *see him* no more; neither shall his place any more behold him.

10 [u]His children shall seek to please the poor, and his hands shall restore their goods.

11 His bones are full *of* [f]*the sin* of his youth, [g]which shall lie down with him in the dust.

12 Though wickedness be sweet in his mouth, *though* he hide it under his tongue;

13 *Though* he spare it, and forsake it not; but keep it still [v]within his mouth:

14 *Yet* his meat in his bowels is turned, *it is* the gall of asps within him.

15 He hath swallowed down riches, and he shall vomit them up again: God shall cast them out of his belly.

16 He shall suck the poison of asps: the viper's tongue shall slay him.

17 He shall not see [h]the rivers, [w]the floods, the brooks of honey and butter.

18 That which he laboured for shall he restore, and shall not swallow *it* down: [x]according to *his* substance *shall* the restitution *be,* and he shall not rejoice *therein.*

19 Because he hath [y]oppressed *and* hath forsaken the poor; *because* he hath violently taken away an house which he builded not;

20 [i]Surely he shall not [z]feel quietness in his belly, he shall not save of that which he desired.

21 [a]There shall none of his meat be left; therefore shall no man look for his goods.

22 In the fulness of his sufficiency he shall be in straits: every hand of the [b]wicked shall come upon him.

23 *When* he is about to fill his belly, *God* shall cast the fury of his wrath upon him, and shall rain *it* upon him while he is eating.

24 [j]He shall flee from the iron weapon, *and* the bow of steel shall strike him through.

25 It is drawn, and cometh out of the body; yea, [k]the glittering sword cometh out of his gall: [l]terrors *are* upon him.

26 All darkness *shall be* hid in his secret places: [m]a fire not blown shall consume him; it shall go ill with him that is left in his tabernacle.

27 The heaven shall reveal his iniquity; and the earth shall rise up against him.

28 The increase of his house shall depart, *and his goods* shall flow away in the day of his wrath.

29 [n]This *is* the portion of a wicked man from God, and the heritage [c]appointed unto him by God.

Job disagrees with his friends

21 BUT JOB answered and said,
2 Hear diligently my speech, and let this be your consolations.

3 Suffer me that I may speak; and after that I have spoken, [o]mock on.

4 As for me, *is* my complaint to man? and if *it were so,* why should not my spirit be [d]troubled?

5 [e]Mark me, and be astonished, [p]and lay *your* hand upon *your* mouth.

6 Even when I remember I am afraid, and trembling taketh hold on my flesh.

7 [q]Wherefore do the wicked live, become old, yea, are mighty in power?

20:5 [c]Ps. 37:35 **20:6** [d]Is. 14:13,14 Obad. 3,4 **20:8** [e]Ps. 73:20 **20:11** [f]ch. 13:26 [g]ch. 21:26 **20:17** [h]Ps. 36:8 Jer. 17:8 **20:20** [i]Eccl. 5:13 **20:24** [j]Is. 24:18 Amos 5:19 **20:25** [k]ch. 16:13 [l]ch. 18:11 **20:26** [m]Ps. 21:9 **20:29** [n]ch. 27:13 **21:3** [o]ch. 16:10 **21:5** [p]Judg. 18:19 ch. 40:4 **21:7** [q]ch. 12:6 Ps. 73:3,12 Jer. 12:1

[s]Heb. *from near* [t]Heb. *cloud* [u]Or, *The poor shall oppress his children* [v]Heb. *in the midst of his palate* [w]Or, *streaming brooks* [x]Heb. *according to the substance of his exchange* [y]Heb. *crushed* [z]Heb. *know* [a]Or, *There shall be none left for his meat* [b]Or, *troublesome* [c]Heb. *of his decree from God* [d]Heb. *shortened?* [e]Heb. *Look unto me.*

21:7 DO THE WICKED LIVE ... ARE MIGHTY IN POWER? Job questioned the inequities of life, especially the prosperity, success, and happiness of many of the wicked. Ps. 73 addressed this theological problem. At times those "of a clean heart" seem "plagued" (Ps. 73:1,14), while the wicked prosper and have no "trouble" (Ps. 73:3–5). God responds by revealing the final outcome of both the godly and the wicked (Ps. 73:16–28). Ultimately God will justly rectify all

DEATH

Job 19:25–26 "For I know that *my redeemer liveth, and* that *he shall stand at the latter* day *upon the earth: And* though *after my skin* worms *destroy this* body, *yet in my flesh shall I see God."*

All humans, believers and unbelievers, are subject to death. The word "death" in the Scriptures, however, has more than one meaning. It is important to understand the believer's relationship to the various meanings of death.

DEATH AS A RESULT OF SIN. Gen. 2—3 teaches that death entered the world because of sin. Our first parents were created with the ability to live forever; when they disobeyed the command of God, they came under the penalty of sin, which is death. (1) Adam and Eve became subject to *physical* death. God had set the tree of life in the Garden of Eden in order that by continually eating from it, humans would never die (see Gen. 2:9, note). But after Adam and Eve ate of the fruit of the tree of knowledge of good and evil, God pronounced these words: "for dust thou *art*, and unto dust shalt thou return" (Gen. 3:19). Though they did not physically die on the day that they ate, they did become subject to the law of death as a result of God's curse.

(2) Adam and Eve also died a *moral* death. God warned Adam that *in the day* he ate of the forbidden fruit, he would surely die (Gen. 2:17). This was a serious warning. Even though Adam and his wife did not die physically on that day, they did die morally, i.e., their nature became sinful. Ever since Adam and Eve, every person has been born with a sinful nature (Rom. 8:5–8), i.e., an innate desire to go his or her own selfish way without concern for God or others (see Gen. 3:6, note; Rom. 3:10–18, note; Eph. 2:3; Col. 2:13).

(3) Adam and Eve also died a *spiritual* death when they disobeyed God in the garden, i.e., their former intimate relationship to God was destroyed (see Gen. 3:6, note). No longer did they look forward to walking and talking with God in the garden; rather, they hid themselves from His presence (Gen. 3:8). Elsewhere, the Scriptures teach that apart from Christ, all are alienated from God and from life in Him (Eph. 4:17–18); they are spiritually dead.

(4) Finally, death as a result of sin involves *eternal* death. Eternal life would have been the consequence of the obedience of Adam and Eve (cf. Gen. 3:22); instead, the principle of eternal death has become operative. Eternal death is eternal condemnation and separation from God as a result of disobedience (see Gen. 3:4, note), i.e., "everlasting destruction from the presence of the Lord" (2 Thes. 1:9; see Rom. 6:16, note).

(5) The only way to escape death in all its multifaceted aspects is through Jesus Christ. He "abolished death, and hath brought life and immortality to light" (2 Tim. 1:10). By His death He has reconciled us with God, thus reversing the spiritual separation and alienation that had come as a result of sin (see Gen. 3:24, note; 2 Cor. 5:18, note). By His resurrection, He overcame and broke the power of Satan, sin, and physical death (see Gen. 3:15, note; Rom. 6:10, note; cf. Rom. 5:18–19; 1 Cor. 15:12–28; 1 John 3:8). That believers will not remain forever in the grave was already a part of the testimony of God's O.T. people (see Job 19:25–26; Ps. 16:9–11; see article on THE RESURRECTION OF THE BODY, p. 1799).

THE MEANING OF PHYSICAL DEATH FOR BELIEVERS. Even though believers in Christ have the assurance of resurrection life, they still go through the experience of physical death. But believers approach death differently than do unbelievers. The following are some Scripturally revealed truths concerning the death of a believer.

(1) Death for the Christian is not the end of life, but a new beginning. Rather than something to be feared (1 Cor. 15:55–57), it is the point of transition to a fuller life.

Death for believers is a release from the afflictions of this world (2 Cor. 4:17) and from an earthly body, in order to be clothed with heavenly life and glory (2 Cor. 5:1–5). Paul speaks of physical death as sleep (1 Cor. 15:6,18,20; 1 Thes. 4:13–15), implying that death is rest from earthly labor and suffering (cf. Rev. 14:13). It means going to be with our godly ancestors who have died before us (see Gen. 25:8, note) and is a door into the presence of the living God (Phil. 1:23).

(2) Scripture also speaks of the death of believers in comforting terms. The death of the godly is "precious in the sight of the LORD" (Ps. 116:15). It is an entrance "into peace" (Is. 57:1–2) and "glory" (Ps. 73:24); a being carried away by the angels "into Abraham's bosom" (Luke 16:22); a going to "paradise" (Luke 23:43); a going to our Father's house with "many mansions" (John 14:2); a blessed departure in order to "be with Christ" (Phil. 1:23); a continual presence "with the Lord" (2 Cor. 5:8); a falling "asleep in Christ" (1 Cor. 15:18; cf. John 11:11; 1 Thes. 4:13); a "gain . . . which is far better" (Phil. 1:21,23); and a time to receive the "crown of righteousness" (see 2 Tim. 4:8, note).

(3) Concerning the time between the believer's death and his or her bodily resurrection, Scripture teaches the following: (a) At the time of death believers are brought into Christ's presence (2 Cor. 5:8; Phil. 1:23). (b) Believers exist in full consciousness (Luke 16:19–31) and experience joy at the kindness and love shown by God (cf. Eph. 2:7). (c) Heaven is like a home, i.e., a haven of rest and security (Rev. 6:11) and a place of community and fellowship with other believers (John 14:2, note). (d) Activities in heaven will include worship and singing (Ps. 87; Rev. 14:2–3; 15:3), assigned tasks (Luke 19:17), and eating and drinking (Luke 14:15; 22:14–18; Rev. 22:2). (e) While awaiting the bodily resurrection, believers are not invisible disembodied spirits, but are clothed with a temporary heavenly form (Luke 9:30–32; 2 Cor. 5:1–4). (f) In heaven believers maintain their personal identity (Mat. 8:11; Luke 9:30–32). (g) Believers who have passed on will continue to be concerned about God's purposes on earth (Rev. 6:9–11).

(4) Even though much hope and joy awaits the believer upon death, believers still grieve when a loved one dies. Upon Jacob's death, for example, Joseph mourned deeply for his father. His reaction to his father's death is a model for all believers who experience the death of a loved one (see Gen. 50:1, note).

8 Their seed is established in their sight with them, and their offspring before their eyes.

9 Their houses [f]*are* safe from fear, [r]neither *is* the rod of God upon them.

10 Their bull gendereth, and faileth not; their cow calveth, and [s]casteth not her calf.

11 They send forth their little ones like a flock, and their children dance.

12 They take the timbrel and harp, and rejoice at the sound of the organ.

13 They [t]spend their days [g]in wealth, and in a moment go down to the grave.

14 [u]Therefore they say unto God, Depart from us; for we desire not the knowledge of thy ways.

15 [v]What *is* the Almighty, that we should serve him? and [w]what profit should we have, if we pray unto him?

16 Lo, their good *is* not in their hand: [x]the counsel of the wicked is far from me.

17 How oft is the [h]candle of the wicked put out! and *how oft* cometh their destruction upon them! *God* [y]distributeth sorrows in his anger.

18 [z]They are as stubble before the wind, and as chaff that the storm [i]carrieth away.

19 God layeth up [j]his iniquity [a]for his children: he rewardeth him, and he shall know *it.*

20 His eyes shall see his destruction, and [b]he shall drink of the wrath of the Almighty.

21 For what pleasure *hath* he in his house after him, when the number of his months is cut off in the midst?

22 [c]Shall *any* teach God knowledge? seeing he judgeth those that are high.

23 One dieth [k]in his full strength, being wholly at ease and quiet.

24 His [l]breasts are full of milk, and his bones are moistened with marrow.

25 And another dieth in the bitterness of his soul, and never eateth with pleasure.

26 They shall [d]lie down alike in the dust, and the worms shall cover them.

27 Behold, I know your thoughts, and the devices *which* ye wrongfully imagine against me.

28 For ye say, Where *is* the house of the prince? and where *are* [m]the dwelling places of the wicked?

29 Have ye not asked them that go by the way? and do ye not know their tokens,

30 [e]That the wicked is reserved to the day of destruction? they shall be brought forth to [n]the day of wrath.

31 Who shall declare his way to his face? and who shall repay him *what* he hath done?

32 Yet shall he be brought to the [o]grave, and shall [p]remain in the tomb.

33 The clods of the valley shall be sweet unto him, and [f]every man shall draw after him, as *there are* innumerable before him.

34 How then comfort ye me in vain, seeing in your answers there remaineth [q]falsehood?

Eliphaz accuses Job again

22 THEN ELIPHAZ the Temanite answered and said,

2 [g]Can a man be profitable unto God, [r]as he that is wise may be profitable unto himself?

3 *Is it* any pleasure to the Almighty, that thou art righteous? or *is it* gain *to him,* that thou makest thy ways perfect?

4 Will he reprove thee for fear of thee? will he enter with thee into judgment?

5 *Is* not thy wickedness great? and thine iniquities infinite?

6 For thou hast [h]taken a pledge from thy brother for nought, and [s]stripped the naked of their clothing.

7 Thou hast not given water to the weary to drink, and thou [i]hast withholden bread from the hungry.

21:9 [r]Ps. 73:5
21:10 [s]Ex. 23:26
21:13 [t]ch. 36:11
21:14 [u]ch. 22:17
21:15 [v]Ex. 5:2 [w]Mal. 3:14
21:16 [x]Ps. 1:1 Prov. 1:10
21:17 [y]Luke 12:46
21:18 [z]Ps. 1:4
21:19 [a]Ex. 20:5
21:20 [b]Ps. 75:8 Is. 51:17
21:22 [c]Is. 40:13
21:26 [d]Eccl. 9:2
21:30 [e]Prov. 16:4
21:33 [f]Heb. 9:27
22:2 [g]Ps. 16:2
22:6 [h]Ex. 22:26
22:7 [i]Deut. 15:7

[f]Heb. are *peace from fear* [g]Or, *in mirth* [h]Or, *lamp* [i]Heb. *stealeth away* [j]i.e. *the punishment of his iniquity* [k]Heb. *in his very perfection,* or, *in the strength of his perfection* [l]Or, *milk pails* [m]Heb. *the tent of the tabernacles of the wicked* [n]Heb. *the day of wraths* [o]Heb. *graves* [p]Heb. *watch in the heap* [q]Heb. *transgression?* [r]Or, *if he may be profitable,* doth his *good success* depend *thereon?* [s]Heb. *stripped the clothes of the naked*

things and render to everyone according to his or her deeds and love of the truth (Rom. 2:5–11). The wicked will not remain unpunished, nor will the righteous be left unvindicated or unrewarded (Rom. 2:5–11; Rev. 2:10).

8 But *as for* [t]the mighty man, he had the earth; and the [u]honourable man dwelt in it.

9 Thou hast sent widows away empty, and the arms of the fatherless have been broken.

10 Therefore snares *are* round about thee, and sudden fear troubleth thee;

11 Or darkness, *that* thou canst not see; and abundance of [j]waters cover thee.

12 *Is* not God in the height of heaven? and behold [v]the height of the stars, how high they are!

13 And thou sayest, [k]How[w] doth God know? can he judge through the dark cloud?

14 Thick clouds *are* a covering to him, that he seeth not; and he walketh in the circuit of heaven.

15 Hast thou marked the old way which wicked men have trodden?

16 Which [l]were cut down out of time, [x]whose foundation was overflown with a flood:

17 [m]Which said unto God, Depart from us: and what can the Almighty do [y]for them?

18 Yet he filled their houses with good *things:* but the counsel of the wicked is far from me.

19 [n]The righteous see *it,* and are glad: and the innocent laugh them to scorn.

20 Whereas our [z]substance is not cut down, but [a]the remnant of them the fire consumeth.

21 Acquaint now thyself [b]with him, and [o]be at peace: thereby good shall come unto thee.

22 Receive, I pray thee, the law from his mouth, and [p]lay up his words in thine heart.

23 If thou return to the Almighty, thou shalt be built up, thou shalt put away iniquity far from thy tabernacles.

24 Then shalt thou [q]lay up gold [c]as dust, and the *gold* of Ophir as the stones of the brooks.

25 Yea, the Almighty shall be thy [d]defence, and thou shalt have [e]plenty of silver.

26 For then shalt thou have thy [r]delight in the Almighty, and shalt lift up thy face unto God.

27 [s]Thou shalt make thy prayer unto him, and he shall hear thee, and thou shalt pay thy vows.

28 Thou shalt also decree a thing, and it shall be established unto thee: and the light shall shine upon thy ways.

29 When *men* are cast down, then thou shalt say, *There is* lifting up; and [t]he shall save [f]the humble person.

30 [g]He shall deliver the island of the innocent: and it is delivered by the pureness of thine hands.

22:11 [j]Ps. 69:1,2
22:13 [k]Ps. 73:11
22:16 [l]ch. 15:32
22:17 [m]ch. 21:14
22:19 [n]Ps. 58:10
22:21 [o]Is. 27:5
22:22 [p]Ps. 119:11
22:24 [q]2 Chr. 1:15
22:26 [r]ch. 27:10
22:27 [s]Is. 58:9
22:29 [t]1 Pet. 5:5

Job's response to Eliphaz

23 THEN JOB answered and said,
2 Even today *is* my complaint bitter: [h]my stroke is heavier than my groaning.

[t]Heb. *the man of arm* [u]Heb. *eminent,* or, *accepted for countenance* [v]Heb. *the head of the stars* [w]Or, *What* [x]Heb. *a flood was poured upon their foundation* [y]Or, *to them?* [z]Or, *estate* [a]Or, *their excellency* [b]i.e. *with God* [c]Or, *on the dust* [d]Or, *gold* [e]Heb. *silver of strength* [f]Heb. *him that hath low eyes* [g]Or, *The innocent shall deliver the island* [h]Heb. *my hand*

22:21–30 THEREBY GOOD SHALL COME UNTO THEE. Eliphaz appealed to Job with a traditional, yet simplistic, doctrine of repentance: if Job was willing to return to God, to receive instruction from His word, to humble himself and remove sin from his life, and to abandon his trust in earthly things and make the Almighty his delight, then God would surely deliver him from all trouble, his prayers would be answered, and success would follow his every endeavor. However, Eliphaz was mistaken in three respects.

(1) Repentance and salvation do not always result in physical and material prosperity. Sometimes men and women of faith, *because of* their faithfulness, are "destitute, afflicted, tormented" (Heb. 11:37); though they believe the promises of God, yet at present they do not receive "the promise" (Heb. 11:39).

(2) In exhorting Job to repent in order to recover his health and prosperity, Eliphaz was unknowingly siding with Satan and his accusations against Job and God. Satan had earlier accused Job of serving God only for what he could get from God (1:9–11). Note that if Job were to repent of some supposed sin in order to gain God's blessing, then he could indeed be accused of serving God simply for personal gain.

(3) Although the words of Eliphaz eloquently express the importance of repentance, they were spoken with wrong motivation. There was no hint of sympathy in his heart for the suffering Job. Eliphaz's failure demonstrates that the message of repentance spoken to the weak and suffering must be accompanied by words of comfort and compassion.

3 Oh that I knew where I might find him! *that* I might come *even* to his seat!

4 I would order *my* cause before him, and fill my mouth with arguments.

5 I would know the words *which* he would answer me, and understand what he would say unto me.

6 [u]Will he plead against me with *his* great power? No; but he would put *strength* in me.

7 There the righteous might dispute with him; so should I be delivered for ever from my judge.

8 [v]Behold, I go forward, but he *is* not *there;* and backward, but I cannot perceive him:

9 On the left hand, where he doth work, but I cannot behold *him:* he hideth himself on the right hand, that I cannot see *him:*

10 But he [w]knoweth [i]the way that I take: *when* [x]he hath tried me, I shall come forth as gold.

11 [y]My foot hath held his steps, his way have I kept, and not declined.

12 Neither have I gone back from the commandment of his lips; [z][j]I have esteemed the words of his mouth more than [k]my necessary *food.*

Ps. 1:1-2

13 But he *is* in one *mind,* and who can turn him? and *what* [a]his soul desireth, even *that* he doeth.

14 For he performeth *the thing that is* [b]appointed for me: and many such *things are* with him.

15 Therefore am I troubled at his presence: when I consider, I am afraid of him.

16 For God [c]maketh my heart soft, and the Almighty troubleth me:

17 Because I was not cut off before the darkness, *neither* hath he covered the darkness from my face.

24 WHY, SEEING [d]times are not hidden from the Almighty, do they that know him not see his days?

2 *Some* remove the [e]landmarks; they violently take away flocks, and [l]feed *thereof.*

3 They drive away the ass of the fatherless, they [f]take the widow's ox for a pledge.

4 They turn the needy out of the way: [g]the poor of the earth hide themselves together.

5 Behold, *as* wild asses in the desert, go they forth to their work; rising betimes for a prey: the wilderness *yieldeth* food for them *and* for *their* children.

6 They reap *every one* his [m]corn in the field: and [n]they gather the vintage of the wicked.

7 They [h]cause the naked to lodge without clothing, that *they have* no covering in the cold.

8 They are wet with the showers of the mountains, and [i]embrace the rock for want of a shelter.

9 They pluck the fatherless from the breast, and take a pledge of the poor.

10 They cause *him* to go naked without clothing, and they take away the sheaf *from* the hungry;

11 *Which* make oil within their

23:6 [u]Is. 57:16 **23:8** [v]ch. 9:11 **23:10** [w]Ps. 139:1-3 [x]Ps. 17:3 & 66:10 Jas. 1:12 **23:11** [y]Ps. 44:18 **23:12** [z]John 4:32,34 **23:13** [a]Ps. 115:3 **23:14** [b]1 Thes. 3:3 **23:16** [c]Ps. 22:14

24:1 [d]Acts 1:7 **24:2** [e]Deut. 19:14 & 27:17 Prov. 22:28 & 23:10 Hos. 5:10 **24:3** [f]Deut. 24:6,10,12, 17 ch. 22:6 **24:4** [g]Prov. 28:28 **24:7** [h]Ex. 22:26 Deut. 24:12,13 ch. 22:6 **24:8** [i]Lam. 4:5

[i] Heb. *the way* that is *with me* [j] Heb. *I have hid,* or, *laid up* [k] Or, *my appointed portion* [l] Or, *feed* them [m] Heb. *mingled corn,* or, *dredge* [n] Heb. *the wicked gather the vintage*

23:3 OH THAT I KNEW WHERE I MIGHT FIND HIM! Throughout the whole experience of Job's suffering, his greatest longing was for the presence of his Lord. (1) He rarely mentioned the loss of prosperity; he barely alluded to his deep sorrow because of the loss of his children; it was the loss of God's presence that he mourned. In all his misery he desired to find God and to have communion with Him again (cf. 13:24; 16:19–21; 29:2–5).

(2) This same longing for God should characterize all true believers. "As the hart panteth after the water brooks, so panteth my soul after thee, O God. My soul thirsteth for God, for the living God" (Ps. 42:1–2). Again: "O God, thou *art* my God; early will I seek thee; my soul thirsteth for thee, my flesh longeth for thee in a dry and thirsty land, where no water is" (Ps. 63:1).

23:10–12 *WHEN* HE HATH TRIED ME. Job felt confident that God still cared about his life and that He knew no adversity would turn Job from faithful adherence to Him. (1) Job saw his suffering as a test of his faith in and love for the Lord. His test was similar to that of Abraham when he was told to sacrifice his son Isaac (Gen. 22).

(2) Jesus Christ Himself was tested by the suffering He underwent (Heb. 5:8), and as a result, He is now our pattern and example (1 Pet. 2:21); we as His followers are required to walk in similar steps (Heb. 13:12–13).

(3) Job's firm conviction that he would pass the test and never abandon his Lord rested on (a) his faithful obedience in the past (vv. 11–12), (b) his love for God's word (v. 12), and (c) his awe and fear of God (vv. 13–15). Likewise, the N.T. believer must resolve never to be swayed from his or her obedience to God, but rather to fear the consequences of unrighteousness and to love God's word more than daily bread (cf. Ps. 40:8; 119:11; see Jas. 1:21, note).

walls, *and* tread *their* winepresses, and
suffer thirst.
12 Men groan from out of the city,
and the soul of the wounded crieth out:
yet God layeth not folly *to them.*
13 They are of those that rebel
against the light; they know not the
ways thereof, nor abide in the paths
thereof.
14 [j]The murderer rising with the
light killeth the poor and needy, and in
the night is as a thief.
15 [k]The eye also of the adulterer
waiteth for the twilight, [l]saying, No
eye shall see me: and [o]disguiseth *his*
face.
16 In the dark they dig through
houses, *which* they had marked for
themselves in the daytime: [m]they
know not the light.
17 For the morning *is* to them even
as the shadow of death: if *one* know
them, they are in the terrors of the shad-
ow of death.
18 He *is* swift as the waters; their
portion is cursed in the earth: he be-
holdeth not the way of the vineyards.
19 Drought and heat [p]consume the
snow waters: *so doth* the grave *those
which* have sinned.
20 The womb shall forget him; the
worm shall feed sweetly on him; [n]he
shall be no more remembered; and
wickedness shall be broken as a tree.
21 He evil entreateth the barren
that beareth not: and doeth not good to
the widow.
22 He draweth also the mighty with
his power: he riseth up, [q]and no *man*
is sure of life.
23 *Though* it be given him *to be* in
safety, whereon he resteth; yet [o]his
eyes *are* upon their ways.
24 They are exalted for a little
while, but [r]are gone and brought low;
they are [s]taken out of the way as all
other, and cut off as the tops of the ears
of corn.
25 And if *it be* not *so* now, who will
make me a liar, and make my speech
nothing worth?

Bildad answers

25 THEN ANSWERED Bildad the
Shuhite, and said,
2 Dominion and fear *are* with him,
he maketh peace in his high places.
3 Is there any number of his ar-
mies? and upon whom doth not [p]his
light arise?

24:14 [j]Ps. 10:8
24:15 [k]Prov. 7:9 [l]Ps. 10:11
24:16 [m]John 3:20
24:20 [n]Prov. 10:7
24:23 [o]Ps. 11:4 Prov. 15:3
25:3 [p]Jas. 1:17
25:4 [q]ch. 4:17 & 15:14
25:6 [r]Ps. 22:6
26:6 [s]Ps. 139:8 Prov. 15:11 Heb. 4:13
26:7 [t]ch. 9:8 Ps. 24:2 & 104:2
26:8 [u]Prov. 30:4
26:10 [v]ch. 38:8 Ps. 33:7 & 104:9
26:12 [w]Ex. 14:21 Is. 51:15 Jer. 31:35
26:13 [x]Ps. 33:6 [y]Is. 27:1
27:2 [z]ch. 34:5

4 [q]How then can man be justified
with God? or how can he be clean *that
is* born of a woman?
5 Behold even to the moon, and it
shineth not; yea, the stars are not pure
in his sight.
6 How much less man, *that is* [r]a
worm? and the son of man, *which is* a
worm?

Job's final speech

26 BUT JOB answered and said,
2 How hast thou helped *him
that is* without power? *how* savest
thou the arm *that hath* no strength?
3 How hast thou counselled *him that
hath* no wisdom? and *how* hast thou
plentifully declared the thing as it is?
4 To whom hast thou uttered
words? and whose spirit came from
thee?
5 Dead *things* are formed from un-
der the waters, [t]and the inhabitants
thereof.
6 [s]Hell *is* naked before him, and
destruction hath no covering.
7 [t]He stretcheth out the north over
the empty place, *and* hangeth the earth
upon nothing.
8 [u]He bindeth up the waters in his
thick clouds; and the cloud is not rent
under them.
9 He holdeth back the face of his
throne, *and* spreadeth his cloud
upon it.
10 [v]He hath compassed the waters
with bounds, [u]until the day and night
come to an end.
11 The pillars of heaven tremble
and are astonished at his reproof.
12 [w]He divideth the sea with his
power, and by his understanding he
smiteth through [v]the proud.
13 [x]By his spirit he hath garnished
the heavens; his hand hath formed
[y]the crooked serpent.
14 Lo, these *are* parts of his ways:
but how little a portion is heard of him?
but the thunder of his power who can
understand?

27 MOREOVER JOB [w]continued
his parable, and said,
2 *As* God liveth, [z]*who* hath taken

[o] Heb. *setteth* his *face in secret* [p] Heb. *violently take* [q] Or, *he trusteth not* his own *life* [r] Heb. *are not* [s] Heb. *closed up* [t] Or, *with the inhabitants* [u] Heb. *until the end of light with darkness* [v] Heb. *pride* [w] Heb. *added to take up*

away my judgment; and the Almighty,
who hath [a]vexed[x] my soul;
3 All the while my breath *is* in me,
and [y]the spirit of God *is* in my nos-
trils;
4 My lips shall not speak wicked-
ness, nor my tongue utter deceit.
5 God forbid that I should justify
you: till I die [b]I will not remove mine
integrity from me.
6 My righteousness I [c]hold fast,
and will not let it go: [d]my heart shall
not reproach *me* [z]so long as I live.
7 Let mine enemy be as the wicked,
and he that riseth up against me as the
unrighteous.
8 [e]For what *is* the hope of the hyp-
ocrite, though he hath gained, when
God taketh away his soul?
9 [f]Will God hear his cry when trou-
ble cometh upon him?
10 [g]Will he delight himself in the
Almighty? will he always call upon
God?
11 I will teach you [a]by the hand of
God: *that* which *is* with the Almighty
will I not conceal.
12 Behold, all ye yourselves have
seen *it;* why then are ye thus altogeth-
er vain?
13 [h]This *is* the portion of a wicked
man with God, and the heritage of op-
pressors, *which* they shall receive of
the Almighty.
14 [i]If his children be multiplied, *it*
is for the sword: and his offspring shall
not be satisfied with bread.
15 Those that remain of him shall
be buried in death: and [j]his widows
shall not weep.
16 Though he heap up silver as the
dust, and prepare raiment as the clay;
17 He may prepare *it,* but [k]the just

27:2 [a]Ruth 1:20 2 Ki. 4:27
27:5 [b]ch. 2:9 & 13:15
27:6 [c]ch. 2:3 [d]Acts 24:16
27:8 [e]Mat. 16:26 Luke 12:20
27:9 [f]ch. 35:12 Prov. 1:28 & 28:9 Is. 1:15 Jer. 14:12 Ezek. 8:18 Mic. 3:4 John 9:31 Jas. 4:3
27:10 [g]See ch. 22:26,27
27:13 [h]ch. 20:29
27:14 [i]Deut. 28:41 Esth. 9:10 Hos. 9:13
27:15 [j]Ps. 78:64
27:17 [k]Prov. 28:8 Eccl. 2:26
27:18 [l]Is. 1:8 Lam. 2:6
27:20 [m]ch. 18:11

shall put *it* on, and the innocent shall
divide the silver.
18 He buildeth his house as a moth,
and [l]as a booth *that* the keeper
maketh.
19 The rich man shall lie down, but
he shall not be gathered: he openeth
his eyes, and he *is* not.
20 [m]Terrors take hold on him as
waters, a tempest stealeth him away in
the night.
21 The east wind carrieth him
away, and he departeth: and as a storm
hurleth him out of his place.
22 For *God* shall cast upon him, and
not spare: [b]he would fain flee out of
his hand.
23 *Men* shall clap their hands at
him, and shall hiss him out of his place.

28 SURELY THERE is [c]a vein for
the silver, and a place for gold
where they refine *it.*
2 Iron is taken out of the [d]earth,
and brass *is* molten *out of* the stone.
3 He setteth an end to darkness,
and searcheth out all perfection: the
stones of darkness, and the shadow of
death.
4 The flood breaketh out from the
inhabitant; *even the waters* forgotten of
the foot: they are dried up, they are
gone away from men.
5 *As for* the earth, out of it cometh
bread: and under it is turned up as it
were fire.
6 The stones of it *are* the place of
sapphires: and it hath [e]dust of gold.
7 *There is* a path which no fowl

[x]Heb. *made my soul bitter* [y]i.e. *the breath which God gave him;* see Gen. 2:7 [z]Heb. *from my days* [a]Or, being *in the hand* [b]Heb. *in fleeing he would flee* [c]Or, *a mine* [d]Or, *dust* [e]Or, *gold ore*

27:4 MY LIPS SHALL NOT SPEAK WICKEDNESS. Job is among the greatest examples of endurance in conviction, adherence to righteousness, and perseverance in the faith (see Jas. 5:11). His unswerving determination to maintain his integrity and remain faithful to God is unparalleled in the salvation history of the faithful. No temptation, suffering, or apparent silence from God could drive him away from allegiance to God and His word. He refused to curse God and die (2:9).

(1) Similarly, N.T. believers must be committed to only one course of action throughout the temptations, sorrows, and dark days of life. With the strongest conviction, they must confidently continue in their faith firm to the end (Col. 1:23); they must never give up as long as they live, holding fast with integrity to God's word and his love. They must determine "to have always a conscience void of offence toward God, and *toward* men" (Acts 24:16; cf. 23:1; 1 Cor. 4:4; 2 Tim. 1:3; 1 John 3:21).

(2) This decision to remain faithful to God and steadfast in faith, hope, and love is not optional for the believer (Heb. 3:14; 10:35–39; Jude 21). Doing so is their safeguard against experiencing shipwreck of their faith when faced with intense persecution, temptations, and assaults from Satan (1 Tim. 1:18–20; cf. 6:11–14; 2 Tim. 4:5–8; see Phil. 3:8–16).

(3) On His part, God promises by His power to guard His faithful people and keep them in His grace, so that they may obtain final "salvation ready to be revealed in the last time" (see 1 Pet. 1:5, note).

knoweth, and which the vulture's eye hath not seen:

8 The lion's whelps have not trodden it, nor the fierce lion passed by it.

9 He putteth forth his hand upon the [f]rock; he overturneth the mountains by the roots.

10 He cutteth out rivers among the rocks; and his eye seeth every precious thing.

11 He bindeth the floods [g]from overflowing; and *the thing that is* hid bringeth he forth to light.

12 [n]But where shall wisdom be found? and where *is* the place of understanding?

13 Man knoweth not the [o]price thereof; neither is it found in the land of the living.

14 [p]The depth saith, It *is* not in me: and the sea saith, *It is* not with me.

15 [h]It [q]cannot be gotten for gold, neither shall silver be weighed *for* the price thereof.

16 It cannot be valued with the gold of Ophir, with the precious onyx, or the sapphire.

17 The gold and the crystal cannot equal it: and the exchange of it *shall not be for* [i]jewels of fine gold.

18 No mention shall be made of [j]coral, or of pearls: for the price of wisdom *is* above rubies.

19 The topaz of Ethiopia shall not equal it, neither shall it be valued with pure gold.

20 [r]Whence then cometh wisdom? and where *is* the place of understanding?

21 Seeing it is hid from the eyes of all living, and kept close from the fowls of the [k]air.

22 [s]Destruction and death say, We have heard the fame thereof with our ears.

23 God understandeth the way thereof, and he knoweth the place thereof.

24 For he looketh to the ends of the earth, *and* [t]seeth under the whole heaven;

25 [u]To make the weight for the winds; and he weigheth the waters by measure.

26 When he [v]made a decree for the rain, and a way for the lightning of the thunder:

27 Then did he see it, and [l]declare it; he prepared it, yea, and searched it out.

28 And unto man he said, Behold, [w]the fear of the Lord, that *is* wisdom; and to depart from evil *is* understanding.

29

MOREOVER JOB [m]continued his parable, and said,

2 Oh that I were as *in* months past, as *in* the days *when* God preserved me;

3 [x]When his [n]candle shined upon my head, *and when* by his light I walked *through* darkness;

4 As I was in the days of my youth, when [y]the secret of God *was* upon my tabernacle;

5 When the Almighty *was* yet with me, *when* my children *were* about me;

6 When [z]I washed my steps with butter, and [a]the rock poured [o]me out rivers of oil;

7 When I went out to the gate

28:12 [n]Eccl. 7:24
28:13 [o]Prov. 3:15
28:14 [p]ver. 22 Rom. 11:33
28:15 [q]Prov. 3:13-15 & 8:10,11,19
28:20 [r]ver. 12
28:22 [s]ver. 14
28:24 [t]Prov. 15:3
28:25 [u]Ps. 135:7
28:26 [v]ch. 38:25
28:28 [w]Deut. 4:6 Prov. 1:7
29:3 [x]ch. 18:6
29:4 [y]Ps. 25:14
29:6 [z]Gen. 49:11 Deut. 32:13 ch. 20:17 [a]Ps. 81:16

[f] Or, *flint* [g] Heb. *from weeping* [h] Heb. *Fine gold shall not be given for it* [i] Or, *vessels of fine gold* [j] Or, *Ramoth* [k] Or, *heaven* [l] Or, *number it* [m] Heb. *added to take up* [n] Or, *lamp* [o] Heb. *with me*

28:28 THE FEAR OF THE LORD, THAT *IS* WISDOM. Fear of and reverence for God are fundamental to the believer's relationship with God (Ps. 61:5; Prov. 1:7). (1) Fearing the Lord makes us concerned and alert that we do not offend our holy God. Without this foundation, no true wisdom exists and no redemptive experience will stand the test of time and temptation.

(2) True fear of God and true Biblical wisdom cause us to turn from evil and result in "the comfort of the Holy Ghost" (see Acts 9:31, note).

(3) To fear God and yet continue in sin is a moral impossibility. The soul that acclaims God's majesty and recognizes His opposition to evil will be characterized by an earnest, decisive, and total endeavor to separate from sin (Ps. 4:4; Prov. 3:7; 8:13; 16:6; Is. 1:16) and follow God's word (Ps. 112:1; 119:63; Prov. 14:2,16; 2 Cor. 7:1; Eph. 5:21; 1 Pet. 1:17; see article on THE FEAR OF THE LORD, p. 282).

29:2 OH THAT I WERE . . . AS *IN* THE DAYS *WHEN* GOD PRESERVED ME. Job persevered in his desire for the communion with God that he had once known (see 23:3, note). He longed for (1) God's special care and protection (cf. Num. 6:24–26; Ps. 91:11; 121:7–8); (2) God's lamp to show him the way in dark or difficult circumstances (v. 3); (3) God's intimate fellowship and love (vv. 4–5; cf. Prov. 3:32); (4) God's grace to help him do good (vv. 12–17); and (5) God's wisdom to share with others (vv. 21–25). What God was to Job, He offers to all those who believe in the Lord Jesus Christ (see John 15:15; Rom. 8:1,31,33; 2 Thes. 3:3; 1 Pet. 3:13).

through the city, *when* I prepared my
seat in the street!
8 The young men saw me, and hid
themselves: and the aged arose, *and*
stood up.
9 The princes refrained talking, and
[b]laid *their* hand on their mouth.
10 [p]The nobles held their peace,
and their [c]tongue cleaved to the roof
of their mouth.
11 When the ear heard *me,* then it
blessed me; and when the eye saw *me,*
it gave witness to me:
12 Because [d]I delivered the poor
that cried, and the fatherless, and *him*
that had none to help him.
13 The blessing of him that was
ready to perish came upon me: and I
caused the widow's heart to sing for
joy.
14 [e]I put on righteousness, and it
clothed me: my judgment *was* as a robe
and a diadem.
15 I was [f]eyes to the blind, and
feet *was* I to the lame.
16 I *was* a father to the poor: and
[g]the cause *which* I knew not I
searched out.
17 And I brake [h]the[q] jaws of the
wicked, and [r]plucked the spoil out of
his teeth.
18 Then I said, [i]I shall die in my
nest, and I shall multiply *my* days as
the sand.
19 [j]My root *was* [s]spread out [k]by
the waters, and the dew lay all night
upon my branch.
20 My glory *was* [t]fresh in me, and
my [l]bow was [u]renewed in my hand.
21 Unto me *men* gave ear, and wait-
ed, and kept silence at my counsel.
22 After my words they spake not
again; and my speech dropped upon
them.
23 And they waited for me as for the
rain; and they opened their mouth wide
as for [m]the latter rain.
24 *If* I laughed on them, they be-
lieved *it* not; and the light of my coun-
tenance they cast not down.
25 I chose out their way, and sat
chief, and dwelt as a king in the army,
as one *that* comforteth the mourners.

30 BUT NOW *they that are* [v]youn-
ger than I have me in derision,
whose fathers I would have disdained
to have set with the dogs of my flock.
2 Yea, whereto *might* the strength
of their hands *profit* me, in whom old
age was perished?

29:9 [b]ch. 21:5
29:10 [c]Ps. 137:6
29:12 [d]Ps. 72:12 Prov. 21:13 & 24:11
29:14 [e]Deut. 24:13 Is. 59:17 & 61:10 Eph. 6:14 1 Thes. 5:8
29:15 [f]Num. 10:31
29:16 [g]Prov. 29:7
29:17 [h]Ps. 58:6 Prov. 30:14
29:18 [i]Ps. 30:6
29:19 [j]ch. 18:16 [k]Ps. 1:3 Jer. 17:8
29:20 [l]Gen. 49:24
29:23 [m]Zech. 10:1

30:9 [n]ch. 17:6 Ps. 35:15 & 69:12 Lam. 3:14
30:10 [o]Num. 12:14 Deut. 25:9 Is. 50:6 Mat. 26:67 & 27:30
30:11 [p]See ch. 12:18
30:12 [q]ch. 19:12
30:16 [r]Ps. 42:4

3 For want and famine *they were*
[w]solitary; fleeing into the wilderness
[x]in former time desolate and waste.
4 Who cut up mallows by the
bushes, and juniper roots *for* their
meat.
5 They were driven forth from
among *men,* (they cried after them as
after a thief;)
6 To dwell in the cliffs of the val-
leys, *in* [y]caves of the earth, and *in* the
rocks.
7 Among the bushes they brayed;
under the nettles they were gathered
together.
8 *They were* children of fools, yea,
children of [z]base men: they were viler
than the earth.
9 [n]And now am I their song, yea, I
am their byword.
10 They abhor me, they flee far
from me, [a]and spare not [o]to spit in
my face.
11 Because he [p]hath loosed my
cord, and afflicted me, they have also
let loose the bridle before me.
12 Upon *my* right *hand* rise the
youth; they push away my feet, and
[q]they raise up against me the ways of
their destruction.
13 They mar my path, they set for-
ward my calamity, they have no helper.
14 They came *upon me* as a wide
breaking in *of waters:* in the desolation
they rolled themselves *upon me.*
15 Terrors are turned upon me:
they pursue [b]my soul as the wind: and
my welfare passeth away as a cloud.
16 [r]And now my soul is poured out
upon me; the days of affliction have
taken hold upon me.
17 My bones are pierced in me in
the night season: and my sinews take
no rest.
18 By the great force *of my disease*
is my garment changed: it bindeth me
about as the collar of my coat.
19 He hath cast me into the mire,
and I am become like dust and ashes.
20 I cry unto thee, and thou dost not
hear me: I stand up, and thou regard-
est me *not.*

[p] Heb. *The voice of the nobles was hid* [q] Heb. *the jawteeth,* or, *the grinders* [r] Heb. *cast* [s] Heb. *opened* [t] Heb. *new* [u] Heb. *changed* [v] Heb. *of fewer days than I* [w] Or, *dark as the night* [x] Heb. *yesternight* [y] Heb. *holes* [z] Heb. *men of no name* [a] Heb. *and withhold not spittle from my face* [b] Heb. *my principal one*

21 Thou art [c]become cruel to me:
with [d]thy strong hand thou opposest
thyself against me.
22 Thou liftest me up to the wind;
thou causest me to ride *upon it*, and
dissolvest my [e]substance.
23 For I know *that* thou wilt bring
me *to* death, and *to* the house [s]appointed
for all living.
24 Howbeit he will not stretch out
his hand to the [f]grave, though they
cry in his destruction.
25 [t]Did not I weep [g]for him that
was in trouble? was *not* my soul
grieved for the poor?
26 [u]When I looked for good, then
evil came *unto me:* and when I waited
for light, there came darkness.
27 My bowels boiled, and rested
not: the days of affliction prevented
me.
28 [v]I went mourning without the
sun: I stood up, *and* I cried in the congregation.
29 [w]I am a brother to dragons, and
a companion to [h]owls.
30 [x]My skin is black upon me, and
[y]my bones are burned with heat.
31 My harp also is *turned* to mourning,
and my organ into the voice of
them that weep.

31 I MADE a covenant with mine
[z]eyes; why then should I think
upon a maid?
2 For what [a]portion of God *is there*
from above? and *what* inheritance of
the Almighty from on high?
3 *Is* not destruction to the wicked?
and a strange *punishment* to the workers
of iniquity?
4 [b]Doth not he see my ways, and
count all my steps?
5 If I have walked with vanity, or if
my foot hath hasted to deceit;
6 [i]Let me be weighed in an even
balance, that God may know mine integrity.
7 If my step hath turned out of the
way, and [c]mine heart walked after
mine eyes, and if any blot hath cleaved
to mine hands;
8 *Then* [d]let me sow, and let another
eat; yea, let my offspring be rooted
out.
9 If mine heart have been deceived
by a woman, or *if* I have laid wait at my
neighbour's door;
10 *Then* let my wife grind unto [e]another,
and let others bow down upon
her.
11 For this *is* an heinous crime; yea,
[f]it *is* an iniquity *to be punished by* the
judges.
12 For it *is* a fire *that* consumeth to
destruction, and would root out all
mine increase.
13 If I did despise the cause of my
manservant or of my maidservant,
when they contended with me;

30:23 [s]Heb. 9:27 **30:25** [t]Ps. 35:13 Rom. 12:15 **30:26** [u]Jer. 8:15 **30:28** [v]Ps. 42:9 **30:29** [w]Ps. 102:6 Mic. 1:8 **30:30** [x]Ps. 119:83 Lam. 4:8 [y]Ps. 102:3 **31:1** [z]Mat. 5:28 **31:2** [a]ch. 20:29 **31:4** [b]2 Chr. 16:9 Prov. 5:21 Jer. 32:19 **31:7** [c]See Num. 15:39 Eccl. 11:9 Ezek. 6:9 Mat. 5:29 **31:8** [d]Lev. 26:16 Deut. 28:30,38 **31:10** [e]2 Sam. 12:11 Jer. 8:10 **31:11** [f]Gen. 38:24 Lev. 20:10 See ver. 28

c Heb. *turned to be cruel* d Heb. *the strength of thy hand* e Or, *wisdom* f Heb. *heap* g Heb. *for him that was hard of day?* h Or, *ostriches* i Heb. *Let him weigh me in balances of justice*

30:20 I CRY UNTO THEE, AND THOU DOST NOT HEAR ME. All God's people have this experience at some point in their walk with God, a time in which they cry out to God for help and He does not seem to answer them. Even the Lord Jesus experienced this (Mat. 27:46). (1) Through this experiece our faith is tested. At such times we must nevertheless persevere in faith (see Mat. 15:21–28; Luke 18:1–7; 1 Pet. 1:7). (2) We know from God's dealing with Job and with faithful believers throughout history that no true follower of the Lord is ever really abandoned by Him (Heb. 13:5), and no earnest prayers ever go unheard (cf. Heb. 10:32–39).

31:1–34 I MADE A COVENANT WITH MY EYES. In this section Job reviewed his firm spiritual integrity, his adherence to God and His ways, and his goodness to others. (1) Job's declarations about God's redemptive work in him embraced every aspect of life. He spoke of his innocence in the sins of the heart, including sexual lust and impure thoughts (vv. 1–4), lying and cheating for gain (vv. 5–8), and marital infidelity (vv. 9–12). He declared his just treatment of workers (vv. 13–15) and his care for the poor and needy (vv. 16–23). He maintained that he was free from covetousness (vv. 24–25), idolatry (vv. 26–28), revenge (vv. 29–32), and hypocrisy (vv. 33–34).

(2) The moral character and purity of heart and life described here serve as a splendid example for every believer. The godly life that Job lived prior to the new covenant can be abundantly experienced by all those who believe in Christ, through the saving power of His death and resurrection (Rom. 8:1–17; Gal. 2:20).

31:1 WHY THEN SHOULD I THINK UPON A MAID? Job was committed to the standard of inner holiness that Christ later articulated in the Sermon on the Mount (Mat. 5:28). Job had made a covenant with his eyes to avoid stimulating lustful desires that come from gazing at a young woman (cf. Gen. 3:6; Num. 15:39). He knew that sensuality would displease His Lord and dissipate the life of God in his soul (vv. 2–4).

31:13 THE CAUSE OF MY MANSERVANT OR OF MY MAIDSERVANT. Job's treatment of his servants exemplifies how employers should care for their employees. He treated his workers

14 What then shall I do when [g]God riseth up? and when he visiteth, what shall I answer him?

15 [h]Did not he that made me in the womb make him? and [j]did not one fashion us in the womb?

16 If I have withheld the poor from *their* desire, or have caused the eyes of the widow to fail;

17 Or have eaten my morsel myself alone, and the fatherless hath not eaten thereof;

18 (For from my youth he was brought up with me, as *with* a father, and I have guided [k]her from my mother's womb;)

19 If I have seen any perish for want of clothing, or any poor without covering;

20 If his loins have not [i]blessed me, and *if* he were *not* warmed with the fleece of my sheep;

21 If I have lifted up my hand [j]against the fatherless, when I saw my help in the gate:

22 *Then* let mine arm fall from my shoulder blade, and mine arm be broken from [l]the bone.

23 For [k]destruction *from* God *was* a terror to me, and by reason of his highness I could not endure.

24 [l]If I have made gold my hope, or have said to the fine gold, *Thou art* my confidence;

25 [m]If I rejoiced because my wealth *was* great, and because mine hand had [m]gotten much;

26 [n]If I beheld [n]the sun when it shined, or the moon walking [o]*in* brightness;

27 And my heart hath been secretly enticed, or [p]my mouth hath kissed my hand:

28 This also *were* an iniquity *to be punished by* the judge: for I should have denied the God *that is* above.

29 [o]If I rejoiced at the destruction of him that hated me, or lifted up myself when evil found him:

30 [p]Neither have I suffered [q]my mouth to sin by wishing a curse to his soul.

31 If the men of my tabernacle said not, Oh that we had of his flesh! we cannot be satisfied.

32 [q]The stranger did not lodge in the street: *but* I opened my doors [r]to the traveller.

33 If I covered my transgressions [r]as[s] Adam, by hiding mine iniquity in my bosom:

34 Did I fear a great [s]multitude, or did the contempt of families terrify me, that I kept silence, *and* went not out of the door?

35 Oh that one would hear me! [t]behold, my desire *is,* [t]*that* the Almighty would answer me, and *that* mine adversary had written a book.

36 Surely I would take it upon my shoulder, *and* bind it *as* a crown to me.

37 I would declare unto him the number of my steps; as a prince would I go near unto him.

38 If my land cry against me, or that the furrows likewise thereof [u]complain;

39 If [u]I have eaten [v]the fruits thereof without money, or [v]have [w]caused the owners thereof to lose their life:

40 Let [w]thistles grow instead of wheat, and [x]cockle instead of barley. The words of Job are ended.

Elihu declares his opinion

32 SO THESE three men ceased [y]to answer Job, because he *was* [x]righteous in his own eyes.

2 Then was kindled the wrath of Eli-

31:14 [g]Ps. 44:21 **31:15** [h]ch. 34:19 **31:20** [i]Deut. 24:13 **31:21** [j]ch. 22:9 **31:23** [k]Is. 13:6 **31:24** [l]Mark 10:24 **31:25** [m]Ps. 62:10 **31:26** [n]Ezek. 8:16 **31:29** [o]Prov. 17:5 **31:30** [p]Mat. 5:44 **31:32** [q]Gen. 19:2,3 **31:33** [r]Prov. 28:13 **31:34** [s]Ex. 23:2 **31:35** [t]ch. 13:22 **31:39** [u]Jas. 5:4 [v]1 Ki. 21:19 **31:40** [w]Gen. 3:18 **32:1** [x]ch. 33:9

[j] Or, *did he not fashion us in one womb?* [k] i.e. *the widow* [l] Or, *the chanelbone* [m] Heb. *found much* [n] Heb. *the light* [o] Heb. *bright* [p] Heb. *my hand hath kissed my mouth* [q] Heb. *my palate* [r] Or, *to the way* [s] Or, *after the manner of men* [t] Or, *behold, my sign* is that *the Almighty will answer me* [u] Heb. *weep* [v] Heb. *the strength thereof* [w] Heb. *caused the soul of the owners thereof to expire,* or, *breathe out* [x] Or, *noisome weeds* [y] Heb. *from answering*

with fairness, kindness, and equality; he listened to them and responded to any just complaint (cf. Lev. 25:42–43,55; Deut. 15:12–15; 16:12). Job knew that one day he would have to give account to God for his treatment of others (v. 14; see Col. 3:25, note).

32:2 ELIHU. A new counselor, Elihu, is introduced here into the narrative. He had refrained from expressing his opinion earlier because he was younger than the others (v. 4). He believed, however, that he had insight into Job's suffering and could instruct him in the correct attitude he should have before God. Elihu's speech differs from the first three in its emphasis that suffering can be God's merciful chastisement in order to enlighten the soul (33:30) and to bring about a more intimate relationship with God (36:7–10). However like the other counselors, Elihu assumed that Job had sinned and therefore deserved his suffering.

hu the son of Barachel the Buzite, of
the kindred of Ram: against Job was
his wrath kindled, because he justified
[z]himself rather than God.
3 Also against his three friends was
his wrath kindled, because they had
found no answer, and *yet* had condemned Job.
4 Now Elihu had [a]waited till Job
had spoken, because they *were* [b]elder
than he.
5 When Elihu saw that *there was* no
answer in the mouth of *these* three
men, then his wrath was kindled.
6 And Elihu the son of Barachel the
Buzite answered and said, I *am*
[c]young, and ye *are* very old; wherefore
I was afraid, and [d]durst not show you
mine opinion.
7 I said, Days should speak, and
multitude of years should teach wisdom.
8 But *there is* a spirit in man: and
[y]the inspiration of the Almighty
giveth them understanding.
9 [z]Great men are not *always* wise:
neither do the aged understand judgment.
10 Therefore I said, Hearken to me;
I also will show mine opinion.
11 Behold, I waited for your words;
I gave ear to your [e]reasons, whilst ye
searched out [f]what to say.
12 Yea, I attended unto you, and,
behold, *there was* none of you that convinced Job, *or* that answered his words:
13 [a]Lest ye should say, We have
found out wisdom: God thrusteth him
down, not man.
14 Now he hath not [g]directed *his*
words against me: neither will I answer him with your speeches.
15 They were amazed, they answered no more: [h]they left off speaking.
16 When I had waited, (for they
spake not, but stood still, *and* answered no more;)
17 *I said,* I will answer also my part,
I also will show mine opinion.
18 For I am full of [f]matter, [i]the
spirit within me constraineth me.

32:8 [y]Prov. 2:6
32:9 [z]1 Cor. 1:26
32:13 [a]Jer. 9:23

19 Behold, my belly *is* as wine *which*
[j]hath no vent; it is ready to burst like
new bottles.
20 I will speak, [k]that I may be refreshed: I will open my lips and answer.
21 Let me not, I pray you, accept
any man's person, neither let me give
flattering titles unto man.
22 For I know not to give flattering
titles; *in so doing* my maker would soon
take me away.

33 WHEREFORE, JOB, I pray
thee, hear my speeches, and
hearken to all my words.
2 Behold, now I have opened my
mouth, my tongue hath spoken [l]in my
mouth.
3 My words *shall be of* the uprightness of my heart: and my lips shall utter knowledge clearly.
4 [b]The spirit of God hath made me,
and the breath of the Almighty hath
given me life.
5 If thou canst answer me, set *thy
words* in order before me, stand up.
6 [c]Behold, I *am* [m]according to thy
wish in God's stead: I also am
[n]formed out of the clay.
7 [d]Behold, my terror shall not
make thee afraid, neither shall my
hand be heavy upon thee.
8 Surely thou hast spoken [o]in
mine hearing, and I have heard the
voice of *thy* words, *saying,*
9 [e]I am clean without transgression, I *am* innocent; neither *is there* iniquity in me.
10 Behold, he findeth occasions
against me, [f]he counteth me for his
enemy,
11 [g]He putteth my feet in the
stocks, he marketh all my paths.
12 Behold, *in* this thou art not just:

33:4 [b]Gen. 2:7
33:6 [c]ch. 9:32,33
33:7 [d]ch. 9:34
33:9 [e]ch. 10:7
33:10 [f]ch. 16:9
33:11 [g]ch. 13:27

[z] Heb. *his soul* [a] Heb. *expected Job in words* [b] Heb. *elder for days* [c] Heb. *few of days* [d] Heb. *feared* [e] Heb. *understandings* [f] Heb. *words* [g] Or, *ordered* his *words* [h] Heb. *they removed speeches from themselves* [i] Heb. *the spirit of my belly* [j] Heb. *is not opened* [k] Heb. *that I may breathe* [l] Heb. *in my palate* [m] Heb. *according to thy mouth* [n] Heb. *cut out of the clay* [o] Heb. *in mine ears*

32:8 A SPIRIT IN MAN. Despite Elihu's claim to spiritual insight from God (cf. 33:4), his statements and theology are not thereby infallible. Some are full of insight; others fall short of Biblical revelation.

33:9 I AM CLEAN WITHOUT TRANSGRESSION. Elihu falsely stated that Job was claiming moral perfection, i.e., that he was "without transgression" all his life. Job had never insisted that he was sinless (see 13:26), but only that he had followed God's ways with all his heart and could never recall having committed a serious transgression that merited such severe punishment (27:5–6; 31:1–40).

I will answer thee, that God is greater than man.

13 Why dost thou [h]strive against him? for [p]he giveth not account of any of his matters.

14 [i]For God speaketh once, yea twice, *yet man* perceiveth it not.

15 [j]In a dream, in a vision of the night, when deep sleep falleth upon men, in slumberings upon the bed;

16 [k]Then [q]he openeth the ears of men, and sealeth their instruction,

17 That he may withdraw man *from his* [r]purpose, and hide pride from man.

18 He keepeth back his soul from the pit, and his life [s]from perishing by the sword.

19 He is chastened also with pain upon his bed, and the multitude of his bones with strong *pain:*

20 [l]So that his life abhorreth bread, and his soul [t]dainty meat.

21 His flesh is consumed away, that it cannot be seen; and his bones *that* were not seen stick out.

22 Yea, his soul draweth near unto the grave, and his life to the destroyers.

23 If there be a messenger with him, an interpreter, one among a thousand, to show unto man his uprightness:

24 Then he is gracious unto him, and saith, Deliver him from going down to the pit: I have found [u]a ransom.

25 His flesh shall be fresher [v]than a child's: he shall return to the days of his youth:

26 He shall pray unto God, and he will be favourable unto him: and he shall see his face with joy: for he will render unto man his righteousness.

27 [w]He looketh upon men, and *if any* [m]say, I have sinned, and perverted *that which was* right, and it [n]profited me not;

28 [x]He will [o]deliver his soul from going into the pit, and his life shall see the light.

29 Lo, all these *things* worketh God [y]oftentimes with man,

30 [p]To bring back his soul from the pit, to be enlightened with the light of the living.

31 Mark well, O Job, hearken unto me: hold thy peace, and I will speak.

32 If thou hast any thing to say, answer me: speak, for I desire to justify thee.

33:13 [h]Is. 45:9
33:14 [i]Ps. 62:11
33:15 [j]Num. 12:6
33:16 [k]ch. 36:10,15
33:20 [l]Ps. 107:18
33:27 [m]2 Sam. 12:13 Prov. 28:13 Luke 15:21 1 John 1:9 [n]Rom. 6:21
33:28 [o]Is. 38:17
33:30 [p]Ps. 56:13
33:33 [q]Ps. 34:11
34:3 [r]ch. 6:30 & 12:11
34:5 [s]ch. 33:9 [t]ch. 27:2
34:6 [u]ch. 9:17
34:7 [v]ch. 15:16
34:9 [w]Mal. 3:14
34:10 [x]ch. 8:3
34:11 [y]Ps. 62:12 Prov. 24:12 Mat. 16:27
34:12 [z]ch. 8:3
34:14 [a]Ps. 104:29
34:15 [b]Gen. 3:19
34:17 [c]2 Sam. 23:3

33 If not, [q]hearken unto me: hold thy peace, and I shall teach thee wisdom.

34

FURTHERMORE ELIHU answered and said,

2 Hear my words, O ye wise *men;* and give ear unto me, ye that have knowledge.

3 [r]For the ear trieth words, as the [z]mouth tasteth meat.

4 Let us choose to us judgment: let us know among ourselves what *is* good.

5 For Job hath said, [s]I am righteous: and [t]God hath taken away my judgment.

6 [u]Should I lie against my right? [a]my wound *is* incurable without transgression.

7 What man *is* like Job, [v]*who* drinketh up scorning like water?

8 Which goeth in company with the workers of iniquity, and walketh with wicked men.

9 For [w]he hath said, It profiteth a man nothing that he should delight himself with God.

10 Therefore hearken unto me, ye [b]men of understanding: [x]far be it from God, *that he should do* wickedness; and *from* the Almighty, *that he should commit* iniquity.

11 [y]For the work of a man shall he render unto him, and cause every man to find according to *his* ways.

12 Yea, surely God will not do wickedly, neither will the Almighty [z]pervert judgment.

13 Who hath given him a charge over the earth? or who hath disposed [c]the whole world?

14 If he set his heart [d]upon man, *if* he [a]gather unto himself his spirit and his breath;

15 [b]All flesh shall perish together, and man shall turn again unto dust.

16 If now *thou hast* understanding, hear this: hearken to the voice of my words.

17 [c]Shall even he that hateth right

[p] Heb. *he answereth not* [q] Heb. *he revealeth,* or, *uncovereth* [r] Heb. *work* [s] Heb. *from passing by the sword* [t] Heb. *meat of desire* [u] Or, *an atonement* [v] Heb. *than childhood* [w] Or, *He shall look upon men, and say, I have sinned* [x] Or, *He hath delivered my soul, &c., and my life* [y] Heb. *twice* and *thrice* [z] Heb. *palate* [a] Heb. *mine arrow* [b] Heb. *men of heart* [c] Heb. *all of it?* [d] Heb. *upon him*

[e]govern? and wilt thou condemn him
that is most just?
18 [d]*Is it fit* to say to a king, *Thou
art* wicked? *and* to princes, *Ye are* un-
godly?
19 *How much less to him* that [e]ac-
cepteth not the persons of princes, nor
regardeth the rich more than the poor?
for [f]they all *are* the work of his hands.
20 In a moment shall they die, and
the people shall be troubled [g]at mid-
night, and pass away: and [f]the
mighty shall be taken away without
hand.
21 [h]For his eyes *are* upon the ways
of man, and he seeth all his goings.
22 [i]*There is* no darkness, nor shad-
ow of death, where the workers of iniq-
uity may hide themselves.
23 For he will not lay upon man
more *than right;* that he should [g]enter
into judgment with God.
24 [j]He shall break in pieces
mighty men [h]without number, and set
others in their stead.
25 Therefore he knoweth their
works, and he overturneth *them* in the
night, so that they are [i]destroyed.
26 He striketh them as wicked men
[j]in the open sight of others;
27 Because they [k]turned back
[k]from him, and [l]would not consider
any of his ways:
28 So that they [m]cause the cry of
the poor to come unto him, and he
[n]heareth the cry of the afflicted.
29 When he giveth quietness, who
then can make trouble? and when he
hideth *his* face, who then can behold
him? whether *it be done* against a na-
tion, or against a man only:
30 That the hypocrite reign not, lest
[o]the people be ensnared.
31 Surely it is meet to be said unto

34:18 [d]Ex. 22:28
34:19 [e]Deut. 10:17 [f]ch. 31:15
34:20 [g]Ex. 12:29
34:21 [h]ch. 31:4
34:22 [i]Ps. 139:12 Amos 9:2,3
34:24 [j]Dan. 2:21
34:27 [k]1 Sam. 15:11 [l]Ps. 28:5 Is. 5:12
34:28 [m]Jas. 5:4 [n]Ex. 22:23
34:30 [o]1 Ki. 12:28,30
34:35 [p]ch. 35:16
35:3 [q]ch. 21:15
35:4 [r]ch. 34:8
35:5 [s]ch. 22:12

God, I have borne *chastisement,* I will
not offend *any more:*
32 *That which* I see not teach thou
me: if I have done iniquity, I will do no
more.
33 [l]*Should it be* according to thy
mind? he will recompense it, whether
thou refuse, or whether thou choose;
and not I: therefore speak what thou
knowest.
34 Let men [m]of understanding tell
me, and let a wise man hearken
unto me.
35 [p]Job hath spoken without
knowledge, and his words *were* without
wisdom.
36 [n]My desire *is that* Job may be
tried unto the end because of *his* an-
swers for wicked men.
37 For he addeth rebellion unto his
sin, he clappeth *his hands* among us,
and multiplieth his words against God.

35 ELIHU SPAKE moreover, and
said,
2 Thinkest thou this to be right, *that*
thou saidst, My righteousness *is* more
than God's?
3 For [q]thou saidst, What advan-
tage will it be unto thee? *and,* What
profit shall I have, [o]*if I be cleansed*
from my sin?
4 [p]I will answer thee, and [r]thy
companions with thee.
5 [s]Look unto the heavens, and see;
and behold the clouds *which* are higher
than thou.
6 If thou sinnest, what doest thou

[e] Heb. *bind?* [f] Heb. *they shall take away the mighty* [g] Heb. *go* [h] Heb. *without searching out* [i] Heb. *crushed* [j] Heb. *in the place of beholders* [k] Heb. *from after him* [l] Heb. Should it be *from with thee?* [m] Heb. *of heart* [n] Or, *My father, let Job be tried* [o] Or, by it *more than by my sin?* [p] Heb. *I will return to thee words*

34:37 HE ADDETH REBELLION UNTO HIS SIN. Elihu believed that Job's questioning of and complaints against God (19:6; 27:2) demonstrated outright rebellion against God. Though it may be true that Job seriously erred in his complaints against God, his heart held steadfastly to Him as his Lord (19:25–27; 23:8–12; 27:1–6). In his zeal to vindicate God, Elihu failed to understand fully the need Job had to express his innermost feelings to God (cf. Ps. 42:9; 43:2).

35:6 IF THOU SINNEST, WHAT DOEST THOU AGAINST HIM? Elihu believed that God is so detached from us (v. 5) that our sins or righteousness have no affect on Him. (1) Elihu's perception is wrong. The Bible reveals that God is not without emotion; He is capable of feeling hurt when men or women reject His love. When they turn against Him and sin, He is deeply grieved (Gen. 6:6; Ps. 78:40; Luke 19:41–44; Eph. 4:30).

(2) On the other hand, when God's people sincerely follow Him in love, obedience, and loyalty, He is greatly pleased (2 Cor. 9:7). God cares for His people with deep feeling, gathering them in His arms like a shepherd (Is. 40:11) and loving them with a tenderness greater than a mother (Is. 49:15). Note the marvelous expression of God's lovingkindness recorded by Isaiah: "In all their affliction he was afflicted, and the angel of his presence saved them: in his love and in his pity he redeemed them; and he bare them, and carried them all the days of old" (Is. 63:9; cf. Is. 53; Heb. 4:14–15).

[t]against him? or *if* thy transgressions be multiplied, what doest thou unto him?

7 [u]If thou be righteous, what givest thou him? or what receiveth he of thine hand?

8 Thy wickedness *may hurt* a man as thou *art;* and thy righteousness *may profit* the son of man.

9 [v]By reason of the multitude of oppressions they make *the oppressed* to cry: they cry out by reason of the arm of the mighty.

10 But none saith, [w]Where *is* God my maker, [x]who giveth songs in the night;

11 Who [y]teacheth us more than the beasts of the earth, and maketh us wiser than the fowls of heaven?

12 [z]There they cry, but none giveth answer, because of the pride of evil men.

13 [a]Surely God will not hear vanity, neither will the Almighty regard it.

14 [b]Although thou sayest thou shalt not see him, *yet* judgment *is* before him; therefore [c]trust thou in him.

15 But now, because *it is* not *so,* [q]he hath [d]visited in his anger; yet [r]he knoweth *it* not in great extremity:

16 [e]Therefore doth Job open his mouth in vain; he multiplieth words without knowledge.

36

ELIHU ALSO proceeded, and said,

2 Suffer me a little, and I will shew thee [s]that *I have* yet to speak on God's behalf.

3 I will fetch my knowledge from afar, and will ascribe righteousness to my Maker.

4 For truly my words *shall* not *be* false: he that is perfect in knowledge *is* with thee.

5 Behold, God *is* mighty, and despiseth not *any:* [f]*he is* mighty in strength *and* [t]wisdom.

6 He preserveth not the life of the wicked: but giveth right to the [u]poor.

7 [g]He withdraweth not his eyes from the righteous: but [h]with kings *are they* on the throne; yea, he doth establish them for ever, and they are exalted.

8 And [i]if *they be* bound in fetters, *and* be holden in cords of affliction;

9 Then he showeth them their work, and their transgressions that they have exceeded.

10 [j]He openeth also their ear to discipline, and commandeth that they return from iniquity.

11 If they obey and serve *him,* they shall [k]spend their days in prosperity, and their years in pleasures.

12 But if they obey not, [v]they shall perish by the sword, and they shall die without knowledge.

13 But the hypocrites in heart [l]heap up wrath: they cry not when he bindeth them.

14 [m]They[w] die in youth, and their life *is* among the unclean.

15 He delivereth the [u]poor in his affliction, and openeth their ears in oppression.

16 Even so would he have removed thee out of the strait [n]*into* a broad place, where *there is* no straitness; and [o]that[x] which should be set on thy table *should be* full of [p]fatness.

17 But thou hast fulfilled the judgment of the wicked: [y]judgment and justice take hold *on thee.*

18 Because *there is* wrath, *beware* lest he take thee away with *his* stroke: then [q]a great ransom cannot [z]deliver thee.

19 [r]Will he esteem thy riches? *no,* not gold, nor all the forces of strength.

20 Desire not the night, when people are cut off in their place.

21 Take heed, [s]regard not iniquity: for [t]this hast thou chosen rather than affliction.

22 Behold, God exalteth by his power: [u]who teacheth like him?

23 [v]Who hath enjoined him his way? or [w]who can say, Thou hast wrought iniquity?

24 Remember that thou [x]magnify his work, which men behold.

25 Every man may see it; man may behold *it* afar off.

26 Behold, God *is* great, and we [y]know *him* not, [z]neither can the number of his years be searched out.

27 For he [a]maketh small the drops of water: they pour down rain according to the vapour thereof:

28 [b]Which the clouds do drop *and* distil upon man abundantly.

29 Also can *any* understand the

35:6 [t]Prov. 8:36 Jer. 7:19 **35:7** [u]Ps. 16:2 Prov. 9:12 **35:9** [v]ch. 34:28 **35:10** [w]Is. 51:13 [x]Ps. 42:8 Acts 16:25 **35:11** [y]Ps. 94:12 **35:12** [z]Prov. 1:28 **35:13** [a]Is. 1:15 Jer. 11:11 **35:14** [b]ch. 9:11 [c]Ps. 37:5,6 **35:15** [d]Ps. 89:32 **35:16** [e]ch. 34:35 **36:5** [f]ch. 9:4 **36:7** [g]Ps. 33:18 [h]Ps. 113:8 **36:8** [i]Ps. 107:10 **36:10** [j]ch. 33:16

36:11 [k]ch. 21:13 Is. 1:19,20 **36:13** [l]Rom. 2:5 **36:14** [m]Ps. 55:23 **36:16** [n]Ps. 18:19 & 31:8 [o]Ps. 23:5 [p]Ps. 36:8 **36:18** [q]Ps. 49:7 **36:19** [r]Prov. 11:4 **36:21** [s]Ps. 66:18 [t]Heb. 11:25 **36:22** [u]Is. 40:13 1 Cor. 2:16 **36:23** [v]ch. 34:13 [w]ch. 34:10 **36:24** [x]Ps. 92:5 Rev. 15:3 **36:26** [y]1 Cor. 13:12 [z]Ps. 90:2 Heb. 1:12 **36:27** [a]Ps. 147:8 **36:28** [b]Prov. 3:20

[q]i.e. *God* [r]i.e. *Job* [s]Heb. *that* there are *yet words for God* [t]Heb. *heart* [u]Or, *afflicted* [v]Heb. *they shall pass away by the sword* [w]Heb. *Their soul dieth* [x]Heb. *the rest of thy table* [y]Or, *judgment and justice should uphold* thee [z]Heb. *turn thee aside*

spreadings of the clouds, *or* the noise
of his tabernacle?
30 Behold, he [c]spreadeth his light
upon it, and covereth [a]the bottom of
the sea.
31 For [d]by them judgeth he the
people; he [e]giveth meat in abundance.
32 [f]With clouds he covereth the
light; and commandeth it *not to shine* by
the cloud that cometh betwixt.
33 [g]The noise thereof showeth
concerning it, the cattle also concern-
ing [b]the vapour.

37 AT THIS also my heart trem-
bleth, and is moved out of his
place.
2 [c]Hear attentively the noise of his
voice, and the sound *that* goeth out of
his mouth.
3 He directeth it under the whole
heaven, and his [d]lightning unto the
[e]ends of the earth.
4 After it [h]a voice roareth: he thun-
dereth with the voice of his excellency;
and he will not stay them when his
voice is heard.
5 God thundereth marvellously with
his voice; [i]great things doeth he,
which we cannot comprehend.
6 For [j]he saith to the snow, Be
thou *on* the earth; [f]likewise to the
small rain, and to the great rain of his
strength.
7 He sealeth up the hand of every
man; [k]that all men may know his
work.
8 Then the beasts [l]go into dens,
and remain in their places.
9 [g]Out of the south cometh the
whirlwind: and cold out of the [h]north.
10 [m]By the breath of God frost is
given: and the breadth of the waters is
straitened.
11 Also by watering he wearieth the
thick cloud: he scattereth [i]his bright
cloud:
12 And it is turned round about by
his counsels: that they may [n]do what-
soever he commandeth them upon the
face of the world in the earth.
13 [o]He causeth it to come, wheth-
er for [j]correction, or [p]for his land, or
[q]for mercy.

Consider his wondrous works

14 Hearken unto this, O Job: stand
still, and [r]consider the wondrous
works of God.
15 Dost thou know when God dis-
posed them, and caused the light of his
cloud to shine?
16 [s]Dost thou know the balanc-
ings of the clouds, the wondrous works
of [t]him which is perfect in knowl-
edge?
17 How thy garments *are* warm,
when he quieteth the earth by the
south *wind?*
18 Hast thou with him [u]spread out
the sky, *which is* strong, *and* as a mol-
ten lookingglass?
19 Teach us what we shall say unto
him; *for* we cannot order *our speech* by
reason of darkness.
20 Shall it be told him that I speak?
if a man speak, surely he shall be swal-
lowed up.
21 And now *men* see not the bright
light which *is* in the clouds: but the
wind passeth, and cleanseth them.
22 [k]Fair weather cometh out of the
north: with God *is* terrible majesty.
23 *Touching* the Almighty, [v]we
cannot find him out: [w]*he is* excellent in
power, and in judgment, and in plenty
of justice: he will not afflict.
24 Men do therefore [x]fear him: he
respecteth not any *that are* [y]wise of
heart.

The LORD speaks

38 THEN THE LORD answered Job
[z]out of the whirlwind, and
said,
2 [a]Who *is* this that darkeneth

36:30 [c]ch. 37:3
36:31 [d]ch. 37:13 [e]Acts 14:17
36:32 [f]Ps. 147:8
36:33 [g]1 Ki. 18:41
37:4 [h]Ps. 29:3
37:5 [i]ch. 5:9
37:6 [j]Ps. 147:16
37:7 [k]Ps. 109:27
37:8 [l]Ps. 104:22
37:10 [m]Ps. 147:17
37:12 [n]Ps. 148:8
37:13 [o]Ex. 9:18 [p]ch. 38:26 [q]2 Sam. 21:10 1 Ki. 18:45
37:14 [r]Ps. 111:2
37:16 [s]ch. 36:29 [t]ch. 36:4
37:18 [u]Gen. 1:6 Is. 44:24
37:23 [v]1 Tim. 6:16 [w]ch. 36:5
37:24 [x]Mat. 10:28 [y]Mat. 11:25
38:1 [z]Ex. 19:16
38:2 [a]ch. 34:35

[a] Heb. *the roots* [b] Heb. *that which goeth up* [c] Heb. *Hear in hearing* [d] Heb. *light* [e] Heb. *wings of the earth* [f] Heb. *and to the shower of rain, and to the showers of rain of his strength* [g] Heb. *Out of the chamber* [h] Heb. *scattering winds* [i] Heb. *the cloud of his light* [j] Heb. *a rod* [k] Heb. *Gold*

38:1 THEN THE LORD ANSWERED JOB. It was God Himself who now addressed Job. He revealed Job's ignorance about the divine role in all that was happening. He humbled Job by revealing how little humans really know and understand about the Almighty. However, through God's response came firsthand revelation to Job of God's presence, mercy, and love. (1) Job's constant prayer and deepest yearning to find God was finally answered (see 23:3, note; 29:2, note), confirming that everything was still all right between himself and his Lord.

(2) The Lord's response to His servant Job illustrates that God will ultimately come to all who sincerely and steadfastly call upon Him; even if our prayers come from hearts of confusion, doubt, frustration, or anger, God will eventually respond

counsel by [b]words without knowledge?

3 [c]Gird up now thy loins like a man; for I will demand of thee, and [1]answer thou me.

4 [d]Where wast thou when I laid the foundations of the earth? declare, [m]if thou hast understanding.

5 Who hath laid the measures thereof, if thou knowest? or who hath stretched the line upon it?

6 Whereupon are the [n]foundations thereof [o]fastened? or who laid the corner stone thereof;

7 When the morning stars sang together, and all [e]the sons of God shouted for joy?

8 [f]Or *who* shut up the sea with doors, when it brake forth, *as if* it had issued out of the womb?

9 When I made the cloud the garment thereof, and thick darkness a swaddlingband for it,

10 And [g]brake[p] up for it my decreed *place,* and set bars and doors,

11 And said, Hitherto shalt thou come, but no further: and here shall [q]thy proud waves [h]be stayed?

12 Hast thou [i]commanded the morning since thy days; *and* caused the dayspring to know his place;

13 That it might take hold of the [r]ends of the earth, that [j]the wicked might be shaken out of it?

14 It is turned as clay *to* the seal; and they stand as a garment.

15 And from the wicked their [k]light is withholden, and [l]the high arm shall be broken.

16 Hast thou [m]entered into the springs of the sea? or hast thou walked in the search of the depth?

17 Have [n]the gates of death been opened unto thee? or hast thou seen the doors of the shadow of death?

18 Hast thou perceived the breadth of the earth? declare if thou knowest it all.

19 Where *is* the way *where* light dwelleth? and *as for* darkness, where *is* the place thereof,

20 That thou shouldest take it [s]to the bound thereof, and that thou shouldest know the paths *to* the house thereof ?

21 Knowest thou *it,* because thou wast then born? or *because* the number of thy days *is* great?

22 Hast thou entered into [o]the treasures of the snow? or hast thou seen the treasures of the hail,

23 [p]Which I have reserved against the time of trouble, against the day of battle and war?

24 By what way is the light parted,

38:2 [b]1 Tim. 1:7
38:3 [c]ch. 40:7
38:4 [d]Ps. 104:5 Prov. 8:29
38:7 [e]ch. 1:6
38:8 [f]Gen. 1:9
38:10 [g]ch. 26:10
38:11 [h]Ps. 89:9
38:12 [i]Ps. 148:5
38:13 [j]Ps. 104:35
38:15 [k]ch. 18:5 [l]Ps. 10:15
38:16 [m]Ps. 77:19
38:17 [n]Ps. 9:13
38:22 [o]Ps. 135:7
38:23 [p]Ex. 9:18 Josh. 10:11 Is. 30:30 Ezek. 13:11,13 Rev. 16:21

[1] Heb. *make me know* [m] Heb. *if thou knowest understanding* [n] Heb. *sockets* [o] Heb. *made to sink?* [p] Or, *established my decree upon it* [q] Heb. *the pride of thy waves* [r] Heb. *wings* [s] Or, *at*

with His presence, comfort, and word.

(3) The most important aspect in our relationship with God is not an intellectual understanding of all of God's ways, but the experience and reality of His divine presence and the assurance that all is right between ourselves and God. In fellowship with God we can endure any trial we are called upon to undergo.

38:3 GIRD UP NOW THY LOINS LIKE A MAN. God's words to Job are remarkable both for what they say and do not say. (1) Amazingly, Job was never told why he suffered. He never learned that his suffering involved such grave matters as the integrity and vindication of God's redemptive work among the fallen human race (see 1:8–9, notes). God's silence in this area indicates that the why of Job's suffering was not the most important issue at stake. (2) Also God did not refer to the careless and extreme statements that Job uttered in his speeches. God did not severely rebuke him or hold his foolishness against him. He understood and sympathized with Job's suffering and weighed his words and feelings with compassion.

38:4 THE FOUNDATIONS OF THE EARTH. God's speeches dealt entirely with the natural world of creation and nature. He described the mystery and complexity of the universe and revealed that His method of ruling the world is far beyond our ability to comprehend. God wanted Job to understand that His activity in the world of nature is analogous to His rule in the moral and spiritual order of the universe, and that complete understanding of God's ways will never be found in this life. But the book of Job does reveal that when all truth is finally known, God's ways and actions will be seen as just and righteous.

38:4 DECLARE, IF THOU HAST UNDERSTANDING. God reproved Job for speaking without knowledge (v. 2) and humbled him by making His suffering servant realize that human reasoning is no match for the infinite and eternal God (cf. 40:1–5). Without rejecting Job's claims to moral integrity, God called into question Job's suggestion that He might not be ruling the world justly (e.g., chs. 21; 24). But God went on to assure Job that in his dialogues with the counselors, he had spoken rightly about God (42:7). In other words, God considered Job's error in judgment as stemming from a lack of understanding, not a failure in faith or in sincere love for His Lord.

which scattereth the east wind upon the earth?

25 Who [q]hath divided a watercourse for the overflowing of waters, or a way for the lightning of thunder;

26 To cause it to rain on the earth, *where* no man *is; on* the wilderness, wherein *there is* no man;

27 [r]To satisfy the desolate and waste *ground;* and to cause the bud of the tender herb to spring forth?

28 [s]Hath the rain a father? or who hath begotten the drops of dew?

29 Out of whose womb came the ice? and the [t]hoary frost of heaven, who hath gendered it?

30 The waters are hid as *with* a stone, and the face of the deep [t]is [u]frozen.

31 Canst thou bind the sweet influences of [v]Pleiades,[u] [v] or loose the bands of [w]Orion?

32 Canst thou bring forth [x]Mazzaroth in his season? or canst thou [y]guide Arcturus with his sons?

33 Knowest thou [w]the ordinances of heaven? canst thou set the dominion thereof in the earth?

34 Canst thou lift up thy voice to the clouds, that abundance of waters may cover thee?

35 Canst thou send lightnings, that they may go, and say unto thee, [z]Here we *are?*

36 [x]Who hath put wisdom in the inward parts? or who hath given understanding to the heart?

37 Who can number the clouds in wisdom? or [a]who can stay the bottles of heaven,

38 [b]When the dust [c]groweth into hardness, and the clods cleave fast together?

39 [y]Wilt thou hunt the prey for the lion? or fill [d]the appetite of the young lions,

40 When they couch in *their* dens, *and* abide in the covert to lie in wait?

41 [z]Who provideth for the raven his food? when his young ones cry unto God, they wander for lack of meat.

38:25 [q]ch. 28:26 **38:27** [r]Ps. 107:35 **38:28** [s]Ps. 147:8 Jer. 14:22 **38:29** [t]Ps. 147:16 **38:30** [u]ch. 37:10 **38:31** [v]ch. 9:9 Amos 5:8 **38:33** [w]Jer. 31:35 **38:36** [x]ch. 32:8 Ps. 51:6 Eccl. 2:26 **38:39** [y]Ps. 104:21 & 145:15 **38:41** [z]Ps. 147:9 Mat. 6:26

39:1 [a]Ps. 29:9 **39:6** [b]ch. 24:5 Jer. 2:24 Hos. 8:9 **39:7** [c]ch. 3:18 **39:9** [d]Num. 23:22 Deut. 33:17 **39:16** [e]Lam. 4:3

39

KNOWEST THOU the time when the wild goats of the rock bring forth? *or* canst thou mark when [a]the hinds do calve?

2 Canst thou number the months *that* they fulfil? or knowest thou the time when they bring forth?

3 They bow themselves, they bring forth their young ones, they cast out their sorrows.

4 Their young ones are in good liking, they grow up with corn; they go forth, and return not unto them.

5 Who hath sent out the wild ass free? or who hath loosed the bands of the wild ass?

6 [b]Whose house I have made the wilderness, and the [e]barren land his dwellings.

7 He scorneth the multitude of the city, neither regardeth he the crying [c]of[f] the driver.

8 The range of the mountains *is* his pasture, and he searcheth after every green thing.

9 Will the [d]unicorn be willing to serve thee, or abide by thy crib?

10 Canst thou bind the unicorn with his band in the furrow? or will he harrow the valleys after thee?

11 Wilt thou trust him, because his strength *is* great? or wilt thou leave thy labour to him?

12 Wilt thou believe him, that he will bring home thy seed, and gather *it into* thy barn?

13 *Gavest thou* the goodly wings unto the peacocks? or [g]wings and feathers unto the ostrich?

14 Which leaveth her eggs in the earth, and warmeth them in dust,

15 And forgetteth that the foot may crush them, or that the wild beast may break them.

16 She is [e]hardened against her

[t] Heb. *is taken* [u] Or, *The seven stars* [v] Heb. *Cimah* [w] Heb. *Cesil?* [x] Or, *The twelve signs* [y] Heb. *guide them* [z] Heb. *Behold us?* [a] Heb. *who can cause to lie down* [b] Or, *When the dust is turned into mire* [c] Heb. *is poured* [d] Heb. *the life* [e] Heb. *salt places* [f] Heb. *of the exactor* [g] Or, *the feathers of the stork and ostrich*

39:1 KNOWEST THOU THE TIME? God continued to interrogate Job with questions he could not answer. By so doing, God showed Job that his desire to debate God was foolish. Job was humbled and silenced, yet he was reassured of the most important thing—God had not abandoned him. The Lord was there, face to face.

39:2 CANST THOU NUMBER THE MONTHS? If God could lead Job to perceive his human limitations in understanding God's ways in the world, then He could persuade Job that He is just and merciful, even when Job did not understand the way in which God was working in his life.

young ones, as though *they were* not
hers: her labour is in vain without fear;
17 Because God hath deprived her
of wisdom, neither hath he [f]imparted
to her understanding.
18 What time she lifteth up herself
on high, she scorneth the horse and his
rider.
19 Hast thou given the horse
strength? hast thou clothed his neck
with thunder?
20 Canst thou make him afraid as a
grasshopper? the glory of his nostrils
is [h]terrible.
21 [i]He paweth in the valley, and
rejoiceth in *his* strength: [g]he goeth on
to meet [j]the armed men.
22 He mocketh at fear, and is not
affrighted; neither turneth he back
from the sword.
23 The quiver rattleth against him,
the glittering spear and the shield.
24 He swalloweth the ground with
fierceness and rage: neither believeth
he that *it is* the sound of the trumpet.
25 He saith among the trumpets,
Ha, ha; and he smelleth the battle afar
off, the thunder of the captains, and
the shouting.
26 Doth the hawk fly by thy wisdom, *and* stretch her wings toward the
south?
27 Doth the eagle mount up [k]at thy
command, and [h]make her nest on
high?
28 She dwelleth and abideth on the
rock, upon the crag of the rock, and the
strong place.
29 From thence she seeketh the
prey, *and* her eyes behold afar off.
30 Her young ones also suck up
blood: and [i]where the slain *are*, there
is she.

40

MOREOVER THE LORD answered Job, and said,
2 Shall he that [j]contendeth with
the Almighty instruct *him?* he that reproveth God, let him answer it.
3 ¶ Then Job answered the LORD,
and said,
4 [k]Behold, I am vile; what shall I
answer thee? [l]I will lay mine hand
upon my mouth.
5 Once have I spoken; but I will not
answer: yea, twice; but I will proceed
no further.
6 ¶ [m]Then answered the LORD unto
Job out of the whirlwind, and said,
7 [n]Gird up thy loins now like a
man: [o]I will demand of thee, and declare thou unto me.
8 [p]Wilt thou also disannul my judg-

h Heb. *terror* i Or, His feet *dig* j Heb. *the armour* k Heb. *by thy mouth*

39:17 [f]ch. 35:11
39:21 [g]Jer. 8:6
39:27 [h]Jer. 49:16; Obad. 4
39:30 [i]Mat. 24:28; Luke 17:37
40:2 [j]ch. 33:13
40:4 [k]Ezra 9:6; ch. 42:6; Ps. 51:4; [l]ch. 29:9; Ps. 39:9
40:6 [m]ch. 38:1
40:7 [n]ch. 38:3; [o]ch. 42:4
40:8 [p]Ps. 51:4; Rom. 3:4

40:2 SHALL HE THAT CONTENDETH WITH THE ALMIGHTY INSTRUCT *HIM*? God once again challenged Job to prove his contention that He was governing the world in an improper manner. (1) If Job could not comprehend the working of God's creation nor understand why things happen as they do, how did he think he could question God about His administration of the affairs of humankind, or even about the suffering God allowed him to experience?

(2) What God was showing His suffering servant was that He had created the world in wisdom and that He was governing it with wisdom and justice. The misfortune that Job had suffered did not mean that God had abandoned His love for His faithful servant.

(3) The suffering of the righteous does not call into question the goodness of God. Their affliction is under the permissive will of God, allowed for His wise, yet often unknown, purpose (see article on THE WILL OF GOD, p. 1060). Adverse circumstances should not destroy our faith in God's love for us; He allows them for our highest good (Rom. 8:28, note).

40:3 THEN JOB ANSWERED THE LORD. Job was now faced with the decision whether to persist in his belief that God had treated him unfairly in view of his years of faithful worship and obedience to His word. Would Job maintain his trust in God in spite of circumstances suggesting that God was unjust and capricious, or would he hold on to the feeling that God had seemingly become his enemy?

40:4 I WILL LAY MINE HAND UPON MY MOUTH. Job was overwhelmed by this new revelation of God. He understood how insignificant humans are before the hidden wisdom of God (cf. 1 Cor. 2:7), and he felt he could speak no more. Still, Job was not quite ready to give up his claim that something had been wrong in God's treatment of him (his final response comes in 42:2–6). Yet Job was coming to the realization that his mysterious and perplexing suffering had not been a mystery to God, and that through it all God could be trusted.

40:6 THEN ANSWERED THE LORD UNTO JOB. In order to bring Job to complete submission to His lordship and ways, God continued His argument. He wanted to overcome Job's remaining resistance and to lead him into a full realization of His love. This loving persistence on God's part reveals His patience, mercy, and genuine care for His suffering people.

40:8 WILT THOU CONDEMN ME? Job's contention that he was innocent and that God had been unjustly punishing him (see 19:6) brought him close to condemning God. The Lord now asked Job specifically whether he would continue to assert his limited perspective of God's administra-

ment? wilt thou condemn me, that thou mayest be righteous?

9 Hast thou an arm like God? or canst thou thunder with [q]a voice like him?

10 [r]Deck thyself now *with* majesty and excellency; and array thyself with glory and beauty.

11 Cast abroad the rage of thy wrath: and behold every one *that is* proud, and abase him.

12 Look on every one *that is* [s]proud, *and* bring him low; and tread down the wicked in their place.

13 Hide them in the dust together; *and* bind their faces in secret.

14 Then will I also confess unto thee that thine own right hand can save thee.

15 ¶ Behold now [l]behemoth, which I made with thee; he eateth grass as an ox.

16 Lo now, his strength *is* in his loins, and his force *is* in the navel of his belly.

17 [m]He moveth his tail like a cedar: the sinews of his stones are wrapped together.

18 His bones *are as* strong pieces of brass; his bones *are* like bars of iron.

19 He *is* the chief of the ways of God: he that made him can make his sword to approach *unto him.*

20 Surely the mountains [t]bring him forth food, where all the beasts of the field play.

21 He lieth under the shady trees, in the covert of the reed, and fens.

22 The shady trees cover him *with* their shadow; the willows of the brook compass him about.

23 Behold, [n]he drinketh up a river, *and* hasteth not: he trusteth that he can draw up Jordan into his mouth.

24 He taketh it with his eyes: *his* nose pierceth through snares.

41 CANST THOU draw out [u]leviathan[o] with an hook? or his tongue with a cord [p]*which* thou lettest down?

2 Canst thou [v]put an hook into his nose? or bore his jaw through with a thorn?

3 Will he make many supplications unto thee? will he speak soft *words* unto thee?

4 Will he make a covenant with thee? wilt thou take him for a servant for ever?

5 Wilt thou play with him as *with* a bird? or wilt thou bind him for thy maidens?

6 Shall the companions make a banquet of him? shall they part him among the merchants?

7 Canst thou fill his skin with barbed irons? or his head with fish spears?

8 Lay thine hand upon him, remember the battle, do no more.

9 Behold, the hope of him is in vain: shall not *one* be cast down even at the sight of him?

10 None *is so* fierce that dare stir him up: who then is able to stand before me?

11 [w]Who hath prevented me, that I should repay *him?* [x]*whatsoever is* under the whole heaven is mine.

12 I will not conceal his parts, nor his power, nor his comely proportion.

13 Who can discover the face of his garment? *or* who can come *to him* [q]with his double bridle?

14 Who can open the doors of his face? his teeth *are* terrible round about.

15 *His* [r]scales *are his* pride, shut up together *as with* a close seal.

16 One is so near to another, that no air can come between them.

17 They are joined one to another, they stick together, that they cannot be sundered.

18 By his sneezings a light doth shine, and his eyes *are* like the eyelids of the morning.

40:9 [q]ch. 37:4 Ps. 29:3,4
40:10 [r]Ps. 93:1 & 104:1
40:12 [s]Is. 2:12 Dan. 4:37
40:20 [t]Ps. 104:14
41:1 [u]Ps. 104:26 Is. 27:1
41:2 [v]Is. 37:29
41:11 [w]Rom. 11:35 [x]Ex. 19:5 Deut. 10:14 Ps. 24:1 & 50:12 1 Cor. 10:26,28

[l]Or, *the elephant,* as some think [m]Or, *He setteth up* [n]Heb. *he oppresseth* [o]i.e. *a whale,* or, *a whirlpool* [p]Heb. which *thou drownest?* [q]Or, *within* [r]Heb. *strong pieces of shields*

tion of the world at the cost of rejecting His justice and goodness?

40:15 THE BEHEMOTH. The behemoth is identified by many commentators as the hippopotamus; the leviathan (ch. 41) is often identified as a giant crocodile or a whale. By these illustrations God emphasized that if Job could not subdue the great creatures of the world, then he was in no position to question and counsel the God who had made these creatures (41:10). Job must trustfully submit to God's rule over the universe, the affairs of humankind, and the lives of His followers. He must trust God and maintain his faith in God—both during the sufferings and afflictions of life and during the times of blessing.

19 Out of his mouth go burning lamps, *and* sparks of fire leap out.

20 Out of his nostrils goeth smoke, as *out* of a seething pot or caldron.

21 His breath kindleth coals, and a flame goeth out of his mouth.

22 In his neck remaineth strength, and [s]sorrow is turned into joy before him.

23 [t]The flakes of his flesh are joined together: they are firm in themselves; they cannot be moved.

24 His heart is as firm as a stone; yea, as hard as a piece of the nether *millstone.*

25 When he raiseth up himself, the mighty are afraid: by reason of breakings they purify themselves.

26 The sword of him that layeth at him cannot hold: the spear, the dart, nor the [u]habergeon.

27 He esteemeth iron as straw, *and* brass as rotten wood.

28 The arrow cannot make him flee: slingstones are turned with him into stubble.

29 Darts are counted as stubble: he laugheth at the shaking of a spear.

30 [v]Sharp stones *are* under him: he spreadeth sharp pointed things upon the mire.

31 He maketh the deep to boil like a pot: he maketh the sea like a pot of ointment.

32 He maketh a path to shine after him; *one* would think the deep *to be* hoary.

33 Upon earth there is not his like, [w]who is made without fear.

34 He beholdeth all high *things:* he *is* a king over all the children of pride.

Job repents in dust and ashes

42 THEN JOB answered the LORD, and said,

2 I know that thou [y]canst do every *thing,* and *that* [x]no thought can be withholden from thee.

3 [z]Who *is* he that hideth counsel without knowledge? therefore have I uttered that I understood not; [a]things too wonderful for me, which I knew not.

4 Hear, I beseech thee, and I will speak: [b]I will demand of thee, and declare thou unto me.

5 I have heard of thee by the hearing of the ear: but now mine eye seeth thee.

6 Wherefore I [c]abhor *myself,* and repent in dust and ashes.

7 ¶ And it was *so,* that after the LORD had spoken these words unto Job, the

42:2 [y]Gen. 18:14 Mat. 19:26 Mark 10:27 & 14:36 Luke 18:27
42:3 [z]ch. 38:2 [a]Ps. 40:5 & 131:1 & 139:6
42:4 [b]ch. 38:3 & 40:7
42:6 [c]Ezra 9:6 ch. 40:4

[s]Heb. *sorrow rejoiceth* [t]Heb. *The fallings* [u]Or, *breastplate* [v]Heb. *Sharp pieces of potsherd* [w]Or, *who behave themselves without fear* [x]Or, *no thought of thine can be hindered*

42:1 THEN JOB ANSWERED THE LORD. Job's final answer to God was one of absolute humility and submission to His revelation. He confessed that (1) God does all things well; (2) that everything that God permits to occur He does so in wisdom and with purpose; and hence (3) even the suffering of the righteous has meaning and divine purpose.

42:3 I UTTERED THAT I UNDERSTOOD NOT. Job admitted that God's ways are beyond human comprehension and that out of misunderstanding he had declared that they were unjust. (1) Note that Job in his suffering and prayers did not sin against God. However, his misunderstanding and complaints against God had led him close to pride and to the belief that God was in some way not perfectly good. Now with the appearance and revelation of his Lord (cf. v. 5), his perspective completely changes.

(2) Job acknowledged his error and was ready to submit to and serve God no matter what happened to him. He would fear and love God for God's own sake, with or without his health, regardless of any personal gain.

(3) By committing himself to God in faith, hope, and love while still suffering and not knowing the why of it all, Job proved Satan's accusation wrong (1:9–11) and thereby vindicated God's power to redeem and reconcile the human race to Himself (see 1:8–9, notes).

42:5 NOW MINE EYE SEETH THEE. Job had earlier prayed to see his Redeemer (19:27); now that longing was fulfilled. God's word and presence brought Job a greater revelation of His ways and character. Through this personal experience, Job was transformed by a sense of forgiveness, a renewed confidence in God's goodness, and a reassuring experience of His love. (1) God's appearance to Job was a vindication of Job's uprightness, and it is an assurance to all faithful believers that the Lord will accept our sincere questions when we are undergoing unexplained adversity and suffering. (2) God is patient with His own and sympathizes with our weaknesses (Heb. 4:15), our misunderstandings, and even our anger. As with Job, if we endure, God will manifest His presence and extend His care to us.

42:6 I . . . REPENT IN DUST AND ASHES. In response to God's revelation, Job humbled himself in repentance. The word "repent" means that Job considered himself and even his moral rightness as mere "dust and ashes" before a holy God (cf. Is. 6). Job did not retract what he had said about his life of righteousness and moral integrity, but he did admit that his accusations and complaints against God were not appropriate for a finite hu-

LORD said to Eliphaz the Temanite, My
wrath is kindled against thee, and
against thy two friends: for ye have not
spoken of me *the thing that is* right, as
my servant Job *hath.*
8 Therefore take unto you now
[d]seven bullocks and seven rams, and
[e]go to my servant Job, and offer up for
yourselves a burnt offering; and my
servant Job shall [f]pray for you: for
[y]him will I accept: lest I deal with you
after your folly, in that ye have not spo-
ken of me *the thing which is* right, like
my servant Job.
9 So Eliphaz the Temanite and Bil-
dad the Shuhite *and* Zophar the Naa-
mathite went, and did according as the
LORD commanded them: the LORD also
accepted [z]Job.

Job's fortunes restored

10 [g]And the LORD turned the cap-
tivity of Job, when he prayed for his
friends: also the LORD [a]gave Job
[h]twice as much as he had before.
11 Then came there unto him [i]all
his brethren, and all his sisters, and all
they that had been of his acquaintance
before, and did eat bread with him in
his house: and they bemoaned him,
and comforted him over all the evil
that the LORD had brought upon him:
every man also gave him a piece of
money, and every one an earring of
gold.
12 So the LORD blessed [j]the latter
end of Job more than his beginning: for
he had [k]fourteen thousand sheep, and
six thousand camels, and a thousand

42:8 [d]Num. 23:1 [e]Mat. 5:24 [f]Gen. 20:17 Jas. 5:15,16 1 John 5:16
42:10 [g]Ps. 14:7 & 126:1 [h]Is. 40:2
42:11 [i]See ch. 19:13
42:12 [j]ch. 8:7 Jas. 5:11 [k]See ch. 1:3

[y] Heb. *his face,* or, *person* [z] Heb. *the face of Job* [a] Heb. *added all that* had been *to Job unto the double*

man to make and repented for doing so (cf. Gen. 18:27).

42:7 AFTER THE LORD HAD SPOKEN. Although the book of Job never gives a final solution to the problem of undeserved suffering by the righteous, the ultimate answer is found not in theological reasoning, but in a personal encounter between God and the faithful sufferer. (1) Only the personal presence of a comforting and caring God will bring confidence in His grace and purpose for our lives. For those who believe in Christ, God sends the Holy Spirit as a Helper and a Comforter (see John 14:16, note). (2) This presence of God through the Holy Spirit teaches us that we may have confidence in God's love, whether in circumstances of adversity or blessing. The Spirit mediates to us the presence of Christ and points us to the cross, by which we have the assurance that God is for us and that He seeks our ultimate good (see Rom. 8:28, note).

42:7 FOR YE HAVE NOT SPOKEN OF ME *THE THING THAT IS* RIGHT. The Lord condemned the three friends of Job for their erroneous theology of prosperity and suffering, evident in their accusations against Job. Their three major errors were: (1) They taught a retributive principle of prosperity and suffering—that the righteous are always blessed and the wicked always experience adversity (see John 9:3, note).

(2) They exhorted Job to admit a sin that he had not committed, so that he might escape his suffering and receive God's blessing. By their counsel they tempted Job to use God for personal gain. If Job had followed their advice, he would have (a) discredited God's faith in him, and (b) confirmed Satan's claim that Job feared God only for blessing and gain.

(3) They had spoken arrogantly in claiming God's sanction for some of their false doctrine and theology.

42:7 RIGHT, AS MY SERVANT JOB *HATH.* God declared that what Job had said was right. He did not mean that everything Job said was completely accurate, but that Job's response to his three friends was completely honest before God and that his attitude was pleasing to Him. God sometimes permits errors in our prayers and allows us to question His ways if our hearts are truly given to Him in sincere commitment.

42:8 MY SERVANT JOB. God calls Job "my servant" (vv. 7–8) and states twice that his prayer was accepted (vv. 8–9). Job was fully restored to God's favor and was given spiritual authority with God. God will hear Job's intercessory prayer for his three friends because of Job's righteous standing with God (vv. 8–9).

42:10 TWICE AS MUCH AS HE HAD BEFORE. The restoration of Job's fortunes reveals God's purpose for all faithful believers. (1) God's redemptive purpose with respect to Job's suffering was accomplished. God had allowed Job to suffer for reasons that Job did not understand. God never allows believers to suffer without a spiritual purpose, even though they may not understand the reasons. We must trust God in such circumstances, knowing that He in His perfect justice will do what is eternally best for us and His kingdom. (2) Job's reconciliation with God and reception of abundant life emphasize that no matter what hardships or pain the faithful must experience, in God's own time, He will reach out to help those who persevere and give them total healing and restoration. "Ye have heard of the patience of Job, and have seen the end of the Lord; that the Lord is very pitiful, and of tender mercy" (Jas. 5:11). (3) Every person who remains faithful to God in the midst of the trials and afflictions of this life will ultimately come to that joyous and blessed state when he or she enjoys the presence of God for all eternity (see 2 Tim. 4:7–8; 1 Pet. 5:10; Rev. 21; 22:1–5).

yoke of oxen, and a thousand she
asses.
13 [l]He had also seven sons and
three daughters.
14 And he called the name of the
first, Jemima; and the name of the sec-
ond, Kezia; and the name of the third,
Keren-happuch.
15 And in all the land were no wom-
en found *so* fair as the daughters of
Job: and their father gave them inheri-
tance among their brethren.
16 After this [m]lived Job an hundred
and forty years, and saw his sons,
and his sons' sons, *even* four genera-
tions.
17 So Job died, *being* old and [n]full
of days.

42:13 [l]ch. 1:2
42:16 [m]ch. 5:26 Prov. 3:16
42:17 [n]Gen. 25:8

PSALMS

Outline

I. Book 1: Psalms 1–41 (41:13)
II. Book 2: Psalms 42–72 (72:19)
III. Book 3: Psalms 73–89 (89:52)
IV. Book 4: Psalms 90–106 (106:48)
V. Book 5: Psalms 107–150 (150:1–6)

Two observations are noteworthy about the above outline. (1) From ancient times, the 150 psalms were organized into these five books, with each book having its own benediction (indicated above in parentheses). Ps. 150 is not only the last psalm and a benediction for Book 5, but also a doxology for the entire Psalter. (2) The following chart provides helpful perspective about the five-book division of the Psalms.

	Book I 1–41	Book II 42–72	Book III 73–89	Book IV 90–106	Book V 107–150
Total Psalms	41	31	17	17	44
Authorship	Mainly David	Mainly David and Sons of Korah	Mainly Asaph	Mainly Anonymous	Mainly David or Anonymous
Predominant Divine Name	*Yahweh* (the "LORD")	*El/Elohim* ("God")	*El/Elohim* ("God")	*Yahweh* (the "LORD")	*Yahweh* (the "LORD")
Frequent Topics	Humans and Creation	Deliverance and Redemption	Worship and Sanctuary	Wilderness and God's Ways	God's Word and Praise
Resemblance to Pentateuch	Genesis	Exodus	Leviticus	Numbers	Deuteronomy

Author: David and Others

Theme: Prayers and Praises

Date of Writing: Largely 10th to 5th centuries B.C.

Background

The Hebrew title for the Psalms is *tehillim*, meaning "praises"; the title in the Septuagint (Greek translation of the O.T., done about 200 B.C.) is *psalmoi*, meaning "songs to the accompaniment of stringed instruments." The English title, "Psalms," is derived from the Septuagint.

Music played an important role in the worship of ancient Israel (cf. Ps. 149–150; 1 Chr. 15:16–22); the psalms were Israel's hymns. Unlike much poetry or songs in the western world that are written with rhyme or meter, O.T. poetry and songs were based on a parallelism of thought, in which the second (or succeeding) line(s) of poetry essentially restates (synonymous parallelism), contrasts (antithetical parallelism), or progressively completes (synthetical parallelism) the first. All three forms of parallelism characterize the

Psalter. The earliest known psalm is from Moses in the fifteenth century B.C. (Ps. 90); the latest ones are from the sixth to fifth centuries B.C. (e.g., Ps. 137). The majority of the psalms, however, were written in the tenth century B.C. during Israel's golden age of poetry.

The editorial titles or superscriptions at the beginning of most psalms, though not an original and inspired part of the psalms, are ancient (before the Septuagint) and significant. The content of these superscriptions varies, covering such categories as (1) author's name (e.g., Ps. 47, "A Psalm for the sons of Korah"), (2) type of psalm (e.g., Ps. 32, a "Maschil," meaning a contemplative or didactic poem), (3) musical terms (e.g., Ps. 4, "To the chief Musician on Neginoth [stringed instruments]"), (4) liturgical notations (e.g., Ps. 45, "A Song of love," i.e., a wedding song), and (5) brief historical notations (e.g., Ps. 3, "A Psalm of David, when he fled from Absalom his son").

Concerning authorship of the psalms, the superscriptions ascribe seventy-three psalms to David, twelve to Asaph (a musically and prophetically gifted Levite, see 1 Chr. 15:16–19; 2 Chr. 29:30), ten to the sons of Korah (a musically gifted family), two to Solomon, one to Heman, one to Ethan, and one to Moses. With the exception of Moses, David, and Solomon, all other designated authors were priests or Levites with musical gifts and responsibilities in sacred worship during David's reign. Fifty psalms are anonymous. Biblical and historical references suggest that David (cf. 1 Chr. 15:16–22), Hezekiah (cf. 2 Chr. 29:25–30; Prov. 25:1), and Ezra (cf. Neh. 10:39; 11:22; 12:27–36,45–47) were each involved at different stages in collecting the psalms for corporate use in Jerusalem. The final compiling of the Psalter most likely occurred during the time of Ezra and Nehemiah (450–400 B.C.).

Purpose

The psalms, as Spirit-inspired prayers and praises, were written, generally speaking, to express the deep inner emotions of the human heart in relation to God. (1) Many were written as prayers to God, expressing (a) trust, love, adoration, thanksgiving, praise, and a longing for close fellowship; (b) discouragement, deep distress, fear, anxiety, humiliation, and a cry for deliverance, healing, or vindication. (2) Others were written as songs expressing praise, thanksgiving, and adoration for who God is and for the great things He has done. (3) Some psalms contain important Messianic sections.

Survey

As an anthology of 150 psalms, the Psalter covers a great breadth of topics, including revelation about God, creation, humankind, salvation, sin and evil, justice and righteousness, worship and praise, prayer, and judgment. It views God in a rich variety of ways: a fortress, rock, shield, shepherd, soldier, creator, ruler, judge, redeemer, sustainer, healer, and avenger; He expresses love, anger, and compassion; He is everywhere present, all-knowing, and almighty. God's people are also described in various ways: as the apple of His eye, sheep, saints, the upright, and the righteous whom He has delivered from the miry pit, placed their feet on the rock, and given them a new song. God directs their steps, satisfies their spiritual longings, forgives all their sins, heals all their diseases, and provides for them an eternal dwelling.

One helpful method for surveying the book is by general categories used for classifying the psalms (with some overlapping). (1) *Hallelujah or Praise Songs*: These magnify the name, majesty, goodness, greatness, and salvation of God (e.g., Ps. 8; 21; 33—34; 103—106; 111—113; 115—117; 135; 145—150). (2) *Thanksgiving Songs*: These acknowledge God's saving help and deliverances on behalf of an individual or Israel as a nation (e.g., Ps. 18; 30; 34; 41; 66; 92; 100; 106; 116; 118; 124; 126; 136; 138). (3) *Prayer and Supplication Psalms*: These include laments and petitions to God, longings for God, and intercession on behalf of God's people (e.g., Ps. 3—6; 13; 43; 54; 67; 69—70; 79—80; 85—86; 88; 90; 102; 141—143). (4) *Penitential Psalms*: These focus on the acknowledgment and confession of sin (e.g., Ps. 32; 38; 51; 130). (5) *Sacred History Songs*: These recount God's dealings with Israel as a nation (e.g., Ps. 78; 105—106; 108; 114; 126; 137). (6) *Enthronement of the Lord Psalms*: These declare boldly that "the LORD reigns" (e.g., Ps. 24; 47; 93; 96—99). (7) *Liturgical Songs*: These were composed for special services or feasts (e.g., Ps. 15; 24; 45; 68; 113—118; these last six were used annually at the Passover). (8) *Trust and De-*

votion Psalms: These express (a) the individual's confidence in God's integrity and the help of His presence, and (b) the heart's devotion to God (e.g., Ps. 11; 16; 23; 27; 31—32; 40; 46; 56; 62—63; 91; 119; 130—131; 139). (9) *Pilgrimage Songs*: Called also "Songs of Zion" or "Songs of Ascent," these were sung by pilgrims during their journey to Jerusalem for the annual feasts of Passover, Pentecost, and Tabernacles (e.g., Ps. 43; 46; 48; 76; 84; 87; 120—134). (10) *Creation Songs*: These acknowledge God's handiwork in the heavens and on the earth (e.g. Ps. 8; 19; 29; 33; 65; 104). (11) *Wisdom and Didactic Psalms*: These reflect on the ways of God and instruct us concerning righteousness (e.g., Ps. 1; 34; 37; 73; 112; 119; 133). (12) *Royal or Messianic Psalms*: These describe certain experiences of King David or Solomon that have prophetic significance and find their ultimate fulfillment in the coming of the Messiah, Jesus Christ (e.g., Ps. 2; 8; 16; 22; 40—41; 45; 68—69; 72; 89; 102; 110; 118). (13) *Imprecatory Psalms*: These psalms invoke God's curse or judgment on the wicked (e.g., Ps. 7; 35; 55; 58; 59; 69; 109; 137; 139:19–22). Since many Christians are perplexed by these psalms, it should be noted that they were written out of zeal for God's name, justice, and righteousness, and from a strong abhorrence of evil, not out of a petty vindictiveness. Essentially they call on God to raise up the righteous and put down the wicked.

Special Features

Nine major features or emphases characterize the Psalms. (1) It is the Bible's longest book and contains the Bible's longest chapter (119:1–176), shortest chapter (117:1–2), and middle verse (118:8). (2) As the Hebrew songbook and devotional book, its spiritual depth and breadth make the psalms the most read and most treasured portion of the O.T. by most believers. (3) "Hallelujah" (translated "Praise ye the LORD" in the King James Bible), a Hebrew term universally recognized among believers, occurs twenty-eight times in the Bible, twenty-four of which are in the Psalms. In the Psalter it reaches its apex in Ps. 150 and conveys complete, rounded, and perfect praise to the Lord. (4) No other book of the Bible so totally expresses the full range of human emotion and needs in relation to God and human life. Its choruses of praise and devotion flow down from the highest mountains, and its cries of desperation arise from the deepest valleys. (5) About half of the psalms involve prayers of faith in times of adversity. (6) It is the O.T. book most frequently quoted in the N.T. (7) It contains many "favorite chapters" of the Bible, such as Ps. 1; 23; 24; 34; 37; 84; 91; 103; 119; 121; 139; and 150. (8) Ps. 119 is unique in the Bible in (a) its length (176 verses), (b) its majestic love for God's Word, and (c) its literary construction involving twenty-two stanzas of eight verses each, with every stanza beginning each of its verses with the same letter and each stanza using a successive letter of the Hebrew alphabet as a memory aid (i.e., an alphabetical acrostic). (9) Its foremost literary feature is a poetic style called parallelism, involving rhythm of thought rather than a rhythm of rhyme or meter. This feature has enabled its message to be translated from one language to another without serious difficulty.

New Testament Fulfillment

There are 186 quotations from the Psalms in the N.T., far more than from any other O.T. book. It is clear that Jesus and the N.T. writers were filled with the psalms and that the Holy Spirit used them often in Jesus' teaching and in other passages where Jesus fulfills Scripture as the prophesied Messiah. For example, the brief Ps 110 (seven verses) is quoted in the N.T. more times than any other O.T. chapter; it contains prophecy about Jesus as the Messiah, as the Son of God, and as a priest forever after the order of Melchizedek. Other Messianic psalms applied to Jesus in the N.T. are: 2; 8; 16; 22; 40; 41; 45; 68; 69; 89; 102; 109; and 118. They are applied to (1) Jesus as prophet, priest, and king; (2) both His first and second advent; (3) His Sonship and character; (4) His sufferings and atoning death; and (5) His resurrection. In summary, the psalms are among the most meticulous of all O.T. prophecies about Christ and are everywhere deeply embedded in the message of the N.T. writers.

Reading Psalms

In order to read the entire Old Testament in one year, the book of Psalms should be read in 44 days, according to the following schedule: ☐ 1–6 ☐ 7–10 ☐ 11–16 ☐ 17–18 ☐ 19–20 ☐ 21–22 ☐ 23–25 ☐ 26–29 ☐ 30–31 ☐ 32–34 ☐ 35–37 ☐ 38–41 ☐ 42–44 ☐ 45–48 ☐ 49–51 ☐ 52–55 ☐ 56–59 ☐ 60–63 ☐ 64–67 ☐ 68–69 ☐ 70–73 ☐ 74–77 ☐ 78 ☐ 79–81 ☐ 82–84 ☐ 85–88 ☐ 89 ☐ 90–93 ☐ 94–98 ☐ 99–101 ☐ 102–103 ☐ 104–106 ☐ 107–108 ☐ 109–112 ☐ 113–116 ☐ 117–118 ☐ 119:1–88 ☐ 119:89–176 ☐ 120–127 ☐ 128–134 ☐ 135–138 ☐ 139–141 ☐ 142–145 ☐ 146–150

NOTES

BOOK I

The way of the righteous

1 BLESSED [a]*IS* the man that walketh not in the counsel of the [a]ungodly, nor standeth in the way of sinners, [b]nor sitteth in the seat of the scornful.

2 But [c]his delight *is* in the law of the LORD; [d]and in his law doth he med-
:6-8 itate day and night.

3 And he shall be like a tree [e]planted by the rivers of water, that bringeth forth his fruit in his season; his leaf also shall not [b]wither; and whatso-
10 ever he doeth shall [f]prosper.

1:1 [a]Prov. 4:14 [b]Ps. 26:4 Jer:15:17
1:2 [c]Ps. 119:35 [d]Josh. 1:8 Ps. 119:1
1:3 [e]Jer. 17:8 Ezek. 47:12 [f]Gen. 39:3 Is. 3:10
1:4 [g]Job 21:18 Is. 17:13
1:6 [h]Ps. 37:18 2 Tim. 2:19
2:1 [i]Acts. 4:25

4 The ungodly *are* not so: but *are* [g]like the chaff which the wind driveth away.

5 Therefore the ungodly shall not stand in the judgment, nor sinners in the congregation of the righteous.

6 For [h]the LORD knoweth the way of the righteous: but the way of the ungodly shall perish.

The triumph of the king

2 WHY[i] DO the heathen [c]rage, and the people [d]imagine a vain thing?

[a] Or, *wicked* [b] Heb. *fade* [c] Or, *tumultuously assemble* [d] Heb. *meditate*

1:1 BLESSED IS THE MAN. Ps. 1 serves as an introduction to the entire book of Psalms. It contrasts the only two kinds of people recognized by God, each with a distinct set of life principles: (1) The godly, who are characterized by righteousness, love, obedience to God's word, and separation from fellowship with the world (vv. 1–2); (2) the ungodly, who represent the ways and counsel of the world, who do not abide in God's word, and who consequently have no part in the assembly of God's people (vv. 4–5). The godly person is known and blessed by God, but the ungodly person has no part in God's kingdom (1 Cor. 6:9) and will perish (v. 6). The separation between these two kinds of people will exist throughout redemptive history and on into eternity.

1:1 THAT WALKETH NOT IN THE COUNSEL OF THE UNGODLY. The first verse of the book of Psalms emphasizes the distinction between the righteous and the wicked. True believers can be distinguished by the things they do not do, the places they do not go, and the company they do not keep. No person can experience God's blessing without turning from those things that are harmful or destructive.

1:2 HIS DELIGHT *IS* IN THE LAW OF THE LORD. Those who are blessed by God not only turn from evil, but also build their lives around the words of the Lord. They seek to obey God's will out of hearts that genuinely take pleasure in God's ways and commandments (see 2 Thes. 2:10, where the wicked perish because they refused to love the truth). What motivates their actions are their redeemed spirits and emotions, captivated by the truth of God as found in His Word.

1:2 IN HIS LAW DOTH HE MEDITATE DAY AND NIGHT. Those seeking to live under God's blessing meditate on God's law (i.e., His Word) in order to shape their thinking, attitudes, and actions. They read the words of Scripture, ponder them, and compare them with other Scriptures. When meditating on a passage in the Bible, questions such as these cross their minds:

Is God's Spirit applying this verse to my present situation?

Is there a promise here for me to claim?

Is this passage revealing a particular sin I must strive to avoid?

Is God issuing a command I must obey?

Is my spirit in harmony with what the Holy Spirit is saying?

Is the passage expressing a truth about God, salvation, sin, the world, or my personal obedience on which I need to be enlightened by the Holy Spirit?

1:3 RIVERS OF WATER. The outcome of those who faithfully seek God and His Word is life in the Spirit. Since water often represents the Spirit of God (e.g., John 7:38–39), those who are instructed by God and abide in His Word will receive an unfailing source of life from the Spirit. The phrase "whatsoever he doeth shall prosper" does not mean that problems or failure will never occur, but rather that a godly person will know God's will and blessing (see 1 John 2, note).

1:4–6 THE UNGODLY. Ps. 1 describes unrepentant sinners with three awful pictures: (1) they are like "chaff" blown away by forces they cannot see (v. 4; see Eph. 2:2, note); (2) they will be condemned before God on the judgment day (v. 5; cf. 76:7; Mal. 3:2; Mat. 25:31–46; Rev. 6:17); (3) they will perish for eternity (v. 6; see Mat. 10:28, note).

2:1–12 WHY DO THE NATIONS RAGE. This psalm consists of four distinct scenes. (1) The psalmist begins by speaking of the peoples and the kings of the world taking a stand against God's Anointed (vv. 1–3; cf. Acts 4:25–27; see next note)—a sad picture of the arrogant rebellion of humankind against God, His law, His redemption, His Messiah, and the moral teaching of His revelation. The N.T. authors likewise see the world in opposition to Christ, the believer, and the Biblical faith (John 15:19; Eph. 6:12).

(2) God responds by deriding the ridiculous efforts of the world to remove Him from the scene (vv. 4–6). The time will come when He will terminate human rebellion and establish His kingdom upon earth (see Rom. 1:18; 1 Thes. 5:1–11; 2 Thes. 2:8; Rev. 19:11–21).

(3) God the Father promises to send His beloved Son (vv. 7–9), the ultimate inheritance of the nations (see Acts 13:33; Heb. 1:5; 5:5; cf. Mat. 3:17; 17:5; 2 Pet. 1:17), to defeat all who oppose His rule. This promise will be fulfilled when Christ

2 The kings of the earth set themselves, and the rulers take counsel together, against the LORD, and against his [j]anointed, *saying,*

3 [k]Let us break their bands asunder, and cast away their cords from us.

4 He that sitteth in the heavens [l]shall laugh: the Lord shall have them in derision.

5 Then shall he speak unto them in his wrath, and [e]vex them in his sore displeasure.

6 Yet have I [f]set my king [m]upon[g] my holy hill of Zion.

7 I will declare [h]the decree: the LORD hath said unto me, [n]Thou *art* my Son; this day have I begotten thee.

8 [o]Ask of me, and I shall give *thee* the heathen *for* thine inheritance, and the uttermost parts of the earth *for* thy possession.

9 [p]Thou shalt break them with a rod of iron; thou shalt dash them in pieces like a potter's vessel.

10 Be wise now therefore, O ye kings: be instructed, ye judges of the earth.

2:2 [j]John 1:41
2:3 [k]Luke 19:14
2:4 [l]Ps. 37:13 Prov. 1:26
2:6 [m]2 Sam. 5:7
2:7 [n]Acts 13:33
2:8 [o]Ps. 22:27
2:9 [p]Ps. 89:23 Rev. 2:27
2:11 [q]Heb. 12:28 [r]Phil. 2:12
2:12 [s]John 5:23 [t]Rev. 6:16 [u]Ps. 34:8 Is. 30:18 Rom. 9:33
3:1 [v]2 Sam. 15-18 [w]2 Sam. 15:12
3:2 [x]Ps. 71:11
3:3 [y]Ps. 28:7 [z]Ps. 27:6
3:4 [a]Ps. 34:4 [b]Ps. 2:6
3:5 [c]Lev. 26:6 Prov. 3:24

11 [q]Serve the LORD with fear, and rejoice [r]with trembling.

12 [s]Kiss the Son, lest he be angry, and ye perish *from* the way, when [t]his wrath is kindled but a little. [u]Blessed *are* all they that put their trust in him.

Confidence facing the enemy

A Psalm of David, [v]when he fled from Absalom his son.

3 LORD, [w]HOW are they increased that trouble me! many *are* they that rise up against me.

2 Many *there be* which say of my soul, [x]*There is* no help for him in God. Selah.

3 But thou, O LORD, *art* [y]a shield [i]for me; my glory, and [z]the lifter up of mine head.

4 I cried unto the LORD with my voice, and [a]he heard me out of his [b]holy hill. Selah.

5 [c]I laid me down and slept; I awaked; for the LORD sustained me.

[e] Or, *trouble* [f] Heb. *anointed* [g] Heb. *upon Zion, the hill of my holiness* [h] Or, *for a decree* [i] Or, *about*

comes to earth at the end of time and destroys the enemies of God (see Rev. 12:5; 19:15). Then all faithful believers will share in His reign over the nations (Rev. 2:26–27).

(4) Through the psalmist, the Holy Spirit exhorts humankind to be wise before Almighty God and to take refuge in Him before that terrible day of God's judgment arrives (vv. 10–12; cf. Heb. 3:7–19).

2:2 HIS ANOINTED. Ps. 2 is a Messianic psalm, i.e., one that prophesies the coming of God's Messiah, Jesus Christ. "Messiah" means "anointed one" and applies to Jesus, whom God anointed to redeem Israel and rule over God's kingdom (see next note; see Mat. 1:1, note).

2:7 THOU *ART* MY SON: THIS DAY HAVE I BEGOTTEN THEE. "Begotten thee" literally translates "brought you forth." It was used of a woman bringing forth a child from the womb, but was also a technical term for a king bringing out his son before the people to proclaim him as king along with his father (cf. 1 Ki. 1:32–34, where David did this for Solomon). Here it applies to Jesus' public proclamation as God's Son and His anointing as prophet, priest, and king (see Mat. 3:12; Acts 13:33; Heb. 1:5; 5:5; 7:28; 2 Pet. 1:13).

2:8 THE HEATHEN *FOR* THINE INHERITANCE. No earthly king was ever given this promise of the nations as an inheritance. It was a promise only to be fulfilled in the Messianic King, Jesus (see Zech. 9:10).

3:1–8 HOW ARE THEY INCREASED THAT TROUBLE ME! This psalm is a lament to God. Nearly a third of the psalms belong to this category. (1) The basic structure of a psalm of lament consists of a fervent calling on God (v. 1), a description of the believer's trouble, suffering, or injustice (vv. 1–2), an affirmation of trust in God (vv. 3–6), a plea for help (v. 7), and an expression of praise or thanksgiving (v. 8). (2) The exceptionally large number of psalms of lament in the Bible indicates that God wants His people to call upon Him in times of need and trouble (see Heb. 4:16).

3:2 SELAH. The meaning of this term is uncertain. It may signal a pause, a musical interlude, or a musical climax.

3:3 THOU, O LORD, *ART* A SHIELD . . . MY GLORY. Believers who live according to the will of God but find themselves confronting affliction and opposition (vv. 1–2; see 2 Sam. 15:12–30) may call upon God with a confidence that He will act on their behalf according to His divine purpose. (1) "Shield" refers to God's protection (see Gen. 15:1, where God is Abraham's shield; Deut. 33:29, where He is Israel's shield). (2) God is the believer's "glory" in that His presence, fellowship, and help are our greatest good. Committing ourselves to God as our provider who bestows glory results in the experience of His grace and presence that enables us to rise above the troubles of life.

3:5 I LAID ME DOWN AND SLEPT. Believers who earnestly call upon God and constantly trust in His faithfulness, with the confidence that He hears (v. 4), may lie down in peace and sleep securely (cf. 4:8). God will sustain them and minister His grace even while they sleep (see 127:2; Prov. 3:24).

6 [d]I will not be afraid of ten thou-
sands of people, that have set *them-
selves* against me round about.
7 Arise, O LORD; save me, O my
God: [e]for thou hast smitten all mine
enemies *upon* the cheek bone; thou
hast broken the teeth of the ungodly.
8 [f]Salvation *belongeth* unto the
LORD: thy blessing *is* upon thy people.
Selah.

Thoughts in the night

To the [j]chief Musician on Neginoth,
A Psalm of David.

4 HEAR ME when I call, O God of
my righteousness: thou hast en-
larged me *when I was* in distress;
[k]have mercy upon me, and hear my
prayer.
2 O ye sons of men, how long *will ye
turn* my glory into shame? *how long* will
ye love vanity, *and* seek after leasing?
Selah.
3 But know that [g]the LORD hath set
apart him that is godly for himself: the
LORD will hear when I call unto him.
4 [h]Stand in awe, and sin not:
[i]commune with your own heart upon
your bed, and be still. Selah.
5 Offer [j]the sacrifices of righ-
teousness, and [k]put your trust in the
LORD.
6 *There be* many that say, Who will
show us *any* good? [l]LORD, lift thou up
the light of thy countenance upon us.
7 Thou hast put [m]gladness in my
heart, more than in the time *that* their
corn and their wine increased.
8 [n]I will both lay me down in

3:6 [d]Ps. 27:3
3:7 [e]Job 16:10 Lam. 3:30
3:8 [f]Is. 43:11
4:3 [g]2 Tim. 2:19 2 Pet. 2:9
4:4 [h]Eph. 4:26 [i]Ps. 77:6
4:5 [j]Deut. 33:19 Ps. 50:14 [k]Ps. 37:3
4:6 [l]Num. 6:26
4:7 [m]Is. 9:3
4:8 [n]Ps. 3:5
[o]Lev. 25:18
5:2 [p]Ps. 3:4
5:3 [q]Ps. 30:5
5:6 [r]Rev. 21:8 [s]Ps. 55:23
5:8 [t]Ps. 25:5
5:9 [u]Luke 11:44 Rom. 3:13

peace, and sleep: [o]for thou, LORD, only
makest me dwell in safety.

A morning prayer

To the chief Musician upon Nehiloth,
A Psalm of David.

5 GIVE EAR to my words, O LORD,
consider my meditation.
2 Hearken unto the [p]voice of my
cry, my King, and my God: for unto
thee will I pray.
3 [q]My voice shalt thou hear in the
morning, O LORD; in the morning will I
direct *my prayer* unto thee, and will
look up.
4 For thou *art* not a God that hath
pleasure in wickedness: neither shall
evil dwell with thee.
5 The foolish shall not stand [l]in
thy sight: thou hatest all workers of
iniquity.
6 [r]Thou shalt destroy them that
speak leasing: [s]the LORD will abhor
[m]the bloody and deceitful man.
7 But as for me, I will come *into* thy
house in the multitude of thy mercy:
and in thy fear will I worship toward
[n]thy holy temple.
8 [t]Lead me, O LORD, in thy righ-
teousness because of [o]mine enemies;
make thy way straight before my face.
9 For *there is* no [p]faithfulness [q]in
their mouth; their inward part *is* [r]very
wickedness; [u]their throat *is* an open

[j] Or, *overseer* [k] Or, *be gracious unto me* [l] Heb. *before thine eyes* [m] Heb. *the man of bloods and deceit* [n] Heb. *the temple of thy holiness* [o] Heb. *those which observe me* [p] Or, *stedfastness* [q] Heb. *in his mouth,* i.e. *in the mouth of any of them* [r] Heb. *wickednesses*

4:1–8 HEAR ME. This psalm reveals the kind of persons who will be heard by God in times of distress. They must have a personal relationship of trust in God (vv. 5,8), an earnest desire for God's help (vv. 1,3,6), and a godly lifestyle (vv. 3–5; see next note).

4:3 THE LORD WILL HEAR WHEN I CALL UNTO HIM. In order to have assurance that God will answer our call for help, we must sincerely endeavor to live a godly life (cf. Prov. 15:29; John 9:31; 15:7). Those who faithfully devote themselves to God have been set apart as His own treasured possession. When we belong to God, we can appeal to Him as our protector and provider (cf. Heb. 10:22; 1 John 3:21–22).

5:3 MY VOICE SHALT THOU HEAR. Firmly determined to seek God with all his heart, David commits himself to three actions. (1) Confident that God will hear his voice, he will persist in prayer and not live without it (vv. 1–2; cf. Deut. 4:29). (2) He will pray to God "in the morning." If we orient our lives around God, morning prayers will be the natural thing to do. Each new morning calls for a renewed dedication of ourselves to God (55:16–17; 88:13; 119:147), fellowship with Him, and a feeding on His Word (cf. 119:9–16). (3) He will "look up" in expectation for answers to his prayer, and throughout the day he will search for signs that God is at work in his life.

5:5–6 THOU HATEST ALL WORKERS OF INIQUITY. Evil does not exist in the abstract. God not only hates sin, but also in some sense hates those who perpetrate evil. On the other hand, the Scriptures also reveal God to be the One who loves sinners, reaches out to them in compassion and mercy, and seeks to redeem them from sin through the cross of Christ (John 3:16).

sepulchre; [v]they flatter with their tongue.

10 [s]Destroy thou them, O God; let them fall [t]by their own counsels; cast them out in the multitude of their transgressions; for they have rebelled against thee.

11 But let all those that put their trust in thee [w]rejoice: let them ever shout for joy, because [u]thou defendest them: let them also that love thy name be joyful in thee.

12 For thou, LORD, wilt bless the righteous; with favour wilt thou [v]compass him as *with* a shield.

Prayer for mercy during trouble

To the chief Musician on Neginoth [x]upon[w] Sheminith, A Psalm of David.

6 O LORD, rebuke me not in thine anger, neither chasten me in thy hot displeasure.

2 Have mercy upon me, O LORD; for I *am* weak: O LORD, [y]heal me; for my bones are vexed.

3 My soul is also sore vexed: but thou, O LORD, how long?

Ps. 41:1-3

4 Return, O LORD, deliver my soul: oh save me for thy mercies' sake.

5 [z]For in death *there is* no remembrance of thee: in the grave who shall give thee thanks?

6 I am weary with my groaning; [x]all the night make I my bed to swim; I water my couch with my tears.

7 [a]Mine eye is consumed because of grief; it waxeth old because of all mine enemies.

8 [b]Depart from me, all ye workers of iniquity; for the LORD hath [c]heard the voice of my weeping.

9 The LORD hath heard my supplication; the LORD will receive my prayer.

10 Let all mine enemies be ashamed and sore vexed: let them return *and* be ashamed suddenly.

The prayer of a wronged man

[d]Shiggaion of David, which he sang unto the LORD, [e]concerning the [y]words of Cush the Benjamite.

7 O LORD my God, in thee do I put my trust: [f]save me from all them that persecute me, and deliver me:

2 [g]Lest he tear my soul like a lion, [h]rending *it* in pieces, while *there is* [z]none to deliver.

3 O LORD my God, [i]if I have done this; if there be [j]iniquity in my hands;

4 If I have rewarded evil unto him

5:9 [v]Ps. 62:4
5:11 [w]Is. 65:13
6:1 [x]1 Chr. 15:21 Ps. 12,title
6:2 [y]Hos. 6:1
6:5 [z]Ps. 30:9
6:7 [a]Job 17:7
6:8 [b]Mat. 25:41 [c]Ps. 3:4
7:1 [d]Hab. 3:1 [e]2 Sam. 16 [f]Ps. 31:15
7:2 [g]Is. 38:13 [h]Ps. 50:22
7:3 [i]2 Sam. 16:7 [j]1 Sam. 24:11

[s] Or, *Make them guilty* [t] Or, *from their counsels* [u] Heb. *thou coverest over,* or, *protectest them* [v] Heb. *crown him* [w] Or, *upon the eighth* [x] Or, *every night* [y] Or, *business* [z] Heb. *not a deliverer*

5:10 DESTROY THOU THEM, O GOD. See Ps. 35:1–38, note on the psalmist's prayer for the destruction of God's enemies.

6:1–10 REBUKE ME NOT IN THINE ANGER. This psalm is one of seven penitential psalms (i.e., psalms of sorrow for sin; the others are Ps. 32; 38; 51; 130; 143). The Holy Spirit inspired this prayer to give encouragement to all who have suffered for a long time under the chastisement of God and who need pardon and healing.

6:2 O LORD, HEAL ME. During a time of physical affliction and divine chastisement that he knows he deserves, the psalmist has lost his sense of the presence of God (v. 4) and spiritual peace (v. 3). He has suffered for a long time and is in intense grief. His prayer is not so much that God will remove all rebuke from him as it is that God's chastening might be mingled with mercy and not be so severe that he dies (cf. Jer. 10:23–24).

6:4 DELIVER MY SOUL. Though the penitent one is concerned about the healing of his body (v. 2), his primary concern is for the healing of his soul and the restoration of the presence and favor of God. He longs for God to be near him and appeals to His mercy and love (vv. 2,4). Since love and mercy are a part of God's character, believers may appeal to Him to be true to His character.

6:6 I AM WEARY WITH MY GROANING. The psalmist's distress and anguish of soul have continued for some time. The statement "but thou, O LORD, how long?" (v. 3), along with vv. 6–7, confirms that God has not immediately restored him to spiritual peace, grace, and His divine presence. Vv. 8–9 teach that in His own time God will hear our supplications and receive our prayer. We need not despair but must wait on God in faith (cf. 13:1; 74:9). In due time He will answer our prayer.

7:1–17 SAVE ME FROM ALL THEM THAT PERSECUTE ME. This psalm serves as a model for all who are unjustly treated, falsely accused, or attacked by those who despise them. The prayer may be applied to our greatest enemy who seeks to tear our souls like a lion (v. 2), i.e., to Satan and his demonic host (Eph. 6:11–12; 1 Pet. 5:8). It is always appropriate to pray for deliverance from the evil one (see Mat. 6:13, note).

7:1 IN THEE DO I PUT MY TRUST. Those who have sincerely committed themselves to God may with all confidence take refuge in the Lord and commit their life situations to Him. In the midst of unjust or troublesome times, we may place ourselves under the protection of God and appeal to Him on the basis of our faithfulness and righteousness (vv. 3–5,8).

that was at peace with me; (yea, [k]I
have delivered him that without cause
is mine enemy:)
5 Let the enemy persecute my soul,
and take *it*; yea, let him tread down my
life upon the earth, and lay mine hon-
our in the dust. Selah.
6 Arise, O LORD, in thine anger,
[l]lift up thyself because of the rage of
mine enemies: and [m]awake for me *to*
the judgment *that* thou hast com-
manded.
7 So shall the congregation of the
people compass thee about: for their
sakes therefore return thou on high.
8 The LORD shall judge the people:
judge me, O LORD, [n]according to my
righteousness, and according to mine
integrity *that is* in me.
9 Oh let the wickedness of the wick-
ed come to an end; but establish the
just: [o]for the righteous God trieth the
hearts and reins.
10 [a]My defence *is* of God, which
saveth the [p]upright in heart.
11 [b]God judgeth the righteous,
and God is angry *with the wicked* every
day.
12 If he turn not, he will [q]whet his
sword; he hath bent his bow, and made
it ready.
13 He hath also prepared for him
the instruments of death; he ordaineth
his arrows against the persecutors.
14 [r]Behold, he travaileth with in-
iquity, and hath conceived mischief,
and brought forth falsehood.
15 [c]He made a pit, and digged it,
[s]and is fallen into the ditch *which* he
made.
16 [t]His mischief shall return upon
his own head, and his violent dealing
shall come down upon his own pate.
17 I will praise the LORD according
to his righteousness: and will sing
praise to the name of the LORD most
high.

7:4 [k]1 Sam. 24:7 **7:6** [l]Ps. 94:2 [m]Ps. 44:23 **7:8** [n]Ps. 18:20 **7:9** [o]1 Sam. 16:7 **7:10** [p]Ps. 125:4 **7:12** [q]Deut. 32:41 **7:14** [r]Job 15:35 **7:15** [s]Job 4:8 **7:16** [t]Esth. 9:25 **8:1** [u]Ps. 81,title & 84,title [v]Ps. 148:13 [w]Ps. 113:4 **8:2** [x]1 Cor. 1:27 [y]Ps. 44:16 **8:3** [z]Ps. 111:2 **8:4** [a]Job 7:17 **8:6** [b]Gen. 1:26

God's glory and man's honour

To the chief Musician [u]upon Gittith,
A Psalm of David.

8 O LORD our Lord, how [v]excel-
lent *is* thy name in all the earth!
who [w]hast set thy glory above the
heavens.
2 [x]Out of the mouth of babes and
sucklings hast thou [d]ordained
strength because of thine enemies,
that thou mightest still [y]the enemy
and the avenger.
3 When I [z]consider thy heavens,
the work of thy fingers, the moon and
the stars, which thou hast ordained;
4 [a]What is man, that thou art
mindful of him? and the son of man,
that thou visitest him?
5 For thou hast made him a little
lower than the angels, and hast
crowned him with glory and honour.
6 [b]Thou madest him to have do-
minion over the works of thy hands;

[a] Heb. *My buckler* is *upon God* [b] Or, *God* is *a righteous judge* [c] Heb. *He hath digged a pit* [d] Heb. *founded*

7:10 GOD, WHICH SAVETH THE UPRIGHT IN HEART. The Holy Spirit teaches that the righteous can expect God to deliver and help them in times of affliction. We may appeal to God on the basis of a clear conscience and our sincere endeavor to maintain uprightness of heart.

(1) We may assert our spiritual integrity before God by praying, "Judge me, O LORD, according to my righteousness" (v. 8; cf. Job 29:14). Such a claim is not self-righteous if it is spoken from a sincere heart, purified by love for God through faith (cf. 1 John 3:21; Jas. 5:16).

(2) What a blessed thing it is to pray for God's help with a repentant heart (Ps. 6). But it is even better when we can pray to God with a clear conscience and with the knowledge that we have wronged no one and have sought sincerely to love God with all our heart.

(3) Note what the apostle Paul states: "Herein do I exercise myself, to have always a conscience void of offence toward God, and *toward* men" (Acts 24:16; cf. 2 Cor. 1:12; 1 Tim. 1:5,19; 2 Tim. 1:3; 1 Pet. 3:21). And Jesus affirms, "If ye abide in me, and my words abide in you, ye shall ask what ye will, and it shall be done unto you" (John 15:7).

8:4–6 THE SON OF MAN. The N.T. quotes these verses from the Septuagint (the Greek translation of the Hebrew O.T.) and applies them to Jesus (Heb. 2:6–8; cf. Eph. 1:19–22). It is only in Him that these truths are perfectly realized. He is the one who, as a representative of the human race, will be given the full dominion over all creation (vv. 6–8; cf. Phil. 2:10).

8:5 WITH GLORY AND HONOUR. This psalm expresses the amazing honor that God has bestowed upon humankind. It affirms that we as humans were created by God for a glorious purpose; we are not just animals, the product of natural evolution and chance (v. 5; see article on CREATION, p. 6). So valuable are we to God that we are special objects of His concern and favor (v. 4). He has honored us by choosing us to rule over His creation (vv. 6–8; cf. Gen. 1:28; 2:15,19). Yet the consciousness of our favored position is no reason for praising ourselves, but a reason for giving thanks and glory to the Creator (v. 9).

[c]thou hast put all *things* under his feet:

7 [e]All sheep and oxen, yea, and the beasts of the field;

8 The fowl of the air, and the fish of the sea, *and whatsoever* passeth through the paths of the seas.

9 [d]O LORD our Lord, how excellent *is* thy name in all the earth!

Praise to God for deliverance

To the chief Musician upon Muth-labben, A Psalm of David.

9 I WILL praise *thee,* O LORD, with my whole heart; I will show forth all thy marvellous works.

2 I will be glad and [e]rejoice in thee: I will sing praise to thy name, O [f]thou most High.

Ps. 34:1-3

3 When mine enemies are turned back, they shall fall and perish at thy presence.

4 For [f]thou hast maintained my right and my cause; thou satest in the throne judging [g]right.

5 Thou hast rebuked the heathen, thou hast destroyed the wicked, thou hast [g]put out their name for ever and ever.

6 [h]O thou enemy, destructions are come to a perpetual end: and thou hast destroyed cities; their memorial is perished with them.

7 [h]But the LORD shall endure for ever: he hath prepared his throne for judgment.

8 And [i]he shall judge the world in righteousness, he shall minister judgment to the people in uprightness.

9 [j]The LORD also will be [i]a refuge for the oppressed, a refuge in times of trouble.

10 And they that [k]know thy name will put their trust in thee: for thou, LORD, hast not forsaken them that seek thee.

11 Sing praises to the LORD, which dwelleth in Zion: [l]declare among the people his doings.

12 [m]When he maketh inquisition for blood, he remembereth them: he forgetteth not the cry of the [j]humble.

13 Have mercy upon me, O LORD; consider my trouble *which I suffer* of them that hate me, thou that liftest me up from the gates of death:

14 That I may show forth all thy praise in the gates of the daughter of Zion: I will [n]rejoice in thy salvation.

15 [o]The heathen are sunk down in the pit *that* they made: in the net which they hid is their own foot taken.

16 The LORD is [p]known *by* the judgment *which* he executeth: the wicked is snared in the work of his own hands. [q]Higgaion. [k] Selah.

17 The wicked shall be turned into hell, *and* all the nations [r]that forget God.

18 [s]For the needy shall not always be forgotten: [t]the expectation of the poor shall *not* perish for ever.

19 Arise, O LORD; let not man prevail: let the heathen be judged in thy sight.

20 Put them in fear, O LORD: *that*

8:6 [c]Heb. 2:8
8:9 [d]ver. 1
9:2 [e]Ps. 5:11 [f]Ps. 83:18
9:5 [g]Prov. 10:7
9:7 [h]Heb. 1:11
9:8 [i]Ps. 96:13
9:9 [j]Ps. 32:7
9:10 [k]Ps. 91:14
9:11 [l]Ps. 107:22
9:12 [m]Gen. 9:5
9:14 [n]Ps. 13:5
9:15 [o]Ps. 7:15,16
9:16 [p]Ex. 7:5 [q]Ps. 92:3
9:17 [r]Job 8:13
9:18 [s]Ps. 12:5 [t]Prov. 23:18

[e] Heb. *Flocks and oxen all of them* [f] Heb. *thou hast made my judgment* [g] Heb. *in righteousness* [h] Or, *The destructions of the enemy are come to a perpetual end: and* their *cities hast thou destroyed* [i] Heb. *an high place* [j] Or, *afflicted* [k] i.e. *Meditation*

9:1–2 I WILL PRAISE *THEE*, O LORD. At the heart of every believer's relationship with God is the requirement to praise Him (see article on PRAISE, p. 816).

9:5 THOU HAST DESTROYED THE WICKED. David speaks as if the events recorded here have already happened — a stylistic feature of prophecy in the psalms. He is so certain that the events will occur that he speaks of them as if they have already been fulfilled (see vv. 15–16).

9:8 HE SHALL JUDGE THE WORLD IN RIGHTEOUSNESS. The psalmist thanks and praises the Lord because He will one day fully deliver those who seek Him (vv. 8–14) and will bring judgment against His enemies (vv. 3–8,15–20). (1) In order to prevent discouragement and despair at the apparent success of evil in the world, God's people must firmly believe and confess that the Lord will one day vindicate those who, in spite of affliction, persevere against all who would destroy their faith in God (vv. 7–1; see Rev. 19 — 21). (2) N.T. believers may apply these verses to the enemies of the Lord and His church. Throughout the N.T. age a conflict rages between the forces of evil and the forces of righteousness. Faithful believers will be opposed by Satan, the world, and false believers within the church (see 2 Tim. 3:12, note).

9:18 THE NEEDY SHALL NOT ALWAYS BE FORGOTTEN. The needy and the afflicted among God's people are objects of His special care (vv. 9–10,12). They have the promise that God will not forsake them (v. 10), that He will remember their prayers (v. 12), and that their hopes will eventually be realized (v. 18).

the nations may know themselves *to be*
but men. Selah.

God hears and acts

10 WHY STANDEST thou afar off,
O LORD? *why* hidest thou *thyself*
in times of trouble?
2 [l]The wicked in *his* pride doth
persecute the poor: [u]let them be tak-
en in the devices that they have imag-
ined.
3 For the wicked [v]boasteth of his
[m]heart's desire, and [w]blesseth[n] the
covetous, *whom* the LORD abhorreth.
4 The wicked, through the pride
of his countenance, will not seek
after God: [o]God *is* not in all his
[x]thoughts.
5 His ways are always grievous; thy
judgments *are* far above out of his
sight: *as for* all his enemies, he puffeth
at them.
6 [y]He hath said in his heart, I shall
not be moved: [z]for *I shall* [p]never *be*
in adversity.
7 [a]His mouth is full of cursing and
[q]deceit and fraud: under his tongue *is*
mischief and [r]vanity.
8 He sitteth in the lurking places of
the villages: in the secret places doth
he murder the innocent: his eyes [s]are
privily set against the poor.
9 He lieth in wait [t]secretly as
a lion in his den: he lieth in wait to
catch the poor: he doth catch the
poor, when he draweth him into his
net.
10 [u]He croucheth, *and* humbleth
himself, that the poor may fall [v]by his
strong ones.
11 He hath said in his heart, God
hath forgotten: [b]he hideth his face; he
will never see *it*.
12 Arise, O LORD; O God, [c]lift up
thine hand: forget not the [w]humble.
13 Wherefore doth the wicked con-
temn God? he hath said in his heart,
Thou wilt not require *it*.
14 Thou hast seen *it;* for thou be-
holdest mischief and spite, to requite *it*
with thy hand: the poor [d]com-
mitteth[x] himself unto thee; [e]thou art
the helper of the fatherless.
15 Break thou the arm of the wick-
ed and the evil *man:* seek out his wick-
edness *till* thou find none.
16 [f]The LORD *is* King for ever and
ever: the heathen are perished out of
his land.
17 LORD, thou hast heard the desire
of the humble: thou wilt [y]prepare
their heart, thou wilt cause thine ear to
hear:
18 To [g]judge the fatherless and
the oppressed, that the man of the
earth may no more [z]oppress.

10:2 [u]Ps. 7:16
10:3 [v]Ps. 94:4 [w]Prov. 28:4
10:4 [x]Ps. 14:1
10:6 [y]Eccl. 8:11 Is. 56:12 [z]Rev. 18:7
10:7 [a]Rom. 3:14
10:11 [b]Job 22:13
10:12 [c]Mic. 5:9
10:14 [d]2 Tim. 1:12 [e]Ps. 68:5
10:16 [f]Ps. 29:10
10:18 [g]Ps. 82:3

[l]Heb. *In the pride of the wicked he doth persecute* [m]Heb. soul's [n]Or, *the covetous blesseth* himself, *he abhorreth the LORD* [o]Or, *all his thoughts* are, There is *no God* [p]Heb. *unto generation and generation* [q]Heb. *deceits* [r]Or, *iniquity* [s]Heb. *hide themselves* [t]Heb. *in the secret places* [u]Heb. *He breaketh himself* [v]Or, *into his strong parts* [w]Or, *afflicted* [x]Heb. *leaveth* [y]Or, *establish* [z]Or, *terrify*

10:1–18 WHY STANDEST THOU AFAR OFF. This prayer wrestles with the question of the seeming delay of the triumph of God's justice (cf. the cry of the martyred saints in Rev. 6:9–10). In this present age injustice and evil run rampant, and God sometimes appears to stand "afar off" and not interfere. God's people must pray that He will stop evil and suffering. Meanwhile, we may be assured that though the day of justice has not arrived, the Lord has heard our prayers and will give strength of heart until the end (vv. 17–18).

10:2 THE WICKED IN *HIS* PRIDE DOTH PERSECUTE. The psalmist grieves over the haughty attitude of cruel and wicked people (vv. 3–11) and their apparent success. (1) He prays that God will overthrow the wicked, help the humble, and reign as king forever in order that sin and terror be abolished from the earth (vv. 12–18). (2) While N.T. believers must always be vitally concerned about the salvation of the wicked, they must also understand that sin and cruelty will never be completely crushed, nor will righteousness fully reign, until Christ returns to destroy all evil (Rev. 19:11—20:10). We must therefore pray that God will soon abolish all evil, that Christ will be crowned king forever, and that on the earth sin and sorrow will cease (see Rev. 19—22).

10:8–10 IN THE SECRET PLACES DOTH HE MURDER THE INNOCENT. These verses can be applied to those who traffic in drugs, alcohol, and abortion, where the result is physical, emotional, and spiritual ruin for many. (1) Out of greed (cf. v. 3), such people draw the poor, the young, and the thoughtless within their nets. Through testimony and advertisement, they craftily emphasize the pleasures of their products while hiding the tragic suffering that comes as a result of their business (v. 9).

(2) These wicked individuals are arrogantly oblivious to their moral accountability before God (vv. 3–4,11,13), and their final end will be disastrous (see Ps. 73). No believer should participate in the promotion of what will harm another human, but rather in love, compassion, and concern seek to help all others avoid such temptations.

PRAISE

Ps. 9:1–2 "I will praise** thee, **O Lord, with my whole heart; I will show forth all thy marvellous works. I will be glad and rejoice in thee: I will sing praise to thy name, O thou most High."

IMPORTANCE OF PRAISE. The Scriptures often exhort God's people to praise the Lord. (1) The writers of the O.T. used three basic words to call Israelites to praise God: the word *barak* (usually translated in the KJV as "to bless" God); the word *halal* (from which "Hallelujah," meaning "praise the Lord," comes); and the word *yadah* (sometimes translated as "give thanks").

(2) The Bible's first song, sung after the Israelites had crossed the Red Sea, was essentially a song of praise and thanksgiving to God (Ex. 15; see v. 2). Moses commanded the Israelites that when they entered the promised land, they were to praise God for His goodness in giving them the promised land (Deut. 8:10). Deborah's song specifically called the people to bless the Lord (Judg. 5:9). David's desire to praise God is recorded both in the story of his life (2 Sam. 22:4,47,50; 1 Chr. 16:4,9,25,35–36; 29:20) and in the psalms he wrote (Ps. 9:1–2; 18:3; 22:23; 52:9; 108:1,3; 145). Other psalmists also call God's people to live their lives praising God (Ps. 33:1–2; 47:6–7; 75:9; 96:1–4; 100; 150). Finally, the O.T. prophets instruct God's people to praise Him (Is. 42:10,12; Jer. 20:13; cf. Is. 12:1; 25:1; Jer. 33:9; Joel 2:26; Hab. 3:3).

(3) The call to praise God reverberates throughout the N.T. Jesus Himself praised His Father in heaven (Mat. 11:25; Luke 10:21). Paul expects all the nations to praise God (Rom. 15:9–11; Eph. 1:3,6,12), and James calls us to praise the Lord (Jas. 3:9; 5:13). And in the end, the picture given in Revelation is of a vast throng of both saints and angels praising God continually (Rev. 4:9–11; 5:8–14; 7:9–12; 11:16–18).

(4) Praising God is one of the main functions of angels (Ps. B 103:20; 148:2) and is the privilege of God's people, both children (Mat. 21:16; cf. Ps. 8:2) and adults (Ps. 30:4; 135:1–2,19–21). Furthermore, God calls all nations to praise Him (Ps. 67:3–5; 117:1; 148:11–13; Is. 42:10–12; Rom. 15:11). In other words, every human being that breathes is called to shout forth the praise of God (Ps. 150:6). As if that is not enough, God also commands inanimate nature to praise Him—such as the sun, moon, and stars (Ps. 148:3–4; cf. Ps. 19:1–2); fire, hail, snow, and wind (Ps. 148:8); mountains, hills, rivers, and seas (Ps. 98:7–8; 148:9; Is. 44:23); all kinds of trees (Ps. 148:9; Is. 55:12); and all kinds of living creatures (Ps. 69:34; 148:10).

METHODS OF PRAISE. Praising God can take place in a variety of ways. (1) Praise is a keynote in the corporate worship of God's people (Ps. 100:4; see article on WORSHIP, p. 730). (2) Both in the corporate worship setting and in other places, the singing of songs, hymns, and spiritual songs is a way to express praise to God (Ps. 96:1–4; 147:1; Eph. 5:19–20; Col. 3:16–17). Praise can be sung with the mind (i.e., in known human languages) or with the Spirit (i.e., in tongues; 1 Cor. 14:14–16, see 14:15, note). (3) Musical praise to God can be expressed through various instruments—horns such as cornets and trumpets (1 Chr. 15:28; Ps. 150:3), wind instruments such as the pipe and flute (1 Sam. 10:5; Ps. 150:4, where the KJV has "organs"), stringed instruments such as the harp and psaltery (1 Chr. 13:8; Ps. 149:3; 150:3), and percussion instruments such as the timbrels (tambourines) and cymbals (Ex. 15:20; Ps. 150:5). (4) We can also communicate God's praise by telling others the wonderful deeds of our God. David, for example, having experienced God's forgiveness, was eager to tell others about what the Lord had done for him (Ps. 51:12–13,15). Other Bible writers exhort us to declare God's glory and praise in the assembly of God's people (Ps. 22:22–25; 111:1; Heb. 2:12) and among the nations (Ps. 18:49; 96:3–4; Is. 42:10–12). Peter calls upon God's chosen people to show forth the "praises of him who hath called you out of darkness into his

marvellous light" (1 Pet. 2:9). Mission work, in other words, is a method of praising God. (5) Finally, a life lived to the glory of God is a way of praising the Lord. Jesus reminds us that if we let our light shine, people will see our good works and give glory and praise to God (Mat. 5:16; cf. John 15:8). Similarly, Paul indicates that a life filled with the fruits of righteousness praises God (Phil. 1:11).

REASONS FOR PRAISE. Why do people praise the Lord? (1) One of the obvious reasons is because of the splendor, glory, and majesty of our God, the One who created the heavens and the earth (Ps. 96:4–6; 145:3; 148:13), the One who is to be exalted in His holiness (Ps. 99:3; Is. 6:3). (2) The experience of God's mighty acts, particularly His acts of salvation and redemption, is a key reason to praise His name (Ps. 96:1–3; 106:1–2; 148:14; 150:2; Luke 1:68–75; 2:14,20). In doing so, we praise God for His unfailing mercy, grace, and love (Ps. 57:9–10; 89:1–2; 117; 145:8–10; Eph. 1:6). (3) We will also naturally want to praise God for any specific acts of deliverance in our lives, such as being rescued from our enemies or healed of our sicknesses (Ps. 9:1–5; 40:1–3; 59:16; 124; Jer. 20:13; Luke 13:13; Acts 3:7–9). (4) Finally, God's continual providential care and provisions for us day by day, both physically and spiritually, are powerful reasons to praise and bless His name (Ps. 68:19; 103; 147; Is. 63:7; see article on THE PROVIDENCE OF GOD, p. 80).

The LORD our refuge

To the chief Musician,
A Psalm of David.

11 IN[h] THE LORD put I my trust: how say ye to my soul, Flee *as* a bird to your mountain?

2 For, lo, [i]the wicked bend *their* bow, they make ready their arrow upon the string, that they may [a]privily shoot at the upright in heart.

3 [j]If the foundations be destroyed, what can the righteous do?

4 The LORD *is* in his holy temple, the LORD's throne *is* in heaven: [k]his eyes behold, his eyelids try, the children of men.

5 The LORD [l]trieth the righteous: but the wicked and him that loveth violence his soul hateth.

6 Upon the wicked he shall rain [b]snares, fire and brimstone, and [c]an horrible tempest: [m]*this shall be* the portion of their cup.

7 For the righteous LORD [n]loveth righteousness; his countenance doth behold the upright.

Good thoughts for bad times

To the chief Musician [o]upon [d]Sheminith, A Psalm of David.

12 HELP,[e] LORD; for the godly man ceaseth; for the faithful fail from among the children of men.

2 [p]They speak vanity every one with his neighbour: *with* flattering lips *and* with [f]a double heart do they speak.

3 The LORD shall cut off all flattering lips, *and* the tongue that speaketh [g]proud things:

4 Who have said, With our tongue will we prevail; our lips [h]*are* our own: who *is* lord over us?

5 For the oppression of the poor, for the sighing of the needy, now will I arise, saith the LORD; I will set *him* in safety *from him that* [i]puffeth at him.

6 The words of the LORD *are* [q]pure words: *as* silver tried in a furnace of earth, purified seven times.

7 Thou shalt keep them, O LORD, thou shalt preserve [j]them from this generation for ever.

8 The wicked walk on every side, when [k]the vilest men are exalted.

The deserted soul

To the [l]chief Musician,
A Psalm of David.

13 HOW LONG wilt thou forget me, O LORD? for ever? [r]how long wilt thou hide thy face from me?

2 How long shall I take counsel in

11:1 [h]Ps. 56:11
11:2 [i]Ps. 64:3,4
11:3 [j]Ps. 82:5
11:4 [k]Ps. 33:13 & 34:15,16
11:5 [l]Gen. 22:1
11:6 [m]Gen. 43:34 1 Sam. 1:4 Ps. 75:8
11:7 [n]Ps. 45:7
12:1 [o]Ps. 6,title
12:2 [p]Ps. 10:7
12:6 [q]2 Sam. 22:31 Ps. 18:30 Prov. 30:5
13:1 [r]Job 13:24

[a] Heb. *in darkness* [b] Or, *quick burning coal* [c] Or, *a burning tempest* [d] Or, *upon the eighth* [e] Or, *Save* [f] Heb. *an heart and an heart* [g] Heb. *great things* [h] Heb. are *with us* [i] Or, *would ensnare him* [j] Heb. *him:* i.e. *every one of them* [k] Heb. *the vilest of the sons of men are exalted* [l] Or, *overseer*

11:1–7 IN THE LORD PUT I MY TRUST. This psalm rebukes those who counsel flight or compromise when Biblical principles are at stake (vv. 1–3). Faithful believers will take refuge in the Lord (v. 1) and remain committed to righteousness even if the moral and spiritual "foundations [are] destroyed" in both society and the church (v. 3). The result will be that the Lord's "countenance doth behold the upright" (v. 7; cf. 16:8–11; 17:15; 23:6).

11:5 HIM THAT LOVETH VIOLENCE HIS SOUL HATETH. Because the Lord "loveth righteousness" (v. 7), He hates those who participate in violence or enjoy being entertained by it. Thus believers must exercise caution concerning the entertainment media and examine themselves to determine whether they take pleasure in and enjoy the portrayal of violence and bloodshed (see Luke 23:35, note; Rom. 1:32, note).

12:1–8 HELP, LORD. This psalm describes a time when the ungodly activity of the wicked is keenly felt by those committed to God and His righteousness. In all ages God's people have experienced this, but in the last days of this age these conditions will be especially prevalent (1 Tim. 4:1). The faithful should know that when they are surrounded by the evils of society and are grieved and oppressed by its immorality, they will be especially protected by the power of God (v. 5). God will "keep them" and "preserve them from this [evil] generation for ever" (v. 7; see 1 Pet. 1:5, note).

13:1 HOW LONG WILT THOU FORGET ME? The psalmist is depressed and discouraged; he is in desperate trouble, yet he feels that God is absent (v. 2) and unwilling to give practical help. Note especially two important lessons: (1) The prayers of the godly may not be answered immediately, for God may appear to pay no attention to our pleas. This feeling of being forsaken by Him may occur in times of sickness, financial need, or severe problems. It may involve family, work, or church. At such times we should pray for the Holy Spirit to give us the assurance that we will yet rejoice in God's salvation (vv. 5–6).

(2) If we are sincerely seeking God's help through genuine faith in Jesus Christ, then God's delay does not mean that we are forsaken by Him. God may instead be planning to accomplish some

my soul, *having* sorrow in my heart dai-
ly? how long shall mine enemy be ex-
alted over me?
3 Consider *and* hear me, O LORD my
God: [s]lighten mine eyes, [t]lest I sleep
the *sleep of* death;
4 Lest mine enemy say, I have pre-
vailed against him; *and* those that trou-
ble me rejoice when I am moved.
5 But I have trusted in thy mercy;
my heart shall rejoice in thy salvation.
6 I will sing unto the LORD, because
:1-3 he hath dealt bountifully with me.

The fate of the fool

14:1–7pp — Ps. 53:1–6

To the chief Musician, *A Psalm* of David.

14 THE [u]FOOL hath said in his
heart, *There is* no God. They are
corrupt, they have done abominable
works, *there is* none that doeth good.
2 [v]The LORD looked down from
heaven upon the children of men, to
see if there were any that did under-
stand, *and* seek God.
3 They are all gone aside, they are
all together become [m]filthy: *there is*
none that doeth good, no, not one.
4 Have all the workers of iniquity no
knowledge? who eat up my people *as*
they eat bread, and [w]call not upon the
LORD.
5 There [n]were they in great fear:
for God *is* in the generation of the righ-
teous.
6 Ye have shamed the counsel of the
poor, because the LORD *is* his [x]refuge.

13:3 [s]Ezra 9:8 [t]Jer. 51:39
14:1 [u]Ps. 10:4
14:2 [v]Ps. 33:13
14:4 [w]Is. 64:7
14:6 [x]Ps. 9:9

7 [y]Oh[o] that the salvation of Israel
were come out of Zion! [z]when the LORD
bringeth back the captivity of his peo-
ple, Jacob shall rejoice, *and* Israel shall
be glad.

The happiness of the holy

A Psalm of David.

15 LORD, [a]WHO shall [p]abide in
thy tabernacle? who shall dwell
in thy holy hill?
2 He that walketh uprightly, and
worketh righteousness, and speaketh
the truth in his heart.
3 *He that* backbiteth not with his
tongue, nor doeth evil to his neighbour,
[b]nor [q]taketh up a reproach against
his neighbour.
4 [c]In whose eyes a vile person is
contemned; but he honoureth them
that fear the LORD. *He that* sweareth to
his own hurt, and changeth not.
5 *He that* putteth not out his money
to usury, nor taketh reward against the
innocent. He that doeth these *things*
[d]shall never be moved.

Joy in God's presence

[e]Michtam[r] of David.

16 PRESERVE ME, O God: for in
thee do I put my trust.
2 *O my soul,* thou hast said unto the

14:7 [y]Ps. 53:6 [z]Job 42:10
15:1 [a]Ps. 24:3
15:3 [b]Ex. 23:1
15:4 [c]Esth. 3:2
15:5 [d]2 Pet. 1:10
16:1 [e]Ps. 56-60

[m] Heb. *stinking* [n] Heb. *they feared a fear* [o] Heb. *Who will give* [p] Heb. *sojourn* [q] Or, *receiveth,* or, *endureth* [r] Or, *A golden* Psalm *of David*

unseen purpose in our lives (cf. 2 Cor. 12:7–10; Heb. 12:10–11; Jas. 1:2–4; 1 Pet. 1:6–7).

13:5 MY HEART SHALL REJOICE IN THY SALVATION. The answer to God's apparent delay is to trust in His lovingkindness and to remember that in the past He has delivered us and blessed us. The Lord's lovingkindness will appear in His own time and way (see Rom. 8:28, note).

14:1–7 THE FOOL. The "fool" is a person who lives as if there is no God. Fools reveal their rebellion against God in two ways. (1) They reject God's revelation, for they do not believe what the Bible says about God. They scorn the moral principles of God's Word and rely on their own ideas to determine right from wrong (vv. 1–3).

(2) They do not seek God, nor do they call on God in prayer for His presence and help.

(3) This psalm describes the depravity of the wicked and teaches that the human race is by nature separated from God (cf. Eph. 2:2–3). Paul quotes the first three verses of this psalm to support the truth that "all have sinned, and come short of the glory of God" (Rom. 3:23; see 3:10–12).

15:1 LORD, WHO SHALL ABIDE IN THY TABERNACLE. This psalm answers the question: "What sort of person experiences the intimate presence and fellowship of God?" It implies that we can cause God to withdraw His presence from our lives through our acts of unrighteousness, deceit, slander, or selfishness. Thus we should examine our actions daily, confess our sins, turn from them, constantly seek through Christ to present ourselves approved to God (2 Tim. 2:15), and realize that to lose communion with God is to lose everything (see 1 John 1:6–7; 2:3–6; 3:21–24).

16:2 MY GOODNESS *EXTENDETH* NOT TO THEE. Apart from God, the psalmist sees no meaning in life and no personal happiness. Nothing in his life is good if the Lord's presence and blessing are absent. Paul expressed this same truth when he said: "For to me to live *is* Christ" (Phil. 1:21; cf. Gal. 2:20).

LORD, Thou *art* my Lord: [f]my goodness *extendeth* not to thee;

3 *But* to the saints that *are* in the earth, and *to* the excellent, in whom *is* all my delight.

4 Their sorrows shall be multiplied *that* [s]hasten *after* another *god:* their drink offerings of blood will I not offer, [g]nor take up their names into my lips.

5 The LORD *is* the portion [t]of mine inheritance and of my cup: thou maintainest my lot.

6 The lines are fallen unto me in pleasant *places;* yea, I have a goodly heritage.

7 I will bless the LORD, who hath given me counsel: my reins also instruct me in the night seasons.

8 I have set the LORD always before me: because *he is* at my right hand, I shall not be moved.

9 Therefore my heart is glad, and my glory rejoiceth: my flesh also shall [u]rest in hope.

10 [h]For thou wilt not leave my soul in hell; neither wilt thou suffer thine Holy One to see corruption.

16:2 [f]Job 35:7
16:4 [g]Ex. 23:13
16:10 [h]Ps. 49:15

11 Thou wilt show me the [i]path of life: in thy presence *is* fulness of joy; at thy right hand *there are* pleasures for evermore.

16:11 [i]Mat. 7:14
17:3 [j]Job 23:10

Deliverance from the wicked

A Prayer of David.

17 HEAR [v]THE right, O LORD, attend unto my cry, give ear unto my prayer, *that goeth* [w]not out of feigned lips.

2 Let my sentence come forth from thy presence; let thine eyes behold the things that are equal.

3 Thou hast proved mine heart; thou hast visited *me* in the night; [j]thou hast tried me, *and* shalt find nothing; I am purposed *that* my mouth shall not transgress.

4 Concerning the works of men, by the word of thy lips I have kept *me from* the paths of the destroyer.

[s] Or, *give gifts to another* [t] Heb. *of my part*
[u] Heb. *dwell confidently* [v] Heb. *justice*
[w] Heb. *without lips of deceit*

16:5 THE LORD . . . MINE INHERITANCE. The "inheritance" and "cup" are the Lord Himself (cf. 73:26; Num. 18:20; Deut. 18:2). An important aspect of our inheritance as N.T. believers is the following: "If a man love me, he will keep my words: and my Father will love him, and we will come unto him, and make our abode with him" (John 14:23). Communion with God is the sure source of blessings and happiness.

16:8 I HAVE SET THE LORD ALWAYS BEFORE ME. Believers should seek and cherish above all else intimate fellowship with God. The Lord's continual presence at our right hand brings His guidance (vv. 7,11), protection (v. 8), joy (v. 9), resurrection (v. 10), and eternal blessings (v. 11).

16:10 THOU WILT NOT LEAVE MY SOUL IN HELL. "Hell" (Heb. *Sheol*) here means the grave. A personal relationship with God will give believers confidence in a future life with God and certainty that He will not abandon them to the grave (cf. 73:26). The apostles Peter and Paul both applied this verse to Christ and His resurrection (Acts 2:25–31; 13:34–37).

(1) *Sheol*, found sixty-five times in the O.T., is translated thirty-one times as "the grave," thirty-one times as "hell,' and three times as "the pit." When the N.T. quotes these passages, it generally translates it with the Greek word *Hades*. Some scholars believe *Sheol* always means "the grave," while others think it never has that meaning alone.

(2) In general, the O.T. views *Sheol* as a place associated with some sort of punishment. (a) When Jacob indicated that he would go to *Sheol* because of the loss of his son Joseph (Gen. 37:35), he felt he must be under the judgment of God; thus he refused to be comforted. There is no evidence that he sought God further until after he heard Joseph was still alive. (b) David clearly indicated that *Sheol* was the place where "the heathen" would go (9:17), and Isaiah said that the heathen king Tiglath-Pileser of Assyria, upon his death, would meet in *Sheol* the kings he conquered (Is. 14:9–10). (c) There are several passages that indicate the Israelites did not expect to go to *Sheol* at all at death, but would instead go where they would enjoy the blessings of God's presence. When David died, for example, he anticipated dwelling in the house of the Lord forever (23:6). Another psalmist believed that God would redeem him from the hand of *Sheol* and receive him to Himself in heaven (49:15; cf. 73:14–15). And Solomon testified that the wise, God-fearing man goes to the place above, "that he may depart from hell beneath" (Prov. 15:24).

17:1 HEAR . . . O LORD. The psalmist's cry to the Lord to hear his prayer is founded not only on God's mercy and grace, but also on his own faithful obedience to God's will and ways (vv. 1–5). God has searched his heart and found that his endeavor to please Him is no pretense (cf. 1 John 3:18–21). That David appeals to God on the basis of his own personal faithfulness expresses the fundamental truth that God has promised to hear the prayers of those who love and honor Him (see John 15:7, note). The first indispensable condition of true prayer is a clear conscience and a pure life (see 1 John 3:22, note; see article on EFFECTIVE PRAYING, p. 540).

5 [k]Hold up my goings in thy paths,
that my footsteps [x]slip not.
6 [l]I have called upon thee, for thou
wilt hear me, O God: incline thine ear
unto me, *and hear* my speech.
7 Show thy marvellous lovingkind-
ness, O thou [y]that savest by thy right
hand them which put their trust *in
thee* from those that rise up *against
them.*
8 Keep me as the apple of the eye,
hide me under the shadow of thy
wings,
9 From the wicked [z]that oppress
me, *from* [a]my deadly enemies, *who*
compass me about.
10 They are inclosed in their own
fat: with their mouth they [m]speak
proudly.
11 They have now compassed us in
our steps: they have set their eyes bow-
ing down to the earth;
12 [b]Like as a lion *that* is greedy of
his prey, and as it were a young lion
[c]lurking in secret places.
13 Arise, O LORD, [d]disappoint
him, cast him down: deliver my
soul from the wicked, [e]*which is* thy
sword:
14 From men [f]*which are* thy hand,
O LORD, from men of the world, *which
have* their portion in *this* life, and
whose belly thou fillest with thy hid
treasure: [g]they are full of children, and
leave the rest of their *substance* to their
babes.
15 As for me, [n]I will behold thy
face in righteousness: [o]I shall be sat-
isfied, when I awake, with thy like-
ness.

17:5 [k]Ps. 119:133
17:6 [l]Ps. 116:2
17:10 [m]1 Sam. 2:3
17:15 [n]1 John 3:2 [o]Ps. 4:6,7 & 16:11

18:1 [p]Ps. 36,title [q]2 Sam. 22 [r]Ps. 144:1
18:2 [s]Heb. 2:13
18:3 [t]Ps. 76:4
18:4 [u]Ps. 116:3
18:7 [v]Acts 4:31

Calling upon God in distress

18:Title–50pp — 2 Sam. 22:1–51

To the chief Musician, *A Psalm* of David, [p]the servant of the LORD, who spake unto the LORD the words of [q]this song in the day *that* the LORD delivered him from the hand of all his enemies, and from the hand of Saul: And he said,

18 I [r]WILL love thee, O LORD,
my strength.
2 The LORD *is* my rock, and my for-
tress, and my deliverer; my God, [h]my
strength, [s]in whom I will trust; my
buckler, and the horn of my salvation,
and my high tower.
3 I will call upon the LORD, [t]*who is
worthy* to be praised: so shall I be
saved from mine enemies. Ps. 27:1
4 [u]The sorrows of death com-
passed me, and the floods of [i]ungodly
men made me afraid.
5 The [j]sorrows of hell compassed
me about: the snares of death prevent-
ed me.
6 In my distress I called upon the
LORD, and cried unto my God: he heard
my voice out of his temple, and my cry
came before him, *even* into his ears.
7 [v]Then the earth shook and trem-

[x]Heb. *be not moved* [y]Or, *that savest them which trust* in thee *from those that rise up against thy right hand* [z]Heb. *that waste me* [a]Heb. *my enemies against the soul* [b]Heb. *The likeness of him* (i.e. *of every one of them)* is *as a lion that desireth to ravin* [c]Heb. *sitting* [d]Heb. *prevent his face* [e]Or, by *thy sword* [f]Or, by *thine hand* [g]Or, their *children are full* [h]Heb. *my rock* [i]Heb. *Belial* [j]Or, *cords*

17:8 THE APPLE OF THE EYE. The psalmist uses two figures which recall God's love and care for His faithful people. (1) "The apple of the eye" is the pupil and is a Hebrew metaphor expressing something greatly valued and dear. (2) "The shadow of thy wings" is a metaphor drawn from the imagery of a hen that protects her young with her wings; hence it expresses tender protection (cf. 36:7; 57:1; 61:4; 63:7). Christ used this metaphor to express His love for Israel (Mat. 23:37). All believers should pray that God will reach out to protect us in times of danger just like someone who instinctively reacts to guard the pupil of the eye from harm (cf. Deut. 32:10; Prov. 7:2; Zech. 2:8), and that the heavenly Father will always be ready to hide and shield us as a mother hen covers her chicks (91:4; Mat. 23:37).

18:1–50 I WILL LOVE THEE, O LORD. This psalm also occurs in 2 Sam. 22 with a few changes. It was probably written early in David's reign (cf. 2 Sam. 8:14), before he committed his terrible sin and suffered greatly under a lifelong chastisement from God (see 2 Sam. 12:1–14). The psalm also prophesies a time when, through the Messiah, all nations will praise the name of God (v. 49; see Rom. 15:9).

18:2 THE LORD, MY ROCK . . . FORTRESS . . . STRENGTH. The metaphors of this verse can be applied to the believer's perpetual struggles against the physical and spiritual forces of this age. God's care is described by six symbols: (1) "my rock" — safety and security in God's immovable strength (cf. 31:2–3; 42:9; 62:7); (2) "my fortress" — a place of refuge and safety where the enemy cannot penetrate; (3) "my deliverer" — a living protector; (4) "my buckler" — a buckler is a type of shield, symbolizing that God comes between us and harm (cf. Gen. 15:1); (5) "horn of my salvation" — strength and victorious power to deliver and save us; (6) "my high tower" — a safe place to lift us above the dangers of life.

bled; the foundations also of the hills moved and were shaken, because he was wroth.

8 There went up a smoke [k]out of his nostrils, and fire out of his mouth devoured: coals were kindled by it.

9 [w]He bowed the heavens also, and came down: and darkness *was* under his feet.

10 [x]And he rode upon a cherub, and did fly: yea, [y]he did fly upon the wings of the wind.

11 He made darkness his secret place; [z]his pavilion round about him *were* dark waters *and* thick clouds of the skies.

12 [a]At the brightness *that was* before him his thick clouds passed, hail *stones* and coals of fire.

13 The LORD also thundered in the heavens, and the Highest gave [b]his voice; hail *stones* and coals of fire.

14 [c]Yea, he sent out his arrows, and scattered them; and he shot out lightnings, and discomfited them.

15 Then the channels of waters were seen, and the foundations of the world were discovered at thy rebuke, O LORD, at the blast of the breath of thy nostrils.

16 [d]He sent from above, he took me, he drew me out of [l]many waters.

17 He delivered me from my strong enemy, and from them which hated me: for they were too strong for me.

18 They prevented me in the day of my calamity: but the LORD was my stay.

19 [e]He brought me forth also into a large place; he delivered me, because he delighted in me.

20 [f]The LORD rewarded me according to my righteousness; according to the cleanness of my hands hath he recompensed me.

21 For I have kept the ways of the LORD, and have not wickedly departed from my God.

22 For all his judgments *were* before me, and I did not put away his statutes from me.

23 I was also upright [m]before him, and I kept myself from mine iniquity.

24 [g]Therefore hath the LORD recompensed me according to my righteousness, according to the cleanness of my hands [n]in his eyesight.

25 [h]With the merciful thou wilt show thyself merciful; with an upright man thou wilt show thyself upright;

26 With the pure thou wilt show thyself pure; and [i]with the froward thou wilt [o]show thyself froward.

27 For thou wilt save the afflicted people; but wilt bring down [j]high looks.

28 [k]For thou wilt light my [p]candle: the LORD my God will enlighten my darkness.

29 For by thee I have [q]run through a troop; and by my God have I leaped over a wall.

30 *As for* God, [l]his way *is* perfect: [m]the word of the LORD is [r]tried: he *is* a buckler [n]to all those that trust in him.

31 [o]For who *is* God save the LORD? or who *is* a rock save our God?

32 *It is* God that [p]girdeth me with strength, and maketh my way perfect.

33 [q]He maketh my feet like hinds' *feet*, and [r]setteth me upon my high places.

34 [s]He teacheth my hands to war, so that a bow of steel is broken by mine arms.

35 Thou hast also given me the shield of thy salvation: and thy right hand hath holden me up, and [s]thy gentleness hath made me great.

36 Thou hast enlarged my steps under me, [t]that [t]my feet did not slip.

37 I have pursued mine enemies, and overtaken them: neither did I turn again till they were consumed.

38 I have wounded them that they were not able to rise: they are fallen under my feet.

39 For thou hast girded me with strength unto the battle: thou hast [u]subdued under me those that rose up against me.

40 Thou hast also given me the necks of mine enemies; that I might destroy them that hate me. Ps. 37:1-

41 They cried, but *there was* none to save *them*: [u]*even* unto the LORD, but he answered them not.

42 Then did I beat them small as the dust before the wind: I did [v]cast them out as the dirt in the streets.

43 Thou hast delivered me from the strivings of the people; *and* [w]thou hast made me the head of the heathen: [x]a people *whom* I have not known shall serve me.

18:9 [w]Ps. 144:5 **18:10** [x]Ps. 99:1 [y]Ps. 104:3 **18:11** [z]Ps. 97:2 **18:12** [a]Ps. 97:3 **18:13** [b]Ps. 29:3 **18:14** [c]Josh. 10:10 Ps. 144:6 Is. 30:30 **18:16** [d]Ps. 144:7 **18:19** [e]Ps. 31:8 & 118:5 **18:20** [f]1 Sam. 24:19 **18:24** [g]1 Sam. 26:23 **18:25** [h]1 Ki. 8:32

18:26 [i]Lev. 26:23,24,27, 28 Prov. 3:34 **18:27** [j]Ps. 101:5 Prov. 6:17 **18:28** [k]Job 18:6 **18:30** [l]Deut. 32:4 Dan. 4:37 Rev. 15:3 [m]Ps. 12:6 & 119:140 Prov. 30:5 [n]Ps. 17:7 **18:31** [o]Deut. 32:31,39 1 Sam. 2:2 Ps. 86:8 Is. 45:5 **18:32** [p]Ps. 91:2 **18:33** [q]2 Sam. 2:18 Hab. 3:19 [r]Deut. 32:13 & 33:29 **18:34** [s]Ps. 144:1 **18:36** [t]Prov. 4:12 **18:41** [u]Job 27:9 Prov. 1:28 Jer. 11:11 **18:42** [v]Zech. 10:5 **18:43** [w]2 Sam. 8 [x]Is. 52:15

[k] Heb. *by his with* [l] Or, *great waters* [m] Heb. [n] Heb. *before his eyes* [o] Or, *wrestle* [p] Or, *lamp* [q] Or, *broken* [r] Or, *refined* [s] Or, *with thy meekness thou hast multiplied me* [t] Heb. *mine ankles* [u] Heb. *caused to bow*

44 [v]As soon as they hear of me,
they shall obey me: [w]the strangers
shall [x] [y]submit themselves unto me.
45 [y]The strangers shall fade away,
and be afraid out of their close places.
46 The LORD liveth; and blessed *be*
my rock; and let the God of my salva-
tion be exalted.
47 *It is* God that [z]avengeth me,
[z]and [a]subdueth the people un-
der me.
48 He delivereth me from mine ene-
mies: yea, [a]thou liftest me up above
those that rise up against me: thou
hast delivered me from the [b]violent
man.
49 [b]Therefore will I [c]give thanks
unto thee, O LORD, among the heathen,
and sing praises unto thy name.
50 [c]Great deliverance giveth he to
his king; and showeth mercy to his
anointed, to David, and to his seed for
evermore.

The works and word of God

To the chief Musician,
A Psalm of David.

19 THE [d]HEAVENS declare the
glory of God; and the firmament
showeth his handiwork.
2 Day unto day uttereth speech, and
night unto night showeth knowledge.
3 *There is* no speech nor language,
[d] [e]*where* their voice is not heard.
4 [e]Their[f] line is gone out through
all the earth, and their words to the
end of the world. In them hath he set
a tabernacle for the sun,
5 Which *is* as a bridegroom coming
out of his chamber, [f]*and* rejoiceth as
a strong man to run a race.
6 His going forth *is* from the end of
the heaven, and his circuit unto the
ends of it: and there is nothing hid from
the heat thereof.
7 [g]The [g]law of the LORD *is* perfect,
[h]converting the soul: the testimony of
the LORD *is* sure, making wise the sim-
ple.
8 The statutes of the LORD *are* right,
rejoicing the heart: the commandment
of the LORD *is* pure, enlightening the
eyes.
9 The fear of the LORD *is* clean, en-
during for ever: the judgments of the
LORD *are* [i]true *and* righteous alto-
gether.
10 More to be desired *are they* than
gold, yea, than much fine gold: sweeter
also than honey and [j]the honeycomb.
11 Moreover by them is thy servant
warned: *and* in keeping of them *there is*
great reward.
12 Who can understand *his* errors?
cleanse thou me from secret *faults.*
13 Keep back thy servant also from
presumptuous *sins;* let them not have
dominion over me: then shall I be up-
right, and I shall be innocent from
[k]the great transgression.
14 Let the words of my mouth, and

18:45 [y]Mic. 7:17
18:47 [z]Ps. 47:3
18:48 [a]Ps. 59:1
18:49 [b]Rom. 15:9
18:50 [c]Ps. 144:10
19:1 [d]Is. 40:22
19:4 [e]Rom. 10:18
19:5 [f]Eccl. 1:5
19:7 [g]Ps. 111:7

[v] Heb. *At the hearing of the ear* [w] Heb. *the sons of the stranger* [x] Or, *yield feigned obedience* [y] Heb. *lie* [z] Heb. *giveth avengements for me* [a] Or, *destroyeth* [b] Heb. *man of violence* [c] Or, *confess* [d] Or, *without these their voice is heard* [e] Heb. *without their voice heard* [f] Or, *Their rule,* or, *direction* [g] Or, *doctrine* [h] Or, *restoring* [i] Heb. *truth* [j] Heb. *the dropping of honeycombs* [k] Or, *much*

19:1 THE HEAVENS DECLARE THE GLORY OF GOD. The Judeo-Christian view is that the physical world declares God's glory and creative power (cf. 148:3–5; cf. Rom. 1:18–20). The view of many unbelievers, in contrast, is that the creation itself is a divine entity (see Deut. 4:19; 2 Ki. 23:5), with a force that controls human destiny (see Is. 47:13; Dan. 4:7); others believe that it came about by chance. The true believer rejects these views, accepts the Scriptural revelation about the universe, and is thus moved to praise the Maker (see 89:5–8, see article on CREATION, p. 6).

19:7–11 THE LAW OF THE LORD IS PERFECT. These verses speak of the nature, benefits, and value of God's law and word. The five facets are: (1) "The law"—a general term for God's revealed will, which directs a person in a right relation to Him (v. 7).

(2) "The testimony"—God's true word which testifies to His character and will (cf. 1 John 5:9), the study of which makes us wise (v. 7).

(3) "The statutes"—definite rules concerning righteous living that are a joy to the godly (v. 8).

(4) "The commandments"—the authoritative source of guiding light for the faithful who seek His way (v. 8; cf. Acts 26:18); the proper response to God's commandment is the "fear of the LORD," which brings freedom from a life of sin (v. 9).

(5) "The judgments"—laws governing social life, which lead to justice and righteousness (v. 9).

19:12 CLEANSE THOU ME FROM SECRET *FAULTS*. Sincere believers endeavor to love and serve God with all their heart (Deut. 6:5). Because they are still imperfect in this life, however, they may fall short of God's will without knowing it and thus need to seek God's forgiveness for their errors and hidden faults (see Lev. 5:2–4). On the other hand, presumptuous or willful sins are a "great transgression" (v. 13) that involve despising God and His word and the loss of a place in His kingdom (see Num. 15:30–31; Gal. 5:19–21).

the meditation of my heart, be acceptable in thy sight, O LORD, [l]my strength, and my [h]redeemer.

19:14 [h]Is. 47:4
21:4 [i]Ps. 61:5,6

A prayer for the king

To the chief Musician,
A Psalm of David.

20 THE LORD hear thee in the day of trouble; the name of the God of Jacob [m]defend thee;
2 Send [n]thee help from the sanctuary, and [o]strengthen thee out of Zion;
3 Remember all thy offerings, and [p]accept thy burnt sacrifice; Selah.
4 Grant thee according to thine own heart, and fulfil all thy counsel.
5 We will rejoice in thy salvation, and in the name of our God we will set up *our* banners: the LORD fulfil all thy petitions.
6 Now know I that the LORD saveth his anointed; he will hear him [q]from his holy heaven [r]with the saving strength of his right hand.
7 Some *trust* in chariots, and some in horses: but we will remember the name of the LORD our God.
8 They are brought down and fallen: but we are risen, and stand upright.
9 Save, LORD: let the king hear us when we call.

Splendor and success of the king

To the chief Musician,
A Psalm of David.

21 THE KING shall joy in thy strength, O LORD; and in thy salvation how greatly shall he rejoice!
2 Thou hast given him his heart's desire, and hast not withholden the request of his lips. Selah.
3 For thou preventest him with the blessings of goodness: thou settest a crown of pure gold on his head.
4 [i]He asked life of thee, *and* thou gavest *it* him, *even* length of days for ever and ever.
5 His glory *is* great in thy salvation: honour and majesty hast thou laid upon him.
6 For thou hast [j]made[s] him most blessed for ever: thou hast [t]made him exceeding glad with thy countenance.
7 For the king trusteth in the LORD, and through the mercy of the most High he shall not be moved.
8 Thine hand shall find out all thine enemies: thy right hand shall find out those that hate thee.
9 Thou shalt make them as a fiery oven in the time of thine anger: the LORD shall swallow them up in his wrath, and the fire shall devour them.
10 Their fruit shalt thou destroy from the earth, and their seed from among the children of men.
11 For they intended evil against thee: they imagined a mischievous device, *which* they are not able *to perform.*
12 Therefore shalt thou make them turn their [u]back, *when* thou shalt make ready *thine arrows* upon thy strings against the face of them.
13 Be thou exalted, LORD, in thine own strength: *so* will we sing and praise thy power.

21:6 [j]Ps. 72:17
22:1 [k]Mark 15:34

A cry of anguish

To the chief Musician upon [v]Aijeleth
Shahar, A Psalm of David.

22 MY [k]GOD, my God, why hast thou forsaken me? *why art thou so* far [w]from helping me, *and from* the words of my roaring?

[l]Heb. *my rock* [m]Heb. *set thee on an high place* [n]Heb. *thy help* [o]Heb. *support thee* [p]Heb. *turn to ashes:* or, *make fat* [q]Heb. *from the heaven of his holiness* [r]Heb. *by the strength of the salvation of his right hand* [s]Heb. *set him* to be *blessings* [t]Heb. *gladded him with joy* [u]Heb. *shoulder* [v]Or, *the hind of the morning* [w]Heb. *from my salvation*

19:14 MY MOUTH . . . HEART, BE ACCEPTABLE IN THY SIGHT. The proper response to the work of salvation in our lives is a constant prayer that God will keep our hearts, words, and lives free from sin and pleasing to Him. Both the meditation of our hearts and the reflection of our minds should be acceptable to God.

20:1–21:13 THE LORD HEAR THEE IN THE DAY OF TROUBLE. Ps. 20 and 21 are companion psalms. They are prayers to God about the warfare of His people against their enemies. Ps. 20 is a prayer before the battle; Ps. 21 is a praise after the battle. For us who believe in Christ, Ps. 20 can be applied to our spiritual warfare. We now struggle against unseen, yet very real, forces of evil, and we yearn for victory over and deliverance from Satan and demonic powers (see Eph. 6:12, note; see article on POWER OVER SATAN AND DEMONS, p. 1486).

22:1–31 MY GOD. This psalm, one of the most quoted in the N.T., is called "the psalm of the cross" because it so precisely portrays Christ's anguished suffering on the cross. Note at least two facts about this psalm: (1) It is a cry of anguish

2 O my God, I cry in the daytime, but thou hearest not; and in the night season, and [x]am not silent.

3 But thou *art* holy, *O thou* that inhabitest the [l]praises of Israel.

4 Our fathers trusted in thee: they trusted, and thou didst deliver them.

5 They cried unto thee, and were delivered: [m]they trusted in thee, and were not confounded.

6 But I *am* [n]a worm, and no man; [o]a reproach of men, and despised of the people.

7 [p]All they that see me laugh me to scorn: they [y]shoot out the lip, [q]they shake the head, *saying,*

8 [r]He[z] trusted on the LORD *that* he would deliver him: [s]let him deliver him, [a]seeing he delighted in him.

9 [t]But thou *art* he that took me out of the womb: thou [b]didst make me hope *when I was* upon my mother's breasts.

10 I was cast upon thee from the womb: [u]thou *art* my God from my mother's belly.

11 Be not far from me; for trouble *is* near; for *there is* [c]none to help.

12 [v]Many bulls have compassed me: strong *bulls* of Bashan have beset me round.

13 [w]They [d]gaped upon me *with* their mouths, *as* a ravening and a roaring lion.

14 I am poured out like water, [x]and all my bones are [e]out of joint: my heart is like wax; it is melted in the midst of my bowels.

15 [y]My strength is dried up like a potsherd; and [z]my tongue cleaveth to my jaws; and thou hast brought me into the dust of death.

16 For dogs have compassed me: the assembly of the wicked have inclosed me: [a]they pierced my hands and my feet.

17 I may tell all my bones: [b]they look *and* stare upon me.

18 [c]They part my garments among them, and cast lots upon my vesture.

19 But be not thou far from me, O LORD: O my strength, haste thee to help me.

20 Deliver my soul from the sword; [d]my[f] darling [g]from the power of the dog.

21 [e]Save me from the lion's mouth: [f]for thou hast heard me from the horns of the unicorns.

A song of praise

22 [g]I will declare thy name unto

22:3 [l]Deut. 10:21
22:5 [m]Is. 49:23
22:6 [n]Job 25:6 [o]Is. 53:3
22:7 [p]Mat. 27:39 [q]Job 16:4
22:8 [r]Mat. 27:43 [s]Ps. 91:14
22:9 [t]Ps. 71:6
22:10 [u]Is. 46:3
22:12 [v]Ps. 68:30
22:13 [w]Lam. 2:16
22:14 [x]Dan. 5:6
22:15 [y]Prov. 17:22 [z]John 19:28
22:16 [a]Mat. 27:35
22:17 [b]Luke 23:27,35
22:18 [c]Luke 23:34
22:20 [d]Ps. 35:17
22:21 [e]2 Tim. 4:17 [f]Is. 34:7
22:22 [g]Heb. 2:12

[x] Heb. there is *no silence to me* [y] Heb. *open* [z] Heb. *He rolled* himself *on the LORD* [a] Or, *if he delight in him* [b] Or, *keptest me in safety* [c] Heb. *not a helper* [d] Heb. *opened their mouths against me* [e] Or, *sundered* [f] Heb. *my only one* [g] Heb. *from the hand*

and grief from a godly sufferer who has not yet been delivered from trials and suffering. In this sense all suffering believers can identify with the words of this prayer. (2) The words of the psalm express an experience far beyond that of any ordinary human experience. Inspired by the Holy Spirit, the psalmist both predicts the suffering of Jesus Christ in His crucifixion and points to His subsequent vindication three days later.

22:1 MY GOD, MY GOD, WHY HAST THOU FORSAKEN ME? Jesus uttered this dreadful cry on the cross when His heavenly Father's caring and protective presence was withdrawn (Is. 53:10–12; 2 Cor. 5:21; see Mat. 27:46, note). Jesus was forsaken by God because He suffered in the sinner's place, having become a curse for us (Gal. 3:13). By quoting this verse, Jesus was also claiming the entire psalm as a description of Himself.

22:2 I CRY . . . BUT THOU HEAREST NOT. The believer, like Jesus Himself, may at times feel forsaken by God. When this occurs, hold fast to your belief in God and in His goodness, and continue to pray and trust (vv. 2–5).

22:7 THEY SHAKE THE HEAD. See Mat. 27:39, which states, "And they that passed by reviled him [Christ], wagging their heads." The very gestures used by Jesus' enemies were predicted in the O.T.

22:8 HE TRUSTED ON THE LORD. This verse recounts the exact words that the enemies of the Lord would say to Him as they witnessed the crucifixion (Mat. 27:43).

22:11–17 *THERE IS* NONE TO HELP. These verses describe the Lord's feelings of helplessness while undergoing the brutality of the scourging and crucifixion.

22:16 THEY PIERCED MY HANDS AND MY FEET. Here is another prophetic reference to the crucifixion (cf. John 20:25; see Mat. 27:35, note).

22:18 THEY PART MY GARMENTS AMONG THEM. The Roman soldiers did exactly as this verse foretold—an amazing fulfillment of prophecy (see Mat. 27:35; Mark 15:24; Luke 23:34; John 19:23–24).

22:22 UNTO MY BRETHREN. Heb. 2:11–12 relates this verse to Jesus Christ; it marks the triumph of the cross. Jesus is now the exalted Redeemer who gathers around Him His "brethren" (i.e., the redeemed who believe in Him and accept His death for them, see John 20:17) and stands "in the midst" of them to praise Him. His death results in help for the afflicted (v. 24), eternal life (v. 26), the preaching of the gospel (vv. 27–29), His rule over all the nations (vv. 28–29), and ultimate exaltation and glory (vv. 30–31).

[h]my brethren: in the midst of the con-
gregation will I praise thee.
23 [i]Ye that fear the LORD, praise
him; all ye the seed of Jacob, glorify
him; and fear him, all ye the seed of
Israel.
24 For he hath not despised nor ab-
horred the affliction of the afflicted;
neither hath he hid his face from him;
but [j]when he cried unto him, he
heard.
25 [k]My praise *shall be* of thee in the
great congregation: [l]I will pay my
vows before them that fear him.
26 The meek shall eat and be satis-
fied: they shall praise the LORD that
seek him: your heart shall live for ever.
27 All the ends of the world shall
remember and turn unto the LORD: and
all the kindreds of the nations shall
worship before thee.
28 [m]For the kingdom *is* the LORD's:
and he *is* the governor among the na-
tions.
29 [n]All *they that be* fat upon earth
shall eat and worship: [o]all they that
go down to the dust shall bow before
him: and none can keep alive his own
soul.
30 A seed shall serve him; [p]it shall
be accounted to the Lord for a genera-
tion.
31 [q]They shall come, and shall de-
clare his righteousness unto a people
that shall be born, that he hath done
this.

22:22 [h]Rom. 8:29
22:23 [i]Ps. 135:19
22:24 [j]Heb. 5:7
22:25 [k]Ps. 35:18 [l]Eccl. 5:4
22:28 [m]Mat. 6:13
22:29 [n]Ps. 45:12 [o]Is. 26:19
22:30 [p]Ps. 87:6
22:31 [q]Ps. 78:6
23:1 [r]Is. 40:11 John 10:11 [s]Phil. 4:19
23:2 [t]Ezek. 34:14 [u]Rev. 7:17
23:3 [v]Ps. 5:8
23:4 [w]Job 10:21,22 Ps. 44:19 [x]Ps. 3:6 [y]Is. 43:2

The shepherd psalm

A Psalm of David.

23 THE LORD *is* [r]my shepherd;
[s]I shall not want.
2 [t]He maketh me to lie down in
[h]green pastures: [u]he leadeth me be-
side the [i]still waters.
3 He restoreth my soul: [v]he
leadeth me in the paths of righteous-
ness for his name's sake.
4 Yea, though I walk through the
valley of [w]the shadow of death, [x]I
will fear no evil: [y]for thou *art* with me;

[h] Heb. *pastures of tender grass* [i] Heb. *waters of quietness*

23:1–6 THE LORD. This psalm, conceived in the mind of the Lord and inspired by the Holy Spirit, expresses His concern and diligent care for those who follow Him. They are the cherished objects of His divine love. He cares for each of them as a father cares for his children and as a shepherd for his sheep.

23:1 THE LORD *IS* MY SHEPHERD. Using a metaphor frequently found in the O.T. (see 28:9; 79:13; 80:1; 95:7; Is. 40:11; Jer. 31:10; Ezek. 34:6–19), God compares Himself to a shepherd in order to illustrate His great love for His people. The Lord Jesus Himself adopted the same metaphor to express His relationship to His people (John 10:11–16; cf. Heb. 13:20; 1 Pet. 5:4). Two truths are emphasized here: (1) God, through Christ and by the Holy Spirit, is so concerned about each of His children that He desires to love, care for, protect, guide, and be near that child, just as a good shepherd does for his own sheep (see John 10:11,14 notes).

(2) Believers are the Lord's sheep. We belong to Him and are the special objects of His affection and attention. Though "all we like sheep have gone astray" (Is. 53:6), the Lord has redeemed us with His shed blood (1 Pet. 1:18–19), and we now belong to Him. As His sheep we can claim the promises of this psalm when we respond to His voice and follow Him (see John 10:3–5; see 10:28, note).

23:1 I SHALL NOT WANT. This means both (1) that I will not lack anything necessary for God's will to be accomplished in my life (see 1 John 2, note), and (2) that I will be content in the Good Shepherd's provision and care of my life, even in times of personal hardship, because I trust in His love and His commitment to me (cf. John 10:11; Phil. 4:11–13).

23:2 HE MAKETH ME TO LIE DOWN. Because of the presence and nearness of the shepherd I can "lie down" in peace, free from all fear. The Holy Spirit as my Comforter, Counselor, and Helper communicates Christ's shepherdly care and presence to me (John 14:16–18; cf. 2 Tim. 1:7). (1) My confident rest in His presence will be experienced in "green pastures," i.e., in Jesus and the Word of God, which are necessary for an abundant life (John 6:32–35,63; 8:31; 10:9; 15:7). (2) "He leadeth me beside the still waters" of His Holy Spirit (see 1:3, note; cf. Jer. 2:13; John 7:37–39).

23:3 HE RESTORETH MY SOUL. When I become discouraged (42:11), the Good Shepherd revives and re-energizes my soul through His power and grace (Prov. 25:13). "He leadeth me" by the Spirit of God (Rom. 8:14) in His chosen paths, ones that conform to His way of holiness (cf. Rom. 8:5–14). My response is obedience: I follow the Shepherd and hear His voice (John 10:3–4); I will not follow "the voice of strangers" (John 10:5).

23:4 THOU *ART* WITH ME. In times of danger, difficulty, and even death, I fear no evil. Why? "For thou art with me" in every situation of life (cf. Mat. 28:20). The "rod" (a short club) is a weapon of defense or discipline, symbolizing God's strength, power, and authority (cf. Ex. 21:20; Job 9:34). The "staff" (a long slender stick with a hook on one end) is used to draw a sheep close to the shepherd, guide it in the right way, or rescue it from trouble. God's rod and staff reassure us of God's love and guidance in our lives (cf. 71:21; 86:17).

thy rod and thy staff they comfort me.
5 Thou preparest a table before me
in the presence of mine enemies: thou
[z]anointest[j] my head with oil; my cup
runneth over.
6 Surely goodness and mercy shall
follow me all the days of my life: and
I will dwell in the house of the LORD
[k]for ever.

Song to the King of glory

A Psalm of David.

24 THE [a]EARTH *is* the LORD'S,
and the fulness thereof; the
world, and they that dwell therein.
2 For he hath founded it upon the
seas, and established it upon the
floods.
3 [b]Who shall ascend into the hill of
the LORD? or who shall stand in his holy
place?
4 [l]He that hath [c]clean hands, and
[d]a pure heart; who hath not lifted up
his soul unto vanity, nor [e]sworn de-
ceitfully.
5 He shall receive the blessing from
the LORD, and righteousness from the
God of his salvation.
6 This *is* the generation of them that
seek him, that [f]seek thy face,
[m]O Jacob. Selah.
7 [g]Lift up your heads, O ye gates;
and be ye lift up, ye everlasting doors;
[h]and the King of glory shall come in.
8 Who *is* this King of glory? The
LORD strong and mighty, the LORD
mighty in battle.
9 Lift up your heads, O ye gates;
even lift *them* up, ye everlasting doors;
and the King of glory shall come in.
10 Who is this King of glory? The
LORD of hosts, he *is* the King of glory.
Selah.

Prayer for guidance and protection

A Psalm of David.

25 UNTO [i]THEE, O LORD, do I lift
up my soul.
2 O my God, I [j]trust in thee: let me
not be ashamed, [k]let not mine ene-
mies triumph over me.
3 Yea, let none that wait on thee be
ashamed: let them be ashamed which
transgress without cause.
4 [l]Show me thy ways, O LORD;
teach me thy paths.
5 Lead me in thy truth, and teach

23:5 [z]Ps. 92:10
24:1 [a]Ex. 9:29; Job 41:11
24:3 [b]Ps. 15:1
24:4 [c]Job 17:9; 1 Tim. 2:8 [d]Mat. 5:8 [e]Ps. 15:4
24:6 [f]Ps. 27:8
24:7 [g]Is. 26:2 [h]Ps. 97:6; Hag. 2:7; Mal. 3:1
25:1 [i]Ps. 86:4
25:2 [j]Ps. 34:8; Is. 28:16 [k]Ps. 13:4
25:4 [l]Ex. 33:13; Ps. 5:8

j Heb. *makest fat* k Heb. *to length of days*
l Heb. *The clean of hands* m Or, O God of Jacob

23:5 PREPAREST A TABLE. God is pictured as caring for my needs in the midst of the forces of evil that attempt to destroy my life and soul (see Rom. 8:31–39). (1) Confronted daily by Satan and surrounded by an ungodly society, I am furnished with sufficient grace to live and rejoice in God's presence (see 2 Cor. 12:9–10). I may eat at the Lord's table in faith, thanksgiving, and hope, fully at peace and protected by the shed blood and broken body of this Good Shepherd (see 1 Cor. 11:23). (2) "Anointest my head with oil" refers to God's special favor and blessing through the anointing of His Holy Spirit upon my body, mind, and spirit (see Eph. 5:18, note). (3) "My cup runneth over" literally translates, "My cup is an abundant drink." It refers to a shepherd's cup, which was a large, hollowed-out stone that could hold forty or fifty gallons and from which the sheep drank.

23:6 GOODNESS AND MERCY. "Mercy" means God's faithful love and kindness. With the Shepherd accompanying me through life's pilgrimage, I will receive constant help, kindness, and support. No matter what happens I can trust the Good Shepherd to work all things together for my good (Rom. 8:28; Jas. 5:11). The goal of my following the Shepherd and experiencing His goodness and mercy is that one day I may be with the Lord forever (1 Thes. 4:17), see His face (Rev. 22:4), and serve Him forever in His house (see Rev. 22:3; cf. John 14:2–3).

24:4 CLEAN HANDS, AND A PURE HEART. David emphasizes that those who want to worship and serve God and receive His blessing must be pursuing a pure heart and a righteous life. "Clean hands" are hands free from external acts of sin (see Is. 1:15; 33:15; 1 Tim. 2:8). A "pure heart" refers to inward holiness, right motives, and goals. Only the pure in heart will see God (Mat. 5:8).

24:5 HE SHALL RECEIVE THE BLESSING. Those who receive a "blessing from the LORD" are those who "seek him" (v. 6) with "clean hands, and a pure heart" (v. 4). We should remind ourselves of this every time we call on God in prayer, worship Him in His house, or seek His grace in the Lord's Supper (see 1 Cor. 11:23–27; 2 Cor. 6:14–18; Heb. 12:14).

24:7–10 KING OF GLORY. These verses are Messianic, for the King of glory is the Lord Jesus (cf. John 1:14). The "generation of them that seek him" (i.e., faithful believers) must pray that the "King of glory shall come." This prayer for God's kingdom to come anticipates Christ's eternal reign and the final destruction of evil (see Zech. 9:9; Mat. 6:10; Rev. 19—22).

25:4 SHOW ME THY WAYS. Like Moses (Ex. 33:13), the psalmist longed intensely to know God's ways. It is possible for believers to know something about God's acts (e.g., salvation, mira-

me: for thou *art* the God of my salva-
tion; on thee do I wait all the day.
6 Remember, O LORD, [m]thy[n] ten-
der mercies and thy lovingkindnesses;
for they *have been* ever of old.
7 Remember not [n]the sins of my
youth, nor my transgressions: [o]ac-
cording to thy mercy remember thou
me for thy goodness' sake, O LORD.
8 Good and upright *is* the LORD:
therefore will he teach sinners in the
way.
9 The meek will he guide in judg-
ment: and the meek will he teach his
way.
10 All the paths of the LORD *are* mer-
cy and truth unto such as keep his cov-
enant and his testimonies.
11 [p]For thy name's sake, O LORD,
pardon mine iniquity; [q]for it *is* great.
12 What man *is* he that feareth the
LORD? [r]him shall he teach in the way
that he shall choose.
13 [s]His soul [o]shall dwell at ease;
and [t]his seed shall inherit the earth.
14 [u]The secret of the LORD *is* with
them that fear him; [p]and he will show
them his covenant.
15 [v]Mine eyes *are* ever toward the
LORD; for he shall [q]pluck my feet out
of the net.
16 [w]Turn thee unto me, and have
mercy upon me; for I *am* desolate and
afflicted.
17 The troubles of my heart are en-
larged: *O* bring thou me out of my dis-
tresses.
18 [x]Look upon mine affliction and
my pain; and forgive all my sins.
19 Consider mine enemies; for they
are many; and they hate me with [r]cru-
el hatred.
20 O keep my soul, and deliver me:
let me not be ashamed; for I put my
trust in thee.
21 Let integrity and uprightness
preserve me; for I wait on thee.
22 [y]Redeem Israel, O God, out of
all his troubles.

25:6 [m]Ps. 103:17 Is. 63:15 **25:7** [n]Job 13:26 Jer. 3:25 [o]Ps. 51:1 **25:11** [p]Ps. 31:3 & 79:9 [q]Rom. 5:20 **25:12** [r]Ps. 37:23 **25:13** [s]Prov. 19:23 [t]Ps. 37:11 **25:14** [u]Prov. 3:32 John 7:17 **25:15** [v]Ps. 141:8 **25:16** [w]Ps. 69:16 **25:18** [x]2 Sam. 16:12 **25:22** [y]Ps. 130:8 **26:1** [z]Ps. 7:8 [a]2 Ki. 20:3 [b]Ps. 28:7 Prov. 29:25

The basis of judgment

A Psalm of David.

26 JUDGE [z]ME, O LORD; for I
have [a]walked in mine integri-
ty: [b]I have trusted also in the LORD;
therefore I shall not slide.

[n] Heb. *thy bowels* [o] Heb. *shall lodge in goodness* [p] Or, *and his covenant to make them know it* [q] Heb. *bring forth* [r] Heb. *hatred of violence*

cles; cf. Ps. 103:7), but never really to know God or to understand His ways (i.e., the principles of wisdom by which He works in us and guides us). The basic principles for knowing God's ways in this psalm are the following: (1) We must have a sincere desire to be led into the righteous ways of God and the truth of His Word (v. 4).

(2) We must be eager to wait upon God "all the day" (v. 5).

(3) We must humbly submit to God (v. 9), commit ourselves to godly living (v. 10), and fear the Lord (vv. 12–14).

(4) Since sin is a barrier to knowing God and His ways, we must forsake sin and be cleansed and forgiven (vv. 4–8). "If I regard iniquity in my heart, the Lord will not hear *me*" (66:18; cf. 1 John 2:1–6).

(5) Adversity in our lives is not necessarily a sign of God's disfavor (cf. 34:19). Knowing God and His ways may lead us into suffering and loss that we would not have otherwise encountered (e.g., Acts 14:22; 20:22–23). The ultimate example of this truth is Jesus Himself, who followed God's will perfectly, yet suffered sorrow, betrayal, and the cross. The believer, abiding in the will of God, must expect the same (Mat. 10:24).

25:12 HIM SHALL HE TEACH. The main theme of this psalm is how God guides the faithful believer in His wisdom. Concerning this guidance, note the following truths: (1) God has a plan for every believer. He had a plan for Adam (Gen. 1:28; 2:18–25), Abraham (Gen. 12:1–3), Joseph (Gen. 45:4–9), and His people, Israel (Gen. 50:24; Ex. 6:6–8). He had a plan for Jesus (Luke 18:31) and Paul (Acts 21:10–14; 22:14–15; 26:16–19; see 21:14, note). God has a definite plan for each of His children (1 Cor. 12; Eph. 1:10; 2:10; 3:11; 4:11–13).

(2) God's plans can be communicated to us by extraordinary means, such as dreams, visions, and prophecy (Acts 2:17; 9:12; 10:3; 13:2; 1 Cor. 14:1; see Acts 21:10, note). However, the usual way He guides us and imparts wisdom to us is through the Holy Scriptures (2 Tim. 3:16) and through the Holy Spirit dwelling in our hearts (Acts 8:29; 10:19; 13:2; 15:28; 16:6; 1 John 2:20,27).

(3) God's plan for believers may be missed if we, by ignoring God's Word or misreading it, make decisions contrary to His will. If the basic convictions, attitudes, and teachings found in the Bible are not deeply embedded in our lives, we will go astray.

(4) A fundamental area of guidance is righteousness (cf. v. 21; Rom. 8:11–14), for God guides us "in the paths of righteousness" (23:3).

25:14 FEAR HIM. Personal knowledge of God and intimate fellowship with Him are reserved for those who fear Him and turn away from evil (cf. Prov. 3:5–7; see article on THE FEAR OF THE LORD, p. 282).

2 [c]Examine me, O LORD, and prove me; try my reins and my heart.

3 For thy lovingkindness *is* before mine eyes: and [d]I have walked in thy truth.

4 [e]I have not sat with vain persons, neither will I go in with dissemblers.

5 I have [f]hated the congregation of evildoers; [g]and will not sit with the wicked.

6 [h]I will wash mine hands in innocency: so will I compass thine altar, O LORD:

7 That I may publish with the voice of thanksgiving, and tell of all thy wondrous works.

8 LORD, [i]I have loved the habitation of thy house, and the place [s]where thine honour dwelleth.

9 [j]Gather[t] not my soul with sinners, nor my life with [u]bloody men:

10 In whose hands *is* mischief, and their right hand is [v]full of [k]bribes.

11 But as for me, I will walk in mine integrity: redeem me, and be merciful unto me.

12 [l]My foot standeth in an [m]even place: [n]in the congregations will I bless the LORD.

David's song of confidence

A Psalm of David.

† Ps. 37:39-40

27 THE LORD *is* [o]my light and [p]my salvation; whom shall I fear? [q]the LORD *is* the strength of my life; of whom shall I be afraid?

2 When the wicked, *even* mine enemies and my foes, [w]came upon me to [r]eat up my flesh, they stumbled and fell.

3 [s]Though an host should encamp against me, my heart shall not fear: though war should rise against me, in this *will* I *be* confident.

4 [t]One *thing* have I desired of the LORD, that will I seek after; that I may [u]dwell in the house of the LORD all the days of my life, to behold [v]the[x] beauty of the LORD, and to inquire in his temple.

5 For [w]in the time of trouble he shall hide me in his pavilion: in the secret of his tabernacle shall he hide me; he shall [x]set me up upon a rock.

6 And now shall [y]mine head be lifted up above mine enemies round about me: therefore will I offer in his tabernacle sacrifices [y]of joy; I will sing, yea, I will sing praises unto the LORD.

7 Hear, O LORD, *when* I cry with my voice: have mercy also upon me, and answer me.

8 [z]*When thou saidst,* Seek ye my face; my heart said unto thee, Thy face, LORD, will I seek.

9 [z]Hide not thy face *far* from me; put not thy servant away in anger: thou hast been my help; leave me not, neither forsake me, O God of my salvation.

10 [a]When my father and my mother forsake me, then the LORD [a]will take me up.

11 [b]Teach me thy way, O LORD, and lead me in [b]a plain path, because of [c]mine enemies.

12 Deliver me not over unto the will of mine enemies: for false witnesses are risen up against me, and such as breathe out cruelty.

13 *I had fainted,* unless I had be-

26:2 [c]Ps. 17:3; 26:3 [d]2 Ki. 20:3; 26:4 [e]Ps. 1:1; 26:5 [f]Ps. 31:6 [g]Ps. 1:1; 26:6 [h]Ps. 73:13; 26:8 [i]Ps. 27:4; 26:9 [j]Ps. 28:3; 26:10 [k]1 Sam. 8:3; 26:12 [l]Ps. 40:2 [m]Ps. 27:11 [n]Ps. 111:1; 27:1 [o]Is. 60:19 [p]Ex. 15:2 [q]Ps. 62:2; 27:2 [r]Ps. 14:4; 27:3 [s]Ps. 3:6; 27:4 [t]Ps. 26:8 [u]Luke 2:37 [v]Ps. 90:17; 27:5 [w]Ps. 91:1 [x]Ps. 40:2; 27:6 [y]Ps. 3:3; 27:9 [z]Ps. 69:17; 27:10 [a]Is. 49:15; 27:11 [b]Ps. 25:4

[s] Heb. *of the tabernacle of thy honour* [t] Or, *Take not away* [u] Heb. *men of blood* [v] Heb. *filled with* [w] Heb. *approached against me* [x] Or, *the delight* [y] Heb. *of shouting* [z] Or, *My heart said unto thee, Let my face seek thy face* [a] Heb. *will gather me* [b] Heb. *a way of plainness* [c] Heb. *those which observe me*

26:8 I HAVE LOVED . . . THY HOUSE. The psalmist's happiness does not come from associating with the world (vv. 4–5,9–10), but from being in the "house" and "congregation" of the Lord (v. 12), i.e., where God's divine presence is manifested among His people and where His glory dwells (see article on THE GLORY OF GOD, p. 1186), and from being with fellow believers who walk in God's truth.

27:4 ONE *THING* HAVE I DESIRED. As in Ps. 26, the psalmist seeks the presence of God. It is the one thing most treasured in his life, and he prays for it with singleness of purpose. God Himself calls all of us to this same purpose: "Seek ye my face" (v. 8). Those who do so, striving to dwell in God's holiness and presence, are given the firm assurance that no matter what trials come to them, the Lord will never forsake them (vv. 9–10). They have no reason for despair; God's goodness is reserved for them (vv. 13–14).

27:13 *I HAD FAINTED*, UNLESS. Trusting in God and experiencing His personal goodness are indispensable for our perseverance in the faith. As believers we may be severely tried, yet nothing can bring us to despair and defeat as long as we keep our eyes on God in faith and hope. In the midst of our darkness we must "wait on the LORD" (v. 14; see 42:5,11; 43:5; 62:5; Is. 40:27–31; Mic. 7:8), draw near to Him, and remain steadfast through His Spirit (see Eph. 6:10; 2 Tim. 2:1; Jas. 5:11).

lieved to see the goodness of the LORD [c]in the land of the living.

14 Wait on the LORD: be of good courage, and he shall strengthen thine heart: wait, I say, on the LORD.

A prayer for help

A *Psalm* of David.

28 UNTO THEE will I cry, O LORD my rock; [d]be not silent [d]to me: [e]lest, *if* thou be silent to me, I become like them that go down into the pit.

2 Hear the voice of my supplications, when I cry unto thee, [f]when I lift up my hands [g]toward[e] thy holy oracle.

3 Draw me not away with the wicked, and with the workers of iniquity, [h]which speak peace to their neighbours, but mischief *is* in their hearts.

4 [i]Give them according to their deeds, and according to the wickedness of their endeavours: give them after the work of their hands; render to them their desert.

5 Because [j]they regard not the works of the LORD, nor the operation of his hands, he shall destroy them, and not build them up.

6 Blessed *be* the LORD, because he hath heard the voice of my supplications.

7 The LORD *is* [k]my strength and my shield; my heart [l]trusted in him, and I am helped: therefore my heart greatly rejoiceth; and with my song will I praise him.

8 The LORD *is* [f]their strength, and he *is* the [m]saving[g] strength of his anointed.

9 Save thy people, and bless [n]thine inheritance: [h]feed them also, [o]and lift them up for ever.

The LORD of the thunderstorm

A Psalm of David.

29 GIVE[p] UNTO the LORD, O [i]ye mighty, give unto the LORD glory and strength.

2 Give unto the LORD [j]the glory due unto his name; worship the LORD [k]in [q]the beauty of holiness.

3 The voice of the LORD *is* upon the waters: [r]the God of glory thundereth: the LORD *is* upon [l]many waters.

4 The voice of the LORD *is* [m]powerful; the voice of the LORD *is* [n]full of majesty.

5 The voice of the LORD breaketh the cedars; yea, the LORD breaketh [s]the cedars of Lebanon.

6 [t]He maketh them also to skip like a calf; Lebanon and [u]Sirion like a young unicorn.

7 The voice of the LORD [o]divideth the flames of fire.

8 The voice of the LORD shaketh the wilderness; the LORD shaketh the wilderness of [v]Kadesh.

9 The voice of the LORD maketh the hinds [p]to calve, and discovereth the forests: and in his temple [q]doth every one speak of *his* glory.

10 The LORD sitteth upon the flood; yea, [w]the LORD sitteth King for ever.

11 [x]The LORD will give strength unto his people; the LORD will bless his people with peace.

The LORD my helper

A Psalm *and* Song [y]*at* the dedication of the house of David.

30 I WILL extol thee, O LORD; for thou hast [z]lifted me up, and hast not made my foes to [a]rejoice over me.

2 O LORD my God, I cried unto thee, and thou hast healed me.

3 O LORD, [b]thou hast brought up my soul from the grave: thou hast kept me alive, that I should not go down to the pit.

4 Sing unto the LORD, O ye saints of his, and give thanks [r]at the remembrance of his holiness.

27:13 [c]Ezek. 26:20
28:1 [d]Ps. 83:1 [e]Ps. 88:4
28:2 [f]Ps. 5:7 [g]Ps. 138:2
28:3 [h]Ps. 12:2
28:4 [i]Rev. 18:6
28:5 [j]Is. 5:12
28:7 [k]Ps. 18:2 [l]Ps. 13:5
28:8 [m]Ps. 20:6
28:9 [n]Deut. 9:29 [o]Ezra 1:4
29:1 [p]1 Chr. 16:28
29:2 [q]2 Chr. 20:21
29:3 [r]Job 37:4,5
29:5 [s]Is. 2:13
29:6 [t]Ps. 114:4 [u]Deut. 3:9
29:8 [v]Num. 13:26
29:10 [w]Ps. 10:16
29:11 [x]Ps. 28:8
30:1 [y]Deut. 20:5 [z]Ps. 28:9 [a]Ps. 25:2
30:3 [b]Ps. 86:13

[d] Heb. *from me* [e] Or, *toward the oracle of thy sanctuary* [f] Or, *his strength* [g] Heb. *strength of salvations* [h] Or, *rule* [i] Heb. *ye sons of the mighty* [j] Heb. *the honour of his name* [k] Or, *in his glorious sanctuary* [l] Or, *great waters* [m] Heb. *in power* [n] Heb. *in majesty* [o] Heb. *cutteth out* [p] Or, *to be in pain* [q] Or, *every whit of it uttereth* [r] Or, *to the memorial*

We can rest assured that, in His own time, God will manifest His goodness to us.

28:1–9 ***IF* THOU BE SILENT.** A faithful believer may at times feel that God is not listening to his or her prayers (vv. 1–3); this experience, however, will not be the norm as long as we continue to draw near to God through Christ (see Heb. 4:16; 7:25). After a period of trial, the Lord will respond and help us as a shepherd cares for his sheep (cf. Is. 40:11).

5 For [c]his[s] anger *endureth but* a
moment; [d]in his favour *is* life: weeping
may endure [t]for a night, but [u]joy
cometh in the morning.
6 And in my prosperity I said, I shall
never be moved.
7 LORD, by thy favour thou hast
[v]made my mountain to stand strong:
[e]thou didst hide thy face, *and* I was
troubled.
8 I cried to thee, O LORD; and unto
the LORD I made supplication.
9 What profit *is there* in my blood,
when I go down to the pit? [f]Shall the
dust praise thee? shall it declare thy
truth?
10 Hear, O LORD, and have mercy
upon me: LORD, be thou my helper.
11 Thou hast turned for me my
mourning into dancing: thou hast put
off my sackcloth, and girded me with
gladness;
12 To the end that [g]*my*[w] glory
may sing praise to thee, and not be si-
lent. O LORD my God, I will give thanks
unto thee for ever.

My times are in thy hand

31:1–4pp — Ps. 71:1–3

To the chief Musician,
A Psalm of David.

31 IN[h] THEE, O LORD, do I put my
trust; let me never be ashamed:
deliver me in thy righteousness.
2 [i]Bow down thine ear to me; de-
liver me speedily: be thou [x]my strong
rock, for an house of defence to
save me.
3 [j]For thou *art* my rock and my for-
tress; therefore [k]for thy name's sake
lead me, and guide me.
4 Pull me out of the net that they
have laid privily for me: for thou *art* my
strength.
5 [l]Into thine hand I commit my
spirit: thou hast redeemed me, O LORD
God of truth.
6 I have hated them [m]that regard
lying vanities: but I trust in the LORD.
7 I will be glad and rejoice in thy
mercy: for thou hast considered my
trouble; thou hast [n]known my soul in
adversities;
8 And hast not [o]shut me up into
the hand of the enemy: thou hast set
my feet in a large room.
9 Have mercy upon me, O LORD, for
I am in trouble: [p]mine eye is con-
sumed with grief, *yea,* my soul and my
belly.
10 For my life is spent with grief,
and my years with sighing: my
strength faileth because of mine iniqui-
ty, and my bones are consumed.
11 [q]I was a reproach among all
mine enemies, but [r]especially among
my neighbours, and a fear to mine ac-
quaintance: [s]they that did see me
without fled from me.
12 [t]I am forgotten as a dead man
out of mind: I am like [y]a broken ves-
sel.
13 [u]For I have heard the slander of
many: [v]fear *was* on every side: while
they [w]took counsel together against
me, they devised to take away my life.
14 But I trusted in thee, O LORD: I
said, Thou *art* my God.
15 My times *are* in thy hand: deliver

30:5 [c]Ps. 103:9 [d]Ps. 63:3 **30:7** [e]Ps. 104:29 **30:9** [f]Ps. 6:5 **30:12** [g]Ps. 57:8 **31:1** [h]Ps. 22:5 **31:2** [i]Ps. 71:2 **31:3** [j]Ps. 18:2 [k]Ps. 23:3

31:5 [l]Luke 23:46 **31:6** [m]Jonah 2:8 **31:7** [n]John 10:27 **31:8** [o]Deut. 32:30 **31:9** [p]Ps. 6:7 **31:11** [q]Is. 53:4 [r]Job 19:13 [s]Ps. 64:8 **31:12** [t]Ps. 88:4,5 **31:13** [u]Jer. 20:10 [v]Lam. 2:22 [w]Mat. 27:1

[s] Heb. there is but *a moment in his anger* [t] Heb. *in the evening* [u] Heb. *singing* [v] Heb. *settled strength for my mountain* [w] i.e. my *tongue,* or, my *soul* [x] Heb. *to me for a rock of strength* [y] Heb. *a vessel that perisheth*

30:6 IN MY PROSPERITY. Secure in his prosperity, the psalmist assumed that his wealth and success made him so strong that nothing could destroy his happiness. God then withdrew His protective hand and brought serious trouble and helplessness into his life, causing him to experience the need for God's continual care and presence (vv. 8–10). All believers who feel secure in themselves, who rely on temporal things, and who give God and His kingdom anything but first place are warned by the words of this psalm.

31:1–24 O LORD . . . DELIVER ME. This psalm is a deeply personal prayer expressing distress and lament because of enemies (vv. 4,8), illness (vv. 9–10), and desertion by friends (vv. 11–13). Jeremiah used a phrase from this psalm (v. 13) to express his sorrow and fear (cf. Jer. 6:25; 20:10); Jesus also quoted from it (the opening words of v. 5) while on the cross (Luke 23:46). This prayer expresses the heartfelt cry of all believers who suffer affliction because of illness, trouble, or oppression from the world or the enemies of righteousness. It reveals that in the times of deep trouble, we can hide "in the secret of thy presence" (v. 20).

31:5 INTO THINE HAND I COMMIT MY SPIRIT. These were Jesus' last words before His death (Luke 23:46); these words have often been used by faithful believers in their dying hours (see Acts 7:59). They express dependence on God and faith in His goodness to His people (see 2 Sam. 24:14; Rom. 8:28). To commit ourselves into God's care is equally appropriate during times of danger and difficulty.

me from the hand of mine enemies, and
from them that persecute me.
16 [x]Make thy face to shine upon
thy servant: save me for thy mercies'
sake.
17 [y]Let me not be ashamed,
O LORD; for I have called upon thee: let
the wicked be ashamed, *and* [z]let[z]
them be silent in the grave.
18 [a]Let the lying lips be put to
silence; which [b]speak [a]grievous
things proudly and contemptuously
against the righteous.
19 [c]*Oh* how great *is* thy goodness,
which thou hast laid up for them that
fear thee; *which* thou hast wrought for
them that trust in thee before the sons
of men!
20 [d]Thou shalt hide them in the se-
cret of thy presence from the pride of
man: [e]thou shalt keep them secret-
ly in a pavilion from the strife of
tongues.
21 Blessed *be* the LORD: for [f]he
hath shown me his marvellous kind-
ness [g]in a [b]strong city.
22 For [h]I said in my haste, [i]I am
cut off from before thine eyes: never-
theless thou heardest the voice of
my supplications when I cried unto
thee.
23 [j]O love the LORD, all ye his
saints: *for* the LORD preserveth the
faithful, and plentifully rewardeth the
proud doer.
24 [k]Be of good courage, and he
shall strengthen your heart, all ye that
hope in the LORD.

31:16 [x]Ps. 4:6
31:17 [y]Ps. 25:2 [z]Ps. 115:17
31:18 [a]Ps. 120:2 [b]Ps. 94:4
31:19 [c]Is. 64:4
31:20 [d]Ps. 27:5 [e]Job 5:21
31:21 [f]Ps. 17:7 [g]1 Sam. 23:7
31:22 [h]Ps. 116:11 [i]Lam. 3:54
31:23 [j]Ps. 34:9
31:24 [k]Ps. 27:14
32:1 [l]Ps. 85:2
32:2 [m]2 Cor. 5:19 [n]John 1. 47
32:4 [o]Job 33:7
32:5 [p]Prov. 28:13
32:6 [q]1 Tim. 1:16 [r]Is. 55:6
32:7 [s]Ps. 9:9 [t]Ex. 15:1

A prayer during distress

[c]*A Psalm* of David, Maschil.

32 BLESSED *IS he whose* [l]trans-
gression *is* forgiven, *whose* sin
is covered.
2 Blessed *is* the man unto whom the
LORD [m]imputeth not iniquity, and [n]in
whose spirit *there is* no guile.
3 When I kept silence, my bones
waxed old through my roaring all the
day long.
4 For day and night thy [o]hand was
heavy upon me: my moisture is turned
into the drought of summer. Selah.
5 I acknowledged my sin unto thee,
and mine iniquity have I not hid. [p]I
said, I will confess my transgressions
unto the LORD; and thou forgavest the
iniquity of my sin. Selah.
6 [q]For this shall every one that is
godly [r]pray unto thee [d]in a time
when thou mayest be found: surely in
the floods of great waters they shall
not come nigh unto him.
7 [s]Thou *art* my hiding place; thou
shalt preserve me from trouble; thou
shalt compass me about with [t]songs
of deliverance. Selah.
8 I will instruct thee and teach thee
in the way which thou shalt go: [e]I will
guide thee with mine eye.

[z] Or, *let them be cut off for the grave* [a] Heb. *a hard thing* [b] Or, *fenced city* [c] Or, A Psalm *of David giving instruction* [d] Heb. *in a time of finding* [e] Heb. *I will counsel* thee, *mine eye* shall be *upon thee*

32:title MASCHIL. This Hebrew word may derive from *sakal*, a Hebrew word meaning "to be wise or skillful." Since *maschil* occurs in the psalm's title, it may indicate that this is a teaching psalm. This particular psalm sets forth the nature of sin and what happens when it is concealed, acknowledged, forsaken, and forgiven. Other *maschil* psalms are Ps. 42; 44; 45; 52 – 55; 74; 78; 88; 89; 142.

32:1 BLESSED *IS HE WHOSE* TRANSGRESSION *IS* FORGIVEN. The only truly happy people are those who have received forgiveness of their sins from God, so that the guilt of their transgressions does not weigh upon their hearts and minds and their consciences are no longer troubled. Such blessedness is open to all sinners who come to the Lord (Mat. 11:28–29). The psalmist describes God's forgiveness in three ways. (1) He forgives the sin, i.e., pardons it. (2) He covers the sin, i.e., puts it out of sight. (3) The sin is not imputed (v. 2), i.e., the guilt is canceled from the record.

32:2 IMPUTETH NOT INIQUITY. Rom. 4:6–8 quotes vv. 1–2 to show that God treats sincerely repentant sinners as righteous, not because righteousness is something they earn through their works, but rather receive as a gift when they confess their sins and believe in the Lord (cf. v. 5).

32:3–4 WHEN I KEPT SILENCE, MY BONES WAXED OLD. These verses describe the agony and penalty that concealed sin brings. When David hid his sin and did not acknowledge it to God, he lost what was most worthwhile in life – his health, peace of mind, happiness, and favor with God. In its place, he experienced guilt and inner torment as God's punishment.

32:5 I ACKNOWLEDGED MY SIN. Acknowledging and confessing sin with an honest, sincere, and repentant heart will always result in God's gracious pardon, the removal of guilt, and the gift of His abiding presence.

32:8 I WILL INSTRUCT THEE. The Lord promises to instruct and guide a forgiven believer who has a teachable spirit, treasures God's presence and counsel (cf. v. 7), trusts in Him (v. 10), rejoices in Him (v. 11), and continues upright in heart (v. 11).

9 [u]Be ye not as the horse, *or* as the mule, *which* have [v]no understanding: whose mouth must be held in with bit and bridle, lest they come near unto thee.

10 [w]Many sorrows *shall be* to the wicked: but [x]he that trusteth in the LORD, mercy shall compass him about.

11 [y]Be glad in the LORD, and rejoice, ye righteous: and shout for joy, all *ye that are* upright in heart.

The LORD provides and delivers

33 REJOICE [z]IN the LORD, O ye righteous: *for* [a]praise is comely for the upright.

2 Praise the LORD with harp: sing unto him with the psaltery [b]*and* an instrument of ten strings.

3 [c]Sing unto him a new song; play skilfully with a loud noise.

4 For the word of the LORD *is* right; and all his works *are done* in truth.

5 [d]He loveth righteousness and judgment: [e]the earth is full of the [f]goodness of the LORD.

6 [f]By the word of the LORD were the heavens made; and all the host of them [g]by the breath of his mouth.

7 [h]He gathereth the waters of the sea together as an heap: he layeth up the depth in storehouses.

8 Let all the earth fear the LORD: let all the inhabitants of the world stand in awe of him.

9 For [i]he spake, and it was *done;* he commanded, and it stood fast.

10 [j]The LORD [g]bringeth the counsel of the heathen to nought: he maketh the devices of the people of none effect.

11 [k]The counsel of the LORD standeth for ever, the thoughts of his heart [h]to all generations.

12 Blessed *is* the nation whose God *is* the LORD; *and* the people *whom* he hath [l]chosen for his own inheritance.

32:9 [u]Prov. 26:3 [v]Job 35:11
32:10 [w]Rom. 2:9 [x]Prov. 16:20
32:11 [y]Ps. 64:10
33:1 [z]Ps. 32:11 [a]Ps. 147:1
33:2 [b]Ps. 92:3
33:3 [c]Ps. 96:1
33:5 [d]Ps. 11:7 [e]Ps. 119:64
33:6 [f]Heb. 11:3 [g]Job 26:13
33:7 [h]Job 26:10
33:9 [i]Gen. 1:3
33:10 [j]Is. 8:10
33:11 [k]Job 23:13
33:12 [l]Ex. 19:5 Deut. 7:6
33:13 [m]Job 28:24 Ps. 11:4
33:15 [n]Jer. 32:19
33:16 [o]Ps. 44:6
33:17 [p]Ps. 20:7 Prov. 21:31
33:18 [q]Job 36:7 Ps. 34:15 [r]Ps. 147:11
33:19 [s]Job 5:20
33:20 [t]Ps. 130:6
33:21 [u]John 16:22
34:1 [v]Eph. 5:20
34:2 [w]Jer. 9:24 [x]Ps. 119:74
34:3 [y]Luke 1:46
34:4 [z]Mat. 7:7

13 [m]The LORD looketh from heaven; he beholdeth all the sons of men.

14 From the place of his habitation he looketh upon all the inhabitants of the earth.

15 He fashioneth their hearts alike; [n]he considereth all their works.

16 [o]There is no king saved by the multitude of an host: a mighty man is not delivered by much strength.

17 [p]An horse *is* a vain thing for safety: neither shall he deliver *any* by his great strength.

18 [q]Behold, the eye of the LORD *is* [r]upon them that fear him, upon them that hope in his mercy;

19 To deliver their soul from death, and [s]to keep them alive in famine.

20 [t]Our soul waiteth for the LORD: he *is* our help and our shield.

21 For our [u]heart shall rejoice in him, because we have trusted in his holy name.

22 Let thy mercy, O LORD, be upon us, according as we hope in thee.

A psalm of praise and trust

A Psalm of David, when he changed his behaviour before [i]Abimelech; who drove him away, and he departed.

34 I WILL [v]bless the LORD at all times: his praise *shall* continually *be* in my mouth.

2 My soul shall make her [w]boast in the LORD: [x]the humble shall hear *thereof,* and be glad.

3 O [y]magnify the LORD with me, and let us exalt his name together. Ps. 92:1-4

4 I [z]sought the LORD, and he heard me, and delivered me from all my fears.

5 [j]They looked unto him, and were

[f] Or, *mercy* [g] Heb. *maketh frustrate* [h] Heb. *to generation and generation* [i] Or, *Achish;* see 1 Sam. 21:13 [j] Or, *They flowed* unto him

33:6 THE WORD OF THE LORD . . . THE BREATH. *Ruach* (here translated "breath") can also mean "spirit"; the breath of God is thus equivalent to the activity of God's Spirit. This verse contains an important Biblical truth: the union of the power of God's word with the power of God's Spirit (through the operation of faith) always releases the creative power of God on behalf of His people.

33:18–19 EYE OF THE LORD *IS* UPON THEM THAT FEAR HIM. While the "eye of the LORD" is on all people (vv. 13–14), it rests in a special way on those who "fear him" (see 34:15). God's "eye" refers to God's caring love and providential oversight of our lives. "To deliver their soul from death, and . . . famine" means that as long as we fear the Lord, hope in Him, wait for Him, and remain in His will, God will watch over and protect us so that we will not die unless it be according to His plan. For more on the Biblical meaning of hope in God, see article on BIBLICAL HOPE, p. 834.

34:1–22 I WILL BLESS THE LORD. The writer of this psalm praises the Lord for a miraculous deliverance from great trouble. His testimony encourages all afflicted believers to believe that they may also experience the goodness of the Lord.

BIBLICAL HOPE

***Ps. 33:18–19** "Behold, the eye of the* LORD *is upon them that fear him, upon them that hope in his mercy; To deliver their soul from death, and to keep them alive in famine."*

DEFINITION OF BIBLICAL HOPE. By its very nature, hope concerns the future (cf. Rom. 8:24–25). However, it involves much more than a mere desire or wish for something in the future; Biblical hope consists of assurance in the heart, even a firm confidence, concerning future things, because these things are based on God's promises and revelation. In other words, Biblical hope is linked inseparably with a firm faith (Rom. 15:13; Heb. 11:1) and a confident trust in God (Ps. 33:21–22). The psalmist puts it most clearly when he parallels "trust" with "hope": "Put not your trust in princes, *nor* in the son of man, in whom *there is* no help. . . . Happy *is he* that *hath* the God of Jacob for his help, whose hope *is* in the LORD his God" (Ps. 146:3–5; cf. Jer. 17:7). Consequently, the sure hope of the believer is a hope that "maketh not ashamed" (Rom. 5:5), i.e., does not disappoint us as empty promises (cf. Ps. 22:4–5; Is. 49:23). Hope, then, is an anchor for the believer in the midst of life (Heb. 6:19–20).

THE BASIS OF THE BELIEVER'S HOPE. The foundation for the believer's confident hope derives from the nature of God, of Jesus Christ, and of God's word. (1) Scripture reveals how God proves Himself mightily on behalf of His people. Ps. 22, for example, reveals David's struggle with a personal situation that threatens his life; when he reflects on God's actions in the past, however, he feels confident that God will deliver him: "Our fathers trusted in thee: they trusted, and thou didst deliver them" (Ps. 22:4). The miraculous power that the Creator God has manifested for His faithful people's benefit is evident in the exodus, the conquest of Canaan, the miracles of Jesus and the apostles, and the like—all of which should build confidence in the Lord God as our helper (cf. Ps. 105; 124:8; Heb. 13:6; see Ex. 6:7, note). On the other hand, those without God have no reason for hope (Eph. 2:12; 1 Thes. 4:13).

(2) The full revelation of the new covenant in Jesus Christ provides even more reason for a confident hope in God. For believers, the Son of God came to destroy the works of the devil (1 John 3:8), the "god of this world" (2 Cor. 4:4; cf. Gal. 1:4; Heb. 2:14; see 1 John 5:19, note; see article on THE SUFFERING OF THE RIGHTEOUS, p. 764). By casting out demons during His earthly ministry, Jesus demonstrated His power over Satan (see article on POWER OVER SATAN AND DEMONS, p. 1486). Moreover, by His death and resurrection He shattered the power of Satan's realm (cf. John 12:31) and exhibited the power of God's kingdom (see article on THE KINGDOM OF GOD, p. 1428). It is little wonder then that Peter exclaims regarding our hope: "Blessed *be* the God and Father of our Lord Jesus Christ, which . . . hath begotten us again unto a lively hope by the resurrection of Jesus Christ from the dead" (1 Pet. 1:3). Jesus is therefore called our hope (Col. 1:27; 1 Tim. 1:1); we must set our hope on Him through the power of the Holy Spirit (Rom. 15:12–13; cf. 1 Pet. 1:13; see Ex. 17:11, note).

(3) God's word is the third basis of hope. God revealed His word through holy prophets and apostles of old, whom He inspired by the Holy Spirit to write without error (2 Tim. 3:16; 2 Pet. 1:19–21; see article on THE INSPIRATION AND AUTHORITY OF SCRIPTURE, p. 1924). Since His word is forever fixed in the heavens (Ps. 119:89), we must therefore place our hope in that word (Ps. 119:49,74,81,114,147; 130:5; cf. Acts 26:6; Rom. 15:4). In fact, everything that we know about God and Jesus Christ is revealed in the infallible Scriptures.

CONTENT OF THE BELIEVER'S HOPE. The believer's ultimate hope and trust must not be in other human beings (Ps. 33:16–17; 147:10–11) or in material possessions or money (Ps. 20:7; Mat. 6:19–21; Luke 12:13–21; 1 Tim. 6:17; see Num. 18:20, note; see article on RICHES AND POVERTY, p. 1568); rather, it must be in God, in His Son Jesus, and in His word. And what does this hope involve? (1) We have hope in God's grace and deliverance in the sufferings that we must undergo in our present lives (Ps. 33:18–19; 42:1–5; 71:1–5,13–14; Jer. 17:17–18). (2) We have hope that the time will come when our sufferings on earth will be finally done away with, when the subjection of the earth to corruption will end, and when the redemption (resurrection) of our bodies will occur (Rom. 8:18–25; cf. Ps. 16:9–10; 2 Pet. 3:12; see Acts 24:15, note; see article on THE RESURRECTION OF THE BODY, p. 1799). (3) We have the hope of the consummation of our salvation (1 Thes. 5:8; see article on BIBLICAL WORDS FOR SALVATION, p. 1726). (4) We have the hope of a residence in the new heaven (2 Cor. 5:1–5; 2 Pet. 3:13; see John 14:2, note), in that city whose builder and maker is God (Heb. 11:10). (5) We have the blessed hope of the glorious appearing of our great God and Savior Jesus Christ (Tit. 2:13), when believers will be caught up from the earth to meet Him in the air (1 Thes. 4:13–18; see article on THE RAPTURE, p. 1889), and when we shall see Him as He is and become like Him (Phil. 3:20–21; 1 John 3:2–3). (6) We have the hope of receiving a crown—of righteousness (2 Tim. 4:8), of glory (1 Pet. 5:4), and of life (Rev. 2:10). (7) Finally, we have the hope of eternal life (Tit. 1:2; 3:7), the life guaranteed to all those who trust and obey the Lord Jesus Christ (John 3:16,36; 6:47; 1 John 5:11–13).

With such great promises in store for those who hope in God and in His Son Jesus, Peter admonishes us: "*be* ready always to *give* an answer to every man that asketh you a reason of the hope that is in you" (1 Pet. 3:15).

lightened: and their faces were not ashamed.

6 [a]This poor man cried, and the LORD heard *him,* and [b]saved him out of all his troubles.

7 [c]The angel of the LORD [d]encampeth round about them that fear him, and delivereth them.

8 O [e]taste and see that the LORD *is* good: [f]blessed *is* the man *that* trusteth in him.

9 O fear the LORD, ye his saints: for *there is* no want to them that fear him.

10 The young lions do lack, and suffer hunger: [g]but they that seek the LORD shall not want any good *thing.*

11 Come, ye children, hearken unto me: [h]I will teach you the fear of the LORD.

12 [i]What man *is he that* desireth life, *and* loveth *many* days, that he may see good?

13 Keep thy tongue from evil, and thy lips from speaking guile.

14 [j]Depart from evil, and do good; [k]seek peace, and pursue it.

15 [l]The eyes of the LORD *are* upon the righteous, and his ears *are open* unto their cry.

16 [m]The face of the LORD *is* against them that do evil, [n]to cut off the remembrance of them from the earth.

17 *The righteous* cry, and [o]the LORD heareth, and delivereth them out of all their troubles.

18 [p]The LORD *is* nigh [q]unto[k] them that are of a broken heart; and saveth such as be [l]of a contrite spirit.

19 [r]Many *are* the afflictions of the righteous: [s]but the LORD delivereth him out of them all.

20 He keepeth all his bones: [t]not one of them is broken.

21 [u]Evil shall slay the wicked: and they that hate the righteous [m]shall be desolate.

22 The LORD [v]redeemeth the soul of his servants: and none of them that trust in him shall be desolate.

A plea for judgment

A Psalm of David.

35 PLEAD [w]*MY cause,* O LORD, with them that strive with me: [x]fight against them that fight against me.

34:6 [a]Ps. 3:4 [b]ver. 17,19 **34:7** [c]Dan. 6:22 [d]2 Ki. 6:17 **34:8** [e]1 Pet. 2:3 [f]Ps. 2:12 **34:10** [g]Ps. 84:11 **34:11** [h]Ps. 32:8 **34:12** [i]1 Pet. 3:10 **34:14** [j]Ps. 37:27 [k]Heb. 12:14 **34:15** [l]Job 36:7 **34:16** [m]Lev. 17:10 [n]Prov. 10:7 **34:17** [o]Ps. 145:19 **34:18** [p]Ps. 145:18 [q]Is. 57:15 **34:19** [r]Prov. 24:16 [s]ver. 6,17 **34:20** [t]John 19:36 **34:21** [u]Ps. 94:23 **34:22** [v]1 Ki. 1:29 Ps. 71:23 **35:1** [w]Ps. 43:1 [x]Ex. 14:25

[k] Heb. *to the broken of heart* [l] Heb. *contrite of spirit* [m] Or, *shall be guilty*

34:7 THE ANGEL OF THE LORD ENCAMPETH ROUND ABOUT. The angel of the Lord probably refers to the angelic host of heaven. They are "ministering spirits, sent forth to minister for them who shall be heirs of salvation" (Heb. 1:14; cf. Gen. 32:1–2; 2 Ki. 6:17; see article on ANGELS AND THE ANGEL OF THE LORD, p. 368). God has appointed His angels to protect and rescue His saints from physical and spiritual harm. This promise of divine intervention is reserved only for those who truly fear God (see next note).

34:9 *THERE IS* NO WANT TO THEM THAT FEAR HIM. Note that the promises in this psalm are conditional, reserved only for those who genuinely fear the Lord. God promises to deliver us from fear (v. 4), save us from trouble (v. 6,17), send angels to encamp around us (v. 7), supply our needs (v. 9), give us abundant life (v. 12), hear our prayers (v. 15), comfort us with His presence (v. 18), and redeem our souls (v. 22)—but only if we seek the Lord (vv. 4,10), cry to Him (v. 6), draw close to Him, fear Him (vv. 7,9), keep our tongues from the evil of lying (v. 13), remain separate from the evil world (v. 14), do good and pursue peace (v. 14), have contrite hearts (v. 18), and become His servants (v. 22).

34:19 MANY *ARE* THE AFFLICTIONS OF THE RIGHTEOUS. In the O.T. God promised blessing and prosperity for those who obeyed His law. Yet alongside this promise is the reality that "many *are* the afflictions of the righteous" (see Heb. 11:33–38; 12:5–10; see article on THE SUFFERING OF THE RIGHTEOUS, p. 764). (1) Believing in God and living righteously will not keep us from trouble and suffering in this life. On the contrary, commitment to God often brings testing and persecution (see Mat. 5:10, note). God has ordained that through many tribulations we must enter the kingdom of God (Acts 14:22; cf. 1 Cor. 15:19; 2 Tim. 3:12). (2) The suffering of the righteous must be counterbalanced by the revelation that the Lord wishes to deliver us out of all our afflictions. When His purpose in permitting affliction is accomplished, He then delivers us from them either by direct supernatural intervention in this life (cf. Heb. 11:33–35) or by victorious death and transference to the life hereafter (cf. Heb. 11:35–37).

35:1–38 FIGHT AGAINST THEM THAT FIGHT AGAINST ME. This psalm is called an imprecatory psalm, meaning that the psalmist prays for God to bring judgment upon the enemies of His people and to overthrow the wicked (see Ps. 35; 69; 109; 137; Neh. 6:14; 13:29; Jer. 15:15; 17:18; Gal. 5:12; 2 Tim. 4:14; Rev. 6:10). Although believers are instructed to forgive their enemies (Luke 23:34) and to pray for their salvation (Mat. 5:39,44), a time comes when we must pray for evil to cease and for justice to be done for the innocent. We should be vitally concerned for the victims of cruelty, oppression, and evil.

More must be said about imprecatory psalms: (1) They are prayers for deliverance from injustice,

2 [y]Take hold of shield and buckler,
and stand up for mine help.
3 Draw out also the spear, and stop
the way against them that persecute
me: say unto my soul, I *am* thy salva-
tion.
4 [z]Let them be confounded and put
to shame that seek after my soul: let
them be turned back and brought to
confusion that devise my hurt.
5 [a]Let them be as chaff before the
wind: and let the angel of the LORD
chase *them*.
6 Let their way be [b]dark[n] and
slippery: and let the angel of the LORD
persecute them.
7 For without cause have they [c]hid
for me their net *in* a pit, *which* without
cause they have digged for my soul.
8 Let [d]destruction come upon him
[o]at unawares; and let his net that he
hath hid catch himself: into that very
destruction let him fall.
9 And my soul shall be joyful in the
LORD: it shall rejoice in his salvation.
10 All my bones shall say, LORD,
[e]who *is* like unto thee, which deliver-
est the poor from him that is too strong
for him, yea, the poor and the needy
from him that spoileth him?
11 [p]False witnesses did rise up;
[q]they laid to my charge *things* that I
knew not.
12 [f]They rewarded me evil for
good *to* the [r]spoiling of my soul.

35:2 [y]Is. 42:13
35:4 [z]Ps. 70:2,3
35:5 [a]Job 21:18 Ps. 1:4
35:6 [b]Ps. 73:18
35:7 [c]Ps. 9:15
35:8 [d]1 Thes. 5:3
35:10 [e]Ex. 15:11
35:12 [f]John 10:32
35:13 [g]Job 30:25
35:15 [h]Job 30:1,8 [i]Job 16:9
35:16 [j]Job 16:9 Lam. 2:16
35:17 [k]Hab. 1:13 [l]Ps. 22:20
35:19 [m]Ps. 13:4 [n]Ps. 38:19 [o]Job 15:12 [p]Ps. 69:4

13 But as for me, [g]when they were
sick, my clothing *was* sackcloth: I
[s]humbled my soul with fasting; and
my prayer returned into mine own bo-
som.
14 I [t]behaved myself [u]as though
he had been my friend *or* brother: I
bowed down heavily, as one that
mourneth *for his* mother.
15 But in mine [v]adversity they re-
joiced, and gathered themselves to-
gether: *yea,* [h]the abjects gathered
themselves together against me, and I
knew *it* not; they did [i]tear *me,* and
ceased not:
16 With hypocritical mockers in
feasts, [j]they gnashed upon me with
their teeth.
17 Lord, how long wilt thou [k]look
on? rescue my soul from their destruc-
tions, [l]my[w] darling from the lions.
18 I will give thee thanks in the
great congregation: I will praise thee
among [x]much people.
19 [m]Let not them that are mine en-
emies [n]wrongfully[y] rejoice over me:
neither [o]let them wink with the eye
[p]that hate me without a cause.
20 For they speak not peace: but

[n] Heb. *darkness and slipperiness* [o] Heb. which *he knoweth not of* [p] Heb. *Witnesses of wrong* [q] Heb. *they asked me* [r] Heb. *depriving* [s] Or, *afflicted* [t] Heb. *walked* [u] Heb. *as a friend, as a brother to me* [v] Heb. *halting* [w] Heb. *my only one* [x] Heb. *strong* [y] Heb. *falsely*

crime, and oppression. Believers have a right to pray for God's protection from evil people.

(2) They are appeals to God to administer justice and to send penalties upon the wicked that are commensurate with their crime (see 28:4). If just retribution is not undertaken by God or human government, violence and chaos will reign in society (see Deut. 25:1–3; Rom. 13:3–4; 1 Pet. 2:13–14).

(3) As you read these prayers, note that the psalmist does not take vengeance into his own hands but commits it to God (cf. Deut. 32:35; Prov. 20:22; Rom. 12:19).

(4) The imprecatory psalms point to the truth that when the iniquity of the wicked reaches a fullness, the Lord in His righteousness does judge and destroy (see Gen. 15:16; Lev. 18:24; Rev. 6:10, 17).

(5) Remember that these prayers are inspired words of the Holy Spirit (cf. 2 Tim. 3:16–17; 2 Pet. 1:19–21) and not just an expression of the human desire of the psalmist.

(6) The ultimate goal of an imprecatory prayer is to see injustice and cruelty come to and end, evil destroyed, Satan defeated, godliness exalted, righteousness established, and the kingdom of God realized. This goal is a dominant concern in the N.T. Christ Himself states that true believers may pray for the vindication of the righteous. The widow's prayer to "avenge me of mine adversary" (Luke 18:3) is answered by Jesus' assurance that God will "avenge his own elect, which cry day and night unto him" (Luke 18:7; cf. Rev. 6:9–10).

(7) Believers must keep two Biblical principles in balance: (a) the desire to see all people come to a saving knowledge of Jesus Christ (cf. 2 Pet. 3:9), and (b) the desire to see evil destroyed and the kingdom of God victorious. We must earnestly pray for the salvation of the lost and weep for those who reject the gospel. Yet we must know also that righteousness, goodness, and love will never be established according to God's purpose until evil is conquered and Satan and his followers are forever put down (see Rev. 6:10,17; 19—21). The faithful must pray, "Come, Lord Jesus" (Rev. 22:20) as God's ultimate and final solution for evil in the world.

35:4 LET THEM BE CONFOUNDED. The N.T. believer may use this prayer as a call to God to contend with our greatest enemy, Satan, and as a testimony of our hatred of sin and evil.

they devise deceitful matters against *them that are* quiet in the land.

21 Yea, they [q]opened their mouth wide against me, *and* said, [r]Aha, aha, our eye hath seen *it.*

22 *This* thou hast [s]seen, O LORD: [t]keep not silence: O Lord, be not [u]far from me.

23 [v]Stir up thyself, and awake to my judgment, *even* unto my cause, my God and my Lord.

24 Judge me, O LORD my God, [w]according to thy righteousness; and let them not rejoice over me.

25 Let them not say in their hearts, [z]Ah, so would we have it: let them not say, [x]We have swallowed him up.

26 Let them be ashamed and brought to confusion together that rejoice at mine hurt: let them be [y]clothed with shame and dishonour that magnify *themselves* against me.

27 [z]Let them shout for joy, and be glad, that favour [a]my righteous cause: yea, let them say continually, Let the LORD be magnified, which hath pleasure in the prosperity of his servant.

28 And my tongue shall speak of thy righteousness *and* of thy praise all the day long.

Wickedness confronts God's love

To the chief Musician, *A Psalm* of David the servant of the LORD.

36 THE TRANSGRESSION of the wicked saith within my heart, *that* [a]*there is* no fear of God before his eyes.

2 For he flattereth himself in his own eyes, [b]until his iniquity be found to be hateful.

3 The words of his mouth *are* iniquity and deceit: [b]he hath left off to be wise, *and* to do good.

4 [c]He deviseth [c]mischief upon his bed; he setteth himself [d]in a way *that is* not good; he abhorreth not evil.

5 Thy mercy, O LORD, *is* in the heavens; *and* thy faithfulness *reacheth* unto the clouds.

6 Thy righteousness *is* like [d]the great mountains; [e]thy judgments *are* a great deep: O LORD, thou preservest man and beast.

7 How [e]excellent *is* thy lovingkindness, O God! therefore the children of men [f]put their trust under the shadow of thy wings.

8 [g]They shall be [f]abundantly satisfied with the fatness of thy house; and thou shalt make them drink of [h]the river of thy pleasures.

9 [i]For with thee *is* the fountain of life: [j]in thy light shall we see light.

10 O [g]continue thy lovingkindness unto them that know thee; and thy righteousness to the upright in heart.

11 Let not the foot of pride come against me, and let not the hand of the wicked remove me.

12 There are the workers of iniquity fallen: they are cast down, and shall not be able to rise.

Blessings to the righteous

A Psalm of David.

37 FRET [k]NOT thyself because of evildoers, neither be thou envious against the workers of iniquity. 

2 For they shall soon be cut down [l]like the grass, and wither as the green herb.

3 Trust in the LORD, and do good; *so* shalt thou dwell in the land, and [h]verily thou shalt be fed.

35:21 [q]Ps. 22:13 [r]Ps. 40:15
35:22 [s]Ex. 3:7 [t]Ps. 28:1 [u]Ps. 10:1
35:23 [v]Ps. 44:23
35:24 [w]2 Thes. 1:6
35:25 [x]Lam. 2:16
35:26 [y]Ps. 109:29
35:27 [z]Rom. 12:15
36:1 [a]Rom. 3:18
36:3 [b]Jer. 4:22
36:4 [c]Prov. 4:16 [d]Is. 65:2
36:6 [e]Rom. 11:33
36:7 [f]Ps. 17:8
36:8 [g]Ps. 65:4 [h]Job 20:17 Rev. 22:1
36:9 [i]Jer. 2:13 [j]1 Pet. 2:9
37:1 [k]Ps. 73:3 Prov. 23:17
37:2 [l]Ps. 90:5,6

[z] Heb. *Ah, ah, our soul* [a] Heb. *my righteousness* [b] Heb. *to find his iniquity to hate* [c] Or, *vanity* [d] Heb. *the mountains of God* [e] Heb. *precious* [f] Heb. *watered* [g] Heb. *draw out at length* [h] Heb. *in truth,* or, *stableness*

36:4 HE ABHORRETH NOT EVIL. The word "evil" refers to basic evil and human depravity; the ungodly do not hate evil. (1) Hatred of sin is an essential feature of God's character (Prov. 6:16; Jer. 44:4; Hab. 1:13). It is a fundamental aspect of Christ's ministry and kingship (45:7; see Heb. 1:9, note). (2) People may be loving and kind, and do good to the poor, yet if they have no indignation against wrong, contempt for the world's immoral ways, zeal for justice, and hatred of evil, they have failed to stand with God or follow the Holy Spirit (cf. Gal. 5:16–24). "Ye that love the LORD, hate evil" (97:10).

37:1–40 FRET NOT THYSELF. This psalm is not a prayer, but a series of proverbial expressions or instructions about godly wisdom. Its theme concerns the believer's attitude toward the apparent success of the wicked and the hardship of the righteous (see also Ps. 49; 73). It teaches that the ungodly will eventually be cast down and lose all they acquired on earth, whereas the righteous who remain loyal to God will have His presence, help, and guidance on earth and will inherit salvation and the promised land. According to the N.T., the believer's inheritance is the "new heaven and . . . earth" (see Rev. 21:1).

4 [m]Delight thyself also in the LORD;
and he shall give thee the desires of
thine heart.
5 [n]Commit[i] thy way unto the
LORD; trust also in him; and he shall
bring *it* to pass.
6 [o]And he shall bring forth thy
righteousness as the light, and thy
judgment as the noonday.
7 [j]Rest in the LORD, [p]and wait pa-
tiently for him: fret not thyself because
of him who prospereth in his way, be-
cause of the man who bringeth wicked
devices to pass.
8 Cease from anger, and forsake
wrath: [q]fret not thyself in any wise to
do evil.
9 For evildoers shall be cut off: but
those that wait upon the LORD, they
shall [r]inherit the earth.
10 For [s]yet for a little while, and
the wicked *shall* not *be*: yea, [t]thou
shalt diligently consider his place, and
it *shall* not *be*.
11 [u]But the meek shall inherit the
earth; and shall delight themselves in
the abundance of peace.
12 The wicked [k]plotteth against
the just, [v]and gnasheth upon him with
his teeth.
13 [w]The Lord shall laugh at him:
for he seeth that [x]his day is coming.
14 The wicked have drawn out the
sword, and have bent their bow, to cast
down the poor and needy, *and* to slay
[l]such as be of upright conversation.
15 [y]Their sword shall enter into
their own heart, and their bows shall
be broken.
16 [z]A little that a righteous man
hath *is* better than the riches of many
wicked.
17 For [a]the arms of the wicked
shall be broken: but the LORD up-
holdeth the righteous.
18 The LORD [b]knoweth the days of
the upright: and their inheritance shall
be [c]for ever.
19 They shall not be ashamed in the
evil time: and [d]in the days of famine
they shall be satisfied.
20 But the wicked shall perish, and
the enemies of the LORD *shall be* as
[m]the fat of lambs: they shall consume;
[e]into smoke shall they consume
away.
21 The wicked borroweth, and
payeth not again: but [f]the righteous
showeth mercy, and giveth.
22 [g]For *such as be* blessed of him
shall inherit the earth; and *they that be*
cursed of him shall be cut off.
23 [h]The steps of a *good* man are
[n]ordered by the LORD: and he de-
lighteth in his way.
24 [i]Though he fall, he shall not be
utterly cast down: for the LORD
upholdeth *him with* his hand.
25 I have been young, and *now* am
old; yet have I not seen the righteous
forsaken, nor his seed [j]begging
bread.
26 [k]*He is* [o]ever merciful, and
lendeth; and his seed *is* blessed.
27 [l]Depart from evil, and do good;
and dwell for evermore.
28 For the LORD [m]loveth judgment,
and forsaketh not his saints; they are
preserved for ever: [n]but the seed of
the wicked shall be cut off.

37:4 [m]Is. 58:14 **37:5** [n]Ps. 55:22 Mat. 6:25 **37:6** [o]Job 11:17 **37:7** [p]Lam. 3:26 **37:8** [q]Ps. 73:3 Eph. 4:26 **37:9** [r]Is. 57:13 **37:10** [s]Heb. 10:36 [t]Job 7:10 **37:11** [u]Mat. 5:5 **37:12** [v]Ps. 35:16 **37:13** [w]Ps. 2:4 [x]1 Sam. 26:10 **37:15** [y]Ps. 9:16 **37:16** [z]Prov. 15:16 **37:17** [a]Ps. 10:15 **37:18** [b]Ps. 1:6 [c]Is. 60:21 **37:19** [d]Ps. 33:19 **37:20** [e]Ps. 102:3 **37:21** [f]Ps. 112:5,9 **37:22** [g]Prov. 3:33 **37:23** [h]1 Sam. 2:9 **37:24** [i]Prov. 24:16 **37:25** [j]Job 15:23 **37:26** [k]Deut. 15:8 **37:27** [l]Ps. 34:14 **37:28** [m]Is. 30:18 [n]Ps. 21:10

[i] Heb. *Roll thy way upon the LORD* [j] Heb. *Be silent to the LORD* [k] Or, *practiseth* [l] Heb. *the upright of way* [m] Heb. *the preciousness of lambs* [n] Or, *established* [o] Heb. *all the day*

37:4 DELIGHT THYSELF ALSO IN THE LORD. To delight yourself in the Lord is to desire and enjoy the nearness of His presence and the truth and righteousness of His word (cf. Job 22:26; 27:10; Is. 58:14). To those who delight themselves in the Lord, God gives the desires of their hearts. (1) God will answer the cry of our hearts if our desires are in accordance with His will (see John 15:7, note). (2) When we delight ourselves in God and His will, God Himself places desires within our hearts that He then sets out to fulfill (see Phil. 2:13).

37:6 HE SHALL BRING FORTH THY RIGHTEOUSNESS AS THE LIGHT. The righteous who are oppressed by sin in the world are promised: (1) answers to their prayers (vv. 4–5); (2) vindication of their righteous standards (v. 6); (3) a heavenly inheritance (vv. 9,11,34); (4) the Lord's sustaining help (vv. 17–19,39); (5) the Lord's guidance, protection, and presence (vv. 23–25, 28); and (6) salvation (v. 39).

37:7 WAIT PATIENTLY FOR HIM. This psalm reveals how the righteous must react when the unrighteous prosper in spite of their evil and immoral ways. We must steadfastly persevere in the faith while waiting for God to bring about justice and to vindicate us (cf. v. 1; 73; Prov. 3:31; 23:17; 24:1; Jer. 12). Patience while undergoing trouble or suffering is possible through the help of the Holy Spirit (Gal. 5:22; Rom. 8:3–4; cf. Eph. 4:1–2; Col. 1:11; 3:12, who assures us that before long, God will reward us and punish the wicked (cf. Rom. 8:28; Heb. 12:1–2,5–13).

29 [o]The righteous shall inherit the land, and dwell therein for ever.

30 [p]The mouth of the righteous speaketh wisdom, and his tongue talketh of judgment.

31 [q]The law of his God *is* in his heart; none of his [p]steps shall slide.

32 The wicked [r]watcheth the righteous, and seeketh to slay him.

33 The LORD [s]will not leave him in his hand, nor [t]condemn him when he is judged.

34 [u]Wait on the LORD, and keep his way, and he shall exalt thee to inherit the land: [v]when the wicked are cut off, thou shalt see *it.*

35 [w]I have seen the wicked in great power, and spreading himself like [q]a green bay tree.

36 Yet he [x]passed away, and, lo, he *was* not: yea, I sought him, but he could not be found.

37 Mark the perfect *man,* and behold the upright: for [y]the end of *that* man *is* peace.

38 [z]But the transgressors shall be destroyed together: the end of the wicked shall be cut off.

✝ 39 But [a]the salvation of the righteous *is* of the LORD: *he is* their strength [b]in the time of trouble.

40 And [c]the LORD shall help them, and deliver them: he shall deliver them from the wicked, and save them, [d]because they trust in him.

Ps. 62:1-8

The burden of suffering

A Psalm of David, [e]to bring to remembrance.

38 O [f]LORD, rebuke me not in thy wrath: neither chasten me in thy hot displeasure.

2 For [g]thine arrows stick fast in me, and [h]thy hand presseth me sore.

3 *There is* no soundness in my flesh because of thine anger; [i]neither *is there any* [r]rest in my bones because of my sin.

4 For [j]mine iniquities are gone over mine head: as an heavy burden they are too [k]heavy for me.

5 My wounds stink *and* are corrupt because of my foolishness.

6 I am [s]troubled; [l]I am bowed down greatly; [m]I go mourning all the day long.

7 For my loins are filled with a [n]loathsome *disease:* and *there is* no soundness in my flesh.

8 I am feeble and sore broken: [o]I have roared by reason of the disquietness of my heart.

9 Lord, all my desire *is* before thee; and my groaning is not hid from thee.

10 My heart panteth, my strength faileth me: as for [p]the light of mine eyes, it also [t]is gone from me.

11 [q]My lovers and my friends [r]stand aloof from my [u]sore; and [v]my kinsmen [s]stand afar off.

12 They also that seek after my life [t]lay snares *for me:* and they that seek my hurt [u]speak mischievous things, and imagine deceits all the day long.

13 But [v]I, as a deaf *man,* heard not; [w]and *I was* as a dumb man *that* openeth not his mouth.

14 Thus I was as a man that heareth not, and in whose mouth *are* no reproofs.

15 For [w]in thee, O LORD, [x]do I hope: thou wilt [x]hear, O Lord my God.

16 For I said, *Hear me,* [y]lest *otherwise* they should rejoice over me: when

37:29 [o]Prov. 2:21
37:30 [p]Mat. 12:35
37:31 [q]Deut. 6:6
37:32 [r]Ps. 10:8
37:33 [s]2 Pet. 2:9 [t]Ps. 109:31
37:34 [u]Ps. 27:14 [v]Ps. 52:5,6
37:35 [w]Job 5:3
37:36 [x]Job 20:5
37:37 [y]Is. 32:17
37:38 [z]Ps. 1:4
37:39 [a]Ps. 3:8 [b]Ps. 9:9
37:40 [c]Is. 31:5 [d]1 Chr. 5:20
38:1 [e]Ps. 70,title [f]Ps. 6:1
38:2 [g]Job 6:4 [h]Ps. 32:4
38:3 [i]Ps. 6:2
38:4 [j]Ezra 9:6 [k]Mat. 11:28
38:6 [l]Ps. 35:14 [m]Job 30:28
38:7 [n]Job 7:5
38:8 [o]Job 3:24
38:10 [p]Ps. 6:7
38:11 [q]Ps. 31:11 [r]Luke 10:31 [s]Luke 23:49
38:12 [t]2 Sam. 17:1 [u]2 Sam. 16:7
38:13 [v]2 Sam. 16:10 [w]Ps. 39:2,9
38:15 [x]Ps. 39:7
38:16 [y]Ps. 13:4

[p] Or, *goings* [q] Or, *a green tree that groweth in his own soil* [r] Heb. *peace,* or, *health* [s] Heb. *wried* [t] Heb. is *not with me* [u] Heb. *stroke* [v] Or, *my neighbours* [w] Or, *thee do I wait for* [x] Or, *answer*

38:1–22 REBUKE ME NOT. This psalm is an anguished prayer for God to withdraw chastisement for sin. David is consumed with a sense of God's displeasure (vv. 1–2). His body is racked by disease and failing strength (vv. 3–10), and he knows that his suffering is the result of his own foolish sin (vv. 3–5,18). He accepts his punishment, confesses his sin, and looks to God for help and salvation (vv. 18,21–22). This prayer may be used by all who have sinned and are suffering from guilt, remorse, and the judgment of God.

38:3 NO SOUNDNESS IN MY FLESH. The psalmist emphasizes two consequences of committing serious sin after knowing the Lord and having received His mercy. (1) Divine anger and judgment. The teaching that God always forgives and forgets sin without ever chastising the repentant believer is not a Biblical teaching. Time may pass before a repentant sinner once again experiences God's favor. Even after forgiveness, there may be temporal consequences that continue for months or even years (see 2 Sam. 12:9–13, notes).

(2) Bodily pain and mental anguish. Sin brings a heavy burden and suffering to the transgressor. God may allow severe sickness or even death as the result of our iniquity (vv. 3–10; cf. Acts 12:21–23; 1 Cor. 11:29–30).

my foot slippeth, they [z]magnify *them-*
selves against me.
17 For I *am* ready [y]to halt, and my
sorrow *is* continually before me.
18 For I will [a]declare mine iniqui-
ty; I will be [b]sorry for my sin.
19 But mine enemies [z]*are* lively,
and they are strong: and they that hate
me wrongfully are multiplied.
20 They also [c]that render evil for
good are mine adversaries; because I
follow *the thing that* good *is.*
21 Forsake me not, O LORD: O my
God, [d]be not far from me.
22 Make haste [a]to help me,
O Lord my salvation.

In time of trouble

To the chief Musician, *even to*
[e]Jeduthun, A Psalm of David.

39 I SAID, I will [f]take heed to
my ways, that I sin not with my
tongue: I will keep [b]my mouth with a
bridle, while the wicked is before
me.
2 [g]I was dumb with silence, I held
my peace, *even* from good; and my sor-
row was [c]stirred.
3 My heart was hot within me, while
I was musing the fire burned: *then*
spake I with my tongue,
4 LORD, make me to know mine end,
and the measure of my days, what it *is;*
that I may know [d]how frail I *am.*
5 Behold, thou hast made my days
as an handbreadth; and mine age *is* as
nothing before thee: verily every man
[e]at his best state *is* altogether vanity.
Selah.
6 Surely every man walketh in [f]a
vain show: surely they are disquieted
in vain: [h]he heapeth up *riches,* and
knoweth not who shall gather them.
7 And now, Lord, what wait I for?
my hope *is* in thee.
8 Deliver me from all my transgres-
sions: make me not [i]the reproach of
the foolish.
9 [j]I was dumb, I opened not my
mouth; because [k]thou didst *it.*
10 Remove thy stroke away from
me: I am consumed by the [g]blow of
thine hand.
11 When thou with rebukes dost
correct man for iniquity, thou makest
[h]his beauty [l]to consume away like a
moth: surely every man *is* vanity.
Selah.
12 Hear my prayer, O LORD, and
give ear unto my cry; hold not thy
peace at my tears: for I *am* a stranger
with thee, *and* a sojourner, [m]as all my
fathers *were.*
13 [n]O spare me, that I may recover
strength, before I go hence, and [o]be
no more.

Delight in the will of the LORD

40:13–17pp — Ps. 70:1–5

To the chief Musician,
A Psalm of David.

40 I [p]WAITED[i] patiently for the
LORD; and he inclined unto me,
and heard my cry.
2 He brought me up also out of [j]an
horrible pit, out of [q]the miry clay, and

38:16 [z]Ps. 35:26
38:18 [a]Prov. 28:13 [b]2 Cor. 7:9
38:20 [c]Ps. 35:12
38:21 [d]Ps. 35:22
39:1 [e]1 Chr. 16:41 Ps. 62,title & 77,title [f]1 Ki. 2:4
39:2 [g]Ps. 38:13
39:6 [h]Luke 12:20
39:8 [i]Ps. 44:13
39:9 [j]Lev. 10:3 [k]Job 2:10
39:11 [l]Job 13:28
39:12 [m]Gen. 47:9
39:13 [n]Job 10:20 [o]Job 14:10
40:1 [p]Ps. 27:14
40:2 [q]Ps. 69:2,14

[y] Heb. *for halting* [z] Heb. being *living, are strong* [a] Heb. *for my help* [b] Heb. *a bridle,* or, *muzzle for my mouth* [c] Heb. *troubled* [d] Or, *what time I have* here [e] Heb. *settled* [f] Heb. *an image* [g] Heb. *conflict* [h] Heb. *that which is to be desired in him to melt away* [i] Heb. *In waiting I waited* [j] Heb. *a pit of noise*

38:21 BE NOT FAR FROM ME. One terrible consequence of willful sin is the loss of God's fellowship and the sense of His presence (cf. 22:19; 35:22; 71:12). It is a grievous and bitter experience to commit willful sin after knowing the mercy of God and the indwelling of the Holy Spirit.

39:1–13 I WILL TAKE HEED TO MY WAYS. This psalm continues the theme of Ps. 38, for the psalmist is still under the severe chastisement of God. He realizes that it is the Lord who is causing his suffering: "I am consumed by the blow of thine hand" (v. 10). He wants to know how long he will live and how long he must continue to suffer such direct punishment from God. He prays that he may not die separated from God and His mercy (vv. 12–13).

39:4–6 MAKE ME TO KNOW MINE END. David prays that the Lord will help him realize the brief span of his life on earth (cf. v. 11; 62:9; 144:4; Job 7:7). This should be the prayerful concern of every believer. God has given each one of us only a short time on earth as a period of testing to determine our faithfulness to God while living in the midst of a perverse generation opposed to God and His word. We may spend the days of our lives living for the things of this world, with little thought that our real home is in heaven with God. Or we may walk in this world as a pilgrim, rejecting the ways of the ungodly, living by God's standards, dedicating ourselves to His ways, and witnessing to the gospel of Christ so that others may be saved. May all of us learn to number our days (90:12) and know that only what is done for God and others will endure eternally (see Luke 12:20; Jas. 4:14).

[r]set my feet upon a rock, *and* estab-
lished my goings.
3 [s]And he hath put a new song in
my mouth, *even* praise unto our God:
many shall see *it,* and fear, and shall
trust in the LORD.
4 [t]Blessed *is* that man that
maketh the LORD his trust, and re-
specteth not the proud, nor such as
turn aside to lies.
5 [u]Many, O LORD my God, *are* thy
wonderful works *which* thou hast done,
[v]and thy thoughts *which are* to us-
ward: [k]they cannot be reckoned up in
order unto thee: *if* I would declare and
speak *of them,* they are more than can
be numbered.
6 Sacrifice and offering thou didst
not desire; mine ears hast thou
[l]opened: burnt offering and sin offer-
ing hast thou not required.
7 Then said I, Lo, I come: in the
volume of the book *it is* written of me,
8 [w]I delight to do thy will, O my
God: yea, thy law *is* [x]within[m] my
heart. (Ps. 78:1-8)
9 [y]I have preached righteousness
in the great congregation: lo, [z]I have
not refrained my lips, O LORD, thou
knowest.
10 [a]I have not hid thy righteous-
ness within my heart; I have declared
thy faithfulness and thy salvation: I
have not concealed thy lovingkindness
and thy truth from the great congrega-
tion.
11 Withhold not thou thy tender
mercies from me, O LORD: [b]let thy lov-
ingkindness and thy truth continually
preserve me.
12 For innumerable evils have com-
passed me about: [c]mine iniquities
have taken hold upon me, so that I am
not able to look up; they are more than
the hairs of mine head: therefore my
heart [n]faileth me.
13 [d]Be pleased, O LORD, to deliver
me: O LORD, make haste to help me.
14 [e]Let them be ashamed and con-
founded together that seek after my
soul to destroy it; let them be driven
backward and put to shame that wish
me evil.
15 Let them be [f]desolate for a re-
ward of their shame that say unto me,
Aha, aha.
16 [g]Let all those that seek thee re-
joice and be glad in thee: let such as
love thy salvation [h]say continually,
The LORD be magnified.
17 [i]But I *am* poor and needy; *yet*
the Lord thinketh upon me: thou *art* my
help and my deliverer; make no tarry-
ing, O my God.

40:2 [r]Ps. 27:5
40:3 [s]Ps. 33:3
40:4 [t]Ps. 34:8
40:5 [u]Job 9:10 [v]Is. 55:8
40:8 [w]John 4:34 [x]Ps. 37:31 Jer. 31:33
40:9 [y]Ps. 22:22 [z]Ps. 119:13
40:10 [a]Acts 20:20
40:11 [b]Ps. 43:3
40:12 [c]Ps. 38:4
40:13 [d]Ps. 70:1
40:14 [e]Ps. 35:4
40:15 [f]Ps. 73:19
40:16 [g]Ps. 70:4 [h]Ps. 35:27
40:17 [i]Ps. 70:5

Psalm of the compassionate

To the chief Musician,
A Psalm of David.

41 BLESSED *IS* he that con-
sidereth [o]the poor: the LORD
will deliver him [p]in time of trouble.

[k] Or, *none can order them unto thee* [l] Heb. *digged* [m] Heb. *in the midst of my bowels* [n] Heb. *forsaketh* [o] Or, *the weak,* or, *sick* [p] Heb. *in the day of evil*

40:6 SACRIFICE AND OFFERING THOU DIDST NOT DESIRE. The psalmist understood that the sacrifices and the symbolic rituals required by God in his law were inadequate by themselves and were no substitute for genuine commitment and heartfelt obedience to Him (see 1 Sam. 15:22; Is. 1:11–17; Jer. 7:22–23; Mic. 6:6–8). Likewise, N.T. believers may participate in water baptism, the Lord's Supper, worship, or songs of praise without a heart truly devoted to God and the commandments of His word. No religious ritual can compensate for the absence of the obedience of faith (cf. Rom. 1:5).

40:8 I DELIGHT TO DO THY WILL, O MY GOD. Heb. 10:5–10 quotes vv. 6–8 of this psalm from the Septuagint and applies them to Jesus Christ. V. 6 speaks of the inadequacy of the old covenant; v. 7 refers to the coming of Christ into the world to bring redemption (cf. Luke 24:27; John 5:46). His obedience to the heavenly Father and His preaching of righteousness are emphasized in vv. 8–10 (cf. Phil. 2:5–8). The motto of Jesus' whole life was, "Lo, I come to do thy will, O God" (Heb. 10:9). It is by Christ's obedience unto death that we have been sanctified (Heb. 10:10) in order that the law of God may be put into our hearts (Heb. 10:16). Thus every believer must also affirm these words of Christ in his or her own life, "Lo, I come to do thy will, O God."

40:8 THY LAW *IS* WITHIN MY HEART. The obedient faith that God desires is a faith that sincerely delights in following God's will and manifests that joy by endeavoring to hide God's word in the heart (cf. 119:11; John 15:7).

41:1 BLESSED *IS* HE THAT CONSIDERETH THE POOR. God has a special concern for the weak and helpless, and He blesses those who show lovingkindness to the needy. Vv. 1–3 expand on the principle, "Blessed *are* the merciful: for they shall obtain mercy" (Mat. 5:7). If we have shared God's pity for those in need, we can pray with confidence that God will deliver us when we are in trouble (v. 1), protect us from harm (v. 2), bless our lives (v. 2), destroy the power of Satan and our enemies (v. 2), and give us His presence and healing when we are sick (v. 3; cf. 72:2,4,12; Deut.

2 The LORD will preserve him, and keep him alive; *and* he shall be blessed upon the earth: [j]and [q]thou wilt not deliver him unto the will of his enemies.

3 The LORD will strengthen him upon the bed of languishing: thou wilt [r]make all his bed in his sickness.

Ps. 103:1-5

4 I said, LORD, be merciful unto me: heal my soul; for I have sinned against thee.

5 Mine enemies speak evil of me, When shall he die, and his name perish?

6 And if he come to see *me,* he speaketh vanity: his heart gathereth iniquity to itself; *when* he goeth abroad, he telleth *it.*

7 All that hate me whisper together against me: against me do they devise [s]my hurt.

8 [t]An evil disease, *say they,* cleaveth fast unto him: and *now* that he lieth he shall rise up no more.

9 [k]Yea, [u]mine own familiar friend, in whom I trusted, [l]which did eat of my bread, hath [v]lifted up *his* heel against me.

10 But thou, O LORD, be merciful unto me, and raise me up, that I may requite them.

11 By this I know that thou favourest me, because mine enemy doth not triumph over me.

12 And as for me, thou upholdest me in mine integrity, and [m]settest me before thy face for ever.

13 [n]Blessed *be* the LORD God of Israel from everlasting, and to everlasting. Amen, and Amen.

41:2 [j]Ps. 27:12
41:9 [k]2 Sam. 15:12; Job 19:19; Ps. 55:12; [l]Obad. 7; John 13:18
41:12 [m]Job 36:7; Ps. 34:15
41:13 [n]Ps. 106:48

BOOK II

Yearning for God

To the chief Musician, [w]Maschil, for the sons of Korah.

42 AS THE hart [x]panteth after the water brooks, so panteth my soul after thee, O God.

2 [o]My soul thirsteth for God, for the living God: when shall I come and appear before God?

3 [p]My tears have been my meat day and night, while they continually say unto me, Where *is* thy God?

4 When I remember these *things,* [q]I pour out my soul in me: for I had gone with the multitude, [r]I went with them to the house of God, with the voice of joy and praise, with a multitude that kept holyday.

5 [s]Why art thou [y]cast down, O my soul? and *why* art thou disquieted in me? [t]hope thou in God: for I shall yet [z]praise him [a]*for* the help of his countenance.

6 O my God, my soul is cast down

42:2 [o]Ps. 63:1
42:3 [p]Ps. 80:5
42:4 [q]Job 30:16; [r]Is. 30:29
42:5 [s]ver. 11; [t]Lam. 3:24

[q] Or, *do not thou deliver* [r] Heb. *turn* [s] Heb. *evil to me* [t] Heb. *A thing of Belial* [u] Heb. *the man of my peace* [v] Heb. *magnified* [w] Or, A Psalm *giving instruction of the sons* [x] Heb. *brayeth* [y] Heb. *bowed down* [z] Or, *give thanks* [a] Or, *his presence* is *salvation*

15:7–11; Prov. 29:14; Is. 11:4; Jer. 22:16; see Mat. 6:30, note).

41:9 LIFTED UP *HIS* HEEL AGAINST ME. Jesus quoted this verse and applied it to His betrayal by Judas Iscariot, who was a trusted friend (Mat. 26:14–16,20–25; John 13:18; see Luke 22:3, note).

42:title THE SONS OF KORAH. These were a Levitical family of singers (cf. 2 Chr. 20:19). For *maschil,* see 32:title, note.

42:2 MY SOUL THIRSTETH FOR GOD. As water is essential for physical life, so God and His presence are essential for satisfaction and wholeness of life. True believers will hunger and thirst for God and His grace, blessing, and supernatural activity in their lives. (1) To stop thirsting for God is to die spiritually; thus we must not allow anything to diminish our intense desire for the things of God. Beware of the cares of this world, the pursuit of earthly things, and the pleasures which choke out hunger and thirst for God and the desire to seek His face in prayer (Mark 4:19).

(2) We should pray that our longing for God's presence might be strengthened, our love for the full manifestation of the Holy Spirit might be greater, and our passion for the fullness of Christ's kingdom and righteousness might be deepened until we cry out to Him day and night in a heartfelt thirst, even as the deer "panteth after the water brooks" in times of drought (v. 1; see Mat. 5:6; 6:33, notes).

42:6 O MY GOD, MY SOUL IS CAST DOWN. Those who thirst for God and yearn for a greater manifestation of His presence may experience delay. Yet the faithful believer will continue thirsting for and seeking after God. The Lord promises to bless those who hunger and thirst after righteousness rather than settle for less than His full blessing (Mat. 5:6). In the midst of God's silence, we must continue to press on to know God and to experience a greater measure of the Holy Spirit (cf. Hos. 6:1–3; Acts 2:38–39; 4:11–13). We must not despair, but put our hope in God and trust in His steadfast love (vv. 8–11).

within me: therefore will I remember thee from the land of Jordan, and of the Hermonites, from [b]the hill Mizar.

7 Deep calleth unto deep at the noise of thy waterspouts: [u]all thy waves and thy billows are gone over me.

8 *Yet* the LORD will command his lovingkindness in the daytime, and [v]in the night his song *shall be* with me, *and* my prayer unto the God of my life.

9 I will say unto God my rock, Why hast thou forgotten me? [w]why go I mourning because of the oppression of the enemy?

10 *As* with a [c]sword in my bones, mine enemies reproach me; [x]while they say daily unto me, Where *is* thy God?

11 [y]Why art thou cast down, O my soul? and why art thou disquieted within me? hope thou in God: for I shall yet praise him, *who is* the health of my countenance, and my God.

A plea for judgment

43 JUDGE[z] ME, O God, and [a]plead my cause against an [d]ungodly nation: O deliver me [e]from the deceitful and unjust man.

2 For thou *art* the God of my strength: why dost thou cast me off? [b]why go I mourning because of the oppression of the enemy?

3 [c]O send out thy light and thy truth: let them lead me; let them bring me unto [d]thy holy hill, and to thy tabernacles.

4 Then will I go unto the altar of God, unto God [f]my exceeding joy: yea, upon the harp will I praise thee, O God my God.

5 [e]Why art thou cast down, O my soul? and why art thou disquieted within me? hope in God: for I shall yet praise him, *who is* the health of my countenance, and my God.

42:7 [u]Ps. 88:7 **42:8** [v]Job 35:10 **42:9** [w]Ps. 38:6 **42:10** [x]Joel 2:17 Mic. 7:10 **42:11** [y]Ps. 43:5 **43:1** [z]Ps. 26:1 [a]Ps. 35:1 **43:2** [b]Ps. 42:9 **43:3** [c]Ps. 40:11 & 57:3 [d]Ps. 3:4 **43:5** [e]Ps. 42:5,11

44:1 [f]Ex. 12:26 Ps. 78:3 **44:2** [g]Ex. 15:17 Deut. 7:1 Ps. 80:8 **44:3** [h]Deut. 8:17 Josh. 24:12 [i]Deut. 7:7,8 **44:4** [j]Ps. 74:12 **44:5** [k]Dan. 8:4 **44:6** [l]Ps. 33:16 **44:7** [m]Ps. 40:14 **44:8** [n]Ps. 34:2 Jer. 9:24 **44:9** [o]Ps. 60:1 **44:10** [p]Lev. 26:17 Deut. 28:25 **44:11** [q]Rom. 8:36 [r]Deut. 28:64 Ps. 60:1 **44:12** [s]Is. 52:3,4 Jer. 15:13 **44:13** [t]Deut. 28:37 **44:14** [u]Jer. 24:9

Appeal to God for deliverance

To the chief Musician for the sons of Korah, Maschil.

44 WE HAVE heard with our ears, O God, [f]our fathers have told us, *what* work thou didst in their days, in the times of old.

2 *How* [g]thou didst drive out the heathen with thy hand, and plantedst them; *how* thou didst afflict the people, and cast them out.

3 For [h]they got not the land in possession by their own sword, neither did their own arm save them: but thy right hand, and thine arm, and the light of thy countenance, [i]because thou hadst a favour unto them.

4 [j]Thou art my King, O God: command deliverances for Jacob.

5 Through thee [k]will we push down our enemies: through thy name will we tread them under that rise up against us.

6 For [l]I will not trust in my bow, neither shall my sword save me.

7 But thou hast saved us from our enemies, and hast [m]put them to shame that hated us.

8 [n]In God we boast all the day long, and praise thy name for ever. Selah.

9 But [o]thou hast cast off, and put us to shame; and goest not forth with our armies.

10 Thou makest us to [p]turn back from the enemy: and they which hate us spoil for themselves.

11 [q]Thou hast given us [g]like sheep *appointed* for meat; and hast [r]scattered us among the heathen.

12 [s]Thou sellest thy people [h]for nought, and dost not increase *thy wealth* by their price.

13 [t]Thou makest us a reproach to our neighbours, a scorn and a derision to them that are round about us.

14 [u]Thou makest us a byword

[b] Or, *the little hill* [c] Or, *killing* [d] Or, *unmerciful* [e] Heb. *from a man of deceit and iniquity* [f] Heb. *the gladness of my joy* [g] Heb. *as sheep of meat* [h] Heb. *without riches*

44:9 BUT THOU HAST CAST OFF. The psalmist believes that God's people are suffering and being defeated because God has forsaken them (vv. 9–16). Yet he is perplexed because he can find no evidence of sin that would account for such rejection, for they have remained faithful to God and His covenant (vv. 17–19). The psalmist reflects the experience of God's children who, though they are upright and blameless like Job, still undergo great adversity, dark periods of testing, and times when God's presence seems to be withdrawn. The answer to that experience is given in v. 22 (see next note).

among the heathen, a [v]shaking of the
head among the people.
15 My confusion *is* continually be-
fore me, and the shame of my face hath
covered me,
16 For the voice of him that re-
proacheth and blasphemeth; [w]by rea-
son of the enemy and avenger.
17 [x]All this is come upon us; yet
have we not forgotten thee, neither
have we dealt falsely in thy covenant.
18 Our heart is not turned back,
[y]neither have our [i]steps declined
from thy way;
19 Though thou hast sore broken us
in [z]the place of dragons, and covered
us [a]with the shadow of death.
20 If we have forgotten the name of
our God, or [b]stretched out our hands
to a strange god;
21 [c]Shall not God search this out?
for he knoweth the secrets of the heart.
22 [d]Yea, for thy sake are we killed
all the day long; we are counted as
sheep for the slaughter.
23 [e]Awake, why sleepest thou,
O Lord? arise, cast *us* not off for ever.
24 [f]Wherefore hidest thou thy
face, *and* forgettest our affliction and
our oppression?
25 For [g]our soul is bowed down to
the dust: our belly cleaveth unto the
earth.
26 Arise [j]for our help, and redeem
us for thy mercies' sake.

44:14 [v]Job 16:4 Ps. 22:7
44:16 [w]Ps. 8:2
44:17 [x]Dan. 9:13
44:18 [y]Job 23:11
44:19 [z]Is. 34:13 [a]Ps. 23:4
44:20 [b]Deut. 6:14 Ps. 88:9
44:21 [c]Job 31:14 Ps. 139:1
44:22 [d]Rom. 8:36
44:23 [e]Ps. 7:6
44:24 [f]Job 13:24 Ps. 13:1
44:25 [g]Ps. 119:25
45:1 [h]Ps. 69,title & 80,title
45:2 [i]Luke 4:22
45:3 [j]Is. 49:2 Heb. 4:12 Rev. 1:16 [k]Is. 9:6
45:4 [l]Rev. 6:2
45:6 [m]Ps. 93:2 Heb. 1:8
45:7 [n]Ps. 33:5 [o]Is. 61:1 [p]1 Ki. 1:39 Ps. 79:4 [q]Ps. 21:6
45:8 [r]Sol. 1:3

The king's marriage

To the chief Musician [h]upon
Shoshannim, for the sons of Korah,
[k]Maschil, A Song of loves.

45 MY HEART [l]is inditing a good
matter: I speak of the things
which I have made touching the king:
my tongue *is* the pen of a ready writer.
2 Thou art fairer than the children
of men: [i]grace is poured into thy lips:
therefore God hath blessed thee for
ever.
3 Gird thy [j]sword upon *thy* thigh,
[k]O *most* mighty, with thy glory and thy
majesty.
4 [l]And in thy majesty [m]ride pros-
perously because of truth and meek-
ness *and* righteousness; and thy right
hand shall teach thee terrible things.
5 Thine arrows *are* sharp in the
heart of the king's enemies; *whereby*
the people fall under thee.
6 [m]Thy throne, O God, *is* for ever
and ever: the sceptre of thy kingdom *is*
a right sceptre.
7 [n]Thou lovest righteousness, and
hatest wickedness: therefore [o]God,[n]
thy God, [p]hath anointed thee with the
oil [q]of gladness above thy fellows.
8 [r]All thy garments *smell* of myrrh,

[i] Or, *goings* [j] Heb. *a help for us* [k] Or, *of instruction* [l] Heb. *boileth*, or, *bubbleth up* [m] Heb. *prosper thou, ride thou* [n] Or, *O God*

44:22 YEA, FOR THY SAKE ARE WE KILLED ALL DAY LONG. The Holy Spirit reveals that some suffering comes to God's faithful people *because* they maintain loyalty to Him in a hostile world. The apostle Paul quotes this verse in Rom. 8:36 to teach that all those who identify with Christ and refuse to conform to the evil world will undergo grief, persecution, and suffering. At the same time, God's people are assured of victory through Jesus Christ, knowing that no adversity can separate them from God's love (see Rom. 8:17, 36, notes).

45:6–7 THY THRONE, O GOD, *IS* FOR EVER. These two verses find their ultimate fulfillment in Jesus Christ. The author of Hebrews applies these verses to the exaltation, prominence, authority, and character of Christ (Heb. 1:8). (1) Christ's dominion will be "for ever and ever" (Rev. 1:6). The Messianic King is called "God" in v. 6 and is distinguished from "thy God" (i.e., the Father) in v. 7. This distinction is consistent with the N.T. teaching that both Christ and the Father are fully God.

(2) In this psalm, the most significant characteristic of Christ is described in terms of loving and hating. (a) He loves righteousness, for it characterizes His kingdom. Since His joy is found in doing His Father's will (Heb. 10:7), He intensely loves righteousness in all its manifestations (cf. Eph. 5:26; Heb. 13:12). (b) As much as He loves righteousness, He hates wickedness. He made this known by dying on the cross to crush evil and to save His people from their sins (Mat. 1:21). While on earth, He confronted all forms of sin: a perverse generation (Mat. 12:39), the satanic strongholds of unrighteousness (Mark 1:34–39), and hypocrisy among God's people (Mat. 23). At the end of this age He will return to establish righteousness upon the earth (Rev. 19—22).

(3) Because Jesus Christ loved righteousness and hated wickedness, God anointed Him above all others. This anointing refers to the glory, blessedness, and authority given to Him by God. The "oil of gladness" is directly related to His anointing with the Holy Spirit (see Mat. 3:16–17; Gal. 5:22–23; see Heb. 1:9, note).

(4) Likewise, the abundant outpouring of the Holy Spirit upon God's people will come only as they share Christ's heartfelt love for righteousness. Furthermore, the right to serve as spiritual leaders of God's people will be based on a Christlike love for righteousness and a persistent resistance to evil (1 Tim. 3:1–7).

and aloes, *and* cassia, out of the ivory
palaces, whereby they have made thee
glad.
9 Kings' daughters *were* among thy
honourable women: [s]upon thy right
hand did stand the queen in gold of
Ophir.
10 Hearken, O daughter, and con-
sider, and incline thine ear; [t]forget
also thine own people, and thy father's
house;
11 So shall the king greatly desire
thy beauty: [u]for he *is* thy Lord; and
worship thou him.
12 And the daughter of Tyre *shall be*
there with a gift; *even* [v]the rich among
the people shall entreat [o]thy favour.
13 [w]The king's daughter *is* all glo-
rious within: her clothing *is* of wrought
gold.
14 [x]She shall be brought unto the
king in raiment of needlework: the vir-
gins her companions that follow her
shall be brought unto thee.
15 With gladness and rejoicing
shall they be brought: they shall enter
into the king's palace.
16 Instead of thy fathers shall be
thy children, [y]whom thou mayest
make princes in all the earth.
17 I will make thy name to be re-
membered in all generations: therefore
shall the people praise thee for ever
and ever.

The presence of God in calamity

To the chief Musician [p]for the sons
of Korah, [z]A Song upon [a]Alamoth.

46 GOD *IS* our refuge and
strength, [b]a very present help
in trouble.

45:9 [s]1 Ki. 2:19
45:10 [t]See Deut. 21:13
45:11 [u]Ps. 95:6 Is. 54:5
45:12 [v]Is. 49:23
45:13 [w]Is. 61:10
45:14 [x]Sol. 1:4
45:16 [y]1 Pet. 2:9 Rev. 1:6 & 20:6
46:1 [z]Ps. 48 & 66 [a]1 Chr. 15:20 [b]Deut. 4:7
46:3 [c]Ps. 93:3,4
46:4 [d]See Is. 8:7 [e]Ps. 48:1,8 Is. 60:14
46:5 [f]Is. 12:6 Ezek. 43:7
46:6 [g]Ps. 2:1 [h]Josh. 2:9
46:7 [i]Ps. 9:9
46:8 [j]Ps. 66:5
46:9 [k]Is. 2:4 [l]Ps. 76:3 [m]Ezek. 39:9
46:10 [n]Is. 2:11,17
47:1 [o]Is. 55:12

2 Therefore will not we fear, though
the earth be removed, and though the
mountains be carried into [q]the midst
of the sea;
3 [c]*Though* the waters thereof roar
and be troubled, *though* the mountains
shake with the swelling thereof. Selah.
4 *There is* [d]a river, the streams
whereof shall make glad [e]the city of
God, the holy *place* of the tabernacles
of the most High.
5 God *is* [f]in the midst of her; she
shall not be moved: God shall help her,
[r]*and that* right early.
6 [g]The heathen raged, the king-
doms were moved: he uttered his voice,
[h]the earth melted.
7 The LORD of hosts *is* with us; the
God of Jacob *is* [i]our[s] refuge. Selah.
8 [j]Come, behold the works of the
LORD, what desolations he hath made in
the earth.
9 [k]He maketh wars to cease unto
the end of the earth; [l]he breaketh the
bow, and cutteth the spear in sunder;
[m]he burneth the chariot in the fire.
10 Be still, and know that I *am* God:
[n]I will be exalted among the heathen,
I will be exalted in the earth.
11 The LORD of hosts *is* with us; the
God of Jacob *is* our refuge. Selah. Is. 28:16

God the King of the earth

To the chief Musician, A Psalm
[p]for the sons of Korah.

47 O [o]CLAP your hands, all ye
people; shout unto God with
the voice of triumph.

[o] Heb. *thy face* [p] Or, *of* [q] Heb. *the heart of the seas* [r] Heb. *when the morning appeareth* [s] Heb. *an high place for us*

46:1–2 OUR REFUGE AND STRENGTH. Although we all experience spiritual barrenness at times (cf. Ps. 44), this is not the norm, for God desires to be near His people with help and comfort. This psalm expresses trust and confidence in God during a time of instability and insecurity. (1) The power and ability to face the uncertainties and adversities of life are found in God. "Refuge" pictures a shelter from danger, indicating that God is our true security in the storms of life (see Is. 4:5–6). "Strength" refers to His might when battling our foes (21:8; Ex. 15:13) and includes His power that works in us (Col. 1:29) and enables us to overcome obstacles in life.

(2) The end result is that He is "a very present help in trouble." God is available to His people and wants us to call upon Him for help in any time of need. (Heb. 4:16). He is sufficient for any situation and never leaves our side. Thus, we need not fear.

46:4 *THERE IS* A RIVER. God's "river" is the continual flow of His grace, glory, and power in the midst of His faithful people (cf. v. 11; Is. 8:6; Ezek. 47:1; Rev. 22:1). This pure life-giving river flows from God the Father (Jer. 2:13), God the Son (Zech. 13:1; John 4:14), and God the Holy Spirit (John 7:38–39). It flows from the throne of God and constantly refreshes believers, both those on earth (John 4:13–14; 7:38) and those in heaven (Rev. 22:1). The most significant blessing of this river is that it brings God into the midst of His people (v. 5): "The LORD of hosts *is* with us" (vv. 7,11).

46:10 BE STILL. The Hebrew here can also be translated "let go," i.e., quit holding on to things that keep you from exalting God and giving Him His proper place in your life.

2 For the LORD most high *is* [p]terrible; [q]*he is* a great King over all the earth.

3 [r]He shall subdue the people under us, and the nations under our feet.

4 He shall choose our [s]inheritance for us, the excellency of Jacob whom he loved. Selah.

5 [t]God is gone up with a shout, the LORD with the sound of a trumpet.

6 Sing praises to God, sing praises: sing praises unto our King, sing praises.

7 [u]For God *is* the King of all the earth: [v]sing ye praises [t]with understanding.

8 [w]God reigneth over the heathen: God sitteth upon the throne of his holiness.

9 [u]The princes of the people are gathered together, *even* the people of the God of Abraham: [x]for the shields of the earth *belong* unto God: he is greatly exalted.

A song to mount Zion

A Song *and* Psalm [v]for the sons of Korah.

48 GREAT *IS* the LORD, and greatly to be praised [y]in the city of our God, *in* the [z]mountain of his holiness.

2 [a]Beautiful for situation, the joy of the whole earth, *is* mount Zion, [b]*on* the sides of the north, [c]the city of the great King.

3 God is known in her palaces for a refuge.

4 For, lo, [d]the kings were assembled, they passed by together.

5 They saw *it, and* so they marvelled; they were troubled, *and* hasted away.

6 Fear [e]took hold upon them there, *and* pain, as of a woman in travail.

47:2 [p]Deut. 7:21 Ps. 76:12 [q]Mal. 1:14 **47:3** [r]Ps. 18:47 **47:4** [s]1 Pet. 1:4 **47:5** [t]Ps. 68:33 **47:7** [u]Zech. 14:9 [v]1 Cor. 14:15 **47:8** [w]1 Chr. 16:31 Ps. 93:1 Rev. 19:6 **47:9** [x]Ps. 89:18 **48:1** [y]Ps. 46:4 [z]Is. 2:2,3 Mic. 4:1 Zech. 8:3 **48:2** [a]Ps. 50:2 Jer. 3:19 [b]Is. 14:13 [c]Mat. 5:35 **48:4** [d]2 Sam. 10:6,14, 16,18,19 **48:6** [e]Ex. 15:15

48:7 [f]Ezek. 27:26 [g]Jer. 18:17 **48:9** [h]Ps. 26:3 **48:10** [i]Deut. 28:58 **49:4** [j]Ps. 78:2 Mat. 13:35

7 Thou [f]breakest the ships of Tarshish [g]with an east wind.

8 As we have heard, so have we seen in the city of the LORD of hosts, in the city of our God: God will establish it for ever. Selah.

9 We have thought of [h]thy lovingkindness, O God, in the midst of thy temple.

10 According to [i]thy name, O God, so *is* thy praise unto the ends of the earth: thy right hand is full of righteousness.

11 Let mount Zion rejoice, let the daughters of Judah be glad, because of thy judgments.

12 Walk about Zion, and go round about her: tell the towers thereof.

13 [w]Mark ye well her bulwarks, [x]consider her palaces; that ye may tell *it* to the generation following.

14 For this God *is* our God for ever and ever: he will be our guide *even* unto death.

The folly of trusting riches

To the chief Musician, A Psalm [v]for the sons of Korah.

49 HEAR THIS, all *ye* people; give ear, all *ye* inhabitants of the world:

2 Both low and high, rich and poor, together.

3 My mouth shall speak of wisdom; and the meditation of my heart *shall be* of understanding.

4 [j]I will incline mine ear to a parable: I will open my dark saying upon the harp.

[t]Or, every one *that hath understanding* [u]Or, *The voluntary of the people are gathered* unto *the people of the God of Abraham* [v]Or, *of* [w]Heb. *Set your heart to her bulwarks* [x]Or, *raise up*

48:1 THE CITY OF OUR GOD. The city of our God and the great king (v. 2) is Jerusalem (Mat. 5:35). It will be established "for ever" (v. 8). What God began in the O.T. He will complete in the New Jerusalem at the end of the ages (Rev. 21:10—22:5; see article on THE CITY OF JERUSALEM, p. 622).

48:14 GOD . . . WILL BE OUR GUIDE *EVEN* UNTO DEATH. The Lord has committed Himself to be the believer's faithful and constant guide throughout life, in the experience of death, and beyond death to the eternal home where we will be with Him forever (John 14:1–3; 1 Thes. 4:17; Rev. 21:3; see Phil. 1:21, note; see article on DEATH, p. 782).

49:1–20 HEAR THIS. This psalm stresses both the futility of trusting in riches and the transitory nature of all that this earth has to offer. The psalmist declares that the person whose life consists in an abundance of possessions or in worldly pleasures or fame (Mat. 6:19–21; Luke 12:15), rather than in seeking after God and His kingdom, will perish (vv. 12–14,16–17); on the other hand, those who live for God will be redeemed from the grave (v. 15; see article on RICHES AND POVERTY, p. 1568).

5 Wherefore should I fear in the days of evil, *when* the iniquity of my heels shall compass me about?

6 They that [k]trust in their wealth, and boast themselves in the multitude of their riches;

7 None *of them* can by any means redeem his brother, nor [l]give to God a ransom for him:

8 (For [m]the redemption of their soul *is* precious, and it ceaseth for ever:)

9 That he should still live for ever, *and* [n]not see corruption.

10 For he seeth *that* [o]wise men die, likewise the fool and the brutish person perish, [p]and leave their wealth to others.

11 Their inward thought *is, that* their houses *shall continue* for ever, *and* their dwelling places [y]to all generations; they [q]call *their* lands after their own names.

12 Nevertheless man *being* in honour abideth not: he is like the beasts *that* perish.

13 This their way *is* their [r]folly: yet their posterity [z]approve their sayings. Selah.

14 Like sheep they are laid in the grave; death shall feed on them; and [s]the upright shall have dominion over them in the morning; [t]and their [a]beauty shall consume [b]in the grave from their dwelling.

15 But God [u]will redeem my soul
Ps. 144 [c]from the power of [d]the grave: for he shall receive me. Selah.

16 Be not thou afraid when one is made rich, when the glory of his house is increased;

17 For when he dieth he shall carry nothing away: his glory shall not descend after him.

18 Though [e]while he lived [v]he blessed his soul: and *men* will praise thee, when thou doest well to thyself.

19 [f]He shall go to the generation of his fathers; they shall never see [w]light.

20 Man *that is* in honour, and understandeth not, [x]is like the beasts *that* perish.

49:6 [k]Mark 10:24
49:7 [l]Job 36:18
49:8 [m]Mat. 16:26
49:9 [n]Ps. 89:48
49:10 [o]Eccl. 2:16 [p]Eccl. 2:18
49:11 [q]Gen. 4:17
49:13 [r]Luke 12:20
49:14 [s]Ps. 47:3 Dan. 7:22 Mal. 4:3 [t]Job 4:21
49:15 [u]Hos. 13:14
49:18 [v]Deut. 29:19
49:19 [w]Job 33:30
49:20 [x]Eccl. 3:19

50:1 [y]1 Chr. 15:17 2 Chr. 29:30 [z]Is. 9:6
50:2 [a]Ps. 80:1
50:3 [b]Ps. 97:3 Dan. 7:10
50:4 [c]Deut. 4:26
50:5 [d]Deut. 33:3 [e]Ex. 24:7
50:6 [f]Ps. 75:7
50:7 [g]Ex. 20:2
50:8 [h]Jer. 7:22 [i]Hos. 6:6
50:9 [j]Acts 17:25
50:12 [k]Job 41:11
50:14 [l]Heb. 13:15 [m]Deut. 23:21
50:15 [n]Job 22:27

True and false religion

A Psalm [y]of[g] Asaph.

50 THE [z]MIGHTY God, *even* the LORD, hath spoken, and called the earth from the rising of the sun unto the going down thereof.

2 Out of Zion, the perfection of beauty, [a]God hath shined.

3 Our God shall come, and shall not keep silence: [b]a fire shall devour before him, and it shall be very tempestuous round about him.

4 [c]He shall call to the heavens from above, and to the earth, that he may judge his people.

5 Gather [d]my saints together unto me; [e]those that have made a covenant with me by sacrifice.

6 And the heavens shall declare his righteousness: for [f]God *is* judge himself. Selah.

7 Hear, O my people, and I will speak; O Israel, and I will testify against thee: [g]I *am* God, *even* thy God.

8 [h]I will not reprove thee [i]for thy sacrifices or thy burnt offerings, *to have been* continually before me.

9 [j]I will take no bullock out of thy house, *nor* he goats out of thy folds.

10 For every beast of the forest *is* mine, *and* the cattle upon a thousand hills.

11 I know all the fowls of the mountains: and the wild beasts of the field *are* [h]mine.

12 If I were hungry, I would not tell thee: [k]for the world *is* mine, and the fulness thereof.

13 Will I eat the flesh of bulls, or drink the blood of goats?

14 [l]Offer unto God thanksgiving; and [m]pay thy vows unto the most High:

15 And [n]call upon me in the day of

[y] Heb. *to generation and generation* [z] Heb. *delight in their mouth* [a] Or, *strength* [b] Or, *the grave* being *an habitation to every one of them* [c] Heb. *from the hand of the grave* [d] Or, *hell* [e] Heb. *in his life* [f] Heb. The soul *shall go* [g] Or, *for Asaph* [h] Heb. *with me*

50:15 CALL UPON ME IN THE DAY OF TROUBLE. The Lord invites all faithful believers to call continually upon Him in times of need and trouble. God desires to hear our prayers, to help us, and to have His name exalted as a God who rescues His people.

trouble: I will deliver thee, and thou shalt [o]glorify me.

16 But unto the wicked God saith, What hast thou to do to declare my statutes, or *that* thou shouldest take my covenant in thy mouth?

17 [p]Seeing thou hatest instruction, and [q]castest my words behind thee.

18 When thou sawest a thief, then thou [r]consentedst with him, and [i]hast been [s]partaker with adulterers.

19 [j]Thou givest thy mouth to evil, and [t]thy tongue frameth deceit.

20 Thou sittest *and* speakest against thy brother; thou slanderest thine own mother's son.

21 These *things* hast thou done, [u]and I kept silence; [v]thou thoughtest that I was altogether *such an one* as thyself: *but* [w]I will reprove thee, and set *them* in order before thine eyes.

22 Now consider this, ye that [x]forget God, lest I tear *you* in pieces, and *there be* none to deliver.

23 [y]Whoso offereth praise glorifieth me: and [z]to him [k]that ordereth *his* conversation *aright* will I show the salvation of God.

50:15 [o]Ps. 22:23
50:17 [p]Rom. 2:21 [q]Neh. 9:26
50:18 [r]Rom. 1:32 [s]1 Tim. 5:22
50:19 [t]Ps. 52:2
50:21 [u]Eccl. 8:11 [v]Ps. 10:11 [w]Ps. 90:8
50:22 [x]Job 8:13 Ps. 9:17 Is. 51:13
50:23 [y]Ps. 27:6 [z]Gal. 6:16
51:1 [a]2 Sam. 12:1 & 11:2,4 [b]Is. 43:25 Col. 2:14
51:2 [c]Heb. 9:14 1 John 1:7
51:4 [d]2 Sam. 12:13 [e]Luke 15:21 [f]Rom. 3:4
51:5 [g]Job 14:4 [h]Job 14:4

The penitent's psalm

To the chief Musician, A Psalm of David, [a]when Nathan the prophet came unto him, after he had gone in to Bath-sheba.

51 HAVE MERCY upon me, O God, according to thy lovingkindness: according unto the multitude of thy tender mercies [b]blot out my transgressions.

2 [c]Wash me thoroughly from mine iniquity, and cleanse me from my sin.

3 For I acknowledge my transgressions: and my sin *is* ever before me.

4 [d]Against thee, thee only, have I sinned, and done *this* evil [e]in thy sight: [f]that thou mightest be justified when thou speakest, *and* be clear when thou judgest.

5 [g]Behold, I was shapen in iniquity; [h]and in sin did my mother [l]conceive me.

6 Behold, thou desirest truth in the inward parts: and in the hidden *part* thou shalt make me to know wisdom.

[i] Heb. *thy portion* was *with adulterers* [j] Heb. *Thou sendest* [k] Heb. *that disposeth* his *way* [l] Heb. *warm me*

50:16–23 WHAT HAST THOU TO DO ... *THAT* THOU SHOULDEST TAKE MY COVENANT IN THY MOUTH? The Lord delivers a stern warning to the wicked hypocrites among His people, threatening to "tear . . . in pieces" (v. 22) those who pretend to be devoted to Him, who claim the covenant salvation and the blessings of His word, and who at the same time ignore His righteous commandments and conform to the ungodliness of a wicked society. They will find no deliverance in the end (v. 22); in fact, such people will receive the greater damnation (Mat. 23:14; see 1 Cor. 11:27, note).

51:Title A PSALM OF DAVID. The title ascribes this psalm of confession to David when Nathan the prophet disclosed his sins of adultery and murder (cf. 2 Sam. 12:1–13). (1) Note that this psalm was written by a believer who deliberately sinned against God in such a serious way that he was cut off from God's life and presence (cf. v. 11). (2) David probably wrote this psalm after he had repented and Nathan had declared God's forgiveness to him (2 Sam. 12:13). He pleads earnestly for a full restoration of salvation, purity, God's presence, spiritual vitality, and joy (vv. 7–13).

51:1–19 HAVE MERCY UPON ME. All those who have sinned greatly and are overwhelmed by feelings of guilt can find forgiveness, cleansing from sin, and restoration to God if they approach Him in the spirit and words of this psalm. David's appeals for forgiveness and restoration are based on God's grace, mercy, lovingkindness, and compassion (v. 1), on a truly broken and repentant heart (v. 17), and ultimately on the atoning death of Christ for our sins (1 John 2:1–2).

51:3 MY SIN *IS* EVER BEFORE ME. At times the assurance of forgiveness and the renewed blessing of God do not come easily. A person who has experienced the joy of salvation and then falls into the depths of immorality may experience a prolonged time of repentance and spiritual struggle before receiving the assurance of pardon and a full restoration to God's favor. David's experience reveals how fearful it is to offend a holy God after having been so richly blessed by Him.

51:4 AGAINST THEE . . . HAVE I SINNED. David is not saying that his sin was not against others, but that it was preeminently against God and His word (see 2 Sam. 12:9–10).

51:5 I WAS SHAPEN IN INIQUITY. David acknowledges that from his infancy he possessed a natural propensity to sin. In other words, he takes responsibility for his own sinful nature. Every person is marred from birth by a selfish inclination to pursue his or her own desires and pleasures, even if it causes pain and suffering for others (see Rom. 5:12, note). This inclination can be purged from our lives only through redemption in Christ and the indwelling Holy Spirit (see article on REGENERATION, p. 1597).

7 [i]Purge me with hyssop, and I shall be clean: wash me, and I shall be [j]whiter than snow.

8 Make me to hear joy and gladness; *that* the bones *which* thou hast broken [k]may rejoice.

9 [l]Hide thy face from my sins, and blot out all mine iniquities.

10 [m]Create in me a clean heart, O God; and renew [m]a right spirit within me.

11 Cast me not away [n]from thy presence; and take not thy [o]holy spirit from me.

Is. 11:1-3a
12 Restore unto me the joy of thy salvation; and uphold me *with thy* [p]free spirit.

13 *Then* will I teach transgressors thy ways; and sinners shall be converted unto thee.

14 Deliver me from [q]bloodguiltiness,[n] O God, thou God of my salvation: *and* [r]my tongue shall sing aloud of thy righteousness.

15 O Lord, open thou my lips: and my mouth shall show forth thy praise.

16 For [s]thou desirest not sacrifice; [o]else would I give *it:* thou delightest not in burnt offering.

17 [t]The sacrifices of God *are* a broken spirit: a broken and a contrite heart, O God, thou wilt not despise.

18 Do good in thy good pleasure unto Zion: build thou the walls of Jerusalem.

19 Then shalt thou be pleased with [u]the sacrifices of righteousness, with burnt offering and whole burnt offering: then shall they offer bullocks upon thine altar.

51:7 [i]Lev. 14:4 Heb. 9:19 [j]Is. 1:18
51:8 [k]Mat. 5:4
51:9 [l]Jer. 16:17
51:10 [m]Ezek. 18:31 Acts 15:19
51:11 [n]Gen 4:14 [o]Luke 11:13 Eph. 4:30
51:12 [p]2 Cor. 3:17
51:14 [q]2 Sam. 12:9 [r]Ps. 35:28
51:16 [s]1 Sam. 15:22 Ps. 40:6 Is. 1:11 Jer. 7:22
51:17 [t]Ps. 34:18 Is. 57:15
51:19 [u]Ps. 4:5 Mal. 3:3

52:1 [v]1 Sam. 22:9 [w]Ezek. 22:9 [x]1 Sam. 21:7
52:2 [y]Ps. 50:19 [z]Ps. 57:4
52:3 [a]Jer. 9:4,5
52:5 [b]Prov. 2:22
52:6 [c]Job 22:19 Ps. 37:34 Mal. 1:5 [d]Ps. 58:10
52:7 [e]Ps. 49:6
52:8 [f]Jer. 11:16 Hos. 14:6
52:9 [g]Ps. 54:6

The fate of the wicked

To the chief Musician, Maschil, *A Psalm* of David, [v]when Doeg the Edomite came and [w]told Saul, and said unto him, David is come to the house of Ahimelech.

52 WHY BOASTEST thou thyself in mischief, O [x]mighty man? the goodness of God *endureth* continually.

2 [y]Thy tongue deviseth mischiefs; [z]like a sharp razor, working deceitfully.

3 Thou lovest evil more than good; *and* [a]lying rather than to speak righteousness. Selah.

4 Thou lovest all devouring words, [p]O *thou* deceitful tongue.

5 God shall likewise [q]destroy thee for ever, he shall take thee away, and pluck thee out of *thy* dwellingplace, and [b]root thee out of the land of the living. Selah.

6 [c]The righteous also shall see, and fear, [d]and shall laugh at him:

7 Lo, *this is* the man *that* made not God his strength; but [e]trusted in the abundance of his riches, *and* strengthened himself in his [r]wickedness.

8 But I *am* [f]like a green olive tree in the house of God: I trust in the mercy of God for ever and ever.

9 I will praise thee for ever, because thou hast done *it:* and I will wait on thy name; [g]for *it is* good before thy saints.

[m] Or, *a constant spirit* [n] Heb. *bloods* [o] Or, *that I should give* it [p] Or, and *the deceitful tongue* [q] Heb. *beat thee down* [r] Or, *substance*

51:10 CREATE IN ME A CLEAN HEART. All believers need God's Spirit to create in them a pure heart that hates iniquity and a renewed spirit that desires to do the will of God. Only God can make us a new creation and restore us to true godliness (John 3:3; 2 Cor. 5:17; see article on REGENERATION, p. 1597).

51:11 TAKE NOT THY HOLY SPIRIT FROM ME. David knows that if God removes the Holy Spirit's convicting and reproving work from his life, then all hope of redemption is gone (see John 16:8, note).

51:12 RESTORE UNTO ME THE JOY OF THY SALVATION. The Lord restored to David the joy of salvation, but note the following about David's life: (1) Scripture clearly teaches that we will reap what we sow: if we sow to the Spirit, we will reap life from the Spirit; if we sow to the flesh, we will reap corruption from the flesh (Gal. 6:7–8). As a result of David's sin, he suffered lifelong consequences in his own life, in his family life, and in his kingdom (2 Sam. 12:1–14). (2) The dreadful consequences of sin that David experienced, even after his sincere confession and repentance, should instill in all God's children a holy fear about choosing to sin in spiteful rebellion against the redemption provided us in Jesus Christ (see 2 Sam. 12, notes).

51:17 A BROKEN AND CONTRITE HEART. God will not turn away a broken and contrite heart that is full of remorse for sin and heavy with grief because of its wickedness. When our self-seeking and proud attitude is brought low and we cry to God for His forgiving grace, we can be sure that we will be accepted by Him (cf. Is. 57:15; Luke 18:10–14).

The fate of the fool

53:1–6pp — Ps. 14:1–7

To the chief Musician upon Mahalath,
Maschil, *A Psalm* of David.

53 THE [s]FOOL hath said in his
heart, *There is* no God. Corrupt
are they, and have done abominable in-
iquity: [h]*there is* none that doeth good.
2 God [i]looked down from heaven
upon the children of men, to see if
there were *any* that did understand,
that did [j]seek God.
3 Every one of them is gone back:
they are altogether become filthy; *there
is* none that doeth good, no, not one.
4 Have the workers of iniquity [k]no
knowledge? who eat up my people *as*
they eat bread: they have not called
upon God.
5 [l]There [t]were they in great fear,
where no fear was: for God hath [m]scat-
tered the bones of him that encampeth
against thee: thou hast put *them* to
shame, because God hath despised
them.
6 [n]Oh[u] that the salvation of Israel
were come out of Zion! When God
bringeth back the captivity of his peo-
ple, Jacob shall rejoice, *and* Israel shall
be glad.

A prayer for deliverance

To the chief Musician on Neginoth,
Maschil, *A Psalm* of David, [o]when
the Ziphims came and said to Saul,
Doth not David hide himself with us?

54 SAVE ME, O God, by thy name,
and judge me by thy strength.
2 Hear my prayer, O God; give ear
to the words of my mouth.
3 For [p]strangers are risen up
against me, and oppressors seek after
my soul: they have not set God before
them. Selah.
4 Behold, God *is* mine helper: [q]the
Lord *is* with them that uphold my soul.
5 He shall reward evil unto [v]mine
enemies: cut them off [r]in thy truth.
6 I will freely sacrifice unto thee: I
will praise thy name, O LORD; [s]for *it is*
good.
7 For he hath delivered me out of all
trouble: [t]and mine eye hath seen *his
desire* upon mine enemies.

The LORD will sustain

To the chief Musician on Neginoth,
Maschil, *A Psalm* of David.

55 GIVE EAR to my prayer,
O God; and hide not thyself
from my supplication.
2 Attend unto me, and hear me: I
[u]mourn in my complaint, and make a
noise;
3 Because of the voice of the enemy,
because of the oppression of the wick-
ed: [v]for they cast iniquity upon me,
and in wrath they hate me.
4 [w]My heart is sore pained within
me: and the terrors of death are fallen
upon me.
5 Fearfulness and trembling are
come upon me, and horror hath [w]over-
whelmed me.
6 And I said, Oh that I had wings
like a dove! *for then* would I fly away,
and be at rest.
7 Lo, *then* would I wander far off,
and remain in the wilderness. Selah.
8 I would hasten my escape from
the windy storm *and* tempest.
9 Destroy, O Lord, *and* divide their

53:1 [h]Rom. 3:10
53:2 [i]Ps. 33:13 [j]2 Chr. 15:2
53:4 [k]Jer. 4:22
53:5 [l]Lev. 26:17 [m]Ezek. 6:5
53:6 [n]Ps. 14:7
54:1 [o]1 Sam. 23:19
54:3 [p]Ps. 86:14
54:4 [q]Ps. 118:7
54:5 [r]Ps. 89:49
54:6 [s]Ps. 52:9
54:7 [t]Ps. 59:10
55:2 [u]Is. 38:14
55:3 [v]2 Sam. 16:7,8
55:4 [w]Ps. 116:3

[s] Ps. 10:4 [t] Heb. *they feared a fear* [u] Heb. *Who will give salvations* [v] Heb. *those that observe me* [w] Heb. *covered me*

53:1–6 THE FOOL. This psalm is almost identical with Ps. 14 (see 14:1–7, note).

54:4 GOD *IS* MINE HELPER. This psalm is an appropriate prayer for believers when facing dangers or imminent disaster. The psalmist calls for help, expecting that God will respond in His saving, delivering, and healing power. Today the Lord sends the Holy Spirit to be our helper on earth and the sustainer of our souls (see John 14:16, note).

55:4 MY HEART IS SORE PAINED WITHIN ME. This psalm may have been written by David after his own son Absalom betrayed him by attempting to usurp the throne. Absalom's rebellion was one of the many dreadful consequences that David suffered because of his sin with Bathsheba (see 2 Sam. 12:11–12, note).

55:6 OH THAT I HAD WINGS LIKE A DOVE . . . WOULD I FLY AWAY. When we are oppressed by evil people or spiritual enemies, or when the troubles of the world bring fear, anguish, and overwhelming anxiety (vv. 2–5), we too often wish to find rest and relief by escaping from our present distress (cf. Jer. 9:2). However, in most cases escape from such situations is not possible. The real solution is found only in seeking refuge in God. We can do as the psalmist did—call upon God evening, morning, and noon (vv. 16–18), and cast our burden upon the Lord by looking to Him to sustain us (v. 22; see next note).

tongues: for I have seen [x]violence and strife in the city.

10 Day and night they go about it upon the walls thereof: mischief also and sorrow *are* in the midst of it.

11 Wickedness *is* in the midst thereof: deceit and guile depart not from her streets.

12 [y]For *it was* not an enemy *that* reproached me; then I could have borne *it:* neither *was it* he that hated me *that* did [z]magnify *himself* against me; then I would have hid myself from him:

13 But *it was* thou, [x]a man mine equal, [a]my guide, and mine acquaintance.

14 [y]We took sweet counsel together, *and* [b]walked unto the house of God in company.

15 Let death seize upon them, *and* let them [c]go down quick into [z]hell: for wickedness *is* in their dwellings, *and* among them.

16 As for me, I will call upon God; and the LORD shall save me.

17 [d]Evening, and morning, and at noon, will I pray, and cry aloud: and he shall hear my voice.

18 He hath delivered my soul in peace from the battle *that was* against me: for [e]there were many with me.

19 God shall hear, and afflict them, [f]even he that abideth of old. Selah. [a]Because they have no changes, therefore they fear not God.

20 He hath [g]put forth his hands against such as [h]be at peace with him: [b]he hath broken his covenant.

21 [i]*The words* of his mouth were smoother than butter, but war *was* in his heart: his words were softer than oil, yet *were* they drawn swords.

22 [j]Cast thy [c]burden upon the LORD, and he shall sustain thee: [k]he shall never suffer the righteous to be moved.

23 But thou, O God, shalt bring them down into the pit of destruction: [l]bloody[d] and deceitful men [m]shall[e] not live out half their days; but I will trust in thee.

55:9 [x]Jer. 6:7 **55:12** [y]Ps. 41:9 [z]Ps. 35:26 **55:13** [a]2 Sam. 15:12 Ps. 41:9 Jer. 9:4 **55:14** [b]Ps. 42:4 **55:15** [c]Num. 16:30 **55:17** [d]Luke 18:1 **55:18** [e]2 Chr. 32:7,8 **55:19** [f]Deut. 33:27 **55:20** [g]Acts 12:1 [h]Ps. 7:4 **55:21** [i]Ps. 28:3 **55:22** [j]Ps. 37:5 Mat. 6:25 [k]Ps. 37:24 **55:23** [l]Ps. 5:6 [m]Job 15:32 Prov. 10:27 Eccl. 7:17 **56:1** [n]1 Sam. 21:11 [o]Ps. 57:1 **56:2** [p]Ps. 57:3 **56:4** [q]Ps. 118:6 Is. 31:3 **56:6** [r]Ps. 59:3 [s]Ps. 71:10

A song for the distressed

To the chief Musician upon Jonath-elem-rechokim, [f]Michtam of David, when the [n]Philistines took him in Gath.

56 BE [o]MERCIFUL unto me, O God: for man would swallow me up; he fighting daily oppresseth me.

2 [g]Mine enemies would daily [p]swallow *me* up: for *they be* many that fight against me, O thou most High.

3 What time I am afraid, I will trust in thee.

4 In God I will praise his word, in God I have put my trust; [q]I will not fear what flesh can do unto me.

5 Every day they wrest my words: all their thoughts *are* against me for evil.

6 [r]They gather themselves together, they hide themselves, they mark my steps, [s]when they wait for my soul.

7 Shall they escape by iniquity? in *thine* anger cast down the people, O God.

8 Thou tellest my wanderings: put

[x] Heb. *a man according to my rank* [y] Heb. *Who sweetened counsel* [z] Or, *the grave* [a] Or, *With whom* also there be *no changes, yet they fear not God* [b] Heb. *he hath profaned* [c] Or, *gift* [d] Heb. *men of bloods and deceit* [e] Heb. *shall not half their days* [f] Or, *A golden* Psalm *of David* [g] Heb. *Mine observers*

55:22 CAST THY BURDEN UPON THE LORD. When facing trials too great to bear, God invites us to cast our burdens and cares upon Him. He then bears the weight of them with us and sustains us in every situation. The Holy Spirit has repeated this invitation throughout redemptive history. Jesus gave this invitation in Mat. 11:28–30. The apostle Peter stated that believers should humble themselves before God, "casting all your care upon him; for he careth for you" (1 Pet. 5:7). And the apostle Paul exhorted us to bring all our anxieties to God in prayer, promising that the peace of God will guard our hearts and minds (see Phil. 4:7, note).

56:4 I WILL PRAISE HIS WORD. In times of fear and trouble, we should praise God for His righteous commandments, His promises, and every sentence He pronounces in all of Scripture (see Ps. 119). As we place our trust in God and His written Word, faith replaces fear (vv. 4,11) and God becomes our helper and deliverer (v. 13). Remember the truth, "God *is* for me" (v. 9; see next note; cf. Rom. 8:31).

56:8 PUT THOU MY TEARS INTO THY BOTTLE . . . IN THY BOOK. God sees, knows, and records in writing all our troubles, distresses, and sufferings (cf. 139:16; Mat. 6:25–32). (1) Every tear shed by a faithful believer is treasured by God and carefully preserved in His memory. He keeps a record so that He can comfort and reward us according to our suffering on earth. For every trial in which we remain faithful to God, we will reap an abundance of joy and glory when we are with Him in heaven (see Rom. 8:17, note; 1 Pet. 4:14,

ble; thou hast broken it: [j]heal the
breaches thereof; for it shaketh.
3 [k]Thou hast shown thy people
hard things: [l]thou hast made us to
drink the wine of astonishment.
4 [m]Thou hast given a banner to
them that fear thee, that it may be dis-
played because of the truth. Selah.
5 [n]That thy beloved may be deliv-
ered; save *with* thy right hand, and
hear me.
6 God hath [o]spoken in his holi-
ness; I will rejoice, I will [p]divide
[q]Shechem, and mete out [r]the valley
of Succoth.
7 Gilead *is* mine, and Manasseh *is*
mine; [s]Ephraim also *is* the strength of
mine head; [t]Judah *is* my lawgiver;
8 Moab *is* my washpot; over Edom
will I cast out my shoe: [u]Philistia,
[a]triumph thou because of me.
9 Who will bring me *into* the
[b]strong city? who will lead me into
Edom?
10 *Wilt* not thou, O God, *which*
[v]hadst cast us off? and *thou*, O God,
which didst [w]not go out with our ar-
mies?
11 Give us help from trouble: for
vain *is* the [c]help of man.
12 Through God [x]we shall do val-
iantly: for he *it is that* shall tread down
our enemies.

60:2 [j]2 Chr. 7:14
60:3 [k]Ps. 71:20 [l]Jer. 25:15
60:4 [m]Ps. 20:5
60:5 [n]Ps. 108:6
60:6 [o]Ps. 89:35 [p]Josh. 1:6 [q]Gen. 12:6 [r]Josh. 13:27
60:7 [s]Deut. 33:17 [t]Gen. 49:10
60:8 [u]2 Sam. 8:1
60:10 [v]Ps. 108:11 [w]Josh. 7:12
60:12 [x]Num. 24:18

The prayer of a troubled heart

To the chief Musician upon Neginah,
A Psalm of David.

61 HEAR MY cry, O God; attend
unto my prayer.
2 From the end of the earth will I
cry unto thee, when my heart is over-
whelmed: lead me to the rock *that* is
higher than I.
3 For thou hast been a shelter for
me, *and* [y]a strong tower from the en-
emy.
4 I will abide in thy tabernacle for
ever: [z]I will [d]trust in the covert of
thy wings. Selah.
5 For thou, O God, hast heard my
vows: thou hast given *me* the heritage
of those that fear thy name.
6 [e]Thou wilt prolong the king's
life: *and* his years [f]as many genera-
tions.
7 He shall abide before God for
ever: O prepare mercy [a]and truth,
which may preserve him.
8 So will I sing praise unto thy
name for ever, that I may daily perform
my vows.

61:3 [y]Prov. 18:10
61:4 [z]Ps. 91:4
61:7 [a]Ps. 40:11
62:1 [b]1 Chr. 25:1 [c]Ps. 33:20
62:2 [d]Ps. 59:9,17
62:3 [e]Is. 30:13
62:4 [f]Ps. 28:3
62:7 [g]Jer. 3:23

Confidence in God

To the chief Musician, to [b]Jeduthun,
A Psalm of David.

62 TRULY[g] [c]MY soul [h]waiteth
upon God: from him *cometh* my
salvation.
2 He only *is* my rock and my salva-
tion; *he is* my [d]defence;[i] I shall not
be greatly moved.
3 How long will ye imagine mischief
against a man? ye shall be slain all of
you: [e]as a bowing wall *shall ye be, and*
as a tottering fence.
4 They only consult to cast *him*
down from his excellency: they delight
in lies: [f]they bless with their mouth,
but they curse [j]inwardly. Selah.
5 My soul, wait thou only upon God;
for my expectation *is* from him.
6 He only *is* my rock and my salva-
tion: *he is* my defence; I shall not be
moved.
7 [g]In God *is* my salvation and my
glory: the rock of my strength, *and* my
refuge, *is* in God.

[a] Or, *triumph thou over me* (by an irony) [b] Heb. *city of strength?* [c] Heb. *salvation* [d] Or, *make my refuge* [e] Heb. *Thou shalt add days to the days of the king* [f] Heb. *as generation and generation* [g] Or, *Only* [h] Heb. *is silent* [i] Heb. *high place* [j] Heb. *in their inward parts*

mity to surrounding society, pride, or the forsaking of Biblical principles of truth and righteousness (see article on CHRIST'S MESSAGE TO THE SEVEN CHURCHES, p. 2036).

61:4 TRUST IN THE COVERT OF THY WINGS. See 35:1–28, note; 57:1, note.

62:1 FROM HIM COMETH MY SALVATION. This psalm expresses a fundamental truth by which every believer should live. In times of trouble, affliction, or opposition from enemies, we should turn to God as our ultimate refuge and deliverer. Every believer who trusts in God should be able to say: (1) I will allow no trouble, crisis, or suffering to shake my confidence in God (vv. 2,6). Not only from Him comes my deliverance (v. 1), but He Himself is my salvation and my strength (vv. 6–7).

(2) In times of anxiety or threat I will commit myself to Him and by earnest prayer tell Him all that is in my heart (see Phil. 4:6, note).

(3) I will wait upon the Lord to act on my behalf, knowing He will respond in mercy and pity toward my plight (vv. 11–12).

8 Trust in him at all times; ye peo-
ple, [h]pour out your heart before him:
Ps. 85:4-7 God *is* a refuge for us. Selah.
9 [i]Surely men of low degree *are*
vanity, *and* men of high degree *are* a lie:
to be laid in the balance, they *are* [k]al-
together *lighter* than vanity.
10 Trust not in oppression, and be-
come not vain in robbery: [j]if riches
increase, set not your heart *upon them.*
11 God hath spoken [k]once; twice
have I heard this; that [l]power *be-
longeth* unto God.
12 Also unto thee, O Lord, *be-
longeth* mercy: for [l]thou renderest to
every man according to his work.

The thirsty soul

A Psalm of David, [m]when he was
in the wilderness of Judah.

63 O GOD, thou *art* my God; early
will I seek thee: [n]my soul
thirsteth for thee, my flesh longeth for
thee in a dry and [m]thirsty land,
[n]where no water is;
2 To see [o]thy power and thy glory,
so *as* I have seen thee in the sanctuary.
3 Because thy lovingkindness *is*
better than life, my lips shall praise
thee.
4 Thus will I bless thee while I live:
I will lift up my hands in thy name.
5 My soul shall be satisfied as *with*
[o]marrow and fatness; and my mouth
shall praise *thee* with joyful lips:
6 When [p]I remember thee upon my
bed, *and* meditate on thee in the *night*
watches.
7 Because thou hast been my help,
therefore in the shadow of thy wings
will I rejoice.
8 My soul followeth hard after thee:
thy right hand upholdeth me.
9 But those *that* seek my soul, to de-
stroy *it,* shall go into the lower parts of
the earth.
10 [p]They shall fall by the sword:
they shall be a portion for foxes.
11 But the king shall rejoice in God;
[q]every one that sweareth by him shall
glory: but the mouth of them that
speak lies shall be stopped.

Appeal for aid against enemies

To the chief Musician,
A Psalm of David.

64 HEAR MY voice, O God, in my
prayer: preserve my life from
fear of the enemy.
2 Hide me from the secret counsel
of the wicked; from the insurrection of
the workers of iniquity:
3 Who whet their tongue like a

62:8 [h]1 Sam. 1:15 Lam. 2:19
62:9 [i]Ps. 39:5 Is. 40:17
62:10 [j]Luke 12:15
62:11 [k]Job 33:14
62:12 [l]Mat. 16:27
63:1 [m]1 Sam. 22:5 [n]Ps. 42:2
63:2 [o]Ps. 27:4
63:6 [p]Ps. 42:8
63:11 [q]Deut. 6:13

[k] Or, *alike* [l] Or, *strength* [m] Heb. *weary* [n] Heb. *without water* [o] Heb. *fatness* [p] Heb. *They shall make him run out* like water *by the hands of the sword*

63:1–11 O GOD ... EARLY WILL I SEEK THEE. Every believer should pray as David did in this psalm. (1) It describes a man's deep longing in his heart for God, one that can only be satisfied by an intimate relationship with Him (see Ps. 42, notes). (2) Those who profess to know God need to examine themselves by asking the following: Do I really possess a strong desire for God and His presence in my life? Or do I go through life largely consumed with secular pursuits and worldly entertainment, while prayer, Bible reading, and a deep hunger and thirst for God and His righteousness have little place or vitality in my life (see Mat. 5:6, note; 6:33, note)?

63:2 TO SEE THY POWER AND GLORY ... IN THE SANCTUARY. Not only should we earnestly seek God's presence in our personal lives, but we should also long for His Spirit, power, and glory to be manifested in His house. We should pray for God to assert Himself in power against satanic dominion, demonic oppression (Mat. 12:28; Mark 1:34,39), sin (Rom. 6), and sickness and infirmities (Mat. 4:23; 9:35; Acts 4:30; 8:7). We should fervently desire that the gospel might convict and save sinners (John 16:8–11; Acts 4:33), sanctify them (John 17:17), and bring them into the Spirit's fullness (Acts 1:8; 2:4; see article on THE KINGDOM OF GOD, p. 1428).

63:6 I REMEMBER THEE ... *AND* MEDITATE ON THEE. Along with prayer and reading God's Word, we should strive to center our thoughts on Him day and night. Remembering God must not be an occasional occurrence, but a repeated experience of looking unto heaven in praise, acknowledging His presence and lordship, and communing with Him. Nothing would be better than that our first thought in the morning and our last thought at night be on His grace, character, love, and plan for us. And when we find it impossible to sleep during the night, we can again turn our minds and hearts to God.

64:1–10 PRESERVE MY LIFE FROM FEAR OF THE ENEMY. The psalmist prays to God for protection from the plots and deception of his enemies. We can apply this prayer to our spiritual battles with Satan. We must pray to be protected from the evil one and those whom he uses against us (see Mat. 6:13, note). In these struggles, we can be confident of God's saving actions on our behalf (vv. 9–10; see article on POWER OVER SATAN AND DEMONS, p. 1486).

sword, [r]*and* bend *their bows to shoot*
their arrows, *even* bitter words:
4 That they may shoot in secret at
the perfect: suddenly do they shoot at
him, and fear not.
5 They encourage themselves *in* an
evil [q]matter: they commune [r]of lay-
ing snares privily; [s]they say, Who
shall see them?
6 They search out iniquities; [s]they
accomplish [t]a diligent search: both
the inward *thought* of every one *of them,*
and the heart, *is* deep.
7 But God shall shoot at them *with*
an arrow; suddenly [u]shall they be
wounded.
8 So they shall make their own
tongue to fall upon themselves: [t]all
that see them shall flee away.
9 And all men shall fear, and shall
[u]declare the work of God; for they
shall wisely consider of his doing.
10 The righteous shall be glad in
the LORD, and shall trust in him; and all
the upright in heart shall glory.

God's provisions for the earth

To the chief Musician, A Psalm *and* Song of David.

65 PRAISE [v]WAITETH[v] for
thee, O God, in Zion: and unto
thee shall the vow be performed.
2 O thou that hearest prayer, [w]unto
thee shall all flesh come.
3 [w]Iniquities prevail against me: *as*
for our transgressions, thou shalt
[x]purge them away.
4 [y]Blessed *is the man whom* thou
[z]choosest, and causest to approach
unto thee, that he may dwell in thy
courts: [a]we shall be satisfied with the
goodness of thy house, *even* of thy holy
temple.
5 *By* terrible things in righteous-
ness wilt thou answer us, O God of our
salvation; *who art* the confidence of all
the ends of the earth, and of them that
are afar off *upon* the sea:
6 Which by his strength setteth fast
the mountains; [b]*being* girded with
power:

64:3 [r]Ps. 58:7
64:5 [s]Ps. 10:11
64:8 [t]Ps. 31:11
64:9 [u]Jer. 50:28 & 51:10
65:1 [v]Ps. 62:1
65:2 [w]Is. 66:23
65:3 [x]Heb. 9:14
65:4 [y]Ps. 33:12 [z]Ps. 4:3 [a]Ps. 36:8
65:6 [b]Ps. 93:1
65:7 [c]Mat. 8:26 [d]Is. 17:13
65:9 [e]Jer. 5:24 [f]Ps. 46:4
65:13 [g]Is. 55:12
66:1 [h]Ps. 100:1
66:3 [i]Ps. 65:5 [j]Ps. 18:44
66:4 [k]Ps. 117:1

7 [c]Which stilleth the noise of the
seas, the noise of their waves, [d]and
the tumult of the people.
8 They also that dwell in the utter-
most parts are afraid at thy tokens:
thou makest the outgoings of the
morning and evening [x]to rejoice.
9 Thou visitest the earth, and [e]wa-
terest[y] it: thou greatly enrichest it
[f]with the river of God, *which* is full of
water: thou preparest them corn, when
thou hast so provided for it.
10 Thou waterest the ridges thereof
abundantly: [z]thou settlest the fur-
rows thereof: [a]thou makest it soft
with showers: thou blessest the
springing thereof.
11 Thou crownest [b]the year with
thy goodness; and thy paths drop fat-
ness.
12 They drop *upon* the pastures of
the wilderness: and the little hills [c]re-
joice on every side.
13 The pastures are clothed with
flocks; [g]the valleys also are covered
over with corn; they shout for joy, they
also sing.

God's power and works

To the chief Musician, A Song *or* Psalm.

66 MAKE[h] A joyful noise unto
God, [d]all ye lands:
2 Sing forth the honour of his name:
make his praise glorious.
3 Say unto God, How [i]terrible *art*
thou in thy works! through the great-
ness of thy power shall thine enemies
[j]submit[e] themselves unto thee.
4 [k]All the earth shall worship thee,

[q] Or, *speech* [r] Heb. *to hide snares* [s] Or, *we are consumed by that which they have thoroughly searched* [t] Heb. *a search searched* [u] Heb. *their wound shall be* [v] Heb. *is silent* [w] Heb. *Words,* or, *Matters of iniquities* [x] Or, *to sing* [y] Or, *after thou hadst made it to desire rain* [z] Or, *thou causest rain to descend* into *the furrows thereof* [a] Heb. *thou dissolvest it* [b] Heb. *the year of thy goodness* [c] Heb. *are girded with joy* [d] Heb. *all the earth* [e] Heb. *lie*

65:4 BLESSED *IS THE MAN WHOM* THOU . . . CAUSETH TO APPROACH *UNTO THEE.* Our greatest joy is to be near God and to enjoy communion with Him. This is now possible for all believers through the sacrifice of Jesus Christ (Heb. 10:10–22) and through the indwelling Holy Spirit (Eph. 5:18). The Bible exhorts us to draw near to God continually, that we might receive His mercy and strength to help us in our times of need (Heb. 4:16; 7:25). Our greatest shame would be to treat lightly this privilege of nearness with God, considering it to be unworthy of our constant endeavor (cf. Heb. 10:36–39).

and shall sing unto thee; they shall
sing *to* thy name. Selah.
5 Come and see the works of God:
he is terrible *in his* doing toward the
children of men.
6 [l]He turned the sea into dry *land:*
they went through the flood on foot:
there did we rejoice in him.
7 He ruleth by his power for ever;
his eyes behold the nations: let not the
rebellious exalt themselves. Selah.
8 O bless our God, ye people, and
make the voice of his praise to be
heard:
9 Which [f]holdeth our soul in life,
and suffereth not our feet to be moved.
10 For [m]thou, O God, hast proved
us: [n]thou hast tried us, as silver is
tried.
11 [o]Thou broughtest us into the
net; thou laidst affliction upon our
loins.
12 [p]Thou hast caused men to ride
over our heads; [q]we went through fire
and through water: but thou brought-
est us out into a [g]wealthy *place.*
13 I will go into thy house with
burnt offerings: [r]I will pay thee my
vows,
14 Which my lips have [h]uttered,
and my mouth hath spoken, when I
was in trouble.
15 I will offer unto thee burnt sacri-
fices of [i]fatlings, with the incense of
rams; I will offer bullocks with goats.
Selah.
16 Come *and* hear, all ye that fear
God, and I will declare what he hath
done for my soul.
17 I cried unto him with my mouth,
and he was extolled with my tongue.
18 [s]If I regard iniquity in my heart,
the Lord will not hear *me:*
19 *But* verily God [t]hath heard *me;*
he hath attended to the voice of my
prayer.
20 Blessed *be* God, which hath not
turned away my prayer, nor his mercy
from me.

God governs the nations

To the chief Musician on Neginoth,
A Psalm *or* Song.

67 GOD BE merciful unto us, and
bless us; *and* [u]cause his face
to shine [j]upon us; Selah.
2 That [v]thy way may be known
upon earth, [w]thy saving health among
all nations.
3 Let the people praise thee, O God;
let all the people praise thee.
4 O let the nations be glad and sing
for joy: for [x]thou shalt judge the peo-
ple righteously, and [k]govern the na-
tions upon earth. Selah.
5 Let the people praise thee, O God;
let all the people praise thee.
6 [y]*Then* shall the earth yield her in-
crease; *and* God, *even* our own God,
shall bless us.

66:6 [l]Ex. 14:21
66:10 [m]Ps. 17:3 Is. 48:10 [n]Zech. 13:9 1 Pet. 1:7
66:11 [o]Lam. 1:13
66:12 [p]Is. 51:23 [q]Is. 43:2
66:13 [r]Eccl. 5:4
66:18 [s]Is. 1:15 John 9:31 Jas. 4:3
66:19 [t]Ps. 116:1,2
67:1 [u]Num. 6:25 Ps. 4:6
67:2 [v]Acts 18:25 [w]Is. 52:10 Tit. 2:11
67:4 [x]Ps. 96:10
67:6 [y]Lev. 26:4 Ps:85:12 Ezek. 34:27

[f]Heb. *putteth* [g]Heb. *moist* [h]Heb. *opened*
[i]Heb. *marrow* [j]Heb. *with us* [k]Heb. *lead*

66:5 COME AND SEE THE WORKS OF GOD. A community of believers must have the works of the Holy Spirit so manifested in their midst that they can glorify God and say to others, "Come and see the works of God" (see article on SPIRITUAL GIFTS FOR BELIEVERS, p. 1790). Nothing short of the full demonstration of God's power among His people will convince the lost of the truth of the gospel of Christ (see article on SIGNS OF BELIEVERS, p. 1516). We must also witness to others on a personal level, giving testimony to God's continual care in our lives (v. 16).

66:18 IF I REGARD INIQUITY ... THE LORD WILL NOT HEAR *ME*. Those who take pleasure in unrighteousness have no hope of answered prayer when they call on God. He wants us separated from sin; only then will He respond to us as a Father to a son (2 Cor. 6:14–18; see Jas. 4:3, note; 1 John 3:22, note; see article on EFFECTIVE PRAYING, p. 540).

67:1–2 GOD ... BLESS US ... THAT THY WAY MAY BE KNOWN UPON EARTH. This psalm speaks of God's plan for His people when He first called Abraham (see Gen. 12:1–3; cf. Num. 6:24). (1) God chose this man so that through his descendants, He might become known to the nations of the world. He intended that Israel's reception and enjoyment of His grace and blessings would cause the heathen nations to take notice, so that they might praise Him and accept His ways of truth and righteousness.

(2) N.T. believers should pray that God will bless them and their families with His presence, love, grace, guidance, salvation, healing power, and fullness of the Spirit, in order that the lost might seek Christ's truth and salvation (Mat. 5:14–16).

(3) The key to effective evangelism and mission work is the blessing of God richly poured out on His people (vv. 2,7). This blessing is described in the N.T. as the promised Holy Spirit (Gal. 3:14), sent forth by the Father into our hearts (Gal. 4:6). Through this Spirit living within us, the proclamation to the nations will achieve its desired results (cf. Acts 1:8).

7 God shall bless us; and all the
ends of the earth shall fear him.

The God of Israel

To the chief Musician, A Psalm *or* Song of David.

68 LET [z]GOD arise, let his enemies be scattered: let them also that hate him flee [l]before him.
2 [a]As smoke is driven away, *so*
drive *them* away: [b]as wax melteth before the fire, *so* let the wicked perish at the presence of God.
3 But [c]let the righteous be glad; let
them rejoice before God: yea, let them [m]exceedingly rejoice.
4 Sing unto God, sing praises to his
name: [d]extol him that rideth upon the heavens [e]by his name JAH, and rejoice before him.
5 [f]A father of the fatherless, and a
judge of the widows, *is* God in his holy habitation.
6 [g]God setteth the solitary [n]in
families: [h]he bringeth out those which are bound with chains: but [i]the rebellious dwell in a dry *land.*
7 O God, [j]when thou wentest forth
before thy people, when thou didst march through the wilderness; Selah:
8 The earth shook, the heavens also
dropped at the presence of God: *even* Sinai itself *was moved* at the presence of God, the God of Israel.
9 [k]Thou, O God, didst [o]send a
plentiful rain, whereby thou didst [p]confirm thine inheritance, when it was weary.
10 Thy congregation hath dwelt
therein: [l]thou, O God, hast prepared of thy goodness for the poor.
11 The Lord gave the word: great
was the [q]company of those that published *it.*
12 [m]Kings of armies [r]did flee
apace: and she that tarried at home divided the spoil.
13 [n]Though ye have lain among
the pots, [o]*yet shall ye be as* the wings of a dove covered with silver, and her feathers with yellow gold.
14 [p]When the Almighty scattered
kings [s]in it, it was *white* as snow in Salmon.
15 The hill of God *is as* the hill of
Bashan; an high hill *as* the hill of Bashan.
16 Why leap ye, ye high hills? [q]*this*
is the hill *which* God desireth to dwell in; yea, the LORD will dwell *in it* for ever.
17 [r]The chariots of God *are* twenty
thousand, [t]*even* thousands of angels: the Lord *is* among them, *as in* Sinai, in the holy *place.*
18 [s]Thou hast ascended on high,
[t]thou hast led captivity captive: [u]thou hast received gifts [u]for men; yea, *for* [v]the rebellious also, [w]that the LORD God might dwell *among them.*
19 Blessed *be* the Lord, *who* daily
loadeth us *with benefits, even* the God of our salvation. Selah.
20 *He that is* our God *is* the God of
salvation; and [x]unto GOD the Lord *belong* the issues from death.
21 But [y]God shall wound the head
of his enemies, [z]*and* the hairy scalp of such an one as goeth on still in his trespasses.
22 The Lord said, I will bring
[a]again from Bashan, I will bring *my people* again [b]from the depths of the sea:
23 [c]That thy foot may be [v]dipped
in the blood of *thine* enemies, [d]*and* the tongue of thy dogs in the same.
24 They have seen thy goings,

68:1 [z]Num. 10:35 Is. 33:3 68:2 [a]Is. 9:18 Hos. 13:3 [b]Mic. 1:4 68:3 [c]Ps. 32:11 68:4 [d]Deut. 33:26 [e]Ex. 6:3 68:5 [f]Ps. 10:14 68:6 [g]1 Sam. 2:5 Ps. 107:4-7 [h]Acts 12:6 [i]Ps. 107:34 68:7 [j]Ex. 13:21 Judg. 4:14 68:9 [k]Deut. 11:11 68:10 [l]Deut. 26:5 Ps. 74:19 68:12 [m]Num. 31:8 Josh. 10:16 68:13 [n]Ps. 81:6 [o]Ps. 105:37 68:14 [p]Josh. 10:10 68:16 [q]Deut. 12:5 1 Ki. 9:3 68:17 [r]Deut. 33:2 68:18 [s]Eph. 4:8 [t]Judg. 5:12 [u]Acts 2:4,33 [v]1 Tim. 1:13 [w]Ps. 78:60 68:20 [x]Deut. 32:39 68:21 [y]Hab. 3:13 [z]Ps. 55:23 68:22 [a]Num. 21:33 [b]Ex. 14:22 68:23 [c]Ps. 58:10 [d]1 Ki. 21:19

[l] Heb. *from his face* [m] Heb. *rejoice with gladness* [n] Heb. *in a house* [o] Heb. *shake out* [p] Heb. *confirm it* [q] Heb. *army* [r] Heb. *did flee, did flee* [s] Or, *for her, she was* [t] Or, *even many thousands* [u] Heb. *in the man* [v] Or, *red*

68:1–35 LET GOD ARISE. This psalm, celebrating God's rule over and care of His people Israel and His victory over His enemies, may foreshadow (1) Christ's destruction of evil and the evil one at the end of the age, and (2) the triumph of all believers in Christ, as they rejoice eternally in the presence of God (Rev. 19—21).

68:5 A FATHER OF THE FATHERLESS. The fatherhood of God for the believer is emphasized in both O.T. and N.T. God delights in protecting the weak, disadvantaged, wronged, and lonely among His people. If you feel alone in this world, you should ask God to put you under His special care and protection (see Luke 7:13, note).

68:18 THOU HAST ASCENDED ON HIGH. This verse describes God's triumphal march in Israel's history, culminating with the establishment of His rule in Jerusalem. It also foreshadows Christ's ascension into heaven to rule as head of the church and to bring many into the kingdom of God (see Eph. 4:8).

68:19 *WHO* DAILY LOADETH US *WITH BENEFITS*. This verse can also be translated, "who daily beareth our burdens" (see 55:22, note).

O God; *even* the goings of my God, my
King, in the sanctuary.
25 [e]The singers went before, the
players on instruments *followed* after;
among *them were* the damsels playing
with timbrels.
26 Bless ye God in the congrega-
tions, *even* the Lord, [w]from [f]the foun-
tain of Israel.
27 There *is* [g]little Benjamin *with*
their ruler, the princes of Judah [x]*and*
their council, the princes of Zebulun,
and the princes of Naphtali.
28 Thy God hath [h]commanded thy
strength: strengthen, O God, that
which thou hast wrought for us.
29 Because of thy temple at Jerusa-
lem [i]shall kings bring presents unto
thee.
30 Rebuke the company of spear-
men, [j]the multitude of the bulls, with
the calves of the people, *till every one*
[k]submit himself with pieces of silver:
[y]scatter thou the people *that* delight
in war.
31 [l]Princes shall come out of
Egypt; [m]Ethiopia shall soon [n]stretch
out her hands unto God.
32 Sing unto God, ye kingdoms of
the earth; O sing praises unto the Lord;
Selah:
33 To him [o]that rideth upon the
heavens of heavens, *which were* of old;
lo, he doth [z]send out his voice, *and*
that a mighty voice.
34 [p]Ascribe ye strength unto God:
his excellency *is* over Israel, and his
strength *is* in the [a]clouds.
35 O God, [q]*thou art* terrible out of
thy holy places: the God of Israel *is* he
that giveth strength and power unto *his*
people. Blessed *be* God.

68:25 [e]1 Chr. 13:8
68:26 [f]Deut. 33:28 Is. 48:1
68:27 [g]1 Sam. 9:21
68:28 [h]Ps. 42:8
68:29 [i]Ps. 72:10
68:30 [j]Ps. 22:12 [k]2 Sam. 8:2
68:31 [l]Is. 19:21 [m]Is. 45:14 [n]Ps. 44:20
68:33 [o]Ps. 18:10
68:34 [p]Ps. 29:1
68:35 [q]Ps. 76:12

69:1 [r]Ps. 45,title [s]Jonah 2:5
69:2 [t]Ps. 40:2
69:3 [u]Ps. 6:6 [v]Ps. 119:82 Is. 38:14
69:4 [w]Ps. 35:19 John 15:25
69:8 [x]Is. 53:3
69:9 [y]John 2:17 [z]Rom. 15:3

The prayer for deliverance

To the chief Musician [r]upon Shoshannim, *A Psalm* of David.

69 SAVE ME, O God; for [s]the wa-
ters are come in unto *my* soul.
2 [t]I sink in [b]deep mire, where
there is no standing: I am come into
[c]deep waters, where the floods over-
flow me.
3 [u]I am weary of my crying: my
throat is dried: [v]mine eyes fail while
I wait for my God.
4 They that [w]hate me without a
cause are more than the hairs of mine
head: they that would destroy me, *be-
ing* mine enemies wrongfully, are
mighty: then I restored *that* which I
took not away.
5 O God, thou knowest my foolish-
ness; and my [d]sins are not hid from
thee.
6 Let not them that wait on thee,
O Lord GOD of hosts, be ashamed for
my sake: let not those that seek thee
be confounded for my sake, O God of
Israel.
7 Because for thy sake I have borne
reproach; shame hath covered my face.
8 [x]I am become a stranger unto my
brethren, and an alien unto my moth-
er's children.
9 [y]For the zeal of thine house hath
eaten me up; [z]and the reproaches of
them that reproached thee are fallen
upon me.

[w] Or, ye that are *of the fountain of Israel*
[x] Or, with *their company* [y] Or, *he scattereth*
[z] Heb. *give* [a] Or, *heavens* [b] Heb. *the mire of depth* [c] Heb. *depth of waters* [d] Heb. *guiltiness*

69:1–36 SAVE ME. This psalm, along with Ps. 22, is one of the most frequently quoted psalms in the N.T. Ps. 69 is quoted as follows: v. 4 - John 15:25; v. 9 - John 2:17; Rom. 15:3; vv. 22–23 - Rom. 11:9–10; v. 25 - Acts 1:20. (1) The author describes a person in the depths of despair, suffering greatly in every possible way because of his faithfulness to God and His righteous ways (vv. 7–12). He wants to worship God in the way God has commanded (vv. 9–12). Tradition assigns this psalm to David (see the psalm title), but it may have been written by Hezekiah (cf. 2 Ki. 18—20; 2 Chr. 29—32), Jeremiah (cf. Jer. 11:19; 12:1), or an unknown Jew desiring to rebuild the temple after the exile (cf. v. 9).

(2) Some portions of this psalm prefigure the sufferings of Jesus. However, the confession of v. 5, as well as the curses of vv. 22–28, cannot be applied to Christ.

69:1–4 SAVE ME, O GOD. This expression of the oppressive sufferings of a righteous person also captures the feelings of the Savior as He underwent persecution from the ungodly and experienced the agony of the cross. Similarly, any righteous believer who undergoes great trouble and sees no way out may cry to God, confident that as God eventually delivered Christ from all His suffering, He will likewise deliver all His children at His own appointed time.

69:9 THE ZEAL OF THINE HOUSE HATH EATEN ME UP. The psalmist bears rejection, shame, and alienation because of his righteous zeal for God's house and kingdom (vv. 6–9). He has spoken against sin and has pleaded for revival, cleansing, and reformation among God's people. For this he has suffered at the hands of those who were comfortable with the spiritual status quo (vv. 9–11).

10 [a]When I wept, *and chastened* my soul with fasting, that was to my reproach.

11 I made sackcloth also my garment; [b]and I became a proverb to them.

12 They that sit in the gate speak against me; and [c]I *was* the song of the [e]drunkards.

13 But as for me, my prayer *is* unto thee, O LORD, [d]*in* an acceptable time: O God, in the multitude of thy mercy hear me, in the truth of thy salvation.

14 Deliver me out of the mire, and let me not sink: [e]let me be delivered from them that hate me, and out of [f]the deep waters.

15 Let not the waterflood overflow me, neither let the deep swallow me up, and let not the pit [g]shut her mouth upon me.

16 Hear me, O LORD; for thy lovingkindness *is* good: [h]turn unto me according to the multitude of thy tender mercies.

17 And [i]hide not thy face from thy servant; for I am in trouble: [f]hear me speedily.

18 Draw nigh unto my soul, *and* redeem it: deliver me because of mine enemies.

19 Thou hast known [j]my reproach, and my shame, and my dishonour: mine adversaries *are* all before thee.

20 Reproach hath broken my heart; and I am full of heaviness: and [k]I looked *for some* [g]to take pity, but *there was* none; and for [l]comforters, but I found none.

21 They gave me also gall for my meat; [m]and in my thirst they gave me vinegar to drink.

22 [n]Let their table become a snare before them: and *that which should have been* for *their* welfare, *let it become* a trap.

23 [o]Let their eyes be darkened, that they see not; and make their loins continually to shake.

24 [p]Pour out thine indignation upon them, and let thy wrathful anger take hold of them.

25 [q]Let [h]their habitation be desolate; *and* [i]let none dwell in their tents.

26 For they persecute [r]*him* whom thou hast smitten; and they talk to the grief of [j]those whom thou hast wounded.

27 [s]Add [k]iniquity unto their iniquity: [t]and let them not come into thy righteousness.

28 Let them [u]be blotted out of the book of the living, [v]and not be written with the righteous.

29 But I *am* poor and sorrowful: let thy salvation, O God, set me up on high.

30 [w]I will praise the name of God with a song, and will magnify him with thanksgiving.

31 [x]*This* also shall please the LORD better than an ox *or* bullock that hath horns and hoofs.

32 [y]The [l]humble shall see *this, and* be glad: and [z]your heart shall live that seek God.

33 For the LORD heareth the poor, and despiseth not [a]his prisoners.

34 [b]Let the heaven and earth praise him, the seas, [c]and every thing that [m]moveth therein.

35 [d]For God will save Zion, and will build the cities of Judah: that they may dwell there, and have it in possession.

36 [e]The seed also of his servants shall inherit it: and they that love his name shall dwell therein.

Deliverance from persecutors

70:1–5pp — Ps. 40:13–17

To the chief Musician,
A Psalm of David,
[f]to bring to remembrance.

70 *MAKE HASTE,* [g]O God, to deliver me; make haste [n]to help me, O LORD.

2 [h]Let them be ashamed and confounded that seek after my soul: let them be turned backward, and put to confusion, that desire my hurt.

3 [i]Let them be turned back for a

69:10 [a]Ps. 35:13
69:11 [b]Jer. 24:9
69:12 [c]Job 30:9
69:13 [d]Is. 49:8
69:14 [e]Ps. 144:7 [f]ver. 1,2,15
69:15 [g]Num. 16:33
69:16 [h]Ps. 25:16
69:17 [i]Ps. 27:9
69:19 [j]Ps. 22:6,7 Is. 53:3
69:20 [k]Is. 63:5 [l]Job 16:2
69:21 [m]Mat. 27:34 Mark 15:23 John 19:29
69:22 [n]Rom. 11:9
69:23 [o]Is. 6:9,10 Rom. 11:10
69:24 [p]1 Thes. 2:16
69:25 [q]Mat. 23:38
69:26 [r]Is. 53:4
69:27 [s]Rom. 1:28 [t]Is. 26:10
69:28 [u]Ex. 32:32 Phil. 4:3 [v]Ezek. 13:9
69:30 [w]Ps. 28:7
69:31 [x]Ps. 50:13
69:32 [y]Ps. 34:2 [z]Ps. 22:26
69:33 [a]Eph. 3:1
69:34 [b]Ps. 96:11 & 148:1 Is. 44:23 [c]Is. 55:12
69:35 [d]Ps. 51:18 Is. 44:26
69:36 [e]Ps. 102:28
70:1 [f]Ps. 38,title [g]Ps. 40:13
70:2 [h]Ps. 35:4,26
70:3 [i]Ps. 40:15

[e] Heb. *drinkers of strong drink* [f] Heb. *make haste to hear me* [g] Heb. *to lament* with me [h] Heb. *their palace* [i] Heb. *let there not be a dweller* [j] Heb. *thy wounded* [k] Or, *punishment of iniquity* [l] Or, *meek* [m] Heb. *creepeth* [n] Heb. *to my help*

69:22–28 LET THEIR TABLE BECOME A SNARE BEFORE THEM. The psalmist prays for judgment to come on those who oppose God and inflict suffering upon the righteous. Paul applied these verses to those Jews who continued to reject Christ and His salvation (Rom. 11:9–10).

reward of their shame that say, Aha,
aha.
4 Let all those that seek thee re-
joice and be glad in thee: and let such
as love thy salvation say continually,
Let God be magnified.
5 [j]But I *am* poor and needy:
[k]make haste unto me, O God: thou *art*
my help and my deliverer; O LORD,
make no tarrying.

The prayer of an aged man

71:1–3pp — Ps. 31:1–4

71 IN [l]THEE, O LORD, do I put my
trust: let me never be put to
confusion.
2 [m]Deliver me in thy righteous-
ness, and cause me to escape: [n]incline
thine ear unto me, and save me.
3 [o]Be[o] thou my strong habitation,
whereunto I may continually resort:
thou hast given [p]commandment to
save me; for thou *art* my rock and my
fortress.
4 [q]Deliver me, O my God, out of
the hand of the wicked, out of the hand
of the unrighteous and cruel man.
5 For thou *art* [r]my hope, O Lord
GOD: *thou art* my trust from my youth.
6 [s]By thee have I been holden up
from the womb: thou art he that took
me out of my mother's bowels: my
praise *shall be* continually of thee.
7 [t]I am as a wonder unto many;
but thou *art* my strong refuge.
8 Let [u]my mouth be filled *with* thy
praise *and with* thy honour all the day.
9 [v]Cast me not off in the time of old
age; forsake me not when my strength
faileth.
10 For mine enemies speak against
me; and they that [p]lay wait for my
soul [w]take counsel together,
11 Saying, God hath forsaken him:
persecute and take him; for *there is*
none to deliver *him*.

70:5 [j]Ps. 40:17 [k]Ps. 141:1 **71:1** [l]Ps. 25:2,3 **71:2** [m]Ps. 31:1 [n]Ps. 17:6 **71:3** [o]Ps. 31:2,3 [p]Ps. 44:4 **71:4** [q]Ps. 140:1,4 **71:5** [r]Jer. 17:7 **71:6** [s]Ps. 22:9,10 Is 46:3 **71:7** [t]Is. 8:18 **71:8** [u]Ps. 35:28 **71:9** [v]ver. 18 **71:10** [w]2 Sam. 17:1 Mat. 27:1

71:12 [x]Ps. 35:22 [y]Ps. 70:1 **71:13** [z]ver. 24 **71:15** [a]Ps. 35:28 [b]Ps. 40:5 **71:18** [c]ver. 9 **71:19** [d]Ps. 57:10 [e]Ps. 35:10 **71:20** [f]Ps. 60:3 [g]Hos. 6:1,2 **71:22** [h]Ps. 92:1-3 [i]2 Ki. 19:22 Is. 60:9 **71:23** [j]Ps. 103:4

12 [x]O God, be not far from me:
O my God, [y]make haste for my help.
13 [z]Let them be confounded *and*
consumed that are adversaries to my
soul; let them be covered *with* reproach
and dishonour that seek my hurt.
14 But I will hope continually, and
will yet praise thee more and more.
15 [a]My mouth shall show forth thy
righteousness *and* thy salvation all the
day; for [b]I know not the numbers
thereof.
16 I will go in the strength of the
Lord GOD: I will make mention of thy
righteousness, *even* of thine only.
17 O God, thou hast taught me from
my youth: and hitherto have I declared
thy wondrous works.
18 [c]Now also [q]when I am old and
grayheaded, O God, forsake me not;
until I have shown [r]thy strength unto
this generation, *and* thy power to every
one *that* is to come.
19 [d]Thy righteousness also,
O God, *is* very high, who hast done
great things: [e]O God, who *is* like unto
thee!
20 [f]*Thou,* which hast shown me
great and sore troubles, [g]shalt
quicken me again, and shalt bring me
up again from the depths of the earth.
21 Thou shalt increase my great-
ness, and comfort me on every side.
22 I will also praise thee [h]with[s]
the psaltery, *even* thy truth, O my God:
unto thee will I sing with the harp, O
thou [i]Holy One of Israel.
23 My lips shall greatly rejoice
when I sing unto thee; and [j]my soul,
which thou hast redeemed.
24 My tongue also shall talk of thy
righteousness all the day long: for they

[o] Heb. *Be thou to me for a rock of habitation*
[p] Heb. *watch,* or, *observe* [q] Heb. *unto old age and gray hairs* [r] Heb. *thine arm* [s] Heb. *with the instrument of psaltery*

71:1–24 I PUT MY TRUST. This psalm contains a prayer by an older person (v. 9) who faces troubles and needs God's help to rescue him from his enemies and afflictions (vv. 1–2,18). He has walked in God's ways since childhood (vv. 5–6,17) and experienced exceptional troubles in life (v. 20), yet he has maintained his faith and confidence in God. He is determined to live the rest of his life with the confidence that God will manifest His power and goodness in his life.

71:9 IN TIMES OF OLD AGE. When strength is failing and the troubles of aging are more evident, we should recall God's guidance in days gone by and look unto Him as our protector, helper, and sustainer for the last days of life. And at the hour of death when physical strength fails, we should know that He will not forsake us but will be near (vv. 12,18) as He brings us by the holy angels into His heavenly presence (Luke 16:22).

71:18 UNTIL I HAVE SHOWN . . THY POWER TO EVERYONE *THAT* IS TO COME. Our hope and purpose in life should be to abide in God and in the fullness of His Spirit, so that His power and goodness might be clearly manifested in our lives. Thus the next generation will be inspired to seek earnestly God's kingdom and His righteousness (Mat. 6:33; cf. Acts 1:8; 4:30–33; 11:24).

are confounded, for they are brought unto shame, that seek my hurt.

A prayer for the king

A Psalm [k]for[t] Solomon.

72 GIVE THE king thy judgments, O God, and thy righteousness unto the king's son.

2 [l]He shall judge thy people with righteousness, and thy poor with judgment.

3 [m]The mountains shall bring peace to the people, and the little hills, by righteousness.

4 [n]He shall judge the poor of the people, he shall save the children of the needy, and shall break in pieces the oppressor.

5 They shall fear thee [o]as long as the sun and moon endure, throughout all generations.

6 [p]He shall come down like rain upon the mown grass: as showers *that* water the earth.

7 In his days shall the righteous flourish; [q]and abundance of peace [u]so long as the moon endureth.

8 [r]He shall have dominion also from sea to sea, and from the river unto the ends of the earth.

9 [s]They that dwell in the wilderness shall bow before him; [t]and his enemies shall lick the dust.

10 [u]The kings of Tarshish and of the isles shall bring presents: the kings of Sheba and Seba shall offer gifts.

11 [v]Yea, all kings shall fall down before him: all nations shall serve him.

12 For he [w]shall deliver the needy when he crieth; the poor also, and *him* that hath no helper.

13 He shall spare the poor and needy, and shall save the souls of the needy.

14 He shall redeem their soul from deceit and violence: and [x]precious shall their blood be in his sight.

15 And he shall live, and to him [v]shall be given of the gold of Sheba: prayer also shall be made for him continually; *and* daily shall he be praised.

16 There shall be an handful of corn in the earth upon the top of the mountains; the fruit thereof shall shake like Lebanon: [y]and *they* of the city shall flourish like grass of the earth.

17 [z]His name [w]shall endure for ever: [x]his name shall be continued as long as the sun: and [a]*men* shall be blessed in him: [b]all nations shall call him blessed.

18 [c]Blessed *be* the LORD God, the God of Israel, [d]who only doeth wondrous things.

19 And [e]blessed *be* his glorious name for ever: [f]and let the whole earth be filled *with* his glory; Amen, and Amen.

20 The prayers of David the son of Jesse are ended.

BOOK III

God delivers the righteous

[y]A Psalm of [g]Asaph.

73 TRULY[z] GOD *is* good to Israel, *even* to such as are [a]of a clean heart.

2 But as for me, my feet were almost gone; my steps had well nigh slipped.

3 [h]For I was envious at the foolish, *when* I saw the prosperity of the wicked.

[t] Or, *of* [u] Heb. *till* there be *no moon*
[v] Heb. one *shall give* [w] Heb. *shall be*
[x] Heb. *shall be as a son to continue his father's name for ever* [y] Or, *A Psalm for Asaph*
[z] Or, *Yet* [a] Heb. *clean of heart*

72:1 [k]Ps. 127,title
72:2 [l]Is. 32:1
72:3 [m]Ps. 85:10 Is. 32:17
72:4 [n]Is. 11:4
72:5 [o]ver. 7:17
72:6 [p]Hos. 6:3
72:7 [q]Is. 2:4 Jer. 33:6 Luke 1:33
72:8 [r]Ex. 23:31 Zech. 9:10
72:9 [s]Ps. 74:14 [t]Is. 49:23
72:10 [u]2 Chr. 9:21
72:11 [v]Is. 49:23
72:12 [w]Job 29:12
72:14 [x]Ps. 116:15
72:16 [y]1 Ki. 4:20
72:17 [z]Ps. 89:36 [a]Gen. 12:3 Jer. 4:2 [b]Luke 1:48
72:18 [c]1 Chr. 29:10 [d]Ex. 15:11
72:19 [e]Neh. 9:5 [f]Num. 14:21 Hab. 2:14
73:1 [g]Ps. 50,title
73:3 [h]Job 21:7 Ps. 37:1

72:1–19 THE KING. According to the title, this psalm is a prayer of Solomon as Israel's king, that his reign will be characterized by justice, righteousness, peace, the destruction of evil, and deliverance for the oppressed and needy. It also points to the reign of Jesus Christ over the world (see Rev. 20—22), since several of its verses apply fully only to Him (vv. 8,11,17; cf. Is. 11:1–5; 60—62). This prayer is similar to the N.T. prayer: "Thy kingdom come. Thy will be done in earth, as *it is* in heaven" (Mat. 6:10). This type of prayer should arise from the hearts of those who desire to see Christ reign as king and His righteousness established on the earth (see Rev. 21:1, note).

73:1–28 GOD *IS* GOOD TO ISRAEL. This psalm deals with a disturbing problem: though God is sovereign and just, the wicked often prosper (vv. 3–12) while those who serve God seem to suffer more (vv. 13–14). The psalmist, who has served God faithfully (vv. 1,13), has become discouraged when he compared his afflictions with the apparent ease and happiness of many of the wicked (vv. 2–3). However, his confidence in God and in His ways is restored when God reveals the tragic end of the wicked and the true blessing of the righteous (vv. 16–28).

4 For *there are* no bands in their death: but their strength *is* [b]firm.

5 [i]They *are* not [c]in trouble *as other* men; neither are they plagued [d]like *other* men.

6 Therefore pride compasseth them about as a chain; violence covereth them [j]*as* a garment.

7 [k]Their eyes stand out with fatness: [e]they have more than heart could wish.

8 [l]They are corrupt, and speak wickedly *concerning* oppression: they [m]speak loftily.

9 They set their mouth [n]against the heavens, and their tongue walketh through the earth.

10 Therefore his people return hither: [o]and waters of a full *cup* are wrung out to them.

11 And they say, [p]How doth God know? and is there knowledge in the most High?

12 Behold, these *are* the ungodly, who prosper in the world; they increase *in* riches.

13 [q]Verily I have cleansed my heart *in* vain, and [r]washed my hands in innocency.

14 For all the day long have I been plagued, and [f]chastened every morning.

15 If I say, I will speak thus; behold, I should offend *against* the generation of thy children.

16 [s]When I thought to know this, [g]it *was* too painful for me;

17 Until [t]I went into the sanctuary of God; *then* understood I [u]their end.

18 Surely [v]thou didst set them in slippery places: thou castedst them down into destruction.

19 How are they *brought* into desolation, as in a moment! they are utterly consumed with terrors.

20 [w]As a dream when *one* awaketh; *so,* O Lord, when thou awakest, thou shalt despise their image.

21 Thus my heart was grieved, and I was pricked in my reins.

22 [x]So foolish *was* I, and [h]ignorant: I was *as* a beast [i]before thee.

23 Nevertheless I *am* continually with thee: thou hast holden *me* by my right hand.

24 [y]Thou shalt guide me with thy counsel, and afterward receive me *to* glory.

25 [z]Whom have I in heaven *but thee?* and *there is* none upon earth *that* I desire beside thee.

26 [a]My flesh and my heart faileth: *but* God *is* the [j]strength of my heart, and my portion for ever.

27 For, lo, [b]they that are far from thee shall perish: thou hast destroyed all them that go a-whoring from thee.

28 But *it is* good for me to [c]draw near to God: I have put my trust in the Lord GOD, that I may declare all thy works.

A plea for relief

[k]Maschil of Asaph.

74 O GOD, why hast thou [d]cast *us* off for ever? *why* doth thine anger [e]smoke against [f]the sheep of thy pasture?

2 Remember thy congregation, *which* thou hast purchased of old; the

73:5 [i]Job 21:9
73:6 [j]Ps. 109:18
73:7 [k]Jer. 5:28
73:8 [l]Ps. 53:1 [m]Jude 16
73:9 [n]Rev. 13:6
73:10 [o]Ps. 75:8
73:11 [p]Job 22:13
73:13 [q]Job 34:9 Mal. 3:14 [r]Ps:26:6
73:16 [s]Eccl. 8:17
73:17 [t]Ps. 77:13 [u]Ps. 37:38
73:18 [v]Ps. 35:6
73:20 [w]Job 20:8 Ps. 90:5
73:22 [x]Ps. 92:6 Prov. 30:2
73:24 [y]Ps. 32:8 & 48:14
73:25 [z]Phil. 3:8
73:26 [a]Ps. 84:2 & 119:81
73:27 [b]Ps. 119:155
73:28 [c]Heb. 10:22
74:1 [d]Ps. 44:9,23 Jer. 31:37 [e]Deut. 29:20 [f]Ps. 95:7

[b] Heb. *fat* [c] Heb. *in the trouble of* other *men* [d] Heb. *with* [e] Heb. *they pass the thoughts of the heart* [f] Heb. *my chastisement* was [g] Heb. *it* was *labour in mine eyes* [h] Heb. *I knew not* [i] Heb. *with thee* [j] Heb. *rock* [k] Or, A Psalm *for Asaph to give instruction*

73:17 UNDERSTOOD I THEIR END. God shows the psalmist the destiny of the wicked. (1) This revelation puts his problem in the perspective both of eternity (vv. 17–20) and of the believer's highest blessing (vv. 25–28). In the end all the righteous will succeed and triumph with God, while the wicked will perish. (2) Given the brief span of our lives, if we evaluate things simply from our limited, earth-bound, human perspective, we will almost certainly become discouraged and filled with despair. We must have God's revealed Word and His Holy Spirit in order to complete our life's journey in faith and confidence in God's goodness and justice.

73:23–28 NEVERTHELESS I *AM* CONTINUALLY WITH THEE. The psalmist discovers the attitude that leads to the triumph of faith. In this life with all its problems, our greatest good is intimate communion with God (v. 28). Let the wicked prosper; our hope, treasure, and life is God Himself—always with us, guiding us by His word and Spirit, upholding us by His power (vv. 23–24), and afterward receiving us into the glories of heaven (v. 24). Like the apostle Paul, our motto as we face the anxieties of life should be: "For me to live *is* Christ, and to die *is* gain" (Phil. 1:21)

74:1–23 O GOD, WHY. The psalmist prays that God's chastisement may not be forever. This prayer is a warning that God's patience will not tolerate sin indefinitely; eventually sorrow and calamity will come.

[1]rod of thine inheritance, *which* thou
hast redeemed; this mount Zion,
wherein thou hast dwelt.
3 Lift up thy feet unto the perpetual
desolations; *even* all *that* the enemy
hath done wickedly in the sanctuary.
4 Thine enemies roar in the midst of
thy congregations; [g]they set up their
ensigns *for* signs.
5 *A man* was famous according as
he had lifted up axes upon the thick
trees.
6 But now they break down the
carved work thereof at once with axes
and hammers.
7 [m]They have cast fire into thy
sanctuary, they have defiled *by casting
down* the dwellingplace of thy name to
the ground.
8 [h]They said in their hearts, Let us
[n]destroy them together: they have
burned up all the synagogues of God in
the land.
9 We see not our signs: [i]*there is* no
more any prophet: neither *is there*
among us any that knoweth how long.
10 O God, how long shall the adver-
sary reproach? shall the enemy blas-
pheme thy name for ever?
11 [j]Why withdrawest thou thy
hand, even thy right hand? pluck *it* out
of thy bosom.
12 For [k]God *is* my King of old,
working salvation in the midst of the
earth.
13 [l]Thou didst [n]divide the sea by
thy strength; [m]thou brakest the heads
of the [o]dragons in the waters.
14 Thou brakest the heads of levia-
than in pieces, *and* gavest him [n]*to be*
meat to the people inhabiting the wil-
derness.
15 [o]Thou didst cleave the fountain
and the flood: [p]thou driedst up
[p]mighty rivers.
16 The day *is* thine, the night also *is*
thine: thou hast prepared the light and
the sun.
17 Thou hast set all the borders of
the earth: [q]thou hast [q]made summer
and winter.
18 [r]Remember this, *that* the ene-
my hath reproached, O LORD, and *that*
[s]the foolish people have blasphemed
thy name.

74:4 [g]Dan. 6:27 **74:8** [h]Ps. 83:4 **74:9** [i]Amos 8:11 **74:11** [j]Lam. 2:3 **74:12** [k]Ps. 44:4 **74:13** [l]Ex. 14:21 [m]Is. 51:9,10 Ezek. 29:3 **74:14** [n]Num. 14:9 **74:15** [o]Ex. 17:5,6 Num. 20:11 [p]Josh. 3:13 **74:17** [q]Gen. 8:22 **74:18** [r]ver. 22 [s]Ps. 39:8

74:19 [t]Sol. 2:14 [u]Ps. 68:10 **74:20** [v]Gen. 17:7,8 Ps. 106:45 **74:22** [w]Ps. 89:51 **74:23** [x]Jonah 1:2 **75:1** [y]Ps. 57,title **75:4** [z]Zech. 1:21 **75:7** [a]Ps. 50:6 [b]1 Sam. 2:7 Dan. 2:21 **75:8** [c]Job 21:20 Jer. 25:15 Rev. 14:10 & 16:19 [d]Prov. 23:30

19 O deliver not the soul [t]of thy
turtledove unto the multitude *of the
wicked:* [u]forget not the congregation
of thy poor for ever.
20 [v]Have respect unto the cov-
enant: for the dark places of the
earth are full of the habitations of
cruelty.
21 O let not the oppressed return
ashamed: let the poor and needy praise
thy name.
22 Arise, O God, plead thine own
cause: [w]remember how the foolish
man reproacheth thee daily.
23 Forget not the voice of thine ene-
mies: the tumult of those that rise up
against thee [x]increaseth[r] continu-
ally.

The justice of God

To the chief Musician,
[y]Al-taschith,[s] A Psalm *or* Song
[t]of Asaph.

75 UNTO THEE, O God, do we
give thanks, *unto thee* do we
give thanks: for *that* thy name is near
thy wondrous works declare.
2 [u]When I shall receive the congre-
gation I will judge uprightly.
3 The earth and all the inhabitants
thereof are dissolved: I bear up the pil-
lars of it. Selah.
4 I said unto the fools, Deal not fool-
ishly: and to the wicked, [z]Lift not up
the horn:
5 Lift not up your horn on high:
speak *not with* a stiff neck.
6 For promotion *cometh* neither
from the east, nor from the west, nor
from the [v]south.
7 But [a]God *is* the judge: [b]he
putteth down one, and setteth up an-
other.
8 For [c]in the hand of the LORD *there
is* a cup, and the wine is red; it is [d]full

[1]Or, *tribe* [m]Heb. *They have sent thy sanctuary into the fire* [n]Heb. *break* [o]Or, *whales* [p]Heb. *rivers of strength* [q]Heb. *made them* [r]Heb. *ascendeth* [s]Or, *Destroy not* [t]Or, *for Asaph* [u]Or, *When I shall take a set time* [v]Heb. *desert*

75:8 IN THE HAND OF THE LORD *THERE IS* A CUP. The picture of God giving the wicked an intoxicating drink is used in Scripture as a symbol of His wrath and punishment. Ps. 60:3 states: "Thou hast made us to drink the wine of astonishment," i.e., wine that makes us stagger (cf. Is. 51:17,22; Jer. 51:7; Rev. 14:10).

of mixture; and he poureth out of the same: [e]but the dregs thereof, all the wicked of the earth shall wring *them* out, *and* drink *them.*

9 But I will declare for ever; I will sing praises to the God of Jacob.

10 [f]All the horns of the wicked also will I cut off; *but* [g]the horns of the righteous shall be exalted.

The victorious power of God

To the chief Musician on Neginoth, A Psalm *or* Song [w]of Asaph.

76 IN [h]JUDAH *is* God known: his name *is* great in Israel.

2 In Salem also is his tabernacle, and his dwellingplace in Zion.

3 [i]There brake he the arrows of the bow, the shield, and the sword, and the battle. Selah.

4 Thou *art* more glorious *and* excellent [j]than the mountains of prey.

5 [k]The stout-hearted are spoiled, [l]they have slept their sleep: and none of the men of might have found their hands.

6 [m]At thy rebuke, O God of Jacob, both the chariot and horse are cast into a dead sleep.

7 Thou, *even* thou, *art* to be feared: and [n]who may stand in thy sight when once thou art angry?

8 [o]Thou didst cause judgment to be heard from heaven; [p]the earth feared, and was still,

9 When God [q]arose to judgment, to save all the meek of the earth. Selah.

10 [r]Surely the wrath of man shall praise thee: the remainder of wrath shalt thou restrain.

11 [s]Vow, and pay unto the LORD your God: [t]let all that be round about him bring presents [x]unto him that ought to be feared.

12 He shall cut off the spirit of princes: [u]*he is* terrible to the kings of the earth.

75:8 [e]Ps. 73:10 **75:10** [f]Ps. 101:8 Jer. 48:25 [g]Ps. 89:17 & 148:14 **76:1** [h]Ps. 48:1 **76:3** [i]Ps. 46:9 Ezek. 39:9 **76:4** [j]Ezek. 38:12 **76:5** [k]Is. 46:12 [l]Ps. 13:3 Jer. 51:39 **76:6** [m]Ex. 15:1,21 Ezek. 39:20 Nah. 2:13 Zech. 12:4 **76:7** [n]Nah. 1:6 **76:8** [o]Ex. 19:10 [p]2 Chr. 20:29,30 **76:9** [q]Ps. 9:7-9 & 72:4 **76:10** [r]Ps. 65:7 Dan. 3:28 **76:11** [s]Eccl. 5:4-6 [t]2 Chr. 32:22,23 Ps. 68:29 **76:12** [u]Ps. 68:35 **77:1** [v]Ps. 39,title & 62,title [w]Ps. 3:4 **77:2** [x]Ps. 50:15 [y]Is. 26:9,16 **77:3** [z]Ps. 143:4 **77:5** [a]Deut. 32:7 Ps. 143:5 Is. 51:9 **77:6** [b]Ps. 42:8 [c]Ps. 4:4 **77:7** [d]Ps. 74:1 [e]Ps. 85:1 **77:8** [f]Rom. 9:6 **77:9** [g]Is. 49:15 **77:10** [h]Ps. 31:22 **77:11** [i]Ps. 143:5 **77:13** [j]Ps. 73:17 [k]Ex. 15:11 **77:15** [l]Ex. 6:6 Deut. 9:29 **77:16** [m]Ex. 14:21

The call to God for help

To the chief Musician, [v]to Jeduthun, A Psalm [w]of Asaph.

77 I [w]CRIED unto God with my voice, *even* unto God with my voice; and he gave ear unto me.

2 [x]In the day of my trouble I [y]sought the Lord: [y]my sore ran in the night, and ceased not: my soul refused to be comforted.

3 I remembered God, and was troubled: I complained, and [z]my spirit was overwhelmed. Selah.

4 Thou holdest mine eyes waking: I am so troubled that I cannot speak.

5 [a]I have considered the days of old, the years of ancient times.

6 I call to remembrance [b]my song in the night: [c]I commune with mine own heart: and my spirit made diligent search.

7 [d]Will the Lord cast off for ever? and will he [e]be favourable no more?

8 Is his mercy clean gone for ever? doth [f]*his* promise fail [z]for evermore?

9 Hath God [g]forgotten to be gracious? hath he in anger shut up his tender mercies? Selah.

10 And I said, This *is* [h]my infirmity: *but I will remember* the years of the right hand of the most High.

11 [i]I will remember the works of the LORD: surely I will remember thy wonders of old.

12 I will meditate also of all thy work, and talk of thy doings.

13 [j]Thy way, O God, *is* in the sanctuary: [k]who *is so* great a God as *our* God?

14 Thou *art* the God that doest wonders: thou hast declared thy strength among the people.

15 [l]Thou hast with *thine* arm redeemed thy people, the sons of Jacob and Joseph. Selah.

16 [m]The waters saw thee, O God,

[w] Or, *for Asaph* [x] Heb. *to fear* [y] Heb. *my hand* [z] Heb. *to generation and generation?*

76:10 THE WRATH OF MAN SHALL PRAISE THEE. The wrath of the wicked can provide the occasion for God to rescue His own and to accomplish great things on their behalf; e.g., Pharaoh's wrath against Israel became God's opportunity to demonstrate His miraculous power in delivering them from Egypt (Ex. 5—12).

77:1–20 I CRIED UNTO GOD. This psalm portrays a person in great trouble who cried unto God but could find no evidence that He was responding (vv. 7–9). Faithful believers sometimes find themselves in a similar situation. If so, they should do as this psalmist did: continue to call on God day and night (vv. 1–2) while remembering God's past deeds of love. In the fullness of God's revelation in His Son, we are reassured that "he . . . spared not his own Son, but delivered him up for us all, how shall he not with him also freely give us all things?" (Rom. 8:32).

the waters saw thee; they were afraid:
the depths also were troubled.
17 [a]The clouds poured out water:
the skies sent out a sound: [n]thine ar-
rows also went abroad.
18 The voice of thy thunder *was* in
the heaven: the lightnings lightened
the world: [o]the earth trembled and
shook.
19 [p]Thy way *is* in the sea, and thy
path in the great waters, [q]and thy
footsteps are not known.
20 [r]Thou leddest thy people like a
flock by the hand of Moses and Aaron.

God's guidance of his people

[s]Maschil[b] of Asaph.

78 GIVE[t] EAR, O my people, *to*
my law: incline your ears to the
words of my mouth.
2 [u]I will open my mouth in a para-
ble: I will utter dark sayings of old:
3 [v]Which we have heard and
known, and our fathers have told us.
4 [w]We will not hide *them* from their
children, [x]showing to the generation
to come the praises of the LORD, and his
strength, and his wonderful works that
he hath done.

77:17 [n]2 Sam. 22:15
77:18 [o]2 Sam. 22:8
77:19 [p]Hab. 3:15 [q]Ex. 14:28
77:20 [r]Ex. 13:21 Is. 63:11,12
78:1 [s]Ps. 74,title [t]Is. 51:4
78:2 [u]Mat. 13:35
78:3 [v]Ps. 44:1
78:4 [w]Deut. 6:7 Joel 1:3 [x]Ex. 13:8,14
78:5 [y]Ps. 147:19 [z]Deut. 4:9
78:6 [a]Ps. 102:18
78:8 [b]2 Ki. 17:14 [c]Ex. 32:9 [d]ver. 37
78:10 [e]2 Ki. 17:15
78:11 [f]Ps. 106:13
78:12 [g]Ex. 7-12

5 For [y]he established a testimony
in Jacob, and appointed a law in Israel,
which he commanded our fathers,
[z]that they should make them known
to their children:
6 [a]That the generation to come
might know *them, even* the children
which should be born; *who* should arise
and declare *them* to their children:
7 That they might set their hope in
God, and not forget the works of God,
but keep his commandments:
8 And [b]might not be as their fa-
thers, [c]a stubborn and rebellious gen-
eration; a generation [d]*that*[c] set not
their heart aright, and whose spirit
was not stedfast with God.
9 The children of Ephraim, *being*
armed, *and* [d]carrying bows, turned
back in the day of battle.
10 [e]They kept not the covenant of
God, and refused to walk in his law;
11 And [f]forgat his works, and his
wonders that he had shown them.
12 [g]Marvellous things did he in the

Ps. 119:1-16

[a] Heb. *The clouds were poured forth with water*
[b] Or, A Psalm *for Asaph to give instruction*
[c] Heb. that *prepared not their heart* [d] Heb. *throwing forth*

78:1 GIVE EAR, O MY PEOPLE. This psalm was written to remind Israel why so many devastating judgments of God came upon them throughout their history. (1) The song warns them to learn from the spiritual failures of their forefathers and to strive diligently to avoid the same unbelief and unfaithfulness. (2) God's people today should pay close attention to this psalm, since many churches and denominations have lost the presence and power of God through unbelief and disobedience to God's word. By failing to make Biblical standards and experience the basis for truth and practice, they have gradually gone astray and turned to their own ways (cf. Is. 53:6).

78:5 THEY SHOULD MAKE THEM KNOWN TO THEIR CHILDREN. Teaching our children the godly principles and precepts of God's Word is not optional; it is a commandment He has given to His people. What God commands, He gives grace to fulfill (see Deut. 6:7, note; see article on PARENTS AND CHILDREN, p. 1880).

78:8 NOT BE AS THEIR FATHERS. God's people are exhorted not to follow in the unfaithful footsteps of their spiritual ancestors. Applied to the N.T. age, churches today should be careful not to pattern themselves after those churches, denominations, or fellowships that have grown cold and have departed from Biblical Christianity. Some errors that have brought spiritual ruin to a church are: (1) failure on the part of leaders to discern, and then warn the people, that they are beginning to imitate the unbiblical ways of former God-fearing churches; (2) failure to make the N.T. revelation of Christ and the apostles the only source of life, truth, and direction for the church (see Eph. 2:20, note); (3) failure to foster church purity in truth, doctrine, and moral matters (see article on OVERSEERS AND THEIR DUTIES, p. 1706); (4) failure to be greatly concerned as the church slides farther and farther from the N.T. norm; (5) failure to keep an intimate devotion to Christ and a fervent life of intercession central in the church's life (Rev. 2:4); (6) toleration of sin in church leaders, teachers, or laypersons that would have been severely dealt with in the past (Rev. 2:14–15,20); (7) substitution of an emphasis on outward success, numbers, and affluence for real spirituality, i.e., purity, righteouness, spiritual wisdom, love, and the Spirit's power manifested among the people (see article on CHRIST'S MESSAGE TO THE SEVEN CHURCHES, p. 2036).

78:8 SET NOT THEIR HEART ARIGHT, AND WHOSE SPIRIT WAS NOT STEDFAST WITH GOD. No generation of believers will inherit the kingdom of God in all its saving purpose and power if they fail to prepare their hearts to seek God and to discern His word and righteous ways. On the other hand, people whose hearts are set steadfastly toward God and who separate themselves from the corrupt world and all unholy compromise will know the glory, strength, and wonder of their God (v. 4; see article on SPIRITUAL SEPARATION FOR BELIEVERS, p. 1814).

78:11 THEY FORGAT HIS WORKS, AND HIS

sight of their fathers, in the land of Egypt, [h]*in* the field of Zoan.

13 [i]He divided the sea, and caused them to pass through; and [j]he made the waters to stand as an heap.

14 [k]In the daytime also he led them with a cloud, and all the night with a light of fire.

15 [l]He clave the rocks in the wilderness, and gave *them* drink as *out of* the great depths.

16 He brought [m]streams also out of the rock, and caused waters to run down like rivers.

17 And they sinned yet more against him by [n]provoking the most High in the wilderness.

18 And [o]they tempted God in their heart by asking meat for their lust.

19 [p]Yea, they spake against God; they said, Can God [e]furnish a table in the wilderness?

20 [q]Behold, he smote the rock, that the waters gushed out, and the streams overflowed; can he give bread also? can he provide flesh for his people?

21 Therefore the LORD heard *this,* and [r]was wroth: so a fire was kindled against Jacob, and anger also came up against Israel;

22 Because they [s]believed not in God, and trusted not in his salvation:

23 Though he had commanded the clouds from above, [t]and opened the doors of heaven,

24 [u]And had rained down manna upon them to eat, and had given them of the corn of heaven.

25 [f]Man did eat angels' food: he sent them meat to the full.

26 [v]He caused an east wind [g]to blow in the heaven: and by his power he brought in the south wind.

78:12 [h]Num. 13:22
78:13 [i]Ex. 14:21 [j]Ex. 15:8
78:14 [k]Ex. 13:21
78:15 [l]Num. 20:11
78:16 [m]Deut. 9:21
78:17 [n]Heb. 3:16
78:18 [o]Ex. 16:2
78:19 [p]Num. 11:4
78:20 [q]Num. 20:11
78:21 [r]Num. 11:1
78:22 [s]Heb. 3:18
78:23 [t]Mal. 3:10
78:24 [u]John 6:31
78:26 [v]Num. 11:31
78:29 [w]Num. 11:20
78:30 [x]Num. 11:33
78:32 [y]Num. 14 & 16 & 17 [z]ver. 22
78:33 [a]Num. 14:29
78:34 [b]Hos. 5:15
78:35 [c]Deut. 32:4,15,31 [d]Is. 41:14 & 63:9
78:36 [e]Ezek. 33:31
78:38 [f]Num. 14:18,20 [g]Is. 48:9 [h]1 Ki. 21:29
78:39 [i]Ps. 103:14 [j]John 3:6 [k]Job 7:7,16

27 He rained flesh also upon them as dust, and [h]feathered fowls like as the sand of the sea:

28 And he let *it* fall in the midst of their camp, round about their habitations.

29 [w]So they did eat, and were well filled: for he gave them their own desire;

30 They were not estranged from their lust. But [x]while their meat *was* yet in their mouths,

31 The wrath of God came upon them, and slew the fattest of them, and [i]smote down the [j]chosen *men* of Israel.

32 For all this [y]they sinned still, and [z]believed not for his wondrous works.

33 [a]Therefore their days did he consume in vanity, and their years in trouble.

34 [b]When he slew them, then they sought him: and they returned and inquired early after God.

35 And they remembered that [c]God *was* their rock, and the high God [d]their redeemer.

36 Nevertheless they did [e]flatter him with their mouth, and they lied unto him with their tongues.

37 For their heart was not right with him, neither were they stedfast in his covenant.

38 [f]But he, *being* full of compassion, forgave *their* iniquity, and destroyed *them* not: yea, many a time [g]turned he his anger away, [h]and did not stir up all his wrath.

39 For [i]he remembered [j]that they *were but* flesh; [k]a wind that

[e]Heb. *order* [f]Or, *Every one did eat the bread of the mighty* [g]Heb. *to go* [h]Heb. *fowl of wing* [i]Heb. *made to bow* [j]Or, *young men*

WONDERS. Israel failed spiritually, at least in part, because they forgot the deeds and miracles God had performed among their founding fathers. Likewise, we must not forget the works and miracles of God done in and through the faithful believers of the N.T. church. The Holy Spirit wants to act today with the same signs, wonders, and miracles that He performed in former days, so that the message of redemption might go forth through our lives and churches with the same power and effectiveness (see Acts 1:8, note; see article on BAPTISM IN THE HOLY SPIRIT, p. 1652).

78:37 THEIR HEART WAS NOT RIGHT . . . NEITHER WERE THEY STEDFAST IN HIS COVENANT. Israel failed to set their hearts to follow God faithfully and completely throughout their lives. Essential to maintaining a right relationship with God is the fundamental resolve to remain steadfast to God and His covenant until our day of final redemption.

78:38 BUT HE, *BEING* FULL OF COMPASSION, FORGAVE. God's patience and mercy are clearly revealed in this psalm. Over and over His people rebelled in unfaithfulness, yet God restrained His anger. God will never abandon His children simply because they fail to please Him perfectly. However, God's longsuffering and forgiveness must not be presumed upon in willful disobedience and rebellion. If we persistently grieve Him by our sin, He will eventually judge us in wrath, just as He did Israel (cf. Heb. 3:7–19).

passeth away, and cometh not again.
40 How oft did they [l]provoke[k]
him in the wilderness, *and* grieve him
in the desert!
41 Yea, [m]they turned back and
tempted God, and limited the Holy One
of Israel.
42 They remembered not his hand,
nor the day when he delivered them
[l]from the enemy.
43 How he had [m]wrought his signs
in Egypt, and his wonders in the field
of Zoan:
44 [n]And had turned their rivers
into blood; and their floods, that they
could not drink.
45 [o]He sent divers sorts of flies
among them, which devoured them;
and [p]frogs, which destroyed them.
46 He gave also their increase unto
the caterpillar, and their labour unto
the locust.
47 [q]He [n]destroyed their vines
with hail, and their sycamore trees
with [o]frost.
48 [r]He[p] gave up their cattle also
to the hail, and their flocks to [q]hot
thunderbolts.
49 He cast upon them the fierce-
ness of his anger, wrath, and indigna-
tion, and trouble, by sending evil an-
gels *among them.*
50 [r]He made a way to his anger;
he spared not their soul from death,
but gave [s]their life over to the pesti-
lence;
51 [s]And smote all the firstborn in
Egypt; the chief of *their* strength in
[t]the tabernacles of Ham:
52 But [u]made his own people to go
forth like sheep, and guided them in
the wilderness like a flock.
53 And he [v]led them on safely, so
that they feared not: but the sea
[w]overwhelmed[t] their enemies.
54 And he brought them to the bor-
der of his [x]sanctuary, *even to* this
mountain, [y]*which* his right hand had
purchased.
55 [z]He cast out the heathen also
before them, and [a]divided them an in-
heritance by line, and made the tribes
of Israel to dwell in their tents.
56 [b]Yet they tempted and pro-
voked the most high God, and kept not
his testimonies:
57 But [c]turned back, and dealt un-
faithfully like their fathers: they were
turned aside [d]like a deceitful bow.
58 [e]For they provoked him to an-
ger with their [f]high places, and
moved him to jealousy with their grav-
en images.
59 When God heard *this,* he was
wroth, and greatly abhorred Israel:
60 So that he forsook the taberna-
cle of Shiloh, the tent *which* he placed
among men;
61 [g]And delivered his strength
into captivity, and his glory into the en-
emy's hand.
62 [h]He gave his people over also
unto the sword; and was wroth with his
inheritance.
63 The fire consumed their young
men; and [i]their maidens were not
[u]given to marriage.
64 [j]Their priests fell by the sword;
and [k]their widows made no lamenta-
tion.
65 Then the Lord awaked as one
out of sleep, *and* [l]like a mighty man
that shouteth by reason of wine.
66 And [m]he smote his enemies in
the hinder parts: he put them to a per-
petual reproach.
67 Moreover he refused the taber-
nacle of Joseph, and chose not the tribe
of Ephraim:
68 But chose the tribe of Judah, the
mount Zion [n]which he loved.
69 And he built his sanctuary like
high *palaces,* like the earth which he
hath [v]established for ever.
70 [o]He chose David also his ser-
vant, and took him from the sheep-
folds:
71 [w]From following [p]the ewes
great with young he brought him [q]to
feed Jacob his people, and Israel his in-
heritance.
72 So he fed them according to the
[r]integrity of his heart; and guided
them by the skilfulness of his hands.

A lament for Jerusalem

A Psalm [x]of Asaph.

79 O GOD, the heathen are come
into [s]thine inheritance; thy
holy temple have they defiled; [t]they
have laid Jerusalem on heaps.
2 [u]The dead bodies of thy servants

78:40 [l]Ps. 95:8-10 Heb. 3:16
78:41 [m]Num. 14:22 Deut. 6:16
78:44 [n]Ex. 7:20 Ps. 105:29
78:45 [o]Ex. 8:24 Ps. 105:31 [p]Ex. 8:6
78:47 [q]Ex. 9:23,25 Ps. 105:33
78:48 [r]Ex. 9:23-25
78:51 [s]Ex. 12:29 [t]Ps. 106:22
78:52 [u]Ps. 77:20
78:53 [v]Ex. 14:19 [w]Ex. 14:27
78:54 [x]Ex. 15:17 [y]Ps. 44:3
78:55 [z]Ps. 44:2 [a]Josh. 13:7
78:56 [b]Judg. 2:11
78:57 [c]Ezek. 20:27 [d]Hos. 7:16
78:58 [e]Deut. 32:16,21 Judg. 2:12 [f]Deut. 12:2
78:61 [g]Judg. 18:30
78:62 [h]1 Sam. 4:10
78:63 [i]Jer. 7:34
78:64 [j]1 Sam. 22:18 [k]Job 27:15
78:65 [l]Is. 42:13
78:66 [m]1 Sam. 5:6
78:68 [n]Ps. 87:2
78:70 [o]1 Sam. 16:11,12
78:71 [p]Is. 40:11 [q]2 Sam. 5:2
78:72 [r]1 Ki. 9:4
79:1 [s]Ps. 74:2 [t]Mic. 3:12
79:2 [u]Jer. 7:33

[k] Or, *rebel against him* [l] Or, *from affliction* [m] Heb. *set* [n] Heb. *killed* [o] Or, *great hailstones* [p] Heb. *He shut up* [q] Or, *lightnings* [r] Heb. *He weighed a path* [s] Or, *their beasts to the murrain* [t] Heb. *covered* [u] Heb. *praised* [v] Heb. *founded* [w] Heb. *From after* [x] Or, *for Asaph*

have they given *to be* meat unto the
fowls of the heaven, the flesh of thy
saints unto the beasts of the earth.
3 Their blood have they shed like
water round about Jerusalem; and *there*
was none to bury *them.*
4 We are become a reproach to our
neighbours, a scorn and derision to
them that are round about us.
5 [v]How long, LORD? wilt thou be an-
gry for ever? shall thy [w]jealousy burn
like fire?
6 [x]Pour out thy wrath upon the
heathen that have [y]not known thee,
and upon the kingdoms that have [z]not
called upon thy name.
7 For they have devoured Jacob, and
laid waste his dwellingplace.
8 [a]O remember not against us
[y]former iniquities: let thy tender mer-
cies speedily prevent us: for we are
brought very low.
9 Help us, O God of our salvation,
for the glory of thy name: and deliver
us, and purge away our sins, [b]for thy
name's sake.
10 [c]Wherefore should the heathen
say, Where *is* their God? let him be
known among the heathen in our sight
by the [z]revenging of the blood of thy
servants *which is* shed.
11 Let [d]the sighing of the prisoner
come before thee; according to the
greatness of [a]thy power [b]preserve
thou those that are appointed to die;
12 And render unto our neighbours
[e]sevenfold into their bosom [f]their re-
proach, wherewith they have re-
proached thee, O Lord.
13 So [g]we thy people and sheep of
thy pasture will give thee thanks for
ever: [h]we will show forth thy praise
[c]to all generations.

79:5 [v]Ps. 74:1,9 [w]Zeph. 3:8 **79:6** [x]Jer. 10:25 Rev. 16:1 [y]Is. 45:4,5 2 Thes. 1:8 [z]Ps. 53:4 **79:8** [a]Is. 64:9 **79:9** [b]Jer. 14:7 **79:10** [c]Ps. 42:10 **79:11** [d]Ps. 102:20 **79:12** [e]Gen. 4:15 Is. 65:6,7 Jer. 32:18 Luke 6:38 [f]Ps. 74:18 **79:13** [g]Ps. 74:1 & 95:7 [h]Is. 43:21

80:1 [i]Ps. 45,title & 69,title [j]Ps. 77:20 [k]Deut. 33:2 Ps. 50:2 **80:3** [l]Lam. 5:21 [m]Num. 6:25 Ps. 4:6 **80:5** [n]Ps. 42:3 Is. 30:20 **80:8** [o]Is. 5:1,7 Jer. 2:21 Ezek. 15:6 [p]Ps. 44:2

A call to God for help

To the chief Musician [i]upon Shoshannim-Eduth, A Psalm [d]of Asaph.

80 GIVE EAR, O Shepherd of Isra-
el, thou that leadest Joseph
[j]like a flock; thou that dwellest *be-*
tween the cherubims, [k]shine forth.
2 Before Ephraim and Benjamin
and Manasseh stir up thy strength, and
[e]come *and* save us.
3 [l]Turn us again, O God, [m]and
cause thy face to shine; and we shall be
saved.
4 O LORD God of hosts, how long
[f]wilt thou be angry against the prayer
of thy people?
5 [n]Thou feedest them with the
bread of tears; and givest them tears to
drink in great measure.
6 Thou makest us a strife unto our
neighbours: and our enemies laugh
among themselves.
7 Turn us again, O God of hosts,
and cause thy face to shine; and we
shall be saved.
8 Thou hast brought [o]a vine out of
Egypt: [p]thou hast cast out the hea-
then, and planted it.
9 Thou preparedst *room* before it,
and didst cause it to take deep root,
and it filled the land.
10 The hills were covered with the
shadow of it, and the boughs thereof
were like [g]the goodly cedars.
11 She sent out her boughs unto the

[y] Or, *the iniquities of them that were before us* [z] Heb. *vengeance* [a] Heb. *thine arm* [b] Heb. *reserve the children of death* [c] Heb. *to generation and generation* [d] Or, *for Asaph* [e] Heb. *come for salvation to us* [f] Heb. *wilt thou smoke* [g] Heb. *the cedars of God*

79:1–13 THE HEATHEN ARE COME. The psalmist here intercedes with God to forgive Israel for her apostasy (vv. 8–9) and to punish the nations that have destroyed Jerusalem and God's temple (vv. 6–7; Jerusalem was destroyed by the Babylonians in 586 B.C.). He acknowledges that the pagan nations were instruments of God's wrath (v. 5), yet what they had done against Israel was executed out of hatred for God and His chosen people (vv. 1–7; cf. Is. 10:5–11; 47:6–7). The psalmist is motivated by concern for God's glory and the promotion of His name among the unbelieving nations (vv. 9–13).

80:1–19 GIVE EAR, O SHEPHERD OF ISRAEL. In this psalm of intercession, the psalmist pleads for the revival and restoration of God's people to their place of full blessing and favor with God. (1) The psalm depicts a people whose divine protection has collapsed, laying them open to assaults from the outside (vv. 12–13). They have eaten the bread of tears and are objects of derision (vv. 5–6). In great humility, the psalmist repeatedly intercedes for God to show His favor once again and to cause His face to shine upon the remnant who call on His name (vv. 1,3,7,14–15,19).

(2) The sentiments of the psalm are characteristic of the plight and prayer of God's people immediately preceding a time of great revival.

(3) This psalm speaks to all believers, individually and corporately, who are not experiencing the full life, power, and righteousness of God as promised in His Word. We must pray that God will revive and renew us by His power and mercy.

sea, and her branches unto the river.
12 Why hast thou *then* [q]broken
down her hedges, so that all they
which pass by the way do pluck her?
13 The boar out of the wood doth
waste it, and the wild beast of the field
doth devour it.
14 Return, we beseech thee, O God
of hosts: [r]look down from heaven, and
behold, and visit this vine;
15 And the vineyard which thy right
hand hath planted, and the branch *that*
thou madest strong for thyself.
16 *It is* burned with fire, *it is* cut
down: [s]they perish at the rebuke of
thy countenance.
17 [t]Let thy hand be upon the man
of thy right hand, upon the son of man
whom thou madest strong for thyself.
18 So will not we go back from thee:
quicken us, and we will call upon thy
name.
19 Turn us again, O LORD God of
hosts, cause thy face to shine; and we
shall be saved.

God's goodness to Israel

To the chief Musician [u]upon Gittith,
A Psalm [h]of Asaph.

81 SING ALOUD unto God our
strength: make a joyful noise
unto the God of Jacob.
2 Take a psalm, and bring hither the
timbrel, the pleasant harp with the
psaltery.
3 Blow up the trumpet in the new
moon, in the time appointed, on our
solemn feast day.
4 For this *was* a statute for Israel,
and a law of the God of Jacob.
5 This he ordained in Joseph *for*
a testimony, when he went out
[i]through the land of Egypt: [v]*where* I
heard a language *that* I understood not.
6 I removed his shoulder from the
burden: his hands [j]were delivered
from the pots.
7 [w]Thou calledst in trouble, and I
delivered thee; [x]I answered thee in
the secret place of thunder: I [y]proved
thee at the waters of [k]Meribah. Selah.
8 [z]Hear, O my people, and I will
testify unto thee: O Israel, if thou wilt
hearken unto me;
9 There shall no [a]strange god be in
thee; neither shalt thou worship any
strange god.
10 [b]I *am* the LORD thy God, which
brought thee out of the land of Egypt:
[c]open thy mouth wide, and I will
fill it.
11 But my people would not heark-
en to my voice; and Israel would
[d]none of me.
12 [e]So I gave them up [l]unto their
own hearts' lust: *and* they walked in
their own counsels.
13 [f]Oh that my people had heark-
ened unto me, *and* Israel had walked in
my ways!
14 I should soon have subdued their
enemies, and turned my hand against
their adversaries.
15 [g]The haters of the LORD should
have [h][m]submitted themselves unto
him: but their time should have en-
dured for ever.
16 He should [i]have fed them also
[n]with the finest of the wheat: and with
honey [j]out of the rock should I have
satisfied thee.

Unjust judgments rebuked

A Psalm [h]of Asaph.

82 GOD [k]STANDETH in the con-
gregation of the mighty; he
judgeth among [l]the gods.
2 How long will ye judge unjustly,
and [m]accept the persons of the wick-
ed? Selah.
3 [o]Defend the poor and fatherless:
[n]do justice to the afflicted and needy.
4 [o]Deliver the poor and needy: rid
them out of the hand of the wicked.
5 They [p]know not, neither will
they understand; they walk on in dark-
ness: [q]all the foundations of the earth
are [p]out of course.
6 [r]I have said, Ye *are* gods; and all
of you *are* children of the most High.

80:12 [q]Is. 5:5 Nah. 2:2 **80:14** [r]Is. 63:15 **80:16** [s]Ps. 39:11 & 76:7 **80:17** [t]Ps. 89:21 **81:1** [u]Ps. 8,title **81:5** [v]Ps. 114:1 **81:7** [w]Ex. 2:23 Ps. 50:15 [x]Ex. 19:19 [y]Ex. 17:6,7 **81:8** [z]Ps. 50:7 **81:9** [a]Deut. 32:12 Is. 43:12 **81:10** [b]Ex. 20:2 [c]Ps. 103:5 **81:11** [d]Ex. 32:1 Deut. 32:15 **81:12** [e]Acts 7:42 **81:13** [f]Deut. 5:29 & 32:29 Is. 48:18 **81:15** [g]Rom. 1:30 [h]Ps. 18:44 **81:16** [i]Deut. 32:14 [j]Job 29:6 **82:1** [k]2 Chr. 19:6 [l]ver. 6 **82:2** [m]Deut. 1:17 **82:3** [n]Jer. 22:3 **82:4** [o]Job 29:12 Prov. 24:11 **82:5** [p]Mic. 3:1 [q]Ps. 11:3 **82:6** [r]Ex. 22:28 John 10:34

[h] Or, *for Asaph* [i] Or, *against* [j] Heb. *passed away* [k] Or, *Strife* [l] Or, *to the hardness of their hearts,* or, *imaginations* [m] Or, *yielded feigned obedience* [n] Heb. *with the fat of wheat* [o] Heb. *Judge* [p] Heb. *moved*

82:6 I HAVE SAID, YE *ARE* GODS. The term "gods" (Heb. *'elohim*) probably refers to human authorities and judges in Israel who were designated as God's representatives in administering justice, protecting the weak, and helping deliver them from their oppressors. The term in no way means that mere humans are potentially gods, but only that they can become God's representatives with power and authority to bring judgment and carry out justice (see John 10:34, note).

7 But [s]ye shall die like men, and
fall like one of the princes.
8 [t]Arise, O God, judge the earth:
[u]for thou shalt inherit all nations.

Prayer for Israel's defence

A Song *or* Psalm [q]of Asaph.

83 KEEP [v]NOT thou silence,
O God: hold not thy peace, and
be not still, O God.
2 For, lo, [w]thine enemies make a
tumult: and they that [x]hate thee have
lifted up the head.
3 They have taken crafty counsel
against thy people, and consulted
[y]against thy hidden ones.
4 They have said, Come, and [z]let
us cut them off from *being* a nation;
that the name of Israel may be no more
in remembrance.
5 For they have consulted together
with one [r]consent: they are confeder-
ate against thee:
6 [a]The tabernacles of Edom, and
the Ishmaelites; of Moab, and the
Hagarenes;
7 Gebal, and Ammon, and Amalek;
the Philistines with the inhabitants of
Tyre;
8 Assur also is joined with them:
[s]they have helped the children of Lot.
Selah.
9 Do unto them as *unto* the Midian-
ites; as *to* [b]Sisera, as *to* Jabin, at the
brook of Kison:
10 *Which* perished at En-dor: [c]they
became *as* dung for the earth.
11 Make their nobles like Oreb, and
like Zeeb: yea, all their princes as [d]Ze-
bah, and as Zalmunna:
12 Who said, Let us take to our-
selves the houses of God in possession.
13 [e]O my God, make them like a
wheel; [f]as the stubble before the
wind.
14 As the fire burneth a wood, and
as the flame [g]setteth the mountains
on fire;
15 So persecute them with thy tem-
pest, and make them afraid with thy
storm.
16 Fill their faces with shame; that
they may seek thy name, O LORD.
17 Let them be confounded and
troubled for ever; yea, let them be put
to shame, and perish:
18 [h]That *men* may know that thou,
whose [i]name alone *is* JEHOVAH, *art*
[j]the most high over all the earth.

Longing for the sanctuary

To the chief Musician [k]upon Gittith,
A Psalm [t]for the sons of Korah.

84 HOW [l]AMIABLE *are* thy tab-
ernacles, O LORD of hosts!
2 [m]My soul longeth, yea, even
fainteth for the courts of the LORD: my
heart and my flesh crieth out for the
living God.
3 Yea, the sparrow hath found an
house, and the swallow a nest for her-
self, where she may lay her young, *even*
thine altars, O LORD of hosts, my King,
and my God.
4 Blessed *are* they that dwell in thy
house: they will be still praising thee.
Selah.
5 Blessed *is* the man whose
strength *is* in thee; in whose heart *are*
the ways *of them.*
6 *Who* passing through the valley
[n]of [u] Baca make it a well; the rain
also [v]filleth the pools.
7 They go [o]from[w] strength to
strength, *every one of them* in Zion [p]ap-
peareth before God.
8 O LORD God of hosts, hear my
prayer: give ear, O God of Jacob. Selah.
9 Behold, [q]O God our shield, and
look upon the face of thine anointed.
10 For a day in thy courts *is* better
than a thousand. [x]I had rather be a
doorkeeper in the house of my God,

82:7 [s]Ps. 49:12 **82:8** [t]Mic. 7:2,7 [u]Ps. 2:8 Rev. 11:15 **83:1** [v]Ps. 28:1 **83:2** [w]Ps. 2:1 [x]Ps. 81:15 **83:3** [y]Ps. 27:5 **83:4** [z]Jer. 11:19 **83:6** [a]See 2 Chr. 20:1, 10,11 **83:9** [b]Judg. 4:15 **83:10** [c]Zeph. 1:17 **83:11** [d]Judg. 8:12 **83:13** [e]Is. 17:13 [f]Ps. 35:5 **83:14** [g]Deut. 32:22 **83:18** [h]Ps. 59:13 [i]Ex. 6:3 [j]Ps. 92:8 **84:1** [k]Ps. 8,title [l]Ps. 27:4 **84:2** [m]Ps. 42:1,2 **84:6** [n]2 Sam. 5:23 **84:7** [o]Prov. 4:18 [p]Deut. 16:16 **84:9** [q]ver. 11

[q] Or, *for Asaph* [r] Heb. *heart* [s] Heb. *they have been an arm to the children of Lot* [t] Or, *of* [u] Or, *of mulberry trees make him a well* [v] Heb. *covereth* [w] Or, *from company to company* [x] Heb. *I would choose rather to sit at the threshold*

84:1–12 HOW AMIABLE *ARE* THY TABERNACLES. This psalm describes believers who are so attached to God that they long above everything else to be in God's house and presence (cf. Ps. 42). Their greatest desire is to experience God's nearness, to worship Him with other faithful believers (v. 10), and to receive His blessings (see v. 4, note).

84:2 MY SOUL LONGETH . . . FOR THE COURTS OF THE LORD. See 42:2,6, notes on hungering and thirsting for the nearness of God.

84:4 BLESSED *ARE* THEY THAT DWELL IN THY HOUSE. Those who go to the house of the Lord seeking His presence will receive His blessing. This blessing includes the nearness of God, a renewed spiritual strength (vv. 5–7), answered prayer (v. 8), and grace, glory, and goodness (v. 11; see Luke 24:50, note).

than to dwell in the tents of wickedness.

11 For the LORD God *is* [r]a sun and [s]shield: the LORD will give grace and glory: [t]no good *thing* will he withhold from them that walk uprightly.

12 O LORD of hosts, [u]blessed *is* the man that trusteth in thee.

Prayer for mercy to Israel

To the chief Musician, A Psalm [v]for[y] the sons of Korah.

85 LORD, THOU hast been [w]favourable[z] unto thy land: thou hast [x]brought back the captivity of Jacob.

2 Thou hast forgiven the iniquity of thy people, thou hast covered all their sin. Selah.

3 Thou hast taken away all thy wrath: [a]thou hast turned *thyself* from the fierceness of thine anger.

✝ 4 [y]Turn us, O God of our salvation, and cause thine anger toward us to cease.

5 [z]Wilt thou be angry with us for ever? wilt thou draw out thine anger to all generations?

6 Wilt thou not [a]revive us again: that thy people may rejoice in thee?

Ps. 98:1-3 7 Show us thy mercy, O LORD, and grant us thy salvation.

8 [b]I will hear what God the LORD will speak: for [c]he will speak peace unto his people, and to his saints: but let them not [d]turn again to folly.

9 Surely [e]his salvation *is* nigh them that fear him; [f]that glory may dwell in our land.

10 Mercy and truth are met together; [g]righteousness and peace have kissed *each other.*

11 Truth shall spring out of the earth; and righteousness shall look down from heaven.

12 [h]Yea, the LORD shall give *that which is* good; and our land shall yield her increase.

13 [i]Righteousness shall go before him; and shall set *us* in the way of his steps.

Prayer for deliverance

[b]A Prayer of David.

86 BOW DOWN thine ear, O LORD, hear me: for I *am* poor and needy.

2 Preserve my soul; for I *am* [c]holy: O thou my God, save thy servant that trusteth in thee.

3 [j]Be merciful unto me, O Lord: for I cry unto thee [d]daily.

4 Rejoice the soul of thy servant: [k]for unto thee, O Lord, do I lift up my soul.

5 [l]For thou, Lord, *art* good, and ready to forgive; and plenteous in mercy unto all them that call upon thee.

6 Give ear, O LORD, unto my prayer; and attend to the voice of my supplications.

7 In the day of my trouble I will call upon thee: for thou wilt answer me.

8 [m]Among the gods *there is* none like unto thee, O Lord; [n]neither *are there any works* like unto thy works.

9 [o]All nations whom thou hast made shall come and worship before thee, O Lord; and shall glorify thy name.

10 For thou *art* great, and [p]doest wondrous things: [q]thou *art* God alone.

11 [r]Teach me thy way, O LORD; I

84:11 [r]Is. 60:19 [s]Gen. 15:1 Ps. 115:9 Prov. 2:7 [t]Ps. 34:9
84:12 [u]Ps. 2:12
85:1 [v]Ps. 42,title [w]Ps. 77:7 [x]Ezra 1:11 Jer. 30:18 Ezek. 39:25 Joel 3:1
85:4 [y]Ps. 80:7
85:5 [z]Ps. 79:5
85:6 [a]Hab. 3:2
85:8 [b]Hab. 2:1 [c]Zech. 9:10 [d]2 Pet. 2:20
85:9 [e]Is. 46:13 [f]Zech. 2:5
85:10 [g]Ps. 72:3 Is. 32:17 Luke 2:14
85:12 [h]Ps. 84:11 Jas. 1:17
85:13 [i]Ps. 89:14
86:3 [j]Ps. 56:1 & 57:1
86:4 [k]Ps. 25:1 & 143:8
86:5 [l]Ps. 130:7 & 145:9 Joel 2:13
86:8 [m]Ex. 15:11 Ps. 89:6 [n]Deut. 3:24
86:9 [o]Ps. 22:31 Is. 43:7 Rev. 15:4
86:10 [p]Ex. 15:11 Ps. 72:18 [q]Deut. 6:4 Mark 12:29
86:11 [r]Ps. 25:4

[y]Or, *of* [z]Or, *well pleased* [a]Or, *thou hast turned thine anger from waxing hot* [b]Or, *A Prayer, being a Psalm of David* [c]Or, *one whom thou favourest* [d]Or, *all the day*

84:11 NO GOOD *THING* WILL HE WITHHOLD. This promise is specifically directed to believers who sincerely endeavor to live godly and righteous lives. What God regards as good relates directly to our fulfilling His purpose for our lives. Our task is to walk uprightly and to trust God to furnish everything that is good—physically and spiritually, temporally and eternally (see 34:10; Mat. 6:33; Rom. 8:28; 1 Cor. 2:9; 1 Tim. 4:8).

85:6 WILT THOU NOT REVIVE US AGAIN. It is right for God's people to pray that He will revive them, both individually and corporately. Salvation and spiritual life are dependent upon God imparting to us His mercy, forgiveness, power, life-giving Spirit, and fervent desire to do His will (see John 3:16; 1 Cor. 15:10; Phil. 2:13; 1 Tim. 1:15–16). When we are at a low point spiritually, not experiencing spiritual blessings as God intended, then we should honestly confess our inner poverty and pray that God will revive us again (see 2 Chr. 17:9, note; 29:5, note; 34:30, note).

86:1 I *AM* POOR AND NEEDY. Prayer that arises out of humility, affliction, and great need is prayer that God will hear and answer. He has a special care for His people who are broken and needy (cf. 35:10; 74:21; Mat. 6:25–34; see Luke 11:3, note).

86:11 TEACH ME THY WAY, O LORD. In the midst of his affliction and trouble, the psalmist humbly asks God to teach him His ways and His

will walk in thy truth: unite my heart
to fear thy name.
12 I will praise thee, O Lord my
God, with all my heart: and I will glorify thy name for evermore.
13 For great *is* thy mercy toward
me: and thou hast delivered my soul
from the lowest [e]hell.
14 O God, the proud are risen
against me, and the assemblies of [f]violent *men* have sought after my soul;
and have not set thee before them.
15 [s]But thou, O Lord, *art* a God
full of compassion, and gracious, longsuffering, and plenteous in mercy and
truth.
16 O turn unto me, and have mercy
upon me; give thy strength unto thy
servant, and save the son of thine
handmaid.
17 Show me a token for good; that
they which hate me may see *it*, and be
ashamed: because thou, LORD, hast
helped me, and comforted me.

Privileges of living in Zion

A Psalm *or* Song [g]for the sons of Korah.

87 HIS FOUNDATION *is* in the holy mountains.
2 [t]The LORD loveth the gates of
Zion more than all the dwellings of Jacob.
3 [u]Glorious things are spoken of
thee, O city of God. Selah.
4 I will make mention of Rahab and
Babylon to them that know me: behold
Philistia, and Tyre, with Ethiopia; this
man was born there.
5 And of Zion it shall be said, This
and that man was born in her: and the
highest himself shall establish her.
6 The LORD shall count, when he
[v]writeth up the people, *that* this *man*
was born there. Selah.
7 As well the singers as the players
on instruments *shall be there:* all my
springs *are* in thee.

Prayer in the face of death

A Song *or* Psalm [g]for the sons of Korah, to the chief Musician upon Mahalath Leannoth, [h]Maschil of [w]Heman the Ezrahite.

88 O LORD [x]God of my salvation, I have cried day *and* night
before thee:
2 Let my prayer come before thee:
incline thine ear unto my cry;
3 For my soul is full of troubles: and
my life [y]draweth nigh unto the grave.
4 [z]I am counted with them that go
down into the pit: I am as a man *that
hath* no strength:
5 Free among the dead, like the
slain that lie in the grave, whom thou
rememberest no more: and they are
[a]cut off [i]from thy hand.
6 Thou hast laid me in the lowest
pit, in darkness, in the deeps.
7 Thy wrath lieth hard upon me, and
[b]thou hast afflicted *me* with all thy
waves. Selah.
8 [c]Thou hast put away mine acquaintance far from me; thou hast
made me an abomination unto them:
[d]*I am* shut up, and I cannot come
forth.
9 [e]Mine eye mourneth by reason of
affliction: LORD, [f]I have called daily
upon thee, [g]I have stretched out my
hands unto thee.
10 [h]Wilt thou show wonders to the

86:15 [s]Ex. 34:6 Neh. 9:17 Ps. 103:8 Joel 2:13
87:2 [t]Ps. 78:68
87:3 [u]See Is. 60
87:6 [v]Ezek. 13:9
88:1 [w]1 Ki. 4:31 1 Chr. 2:6 [x]Ps. 27:9
88:3 [y]Ps. 107:18
88:4 [z]Ps. 28:1
88:5 [a]Is. 53:8
88:7 [b]Ps. 42:7
88:8 [c]Job 19:13 [d]Lam. 3:7
88:9 [e]Ps. 38:10 [f]Ps. 86:3 [g]Ps. 143:6
88:10 [h]Ps. 6:5 Is. 38:18

[e] Or, *grave* [f] Heb. *terrible* [g] Or, *of* [h] Or, A Psalm *of Heman the Ezrahite, giving instruction* [i] Or, *by thy hand*

truth, that he might fear God from the heart. When we are experiencing trials and difficulties, we must cry out to God for wisdom to walk in His ways and for a heart that truly fears and delights in His truth.

88:1–18 I HAVE CRIED DAY *AND* NIGHT. Some regard this as the saddest of all psalms. The supplicant has suffered much (v. 3), perhaps as a leper (cf. v. 8). He feels that he is nearing death and that God has rejected him (vv. 7,14,16–18). He has cried day and night unto God and appears to have received no answer (vv. 1–2,13). He is dejected and has little hope. Yet in faith he will not let go of God; he confesses that the Lord is still the God of his salvation (v. 1). (1) The psalmist's experience is much like that of Job, though in this case we are not told the reason behind his suffering and apparent silence of God.

(2) This psalm reveals that God occasionally permits times of sadness and despair in a believer's life. It is a dark experience when there is no apparent reason for our problems and when God seems far away. Throughout such suffering, a measure of mystery will remain until we are with God in heaven. In the meantime, both faith in God as our salvation and our right relationship with Him are essential to get us through, and we must never forget that in the final analysis, "neither death, nor life . . . nor things present, nor things to come . . . shall be able to separate us from the love of God, which is in Christ Jesus our Lord" (Rom. 8:38–39).

dead? shall the dead arise *and* praise
thee? Selah.
11 Shall thy lovingkindness be de-
clared in the grave? *or* thy faithfulness
in destruction?
12 [i]Shall thy wonders be known in
the dark? and thy righteousness in the
land of forgetfulness?
13 But unto thee have I cried,
O LORD; and [j]in the morning shall my
prayer prevent thee.
14 LORD, why castest thou off my
soul? *why* [k]hidest thou thy face
from me?
15 I *am* afflicted and ready to die
from *my* youth up: *while* [l]I suffer thy
terrors I am distracted.
16 Thy fierce wrath goeth over me;
thy terrors have cut me off.
17 They came round about me
[j]daily like water; they [m]compassed
me about together.
18 [n]Lover and friend hast thou put
far from me, *and* mine acquaintance
into darkness.

God's covenant with David

[k]Maschil of [o]Ethan the Ezrahite.

89 I [p] WILL sing of the mercies
of the LORD for ever: with my
mouth will I make known thy faithful-
ness [q]to[1] all generations.
2 For I have said, Mercy shall be
built up for ever: [r]thy faithfulness
shalt thou establish in the very heav-
ens.
3 [s]I have made a covenant with my
chosen, I have [t]sworn unto David my
servant,
4 Thy seed will I establish for ever,
and build up thy throne [u]to all genera-
tions. Selah.
5 And [v]the heavens shall praise
thy wonders, O LORD: thy faithfulness
also in the congregation of the saints.
6 For who in the heaven can be com-
pared unto the LORD? *who* among the
sons of the mighty can be likened unto
the LORD?
7 [w]God is greatly to be feared in the
assembly of the saints, and to be had
in reverence of all *them that are* about
him.
8 O LORD God of hosts, who *is* a
strong LORD like unto thee? or to thy
faithfulness round about thee?
9 [x]Thou rulest the raging of the
sea: when the waves thereof arise,
thou stillest them.
10 [y]Thou hast broken [m]Rahab in
pieces, as one that is slain; thou hast
scattered thine enemies [n]with thy
strong arm.
11 [z]The heavens *are* thine, the
earth also *is* thine: *as for* the world and
the fulness thereof, thou hast founded
them.
12 The north and the south thou
hast created them: [a]Tabor and [b]Her-
mon shall rejoice in thy name.
13 Thou hast [o]a mighty arm:
strong is thy hand, *and* high is thy right
hand.
14 Justice and judgment *are* the
[p]habitation of thy throne: mercy and
truth shall go before thy face.
15 Blessed *is* the people that know
the [c]joyful sound: they shall walk,
O LORD, in the light of thy counte-
nance.
16 In thy name shall they rejoice all

88:12 [i]Job 10:21
88:13 [j]Ps. 5:3
88:14 [k]Job 13:24 Ps. 13:1
88:15 [l]Job 6:4
88:17 [m]Ps. 22:16
88:18 [n]Job 19:13
89:1 [o]1 Ki. 4:31 1 Chr. 2:6 [p]Ps. 101:1 [q]ver. 4 Ps. 119:90
89:2 [r]Ps. 119:89
89:3 [s]1 Ki. 8:16 1 Chr. 28:4 [t]2 Sam. 7:13
89:4 [u]Luke 1:33
89:5 [v]Ps. 19:1
89:7 [w]Ps. 76:7,11
89:9 [x]Ps. 65:7
89:10 [y]Ps. 87:4
89:11 [z]Gen. 1:1
89:12 [a]Josh. 19:22 [b]Josh. 12:1
89:15 [c]Ps. 98:6

[j] Or, *all the day* [k] Or, A Psalm *for Ethan the Ezrahite, to give instruction* [1] Heb. *to generation and generation* [m] Or, *Egypt* [n] Heb. *with the arm of thy strength* [o] Heb. *an arm with might* [p] Or, *establishment*

89:1–52 THY FAITHFULNESS. This psalm is a prayer dealing with the destruction of Jerusalem and the fallen dynasty of David, and with God's promise that David's line will remain forever (vv. 29,34–37; cf. 2 Sam. 7:8–16). The author questions whether God has failed to keep His pledge. He prays that God will restore His people and the throne of David, and remove His wrath from Israel (vv. 46–52). What the psalmist did not know was that even though God had punished Israel for her sins, He would keep His promise through Jesus Christ, who was of the line of David and whose kingdom will have no end (Luke 1:31–33).

89:4 THY SEED WILL I ESTABLISH FOR EVER. God's covenant promise to David was that his "seed," i.e., line, would rule on the throne forever (see also vv. 29,36–37). (1) It is obvious that God's promise did not involve all of David's descendants. When the Davidic kings disobeyed God, He removed them just as He delivered the northern kingdom over to its enemies and to captivity when the people persisted in apostasy (see vv. 38–51).

(2) The N.T. sees the fulfillment of this verse in the Lord Jesus Christ. The apostle Peter states: "Of the man's [David's] seed hath God according to *his* promise raised unto Israel a Saviour, Jesus" (Acts 13:23). And the angel Gabriel revealed to Mary: "and the Lord God shall give unto him [Jesus] the throne of his father David . . . and of his kingdom there shall be no end" (Luke 1:32–33; cf. 1:69).

the day: and in thy righteousness shall they be exalted.

17 For thou *art* the glory of their strength: and in thy favour our horn shall be exalted.

18 For [d]the[q] LORD *is* our defence; and the Holy One of Israel *is* our king.

19 Then thou spakest in vision to thy holy one, and saidst, I have laid help upon *one that is* mighty; I have exalted *one* [e]chosen out of the people.

20 [f]I have found David my servant; with my holy oil have I anointed him:

21 [g]With whom my hand shall be established: mine arm also shall strengthen him.

22 [h]The enemy shall not exact upon him; nor the son of wickedness afflict him.

23 [i]And I will beat down his foes before his face, and plague them that hate him.

24 But [j]my faithfulness and my mercy *shall be* with him: and in my name shall his horn be exalted.

25 I will set his hand also in the sea, and his right hand in the rivers.

26 He shall cry unto me, Thou *art* [k]my father, my God, and [l]the rock of my salvation.

27 Also I will make him [m]*my* firstborn, [n]higher than the kings of the earth.

28 [o]My mercy will I keep for him for evermore, and my covenant shall stand fast with him.

29 His seed also will I make *to endure* for ever, [p]and his throne [q]as the days of heaven.

30 [r]If his children [s]forsake my law, and walk not in my judgments;

31 If they [r]break my statutes, and keep not my commandments;

32 Then [t]will I visit their transgression with the rod, and their iniquity with stripes.

33 [u]Nevertheless my lovingkindness [s]will I not utterly take from him, nor suffer my faithfulness [t]to fail.

34 My covenant will I not break, nor alter the thing that is gone out of my lips.

35 Once have I sworn [v]by my holiness [u]that I will not lie unto David.

36 [w]His seed shall endure for ever, and his throne [x]as the sun before me.

37 It shall be established for ever as the moon, and *as* a faithful witness in heaven. Selah.

38 But thou hast [y]cast off and [z]abhorred, thou hast been wroth with thine anointed.

39 Thou hast made void the covenant of thy servant: [a]thou hast profaned his crown *by casting it* to the ground.

40 Thou hast broken down all his hedges; thou hast brought his strong holds to ruin.

41 All that pass by the way spoil him: he is [b]a reproach to his neighbours.

42 Thou hast set up the right hand of his adversaries; thou hast made all his enemies to rejoice.

43 Thou hast also turned the edge of his sword, and hast not made him to stand in the battle.

44 Thou hast made his [v]glory to cease, and cast his throne down to the ground.

45 The days of his youth hast thou shortened: thou hast covered him with shame. Selah.

46 [c]How long, LORD? wilt thou hide thyself for ever? shall thy wrath burn like fire?

47 [d]Remember how short my time is: wherefore hast thou made all men in vain?

48 [e]What man *is he that* liveth, and shall not [f]see death? shall he deliver his soul from the hand of the grave? Selah.

49 Lord, where *are* thy former lo-

89:18 [d]Ps. 47:9
89:19 [e]1 Ki. 11:34
89:20 [f]1 Sam. 16:1
89:21 [g]Ps. 80:17
89:22 [h]2 Sam. 7:10
89:23 [i]2 Sam. 7:9
89:24 [j]2 Sam. 7:15
89:26 [k]1 Chr. 22:10 [l]2 Sam. 22:47
89:27 [m]Col. 1:15 [n]Num. 24:7
89:28 [o]Is. 55:3
89:29 [p]Jer. 33:17 [q]Deut. 11:21
89:30 [r]2 Sam. 7:14 [s]Ps. 119:53 Jer. 9:13
89:32 [t]2 Sam. 7:14
89:33 [u]2 Sam. 7:15
89:35 [v]Amos 4:2
89:36 [w]Luke 1:33 [x]Ps. 72:17
89:38 [y]1 Chr. 28:9 [z]Deut. 32:19
89:39 [a]Lam. 5:16
89:41 [b]Ps. 44:13
89:46 [c]Ps. 79:5
89:47 [d]Job 7:7
89:48 [e]Ps. 49:9 [f]Heb. 11:5

[q] Or, *our shield* is *of the LORD, and our king* is *of the Holy One of Israel* [r] Heb. *profane my statutes* [s] Heb. *I will not make void from him* [t] Heb. *to lie* [u] Heb. *if I lie* [v] Heb. *brightness*

89:19–37 I HAVE EXALTED *ONE* CHOSEN. The psalmist reminds God of His election of David's line to rule over Israel and of His promise that David's dynasty would endure forever (vv. 27–29), in spite of the unfaithfulness of Israel (see previous note).

89:30 IF HIS CHILDREN FORSAKE MY LAW. God's promises in vv. 30–37 did not ensure the reign of David's descendants as kings forever, nor do they address the issue of the personal salvation of these kings. Rather, the promises were given to David to assure him that the unfaithfulness of Israel and her kings would not interfere with God's purpose to establish one of his descendants (i.e., Jesus) upon an everlasting throne (vv. 36–37).

vingkindnesses, *which* thou [g]swarest
unto David [h]in thy truth?
50 Remember, Lord, the reproach
of thy servants; [i]*how* I do bear in my
bosom *the reproach of* all the mighty
people;
51 [j]Wherewith thine enemies have
reproached, O LORD; wherewith they
have reproached the footsteps of thine
anointed.
52 [k]Blessed *be* the LORD for ever-
more. Amen, and Amen.

BOOK IV

Eternal God and mortal man

[w]A Prayer [l]of Moses
the man of God.

90 LORD, [m]THOU hast been our
dwellingplace [x]in all genera-
tions.
2 [n]Before the mountains were
brought forth, or ever thou hadst
formed the earth and the world, even
from everlasting to everlasting, thou
art God.
3 Thou turnest man to destruction;
and sayest, [o]Return, ye children of
men.
4 [p]For a thousand years in thy
sight *are but* as yesterday [y]when it is
past, and *as* a watch in the night.
5 Thou carriest them away as with
a flood; [q]they are *as* a sleep: in the
morning [r]*they are* like grass *which*
[z]groweth up.
6 In the morning it flourisheth, and
groweth up; in the evening it is cut
down, and withereth.
7 For we are consumed by thine an-
ger, and by thy wrath are we troubled.
8 [s]Thou hast set our iniquities be-
fore thee, our [t]secret *sins* in the light
of thy countenance.
9 For all our days are [a]passed
away in thy wrath: we spend our years
[b]as a tale *that is told.*
10 [c]The days of our years *are*
threescore years and ten; and if by rea-
son of strength *they be* fourscore years,
yet *is* their strength labour and sorrow;
for it is soon cut off, and we fly away.
11 Who knoweth the power of thine
anger? even according to thy fear, *so is*
thy wrath.
12 [u]So teach *us* to number our
days, that we may [d]apply *our* hearts
unto wisdom.
13 Return, O LORD, how long? and
let it [v]repent thee concerning thy ser-
vants.
14 O satisfy us early with thy mer-
cy; [w]that we may rejoice and be glad
all our days.
15 Make us glad according to the
days *wherein* thou hast afflicted us, *and*
the years *wherein* we have seen evil.
16 Let [x]thy work appear unto thy
servants, and thy glory unto their chil-
dren.
17 [y]And let the beauty of the LORD
our God be upon us: and [z]establish
thou the work of our hands upon us;
yea, the work of our hands establish
thou it.

89:49 [g]2 Sam. 7:15 [h]Ps. 54:5 **89:50** [i]Ps. 69:9,19 **89:51** [j]Ps. 74:22 **89:52** [k]Ps. 41:13 **90:1** [l]Deut. 33:1 [m]Ezek. 11:16 **90:2** [n]Prov. 8:25 **90:3** [o]Gen. 3:19 **90:4** [p]2 Pet. 3:8 **90:5** [q]Ps. 73:20 [r]Is. 40:6 **90:8** [s]Ps. 50:21 [t]Ps. 19:12 **90:12** [u]Ps. 39:4 **90:13** [v]Deut. 32:36 Ps. 135:14 **90:14** [w]Ps. 85:6 **90:16** [x]Hab. 3:2 **90:17** [y]Ps. 27:4 [z]Is. 26:12

[w]Or, *A Prayer,* being a Psalm *of Moses* [x]Heb. *in generation and generation* [y]Or, *when he hath passed* them [z]Or, *is changed* [a]Heb. *turned away* [b]Or, *as a meditation* [c]Heb. As for *the days of our years, in them* are *seventy years* [d]Heb. *cause to come*

90:1–17 LORD, THOU HAST BEEN OUR DWELLINGPLACE. This prayer, ascribed to Moses, was probably written during the forty years that God made Israel wander in the wilderness as punishment for their unfaithfulness (Deut. 8:15). A generation of disobedient Israelites died during this time (cf. vv. 7–11; see Num. 14:22–33). After acknowledging their iniquities and God's punishment, Moses prays for the restoration of God's favor and blessing.

90:2 FROM EVERLASTING TO EVERLASTING. This phrase refers to God's eternal existence, having neither beginning nor end. (1) "Everlasting" (Heb. *olam*) does not necessarily mean that God transcends time, but rather connotes His endless duration in time (cf. 48:14; Gen. 21:33; Job 10:5; 36:26). Scripture does not teach that God exists in some kind of eternal present, where there is neither past nor future. (2) Those passages in Scripture that affirm God's eternity do so in terms of continuation, not timelessness. God knows the past as past, the present as present, and the future as future.

90:12 TEACH *US* TO NUMBER OUR DAYS. Our days upon this earth, at best seventy to eighty years (cf. v. 10), are few when compared to eternity. We should pray for a sober understanding of the brevity of our lives so as to present to God a heart of wisdom in how we use each day He gives us (cf. 39:4). This life should be a preparation for the next life, and we should determine what God wants to accomplish for Himself, our families, and others through our faithful service. When our time here is over and we reach heaven, how we lived or did not live in dedication to God will be evaluated. In that light, we must pray for a heart of wisdom, a righteous fear of God (v. 11), and the favor of God in our lives and in our work for Him (vv. 13–17).

The security of the godly

91 HE [a]THAT dwelleth in the se-
cret place of the most High
shall [e]abide [b]under the shadow of
the Almighty.
2 [c]I will say of the LORD, *He is* my
refuge and my fortress: my God; in him
will I trust.
3 Surely [d]he shall deliver thee
from the snare of the fowler, *and* from
the noisome pestilence.
4 [e]He shall cover thee with his
feathers, and under his wings shalt
thou trust: his truth *shall be thy* shield
and buckler.
5 [f]Thou shalt not be afraid for the
terror by night; *nor* for the arrow *that*
flieth by day;
6 *Nor* for the pestilence *that*
walketh in darkness; *nor* for the de-
struction *that* wasteth at noonday.
7 A thousand shall fall at thy side,
and ten thousand at thy right hand; *but*
it shall not come nigh thee.
8 Only [g]with thine eyes shalt thou
behold and see the reward of the
wicked.
9 Because thou hast made the LORD,
which is [h]my refuge, *even* the most
High, [i]thy habitation;
10 [j]There shall no evil befall thee,
neither shall any plague come nigh thy
dwelling.
11 [k]For he shall give his angels
charge over thee, to keep thee in all thy
ways.
12 They shall bear thee up in *their*
hands, [l]lest thou dash thy foot
against a stone.
13 Thou shalt tread upon the lion
and [f]adder: the young lion and the
dragon shalt thou trample under feet.
14 Because he hath set his love
upon me, therefore will I deliver him:
I will set him on high, because he hath
[m]known my name.
15 [n]He shall call upon me, and I
will answer him: [o]I *will be* with him in
trouble; I will deliver him, and [p]hon-
our him.
16 With [q]long[g] life will I satisfy
him, and show him my salvation.

Praise for the LORD's goodness

A Psalm *or* Song for the sabbath day.

92 *IT IS a* [r]good *thing* to give
thanks unto the LORD, and to
sing praises unto thy name, O most
High:

91:1 [a]Ps. 31:20 [b]Ps. 17:8
91:2 [c]Ps. 142:5
91:3 [d]Ps. 124:7
91:4 [e]Ps. 17:8
91:5 [f]Job 5:19 Ps. 112:7 Prov. 3:23 Is. 43:2
91:8 [g]Mal. 1:5
91:9 [h]ver. 2 [i]Ps. 90:1
91:10 [j]Prov. 12:21
91:11 [k]Ps. 34:7 & 71:3 Mat. 4:6 Luke 4:10 Heb. 1:14
91:12 [l]Job 5:23 Ps. 37:24
91:14 [m]Ps. 9:10
91:15 [n]Ps. 50:15 [o]Is. 43:2 [p]1 Sam. 2:30
91:16 [q]Prov. 3:2
92:1 [r]Ps. 147:1

[e] Heb. *lodge* [f] Or, *asp* [g] Heb. *length of days*

91:1–16 UNDER THE SHADOW OF THE ALMIGHTY. This psalm expresses the security of those who trust fully in God. It assures us that God will be our refuge and that we may seek His protection in times of spiritual and physical danger.

91:1 HE THAT DWELLETH IN THE SECRET PLACE OF THE MOST HIGH. This psalm offers security for the children of God, i.e., those who commit themselves to the will and protection of the Almighty and daily seek to dwell in God's presence. The more fully we abide in Christ and His word, making Him our life and dwellingplace, the fuller will be our peace and the greater our deliverance in times of danger (cf. 17:8; Mat. 23:37; John 15:1–11).

91:1–2 THE MOST HIGH. The four names for God in this psalm describe different aspects of His protection. (1) "Most High" shows Him to be greater than any threat we face (cf. Gen. 14:19); (2) "Almighty" emphasizes His power to confront and destroy every enemy (cf. Ex. 6:3); (3) "the LORD" assures us that His presence is always with us; and (4) "my God" expresses the truth that God has chosen to associate intimately with those who trust in Him.

91:10 THERE SHALL NO EVIL BEFALL THEE. Nothing can happen to a faithful servant except by God's permission (cf. vv. 7–10). This truth does not mean that there will never be unpleasant or difficult times (cf. Rom. 8:35–36), but that as long as we make God our Lord and refuge, everything that happens to us will work out for our good (see Rom. 8:28, note).

91:11 HE SHALL GIVE HIS ANGELS CHARGE OVER THEE. God commissions angels to watch carefully over the lives and interests of the faithful. (1) They take special note of all those who seek continually to dwell in the presence of God, and they guard the body, soul, and spirit of these believers. (2) The protection includes all our ways. There is no limit as long as we walk in the shadow of the Almighty. They bear us up in our troubles (v. 12) and give us support as we face our spiritual enemies (Eph. 6:10–12; 1 Pet. 5:8; see Mat. 18:10, note; see article on ANGELS AND THE ANGEL OF THE LORD, p. 368).

91:14 BECAUSE HE HATH SET HIS LOVE UPON ME. Here the Lord Himself addresses His faithful followers. Because they truly love Him, He Himself promises to come to their aid in times of trouble. The secret for receiving God's protective care is a heart that is intimately attached to the Lord in gratitude and affection. He knows who such believers are and He will be with them in trouble, hear their prayers, and give them lives full of His divine presence and provision (see John 14:12–21; 15:1–10).

92:1 *IT IS A* GOOD *THING* TO GIVE THANKS UNTO THE LORD. Thanksgiving and gratitude to God are basic elements in the believer's life (cf.

2 To [s]show forth thy lovingkindness in the morning, and thy faithfulness [h]every night,

3 [t]Upon an instrument of ten strings, and upon the psaltery; [i]upon the harp with [j]a solemn sound.

4 For thou, LORD, hast made me glad through thy work: I will triumph in the works of thy hands.

5 [u]O LORD, how great are thy works! *and* [v]thy thoughts are very deep.

6 [w]A brutish man knoweth not; neither doth a fool understand this.

7 When [x]the wicked spring as the grass, and when all the workers of iniquity do flourish; *it is* that they shall be destroyed for ever:

8 [y]But thou, LORD, *art most* high for evermore.

9 For, lo, thine enemies, O LORD, for, lo, thine enemies shall perish; all the workers of iniquity shall [z]be scattered.

10 But [a]my horn shalt thou exalt like *the horn of* an unicorn: I shall be [b]anointed with fresh oil.

11 [c]Mine eye also shall see *my desire* on mine enemies, *and* mine ears shall hear *my desire* of the wicked that rise up against me.

12 [d]The righteous shall flourish like the palm tree: he shall grow like a cedar in Lebanon.

13 Those that be planted in the house of the LORD shall flourish [e]in the courts of our God.

14 They shall still bring forth fruit in old age; they shall be fat and [k]flourishing;

15 To show that the LORD *is* upright: [f]*he is* my rock, and [g]*there is* no unrighteousness in him.

The majesty of the LORD

93 THE [h]LORD reigneth, [i]he is clothed with majesty; the LORD is clothed with strength, [j]*wherewith* he hath girded himself: the world also is stablished, that it cannot be moved.

2 [k]Thy throne *is* established [l]of old: thou *art* from everlasting.

3 The floods have lifted up, O LORD, the floods have lifted up their voice; the floods lift up their waves.

4 [l]The LORD on high *is* mightier than the noise of many waters, *yea, than* the mighty waves of the sea.

5 Thy testimonies are very sure: holiness becometh thine house, O LORD, [m]for ever.

An appeal for God to avenge

94 O LORD [n]God, [m]to whom vengeance belongeth; O God, to whom vengeance belongeth, [o]show thyself.

2 [n]Lift up thyself, thou [o]judge of the earth: render a reward to the proud.

3 LORD, [p]how long shall the wicked, how long shall the wicked triumph?

4 *How long* shall they [q]utter *and* speak hard things? *and* all the workers of iniquity boast themselves?

5 They break in pieces thy people, O LORD, and afflict thine heritage.

6 They slay the widow and the stranger, and murder the fatherless.

7 [r]Yet they say, The LORD shall not see, neither shall the God of Jacob regard *it*.

8 [s]Understand, ye brutish among the people: and *ye* fools, when will ye be wise?

9 [t]He that planted the ear, shall he not hear? he that formed the eye, shall he not see?

10 He that chastiseth the heathen, shall not he correct? he that [u]teacheth man knowledge, *shall not he know?*

11 [v]The LORD knoweth the thoughts of man, that they *are* vanity.

92:2 [s]Ps. 89:1
92:3 [t]1 Chr. 23:5; Ps. 33:2
92:5 [u]Ps. 40:5; [v]Is. 28:29; Rom. 11:33
92:6 [w]Ps. 73:22
92:7 [x]Job 12:6 & 21:7; Ps. 37:1,2; Jer. 12:1,2; Mal. 3:15
92:8 [y]Ps. 83:18
92:9 [z]Ps. 68:1
92:10 [a]Ps. 89:17; [b]Ps. 23:5
92:11 [c]Ps. 54:7 & 59:10
92:12 [d]Ps. 52:8; Is. 65:22; Hos. 14:5,6
92:13 [e]Ps. 100:4
92:15 [f]Deut. 32:4; [g]Rom. 9:14
93:1 [h]Ps. 96:10 & 97:1; Is. 52:7; Rev. 19:6; [i]Ps. 104:1; [j]Ps. 65:6
93:2 [k]Ps. 45:6; Prov. 8:22
93:4 [l]Ps. 65:7 & 89:9
94:1 [m]Nah. 1:2
94:2 [n]Ps. 7:6; [o]Gen. 18:25
94:3 [p]Job 20:5
94:4 [q]Ps. 31:18; Jude 15
94:7 [r]Ps. 10:11
94:8 [s]Ps. 73:22 & 92:6
94:9 [t]Ex. 4:11
94:10 [u]Job 35:11; Is. 28:26
94:11 [v]1 Cor. 3:20

[h] Heb. *in the nights* [i] Or, *upon the solemn sound with the harp* [j] Heb. *Higgaion;* see Ps. 9:16 [k] Heb. *green* [l] Heb. *from then* [m] Heb. *to length of days* [n] Heb. *God of revenges* [o] Heb. *shine forth;* see Ps. 80:1

Phil. 4:6; Col. 4:2; 1 Tim. 2:1). We must thank the Lord morning and evening for salvation through His Son, Jesus (Col. 1:12), for His lovingkindness and grace, and for His faithful guidance and care (v. 2). We should express our gratitude for the word of God (1 Thes. 2:13) and for His spiritual gifts (1 Cor. 14:18). N.T. believers must give thanks in the name of the Lord Jesus Christ (Col. 3:17).

94:1–23 O LORD GOD, TO WHOM VENGEANCE BELONGETH. Believers should be so grieved because of all the injustice, brutality, and wickedness in the world that they pray continually for God to stop the triumph of evil and avenge the wrong. Jesus states that His elect should "cry day and night" unto God that He might "avenge them speedily" (Luke 18:7–8; see also Rev. 6:10–11). Commitment to justice and sympathy for those who are wrongfully treated should cause us to pray for the return of Christ that He might rule the earth in righteousness (Mat. 6:10).

12 [w]Blessed *is* the man whom thou chastenest, O LORD, and teachest him out of thy law;

13 That thou mayest give him rest from the days of adversity, until the pit be digged for the wicked.

14 [x]For the LORD will not cast off his people, neither will he forsake his inheritance.

15 But judgment shall return unto righteousness: and all the upright in heart [p]shall follow it.

16 Who will rise up for me against the evildoers? *or* who will stand up for me against the workers of iniquity?

17 [y]Unless the LORD *had been* my help, my soul had [q]almost dwelt in silence.

18 When I said, [z]My foot slippeth; thy mercy, O LORD, held me up.

19 In the multitude of my thoughts within me thy comforts delight my soul.

20 Shall [a]the throne of iniquity have fellowship with thee, which [b]frameth mischief by a law?

21 [c]They gather themselves together against the soul of the righteous, and [d]condemn the innocent blood.

22 But the LORD is [e]my defence; and my God *is* the rock of my refuge.

23 And [f]he shall bring upon them their own iniquity, and shall cut them off in their own wickedness; *yea,* the LORD our God shall cut them off.

A call to praise the LORD

95 O COME, let us sing unto the LORD: [g]let us make a joyful noise to [h]the rock of our salvation.

2 Let us [r]come before his presence with thanksgiving, and make a joyful noise unto him with psalms.

3 For [i]the LORD *is* a great God, and a great King above all gods.

4 [s]In his hand *are* the deep places of the earth: [t]the strength of the hills *is* his also.

5 [j]The[u] sea *is* his, and he made it: and his hands formed the dry *land.*

6 O come, let us worship and bow down: let [k]us kneel before the LORD our maker.

7 For he *is* our God; and [l]we *are* the people of his pasture, and the sheep of his hand. [m]Today if ye will hear his voice,

8 Harden not your heart, [n]as in the [v]provocation, *and* as *in* the day of temptation in the wilderness:

9 When [o]your fathers tempted me, proved me, and [p]saw my work.

10 [q]Forty years long was I grieved with *this* generation, and said, It *is* a people that do err in their heart, and they have not known my ways:

11 Unto whom [r]I sware in my wrath [w]that they should not enter into my rest.

A call to worship the LORD

96:1–13pp — 1 Chr. 16:23–33

96 O [s]SING unto the LORD a new song: sing unto the LORD, all the earth.

2 Sing unto the LORD, bless his name; show forth his salvation from day to day.

94:12 [w]Job 5:17; Heb. 12:5 **94:14** [x]1 Sam. 12:22; Rom. 11:1 **94:17** [y]Ps. 124:1,2 **94:18** [z]Ps. 38:16 **94:20** [a]Amos 6:3 [b]Is. 10:1 **94:21** [c]Mat. 27:1 [d]Prov. 17:15 **94:22** [e]Ps. 59:9 **94:23** [f]Ps. 7:16; Prov. 2:22 **95:1** [g]Ps. 100:1 [h]Deut. 32:15; 2 Sam. 22:47 **95:3** [i]Ps. 96:4 **95:5** [j]Gen. 1:9,10 **95:6** [k]Phil. 2:10 **95:7** [l]Ps. 79:13 & 100:3 [m]Heb. 3:7 **95:8** [n]Ex. 17:2,7 **95:9** [o]Ps. 78:18; 1 Cor. 10:9 [p]Num. 14:22 **95:10** [q]Heb. 3:10 **95:11** [r]Heb. 4:3,5 **96:1** [s]1 Chr. 16:23-33

[p] Heb. shall be *after it* [q] Or, *quickly* [r] Heb. *prevent his face* [s] Heb. *In whose* [t] Or, *the heights of the hills* are *his* [u] Heb. *Whose the sea* is [v] Heb. *contention* [w] Heb. *if they enter into my rest*

94:12 BLESSED *IS* THE MAN WHOM THOU CHASTENEST. See Heb. 12:5, note on God's chastisement of His children.

95:1–11 O COME, LET US SING. This psalm calls us to make sure that our worship and praise are accompanied by hearts that are obedient to the Lord. It sets forth Israel's sin and rebellion in the wilderness as an example of those who err in what they desire, do not know God's righteous ways, and therefore fail to receive what God has promised (see Num. 14:22–23,28,30; Deut. 1:34–35).

95:7–11 TODAY IF YE WILL HEAR HIS VOICE. The N.T. applies these verses to believers in Christ; the "rest" mentioned in v. 11 is no longer Canaan, but our salvation in Him (see Heb. 3:7—4:12, notes).

95:8 HARDEN NOT YOUR HEART. Those who worship and praise the Lord must also hear and obey His voice (vv. 7,10). To ignore the voice of the Holy Spirit results in a hardening of our hearts so that we become less and less sensitive to the desires of the Spirit (see Heb. 3:8, note); the result is God's wrath coming upon a church or individual (vv. 10–11).

96:2–3 DECLARE HIS GLORY AMONG THE HEATHEN. Those of us who have received God's salvation and experienced His wonderful deeds must be eager to tell others that He can deliver and save them. The command to declare His glory among the nations looks forward to the Great Commission that Jesus gave, i.e., to go into all the world and preach the gospel to all nations (see Mat. 28:19, note).

3 Declare his glory among the heathen, his wonders among all people.

4 For [t]the LORD *is* great, and [u]greatly to be praised: [v]he *is* to be feared above all gods.

5 For [w]all the gods of the nations *are* idols: [x]but the LORD made the heavens.

6 Honour and majesty *are* before him: strength and [y]beauty *are* in his sanctuary.

7 [z]Give unto the LORD, O ye kindreds of the people, give unto the LORD glory and strength.

8 Give unto the LORD the glory [x]*due unto* his name: bring an offering, and come into his courts.

9 O worship the LORD [a]in[y] the beauty of holiness: fear before him, all the earth.

10 Say among the heathen *that* [b]the LORD reigneth: the world also shall be established that it shall not be moved: [c]he shall judge the people righteously.

11 [d]Let the heavens rejoice, and let the earth be glad; [e]let the sea roar, and the fulness thereof.

12 Let the field be joyful, and all that *is* therein: then shall all the trees of the wood rejoice

13 Before the LORD: for he cometh, for he cometh to judge the earth: [f]he shall judge the world with righteousness, and the people with his truth.

Prov. 11:30

The LORD's power and dominion

97 THE [g]LORD reigneth; let the earth rejoice; let the [z]multitude of [h]isles be glad *thereof.*

2 [i]Clouds and darkness *are* round about him: [j]righteousness and judgment *are* the [a]habitation of his throne.

3 [k]A fire goeth before him, and burneth up his enemies round about.

4 [l]His lightnings enlightened the world: the earth saw, and trembled.

5 [m]The hills melted like wax at the presence of the LORD, at the presence of the Lord of the whole earth.

6 [n]The heavens declare his righteousness, and all the people see his glory.

7 [o]Confounded be all they that serve graven images, that boast themselves of idols: [p]worship him, all *ye* gods.

8 Zion heard, and was glad; and the daughters of Judah rejoiced because of thy judgments, O LORD.

9 For thou, LORD, *art* [q]high above all the earth: [r]thou art exalted far above all gods.

10 Ye that love the LORD, [s]hate evil: [t]he preserveth the souls of his saints; [u]he delivereth them out of the hand of the wicked.

11 [v]Light is sown for the righteous, and gladness for the upright in heart.

12 [w]Rejoice in the LORD, ye righteous; [x]and give thanks [b]at the remembrance of his holiness.

Praise to a righteous LORD

A Psalm.

98 O [y]SING unto the LORD a new song; for [z]he hath done marvellous things: [a]his right hand, and his holy arm, hath gotten him the victory.

2 [b]The LORD hath made known his salvation: [c]his righteousness hath he [c]openly shown in the sight of the heathen.

x Heb. *of his name* y Or, *in the glorious sanctuary* z Heb. *many,* or, *great isles* a Or, *establishment* b Or, *to the memorial* c Or, *revealed*

96:4 [t]Ps. 145:3 [u]Ps. 18:3 [v]Ps. 95:3
96:5 [w]Jer. 10:11 [x]Ps. 115:15 Is. 42:5
96:6 [y]Ps. 29:2
96:7 [z]Ps. 29:1,2
96:9 [a]Ps. 29:2
96:10 [b]Ps. 97:1 [c]Ps. 67:4
96:11 [d]Ps. 69:34 [e]Ps. 98:7
96:13 [f]Rev. 19:11
97:1 [g]Ps. 96:10 [h]Is. 60:9
97:2 [i]Ps. 18:11 [j]Ps. 89:14
97:3 [k]Ps. 18:8
97:4 [l]Ex. 19:18
97:5 [m]Mic. 1:4
97:6 [n]Ps. 19:1
97:7 [o]Ex. 20:4 Lev. 26:1 [p]Heb. 1:6
97:9 [q]Ps. 83:18 [r]Ex. 18:11 Ps. 95:3
97:10 [s]Ps. 34:14 Amos 5:15 [t]Prov. 2:8 [u]Ps. 37:39 Dan. 3:28
97:11 [v]Job 22:28 Prov. 4:18
97:12 [w]Ps. 33:1 [x]Ps. 30:4
98:1 [y]Ps. 96:1 Is. 42:10 [z]Ex. 15:11 Ps. 77:14 [a]Ex. 15:6 Is. 63:5
98:2 [b]Is. 52:10 Luke 2:30 [c]Is. 62:2

97:1–12 THE LORD REIGNETH. This psalm describes four elements of God's kingdom: righteousness and justice as the foundation of His throne (v. 2), His ruling power over all the earth (vv. 1–6,9), His victory over false gods (v. 7), and the subsequent joy of the righteous (vv. 8–12). It prophesies the ultimate revelation of Christ and His kingdom rule at the end of history (Rev. 19—22), an event that will call forth great joy among the redeemed (cf. Is. 25:9; Rev. 11:15–17; 18:20; 19:1–3).

97:10 YE THAT LOVE THE LORD, HATE EVIL. Those who claim to love the Lord will be tested by how much they hate evil while living upon this earth. A truly regenerated believer, made one with Christ and indwelt by the Holy Spirit, will love what God loves and hate what He hates. We should be vexed by the wickedness, brutality, and ungodliness in the world, and grieved by the lives being destroyed by its evil; furthermore, we should be deeply distressed when sin and immorality are tolerated in the house of God (see 1 Cor. 5:2, note; Heb. 1:9, note).

98:1–9 A NEW SONG. This psalm is a prophetic song of praise for the victory of the Lord and for His salvation made known to Israel and all the nations (vv. 1–3). This prophecy is now being fulfilled through the outpouring of the Holy Spirit upon believers and the Spirit-empowered proclamation of the gospel (Acts 1:8; 2:4).

Ps. 116:1-13

3 He hath [d]remembered his mercy and his truth toward the house of Israel: [e]all the ends of the earth have seen the salvation of our God.

4 [f]Make a joyful noise unto the LORD, all the earth: make a loud noise, and rejoice, and sing praise.

5 Sing unto the LORD with the harp; with the harp, and the voice of a psalm.

6 [g]With trumpets and sound of cornet make a joyful noise before the LORD, the King.

7 Let the sea roar, and the fulness thereof; the world, and they that dwell therein.

8 Let the floods [h]clap *their* hands: let the hills be joyful together

9 Before the LORD; [i]for he cometh to judge the earth: with righteousness shall he judge the world, and the people with equity.

Is. 11:3b-4

Praise to a holy God

99 THE LORD reigneth; let the people tremble: [j]he sitteth *between* the cherubims; let the earth [d]be moved.

2 The LORD *is* great in Zion; and he *is* [k]high above all the people.

3 Let them praise thy great and terrible name; *for* it *is* holy.

4 [l]The king's strength also loveth judgment; thou dost establish equity, thou executest judgment and righteousness in Jacob.

5 Exalt ye the LORD our God, and worship at [m]his footstool; *for* [n]he[e] *is* holy.

6 [o]Moses and Aaron among his priests, and Samuel among them that call upon his name; they [p]called upon the LORD, and he answered them.

7 [q]He spake unto them in the cloudy pillar: they kept his testimonies, and the ordinance *that* he gave them.

8 Thou answeredst them, O LORD our God: [r]thou wast a God that forgavest them, though [s]thou tookest vengeance of their inventions.

9 [t]Exalt the LORD our God, and worship at his holy hill; for the LORD our God *is* holy.

A song of praise and joy

[u]A Psalm of [f]praise.

100 MAKE [v]A joyful noise unto the LORD, [g]all ye lands.

2 Serve the LORD with gladness: come before his presence with singing.

3 Know ye that the LORD he *is* God: [w]*it is* he *that* hath made us, [h]and not we ourselves; [x]*we are* his people, and the sheep of his pasture.

4 [y]Enter into his gates with thanksgiving, *and* into his courts with praise: be thankful unto him, *and* bless his name.

5 For the LORD *is* good; [z]his mercy *is* everlasting; and his truth *endureth* [a]to[i] all generations.

Ps. 113

98:3 [d]Luke 1:54 [e]Is. 49:6 98:4 [f]Ps. 95:1 98:6 [g]Num. 10:10 98:8 [h]Is. 55:12 98:9 [i]Ps. 96:10 99:1 [j]Ex. 25:22 99:2 [k]Ps. 97:9 99:4 [l]Job 36:5-7 99:5 [m]Ps. 132:7 [n]Lev. 19:2 99:6 [o]Jer. 15:1 [p]Ex. 14:15 1 Sam. 7:9 99:7 [q]Ex. 33:9 99:8 [r]Num. 14:20 [s]Deut. 9:20 99:9 [t]Ps. 34:3 100:1 [u]Ps. 145,title [v]Ps. 95:1 100:3 [w]Eph. 2:10 [x]Ezek. 34:31 100:4 [y]Ps. 116:17 100:5 [z]Ps. 136:1 [a]Ps. 89:1

[d]Heb. *stagger* [e]Or, *it is holy* [f]Or, *thanksgiving* [g]Heb. *all the earth* [h]Or, *and his we are* [i]Heb. *to generation and generation*

98:9 HE COMETH TO JUDGE THE EARTH. This verse will find its ultimate fulfillment in our Lord's return to judge the world (see Rev. 19–22), eliminate sin and sorrow, and renew the heavens and earth. Nature itself will rejoice at that time (v. 8), as it participates in the final redemption when Christ rules the earth in righteousness and justice (see Is. 55:12–13; Rom. 8:19–22).

99:3 THY GREAT AND TERRIBLE NAME; *FOR* IT *IS* HOLY. The Lord God is so awesome and holy that even His name must be treated with the utmost reverence and respect. God may never be treated lightly, since He is enthroned far above humans in strength, justice, purity, and greatness. We must both love and fear God (vv. 1–3), and beware of adopting the world's casual use of His name (see Ex. 20:7, note; Mat. 6:9, note).

99:6 THEY CALLED UPON THE LORD, AND HE ANSWERED THEM. Although God is holy and to be feared (vv. 1–2), He has come down to us through Jesus Christ. He seeks our fellowship and delights in hearing and answering His people's prayers. Moses, Aaron, and Samuel are listed as those who had a special relationship with God through their intercessory prayers.

99:8 THOU ... FORGAVEST THEM ... THOU TOOK VENGEANCE OF THEIR INVENTIONS. God can pardon and punish an individual at the same time. We must distinguish between being restored in our relationship with God and still experiencing the consequences of sins we have committed (see 2 Sam. 12:13, note; 1 Chr. 21:14, note).

100:2 COME BEFORE HIS PRESENCE WITH SINGING. Individual and congregational singing should be done primarily "unto the LORD" (v. 1), with joy and out of a conscious awareness of His presence. In song we remember that He created us and redeemed us, and that we are now His people and He is our shepherd (v. 3). We sing of His love, faithfulness, and truth that will endure forever (v. 5; see Eph. 5:19, note).

A perfect heart

A Psalm of David.

101 I WILL sing of mercy and judgment: unto thee, O LORD, will I sing.

2 I will [b]behave myself wisely in a perfect way. O when wilt thou come unto me? I will [c]walk within my house with a perfect heart.

3 I will set no [j]wicked thing before mine eyes: [d]I hate the work of them [e]that turn aside; *it* shall not cleave to me.

4 A froward heart shall depart from me: I will not [f]know a wicked *person.*

5 Whoso privily slandereth his neighbour, him will I cut off: [g]him that hath an high look and a proud heart will not I suffer.

6 Mine eyes *shall be* upon the faithful of the land, that they may dwell with me: he that walketh [k]in a perfect way, he shall serve me.

7 He that worketh deceit shall not dwell within my house: he that telleth lies [l]shall not tarry in my sight.

8 I will [h]early destroy all the wicked of the land; that I may cut off all wicked doers [i]from the city of the LORD.

God's years and man's days

A Prayer [m]of the afflicted, [j]when he is overwhelmed, and poureth out his complaint before the LORD.

102 HEAR MY prayer, O LORD, and let my cry [k]come unto thee.

101:2 [b]1 Sam. 18:14 [c]1 Ki. 11:4
101:3 [d]Ps. 97:10 [e]Josh. 23:6
101:4 [f]Ps. 119:115
101:5 [g]Prov. 6:17
101:8 [h]Ps. 75:10 Jer. 21:12 [i]Ps. 48:2,8
102:1 [j]Ps. 61:2 [k]Ps. 18:6
102:2 [l]Ps. 69:17 [m]Ps. 71:2
102:3 [n]Jas. 4:14 [o]Job 30:30 Ps. 31:10
102:4 [p]Ps. 37:2
102:5 [q]Job 19:20
102:6 [r]Job. 30:29 [s]Is. 34:11
102:7 [t]Ps. 77:4 [u]Ps. 38:11
102:8 [v]Acts 26:11 [w]Acts 23:12
102:9 [x]Ps. 42:3
102:10 [y]Ps. 30:7
102:11 [z]Eccl. 6:12 [a]Is. 40:6-8 Jas. 1:10
102:12 [b]Ps. 9:7 [c]Ps. 135:13
102:13 [d]Is. 60:10 [e]Is. 40:2
102:14 [f]Ps. 79:1

2 [l]Hide not thy face from me in the day *when* I am in trouble; [m]incline thine ear unto me: in the day *when* I call answer me speedily.

3 [n]For my days are consumed [n]like smoke, and [o]my bones are burned as an hearth.

4 My heart is smitten, and [p]withered like grass; so that I forget to eat my bread.

5 By reason of the voice of my groaning [q]my bones cleave to my [o]skin.

6 [r]I am like [s]a pelican of the wilderness: I am like an owl of the desert.

7 I [t]watch, and am as a sparrow [u]alone upon the house top.

8 Mine enemies reproach me all the day; *and* they that are [v]mad against me are [w]sworn against me.

9 For I have eaten ashes like bread, and [x]mingled my drink with weeping,

10 Because of thine indignation and thy wrath: for [y]thou hast lifted me up, and cast me down.

11 [z]My days *are* like a shadow that declineth; and [a]I am withered like grass.

12 But [b]thou, O LORD, shalt endure for ever; and [c]thy remembrance unto all generations.

13 Thou shalt arise, *and* [d]have mercy upon Zion: for the time to favour her, yea, the [e]set time, is come.

14 For thy servants take pleasure in [f]her stones, and favour the dust thereof.

[j] Heb. *thing of Belial* [k] Or, *perfect in the way*
[l] Heb. *shall not be established* [m] Or, *for*
[n] Or, (as some read) *into smoke* [o] Or, *flesh*

101:1–8 OF MERCY AND JUDGMENT. This psalm pictures the kind of heart that the king of Israel must have if he desires to rule according to the will of God. The attitudes expressed in this psalm also apply to those who rule in the church of God (cf. Acts 20:28; 24:16).

101:2 I WILL WALK WITHIN MY HOUSE WITH A PERFECT HEART. Faithful believers will make it a priority to please God in their own homes. Family relationships are where true godliness must first be manifested and developed. The very purpose and direction of our hearts must be to seek God in prayer, to study His Word, to have family devotions, to show love and care toward the members of our family, to walk blamelessly, and to have eyes that refuse to look on evil (see next note).

101:3 I WILL SET NO WICKED THING BEFORE MINE EYES. Today the ungodly are consumed with using their eyes to view immorality, wickedness, brutality, violence, pornography, and all kinds of evil as a means to gratify their lust and desire for perverted pleasure. Through television, movies, videos, books, and magazines, people can observe every kind of wickedness. However, those committed to God and His righteousness will hate and shun evil (see 97:10, note) and will guard their lives and families by setting nothing before their eyes that would displease or grieve the Holy Spirit (see previous note; Rom. 1:32, note).

102:2 IN THE DAY *WHEN* I AM IN TROUBLE. During times of great trouble in life, when nearly everything seems to be going wrong and we find ourselves helpless to change the situation, our only hope is to call upon God and place our lives and circumstances in His hands (cf. 39:12; 54:2; 61:1; 64:1). The psalmist does this by crying out to the Lord for mercy and asking for His intervention. He is confident that God will answer his prayer and not forsake him.

15 So the heathen shall [g]fear the name of the LORD, and all the kings of the earth thy glory.

16 When the LORD shall build up Zion, [h]he shall appear in his glory.

17 [i]He will regard the prayer of the destitute, and not despise their prayer.

18 This shall be [j]written for the generation to come: and [k]the people which shall be created shall praise the LORD.

19 For he hath [l]looked down from the height of his sanctuary; from heaven did the LORD behold the earth;

20 [m]To hear the groaning of the prisoner; to loose [p]those that are appointed to death;

21 To [n]declare the name of the LORD in Zion, and his praise in Jerusalem;

22 When the people are gathered together, and the kingdoms, to serve the LORD.

23 He [q]weakened my strength in the way; he [o]shortened my days.

24 [p]I said, O my God, take me not away in the midst of my days: [q]thy years *are* throughout all generations.

25 [r]Of old hast thou laid the foundation of the earth: and the heavens *are* the work of thy hands.

26 [s]They shall perish, but thou shalt [r]endure: yea, all of them shall wax old like a garment; as a vesture shalt thou change them, and they shall be changed:

27 But [t]thou *art* the same, and thy years shall have no end.

28 [u]The children of thy servants shall continue, and their seed shall be established before thee.

102:15 [g]1 Ki. 8:43
102:16 [h]Is. 60:1,2
102:17 [i]Neh. 1:6
102:18 [j]Rom. 15:4 [k]Ps. 22:31
102:19 [l]Deut. 26:15
102:20 [m]Ps. 79:11
102:21 [n]Ps. 22:22
102:23 [o]Job 21:21
102:24 [p]Is. 38:10 [q]Ps. 90:2
102:25 [r]Heb. 1:10
102:26 [s]Is. 34:4
102:27 [t]Mal. 3:6 Heb. 13:8
102:28 [u]Ps. 69:36
103:1 [v]Ps. 104:1
103:3 [w]Ps. 130:8 Is. 33:24 [x]Ex. 15:26
103:4 [y]Ps. 5:12
103:5 [z]Is. 40:31
103:7 [a]Ps. 147:19
103:8 [b]Ex. 34:6,7
103:9 [c]Ps. 30:5
103:10 [d]Ezra 9:13
103:12 [e]Is. 43:25
103:13 [f]Mal. 3:17

The benefits of the LORD

A Psalm of David.

103 BLESS [v]THE LORD, O my soul: and all that is within me, *bless* his holy name.

2 Bless the LORD, O my soul, and forget not all his benefits:

3 [w]Who forgiveth all thine iniquities; who [x]healeth all thy diseases;

4 Who redeemeth thy life from destruction; [y]who crowneth thee with lovingkindness and tender mercies;

5 Who satisfieth thy mouth with good *things; so that* [z]thy youth is renewed like the eagle's.

6 The LORD executeth righteousness and judgment for all that are oppressed.

7 [a]He made known his ways unto Moses, his acts unto the children of Israel.

8 [b]The LORD *is* merciful and gracious, slow to anger, and [s]plenteous in mercy.

9 [c]He will not always chide: neither will he keep *his anger* for ever.

10 [d]He hath not dealt with us after our sins; nor rewarded us according to our iniquities.

11 For [t]as the heaven is high above the earth, *so* great is his mercy toward them that fear him.

12 As far as the east is from the west, *so* far hath he [e]removed our transgressions from us.

13 [f]Like as a father pitieth *his* chil-

[p] Heb. *the children of death* [q] Heb. *afflicted* [r] Heb. *stand* [s] Heb. *great of mercy* [t] Heb. *according to the height of the heaven*

102:25–26 HAST THOU LAID THE FOUNDATIONS. These verses, quoted in Heb. 1:10–12, imply that the experiences of trouble described by the psalmist apply to Jesus Christ as well (vv. 1–11). Vv. 12–28 speak about the Lord's kingdom on earth, His work in creation, and His eternity. The present heavens and earth will be exchanged for a brand new heaven and earth (as the figure of changing clothes shows). But God will not change; He remains the same.

103:1–2 BLESS THE LORD, O MY SOUL. "To bless" carries the meaning of "to praise." This psalm thus expresses thanksgiving and praise to the Lord for the benefits and blessings that He bestows on the believing covenant people. We must never forget God's goodness to us (cf. Deut. 8:12–14; 2 Chr. 32:25) or fail to be thankful for His blessings showered upon us through the Holy Spirit (see next note; cf. Acts 2:38–39; 9:17–18; see John 14:16, note).

103:3–16 FORGIVETH ... HEALETH. The fall of Adam into sin led the human race into the universal experience of sin, sickness, and death. In contrast, the psalmist lists God's blessings for His people: forgiveness of our sins, healing for our diseases, and the gifts of redemption and eternal life. Forgiveness is the first and most important gift we can receive from God. Through it we are restored to God and redeemed from destruction (v. 4). Healing of diseases that come to us because of sin and Satan is likewise part of the salvation that God makes available to His people (see Jas. 5:15–16, notes; see article on DIVINE HEALING, p. 1418).

103:13 THE LORD PITIETH THEM THAT FEAR HIM. God shows mercy to those who truly fear Him. The fear of God is a redeeming fear that motivates us to turn away from evil, to keep God's

dren, *so* the LORD pitieth them that fear him.

14 For he knoweth our frame; he remembereth that we *are* [g]dust.

15 *As for* man, [h]his days *are* as grass: [i]as a flower of the field, so he flourisheth.

16 For the wind passeth over it, and [u]it is gone; and [j]the place thereof shall know it no more.

17 But the mercy of the LORD *is* from everlasting to everlasting upon them that fear him, and his righteousness unto children's children;

18 [k]To such as keep his covenant, and to those that remember his commandments to do them.

19 The LORD hath prepared his throne in the heavens; and [l]his kingdom ruleth over all.

20 [m]Bless the LORD, ye his angels, [v]that excel in strength, that [n]do his commandments, hearkening unto the voice of his word.

21 Bless ye the LORD, all *ye* [o]his hosts; [p]ye ministers of his, that do his pleasure.

22 Bless the LORD, all his works in all places of his dominion: bless the LORD, O my soul.

God the creator of the earth

104 BLESS [q]THE LORD, O my soul. O LORD my God, thou art very great; thou art clothed with honour and majesty.

2 [r]Who coverest *thyself* with light as *with* a garment: [s]who stretchest out the heavens like a curtain:

3 [t]Who layeth the beams of his chambers in the waters: [u]who maketh the clouds his chariot: [v]who walketh upon the wings of the wind:

4 [w]Who maketh his angels spirits; his ministers a flaming fire:

5 [x]*Who*[w] laid the foundations of the earth, *that* it should not be removed for ever.

6 [y]Thou coveredst it with the deep as *with* a garment: the waters stood above the mountains.

7 At thy rebuke they fled; at the voice of thy thunder they hasted away.

8 [z]They[x] go up by the mountains; they go down by the valleys unto the place which thou hast founded for them.

9 [a]Thou hast set a bound that they may not pass over; [b]that they turn not again to cover the earth.

10 [y]He sendeth the springs into the valleys, *which* [z]run among the hills.

11 They give drink to every beast of the field: the wild asses [a]quench their thirst.

12 By them shall the fowls of the heaven have their habitation, *which* [b]sing among the branches.

13 [c]He watereth the hills from his chambers: the earth is satisfied with [d]the fruit of thy works.

14 [e]He causeth the grass to grow for the cattle, and herb for the service of man: that he may bring forth [f]food out of the earth;

15 And [g]wine *that* maketh glad the

103:14 [g]Eccl. 12:7
103:15 [h]1 Pet. 1:24 [i]Job 14:1,2
103:16 [j]Job 7:10
103:18 [k]Deut. 7:9
103:19 [l]Ps. 47:2 Dan. 4:25
103:20 [m]Ps. 148:2 [n]Mat. 6:10
103:21 [o]Gen. 32:2 [p]Heb. 1:14
104:1 [q]Ps. 103:1
104:2 [r]Dan. 7:9 [s]Is. 40:22
104:3 [t]Amos 9:6 [u]Is. 19:1 [v]Ps. 18:10
104:4 [w]Heb. 1:7
104:5 [x]Job 26:7
104:6 [y]Gen. 7:19
104:8 [z]Gen. 8:5
104:9 [a]Job 26:10 [b]Gen. 9:11
104:13 [c]Ps. 147:8 [d]Jer. 10:13
104:14 [e]Gen. 1:29 [f]Job 28:5 Ps. 136:25
104:15 [g]Judg. 9:13

[u]Heb. *it is not* [v]Heb. *mighty in strength*
[w]Heb. *He hath founded the earth upon her bases*
[x]Or, *The mountains ascend, the valleys descend*
[y]Heb. *Who sendeth* [z]Heb. *walk* [a]Heb. *break* [b]Heb. *give a voice*

---

precepts, and to seek the Lord's nearness and grace (see article on THE FEAR OF THE LORD, p. 282). The blessings God gives to those who fear Him are: (1) His mercy, lovingkindness, and forgiveness (vv. 11–12,17; cf. Is. 1:18; 38:17; Jer. 31:14); (2) His fatherly love and compassion (vv. 13–14); and (3) His faithfulness and goodness to their children (v. 17).

103:14 FOR HE KNOWETH OUR FRAME. God pities His children because He knows their weaknesses and infirmities. Even the best of His followers stand in need of His compassion. As a father has deep compassion for his children when they fail, suffer, or are mistreated, so also the heavenly Father hurts when His own are hurting. In the midst of trouble, failure, and struggle, we must not think that God is aloof or uncaring; rather, we must remember that His eyes look on us with compassion, and He will help us according to our need (cf. Luke 7:12–13).

104:1–35 GOD, THOU ART VERY GREAT. This psalm is a hymn about God's creation of all things and His providential care over all His works. It emphasizes His involvement with all He has made, for He dwells in the world and sustains it (see article on THE PROVIDENCE OF GOD, p. 80). What God continues to do in the universe reflects His glory. Yet God's creation is marred because of sin and evil; thus the psalm ends with a prayer for God to remove from it all things that are wicked and all those who do iniquity (cf. Rom. 8:19–23; see Gen. 1—2, notes).

104:15 WINE THAT MAKETH GLAD. The word "wine" (Heb. *yayin*) refers here to that which comes directly from the "herb" (i.e., plants or vines, v. 14), not that which humans have permitted to ferment. Natural grape juice is delicious in taste, nutritious as a food, and fully approved by God (cf. Amos 9:14; see article on WINE IN THE OLD TESTAMENT, p. 220)

heart of man, *and* [c]oil to make *his* face to shine, and bread *which* strengtheneth man's heart.

16 The trees of the LORD are full *of sap;* the cedars of Lebanon, which he hath planted;

17 Where the birds make their nests: *as for* the stork, the fir trees *are* her house.

18 The high hills *are* a refuge for the wild goats; *and* the rocks for the conies.

19 [h]He appointed the moon for seasons: the sun knoweth his going down.

20 [i]Thou makest darkness, and it is night: wherein [d]all the beasts of the forest do creep *forth.*

21 [j]The young lions roar after their prey, and seek their meat from God.

22 The sun ariseth, they gather themselves together, and lay them down in their dens.

23 Man goeth forth unto [k]his work and to his labour until the evening.

24 [l]O LORD, how manifold are thy works! in wisdom hast thou made them all: the earth is full of thy riches.

25 *So is* this great and wide sea, wherein *are* things creeping innumerable, both small and great beasts.

26 There go the ships: *there is* that [m]leviathan, *whom* thou hast [e]made to play therein.

27 [n]These wait all upon thee; that thou mayest give *them* their meat in due season.

28 *That* thou givest them they gather: thou openest thine hand, they are filled with good.

29 Thou hidest thy face, they are troubled: [o]thou takest away their breath, they die, and return to their dust.

30 [p]Thou sendest forth thy spirit, they are created: and thou renewest the face of the earth.

31 The glory of the LORD [f]shall endure for ever: the LORD [q]shall rejoice in his works.

32 He looketh on the earth, and it [r]trembleth: [s]he toucheth the hills, and they smoke.

33 [t]I will sing unto the LORD as long as I live: I will sing praise to my God while I have my being.

34 My meditation of him shall be sweet: I will be glad in the LORD.

35 Let [u]the sinners be consumed out of the earth, and let the wicked be no more. Bless thou the LORD, O my soul. Praise ye the LORD.

The LORD remembers his covenant

105:1–15pp — 1 Chr. 16:8–22

105 O [v]GIVE thanks unto the LORD; call upon his name: [w]make known his deeds among the people.

2 Sing unto him, sing psalms unto him: [x]talk ye of all his wondrous works.

3 Glory ye in his holy name: let the heart of them rejoice that seek the LORD.

4 Seek the LORD, and his strength: [y]seek his face evermore.

5 [z]Remember his marvellous works that he hath done; his wonders, and the judgments of his mouth;

6 O ye seed of Abraham his servant, ye children of Jacob his chosen.

7 He *is* the LORD our God: [a]his judgments *are* in all the earth.

8 He hath [b]remembered his cov-

104:19 [h]Gen. 1:14 **104:20** [i]Is. 45:7 **104:21** [j]Job 38:39 **104:23** [k]Gen. 3:19 **104:24** [l]Prov. 3:19 **104:26** [m]Job 41:1 **104:27** [n]Ps. 136:25 **104:29** [o]Job 34:15 Eccl. 12:7 **104:30** [p]Is. 32:15 Ezek. 37:9 **104:31** [q]Gen. 1:31 **104:32** [r]Hab. 3:10 [s]Ps. 144:5 **104:33** [t]Ps. 63:4 **104:35** [u]Ps. 37:38 Prov. 2:22 **105:1** [v]1 Chr. 16:8 Is. 12:4 [w]Ps. 145:5 **105:2** [x]Ps. 119:27 **105:4** [y]Ps. 27:8 **105:5** [z]Ps. 77:11 **105:7** [a]Is. 26:9 **105:8** [b]Luke 1:72

[c]Heb. *to make* his *face shine with oil,* or, *more than oil* [d]Heb. *all the beasts thereof do trample on the forest* [e]Heb. *formed* [f]Heb. *shall be*

105:1–45 GIVE THANKS UNTO THE LORD. This psalm calls Israel to worship, praise, obey, and seek the Lord (vv. 1–4) because He has miraculously directed their personal and corporate history in order to create and preserve the nation of Israel as a holy people who observe His righteous laws (vv. 5–45). The psalmist intends to inspire in the people gratitude for the Lord's care in their lives, joy in their possession of the holy land, and faithfulness to Him and His word. Likewise, we as believers should look back and remember God's history with us; to do so should elicit thankfulness and a greater loyalty to Him who gave Himself for us (Rom. 8:32; Gal. 2:20).

105:4 SEEK THE LORD, AND HIS STRENGTH. We are invited not only to seek the Lord's presence, but also the power and strength of His grace. (1) We all need divine strength in order to persevere in salvation, live a life pleasing unto God, and witness in the power of the Holy Spirit (see Acts 1:8, note; 2:4, note; see article on FAITH AND GRACE, p. 1738). (2) We must daily look to God and His grace, or we will face spiritual weakness and defeat. Thus we must stir ourselves up constantly to seek Him earnestly with our whole heart (see Mat. 7:7–8, note; Luke 18:1,7, notes) and to expect signs of His presence and power in our lives (see Deut. 4:29, note; 2 Chr. 26:5, note; Mat. 7:7; Heb. 11:6).

enant for ever, the word *which* he commanded to a thousand generations.

9 [c]Which *covenant* he made with Abraham, and his oath unto Isaac;

10 And confirmed the same unto Jacob for a law, *and* to Israel *for* an everlasting covenant:

11 Saying, [d]Unto thee will I give the land of Canaan, [g]the lot of your inheritance:

12 [e]When they were *but* a few men in number; yea, very few, [f]and strangers in it.

13 When they went from one nation to another, from *one* kingdom to another people;

14 [g]He suffered no man to do them wrong: yea, [h]he reproved kings for their sakes;

15 *Saying,* Touch not mine anointed, and do my prophets no harm.

16 Moreover [i]he called for a famine upon the land: he brake the whole [j]staff of bread.

17 [k]He sent a man before them, *even* Joseph, *who* [l]was sold for a servant:

18 [m]Whose feet they hurt with fetters: [h]he was laid in iron:

19 Until the time that his word came: [n]the word of the LORD tried him.

20 [o]The king sent and loosed him; *even* the ruler of the people, and let him go free.

21 [p]He made him lord of his house, and ruler of all his [i]substance:

22 To bind his princes at his pleasure; and teach his senators wisdom.

23 [q]Israel also came into Egypt; and Jacob sojourned [r]in the land of Ham.

24 And [s]he increased his people greatly; and made them stronger than their enemies.

25 [t]He turned their heart to hate his people, to deal subtly with his servants.

26 [u]He sent Moses his servant; *and* Aaron whom he had chosen.

27 [v]They showed [j]his signs among them, [w]and wonders in the land of Ham.

28 [x]He sent darkness, and made it dark; and [y]they rebelled not against his word.

105:9 [c]Gen. 17:2 & 22:16
105:11 [d]Gen. 13:15 & 15:18
105:12 [e]Gen. 34:30 Deut. 7:7 [f]Heb. 11:9
105:14 [g]Gen. 35:5 [h]Gen. 12:17
105:16 [i]Gen. 41:54 [j]Lev. 26:26 Is. 3:1
105:17 [k]Gen. 45:5 [l]Gen. 37:28
105:18 [m]Gen. 40:15
105:19 [n]Gen. 41:25
105:20 [o]Gen. 41:14
105:21 [p]Gen. 41:40
105:23 [q]Gen. 46:6 [r]Ps. 78:51
105:24 [s]Ex. 1:7
105:25 [t]Ex. 1:8
105:26 [u]Ex. 3:10
105:27 [v]Ex. 7-12 [w]Ps. 106:22
105:28 [x]Ex. 10:22 [y]Ps. 99:7
105:29 [z]Ex. 7:20 Ps. 78:44
105:30 [a]Ex. 8:6 Ps. 78:45
105:31 [b]Ex. 8:17 Ps. 78:45
105:32 [c]Ex. 9:23 Ps. 78:48
105:33 [d]Ps. 78:47
105:34 [e]Ex. 10:4 Ps. 78:46
105:36 [f]Ex. 12:29 Ps. 78:51 [g]Gen. 49:3
105:37 [h]Ex. 12:35
105:38 [i]Ex. 12:33
105:39 [j]Ex. 13:21 Neh. 9:12
105:40 [k]Ex. 16:12 Ps. 78:18 [l]Ps. 78:24
105:41 [m]Ex. 17:6 Ps. 78:15 1 Cor. 10:4
105:42 [n]Gen. 15:14

29 [z]He turned their waters into blood, and slew their fish.

30 [a]Their land brought forth frogs in abundance, in the chambers of their kings.

31 [b]He spake, and there came divers sorts of flies, *and* lice in all their coasts.

32 [c]He[k] gave them hail for rain, *and* flaming fire in their land.

33 [d]He smote their vines also and their fig trees; and brake the trees of their coasts.

34 [e]He spake, and the locusts came, and caterpillars, and that without number,

35 And did eat up all the herbs in their land, and devoured the fruit of their ground.

36 [f]He smote also all the firstborn in their land, [g]the chief of all their strength.

37 [h]He brought them forth also with silver and gold: and *there was* not one feeble *person* among their tribes.

38 [i]Egypt was glad when they departed: for the fear of them fell upon them.

39 [j]He spread a cloud for a covering; and fire to give light in the night.

40 [k]*The people* asked, and he brought quails, and [l]satisfied them with the bread of heaven.

41 [m]He opened the rock, and the waters gushed out; they ran in the dry places *like* a river.

42 For he remembered [n]his holy promise, *and* Abraham his servant.

43 And he brought forth his people with joy, *and* his chosen with [l]gladness:

44 [o]And gave them the lands of the heathen: and they inherited the labour of the people;

45 [p]That they might observe his statutes, and keep his laws. [m]Praise ye the LORD.

105:44 [o]Josh. 13:7 105:45 [p]Deut. 4:1 & 6:21-25

[g] Heb. *the cord* [h] Heb. *his soul came into iron*
[i] Heb. *possession* [j] Heb. *words of his signs*
[k] Heb. *He gave their rain hail* [l] Heb. *singing*
[m] Heb. *Hallelujah*

105:15 TOUCH NOT MINE ANOINTED. In this context, the anointed ones are Abraham, Isaac, Jacob (with his new name, Israel), and Joseph (vv. 9–10,17); we may not conclude from this verse, however, that we should give heed to every person who claims to be anointed.

God's mercy to Israel

106:1,47–48pp — 1 Chr. 16:34–36

106 PRAISE[n] YE the LORD. [q]O
give thanks unto the LORD;
for *he is* good: for his mercy *endureth* for
ever.
2 Who can utter the mighty acts of
the LORD? *who* can show forth all his
praise?
3 Blessed *are* they that keep judg-
ment, *and* he that [r]doeth righteous-
ness at [s]all times.
4 [t]Remember me, O LORD, with the
favour *that thou bearest unto* thy people:
O visit me with thy salvation;
5 That I may see the good of thy
chosen, that I may rejoice in the glad-
ness of thy nation, that I may glory
with thine inheritance.
6 [u]We have sinned with our fa-
thers, we have committed iniquity, we
have done wickedly.
7 Our fathers understood not thy
wonders in Egypt; they remembered
not the multitude of thy mercies; [v]but
provoked *him* at the sea, *even* at the
Red sea.
8 Nevertheless he saved them for
his name's sake, [w]that he might make
his mighty power to be known.
9 [x]He rebuked the Red sea also,
and it was dried up: so [y]he led them
through the depths, as through the wil-
derness.
10 And he [z]saved them from the
hand of him that hated *them,* and re-
deemed them from the hand of the en-
emy.
11 [a]And the waters covered their
enemies: there was not one of them
left.
12 [b]Then believed they his words;
they sang his praise.
13 [c]They[o] soon forgat his works;
they waited not for his counsel:
14 [d]But [p]lusted exceedingly in

106:1 [q]1 Chr. 16:34
106:3 [r]Ps. 15:2 [s]Gal. 6:9
106:4 [t]Ps. 119:132
106:6 [u]Dan. 9:5
106:7 [v]Ex. 14:11
106:8 [w]Ex. 9:16
106:9 [x]Ex. 14:21 Ps. 18:15 Nah. 1:4 [y]Is. 63:11
106:10 [z]Ex. 14:30
106:11 [a]Ex. 14:27
106:12 [b]Ex. 15:1
106:13 [c]Ex. 15:24
106:14 [d]1 Cor. 10:6
106:15 [e]Num. 11:31 [f]Is. 10:16
106:16 [g]Num. 16:1
106:17 [h]Deut. 11:6
106:18 [i]Num. 16:35,46
106:19 [j]Ex. 32:4
106:20 [k]Jer. 2:11 Rom. 1:23
106:21 [l]Ps. 78:11
106:22 [m]Ps. 78:51
106:23 [n]Ex. 32:10 Deut. 9:19 [o]Ezek. 22:30
106:24 [p]Deut. 8:7 Ezek. 20:6 [q]Heb. 3:18
106:25 [r]Num. 14:2
106:26 [s]Ezek. 20:15 [t]Num. 14:29
106:27 [u]Lev. 26:33
106:28 [v]Hos. 9:10

the wilderness, and tempted God in the
desert.
15 [e]And he gave them their re-
quest; but [f]sent leanness into their
soul.
16 [g]They envied Moses also in the
camp, *and* Aaron the saint of the LORD.
17 [h]The earth opened and swal-
lowed up Dathan, and covered the com-
pany of Abiram.
18 [i]And a fire was kindled in their
company; the flame burned up the
wicked.
19 [j]They made a calf in Horeb, and
worshipped the molten image.
20 Thus [k]they changed their glory
into the similitude of an ox that eateth
grass.
21 They [l]forgat God their saviour,
which had done great things in Egypt;
22 Wondrous works in [m]the land of
Ham, *and* terrible things by the Red
sea.
23 [n]Therefore he said that he
would destroy them, had not Moses his
chosen [o]stood before him in the
breach, to turn away his wrath, lest he
should destroy *them.*
24 Yea, they despised [p]the[q]
pleasant land, they [q]believed not his
word:
25 [r]But murmured in their tents,
and hearkened not unto the voice of the
LORD.
26 [s]Therefore he lifted up his hand
against them, [t]to overthrow them in
the wilderness:
27 [u]To[r] overthrow their seed also
among the nations, and to scatter them
in the lands.
28 [v]They joined themselves also
unto Baal-peor, and ate the sacrifices
of the dead.
29 Thus they provoked *him* to anger

[n] Heb. *Hallelujah* [o] Heb. *They made haste, they forgat* [p] Heb. *lusted a lust* [q] Heb. *a land of desire* [r] Heb. *To make them fall*

106:1–48 FOR HIS MERCY *ENDURETH* FOR EVER. This psalm recounts Israel's recurring rebellion and apostasy with respect to God's word and ways. The psalmist confesses their sins and unfaithfulness and prays that God will once again visit His repentant people with full salvation and blessings. God's people individually and collectively should confess their shortcomings before the Lord. When we recognize our spiritual failure and then repent, real revival and reformation can take place (see article on CHRIST'S MESSAGE TO THE SEVEN CHURCHES, p. 2036).

106:15 HE GAVE THEM THEIR REQUEST; BUT SENT LEANNESS. We must beware of desiring and pursuing what is not in the will of God. When we insist on satisfying our selfish desires, God sometimes lets us have our own way, but with it comes spiritual leanness or physical calamity. God may allow us to pursue things contrary to His revealed will, such as an unholy vocational ambition, an unholy love affair, worldly pleasures, covetous desires, or ungodly fellowship with unbelievers, but in the end those things have destructive consequences (e.g., Gen. 13:12–13; 19; Hos. 13:11).

with their inventions: and the plague brake in upon them.

30 [w]Then stood up Phinehas, and executed judgment: and *so* the plague was stayed.

31 And that was counted unto him [x]for righteousness unto all generations for evermore.

32 [y]They angered *him* also at the waters of strife, so that it went ill with Moses for their sakes:

33 [z]Because they provoked his spirit, so that he spake unadvisedly with his lips.

34 [a]They did not destroy the nations, [b]concerning whom the LORD commanded them:

35 [c]But were mingled among the heathen, and learned their works.

36 And [d]they served their idols: [e]which were a snare unto them.

37 Yea, [f]they sacrificed their sons and their daughters unto [g]devils,

38 And shed innocent blood, *even* the blood of their sons and of their daughters, whom they sacrificed unto the idols of Canaan: and [h]the land was polluted with blood.

39 Thus were they [i]defiled with their own works, and [j]went a-whoring with their own inventions.

40 Therefore [k]was the wrath of the LORD kindled against his people, insomuch that he abhorred [l]his own inheritance.

41 And [m]he gave them into the hand of the heathen; and they that hated them ruled over them.

42 Their enemies also oppressed them, and they were brought into subjection under their hand.

43 [n]Many times did he deliver them; but they provoked *him* with their counsel, and were [s]brought low for their iniquity.

44 Nevertheless he regarded their affliction, when [o]he heard their cry:

45 [p]And he remembered for them his covenant, and [q]repented [r]according to the multitude of his mercies.

46 [s]He made them also to be pitied of all those that carried them captives.

47 [t]Save us, O LORD our God, and gather us from among the heathen, to give thanks unto thy holy name, *and* to triumph in thy praise.

48 [u]Blessed *be* the LORD God of Israel from everlasting to everlasting: and let all the people say, Amen. [t]Praise ye the LORD.

BOOK V

The LORD's goodness to men

107 O [v]GIVE thanks unto the LORD, for [w]*he is* good: for his mercy *endureth* for ever.

2 Let the redeemed of the LORD say *so,* [x]whom he hath redeemed from the hand of the enemy;

3 And [y]gathered them out of the lands, from the east, and from the west, from the north, and [u]from the south.

4 They wandered in [z]the wilderness in a solitary way; they found no city to dwell in.

5 Hungry and thirsty, their soul fainted in them.

6 [a]Then they cried unto the LORD in

[s] Or, *impoverished,* or, *weakened* [t] Heb. *Hallelujah* [u] Heb. *from the sea*

106:30 [w]Num. 25:7 **106:31** [x]Num. 25:11 **106:32** [y]Num. 20:3 Ps. 81:7 **106:33** [z]Num. 20:10 **106:34** [a]Judg. 1:21 [b]Deut. 7:2 Judg. 2:2 **106:35** [c]Judg. 3:5,6 Is. 2:6 **106:36** [d]Judg. 2:12 [e]Deut. 7:16 **106:37** [f]2 Ki. 16:3 [g]Lev. 17:7 **106:38** [h]Num. 35:33 **106:39** [i]Ezek. 20:18 [j]Lev. 17:7 Num. 15:39 Ezek. 20:30 **106:40** [k]Judg. 2:14 [l]Deut. 9:29 **106:41** [m]Judg. 2:14 Neh. 9:27 **106:43** [n]Judg. 2:16 Neh. 9:27 **106:44** [o]Judg. 10:10 **106:45** [p]Lev. 26:41 [q]Judg. 2:18 [r]Ps. 69:16 **106:46** [s]Ezra 9:9 Jer. 42:12 **106:47** [t]1 Chr. 16:35 **106:48** [u]Ps. 41:13 **107:1** [v]Ps. 106:1 [w]Ps. 119:68 **107:2** [x]Ps. 106:10 **107:3** [y]Ps. 106:47 **107:4** [z]Deut. 32:10 **107:6** [a]Ps. 50:15 Hos. 5:15

106:37 THEY SACRIFICED THEIR SONS AND THEIR DAUGHTERS UNTO DEVILS. Those who served idols in O.T. times were in actuality dealing with demons, for behind all false religions are demonic manifestations, powers, and influence (see article on THE NATURE OF IDOLATRY, p. 428). (1) Likewise, when a believer in Christ conforms to the world and adopts its ungodly customs and ways, he or she is in reality submitting to demonic influences (1 Cor. 10:19–22; see Eph. 2:2, note). (2) Today some in the church unknowingly sacrifice their children to demons by allowing them to be influenced by the ungodliness and immorality of the world through the entertainment media, unbelieving companions, or instruction contrary to Biblical truth.

107:1–43 GIVE THANKS UNTO THE LORD. This psalm exhorts the redeemed to praise the Lord for deliverance from desperate and dangerous situations. The psalmist uses four examples to illustrate that God responds to the extreme troubles of His people when they pray: hunger and thirst (vv. 4–9), slavery (vv. 10–16), illness almost to death (vv. 17–22), and the danger of storm (vv. 23–32). This psalm is relevant today for all believers who in misery and affliction cry out to the Lord. It builds up our faith and encourages us during those times when we need God to intervene specifically in our lives.

107:6 THEY CRIED UNTO THE LORD. Four times the psalmist uses this phrase, and four times it is stated that God "delivered them out of their distresses" (v. 6;cf. vv. 13,19,28). God frequently brings His children to a place where their own self-sufficiency fails and where no human being can help, in order that they might cry out to Him in humble and childlike faith.

their trouble, *and* he delivered them out of their distresses.

7 And he led them forth by the [b]right way, that they might go to a city of habitation.

8 [c]Oh that *men* would praise the LORD *for* his goodness, and *for* his wonderful works to the children of men!

9 For [d]he satisfieth the longing soul, and filleth the hungry soul with goodness.

10 Such as [e]sit in darkness and in the shadow of death, *being* [f]bound in affliction and iron;

11 Because they [g]rebelled against the words of God, and contemned [h]the counsel of the most High:

12 Therefore he brought down their heart with labour; they fell down, and *there was* [i]none to help.

13 Then they cried unto the LORD in their trouble, *and* he saved them out of their distresses.

14 [j]He brought them out of darkness and the shadow of death, and brake their bands in sunder.

15 [k]Oh that *men* would praise the LORD *for* his goodness, and *for* his wonderful works to the children of men!

16 For he hath [l]broken the gates of brass, and cut the bars of iron in sunder.

17 Fools [m]because of their transgression, and because of their iniquities, are afflicted.

18 [n]Their soul abhorreth all manner of meat; and they [o]draw near unto the gates of death.

19 Then they cry unto the LORD in their trouble, *and* he saveth them out of their distresses.

20 [p]He sent his word, and [q]healed them, and [r]delivered *them* from their destructions.

21 Oh that *men* would praise the LORD *for* his goodness, and *for* his wonderful works to the children of men!

22 [s]And let them sacrifice the sacrifices of thanksgiving, and [t]declare his works with [v]rejoicing.

23 They that go down to the sea in ships, that do business in great waters;

24 These see the works of the LORD, and his wonders in the deep.

25 For he commandeth, and [u]raiseth[w] the stormy wind, which lifteth up the waves thereof.

26 They mount up to the heaven, they go down again to the depths: [v]their soul is melted because of trouble.

27 They reel to and fro, and stagger like a drunken man, and [x]are at their wit's end.

28 [w]Then they cry unto the LORD in their trouble, and he bringeth them out of their distresses.

29 [x]He maketh the storm a calm, so that the waves thereof are still.

30 Then are they glad because they be quiet; so he bringeth them unto their desired haven.

31 [y]Oh that *men* would praise the LORD *for* his goodness, and *for* his wonderful works to the children of men!

32 Let them exalt him also [z]in the congregation of the people, and praise him in the assembly of the elders.

33 He [a]turneth rivers into a wilderness, and the watersprings into dry ground;

34 A [b]fruitful land into [y]barrenness, for the wickedness of them that dwell therein.

35 [c]He turneth the wilderness into a standing water, and dry ground into watersprings.

36 And there he maketh the hungry to dwell, that they may prepare a city for habitation;

37 And sow the fields, and plant vineyards, which may yield fruits of increase.

38 [d]He blesseth them also, so that they [e]are multiplied greatly; and suffereth not their cattle to decrease.

39 Again, they are [f]minished and brought low through oppression, affliction, and sorrow.

40 [g]He poureth contempt upon princes, and causeth them to wander in the [z]wilderness, *where there is* no way.

41 [h]Yet setteth he the poor on high [a]from affliction, and [i]maketh *him* families like a flock.

42 [j]The righteous shall see *it*, and

107:7 [b]Ezra 8:21
107:8 [c]ver. 15,21
107:9 [d]Ps. 34:10 Luke 1:53
107:10 [e]Luke 1:79 [f]Job 36:8
107:11 [g]Lam. 3:42 [h]Ps. 73:24 Luke 7:30 Acts 20:27
107:12 [i]Ps. 22:11 Is. 63:5
107:14 [j]Ps. 68:6 Acts 12:7
107:15 [k]ver. 8,21,31
107:16 [l]Is. 45:2
107:17 [m]Lam. 3:39
107:18 [n]Job 33:20 [o]Job 33:22 Ps. 9:13
107:20 [p]Mat. 8:8 [q]Ps. 30:2 & 103:3 [r]Job 33:28 Ps. 30:3 & 49:15
107:22 [s]Lev. 7:12 Ps. 116:17 Heb. 13:15 [t]Ps. 9:11 & 73:28 & 118:17
107:25 [u]Jonah 1:4
107:26 [v]Ps. 22:14
107:28 [w]ver. 6,13,19
107:29 [x]Ps. 89:9 Mat. 8:26
107:31 [y]ver. 8,15,21
107:32 [z]Ps. 22:22,25
107:33 [a]1 Ki. 17:1,7
107:34 [b]Gen. 13:10 & 14:3 & 19:25
107:35 [c]Ps. 114:8 Is. 41:18
107:38 [d]Gen. 12:2 & 17:16,20 [e]Ex. 1:7
107:39 [f]2 Ki. 10:32
107:40 [g]Job 12:21,24
107:41 [h]1 Sam. 2:8 Ps. 113:7,8 [i]Ps. 78:52
107:42 [j]Job 5:15,16

[v] Heb. *singing* [w] Heb. *maketh to stand*
[x] Heb. *all their wisdom is swallowed up*
[y] Heb. *saltness* [z] Or, *void place* [a] Or, *after*

107:13 HE SAVED THEM OUT OF THEIR DISTRESSES. Note that even when we have only ourselves to blame for our troubles, God desires to deliver us (vv. 1–13,17–22). Hence, even if we are experiencing great distress, knowing that God may be judging us, we can still put our hope in His mercy and call to Him in faith for His forgiveness and help.

rejoice: and all [k]iniquity shall stop her
mouth.
43 [l]Whoso *is* wise, and will ob-
serve these *things,* even they shall un-
derstand the lovingkindness of the
LORD.

A song of confidence in God

108:1–5pp — Ps. 57:7–11
108:6–13pp — Ps. 60:5–12

A Song *or* Psalm of David.

108 O [m]GOD, my heart is fixed;
I will sing and give praise,
even with my glory.
2 [n]Awake, psaltery and harp: I *my-*
self will awake early.
3 I will praise thee, O LORD, among
the people: and I will sing praises unto
thee among the nations.
4 For thy mercy *is* great above the
heavens: and thy truth *reacheth* unto
the [b]clouds.
5 [o]Be thou exalted, O God, above
the heavens: and thy glory above all
the earth;
6 [p]That thy beloved may be deliv-
ered: save *with* thy right hand, and an-
swer me.
7 God hath spoken in his holiness;
I will rejoice, I will divide Shechem,
and mete out the valley of Succoth.
8 Gilead *is* mine; Manasseh *is* mine;
Ephraim also *is* the strength of mine
head; [q]Judah *is* my lawgiver;
9 Moab *is* my washpot; over Edom
will I cast out my shoe; over Philistia
will I triumph.
10 [r]Who will bring me into the
strong city? who will lead me into
Edom?
11 *Wilt* not *thou,* O God, *who* hast
cast us off? and wilt not thou, O God,
go forth with our hosts?
12 Give us help from trouble: for
vain *is* the help of man.
13 [s]Through God we shall do val-
iantly: for he *it is that* shall tread down
our enemies.

107:42 [k]Job 5:16; Ps. 63:11; Prov. 10:11; Rom. 3:19
107:43 [l]Ps. 64:9; Jer. 9:12; Hos. 14:9
108:1 [m]Ps. 57:7
108:2 [n]Ps. 57:8-11
108:5 [o]Ps. 57:5,11
108:6 [p]Ps. 60:5
108:8 [q]Gen. 49:10
108:10 [r]Ps. 60:9
108:13 [s]Ps. 60:12
109:1 [t]Ps. 83:1
109:3 [u]Ps. 35:7 & 69:4; John 15:25
109:5 [v]Ps. 35:7,12 & 38:20
109:6 [w]Zech. 3:1
109:7 [x]Prov. 28:9
109:8 [y]Acts 1:20
109:9 [z]Ex. 22:24
109:11 [a]Job 5:5 & 18:9
109:13 [b]Job 18:19; Ps. 37:28; [c]Prov. 10:7
109:14 [d]Ex. 20:5; [e]Neh. 4:5; Jer. 18:23

A cry to God for help

To the chief Musician,
A Psalm of David.

109 HOLD [t]NOT thy peace,
O God of my praise;
2 For the mouth of the wicked and
the [c]mouth of the deceitful [d]are
opened against me: they have spoken
against me with a lying tongue.
3 They compassed me about also
with words of hatred; and fought
against me [u]without a cause.
4 For my love they are my adversar-
ies: but I *give myself unto* prayer.
5 And [v]they have rewarded me evil
for good, and hatred for my love.
6 Set thou a wicked man over him:
and let [w]Satan[e] stand at his right
hand.
7 When he shall be judged, let him
[f]be condemned: and [x]let his prayer
become sin.
8 Let his days be few; *and* [y]let an-
other take his [g]office.
9 [z]Let his children be fatherless,
and his wife a widow.
10 Let his children be continually
vagabonds, and beg: let them seek *their*
bread also out of their desolate places.
11 [a]Let the extortioner catch all
that he hath; and let the strangers
spoil his labour.
12 Let there be none to extend mer-
cy unto him: neither let there be any to
favour his fatherless children.
13 [b]Let his posterity be cut off; *and*
in the generation following let their
[c]name be blotted out.
14 [d]Let the iniquity of his fathers
be remembered with the LORD; and let
not the sin of his mother [e]be blotted
out.
15 Let them be before the LORD con-

[b] Or, *skies* [c] Heb. *mouth of deceit* [d] Heb. *have opened* themselves [e] Or, *an adversary* [f] Heb. *go out guilty,* or, *wicked* [g] Or, *charge*

108:1–13 MY HEART IS FIXED. This psalm combines the words from 57:7–11 and 60:4–12. The psalmist is confident that ultimately God will deliver His people and give them victory over all their enemies.

108:9 MOAB ... EDOM ... PHILISTIA. Moab, Edom, and Philistia were enemies of Israel on her eastern, southern, and western borders.

109:1–31 HOLD NOT THY PEACE, O GOD. This psalm appeals to God to judge and punish those who are wicked and deceitful. This prayer reflects a concern that justice be done on earth through the righteous punishment of serious criminals who hurt others for personal gain. In this age, to carry out just retribution is the only way to protect the innocent and assure that lawlessness will be held in check in society (see Rom. 13:1,4, notes). The psalmist's prayer will find ultimate fulfillment only when God again sends His Son Jesus to earth to destroy all evil and to reign upon the earth (Rev. 19—22; see also Ps. 35:1–38, note).

tinually, that he may [f]cut off the memory of them from the earth.

16 Because that he remembered not to show mercy, but persecuted the poor and needy man, that he might even slay the [g]broken in heart.

17 [h]As he loved cursing, so let it come unto him: as he delighted not in blessing, so let it be far from him.

18 As he clothed himself with cursing like as with his garment, so let it [i]come **[h]**into his bowels like water, and like oil into his bones.

19 Let it be unto him as the garment *which* covereth him, and for a girdle wherewith he is girded continually.

20 *Let* this *be* the reward of mine adversaries from the LORD, and of them that speak evil against my soul.

21 But do thou for me, O GOD the Lord, for thy name's sake: because thy mercy *is* good, deliver thou me.

22 For I *am* poor and needy, and my heart is wounded within me.

23 I am gone [j]like the shadow when it declineth: I am tossed up and down as the locust.

24 My [k]knees are weak through fasting; and my flesh faileth of fatness.

25 I became also [l]a reproach unto them: *when* they looked upon me [m]they shaked their heads.

26 Help me, O LORD my God: O save me according to thy mercy:

27 [n]That they may know that this *is* thy hand; *that* thou, LORD, hast done it.

28 [o]Let them curse, but bless thou: when they arise, let them be ashamed; but let [p]thy servant rejoice.

29 [q]Let mine adversaries be clothed with shame, and let them cover themselves with their own confusion, as with a mantle.

30 I will greatly praise the LORD with my mouth; yea, [r]I will praise him among the multitude.

109:15 [f]Job 18:17 Ps. 34:16
109:16 [g]Ps. 34:18
109:17 [h]Prov. 14:14 Ezek. 35:6
109:18 [i]Num. 5:22
109:23 [j]Ps. 102:11
109:24 [k]Heb. 12:12
109:25 [l]Ps. 22:6,7 [m]Mat. 27:39
109:27 [n]Job 37:7
109:28 [o]2 Sam. 16:11 [p]Is. 65:14
109:29 [q]Ps. 35:26 & 132:18
109:30 [r]Ps. 35:18 & 111:1
109:31 [s]Ps. 16:8 & 73:23
110:1 [t]Mat. 22:44 Mark 12:36 Luke 20:42 Acts 2:34 1 Cor. 15:25
110:3 [u]Judg. 5:2 [v]Ps. 96:9
110:4 [w]Num. 23:19
110:5 [x]Ps. 16:8 [y]Ps. 2:5,12 Rom. 2:5
110:6 [z]Ps. 68:21 Hab. 3:13
110:7 [a]Is. 53:12
111:1 [b]Ps. 35:18 & 89:5 & 107:32
111:2 [c]Job 38-41 Ps. 92:5 [d]Ps. 143:5
111:3 [e]Ps. 145:4

31 For [s]he shall stand at the right hand of the poor, to save *him* **[i]**from those that condemn his soul.

The king as priest and victor

A Psalm of David.

110 THE [t]LORD said unto my Lord, Sit thou at my right hand, until I make thine enemies thy footstool.

2 The LORD shall send the rod of thy strength out of Zion: rule thou in the midst of thine enemies.

3 [u]Thy people *shall be* willing in the day of thy power, [v]in the beauties of holiness **[j]**from the womb of the morning: thou hast the dew of thy youth.

4 The LORD hath sworn, and [w]will not repent, Thou *art* a priest for ever after the order of Melchizedek.

5 The Lord [x]at thy right hand shall strike through kings [y]in the day of his wrath.

6 He shall judge among the heathen, he shall fill *the places* with the dead bodies; [z]he shall wound the heads over **[k]**many countries.

7 He shall drink of the brook in the way: [a]therefore shall he lift up the head.

The LORD's wonderful works

111 PRAISE[1] YE the LORD. [b]I will praise the LORD with *my* whole heart, in the assembly of the upright, and *in* the congregation.

2 [c]The works of the LORD *are* great, [d]sought out of all them that have pleasure therein.

3 His work *is* [e]honourable and glo-

h Heb. *within him* **i** Heb. *from the judges of his soul* **j** Or, *more than the womb of the morning: thou shalt have* **k** Or, *great* **l** Heb. *Hallelujah*

110:1–7 THE LORD SAID UNTO MY LORD. This psalm speaks of the lordship of the Messiah, His priesthood, His destruction of the wicked, and His reign on earth. It clearly prophesies about Jesus Christ (the psalm is cited seven times in the N.T.). Jesus applied v. 1 to Himself in making His claim to deity (Mat. 22:44), and the apostle Peter quoted v. 1 to emphasize Christ's lordship (Acts 2:33–35; 5:30–31; cf. Rom. 8:34; Heb. 10:13). Heb. 5:6 and 6:20—7:28 quote v. 4 to prove that God made Christ a priest forever.

110:4 THOU *ART* A PRIEST FOR EVER. See Heb. 5:5–10; 6:19—7:28, for comments on how this is fulfilled in Christ.

110:6 HE SHALL JUDGE AMONG THE HEATHEN. This verse pictures Christ coming to the earth as a warrior to defeat and judge all those who oppose God's kingdom and His righteousness (see Rev. 19:11–21).

111:1–10 I WILL PRAISE THE LORD. This psalm praises the Lord for His physical and spiritual blessings and for His providential care over those who love and fear Him. The psalmist has determined to praise God not only privately but also "in the congregation" (v. 1). It is Biblical to praise God spontaneously and aloud in church.

rious: and his righteousness endureth for ever.

4 He hath made his wonderful works to be remembered: [f]the LORD *is* gracious and full of compassion.

5 He hath given [g]meat[m] unto them that fear him: he will ever be mindful of his covenant.

6 He hath shown his people the power of his works, that he may give them the heritage of the heathen.

7 The works of his hands *are* [h]verity and judgment; [i]all his commandments *are* sure.

8 [j]They [n]stand fast for ever and ever, *and are* [k]done in truth and uprightness.

9 [l]He sent redemption unto his people: he hath commanded his covenant for ever: [m]holy and reverend *is* his name.

10 [n]The fear of the LORD *is* the beginning of wisdom: [o]a[o] good understanding have all they [p]that do *his commandments:* his praise endureth for ever.

The prosperity of the righteous

112 PRAISE[q] YE the LORD. Blessed *is* the man *that* feareth the LORD, *that* [p]delighteth greatly in his commandments.

2 [q]His seed shall be mighty upon earth: the generation of the upright shall be blessed.

3 [r]Wealth and riches *shall be* in his house: and his righteousness endureth for ever.

4 [s]Unto the upright there ariseth light in the darkness: *he is* gracious, and full of compassion, and righteous.

111:4 [f]Ps. 86:5 & 103:8
111:5 [g]Mat. 6:26
111:7 [h]Rev. 15:3 [i]Ps. 19:7
111:8 [j]Is. 40:8 [k]Rev:15:3
111:9 [l]Luke 1:68 [m]Luke 1:49
111:10 [n]Eccl. 12:13 [o]Prov. 3:4
112:1 [p]Ps. 119:16
112:2 [q]Ps. 102:28
112:3 [r]Mat. 6:33
112:4 [s]Job 11:17 Ps. 97:11
112:5 [t]Ps. 37:26 [u]Eph. 5:15 Col. 4:5
112:6 [v]Prov. 10:7
112:7 [w]Prov. 1:33 [x]Ps. 57:7 [y]Ps. 64:10
112:8 [z]Prov. 1:33 [a]Ps. 59:10 & 118:7
112:9 [b]2 Cor. 9:9 [c]Ps. 75:10
112:10 [d]Luke 13:28 [e]Ps. 37:12 [f]Ps. 58:7,8 [g]Prov. 11:7
113:1 [h]Ps. 135:1
113:2 [i]Dan. 2:20
113:3 [j]Is. 59:19 Mal. 1:11
113:4 [k]Ps. 97:9 & 99:2 [l]Ps. 8:1
113:5 [m]Ps. 89:6

5 [t]A good man showeth favour, and lendeth: he will guide his affairs [u]with [r]discretion.

6 Surely he shall not be moved for ever: [v]the righteous shall be in everlasting remembrance.

7 [w]He shall not be afraid of evil tidings: his [x]heart is fixed, [y]trusting in the LORD.

8 His heart *is* established, [z]he shall not be afraid, until he [a]see *his desire* upon his enemies.

9 [b]He hath dispersed, he hath given to the poor; his righteousness endureth for ever; [c]his horn shall be exalted with honour.

10 [d]The wicked shall see *it,* and be grieved; [e]he shall gnash with his teeth, and [f]melt away: [g]the desire of the wicked shall perish.

A hymn of praise to God

113 PRAISE[q] YE the LORD. [h]Praise, O ye servants of the LORD, praise the name of the LORD.

2 [i]Blessed be the name of the LORD from this time forth and for evermore.

3 [j]From the rising of the sun unto the going down of the same the LORD's name *is* to be praised.

4 The LORD *is* [k]high above all nations, *and* [l]his glory above the heavens.

5 [m]Who *is* like unto the LORD our God, who [s]dwelleth on high,

[m] Heb. *prey* [n] Heb. are *established* [o] Or, *good success* [p] Heb. *that do them* [q] Heb. *Hallelujah* [r] Heb. *judgment* [s] Heb. *exalteth* himself *to dwell*

111:10 THE FEAR OF THE LORD *IS* THE BEGINNING OF WISDOM. This truth serves as the foundation for O.T. wisdom literature (see Job 28:28; Prov. 1:7; 9:10; Eccl. 12:13; see article on THE FEAR OF THE LORD, p. 282).

112:1–10 BLESSED *IS* THE MAN. This psalm speaks of the blessings in store for a God-fearing and righteous person. God promises to bless those who fear Him and delight in His commandments and written Word (v. 1; cf. Ps. 119).

112:1 DELIGHTETH GREATLY IN HIS COMMANDMENTS. What matters most in the life of a God-fearing person is that God's will be done on earth (cf. Mat. 6:10). Such people love God's laws because His commands represent the righteousness scorned by the world (v. 10; see Heb. 1:9, note).

112:3 WEALTH AND RICHES. See 1 John 2, note on the well-being of God's faithful people.

112:7 HE SHALL NOT BE AFRAID OF EVIL TIDINGS. The psalmist is not moved by fear and anxiety in times of trouble because his trust is in the Lord and not in himself or in external circumstances (cf. Ps. 37).

113–118 PASSOVER PSALMS. These psalms were used by Jews at the yearly Passover celebration. The first two were sung before the meal and the remaining four after the meal. Thus these were probably the last songs Jesus Christ sang before His death. Since these psalms begin in Hebrew with the word "Hallelujah" (113:1), Jews came to call them "The Hallel [Praise]."

113:1–9 PRAISE YE THE LORD. This psalm reiterates the twofold Biblical principle that God gives grace to the humble (cf. Jas. 4:6,10; 1 Pet. 5:5–7) and has compassion on the poor and needy (see Luke 7:13, note; 1 Tim. 5:9, note; see article on THE CARE OF THE POOR AND NEEDY, p. 1312).

6 [n]Who humbleth *himself* to behold *the things that are* in heaven, and in the earth!

7 [o]He raiseth up the poor out of the dust, *and* lifteth the needy out of the dunghill;

8 That he may [p]set *him* with princes, *even* with the princes of his people.

9 [q]He maketh the barren woman [t]to keep house, *and to be* a joyful mother of children. Praise ye the LORD.

[Ps. 135:1-4]

The God of the exodus

114 WHEN [r]ISRAEL went out of Egypt, the house of Jacob [s]from a people of strange language;

2 [t]Judah was his sanctuary, *and* Israel his dominion.

3 [u]The sea saw *it,* and fled: [v]Jordan was driven back.

4 [w]The mountains skipped like rams, *and* the little hills like lambs.

5 [x]What *ailed* thee, O thou sea, that thou fleddest? thou Jordan, *that* thou wast driven back?

6 Ye mountains, *that* ye skipped like rams; *and* ye little hills, like lambs?

7 Tremble, thou earth, at the presence of the Lord, at the presence of the God of Jacob;

8 [y]Which turned the rock *into* a standing water, the flint into a fountain of waters.

To God alone belongs glory

115:4–11pp — Ps. 135:15–20

115 NOT [z]UNTO us, O LORD, not unto us, but unto thy name give glory, for thy mercy, *and* for thy truth's sake.

2 Wherefore should the heathen say, [a]Where *is* now their God?

3 [b]But our God *is* in the heavens: he hath done whatsoever he hath pleased.

4 [c]Their idols *are* silver and gold, the work of men's hands.

5 They have mouths, but they speak not: eyes have they, but they see not:

113:6 [n]Ps. 11:4 & 138:6 Is. 57:15
113:7 [o]1 Sam. 2:8 Ps. 107:41
113:8 [p]Job 36:7
113:9 [q]1 Sam. 2:5 Ps. 68:6 Is. 54:1 Gal. 4:27
114:1 [r]Ex. 13:3 [s]Ps. 81:5
114:2 [t]Ex. 6:7 Deut. 27:9
114:3 [u]Ex. 14:21 Ps. 77:16 [v]Josh. 3:13
114:4 [w]Ps. 29:6 & 68:16
114:5 [x]Hab. 3:8
114:8 [y]Ex. 17:6 Num. 20:11 Ps. 107:35
115:1 [z]Is. 48:11 Ezek. 36:32
115:2 [a]Ps. 42:3,10 & 79:10 Joel 2:17
115:3 [b]1 Chr. 16:26 Ps. 135:6 Dan. 4:35
115:4 [c]Deut. 4:28 Ps. 135:15 Jer. 10:3
115:8 [d]Ps. 135:18 Is. 44:9-11
115:9 [e]Ps. 118:2,3 [f]Ps. 33:20
115:13 [g]Ps. 128:1
115:15 [h]Gen. 14:19 [i]Gen. 1:1 Ps. 96:5
115:17 [j]Ps. 6:5 & 88:10-12 Is. 38:18
115:18 [k]Ps. 113:2 Dan. 2:20
116:1 [l]Ps. 18:1
116:3 [m]Ps. 18:4-6

6 They have ears, but they hear not: noses have they, but they smell not:

7 They have hands, but they handle not: feet have they, but they walk not: neither speak they through their throat.

8 [d]They that make them are like unto them; *so is* every one that trusteth in them.

9 [e]O Israel, trust thou in the LORD: [f]he *is* their help and their shield.

10 O house of Aaron, trust in the LORD: he *is* their help and their shield.

11 Ye that fear the LORD, trust in the LORD: he *is* their help and their shield.

12 The LORD hath been mindful of us: he will bless *us;* he will bless the house of Israel; he will bless the house of Aaron.

13 [g]He will bless them that fear the LORD, *both* small [u]and great.

14 The LORD shall increase you more and more, you and your children.

15 Ye *are* [h]blessed of the LORD [i]which made heaven and earth.

16 The heaven, *even* the heavens, *are* the LORD's: but the earth hath he given to the children of men.

17 [j]The dead praise not the LORD, neither any that go down into silence.

18 [k]But we will bless the LORD from this time forth and for evermore. Praise the LORD.

Deliverance from death

116 I [l]LOVE the LORD, because he hath heard my voice *and* my supplications. ✝

2 Because he hath inclined his ear unto me, therefore will I call upon *him* [v]as long as I live.

3 [m]The sorrows of death compassed me, and the pains of hell [w]gat hold upon me: I found trouble and sorrow.

[t]Heb. *to dwell in an house* [u]Heb. *with*
[v]Heb. *in my days* [w]Heb. *found me*

115:1 NOT UNTO US ... BUT UNTO THY NAME GIVE GLORY. We must never seek glory for ourselves, but rather always desire to manifest God's glory and honor His name before the world. We must determine to live in such a way that we will not bring shame or reproach upon the name of Christ or His church (cf. Mat. 5:14–16; 1 Cor. 6:20).

115:9 TRUST THOU IN THE LORD. Those who trust in the Lord rather than in things that can be seen (vv. 4–8) receive the Lord as their help and shield (vv. 9–11). He remembers those who fear Him and promises to bless them (vv. 12–15). God rules in the heavens, but He has delegated the rule of the earth to "the children of men" (v. 16).

116:1–19 I LOVE THE LORD. This psalm expresses thanksgiving to the Lord for deliverance from death and declares the praise of all afflicted believers who have been rescued by the Lord and have been spared death or great calamity.

4 Then called I upon the name of the LORD; O LORD, I beseech thee, deliver my soul.

5 [n]Gracious *is* the LORD, and [o]righteous; yea, our God *is* merciful.

6 The LORD preserveth the simple: I was brought low, and he helped me.

7 Return unto thy [p]rest, O my soul; for [q]the LORD hath dealt bountifully with thee.

8 [r]For thou hast delivered my soul from death, mine eyes from tears, *and* my feet from falling.

9 I will walk before the LORD [s]in the land of the living.

10 [t]I believed, therefore have I spoken: I was greatly afflicted:

11 [u]I said in my haste, [v]All men *are* liars.

12 What shall I render unto the LORD *for* all his benefits toward me?

13 I will take the cup of salvation, and call upon the name of the LORD.

s. 12:1-3

14 [w]I will pay my vows unto the LORD now in the presence of all his people.

15 [x]Precious in the sight of the LORD *is* the death of his saints.

16 O LORD, truly [y]I *am* thy servant; I *am* thy servant, *and* [z]the son of thine handmaid: thou hast loosed my bonds.

17 I will offer to thee [a]the sacrifice of thanksgiving, and will call upon the name of the LORD.

18 I will pay my vows unto the LORD now in the presence of all his people,

19 In the [b]courts of the LORD's house, in the midst of thee, O Jerusalem. Praise ye the LORD.

116:5 [n]Ps. 103:8 [o]Ezra 9:15 Neh. 9:8 Ps. 119:137 & 145:17
116:7 [p]Jer. 6:16 Mat. 11:29 [q]Ps. 13:6 & 119:17
116:8 [r]Ps. 56:13
116:9 [s]Ps. 27:13
116:10 [t]2 Cor. 4:13
116:11 [u]Ps. 31:22 [v]Rom. 3:4
116:14 [w]ver. 18 Ps. 22:25 Jonah 2:9
116:15 [x]Ps. 72:14
116:16 [y]Ps. 119:125 & 143:12 [z]Ps. 86:16
116:17 [a]Lev. 7:12 Ps. 50:14 & 107:22
116:19 [b]Ps. 96:8 & 100:4
117:1 [c]Rom. 15:11
117:2 [d]Ps. 100:5
118:1 [e]1 Chr. 16:8 Ps. 106:1 & 107:1
118:2 [f]Ps. 115:9
118:5 [g]Ps. 120:1 [h]Ps. 18:19
118:6 [i]Ps. 27:1 Heb. 13:6
118:7 [j]Ps. 54:4 [k]Ps. 59:10
118:8 [l]Ps. 40:4 & 62:8,9
118:9 [m]Ps. 146:3
118:11 [n]Ps. 88:17

Praise for God's steadfast love

117 O [c]PRAISE the LORD, all ye nations: praise him, all ye people.

2 For his merciful kindness is great toward us: and [d]the truth of the LORD *endureth* for ever. Praise ye the LORD.

The LORD's mercy

118 O [e]GIVE thanks unto the LORD; for *he is* good: because his mercy *endureth* for ever.

2 [f]Let Israel now say, that his mercy *endureth* for ever.

3 Let the house of Aaron now say, that his mercy *endureth* for ever.

4 Let them now that fear the LORD say, that his mercy *endureth* for ever.

5 [g]I called upon the LORD [x]in distress: the LORD answered me, *and* [h]*set me* in a large place.

6 [i]The LORD *is* [y]on my side; I will not fear: what can man do unto me?

7 [j]The LORD taketh my part with them that help me: therefore shall [k]I see *my desire* upon them that hate me.

8 [l]*It is* better to trust in the LORD than to put confidence in man.

9 [m]*It is* better to trust in the LORD than to put confidence in princes.

10 All nations compassed me about: but in the name of the LORD will I [z]destroy them.

11 They [n]compassed me about; yea, they compassed me about: but in the name of the LORD I will destroy them.

[x] Heb. *out of distress* [y] Heb. *for me* [z] Heb. *cut them off*

116:12 WHAT SHALL I RENDER UNTO THE LORD *FOR* ALL HIS BENEFITS. Gratitude flows from the hearts of all those who have experienced salvation from the Lord. They will express it by their love (v. 1), loyalty (v. 2), righteous living (v. 9), thanksgiving, and a firm resolve to obey the Lord (v. 14).

116:15 PRECIOUS ... *IS* THE DEATH OF HIS SAINTS. (1) The Lord carefully watches over the lives of his faithful people. (2) He exercises control over the circumstances of their death (Rom. 8:28,35–39). (3) When they are dying, He is there with them. (4) Their death, which is of great value to Him, is the occasion when they are delivered from all evil, are taken from this life to blessed victory, and are brought into heaven to see Jesus face to face (see Phil. 1:21, note; see article on DEATH, p. 782).

117:1 ALL YE NATIONS. Paul quotes this verse in Rom. 15:11 to prove that the O.T. anticipated God's offer of salvation to people of all nations (cf. Ps. 67).

118:1–29 HIS MERCY *ENDURETH* FOR EVER. This psalm praises the Lord for His everlasting love for His people. It may have been the last words sung by Jesus and His disciples before He went to the Garden of Gethsemane, where He was arrested and led to His death (cf. Mat. 26:30; Mark 14:26). It will also be sung before the return of Christ at the end of the age (compare v. 26 with Mat. 23:39). When reading this psalm, meditate on what might have been in Christ's mind when He sang it for the last time.

118:6 THE LORD *IS* ON MY SIDE. Those who take refuge in the Lord are assured that He is for them and with them to give help and strength (vv. 7,14; see Ex. 3:14, note; Josh. 1:9; Jer. 1:8).

12 They compassed me about [o]like
bees; they are quenched [p]as the fire of
thorns: for in the name of the LORD I
will [a]destroy them.
13 Thou hast thrust sore at me that
I might fall: but the LORD helped me.
14 [q]The LORD *is* my strength and
song, and is become my salvation.
15 The voice of rejoicing and salva-
tion *is* in the tabernacles of the righ-
teous: the right hand of the LORD doeth
valiantly.
16 [r]The right hand of the LORD is
exalted: the right hand of the LORD
doeth valiantly.
17 [s]I shall not die, but live, and
[t]declare the works of the LORD.
18 The LORD hath [u]chastened me
sore: but he hath not given me over
unto death.
19 [v]Open to me the gates of righ-
teousness: I will go into them, *and* I
will praise the LORD:
20 [w]This gate of the LORD, [x]into
which the righteous shall enter.
21 I will praise thee: for thou hast
[y]heard me, and [z]art become my sal-
vation.
22 [a]The stone *which* the builders
refused is become the head *stone* of the
corner.
23 [b]This is the LORD's doing; it *is*
marvellous in our eyes.
24 This *is* the day *which* the LORD
hath made; we will rejoice and be glad
in it.
25 Save now, I beseech thee,
O LORD: O LORD, I beseech thee, send
now prosperity.
26 [b]Blessed *be* he that cometh in
the name of the LORD: we have blessed
you out of the house of the LORD.
27 God *is* the LORD, which hath
shown us [c]light: bind the sacrifice
with cords, *even* unto the horns of the
altar.
28 Thou *art* my God, and I will
praise thee: [d]*thou art* my God, I will
exalt thee.
29 [e]O give thanks unto the LORD;
for *he is* good: for his mercy *endureth* for
ever.

118:12 [o]Deut. 1:44 [p]Eccl. 7:6 Nah. 1:10 **118:14** [q]Ex. 15:2 Is. 12:2 **118:16** [r]Ex. 15:6 **118:17** [s]Ps. 6:5 Hab. 1:12 [t]Ps. 73:28 **118:18** [u]2 Cor. 6:9 **118:19** [v]Is. 26:2 **118:20** [w]Ps. 24:7 [x]Is. 35:8 Rev. 22:14 **118:21** [y]Ps. 116:1 [z]ver. 14 **118:22** [a]Mat. 21:42 Mark 12:10 Luke 20:17 Acts 4:11 **118:26** [b]Mat. 21:9 Mark 11:9 Luke 19:38 See Zech. 4:7 **118:27** [c]Esth. 8:16 1 Pet. 2:9 **118:28** [d]Ex. 15:2 Is. 25:1 **118:29** [e]ver. 1 **119:1** [f]Ps. 128:1 **119:3** [g]1 John 3:9 & 5:18

Keepers of God's law

ALEPH.

119 BLESSED *ARE* the [c]un-
defiled in the way, [f]who
walk in the law of the LORD.
2 Blessed *are* they that keep his tes-
timonies, *and that* seek him with the
whole heart.
3 [g]They also do no iniquity: they
walk in his ways.
4 Thou hast commanded *us* to keep
thy precepts diligently.

[a] Heb. *cut down* [b] Heb. *This is from the LORD* [c] Or, *perfect*, or, *sincere*

118:22–23 THE STONE . . . REFUSED. Jesus applied these verses to Himself because He was cast aside by His own people, but afterwards became the principal stone of God's new house, the church (Mat. 21:42; Mark 12:10; Luke 20:17; Acts 4:11; Eph. 2:20; 1 Pet. 2:7).

118:24 THIS IS THE DAY. The context shows the day referred to here is a day of salvation or redemption.

118:25 SAVE NOW. This phrase (Heb. *hosh'iana'*) becomes "Hosanna" in the Greek translation of the O.T.; it prophesies the salvation through Christ's sacrifice (cf. vv. 26–27) and was sung by the crowds during Jesus' triumphal entry into Jerusalem (cf. Mat. 21:9).

119:1–176 BLESSED *ARE* THE UNDEFILED. This psalm expresses a majestic love for God's written Word. It deals with the Word as promise, commandment, guide, testimony, teaching, wisdom, truth, righteousness, and reproof. It is presented as the psalmist's comfort, protection, treasure, rule for life, delight to his heart and soul, and resource for all his needs. (1) The psalmist expresses a profound love for God by reading, meditating upon, and praying over His Word. He teaches us that we will grow in grace and righteousness only as love for that Word increases in us.

(2) This psalm is called an alphabetical acrostic because its twenty-two stanzas (or paragraphs) of eight verses each correspond to the twenty-two letters of the Hebrew alphabet. Each verse in the paragraphs begins with the letter characteristic of its stanza.

119:1 BLESSED. God promises to pour out His blessing on those who have chosen to live by His Word with all its standards and directives. They will have His personal presence (cf. Gen. 26:3), bringing them strength, help, and protection (Eph. 3:16; Col. 1:11; see Luke 24:50, note).

119:1 THE LAW. The law (Heb. *torah*) represents God's entire instruction to His people. It can also refer to the Pentateuch (the first five books of the O.T.) or to the O.T. as a whole.

119:2 TESTIMONIES. God's testimonies (Heb. *'edot*) represent the covenant stipulations or requirements that are declared as His will.

119:3 WAYS. God's ways (Heb. *derek*) represent those principles and means of operation by which God relates to His people and advances His redemption in the earth. His ways are contrary to humanistic wisdom and values (see Is. 55.8–9).

119:4 PRECEPTS. God's precepts (Heb. *piqqudim*) involve detailed instruction from the Lord.

5 O that my ways were directed to keep thy statutes!

6 [h]Then shall I not be ashamed, when I have respect unto all thy commandments.

7 [i]I will praise thee with uprightness of heart, when I shall have learned [d]thy righteous judgments.

8 I will keep thy statutes: O forsake me not utterly.

BETH.

Purity, the fruit of the law

9 Wherewithal shall a young man cleanse his way? by taking heed *thereto* according to thy word.

10 With my whole heart have I [j]sought thee: O let me not [k]wander from thy commandments.

11 [l]Thy word have I hid in mine heart, that I might not sin against thee.

12 Blessed *art* thou, O LORD: [m]teach me thy statutes.

13 With my lips have I [n]declared all the judgments of thy mouth.

14 I have rejoiced in the way of thy testimonies, as *much as* in all riches.

15 I will [o]meditate in thy precepts, and have respect unto thy ways.

Prov. 3:1-6 16 I will [p]delight myself in thy statutes: I will not forget thy word.

119:6 [h]Job 22:26 1 John 2:28
119:7 [i]ver. 171
119:10 [j]2 Chr. 15:15 [k]ver. 21,118
119:11 [l]Ps. 37:31 Luke 2:19
119:12 [m]ver. 26,33 Ps. 25:4
119:13 [n]Ps. 34:11
119:15 [o]ver. 23,48 Ps. 1:2
119:16 [p]Ps. 1:2
119:17 [q]Ps. 116:7
119:19 [r]Gen. 47:9 1 Chr. 29:15 Ps. 39:12 2 Cor. 5:6 Heb. 11:13
119:20 [s]Ps. 42:1,2 & 63:1 & 84:2
119:21 [t]ver. 10,110
119:22 [u]Ps. 39:8
119:23 [v]ver. 15
119:24 [w]ver. 77,92
119:25 [x]Ps. 44:25 [y]Ps. 143:11

GIMEL.

Eyes to see God's law

17 [q]Deal bountifully with thy servant, *that* I may live, and keep thy word.

18 [e]Open thou mine eyes, that I may behold wondrous things out of thy law.

19 [r]I *am* a stranger in the earth: hide not thy commandments from me.

20 [s]My soul breaketh for the longing *that it hath* unto thy judgments at all times.

21 Thou hast rebuked the proud *that are* cursed, which do [t]err from thy commandments.

22 [u]Remove from me reproach and contempt; for I have kept thy testimonies.

23 Princes also did sit *and* speak against me: *but* thy servant did [v]meditate in thy statutes.

24 [w]Thy testimonies also *are* my delight *and* [f]my counsellors.

DALETH.

Prayer for understanding the law

25 [x]My soul cleaveth unto the dust: [y]quicken thou me according to thy word.

26 I have declared my ways, and

[d] Heb. *judgments of thy righteousness* [e] Heb. *Reveal* [f] Heb. *men of my counsel*

119:5 STATUTES. God's statutes (Heb. *huqqim*) consist of regulations for His people individually and collectively.

119:5 O THAT MY WAYS WERE DIRECTED TO KEEP THY STATUTES! Believers should ask God continually for the grace needed to follow His will and be established in His ways. Such a petition is necessary because we cannot remain faithful to God's laws without His sustaining help and the work of the Holy Spirit in our hearts (see Mat. 7:21, note).

119:6 COMMANDMENTS. God's commandments (Heb. *miswot*) refer to rules and regulations that express God's authority and will for His people and that He expects us to obey.

119:7 JUDGMENTS. God's judgments (Heb. *mishpatim*) are His verdicts as divine Judge regarding the actions of people with one another.

119:9 WORD. God's word (Heb. *dabar*) represents both His revelation in general and His commandments and promises.

119:9 WHEREWITHAL SHALL A YOUNG MAN CLEANSE HIS WAY? How may believers keep their lives pure, resisting the immoral influences that characterize the ungodly environment in which we live? The second stanza of this psalm lists the following eight ways, one in each verse: (1) by making an irreversible decision to remain loyal to God's written Word for the rest of our lives; (2) by seeking the Lord in prayer; (3) by committing God's Word to memory; (4) by looking to God for guidance; (5) by taking an open stand for God's truth; (6) by rejoicing and delighting in what God says; (7) by considering the outcome of God's ways as opposed to the ways of the world; and (8) by never becoming too busy to read and study God's Word.

119:23 PRINCES ALSO DID SIT *AND* SPEAK AGAINST ME. The psalmist testifies that he has suffered much scorn, contempt, and slander as he attempted to live a righteous life in accordance with God's Word; this opposition, however, did not deter him from following God's way. Today those who are faithful to Christ and His Word must also expect to be criticized and ridiculed. They may be called legalists or extremists by those who conform to the worldly ways of an ungodly society (see Mat. 5:10, note; Luke 6:22, note).

thou heardest me: [z]teach me thy statutes.

27 Make me to understand the way of thy precepts: so [a]shall I talk of thy wondrous works.

28 [b]My soul [g]melteth for heaviness: strengthen thou me according unto thy word.

29 Remove from me the way of lying: and grant me thy law graciously.

30 I have chosen the way of truth: thy judgments have I laid *before me.*

31 I have stuck unto thy testimonies: O LORD, put me not to shame.

32 I will run the way of thy commandments, when thou shalt [c]enlarge my heart.

HE.

Living the LORD's way

33 [d]Teach me, O LORD, the way of thy statutes; and I shall keep it [e]*unto* the end.

34 Give me understanding, and I shall keep thy law; yea, I shall observe it with *my* whole heart.

35 Make me to go in the path of thy commandments; for therein do I [f]delight.

36 Incline my heart unto thy testimonies, and not to [g]covetousness.

37 [h]Turn[h] away mine eyes from [i]beholding vanity; *and* quicken thou me in thy way.

38 [j]Stablish thy word unto thy servant, who *is devoted* to thy fear.

39 Turn away my reproach which I fear: for thy judgments *are* good.

40 Behold, I have [k]longed after thy precepts: [l]quicken me in thy righteousness.

119:26 [z]Ps. 25:4 & 27:11 & 86:11 **119:27** [a]Ps. 145:5,6 **119:28** [b]Ps. 107:26 **119:32** [c]1 Ki. 4:29 Is. 60:5 2 Cor. 6:11 **119:33** [d]ver. 12 [e]Mat. 10:22 Rev. 2:26 **119:35** [f]ver. 16 **119:36** [g]Ezek. 33:31 Mark 7:21 Luke 12:15 Heb. 13:5 **119:37** [h]Is. 33:15 [i]Prov. 23:5 **119:38** [j]2 Sam. 7:25 **119:40** [k]ver. 20 [l]ver. 25,37

119:41 [m]ver. 77 Ps. 106:4 **119:46** [n]Ps. 138:1 Mat. 10:18 Acts 26 **119:47** [o]ver. 16 **119:48** [p]ver. 15 **119:49** [q]ver. 74,81 **119:50** [r]Rom. 15:4 **119:51** [s]Jer. 20:7 [t]ver. 157 Job 23:11 Ps. 44:18

VAU.

Salvation through God's law

41 [m]Let thy mercies come also unto me, O LORD, *even* thy salvation, according to thy word.

42 [i]So shall I have wherewith to answer him that reproacheth me: for I trust in thy word.

43 And take not the word of truth utterly out of my mouth; for I have hoped in thy judgments.

44 So shall I keep thy law continually for ever and ever.

45 And I will walk [j]at liberty: for I seek thy precepts.

46 [n]I will speak of thy testimonies also before kings, and will not be ashamed.

47 And I will [o]delight myself in thy commandments, which I have loved.

48 My hands also will I lift up unto thy commandments, which I have loved; and I will [p]meditate in thy statutes.

ZAIN.

Comfort in God's law

49 Remember the word unto thy servant, upon which thou hast caused me to [q]hope.

50 This *is* my [r]comfort in my affliction: for thy word hath quickened me.

51 The proud have had me greatly [s]in derision: *yet* have I not [t]declined from thy law.

52 I remembered thy judgments of old, O LORD; and have comforted myself.

[g] Heb. *droppeth* [h] Heb. *Make to pass* [i] Or, *So shall I answer him that reproacheth me in a thing* [j] Heb. *at large*

119:27 MAKE ME TO UNDERSTAND THE WAY OF THY PRECEPTS. God's Word can only be understood fully with His help (vv. 26–27,29). Thus we should continually pray for God, through His Holy Spirit, to draw near to us, to increase our understanding, and to teach us His truth (see John 14:17, note; 1 John 2:27, note).

119:47–48 I WILL DELIGHT . . . I HAVE LOVED . . . THY COMMANDMENTS. A major emphasis of Ps. 119 is the psalmist's delight in and heartfelt love for the Word of God. (1) Joy comes to his heart as he reads and obeys God's Word. Likewise, when we read the Bible with an earnest desire to understand and keep Christ's commandments (vv. 20,24,40,60), the Holy Spirit imparts God's love to our hearts (see John 14:15–17,21,23; Rom. 5:5, note), helps us to discern the truth of God's Word, and brings us great joy and delight (cf. John 15:10–11).

(2) Delighting in God's Word develops into an even deeper love for all God's ways. Because we have come to love Him (v. 132), we love the Scriptures that reveal Him and His will to us. As a result, we have been made one with Him (Rom. 6:5), and our hearts now have a profound love and devotion for His revealed truth.

119:50 MY COMFORT IN MY AFFLICTION . . . THY WORD. God has ordained that His Word, made powerful by the Spirit, will bring comfort, hope, and strength to His faithful as we experience trouble and sorrow. Because God's Word is living (cf. Heb. 4:12), it has power to revive and restore us who abide in it and in God (cf. John 14:27). When in trouble, turn to the Lord and His Word and wait for His Spirit to give peace to your heart (cf. Phil. 4:6–9).

53 [u]Horror hath taken hold upon me because of the wicked that forsake thy law.

54 Thy statutes have been my songs in the house of my pilgrimage.

55 [v]I have remembered thy name, O LORD, in the night, and have kept thy law.

56 This I had, because I kept thy precepts.

CHETH.

The LORD our portion

57 [w]*Thou art* my portion, O LORD: I have said that I would keep thy words.

58 I entreated thy favour with *my* whole heart: be merciful unto me [x]according to thy word.

59 I [y]thought on my ways, and turned my feet unto thy testimonies.

60 I made haste, and delayed not to keep thy commandments.

61 The [k]bands of the wicked have robbed me: *but* I have not forgotten thy law.

62 [z]At midnight I will rise to give thanks unto thee because of thy righteous judgments.

63 I *am* a companion of all *them* that fear thee, and of them that keep thy precepts.

64 [a]The earth, O LORD, is full of thy mercy: [b]teach me thy statutes.

TETH.

God's law taught by affliction

65 Thou hast dealt well with thy servant, O LORD, according unto thy word.

66 Teach me good judgment and knowledge: for I have believed thy commandments.

67 [c]Before I was afflicted I went astray: but now have I kept thy word.

68 Thou *art* [d]good, and doest good; [e]teach me thy statutes.

69 The proud have [f]forged a lie against me: *but* I will keep thy precepts with *my* whole heart.

70 [g]Their heart is as fat as grease; *but* I [h]delight in thy law.

71 [i]*It is* good for me that I have been afflicted; that I might learn thy statutes.

72 [j]The law of thy mouth *is* better unto me than thousands of gold and silver.

JOD.

Confidence in the law

73 [k]Thy hands have made me and fashioned me: [l]give me understanding, that I may learn thy commandments.

74 [m]They that fear thee will be glad when they see me; because [n]I have hoped in thy word.

75 I know, O LORD, that thy judgments *are* [1]right, and [o]*that* thou in faithfulness hast afflicted me.

76 Let, I pray thee, thy merciful kindness be [m]for my comfort, according to thy word unto thy servant.

77 [p]Let thy tender mercies come unto me, that I may live: for [q]thy law *is* my delight.

78 Let the proud [r]be ashamed; [s]for they dealt perversely with me without a cause: *but* I will [t]meditate in thy precepts.

79 Let those that fear thee turn unto me, and those that have known thy testimonies.

80 Let my heart be sound in thy statutes; that I be not ashamed.

CAPH.

A longing for comfort

81 [u]My soul fainteth for thy salvation: *but* [v]I hope in thy word.

82 [w]Mine eyes fail for thy word, saying, When wilt thou comfort me?

83 For [x]I am become like a bottle in the smoke; *yet* do I not forget thy statutes.

84 [y]How many *are* the days of thy servant? [z]when wilt thou execute judgment on them that persecute me?

119:53 [u]Ezra 9:3 **119:55** [v]Ps. 63:6 **119:57** [w]Ps. 16:5 Jer. 10:16 Lam. 3:24 **119:58** [x]ver. 41 **119:59** [y]Luke 15:17 **119:62** [z]Acts 16:25 **119:64** [a]Ps. 33:5 [b]ver. 12,26 **119:67** [c]ver. 71 Jer. 31:18 Heb. 12:11 **119:68** [d]Ps. 106:1 & 107:1 Mat. 19:17 [e]ver. 12,26 **119:69** [f]Job 13:4 Ps. 109:2 **119:70** [g]Ps. 17:10 Is. 6:10 Acts 28:27 [h]ver. 35

119:71 [i]ver. 67 Heb. 12:10 **119:72** [j]Ps. 19:10 Prov. 8:10,11,19 **119:73** [k]Job 10:8 Ps. 100:3 & 138:8 & 139:14 [l]ver. 34,144 **119:74** [m]Ps. 34:2 [n]ver. 49,147 **119:75** [o]Heb. 12:10 **119:77** [p]ver. 41 [q]ver. 24,47 **119:78** [r]Ps. 25:3 [s]ver. 86 [t]ver. 23 **119:81** [u]Ps. 73:26 & 84:2 [v]ver. 74,114 **119:82** [w]ver. 123 Ps. 69:3 **119:83** [x]Job 30:30 **119:84** [y]Ps. 39:4 [z]Rev. 6:10

[k] Or, *companies* [1] Heb. *righteousness* [m] Heb. *to comfort me*

119:57 *THOU ART* MY PORTION, O LORD. The psalmist's life centers around God and His Word. If we desire to know God and His love (vv. 57–64), we must abide in His Word (v. 57), seek His favor and grace with our whole heart (v. 58), hasten to keep His Word (v. 60), pray often (v. 62), associate with those who fear Him (v. 63), look for His love (v. 64), and pray to know and do His will (v. 64). We cannot abide in Christ without abiding in His Word (John 15:1–10).

119:67 I WAS AFFLICTED . . . NOW HAVE I KEPT THY WORD. God sometimes allows us to experience hardships and troubles in order to draw us closer to His Word (cf. 94:12; Prov. 3:11–12; see Heb. 12:5, note).

85 [a]The proud have digged pits for me, which *are* not after thy law.

86 All thy commandments *are* [n]faithful: [b]they persecute me [c]wrongfully; help thou me.

87 They had almost consumed me upon earth; but I forsook not thy precepts.

88 [d]Quicken me after thy lovingkindness; so shall I keep the testimony of thy mouth.

LAMED.

God's unchangeable law

89 [e]For ever, O LORD, thy word is settled in heaven.

90 Thy faithfulness *is* [o]unto all generations: thou hast established the earth, and it [p]abideth.

91 They continue this day according to [f]thine ordinances: for all *are* thy servants.

92 Unless [g]thy law *had been* my delights, I should then have perished in mine affliction.

93 I will never forget thy precepts: for with them thou hast quickened me.

94 I *am* thine, save me; for I have sought thy precepts.

95 The wicked have waited for me to destroy me: *but* I will consider thy testimonies.

96 [h]I have seen an end of all perfection: *but* thy commandment *is* exceeding broad.

MEM.

The love of God's law

97 O how love I thy law! [i]it *is* my meditation all the day.

98 Thou through thy commandments hast made me [j]wiser than mine enemies: for [q]they *are* ever with me.

99 I have more understanding than all my teachers: [k]for thy testimonies *are* my meditation.

100 [l]I understand more than the ancients, because I keep thy precepts.

119:85 [a]Ps. 35:7 Prov. 16:27
119:86 [b]ver. 78 [c]Ps. 35:19
119:88 [d]ver. 40
119:89 [e]Ps. 89:2 Mat. 24:34 1 Pet. 1:25
119:91 [f]Jer. 33:25
119:92 [g]ver. 24
119:96 [h]Mat. 5:18
119:97 [i]Ps. 1:2
119:98 [j]Deut. 4:6
119:99 [k]2 Tim. 3:15
119:100 [l]Job 32:7-9

101 I have [m]refrained my feet from every evil way, that I might keep thy word.

102 I have not departed from thy judgments: for thou hast taught me.

103 [n]How sweet are thy words unto my [r]taste! *yea, sweeter* than honey to my mouth!

104 Through thy precepts I get understanding: therefore [o]I hate every false way.

NUN.

God's law a lamp to the feet

105 [p]Thy word *is* a [s]lamp unto my feet, and a light unto my path.

106 [q]I have sworn, and I will perform *it*, that I will keep thy righteous judgments.

107 I am afflicted very much: [r]quicken me, O LORD, according unto thy word.

108 Accept, I beseech thee, [s]the freewill offerings of my mouth, O LORD, and [t]teach me thy judgments.

109 [u]My soul *is* continually in my hand: yet do I not forget thy law.

110 [v]The wicked have laid a snare for me: yet I [w]erred not from thy precepts.

111 [x]Thy testimonies have I taken as an heritage for ever: for [y]they *are* the rejoicing of my heart.

112 I have inclined mine heart [t]to perform thy statutes always, [z]*even unto* the end.

SAMECH.

God's law a hiding place

113 I hate *vain* thoughts: but thy law do I love.

114 [a]Thou *art* my hiding place and my shield: [b]I hope in thy word.

115 [c]Depart from me, ye evildoers:

119:101 [m]Prov. 1:15
119:103 [n]Ps. 19:10 Prov. 8:11
119:104 [o]ver. 128
119:105 [p]Prov. 6:23
119:106 [q]Neh. 10:29
119:107 [r]ver. 88
119:108 [s]Hos. 14:2 Heb. 13:15 [t]ver. 12,26
119:109 [u]Job 13:14
119:110 [v]Ps. 140:5 [w]ver. 10,21
119:111 [x]Deut. 33:4 [y]ver. 77,92
119:112 [z]ver. 33
119:114 [a]Ps. 32:7 [b]ver. 81
119:115 [c]Ps. 6:8 Mat. 7:23

[n] Heb. *faithfulness* [o] Heb. *to generation and generation* [p] Heb. *standeth* [q] Heb. *it is ever with me* [r] Heb. *palate* [s] Or, *candle* [t] Heb. *to do*

119:89 THY WORD IS SETTLED IN HEAVEN. See article on THE INSPIRATION AND AUTHORITY OF SCRIPTURE, p. 1924.

119:98 THY COMMANDMENT HAS MADE ME WISER. Through our devotion to God's Word we learn to see life as God sees it, value what He values, and love what He loves. We attune ourselves to the thoughts of God (see 1 Cor. 2:16, note).

119:105 THY WORD *IS* . . . A LIGHT UNTO MY PATH. God's Word contains the spiritual principles that will help us avoid many sorrows, pitfalls, and tragedies brought on by wrong decisions and choices. Consequently, we must treasure its wisdom and steadfastly hold on to its precepts in all life's situations (vv. 106,112).

119:113 I HATE *VAIN* THOUGHTS . . . THY LAW DO I LOVE. We really cannot love God's Word without hating evil (vv. 113,115, 119,128; see Heb. 1:9, note) and maintaining a holy and reverent fear of God and His judgments.

for I will keep the commandments of my God.

116 Uphold me according unto thy word, that I may live: and let me not [d]be ashamed of my hope.

117 Hold thou me up, and I shall be safe: and I will have respect unto thy statutes continually.

118 Thou hast trodden down all them that [e]err from thy statutes: for their deceit *is* falsehood.

119 Thou [u]puttest away all the wicked of the earth [f]*like* dross: therefore I love thy testimonies.

120 [g]My flesh trembleth for fear of thee; and I am afraid of thy judgments.

AIN.

The psalmist loves God's law

121 I have done judgment and justice: leave me not to mine oppressors.

122 Be [h]surety for thy servant for good: let not the proud oppress me.

123 [i]Mine eyes fail for thy salvation, and for the word of thy righteousness.

124 Deal with thy servant according unto thy mercy, and [j]teach me thy statutes.

125 [k]I *am* thy servant; give me understanding, that I may know thy testimonies.

126 *It is* time for *thee*, LORD, to work: *for* they have made void thy law.

127 [l]Therefore I love thy commandments above gold; yea, above fine gold.

128 Therefore I esteem all *thy* precepts *concerning* all *things to be* right; *and* I [m]hate every false way.

PE.

The psalmist keeps God's law

129 Thy testimonies *are* wonderful: therefore doth my soul keep them.

130 The entrance of thy words giveth light; [n]it giveth understanding unto the simple.

131 I opened my mouth, and panted: for I [o]longed for thy commandments.

119:116 [d]Ps. 25:2 Rom. 5:5
119:118 [e]ver. 21
119:119 [f]Ezek. 22:18
119:120 [g]Hab. 3:16
119:122 [h]Heb. 7:22
119:123 [i]ver. 81,82
119:124 [j]ver. 12
119:125 [k]Ps. 116:16
119:127 [l]Ps. 19:10
119:128 [m]ver. 104
119:130 [n]Ps. 19:7
119:131 [o]ver. 20
119:132 [p]Ps. 106:4 [q]2 Thes. 1:6
119:133 [r]Ps. 17:5 [s]Ps. 19:13 Rom. 6:12
119:134 [t]Luke 1:74
119:135 [u]Ps. 4:6 [v]ver. 12,26
119:136 [w]Jer. 9:1 Ezek. 9:4
119:137 [x]Neh. 9:33
119:138 [y]Ps. 19:7-9
119:139 [z]Ps. 69:9 John 2:17
119:140 [a]Ps. 12:6
119:142 [b]Ps. 19:9
119:143 [c]ver. 77
119:144 [d]ver. 34,73

132 [p]Look thou upon me, and be merciful unto me, [q]as[v] thou usest to do unto those that love thy name.

133 [r]Order my steps in thy word: and [s]let not any iniquity have dominion over me.

134 [t]Deliver me from the oppression of man: so will I keep thy precepts.

135 [u]Make thy face to shine upon thy servant; and [v]teach me thy statutes.

136 [w]Rivers of waters run down mine eyes, because they keep not thy law.

TZADDI.

God's law is true

137 [x]Righteous *art* thou, O LORD, and upright *are* thy judgments.

138 [y]Thy testimonies *that* thou hast commanded *are* [w]righteous and very [x]faithful.

139 [z]My zeal hath [y]consumed me, because mine enemies have forgotten thy words.

140 [a]Thy word *is* very [z]pure: therefore thy servant loveth it.

141 I *am* small and despised: *yet* do not I forget thy precepts.

142 Thy righteousness *is* an everlasting righteousness, and thy law *is* [b]the truth.

143 Trouble and anguish have [a]taken hold on me: *yet* thy commandments *are* [c]my delights.

144 The righteousness of thy testimonies *is* everlasting: [d]give me understanding, and I shall live.

KOPH.

A cry for salvation

145 I cried with *my* whole heart; hear me, O LORD: I will keep thy statutes.

[u] Heb. *causest to cease* [v] Heb. *according to the custom towards those* [w] Heb. *righteousness* [x] Heb. *faithfulness* [y] Heb. *cut me off* [z] Heb. *tried*, or, *refined* [a] Heb. *found me*

119:121 LEAVE ME NOT TO MINE OPPRESSORS. Like the psalmist, believers may appeal for God's help, based on (1) obedience to and love for His Word (vv. 121–122), (2) God's promises in His sure Word (v. 123), (3) God's mercy and steadfast love (v. 124), (4) our commitment to serve Him (v. 125), and (5) the urgent needs we have in our lives (v. 126).

119:136 WATERS RUN DOWN MINE EYES, BECAUSE THEY KEEP NOT THY LAW. Those who love God's Word will experience grief and sorrow, even anger (v. 53), when they see God's laws rejected and scorned by the ungodly; these feelings will undoubtedly continue until the return of Christ (see Luke 19:45, note; 2 Pet. 2:8, note).

146 I cried unto thee; save me, [b]and I shall keep thy testimonies.

147 [e]I prevented the dawning of the morning, and cried: [f]I hoped in thy word.

148 [g]Mine eyes prevent the *night* watches, that I might meditate in thy word.

149 Hear my voice according unto thy lovingkindness: O LORD, [h]quicken me according to thy judgment.

150 They draw nigh that follow after mischief: they are far from thy law.

151 Thou *art* [i]near, O LORD; [j]and all thy commandments *are* truth.

152 Concerning thy testimonies, I have known of old that thou hast founded them [k]for ever.

RESH.

Keeping God's law in adversity

153 [l]Consider mine affliction, and deliver me: for I do not forget thy law.

154 [m]Plead my cause, and deliver me: [n]quicken me according to thy word.

155 [o]Salvation *is* far from the wicked: for they seek not thy statutes.

156 [c]Great *are* thy tender mercies, O LORD: [p]quicken me according to thy judgments.

157 Many *are* my persecutors and mine enemies; *yet* do I not [q]decline from thy testimonies.

158 I beheld the transgressors, and [r]was grieved; because they kept not thy word.

159 Consider how I love thy precepts: [s]quicken me, O LORD, according to thy lovingkindness.

160 [d]Thy word *is* true *from* the beginning: and every one of thy righteous judgments *endureth* for ever.

SCHIN.

Peace in keeping God's law

161 [t]Princes have persecuted me without a cause: but my heart standeth in awe of thy word.

119:147 [e]Ps. 5:3 [f]ver. 74 **119:148** [g]Ps. 63:1,6 **119:149** [h]ver. 40 **119:151** [i]Ps. 145:18 [j]ver. 142 **119:152** [k]Luke 21:33 **119:153** [l]Lam. 5:1 **119:154** [m]1 Sam. 24:15 [n]ver. 40 **119:155** [o]Job 5:4 **119:156** [p]ver. 149 **119:157** [q]Ps. 44:18 **119:158** [r]Ezek. 9:4 **119:159** [s]ver. 88 **119:161** [t]1 Sam. 24:11

119:165 [u]Prov. 3:2 Is. 32:17 **119:166** [v]Gen. 49:18 **119:168** [w]Prov. 5:21 **119:169** [x]ver. 144 **119:171** [y]ver. 7 **119:173** [z]Josh. 24:22 **119:174** [a]ver. 166 [b]ver. 16,24 **119:176** [c]Is. 53:6

162 I rejoice at thy word, as one that findeth great spoil.

163 I hate and abhor lying: *but* thy law do I love.

164 Seven times a day do I praise thee because of thy righteous judgments.

165 [u]Great peace have they which love thy law: and [e]nothing shall offend them.

166 [v]LORD, I have hoped for thy salvation, and done thy commandments.

167 My soul hath kept thy testimonies; and I love them exceedingly.

168 I have kept thy precepts and thy testimonies: [w]for all my ways *are* before thee.

TAU

A prayer for understanding

169 Let my cry come near before thee, O LORD: [x]give me understanding according to thy word.

170 Let my supplication come before thee: deliver me according to thy word.

171 [y]My lips shall utter praise, when thou hast taught me thy statutes.

172 My tongue shall speak of thy word: for all thy commandments *are* righteousness.

173 Let thine hand help me; for [z]I have chosen thy precepts.

174 [a]I have longed for thy salvation, O LORD; and [b]thy law *is* my delight.

175 Let my soul live, and it shall praise thee; and let thy judgments help me.

176 [c]I have gone astray like a lost sheep; seek thy servant; for I do not forget thy commandments.

[b] Or, *that I may keep* [c] Or, *Many* [d] Heb. *The beginning of thy word* is *true* [e] Heb. *they shall have no stumblingblock*

119:151 THOU *ART* NEAR, O LORD. The psalmist experiences God's nearness in times of trouble because he loves the Lord and is devoted to meditating on His Word (v. 148; cf. vv. 153–160). The Lord is near to all who love Him and His Word. If you have trouble in your life, take your Bible and in the presence of God, use it to revitalize your relationship with Him.

119:176 I HAVE GONE ASTRAY LIKE A LOST SHEEP. The writer cannot mean that he has departed from the Lord and rejected His Word, for he has declared the contrary over and over in this psalm; his concluding words remain, "I do not forget thy commandments." The psalmist here may simply be acknowledging that he is prone to error apart from being guided by God's Word.

A prayer for deliverance

A Song of degrees.

120 IN [d]MY distress I cried
unto the LORD, and he
heard me.
2 Deliver my soul, O LORD, from ly-
ing lips, *and* from a deceitful tongue.
3 [f]What shall be given unto thee?
or what shall be [g]done unto thee, thou
false tongue?
4 [h]Sharp arrows of the mighty,
with coals of juniper.
5 Woe is me, that I sojourn in [e]Me-
sech, [f]*that* I dwell in the tents of Ke-
dar!
6 My soul hath long dwelt with him
that hateth peace.
7 I *am* [i]*for* peace: but when I
speak, they *are* for war.

Help from the LORD

A Song of degrees.

121 I [g]WILL[j] lift up mine
eyes unto the hills, from
whence cometh my help.
2 [h]My help *cometh* from the LORD,
which made heaven and earth.
3 [i]He will not suffer thy foot to be
moved: [j]he that keepeth thee will not
slumber.
4 Behold, he that keepeth Israel
shall neither slumber nor sleep.
5 The LORD *is* thy keeper: the LORD
is [k]thy shade [l]upon thy right hand.

120:1 [d]Jonah 2:2
120:5 [e]Gen. 10:2; Ezek. 27:13; [f]Gen. 25:13; 1 Sam. 25:1; Jer. 49:28
121:1 [g]Jer. 3:23
121:2 [h]Ps. 124:8
121:3 [i]1 Sam. 2:9; [j]Ps. 127:1; Is. 27:3
121:5 [k]Is. 25:4; [l]Ps. 16:8
121:6 [m]Ps. 91:5; Is. 49:10
121:7 [n]Ps. 41:2
121:8 [o]Deut. 28:6
122:1 [p]Is. 2:3; Zech. 8:21
122:3 [q]See 2 Sam. 5:9
122:4 [r]Ex. 23:17; Deut. 16:16; [s]Ex. 16:34
122:5 [t]Deut. 17:8; 2 Chr. 19:8
122:6 [u]Ps. 51:18

6 [m]The sun shall not smite thee by
day, nor the moon by night.
7 The LORD shall preserve thee from
all evil: he shall [n]preserve thy soul.
8 The LORD shall [o]preserve thy go-
ing out and thy coming in from this
time forth, and even for evermore.

The peace of Jerusalem

A Song of degrees of David.

122 I WAS glad when they said
unto me, [p]Let us go into
the house of the LORD.
2 Our feet shall stand within thy
gates, O Jerusalem.
3 Jerusalem is builded as a city that
is [q]compact together:
4 [r]Whither the tribes go up, the
tribes of the LORD, unto [s]the testimony
of Israel, to give thanks unto the name
of the LORD.
5 [t]For there [k]are set thrones of
judgment, the thrones of the house of
David.
6 [u]Pray for the peace of Jerusalem:
they shall prosper that love thee.
7 Peace be within thy walls, *and*
prosperity within thy palaces.

[f] Or, *What shall* the deceitful tongue *give unto thee?* or, *What shall it profit thee?* [g] Heb. *added* [h] Or, It is as *the sharp arrows of the mighty* man, *with coals of juniper* [i] Or, a man *of peace* [j] Or, *Shall I lift up mine eyes to the hills? whence should my help come?* [k] Heb. *do sit*

120—134 SONGS OF DEGREES. These fifteen psalms are entitled "Songs of Degrees" or "Songs of Ascents" (i.e, of Steps). Some believe this phrase refers to the steps on the stairlike sundial of King Ahaz where the shadow went back ten degrees as a guarantee that God would give King Hezekiah fifteen added years of peaceful reign. These psalms were then compiled to celebrate that promise (2 Ki. 20:6–10; Is. 38:5–8). Most believe that the phrase "Songs of Ascents" refers to those psalms that the Jews would sing together as they "went up" to Jerusalem as pilgrims to the sacred feasts.

120:1–7 HE HEARD ME. The grand thought of this pilgrim psalm is that the God who created the heavens and earth takes the time to watch over and care for all those who trust Him and His word. No evil will be allowed to destroy their fellowship with Him (see also Rom. 8:28–39).

121:1–2 FROM WHENCE COMETH MY HELP. The first verse of this psalm likely should be read as a rhetorical question with a negative answer. "Shall I look to the mountains for help? No! My help cometh from the LORD."

121:2 MY HELP *COMETH* FROM THE LORD. Family, friends, or wealth must never be viewed as our ultimate source of help in this life. That belongs to God, the only source for meeting our needs physically and spiritually. We must trust in Him with all our hearts and seek Him for grace "to help in time of need" (see Heb. 4:16, note).

121:5 THE LORD *IS* THY KEEPER. The faithful child of God is always under the Lord's protection, defense, and watchful care (see 1 Pet. 1:5, note). Jesus emphasized this truth when He said, "The very hairs of your head are all numbered. Fear ye not therefore" (Mat. 10:30–31).

121:8 PRESERVE THY GOING OUT AND THY COMING IN. This text may be applied both to our Christian lives from spiritual birth until we leave this earth and to our physical lives as we go out in the morning to work and come home to rest. God will preserve us; He is our constant guard.

122:1 THE HOUSE OF THE LORD. God's house should be a place where the believer joyfully experiences intimate communion with the Lord, the fellowship of the Spirit, and the love of fellow believers.

8 For my brethren and companions' sakes, I will now say, Peace *be* within thee.

9 Because of the house of the LORD our God I will [v]seek thy good.

A song of confidence in God

A Song of degrees.

123 UNTO THEE [w]lift I up mine eyes, O thou [x]that dwellest in the heavens.

2 Behold, as the eyes of servants *look* unto the hand of their masters, *and* as the eyes of a maiden unto the hand of her mistress; so our eyes *wait* upon the LORD our God, until that he have mercy upon us.

3 Have mercy upon us, O LORD, have mercy upon us: for we are exceedingly filled with contempt.

4 Our soul is exceedingly filled with the scorning of those that are at ease, *and* with the contempt of the proud.

God's deliverance

A Song of degrees of David.

124 IF *IT had not been* the LORD who was on our side, [y]now may Israel say;

2 If *it had not been* the LORD who was on our side, when men rose up against us:

3 Then they had [z]swallowed us up quick, when their wrath was kindled against us:

4 Then the waters had overwhelmed us, the stream had gone over our soul:

5 Then the proud waters had gone over our soul.

122:9 [v]Neh. 2:10
123:1 [w]Ps. 121:1 & 141:8 [x]Ps. 2:4 & 11:4 & 115:3
124:1 [y]Ps. 129:1
124:3 [z]Ps. 56:1,2 & 57:3 Prov. 1:12
124:7 [a]Ps. 91:3 Prov. 6:5
124:8 [b]Ps. 121:2 [c]Gen. 1:1 Ps. 134:3
125:3 [d]Prov. 22:8 Is. 14:5
125:5 [e]Prov. 2:15 [f]Ps. 128:6
126:1 [g]Ps. 53:6 & 85:1 Hos. 6:11 Joel 3:1 [h]Acts 12:9
126:2 [i]Job 8:21

6 Blessed *be* the LORD, who hath not given us *as* a prey to their teeth.

7 Our soul is escaped [a]as a bird out of the snare of the fowlers: the snare is broken, and we are escaped.

8 [b]Our help *is* in the name of the LORD, [c]who made heaven and earth.

The LORD the protector

A Song of degrees.

125 THEY THAT trust in the LORD *shall be* as mount Zion, *which* cannot be removed, *but* abideth for ever.

2 *As* the mountains *are* round about Jerusalem, so the LORD *is* round about his people from henceforth even for ever.

3 For [d]the rod of [1]the wicked shall not rest upon the lot of the righteous; lest the righteous put forth their hands unto iniquity.

4 Do good, O LORD, unto *those that be* good, and to *them that are* upright in their hearts.

5 As for such as turn aside unto their [e]crooked ways, the LORD shall lead them forth with the workers of iniquity: *but* [f]peace *shall be* upon Israel.

Zion's captivity

A Song of degrees.

126 WHEN THE LORD [g]turned[m] again the captivity of Zion, [h]we were like them that dream.

2 Then [i]was our mouth filled with laughter, and our tongue with singing: then said they among the heathen,

[1] Heb. *wickedness* [m] Heb. *returned the returning of Zion*

123:1 UNTO THEE LIFT I UP MY EYES. This psalm describes humble believers who look continually and expectantly to God to put an end to the contempt and scorn shown towards them. It expresses the cry of those who are always watching for and desiring Christ's return to save His people from an ungodly and hostile world (see Heb. 12:2; 2 Pet. 3:12; see Mat. 24:42, note; Tit. 2:13, note).

124:1 IF *IT HAD NOT BEEN* THE LORD WHO WAS ON OUR SIDE. If God is not with us, we have no chance to escape the pitfalls of life or ward off our spiritual enemy. The dangers and troubles we face may seem so overwhelming that no one but God and His miraculous power can save us. On the other hand, "if God *be* for us, who *can be* against us" (Rom. 8:31). No foe or situation can defeat us when God is on our side.

126:1 WHEN THE LORD TURNED AGAIN THE CAPTIVITY OF ZION. This is a technical phrase that means, "When the LORD restored the prosperity of Zion" (cf. Job 42:10). This restoration took place partially in 701 B.C., when Sennacherib's threat to take Jerusalem was turned back in fulfillment of prophecy, and the surrounding nations sent presents to Hezekiah (2 Chr. 32:22–23). It was fulfilled in even greater measure when the Jews returned to Jerusalem from the Babylonian captivity in 538–537 B.C.

The LORD [n]hath done great things for
them.
3 The LORD hath done great things
for us; *whereof* we are glad.
4 Turn again our captivity, O LORD,
as the streams in the south.
5 [j]They that sow in tears shall
reap in [o]joy.
6 He that goeth forth and weepeth,
bearing [p]precious seed, shall doubt-
less come again with rejoicing, bring-
ing his sheaves *with him*.

The vanity of work without God

A Song of degrees [q]for Solomon.

127 EXCEPT THE LORD build
the house, they labour in
vain [r]that build it: except [k]the LORD
keep the city, the watchman waketh
but in vain.
2 *It is* vain for you to rise up early,
to sit up late, to [l]eat the bread of sor-
rows: *for* so he giveth his beloved
sleep.
3 Lo, [m]children *are* an heritage of
the LORD *and* [n]the fruit of the womb *is*
his reward.
4 As arrows *are* in the hand of a
mighty man; so *are* children of the
youth.
5 Happy *is* the man that [s]hath his
quiver full of them: [o]they shall not be
ashamed, but they [t]shall speak with
the enemies in the gate.

126:5 [j]See Jer. 31:9
127:1 [k]Ps. 121:3-5
127:2 [l]Gen. 3:17,19
127:3 [m]Gen. 33:5 & 48:4 Josh. 24:3,4 [n]Deut. 28:4
127:5 [o]Job 5:4 Prov. 27:11
128:1 [p]Ps. 119:1
128:2 [q]Is. 3:10
128:3 [r]Ezek. 19:10 [s]Ps. 52:8 & 144:12
128:5 [t]Ps. 134:3
128:6 [u]Gen. 50:23 Job 42:16 [v]Ps. 125:5
129:1 [w]Ezek. 23:3 Hos. 2:15 [x]Ps. 124:1

The God-fearing family

A Song of degrees.

128 BLESSED [p]*IS* every one
that feareth the LORD; that
walketh in his ways.
2 [q]For thou shalt eat the labour of
thine hands: happy *shalt* thou *be*, and *it*
shall be well with thee.
3 Thy wife *shall be* [r]as a fruitful
vine by the sides of thine house: thy
children [s]like olive plants round
about thy table.
4 Behold, that thus shall the man be
blessed that feareth the LORD.
5 [t]The LORD shall bless thee out of
Zion: and thou shalt see the good of
Jerusalem all the days of thy life.
6 Yea, thou shalt [u]see thy chil-
dren's children, *and* [v]peace upon Is-
rael.

Israel's enemies

A Song of degrees.

129 MANY[u] A time have they
afflicted me from [w]my
youth, [x]may Israel now say:
2 Many a time have they afflicted

[n] Heb. *hath magnified to do with them*
[o] Or, *singing* [p] Or, *seed basket* [q] Or, *of Solomon;* see Ps. 72, title [r] Heb. that are *builders of it in it* [s] Heb. *hath filled his quiver with them* [t] Or, *shall subdue,* or, *destroy*
[u] Or, *Much*

126:5–6 THEY THAT SOW IN TEARS SHALL REAP IN JOY. Heartfelt brokenness and faithful sowing in agonizing prayer will bring from God the blessings of renewal, revival, and miraculous works (cf. Mat. 5:4; 2 Cor. 9:6). Believers are assured that what they now diligently sow will be abundantly blessed by God in the future. So let us sow unto God faithfulness, righteousness, and intercession, regardless of whatever pain we may be experiencing, knowing that there will be a great harvest of God's blessings (cf. Jer. 31:9).

127:1–5 EXCEPT THE LORD BUILD. Only what is from God and has His blessing is truly valuable in life. Conversely, if God is not in our lives, activities, goals, and families, then all is in vain and will end in frustration and disappointment. Thus we should seek God's blessing and guidance in all things from the very beginning of our lives (see Luke 24:50, note).

127:1 EXCEPT THE LORD BUILD THE HOUSE. As we labor to build God's house on earth, we must make sure we build it according to His pattern and by His Spirit, not according to mere human ideas, plans, and efforts (cf. Ex. 25:9,40; see Acts 7:44, note).

127:2 *FOR* SO HE GIVETH HIS BELOVED SLEEP. It is God's will that we enjoy peaceful sleep and anxiety-free lives (see Mat. 6:25–34; Phil. 4:6). The text also implies that God keeps on giving even when we are asleep.

127:3 CHILDREN *ARE* AN HERITAGE OF THE LORD. Under the old covenant a large family was considered a blessing, while not having children was considered a curse (Gen. 30:2,18; 33:5; 48:9; Deut. 7:13). Under the new covenant the presence of many children is not necessarily evidence of divine favor, nor is their absence to be viewed as a curse. A large family may be a misfortune if the children are not properly cared for and brought to salvation in Christ; having no children can be a blessing if one dedicates his or her life and time to the Lord's service (1 Cor. 7:7–8, 32–33).

All children of believers must be viewed as gifts of God requiring wise and faithful stewardship. Only as the Lord's ways and commandments are accepted, taught, and followed by the parents and children will they experience God's full blessing (see Ps. 128; see article on PARENTS AND CHILDREN, p. 1880).

me from my youth: yet they have not prevailed against me.

3 The plowers plowed upon my back: they made long their furrows.

4 The LORD *is* righteous: he hath cut asunder the cords of the wicked.

5 Let them all be confounded and turned back that hate Zion.

6 Let them be as [y]the grass *upon* the housetops, which withereth afore it groweth up:

7 Wherewith the mower filleth not his hand; nor he that bindeth sheaves his bosom.

8 Neither do they which go by say, [z]The blessing of the LORD *be* upon you: we bless you in the name of the LORD.

Waiting on the LORD

A Song of degrees.

130 OUT [a]OF the depths have I cried unto thee, O LORD.

2 Lord, hear my voice: let thine ears be attentive to the voice of my supplications.

3 [b]If thou, LORD, shouldest mark iniquities, O Lord, who shall stand?

4 But *there is* [c]forgiveness with thee, that [d]thou mayest be feared.

5 [e]I wait for the LORD, my soul doth wait, and [f]in his word do I hope.

6 [g]My soul *waiteth* for the Lord more than they that watch for the morning: [v]*I say, more than* they that watch for the morning.

7 [h]Let Israel hope in the LORD: for [i]with the LORD *there is* mercy, and with him *is* plenteous redemption.

8 And [j]he shall redeem Israel from all his iniquities.

A song of the humble

A Song of degrees of David.

131 LORD, MY heart is not haughty, nor mine eyes lofty: [k]neither do I [w]exercise myself in great matters, or in things too [l]high[x] for me.

2 Surely I have behaved and quieted [y]myself, [m]as a child that is weaned of his mother: my soul *is* even as a weaned child.

3 [n]Let Israel hope in the LORD [z]from henceforth and for ever.

The promise to David and Zion

132:8–10pp — 2 Chr. 6:41–42

A Song of degrees.

132 LORD, REMEMBER David, *and* all his afflictions:

2 How he sware unto the LORD, [o]*and* vowed unto [p]the mighty *God* of Jacob;

3 Surely I will not come into the tabernacle of my house, nor go up into my bed;

4 I will [q]not give sleep to mine eyes, *or* slumber to mine eyelids,

5 Until I [r]find out a place for the LORD, [a]an habitation for the mighty *God* of Jacob.

6 Lo, we heard of it [s]at Ephratah: [t]we found it [u]in the fields of the wood.

7 We will go into his tabernacles: [v]we will worship at his footstool.

8 [w]Arise, O LORD, into thy rest; thou, and [x]the ark of thy strength.

9 Let thy priests [y]be clothed with righteousness; and let thy saints shout for joy.

10 For thy servant David's sake turn not away the face of thine anointed.

11 [z]The LORD hath sworn *in* truth unto David; he will not turn from it; [a]Of the fruit of [b]thy body will I set upon thy throne.

12 If thy children will keep my covenant and my testimony that I shall teach them, their children shall also sit upon thy throne for evermore.

13 [b]For the LORD hath chosen Zion; he hath desired *it* for his habitation.

129:6 [y]Ps. 37:2 **129:8** [z]Ruth 2:4 Ps. 118:26 **130:1** [a]Lam. 3:55 Jonah 2:2 **130:3** [b]Ps. 143:2 Rom. 3:20 **130:4** [c]Ex. 34:7 [d]1 Ki. 8:40 Ps. 2:11 Jer. 33:8 **130:5** [e]Ps. 27:14 Is. 8:17 [f]Ps. 119:81 **130:6** [g]Ps:119:147 **130:7** [h]Ps. 131:3 [i]Ps. 86:5 Is. 55:7 **130:8** [j]Ps. 103:3,4 Mat. 1:21 **131:1** [k]Rom. 12:16 [l]Job 42:3 Ps. 139:6 **131:2** [m]Mat. 18:3 1 Cor. 14:20 **131:3** [n]Ps. 130:7 **132:2** [o]Ps. 65:1 [p]Gen. 49:24 **132:4** [q]Prov. 6:4 **132:5** [r]Acts 7:46 **132:6** [s]1 Sam. 17:12 [t]1 Sam. 7:1 [u]1 Chr. 13:5 **132:7** [v]Ps. 5:7 & 99:5 **132:8** [w]Num. 10:35 2 Chr. 6:41 [x]Ps. 78:61 **132:9** [y]Job 29:14 Is. 61:10 **132:11** [z]Ps. 89:3,4 [a]2 Sam. 7:12 1 Ki. 8:25 **132:13** [b]Ps. 48:1,2

[v] Or, *which watch unto the morning* [w] Heb. *walk* [x] Heb. *wonderful* [y] Heb. *my soul* [z] Heb. *from now* [a] Heb. *habitations* [b] Heb. *thy belly*

130:1 OUT OF THE DEPTHS HAVE I CRIED. Those who reap the misery and torment of their own sins can cry out to God with assurance that God will forgive, heal, and bring them back into fellowship with Himself. God desires to show mercy to all who are in trouble, saving them from the slavery of sin so that they might know His love, care, and goodness (v. 4; see Mat. 26:28, note).

132:1–18 REMEMBER DAVID. This psalm petitions God to bless David's sons as they rule Israel (cf. 2 Sam. 7:8–29; see article on GOD'S COVENANT WITH DAVID, p. 470). This blessing will become a reality only when God abides in His temple and among His people (vv. 13–18).

14 [c]This *is* my rest for ever: here will I dwell; for I have desired it.

15 [d]I will [c]abundantly bless her provision: I will satisfy her poor with bread.

16 [e]I will also clothe her priests with salvation: [f]and her saints shall shout aloud for joy.

17 [g]There will I make the horn of David to bud: [h]I have ordained a [d]lamp for mine anointed.

18 His enemies will I [i]clothe with shame: but upon himself shall his crown flourish.

Brotherly unity

A Song of degrees of David.

133 BEHOLD, HOW good and how pleasant *it is* for [j]brethren to dwell [e]together in unity!

2 *It is* like [k]the precious ointment upon the head, that ran down upon the beard, *even* Aaron's beard: that went down to the skirts of his garments;

3 As the dew of [l]Hermon, *and as the dew* that descended upon the mountains of Zion: for [m]there the LORD commanded the blessing, *even* life for evermore.

Blessing for the night watch

A Song of degrees.

134 BEHOLD, BLESS ye the LORD, [n]all *ye* servants of the LORD, [o]which by night stand in the house of the LORD.

2 [p]Lift up your hands [f]*in* the sanctuary, and bless the LORD.

3 [q]The LORD that made heaven and earth [r]bless thee out of Zion.

Praise to the LORD

135:15–20pp — Ps. 115:4–11

135 PRAISE YE the LORD. Praise ye the name of the LORD; [s]praise *him*, O ye servants of the LORD.

2 [t]Ye that stand in the house of the LORD, in [u]the courts of the house of our God,

3 Praise the LORD; for [v]the LORD *is* good: sing praises unto his name; [w]for *it is* pleasant.

4 For [x]the LORD hath chosen Jacob unto himself, *and* Israel for his peculiar treasure. Ps. 146

5 For I know that [y]the LORD *is* great, and *that* our Lord *is* above all gods.

6 [z]Whatsoever the LORD pleased, *that* did he in heaven, and in earth, in the seas, and all deep places.

7 [a]He causeth the vapours to ascend from the ends of the earth; [b]he maketh lightnings for the rain; he bringeth the wind out of his [c]treasuries.

8 [d]Who smote the firstborn of Egypt, [g]both of man and beast.

9 [e]*Who* sent tokens and wonders into the midst of thee, O Egypt, [f]upon Pharaoh, and upon all his servants.

10 [g]Who smote great nations, and slew mighty kings;

132:14 [c]Ps. 68:16 **132:15** [d]Ps. 147:14 **132:16** [e]2 Chr. 6:41 [f]Hos. 11:12 **132:17** [g]Ezek. 29:21 Luke 1:69 [h]1 Ki. 11:36 **132:18** [i]Ps. 35:26 & 109:29 **133:1** [j]Gen. 13:8 Heb:13:1 **133:2** [k]Ex. 30:25 **133:3** [l]Deut. 4:48 [m]Lev. 25:21 Deut. 28:8 Ps. 42:8 **134:1** [n]Ps. 135:1,2 [o]1 Chr. 9:33 **134:2** [p]1 Tim. 2:8 **134:3** [q]Ps. 124:8 [r]Ps. 128:5 & 135:21 **135:1** [s]Ps. 113:1 & 134:1 **135:2** [t]Luke 2:37 [u]Ps. 116:19 **135:3** [v]Ps. 119:68 [w]Ps. 147:1 **135:4** [x]Ex. 19:5 Deut. 7:6,7 **135:5** [y]Ps. 95:3 & 97:9 **135:6** [z]Ps. 115:3 **135:7** [a]Jer. 10:13 [b]Job 28:25 Zech. 10:1 [c]Job 38:22 **135:8** [d]Ex. 12:12 Ps. 78:51 **135:9** [e]Ex. 7-10 [f]Ps. 136:15 **135:10** [g]Num. 21:24 Ps. 136:17

[c] Or, *surely* [d] Or, *candle* [e] Heb. *even together* [f] Or, in *holiness* [g] Heb. *from man unto beast*

132:17 THERE WILL I MAKE THE HORN OF DAVID TO BUD. The expectations of this prayer were never fulfilled through David's descendants who were kings of Israel and Judah. Because the Israelites forsook the Lord (cf. v. 12), God destroyed Jerusalem and the temple in 586 B.C. The longings of this prayer will be fulfilled only in Jesus Christ, the greatest Son of David, of whose "kingdom there shall be no end" (Luke 1:32–33; cf. Mat. 1:1; Luke 1:68–79).

133:1–3 BRETHREN TO DWELL TOGETHER IN UNITY! This psalm expresses the same spiritual truth as John 17, where Jesus prayed that His followers would be established in love, holiness, and unity. He knew that the Holy Spirit could not operate in their midst if there were divisions based on sin and selfish ambitions (see 1 Cor. 1:10–13; 3:1–3). But fervent love for God and for one another, along with sanctification in the truth of God's word, will bring God's nearness to and His anointing on His people (see John 17:21, note; Eph. 4:3, note).

134:1–3 WHICH BY NIGHT STAND IN THE HOUSE OF THE LORD. This psalm speaks of all-night worship and intercession in God's house. Should not God's people under the new covenant be equally zealous for being involved in all-night services devoted to spiritual worship and earnest intercession for revival in the church and salvation for the lost?

135:1–21 PRAISE YE THE LORD. This call to praise God is based on three facts: (1) God has brought Israel into a saving covenant relationship with Him (vv. 1–4; cf. Ex. 19:5); (2) God is a living God, active in the affairs of the world and His people (vv. 5–13); (3) God is near His people, feeling compassion for those who serve Him (v. 14).

11 Sihon king of the Amorites, and Og king of Bashan, and [h]all the kingdoms of Canaan:

12 [i]And gave their land *for* an heritage, an heritage unto Israel his people.

13 [j]Thy name, O LORD, *endureth* for ever; *and* thy memorial, O LORD, [h]throughout all generations.

14 [k]For the LORD will judge his people, and he will repent himself concerning his servants.

15 [l]The idols of the heathen *are* silver and gold, the work of men's hands.

16 They have mouths, but they speak not; eyes have they, but they see not;

17 They have ears, but they hear not; neither is there *any* breath in their mouths.

18 They that make them are like unto them: *so is* every one that trusteth in them.

19 [m]Bless the LORD, O house of Israel: bless the LORD, O house of Aaron:

20 Bless the LORD, O house of Levi: ye that fear the LORD, bless the LORD.

21 Blessed be the LORD [n]out of Zion, which dwelleth at Jerusalem. Praise ye the LORD.

A litany of God's wonders

136 O [o]GIVE thanks unto the LORD; for *he is* good: [p]for his mercy *endureth* for ever.

2 O give thanks unto [q]the God of gods: for his mercy *endureth* for ever.

3 O give thanks to the Lord of lords: for his mercy *endureth* for ever.

4 To him [r]who alone doeth great wonders: for his mercy *endureth* for ever.

5 [s]To him that by wisdom made the heavens: for his mercy *endureth* for ever.

6 [t]To him that stretched out the earth above the waters: for his mercy *endureth* for ever.

7 [u]To him that made great lights: for his mercy *endureth* for ever:

8 [v]The sun [i]to rule by day: for his mercy *endureth* for ever:

9 The moon and stars to rule by night: for his mercy *endureth* for ever.

10 [w]To him that smote Egypt in their firstborn: for his mercy *endureth* for ever:

11 [x]And brought out Israel from among them: for his mercy *endureth* for ever:

12 [y]With a strong hand, and with a stretched out arm: for his mercy *endureth* for ever.

13 [z]To him which divided the Red sea into parts: for his mercy *endureth* for ever:

14 And made Israel to pass through the midst of it: for his mercy *endureth* for ever:

15 [a]But [j]overthrew Pharaoh and his host in the Red sea: for his mercy *endureth* for ever.

16 [b]To him which led his people through the wilderness: for his mercy *endureth* for ever.

17 [c]To him which smote great kings: for his mercy *endureth* for ever:

18 [d]And slew famous kings: for his mercy *endureth* for ever:

19 [e]Sihon king of the Amorites: for his mercy *endureth* for ever:

20 [f]And Og the king of Bashan: for his mercy *endureth* for ever:

21 [g]And gave their land for an heritage: for his mercy *endureth* for ever:

22 *Even* an heritage unto Israel his servant: for his mercy *endureth* for ever.

23 Who [h]remembered us in our low estate: for his mercy *endureth* for ever:

24 And hath redeemed us from our enemies: for his mercy *endureth* for ever.

25 [i]Who giveth food to all flesh: for his mercy *endureth* for ever.

26 O give thanks unto the God of heaven: for his mercy *endureth* for ever.

Captives in Babylon

137 BY THE rivers of Babylon, there we sat down, yea, we wept, when we remembered Zion.

2 We hanged our harps upon the willows in the midst thereof.

3 For there they that carried us away captive required of us [k]a song; and they that [j]wasted[l] us *required of*

135:11 [h]Josh. 12:7
135:12 [i]Ps. 78:55 & 136:21,22
135:13 [j]Ex. 3:15 Ps. 102:12
135:14 [k]Deut. 32:36
135:15 [l]Ps. 115:4-8
135:19 [m]Ps. 115:9
135:21 [n]Ps. 134:3
136:1 [o]Ps. 106:1 [p]1 Chr. 16:34
136:2 [q]Deut. 10:17
136:4 [r]Ps. 72:18
136:5 [s]Gen. 1:1 Prov. 3:19 Jer. 51:15
136:6 [t]Gen. 1:9 Ps. 24:2 Jer. 10:12
136:7 [u]Gen. 1:14
136:8 [v]Gen. 1:16
136:10 [w]Ex. 12:29 Ps. 135:8
136:11 [x]Ex. 12:51
136:12 [y]Ex. 6:6
136:13 [z]Ex. 14:21 Ps. 78:13
136:15 [a]Ex. 14:27 Ps. 135:9
136:16 [b]Ex. 13:18
136:17 [c]Ps. 135:10
136:18 [d]Deut. 29:7
136:19 [e]Num. 21:21
136:20 [f]Num. 21:33
136:21 [g]Josh. 12:1 Ps. 135:12
136:23 [h]Gen. 8:1 Deut. 32:36 Ps. 113:7
136:25 [i]Ps. 104:27 & 145:15
137:3 [j]Ps. 79:1

h Heb. *to generation and generation* i Heb. *for the rulings by day* j Heb. *shaked off* k Heb. *the words of song* l Heb. *laid us on heaps*

136:1–26 FOR HIS MERCY *ENDURETH* FOR EVER. This repeated refrain teaches us that God's mercy and love are the foundation of all His works on our behalf and the fountainhead of all our thanksgiving. His mercy includes His faithfulness and kindness.

us mirth, *saying,* Sing us *one* of the
songs of Zion.
4 How shall we sing the LORD's song
in a [m]strange land?
5 If I forget thee, O Jerusalem, let
my right hand forget *her cunning.*
6 If I do not remember thee, let my
[k]tongue cleave to the roof of my
mouth; if I prefer not Jerusalem above
[n]my chief joy.
7 Remember, O LORD, [l]the chil-
dren of Edom in the day of Jerusalem;
who said, [o]Rase *it,* rase *it, even* to the
foundation thereof.
8 O daughter of Babylon, [m]who art
to be [p]destroyed; happy *shall he be,*
[n]that[q] rewardeth thee as thou hast
served us.
9 Happy *shall he be,* that taketh and
[o]dasheth thy little ones against [r]the
stones.

The LORD a faithful God

A *Psalm* of David.

138 I WILL praise thee with my
whole heart: [p]before the
gods will I sing praise unto thee.
2 [q]I will worship [r]toward thy holy
temple, and praise thy name for thy
lovingkindness and for thy truth: for
thou hast [s]magnified thy word above
all thy name.
3 In the day when I cried thou an-
sweredst me, *and* strengthenedst me
with strength in my soul.
4 [t]All the kings of the earth shall
praise thee, O LORD, when they hear
the words of thy mouth.
5 Yea, they shall sing in the ways of

137:6 [k]Ezek. 3:26
137:7 [l]Jer. 49:7 Lam. 4:22 Ezek. 25:12 Obad. 10
137:8 [m]Is. 13:1,6 Jer. 25:12 [n]Jer. 50:15 Rev. 18:6
137:9 [o]Is. 13:16
138:1 [p]Ps. 119:46
138:2 [q]Ps. 28:2 [r]1 Ki. 8:29 Ps. 5:7 [s]Is. 42:21
138:4 [t]Ps. 102:15
138:6 [u]Ps. 113:5,6 Is. 57:15 [v]Prov. 3:34 Jas. 4:6 1 Pet. 5:5
138:7 [w]Ps. 23:3,4
138:8 [x]Ps. 57:2 Phil. 1:6 [y]Job 10:3,8
139:1 [z]Ps. 17:3 Jer. 12:3
139:2 [a]2 Ki. 19:27 [b]Mat. 9:4 John 2:24
139:3 [c]Job 31:4
139:4 [d]Heb. 4:13
139:6 [e]Job 42:3 Ps. 40:5

the LORD: for great *is* the glory of the
LORD.
6 [u]Though the LORD *be* high, yet
[v]hath he respect unto the lowly: but
the proud he knoweth afar off.
7 [w]Though I walk in the midst of
trouble, thou wilt revive me: thou shalt
stretch forth thine hand against the
wrath of mine enemies, and thy right
hand shall save me.
8 [x]The LORD will perfect *that which*
concerneth me: thy mercy, O LORD, *en-
dureth* for ever: [y]forsake not the
works of thine own hands.

The prayer of a believing heart

To the chief Musician,
A Psalm of David.

139 O LORD, [z]thou hast
searched me, and known
me.
2 [a]Thou knowest my downsitting
and mine uprising, thou [b]understand-
est my thought afar off.
3 [c]Thou [s]compassest my path
and my lying down, and art acquainted
with all my ways.
4 For *there is* not a word in my
tongue, *but,* lo, O LORD, [d]thou knowest
it altogether.
5 Thou hast beset me behind and
before, and laid thine hand upon me.
6 [e]*Such* knowledge *is* too wonder-
ful for me; it is high, I cannot *attain*
unto it.

[m] Heb. *land of a stranger?* [n] Heb. *the head of my joy* [o] Heb. *Make bare* [p] Heb. *wasted* [q] Heb. *that recompenseth unto thee thy deed which thou didst to us* [r] Heb. *the rock* [s] Or, *winnowest*

137:9 DASHETH THY LITTLE ONES. When the Babylonians captured Jerusalem in 586 B.C., they had taken helpless babies from their mothers and dashed them against the nearest wall. God will punish their cruelty by causing them to reap what they had sown (see Is. 13:16; Jer. 23:2). The cruel violence they had unmercifully perpetrated on others will return to them. Note two things about this cry for appropriate retribution: (1) Divine retribution rests mostly on the cruel adults. They are the ones who will suffer the most. The innocent children who die in times of war or divine judgments are accepted by God and not condemned. God does not impute sin to an individual until he or she rejects God's law written in the human heart or in Scripture (see 1 Sam. 15:3, note; Rom. 5:12,14, notes; 7:9–11, note).

(2) Although the N.T. emphasizes forgiving one's enemies and praying for their salvation (Mat. 5:43–48), there will come a time at the end of history when the Holy Spirit will lead His people to pray for divine retribution upon the arrogant, unrepentant, and ungodly (see Rev. 6:10).

139:1–24 LORD, THOU HAS SEARCHED ME. This psalm describes various aspects of God's attributes, especially His omnipresence and omniscience as these characteristics relate to His care for His people (see article on THE ATTRIBUTES OF GOD, p. 912). The God of heaven and earth created us and has perfect knowledge of us; He is always with us, and His thoughts are always directed toward us in every situation.

139:1–6 O LORD, THOU HAST . . . KNOWN *ME*. God knows all our inward thoughts, motives, desires, and fears, as well as our outward habits and actions. He knows all we do from the beginning of the day to its end. In everything that we do, He encircles us with His care and lays His hand of favor upon our heads (v. 5).

7 [f]Whither shall I go from thy spirit? or whither shall I flee from thy presence?

8 [g]If I ascend up into heaven, thou *art* there: [h]if I make my bed in hell, behold, thou *art there.*

9 *If* I take the wings of the morning, *and* dwell in the uttermost parts of the sea;

10 Even there shall thy hand lead me, and thy right hand shall hold me.

11 If I say, Surely the darkness shall cover me; even the night shall be light about me.

12 Yea, [i]the darkness [t]hideth not from thee; but the night shineth as the day: [u]the darkness and the light *are* both alike *to thee.*

13 For thou hast possessed my reins: thou hast covered me in my mother's womb.

14 I will praise thee; for I am fearfully *and* wonderfully made: marvellous *are* thy works; and *that* my soul knoweth [v]right well.

15 [j]My [w]substance was not hid from thee, when I was made in secret, *and* curiously wrought in the lowest parts of the earth.

16 Thine eyes did see my substance, yet being unperfect; and in thy book [x]all *my members* were written, [y]*which* in continuance were fashioned, when *as yet there was* none of them.

17 [k]How precious also are thy thoughts unto me, O God! how great is the sum of them!

18 *If* I should count them, they are more in number than the sand: when I awake, I am still with thee.

19 Surely thou wilt [l]slay the wicked, O God: [m]depart from me therefore, ye bloody men.

20 For they [n]speak against thee wickedly, *and* thine enemies take *thy name* in vain.

21 [o]Do not I hate them, O LORD, that hate thee? and am not I grieved with those that rise up against thee?

22 I hate them with perfect hatred: I count them mine enemies.

23 [p]Search me, O God, and know my heart: try me, and know my thoughts:

139:7 [f]Jer. 23:24 Jonah 1:3
139:8 [g]Amos 9:2 [h]Prov. 15:11
139:12 [i]Job 34:22
139:15 [j]Job 10:8,9
139:17 [k]Ps. 40:5
139:19 [l]Is. 11:4 [m]Ps. 119:115
139:20 [n]Jude 15
139:21 [o]2 Chr. 19:2
139:23 [p]Job 31:6

[t] Heb. *darkeneth not* [u] Heb. *as is the darkness, so is the light* [v] Heb. *greatly* [w] Or, *strength,* or, *body* [x] Heb. *all of them* [y] Or, what *days they should be fashioned*

139:7–12 WHITHER SHALL I GO FROM THY SPIRIT. The child of God can never move beyond God's care, guidance, and supporting strength (see v. 10 as the key to understanding v. 7). He is with us in all situations, in whatever the present and the future brings.

139:13 THOU HAST COVERED ME IN MY MOTHER'S WOMB. God is creatively and actively involved in the development of human life. He personally cares for a baby from the moment of its conception; His regard for a fetus extends to a plan for his or her life (see next note). For this reason God considers the abortion of an unborn infant as the murder of a human life (see Ex. 21:22–23, note).

139:16 IN THY BOOK ALL *MY MEMBERS* WERE WRITTEN. God does not bring us into life without a purpose. (1) The statement about the days ordained for us probably refers to our alloted time on earth, i.e., generally seventy or eighty years (see Ps. 90:10), though one may die before his or her time (see 55:23; Job 22:16; Prov. 10:27; Eccl. 7:17).

(2) The time mentioned in this psalm refers not only to days, but also to God's plan for our lives as a whole. In his plan, He is "not willing that any should perish, but that all should come to repentance" (2 Pet. 3:9; cf. 1 Tim. 2:4). Thus God intends for us to accept Jesus as our Lord and Savior and fulfill His will in a life of service to Him.

139:17 HOW PRECIOUS ALSO ARE THY THOUGHTS UNTO ME. We can be comforted knowing that God is continually aware of our needs, troubles, and suffering, and that He plans for our care, forgiveness, salvation, and sanctification. His thoughts for us are unfathomable and immeasurable. As the apostle Paul writes, "Eye hath not seen, nor ear heard, neither have entered into the heart of man, the things which God hath prepared for them that love him" (1 Cor. 2:9).

139:21 AM NOT I GRIEVED WITH THOSE THAT RISE UP AGAINST THEE? Having meditated on God's great love for him, the psalmist reciprocates with great love and loyalty to His Lord. His anger is stirred against those who oppose and blaspheme God's wonderful name. In deep sympathy with God and His cause, he so identifies himself with the Lord that he hates what God hates and loves what God loves (see Heb. 1:9, note). He is grieved and distressed by all the evil and immorality around him (see 2 Pet. 2:7–8). We too who have truly seen the Lord's salvation, love, and goodness should find no love within ourselves for the world and its ways (see 1 John 2:15–16).

139:23–24 SEARCH ME, O GOD. This is an appropriate prayer for every believer. Not only must we hate unrighteousness in the world (vv. 19–22), but we must also be aware that there may be something in us that grieves God. We should be willing to ask God to put us through any test that would further His work of sanctification in us. If anything offensive is found, we must turn from it in repentance (see Col. 3:17, note).

24 And see if *there be any* [z]wicked
way in me, and [q]lead me in the way
everlasting.

For protection against enemies

To the chief Musician,
A Psalm of David.

140 DELIVER ME, O LORD, from
the evil man: preserve me
from the [a]violent man;
2 Which imagine mischiefs in *their*
heart; [r]continually are they gathered
together *for* war.
3 They have sharpened their
tongues like a serpent; [s]adders' poi-
son *is* under their lips. Selah.
4 [t]Keep me, O LORD, from the
hands of the wicked; preserve me from
the violent man; who have purposed to
overthrow my goings.
5 [u]The proud have hid a snare for
me, and cords; they have spread a net
by the wayside; they have set gins for
me. Selah.
6 I said unto the LORD, Thou *art* my
God: hear the voice of my supplica-
tions, O LORD.
7 O GOD the Lord, the strength of my
salvation, thou hast covered my head
in the day of battle.
8 Grant not, O LORD, the desires of
the wicked: further not his wicked de-
vice; [v]*lest*[b] they exalt themselves.
Selah.
9 *As for* the head of those that com-
pass me about, [w]let the mischief of
their own lips cover them.
10 [x]Let burning coals fall upon
them: let them be cast into the fire;
into deep pits, that they rise not up
again.
11 Let not [c] [d]an evil speaker be
established in the earth: evil shall hunt
the violent man to overthrow *him*.
12 I know that the LORD will [y]main-
tain the cause of the afflicted, *and* the
right of the poor.
13 Surely the righteous shall give
thanks unto thy name: the upright
shall dwell in thy presence.

139:24 [q]Ps. 5:8
140:2 [r]Ps. 56:6
140:3 [s]Ps. 58:4
140:4 [t]Ps. 71:4
140:5 [u]Jer. 18:22
140:8 [v]Deut. 32:27
140:9 [w]Ps. 7:16
140:10 [x]Ps. 11:6
140:12 [y]Ps. 9:4

Conduct amidst trial

A Psalm of David.

141 LORD, I cry unto thee:
[z]make haste unto me; give
ear unto my voice, when I cry unto
thee.
2 Let [a]my prayer be [e]set forth be-
fore thee [b]*as* incense; *and* [c]the lifting
up of my hands *as* [d]the evening sacri-
fice.
3 Set a watch, O LORD, before my
mouth; keep the door of my lips.
4 Incline not my heart to *any* evil
thing, to practise wicked works with
men that work iniquity: [e]and let me
not eat of their dainties.
5 [f]Let[f] the righteous smite me; *it
shall be* a kindness: and let him reprove
me; *it shall be* an excellent oil, *which*
shall not break my head: for yet my
prayer also *shall be* in their calamities.
6 When their judges are overthrown
in stony places, they shall hear my
words; for they are sweet.
7 Our bones are scattered at the
grave's mouth, as when one cutteth
and cleaveth *wood* upon the earth.
8 But [g]mine eyes *are* unto thee, O
GOD the Lord: in thee is my trust;
[g]leave not my soul destitute.
9 Keep me from [h]the snares *which*

141:1 [z]Ps. 70:5
141:2 [a]Rev. 5:8 [b]Rev. 8:3 [c]1 Tim. 2:8 [d]Ex. 29:39
141:4 [e]Prov. 23:6
141:5 [f]Prov. 9:8
141:8 [g]Ps. 25:15
141:9 [h]Ps. 119:110

[z] Heb. *way of pain* [a] Heb. *man of violences* [b] Or, *let them not be exalted* [c] Heb. *a man of tongue* [d] Or, *an evil speaker, a wicked man of violence, be established in the earth: let him be hunted to his overthrow* [e] Heb. *directed* [f] Or, *Let the righteous smite me kindly, and reprove me; let not their precious oil break my head* [g] Heb. *make not my soul bare*

140:1–13 DELIVER ME, O LORD, FROM THE EVIL MAN. We should ask God to deliver us not only from evil people but also from the "evil one," i.e., Satan. As our greatest enemy, he seeks to snare and destroy us (see Mat. 4:10, note; 6:13, note; see article on POWER OVER SATAN AND DEMONS, p. 1486).

141:4 INCLINE NOT MY HEART TO *ANY* EVIL THING. Those who love the Lord should pray that God will keep them from desiring, speaking, or doing any evil (cf. Mat. 6:13; John 14:15, 21). We must shun all compromise with wicked persons and refuse to be entertained by their "dainties," i.e., seductive pleasures (see Rom. 1:32, note; see article on SANCTIFICATION, p. 1982).

141:5 LET THE RIGHTEOUS SMITE ME. If we sincerely desire to please our Lord, we will welcome rebuke that convicts us of anything contrary to the holiness of God. When a righteous person cries out fervently against sin and compromise in the church, he or she should be supported, not rejected (see Prov. 15:5,32; John 16:8; Eph. 5:11; 2 Tim. 4:2). Our attitude towards such servants of God reveals our own spiritual state (see 2 Tim. 4:3–4, note).

THE ATTRIBUTES OF GOD

Ps. 139:7–8 "Whither shall I go from thy spirit? or whither shall I flee from thy presence? If I ascend up into heaven, thou art *there: if I make my bed in hell, behold, thou* art *there."*

The Bible does not seek to prove that God exists. Rather, it assumes His existence and describes numerous attributes that characterize Him. Some of these attributes are unique to Him as God; others we see in human beings, as a result of their being created in the image of God.

UNIQUE ATTRIBUTES OF GOD. (1) God is omnipresent—i.e., He is present everywhere at the same time. The psalmist states that no matter where we go, God is there (Ps. 139:7–12; cf. Jer. 23:23–24; Acts 17:27–28); He observes everything that we do.

(2) God is omniscient—i.e., He knows everything (Ps. 139:1–6; 147:5). He knows not only our actions, but also our very thoughts (1 Sam. 16:7; 1 Ki. 8:39; Ps. 44:21; Jer. 17:9–10). When the Bible speaks about God's foreknowledge (Is. 42:9; Acts 2:23; 1 Pet. 1:2), it means that He knows all things possible as possible, all things certain as certain, all things contingent as contingent, all things future as future, all things past as past, all things foreordained as predestined certainties (cf. 1 Sam. 23:10–13; Jer. 38:17–20). Biblical foreknowledge does not entail philosophical determinism. God remains free to make decisions and alter His purposes in time and history, according to His own will and wisdom. In other words, God is not a prisoner of His own foreknowledge (see Num. 14:11–20; 2 Ki. 20:1–7; see article on ELECTION AND PREDESTINATION, p. 1846).

(3) God is omnipotent—i.e., He is all-powerful and has ultimate authority over all things and all creatures (Ps. 147:13–18; Jer. 32:17; Mat. 19:26; Luke 1:37). This does not mean, however, that God uses all His power and authority at all times; for example, God has the power to destroy all sin, but He has chosen not to do so until the end of history (see 1 John 5:19, note). In many cases, God limits His power, channeling it through His people (2 Cor. 12:7–10); in these cases, His power is dependent on our degree of availability and submission to Him (see Eph. 3:20, note; see article on THE PROVIDENCE OF GOD, p. 80).

(4) God is transcendent—i.e., He is different and independent from His creation (see Ex. 24:9–18; Is. 6:1–3; 40:12–26; 55:8–9). His being and existence are infinitely greater and higher than the created order (1 Ki. 8:27; Is. 66:1–2; Acts 17:24–25). He dwells in perfect and pure existence, far above what He has made. He Himself is uncreated and exists apart from creation (see 1 Tim. 6:16, note). Transcendence does not entail, however, that God is incapable of dwelling among His people as their God (Lev. 26:11–12; Ezek. 37:27; 43:7; 2 Cor. 6:16).

(5) God is eternal—i.e., He is from everlasting to everlasting (Ps. 90:1–2; 102:12; Is. 57:15). There was never a time, either in the past or the future, when God did not or will not exist. He is not bound by human time (cf. Ps. 90:4; 2 Pet. 3:8) and is, therefore, best described as "I am" (cf. Ex. 3:14; John 8:58).

(6) God is unchangeable—i.e., there is no change in the attributes of God, in His perfections, or in His purpose for humankind (Num. 23:19; Ps. 102:26–28; Is. 41:4; Mal. 3:6; Heb. 1:11–12; Jas. 1:17); this does not mean, however, that God never alters his temporary purposes in response to the actions of humans. He may, for example, alter his intentions of judgment because of the sincere repentance of sinners (cf. Jonah 3:6–10). Furthermore, He remains free to respond to the needs of human beings and to the prayers of His people. The Scriptures often speak about God as changing His mind as a result of the diligent prayers of the righteous (e.g., Num. 14:1–20; 2 Ki. 20:2–6; Is. 38:2–6; Luke 18:1–8; see articles on ELECTION AND PREDESTINATION, p. 1846, and EFFECTIVE PRAYING, p. 540).

(7) God is perfect and holy—i.e., He is completely without sin and absolutely righteous (Lev. 11:44–45; Ps. 85:13; 145:17; Mat. 5:48). Adam and Eve were created without sin (cf. Gen. 1:31), but with the capability of sinning. God, on the other hand, cannot sin (Num. 23:19; 2 Tim. 2:13; Tit. 1:2; Heb. 6:18). His holiness also includes His dedication to carrying out His purpose and plan.

(8) God is triune—i.e., He is one God (Deut. 6:4; Is. 45:21; 1 Cor. 8:5–6; Eph. 4:6; 1 Tim. 2:5) who has manifested Himself in three divine persons: Father, Son, and Holy Spirit (e.g., Mat. 28:19; 2 Cor. 13:14; 1 Pet. 1:2). Each person is fully divine, equal with the other two; yet they are not three Gods, but one (see Mat. 3:17, note; Mark 1:11, note).

MORAL ATTRIBUTES OF GOD. Many characteristics of the one true God, particularly His moral attributes, bear similarity to human qualities; however, His attributes all exist to a degree incomparably greater than they do in us. For example, even though both God and humans have the ability to love, no human is able to love to the degree and intensity that God does. Moreover, it must be stressed that our ability to exercise these characteristics is related to our being created in God's image (Gen. 1:26–27). In other words, we are like Him, not He like us.

(1) God is good (Ps. 25:8; 106:1; Mark 10:18). All that God originally created was good, an extension of His own nature (Gen. 1:4,10,12,18,21,25,31). He continues to be good to His creation by sustaining it on behalf of all His creatures (Ps. 104:10–28; 145:9; see article on THE PROVIDENCE OF GOD, p. 80); he even provides for the ungodly (Mat. 5:45; Acts 14:17). God is especially good to His people who call upon him in truth (Ps. 145:18–20).

(2) God is love (1 John 4:8). His love is a selfless love that embraces the entire world of sinful humankind (John 3:16; Rom. 5:8). The chief expression of that love was His sending of His only Son Jesus to die for sinners (1 John 4:9–10). In addition, God has a special family love for those who through Jesus are reconciled to Him (see John 16:27, note).

(3) God is merciful and gracious (Ex 34:6; 2 Chr. 30:9; Ps. 103:8; 145:8; Joel 2:13). He does not cut off and destroy humanity as our sins deserve (Ps. 103:10), but offers forgiveness as a free gift to be received through faith in Jesus Christ (Ps. 103:11–12; Rom. 6:23; 1 Cor. 1:3–4; Eph. 2:8–9; Tit. 2:11; 3:4–5; see article on FAITH AND GRACE, p. 1738).

(4) God is compassionate (2 Ki. 13:23; Ps. 86:15; 112:4). To be compassionate means to feel sorrow for someone else's suffering, with a desire to help. Out of His compassion for humanity, God provided forgiveness and salvation (cf. Ps. 78:38). Likewise, Jesus the Son of God manifested compassion for the multitudes when He preached the gospel to the poor, proclaimed release to the captives and recovery of sight to the blind, and set free the downtrodden (Luke 4:18; cf. Mat. 9:36; 14:14; 15:32; 20:34; Mark 1:41; see Mark 6:34, note).

(5) God is patient and longsuffering (Ex. 34:6; Num. 14:18; Rom. 2:4; 1 Tim. 1:16). God first expressed this characteristic in the Garden of Eden after Adam and Eve's sin, when He did not destroy the human race as He had a right to do (cf. Gen. 2:16–17). God was also patient in the days of Noah, while the ark was being built (1 Pet. 3:20). And God is still longsuffering with the sinful human race; He does not presently judge so as to destroy the world because He is patiently giving everyone the opportunity to repent and be saved (2 Pet. 3:9).

(6) God is truth (Ex. 34:6; Deut. 32:4; Ps. 31:5; Is. 65:16). Jesus called Himself "the truth" (John 14:6), and the Spirit is known as the "Spirit of truth" (John 14:17; cf. 1 John 5:6). Since God is entirely trustworthy and true in all He says and does, His word is also described as truth (2 Sam. 7:28; Ps. 119:43; Is. 45:19; John 17:17). In keeping with this fact, the Bible makes it plain that God does not tolerate lies or falsehood of any kind (Num. 23:19; Tit. 1:2; Heb. 6:18).

(7) God is faithful (Deut. 7:9; Is. 49:7; Lam. 3:23; Heb. 10:23). God will do what He has revealed in His Word, carrying out both His promises and His warnings (Num.

14:32–35; 2 Sam. 7:28; Job 34:12; Acts 13:23,32–33; see 2 Tim. 2:13, note). God's faithfulness should bring unspeakable comfort to believers and great fear of His judgment to all who do not repent and believe in the Lord Jesus (Heb. 6:4–8; 10:26–31).

(8) Finally, God is just (Deut. 32:4; Is. 45:21; 1 John 1:9); to be just means that God upholds the moral order of the universe, and is righteous and without sin in the manner in which He treats humankind (Neh. 9:33; Dan. 9:14). God's determination to punish sinners with death (Rom. 5:12; see article on DEATH, p. 782) proceeds from His justice (Rom. 6:23; cf. Gen. 2:16–17); He is angry at sin because of His love for righteousness (Rom. 3:5–6; see Judg. 10:7, note). He reveals His wrath against every form of wickedness (Rom. 1:18), especially idolatry (1 Ki. 14:9,15,22), unbelief (Ps. 78:21–22; John 3:36), and unjust treatment of other people (Is. 10:1–4; Amos 2:6–7). Jesus Christ, who is called the "Just One" (Acts 7:52; 22:14; cf. Acts 3:14), also loves righteousness and hates evil (see Mark 3:5; Rom. 1:18, note; Heb. 1:9, note). Note that God's justice is not opposed to His love. On the contrary, it was to satisfy His justice that He sent Jesus into the world as His gift of love (John 3:16; 1 John 4:9–10) and as His sacrifice for sin on our behalf (Is. 53:5–6; Rom. 4:25; 1 Pet. 3:18), in order to reconcile us to Himself (2 Cor. 5:18–21; see notes).

God's final revelation of Himself is in Jesus Christ (cf. John 1:18; Heb. 1:1–4). In other words, if we want to understand completely the personhood of God, we must look at Christ, for in Him all the fullness of the Godhead dwells (Col. 2:9).

they have laid for me, and the gins of the workers of iniquity.

10 [i]Let the wicked fall into their own nets, whilst that I withal [h]escape.

The prisoner's prayer

[j]Maschil[i] of David; A Prayer [k]when he was in the cave.

142 I CRIED unto the LORD with my voice; with my voice unto the LORD did I make my supplication.

2 [l]I poured out my complaint before him; I showed before him my trouble.

3 [m]When my spirit was overwhelmed within me, then thou knewest my path. [n]In the way wherein I walked have they privily laid a snare for me.

4 [o]I[j] looked on *my* right hand, and beheld, but [p]*there was* no man that would know me: refuge [k]failed me; [l]no man cared for my soul.

5 I cried unto thee, O LORD: I said, [q]Thou *art* my refuge *and* [r]my portion [s]in the land of the living.

6 Attend unto my cry; for I am [t]brought very low: deliver me from my persecutors; for they are stronger than I.

7 Bring my soul out of prison, that I may praise thy name: [u]the righteous shall compass me about; [v]for thou shalt deal bountifully with me.

The prayer of a soul in distress

A Psalm of David.

143 HEAR MY prayer, O LORD, give ear to my supplications: [w]in thy faithfulness answer me, *and* in thy righteousness.

2 And [x]enter not into judgment with thy servant: for [y]in thy sight shall no man living be justified.

3 For the enemy hath persecuted my soul; he hath smitten my life down to the ground; he hath made me to dwell in darkness, as those that have been long dead.

4 [z]Therefore is my spirit overwhelmed within me; my heart within me is desolate.

5 [a]I remember the days of old; I meditate on all thy works; I muse on the work of thy hands.

6 [b]I stretch forth my hands unto thee: [c]my soul *thirsteth* after thee, as a thirsty land. Selah.

7 Hear me speedily, O LORD: my spirit faileth: hide not thy face from me, [d]lest[m] I be like unto them that go down into the pit.

8 Cause me to hear thy lovingkindness [e]in the morning; for in thee do I trust: cause me to know the way wherein I should walk; for [f]I lift up my soul unto thee.

9 Deliver me, O LORD, from mine enemies: I [n]flee unto thee to hide me.

10 [g]Teach me to do thy will; for thou *art* my God: [h]thy spirit *is* good; lead me into [i]the land of uprightness.

11 [j]Quicken me, O LORD, for thy name's sake: for thy righteousness' sake bring my soul out of trouble.

12 And of thy mercy [k]cut off mine enemies, and destroy all them that afflict my soul: for I *am* thy servant.

The warrior's psalm

A Psalm of David.

144 BLESSED *BE* the LORD [l]my[o] strength, [m]which teacheth my hands [p]to war, *and* my fingers to fight:

141:10 [i]Ps. 35:8
142:1 [j]Ps. 57,title [k]1 Sam. 22:1
142:2 [l]Is. 26:16
142:3 [m]Ps. 143:4 [n]Ps. 140:5
142:4 [o]Ps. 69:20 [p]Ps. 31:11
142:5 [q]Ps. 46:1 [r]Lam. 3:24 [s]Ps. 27:13
142:6 [t]Ps. 116:6
142:7 [u]Ps. 34:2 [v]Ps. 13:6
143:1 [w]Ps. 31:1
143:2 [x]Job 14:3 [y]Ex. 34:7
143:4 [z]Ps. 77:3
143:5 [a]Ps. 77:5
143:6 [b]Ps. 88:9 [c]Ps. 63:1
143:7 [d]Ps. 28:1
143:8 [e]Ps. 46:5 [f]Ps. 25:1
143:10 [g]Ps. 25:4,5 [h]Neh. 9:20 [i]Is. 26:10
143:11 [j]Ps. 119:25
143:12 [k]Ps. 54:5
144:1 [l]Ps. 18:2,31 [m]2 Sam. 22:35 Ps. 18:34

---

[h] Heb. *pass over* [i] Or, A Psalm *of David, giving instruction* [j] Or, *Look on the right hand, and see* [k] Heb. *perished from me* [l] Heb. *no man sought after my soul* [m] Or, *for I am become like* [n] Heb. *hide me with thee* [o] Heb. my *rock* [p] Heb. *to the war*

142:1–7 I CRIED UNTO THE LORD. This psalm comes from one who is deeply troubled and overwhelmed by a desperate situation. Although the psalmist is experiencing loneliness without any supporting human companionship or sympathy, the Lord still remains his refuge, friend, and helper. When believers are afflicted and oppressed, rather than remaining silent, they should cry out to God, who has pledged Himself to be our comforter and helper in time of need (see John 14:16–26; 2 Cor. 1:4–5).

143:1–12 HEAR MY PRAYER, O LORD. Like the preceding psalm, this one describes a believer who is facing overwhelming troubles and feels he has reached the end of his endurance (vv. 3–4,7; cf. 104:29). All he has left is prayerful hope that God will revive him again and deliver him out of his great trial (vv. 10–11; see previous note).

144:1–15 BLESSED BE THE LORD, MY ROCK. God is an immovable rock, stronghold, shield, and deliverer for those who take refuge in Him (cf. Ps. 140 — 143). He trains the hands of the

2 [q]My goodness, and my fortress; my high tower, and my deliverer; my shield, and *he* in whom I trust; who subdueth my people under me.

3 [n]LORD, what *is* man, that thou takest knowledge of him! *or* the son of man, that thou makest account of him!

4 [o]Man is like to vanity: [p]his days *are* as a shadow that passeth away.

5 [q]Bow thy heavens, O LORD, and come down: [r]touch the mountains, and they shall smoke.

6 [s]Cast forth lightning, and scatter them: shoot out thine arrows, and destroy them.

7 Send thine [r]hand from above; rid me, and deliver me out of great waters, from the hand of strange children;

8 Whose mouth [t]speaketh vanity, and their right hand *is* a right hand of falsehood.

9 I will [u]sing a new song unto thee, O God: upon a psaltery *and* an instrument of ten strings will I sing praises unto thee.

10 [v]*It is he* that giveth [s]salvation unto kings: who delivereth David his servant from the hurtful sword.

11 Rid me, and deliver me from the hand of strange children, whose mouth speaketh vanity, and their right hand *is* a right hand of falsehood:

12 That our sons *may be* [w]as plants grown up in their youth; *that* our daughters *may be* as corner stones, [t]polished *after* the similitude of a palace:

13 *That* our garners *may be* full, affording [u]all manner of store: *that* our sheep may bring forth thousands and ten thousands in our streets:

14 *That* our oxen *may be* [v]strong to labour; *that there be* no breaking in, nor going out; that *there be* no complaining in our streets.

15 [x]Happy *is that* people, that is in such a case: *yea,* happy *is that* people, whose God *is* the LORD.

144:3 [n]Job 7:17 Ps. 8:4 Heb. 2:6 **144:4** [o]Job 4:19 [p]Ps. 102:11 **144:5** [q]Ps. 18:9 [r]Ps. 104:32 **144:6** [s]Ps. 18:13 **144:8** [t]Ps. 12:2 **144:9** [u]Ps. 33:2,3 **144:10** [v]Ps. 18:50 **144:12** [w]Ps. 128:3 **144:15** [x]Ps. 33:12 **145:1** [y]Ps. 100,title **145:3** [z]Ps. 147:5 [a]Rom. 11:33 **145:4** [b]Is. 38:9 **145:8** [c]Num. 14:18 **145:9** [d]Nah. 1:7 **145:10** [e]Ps. 19:1

The goodness of the LORD

David's [y]*Psalm* of praise.

145 I WILL extol thee, my God, O king; and I will bless thy name for ever and ever.

2 Every day will I bless thee; and I will praise thy name for ever and ever.

3 [z]Great *is* the LORD, and greatly to be praised; [w]and [a]his greatness *is* unsearchable.

4 [b]One generation shall praise thy works to another, and shall declare thy mighty acts.

5 I will speak of the glorious honour of thy majesty, and of thy wondrous [x]works.

6 And *men* shall speak of the might of thy terrible acts: and I will [y]declare thy greatness.

7 They shall abundantly utter the memory of thy great goodness, and shall sing of thy righteousness.

8 [c]The LORD *is* gracious, and full of compassion; slow to anger, and [z]of great mercy.

9 [d]The LORD *is* good to all: and his tender mercies *are* over all his works.

10 [e]All thy works shall praise

[q] Or, *My mercy* [r] Heb. *hands* [s] Or, *victory* [t] Heb. *cut* [u] Heb *from kind to kind* [v] Heb. *able to bear burdens,* or, *loaden* with flesh [w] Heb. *and of his greatness* there is *no search* [x] Heb. *things,* or, *words* [y] Heb. *declare it* [z] Heb. *great in mercy*

righteous for war and their fingers for battle in all areas of spiritual conflict (see next note).

144:1 TEACHETH MY HANDS TO WAR. The psalmist was called upon to wage war for the nation of Israel. We can apply this message to believers in Christ, whom God calls to wage spiritual battle against Satan, the world, and the flesh. We must advance His kingdom by proclaiming the gospel in the power of the Holy Spirit, by bringing down Satan's strongholds, and by leading people to salvation in Christ (see Eph. 6:11–18, notes). Warriors who depend on God's strength and training will be victorious.

144:5 O LORD . . . COME DOWN. God has trained the psalmist to trust Him for battle and for any time of crisis (vv. 1–2). Moreover, the psalmist must continue to trust God for the battle, as there are still many dangers to face (v. 7). After experiencing salvation in Christ and the baptism in the Holy Spirit, believers also continue to need God's daily strength and grace to face the battles of temptations and spiritual warfare encountered in following Christ. Seeking God's face for heaven's help is an ongoing cry for all who are members of God's kingdom (Mat. 6:33; Heb. 7:25; 11:6).

145:2 EVERY DAY I WILL BLESS THEE. No day should pass without praising and thanking God for His blessings and gifts to us. He is our Maker, Redeemer, and Provider (cf. 34:1).

145:8 THE LORD *IS* GRACIOUS. This oft-repeated refrain expresses God's delight in showing mercy (cf. Ex. 34:6–7). When He sees misery, it moves His heart to compassion. He is slow to become angry at our offenses and quickly shows mercy when forgiveness is requested (cf. Ex. 3:7; Judg. 2:18).

thee, O LORD; and thy saints shall bless thee.

11 They shall speak of the glory of thy kingdom, and talk of thy power;

12 To make known to the sons of men his mighty acts, and the glorious majesty of his kingdom.

13 [f]Thy kingdom *is* [a]an everlasting kingdom, and thy dominion *endureth* throughout all generations.

14 The LORD upholdeth all that fall, and [g]raiseth up all *those that be* bowed down.

15 [h]The eyes of all [b]wait upon thee; and [i]thou givest them their meat in due season.

16 Thou openest thine hand, [j]and satisfiest the desire of every living thing.

17 The LORD *is* righteous in all his ways, and [c]holy in all his works.

18 [k]The LORD *is* nigh unto all them that call upon him, to all that call upon him [l]in truth.

19 He will fulfil the desire of them that fear him: he also will hear their cry, and will save them.

20 [m]The LORD preserveth all them that love him: but all the wicked will he destroy.

21 My mouth shall speak the praise of the LORD: and let all flesh bless his holy name for ever and ever.

An exhortation to trust God

146 PRAISE[d] YE the LORD. [n]Praise the LORD, O my soul.

2 [o]While I live will I praise the LORD: I will sing praises unto my God while I have any being.

3 [p]Put not your trust in princes, *nor* in the son of man, in whom *there is* no [e]help.

4 [q]His breath goeth forth, he returneth to his earth; in that very day [r]his thoughts perish.

5 [s]Happy *is he* that *hath* the God of Jacob for his help, whose hope *is* in the LORD his God:

6 [t]Which made heaven, and earth, the sea, and all that therein *is:* which keepeth truth for ever:

7 [u]Which executeth judgment for the oppressed: [v]which giveth food to the hungry. [w]The LORD looseth the prisoners:

8 [x]The LORD openeth *the eyes of* the blind: [y]the LORD raiseth them that are bowed down: the LORD loveth the righteous:

9 [z]The LORD preserveth the strangers; he relieveth the fatherless and widow: [a]but the way of the wicked he turneth upside down.

10 [b]The LORD shall reign for ever, *even* thy God, O Zion, unto all generations. Praise ye the LORD. Ps. 150

The might and grace of the LORD

147 PRAISE YE the LORD: for [c]*it is* good to sing praises unto our God; [d]for *it is* pleasant; *and* [e]praise is comely.

2 The LORD doth [f]build up Jerusalem: [g]he gathereth together the outcasts of Israel.

3 [h]He healeth the broken in heart, and bindeth up their [f]wounds.

4 [i]He telleth the number of the stars; he calleth them all by *their* names.

5 [j]Great *is* our Lord, and of [k]great power: [l]his[g] understanding *is* infinite.

6 [m]The LORD lifteth up the meek: he

145:13 [f]1 Tim. 1:17
145:14 [g]Ps. 146:8
145:15 [h]Ps. 104:27 [i]Ps. 136:25
145:16 [j]Ps. 104:21
145:18 [k]Deut. 4:7 [l]John 4:24
145:20 [m]Ps. 31:23
146:1 [n]Ps. 103:1
146:2 [o]Ps. 104:33
146:3 [p]Is. 2:22
146:4 [q]Eccl. 12:7 [r]1 Cor. 2:6
146:5 [s]Jer. 17:7
146:6 [t]Rev. 14:7
146:7 [u]Ps. 103:6 [v]Ps. 107:9 [w]Ps. 107:10
146:8 [x]Mat. 9:30 [y]Luke 13:13
146:9 [z]Deut. 10:18 Ps. 68:5 [a]Ps. 147:6
146:10 [b]Ex. 15:18 Ps. 10:16
147:1 [c]Ps. 92:1 [d]Ps. 135:3 [e]Ps. 33:1
147:2 [f]Ps. 102:16 [g]Deut. 30:3
147:3 [h]Ps. 51:17
147:4 [i]Is. 40:26
147:5 [j]Ps. 48:1 [k]Nah. 1:3 [l]Is. 40:28
147:6 [m]Ps. 146:8

[a] Heb. *a kingdom of all ages* [b] Or, *look unto thee* [c] Or, *merciful,* or, *bountiful* [d] Heb. *Hallelujah* [e] Or, *salvation* [f] Heb. *griefs* [g] Heb. *of his understanding* there is *no number*

145:18 NIGH UNTO ALL THEM THAT CALL UPON HIM. All who call upon God in truth (i.e., with a sincere and upright heart) may be assured that He is near. He will hear their prayer, fulfill their desire for help, and work for their deliverance (v. 19).

146–150 PRAISE YE THE LORD. These psalms begin and end with "Praise ye the LORD" (Heb. *Hallelujah*), bringing the book of Psalms to a fitting climax. Note that the Jews called the entire book of Psalms *Tehillim* ("Praises"). Every worship service should include praise to God (see article on PRAISE, p. 816).

147:6 THE LORD LIFTETH UP THE MEEK. The term "meek" (Heb. *anawah*) often includes the idea of suffering and refers to those who are afflicted. Because such people cannot cope with all of life's problems and responsibilities by themselves, in humility they call upon God for His help and strength. (1) God lifts up the meek and gives them support. The psalmist assures them of God's help and ultimate victory (cf. 22:26; 25:9; 37:11). (2) As God supported the meek in O.T. times, Jesus ministers to the afflicted and humble under the new covenant (Mat. 11:28–30; cf. Is. 11:4; 29:19; Zeph. 2:3). (3) Since God delights in those who are of a humble spirit, all believers should earnestly pray for a spirit of humility so that they may be pleasing to Him (Gal. 5:23; Eph. 4:2; Col. 3:12; Tit. 3:2).

casteth the wicked down to the ground.

7 Sing unto the LORD with thanksgiving; sing praise upon the harp unto our God:

8 [n]Who covereth the heaven with clouds, who prepareth rain for the earth, who maketh grass to grow upon the mountains.

9 [o]He giveth to the beast his food, *and* [p]to the young ravens which cry.

10 [q]He delighteth not in the strength of the horse: he taketh not pleasure in the legs of a man.

11 The LORD taketh pleasure in them that fear him, in those that hope in his mercy.

12 Praise the LORD, O Jerusalem; praise thy God, O Zion.

13 For he hath strengthened the bars of thy gates; he hath blessed thy children within thee.

14 [r]He[h] maketh peace *in* thy borders, *and* [s]filleth thee with the [i]finest of the wheat.

15 [t]He sendeth forth his commandment *upon* earth: his word runneth very swiftly.

16 [u]He giveth snow like wool: he scattereth the hoarfrost like ashes.

17 He casteth forth his ice like morsels: who can stand before his cold?

18 [v]He sendeth out his word, and melteth them: he causeth his wind to blow, *and* the waters flow.

19 [w]He showeth [j]his word unto Jacob, [x]his statutes and his judgments unto Israel.

20 [y]He hath not dealt so with any nation: and *as for his* judgments, they have not known them. Praise ye the LORD.

Nature's praise of the LORD

148 PRAISE[k] YE the LORD. Praise ye the LORD from the heavens: praise him in the heights.

2 Praise ye him, all his angels: praise ye him, all his hosts.

3 Praise ye him, sun and moon: praise him, all ye stars of light.

4 Praise him, [z]ye heavens of heavens, and [a]ye waters that *be* above the heavens.

5 Let them praise the name of the LORD: for [b]he commanded, and they were created.

6 [c]He hath also stablished them for ever and ever; he hath made a decree which shall not pass.

7 Praise the LORD from the earth, [d]ye dragons, and all deeps:

8 Fire, and hail; snow, and vapour; stormy wind [e]fulfilling his word:

9 [f]Mountains, and all hills; fruitful trees, and all cedars:

10 Beasts, and all cattle; creeping things, and [l]flying fowl:

11 Kings of the earth, and all people; princes, and all judges of the earth:

12 Both young men, and maidens; old men, and children:

13 Let them praise the name of the LORD: for [g]his name alone is [m]excellent; [h]his glory *is* above the earth and heaven.

14 [i]He also exalteth the horn of his people, [j]the praise of all his saints; *even* of the children of Israel, [k]a people near unto him. Praise ye the LORD.

The LORD's love of Israel

149 PRAISE[k] YE the LORD. [l]Sing unto the LORD a new song, *and* his praise in the congregation of saints.

2 Let Israel rejoice in [m]him that made him: let the children of Zion be joyful in their [n]King.

3 [o]Let them praise his name [n]in the dance: let them sing praises unto him with the timbrel and harp.

4 For [p]the LORD taketh pleasure in his people: [q]he will beautify the meek with salvation.

5 Let the saints be joyful in glory: let them [r]sing aloud upon their beds.

6 *Let* the high *praises* of God *be* [o]in

147:8 [n]Job 38:26; Ps. 104:13 **147:9** [o]Job 38:41; Ps. 104:27 [p]Mat. 6:26 **147:10** [q]Ps. 33:16; Hos. 1:7 **147:14** [r]Is. 60:17,18 [s]Ps. 132:15 **147:15** [t]Ps. 107:20 **147:16** [u]Job 37:6 **147:18** [v]Job 37:10 **147:19** [w]Deut. 33:4; Ps. 76:1 [x]Mal. 4:4 **147:20** [y]Rom. 3:1,2 **148:4** [z]1 Ki. 8:27; 2 Cor. 12:2

[a]Gen. 1:7 **148:5** [b]Gen. 1:1,6; Ps. 33:6,9 **148:6** [c]Ps. 89:37; Jer. 33:25 **148:7** [d]Is. 43:20 **148:8** [e]Ps. 147:15-18 **148:9** [f]Is. 44:23 **148:13** [g]Is. 12:4 [h]Ps. 113:4 **148:14** [i]Ps. 75:10 [j]Ps. 149:9 [k]Eph. 2:17 **149:1** [l]Ps. 33:3; Is. 42:10 **149:2** [m]Job 35:10; Ps. 100:3; Is. 54:5 [n]Zech. 9:9; Mat. 21:5 **149:3** [o]Ps. 81:2 **149:4** [p]Ps. 35:27 [q]Ps. 132:16 **149:5** [r]Job 35:10

[h] Heb. *Who maketh thy border peace* [i] Heb. *fat of wheat* [j] Heb. *his words* [k] Heb. *Hallelujah* [l] Heb. *birds of wing* [m] Heb. *exalted* [n] Or, *with the pipe* [o] Heb. *in their throat*

149:6 *PRAISES* . . . A TWOEDGED SWORD IN THEIR HAND. This verse addresses the activity of the righteous in two areas: worship and spiritual warfare. Our desire to praise God must be accompanied by the desire to aggressively oppose Satan's kingdom and all evil. God's kingdom will never be fully realized until the hostile forces of darkness are destroyed. We must take our stand against the powers of evil by living a righteous life in faith, taking the sword of the Spirit (i.e., the word of God), and praying in the Spirit (see Eph. 6:11–18, notes). At the end of the age we will, to

their mouth, and [s]a twoedged sword
in their hand;
7 To execute vengeance upon the
heathen, *and* punishments upon the
people;
8 To bind their kings with chains,
and their nobles with fetters of iron;
9 [t]To execute upon them the judg-
ment written: [u]this honour have all
his saints. Praise ye the LORD.

Let every thing praise the LORD

150 PRAISE[p] YE the LORD.
Praise God in his sanctuary:
praise him in the firmament of his
power.

2 [v]Praise him for his mighty acts;
praise him according to his excellent
[w]greatness.
3 Praise him with the sound of the
[x]trumpet:[q] [y]praise him with the
psaltery and harp.
4 Praise him [z]with the timbrel and
[a]dance:[r] praise him with [b]stringed
instruments and organs.
5 Praise him upon the loud [c]cym-
bals: praise him upon the high sound-
ing cymbals.
6 Let every thing that hath breath
praise the LORD. Praise ye the LORD. Is. 12:4-6

149:6 [s]Heb. 4:12 Rev. 1:16
149:9 [t]Deut. 7:1,2 [u]Ps. 148:14
150:2 [v]Ps. 145:5 [w]Deut. 3:24
150:3 [x]Ps. 98:6 [y]Ps. 81:2
150:4 [z]Ex. 15:20 [a]Ps. 149:3 [b]Ps. 33:2 Is. 38:20
150:5 [c]1 Chr. 15:16,19, 28

[p] Heb. *Hallelujah* [q] Or, *cornet* [r] Or, *pipe*

the praise of God, participate in His judgment upon the unrepentant world of the antichrist (1 Cor. 6:2–3; Rev. 18:20; 19:1–4,11–21).

150:1 PRAISE YE THE LORD. True praise of God will not be confined to the sanctuary (vv. 1–2,6). We can truly praise God only when we see His full greatness and goodness, and recall and meditate upon all that He has done in creation and redemption and in our personal lives. In this way praise becomes a powerful response of the heart expressing joy, gratitude, and the desire for communion with our Lord. In addition to praising God with our songs and instruments in the sanctuary, we can praise God with a life of love and joy (1 John 4:19), with faith in Christ (John 1:7), with victory over the powers of Satan (Eph. 6:10–18), with a spiritual hunger for His kingdom and His righteousness (Mat. 6:33), with devotion to His Word (Ps. 119), with the love of God poured into our hearts by the Holy Spirit (Rom. 5:5), with the proclamation of His gospel (Rom. 1:16), and with the expectation of His imminent return (2 Tim. 4:8; Tit. 2:13; see article on PRAISE, p. 816).

OLD TESTAMENT PROPHECIES FULFILLED IN CHRIST

O.T. Text	N.T. Text	Subject
Gen. 3:15	Luke 22:53	Satan against Jesus
Gen. 3:15	Heb. 2:14; 1 John 3:8	Jesus' victory over Satan
Gen. 12:3	Acts 3:25; Gal. 3:8	Gentiles blessed through Christ as the seed of Abraham
Gen. 13:15	Gal. 3:15–16, 19	Messiah as the seed of Abraham
Gen. 14:18–20	Heb. 7	Jesus' priesthood according to the likeness of Melchizedek
Gen. 18:18	Acts 3:25; Gal. 3:8	Gentiles blessed through Christ as the seed of Abraham
Gen. 22:18	Acts 3:25; Gal. 3:8	Gentiles blessed through Christ as the seed of Abraham
Gen. 26:4	Acts 3:25; Gal. 3:8	Gentiles blessed through Christ as the seed of Abraham
Gen. 49:10	Luke 1:32–33	Coming ruler from Judah
Ex. 12:1–14,46	John 19:31–36; 1 Cor. 5:7; 1 Pet. 1:19	The Messiah as the Passover Lamb
Ex. 16:4	John 6:31–33	Messiah to give true bread from heaven
Ex. 24:8	Heb. 9:11–28	The Messiah's blood to be shed as sacrifice
Lev. 16:15–17	Rom. 3:25; Heb. 9:1–14,24; 1 John 2:2	Atoning sacrifice of blood
Num. 21:8–9	John 3:14–15	Life through looking at one on a cross
Num. 24:17	Luke 1:32–33	Coming ruler from Jacob
Num. 24:17	Rev. 22; 16	Coming Star out of Jacob
Deut. 18:17	John 6:14; 12:49–50; Acts 3:22–23	Coming prophet sent from God
Deut. 21:23	Gal. 3:13	Messiah cursed for hanging on a tree
Deut. 30:12–14	Rom. 10:6–8	Jesus is God's word near to us
2 Sam. 7:14	Heb. 1:5	Messiah to be God's Son
2 Sam. 7:16	Luke 1:32–33; Rev. 19:11–16	David's Son as eternal king
1 Chr. 17:13	Heb. 1:5	Messiah to be God's Son
1 Chr. 17:14	Luke 1:32–33; Rev. 19:11–16	David's Son as eternal king
Ps. 2:7	Mat. 3:17; 17:5; Mark 1:11; 9:7; Luke 3:22; 9:35; Acts 13:33; Heb 1:5	God's address to His Son
Ps. 2:9	Rev. 2:27	Messiah to rule the nations with power
Ps. 8:2	Mat. 21:16	Children to praise God's Son
Ps. 8:4–5	Heb. 2:6–9	Jesus lower than the angels
Ps. 8:6	1 Cor. 15:27–28; Eph. 1:22	Everything subject to God's Son

O.T. Text	N.T. Text	Subject
Ps. 16:8–11	Acts 2:25–32; 13:35–37	David's Son to be raised from the dead
Ps. 22:1	Mat. 27:46; Mark 15:34	God-forsaken cry by the Messiah
Ps. 22:7–8	Mat. 27:29,41–44; Mark 15:18,29–32; Luke 23:35–39	Messiah mocked by a crowd
Ps. 22:18	Mat. 27:35; Mark 15:24; Luke 23:34; John 19:24	Casting lots for Jesus' clothes
Ps. 22:22	Heb. 2:12	Jesus to declare his name in the church
Ps. 31:5	Luke 23:46	Messiah to commit his spirit to God
Ps. 34:20	John 19:31–36	Messiah to have no broken bones
Ps. 35:19	John 15:25	Messiah experiencing hatred for no reason
Ps. 40:6–8	John 6:38; Heb. 10:5–9	Messiah to do God's perfect will
Ps. 41:9	John 13:18	The Messiah's betrayal by a friend
Ps. 45:6–7	Heb. 1:8–9	Characteristics of the coming King
Ps. 68:18	Eph. 4:7–11	Ascension and giving gifts to humans
Ps. 69:4	John 15:25	Messiah experiencing hatred for no reason
Ps. 69:9	John 2:14–22	The Messiah's zeal for God's house
Ps. 69:21	John 19:29	The thirst of the suffering Messiah
Ps. 69:25	Acts 1:20	Judgment on the Messiah's persecutor
Ps. 78:2	Mat. 13:34–35	Messiah to speak in parables
Ps. 102:25–27	Heb. 1:10–12	Characteristics of the coming King
Ps. 110:1	Acts 2:34–35; 1 Cor. 15:25; Eph 1:20–22; Heb. 1:13; 10:12–13	Jesus exalted in power at God's right hand
Ps. 110:1	Mat. 22:41–45; Mark 12:35–37; Luke 20:41–44	Jesus as Son and Lord of David
Ps. 110:4	Heb. 5:6; 7:11–22	Jesus' priesthood after Melchizedek
Ps. 118:22–23	Mat. 21:42–44; Mark 12:10–12; Luke 20:17–19; Acts 4:10–11; 1 Pet. 2:7–8	Rejected stone to become head of the corner
Ps. 118:26	Mat. 21:9; Mark 11:9; Luke 19:38; John 12:13	Messiah to come in the name of the Lord
Is. 6:9–10	Mat. 13:14–15; Mark 4:12; Luke 8:10; John 12:37–41	Hearts to be closed to the gospel
Is. 7:14	Mat. 1:18–23; Luke 1:26–35	Virgin birth of the Messiah
Is. 8:14	Rom. 9:32–33; 1 Pet. 2:7–8	A stone on which people stumble
Is. 9:1–2	Mat. 4:13–16; Mark 1:14–15; Luke 4:14–15	Ministry to begin in Galilee
Is. 9:6–7	Luke 1:32–33	David's Son as eternal king
Is. 9:7	John 1:1,18	The Messiah to be God

O.T. Text	N.T. Text	Subject
Is. 9:7	Eph. 2:14–17	The Messiah to be a man of peace
Is. 11:1–2	Mat. 3:16; Mark 1:10; Luke 3:21–22	Rod of Jesse (David) to receive the Spirit
Is. 11:10	Luke 1:32–33	Rod of Jesse (David) as coming ruler
Is. 11:10	Rom. 15:12	Salvation to be available for Gentiles
Is. 22:22	Rev. 3:7	Jesus to receive the key of David
Is. 25:8	1 Cor. 15:54	Death to be swallowed up in victory
Is. 28:16	Rom. 9:32–33; 1 Pet. 2:6	Messiah to be the chief corner stone
Is. 35:5–6	Mat. 11:4–6; Luke 7:22	Messiah to be a mighty worker of miracles
Is. 40:3–5	Mat. 3:3; Mark 1:3; Luke 3:4–6; John 1:23	Jesus' forerunner, a voice in the wilderness
Is. 42:1–4	Mat. 12:15–21	Messiah as the chosen servant of the Lord
Is. 45:23	Rom 14:11; Phil. 2:10	Every knee to bow before the Messiah
Is. 49:6	Acts 13:46–47	Messiah as a light to the Gentiles
Is. 50:6	Mat. 27:26–30; Mark 14:65; 15:15,19; Luke 22:63; John 19:1,3	Beating God's servant
Is. 50:6	Mat. 26:67; Mark 14:65	Spitting on God's servant
Is. 53:1	John 12:38; Rom. 10:16	Israel not to believe in the Messiah
Is. 53:3	John 1:11	Messiah to be rejected by His own people
Is. 53:4–5	Mat. 8:16–17; Mark 1:32–34; Luke 4:40–41; 1 Pet. 2:24	Healing ministry of God's servant
Is. 53:7–8	John 1:29,36; Acts 8:30–35; 1 Pet. 1:19; Rev. 5:6,12	Suffering Lamb of God
Is. 53:9	Heb. 4:15; 1 Pet. 2:22	The sinless servant of God
Is. 53:9	Mat. 27:57–60	Messiah to be buried in a rich man's grave
Is. 53:12	Mat. 27:38; Mark 15:27–28; Luke 22:37; 23:33; John 19:18	God's servant numbered with transgressors
Is. 55:3	Luke 22:20; 1 Cor. 11:25	Everlasting covenant through the Messiah
Is. 55:3	Acts 13:33	Blessings of David given to the Messiah
Is. 59:20–21	Rom. 11:26–27	Israel's Deliverer to come from Zion
Is. 60:1–3	Mat. 2:11; Rom. 15:8–12	Gentiles coming to worship the Messiah
Is. 61:1–2	Mat. 3:16; Mark 1:10; Luke 4:18–21	The Messiah anointed by the Holy Spirit
Is. 65:1	Rom. 10:20	Gentiles would believe in the Messiah
Is. 65:2	Rom. 10:21	Israel would reject the Messiah
Jer. 23:5	Luke 1:32–33	David's Son to be a great King
Jer. 23:6	Mat. 1:21	David's Son to be Savior
Jer. 23:6	1 Cor. 1:30	Messiah to be named "Our Righteousness"

O.T. Text	N.T. Text	Subject
Jer. 31:15	Mat. 2:16–18	Rachel weeping when God's Son is born
Jer. 31:31–34	Luke 22:20; 1 Cor. 11:25; Heb. 8:8–12; 10:15–18	Jesus and the new covenant
Jer. 32:40	Luke 22:20; 1 Cor. 11:25	Everlasting covenant through the Messiah
Jer. 33:15	Luke 1:32–33	David's Son to be a great King
Jer. 33:16	Mat. 1:21	David's Son to be Savior
Jer. 33:16	1 Cor. 1:30	Messiah to be named "Our Righteousness"
Ezek. 21:26–27	Luke 1:32–33	A rightful crown for the Messiah
Ezek. 34:23–24	John 10:11,14,16; Heb. 13:20; 1 Pet. 5:4	The coming good shepherd
Ezek. 37:24–25	Luke 1:32–33	Messiah to be David's Son and a king
Ezek. 37:24–25	John 10:11,14,16; Heb. 13:20; 1 Pet. 5:4	The coming good shepherd
Ezek. 37:26	Luke 22:20; 1 Cor. 11:25	Messiah's everlasting covenant of peace
Dan. 7:13–14	Mat. 24:30; 26:64; Mark 13:26; 14:62; Luke 21:27; Rev. 1:13; 14:14	The coming of the Son of Man
Dan. 7:27	Rev. 11:15	The coming everlasting kingdom of the Messiah
Dan. 9:24–26	Gal. 4:4	Timetable for the Messiah's coming
Hos. 11:1	Mat. 2:14–15	Jesus to return from Egypt
Joel 2:28–32	Acts 2:14–21	God's Spirit to be poured out
Am. 9:11–12	Acts 15:13–18	Gentiles would believe in the Messiah
Jonah 1:17	Mat. 12:39–40	Messiah to be three days and nights in grave
Mic. 5:2	Mat. 2:1–6	The Messiah to be born in Bethlehem
Mic. 5:2	Luke 1:32–33	The Messiah as an eternal king
Mic. 5:4	John 10:11,14	The coming shepherd of God's flock
Mic. 5:5	Eph. 2:14–17	The Messiah to be a man of peace
Zech. 9:9	Mat. 21:1–9; Mark 11:1–10; Luke 19:28–38; John 12:12–16	The coming ruler on a donkey
Zech. 11:12–13	Mat. 27:1–10	Thirty pieces of silver for a potter's field
Zech. 12:10	John 19:37; Rev. 1:7	Looking on the pierced Messiah
Zech. 13:7	Mat. 26:31; 26:55–56; Mark 14:27; 14:48–50	Striking the coming shepherd; the sheep flee
Mal. 3:1	Mat. 11:7–10; Mark 1:2–4; Luke 7:24–27	The forerunner to the Messiah
Mal. 4:5–6	Mat. 11:14; 17:11–13; Mark 9:11–13; Luke 1:16–17	The forerunner as Elijah returned

PROVERBS

Outline

I. Prologue: Purpose and Themes of Proverbs (1:1–7)
II. Thirteen Wisdom Discourses for Youth (1:8—9:18)
  A. Obey Your Parents and Heed Their Counsel (1:8–9)
  B. Say "No" to All Enticements of Sinners (1:10–19)
  C. Submit to Wisdom and the Fear of the Lord (1:20–33)
  D. Pursue Wisdom with Its Discernment and Virtue (2:1–22)
  E. Characteristics and Benefits of True Wisdom (3:1–35)
  F. Wisdom as a Family Treasure (4:1–13,20–27)
  G. Wisdom and the Two Paths in Life (4:14–19)
  H. The Enticement and Folly of Sexual Immorality (5:1–14)
  I. Exhortation Concerning Marital Faithfulness (5:15–23)
  J. Avoid Surety, Laziness, and Deceit (6:1–19)
  K. The Crass Folly of All Forms of Sexual Immorality (6:20—7:27)
  L. Wisdom's Appeal (8:1–36)
  M. Wisdom and Folly Contrasted (9:1–18)
III. The Main Collection of Solomon's Proverbs (10:1—22:16)
  A. Proverbs Contrasting the Righteous and the Wicked (10:1—15:33)
  B. Proverbs Encouraging a Righteous Life (16:1—22:16)
IV. Additional Words of Wise Men (22:17—24:34)
V. Solomon's Proverbs Recorded by Hezekiah's Men (25:1—29:27)
  A. Proverbs Concerning Various Kinds of People (25:1—26:28)
  B. Proverbs Concerning Various Activities (27:1—29:27)
VI. Final Words of Wisdom (30:1—31:31)
  A. By Agur (30:1–33)
  B. By Lemuel (31:1–9)
  C. About a Wife Who is Wise (31:10–31)

Author: Solomon and Others

Theme: Wisdom for Right Living

Date of Writing: c. 970–700 B.C.

Background

The Hebrew O.T. was typically divided into three categories: The Law, the Prophets, and the Writings (cf. Luke 24:44). Included under the third category were the Poetic and Wisdom books, such as Job, Psalms, Proverbs, and Ecclesiastes. In a similar manner, ancient Israel had three categories of ministers: the priests, the prophets, and the sages ("the wise men"). The latter were especially gifted with godly wisdom and counsel concerning both practical and philosophical issues of life. Proverbs represents the inspired wisdom of the sages.

The Hebrew term *mashal*, translated "proverb," variously means "oracle," "parable," or "wise saying." Thus there are some longer discourses (oracles) in the book of Proverbs (e.g., 1:20–33; 2:1–22; 5:1–14), as well as many short, pithy statements containing wisdom

for living a prudent and righteous life. Whereas Proverbs represents a form of proverbial teaching common in the ancient Near East, its wisdom is distinctive in that it is given in the context of God and His righteous standards for His covenant people. Reasons for the popularity of proverbial teaching in ancient times were its crisp clarity and its capability of being easily memorized and passed on from generation to generation.

Just as David is the fountainhead of the psalmic tradition in Israel, so Solomon is the fountainhead of the wisdom tradition in Israel (see 1:1; 10:1; 25:1). According to 1 Ki. 4:32, Solomon produced 3,000 proverbs and 1,005 songs in his lifetime. Other authors mentioned by name in Proverbs are Agur (30:1–33) and King Lemuel (31:1–9), both of whom are unknown to us. Additional authors are implied in 22:17 and 24:23. Though most of the Proverbs originated in the 10th century B.C., the earliest possible date for completing this book would be during the reign of Hezekiah (i.e., c. 700 B.C.). The involvement of Hezekiah's men in compiling Solomon's proverbs (25:1—29:27) can be dated to 715–686 B.C., during a time of spiritual revival led by this God-fearing king. Most likely the proverbs of Agur, Lemuel, and the additional "sayings of the wise" (i.e., the sages) were collected together at this time as well.

Purpose

The book's purpose is forthrightly stated in 1:2–7: to provide wisdom and understanding concerning wise behavior, righteousness, justice, and equity (1:2–3), so that (1) simple people can be prudent (1:4), (2) youth can obtain knowledge and discretion (1:4), and (3) the wise might become wiser (1:5–6). Though Proverbs is essentially a wisdom handbook on living rightly and prudently, the necessary foundation of that wisdom is explicitly stated as being "the fear of the LORD" (1:7).

Survey

The unifying theme of Proverbs is "wisdom for right living," a wisdom that begins with humble submission to God and then flows to every area of life. The wisdom in Proverbs (1) admonishes concerning the family, youth, sexual purity, marital faithfulness, honesty, hard work, generosity, friendship, justice, righteousness, and discipline; (2) warns about the folly of sin, strife, dangers of the tongue, foolishness, alcohol, gluttony, lust, immorality, falsehood, slothfulness, and wrong company; (3) contrasts discretion and folly, the righteous and the wicked, pride and humility, laziness and diligence, poverty and wealth, love and lust, right and wrong, and life and death.

Although Proverbs, like Psalms, is not as easily summarized as other books of the Bible, there is some discernible structure (see "Outline"). This is especially true in chs. 1–9, which contain a series of thirteen discourses such as a father would give to his son upon entering the teen years. Except for three discourses (see 1:30; 8:1; 9:1), each one begins with "my son" or "my sons." These thirteen discourses contain numerous important precepts of wisdom for youth. Beginning with ch. 10, Proverbs contains important directives concerning family relationships (e.g., 10:1; 12:4; 17:21,25: 18:22; 19:14,26; 20:7; 21:9,19; 22:6,28; 23:13–14,22,24–25; 25:24; 27:15–16; 29:15–17; 30:11; 31:10–31). Although Proverbs is an intensely practical book, it also contains a profound view of God. God is wisdom personified (e.g., 8:22–31) and the Creator (e.g., 3:19–20; 8:22–31; 14:31; 22:2); He is characterized as omniscient (e.g., 5:21; 15:3,11; 21:2), just (e.g., 11:1; 15:25–27,29; 19:17; 21:2–3), and sovereign (e.g., 16:9,33; 19:21, 21:1). Proverbs concludes with an impressive tribute to a wife of noble character (31:10–31).

Special Features

Eight major features or emphases characterize Proverbs. (1) Wisdom, rather than being tied to intelligence or vast knowledge, is directly related to "the fear of the LORD" (1:7). Thus the wise are those who know God and keep His commandments. The fear of the Lord is a recurring emphasis in the book (1:7,29; 2:5; 3:7; 8:13; 9:10; 10:27; 14:26–27; 15:16,33; 16:6; 19:23; 22:4; 23:17; 24:21). (2) Much of the wise counsel presented in Proverbs is in the format of a father's godly advice to his young son or sons. (3) It is the most thoroughly

practical book in the O.T., as it touches upon a broad range of basic principles for right relationships and behavior in everyday life—principles that are applicable to all generations and cultures. (4) Its practical wisdom, godly precepts, and basic principles for life are conveyed in short, pungent statements that are easily memorized and remembered by youth as guidelines for their lives. (5) The family occupies a place of pivotal importance in Proverbs, even as it did in God's covenant with Israel (cf. Ex. 20:12,14,17; Deut. 6:1–9). Sins that violate God's purpose for the family are especially exposed and warned against. (6) Prominent literary features of the proverbs are their prolific use of vivid, figurative language (e.g., similes and metaphors), comparisons and contrasts, concise precepts, and repetition. (7) The wise wife and mother portrayed at the book's end (ch. 31) is unique in ancient literature in terms of the high and noble manner in which a good woman is viewed. (8) Wisdom exhortations in Proverbs are the O.T. forerunner to the many practical exhortations in the N.T. letters.

New Testament Fulfillment

Wisdom is personified in ch. 8 in a way similar to the personification of *logos* ("Word") in the Gospel of John (ch. 1:1–18). Wisdom is (1) involved in creation (3:19–20; 8:22–31), (2) related to the origin of both biological and spiritual life (3:19; 8:35), (3) applicable to righteous and moral living (8:8–9), and (4) available to those who seek for her (2:1–10; 3:13–18; 4:7–9; 8:35–36). The wisdom of Proverbs finds its ultimate expression in Jesus Christ, someone "greater than Solomon" (Luke 11:31), who "is made unto us wisdom" (1 Cor. 1:30) and "in whom are hid all the treasures of wisdom and knowledge" (Col. 2:3).

Reading Proverbs

In order to read the entire Old Testament in one year, the book of Proverbs should be read in 14 days, according to the following schedule: □ 1–2 □ 3–4 □ 5–7 □ 8–9 □ 10–11 □ 12–13 □ 14–15 □ 16–17 □ 18–19 □ 20–21 □ 22–23 □ 24–26 □ 27–28 □ 29–31

NOTES

The purpose of Proverbs

1 THE [a]PROVERBS of Solomon the son of David, king of Israel;

2 To know wisdom and instruction; to perceive the words of understanding;

3 To receive the instruction of wisdom, justice, and judgment, and [a]equity;

4 To give subtlety to the simple, to the young man knowledge and [b]discretion.

5 [b]A wise *man* will hear, and will increase learning; and a man of understanding shall attain unto wise counsels:

6 To understand a proverb, and [c]the interpretation; the words of the wise, and their [c]dark sayings.

7 ¶ [d]The fear of the LORD *is* [d]the beginning of knowledge: *but* fools despise wisdom and instruction.

8 [e]My son, hear the instruction of thy father, and forsake not the law of thy mother:

9 For they *shall be* [e]an ornament of grace unto thy head, and chains about thy neck.

Warnings against violence

10 ¶ My son, if sinners entice thee, [f]consent thou not.

11 If they say, Come with us, let us [g]lay wait for blood, let us lurk privily for the innocent without cause:

12 Let us swallow them up alive as the grave; and whole, [h]as those that go down into the pit:

13 We shall find all precious substance, we shall fill our houses with spoil:

14 Cast in thy lot among us; let us all have one purse:

15 My son, [i]walk not thou in the way with them; [j]refrain thy foot from their path:

16 [k]For their feet run to evil, and make haste to shed blood.

17 Surely in vain the net is spread [f]in the sight of any bird.

18 And they lay wait for their *own* blood; they lurk privily for their *own* lives.

19 [l]So *are* the ways of every one that is greedy of gain; *which* taketh away the life of the owners thereof.

Result of rejecting wisdom

20 ¶ [m]Wisdom[g] crieth without; she uttereth her voice in the streets:

1:1 [a]1 Ki. 4:32 Eccl. 12:9
1:5 [b]ch. 9:9
1:6 [c]Ps. 78:2
1:7 [d]Job 28:28 Ps. 111:10 Eccl. 12:13
1:8 [e]ch. 4:1
1:10 [f]Gen. 39:7
1:11 [g]Jer. 5:26
1:12 [h]Ps. 28:1
1:15 [i]Ps. 1:1 [j]Ps. 119:101
1:16 [k]Is. 59:7
1:19 [l]1 Tim. 6:10
1:20 [m]John 7:37

[a] Heb. *equities* [b] Or, *advisement* [c] Or, *an eloquent speech* [d] Or, *the principal part* [e] Heb. *an adding* [f] Heb. *in the eyes of every thing that hath a wing* [g] Heb. *Wisdoms,* i.e. *Excellent wisdom*

1:1 THE PROVERBS. A proverb is a short, compact saying, comparison, or question that expresses a principle or an observation about human behavior from God's point of view. These proverbs were written to instruct God's people (especially young people) how to live to please Him, have a happy and successful life, and avoid the tragedies resulting from sin (vv. 2–6,15–19).

1:1 SOLOMON. Solomon, the third king of Israel, wrote many of these proverbs. Early in his reign he prayed for wisdom, and God granted his request (1 Ki. 3:5–14; 4:29–32). Later in life, however, Solomon himself did not follow the wisdom God gave him. Failing to persevere in the fear of the Lord, he turned his heart away from God (1 Ki. 11:1–11; see 11:1, note). Thus merely knowing or teaching moral principles from God's Word is not adequate to ensure spiritual life; there must also be an ongoing fear of, dependence on, and responsibility to God (v. 7).

1:2 WISDOM. As used in this book, wisdom means living and thinking according to God's truth, ways, and design. It means to approach all of life from God's point of view, believing that everything God says is right and true and the only worthy standard by which to live. Gaining wisdom is far better than possessing silver and gold (3:13–14). It comes only to those who seek it through a proper relationship with God (v. 7) and a diligent study of His Word (3:1–3). Christ, whom the N.T. says is the ultimate wisdom of God (1 Cor. 1:30; Col. 2:3), teaches us that we gain wisdom by abiding in His word, by allowing His words to abide in us (John 15:7), and by yielding our hearts and minds to the indwelling Holy Spirit (John 14:16–26).

1:7 THE FEAR OF THE LORD. A reverent awe of God's power, majesty, and holiness produces in us a holy fear of transgressing His revealed will; such reverence is essential to gaining a heart of wisdom. The N.T. indicates that the sincere fear of the Lord in our hearts will be accompanied by the comfort of the Holy Spirit (see Acts 9:31, note; see article on THE FEAR OF THE LORD, p. 282).

1:10 MY SON, IF SINNERS ENTICE THEE. Early in life young people face enticements to sin. Peer pressure will tempt them to join with the majority and enjoy sinful pleasures. Young people can resist such temptations to turn from God and His way by developing a close relationship with God as their Lord, by a willingness to stand alone, if need be, in their commitment to God's righteous ways (vv. 15–16), and by knowing that the way of compromise and sinful pleasure leads to heartache, distress, calamity, and destruction (v. 27; see Mat. 4:1–11, note).

21 She crieth in the chief place of concourse, in the openings of the gates: in the city she uttereth her words, *saying,*

22 How long, ye simple ones, will ye love simplicity? and the scorners delight in their scorning, and fools hate knowledge?

23 Turn you at my reproof: behold, [n]I will pour out my spirit unto you, I will make known my words unto you.

24 ¶ [o]Because I have called, and ye refused; I have stretched out my hand, and no man regarded;

25 But ye [p]have set at nought all my counsel, and would none of my reproof:

26 [q]I also will laugh at your calamity; I will mock when your fear cometh;

27 When [r]your fear cometh as desolation, and your destruction cometh as a whirlwind; when distress and anguish cometh upon you.

28 [s]Then shall they call upon me, but I will not answer; they shall seek me early, but they shall not find me:

29 For that they [t]hated knowledge, and did not [u]choose the fear of the LORD:

30 [v]They would none of my counsel: they despised all my reproof.

31 Therefore [w]shall they eat of the fruit of their own way, and be filled with their own devices.

32 For the [h]turning away of the simple shall slay them, and the prosperity of fools shall destroy them.

33 But [x]whoso hearkeneth unto me shall dwell safely, and [y]shall be quiet from fear of evil.

1:23 [n]Joel 2:28 **1:24** [o]Is. 66:4 Jer. 7:13 Zech. 7:11 **1:25** [p]Ps. 107:11 Luke 7:30 **1:26** [q]Ps. 2:4 **1:27** [r]ch. 10:24 **1:28** [s]Job 27:9 Is. 1:15 Jer. 14:12 Ezek. 8:18 Mic. 3:4 Zech. 7:13 Jas. 4:3 **1:29** [t]Job 21:14 [u]Ps:119:173 **1:30** [v]Ps. 81:11 **1:31** [w]Job 4:8 Is. 3:11 Jer. 6:19 **1:33** [x]Ps. 25:12 [y]Ps. 112:7

2:1 [z]ch. 4:21 **2:4** [a]ch. 3:14 Mat. 13:44 **2:6** [b]1 Ki. 3:9 Jas. 1:5 **2:7** [c]Ps. 84:11 **2:8** [d]1 Sam. 2:9 Ps. 66:9 **2:11** [e]ch. 6:22

The reward of wisdom

2 MY SON, if thou wilt receive my words, and [z]hide my commandments with thee;

2 So that thou incline thine ear unto wisdom, *and* apply thine heart to understanding;

3 Yea, if thou criest after knowledge, *and* [i]liftest up thy voice for understanding;

4 [a]If thou seekest her as silver, and searchest for her as *for* hid treasures;

5 Then shalt thou understand the fear of the LORD, and find the knowledge of God.

6 [b]For the LORD giveth wisdom: out of his mouth *cometh* knowledge and understanding.

7 He layeth up sound wisdom for the righteous: [c]*he is* a buckler to them that walk uprightly.

8 He keepeth the paths of judgment, and [d]preserveth the way of his saints.

9 Then shalt thou understand righteousness, and judgment, and equity; *yea,* every good path.

10 ¶ When wisdom entereth into thine heart, and knowledge is pleasant unto thy soul;

11 Discretion shall preserve thee, [e]understanding shall keep thee:

12 To deliver thee from the way of the evil *man,* from the man that speaketh froward things;

13 Who leave the paths of upright-

[h] Or, *ease of the simple* [i] Heb. *givest thy voice*

1:26 YOUR CALAMITY. The book of Proverbs emphasizes that God has appointed absolute standards of right and wrong; to disregard them will bring tragic results in our lives. One of the greatest truths we can learn in our youth is that we will indeed reap what we sow (Gal. 6:7–9). The eventual price we pay for sin is anguish, suffering, and even disaster (v. 27).

2:1 HIDE MY COMMANDMENTS WITH THEE. Only by putting God's word into our minds will we learn to live wisely and righteously in our relationship with God (v. 5). We can become victorious over sin with God's commandments in our hearts (Ps. 119:11) and Christ's word abiding within us (John 15:7; Jas. 1:21).

2:3 IF THOU CRIEST AFTER KNOWLEDGE. The study of God's word (see previous note) must be accompanied with a spirit of prayer that earnestly cries out for wisdom and discernment. Study alone may make a Bible scholar, but prayer along with the study of God's word allows the Holy Spirit to take that revelation and transform us into spiritual people. Pray over the verses of Scripture you read, hungering for divine illumination and understanding (vv. 5–7).

2:10 WHEN WISDOM ENTERETH INTO THINE HEART. Only when God's wisdom enters our hearts—i.e., our inward motives, desires, and thoughts—will it produce life and power (cf. 4:23). To accomplish this, the Spirit of truth must work within our souls (John 16:13–14) to make God's commandments and ways a delight to us (Ps. 119:47–48).

ness, to [f]walk in the ways of dark-
ness;
14 Who [g]rejoice to do evil, *and*
[h]delight in the frowardness of the
wicked;
15 [i]Whose ways *are* crooked, and
they froward in their paths:
16 To deliver thee from [j]the
strange woman, [k]*even* from the
stranger *which* flattereth with her
words;
17 [l]Which forsaketh the guide of
her youth, and forgetteth the covenant
of her God.
18 For [m]her house inclineth unto
death, and her paths unto the dead.
19 None that go unto her return
again, neither take they hold of the
paths of life.
20 That thou mayest walk in the
way of good *men,* and keep the paths of
the righteous.
21 [n]For the upright shall dwell in
the land, and the perfect shall remain
in it,
22 [o]But the wicked shall be cut off
from the earth, and the transgressors
shall be [j]rooted out of it.

2:13 [f]John 3:19
2:14 [g]Jer. 11:15 [h]Rom. 1:32
2:15 [i]Ps. 125:5
2:16 [j]ch. 5:20 [k]ch. 5:3
2:17 [l]See Mal. 2:14,15
2:18 [m]ch. 7:27
2:21 [n]Ps. 37:29
2:22 [o]Job 18:17 Ps. 37:28
3:1 [p]Deut. 8:1
3:2 [q]Ps. 119:165
3:3 [r]Ex. 13:9 Deut. 6:8 [s]2 Cor. 3:3
3:4 [t]Rom. 14:18
3:5 [u]Ps. 37:3,5 [v]Jer. 9:23
3:6 [w]1 Chr. 28:9 [x]Jer. 10:23
3:7 [y]Rom. 12:16 [z]ch. 16:6
3:8 [a]Job 21:24
3:9 [b]Ex. 22:29

The blessing of wisdom

3 MY SON, forget not my law; [p]but
let thine heart keep my command-
ments:
2 For length of days, and [k]long life,
and [q]peace, shall they add to thee.
3 Let not mercy and truth forsake
thee: [r]bind them about thy neck;
[s]write them upon the table of thine
heart:
4 [t]So shalt thou find favour and
[l]good understanding in the sight of
God and man.
5 ¶ [u]Trust in the LORD with all
thine heart; [v]and lean not unto thine
own understanding.
6 [w]In all thy ways acknowledge
him, and he shall [x]direct thy paths. Eccl. 12:13-14
7 ¶ [y]Be not wise in thine own eyes:
[z]fear the LORD, and depart from evil.
8 It shall be [m]health to thy navel,
and [a]marrow[n] to thy bones.
9 [b]Honour the LORD with thy sub-
stance, and with the firstfruits of all
thine increase:

[j] Or, *plucked up* [k] Heb. *years of life* [l] Or, *good success* [m] Heb. *medicine* [n] Heb. *watering,* or, *moistening*

2:20 WALK IN THE WAY OF GOOD *MEN*, AND KEEP THE PATHS OF THE RIGHTEOUS. The blessings of gaining wisdom include: (1) learning to fear the Lord and thereby being guarded from evil along life's path (vv. 5–8); (2) having the ability to discern good from evil and thereby avoiding the tragedies of sin (v. 11); (3) desiring to avoid evil people and associating with those who are good and righteous (vv. 12–15,20); (4) abstaining from sexual immorality (vv. 16–19); and (5) gaining the promised blessings of God (v. 21).

3:2 LONG LIFE, AND PEACE. Generally speaking, obeying God and living by His holy principles will result in better health (v. 8), a longer life, and a happier and more prosperous life (cf. v. 16). However, this general principle must not be taken as an absolute guarantee to which there are no exceptions. At times the righteous are afflicted (Job 1—2) and do not live long lives (Acts 7:59–60); conversely, sometimes it is the wicked who are healthy and prosperous (Ps. 73:3,12; Jas. 5:5), though their final judgment is sure (Ps. 73:17–20: Jas. 5:1–4).

3:5 TRUST IN THE LORD. Trusting in the Lord with all our heart is the opposite of doubting God and His word. Such trust is fundamental to our relationship with God and is based on the premise that He is trustworthy. As God's children we can be assured that our heavenly Father loves us and will faithfully care for us (see Mat. 10:31, note), guide us rightly, give us grace, and keep His promises. In the most difficult times of our lives, we can commit our way to the Lord (cf. Ps. 37:5) and trust Him to work on our behalf.

3:5 THINE OWN UNDERSTANDING. Our own understanding is limited, fallible, and subject to error (Eph. 4:18). It must therefore be enlightened by God's word and led by the Holy Spirit (Rom. 8:9–16). Rather than relying on our own judgment (v. 7), we must pray for God's wisdom and will in all our decisions and goals of life (see 2:3, note).

3:6 IN ALL THY WAYS ACKNOWLEDGE HIM. In all our plans, decisions, and activities, we should acknowledge God as Lord and His will as our supreme desire. Every day we must live in a close, trusting relationship with God, always looking to Him for direction "by prayer and supplication with thanksgiving" (see Phil. 4:6, note). When we do this, God promises to direct our paths; i.e., He will lead us to His goal for our lives, remove all obstacles, and enable us to make the right choices (see 11:5; Is. 45:13).

3:9 HONOUR THE LORD WITH THY SUBSTANCE. The Israelites brought the first portion of their harvest to the Lord God to acknowledge that He was owner of the land (Lev. 23:10; 25:23; Num. 18:12–13). We also should give God the firstfruits of our income so that we may honor Him as Lord of our lives and possessions. God will then open the way to pour out His blessings upon us (see Mal. 3:10, note; 2 Cor. 9:6, note). "Them that honour me I will honour" (1 Sam. 2:30) is God's promise to all who faithfully and generously give of their finances.

10 [c]So shall thy barns be filled with plenty, and thy presses shall burst out with new wine.

11 ¶ [d]My son, despise not the chastening of the LORD; neither be weary of his correction:

12 For whom the LORD loveth he correcteth; [e]even as a father the son *in whom* he delighteth.

13 ¶ [f]Happy *is* the man *that* findeth wisdom, and [o]the man *that* getteth understanding.

14 [g]For the merchandise of it *is* better than the merchandise of silver, and the gain thereof than fine gold.

15 She *is* more precious than rubies: and [h]all the things thou canst desire are not to be compared unto her.

16 [i]Length of days *is* in her right hand; *and* in her left hand riches and honour.

17 [j]Her ways *are* ways of pleasantness, and all her paths *are* peace.

18 She *is* [k]a tree of life to them that lay hold upon her: and happy *is every one* that retaineth her.

19 [l]The LORD by wisdom hath founded the earth; by understanding hath he [p]established the heavens.

20 [m]By his knowledge the depths are broken up, and [n]the clouds drop down the dew.

21 ¶ My son, let not them depart from thine eyes: keep sound wisdom and discretion:

22 So shall they be life unto thy soul, and [o]grace to thy neck.

23 [p]Then shalt thou walk in thy way safely, and thy foot shall not stumble.

24 [q]When thou liest down, thou shalt not be afraid: yea, thou shalt lie down, and thy sleep shall be sweet.

25 [r]Be not afraid of sudden fear, neither of the desolation of the wicked, when it cometh.

26 For the LORD shall be thy confidence, and shall keep thy foot from being taken.

27 ¶ [s]Withhold not good from [q]them to whom it is due, when it is in the power of thine hand to do *it.*

28 [t]Say not unto thy neighbour, Go, and come again, and tomorrow I will give; when thou hast it by thee.

29 [r]Devise not evil against thy neighbour, seeing he dwelleth securely by thee.

30 ¶ [u]Strive not with a man without cause, if he have done thee no harm.

31 ¶ [v]Envy thou not [s]the oppressor, and choose none of his ways.

32 For the froward *is* abomination to the LORD: [w]but his secret *is* with the righteous.

33 ¶ [x]The curse of the LORD *is* in the house of the wicked: but [y]he blesseth the habitation of the just.

34 [z]Surely he scorneth the scorners: but he giveth grace unto the lowly.

35 The wise shall inherit glory: but shame [t]shall be the promotion of fools.

The command to obtain wisdom

4 HEAR, [a]YE children, the instruction of a father, and attend to know understanding.

2 For I give you good doctrine, forsake ye not my law.

3 For I was my father's son, [b]tender and only *beloved* in the sight of my mother.

4 [c]He taught me also, and said

3:10 [c]Deut. 28:8
3:11 [d]Job 5:17 Ps. 94:12
3:12 [e]Deut. 8:5
3:13 [f]ch. 8:34,35
3:14 [g]Job 28:13 Ps. 19:10
3:15 [h]Mat. 13:44
3:16 [i]1 Tim. 4:8
3:17 [j]Mat. 11:29
3:18 [k]Gen. 2:9
3:19 [l]Ps. 104:24
3:20 [m]Gen. 1:9 [n]Deut. 33:28 Job 36:28
3:22 [o]ch. 1:9
3:23 [p]Ps. 37:24
3:24 [q]Lev. 26:6 Ps. 3:5
3:25 [r]Ps. 91:5
3:27 [s]Rom. 13:7 Gal. 6:10
3:28 [t]Lev. 19:13
3:30 [u]Rom. 12:18
3:31 [v]Ps. 37:1
3:32 [w]Ps. 25:14
3:33 [x]Zech. 5:3,4 Mal. 2:2 [y]Ps. 1:3
3:34 [z]Jas. 4:6 1 Pet. 5:5
4:1 [a]Ps. 34:11 ch. 1:8
4:3 [b]1 Chr. 29:1
4:4 [c]1 Chr. 28:9 Eph. 6:4

[o] Heb. *the man that draweth out understanding*
[p] Or, *prepared* [q] Heb. *the owners thereof*
[r] Or, *Practise no evil* [s] Heb. *a man of violence*
[t] Heb. *exalteth the fools*

3:11–12 DESPISE NOT THE CHASTENING OF THE LORD. At times God allows us to pass through trials and difficulties in order to conform us more perfectly to His holiness and to His will for our lives (cf. Job 5:17). The N.T. uses these verses to offer encouragement to believers who are enduring pain and affliction (see Heb. 12:5, note).

3:16 RICHES AND HONOUR. Earthly riches and honor do not always come to us even though we are living according to God's wisdom. But we can be sure that we will receive everlasting riches and honor from God as our future inheritance (Luke 16:11; Eph. 1:18; 3:8).

3:23 WALK IN THY WAY SAFELY. Wisdom gives security because it keeps us walking safely in God's good, acceptable, and perfect will (cf. 10:9; Rom. 12:2). God will not allow those who trust in Him to be caught or destroyed by the traps set by the enemy (vv. 25–26).

4:1–4 HEAR, YE CHILDREN, THE INSTRUCTION OF A FATHER. Solomon had learned about God's ways from his father and was now passing instruction on to his sons. God wants true godliness and commitment to His ways to be learned primarily through the teaching of parents and the examples provided in the home, and not by delegating that responsibility to church education programs (Deut. 6:7; see article on PARENTS AND CHILDREN, p. 1880).

unto me, Let thine heart retain my
words: [d]keep my commandments, and
live.
5 [e]Get wisdom, get understanding:
forget *it* not; neither decline from the
words of my mouth.
6 Forsake her not, and she shall
preserve thee: [f]love her, and she shall
keep thee.
7 [g]Wisdom *is* the principal thing;
therefore get wisdom: and with all thy
getting get understanding.
8 [h]Exalt her, and she shall pro-
mote thee: she shall bring thee to hon-
our, when thou dost embrace her.
9 She shall give to thine head [i]an
ornament of grace: [u]a crown of glory
shall she deliver to thee.
10 Hear, O my son, and receive my
sayings; [j]and the years of thy life
shall be many.
11 I have taught thee in the way of
wisdom; I have led thee in right paths.
12 When thou goest, [k]thy steps
shall not be straitened; [l]and when
thou runnest, thou shalt not stumble.
13 Take fast hold of instruction; let
her not go: keep her; for she *is* thy life.
14 ¶ [m]Enter not into the path of the
wicked, and go not in the way of evil
men.
15 Avoid it, pass not by it, turn from
it, and pass away.
16 [n]For they sleep not, except they
have done mischief; and their sleep is
taken away, unless they cause *some* to
fall.
17 For they eat the bread of wicked-
ness, and drink the wine of violence.
18 [o]But the path of the just [p]*is* as
the shining light, that shineth more
and more unto the perfect day.
19 [q]The way of the wicked *is* as
darkness: they know not at what they
stumble.
20 ¶ My son, attend to my words;
incline thine ear unto my sayings.
21 [r]Let them not depart from thine
eyes; [s]keep them in the midst of thine
heart.
22 For they *are* life unto those that
find them, and [t]health[v] to all their
flesh.
23 ¶ Keep thy heart [w]with all dili-
gence; for out of it *are* the issues of life.
24 Put away from thee [x]a froward
mouth, and perverse lips put far from
thee.
25 Let thine eyes look right on, and
let thine eyelids look straight before
thee.
26 Ponder the path of thy feet, and
[y]let all thy ways be established.

4:4 [d]ch. 7:2
4:5 [e]ch. 2:2,3
4:6 [f]2 Thes. 2:10
4:7 [g]Mat. 13:44 Luke 10:42
4:8 [h]1 Sam. 2:30
4:9 [i]ch. 1:9 & 3:22
4:10 [j]ch. 3:2
4:12 [k]Ps. 18:36 [l]Ps. 91:11,12
4:14 [m]Ps. 1:1 ch. 1:10,15
4:16 [n]Ps. 36:4 Is. 57:20
4:18 [o]Mat. 5:14,45 Phil. 2:15 [p]2 Sam. 23:4
4:19 [q]1 Sam. 2:9 Job 18:5,6 Is. 59:9,10 Jer. 23:12 John 12:35
4:21 [r]ch. 3:3,21 [s]ch. 2:1
4:22 [t]ch. 3:8 & 12:18

[u] Or, *she shall compass thee with a crown of glory* [v] Heb. *medicine* [w] Heb. *above all keeping* [x] Heb. *frowardness of mouth, and perverseness of lips* [y] Or, *all thy ways shall be ordered aright*

4:5 GET WISDOM, GET UNDERSTANDING. The wisdom of God is essential for a meaningful and godly life (vv. 20–22; 3:21–22). Therefore, we must seek it above all things. However, to attain such wisdom is not easy, for it is given only to those who diligently pay the price for it. Wisdom comes through two avenues. (1) Instruction. Through instruction, a person will experience a spiritual transformation of turning from evil and turning to a knowledge of God. A personal relationship with God is the first step in obtaining true wisdom. Believers must fear the Lord and hate evil (8:13; 9:10).

(2) Devotion. Wisdom is for the person who sees its value and therefore diligently seeks it (8:17). The wise person learns from instruction (9:9) and from God's discipline (3:11), accepts the commandments of God (10:8), listens to the godly counsel of parents and others (v. 1; 13:10), and treasures wisdom as more valuable than silver, gold, or precious jewels (3:14–15; 23:23).

Jesus Christ is the supreme manifestation of the wisdom of God (1 Cor. 1:30; Col. 2:2–3). Thus, this O.T. exhortation is equivalent to a call to commit our lives to Jesus Christ. We must turn from sin and self to Him, sacrificing all that is necessary in order to follow Him as His disciples (Mat. 13:44–46; Luke 14:33).

4:13 FOR SHE *IS* THY LIFE. In Proverbs wisdom brings life and is life. To live as God has designed brings (1) a good and joyful life (15:23,27), (2) normally a longer physical life (v. 10; 3:2; 9:11), (3) a moral and spiritual life (8:35; 9:6; 10:16; 19:23), and (4) the hope of life after death (compare 11:7 with 14:32). Christ, who is our wisdom (see previous note), is the fulfillment of this O.T. ideal of wisdom; He is now our life (John 5:40; 11:25; 14:6), and those who have Him have life (1 John 5:12).

4:23 KEEP THY HEART WITH ALL DILIGENCE. The heart is the wellspring of desire and decision (see article on THE HEART, p. 932). Following God and knowing His ways involve a resolute decision to remain committed to Him, seeking first His kingdom and His righteousness (Mat. 6:33). If we find that our hunger and thirst for God and His kingdom are declining, we should reevaluate our priorities, honestly acknowledge our lukewarmness, and earnestly pray for a renewed desire for God and His favor. Failure to "keep" our hearts results in a departure from the path of safety and entrapment in a destructive snare (cf. 7:24–27); to watch over our hearts with all diligence results in all our ways being established in His favor and grace (vv. 25–27).

THE HEART

***Prov. 4:23** "Keep thy heart with all diligence; for out of it* are *the issues of life."*

DEFINITION OF THE HEART. Contemporary people generally consider the head with its brain to be the center and the director of human activity. However, the Bible speaks of the heart as the center; "out of it *are* the issues of life" (Prov. 4:23; cf. Luke 6:45). Biblically, the heart may be seen as containing the totality of one's intellect, emotion, and volition (see Mark 7:20–23, note).

(1) The heart is the center of the intelleot. People consider things in their heart (Deut. 8:5), meditate in their heart (Ps. 19:14), commune with themselves (Ps. 77:6) or with God (1 Sam. 1:12–13) in their heart, hide God's word in their heart (Ps. 119:11), keep things in their heart (Prov. 4:21), imagine things in their heart (Ps. 140:2), reason in their heart (Mark 2:8), doubt in their heart (Mark 11:23), ponder in their heart (Luke 2:19), believe in their heart (Rom. 10:9), and sing in their heart (Eph. 5:19). All of these actions of the heart are primarily issues involving the mind.

(2) The heart is the center of the emotions. Thus the Scriptures speak about the glad heart (Ex. 4:14; Jer. 15:16), the loving heart (Deut. 6:5), the fearful heart (Josh. 5:1), the courageous heart (Ps. 27:14), the repentant heart (Ps. 51:17), the heavy heart (Prov. 12:25; Rom. 9:2), the angry heart (Prov. 19:3), the revived heart (Isa 57:15), the pained heart (Jer. 4:19), the grieving heart (Lam. 2:18), the humble heart (Mat. 11:29), the excited or burning heart (Luke 24:32), and the troubled heart (John 14:1). All of these actions of the heart are primarily emotional in character.

(3) Finally, the heart is the center of the human will. Thus we read in the Scriptures about the hardened heart that refuses to do what God commands (Ex. 4:21), the heart that is inclined to cling to God (Josh. 24:23) and to obey His testimonies (Ps. 119:36), the heart that intends to do something (2 Chr. 6:7), the heart that is set to seek the Lord (1 Chr. 22:19), the heart that decides (2 Chr. 6:7), the heart that wants to receive from the Lord (Ps. 21:1–2), and the heart that desires to do something (Rom. 10:1). All of these activities take place in the human will.

THE NATURE OF THE HEART APART FROM GOD. When Adam and Eve chose to follow the temptation of the serpent to eat of the tree of knowledge of good and evil, their decision drastically affected the human heart—it became filled with evil. At present, therefore, according to the testimony of Jeremiah, "the heart *is* deceitful above all *things*, and desperately wicked: who can know it?" (Jer. 17:9). Jesus confirmed Jeremiah's diagnosis when he said that what defiles a person before God is not the failure to follow some ceremonial law, but the willingness to listen to wicked inclinations lodged in one's heart such as "evil thoughts, adulteries, fornications, murders, thefts, covetousness, wickedness, deceit, lasciviousness, an evil eye, blasphemy, pride, foolishness" (Mark 7:21–22). Jesus taught about the seriousness of sin in the heart when he said that the sin of anger and hatred is tantamount to murder (Mat. 5:21–22) and the sin of lust is just as sinful as actual adultery (Mat. 5:27–28; see Ex. 20:14, note; Mat. 5:28, note).

Hearts that are bent upon doing evil run the grave risk of becoming hardened. Those who persistently refuse to listen to God's Word and to obey what He commands, and instead follow the wicked desires of their hearts will find that God will eventually harden their hearts so that they lose all sensitivity to His Word and to the desires of the Holy Spirit (see Ex. 7:3, note; Heb. 3:8, note). The primary example of this in the Scriptures is the heart of the Pharaoh at the time of the exodus (see Ex. 7:3,13,22–23; 8:15,32; 9:12; 10:1; 11:10; 14:17). Paul saw the same general principle operative in the Roman Empire (cf. Rom. 1:24,26,28) and predicted that it would also occur during the days of the antichrist (2 Thes. 2:11–12). The writer of Hebrews filled his letter with warnings

to believers not to harden their hearts (e.g., Heb. 3:8–12; see article on PERSONAL APOSTASY, p. 1946, for a description of the steps leading to hardheartedness). Anyone who continues to reject God's word will eventually have a hardened heart.

THE REGENERATED HEART. God's answer to the sinfulness of the human heart is *regeneration*, which comes to all those who repent of their sins, turn to God, and place a personal faith in Jesus as Lord and Savior. (1) Regeneration is a matter of the heart. The person who repents from his heart of all sin and confesses in his heart that Jesus is Lord (Rom. 10:9) is born again and receives a new heart from God (cf. Ps. 51:10; Ezek. 11:19).

(2) Within the hearts of those who experience spiritual birth, God creates a desire to love Him and to obey Him (see article on REGENERATION, p. 1597). Repeatedly God emphasized to His people the necessity of a love which comes from the heart (see Deut. 4:29, note; 6:6, note). Such love for and devotion to God cannot be separated from obedience to His law (cf. Ps. 119:34,69,112); Jesus taught that love for God with the whole heart and love for one's neighbor summarize the entire law of God (Mat. 22:37–40).

(3) Love from the heart is the essential ingredient in obedience to God. All too often God's people tried to substitute obedience to mere outward religious forms (such as feast days, offerings, and sacrifices) for genuine love from the heart (see Is. 1:10–17; Amos 5:21–26; Mic. 6:6–8; see Deut. 10:12, note). Outward observance without an inner desire to serve God is hypocrisy and is severely condemned by our Lord (see Mat. 23:13–28; see Luke 21:1–4, note).

(4) Many other spiritual activities take place in the hearts of regenerated believers. They praise God from their heart (Ps. 9:1), meditate on God's word continually in their heart (Ps. 19:14), cry out to God from the heart (Ps. 84:2), seek God with all their heart (Ps. 119:2,10), hide God's word in their heart (Ps. 119:11; see Deut. 6:6, note), trust in the Lord with their whole heart (Prov. 3:5), experience the love of God poured out into their heart (Rom. 5:5), and sing to God from their heart (Eph. 5:19; Col. 3:16).

27 [u]Turn not to the right hand nor to the left: [v]remove thy foot from evil.

Warning against unchastity

5 MY SON, attend unto my wisdom, *and* bow thine ear to my understanding:

2 That thou mayest regard discretion, and *that* thy lips may [w]keep knowledge.

3 ¶ [x]For the lips of a strange woman drop *as* an honeycomb, and her [z]mouth *is* [y]smoother than oil:

4 But her end is [z]bitter as wormwood, [a]sharp as a twoedged sword.

5 [b]Her feet go down to death; her steps take hold on hell.

6 Lest thou shouldest ponder the path of life, her ways are moveable, *that* thou canst not know *them.*

7 Hear me now therefore, O ye children, and depart not from the words of my mouth.

8 Remove thy way far from her, and come not nigh the door of her house:

9 Lest thou give thine honour unto others, and thy years unto the cruel:

10 Lest strangers be filled with [a]thy wealth; and thy labours *be* in the house of a stranger;

11 And thou mourn at the last, when thy flesh and thy body are consumed,

12 And say, How have I [c]hated instruction, and my heart [d]despised reproof;

13 And have not obeyed the voice of my teachers, nor inclined mine ear to them that instructed me!

14 I was almost in all evil in the midst of the congregation and assembly.

15 ¶ Drink waters out of thine own cistern, and running waters out of thine own well.

16 Let thy fountains be dispersed abroad, *and* rivers of waters in the streets.

17 Let them be only thine own, and not strangers' with thee.

18 Let thy fountain be blessed: and rejoice with [e]the wife of thy youth.

19 [f]*Let her be as* the loving hind and pleasant roe; let her breasts [b]satisfy thee at all times; and [c]be thou ravished always with her love.

20 And why wilt thou, my son, be ravished with [g]a strange woman, and embrace the bosom of a stranger?

21 [h]For the ways of man *are* before the eyes of the LORD, and he pondereth all his goings.

22 ¶ [i]His own iniquities shall take the wicked himself, and he shall be holden with the cords of his [d]sins.

23 [j]He shall die without instruction; and in the greatness of his folly he shall go astray.

Warnings against idleness

6 MY SON, [k]if thou be surety for thy friend, *if* thou hast stricken thy hand with a stranger,

2 Thou art snared with the words of

4:27 [u]Deut. 5:32 & 28:14 Josh. 1:7 [v]Is. 1:16 Rom. 12:9
5:2 [w]Mal. 2:7
5:3 [x]ch. 2:16 & 6:24 [y]Ps. 55:21
5:4 [z]Eccl. 7:26 [a]Heb. 4:12
5:5 [b]ch. 7:27
5:12 [c]ch. 1:29 [d]ch. 1:25 & 12:1
5:18 [e]Mal. 2:14
5:19 [f]Sol. 2:9 & 4:5
5:20 [g]ch. 2:16
5:21 [h]2 Chr. 16:9 Job 31:4 ch. 15:3 Jer. 16:17 Hos. 7:2 Heb. 4:13
5:22 [i]Ps. 9:15
5:23 [j]Job 4:21 & 36:12
6:1 [k]ch. 11:15

[z] Heb. *palate* [a] Heb. *thy strength* [b] Heb. *water thee* [c] Heb. *err thou always in her love* [d] Heb. *sin*

5:3 THE LIPS OF A STRANGE WOMAN. The book of Proverbs repeatedly warns about the destructiveness of sexual immorality. Solomon emphasizes that though immorality's deceptive pleasures are attractive, giving in to them will lead to ruin (vv. 7–14). Violations of God's standards of sexual purity and chastity are found in this chapter and in 2:16–19; 6:20–35; 22:14; 23:27–28; 29:3; 30:20; 31:3. The alternative to sexual immorality is commitment to God (vv. 1), disciplined restraint prior to marriage, and the fulfillment of natural sexual desire through a holy love life in marriage (vv. 15–23; see article on STANDARDS OF SEXUAL MORALITY, p. 1964).

5:14 I WAS ALMOST IN ALL EVIL. God has ordained that those who give in to sexual immorality will experience regret and remorse—both in the breakdown of family life and in personal suffering. Premarital sex and marital infidelity have deadly consequences (vv. 5,11). What may begin as a taste of honey (v. 3) will end with the taste of bitterness. God will not be mocked (v. 21); what is sown will be reaped.

5:15 DRINK WATERS OUT OF THINE OWN CISTERN. A man's source of affectionate love (vv. 18–20) should be his own wife (cf. Ex. 20:17). Note that sexual delight in marriage is legitimate and God-given (cf. Gen. 2:20–25). A spouse should be considered a special gift from God and cherished with pleasure, purity, and thanksgiving (19:14).

5:21 THE WAYS OF MAN *ARE* BEFORE THE EYES OF THE LORD. One reason Proverbs gives for resisting sexual immorality is that God sees and knows our ungodly ways (cf. 15:3; Job 31:4; 34:21; Jer. 16:17) and will judge us accordingly. He "will be a swift witness against . . . adulterers" (Mal. 3:5). Since our activities are "before the eyes of the LORD," no one guilty of adultery will escape its terrible consequences (see 2 Sam. 12:9–13, notes).

6:1 IF THOU BE SURETY FOR THY FRIEND. This verse is a warning against becoming a "surety" for a friend (cf. 11:15; 17:18; 22:26). Surety

thy mouth, thou art taken with the
words of thy mouth.
3 Do this now, my son, and deliver
thyself, when thou art come into the
hand of thy friend; go, humble thyself,
[e]and make sure thy friend.
4 [l]Give not sleep to thine eyes, nor
slumber to thine eyelids.
5 Deliver thyself as a roe from the
hand *of the hunter,* and as a bird from
the hand of the fowler.
6 ¶ [m]Go to the ant, thou sluggard;
consider her ways, and be wise:
7 Which having no guide, overseer,
or ruler,
8 Provideth her meat in the sum-
mer, *and* gathereth her food in the har-
vest.
9 [n]How long wilt thou sleep, O
sluggard? when wilt thou arise out of
thy sleep?
10 *Yet* a little sleep, a little slumber,
a little folding of the hands to sleep:
11 [o]So shall thy poverty come as
one that travelleth, and thy want as an
armed man.

Warning against sowing discord

12 ¶ A naughty person, a wicked
man, walketh with a froward mouth.
13 [p]He winketh with his eyes, he
speaketh with his feet, he teacheth
with his fingers;
14 Frowardness *is* in his heart, [q]he
deviseth mischief continually; [r]he
[f]soweth discord.
15 Therefore shall his calamity
come suddenly; suddenly shall he [s]be
broken [t]without remedy.
16 ¶ These six *things* doth the LORD
hate: yea, seven *are* an abomination
[g]unto him:
17 [u]A[h] proud look, [v]a lying

6:4 [l]Ps. 132:4
6:6 [m]Job 12:7
6:9 [n]ch. 24:33
6:11 [o]ch. 10:4
6:13 [p]Job 15:12 ch. 10:10
6:14 [q]Mic. 2:1 [r]ver. 19
6:15 [s]Jer. 19:11 [t]2 Chr. 36:16
6:17 [u]Ps. 101:5 [v]Ps. 120:2,3
[w]Is. 1:15
6:18 [x]Gen. 6:5 [y]Is. 59:7
6:19 [z]Ps. 27:12 [a]ver. 14
6:20 [b]Eph. 6:1
6:21 [c]ch. 3:3
6:22 [d]ch. 3:23 [e]ch. 2:11
6:23 [f]Ps. 19:8
6:24 [g]ch. 2:16
6:25 [h]Mat. 5:28
6:26 [i]ch. 29:3 [j]Gen. 39:14 [k]Ezek. 13:18

tongue, and [w]hands that shed inno-
cent blood,
18 [x]An heart that deviseth wicked
imaginations, [y]feet that be swift in
running to mischief,
19 [z]A false witness *that* speaketh
lies, and he [a]that soweth discord
among brethren.

Warning against adultery

20 ¶ [b]My son, keep thy father's
commandment, and forsake not the
law of thy mother:
21 [c]Bind them continually upon
thine heart, *and* tie them about thy
neck.
22 [d]When thou goest, it shall lead
thee; when thou sleepest, [e]it shall
keep thee; and *when* thou awakest, it
shall talk with thee.
23 [f]For the commandment *is* a
[i]lamp; and the law *is* light; and re-
proofs of instruction *are* the way of life:
24 [g]To keep thee from the evil
woman, from the flattery [j]of the
tongue of a strange woman.
25 [h]Lust not after her beauty in
thine heart; neither let her take thee
with her eyelids.
26 For [i]by means of a whorish
woman *a man is brought* to a piece of
bread: [j]and [k]the adulteress will
[k]hunt for the precious life.
27 Can a man take fire in his bosom,
and his clothes not be burned?
28 Can one go upon hot coals, and
his feet not be burned?
29 So he that goeth in to his neigh-

[e] Or, *so shalt thou prevail with thy friend*
[f] Heb. *casteth forth* [g] Heb. *of his soul*
[h] Heb. *Haughty eyes* [i] Or, *candle* [j] Or, *of the strange tongue* [k] Heb. *the woman of a man,* or, *a mans wife*

means accepting responsibility for someone's debt if he or she fails to pay it. This makes the financial situation of a co-signer dependent upon the actions of the friend and subject to events beyond his or her control. It can lead to poverty (cf. 22:26–27) and the loss of lifelong friendships. This does not mean, however, that we should refuse to help someone who is in real need of the basic necessities of life (Ex. 22:14; Lev. 25:35; Mat. 5:42). But we should give to the poor rather than lend to them (cf. Mat. 14:21; Mark 10:21; see Prov. 19:17, note).

6:6 THOU SLUGGARD. The sluggard or lazy person is one who (1) puts off beginning what he or she should do (vv. 9–10; cf. 22:13), (2) does not finish what has been started (12:27), and (3) follows the least difficult course of action (20:4). Slothfulness, or laziness, is even more tempting in the spiritual realm than it is in the physical. God exhorts us to make our calling and election sure with all diligence (2 Pet. 1:10; cf. 2 Cor. 8:7; 2 Pet. 1:5).

6:20 SON ... FATHER ... MOTHER. The book of Proverbs places supreme value upon the family. (1) A family is made up of a father and a mother, with a child or children. (2) Both parents must share in the spiritual training of their children (1:8–9; 4:1–5). (3) Wise children will obey and honor their parents (1:8; 2:1; 3:1; 10:1). (4) Marital fidelity and mutual love are exalted (5:15–20).

bour's wife; whosoever toucheth her shall not be innocent.

30 *Men* do not despise a thief, if he steal to satisfy his soul when he is hungry;

31 But *if* he be found, [l]he shall restore sevenfold; he shall give all the substance of his house.

32 *But* whoso committeth adultery with a woman [m]lacketh [1]understanding: he *that* doeth it destroyeth his own soul.

33 A wound and dishonour shall he get; and his reproach shall not be wiped away.

34 For jealousy *is* the rage of a man: therefore he will not spare in the day of vengeance.

35 [m]He will not regard any ransom; neither will he rest content, though thou givest many gifts.

7 MY SON, keep my words, and [n]lay up my commandments with thee.

2 [o]Keep my commandments, and live; [p]and my law as the apple of thine eye.

3 [q]Bind them upon thy fingers, write them upon the table of thine heart.

4 Say unto wisdom, Thou *art* my sister; and call understanding *thy* kinswoman:

5 [r]That they may keep thee from the strange woman, from the stranger *which* flattereth with her words.

6 ¶ For at the window of my house I looked through my casement,

7 And beheld among the simple ones, I discerned among [n]the youths, a young man [s]void of understanding,

8 Passing through the street near her corner; and he went the way to her house,

9 [t]In the twilight, [o]in the evening, in the black and dark night:

10 And, behold, there met him a woman *with* the attire of an harlot, and subtle of heart.

11 ([u]She *is* loud and stubborn; [v]her feet abide not in her house:

12 Now *is she* without, now in the streets, and lieth in wait at every corner.)

13 So she caught him, and kissed him, *and* [p]with an impudent face said unto him,

14 [q]*I have* peace offerings with me; this day have I paid my vows.

15 Therefore came I forth to meet thee, diligently to seek thy face, and I have found thee.

16 I have decked my bed with coverings of tapestry, with carved *works*, with [w]fine linen of Egypt.

17 I have perfumed my bed with myrrh, aloes, and cinnamon.

18 Come, let us take our fill of love until the morning: let us solace ourselves with loves.

19 For the goodman *is* not at home, he is gone a long journey:

20 He hath taken a bag of money [r]with him, *and* will come home at [s]the day appointed.

21 With [x]her much fair speech she caused him to yield, [y]with the flattering of her lips she forced him.

22 He goeth after her [t]straightway, as an ox goeth to the slaughter,

6:31 [l]Ex. 22:1 **6:32** [m]ch. 7:7 **7:1** [n]ch. 2:1 **7:2** [o]Lev. 18:5 ch. 4:4 [p]Deut. 32:10 **7:3** [q]Deut. 6:8 & 11:18 ch. 3:3 & 6:21 **7:5** [r]ch. 2:16 & 5:3 & 6:24 **7:7** [s]ch. 6:32 & 9:4,16

7:9 [t]Job 24:15 **7:11** [u]ch. 9:13 [v]1 Tim. 5:13 Tit. 2:5 **7:16** [w]Is. 19:9 **7:21** [x]ch. 5:3 [y]Ps. 12:2

[1] Heb. *heart* [m] Heb. *He will not accept the face of any ransom* [n] Heb. *the sons* [o] Heb. *in the evening of the day* [p] Heb. *she strengthened her face and said* [q] Heb. *Peace offerings* are *upon me* [r] Heb. *in his hand* [s] Or, *the new moon* [t] Heb. *suddenly*

6:32–33 WHOSO COMMITTETH ADULTERY. Covenant children of God who commit adultery will experience trouble and dishonor; moreover, their reproach shall never be taken away. (1) Adultery is a grave and heinous sin against God (2 Sam. 12:9–10) and against the innocent partner who has been defrauded; the shame and disgrace of that sin remain with the guilty party for life. Though the guilt of adultery may be forgiven by repentance, its reproach will remain and its scars are never completely removed. Amends can never be adequately made (see 2 Sam. 12:10; 13:13,22; 1 Ki. 15:5; Neh. 13:26; Mat. 1:6).

(2) Because of the far-reaching and fearful consequences of adultery on all involved, we should run from every temptation and shun all associations that might lead to this sin. We should pray to be delivered from temptation (Mat. 6:13) and soberly recall the words of Scripture when tempted: "Let him that thinketh he standeth take heed lest he fall" (1 Cor. 10:12).

7:1–27 KEEP MY WORDS. Once more Proverbs warns against immorality committed in the name of love (v. 18), emphasizing its disastrous results (vv. 25–27; see 5:5; 5:14, note; 6:32–33, note). Sexual immorality can be avoided (1) by being firmly commited to all that God says is right and good (vv. 1–5), (2) by not allowing our thoughts to dwell on lustful pleasures (v. 25), and (3) by knowing that this sin leads to sorrow, regret, and death (vv. 26–27).

or as a fool to the correction of the stocks;

23 Till a dart strike through his liver; [z]as a bird hasteth to the snare, and knoweth not that it *is* for his life.

24 ¶ Hearken unto me now therefore, O ye children, and attend to the words of my mouth.

25 Let not thine heart decline to her ways, go not astray in her paths.

26 For she hath cast down many wounded: yea, [a]many strong *men* have been slain by her.

27 [b]Her house *is* the way to hell, going down to the chambers of death.

The call of wisdom

8 DOTH NOT [c]wisdom cry? and understanding put forth her voice?

2 She standeth in the top of high places, by the way in the places of the paths.

3 She crieth at the gates, at the entry of the city, at the coming in at the doors.

4 Unto you, O men, I call; and my voice *is* to the sons of man.

5 O ye simple, understand wisdom: and, ye fools, be ye of an understanding heart.

6 Hear; for I will speak of [d]excellent things; and the opening of my lips *shall be* right things.

7 For my mouth shall speak truth; and wickedness *is* [u]an abomination to my lips.

8 All the words of my mouth *are* in righteousness; *there is* nothing [v]froward or perverse in them.

9 They *are* all plain to him that understandeth, and right to them that find knowledge.

10 Receive my instruction, and not silver; and knowledge rather than choice gold.

11 [e]For wisdom *is* better than rubies; and all the things that may be desired are not to be compared to it.

12 I wisdom dwell with [w]prudence, and find out knowledge of witty inventions.

13 [f]The fear of the LORD *is* to hate evil: [g]pride, and arrogancy, and the evil way, and [h]the froward mouth, do I hate.

14 Counsel *is* mine, and sound wisdom: I *am* understanding; [i]I have strength.

15 [j]By me kings reign, and princes decree justice.

16 By me princes rule, and nobles, *even* all the judges of the earth.

17 [k]I love them that love me; and [l]those that seek me early shall find me.

18 [m]Riches and honour *are* with me; *yea,* durable riches and righteousness.

19 [n]My fruit *is* better than gold, yea, than fine gold; and my revenue than choice silver.

20 I [x]lead in the way of righteousness, in the midst of the paths of judgment:

21 That I may cause those that love me to inherit substance; and I will fill their treasures.

22 [o]The LORD possessed me in the beginning of his way, before his works of old.

23 [p]I was set up from everlasting, from the beginning, or ever the earth was.

24 When *there were* no depths, I was brought forth; when *there were* no fountains abounding with water.

25 [q]Before the mountains were settled, before the hills was I brought forth:

26 While as yet he had not made the earth, nor the [y]fields, nor [z]the highest part of the dust of the world.

27 When he prepared the heavens, I *was* there: when he set [a]a compass upon the face of the depth:

28 When he established the clouds above: when he strengthened the fountains of the deep:

29 [r]When he gave to the sea his decree, that the waters should not pass his commandment: when [s]he appointed the foundations of the earth:

30 [t]Then I was by him, *as* one brought up *with him:* [u]and I was daily *his* delight, rejoicing always before him;

31 Rejoicing in the habitable part of

7:23 [z]Eccl. 9:12
7:26 [a]Neh. 13:26
7:27 [b]ch. 2:18 & 5:5 & 9:18
8:1 [c]ch. 1:20 & 9:3
8:6 [d]ch. 22:20
8:11 [e]Job 28:15 Ps. 19:10 & 119:127 ch. 3:14,15 & 4:5,7 & 16:16
8:13 [f]ch. 16:6 [g]ch. 6:17 [h]ch. 4:24
8:14 [i]Eccl. 7:19
8:15 [j]Dan. 2:21 Rom. 13:1
8:17 [k]1 Sam. 2:30 Ps. 91:14 John 14:21 [l]Jas. 1:5
8:18 [m]ch. 3:16 Mat. 6:33
8:19 [n]ver. 10 ch. 3:14
8:22 [o]ch. 3:19
8:23 [p]Ps. 2:6
8:25 [q]Job 15:7,8
8:29 [r]Gen. 1:9,10 Job 38:10 Jer. 5:22 [s]Job 38:4
8:30 [t]John 1:1,2 [u]Mat. 3:17 Col. 1:13

[u] Heb. *the abomination of my lips* [v] Heb. *wreathed* [w] Or, *subtlety* [x] Or, *walk* [y] Or, *open places* [z] Or, *the chief part* [a] Or, *a circle*

8:13 THE FEAR OF THE LORD *IS* TO HATE EVIL. The fear of God should cause us to depart from evil (16:6) and to hate sin that displeases Him and destroys us and those we love (see article on THE FEAR OF THE LORD, p. 282).

his earth; and [v]my delights *were* with
the sons of men.
32 Now therefore hearken unto me,
O ye children: for [w]blessed *are they*
that keep my ways.
33 Hear instruction, and be wise,
and refuse it not.
34 [x]Blessed *is* the man that hear-
eth me, watching daily at my gates,
waiting at the posts of my doors.
35 For whoso findeth me findeth
life, and shall [y]obtain[b] favour of the
LORD.
36 But he that sinneth against me
[z]wrongeth his own soul: all they that
hate me love death.

Wisdom and folly contrasted

9 WISDOM HATH [a]builded her
house, she hath hewn out her sev-
en pillars:
2 [b]She hath killed [c]her beasts;
[c]she hath mingled her wine; she hath
also furnished her table.
3 She hath [d]sent forth her maid-
ens; [e]she crieth [f]upon the highest
places of the city,
4 [g]Whoso *is* simple, let him turn in
hither: *as for* him that wanteth under-
standing, she saith to him,
5 [h]Come, eat of my bread, and
drink of the wine *which* I have mingled.
6 Forsake the foolish, and live; and
go in the way of understanding.
7 He that reproveth a scorner
getteth to himself shame: and he that
rebuketh a wicked *man getteth* himself
a blot.
8 [i]Reprove not a scorner, lest he
hate thee: [j]rebuke a wise man, and he
will love thee.
9 Give *instruction* to a wise *man,* and
he will be yet wiser: teach a just *man,*
[k]and he will increase in learning.
10 [l]The fear of the LORD *is* the be-

8:31 [v]Ps. 16:3
8:32 [w]Ps. 119:1,2; Luke 11:28
8:34 [x]ch. 3:13,18
8:35 [y]ch. 12:2
8:36 [z]ch. 20:2
9:1 [a]Mat. 16:18; Eph. 2:20; 1 Pet. 2:5
9:2 [b]Mat. 22:4 [c]ch. 23:30
9:3 [d]Rom. 10:15 [e]ch. 8:1,2 [f]ver. 14
9:4 [g]Ps. 19:7; ch. 6:32
9:5 [h]Sol. 5:1; Is. 55:1; John 6:27
9:8 [i]Mat. 7:6 [j]Ps. 141:5
9:9 [k]Mat. 13:12
9:10 [l]Job 28:28; ch. 1:7
9:11 [m]ch. 3:2,16
9:12 [n]Job 35:6,7; ch. 16:26
9:13 [o]ch. 7:11
9:14 [p]ver. 3
9:16 [q]ch. 7:7,8
9:17 [r]ch. 20:17
9:18 [s]ch. 2:18
10:1 [t]ch. 15:20
10:2 [u]Ps. 49:6; Luke 12:20 [v]Dan. 4:27
10:3 [w]Ps. 10:14
10:4 [x]ch. 19:15 [y]ch. 13:4

ginning of wisdom: and the knowledge
of the holy *is* understanding.
11 [m]For by me thy days shall be
multiplied, and the years of thy life
shall be increased.
12 [n]If thou be wise, thou shalt be
wise for thyself: but *if* thou scornest,
thou alone shalt bear *it.*
13 ¶ [o]A foolish woman *is* clamor-
ous: *she is* simple, and knoweth noth-
ing.
14 For she sitteth at the door of her
house, on a seat [p]in the high places of
the city,
15 To call passengers who go right
on their ways:
16 [q]Whoso *is* simple, let him turn
in hither: and *as for* him that wanteth
understanding, she saith to him,
17 [r]Stolen waters are sweet, and
bread [d]*eaten* in secret is pleasant.
18 But he knoweth not that [s]the
dead *are* there; *and that* her guests *are*
in the depths of hell.

Proverbs of Solomon

10 THE PROVERBS of Solomon.
[t]A wise son maketh a glad fa-
ther: but a foolish son *is* the heaviness
of his mother.
2 [u]Treasures of wickedness profit
nothing: [v]but righteousness deliver-
eth from death.
3 [w]The LORD will not suffer the soul
of the righteous to famish: but he
casteth away [e]the substance of the
wicked.
4 [x]He becometh poor that dealeth
with a slack hand: but [y]the hand of the
diligent maketh rich.
5 He that gathereth in summer *is* a

[b] Heb. *bring forth* [c] Heb. *her killing* [d] Heb. *of secrecies* [e] Or, *the wicked for* their *wickedness*

9:8 REBUKE A WISE MAN, AND HE WILL LOVE THEE. If we are truly wise people who want to please God, we will welcome reproof and criticism (27:6; 28:23). Admonition and correction from a friend, family member, or pastor are some of the ways God uses to mold our character according to His holy will (see John 16:8; Eph. 5:11; 2 Tim. 4:2; Tit. 2:15; Rev. 3:19). The church that receives with humility and obedience the reproof of a loving pastor will indeed be blessed by the Holy Spirit.

10:2–7 RIGHTEOUSNESS DELIVERETH FROM DEATH. These verses contrast the blessings of righteous living with the unhappiness of wicked living.

10:3 THE LORD WILL NOT SUFFER THE SOUL OF THE RIGHTEOUS TO FAMISH. This proverb describes the general providence and provision of God in meeting the physical needs of His people (cf. Mat. 6:11,33). This truth does not deny that there may be times when we will find it difficult to provide for the needs of ourselves or our families. Times of war, famine, or devastating economic or social conditions, as well as periods of persecution, may result in severe hardship for the righteous (see 1 John 2, note); nevertheless, God will never abandon His children who trust fully in Him.

10:5 HE THAT SLEEPETH IN HARVEST. How shameful it is to be lazy when there is physi-

wise son: *but* he that sleepeth in harvest *is* [z]a son that causeth shame.

6 Blessings *are* upon the head of the just: but [a]violence covereth the mouth of the wicked.

7 [b]The memory of the just *is* blessed: but the name of the wicked shall rot.

8 The wise in heart will receive commandments: [c]but [f]a prating fool [g]shall fall.

9 [d]He that walketh uprightly walketh surely: but he that perverteth his ways shall be known.

10 [e]He that winketh with the eye causeth sorrow: [f]but a prating fool [g]shall fall.

11 [g]The mouth of a righteous *man is* a well of life: but [h]violence covereth the mouth of the wicked.

12 Hatred stirreth up strifes: but [i]love covereth all sins.

13 In the lips of him that hath understanding wisdom is found: but [j]a rod *is* for the back of him that is void of [h]understanding.

14 Wise *men* lay up knowledge: but [k]the mouth of the foolish *is* near destruction.

15 [l]The rich man's wealth *is* his strong city: the destruction of the poor *is* their poverty.

16 The labour of the righteous *tendeth* to life: the fruit of the wicked to sin.

17 He *is in* the way of life that keepeth instruction: but he that refuseth reproof [i]erreth.

18 He that hideth hatred *with* lying lips, and [m]he that uttereth a slander, *is* a fool.

19 [n]In the multitude of words there wanteth not sin: but [o]he that refraineth his lips *is* wise.

20 The tongue of the just *is as* choice silver: the heart of the wicked *is* little worth.

21 The lips of the righteous feed many: but fools die for want [j]of wisdom.

22 [p]The blessing of the LORD, it maketh rich, and he addeth no sorrow with it.

23 [q]*It is* as sport to a fool to do mischief: but a man of understanding hath wisdom.

24 [r]The fear of the wicked, it shall come upon him: but [s]the desire of the righteous shall be granted.

25 As the whirlwind passeth, [t]so *is* the wicked no *more:* but [u]the righteous *is* an everlasting foundation.

26 As vinegar to the teeth, and as smoke to the eyes, so *is* the sluggard to them that send him.

27 [v]The fear of the LORD [k]prolongeth days: but [w]the years of the wicked shall be shortened.

28 The hope of the righteous *shall be* gladness: but the [x]expectation of the wicked shall perish.

29 The way of the LORD *is* strength to the upright: [y]but destruction *shall be* to the workers of iniquity.

30 [z]The righteous shall never be removed: but the wicked shall not inhabit the earth.

31 [a]The mouth of the just bringeth forth wisdom: but the froward tongue shall be cut out.

10:5 [z]ch. 19:26 **10:6** [a]ver:11 **10:7** [b]Ps. 112:6 Eccl. 8:10 **10:8** [c]ver. 10 **10:9** [d]Ps. 23:4 ch. 28:18 Is. 33:15,16 **10:10** [e]ch. 6:13 [f]ver. 8 **10:11** [g]Ps. 37:30 [h]Ps. 107:42 **10:12** [i]1 Cor. 13:7 1 Pet. 4:8 **10:13** [j]ch. 26:3 **10:14** [k]ch. 18:7 **10:15** [l]Job 31:24 1 Tim. 6:17 **10:18** [m]Ps. 15:3 **10:19** [n]Eccl. 5:3 [o]Jas. 3:2 **10:22** [p]Gen. 24:35 Ps. 37:22 **10:23** [q]ch. 15:21 **10:24** [r]Job 15:21 [s]Ps. 145:19 Mat. 5:6 1 John 5:14 **10:25** [t]Ps. 37:9,10 [u]Ps. 15:5 Mat:16:18 **10:27** [v]ch. 9:11 [w]Job 15:32 **10:28** [x]Job 8:13 **10:29** [y]Ps. 1:6 **10:30** [z]Ps. 37:22 **10:31** [a]Ps. 37:30

[f]Heb. *a fool of lips* [g]Or, *shall be beaten* [h]Heb. *heart* [i]Or, *causeth to err* [j]Heb. *of heart* [k]Heb. *addeth*

cal work to be done (cf. 6:9–11; 19:15). How much more shameful is it to refuse selfishly to work for the harvest of souls. We must heed the words of Jesus and labor with Him for the salvation of the world (Mat. 9:37–38).

10:11 A RIGHTEOUS *MAN IS* A WELL OF LIFE. Those who know and follow God's ways will lead others into the full life given by God. Compare Ezek. 47:1–12 and John 4:14; 7:38, where the Spirit living in the believer is regarded as the source of living water. As this living water flows through the believer, it brings eternal life to others. Believers should pray that the Holy Spirit will enable them to carry out that great task (see 1 Cor. 12:4–10; 14:1–40).

10:15 THE RICH MAN'S WEALTH *IS* HIS STRONG CITY. This proverb observes the apparent advantages of riches (cf. 14:20; 19:4) and the disadvantages of poverty (cf. 18:23; 19:4,7). It may appear to the casual observer that the rich are secure (see 11:4). Yet in God's sight, the "treasures of wickedness profit nothing" (v. 2). The N.T. sheds clearer light on the state of the rich and poor. "Hath not God chosen the poor of this world rich in faith, and heirs of the kingdom?" (Jas. 2:5; cf. Luke 2:7–12; 4:22). Like the other O.T. books, Proverbs must be read in the light of God's complete revelation in His Son recorded in the N.T. (Heb. 1:1–3; see article on CHRIST IN THE OLD TESTAMENT, p. 562).

10:22 THE BLESSING OF THE LORD, IT MAKETH RICH. All too often material wealth in this world is gained through wickedness and greed and is therefore not from God (v. 2). True riches consist in the blessing of the Lord. Whether we are poor or rich, the Lord's presence and favor are our greatest wealth.

32 The lips of the righteous know what is acceptable: but the mouth of the wicked *speaketh* [l]frowardness.

11

A [b]FALSE[m] balance *is* abomination to the LORD: but [n]a just weight *is* his delight.

2 [c]*When* pride cometh, then cometh shame: but with the lowly *is* wisdom.

3 [d]The integrity of the upright shall guide them: but the perverseness of transgressors shall destroy them.

4 [e]Riches profit not in the day of wrath: but [f]righteousness delivereth from death.

5 The righteousness of the perfect shall [o]direct his way: but the wicked shall fall by his own wickedness.

6 The righteousness of the upright shall deliver them: but [g]transgressors shall be taken in *their own* naughtiness.

7 [h]When a wicked man dieth, *his* expectation shall perish: and the hope of unjust *men* perisheth.

8 [i]The righteous is delivered out of trouble, and the wicked cometh in his stead.

9 An hypocrite with *his* mouth destroyeth his neighbour: but through knowledge shall the just be delivered.

10 [j]When it goeth well with the righteous, the city rejoiceth: and when the wicked perish, *there is* shouting.

11 [k]By the blessing of the upright the city is exalted: but it is overthrown by the mouth of the wicked.

12 He that is [p]void of wisdom despiseth his neighbour: but a man of understanding holdeth his peace.

13 [l]A[q] talebearer revealeth secrets: but he that is of a faithful spirit concealeth the matter.

14 [m]Where no counsel *is*, the people fall: but in the multitude of counsellors *there is* safety.

15 [n]He that is surety for a stranger [r]shall smart *for it:* and he that hateth [s]suretyship is sure.

16 [o]A gracious woman retaineth honour: and strong *men* retain riches.

17 [p]The merciful man doeth good to his own soul: but *he that is* cruel troubleth his own flesh.

18 The wicked worketh a deceitful work: but [q]to him that soweth righteousness *shall be* a sure reward.

19 As righteousness *tendeth* to life: so he that pursueth evil *pursueth it* to his own death.

20 They that are of a froward heart *are* abomination to the LORD: but *such as are* upright in *their* way *are* his delight.

21 [r]*Though* hand *join* in hand, the wicked shall not be unpunished: but [s]the seed of the righteous shall be delivered.

22 *As* a jewel of gold in a swine's snout, *so is* a fair woman which [t]is without discretion.

23 The desire of the righteous *is* only good: *but* the expectation of the wicked [t]*is* wrath.

24 There is that [u]scattereth, and yet increaseth; and *there is* that withholdeth more than is meet, but *it tendeth* to poverty.

25 [v]The[u] liberal soul shall be made fat: [w]and he that watereth shall be watered also himself.

26 [x]He that withholdeth corn, the

11:1 [b]Lev. 19:35 Deut. 25:13 **11:2** [c]ch. 16:18 **11:3** [d]ch. 13:6 **11:4** [e]Ezek. 7:19 Zeph. 1:18 [f]Gen. 7:1 **11:6** [g]Eccl. 10:8 **11:7** [h]ch. 10:28 **11:8** [i]ch. 21:18 **11:10** [j]Esth. 8:15 **11:11** [k]ch. 29:8 **11:13** [l]Lev. 19:16 ch. 20:19 **11:14** [m]1 Ki. 12:1 **11:15** [n]ch. 6:1 **11:16** [o]ch. 31:30 **11:17** [p]Mat. 5:7 **11:18** [q]Hos. 10:12 **11:21** [r]ch. 16:5 [s]Ps. 112:2 **11:23** [t]Rom. 2:8,9 **11:24** [u]Ps. 112:9 **11:25** [v]2 Cor. 9:6 [w]Mat. 5:7 **11:26** [x]Amos 8:5,6

[l] Heb. *frowardnesses* [m] Heb. *Balances of deceit* [n] Heb. *a perfect stone* [o] Heb. *rectify* [p] Heb. *destitute of heart* [q] Heb. *He that walketh, being a talebearer* [r] Heb. *shall be sore broken* [s] Heb. *those that strike* hands [t] Heb. *departeth from* [u] Heb. *The soul of blessing*

11:1 A FALSE BALANCE *IS* ABOMINATION TO THE LORD. The use of inaccurate scales to cheat someone is condemned by God (cf. Lev. 19:35). He commands that we deal honestly with all people, both in financial matters and in other circumstance where cheating is possible. We must always keep in mind that the Lord's "countenance doth behold the upright" (Ps. 11:7); they only "shall dwell in [his] presence" (Ps. 140:13; cf. 24:3–5).

11:8 THE RIGHTEOUS IS DELIVERED OUT OF TROUBLE. As a general principle, righteous living results in less problems than wicked living (cf. vv. 3–9). This does not mean that those who follow God will never have any problems. But the righteous may be assured that when they suffer afflictions, they will ultimately be delivered in God's own time.

11:19 RIGHTEOUSNESS TENDETH TO LIFE. See 10:11, note.

11:19 HE THAT PURSUETH EVIL ... DEATH. God has decreed penalties for actions that violate His laws. The unrighteous will ultimately pay for their sins and their disregard of God and others (see 6:29; Gen. 34:25–30; 49:7; Rom. 6:23; Jas. 1:15).

11:24–25 SCATTERETH, AND YET INCREASETH. God promises that those who give generously will receive back more than they give. He blesses those who are kind and generous, whether it be in their finances or in giving of themselves. The N.T. teaches that we are stewards of God's gifts and must use them for His cause and for the benefit of those in need (Mat. 25:26–27; see 2 Cor. 8:2, note; 9:8, note).

people shall curse him: but [y]blessing *shall be* upon the head of him that selleth *it*.

27 He that diligently seeketh good procureth favour: [z]but he that seeketh mischief, it shall come unto him.

28 [a]He that trusteth in his riches shall fall: but [b]the righteous shall flourish as a branch.

29 He that troubleth his own house [c]shall inherit the wind: and the fool *shall be* servant to the wise of heart.

30 The fruit of the righteous *is* a tree of life; and [d]he that [v]winneth souls *is* wise.

31 [e]Behold, the righteous shall be recompensed in the earth: much more the wicked and the sinner.

12 WHOSO LOVETH instruction loveth knowledge: but he that hateth reproof *is* brutish.

2 A good *man* obtaineth favour of the LORD: but a man of wicked devices will he condemn.

3 A man shall not be established by wickedness: but the [f]root of the righteous shall not be moved.

4 [g]A virtuous woman *is* a crown to her husband: but she that maketh ashamed *is* [h]as rottenness in his bones.

5 The thoughts of the righteous *are* right: *but* the counsels of the wicked *are* deceit.

6 [i]The words of the wicked *are* to lie in wait for blood: [j]but the mouth of the upright shall deliver them.

7 [k]The wicked are overthrown, and *are* not: but the house of the righteous shall stand.

8 A man shall be commended according to his wisdom: [l]but he that is [w]of a perverse heart shall be despised.

9 [m]*He that is* despised, and hath a servant, *is* better than he that honoureth himself, and lacketh bread.

11:26 [y]Job 29:13 **11:27** [z]Esth. 7:10 Ps. 7:15,16 **11:28** [a]Job. 31:24 Mark 10:24 Luke 12:21 1 Tim. 6:17 [b]Ps. 1:3 Jer. 17:8 **11:29** [c]Eccl. 5:16 **11:30** [d]Dan. 12:3 Jas. 5:20 **11:31** [e]Jer. 25:29 **12:3** [f]ch. 10:25 **12:4** [g]1 Cor. 11:7 [h]ch. 14:30 **12:6** [i]ch. 1:11,18 [j]ch. 14:3 **12:7** [k]Ps. 37:36 **12:8** [l]1 Sam. 25:17 **12:9** [m]ch. 13:7

12:10 [n]Deut. 25:4 **12:11** [o]Gen. 3:19 ch. 28:19 [p]ch. 6:32 **12:13** [q]ch. 18:7 [r]2 Pet. 2:9 **12:14** [s]ch. 13:2 [t]Is. 3:10,11 **12:15** [u]Luke 18:11 **12:16** [v]ch. 29:11 **12:17** [w]ch. 14:5 **12:18** [x]Ps. 57:4 & 64:3 **12:19** [y]ch. 19:5,9 **12:22** [z]Rev. 22:15 **12:23** [a]ch. 13:16

10 [n]A righteous *man* regardeth the life of his beast: but the [x]tender mercies of the wicked *are* cruel.

11 [o]He that tilleth his land shall be satisfied with bread: but he that followeth vain *persons* [p]*is* void of understanding.

12 The wicked desireth [y]the net of evil *men:* but the root of the righteous yieldeth *fruit.*

13 [q]The[z] wicked is snared by the transgression of *his* lips: [r]but the just shall come out of trouble.

14 [s]A man shall be satisfied with good by the fruit of *his* mouth: [t]and the recompence of a man's hands shall be rendered unto him.

15 [u]The way of a fool *is* right in his own eyes: but he that hearkeneth unto counsel *is* wise.

16 [v]A fool's wrath is [a]presently known: but a prudent *man* covereth shame.

17 [w]*He that* speaketh truth showeth forth righteousness: but a false witness deceit.

18 [x]There is that speaketh like the piercings of a sword: but the tongue of the wise *is* health.

19 The lip of truth shall be established for ever: [y]but a lying tongue *is* but for a moment.

20 Deceit *is* in the heart of them that imagine evil: but to the counsellors of peace *is* joy.

21 There shall no evil happen to the just: but the wicked shall be filled with mischief.

22 [z]Lying lips *are* abomination to the LORD: but they that deal truly *are* his delight.

23 [a]A prudent man concealeth

[v]Heb. *taketh* [w]Heb. *perverse of heart* [x]Or, *bowels* [y]Or, *the fortress* [z]Heb. *The snare of the wicked* is *in the transgression of lips* [a]Heb. *in that day*

11:30 HE THAT WINNETH SOULS *IS* WISE. Influencing people for righteousness is wise. The N.T. emphasizes that believers should lead people to Christ, salvation, and lives of righteousness (see John 14:6; 1 Cor. 9:20–22; 10:33; 1 Pet. 3:1–2; Jas. 5:19–20).

12:1 HE THAT HATETH REPROOF IS BRUTISH. At times we all need reproof and correction. A proud person hates to be corrected, but the humble person will honestly receive criticism and profit from it (cf. 1:7; 6:23; 10:17).

12:4 A VIRTUOUS WOMAN *IS* A CROWN TO HER HUSBAND. Normally the most important human relationship we will ever have is with a wife or husband. A good spouse will help bring happiness, joy, and success, while a bad spouse will cause much sorrow and misery. When seeking a marriage partner, we should consider the person's character and his or her commitment to Christ and His standards of holy living, lest we marry the wrong person and suffer a lifetime of regret (see 1 Cor. 7:3,14, notes).

12:10 A RIGHTEOUS *MAN* . . . HIS BEAST. God's way of righteous living includes kindness even to animals. Animals are useful to humans for companionship, work, and food, and they should never be mistreated or used in a cruel manner (Gen. 1:28; 9:3; 24:32; Deut. 25:4).

knowledge: but the heart of fools pro-
claimeth foolishness.
24 [b]The hand of the diligent shall
bear rule: but the [b]slothful shall be
under tribute.
25 [c]Heaviness in the heart of man
maketh it stoop: but [d]a good word
maketh it glad.
26 The righteous *is* more [c]excel-
lent than his neighbour: but the way of
the wicked seduceth them.
27 The slothful *man* roasteth not
that which he took in hunting: but the
substance of a diligent man *is* precious.
28 In the way of righteousness *is*
life; and *in* the pathway *thereof there is*
no death.

13 A WISE son *heareth* his fa-
ther's instruction: [e]but a
scorner heareth not rebuke.
2 [f]A man shall eat good by the
fruit of *his* mouth: but the soul of the
transgressors *shall eat* violence.
3 [g]He that keepeth his mouth
keepeth his life: *but* he that openeth
wide his lips shall have destruction.
4 [h]The soul of the sluggard
desireth, and *hath* nothing: but the soul
of the diligent shall be made fat.
5 A righteous *man* hateth lying: but
a wicked *man* is loathsome, and com-
eth to shame.
6 [i]Righteousness keepeth *him that*
is upright in the way: but wickedness
overthroweth [d]the sinner.
7 [j]There is that maketh himself
rich, yet *hath* nothing: *there is* that
maketh himself poor, yet *hath* great
riches.
8 The ransom of a man's life *are* his
riches: but the poor heareth not re-
buke.
9 The light of the righteous re-
joiceth: [k]but the [e]lamp of the wicked
shall be put out.
10 Only by pride cometh conten-
tion: but with the well advised *is* wis-
dom.
11 [l]Wealth *gotten* by vanity shall
be diminished: but he that gathereth
[f]by labour shall increase.
12 Hope deferred maketh the heart
sick: but [m]*when* the desire cometh, *it*
is a tree of life.
13 Whoso [n]despiseth the word
shall be destroyed: but he that feareth
the commandment [g]shall be re-
warded.
14 [o]The law of the wise *is* a foun-
tain of life, to depart from [p]the snares
of death.
15 Good understanding giveth fa-
vour: but the way of transgressors *is*
hard.
16 [q]Every prudent *man* dealeth
with knowledge: but a fool [h]layeth
open *his* folly.
17 A wicked messenger falleth into
mischief: but [r]a[i] faithful ambassa-
dor *is* health.
18 Poverty and shame *shall be to*
him that refuseth instruction: but [s]he
that regardeth reproof shall be hon-
oured.
19 [t]The desire accomplished is
sweet to the soul: but *it is* abomination
to fools to depart from evil.
20 He that walketh with wise *men*
shall be wise: but a companion of fools
[j]shall be destroyed.
21 [u]Evil pursueth sinners: but to
the righteous good shall be repaid.
22 A good *man* leaveth an inheri-
tance to his children's children: and
[v]the wealth of the sinner *is* laid up for
the just.
23 [w]Much food *is in* the tillage of

12:24 [b]ch. 10:4 **12:25** [c]ch. 15:13 [d]Is. 50:4 **13:1** [e]Is. 28:15 **13:2** [f]ch. 12:14 **13:3** [g]Ps. 39:1 ch. 21:23 Jas. 3:2 **13:4** [h]ch. 10:4 **13:6** [i]ch. 11:3,5,6 **13:7** [j]ch. 12:9 **13:9** [k]Job 18:5,6 & 21:17 ch. 24:20 **13:11** [l]ch. 10:2 & 20:21 **13:12** [m]ver. 19 **13:13** [n]2 Chr. 36:16 **13:14** [o]ch. 10:11 & 14:27 & 16:22 [p]2 Sam. 22:6 **13:16** [q]ch. 12:23 & 15:2 **13:17** [r]ch. 25:13 **13:18** [s]ch. 15:5,31 **13:19** [t]ver. 12 **13:21** [u]Ps. 32:10 **13:22** [v]Job 27:17 ch. 28:8 Eccl. 2:26 **13:23** [w]ch. 12:11

[b] Or, *deceitful* [c] Or, *abundant* [d] Heb. *sin* [e] Or, *candle* [f] Heb. *with the hand* [g] Or, *shall be in peace* [h] Heb. *spreadeth* [i] Heb. *an ambassador of faithfulness* [j] Heb. *shall be broken*

13:3 HE THAT KEEPETH HIS MOUTH KEEPETH HIS LIFE. Careless speech and an unbridled tongue can undermine our influence for righteousness, cause us to sin (Eccl. 5:6), and affect our relationship with God (Eccl. 5:7). A perfect person carefully controls his or her speech (8:6–8; Jas. 3:2). We should ask God for help in controlling our tongues (see Ps. 141:3; cf. Prov. 10:14,19; 18:7; 2 Tim. 3:3; Jas. 3:2–13).

13:5 A RIGHTEOUS *MAN* HATETH LYING. A righteous person would rather experience pain by telling the truth than avoid suffering by lying (Dan. 3:16–18). Such people know that to give in to the habit of lying is to sin against the Lord (12:22); to do so will exclude them from the kingdom of God (John 8:44; see Rev. 22:15, note).

13:10 ONLY BY PRIDE COMETH CONTENTION. Often people quarrel and contend for their own ideas because of pride. In so doing they may desire preeminence (Luke 22:24), be rebellious against authority (Num. 12:2) or Biblical truth (2 Tim. 4:3–4), or be driven by a spirit of sectarianism (1 Cor. 3:3–4). When arguments occur, we need to ask ourselves whether pride is involved or whether we are honestly contending for the truth (Gal. 2:5; 1 Thes. 2:2; Jude 3).

13:23 DESTROYED FOR WANT OF JUDGMENT. "Judgment" (Heb. *mispat*) may also be ren-

the poor: but there is *that is* destroyed for want of judgment.

24 [x]He that spareth his rod hateth his son: but he that loveth him chasteneth him betimes.

25 [y]The righteous eateth to the satisfying of his soul: but the belly of the wicked shall want.

14

EVERY WISE woman buildeth her house: but the foolish plucketh it down with her hands.

2 He that walketh in his uprightness feareth the LORD: [z]but *he that is* perverse in his ways despiseth him.

3 In the mouth of the foolish *is* a rod of pride: [a]but the lips of the wise shall preserve them.

4 Where no oxen *are,* the crib *is* clean: but much increase *is* by the strength of the ox.

5 [b]A faithful witness will not lie: but a false witness will utter lies.

6 A scorner seeketh wisdom, and *findeth it* not: but [c]knowledge *is* easy unto him that understandeth.

7 Go from the presence of a foolish man, when thou perceivest not *in him* the lips of knowledge.

8 The wisdom of the prudent *is* to understand his way: but the folly of fools *is* deceit.

9 [d]Fools make a mock at sin: but among the righteous *there is* favour.

10 The heart knoweth [k]his own bitterness; and a stranger doth not intermeddle with his joy.

11 [e]The house of the wicked shall be overthrown: but the tabernacle of the upright shall flourish.

12 [f]There is a way which seemeth right unto a man, but [g]the end thereof *are* the ways of death.

13 Even in laughter the heart is sorrowful; and [h]the end of that mirth *is* heaviness.

14 The backslider in heart shall be [i]filled with his own ways: and a good man *shall be satisfied* from himself.

15 The simple believeth every word: but the prudent *man* looketh well to his going.

16 [j]A wise *man* feareth, and departeth from evil: but the fool rageth, and is confident.

17 *He that is* soon angry dealeth foolishly: and a man of wicked devices is hated.

18 The simple inherit folly: but the prudent are crowned with knowledge.

19 The evil bow before the good; and the wicked at the gates of the righteous.

20 [k]The poor is hated even of his own neighbour: but [l]the rich *hath* many friends.

21 He that despiseth his neighbour sinneth: [l]but he that hath mercy on the poor, happy *is* he.

22 Do they not err that devise evil? but mercy and truth *shall be* to them that devise good.

23 In all labour there is profit: but the talk of the lips *tendeth* only to penury.

24 The crown of the wise *is* their

13:24 [x]ch. 19:18 & 22:15 & 23:13 & 29:15,17
13:25 [y]Ps. 34:10 & 37:3
14:2 [z]Rom. 2:4
14:3 [a]ch. 12:6
14:5 [b]ver. 25 Ex. 20:16 & 23:1 ch. 6:19 & 12:17
14:6 [c]ch. 8:9 & 17:24
14:9 [d]ch. 10:23
14:11 [e]Job 8:15
14:12 [f]ch. 16:25 [g]Rom. 6:21
14:13 [h]ch. 5:4 Eccl. 2:2
14:14 [i]ch. 1:31 & 12:14
14:16 [j]ch. 22:3
14:20 [k]ch. 19:7
14:21 [l]Ps. 41:1 & 112:9

k Heb. *the bitterness of his soul* **l** Heb. *many are the lovers of the rich*

dered "justice." Some people are poor and remain so because they are victims of injustice in society (cf. Ps. 35:10; see Jas. 5:1–6).

13:24 HE THAT SPARETH HIS ROD HATETH HIS SON. Scripture instructs parents to discipline their children with the "rod" during their formative years. Spanking should be done only for willful disobedience or defiance; it has as its goal the elimination of folly, rebellion, and disrespect for parents (22:15). Adequate parental discipline administered in a wise, loving, and considerate manner helps children to learn that wrong behavior carries unpleasant consequences and may involve suffering (29:15). Such discipline is necessary lest children form attitudes that will later bring them to ruin and death (19:18; 23:13–14). Godly discipline in a family will bring happiness and peace to the home (29:17). It must always be administered out of love, just as our heavenly Father does (Heb. 12:6–7; Rev. 3:19).

14:1 EVERY WISE WOMAN BUILDETH HER HOUSE. A wise and godly woman makes her home a place of refuge, peace, and joy, whereas a foolish woman neglects her home and family (see 1 Tim. 2:15, note; Tit. 2:4–5, note).

14:2 DESPISETH HIM. To despise God is to sin against Him and treat Him with contempt.

14:12 SEEMETH RIGHT. Humanistic wisdom is a poor basis for determining what is true or false, right or wrong, worthy or unworthy. God's written revelation is the only infallible source for determining the right path of life. The human way has in it the seeds of death; God's way leads to eternal life.

14:14 THE BACKSLIDER IN HEART. Backsliders are those who have turned their hearts away from God to go their own selfish way (see article on PERSONAL APOSTASY, p. 1946). Such persons will reap the fruit of their decision in heartache and misery (cf. 1:31; 12:14; Gal. 6:7). Those who remain faithful to God (i.e., "the prudent *man*," v. 15) will reap the rewards of righteousness, both in this life and in the next (see Rev. 2:7, note).

riches: *but* the foolishness of fools *is*
folly.
25 [m]A true witness delivereth
souls: but a deceitful *witness* speaketh
lies.
26 In the fear of the LORD *is* strong
confidence: and his children shall have
a place of refuge.
27 [n]The fear of the LORD *is* a foun-
tain of life, to depart from the snares
of death.
28 In the multitude of people *is* the
king's honour: but in the want of peo-
ple *is* the destruction of the prince.
29 [o]*He that is* slow to wrath *is* of
great understanding: but *he that is*
[m]hasty of spirit exalteth folly.
30 A sound heart *is* the life of the
flesh: but [p]envy [q]the rottenness of
the bones.
31 [r]He that oppresseth the poor
reproacheth [s]his Maker: but he that
honoureth him hath mercy on the poor.
32 The wicked is driven away in his
wickedness: but [t]the righteous hath
hope in his death.
33 Wisdom resteth in the heart of
him that hath understanding: but
[u]*that which is* in the midst of fools is
made known.
34 Righteousness exalteth a na-
tion: but sin *is* a reproach [n]to any peo-
ple.
35 [v]The king's favour *is* toward a
wise servant: but his wrath is *against*
him that causeth shame.

15

15 A [w]SOFT answer turneth
away wrath: but [x]grievous
words stir up anger.
2 The tongue of the wise useth
knowledge aright: [y]but the mouth of
fools [o]poureth out foolishness.
3 [z]The eyes of the LORD *are* in every
place, beholding the evil and the good.
4 [p]A wholesome tongue *is* a tree of
life: but perverseness therein *is* a
breach in the spirit.
5 [a]A fool despiseth his father's in-
struction: [b]but he that regardeth re-
proof is prudent.
6 In the house of the righteous *is*
much treasure: but in the revenues of
the wicked is trouble.
7 The lips of the wise disperse
knowledge: but the heart of the foolish
doeth not so.
8 [c]The sacrifice of the wicked *is* an
abomination to the LORD: but the prayer
of the upright *is* his delight.
9 The way of the wicked *is* an abom-
ination unto the LORD: but he loveth
him that [d]followeth after righteous-
ness.
10 [q]Correction *is* [e]grievous unto
him that forsaketh the way: *and* [f]he
that hateth reproof shall die.
11 [g]Hell and destruction *are* before
the LORD: how much more then [h]the
hearts of the children of men?
12 [i]A scorner loveth not one that
reproveth him: neither will he go unto
the wise.
13 [j]A merry heart maketh a cheer-
ful countenance: but [k]by sorrow of the
heart the spirit is broken.
14 The heart of him that hath un-

14:25 [m]ver. 5
14:27 [n]ch. 13:14
14:29 [o]Jas. 1:19
14:30 [p]Ps. 112:10 [q]ch. 12:4
14:31 [r]ch. 17:5 Mat. 25:40 [s]ch. 22:2
14:32 [t]Job 13:15 Ps. 23:4 2 Cor. 1:9 2 Tim. 4:18
14:33 [u]ch. 12:16
14:35 [v]Mat. 24:45
15:1 [w]ch. 25:15 [x]1 Sam. 25:10
15:2 [y]ch. 12:23
15:3 [z]Job 34:21 Heb. 4:13
15:5 [a]ch. 10:1 [b]ch. 13:18
15:8 [c]Is. 1:11 Jer. 6:20 Amos 5:22
15:9 [d]ch. 21:21 1 Tim. 6:11
15:10 [e]1 Ki. 22:8 [f]ch. 5:12
15:11 [g]Job 26:6 Ps. 139:8 [h]2 Chr. 6:30 John 2:24
15:12 [i]Amos 5:10 2 Tim. 4:3
15:13 [j]ch. 17:22 [k]ch. 12:25

[m] Heb. *short of spirit* [n] Heb. *to nations*
[o] Heb. *belcheth*, or, *bubbleth* [p] Heb. *The healing of the tongue* [q] Or, *Instruction*

14:31 HE THAT OPPRESSETH THE POOR. Whosoever mistreats or takes advantage of a poor person offends God and shows contempt for Him. The poor also are made in the image of God (Gen. 9:6) and are objects of His special mercy and concern (Deut. 15:11). The N.T. reveals that the gospel must be proclaimed to the poor (Mat. 11:5; Acts 4:13; Jas. 2:5); note that Jesus Christ identified Himself with the poor (Luke 2:7; 2 Cor. 8:9; Phil. 2:7).

14:32 THE RIGHTEOUS HATH HOPE IN HIS DEATH. Although the O.T. contains no fully developed doctrine of what happens after death, Proverbs does reveal that the righteous have the hope of life after death. When the wicked die, they have no hope, only dread of final ruin. When the righteous die, they commit themselves to God as their refuge and hope beyond death (cf. 12:28; Ps. 49:14–15; 73:24). Further revelation concerning the eternal destiny of the righteous and the wicked is provided in the N.T. teachings of Christ and the apostles.

15:1 A SOFT ANSWER. When facing anger, a soft answer will encourage reconciliation and peace (cf. 1 Sam. 25:21–34), while harsh words stir up more anger and hostility (see Col. 4:5–6).

15:6 IN THE HOUSE OF THE RIGHTEOUS *IS* MUCH TREASURE. Though the home of the righteous (individually or corporately) may lack earthly riches, it does contain spiritual treasures that greatly enrich and sustain the lives of God's people (cf. vv. 16–17). By contrast, the home of the wicked is filled with much trouble and strife (cf. v. 27; 1:10–19; 10:2).

15:8–9 THE SACRIFICE OF THE WICKED. Only those who are upright and who strive to follow the ways of God are accepted by Him (see 28:9, note).

15:14 THE MOUTH OF FOOLS FEEDETH ON FOOLISHNESS. In this day of high technology in communication media and entertainment, we must carefully guard our hearts and minds. We prove

derstanding seeketh knowledge: but
the mouth of fools feedeth on foolish-
ness.
15 All the days of the afflicted *are*
evil: [l]but he that is of a merry heart
hath a continual feast.
16 [m]Better *is* little with the fear of
the LORD than great treasure and trou-
ble therewith.
17 [n]Better *is* a dinner of herbs
where love is, than a stalled ox and ha-
tred therewith.
18 [o]A wrathful man stirreth up
strife: but *he that is* slow to anger ap-
peaseth strife.
19 [p]The way of the slothful *man is*
as an hedge of thorns: but the way of
the righteous [r]*is* made plain.
20 [q]A wise son maketh a glad fa-
ther: but a foolish man despiseth his
mother.
21 [r]Folly *is* joy to *him that is* [s]des-
titute of wisdom: [s]but a man of under-
standing walketh uprightly.
22 [t]Without counsel purposes are
disappointed: but in the multitude of
counsellors they are established.
23 A man hath joy by the answer of
his mouth: and [u]a word *spoken* [t]in
due season, how good *is it!*
24 [v]The way of life *is* above to the
wise, that he may depart from hell be-
neath.
25 [w]The LORD will destroy the
house of the proud: but [x]he will estab-
lish the border of the widow.
26 [y]The thoughts of the wicked *are*
an abomination to the LORD: [z]but *the*
words of the pure *are* [u]pleasant words.
27 [a]He that is greedy of gain trou-
bleth his own house; but he that hateth
gifts shall live.
28 The heart of the righteous [b]stu-
dieth to answer: but the mouth of the
wicked poureth out evil things.
29 [c]The LORD *is* far from the wick-
ed: but [d]he heareth the prayer of the
righteous.
30 The light of the eyes rejoiceth
the heart: *and* a good report maketh
the bones fat.
31 [e]The ear that heareth the re-
proof of life abideth among the wise.
32 He that refuseth [v]instruction
despiseth his own soul: but he that
[w]heareth reproof [x]getteth under-
standing.
33 [f]The fear of the LORD *is* the in-
struction of wisdom; and [g]before hon-
our *is* humility.

16 THE [h]PREPARATIONS[y] of
the heart in man, [i]and the an-
swer of the tongue, *is* from the LORD.
2 [j]All the ways of a man *are* clean
in his own eyes; but [k]the LORD
weigheth the spirits.
3 [l]Commit[z] thy works unto the
LORD, and thy thoughts shall be estab-
lished.
4 [m]The LORD hath made all *things*

15:15 [l]ch. 17:22 **15:16** [m]Ps. 37:16 1 Tim. 6:6 **15:17** [n]ch. 17:1 **15:18** [o]ch. 26:21 **15:19** [p]ch. 22:5 **15:20** [q]ch. 10:1 **15:21** [r]ch. 10:23 [s]Eph. 5:15 **15:22** [t]ch. 11:14 **15:23** [u]ch. 25:11 **15:24** [v]Phil. 3:20 Col. 3:1,2 **15:25** [w]ch. 12:7 [x]Ps. 68:5,6 **15:26** [y]ch. 6:16,18 [z]Ps. 37:30

15:27 [a]Is. 5:8 **15:28** [b]1 Pet. 3:15 **15:29** [c]Ps. 10:1 & 34:16 [d]Ps. 145:18 **15:31** [e]ver. 5 **15:33** [f]ch. 1:7 [g]ch. 18:12 **16:1** [h]Jer. 10:23 [i]Mat. 10:19 **16:2** [j]ch. 21:2 [k]1 Sam. 16:7 **16:3** [l]Ps. 37:5 **16:4** [m]Is. 43:7

r Heb. *is raised up* s Heb. *void of heart*
t Heb. *in his season* u Heb. *words of pleasantness* v Or, *correction* w Or, *obeyeth*
x Heb. *possesseth an heart* y Or, *disposings*
z Heb. *Roll*

ourselves to be fools if we feed on what offends the Holy Spirit and profanes the righteousness of God (see Rom. 1:32, note). Wise persons will fill their thoughts only with what is good, true, and pure (Phil. 4:8).

15:22 WITHOUT COUNSEL. Proverbs frequently emphasizes the wisdom of seeking the advice of others with regard to our plans and purposes (see also 11:14; 20:18; 24:6).

15:24 THE WAY OF LIFE *IS* ABOVE TO THE WISE. Here is another O.T. glimpse of a future hope. Literally, this verse translates: "The path of life is to the place above for the wise, that he may avoid hell (Heb. *Sheol*) beneath." *Sheol* (sometimes translated as "the grave") can also mean a place of punishment after death (cf. N.T. "Hades"; see Ps. 16:10, note). Thus the godly will go to the place above (heaven) after death and avoid *Sheol* altogether (cf. Ps. 23:6; 73:24–25).

15:29 HE HEARETH THE PRAYER OF THE RIGHTEOUS. See 1 John 3:22, note on prayer and keeping God's commandments.

16:1 THE ANSWER OF THE TONGUE. We as humans may make plans, but the ability to carry out those plans rightly comes from God (cf. vv. 9,33; 21:31).

16:2 CLEAN IN HIS OWN EYES. Believers are often blind to their own faults and their spiritual poverty. If we are honest when we come to God in prayer, He will reveal the real condition of our hearts so that we might be truly clean and better follow the Holy Spirit (Luke 16:15; 1 Cor. 4:4–5; Heb. 4:12).

16:3 COMMIT THY WORKS UNTO THE LORD. Believers should not undertake anything presumptuously, but in all things search for the Lord's will (Jas. 4:14–16). If our works and motives are right, then we can commit them to the Lord and be assured that He will establish them and bless us (see 3:6; Ps. 37:5; 90:16–17; 1 Pet. 5:7).

16:4 THE WICKED FOR THE DAY OF EVIL. Everything will meet with its proper end, and those who do evil will suffer the just punishment of God (cf. v. 5). This passage stresses that God will deal justly with the wicked; He does not create

for himself: [n]yea, even the wicked for the day of evil.

5 [o]Every one *that is* proud in heart *is* an abomination to the LORD: [p]*though* hand *join* in hand, he shall not be [a]unpunished.

6 [q]By mercy and truth iniquity is purged: and [r]by the fear of the LORD *men* depart from evil.

Is. 44:24-25 7 When a man's ways please the LORD, he maketh even his enemies to be at peace with him.

8 [s]Better *is* a little with righteousness than great revenues without right.

9 [t]A man's heart deviseth his way: [u]but the LORD directeth his steps.

10 [b]A divine sentence *is* in the lips of the king: his mouth transgresseth not in judgment.

11 [v]A just weight and balance *are* the LORD'S: [c]all the weights of the bag *are* his work.

12 *It is* an abomination to kings to commit wickedness: for [w]the throne is established by righteousness.

13 [x]Righteous lips *are* the delight of kings; and they love him that speaketh right.

14 [y]The wrath of a king *is as* messengers of death: but a wise man will pacify it.

15 In the light of the king's countenance *is* life; and [z]his favour *is* [a]as a cloud of the latter rain.

16 [b]How much better *is it* to get wisdom than gold! and to get understanding rather to be chosen than silver!

17 The highway of the upright *is* to depart from evil: he that keepeth his way preserveth his soul.

18 Pride *goeth* before destruction, and an haughty spirit before a fall.

19 Better *it is to be* of an humble spirit with the lowly, than to divide the spoil with the proud.

20 [d]He that handleth a matter wisely shall find good: and whoso [c]trusteth in the LORD, happy *is* he.

16:4 [n]Job 21:30
16:5 [o]ch. 8:13 [p]ch. 11:21
16:6 [q]Dan. 4:27 [r]ch. 14:16
16:8 [s]Ps. 37:16
16:9 [t]ch. 19:21 [u]Jer. 10:23
16:11 [v]Lev. 19:36
16:12 [w]ch. 25:5
16:13 [x]ch. 14:35
16:14 [y]ch. 19:12
16:15 [z]ch. 19:12 [a]Job 29:23
16:16 [b]ch. 8:11,19
16:20 [c]Ps. 34:8
16:22 [d]ch. 13:14
16:25 [e]ch. 14:12
16:26 [f]Eccl. 6:7
16:28 [g]ch. 15:18 [h]ch. 17:9
16:29 [i]ch. 1:10
16:31 [j]ch. 20:29
16:32 [k]ch. 19:11
17:1 [l]ch. 15:17
17:2 [m]ch. 10:5

21 The wise in heart shall be called prudent: and the sweetness of the lips increaseth learning.

22 [d]Understanding *is* a wellspring of life unto him that hath it: but the instruction of fools *is* folly.

23 The heart of the wise [e]teacheth his mouth, and addeth learning to his lips.

24 Pleasant words *are as* an honeycomb, sweet to the soul, and health to the bones.

25 [e]There is a way that seemeth right unto a man, but the end thereof *are* the ways of death.

26 [f]He[f] that laboureth laboureth for himself; for his mouth [g]craveth it of him.

27 [h]An ungodly man diggeth up evil: and in his lips *there is* as a burning fire.

28 [g]A froward man [i]soweth strife: and [h]a whisperer separateth chief friends.

29 A violent man [i]enticeth his neighbour, and leadeth him into the way *that is* not good.

30 He shutteth his eyes to devise froward things: moving his lips he bringeth evil to pass.

31 [j]The hoary head *is* a crown of glory, *if* it be found in the way of righteousness.

32 [k]*He that is* slow to anger *is* better than the mighty; and he that ruleth his spirit than he that taketh a city.

33 The lot is cast into the lap; but the whole disposing thereof *is* of the LORD.

17

BETTER *IS* [l]a dry morsel, and quietness therewith, than an house full of [j]sacrifices *with* strife.

2 A wise servant shall have rule over [m]a son that causeth shame, and

[a] Heb. *held innocent* [b] Heb. *Divination* [c] Heb. *all the stones* [d] Or, *He that understandeth a matter* [e] Heb. *maketh wise* [f] Heb. *The soul of him that laboureth* [g] Heb. *boweth unto him* [h] Heb. *A man of Belial* [i] Heb. *sendeth forth* [j] Or, *good cheer*

---

or encourage wickedness (see Jas. 1:13,17).

16:5 PROUD IN HEART. See Jas. 4:6,16, notes.

16:7 HIS ENEMIES TO BE AT PEACE. This phrase applies to God's promise to Israel that their land would be preserved from hostile attack if they would do His will (Ex. 34:24; 2 Chr. 17:10). N.T. believers, however, will experience the hostility of their enemies — Satan and the world — because in many cases they are doing the will of God (cf. Mat. 5:10; Luke 21:17–18; John 15:20; Acts 14:19).

16:33 LOT IS CAST INTO THE LAP. Like vv. 1,9, this verse refers to God's providence and guidance in the life of the righteous. It does not mean that God directly controls and determines every flip of the coin in life. Rather, it simply states the spiritual principle that a righteous person who commits his or her way to the Lord (vv. 3,9) and acknowledges Him will be directed by the Lord (see 3:5–6, notes).

shall have part of the inheritance among the brethren.

3 The refining pot *is* for silver, and the furnace for gold: [n]but the LORD trieth the hearts.

4 A wicked doer giveth heed to false lips; *and* a liar giveth ear to a naughty tongue.

5 [o]Whoso mocketh the poor reproacheth his Maker: *and* he that is glad at calamities shall not be [k]unpunished.

6 Children's children *are* the crown of old men; and the glory of children *are* their fathers.

7 [l]Excellent speech becometh not a fool: much less do [m]lying lips a prince.

8 A gift *is as* [n]a precious stone in the eyes of him that hath it: whithersoever it turneth, it prospereth.

9 [p]He that covereth a transgression [o]seeketh love; but [q]he that repeateth a matter separateth *very* friends.

10 [p]A reproof entereth more into a wise man than an hundred stripes into a fool.

11 An evil *man* seeketh only rebellion: therefore a cruel messenger shall be sent against him.

12 Let [r]a bear robbed of her whelps meet a man, rather than a fool in his folly.

13 Whoso [s]rewardeth evil for good, evil shall not depart from his house.

14 The beginning of strife *is as* when one letteth out water: therefore [t]leave off contention, before it be meddled with.

15 [u]He that justifieth the wicked, and he that condemneth the just, even they both *are* abomination to the LORD.

16 Wherefore *is there* a price in the hand of a fool to get wisdom, [v]seeing *he hath* no heart *to it?*

17:3 [n]Jer. 17:10
17:5 [o]ch. 14:31
17:9 [p]ch. 10:12 [q]ch. 16:28
17:12 [r]Hos. 13:8
17:13 [s]Ps. 109:4,5 Jer. 18:20
17:14 [t]ch. 20:3
17:15 [u]Ex. 23:7 Is. 5:23
17:16 [v]ch. 21:25,26
17:17 [w]Ruth 1:16
17:18 [x]ch. 6:1
17:19 [y]ch. 16:18
17:20 [z]Jas. 3:8
17:21 [a]ch. 10:1
17:22 [b]ch. 12:25 [c]Ps. 22:15
17:23 [d]Ex. 23:8
17:24 [e]Eccl. 2:14
17:25 [f]ch. 10:1
17:26 [g]ch:18:5
17:27 [h]Jas. 1:19
17:28 [i]Job 13:5

17 [w]A friend loveth at all times, and a brother is born for adversity.

18 [x]A man void of [q]understanding striketh hands, *and* becometh surety in the presence of his friend.

19 He loveth transgression that loveth strife: *and* [y]he that exalteth his gate seeketh destruction.

20 [r]He that hath a froward heart findeth no good: and he that hath [z]a perverse tongue falleth into mischief.

21 [a]He that begetteth a fool *doeth it* to his sorrow: and the father of a fool hath no joy.

22 [b]A merry heart doeth good [s]*like* a medicine: [c]but a broken spirit drieth the bones.

23 A wicked *man* taketh a gift out of the bosom [d]to pervert the ways of judgment.

24 [e]Wisdom *is* before him that hath understanding; but the eyes of a fool *are* in the ends of the earth.

25 [f]A foolish son *is* a grief to his father, and bitterness to her that bare him.

26 Also [g]to punish the just *is* not good, *nor* to strike princes for equity.

27 [h]He that hath knowledge spareth his words: *and* a man of understanding is of [t]an excellent spirit.

28 [i]Even a fool, when he holdeth his peace, is counted wise: *and* he that shutteth his lips *is esteemed* a man of understanding.

18 THROUGH [u]DESIRE a man, having separated himself, seeketh *and* intermeddleth with all wisdom.

2 A fool hath no delight in under-

[k] Heb. *held innocent* [l] Heb. *A lip of excellency* [m] Heb. *a lip of lying* [n] Heb. *a stone of grace* [o] Or, *procureth* [p] Or, *A reproof aweth more a wise man, than to strike a fool an hundred times* [q] Heb. *heart* [r] Heb. *The froward of heart* [s] Or, *to a medicine* [t] Or, *a cool spirit* [u] Or, *He that separateth himself seeketh according to his desire and intermeddleth in every business*

17:5 WHOSO MOCKETH THE POOR. See 14:31, note.

17:8 A GIFT. A gift (i.e., bribe) will sometimes bring temporary success and wealth. Bribery, however, is sin; it is therefore condemned in Scripture because it hinders justice from being realized (v. 23; 15:27; 1 Sam. 12:3; Is. 1:23; 1 Tim. 6:10).

17:13 EVIL SHALL NOT DEPART FROM HIS HOUSE. This truth is illustrated in the life of David. He "rewarded" Uriah's integrity and faithfulness with evil. From that point on, evil did not depart from David's own house (2 Sam. 12:10–12).

17:17 A BROTHER IS BORN FOR ADVERSITY. A brother is born to help us in time of need.

17:18 BECOMETH SURETY. See 6:1, note.

17:27 HE THAT HATH KNOWLEDGE SPARETH HIS WORDS. The wise will restrain their speech and be cautious in what they say. They will not exaggerate the truth or harm others when speaking; rather, they will be careful to speak accurately and to edify others (cf. Ps. 39:1–2).

standing, but that his heart may discover itself.

3 When the wicked cometh, *then* cometh also contempt, and with ignominy reproach.

4 [j]The words of a man's mouth *are as* deep waters, [k]*and* the wellspring of wisdom *as* a flowing brook.

5 [l]*It is* not good to accept the person of the wicked, to overthrow the righteous in judgment.

6 A fool's lips enter into contention, and his mouth calleth for strokes.

7 [m]A fool's mouth *is* his destruction, and his lips *are* the snare of his soul.

8 [n]The words of a [v]talebearer *are* [w]as wounds, and they go down into the [x]innermost parts of the belly.

9 He also that is slothful in his work is [o]brother to him that is a great waster.

10 [p]The name of the LORD *is* a strong tower: the righteous runneth into it, and [y]is safe.

11 [q]The rich man's wealth *is* his strong city, and as an high wall in his own conceit.

12 [r]Before destruction the heart of man is haughty, and before honour *is* humility.

13 He that [z]answereth a matter [s]before he heareth *it*, it *is* folly and shame unto him.

14 The spirit of a man will sustain his infirmity; but a wounded spirit who can bear?

15 The heart of the prudent getteth knowledge; and the ear of the wise seeketh knowledge.

16 [t]A man's gift maketh room for him, and bringeth him before great men.

17 *He that is* first in his own cause *seemeth* just; but his neighbour cometh and searcheth him.

18 The lot causeth contentions to cease, and parteth between the mighty.

19 A brother offended *is harder to be won* than a strong city: and *their* contentions *are* like the bars of a castle.

20 [u]A man's belly shall be satisfied with the fruit of his mouth; *and* with the increase of his lips shall he be filled.

21 [v]Death and life *are* in the power of the tongue: and they that love it shall eat the fruit thereof.

22 [w]*Whoso* findeth a wife findeth a good *thing*, and obtaineth favour of the LORD.

23 The poor useth entreaties; but the rich answereth [x]roughly.

24 A man *that hath* friends must show himself friendly: [y]and there is a friend *that* sticketh closer than a brother.

19 BETTER [z]*IS* the poor that walketh in his integrity, than *he that is* perverse in his lips, and is a fool.

2 Also, *that* the soul *be* without knowledge, *it is* not good; and he that hasteth with *his* feet sinneth.

3 The foolishness of man perverteth his way: [a]and his heart fretteth against the LORD.

4 [b]Wealth maketh many friends; but the poor is separated from his neighbour.

5 [c]A false witness shall not be [a]unpunished, and *he that* speaketh lies shall not escape.

6 [d]Many will entreat the favour of the prince: and [e]every man *is* a friend to [b]him that giveth gifts.

7 [f]All the brethren of the poor do hate him: how much more do his friends go [g]far from him? he pursueth *them with* words, *yet* they *are* wanting *to him*.

18:4 [j]ch. 10:11 [k]Jas. 3:17 **18:5** [l]Lev. 19:15 **18:7** [m]ch. 10:14 **18:8** [n]ch. 12:18 **18:9** [o]ch. 28:24 **18:10** [p]2 Sam. 22:3 **18:11** [q]ch. 10:15 **18:12** [r]ch. 16:18 **18:13** [s]John 7:51 **18:16** [t]Gen. 32:20 1 Sam. 25:27

18:20 [u]ch. 12:14 **18:21** [v]Mat. 12:37 **18:22** [w]ch. 31:10 **18:23** [x]Jas. 2:3 **18:24** [y]ch. 17:17 **19:1** [z]ch. 28:6 **19:3** [a]Ps. 37:7 **19:4** [b]ch. 14:20 **19:5** [c]Ex. 23:1 **19:6** [d]ch. 29:26 [e]ch. 17:8 **19:7** [f]ch. 14:20 [g]Ps. 38:11

[v] Or, *whisperer* [w] Or, *like as when men are wounded* [x] Heb. *chambers* [y] Heb. *is set aloft* [z] Heb. *returneth a word* [a] Heb. *held innocent* [b] Heb. *a man of gifts*

18:10–11 THE NAME OF THE LORD. The name of the Lord represents His person, authority, and character (cf. Ex. 3:14–15; Acts 4:12). The righteous turn to the Lord for refuge and help in trouble. However, the misguided rich believe money is their source of security during the storms of life (see article on RICHES AND POVERTY, p. 1568).

18:12 HEART OF MAN IS HAUGHTY. Pride is a spirit of self-importance that involves trusting in ourselves. Boasting and arrogance are sins associated with pride, and they will bring us to destruction (cf. 15:33; 16:18). Pride is deceptive (Jer. 49:16), making a humble response to God and others impossible. God opposes the proud, but gives grace and honor to the humble (Jas. 4:6).

19:4 WEALTH MAKETH MANY FRIENDS. This proverb speaks of what often is, not of the way things should be. Though superficial friends are attracted to the wealthy as flies are drawn to honey, a poor person has few friends because he or she cannot provide anyone with financial or personal gain (cf. v. 6). The N.T. warns against this attitude among believers (Jas. 2:1–9).

8 He that getteth [c]wisdom loveth
his own soul: he that keepeth under-
standing [h]shall find good.
9 [i]A false witness shall not be un-
punished, and *he that* speaketh lies
shall perish.
10 Delight is not seemly for a fool;
much less [j]for a servant to have rule
over princes.
11 [k]The [d]discretion of a man de-
ferreth his anger; [l]and *it is* his glory
to pass over a transgression.
12 [m]The king's wrath *is* as the
roaring of a lion; but his favour *is* [n]as
dew upon the grass.
13 [o]A foolish son *is* the calamity of
his father: [p]and the contentions of a
wife *are* a continual dropping.
14 [q]House and riches *are* the inher-
itance of fathers: and [r]a prudent wife
is from the LORD.
15 [s]Slothfulness casteth into a
deep sleep; and an idle soul shall [t]suf-
fer hunger.
16 [u]He that keepeth the command-
ment keepeth his own soul; *but* he that
despiseth his ways shall die.
17 [v]He that hath pity upon the
poor lendeth unto the LORD; and [e]that
which he hath given will he pay him
again.
18 [w]Chasten thy son while there is
hope, and let not thy soul spare [f]for
his crying.
19 A man of great wrath shall suffer
punishment: for if thou deliver *him*, yet
thou must [g]do it again.
20 Hear counsel, and receive in-
struction, that thou mayest be wise
[x]in thy latter end.
21 *There are* many devices in a
man's heart; [y]nevertheless the coun-
sel of the LORD, that shall stand.
22 The desire of a man *is* his kind-
ness: and a poor man *is* better than a
liar.
23 [z]The fear of the LORD *tendeth* to
life: and *he that hath it* shall abide satis-
fied; he shall not be visited with evil.
24 [a]A slothful *man* hideth his hand
in *his* bosom, and will not so much as
bring it to his mouth again.
25 Smite a scorner, and the simple
[b]will[h] beware: and [c]reprove one
that hath understanding, *and* he will
understand knowledge.
26 He that wasteth *his* father, *and*
chaseth away *his* mother, *is* [d]a son
that causeth shame, and bringeth re-
proach.
27 Cease, my son, to hear the in-
struction *that causeth* to err from the
words of knowledge.
28 [i]An ungodly witness scorneth
judgment: and [e]the mouth of the
wicked devoureth iniquity.
29 Judgments are prepared for
scorners, [f]and stripes for the back of
fools.

20
WINE [g]*IS* a mocker, strong
drink *is* raging: and whosoever
is deceived thereby is not wise.

19:8 [h]ch. 16:20 **19:9** [i]ver. 5 **19:10** [j]ch. 30:22 **19:11** [k]Jas. 1:19 [l]ch. 16:32 **19:12** [m]ch. 16:14 [n]Hos. 14:5 **19:13** [o]ch. 10:1 [p]ch. 21:9,19 **19:14** [q]2 Cor. 12:14 [r]ch. 18:22 **19:15** [s]ch. 6:9 [t]ch. 10:4 **19:16** [u]Luke 10:28 **19:17** [v]2 Cor. 9:6 **19:18** [w]ch. 13:24 **19:20** [x]Ps. 37:37 **19:21** [y]Heb. 6:17 **19:23** [z]1 Tim. 4:8 **19:24** [a]ch. 15:19 **19:25** [b]Deut. 13:11 [c]ch. 9:8 **19:26** [d]ch. 17:2 **19:28** [e]Job 15:16 **19:29** [f]ch. 26:3 **20:1** [g]Gen. 9:21

[c] Heb. *an heart* [d] Or, *prudence* [e] Or, *his deed* [f] Or, *to his destruction:* or, *to cause him to die* [g] Heb. *add* [h] Heb. *will be cunning* [i] Heb. *A witness of Belial*

19:14 A PRUDENT WIFE *IS* FROM THE LORD. When seeking a marriage partner, prudence is more important than appearance. God's wisdom, guidance, and blessing are essential if we want to have a happy marriage. A believer should seek to marry someone who is deeply committed to the Lord Jesus, His word, and the standards of His kingdom. Marriage to a person of godly character is a special blessing of God (cf. 18:22; Gen. 24:14). To enter into marriage without the guidance of God is to invite suffering, regret, and disaster.

19:17 LENDETH TO THE LORD. Graciously giving of what we have to help the poor is a way of serving the Lord. He will repay those who do this (see 6:1, note).

19:18 CHASTEN THY SON. Children should be disciplined at a young age while there is opportunity to mold their lives for good and to teach them godly ways. When parents fail to do so, they become partially responsible for subsequent ruin that comes to the lives of their children (see 13:24, note).

20:1 WINE *IS* A MOCKER, STRONG DRINK *IS* RAGING. This verse describes the nature and potential evil of fermented drink. Note that the intoxicating drink itself is condemned along with its effects. (1) Wine as "a mocker" frequently leads to scorn and disdain for what is good (cf. 9:7–8; 13:1; 14:6; 15:12). Alcoholic beverages as "raging" often cause disturbances, hostility, and conflict in families and society.

(2) Wine and intoxicating drink are labeled a mocker and raging regardless of the quantity used.

(3) "Whosoever is deceived" into thinking that intoxicating beverages are acceptable, good, healthy, or safe when taken moderately ignores the clear warning of Scripture (23:29–35).

(4) This condemnation of intoxicating drink does not mean the Bible condemns the use of all wine. *Yayin*, the common Hebrew word for "wine" in the O.T., often refers to unfermented grape juice; the Bible does not condemn the consumption of unfermented wine (see 23:29–35, notes; see article on WINE IN THE OLD TESTAMENT, p. 220).

2 [h]The fear of a king *is* as the roaring of a lion: *whoso* provoketh him to anger [i]sinneth *against* his own soul.

3 [j]*It is* an honour for a man to cease from strife: but every fool will be meddling.

4 [k]The sluggard will not plow by reason of the [j]cold; [l]*therefore* shall he beg in harvest, and *have* nothing.

5 Counsel in the heart of man *is like* deep water; but a man of understanding will draw it out.

6 [m]Most men will proclaim every one his own [k]goodness: but [n]a faithful man who can find?

7 [o]The just *man* walketh in his integrity: [p]his children *are* blessed after him.

8 [q]A king that sitteth in the throne of judgment scattereth away all evil with his eyes.

9 [r]Who can say, I have made my heart clean, I am pure from my sin?

10 [s]Divers[l] weights, *and* [m]divers measures, both of them *are* alike abomination to the LORD.

11 Even a child is [t]known by his doings, whether his work *be* pure, and whether *it be* right.

12 [u]The hearing ear, and the seeing eye, the LORD hath made even both of them.

13 [v]Love not sleep, lest thou come to poverty; open thine eyes, *and* thou shalt be satisfied with bread.

14 *It is* naught, *it is* naught, saith the buyer: but when he is gone his way, then he boasteth.

15 There is gold, and a multitude of rubies: but [w]the lips of knowledge *are* a precious jewel.

16 [x]Take his garment that is surety *for* a stranger: and take a pledge of him for a strange woman.

20:2 [h]ch. 19:12 [i]ch. 8:36
20:3 [j]ch. 17:14
20:4 [k]ch. 10:4 [l]ch. 19:15
20:6 [m]Mat. 6:2 Luke 18:11 [n]Luke 18:8
20:7 [o]2 Cor. 1:12 [p]Ps. 37:26
20:8 [q]ver. 26
20:9 [r]1 Ki. 8:46
20:10 [s]Deut. 25:13
20:11 [t]Mat. 7:16
20:12 [u]Ex. 4:11
20:13 [v]Rom. 12:11
20:15 [w]ch. 3:15
20:16 [x]ch. 22:26
20:17 [y]ch. 9:17
20:18 [z]ch. 24:6 [a]Luke 14:31
20:19 [b]ch. 11:13 [c]Rom. 16:18
20:20 [d]Mat. 15:4 [e]Job 18:5,6
20:21 [f]ch. 28:20 [g]Hab. 2:6
20:22 [h]Rom. 12:17 [i]2 Sam. 16:12
20:23 [j]ver. 10
20:24 [k]Ps. 37:23
20:25 [l]Eccl. 5:4,5
20:26 [m]Ps. 101:8
20:27 [n]1 Cor. 2:11
20:28 [o]Ps. 101:1

17 [y]Bread[n] of deceit *is* sweet to a man; but afterwards his mouth shall be filled with gravel.

18 [z]*Every* purpose is established by counsel: [a]and with good advice make war.

19 [b]He that goeth about *as* a talebearer revealeth secrets: therefore meddle not with him [c]that [o]flattereth with his lips.

20 [d]Whoso curseth his father or his mother, [e]his [p]lamp shall be put out in obscure darkness.

21 [f]An inheritance *may be* gotten hastily at the beginning; [g]but the end thereof shall not be blessed.

22 [h]Say not thou, I will recompense evil; *but* [i]wait on the LORD, and he shall save thee.

23 [j]Divers weights *are* an abomination unto the LORD; and [q]a false balance *is* not good.

24 [k]Man's goings *are* of the LORD; how can a man then understand his own way?

25 *It is* a snare to the man *who* devoureth *that which is* holy, and [l]after vows to make inquiry.

26 [m]A wise king scattereth the wicked, and bringeth the wheel over them.

27 [n]The spirit of man *is* the [r]candle of the LORD, searching all the inward parts of the belly.

28 [o]Mercy and truth preserve the king: and his throne is upholden by mercy.

29 The glory of young men *is* their

j Or, *winter* **k** Or, *bounty* **l** Heb. *A stone and a stone* **m** Heb. *an ephah and an ephah* **n** Heb. *Bread of lying,* or, *falsehood* **o** Or, *enticeth* **p** Or, *candle* **q** Heb. *balances of deceit* **r** Or, *lamp*

20:9 WHO CAN SAY . . . CLEAN . . . PURE. Apart from having been redeemed, no one has kept his or her heart clean and free from the guilt of sin (cf. Rom. 3:9–12). Those who have come to God for forgiveness and cleansing have "clean hands, and a pure heart" (Ps. 24:4). Only by God's grace and redemption can anyone live a life "void of offence toward God, and *toward* men" (see Acts 24:16, note).

20:22 I WILL RECOMPENSE EVIL. When mistreated, we must not take vengeance into our own hands (cf. Deut. 32:35; Rom. 12:19; Heb. 10:30). Rather, we must take our suffering to the Lord and entrust ourselves to our faithful God (cf. 1 Pet. 2:23; 4:19). He will in His own time avenge the injustices experienced by the righteous who cry day and night unto Him (Luke 18:7–8).

20:24 HOW CAN A MAN THEN UNDERSTAND HIS OWN WAY? God sometimes directs the path of the righteous in such a way that they find it difficult to understand what is happening. We may be unable to see good in some circumstances, but the Bible encourages us to believe that God is nevertheless working behind the scenes for our good (see Rom. 8:28, note; cf. Ps. 37:23).

20:27 THE SPIRIT OF MAN *IS* THE CANDLE OF THE LORD. The human spirit is the center of conscience and discernment, providing a window for God's light to bring spiritual understanding to our inner life (cf. Job 32:8; Mat. 6:23).

strength: and [p]the beauty of old men *is* the gray head.

30 The blueness of a wound [s]cleanseth away evil: so *do* stripes the inward parts of the belly.

21

THE KING'S heart *is* in the hand of the LORD, *as* the rivers of water: he turneth it whithersoever he will.

2 [q]Every way of a man *is* right in his own eyes: [r]but the LORD pondereth the hearts.

3 [s]To do justice and judgment *is* more acceptable to the LORD than sacrifice.

4 [t]An[t] high look, and a proud heart, *and* [u]the plowing of the wicked, *is* sin.

5 [u]The thoughts of the diligent *tend* only to plenteousness; but of every one *that is* hasty only to want.

6 [v]The getting of treasures by a lying tongue *is* a vanity tossed to and fro of them that seek death.

7 The robbery of the wicked shall [v]destroy them; because they refuse to do judgment.

8 The way of man *is* froward and strange: but *as for* the pure, his work *is* right.

9 *It is* better to dwell in a corner of the housetop, than with [w]a brawling woman in [x]a wide house.

10 [w]The soul of the wicked desireth evil: his neighbour [y]findeth no favour in his eyes.

11 [x]When the scorner is punished, the simple is made wise: and when the wise is instructed, he receiveth knowledge.

12 The righteous *man* wisely considereth the house of the wicked: *but* *God* overthroweth the wicked for *their* wickedness.

13 [y]Whoso stoppeth his ears at the cry of the poor, he also shall cry himself, but shall not be heard.

14 A gift in secret pacifieth anger: and a reward in the bosom strong wrath.

15 *It is* joy to the just to do judgment: but destruction *shall be* to the workers of iniquity.

16 The man that wandereth out of the way of understanding shall remain in the congregation of the dead.

17 He that loveth [z]pleasure *shall be* a poor man: he that loveth wine and oil shall not be rich.

18 The wicked *shall be* a ransom for the righteous, and the transgressor for the upright.

19 *It is* better to dwell [a]in the wilderness, than with a contentious and an angry woman.

20 [z]*There is* treasure to be desired and oil in the dwelling of the wise; but a foolish man spendeth it up.

21 [a]He that followeth after righteousness and mercy findeth life, righteousness, and honour.

22 [b]A wise *man* scaleth the city of the mighty, and casteth down the strength of the confidence thereof.

23 [c]Whoso keepeth his mouth and his tongue keepeth his soul from troubles.

24 Proud *and* haughty scorner *is* his

20:29 [p]ch. 16:31
21:2 [q]ch. 16:2 [r]ch. 24:12 Luke 16:15
21:3 [s]1 Sam. 15:22
21:4 [t]ch. 6:17
21:5 [u]ch. 10:4
21:6 [v]2 Pet. 2:3
21:10 [w]Jas. 4:5
21:11 [x]ch. 19:25
21:13 [y]Mat. 7:2
21:20 [z]Ps. 112:3 Mat. 25:3,4
21:21 [a]Mat. 5:6
21:22 [b]Eccl. 9:14
21:23 [c]ch. 12:13 Jas. 3:2

[s]Heb. is *a purging medicine against evil* [t]Heb. *Haughtiness of eyes* [u]Or, *the light of the wicked* [v]Heb. *saw them,* or, *dwell with them* [w]Heb. *a woman of contentions* [x]Heb. *an house of society* [y]Heb. *is not favoured* [z]Or, *sport* [a]Heb. *in the land of the desert*

21:1 THE KING'S HEART *IS* IN THE HAND OF THE LORD. This verse does not mean that everything a national leader desires or does comes directly from the Lord. God is certainly not the author of the evil perpetrated by rulers (Jas. 1:13–15). Rather, God has ultimate authority over the rulers of the world and at times chooses to influence their decisions so as to further His redemptive purpose in history (cf. Ex. 10:1–2; Ezra 7:21; Is. 10:5–7; 45:1–6). The N.T. teaches that the prayers of God's people influence the Lord to direct the decisions of rulers more fully in accordance with His will (1 Tim. 2:1–3).

21:3 MORE ACCEPTABLE . . . THAN SACRIFICE. God desires His people to be righteous and just rather than to be merely involved in religious activities. Sacrifice, worship, and offerings are unacceptable to Him if we are not living according to His will (cf. Hos. 6:6; Mic. 6:7–8; Rom. 12:1–2; Heb. 10:5–9). Gifts offered to God should be accompanied by holy living; otherwise, they are detestable to Him (v. 27).

21:13 THE CRY OF THE POOR. If we want God to hear our prayers when we are in need, then we must also hear and respond in love to the needs of others (cf. Mat. 25:31–46; Luke 16:19–31; Jas. 2:13).

21:20 A FOOLISH MAN SPENDETH IT UP. Those who are wise and prudent will have the necessities of life, while the foolish spend all they have to acquire nonessential things for pleasure (v. 17). Today many foolishly use easy credit, which often proves to be their undoing. God is pleased with those who wisely accept a lower standard of living rather than go into debt and live beyond their means.

name, who dealeth [b]in proud wrath.

25 The desire of the slothful killeth him; for his hands refuse to labour.

26 He coveteth greedily all the day long: but the righteous giveth and spareth not.

27 [d]The sacrifice of the wicked *is* abomination: how much more, *when* he bringeth it [c]with a wicked mind?

28 [d]A false witness shall perish: but the man that heareth speaketh constantly.

29 A wicked man hardeneth his face: but *as for* the upright, he [e]directeth his way.

30 [e]*There is* no wisdom nor understanding nor counsel against the LORD.

31 The horse *is* prepared against the day of battle: but [f]safety[f] *is* of the LORD.

22 A [g]*GOOD* name *is* rather to be chosen than great riches, *and* [g]loving favour rather than silver and gold.

2 The rich and poor meet together: the LORD *is* the maker of them all.

3 A prudent *man* foreseeth the evil, and hideth himself: but the simple pass on, and are punished.

4 [h]By humility *and* the fear of the LORD *are* riches, and honour, and life.

5 Thorns *and* snares *are* in the way of the froward: he that doth keep his soul shall be far from them.

6 [h]Train[i] up a child [j]in the way he should go: and when he is old, he will not depart from it.

7 The rich ruleth over the poor, and the borrower *is* servant [k]to the lender.

21:27 [d]Jer. 6:20
21:30 [e]Is. 8:9,10 Jer. 9:23 Acts 5:39
21:31 [f]Ps. 3:8
22:1 [g]Eccl. 7:1
22:6 [h]Eph. 6:4 2 Tim. 3:15
22:9 [i]2 Cor. 9:6
22:10 [j]Ps. 101:5
22:11 [k]Ps. 101:6
22:13 [l]ch. 26:13
22:14 [m]ch. 2:16 & 5:3 & 7:5 [n]Eccl. 7:26
22:15 [o]ch. 13:24

8 He that soweth iniquity shall reap vanity: [l]and the rod of his anger shall fail.

9 [i]He[m] that hath a bountiful eye shall be blessed; for he giveth of his bread to the poor.

10 [j]Cast out the scorner, and contention shall go out; yea, strife and reproach shall cease.

11 [k]He that loveth pureness of heart, [n]*for* the grace of his lips the king *shall be* his friend.

12 The eyes of the LORD preserve knowledge, and he overthroweth [o]the words of the transgressor.

13 [l]The slothful *man* saith, *There is* a lion without, I shall be slain in the streets.

14 [m]The mouth of strange women *is* a deep pit: [n]he that is abhorred of the LORD shall fall therein.

15 Foolishness *is* bound in the heart of a child; *but* [o]the rod of correction shall drive it far from him.

16 He that oppresseth the poor to increase his *riches, and* he that giveth to the rich, *shall* surely *come* to want.

Hear the words of the wise

17 Bow down thine ear, and hear

[b] Heb. *in the wrath of pride* [c] Heb. *in wickedness?* [d] Heb. *A witness of lies* [e] Or, *considereth* [f] Or, *victory* [g] Or, *favour is better than* [h] Or, *The reward of humility* [i] Or, *Catechise* [j] Heb. *in his way* [k] Heb. *to the man that lendeth* [l] Or, *and with the rod of his anger he shall be consumed* [m] Heb. *Good of eye* [n] Or, and hath *grace in his lips* [o] Or, *the matters*

22:4 RICHES, AND HONOUR, AND LIFE. Those who remain faithful to God will receive these blessings at His own appointed time. All God's people will be among those who "inherit the earth" (Mat. 5:5). Even now God's poor are considered rich in spiritual wealth and honor (Rev. 2:9).

22:6 TRAIN UP A CHILD IN THE WAY HE SHOULD GO. Parents must commit themselves to the godly training and discipline of their children (cf. v. 15; 13:24; 19:18; 23:13–14; 29:17). (1) The Hebrew word for "train" means to "dedicate." Thus Christian training has as its purpose the dedication of our children to God and His will, accomplished by separating them from evil influences of the world and by instructing them in godly conduct. The same root word can also mean to "cultivate a taste for"; parents must encourage their children to seek God for themselves and thus to enjoy genuine spiritual experiences they will never forget.

(2) "He will not depart from it." The general principle is that a properly trained child will not depart from the godly ways taught by his or her parents. However, this is not an absolute guarantee that all children of God-fearing parents will remain true to God and His word. When living in an evil society where many of God's people are themselves unfaithful, the children of godly parents can be influenced to sin and to give in to temptation (see Ezek. 14:14–20, where God speaks of an apostasy so great that even righteous men like Noah, Daniel, and Job could not save their own sons or daughters).

22:7 BORROWER *IS* SERVANT TO THE LENDER. Those who live beyond their means end up enslaved to their creditors (see 21:20, note).

22:9 BOUNTIFUL EYE SHALL BE BLESSED. God blesses those who are generous (see 11:24–25, note).

22:14 HE THAT IS ABHORRED OF THE LORD. Those who turn from God, seek their own way, and resent reproof fall under God's wrath and curse. He turns them over to sexual impurity and shameful lust (see Rom. 1:18–21, notes).

the words of the wise, and apply thine heart unto my knowledge.
18 For *it is* a pleasant thing if thou keep them [p]within thee; they shall withal be fitted in thy lips.
19 That thy trust may be in the LORD, I have made known to thee this day, [q]even to thee.
20 Have not I written to thee excellent things in counsels and knowledge,
21 [p]That I might make thee know the certainty of the words of truth; [q]that thou mightest answer the words of truth [r]to them that send unto thee?
22 Rob not the poor, because he *is* poor: neither oppress the afflicted in the gate:
23 [r]For the LORD will plead their cause, and spoil the soul of those that spoiled them.
24 Make no friendship with an angry man; and with a furious man thou shalt not go:
25 Lest thou learn his ways, and get a snare to thy soul.
26 [s]Be not thou *one* of them that strike hands, *or* of them that are sureties for debts.
27 If thou hast nothing to pay, why should he take away thy bed from under thee?
28 [t]Remove not the ancient [s]landmark, which thy fathers have set.
29 Seest thou a man diligent in his business? he shall stand before kings; he shall not stand before [t]mean *men.*

23 WHEN THOU sittest to eat with a ruler, consider diligently what *is* before thee:
2 And put a knife to thy throat, if thou *be* a man given to appetite.
3 Be not desirous of his dainties: for they *are* deceitful meat.
4 [u]Labour not to be rich: [v]cease from thine own wisdom.
5 [u]Wilt thou set thine eyes upon that which is not? for *riches* certainly make themselves wings; they fly away as an eagle toward heaven.
6 Eat thou not the bread of *him that hath* [w]an evil eye, neither desire thou his dainty meats:
7 For as he thinketh in his heart, so *is* he: Eat and drink, [x]saith he to thee; but his heart *is* not with thee.
8 The morsel *which* thou hast eaten shalt thou vomit up, and lose thy sweet words.
9 [y]Speak not in the ears of a fool: for he will despise the wisdom of thy words.
10 Remove not the old [s]landmark; and enter not into the fields of the fatherless:
11 [z]For their redeemer *is* mighty; he shall plead their cause with thee.
12 Apply thine heart unto instruction, and thine ears to the words of knowledge.
13 [a]Withhold not correction from the child: for *if* thou beatest him with the rod, he shall not die.
14 Thou shalt beat him with the rod, and shalt deliver his soul from hell.
15 My son, if thine heart be wise, my heart shall rejoice, [v]even mine.
16 Yea, my reins shall rejoice, when thy lips speak right things.
17 [b]Let not thine heart envy sinners: but [c]*be thou* in the fear of the LORD all the day long.
18 [d]For surely there is an [w]end; and thine expectation shall not be cut off.
19 Hear thou, my son, and be wise, and guide thine heart in the way.
20 [e]Be not among winebibbers; among riotous eaters [x]of flesh:
21 For the drunkard and the glutton shall come to poverty: and drowsiness shall clothe *a man* with rags.
22 [f]Hearken unto thy father that begat thee, and despise not thy mother when she is old.
23 [g]Buy the truth, and sell *it* not; *also* wisdom, and instruction, and understanding.
24 [h]The father of the righteous shall greatly rejoice: and he that begetteth a wise *child* shall have joy of him.
25 Thy father and thy mother shall be glad, and she that bare thee shall rejoice.
26 My son, give me thine heart, and let thine eyes observe my ways.

22:21 [p]Luke 1:3,4 [q]1 Pet. 3:15
22:23 [r]1 Sam. 24:12 Ps. 12:5
22:26 [s]ch. 11:15
22:28 [t]Deut. 19:14
23:4 [u]1 Tim. 6:9 [v]Rom. 12:16
23:6 [w]Deut. 15:9
23:7 [x]Ps. 12:2
23:9 [y]ch. 9:8 Mat. 7:6
23:11 [z]ch. 22:23
23:13 [a]ch. 13:24
23:17 [b]Ps. 37:1 [c]ch. 28:14
23:18 [d]Ps. 37:37
23:20 [e]Is. 5:22
23:22 [f]ch. 1:8 Eph. 6:1,2
23:23 [g]Mat. 13:44
23:24 [h]ch. 10:1

[p] Heb. *in thy belly* [q] Or, trust *thou also* [r] Or, *to those that send thee?* [s] Or, *bound* [t] Heb. *obscure* men [u] Heb. *Wilt thou cause thine eyes to fly upon* [v] Or, *even I* will rejoice [w] Or, *reward* [x] Heb. *of their flesh*

23:4 LABOUR NOT TO BE RICH. This command is repeated in the N.T. (Mat. 6:19; 1 Tim. 6:9–11; Heb. 13:5; see article on RICHES AND POVERTY, p. 1568).

27 [i]For a whore *is* a deep ditch;
and a strange woman *is* a narrow pit.
28 [j]She also lieth in wait [y]as *for*
a prey, and increaseth the transgres-
sors among men.
29 [k]Who hath woe? who hath sor-
row? who hath contentions? who hath
babbling? who hath wounds without
cause? who [l]hath redness of eyes?
30 [m]They that tarry long at the
wine; they that go to seek [n]mixed
wine.
31 Look not thou upon the wine
when it is red, when it giveth his colour
in the cup, *when* it moveth itself aright.
32 At the last it biteth like a ser-
pent, and stingeth like [z]an adder.
33 Thine eyes shall behold strange
women, and thine heart shall utter per-
verse things.
34 Yea, thou shalt be as he that
lieth down [a]in the midst of the sea, or
as he that lieth upon the top of a mast.
35 [o]They have stricken me, *shalt
thou say, and* I was not sick; they have
beaten me, *and* [p]I[b] felt *it* not: when
shall I awake? I will seek it yet again.

24 BE NOT thou [q]envious against
evil men, neither desire to be
with them.

23:27 [i]ch. 22:14
23:28 [j]ch. 7:12 Eccl. 7:26
23:29 [k]Is. 5:11,22 [l]Gen. 49:12
23:30 [m]Eph. 5:18 [n]Ps. 75:8
23:35 [o]Jer. 5:3 [p]Eph. 4:19
24:1 [q]Ps. 37:1 & 73:3 ch. 3:31
24:5 [r]ch. 21:22
24:6 [s]Luke 14:31
24:7 [t]Ps. 10:5
24:8 [u]Rom. 1:30
24:11 [v]Ps. 82:4 Is. 58:6,7 1 John 3:16

2 For their heart studieth destruc-
tion, and their lips talk of mischief.
3 Through wisdom is an house
builded; and by understanding it is es-
tablished:
4 And by knowledge shall the cham-
bers be filled with all precious and
pleasant riches.
5 [r]A wise man [c]*is* strong; yea, a
man of knowledge [d]increaseth
strength.
6 [s]For by wise counsel thou shalt
make thy war: and in multitude of
counsellors *there is* safety.
7 [t]Wisdom *is* too high for a fool: he
openeth not his mouth in the gate.
8 He that [u]deviseth to do evil shall
be called a mischievous person.
9 The thought of foolishness *is* sin:
and the scorner *is* an abomination to
men.
10 *If* thou faint in the day of adversi-
ty, thy strength *is* [e]small.
11 [v]If thou forbear to deliver *them
that are* drawn unto death, and *those
that are* ready to be slain;

[y] Or, *as a robber* [z] Or, *a cockatrice* [a] Heb. *in the heart of the sea* [b] Heb. *I knew* it not [c] Heb. is *in strength* [d] Heb. *strengtheneth might* [e] Heb. *narrow*

23:29–35 MIXED WINE. These verses contain the first unambiguous commandment in God's progressive revelation that clearly forbids all His people to desire and to drink fermented wine (see next note). God instructs us here regarding alcoholic beverages and their corrupting influence (for an extended discussion of this issue, see article on WINE IN THE OLD TESTAMENT, p. 220).

23:31 LOOK NOT UPON THE WINE. This verse warns of the danger of wine (Heb. *yayin*) when it is in the process of fermentation. Hence, the *yayin* spoken of in this passage must be distinguished from unfermented *yayin* (see Is. 16:10; see article on WINE IN THE OLD TESTAMENT, p. 220). Fermentation is the process whereby sugar in grape juice is converted into alcohol and carbon dioxide. (1) The word "look" (Heb. *ra'ah*) is a common word meaning to "see, look at, examine" (cf. Gen. 27:1); *ra'ah* can be used in the sense of to "choose," suggesting that fermented wine must not be looked on with desire. God instructs His people not even to think about drinking fermented wine; no allowance is made for moderate drinking.

(2) The adjective "red" (Heb. *'adem*) means "red, ruddy, or rosy." According to Gesenius's *Lexicon*, it refers to the "sparkle" of wine in a cup, i.e., to the issue of fermentation.

(3)The next phrase, "giveth his colour in the cup" is literally, "when it gives in the cup its eye." This either refers to the bubbles of carbon dioxide generated by fermentation or to the sparkling appearance of fermented wine.

23:32 AT THE LAST IT BITETH LIKE A SERPENT. God commands His people not to look upon wine when it is red because fermented wine destroys a person like a snake and poisons him or her like an adder. The effects of alcohol are demonic and destructive; they include red eyes, blurred vision, a confused mind, and perverse and deceitful words (vv. 29,33). Consuming alcohol opens one's life to drunkenness (v. 34), woe, sorrow, violence, contention, physical harm (vv. 29, 35), and addiction (v. 35; see next note; see Rom. 14:21, note).

23:35 I WILL SEEK IT YET AGAIN. This passage describes the addictive effects of fermented wine. Oftentimes, the one who drinks will seek more and more until he or she can no longer control the drinking. That is why God says, "Look not upon *such* wine." Believers must not drink, or even think about drinking, any intoxicating beverage. This instruction is normative and authoritative for God's people today. We must not rationalize and relativize God's teaching in vv. 29–35 so that it doesn't apply to modern Christians. Beware of those who reinterpret v. 31 to mean, "Look on the wine with self-control and moderation when it sparkles in the cup."

24:10 THE DAY OF ADVERSITY. Trouble and distress will come to all of us at some time in this life (Job 7:7; Jas. 1:4). When they do, we as believers must be strong in the Lord, look to Him as our refuge (Deut. 33:27), and call upon Him, confident that His promise never to forsake us is true (Heb.

12 If thou sayest, Behold, we knew it not; doth not [w]he that pondereth the heart consider *it?* and he that keepeth thy soul, doth *not* he know *it?* and shall *not* he render to *every* man [x]according to his works?

13 My son, [y]eat thou honey, because *it is* good; and the honeycomb, *which is* sweet [f]to thy taste:

14 [z]So *shall* the knowledge of wisdom *be* unto thy soul: when thou hast found *it,* then there shall be a reward, and thy expectation shall not be cut off.

15 Lay not wait, O wicked *man,* against the dwelling of the righteous; spoil not his resting place:

16 [a]For a just *man* falleth seven times, and riseth up again: [b]but the wicked shall fall into mischief.

17 [c]Rejoice not when thine enemy falleth, and let not thine heart be glad when he stumbleth:

18 Lest the LORD see *it,* and [g]it displease him, and he turn away his wrath from him.

19 [d]Fret[h] not thyself because of evil *men,* neither be thou envious at the wicked;

20 For there shall be no reward to the evil *man;* the [i]candle of the wicked shall be put out.

21 My son, [e]fear thou the LORD and the king: *and* meddle not with [j]them that are given to change:

22 For their calamity shall rise suddenly; and who knoweth the ruin of them both?

Sayings of the wise

23 These *things* also *belong* to the wise. [f]*It is* not good to have respect of persons in judgment.

24 [g]He that saith unto the wicked, Thou *art* righteous; him shall the people curse, nations shall abhor him:

25 But to them that rebuke *him*

24:12 [w]ch. 21:2 [x]Ps. 62:12
24:13 [y]Sol. 5:1
24:14 [z]Ps. 19:10
24:16 [a]Ps. 34:19 Mic. 7:8 [b]Esth. 7:10 Amos 5:2
24:17 [c]Job 31:29 Obad. 12
24:19 [d]Ps. 37:1
24:21 [e]Rom. 13:7 1 Pet. 2:17
24:23 [f]Lev. 19:15 Deut. 16:19
24:24 [g]Is. 5:23
24:27 [h]1 Ki. 5:17
24:28 [i]Eph. 4:25
24:29 [j]Mat. 5:39
24:31 [k]Gen. 3:18
24:33 [l]ch. 6:9
25:1 [m]1 Ki. 4:32
25:2 [n]Rom. 11:33 [o]Job 29:16
25:4 [p]2 Tim. 2:21

shall be delight, and [k]a good blessing shall come upon them.

26 *Every man* shall kiss *his* lips [l]that giveth a right answer.

27 [h]Prepare thy work without, and make it fit for thyself in the field; and afterwards build thine house.

28 [i]Be not a witness against thy neighbour without cause; and deceive *not* with thy lips.

29 [j]Say not, I will do so to him as he hath done to me: I will render to the man according to his work.

30 I went by the field of the slothful, and by the vineyard of the man void of understanding;

31 And, lo, [k]it was all grown over with thorns, *and* nettles had covered the face thereof, and the stone wall thereof was broken down.

32 Then I saw, *and* [m]considered *it* well: I looked upon *it, and* received instruction.

33 [l]*Yet* a little sleep, a little slumber, a little folding of the hands to sleep:

34 So shall thy poverty come *as* one that travelleth; and thy want as [n]an armed man.

More proverbs of Solomon

25 THESE[m] *ARE* also proverbs of Solomon, which the men of Hezekiah king of Judah copied out.

2 [n]*It is* the glory of God to conceal a thing: but the honour of kings *is* [o]to search out a matter.

3 The heaven for height, and the earth for depth, and the heart of kings [o]*is* unsearchable.

4 [p]Take away the dross from the

[f] Heb. *upon thy palate* [g] Heb. *it be evil in his eyes* [h] Or, *Keep not company with the wicked* [i] Or, *lamp* [j] Heb. *changers* [k] Heb. *a blessing of good* [l] Heb. *that answereth right words* [m] Heb. *set my heart* [n] Heb. *a man of shield* [o] Heb. there is *no searching*

13:5). To those who faithfully trust in Him, God gives sufficient strength and grace to endure the time of trouble (Is. 40:29; 2 Cor. 12:9; Col. 1:11).

24:16 A JUST *MAN* . . . RISETH UP AGAIN. When adversity, trials, and setbacks occur in the life of the righteous, they will bounce back because God's grace lifts them up (see previous note). God does not guarantee us trouble-free lives, but He does promise to sustain us, no matter what happens. "*We are* troubled on every side, yet not distressed; *we are* perplexed, but not in despair; persecuted, but not forsaken; cast down, but not destroyed" (2 Cor. 4:8–9; see 4:7, note).

25:1 HEZEKIAH. Hezekiah ruled as king over Israel 200 years after Solomon (c. 715–686 B.C.); see 2 Ki 18—20; 2 Chr. 29—32; Is. 36—39 for information on his reign.

25:2 TO CONCEAL A THING. God has chosen not to reveal all things clearly (cf. Rom. 11:33). He has left much concealed beneath a surface reading of the Scriptures that only those who pursue Him diligently will discover. Leaders of God's people should eagerly search the depths of God's revelation in His Word (see 1 Cor. 2:6–16).

silver, and there shall come forth a vessel for the refiner.

5 [q]Take away the wicked *from* before the king, and [r]his throne shall be established in righteousness.

6 [p]Put not forth thyself in the presence of the king, and stand not in the place of great *men:*

7 [s]For better *it is* that it be said unto thee, Come up hither; than that thou shouldest be put lower in the presence of the prince whom thine eyes have seen.

8 [t]Go not forth hastily to strive, lest *thou know not* what to do in the end thereof, when thy neighbour hath put thee to shame.

9 [u]Debate thy cause with thy neighbour *himself;* and [q]discover not a secret to another:

10 Lest he that heareth *it* put thee to shame, and thine infamy turn not away.

11 [v]A word [r]fitly spoken *is like* apples of gold in pictures of silver.

12 *As* an earring of gold, and an ornament of fine gold, *so is* a wise reprover upon an obedient ear.

13 [w]As the cold of snow in the time of harvest, *so is* a faithful messenger to them that send him: for he refresheth the soul of his masters.

14 [x]Whoso boasteth himself [s]of a false gift *is like* [y]clouds and wind without rain.

15 [z]By long forbearing is a prince persuaded, and a soft tongue breaketh the bone.

16 [a]Hast thou found honey? eat so much as is sufficient for thee, lest thou be filled therewith, and vomit it.

17 [t]Withdraw thy foot from thy neighbour's house; lest he be [u]weary of thee, and *so* hate thee.

18 [b]A man that beareth false witness against his neighbour *is* a maul, and a sword, and a sharp arrow.

19 Confidence in an unfaithful man in time of trouble *is like* a broken tooth, and a foot out of joint.

20 *As* he that taketh away a garment in cold weather, *and as* vinegar upon nitre, so *is* he that [c]singeth songs to an heavy heart.

21 [d]If thine enemy be hungry, give him bread to eat; and if he be thirsty, give him water to drink:

22 For thou shalt heap coals of fire upon his head, [e]and the LORD shall reward thee.

23 [f]The[v] north wind driveth away rain: so *doth* an angry countenance [g]a backbiting tongue.

24 [h]*It is* better to dwell in the corner of the housetop, than with a brawling woman and in a wide house.

25 *As* cold waters to a thirsty soul, so *is* good news from a far country.

26 A righteous man falling down before the wicked *is as* a troubled fountain, and a corrupt spring.

27 [i]*It is* not good to eat much honey: so *for men* [j]to search their own glory *is not* glory.

28 [k]He that *hath* no rule over his own spirit *is like* a city *that is* broken down, *and* without walls.

26 AS SNOW in summer, [l]and as rain in harvest, so honour is not seemly for a fool.

2 As the bird by wandering, as the swallow by flying, so [m]the curse causeless shall not come.

3 [n]A whip for the horse, a bridle for the ass, and a rod for the fool's back.

4 Answer not a fool according to his folly, lest thou also be like unto him.

5 [o]Answer a fool according to his folly, lest he be wise in [w]his own conceit.

6 He that sendeth a message by the hand of a fool cutteth off the feet, *and* drinketh [x]damage.

7 The legs of the lame [y]are not equal: so *is* a parable in the mouth of fools.

8 [z]As he that bindeth a stone in a sling, so *is* he that giveth honour to a fool.

9 *As* a thorn goeth up into the hand of a drunkard, so *is* a parable in the mouth of fools.

10 [a]The great *God* that formed all

25:5 [q]ch. 20:8 [r]ch. 16:12
25:7 [s]Luke 14:10
25:8 [t]Mat. 5:25
25:9 [u]Mat. 5:25
25:11 [v]ch. 15:23
25:13 [w]ch. 13:17
25:14 [x]ch. 20:6 [y]Jude 12
25:15 [z]ch. 15:1
25:16 [a]ver. 27
25:18 [b]Ps. 57:4
25:20 [c]Dan. 6:18
25:21 [d]Mat. 5:44
25:22 [e]2 Sam. 16:12
25:23 [f]Job 37:22 [g]Ps. 101:5
25:24 [h]ch. 19:13
25:27 [i]ver. 16 [j]ch. 27:2
25:28 [k]ch. 16:32
26:1 [l]1 Sam. 12:17
26:2 [m]Deut. 23:5
26:3 [n]Ps. 32:9
26:5 [o]Mat. 16:1-4

[p] Heb. *Set not out thy glory* [q] Or, *discover not the secret of another* [r] Heb. *spoken upon his wheels* [s] Heb. *in a gift of falsehood* [t] Or, *Let thy foot be seldom in thy neighbour's house* [u] Heb. *full of thee* [v] Or, *The north wind bringeth forth rain: so doth a backbiting tongue an angry countenance* [w] Heb. *his own eyes* [x] Or, *violence* [y] Heb. *are lifted up* [z] Or, *As he that putteth a precious stone in an heap of stones* [a] Or, *A great man grieveth all, and he hireth the fool, he hireth also transgressors*

25:21–22 IF THINE ENEMY BE HUNGRY. Doing good to our enemies may cause them to experience shame and eventually bring them to God and salvation (see Rom. 12:20).

things both rewardeth the fool, and re-
wardeth transgressors.
11 [p]As a dog returneth to his vom-
it, [q]*so* a fool [b]returneth to his folly.
12 [r]Seest thou a man wise in his
own conceit? *there is* more hope of a
fool than of him.
13 The slothful *man* saith, *There is* a
lion in the way; a lion *is* in the streets.
14 *As* the door turneth upon his
hinges, so *doth* the slothful upon his
bed.
15 The slothful hideth his hand in
his bosom; [c]it grieveth him to bring it
again to his mouth.
16 The sluggard *is* wiser in his own
conceit than seven men that can ren-
der a reason.
17 He that passeth by, *and* [d]med-
dleth with strife *belonging* not to him,
is like one that taketh a dog by the ears.
18 As a mad *man* who casteth
[e]firebrands, arrows, and death,
19 So *is* the man *that* deceiveth his
neighbour, and saith, [s]Am not I in
sport?
20 [f]Where no wood is, *there* the
fire goeth out: so where *there is* no
[g]talebearer, the strife [h]ceaseth.
21 [t]*As* coals *are* to burning coals,
and wood to fire; so *is* a contentious
man to kindle strife.
22 The words of a talebearer *are* as
wounds, and they go down into the
[i]innermost parts of the belly.
23 Burning lips and a wicked heart
are like a potsherd covered with silver
dross.
24 He that hateth [j]dissembleth
with his lips, and layeth up deceit with-
in him;
25 [u]When he [k]speaketh fair, be-

26:11 [p]2 Pet. 2:22 [q]Ex. 8:15
26:12 [r]Rev. 3:17
26:19 [s]Eph. 5:4
26:21 [t]ch. 15:18
26:25 [u]Ps. 28:3
26:27 [v]Ps. 7:15

lieve him not: for *there are* seven abomi-
nations in his heart.
26 *Whose* [l]hatred is covered by de-
ceit, his wickedness shall be shown be-
fore the *whole* congregation.
27 [v]Whoso diggeth a pit shall fall
therein: and he that rolleth a stone, it
will return upon him.
28 A lying tongue hateth *those that*
are afflicted by it; and a flattering
mouth worketh ruin.

27 BOAST NOT thyself of [m]to-
morrow; for thou knowest not
what a day may bring forth.
2 Let another man praise thee, and
not thine own mouth; a stranger, and
not thine own lips.
3 A stone *is* [n]heavy, and the sand
weighty; but a fool's wrath *is* heavier
than them both.
4 [o]Wrath *is* cruel, and anger *is* out-
rageous; but who *is* able to stand be-
fore [p]envy?
5 Open rebuke *is* better than secret
love.
6 Faithful *are* the wounds of a
friend; but the kisses of an enemy *are*
[q]deceitful.
7 The full soul [r]loatheth an honey-
comb; but to the hungry soul every bit-
ter thing is sweet.
8 As a bird that wandereth from her
nest, so *is* a man that wandereth from
his place.
9 Ointment and perfume rejoice the

[b]Heb. *iterateth his folly* [c]Or, *he is weary* [d]Or, *is enraged* [e]Heb. *flames*, or, *sparks* [f]Heb. *Without wood* [g]Or, *whisperer* [h]Heb. *is silent* [i]Heb. *chambers* [j]Or, *is known* [k]Heb. *maketh his voice gracious* [l]Or, *hatred is covered in secret* [m]Heb. *tomorrow day* [n]Heb. *heaviness* [o]Heb. *Wrath* is *cruelty, and anger an overflowing* [p]Or, *jealousy?* [q]Or, *earnest*, or, *frequent* [r]Heb. *treadeth under foot*

26:11 A DOG RETURNETH TO HIS VOMIT. Peter applied this proverb to those who once followed Christ, knew the way of righteousness, and then turned back from God and His holy commandments to live in sin again (2 Pet. 2:20–22).

26:12 WISE IN HIS OWN CONCEIT. Pride and self-importance cause people to seem wise in their own estimation and therefore arrogantly confident in their own ideas. Wisdom and truth are formed not by human reasoning, however, but by accepting what God has said and revealed in all Scripture. In honestly acknowledging the potential for deceit within our hearts, we must not automatically assume that our standards of right or wrong are God's standards (see Jer. 17:9, note). Rather, God calls us humbly to bring all our thoughts into submission to the authority of His revelation and the ministry of the Holy Spirit (John 16:8–14), asking Him to convict and correct us in the areas where we are wrong (cf. Rev. 3:17).

27:1 BOAST NOT THYSELF OF TOMORROW. James may have had this verse in mind when he wrote, "Ye know not what *shall be* on the morrow. For what *is* your life? It is even a vapour, that appeareth for a little time, and then vanisheth away" (Jas. 4:14). Because of the brevity and uncertainty of life, our plans should always be contingent upon what the Lord wills (Jas. 4:15) and not on our assumptions. Christ applied this truth about the uncertainty of the future to the necessity of always being ready for the hour of His return (see Mark 13:35, note; Luke 12:35–40, note; 21:34, note).

heart: so *doth* the sweetness of a man's friend [s]by hearty counsel.

10 Thine own friend, and thy father's friend, forsake not; neither go into thy brother's house in the day of thy calamity: *for* [w]better *is* a neighbour *that is* near than a brother far off.

11 My son, be wise, and make my heart glad, [x]that I may answer him that reproacheth me.

12 A prudent *man* foreseeth the evil, *and* hideth himself; *but* the simple pass on, *and* are punished.

13 Take his garment that is surety for a stranger, and take a pledge of him for a strange woman.

14 He that blesseth his friend with a loud voice, rising early in the morning, it shall be counted a curse to him.

15 A continual dropping in a very rainy day and a contentious woman are alike.

16 Whosoever hideth her hideth the wind, and the ointment of his right hand, *which* betrayeth *itself*.

17 Iron sharpeneth iron; so a man sharpeneth the countenance of his friend.

18 [y]Whoso keepeth the fig tree shall eat the fruit thereof: so he that waiteth on his master shall be honoured.

19 As in water face *answereth* to face, so the heart of man to man.

20 [z]Hell and destruction are [t]never full; so [a]the eyes of man are never satisfied.

21 [b]*As* the refining pot for silver, and the furnace for gold; so *is* a man to his praise.

22 [c]Though thou shouldest bray a fool in a mortar among wheat with a pestle, *yet* will not his foolishness depart from him.

23 Be thou diligent to know the state of thy flocks, *and* [u]look well to thy herds.

27:10 [w]ch. 17:17
27:11 [x]Ps. 127:5
27:18 [y]1 Cor. 9:7
27:20 [z]Hab. 2:5 [a]Eccl. 1:8
27:21 [b]ch. 17:3
27:22 [c]Jer. 5:3
27:25 [d]Ps. 104:14
28:1 [e]Ps. 53:5
28:3 [f]Mat. 18:28
28:4 [g]Rom. 1:32 [h]1 Ki. 18:18
28:5 [i]Ps. 92:6 [j]John 7:17
28:6 [k]ch. 19:1
28:7 [l]ch. 29:3
28:8 [m]ch. 13:22
28:9 [n]Ps. 66:18
28:10 [o]ch. 26:27

24 For [v]riches *are* not for ever: and doth the crown *endure* [w]to every generation?

25 [d]The hay appeareth, and the tender grass showeth itself, and herbs of the mountains are gathered.

26 The lambs *are* for thy clothing, and the goats *are* the price of the field.

27 And *thou shalt have* goats' milk enough for thy food, for the food of thy household, and *for* the [x]maintenance for thy maidens.

28 THE [e]WICKED flee when no man pursueth: but the righteous are bold as a lion.

2 For the transgression of a land many *are* the princes thereof: but [y]by a man of understanding *and* knowledge the state *thereof* shall be prolonged.

3 [f]A poor man that oppresseth the poor *is like* a sweeping rain [z]which leaveth no food.

4 [g]They that forsake the law praise the wicked: [h]but such as keep the law contend with them.

5 [i]Evil men understand not judgment: but [j]they that seek the LORD understand all *things*.

6 [k]Better *is* the poor that walketh in his uprightness, than *he that is* perverse *in his* ways, though he *be* rich.

7 [l]Whoso keepeth the law *is* a wise son: but he that [a]is a companion of riotous *men* shameth his father.

8 [m]He that by usury and [b]unjust gain increaseth his substance, he shall gather it for him that will pity the poor.

9 He that turneth away his ear from hearing the law, [n]even his prayer *shall be* abomination.

10 [o]Whoso causeth the righteous

[s] Heb. *from the counsel of the soul* [t] Heb. *not* [u] Heb. *set thy heart* [v] Heb. *strength* [w] Heb. *to generation and generation?* [x] Heb. *life* [y] Or, *by men of understanding* and *wisdom shall they likewise be prolonged* [z] Heb. *without food* [a] Or, *feedeth gluttons* [b] Heb. *by increase*

27:21 A MAN TO HIS PRAISE. The praise we receive from others tests us as to how we will respond—either in pride or in humility. An attitude of pride reveals self-deception in our hearts, for we do not realize that what we are and what we have done are largely due to God and others (see Phil. 2:3, note). Our actions must never be done for praise or self-glory, but must flow from our commitment to God, His word, and His kingdom. When we pass the test of praise, it confirms that we are living to please God rather than other humans and that our hearts are pure and our spirits one with God.

28:5 THEY THAT SEEK THE LORD. See 2 Chr. 14:4, note; 26:5, note.

28:9 HIS PRAYER *SHALL BE* ABOMINATION. God will not answer the prayers of those who have no sincere commitment to obey Him and His word. To compromise our commitment to God and His word by participating in even a few sinful pleasures will render our prayers ineffective (cf. 15:29; Ps. 66:18; Is. 59:2; see article on EFFECTIVE PRAYING, p. 540). Prayer without love for God's word and law is hypocrisy and is insulting to Him (see 1 John 3:22, note).

to go astray in an evil way, he shall fall
himself into his own pit: [p]but the up-
right shall have good *things* in posses-
sion.
11 The rich man *is* wise [c]in his
own conceit; but the poor that hath un-
derstanding searcheth him out.
12 [q]When righteous *men* do re-
joice, *there is* great glory: but when the
wicked rise, a man is [d]hidden.
13 [r]He that covereth his sins shall
not prosper: but whoso confesseth and
forsaketh *them* shall have mercy.
14 Happy *is* the man [s]that feareth
always: [t]but he that hardeneth his
heart shall fall into mischief.
15 [u]*As* a roaring lion, and a rang-
ing bear; [v]*so is* a wicked ruler over the
poor people.
16 The prince that wanteth under-
standing *is* also a great oppressor: *but*
he that hateth covetousness shall pro-
long *his* days.
17 [w]A man that doeth violence to
the blood of *any* person shall flee to the
pit; let no man stay him.
18 [x]Whoso walketh uprightly shall
be saved: but [y]*he that is* perverse *in his*
ways shall fall at once.
19 [z]He that tilleth his land shall
have plenty of bread: but he that fol-
loweth after vain *persons* shall have
poverty enough.
20 A faithful man shall abound with
blessings: [a]but he that maketh haste
to be rich shall not be [e]innocent.
21 [b]To have respect of persons *is*
not good: for [c]for a piece of bread *that*
man will transgress.
22 [d]He[f] that hasteth to be rich
hath an evil eye, and considereth not
that poverty shall come upon him.
23 [e]He that rebuketh a man after-
wards shall find more favour than he
that flattereth with the tongue.
24 Whoso robbeth his father or his
mother, and saith, *It is* no transgres-
sion; the same [f]*is* the companion of
[g]a destroyer.
25 [g]He that is of a proud heart
stirreth up strife: [h]but he that putteth
his trust in the LORD shall be made fat.
26 He that trusteth in his own heart
is a fool: but whoso walketh wisely, he
shall be delivered.
27 [i]He that giveth unto the poor
shall not lack: but he that hideth his
eyes shall have many a curse.
28 [j]When the wicked rise, [k]men
hide themselves: but when they perish,
the righteous increase.
29 HE,[l] [h] THAT being often re-
proved hardeneth *his* neck,
shall suddenly be destroyed, and that
without remedy.
2 [m]When the righteous are [i]in au-
thority, the people rejoice: but when
the wicked beareth rule, [n]the people
mourn.
3 [o]Whoso loveth wisdom rejoiceth
his father: [p]but he that keepeth com-
pany with harlots spendeth *his* sub-
stance.
4 The king by judgment esta-
blisheth the land: but [j]he that re-
ceiveth gifts overthroweth it.
5 A man that flattereth his neigh-
bour spreadeth a net for his feet.
6 In the transgression of an evil
man *there is* a snare: but the righteous
doth sing and rejoice.
7 [q]The righteous considereth the

28:10 [p]Mat. 6:33
28:12 [q]ch. 11:10
28:13 [r]Ps. 32:3,5
28:14 [s]Ps. 16:8 [t]Rom. 2:5
28:15 [u]1 Pet. 5:8 [v]Mat. 2:16
28:17 [w]Gen. 9:6
28:18 [x]ch. 10:9,25 [y]ver. 6
28:19 [z]ch. 12:11
28:20 [a]1 Tim. 6:9
28:21 [b]ch. 18:5 [c]Ezek. 13:19
28:22 [d]ver:20
28:23 [e]ch. 27:5,6
28:24 [f]ch. 18:9
28:25 [g]ch. 13:10 [h]1 Tim. 6:6
28:27 [i]Deut. 15:7
28:28 [j]ver. 12 [k]Job 24:4
29:1 [l]2 Chr. 36:16
29:2 [m]Esth. 8:15 [n]Esth. 3:15
29:3 [o]ch. 10:1 [p]Luke 15:13
29:7 [q]Job 29:16 Ps. 41:1

[c] Heb. *in his eyes* [d] Or, *sought for* [e] Or, *unpunished* [f] Or, *He that hath an evil eye hasteth to be rich* [g] Heb. *a man destroying* [h] Heb. *A man of reproofs* [i] Or, *increased* [j] Heb. *a man of oblations*

28:13 HE THAT COVERETH HIS SINS. Those who attempt to deny their sin or keep it hidden rather than acknowledge, confess, and forsake their sin will make no spiritual progress. God's forgiveness and mercy are available, however, for all those who come to God in sincere repentance (see Mat. 3:2, note).

28:20 A FAITHFUL MAN ... BLESSINGS. See Luke 24:50, note.

28:27 GIVING UNTO THE POOR. God will take care of those who give to the poor and needy (cf. 11:24–25; 14:21; 19:17; 21:26; see article on THE CARE OF THE POOR AND NEEDY, p. 1312). The blessings of God abound to those who give to help meet the physical or spiritual needs of others (see 2 Cor. 8:2, note; 9:6–8, notes).

29:1 DESTROYED, AND THAT WITHOUT REMEDY. Those who repeatedly reject the clear reproof and conviction of the Holy Spirit (John 16:8–11) and despise His chastening and correction (Heb. 12:5–11,25) run the risk of hardening their hearts to the point of being cut off from God's mercy and of being judged by Him. No one can continue in sin and reject God's grace, mercy, and love without eventually suffering irreparably for it (cf. 1 Sam. 2:25; see article on PERSONAL APOSTASY, p. 1946).

29:7 CONSIDERETH THE CAUSE OF THE POOR. Concern for the poor and needy was revealed to Israel as God's standard of righteousness under the old covenant (see 28:27, note). True followers of Christ will likewise share His

cause of the poor: *but* the wicked regardeth not to know *it.*

8 [r]Scornful men [k]bring a city into a snare: but wise *men* [s]turn away wrath.

9 *If* a wise man contendeth with a foolish man, [t]whether he rage or laugh, *there is* no rest.

10 [u]The[1] bloodthirsty hate the upright: but the just seek his soul.

11 A [v]fool uttereth all his mind: but a wise *man* keepeth it in till afterwards.

12 If a ruler hearken to lies, all his servants *are* wicked.

13 The poor and [m]the deceitful man meet together: [w]the LORD lighteneth both their eyes.

14 [x]The king that faithfully judgeth the poor, his throne shall be established for ever.

15 The rod and reproof give wisdom: but [y]a child left *to himself* bringeth his mother to shame.

16 When the wicked are multiplied, transgression increaseth: [z]but the righteous shall see their fall.

17 [a]Correct thy son, and he shall give thee rest; yea, he shall give delight unto thy soul.

18 [b]Where *there is* no vision, the people [n]perish: but [c]he that keepeth the law, happy *is* he.

19 A servant will not be corrected by words: for though he understand he will not answer.

20 Seest thou a man *that is* hasty [o]in his words? [d]*there is* more hope of a fool than of him.

21 He that delicately bringeth up his servant from a child shall have him become *his* son at the length.

22 [e]An angry man stirreth up strife, and a furious man aboundeth in transgression.

23 [f]A man's pride shall bring him low: but honour shall uphold the humble in spirit.

24 Whoso is partner with a thief hateth his own soul: [g]he heareth cursing, and betrayeth *it* not.

25 [h]The fear of man bringeth a snare: but whoso putteth his trust in the LORD [p]shall be safe.

26 [i]Many seek [q]the ruler's favour; but *every* man's judgment *cometh* from the LORD.

27 An unjust man *is* an abomination to the just: and *he that is* upright in the way *is* abomination to the wicked.

Observations of Agur

30 THE WORDS of Agur the son of Jakeh, *even* the prophecy: the man spake unto Ithiel, even unto Ithiel and Ucal,

2 [j]Surely I *am* more brutish than *any* man, and have not the understanding of a man.

3 I neither learned wisdom, nor [r]have the knowledge of the holy.

4 [k]Who hath ascended up into heaven, or descended? [l]who hath gathered the wind in his fists? who hath bound the waters in a garment? who hath established all the ends of the earth? what *is* his name, and what *is* his son's name, if thou canst tell?

5 [m]Every word of God *is* [s]pure: [n]he *is* a shield unto them that put their trust in him.

6 [o]Add thou not unto his words,

k Or, *set a city on fire* **1** Heb. *Men of blood* **m** Or, *the usurer* **n** Or, *is made naked* **o** Or, *in his matters?* **p** Heb. *shall be set on high* **q** Heb. *the face of a ruler* **r** Heb. *know* **s** Heb. *purified*

29:8 [r]ch. 11:11 [s]Ezek. 22:30
29:9 [t]Mat. 11:17
29:10 [u]1 John 3:12
29:11 [v]ch. 12:16
29:13 [w]Mat. 5:45
29:14 [x]ch. 20:28
29:15 [y]ch. 17:21,25
29:16 [z]Ps. 37:36
29:17 [a]ch. 19:18
29:18 [b]1 Sam. 3:1 Amos 8:11 [c]John 13:17
29:20 [d]ch. 26:12
29:22 [e]ch. 26:21
29:23 [f]Job 22:29 Is. 66:2 Dan. 4:30 Mat. 23:12
29:24 [g]Lev. 5:1
29:25 [h]Gen. 12:12
29:26 [i]Ps. 20:9
30:2 [j]Ps. 73:22
30:4 [k]John 3:13 [l]Job 38:4 Ps. 104:3 Is. 40:12
30:5 [m]Ps. 12:6 [n]Ps. 18:30
30:6 [o]Deut. 4:2 Rev. 22:18

---

concern that the poor be treated fairly and compassionately (see Luke 6:20–21; Acts 4:34–35; 6:1–6; 20:38; 1 Cor. 16:2; see Jas. 1:27, note).

29:15 ROD AND REPROOF. Children who are not trained, disciplined, and restrained by their parents will later bring shame to them and harm to themselves. Sometimes words of reproof alone are adequate; at other times they must be accompanied by the rod of correction (cf. v. 17; see 13:24, note). If physical discipline is used, it is important that it be accompanied by an explanation so that the child clearly understands why the rod was used and what conduct is required.

29:18 WHERE *THERE IS* NO VISION. "Vision" (Heb. *hazon*) means "revelation." When there is no clear revelation and bold declaration of God's will and standards, God's people lose their Biblical convictions, cast off their moral restraints, and subsequently perish (cf. Ex. 32:25). The revealed will of God and His righteous demands as expressed in Scripture must be repeatedly kept before the congregation, or many will begin to conform to the world (cf. Rom. 12:1–2) and transgress God's law.

30:5 EVERY WORD OF GOD *IS* PURE. See article on THE INSPIRATION AND AUTHORITY OF SCRIPTURE, p. 1924.

30:6 ADD THOU NOT UNTO HIS WORD. God's Word must not be mixed with human ideas and speculations, such as those found in worldly philosophy, psychology, sorcery, or spiritism. God's revealed truth is fully adequate to meet the

lest he reprove thee, and thou be found a liar.

7 Two *things* have I required of thee; [t]deny me *them* not before I die:

8 Remove far from me vanity and lies: give me neither poverty nor riches; [p]feed me with food [u]convenient for me:

9 [q]Lest I be full, and [v]deny *thee,* and say, Who *is* the LORD? or lest I be poor, and steal, and take the name of my God *in vain.*

10 [w]Accuse not a servant unto his master, lest he curse thee, and thou be found guilty.

11 *There is* a generation *that* curseth their father, and doth not bless their mother.

12 *There is* a generation [r]*that are* pure in their own eyes, and *yet* is not washed from their filthiness.

13 *There is* a generation, O how [s]lofty are their eyes! and their eyelids are lifted up.

14 [t]*There is* a generation, whose teeth *are as* swords, and their jaw teeth *as* knives, [u]to devour the poor from off the earth, and the needy from *among* men.

15 The horseleach hath two daughters, *crying,* Give, give. There are three *things that* are never satisfied, *yea,* four *things* say not, [x]*It is* enough:

16 [v]The grave; and the barren womb; the earth *that* is not filled with water; and the fire *that* saith not, *It is* enough.

17 [w]The eye *that* mocketh at *his* father, and despiseth to obey *his* mother, the ravens of [y]the valley shall pick it out, and the young eagles shall eat it.

18 There be three *things which* are too wonderful for me, yea, four which I know not:

19 The way of an eagle in the air; the way of a serpent upon a rock; the way of a ship in the [z]midst of the sea; and the way of a man with a maid.

20 Such *is* the way of an adulterous woman; she eateth, and wipeth her mouth, and saith, I have done no wickedness.

21 For three *things* the earth is disquieted, and for four *which* it cannot bear:

22 [x]For a servant when he reigneth; and a fool when he is filled with meat;

23 For an odious *woman* when she is married; and an handmaid that is heir to her mistress.

24 There be four *things which are* little upon the earth, but they *are* [a]exceeding wise:

25 [y]The ants *are* a people not strong, yet they prepare their meat in the summer;

26 [z]The conies *are but* a feeble folk, yet make they their houses in the rocks;

27 The locusts have no king, yet go they forth all of them [b]by bands;

28 The spider taketh hold with her hands, and is in kings' palaces.

29 There be three *things* which go well, yea, four are comely in going:

30 A lion *which is* strongest among beasts, and turneth not away for any;

31 A [c] [d]greyhound; an he goat also; and a king, against whom *there is* no rising up.

32 If thou hast done foolishly in lifting up thyself, or if thou hast thought evil, [a]*lay* thine hand upon thy mouth.

33 Surely the churning of milk bringeth forth butter, and the wringing of the nose bringeth forth blood: so the forcing of wrath bringeth forth strife.

Words of king Lemuel

31 THE WORDS of king Lemuel, the prophecy that his mother taught him.

2 What, my son? and what, [b]the son of my womb? and what, the son of my vows?

3 [c]Give not thy strength unto wom-

30:8 [p]Mat. 6:11 **30:9** [q]Deut. 8:12 **30:12** [r]Luke 18:11 **30:13** [s]Ps. 131:1 ch. 6:17 **30:14** [t]Job 29:17 Ps. 52:2 [u]Ps. 14:4 Amos 8:4 **30:16** [v]ch. 27:20 Hab. 2:5 **30:17** [w]Gen. 9:22 Lev. 20:9 ch. 20:20 & 23:22

30:22 [x]ch. 19:10 Eccl. 10:7 **30:25** [y]ch. 6:6 **30:26** [z]Ps. 104:18 **30:32** [a]Job 21:5 & 40:4 Mic. 7:16 **31:2** [b]Is. 49:15 **31:3** [c]ch. 5:9

[t]Heb. *withhold not from me* [u]Heb. *of my allowance* [v]Heb. *belie* thee [w]Heb. *Hurt not with thy tongue* [x]Heb. *Wealth* [y]Or, *the brook* [z]Heb. *heart* [a]Heb. *wise, made wise* [b]Heb. *gathered together* [c]Or, *horse* [d]Heb. *girt in the loins*

spiritual needs of humankind. Those who teach that something must be added to Biblical truth in order to fulfill our lives in Christ are liars (cf. Rev. 22:18; see 2 Pet. 1:3, note).

30:8 NEITHER POVERTY NOR RICHES. We should pray to have adequate income to meet personal and family needs, to support God's work, and to give to those in need (see 2 Cor. 9:8–12).

30:17 MOCKETH AT *HIS* FATHER, AND DESPISETH TO OBEY *HIS* MOTHER. God requires of young people that they respect and obey their parents. To honor our fathers and mothers will bring God's blessing (Ex. 20:12; Deut. 5:16; Eph. 6:1–3); to disobey and scorn them and their instruction will bring God's curse.

en, nor thy ways [d]to that which destroyeth kings.
4 [e]*It is* not for kings, O Lemuel, *it is* not for kings to drink wine; nor for princes strong drink:
5 [f]Lest they drink, and forget the law, and [e]pervert the judgment [f]of any of the afflicted.
6 [g]Give strong drink unto him that is ready to perish, and wine unto those that be [g]of heavy hearts.
7 Let him drink, and forget his poverty, and remember his misery no more.
8 [h]Open thy mouth for the dumb in the cause of all [h]such as are appointed to destruction.
9 Open thy mouth, [i]judge righteously, and [j]plead the cause of the poor and needy.

The virtuous woman

10 ¶ [k]Who can find a virtuous woman? for her price *is* far above rubies.
11 The heart of her husband doth safely trust in her, so that he shall have no need of spoil.
12 She will do him good and not evil all the days of her life.
13 She seeketh wool, and flax, and worketh willingly with her hands.

31:3 [d]Deut. 17:17 Neh. 13:26 ch. 7:26 Hos. 4:11 **31:4** [e]Eccl. 10:17 **31:5** [f]Hos. 4:11 **31:6** [g]Ps. 104:15 **31:8** [h]See Job 29:15,16 **31:9** [i]Lev. 19:15 Deut. 1:16 [j]Job 29:12 Is. 1:17 Jer. 22:16 **31:10** [k]ch. 12:4 & 18:22 & 19:14

14 She is like the merchants' ships; she bringeth her food from afar.
15 [l]She riseth also while it is yet night, and [m]giveth meat to her household, and a portion to her maidens.
16 She considereth a field, and [i]buyeth it: with the fruit of her hands she planteth a vineyard.
17 She girdeth her loins with strength, and strengtheneth her arms.
18 [j]She perceiveth that her merchandise *is* good: her candle goeth not out by night.
19 She layeth her hands to the spindle, and her hands hold the distaff.
20 [n]She[k] stretcheth out her hand to the poor; yea, she reacheth forth her hands to the needy.
21 She is not afraid of the snow for her household: for all her household *are* clothed with [l]scarlet.
22 She maketh herself coverings of tapestry; her clothing *is* silk and purple.

31:15 [l]Rom. 12:11 [m]Luke 12:42 **31:20** [n]Eph. 4:28 Heb. 13:16

[e] Heb. *alter* [f] Heb. *of all the sons of affliction* [g] Heb. *bitter of soul* [h] Heb. *the sons of destruction* [i] Heb. *taketh* [j] Heb. *She tasteth* [k] Heb. *She spreadeth* [l] Or, *double garments*

31:4–5 *IT IS* NOT FOR KINGS TO DRINK WINE. God had a high standard for the kings and rulers of His people, especially with respect to drinking fermented wine and intoxicating beverages. (1) The Hebrew literally says: "Let there be no drinking"; this passage makes no allowance for moderate drinking (see 20:1, note; 23:29–35, notes; see article on WINE IN THE OLD TESTAMENT, p. 220).

(2) The reason that kings and rulers are not to drink intoxicating drink is that they might otherwise forget the law. Such drinking would weaken them morally and lead them to disobey God's law and pervert justice. This text led the Jewish rabbis to decree that a judge who drank a *renuth* (i.e., a glass of wine) was "not permitted to sit in judgment, nor in a school, or under similar circumstances permitted to teach" (Koplowitz, *Midrush, yayin*, p. 30).

(3) The same principle applied in the O.T. to priests and Levites who ministered before God on behalf of the people (Lev. 10:8–11; see 10:9, note).

(4) All N.T. believers are regarded as kings and priests unto God, who rule in God's spiritual kingdom (1 Pet. 2:9). Therefore, God's standard for kings and priests with respect to not drinking intoxicating beverages applies equally to us (see Num. 6:1–3; Eph. 5:18, note; 1 Tim. 3:3, note).

31:6–7 GIVE STRONG DRINK UNTO HIM THAT IS READY TO PERISH. It is improbable that the inspired writer intended to sanction or command intoxication as a way of forgetting one's troubles as death approaches. God's prescription for affliction is to turn to Him in prayer, not to intoxicating drink (Ps. 12; 25; 30; 34). (1) These words may be interpreted as an ironic expression that intoxicating drink is for those who have already ruined their lives and are without hope, unlike wise kings and rulers who must be total abstainers (vv. 4–5).

(2) Vv. 8–9 follow with the proper action to be taken toward those who are suffering because their rights have been violated (cf. v. 5): the righteous must defend the rights of the afflicted. To recommend drunkenness in order to help them forget their troubles would resolve no problems, but only create new ones. To attempt to alleviate problems through intoxication may be the world's way, but it is not God's way.

31:10–31 A VIRTUOUS WOMAN. These verses describe the ideal wife and mother. Her whole life is centered around a reverent fear for God (v. 30), compassion for those in need (vv. 19–20), and faithfulness and love toward her family (v. 27). All the ideals set forth here will probably not be fulfilled in any one wife and mother. But each wife can seek to serve God, her family, and others with the ability and material resources that God has given her (see Eph. 5:22, note; 1 Tim. 2:15, note).

23 [o]Her husband is known in the gates, when he sitteth among the elders of the land.

24 She maketh fine linen, and selleth *it;* and delivereth girdles unto the merchant.

25 Strength and honour *are* her clothing; and she shall rejoice in time to come.

26 She openeth her mouth with wisdom; and in her tongue *is* the law of kindness.

27 She looketh well to the ways of her household, and eateth not the bread of idleness.

31:23
[o] ch. 12:4

28 Her children arise up, and call her blessed; her husband *also,* and he praiseth her.

29 Many daughters [m]have done virtuously, but thou excellest them all.

30 Favour *is* deceitful, and beauty *is* vain: *but* a woman *that* feareth the LORD, she shall be praised.

31 Give her of the fruit of her hands; and let her own works praise her in the gates.

[m] Or, *have gotten riches*

ECCLESIASTES

Outline

Title (1:1)

I. Introduction: The General Futility of Life (1:2–11)

II. The Futility of a Self-centered Life Illustrated from Personal Experience (1:12—2:26)
   - A. The Uselessness of Human Wisdom and Philosophy (1:12–18)
   - B. The Emptiness of Pleasure and Wealth (2:1–11)
   - C. The Vanity of Great Accomplishments (2:12–17)
   - D. The Inequity of Hard Work (2:18–23)
   - E. Conclusion: Enjoyment Comes Only from God (2:24–26)

III. Various Reflections on Life's Experiences (3:1—11:6)
   - A. Perspectives on the Created Order (3:1–22)
     1. A Time Created for Everything (3:1–8)
     2. The Beauty of Creation (3:9–14)
     3. God Is Judge of All (3:15–22)
   - B. Futile Experiences of Life (4:1–16)
     1. Experiencing Oppression (4:1–3)
     2. Competitive Work (4:4–6)
     3. Having No Friends (4:7–12)
     4. Failing to Accept Advice (4:13–16)
   - C. Warnings to the Reader (5:1—6:12)
     1. About Approaching God (5:1–7)
     2. About Accumulating Possessions (5:8–20)
     3. About Living and Dying (6:1–12)
   - D. Miscellaneous Proverbs on Wisdom (7:1—8:1)
   - E. Matters of Justice (8:2—9:12)
     1. Obedience to the King (8:2–8)
     2. Crime and Punishment (8:9–13)
     3. The Problem of True Justice (8:14–17)
     4. Ultimate Justice for Everyone (9:1–6)
     5. The Remedy of Faith (9:7–12)
   - F. More Miscellaneous Proverbs on Wisdom (9:13—11:6)

IV. Concluding Exhortations (11:7—12:14)
   - A. Rejoice in Your Youth (11:7–10)
   - B. Remember God in Your Youth (12:1–8)
   - C. Cling to One Book (12:9–12)
   - D. Fear God and Keep His Commandments (12:13–14)

Author: Solomon

Theme: The Vanity of Life Apart from God

Date of Writing: c. 935 B.C.

Background

The title of this book in the Hebrew O.T. is *qoheleth* (from Heb. *qahal*, "to assemble"); literally, it means "one who holds and addresses an assembly." This word occurs seven times in the book (1:1,2,12; 7:27; 12:8–10) and is generally translated as "Preacher" or "Teacher." The corresponding word in the Septuagint is *ekklesiastēs*, from which the English title Ecclesiastes is derived. The entire work, therefore, is a series of teachings by a well-known public speaker.

The author is generally believed to be Solomon, even though his name does not occur in this book as it does in Proverbs (e.g., Prov. 1:1; 10:1; 25:1) and the Song of Solomon (cf. Sol. 1:1). Several passages, however, suggest his authorship. (1) The author identifies himself as a son of David who was king in Jerusalem (1:1,12). (2) He refers to himself as the wisest ruler of God's people (1:16) and the writer of many proverbs (12:9). (3) His kingdom was known for its wealth and affluent grandeur (2:4–9). All of these elements fit the Biblical description of King Solomon (cf. 1 Ki. 2:9; 3:12; 4:29–34; 5:12; 10:1–8). Furthermore, we know Solomon occasionally gathered an assembly of Israelites and addressed them (e.g., 1 Ki. 8:1). Jewish tradition ascribes the book to Solomon. On the other hand, the fact that his name is not explicitly recorded in Ecclesiastes (as in his other two books) may suggest that someone else was involved in putting the book together. It is best to regard the book as coming from the hand of Solomon, but perhaps as gathered together into its present form by some later person, similar to the way certain parts of the book of Proverbs were collated (cf. Prov. 25:1).

Liturgically, the book of Ecclesiastes became one of the five scrolls from the third part of the Hebrew Bible, the *Hagiographa* ("Holy Writings"), each of which was read publicly each year at one of the Jewish feasts. Ecclesiastes was assigned to be read at the Feast of Tabernacles.

Purpose

According to Jewish tradition, Solomon wrote the Song of Solomon during his younger years, Proverbs in his middle years, and Ecclesiastes during the last years of his life. The accumulative effect of Solomon's spiritual decline, idolatry, and life of self-indulgence left him at the end disillusioned with pleasure and materialism as a way to happiness. Ecclesiastes records his cynical reflections about the futility and emptiness of seeking happiness in life apart from God and His Word. He had experienced wealth, power, honor, fame, and sensual pleasure—all in great abundance—yet they added up in the end to emptiness and disillusionment: "Vanity of vanities; all *is* vanity" (1:2). His primary purpose in writing Ecclesiastes may have been to share his regrets and firsthand testimony with others before he died, especially with young people, so that they would not make the same mistakes he had. He establishes forever the utter futility of basing one's values in life on earthly possessions and personal ambition. Though young people should enjoy their youth (11:9–10), it is more important to commit themselves to their Creator (12:1) and to resolve to fear God and keep His commandments (12:13–14). Such is the only path to meaning in life.

Survey

It is difficult to provide an orderly analysis of the contents of Ecclesiastes; no outline easily accounts for every verse or paragraph. In some ways, Ecclesiastes reads like excerpts from a philosopher's personal journal during the latter and disappointing years of his life. He begins by stating his underlying theme that all of life is vanity and vexation of spirit (1:1–11). The book's first major block of material is strictly autobiographical; Solomon describes the highlights of his intensely self-centered life of affluence, pleasure, and worldly success (1:12—2:23). The pursuit of happiness through these means had ended for him in dissatisfaction and emptiness. The bulk of the book contains a series of random thoughts that underscore the futility and perplexity of life without God at its center. Life "under the sun" (a phrase that occurs twenty-nine times in the book) is life as seen through

the eyes of the unredeemed and is characterized by inequities, uncertainties, unpredictable changes in fortune, and violations of justice. Solomon can find ultimate meaning in life only when he looks "above the sun" to God. Pleasure-seeking is superficial and foolish; one's youth is too brief and life too fleeting to be squandered foolishly. The unpredictability of life and the certainty of death cause Solomon to be cynical about God's purposes and ways. The book concludes by instructing youth to remember God while they are young, so that they do not grow old with bitter regrets and the sad task of giving an account to God for a wasted life.

Special Features

Five major features or emphases characterize Ecclesiastes. (1) It is an intensely personal book, with the author frequently using the personal pronoun "I" throughout the first ten chapters. (2) Through the underlying pessimism of the author, the book reveals that life apart from God is unpredictable and filled with vanity (the word "vanity" occurs thirty-seven times). Solomon observes cynically the various paradoxes and perplexities of life (see, e.g., 2:23 and 2:24; 8:12 and 8:13; 7:3 and 8:15). (3) The heart of Solomon's advice in the book occurs in the last two verses: "Fear God, and keep his commandments: for this *is* the whole *duty* of man" (12:13–14). (4) The literary style of the book is disjointed; its vocabulary and syntax are among the most difficult Hebrew in the O.T. and do not fit easily into any particular era of Hebrew literature. (5) It contains the most picturesque allegory in the Bible about a person growing older (12:2–7).

New Testament Fulfillment

Although only one passage from Ecclesiastes seems to be quoted in the N.T. (7:20 in Rom. 3:10, on the universality of sin), yet there appear to be several allusions: Eccl. 3:17; 11:9; 12:14 in Mat. 16:27; Rom. 2:6–8; 2 Cor. 5:10; 2 Thes. 1:6–7; Eccl. 5:15 in 1 Tim. 6:7. The author's conclusion about the futility of pursuing worldly possessions was reiterated by Jesus when He said (1) that we should not lay up treasures on earth (Mat. 6:19–21,24), and (2) that it is senseless to gain the whole world and lose one's soul (Mat. 16:26). The theme of Ecclesiastes, i.e., that life apart from God is vanity and futility, sets the stage for the N.T. message of grace: joy, salvation, and eternal life come only as a gift from God (cf. John 10:10; Rom. 6:23).

In several ways, this book prepared the way for N.T. revelation in reverse fashion. Its frequent references to the futility of life and the certainty of death prepare the reader for God's answer to death and judgment, i.e., eternal life through Jesus Christ. Since the wisest man in the O.T. was unable to find satisfactory answers to the problems of life through his pursuit of self-centered pleasure, wealth, and accumulated knowledge, we must look for answers in One whom the N.T. says is "greater than Solomon" (Mat. 12:42), even Jesus Christ, "in whom are hid all the treasures of wisdom and knowledge" (Col. 2:3).

Reading Ecclesiastes

In order to read the entire Old Testament in one year, the book of Ecclesiastes should be read in 4 days, according to the following schedule: ☐ 1–2 ☐ 3–5 ☐ 6–8 ☐ 9–12

NOTES

Vanity of human wisdom

1 THE WORDS [a]of the Preacher,
the son of David, king in Jerusa-
lem.
2 [b]Vanity of vanities, saith the
Preacher, vanity of vanities; [c]all *is*
vanity.
3 [d]What profit hath a man of all his
labour which he taketh under the sun?
4 *One* generation passeth away, and
another generation cometh: [e]but the
earth abideth for ever.
5 [f]The sun also ariseth, and the
sun goeth down, and [a]hasteth to his
place where he arose.
6 [g]The wind goeth toward the
south, and turneth about unto the
north; it whirleth about continually,
and the wind returneth again accord-
ing to his circuits.
7 [h]All the rivers run into the sea;
yet the sea *is* not full; unto the place
from whence the rivers come, thither
they [b]return again.
8 All things *are* full of labour; man
cannot utter *it:* [i]the eye is not satis-
fied with seeing, nor the ear filled with
hearing.
9 [j]The thing that hath been, it *is*
that which shall be; and that which is
done *is* that which shall be done: and
there is no new *thing* under the sun.
10 Is there *any* thing whereof it may
be said, See, this *is* new? it hath been
already of old time, which was be-
fore us.
11 *There is* no remembrance of for-
mer *things;* neither shall there be *any*
remembrance of *things* that are to
come with *those* that shall come after.
12 ¶ [k]I the Preacher was king over
Israel in Jerusalem.
13 And I gave my heart to seek and
search out by wisdom concerning all
things that are done under heaven:
[l]this sore travail hath God given to
the sons of man [c]to be exercised
therewith.
14 I have seen all the works that
are done under the sun; and, behold,
all *is* vanity and vexation of spirit.
15 [m]*That which is* crooked cannot
be made straight: and [d]that which is
wanting cannot be numbered.
16 I communed with mine own
heart, saying, Lo, I am come to great
estate, and have gotten [n]more wis-
dom than all *they* that have been before
me in Jerusalem: yea, my heart [e]had
great experience of wisdom and knowl-
edge.
17 [o]And I gave my heart to know
wisdom, and to know madness and fol-
ly: I perceived that this also is vexation
of spirit.
18 For [p]in much wisdom *is* much
grief: and he that increaseth knowl-
edge increaseth sorrow.

Vanity of pleasure and wealth

2 I [q]SAID in mine heart, Go to
now, I will prove thee with mirth,
therefore enjoy pleasure: and, behold,
[r]this also *is* vanity.

1:1 [a]ver. 12 ch. 7:27 & 12:8-10
1:2 [b]Ps. 39:5,6 & 62:9 & 144:4 ch. 12:8 [c]Rom. 8:20
1:3 [d]ch. 2:22
1:4 [e]Ps. 104:5 & 119:90
1:5 [f]Ps. 19:4-6
1:6 [g]John 3:8
1:7 [h]Ps. 104:8,9 Jer. 5:22
1:8 [i]Prov. 27:20
1:9 [j]ch. 3:15
1:12 [k]ver. 1
1:13 [l]Gen. 3:19 ch. 3:10
1:15 [m]ch. 7:13
1:16 [n]1 Ki. 3:12,13
1:17 [o]ch. 2:3,12
1:18 [p]ch. 12:12
2:1 [q]Luke 12:19 [r]ch. 1:2

[a] Heb. *panteth* [b] Heb. *return to go* [c] Or, *to afflict them* [d] Heb. *defect* [e] Heb. *had seen much*

1:2 ALL *IS* VANITY. This verse states the theme of Ecclesiastes, i.e., all our activities on earth are meaningless and purposeless when carried out apart from God's will, His fellowship, and His loving activity in our lives. The book also emphasizes that creation itself is subject to vanity and corruption. (1) The author's concern is to destroy the false hopes that people place in a completely secular world. He wants them to see the solemn facts of evil, injustice, and death, and to realize that life apart from God has no meaning and cannot produce true happiness.

(2) The solution to the problem is found in faith and trust in God; only this makes life worthwhile. We must look beyond earthly things into the heavenlies to receive hope, joy, and peace (3:12–17; 8:12–13; 12:13–14).

1:5–11 THE SUN ALSO ARISETH. The earth appears to go its own predetermined way with nothing changing. Human beings cannot look to nature to find meaning for their existence on earth, nor can they find total satisfaction in it.

1:9 *THERE IS* NO NEW *THING* UNDER THE SUN. This verse does not mean that there are no new inventions, but only that there is no new type of activity. The pursuits, goals, and desires of humankind remain the same.

1:12–18 I THE PREACHER ... SEARCH OUT BY WISDOM. Humans cannot find purpose in life in and by themselves, nor can people use their own human achievement to set right all that appears wrong in the world (v. 15). The solution calls for something higher than human wisdom, philosophy, or ideas. That wisdom is "from above" (Jas. 3:17), "the hidden *wisdom*, which God ordained before the world" (1 Cor. 2:7).

2:1–11 PLEASURE ... THIS ALSO *IS* VANITY. Solomon relates how he tried pleasure, wealth, and cultural delights in an effort to find fulfillment and the good life; yet these things did not result in true happiness — life was still void of satisfaction (v. 11). We can only find lasting peace, fulfillment, and joy if we look for our happiness in God and His will.

2 I said of laughter, *It is* mad: and
of mirth, What doeth it?
3 [s]I sought in mine heart [f]to give
myself unto wine, yet acquainting mine
heart with wisdom; and to lay hold on
folly, till I might see what *was* that
good for the sons of men, which they
should do under the heaven [g]all the
days of their life.
4 I made me great works; I builded
me houses; I planted me vineyards:
5 I made me gardens and orchards,
and I planted trees in them of all *kind*
of fruits:
6 I made me pools of water, to water
therewith the wood that bringeth forth
trees:
7 I got *me* servants and maidens,
and had [h]servants born in my house;
also I had great possessions of great
and small cattle above all that were in
Jerusalem before me:
8 [t]I gathered me also silver and
gold, and the peculiar treasure of kings
and of the provinces: I gat me men
singers and women singers, and the
delights of the sons of men, *as* [i]musi-
cal instruments, and that of all sorts.
9 So I was great, and increased
more than all that were before me in
Jerusalem: also my wisdom remained
with me.
10 And whatsoever mine eyes de-
sired I kept not from them, I withheld
not my heart from any joy; for my heart
rejoiced in all my labour: and [u]this
was my portion of all my labour.
11 Then I looked on all the works
that my hands had wrought, and on the
labour that I had laboured to do: and,
behold, all *was* [v]vanity and vexation of
spirit, and *there was* no profit under the
sun.

The fool and the wise must die

12 ¶ And I turned myself to behold
wisdom, [w]and madness, and folly: for
what *can* the man *do* that cometh after
the king? [j]*even* that which hath been
already done.
13 Then I saw [k]that wisdom ex-
celleth folly, as far as light excelleth
darkness.

2:3 [s]ch. 1:17
2:8 [t]1 Ki. 9:28 & 10:10,14,21
2:10 [u]ch. 3:22 & 5:18 & 9:9
2:11 [v]ch. 1:3,14
2:12 [w]ch. 1:17 & 7:25

2:14 [x]Prov. 17:24 ch. 8:1 [y]Ps. 49:10 ch. 9:2,3,11
2:18 [z]Ps. 49:10
2:22 [a]ch. 1:3 & 3:9
2:23 [b]Job 5:7 & 14:1

14 [x]The wise man's eyes *are* in his
head; but the fool walketh in darkness:
and I myself perceived also that [y]one
event happeneth to them all.
15 Then said I in my heart, As it
happeneth to the fool, so it [l]hap-
peneth even to me; and why was I then
more wise? Then I said in my heart,
that this also *is* vanity.
16 For *there is* no remembrance of
the wise more than of the fool for ever;
seeing that which now *is* in the days to
come shall all be forgotten. And how
dieth the wise *man?* as the fool.
17 Therefore I hated life; because
the work that is wrought under the sun
is grievous unto me: for all *is* vanity
and vexation of spirit.

The futility of labour

18 ¶ Yea, I hated all my labour
which I had [m]taken under the sun: be-
cause [z]I should leave it unto the man
that shall be after me.
19 And who knoweth whether he
shall be a wise *man* or a fool? yet shall
he have rule over all my labour wherein
I have laboured, and wherein I have
shown myself wise under the sun. This
is also vanity.
20 Therefore I went about to cause
my heart to despair of all the labour
which I took under the sun.
21 For there is a man whose labour
is in wisdom, and in knowledge, and in
equity; yet to a man that hath not la-
boured therein shall he [n]leave it *for*
his portion. This also *is* vanity and a
great evil.
22 [a]For what hath man of all his
labour, and of the vexation of his heart,
wherein he hath laboured under the
sun?
23 For all his days *are* [b]sorrows,
and his travail grief; yea, his heart

[f]Heb. *to draw my flesh with wine* [g]Heb. *the number of the days of their life* [h]Heb. *sons of my house* [i]Heb. *musical instrument and instruments* [j]Or, *in those things which have been already done* [k]Heb. *that there is an excellency in wisdom more than in folly* [l]Heb. *happeneth to me, even to me* [m]Heb. *laboured* [n]Heb. *give*

2:12–17 WISDOM . . . AND FOLLY. Solomon saw a temporary advantage of living wisely upon the earth, for the wise person has less trouble than the fool. But all advantages are canceled out at death. Thus earthly wisdom has no real permanent worth.

2:18–23 I HATED ALL MY LABOUR. Human labor, if not dedicated to God, has no permanent value (see Col. 3:23, note). Even what is left of one's possessions after death may be squandered foolishly by someone else.

taketh not rest in the night. This is also
vanity.
24 ¶ [c]*There is* nothing better for a
man, *than* that he should eat and drink,
and *that* he [o]should make his soul en-
joy good in his labour. This also I saw,
that it *was* from the hand of God.
25 For who can eat, or who else can
hasten *hereunto,* more than I?
26 For *God* giveth to a man that *is*
good [p]in his sight wisdom, and knowl-
edge, and joy: but to the sinner he
giveth travail, to gather and to heap
up, that [d]he may give to *him that is*
good before God. This also *is* vanity
and vexation of spirit.

A time for everything

3 TO EVERY *thing there is* a season,
and a [e]time to every purpose un-
der the heaven:
2 A time [q]to be born, and [f]a time
to die; a time to plant, and a time to
pluck up *that which is* planted;
3 A time to kill, and a time to heal;
a time to break down, and a time to
build up;
4 A time to weep, and a time to
laugh; a time to mourn, and a time to
dance;
5 A time to cast away stones, and a
time to gather stones together; a time
to embrace, and [g]a time [r]to refrain
from embracing;
6 A time to [s]get, and a time to lose;
a time to keep, and a time to cast away;
7 A time to rend, and a time to sew;
[h]a time to keep silence, and a time to
speak;
8 A time to love, and a time to
[i]hate; a time of war, and a time of
peace.
9 [j]What profit hath he that
worketh in that wherein he laboureth?
10 [k]I have seen the travail, which
God hath given to the sons of men to
be exercised in it.
11 He hath made every *thing* beauti-
ful in his time: also he hath set the
world in their heart, so that [l]no man
can find out the work that God maketh
from the beginning to the end.
12 I know that *there is* no good in
them, but for *a man* to rejoice, and to
do good in his life.
13 And also [m]that every man
should eat and drink, and enjoy the
good of all his labour, it *is* the gift of
God.
14 I know that, whatsoever God
doeth, it shall be for ever: [n]nothing
can be put to it, nor anything taken
from it: and God doeth *it,* that *men*
should fear before him.
15 [o]That which hath been is now;
and that which is to be hath already
been; and God requireth [t]that which
is past.

The vanity of all life

16 ¶ And moreover [p]I saw under
the sun the place of judgment, *that*
wickedness *was* there; and the place of
righteousness, *that* iniquity *was* there.
17 I said in mine heart, [q]God shall
judge the righteous and the wicked: for
there is [r]a time there for every purpose
and for every work.
18 I said in mine heart concerning
the estate of the sons of men, [u]that
God might manifest them, and that
they might see that they themselves
are beasts.
19 [s]For that which befalleth the

2:24 [c]ch. 3:12,13,22 & 5:18 & 8:15
2:26 [d]Job 27:16,17 Prov. 28:8
3:1 [e]ver. 17 ch. 8:6
3:2 [f]Heb. 9:27
3:5 [g]Joel 2:16 1 Cor. 7:5
3:7 [h]Amos 5:13
3:8 [i]Luke 14:26
3:9 [j]ch. 1:3
3:10 [k]ch. 1:13
3:11 [l]ch. 8:17 Rom. 11:33
3:13 [m]ch. 2:24
3:14 [n]Jas. 1:17
3:15 [o]ch. 1:9
3:16 [p]ch. 5:8
3:17 [q]Rom. 2:6-8 2 Cor. 5:10 2 Thes. 1:6 [r]ver. 1
3:19 [s]Ps. 49:12,20 & 73:22 ch. 2:16

[o] Or, *delight his senses* [p] Heb. *before him* [q] Heb. *to bear* [r] Heb. *to be far from* [s] Or, *seek* [t] Heb. *that which is driven away* [u] Or, *that they might clear God, and see*

2:24–26 FROM THE HAND OF GOD. The author reaches two conclusions: (1) Eating, drinking, and working—in fact, all activities in life—can bring satisfaction only if one has a personal relationship with God. Only He enables us to find enjoyment in life. (2) God gives true wisdom, knowledge, and joy to those who in faith please Him (cf. 3:12–13,22; 5:18–20; 8:15; 9:7). Thus we must see life as a gift from God and look to Him to work out His purpose for us (see Phil. 2:13, note).

3:1–8 TO EVERY *THING THERE IS* A SEASON . . . PURPOSE. God has an eternal plan that includes the purposes and activities of every person on earth. We must give ourselves to God as holy sacrifices, allow the Holy Spirit to accomplish God's plan for us, and be careful not to be out of God's will and miss God's timing and purpose for our lives (see Rom. 12:1–2, notes).

3:13 THE GIFT OF GOD. The ability to enjoy life and live it properly is a gift from God that comes only when we are brought into a right relationship with Him and sincerely submit ourselves to Him as our Lord and God. He then gives us joy in what we do.

3:16–17 WICKEDNESS *WAS* THERE. In this world the perfection of God's purposes is marred by injustice and wickedness. But, Solomon adds, we can be assured that God will, in His own time, judge the wicked and reward the righteous (cf. Rom. 2:5–11).

3:19 SO DIETH THE OTHER. Biologically, hu-

sons of men befalleth beasts; even one
thing befalleth them: as the one dieth,
so dieth the other; yea, they have all
one breath; so that a man hath no
preeminence above a beast: for all *is*
vanity.
20 All go unto one place; [t]all are of
the dust, and all turn to dust again.
21 [u]Who knoweth the spirit [v]of
man that [w]goeth upward, and the spir-
it of the beast that goeth downward to
the earth?
22 [v]Wherefore I perceive that *there*
is nothing better, than that a man
should rejoice in his own works; for
[w]that *is* his portion: [x]for who shall
bring him to see what shall be after
him?
4 SO I returned, and considered all
the [y]oppressions that are done
under the sun: and behold the tears of
such as were oppressed, and they had
no comforter; and on the [x]side of their
oppressors *there was* power; but they
had no comforter.
2 [z]Wherefore I praised the dead
which are already dead more than the
living which are yet alive.
3 [a]Yea, better *is he* than both they,
which hath not yet been, who hath not
seen the evil work that is done under
the sun.

Travail of the wise and foolish

4 ¶ Again, I considered all travail,
and [y]every right work, that [z]for this
a man is envied of his neighbour. This
is also vanity and vexation of spirit.
5 [b]The fool foldeth his hands to-
gether, and eateth his own flesh.
6 [c]Better *is* an handful *with* quiet-
ness, than both the hands full *with* tra-
vail and vexation of spirit.
7 ¶ Then I returned, and I saw vani-
ty under the sun.
8 There is one *alone,* and *there is* not
a second; yea, he hath neither child nor
brother: yet *is there* no end of all his
labour; neither is his [d]eye satisfied
with riches; [e]neither *saith he,* For
whom do I labour, and bereave my soul
of good? This *is* also vanity, yea, it *is*
a sore travail.
9 ¶ Two *are* better than one; be-
cause they have a good reward for their
labour.
10 For if they fall, the one will lift up
his fellow: but woe to him *that is* alone
when he falleth; for *he hath* not another
to help him up.
11 Again, if two lie together, then
they have heat: but how can one be
warm *alone?*
12 And if one prevail against him,
two shall withstand him; and a three-
fold cord is not quickly broken.
13 ¶ Better *is* a poor and a wise

3:20 [t]Gen. 3:19
3:21 [u]ch. 12:7
3:22 [v]ver. 12; ch. 2:24 & 5:18 & 11:9; [w]ch. 2:10; [x]ch. 6:12 & 8:7 & 10:14
4:1 [y]ch. 3:16 & 5:8
4:2 [z]Job 3:17
4:3 [a]Job 3:11,16,21; ch. 6:3
4:5 [b]Prov. 6:10 & 24:33
4:6 [c]Prov. 15:16,17 & 16:8
4:8 [d]Prov. 27:20; 1 John 2:16; [e]Ps. 39:6

[v]Heb. *of the sons of man* [w]Heb. *is ascending*
[x]Heb. *hand* [y]Heb. *all the rightness of work*
[z]Heb. *this is the envy of a man from his neighbour*

mans die just like the animals. This fact shows our weakness and frailty and should cause us to fear and obey God (12:13).

3:21 THE SPIRIT OF MAN THAT GOETH UPWARD. By physical observation no one can determine if a person's spirit goes "upward." Solomon revealed the meaning of this verse when he said in 12:7: "the spirit shall return unto God who gave it" (cf. Ps. 16:9–11; 49:15; 73:23–26; Is. 26:19; Dan. 12:2–3).

4:1 THEY HAD NO COMFORTER. Looking around at a world that was rejecting God's ways, Solomon saw oppression everywhere, and the oppressed had no comforter. It is still true that there is much oppression in the world—but comfort is available, for our God is "the God of all comfort" (2 Cor. 1:3). God the Father comforted His people in O.T. times when they looked to Him (Ps. 86:17; Is. 51:3,12), Jesus brought comfort and healing while on earth (Mat. 9:22), and the Holy Spirit was promised as another Comforter (John 14:16). Believers are also instructed to comfort one another (1 Thes. 5:11).

4:4–8 BETTER *IS* AN HANDFUL *WITH* QUIETNESS, THAN BOTH HANDS FULL *WITH* TRAVAIL. Hard work and the development of skill are often spurred on by jealous rivalry with one's neighbor and the spirit of selfish competition; those motivations are self-destructive (v. 5). God wants us instead to seek a life of moderation—to do good work and to live in a quiet, godly manner. We must work together (v. 9) and help each other (vv. 10–11).

4:9–12 TWO *ARE* BETTER THAN ONE. Companionship has many advantages, for God did not create us to live without fellowship (Gen. 2:18). We all need the love, help, and support of friends, family, and fellow believers (Acts 2:42). Yet even this is insufficient without the daily companionship of God the Father, the Son, and the Holy Spirit (1 Cor. 1:9; 2 Cor. 13:14; Phil. 2:1; 1 John 1:3, 6–7).

4:13–16 THEY ALSO THAT COME AFTER SHALL NOT REJOICE IN HIM. This contrast between a wise boy and a foolish old king who refuses advice shows how sad it is when a ruler becomes arrogant and no longer knows how to be the servant-leader of his people (v. 13).

child than an old and foolish king,
[a]who will no more be admonished.
14 For out of prison he cometh to
reign; whereas also *he that is* born in
his kingdom becometh poor.
15 I considered all the living which
walk under the sun, with the second
child that shall stand up in his stead.
16 *There is* no end of all the people,
even of all that have been before them:
they also that come after shall not re-
joice in him. Surely this also *is* vanity
and vexation of spirit.

The vanity of vows

5 KEEP [f]THY foot when thou goest
to the house of God, and be more
ready to hear, [g]than to give the sacri-
fice of fools: for they consider not that
they do evil.
2 Be not rash with thy mouth, and
let not thine heart be hasty to utter *any*
[b]thing before God: for God *is* in heav-
en, and thou upon earth: therefore let
thy words [h]be few.
3 For a dream cometh through the
multitude of business; and [i]a fool's
voice *is known* by multitude of words.
4 [j]When thou vowest a vow unto
God, defer not to pay it; for *he hath* no
pleasure in fools: pay that which thou
hast vowed.
5 [k]Better *is it* that thou shouldest
not vow, than that thou shouldest vow
and not pay.
6 Suffer not thy mouth to cause thy
flesh to sin; [l]neither say thou before
the angel, that it *was* an error: where-
fore should God be angry at thy voice,
and destroy the work of thine hands?
7 For in the multitude of dreams
and many words *there are* also *divers*
vanities: but [m]fear thou God.

5:1 [f]See Ex. 3:5 Is. 1:12 [g]1 Sam. 15:22 Ps. 50:8 Prov. 15:8 & 21:27 Hos. 6:6
5:2 [h]Prov. 10:19 Mat. 6:7
5:3 [i]Prov. 10:19
5:4 [j]Num. 30:2 Deut. 23:21
5:5 [k]Prov. 20:25 Acts 5:4
5:6 [l]1 Cor. 11:10
5:7 [m]ch. 12:13
5:8 [n]ch. 3:16 [o]Ps. 12:5 & 58:11 & 82:1
5:13 [p]ch. 6:1
5:15 [q]Job 1:21 Ps. 49:17 1 Tim. 6:7
5:16 [r]ch. 1:3 [s]Prov. 11:29
5:17 [t]Ps. 127:2

The vanity of riches

8 ¶ If thou [n]seest the oppression of
the poor, and violent perverting of
judgment and justice in a province,
marvel not [c]at the matter: for [o]*he
that is* higher than the highest re-
gardeth; and *there be* higher than they.
9 ¶ Moreover the profit of the earth
is for all: the king *himself* is served by
the field.
10 He that loveth silver shall not be
satisfied with silver; nor he that loveth
abundance with increase: this *is* also
vanity.
11 When goods increase, they are
increased that eat them: and what
good *is there* to the owners thereof, sav-
ing the beholding *of them* with their
eyes?
12 The sleep of a labouring man *is*
sweet, whether he eat little or much:
but the abundance of the rich will not
suffer him to sleep.
13 [p]There is a sore evil *which* I
have seen under the sun, *namely,*
riches kept for the owners thereof to
their hurt.
14 But those riches perish by evil
travail: and he begetteth a son, and
there is nothing in his hand.
15 [q]As he came forth of his moth-
er's womb, naked shall he return to go
as he came, and shall take nothing of
his labour, which he may carry away in
his hand.
16 And this also *is* a sore evil, *that*
in all points as he came, so shall he go:
and [r]what profit hath he [s]that hath
laboured for the wind?
17 All his days also [t]he eateth in

[a] Heb. *who knoweth not to be admonished*
[b] Or, *word* [c] Heb. *at the will,* or, *purpose*

5:1 KEEP THY FOOT WHEN THOU GOEST TO THE HOUSE OF GOD. Entering the house of God should be done reverently rather than carelessly. Be spiritually prepared before coming; then be ready to hear and obey what you hear.

5:4–6 PAY THAT WHICH THOU HAST VOWED. A vow is a solemn promise to God that must be kept. It is better not to vow at all than to vow and not fulfill it. N.T. believers make a vow to live separated from sin and dedicated to God when they partake of the Lord's Supper (see 1 Cor. 11:20, note). To seek the pleasures of sin after making this vow to God brings His anger and judgment, for it means that the vow was really a lie. Lying to God may bring severe punishment (e.g., Ananias and Sapphira, see Acts 5:1–11).

5:8 *THERE BE* HIGHER THAN THEY. Observing again the oppression of the poor and the prevailing lack of justice, Solomon reminds the oppressors that God is the highest Judge. He is above everyone, and He will give the final verdict on the judgment day.

5:10–17 HE THAT LOVETH SILVER SHALL NOT BE SATISFIED WITH SILVER. Money and the abundance of material things do not give life meaning and thus cannot bring real happiness. In general, the honest working person who comes in after a good day's work sleeps peacefully, while wealthy individuals can't sleep for fear that some calamity or a mistake on their part will cause them to lose everything. But even if they do not lose anything, they will take nothing with them when they die. It is sad that so many people work so hard for an abundance of possessions, when it is much better to lay up treasures in heaven (Mat. 6:19–21).

darkness, and *he hath* much sorrow
and wrath with his sickness.
18 ¶ Behold *that* which I have seen:
[u]*it*[d] *is* good and comely *for one* to eat
and to drink, and to enjoy the good of
all his labour that he taketh under the
sun [e]all the days of his life, which God
giveth him: [v]for it *is* his portion.
19 [w]Every man also to whom God
hath given riches and wealth, and hath
given him power to eat thereof, and to
take his portion, and to rejoice in his
labour; this *is* the gift of God.
20 [f]For he shall not much remem-
ber the days of his life; because God
answereth *him* in the joy of his heart.

6 THERE[x] IS an evil which I have
seen under the sun, and it *is* com-
mon among men:
2 A man to whom God hath given
riches, wealth, and honour, [y]so that
he wanteth nothing for his soul of all
that he desireth, [z]yet God giveth him
not power to eat thereof, but a stranger
eateth it: this *is* vanity, and it *is* an evil
disease.
3 ¶ If a man beget an hundred *chil-
dren,* and live many years, so that the
days of his years be many, and his soul
be not filled with good, and [a]also *that*
he have no burial; I say, *that* [b]an un-
timely birth *is* better than he.
4 For he cometh in with vanity, and
departeth in darkness, and his name
shall be covered with darkness.
5 Moreover he hath not seen the
sun, nor known *any thing:* this hath
more rest than the other.

5:18
[u]ch. 2:24
& 3:12,13
& 9:7
& 11:9
1 Tim. 6:17
[v]ch. 2:10
& 3:22
5:19
[w]ch. 2:24
& 3:13
6:1
[x]ch. 5:13
6:2
[y]Job 21:10
Ps. 17:14
& 73:7
[z]Luke 12:20
6:3
[a]2 Ki. 9:35
Is. 14:19,20
Jer. 22:19
[b]Job 3:16
Ps. 58:8
ch. 4:3

6:7
[c]Prov. 16:26
6:10
[d]Job 9:32
Is. 45:9
Jer. 49:19
6:12
[e]Ps. 102:11
& 144:4
Jas. 4:14
[f]Ps. 39:6
ch. 8:7
7:1
[g]Prov. 22:1

6 ¶ Yea, though he live a thousand
years twice *told,* yet hath he seen no
good: do not all go to one place?
7 [c]All the labour of man *is* for his
mouth, and yet the [g]appetite is not
filled.
8 For what hath the wise more than
the fool? what hath the poor, that
knoweth to walk before the living?
9 ¶ Better *is* the sight of the eyes
[h]than the wandering of the desire:
this *is* also vanity and vexation of
spirit.
10 That which hath been is named
already, and it is known that it *is* man:
[d]neither may he contend with him
that is mightier than he.
11 ¶ Seeing there be many things
that increase vanity, what *is* man the
better?
12 For who knoweth what *is* good
for man in *this* life, [i]all the days of his
vain life which he spendeth as [e]a
shadow? for [f]who can tell a man what
shall be after him under the sun?

Choosing wisdom

7 A [g]GOOD name *is* better than
precious ointment; and the day of
death than the day of one's birth.
2 ¶ *It is* better to go to the house of
mourning, than to go to the house of
feasting: for that *is* the end of all men;

[d] Heb. there is *a good which is comely* [e] Heb. *the number of the days* [f] Or, *Though* he give *not much,* yet *he remembereth* [g] Heb. *soul* [h] Heb. *than the walking of the soul* [i] Heb. *the number of the days of the life of his vanity*

5:18–20 REJOICE IN HIS LABOR; THIS *IS* THE GIFT OF GOD. When God allows us to enjoy our work and to gain in a just manner more than we need for our necessities, we must consider that what we have is a gift from God to be used to help others and God's cause upon the earth.

6:2 A STRANGER EATETH IT. A person may have everything he or she needs to enjoy life, but still be unable to do so. The ability to enjoy what we have depends on a right relationship with God. If we are committed to Him and His kingdom, God will enable us to enjoy His material gifts.

6:3–6 THOUGH HE LIVE A THOUSAND YEARS TWICE *TOLD*. Death at an early age is sad; however, long life does not guarantee that a person will enjoy what God has given him or her. A life filled with trouble makes people wish they had died at birth and avoided all the suffering (cf. Job 3). In the light of eternity, the important thing is whether we live our lives for God (cf. 12:13–14).

6:10 NEITHER MAY HE CONTEND WITH HIM THAT IS MIGHTIER THAN HE. Almighty God knows everything that exists, and He knows all about us as human beings. How foolish it is to contend with Him. We ourselves often do not know what is good for us, nor do we know what will happen after we die. How much better it is to trust God and humbly live for Him.

7:1 A GOOD NAME *IS* BETTER THAN PRECIOUS OINTMENT. A good name means more than good social standing; it represents genuine goodness of character. Such a person has a more permanent influence on others than the person who is concerned only about social status.

7:1 THE DAY OF DEATH. The day of a believer's death is better than the day of his or her birth, for it marks the beginning of a far better life with God (2 Cor. 5:1–10; Phil. 1:21–23; see article on DEATH, p. 782).

7:2–6 SORROW *IS* BETTER THAN LAUGHTER. Solomon contrasts the sober effects of sorrow and the grief caused by a wise rebuke with the silly laughter and frivolous joking of fools. Those who are reprimanded may feel sad, but such sorrow often results in their repentance. Because they are now confronted with the real issues of life,

and the living will lay *it* to his heart.

3 [j]Sorrow *is* better than laughter: [h]for by the sadness of the countenance the heart is made better.

4 The heart of the wise *is* in the house of mourning; but the heart of fools *is* in the house of mirth.

5 [i]*It is* better to hear the rebuke of the wise, than for a man to hear the song of fools.

6 [j]For as the [k]crackling of thorns under a pot, so *is* the laughter of the fool: this also *is* vanity.

7 ¶ Surely oppression maketh a wise man mad; [k]and a gift destroyeth the heart.

8 Better *is* the end of a thing than the beginning thereof: *and* [l]the patient in spirit *is* better than the proud in spirit.

9 [m]Be not hasty in thy spirit to be angry: for anger resteth in the bosom of fools.

10 Say not thou, What is *the cause* that the former days were better than these? for thou dost not inquire [l]wisely concerning this.

11 ¶ Wisdom *is* [m]good with an inheritance: and *by it there is* profit [n]to them that see the sun.

12 For wisdom *is* a [n]defence, *and* money *is* a defence: but the excellency of knowledge *is, that* wisdom giveth life to them that have it.

13 Consider the work of God: for [o]who can make *that* straight, which he hath made crooked?

14 [p]In the day of prosperity be joyful, but in the day of adversity consider: God also hath [o]set the one over against the other, to the end that man should find nothing after him.

15 All *things* have I seen in the days of my vanity: [q]there is a just *man* that perisheth in his righteousness, and there is a wicked *man* that prolongeth *his life* in his wickedness.

16 [r]Be not righteous over much; [s]neither make thyself over wise: why shouldest thou [p]destroy thyself?

17 Be not over much wicked, neither be thou foolish: [t]why shouldest thou die [q]before thy time?

18 *It is* good that thou shouldest take hold of this; yea, also from this withdraw not thine hand: for he that feareth God shall come forth of them all.

19 [u]Wisdom strengtheneth the wise more than ten mighty *men* which are in the city.

20 [v]For *there is* not a just man upon earth, that doeth good, and sinneth not.

21 Also [r]take no heed unto all words that are spoken; lest thou hear thy servant curse thee:

22 For oftentimes also thine own heart knoweth that thou thyself likewise hast cursed others.

23 ¶ All this have I proved by wisdom: [w]I said, I will be wise; but it *was* far from me.

24 [x]That which is far off, and [y]exceeding deep, who can find it out?

7:3 [h]2 Cor. 7:10 **7:5** [i]Ps. 141:5 Prov. 15:31 **7:6** [j]ch. 2:2 **7:7** [k]Ex. 23:8 Deut. 16:19 **7:8** [l]Prov. 14:29 **7:9** [m]Prov. 14:17 Jas. 1:19 **7:11** [n]ch. 11:7 **7:13** [o]Job 12:14 ch. 1:15 **7:14** [p]Deut. 28:47 **7:15** [q]ch. 8:14 **7:16** [r]Prov. 25:16 [s]Rom. 12:3 **7:17** [t]Job 15:32 Ps. 55:23 **7:19** [u]Prov. 21:22 ch. 9:16,18 **7:20** [v]1 Ki. 8:46 2 Chr. 6:36 Prov. 20:9 1 John 1:8 **7:23** [w]Rom. 1:22 **7:24** [x]Job 28:12 1 Tim. 6:16 [y]Rom. 11:33

[j] Or, *Anger* [k] Heb. *sound* [l] Heb. *out of wisdom* [m] Or, *as good as an inheritance, yea, better too* [n] Heb. *shadow* [o] Heb. *made* [p] Heb. *be desolate?* [q] Heb. *not in thy time?* [r] Heb. *give not thine heart*

such sorrow is better than laughter and "good times."

7:8–14 CONSIDER THE WORK OF GOD. Solomon calls for persevering toward God-given goals (cf. Phil. 3:13–14) while accepting the path God provides, whether it seems rough or smooth. By acknowledging that God is at work in us, we can rejoice in prosperity and learn to trust God in adversity. Like the apostle Paul we must learn to be content—whether living in plenty or in want (Phil. 4:12).

7:16 BE NOT RIGHTEOUS OVER MUCH; NEITHER MAKE THYSELF OVER WISE. This verse must be interpreted in the light of Prov. 3:7, "Be not wise in thine own eyes: fear the LORD, and depart from evil." Those who depend on their own good deeds for salvation and those who imagine themselves to be wise will only destroy themselves. We need true righteousness from God to regenerate our hearts and true wisdom from the Holy Spirit to understand God's Word.

7:20–22 *THERE IS* NOT A JUST MAN UPON EARTH, THAT DOETH GOOD, AND SINNETH NOT. This verse does not contradict God's statement about Job's blamelessness (see Job 1:8; 2:3); rather, it states the truth that "all have sinned, and come short of the glory of God" (Rom. 3:23; cf. 3:10–18).

7:23–28 I SAID, I WILL BE WISE; BUT IT *WAS* FAR FROM ME. Those who seek wisdom by their own efforts and reasoning fail to find it. The hindrance comes from "the woman" (v. 26), who is the personification of the seduction of immorality and wickedness. She is the exact opposite of the woman personified as wisdom in Prov. 8:1–4. Sinners cannot find wisdom because they are ensnared by wickedness, but those who please God by their faith and obedience receive God's wisdom and escape a life of sin.

25 [z]I[s] applied mine heart to
know, and to search, and to seek out
wisdom, and the reason *of things,* and
to know the wickedness of folly, even
of foolishness *and* madness:
26 [a]And I find more bitter than
death the woman, whose heart *is*
snares and nets, *and* her hands *as*
bands: [t]whoso pleaseth God shall es-
cape from her; but the sinner shall be
taken by her.
27 Behold, this have I found, saith
[b]the preacher, [u]*counting* one by one,
to find out the account:
28 Which yet my soul seeketh, but
I find not: [c]one man among a thou-
sand have I found; but a woman among
all those have I not found.
29 Lo, this only have I found, [d]that
God hath made man upright; but [e]they
have sought out many inventions.

Obedience to authority

8 WHO *IS* as the wise *man?* and who
knoweth the interpretation of a
thing? [f]a man's wisdom maketh his
face to shine, and [g]the[v] boldness of
his face shall be changed.
2 I *counsel thee* to keep the king's
commandment, [h]and *that* in regard of
the oath of God.
3 [i]Be not hasty to go out of his
sight: stand not in an evil thing; for he
doeth whatsoever pleaseth him.
4 Where the word of a king *is, there*
is power: and [j]who may say unto him,
What dost thou?
5 Whoso keepeth the command-
ment [w]shall feel no evil thing: and a
wise man's heart discerneth both time
and judgment.
6 ¶ Because [k]to every purpose
there is time and judgment, therefore
the misery of man *is* great upon him.
7 [l]For he knoweth not that which
shall be: for who can tell him [x]when
it shall be?
8 [m]*There is* no man that hath power
over the spirit to retain the spirit; nei-
ther *hath he* power in the day of death:
and *there is* no [y]discharge in *that* war;
neither shall wickedness deliver those
that are given to it.
9 All this have I seen, and applied
my heart unto every work that is done
under the sun: *there is* a time wherein
one man ruleth over another to his own
hurt.
10 And so I saw the wicked buried,
who had come and gone from the place
of the holy, and they were forgotten in
the city where they had so done: this *is*
also vanity.
11 [n]Because sentence against an
evil work is not executed speedily,
therefore the heart of the sons of men
is fully set in them to do evil.
12 ¶ [o]Though a sinner do evil an
hundred times, and his *days* be pro-
longed, yet surely I know that [p]it shall
be well with them that fear God, which
fear before him:
13 But it shall not be well with the
wicked, neither shall he prolong *his*
days, *which are* as a shadow; because
he feareth not before God.
14 There is a vanity which is done
upon the earth; that there be just *men,*
unto whom it [q]happeneth according to
the work of the wicked; again, there be
wicked *men,* to whom it happeneth ac-
cording to the work of the righteous: I
said that this also *is* vanity.
15 [r]Then I commended mirth, be-
cause a man hath no better thing under
the sun, than to eat, and to drink, and
to be merry: for that shall abide with
him of his labour the days of his life,
which God giveth him under the sun.
16 ¶ When I applied mine heart to
know wisdom, and to see the business
that is done upon the earth: (for also
there is that neither day nor night seeth
sleep with his eyes:)
17 Then I beheld all the work of

7:25 [z]ch. 1:17 **7:26** [a]Prov. 5:3,4 **7:27** [b]ch. 1:1,2 **7:28** [c]Job 33:23 Ps. 12:1 **7:29** [d]Gen. 1:27 [e]Gen. 3:6,7 **8:1** [f]Prov. 4:8,9 Acts 6:15 [g]Deut. 28:50 **8:2** [h]1 Chr. 29:24 Ezek. 17:18 **8:3** [i]ch. 10:4 **8:4** [j]Job 34:18 **8:6** [k]ch. 3:1 **8:7** [l]Prov. 24:22 ch. 6:12 & 9:12 & 10:14 **8:8** [m]Ps. 49:6,7 **8:11** [n]Ps. 10:6 & 50:21 Is. 26:10 **8:12** [o]Is. 65:20 Rom. 2:5 [p]Ps. 37:11,18,19 Prov. 1:32,33 Is. 3:10,11 Mat. 25:34,41 **8:14** [q]Ps. 73:14 ch. 2:14 & 7:15 & 9:1-3 **8:15** [r]ch. 2:24 & 3:12,22 & 5:18 & 9:7

[s]Heb. *I and my heart compassed* [t]Heb. he that is *good before God* [u]Or, weighing *one thing after another, to find out the reason* [v]Heb. *the strength* [w]Heb. *shall know* [x]Or, *how it shall be?* [y]Or, *casting off* weapons

8:2 KEEP THE KING'S COMMANDMENT, AND *THAT* IN REGARD OF THE OATH OF GOD. The king here represents human government as instituted by God. Government officials who follow God's principles of living encourage righteous living. Our Lord wants us to obey the just laws of government (see Rom. 13:1, note; Tit. 3:1; 1 Pet. 2:13–18).

8:13 IT SHALL NOT BE WELL WITH THE WICKED. In the world it often seems that evil triumphs and sinners go unpunished (cf. Ps. 73). Yet God assures us that He will eventually punish evildoers according to what they deserve.

8:17 I BEHELD ALL THE WORK OF GOD, THAT A MAN CANNOT FIND OUT. Solomon recognized that no matter how wise we are, we cannot by our own wisdom explain all the works of God or the ways of His providence. Like Job, we do not have to know all the reasons; we simply need to trust in the Lord and believe that He does

God, that [s]a man cannot find out the
work that is done under the sun: be-
cause though a man labour to seek *it*
out, yet he shall not find *it;* yea further;
though a wise *man* think to know *it,* yet
shall he not be able to find *it.*

Make the best of this life

9 FOR ALL this [z]I considered in my
heart even to declare all this,
[t]that the righteous, and the wise, and
their works, *are* in the hand of God: no
man knoweth either love or hatred *by*
all *that is* before them.
2 [u]All *things come* alike to all: *there*
is one event to the righteous, and to the
wicked; to the good and to the clean,
and to the unclean; to him that sacri-
ficeth, and to him that sacrificeth not:
as *is* the good, so *is* the sinner; *and* he
that sweareth, as *he* that feareth an
oath.
3 This *is* an evil among all *things*
that are done under the sun, that *there*
is one event unto all: yea, also the
heart of the sons of men is full of evil,
and madness *is* in their heart while
they live, and after that *they go* to the
dead.
4 ¶ For to him that is joined to all
the living there is hope: for a living dog
is better than a dead lion.
5 For the living know that they shall
die: but [v]the dead know not any thing,
neither have they any more a reward;
for [w]the memory of them is forgotten.
6 Also their love, and their hatred,
and their envy, is now perished; nei-
ther have they any more a portion for
ever in any *thing* that is done under the
sun.
7 ¶ Go thy way, [x]eat thy bread with
joy, and drink thy wine with a merry
heart; for God now accepteth thy
works.

8:17 [s]Job 5:9 ch. 3:11 Rom. 11:33
9:1 [t]ch. 8:14
9:2 [u]Job 21:7 Ps. 73:3,12,13 Mal. 3:15
9:5 [v]Job 14:21 Is. 63:16 [w]Job 7:8-10 Is. 26:14
9:7 [x]ch. 8:15
9:9 [y]ch. 2:10,24 & 3:13,22 & 5:18
9:11 [z]Amos 2:14,15 Jer. 9:23
9:12 [a]ch. 8:7 [b]Prov. 29:6 Luke 12:20,39 & 17:26 1 Thes. 5:3
9:14 [c]See 2 Sam. 20:16-22
9:16 [d]ver. 18 Prov. 21:22 & 24:5 ch. 7:19 [e]Mark 6:2

8 Let thy garments be always white;
and let thy head lack no ointment.
9 [a]Live joyfully with the wife
whom thou lovest all the days of the
life of thy vanity, which he hath given
thee under the sun, all the days of thy
vanity: [y]for that *is* thy portion in *this*
life, and in thy labour which thou tak-
est under the sun.
10 Whatsoever thy hand findeth to
do, do *it* with thy might; for *there is* no
work, nor device, nor knowledge, nor
wisdom, in the grave, whither thou go-
est.
11 ¶ I returned, [z]and saw under
the sun, that the race *is* not to the
swift, nor the battle to the strong, nei-
ther yet bread to the wise, nor yet
riches to men of understanding, nor yet
favour to men of skill; but time and
chance happeneth to them all.
12 For [a]man also knoweth not his
time: as the fishes that are taken in an
evil net, and as the birds that are
caught in the snare; so *are* the sons of
men [b]snared in an evil time, when it
falleth suddenly upon them.

The wise man and the fool

13 ¶ This wisdom have I seen also
under the sun, and it *seemed* great
unto me:
14 [c]*There was* a little city, and few
men within it; and there came a great
king against it, and besieged it, and
built great bulwarks against it:
15 Now there was found in it a poor
wise man, and he by his wisdom deliv-
ered the city; yet no man remembered
that same poor man.
16 [d]Then said I, Wisdom *is* better
than strength: nevertheless [e]the poor

[z] Heb. *I gave,* or, *set to my heart* [a] Heb. *See,* or, *Enjoy life*

---

all things well. If we are His children, we are in His hands (9:1).

9:2 ALL *THINGS COME* ALIKE TO ALL. Solomon looks at the inevitability of death from the point of view of this life only. From that standpoint, it does not seem fair that death comes indiscriminately to all, both the godly and the wicked.

9:7 EAT THY BREAD WITH JOY, AND DRINK THY WINE WITH A MERRY HEART. Though death comes to all and time and chance happen to everyone (v. 11), we who are acceptable to God (cf. Rom. 12:2) should not stop enjoying what He has given us. The "wine" (Heb. *yayin*) referred to here undoubtedly means sweet, freshly squeezed grape juice (see article on WINE IN THE OLD TESTAMENT, p. 220).

9:10 DO *IT* WITH THY MIGHT. Whatever work we do, we should undertake it with all our heart as unto the Lord (see Col. 3:23).

9:15 NO MAN REMEMBERED THAT SAME POOR MAN. In this parable, a little city besieged by a great army seemed in a hopeless situation (v. 14). But a poor wise man devised a plan and the city was saved. Apparently someone else took the credit for saving the city, however, and the wise man, probably because he was poor, was forgotten. Believers should recognize that while they are on earth, justice and fairness will be imperfect at best; but in life after death, God will right all wrongs and reward all righteous deeds.

man's wisdom *is* despised, and his
words are not heard.
17 The words of wise *men are* heard
in quiet more than the cry of him that
ruleth among fools.
18 [f]Wisdom *is* better than weap-
ons of war: but [g]one sinner destroyeth
much good.
10 DEAD [b]FLIES cause the oint-
ment of the apothecary to send
forth a stinking savour: *so doth* a little
folly him that is in reputation for wis-
dom *and* honour.
2 A wise man's heart *is* at his right
hand; but a fool's heart at his left.
3 Yea also, when he that is a fool
walketh by the way, [c]his wisdom
faileth *him*, [h]and he saith to every one
that he *is* a fool.
4 If the spirit of the ruler rise up
against thee, [i]leave not thy place; for
[j]yielding pacifieth great offences.
5 There is an evil *which* I have seen
under the sun, as an error *which* pro-
ceedeth [d]from the ruler:
6 [k]Folly is set [e]in great dignity,
and the rich sit in low place.
7 I have seen servants [l]upon
horses, and princes walking as ser-
vants upon the earth.
8 [m]He that diggeth a pit shall fall
into it; and whoso breaketh an hedge,
a serpent shall bite him.
9 Whoso removeth stones shall be
hurt therewith; *and* he that cleaveth
wood shall be endangered thereby.
10 If the iron be blunt, and he do not
whet the edge, then must he put to
more strength: but wisdom *is* profit-
able to direct.
11 Surely the serpent will bite
[n]without enchantment; and [f]a bab-
bler is no better.
12 [o]The words of a wise man's
mouth *are* [g]gracious; but [p]the lips of
a fool will swallow up himself.
13 The beginning of the words of his
mouth *is* foolishness: and the end of
[h]his talk *is* mischievous madness.
14 [q]A fool also [i]is full of words:
a man cannot tell what shall be; and
[r]what shall be after him, who can tell
him?
15 The labour of the foolish weari-
eth every one of them, because he
knoweth not how to go to the city.
16 ¶ [s]Woe to thee, O land, when
thy king *is* a child, and thy princes eat
in the morning!
17 Blessed *art* thou, O land, when
thy king *is* the son of nobles, and [t]thy
princes eat in due season, for strength,
and not for drunkenness!
18 ¶ By much slothfulness the
building decayeth; and through idle-
ness of the hands the house droppeth
through.
19 ¶ A feast is made for laughter,
and [u]wine [j]maketh merry: but mon-
ey answereth all *things*.
20 ¶ [v]Curse not the king, no not in
thy [k]thought; and curse not the rich
in thy bedchamber: for a bird of the air
shall carry the voice, and that which
hath wings shall tell the matter.

The investment of a life

11 CAST THY bread [w]upon[l] the
waters: [x]for thou shalt find it
after many days.
2 [y]Give a portion [z]to seven, and
also to eight; [a]for thou knowest not
what evil shall be upon the earth.

9:18 [f]ver. 16 [g]Josh. 7:1 **10:3** [h]Prov. 13:16 & 18:2 **10:4** [i]ch. 8:3 [j]1 Sam. 25:24 Prov. 25:15 **10:6** [k]Esth. 3:1 **10:7** [l]Prov. 19:10 & 30:22 **10:8** [m]Ps. 7:15 Prov. 26:27 **10:11** [n]Ps. 58:4,5 Jer. 8:17 **10:12** [o]Prov. 10:32 [p]Prov. 10:14 **10:14** [q]Prov. 15:2 [r]ch. 3:22 & 8:7 **10:16** [s]Is. 3:4,5 & 5:11 **10:17** [t]Prov. 31:4 **10:19** [u]Ps. 104:15 **10:20** [v]Ex. 22:28 Acts 23:5 **11:1** [w]See Is. 32:20 [x]Deut. 15:10 Prov. 19:17 Mat. 10:42 **11:2** [y]Ps. 112:9 1 Tim. 6:18 [z]Mic. 5:5 [a]Eph. 5:16

[b] Heb. *Flies of death* [c] Heb. *his heart* [d] Heb. *from before* [e] Heb. *in great heights* [f] Heb. *the master of the tongue* [g] Heb. *grace* [h] Heb. *his mouth* [i] Heb. *multiplieth words* [j] Heb. *maketh glad the life* [k] Or, *conscience* [l] Heb. *upon the face of the waters*

10:1 DEAD FLIES CAUSE THE OINTMENT . . . TO SEND FORTH A STINKING SAVOUR. Just as dead flies by their decay spoil a batch of perfume, so a little foolishness can counteract the effects of great wisdom. Wise plans can be laid out, but someone who makes a foolish mistake can spoil them all (see 2 Ki. 20:12–19).

10:8–10 HE THAT DIGGETH A PIT. Wisdom takes into account the risks and difficulties of life and its ordinary tasks. The wise person is kept from harm because he or she knows what could happen and is careful to avoid pitfalls .

10:16 WOE TO THEE, O LAND, WHEN THY KING *IS* A CHILD. It is a sad state of affairs when rulers and leaders are childish and when their princes and their assistants begin the day by satisfying their appetites (probably in drinking parties). How tragic it is throughout history that intoxicating drink has flowed so freely in the capital cities of the world. We need godly leaders that set a good example (v. 17).

11:1 CAST THY BREAD UPON THE WATERS. One meaning of the Hebrew word for "bread" is "grain" that can be used for bread. The picture may be that of Egyptians scattering grain on the water that flooded their lands when the Nile rose every year. It would appear to sink down and be forgotten, but in due time there would be a harvest. We may apply this to our willingness to be generous and helpful (v. 2). We must give liberally, since one day we ourselves may be in great need (cf. 2 Cor. 8:10–15).

3 If the clouds be full of rain, they
empty *themselves* upon the earth: and if
the tree fall toward the south, or to-
ward the north, in the place where the
tree falleth, there it shall be.
4 He that observeth the wind shall
not sow; and he that regardeth the
clouds shall not reap.
5 As [b]thou knowest not what *is* the
way of the spirit, [c]*nor* how the bones
do grow in the womb of her that is with
child: even so thou knowest not the
works of God who maketh all.
6 In the morning sow thy seed, and
in the evening withhold not thine hand:
for thou knowest not whether [m]shall
prosper, either this or that, or whether
they both *shall be* alike good.
7 ¶ Truly the light *is* sweet, and a
pleasant *thing it is* for the eyes [d]to be-
hold the sun:
8 But if a man live many years, *and*
rejoice in them all; yet let him remem-
ber the days of darkness; for they shall
be many. All that cometh *is* vanity.
9 ¶ Rejoice, O young man, in thy
youth; and let thy heart cheer thee in
the days of thy youth, [e]and walk in the
ways of thine heart, and in the sight of
thine eyes: but know thou, that for all
these *things* [f]God will bring thee into
judgment.
10 Therefore remove [n]sorrow from
thy heart, and [g]put away evil from thy
flesh: [h]for childhood and youth *are*
vanity.

The span of a life

12 REMEMBER [i]NOW thy Cre-
ator in the days of thy youth,
while the evil days come not, nor the
years draw nigh, [j]when thou shalt
say, I have no pleasure in them;
2 While the sun, or the light, or the
moon, or the stars, be not darkened,
nor the clouds return after the rain:
3 In the day when the keepers of the
house shall tremble, and the strong
men shall bow themselves, and [o]the
grinders cease because they are few,
and those that look out of the windows
be darkened,
4 And the doors shall be shut in the
streets, when the sound of the grinding
is low, and he shall rise up at the voice
of the bird, and all [k]the daughters of
music shall be brought low;
5 Also *when* they shall be afraid of
that which is high, and fears *shall be* in
the way, and the almond tree shall
flourish, and the grasshopper shall be
a burden, and desire shall fail: because
man goeth to [l]his long home, and
[m]the mourners go about the streets:
6 Or ever the silver cord be loosed,
or the golden bowl be broken, or the
pitcher be broken at the fountain, or
the wheel broken at the cistern.
7 [n]Then shall the dust return to
the earth as it was: [o]and the spirit
shall return unto God [p]who gave it.
8 ¶ [q]Vanity of vanities, saith the
preacher; all *is* vanity.

The whole duty of man

9 And [p]moreover, because the

11:5 [b]John 3:8 [c]Ps. 139:14
11:7 [d]ch. 7:11
11:9 [e]Num. 15:39 [f]ch. 12:14
11:10 [g]2 Cor. 7:1 [h]Ps. 39:5
12:1 [i]Lam. 3:27 [j]2 Sam. 19:35
12:4 [k]2 Sam. 19:35
12:5 [l]Job 17:13 [m]Jer. 9:17
12:7 [n]Gen. 3:19 [o]ch. 3:21 [p]Num. 16:22 Job 34:14 Zech. 12:1
12:8 [q]Ps. 62:9

[m] Heb. *shall be right* [n] Or, *anger* [o] Or, *the grinders fail, because they grind little* [p] Or, *the more wise the preacher was*

11:4 HE THAT OBSERVETH THE WIND SHALL NOT SOW. We are in a world where always waiting for the most favorable conditions will accomplish nothing (cf. Mat. 24:7–14). Conditions will never be ideal during this present age. We must persevere in praying and in reading our Bibles daily. We must live by God's righteous standards, even if everyone around us pursues sinful pleasures.

11:9 FOR ALL THESE *THINGS* GOD WILL BRING THEE INTO JUDGMENT. God wants His people to rejoice and young people to enjoy their youth. But all such rejoicing must be tempered with the recognition that God holds us accountable for our sinful actions. If we allow our lives to degenerate into superficial levity and the enjoyment of sinful things, the end result will be trouble and suffering in this life and judgment in the next.

12:1–7 REMEMBER NOW THY CREATOR IN THE DAYS OF THY YOUTH. "Remember" in the Bible always implies action; e.g., when God "remembered" Abraham (Gen. 19:29), He became involved in his life for his good. Therefore, remembering our Creator means acting in the way He intended us to act when He created us. He has given us life and the opportunities that come with youth. We can "remember" God only by the help of the Holy Spirit, as we "put on the new man, which after God is created in righteousness and true holiness" (Eph. 4:24); and we must do so before death comes. Vv. 3–7 give a dramatic picture of the aging process of the physical body, leading to death. We can be comforted, however, by the fact that the inner person can still be "renewed day by day" (2 Cor. 4:16).

12:7 DUST RETURN TO THE EARTH … THE SPIRIT SHALL RETURN TO GOD. This verse distinguishes between that aspect of the human person which remains at the time of death and that aspect which returns to God. For more on this, see article on HUMAN PERSONHOOD, p. 978.

12:8 ALL *IS* VANITY. See 1:2, note.

HUMAN PERSONHOOD

Eccl. 12:6–7 "Or ever the silver cord be loosed, or the golden bowl be broken, or the pitcher be broken at the fountain, or the wheel broken at the cistern. Then shall the dust return to the earth as it was: and the spirit shall return unto God who gave it."

Of all the creatures God made, the human being is by far the highest and most complex. Because of pride, however, humans often forget that God is their Creator, that they are created beings, and that they are therefore dependent on God. This article examines the Biblical perspective on human personhood.

HUMAN PERSONHOOD IN THE IMAGE OF GOD. (1) The Scriptures state clearly that the human race, by a special decision of God, was created in God's image and after His likeness (Gen. 1:26–27). Hence both Adam and Eve were not products of evolution (Gen. 1:27; Mat. 19:4; Mark 10:6; see article on CREATION, p. 6). Because they were created in the likeness of God, they were able to respond to and have fellowship with God, and to reflect His love, glory, and holiness (see Gen. 1:26, note).

(2) Note at least three different aspects of the image of God in humankind (see Gen. 1:26, note): Adam and Eve possessed a *moral* likeness to God, in that they were righteous and holy (cf. Eph. 4:24), with hearts capable of loving and of wanting to do what was right. They possessed a likeness to God in *intelligence*, for they were created with spirit, mind, emotions, and power of choice (Gen. 2:19–20; 3:6–7). In some sense their *physical* makeup was in God's image in a way not true of animals. God gave to human beings the image in which He was to appear visibly in the O.T. (Gen. 18:1–2) and the form that His Son would one day assume (Luke 1:35; Phil. 2:7).

(3) When Adam and Eve sinned, this image of God in them was seriously corrupted, but not totally destroyed. (a) Certainly their moral likeness to God was corrupted when they sinned (cf. Gen. 6:5), so that they were no longer perfect and holy, but now had a tendency toward sin which they passed on to their children (cf. Gen. 4; see Rom. 5:12, note). The N.T. confirms the corruption of the image of God when it says that redeemed believers must be renewed to the original moral likeness of God (cf. Eph. 4:22–24; Col. 3:10). (b) At the same time, sinful humans still have many of the aspects of the likeness to God in intelligence, with a capacity for fellowship and communication with Him (cf. Gen. 3:8–19; Acts 17:27–28). This dimension of the image of God was also marred but not totally obliterated when Adam and Eve sinned in the Garden of Eden (cf. Gen. 9:6; Jas. 3:9).

COMPONENTS OF HUMAN PERSONHOOD. The Bible reveals that human personhood, made in the image of God, is a triunity involving the components of spirit, soul, and body (1 Thes. 5:23; Heb. 4:12). (1) God formed Adam out of the dust of the ground (body) and breathed into his nostrils the breath of life (spirit), and he became "a living soul" (Gen. 2:7). God intended that by eating of the tree of life and by obeying His command not to eat of the tree of knowledge of good and evil, humankind would never die but would live forever (cf. Gen. 2:16–17; 3:22–24). Only after death entered the world as a result of human sin do we read about the separation of a person into the dust of the earth and the spirit, which returns to God (Gen. 3:19; 35:18; Eccl. 12:7; Rev. 6:9; see article on DEATH, p. 782). In other words, the separation of the body from the spirit and soul is the result of God's curse on the human race because of sin and will eventually be remedied only at the resurrection of the body on the last day (see article on THE RESURRECTION OF THE BODY, p. 1799).

(2) The soul (Heb. *nephesh*; Gk. *psychē*) may be briefly defined as the nonmaterial aspects of mind, emotions, and will in human personhood that result from the union of spirit and body. The soul along with the human spirit will continue to live when an

individual physically dies. The soul is so closely linked with one's inner personhood that it is sometimes used as a synonym for "person" (e.g., Lev. 4:2; 7:20; Acts 7:14; Rom. 13:1). The body (Heb. *basar*; Gk. *sōma*) may be briefly defined as that material element in an individual that returns to the dust when he or she dies (sometimes also called "flesh"). The spirit (Heb. *ruach*; Gk. *pneuma*) may be briefly defined as the nonmaterial life component of the human being, wherein resides our spiritual capacity and conscience; that aspect is the one whereby we are most in contact with God's Spirit.

(3) Of these three components that constitute the "whole" of human personhood, only the spirit and the soul are indestructible and survive death, either to live in heaven (Rev. 6:9; 20:4) or in hell (cf. Ps. 16:10; Mat. 16:26). However, the Bible is insistent that as long as we are alive, believers must take good care of their bodies by keeping them free from immorality and evil (Rom. 6:6,12–13; 1 Cor. 6:13–20; 1 Thes. 4:3–4) and by dedicating them to the service of God (Rom. 6:13; 12:1; see article on STANDARDS OF SEXUAL MORALITY, p. 1964). The body will also experience transformation on the day of resurrection, so that human personhood is totally redeemed in the end for those who are in Christ Jesus.

THE RESPONSIBILITIES OF HUMAN PERSONHOOD. When God created human beings, he entrusted them with several responsibilities. (1) God made them in His own image so that He could develop a loving, personal relationship with them for all eternity and so that they would glorify Him as Lord. So much did God desire a people to enjoy Him, glorify Him, and live in righteousness and holiness before Him that when Satan succeeded in tempting Adam and Eve to rebel against and disobey God, the Lord promised to send a Savior to redeem the world (see Gen. 3:15, note; see article on CREATION, p. 6).

(2) It was God's will that human beings love Him above all and love their neighbors as themselves. This twofold commandment of love summarizes the entire law of God (Lev. 19:18; Deut. 6:4–5; Mat. 22:37–40; Rom. 13:9–10).

(3) God also established the institution of marriage in the Garden of Eden (Gen. 2:21–24). He intended that marriage should be monogamous, a lifelong relationship between husband and wife (cf. Mat. 19:5–9; Eph. 5:22–33). Within the context of marriage, God commanded that the human race "be fruitful, and multiply, and replenish the earth" (Gen. 1:28; 9:7). Man and woman were to reproduce godly offspring in a family context. God considers a godly family and the raising of children within healthy family relationships as a high priority in the world (see Gen. 1:28, note).

(4) God also charged Adam and all of his descendants to "subdue" the earth and to "have dominion over the fish of the sea, and over the fowl of the air, and over every living thing that moveth upon the earth" (Gen. 1:28). Already in the Garden of Eden Adam was given the responsibility of dressing and keeping the garden and of naming the animals (Gen. 2:15,19–20).

(5) Note that when Adam and Eve sinned by eating of the forbidden fruit, some of their dominion over the world was lost to Satan, who now as "the god of this world" (2 Cor. 4:4) controls this present evil age (see 1 John 5:19, note; cf. Gal. 1:4; Eph. 6:12; see article on THE PROVIDENCE OF GOD, p. 80). But God still expects believers to fulfill His divine purpose by taking good care of His world, by consecrating all things in the earth to Him, and by managing His creation in a God-glorifying way (cf. Ps. 8:6–8; Heb. 2:7–8).

(6) Because of the presence of sin in the world, God sent His Son Jesus to redeem the world. The awesome task of bringing that message of God's redemptive love has been given to God's people, whom he has called to be witnesses of Christ and His salvation to the ends of the earth (Mat. 28:18–20; Acts 1:8) and to be the light and salt of the earth (Mat. 5:13–16).

preacher was wise, he still taught the people knowledge; yea, he gave good heed, and sought out, *and* [r]set in order many proverbs.

10 The preacher sought to find out [q]acceptable words: and *that which was* written *was* upright, *even* words of truth.

11 The words of the wise *are* as goads, and as nails fastened *by* the masters of assemblies, *which* are given from one shepherd.

12 And further, by these, my son, be admonished: of making many books *there is* no end; and [s]much [r]study *is* a weariness of the flesh.

13 ¶ [s]Let us hear the conclusion of the whole matter: [t]Fear God, and keep his commandments: for this *is* the whole *duty* of man.

14 For [u]God shall bring every work into judgment, with every secret thing, whether *it be* good, or whether *it be* evil.

12:9 [r]1 Ki. 4:32
12:12 [s]ch. 1:18
12:13 [t]Deut. 10:12
12:14 [u]Mat. 12:36

Is. 2:3-5

[q] Heb. *words of delight* [r] Or, *reading* [s] Or, *The end of the matter,* even *all that hath been heard,* is

12:11 THE WORDS OF THE WISE *ARE* AS GOADS. The wise words of truth that come from the one divine Shepherd act (1) as goads (i.e., pointed sticks) to prod us on in the right way, and (2) as nails to secure the truth in our minds. God's Word, therefore, is far more valuable than all the many books of human wisdom.

12:13 FOR THIS *IS* THE WHOLE *DUTY* OF MAN. The entire book of Ecclesiastes must be understood in the light of this concluding verse. Solomon began with a cynical appraisal of life as vanity, emptiness, meaninglessness, but he ends with serious counsel about where meaning can be found. Fear of God, love for Him and His Word, and obedience to His commandments bring purpose and satisfaction that cannot be found in any other way.

12:14 FOR GOD SHALL BRING EVERY WORK INTO JUDGMENT. As a final word, Solomon reminds us of a solemn and enduring truth: we are fully accountable to God for our deeds. The Lord will evaluate each of us, believer and unbeliever alike, and will judge all our deeds, whether they are good or evil (cf. Rom. 14:10,12; 2 Cor. 5:10; Rev. 20:12–13). We will not be justified on the judgment day if we have neglected or rejected God's grace (see article on THE JUDGMENT OF BELIEVERS, p. 1811).

SONG OF SOLOMON

Outline

Title (1:1)

I. The First Poem: The Bride Longs for the Bridegroom (1:2—2:7)
   - A. Her Longing Expressed (1:2–4a)
   - B. Support from Her Friends (1:4b)
   - C. Her Question (1:5–7)
   - D. Advice from Her Friends (1:8)
   - E. The Bridegroom Appears and Speaks (1:9–11)
   - F. Exchange of Affection Between Bride and Bridegroom (1:12—2:7)

II. The Second Poem: The Lovers Seek and Find Each Other (2:8—3:5)
   - A. The Bride Spots Her Bridegroom Coming (2:8–9)
   - B. The Bridegroom's Overtures (2:10–15)
   - C. The Bride's Expression of Exclusive Love (2:16–17)
   - D. The Bridegroom Lost and Found Again (3:1–5)

III. The Third Poem: The Wedding Procession (3:6—5:1)
   - A. The Bridegroom Approaches (3:6–11)
   - B. The Bridegroom's Affection for His Bride (4:1–15)
   - C. The Bride and Bridegroom Come Together (4:16—5:1)

IV. The Fourth Poem: The Bride Fears Losing the Bridegroom (5:2—6:3)
   - A. The Bride's Dream at Night (5:2–7)
   - B. The Bride and Her Friends Discuss the Bridegroom (5:8–16)
   - C. The Place Where the Bridegroom Has Gone (6:1–3)

V. The Fifth Poem: The Beauty of the Bride (6:4—8:4)
   - A. The Bridegroom's Description of the Bride (6:4–9)
   - B. The Bridegroom and His Friends Discuss the Bride (6:10–13)
   - C. The Further Description of the Bride (7:1–8)
   - D. The Bride's Affection for the Bridegroom (7:9—8:4)

VI. The Sixth Poem: The Ultimate Beauty of Love (8:5–14)
   - A. The Intensity of Love (8:5–7)
   - B. The Expansion of Love (8:8–9)
   - C. The Contentment of Love (8:10–14)

Author: Solomon

Theme: Wedded Love

Date of Writing: c. 960 B.C.

Background

The Hebrew name for this book translates literally as "The Song of Songs," an expression that means "The Greatest Song" (just as "King of kings" means "The Greatest King"). It was regarded, therefore, as the greatest of wedding songs ever penned. The title "Song of Solomon" in the KJV derives from the belief that Solomon wrote "the song of songs" (1:1).

Solomon was a prolific songwriter of 1005 songs (1 Ki. 4:32). His name appears in the title verse as the author (1:1), and at six other places throughout the song (1:5; 3:7,9,11;

8:11–12). He is also identified as the bridegroom; originally the book may have been a series of poems between him and his bride. The book's eight chapters contain references to at least fifteen different species of animals and twenty-one varieties of plant life; both of these groups were investigated and mentioned by Solomon in numerous songs (1 Ki. 4:33). Finally, geographical references in the book indicate places all throughout the land of Israel, suggesting the book was composed before the division of the nation into the northern and southern kingdoms.

Solomon must have composed the book early in his life as the king of Israel, long before he had 700 wives and 300 concubines (1 Ki. 11:3). But the question arises: how could Solomon have used such monogamous language if he already may have had wives and concubines (6:8)? The answer may lie in the fact that the Shulammite maiden (6:13) was Solomon's first wife from his youth, before he became king (3:11); 6:8 may reflect only the state of things at the time the book was formally written for publication. The Shulammite is described in this song as a common girl from the countryside, attractive and beautiful, to whom Solomon was deeply and emotionally committed as one would be to his first love and bride.

Liturgically, the Song of Solomon became one of the five scrolls of the third part of the Hebrew Bible, the *Hagiographa* ("Holy Writings"), each of which was read publicly at one of the annual Jewish feasts. This one was assigned to be read at the Passover.

Purpose

This book was inspired by the Holy Spirit and incorporated into the Scriptures to underscore the divine origin of the joy and dignity of human love in marriage. Genesis reveals that human sexuality and marriage preceded the fall of humankind into sin (Gen. 2:18–25). Though sin has marred this important area of human experience, God wants us to know that it can be pure, wholesome, and beautiful. The Song of Solomon, therefore, provides a corrective model between two extremes in history: (1) the abandonment of married love for sexual perversion (i.e., homosexual or lesbian relationships) and fleeting unmarried heterosexual encounters, and (2) an asceticism, often mistaken as the Christian view of sex, that denies the goodness of physical love in the marriage relationship.

Survey

The content of the Song of Solomon is not easily analyzed. Rather than moving in a methodical and logical manner from the first chapter to the last, it moves in a series of interlocking circles revolving around a central theme of love. As a song, it has six stanzas or poems, each one dealing with some aspect of the courtship and wedded love of Solomon and his bride (1:2—2:7; 2:8—3:5; 3:6—5:1; 5:2—6:3; 6:4—8:4; 8:5–14). The virginity of the bride is described as "a garden inclosed" (4:12), and the consummation of the marriage as entering the garden to enjoy its pleasant fruit (4:16; 5:1). Most of the conversations are between the bride (a Shulammite maiden), Solomon the king, and a chorus of friends of the bride and bridegroom called the "daughters of Jerusalem." When the bride and bridegroom are together, they are mutually fulfilled; when they are apart, they experience a longing for each other's presence. The literary climax of the Song of Solomon is 8:6–7.

Special Features

Four major features or emphases characterize the Song of Solomon. (1) It is the only book in the Bible that deals exclusively with the unique love of a bride and a bridegroom. Throughout it describes courtship and married love, especially the bliss of newlyweds. (2) It is a unique literary masterpiece full of discreet but sensuous imagery, primarily drawn from the world of nature. The various metaphors and descriptive language portray the emotion, power, and beauty of romantic and wedded love, which was considered pure and chaste in Bible times. (3) It is one of a small number of O.T. books that are neither quoted nor alluded to in the N.T. (4) It is one of two books in the O.T. (cf. the book of Esther) that do not explicitly mention God in the text (though some manuscripts contain a reference to "the LORD" in 8:6).

New Testament Fulfillment

(1) The Song of Solomon prefigures a N.T. theme revealed to the writer of Hebrews: "Marriage *is* honourable in all, and the bed undefiled" (Heb 13:4). Christians may, and even should, enjoy romantic love within the bonds of the marriage relationship. (2) Many past interpreters have seen this book as primarily or exclusively a prophetic allegory describing the love relationship between God and Israel, or between Christ and the church, His bride. Since the N.T. itself nowhere views the Song of Solomon in this manner, nor even quotes from it, this interpretation is highly unlikely. The Bible nowhere indicates that any aspect of Solomon's married life is a divinely intended "type" of Christ. However, since several crucial N.T. passages describe Christ's love for the church in terms of the marriage relationship (e.g., 2 Cor. 11:2; Eph. 5:22–33; Rev. 19:7–9; 21:1–2,9), the Song of Solomon may be viewed as *illustrating* the quality of love that exists between Christ and His bride, the church. It is an exclusive, committed, and intensely personal love that allows for no other courtships.

Reading Song of Solomon

In order to read the entire Old Testament in one year, the book of Song of Solomon should be read in 3 days, according to the following schedule: ☐ 1–2 ☐ 3–5 ☐ 6–8

NOTES

1

THE [a]SONG of songs, which *is* Solomon's.

In the chambers of the king

2 Let him kiss me with the kisses of his mouth: [b]for [a]thy love *is* better than wine.

3 Because of the savour of thy good ointments thy name *is as* ointment poured forth, therefore do the virgins love thee.

4 [c]Draw me, [d]we will run after thee: the king [e]hath brought me into his chambers: we will be glad and rejoice in thee, we will remember thy love more than wine: [b]the upright love thee.

5 I *am* black, but comely, O ye daughters of Jerusalem, as the tents of Kedar, as the curtains of Solomon.

6 Look not upon me, because I *am* black, because the sun hath looked upon me: my mother's children were angry with me; they made me the keeper of the vineyards; *but* mine own vineyard have I not kept.

7 Tell me, O thou whom my soul loveth, where thou feedest, where thou makest *thy flock* to rest at noon: for why should I be [c]as one that turneth aside by the flocks of thy companions?

8 ¶ If thou know not, [f]O thou fairest among women, go thy way forth by the footsteps of the flock, and feed thy kids beside the shepherds' tents.

9 I have compared thee, [g]O my love, [h]to a company of horses in Pharaoh's chariots.

10 [i]Thy cheeks are comely with rows *of jewels,* thy neck with chains *of gold.*

11 We will make thee borders of gold with studs of silver.

12 ¶ While the king *sitteth* at his table, my spikenard sendeth forth the smell thereof.

13 A bundle of myrrh *is* my wellbeloved unto me; he shall lie all night betwixt my breasts.

14 My beloved *is* unto me *as* a cluster of [j]camphire[d] in the vineyards of En-gedi.

15 [k]Behold, thou *art* fair, [e]my love; behold, thou *art* fair; thou *hast* doves' eyes.

16 Behold, thou *art* fair, my beloved, yea, pleasant: also our bed *is* green.

17 The beams of our house *are* cedar, *and* our [f]rafters of fir.

The rose of Sharon

2

I AM the rose of Sharon, *and* the lily of the valleys.

1:1 [a]1 Ki. 4:32
1:2 [b]ch. 4:10
1:4 [c]Hos. 11:4 John 6:44 & 12:32 [d]Phil. 3:12-14 [e]Ps. 45:14,15 John 14:2 Eph. 2:6
1:8 [f]ch. 5:9
1:9 [g]ch. 2:2,10,13 & 4:1,7 John 15:14 [h]2 Chr. 1:16
1:10 [i]Ezek. 16:11
1:14 [j]ch. 4:13
1:15 [k]ch. 4:1 & 5:12

[a] Heb. *thy loves* [b] Or, *they love thee uprightly*
[c] Or, *as one that is veiled* [d] Or, *cypress*
[e] Or, *my companion* [f] Or, *galleries*

1:1 THE SONG OF SONGS. This is the book's own title in the Hebrew text. It means the best or greatest song. Solomon wrote 1,005 songs (1 Ki. 4:32).

1:5 AS THE TENTS OF KEDAR. Tents were usually made of black goat hair. Kedar was an Arabian tribe descended from Ishmael (Gen. 25:13; cf. Is. 21:16–17); thus some have suggested that the bride was an Arabian princess.

1:6 MINE OWN VINEYARD HAVE I NOT KEPT. The cruel brothers of the maiden forced her to guard and care for their vineyards, something she had not done for her own. This outdoor work may be the reason her skin was so dark, a marked contrast to the sun-bonnetted beauties of Jerusalem—though hard work had not destroyed her real beauty (v. 5). In view of these verses it is hard to see how some suppose the speaker here was the daughter of Pharaoh (1 Ki. 3:1). This Shulamite maiden was probably the princess Solomon first loved and married before he began to enter marriages for the sake of political alliances.

1:9 MY LOVE. The Hebrew means "my companion" in the sense of "my friend" (see also 2:10, 4:1,7, etc.). It was a term of endearment used before marriage. The comparison to horses was considered a compliment in those days.

1:11 BORDERS OF GOLD WITH STUDS OF SILVER. In contrast to her humble shepherd's attire, she would be decorated with jewels and strings of golden beads with points of silver.

1:12 MY SPIKENARD. Nard is an ointment from an aromatic Himalayan herb.

1:13 A BUNDLE OF MYRRH *IS* MY WELL-BELOVED UNTO ME. Myrrh is an aromatic resin from the bark of a balsam tree found in Arabia and India. The bundle of myrrh was probably in a perfume bag. The Hebrew in the rest of the verse indicates that the myrrh, *not the beloved*, would lie between her breasts. In other words, thoughts of him would be with her, refreshing her as myrrh would do.

1:14 CAMPHIRE. These are henna flowers, which produce an orange dye and have a pleasant fragrance.

1:15 DOVES' EYES. This comparison seems to refer to innocence. The Shulamite does not use seductive glances to try to stir up base emotions.

2:1 I AM THE ROSE OF SHARON, *AND* THE LILY OF THE VALLEYS. This is the Shulamite maiden speaking; she compares herself to simple wild flowers of the fields, for she is not accustomed to the luxuries of Jerusalem. Sharon is the coastal plain just south of Mount Carmel.

2 As the lily among thorns, so *is* my
love among the daughters.
3 As the apple tree among the trees
of the wood, so *is* my beloved among
the sons. [g]I sat down under his shad-
ow with great delight, [l]and his fruit
was sweet to my [h]taste.
4 He brought me to the [i]banquet-
ing house, and his banner over me *was*
love.
5 Stay me with flagons, [j]comfort
me with apples: for I *am* sick of love.
6 [m]His left hand *is* under my head,
and his right hand doth embrace me.
7 [n]I[k] charge you, O ye daughters
of Jerusalem, by the roes, and by the
hinds of the field, that ye stir not up,
nor awake *my* love, till he please.
8 ¶ The voice of my beloved! behold,
he cometh leaping upon the moun-
tains, skipping upon the hills.
9 [o]My beloved is like a roe or a
young hart: behold, he standeth behind
our wall, he looketh forth at the win-
dows, [1]showing himself through the
lattice.
10 My beloved spake, and said unto
me, [p]Rise up, my love, my fair one,
and come away.
11 For, lo, the winter is past, the
rain is over *and* gone;
12 The flowers appear on the earth;
the time of the singing *of birds* is come,
and the voice of the turtle is heard in
our land;
13 The fig tree putteth forth her
green figs, and the vines *with* the ten-
der grape give a *good* smell. [q]Arise,
my love, my fair one, and come away.
14 ¶ O my dove, *that art* in the clefts
of the rock, in the secret *places* of the
stairs, let me see thy countenance,
[r]let me hear thy voice; for sweet *is* thy
voice, and thy countenance *is* comely.
15 Take us [s]the foxes, the little
foxes, that spoil the vines: for our vines
have tender grapes.
16 ¶ [t]My beloved *is* mine, and I *am*
his: he feedeth among the lilies.
17 [u]Until the day break, and the
shadows flee away, turn, my beloved,
and be thou [v]like a roe or a young hart
upon the mountains [m]of Bether.

The maiden's search

3 BY [w]NIGHT on my bed I sought
him whom my soul loveth: I sought
him, but I found him not.
2 I will rise now, and go about the
city in the streets, and in the broad
ways I will seek him whom my soul
loveth: I sought him, but I found him
not.
3 [x]The watchmen that go about
the city found me: *to whom I said,* Saw
ye him whom my soul loveth?
4 *It was* but a little that I passed
from them, but I found him whom my
soul loveth: I held him, and would not
let him go, until I had brought him into
my mother's house, and into the cham-
ber of her that conceived me.
5 [y]I charge you, O ye daughters of
Jerusalem, by the roes, and by the
hinds of the field, that ye stir not up,
nor awake *my* love, till he please.
6 ¶ [z]Who *is* this that cometh out of
the wilderness like pillars of smoke,
perfumed with myrrh and frankin-

2:3 [l]Rev. 22:1,2 **2:6** [m]ch. 8:3 **2:7** [n]ch. 3:5 & 8:4 **2:9** [o]ver:17 **2:10** [p]ver. 13 **2:13** [q]ver:10 **2:14** [r]ch. 8:13 **2:15** [s]Ps. 80:13 Ezek:13:4 Luke 13:32 **2:16** [t]ch. 6:3 **2:17** [u]ch. 4:6 [v]ver. 9 ch. 8:14 **3:1** [w]Is. 26:9 **3:3** [x]ch. 5:7 **3:5** [y]ch. 2:7 & 8:4 **3:6** [z]ch. 8:5

[g]Heb. *I delighted and sat down* [h]Heb. *palate* [i]Heb. *house of wine* [j]Heb. *straw me with apples* [k]Heb. *I adjure you* [1]Heb. *flourishing* [m]Or, *of division*

2:5 STAY ME WITH FLAGONS, COMFORT ME WITH APPLES. In a weakened, lovesick condition (possibly involving disappointment) she wants to be refreshed with "flagons" (i.e., raisin cakes, which were full of energy). "Comfort" is another word meaning "refresh."

2:7 THAT YE STIR NOT UP, NOR AWAKE *MY* LOVE, TILL HE PLEASE. This phrase occurs three times in the Song of Solomon (see 3:5; 8:4). It is spoken by the maiden and refers to physical intimacy between her and her lover. She does not want any intimacy to occur until the situation is appropriate, i.e., until she and Solomon are married. The Bible allows for sexual relations only between a husband and a wife (see 4:12, note; see article on STANDARDS OF SEXUAL MORALITY, p. 1964).

2:12 THE VOICE OF THE TURTLE. "Turtle" is the turtle-dove.

2:14 THE STAIRS. These are steps cut in the rock cliff leading to a mountain path.

2:16 MY BELOVED *IS* MINE, AND I *AM* HIS. The love the two lovers have for each other is genuine and monogamous. There is no desire or room for any other person. In marriage, there must be such a love for and commitment to each other that faithfulness to a spouse is of highest importance in our lives.

3:1–4 BY NIGHT . . . I SOUGHT HIM, BUT I FOUND HIM NOT. "Night" is plural in the Hebrew and means "night after night"; the Shulamite may have been dreaming (v. 5) night after night that she was searching for her lover but not finding him.

3:6 WHO *IS* THIS THAT COMETH. "This" is feminine in the Hebrew; the verbs that follow refer to the bride's coming.

cense, with all powders of the merchant?

7 Behold his bed, which *is* Solomon's; threescore valiant men *are* about it, of the valiant of Israel.

8 They all hold swords, *being* expert in war: every man *hath* his sword upon his thigh because of fear in the night.

9 King Solomon made himself [n]a chariot of the wood of Lebanon.

10 He made the pillars thereof *of* silver, the bottom thereof *of* gold, the covering of it *of* purple, the midst thereof being paved *with* love, for the daughters of Jerusalem.

11 Go forth, O ye daughters of Zion, and behold king Solomon with the crown wherewith his mother crowned him in the day of his espousals, and in the day of the gladness of his heart.

The king offers his love

4 BEHOLD, [a]THOU *art* fair, my love; behold, thou *art* fair; thou *hast* doves' eyes within thy locks: thy hair *is* as a [b]flock of goats, [o]that appear from mount Gilead.

2 [c]Thy teeth *are* like a flock *of sheep that are even* shorn, which came up from the washing; whereof every one bear twins, and none *is* barren among them.

3 Thy lips *are* like a thread of scarlet, and thy speech *is* comely: [d]thy temples *are* like a piece of a pomegranate within thy locks.

4 [e]Thy neck *is* like the tower of David builded [f]for an armoury, whereon there hang a thousand bucklers, all shields of mighty men.

4:1 [a]ch. 1:15 & 5:12 [b]ch. 6:5
4:2 [c]ch. 6:6
4:3 [d]ch. 6:7
4:4 [e]ch. 7:4 [f]Neh. 3:19
4:5 [g]See Prov. 5:19 ch:7:3
4:6 [h]ch. 2:17
4:7 [i]Eph. 5:27
4:8 [j]Deut. 3:9
4:10 [k]ch. 1:2
4:11 [l]Prov. 24:13,14 ch. 5:1 [m]Gen. 27:27 Hos. 14:6,7

5 [g]Thy two breasts *are* like two young roes that are twins, which feed among the lilies.

6 [h]Until the day [p]break, and the shadows flee away, I will get me to the mountain of myrrh, and to the hill of frankincense.

7 [i]Thou *art* all fair, my love; *there is* no spot in thee.

8 ¶ Come with me from Lebanon, *my* spouse, with me from Lebanon: look from the top of Amana, from the top of Shenir [j]and Hermon, from the lions' dens, from the mountains of the leopards.

9 Thou hast [q]ravished my heart, my sister, *my* spouse; thou hast ravished my heart with one of thine eyes, with one chain of thy neck.

10 How fair is thy love, my sister, *my* spouse! [k]how much better is thy love than wine! and the smell of thine ointments than all spices!

11 Thy lips, O *my* spouse, drop *as* the honeycomb: [l]honey and milk *are* under thy tongue; and the smell of thy garments *is* [m]like the smell of Lebanon.

12 A garden [r]inclosed *is* my sister, *my* spouse; a spring shut up, a fountain sealed.

13 Thy plants *are* an orchard of pomegranates, with pleasant fruits; [s]camphire, with spikenard,

14 Spikenard and saffron; calamus and cinnamon, with all trees of frank-

[n] Or, *a bed* [o] Or, *that eat of* [p] Heb. *breathe* [q] Or, *taken away my heart* [r] Heb. *barred* [s] Or, *cypress*

3:11 GO FORTH . . . AND BEHOLD KING SOLOMON. Because of the intercession of Bathsheba, Solomon's mother, and the prophet Nathan, Solomon was brought out and publicly anointed king (1 Ki. 1:22–40). "The day of his espousals" is his wedding day. It appears that when Solomon was brought out and anointed king, he was already married and was wearing the crown with which his mother crowned him. In view also are the covenant promises given by God (2 Sam. 7:13–16; see article on GOD'S COVENANT WITH DAVID, p. 470).

4:7 THOU *ART* ALL FAIR . . . *THERE IS* NO SPOT IN THEE. Everything about the Shulamite was beautiful and without blemish. "Spot" can also refer to moral blemishes; thus she is physically and morally pure.

4:8 AMANA . . . SHENIR . . . HERMON. Amana is the name for a mountain in the Anti-Lebanon mountain range; at their southern end are the peaks of Shenir (also spelled Senir) and Mount Hermon, northeast of Galilee.

4:9 THOU HAST RAVISHED MY HEART, MY SISTER, *MY* SPOUSE. "Sister" here means "beloved"; "spouse" means "bride." Solomon's beloved bride has captured his heart and stolen it away.

4:12 A GARDEN INCLOSED. The three figures of speech in this verse emphasize the fact the Shulamite had retained her virginity and was sexually pure on her wedding night. Virginity until marriage is God's sexual standard of purity for all young people, male and female. To violate God's holy standard defiles one's spirit and conscience and cheapens the moment of marriage consummation (see article on STANDARDS OF SEXUAL MORALITY, p. 1964).

4:14 SAFFRON. This is a plant whose violet flowers yielded a yellow dye. A fragrant ointment was made by mixing it with olive oil.

4:14 CALAMUS . . . ALOES. Calamus is an aromatic spice; aloes is an aromatic wood from Bangladesh and China.

incense; myrrh and aloes, with all the
chief spices:
15 A fountain of gardens, a well of
[n]living waters, and streams from Leb-
anon.
16 ¶ Awake, O north wind; and
come, thou south; blow upon my gar-
den, *that* the spices thereof may flow
out. [o]Let my beloved come into his
garden, and eat his pleasant fruits.

5 I [p]AM come into my garden, my
sister, *my* spouse: I have gathered
my myrrh with my spice; [q]I have eaten
my honeycomb with my honey; I have
drunk my wine with my milk: eat, O
[r]friends; drink, [t]yea, drink abun-
dantly, O beloved.

The torment of separation

2 ¶ I sleep, but my heart waketh: *it*
is the voice of my beloved [s]that
knocketh, *saying*, Open to me, my sis-
ter, my love, my dove, my undefiled: for
my head is filled with dew, *and* my
locks with the drops of the night.
3 I have put off my coat; how shall
I put it on? I have washed my feet; how
shall I defile them?
4 My beloved put in his hand by the
hole *of the door*, and my bowels were
moved [u]for him.
5 I rose up to open to my beloved;
and my hands dropped *with* myrrh, and
my fingers *with* [v]sweetsmelling
myrrh, upon the handles of the lock.
6 I opened to my beloved; but my
beloved had withdrawn himself, *and*
was gone: my soul failed when he
spake: [t]I sought him, but I could not
find him; I called him, but he gave me
no answer.
7 [u]The watchmen that went about
the city found me, they smote me, they
wounded me; the keepers of the walls
took away my veil from me.
8 I charge you, O daughters of Jeru-
salem, if ye find my beloved, [w]that ye
tell him, that I *am* sick of love.
9 ¶ What *is* thy beloved more than
another beloved, [v]O thou fairest
among women? what *is* thy beloved
more than *another* beloved, that thou
dost so charge us?
10 My beloved *is* white and ruddy,
[x]the chiefest among ten thousand.
11 His head *is as* the most fine gold,
his locks *are* [y]bushy, *and* black as a
raven.
12 [w]His eyes *are* as *the eyes* of
doves by the rivers of waters, washed
with milk, *and* [z]fitly set.
13 His cheeks *are* as a bed of spices,
as [a]sweet flowers: his lips *like* lilies,
dropping sweetsmelling myrrh.
14 His hands *are as* gold rings set
with the beryl: his belly *is as* bright ivo-
ry overlaid *with* sapphires.
15 His legs *are as* pillars of marble,
set upon sockets of fine gold: his coun-
tenance *is* as Lebanon, excellent as the
cedars.
16 [b]His mouth *is* most sweet: yea,
he *is* altogether lovely. This *is* my be-
loved, and this *is* my friend, O daugh-
ters of Jerusalem.

6 WHITHER IS thy beloved gone,
[x]O thou fairest among women?
whither is thy beloved turned aside?
that we may seek him with thee.
2 My beloved is gone down into his
garden, to the beds of spices, to feed in
the gardens, and to gather lilies.
3 [y]I *am* my beloved's, and my be-
loved *is* mine: he feedeth among the lil-
ies.

The maiden's beauty

4 ¶ Thou *art* beautiful, O my love, as
Tirzah, comely as Jerusalem, [z]terrible
as *an army* with banners.
5 Turn away thine eyes from me, for
[c]they have overcome me: thy hair *is*
[a]as a flock of goats that appear from
Gilead.
6 [b]Thy teeth *are* as a flock of sheep
which go up from the washing, whereof

4:15 [n]John 4:10 & 7:38 **4:16** [o]ch. 5:1 **5:1** [p]ch. 4:16 [q]ch. 4:11 [r]Luke 15:7,10 **5:2** [s]Rev. 3:20 **5:6** [t]ch. 3:1 **5:7** [u]ch. 3:3 **5:9** [v]ch. 1:8 **5:12** [w]ch. 1:15 & 4:1 **6:1** [x]ch. 1:8 **6:3** [y]ch. 2:16 & 7:10 **6:4** [z]ver. 10 **6:5** [a]ch. 4:1 **6:6** [b]ch. 4:2

[t] Or, *and be drunken with loves* [u] Or, (as some read) *in me* [v] Heb. *passing*, or, *running about* [w] Heb. *what* [x] Heb. *a standard bearer* [y] Or, *curled* [z] Heb. *sitting in fulness*, i.e. *fitly placed, and set as a precious stone in the foil of a ring* [a] Or, *towers of perfumes* [b] Heb. *His palate* [c] Or, *they have puffed me up*

5:4 MY BOWELS WERE MOVED FOR HIM. "Bowels" (i.e., the belly, intestines, and inner parts) were considered the seat of emotions, especially feelings of affection. The maiden's entire body quivered when she thought of her lover.

5:14 SAPPHIRES. A sapphire is a semiprecious stone of rich azure blue.

5:16 HE *IS* ALTOGETHER LOVELY. Everything about the bridegroom is precious, desirable, and delightful.

6:4 TERRIBLE AS *AN ARMY* WITH BANNERS. The bridegroom regarded his darling to be as awe-inspiring as an army with banners. Others take this to mean as awesome as a host of stars (such as the Milky Way).

every one beareth twins, and *there is* not one barren among them.

7 [c]As a piece of a pomegranate *are* thy temples within thy locks.

8 There are threescore queens, and fourscore concubines, and virgins without number.

9 My dove, my undefiled is *but* one; she *is* the *only* one of her mother, she *is* the choice *one* of her that bare her. The daughters saw her, and blessed her; *yea,* the queens and the concubines, and they praised her.

10 ¶ Who *is* she *that* looketh forth as the morning, fair as the moon, clear as the sun, [d]*and* terrible as *an army* with banners?

11 I went down into the garden of nuts to see the fruits of the valley, *and* [e]to see whether the vine flourished, *and* the pomegranates budded.

12 [d]Or ever I was aware, my soul [e]made me *like* the chariots of Amminadib.

13 Return, return, O Shulamite; return, return, that we may look upon thee. What will ye see in the Shulamite? As it were the company of two armies.

7 HOW BEAUTIFUL are thy feet with shoes, [f]O prince's daughter! the joints of thy thighs *are* like jewels, the work of the hands of a cunning workman.

2 Thy navel *is like* a round goblet, *which* wanteth not [f]liquor: thy belly *is like* an heap of wheat set about with lilies.

3 [g]Thy two breasts *are* like two young roes *that are* twins.

4 [h]Thy neck *is* as a tower of ivory; thine eyes *like* the fishpools in Heshbon, by the gate of Bath-rabbim: thy nose *is* as the tower of Lebanon which looketh toward Damascus.

5 Thine head upon thee *is* like [g]Carmel, and the hair of thine head like purple; the king *is* [h]held in the galleries.

6 How fair and how pleasant art thou, O love, for delights!

7 This thy stature is like to a palm tree, and thy breasts to clusters *of grapes.*

8 I said, I will go up to the palm tree, I will take hold of the boughs thereof: now also thy breasts shall be as clusters of the vine, and the smell of thy nose like apples;

9 And the roof of thy mouth like the best wine for my beloved, that goeth *down* [i]sweetly, causing the lips [j]of those that are asleep to speak.

The maiden desires her beloved

10 ¶ [i]I *am* my beloved's, and [j]his desire *is* toward me.

11 Come, my beloved, let us go forth into the field; let us lodge in the villages.

12 Let us get up early to the vineyards; let us [k]see if the vine flourish, *whether* the tender grape [k]appear, *and* the pomegranates bud forth: there will I give thee my loves.

13 The [l]mandrakes give a smell, and at our gates [m]*are* all manner of pleasant *fruits,* new and old, *which* I have laid up for thee, O my beloved.

8 O THAT thou *wert* as my brother, that sucked the breasts of my mother! *when* I should find thee without, I would kiss thee; yea, [l]I should not be despised.

2 I would lead thee, *and* bring thee into my mother's house, *who* would instruct me: I would cause thee to drink of [n]spiced wine of the juice of my pomegranate.

3 [o]His left hand *should be* under my head, and his right hand should embrace me.

4 [p]I charge you, O daughters of Jerusalem,

6:7 [c]ch. 4:3 **6:10** [d]ver. 4 **6:11** [e]ch. 7:12 **7:1** [f]Ps. 45:13 **7:3** [g]ch. 4:5 **7:4** [h]ch. 4:4 **7:10** [i]ch. 2:16 & 6:3 [j]Ps. 45:11 **7:12** [k]ch. 6:11 **7:13** [l]Gen. 30:14 [m]Mat. 13:52 **8:2** [n]Prov. 9:2 **8:3** [o]ch. 2:6 **8:4** [p]ch. 2:7 & 3:5

[d]Heb. *I knew not* [e]Or, *set me on the chariots of my willing people* [f]Heb. *mixture* [g]Or, *crimson* [h]Heb. *bound* [i]Heb. *straightly* [j]Or, *of the ancient* [k]Heb. *open* [l]Heb. *they should not despise me*

6:8 THREESCORE QUEENS, AND FOURSCORE CONCUBINES, AND VIRGINS WITHOUT NUMBER. The women of Jerusalem are classified as queens, concubines, and virgins (Heb. *alamoth,* virgins of marriageable age). But the Shulamite cannot be compared with any of them; she is one of a kind, in a class by herself.

6:13 RETURN, O SHULAMITE. Some take "Shulamite" to mean a woman of Shunem. Others take it to be a feminine form of Solomon as a title, i.e., a "Solomonitess," or Solomon's girl.

7:4 FISHPOOLS IN HESHBON ... BATH-RABBIM. These are reservoirs outside the walls of Heshbon, about five miles northeast of Mount Nebo. Bath-rabbim (lit. "daughter of multitudes") was probably the name of one of the gates of Heshbon.

7:13 MANDRAKES. These herbs were considered to be an aphrodisiac, i.e., something that excites sexual desire (cf. Gen. 30:14–17).

8:4 THAT YE STIR NOT UP, NOR AWAKE *MY* LOVE, TILL HE PLEASE. See 2:7, note.

rusalem, [m]that ye stir not up, nor
awake *my* love, until he please.
5 [q]Who *is* this that cometh up from
the wilderness, leaning upon her be-
loved? I raised thee up under the apple
tree: there thy mother brought thee
forth: there she brought thee forth *that*
bare thee.
6 ¶ [r]Set me as a seal upon thine
heart, as a seal upon thine arm: for
love *is* strong as death; jealousy *is*
[n]cruel as the grave: the coals thereof
are coals of fire, *which hath* a most
vehement flame.
7 Many waters cannot quench love,
neither can the floods drown it: [s]if a
man would give all the substance of his
house for love, it would utterly be con-
temned.
8 ¶ [t]We have a little sister, and she
hath no breasts: what shall we do for
our sister in the day when she shall be
spoken for?
9 If she *be* a wall, we will build upon
her a palace of silver: and if she *be* a
door, we will inclose her with boards of
cedar.
10 I *am* a wall, and my breasts like
towers: then was I in his eyes as one
that found [o]favour.
11 Solomon had a vineyard at Baal-
hamon; [u]he let out the vineyard unto
keepers; every one for the fruit thereof
was to bring a thousand *pieces* of silver.
12 My vineyard, which *is* mine, *is*
before me: thou, O Solomon, *must have*
a thousand, and those that keep the
fruit thereof two hundred.
13 Thou that dwellest in the gar-
dens, the companions hearken to thy
voice: [v]cause me to hear *it*.
14 ¶ [w]Make[p] haste, my beloved,
and [x]be thou like to a roe or to a young
hart upon the mountains of spices.

8:5 [q]ch. 3:6
8:6 [r]Is. 49:16 Jer. 22:24 Hag. 2:23
8:7 [s]Prov. 6:35
8:8 [t]Ezek. 23:33
8:11 [u]Mat. 21:33
8:13 [v]ch. 2:14
8:14 [w]See Rev. 22:17, 20 [x]ch. 2:17

[m] Heb. *why should ye stir up,* or, *why* [n] Heb. *hard* [o] Heb. *peace* [p] Heb. *flee away*

8:6–7 LOVE *IS* AS STRONG AS DEATH ... MANY WATERS CANNOT QUENCH LOVE. There is nothing more powerful and beautiful than expressing mutual love between a man and woman who are truly committed to each other.

8:6 JEALOUSY *IS* CRUEL AS THE GRAVE. Jealousy here can be translated "ardent love." It is as inflexible as "*Sheol*" or the grave, a place from which no one can escape (see Ps. 16:10, note).

8:7 IF A MAN WOULD GIVE ALL THE SUBSTANCE OF HIS HOUSE FOR LOVE, IT WOULD UTTERLY BE CONTEMNED. Trying to buy love for money is something to be scorned; it cannot be done. Similarly, any marriage that is based on the attractiveness of the earthly possessions of either the husband or the wife is doomed to failure.

8:9 IF SHE *BE* A WALL ... IF SHE *BE* A DOOR. If the little sister is a wall resisting temptation, the daughters of Jerusalem will adorn her (i.e., prepare her for marriage). If she is a door ready to succumb to temptation, they will do whatever is needed to protect her from such defilement.

8:11 BAAL-HAMON. This is a place where Solomon rented his vineyards to tenant farmers.

8:12 MY VINEYARD ... *IS* BEFORE ME. In contrast to Solomon's many vineyards, she has her own single vineyard. Solomon can have the income from his, and his keepers can have their portion, but her vineyard is something better.

ISAIAH

Outline

I. Prophecies of Judgment and Rebuke (1:1—35:10)
   A. The Setting for Isaiah's Prophecy (1:1–31)
   B. Isaiah's Early Prophecies (2:1—5:30)
      1. The Day of the Lord (2:1–22)
      2. Judgment Against Judah and Jerusalem (3:1—4:1)
      3. Predictions of Judgment and Glory (4:2–6)
      4. Parable About Judah's Judgment and Exile (5:1–30)
   C. Isaiah's Cleansing and Commissioning by God (6:1–13)
   D. Isaiah's Early Messianic Prophecies (7:1—12:6)
      1. The Sign of Immanuel (7:1–25)
      2. Foreshadowings of Messianic Deliverance (8:1—9:7)
      3. Prophecies of Judgment Against Israel (Northern Kingdom) and Assyria (9:8—10:34)
      4. The Davidic Messiah and His Kingdom (11:1—12:6)
   E. Isaiah's Prophecies of Judgment Against the Nations (13:1—23:18)
      1. Against Babylon (13:1—14:23)
      2. Against Assyria (14:24–27)
      3. Against Philistia (14:28–32)
      4. Against Moab (15:1—16:14)
      5. Against Damascus and Samaria (17:1–14)
      6. Against Ethiopia (18:1–7)
      7. Against Egypt (19:1—20:6)
      8. Against Babylon (Second Oracle) (21:1–10)
      9. Against Edom (21:11–12)
      10. Against Arabia (21:13–17)
      11. Against Jerusalem (22:1–25)
      12. Against Tyre (23:1–18)
   F. Prophecies About the Consummation of History (24:1—27:13)
   G. Prophecies of Woe Intertwined with Prophetic Hope of Salvation (28:1—35:10)

II. Historical Interlude Concerning Hezekiah (36:1—39:8)
   A. Hezekiah's Deliverance from Assyria (36:1—37:38)
   B. Hezekiah's Sickness and Healing (38:1–22)
   C. Hezekiah's Foolish Pride (39:1–8)

III. Prophecies of Salvation and Hope (40:1—66:24)
   A. Prophetic Promises of Restoration for God's People (40:1—48:22)
      1. The Glory of the Lord and His Servant Will be Revealed (40:1—42:25)
      2. The Restoration of a Redeemed Remnant (43:1—45:25)
      3. Lessons of Faith for Judah When God Judges Babylon (46:1—48:22)
   B. Prophetic Promises Concerning the Suffering Servant Messiah (49:1—53:12)
      1. His Mission and Obedience (49:1—50:11)
      2. His Encouragement and Exhortation for the Remnant (51:1—52:12)
      3. His Suffering and Atoning Death (52:13—53:12)
   C. Further Prophetic Revelation Concerning Restoration and Redemption (54:1—59:21)

D. Prophetic Visions of a Glorious Future for Zion (60:1–66:24)
1. Zion's Prosperity and Peace (60:1–22)
2. The Messiah's Anointing and Mission (61:1–11)
3. Prophetic Intercession for Zion's Restoration and Glory (62:1–64:12)
4. God's Answer of Mercy and Glorious Consummation (65:1–66:24)

Author: Isaiah

Theme: Judgment and Salvation

Date of Writing: c. 700–680 B.C.

Background

The historical setting for the prophetic ministry of Isaiah, son of Amoz, was Jerusalem during the reign of four kings of Judah: Uzziah, Jotham, Ahaz, and Hezekiah (1:1). Since King Uzziah died in 740 B.C. (cf. 6:1) and Hezekiah in 687 B.C., Isaiah's ministry spanned more than half a century of Judah's history. According to Hebrew tradition, Isaiah was martyred by being sawn in two (cf. Heb. 11:37) by Hezekiah's wicked son and successor to the throne, King Manasseh (c. 680 B.C.).

Isaiah apparently came from an influential upper-class family in Jerusalem; he was educated, had gifts as a poet and prophet, was acquainted with royalty, and gave prophetic counsel to kings concerning the foreign affairs of Judah. He is usually regarded as the most literary and influential of the writing prophets. He was married to a wife gifted as a prophetess, and they had two sons whose names contained a symbolic message for the nation.

Isaiah was a contemporary of Hosea and Micah; he prophesied during the threatening expansion of the Assyrian empire, the final collapse of Israel (the northern kingdom), and the spiritual and moral decline of Judah (the southern kingdom). Isaiah warned Judah's King Ahaz not to look to Assyria for help against Israel and Syria; he warned King Hezekiah, after Israel's fall in 722 B.C., not to make alliances with foreign nations against Assyria. He exhorted both kings to place their trust solely in the Lord as their security (7:3–7; 30:1–17). Isaiah enjoyed his greatest influence during the reign of King Hezekiah.

Some scholars question whether Isaiah wrote the entire book that bears his name. These scholars assign only chs. 1–39 to Isaiah of Jerusalem; they typically attribute chs. 40–66 to another author or authors more than a century and a half later. There is no Biblical data, however, that requires one to reject Isaiah's authorship of the entire book. Isaiah's prophetic messages in chs. 40–66 for the Jewish exiles in Babylon long after his death emphasize God's ability to reveal specific future events through His prophets (e.g. 42:8–9; 44:6–8; 45:1; 47:1–11; 53:1–12). If one accepts the phenomena of prophetic visions and revelations (cf. Rev. 1:1; 4:1–22:21), then the major obstacle to believing that Isaiah wrote the entire book is removed. Positive supporting evidence is plentiful and falls under two broad categories. (1) Internal evidence from the book itself includes the superscription in 1:1 (which stands for the entire book) and the numerous striking parallels of expression and thought between both major sections of the book. One notable example is the expression "the Holy One of Israel," which occurs twelve times in chs. 1–39, fourteen times in chs. 40–66, and only six times in the rest of the O.T. combined. No less than twenty-five Hebrew word-forms appear in both major divisions of Isaiah but nowhere else in O.T. prophetic books. (2) External evidence includes the testimony of the Jewish Talmud and the N.T. itself, which attributes all parts of the book to the prophet Isaiah (e.g., cf. Mat. 12:17–21 with Is. 42:1–4; Mat. 3:3 and Luke 3:4 with Is. 40:3; John 12:37–41 with Is. 6:9–10 and 53:1; Acts 8:28–33 with Is. 53:7–9; Rom. 9:27 and 10:16–21 with Is. 10, 53, and 65).

Purpose

A threefold purpose is apparent in the writing of Isaiah. (1) The prophet first confronted his own nation and other contemporary nations with the word of the Lord concerning their

sin and God's coming judgment. (2) Then, by revelatory visions and the Spirit of prophecy, Isaiah prophesied hope to a whole future generation of Jewish exiles who would in time be restored from captivity and whom God would redeem as a light to the Gentiles. (3) Finally, Isaiah prophesied that God was going to send forth the Davidic Messiah, whose salvation would eventually encompass all the nations of the earth, thus providing hope for God's people under both the old and new covenants.

Survey

Most scholars agree that the sixty-six chapters of Isaiah divide naturally into two major sections: chs. 1—39 and chs. 40—66. In certain respects Isaiah is like the Bible in miniature: (1) Isaiah's twofold division stressed the general themes of judgment and salvation, corresponding to the overall general themes of the O.T. and N.T.; and (2) in both divisions of Isaiah and the Bible, the thread that ties them together is the redemptive work of Christ.

(1) Section one of Isaiah (chs. 1—39) contains four large blocks of material. (a) In chs. 1—12, Isaiah warns and denounces Judah for her idolatry, immorality, and social injustices during a time of deceptive prosperity. Intertwined with the message of coming judgment are important Messianic prophecies (e.g. 2:4; 7:14; 9:6–7; 11:1–9), and Isaiah's testimony of his own cleansing from sin and divine commissioning for the prophetic ministry (ch. 6). (b) In chs. 13—23, Isaiah prophesies to nations contemporary with Judah about their sin and God's coming judgment. (c) Chs. 24—35 contain an assortment of prophetic promises of future salvation and judgment. (d) Chs. 36—39 record selective history from the life of King Hezekiah, which parallels 2 Ki. 18:13—20:21.

(2) The second major section (chs. 40—66) contains some of the most profound prophecies in the Bible about the greatness of God and the vastness of His redemptive plan. These chapters inspired hope and comfort in God's people during the remaining years of Hezekiah's reign (38:5) and for centuries afterward. They are full of prophetic revelation of God's glory and power, and of His promises to restore a righteous and fruit-bearing remnant in Israel and among the nations in full demonstration of His redemptive love. These promises and their fulfillment are especially connected to the theme of suffering and contain Isaiah's "servant songs" (see 42:1–4; 49:1–6; 50:4–9; 52:13—53:12), which point beyond the experience of the Jewish exiles to the future coming of Jesus Christ and His atoning death (ch. 53). The prophet predicts that the coming Messiah will enable righteousness to shine brightly and salvation to go forth to the nations like a torch that is burning (chs. 60—66). He condemns spiritual blindness concerning God's ways (42:18–25) and commends intercessory prayer and spiritual travail by God's people as necessary in order that all things may be fulfilled (cf. 56:6–8; 62:1–2,6–7; 66:7–18).

Special Features

Eight major features or emphases characterize the book of Isaiah. (1) It is largely written in Hebrew poetic form and stands unsurpassed as a literary gem in the beauty, power, and versatility of its poetry. Isaiah's rich vocabulary surpasses that of all other O.T. writers. (2) Isaiah is called "the evangelical prophet," because, of all the O.T. books, his Messianic prophecies contain the fullest and clearest declaration of the gospel of Jesus Christ. (3) His vision of the cross in ch. 53 is the most specific and detailed prophecy in the whole Bible about Jesus' atoning death for sinners. (4) It is the most theological and comprehensive of all O.T. prophetic books. It reaches back in time to God's creation of the heavens and earth and human life (e.g., 42:5) and looks forward in time to God's consummation of history and the creation of a new heavens and a new earth (e.g., 65:17; 66:22). (5) It contains more revelation about the nature, majesty, and holiness of God than any other O.T. prophetic book. Isaiah's God is holy and all-powerful, the One who will judge sin and unrighteousness among humans and the nations. His favorite expression for God is "the Holy One of Israel." (6) Isaiah—whose name means "The LORD is salvation" or "The LORD saves"—is the prophet of salvation. He uses the specific term "salvation" nearly three times more than all other O.T. prophetic books combined. Isaiah reveals that God's full purpose of salvation will be realized only in connection with the Messiah. (7) Isaiah frequently refers back to

earlier redemptive events in Israel's history: e.g., the exodus (4:5–6; 11:15; 31:5; 43:16–17), the destruction of Sodom and Gomorrah (1:9), and Gideon's victory over the Midianites (9:4; 10:26; 28:21); he also draws from Moses' prophetic song in Deut. 32 (1:2; 30:17; 43:11,13). (8) Isaiah joins Deuteronomy and the Psalms as one of the three O.T. books most often quoted and referred to in the N.T.

New Testament Fulfillment

Isaiah prophesies about John the Baptist as the appointed forerunner to the Messiah (40:3–5; cf. Mat. 3:1–3). The following are some of Isaiah's many Messianic prophecies and their N.T. application in the life and ministry of Jesus Christ: His incarnation and deity (Is. 7:14; see Mat. 1:22–23 and Luke 1:34–35; Is. 9:6–7; see Luke 1:32–33; 2:11); His youth (Is. 7:15–16 and 11:1; see Luke 3:23,32 and Acts 13:22–23); His mission (Is. 11:2–5; 42:1–4; 60:1–3; and 61:1; see Luke 4:17–19,21); His obedience (Is. 50:5; see Heb. 5:8); His message and anointing by the Spirit (Is. 11:2; 42:1; and 61:1; see Mat. 12:15–21); His miracles (Is. 35:5–6; see Mat. 11:2–5); His suffering (Is. 50:6; see Mat. 26:67 and 27:26,30; Is. 53:4–5,11; see Acts 8:28–33); His rejection (Is. 53:1–3; see Luke 23:18; John 1:11 and 7:5); His shame (Is. 52:14; see Phil. 2:7–8); His atoning death (Is. 53:4–12; see Rom. 5:6); His ascension (Is. 52:13; see Phil. 2:9–11); and His second advent (Is. 26:20–21; see Jude 14; Is. 61:2–3; see 2 Thes. 1:5–12; Is. 65:17–25; see 2 Pet. 3:13).

Reading Isaiah

In order to read the entire Old Testament in one year, the book of Isaiah should be read in 28 days, according to the following schedule: ☐ 1–2 ☐ 3–5 ☐ 6–8 ☐ 9–10 ☐ 11–12 ☐ 13–14 ☐ 15–18 ☐ 19–22 ☐ 23–24 ☐ 25–26 ☐ 27–28 ☐ 29–30 ☐ 31–32 ☐ 33–34 ☐ 35–37 ☐ 38–39 ☐ 40–41 ☐ 42–43 ☐ 44–45 ☐ 46–47 ☐ 48–49 ☐ 50–51 ☐ 52–53 ☐ 54–56 ☐ 57–58 ☐ 59–60 ☐ 61–63 ☐ 64–66

NOTES

1 THE [a]VISION of Isaiah the son of
Amoz, which he saw concerning
Judah and Jerusalem in the days of Uz-
ziah, Jotham, Ahaz, *and* Hezekiah,
kings of Judah.

Israel's rebellion

2 [b]Hear, O heavens, and give ear,
O earth: for the LORD hath spoken, I
have nourished and brought up chil-
dren, and they have rebelled
against me.
3 [c]The ox knoweth his owner, and
the ass his master's crib: *but* Israel
[d]doth not know, my people doth not
consider.
4 Ah sinful nation, a people [a]laden
with iniquity, [e]a seed of evildoers,
children that are corrupters: they have
forsaken the LORD, they have provoked
the Holy One of Israel unto anger, they
are [b]gone away backward.
5 ¶ [f]Why should ye be stricken any
more? ye will [c]revolt more and more:
the whole head is sick, and the whole
heart faint.
6 From the sole of the foot even
unto the head *there is* no soundness in
it; *but* wounds, and bruises, and putri-
fying sores: they have not been closed,
neither bound up, neither mollified
with [d]ointment.
7 [g]Your country *is* desolate, your
cities *are* burned with fire: your land,
strangers devour it in your presence,
and *it is* desolate, [e]as overthrown by
strangers.
8 And the daughter of Zion is left
[h]as a cottage in a vineyard, as a lodge
in a garden of cucumbers, [i]as a be-
sieged city.
9 [j]Except the LORD of hosts had
left unto us a very small remnant, we
should have been as [k]Sodom, *and* we
should have been like unto Gomorrah.
10 ¶ Hear the word of the LORD, ye
rulers [l]of Sodom; give ear unto the
law of our God, ye people of Gomorrah.
11 To what purpose *is* the multitude
of your [m]sacrifices unto me? saith the
LORD: I am full of the burnt offerings of

1:1 [a]Num. 12:6 **1:2** [b]Jer. 2:12 **1:3** [c]Jer. 8:7 [d]Jer. 9:3,6 **1:4** [e]Mat. 3:7 **1:5** [f]ch. 9:13 **1:7** [g]Deut. 28:51 **1:8** [h]Job 27:18 [i]Jer. 4:17 **1:9** [j]Lam. 3:22 [k]Gen. 19:24 **1:10** [l]Deut. 32:32 **1:11** [m]1 Sam. 15:22

[a] Heb. *of heaviness* [b] Heb. *alienated,* or, *separated* [c] Heb. *increase revolt* [d] Or, *oil* [e] Heb. *as the overthrow of strangers*

1:1 THE VISION. Isaiah did not prophesy about or record his own ideas; rather, he received visions from God inspired by the Holy Spirit (cf. 2 Pet. 1:20–21). He was allowed to see coming events in God's plan of salvation through an unerring communication from God Himself.

1:1 ISAIAH. The name "Isaiah" means "the LORD saves." As a prophet commissioned by God, Isaiah began his ministry in 740 B.C., the year King Uzziah died (see 6:1). He prophesied forty or more years and probably died about 680 B.C. (see the introduction to Isaiah for more about him).

1:1 CONCERNING JUDAH. Isaiah's long prophetic ministry took place during the time of the divided kingdom (see 1 Ki. 12:20, note; 2 Chr. 10:1, note). The northern kingdom—variously called "Israel," "Samaria," or "Ephraim"—included ten tribes of the Israelites. The southern kingdom—usually called "Judah," with its capital at Jerusalem—consisted of the tribes of Judah and Benjamin. Both kingdoms had turned from God and His law to heathen nations and their false gods to deliver them from their enemies. The northern kingdom was conquered and destroyed by Assyria in 722 B.C. Isaiah warned Judah that they too would be destroyed because of their sin and apostasy (39:6).

1:2 THEY HAVE REBELLED AGAINST ME. Judah and Israel had received God's covenant, His law, His temple, and His many promises; yet they lived sinful lives, disregarded that covenant, and failed to acknowledge God as the source of their salvation and blessing. Hence, God was sending judgment (vv. 5–8).

1:3 ISRAEL. Here "Israel" refers to all the twelve tribes, including Judah.

1:4 THE HOLY ONE OF ISRAEL. This expression as a title for God occurs twenty-six times in Isaiah; five additional times God is referred to simply as "the Holy One." By using this name for God, undoubtedly derived in part from Isaiah's powerful vision of God in His holiness (ch. 6), the prophet not only emphasizes God's distinctively holy character, but also that God's people must be holy if they are to continue in a covenant relationship with Him.

1:7 YOUR COUNTRY *IS* DESOLATE. In an effort to bring Judah to repentance, God allowed their land to be plundered by foreigners (see 2 Chr. 28:5–18). The people's sin had cut them off from God's blessing and protection, and judgment had already begun. The land and people would ultimately be destroyed by Nebuchadnezzar and his Babylonian army (605–586 B.C.). Persistent sin by unrepentant sinners will always bring God's judgment and eventual destruction.

1:9–10 SODOM . . . GOMORRAH. The cities of Sodom and Gomorrah were completely destroyed because of their great sin (Gen. 19:1–25). Isaiah equates Judah with these cities because of its great unfaithfulness.

1:11 TO WHAT PURPOSE . . . YOUR SACRIFICES UNTO ME? Isaiah condemns the people for participating in evil deeds and injustices (vv. 16–17), while continuing to bring offerings and sacrifices to God and to pray to and worship Him. Worship and praise become an abomination to Him if our hearts are not sincerely devoted to Him and His holy ways (cf. 66:3; Jer. 7:21–26; Hos. 6:6; Amos 5:21–24; Mic. 6:6–8).

rams, and the fat of fed beasts; and I
delight not in the blood of bullocks, or
of lambs, or of [f]he goats.
12 When ye come [n]to[g] appear be-
fore me, who hath required this at your
hand, to tread my courts?
13 Bring no more [o]vain oblations;
incense is an abomination unto me; the
new moons and sabbaths, [p]the calling
of assemblies, I cannot away with; *it is*
[h]iniquity, even the solemn meeting.
14 Your [q]new moons and your
[r]appointed feasts my soul hateth:
they are a trouble unto me; [s]I am wea-
ry to bear *them*.
15 And [t]when ye spread forth your
hands, I will hide mine eyes from you:
[u]yea, when ye [i]make many prayers,
I will not hear: your hands are full of
[j]blood.
16 ¶ [v]Wash you, make you clean;
put away the evil of your doings from
before mine eyes; [w]cease to do evil;
17 Learn to do well; seek judgment,
[k]relieve the oppressed, judge the fa-
therless, plead for the widow.
18 Come now, and [x]let us reason
together, saith the LORD: though your
sins be as scarlet, [y]they shall be as
white as snow; though they be red like
crimson, they shall be as wool.
19 If ye be willing and obedient, ye
shall eat the good of the land:
20 But if ye refuse and rebel, ye
shall be devoured with the sword: [z]for
the mouth of the LORD hath spoken *it*.
21 ¶ [a]How is the faithful city be-
come an harlot! it was full of judgment;
righteousness lodged in it; but now
murderers.
22 [b]Thy silver is become dross, thy
wine mixed with water:
23 [c]Thy princes *are* rebellious, and
[d]companions of thieves: [e]every one
loveth gifts, and followeth after re-
wards: they [f]judge not the fatherless,
neither doth the cause of the widow
come unto them.
24 Therefore saith the Lord, the
LORD of hosts, the mighty One of Israel,
Ah, [g]I will ease me of mine adversar-
ies, and avenge me of mine enemies:
25 ¶ And I will turn my hand upon
thee, and [h]purely[l] purge away thy
dross, and take away all thy tin:
26 And I will restore thy judges
[i]as at the first, and thy counsellors as
at the beginning: afterward [j]thou
shalt be called, The city of righteous-
ness, the faithful city.
27 Zion shall be redeemed with
judgment, and [m]her converts with
righteousness.
28 ¶ And the [k]destruction[n] of the
transgressors and of the sinners *shall
be* together, and they that forsake the
LORD shall be consumed.
29 For they shall be ashamed of
[l]the oaks which ye have desired,
[m]and ye shall be confounded for the
gardens that ye have chosen.
30 For ye shall be as an oak whose
leaf fadeth, and as a garden that hath
no water.
31 [n]And the strong shall be [o]as
tow, [o]and the maker of it as a spark,
and they shall both burn together, and
none shall quench *them*.

God's kingdom to triumph

2:1–4pp — Mic. 4:1–3

2 THE WORD that Isaiah the son of
Amoz saw concerning Judah and
Jerusalem.
2 And [p]it shall come to pass [q]in

1:12 [n]Ex. 23:17
1:13 [o]Mat. 15:9 [p]Joel 1:14
1:14 [q]Num. 28:11 [r]Lam. 2:6 [s]ch. 43:24
1:15 [t]Prov. 1:28 Mic. 3:4 [u]Ps. 66:18
1:16 [v]Jer. 4:14 [w]Rom. 12:9
1:18 [x]ch. 43:26 [y]Ps. 51:7 Rev. 7:14
1:20 [z]Tit. 1:2
1:21 [a]Jer. 2:20
1:22 [b]Jer. 6:28
1:23 [c]Hos. 9:15 [d]Prov. 29:24 [e]Jer. 22:17 Ezek. 22:12
[f]Jer. 5:28 Zech. 7:10
1:24 [g]Deut. 28:63
1:25 [h]Mal. 3:3
1:26 [i]Jer. 33:7 [j]Zech. 8:3
1:28 [k]Job 31:3
1:29 [l]ch. 57:5 [m]ch. 65:3
1:31 [n]Ezek. 32:21 [o]ch. 43:17
2:2 [p]Mic. 4:1 [q]Gen. 49:1 Jer. 23:20

[f] Heb. *great he goats* [g] Heb. *to be seen* [h] Or, *grief* [i] Heb. *multiply prayer* [j] Heb. *bloods* [k] Or, *righten* [l] Heb. *according to pureness* [m] Or, *they that return of her* [n] Heb. *breaking* [o] Or, *and his work*

1:15 I WILL NOT HEAR. Sin in our lives will cause God to turn away from our prayers (see Jas. 4:3, note; 1 John 3:22, note; see article on EFFECTIVE PRAYING, p. 540).

1:18 COME NOW, AND LET US REASON. God did not want to condemn and destroy His people. He offered full forgiveness if they would only repent, put away evil, strive to do good, and obey His word (vv. 16–19). God's forgiveness is now available for all who, though they have sinned, confess their sins, repent, and accept God's cleansing through the blood of Jesus Christ (Luke 24:46–47; 1 John 1:9). Those who refuse God's mercy and choose instead to cling rebelliously to their own ways will be destroyed (v. 20).

1:25 PURGE AWAY THY DROSS. God intended to purge away evil from His people and to restore a remnant who repented (vv. 18–19,26–27). He was not yet finished with Judah (cf. Ezra 1; 5:2,14–16), for the Redeemer of the entire human race still had to come through these chosen people. Although "Zion" (v. 27, i.e., Jerusalem) would be restored, only those who truly turned to God would be saved and not destroyed (cf. 65:8–16).

2:2 IN THE LAST DAYS. The N.T. defines the last days as the period of time between the first and second comings of Christ (see Acts 2:17, note). What Isaiah describes in vv. 1–5 will reach its fulfillment at Christ's second coming, when He establishes the kingdom of God upon earth.

the last days, [r]*that* the mountain of the LORD's house shall be [p]established in the top of the mountains, and shall be exalted above the hills; [s]and all nations shall flow unto it.

3 And many people shall go and say, [t]Come ye, and let us go up to the mountain of the LORD, to the house of the God of Jacob; and he will teach us of his ways, and we will walk in his paths: [u]for out of Zion shall go forth the law, and the word of the LORD from Jerusalem.

4 And he shall judge among the nations, and shall rebuke many people: and [v]they shall beat their swords into plowshares, and their spears into [q]pruninghooks: nation shall not lift up sword against nation, [w]neither shall they learn war any more.

The day of the LORD

5 O house of Jacob, come ye, and let
Is. 35:8-9 us [x]walk in the light of the LORD.

6 ¶ Therefore thou hast forsaken thy people the house of Jacob, because they be replenished [y]from[r] the east, and [z]*are* soothsayers like the Philistines, [a]and they [s]please themselves in the children of strangers.

7 [b]Their land also is full of silver and gold, neither *is there any* end of their treasures; their land is also full of horses, neither *is there any* end of their chariots:

8 [c]Their land also is full of idols; they worship the work of their own hands, that which their own fingers have made:

9 And the mean man boweth down, and the great man humbleth himself: therefore forgive them not.

10 ¶ [d]Enter into the rock, and hide thee in the dust, for fear of the LORD, and for the glory of his majesty.

11 The [e]lofty looks of man shall be humbled, and the haughtiness of men shall be bowed down, and the LORD alone shall be exalted [f]in that day.

12 For the day of the LORD of hosts *shall be* upon every *one that is* proud and lofty, and upon every *one that is* lifted up; and he shall be brought low:

13 And upon all [g]the cedars of Lebanon, *that are* high and lifted up, and upon all the oaks of Bashan,

14 And [h]upon all the high mountains, and upon all the hills *that are* lifted up,

15 And upon every high tower, and upon every fenced wall,

16 [i]And upon all the ships of Tar-

2:2 [r]Ps. 68:15 [s]Ps. 72:8
2:3 [t]Jer. 50:5 Zech. 8:21 [u]Luke 24:47
2:4 [v]Ps. 46:9 [w]Ps. 72:3,7
2:5 [x]Eph. 5:8
2:6 [y]Num. 23:7 [z]Deut. 18:14 [a]Ps. 106:35 Jer. 10:2
2:7 [b]Deut. 17:16
2:8 [c]Jer. 2:28
2:10 [d]Rev. 6:15
2:11 [e]ch. 5:15 [f]Hos. 2:16 Zech. 9:16
2:13 [g]ch. 14:8 Ezek. 31:3 Zech. 11:1
2:14 [h]ch. 30:25
2:16 [i]1 Ki. 10:22

[p]Or, *prepared* [q]Or, *scythes* [r]Or, *more than the east* [s]Or, *abound with the children*

2:2–5 THE LORD'S HOUSE SHALL BE ESTABLISHED. Isaiah prophesies of a time when God's rule will be established over all the earth (cf. Mic. 4:1–3). All evil, injustice, and rebellion directed against God and His law will be put down, and righteousness will reign (cf. 59:20—60:3,14; Jer. 33:14–16; Zech. 2:10–12). "All nations," Jews and Gentiles, will worship and serve the Lord. This prophecy reflects God's final purpose for Israel and the human race; it is fulfilled in Jesus Christ Himself, who executes justice and righteousness upon the earth (9:1–7; 11:3–5).

2:3 TEACH US OF HIS WAYS ... HIS PATHS. The primary concern of all who come to the Lord should be to know and to obey God's will as citizens of His kingdom. It is important that we who proclaim God's message take supreme care that our preaching and teaching are the word of God—based upon the inspired Scriptures as the revelation of the O.T. prophets, Christ, and the N.T. apostles (see Eph. 2:20, note). All people, both the lost and the saved, need to hear God's truth proclaimed from the lips of those anointed by the Holy Spirit and committed to the righteousness of God's ways.

2:6–9 THOU HAST FORSAKEN THY PEOPLE. These verses describe the apostasy and worldliness of the nation of Judah. They had rejected God, accepted idols and the occult, taken pleasure in the ungodly ways of the heathen, and looked for their security in money, foreign alliances, and military might. Thus Isaiah prayed that they would not be forgiven until God had dealt with them so severely that they genuinely repented (vv. 17–21). He knew that the superficial forgiveness of religious ritual would only make matters worse. True repentance must precede forgiveness (1:16–20).

2:11 THE HAUGHTINESS OF MEN SHALL BE BOWED DOWN. One serious consequence of human pride is the belief that we can decide for ourselves, independent of God, how to live and what to consider as right and wrong. On the day of judgment, God will bring this attitude of haughtiness to the lowest shame and abasement.

2:12 THE DAY OF THE LORD. According to Isaiah, a time of judgment was coming. The immediate fulfillment of his prophecy was God's devastation of the land of Israel through the armies of the Assyrians and Babylonians as His agents of wrath (39:6). In the larger prophetic perspective, "the day of the LORD" refers to the time when God will cast down all evil on the earth (cf. Joel 2:31; see 1 Thes. 5:2, notes; see Rev. 4—19, notes; see article on THE GREAT TRIBULATION, p. 1456).

shish, and upon all [t]pleasant pictures.

17 [j]And the loftiness of man shall be bowed down, and the haughtiness of men shall be made low: and the LORD alone shall be exalted [k]in that day.

18 And [u]the idols he shall utterly abolish.

19 And they shall go into the [l]holes of the rocks, and into the caves of [v]the earth, [m]for fear of the LORD, and for the glory of his majesty, when he ariseth [n]to shake terribly the earth.

20 In that day a man shall cast [w]his idols of silver, and his idols of gold, [x]which they made *each one* for himself to worship, to the moles and to the bats;

21 [o]To go into the clefts of the rocks, and into the tops of the ragged rocks, [p]for fear of the LORD, and for the glory of his majesty, when he ariseth to shake terribly the earth.

22 [q]Cease ye from man, whose [r]breath *is* in his nostrils: for wherein is he to be accounted of?

The judgment of the LORD

3 FOR, BEHOLD, the Lord, the LORD of hosts, [s]doth take away from Jerusalem and from Judah [t]the stay and the staff, the whole stay of bread, and the whole stay of water,

2 [u]The mighty man, and the man of war, the judge, and the prophet, and the prudent, and the ancient,

3 The captain of fifty, and [y]the honourable man, and the counsellor, and the cunning artificer, and the [z]eloquent orator.

4 And I will give [v]children *to be* their princes, and babes shall rule over them.

5 And the people shall be oppressed, every one by another, and every one by his neighbour: the child shall behave himself proudly against the ancient, and the base against the honourable.

6 When a man shall take hold of his brother of the house of his father, *saying,* Thou hast clothing, be thou our ruler, and *let* this ruin *be* under thy hand:

7 In that day shall he swear, saying, I will not be an [a]healer; for in my house *is* neither bread nor clothing: make me not a ruler of the people.

8 For [w]Jerusalem is ruined, and Judah is fallen: because their tongue and their doings *are* against the LORD, to provoke the eyes of his glory.

9 ¶ The show of their countenance doth witness against them; and they declare their sin as [x]Sodom, they hide *it* not. Woe unto their soul! for they have rewarded evil unto themselves.

10 Say ye to the righteous, [y]that *it shall be* well *with him:* [z]for they shall eat the fruit of their doings. Is. 27:6

11 Woe unto the wicked! [a]*it shall be* ill *with him:* for the reward of his hands shall be [b]given him.

12 ¶ *As for* my people, [b]children *are* their oppressors, and women rule over them. O my people, [c]they[c] which lead thee cause *thee* to err, and [d]destroy the way of thy paths.

13 The LORD standeth up [d]to plead, and standeth to judge the people.

14 The LORD will enter into judgment with the ancients of his people, and the princes thereof: for ye have [e]eaten up [e]the vineyard; the spoil of the poor *is* in your houses.

15 What mean ye *that* ye [f]beat my

2:17 [j]ver. 11 [k]ver:11
2:19 [l]Hos. 10:8 Rev. 9:6 [m]2 Thes. 1:9 [n]Hag. 2:6,21
2:21 [o]ver. 19 [p]ver. 10,19
2:22 [q]Ps. 146:3 [r]Job 27:3
3:1 [s]Jer. 37:21 [t]Lev. 26:26
3:2 [u]2 Ki. 24:14
3:4 [v]Eccl. 10:16
3:8 [w]Mic. 3:12
3:9 [x]Gen. 13:13
3:10 [y]Eccl. 8:12 [z]Ps. 128:2
3:11 [a]Ps. 11:6
3:12 [b]ver. 4 [c]ch. 9:16
3:13 [d]Mic. 6:2
3:14 [e]Mat. 21:33
3:15 [f]Mic. 3:2,3

[t] Heb. *pictures of desire* [u] Or, *the idols shall utterly pass away* [v] Heb. *the dust* [w] Heb. *the idols of his silver* [x] Or, *which they made for him* [y] Heb. *a man eminent in countenance* [z] Or, *skilful of speech* [a] Heb. *binder up* [b] Heb. *done to him* [c] Or, *they which call thee blessed* [d] Heb. *swallow up* [e] Or, *burnt*

3:1 TAKE AWAY FROM JERUSALEM. As a result of the people's sins, God's judgment would touch every part of society and all classes of people would suffer (vv. 2–3).

3:5 OPPRESSED ... EVERY ONE BY HIS NEIGHBOUR. The rejection of God's ways in a society opens the way for injustice, cruel oppression, violence, disrespect for parents by rebellious youth, and the casting off of all moral restraint (see Mat. 24:12, note; 2 Tim. 3:1–5, notes). All people suffer as society disintegrates.

3:10 SAY YE TO THE RIGHTEOUS. Isaiah was told to encourage those who remained faithful to God in the midst of an unrighteous people. Although they might suffer for righteousness' sake now, it would ultimately go well for them and God would richly reward them. To the wicked, however, God guarantees punishment (see Mat. 5:10, note).

3:14 THE SPOIL OF THE POOR. God hates the mistreatment of the less fortunate in society. In the church too, He makes members accountable for the way they treat one another (see Col. 3:25, note). God demands that we show love, justice, and compassion in our relations with others.

people to pieces, and grind the faces of the poor? saith the Lord GOD of hosts.

16 ¶ Moreover the LORD saith, Because the daughters of Zion are haughty, and walk with stretched forth necks and [f]wanton eyes, walking and [g]mincing *as* they go, and making a tinkling with their feet:

17 Therefore the Lord will smite with [g]a scab the crown of the head of the daughters of Zion, and the LORD will [h]discover[h] their secret parts.

18 In that day the Lord will take away the bravery of *their* tinkling ornaments *about their feet,* and *their* [i]cauls, and *their* [i]round tires like the moon,

19 The [j]chains, and the bracelets, and the [k]mufflers,

20 The bonnets, and the ornaments of the legs, and the headbands, and the [l]tablets, and the earrings,

21 The rings, and nose jewels,

22 The changeable suits of apparel, and the mantles, and the wimples, and the crisping pins,

23 The glasses, and the fine linen, and the hoods, and the veils.

24 And it shall come to pass, *that* instead of sweet smell there shall be stink; and instead of a girdle a rent; and instead of well set hair [j]baldness; and instead of a stomacher a girding of sackcloth; *and* burning instead of beauty.

25 Thy men shall fall by the sword, and thy [m]mighty in the war.

26 [k]And her gates shall lament and mourn; and she *being* [n] [o]desolate [l]shall sit upon the ground.

4 AND [m]IN that day seven women shall take hold of one man, saying, We will [n]eat our own bread, and wear our own apparel: only [p]let us be called by thy name, [q]to take away [o]our reproach.

Blessings under the Messiah

2 In that day shall [p]the branch of the LORD be [r]beautiful and glorious, and the fruit of the earth *shall be* excellent and comely [s]for them that are escaped of Israel.

3 And it shall come to pass, *that he that is* left in Zion, and *he that* remaineth in Jerusalem, [q]shall be called holy, *even* every one that is [r]written [t]among the living in Jerusalem:

4 When [s]the Lord shall have washed away the filth of the daughters of Zion, and shall have purged the blood of Jerusalem from the midst thereof by the spirit of judgment, and by the spirit of burning.

5 And the LORD will create upon every dwellingplace of mount Zion, and upon her assemblies, [t]a cloud and smoke by day, and [u]the shining of a flaming fire by night: for [u]upon all the glory *shall be* [v]a defence.

6 And there shall be a tabernacle for a shadow in the daytime from the heat, and [v]for a place of refuge, and for a covert from storm and from rain.

The parable of the vineyard

5 NOW WILL I sing to my wellbeloved a song of my beloved

3:17 [g]Deut. 28:27 [h]Jer. 13:22
3:18 [i]Judg. 8:21
3:24 [j]ch. 22:12
3:26 [k]Jer. 14:2 [l]Lam. 2:10
4:1 [m]ch. 2:11,17 [n]2 Thes. 3:12
[o]Luke 1:25
4:2 [p]Jer. 23:5
4:3 [q]ch. 60:21 [r]Phil. 4:3
4:4 [s]Mal. 3:2,3
4:5 [t]Ex. 13:21 [u]Zech. 2:5
4:6 [v]ch. 25:4

[f]Heb. *deceiving with their eyes* [g]Or, *tripping nicely* [h]Heb. *make naked* [i]Or, *networks* [j]Or, *sweet balls* [k]Or, *spangled ornaments* [l]Heb. *houses of the soul* [m]Heb. *might* [n]Or, *emptied* [o]Heb. *cleansed* [p]Heb. *let thy name be called upon us* [q]Or, *take thou away* [r]Heb. *beauty and glory* [s]Heb. *for the escaping of Israel* [t]Or, *to life* [u]Or, *above* [v]Heb. *a covering*

3:16–26 THE DAUGHTERS OF ZION. In the midst of spiritual, moral, and political decline, the women of Judah were characterized by their devotion to all kinds of things related to fashionable and external appearance rather than to inward holiness and love for God. They were self-centered women, searching for sexual attractiveness and thinking only of their wants, but showing no concern for the oppressed, the poor, or the tragic spiritual condition of their families and people. God threatened to bring them to shame and disgrace by making them miserable slaves of their conquerors (vv. 17,24). God still demands humility, modesty, and holiness in believing women (see 1 Cor. 11:6, note; 1 Tim. 2:9, note; cf. 1 Pet. 3:3–4).

4:2 THE BRANCH OF THE LORD. This is a title for the Messiah (i.e., the Christ). He will come forth as a branch from the root of David (see 11:1; 53:2; Jer. 23:5; 33:15; Zech. 3:8; 6:12; Rom. 15:12; Rev. 5:5; 22:16). Vv. 2–6 refer to a time of both judgment and salvation, a time when Christ will rule over His faithful remnant in Jerusalem (v. 4) and care for them with great concern and love (cf. 38:5–8,15–17; 65:18).

4:3 SHALL BE CALLED HOLY. Those who survive the coming judgment will be "holy," i.e., they will have the character of God, who is "the Holy One of Israel" (1:4). In other words, they will be separated from the sinful world, cleansed from all defilement by the blood of Christ, and regenerated by the Holy Spirit. Over them will hover the glory of God like a canopy (v. 5).

5:1–7 A VINEYARD. This parable of the vineyard demonstrates that God did everything possible to make Judah a righteous and fruitful nation. Only when they failed to become what He wanted

touching [w]his vineyard. My well-beloved hath a vineyard in [w]a very fruitful hill:

2 And he [x]fenced it, and gathered out the stones thereof, and planted it with the choicest vine, and built a tower in the midst of it, and also [y]made a winepress therein: [x]and he looked that it should bring forth grapes, and it brought forth wild grapes.

3 And now, O inhabitants of Jerusalem, and men of Judah, [y]judge, I pray you, betwixt me and my vineyard.

4 What could have been done more to my vineyard, that I have not done in it? wherefore, when I looked that it should bring forth grapes, brought it forth wild grapes?

5 And now go to; I will tell you what I will do to my vineyard: [z]I will take away the hedge thereof, and it shall be eaten up; *and* break down the wall thereof, and it shall be [z]trodden down:

6 And I will lay it waste: it shall not be pruned, nor digged; but there shall come up briers and thorns: I will also command the clouds that they rain no rain upon it.

7 For the vineyard of the LORD of hosts *is* the house of Israel, and the men of Judah [a]his pleasant plant: and he looked for judgment, but behold [b]oppression; for righteousness, but behold a cry.

God's judgment against Judah

8 ¶ Woe unto them that join [a]house to house, *that* lay field to field, till *there be* no place, that [c]they may be placed alone in the midst of the earth!

9 [b]In[d] mine ears *said* the LORD of hosts, [e]Of a truth many houses shall be desolate, *even* great and fair, without inhabitant.

10 Yea, ten acres of vineyard shall yield one [c]bath, and the seed of an homer shall yield an ephah.

11 ¶ [d]Woe unto them that rise up early in the morning, *that* they may follow strong drink; that continue until night, *till* wine [f]inflame them!

12 And [e]the harp, and the viol, the tabret, and pipe, and wine, are in their feasts: but [f]they regard not the work of the LORD, neither consider the operation of his hands.

13 ¶ [g]Therefore my people are gone into captivity, because *they have* no knowledge: and [g]their honourable men *are* famished, and their multitude dried up with thirst.

14 Therefore hell hath enlarged herself, and opened her mouth without measure: and their glory, and their multitude, and their pomp, and he that rejoiceth, shall descend into it.

15 And [h]the mean man shall be brought down, and the mighty man shall be humbled, and the eyes of the lofty shall be humbled:

16 But the LORD of hosts shall be exalted in judgment, and [h] [i]God that is holy shall be sanctified in righteousness.

17 Then shall the lambs feed after their manner, and the waste places of [i]the fat ones shall strangers eat.

18 Woe unto them that draw iniquity with cords of vanity, and sin as it were with a cart rope:

19 [j]That say, Let him make speed, *and* hasten his work, that we may see *it:* and let the counsel of the Holy One of Israel draw nigh and come, that we may know *it!*

20 ¶ Woe unto them that [j]call evil good, and good evil; that put darkness

5:1 [w]Ps. 80:8; Jer. 2:21; Mat. 21:33; Mark 12:1
5:2 [x]Deut. 32:6
5:3 [y]Rom. 3:4
5:5 [z]Ps. 80:12
5:8 [a]Mic. 2:2
5:9 [b]ch. 22:14
5:10 [c]Ezek. 45:11
5:11 [d]Prov. 23:29
5:12 [e]Amos 6:5; [f]Job 34:27; Ps. 28:5
5:13 [g]Hos. 4:6
5:15 [h]ch. 2:9,11
5:17 [i]ch. 10:16
5:19 [j]Jer. 17:15; Amos 5:18

[w] Heb. *the horn of the son of oil* [x] Or, *made a wall about it* [y] Heb. *hewed* [z] Heb. *for a treading* [a] Heb. *plant of his pleasures* [b] Heb. *a scab* [c] Heb. *ye* [d] Or, *This is in mine ears,* saith *the LORD* [e] Heb. *If not* [f] Or, *pursue them* [g] Heb. *their glory* are *men of famine* [h] Or, *the holy God* [i] Heb. *the God the holy* [j] Heb. *that say concerning evil,* It is *good*

them to become did God destroy His vineyard (compare Jesus' parable of the tenants in Mat. 21:33–44). Isaiah's parable points historically to the destruction of Jerusalem and the kingdom of Judah in 586 B.C.

5:8–32 WOE UNTO THEM. Six woes (i.e., statements of judgment) are pronounced upon six types of sins: (1) selfish greed (v. 8), (2) drunken conduct (vv. 11–12), (3) mockery at God's power to judge their sin (vv. 18–19), (4) distortion of God's moral standards (v. 20), (5) arrogance and pride (v. 21), and (6) perversion of justice (vv. 22–23; cf. Christ's woes upon religious hypocrites; see Mat. 23, notes).

5:20 CALL EVIL GOOD. On the one hand, society often exalts sin by calling depravity manly strength, or calling immorality and perversion true virtue and commendable freedom. On the other hand, society opposes righteousness by calling it evil. Note these two common examples where this pattern occurs: (1) Sexual perversion (e.g., homosexuality and lesbianism) is called a legitimate alternative lifestyle that should be openly accepted, while opponents of such conduct who accept the

for light, and light for darkness; that
put bitter for sweet, and sweet for bit-
ter!
21 Woe unto *them that are* [k]wise in
their own eyes, and prudent [k]in their
own sight!
22 Woe unto *them that are* mighty to
drink wine, and men of strength to
mingle strong drink:
23 Which [l]justify the wicked for
reward, and take away the righteous-
ness of the righteous from him!
24 Therefore [m]as [l]the fire devour-
eth the stubble, and the flame con-
sumeth the chaff, *so* [n]their root shall
be as rottenness, and their blossom
shall go up as dust: because they have
cast away the law of the LORD of hosts,
and despised the word of the Holy One
of Israel.
25 [o]Therefore is the anger of the
LORD kindled against his people, and he
hath stretched forth his hand against
them, and hath smitten them: and
[p]the hills did tremble, and their car-
cases *were* [m]torn in the midst of the
streets. [q]For all this his anger is not
turned away, but his hand *is* stretched
out still.
26 ¶ [r]And he will lift up an ensign
to the nations from far, and will [s]hiss
unto them from [t]the end of the earth:
and, behold, [u]they shall come with
speed swiftly:
27 None shall be weary nor stumble

5:21 [k]Rom. 1:22
5:23 [l]Prov. 17:15
5:24 [m]Ex. 15:7 [n]Job 18:16
5:25 [o]2 Ki. 22:13 [p]Jer. 4:24 [q]ch. 9:12,17
5:26 [r]ch. 11:12 [s]ch. 7:18 [t]Mal. 1:11 [u]Joel 2:7
5:27 [v]Dan. 5:6
5:28 [w]Jer. 5:16
5:30 [x]ch. 8:22
6:1 [y]John 12:41
6:2 [z]Ezek. 1:11

among them; none shall slumber nor
sleep; neither [v]shall the girdle of their
loins be loosed, nor the latchet of their
shoes be broken:
28 [w]Whose arrows *are* sharp, and
all their bows bent, their horses' hoofs
shall be counted like flint, and their
wheels like a whirlwind:
29 Their roaring *shall be* like a lion,
they shall roar like young lions: yea,
they shall roar, and lay hold of the
prey, and shall carry *it* away safe, and
none shall deliver *it*.
30 And in that day they shall roar
against them like the roaring of the
sea: and if *one* [x]look unto the land,
behold darkness *and* [n]sorrow, [o]and
the light is darkened in the heavens
thereof.

Isaiah commissioned

6 IN THE year that king Uzziah died
I [y]saw also the Lord sitting upon
a throne, high and lifted up, and [p]his
train filled the temple.
2 Above it stood the seraphims:
each one had six wings; with twain he
covered his face, and [z]with twain he
covered his feet, and with twain he did
fly.

[k]Heb. *before their face* [l]Heb. *the tongue of fire* [m]Or, *as dung* [n]Or, *distress* [o]Or, *when it is light, it shall be dark in the destructions thereof* [p]Or, *the skirts thereof*

Biblical standards of sexual morality are called bigots who perpetuate oppressive prejudice (see article on STANDARDS OF SEXUAL MORALITY, p. 1964). (2) Pro-abortion advocates are called "sensitive" persons with a deep commitment to the rights of women, while active pro-life supporters are called "extremists" or "religious fanatics." Believers, however, must commit themselves wholeheartedly and irreversibly to God's standards of good and evil as revealed in His written Word.

5:24 FOR THEY HAVE CAST AWAY THE LAW OF THE LORD. Isaiah teaches the doctrine of just retribution for sin. Rejecting God's laws and despising His word will result in people being given over to the consequences of their sins and to divine punishment (v. 25; cf. Hos. 4:6).

5:26 THE NATIONS FROM FAR. Isaiah describes Judah's coming destruction by a distant nation. It was imminent and certain, and Judah would have no power to turn back the enemy. Isaiah undoubtedly foresaw the invasions of the Assyrians, whose armies plundered Judah in 701 B.C., and the Babylonians, who began aggression in 605 B.C. God has often used other nations to punish the apostasy of His people (see also Mat. 5:13, note).

6:1 THE YEAR THAT KING UZZIAH DIED. The year was approximately 740 B.C. (cf. 2 Chr. 26:16–21). Though Isaiah may have prophesied earlier (chs. 1–5), he now received a vision of God, was cleansed, and was given a specific commission to proclaim God's word to a spiritually blind, deaf, and insensitive people (vv. 9–10).

6:1 I SAW ALSO THE LORD. This vision gave Isaiah a proper understanding of his message and call. It revealed one of this book's major concerns, namely, that God's glory, majesty, and holiness demand that those who serve Him also must be holy. Churches today likewise need a vision of God in their midst as the holy Lord and Judge of all. The recognition of the need for His sanctifying work in our lives will inevitably accompany such a vision. The result could well be similar to that of Isaiah—earnest confession, glorious cleansing, and powerful commissioning by God in regard to His will and call (vv. 5–8; cf. Rev. 1:13–17).

6:2 SERAPHIMS. These are angelic beings of high order; "seraphims" may be another designation for the living creatures revealed elsewhere in Scripture (e.g., Rev. 4:6–9). Their title (literally, "burning ones") may signify their purity as those who serve God around His throne. They so reflected the glory of God that they seemed to be on fire.

3 And [q]one cried unto another, and
said, [a]Holy, holy, holy, *is* the LORD of
hosts: [b]the[r] whole earth *is* full of his
glory.
4 And the posts of the [s]door moved
at the voice of him that cried, and the
house was filled with smoke.
5 ¶ Then said I, Woe *is* me! for I am
[t]undone; because I *am* a man of un-
clean lips, and I dwell in the midst of
a people of unclean lips: for mine eyes
have seen the King, the LORD of hosts.
6 Then flew one of the seraphims
unto me, [u]having a live coal in his
hand, *which* he had taken with the
tongs from off [c]the altar:
7 And he [d]laid[v] *it* upon my mouth,
and said, Lo, this hath touched thy
lips; and thine iniquity is taken away,
and thy sin purged.
8 Also I heard the voice of the Lord,
saying, Whom shall I send, and who
will go for [e]us? Then said I, [w]Here *am*
Is. 42:6-7 I; send me.
9 ¶ And he said, Go, and tell this
people, Hear ye [x] [y]indeed, but un-
derstand not; and see ye [z]indeed, but
perceive not.
10 Make [f]the heart of this people
fat, and make their ears heavy, and
shut their eyes; [g]lest they see with
their eyes, and hear with their ears,
and understand with their heart, and
convert, and be healed.
11 Then said I, Lord, how long? And
he answered, [h]Until the cities be
wasted without inhabitant, and the
houses without man, and the land be
[a]utterly desolate,
12 [i]And the LORD have removed
men far away, and *there be* a great for-
saking in the midst of the land.
13 ¶ But yet in it *shall be* a tenth,
[b]and *it* shall return, and shall be eat-
en: as a teil tree, and as an oak, whose
[c]substance *is* in them, when they cast
their leaves: so [j]the holy seed *shall be*
the substance thereof.

The sign of Immanuel

7 AND IT came to pass in the days
of Ahaz the son of Jotham, the son

6:3 [a]Rev. 4:8 [b]Ps. 72:19
6:6 [c]Rev. 8:3
6:7 [d]Jer. 1:9
6:8 [e]Gen. 1:26
6:10 [f]Ps. 119:70 [g]Jer. 5:21
6:11 [h]Mic. 3:12
6:12 [i]2 Ki. 25:21
6:13 [j]Ezra 9:2

[q] Heb. *this cried to this* [r] Heb. *his glory is the fulness of the whole earth* [s] Heb. *thresholds* [t] Heb. *cut off* [u] Heb. *and in his hand a live coal* [v] Heb. *caused it to touch* [w] Heb. *Behold me* [x] Or, *without ceasing* [y] Heb. *hear ye in hearing* [z] Heb. *in seeing* [a] Heb. *desolate with desolation* [b] Or, *when it is returned, and hath been broused* [c] Or, *stock,* or, *stem*

6:3 HOLY, HOLY, HOLY, *IS* THE LORD. The foremost characteristic of God revealed to Isaiah is His holiness, signifying His purity of character, separation from sin, and opposition to all that is evil (see article on THE ATTRIBUTES OF GOD, p. 912). God's absolute holiness must be proclaimed in the churches as it is proclaimed in the heavens.

6:5 WOE *IS* ME! In full view of God's holiness, Isaiah instantly realized his own imperfection and uncleanness, especially with respect to his speech (cf. Jas. 3:1–6). He also recognized the consequences of seeing God face to face (cf. Ex. 33:20) and was frightened. God then cleansed his mouth and heart (cf. Lev. 16:12; Jer. 1:9) and made him fit to remain in His presence as a servant and prophet of the Holy One of Israel. All who approach God must have their sins forgiven and their hearts cleansed by the Holy Spirit (cf. Heb. 10:19–22), for only God can furnish the purity that He demands (see article on REGENERATION, p. 1597).

6:8 WHOM SHALL I SEND. Only after receiving his cleansing was Isaiah commissioned as a prophet (see article on THE PROPHET IN THE OLD TESTAMENT, p. 1002). This passage reminds us of the Great Commission of our risen Lord to proclaim the gospel of salvation to all the world (Mat. 28:18–20). If that command to go out grips our hearts, we must respond in the same way as Isaiah did, "Here *am* I; send me."

6:9 GO, AND TELL THIS PEOPLE. God told Isaiah that the people would reject his message and remain indifferent to the prophetic call for repentance. His preaching would in fact turn hearts even more against the Lord (vv. 9–10; cf. Mat. 13:14–15; Mark 4:12; Luke 8:10). Nevertheless, Isaiah had to preach faithfully the unpopular message of judgment (cf. Jer. 1:8,19; Ezek. 2:3–4). There would be a limit, however, to his heartrending ministry. The judgments brought through Sennacherib in 701 B.C. (vv. 11–12) would bring Jerusalem to faith and obedience (36:21; 37:7); as a result, Isaiah would be able to have a new ministry, during the additional fifteen added years granted to Hezekiah (38:5).

6:13 THE HOLY SEED. God encouraged Isaiah by telling him that a small remnant of people would believe and be preserved. A new Judah that would be called holy would come forth, through whom God would work His plan of salvation for the world. Likewise, under the new covenant God will judge an apostate church and raise up a holy remnant that will remain faithful to Him and His Word (see article on CHRIST'S MESSAGE TO THE SEVEN CHURCHES, p. 2036).

7:1–25 IN THE DAYS OF AHAZ. About 735/734 B.C., the kings of Israel and Syria attacked Judah. King Ahaz of Judah was told by Isaiah to trust God for deliverance. Yet Ahaz refused to accept God's offer of a miraculous sign, and he sought help from Assyria instead (see 2 Ki. 16:5–18; 2 Chr. 28:16–21). God gave a sign anyway to the whole house of David—the birth of Immanuel (vv. 13–17). Though the Syrian and

THE PROPHET IN THE OLD TESTAMENT

Is. 6:8–9 "Also I heard the voice of the Lord, saying, Whom shall I send, and who will go for us? Then said I, Here am I; send me. And he said, Go, and tell this people, Hear ye indeed, but understand not; and see ye indeed, but perceive not."

THE PLACE OF THE PROPHETS IN HEBREW HISTORY. (1) The O.T. prophets were men and women of God who towered spiritually over their contemporaries. No category of people in all literature presents a more dramatic picture than do the O.T. prophets. Priests, judges, kings, wise counselors, and psalmists each had a distinctive place in Israel's history, but none of these ever rose to the stature of the prophets or continued to exert as much influence on the subsequent history of redemption.

(2) The prophets exerted a major influence in the composition of the O.T. itself. This is evident in the threefold division of the Hebrew Bible: The Torah, The Prophets, and The Writings (cf. Luke 24:44). The category known as The Prophets included six historical books written from the prophetic perspective: Joshua, Judges, 1 and 2 Samuel, and 1 and 2 Kings. It is likely that the authors of these books were prophets. Secondly, there were the sixteen specific prophetic books (Isaiah to Malachi). Finally, Moses, the author of the first five books of the Bible (the Torah), was a prophet (Deut. 18:15). Thus a full two-thirds of the O.T. was written by prophets.

HEBREW WORDS FOR THE PROPHETS. (1) *Ro'eh*. This Hebrew noun, translated "seer" in English, indicates a special ability to see into the spiritual realm and foresee future events. The title suggests that the prophet was not deceived by the external appearance of things; rather, he saw issues as they really were from the perspective of God Himself. As a seer, the prophet received dreams, visions, and revelations from God which enabled him to convey spiritual realities to God's people.

(2) *Nabi'*. (a) This is the main Hebrew word for "prophet," occurring 309 times in the O.T. (*nabi'im* is its plural form). Although the origin of this word is unclear, the meaning of the Hebrew verb "to prophesy" meant: "to put forth words abundantly from God's mind and by God's Spirit" (Gesenius, *Hebrew Lexicon*). Thus a *nabi'* was a spokesperson who poured forth words under the impelling power of God's Spirit. The Greek term *prophētēs*, from which our English word "prophet" is derived, means "one who speaks on behalf of another." The prophets spoke for God to the covenant people, based on what they heard, saw, and received from Him. (b) In the O.T., the prophet was also designated by such terms as "man of God" (see 2 Ki. 4:21, note), "servant of the LORD" (cf. Is. 20:3; Dan. 6:20), "man of the Spirit" (cf. Is. 61:1–3), "watchman" (Ezek. 3:17), and "the LORD's messenger" (Hag. 1:13). The prophet also interpreted prophetic dreams (e.g., Joseph, Daniel) and provided an understanding of history—both the present and the future—from a prophetic perspective.

MEN OF THE SPIRIT AND THE WORD. The prophet was not simply another religious leader in Hebrew history, but one into whom God's Spirit and God's word had entered and taken possession (Ezek. 37:1,4). Because the Spirit and the word were in him, the O.T. prophet manifested the following three characteristics: (1) *Divinely revealed knowledge*. The prophet experienced God-given knowledge with respect to people, events, and redemptive truth. The primary purpose of this knowledge was to encourage God's people to remain faithful to Him and His covenant. The distinguishing feature of O.T. prophecy was that it made clear the will of God for His people by way of instruction, correction, and warning. God used the prophets to pronounce His judgment before it occurred. Out of the soil of Israel's and Judah's dark history came specific prophecy about the Messiah and the kingdom of God, as well as prediction about future world events.

(2) *Divinely given powers*. The prophets were drawn into the sphere of the miraculous as they were filled with God's Spirit. Through the prophets the life and power of God were manifested in supernatural ways in a world otherwise sealed against it.

(3) *A distinctive lifestyle*. The prophets by and large abandoned the ordinary pursuits of life to live exclusively for God. They protested intensely against idolatry, immorality, and all manner of evil among God's people, as well as against corruption in the lives of kings and priests. They were activists for holy and righteous changes in Israel. The prophets, always on the offense for God's kingdom and His righteousness, championed the will of God without thought of personal risk.

EIGHT CHARACTERISTICS OF THE OLD TESTAMENT PROPHET. What sort of a person was the O.T. prophet? (1) He was a person who had a close relationship with God and who became God's confidant (Amos 3:7). The prophet saw the world and the covenant people from God's perspective, not from a human point of view.

(2) Since he was close to God, the prophet was in sympathy with God and with what God was suffering because of the sins of His people. Since he understood God's purpose, will, and desires better than anyone else, he experienced the same emotional reactions as God did. In other words, the prophet not only heard God's voice but also felt His heart (Jer 6:11; 15:16–17; 20:9).

(3) Also like God, the prophet deeply loved God's people. When the people were hurting, the prophet felt deep pain (see the book of Lamentations). He wanted God's best for them (Ezek. 18:23), and thus his messages included not only warnings but also words of hope and comfort.

(4) The prophet sought the highest good for the people, i.e., complete trust in and loyalty to God. Therefore, he warned against trusting in other things, such as human wisdom, wealth, power, or other gods (Jer. 8:9–10; Hos. 10:13–14; Amos 6:8). The prophets continually exhorted the people to live by God's covenant obligations in order to receive God's redemptive blessings.

(5) The prophet had a deep sensitivity to sin and evil (Jer. 2:12–13,19; 25:3–7; Amos 8:4–7; Mic 3:8). He was impatient with cruelty, crime, immorality, and injustice. What might appear as a slight deviation from God's law to the common people was seen as a disaster by the prophet. He had little tolerance for all their compromises, complacency, pretenses, and excuses (Is. 32:11; Jer. 6:20; 7:8–15,21–23; Amos 4:1; 6:1). He shared better than anyone God's love of righteousness and hatred of iniquity (cf. Heb. 1:9, note).

(6) The prophet constantly challenged the shallow and superficial holiness of God's people and tried desperately to encourage heartfelt obedience to every word that God had revealed in His law. He was totally dedicated to God; he hated halfhearted commitment, shunned the middle road, and demanded complete faithfulness to God. He accepted nothing less than the fullness of God's kingdom and His righteousness manifested among God's people.

(7) The prophet had a vision for the future—expressed in predictions of doom and destruction (e.g., Is. 63:1–6; Jer. 11:22–23; 13:15–21; Ezek. 14:12–21; Amos 5:16–20,27), as well as in visions of restoration and renewal (e.g., Is. 61—62; 65:17—66:24; Jer. 33; Ezek. 37). The prophets spoke numerous prophecies regarding the coming of the Messiah (see chart on OLD TESTAMENT PROPHECIES FULFILLED IN CHRIST, p. 920).

(8) Finally, the prophet was often a man of loneliness and sorrow (Jer. 14:17–18; 20:14–18; Amos 7:10–13; Jonah 3—4), frequently persecuted by the false prophets who were predicting peace, prosperity, and security for God's sinful people (Jer. 15:15; 20:1–6; 26:8–11; Amos 5:10; cf. Mat. 23:29–36; Acts 7:51–53). At the same time, however, the true prophet was such a man of God that the people and their leaders could not ignore his character or his message (Ezek. 3:8–11).

THE PROPHET AND THE PRIEST. During most of Israel's history, the priests and prophets invariably collided. God had intended them to work together, but the priests tended to compromise by not standing against the corruption of God's people. (1) The priests were usually tied to the status quo, finding it difficult to worship God except

through ceremonies and liturgy. Though morality had a place in their theology, it was not emphasized in their practice.

(2) The prophet, on the other hand, placed emphasis on lifestyle, conduct, and moral issues. He constantly confronted persons who depended on mere performance of religious duties. He irritated, prodded, denounced, stood alone in his righteous demands, and insisted on applying God's eternal principles to life. The prophet was an ethical teacher, a moral reformer, and a disturber of the human mind. He constantly exposed sin and apostasy, seeking to stir the people to holy living.

THE MESSAGE OF THE O.T. PROPHETS. The prophets' message emphasized three major themes: (1) *The nature of God*. (a) They revealed and declared God to be the Creator and Almighty Ruler of the universe (e.g., Is. 40:28), and the sovereign Lord of history who makes the events of history serve His ultimate purposes of salvation and judgment (cf. Is. 44:28; 45:1; Amos 5:27; Hab. 1:6). (b) They emphasized that God is a holy, righteous, and just God, who is repelled by sin, unrighteousness, and injustice. Since His holiness is tempered by mercy, He is longsuffering and slow to act in wrath and judgment. Because He is holy by nature, He requires His people to be consecrated as HOLINESS TO THE LORD (Zech. 14:20; cf. Is. 29:22–24; Jer. 2:3). As the covenant-making God who entered into a unique relationship with Israel, He requires His people to obey His commandments as part of that relational contract.

(2) *Sin and repentance*. The O.T. prophets shared God's grief at the continual disobedience, unfaithfulness, idolatry, and immorality of His covenant people; they spoke stern words of righteous judgment against them. Their message was the same as the message of John the Baptist and Jesus—"repent or perish." They predicted such major catastrophic judgments as the destruction of Samaria by Assyria (e.g., Hos. 5:8–12; 9:3–7; 10:6–15) and the destruction of Jerusalem by Babylon (e.g., Jer. 19:7–15; 32:28–36; Ezek. 5:5–12; 21:2,24–27).

(3) *Prediction and Messianic hope*. (a) Although the covenant people as a whole were unfaithful to God and their covenant vows, the prophets never ceased to have a message of hope. They knew that God would fulfill the Abrahamic covenant and promises (see article on GOD'S COVENANT WITH ABRAHAM, ISAAC, AND JACOB, p. 48) through a faithful and God-fearing remnant. Eventually the Messiah would come, and through Him God would offer salvation to all the peoples of the earth. (b) The prophets stood between the spiritual collapse of their own generation and the emerging hope of a Messianic age. The prophetic dilemma was that they had to speak the word of God to an obstinate people, even though they knew it would be rejected and unheeded until the new order emerged (cf. Is. 6:9–13). The prophets were both champions of the old covenant and forerunners of the new covenant. They lived in the present but pointed to the future.

THE FALSE PROPHETS. There are numerous references to false prophets in the O.T. For example, four hundred false prophets were summoned together by King Ahab (2 Chr. 18:4–7); the Bible records that a deceiving spirit was in their mouths (2 Chr. 18:18–22). According to the O.T., a prophet was considered false (1) if he turned people away from the true God toward some form of idolatry (Deut. 13:1–5); (2) if he practiced divination, astrology, sorcery, witchcraft, and the like (see Deut. 18:10–11, notes); (3) if his prophecies departed from or conflicted with the clear message of God in Scripture (Deut. 13:1–5); (4) if he did not expose the sins of God's people (Jer. 23:9–18); or (5) if he predicted specific things that did not come to pass (Deut. 18:20–22). Concerning this last criterion, note that prophets under the new covenant did not speak with the same finality or infallibility as did the O.T. prophets, who were God's primary voice of revelation to Israel. In the N.T., the prophet is only one of five major ministry gifts in the church (see article on THE MINISTRY GIFTS OF THE CHURCH, p. 1852). The N.T. prophets had limitations that the O.T. prophets did not (cf. 1 Cor. 14:29–33) because of the multifaceted and interdependent nature of ministry in N.T. times (see article on SPIRITUAL GIFTS FOR BELIEVERS, p. 1790).

of Uzziah, king of Judah, *that* Rezin the king of Syria, and Pekah the son of Remaliah, king of Israel, went up toward Jerusalem to war against it, but could not prevail against it.

2 And it was told the house of David, saying, Syria [d]is confederate with Ephraim. And his heart was moved, and the heart of his people, as the trees of the wood are moved with the wind.

3 Then said the LORD unto Isaiah, Go forth now to meet Ahaz, thou, and [e]Shear-jashub thy son, at the end of the conduit of the upper pool in the [f]highway of the fuller's field;

4 And say unto him, Take heed, and be quiet; fear not, [g]neither be fainthearted for the two tails of these smoking firebrands, for the fierce anger of Rezin with Syria, and of the son of Remaliah.

5 Because Syria, Ephraim, and the son of Remaliah, have taken evil counsel against thee, saying,

6 Let us go up against Judah, and [h]vex it, and let us make a breach therein for us, and set a king in the midst of it, *even* the son of Tabeal:

7 Thus saith the Lord GOD, [k]It shall not stand, neither shall it come to pass.

8 [l]For the head of Syria *is* Damascus, and the head of Damascus *is* Rezin; and within threescore and five years shall Ephraim be broken, [i]that it be not a people.

9 And the head of Ephraim *is* Samaria, and the head of Samaria *is* Remaliah's son. [m]If[j] ye will not believe, surely ye shall not be established.

10 ¶ [k]Moreover the LORD spake again unto Ahaz, saying,

11 [n]Ask thee a sign of the LORD thy God; [l]ask it either in the depth, or in the height above.

12 But Ahaz said, I will not ask, neither will I tempt the LORD.

13 And he said, Hear ye now, O house of David; *Is it* a small thing for you to weary men, but will ye weary my God also?

14 Therefore the Lord himself shall give you a sign; [o]Behold, a virgin shall conceive, and bear [p]a son, and shall call his name [q]Immanuel.

15 Butter and honey shall he eat, that he may know to refuse the evil, and choose the good.

16 [r]For before the child shall know to refuse the evil, and choose the good, the land that thou abhorrest shall be forsaken of [s]both her kings.

17 ¶ [t]The LORD shall bring upon thee, and upon thy people, and upon thy father's house, days that have not come, from the day that [u]Ephraim departed from Judah; *even* the king of Assyria.

18 And it shall come to pass in that day, *that* the LORD [v]shall hiss for the fly that *is* in the uttermost part of the rivers of Egypt, and for the bee that *is* in the land of Assyria.

19 And they shall come, and shall rest all of them in the desolate valleys, and in [w]the holes of the rocks, and

7:7 [k]ch. 8:10
7:8 [l]2 Sam. 8:6
7:9 [m]2 Chr. 20:20
7:11 [n]Mat. 12:38
7:14 [o]Mat. 1:23 [p]ch. 9:6 [q]ch. 8:8
7:16 [r]See ch. 8:4 [s]2 Ki. 15:30
7:17 [t]2 Chr. 28:19 [u]1 Ki. 12:16
7:18 [v]ch. 5:26
7:19 [w]Jer. 16:16

[d]Heb. *resteth on Ephraim* [e]i.e. *The remnant shall return* [f]Or, *causeway* [g]Heb. *let not thy heart be tender* [h]Or, *waken* [i]Heb. *from a people* [j]Or, *Do ye not believe?* it is *because ye are not stable* [k]Heb. *And the LORD added to speak* [l]Or, *make* thy *petition deep*

Israelite invasion would fail, God would later send the Assyrians and Babylonians to devastate the land.

7:3 SHEAR-JASHUB. The name of Isaiah's oldest son means "a remnant will return." This name highlighted God's intention to preserve a faithful remnant of the people to carry out His plan of salvation (cf. 11:11–12,16; 37:4,31).

7:8 WITHIN THREESCORE AND FIVE YEARS. Israel (also called Ephraim) was defeated in 722 B.C. by Assyria, who brought foreigners to the land to intermarry with the few remaining Israelites; the resulting racial mixture came to be called Samaritans (see 2 Ki. 17:24–34; cf. John 4:7–42).

7:12 AHAZ SAID, I WILL NOT ASK. Ahaz rejected the counsel of the prophet Isaiah to trust in God for deliverance. Instead, he trusted his own limited understanding and sought the help of Assyria (see 2 Ki. 16:5–18; 2 Chr. 28:16–21).

7:14 A VIRGIN SHALL CONCEIVE . . . IMMANUEL. "Virgin" (Heb. *almah*) can mean either "virgin" or "a young woman before marriage." (1) The immediate application of this sign was to a new bride, who would have been a virgin until the time of her marriage. Before her son was old enough to know right from wrong, the kings of Syria and Israel would be destroyed (v. 16). (2) The ultimate fulfillment of this prophecy was realized in the birth of Jesus Christ by the virgin Mary (Mat. 1:23). Mary was a virgin and remained a virgin until after the birth of Jesus (Mat. 1:18,25). The conception of her son came about by a miracle of the Holy Spirit rather than through the act of a man (see Mat. 1:16,23, notes; Luke 1:35, note). (3) The virgin's son was to be called "Immanuel," i.e., "God with us" (Mat. 1:23). That name acquired a new depth of meaning in the personal coming into the world of God's only begotten Son (cf. John 3:16).

upon all thorns, and upon all [m]bushes.
20 In the same day shall the Lord
shave with a [x]razor that is hired,
namely, by them beyond the river, by
the king of Assyria, the head, and the
hair of the feet: and it shall also con-
sume the beard.
21 And it shall come to pass in that
day, *that* a man shall nourish a young
cow, and two sheep;
22 And it shall come to pass, for the
abundance of milk *that* they shall give
he shall eat butter: for butter and hon-
ey shall every one eat that is left [n]in
the land.
23 And it shall come to pass in that
day, *that* every place shall be, where
there were a thousand vines at a thou-
sand silverlings, [y]it shall *even* be for
briers and thorns.
24 With arrows and with bows shall
men come thither; because all the land
shall become briers and thorns.
25 And *on* all hills that shall be
digged with the mattock, there shall
not come thither the fear of briers and
thorns: but it shall be for the sending
forth of oxen, and for the treading of
lesser cattle.

The coming war and deliverer

8 MOREOVER THE LORD said unto
me, Take thee a great roll, and
[z]write in it with a man's pen concern-
ing [o]Maher-shalal-hash-baz.
2 And I took unto me faithful wit-
nesses to record, [a]Uriah the priest,
and Zechariah the son of Jeberechiah.
3 And I [p]went unto the prophet-
ess; and she conceived, and bare a son.
Then said the LORD to me, Call his
name Maher-shalal-hash-baz.
4 [b]For before the child shall have
knowledge to cry, My father, and my
mother, [c]the[q] riches of Damascus
and the spoil of Samaria shall be taken
away before the king of Assyria.
5 ¶ The LORD spake also unto me
again, saying,
6 Forasmuch as this people refus-
eth the waters of [d]Shiloah that go
softly, and rejoice [e]in Rezin and Rem-
aliah's son;
7 Now therefore, behold, the Lord
bringeth up upon them the waters of
the river, strong and many, *even* the
king of Assyria, and all his glory: and
he shall come up over all his channels,
and go over all his banks:
8 And he shall pass through Judah;
he shall overflow and go over, [f]he
shall reach *even* to the neck; and [r]the
stretching out of his wings shall fill the
breadth of thy land, O [g]Immanuel.
9 ¶ [h]Associate yourselves, O ye
people, [s]and ye shall be broken in
pieces; and give ear, all ye of far coun-
tries: gird yourselves, and ye shall be
broken in pieces; gird yourselves, and
ye shall be broken in pieces.
10 [i]Take counsel together, and it
shall come to nought; speak the word,
[j]and it shall not stand: [k]for God *is*
with us.
11 ¶ For the LORD spake thus to me
[t]with a strong hand, and instructed
me that I should not walk in the way
of this people, saying,
12 Say ye not, A confederacy, to all

7:20 [x]2 Ki. 16:7 **7:23** [y]ch. 5:6 **8:1** [z]Hab. 2:2 **8:2** [a]2 Ki. 16:10 **8:4** [b]ch. 7:16 [c]2 Ki. 15:29 **8:6** [d]John 9:7 [e]ch. 7:1,2 **8:8** [f]ch. 30:28 [g]ch. 7:14 **8:9** [h]Joel 3:9 **8:10** [i]Job 5:12 [j]ch. 7:7 [k]ch. 7:14 Rom. 8:31

[m] Or, *commendable trees* [n] Heb. *in the midst of the land* [o] Heb. *In making speed to the spoil he hasteneth the prey,* or, *Make speed* [p] Heb. *approached unto* [q] Or, he that is *before the king of Assyria shall take away the riches* [r] Heb. *the fulness of the breadth of thy land shall be the stretchings out of his wings* [s] Or, *yet* [t] Heb. *in strength of hand*

8:1 MAHER-SHALAL-HASH-BAZ. The meaning of the name of Isaiah's second son (cf. 7:3, note) is "plundering and despoiling will come quickly." That name predicted not only Syria's destruction and fall at the hands of Assyria (732 B.C.), but Israel's as well (722 B.C.).

8:6 THE WATERS OF SHILOAH. The "waters of Shiloah" (known in the N.T. as the pool of Siloam, John 9:7) were fed by a gentle spring which served as Jerusalem's underground source of water in times of siege by a hostile nation. They symbolized God's gracious and gentle rule over Israel through His kingly representatives—i.e., the godly Davidic kings. Since Judah and Jerusalem were rejecting God's beneficent rule, they would instead experience the destructive waters from the region of the Euphrates, i.e., the mighty flood of invading Assyrian soldiers (vv. 7–10).

8:8 O IMMANUEL. In the midst of Isaiah's prophecy, the Spirit of prophecy pointed to a hope for the future. No matter what happened, those who were faithful to God did not need to fear, for Immanuel ("God with us," cf. v. 10) was the confidence of all who trusted in Him. "Immanuel" is thus the enduring watchword for God's people throughout history—past, present, and future (Mat. 1:23).

8:12 A CONFEDERACY. Isaiah had been attempting to persuade Judah to seek God rather than foreign help. He was accused of conspiracy and treason. Likewise, throughout the history of the church, those who have attempted to call the church away from human programs and non-biblical Christianity and back to its original power, ho-

them to whom [l]this people shall say,
A confederacy; [m]neither fear ye their
fear, nor be afraid.
13 [n]Sanctify the LORD of hosts him-
self; and [o]*let* him *be* your fear, and *let*
him *be* your dread.
14 And [p]he shall be for a sanctu-
ary; but for [q]a stone of stumbling and
for a rock of offence to both the houses
of Israel, for a gin and for a snare to the
inhabitants of Jerusalem.
15 And many among them shall
[r]stumble, and fall, and be broken, and
be snared, and be taken.

Command to trust the LORD

16 Bind up the testimony, seal the
law among my disciples.
17 And I will wait upon the LORD,
that [s]hideth his face from the house of
Jacob, and I [t]will look for him.
18 [u]Behold, I and the children
whom the LORD hath given me [v]*are* for
signs and for wonders in Israel from
the LORD of hosts, which dwelleth in
mount Zion.
19 ¶ And when they shall say unto
you, [w]Seek unto them that have famil-
iar spirits, and unto wizards [x]that
peep, and that mutter: should not a
people seek unto their God? for the liv-
ing [y]to the dead?
20 [z]To the law and to the testimo-
ny: if they speak not according to this
word, *it is* because [a]*there is* [u]no light
in them.
21 And they shall pass through it,
hardly bestead and hungry: and it shall
come to pass, that when they shall be

8:12 [l]ch. 7:2 [m]1 Pet. 3:14
8:13 [n]Num. 20:12 [o]Ps. 76:7 Luke 12:5
8:14 [p]Ezek. 11:16 [q]Luke 2:34 Rom. 9:33 1 Pet. 2:8
8:15 [r]Mat. 21:44 Luke 20:18 Rom. 11:25
8:17 [s]ch. 54:8 [t]Hab. 2:3 Luke 2:25
8:18 [u]Heb. 2:13 [v]Ps. 71:7 Zech. 3:8
8:19 [w]1 Sam. 28:8 [x]ch. 29:4 [y]Ps. 106:28
8:20 [z]Luke 16:29 [a]Mic. 3:6
8:21 [b]Rev. 16:11
8:22 [c]ch. 5:30 [d]ch. 9:1
9:1 [e]ch. 8:22 [f]2 Ki. 15:29 2 Chr. 16:4 [g]Lev. 26:24 2 Ki. 17:5 1 Chr. 5:26
9:2 [h]Mat. 4:16 Eph. 5:8,14
9:3 [i]Judg. 5:30
9:4 [j]ch. 10:5 [k]Judg. 7:22 Ps. 83:9
9:5 [l]ch. 66:15
9:6 [m]ch. 7:14 Luke 2:11

hungry, they shall fret themselves, and
[b]curse their king and their God, and
look upward.
22 And [c]they shall look unto the
earth; and behold trouble and dark-
ness, [d]dimness of anguish; and *they*
shall be driven to darkness.

The birth of the messianic king

9 NEVERTHELESS [e]THE dimness
shall not *be* such as *was* in her vex-
ation, when at the [f]first he lightly af-
flicted the land of Zebulun and the land
of Naphtali, and [g]afterward did more
grievously afflict *her by* the way of the
sea, beyond Jordan, in Galilee [v]of the
nations.
2 [h]The people that walked in dark-
ness have seen a great light: they that
dwell in the land of the shadow of
death, upon them hath the light shined.
3 Thou hast multiplied the nation,
and [w]not increased the joy: they joy
before thee according to the joy in har-
vest, *and* as *men* rejoice [i]when they
divide the spoil.
4 [x]For thou hast broken the yoke
of his burden, and [j]the staff of his
shoulder, the rod of his oppressor, as
in the day of [k]Midian.
5 [y]For every battle of the warrior *is*
with confused noise, and garments
rolled in blood; [l]but[z] *this* shall be
with burning *and* [a]fuel of fire.
6 [m]For unto us a child is born, unto

[u] Heb. *no morning* [v] Or, *populous* [w] Or, *to him* [x] Or, *When thou brakest* [y] Or, *When the whole battle of the warrior was* [z] Or, *and it was* [a] Heb. *meat*

liness, and mission, have often met with persecution and disfavor. Rather than fearing other people, the prophet was exhorted to fear only the Lord of hosts (vv. 12–13).

8:13 *LET* HIM *BE* YOUR FEAR. In times of danger and trial, God alone is the One whom we must fear and look to for our deliverance (cf. Mat. 10:28). Through a proper reverence and love for Him, He will be present with us and be our sanctuary and protection (v. 14).

8:16 SEAL THE LAW AMONG MY DISCIPLES. The great majority of God's people were living in apostasy, but there remained a faithful remnant—disciples who followed the will of the Lord. They were the ones called to preserve God's word. In every age, the true disciples of the Lord, those whose hearts have been set on His word, must contend for God's unalterable truth (see Jude 3) and pass it along to the next generation.

9:1–7 THE DIMNESS *SHALL* NOT *BE* SUCH AS *WAS*. Isaiah speaks of a coming deliverer who would one day lead God's people to joy, peace, righteousness, and justice. This person is the Messiah—Jesus Christ, the Son of God. This prophecy reveals several important truths about the coming Messiah. (1) For the most part, He would minister in Galilee (v. 1; cf. Mat. 4:13–14). (2) He would bring the light of salvation and hope (v. 2; cf. 42:6; 49:6; Mat. 4:15–16). (3) He would enlarge the community of God's people, primarily by the inclusion of Gentiles in the household of faith (v. 3; cf. Acts 15:13–18). (4) He would bring peace by delivering His people from the yoke of oppression and crushing their enemies (vv. 4–5). (5) The Messiah would come from the nation of Israel and be called Wonderful, Counsellor, mighty God, everlasting Father, and the Prince of Peace (see v. 6, note). (6) He would rule over God's people forever (v. 7; cf. 2 Sam. 7:16).

9:6 FOR UNTO US A CHILD IS BORN. This foretells the birth of the Messiah, Jesus Christ (see also 7:14, note). His birth would be at a definite time and place in history, and this Messianic Son would be born in a unique and marvelous way. Isa-

us a [n]son is given: and [o]the government shall be upon his shoulder: and his name shall be called [p]Wonderful, Counsellor, [q]The mighty God, The everlasting Father, [r]The Prince of Peace.

7 Of the increase of *his* government and peace [s]*there shall be* no end, upon the throne of David, and upon his kingdom, to order it, and to establish it with judgment and with justice from henceforth even for ever. The [t]zeal of the LORD of hosts will perform this.

The LORD's anger against Israel

8 ¶ The Lord sent a word into Jacob, and it hath lighted upon Israel.

9 And all the people shall know, *even* Ephraim and the inhabitant of Samaria, that say in the pride and stoutness of heart,

10 The bricks are fallen down, but we will build with hewn stones: the sycamores are cut down, but we will change *them into* cedars.

11 Therefore the LORD shall set up the adversaries of Rezin against him, and [b]join his enemies together;

12 The Syrians before, and the Philistines behind; and they shall devour Israel [c]with open mouth. [u]For all this his anger is not turned away, but his hand *is* stretched out still.

13 ¶ For [v]the people turneth not unto him that smiteth them, neither do they seek the LORD of hosts.

14 Therefore the LORD will cut off from Israel head and tail, branch and rush, [w]in one day.

15 The ancient and honourable, he *is* the head; and the prophet that teacheth lies, he *is* the tail.

16 For [x]the[d] leaders of this people cause *them* to err; and [e]*they that are* led of them *are* [f]destroyed.

17 Therefore the Lord [y]shall have no joy in their young men, neither shall have mercy on their fatherless and widows: for every one *is* an hypocrite and an evildoer, and every mouth speaketh [g]folly. [z]For all this his anger is not turned away, but his hand *is* stretched out still.

18 ¶ For wickedness [a]burneth as the fire: it shall devour the briers and thorns, and shall kindle in the thickets of the forest, and they shall mount up *like* the lifting up of smoke.

19 Through the wrath of the LORD of hosts is [b]the land darkened, and the people shall be as the [h]fuel of the fire: [c]no man shall spare his brother.

20 And he shall [i]snatch on the right hand, and be hungry; and he shall eat on the left hand, [d]and they shall not be satisfied: [e]they shall eat every man the flesh of his own arm:

21 Manasseh, Ephraim; and Ephraim, Manasseh: *and* they together *shall be* against Judah. [f]For all this his anger is not turned away, but his hand *is* stretched out still.

10 WOE UNTO them that [g]decree unrighteous decrees, and [j]that write grievousness *which* they have prescribed;

2 To turn aside the needy from judgment, and to take away the right from

9:6 [n]John 3:16 [o]Mat. 28:18 1 Cor. 15:25 [p]Judg. 13:18 [q]Tit. 2:13 [r]Eph. 2:14 **9:7** [s]Dan. 2:44 Luke 1:32 [t]ch. 37:32 **9:12** [u]Jer. 4:8 **9:13** [v]Jer. 5:3 **9:14** [w]Rev. 18:8

9:16 [x]ch. 3:12 **9:17** [y]Ps. 147:10 [z]ch. 5:25 **9:18** [a]Mal. 4:1 **9:19** [b]ch. 8:22 [c]Mic. 7:2,6 **9:20** [d]Lev. 26:26 [e]Jer. 19:9 **9:21** [f]ver. 12,17 **10:1** [g]Ps. 58:2

[b] Heb. *mingle* [c] Heb. *with whole mouth* [d] Or, *they that call them blessed* [e] Or, *they that are called blessed of them* [f] Heb. *swallowed up* [g] Or, *villany* [h] Heb. *meat* [i] Heb. *cut* [j] Or, *to the writers that write grievousness*

iah records five names that would characterize His function as Messiah. (1) Wonderful. The Messiah would Himself be a supernatural wonder. The Hebrew word (*pele'*) is only used of God and never of humans or human works (cf. Is. 28:29). The Messiah would show His character by His deeds and miracles. (2) Counsellor. The Messiah would be the incarnation of perfect wisdom and have the words of eternal life. As counsellor he would disclose the perfect plan of salvation (cf. ch. 11;). (3) Mighty God. In the Messiah all the fullness of deity would exist in bodily form (Col. 2:9; cf. John 1:1, 14). (4) Everlasting Father. He not only would come to reveal the heavenly Father, but He Himself would act toward His people eternally as a compassionate father who loves, guards, and supplies the needs of His children (cf. Ps. 103:13). (5) Prince of Peace. His rule would bring peace with God for humankind through deliverance from sin and death (11:6–9; cf. Rom. 5:1; 8:2).

9:7 GOVERNMENT AND PEACE *THERE SHALL* BE NO END. In this prophetic statement concerning the establishment of Christ's reign, no distinction is made between a first and second coming. At this point in human history, Christ's entire redemptive work and rule is viewed as occurring in one distant coming. Nowhere does the O.T. clearly reveal that Christ's rule on earth would involve a first and second advent in history. Likewise in the N.T., time gaps between end-time events are not always clearly distinguished (see Mat. 24:42–44, notes).

9:8—10:4 A WORD INTO JACOB. These verses describe Israel's arrogance and persistent impenitence, and God's anger and judgment against them. Even in their great trouble they would not humble themselves and turn to God with a contrite and broken heart.

the poor of my people, that widows may be their prey, and *that* they may rob the fatherless!

3 And [h]what will ye do in [i]the day of visitation, and in the desolation *which* shall come from far? to whom will ye flee for help? and where will ye leave your glory?

4 Without me they shall bow down under the prisoners, and they shall fall under the slain. [j]For all this his anger is not turned away, but his hand *is* stretched out still.

Assyria to be destroyed

5 ¶ [k]O [l]Assyrian, [k]the rod of mine anger, [m]and the staff in their hand is mine indignation.

6 I will send him against [l]an hypocritical nation, and against the people of my wrath will I [m]give him a charge, to take the spoil, and to take the prey, and [n]to tread them down like the mire of the streets.

7 [n]Howbeit he meaneth not so, neither doth his heart think so; but *it is* in his heart to destroy and cut off nations not a few.

8 [o]For he saith, *Are* not my princes altogether kings?

9 *Is* not [p]Calno [q]as Carchemish? *is* not Hamath as Arpad? *is* not Samaria [r]as Damascus?

10 As my hand hath found the kingdoms of the idols, and whose graven images did excel them of Jerusalem and of Samaria;

11 Shall I not, as I have done unto Samaria and her idols, so do to Jerusalem and her idols?

12 Wherefore it shall come to pass, *that* when the Lord hath performed his whole work [s]upon mount Zion and on Jerusalem, [t]I will [o]punish the fruit [p]of the stout heart of the king of Assyria, and the glory of his high looks.

13 [u]For he saith, By the strength of my hand I have done *it,* and by my wisdom; for I am prudent: and I have removed the bounds of the people, and have robbed their treasures, and I have put down the inhabitants [q]like a valiant *man:*

14 And [v]my hand hath found as a nest the riches of the people: and as one gathereth eggs *that are* left, have I gathered all the earth; and there was none that moved the wing, or opened the mouth, or peeped.

15 Shall [w]the axe boast itself against him that heweth therewith? *or* shall the saw magnify itself against him that shaketh it? [r]as if the rod should shake *itself* against them that lift it up, *or* as if the staff should lift up [s]*itself, as if it were* no wood.

16 Therefore shall the Lord, the Lord of hosts, send among his fat ones leanness; and under his glory he shall kindle a burning like the burning of a fire.

17 And the light of Israel shall be for a fire, and his Holy One for a flame: [x]and it shall burn and devour his thorns and his briers in one day;

18 And shall consume the glory of his forest, and of [y]his fruitful field, [t]both soul and body: and they shall be as when a standardbearer fainteth.

19 And the rest of the trees of his forest shall be [u]few, that a child may write them.

A remnant of Israel to be saved

20 ¶ And it shall come to pass in that day, *that* the remnant of Israel, and such as are escaped of the house of Jacob, [z]shall no more again stay upon him that smote them; but shall stay upon the LORD, the Holy One of Israel, in truth.

21 The remnant shall return, *even* the remnant of Jacob, unto the mighty God.

10:3 [h]Job 31:14 [i]Hos. 9:7
10:4 [j]ch. 5:25
10:5 [k]Jer. 51:20
10:6 [l]ch. 9:17 [m]Jer. 34:22
10:7 [n]Gen. 50:20
10:8 [o]2 Ki. 19:10
10:9 [p]Amos 6:2 [q]2 Chr. 35:20 [r]2 Ki. 16:9
10:12 [s]2 Ki. 19:31 [t]Jer. 50:18
10:13 [u]Is. 37:24
10:14 [v]Job 31:25
10:15 [w]Jer. 51:20
10:17 [x]ch. 9:18
10:18 [y]2 Ki. 19:23
10:20 [z]2 Ki. 16:7

[k]Or, *Woe to the Assyrian* [l]Heb. *Asshur* [m]Or, *though* [n]Heb. *to lay them a treading* [o]Heb. *visit upon* [p]Heb. *of the greatness of the heart* [q]Or, *like many people* [r]Or, *as if a rod should shake them that lift it up* [s]Or, that which is *not wood* [t]Heb. *from the soul, and even to the flesh* [u]Heb. *number*

10:5 O ASSYRIAN. God had used the Assyrians to punish His godless people. Now God would punish Assyria for their pride and arrogance (vv. 8–14). Thus Isaiah prophesied destruction for the Assyrians (vv. 16–19). This specific prophecy was fulfilled when God's angel put to death 185,000 soldiers in the Assyrian camp surrounding Jerusalem (see ch. 37).

10:20 THE REMNANT OF ISRAEL. Isaiah again assures the faithful believers that after God had judged Israel, a godly remnant who trusted in the Lord would be preserved and restored; this remnant would be the true Israel (cf. Rom. 9:6–9). God's plan of salvation for the world will always be carried out by the remnant who truly believe and obey His word, not by those who merely profess to believe (see 6:13, note; 8:16, note; cf. Rom. 4:16; 9:27; 11:5; Rev. 3:4–5).

22 [a]For though thy people Israel
be as the sand of the sea, [b]*yet* a rem-
nant [v]of them shall return: the con-
sumption decreed shall overflow
[w]with righteousness.
23 [c]For the Lord GOD of hosts shall
make a consumption, even determined,
in the midst of all the land.
24 ¶ Therefore thus saith the Lord
GOD of hosts, O my people that dwell-
est in Zion, [d]be not afraid of the As-
syrian: he shall smite thee with a rod,
[x]and shall lift up his staff against
thee, after the manner of [e]Egypt.
25 For yet a very little while, [f]and
the indignation shall cease, and mine
anger in their destruction.
26 And the LORD of hosts shall stir
up [g]a scourge for him according to the
slaughter of [h]Midian at the rock of
Oreb: and [i]*as* his rod *was* upon the
sea, so shall he lift it up after the man-
ner of Egypt.
27 And it shall come to pass in that
day, *that* his burden [y]shall be taken
away from off thy shoulder, and his
yoke from off thy neck, and the yoke
shall be destroyed because of [j]the
anointing.
28 He is come to Aiath, he is passed
to Migron; at Michmash he hath laid up
his carriages:
29 They are gone over [k]the pas-
sage: they have taken up their lodging
at Geba; Ramah is afraid; [l]Gibeah of
Saul is fled.
30 [z]Lift up thy voice, O daughter

10:22 [a]Rom. 9:27 [b]ch. 6:13
10:23 [c]Dan. 9:27 Rom. 9:28
10:24 [d]ch. 37:6 [e]Ex. 14
10:25 [f]Dan. 11:36
10:26 [g]2 Ki. 19:35 [h]ch. 9:4 [i]Ex. 14:26
10:27 [j]Ps. 105:15 1 John 2:20
10:29 [k]1 Sam. 13:23 [l]1 Sam. 11:4

[m]of Gallim: cause it to be heard unto
[n]Laish, O poor Anathoth.
31 [o]Madmenah is removed; the in-
habitants of Gebim gather themselves
to flee.
32 As yet shall he remain [p]at Nob
that day: he shall [q]shake his hand
against the mount of [r]the daughter of
Zion, the hill of Jerusalem.
33 Behold, the Lord, the LORD of
hosts, shall lop the bough with terror:
and [s]the high ones of stature *shall be*
hewn down, and the haughty shall be
humbled.
34 And he shall cut down the thick-
ets of the forest with iron, and Lebanon
shall fall [a]by a mighty one.

The branch out of Jesse

11 AND [t]THERE shall come
forth a rod out of the stem of
[u]Jesse, and [v]a Branch shall grow out
of his roots:
2 [w]And the spirit of the LORD shall
rest upon him, the spirit of wisdom and
understanding, the spirit of counsel
and might, the spirit of knowledge and
of the fear of the LORD;
3 And shall make him of [b]quick
understanding in the fear of the LORD: Is. 32:1
and he shall not judge after the sight
of his eyes, neither reprove after the
hearing of his ears:

10:30 [m]1 Sam. 25:44 [n]Judg. 18:7
10:31 [o]Josh. 15:31
10:32 [p]1 Sam. 21:1 Neh. 11:32 [q]ch. 13:2 [r]ch. 37:22
10:33 [s]Amos 2:9
11:1 [t]Zech. 6:12 Rev. 5:5 [u]Acts 13:23 [v]ch. 4:2
11:2 [w]ch. 61:1 John 1:32

[v]Heb. *in,* or, *among* [w]Or, *in* [x]Or, *but he shall lift up his staff for thee* [y]Heb. *shall remove* [z]Heb. *Cry shrill with thy voice* [a]Or, *mightily* [b]Heb. *scent,* or, *smell*

10:28–34 HE IS COME TO AIATH. Isaiah foretells the route the Assyrian invaders would take as they sought to plunder Jerusalem. God Himself would cut them down (cf. 37:33–38).

11:1 A BRANCH SHALL GROW OUT OF HIS ROOTS. Isaiah gives a glorious picture of a future new world governed by the Branch (i.e., Jesus Christ). The Hebrew word *netzer* ("Branch") is likely the root word from which the name "Nazareth" is derived. Jesus was called a Nazarene (Mat. 2:23), which can mean either "a man of Nazareth" or "a man of the Branch." He would come forth as a branch from the root of Jesse, i.e., David's father (see 4:2, note; cf. 4:2–6; 7:14; 9:1–7; Rom. 15:12) and would become ruler of a world restored to peace, righteousness, and goodness. The initial fulfillment of this prophecy came 700 years later when Jesus Christ was born, while its completion awaits the second coming of Christ (see 9:7, note).

11:2 THE SPIRIT OF THE LORD SHALL REST UPON HIM. The Messiah would be mightily anointed by the Holy Spirit in order to carry out the will of the Father and to bring full salvation to the nations (Is. 61:1; Mat. 3:16–17; John 1:33–34; see article on JESUS AND THE HOLY SPIRIT, p. 1550). In order to carry out His plan of salvation, the Messiah would also baptize and anoint His followers in the Holy Spirit. This is an essential requirement in the ongoing work of redemption (see Mat. 3:11, note; Luke 3:16, note; Acts 1:5, note; see article on BAPTISM IN THE HOLY SPIRIT, p. 1652).

11:2–3 THE SPIRIT. Isaiah mentions the Holy Spirit more often than any other O.T. prophet (11:2; 30:1; 32:15; 34:16; 40:13; 42:1; 44:3; 48:16; 59:21; 61:1; 63:10–11,14; see article on THE SPIRIT IN THE OLD TESTAMENT, p. 1302). This prophetic description of the Messiah's anointing relates to His spiritual character and stature (see 61:1–3, note). The Messiah is filled with the Spirit, and His charismatic gifts are described as (1) the Spirit (v. 1), (2) wisdom (v. 2), (3) understanding (v. 2), (4) counsel (v. 2), (5) strength (v. 2), (6) knowledge (v. 2), and (7) the fear of the Lord. The fullness of this description is unprecedented in Scripture. The sevenfold gift signifies the fullness of the gift.

4 But [x]with righteousness shall he judge the poor, and [c]reprove with equity for the meek of the earth: and he shall [y]smite the earth with the rod of his mouth, and with the breath of his lips shall he slay the wicked.

5 And righteousness shall be the girdle of his loins, and faithfulness the girdle of his reins.

6 [z]The wolf also shall dwell with the lamb, and the leopard shall lie down with the kid; and the calf and the young lion and the fatling together; and a little child shall lead them.

7 And the cow and the bear shall feed; their young ones shall lie down together: and the lion shall eat straw like the ox.

8 And the sucking child shall play on the hole of the asp, and the weaned child shall put his hand on the [d]cockatrice's den.

9 [a]They shall not hurt nor destroy in all my holy mountain: for [b]the earth shall be full of the knowledge of the LORD, as the waters cover the sea.

10 ¶ [c]And in that day [d]there shall be a root of Jesse, which shall stand for an ensign of the people; to it shall the [e]Gentiles seek: and his rest shall be [e]glorious.

11 And it shall come to pass in that day, *that* the Lord shall set his hand again the second time to recover the remnant of his people, which shall be left, [f]from Assyria, and from Egypt, and from Pathros, and from Cush, and from Elam, and from Shinar, and from Hamath, and from the islands of the sea.

12 And he shall set up an ensign for the nations, and shall assemble the outcasts of Israel, and gather together the [g]dispersed of Judah from the four [f]corners of the earth.

13 [h]The envy also of Ephraim shall depart, and the adversaries of Judah shall be cut off: Ephraim shall not envy Judah, and Judah shall not vex Ephraim.

14 But they shall fly upon the shoulders of the Philistines toward the west; they shall spoil [g]them of the east together: [i]they[h] shall lay their hand upon Edom and Moab; [i]and the children of Ammon shall obey them.

15 And the LORD [j]shall utterly destroy the tongue of the Egyptian sea; and with his mighty wind shall he shake his hand over the river, and shall smite it in the seven streams, [k]and make *men* go over [j]dryshod.

16 And [l]there shall be an highway for the remnant of his people, which shall be left, from Assyria; [m]like as it was to Israel in the day that he came up out of the land of Egypt.

11:4 [x]Rev. 19:11 [y]Job 4:9 Mal. 4:6 2 Thes. 2:8
11:6 [z]Hos. 2:18
11:9 [a]Job 5:23 [b]Hab. 2:14
11:10 [c]ch. 2:11 [d]Rom. 15:12 [e]Rom. 15:10
11:11 [f]Zech. 10:10
11:12 [g]John 7:35
11:13 [h]Jer. 3:18 Ezek. 37:16,17,22
11:14 [i]Dan. 11:41
11:15 [j]Zech. 10:11 [k]Rev. 16:12
11:16 [l]ch. 19:23 [m]Ex. 14:29
12:1 [n]ch. 2:11

Thanksgiving for God's salvation

12 AND [n]IN that day thou shalt say, O LORD, I will praise thee:

[c] Or, *argue* [d] Or, *adder's* [e] Heb. *glory* [f] Heb. *wings* [g] Heb. *the children of the east* [h] Heb. *Edom and Moab* shall be *the laying on of their hand* [i] Heb. *the children of Ammon their obedience* [j] Heb. *in shoes*

11:4 HE SHALL SMITE THE EARTH. This verse refers to Christ's return to earth in judgment and His destruction of all the wicked (cf. 2 Thes. 1:6–10; 2:8; Rev. 19). This return in just retribution is necessary in order to establish His perfect and righteous rule.

11:5 RIGHTEOUSNESS ... FAITHFULNESS. Righteousness and faithfulness are integral qualities of the reign of the Messiah. They are also requirements for all who would rule in the Messiah's church (see article on MORAL QUALIFICATIONS FOR OVERSEERS, p. 1908).

11:6–9 THE WOLF ALSO SHALL DWELL WITH THE LAMB. The Messianic age will be characterized by the absence of enmity, brutality, and hostility, here symbolized by tranquility among animals. The Messiah will bring peace to earth and transform believers and nature as the final fruit of redemption (cf. 35:9; 65:20–25; Ezek. 34:25–29).

11:10–16 IN THAT DAY. The final days of the Messianic kingdom will be preceded by a regathering of Jews who accept Jesus Christ as the Messiah. This restoration of Israel and Judah will involve the following: (1) the faithful remnant that is left (vv. 11–12; cf. Deut. 30:3–5; Jer. 31:1,8,10; Ezek. 39:22,28); (2) a gathering to the Messiah (11:10,12; Jer. 23:5–8; Ezek. 37:21–25); (3) a total cleansing for Israel (Deut. 30:3–6; Jer. 32:37–41; Ezek. 11:17–20); (4) blessing and prosperity in the land (Jer. 31:8,10,12–13,28; 32:37–41; Ezek. 28:25–26; 39:25–29; Amos 9:11–15); (5) blessing for all people, Gentiles as well as Jews (v. 12; 55:3–5; 60:1–5,10–14; Jer. 16:15,19- 21; Zech. 2:10–12; Mic. 4:1–4); (6) judgment on the ungodly (vv. 14–16; Jer. 25:29–33; Joel 3:1-2,12–14); and (7) ultimate restoration in "the latter days" (Hos. 3:4–5; see Rom. 11:26, note; see article on ISRAEL IN GOD'S PLAN OF SALVATION, p. 1748).

12:1–6 IN THAT DAY. God's people will praise Him when the universal reign of the Messiah begins. Even now we must pray for and anticipate in faith and hope the return of our Lord and the establishment of His eternal reign in righteousness. When that day comes, we will

though thou wast angry with me, thine
anger is turned away, and thou comfor-
tedst me.
2 Behold, God *is* my salvation; I will
trust, and not be afraid: for the LORD
[o]JEHOVAH *is* my [p]strength and *my*
song; he also is become my salvation.
3 Therefore with joy shall ye draw
Is. 25:9 [q]water out of the wells of salvation.
4 And in that day shall ye say,
[r]Praise the LORD, [k]call upon his
name, [s]declare his doings among the
people, make mention that his [t]name
is exalted.
5 [u]Sing unto the LORD; for he hath
done excellent things: this *is* known in
all the earth.
6 [v]Cry out and shout, thou [l]in-
habitant of Zion: for great *is* [w]the Holy
Is. 26:1-4 One of Israel in the midst of thee.

The doom of Babylon

13 THE [x]BURDEN of Babylon,
which Isaiah the son of Amoz
did see.
2 [y]Lift ye up a banner [z]upon the
high mountain, exalt the voice unto
them, [a]shake the hand, that they may
go into the gates of the nobles.
3 I have commanded my sanctified
ones, I have also called [b]my mighty
ones for mine anger, *even* them that
[c]rejoice in my highness.
4 The noise of a multitude in the
mountains, [m]like as of a great people;
a tumultuous noise of the kingdoms of
nations gathered together: the LORD of
hosts mustereth the host of the battle.
5 They come from a far country,
from the end of heaven, *even* the LORD,
and the weapons of his indignation, to
destroy the whole land.
6 ¶ Howl ye; [d]for the day of the
LORD *is* at hand; [e]it shall come as a
destruction from the Almighty.
7 Therefore shall all hands [n]be
faint, and every man's heart shall melt:
8 And they shall be afraid: [f]pangs
and sorrows shall take hold of them;
they shall be in pain as a woman that
travaileth: they shall [o]be amazed
[p]one at another; their faces *shall be as*
[q]flames.
9 Behold, [g]the day of the LORD com-
eth, cruel both with wrath and fierce
anger, to lay the land desolate: and he
shall destroy [h]the sinners thereof out
of it.
10 For the stars of heaven and the
constellations thereof shall not give
their light: the sun shall be [i]darkened
in his going forth, and the moon shall
not cause her light to shine.
11 And I will punish the world for
their evil, and the wicked for their iniq-
uity; [j]and I will cause the arrogancy
of the proud to cease, and will lay low
the haughtiness of the terrible.
12 I will make a man more precious
than fine gold; even a man than the
golden wedge of Ophir.
13 [k]Therefore I will shake the
heavens, and the earth shall remove
out of her place, in the wrath of the
LORD of hosts, and in [l]the day of his
fierce anger.
14 And it shall be as the chased roe,
and as a sheep that no man taketh up:
[m]they shall every man turn to his own

12:2 [o]Ps. 83:18 [p]Ex. 15:2 Ps. 118:14 **12:3** [q]John 4:10 **12:4** [r]1 Chr. 16:8 Ps. 105:1 [s]Ps. 145:4-6 [t]Ps. 34:3 **12:5** [u]Ex. 15:1 Ps. 98:1 **12:6** [v]Zeph. 3:14 [w]Ps. 89:18 **13:1** [x]Jer. 50 & 51 **13:2** [y]ch. 18:3 [z]Jer. 51:25 [a]ch. 10:32 **13:3** [b]Joel 3:11 [c]Ps. 149:2 **13:6** [d]Zeph. 1:7 Rev. 6:17 [e]Job 31:23 Joel 1:15 **13:8** [f]Ps. 48:6 **13:9** [g]Mal. 4:1 [h]Ps. 104:35 Prov. 2:22 **13:10** [i]Ezek. 32:7 Joel 2:31 Mat. 24:29 Mark 13:24 **13:11** [j]ch. 2:17 **13:13** [k]Hag. 2:6 [l]Ps. 110:5 Lam. 1:12 **13:14** [m]Jer. 50:16

[k] Or, *proclaim his name* [l] Heb. *inhabitress* [m] Heb. *the likeness of* [n] Or, *fall down* [o] Heb. *wonder* [p] Heb. *every man at his neighbour* [q] Heb. *faces of the flames*

sing this song of praise.

13:1—23:18 BURDEN. These chapters record judgments pronounced upon foreign nations and apostate Jerusalem. Isaiah starts with Babylon (13:1—14:23) and Assyria (14:24–27), and continues with prophecies against smaller nations. These chapters teach that all nations and peoples are accountable to God; those who oppose Him and His divine plan of salvation will be judged and destroyed, and those who believe in Him will ultimately triumph.

13:1 BABYLON. Isaiah prophesies that Babylon would be overthrown like Sodom and Gomorrah. Babylon was a center of pagan culture, opposing God and His ways from very early in human history (cf. Gen. 11:1–9). Ironically it served as God's instrument of wrath against Jerusalem, taking its residents into captivity. In the N.T. Babylon symbolizes the world's religious and political center in opposition to God and His people (see Rev. 17:1, note). The ruins of Babylon are in modern-day Iraq.

13:4 THE BATTLE. The fulfillment of the prophecy about the fall of Babylon went through various stages. The first was the Assyrian attack on Babylon in 689 B.C., when Sennacherib overthrew it. After it rose to power again under Nebuchadnezzar, Babylon was captured in 539 B.C. by Cyrus of the Medo-Persian empire (cf. v. 17). In 518 B.C. the city was ravaged again, its walls were torn down, and it fell into total ruin.

13:6–13 THE DAY OF THE LORD *IS* AT HAND. The destruction of Babylon is a type of the end-time destruction of all God's enemies and the final judgment to come over all the earth during the period of the tribulation. Isaiah puts them both together here (cf. Ezek. 32:7; Joel 2:10; 3:16; Hag. 2:6–7,21–22; Zech. 14:6–7).

people, and flee every one into his own
land.
15 Every one that is found shall be
thrust through; and every one that is
joined *unto them* shall fall by the sword.
16 Their children also shall be
[n]dashed to pieces before their eyes;
their houses shall be spoiled, and their
wives ravished.
17 [o]Behold, I will stir up the
Medes against them, which shall not
regard silver; and *as for* gold, they shall
not delight in it.
18 *Their* bows also shall dash the
young men to pieces; and they shall
have no pity on the fruit of the womb;
their eye shall not spare children.
19 ¶ [p]And Babylon, the glory of
kingdoms, the beauty of the Chaldees'
excellency, shall be [r]as when God
overthrew [q]Sodom and Gomorrah.
20 [r]It shall never be inhabited, nei-
ther shall it be dwelt in from genera-
tion to generation: neither shall the
Arabian pitch tent there; neither shall
the shepherds make their fold there.
21 [s]But [s]wild beasts of the desert
shall lie there; and their houses shall
be full of [t]doleful creatures; and
[u] [v]owls shall dwell there, and satyrs
shall dance there.
22 And [w]the wild beasts of the is-
lands shall cry in their [x]desolate
houses, and dragons in *their* pleasant
palaces: [t]and her time *is* near to
come, and her days shall not be pro-
longed.

14 FOR THE LORD [u]will have mer-
cy on Jacob, and [v]will yet
choose Israel, and set them in their
own land: [w]and the strangers shall be
joined with them, and they shall cleave
to the house of Jacob.
2 And the people shall take them,
[x]and bring them to their place: and
the house of Israel shall possess them
in the land of the LORD for servants and
handmaids: and they shall take them
captives, [y]whose captives they were;
[y]and they shall rule over their oppres-
sors.
3 And it shall come to pass in the
day that the LORD shall give thee rest
from thy sorrow, and from thy fear, and
from the hard bondage wherein thou
wast made to serve,
4 ¶ That thou [z]shalt take up this
[z]proverb against the king of Babylon,
and say, How hath the oppressor
ceased! the [a]golden[a] city ceased!
5 The LORD hath broken [b]the staff
of the wicked, *and* the sceptre of the
rulers.
6 He who smote the people in wrath
with [b]a continual stroke, he that
ruled the nations in anger, is persecut-
ed, *and* none hindereth.
7 The whole earth is at rest, *and* is
quiet: they break forth into singing.
8 [c]Yea, the fir trees rejoice at thee,
and the cedars of Lebanon, *saying,*
Since thou art laid down, no feller is
come up against us.
9 [d]Hell[c] from beneath is moved
for thee to meet *thee* at thy coming: it
stirreth up the dead for thee, *even* all
the [d] [e]chief ones of the earth; it hath
raised up from their thrones all the
kings of the nations.
10 All they shall speak and say unto
thee, Art thou also become weak as
we? art thou become like unto us?
11 Thy pomp is brought down to the
grave, *and* the noise of thy viols:
the worm is spread under thee, and
the worms cover thee.
12 [e]How art thou fallen from heav-
en, [f]O Lucifer, son of the morning!
how art thou cut down to the ground,
which didst weaken the nations!

13:16 [n]Ps. 137:9 Nah. 3:10 Zech. 14:2 **13:17** [o]Jer. 51:11 Dan. 5:28 **13:19** [p]ch. 14:4 [q]Gen. 19:24 Deut. 29:23 Jer. 50:40 **13:20** [r]Jer. 50:3 **13:21** [s]ch. 34:11 **13:22** [t]Jer. 51:33 **14:1** [u]Ps. 102:13 [v]Zech. 1:17 [w]ch. 60:4,5,10 **14:2** [x]ch. 49:22 & 60:9 & 66:20 [y]ch. 60:14 **14:4** [z]ch. 13:19 Hab. 2:6 [a]Rev. 18:16 **14:5** [b]Ps. 125:3 **14:8** [c]ch. 55:12 Ezek. 31:16 **14:9** [d]Ezek. 32:21 **14:12** [e]ch. 34:4

[r] Heb *as the overthrowing* [s] Heb. *Ziim* [t] Heb. *Ochim* [u] Or, *ostriches* [v] Heb. *daughters of the owl* [w] Heb. *Iim* [x] Or, *palaces* [y] Heb. *that had taken them captives* [z] Or, *taunting speech* [a] Or, *exactress of gold* [b] Heb. *a stroke without removing* [c] Or, *The grave* [d] Heb. *leaders* [e] Or, *great goats* [f] Or, *O day star*

13:20 IT SHALL NEVER BE INHABITED. This verse emphasizes that no monument to human glory and achievement has any permanence in itself. One day all things made by humans will rust or fade away (cf. Mat. 6:19), while God's glory will fill the earth.

14:4–21 PROVERB AGAINST THE KING OF BABYLON. This taunting prophetic hymn was to be sung by those who saw the downfall of the king of Babylon. The king would be cut down and "brought down to hell" (v. 15). These verses ultimately apply to all rulers and people who defy God and oppose the principles of His kingdom.

14:12–15 O LUCIFER. Some believe that these verses not only refer to the king of Babylon, but are also a veiled reference to Satan (cf. Christ's statement in Luke 10:18). Others think they may refer to the end-time antichrist who will rule over "Babylon" (see Rev. 17:1–3, notes) in opposition to God and His people (cf. Rev. 13:4; see article on THE AGE OF THE ANTICHRIST, p. 1896).

13 For thou hast said in thine heart, [f]I will ascend into heaven, [g]I will exalt my throne above the stars of God: I will sit also upon the mount of the congregation, [h]in the sides of the north:

14 I will ascend above the heights of the clouds: [i]I will be like the most High.

15 Yet thou [j]shalt be brought down to hell, to the sides of the pit.

16 They that see thee shall narrowly look upon thee, *and* consider thee, *saying, Is* this the man that made the earth to tremble, that did shake kingdoms;

17 *That* made the world as a wilderness, and destroyed the cities thereof; *that* [g]opened not the house of his prisoners?

18 All the kings of the nations, *even* all of them, lie in glory, every one in his own house.

19 But thou art cast out of thy grave like an abominable branch, *and as* the raiment of those that are slain, thrust through with a sword, that go down to the stones of the pit; as a carcase trodden under feet.

20 Thou shalt not be joined with them in burial, because thou hast destroyed thy land, *and* slain thy people:
Is. 24:21-23 [k]the seed of evildoers shall never be renowned.

21 Prepare slaughter for his children [l]for the iniquity of their fathers; that they do not rise, nor possess the land, nor fill the face of the world with cities.

22 For I will rise up against them, saith the LORD of hosts, and cut off from Babylon [m]the name, and [n]remnant, [o]and son, and nephew, saith the LORD.

23 [p]I will also make it a possession for the bittern, and pools of water: and I will sweep it with the besom of destruction, saith the LORD of hosts.

The overthrow of Assyria

24 ¶ The LORD of hosts hath sworn, saying, Surely as I have thought, so shall it come to pass; and as I have purposed, *so* shall it stand:

25 That I will break the Assyrian in my land, and upon my mountains tread him under foot: then shall [q]his yoke depart from off them, and his burden depart from off their shoulders.

26 This *is* the purpose that is purposed upon the whole earth: and this *is* the hand that is stretched out upon all the nations.

27 For the LORD of hosts hath [r]purposed, and who shall disannul *it?* and his hand *is* stretched out, and who shall turn it back?

A burden about Palestina

28 In the year that [s]king Ahaz died was this burden.

29 ¶ Rejoice not thou, whole Palestina, [t]because the rod of him that smote thee is broken: for out of the serpent's root shall come forth a [h]cockatrice, [u]and his fruit *shall be* a fiery flying serpent.

30 And the firstborn of the poor shall feed, and the needy shall lie down in safety: and I will kill thy root with famine, and he shall slay thy remnant.

31 Howl, O gate; cry, O city; thou, whole Palestina, *art* dissolved: for there shall come from the north a smoke, and [i]none *shall be* alone in his [j]appointed times.

32 What shall *one* then answer the messengers of the nation? That [v]the LORD hath founded Zion, and [w]the poor of his people shall [k]trust in it.

Moab's devastation

16:6–12pp — Jer. 48:29–36

15 THE [x]BURDEN of Moab. Because in the night [y]Ar of Moab is laid waste, *and* [l]brought to silence; because in the night Kir of Moab is laid waste, *and* brought to silence;

2 He is gone up to Bajith, and to Dibon, the high places, to weep: Moab

14:13 [f]Mat. 11:23 [g]Dan. 8:10 [h]Ps. 48:2
14:14 [i]ch. 47:8 2 Thes. 2:4
14:15 [j]Mat. 11:23
14:20 [k]Job 18:19 Ps. 21:10 & 37:28 & 109:13
14:21 [l]Ex. 20:5 Mat. 23:35
14:22 [m]Prov. 10:7 Jer. 51:62 [n]1 Ki. 14:10 [o]Job 18:19
14:23 [p]ch. 34:11 Zeph. 2:14
14:25 [q]ch. 10:27
14:27 [r]2 Chr. 20:6 Job 9:12 & 23:13 Ps. 33:11 Prov. 19:21 & 21:30 ch. 43:13 Dan. 4:31,35
14:28 [s]2 Ki. 16:20
14:29 [t]2 Chr. 26:6 [u]2 Ki. 18:8
14:32 [v]Ps. 87:1,5 [w]Zech. 11:11
15:1 [x]Jer. 48:1 [y]Num. 21:28

[g] Or, *did not let his prisoners loose homewards?*
[h] Or, *adder* [i] Or, he shall *not* be *alone*
[j] Or, *assemblies* [k] Or, *betake themselves unto it*
[l] Or, *cut off*

14:24–27 I WILL BREAK THE ASSYRIAN. This prophecy concerns Judah's immediate threat from Assyria; God would crush the Assyrian army (see 37:21–36; 2 Ki. 19).

14:29 PALESTINA. Isaiah prophesies the defeat of Philistia in Palestine (v. 30). Judah should not accept the offer of the messengers of Philistia for an alliance, but must trust in the Lord instead (v. 32).

15:1 MOAB. Located immediately east of the Dead Sea, Moab had always been an enemy of Israel (cf. 25:10; 2 Ki. 3:4–5; 13:20; Ezek. 25:8–11). Like the other hostile nations, they too would be destroyed.

shall howl over Nebo, and over Mede-
ba: [z]on all their heads *shall be* bald-
ness, *and* every beard cut off.
3 In their streets they shall gird
themselves with sackcloth: on the tops
of their houses, and in their streets, ev-
ery one shall howl, [m]weeping abun-
dantly.
4 And Heshbon shall cry, and Elea-
leh: their voice shall be heard *even* unto
Jahaz: therefore the armed soldiers of
Moab shall cry out; his life shall be
grievous unto him.
5 [a]My heart shall cry out for Moab;
[n]his fugitives *shall flee* unto Zoar, an
heifer of three years old: for [b]by the
mounting up of Luhith with weeping
shall they go it up; for in the way of
Horonaim they shall raise up a cry of
[o]destruction.
6 For the waters [c]of Nimrim shall
be [p]desolate: for the hay is withered
away, the grass faileth, there is no
green thing.
7 Therefore the abundance they
have gotten, and that which they have
laid up, shall they carry away to the
[q]brook of the willows.
8 For the cry is gone round about
the borders of Moab; the howling
thereof unto Eglaim, and the howling
thereof unto Beer-elim.
9 For the waters of Dimon shall be
full of blood: for I will bring [r]more
upon Dimon, [d]lions upon him that es-
capeth of Moab, and upon the remnant
of the land.

16 SEND [e]YE the lamb to the rul-
er of the land [f]from [s]Sela to
the wilderness, unto the mount of the
daughter of Zion.
2 For it shall be, *that,* as a wander-
ing bird [t]cast out of the nest, *so* the
daughters of Moab shall be at the fords
of [g]Arnon.
3 [u]Take counsel, execute judg-
ment; make thy shadow as the night in
the midst of the noonday; hide the out-
casts; betray not him that wandereth.
4 Let mine outcasts dwell with
thee, Moab; be thou a covert to them
from the face of the spoiler: for the
[v]extortioner is at an end, the spoiler
ceaseth, [w]the oppressors are con-
sumed out of the land.
5 And in mercy [h]shall the throne
be [x]established: and he shall sit upon
it in truth in the tabernacle of David,
[i]judging, and seeking judgment, and
hasting righteousness.
6 ¶ We have heard of the [j]pride of
Moab; *he is* very proud: *even* of his
haughtiness, and his pride, and his
wrath: [k]*but* his lies *shall* not *be* so.
7 Therefore shall Moab [l]howl for
Moab, every one shall howl: for the
foundations [m]of Kir-hareseth shall ye
[y]mourn; surely *they are* stricken.
8 For [n]the fields of Heshbon lan-
guish, *and* [o]the vine of Sibmah: the
lords of the heathen have broken down
the principal plants thereof, they are
come *even* unto Jazer, they wandered
through the wilderness: her branches
are [z]stretched out, they are gone over
the sea.
9 ¶ Therefore I will bewail with the
weeping of Jazer the vine of Sibmah: I
will water thee with my tears, [p]O
Heshbon, and Elealeh: for [a]the shout-
ing for thy summer fruits and for thy
harvest is fallen.
10 And [q]gladness is taken away,
and joy out of the plentiful field; and in

15:2 [z]Lev. 21:5 **15:5** [a]Jer. 48:31 [b]Jer. 48:5 **15:6** [c]Num. 32:36 **15:9** [d]2 Ki. 17:25 **16:1** [e]2 Ki. 3:4 [f]2 Ki. 14:7 **16:2** [g]Num. 21:13 **16:5** [h]Luke 1:33 [i]Ps. 72:2 **16:6** [j]Jer. 48:29 [k]ch. 28:15 **16:7** [l]Jer. 48:20 [m]2 Ki. 3:25 **16:8** [n]ch. 24:7 [o]ver. 9 **16:9** [p]ch. 15:4 **16:10** [q]ch. 24:8 Jer. 48:33

[m]Heb. *descending into weeping,* or, *coming down with weeping* [n]Or, *to the borders thereof, even to Zoar,* as *an heifer* [o]Heb. *breaking* [p]Heb. *desolations* [q]Or, *valley of the Arabians* [r]Heb. *additions* [s]Or, *Petra* Heb. *A rock* [t]Or, *a nest forsaken* [u]Heb. *Bring* [v]Heb. *wringer* [w]Heb. *the treaders down* [x]Or, *prepared* [y]Or, *mutter* [z]Or, *plucked up* [a]Or, *the alarm is fallen upon*

15:5 MY HEART SHALL CRY OUT FOR MOAB. Seeing the terrible suffering of this enemy of God's people, Isaiah cried out in compassion for the Moabite victims (cf. 21:2–4; 22:4). In like manner, we should feel compassion and pity for those who destroy themselves by pursuing sin and evil (see Luke 19:41, note).

16:1–5 UNTO THE MOUNT . . . OF ZION. The fugitives and refugees of Moab were told to seek shelter in Judah and to submit to the king of Jerusalem.

16:4–5 THE EXTORTIONER IS AT AN END. Looking to the future, Isaiah saw the Messianic kingdom and the end of all oppression.

16:6–13 THE PRIDE OF MOAB. Although war and destruction would someday cease (see previous note), the Moabites of Isaiah's day would face judgment because of their pride and their failure to acknowledge God and His righteousness.

16:10 NO WINE IN THEIR PRESSES. Here the fresh, unfermented juice of the grape that is still in the presses is called "wine" (Heb. *yayin*), as it is elsewhere in the O.T. (see article on WINE IN THE OLD TESTAMENT, p. 220). The N.T. Greek equivalent of *yayin* is *oinos* (see articles on WINE IN NEW TESTAMENT TIMES, (1) and (2), p. 1538, and p. 1594).

the vineyards there shall be no singing,
neither shall there be shouting: the
treaders shall tread out no wine in *their*
presses; I have made *their vintage*
shouting to cease.
11 Wherefore [r]my bowels shall
sound like an harp for Moab, and mine
inward parts for Kir-haresh.
12 ¶ And it shall come to pass,
when it is seen that Moab is weary on
[s]the high place, that he shall come to
his sanctuary to pray; but he shall not
prevail.
13 This *is* the word that the LORD
hath spoken concerning Moab since
that time.
14 But now the LORD hath spoken,
saying, Within three years, [t]as the
years of an hireling, and the glory of
Moab shall be contemned, with all that
great multitude; and the remnant *shall*
be very small *and* [b]feeble.

Crushing of Damascus

17 THE [u]BURDEN of Damascus.
Behold, Damascus is taken
away from *being* a city, and it shall be
a ruinous heap.
2 The cities of Aroer *are* forsaken:
they shall be for flocks, which shall lie
down, and [v]none shall make *them*
afraid.
3 [w]The fortress also shall cease
from Ephraim, and the kingdom from
Damascus, and the remnant of Syria:
they shall be as the glory of the
children of Israel, saith the LORD of
hosts.
4 And in that day it shall come to
pass, *that* the glory of Jacob shall be
made thin, and [x]the fatness of his
flesh shall wax lean.
5 [y]And it shall be as when the har-
vestman gathereth the corn, and
reapeth the ears with his arm; and it
shall be as he that gathereth ears in
the valley of Rephaim.
6 ¶ [z]Yet gleaning grapes shall be
left in it, as the shaking of an olive tree,
two *or* three berries in the top of the
uppermost bough, four *or* five in the
outmost fruitful branches thereof,
saith the LORD God of Israel.
7 At that day shall a man [a]look to
his Maker, and his eyes shall have re-
spect to the Holy One of Israel.
8 And he shall not look to the al-
tars, the work of his hands, neither
shall respect *that* which his fingers
have made, either the groves, or the
[c]images.
9 ¶ In that day shall his strong cit-
ies be as a forsaken bough, and an up-
permost branch, which they left be-
cause of the children of Israel: and
there shall be desolation.
10 Because thou hast forgotten
[b]the God of thy salvation, and hast not
been mindful of the rock of thy
strength, therefore shalt thou plant
pleasant plants, and shalt set it with
strange slips:
11 In the day shalt thou make thy
plant to grow, and in the morning shalt
thou make thy seed to flourish: *but* the
harvest *shall be* [d]a heap in the day of
grief and of desperate sorrow.
12 ¶ Woe to the [e]multitude of
many people, *which* make a noise
[c]like the noise of the seas; and to
the rushing of nations, *that* make a
rushing like the rushing of [f]mighty
waters!
13 The nations shall rush like the
rushing of many waters: but *God* shall
[d]rebuke them, and they shall flee far
off, and [e]shall be chased as the chaff
of the mountains before the wind, and
like [g]a rolling thing before the whirl-
wind.
14 And behold at eveningtide trou-
ble; *and* before the morning he *is* not.
This *is* the portion of them that spoil
us, and the lot of them that rob us.

16:11 [r]Jer. 48:36
16:12 [s]ch. 15:2
16:14 [t]ch. 21:16
17:1 [u]Jer. 49:23 Amos 1:3 Zech. 9:1
17:2 [v]Jer. 7:33
17:3 [w]ch. 7:16 & 8:4
17:4 [x]ch. 10:16
17:5 [y]Jer. 51:33
17:6 [z]ch. 24:13
17:7 [a]Mic. 7:7
17:10 [b]Ps. 68:19
17:12 [c]Jer. 6:23
17:13 [d]Ps. 9:5 [e]Ps. 88:13 Hos. 13:3

[b] Or, *not many* [c] Or, *sun images* [d] Or, *removed in the day of inheritance, and* there shall be *deadly sorrow* [e] Or, *noise* [f] Or, *many* [g] Or, *thistledown*

17:1–6 DAMASCUS IS TAKEN AWAY. Damascus, the capital of Syria (v. 3), would be overthrown. Ephraim (i.e., Israel, or the northern kingdom) would also suffer because of its alliance with Damascus against Assyria.

17:7 LOOK TO HIS MAKER. The judgments of God on Israel would cause a remnant to turn away from idolatry back to the Lord God their Maker. They would realize how useless their idols were in times of trouble and war.

17:10 THOU HAST FORGOTTEN THE GOD OF THY SALVATION. Forgetting God is not a sin limited to Israel. Jesus warns that the cares of this world, the deception of riches, the pursuit of material things, and the pleasure of sin can choke God's word in the lives of believers (cf. Mark 4:3–9,14–20) and cause them to forget Him, to stop praying daily, and no longer to delight in Him or His word. When this happens, we lose the blessing and presence of God.

An oracle about Ethiopia

18 WOE [f]TO the land shadowing
with wings, which *is* beyond the
rivers of Ethiopia:
2 That sendeth ambassadors by the
sea, even in vessels of bulrushes upon
the waters, *saying,* Go, ye swift mes-
sengers, to [g]a nation [h]scattered and
peeled, to a people terrible from their
beginning hitherto; [i] [j]a nation met-
ed out and trodden down, [k]whose
land the rivers have spoiled!
3 All ye inhabitants of the world,
and dwellers on the earth, see ye,
[h]when he lifteth up an ensign on the
mountains; and when he bloweth a
trumpet, hear ye.
4 For so the LORD said unto me, I
will take my rest, and I will [l]consider
in my dwellingplace like a clear heat
[m]upon herbs, *and* like a cloud of dew
in the heat of harvest.
5 For afore the harvest, when the
bud is perfect, and the sour grape is
ripening in the flower, he shall both cut
off the sprigs with pruning hooks, and
take away *and* cut down the branches.
6 They shall be left together unto
the fowls of the mountains, and to the
beasts of the earth: and the fowls shall
summer upon them, and all the beasts
of the earth shall winter upon them.
7 ¶ In that time [i]shall the present
be brought unto the LORD of hosts of a
people [j]scattered[h] and peeled, and
from a people terrible from their begin-
ning hitherto; a nation meted out and
trodden under foot, whose land the riv-
ers have spoiled, to the place of the
name of the LORD of hosts, the mount
Zion.

The doom of Egypt

19 THE [k]BURDEN of Egypt. Be-
hold, the LORD [l]rideth upon a
swift cloud, and shall come into Egypt:
and [m]the idols of Egypt shall be moved
at his presence, and the heart of Egypt
shall melt in the midst of it.
2 And I will [n]set[n] the Egyptians
against the Egyptians: and they shall
fight every one against his brother, and
every one against his neighbour; city

18:1 [f]ch. 20:4,5 Ezek. 30:4,5,9 Zeph. 2:12 & 3:10
18:2 [g]ver. 7
18:3 [h]ch. 5:26
18:7 [i]See Ps. 68:31 & 72:10 ch. 16:1 Zeph. 3:10 Mal. 1:11 [j]ver. 2
19:1 [k]Jer. 46:13 Ezek. 29 & 30 [l]Ps. 18:10 & 104:3 [m]Ex. 12:12 Jer. 43:12
19:2 [n]Judg. 7:22 1 Sam. 14:16,20 2 Chr. 20:23
19:3 [o]ch. 8:19 & 47:12
19:4 [p]ch. 20:4 Jer. 46:26 Ezek. 29:19
19:5 [q]Jer. 51:36 Ezek. 30:12
19:6 [r]2 Ki. 19:24
19:9 [s]1 Ki. 10:28 Prov. 7:16
19:11 [t]Num. 13:22
19:12 [u]1 Cor. 1:20
19:13 [v]Jer. 2:16

against city, *and* kingdom against
kingdom.
3 And the spirit of Egypt [o]shall fail
in the midst thereof; and I will [p]de-
stroy the counsel thereof: and they
shall [o]seek to the idols, and to the
charmers, and to them that have famil-
iar spirits, and to the wizards.
4 And the Egyptians will I [q]give
over [p]into the hand of a cruel lord; and
a fierce king shall rule over them, saith
the Lord, the LORD of hosts.
5 [q]And the waters shall fail from
the sea, and the river shall be wasted
and dried up.
6 And they shall turn the rivers far
away; *and* the brooks [r]of defence
shall be emptied and dried up: the
reeds and flags shall wither.
7 The paper reeds by the brooks, by
the mouth of the brooks, and every
thing sown by the brooks, shall wither,
be driven away, [r]and be no *more.*
8 The fishers also shall mourn, and
all they that cast angle into the brooks
shall lament, and they that spread nets
upon the waters shall languish.
9 Moreover they that work in [s]fine
flax, and they that weave [s]networks,
shall be confounded.
10 And they shall be broken in the
[t]purposes thereof, all that make
sluices *and* ponds [u]for fish.
11 ¶ Surely the princes of [t]Zoan
are fools, the counsel of the wise coun-
sellors of Pharaoh is become brutish:
how say ye unto Pharaoh, I *am* the son
of the wise, the son of ancient kings?
12 [u]Where *are* they? where *are* thy
wise *men?* and let them tell thee now,
and let them know what the LORD of
hosts hath purposed upon Egypt.
13 The princes of Zoan are become
fools, [v]the princes of Noph are de-

[h] Or, *outspread and polished* [i] Or, *a nation that meteth out, and treadeth down* [j] Heb. *a nation of line, line, and treading under foot* [k] Or, *whose land the rivers despise* [l] Or, *regard my set dwelling* [m] Or, *after rain* [n] Heb. *mingle* [o] Heb. *shall be emptied* [p] Heb. *swallow up* [q] Or, *shut up* [r] Heb. *and shall not be foundations* [s] Or, *white works* [t] Heb. *foundations* [u] Heb. *of living things*

18:1 ETHIOPIA. Ethiopia (or Cush) was south of Egypt. Its king at that time ruled all of Egypt. He evidently had sent messengers to Israel in order to seek an alliance against Assyria (v. 2). God Himself would defeat the Assyrian enemy in His own time (vv. 3–6). After the Assyrian defeat, the people of Cush would bring gifts to Jerusalem (v. 7).

19:1–15 EGYPT. Isaiah foretells a judgment of God coming upon Egypt. Consequently, it would do Judah no good to align herself with Egypt against the invading Assyrians.

ceived; they have also seduced Egypt, *even* [v] [w]*they that are* the stay of the tribes thereof.

14 The LORD hath mingled [w]a[x] perverse spirit in the midst thereof: and they have caused Egypt to err in every work thereof, as a drunken *man* staggereth in his vomit.

15 Neither shall there be *any* work for Egypt, which [x]the head or tail, branch or rush, may do.

16 In that day shall Egypt [y]be like unto women: and it shall be afraid and fear because of the shaking of the hand of the LORD of hosts, [z]which he shaketh over it.

17 And the land of Judah shall be a terror unto Egypt, every one that maketh mention thereof shall be afraid in himself, because of the counsel of the LORD of hosts, which he hath determined against it.

18 ¶ In that day shall five cities in the land of Egypt [a]speak [y]the language of Canaan, and swear to the LORD of hosts; one shall be called, The city [z]of destruction.

19 In that day [b]shall there be an altar to the LORD in the midst of the land of Egypt, and a pillar at the border thereof to the LORD.

20 And [c]it shall be for a sign and for a witness unto the LORD of hosts in the land of Egypt: for they shall cry unto the LORD because of the oppressors, and he shall send them a saviour, and a great one, and he shall deliver them.

21 And the LORD shall be known to Egypt, and the Egyptians shall know the LORD in that day, and [d]shall do sacrifice and oblation; yea, they shall vow a vow unto the LORD, and perform *it.*

22 And the LORD shall smite Egypt: he shall smite and heal *it:* and they shall return *even* to the LORD, and he shall be entreated of them, and shall heal them.

23 ¶ In that day [e]shall there be a highway out of Egypt to Assyria, and the Assyrian shall come into Egypt, and the Egyptian into Assyria, and the Egyptians shall serve with the Assyrians.

24 In that day shall Israel be the third with Egypt and with Assyria, *even* a blessing in the midst of the land:

25 Whom the LORD of hosts shall bless, saying, Blessed *be* Egypt my people, and Assyria [f]the work of my hands, and Israel mine inheritance.

20 IN THE year that [g]Tartan came unto Ashdod, (when Sargon the king of Assyria sent him,) and fought against Ashdod, and took it;

2 At the same time spake the LORD [a]by Isaiah the son of Amoz, saying, Go and loose [h]the sackcloth from off thy loins, and put off thy shoe from thy foot. And he did so, [i]walking naked and barefoot.

3 And the LORD said, Like as my servant Isaiah hath walked naked and

19:14 [w]1 Ki. 22:22 ch. 29:10
19:15 [x]ch. 9:14
19:16 [y]Jer. 51:30 Nah. 3:13 [z]ch. 11:15
19:18 [a]Zeph. 3:9
19:19 [b]Gen. 28:18 Ex. 24:4 Josh. 22:10,26,27
19:20 [c]Josh. 4:20 & 22:27
19:21 [d]Mal. 1:11
19:23 [e]ch. 11:16
19:25 [f]Ps. 100:3 ch. 29:23 Hos. 2:23 Eph. 2:10
20:1 [g]2 Ki. 18:17
20:2 [h]Zech. 13:4 [i]1 Sam. 19:24 Mic. 1:8,11

[v] Or, *governors* [w] Heb. *corners* [x] Heb. *a spirit of perverseness* [y] Heb. *the lip* [z] Or, *of Heres,* or, *of the sun* [a] Heb. *by the hand of Isaiah*

19:16–25 IN THAT DAY. Isaiah gives four prophecies to be fulfilled "in that day." (1) The Egyptians would fear Judah when they realized their judgment had come from God (vv. 16–17). (2) After a time of affliction, cities in Egypt would worship the Lord and altars would be erected to Him (vv. 18–19). (3) The Egyptians would cry out to God, who would send them a Savior, and many would turn to the Lord (vv. 20–22). (4) Egypt, Assyria, and Israel would all worship the Lord together (vv. 23–25). Though "that day" is not clearly identified here, other Scriptures suggest that it refers to end-time events associated with the tribulation period (cf. Rev. 4—19) and the millennial rule of Christ (cf. Rev. 20).

19:25 THE LORD OF HOSTS SHALL BLESS . . . EGYPT . . . ASSYRIA . . . ISRAEL. This will ultimately be fulfilled at the end of the age when all nations of the earth will be blessed (Gen. 12:3) during the righteous reign of the Messiah, Jesus Christ (cf. 2:2–4; 11:1–10). One day the God of Israel will be the God of Arabs, Jews, and all other peoples and nations.

20:1 ASHDOD. The attack on this Philistine city probably occurred in 711 B.C.

20:2 WALKING NAKED AND BAREFOOTED. Isaiah was to appear in public stripped of his outer clothes for three years as an enacted parable or sign of what would happen to Egypt and Cush when Assyria carried them into captivity. The message was intended to warn Judah not to trust in an alliance with Egypt, but rather to look to the Lord their God. Isaiah may not have been completely naked (see 2 Sam. 6:20, note; John 21:7, note), but rather stripped to a loin cloth. Perhaps he conducted himself in this humiliating manner only a portion of each day.

20:3 ISAIAH . . . A SIGN AND WONDER. Isaiah obeyed God even though it meant shame and embarrassment to him for three years. If our obedience to God and our separation from ungodly ways are as they should be, then we can also expect sometimes to suffer reproach, embarrassment, and humiliation. Righteousness and persecution

barefoot three years [j]*for* a sign and
wonder upon Egypt and upon Ethiopia;
4 So shall the king of Assyria lead
away [b]the Egyptians prisoners, and
the Ethiopians captives, young and
old, naked and barefoot, [k]even with
their buttocks uncovered, to the
[c]shame of Egypt.
5 [l]And they shall be afraid and
ashamed of Ethiopia their expectation,
and of Egypt their glory.
6 And the inhabitant of this [d]isle
shall say in that day, Behold, such *is*
our expectation, whither we flee for
help to be delivered from the king of
Assyria: and how shall we escape?

Elam and Media defeat Babylon

21 THE BURDEN of the desert of
the sea. As [m]whirlwinds in the
south pass through; *so* it cometh from
the desert, from a terrible land.
2 A [e]grievous vision is declared
unto me; [n]the treacherous dealer
dealeth treacherously, and the spoiler
spoileth. [o]Go up, O Elam: besiege, O
Media; all the sighing thereof have I
made to cease.
3 Therefore [p]are my loins filled
with pain: [q]pangs have taken hold
upon me, as the pangs of a woman that
travaileth: I was bowed down at the
hearing *of it;* I was dismayed at the see-
ing *of it.*
4 [f]My heart panted, fearfulness af-
frighted me: [r]the night of my pleasure
hath he [g]turned into fear unto me.
5 [s]Prepare the table, watch in the
watchtower, eat, drink: arise, ye
princes, *and* anoint the shield.
6 For thus hath the Lord said unto
me, Go, set a watchman, let him de-
clare what he seeth.
7 [t]And he saw a chariot *with* a cou-
ple of horsemen, a chariot of asses, *and*
a chariot of camels; and he hearkened
diligently with much heed:
8 And [h]he cried, A lion: My lord, I
stand continually upon the [u]watch-
tower in the daytime, and I am set in
my ward [i]whole nights:
9 And, behold, here cometh a chari-
ot of men, *with* a couple of horsemen.
And he answered and said, [v]Babylon
is fallen, is fallen; and [w]all the graven
images of her gods he hath broken
unto the ground.
10 [x]O my threshing, and the
[j]corn of my floor: that which I have
heard of the LORD of hosts, the God of
Israel, have I declared unto you.
11 ¶ [y]The burden of Dumah. He
calleth to me out of Seir, Watchman,
what of the night? Watchman, what of
the night?
12 The watchman said, The morn-
ing cometh, and also the night: if ye
will inquire, inquire ye: return, come.
13 ¶ [z]The burden upon Arabia. In
the forest in Arabia shall ye lodge,
O ye travelling companies [a]of Deda-
nim.
14 The inhabitants of the land of
Tema [k]brought water to him that was
thirsty, they prevented with their
bread him that fled.
15 For they fled [l] [m]from the
swords, from the drawn sword, and
from the bent bow, and from the griev-
ousness of war.
16 For thus hath the Lord said unto

20:3 [j]ch. 8:18 **20:4** [k]2 Sam. 10:4 ch. 3:17 Jer. 13:22 Mic. 1:11 **20:5** [l]2 Ki. 18:21 **21:1** [m]Zech. 9:14 **21:2** [n]ch. 33:1 [o]ch. 13:17 Jer. 49:34 **21:3** [p]ch. 15:5 & 16:11 [q]ch. 13:8 **21:4** [r]Deut. 28:67 **21:5** [s]Dan. 5:5 **21:7** [t]ver. 9 **21:8** [u]Hab. 2:1 **21:9** [v]Jer. 51:8 Rev. 14:8 & 18:2 [w]ch. 46:1 Jer. 50:2 & 51:44 **21:10** [x]Jer. 51:33 **21:11** [y]1 Chr. 1:30 Jer. 49:7,8 Ezek. 35:2 Obad. 1 **21:13** [z]Jer. 49:28 [a]1 Chr. 1:9

[b]Heb. *the captivity of Egypt* [c]Heb. *nakedness* [d]Or, *country* [e]Heb. *hard* [f]Or, *My mind wandered* [g]Heb. *put* [h]Or, *cried as a lion* [i]Or, *every night* [j]Heb. *son* [k]Or, *bring ye* [l]Or, *for fear* [m]Heb. *from the face*

often go together (see Mat. 5:10, note).

21:1–10 THE DESERT OF THE SEA. God gives Isaiah a second vision of the downfall and destruction of Babylon, which lay just north of the Persian Gulf (see ch. 13, notes).

21:2 ELAM. Elam was located east of the Tigris River and Babylon, bordered on the north by Media and Assyria and on the south by the Persian Gulf. The Elamites were allied with the Medo-Persian army when Babylon was conquered in 539 B.C. The Elamite city of Susa became an important capital of the Persian empire.

21:9 BABYLON IS FALLEN. Babylon, the enemy of God's people, would fall, its reliance on false gods shattered; this fall first took place in 689 B.C., when Sennacherib smashed their idols (except for Bel and Nebo, see ch. 46). The apostle John heard the same words in his visions (Rev. 14:8; 18:1–2), prophesying that the end-time Babylon, a symbol of all that opposes Christ and His people in this world, would be destroyed. At that time, Christ will complete the redemption of His people. Believers must pray for the fall and destruction of end-time Babylon (see Rev. 17:1–5, notes; 18:2–21, notes).

21:11 DUMAH. Dumah is an alternate name for Edom, the land of Esau's descendants. Edom was located immediately south of Judah and the Dead Sea (see also 34:5–15).

21:13 ARABIA. Arabia was located between Edom and Babylon. It would experience warfare and defeat at the hands of invaders, fulfilled when the Assyrians attacked the Arabians in 732 and 725 B.C. (cf. Jer. 25:17,24); Sennarcherib also conquered Arabia in 688 B.C. and took the title "King of Arabia."

me, Within a year, [b]according to the
years of an hireling, and all the glory
of [c]Kedar shall fail:
17 And the residue of the number of
[n]archers, the mighty men of the chil-
dren of Kedar, shall be diminished: for
the LORD God of Israel hath spoken *it.*

A burden about Jerusalem

22 THE BURDEN of the valley of
vision. What aileth thee now,
that thou art wholly gone up to the
housetops?
2 Thou that art full of stirs, a tumul-
tuous city, [d]a joyous city: thy slain
men are not slain with the sword, nor
dead in battle.
3 All thy rulers are fled together,
they are bound [o]by the archers: all
that are found in thee are bound to-
gether, *which* have fled from far.
4 Therefore said I, Look away from
me; [e]I[p] will weep bitterly, labour not
to comfort me, because of the spoiling
of the daughter of my people.
5 [f]For *it is* a day of trouble, and of
treading down, and of perplexity [g]by
the Lord GOD of hosts in the valley of
vision, breaking down the walls, and of
crying to the mountains.
6 [h]And Elam bare the quiver with
chariots of men *and* horsemen, and
[i]Kir [q]uncovered the shield.
7 And it shall come to pass, *that*
[r]thy choicest valleys shall be full of
chariots, and the horsemen shall set
themselves in array [s]at the gate.
8 ¶ And he discovered the covering
of Judah, and thou didst look in that
day to the armour [j]of the house of the
forest.
9 [k]Ye have seen also the breaches
of the city of David, that they are many:
and ye gathered together the waters of
the lower pool.
10 And ye have numbered the
houses of Jerusalem, and the houses
have ye broken down to fortify the
wall.
11 [l]Ye made also a ditch between
the two walls for the water of the old
pool: but ye have not looked unto the
maker thereof, neither had respect
unto him that fashioned it long ago.
12 And in that day did the Lord GOD
of hosts [m]call to weeping, and to
mourning, and [n]to baldness, and to
girding with sackcloth:
13 And behold joy and gladness,
slaying oxen, and killing sheep, eating
flesh, and drinking wine: [o]let us eat
and drink; for tomorrow we shall die.
14 [p]And it was revealed in mine
ears by the LORD of hosts, Surely this
iniquity [q]shall not be purged from you
till ye die, saith the Lord GOD of hosts.
15 ¶ Thus saith the Lord GOD of
hosts, Go, get thee unto this treasurer,
even unto [r]Shebna, which *is* over the
house, *and say,*
16 What hast thou here? and whom
hast thou here, that thou hast hewed
thee out a sepulchre here, [t]*as* he
[s]that heweth him out a sepulchre on
high, *and* that graveth an habitation for
himself in a rock?
17 Behold, [u]the LORD will carry
thee away with [v]a mighty captivity,
[t]and will surely cover thee.
18 He will surely violently turn and
toss thee *like* a ball into a [w]large coun-
try: there shalt thou die, and there the
chariots of thy glory *shall be* the shame
of thy lord's house.
19 And I will drive thee from thy
station, and from thy state shall he pull
thee down.

21:16 [b]ch. 16:14 [c]Ps. 120:5 ch. 60:7
22:2 [d]ch. 32:13
22:4 [e]Jer. 4:19
22:5 [f]ch. 37:3 [g]Lam. 1:5
22:6 [h]Jer. 49:35 [i]ch. 15:1
22:8 [j]1 Ki. 7:2 & 10:17
22:9 [k]2 Ki. 20:20 2 Chr. 32:4
22:11 [l]Neh. 3:16
22:12 [m]Joel 1:13 [n]See Ezra 9:3 ch. 15:2 Mic. 1:16
22:13 [o]ch. 56:12 1 Cor. 15:32
22:14 [p]ch. 5:9 [q]1 Sam. 3:14 Ezek. 24:13
22:15 [r]2 Ki. 18:37 ch. 36:3
22:16 [s]See 2 Sam. 18:18 Mat. 27:60
22:17 [t]Esth. 7:8

[n] Heb. *bows* [o] Heb. *of the bow* [p] Heb. *I will be bitter in weeping* [q] Heb. *made naked* [r] Heb. *the choice of thy valleys* [s] Or, *toward* [t] Or, *O he* [u] Or, *the LORD who covered thee with an excellent covering, and clothed thee gorgeously, shall surely* [v] Heb. *the captivity of a man* [w] Heb. *large of spaces*

22:1 THE VALLEY OF VISION. This name refers to Jerusalem or to the valley near Jerusalem where God had revealed Himself in prophetic visions. God here rebukes the inhabitants of Jerusalem for their frivolous attitude in the midst of grave danger and apostasy (vv. 1–14).

22:4 I WILL WEEP BITTERLY. Isaiah, a true prophet, felt deeply the tragedy of a fallen and apostate people. God's people were being destroyed, and he grieved for them and for his betrayed God. While others were experiencing joy and revelry (vv. 12–13), the prophet had to share the sorrow of God (see next note).

22:12–13 CALL TO WEEPING. When God's people compromise with the world and turn away from obeying God's righteous ways, He calls them to repent, confess their spiritual poverty, and seek His face. Christ wants all churches to examine their spiritual state in the light of the N.T. and its standards (cf. Rev. 2—3). Like Isaiah, today's prophets should call for repentance, humility, tears, prayer, and fasting, rather than for frivolity.

22:15–25 SHEBNA. God pronounces judgment against a corrupt government official named Shebna, who was to be replaced by Eliakim, a godly ruler (cf. v. 20).

20 ¶ And it shall come to pass in
that day, that I will call my servant
[u]Eliakim the son of Hilkiah:
21 And I will clothe him with thy
robe, and strengthen him with thy gir-
dle, and I will commit thy government
into his hand: and he shall be a father
to the inhabitants of Jerusalem, and to
the house of Judah.
22 And the key of the house of Da-
vid will I lay upon his shoulder; so he
shall [v]open, and none shall shut; and
he shall shut, and none shall open.
23 And I will fasten him *as* [w]a nail
in a sure place; and he shall be for a
glorious throne to his father's house.
24 And they shall hang upon him all
the glory of his father's house, the off-
spring and the issue, all vessels of
small quantity, from the vessels of
cups, even to all the [x]vessels of flag-
ons.
25 In that day, saith the LORD of
hosts, shall the nail that is fastened in
the sure place be removed, and be cut
down, and fall; and the burden that *was*
upon it shall be cut off: for the LORD
hath spoken *it.*

A burden about Tyre

23 THE [x]BURDEN of Tyre. Howl,
ye ships of Tarshish; for it is
laid waste, so that there is no house,
no entering in: [y]from the land of Chit-
tim it is revealed to them.
2 Be [y]still, ye inhabitants of the
isle; thou whom the merchants of Zi-
don, that pass over the sea, have re-
plenished.
3 And by great waters the seed of
Sihor, the harvest of the river, *is* her
revenue; and [z]she is a mart of na-
tions.
4 Be thou ashamed, O Zidon: for the
sea hath spoken, *even* the strength of
the sea, saying, I travail not, nor bring
forth children, neither do I nourish up
young men, *nor* bring up virgins.
5 [a]As at the report concerning
Egypt, *so* shall they be sorely pained at
the report of Tyre.
6 Pass ye over to Tarshish; howl, ye
inhabitants of the isle.
7 *Is* this your [b]joyous *city,* whose
antiquity *is* of ancient days? her own
feet shall carry her [z]afar off to so-
journ.
8 Who hath taken this counsel
against Tyre, [c]the crowning *city,*
whose merchants *are* princes, whose
traffickers *are* the honourable of the
earth?
9 The LORD of hosts hath purposed
it, [a]to stain the pride of all glory, *and*
to bring into contempt all the honour-
able of the earth.
10 Pass through thy land as a river,
O daughter of Tarshish: *there is* no
more [b]strength.
11 He stretched out his hand over
the sea, he shook the kingdoms: the
LORD hath given a commandment
[c]against [d]the merchant *city,* to de-
stroy the [e]strong holds thereof.
12 And he said, [d]Thou shalt no
more rejoice, O thou oppressed virgin,
daughter of Zidon: arise, [e]pass over to
Chittim; there also shalt thou have no
rest.
13 Behold the land of the Chalde-
ans; this people was not, *till* the Assyr-
ian founded it for [f]them that dwell in
the wilderness: they set up the towers
thereof, they raised up the palaces
thereof; *and* he brought it to ruin.
14 Howl, ye ships of Tarshish: for
your strength is laid waste.
15 And it shall come to pass in that
day, that Tyre shall be forgotten seven-
ty years, according to the days of one
king: after the end of seventy years
[f]shall Tyre sing as an harlot.
16 Take an harp, go about the city,
thou harlot that hast been forgotten;
make sweet melody, sing many songs,
that thou mayest be remembered.
17 ¶ And it shall come to pass after

22:20 [u]2 Ki. 18:18
22:22 [v]Job 12:14
22:23 [w]Ezra 9:8
23:1 [x]Jer. 25:22 & 47:4 Ezek. 26 & 27 & 28 Amos 1:9 Zech. 9:2,4 [y]ver. 12
23:3 [z]Ezek. 27:3
23:5 [a]ch. 19:16
23:7 [b]ch. 22:2
23:8 [c]See Ezek. 28:2, 12
23:12 [d]Rev. 18:22 [e]ver. 1
23:13 [f]Ps. 72:9

[x] Or, *instruments of viols* [y] Heb. *silent*
[z] Heb. *from afar off* [a] Heb. *to pollute*
[b] Heb. *girdle* [c] Or, *concerning a merchantman*
[d] Heb. *Canaan* [e] Or, *strengths* [f] Heb. *it shall be unto Tyre as the song of an harlot*

23:1 TYRE. Tyre was a Phoenician center for world commerce on the east coast of the Mediterranean Sea just north of Palestine. Its citizens were wealthy, but also evil and full of pride. Thus Isaiah prophesied that God would bring that city down for seventy years and then restore it for a time (vv. 8–9,17–18). God's people would once again engage in trade with Tyre.

23:13 THE LAND OF THE CHALDEANS. The land of Chaldea was the region of which Babylon was the chief city. Nebuchadnezzar, one of its kings, invaded Tyre in 572 B.C., approximately one hundred years after Isaiah made this prophecy.

23:17 SHALL COMMIT FORNICATION. Tyre would "commit fornication" with the nations by using sinful and dishonest commercial practices, accompanied by immoral activity, to gain wealth from other nations.

the end of seventy years, that the LORD
will visit Tyre, and she shall turn to her
hire, and [g]shall commit fornication
with all the kingdoms of the world
upon the face of the earth.
18 And her merchandise and her
hire [h]shall be holiness to the LORD: it
shall not be treasured nor laid up; for
her merchandise shall be for them that
dwell before the LORD, to eat sufficiently, and for [g]durable clothing.

Judgment for universal sin

24 BEHOLD, THE LORD maketh
the earth empty, and maketh it
waste, and [h]turneth it upside down,
and scattereth abroad the inhabitants
thereof.
2 And it shall be, as with the people,
so with the [i]priest;[i] as with the servant, so with his master; as with the
maid, so with her mistress; [j]as with
the buyer, so with the seller; as with
the lender, so with the borrower; as
with the taker of usury, so with the giver of usury to him.
3 The land shall be utterly emptied,
and utterly spoiled: for the LORD hath
spoken this word.
4 The earth mourneth *and* fadeth
away, the world languisheth *and* fadeth
away, [j]the haughty people of the
earth do languish.
5 [k]The earth also is defiled under
the inhabitants thereof; because they
have transgressed the laws, changed
the ordinance, broken the everlasting
covenant.

6 Therefore hath [l]the curse devoured the earth, and they that dwell
therein are desolate: therefore the inhabitants of the earth are burned, and
few men left.
7 [m]The new wine mourneth, the
vine languisheth, all the merryhearted
do sigh.
8 The mirth [n]of tabrets ceaseth,
the noise of them that rejoice endeth,
the joy of the harp ceaseth.
9 They shall not drink wine with a
song; strong drink shall be bitter to
them that drink it.
10 The city of confusion is broken
down: every house is shut up, that no
man may come in.
11 *There is* a crying for wine in the
streets; all joy is darkened, the mirth
of the land is gone.
12 In the city is left desolation, and
the gate is smitten with destruction.
13 ¶ When thus it shall be in the
midst of the land among the people,
[o]*there shall be* as the shaking of an olive tree, *and* as the gleaning grapes
when the vintage is done.
14 They shall lift up their voice,
they shall sing for the majesty of the
LORD, they shall cry aloud from the sea.
15 Wherefore glorify ye the LORD in
the [k]fires, *even* [p]the name of the LORD
God of Israel in the isles of the sea.
16 ¶ From the [l]uttermost part of
the earth have we heard songs, *even*

23:17 [g]Rev. 17:2 **23:18** [h]Zech. 14:20,21 **24:2** [i]Hos. 4:9 [j]Ezek. 7:12,13 **24:5** [k]Gen. 3:17 Num. 35:33 **24:6** [l]Mal. 4:6 **24:7** [m]ch. 16:8,9 Joel 1:10,12 **24:8** [n]Jer. 7:34 & 16:9 & 25:10 Ezek. 26:13 Hos. 2:11 Rev. 18:22 **24:13** [o]ch. 17:5,6 **24:15** [p]Mal. 1:11

[g] Heb. *old* [h] Heb. *perverteth the face thereof* [i] Or, *prince* [j] Heb. *the height of the people* [k] Or, *valleys* [l] Heb. *wing*

24:1—27:13 BEHOLD. These chapters deal with end-time events in apocalyptic language, the type of language used in the book of Revelation. They speak of God's judgment against the world for its sin and of the blessings He has prepared for His people.

24:1 THE LORD MAKETH THE EARTH EMPTY. This chapter describes God's coming judgment upon the whole earth and its inhabitants. He will completely destroy most of the earth and its inhabitants. This time of world desolation is called the great tribulation in the N.T. (cf. Mat. 24:15–21; 1 Thes. 5:1–3; Rev. 6; 8—9; 15—16; 18—19; see article on THE GREAT TRIBULATION, p. 1456). After this worldwide judgment, Christ will return to rule over the righteous of the earth (Rev. 19—20).

24:5 THE EARTH IS ALSO DEFILED. God's wrath will come upon the world because humankind has defiled the earth with sin, immorality, and wickedness. At the present time, sin predominates, but at the end time God ordains a dreadful and inescapable doom to come upon all those who take pleasure in unrighteousness (see 1 Thes. 5:2, note; 2 Thes. 2:12, note).

24:6 THE INHABITANTS OF THE EARTH ARE BURNED. The wages of sin are death and destruction (cf. Rom. 6:23). This truth is demonstrated on an international scale at the end of time when all who do not repent and turn to God will be destroyed. The devastation will be like that of a fire that burns and devours completely (cf. 1:31; 5:24; 9:18; 10:16–17; 29:6; 30:27; Zech. 5:3–4; Rev. 19:11–21).

24:14 THEY SHALL LIFT UP THEIR VOICE ... SING. The righteous who remain faithful to God will rejoice and give Him glory when they see the destruction of this corrupt world system. They will delight in the defeat of sin and evil (see Rev. 18:20, where the angels and believers are commanded to rejoice in God's righteous judgment against Satan's system and the wickedness of humankind).

24:16 WOE UNTO ME! In contrast to the rejoicing about the coming victory over evil, Isaiah is distressed by the sin and treachery around him.

glory to the righteous. But I said, [m]My
leanness, my leanness, woe unto me!
[q]the treacherous dealers have dealt
treacherously; yea, the treacherous
dealers have dealt very treacherously.
17 [r]Fear, and the pit, and the
snare, *are* upon thee, O inhabitant of
the earth.
18 And it shall come to pass, *that* he
who fleeth from the noise of the fear
shall fall into the pit; and he that com-
eth up out of the midst of the pit
shall be taken in the snare: for [s]the
windows from on high are open,
and [t]the foundations of the earth do
shake.
19 [u]The earth is utterly broken
down, the earth is clean dissolved, the
earth is moved exceedingly.
20 The earth shall [v]reel to and fro
like a drunkard, and shall be removed
like a cottage; and the transgression
thereof shall be heavy upon it; and it
shall fall, and not rise again.
21 And it shall come to pass in that
day, *that* the LORD shall [n]punish the
host of the high ones *that are* on high,
[w]and the kings of the earth upon the
earth.
22 And they shall be gathered to-
gether, [o]*as* prisoners are gathered in
the [p]pit, and shall be shut up in the
prison, and after many days shall they
be [q]visited.
23 Then the [x]moon shall be con-
founded, and the sun ashamed, when
the LORD of hosts shall [y]reign in

24:16 [q]Jer. 5:11
24:17 [r]See Jer. 48:43,44
24:18 [s]Gen. 7:11 [t]Ps. 18:7
24:19 [u]Jer. 4:23
24:20 [v]ch. 19:14
24:21 [w]Ps. 76:12
24:23 [x]ch. 13:10 & 60:19 Ezek. 32:7 Joel 2:31 & 3:15 [y]Rev. 19:4,6 [z]Heb. 12:22
25:1 [a]Ex. 15:2 [b]Ps. 98:1 [c]Num. 23:19
25:2 [d]ch. 21:9 & 23:13 Jer. 51:37
25:3 [e]Rev. 11:13
25:4 [f]ch. 4:6
25:6 [g]ch. 2:2,3 [h]Prov. 9:2 Mat. 22:4 [i]Dan. 7:14 Mat. 8:11

[z]mount Zion, and in Jerusalem, and
[r]before his ancients gloriously. Dan. 10:11

Praise the LORD

25 O LORD, thou *art* my God; [a]I
will exalt thee, I will praise thy
name; [b]for thou hast done wonderful
things; [c]*thy* counsels of old *are* faith-
fulness *and* truth.
2 For thou hast made [d]of a city an
heap; *of* a defenced city a ruin: a palace
of strangers to be no city; it shall never
be built.
3 Therefore shall the strong people
[e]glorify thee, the city of the terrible
nations shall fear thee.
4 For thou hast been a strength to
the poor, a strength to the needy in his
distress, [f]a refuge from the storm, a
shadow from the heat, when the blast
of the terrible ones *is* as a storm *against*
the wall.
5 Thou shalt bring down the noise
of strangers, as the heat in a dry place;
even the heat with the shadow of a
cloud: the branch of the terrible ones
shall be brought low.
6 ¶ And in [g]this mountain shall
[h]the LORD of hosts make unto [i]all
people a feast of fat things, a feast of
wines on the lees, of fat things full of

[m] Heb. *Leanness to me,* or, *My secret to me* [n] Heb. *visit upon* [o] Heb. *with the gathering of prisoners* [p] Or, *dungeon* [q] Or, *found wanting* [r] Or, there shall be *glory before his ancients*

24:17 FEAR, AND THE PIT . . . *ARE* UPON THEE. Jesus taught that the only way believers can escape "all these things that shall come to pass" (Luke 21:36) is by guarding against sin in their lives and persevering in prayer for the grace of God (see Luke 21:34,36, notes).

24:21 PUNISH THE HOST OF THE HIGH ONES. These powers are satanic and demonic spiritual forces opposed to God (see Eph. 6:11–12; Rev. 20:1–3; see Rev. 12:7–9, note). At the end of history, they will be shut up in prison (see Rev. 20:1–3), judged, and punished (Rev. 20:11–15,20).

24:23 THE LORD OF HOSTS SHALL REIGN. After casting down all evil powers, God's kingdom will come to the earth and the Lord will reign there (cf. Rev. 20:1–4; 21:1–9). Only then will God receive the honor and glory due Him.

25:1–12 I WILL PRAISE THY NAME. Isaiah praises the Lord for the defeat of everyone and everything that opposed His righteous purpose and kingdom, and for His role as the deliverer and comforter of His people.

25:6 THIS MOUNTAIN. Isaiah prophesies about the future kingdom and salvation that will come after Christ's return to earth (vv. 6–12; cf. Rev. 19—21). This "mountain" refers to Mount Zion, or Jerusalem (cf. 2:1–4; 24:23; Rev. 21:1–2); "all people" indicates the success of the proclamation of the gospel around the world.

25:6 FAT THINGS . . . WINES ON THE LEES. The lavish banquet to be enjoyed in the kingdom of God represents the wonderful blessings that believers will experience in His presence. "Lees" (Heb. *shemarim*) originally signified "holders" or "preservers." Thus "a feast of wines on the lees" literally translates "a feast of preserves," probably referring to the juice of the grape that had been preserved and kept for a long period of time. Note Jer. 48:11–12, where God compares Moab to juice remaining on his lees and therefore "his taste remained in him, and his scent is not changed"—meaning that God's blessings kept in store for centuries for His faithful people will not change in purpose from His original intention (see article on WINE IN THE OLD TESTAMENT, p. 220).

marrow, of wines on the lees well refined.

7 And he will [s]destroy in this mountain the face of the covering [t]cast over all people, and [j]the veil that is spread over all nations.

8 He will [k]swallow up death in victory; and the Lord GOD will [l]wipe away tears from off all faces; and the rebuke of his people shall he take away from off all the earth: for the LORD hath spoken *it.*

Is. 43:11-13 9 ¶ And it shall be said in that day, Lo, this *is* our God; [m]we have waited for him, and he will save us: this *is* the LORD; we have waited for him, [n]we will be glad and rejoice in his salvation.

10 For in this mountain shall the hand of the LORD rest, and Moab shall be [u]trodden down under him, even as straw is [v]trodden down for the dunghill.

11 And he shall spread forth his hands in the midst of them, as he that swimmeth spreadeth forth *his hands* to swim: and he shall bring down their pride together with the spoils of their hands.

12 And the [o]fortress of the high fort of thy walls shall he bring down, lay low, *and* bring to the ground, *even* to the dust.

Song of rejoicing in Judah

26 IN [p]THAT day shall this song be sung in the land of Judah; We have a strong city; [q]salvation will *God* appoint *for* walls and bulwarks.

2 [r]Open ye the gates, that the righteous nation which keepeth the [w]truth may enter in.

3 Thou wilt keep *him* in [x]perfect peace, *whose* [y]mind *is* stayed *on thee:* because he trusteth in thee.

4 Trust ye in the LORD for ever: [s]for in the LORD JEHOVAH *is* [t]everlasting[z] strength: Is. 42:10-12

5 ¶ For he bringeth down them that dwell on high; [u]the lofty city, he layeth it low; he layeth it low, *even* to the ground; he bringeth it *even* to the dust.

6 The foot shall tread it down, *even* the feet of the poor, *and* the steps of the needy.

7 The way of the just *is* uprightness: [v]thou, most upright, dost weigh the path of the just.

8 Yea, [w]in the way of thy judgments, O LORD, have we waited for thee; the desire of *our* soul *is* to thy name, and to the remembrance of thee.

9 [x]With my soul have I desired thee in the night; yea, with my spirit within me will I seek thee early: for when thy judgments *are* in the earth,

25:7 [j]2 Cor. 3:15 Eph. 4:18 **25:8** [k]Hos. 13:14 1 Cor. 15:54 [l]Rev. 7:17 & 21:4 **25:9** [m]Gen. 49:18 Tit. 2:13 [n]Ps. 20:5 **25:12** [o]ch. 26:5 **26:1** [p]ch. 2:11 [q]ch. 60:18 **26:2** [r]Ps. 118:19,20 **26:4** [s]ch. 45:17 [t]Deut. 32:4 **26:5** [u]ch. 25:12 & 32:19 **26:7** [v]Ps. 37:23 **26:8** [w]ch. 64:5 **26:9** [x]Ps. 63:6 Sol. 3:1

[s] Heb. *swallow up* [t] Heb. *covered* [u] Or, *threshed* [v] Or, *threshed in Madmenah* [w] Heb. *truths* [x] Heb. *peace, peace;* see ch. 57:19 [y] Or, *thought,* or, *imagination* [z] Heb. *the rock of ages*

25:8 SWALLOW UP DEATH IN VICTORY . . . WIPE AWAY TEARS. In God's future kingdom all the sorrow, misery, and death that now prevail on the earth will be removed and never again reappear (see the N.T. expression of this truth in 1 Cor. 15:54; Rev. 21:4). Like a caring parent, God Himself will wipe away all the tears from the eyes of His children, and there will never again be a reason for tears and grief. These glorious blessings will occur only when Christ returns to earth, triumphs over evil, and reigns over all creation. Such promises should lead us to see the Lord's great love and compassion for us and cause us to pray earnestly and ceaselessly for the glorious consummation of redemption through Christ.

25:9 WE HAVE WAITED FOR HIM. Isaiah describes the faithful in God's kingdom as those who have waited for the Lord. All believers should wait expectantly for the return of our Lord and the fulfillment of all His promises (see Luke 2:25, note; 1 Cor. 1:7; Tit. 2:13).

26:1–21 THIS SONG. Confident that God will accomplish His redemptive purpose, the saints break forth into praise and prayer. Their song concerns God's triumphant destruction of all evil and the establishment of His kingdom.

26:3 PEACE, *WHOSE* MIND *IS* STAYED *ON THEE.* As the trying and stressful days of the end of history occur, God will keep in perfect peace the remnant who remain steadfast and faithful to their Lord. In times of trouble we must continually strive to keep our minds turned to the Lord in prayer, trust, and hope. We must place our trust in Him because He is a Rock who endures forever (v. 4); He is a sure and firm foundation.

26:8–9 WE WAITED FOR THEE. During the final days of history the righteous will wait (i.e., long for) the appearing of their Lord. (1) Isaiah describes that longing as an earnest yearning for the final manifestation of the presence of God and His righteousness upon earth. (2) Faithful believers in Christ should long and pray for the return of their Lord to catch them away from the earth so that they might be with Him forever (see article on THE RAPTURE, p. 1889). They desire (a) the judgments of the Lord to begin so that the ungodly will learn what justice and righteousness are, and (b) the Lord to reign triumphantly forever (cf. Rev. 20—21).

the inhabitants of the world will learn
righteousness.
10 [y]Let favour be shown to the
wicked, *yet* will he not learn righteous-
ness: in [z]the land of uprightness will
he deal unjustly, and will not behold
the majesty of the LORD.
11 LORD, *when* thy hand is lifted up,
[a]they will not see: *but* they shall see,
and be ashamed for *their* envy [a]at the
people; yea, the fire of thine enemies
shall devour them.
12 ¶ LORD, thou wilt ordain peace for
us: for thou also hast wrought all our
works [b]in us.
13 O LORD our God, [b]*other* lords be-
side thee have had dominion over us:
but by thee only will we make mention
of thy name.
14 *They are* dead, they shall not live;
they are deceased, they shall not rise:
therefore hast thou visited and de-
stroyed them, and made all their mem-
ory to perish.
15 Thou hast increased the nation,
O LORD, thou hast increased the na-
tion: thou art glorified: thou hadst re-
moved *it* far *unto* all the ends of the
earth.
16 LORD, [c]in trouble have they vis-
ited thee, they poured out a [c]prayer
when thy chastening *was* upon them.
17 Like as [d]a woman with child,
that draweth near the time of her deliv-
ery, is in pain, *and* crieth out in her
pangs; so have we been in thy sight,
O LORD.
18 We have been with child, we
have been in pain, we have as it were
brought forth wind; we have not
wrought any deliverance in the earth;
neither have [e]the inhabitants of the
world fallen.
19 [f]Thy dead *men* shall live, *togeth-
er with* my dead body shall they arise.
[g]Awake and sing, ye that dwell in
dust: for thy dew *is as* the dew of herbs,
and the earth shall cast out the dead.
20 ¶ Come, my people, [h]enter thou
into thy chambers, and shut thy doors
about thee: hide thyself as it were [i]for
a little moment, until the indignation
be overpast.
21 For, behold, the LORD [j]cometh
out of his place to punish the inhabi-
tants of the earth for their iniquity: the
earth also shall disclose her [d]blood,
and shall no more cover her slain.

26:10 [y]Eccl. 8:12 Rom 2:4 [z]Ps. 143:10 **26:11** [a]Job 34:27 Ps. 28:5 ch. 5:12 **26:13** [b]2 Chr. 12:8 **26:16** [c]Hos. 5:15 **26:17** [d]ch. 13:8 John 16:21 **26:18** [e]Ps. 17:14 **26:19** [f]Ezek. 37:1 [g]Dan. 12:2 **26:20** [h]Ex. 12:22,23 [i]Ps. 30:5 ch. 54:7,8 2 Cor. 4:17 **26:21** [j]Mic. 1:3 Jude 14 **27:1** [k]Ps. 74:13,14 [l]ch. 51:9 Ezek. 29:3 & 32:2 **27:2** [m]ch. 5:1 [n]Ps. 80:8 Jer. 2:21 **27:3** [o]Ps. 121:4,5 **27:4** [p]2 Sam. 23:6 ch. 9:18 **27:5** [q]ch. 25:4 [r]Job 22:21 **27:6** [s]ch. 37:31 Hos. 14:5,6

Israel to be delivered

27 IN THAT day the LORD with his
sore and great and strong
sword shall punish leviathan the
[e]piercing serpent, [k]even leviathan
that crooked serpent; and he shall slay
[l]the dragon that *is* in the sea.
2 In that day [m]sing ye unto her, [n]A
vineyard of red wine.
3 [o]I the LORD do keep it; I will wa-
ter it every moment: lest *any* hurt it, I
will keep it night and day.
4 Fury *is* not in me: who would set
[p]the briers *and* thorns against me in
battle? I would [f]go through them, I
would burn them together.
5 Or let him take hold [q]of my
strength, *that* he may [r]make peace
with me; *and* he shall make peace
with me.
6 He shall cause them that come of
Jacob [s]to take root: Israel shall blos-
som and bud, and fill the face of the
world with fruit. [Is. 32:16-18]
7 ¶ Hath he smitten him, [g]as he

[a] Or, *toward* thy *people* [b] Or, *for us* [c] Heb. *secret speech* [d] Heb. *bloods* [e] Or, *crossing like a bar* [f] Or, *march against* [g] Heb. *according to the stroke of those*

26:16–19 THEY POURED OUT A PRAYER. Isaiah recalls the times when God chastened Israel, and those who remained loyal to God called upon Him in earnest prayer. Although these faithful ones have died, they will rise from the dead and live again upon the earth (see next note).

26:19 MY DEAD BODY SHALL . . . ARISE. This is one of the strongest O.T. declarations of the doctrine of the resurrection of the body (cf. Job 19:26; Ps. 16:10; Dan. 12:2). Those who have faithfully served God (vv. 2–3) will rise from the dead and live again after death (see John 5:28–29; 1 Cor. 15:50–53; Phil. 3:21; see article on THE RESURRECTION OF THE BODY, p. 1799).

26:20–21 ENTER THOU INTO THY CHAMBERS. During the great tribulation, when God punishes the inhabitants of the earth (cf. Mic. 1:3), those who remain faithful to Him will hide themselves and wait before the Lord in prayer until He has accomplished His purposes and the final redemption arrives (see article on THE GREAT TRIBULATION, p. 1456).

27:1 LEVIATHAN . . . SERPENT. This imagery symbolizes evil and the sinful world in revolt against God. At the end of time, all who oppose God will be destroyed (see Rev. 19:11–20, notes).

27:2–6 A VINEYARD. This prophetic song emphasizes God's desire to make Israel a fruitful vineyard. In the kingdom age, Israel will influence the whole earth for God and for righteousness (v. 6).

27:7–11 HATH HE SMITTEN HIM. God

smote those that smote him? *or* is he slain according to the slaughter of them that are slain by him?

8 [t]In measure, [h]when it shooteth forth, thou wilt debate with it: [u]he[i] stayeth his rough wind in the day of the east wind.

9 By this therefore shall the iniquity of Jacob be purged; and this *is* all the fruit to take away his sin; when he maketh all the stones of the altar as chalkstones that are beaten in sunder, the groves and [j]images shall not stand up.

10 Yet the defenced city *shall be* desolate, *and* the habitation forsaken, and left like a wilderness: [v]there shall the calf feed, and there shall he lie down, and consume the branches thereof.

11 When the boughs thereof are withered, they shall be broken off: the women come, *and* set them on fire: for [w]it *is* a people of no understanding: therefore he that made them will not have mercy on them, and [x]he that formed them will show them no favour.

12 ¶ And it shall come to pass in that day, *that* the LORD shall beat off from the channel of the river unto the stream of Egypt, and ye shall be gathered one by one, O ye children of Israel.

13 [y]And it shall come to pass in that day, [z]*that* the great trumpet shall be blown, and they shall come which were ready to perish in the land of Assyria, and the outcasts in the land of Egypt, and shall worship the LORD in the holy mount at Jerusalem.

Woe to Ephraim

28 WOE TO [a]the crown of pride, to the drunkards of Ephraim, whose [b]glorious beauty *is* a fading flower, which *are* on the head of the fat valleys of them that are [k]overcome with wine!

2 Behold, the Lord hath a mighty and strong one, [c]*which* as a tempest of hail *and* a destroying storm, as a flood of mighty waters overflowing, shall cast down to the earth with the hand.

3 [d]The crown of pride, the drunkards of Ephraim, shall be trodden [l]under feet:

4 And [e]the glorious beauty, which *is* on the head of the fat valley, shall be a fading flower, *and* as the hasty fruit before the summer; which *when* he that looketh upon it seeth, while it is yet in his hand he [m]eateth it up.

5 ¶ In that day shall the LORD of hosts be for a crown of glory, and for a diadem of beauty, unto the residue of his people,

6 And for a spirit of judgment to him that sitteth in judgment, and for strength to them that turn the battle to the gate.

7 ¶ But they also [f]have erred through wine, and through strong drink are out of the way; [g]the priest and the prophet have erred through strong drink, they are swallowed up of wine, they are out of the way through strong drink; they err in vision, they stumble *in* judgment.

8 For all tables are full of vomit *and* filthiness, *so that there is* no place *clean*.

9 ¶ [h]Whom shall he teach knowledge? and whom shall he make to understand [n]doctrine? *them that are* weaned from the milk, *and* drawn from the breasts.

10 For precept [o]*must be* upon precept, precept upon precept; line upon

27:8 [t]Job 23:6 Ps. 6:1 Jer. 10:24 & 30:11 & 46:28 1 Cor. 10:13 [u]Ps. 78:38
27:10 [v]See ch. 17:2 & 32:14
27:11 [w]Deut. 32:28 ch. 1:3 Jer. 8:7 [x]Deut. 32:18 ch. 43:1,7 & 44:2,21,24
27:13 [y]ch. 2:11 [z]Mat. 24:31 Rev. 11:15
28:1 [a]ver. 3 [b]ver. 4
28:2 [c]ch. 30:30 Ezek. 13:11
28:3 [d]ver. 1
28:4 [e]ver. 1
28:7 [f]Prov. 20:1 Hos. 4:11 [g]ch. 56:10,12
28:9 [h]Jer. 6:10

[h] Or, *when thou sendest it forth* [i] Or, *when he removeth it* [j] Or, *sun images* [k] Heb. *broken* [l] Heb. *with feet* [m] Heb. *swalloweth* [n] Heb. *the hearing?* [o] Or, hath been

promises not to destroy Israel completely as He will do to many of their enemies. Yet punishment will surely come to many Israelites because of their transgression and their need to be pruned in order to bear fruit again.

27:12–13 YE SHALL BE GATHERED. At the end of time a remnant of Jews will accept Christ as the Messiah and will gather in Jerusalem to worship the Lord (cf. 11:11–16; see Mat. 23:39, note; Rom. 11:1,26, notes; Rev. 12:6, note).

28:1–29 EPHRAIM. In chs. 28—33, Isaiah returns to his own day to prophesy concerning Israel (called Ephraim) and Judah. He denounces their sin and apostasy and reveals God's coming judgment. Yet the judgment will be no more severe than necessary to purify God's chosen people and bring forth a holy remnant.

28:7 ERRED THROUGH WINE. Isaiah describes Israel's iniquity in terms of their despicable and shameful conduct resulting from the use of intoxicating wine (cf. Amos 4:1; 6:1,6). Both the people and religious leaders had traded truth and righteousness for filthy vomit and gross disorientation. Their drunken debauchery demonstrated a clear rejection of God's commandments (see Prov. 23:31, note). The righteous should be filled with the Spirit rather than with intoxicating wine (see Eph. 5:18, note).

line, line upon line; here a little, *and*
there a little:
11 For with [i]stammering[p] lips
and another tongue [q]will he speak to
this people.
12 To whom he said, This *is* the rest
wherewith ye may cause the weary to
rest; and this *is* the refreshing: yet they
would not hear.
13 But the word of the LORD was
unto them precept upon precept, pre-
cept upon precept; line upon line, line
upon line; here a little, *and* there a lit-
tle; that they might go, and fall back-
ward, and be broken, and snared, and
taken.
14 ¶ Wherefore hear the word of the
LORD, ye scornful men, that rule this
people which *is* in Jerusalem.
15 Because ye have said, We have
made a covenant with death, and
with hell are we at agreement; when
the overflowing scourge shall pass
through, it shall not come unto us:
[j]for we have made lies our refuge, and
under falsehood have we hid our-
selves:
16 ¶ Therefore thus saith the Lord
GOD, Behold, I lay in Zion for a founda-
tion [k]a stone, a tried stone, a precious
corner *stone,* a sure foundation: he that
Dan. 3:1-27 believeth shall not make haste.
17 Judgment also will I lay to the
line, and righteousness to the plum-
met: and the hail shall sweep away
[l]the refuge of lies, and the waters
shall overflow the hiding place.
18 ¶ And your covenant with death
shall be disannulled, and your agree-
ment with hell shall not stand; when
the overflowing scourge shall pass
through, then ye shall be [r]trodden
down by it.
19 From the time that it goeth forth
it shall take you: for morning by morn-
ing shall it pass over, by day and by
night: and it shall be a vexation only
[s]*to* understand the report.
20 For the bed is shorter than that
a man can stretch himself *on it:* and the
covering narrower than that he can
wrap himself *in it.*
21 For the LORD shall rise up as *in*
mount [m]Perazim, he shall be wroth as
in the valley of [n]Gibeon, that he may
do his work, [o]his strange work; and
bring to pass his act, his strange act.
22 Now therefore be ye not mock-
ers, lest your bands be made strong:
for I have heard from the Lord GOD of
hosts [p]a consumption, even deter-
mined upon the whole earth.
23 ¶ Give ye ear, and hear my voice;
hearken, and hear my speech.
24 Doth the plowman plow all day
to sow? doth he open and break the
clods of his ground?
25 When he hath made plain the
face thereof, doth he not cast abroad
the fitches, and scatter the cummin,
and cast in [t]the principal wheat and
the appointed barley and the [u]rie in
their [v]place?
26 [w]For his God doth instruct him
to discretion, *and* doth teach him.
27 For the fitches are not threshed
with a threshing instrument, neither is
a cart wheel turned about upon the
cummin; but the fitches are beaten out
with a staff, and the cummin with a
rod.
28 Bread *corn* is bruised; because
he will not ever be threshing it, nor

28:11 [i]1 Cor. 14:21
28:15 [j]Amos 2:4
28:16 [k]Gen. 49:24 Ps. 118:22 Mat. 21:42 Acts. 4:11 Rom. 9:33 & 10:11 Eph. 2:20 1 Pet. 2:6-8
28:17 [l]ver. 15
28:21 [m]2 Sam. 5:20 1 Chr. 14:11 [n]Josh. 10:10,12 2 Sam. 5:25 1 Chr. 14:16 [o]Lam. 3:33
28:22 [p]ch. 10:22 Dan 9:27

[p] Heb. *stammerings of lips* [q] Or, *he hath spoken* [r] Heb. *a treading down to it* [s] Or, when *he shall make you to understand doctrine* [t] Or, *the wheat in the principal* place, *and barley in the appointed* place [u] Or, *spelt* [v] Heb. *border?* [w] Or, *And he bindeth it in such sort as his God doth teach him*

28:11 ANOTHER TONGUE. If the Israelites refused to hear Isaiah, God would force them to listen through the military might of a foreign power, e.g., the Assyrians, who spoke a language they could not understand.

28:13 THAT THEY MIGHT . . . BE BROKEN. Because they rejected the prophet's word, God would now use the message to harden them, thus ensuring their judgment and capture (see 6:9, note).

28:15 A COVENANT WITH DEATH. The people were choosing their own way by worshiping other gods (cf. 8:19). They felt secure in their agreement with these demonic powers (see article on THE NATURE OF IDOLATRY, p. 428), thinking these powers would provide immunity from harm; in reality, however, they were making a covenant with death.

28:16 I LAY IN ZION . . . A STONE. The stone is the Lord Himself (cf. 8:14; 17:10; Gen. 49:24); faith in Him alone provided hope for salvation. The N.T. declares that the ultimate fulfillment of this verse is found in Jesus Christ (Rom. 9:33; 1 Cor. 3:11; Eph. 2:20; 1 Pet. 2:4–6). On Christ as the foundation God is building a new people, whose commitment must be to righteousness and justice (v. 17; cf. Ps. 118:22).

28:23–29 HEAR MY VOICE. God would act in such a way that He would bring forth a righteous remnant from the crucible of judgment.

break *it with* the wheel of his cart, nor
bruise it *with* his horsemen.
29 This also cometh forth from the
LORD of hosts, [q]*which* is wonderful in
counsel, *and* excellent in working.

Doom to the city of Jerusalem

29 WOE [r]TO[x] Ariel, to Ariel,
[y]the city [s]*where* David dwelt!
add ye year to year; let them [z]kill sac-
rifices.
2 Yet I will distress Ariel, and there
shall be heaviness and sorrow: and it
shall be unto me as Ariel.
3 And I will camp against thee
round about, and will lay siege against
thee with a mount, and I will raise forts
against thee.
4 And thou shalt be brought down,
and shalt speak out of the ground, and
thy speech shall be low out of the dust,
and thy voice shall be, as of one that
hath a familiar spirit, [t]out of the
ground, and thy speech shall [a]whis-
per out of the dust.
5 Moreover the multitude of thy
[u]strangers shall be like small dust,
and the multitude of the terrible ones
shall be [v]as chaff that passeth away:
yea, it shall be [w]at an instant sud-
denly.
6 [x]Thou shalt be visited of the LORD
of hosts with thunder, and with earth-
quake, and great noise, with storm and
tempest, and the flame of devouring
fire.
7 ¶ [y]And the multitude of all the
nations that fight against Ariel, even
all that fight against her and her muni-
tion, and that distress her, shall be
[z]as a dream of a night vision.

28:29 [q]Ps. 92:5 Jer. 32:19
29:1 [r]Ezek. 43:15,16 [s]2 Sam. 5:9
29:4 [t]ch. 8:19
29:5 [u]ch. 25:5 [v]Job 21:18 ch. 17:13 [w]ch. 30:13
29:6 [x]ch. 28:2 & 30:30
29:7 [y]ch. 37:36 [z]Job 20:8
29:8 [a]Ps. 73:20
29:9 [b]See ch. 28:7,8 [c]ch. 51:21
29:10 [d]Rom. 11:8 [e]Ps. 69:23 ch. 6:10 [f]1 Sam. 9:9
29:11 [g]ch. 8:16 [h]Dan. 12:4 Rev. 5:1-5,9
29:13 [i]Ezek. 33:31 Mat. 15:8,9 Mark 7:6,7 [j]Col. 2:22
29:14 [k]Hab. 1:5

8 [a]It shall even be as when an hun-
gry *man* dreameth, and, behold, he
eateth; but he awaketh, and his soul is
empty: or as when a thirsty man
dreameth, and, behold, he drinketh;
but he awaketh, and, behold, *he is* faint,
and his soul hath appetite: so shall the
multitude of all the nations be, that
fight against mount Zion.
9 ¶ Stay yourselves, and wonder;
[b]cry ye out, and cry: [b]they are drunk-
en, [c]but not with wine; they stagger,
but not with strong drink.
10 For [d]the LORD hath poured out
upon you the spirit of deep sleep, and
hath [e]closed your eyes: the prophets
and your [c]rulers, [f]the seers hath he
covered.
11 And the vision of all is become
unto you as the words of a [d]book
[g]that is sealed, which *men* deliver to
one that is learned, saying, Read this,
I pray thee: [h]and he saith, I cannot;
for it *is* sealed:
12 And the book is delivered to him
that is not learned, saying, Read this,
I pray thee: and he saith, I am not
learned.
13 ¶ Wherefore the Lord said,
[i]Forasmuch as this people draw near
me with their mouth, and with their lips
do honour me, but have removed their
heart far from me, and their fear to-
ward me is taught by [j]the precept of
men:
14 [k]Therefore, behold, [e]I will pro-
ceed to do a marvellous work among

[x] Or, *O Ariel,* i.e. *the lion of God* [y] Or, *of the city* [z] Heb. *cut off the heads* [a] Heb. *peep,* or, *chirp* [b] Or, *take your pleasure, and riot* [c] Heb. *heads* [d] Or, *letter* [e] Heb. *I will add*

29:1–4 WOE TO ARIEL. Ariel (meaning "lion of God") is a symbolic name for Jerusalem. Although the inhabitants of Jerusalem felt secure and continued their religious festivals as usual, God would bring devastating judgment upon them because of their sin. When God's people do not recognize their spiritual poverty and their need to cry out to Him in repentance and prayer, He eventually has to remove them from their place in His kingdom (see Rev. 2:5, note).

29:5–8 THY STRANGERS. Although terrible judgment was coming upon Jerusalem, it would not involve total destruction. God would deliver His people and destroy Jerusalem's enemies. Isaiah's description likely refers to their deliverance from Assyria during Sennacherib's invasion (see 10:5–19). Unfortunately, even this miracle of God did not accomplish a thorough repentance and true obedience in His people. Thus a more devastating judgment came later, during the Babylonian invasions (605, 597, and 586 B.C.).

29:13 REMOVED THEIR HEART FAR FROM ME. God's people were coming before Him in prayer, worship, song, and praise, even though their hearts were not committed to Him or His word. They acted as if God's revelation and His righteous standards were not obligatory. Instead of cherishing God and His word, they filled their lives with the religious rituals and traditions taught by their leaders, and in false security they lived for themselves (cf. Jer. 4:3–4; 24:7; 31:31–34). A similar destructive spiritual condition exists in some churches today. People praise and honor God with their lips, while they have no real love for God or His righteous precepts. When their worship service is over, they seek the pleasures of sin and the world to satisfy their carnal desires (see Mark 7:6,8, notes). The result is spiritual blindness and deception (v. 14).

this people, *even* a marvellous work
and a wonder: [l]for the wisdom of their
wise *men* shall perish, and the under-
standing of their prudent *men* shall be
hid.
15 [m]Woe unto them that seek deep
to hide their counsel from the LORD,
and their works are in the dark, and
[n]they say, Who seeth us? and who
knoweth us?
16 Surely your turning of things up-
side down shall be esteemed as the
potter's clay: for shall the [o]work say
of him that made it, He made me not?
or shall the thing framed say of him
that framed it, He had no understand-
ing?
17 *Is* it not yet a very little while,
and [p]Lebanon shall be turned into a
fruitful field, and the fruitful field shall
be esteemed as a forest?
18 ¶ And [q]in that day shall the deaf
hear the words of the book, and the
eyes of the blind shall see out of ob-
scurity, and out of darkness.
19 [r]The meek also [f]shall in-
crease *their* joy in the LORD, and [s]the
poor among men shall rejoice in the
Holy One of Israel.
20 For the terrible one is brought to
nought, and [t]the scorner is con-
sumed, and all that [u]watch for iniqui-
ty are cut off:
21 That make a man an offender for
a word, and [v]lay a snare for him that
reproveth in the gate, and turn aside
the just [w]for a thing of nought.
22 Therefore thus saith the LORD,
[x]who redeemed Abraham, concerning
the house of Jacob, Jacob shall not now
be ashamed, neither shall his face now
wax pale.
23 But when he seeth his children,
[y]the work of mine hands, in the midst
of him, they shall sanctify my name,
and sanctify the Holy One of Jacob, and
shall fear the God of Israel.
24 They also [z]that erred in spirit
[g]shall come to understanding, and
they that murmured shall learn doc-
trine.

Rebellious Judah to be crushed

30 WOE TO the rebellious chil-
dren, saith the LORD, [a]that
take counsel, but not of me; and that
cover with a covering, but not of my
spirit, [b]that they may add sin to sin:
2 [c]That walk to go down into
Egypt, and [d]have not asked at my
mouth; to strengthen themselves in
the strength of Pharaoh, and to trust in
the shadow of Egypt!
3 [e]Therefore shall the strength of
Pharaoh be your shame, and the trust
in the shadow of Egypt *your* confusion.
4 For his princes were at [f]Zoan,
and his ambassadors came to Hanes.
5 [g]They were all ashamed of a peo-
ple *that* could not profit them, nor be an
help nor profit, but a shame, and also
a reproach.
6 [h]The burden of the beasts of the
south: into the land of trouble and an-
guish, from whence *come* the young
and old lion, [i]the viper and fiery flying
serpent, they will carry their riches
upon the shoulders of young asses, and
their treasures upon the bunches of
camels, to a people *that* shall not profit
them.
7 [j]For the Egyptians shall help in
vain, and to no purpose: therefore
have I cried [h]concerning this, [k]Their
strength *is* to sit still.
8 ¶ Now go, [l]write it before them
in a table, and note it in a book, that it

29:14 [l]Jer. 49:7 Obad. 8 1 Cor. 1:19
29:15 [m]ch. 30:1 [n]Ps. 94:7
29:16 [o]ch. 45:9 Rom. 9:20
29:17 [p]ch. 32:15
29:18 [q]ch. 35:5
29:19 [r]ch. 61:1 [s]Jas. 2:5
29:20 [t]ch. 28:14,22 [u]Mic. 2:1
29:21 [v]Amos 5:10,12 [w]Prov. 28:21
29:22 [x]Josh. 24:3
29:23 [y]ch. 19:25 & 45:11 & 60:21 Eph. 2:10
29:24 [z]ch. 28:7
30:1 [a]ch. 29:15 [b]Deut. 29:19
30:2 [c]ch. 31:1 [d]Num. 27:21 Josh. 9:14 1 Ki. 22:7 Jer. 21:2 & 42:2,20
30:3 [e]ch. 20:5 Jer. 37:5,7
30:4 [f]ch. 19:11
30:5 [g]Jer. 2:36
30:6 [h]ch. 57:9 Hos. 8:9 & 12:1 [i]Deut. 8:15
30:7 [j]Jer. 37:7 [k]ver. 15
30:8 [l]Hab. 2:2

[f] Heb. *shall add* [g] Heb. *shall know*
understanding [h] Or, *to her*

29:17–24 A FRUITFUL FIELD. Isaiah's prophecies of judgment are never without hope, for they characteristically include the theme of Israel's restoration. These verses envision the last days of this age when the humble and poor of Israel will turn to God (vv. 18–19) and the wicked will be destroyed (vv. 20–21). Israel's full restoration will occur shortly before Christ's return to earth to reign (see Rom. 11:26, note; Rev. 12:6, note; see article on ISRAEL IN GOD'S PLAN OF SALVATION, p. 1748). The blessings of sight for the blind and hearing for the deaf (v. 18; cf. 32:3; 35:5) accompanied Christ's first coming; God's people will receive full redemption at His second coming.

30:1–5 TAKE COUNSEL, BUT NOT OF ME. Judah had sought an alliance with Egypt to gain protection from Assyria (cf. 2 Ki. 18:21), thereby rejecting God's counsel, refusing to believe His promises, and casting aside His principles of holy living. They were guilty of despising the Lord and preferring the might of human achievement to the power of the Spirit (see Zech. 4:6, note).

30:6–7 THE SOUTH. The south (Heb. *Negev*) was the rugged and dangerous area of southern Palestine, filled with wild animals. Delegations from Judah had to pass through this region in order to take their merchandise and riches to Egypt. Isaiah prophesies that their journey to Egypt would do them no good; the Egyptians could not help them.

may be for [i]the time to come for ever and ever:

9 That [m]this *is* a rebellious people, lying children, children *that* will not hear the law of the LORD:

10 [n]Which say to the seers, See not; and to the prophets, Prophesy not unto us right things, [o]speak unto us smooth things, prophesy deceits:

11 Get you out of the way, turn aside out of the path, cause the Holy One of Israel to cease from before us.

12 Wherefore thus saith the Holy One of Israel, Because ye despise this word, and trust in [j]oppression and perverseness, and stay thereon:

13 Therefore this iniquity shall be to you [p]as a breach ready to fall, swelling out in a high wall, whose breaking [q]cometh suddenly at an instant.

14 And [r]he shall break it as the breaking of [k]the potters' vessel that is broken in pieces; he shall not spare: so that there shall not be found in the bursting of it a sherd to take fire from the hearth, or to take water *withal* out of the pit.

15 For thus saith the Lord GOD, the Holy One of Israel; [s]In returning and rest shall ye be saved; in quietness and in confidence shall be your strength: [t]and ye would not.

16 But ye said, No; for we will flee upon horses; therefore shall ye flee: and, We will ride upon the swift; therefore shall they that pursue you be swift.

17 [u]One thousand *shall flee* at the rebuke of one; at the rebuke of five shall ye flee: till ye be left as [l]a beacon upon the top of a mountain, and as an ensign on an hill.

18 ¶ And therefore will the LORD wait, that he may be gracious unto you, and therefore will he be exalted, that he may have mercy upon you: for the LORD *is* a God of judgment: [v]blessed *are* all they that wait for him.

19 For the people [w]shall dwell in Zion at Jerusalem: thou shalt weep no more: he will be very gracious unto thee at the voice of thy cry; when he shall hear it, he will answer thee.

20 And *though* the Lord give you [x]the bread of adversity, and the water of [m]affliction, yet shall not [y]thy teachers be removed into a corner any more, but thine eyes shall see thy teachers:

21 And thine ears shall hear a word behind thee, saying, This *is* the way, walk ye in it, when ye [z]turn to the right hand, and when ye turn to the left.

22 [a]Ye shall defile also the covering of [n]thy graven images of silver, and the ornament of thy molten images of gold: thou shalt [o]cast them away as a menstruous cloth; [b]thou shalt say unto it, Get thee hence.

23 [c]Then shall he give the rain of thy seed, that thou shalt sow the ground withal; and bread of the increase of the earth, and it shall be fat and plenteous: in that day shall thy cattle feed in large pastures.

24 The oxen likewise and the young asses that ear the ground shall eat [p] [q]clean provender, which hath been winnowed with the shovel and with the fan.

25 And there shall be [d]upon every

30:9 [m]Deut. 32:20 ch. 1:4
30:10 [n]Jer. 11:21 Amos 2:12 Mic. 2:6 [o]1 Ki. 22:13 Mic. 2:11
30:13 [p]Ps. 62:3 [q]ch. 29:5
30:14 [r]Ps. 2:9 Jer. 19:11
30:15 [s]ch. 7:4 [t]Mat. 23:37
30:17 [u]Lev. 26:8 Deut. 28:25 Josh. 23:10
30:18 [v]Ps. 2:12 & 34:8 Prov. 16:20 Jer. 17:7
30:19 [w]ch. 65:9
30:20 [x]1 Ki. 22:27 Ps. 127:2 [y]Ps. 74:9 Amos 8:11
30:21 [z]Josh. 1:7
30:22 [a]2 Chr. 31:1 ch. 31:7 [b]Hos. 14:8
30:23 [c]Mat. 6:33 1 Tim. 4:8
30:25 [d]ch. 2:14,15

[i] Heb. *the latter day* [j] Or, *fraud* [k] Heb. *the bottle of potters* [l] Or, *a tree bereft of branches,* or, *boughs:* or, *a mast* [m] Or, *oppression* [n] Heb. *the graven images of thy silver* [o] Heb. *scatter* [p] Or, *savoury* [q] Heb. *leavened*

30:10 SPEAK UNTO US SMOOTH THINGS. The people could not bear to hear prophetic words that condemned their sinful lifestyle. (1) They were tired of hearing about God and the holy lifestyle He required. They wanted to hear encouraging, pleasant, and inoffensive messages. (2) Paul states that in the last days a similar state of mind will prevail among some within the churches. These people will reject God's messengers who proclaim the truth and instead choose leaders who preach what they want to hear. They will insist on pleasant and flattering messages that do not expose their sin and worldliness, but rather assure them of their security and God's love no matter what they do (see 2 Tim. 4:3–4, note).

30:15 IN RETURNING . . . SHALL YE BE SAVED. Judah could be saved if only its rulers and people would return to God and put their confidence in Him. Since they would not, however, they would be defeated and stand alone as a beacon on a hill, a stark example of the consequences of forsaking God (v. 17).

30:18–26 THAT HE MAY BE GRACIOUS. The Lord desires to be gracious to His people and to bless all who long for Him (see Ps. 42:2, note). He will pour out these blessings on the believing remnant when He restores them to a place of favor alongside the Messiah.

30:25 THE DAY OF THE GREAT SLAUGHTER. The long-range application of this prophecy may be to the battle of Armageddon, when God destroys all the wicked (see Rev. 16:16,

high mountain, and upon every [r]high
hill, rivers *and* streams of waters in the
day of the great slaughter, when the
towers fall.
26 Moreover [e]the light of the moon
shall be as the light of the sun, and the
light of the sun shall be sevenfold, as
the light of seven days, in the day that
the LORD bindeth up the breach of his
people, and healeth the stroke of their
wound.
27 ¶ Behold, the name of the LORD
cometh from far, burning *with* his
anger, [s]and the burden *thereof is*
[t]heavy: his lips are full of indigna-
tion, and his tongue as a devouring
fire:
28 And [f]his breath, as an over-
flowing stream, [g]shall reach to the
midst of the neck, to sift the nations
with the sieve of vanity: and *there shall*
be [h]a bridle in the jaws of the people,
causing *them* to err.
29 Ye shall have a song, as in
the night *when* a holy solemnity is
kept; and gladness of heart, as when
one goeth with a pipe to come into
[i]the mountain of the LORD, to the
[j]mighty[u] One of Israel.
30 [k]And the LORD shall cause [v]his
glorious voice to be heard, and shall
show the lighting down of his arm, with
the indignation of *his* anger, and *with*
the flame of a devouring fire, *with*
scattering, and tempest, [l]and hail-
stones.
31 For [m]through the voice of the
LORD shall the Assyrian be beaten
down, [n]*which* smote with a rod.
32 And [w]*in* every place where the
grounded staff shall pass, which the
LORD shall [x]lay upon him, *it* shall
be with tabrets and harps: and in
battles of [o]shaking will he fight
[y]with it.
33 [p]For Tophet *is* ordained [z]of
old; yea, for the king it is prepared; he
hath made *it* deep *and* large: the pile
thereof *is* fire and much wood; the
breath of the LORD, like a stream of
brimstone, doth kindle it.

30:26 [e]ch. 60:19,20 **30:28** [f]ch. 11:4 [g]ch. 8:8 [h]ch. 37:29 **30:29** [i]ch. 2:3 [j]Deut. 32:4 **30:30** [k]ch. 29:6 [l]ch. 28:2 **30:31** [m]ch. 37:36 [n]ch. 10:5,24 **30:32** [o]ch. 11:15 **30:33** [p]Jer. 7:31

31:1 [q]ch. 30:2 [r]Ps. 20:7 [s]Dan. 9:13 **31:2** [t]Num. 23:19 **31:4** [u]Amos 3:8 **31:5** [v]Deut. 32:11 **31:7** [w]ch. 2:20 [x]1 Ki. 12:30 **31:8** [y]2 Ki. 19:35,36

The folly of reliance upon Egypt

31 WOE TO them [q]that go down
to Egypt for help; and [r]stay on
horses, and trust in chariots, because
they are many; and in horsemen, be-
cause they are very strong; but they
look not unto the Holy One of Israel,
[s]neither seek the LORD!
2 Yet he also *is* wise, and will bring
evil, and [t]will not [a]call back his
words: but will arise against the house
of the evildoers, and against the help of
them that work iniquity.
3 Now the Egyptians *are* men, and
not God; and their horses flesh, and
not spirit. When the LORD shall stretch
out his hand, both he that helpeth shall
fall, and he that is helped shall fall
down, and they all shall fail together.
4 For thus hath the LORD spoken
unto me, [u]Like as the lion and the
young lion roaring on his prey, when a
multitude of shepherds is called forth
against him, *he* will not be afraid of
their voice, nor abase himself for the
[b]noise of them: so shall the LORD of
hosts come down to fight for mount
Zion, and for the hill thereof.
5 [v]As birds flying, so will the LORD
of hosts defend Jerusalem; defending
also he will deliver *it; and* passing over
he will preserve *it*.
6 ¶ Turn ye unto *him from* whom the
children of Israel have deeply revolted.
7 For in that day every man shall
[w]cast away his idols of silver, and
[c]his idols of gold, which your own
hands have made unto you *for* [x]a sin.
8 ¶ Then shall the Assyrian [y]fall
with the sword, not of a mighty man;
and the sword, not of a mean man,
shall devour him: but he shall flee

[r] Heb. *lifted up* [s] Or, *and the grievousness of flame* [t] Heb. *heaviness* [u] Heb. *Rock* [v] Heb. *the glory of his voice* [w] Heb. *every passing of the rod founded* [x] Heb. *cause to rest upon him* [y] Or, *against them* [z] Heb. *from yesterday* [a] Heb. *remove* [b] Or, *multitude* [c] Heb. *the idols of his gold*

note; 19:17, note).

30:27–33 BURNING *WITH* HIS ANGER. This prophecy concerns the overthrow of the Assyrian army (v. 31; cf. 37:36).

31:1 WOE TO THEM. Isaiah pronounces a woe upon the evildoers (v. 2) who were trusting in Egypt's horses and chariots rather than in the Lord (cf. Deut. 17:16). Believers today must be careful not to commit the same sin as Judah. We must put our faith in God, revere His commandments, and seek Him daily for His grace and help in all our needs (cf. Heb. 4:16).

31:4–9 THE LORD . . . TO FIGHT FOR MOUNT ZION. God would come as a lion, fight the Assyrians as a champion warrior, and defend Jerusalem (cf. 37:36). Thus Isaiah called upon the Israelites to throw away their idols and turn to the Lord in faith.

[d]from the sword, and his young men
shall be [e] [f]discomfited.
9 And [z]he[g] shall pass over to
[h]his strong hold for fear, and his
princes shall be afraid of the ensign,
saith the LORD, whose fire *is* in Zion,
and his furnace in Jerusalem.

Israel's ultimate deliverance

32 BEHOLD, [a]A king shall reign
in righteousness, and princes
shall rule in judgment.
2 And a man shall be as an hiding
place from the wind, and [b]a covert
from the tempest; as rivers of water in
a dry place, as the shadow of a [i]great
rock in a weary land.
3 And [c]the eyes of them that see
shall not be dim, and the ears of them
that hear shall hearken.
4 The heart also of the [j]rash shall
understand knowledge, and the tongue
of the stammerers shall be ready to
speak [k]plainly.
5 The vile person shall be no more
called liberal, nor the churl said *to be*
bountiful.
6 For the vile person will speak vil-
lany, and his heart will work iniquity,
to practise hypocrisy, and to utter er-
ror against the LORD, to make empty
the soul of the hungry, and he will
cause the drink of the thirsty to
fail.
7 The instruments also of the churl
are evil: he deviseth wicked devices to
destroy the poor with lying words, even
[l]when the needy speaketh right.
8 But the liberal deviseth liberal
things; and by liberal things shall he
[m]stand.

After calamity, restoration

9 ¶ Rise up, ye women [d]that are at
ease; hear my voice, ye careless
daughters; give ear unto my speech.
10 [n]Many days and years shall ye
be troubled, ye careless women: for the
vintage shall fail, the gathering shall
not come.
11 Tremble, ye women that are at
ease; be troubled, ye careless ones:
strip you, and make you bare, and gird
sackcloth upon *your* loins.
12 They shall lament for the teats,
for [o]the pleasant fields, for the fruit-
ful vine.
13 [e]Upon the land of my people
shall come up thorns *and* briers; [p]Yea,
upon all the houses of joy *in* [f]the joy-
ous city:
14 [g]Because the palaces shall be
forsaken; the multitude of the city
shall be left; the [q]forts and towers
shall be for dens for ever, a joy of wild
asses, a pasture of flocks;
15 Until [h]the spirit be poured upon
us from on high, and [i]the wilderness
be a fruitful field, and the fruitful field
be counted for a forest. Is. 42:1
16 Then judgment shall dwell in the
wilderness, and righteousness remain
in the fruitful field.
17 [j]And the work of righteousness
shall be peace; and the effect of righ-
teousness quietness and assurance for
ever.
18 And my people shall dwell in a
peaceable habitation, and in sure Ezek.
dwellings, and in quiet resting places; 17:22
24
19 [k]When it shall hail, coming

31:9 [z]ch. 37:37
32:1 [a]Ps. 45:1
32:2 [b]ch. 4:6
32:3 [c]ch. 29:18
32:9 [d]Amos 6:1
32:13 [e]Hos. 9:6 [f]ch. 22:2
32:14 [g]ch. 27:10
32:15 [h]Joel 2:28 [i]ch. 29:17
32:17 [j]Jas. 3:18
32:19 [k]ch. 30:30

[d] Or, *for fear of the sword* [e] Or, *tributary* [f] Heb. *for melting*, or, *tribute* [g] Heb. *his rock shall pass away for fear* [h] Or, *his strength* [i] Heb. *heavy* [j] Heb. *hasty* [k] Or, *elegantly* [l] Or, *when he speaketh* against *the poor in judgment* [m] Or, *be established* [n] Heb. *Days above a year* [o] Heb. *the fields of desire* [p] Or, *burning upon* [q] Or, *clifts and watchtowers*

32:1–8 A KING SHALL REIGN IN RIGHTEOUSNESS. This prophecy foresees the worldwide reign of Christ (cf. 9:7; 11:4; 16:5), characterized by righteousness and by people who live in accordance with the word of God.

32:9–14 WOMEN THAT ARE AT EASE. Many Israelites were complacent about sin, even though it was destroying their families and nation; instead, Isaiah told them that they should beat their breasts (v. 12), tremble (v. 11), be dressed in sackcloth (v. 11), and be distressed (v. 11) as they cry out to God until He pours out the Spirit from heaven (v. 15). Today, whenever sin, Satan, and the world gain inroads into the church, we too should mourn and cry out for God to restore righteousness and the fullness of the Spirit in His house (vv. 15–16; cf. ch. 35).

32:15–20 UNTIL THE SPIRIT BE POURED UPON US. Isaiah returns to the theme of the righteous reign of the king (see vv. 1–8, note). (1) The righteousness and blessing of the kingdom age will come about because the Spirit will be poured out upon the people and will work in the hearts of the people (cf. 44:3). (2) In the present age, the blessings of redemption come to us through the Spirit, who has been poured out upon believers (cf. Joel 2:28–32; Acts 1:8 and 2:4, notes). Yet this outpouring is only partial; we await and pray for the fullness of redemption and the full outpouring of the Holy Spirit at the end of history.

down [l]on the forest; [r]and the city
shall be low in a low place.
20 Blessed *are* ye that sow beside
all waters, that send forth *thither* the
feet of [m]the ox and the ass.

The distress of Judah

33 WOE TO thee [n]that spoilest,
and thou *wast* not spoiled; and
dealest treacherously, and they dealt
not treacherously with thee! [o]when
thou shalt cease to spoil, thou shalt be
spoiled; *and* when thou shalt make an
end to deal treacherously, they shall
deal treacherously with thee.
2 O LORD, be gracious unto us; [p]we
have waited for thee: be thou their arm
every morning, our salvation also in
the time of trouble.
3 At the noise of the tumult the peo-
ple fled; at the lifting up of thyself the
nations were scattered.
4 And your spoil shall be gathered
like the gathering of the caterpillar: as
the running to and fro of locusts shall
he run upon them.
5 [q]The LORD is exalted; for he
dwelleth on high: he hath filled Zion
with judgment and righteousness.
6 And wisdom and knowledge shall
be the stability of thy times, *and*
strength of [s]salvation: the fear of the
LORD *is* his treasure.
7 Behold, their [t]valiant ones shall
cry without: [r]the ambassadors of
peace shall weep bitterly.
8 [s]The highways lie waste, the
wayfaring man ceaseth: [t]he hath bro-
ken the covenant, he hath despised the
cities, he regardeth no man.
9 [u]The earth mourneth *and* lan-
guisheth: Lebanon is ashamed *and*
[u]hewn down: Sharon is like a wilder-
ness; and Bashan and Carmel shake off
their fruits.
10 [v]Now will I rise, saith the LORD;
now will I be exalted; now will I lift up
myself.

32:19 [l]Zech. 11:2
32:20 [m]ch. 30:24
33:1 [n]ch. 21:2 Hab. 2:8 [o]Rev. 13:10
33:2 [p]ch. 25:9
33:5 [q]Ps. 97:9
33:7 [r]2 Ki. 18:18,37
33:8 [s]Judg. 5:6 [t]2 Ki. 18:14-17
33:9 [u]ch. 24:4
33:10 [v]Ps. 12:5
33:11 [w]Ps. 7:14 ch. 59:4
33:12 [x]ch. 9:18
33:13 [y]ch. 49:1
33:15 [z]Ps. 15:2 & 24:4 [a]Ps. 119:37
33:18 [b]1 Cor. 1:20
33:19 [c]2 Ki. 19:32 [d]Deut. 28:49,50 Jer. 5:15
33:20 [e]Ps. 48:12 [f]Ps. 46:5 & 125:1,2

11 [w]Ye shall conceive chaff, ye
shall bring forth stubble: your breath,
as fire, shall devour you.
12 And the people shall be *as* the
burnings of lime: [x]*as* thorns cut up
shall they be burned in the fire.
13 ¶ Hear, [y]ye *that are* far off, what
I have done; and, ye *that are* near, ac-
knowledge my might.
14 The sinners in Zion are afraid;
fearfulness hath surprised the hypo-
crites. Who among us shall dwell with
the devouring fire? who among us shall
dwell with everlasting burnings?
15 He that [z]walketh [v]righteous-
ly, and speaketh [w]uprightly; he that
despiseth the gain of [x]oppressions,
that shaketh his hands from holding of
bribes, that stoppeth his ears from
hearing of [y]blood, and [a]shutteth his
eyes from seeing evil;
16 He shall dwell on [z]high: his
place of defence *shall be* the munitions
of rocks: bread shall be given him; his
waters *shall be* sure.

Safety and joy under the Messiah

17 Thine eyes shall see the king in
his beauty: they shall behold [a]the
land that is very far off.
18 Thine heart shall meditate ter-
ror. [b]Where *is* the scribe? where *is* the
[b]receiver? where *is* he that counted
the towers?
19 [c]Thou shalt not see a fierce
people, [d]a people of a deeper speech
than thou canst perceive; of a [c]stam-
mering tongue, *that thou canst* not un-
derstand.
20 [e]Look upon Zion, the city of our
solemnities: thine eyes shall see [f]Je-

[r] Or, *and the city shall be utterly abased* [s] Heb. *salvations* [t] Or, *messengers* [u] Or, *withered away* [v] Heb. *in righteousnesses* [w] Heb. *uprightnesses* [x] Or, *deceits* [y] Heb. *bloods* [z] Heb. *heights,* or, *high places* [a] Heb. *the land of far distances* [b] Heb. *weigher?* [c] Or, *ridiculous*

33:1 TO THEE THAT SPOILEST. The immediate application is to the Assyrians; the ultimate application is to the antichrist and to Satan himself (see Rev. 19:20; 20:10).

33:2–9 O LORD, BE GRACIOUS UNTO US. This is the prayer of the righteous remnant for deliverance from the hand of their enemy.

33:14–16 WHO ... SHALL DWELL WITH THE DEVOURING FIRE? Isaiah describes those among God's people who will come through the fire of His judgment. Note that it will be only those who live godly lives that flow from hearts that are right with God. That godly person is described as one who: (1) conforms to the righteous requirements of God's law, (2) speaks sincerely without deceit, (3) rejects making money by unjust means, (4) refuses to be involved in criminal violence, and (5) refuses to look upon evil with pleasure or to delight in the wicked actions of others.

33:17–24 THE KING. This is probably a prophecy concerning God's future kingdom on earth. Therefore, the reigning king will be the Messiah—Jesus Christ.

rusalem a quiet habitation, a tabernacle *that* shall not be taken down; [g]not one of [h]the stakes thereof shall ever be removed, neither shall any of the cords thereof be broken.

21 But there the glorious LORD *will be* unto us a place [d]of broad rivers *and* streams; wherein shall go no galley with oars, neither shall gallant ship pass thereby.

22 For the LORD *is* our judge, the LORD *is* our [i]lawgiver,[e] [j]the LORD *is* our king; he will save us.

23 [f]Thy tacklings are loosed; they could not well strengthen their mast, they could not spread the sail: then is the prey of a great spoil divided; the lame take the prey.

24 And the inhabitant shall not say, I am sick: [k]the people that dwell therein *shall be* forgiven *their* iniquity.

The judgment on the nations

34 COME[l] NEAR, ye nations, to hear; and hearken, ye people: [m]let the earth hear, and [g]all that is therein; the world, and all things that come forth of it.

2 For the indignation of the LORD *is* upon all nations, and *his* fury upon all their armies: he hath utterly destroyed them, he hath delivered them to the slaughter.

3 Their slain also shall be cast out, and [n]their stink shall come up out of their carcases, and the mountains shall be melted with their blood.

4 And [o]all the host of heaven shall be dissolved, and the heavens shall be rolled together as a scroll: [p]and all their host shall fall down, as the leaf falleth off from the vine, and as a [q]falling *fig* from the fig tree.

5 For [r]my sword shall be bathed in heaven: behold, it [s]shall come down upon Idumea, and upon the people of my curse, to judgment.

6 The sword of the LORD is filled with blood, it is made fat with fatness, *and* with the blood of lambs and goats, with the fat of the kidneys of rams: for [t]the LORD hath a sacrifice in Bozrah, and a great slaughter in the land of Idumea.

7 And the [h]unicorns shall come down with them, and the bullocks with the bulls; and their land shall be [i]soaked with blood, and their dust made fat with fatness.

8 For *it is* the day of the LORD's [u]vengeance, *and* the year of recompences for the controversy of Zion.

9 [v]And the streams thereof shall be turned into pitch, and the dust thereof into brimstone, and the land thereof shall become burning pitch.

10 It shall not be quenched night nor day; [w]the smoke thereof shall go up for ever: [x]from generation to generation it shall lie waste; none shall pass through it for ever and ever.

11 ¶ [y]But the [j]cormorant and the bittern shall possess it; the owl also and the raven shall dwell in it: and [z]he shall stretch out upon it the line of confusion, and the stones of emptiness.

12 They shall call the nobles thereof to the kingdom, but none *shall be* there, and all her princes shall be nothing.

13 And [a]thorns shall come up in her palaces, nettles and brambles in the fortresses thereof: and [b]it shall be an habitation of dragons, *and* a court for [k] [l]owls.

14 [m]The wild beasts of the desert shall also meet with [n]the wild beasts of the island, and the satyr shall cry to his fellow; the [o]screech owl also shall rest there, and find for herself a place of rest.

15 There shall the great owl make her nest, and lay, and hatch, and gath-

33:20 [g]ch. 37:33 [h]ch. 54:2
33:22 [i]Jas. 4:12 [j]Ps. 89:18
33:24 [k]Jer. 50:20
34:1 [l]Ps. 49:1 [m]Deut. 32:1
34:3 [n]Joel 2:20
34:4 [o]Ps. 102:26 Ezek. 32:7,8 Joel 2:31 Mat. 24:29 2 Pet. 3:10 [p]ch. 14:12 [q]Rev. 6:13
34:5 [r]Jer. 46:10 [s]Jer. 49:7 Mal. 1:4
34:6 [t]Zeph. 1:7
34:8 [u]ch. 63:4
34:9 [v]Deut. 29:23
34:10 [w]Rev. 14:11 & 18:18 & 19:3 [x]Mal. 1:4
34:11 [y]ch. 14:23 Zeph. 2:14 Rev. 18:2 [z]2 Ki. 21:13 Lam. 2:8
34:13 [a]ch. 32:13 Hos. 9:6 [b]ch. 13:21

[d] Heb. *broad of spaces,* or, *hands* [e] Heb. *statutemaker* [f] Or, *They have forsaken thy tacklings* [g] Heb. *the fulness thereof* [h] Or, *rhinocerots* [i] Or, *drunken* [j] Or, *pelican* [k] Or, *ostriches* [l] Heb. *daughters of the owl* [m] Heb. *Ziim* [n] Heb. *Ijim* [o] Or, *night monster*

34:1–7 ALL NATIONS ... UTTERLY DESTROYED. These verses depict the terrible judgment to fall on all nations at the end of time. They emphasize God's wrath against all sin and rebellion (see Rev. 16:16, note; 19:17, note); this judgment will involve disturbances in the heavens (v. 4; cf. Mat. 24:29; Rev. 6:13–14) and is linked with Christ's return to set up His kingdom on earth (Rev. 19—20). At the present time, nations may ridicule and reject God's way, but at a time known only to God, great tribulation and judgment will shake the nations.

34:8–17 THE YEAR OF RECOMPENCES. Though speaking in the context of a destruction coming from God on the Edomites as enemies of Him and His people (cf. 2 Sam. 8:13–14; Ps. 137:7; Lam. 4:21), Isaiah prophesies a coming judgment on all the unregenerate, i.e., all those hostile to God and His word.

er under her shadow: there shall the
vultures also be gathered, every one
with her mate.
16 ¶ Seek ye out of [c]the book of the
LORD, and read: no one of these shall
fail, none shall want her mate: for my
mouth it hath commanded, and his
spirit it hath gathered them.
17 And he hath cast the lot for
them, and his hand hath divided it unto
them by line: they shall possess it for
ever, from generation to generation
shall they dwell therein.

The return to Zion promised

35 THE [d]WILDERNESS and the
solitary place shall be glad for
them; and the desert shall rejoice, and
blossom as the rose.
2 [e]It shall blossom abundantly,
and rejoice even with joy and singing:
the glory of Lebanon shall be given
unto it, the excellency of Carmel and
Sharon, they shall see the glory of the
LORD, *and* the excellency of our God.
3 ¶ [f]Strengthen ye the weak
hands, and confirm the feeble knees.
4 Say to them *that are* of a [p]fearful
heart, Be strong, fear not: behold, your
God will come *with* vengeance, *even*
God *with* a recompence; he will come
and save you.
5 Then the [g]eyes of the blind shall
be opened, and [h]the ears of the deaf
shall be unstopped.
6 Then shall the [i]lame *man* leap as
an hart, and the [j]tongue of the dumb
sing: for in the wilderness shall [k]wa-
ters break out, and streams in the
desert.
7 And the parched ground shall be-
come a pool, and the thirsty land
springs of water: in [l]the habitation of
dragons, where each lay, *shall be*
[q]grass with reeds and rushes.
8 And an highway shall be there,
and a way, and it shall be called The
way of holiness; [m]the unclean shall
not pass over it; [r]but it *shall be* for
those: the wayfaring men, though
fools, shall not err *therein.*
9 [n]No lion shall be there, nor *any*
ravenous beast shall go up thereon, it
shall not be found there; but the re-
deemed shall walk *there:*
10 And the [o]ransomed of the LORD
shall return, and come to Zion with
songs and everlasting joy upon their
heads: they shall obtain joy and glad-
ness, and [p]sorrow and sighing shall
flee away.

Is. 40:10-11

Is. 58:1-8

Sennacherib taunts Hezekiah

36:1–22pp — 2 Ki. 18:13,17–37; 2 Chr. 32:9–19

36 NOW [q]IT came to pass in the
fourteenth year of king Hezeki-
ah, *that* Sennacherib king of Assyria
came up against all the defenced cities
of Judah, and took them.
2 And the king of Assyria sent Rab-
shakeh from Lachish to Jerusalem
unto king Hezekiah with a great army.
And he stood by the conduit of the up-
per pool in the highway of the fuller's
field.
3 Then came forth unto him Elia-
kim, Hilkiah's son, which was over the
house, and Shebna the [s]scribe, and
Joah, Asaph's son, the recorder.

34:16 [c]Mal. 3:16 **35:1** [d]ch. 55:12 **35:2** [e]ch. 32:15 **35:3** [f]Job 4:3,4 Heb. 12:12 **35:5** [g]ch. 29:18 Mat. 9:27 & 11:5 John 9:6,7 [h]Mat. 11:5 **35:6** [i]Mat. 11:5 & 15:30 John 5:8,9 Acts 8:7 [j]ch. 32:4 Mat. 9:32 & 12:22 [k]ch. 41:18 John 7:38 **35:7** [l]ch. 34:13 **35:8** [m]ch. 52:1 Rev. 21:27 **35:9** [n]Lev. 26:6 ch. 11:9 Ezek. 34:25 **35:10** [o]ch. 51:11 [p]ch. 25:8 Rev. 7:17 & 21:4 **36:1** [q]2 Ki. 18:13,17 2 Chr. 32:1

[p] Heb. *hasty* [q] Or, *a court for reeds* [r] Or, *for he* shall be *with them* [s] Or, *secretary*

35:1 THE DESERT SHALL REJOICE. Whereas the preceding chapter described God's judgment through the destruction of the wicked, this chapter predicts a day of God's redemption when the earth will blossom profusely with righteousness and manifest His glory amidst great rejoicing by His people. This chapter has several levels of application, beginning with the first coming of Jesus Christ and reaching its full realization at His second coming (see Rev. 19—22).

35:4 YOUR GOD WILL COME *WITH* VENGEANCE. God will one day come to recompense the world for its evil and to reward the righteous with His great salvation (cf. 2 Thes. 1:6–10). At that time the redeemed will be completely saved from sin and all its consequences (see article on THE RAPTURE, p. 1889).

35:5–6 EYES OF THE BLIND SHALL BE OPENED. Jesus Christ refers to these verses as evidence of His Messiahship (Mat. 11:4–5; Luke 7:22). When the church of Jesus Christ is truly empowered by the Holy Spirit to do the "greater works" (John 14:12), the signs and wonders of Is. 35 will again occur, just as they did during the time described in the book of Acts.

35:8–11 THE WAY OF HOLINESS. Whenever the Spirit is poured out from on high (32:15), resulting in a powerful revelation of God's glory and majesty (v. 2), then the way of holiness will become so clear that even a fool will not miss it (v. 8). All the redeemed will then walk in complete holiness (v. 10).

36:1 KING HEZEKIAH. With chs. 36—39 (paralleling 2 Ki. 18—20), Isaiah moves from prophecy to the history of King Hezekiah. Hezekiah was a godly king of Judah who trusted in the Lord and served Him (see 2 Ki. 18:5, note). "The fourteenth year" of his reign was 701 B.C., when Sennacherib, king of Assyria, invaded Judah with the intention of capturing Jerusalem.

4 ¶ [r]And Rab-shakeh said unto them, Say ye now to Hezekiah, Thus saith the great king, the king of Assyria, What confidence *is* this wherein thou trustest?

5 I say, *sayest thou,* (but *they are but* [t]vain words) [u]*I have* counsel and strength for war: now on whom dost thou trust, that thou rebellest against me?

6 Lo, thou trustest in the [s]staff of this broken reed, on Egypt; whereon if a man lean, it will go into his hand, and pierce it: so *is* Pharaoh king of Egypt to all that trust in him.

7 But if thou say to me, We trust in the LORD our God: *is it* not he, whose high places and whose altars Hezekiah hath taken away, and said to Judah and to Jerusalem, Ye shall worship before this altar?

8 Now therefore give [v]pledges, I pray thee, to my master the king of Assyria, and I will give thee two thousand horses, if thou be able on thy part to set riders upon them.

9 How then wilt thou turn away the face of one captain of the least of my master's servants, and put thy trust on Egypt for chariots and for horsemen?

10 And am I now come up without the LORD against this land to destroy it? the LORD said unto me, Go up against this land, and destroy it.

11 ¶ Then said Eliakim and Shebna and Joah unto Rab-shakeh, Speak, I pray thee, unto thy servants in the Syrian language; for we understand *it:* and speak not to us in the Jews' language, in the ears of the people that *are* on the wall.

12 ¶ But Rab-shakeh said, Hath my master sent me to thy master and to thee to speak these words? *hath he* not *sent me* to the men that sit upon the wall, that they may eat their own dung, and drink their own piss with you?

13 Then Rab-shakeh stood, and cried with a loud voice in the Jews' language, and said, Hear ye the words of the great king, the king of Assyria.

14 Thus saith the king, Let not Hezekiah deceive you: for he shall not be able to deliver you.

15 Neither let Hezekiah make you trust in the LORD, saying, The LORD will surely deliver us: this city shall not be delivered into the hand of the king of Assyria.

16 Hearken not to Hezekiah: for thus saith the king of Assyria, [w,x]Make *an agreement* with me *by* a present, and come out to me: [t]and eat ye every one of his vine, and every one of his fig tree, and drink ye every one the waters of his own cistern;

17 Until I come and take you away to a land like your own land, a land of corn and wine, a land of bread and vineyards.

18 *Beware* lest Hezekiah persuade you, saying, The LORD will deliver us. Hath any of the gods of the nations delivered his land out of the hand of the king of Assyria?

19 Where *are* the gods of Hamath and Arphad? where *are* the gods of Sepharvaim? and have they delivered Samaria out of my hand?

20 Who *are they* among all the gods of these lands, that have delivered their land out of my hand, that the LORD should deliver Jerusalem out of my hand?

21 But they held their peace, and answered him not a word: for the king's commandment was, saying, Answer him not.

22 ¶ Then came Eliakim, the son of Hilkiah, that *was* over the household, and Shebna the scribe, and Joah, the son of Asaph, the recorder, to Hezekiah with *their* clothes rent, and told him the words of Rab-shakeh.

36:4 [r]2 Ki. 18:19
36:6 [s]Ezek. 29:6,7
36:16 [t]Zech. 3:10

[t]Heb. *a word of lips* [u]Or, but *counsel and strength* are *for the war* [v]Or, *hostages* [w]Or, *Seek my favour by a present* [x]Heb. *Make with me a blessing*

36:4–10 RAB-SHAKEH SAID. The field commander of Sennacherib's army attempted to undermine the people's confidence in the Lord through intimidation, lies, and arguments that the God of Judah was not strong enough to deliver them (cf. 2 Ki. 19:6–13).

36:20 THE LORD SHOULD DELIVER JERUSALEM OUT OF MY HAND? Rab-shakeh mockingly suggested that the God of Judah was not powerful enough to deliver Jerusalem from his army. He implied that it would take a miracle and that this was no time to expect such a thing. Satan still uses such tactics on God's children; he tells them that when they are in great need, they should not expect or seek a miracle from God. Note, however, that God did work a miracle for Judah and defeated Rab-shakeh and his army (37:36–38).

Isaiah's message to Hezekiah

37:1–13pp — 2 Ki. 19:1–13

37 AND [u]IT came to pass, when king Hezekiah heard *it,* that he rent his clothes, and covered himself with sackcloth, and went into the house of the LORD.

2 And he sent Eliakim, who *was* over the household, and Shebna the scribe, and the elders of the priests covered with sackcloth, unto Isaiah the prophet the son of Amoz.

3 And they said unto him, Thus saith Hezekiah, This day *is* a day of trouble, and of rebuke, and of [y]blasphemy: for the children are come to the birth, and *there is* not strength to bring forth.

4 It may be the LORD thy God will hear the words of Rab-shakeh, whom the king of Assyria his master hath sent to reproach the living God, and will reprove the words which the LORD thy God hath heard: wherefore lift up *thy* prayer for the remnant that is [z]left.

5 So the servants of king Hezekiah came to Isaiah.

6 ¶ And Isaiah said unto them, Thus shall ye say unto your master, Thus saith the LORD, Be not afraid of the words that thou hast heard, wherewith the servants of the king of Assyria have blasphemed me.

7 Behold, I will [a]send a blast upon him, and he shall hear a rumour, and return to his own land; and I will cause him to fall by the sword in his own land.

8 ¶ So Rab-shakeh returned, and found the king of Assyria warring against Libnah: for he had heard that he was departed from Lachish.

9 And he heard say concerning Tirhakah king of Ethiopia, He is come forth to make war with thee. And when he heard *it,* he sent messengers to Hezekiah, saying,

10 Thus shall ye speak to Hezekiah king of Judah, saying, Let not thy God, in whom thou trustest, deceive thee, saying, Jerusalem shall not be given into the hand of the king of Assyria.

11 Behold, thou hast heard what the kings of Assyria have done to all lands by destroying them utterly; and shalt thou be delivered?

12 Have the gods of the nations delivered them which my fathers have destroyed, *as* Gozan, and Haran, and Rezeph, and the children of Eden which *were* in Telassar?

13 Where *is* the king of [v]Hamath, and the king of Arphad, and the king of the city of Sepharvaim, Hena, and Ivah?

Hezekiah's prayer to the LORD

37:14–20pp — 2 Ki. 19:14–19

14 ¶ And Hezekiah received the letter from the hand of the messengers, and read it: and Hezekiah went up unto the house of the LORD, and spread it before the LORD.

15 And Hezekiah prayed unto the LORD, saying,

16 O LORD of hosts, God of Israel, that dwellest *between* the cherubims, thou *art* the God, *even* thou alone, of all the kingdoms of the earth: thou hast made heaven and earth.

17 [w]Incline thine ear, O LORD, and hear; open thine eyes, O LORD, and see: and hear all the words of Sennacherib, which hath sent to reproach the living God.

18 Of a truth, LORD, the kings of Assyria have laid waste all the [b]nations, and their countries,

19 And have [c]cast their gods into the fire: for they *were* no gods, but the

37:1 [u]2 Ki. 19:1
37:13 [v]Jer. 49:23
37:17 [w]Dan. 9:18

[y] Or, *provocation* [z] Heb. *found* [a] Or, *put a spirit into him* [b] Heb *lands* [c] Heb. *given*

37:1 HEZEKIAH ... WENT INTO THE HOUSE OF THE LORD. Rab-shakeh's intimidation and accusations were unworthy of a response (36:21), but they were worthy of earnest intercession. Hezekiah, a man of God, turned to God in humble and contrite prayer and sought to know His word through the mouth of Isaiah the prophet (v. 2; see 2 Ki. 19:1, note). In times of trouble, the best thing we can do is seek the face of God and ask Him to speak to us through His written or prophetic word.

37:7 I WILL SEND A BLAST UPON HIM. This verse refers to an inner voice sent by God to influence a person's conduct and thought. Concerning the prediction that the king of Assyria would "fall by the sword," see vv. 37–38.

37:10 THY GOD. Sennacherib attempted in every way to destroy Hezekiah's confidence in the Lord. The Assyrian king arrogantly believed that his royal power surpassed that of the God of Judah or any god.

37:14–20 HEZEKIAH PRAYED. See 2 Ki. 19:15, note.

work of men's hands, wood and stone: therefore they have destroyed them.

20 Now therefore, O LORD our God, save us from his hand, that all the kingdoms of the earth may know that thou *art* the LORD, *even* thou only.

The promise of deliverance

37:21–38pp — 2 Ki. 19:20–37; 2 Chr. 32:20–21

21 ¶ Then Isaiah the son of Amoz sent unto Hezekiah, saying, Thus saith the LORD God of Israel, Whereas thou hast prayed to me against Sennacherib king of Assyria:

22 This *is* the word which the LORD hath spoken concerning him; The virgin, the daughter of Zion, hath despised thee, *and* laughed thee to scorn; the daughter of Jerusalem hath shaken her head at thee.

23 Whom hast thou reproached and blasphemed? and against whom hast thou exalted *thy* voice, and lifted up thine eyes on high? *even* against the Holy One of Israel.

24 [d]By thy servants hast thou reproached the Lord, and hast said, By the multitude of my chariots am I come up to the height of the mountains, to the sides of Lebanon; and I will cut down [e]the tall cedars thereof, *and* the choice fir trees thereof: and I will enter into the height of his border, *and* [f]the forest of his Carmel.

25 I have digged, and drunk water; and with the sole of my feet have I dried up all the rivers of the [g]besieged places.

26 [x]Hast[h] thou not heard long ago, *how* I have done it; *and* of ancient times, that I have formed it? now have I brought it to pass, that thou shouldest be to lay waste defenced cities *into* ruinous heaps.

27 Therefore their inhabitants *were* [i]of small power, they were dismayed and confounded: they were *as* the grass of the field, and *as* the green herb, *as* the grass on the housetops, and *as corn* blasted before it be grown up.

28 But I know thy [j]abode, and thy going out, and thy coming in, and thy rage against me.

29 Because thy rage against me, and thy tumult, is come up into mine ears, therefore [y]will I put my hook in thy nose, and my bridle in thy lips, and I will turn thee back by the way by which thou camest.

30 And this *shall be* a sign unto thee, Ye shall eat *this* year such as growth of itself; and the second year that which springeth of the same: and in the third year sow ye, and reap, and plant vineyards, and eat the fruit thereof.

31 And [k]the remnant that is escaped of the house of Judah shall again take root downward, and bear fruit upward:

32 For out of Jerusalem shall go forth a remnant, and [l]they that escape out of mount Zion: the [z]zeal of the LORD of hosts shall do this.

33 Therefore thus saith the LORD concerning the king of Assyria, He shall not come into this city, nor shoot an arrow there, nor come before it with [m]shields, nor cast a bank against it.

34 By the way that he came, by the same shall he return, and shall not come into this city, saith the LORD.

35 For I will [a]defend this city to save it for mine own sake, and for my servant David's sake.

36 Then the [b]angel of the LORD went forth, and smote in the camp of the Assyrians a hundred and fourscore and five thousand: and when they arose early in the morning, behold, they *were* all dead corpses.

37 ¶ So Sennacherib king of Assyria departed, and went and returned, and dwelt at Nineveh.

38 And it came to pass, as he was worshipping in the house of Nisroch his god, that Adrammelech and Sharezer his sons smote him with the sword; and they escaped into the land of [n]Ar-

37:26 [x]2 Ki. 19:25
37:29 [y]ch. 30:28 Ezek. 38:4
37:32 [z]2 Ki. 19:31 ch. 9:7
37:35 [a]2 Ki. 20:6 ch. 38:6
37:36 [b]2 Ki. 19:35

[d]Heb. *By the hand of thy servants* [e]Heb. *the tallness of the cedars thereof,* and *the choice of the fir trees thereof* [f]Or, *the forest* and *his fruitful field* [g]Or, *fenced and closed* [h]Or, *Hast thou not heard* how *I have made it long ago,* and *formed it of ancient times? should I now bring it to be laid waste,* and *defenced cities* to be *ruinous heaps?* [i]Heb. *short of hand* [j]Or, *sitting* [k]Heb. *the escaping of the house of Judah that remaineth* [l]Heb. *the escaping* [m]Heb. *shield* [n]Heb. *Ararat*

37:20 THAT . . . THE EARTH MAY KNOW THAT THOU *ART* THE LORD. See 2 Ki. 19:19, note.

37:36 THE ANGEL OF THE LORD. This destruction of the Assyrian army was foretold in 10:3–34; 30:31; 31:8 (see 2 Ki. 19:35, note on this miraculous deliverance of God's people).

menia: and Esar-haddon his son
reigned in his stead.

Hezekiah's sickness

38:1–8pp — 2 Ki. 20:1–11; 2 Chr. 32:24–26

38 IN [c]THOSE days was Hezeki-
ah sick unto death. And Isaiah
the prophet the son of Amoz came unto
him, and said unto him, Thus saith the
LORD, [d]Set[o] thine house in order: for
thou shalt die, and not live.
2 Then Hezekiah turned his face to-
ward the wall, and prayed unto the
LORD,
3 And said, [e]Remember now,
O LORD, I beseech thee, how I have
walked before thee in truth and with a
perfect heart, and have done *that which*
is good in thy sight. And Hezekiah
wept [p]sore.
4 ¶ Then came the word of the LORD
to Isaiah, saying,
5 Go, and say to Hezekiah, Thus
saith the LORD, the God of David thy
father, I have heard thy prayer, I have
seen thy tears: behold, I will add unto
thy days fifteen years.
6 And I will deliver thee and this
city out of the hand of the king of As-
syria: and [f]I will defend this city.
7 And this *shall be* [g]a sign unto
thee from the LORD, that the LORD will
do this thing that he hath spoken;
8 Behold, I will bring again the
shadow of the degrees, which is gone
down in the [q]sun dial of Ahaz, ten de-
grees backward. So the sun returned
ten degrees, by which degrees it was
gone down.
9 ¶ The writing of Hezekiah king of
Judah, when he had been sick, and was
recovered of his sickness:
10 I said in the cutting off of my
days, I shall go to the gates of the
grave; I am deprived of the residue of
my years.
11 I said, I shall not see the LORD,
even the LORD, [h]in the land of the liv-
ing: I shall behold man no more with
the inhabitants of the world.
12 [i]Mine age is departed, and is
removed from me as a shepherd's tent:
I have cut off like a weaver my life: he
will cut me off [r]with pining sickness:
from day *even* to night wilt thou make
an end of me.
13 I reckoned till morning, *that,* as
a lion, so will he break all my bones:
from day *even* to night wilt thou make
an end of me.
14 Like a crane *or* a swallow, so did
I chatter: [j]I did mourn as a dove: mine
eyes fail *with looking* upward: O LORD,
I am oppressed; [s]undertake for me.
15 What shall I say? he hath both
spoken unto me, and himself hath done
it: I shall go softly all my years [k]in the
bitterness of my soul.
16 O Lord, by these *things men* live,
and in all these *things is* the life of my
spirit: so wilt thou recover me, and
make me to live.
17 Behold, [t]for peace I had great
bitterness: but [u]thou hast in love to
my soul *delivered it* from the pit of cor-

38:1 [c]2 Ki. 20:1 2 Chr. 32:24 [d]2 Sam. 17:23
38:3 [e]Neh. 13:14
38:6 [f]ch. 37:35
38:7 [g]2 Ki. 20:8 ch. 7:11
38:11 [h]Ps. 27:13 & 116:9
38:12 [i]Job 7:6
38:14 [j]ch. 59:11
38:15 [k]Job 7:11

[o] Heb. *Give charge concerning thy house* [p] Heb. *with great weeping* [q] Heb. *degrees by,* or, *with the sun* [r] Or, *from the* thrum [s] Or, *ease me* [t] Or, *on my peace came great bitterness* [u] Heb. *thou hast loved my soul from the pit*

38:1 THOU SHALT DIE. Through Isaiah God prophesied that Hezekiah would die as the inevitable physical consequence of his sickness. However, much prophecy is conditional (e.g., see Jer. 18:7–10); God does not act deceitfully (Heb. 6:18), but He can change His plans as a result of our response to His word. God's word to Hezekiah was a direct and unequivocable statement expressing a genuine possibility. But because Hezekiah responded in earnest prayer and in confidence in God's ability to heal his physical malady, God in mercy answered his prayer and added fifteen years to his life.

38:5 I HAVE HEARD THY PRAYER. God's statement that Hezekiah must prepare for death and Hezekiah's prayer to God (v. 2) have important implications for our relationship to God. (1) All the things that God declares about the future are not necessarily irrevocable (cf. Jonah 3:1–10). When believers are confronted with tragedy, we can rest assured that God cares about what happens to us. He is compassionate and sensitive to our experiences.

(2) Our prayers do have an effect on God, His purposes, and the outworking of His sovereign plan. Thus what happens in our lives or in the life of the church is determined by both God's plan and our prayers. We must always maintain the Scriptural conviction that prayer does change things (vv. 4–7; cf. 1 Ki. 21:29; Ezek. 33:13–16; Jas. 5:14–15).

38:8 THE SUN RETURNED TEN DEGREES. The exact nature of the sun's shadow being reversed on the stairway is not explained; what is clear is that it did occur by God's powerful word as a prophetic sign to Hezekiah that God had heard his prayer and seen his tears, and would heal him.

ruption: for thou hast cast all my sins
behind thy back.
18 For [l]the grave cannot praise
thee, death can *not* celebrate thee: they
that go down into the pit cannot hope
for thy truth.
19 The living, the living, he shall
praise thee, as I *do* this day: [m]the fa-
ther to the children shall make known
thy truth.
20 The LORD *was ready* to save me:
therefore we will sing my songs to the
stringed instruments all the days of
our life in the house of the LORD.
21 For [n]Isaiah had said, Let them
Is. 53:4-5 take a lump of figs, and lay *it* for a plas-
ter upon the boil, and he shall recover.
22 [o]Hezekiah also had said, What
is the sign that I shall go up to the
house of the LORD?

Hezekiah's folly and exile

39:1–8pp — 2 Ki. 20:12–19

39 AT [p]THAT time Merodach-
baladan, the son of Baladan,
king of Babylon, sent letters and a
present to Hezekiah: for he had heard
that he had been sick, and was recov-
ered.
2 [q]And Hezekiah was glad of them,
and showed them the house of his
[v]precious things, the silver, and the
gold, and the spices, and the precious
ointment, and all the house of his
[w,x]armour, and all that was found in
his treasures: there was nothing in his
house, nor in all his dominion, that
Hezekiah showed them not.
3 ¶ Then came Isaiah the prophet
unto king Hezekiah, and said unto him,
What said these men? and from
whence came they unto thee? And Hez-
ekiah said, They are come from a far
country unto me, *even* from Babylon.
4 Then said he, What have they
seen in thine house? And Hezekiah an-
swered, All that *is* in mine house have
they seen: there is nothing among my
treasures that I have not shown them.
5 Then said Isaiah to Hezekiah,
Hear the word of the LORD of hosts:
6 Behold, the days come, [r]that all
that *is* in thine house, and *that* which
thy fathers have laid up in store until
this day, shall be carried to Babylon:
nothing shall be left, saith the LORD.
7 And of thy sons that shall issue
from thee, which thou shalt beget,
shall they take away; and [y]they shall
be eunuchs in the palace of the king of
Babylon.
8 Then said Hezekiah to Isaiah,
[s]Good *is* the word of the LORD which
thou hast spoken. He said moreover,
For there shall be peace and truth in
my days.

Comfort for God's people

40 COMFORT YE, comfort ye my
people, saith your God.

38:18 [l]Ps. 6:5 & 30:9 & 88:11 & 115:17 Eccl. 9:10 **38:19** [m]Deut. 4:9 & 6:7 Ps. 78:3,4 **38:21** [n]2 Ki. 20:7 **38:22** [o]2 Ki. 20:8 **39:1** [p]2 Ki. 20:12 **39:2** [q]2 Chr. 32:31 **39:6** [r]Jer. 20:5 **39:8** [s]1 Sam. 3:18

[v] Or, *spicery* [w] Or, *jewels* [x] Heb. *vessels,* or, *instruments* [y] Fulfilled in Dan. 1:2,3

39:1 KING OF BABYLON. Babylon was attempting to free itself from the dominance of Assyria at this time. Thus this visit by the king of Babylon to Jerusalem was clearly to seek political alliance with Judah. By his reaction to the gifts and flattery of the delegation, Hezekiah demonstrated foolish presumption and a lack of faith in God. Isaiah later told him that the Babylonians would someday destroy Jerusalem (v. 6). We must remember that whatever we trust instead of God will one day turn on us and destroy us.

39:6 SHALL BE CARRIED TO BABYLON. When the Babylonians would conquer Jerusalem, they would carry off its people and treasures to their own country (cf. 14:3–4). In the final analysis, the cause of the Babylonian captivity was not Hezekiah's foolishness in showing the temple treasures, but the sins of the people and especially of Hezekiah's son Manasseh (cf. 2 Ki. 21). After Hezekiah's death the nation once again rebuilt the centers of idol worship (see 2 Chr. 33:11; 36:18, for the fulfillment of the prophecy).

40—66 COMFORT YE. These chapters were written during the later years of Isaiah's life. God revealed these prophecies in order to offer hope and comfort to His people during their captivity in Babylon 150 years after the time of Isaiah (see 39:5–8); they are filled with prophetic revelation about the coming Messiah and His future kingdom on earth. Some predicted events were fulfilled in connection with Judah's Babylonian captivity and restoration, many relate more specifically to the appearing of Jesus Christ on earth, and still others await fulfillment. In general, chs. 40—48 emphasize deliverance, chs. 49—57 redemption, and chs. 58—66 glory.

40:1 COMFORT YE MY PEOPLE. Isaiah comforts God's people by prophesying to a future generation the good news that God's period of chastisement was nearly over and salvation and blessing were coming. If you are experiencing great difficulty in your life and you know that Christ is your Savior, you can pray for God to deliver you from such trouble or to be with you and help you in the midst of it. To give us comfort is a task of the triune God: God the Father is called "the God of all comfort" (2 Cor. 1:3), "to comfort all that mourn" is a characteristic of the ministry of the Son of God (Is. 61:2), and the Holy Spirit is called "the Comforter" (John 14:16,26; 15:26; 16:7).

2 Speak ye [z]comfortably to Jerusa-
lem, and cry unto her, that her [a]war-
fare is accomplished, that her iniquity
is pardoned: [t]for she hath received of
the LORD's hand double for all her sins.
3 ¶ [u]The voice of him that crieth in
the wilderness, [v]Prepare ye the way
of the LORD, [w]make straight in the
desert a highway for our God.
4 Every valley shall be exalted, and
every mountain and hill shall be made
low: [x]and the crooked shall be made
[b]straight, and the rough places
[c]plain:
5 And the glory of the LORD shall be
revealed, and all flesh shall see *it* to-
gether: for the mouth of the LORD hath
spoken *it*.
6 The voice said, Cry. And he said,
What shall I cry? [y]All flesh *is* grass,
and all the goodliness thereof *is* as the
flower of the field:
7 The grass withereth, the flower
fadeth: because the spirit of the LORD
bloweth upon it: surely the people *is*
grass.
8 The grass withereth, the flower
fadeth: but [z]the word of our God shall
stand for ever.
9 ¶ [a]O[d] Zion, that bringest good
tidings, get thee up into the high moun-
tain; [e]O Jerusalem, that bringest good
tidings, lift up thy voice with strength;
lift *it* up, be not afraid; say unto the
cities of Judah, Behold your God!
10 Behold, the Lord GOD will come
[f]with strong *hand*, and [b]his arm
shall rule for him: behold, [c]his reward
is with him, and [d]his[g] work before
him.
11 He shall [e]feed his flock like a
shepherd: he shall gather the lambs
with his arm, and carry *them* in his bo-
som, *and* shall gently lead those [h]that Is. 62:11-12
are with young.
12 ¶ [f]Who hath measured the wa-
ters in the hollow of his hand, and met-
ed out heaven with the span, and com-
prehended the dust of the earth in [i]a
measure, and weighed the mountains
in scales, and the hills in a balance?
13 [g]Who hath directed the spirit of
the LORD, or *being* [j]his counsellor hath
taught him?
14 With whom took he counsel, and
who [k]instructed him, and taught him
in the path of judgment, and taught

40:2 [t]ch. 61:7 **40:3** [u]Mat. 3:3 [v]Mal. 3:1 [w]Ps. 68:4 **40:4** [x]ch. 45:2 **40:6** [y]Job 14:2 **40:8** [z]John 12:34 **40:9** [a]ch. 41:27 **40:10** [b]ch. 59:16 [c]ch. 62:11 [d]ch. 49:4 **40:11** [e]Ezek. 34:23 John 10:11 Heb. 13:20 1 Pet. 2:25 **40:12** [f]Prov. 30:4 **40:13** [g]Job 21:22 1 Cor. 2:16

[z] Heb. *to the heart* [a] Or, *appointed time*
[b] Or, *a straight place* [c] Or, *a plain place*
[d] Or, *O thou that tellest good tidings to Zion*
[e] Or, *O thou that tellest good tidings to Jerusalem*
[f] Or, *against the strong* [g] Or, *recompence for his work* [h] Or, *that give suck* [i] Heb. *a tierce* [j] Heb. *man of his counsel* [k] Heb. *made him understand*

40:3–8 THE VOICE OF HIM THAT CRIETH IN THE WILDERNESS. These verses, like much prophecy in Isaiah, have several levels of application: (1) to the Jews' restoration from exile, (2) to the coming of the Messiah and His salvation, and (3) to the consummation of redemption in the new heaven and earth. The N.T. sees the fulfillment of v. 3 in John the Baptist—the forerunner of the Messiah (Mat. 3:1–4; Mark 1:1–4; Luke 1:76–78; John 1:23). John made clear that the way to prepare for the Lord's coming was through repentance (Mat. 3:1–8).

40:5 THE GLORY OF THE LORD SHALL BE REVEALED. Israel would see the glory of the Lord when He delivered them from Babylonian captivity. But God would reveal His glory and power in even greater ways in the person of Jesus Christ (John 1:14; 11:4,40; Heb. 1:3) and at Christ's return from heaven (Mat. 16:27; 24:30; Rev. 1:7).

40:8 THE WORD OF OUR GOD SHALL STAND FOR EVER. All created life is frail and weak and will ultimately come to an end (cf. 37:27; Ps. 90:5; 103:15), but God's word endures forever. God's promises will be fulfilled; His redemptive truth cannot be annulled or changed (see article on THE INSPIRATION AND AUTHORITY OF SCRIPTURE, p. 1924).

40:10 THE LORD GOD WILL COME WITH STRONG *HAND*. Salvation, blessing, and comfort are all associated with the coming of the Lord to His faithful people. He comes with power and authority like a mighty ruler; yet His presence is like that of a caring shepherd tending His lambs (v. 11; cf. Gen. 49:24; Ezek. 34:23; 37:24; John 10:11,14; Heb. 13:20; 1 Pet. 5:4). This truth should fill God's people with faith, hope, and prayerful longing for His nearness and special visitation, while they look for the day of His return and of final redemption (1 Thes. 4:14–18).

40:11 GATHER THE LAMBS WITH HIS ARM. God is described as one who picks up an individual lamb in order to protect it and carry it close to His heart (cf. Mat. 6:24–34). Although God is all-powerful (v. 10) and the nations are as dust before Him (v. 15), He still cares for each of His own in a personal way. We must never think that God is so majestic that He ignores the needs and problems of the individual believer.

40:12–31 WHO HATH MEASURED. These verses emphasize God's wisdom, greatness, majesty, and creative power (see article on THE ATTRIBUTES OF GOD, p. 912). The truths expressed here inspire His people to trust in Him, the One who can deliver them and establish His kingdom forever.

him knowledge, and showed to him the
way of [1]understanding?
15 Behold, the nations *are* as a drop
of a bucket, and are counted as the
small dust of the balance: behold, he
taketh up the isles as a very little
thing.
16 And Lebanon *is* not sufficient to
burn, nor the beasts thereof sufficient
for a burnt offering.
17 All nations before him *are* as
[h]nothing; and [i]they are counted to
him less than nothing, and vanity.
18 ¶ To whom then will ye [j]liken
God? or what likeness will ye compare
unto him?
19 [k]The workman melteth a grav-
en image, and the goldsmith spreadeth
it over with gold, and casteth silver
chains.
20 He that [m]*is* so impoverished
that he hath no oblation chooseth a
tree *that* will not rot; he seeketh unto
him a cunning workman [l]to prepare a
graven image, *that* shall not be moved.
21 [m]Have ye not known? have ye
not heard? hath it not been told you
from the beginning? have ye not under-
stood from the foundations of the
earth?
22 [n]*It is* he that sitteth upon the
circle of the earth, and the inhabitants
thereof *are* as grasshoppers; that
[n]stretcheth out the heavens as a cur-
tain, and spreadeth them out as a tent
to dwell in:
23 That bringeth the [o]princes to
nothing; he maketh the judges of the
earth as vanity.
24 Yea, they shall not be planted;
yea, they shall not be sown: yea,
their stock shall not take root in the
earth: and he shall also blow upon
them, and they shall wither, and the
whirlwind shall take them away as
stubble.
25 [p]To whom then will ye liken me,
or shall I be equal? saith the Holy One.
26 Lift up your eyes on high, and be-
hold who hath created these *things*,
that bringeth out their host by number:
[q]he calleth them all by names by the
greatness of his might, for that *he is*
strong in power; not one faileth.
27 Why sayest thou, O Jacob, and
speakest, O Israel, My way is hid from
the LORD, and my judgment is passed
over from my God?
28 ¶ Hast thou not known? hast
thou not heard, *that* the everlasting
God, the LORD, the Creator of the ends
of the earth, fainteth not, neither is
weary? [r]*there is* no searching of his
understanding.
29 He giveth power to the faint; and
to *them that have* no might he in-
creaseth strength.
30 Even the youths shall faint and
be weary, and the young men shall ut-
terly fall:
31 But they that wait upon the LORD
[s]shall [o]renew *their* strength; they
shall mount up with wings as eagles;
they shall run, and not be weary; *and*
they shall walk, and not faint.

God will help Israel

41 KEEP[t] SILENCE before me, O
islands; and let the people re-
new *their* strength: let them come near;
then let them speak: let us come near
together to judgment.
2 Who raised up [p]the righteous
man [u]from the east, called him to his
foot, [v]gave the nations before him,

40:17 [h]Dan. 4:35 [i]Ps. 62:9
40:18 [j]ch. 46:5 Acts 17:29
40:19 [k]ch. 41:6,7 & 44:12 Jer. 10:3
40:20 [l]ch. 41:7 Jer. 10:4
40:21 [m]Ps. 19:1 Acts 14:17 Rom. 1:19
40:22 [n]Job 9:8 Ps. 104:2 ch. 42:5 & 51:13 Jer. 10:12
40:23 [o]Job 12:21 Ps. 107:40
40:25 [p]ver. 18
40:26 [q]Ps. 147:4
40:28 [r]Ps. 147:5 Rom. 11:33
40:31 [s]Ps. 103:5
41:1 [t]Zech. 2:13
41:2 [u]ch. 46:11 [v]Gen. 14:14 ch. 45:1

[1] Heb. *understandings?* [m] Heb. is *poor of oblation* [n] Or, *Him that sitteth* [o] Heb. *change* [p] Heb. *righteousness*

40:26 WHO HATH CREATED THESE *THINGS*. See article on CREATION, p. 6.

40:31 THEY THAT WAIT UPON THE LORD SHALL RENEW *THEIR* STRENGTH. To wait on the Lord is to trust Him fully with our lives. It involves looking to Him as our source of help and grace in time of need (cf. Ps. 25:3–5; 27:14; Luke 2:25,38). Those who wait upon the Lord are promised: (1) the strength of God to revive them in the midst of exhaustion and weakness, of suffering and trial; (2) the ability to rise above their difficulties as an eagle that soars into the sky; and (3) the ability to run spiritually without tiring and to walk steadily forward without fainting at God's delays. God promises that if His people will patiently trust Him, He will provide whatever is needed to sustain them constantly (1 Pet. 1:5).

41:1 LET US COME NEAR TOGETHER TO JUDGMENT. In this chapter the nations are challenged to demonstrate that they have the same power, wisdom, and foreknowledge as the God of Israel.

41:2 THE RIGHTEOUS *MAN* FROM THE EAST. More than 150 years before the birth of Cyrus, Isaiah foresaw that God would raise up a man to do His will by conquering the nations and protecting Israel. This man was Cyrus, the king of Persia (559–530 B.C.; see 44:28; 45:1), the one who freed the Jews from their Babylonian exile. He was called righteous, not because he himself was righteous, but because he would carry out God's righteous plan of redemption on the earth.

and made *him* rule over kings? he gave *them* as the dust to his sword, *and* as driven stubble to his bow.

3 He pursued them, *and* passed [q]safely; *even* by the way *that* he had not gone with his feet.

4 [w]Who hath wrought and done *it,* calling the generations from the beginning? I the LORD, the [x]first, and with the last; I *am* he.

5 The isles saw *it,* and feared; the ends of the earth were afraid, drew near, and came.

6 [y]They helped every one his neighbour; and *every one* said to his brother, [r]Be of good courage.

7 [z]So the carpenter encouraged the [s]goldsmith, *and* he that smootheth *with* the hammer [t]him that smote the anvil, [u]saying, It *is* ready for the soldering: and he fastened it with nails, [a]*that* it should not be moved.

8 But thou, Israel, *art* my servant, Jacob whom I have [b]chosen, the seed of Abraham my [c]friend.

9 *Thou* whom I have taken from the ends of the earth, and called thee from the chief men thereof, and said unto thee, Thou *art* my servant; I have chosen thee, and not cast thee away.

10 ¶ [d]Fear thou not; [e]for I *am* with thee: be not dismayed; for I *am* thy God: I will strengthen thee; yea, I will help thee; yea, I will uphold thee with the right hand of my righteousness.

11 Behold, all they that were incensed against thee shall be [f]ashamed and confounded: they shall be as nothing; and [v]they that strive with thee shall perish.

12 Thou shalt seek them, and shalt not find them, *even* [w]them that contended with thee: [x]they that war against thee shall be as nothing, and as a thing of nought.

41:4 [w]ver. 26 [x]ch. 44:6 Rev. 1:17 & 22:13
41:6 [y]ch. 40:19
41:7 [z]ch. 40:19 [a]ch. 40:20
41:8 [b]Deut. 7:6 & 10:15 Ps. 135:4 ch. 43:1 [c]2 Chr. 20:7 Jas. 2:23
41:10 [d]ver. 13,14 ch. 43:5 [e]Deut. 31:6
41:11 [f]Ex. 23:22 ch. 45:24 & 60:12 Zech. 12:3
41:15 [g]Mic. 4:13 2 Cor. 10:4
41:16 [h]Jer. 51:2 [i]ch. 45:25
41:18 [j]ch. 35:6,7 & 43:19 & 44:3 [k]Ps. 107:35
41:20 [l]Job 12:9

13 For I the LORD thy God will hold thy right hand, saying unto thee, Fear not; I will help thee.

14 Fear not, thou worm Jacob, *and* ye [y]men of Israel; I will help thee, saith the LORD, and thy redeemer, the Holy One of Israel.

15 Behold, [g]I will make thee a new sharp threshing instrument having [z]teeth: thou shalt thresh the mountains, and beat *them* small, and shalt make the hills as chaff.

16 Thou shalt [h]fan them, and the wind shall carry them away, and the whirlwind shall scatter them: and thou shalt rejoice in the LORD, *and* [i]shalt glory in the Holy One of Israel.

17 *When* the poor and needy seek water, and *there is* none, *and* their tongue faileth for thirst, I the LORD will hear them, *I* the God of Israel will not forsake them.

18 I will open [j]rivers in high places, and fountains in the midst of the valleys: I will make the [k]wilderness a pool of water, and the dry land springs of water.

19 I will plant in the wilderness the cedar, the shittah tree, and the myrtle, and the oil tree; I will set in the desert the fir tree, *and* the pine, and the box tree together:

20 [l]That they may see, and know, and consider, and understand together, that the hand of the LORD hath done this, and the Holy One of Israel hath created it.

21 [a]Produce your cause, saith the

[q]Heb. *in peace* [r]Heb. *Be strong* [s]Or, *founder* [t]Or, *the smiting* [u]Or, *saying of the soder, It* is *good* [v]Heb. *the men of thy strife* [w]Heb. *the men of thy contention* [x]Heb. *the men of thy war* [y]Or, *few men* [z]Heb. *mouths* [a]Heb. *Cause to come near*

41:6 THEY HELPED EVERY ONE HIS NEIGHBOUR. Alliances among nations would not stop the advance of Cyrus as the instrument of God's purpose.

41:8 ISRAEL ... I HAVE CHOSEN. Israel must not fear destruction, because God had chosen them as His channel to carry out the promise of redemption He had made to their ancestors. Through the nation of Israel would come both the Messiah and the written revelation of God, by which salvation would go to all the nations of the earth (see article on GOD'S COVENANT WITH ABRAHAM, ISAAC, AND JACOB, p. 48).

41:10–11 I *AM* WITH THEE. N.T. believers have also become the chosen servants of God (Eph. 1:3–12; 1 Pet. 2:9). We can therefore claim the promises of these verses for ourselves. We must not fear other humans because God is with us (cf. 40:9; 43:2,5; Gen. 15:1; Acts 18:9–10): (1) to impart the grace and strength needed to face all the circumstances of life; (2) to help us through times of crises as our source of peace; and (3) to sustain us and be our advocate.

41:21–24 PRODUCE YOUR CAUSE. God challenges the nations to foretell the future by their idols as accurately as Isaiah has done by the Spirit of the Lord.

LORD; bring forth your strong *reasons,* saith the King of Jacob.

22 [m]Let them bring *them* forth, and show us what shall happen: let them show the former things, what they *be,* that we may [b]consider them, and know the latter end of them; or declare us things for to come.

23 [n]Show the things that are to come hereafter, that we may know that ye *are* gods: yea, [o]do good, or do evil, that we may be dismayed, and behold *it* together.

24 Behold, [p]ye *are* [c]of nothing, and your work [d]of nought: an abomination *is he that* chooseth you.

25 I have raised up *one* from the north, and he shall come: from the rising of the sun [q]shall he call upon my name: [r]and he shall come upon princes as *upon* mortar, and as the potter treadeth clay.

26 [s]Who hath declared from the beginning, that we may know? and beforetime, that we may say, *He is* righteous? yea, *there is* none that showeth, yea, *there is* none that declareth, yea, *there is* none that heareth your words.

27 [t]The first [u]*shall say* to Zion, Behold, behold them: and I will give to Jerusalem one that bringeth good tidings.

28 [v]For I beheld, and *there was* no man; even among them, and *there was* no counsellor, that, when I asked of them, could [e]answer a word.

29 [w]Behold, they *are* all vanity; their works *are* nothing: their molten images *are* wind and confusion.

41:22 [m]ch. 45:21 **41:23** [n]ch. 42:9 & 44:7,8 & 45:3 John 13:19 [o]Jer. 10:5 **41:24** [p]Ps. 115:8 ch. 44:9 1 Cor. 8:4 **41:25** [q]Ezra 1:2 [r]ver. 2 **41:26** [s]ch. 43:9 **41:27** [t]ver. 4 [u]ch. 40:9 **41:28** [v]ch. 63:5 **41:29** [w]ver. 24

42:1 [x]ch. 43:10 & 49:3,6 Mat. 12:18 Phil. 2:7 [y]Mat. 3:17 & 17:5 Eph. 1:6 [z]ch. 11:2 John 3:34 **42:4** [a]Gen. 49:10 **42:5** [b]ch. 44:24 Zech. 12:1 [c]Acts 17:25 **42:6** [d]ch. 43:1 [e]ch. 49:8 [f]ch. 49:6 Luke 2:32 Acts 13:47 **42:7** [g]ch. 35:5 [h]ch. 61:1 Luke 4:18 2 Tim. 2:26 Heb. 2:14 [i]ch. 9:2 **42:8** [j]ch. 48:11

The mission of God's servant

42 BEHOLD [x]MY servant, whom I uphold; mine elect, *in whom* my soul [y]delighteth; [z]I have put my spirit upon him: he shall bring forth judgment to the Gentiles. Is. 44:3

2 He shall not cry, nor lift up, nor cause his voice to be heard in the street.

3 A bruised reed shall he not break, and the [f]smoking flax shall he not [g]quench: he shall bring forth judgment unto truth.

4 He shall not fail nor be [h]discouraged, till he have set judgment in the earth: [a]and the isles shall wait for his law.

5 ¶ Thus saith God the LORD, [b]he that created the heavens, and stretched them out; he that spread forth the earth, and that which cometh out of it; [c]he that giveth breath unto the people upon it, and spirit to them that walk therein:

6 [d]I the LORD have called thee in righteousness, and will hold thine hand, and will keep thee, [e]and give thee for a covenant of the people, for [f]a light of the Gentiles;

7 [g]To open the blind eyes, to [h]bring out the prisoners from the prison, *and* them that sit in [i]darkness out of the prison house. Is. 43:9-10

8 I *am* the LORD: that *is* my name: and my [j]glory will I not give to an-

[b] Heb. *set our heart* upon them [c] Or, worse *than nothing* [d] Or, worse *than of a viper* [e] Heb. *return* [f] Or, *dimly burning* [g] Heb. *quench it* [h] Heb. *broken*

41:25 *ONE* FROM THE NORTH. This phrase describes Cyrus (see v. 2, note). North is the direction from which invasions into Israel usually came (cf. Jer. 1:14; 6:22; 25:9; 46:20; 47:2; 50:3). Although Cyrus was not a worshiper of the Lord, he did use the name of the Lord in his decree to allow the exiles to return to the promised land (Ezra 1:2).

42:1–7 BEHOLD MY SERVANT. These verses are quoted in part in the N.T. (see Mat. 12:18–21); clearly the servant about whom the prophet writes is Jesus Christ, the Messiah.

42:1 I HAVE PUT MY SPIRIT UPON HIM. The Messiah would be anointed with the Holy Spirit in order to perform His task of redemption (cf. 61:1; see article on JESUS AND THE HOLY SPIRIT, p. 1550). His followers, who would continue what Jesus had begun, also needed the Holy Spirit poured out upon them (Acts 1:8; 2:4). Only the Spirit can enable believers to minister with the necessary wisdom, revelation, and power.

42:1 BRING FORTH JUDGMENT TO THE GENTILES. By the power of the Holy Spirit, the Messiah would bring the standards of holy justice and the principles of divine truth to all the nations. His work was therefore missionary in nature. Today this same task is the responsibility of those who bear the name of Christ. He baptizes His followers in the Holy Spirit so that they may carry out this commission (see Acts 1:8, note).

42:6 A LIGHT OF THE GENTILES. The Messiah's mission would include bringing the covenant of salvation to the Gentiles as well as to the Jews. The new covenant would be established by His death (Jer. 31:31–34; Heb. 8:6–13; 9:15; see article on THE OLD COVENANT AND THE NEW COVENANT, p. 1954).

42:7 TO OPEN THE BLIND EYES. By His death and the power of the Holy Spirit, the Messiah would free all believers from the darkness of sin and guilt (see Rom. 5:12, note) and release them from the power of Satan (cf. 1 John 3:8).

other, neither my praise to graven
images.
9 Behold, the former things are
come to pass, and new things do I de-
clare: before they spring forth I tell you
of them.

Song of praise to the LORD

10 [k]Sing unto the LORD a new song,
and his praise from the end of the
earth, [l]ye that go down to the sea, and
[i]all that is therein; the isles, and the
inhabitants thereof.
11 Let the wilderness and the
cities thereof lift up *their voice*, the
villages *that* Kedar doth inhabit: let
the inhabitants of the rock sing,
let them shout from the top of the
mountains.
12 Let them give glory unto the
LORD, and declare his praise in the is-
lands.
13 The LORD shall go forth as a
mighty man, he shall stir up jealousy
like a man of war: he shall cry, [m]yea,
roar; he shall [j]prevail against his ene-
mies.
14 I have long time holden my
peace; I have been still, *and* refrained
myself: *now* will I cry like a travailing
woman; I will destroy and [k]devour at
once.
15 I will make waste mountains and
hills, and dry up all their herbs; and I
will make the rivers islands, and I will
dry up the pools.
16 And I will bring the blind by a
way *that* they knew not; I will lead
them in paths *that* they have not
known: I will make darkness light be-
fore them, and crooked things
[l]straight. These things will I do unto
them, and not forsake them.
17 ¶ They shall be [n]turned back,
they shall be greatly ashamed, that
trust in graven images, that say to the
molten images, Ye *are* our gods.

42:10 [k]Ps. 33:3 & 40:3 & 98:1 [l]Ps. 107:23
42:13 [m]ch. 31:4
42:17 [n]Ps. 97:7 ch. 1:29 & 44:11 & 45:16
42:19 [o]ch. 43:8 Ezek. 12:2 See John 9:39,41
42:20 [p]Rom. 2:21
42:25 [q]2 Ki. 25:9 [r]Hos. 7:9
43:1 [s]ver. 7 [t]ver. 21 ch. 44:2,21 [u]ch. 44:6 [v]ch. 42:6 & 45:4
43:2 [w]Ps. 66:12 & 91:3 [x]Deut. 31:6

The nation's sin and punishment

18 Hear, ye deaf; and look, ye blind,
that ye may see.
19 [o]Who *is* blind, but my servant?
or deaf, as my messenger *that* I sent?
who *is* blind as *he that is* perfect, and
blind as the LORD'S servant?
20 Seeing many things, [p]but thou
observest not; opening the ears, but he
heareth not.
21 The LORD is well pleased for his
righteousness' sake; he will magnify
the law, and make [m]*it* honourable.
22 But this *is* a people robbed and
spoiled; [n]*they are* all of them snared in
holes, and they are hid in prison
houses: they are for a prey, and none
delivereth; for [o]a spoil, and none
saith, Restore.
23 Who among you will give ear to
this? *who* will hearken and hear [p]for
the time to come?
24 Who gave Jacob for a spoil, and
Israel to the robbers? did not the LORD,
he against whom we have sinned? for
they would not walk in his ways, nei-
ther were they obedient unto his law.
25 Therefore he hath poured upon
him the fury of his anger, and the
strength of battle: [q]and it hath set him
on fire round about, [r]yet he knew not;
and it burned him, yet he laid *it* not to
heart.

God will redeem his people

43 BUT NOW thus saith the LORD
[s]that created thee, O Jacob,
[t]and he that formed thee, O Israel,
Fear not: [u]for I have redeemed thee,
[v]I have called *thee* by thy name; thou
art mine.
2 [w]When thou passest through the
waters, [x]I *will be* with thee; and

[i] Heb. *the fulness thereof* [j] Or, *behave himself mightily* [k] Heb. *swallow*, or, *sup up* [l] Heb. *into straightness* [m] Or, him [n] Or, *in snaring all the young men of them* [o] Heb. *a treading* [p] Heb. *for the after time?*

42:10–17 SING UNTO THE LORD. Isaiah foresees a time when the Gentiles and faithful Israel will sing the praise of their Lord to the ends of the earth because of the glorious redemption and victory they have experienced through Him.

42:18–25 YE DEAF . . . YE BLIND. Because of the spiritual blindness and deafness of God's people, they were being plundered and despoiled by their enemy; there was no one to deliver and restore them.

43:1–28 BUT NOW. This chapter speaks about Israel's deliverance from Babylonian captivity because of God's love for His people.

43:1–7 THUS SAITH THE LORD. In this section, God expresses His love for Israel and the benefits of that love. All the blessings mentioned here apply even more to those who are children of God through faith in Christ. God has created and redeemed us; we belong to Him, and He knows each one of us by name (v. 1). When we pass through trouble and affliction, we will not be destroyed, for He is with us (vv. 2,5). We are precious and honored in His sight, objects of His great love (v. 4).

through the rivers, they shall not overflow thee: when thou [y]walkest through the fire, thou shalt not be burned; neither shall the flame kindle upon thee.

3 For I *am* the LORD thy God, the Holy One of Israel, thy Saviour: [z]I gave Egypt *for* thy ransom, Ethiopia and Seba for thee.

4 Since thou wast precious in my sight, thou hast been honourable, and I have loved thee: therefore will I give men for thee, and people for thy [q]life.

5 [a]Fear not: for I *am* with thee: I will bring thy seed from the east, and gather thee from the west;

6 I will say to the north, Give up; and to the south, Keep not back: bring my sons from far, and my daughters from the ends of the earth;

7 *Even* every one that is [b]called by my name: for [c]I have created him for my glory, [d]I have formed him; yea, I have made him.

8 ¶ [e]Bring forth the blind people that have eyes, and the deaf that have ears.

9 Let all the nations be gathered together, and let the people be assembled: [f]who among them can declare this, and show us former things? let them bring forth their witnesses, that they may be justified: or let them hear, and say, *It is* truth.

10 [g]Ye *are* my witnesses, saith the LORD, [h]and my servant whom I have chosen: that ye may know and believe me, and understand that I *am* he: [i]before me there was [r]no God formed, neither shall there be after me.

Is. 45:22-23

11 I, *even* I, [j]*am* the LORD; and beside me *there is* no saviour.

12 I have declared, and have saved, and I have shown, when *there was* no [k]strange *god* among you: [l]therefore ye *are* my witnesses, saith the LORD, that I *am* God.

13 [m]Yea, before the day *was* I *am* he; and *there is* none that can deliver out of my hand: I will work, and who shall [n]let[s] it?

Is. 51:4-6

14 ¶ Thus saith the LORD, your redeemer, the Holy One of Israel; For your sake I have sent to Babylon, and have brought down all their [t]nobles, and the Chaldeans, whose cry *is* in the ships.

15 I *am* the LORD, your Holy One, the creator of Israel, your King.

16 Thus saith the LORD, which [o]maketh a way in the sea, and a [p]path in the mighty waters;

17 Which [q]bringeth forth the chariot and horse, the army and the power; they shall lie down together, they shall not rise: they are extinct, they are quenched as tow.

18 ¶ [r]Remember ye not the former things, neither consider the things of old.

19 Behold, I will do a [s]new thing; now it shall spring forth; shall ye not know it? [t]I will even make a way in the wilderness, *and* rivers in the desert.

20 The beast of the field shall honour me, the dragons and the [u] [v]owls: because [u]I give waters in the wilderness, *and* rivers in the desert, to give drink to my people, my chosen.

21 [v]This people have I formed for myself; they shall show forth my praise.

Israel's sin of ingratitude

22 ¶ But thou hast not called upon me, O Jacob; but thou [w]hast been weary of me, O Israel.

23 [x]Thou hast not brought me the [w]small cattle of thy burnt offerings; neither hast thou honoured me with thy sacrifices. I have not caused thee to serve with an offering, nor wearied thee with incense.

24 Thou hast bought me no sweet cane with money, neither hast thou [x]filled me with the fat of thy sacri-

43:2 [y]Dan. 3:25
43:3 [z]Prov. 11:8 & 21:18
43:5 [a]ch. 41:10 & 44:2 Jer. 30:10 & 46:27,28
43:7 [b]ch. 63:19 Jas. 2:7 [c]Ps. 100:3 ch. 29:23 John 3:3,5 2 Cor. 5:17 Eph. 2:10 [d]ver. 1
43:8 [e]ch. 6:9 & 42:19 Ezek. 12:2
43:9 [f]ch. 41:21,22,26
43:10 [g]ch. 44:8 [h]ch. 55:4 [i]ch. 44:6
43:11 [j]ch. 45:21 Hos. 13:4
43:12 [k]Deut. 32:16 Ps. 81:9 [l]ch. 44:8
43:13 [m]Ps. 90:2 John 8:58 [n]Job 9:12 ch. 14:27
43:16 [o]Ex. 14:16 Ps. 77:19 ch. 51:10 [p]Josh. 3:13
43:17 [q]Ex. 14:4-9,25
43:18 [r]Jer. 16:14
43:19 [s]2 Cor. 5:17 Rev. 21:5 [t]Ex. 17:6 Num. 20:11 Deut. 8:15 Ps. 78:16
43:20 [u]ch. 48:21
43:21 [v]Ps. 102:18 Eph. 1:5,6
43:22 [w]Mal. 1:13
43:23 [x]Amos 5:25

[q] Or, *person* [r] Or, *nothing formed of God* [s] Heb. *turn it back?* [t] Heb. *bars* [u] Or, *ostriches* [v] Heb. *daughters of the owl* [w] Heb. *lambs,* or, *kids* [x] Heb. *made me drunk,* or, *abundantly moistened*

43:8–13 BRING FORTH THE BLIND. Although Israel was still spiritually blind, God had a future for them in His plan of redemption; they would still be His witnesses and His servants (v. 10; see article on ISRAEL IN GOD'S PLAN OF SALVATION, p. 1748).

43:14–21 BABYLON. God would judge the Babylonians and deliver His people. They would receive a "new thing" (v. 19), i.e., a new time of forgiveness, blessing, restoration, and God's presence. For this they would praise their God (v. 21).

43:22–28 BUT THOU HAST NOT CALLED UPON ME. At the time of Isaiah's writing, Judah was not yet calling upon God for forgiveness and help; they continued to wallow in their sins (v. 24). If they would not repent, they would go into captivity under God's curse for a prescribed period of time (v. 28).

fices: but thou hast made me to serve with thy sins, thou hast [y]wearied me with thine iniquities.

25 I, *even* I, *am* he that [z]blotteth out thy transgressions [a]for mine own sake, [b]and will not remember thy sins.

26 Put me in remembrance: let us plead together: declare thou, that thou mayest be justified.

27 Thy first father hath sinned, and thy [c]teachers[y] have transgressed against me.

28 Therefore [d]I have profaned the [z]princes of the sanctuary, [e]and have given Jacob to the curse, and Israel to reproaches.

God's blessings upon the nation

44 YET NOW hear, [f]O Jacob my servant; and Israel, whom I have chosen:

2 Thus saith the LORD that made thee, [g]and formed thee from the womb, *which* will help thee; Fear not, O Jacob, my servant; and thou, [h]Jesurun, whom I have chosen.

3 For I will [i]pour water upon him that is thirsty, and floods upon the dry ground: I will pour my spirit upon thy seed, and my blessing upon thine off-
Is. 59:21 spring:

4 And they shall spring up *as* among the grass, as willows by the water courses.

5 One shall say, I *am* the LORD's; and another shall call *himself* by the name of Jacob; and another shall subscribe *with* his hand unto the LORD, and surname *himself* by the name of Israel.

Judgment upon idol worship

6 Thus saith the LORD the King of Israel, and his redeemer the LORD of hosts; [j]I *am* the first, and I *am* the last; and beside me *there is* no God.

7 And [k]who, as I, shall call, and shall declare it, and set it in order for me, since I appointed the ancient people? and the things that are coming, and shall come, let them show unto them.

8 Fear ye not, neither be afraid: [l]have not I told thee from that time, and have declared *it?* [m]ye *are* even my witnesses. Is there a God beside me? yea, [n]*there is* no [a]God; I know not *any.*

9 ¶ [o]They that make a graven image *are* all of them vanity; and their [b]delectable things shall not profit; and they *are* their own witnesses; [p]they see not, nor know; that they may be ashamed.

10 Who hath formed a god, or molten a graven image [q]*that* is profitable for nothing?

11 Behold, all his fellows shall be [r]ashamed: and the workmen, they *are* of men: let them all be gathered together, let them stand up; *yet* they shall fear, *and* they shall be ashamed together.

12 [s]The smith [c]with the tongs both worketh in the coals, and fashioneth it with hammers, and worketh it with the strength of his arms: yea, he is hungry, and his strength faileth: he drinketh no water, and is faint.

13 The carpenter stretcheth out *his* rule; he marketh it out with a line; he fitteth it with planes, and he marketh it out with the compass, and maketh it after the figure of a man, according to the beauty of a man; that it may remain in the house.

14 He heweth him down cedars, and taketh the cypress and the oak, which

43:24 [y]ch. 1:14 Mal. 2:17
43:25 [z]ch. 44:22 Jer. 50:20 Acts 3:19 [a]Ezek. 36:22 [b]ch. 1:18 Jer. 31:34
43:27 [c]Mal. 2:7,8
43:28 [d]ch. 47:6 Lam. 2:2,6 [e]Ps. 79:4 Jer. 24:9 Dan. 9:11 Zech. 8:13
44:1 [f]ver. 21 Jer. 30:10 & 46:27,28
44:2 [g]ch. 43:1,7 [h]Deut. 32:15
44:3 [i]ch. 35:7 Joel 2:28 John 7:38 Acts 2:18
44:6 [j]ch. 41:4 Rev. 1:8,17 & 22:13
44:7 [k]ch. 41:4,22
44:8 [l]ch. 41:22 [m]ch. 43:10 [n]Deut. 4:35 & 32:39 1 Sam. 2:2 2 Sam. 22:32
44:9 [o]ch. 41:24 [p]Ps. 115:4
44:10 [q]Jer. 10:5 Hab. 2:18
44:11 [r]Ps. 97:7 ch. 1:29 & 42:17
44:12 [s]ch. 40:19 Jer. 10:3

[y] Heb. *interpreters* [z] Or, *holy princes* [a] Heb. *rock;* see Deut. 32:4 [b] Heb. *desirable* [c] Or, *with an axe*

44:3 I WILL POUR MY SPIRIT UPON THY SEED. Although Israel was largely an apostate nation in Isaiah's time, he prophesied that the day would come when the Holy Spirit would be poured out upon a future generation (cf. 32:15; Jer. 31:33–34; Ezek. 36:26–27; 39:29; Zech. 12:10—13:1). This prophecy finds partial fulfillment on the day of Pentecost (cf. Joel 2:25–29; Acts 2:17–18; see Acts 1:8 and 2:4, notes) and awaits complete fulfillment for Israel after they accept Christ as the Messiah (see Rom. 11:25–26, notes). The outpouring of God's Spirit upon His people is associated with restoration, blessing, and fruitfulness (vv. 3–4).

44:5 I *AM* THE LORD'S. A prominent result of the Spirit being poured out upon us is our testimony that we belong to the Lord and that He is our heavenly Father. The Spirit creates in us the confidence that we belong to God and that we have all the rights and privileges of being His children (see Rom. 8:16, note; Gal. 4:6, note).

44:6–20 THUS SAITH THE LORD. God exposes the foolishness of making an idol or a god out of material substance and then praying to it for help (vv. 12,17); even today people make all kinds of statues and idols and bow before them in prayer and adoration, hoping that the spirit whom the image represents will help and deliver them (v. 17).

he [d]strengtheneth for himself among
the trees of the forest: he planteth an
ash, and the rain doth nourish *it.*
15 Then shall it be for a man to
burn: for he will take thereof, and
warm himself; yea, he kindleth *it,* and
baketh bread; yea, he maketh a god,
and worshippeth *it;* he maketh it a
graven image, and falleth down
thereto.
16 He burneth part thereof in the
fire; with part thereof he eateth flesh;
he roasteth roast, and is satisfied: yea,
he warmeth *himself,* and saith, Aha, I
am warm, I have seen the fire:
17 And the residue thereof he
maketh a god, *even* his graven image:
he falleth down unto it, and wor-
shippeth *it,* and prayeth unto it, and
saith, Deliver me; for thou *art* my god.
18 [t]They have not known nor un-
derstood: for [u]he hath [e]shut their
eyes, that they cannot see; *and* their
hearts, that they cannot understand.
19 And none [v]considereth[f] in his
heart, neither *is there* knowledge nor
understanding to say, I have burned
part of it in the fire; yea, also I have
baked bread upon the coals thereof; I
have roasted flesh, and eaten *it:* and
shall I make the residue thereof an
abomination? shall I fall down to [g]the
stock of a tree?
20 He feedeth on ashes: [w]a de-
ceived heart hath turned him aside,
that he cannot deliver his soul, nor say,
Is there not a lie in my right hand?
21 ¶ Remember these, O Jacob and
Israel; for [x]thou *art* my servant: I have
formed thee; thou *art* my servant: O Is-
rael, thou shalt not be forgotten of me.
22 [y]I have blotted out, as a thick
cloud, thy transgressions, and, as a
cloud, thy sins: return unto me; for [z]I
have redeemed thee.
23 [a]Sing, O ye heavens; for the
LORD hath done *it:* shout, ye lower parts
of the earth: break forth into singing,
ye mountains, O forest, and every tree
therein: for the LORD hath redeemed Ja-
cob, and glorified himself in Israel.

Cyrus to restore Jerusalem

24 Thus saith the LORD, [b]thy re-
deemer, and [c]he that formed thee
from the womb, I *am* the LORD that
maketh all *things;* [d]that stretch-
eth forth the heavens alone; that
spreadeth abroad the earth by myself;
25 That [e]frustrateth the tokens
[f]of the liars, and maketh diviners
mad; that turneth wise *men* backward, Jer. 1:18-19
[g]and maketh their knowledge foolish;
26 [h]That confirmeth the word of
his servant, and performeth the coun-
sel of his messengers; that saith to Je-
rusalem, Thou shalt be inhabited; and
to the cities of Judah, Ye shall be built,
and I will raise up the [h]decayed
places thereof:
27 [i]That saith to the deep, Be dry,
and I will dry up thy rivers:
28 That saith of Cyrus, *He is* my
shepherd, and shall perform all my
pleasure: even saying to Jerusalem,
[j]Thou shalt be built; and to the tem-
ple, Thy foundation shall be laid.

45 THUS SAITH the LORD to his
anointed, to Cyrus, whose
[k]right hand I [i]have holden, [l]to sub-
due nations before him; and I will loose
the loins of kings, to open before him
the two leaved gates; and the gates
shall not be shut;
2 I will go before thee, [m]and make
the crooked places straight: [n]I will
break in pieces the gates of brass, and
cut in sunder the bars of iron:
3 And I will give thee the treasures
of darkness, and hidden riches of se-
cret places, [o]that thou mayest know
that I, the LORD, which [p]call *thee* by thy
name, *am* the God of Israel.

44:18 [t]ch. 45:20 [u]2 Thes. 2:11
44:19 [v]ch. 46:8
44:20 [w]Hos. 4:12 Rom. 1:21 2 Thes. 2:11
44:21 [x]ver. 1,2
44:22 [y]ch. 43:25 [z]ch. 43:1 1 Cor. 6:20 1 Pet. 1:18
44:23 [a]Ps. 69:34 ch. 42:10 & 49:13 Jer. 51:48 Rev. 18:20
44:24 [b]ch. 43:14 [c]ch. 43:1 [d]Job 9:8
44:25 [e]ch. 47:13 [f]Jer. 50:36 [g]1 Cor. 1:20
44:26 [h]Zech. 1:6
44:27 [i]Jer. 50:38 & 51:32,36
44:28 [j]2 Chr. 36:22 Ezra 1:1 ch. 45:13
45:1 [k]ch. 41:13 [l]Dan. 5:30
45:2 [m]ch. 40:4 [n]Ps. 107:16
45:3 [o]ch. 41:23 [p]Ex. 33:12

[d] Or, *taketh courage* [e] Heb. *daubed* [f] Heb. *setteth to his heart* [g] Heb. *that which comes of a tree?* [h] Heb. *wastes* [i] Or, *strengthened*

44:24 THAT MAKETH ALL *THINGS*. See article on CREATION, p. 6.

44:28 CYRUS . . . TEMPLE. Isaiah identifies Cyrus by name as the very one who would initiate the release of the Jews from captivity (v. 28). This prophecy was made 150 years before its fulfillment. In 538 B.C., Cyrus issued a decree permitting the Jews to return to Jerusalem to rebuild their city and temple (Ezra 1:1–2). God so ordered events in the birth and life of Cyrus that His plans and purposes were fulfilled to the letter (see 41:2, note).

45:1 ANOINTED . . . CYRUS. Although not a worshiper of God (vv. 4–5), Cyrus is called "the anointed one," the same title God later gave to His Son (the Messiah, or Christ). Cyrus (550–530 B.C.) was anointed in the sense that he was used by God to perform the important task of setting Israel free from bondage, so that God could complete His plan to use Israel to bring about the salvation of the human race. Cyrus founded the Persian Empire, which lasted for two centuries. He captured Babylonia in 539 B.C. and then allowed the Jews to return to their land (see Ezra 1).

4 For [q]Jacob my servant's sake, and Israel mine elect, I have even called thee by thy name: I have surnamed thee, though thou hast not known me.

5 ¶ I [r]*am* the LORD, and [s]*there is* none else, *there is* no God beside me: [t]I girded thee, though thou hast not known me:

6 [u]That they may know from the rising of the sun, and from the west, that *there is* none beside me. I *am* the LORD, and *there is* none else.

7 I form the light, and create darkness: I make peace, and [v]create evil: I the LORD do all these *things.*

8 [w]Drop down, ye heavens, from above, and let the skies pour down righteousness: let the earth open, and let them bring forth salvation, and let righteousness spring up together; I the LORD have created it.

9 Woe unto him that striveth with [x]his Maker! *Let* the potsherd *strive* with the potsherds of the earth. [y]Shall the clay say to him that fashioneth it, What makest thou? or thy work, He hath no hands?

10 Woe unto him that saith unto *his* father, What begettest thou? or to the woman, What hast thou brought forth?

11 Thus saith the LORD, the Holy One of Israel, and his Maker, Ask me of things to come concerning [z]my sons, and concerning [a]the work of my hands command ye me.

12 [b]I have made the earth, and [c]created man upon it: I, *even* my hands, have stretched out the heavens, and [d]all their host have I commanded.

13 [e]I have raised him up in righteousness, and I will [j]direct all his ways: he shall [f]build my city, and he shall let go my captives, [g]not for price nor reward, saith the LORD of hosts.

14 Thus saith the LORD, [h]The labour of Egypt, and merchandise of Ethiopia and of the Sabeans, men of stature, shall come over unto thee, and they shall be thine: they shall come after thee; [i]in chains they shall come over, and they shall fall down unto thee, they shall make supplication unto thee, *saying,* [j]Surely God *is* in thee; and [k]*there is* none else, *there is* no God.

15 Verily thou *art* a God [l]that hidest thyself, O God of Israel, the Saviour.

16 They shall be ashamed, and also confounded, all of them: they shall go to confusion together *that are* [m]makers of idols.

17 [n]*But* Israel shall be saved in the LORD with an everlasting salvation: ye shall not be ashamed nor confounded world without end.

18 For thus saith the LORD [o]that created the heavens; God himself that formed the earth and made it; he hath established it, he created it not in vain, he formed it to be inhabited: [p]I *am* the LORD; and *there is* none else.

19 I have not spoken in [q]secret, in a dark place of the earth: I said not unto the seed of Jacob, Seek ye me in vain: [r]I the LORD speak righteousness, I declare things that are right.

20 ¶ Assemble yourselves and come; draw near together, ye *that are* escaped of the nations: [s]they have no knowledge that set up the wood of their graven image, and pray unto a god *that* cannot save.

21 Tell ye, and bring *them* near; yea, let them take counsel together: [t]who hath declared this from ancient time? *who* hath told it from that time? *have* not I the LORD? [u]and *there is* no God else beside me; a just God and a Saviour; *there is* none beside me.

22 [v]Look unto me, and be ye saved, all the ends of the earth: for I *am* God, and *there is* none else.

23 [w]I have sworn by myself, the word is gone out of my mouth *in* righteousness, and shall not return, That

45:4 [q]ch. 44:1
45:5 [r]Deut. 4:35 & 32:39 ch. 44:8 [s]ver. 14,18 [t]Ps. 18:32
45:6 [u]Ps. 102:15 Mal. 1:11
45:7 [v]Amos 3:6
45:8 [w]Ps. 85:11
45:9 [x]ch. 64:8 [y]ch. 29:16 Jer. 18:6 Rom. 9:20
45:11 [z]Jer. 31:9 [a]Is. 29:23
45:12 [b]ch. 42:5 [c]Gen. 1:26 [d]Gen. 2:1
45:13 [e]ch. 41:2 [f]2 Chr. 36:22 [g]Rom. 3:24
45:14 [h]Ps. 68:31 Zech. 8:22 [i]Ps. 149:8 [j]1 Cor. 14:25 [k]ver. 5
45:15 [l]Ps. 44:24 ch. 57:17
45:16 [m]ch. 44:11
45:17 [n]ch. 26:4
45:18 [o]ch. 42:5 [p]ver. 5
45:19 [q]Deut. 30:11 [r]Ps. 19:8
45:20 [s]ch. 46:7
45:21 [t]ch. 41:22 & 43:9 [u]ch. 44:8
45:22 [v]Ps. 22:27 & 65:5
45:23 [w]Heb. 6:13

[j] Or, *make straight*

45:14–17 SURELY GOD *IS* IN THEE. A day will come when all the nations will acknowledge that the God of Israel is the only God and when Israel will never again be shamed (see Rev. 20:4, note).

45:22 BE YE SAVED, ALL THE ENDS OF THE EARTH. God gives an invitation to all individuals upon the earth to repent and turn to Him for salvation. The gospel of Christ contains the same invitation, and God has commanded that His church take this good news to all the world (Mat. 28:19–20; Acts 1:8; see Is. 42:1, note). The Lord desires the conversion of all people (2 Pet. 3:9).

45:23 EVERY KNEE SHALL BOW. Paul quotes this verse in Rom. 14:11 and Phil. 2:10–11 to show that although not every person turns to the Lord in true repentance during this life, all people will one day, either voluntarily or involuntarily, bow before Christ and confess that He is Lord.

Is. 49:5-6 unto me every [x]knee shall bow, [y]ev-
ery tongue shall swear.
24 [k]Surely, shall *one* say, in the
LORD have I [z]righteousness[1] and
strength: *even* to him shall *men* come;
and [a]all that are incensed against him
shall be ashamed.
25 [b]In the LORD shall all the seed of
Israel be justified, and [c]shall glory.

Babylon's idols and the LORD

46 BEL [d]BOWETH down, Nebo
stoopeth, their idols were upon
the beasts, and upon the cattle: your
carriages *were* heavy laden; [e]*they are*
a burden to the weary *beast.*
2 They stoop, they bow down to-
gether; they could not deliver the bur-
den, [f]but [m]themselves are gone into
captivity.
3 ¶ Hearken unto me, O house of Ja-
cob, and all the remnant of the house
of Israel, [g]which are borne *by me* from
the belly, which are carried from the
womb:
4 And *even* to *your* old age [h]I *am* he;
and *even* to hoar hairs [i]will I carry
you: I have made, and I will bear; even
I will carry, and will deliver *you.*
5 ¶ [j]To whom will ye liken me, and
make *me* equal, and compare me, that
we may be like?
6 [k]They lavish gold out of the bag,
and weigh silver in the balance, *and*
hire a goldsmith; and he maketh it a
god: they fall down, yea, they worship.
7 [l]They bear him upon the shoul-
der, they carry him, and set him in his
place, and he standeth; from his place
shall he not remove: yea, [m]*one* shall
cry unto him, yet can he not answer,
nor save him out of his trouble.
8 Remember this, and show your-
selves men: [n]bring *it* again to mind,
O ye transgressors.
9 [o]Remember the former things of
old: for I *am* God, and [p]*there is* none

45:23 [x]Phil. 2:10 [y]Ps. 63:11
45:24 [z]Jer. 23:5 1 Cor. 1:30 [a]ch. 41:11
45:25 [b]ver. 17 [c]1 Cor. 1:31
46:1 [d]ch. 21:9 Jer. 50:2 [e]Jer. 10:5
46:2 [f]Jer. 48:7
46:3 [g]Deut. 32:11 Ps. 71:6
46:4 [h]Mal. 3:6 [i]Ps. 48:14
46:5 [j]ch. 40:18
46:6 [k]ch. 40:19 & 41:6 Jer. 10:3
46:7 [l]Jer. 10:5 [m]ch. 45:20
46:8 [n]ch. 44:19
46:9 [o]Deut. 32:7 [p]ch. 45:5,21
46:10 [q]ch. 45:21 [r]Ps. 33:11 Prov. 19:21 Acts 5:39 Heb. 6:17
46:11 [s]ch. 41:2,25 [t]ch. 44:28 [u]Num. 23:19
46:12 [v]Ps. 76:5 [w]Rom. 10:3
46:13 [x]Rom. 1:17 [y]Hab. 2:3 [z]ch. 62:11
47:1 [a]Jer. 48:18 [b]ch. 3:26
47:2 [c]Ex. 11:5 Judg. 16:21 Mat. 24:41
47:3 [d]ch. 3:17 & 20:4 Jer. 13:22 Nah. 3:5 [e]Rom. 12:19
47:4 [f]Jer. 50:34
47:5 [g]1 Sam. 2:9 [h]Dan. 2:37

else; *I am* God, and *there is* none
like me,
10 [q]Declaring the end from the be-
ginning, and from ancient times *the
things* that are not *yet* done, saying,
[r]My counsel shall stand, and I will do
all my pleasure:
11 Calling a ravenous bird [s]from
the east, [n]the man [t]that executeth
my counsel from a far country: yea, [u]I
have spoken *it,* I will also bring it to
pass; I have purposed *it,* I will also
do it.
12 ¶ Hearken unto me, ye [v]stout-
hearted, [w]that *are* far from righteous-
ness:
13 [x]I bring near my righteousness;
it shall not be far off, and my salvation
[y]shall not tarry: and I will place [z]sal-
vation in Zion for Israel my glory.

Judgment against Babylon

47 COME [a]DOWN, and [b]sit in
the dust, O virgin daughter of
Babylon, sit on the ground: *there is* no
throne, O daughter of the Chaldeans:
for thou shalt no more be called tender
and delicate.
2 [c]Take the millstones, and grind
meal: uncover thy locks, make bare the
leg, uncover the thigh, pass over the
rivers.
3 [d]Thy nakedness shall be uncov-
ered, yea, thy shame shall be seen: [e]I
will take vengeance, and I will not
meet *thee as* a man.
4 *As for* [f]our redeemer, the LORD of
hosts *is* his name, the Holy One of Is-
rael.
5 Sit thou [g]silent, and get thee into
darkness, O daughter of the Chalde-
ans: [h]for thou shalt no more be called,
The lady of kingdoms.

[k] Or, *Surely he shall say of me, In the LORD is all righteousness and strength* [1] Heb. *righteousnesses* [m] Heb. *their soul* [n] Heb. *the man of my counsel*

46:1 BEL . . . NEBO. Bel, also called Merodach (cf. Jer. 50:2), was the chief deity of Babylon; Nebo was the god of learning, writing, and astronomy. These gods could not keep Babylon from being destroyed.

46:4 I WILL CARRY . . . *YOU*. In contrast to gods made with human hands (44:12–17) which have to be carried by those who create them (v. 1), the Lord, our Creator, is able to carry us. He has cared for us from the beginning of our lives, continues to act on our behalf, and will sustain us even to the end.

47:1–15 O VIRGIN DAUGHTER OF BABYLON. This chapter prophesies the doom and fall of Babylon. Babylon represented a pagan culture, self-centered and proud (vv. 8,10); its inhabitants lived in sensual pleasure and trusted in their own wisdom and knowledge, and in magic (vv. 10, 12–13). Such people were destined for a sudden and overwhelming judgment (vv. 9,11). In the last days of the tribulation, Babylon, representing all pagan and humanistic cultures of the unregenerate world, will be overthrown by God in His wrath (see Rev. 17:1, notes; 18:2, note).

6 ¶ [i]I was wroth with my people, [j]I have polluted mine inheritance, and given them into thine hand: thou didst show them no mercy; [k]upon the ancient hast thou very heavily laid thy yoke.

7 ¶ And thou saidst, I shall be [l]a lady for ever: *so* that thou didst not [m]lay these *things* to thy heart, [n]neither didst remember the latter end of it.

8 Therefore hear now this, *thou that art* given to pleasures, that dwellest carelessly, that sayest in thine heart, [o]I *am*, and none else beside me; [p]I shall not sit *as* a widow, neither shall I know the loss of children:

9 But [q]these two *things* shall come to thee [r]in a moment in one day, the loss of children, and widowhood: they shall come upon thee in their perfection [s]for the multitude of thy sorceries, *and* for the great abundance of thine enchantments.

10 ¶ For thou [t]hast trusted in thy wickedness: [u]thou hast said, None seeth me. Thy wisdom and thy knowledge, it hath [o]perverted thee; [v]and thou hast said in thine heart, I *am*, and none else beside me.

11 ¶ Therefore shall evil come upon thee; thou shalt not know [p]from whence it riseth: and mischief shall fall upon thee; thou shalt not be able to [q]put it off: and [w]desolation shall come upon thee suddenly, *which* thou shalt not know.

12 Stand now with thine enchantments, and with the multitude of thy sorceries, wherein thou hast laboured from thy youth; if so be thou shalt be able to profit, if so be thou mayest prevail.

13 [x]Thou art wearied in the multitude of thy counsels. Let now [y]the [r]astrologers, the stargazers, [s]the monthly prognosticators, stand up, and save thee from *these things* that shall come upon thee.

14 Behold, they shall be [z]as stubble; the fire shall burn them; they shall not deliver [t]themselves from the power of the flame: *there shall* not *be* a coal to warm at, *nor* fire to sit before it.

15 Thus shall they be unto thee with whom thou hast laboured, *even* [a]thy merchants, from thy youth: they shall wander every one to his quarter; none shall save thee.

Obstinate Israel

48 HEAR YE this, O house of Jacob, which are called by the name of Israel, and [b]are come forth out of the waters of Judah, [c]which swear by the name of the LORD, and make mention of the God of Israel, [d]*but* not in truth, nor in righteousness.

2 For they call themselves [e]of the holy city, and [f]stay themselves upon the God of Israel; The LORD of hosts *is* his name.

3 [g]I have declared the former things from the beginning; and they went forth out of my mouth, and I showed them; I did *them* suddenly, [h]and they came to pass.

4 Because I knew that thou *art* [u]obstinate, and [i]thy neck *is* an iron sinew, and thy brow brass;

5 [j]I have even from the beginning declared *it* to thee; before it came to pass I showed *it* thee: lest thou shouldest say, Mine idol hath done them, and my graven image, and my molten image, hath commanded them.

6 Thou hast heard, see all this; and will not ye declare *it?* I have shown thee new things from this time, even hidden things, and thou didst not know them.

7 They are created now, and not from the beginning; even before the day when thou heardest them not; lest thou shouldest say, Behold, I knew them.

8 Yea, thou heardest not; yea, thou

47:6 [i]See 2 Sam. 24:14; 2 Chr. 28:9; Zech. 1:15 [j]ch. 43:28 [k]Deut. 28:50 **47:7** [l]Rev. 18:7 [m]ch. 46:8 [n]Deut. 32:29 **47:8** [o]Zeph. 2:15 [p]Rev. 18:7 **47:9** [q]ch. 51:19 [r]1 Thes. 5:3 [s]Nah. 3:4 **47:10** [t]Ps. 52:7 [u]ch. 29:15; Ezek. 8:12 [v]ver. 8 **47:11** [w]1 Thes. 5:3 **47:13** [x]ch. 57:10 [y]Dan. 2:2 **47:14** [z]Nah. 1:10; Mal. 4:1 **47:15** [a]Rev. 18:11 **48:1** [b]Ps. 68:26 [c]Deut. 6:13; Zeph. 1:5 [d]Jer. 4:2 **48:2** [e]ch. 52:1 [f]Mic. 3:11; Rom. 2:17 **48:3** [g]ch. 44:7,8 [h]Josh. 21:45 **48:4** [i]Ex. 32:9; Deut. 31:27 **48:5** [j]ver. 3

[o] Or, *caused thee to turn away* [p] Heb. *the morning thereof* [q] Heb. *expiate* [r] Heb. *viewers of the heavens* [s] Heb. *that give knowledge concerning the months* [t] Heb. *their souls* [u] Heb. *hard*

48:1–22 *BUT* NOT IN TRUTH, NOR IN RIGHTEOUSNESS. This chapter reveals that Judah was a people who professed to follow God and call upon His name, but who in reality rejected the truths of His word and refused to live righteously before Him. They had a form of religion, yet they denied God His rightful place in their lives (see Mat. 23:13, note on hypocrisy; 2 Tim. 3:5, note).

48:5 FROM THE BEGINNING DECLARED *IT*. Through the prophets, God foretold Israel's captivity and release, proving that He is the one true God. No worshiper of idols or demons can accurately predict the future or foretell specific events as the God of Israel can.

48:6 NEW THINGS. The "new things" include the coming Messiah and the new heavens and new earth (ch. 53; 65:17).

knewest not; yea, from that time *that*
thine ear was not opened: for I knew
that thou wouldest deal very treacher-
ously, and wast called [k]a transgres-
sor from the womb.
9 ¶ [l]For my name's sake [m]will I
defer mine anger, and for my praise
will I refrain for thee, that I cut thee
not off.
10 Behold, [n]I have refined thee,
but not [v]with silver; I have chosen
thee in the furnace of affliction.
11 [o]For mine own sake, *even* for
mine own sake, will I do *it:* for [p]how
should *my name* be polluted? and [q]I
will not give my glory unto another.

The Redeemer of Israel

12 ¶ Hearken unto me, O Jacob and
Israel, my called; [r]I *am* he; I *am* the
[s]first, I also *am* the last.
13 [t]Mine hand also hath laid the
foundation of the earth, and [w]my right
hand hath spanned the heavens: *when*
[u]I call unto them, they stand up to-
gether.
14 All ye, assemble yourselves, and
hear; which among them hath declared
these *things?* [v]The LORD hath loved
him: [w]he will do his pleasure on Bab-
ylon, and his arm *shall be on* the Chal-
deans.
15 I, *even* I, have spoken; yea, [x]I
have called him: I have brought him,
and he shall make his way prosperous.
16 ¶ Come ye near unto me, hear ye
this; [y]I have not spoken in secret from
the beginning; from the time that it
was, there *am* I: and now [z]the Lord
GOD, and his spirit, hath sent me.
17 Thus saith [a]the LORD, thy Re-
deemer, the Holy One of Israel; I *am*
the LORD thy God which teacheth thee

48:8 [k]Ps. 58:3
48:9 [l]Ps. 79:9 & 106:8 Ezek. 20:9 [m]Ps. 78:38
48:10 [n]Ps. 66:10
48:11 [o]ver. 9 [p]Deut. 32:26 Ezek. 20:9 [q]ch. 42:8
48:12 [r]Deut. 32:39 [s]ch. 44:6 Rev. 22:13
48:13 [t]Ps. 102:25 [u]ch. 40:26
48:14 [v]ch. 45:1 [w]ch. 44:28
48:15 [x]ch. 45:1,2
48:16 [y]ch. 45:19 [z]Zech. 2:8
48:17 [a]ch. 43:14 [b]Ps. 32:8
48:18 [c]Deut. 32:29 Ps. 81:13 [d]Ps. 119:165
48:19 [e]Gen. 22:17 Hos. 1:10
48:20 [f]Jer. 50:8 [g]Ex. 19:4-6
48:21 [h]ch. 41:17,18 [i]Ex. 17:6 Ps. 105:41
48:22 [j]ch. 57:21
49:1 [k]ch. 41:1 [l]Jer. 1:5 Mat. 1:20 John 10:36
49:2 [m]ch. 11:4 Hos. 6:5 Rev. 1:16 [n]ch. 51:16 [o]Ps. 45:5
49:3 [p]ch. 42:1 Zech. 3:8 [q]John 15:8 Eph. 1:6

to profit, [b]which leadeth thee by the
way *that* thou shouldest go.
18 [c]O that thou hadst hearkened
to my commandments! [d]then had thy
peace been as a river, and thy righ-
teousness as the waves of the sea:
19 [e]Thy seed also had been as the
sand, and the offspring of thy bowels
like the gravel thereof; his name
should not have been cut off nor de-
stroyed from before me.
20 ¶ [f]Go ye forth of Babylon, flee
ye from the Chaldeans, with a voice of
singing declare ye, tell this, utter it
even to the end of the earth; say ye, The
LORD hath [g]redeemed his servant Ja-
cob.
21 And they [h]thirsted not *when* he
led them through the deserts: he
[i]caused the waters to flow out of the
rock for them: he clave the rock also,
and the waters gushed out.
22 [j]*There is* no peace, saith the
LORD, unto the wicked.

The servant's call

49 LISTEN, [k]O isles, unto me;
and hearken, ye people, from
far; [l]The LORD hath called me from the
womb; from the bowels of my mother
hath he made mention of my name.
2 And he hath made [m]my mouth
like a sharp sword; [n]in the shadow of
his hand hath he hid me, and made me
[o]a polished shaft; in his quiver hath
he hid me;
3 And said unto me, [p]Thou *art* my
servant, O Israel, [q]in whom I will be
glorified.

[v] Or, *for silver;* see Ezek. 22:20-22 [w] Or, *the palm of my right hand hath spread out*

48:12–15 HEARKEN UNTO ME, O JACOB. This prophecy again alludes to Cyrus as God's chosen instrument to overthrow Babylon (see 41:2, note; 45:1, note).

48:16 HIS SPIRIT, HATH SENT ME. This verse refers to the coming Messiah, who is empowered by the Holy Spirit (cf. 61:1).

48:20 GO YE FORTH OF BABYLON. This declaration would take on great importance for the Jews toward the end of their seventy-year captivity in Babylon (539 B.C.), as they prepared to leave that country and return to Judah according to Cyrus's decree (cf. Rev. 18:4).

49–57 LISTEN . . . UNTO ME. These chapters contain many prophecies about the "Servant of the LORD," who ultimately is Jesus Christ. His ministry brings atonement for sin, salvation to all the nations, the restoration of Israel, and judgment upon the ungodly.

49:1 THE LORD HATH CALLED ME. The Messianic calling of Jesus Christ is pictured as being "from the womb," i.e., the womb of the virgin Mary (see Luke 1:31–33).

49:2 SWORD . . . SHAFT. The words of the coming Messiah would be like a sharp sword that pierces the consciences of all who hear (cf. Rev. 1:16; 2:12,16). The "shaft" or arrow may symbolize God's judgment on those who do not accept His word.

49:3 MY SERVANT, O ISRAEL. This designation cannot be restricted to the nation of Israel, since the servant's task was that of bringing Jacob (i.e., Israel) back to God (v. 5). God's Servant-Son, Jesus, embodied the ideal Israel, and He fulfilled all that God had required from national Israel.

4 [r]Then I said, I have laboured in
vain, I have spent my strength for
nought, and in vain: *yet* surely my judg-
ment *is* with the LORD, and [s]my[x]
work with my God.
5 ¶ And now, saith the LORD [t]that
formed me from the womb *to be* his ser-
vant, to bring Jacob again to him,
[y]Though Israel [u]be not gathered,
yet shall I be glorious in the eyes of
the LORD, and my God shall be my
strength.
6 And he said, [z]It is a light thing
that thou shouldest be my servant to
raise up the tribes of Jacob, and to re-
store the [a]preserved of Israel: I will
also give thee for a [v]light to the Gen-
tiles, that thou mayest be my salvation
unto the end of the earth.
7 Thus saith the LORD, the Redeem-
er of Israel, *and* his Holy One, [w]to[b]
him whom man despiseth, to him
whom the nation abhorreth, to a ser-
vant of rulers, [x]Kings shall see and
arise, princes also shall worship, be-
cause of the LORD that is faithful, *and*
the Holy One of Israel, and he shall
choose thee.

Is. 52:7-10

The restoration of Israel

8 Thus saith the LORD, [y]In an ac-
ceptable time have I heard thee, and in
a day of salvation have I helped thee:
and I will preserve thee, [z]and give
thee for a covenant of the people, to
[c]establish the earth, to cause to in-
herit the desolate heritages;
9 That thou mayest say [a]to the
prisoners, Go forth; to them that *are* in
darkness, Show yourselves. They shall
feed in the ways, and their pastures
shall be in all high places.
10 They shall not [b]hunger nor
thirst; [c]neither shall the heat nor sun
smite them: for he that hath mercy on
them [d]shall lead them, even by the
springs of water shall he guide them.
11 [e]And I will make all my moun-
tains a way, and my highways shall be
exalted.
12 Behold, [f]these shall come from
far: and, lo, these from the north and
from the west; and these from the land
of Sinim.
13 ¶ [g]Sing, O heavens; and be joy-
ful, O earth; and break forth into sing-
ing, O mountains: for the LORD hath
comforted his people, and will have
mercy upon his afflicted.
14 [h]But Zion said, The LORD hath
forsaken me, and my Lord hath forgot-
ten me.
15 [i]Can a woman forget her suck-
ing child, [d]that she should not have
compassion on the son of her womb?

49:4 [r]Ezek. 3:19 [s]ch. 40:10 **49:5** [t]ver. 1 [u]Mat. 23:37 **49:6** [v]Luke 2:32 **49:7** [w]Mat. 26:67 [x]Ps. 72:10 **49:8** [y]Ps. 69:13 2 Cor. 6:2 [z]ch. 42:6 **49:9** [a]Zech. 9:12 **49:10** [b]Rev. 7:16 [c]Ps. 121:6 [d]Ps. 23:2 **49:11** [e]ch. 40:4 **49:12** [f]ch. 43:5,6 **49:13** [g]ch. 44:23 **49:14** [h]ch. 40:27 **49:15** [i]Ps. 103:13 Mal. 3:17 Mat. 7:11

[x] Or, *my reward* [y] Or, *That Israel may be gathered to him, and I may* [z] Or, Art thou *lighter than that thou shouldest* [a] Or, *desolations* [b] Or, *to him that is despised in soul* [c] Or, *raise up* [d] Heb. *from having compassion*

49:4 I HAVE LABOURED IN VAIN. The ministry of the prophets as God's servants was full of disappointments and hostile opposition from many in Israel. Likewise, the mission of *the* Servant, Jesus Christ, appeared to have failed when He died on the cross (see 50:6–9; 52:13—53:12 for more on the suffering of God's Servant).

49:5–6 TO BRING JACOB AGAIN TO HIM. This prophecy describes two important aspects of Jesus' mission: (1) To bring Israel back to God—i.e., the Jewish converts of the N.T. church and of the present age, as well as the remnant of Israel to be restored in the final age; and (2) to bring God's light and message of salvation to all the nations (see next note).

49:6 SALVATION UNTO THE END OF THE EARTH. The Messiah's mission is that all nations hear the gospel and have an opportunity to believe in God's Servant-Son. This verse is sometimes called the "great commission of the Old Testament." This commission will not be fulfilled until the gospel is adequately preached throughout the whole world. When this occurs, "then shall the end come" (see Mat. 24:14, note). The task of N.T. believers is to preach the gospel faithfully, taking it to all nations until the Lord returns.

49:7 MAN DESPISETH ... ABHORRETH. Christ would be despised and hated by many (cf. 53:3), yet His former enemies would bow before Him.

49:8–13 THUS SAITH THE LORD. These verses describe the joyful and blessed condition of those who find deliverance and salvation in Christ.

49:14–17 THE LORD HATH FORSAKEN ME. These are the words of the Israelites, who experienced great adversity and thus felt abandoned and forgotten by God. God's response gives divine assurance to any believer going through trying times. (1) His love for us is greater than the natural affection of a loving mother for her children. It is therefore unthinkable that He will ever forget us, especially in our times of despair and grief (cf. Jer. 31:20). (2) His compassion for us will never fail, regardless of life's circumstances. He watches over us with great tenderness and love, and we may rest in the conviction that He will never leave us. (3) The evidence of God's great love is that He has engraven us on the palms of His own hands, so that He can never forget us. The scars in His hands are ever before His eyes as a reminder of the great love He has showered on us and of His desire to care for us.

yea, they may forget, [j]yet will I not
forget thee.
16 Behold, [k]I have graven thee
upon the palms of *my* hands; thy walls
are continually before me.
17 Thy children shall make haste;
[l]thy destroyers and they that made
thee waste shall go forth of thee.
18 ¶ [m]Lift up thine eyes round
about, and behold: all these gather
themselves together, *and* come to thee.
As I live, saith the LORD, thou shalt
surely clothe thee with them all, [n]as
with an ornament, and bind them *on
thee,* as a bride *doeth.*
19 For thy waste and thy desolate
places, and the land of thy destruction,
[o]shall even now be too narrow by rea-
son of the inhabitants, and they that
swallowed thee up shall be far away.
20 [p]The children which thou shalt
have, [q]after thou hast lost the other,
shall say again in thine ears, The place
is too strait for me: give place to me
that I may dwell.
21 Then shalt thou say in thine
heart, Who hath begotten me these,
seeing I have lost my children, and am
desolate, a captive, and removing to
and fro? and who hath brought up
these? Behold, I was left alone; these,
where *had* they *been?*
22 [r]Thus saith the Lord GOD, Be-
hold, I will lift up mine hand to the
Gentiles, and set up my standard to the
people: and they shall bring thy sons in
their [e]arms, and thy daughters shall
be carried upon *their* shoulders.
23 [s]And kings shall be thy [f]nurs-
ing fathers, and their [g]queens thy
nursing mothers: they shall bow down
to thee with *their* face toward the earth,
and [t]lick up the dust of thy feet; and
thou shalt know that I *am* the LORD: for
[u]they shall not be ashamed that wait
for me.
24 ¶ [v]Shall the prey be taken from
the mighty, or [h]the lawful captive de-
livered?
25 But thus saith the LORD, Even the
[i]captives of the mighty shall be taken
away, and the prey of the terrible shall
be delivered: for I will contend with
him that contendeth with thee, and I
will save thy children.
26 And I will [w]feed them that op-
press thee with their own flesh; and
they shall be drunken with their own
[x]blood, as with [j]sweet wine: and all
flesh [y]shall know that I the LORD *am*
thy Saviour and thy Redeemer, the
mighty One of Jacob.

49:15 [j]Rom. 11:29
49:16 [k]Ex. 13:9; Sol. 8:6
49:17 [l]ver. 19
49:18 [m]ch. 60:4; [n]Prov. 17:6
49:19 [o]ch. 54:1,2; Zech. 10:10
49:20 [p]ch. 60:4; [q]Mat. 3:9; Rom. 11:11
49:22 [r]ch. 60:4
49:23 [s]Ps. 72:11; ch. 52:15 & 60:16; [t]Ps. 72:9; Mic. 7:17; [u]Ps. 34:22; Rom. 5:5 & 9:33
49:24 [v]Mat. 12:29; Luke 11:21,22
49:26 [w]ch. 9:20; [x]Rev. 14:20 & 16:6; [y]Ps. 9:16; ch. 60:16

Sin separates Israel from God

50 THUS SAITH the LORD, Where
is [z]the bill of your mother's di-
vorcement, whom I have put away? or
which of my [a]creditors *is it* to whom
I have sold you? Behold, for your iniq-
uities [b]have ye sold yourselves, and
for your transgressions is your mother
put away.
2 Wherefore, when I came, *was there*
no man? [c]when I called, *was there*
none to answer? [d]Is my hand short-
ened at all, that it cannot redeem? or
have I no power to deliver? behold, [e]at
my rebuke I [f]dry up the sea, I make
the [g]rivers a wilderness: [h]their fish
stinketh, because *there is* no water, and
dieth for thirst.
3 [i]I clothe the heavens with black-
ness, [j]and I make sackcloth their cov-
ering.

Obedient response of the servant

4 [k]The Lord GOD hath given me the
tongue of the learned, that I should
know how to speak a word in season to
him that is [l]weary: he wakeneth morn-
ing by morning, he wakeneth mine ear
to hear as the learned.
5 ¶ The Lord GOD [m]hath opened
mine ear, and I was not [n]rebellious,
neither turned away back.
6 [o]I gave my back to the smiters,

50:1 [z]Deut. 24:1; Jer. 3:8; Hos. 2:2; [a]2 Ki. 4:1; Mat. 18:25; [b]ch. 52:3
50:2 [c]Prov. 1:24; ch. 65:12; Jer. 35:15; [d]Num. 11:23; [e]Ps. 106:9; Nah. 1:4; [f]Ex. 14:21; [g]Josh. 3:16; [h]Ex. 7:18
50:3 [i]Ex. 10:21; [j]Rev. 6:12
50:4 [k]Ex. 4:11; [l]Mat. 11:28
50:5 [m]Ps. 40:6-8; [n]Mat. 26:39; John 14:31; Heb. 10:5
50:6 [o]Mat. 26:67

[e] Heb. *bosom* [f] Heb. *nourishers* [g] Heb. *princesses* [h] Heb. *the captivity of the just* [i] Heb. *captivity* [j] Or, *new wine*

49:22–26 GENTILES . . . SHALL BRING THY SONS. These verses foresee a time when Israel would be restored to God and the Gentiles converted. The Gentiles would in fact lead a future generation of Jews back to the Lord (cf. 14:2; 43:6; 60:9; see article on ISRAEL IN GOD'S PLAN OF SALVATION, p. 1748).

50:4–11 THE LORD GOD HATH GIVEN. Intertwined with the prophet's own experiences and exhortations in these verses are prophetic words of the character and suffering of the Messiah.

50:4 SPEAK . . . TO *HIM THAT IS* WEARY. The Messiah would comfort the weak and the troubled (cf. 42:3; Mat. 11:28); He Himself would commune "morning by morning" with His Father (cf. Mark 1:35).

50:6 I GAVE MY BACK TO THE SMITERS. The Messiah would endure suffering, humiliation, and disgrace in fulfilling His task of redeeming the human race (cf. Mat. 27:26,30; Mark 14:65;

and [p]my cheeks to them that plucked
off the hair: I hid not my face from
shame and spitting.
7 ¶ For the Lord GOD will help me;
therefore shall I not be confounded:
therefore have [q]I set my face like a
flint, and I know that I shall not be
ashamed.
8 [r]*He is* near that justifieth me;
who will contend with me? let us stand
together: who *is* [k]mine adversary? let
him come near to me.
9 Behold, the Lord GOD will help me;
who *is* he *that* shall condemn me? [s]lo,
they all shall wax old as a garment;
[t]the moth shall eat them up.
10 ¶ Who *is* among you that feareth
the LORD, that obeyeth the voice of his
servant, that [u]walketh *in* darkness,
and hath no light? [v]let him trust in the
name of the LORD, and stay upon his
God.
11 Behold, all ye that kindle a fire,
that compass *yourselves* about with
sparks: walk in the light of your fire,
and in the sparks *that* ye have kindled.
[w]This shall ye have of mine hand; ye
shall lie down [x]in sorrow.

The LORD will deliver his people

51 HEARKEN TO me, [y]ye that
follow after righteousness, ye
that seek the LORD: look unto the rock
whence ye are hewn, and to the hole of
the pit *whence* ye are digged.
2 [z]Look unto Abraham your fa-
ther, and unto Sarah *that* bare you:
[a]for I called him alone, and [b]blessed
him, and increased him.
3 For the LORD [c]shall comfort Zion:
he will comfort all her waste places;
and he will make her wilderness like
Eden, and her desert [d]like the garden
of the LORD; joy and gladness shall be
found therein, thanksgiving, and the
voice of melody.
4 ¶ Hearken unto me, my people;
and give ear unto me, O my nation:
[e]for a law shall proceed from me, and
I will make my judgment to rest [f]for
a light of the people.
5 [g]My righteousness *is* near; my
salvation is gone forth, [h]and mine
arms shall judge the people; [i]the isles
shall wait upon me, and [j]on mine arm
shall they trust.
6 [k]Lift up your eyes to the heav-
ens, and look upon the earth beneath:
for [l]the heavens shall vanish away
like smoke, [m]and the earth shall wax
old like a garment, and they that dwell
therein shall die in like manner: but my
salvation shall be for ever, and my
righteousness shall not be abolished. Is. 53:6-12
7 ¶ [n]Hearken unto me, ye that
know righteousness, the people [o]in
whose heart *is* my law; [p]fear ye not
the reproach of men, neither be ye
afraid of their revilings.
8 For [q]the moth shall eat them up
like a garment, and the worm shall eat
them like wool: but my righteousness
shall be for ever, and my salvation from
generation to generation.
9 ¶ [r]Awake, awake, [s]put on
strength, O arm of the LORD; awake,

[k] Heb. *the master of my cause?*

50:6 [p]Lam. 3:30 **50:7** [q]Ezek. 3:8,9 **50:8** [r]Rom. 8:32 **50:9** [s]Job 13:28 Ps. 102:26 ch. 51:6 [t]ch. 51:8 **50:10** [u]Ps. 23:4 [v]2 Chr. 20:20 Ps. 20:7 **50:11** [w]John 9:39 [x]Ps. 16:4 **51:1** [y]Rom. 9:30-32 **51:2** [z]Rom. 4:1 Heb. 11:11 [a]Gen. 12:1 [b]Gen. 24:35 **51:3** [c]ver. 12 ch. 52:9 [d]Gen. 13:10 Joel 2:3 **51:4** [e]ch. 2:3 [f]ch. 42:6 **51:5** [g]ch. 46:13 Rom. 1:16 [h]Ps. 67:4 [i]ch. 60:9 [j]Rom. 1:16 **51:6** [k]ch. 40:26 [l]Ps. 102:26 Mat. 24:35 2 Pet. 3:10 [m]ch. 50:9 **51:7** [n]ver. 1 [o]Ps. 37:31 [p]Mat. 10:28 Acts 5:41 **51:8** [q]ch. 50:9 **51:9** [r]Ps. 44:23 [s]Ps. 93:1

15:16–20; John 19:1).

50:7 I SET MY FACE LIKE A FLINT. Because Christ knew that His suffering and death would result in the redemption of all who would believe in Him, "he steadfastly set his face to go to Jerusalem" (Luke 9:51).

50:10–11 YOU THAT FEARETH THE LORD. The prophet Isaiah calls upon those who trust in the Lord to remain faithful to Him even though they may have to walk in the darkness of the apostasy of the nation. Those who kindle a fire, i.e., walk in the light of their own fire — their own ideas and ways — rather than submitting to God and the revelation of His word, will "lie down in sorrow."

51:1–3 YE THAT FOLLOW AFTER RIGHTEOUSNESS. God encourages the faithful remnant who seek Him and His righteousness (cf. Mat. 5:6) to have full confidence that He will one day establish His kingdom on earth. This promise is repeated in the N.T. (Rev. 11:15; 19—22). Although sin and Satan now have much of the world under their control (John 12:31; Eph. 2:1–3), the Lord will return to destroy evil and establish His kingdom on this earth.

51:4–5 A LIGHT OF THE PEOPLE. God's kingdom on earth at the end of time will bring salvation and righteousness to all the nations of the world (cf. 2:2–4; 42:4).

51:6 THE HEAVENS SHALL VANISH. The establishment of God's eternal kingdom on earth will involve the destruction of the present heaven and earth and the death of all who oppose God and His righteousness (24:4; 34:4; 50:9; Heb. 1:10–11; Rev. 19). Thereupon our Lord will create a new heaven and earth for the saints (65:17; 66:22; Rev. 21:1), where He will dwell forever with those whom He has redeemed (2 Pet. 3:13).

51:9–11 AWAKE ... ARM OF THE LORD. We must respond to God's promises for the final redemption of His faithful people and the earth by fervently desiring and praying that those things come to pass. The apostle Peter teaches that our prayers can hasten that day: "We, according to his promise, look for new heavens and a new earth,

[t]as in the ancient days, in the generations of old. [u]*Art* thou not it that hath cut [v]Rahab, *and* wounded the [w]dragon?

10 *Art* thou not it which hath [x]dried the sea, the waters of the great deep; that hath made the depths of the sea a way for the ransomed to pass over?

11 Therefore [y]the redeemed of the LORD shall return, and come with singing unto Zion; and everlasting joy *shall be* upon their head: they shall obtain gladness and joy; *and* sorrow and mourning shall flee away.

12 I, *even* I, *am* he [z]that comforteth you: who *art* thou, that thou shouldest be afraid [a]of a man *that* shall die, and of the son of man *which* shall be made [b]*as* grass;

13 And forgettest the LORD thy maker, [c]that hath stretched forth the heavens, and laid the foundations of the earth; and hast feared continually every day because of the fury of the oppressor, as if he [1]were ready to destroy? [d]and where *is* the fury of the oppressor?

14 The captive exile hasteneth that he may be loosed, [e]and that he should not die in the pit, nor that his bread should fail.

15 But I *am* the LORD thy God, that [f]divided the sea, whose waves roared: The LORD of hosts *is* his name.

16 And [g]I have put my words in thy mouth, and [h]I have covered thee in the shadow of mine hand, [i]that I may plant the heavens, and lay the foundations of the earth, and say unto Zion, Thou *art* my people.

The cup of God's fury

17 ¶ [j]Awake, awake, stand up, O Jerusalem, which [k]hast drunk at the hand of the LORD the cup of his fury; [l]thou hast drunken the dregs of the cup of trembling, *and* wrung *them* out.

18 *There is* none to guide her among all the sons *whom* she hath brought forth; neither *is there any* that taketh her by the hand of all the sons *that* she hath brought up.

19 [m]These two *things* [m]are come unto thee; who shall be sorry for thee? desolation, and [n]destruction, and the famine, and the sword: [n]by whom shall I comfort thee?

20 [o]Thy sons have fainted, they lie at the head of all the streets, as a wild bull in a net: they are full of the fury of the LORD, the rebuke of thy God.

21 ¶ Therefore hear now this, thou afflicted, and drunken, [p]but not with wine:

22 Thus saith thy Lord the LORD, and thy God [q]*that* pleadeth the cause of his people, Behold, I have taken out of thine hand the cup of trembling, *even* the dregs of the cup of my fury; thou shalt no more drink it again:

23 But [r]I will put it into the hand of them that afflict thee; [s]which have said to thy soul, Bow down, that we may go over: and thou hast laid thy body as the ground, and as the street, to them that went over.

God will restore Jerusalem

52 AWAKE, [t]AWAKE; put on thy strength, O Zion; put on thy beautiful garments, O Jerusalem, [u]the holy city: for [v]henceforth there shall no more come into thee the uncircumcised [w]and the unclean.

2 [x]Shake thyself from the dust; arise, *and* sit down, O Jerusalem: [y]loose thyself from the bands of thy neck, O captive daughter of Zion.

3 For thus saith the LORD, [z]Ye have sold yourselves for nought; and ye shall be redeemed without money.

4 For thus saith the Lord GOD, My people went down aforetime into [a]Egypt to sojourn there; and the Assyrian oppressed them without cause.

5 Now therefore, what have I here, saith the LORD, that my people is taken away for nought? they that rule over them make them to howl, saith the

51:9 [t]Ps. 44:1 [u]Job 26:12 [v]Ps. 87:4 & 89:10 [w]Ps. 74:13 Ezek. 29:3
51:10 [x]Ex. 14:21 ch. 43:16
51:11 [y]ch. 35:10
51:12 [z]2 Cor. 1:3 [a]Ps. 118:6 [b]1 Pet. 1:24
51:13 [c]Ps. 104:2 [d]Job 20:7
51:14 [e]Zech. 9:11
51:15 [f]Job 26:12 Ps. 74:13 Jer. 31:35
51:16 [g]Deut. 18:18 ch. 59:21 John 3:34 [h]ch. 49:2 [i]ch. 65:17
51:17 [j]ch. 52:1 [k]Job 21:20 Jer. 25:15 [l]See Deut. 28:28, 34 Ps. 60:3 Ezek. 23:32-34
51:19 [m]ch. 47:9 [n]Amos 7:2
51:20 [o]Lam. 2:11
51:21 [p]See ver. 17 Lam. 3:15
51:22 [q]Jer. 50:34
51:23 [r]Jer. 25:17 Zech. 12:2 [s]Ps. 66:11
52:1 [t]ch. 51:9,17 [u]Neh. 11:1 Mat. 4:5 Rev. 21:2 [v]Nah. 1:15 [w]Rev. 21:27
52:2 [x]ch. 3:26 [y]Zech. 2:7
52:3 [z]Ps. 44:12
52:4 [a]Gen. 46:6

[1] Or, *made* himself *ready* [m] Heb. *happened*
[n] Heb. *breaking*

wherein dwelleth righteousness" (2 Pet. 3:13; see 3:12, note).

51:17–23 O JERUSALEM. In these verses Isaiah prophesies concerning Israel's exile because of God's wrath and goes on to proclaim God's promise of future deliverance. He foresees a time when God's judgment of His people would end and their anguish cease. God would then judge those who afflicted them.

52:1–6 PUT ON THY STRENGTH. Isaiah envisions a time when God would restore His exiled people for His name's sake and when Jerusalem would be rebuilt.

LORD; and my name continually every day *is* [b]blasphemed.

6 Therefore my people shall know my name: therefore *they shall know* in that day that I *am* he that doth speak: behold, *it is* I.

7 ¶ [c]How beautiful upon the mountains are the feet of him that bringeth good tidings, that publisheth peace; that bringeth good tidings of good, that publisheth salvation; that saith unto Zion, [d]Thy God reigneth!

8 Thy watchmen shall lift up the voice; with the voice together shall they sing: for they shall see eye to eye, when the LORD shall bring again Zion.

9 ¶ Break forth into joy, sing together, ye waste places of Jerusalem: for the LORD hath comforted his people, he hath redeemed Jerusalem.

10 [e]The LORD hath made bare his holy arm in the eyes of all the nations; and [f]all the ends of the earth shall see the salvation of our God.

Ezek. 3:10-11

11 ¶ [g]Depart ye, depart ye, go ye out from thence, touch no unclean *thing;* go ye out of the midst of her; [h]be ye clean, that bear the vessels of the LORD.

12 For [i]ye shall not go out with haste, nor go by flight: [j]for the LORD will go before you; [k]and the God of Israel *will* [o]*be* your rearward.

The servant of the LORD

13 ¶ Behold, [l]my servant shall [m]deal[p] prudently, [n]he shall be exalted and extolled, and be very high.

14 As many were astonied at thee; his [o]visage was so marred more than any man, and his form more than the sons of men:

15 [p]So shall he sprinkle many nations; the kings shall shut their mouths at him: for *that* [q]which had not been told them shall they see; and *that* which they had not heard shall they consider.

53 WHO [r]HATH believed our [q] [r]report? and to whom is the arm of the LORD revealed?

2 For he shall grow up before him as a tender plant, and as a root out of a dry ground: he hath no form nor comeliness; and when we shall see him, *there is* no beauty that we should desire him.

3 [s]He is despised and rejected of men; a man of sorrows, and [t]ac-

52:5 [b]Ezek. 36:20
52:7 [c]Rom. 10:15 [d]Ps. 93:1
52:10 [e]Ps. 98:2,3 [f]Luke 3:6
52:11 [g]ch. 48:20 [h]Lev. 22:2
52:12 [i]Ex. 12:33 [j]Mic. 2:13 [k]Ex. 14:19
52:13 [l]ch. 42:1 [m]Jer. 23:5 [n]Phil. 2:9
52:14 [o]Ps. 22:6,7
52:15 [p]Ezek. 36:25 [q]Eph. 3:5,9
53:1 [r]John 12:38 Rom. 10:16
53:3 [s]Ps. 22:6 [t]Heb. 4:15

[o] Heb. *gather you up* [p] Or, *prosper* [q] Or, *doctrine?* [r] Heb. *hearing?*

52:7 HOW BEAUTIFUL . . . ARE THE FEET. This verse refers first to those who proclaimed release to the captives in Babylon. It also foreshadows the announcement of salvation through the coming Messiah (see Rom. 10:15; Eph. 6:15). The focus of the proclaimed message is, "Thy God reigneth," i.e., the kingdom of God has come to earth (cf. Mark 1:14–15; see article on THE KINGDOM OF GOD, p. 1428).

52:11 GO YE OUT . . . TOUCH NO UNCLEAN *THING*. The exodus from Babylon, like the exodus from Egypt, pictured deliverance from the world and all that is unclean. The redeemed people were specifically instructed to purify themselves from all uncleanness. Likewise, when individuals accept Christ as Lord and Savior, they must separate themselves from the world and purify themselves from all evil (see article on SPIRITUAL SEPARATION FOR BELIEVERS, p. 1814).

52:13—53:12 THE SUFFERING SERVANT. This section concerns the suffering and rejection of the Servant-Messiah, Jesus Christ. Isaiah prophesies that through His suffering many would be forgiven, justified, redeemed, and healed. His suffering would also lead to His exaltation and glory. The N.T. quotes from this portion of Scripture more than from any other O.T. section.

52:13 BEHOLD, MY SERVANT. Jesus the Messiah, the Servant of God, would do the will of God perfectly and be highly exalted as a result (cf. Acts 2:33; Phil. 2:9; Col. 3:1; Heb. 1:3; 8:1).

52:14 HIS VISAGE WAS SO MARRED. This verse describes Jesus' mistreatment by the Jews and the Roman soldiers at His trial and crucifixion (cf. Ps. 22:6–8; see Mat. 26:67, note).

52:15 SPRINKLE MANY NATIONS. This phrase refers to the spiritual cleansing and purification (cf. Ex. 29:21; Lev. 8:11,30) that people from all nations would experience when they received the message of the Servant-Messiah. This cleansing would come by the sprinkled blood of Christ.

53:1 WHO HATH BELIEVED OUR REPORT? Although Jesus is God's Messiah, many would choose not to believe in Him and would therefore fail to receive the salvation of the Lord (see John 12:38; Rom. 10:16). There were relatively few true believers among the Jews at His first coming.

53:2 ROOT OUT OF A DRY GROUND. Jesus not only had humble beginnings, but He came to earth at a time of great spiritual drought. John the Baptist began to awaken the people shortly before Jesus began His public ministry.

53:2 *THERE IS* NO BEAUTY THAT WE SHOULD DESIRE HIM. The Messiah would lack earthly grandeur and physical attractiveness. God's greatest concern is always a person's character, godliness, and obedience, not earthly status or physical beauty (cf. 1 Sam. 16:7; see Luke 22:24–30, note).

53:3 DESPISED AND REJECTED. Instead of being accepted by Israel, Jesus Christ would be

quainted with grief: and [s] [t]we hid as it were *our* faces from him; he was despised, and [u]we esteemed him not.

4 ¶ Surely [v]he hath borne our griefs, and carried our sorrows: yet we did esteem him stricken, smitten of God, and afflicted.

5 But he *was* [w]wounded[u] for our transgressions, *he was* bruised for our iniquities: the chastisement of our peace *was* upon him; and with his [x]stripes[v] we are healed.

Is. 57:18-19

6 All we like sheep have gone astray; we have turned every one to his own way; and the LORD [w]hath laid on him the iniquity of us all.

7 He was oppressed, and he was afflicted, yet [y]he opened not his mouth: [z]he is brought as a lamb to the slaughter, and as a sheep before her shearers is dumb, so he openeth not his mouth.

8 [x]He was taken from prison and from judgment: and who shall declare his generation? for [a]he was cut off out of the land of the living: for the transgression of my people [y]was he stricken.

9 [b]And he made his grave with the wicked, and with the rich in his [z]death; because he had done no violence, neither *was any* [c]deceit in his mouth.

10 ¶ Yet it pleased the LORD to bruise him; he hath put *him* to grief: [a]when thou shalt make his soul [d]an offering for sin, he shall see *his* seed, he shall prolong *his* days, and the pleasure of the LORD shall prosper in his hand.

11 He shall see of the travail of his soul, *and* shall be satisfied: by his knowledge shall [e]my righteous [f]servant [g]justify many; for he shall bear their iniquities.

12 [h]Therefore will I divide him *a portion* with the great, [i]and he shall divide the spoil with the strong; be-

53:3 [u]John 1:10 **53:4** [v]Mat. 8:17 Heb. 9:28 **53:5** [w]Rom. 4:25 [x]1 Pet. 2:24 **53:7** [y]Mat. 26:63 [z]Acts 8:32 **53:8** [a]Dan. 9:26 **53:9** [b]Mat. 27:57 [c]1 John 3:5 **53:10** [d]2 Cor. 5:21 **53:11** [e]1 John 2:1 [f]ch. 42:1 [g]Rom 5:18 **53:12** [h]Ps. 2:8 [i]Col. 2:15

[s] Or, *he hid as it were* his *face from us* [t] Heb. *as an hiding of faces from him,* or, *from us* [u] Or, *tormented* [v] Heb. *bruise* [w] Heb. *hath made the iniquity of us all to meet on him* [x] Or, *He was taken away by distress and judgment: but* [y] Heb. was *the stroke upon him* [z] Heb. *deaths* [a] Or, *when his soul shall make an offering*

hated and rejected by its rulers (see 52:14, note; Mat. 26:57, note).

53:3 A MAN OF SORROWS. Jesus' mission would involve great pain, suffering, disappointment, and grief because of the sins of humankind. Likewise, all those who follow Jesus will likely experience a measure of suffering and disappointment (see 2 Cor. 11:23, note).

53:4 BORNE OUR GRIEFS. This verse is quoted in Mat. 8:17 with reference to Jesus' ministry of healing the sick—both the physically and the spiritually sick. The word translated "griefs" (Heb. *choli*) is literally "sickness" or "infirmities." Thus the Messiah would endure punishment in order that we may be delivered from our diseases and sicknesses as well as from our sins. It is therefore right and good for us to pray for physical healing. As He bore our sins, He also takes the sickness and grief that belong to us, lifts them upon Himself, and carries them (see next two notes).

53:5 WOUNDED FOR OUR TRANSGRESSIONS. Christ was crucified because we have sinned and are guilty before God (cf. Ps. 22:16; Zech. 12:10; John 19:34). As our substitute, He took the punishment due us and paid the penalty for our sins—the penalty of death (Rom. 6:23). Therefore, we can be forgiven and have peace with God (cf. Rom. 5:1).

53:5 WITH HIS STRIPES WE ARE HEALED. This healing refers to salvation with all its benefits, spiritual and physical. Sickness and disease are the result of the fall and Satan's activity in the world (see article on DIVINE HEALING, p. 1418). "For this purpose the Son of God was manifested, that he might destroy the works of the devil" (1 John 3:8). Christ gave gifts of healing to His church (1 Cor. 12:9) and commanded His followers to heal the sick as part of their proclamation of the kingdom of God (Luke 9:1–2,6; 10:1,8–9,19).

53:6 ALL WE LIKE SHEEP HAVE GONE ASTRAY. Every person at one time or another has preferred following his or her own selfish and sinful way to obeying God's righteous commandments (see Rom. 6:1, notes). We are all guilty, and therefore we need Christ to die in our place.

53:7 AS A LAMB TO THE SLAUGHTER. Jesus endured His suffering for us patiently and voluntarily (1 Pet. 2:23; cf. John 1:29,36; Rev. 5:6).

53:9 HIS GRAVE WITH THE WICKED. This phrase may simply indicate that Jesus Christ would die alongside the wicked, or that the Roman soldiers intended to bury Him with the two thieves. Yet, as here prophesied, He was buried in the grave of a rich man (Mat. 27:57–60).

53:10 IT PLEASED THE LORD TO BRUISE HIM. It was the will of God the Father that His Son be sent to die on the cross for a lost world (see John 3:16, note; see article on THE WILL OF GOD, p. 1060). By making Christ an atoning sacrifice for all transgressions (cf. Lev. 5:15; 6:5; 19:21; see article on THE DAY OF ATONEMENT, p. 188), God's redemptive purpose of bringing many people to salvation has been accomplished. "He shall prolong *his* days" means, "He shall rise from the dead and live forever."

53:11 TRAVAIL OF HIS SOUL. The suffering of the Messiah would accomplish God's purpose and result in salvation for the "many" who believe.

53:12 *A PORTION* WITH THE GREAT. God

(3) Believers are called to pray that God's will may be done (cf. Mat. 6:10; 26:42; Luke 11:2; Rom. 15:30–32; Jas. 4:13–15): we must sincerely desire God's perfect will and intend to fulfill it in our lives and in the lives of our families (see Mat. 6:10, note). If this is our prayer and commitment, then we can rest assured that our present and future are in the protective care of our heavenly Father (cf. Acts 18:21; 1 Cor. 4:19; 16:7). However, if there is deliberate sin in our lives and rebellion against His word, then we must realize that God will not answer our prayers (see article on EFFECTIVE PRAYING, p. 540). We cannot expect God's will to be done on earth as it is in heaven unless we ourselves are attempting to do His will in our own lives.

(4) Finally, we must not use the will of God as an excuse for passivity or irresponsibility with respect to His call to battle sin, evil, and spiritual lukewarmness. It is Satan, not God, who is responsible for this present evil age with its cruelty, evil, and injustice (see 1 John 5:19, note), and it is Satan who causes much of the pain and suffering in the world (cf. Job 1:6–12; 2:1–6; Luke 13:16; 2 Cor. 12:7). Just as Jesus came to destroy the works of the devil (1 John 3:8), so it is God's explicit will for us as believers to wage war against those spiritual hosts of wickedness through the Holy Spirit (Eph. 6:10–20; 1 Thes. 5:8; see article on THE CHRISTIAN'S RELATIONSHIP TO THE WORLD, p. 2004).

JERUSALEM DURING TIME OF THE PROPHETS

c. 750–586 B.C.

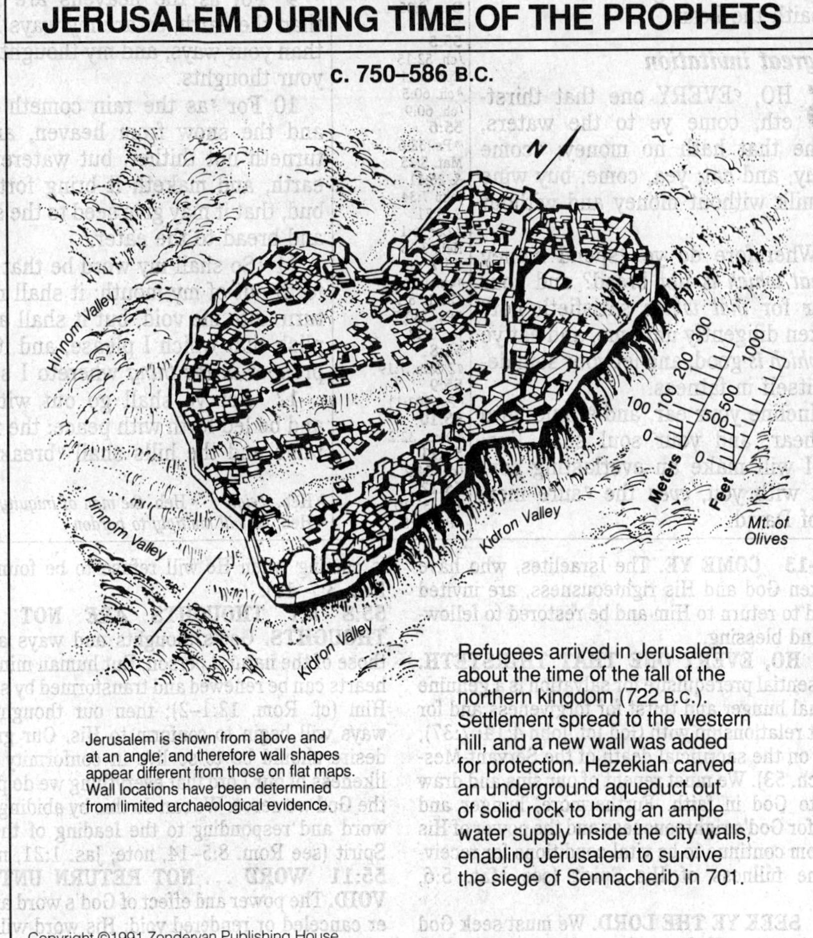

Jerusalem is shown from above and at an angle; and therefore wall shapes appear different from those on flat maps. Wall locations have been determined from limited archaeological evidence.

Refugees arrived in Jerusalem about the time of the fall of the northern kingdom (722 B.C.). Settlement spread to the western hill, and a new wall was added for protection. Hezekiah carved an underground aqueduct out of solid rock to bring an ample water supply inside the city walls, enabling Jerusalem to survive the siege of Sennacherib in 701.

[z]taught of the LORD; and [a]great *shall be* the peace of thy children.

14 In righteousness shalt thou be established: thou shalt be far from oppression; for thou shalt not fear: and from terror; for it shall not come near thee.

15 Behold, they shall surely gather together, *but* not by me: whosoever shall gather together against thee shall fall for thy sake.

16 Behold, I have created the smith that bloweth the coals in the fire, and that bringeth forth an instrument for his work; and I have created the waster to destroy.

17 ¶ No weapon that is formed against thee shall prosper; and every tongue *that* shall rise against thee in judgment thou shalt condemn. This *is* the heritage of the servants of the LORD, [b]and their righteousness *is* of me, saith the LORD.

The great invitation

55 HO, [c]EVERY one that thirsteth, come ye to the waters, and he that hath no money; [d]come ye, buy, and eat; yea, come, buy wine and milk without money and without price.

2 Wherefore do ye [b]spend money for *that which is* not bread? and your labour for *that which* satisfieth not? hearken diligently unto me, and eat ye *that which is* good, and let your soul delight itself in fatness.

3 Incline your ear, and [e]come unto me: hear, and your soul shall live; [f]and I will make an everlasting covenant with you, *even* the [g]sure mercies of David.

4 Behold, I have given him *for* [h]a witness to the people, [i]a leader and commander to the people.

5 [j]Behold, thou shalt call a nation *that* thou knowest not, [k]and nations *that* knew not thee shall run unto thee because of the LORD thy God, and for the Holy One of Israel; [l]for he hath glorified thee.

6 ¶ [m]Seek ye the LORD while he may be found, call ye upon him while he is near:

7 [n]Let the wicked forsake his way, and [c]the unrighteous man [o]his thoughts: and let him return unto the LORD, [p]and he will have mercy upon him; and to our God, for [d]he will abundantly pardon.

8 ¶ [q]For my thoughts *are* not your thoughts, neither *are* your ways my ways, saith the LORD.

9 [r]For *as* the heavens are higher than the earth, so are my ways higher than your ways, and my thoughts than your thoughts.

10 For [s]as the rain cometh down, and the snow from heaven, and returneth not thither, but watereth the earth, and maketh it bring forth and bud, that it may give seed to the sower, and bread to the eater:

11 [t]So shall my word be that goeth forth out of my mouth: it shall not return unto me void, but it shall accomplish that which I please, and it shall prosper *in the thing* whereto I sent it.

12 [u]For ye shall go out with joy, and be led forth with peace: the mountains and the hills shall [v]break forth

Is. 59: 17

54:13 [z]ch. 11:9 Jer. 31:34 John 6:45 1 Cor. 2:10 1 Thes. 4:9 1 John 2:20 [a]Ps. 119:165
54:17 [b]ch. 45:24,25
55:1 [c]John 4:14 [d]Mat. 13:44 Rev. 3:18
55:3 [e]Mat. 11:28 [f]ch. 54:8 & 61:8 Jer. 32:40 [g]2 Sam. 7:8 Ps. 89:28 Acts 13:34
55:4 [h]John 18:37 Rev. 1:5 [i]Jer. 30:9 Ezek. 34:23 Dan. 9:25 Hos. 3:5
55:5 [j]ch. 52:15 Eph. 2:11 [k]ch. 60:5 [l]ch. 60:9
55:6 [m]Ps. 32:6 Mat. 5:25 & 25:11 John 7:34 & 8:21 2 Cor. 6:1 Heb. 3:13
55:7 [n]ch. 1:16 [o]Zech. 8:17 [p]Ps. 130:7 Jer. 3:12
55:8 [q]2 Sam. 7:19
55:9 [r]Ps. 103:11
55:10 [s]Deut. 32:2
55:11 [t]ch. 54:9
55:12 [u]ch. 35:10 [v]Ps. 98:8

b Heb. *weigh* c Heb. *the man of iniquity*
d Heb. *he will multiply to pardon*

55:1–13 COME YE. The Israelites, who have forsaken God and His righteousness, are invited by God to return to Him and be restored to fellowship and blessing.

55:1 HO, EVERY ONE THAT THIRSTETH. An essential prerequisite for salvation is a genuine spiritual hunger and thirst for forgiveness and for a right relationship with God (cf. John 4:14; 7:37), based on the sacrificial death of the Servant-Messiah (ch. 53). We must repent of our sins and draw near to God in faith. Furthermore, hunger and thirst for God's righteousness and the power of His kingdom continue to be vital conditions for receiving the fullness of His Spirit (see Mat. 5:6, note).

55:6 SEEK YE THE LORD. We must seek God while there is still the promise of His response (cf. Jer. 29:13–14; Hos. 3:5; Amos 5:4,6,14). God's time of salvation is limited (cf. 2 Cor. 6:1–2); a day is coming when He will refuse to be found (see Heb. 3:7–11).

55:8 MY THOUGHTS *ARE* NOT YOUR THOUGHTS. God's thoughts and ways are not those of the natural person. But human minds and hearts can be renewed and transformed by seeking Him (cf. Rom. 12:1–2); then our thoughts and ways will begin to conform to His. Our greatest desire should be to so live in conformity to the likeness of our Lord that everything we do pleases the God we serve. We can do this by abiding in His word and responding to the leading of the Holy Spirit (see Rom. 8:5–14, note; Jas. 1:21, note).

55:11 WORD ... NOT RETURN UNTO ME VOID. The power and effect of God's word are never canceled or rendered void; His word will bring either spiritual life to those who receive it or just condemnation for those who reject it (see article on THE WORD OF GOD, p. 1064).

before you into singing, and [w]all the
trees of the field shall clap *their* hands.
13 [x]Instead of [y]the thorn shall
come up the fir tree, and instead of the
brier shall come up the myrtle tree:
and it shall be to the LORD [z]for a name,
for an everlasting sign *that* shall not be
cut off.

Strangers included in the blessing

56 THUS SAITH the LORD, Keep ye
[e]judgment, and do justice:
[a]for my salvation *is* near to come, and
my righteousness to be revealed.
2 Blessed *is* the man *that* doeth this,
and the son of man *that* layeth hold on
it; [b]that keepeth the sabbath from pol-
luting it, and keepeth his hand from do-
ing any evil.
3 ¶ Neither let [c]the son of the
stranger, that hath joined himself to
the LORD, speak, saying, The LORD hath
utterly separated me from his people:
neither let the eunuch say, Behold, I
am a dry tree.
4 For thus saith the LORD unto the
eunuchs that keep my sabbaths, and
choose *the things* that please me, and
take hold of my covenant;
5 Even unto them will I give in
[d]mine house and within my walls a
place [e]and a name better than of sons
and of daughters: I will give them an
everlasting name, that shall not be cut
off.
6 Also the sons of the stranger, that
join themselves to the LORD, to serve
him, and to love the name of the LORD,
to be his servants, every one that
keepeth the sabbath from polluting it,
and taketh hold of my covenant;
7 Even them will I [f]bring to my
holy mountain, and make them joyful
in my house of prayer: [g]their burnt of-
ferings and their sacrifices *shall be* ac-
cepted upon mine altar; for [h]mine
house shall be called an house of
prayer [i]for all people.
8 The Lord GOD [j]which gathereth
the outcasts of Israel saith, [k]Yet will
I gather *others* to him, [f]beside those
that are gathered unto him.

The failure of Israel's leaders

9 ¶ [l]All ye beasts of the field, come
to devour, *yea,* all ye beasts in the for-
est.
10 His watchmen *are* [m]blind: they
are all ignorant, [n]they *are* all dumb
dogs, they cannot bark; [g]sleeping, ly-
ing down, loving to slumber.
11 Yea, *they are* [o]greedy[h] dogs
which [p]can[i] never have enough, and
they *are* shepherds *that* cannot under-
stand: they all look to their own way,
every one for his gain, from his quar-
ter.
12 Come ye, *say they,* I will fetch
wine, and we will fill ourselves with
strong drink; [q]and tomorrow shall be
as this day, *and* much more abundant.
57 THE RIGHTEOUS perisheth,
and no man layeth *it* to heart:
and [r]merciful[j] men *are* taken away,
[s]none considering that the righteous
is taken away [k]from the evil *to come.*
2 He shall [t]enter[l] into peace:
they shall rest in [u]their beds, *each one*
walking [m]*in* his uprightness.
3 ¶ But draw near hither, [v]ye sons

55:12 [w]1 Chr. 16:33
55:13 [x]ch. 41:19 [y]Mic. 7:4 [z]Jer. 13:11
56:1 [a]Mat. 4:17
56:2 [b]ch. 58:13
56:3 [c]Acts 8:27
56:5 [d]1 Tim. 3:15 [e]1 John 3:1
56:7 [f]ch. 2:2 [g]Rom. 12:1 Heb. 13:15 1 Pet. 2:5 [h]Mat. 21:13 [i]Mal. 1:11
56:8 [j]ch. 11:12 [k]John 10:16
56:9 [l]Jer. 12:9
56:10 [m]Mat. 15:14 [n]Phil. 3:2
56:11 [o]Mic. 3:11 [p]Ezek. 34:2
56:12 [q]Ps. 10:6 Prov. 23:35 Luke 12:19
57:1 [r]Ps. 12:1 [s]1 Ki. 14:13
57:2 [t]Luke 2:29 [u]2 Chr. 16:14
57:3 [v]Mat. 16:4

[e] Or, *equity* [f] Heb. *to his gathered* [g] Or, *dreaming,* or, *talking in their sleep* [h] Heb. *strong of appetite* [i] Heb. *know not to be satisfied* [j] Heb. *men of kindness,* or, *godliness* [k] Or, *from that which is evil* [l] Or, *go in peace* [m] Or, *before him*

56:1–2 DO JUSTICE ... SALVATION *IS* NEAR. Justice and righteousness are the fruit of salvation, directly linked to the influence of God's kingdom. They cannot be separated.

56:3–8 STRANGER . . . EUNUCH. In the Messiah's kingdom all foreigners and eunuchs who turn to the Lord are accepted with the same rights and privileges as the rest of the covenant community (see Ex. 12:43; Deut. 23:1, where they were once excluded from public worship). Regardless of one's nationality, societal status, or personal disabilities, God loves and accepts each believer as one of His precious children.

56:7 MINE HOUSE SHALL BE CALLED AN HOUSE OF PRAYER. The linking together of prayer and God's house reveals that the central purpose of worship is to bring worshipers near to Him in communion, praise, intercession, and petition; to attend church without fervent and intense communion with God is to miss the essential nature and purpose of worship. Jesus cited this verse when He drove the moneychangers out of God's temple (see Mark 11:17, note; Luke 19:45, note).

56:10–12 WATCHMEN *ARE* BLIND. God condemned the corrupt leaders and priests of Israel, for they did not know His word, were greedy for selfish gain, and could not stay away from alcoholic beverages.

57:1–2 THE RIGHTEOUS PERISHETH. Righteous believers were being mistreated at the hands of the cruel and corrupt leaders of Judah and were perishing (cf. 2 Ki. 21:16). But by their death, these martyrs were spared the terrible horrors of God's judgment that would soon come upon His people.

57:3–14 YE SONS OF THE SORCERESS. The

THE WORD OF GOD

***Is. 55:10–11** "For as the rain cometh down, and the snow from heaven, and returneth not thither, but watereth the earth, and maketh it bring forth and bud, that it may give seed to the sower, and bread to the eater: So shall my word be that goeth forth out of my mouth: it shall not return unto me void, but it shall accomplish that which I please, and it shall prosper* in the thing *whereto I sent it."*

THE NATURE OF THE WORD OF GOD. The phrase "the word of God" (also "the word of the LORD," or even simply "the Word") refers to a variety of situations in the Scriptures. (1) It obviously refers first of all to anything that God has spoken directly. When God spoke to Adam and Eve (e.g., Gen. 2:16–17; Gen. 3:9–19), what He said was the word of God. In a similar way, God spoke His word to Abraham (e.g., Gen. 12:1–3), Isaac (e.g., Gen. 26:1–5), Jacob (e.g., Gen. 28:13–15), and Moses (e.g., Ex. 3—4). God also spoke to the entire nation of Israel at Mount Sinai when he recited the Ten Commandments (see Ex. 20:1–19); the words that they heard were His words.

(2) In addition to direct speech, God also spoke through the prophets (see article on THE PROPHET IN THE OLD TESTAMENT, p. 1002). When they addressed God's people, they usually prefaced their statements with "Thus saith the LORD" or "The word of the LORD came to me." Thus, when the Israelites were listening to the words of a prophet, they were listening to the word of God.

(3) The same is true for what the apostles said in the N.T. Even though they did not preface their comments with "This is what the Lord says," what they spoke and proclaimed was indeed the word of God. For example, Paul's sermon that he preached to the people of Antioch in Pisidia (Acts 13:16–41) created such a stir that "the next sabbath day came almost the whole city together to hear the word of God" (Acts 13:44). Paul himself said to the Thessalonians that "when ye received the word of God which ye heard of us, ye received *it* not *as* the word of men, but as it is in truth, the word of God" (1 Thes. 2:13; cf. Acts 8:25).

(4) Furthermore, everything that Jesus spoke was the word of God, for He is, after all, God (John 1:1,18; 10:30; 1 John 5:20). Luke, the writer of the third Gospel, states explicitly that when people heard Jesus, they heard the word of God (Luke 5:1). Note how in contrast to the O.T. prophets, who usually began with some form of "This is what the Lord says," Jesus introduced His sayings with "I say unto you" (e.g., Mat. 5:18,20,22,32,39; 11:22,24; Mark 9:1; 10:15; Luke 10:12; 12:4; John 5:19; 6:26; 8:34). In other words, He had divine authority within Himself to speak the word of God. So important is it to listen to Jesus' words that "He that heareth my word, and believeth on him that sent me, hath everlasting life, and shall not come into condemnation" (John 5:24). Indeed, Jesus is so closely identified with the word of God that He is actually called "the Word" (John 1:1,14; 1 John 1:1; Rev. 19:13–16; see John 1:1, note).

(5) The word of God is the written record of what the prophets, apostles, and Jesus have spoken—i.e., the Scriptures. In the N.T., whether a writer used the phrase "Moses said," "David said," "the Holy Ghost says," or "God says" made no difference (see Acts 3:22; Rom. 10:5,19; Heb. 3:7; 4:7); what was written in the Bible was the word of God (see article on THE INSPIRATION AND AUTHORITY OF SCRIPTURE, p. 1924).

(6) Though not on the same level of authority as Scripture itself, the spoken proclamation by preachers or prophets in the church today may be called the word of God. (a) Peter indicated that what his readers received through the preaching of the word was the word of God (1 Pet. 1:25), and Paul instructed Timothy to "preach the word" (2 Tim. 4:2). Such preaching must never stand independent of the written Word of God, however. In fact, the test to determine whether God's word is being spoken to us in a sermon or

message is whether it corresponds to the written Word of God (see article on FALSE TEACHERS, p. 1508). (b) What about a person who receives a prophecy or revelation in a worship setting (1 Cor. 14:26–32); is he or she receiving the word of God? The answer to this question is a qualified "Yes." Paul asserts that such messages are subject to evaluation by other prophets; thus it is possible that such prophecies may not be the word of God (see 1 Cor. 14:29, note). Only in a secondary sense can we speak of prophets today speaking under the inspiration of the Holy Spirit; the revelation of a prophet today must never be elevated to the point of inerrancy (see 1 Cor. 14:31, note; see articles on SPIRITUAL GIFTS FOR BELIEVERS, p. 1790, and THE MINISTRY GIFTS OF THE CHURCH, p. 1852).

THE POWER OF THE WORD OF GOD. The word of God is eternally fixed in heaven (Ps. 119:89; Is. 40:8; 1 Pet. 1:24–25). Yet it is not a static word; it is dynamic and powerful (cf. Heb. 4:12), and it accomplishes great things (Is. 55:11). (1) The word of God is the creative word. According to the creation account, things came into being when God spoke his word (e.g., Gen. 1:3–4,6–7,9). This process is summarized by the psalmist who wrote, "By the word of the LORD were the heavens made" (Ps. 33:6; cf. v. 9), and by the writer to Hebrews, "Through faith we understand that the worlds were framed by the word of God" (Heb. 11:3; cf. 2 Pet. 3:5). Note that according to John, the Word that God used to create all things was Jesus Christ (John 1:1–3; see article on CREATION, p. 6).

(2) The word of God also has the power to sustain creation. Again, using the words of the writer to the Hebrews, God upholds "all things by the word of his power" (Heb. 1:3; see also Ps. 147:15–18). Like the creative word, this word is related to Jesus Christ, for Paul insists that "by him [Jesus] all things consist" (i.e., are held together, Col. 1:17).

(3) The word of God has the power to impart new life. Peter testifies that we are born again "by the word of God, which liveth and abideth for ever" (1 Pet. 1:23; cf. 2 Tim. 3:15; Jas. 1:18). It is for this reason that Jesus Himself is called "the Word of life" (1 John 1:1).

(4) The word of God also releases grace, power, and revelation by which believers grow in their faith and in their commitment to Jesus Christ. Isaiah uses a powerful picture: just as water from the sky causes things to grow physically, so also the word that proceeds out of the mouth of God causes us to grow spiritually (Is. 55:10–11). Peter echoes the same thought when he writes that by drinking the pure milk of the word of God, we grow in our salvation (1 Pet. 2:2).

(5) The word of God is likewise the sword that God has given us whereby we may fight Satan (Eph. 6:17; cf. Rev. 19:13–15). Note how in the story of Jesus' victory over the temptations of Satan, each time He defeated Satan by declaring, "It is written" (i.e., "It stands as God's infallible Word"; cf. Luke 4:1–11; see Mat. 4:1–11, note).

(6) Finally, the word of God has the power to judge us. The O.T. prophets and the N.T. apostles frequently spoke words of judgment received from the Lord. Jesus Himself said what will judge us in the last day is His word (John 12:48), and the writer to the Hebrews writes that the powerful word of God discerns (i.e., judges) "the thoughts and intents of the heart" (see Heb. 4:12, note). In other words, those who choose to ignore God's word will one day experience it as a word of condemnation.

OUR REACTION TO THE WORD OF GOD. The Bible describes in clear and unmistakable language how we should react to the word of God in all its different forms. We must eagerly hear God's word (Is. 1:10; Jer. 7:1–2; Acts 17:11) and seek to understand it (Mat. 13:23). We must praise God's word (Ps. 56:4,10), love it (Ps. 119:47,113), and let it be our joy and delight (Ps. 119:16,47). We must accept what the word of God says (Mark 4:20; Acts 2:41; 1 Thes. 2:13), hide it deep within our hearts (Ps. 119:11), trust it (Ps. 119:42), and place our hope in its promises (Ps. 119:74,81,114; 130:5). Above all, we must obey what it commands (Ps. 119:17,67; Jas. 1:22–24) and live according to it (Ps. 119:9). God calls those who minister the word (cf. 1 Tim. 5:17) to handle it rightly (2 Tim. 2:15) and to preach it faithfully (2 Tim. 4:2). All believers are called to proclaim the message of God's word wherever they go (Acts 8:4).

of the sorceress, the seed of the adulterer and the whore.

4 Against whom do ye sport yourselves? against whom make ye a wide mouth, *and* draw out the tongue? *are* ye not children of transgression, a seed of falsehood,

5 Enflaming yourselves [n]with idols [w]under every green tree, [x]slaying the children in the valleys under the clefts of the rocks?

6 Among the smooth *stones* of the stream *is* thy portion; they, they *are* thy lot: even to them hast thou poured a drink offering, thou hast offered a meat offering. Should I receive comfort in these?

7 [y]Upon a lofty and high mountain hast thou set [z]thy bed: even thither wentest thou up to offer sacrifice.

8 Behind the doors also and the posts hast thou set up thy remembrance: for thou hast discovered *thyself to another* than me, and art gone up; thou hast enlarged thy bed, and [o]made thee *a covenant* with them; [a]thou lovedst their bed [p]where thou sawest *it.*

9 And [b]thou[q] wentest to the king with ointment, and didst increase thy perfumes, and didst send thy messengers far off, and didst debase *thyself even* unto hell.

10 Thou art wearied in the greatness of thy way; [c]*yet* saidst thou not, There is no hope: thou hast found the [r]life of thine hand; therefore thou wast not grieved.

11 And [d]of whom hast thou been afraid or feared, that thou hast lied, and hast not remembered me, nor laid *it* to thy heart? [e]have not I held my peace even of old, and thou fearest me not?

12 I will declare thy righteousness, and thy works; for they shall not profit thee.

13 ¶ When thou criest, let thy companies deliver thee; but the wind shall carry them all away; vanity shall take *them:* but he that putteth his trust in me shall possess the land, and shall inherit my holy mountain;

Compassion for the repentant

14 And shall say, [f]Cast ye up, cast ye up, prepare the way, take up the stumblingblock out of the way of my people.

15 For thus saith the high and lofty One that inhabiteth eternity, [g]whose name *is* Holy; [h]I dwell in the high and holy *place,* [i]with him also *that is* of a contrite and humble spirit, [j]to revive the spirit of the humble, and to revive the heart of the contrite ones.

16 [k]For I will not contend for ever, neither will I be always wroth: for the spirit should fail before me, and the souls [l]*which* I have made.

17 For the iniquity of [m]his covetousness was I wroth, and smote him: [n]I hid me, and was wroth, [o]and he went on [s]frowardly in the way of his heart.

18 I have seen his ways, and [p]will heal him: I will lead him also, and restore comforts unto him and to [q]his mourners.

19 I create [r]the fruit of the lips; Peace, peace [s]to *him that is* far off, and to *him that is* near, saith the LORD; and I will heal him.

20 [t]But the wicked *are* like the troubled sea, when it cannot rest, whose waters cast up mire and dirt.

21 [u]*There is* no peace, saith my God, to the wicked.

Jer. 17:1

57:5 [w]2 Ki. 16:4 [x]Lev. 18:21 2 Ki. 16:3 Jer. 7:31 Ezek. 16:20
57:7 [y]Ezek. 16:16 [z]Ezek. 23:41
57:8 [a]Ezek. 16:26
57:9 [b]Hos. 7:11
57:10 [c]Jer. 2:25
57:11 [d]ch. 51:12 [e]Ps. 50:21
57:14 [f]ch. 40:3
57:15 [g]Job 6:10 Luke 1:49 [h]Zech. 2:13 [i]Ps. 34:18 & 51:17 [j]Ps. 147:3 ch. 61:1
57:16 [k]Ps. 85:5 & 103:9 Mic. 7:18 [l]Num. 16:22 Job 34:14 Heb. 12:9
57:17 [m]Jer. 6:13 [n]ch. 8:17 & 45:15 [o]ch. 9:13
57:18 [p]Jer. 3:22 [q]ch. 61:2
57:19 [r]Heb. 13:15 [s]Acts 2:39 Eph. 2:17
57:20 [t]Job 15:20 Prov. 4:16
57:21 [u]ch. 48:22

[n] Or, *among the oaks* [o] Or, *hewed it for thyself* larger *than theirs* [p] Or, *thou providedst room* [q] Or, *thou respectedst the king* [r] Or, *living* [s] Heb. *turning away*

people of Judah forsook the Lord and chose instead to worship the gods of heathen nations. This worship involved immorality, prostitution, sorcery, and human sacrifices. But God would let no one get away with sin. Those who transgressed His law would reap what they had sown and lose much more than they had hoped to gain by their wickedness.

57:15 A CONTRITE AND HUMBLE SPIRIT. To those who were humble and repentant, the Lord God came with a gracious promise: He who dwelt in "the high and holy *place*" would personally live with those of a "contrite and humble spirit." "Contrite" refers to any who are oppressed by the burden of sin and want to find freedom from its enslavement; "humble spirit" refers to the broken in heart because of the calamities and afflictions of life (cf. Ps. 34:18–19). God comes to live with such people in order to revive their spirits, give new life, and provide the comfort of His presence.

57:21 NO PEACE . . . TO THE WICKED. God has so structured the human conscience that there will never be real peace for those who live wickedly—neither inward peace nor outward peace. As long as they sin, their lives will be like the troubled sea, full of turmoil and mud (v. 20). God is opposed

Right and wrong fasting

58 CRY [t]ALOUD, spare not, lift
up thy voice like a trumpet,
and show my people their transgres-
sion, and the house of Jacob their
sins.
2 Yet they seek me daily, and de-
light to know my ways, as a nation that
did righteousness, and forsook not the
ordinance of their God: they ask of me
the ordinances of justice; they take de-
light in approaching to God.
3 ¶ [v]Wherefore have we fasted, *say
they,* and thou seest not? *wherefore*
have we [w]afflicted our soul, and thou
takest no knowledge? Behold, in the
day of your fast ye find pleasure, and
exact all your [u] [v]labours.
4 [x]Behold, ye fast for strife and de-
bate, and to smite with the fist of wick-
edness: [w]ye shall not fast as *ye do this*
day, to make your voice to be heard on
high.
5 Is it [y]such a fast that I have cho-
sen? [z]a[x] day for a man to afflict his
soul? *is it* to bow down his head as a
bulrush, and [a]to spread sackcloth and
ashes *under him?* wilt thou call this a
fast, and an acceptable day to the
LORD?
6 *Is* not this the fast that I have cho-
sen? to loose the bands of wickedness,
[b]to undo [y]the heavy burdens, and
[c]to let the [z]oppressed go free, and
that ye break every yoke?
7 *Is it* not [d]to deal thy bread to the
hungry, and that thou bring the poor
that are [a]cast out to thy house?
[e]when thou seest the naked, that thou
cover him; and that thou hide not thy-
self from [f]thine own flesh?
8 ¶ [g]Then shall thy light break
forth as the morning, and thine health
shall spring forth speedily: and thy
righteousness shall go before thee;
[h]the glory of the LORD [b]shall be thy
rearward. Jer. 11:1-5
9 Then shalt thou call, and the LORD
shall answer; thou shalt cry, and he
shall say, Here I *am.* If thou take away
from the midst of thee the yoke, the
putting forth of the finger, and
[i]speaking vanity;
10 And *if* thou draw out thy soul to
the hungry, and satisfy the afflicted
soul; then shall thy light rise in ob-
scurity, and thy darkness *be* as the
noonday:
11 And the LORD shall guide thee
continually, and satisfy thy soul in
[c]drought, and make fat thy bones:

58:3 [v]Mal. 3:14 [w]Lev. 16:29 & 23:27 **58:4** [x]1 Ki. 21:9 **58:5** [y]Zech. 7:5 [z]Lev. 16:29 [a]Esth. 4:3 Job 2:8 Dan. 9:3 **58:6** [b]Neh. 5:10 [c]Jer. 34:9 **58:7** [d]Ezek. 18:7 Mat. 25:35 [e]Job 31:19 [f]Gen. 29:14 Neh. 5:5 **58:8** [g]Job 11:17 [h]Ex. 14:19 ch. 52:12 **58:9** [i]Ps. 12:2

[t] Heb. *with the throat* [u] Or, *things wherewith ye grieve others* [v] Heb. *griefs* [w] Or, *ye fast not as this day* [x] Or, *to afflict his soul for a day?* [y] Heb. *the bundles of the yoke* [z] Heb. *broken* [a] Or, *afflicted* [b] Heb. *shall gather thee up* [c] Heb. *droughts*

to them, while desiring that they will repent and be saved (cf. 2 Pet. 3:9).

58:1 CRY ALOUD, SPARE NOT. The prophet cries out against the people's sins like a mighty trumpet blast; the transgressions and hypocrisy of God's people must be revealed. If God's messengers fail to point out the sins of His people, they are not faithful to God's call.

58:2 THEY SEEK ME DAILY. Judah was seeking God every day as though they desired to know His ways; yet, at the same time, they were living in sin and in indifference to His righteous commands. Today congregations may worship the Lord outwardly, appear to delight in praising Him, and seem eager to know His ways; at the same time, they may be conforming to the ways of the world and neglecting the diligent study of His written Word. Such "worship" is an insult and an abomination to God.

58:3 IN THE DAY OF YOUR FAST. God's people were complaining that He would not help them. But God knew that their worship and their fasting were hypocritical. He tells them that no religious act has any value to Him if it does not come from those who humbly seek to obey His commandments and who compassionately reach out to those in need.

58:6 THE FAST THAT I HAVE CHOSEN. The fast that God approves is one accompanied by love for Him and genuine concern for those who are oppressed. Believers must understand that the giving of tithes and offerings to the church does not free them from their responsibility to give to the poor. We should share our food with the hungry and provide clothing for those who have none. We must make a sincere effort to determine the needs of others, especially within our local congregations, and to commit ourselves to helping in whatever way we can (cf. Gal. 6:10; see article on THE CARE OF THE POOR AND NEEDY, p. 1312). The blessings of v. 8 (see next note) are given to those who have the heart of v. 6 and are committed to the course of action in v. 7.

58:8–12 THEN SHALL THY LIGHT BREAK FORTH. When there is true love for God and sincere concern for the welfare of others, a channel is opened for God's full blessing to come into our lives. The rewards for such love are stated here: (1) the light of God and the full joy of salvation and healing, (2) God's protection and presence manifested in our lives, (3) God's help in trouble through answered prayer, (4) the lifting of darkness and oppression, (5) God's guidance, strength, and fruitfulness, and (6) true restoration, with the revival of God's standards and ideals.

and thou shalt be like a watered garden, and like a spring of water, whose waters [d]fail not.

12 And *they that shall be* of thee [j]shall build the old waste places: thou shalt raise up the foundations of many generations; and thou shalt be called, The repairer of the breach, The restorer of paths to dwell in.

13 ¶ If [k]thou turn away thy foot from the sabbath, *from* doing thy pleasure on my holy day; and call the sabbath a delight, the holy of the LORD, honourable; and shalt honour him, not doing thine own ways, nor finding thine own pleasure, nor speaking *thine own* words:

14 [l]Then shalt thou delight thyself in the LORD; and I will cause thee to [m]ride upon the high places of the earth, and feed thee with the heritage of Jacob thy father: [n]for the mouth of the LORD hath spoken *it.*

Sin, confession and redemption

59 BEHOLD, THE LORD'S hand is not [o]shortened, that it cannot save; neither his ear heavy, that it cannot hear:

2 But your iniquities have separated between you and your God, and your sins [e]have hid *his* face from you, that he will not hear.

3 For [p]your hands are defiled with blood, and your fingers with iniquity; your lips have spoken lies, your tongue hath muttered perverseness.

4 None calleth for justice, nor *any* pleadeth for truth: they trust in vanity, and speak lies; [q]they conceive mischief, and bring forth iniquity.

5 They hatch [f]cockatrice' eggs, and weave the spider's web: he that eateth of their eggs dieth, and [g]that which is crushed breaketh out into a viper.

6 [r]Their webs shall not become garments, neither shall they cover themselves with their works: their works *are* works of iniquity, and the act of violence *is* in their hands.

7 [s]Their feet run to evil, and they make haste to shed innocent blood: their thoughts *are* thoughts of iniquity; wasting and [h]destruction *are* in their paths.

8 The way of peace they know not; and *there is* no [i]judgment in their goings: [t]they have made them crooked paths: whosoever goeth therein shall not know peace.

9 ¶ Therefore is judgment far from us, neither doth justice overtake us: [u]we wait for light, but behold obscurity; for brightness, *but* we walk in darkness.

10 [v]We grope for the wall like the blind, and we grope as if *we had* no eyes: we stumble at noonday as in the night; *we are* in desolate places as dead *men.*

11 We roar all like bears, and [w]mourn sore like doves: we look for judgment, but *there is* none; for salvation, *but* it is far off from us.

12 For our transgressions are multiplied before thee, and our sins testify against us: for our transgressions *are* with us; and *as for* our iniquities, we know them;

13 In transgressing and lying against the LORD, and departing away from our God, speaking oppression and revolt, conceiving and uttering [x]from the heart words of falsehood.

14 And judgment is turned away backward, and justice standeth afar off: for truth is fallen in the street, and equity cannot enter.

58:12 [j]ch. 61:4
58:13 [k]ch. 56:2
58:14 [l]Job 22:26 [m]Deut. 32:13 & 33:29 [n]ch. 1:20 & 40:5 Mic. 4:4
59:1 [o]Num. 11:23 ch. 50:2
59:3 [p]ch. 1:15
59:4 [q]Job 15:35 Ps. 7:14
59:6 [r]Job 8:14
59:7 [s]Prov. 1:16 Rom. 3:15
59:8 [t]Ps. 125:5 Prov. 2:15
59:9 [u]Jer. 8:15
59:10 [v]Deut. 28:29 Job 5:14 Amos 8:9
59:11 [w]ch. 38:14 Ezek. 7:16
59:13 [x]Mat. 12:34

[d] Heb. *lie,* or, *deceive* [e] Or, *have made* him *hide* [f] Or, *adders'* [g] Or, *that which is sprinkled* is as if *there brake out a viper*
[h] Heb. *breaking* [i] Or, *right*

58:13 THE SABBATH. God has ordained from creation that one day in seven should be set aside as "holy" unto Him, a day for God's people to cease their usual activities and devote themselves to physical rest and spiritual renewal (see Ex. 20:8, note; Mat. 12:1, note); doing so will increase our delight in the Lord and enable us to attain new spiritual heights (v. 14).

59:1–8 THE LORD'S HAND ... SHORTENED. This passage describes additional sins that have prevented the people from receiving God's promised blessings (see previous two notes).

59:2 INIQUITIES HAVE SEPARATED BETWEEN YOU AND YOUR GOD. Sin and wickedness in our lives put a wall between us and God. Because of this barrier, we can no longer experience God's favor, protection, help, or salvation. Thus our prayers will not be answered (Ps. 66:18).

59:5 COCKATRICE'S EGGS. These are the eggs of a poisonous snake, also called an adder.

59:9–14 THEREFORE IS JUDGMENT FAR FROM US. Isaiah describes true intercessors as those who know that they are sinners, who confess their sin, and who are deeply grieved over their seemingly hopeless condition.

15 Yea, truth faileth; and he *that* de-
parteth from evil [j]maketh himself a
prey: and the LORD saw *it*, and [k]it dis-
pleased him that *there was* no judg-
ment.
16 ¶ [y]And he saw that *there was* no
man, and [z]wondered that *there was*
no intercessor: [a]therefore his arm
brought salvation unto him; and his
righteousness, it sustained him.
17 [b]For he put on righteousness as
a breastplate, and an helmet of salva-
tion upon his head; and he put on the
garments of vengeance *for* clothing,
:10 and was clad with zeal as a cloak.
18 [c]According to *their* [l]deeds, ac-
cordingly he will repay, fury to his ad-
versaries, recompence to his enemies;
to the islands he will repay recom-
pence.
19 [d]So shall they fear the name of
the LORD from the west, and his glory
from the rising of the sun. When the
enemy shall come in [e]like a flood, the
spirit of the LORD shall [m]lift up a stan-
dard against him.
20 ¶ And [f]the Redeemer shall
come to Zion, and unto them that turn
from transgression in Jacob, saith the
LORD.
21 [g]As for me, this *is* my covenant
with them, saith the LORD; My spirit
that *is* upon thee, and my words which
I have put in thy mouth, shall not de-
part out of thy mouth, nor out of the
mouth of thy seed, nor out of the mouth
of thy seed's seed, saith the LORD, from Ezek. 2:1-2
henceforth and for ever.

59:16 [y]Ezek. 22:30 [z]Mark 6:6 [a]Ps. 98:1 ch. 63:5 **59:17** [b]Eph. 6:14,17 1 Thes. 5:8 **59:18** [c]ch. 63:6 **59:19** [d]Ps. 113:3 Mal. 1:11 [e]Rev. 12:15 **59:20** [f]Rom. 11:26 **59:21** [g]Heb. 8:10 & 10:16

The dawn of Zion's glory

60 ARISE, [h]SHINE;[n] for thy
light is come, and [i]the glory of
the LORD is risen upon thee.
2 For, behold, the darkness shall
cover the earth, and gross darkness
the people: but the LORD shall arise
upon thee, and his glory shall be seen
upon thee.
3 And the [j]Gentiles shall come to
thy light, and kings to the brightness
of thy rising.
4 [k]Lift up thine eyes round about,
and see: all they gather themselves to-
gether, [l]they come to thee: thy sons
shall come from far, and thy daughters
shall be nursed at *thy* side.
5 Then thou shalt see, and flow to-
gether, and thine heart shall fear, and
be enlarged; because [m]the [o]abun-
dance of the sea shall be converted
unto thee, the [p]forces of the Gentiles
shall come unto thee.
6 The multitude of camels shall cov-
er thee, the dromedaries of Midian and
[n]Ephah; all they from [o]Sheba shall
come: they shall bring [p]gold and in-

60:1 [h]Eph. 5:14 [i]Mal. 4:2 **60:3** [j]ch. 49:6,23 Rev. 21:24 **60:4** [k]ch. 49:18 [l]ch. 49:20-22 & 66:12 **60:5** [m]Rom. 11:25 **60:6** [n]Gen. 25:4 [o]Ps. 72:10 [p]ch. 61:6 Mat. 2:11

[j] Or, *is accounted mad* [k] Heb. *it was evil in his eyes* [l] Heb. *recompences* [m] Or, *put him to flight* [n] Or, *be enlightened; for thy light cometh* [o] Or, *noise of the sea shall be turned toward thee* [p] Or, *wealth;* see ver. 11; ch. 61:6

59:16 HE SAW THAT *THERE WAS* NO MAN. The Lord saw the magnitude of Israel's sins and recognized that there was no intercessor to turn the tide. Then He Himself decided to stretch forth "his arm" to save His people, which ultimately happened in the coming of Jesus Christ. Even now it is the Lord Jesus Christ who Himself personally intercedes for us in heaven (Heb. 7:25); He looks for intercessors on earth to join Him in standing "in the gap" (Ezek. 22:30) on behalf of His church, which needs revival, and of the lost, who need salvation.

59:17–18 RIGHTEOUSNESS AS A BREASTPLATE. Paul cited two phrases from this verse in his description of the believer's armor: "the breastplate of righteousness" and "the helmet of salvation" (Eph. 6:14–17). Isaiah's mention of "garments of vengeance" and "fury to his adversaries" (v. 18), envisions God's great day of wrath at the end of the age (see Rev. 19, notes).

59:20 REDEEMER SHALL COME TO ZION. This Redeemer is Jesus Christ (cf. 35:4; 40:9; 52:7); He will come to those who genuinely turn from their transgression and serve the Lord, i.e., to the true Israel.

59:21 MY SPIRIT . . . MY WORDS. God promises those who turn from their sins and accept the Messiah that His Spirit will come upon them (cf. John 16:13; Acts 2:4) and His word will not depart from their mouths. The Spirit and the word of the Lord will endorse the witness of the true church and her seed forever. God's people must declare the gospel in the power and righteousness of the Holy Spirit (see Acts 1:8, notes; see article on BAPTISM IN THE HOLY SPIRIT, p. 1652).

60:1–3 FOR THY LIGHT IS COME. This chapter prophesies that with the advent of the Messiah, the glory of the Lord would come among His people and many Gentiles would come to the light. The N.T. applies these verses to Jesus' anointed ministry in Galilee (see Mat. 4:16–17). Ever since the great missionary thrust of the gospel began in the N.T., this prophecy is being fulfilled.

60:4–9 THEY COME TO THEE. These verses describe the coming Messianic kingdom of our Lord. Isaiah sees God's glory coming to Israel and other nations coming to them to receive that light and salvation (cf. 49:23); these nations will bring offerings from their wealth unto the Lord (cf. 61:6; 66:12).

cense; and they shall show forth the praises of the LORD.

7 All the flocks of [q]Kedar shall be gathered together unto thee, the rams of Nebaioth shall minister unto thee: they shall come up with acceptance on mine altar, and [r]I will glorify the house of my glory.

8 Who *are* these *that* fly as a cloud, and as the doves to their windows?

9 [s]Surely the isles shall wait for me, and the ships of Tarshish first, [t]to bring thy sons from far, [u]their silver and their gold with them, [v]unto the name of the LORD thy God, and to the Holy One of Israel, [w]because he hath glorified thee.

10 And [x]the sons of strangers shall build up thy walls, [y]and their kings shall minister unto thee: for [z]in my wrath I smote thee, [a]but in my favour have I had mercy on thee.

11 Therefore thy gates [b]shall be open continually; they shall not be shut day nor night; that *men* may bring unto thee the ¶forces of the Gentiles, and *that* their kings *may be* brought.

12 [c]For the nation and kingdom that will not serve thee shall perish; yea, *those* nations shall be utterly wasted.

13 [d]The glory of Lebanon shall come unto thee, the fir tree, the pine tree, and the box together, to beautify the place of my sanctuary; and I will make [e]the place of my feet glorious.

14 The sons also of them that afflicted thee shall come bending unto thee; and all they that despised thee shall [f]bow themselves down at the soles of thy feet; and they shall call thee, The city of the LORD, [g]The Zion of the Holy One of Israel.

15 Whereas thou hast been forsaken and hated, so that no man went through *thee*, I will make thee an eternal excellency, a joy of many generations.

16 Thou shalt also suck the milk of the Gentiles, [h]and shalt suck the breast of kings: and thou shalt know that [i]I the LORD *am* thy Saviour and thy Redeemer, the mighty One of Jacob.

17 For brass I will bring gold, and for iron I will bring silver, and for wood brass, and for stones iron: I will also make thy officers peace, and thine exactors righteousness.

18 Violence shall no more be heard in thy land, wasting nor destruction within thy borders; but thou shalt call [j]thy walls Salvation, and thy gates Praise.

19 The [k]sun shall be no more thy light by day; neither for brightness shall the moon give light unto thee: but the LORD shall be unto thee an everlasting light, and [l]thy God thy glory.

20 [m]Thy sun shall no more go down; neither shall thy moon withdraw itself: for the LORD shall be thine everlasting light, and the days of thy mourning shall be ended.

21 [n]Thy people also *shall be* all righteous: [o]they shall inherit the land for ever, [p]the branch of my planting, [q]the work of my hands, that I may be glorified.

22 [r]A little one shall become a thousand, and a small one a strong nation: I the LORD will hasten it in his time.

Good tidings of salvation

61 THE [s]SPIRIT of the Lord GOD *is* upon me; because the LORD

60:7 [q]Gen. 25:13 [r]Hag. 2:7,9
60:9 [s]Ps. 72:10 ch. 51:5 [t]Gal. 4:26 [u]Ps. 68:30 Zech. 14:14 [v]Jer. 3:17 [w]ch. 55:5
60:10 [x]Zech. 6:15 [y]ch. 49:23 Rev. 21:24 [z]ch. 57:17 [a]ch. 54:7,8
60:11 [b]Rev. 21:25
60:12 [c]Zech. 14:17 Mat. 21:44
60:13 [d]ch. 35:2 [e]1 Chr. 28:2 Ps. 132:7
60:14 [f]ch. 49:23 Rev. 3:9 [g]Heb. 12:22 Rev. 14:1
60:16 [h]ch. 49:23 & 61:6 [i]ch. 43:3
60:18 [j]ch. 26:1
60:19 [k]Rev. 21:23 [l]Zech. 2:5
60:20 [m]Amos 8:9
60:21 [n]ch. 52:1 ch. 52:1 Rev. 21:27 [o]Ps. 37:11 Mat. 5:5 [p]ch. 61:3 Mat. 15:13 John 15:2 [q]ch. 29:23 Eph. 2:10
60:22 [r]Mat. 13:31
61:1 [s]Luke 4:18 John 1:32 & 3:34

¶Or, *wealth;* see ver. 5

60:10 SHALL BUILD UP THY WALLS. The nations will contribute financially to the establishment of the rule of God in Jerusalem. Those who oppose the Messianic kingdom will be destroyed (v. 12).

60:19 THE SUN SHALL BE NO MORE THY LIGHT. This verse looks forward to the Jerusalem of the new heaven and new earth, in which God and the Lamb will be the everlasting light of His people (see Rev. 21:23; 22:3–5; cf. Zech. 2:5).

60:21 *SHALL BE* . . . RIGHTEOUS. During the Messianic kingdom, Israel will be characterized by faithfulness and righteousness rather than by the unfaithfulness and apostasy of her past history.

61:1–3 THE SPIRIT OF THE LORD GOD *IS* UPON ME. This description of the Messiah and His anointing relate to His mission or ministry (see 11:2–3, note, where Isaiah describes more directly His spiritual character and stature). When Jesus began His ministry, He quoted these verses and applied them to Himself (Luke 4:18–19). In order to fulfill His ministry, Jesus was anointed with the Holy Spirit (cf. 11:2; 42:1). His anointed ministry involved (1) preaching the gospel to the poor, the meek, and the afflicted; (2) healing and binding up the spiritually and physically sick and brokenhearted; (3) breaking the bonds of evil and proclaiming freedom from sin and satanic dominion; and (4) opening the spiritual eyes of the lost that they might see the light of the gospel and be saved. This fourfold purpose characterized the entire ministry of Jesus Christ, and it will continue to be

[t]hath anointed me to preach good tid-
ings unto the meek; he hath sent me
[u]to bind up the brokenhearted, to pro-
claim [v]liberty to the captives, and the
opening of the prison to *them that are*
bound;
2 [w]To proclaim the acceptable year
of the LORD, and [x]the day of vengeance
of our God; [y]to comfort all that
mourn;
3 To appoint unto them that mourn
in Zion, [z]to give unto them beauty for
ashes, the oil of joy for mourning, the
garment of praise for the spirit of
heaviness; that they might be called
trees of righteousness, [a]the planting
of the LORD, [b]that he might be glori-
fied.
4 ¶ And they shall [c]build the old
wastes, they shall raise up the former
desolations, and they shall repair the
waste cities, the desolations of many
generations.
5 And [d]strangers shall stand and
feed your flocks, and the sons of the
alien *shall be* your plowmen and your
vinedressers.
6 [e]But ye shall be named the
Priests of the LORD: *men* shall call you
the Ministers of our God: [f]ye shall eat
the riches of the Gentiles, and in their
glory shall ye boast yourselves.
7 ¶ [g]For your shame *ye shall have*
double; and *for* confusion they shall re-
joice in their portion: therefore in their
land they shall possess the double:
everlasting joy shall be unto them.
8 For [h]I the LORD love judgment,
[i]I hate robbery for burnt offering; and
I will direct their work in truth, [j]and
I will make an everlasting covenant
with them.
9 And their seed shall be known

Ezek.
3-4

61:1 [t]Ps. 45:7 [u]Ps. 147:3 ch. 57:15 [v]ch. 42:7 Jer. 34:8
61:2 [w]Lev. 25:9 [x]ch. 34:8 Mal. 4:1,3 2 Thes. 1:7 [y]ch. 57:18 Mat. 5:4
61:3 [z]Ps. 30:11 [a]ch. 60:21 [b]John 15:8
61:4 [c]ch. 49:8 Ezek. 36:33
61:5 [d]Eph. 2:12
61:6 [e]Ex. 19:6 ch. 60:17 1 Pet. 2:5 Rev. 1:6 & 5:10 [f]ch. 60:5
61:7 [g]ch. 40:2 Zech. 9:12
61:8 [h]Ps. 11:7 [i]ch. 1:11,13 [j]ch. 55:3
61:9 [k]ch. 65:23
61:10 [l]Hab. 3:18 [m]Ps. 132:9,16 [n]ch. 49:18 Rev. 21:2
61:11 [o]Ps. 72:3 & 85:11 [p]ch. 60:18 & 62:7
62:2 [q]ch. 60:3 [r]See ver. 4,12
62:3 [s]Zech. 9:16
62:4 [t]Hos. 1:10 [u]ch. 49:14 & 54:6,7 [v]ch. 54:1

among the Gentiles, and their offspring
among the people: all that see them
shall acknowledge them, [k]that they
are the seed *which* the LORD hath
blessed.
10 [l]I will greatly rejoice in the
LORD, my soul shall be joyful in my God;
for [m]he hath clothed me with the gar-
ments of salvation, he hath covered me
with the robe of righteousness, [n]as a
bridegroom [r]decketh *himself* with or-
naments, and as a bride adorneth *her-
self* with her jewels. Is. 63:1-6
11 For as the earth bringeth forth
her bud, and as the garden causeth the
things that are sown in it to spring
forth; so the Lord GOD will cause
[o]righteousness and [p]praise to spring
forth before all the nations.

The restoration of Zion

62 FOR ZION'S sake will I not
hold my peace, and for Jerusa-
lem's sake I will not rest, until the
righteousness thereof go forth as
brightness, and the salvation thereof
as a lamp *that* burneth.
2 [q]And the Gentiles shall see thy
righteousness, and all kings thy glory:
[r]and thou shalt be called by a new
name, which the mouth of the LORD
shall name.
3 Thou shalt also be [s]a crown of
glory in the hand of the LORD, and a
royal diadem in the hand of thy God.
4 [t]Thou shalt no more be termed
[u]Forsaken; neither shall thy land any
more be termed [v]Desolate: but thou
shalt be called [s]Hephzibah, and thy
land [t]Beulah: for the LORD delighteth

[r] Heb. *decketh as a priest* [s] i.e. *My delight is in her* [t] i.e. *Married*

fulfilled by the church as long as it is on the earth.

61:1 THE SPIRIT . . . GOD . . . ME. There is a hint in this O.T. passage of the doctrine of the Trinity: the "Lord GOD," the "Spirit," and "me" (i.e., Jesus; see Mark 1:11, note).

61:2 THE DAY OF VENGEANCE. Jesus did not include this phrase when he quoted this prophecy (Luke 4:18–19), since the "day of vengeance" would not occur until His second coming. Final judgment upon the wicked will take place during the great tribulation and at Christ's return to earth (Rev. 5—19; cf. Is. 34:8; Mat. 24:30).

61:4–9 SHALL BUILD THE OLD WASTES. After the second coming of Christ at the end of the age, Israel will be rebuilt and other nations will work among them and worship the Lord with them (vv. 5–6). Israelites will function as priests and ministers, teaching and mediating the word of God to others (v. 6).

61:10–11 I WILL GREATLY REJOICE IN THE LORD. After the return of Christ all those who are a part of His kingdom will rejoice. They will be clothed with "salvation" (i.e., they will belong to God's redeemed) and "righteousness" (i.e., they will live by God's standards).

62:1–12 ZION . . . JERUSALEM. This chapter speaks of a day when Jerusalem will be filled with the glory and righteousness of the Lord; God's people will dwell within its walls in peace and joy, and all the world will benefit from its exaltation. This day will take place after the Savior comes at the end of the age (v. 11).

62:4 HEPHZIBAH . . . BEULAH. Hephzibah means "my delight is in her," and Beulah means "married one"; these names signify that God has renewed His covenant with Jerusalem.

in thee, and thy land shall be married.

5 ¶ For *as* a young man marrieth a virgin, *so* shall thy sons marry thee: and [u]*as* the bridegroom rejoiceth over the bride, *so* [w]shall thy God rejoice over thee.

6 [x]I have set watchmen upon thy walls, O Jerusalem, *which* shall never hold their peace day nor night: [v]ye that make mention of the LORD, keep not silence,

7 And give him no [w]rest, till he establish, and till he make Jerusalem [y]a praise in the earth.

8 The LORD hath sworn by his right hand, and by the arm of his strength, [x]Surely I will no more [z]give thy corn *to be* meat for thine enemies; and the sons of the stranger shall not drink thy wine, for the which thou hast laboured:

9 But they that have gathered it shall eat it, and praise the LORD; and they that have brought it together shall drink it [a]in the courts of my holiness.

10 ¶ Go through, go through the gates; [b]prepare ye the way of the people; cast up, cast up the highway; gather out the stones; [c]lift up a standard for the people.

Is. 66:15-16

11 Behold, the LORD hath proclaimed unto the end of the world, [d]Say ye to the daughter of Zion, Behold, thy salvation cometh; behold, his [e]reward *is* with him, and his [y]work before him.

12 And they shall call them, The holy people, The redeemed of the LORD: and thou shalt be called, Sought out, A city [f]not forsaken.

62:5 [w]ch. 65:19 **62:6** [x]Ezek. 3:17 **62:7** [y]ch. 61:11 Zeph. 3:20 **62:8** [z]Deut. 28:31 Jer. 5:17 **62:9** [a]See Deut. 12:12 & 14:23,26 & 16:11,14 **62:10** [b]ch. 40:3 & 57:14 [c]ch. 11:12 **62:11** [d]Zech. 9:9 Mat. 21:5 John 12:15 [e]ch. 40:10 Rev. 22:12 **62:12** [f]ver. 4

63:2 [g]Rev. 19:13 **63:3** [h]Lam. 1:15 Rev. 14:19,20 & 19:15 **63:4** [i]ch. 34:8 & 61:2 **63:5** [j]ch. 41:28 & 59:16 [k]John 16:32 [l]Ps. 98:1 ch. 59:16

Vengeance and redemption

63 WHO *IS* this that cometh from Edom, with dyed garments from Bozrah? this *that is* [z]glorious in his apparel, travelling in the greatness of his strength? I that speak in righteousness, mighty to save.

2 Wherefore [g]*art thou* red in thine apparel, and thy garments like him that treadeth in the winevat?

3 I have [h]trodden the winepress alone; and of the people *there was* none with me: for I will tread them in mine anger, and trample them in my fury; and their blood shall be sprinkled upon my garments, and I will stain all my raiment.

4 For the [i]day of vengeance *is* in mine heart, and the year of my redeemed is come.

5 [j]And I looked, and [k]*there was* none to help; and I wondered that *there was* none to uphold: therefore mine own [l]arm brought salvation unto me; and my fury, it upheld me.

6 And I will tread down the people in mine anger, and make them drunk in my fury, and I will bring down their strength to the earth.

Jer. 23:5

Praise to the LORD

7 ¶ I will mention the lovingkindnesses of the LORD, *and* the praises of the LORD, according to all that the LORD hath bestowed on us, and the great goodness toward the house of Israel, which he hath bestowed on them ac-

[u] Heb. *with the joy of the bridegroom* [v] Or, *ye that are the LORD's remembrancers* [w] Heb. *silence* [x] Heb. *If I give* [y] Or, *recompence* [z] Heb. *decked*

62:6 WATCHMEN . . . NEVER HOLD THEIR PEACE. God has appointed watchmen on the walls of Zion, i.e., prophets and faithful intercessors who never stop praying for the establishment of God's kingdom on earth and for the glory of Jerusalem. Similarly, N.T. believers must make it a practice to intercede unceasingly for the establishment of God's kingdom and Christ's righteous rule over the earth (see Mat. 6:10, note). In all things that we know to be God's will, we must continually cry out to Him and "give him no rest" (v. 7), until He brings to pass all that He has promised.

62:11 THY SALVATION COMETH. This verse refers to Christ's second coming to establish righteousness upon the earth and bring praise to Jerusalem for His name's sake; "his reward *is* with him" (cf. Rev. 22:12).

63:1–6 FROM EDOM, WITH DYED GARMENTS. These verses depict God's future judgment upon an ungodly world. "Edom" represents all the world powers that are opposed to God and His people. The Lord's garments are stained red with the blood of the wicked. Note Rev. 19:13, where Christ's robe is pictured as "dipped in blood" as He returns to the earth to destroy the wicked.

63:3 TRODDEN THE WINEPRESS ALONE. God Himself will wage war against the nations and defeat them. He will trample them as people trample grapes in the winepress (cf. Joel 3:13; Rev. 14:17–20; 19:15).

63:7 — 64:12 LOVINGKINDNESSES OF THE LORD. Isaiah praises God's lovingkindness and past mercy, confesses Israel's sin, and intercedes for their deliverance from judgment and for God's promised redemption.

cording to his mercies, and according
to the multitude of his lovingkind-
nesses.
8 For he said, Surely they *are* my
people, children *that* will not lie: so he
was their Saviour.
9 [m]In all their affliction he was af-
flicted, [n]and the angel of his presence
saved them: [o]in his love and in his pity
he redeemed them; and [p]he bare
them, and carried them all the days of
old.
10 ¶ But they [q]rebelled, and
[r]vexed his holy spirit: [s]therefore he
was turned to be their enemy, *and* he
fought against them.
11 Then he remembered the days of
old, Moses, *and* his people, *saying,*
Where *is* he that [t]brought them up out
of the sea with the [u]shepherd[a] of his
flock? [v]where *is* he that put his holy
spirit within him?
12 That led *them* by the right hand
of Moses [w]with his glorious arm, [x]di-
viding the water before them, to make
himself an everlasting name?
13 [y]That led them through the
deep, as an horse in the wilderness,
that they should not stumble?
14 As a beast goeth down into the
valley, the spirit of the LORD caused
him to rest: so didst thou lead thy peo-
ple, [z]to make thyself a glorious name.

Judah appeals to God

15 ¶ [a]Look down from heaven, and
behold [b]from the habitation of thy ho-
liness and of thy glory: where *is* thy
zeal and thy strength, [b]the sounding
[c]of thy bowels and of thy mercies to-
ward me? are they restrained?
16 [d]Doubtless thou *art* our father,
though Abraham [e]be ignorant of us,
and Israel acknowledge us not: thou,
O LORD, *art* our father, [c]our redeemer;
thy name *is* from everlasting.
17 ¶ O LORD, why hast thou [f]made
us to err from thy ways, *and* [g]hard-
ened our heart from thy fear? [h]Return
for thy servants' sake, the tribes of
thine inheritance.
18 [i]The people of thy holiness
have possessed *it* but a little while:
[j]our adversaries have trodden down
thy sanctuary.
19 We are *thine:* thou never barest
rule over them; [d]they were not called
by thy name.

64 OH THAT thou wouldest
[k]rend the heavens, that thou
wouldest come down, that [l]the moun-
tains might flow down at thy presence,
2 As *when* [e]the melting fire burn-
eth, the fire causeth the waters to boil,
to make thy name known to thine ad-
versaries, *that* the nations may tremble
at thy presence!
3 When [m]thou didst terrible things
which we looked not for, thou camest
down, the mountains flowed down at
thy presence.
4 For since the beginning of the
world [n]*men* have not heard, nor per-
ceived by the ear, neither hath the eye
[f]seen, O God, beside thee, *what* he
hath prepared for him that waiteth for
him.
5 Thou meetest him that rejoiceth
[o]and worketh righteousness, [p]*those*
that remember thee in thy ways: be-
hold, thou art wroth; for we have
sinned: [q]in those is continuance, and
we shall be saved.
6 But we are all as an unclean *thing,*
and all [r]our righteousnesses *are* as
filthy rags; and we all do [s]fade as a
leaf; and our iniquities, like the wind,
have taken us away.
7 And *there is* none that calleth upon

63:9 [m]Judg. 10:16; Acts 9:4 [n]Ex. 14:19; Acts 12:11 [o]Deut. 7:7 [p]Ex. 19:4
63:10 [q]Ex. 15:24; Ps. 95:9 [r]Ps. 78:40; Acts 7:51 [s]Ex. 23:21
63:11 [t]Ex. 14:30 [u]Ps. 77:20 [v]Num. 11:17
63:12 [w]Ex. 15:6 [x]Josh. 3:16
63:13 [y]Ps. 106:9
63:14 [z]2 Sam. 7:23
63:15 [a]Deut. 26:15; Ps. 80:14 [b]Ps. 33:14 [c]Jer. 31:20; Hos. 11:8
63:16 [d]Deut. 32:6 [e]Job 14:21
63:17 [f]Ps. 119:10 [g]ch. 6:10 with John 12:40 [h]Ps. 90:13
63:18 [i]Deut. 7:6 [j]Ps. 74:7
64:1 [k]Ps. 144:5 [l]Mic. 1:4
64:3 [m]Ex. 34:10; Ps. 68:8
64:4 [n]Ps. 31:19; 1 Cor. 2:9
64:5 [o]Acts 10:35 [p]ch. 26:8 [q]Mal. 3:6
64:6 [r]Phil. 3:9 [s]Ps. 90:5,6

[a] Or, *shepherds* [b] Or, *the multitude* [c] Or, *our redeemer from everlasting* is *thy name*
[d] Or, *thy name was not called upon them*
[e] Heb. *the fire of meltings* [f] Or, *seen a God beside thee,* which *doeth* so *for him*

63:9 ANGEL OF HIS PRESENCE. This angel is probably the angel of the Lord, who is really the Lord Himself (see Gen. 16:7, note; Ex. 3:2, note; see article on ANGELS AND THE ANGEL OF THE LORD, p. 368).

63:10 VEXED HIS HOLY SPIRIT. "Vexed" suggests the violation of the Holy Spirit's love and a rebellion against His ways. The Spirit is a divine person who can be hurt and grieved (cf. Eph. 4:30); "holy" refers to His majestic holiness and spotless purity. The Holy Spirit has been given to all believers to bring them into God's grace, revelation, power, love, presence, guidance, and holiness.

64:1–4 REND THE HEAVENS ... COME DOWN. As a representative of God's people, Isaiah entreats the Lord to intervene in the affairs of the world, to defeat His enemies, and to save all those who call upon Him. N.T. believers should pray this prayer daily. God promises to act on behalf of those who wait for Him (v. 4).

64:4 PREPARED FOR HIM THAT WAITETH FOR HIM. God promises to do great things for those who wait for Him. He can intervene in the events of human history so as to cause people to perform His will. Believers must look to Him and persevere in hope, confidence, and patience.

thy name, that stirreth up himself to take hold of thee: for thou hast hid thy face from us, and hast [g]consumed us, because of our iniquities.

8 [t]But now, O LORD, thou *art* our father; we *are* the clay, [u]and thou our potter; and we all *are* [v]the work of thy hand.

9 ¶ Be not [w]wroth very sore, O LORD, neither remember iniquity for ever: behold, see, we beseech thee, [x]we *are* all thy people.

10 Thy holy cities are a wilderness, Zion is a wilderness, [y]Jerusalem a desolation.

11 [z]Our holy and our beautiful house, where our fathers praised thee, is burned up with fire: and all [a]our pleasant things are laid waste.

12 [b]Wilt thou refrain thyself for these *things,* O LORD? [c]wilt thou hold thy peace, and afflict us very sore?

Judgment and salvation

65 I [d]AM sought of *them that* asked not *for me;* I am found of *them that* sought me not: I said, Behold me, behold me, unto a nation *that* [e]was not called by my name.

2 [f]I have spread out my hands all the day unto a rebellious people, which walketh in a way *that was* not good, after their own thoughts;

3 A people [g]that provoketh me to anger continually to my face; [h]that sacrificeth in gardens, and burneth incense [h]upon altars of brick;

4 [i]Which remain among the graves, and lodge in the monuments, [j]which eat swine's flesh, and [i]broth of abominable *things is in* their vessels;

5 [k]Which say, Stand by thyself, come not near to me; for I am holier than thou. These *are* a smoke in my [j]nose, a fire that burneth all the day.

6 Behold, [l]*it is* written before me: [m]I will not keep silence, [n]but will recompense, even recompense into their bosom,

7 Your iniquities, and [o]the iniquities of your fathers together, saith the LORD, [p]which have burned incense upon the mountains, [q]and blasphemed me upon the hills: therefore will I measure their former work into their bosom.

8 ¶ Thus saith the LORD, As the new wine is found in the cluster, and *one* saith, Destroy it not; for [r]a blessing *is* in it: so will I do for my servants' sakes, that I may not destroy them all.

9 And I will bring forth a seed out of Jacob, and out of Judah an inheritor of my mountains: and mine [s]elect shall inherit it, and my servants shall dwell there.

10 And [t]Sharon shall be a fold of flocks, and [u]the valley of Achor a place for the herds to lie down in, for my people that have sought me.

11 ¶ But ye *are* they that forsake the LORD, that forget [v]my holy mountain, that prepare [w]a table for that [k]troop, and that furnish the drink offering unto that [l]number.

12 Therefore will I number you to the sword, and ye shall all bow down to the slaughter: [x]because when I called, ye did not answer; when I spake, ye did not hear; but did evil before mine eyes, and did choose *that* wherein I delighted not.

13 Therefore thus saith the Lord GOD, Behold, my servants shall eat, but ye shall be hungry: behold, my servants shall drink, but ye shall be thirsty: behold, my servants shall rejoice, but ye shall be ashamed:

14 Behold, my servants shall sing for joy of heart, but ye shall cry for sorrow of heart, and [y]shall howl for [m]vexation of spirit.

64:8 [t]ch. 63:16 [u]ch. 29:16 [v]Eph. 2:10 **64:9** [w]Ps. 74:1,2 [x]Ps. 79:13 **64:10** [y]Ps. 79:1 **64:11** [z]Ps. 74:7 [a]Ezek. 24:21 **64:12** [b]ch. 42:14 [c]Ps. 83:1 **65:1** [d]Rom. 9:24 Eph. 2:12 [e]ch. 63:19 **65:2** [f]Rom. 10:21 **65:3** [g]Deut. 32:21 [h]ch. 1:29 Lev. 17:5 **65:4** [i]Deut. 18:11 [j]ch. 66:17 **65:5** [k]Mat. 9:11 Luke 18:11 Jude 19 **65:6** [l]Deut. 32:34 Mal. 3:16 [m]Ps. 50:3 [n]Ps. 79:12 Jer. 16:18 Ezek. 11:21 **65:7** [o]Ex. 20:5 [p]Ezek. 18:6 [q]Ezek. 20:27 **65:8** [r]Joel 2:14 **65:9** [s]Mat. 24:22 **65:10** [t]ch. 33:9 [u]Josh. 7:24 Hos. 2:15 **65:11** [v]ch. 56:7 [w]Ezek. 23:41 1 Cor. 10:21 **65:12** [x]2 Chr. 36:15,16 Prov. 1:24 Jer. 7:13 **65:14** [y]Mat. 8:12 Luke 13:28

[g]Heb. *melted* [h]Heb. *upon bricks* [i]Or, *pieces* [j]Or, *anger* [k]Or, *God* [l]Or, *Meni* [m]Heb. *breaking*

65:1–7 SOUGHT OF *THEM THAT* ASKED NOT *FOR ME*. In these verses, God responds to Isaiah's prayer by describing His continual appeal to the rebellious nation to return to Him. Because of their wickedness, God would recompense them with judgment (vv. 6–7), accomplished largely in the Assyrian invasion (chs. 1—37) and the Babylonian captivity (chs. 38—66).

65:8 NEW WINE IS FOUND IN THE CLUSTER. This word for "wine" (Heb. *tirosh*) generally refers to the unfermented fruit of the vine (see article on WINE IN THE OLD TESTAMENT, p. 220). Note that it is this type of wine that God says is a blessing.

65:9 BRING FORTH A SEED OUT OF JACOB. Although God would judge Israel (vv. 6–7), He would also save a remnant of true believers who would return to the land and carry on His redemptive mission in the world. They would experience His joy and blessings (vv. 13–16).

65:12 I NUMBER YOU TO THE SWORD. Those among God's people who refused to listen to God and persisted in sinning were destined for slaughter, famine, and destruction.

15 And ye shall leave your name [z]for a curse unto [a]my chosen: for the Lord GOD shall slay thee, and [b]call his servants by another name:

16 [c]That he who blesseth himself in the earth shall bless himself in the God of truth; and [d]he that sweareth in the earth shall swear by the God of truth; because the former troubles are forgotten, and because they are hid from mine eyes.

The joy of the new age

17 ¶ For, behold, I create [e]new heavens and a new earth: and the former shall not be remembered, nor [n]come into mind.

18 But be ye glad and rejoice for ever *in that* which I create: for, behold, I create Jerusalem a rejoicing, and her people a joy.

19 And [f]I will rejoice in Jerusalem, and joy in my people: and the [g]voice of weeping shall be no more heard in her, nor the voice of crying.

20 There shall be no more thence an infant of days, nor an old man that hath not filled his days; for the child shall die an hundred years old; [h]but the sinner *being* an hundred years old shall be accursed.

21 And they shall build houses, and inhabit *them;* and they shall plant vineyards, and eat the fruit of them.

22 They shall not build, and another inhabit; they shall not plant, and another eat: for [i]as the days of a tree *are* the days of my people, and [j]mine elect [o]shall long enjoy the work of their hands.

23 They shall not labour in vain, [k]nor bring forth for trouble; for [l]they *are* the seed of the blessed of the LORD, and their offspring with them.

24 And it shall come to pass, that [m]before they call, I will answer; and while they are yet speaking, I will hear.

25 The [n]wolf and the lamb shall feed together, and the lion shall eat straw like the bullock: [o]and dust *shall be* the serpent's meat. They shall not hurt nor destroy in all my holy mountain, saith the LORD.

65:15 [z]Jer. 29:22 Zech. 8:13 [a]ver. 9,22 [b]Acts 11:26 **65:16** [c]Ps. 72:17 Jer. 4:2 [d]Deut. 6:13 Zeph. 1:5 **65:17** [e]2 Pet. 3:13 Rev. 21:1 **65:19** [f]ch. 62:5 [g]ch. 35:10 Rev. 7:17 **65:20** [h]Eccl. 8:12 **65:22** [i]Ps. 92:12 [j]ver. 9,15 **65:23** [k]Hos. 9:12 [l]ch. 61:9 **65:24** [m]Dan. 9:21 **65:25** [n]ch. 11:6 [o]Gen. 3:14 **66:1** [p]1 Ki. 8:27 2 Chr. 6:18 Mat. 5:34 Acts 17:24 **66:2** [q]ch. 57:15 & 61:1 [r]Ps. 34:18 & 51:17 [s]ver. 5 Ezra 9:4 & 10:3 Prov. 28:14 **66:3** [t]ch. 1:11 [u]Deut. 23:18 **66:4** [v]Prov. 1:24 ch. 65:12 Jer. 7:13

Judgment and hope

66 THUS SAITH the LORD, [p]The heaven *is* my throne, and the earth *is* my footstool: where *is* the house that ye build unto me? and where *is* the place of my rest?

2 For all those *things* hath mine hand made, and all those *things* have been, saith the LORD: [q]but to this *man* will I look, [r]*even* to *him that is* poor and of a contrite spirit, and [s]trembleth at my word.

3 [t]He that killeth an ox *is as if* he slew a man; he that sacrificeth a [p]lamb, *as if* he [u]cut off a dog's neck; he that offereth an oblation, *as if he offered* swine's blood; he that [q]burneth incense, *as if* he blessed an idol. Yea, they have chosen their own ways, and their soul delighteth in their abominations.

4 I also will choose their [r]delusions, and will bring their fears upon them; [v]because when I called, none did answer; when I spake, they did not

[n] Heb. *come upon the heart* [o] Heb. *shall make them continue long,* or, *shall wear out* [p] Or, *kid* [q] Heb. *maketh a memorial of;* see Lev. 2:2 [r] Or, *devices*

65:17–25 I CREATE NEW HEAVENS AND A NEW EARTH. This prophecy foresees God's future kingdom on earth. Isaiah blends the age of eternity where sin and death shall be no more (vv. 17–19) with the Messianic age (i.e., the millennial kingdom) that precedes it (vv. 19–25; Rev. 20:4–6). Note that v. 18 begins with a strong adversative ("But"): there will indeed be new heavens and a new earth, *but* God also has plans for the present Jerusalem in His millennial kingdom.

65:20 NO MORE THENCE AN INFANT OF DAYS. Although death will exist in the millennial kingdom, life spans will be much longer than they are now. A one hundred-year-old person will still be considered a youth and those who die before that age will be considered accursed.

65:24 BEFORE THEY CALL, I WILL ANSWER. No longer will God's people need to persevere in prayer for their daily needs; the Lord will answer their prayers without delay.

65:25 THE WOLF AND THE LAMB SHALL FEED TOGETHER. Peace and safety will characterize the Messianic kingdom. Once-wild animals will be tame, and perfect harmony will exist among them (cf. 11:6–9).

66:2 TO THIS *MAN* WILL I LOOK. God is not impressed with the splendor of any building that humans construct for Him, but He does delight in a certain kind of person (vv. 1–2) — those who are humble in spirit, who recognize their need for His continuing help and grace, and who seek to follow His word with all their heart (see 57:15, note).

66:3 HE THAT KILLETH AN OX. Those who worship God while choosing to live in their own ways and not in accordance with His word (v. 2) are an abomination to Him. Such people will receive harsh retribution from the Lord.

hear: but they did evil before mine eyes, and chose *that* in which I delighted not.

5 ¶ Hear the word of the LORD, [w]ye that tremble at his word; Your brethren that hated you, that cast you out for my name's sake, said, [x]Let the LORD be glorified: but [y]he shall appear to your joy, and they shall be ashamed.

6 A voice of noise from the city, a voice from the temple, a voice of the LORD that rendereth recompence to his enemies.

7 Before she travailed, she brought forth; before her pain came, she was delivered of a man child.

8 Who hath heard such a thing? who hath seen such things? Shall the earth be made to bring forth in one day? *or* shall a nation be born at once? for as soon as Zion travailed, she brought forth her children.

9 Shall I bring to the birth, and not [s]cause to bring forth? saith the LORD: shall I cause to bring forth, and shut *the womb?* saith thy God.

10 Rejoice ye with Jerusalem, and be glad with her, all ye that love her: rejoice for joy with her, all ye that mourn for her:

11 That ye may suck, and be satisfied with the breasts of her consolations; that ye may milk out, and be delighted with the [t]abundance of her glory.

12 For thus saith the LORD, Behold, [z]I will extend peace to her like a river, and the glory of the Gentiles like a flowing stream: then shall ye [a]suck, ye shall be [b]borne upon *her* sides, and be dandled upon *her* knees.

13 As one whom his mother comforteth, so will I comfort you; and ye shall be comforted in Jerusalem.

14 And when ye see *this,* your heart shall rejoice, and [c]your bones shall flourish like an herb: and the hand of the LORD shall be known toward his servants, and *his* indignation toward his enemies.

15 [d]For, behold, the LORD will come with fire, and with his chariots like a whirlwind, to render his anger with fury, and his rebuke with flames of fire.

16 For by fire and by [e]his sword will the LORD plead with all flesh: and the slain of the LORD shall be many.

17 [f]They that sanctify themselves, and purify themselves in the gardens [u]behind one *tree* in the midst, eating swine's flesh, and the abomination, and the mouse, shall be consumed together, saith the LORD.

18 For I *know* their works and their thoughts: it shall come, that I will gather all nations and tongues; and they shall come, and see my glory.

19 [g]And I will set a sign among them, and I will send those that escape of them unto the nations, *to* Tarshish, Pul, and Lud, that draw the bow, *to* Tubal, and Javan, *to* the isles afar off, that have not heard my fame, neither have seen my glory; [h]and they shall declare my glory among the Gentiles.

20 And they shall bring all your brethren [i]*for* an offering unto the LORD out of all nations upon horses, and in chariots, and in [v]litters, and upon mules, and upon swift beasts, to my holy mountain Jerusalem, saith the LORD, as the children of Israel bring an offering in a clean vessel into the house of the LORD.

21 And I will also take of them for [j]priests *and* for Levites, saith the LORD.

22 For as [k]the new heavens and

66:5 [w]ver. 2 [x]ch. 5:19 [y]2 Thes. 1:10 Tit. 2:13
66:12 [z]ch. 48:18 & 60:5 [a]ch. 60:16 [b]ch. 49:22 & 60:4
66:14 [c]See Ezek. 37:1
66:15 [d]ch. 9:5
66:16 [e]ch. 27:1
66:17 [f]ch. 65:3,4
66:19 [g]Luke 2:34 [h]Mal. 1:11
66:20 [i]Rom. 15:16
66:21 [j]Ex. 19:6 ch. 61:6 1 Pet. 2:9 Rev. 1:6
66:22 [k]ch. 65:17 2 Pet. 3:13 Rev. 21:1

[s] Or, *beget?* [t] Or, *brightness* [u] Or, *one after another* [v] Or, *coaches*

66:7–14 SHE BROUGHT FORTH. Isaiah envisions the rebirth of Israel as God's people during the Messianic kingdom; the birth will be remarkably quick and will bring joy (v. 10), peace (v. 12; cf. 48:18), and prosperity (v. 11).

66:10–14 REJOICE YE WITH JERUSALEM. Jerusalem is compared to a mother who feeds and ministers to her children. Jerusalem will have peace and be a comfort to all who love God, including Gentiles who come to her.

66:15 THE LORD WILL COME WITH FIRE. When God establishes Jerusalem and the Messianic kingdom, He also will come with judgment upon His enemies (cf. Zech. 14:3; 2 Thes. 1:7–9; Rev. 19:11–21).

66:18–21 I WILL GATHER ALL NATIONS. Believers from all nations will be gathered to see the glory of God. Having survived His judgment, they will be sent to the nations to bring all remaining Jews to the Lord, the God of Israel; this gathering will occur at the end of the age.

66:22–24 THE NEW HEAVENS AND NEW EARTH. At the end of history, i.e., at the end of the Messianic kingdom, God will create the new heavens and the new earth (see 65:17–25, note; Rev. 21:1). All believers will be with the Lord forever (cf. Rev. 21—22), while all those who rebelled against Him and His word will spend eternity in hell (cf. 50:11; 57:21; Mark 9:45; see Mat. 10:28, note).

the new earth, which I will make, shall
remain before me, saith the LORD, so
shall your seed and your name remain.
23 And [l]it shall come to pass, *that*
[w]from one new moon to another, and
from one sabbath to another, [m]shall
all flesh come to worship before me,
saith the LORD.
24 And they shall go forth, and look
upon [n]the carcases of the men that
have transgressed against me: for
their [o]worm shall not die, neither
shall their fire be quenched; and they
shall be an abhorring unto all flesh.

66:23 [l]Zech. 14:16 [m]Ps. 65:2

66:24 [n]ver. 16 [o]Mark 9:44,46,48

[w] Heb. *from new moon to his new moon, and from sabbath to his sabbath*

JEREMIAH

Outline

I. Jeremiah's Call and Commissioning (1:1–19)
II. Jeremiah's Prophetic Word to Judah (2:1—33:26)
  A. Prophecies About Judgment (2:1—29:32)
    1. Judah's Deliberate Apostasy and Approaching Destruction (2:1—6:30)
    2. Judah's Folly and Religious Hypocrisy (7:1—10:25)
    3. Judah's Unfaithfulness to the Covenant (11:1—13:27)
    4. Judgments Predicted, Intercession and Loneliness, and Judah's Sins (14:1—17:27)
    5. Two Prophetic Parables and a Lament (18:1—20:18)
    6. Condemnation of Wicked Kings, False Prophets, and Rotten Judah (21:1—24:10)
    7. The Coming Babylonian Captivity (25:1—29:32)
  B. Prophecies About Restoration (30:1—33:26)
    1. Dimensions of God's Restoration of His People (30:1—31:26)
    2. Promise of a New Covenant and an Illustration of Faith (31:27—32:44)
    3. The Righteous Branch of David (33:1–26)
III. Jeremiah's Role as Prophetic Watchman (34:1—45:5)
  A. Declaration to King Zedekiah of Coming Captivity (34:1–22)
  B. The Lesson of the Rechabites (35:1–19)
  C. Jeremiah's Scroll Burned and the Prophet Twice Incarcerated (36:1—38:28)
  D. Jeremiah's Prophecy Fulfilled About the Fall of Jerusalem (39:1–18)
  E. Jeremiah's Ministry after the Fall of Jerusalem (40:1—45:5)
IV. Jeremiah's Prophetic Word to the Nations (46:1—51:64)
  A. Egypt (46:1–28)
  B. Philistia (47:1–7)
  C. Moab (48:1–47)
  D. Ammon (49:1–6)
  E. Edom (49:7–22)
  F. Damascus (49:23–27)
  G. Arabia (49:28–33)
  H. Elam (49:34–39)
  I. Babylon (50:1—51:64)
V. Historical Addendum About Jerusalem's Fall (52:1–34)

Author: Jeremiah

Theme: God's Inescapable Judgment for Unrepentant Judah

Date of Writing: c. 585–580 B.C.

Background

Jeremiah's prophetic ministry was directed to the southern kingdom of Judah during the last forty years of its history (626–586 B.C.). He lived to witness the Babylonian invasions of Judah that resulted in the destruction of Jerusalem and the temple. Since it was

Jeremiah's lot to prophesy to the nation during the final years of its decline and fall, his book is understandably filled with much gloom and foreboding.

Jeremiah, the son of a priest, was born and raised in the priestly village of Anathoth (four miles northeast of Jerusalem) during the reign of wicked King Manasseh. Jeremiah began his prophetic ministry during the thirteenth year of the reign of good King Josiah, and he supported Josiah's reform movement. He soon saw, however, that it was not resulting in a genuine change of heart among the people. Jeremiah warned that unless there was true national repentance, judgment and destruction would come suddenly.

In 612 B.C., Assyria was conquered by a Babylonian coalition. About four years after King Josiah's death, Egypt was defeated by Babylon at the battle of Carchemish (605 B.C.; see 46:2). That same year Nebuchadnezzar's Babylonian army invaded Palestine, captured Jerusalem, and deported some of Jerusalem's choicest youth to Babylon, among whom were Daniel and his three friends. A second campaign against Jerusalem occurred in 597 B.C., with 10,000 captives being taken to Babylon, among whom was Ezekiel. All this time Jeremiah's prophetic warning about God's impending judgment went unheeded. The final devastation came to Jerusalem, the temple, and the entire kingdom of Judah in 586 B.C.

This prophetic book reveals that Jeremiah, often called "the weeping prophet," was a man with a harsh message but a sensitive and broken heart (e.g., 8:21—9:1). His tender spirit made his suffering more intense as God's prophetic word was spurned by family and friends, by priests and kings, and by the people of Judah as a whole. Though lonely and rejected all his life, Jeremiah was nevertheless one of the boldest and bravest of all the prophets. In spite of great opposition, he faithfully carried out his prophetic call to warn his fellow citizens that God's judgment was at hand. In summarizing Jeremiah's life, one writer says: "A more crushing burden was never laid upon mortal man. In the whole history of the Jewish race there has been no such example of intense sincerity, unrelieved suffering, fearless proclamation of God's message, and unwearying intercession of a prophet for his people as is found in the life of Jeremiah. But the tragedy of his life was this: he preached to deaf ears and reaped only hate in return for his love to his fellow countrymen" (Farley).

The book's author is clearly stated to be Jeremiah (1:1). After twenty years of prophesying to Judah, Jeremiah was instructed by God to put his messages in written form. He did so by dictating his prophecies to his faithful secretary, Baruch (36:1–4). Since Jeremiah was banned from appearing before the king, Jeremiah sent Baruch to read the prophecies in the temple, after which Jehudi read them to King Jehoiakim. The king demonstrated his contempt for Jeremiah and the Lord's word by cutting the scroll in pieces and throwing it into the fire (36:22–23). Jeremiah again dictated his prophecies to Baruch, this time including even more than were in the first scroll. Most likely, Baruch put Jeremiah's book in its final form shortly after Jeremiah's death (c. 585–580 B.C.).

Purpose

The book was written (1) to provide an enduring record of Jeremiah's prophetic ministry and message, (2) to reveal the inevitable and inescapable judgment of God when His people broke the covenant and persisted in rebellion against God and His word, and (3) to demonstrate the authenticity and authority of the prophetic word. Many of Jeremiah's prophecies were fulfilled in his own lifetime (e.g., 16:9; 20:4; 25:1–14; 27:19–22; 28:15–17; 32:10–13; 34:1–5); other prophecies involving the far-distant future were fulfilled later or are yet to be fulfilled (e.g., 23:5–6; 30:8–9; 31:31–34; 33:14–16).

Survey

The book is essentially a collection of prophecies by Jeremiah, addressed primarily to Judah (chs. 2—29) but also to nine foreign nations (chs. 46—51); these prophecies focus mainly on judgment, though there are some that concern restoration (see especially chs. 30—33). These prophecies are not strictly arranged chronologically or thematically, though the book of Jeremiah has the overall structure indicated in the preceding outline. Part of the book is written in poetry, while other parts are written in a prose or narrative format. Its prophetic messages are interlaced with historical glimpses of (1) the prophet's personal life and ministry (e.g., chs. 1; 34—38; 40—45), (2) Judah's history primarily during the time

of kings Josiah (chs. 1—6), Jehoiakim (chs. 7—20), and Zedekiah (chs. 21—25; 34), including the fall of Jerusalem (ch. 39), and (3) international events involving Babylon and other nations (chs. 25—29; 46—52).

Like Ezekiel, Jeremiah uses a variety of parabolic and symbolic actions to illustrate graphically his prophetic message: e.g., the worthless girdle or waistband (13:1–14), the drought (14:1–9), his being forbidden by God to marry or have children (16:1–9), the potter and the clay (18:1–11), the potter's smashed jar (19:1–13), the two baskets of figs (24:1–10), the yoke around his neck (27:1–11), buying a plot of ground in his hometown (32:6–15), and large stones placed in Pharaoh's brick pavement (43:8–13). Jeremiah's clear understanding of his prophetic call (1:17), along with God's frequent reaffirmations (e.g., 3:12; 7:2,27–28; 11:2,6; 13:12–13; 17:19–20), enabled him to proclaim boldly and faithfully the prophetic word to Judah in spite of her continual response of hostility, rejection, and persecution (e.g., 15:20–21). After the destruction of Jerusalem, Jeremiah was taken against his will to Egypt, where he continued to prophesy until his death (chs. 43—44).

Special Features

Seven major features or emphases characterize the book of Jeremiah. (1) It is the second longest book in the Bible, containing more words (not chapters) than any other book except the Psalms. (2) The personal life and struggles of Jeremiah as a prophet are revealed in greater depth and detail than those of any other O.T. prophet. (3) It is permeated with the sadness, heartaches, and sobs of the "weeping prophet" over the rebellion of Judah. In spite of Jeremiah's harsh message, he felt deep grief and brokenness for God's people. Yet his greatest loyalty was to God, and his deepest grief was God's hurt. (4) Its key word is "backsliding" (used thirteen times), and its perpetual theme is God's inescapable judgment for rebellion and apostasy. (5) Its greatest single theological revelation is the concept of the "new covenant," which God would establish with His faithful people at a future time of restoration (31:31–34). (6) Its poetry is as eloquent and lyrical as any in the Bible, with an abundance of striking metaphors, vivid phrases, and memorable passages. (7) There are more references to the nation of Babylon in Jeremiah's prophecies (164) than in the remainder of the Bible.

New Testament Fulfillment

The foremost use of Jeremiah in the N.T. concerns his prophecy of a "new covenant" (31:31–34). Though Israel and Judah repeatedly broke God's covenants and subsequently were broken in judgment for their backslidings, Jeremiah prophesied about a day when God would make a new covenant with them (31:31). The N.T. makes clear that this new covenant was instituted with the death and resurrection of Christ (Luke 22:20; cf. Mat. 26:26–29; Mark 14:22–25), is now being fulfilled in the church as the new covenant people of God (Heb. 8:8–13), and will reach its climax in the great salvation of Israel (Rom. 11:27). Other Messianic passages from Jeremiah that are applied to Jesus Christ in the N.T. are: (1) the Messiah as the good shepherd and the righteous Branch of David (Jer. 23:1–8; see Mat. 21:8–9; John 10:1–18; 1 Cor. 1:30; 2 Cor. 5:21); (2) bitter weeping in Ramah (Jer. 31:15), fulfilled at the time that Herod attempted to destroy the baby Jesus (see Mat. 2:17–18); and (3) Messianic zeal for the purity of God's house (Jer. 7:11), demonstrated in Jesus' cleansing of the temple (see Mat. 21:13; Mark 11:17; Luke 19:46).

Reading Jeremiah

In order to read the entire Old Testament in one year, the book of Jeremiah should be read in 23 days, according to the following schedule: □ 1–2 □ 3–4 □ 5–6 □ 7–8 □ 9–10 □ 11–12 □ 13–14 □ 15–16 □ 17–18 □ 19–22 □ 23–25 □ 26–28 □ 29–30 □ 31–32 □ 33 □ 34–35 □ 36–37 □ 38–40 □ 41–43 □ 44–47 □ 48–49 □ 50–51 □ 52

NOTES

The prophet's call

1 THE WORDS of Jeremiah the son
of Hilkiah, of the priests that
were [a]in Anathoth in the land of Ben-
jamin:
2 To whom the word of the LORD
came in the days of Josiah the son of
Amon king of Judah, [b]in the thirteenth
year of his reign.
3 It came also in the days of Jehoia-
kim the son of Josiah king of Judah,
[c]unto the end of the eleventh year of
Zedekiah the son of Josiah king of Ju-
dah, [d]unto the carrying away of Jeru-
salem captive [e]in the fifth month.
4 Then the word of the LORD came
unto me, saying,
5 Before I [f]formed thee in the belly
[g]I knew thee; and before thou camest
forth out of the womb I [h]sanctified
thee, *and* I [a]ordained thee a prophet
unto the nations.
6 Then said I, [i]Ah, Lord GOD! be-
hold, I cannot speak: for I *am* a child.
7 ¶ But the LORD said unto me, Say
not, I *am* a child: for thou shalt go to
all that I shall send thee, and [j]what-
soever I command thee thou shalt
speak.
8 [k]Be not afraid of their faces: for
[l]I *am* with thee to deliver thee, saith
the LORD.
9 Then the LORD put forth his hand,
and [m]touched my mouth. And the LORD
said unto me, Behold, I have [n]put my
words in thy mouth.
10 [o]See, I have this day set thee
over the nations and over the king-
doms, to [p]root out, and to pull down,
and to destroy, and to throw down, to
build, and to plant.
11 ¶ Moreover the word of the LORD
came unto me, saying, Jeremiah, what
seest thou? And I said, I see a rod of
an almond tree.
12 Then said the LORD unto me,
Thou hast well seen: for I will hasten
my word to perform it.
13 And the word of the LORD came
unto me the second time, saying, What
seest thou? And I said, I see [q]a seeth-
ing pot; and the face thereof *is* [b]to-
ward the north.
14 Then the LORD said unto me, Out
of the [r]north an evil [c]shall break
forth upon all the inhabitants of the
land.
15 For, lo, I will [s]call all the fami-

1:1 [a]Josh. 21:18 1 Chr. 6:60 ch. 32:7,8
1:2 [b]ch. 25:3
1:3 [c]ch. 39:2 [d]ch. 52:12 [e]2 Ki. 25:8
1:5 [f]Is. 49:1,5 [g]Ex. 33:12 [h]Luke 1:15 Gal. 1:15
1:6 [i]Ex. 4:10 & 6:12,30
1:7 [j]Num. 22:20,38 Mat. 28:20
1:8 [k]Ezek. 2:6 & 3:9 [l]Ex. 3:12 Deut. 31:6 Josh. 1:5 ch. 15:20 Acts 26:17 Heb. 13:6
1:9 [m]Is. 6:7 [n]Is. 51:16 ch. 5:14
1:10 [o]1 Ki. 19:17 [p]ch. 18:7 2 Cor. 10:4
1:13 [q]Ezek. 11:3 & 24:3
1:14 [r]ch. 6:1
1:15 [s]ch. 6:22

[a] Heb. *gave* [b] Heb. *from the face of the north* [c] Heb. *shall be opened*

1:1 JEREMIAH. Jeremiah was called by God to be a prophet to the southern kingdom of Judah. His ministry spanned its last forty years, including the days immediately before the destruction of Jerusalem and the carrying away of God's people to Babylon (627–586 B.C.). He ministered during the reigns of Josiah, Jehoahaz, Jehoiakim, Jehoiachin, and Zedekiah. During that time the nation was rebelling against God and relying on political alliances to gain deliverance from its enemies. Jeremiah urged the people to repent of their sins and warned them that they would indeed suffer punishment for rejecting God and His law. Because of his message and his devotion to the Lord, Jeremiah experienced much opposition and suffering.

1:5 BEFORE I FORMED THEE ... I ORDAINED THEE. Before Jeremiah was born, God had already determined that he would be a prophet. Just as God had a life plan for Jeremiah, so He does for every person. His goal is for us to live according to His will and to allow Him to fulfill His plan in us. As with Jeremiah, living according to God's plan may involve suffering; nevertheless, God always works for our greatest good (see Rom. 8:28, note).

1:8 BE NOT AFRAID. Jeremiah was only a youth at the time of his call; he experienced intense anxiety and fear at the awesome thought of speaking the word of the Lord to the elders of Judah (v. 7). God responded by promising to be with him and to empower him to fulfill that calling. No matter what your task is in life, God always promises His abiding presence and help if you remain steadfast in your faith.

1:9 MY WORDS IN THY MOUTH. God assures Jeremiah that his prophetic message would be inspired by God; his words would be God's words (cf. Rom. 10:8). Convinced of this, Jeremiah never compromised or modified God's word (see 37:16–17).

1:10 TO ROOT OUT, AND TO PULL DOWN. Jeremiah's message had elements of both judgment and restoration; however, because of his place in Judah's history, his message focused primarily on judgment and doom. The corrupt nation of Israel had to be torn down before God could plant and build anew.

1:11 A ROD OF AN ALMOND TREE. The almond tree is the first tree to bud in spring. This vision implied two things: (1) God's spoken word through Jeremiah would be rapidly fulfilled, and (2) the people would recognize that God was alive and was guiding the course of history to fulfill His purposes (cf. Aaron's almond rod that budded, Num. 17:1–10).

1:14 OUT OF THE NORTH AN EVIL SHALL BREAK FORTH. This verse refers to the Babylonian campaigns against Judah and the siege of Jerusalem. A massive invasion would come from the north because God's people had forsaken Him, offered sacrifices to other gods, and worshiped the works of their own hands (v. 16).

lies of the kingdoms of the north, saith
the LORD; and they shall come, and they
shall [t]set every one his throne at the
entering of the gates of Jerusalem, and
against all the walls thereof round
about, and against all the cities of Ju-
dah.
16 And I will utter my judgments
against them touching all their wicked-
ness, [u]who have forsaken me, and
have burned incense unto other gods,
and worshipped the works of their own
hands.
17 ¶ Thou therefore [v]gird up thy
loins, and arise, and speak unto them
all that I command thee: [w]be not dis-
mayed at their faces, lest I [d]confound
thee before them.
18 For, behold, I have made thee
this day [x]a defenced city, and an iron
pillar, and brasen walls against the
whole land, against the kings of Judah,
against the princes thereof, against the
priests thereof, and against the people
of the land.
19 And they shall fight against
thee; but they shall not prevail against
thee; [y]for I *am* with thee, saith the
LORD, to deliver thee.

Ezek. ...:4

1:15 [t]ch. 39:3
1:16 [u]Deut. 28:20 ch. 17:13
1:17 [v]2 Ki. 4:29 Job 38:3 Luke 12:35 1 Pet. 1:13 [w]Ex. 3:12 Ezek. 2:6
1:18 [x]Is. 50:7 ch. 6:27 & 15:20
1:19 [y]ver. 8

Israel's faithlessness

2 MOREOVER THE word of the
LORD came to me, saying,
2 Go and cry in the ears of Jerusa-
lem, saying, Thus saith the LORD; I re-
member [e]thee, the kindness of thy
[z]youth, the love of thine espousals,
[a]when thou wentest after me in the
wilderness, in a land *that was* not sown.
3 [b]Israel *was* holiness unto the
LORD, *and* [c]the firstfruits of his in-
crease: [d]all that devour him shall of-
fend; evil shall come upon them, saith
the LORD.
4 Hear ye the word of the LORD,
O house of Jacob, and all the families
of the house of Israel:
5 ¶ Thus saith the LORD, [e]What in-
iquity have your fathers found in me,
that they are gone far from me, [f]and
have walked after vanity, and are be-
come vain?
6 Neither said they, Where *is* the
LORD that [g]brought us up out of the
land of Egypt, that led us through
[h]the wilderness, through a land of
deserts and of pits, through a land of
drought, and of the shadow of death,
through a land that no man passed
through, and where no man dwelt?
7 And I brought you into [i]a [f] plen-
tiful country, to eat the fruit thereof
and the goodness thereof; but when ye
entered, ye [j]defiled my land, and
made mine heritage an abomination.
8 The priests said not, Where *is* the

2:2 [z]Ezek. 16:8,22,60 & 23:3,8 Hos. 2:15 [a]Deut. 2:7
2:3 [b]Ex. 19:5,6 [c]Jas. 1:18 Rev. 14:4 [d]ch. 12:14 See ch. 50:7
2:5 [e]Is. 5:4 Mic. 6:3 [f]2 Ki. 17:15 Jonah 2:8
2:6 [g]Is. 63:9 [h]Deut. 8:15
2:7 [i]Num. 13:27 [j]Num. 35:33

[d] Or, *break to pieces* [e] Or, *for thy sake*
[f] Or, *the land of Carmel*

1:18 I HAVE MADE THEE . . . A DEFENCED CITY, AND AN IRON PILLAR. Though Jeremiah was a sensitive young man, God put some spiritual iron into his backbone, enabling him to become the strongest, boldest, and bravest of all the prophets. God can use us in ways far beyond our own natural tendencies and abilities.

1:19 THEY SHALL FIGHT AGAINST THEE. Jeremiah was told that Judah's kings, state officials, priests, and even the people would stand against him and the message he had been called to proclaim (v. 18). But the prophet was encouraged to speak out boldly and to stand firm in his convictions, for God promised to be with him; He assured him that his enemies would not overcome him. God always stands with His faithful servants who declare the truth to those who have departed from His word and are conformed to the world.

2:2 I REMEMBER THEE. Early in Israel's history God's people trusted in the Lord with deep devotion. So intimate was their relationship that the nation was considered the wife of the Lord (cf. 3:14; 31:32; Is. 54:5). But now the whole house of Israel had forsaken God and gone after other gods (vv. 4–5,25).

2:5 THEY ARE GONE FAR FROM ME. Israel had turned its back on the Lord, even though He had remained faithful to them. All believers are confronted with the same temptation of forgetting the goodness and redemption of God while pursuing their own desires and the sinful pleasures of the world.

2:8 WHERE *IS* THE LORD. The priests were so insensitive to the presence and power of God that they did not notice He had left them. They never wondered why the Lord's presence and blessing were missing in Israel. Today spiritual leaders should be greatly concerned when God's presence and the manifestations of the Holy Spirit are not evident in their congregations. A true servant of God will ask, "Where is the Lord?"

2:8 THEY THAT HANDLE THE LAW KNEW ME NOT. How sad it is that one can be a student or teacher of God's Word and yet not know the Lord as a personal Savior and an intimate friend (see article on BIBLE TRAINING FOR CHRISTIANS, p. 1920).

2:8 THE PROPHETS PROPHESIED BY BAAL. The prophets were expected to point the people back to God's word and to call for repentance (see article on THE PROPHET IN THE OLD TESTAMENT, p. 1002). They were to speak only the word of God. Yet many of Judah's prophets were so backslidden that they prophesied by the

LORD? and they that handle the [k]law knew me not: the pastors also transgressed against me, [l]and the prophets prophesied by Baal, and walked after *things that* do not profit.

9 ¶ Wherefore [m]I will yet plead with you, saith the LORD, and with your children's children will I plead.

10 For pass [g]over the isles of Chittim, and see; and send unto Kedar, and consider diligently, and see if there be such a thing.

11 [n]Hath a nation changed *their* gods, which *are* [o]yet no gods? [p]but my people have changed their glory for *that which* doth not profit.

12 Be astonished, O ye heavens, at this, and be horribly afraid, be ye very desolate, saith the LORD.

13 For my people have committed two evils; they have forsaken me the [q]fountain of living waters, *and* hewed them out cisterns, broken cisterns, that can hold no water.

14 ¶ *Is* Israel [r]a servant? *is* he a homeborn *slave?* why is he [h]spoiled?

15 [s]The young lions roared upon him, *and* [i]yelled, and they made his land waste: his cities are burned without inhabitant.

16 Also the children of Noph and [t]Tahapanes [j]have broken the crown of thy head.

17 [u]Hast thou not procured this unto thyself, in that thou hast forsaken the LORD thy God, when [v]he led thee by the way?

18 And now what hast thou to do [w]in the way of Egypt, to drink the waters of [x]Sihor? or what hast thou to do in the way of Assyria, to drink the waters of the river?

19 Thine own wickedness shall correct thee, and thy backslidings shall reprove thee: know therefore and see that *it is* an evil *thing* and bitter, that thou hast forsaken the LORD thy God, and that my fear *is* not in thee, saith the Lord GOD of hosts.

20 ¶ For of old time I have broken thy yoke, *and* burst thy bands; and [y]thou saidst, I will not [k]transgress; when [z]upon every high hill and under every green tree thou wanderest, [a]playing the harlot.

21 Yet I had [b]planted thee a noble vine, wholly a right seed: how then art thou turned into [c]the degenerate plant of a strange vine unto me?

22 For though thou wash thee with nitre, and take thee much soap, *yet* thine iniquity is marked before me, saith the Lord GOD.

23 [d]How canst thou say, I am not polluted, I have not gone after Baalim? see thy way in the valley, know what thou hast done: [l]*thou art* a swift dromedary traversing her ways;

24 [m]A wild ass [n]used to the wilderness, *that* snuffeth up the wind at [o]her pleasure; in her occasion who can [p]turn her away? all they that seek her will not weary themselves; in her month they shall find her.

25 Withhold thy foot from being unshod, and thy throat from thirst: but thou saidst, [q]There is no hope: no; for I have loved [e]strangers, and after them will I go.

26 As the thief is ashamed when he is found, so is the house of Israel

2:8 [k]Rom. 2:20 [l]ch. 23:13
2:9 [m]Ezek. 20:35,36 Mic. 6:2
2:11 [n]Mic. 4:5 [o]Ps. 115:4 Is. 37:19 [p]Ps. 106:20 Rom. 1:23
2:13 [q]Ps. 36:9 John 4:14
2:14 [r]Ex. 4:22
2:15 [s]Is. 1:7
2:16 [t]ch. 43:7-9
2:17 [u]ch. 4:18 [v]Deut. 32:10
2:18 [w]Is. 30:1,2 [x]Josh. 13:3
2:20 [y]Judg. 10:16 [z]Deut. 12:2 [a]Ex. 34:15
2:21 [b]Ex. 15:17 [c]Is. 5:4
2:23 [d]Prov. 30:12
2:25 [e]ch. 3:13

[g] Or, *over to* [h] Heb. become *a spoil?* [i] Heb. *gave out their voice* [j] Or, *feed on thy crown* [k] Or, *serve* [l] Or, *O swift dromedary* [m] Or, *O wild ass* [n] Heb. *taught* [o] Heb. *the desire of her heart* [p] Or, *reverse it?* [q] Or, *Is the case desperate?*

demonic powers of idols (see article on THE NATURE OF IDOLATRY, p. 428). If pastors and leaders preach the humanistic ideas found in much contemporary psychology, philosophy, and liberal theology, rather than the word of God, they themselves become as guilty as the false prophets of Jeremiah's day.

2:13 COMMITTED TWO EVILS. God's people under the old covenant committed two fundamental sins: (1) they forsook the Lord, the only One who could give them a truly abundant life (cf. 17:13; Ps. 36:9; John 10:10), and (2) they sought life and pleasure in the idolatrous things of the world, things that had no real or lasting value. In doing so, they lost their purpose and destiny as a redeemed people (v. 11). True "living water" (cf. John 4:10–14; 7:37–39) is found only in a personal, devoted relationship with God through Christ.

2:19 THINE OWN WICKEDNESS SHALL CORRECT THEE. Sin often brings its own punishment. When believers forsake the Lord, they lose God's protection and blessing and open themselves up to destructive temptations. Sin enslaves them, and many evil and bitter things may happen to them.

2:20–30 PLAYING THE HARLOT. Jeremiah often used the analogy of an immoral, adulterous prostitute to illustrate the depth of Judah's unfaithfulness to God as her husband. Using a similar metaphor, the N.T. calls the church the bride of Christ (see 2 Cor. 11:2; Eph. 5:25–27; Rev. 19:7). Believers should likewise be careful to remain faithful to their Lord and not to abandon Him for other lovers (cf. v. 33).

ashamed; they, their kings, their
princes, and their priests, and their
prophets,
27 Saying to a stock, Thou *art* my
father; and to a stone, Thou hast
[r]brought me forth: for they have
turned [s]*their* back unto me, and not
their face: but in the time of their
[f]trouble they will say, Arise, and
save us.
28 But [g]where *are* thy gods that
thou hast made thee? let them arise, if
they [h]can save thee in the time of thy
[t]trouble: for [i]*according to* the num-
ber of thy cities are thy gods, O Judah.
29 Wherefore will ye plead with me?
ye all have transgressed against me,
saith the LORD.
30 In vain have I [j]smitten your
children; they received no correction:
your own sword hath [k]devoured your
prophets, like a destroying lion.
31 ¶ O generation, see ye the word
of the LORD. Have I been a wilderness
unto Israel? a land of darkness? where-
fore say my people, [u]We are lords;
[l]we will come no more unto thee?
32 Can a maid forget her orna-
ments, *or* a bride her attire? yet my
people [m]have forgotten me days with-
out number.
33 Why trimmest thou thy way to
seek love? therefore hast thou also
taught the wicked ones thy ways.
34 Also in thy skirts is found [n]the
blood of the souls of the poor inno-
cents: I have not found it by [v]secret
search, but upon all these.
35 [o]Yet thou sayest, Because I am
innocent, surely his anger shall turn
from me. Behold, [p]I will plead with
thee, [q]because thou sayest, I have not
sinned.
36 [r]Why gaddest thou about so
much to change thy way? [s]thou also
shalt be ashamed of Egypt, [t]as thou
wast ashamed of Assyria.

2:27 [f]Is. 26:16
2:28 [g]Judg. 10:14 [h]Is. 45:20 [i]ch. 11:13
2:30 [j]Is. 9:13 [k]Acts 7:52
2:31 [l]Deut. 32:15
2:32 [m]Ps. 106:21
2:34 [n]Ps. 106:38
2:35 [o]ver. 23,29 [p]ver. 9 [q]Prov. 28:13
2:36 [r]Hos. 12:1 [s]Is. 30:3 [t]2 Chr. 28:16
2:37 [u]2 Sam. 13:19
3:1 [v]Deut. 24:4 [w]ch. 2:7 [x]ch. 2:20 Ezek. 16:26 [y]Zech. 1:3
3:2 [z]Deut. 12:2 [a]Prov. 23:28 [b]ch. 2:7
3:3 [c]Lev. 26:19 [d]Zeph. 3:5
3:4 [e]Prov. 2:17 [f]Hos. 2:15
3:5 [g]Ps. 103:9 Is. 57:16
3:6 [h]ch. 7:24 [i]ch. 2:20
3:7 [j]2 Ki. 17:13 [k]Ezek. 16:46
3:8 [l]Ezek. 23:9

37 Yea, thou shalt go forth from
him, and [u]thine hands upon thine
head: for the LORD hath rejected thy
confidences, and thou shalt not pros-
per in them.

3 THEY [w]SAY, If a man put away
his wife, and she go from him, and
become another man's, [v]shall he re-
turn unto her again? shall not that
[w]land be greatly polluted? but thou
hast [x]played the harlot with many lov-
ers; [y]yet return again to me, saith the
LORD.
2 Lift up thine eyes unto [z]the high
places, and see where thou hast not
been lain with. [a]In the ways hast thou
sat for them, as the Arabian in the wil-
derness; [b]and thou hast polluted the
land with thy whoredoms and with thy
wickedness.
3 Therefore the [c]showers have
been withholden, and there hath been
no latter rain; and thou hadst a
[d]whore's forehead, thou refusedst to
be ashamed.
4 Wilt thou not from this time cry
unto me, My father, thou *art* [e]the
guide of [f]my youth?
5 [g]Will he reserve *his anger* for
ever? will he keep *it* to the end? Be-
hold, thou hast spoken and done evil
things as thou couldest.
6 ¶ The LORD said also unto me in
the days of Josiah the king, Hast thou
seen *that* which [h]backsliding Israel
hath done? she is [i]gone up upon every
high mountain and under every green
tree, and there hath played the harlot.
7 [j]And I said after she had done all
these *things*, Turn thou unto me. But
she returned not. And her treacherous
[k]sister Judah saw *it*.
8 And I saw, when [l]for all the
causes whereby backsliding Israel

[r] Or, *begotten me* [s] Heb. *the hinder part of the neck* [t] Heb. *evil* [u] Heb. *We have dominion* [v] Heb. *digging* [w] Heb. *Saying*

2:32 MY PEOPLE HAVE FORGOTTEN ME. Jeremiah reveals the intense grief and sorrow of God because of His people's unfaithfulness. They had done the unthinkable in forgetting the One who had redeemed them from Egypt and cared for them in the wilderness.

3:1–5 THOU HAST PLAYED THE HARLOT. Judah's turning to other gods is equivalent to spiritual adultery against the Lord; this unfaithfulness often came to expression in immorality in the natural realm as the people became involved in cult prostitution. In spite of God's word to them through His servant Jeremiah, the people continued in their evil ways. The N.T. often warns against idolatry and immorality, lest those who live under the new covenant repeat the mistakes of those who lived under the old (cf. 1 Cor. 6:9–11).

3:6 WHICH BACKSLIDING ISRAEL HATH DONE. Israel, the northern kingdom, had been unfaithful to God; as a result, they had been carried away into captivity by Assyria in 722–721 B.C. Judah, the southern kingdom, should have learned from her sister's tragic experience, but did not. She too gave herself to spiritual harlotry and wickedness.

committed adultery I had [m]put her
away, and given her a bill of divorce;
[n]yet her treacherous sister Judah
feared not, but went and played the
harlot also.
9 And it came to pass through the
[x]lightness of her whoredom, that she
[o]defiled the land, and committed adul-
tery with [p]stones and with stocks.
10 And yet for all this her treacher-
ous sister Judah hath not turned unto
me [q]with her whole heart, but
[y]feignedly, saith the LORD.
11 And the LORD said unto me,
[r]The backsliding Israel hath justified
herself more than treacherous Judah.
12 ¶ Go and proclaim these words
toward [s]the north, and say, Return,
thou backsliding Israel, saith the LORD;
and I will not cause mine anger to fall
upon you: for I *am* [t]merciful, saith the
LORD, *and* I will not keep *anger* for ever.
13 [u]Only acknowledge thine iniq-
uity, that thou hast transgressed
against the LORD thy God, and hast
[v]scattered thy ways to the [w]strang-
ers [x]under every green tree, and ye
have not obeyed my voice, saith the
LORD.
14 Turn, O backsliding children,
saith the LORD; [y]for I am married unto
you: and I will take you [z]one of a city,
and two of a family, and I will bring you
to Zion:
15 And I will give you [a]pastors ac-
cording to mine heart, which shall
[b]feed you with knowledge and under-
standing.
16 And it shall come to pass, when
ye be multiplied and increased in the
land, in those days, saith the LORD, they
shall say no more, The ark of the cov-
enant of the LORD: [c]neither shall it
[z]come to mind: neither shall they re-
member it; neither shall they visit *it;*
neither shall [a]*that* be done any more.
17 At that time they shall call Jeru-
salem the throne of the LORD; and all

3:8 [m]2 Ki. 17:6 [n]Ezek. 23:11
3:9 [o]ch. 2:7 [p]ch. 2:27
3:10 [q]Hos. 7:14
3:11 [r]Ezek. 16:51
3:12 [s]2 Ki. 17:6 [t]Ps. 86:15
3:13 [u]Deut. 30:1 [v]Ezek. 16:15 [w]ch. 2:25 [x]Deut. 12:2
3:14 [y]Hos. 2:19 [z]Rom. 11:5
3:15 [a]Ezek. 34:23 Eph. 4:11 [b]Acts 20:28
3:16 [c]Is. 65:17
3:17 [d]Is. 60:9 [e]ch. 11:8
3:18 [f]Is. 11:13 Hos. 1:11 [g]ch. 31:8 [h]Amos. 9:15
3:19 [i]Ps. 106:24 [j]Is. 63:16
3:20 [k]Is. 48:8
3:21 [l]Is. 15:2
3:22 [m]ver. 14 Hos. 14:1 [n]Hos. 6:1 & 14:4
3:23 [o]Ps. 121:1,2 [p]Ps. 3:8
3:24 [q]ch. 11:13 Hos. 9:10
3:25 [r]Ezra 9:7

the nations shall be gathered unto it,
[d]to the name of the LORD, to Jerusa-
lem: neither shall they [e]walk any
more after the [b]imagination of their
evil heart.
18 In those days [f]the house of Ju-
dah shall walk [c]with the house of Is-
rael, and they shall come together out
of the land of [g]the north to [h]the land
that I have [d]given for an inheritance
unto your fathers.
19 But I said, How shall I put thee
among the children, and give thee [i]a
[e]pleasant land, [f]a goodly heritage of
the hosts of nations? and I said, Thou
shalt call me, [j]My father; and shalt
not turn away [g]from me.
20 ¶ Surely *as* a wife treacherously
departeth from her [h]husband, so
[k]have ye dealt treacherously with me,
O house of Israel, saith the LORD.
21 A voice was heard upon [l]the
high places, weeping *and* supplications
of the children of Israel: for they have
perverted their way, *and* they have for-
gotten the LORD their God.
22 [m]Return, ye backsliding chil-
dren, *and* [n]I will heal your backslid-
ings. Behold, we come unto thee; for
thou *art* the LORD our God.
23 [o]Truly in vain *is salvation hoped*
for from the hills, *and from* the multi-
tude of mountains: [p]truly in the LORD
our God *is* the salvation of Israel.
24 [q]For shame hath devoured the
labour of our fathers from our youth;
their flocks and their herds, their sons
and their daughters.
25 We lie down in our shame, and
our confusion covereth us: [r]for we
have sinned against the LORD our God,

[x] Or, *fame* [y] Heb. *in falsehood* [z] Heb. *come upon the heart* [a] Or, *it be magnified* [b] Or, *stubbornness* [c] Or, *to* [d] Or, *caused your fathers to possess* [e] Heb. *land of desire* [f] Heb. *an heritage of glory,* or, *beauty* [g] Heb. *from after me* [h] Heb. *friend*

3:12 PROCLAIM THESE WORDS TOWARD THE NORTH. The remnant of Israel living in Assyrian captivity were told that they could still repent. God remains merciful and does not want to punish forever. Jeremiah went on to prophesy that a remnant would someday return to God and to the promised land (v. 14).

3:15 PASTORS ACCORDING TO MINE HEART. Jeremiah pictures a day when Israel would have pastors who lived according to God's word and imparted life through their understanding of it. Because they knew God's heart, they would know how to shepherd God's people. That type of knowledge in leaders is essential for the spiritual vitality and ethical purity of God's people (see article on MORAL QUALIFICATIONS FOR OVERSEERS, p. 1908).

3:16–19 IN THOSE DAYS. Jeremiah prophesies here of the Messianic age when Christ will reign over His people. The ark, which had earlier symbolized God's presence, would no longer be needed, for the Messiah would be visibly present. Jerusalem would be called God's throne and all nations would worship Him. (v. 17).

we and our fathers, from our youth
even unto this day, and [s]have not
obeyed the voice of the LORD our God.

4 IF THOU wilt return, O Israel,
saith the LORD, [t]return unto me:
and if thou wilt put away thine abomi-
nations out of my sight, then shalt thou
not remove.

2 [u]And thou shalt swear, The LORD
liveth, [v]in truth, in judgment, and in
righteousness; [w]and the nations shall
bless themselves in him, and in him
shall they [x]glory.

3 ¶ For thus saith the LORD to the
men of Judah and Jerusalem, [y]Break
up your fallow ground, and [z]sow not
among thorns.

4 [a]Circumcise yourselves to the
LORD, and take away the foreskins of
your heart, ye men of Judah and inhabi-
tants of Jerusalem: lest my fury come
forth like fire, and burn that none can
quench *it,* because of the evil of your
doings.

Judgment from the north

5 Declare ye in Judah, and publish
in Jerusalem; and say, Blow ye the
trumpet in the land: cry, gather togeth-
er, and say, [b]Assemble yourselves,
and let us go into the defenced cities.

6 Set up the standard toward Zion:
[i]retire, stay not: for I will bring evil
from the [c]north, and a great [j]de-
struction.

7 [d]The lion is come up from his
thicket, and [e]the destroyer of the
Gentiles is on his way; he is gone forth
from his place [f]to make thy land deso-
late; *and* thy cities shall be laid waste,
without an inhabitant.

8 For this [g]gird you with sack-
cloth, lament and howl: for the fierce
anger of the LORD is not turned back
from us.

9 And it shall come to pass at that
day, saith the LORD, *that* the heart of
the king shall perish, and the heart of
the princes; and the priests shall be as-
tonished, and the prophets shall won-
der.

10 Then said I, Ah, Lord GOD!
[h]surely thou hast greatly deceived
this people and Jerusalem, [i]saying,
Ye shall have peace; whereas the
sword reacheth unto the soul.

11 At that time shall it be said to
this people and to Jerusalem, [j]A dry
wind of the high places in the wilder-
ness toward the daughter of my people,
not to fan, nor to cleanse,

12 *Even* [k]a full wind from those
places shall come unto me: now also
[k]will I [l]give sentence against them.

13 Behold, he shall come up as
clouds, and [l]his chariots *shall be* as a
whirlwind: [m]his horses are swifter
than eagles. Woe unto us! for we are
spoiled.

14 O Jerusalem, [n]wash thine heart
from wickedness, that thou mayest be
saved. How long shall thy vain
thoughts lodge within thee?

15 For a voice declareth [o]from
Dan, and publisheth affliction from
mount Ephraim.

16 Make ye mention to the nations;
behold, publish against Jerusalem, *that*
watchers come from a far country, and
give out their voice against the cities of
Judah.

17 [p]As keepers of a field, are they
against her round about; because she
hath been rebellious against me, saith
the LORD.

18 [q]Thy way and thy doings have
procured these *things* unto thee; this *is*
thy wickedness, because it is bitter, be-
cause it reacheth unto thine heart.

19 ¶ My [r]bowels, my bowels! I am

3:25 [s]ch. 22:21
4:1 [t]ch. 3:1,22 Joel 2:12
4:2 [u]Deut. 10:20 Is. 45:23 & 65:16 See ch. 5:2 [v]Is. 48:1 Zech. 8:8 [w]Gen. 22:18 Ps. 72:17 Gal. 3:8 [x]1 Cor. 1:31
4:3 [y]Hos. 10:12 [z]Mat. 13:7
4:4 [a]Deut. 10:16 ch. 9:26 Rom. 2:28
4:5 [b]ch. 8:14
4:6 [c]ch. 1:13-15 & 6:1,22
4:7 [d]2 Ki. 24:1 ch. 5:6 Dan. 7:4 [e]ch. 25:9 [f]Is. 1:7
4:8 [g]Is. 22:12
4:10 [h]Ezek. 14:9 2 Thes. 2:11 [i]ch. 14:13
4:11 [j]ch. 51:1 Ezek. 17:10 Hos. 13:15
4:12 [k]ch. 1:16
4:13 [l]Is. 5:28 [m]Deut. 28:49 Lam. 4:19 Hos. 8:1 Hab. 1:8
4:14 [n]Is. 1:16 Jas. 4:8
4:15 [o]ch. 8:16
4:17 [p]2 Ki. 25:1
4:18 [q]Ps. 107:17 Is. 50:1 ch. 2:17,19
4:19 [r]Is. 15:5 & 16:11 & 21:3 See Luke 19:42

[i] Or, *strengthen* [j] Heb. *breaking* [k] Or, *a fuller wind than those* [l] Heb. *utter judgments*

4:3–31 THUS SAITH THE LORD. Ch. 4 describes the desolation that would soon come upon God's people because of their sin and apostasy. They would learn how evil and bitter it was to forsake the Lord (cf. 2:19).

4:4 THE FORESKINS OF YOUR HEART. To avoid the terrible calamity coming upon them, the people of Judah had to undergo a complete moral renewal by committing themselves to truth, justice, and righteousness. They must be open to the conviction of the Spirit, repent of their sins, and break up the hardened soil of their hearts (v. 3). The evil in their heart must be removed as surely as the foreskin was removed in physical circumcision.

4:6 I WILL BRING EVIL FROM THE NORTH, AND A GREAT DESTRUCTION. In His anger against His people, God would cause the Babylonians to invade Judah and allow them to devastate the land (see 1:14, note).

4:10 THOU HAST GREATLY DECEIVED THIS PEOPLE. Many of Judah's prophets had spoken deceptively to God's people by giving them false hopes of peace and security, while ignoring their sinful ways (cf. 14:13–16; 23:17; 1 Ki. 22:20–23). God had permitted the people to believe a lie because they had no love for the truth and took pleasure in sin (cf. 2 Thes. 2:9–12).

pained at [m]my very heart; my heart maketh a noise in me; I cannot hold my peace, because thou hast heard, O my soul, the sound of the trumpet, the alarm of war.

20 [s]Destruction upon destruction is cried; for the whole land is spoiled: suddenly are [t]my tents spoiled, *and* my curtains in a moment.

21 How long shall I see the standard, *and* hear the sound of the trumpet?

22 For my people *is* foolish, they have not known me; they *are* sottish children, and they have none understanding: [u]they *are* wise to do evil, but to do good they have no knowledge.

23 I [v]beheld the earth, and, lo, *it was* [w]without form, and void; and the heavens, and they *had* no light.

24 [x]I beheld the mountains, and, lo, they trembled, and all the hills moved lightly.

25 I beheld, and, lo, *there was* no man, and [y]all the birds of the heavens were fled.

26 I beheld, and, lo, the fruitful place *was* a wilderness, and all the cities thereof were broken down at the presence of the LORD, *and* by his fierce anger.

27 For thus hath the LORD said, The whole land shall be desolate; [z]yet will I not make a full end.

28 For this [a]shall the earth mourn, and [b]the heavens above be black: because I have spoken *it,* I have purposed *it,* and [c]will not repent, neither will I turn back from it.

29 The whole city shall flee for the noise of the horsemen and bowmen; they shall go into thickets, and climb up upon the rocks: every city *shall be* forsaken, and not a man dwell therein.

30 And *when* thou *art* spoiled, what wilt thou do? Though thou clothest thyself with crimson, though thou deckest thee with ornaments of gold, [d]though thou rentest thy [n]face with painting, in vain shalt thou make thyself fair; [e]*thy* lovers will despise thee, they will seek thy life.

31 For I have heard a voice as of a woman in travail, *and* the anguish as of her that bringeth forth her first child, the voice of the daughter of Zion, *that* bewaileth herself, *that* [f]spreadeth her hands, *saying,* Woe *is* me now! for my soul is wearied because of murderers.

4:20 [s]Ps. 42:7 Ezek. 7:26 [t]ch. 10:20
4:22 [u]Rom. 16:19
4:23 [v]Is. 24:19 [w]Gen. 1:2
4:24 [x]Is. 5:25 Ezek. 38:20
4:25 [y]Zeph. 1:3
4:27 [z]ch. 5:10,18 & 30:11 & 46:28
4:28 [a]Hos. 4:3 [b]Is. 5:30 & 50:3 [c]Num. 23:19 ch. 7:16
4:30 [d]2 Ki. 9:30 [e]ch. 22:20,22
4:31 [f]Is. 1:15 Lam. 1:17
5:1 [g]Ezek. 22:30 [h]Gen. 18:23 [i]Gen. 18:26
5:2 [j]Tit. 1:16 [k]ch. 4:2 [l]ch. 7:9
5:3 [m]2 Chr. 16:9 [n]Is. 1:5 & 9:13 ch. 2:30 [o]ch. 7:28 Zeph. 3:2
5:4 [p]ch. 8:7
5:5 [q]Mic. 3:1 [r]Ps. 2:3
5:6 [s]ch. 4:7 [t]Ps. 104:20 Hab. 1:8 Zeph. 3:3 [u]Hos. 13:7

Futile search for an upright man

5 RUN YE to and fro through the streets of Jerusalem, and see now, and know, and seek in the broad places thereof, [g]if ye can find a man, [h]if there be *any* that executeth judgment, that seeketh the truth; [i]and I will pardon it.

2 And [j]though they say, [k]The LORD liveth; surely they [l]swear falsely.

3 O LORD, *are* not [m]thine eyes upon the truth? thou hast [n]stricken them, but they have not grieved; thou hast consumed them, *but* [o]they have refused to receive correction: they have made their faces harder than a rock; they have refused to return.

4 Therefore I said, Surely these *are* poor; they are foolish: for [p]they know not the way of the LORD, *nor* the judgment of their God.

5 I will get me unto the great men, and will speak unto them; for [q]they have known the way of the LORD, *and* the judgment of their God: but these have altogether [r]broken the yoke, *and* burst the bonds.

6 Wherefore [s]a lion out of the forest shall slay them, [t]*and* a wolf of the [o]evenings shall spoil them, [u]a leopard shall watch over their cities: every one that goeth out thence shall be torn in pieces: because their transgressions

[m] Heb. *the walls of my heart* [n] Heb. *eyes*
[o] Or, *deserts*

4:19–22 I AM PAINED AT MY VERY HEART. Jeremiah experienced God's agony for Judah and expressed the pain and sorrow that the Lord felt at the coming desolation. Likewise, believers should feel sorrow at the thought of men and women being taken captive and destroyed by sin and Satan. The terrible future of the lost should cause us to lament as Jesus did when He expressed intense grief over the lost spiritual condition of Jerusalem (Luke 13:34).

4:23 THE EARTH . . . VOID. Jeremiah's vision of the utter devastation coming upon his people made it appear as if the whole universe had been laid waste and changed into the same formlessness it had in the beginning before God began to shape the world (cf. Gen. 1:2).

5:1–9 *ANY* . . . THAT SEEKETH THE TRUTH. Judah's corruption had reached such a degree that few could be found who loved God's truth and righteousness. The nation was guilty; therefore, God determined to bring judgment upon His faithless people.

are many, *and* their backslidings [p]are
increased.
7 ¶ How shall I pardon thee for this?
thy children have forsaken me, and
[v]sworn by *them* [w]*that are* no gods:
[x]when I had fed them to the full, they
then committed adultery, and assem-
bled themselves by troops in the har-
lots' houses.
8 [y]They were *as* fed horses in the
morning: every one neighed after his
neighbour's wife.
9 [z]Shall I not visit for these *things?*
saith the LORD: [a]and shall not my soul
be avenged on such a nation as this?
10 ¶ [b]Go ye up upon her walls, and
destroy; [c]but make not a full end:
take away her battlements; for they *are*
not the LORD's.
11 For [d]the house of Israel and the
house of Judah have dealt very treach-
erously against me, saith the LORD.
12 [e]They have belied the LORD, and
said, [f]*It is* not he; neither shall evil
come upon us; [g]neither shall we see
sword nor famine:
13 And the prophets shall become
wind, and the word *is* not in them: thus
shall it be done unto them.
14 Wherefore thus saith the LORD
God of hosts, Because ye speak this
word, [h]behold, I will make my words
in thy mouth fire, and this people
wood, and it shall devour them.
15 Lo, I will bring a [i]nation upon
you [j]from far, O house of Israel, saith
the LORD: it *is* a mighty nation, it *is* an
ancient nation, a nation whose lan-
guage thou knowest not, neither un-
derstandest what they say.
16 Their quiver *is* as an open sepul-
chre, they *are* all mighty men.
17 And they shall eat up thine
[k]harvest, and thy bread, *which* thy
sons and thy daughters should eat:
they shall eat up thy flocks and thine
herds: they shall eat up thy vines and
thy fig trees: they shall impoverish thy
fenced cities, wherein thou trustedst,
with the sword.
18 Nevertheless in those days, saith
the LORD, I [l]will not make a full end
with you.
19 ¶ And it shall come to pass,
when ye shall say, [m]Wherefore doeth
the LORD our God all these *things* unto
us? then shalt thou answer them, Like
as ye have [n]forsaken me, and served
strange gods in your land, so [o]shall ye
serve strangers in a land *that is* not
yours.
20 Declare this in the house of Ja-
cob, and publish it in Judah, saying,
21 Hear now this, O [p]foolish peo-
ple, and without [q]understanding;
which have eyes, and see not; which
have ears, and hear not:
22 [q]Fear ye not me? saith the LORD:
will ye not tremble at my presence,
which have placed the sand *for* the
[r]bound of the sea by a perpetual de-
cree, that it cannot pass it: and though
the waves thereof toss themselves, yet
can they not prevail; though they roar,
yet can they not pass over it?
23 But this people hath a revolting
and a rebellious heart; they are revolt-
ed and gone.
24 Neither say they in their heart,
Let us now fear the LORD our God,
[s]that giveth rain, both the [t]former
and the latter, in his season: [u]he re-
serveth unto us the appointed weeks of
the harvest.
25 ¶ [v]Your iniquities have turned
away these *things*, and your sins have
withholden good *things* from you.
26 For among my people are found
wicked *men:* [r]they [w]lay wait, as he
that setteth snares; they set a trap,
they catch men.
27 As a [s]cage is full of birds, so *are*
their houses full of deceit: therefore
they are become great, and waxen rich.

5:7 [v]Josh. 23:7 Zeph:1:5 [w]Deut. 32:21 Gal. 4:8 [x]Deut. 32:15
5:8 [y]Ezek. 22:11
5:9 [z]ver. 29 ch. 9:9 [a]ch. 44:22
5:10 [b]ch. 39:8 [c]ver. 18 ch. 4:27
5:11 [d]ch. 3:20
5:12 [e]2 Chr. 36:16 ch. 4:10 [f]Is. 28:15 [g]ch. 14:13
5:14 [h]ch. 1:9
5:15 [i]Deut. 28:49 Is. 5:26 ch. 1:15 & 6:22 [j]Is. 39:3 ch. 4:16
5:17 [k]Lev. 26:16 Deut. 28:31,33
5:18 [l]ch. 4:27
5:19 [m]Deut. 29:24 1 Ki. 9:8,9 ch. 13:22 & 16:10 [n]ch. 2:13 [o]Deut. 28:48
5:21 [p]Is. 6:9 Ezek. 12:2 Mat. 13:14 John 12:40 Acts 28:26 Rom. 11:8
5:22 [q]Rev. 15:4 [r]Job 26:10 Prov. 8:29
5:24 [s]Ps. 147:8 Acts 14:17 [t]Joel 2:23 [u]Gen. 8:22
5:25 [v]ch. 3:3
5:26 [w]Prov. 1:11 Hab. 1:15

[p] Heb. *are strong* [q] Heb. *heart* [r] Or, *they pry as fowlers lie in wait* [s] Or, *coop*

5:10 THEY *ARE* NOT THE LORD'S. The people professed to be the Lord's (cf. 3:4), but God testified that they were not His people. Likewise, anyone who claims to be a born-again believer, yet is given over to the sins described in this chapter (e.g., lying, dishonesty, adultery), does not belong to the Lord; like many in Judah, such people have been deceived into believing that their unfaithfulness to God will not bring His ultimate condemnation.

5:12 NEITHER SHALL EVIL COME UPON US. The temptation is always strong to believe that God will overlook our sins and not send the judgment about which His Word warns. Many of God's people tend to claim the promises but doubt the warnings.

5:22 FEAR YE NOT ME? The people did not obey God because they had no fear of Him and did not tremble at the reality of His presence (see article on THE FEAR OF THE LORD, p. 282).

28 They are waxen [x]fat, they shine: yea, they overpass the deeds of the wicked: they judge not [y]the cause, the cause of the fatherless, [z]yet they prosper; and the right of the needy do they not judge.

29 [a]Shall I not visit for these *things?* saith the LORD: shall not my soul be avenged on such a nation as this?

30 ¶ [t]A wonderful and [b]horrible thing is committed in the land;

31 The prophets prophesy [c]falsely, and the priests [u]bear rule by their means; and my people [d]love *to have it* so: and what will ye do in the end thereof?

Jerusalem under siege

6 O YE children of Benjamin, gather yourselves to flee out of the midst of Jerusalem, and blow the trumpet in Tekoa, and set up a sign of fire in [e]Beth-haccerem: [f]for evil appeareth out of the north, and great destruction.

2 I have likened the daughter of Zion to a [v]comely and delicate *woman.*

3 The shepherds with their flocks shall come unto her; [g]they shall pitch *their* tents against her round about; they shall feed every one in his place.

4 [h]Prepare ye war against her; arise, and let us go up [i]at noon. Woe unto us! for the day goeth away, for the shadows of the evening are stretched out.

5 Arise, and let us go by night, and let us destroy her palaces.

6 ¶ For thus hath the LORD of hosts said, Hew ye down trees, and [w]cast a mount against Jerusalem: this *is* the city to be visited; she *is* wholly oppression in the midst of her.

7 [j]As a fountain casteth out her waters, so she casteth out her wickedness: [k]violence and spoil is heard in her; before me continually *is* grief and wounds.

8 Be thou instructed, O Jerusalem, lest [l]my soul [x]depart from thee; lest I make thee desolate, a land not inhabited.

9 ¶ Thus saith the LORD of hosts, They shall thoroughly glean the remnant of Israel as a vine: turn back thine hand as a grapegatherer into the baskets.

10 To whom shall I speak, and give warning, that they may hear? behold, their [m]ear *is* uncircumcised, and they cannot hearken: behold, [n]the word of the LORD is unto them a reproach; they have no delight in it.

11 Therefore I am full of the fury of the LORD; [o]I am weary with holding in: I will pour it out [p]upon the children abroad, and upon the assembly of young men together: for even the husband with the wife shall be taken, the aged with *him that is* full of days.

12 And [q]their houses shall be turned unto others, *with their* fields and wives together: for I will stretch out my hand upon the inhabitants of the land, saith the LORD.

13 For from the least of them even unto the greatest of them every one *is* given to [r]covetousness; and from the prophet even unto the priest every one dealeth falsely.

14 They have [s]healed also the [y]hurt *of the daughter* of my people slightly, [t]saying, Peace, peace; when *there is* no peace.

5:28 [x]Deut. 32:15 [y]Is. 1:23 Zech. 7:10 [z]Job 12:6 Ps. 73:12
5:29 [a]Mal. 3:5
5:30 [b]Hos. 6:10
5:31 [c]ch. 14:14 & 23:25,26 Ezek. 13:6 [d]Mic. 2:11
6:1 [e]Neh. 3:14 [f]ch. 4:6
6:3 [g]2 Ki. 25:1
6:4 [h]Joel 3:9 [i]ch. 15:8
6:7 [j]Is. 57:20 [k]Ps. 55:9 ch. 20:8 Ezek. 7:11
6:8 [l]Hos. 9:12
6:10 [m]Acts 7:51 See Ex. 6:12 [n]ch. 20:8
6:11 [o]ch. 20:9 [p]ch. 9:21
6:12 [q]Deut. 28:30 ch. 8:10
6:13 [r]Is. 56:11 ch. 8:10 Mic. 3:5,11
6:14 [s]ch. 8:11 Ezek. 13:10 [t]ch. 4:10 & 23:17

[t] Or, *Astonishment and filthiness* [u] Or, *take into their hands* [v] Or, *dwelling at home* [w] Or, *pour out the engine of shot* [x] Heb. *be loosed,* or, *disjointed* [y] Heb. *bruise,* or, *breach*

5:31 THE PROPHETS PROPHESY FALSELY. Those who had been entrusted with the spiritual well-being of the nation were guilty of treachery against their God. (1) The prophets had rejected God's word and prophesied only good things to come. They made few moral demands on the people, and the people were happy to have it that way. (2) The priests governed the people by their own ideas rather than by God's word. The prophets and priests thus lulled the nation into a false security. Jeremiah proclaimed that there was no real security before God apart from sincere repentance and a commitment to obey His word.

6:1–30 FLEE OUT OF THE MIDST OF JERUSALEM. This chapter describes the great destruction soon to be inflicted upon Jerusalem and its impenitent people. This word was fulfilled in Jeremiah's lifetime. Jeremiah both warned Judah and Jerusalem and called them to repentance. If the people would only turn to God and renew their covenant with Him, they would have an opportunity to escape ruin. Jeremiah's constant plea was rebuffed in scorn; thus judgment was imminent.

6:3 SHEPHERDS WITH THEIR FLOCKS. The Babylonian commanders are compared to shepherds and their troops to flocks who would lay bare the land.

6:14 PEACE; WHEN *THERE* IS NO PEACE. The false prophets were preaching a message of false security. Instead of warning the people of coming judgment and of the need to repent, they told them that there was nothing to fear.

15 Were they [u]ashamed when they had committed abomination? nay, they were not at all ashamed, neither could they blush: therefore they shall fall among them that fall: at the time *that* I visit them they shall be cast down, saith the LORD.

16 Thus saith the LORD, Stand ye in the ways, and see, and ask for the [v]old paths, where *is* the good way, and walk therein, and ye shall find [w]rest for your souls. But they said, We will not walk *therein.*

17 Also I set [x]watchmen over you, *saying,* Hearken to the sound of the trumpet. But they said, We will not hearken.

18 ¶ Therefore hear, ye nations, and know, O congregation, what *is* among them.

19 [y]Hear, O earth: behold, I will bring evil upon this people, *even* [z]the fruit of their thoughts, because they have not hearkened unto my words, nor to my law, but rejected it.

20 [a]To what purpose cometh there to me incense [b]from Sheba, and the sweet cane from a far country? [c]your burnt offerings *are* not acceptable, nor your sacrifices sweet unto me.

21 Therefore thus saith the LORD, Behold, I will lay stumblingblocks before this people, and the fathers and the sons together shall fall upon them; the neighbour and his friend shall perish.

22 Thus saith the LORD, Behold, a people cometh from the [d]north country, and a great nation shall be raised from the sides of the earth.

23 They shall lay hold on bow and spear; they *are* cruel, and have no mercy; their voice [e]roareth like the sea; and they ride upon horses, set in array as men for war against thee, O daughter of Zion.

24 We have heard the fame thereof: our hands wax feeble: [f]anguish hath taken hold of us, *and* pain, as of a woman in travail.

25 Go not forth into the field, nor walk by the way; for the sword of the enemy *and* fear *is* on every side.

26 ¶ O daughter of my people, [g]gird *thee* with sackcloth, [h]and wallow thyself in ashes: [i]make thee mourning, *as for* an only son, most bitter lamentation: for the spoiler shall suddenly come upon us.

27 I have set thee *for* a tower *and* [j]a fortress among my people, that thou mayest know and try their way.

28 [k]They *are* all grievous revolters, [l]walking with slanders: *they are* [m]brass and iron; they *are* all corrupters.

29 The bellows are burned, the lead is consumed of the fire; the founder melteth in vain: for the wicked are not plucked away.

30 [n]Reprobate[z] silver shall *men* call them, because the LORD hath rejected them.

6:15 [u]ch. 3:3 **6:16** [v]Is. 8:20 ch. 18:15 Mal. 4:4 Luke 16:29 [w]Mat. 11:29 **6:17** [x]Is. 21:11 & 58:1 ch. 25:4 Ezek. 3:17 Hab. 2:1 **6:19** [y]Is. 1:2 [z]Prov. 1:31 **6:20** [a]Ps. 40:6 & 50:7-9 Is. 1:11 & 66:3 Amos 5:21 Mic. 6:6 [b]Is. 60:6 [c]ch. 7:21 **6:22** [d]ch. 1:15 & 10:22 **6:23** [e]Is. 5:30 **6:24** [f]ch. 4:31 & 13:21 & 49:24 & 50:43 **6:26** [g]ch. 4:8 [h]ch. 25:34 Mic. 1:10 [i]Zech. 12:10 **6:27** [j]ch. 1:18 & 15:20 **6:28** [k]ch. 5:23 [l]ch. 9:4 [m]Ezek. 22:18 **6:30** [n]Is. 1:22 **7:2** [o]ch. 26:2 **7:3** [p]ch. 18:11 & 26:13 **7:4** [q]Mic. 3:11 **7:5** [r]ch. 22:3 **7:6** [s]Deut. 6:14,15 & 8:19 ch:13:10 **7:7** [t]Deut. 4:40

Judah's idolatry and immorality

7 THE WORD that came to Jeremiah from the LORD, saying,

2 [o]Stand in the gate of the LORD'S house, and proclaim there this word, and say, Hear the word of the LORD, all *ye of* Judah, that enter in at these gates to worship the LORD.

3 Thus saith the LORD of hosts, the God of Israel, [p]Amend your ways and your doings, and I will cause you to dwell in this place.

4 [q]Trust ye not in lying words, saying, The temple of the LORD, The temple of the LORD, The temple of the LORD, *are* these.

5 For if ye thoroughly amend your ways and your doings; if ye thoroughly [r]execute judgment between a man and his neighbour;

6 *If* ye oppress not the stranger, the fatherless, and the widow, and shed not innocent blood in this place, [s]neither walk after other gods to your hurt:

7 [t]Then will I cause you to dwell in

[z] Or, *Refuse silver*

6:16 ASK FOR THE OLD PATHS. God's people had strayed from the way of righteousness into idolatry and wickedness, and He called them back to the former paths of the covenant and the law of Moses. Likewise, the church must always examine itself to see if it has strayed from the path of the Spirit's power and the righteousness proclaimed in the N.T. The full blessing of God will be enjoyed only by those who ask, seek, and knock for His best (cf. Luke 11:5–13) and who are committed to live according to the pattern set forth in the N.T. (see Acts 7:44, note).

7:3 AMEND YOUR WAYS. God gives yet another call to the people to repent of their evil ways; however, as long as they believed they were secure simply because of the temple and its ritual, they saw no need to repent (v. 4; see next note).

this place, in [u]the land that I gave to your fathers, for ever and ever.

8 ¶ Behold, [v]ye trust in [w]lying words, that cannot profit.

9 [x]Will ye steal, murder, and commit adultery, and swear falsely, and burn incense unto Baal, and [y]walk after other gods whom ye know not;

10 [z]And come and stand before me in this house, [a]which[a] is called by my name, and say, We are delivered to do all these abominations?

11 Is [b]this house, which is called by my name, become a [c]den of robbers in your eyes? Behold, even I have seen *it,* saith the LORD.

12 But go ye now unto [d]my place which *was* in Shiloh, [e]where I set my name at the first, and see [f]what I did to it for the wickedness of my people Israel.

13 And now, because ye have done all these works, saith the LORD, and I spake unto you, [g]rising up early and speaking, but ye heard not; and I [h]called you, but ye answered not;

14 Therefore will I do unto *this* house, which is called by my name, wherein ye trust, and unto the place which I gave to you and to your fathers, as I have done to [i]Shiloh.

15 And I will cast you out of my sight, [j]as I have cast out all your brethren, [k]*even* the whole seed of Ephraim.

16 Therefore [l]pray not thou for this people, neither lift up cry nor prayer for them, neither make intercession to me: [m]for I will not hear thee.

17 ¶ Seest thou not what they do in the cities of Judah and in the streets of Jerusalem?

18 [n]The children gather wood, and the fathers kindle the fire, and the women knead *their* dough, to make cakes to the [b]queen of heaven, and to [o]pour out drink offerings unto other gods, that they may provoke me to anger.

19 [p]Do they provoke me to anger? saith the LORD: *do they* not *provoke* themselves to the confusion of their own faces?

20 Therefore thus saith the Lord GOD; Behold, mine anger and my fury shall be poured out upon this place, upon man, and upon beast, and upon the trees of the field, and upon the fruit of the ground; and it shall burn, and shall not be quenched.

21 ¶ Thus saith the LORD of hosts, the God of Israel; [q]Put your burnt offerings unto your sacrifices, and eat flesh.

22 [r]For I spake not unto your fathers, nor commanded them in the day that I brought them out of the land of Egypt, [c]concerning burnt offerings or sacrifices:

23 But this thing commanded I them, saying, [s]Obey my voice, and [t]I will be your God, and ye shall be my people: and walk ye in all the ways that I have commanded you, that it may be well unto you.

24 [u]But they hearkened not, nor inclined their ear, but [v]walked in the counsels *and* in the [d]imagination of their evil heart, and [w]went[e] backward, and not forward.

25 Since the day that your fathers came forth out of the land of Egypt

7:7 [u]ch. 3:18
7:8 [v]ver. 4 [w]ch. 5:31 & 14:13,14
7:9 [x]1 Ki. 18:21 Hos. 4:1,2 Zeph. 1:5 [y]Ex. 20:3
7:10 [z]Ezek. 23:39 [a]ver. 11,14 ch. 32:34 & 34:15
7:11 [b]Is. 56:7 [c]Mat. 21:13 Mark 11:17 Luke 19:46
7:12 [d]Josh. 18:1 Judg. 18:31 [e]Deut. 12:11 [f]1 Sam. 4:10 Ps. 78:60 ch. 26:6
7:13 [g]2 Chr. 36:15 ch. 11:7 [h]Prov. 1:24 Is. 65:12 & 66:4
7:14 [i]1 Sam. 4:10 Ps. 78:60
7:15 [j]2 Ki. 17:23 [k]Ps. 78:67
7:16 [l]Ex. 32:10 [m]ch. 15:1
7:18 [n]ch. 44:17 [o]ch. 19:13
7:19 [p]Deut. 32:16,21
7:21 [q]Is. 1:11 Amos 5:21 Hos. 8:13
7:22 [r]1 Sam. 15:22 Ps. 51:16 Hos. 6:6
7:23 [s]Ex. 15:26 Deut. 6:3 [t]Ex. 19:5 Lev. 26:12
7:24 [u]Ps. 81:11 [v]Ps. 81:12 [w]ch. 32:33

[a] Heb. *whereupon my name is called* [b] Or, *frame,* or, *workmanship of heaven* [c] Heb. *concerning the matter of* [d] Or, *stubbornness* [e] Heb. *were*

7:9–10 STEAL, MURDER ... AND STAND BEFORE ME. The people were committing all kinds of sins (vv. 5–9); then on the Sabbath they came to the temple and stood before God, deluding themselves into thinking they were secure in God's love for them. This same sort of theology is in evidence today when people who live in rebellion against God and His commands feel secure because they believe in "the blood of Christ." In Jeremiah's words, they are trusting "in lying [i.e., deceptive] words, that cannot profit" (v. 8).

7:11 DEN OF ROBBERS. Robbers often used a den to hide in and to plan their next crime. Jeremiah adopts this picture to depict people who were coming to the temple to offer sacrifices that they thought would hide their sin from God. At the same time, they were planning to continue in their sinful ways. Jesus quoted part of this verse in His indictment of the Jewish leaders of His day (see Mat. 21:13; Mark 11:17; Luke 19:46).

7:12 SHILOH. Shiloh, about eighteen miles north of Jerusalem, housed the tabernacle during the time of the judges (Josh. 18:1). Jeremiah maintains that Shiloh was destroyed because of the sins of the people (7:12,14; 26:6); the same fate awaited Jerusalem and its temple if the people did not change their sinful ways.

7:18 QUEEN OF HEAVEN. The "queen of heaven" is either the the Babylonian fertility goddess Ishtar or the Phoenician goddess Ashtoreth. Her images have been found in Palestine. Women were especially involved in her worship.

unto this day I have even [x]sent unto
you all my servants the prophets,
[y]daily rising up early and sending
them:
26 [z]Yet they hearkened not unto
me, nor inclined their ear, but [a]hard-
ened their neck: [b]they did worse than
their fathers.
27 Therefore [c]thou shalt speak all
these words unto them; but they will
not hearken to thee: thou shalt also
call unto them; but they will not an-
swer thee.
28 But thou shalt say unto them,
This *is* a nation that obeyeth not the
voice of the LORD their God, [d]nor re-
ceiveth [f]correction: [e]truth is per-
ished, and is cut off from their mouth.
29 ¶ [f]Cut off thine hair, *O Jerusa-
lem*, and cast *it* away, and take up a
lamentation on high places; for the
LORD hath rejected and forsaken the
generation of his wrath.

The terrible days to come

30 For the children of Judah have
done evil in my sight, saith the LORD:
[g]they have set their abominations in
the house which is called by my name,
to pollute it.
31 And they have built the [h]high
places of Tophet, which *is* in the valley
of the son of Hinnom, to [i]burn their
sons and their daughters in the fire;
[j]which I commanded *them* not, nei-
ther [g]came it into my heart.
32 ¶ Therefore, behold, [k]the days
come, saith the LORD, that it shall no
more be called Tophet, nor the valley
of the son of Hinnom, but the valley of
slaughter: [l]for they shall bury in To-
phet, till there be no place.
33 And the [m]carcases of this peo-
ple shall be meat for the fowls of the
heaven, and for the beasts of the earth;
and none shall fray *them* away.

7:25 [x]2 Chr. 36:15 [y]ver. 13
7:26 [z]ch. 11:8 [a]Neh. 9:17 [b]ch. 16:12
7:27 [c]Ezek. 2:7
7:28 [d]ch. 5:3 [e]ch. 9:3
7:29 [f]Job 1:20 Is. 15:2 Mic 1:16
7:30 [g]2 Ki. 21:4 2 Chr. 33:4 Ezek. 7:20 Dan. 9:27
7:31 [h]2 Ki. 23:10 [i]Ps. 106:38 [j]Deut. 17:3
7:32 [k]ch. 19:6 [l]2 Ki. 23:10 ch. 19:11
7:33 [m]Deut. 28:26
7:34 [n]Is. 24:7,8 Ezek. 26:13 Hos. 2:11 Rev. 18:23 [o]Lev. 26:33
8:2 [p]2 Ki. 23:5 Ezek. 8:16 [q]ch. 22:19
8:3 [r]Job 3:21 & 7:15,16 Rev. 9:6
8:5 [s]ch. 7:24 [t]ch. 9:6 [u]ch. 5:3
8:6 [v]2 Pet. 3:9
8:7 [w]Is. 1:3

34 Then will I cause to [n]cease from
the cities of Judah, and from the streets
of Jerusalem, the voice of mirth, and
the voice of gladness, the voice of the
bridegroom, and the voice of the bride:
for [o]the land shall be desolate.
8 AT THAT time, saith the LORD,
they shall bring out the bones of
the kings of Judah, and the bones of his
princes, and the bones of the priests,
and the bones of the prophets, and the
bones of the inhabitants of Jerusalem,
out of their graves:
2 And they shall spread them before
the sun, and the moon, and all the host
of heaven, whom they have loved, and
whom they have served, and after
whom they have walked, and whom
they have sought, and [p]whom they
have worshipped: they shall not be
gathered, [q]nor be buried; they shall be
for dung upon the face of the earth.
3 And [r]death shall be chosen rath-
er than life by all the residue of them
that remain of this evil family, which
remain in all the places whither I have
driven them, saith the LORD of hosts.

Punishment of sinful Israel

4 ¶ Moreover thou shalt say unto
them, Thus saith the LORD; Shall they
fall, and not arise? shall he turn away,
and not return?
5 Why *then* is this people of Jerusa-
lem [s]slidden back by a perpetual
backsliding? [t]they hold fast deceit,
[u]they refuse to return.
6 [v]I hearkened and heard, *but* they
spake not aright: no man repented him
of his wickedness, saying, What have I
done? every one turned to his course,
as the horse rusheth into the battle.
7 Yea, [w]the stork in the heaven
knoweth her appointed times; and

[f] Or, *instruction* [g] Heb. *came it upon my heart*

7:31 VALLEY OF THE SON OF HINNOM. This valley on the southern perimeter of Jerusalem was used as a garbage dump and as a place to worship idols and to sacrifice children by fire (a practice strictly forbidden under the Mosaic Law; see Lev. 18:21; 20:2–5). Some of the worst sins in Jewish history were committed in this location. From the name "Valley of Hinnom" (Heb. *ge'hinnom*) comes the Greek *gehenna*, translated "hell" in the N.T., the place of God's eternal judgment (Mat. 18:9; Mark 9:47–48; see Mat. 10:28, note).

8:1–22 AT THAT TIME. Jeremiah refers to the impending desolation of Judah and Jerusalem as if it had already occurred. Their fate would be the result of the people's stubborn rebellion and sin (cf. 7:24). Jeremiah's vision of desolation caused him great sorrow (vv. 18–22). Yet while he was prophesying doom, false prophets were predicting peace (vv. 10–11).

8:1–2 BONES . . . ALL THE HOST OF HEAVEN. In O.T. times, it was considered the ultimate sacrilege to leave the dead unburied. As a fitting punishment for their idolatry, God announced His intention of allowing the bones of the people to lay open before the stars they loved to worship.

8:7 MY PEOPLE KNOW NOT THE JUDGMENT OF THE LORD. The people were ignorant of God's law. Moreover, their leaders so distorted

[x]the turtle and the crane and the
swallow observe the time of their com-
ing; but [y]my people know not the
judgment of the LORD.
8 How do ye say, We *are* wise, [z]and
the law of the LORD *is* with us? Lo, cer-
tainly [a]in[h] vain made he *it;* the pen
of the scribes *is* in vain.
9 [b]The[i] wise *men* are ashamed,
they are dismayed and taken: lo, they
have rejected the word of the LORD; and
[j]what wisdom *is* in them?
10 Therefore [c]will I give their
wives unto others, *and* their fields to
them that shall inherit *them:* for every
one from the least even unto the great-
est is given to [k]covetousness, from
the prophet even unto the priest every
one dealeth falsely.
11 For they have [d]healed the hurt
of the daughter of my people slightly,
saying, [e]Peace, peace; when *there is*
no peace.
12 Were they [f]ashamed when they
had committed abomination? nay, they
were not at all ashamed, neither could
they blush: therefore shall they fall
among them that fall: in the time of
their visitation they shall be cast down,
saith the LORD.
13 ¶ [l]I will surely consume them,
saith the LORD: *there shall be* no grapes
[g]on the vine, nor figs on the [h]fig tree,
and the leaf shall fade; and *the things
that* I have given them shall pass away
from them.
14 Why do we sit still? [i]assemble
yourselves, and let us enter into the
defenced cities, and let us be silent
there: for the LORD our God hath put us
to silence, and given us [j]water of
[m]gall to drink, because we have
sinned against the LORD.

8:7 [x]Sol. 2:12 [y]ch. 5:4,5
8:8 [z]Rom. 2:17 [a]Is. 10:1
8:9 [b]ch. 6:15
8:10 [c]Zeph. 1:13
8:11 [d]ch. 6:14 [e]Ezek. 13:10
8:12 [f]ch. 3:3
8:13 [g]Joel 1:7 [h]Mat. 21:19
8:14 [i]ch. 4:5 [j]ch. 9:15
8:15 [k]ch. 14:19
8:16 [l]ch. 4:15 [m]ch. 47:3
8:17 [n]Ps. 58:4,5
8:19 [o]Is. 39:3
8:21 [p]ch. 9:1 [q]Joel 2:6
8:22 [r]ch. 46:11
9:1 [s]Is. 22:4

15 We [k]looked for peace, but no
good *came; and* for a time of health, and
behold trouble!
16 The snorting of his horses was
heard from [l]Dan: the whole land
trembled at the sound of the neighing
of his [m]strong ones; for they are come,
and have devoured the land, and [n]all
that is in it; the city, and those that
dwell therein.
17 For, behold, I will send serpents,
cockatrices, among you, which *will* not
be [n]charmed, and they shall bite you,
saith the LORD.
18 ¶ *When* I would comfort myself
against sorrow, my heart *is* faint
[o]in me.
19 Behold the voice of the cry of the
daughter of my people [p]because of
them that dwell in [o]a far country: *Is*
not the LORD in Zion? *is* not her king in
her? Why have they provoked me to an-
ger with their graven images, *and* with
strange vanities?
20 The harvest is past, the summer
is ended, and we are not saved.
21 [p]For the hurt of the daughter of
my people am I hurt; I am [q]black; as-
tonishment hath taken hold on me.
22 *Is there* no [r]balm in Gilead; *is
there* no physician there? why then is
not the health of the daughter of my
people [q]recovered?
9 OH [s]THAT[r] my head were wa-
ters, and mine eyes a fountain of

[h] Or, *the false pen of the scribes worketh for falsehood* [i] Or, *Have they been ashamed* [j] Heb. *the wisdom of what thing* [k] Is. 56:11 [l] Or, *In gathering I will consume* [m] Or, *poison* [n] Heb. *the fulness thereof* [o] Heb. *upon* [p] Heb. *because of the country of them that are far off* [q] Heb. *gone up?* [r] Heb. *Who will give my head*

the word of God and falsified its message that the people were assured they could sin without condemnation (v. 8). In a similar manner, the apostle Peter speaks of those who twist the word of God to their own destruction and to the destruction of others (cf. 2 Pet. 3:16). We must beware of any ministers who teach that those who willfully continue in sin and rebellion against God will still inherit salvation and the kingdom of God (see 1 Cor. 6:9, note).

8:12 THEY WERE NOT AT ALL ASHAMED. The people had reached a stage of apostasy where they would never repent; all shame and remorse for sin was gone. Their impending judgment awaited only the day of God's visitation. Churches today reach this same stage of apostasy when they reject God's word and commit the sort of abominable sins described by Paul in Rom. 1:24–32 (see Rom. 1:27, note).

8:18–23 MY HEART *IS* FAINT. These words reveal the prophet's profound grief over the sin and the destruction of God's people. He is torn by his loyalty to God and his deep ties to the people. He is in such anguish that he wants to leave the people forever (9:2). Believers experience this same kind of grief when they see their loved ones live in rebellion against God and His righteous ways. Vicariously, they experience the suffering of God as they anticipate the disaster awaiting those who will not repent.

9:1–26 MY EYES A FOUNTAIN OF TEARS. Jeremiah continues to express his anguish over God's rebellious people and their refusal to repent and thereby escape from the coming destruction. He wanted to weep, but his pain was too deep for tears. Cries of woe, charges of guilt, and warnings

tears, that I might weep day and night
for the slain of the daughter of my peo-
ple!
2 Oh that I had in the wilderness a
lodging place of wayfaring men; that I
might leave my people, and go from
them! for [t]they *be* all adulterers, an
assembly of treacherous men.
3 And [u]they bend their tongues *like*
their bow *for* lies: but they are not val-
iant for the truth upon the earth; for
they proceed from evil to evil, and they
[v]know not me, saith the LORD.
4 [w]Take ye heed every one of his
[s]neighbour, and trust ye not in any
brother: for every brother will utterly
supplant, and every neighbour will
[x]walk with slanders.
5 And they will [t]deceive every one
his neighbour, and will not speak the
truth: they have taught their tongue to
speak lies, *and* weary themselves to
commit iniquity.
6 Thine habitation *is* in the midst of
deceit; through deceit they refuse to
know me, saith the LORD.
7 Therefore thus saith the LORD of
hosts, Behold, [y]I will melt them, and
try them; [z]for how shall I do for the
daughter of my people?
8 Their tongue *is as* an arrow shot
out; it speaketh [a]deceit: *one* speaketh
[b]peaceably to his neighbour with his
mouth, but [c]in heart he layeth [u]his
wait.
9 ¶ [d]Shall I not visit them for these
things? saith the LORD: shall not my
soul be avenged on such a nation as
this?
10 For the mountains will I take up
a weeping and wailing, and [e]for the
[v]habitations of the wilderness a lam-
entation, because they are [w]burned
up, so that none can pass through
them; neither can *men* hear the voice of
the cattle; [f]both[x] the fowl of the
heavens and the beast are fled; they
are gone.
11 And I will make Jerusalem
[g]heaps, *and* [h]a den of dragons; and I
will make the cities of Judah [y]deso-
late, without an inhabitant.
12 ¶ [i]Who *is* the wise man, that
may understand this? and *who is he* to

9:2 [t]ch. 5:7,8
9:3 [u]Ps. 64:3 [v]1 Sam. 2:12
9:4 [w]Mic. 7:5,6 [x]ch. 6:28
9:7 [y]Is. 1:25 [z]Hos. 11:8
9:8 [a]Ps. 12:2 [b]Ps. 55:21 [c]Heb. *in the midst of him*
9:9 [d]ch. 5:9,29
9:10 [e]Hos. 4:3 [f]ch. 4:25
9:11 [g]Is. 25:2 [h]Is. 13:22 & 34:13
9:12 [i]Hos. 14:9
9:14 [j]ch. 7:24 [k]Or, *stubbornness* [l]Gal. 1:14
9:15 [m]Ps. 80:5 [n]ch. 8:14 Lam. 3:19
9:16 [o]Lev. 26:33 Deut. 28:64 [p]Lev. 26:33 ch. 44:27 Ezek. 5:2
9:17 [q]2 Chr. 35:25 Job 3:8 Eccl. 12:5 Amos 5:16 Mat. 9:23
9:18 [r]ch. 14:17
9:19 [s]Lev. 18:28
9:21 [t]ch. 6:11
9:22 [u]ch. 8:2

whom the mouth of the LORD hath spo-
ken, that he may declare it, for what
the land perisheth *and* is burned up
like a wilderness, that none passeth
through?
13 And the LORD saith, Because
they have forsaken my law which I set
before them, and have not obeyed my
voice, neither walked therein;
14 But have [j]walked after the
[k]imagination of their own heart, and
after Baalim, [l]which their fathers
taught them:
15 Therefore thus saith the LORD of
hosts, the God of Israel; Behold, I will
[m]feed them, *even* this people, [n]with
wormwood, and give them water of gall
to drink.
16 I will [o]scatter them also among
the heathen, whom neither they nor
their fathers have known: [p]and I will
send a sword after them, till I have
consumed them.
17 ¶ Thus saith the LORD of hosts,
Consider ye, and call for [q]the mourn-
ing women, that they may come; and
send for cunning *women,* that they may
come:
18 And let them make haste, and
take up a wailing for us, that [r]our
eyes may run down with tears, and our
eyelids gush out with waters.
19 For a voice of wailing is heard
out of Zion, How are we spoiled! we are
greatly confounded, because we have
forsaken the land, because [s]our
dwellings have cast *us* out.
20 Yet hear the word of the LORD,
O ye women, and let your ear receive
the word of his mouth, and teach your
daughters wailing, and every one her
neighbour lamentation.
21 For death is come up into our
windows, *and* is entered into our pal-
aces, to cut off [t]the children from
without, *and* the young men from the
streets.
22 Speak, Thus saith the LORD,
Even the carcases of men shall fall
[u]as dung upon the open field, and as

[s]Or, *friend* [t]Or, *mock* [u]Or, *wait for him* [v]Or, *pastures* [w]Or, *desolate* [x]Heb. *from the fowl even to* [y]Heb. *desolation*

of inescapable judgment are interspersed throughout the chapter. Jeremiah is often called the "weeping prophet" (cf. 14:17), weeping night and day for a people too hardhearted to realize the impending doom coming upon them. Because of his intense emotions of sorrow, Jeremiah is traditionally considered to be the author of the book of Lamentations (see the introduction to Lamentations).

the handful after the harvestman, and none shall gather *them*.

23 ¶ Thus saith the LORD, [v]Let not the wise *man* glory in his wisdom, neither let the mighty *man* glory in his might, let not the rich *man* glory in his riches:

24 But [w]let him that glorieth glory in this, that he understandeth and knoweth me, that I *am* the LORD which exercise lovingkindness, judgment, and righteousness, in the earth: [x]for in these *things* I delight, saith the LORD.

25 ¶ Behold, the days come, saith the LORD, that [y]I will [z]punish all *them which are* circumcised with the uncircumcised;

26 Egypt, and Judah, and Edom, and the children of Ammon, and Moab, and all *that are* [a]in the [z]utmost corners, that dwell in the wilderness: for all *these* nations *are* uncircumcised, and all the house of Israel *are* [a]uncircumcised in the heart.

The living God and dead gods

10:12–16pp — Jer. 51:15–19

10 HEAR YE the word which the LORD speaketh unto you, O house of Israel:

2 Thus saith the LORD, [b]Learn not the way of the heathen, and be not dismayed at the signs of heaven; for the heathen are dismayed at them.

3 For the [b]customs of the people *are* vain: for [c]*one* cutteth a tree out of the forest, the work of the hands of the workman, with the axe.

4 They deck it with silver and with gold; they [d]fasten it with nails and with hammers, that it move not.

5 They *are* upright as the palm tree, [e]but speak not: they must needs be [f]borne, because they cannot go. Be not afraid of them; for [g]they cannot do evil, neither also *is it* in them to do good.

6 Forasmuch as *there is* none [h]like unto thee, O LORD; thou *art* great, and thy name *is* great in might.

9:23 [v]Eccl. 9:11
9:24 [w]1 Cor. 1:31; 2 Cor. 10:17; [x]Mic. 7:18
9:25 [y]Rom. 2:8,9
9:26 [z]ch. 25:23; [a]Lev. 26:41; Ezek. 44:7; Rom. 2:28
10:2 [b]Lev. 18:3
10:3 [c]Is. 40:19 & 45:20
10:4 [d]Is. 41:7
10:5 [e]Ps. 115:5; Hab. 2:19; 1 Cor. 12:2; [f]Ps. 115:7; Is. 46:1,7; [g]Is. 41:23
10:6 [h]Ex. 15:11; Ps. 86:8,10
10:7 [i]Rev. 15:4; [j]Ps. 89:6
10:8 [k]Ps. 115:8; Hab. 2:18
10:9 [l]Dan. 10:5; [m]Ps. 115:4
10:10 [n]Ps. 31:5; [o]1 Tim. 6:17; [p]Ps. 10:16
10:11 [q]Ps. 96:5; [r]Zech. 13:2
10:12 [s]Gen. 1:1,6; Ps. 136:5; [t]Ps. 93:1; [u]Job 9:8; Ps. 104:2; Is. 40:22
10:13 [v]Job 38:34; [w]Ps. 135:7
10:14 [x]ch. 51:17; [y]Prov. 30:2; [z]Is. 42:17 & 44:11; [a]Hab. 2:18

7 [i]Who would not fear thee, O King of nations? for [c]to thee doth it appertain: forasmuch as [j]among all the wise *men* of the nations, and in all their kingdoms, *there is* none like unto thee.

8 But they are [d]altogether [k]brutish and foolish: the stock *is* a doctrine of vanities.

9 Silver spread into plates is brought from Tarshish, and [l]gold from Uphaz, the work of the workman, and of the hands of the founder: blue and purple *is* their clothing: they *are* all [m]the work of cunning *men*.

10 But the LORD *is* the [n]true[e] God, he *is* [o]the living God, and an [p]everlasting[f] king: at his wrath the earth shall tremble, and the nations shall not be able to abide his indignation.

11 [g]Thus shall ye say unto them, [q]The gods that have not made the heavens and the earth, *even* [r]they shall perish from the earth, and from under these heavens.

12 He [s]hath made the earth by his power, he hath [t]established the world by his wisdom, and [u]hath stretched out the heavens by his discretion.

13 [v]When he uttereth his voice, *there is* a [h]multitude of waters in the heavens, and [w]he causeth the vapours to ascend from the ends of the earth; he maketh lightnings [i]with rain, and bringeth forth the wind out of his treasures.

14 [x]Every man [j]is [y]brutish in *his* knowledge: [z]every founder is confounded by the graven image: [a]for his molten image *is* falsehood, and *there is* no breath in them.

15 They *are* vanity, *and* the work of

[z] Heb. *visit upon* [a] Heb. *cut off into corners,* or, *having the corners* of their hair *polled* [b] Heb. *statutes,* or, *ordinances are vanity* [c] Or, *it liketh thee* [d] Heb. *in one, or, at once* [e] Heb. *God of truth* [f] Heb. *king of eternity* [g] Ver. 11 is in the Chaldean language [h] Or, *noise* [i] Or, *for rain* [j] Or, *is more brutish than to know*

9:24 LET HIM THAT GLORIETH GLORY IN THIS. We must not boast in worldly knowledge, human ability, or earthly riches (v. 23); instead, we must exult and rejoice only in our personal relationship with the Lord and in His grace, which enables us to live righteously. All earthly values pale in significance when compared to the joy of knowing God. True worth consists in committing ourselves to the Lord God and His standards and in allowing Him to fill us with His Holy Spirit.

10:2–16 LEARN NOT THE WAY OF THE HEATHEN. Because of the threat of the Babylonian invasion, the people turned more and more to idols and to the astrology and spiritism of the surrounding nations. Jeremiah warns the people against such action, declaring that the Lord God is the one true God who created all things (vv. 10–12).

errors: in the time of their visitation
they shall perish.
16 [b]The portion of Jacob *is* not like
them: for he *is* the former of all *things;*
and [c]Israel *is* the rod of his inheri-
tance: [d]The LORD of hosts *is* his name.

Coming distress

17 ¶ [e]Gather up thy wares out of
the land, O [k]inhabitant of the fortress.
18 For thus saith the LORD, Behold,
I will [f]sling out the inhabitants of the
land at this once, and will distress
them, [g]that they may find *it so.*
19 ¶ [h]Woe is me for my hurt! my
wound is grievous: but I said, [i]Truly
this *is* a grief, and [j]I must bear it.
20 [k]My tabernacle is spoiled, and
all my cords are broken: my children
are gone forth of me, and they *are* not:
there is none to stretch forth my tent
any more, and to set up my curtains.
21 For the pastors are become brut-
ish, and have not sought the LORD:
therefore they shall not prosper, and
all their flocks shall be scattered.
22 Behold, the noise of the bruit is
come, and a great commotion out of the
[l]north country, to make the cities of
Judah desolate, *and* a [m]den of dragons.
23 ¶ O LORD, I know that the [n]way
of man *is* not in himself: *it is* not in man
that walketh to direct his steps.
24 O LORD, [o]correct me, but with
judgment; not in thine anger, lest thou
[1]bring me to nothing.
25 [p]Pour out thy fury upon the
heathen [q]that know thee not, and
upon the families that call not on thy
name: for they have eaten up Jacob,
and [r]devoured him, and consumed
him, and have made his habitation des-
olate.

Judah has broken the covenant

11 THE WORD that came to Jere-
miah from the LORD, saying,
2 Hear ye the words of this cov-
enant, and speak unto the men of Ju-
dah, and to the inhabitants of Jerusa-
lem;
3 And say thou unto them, Thus
saith the LORD God of Israel; [s]Cursed
be the man that obeyeth not the words
of this covenant,
4 Which I commanded your fathers
in the day *that* I brought them forth out
of the land of Egypt, [t]from the iron
furnace, saying, [u]Obey my voice, and
do them, according to all which I com-
mand you: so shall ye be my people,
and I will be your God:
5 That I may perform the [v]oath
which I have sworn unto your fathers,
to give them a land flowing with milk
and honey, as *it is* this day. Then an- Ezek.
swered I, and said, [m]So be it, O LORD. 20:39-44
6 Then the LORD said unto me, Pro-
claim all these words in the cities of
Judah, and in the streets of Jerusalem,
saying, Hear ye the words of this cov-
enant, [w]and do them.
7 For I earnestly protested unto
your fathers in the day *that* I brought
them up out of the land of Egypt, *even*
unto this day, [x]rising early and pro-
testing, saying, Obey my voice.
8 [y]Yet they obeyed not, nor in-
clined their ear, but [z]walked every
one in the [n]imagination of their evil
heart: therefore I will bring upon them
all the words of this covenant, which I
commanded *them* to do; but they did
them not.
9 And the LORD said unto me, [a]A
conspiracy is found among the men of
Judah, and among the inhabitants of Je-
rusalem.
10 They are turned back to [b]the in-
iquities of their forefathers, which re-
fused to hear my words; and they went
after other gods to serve them: the
house of Israel and the house of Judah
have broken my covenant which I
made with their fathers.

10:16 [b]Lam. 3:24 [c]Deut. 32:9 [d]Is. 47:4 & 54:5
10:17 [e]ch. 6:1 Ezek. 12:3
10:18 [f]1 Sam. 25:29 [g]Ezek. 6:10
10:19 [h]ch. 8:21 [i]Ps. 77:10 [j]Mic. 7:9
10:20 [k]ch. 4:20
10:22 [l]ch. 5:15 [m]ch. 9:11
10:23 [n]Prov. 16:1
10:24 [o]ch. 30:11
10:25 [p]Ps. 79:6 [q]Job 18:21 [r]ch. 8:16
11:3 [s]Deut. 27:26
11:4 [t]Deut. 4:20 [u]Lev. 26:12 ch. 7:23
11:5 [v]Deut. 7:12 Ps. 105:9
11:6 [w]Rom. 2:13 Jas. 1:22
11:7 [x]ch. 35:15
11:8 [y]ch. 7:26 [z]ch. 9:14
11:9 [a]Ezek. 22:25
11:10 [b]Ezek. 20:18

[k] Heb. *inhabitress* [1] Heb. *diminish me* [m] Heb. *Amen* [n] Or, *stubbornness*

10:17–22 GATHER UP THY WARES. The invasion of the Babylonians was so imminent and the accompanying disaster so real to Jeremiah that he uttered words of lament that the people would wail in exile (vv. 19–20).

10:25 POUR OUT THY FURY UPON THE HEATHEN. Jeremiah prays that the invaders who had so cruelly preyed upon the Israelites would themselves experience the full tide of God's wrath, which they so richly deserved (cf. Ps. 79:6–7).

11:3 CURSED *BE* THE MAN THAT OBEYETH NOT. Israel had made a covenant with God, promising to obey Him as their Lord and God. In return God would be their God and would give them the deed to the land of Canaan and the protection that they needed (see article on GOD'S COVENANT WITH THE ISRAELITES, p. 314). But the people had persisted in disobedience and turned to other gods. Hence the covenant curses pronounced for disobedience would go into effect (cf. Deut. 28).

11 ¶ Therefore thus saith the LORD, Behold, I will bring evil upon them, which they shall not be able [o]to escape; and [c]though they shall cry unto me, I will not hearken unto them.

12 Then shall the cities of Judah and inhabitants of Jerusalem go, and [d]cry unto the gods unto whom they offer incense: but they shall not save them at all in the time of their [p]trouble.

13 For *according to* the number of thy [e]cities were thy gods, O Judah; and *according to* the number of the streets of Jerusalem have ye set up altars to *that* [f]shameful[q] thing, *even* altars to burn incense unto Baal.

14 Therefore [g]pray not thou for this people, neither lift up a cry or prayer for them: for I will not hear *them* in the time that they cry unto me for their [p]trouble.

15 [h]What[r] hath my beloved to do in mine house, *seeing* she hath [i]wrought lewdness with many, and [j]the holy flesh is passed from thee? [s]when thou doest evil, then thou [k]rejoicest.

16 The LORD called thy name, [l]A green olive tree, fair, *and* of goodly fruit: with the noise of a great tumult he hath kindled fire upon it, and the branches of it are broken.

17 For the LORD of hosts, [m]that planted thee, hath pronounced evil against thee, for the evil of the house of Israel and of the house of Judah, which they have done against themselves to provoke me to anger in offering incense unto Baal.

The certainty of doom

18 ¶ And the LORD hath given me knowledge *of it,* and I know *it:* then thou showedst me their doings.

19 But I *was* like a lamb *or* an ox *that* is brought to the slaughter; and I knew not that they had devised devices against me, *saying,* Let us destroy [t]the tree with the fruit thereof, [n]and let us cut him off from [o]the land of the living, that his name may be no more remembered.

20 But, O LORD of hosts, that judgest righteously, that [p]triest the reins and the heart, let me see thy vengeance on them: for unto thee have I revealed my cause.

21 Therefore thus saith the LORD of the men of Anathoth, [q]that seek thy life, saying, [r]Prophesy not in the name of the LORD, that thou die not by our hand:

22 Therefore thus saith the LORD of hosts, Behold, I will [u]punish them: the young men shall die by the sword; their sons and their daughters shall die by famine:

23 And there shall be no remnant of them: for I will bring evil upon the men of Anathoth, *even* [s]the year of their visitation.

Jeremiah's prayer

12 RIGHTEOUS [t]*ART* thou, O LORD, when I plead with thee: yet [v]let me talk with thee of *thy* judgments: [u]Wherefore doth the way of the wicked prosper? *wherefore* are all they happy that deal very treacherously?

2 Thou hast planted them, yea, they have taken root: [w]they grow, yea, they bring forth fruit: [v]thou *art* near in

11:11 [c]Ps. 18:41 Prov. 1:28
11:12 [d]Deut. 32:37
11:13 [e]ch. 2:28 [f]ch. 3:24
11:14 [g]Ex. 32:10
11:15 [h]Ps. 50:16 [i]Ezek. 16:25 [j]Tit. 1:15 [k]Prov. 2:14
11:16 [l]Ps. 52:8
11:17 [m]Is. 5:2
11:19 [n]Ps. 83:4 [o]Ps. 27:13
11:20 [p]1 Chr. 28:9 Ps. 7:9
11:21 [q]ch. 12:5,6 [r]Mic. 2:6
11:23 [s]ch. 23:12
12:1 [t]Ps. 51:4 [u]Mal. 3:15
12:2 [v]Mat. 15:8

[o]Heb. *to go forth of* [p]Heb. *evil* [q]Heb. *shame* [r]Heb. *What is to my beloved in my house* [s]Or, *when thy evil is* [t]Heb. *the stalk with his bread* [u]Heb. *visit upon* [v]Or, *let me reason the case with thee* [w]Heb. *they go on*

11:14 PRAY NOT THOU FOR THIS PEOPLE. Several times God instructed Jeremiah not to pray or intercede for the people (cf. 7:16; 14:11). The people so persisted in rebellion against the Lord and were so attached to their idols that prayer for them would do no good. God had resolved to give them no help when their time of destruction came. This passage warns us that our prayers might not be answered by God if we are not making a sincere effort to obey Him and follow His ways (see article on EFFECTIVE PRAYING, p. 540).

11:19–23 DEVISED DEVICES AGAINST ME. A number of men of Anathoth (Jeremiah's hometown) plotted against Jeremiah; they wanted to kill him because he had remained faithful to the Lord God and exposed their sins and idolatry. God assured the prophet that the conspirators would neither succeed in their plot nor survive the day of punishment. Jeremiah continued to proclaim God's word despite persecution.

12:1–4 WHEREFORE DOTH THE WAY OF THE WICKED PROSPER? Jeremiah contrasted his own suffering with the prosperity of the wicked. He was confused by the delay of God's judgment on such people. The material success of the wicked was a recurring problem for O.T. saints, for they thought mainly in terms of temporal rewards and punishments (see Job 21:7–15; Ps. 10: 37; 73; 94; Hab. 1:5–13; Mal. 3:15).

their mouth, and far from their reins.
3 But thou, O LORD, [w]knowest me:
thou hast seen me, and [x]tried mine
heart [x]toward thee: pull them out like
sheep for the slaughter, and prepare
them for [y]the day of slaughter.
4 How long shall [z]the land mourn,
and the herbs of every field wither,
[a]for the wickedness of them that
dwell therein? [b]the beasts are con-
sumed, and the birds; because they
said, He shall not see our last end.

God's answer

5 ¶ If thou hast run with the foot-
men, and they have wearied thee, then
how canst thou contend with horses?
and *if* in the land of peace, *wherein* thou
trustedst, *they wearied thee,* then how
wilt thou do in [c]the swelling of Jor-
dan?
6 For even [d]thy brethren, and the
house of thy father, even they have
dealt treacherously with thee; yea,
[y]they have called a multitude after
thee: [e]believe them not, though they
speak [z]fair words unto thee.
7 ¶ I have forsaken mine house, I
have left mine heritage; I have given
[a]the dearly beloved of my soul into
the hand of her enemies.
8 Mine heritage is unto me as a lion
in the forest; it [b] [c]crieth out against
me: therefore have I hated it.
9 Mine heritage *is* unto me *as* a
[d]speckled bird, the birds round about
are against her; come ye, assemble all
the beasts of the field, [f]come[e] to de-
vour.
10 Many [g]pastors have destroyed
[h]my vineyard, they have [i]trodden my
portion under foot, they have made my
[f]pleasant portion a desolate wilder-
ness.
11 They have made it desolate, *and*
being desolate [j]it mourneth unto me;
the whole land is made desolate, be-
cause [k]no man layeth *it* to heart.
12 The spoilers are come upon all
high places through the wilderness: for
the sword of the LORD shall devour from
the *one* end of the land even to the *other*
end of the land: no flesh shall have
peace.
13 [l]They have sown wheat, but
shall reap thorns: they have put them-
selves to pain, *but* shall not profit: and
[g]they shall be ashamed of your reve-
nues because of the fierce anger of the
LORD.
14 ¶ Thus saith the LORD against all
mine evil neighbours, that [m]touch the
inheritance which I have caused my
people Israel to inherit; Behold, I will
[n]pluck them out of their land, and
pluck out the house of Judah from
among them.
15 [o]And it shall come to pass, after
that I have plucked them out I will re-
turn, and have compassion on them,
[p]and will bring them again, every man
to his heritage, and every man to his
land.
16 And it shall come to pass, if they
will diligently learn the ways of my
people, [q]to swear by my name, The
LORD liveth; as they taught my people
to swear by Baal; then shall they be
[r]built in the midst of my people.
17 But if they will not [s]obey, I will
utterly pluck up and destroy that na-
tion, saith the LORD.

The parable of the girdle

13 THUS SAITH the LORD unto me,
Go and get thee a linen girdle,

12:3 [w]Ps. 17:3 [x]ch. 11:20 [y]Jas. 5:5 **12:4** [z]Hos. 4:3 [a]Ps. 107:34 [b]ch. 9:10 **12:5** [c]Josh. 3:15 1 Chr. 12:15 **12:6** [d]ch. 9:4 [e]Prov. 26:25 **12:9** [f]Is. 56:9 **12:10** [g]ch. 6:3 [h]Is. 5:1,5 [i]Is. 63:18 **12:11** [j]ver. 4 [k]Is. 42:25 **12:13** [l]Lev. 26:16 Deut. 28:38 Mic. 6:15 Hag. 1:6 **12:14** [m]Zech. 2:8 [n]Deut. 30:3 ch. 32:37 **12:15** [o]Ezek. 28:25 [p]Amos 9:14 **12:16** [q]ch. 4:2 [r]Eph. 2:20,21 1 Pet. 2:5 **12:17** [s]Is. 60:12

[x] Heb. *with thee* [y] Or, *they cried after thee fully* [z] Heb. *good things* [a] Heb. *the love* [b] Or, *yelleth* [c] Heb. *giveth out his voice* [d] Or, *taloned* [e] Or, *cause them to come* [f] Heb. *portion of desire* [g] Or, *ye*

12:5 THEY HAVE WEARIED THEE. What Jeremiah endured at the hands of the priests in Anathoth was nothing compared to the persecutions yet to come. Therefore, he was to prepare himself with faith and courage to face the greater trials ahead.

12:6 EVEN THY BRETHREN. Evidently some of Jeremiah's own family had turned against him and dealt treacherously with him.

12:7–13 I HAVE FORSAKEN MINE HOUSE. The Lord Himself laments the deplorable spiritual condition of the people and the desolation coming upon the land. God experiences immense pain and sorrow whenever He must deliver His people over to the consequences of their sins.

12:16–17 IT SHALL COME TO PASS. Jeremiah has the Messianic age in view here. The nations will be given an inheritance among God's people if they learn the ways of God and worship Him in truth. If they rebel, however, they will be destroyed.

13:1–11 A LINEN GIRDLE. Jeremiah's symbolic act involving the linen girdle gave the people a parabolic object lesson. Israel and Judah were the linen girdle worn by the Lord, symbolizing the close relationship that He once had with them when they were faithful to Him. Now the people had become worthless and must be cast off, just

and put it upon thy loins, and put it not in water.

2 So I got a girdle according to the word of the LORD, and put *it* on my loins.

3 And the word of the LORD came unto me the second time, saying,

4 Take the girdle that thou hast got, which *is* upon thy loins, and arise, go to Euphrates, and hide it there in a hole of the rock.

5 So I went, and hid it by Euphrates, as the LORD commanded me.

6 And it came to pass after many days, that the LORD said unto me, Arise, go to Euphrates, and take the girdle from thence, which I commanded thee to hide there.

7 Then I went to Euphrates, and digged, and took the girdle from the place where I had hid it: and, behold, the girdle was marred, it was profitable for nothing.

8 Then the word of the LORD came unto me, saying,

9 Thus saith the LORD, After this manner [t]will I mar the pride of Judah, and the great pride of Jerusalem.

10 This evil people, which refuse to hear my words, which [u]walk in the [h]imagination of their heart, and walk after other gods, to serve them, and to worship them, shall even be as this girdle, which is good for nothing.

11 For as the girdle cleaveth to the loins of a man, so have I caused to cleave unto me the whole house of Israel and the whole house of Judah, saith the LORD; that [v]they might be unto me for a people, and [w]for a name, and for a praise, and for a glory: but they would not hear.

The parable of the bottles

12 ¶ Therefore thou shalt speak unto them this word; Thus saith the LORD God of Israel, Every bottle shall be filled with wine: and they shall say unto thee, Do we not certainly know that every bottle shall be filled with wine?

13 Then shalt thou say unto them, Thus saith the LORD, Behold, I will fill all the inhabitants of this land, even the kings that sit upon David's throne, and the priests, and the prophets, and all the inhabitants of Jerusalem, [x]with drunkenness.

14 And [y]I will dash them [i]one against another, even the fathers and the sons together, saith the LORD: I will not pity, nor spare, nor have mercy, [j]but destroy them.

The pride and shame of Jerusalem

15 ¶ Hear ye, and give ear; be not proud: for the LORD hath spoken.

16 Give glory to the LORD your God, before he cause [z]darkness, and before your feet stumble upon the dark mountains, and, while ye [a]look for light, he turn it into [b]the shadow of death, *and* make *it* gross darkness.

17 But if ye will not hear it, my soul shall weep in secret places for *your* pride; and [c]mine eye shall weep sore, and run down with tears, because the LORD's flock is carried away captive.

18 Say unto [d]the king and to the queen, Humble yourselves, sit down: for your [k]principalities shall come down, *even* the crown of your glory.

19 The cities of the south shall be shut up, and none shall open *them:* Judah shall be carried away captive all of it, it shall be wholly carried away captive.

20 Lift up your eyes, and behold them [e]that come from the north: where *is* the flock *that* was given thee, thy beautiful flock?

21 What wilt thou say when he shall [l]punish thee? for thou hast taught them *to be* captains, *and* as chief over thee: shall not [f]sorrows take thee, as a woman in travail?

22 ¶ And if thou say in thine heart, [g]Wherefore come these things upon me? For the greatness of thine iniquity

13:9 [t]Lev. 26:19
13:10 [u]ch. 9:14 & 11:8 & 16:12
13:11 [v]Ex. 19:5 [w]ch. 33:9
13:13 [x]Is. 51:17,21 & 63:6 ch. 25:27 & 51:7
13:14 [y]Ps. 2:9
13:16 [z]Is. 5:30 & 8:22 Amos 8:9 [a]Is. 59:9 [b]Ps. 44:19
13:17 [c]ch. 9:1 & 14:17 Lam. 1:2,16 & 2:18
13:18 [d]2 Ki. 24:12 ch. 22:26
13:20 [e]ch. 6:22
13:21 [f]ch. 6:24
13:22 [g]ch. 16:10

[h] Or, *stubbornness* [i] Heb. *a man against his brother* [j] Heb. *from destroying them* [k] Or, *head tires* [l] Heb. *visit upon*

as Jeremiah did with the linen cloth. During the people's exile in the area of the Euphrates, they would be worthless because of their sin. All their glory and pride would disappear.

13:12–14 EVERY BOTTLE SHALL BE FILLED WITH WINE. The empty bottles are the people of Judah. They would be filled with "drunkenness," i.e., judgment and confusion (cf. 25:15–16; Is. 49:26; 63:6), and then they would be broken and destroyed.

13:22 THE GREATNESS OF THINE INIQUITY. When judgment came, the people had to know that it was happening to them because of their many sins. They were so accustomed to doing evil that they could not change (v. 23).

are [h]thy skirts discovered, *and* thy
heels [m]made bare.
23 Can the Ethiopian change his
skin, or the leopard his spots? *then* may
ye also do good, that are [n]accustomed
to do evil.
24 Therefore will I scatter them
[i]as the stubble that passeth away by
the wind of the wilderness.
25 [j]This *is* thy lot, the portion of
thy measures from me, saith the LORD;
because thou hast forgotten me, and
trusted in [k]falsehood.
26 Therefore [l]will I discover thy
skirts upon thy face, that thy shame
may appear.
27 I have seen thine adulteries, and
thy [m]neighings, the lewdness of thy
whoredom, *and* thine abominations
[n]on the hills in the fields. Woe unto
thee, O Jerusalem! wilt thou not be
made clean? [o]when *shall it* once *be?*

Judah beyond deliverance

14 THE WORD of the LORD that
came to Jeremiah concerning
[p]the dearth.
2 Judah mourneth, and [o]the gates
thereof languish; they are [p]black unto
the ground; and [q]the cry of Jerusalem
is gone up.
3 And their nobles have sent their
little ones to the waters: they came to
the pits, *and* found no water; they re-
turned with their vessels empty; they
were [r]ashamed and confounded,
[s]and covered their heads.
4 Because the ground is chapt, for
there was no rain in the earth, the
plowmen were ashamed, they covered
their heads.
5 Yea, the hind also calved in the
field, and forsook *it*, because there was
no grass.
6 And [t]the wild asses did stand in
the high places, they snuffed up the
wind like dragons; their eyes did fail,
because *there was* no grass.
7 ¶ O LORD, though our iniquities
testify against us, do thou *it* [u]for thy
name's sake: for our backslidings are
many; we have sinned against thee.
8 [v]O the hope of Israel, the saviour
thereof in time of trouble, why should-
est thou be as a stranger in the land,
and as a wayfaring man *that* turneth
aside to tarry for a night?
9 Why shouldest thou be as a man
astonied, as a mighty man [w]*that* can-
not save? yet thou, O LORD, [x]*art* in the
midst of us, and [q]we are called by thy
name; leave us not.
10 ¶ Thus saith the LORD unto this
people, [y]Thus have they loved to wan-
der, they have not refrained their feet,
therefore the LORD doth not accept
them; [z]he will now remember their in-
iquity, and visit their sins.
11 Then said the LORD unto me,
[a]Pray not for this people for *their*
good.
12 [b]When they fast, I will not hear
their cry; and [c]when they offer burnt
offering and an oblation, I will not ac-
cept them: but [d]I will consume them
by the sword, and by the famine, and by
the pestilence.
13 ¶ [e]Then said I, Ah, Lord GOD!
behold, the prophets say unto them, Ye
shall not see the sword, neither shall
ye have famine; but I will give you
[r]assured peace in this place.
14 Then the LORD said unto me,
[f]The prophets prophesy lies in my
name: [g]I sent them not, neither have
I commanded them, neither spake unto
them: they prophesy unto you a false
vision and divination, and a thing of
nought, and the deceit of their heart.
15 Therefore thus saith the LORD
concerning the prophets that prophesy
in my name, and I sent them not, [h]yet

13:22 [h]Is. 3:17 & 47:2,3 Ezek. 16:37-39 Nah. 3:5 **13:24** [i]Ps. 1:4 Hos. 13:3 **13:25** [j]Job 20:29 Ps. 11:6 [k]ch. 10:14 **13:26** [l]Lam. 1:8 Ezek. 16:37 Hos. 2:10 **13:27** [m]ch. 5:8 [n]Is. 65:7 ch. 2:20 **14:2** [o]Is. 3:26 [p]ch. 8:21 [q]1 Sam. 5:12 **14:3** [r]Ps. 40:14 [s]2 Sam. 15:30 **14:6** [t]ch. 2:24 **14:7** [u]Ps. 25:11 **14:8** [v]ch. 17:13 **14:9** [w]Is. 59:1 [x]Ex. 29:45 Lev. 26:11 **14:10** [y]See ch. 2:23-25 [z]Hos. 8:13 **14:11** [a]Ex. 32:10 **14:12** [b]Prov. 1:28 Is. 1:15 Ezek. 8:18 Zech. 7:13 [c]ch. 6:20 [d]ch. 9:16 **14:13** [e]ch. 4:10 **14:14** [f]ch. 27:10 [g]ch. 29:8,9 **14:15** [h]ch. 5:12

[m] Or, *shall be violently taken away* [n] Heb. *taught* [o] Heb. *after when yet?* [p] Heb. *the words of the dearths,* or, *restraints* [q] Heb. *thy name is called upon us* [r] Heb. *peace of truth*

14:1 CONCERNING THE DEARTH. This chapter speaks of the disastrous effects of a drought on the people and the land. God sent this natural disaster upon Judah during its final years because of their unfaithfulness to Him and His covenant (cf. Lev. 26:18–19; Deut. 28:22–24). The people had rejected God—the spring of living water (2:13)—and now they would lose their supply of natural water.

14:7–12 O LORD . . . OUR INIQUITIES TESTIFY AGAINST US. The people cried to God for rain, yet the Lord refused to answer these prayers as a testimony to the inescapable judgment they had to bear because of their sin. All who continue in sin should realize that a time may come when God refuses to hear their prayers and sends the punishment their sins deserve.

14:14 THE PROPHETS PROPHESY LIES. God's people must be aware that some prophets in their midst may prophesy lies and falsely claim to have received visions from the Lord. For this reason all prophets must be tested according to Biblical standards (see 1 Cor. 14:29, note; see article on FALSE TEACHERS, p. 1508).

they say, Sword and famine shall not be in this land; By sword and famine shall those prophets be consumed.

16 And the people to whom they prophesy shall be cast out in the streets of Jerusalem because of the famine and the sword; [i]and they shall have none to bury them, them, their wives, nor their sons, nor their daughters: for I will pour their wickedness upon them.

17 ¶ Therefore thou shalt say this word unto them; [j]Let mine eyes run down with tears night and day, and let them not cease: [k]for the virgin daughter of my people is broken with a great breach, with a very grievous blow.

18 If I go forth into [l]the field, then behold the slain with the sword! and if I enter into the city, then behold them that are sick with famine! yea, both the prophet and the priest [m]go[s] about into a land that they know not.

19 [n]Hast thou utterly rejected Judah? hath thy soul loathed Zion? why hast thou smitten us, and [o]*there is* no healing for us? [p]we looked for peace, and *there is* no good; and for the time of healing, and behold trouble!

20 We acknowledge, O LORD, our wickedness, *and* the iniquity of our fathers: for [q]we have sinned against thee.

21 Do not abhor *us,* for thy name's sake, do not disgrace the throne of thy glory: [r]remember, break not thy covenant with us.

22 [s]Are there *any* among [t]the vanities of the Gentiles that can cause rain? or can the heavens give showers? [u]*art* not thou he, O LORD our God? therefore we will wait upon thee: for thou hast made all these *things.*

15

THEN SAID the LORD unto me, [v]Though [w]Moses and [x]Samuel stood before me, *yet* my mind *could* not *be* toward this people: cast *them* out of my sight, and let them go forth.

2 And it shall come to pass, if they say unto thee, Whither shall we go forth? then thou shalt tell them, Thus saith the LORD; [y]Such as *are* for death, to death; and such as *are* for the sword, to the sword; and such as *are* for the famine, to the famine; and such as *are* for the captivity, to the captivity.

3 And I will [z]appoint over them four [t]kinds, saith the LORD: the sword to slay, and the dogs to tear, and [a]the fowls of the heaven, and the beasts of the earth, to devour and destroy.

4 And [u]I will cause them to be [b]removed into all kingdoms of the earth, because of [c]Manasseh the son of Hezekiah king of Judah, for *that* which he did in Jerusalem.

5 For who shall have pity upon thee, O Jerusalem? or who shall bemoan thee? or who shall go aside [v]to ask how thou doest?

6 [d]Thou hast forsaken me, saith the LORD, thou art [e]gone backward: therefore will I stretch out my hand against thee, and destroy thee; [f]I am weary with repenting.

7 And I will fan them with a fan in the gates of the land; I will bereave *them* of [w]children, I will destroy my people, *since* they return not from their ways.

8 Their widows are increased to me above the sand of the seas: I have brought upon them [x]against the mother of the young men a spoiler at noonday: I have caused *him* to fall upon it suddenly, and terrors upon the city.

9 [g]She that hath borne seven lan-

14:16 [i]Ps. 79:3 **14:17** [j]ch. 9:1 [k]ch. 8:21 **14:18** [l]Ezek. 7:15 [m]ch. 5:31 **14:19** [n]Lam. 5:22 [o]ch. 15:18 [p]ch. 8:15 **14:20** [q]Ps. 106:6 Dan. 9:8 **14:21** [r]Ps. 106:45 **14:22** [s]Zech. 10:1 [t]Deut. 32:21 [u]Ps. 135:7 **15:1** [v]Ezek. 14:14 [w]Ex. 32:11 Ps. 99:6 [x]1 Sam. 7:9 **15:2** [y]Ezek. 5:2 Zech. 11:9 **15:3** [z]Lev. 26:16 [a]Deut. 28:26 **15:4** [b]Deut. 28:25 [c]2 Ki. 24:3,4 **15:6** [d]ch. 2:13 [e]ch. 7:24 [f]Hos. 13:14 **15:9** [g]1 Sam. 2:5

[s] Or, *make merchandise against a land, and* men *acknowledge* it *not* [t] Heb. *families* [u] Heb. *I will give them for a removing* [v] Heb. *to ask of thy peace?* [w] Or, *whatsoever is dear* [x] Or, *against the mother* city *a young man spoiling* or, *against the mother* and *the young men*

14:17 LET MINE EYES RUN DOWN WITH TEARS. Once again, Jeremiah expresses deep sorrow over the coming judgment of God's people and the promised land (cf. 9:18; 13:17; see 9:1–26, note).

15:1–9 THEN THE LORD SAID TO ME. God responds to Jeremiah's intercession in 14:19–22. Because the people had rejected Him and kept on backsliding, the destruction of Jerusalem and the exile to Babylon were inevitable. God said He would ignore even the intercession of Moses and Samuel if they were to stand before Him on behalf of the people (see next note).

15:1 MOSES AND SAMUEL. These were two great intercessors who in the past had pleaded with God on behalf of the children of Israel (cf. Ex. 32:11–14,30–32; Num. 14:13–20; Deut. 9:13–29; 1 Sam. 7:8–9; 12:19–25).

15:4 BECAUSE OF MANASSEH. Manasseh was Judah's most evil king, the one who had led the people into great apostasy (2 Ki. 21:10–15; 23:26; 24:3). He was now dead, but the effects of his sins remained. Judgment would come because of the people's willingness to persist in the unfaithfulness and rebellion inspired by Manasseh.

guisheth: she hath given up the ghost;
[h]her sun is gone down while *it was* yet
day: she hath been ashamed and con-
founded: and the residue of them will
I deliver to the sword before their ene-
mies, saith the LORD.
10 ¶ [i]Woe is me, my mother, that
thou hast borne me a man of strife and
a man of contention to the whole earth!
I have neither lent on usury, nor men
have lent to me on usury; *yet* every one
of them doth curse me.
11 The LORD said, Verily it shall be
well with thy remnant; verily [y]I will
cause [j]the enemy to entreat thee *well*
in the time of evil and in the time of
affliction.
12 Shall iron break the northern
iron and the steel?
13 Thy substance and thy treasures
will I give to the [k]spoil without price,
and *that* for all thy sins, even in all thy
borders.
14 And I will make *thee* to pass with
thine enemies [l]into a land *which* thou
knowest not: for a [m]fire is kindled in
mine anger, *which* shall burn upon you.
15 ¶ O LORD, [n]thou knowest: re-
member me, and visit me, and [o]re-
venge me of my persecutors; take me
not away in thy longsuffering: know
that [p]for thy sake I have suffered re-
buke.
16 Thy words were found, and I did
[q]eat them; and [r]thy word was unto
me the joy and rejoicing of mine heart:
for [z]I am called by thy name, O LORD
God of hosts.
17 [s]I sat not in the assembly of the
mockers, nor rejoiced; I sat alone be-
cause of thy hand: for thou hast filled
me with indignation.

15:9 [h]Amos 8:9
15:10 [i]Job 3:1
15:11 [j]ch. 40:4,5
15:13 [k]Ps. 44:12
15:14 [l]ch. 16:13 [m]Deut. 32:22
15:15 [n]ch. 12:3 [o]ch. 20:12 [p]Ps. 69:7
15:16 [q]Ezek. 3:1,3 Rev. 10:9 [r]Job 23:12 Ps. 119:72
15:17 [s]Ps. 26:4,5
15:18 [t]ch. 30:15 [u]ch. 1:18,19
15:19 [v]Zech. 3:7 [w]ver. 1 [x]Ezek. 22:26
15:20 [y]ch. 20:11
16:4 [z]ch. 15:2 [a]ch. 22:18 & 25:33 [b]Ps. 83:10 ch. 8:2 & 9:22

18 Why is my [t]pain perpetual, and
my wound incurable, *which* refuseth to
be healed? wilt thou be altogether unto
me [u]as a liar, *and as* waters *that*
[a]fail?
19 ¶ Therefore thus saith the LORD,
[v]If thou return, then will I bring thee
again, *and* thou shalt [w]stand before
me: and if thou [x]take forth the pre-
cious from the vile, thou shalt be as my
mouth: let them return unto thee; but
return not thou unto them.
20 And I will make thee unto this
people a fenced brasen wall: and they
shall fight against thee, but [y]they
shall not prevail against thee: for I *am*
with thee to save thee and to deliver
thee, saith the LORD.
21 And I will deliver thee out of the
hand of the wicked, and I will redeem
thee out of the hand of the terrible.

Punishment and promise

16 THE WORD of the LORD came
also unto me, saying,
2 Thou shalt not take thee a wife,
neither shalt thou have sons or daugh-
ters in this place.
3 For thus saith the LORD concern-
ing the sons and concerning the daugh-
ters that are born in this place, and
concerning their mothers that bare
them, and concerning their fathers
that begat them in this land;
4 They shall die of [z]grievous
deaths; they shall not be [a]lamented;
neither shall they be buried; *but* they
shall be [b]as dung upon the face of the

[y] Or, *I will entreat the enemy for thee* [z] Heb. *thy name is called upon me* [a] Heb. *be not sure?*

15:10 WOE IS ME. Jeremiah complained to the Lord that he was being cursed by all the people of the land. The Lord responded (vv. 11–14) by telling him that when the judgment came, his enemies would plead with him for help (cf. 21:1–7; 37:1–10,17–20; 38:14–18).

15:16 THY WORDS . . . JOY AND REJOICING OF MINE HEART. Jeremiah differed from the people in two fundamental ways. (1) He loved the word of the Lord; it was a joy and delight to his heart. One sure sign that we are children of God is an intense love for the inspired Word of God (see Ps. 119, notes; see article on THE WORD OF GOD, p. 1064). (2) He remained separated from the sinful actions of the wicked (v. 17). The resulting experience of isolation and loneliness was the price he had to pay for loyalty to God and His righteousness (cf. Ps. 26:3–5).

15:19–21 IF THOU RETURN. Jeremiah accused God of not being as faithful to him as He should have been (v. 18). God told him to repent of such words and went on to give him a promise and a renewal of his call.

16:2–10 THOU SHALT NOT TAKE THEE A WIFE. Certain restrictions were put on Jeremiah's life and ministry that would serve as object lessons for the people when the hour of judgment arrived. (1) The first restriction was the command not to marry and have children, illustrating that in the coming affliction many families would die (vv. 1–4). (2) The second was not to show mourning or sympathy at a funeral meal, revealing that God had withdrawn His blessing, love, and compassion from the people (vv. 5–7). (3) The third was not to take part in festive occasions, showing that God would bring an end in Judah to all joy and gladness (vv. 8–9).

earth: and they shall be consumed by
the sword, and by famine; and their
[c]carcases shall be meat for the fowls
of heaven, and for the beasts of the
earth.
5 For thus saith the LORD, [d]Enter
not into the house of [b]mourning, nei-
ther go to lament nor bemoan them: for
I have taken away my peace from this
people, saith the LORD, *even* lovingkind-
ness and mercies.
6 Both the great and the small shall
die in this land: they shall not be bur-
ied, [e]neither shall *men* lament for
them, nor [f]cut themselves, nor
[g]make themselves bald for them:
7 Neither shall *men* [h]tear[c] *them-
selves* for them in mourning, to comfort
them for the dead; neither shall *men*
give them the cup of consolation to
[i]drink for their father or for their
mother.
8 Thou shalt not also go into the
house of feasting, to sit with them to
eat and to drink.
9 For thus saith the LORD of hosts,
the God of Israel; Behold, [j]I will
cause to cease out of this place in your
eyes, and in your days, the voice of
mirth, and the voice of gladness, the
voice of the bridegroom, and the voice
of the bride.
10 ¶ And it shall come to pass,
when thou shalt show this people all
these words, and they shall say unto
thee, [k]Wherefore hath the LORD pro-
nounced all this great evil against us?
or what *is* our iniquity? or what *is* our
sin that we have committed against the
LORD our God?
11 Then shalt thou say unto them,
[l]Because your fathers have forsaken
me, saith the LORD, and have walked
after other gods, and have served
them, and have worshipped them, and
have forsaken me, and have not kept
my law;
12 And ye have done [m]worse than
your fathers; for, behold, [n]ye walk ev-
ery one after the [d]imagination of his
evil heart, that they may not hearken
unto me:

16:4 [c]Ps. 79:2 ch. 7:33 & 34:20
16:5 [d]Ezek. 24:17,22, 23
16:6 [e]ch. 22:18 [f]Lev. 19:28 Deut. 14:1 ch. 41:5 & 47:5 [g]Is. 22:12 ch. 7:29
16:7 [h]Ezek. 24:17 Hos. 9:4 See Deut. 26:14 Job 42:11 [i]Prov. 31:6
16:9 [j]Is. 24:7,8 Ezek. 26:13 Hos. 2:11 Rev. 18:23
16:10 [k]Deut. 29:24 ch. 5:19
16:11 [l]Deut. 29:25 ch. 22:9
16:12 [m]ch. 7:26 [n]ch. 13:10
16:13 [o]Deut. 4:26 & 28:36,63 [p]ch. 15:14
16:14 [q]Is. 43:18 ch. 23:7,8
16:15 [r]ch. 24:6 & 30:3 & 32:37
16:16 [s]Amos 4:2 Hab. 1:15
16:17 [t]Job 34:21 Prov. 5:21 & 15:3 ch. 32:19
16:18 [u]Is. 40:2 ch. 17:18 [v]Ezek. 43:7
16:19 [w]Ps. 18:2 [x]ch. 17:17 [y]Is. 44:10 ch. 10:5
16:20 [z]Is. 37:19 ch. 2:11 Gal. 4:8
16:21 [a]Ex. 15:3 ch. 33:2 Amos 5:8

13 [o]Therefore will I cast you out of
this land [p]into a land that ye know
not, *neither* ye nor your fathers; and
there shall ye serve other gods day and
night; where I will not show you fa-
vour.
14 ¶ Therefore, behold, the [q]days
come, saith the LORD, that it shall no
more be said, The LORD liveth, that
brought up the children of Israel out of
the land of Egypt;
15 But, The LORD liveth, that
brought up the children of Israel from
the land of the north, and from all the
lands whither he had driven them: and
[r]I will bring them again into their land
that I gave unto their fathers.
16 ¶ Behold, I will send for many
[s]fishers, saith the LORD, and they shall
fish them; and after will I send for
many hunters, and they shall hunt
them from every mountain, and from
every hill, and out of the holes of the
rocks.
17 For mine [t]eyes *are* upon all
their ways: they are not hid from my
face, neither is their iniquity hid from
mine eyes.
18 And first I will recompense their
iniquity and their sin [u]double; be-
cause [v]they have defiled my land,
they have filled mine inheritance with
the carcases of their detestable and
abominable things.
19 O LORD, [w]my strength, and my
fortress, and [x]my refuge in the day of
affliction, the Gentiles shall come unto
thee from the ends of the earth, and
shall say, Surely our fathers have in-
herited lies, vanity, and *things*
[y]wherein *there is* no profit.
20 Shall a man make gods unto
himself, and [z]they *are* no gods?
21 Therefore, behold, I will this
once cause them to know, I will cause
them to know mine hand and my
might; and they shall know that [a]my
name *is* [e]The LORD.

[b] Or, *mourning feast* [c] Or, *break bread for them* [d] Or, *stubbornness* [e] Or, *JEHOVAH;* see Ps. 83:18

16:15 I WILL BRING THEM AGAIN INTO THEIR LAND. Although the people would be carried away into exile, their punishment would not be permanent. A remnant would again be restored to their homeland in order to carry out God's plan of redemption centered in the coming Messiah.

16:18 RECOMPENSE . . . DOUBLE. The Hebrew term translated "double" can also mean "equivalent." God would pay the people back in full for their sin and wickedness.

16:19 THE GENTILES SHALL COME UNTO THEE FROM THE ENDS OF THE EARTH. Jeremiah foresaw a day when the nations of the earth would come and worship the Lord and would renounce their false gods as worthless idols (cf. Is. 2:1–4; 45:14; Zech. 8:20–23).

God, the hope of Israel

17 THE SIN of Judah *is* written
with a [b]pen of iron, *and* with
the [f]point of a diamond: *it is* [c]graven
upon the table of their heart, and upon
the horns of your altars;
2 Whilst their children remember
their altars and their [d]groves by the
green trees upon the high hills.
3 O my mountain in the field, I will
give thy substance *and* all thy trea-
sures to the spoil, *and* thy high places
for sin, throughout all thy borders.
4 And thou, even [g]thyself, shalt
discontinue from thine heritage that I
gave thee; and I will cause thee to
serve thine enemies in [e]the land
which thou knowest not: for [f]ye have
kindled a fire in mine anger, *which*
shall burn for ever.
5 ¶ Thus saith the LORD; [g]Cursed *be*
the man that trusteth in man, and
maketh [h]flesh his arm, and whose
heart departeth from the LORD.
6 For he shall be [i]like the heath in
the desert, and [j]shall not see when
good cometh; but shall inhabit the
parched places in the wilderness, [k]*in*
a salt land and not inhabited.
7 [l]Blessed *is* the man that trusteth
in the LORD, and whose hope the
LORD is.
8 For he shall be [m]as a tree planted
by the waters, and *that* spreadeth out
her roots by the river, and shall not see
when heat cometh, but her leaf shall be
green; and shall not be careful in the
year of [h]drought, neither shall cease
from yielding fruit.
9 ¶ The heart *is* deceitful above all
things, and desperately wicked: who
can know it?
10 I the LORD [n]search the heart, *I*
try the reins, [o]even to give every man
according to his ways, *and* according to
the fruit of his doings.
11 *As* the partridge [i]sitteth *on*
eggs, and hatcheth *them* not; *so* he that
getteth riches, and not by right, [p]shall
leave them in the midst of his days, and
at his end shall be [q]a fool.
12 ¶ A glorious high throne from
the beginning *is* the place of our sanc-
tuary.
13 O LORD, [r]the hope of Israel,
[s]all that forsake thee shall be
ashamed, *and* they that depart from me
shall be [t]written in the earth, because
they have forsaken the LORD, the
[u]fountain of living waters.
14 Heal me, O LORD, and I shall be
healed; save me, and I shall be saved:
for [v]thou *art* my praise. Jer. 30:17
15 ¶ Behold, they say unto me,
[w]Where *is* the word of the LORD? let it
come now.
16 As for me, [x]I have not hastened
from *being* a pastor [j]to follow thee:
neither have I desired the woeful day;
thou knowest: that which came out of
my lips was *right* before thee.
17 Be not a terror unto me: [y]thou
art my hope in the day of evil.
18 [z]Let them be confounded that
persecute me, but [a]let not me be con-
founded: let them be dismayed, but let
not me be dismayed: bring upon them
the day of evil, and [b]destroy[k] them
with double destruction.

17:1 [b]Job 19:24 [c]Prov. 3:3 2 Cor. 3:3 **17:2** [d]Judg. 3:7 2 Chr. 24:18 & 33:3,19 ch. 2:20 **17:4** [e]ch. 16:13 [f]ch. 15:14 **17:5** [g]Is. 30:1,2 & 31:1 [h]See Is. 31:3 **17:6** [i]ch. 48:6 [j]Job 20:17 [k]Deut. 29:23 **17:7** [l]Ps. 2:12 & 34:8 Prov. 16:20 Is. 30:18 **17:8** [m]Job 8:16 Ps. 1:3 **17:10** [n]1 Sam. 16:7 1 Chr. 28:9 Ps. 7:9 & 139:23,24 Prov. 17:3 ch. 20:12 Rom. 8:27 Rev. 2:23 [o]Ps. 62:12 ch. 32:19 Rom. 2:6 **17:11** [p]Ps. 55:23 [q]Luke 12:20 **17:13** [r]ch. 14:8 [s]Ps. 73:27 Is. 1:28 [t]See Luke 10:20 [u]ch. 2:13 **17:14** [v]Deut. 10:21 Ps. 109:1 & 148:14 **17:15** [w]Is. 5:19 Ezek. 12:22 Amos 5:18 2 Pet. 3:4 **17:16** [x]ch. 1:4 **17:17** [y]ch. 16:19 **17:18** [z]Ps. 35:4 & 70:2 [a]Ps. 25:2 [b]ch. 11:20

[f] Heb. *nail* [g] Heb. *in thyself* [h] Or, *restraint* [i] Or, *gathereth* young *which she hath not brought forth* [j] Heb. *after thee* [k] Heb. *break them with a double breach*

17:1 THE SIN OF JUDAH. Jeremiah indicts the nation for its great wickedness. The people's sin was so deeply etched into their nature that idolatry and evil had become an integral part of their lives. For their infidelity they would lose their land and become slaves (v. 4).

17:5–8 CURSED *BE* THE MAN. Those whose trust centers in themselves and in human resources are destined for disappointment, spiritual poverty, and ultimate loss. On the contrary, those who fully trust in the Lord will be blessed and ultimately rewarded with a godly inheritance. They will not fear or be anxious in any of life's circumstances because their roots go down deep into God.

17:9 THE HEART *IS* DECEITFUL . . . DESPERATELY WICKED. The heart is the inner being of a person and includes one's desires, feelings, and thoughts (see article on THE HEART, p. 932). Above all, it is desperately evil and corrupt; as a result, people turn to selfishness and evil rather than to God's way of righteousness. The corrupt human heart cannot be changed by itself. The only remedy is to experience God's grace, be born again through faith in Christ, and receive a new heart—one that hates evil and delights in doing God's will (cf. 24:7; Ezek. 11:19–20; Mat. 5:8).

17:14–18 HEAL ME . . . SAVE ME. In the face of persecution and opposition, Jeremiah prays for God's grace to help him continue his prophetic ministry. The people and the false prophets had been taunting him and scoffing at his prophecies because his predictions had not yet been fulfilled (v. 15). In spite of this suffering, Jeremiah refused to turn from his ministry, but continued to look to God for strength and help.

Sabbath observance stressed

19 ¶ Thus said the LORD unto me; Go and stand in the gate of the children of the people, whereby the kings of Judah come in, and by the which they go out, and in all the gates of Jerusalem;

20 And say unto them, [c]Hear ye the word of the LORD, ye kings of Judah, and all Judah, and all the inhabitants of Jerusalem, that enter in by these gates:

21 Thus saith the LORD; [d]Take heed to yourselves, and bear no burden on the sabbath day, nor bring *it* in by the gates of Jerusalem;

22 Neither carry forth a burden out of your houses on the sabbath day, neither do ye any work, but hallow ye the sabbath day, as I [e]commanded your fathers.

23 [f]But they obeyed not, neither inclined their ear, but made their neck stiff, that they might not hear, nor receive instruction.

24 And it shall come to pass, if ye diligently hearken unto me, saith the LORD, to bring in no burden through the gates of this city on the sabbath day, but hallow the sabbath day, to do no work therein;

25 [g]Then shall there enter into the gates of this city kings and princes sitting upon the throne of David, riding in chariots and on horses, they, and their princes, the men of Judah, and the inhabitants of Jerusalem: and this city shall remain for ever.

26 And they shall come from the cities of Judah, and from [h]the places about Jerusalem, and from the land of Benjamin, and from [i]the plain, and from the mountains, and from [j]the south, bringing burnt offerings, and sacrifices, and meat offerings, and incense, and bringing [k]sacrifices of praise, unto the house of the LORD.

27 But if ye will not hearken unto me to hallow the sabbath day, and not to bear a burden, even entering in at the gates of Jerusalem on the sabbath day; then [l]will I kindle a fire in the gates thereof, [m]and it shall devour the palaces of Jerusalem, and it shall not be quenched.

The parable of potter and clay

18 THE WORD which came to Jeremiah from the LORD, saying,

2 Arise, and go down to the potter's house, and there I will cause thee to hear my words.

3 Then I went down to the potter's house, and, behold, he wrought a work on the [1]wheels.

4 And the vessel [m]that he made of clay was marred in the hand of the potter: so he [n]made it again another vessel, as seemed good to the potter to make *it*.

5 Then the word of the LORD came to me, saying,

6 O house of Israel, [n]cannot I do with you as this potter? saith the LORD. Behold, [o]as the clay *is* in the potter's hand, so *are* ye in mine hand, O house of Israel.

7 *At what* instant I shall speak concerning a nation, and concerning a kingdom, to [p]pluck up, and to pull down, and to destroy *it;*

8 [q]If that nation, against whom I have pronounced, turn from their evil,

17:20 [c]ch. 19:3 **17:21** [d]Num. 15:32 Neh. 13:19 **17:22** [e]Ex. 20:8 & 31:13 Ezek. 20:12 **17:23** [f]ch. 7:24,26 **17:25** [g]ch. 22:4 **17:26** [h]ch. 33:13 [i]Zech. 7:7 [j]Zech. 7:7 [k]Ps. 107:22 & 116:17 **17:27** [l]ch. 21:14 Lam. 4:11 Amos 1:4,7,10,12 [m]2 Ki. 25:9 ch. 52:13 **18:6** [n]Is. 45:9 Rom. 9:20 [o]Is. 64:8 **18:7** [p]ch. 1:10 **18:8** [q]Ezek. 18:21 & 33:11

[1] Or, *frames,* or, *seats* [m] Or, *that he made was marred, as clay in the hand of the potter* [n] Heb. *returned and made*

17:19–23 GO AND STAND IN THE GATE. These verses on keeping the Sabbath day demonstrate that even Jeremiah's prophecies of doom were conditional in nature. If the people would only turn to God, keep the Sabbath, and do right, then they would avoid captivity (vv. 24–26). A way of salvation was still open for Judah.

18:2 THE POTTER'S HOUSE. Jeremiah was told to go to a potter's house, where he observed a potter fashioning a vessel out of clay. Because the vessel was not suitable for what the potter intended, he had to remold it into something other than what he had first designed. This parable contains several important principles for God's work in our lives. (1) Our submission to God as the One who molds both our character and our service to Him determines to a large extent what He can do with us. (2) A lack of fervent commitment to God can frustrate His original purpose for us (cf. v. 10). (3) God remains free to change His intentions for our lives. If He has planned goodness and blessing for us and if we rebel against Him, He may then shape us into a vessel for destruction (vv. 7–11; cf. 19:10–11; Rom. 9:22). On the other hand, if we are, through our own stubbornness, vessels headed for destruction, but we repent, God will begin to shape us into vessels of honor and blessing (cf. 2 Tim. 2:20–21).

18:8 I WILL REPENT. The word "repent" here means to relent, to change one's mind and purpose, or to reconsider. God remains free to change His pronounced decisions and to regulate His dealings with us according to our response to His offer of forgiveness or to His threat of judgment. Things are not predetermined and unalterable, not even in the mind of God; He takes into account spiritual

[r]I will repent of the evil that I thought to do unto them.

9 And *at what* instant I shall speak concerning a nation, and concerning a kingdom, to build and to plant *it;*

10 If it do evil in my sight, that it obey not my voice, then I will repent of the good, wherewith I said I would benefit them.

11 ¶ Now therefore go to, speak to the men of Judah, and to the inhabitants of Jerusalem, saying, Thus saith the LORD; Behold, I frame evil against you, and devise a device against you: [s]return ye now every one from his evil way, and make your ways and your doings good.

12 And they said, [t]There is no hope: but we will walk after our own devices, and we will every one do the imagination of his evil heart.

13 Therefore thus saith the LORD; [u]Ask ye now among the heathen, who hath heard such things: the virgin of Israel hath done [v]a very horrible thing.

14 Will *a man* leave [o]the snow of Lebanon *which cometh* from the rock of the field? *or* shall the cold flowing waters that come from another place be forsaken?

15 Because my people hath forgotten [w]me, they have burned incense to vanity, and they have caused them to stumble in their ways *from* the [x]ancient paths, to walk in paths, *in* a way not cast up;

16 To make their land [y]desolate, *and* a perpetual [z]hissing; every one that passeth thereby shall be astonished, and wag his head.

17 [a]I will scatter them [b]as with an east wind before the enemy; [c]I will show them the back, and not the face, in the day of their calamity.

18 ¶ Then said they, [d]Come, and let us devise devices against Jeremiah; [e]for the law shall not perish from the priest, nor counsel from the wise, nor the word from the prophet. Come, and let us smite him [p]with the tongue, and let us not give heed to any of his words.

19 Give heed to me, O LORD, and hearken to the voice of them that contend with me.

20 [f]Shall evil be recompensed for good? for [g]they have digged a pit for my soul. Remember that I stood before thee to speak good for them, *and* to turn away thy wrath from them.

21 Therefore [h]deliver up their children to the famine, and [q]pour out their *blood* by the force of the sword; and let their wives be bereaved of their children, and *be* widows; and let their men be put to death; *let* their young men *be* slain by the sword in battle.

22 Let a cry be heard from their houses, when thou shalt bring a troop suddenly upon them: for [i]they have digged a pit to take me, and hid snares for my feet.

23 Yet, LORD, thou knowest all their counsel against me [r]to slay *me:* [j]forgive not their iniquity, neither blot out their sin from thy sight, but let them be overthrown before thee; deal *thus* with them in the time of thine anger.

19 THUS SAITH the LORD, Go and get a potter's earthen bottle, and *take* of the ancients of the people, and of the ancients of the priests;

2 And go forth unto [k]the valley of the son of Hinnom, which *is* by the entry of [s]the east gate, and proclaim there the words that I shall tell thee,

3 [l]And say, Hear ye the word of the LORD, O kings of Judah, and inhabitants of Jerusalem; Thus saith the LORD of hosts, the God of Israel; Behold, I will bring evil upon this place, the which whosoever heareth, his ears shall [m]tingle.

4 Because they [n]have forsaken me, and have estranged this place, and have burned incense in it unto other gods, whom neither they nor their fa-

18:8 [r]ch. 26:3 Jonah 3:10 **18:11** [s]2 Ki. 17:13 ch. 7:3 **18:12** [t]ch. 2:25 **18:13** [u]ch 2:10 1 Cor. 5:1 [v]ch. 5:30 **18:15** [w]ch. 2:13,32 [x]ch. 6:16 **18:16** [y]ch. 19:8 [z]1 Ki. 9:8 Lam. 2:15 Mic. 6:16 **18:17** [a]ch. 13:24 [b]Ps. 48:7 [c]See ch. 2:27 **18:18** [d]ch. 11:19 [e]Lev. 10:11 Mal. 2:7 John 7:48 **18:20** [f]Ps. 109:4 [g]ver. 22 Ps. 35:7 **18:21** [h]Ps. 109:9 **18:22** [i]ver. 20 **18:23** [j]Ps. 35:4 & 109:14 ch. 11:20 **19:2** [k]Josh. 15:8 2 Ki. 23:10 **19:3** [l]ch. 17:20 [m]1 Sam. 3:11 2 Ki. 21:12 **19:4** [n]Deut. 28:20 Is. 65:11

[o] Or, *my fields for a rock,* or for *the snow of Lebanon? shall the running waters be forsaken for the strange cold* waters? [p] Or, *for the tongue* [q] Heb. *pour them out* [r] Heb. *for death* [s] Heb. *the sun gate*

changes in people. Although God does not change within Himself (Num. 23:19; Jas. 1:17), He retains the right to change His mind and alter His declared promises and threats. We should never accept a theology that denies God this sovereign freedom (cf. Ezek. 18:21–28; 33:13–16).

19:1–15 A POTTER'S EARTHEN BOTTLE. Through a dramatic parable, Jeremiah reveals that Jerusalem and Judah would experience such a devastating judgment that they would be broken in pieces.

19:2 VALLEY OF THE SON OF HINNOM. God instructed Jeremiah to take some of the leaders (v. 1) to the place where they burned incense to other gods and sacrificed their children by fire (see 7:31, note). There he proclaimed the word of the Lord concerning the coming calamity (v. 3).

thers have known, nor the kings of Ju-
dah, and have filled this place with
[o]the blood of innocents;
5 [p]They have built also the high
places of Baal, to burn their sons with
fire *for* burnt offerings unto Baal,
[q]which I commanded not, nor spake
it, neither came *it* into my mind:
6 Therefore, behold, the days come,
saith the LORD, that this place shall no
more be called Tophet, nor [r]The val-
ley of the son of Hinnom, but The val-
ley of slaughter.
7 And I will make void the counsel
of Judah and Jerusalem in this place;
[s]and I will cause them to fall by the
sword before their enemies, and by the
hands of them that seek their lives:
and their [t]carcases will I give to be
meat for the fowls of the heaven, and
for the beasts of the earth.
8 And I will make this city [u]deso-
late, and an hissing; every one that
passeth thereby shall be astonished
and hiss because of all the plagues
thereof.
9 And I will cause them to eat the
[v]flesh of their sons and the flesh of
their daughters, and they shall eat ev-
ery one the flesh of his friend in the
siege and straitness, wherewith their
enemies, and they that seek their lives,
shall straiten them.
10 [w]Then shalt thou break the bot-
tle in the sight of the men that go with
thee,
11 And shalt say unto them, Thus
saith the LORD of hosts; [x]Even so will
I break this people and this city, as *one*
breaketh a potter's vessel, that cannot
[t]be made whole again: and they shall
[y]bury *them* in Tophet, till *there be* no
place to bury.
12 Thus will I do unto this place,
saith the LORD, and to the inhabitants
thereof, and *even* make this city as To-
phet:
13 And the houses of Jerusalem,
and the houses of the kings of Judah,
shall be defiled [z]as the place of To-
phet, because of all the houses upon
whose [a]roofs they have burned in-

19:4 [o]2 Ki. 21:16 ch. 2:34
19:5 [p]ch. 7:31 & 32:35 [q]Lev. 18:21
19:6 [r]Josh. 15:8
19:7 [s]Lev. 26:17 Deut. 28:25 [t]Ps. 79:2 ch. 7:33 & 16:4 & 34:20
19:8 [u]ch. 18:16 & 49:13 & 50:13
19:9 [v]Lev. 26:29 Deut. 28:53 Is. 9:20 Lam. 4:10
19:10 [w]ch. 51:63,64
19:11 [x]Ps. 2:9 Is. 30:14 Lam. 4:2 [y]ch. 7:32
19:13 [z]2 Ki. 23:10 [a]2 Ki. 23:12 ch. 32:29 Zeph. 1:5
[b]ch. 7:18
19:14 [c]See 2 Chr. 20:5
19:15 [d]ch. 7:26 & 17:23
20:1 [e]1 Chr. 24:14
20:5 [f]2 Ki. 20:17 & 24:12-16 & 25:13 ch. 3:24

cense unto all the host of heaven, and
[b]have poured out drink offerings unto
other gods.
14 Then came Jeremiah from To-
phet, whither the LORD had sent him to
prophesy; and he stood in [c]the court
of the LORD's house; and said to all the
people,
15 Thus saith the LORD of hosts, the
God of Israel; Behold, I will bring upon
this city and upon all her towns all the
evil that I have pronounced against it,
because [d]they have hardened their
necks, that they might not hear my
words.

Jeremiah and Pashur

20 NOW PASHUR the son of [e]Im-
mer the priest, who *was* also
chief governor in the house of the LORD,
heard that Jeremiah prophesied these
things.
2 Then Pashur smote Jeremiah the
prophet, and put him in the stocks that
were in the high gate of Benjamin,
which *was* by the house of the LORD.
3 And it came to pass on the mor-
row, that Pashur brought forth Jeremi-
ah out of the stocks. Then said Jeremi-
ah unto him, The LORD hath not called
thy name Pashur, but [u]Magor-missa-
bib.
4 For thus saith the LORD, Behold, I
will make thee a terror to thyself, and
to all thy friends: and they shall fall by
the sword of their enemies, and thine
eyes shall behold *it*: and I will give all
Judah into the hand of the king of Bab-
ylon, and he shall carry them captive
into Babylon, and shall slay them with
the sword.
5 Moreover I [f]will deliver all the
strength of this city, and all the labours
thereof, and all the precious things
thereof, and all the treasures of the
kings of Judah will I give into the hand
of their enemies, which shall spoil
them, and take them, and carry them
to Babylon.

[t]Heb. *be healed* [u]i.e. *Fear round about;* see Ps. 31:13; ver. 10; ch. 6:25 & 46:5 & 49:29

19:9 EAT THE FLESH OF THEIR SONS. During the siege of the Babylonians in 586 B.C., some of the people resorted to cannibalism, thus showing the severity of the siege that God had brought upon them and the depth of depravity to which they had fallen (see Lam. 2:20; 4:10; Ezek. 5:10).

20:2–3 PASHUR SMOTE JEREMIAH THE PROPHET. Jeremiah was beaten, probably with forty lashes (see Deut. 25:2–3), and imprisoned in the stocks. However, the prophet refused to yield to physical pain and continued to announce the nation's doom. He gave Pashur a new name, "Magor-missabib," meaning "terror all around." Pashur and the nation would soon experience terror all around.

6 And thou, Pashur, and all that
dwell in thine house shall go into cap-
tivity: and thou shalt come to Babylon,
and there thou shalt die, and shalt be
buried there, thou, and all thy friends,
to whom thou hast [g]prophesied lies.

Jeremiah complains to the LORD

7 ¶ O LORD, thou hast deceived
me, and I was [v]deceived: [h]thou art
stronger than I, and hast prevailed:
[i]I am in derision daily, every one
mocketh me.
8 For since I spake, I cried out, [j]I
cried violence and spoil; because the
word of the LORD was made a reproach
unto me, and a derision, daily.
9 Then I said, I will not make men-
tion of him, nor speak any more in his
name. But *his word* was in mine heart
as a [k]burning fire shut up in my bones,
and I was weary with forbearing, and
[l]I could not *stay.*
10 ¶ [m]For I heard the defaming of
many, fear on every side. Report, *say*
they, and we will report it. [n]All[w] my
familiars watched for my halting, *say-*
ing, Peradventure he will be enticed,
and we shall prevail against him, and
we shall take our revenge on him.
11 But the LORD *is* with me as a
mighty terrible one: therefore my per-
secutors shall stumble, and they shall
not [o]prevail: they shall be greatly
ashamed; for they shall not prosper:
their [p]everlasting confusion shall nev-
er be forgotten.
12 But, O LORD of hosts, that [q]tri-
est the righteous, *and* seest the reins
and the heart, [r]let me see thy ven-
geance on them: for unto thee have I
opened my cause.
13 Sing unto the LORD, praise ye the
LORD: for [s]he hath delivered the soul
of the poor from the hand of evildoers. Jer. 31:7
14 ¶ [t]Cursed *be* the day wherein I
was born: let not the day wherein my
mother bare me be blessed.
15 Cursed *be* the man who brought
tidings to my father, saying, A man
child is born unto thee; making him
very glad.
16 And let that man be as the cities
which the LORD [u]overthrew, and re-
pented not: and let him [v]hear the cry
in the morning, and the shouting at
noontide;
17 [w]Because he slew me not from
the womb; or that my mother might
have been my grave, and her womb *to*
be always great *with me.*
18 [x]Wherefore came I forth out of
the womb to [y]see labour and sorrow,
that my days should be consumed with
shame?

Zedekiah's prayer; God's answer

21 THE WORD which came unto
Jeremiah from the LORD, when
king Zedekiah sent unto him [z]Pashur
the son of Melchiah, and [a]Zephaniah
the son of Maaseiah the priest, saying,
2 [b]Inquire, I pray thee, of the LORD
for us; for Nebuchadrezzar king of Bab-
ylon maketh war against us; if so be
that the LORD will deal with us accord-
ing to all his wondrous works, that he
may go up from us.
3 ¶ Then said Jeremiah unto them,
Thus shall ye say to Zedekiah:
4 Thus saith the LORD God of Israel;
Behold, I will turn back the weapons of
war that *are* in your hands, wherewith
ye fight against the king of Babylon,

20:6 [g]ch. 14:13,14 & 28:15 & 29:21 **20:7** [h]ch. 1:6,7 [i]Lam. 3:14 **20:8** [j]ch. 6:7 **20:9** [k]Job 32:18,19 Ps. 39:3 [l]Job 32:18 Acts 18:5 **20:10** [m]Ps. 31:13 [n]Job 19:19 Ps. 41:9 & 55:13,14 Luke 11:53,54 **20:11** [o]ch. 15:20 & 17:18 [p]ch. 23:40 **20:12** [q]ch. 11:20 & 17:10 [r]Ps. 54:7 & 59:10 **20:13** [s]Ps. 35:9,10 & 109:30,31 **20:14** [t]Job 3:3 ch. 15:10 **20:16** [u]Gen. 19:25 [v]ch. 18:22 **20:17** [w]Job 3:10,11 **20:18** [x]Job 3:20 [y]Lam. 3:1 **21:1** [z]ch. 38:1 [a]2 Ki. 25:18 ch. 29:25 & 37:3 **21:2** [b]ch. 37:3,7

[v]Or, *enticed* [w]Heb. *Every man of my peace*

20:7–18 O LORD. Jeremiah expresses to God the conflicting emotions of intense grief and deep depression on the one hand, and persistent faith and trust in God on the other.

20:7 THOU HAST DECEIVED ME. Jeremiah was not accusing God of lying. The Hebrew word translated "deceived" means literally "reduced" or "overpowered." Jeremiah was maintaining that he had been forced into becoming a prophet by divine compulsion and that this had reduced him to shame and ridicule. His message, which had not yet been fulfilled, was continually being laughed at and mocked, and he himself was being treated with contempt by his fellow citizens.

20:9 *HIS WORD* . . . A BURNING FIRE. No matter how hard Jeremiah tried, he was unable to suppress the divine message within him. He sympathized fully with the divine anger against the sins of the people. The prophet felt such a oneness with God and His cause that he had to proclaim God's word, even though it brought him excruciating pain and suffering.

20:14–18 CURSED *BE* THE DAY. Jeremiah's sufferings and his feelings of frustration and failure made him wish he had never been born (cf. Job 3). Yet he continued to declare God's word, sustained by God's grace in his darkest hours (vv. 11–13).

21:1 ZEDEKIAH. Zedekiah, the last king of Judah, was reigning when Jerusalem fell. His revolt against Babylon brought about the invasion of Judah and Jerusalem's subsequent destruction; the underlying spiritual cause behind the nation's fall, however, was God's decree against His people because of Manasseh's sin and Judah's apostasy (15:4).

and *against* the Chaldeans, which be-
siege you without the walls, and [c]I
will assemble them into the midst of
this city.
5 And I myself will fight against you
with an [d]outstretched hand and with
a strong arm, even in anger, and in
fury, and in great wrath.
6 And I will smite the inhabitants of
this city, both man and beast: they
shall die of a great pestilence.
7 And afterward, saith the LORD, [e]I
will deliver Zedekiah king of Judah,
and his servants, and the people, and
such as are left in this city from the
pestilence, from the sword, and from
the famine, into the hand of Nebu-
chadrezzar king of Babylon, and into
the hand of their enemies, and into
the hand of those that seek their life:
and he shall smite them with the edge
of the sword; [f]he shall not spare
them, neither have pity, nor have
mercy.
8 ¶ And unto this people thou shalt
say, Thus saith the LORD; Behold, [g]I
set before you the way of life, and the
way of death.
9 He that [h]abideth in this city shall
die by the sword, and by the famine,
and by the pestilence: but he that goeth
out, and falleth to the Chaldeans that
besiege you, he shall live, and [i]his life
shall be unto him for a prey.
10 For I have [j]set my face against
this city for evil, and not for good, saith
the LORD: [k]it shall be given into the
hand of the king of Babylon, and he
shall [l]burn it with fire.
11 ¶ And touching the house of the

21:4 [c]Is. 13:4
21:5 [d]Ex. 6:6
21:7 [e]ch. 37:17 & 39:5 & 52:9 [f]Deut. 28:50 2 Chr. 36:17
21:8 [g]Deut. 30:19
21:9 [h]ch. 38:2,17,18 [i]ch. 39:18 & 45:5
21:10 [j]Lev. 17:10 ch. 44:11 Amos 9:4 [k]ch. 38:3 [l]ch. 34:2,22 & 37:10 & 38:18,23 & 52:13
21:12 [m]ch. 22:3 Zech. 7:9 [n]Ps. 101:8
21:13 [o]Ezek. 13:8 [p]ch. 49:4
21:14 [q]Prov. 1:31 Is. 3:10,11 [r]2 Chr. 36:19 ch. 52:13
22:2 [s]ch. 17:20
22:3 [t]ch. 21:12

king of Judah, *say,* Hear ye the word of
the LORD;
12 O house of David, thus saith the
LORD; [m]Execute[x] judgment [n]in the
morning, and deliver *him that is* spoiled
out of the hand of the oppressor, lest
my fury go out like fire, and burn that
none can quench *it,* because of the evil
of your doings.
13 Behold, [o]I *am* against thee, O
[y]inhabitant of the valley, *and* rock of
the plain, saith the LORD; which say,
[p]Who shall come down against us? or
who shall enter into our habitations?
14 But I will [z]punish you accord-
ing to the [q]fruit of your doings, saith
the LORD: and I will kindle a fire in the
forest thereof, and [r]it shall devour all
things round about it.

A burden about evil kings

22 THUS SAITH the LORD; Go
down to the house of the king of
Judah, and speak there this word,
2 And say, [s]Hear the word of the
LORD, O king of Judah, that sittest upon
the throne of David, thou, and thy ser-
vants, and thy people that enter in by
these gates:
3 Thus saith the LORD; [t]Execute ye
judgment and righteousness, and de-
liver the spoiled out of the hand of the
oppressor: and do no wrong, do no vio-
lence to the stranger, the fatherless,
nor the widow, neither shed innocent
blood in this place.
4 For if ye do this thing indeed,

[x] Heb. *Judge* [y] Heb. *inhabitress* [z] Heb. *visit upon*

21:5 I MYSELF WILL FIGHT AGAINST YOU. Zedekiah sent two priests to ask Jeremiah if God would cause Nebuchadnezzar to retreat (vv. 1–3). Through the prophet God declared an emphatic "No." In fact, God Himself would fight against Judah and deliver His people into the hands of their enemies. All their resistance would prove useless.

21:7 ZEDEKIAH . . . INTO THE HAND OF NEBUCHADREZZAR. Jeremiah's prophecy was literally fulfilled in 586 B.C. (cf. 52:9–11,24–27). Zedekiah's sons were slaughtered before his eyes by the king of Babylon; then Zedekiah's own eyes were blinded, and in pitiful humiliation he was led away in chains to Babylon, where he died in exile (39:5–7).

21:8–10 WAY OF LIFE . . . WAY OF DEATH. Jeremiah prophesied to the people that if they did not submit to God's decreed judgment and surrender to the Chaldeans (i.e., the Babylonians), they would die in the city.

21:11–14 HOUSE OF THE KING. Jeremiah prophesies to the royal family of Judah that God had expected them to administer justice to the people. But because they had encouraged sin and done nothing for the oppressed, God's wrath would burn against them like fire.

22:1–30 THE KING OF JUDAH. Jeremiah's prophecies are not organized in strict chronological order. In this chapter he prophesies to the three kings who preceded King Zedekiah (see 21:1, note) about God's judgment against them. He predicted that God would punish the house of David (21:12) and judge the following kings: Shallum (vv. 1–12), Jehoiakim (vv. 13–23), and Coniah (i.e., Jehoiachin; vv. 24–30).

22:1–6 GO DOWN TO . . . THE KING. Jeremiah exhorted Judah's King Shallum (v. 11; see next note) to practice justice and righteousness and to help the oppressed and needy. If only the king would do this, he would not experience the desolation described in vv. 6–9.

[u]then shall there enter in by the gates
of this house kings sitting [a]upon the
throne of David, riding in chariots and
on horses, he, and his servants, and his
people.
5 But if ye will not hear these
words, [v]I swear by myself, saith the
LORD, that this house shall become a
desolation.
6 For thus saith the LORD unto the
king's house of Judah; Thou *art* Gilead
unto me, *and* the head of Lebanon: *yet*
surely I will make thee a wilderness;
and cities *which* are not inhabited.
7 And I will prepare destroyers
against thee, every one with his weap-
ons: and they shall cut down [w]thy
choice cedars, [x]and cast *them* into the
fire.
8 And many nations shall pass by
this city, and they shall say every man
to his neighbour, [y]Wherefore hath the
LORD done thus unto this great city?
9 Then they shall answer, [z]Be-
cause they have forsaken the covenant
of the LORD their God, and worshipped
other gods, and served them.
10 ¶ Weep ye not for [a]the dead,
neither bemoan him: *but* weep sore for
him [b]that goeth away: for he shall re-
turn no more, nor see his native coun-
try.
11 For thus saith the LORD touching
[c]Shallum the son of Josiah king of Ju-
dah, which reigned instead of Josiah
his father, [d]which went forth out of
this place; He shall not return thither
any more:
12 But he shall die in the place
whither they have led him captive, and
shall see this land no more.
13 ¶ [e]Woe unto him that buildeth
his house by unrighteousness, and his
chambers by wrong; [f]*that* useth his
neighbour's service without wages,
and giveth him not for his work;
14 That saith, I will build me a wide
house and large chambers, and cutteth
him out [b]windows; and *it is* ceiled
with cedar, and painted with vermilion.
15 Shalt thou reign, because thou
closest *thyself* in cedar? did not thy fa-
ther eat and drink, and do judgment
and justice, *and* then [g]*it was* well with
him?
16 He judged the cause of the poor
and needy; then *it was* well *with him:*
was not this to know me? saith the
LORD.
17 [h]But thine eyes and thine heart
are not but for thy covetousness, and
for to shed innocent blood, and for op-
pression, and for [c]violence, to do *it.*
18 Therefore thus saith the LORD
concerning Jehoiakim the son of Josiah
king of Judah; [i]They shall not lament
for him, *saying,* [j]Ah my brother! or,
Ah sister! they shall not lament for
him, *saying,* Ah lord! or, Ah his glory!
19 [k]He shall be buried with the
burial of an ass, drawn and cast forth
beyond the gates of Jerusalem.
20 ¶ Go up to Lebanon, and cry; and
lift up thy voice in Bashan, and cry
from the passages: for all thy lovers
are destroyed.
21 I spake unto thee in thy [d]pros-
perity; *but* thou saidst, I will not hear.
[l]This *hath been* thy manner from thy
youth, that thou obeyedst not my voice.
22 The wind shall eat up all [m]thy
pastors, and thy lovers shall go into
captivity: surely then shalt thou be
ashamed and confounded for all thy
wickedness.
23 O [e]inhabitant of Lebanon, that
makest thy nest in the cedars, how gra-
cious shalt thou be when pangs come
upon thee, [n]the pain as of a woman in
travail!
24 *As* I live, saith the LORD,

22:4 [u]ch. 17:25 **22:5** [v]Heb. 6:13,17 **22:7** [w]Is. 37:24 [x]ch. 21:14 **22:8** [y]Deut. 29:24,25 1 Ki. 9:8,9 **22:9** [z]2 Ki. 22:17 2 Chr. 34:25 **22:10** [a]2 Ki. 22:20 [b]ver. 11 **22:11** [c]See 1 Chr. 3:15, with 2 Ki. 23:30 [d]2 Ki. 23:34 **22:13** [e]ver. 18 2 Ki. 23:35 [f]Lev. 19:13 Deut. 24:14,15 Mic. 3:10 Hab. 2:9 Jas. 5:4 **22:15** [g]Ps. 128:2 Is. 3:10 **22:17** [h]Ezek. 19:6 **22:18** [i]ch. 16:4,6 [j]See 1 Ki. 13:30 Fulfilled **22:19** [k]2 Chr. 36:6 ch. 36:30 **22:21** [l]ch. 3:25 & 7:23 **22:22** [m]ch. 23:1 **22:23** [n]ch. 6:24

[a] Heb. *for David upon his throne* [b] Or, *my windows* [c] Or, *incursion* [d] Heb. *prosperities* [e] Heb. *inhabitress*

22:11–12 SHALLUM. Shallum, also called Jehoahaz (see 2 Ki. 23:31; 2 Chr. 36:1–4), was the fourth son of Josiah (1 Chr. 3:15). He was king for three months before being carried off to Egypt, where he died.

22:13–19 WOE UNTO HIM. This prophecy scathingly condemned King Jehoiakim (v. 18) for his sins of injustice and oppression. During Nebuchadnezzar's first invasion of Jerusalem, Jehoiakim was taken captive to Babylon (see 2 Chr. 36:5–8); he was later released and given a dishonorable burial outside of Jerusalem (vv. 18–19).

22:16 THE POOR AND NEEDY. The apostle James emphasizes this same truth: the kind of faith God accepts is one that expresses itself in a genuine care for those in need (see Jas. 1:27, note). If we help the needy and the oppressed, we will receive the blessing and commendation of God (cf. Gal. 6:10; see article on THE CARE OF THE POOR AND NEEDY, p. 1312).

22:24–30 CONIAH. Also known as Jehoiachin (2 Chr. 36:9–10), Coniah ruled for only three months before he was taken to Babylon during Nebuchadnezzar's second invasion of Jerusalem (cf. 24:1; 29:2).

[o]though Coniah the son of Jehoiakim
king of Judah [p]were the signet upon
my right hand, yet would I pluck thee
thence;
25 [q]And I will give thee into the
hand of them that seek thy life, and
into the hand *of them* whose face thou
fearest, even into the hand of Nebu-
chadrezzar king of Babylon, and into
the hand of the Chaldeans.
26 [r]And I will cast thee out, and
thy mother that bare thee, into another
country, where ye were not born; and
there shall ye die.
27 But to the land whereunto they
[f]desire to return, thither shall they
not return.
28 *Is* this man Coniah a despised
broken idol? *is he* [s]a vessel wherein *is*
no pleasure? wherefore are they cast
out, he and his seed, and are cast into
a land which they know not?
29 [t]O earth, earth, earth, hear the
word of the LORD.
30 Thus saith the LORD, Write ye
this man [u]childless, a man *that* shall
not prosper in his days: for no man of
his seed shall prosper, [v]sitting upon
the throne of David, and ruling any
more in Judah.

The remnant and the true king

23 WOE [w]BE unto the pastors
that destroy and scatter the
sheep of my pasture! saith the LORD.
2 Therefore thus saith the LORD God
of Israel against the pastors that feed
my people; Ye have scattered my flock,
and driven them away, and have not
visited them: [x]behold, I will visit upon
you the evil of your doings, saith the
LORD.
3 And [y]I will gather the remnant of
my flock out of all countries whither I
have driven them, and will bring them
again to their folds; and they shall be
fruitful and increase.
4 And I will set up [z]shepherds over
them which shall feed them: and they
shall fear no more, nor be dismayed,
neither shall they be lacking, saith the
LORD.
5 ¶ Behold, [a]the days come, saith
the LORD, that I will raise unto David a
righteous Branch, and a King shall
reign and prosper, [b]and shall execute
judgment and justice in the earth.
6 [c]In his days Judah shall be
saved, and Israel [d]shall dwell safely:
and [e]this *is* his name whereby he shall
be called, [g]THE LORD OUR RIGH- Ezek.
TEOUSNESS. 3:16-21
7 Therefore, behold, [f]the days
come, saith the LORD, that they shall no
more say, The LORD liveth, which
brought up the children of Israel out of
the land of Egypt;
8 But, The LORD liveth, which
brought up and which led the seed of
the house of Israel out of the north
country, [g]and from all countries
whither I had driven them; and they
shall dwell in their own land.

False prophets

9 ¶ Mine heart within me is broken
because of the prophets; [h]all my
bones shake; I am like a drunken man,
and like a man whom wine hath over-
come, because of the LORD, and be-
cause of the words of his holiness.
10 For [i]the land is full of adulter-
ers; for [j]because of [h]swearing the

22:24 [o]See 2 Ki. 24:6,8 1 Chr. 3:16 ch. 37:1 [p]Sol. 8:6 Hag. 2:23 **22:25** [q]ch. 34:20 **22:26** [r]2 Ki. 24:15 2 Chr. 36:10 **22:28** [s]Ps. 31:12 ch. 48:38 Hos. 8:8 **22:29** [t]Deut. 32:1 Is. 1:2 & 34:1 Mic. 1:2 **22:30** [u]See 1 Chr. 3:16, 17 Mat. 1:12 [v]ch. 36:30 **23:1** [w]ch. 10:21 22:22 Ezek. 34:2 **23:2** [x]Ex. 32:34 **23:3** [y]ch. 32:37 Ezek. 34:13 **23:4** [z]ch. 3:15 Ezek. 34:23 **23:5** [a]Is. 4:2 & 11:1 & 40:10,11 ch. 33:14 Dan. 9:24 Zech. 6:12 John 1:45 [b]Ps. 72:2 Is. 9:7 & 32:1,18 **23:6** [c]Deut. 33:28 Zech. 14:11 [d]ch. 32:37 [e]ch. 33:16 1 Cor. 1:30 **23:7** [f]ch. 16:14 **23:8** [g]Is. 43:5,6 **23:9** [h]See Hab. 3:16 **23:10** [i]ch. 9:2 [j]Hos. 4:2,3

[f]Heb. *lift up their mind* [g]Heb. *Jehovah-tsidkenu* [h]Or, *cursing*

23:1 WOE BE UNTO THE PASTORS. In this chapter Jeremiah prophesies woe and judgment on Judah's spiritual leaders (the priests and the false prophets), who were selfishly enriching themselves while not caring at all about the condition of the people (cf. Ezek. 34). They would be destroyed and the people sent into exile. What would God do then? He Himself would "gather the remnant . . . and . . . bring them again to their folds" (v. 3), and give them shepherds who would rightly care for them; the ultimate Shepherd would be the "righteous Branch" (v. 5), i.e., the Messiah.

23:5–6 A RIGHTEOUS BRANCH. The branch (i.e., the kingly line) of David was cut off when God destroyed the Davidic monarchy in 586 B.C. (1) God did promise, however, to raise up a king from the line of David who would be a righteous Branch; this King would finally and fully do what was just and right (cf. Zech. 3:8). This prophecy points to the Messiah, Jesus Christ. (2) His full execution of judgment will occur after His second coming and before His millennial reign on the earth. (3) He will be called "THE LORD OUR RIGHTEOUSNESS" (v. 6). The believing remnant will "be found in him, not having [their] own righteousness, which is of the law, but that which is through the faith of Christ, the righteousness which is of God by faith" (Phil. 3:9).

23:9–40 THE PROPHETS. Jeremiah denounces the sins of the false prophets, who had opposed his message of doom (6:13–14; 14:14–16; 29:8–9) and proclaimed only peace and prosperity (see 6:14, note). Jeremiah placed the responsibility for Judah's deplorable moral state on the shoulders of these wicked prophets.

land mourneth; [k]the pleasant places
of the wilderness are dried up, and
their [i]course is evil, and their force *is*
not right.
11 For [l]both prophet and priest
are profane; yea, [m]in my house have I
found their wickedness, saith the LORD.
12 [n]Wherefore their way shall be
unto them as slippery *ways* in the dark-
ness: they shall be driven on, and fall
therein: for I [o]will bring evil upon
them, *even* the year of their visitation,
saith the LORD.
13 And I have seen [j,k]folly in the
prophets of Samaria; [p]they prophe-
sied in Baal, and [q]caused my people
Israel to err.
14 I have seen also in the prophets
of Jerusalem [l]an horrible thing:
[r]they commit adultery, and [s]walk in
lies: they [t]strengthen also the hands
of evildoers, that none doth return
from his wickedness: they are all of
them unto me as [u]Sodom, and the in-
habitants thereof as Gomorrah.
15 Therefore thus saith the LORD of
hosts concerning the prophets; Be-
hold, I will feed them with [v]worm-
wood, and make them drink the water
of gall: for from the prophets of Jerusa-
lem is [m]profaneness gone forth into
all the land.
16 Thus saith the LORD of hosts,
Hearken not unto the words of the
prophets that prophesy unto you: they
make you vain: [w]they speak a vision of
their own heart, *and* not out of the
mouth of the LORD.
17 They say still unto them that de-
spise me, The LORD hath said, [x]Ye
shall have peace; and they say unto ev-
ery one that walketh after the [n]imagi-
nation of his own heart, [y]No evil shall
come upon you.
18 For [z]who hath stood in the
[o]counsel of the LORD, and hath per-
ceived and heard his word? who hath
marked his word, and heard *it*?
19 Behold, a [a]whirlwind of the
LORD is gone forth in fury, even a griev-
ous whirlwind: it shall fall grievously
upon the head of the wicked.
20 The [b]anger of the LORD shall not
return, until he have executed, and till
he have performed the thoughts of his
heart: [c]in the latter days ye shall con-
sider it perfectly.
21 [d]I have not sent these prophets,
yet they ran: I have not spoken to
them, yet they prophesied.
22 But if they had [e]stood in my
counsel, and had caused my people to
hear my words, then they should have
[f]turned them from their evil way, and
from the evil of their doings.
23 *Am* I a God at hand, saith the
LORD, and not a God afar off?
24 Can any [g]hide himself in secret
places that I shall not see him? saith
the LORD. [h]Do not I fill heaven and
earth? saith the LORD.
25 I have heard what the prophets
said, that prophesy lies in my name,
saying, I have dreamed, I have
dreamed.
26 How long shall *this* be in the
heart of the prophets that prophesy
lies? yea, *they are* prophets of the de-
ceit of their own heart;
27 Which think to cause my people
to forget my name by their dreams
which they tell every man to his neigh-
bour, [i]as their fathers have forgotten
my name for Baal.
28 The prophet [p]that hath a
dream, let him tell a dream; and he that
hath my word, let him speak my word

23:10 [k]ch. 9:10
23:11 [l]Zeph. 3:4 [m]ch. 7:30 Ezek. 8:11 & 23:39
23:12 [n]Ps. 35:6 Prov. 4:19 ch. 13:16 [o]ch. 11:23
23:13 [p]ch. 2:8 [q]Is. 9:16
23:14 [r]ch. 29:23 [s]ver. 26 [t]Ezek. 13:22 [u]Is. 1:9,10
23:15 [v]ch. 9:15
23:16 [w]ch. 14:14
23:17 [x]ch. 8:11 Ezek. 13:10 Zech. 10:2 [y]Mic. 3:11
23:18 [z]Job 15:8 1 Cor. 2:16
23:19 [a]ch. 25:32 & 30:23
23:20 [b]ch. 30:24 [c]Gen. 49:1
23:21 [d]ch:14:14
23:22 [e]ver. 18 [f]ch. 25:5
23:24 [g]Ps. 139:7 Amos 9:2,3 [h]1 Ki. 8:27 Ps. 139:7
23:27 [i]Judg. 3:7

[i] Or, *violence* [j] Or, *an absurd thing* [k] Heb. *unsavoury* [l] Or, *filthiness* [m] Or, *hypocrisy* [n] Or, *stubbornness* [o] Or, *secret* [p] Heb. *with whom* is

23:14 IN THE PROPHETS ... AN HORRIBLE THING. God calls the spiritual adultery of the false prophets a terrible thing. They were supposed to be his righteous representatives, but instead they lived like the people of Sodom and Gomorrah. The example of these "spiritual leaders" contributed greatly to the increase of immorality and the hardening of the people's hearts against repentance. When a minister of God commits adultery, it is especially an abomination before God. Not only does such a sin reflect unfaithfulness to God, but it shows contempt for Him and His word (see 2 Sam. 12:9–12, notes) and disqualifies this leader as a servant of the Lord and his flock (see article on MORAL QUALIFICATIONS FOR OVERSEERS, p. 1908).

23:17 THEY SAY ... YE SHALL HAVE PEACE. False prophets hold out to God's people a false hope and security (see vv. 9–40, note). (1) Those who maintain that the immoral and disobedient among God's people will not be condemned for their evil and do not need to fear God's wrath and judgment prove themselves to be false messengers. (2) Prophets with this message existed not only in O.T. times but also in N.T. times. The apostle Paul warned the Ephesians not to be deceived by such teachers (Eph. 5:4–6; see 1 Cor. 6:9, note; Gal. 5:21, note).

faithfully. What *is* the chaff to the wheat? saith the LORD.

29 *Is* not my word like as a fire? saith the LORD; and like a hammer *that* breaketh the rock in pieces?

30 Therefore, behold, [j]I *am* against the prophets, saith the LORD, that steal my words every one from his neighbour.

31 Behold, I *am* against the prophets, saith the LORD, [q]that use their tongues, and say, He saith.

32 Behold, I *am* against them that prophesy false dreams, saith the LORD, and do tell them, and cause my people to err by their lies, and by [k]their lightness; yet I sent them not, nor commanded them: therefore they shall not profit this people at all, saith the LORD.

The burden of the LORD

33 ¶ And when this people, or the prophet, or a priest, shall ask thee, saying, What *is* [l]the burden of the LORD? thou shalt then say unto them, What burden? [m]I will even forsake you, saith the LORD.

34 And *as for* the prophet, and the priest, and the people, that shall say, The burden of the LORD, I will even [r]punish that man and his house.

35 Thus shall ye say every one to his neighbour, and every one to his brother, What hath the LORD answered? and, What hath the LORD spoken?

36 And the burden of the LORD shall ye mention no more: for every man's word shall be his burden; for ye have perverted the words of the living God, of the LORD of hosts our God.

37 Thus shalt thou say to the prophet, What hath the LORD answered thee? and, What hath the LORD spoken?

23:30 [j]Deut. 18:20 ch. 14:14,15
23:32 [k]Zeph. 3:4
23:33 [l]Mal. 1:1 [m]ver. 39

23:39 [n]Hos. 4:6 [o]ver. 33
23:40 [p]ch. 20:11
24:1 [q]Amos 7:1,4 & 8:1 [r]2 Ki. 24:12 2 Chr. 36:10 [s]See ch. 22:24 & 29:2

38 But since ye say, The burden of the LORD; therefore thus saith the LORD; Because ye say this word, The burden of the LORD, and I have sent unto you, saying, Ye shall not say, The burden of the LORD;

39 Therefore, behold, I, even I, [n]will utterly forget you, and [o]I will forsake you, and the city that I gave you and your fathers, *and cast you* out of my presence:

40 And I will bring [p]an everlasting reproach upon you, and a perpetual shame, which shall not be forgotten.

Sign of the good and evil figs

24 THE [q]LORD showed me, and, behold, two baskets of figs *were* set before the temple of the LORD, after that Nebuchadrezzar [r]king of Babylon had carried away captive [s]Jeconiah the son of Jehoiakim king of Judah, and the princes of Judah, with the carpenters and smiths, from Jerusalem, and had brought them to Babylon.

2 One basket *had* very good figs, *even* like the figs *that are* first ripe: and the other basket *had* very naughty figs, which could not be eaten, [s]they were so bad.

3 Then said the LORD unto me, What seest thou, Jeremiah? And I said, Figs; the good figs, very good; and the evil, very evil, that cannot be eaten, they are so evil.

4 ¶ Again the word of the LORD came unto me, saying,

5 Thus saith the LORD, the God of Israel; Like these good figs, so will I acknowledge [t]them that are carried

[q] Or, *that smooth their tongues* [r] Heb. *visit upon* [s] Heb. *for badness* [t] Heb. *the captivity*

23:31–32 I AM AGAINST THE PROPHETS. God's word to Jeremiah warns us how dangerous it is to declare, "Thus saith the LORD," if we are not sure that the word is from the Lord. The prophetic office must be undertaken only with the utmost seriousness (cf. vv. 33–40).

24:1–10 AFTER THAT NEBUCHADREZZAR ... HAD CARRIED AWAY CAPTIVE. The historical background for the parable of the two baskets of figs is the beginning of Zedekiah's reign. Nebuchadnezzar had just deported Jehoiachin and many other Israelites to Babylon (597 B.C.). Zedekiah and those who remained behind had been spared the judgment of God; thus they believed Jeremiah's prophecies of total destruction were misguided. Jeremiah's parable warned that those left in Jerusalem would experience a far more devastating judgment than those who had already gone into exile in Babylon.

24:1 TWO BASKETS OF FIGS. The first basket of figs (i.e., the exiles of 597 B.C.) was considered to contain good figs, good in that God would purify them through the suffering of the exile (v. 5). After their exile they would be brought back into the land (v. 6) and would turn from idolatry to God with all their hearts (v. 7). God would use them to accomplish His redemptive purpose in the world. The second basket of figs had bad figs (v. 2) and represented King Zedekiah and those who remained in Jerusalem after that recent deportation. They would continue to oppose Jeremiah and his message and thus experience the incredible horrors of the fall of Jerusalem in 586 B.C., bringing great disgrace.

away captive of Judah, whom I have sent out of this place into the land of the Chaldeans for *their* good.

6 For I will set mine eyes upon them for good, and [t]I will bring them again to this land: and [u]I will build them, and not pull *them* down; and I will plant them, and not pluck *them* up.

7 And I will give them [v]an heart to know me, that I *am* the LORD: and they shall be [w]my people, and I will be their God: for they shall return unto me [x]with their whole heart.

8 ¶ And as the evil [y]figs, which cannot be eaten, they are so evil; surely thus saith the LORD, So will I give Zedekiah the king of Judah, and his princes, and the residue of Jerusalem, that remain in this land, and [z]them that dwell in the land of Egypt:

9 And I will deliver them [u]to [a]be removed into all the kingdoms of the earth for *their* hurt, [b]*to be* a reproach and a proverb, a taunt and a curse, in all places whither I shall drive them.

10 And I will send the sword, the famine, and the pestilence, among them, till they be consumed from off the land that I gave unto them and to their fathers.

Judah's captivity

25 THE WORD that came to Jeremiah concerning all the people of Judah [c]in the fourth year of Jehoiakim the son of Josiah king of Judah, that *was* the first year of Nebuchadrezzar king of Babylon;

2 The which Jeremiah the prophet spake unto all the people of Judah, and to all the inhabitants of Jerusalem, saying,

3 [d]From the thirteenth year of Josiah the son of Amon king of Judah, even unto this day, that *is* the three and twentieth year, the word of the LORD hath come unto me, and I have spoken unto you, rising early and speaking; [e]but ye have not hearkened.

4 And the LORD hath sent unto you all his servants the prophets, [f]rising early and sending *them;* but ye have not hearkened, nor inclined your ear to hear.

5 They said, [g]Turn ye again now every one from his evil way, and from the evil of your doings, and dwell in the land that the LORD hath given unto you and to your fathers for ever and ever:

6 And go not after other gods to serve them, and to worship them, and provoke me not to anger with the works of your hands; and I will do you no hurt.

7 Yet ye have not hearkened unto me, saith the LORD; that ye might [h]provoke me to anger with the works of your hands to your own hurt.

8 ¶ Therefore thus saith the LORD of hosts; Because ye have not heard my words,

9 Behold, I will send and take [i]all the families of the north, saith the LORD, and Nebuchadrezzar the king of Babylon, [j]my servant, and will bring them against this land, and against the inhabitants thereof, and against all these nations round about, and will utterly destroy them, and [k]make them an astonishment, and an hissing, and perpetual desolations.

10 Moreover [v]I will take from them the [l]voice of mirth, and the voice of gladness, the voice of the bridegroom, and the voice of the bride, [m]the sound of the millstones, and the light of the candle.

11 And this whole land shall be a

[u] Heb. *for removing,* or, *vexation* [v] Heb. *I will cause to perish from them*

24:6 [t]ch. 12:15 & 29:10 [u]ch. 32:41 & 33:7 & 42:10 **24:7** [v]Deut. 30:6 ch. 32:39 Ezek. 11:19 & 36:26,27 [w]ch. 30:22 & 31:33 & 32:38 [x]ch. 29:13 **24:8** [y]ch. 29:17 [z]See ch. 43 & 44 **24:9** [a]Deut. 28:25,37 1 Ki. 9:7 2 Chr. 7:20 ch. 15:4 & 29:18 & 34:17 [b]Ps. 44:13,14 **25:1** [c]ch 36:1 **25:3** [d]ch. 1:2 [e]ch. 7:13 & 11:7,8,10 **25:4** [f]ch. 7:13,25 **25:5** [g]ch. 18:11 Jonah 3:8 **25:7** [h]Deut. 32:21 **25:9** [i]ch. 1:15 [j]ch. 27:6 Is. 45:1 [k]ch. 18:16 **25:10** [l]Is. 24:7 Hos. 2:11 Rev. 18:23 [m]Eccl. 12:4

25:1 THE FIRST YEAR OF NEBUCHADREZZAR. This year was 605 B.C., an important date because Nebuchadnezzar's reign marks the beginning of four successive kingdoms that were to have world dominion (see Dan. 2; 7).

25:3 THREE AND TWENTIETH YEAR. Jeremiah had preached earnestly for twenty-three years, but the people had not listened. He had exhorted them to turn from their worship of idols and from their sinful ways, but they had remained obstinate. God had even sent other prophets to warn Judah (v. 4), among whom were Urijah, Zephaniah, and Habakkuk. Jeremiah's experience underscores the truth that no matter how faithful we are in witnessing to the saving gospel of Christ, some will refuse to heed God's word and go on to their own destruction. Furthermore, in the last days, those in the church who remain faithful to God and His word will be grieved as they see many abandon Biblical faith and God's righteous standards (see 1 Tim. 4:1, note).

25:11 SEVENTY YEARS. Judah would remain in exile for approximately seventy years. The seventy years began in the fourth year of King Jehoiakim (605 B.C.), when the first set of exiles were carried off, and continued to the first return of exiles in 538 B.C., following the decree of Cyrus (see Ezra 1:1, note; 2:1, note; cf. 2 Chr. 36:21–23; Dan. 9:2).

desolation, *and* an astonishment; and these nations shall serve the king of Babylon seventy years.

12 ¶ And it shall come to pass, [n]when seventy years are accomplished, *that* I will [w]punish the king of Babylon, and that nation, saith the LORD, for their iniquity, and the land of the Chaldeans, [o]and will make it perpetual desolations.

13 And I will bring upon that land all my words which I have pronounced against it, *even* all that is written in this book, which Jeremiah hath prophesied against all the nations.

14 [p]For many nations [q]and great kings shall [r]serve themselves of them also: [s]and I will recompense them according to their deeds, and according to the works of their own hands.

The cup of fury

15 ¶ For thus saith the LORD God of Israel unto me; Take the [t]wine cup of this fury at my hand, and cause all the nations, to whom I send thee, to drink it.

16 And [u]they shall drink, and be moved, and be mad, because of the sword that I will send among them.

17 Then took I the cup at the LORD's hand, and made all the nations to drink, unto whom the LORD had sent me:

18 *To wit,* Jerusalem, and the cities of Judah, and the kings thereof, and the princes thereof, to make them [v]a desolation, an astonishment, an hissing, and [w]a curse; as *it is* this day;

19 Pharaoh king of Egypt, and his servants, and his princes, and all his people;

20 And all the mingled people, and all the kings of [x]the land of Uz, and all the kings of the land of the Philistines, and Ashkelon, and Azzah, and Ekron, and [y]the remnant of Ashdod,

21 [z]Edom, and Moab, and the children of Ammon,

22 And all the kings of [a]Tyrus, and all the kings of Zidon, and the kings of the [x]isles which *are* beyond the [b]sea,

23 [c]Dedan, and Tema, and Buz, and all [y]*that are* in the utmost corners,

24 And all the kings of Arabia, and all the kings of the [d]mingled people that dwell in the desert,

25 And all the kings of Zimri, and all the kings of Elam, and all the kings of the Medes,

26 [e]And all the kings of the north, far and near, one with another, and all the kingdoms of the world, which *are* upon the face of the earth: and the king of Sheshach shall drink after them.

27 Therefore thou shalt say unto them, Thus saith the LORD of hosts, the God of Israel; [f]Drink ye, and [g]be drunken, and spew, and fall, and rise no more, because of the sword which I will send among you.

28 And it shall be, if they refuse to take the cup at thine hand to drink, then shalt thou say unto them, Thus saith the LORD of hosts; Ye shall certainly drink.

29 For, lo, [h]I begin to bring evil on the city [i]which[z] is called by my name, and should ye be utterly unpunished? Ye shall not be unpunished: for [j]I will call for a sword upon all the inhabitants of the earth, saith the LORD of hosts.

30 Therefore prophesy thou against them all these words, and say unto them, The LORD shall [k]roar from on high, and utter his voice from [l]his holy habitation; he shall mightily roar upon [m]his habitation; he shall give [n]a shout, as they that tread *the grapes,* against all the inhabitants of the earth.

31 A noise shall come *even* to the ends of the earth; for the LORD hath [o]a controversy with the nations, [p]he will plead with all flesh; he will give them *that are* wicked to the sword, saith the LORD.

32 Thus saith the LORD of hosts, Behold, evil shall go forth from nation to nation, and [q]a great whirlwind shall be raised up from the coasts of the earth.

33 [r]And the slain of the LORD shall

25:12 [n]2 Chr. 36:21,22 Ezra 1:1 Dan. 9:2 [o]Is. 21:1 ch. 50:3
25:14 [p]ch. 50:9 & 51:27,28 [q]ch. 51:27 [r]ch. 27:7 [s]ch. 50:29 & 51:6,24
25:15 [t]Job 21:20 Ps. 75:8 Is. 51:17 Rev. 14:10
25:16 [u]ch. 51:7 Ezek. 23:34 Nah. 3:11
25:18 [v]ver. 9,11 [w]ch. 24:9
25:20 [x]Job 1:1 [y]Is. 20:1
25:21 [z]ch. 49:7
25:22 [a]ch. 47:4 [b]ch. 49:23
25:23 [c]ch. 49:8
25:24 [d]Ezek. 30:5
25:26 [e]ch. 50:9
25:27 [f]Hab. 2:16 [g]Is. 63:6
25:29 [h]Ezek. 9:6 Luke 23:31 1 Pet. 4:17 [i]Dan. 9:18 [j]Ezek. 38:21
25:30 [k]Is. 42:13 Joel 3:16 Amos 1:2 [l]Ps. 11:4 [m]1 Ki. 9:3 Ps. 132:14 [n]Is. 16:9 ch. 48:33
25:31 [o]Hos. 4:1 Mic. 6:2 [p]Is. 66:16 Joel 3:2
25:32 [q]ch. 23:19 & 30:23
25:33 [r]Is. 66:16

[w] Heb. *visit upon* [x] Or, *region by the sea side* [y] Heb. *cut off into corners,* or, *having the corners of the hair polled;* see ch. 9:26 [z] Heb. *upon which my name is called*

25:12 I WILL PUNISH THE KING OF BABYLON. Jeremiah prophesies that God would repay Babylon for its cruel and sinful deeds. Babylon was defeated by the Medes and Persians under Cyrus in 539 B.C. (cf. Dan. 5:30–31).

25:15 THE WINE CUP OF THIS FURY. Intoxicating wine is often used in Scripture to signify God's wrath (see 49:12; 51:7; Job 21:20; Ps. 60:3; Is. 51:17,22; Ezek. 23:31; Rev. 14:8,10; 16:19; 18:6).

be at that day from *one* end of the earth
even unto the *other* end of the earth:
they shall not be [s]lamented, [t]neither
gathered, nor buried; they shall be
dung upon the ground.
34 ¶ [u]Howl, ye shepherds, and cry;
and wallow yourselves *in the ashes,* ye
principal of the flock: for [a]the days of
your slaughter and of your dispersions
are accomplished; and ye shall fall like
[b]a pleasant vessel.
35 And the shepherds shall have no
way to flee, nor the principal of the
flock to escape.
36 A voice of the cry of the shep-
herds, and an howling of the principal
of the flock, *shall be heard:* for the LORD
hath spoiled their pasture.
37 And the peaceable habitations
are cut down because of the fierce an-
ger of the LORD.
38 He hath forsaken his covert, as
the lion: for their land is [c]desolate be-
cause of the fierceness of the oppres-
sor, and because of his fierce anger.

Jeremiah arrested and released

26 IN THE beginning of the reign
of Jehoiakim the son of Josiah
king of Judah came this word from the
LORD, saying,
2 Thus saith the LORD; Stand in
[v]the court of the LORD's house, and
speak unto all the cities of Judah,
which come to worship in the LORD's
house, [w]all the words that I command
thee to speak unto them; [x]diminish
not a word:
3 [y]If so be they will hearken, and
turn every man from his evil way, that
I may [z]repent me of the evil, which I
purpose to do unto them because of the
evil of their doings.
4 And thou shalt say unto them,
Thus saith the LORD; [a]If ye will not
hearken to me, to walk in my law,
which I have set before you,
5 To hearken to the words of my
servants the prophets, [b]whom I sent
unto you, both rising up early, and
sending *them,* but ye have not heark-
ened;
6 Then will I make this house like
[c]Shiloh, and will make this city [d]a
curse to all the nations of the earth.
7 So the priests and the prophets
and all the people heard Jeremiah
speaking these words in the house of
the LORD.
8 ¶ Now it came to pass, when Jere-
miah had made an end of speaking all
that the LORD had commanded *him* to
speak unto all the people, that the
priests and the prophets and all the
people took him, saying, Thou shalt
surely die.
9 Why hast thou prophesied in the
name of the LORD, saying, This house
shall be like Shiloh, and this city shall
be desolate without an inhabitant? And
all the people were gathered against
Jeremiah in the house of the LORD.
10 ¶ When the princes of Judah
heard these things, then they came up
from the king's house unto the house
of the LORD, and sat down [d]in the en-
try of the new gate of the LORD's *house.*
11 Then spake the priests and the
prophets unto the princes and to all the
people, saying, [e]This man *is* worthy to
die; [e]for he hath prophesied against
this city, as ye have heard with your
ears.
12 ¶ Then spake Jeremiah unto all
the princes and to all the people, say-
ing, The LORD sent me to prophesy

25:33 [s]ch. 16:4,6 [t]Ps. 79:3 ch. 8:2 Rev. 11:9 **25:34** [u]ch. 4:8 & 6:26 **26:2** [v]ch. 19:14 [w]Ezek. 3:10 Mat. 28:20 [x]Acts 20:27 **26:3** [y]ch. 36:3 [z]ch. 18:8 Jonah 3:8,9 **26:4** [a]Lev. 26:14 Deut. 28:15 **26:5** [b]ch. 7:13,25 & 11:7 & 25:3,4 **26:6** [c]1 Sam. 4:10,11 Ps. 78:60 ch. 7:12,14 [d]Is. 65:15 ch. 24:9 **26:11** [e]ch. 38:4

[a] Heb. *your days for slaughter* [b] Heb. *a vessel of desire* [c] Heb. *a desolation* [d] Or, *at the door* [e] Heb. *The judgment of death* is *for this man*

26:2 ALL THE WORDS THAT I COMMAND THEE. Knowing that his prophecy would offend people and cause hostility and opposition, Jeremiah may have been tempted to hold back some particularly severe words given him by the Lord; the Lord told him not to omit a single word. The entire message of God must be proclaimed. Faithful ministers should not avoid speaking the harsh words of God's commands and warnings, even though they know some will turn away from them. Those who ignore parts of God's word and accommodate the sins of the congregation are unworthy ministers.

26:8 THOU SHALT SURELY DIE. Because of his proclamation of the word of the Lord, Jeremiah was seized by the religious establishment (i.e., the priests and false prophets), who demanded his death. Religious leaders are often the ones who consistently oppose those who call for a return to Biblical faith and genuine righteousness. This was true in Jesus' day; it will also be true in the last days before His return.

26:12–15 THEN SPAKE JEREMIAH. Jeremiah refused to retract his message of doom when threatened with death. Rather, he emphasized that his authority came from God, and he then called on the sinful people to repent. He remained faithful to God and His word despite a possible dangerous outcome.

against this house and against this city all the words that ye have heard.

13 Therefore now [f]amend your ways and your doings, and obey the voice of the LORD your God; and the LORD will [g]repent him of the evil that he hath pronounced against you.

14 As for me, behold, [h]I *am* in your hand: do with me [f]as seemeth good and meet unto you.

15 But know ye for certain, that if ye put me to death, ye shall surely bring innocent blood upon yourselves, and upon this city, and upon the inhabitants thereof: for of a truth the LORD hath sent me unto you to speak all these words in your ears.

16 ¶ Then said the princes and all the people unto the priests and to the prophets; This man *is* not worthy to die: for he hath spoken to us in the name of the LORD our God.

17 [i]Then rose up certain of the elders of the land, and spake to all the assembly of the people, saying,

18 [j]Micah the Morasthite prophesied in the days of Hezekiah king of Judah, and spake to all the people of Judah, saying, Thus saith the LORD of hosts; [k]Zion shall be plowed *like* a field, and Jerusalem shall become heaps, and the mountain of the house as the high places of a forest.

19 Did Hezekiah king of Judah and all Judah put him at all to death? [l]did he not fear the LORD, and besought [g]the LORD, and the LORD [m]repented him of the evil which he had pronounced against them? [n]Thus might we procure great evil against our souls.

20 And there was also a man that prophesied in the name of the LORD, Urijah the son of Shemaiah of Kirjath-jearim, who prophesied against this city and against this land according to all the words of Jeremiah:

21 And when Jehoiakim the king, with all his mighty men, and all the princes, heard his words, the king sought to put him to death: but when Urijah heard it, he was afraid, and fled, and went into Egypt;

22 And Jehoiakim the king sent men into Egypt, *namely,* Elnathan the son of Achbor, and *certain* men with him into Egypt.

23 And they fetched forth Urijah out of Egypt, and brought him unto Jehoiakim the king; who slew him with the sword, and cast his dead body into the graves of the [h]common people.

24 Nevertheless [o]the hand of Ahikam the son of Shaphan was with Jeremiah, that they should not give him into the hand of the people to put him to death.

Nebuchadnezzar's victory

27 IN THE beginning of the reign of Jehoiakim the son of Josiah [p]king of Judah came this word unto Jeremiah from the LORD, saying,

2 Thus [i]saith the LORD to me; Make thee bonds and yokes, [q]and put them upon thy neck,

3 And send them to the king of Edom, and to the king of Moab, and to the king of the Ammonites, and to the king of Tyrus, and to the king of Zidon, by the hand of the messengers which come to Jerusalem unto Zedekiah king of Judah;

4 And command them [j]to say unto their masters, Thus saith the LORD of hosts, the God of Israel; Thus shall ye say unto your masters;

5 [r]I have made the earth, the man and the beast that *are* upon the ground, by my great power and by my outstretched arm, and [s]have given it unto whom it seemed meet unto me.

6 [t]And now have I given all these lands into the hand of Nebuchadnezzar

26:13 [f]ch. 7:3 [g]ver. 3,19
26:14 [h]ch. 38:5
26:17 [i]See Acts 5:34
26:18 [j]Mic. 1:1 [k]Mic. 3:12
26:19 [l]2 Chr. 32:26 [m]Ex. 32:14 2 Sam. 24:16 [n]Acts 5:39
26:24 [o]2 Ki. 22:12,14 ch. 39:14
27:1 [p]See ver. 3,12,20 ch. 28:1
27:2 [q]ch. 28:10,12 Ezek. 4:1 & 12:3 & 24:3
27:5 [r]Ps. 115:15 & 146:6 Is. 45:12 [s]Ps. 115:16 Dan. 4:17,25,32
27:6 [t]ch. 28:14

[f]Heb. *as it is good and right in your eyes* [g]Heb. *the face of the LORD* [h]Heb. *sons of the people* [i]Or, *hath the LORD said* [j]Or, *concerning their masters, saying*

26:16–24 THIS MAN *IS* NOT WORTHY TO DIE. After hearing Jeremiah's defense (vv. 12–15), the officials and people sided with him against the priests and prophets. Some elders defended Jeremiah by giving examples of the actions of a righteous king, Hezekiah, and an evil king, Jehoiakim.

26:23 URIJAH . . . DEAD BODY. Jeremiah was delivered from death, while another righteous prophet named Urijah was not. Why God allows some of His people to suffer a martyr's death and others to die a natural death is not explained in Scripture (cf. Acts 12:1–17). But we do know that God has an eternal purpose in what He permits to happen to His faithful followers and that He works all things together for their good (see Rom. 8:28, note).

27:6 NEBUCHADNEZZAR . . . MY SERVANT. Nebuchadnezzar is called God's servant, not because he was righteous, but because God would use him and his army to punish many nations, including God's nation of Judah, for their sins. How-

the king of Babylon, [u]my servant; and [v]the beasts of the field have I given him also to serve him.

7 [w]And all nations shall serve him, and his son, and his son's son, [x]until the very time of his land come: [y]and then many nations and great kings shall serve themselves of him.

8 And it shall come to pass, *that* the nation and kingdom which will not serve the same Nebuchadnezzar the king of Babylon, and that will not put their neck under the yoke of the king of Babylon, that nation will I punish, saith the LORD, with the sword, and with the famine, and with the pestilence, until I have consumed them by his hand.

9 Therefore hearken not ye to your prophets, nor to your diviners, nor to your [k]dreamers, nor to your enchanters, nor to your sorcerers, which speak unto you, saying, Ye shall not serve the king of Babylon:

10 [z]For they prophesy a lie unto you, to remove you far from your land; and that I should drive you out, and ye should perish.

11 But the nations that bring their neck under the yoke of the king of Babylon, and serve him, those will I let remain still in their own land, saith the LORD; and they shall till it, and dwell therein.

12 ¶ I spake also to [a]Zedekiah king of Judah according to all these words, saying, Bring your necks under the yoke of the king of Babylon, and serve him and his people, and live.

13 [b]Why will ye die, thou and thy people, by the sword, by the famine, and by the pestilence, as the LORD hath spoken against the nation that will not serve the king of Babylon?

14 Therefore hearken not unto the words of the prophets that speak unto you, saying, Ye shall not serve the king of Babylon: for they prophesy [c]a lie unto you.

15 For I have not sent them, saith the LORD, yet they prophesy [l]a lie in my name; that I might drive you out, and that ye might perish, ye, and the prophets that prophesy unto you.

16 Also I spake to the priests and to all this people, saying, Thus saith the LORD; Hearken not to the words of your prophets that prophesy unto you, saying, Behold, [d]the vessels of the LORD's house shall now shortly be brought again from Babylon: for they prophesy a lie unto you.

17 Hearken not unto them; serve the king of Babylon, and live: wherefore should this city be laid waste?

18 But if they *be* prophets, and if the word of the LORD be with them, let them now make intercession to the LORD of hosts, that the vessels which are left in the house of the LORD, and *in* the house of the king of Judah, and at Jerusalem, go not to Babylon.

19 ¶ For thus saith the LORD of hosts [e]concerning the pillars, and concerning the sea, and concerning the bases, and concerning the residue of the vessels that remain in this city,

20 Which Nebuchadnezzar king of Babylon took not, when he carried away [f]captive Jeconiah the son of Jehoiakim king of Judah from Jerusalem to Babylon, and all the nobles of Judah and Jerusalem;

21 Yea, thus saith the LORD of hosts, the God of Israel, concerning the vessels that remain *in* the house of the LORD, and *in* the house of the king of Judah and of Jerusalem;

22 They shall be [g]carried to Babylon, and there shall they be until the day that I [h]visit them, saith the LORD; then [i]will I bring them up, and restore them to this place.

27:6 [u]ch. 25:9 & 43:10 Ezek. 29:18,20 [v]ch. 28:14 Dan. 2:38 **27:7** [w]2 Chr. 36:20 [x]ch. 25:12 & 50:27 Dan. 5:26 [y]ch. 25:14 **27:10** [z]ver. 14 **27:12** [a]ch. 28:1 & 38:17 **27:13** [b]Ezek. 18:31 **27:14** [c]ch. 14:14 & 23:21 & 29:8,9 **27:16** [d]2 Chr. 36:7,10 ch. 28:3 Dan. 1:2 **27:19** [e]2 Ki. 25:13 ch. 52:17,20,21 **27:20** [f]2 Ki. 24:14,15 ch. 24:1 **27:22** [g]2 Ki. 25:13 2 Chr. 36:18 [h]2 Chr. 36:21 ch. 29:10 & 32:5 [i]Ezra 1:7 & 7:19

[k]Heb. *dreams* [l]Heb. *in a lie*, or, *lyingly*

ever, God would also overthrow Babylon in His own set time (v. 7).

27:8 THE NATION ... WHICH WILL NOT SERVE. Jeremiah's prophetic counsel to Judah was to submit to Babylon's dominion and not resist the will of God for them. However, if they rebelled and fought against Babylon, Jeremiah warned that they would experience great suffering and defeat.

27:9 HEARKEN NOT YE TO YOUR PROPHETS. The false prophets were predicting a successful rebellion against their enemies and encouraging the people to throw off the yoke of Babylon. Jeremiah, on the other hand, instructed the people not to listen to them; he prophesied that Babylon would dominate Judah and the surrounding nations.

27:16 THE VESSELS OF THE LORD'S HOUSE. Some temple objects had been carried off to Babylon in 605 B.C. (see Dan. 1:1–2), others in 597 B.C. (2 Ki. 24:13).

Jeremiah exposes Hananiah

28 AND [j]IT came to pass the
same year, in the beginning of
the reign of Zedekiah king of Judah, in
the fourth year, *and* in the fifth month,
that Hananiah the son of Azur the
prophet, which *was* of Gibeon, spake
unto me in the house of the LORD, in the
presence of the priests and of all the
people, saying,
2 Thus speaketh the LORD of hosts,
the God of Israel, saying, I have broken
[k]the yoke of the king of Babylon.
3 [l]Within [m]two full years will I
bring again into this place all the ves-
sels of the LORD's house, that Nebu-
chadnezzar king of Babylon took away
from this place, and carried them to
Babylon:
4 And I will bring again to this place
Jeconiah the son of Jehoiakim king of
Judah, with all the [n]captives of Judah,
that went into Babylon, saith the LORD:
for I will break the yoke of the king of
Babylon.
5 ¶ Then the prophet Jeremiah said
unto the prophet Hananiah in the pres-
ence of the priests, and in the presence
of all the people that stood in the house
of the LORD,
6 Even the prophet Jeremiah said,
[m]Amen: the LORD do so: the LORD per-
form thy words which thou hast proph-
esied, to bring again the vessels of the
LORD's house, and all that is carried
away captive, from Babylon into this
place.
7 Nevertheless hear thou now this
word that I speak in thine ears, and in
the ears of all the people;
8 The prophets that have been be-
fore me and before thee of old prophe-
sied both against many countries, and
against great kingdoms, of war, and of
evil, and of pestilence.
9 [n]The prophet which prophesieth
of peace, when the word of the prophet
shall come to pass, *then* shall the
prophet be known, that the LORD hath
truly sent him.
10 ¶ Then Hananiah the prophet
took the [o]yoke from off the prophet
Jeremiah's neck, and brake it.
11 And Hananiah spake in the pres-
ence of all the people, saying, Thus
saith the LORD; Even so will I break the
yoke of Nebuchadnezzar king of Bab-
ylon [p]from the neck of all nations
within the space of two full years.
And the prophet Jeremiah went his
way.
12 ¶ Then the word of the LORD
came unto Jeremiah *the prophet,* after
that Hananiah the prophet had broken
the yoke from off the neck of the proph-
et Jeremiah, saying,
13 Go and tell Hananiah, saying,
Thus saith the LORD; Thou hast broken
the yokes of wood; but thou shalt make
for them yokes of iron.
14 For thus saith the LORD of hosts,
the God of Israel; [q]I have put a yoke
of iron upon the neck of all these na-
tions, that they may serve Nebuchad-
nezzar king of Babylon; and they shall
serve him: and [r]I have given him the
beasts of the field also.
15 ¶ Then said the prophet Jeremi-
ah unto Hananiah the prophet, Hear
now, Hananiah; The LORD hath not sent
thee; but [s]thou makest this people to
trust in a lie.
16 Therefore thus saith the LORD;
Behold, I will cast thee from off the
face of the earth: this year thou shalt
die, because thou hast taught [t]rebel-
lion[o] against the LORD.
17 So Hananiah the prophet died
the same year in the seventh month.

28:1 [j]ch. 27:1
28:2 [k]ch. 27:12
28:3 [l]ch. 27:16
28:6 [m]1 Ki. 1:36
28:9 [n]Deut. 18:22
28:10 [o]ch. 27:2
28:11 [p]ch. 27:7
28:14 [q]Deut. 28:48 ch. 27:7 [r]ch. 27:6
28:15 [s]ch. 29:31 Ezek. 13:22
28:16 [t]Deut. 13:5 ch. 29:32

[m] Heb. *two years of days* [n] Heb. *captivity*
[o] Heb. *revolt*

28:1 HANANIAH . . . THE PROPHET. Hananiah, who opposed Jeremiah's message of doom, was a false prophet who predicted the fall of Babylon and the return of exiles and temple treasures within two years. False religious leaders often predict that the blessings of God come unconditionally, without the need for repentance or holy living. Such a message always has popular appeal.

28:6–9 JEREMIAH SAID, AMEN. Jeremiah's "Amen" shows he also desired the return of the captives; however, first he prophesied further disaster for the people. Time would show Hananiah to be a false prophet and Jeremiah a true one. Jeremiah here did not immediately give a new prophecy; rather, he referred to the word of God already given through older prophets (like Isaiah).

28:13–17 GO AND TELL HANANIAH. Hananiah had deceived the people into believing lies. As a result, Jeremiah received a word from the Lord that predicted Hananiah's death. Within two months the false prophet died, confirming Jeremiah's prophecy. The penalty for apostasy and false prophecy is high. All leaders within the church who are not genuine servants of God will someday encounter the same severe judgment of God.

A letter to the captives

29 NOW THESE *are* the words of
the letter that Jeremiah the
prophet sent from Jerusalem unto the
residue of the elders which were car-
ried away captives, and to the priests,
and to the prophets, and to all the peo-
ple whom Nebuchadnezzar had carried
away captive from Jerusalem to Bab-
ylon;

2 (After that [u]Jeconiah the king,
and the queen, and the [p]eunuchs, the
princes of Judah and Jerusalem, and
the carpenters, and the smiths, were
departed from Jerusalem;)

3 By the hand of Elasah the son of
Shaphan, and Gemariah the son of Hil-
kiah, (whom Zedekiah king of Judah
sent unto Babylon to Nebuchadnezzar
king of Babylon) saying,

4 Thus saith the LORD of hosts, the
God of Israel, unto all that are carried
away captives, whom I have caused to
be carried away from Jerusalem unto
Babylon;

5 [v]Build ye houses, and dwell *in
them;* and plant gardens, and eat the
fruit of them;

6 Take ye wives, and beget sons
and daughters; and take wives for your
sons, and give your daughters to hus-
bands, that they may bear sons and
daughters; that ye may be increased
there, and not diminished.

7 And seek the peace of the city
whither I have caused you to be carried
away captives, [w]and pray unto the
LORD for it: for in the peace thereof
shall ye have peace.

8 ¶ For thus saith the LORD of hosts,
the God of Israel; Let not your proph-
ets and your diviners, that *be* in the
midst of you, [x]deceive you, neither
hearken to your dreams which ye
cause to be dreamed.

9 [y]For they prophesy [q]falsely
unto you in my name: I have not sent
them, saith the LORD.

10 ¶ For thus saith the LORD, That
after [z]seventy years be accomplished
at Babylon I will visit you, and perform
my good word toward you, in causing
you to return to this place.

11 For I know the thoughts that I
think toward you, saith the LORD,
thoughts of peace, and not of evil, to
give you an [r]expected end.

12 Then shall ye [a]call upon me,
and ye shall go and pray unto me, and
I will hearken unto you.

13 And [b]ye shall seek me, and find
me, when ye shall search for me [c]with
all your heart.

14 And [d]I will be found of you,
saith the LORD: and I will turn away
your captivity, and [e]I will gather you
from all the nations, and from all the
places whither I have driven you, saith
the LORD; and I will bring you again into
the place whence I caused you to be
carried away captive.

15 ¶ Because ye have said, The
LORD hath raised us up prophets in
Babylon;

29:2 [u]2 Ki. 24:12 ch. 22:26 & 28:4
29:5 [v]ver. 28
29:7 [w]Ezra 6:10 1 Tim. 2:2
29:8 [x]ch. 14:14 & 23:21 & 27:14,15 Eph. 5:6
29:9 [y]ver. 31
29:10 [z]2 Chr. 36:21,22 Ezra 1:1 ch. 25:12 & 27:22 Dan. 9:2
29:12 [a]Dan. 9:3
29:13 [b]Lev. 26:39,40 Deut. 30:1 [c]ch. 24:7
29:14 [d]Deut. 4:7 Ps. 32:6 & 46:1 Is. 55:6 [e]ch. 23:3,8 & 30:3 & 32:37

[p] Or, *chamberlains* [q] Heb. *in a lie* [r] Heb. *end and expectation*

29:1–23 THE LETTER. Jeremiah's letter to the Jewish exiles taken captive in 597 B.C. was probably written a year or two after they arrived in Babylon. He gave them the following instructions: (1) They must live normal lives, build houses, marry, and seek the peace or well-being of the city where God had providentially placed them, for they would not be returning to the promised land until the end of seventy years (vv. 7,10). (2) They must not listen to the false prophets who were predicting the exile would be short (vv. 8–9). (3) Those who remained in Jerusalem would suffer greatly for their persistence in rebelling against God (vv. 15–19). (4) Two false prophets would be killed because they were living in adultery and falsely representing God's word (vv. 21–23). (5) At the end of the seventy years of captivity, the remnant would seek God earnestly for restoration; He would answer their intercession because of His plans for them (vv. 10–14).

29:10 AFTER SEVENTY YEARS BE ACCOMPLISHED AT BABYLON. See 25:11, note.

29:12–13 THEN SHALL YE CALL . . . AND I WILL HEARKEN. Strategic timing is often involved in the fulfillment of God's promises (cf. Paul's reference to "the fulness of the time" in Gal. 4:4). God fulfills His word and promises both in relation to the fullness of His redemptive purpose (cf. v. 10) and in response to the earnest prayers of His faithful people (cf. Amos 5:4–6; see Dan. 9:2,5, notes). Jeremiah prophesied that at the end of the seventy-year captivity, a new fullness of time would occur; God would then move within a holy remnant so that they would seek Him in prayer with all their hearts. Thereupon God would listen, answer from heaven, and fulfill His promises of restoration (vv. 13–14). Note two principles: (1) when God desires to do great things for His people, He moves His people to great praying; and (2) the timing of God's answers to their prayers is often linked to God's purposes for His people as a whole.

THE PEACE OF GOD

Jer. 29:7 "And seek the peace of the city whither I have caused you to be carried away captives, and pray unto the Lord for it: for in the peace thereof shall ye have peace."

DEFINITION OF PEACE. The Hebrew word for peace is *shalom*. It denotes far more than the absence of war and conflict; the basic meaning of *shalom* is harmony, wholeness, soundness, well-being, and success in all areas of life. (1) It can refer to tranquility in international relationships, such as peace between warring nations (e.g., 1 Sam. 7:14; 1 Ki. 4:24; 1 Chr. 19:19). (2) It can also be experienced as a settled feeling within a nation, during times of prosperity and no civil war (2 Sam. 3:21–23; 1 Chr. 22:9; Ps. 122:6–7). (3) Peace can likewise be seen as wholeness and harmony in human relationships, both inside the home (Prov. 17:1; 1 Cor. 7:15) and outside the home (Rom. 12:18; Heb. 12:14; 1 Pet. 3:11). (4) And peace can refer to one's personal sense of wholeness and well-being, a being free from anxiety and at peace within our own souls (Ps. 4:8; 119:165; cf. Job 3:26) and with God (Num. 6:26; Rom. 5:1). (5) Finally, even though the word *shalom* is not used in Gen. 1—2, *shalom* describes the original created world that existed in perfect harmony and wholeness. When God created the heavens and the earth, he created a world at peace. The total well-being of creation is reflected in the summary statement: after God had finished creating the world, "every thing . . . *was* very good" (Gen. 1:31).

THE DISRUPTION OF PEACE. When Adam and Eve listened to the voice of the serpent and ate of the forbidden tree (Gen. 3:1–7), their disobedience introduced sin and disrupted creation's original harmony. (1) At that time, Adam and Eve experienced, for the first time, guilt and shame before God (Gen. 3:8) and a loss of inner peace.

(2) Adam and Eve's sin in the Garden of Eden destroyed their harmonious relationship with God. Before partaking of that fruit, they had intimate fellowship with God in the garden (cf. Gen. 3:8), but afterwards they "hid themselves from the presence of the Lord God amongst the trees of the garden" (Gen. 3:8). Instead of looking forward to talking with God, they were now afraid of his voice (Gen. 3:10).

(3) Furthermore, the harmonious relationship between Adam and Eve as husband and wife was disrupted. When God began discussing their sin with them, Adam blamed Eve (Gen. 3:12), and God pronounced that strife would continue between man and woman (Gen. 3:16). Thus began all the social conflict that is now part of our human predicament, from arguments and violence in our homes (cf. 1 Sam. 1:1–8; Prov. 15:18; 17:1) to international conflicts and wars.

(4) Finally, sin disrupted the harmony and unity between humankind and nature. Before Adam sinned, he joyfully worked in the Garden of Eden (Gen. 2:15) and freely walked among the animals, giving each one a name (Gen. 2:19–20). Part of God's curse after the fall included enmity between Adam and Eve and the serpent (Gen. 3:15), as well as the reality that work would entail sweat and drudgery (Gen. 3:17–19). Where there had been harmony between the human race and the environment, there was now struggle and conflict, so that "the whole creation groaneth and travaileth in pain together until now" (see Rom. 8:22, note).

THE RESTORATION OF PEACE. Though the result of the fall was the destruction of peace and well-being for humankind and indeed for the entire created world, God has planned to restore *shalom*. Thus, the story of regaining peace is the story of redemption in Christ. (1) Insofar as Satan initiated the destruction of peace into our world in the Garden of Eden, the reestablishment of peace must involve the destruction of Satan and his power. In fact, many of the O.T. promises regarding the coming of the Messiah were promises of a coming victory and peace. David prophesied that the Son of God would rule the nations (Ps. 2:8–9; cf. Rev. 2:26–27; 19:15). Isaiah prophesied that the Messiah

would reign as the Prince of Peace (Is. 9:6–7). Ezekiel predicted that the new covenant God planned to establish through the Messiah would be a covenant of peace (Ezek. 34:25; 37:26). And Micah, in prophesying of the birth of the coming ruler in Bethlehem, stated that "this *man* shall be the peace" (Mic. 5:5).

(2) At Jesus' birth, the angels proclaimed that God's peace had now come to the earth (Luke 2:14). Jesus Himself came to destroy the works of the devil (1 John 3:8) and to break down all barriers of conflict that are a part of our lives, thus making peace (Eph. 2:12–17). Jesus gave His disciples His peace as a lasting legacy before He went to the cross (John 14:27; 16:33). By His death and resurrection, Jesus disarmed the hostile principalities and powers and thereby made peace possible (Col. 1:20; 2:14–15; cf. Is. 53:4–5). Therefore, when we believe in Jesus Christ, we are justified by faith and have peace with God (Rom. 5:1). The message that Christians proclaim is the good news of peace (Acts 10:36; cf. Is. 52:7).

(3) Merely knowing that Christ came as the Prince of Peace does not mean that peace will automatically become part of our lives; to experience peace requires that we be united with Christ in an active faith. The first step is to believe in the Lord Jesus Christ. When we do, we are justified by faith (Rom. 3:21–28; 4:1–13; Gal. 2:16) and so have peace with God (Rom. 5:1). Along with faith, we must walk in obedience to His commandments in order to live in peace (Lev. 26:3,6). The O.T. prophets frequently declare that there is no peace for the wicked (Is. 57:21; 59:8; Jer. 6:14; 8:11; Ezek. 13:10,16). To know God's peace, He has given us the Holy Spirit, who begins to work His fruit in us—one aspect of which is peace (Gal. 5:22; cf. Rom. 14:17; Eph. 4:3). With the Spirit's help, we must pray for peace (Ps. 122:6–7; Jer. 29:7; see Phil. 4:7, note), let peace rule in our hearts (Col. 3:15), seek peace and pursue it (Ps. 34:14; Jer. 29:7; 2 Tim. 2:22; 1 Pet. 3:11), and do our best to live in peace with others (Rom. 12:18; 2 Cor. 13:11; 1 Thes. 5:13; Heb. 12:14).

16 *Know* that thus saith the LORD of the king that sitteth upon the throne of David, and of all the people that dwelleth in this city, *and* of your brethren that are not gone forth with you into captivity;

17 Thus saith the LORD of hosts; Behold, I will send upon them the sword, the famine, and the pestilence, and will make them like [f]vile figs, that cannot be eaten, they are so evil.

18 And I will persecute them with the sword, with the famine, and with the pestilence, and [g]will deliver them to be removed to all the kingdoms of the earth, [s]to be [h]a curse, and an astonishment, and an hissing, and a reproach, among all the nations whither I have driven them:

19 Because they have not hearkened to my words, saith the LORD, which [i]I sent unto them by my servants the prophets, rising up early and sending *them;* but ye would not hear, saith the LORD.

20 ¶ Hear ye therefore the word of the LORD, all ye of the captivity, whom I have sent from Jerusalem to Babylon:

21 Thus saith the LORD of hosts, the God of Israel, of Ahab the son of Kolaiah, and of Zedekiah the son of Maaseiah, which prophesy a lie unto you in my name; Behold, I will deliver them into the hand of Nebuchadrezzar king of Babylon; and he shall slay them before your eyes;

22 [j]And of them shall be taken up a curse by all the captivity of Judah which *are* in Babylon, saying, The LORD make thee like Zedekiah and like Ahab, [k]whom the king of Babylon roasted in the fire;

23 Because [l]they have committed villainy in Israel, and have committed adultery with their neighbours' wives, and have spoken lying words in my name, which I have not commanded them; even I know, and *am* a witness, saith the LORD.

29:17 [f]ch. 24:8
29:18 [g]Deut. 28:25 2 Chr. 29:8 ch. 15:4 & 24:9 & 34:17 [h]ch. 26:6 & 42:18
29:19 [i]ch. 25:4 & 32:33
29:22 [j]See Gen. 48:20 Is. 65:15 [k]Dan. 3:6
29:23 [l]ch. 23:14
29:25 [m]2 Ki. 25:18 ch. 21:1
29:26 [n]ch. 20:1 [o]2 Ki. 9:11 Acts 26:24 [p]ch. 20:2
29:28 [q]ver. 5
29:31 [r]ch. 28:15
29:32 [s]ch. 28:16

A letter to Shemaiah

24 ¶ *Thus* shalt thou also speak to Shemaiah the [t]Nehelamite, saying,

25 Thus speaketh the LORD of hosts, the God of Israel, saying, Because thou hast sent letters in thy name unto all the people that *are* at Jerusalem, [m]and to Zephaniah the son of Maaseiah the priest, and to all the priests, saying,

26 The LORD hath made thee priest in the stead of Jehoiada the priest, that ye should be [n]officers in the house of the LORD, for every man *that is* [o]mad, and maketh himself a prophet, that thou shouldest [p]put him in prison, and in the stocks.

27 Now therefore why hast thou not reproved Jeremiah of Anathoth, which maketh himself a prophet to you?

28 For therefore he sent unto us *in* Babylon, saying, This *captivity is* long: [q]build ye houses, and dwell *in them;* and plant gardens, and eat the fruit of them.

29 And Zephaniah the priest read this letter in the ears of Jeremiah the prophet.

30 ¶ Then came the word of the LORD unto Jeremiah, saying,

31 Send to all them of the captivity, saying, Thus saith the LORD concerning Shemaiah the Nehelamite; Because that Shemaiah hath prophesied unto you, [r]and I sent him not, and he caused you to trust in a lie:

32 Therefore thus saith the LORD; Behold, I will punish Shemaiah the Nehelamite, and his seed: he shall not have a man to dwell among this people; neither shall he behold the good that I will do for my people, saith the LORD; [s]because he hath taught [u]rebellion against the LORD.

Restoration of Israel

30 THE WORD that came to Jeremiah from the LORD, saying,

[s] Heb. *for a curse* [t] Or, *dreamer* [u] Heb. *revolt*

29:23 COMMITTED VILLANY IN ISRAEL. God considers it outrageous to proclaim His message and at the same time commit adultery and other immoral acts. For this reason, the two prophets Ahab and Zedekiah (v. 21) would be put to death before all the people. Church leaders today who proclaim God's word while living in adultery will also have to face His severe judgment (see article on MORAL QUALIFICATIONS FOR OVERSEERS, p. 1908).

29:24–32 SHEMAIAH. Shemaiah was a false prophet in Babylon who had written a letter to Zephaniah, a priest in Jerusalem, urging him to imprison Jeremiah. Evidently Jeremiah's letters to the exiles had angered the false prophets in Babylon. God responded by asserting that neither Shemaiah nor his descendants would participate in the return to Jerusalem.

30:1—33:26 THE WORD ... FROM THE LORD. Chs. 30—33 contain prophecies about the

2 Thus speaketh the LORD God of Is-
rael, saying, Write thee all the words
that I have spoken unto thee in a book.
3 For, lo, the days come, saith the
LORD, that [t]I will bring again the cap-
tivity of my people Israel and Judah,
saith the LORD: [u]and I will cause them
to return to the land that I gave to their
fathers, and they shall possess it.
4 ¶ And these *are* the words that the
LORD spake concerning Israel and con-
cerning Judah.
5 For thus saith the LORD; We have
heard a voice of trembling, [v]of fear,
and not of peace.
6 Ask ye now, and see whether [w]a
man doth travail with child? wherefore
do I see every man with his hands on
his loins, [v]as a woman in travail, and
all faces are turned into paleness?
7 [w]Alas! for that day *is* great, [x]so
that none *is* like it: it *is* even the time
of Jacob's trouble; but he shall be
saved out of it.
8 For it shall come to pass in that
day, saith the LORD of hosts, *that* I will
break his yoke from off thy neck, and
will burst thy bonds, and strangers
shall no more serve themselves of him:
9 But they shall serve the LORD their
God, and [y]David their king, whom I
will [z]raise up unto them.
10 ¶ Therefore [a]fear thou not,
O my servant Jacob, saith the LORD;
neither be dismayed, O Israel: for, lo,
I will save thee from afar, and thy seed
[b]from the land of their captivity; and
Jacob shall return, and shall be in rest,
and be quiet, and none shall make *him*
afraid.
11 For I *am* with thee, saith the
LORD, to save thee: [c]though I make a
full end of all nations whither I have
scattered thee, [d]yet will I not make a
full end of thee: but I will correct thee
[e]in measure, and will not leave thee
altogether unpunished.
12 For thus saith the LORD, [f]Thy
bruise *is* incurable, *and* thy wound *is*
grievous.
13 *There is* none to plead thy cause,
[x]that thou mayest be bound up:
[g]thou hast no healing medicines.
14 [h]All thy lovers have forgotten
thee; they seek thee not; for I have
wounded thee with the wound [i]of an
enemy, with the chastisement [j]of a
cruel one, for the multitude of thine in-
iquity; [k]*because* thy sins were in-
creased.
15 Why [l]criest thou for thine af-
fliction? thy sorrow *is* incurable for the
multitude of thine iniquity: *because* thy
sins were increased, I have done these
things unto thee.
16 Therefore all they that devour
thee [m]shall be devoured; and all thine
adversaries, every one of them, shall
go into captivity; and they that spoil
thee shall be a spoil, and all that prey
upon thee will I give for a prey.
17 [n]For I will restore health unto
thee, and I will heal thee of thy
wounds, saith the LORD; because they
called thee an Outcast, *saying,* This *is*
Zion, whom no man seeketh after. Ezek. 47:12
18 ¶ Thus saith the LORD; Behold,
[o]I will bring again the captivity of Ja-

30:3 [t]ver. 18 ch. 32:44 Ezek. 39:25 Amos 9:14,15 [u]ch. 16:15 **30:6** [v]ch. 4:31 & 6:24 **30:7** [w]Joel 2:11,31 Amos 5:18 Zeph. 1:14 [x]Dan. 12:1 **30:9** [y]Is. 55:3,4 Ezek. 34:23 & 37:24 Hos. 3:5 [z]Luke 1:69 Acts 2:30 & 13:23 **30:10** [a]Is. 41:13 & 43:5 & 44:2 ch. 46:27,28 [b]ch. 3:18 **30:11** [c]Amos 9:8 [d]ch. 4:27 [e]Ps. 6:1 Is. 27:8 ch. 10:24 & 46:28 **30:12** [f]2 Chr. 36:16 ch. 15:18 **30:13** [g]ch. 8:22 **30:14** [h]Lam. 1:2 [i]Job 13:24 & 16:9 & 19:11 [j]Job 30:21 [k]ch. 5:6 **30:15** [l]ch. 15:18 **30:16** [m]Ex. 23:22 Is. 33:1 & 41:11 ch. 10:25 **30:17** [n]ch. 33:6 **30:18** [o]ver. 3 ch. 33:7,11

[v]Or, there is *fear, and not peace* [w]Heb. *a male* [x]Heb. *for binding up,* or, *pressing*

future restoration and redemption of both Israel (the northern kingdom) and Judah (the southern kingdom). Jeremiah's prophecies encompass the near-at-hand restoration of the Jews from the Babylonian exile and the far-distant events related to the Messiah at the end of the age, when Christ will reign over His people. Jeremiah assures the Jewish exiles who were facing an apparently hopeless future that God's chosen people would not become extinct; a remnant would remain, through whom God would accomplish His will for the world.

30:3 RETURN TO THE LAND. Jeremiah had good news for the exiles—the promise of restoration and repossession of their homeland. The promise was made to both the northern kingdom (Israel) and the southern kingdom (Judah). From the exiles who had been displaced and refined by their experience of deportation would come God's remnant, who would in turn give hope to all humankind.

30:7 THE TIME OF JACOB'S TROUBLE. The verses that follow this phrase indicate that Jeremiah is speaking about the time of future tribulation for the Jewish people (cf. Is. 2:12–21; Ezek. 30:3; Dan. 9:27; Joel 1:15; Zech. 14:1–8,12–15; Mat. 24:21). From this time of great trouble a remnant of Israel would be saved; they would be freed from their oppressors (v. 8) to serve God and the Messiah (v. 9). Jacob's trouble would end at the appearing of Christ to establish His kingdom on earth (Rev. 19:11–21; 20:4–6).

30:9–10 DAVID THEIR KING. The person whom the people will serve is Jesus the Messiah, the descendant of David (cf. Hos. 3:5; Ezek. 37:24–25). "Jacob" refers to a righteous remnant from both Israel and Judah; they will live in peace and security, and the nations that opposed God and persecuted those serving Him will be destroyed (v. 11).

cob's tents, and [p]have mercy on his dwellingplaces; and the city shall be builded upon her own [y]heap, and the palace shall remain after the manner thereof.

19 And [q]out of them shall proceed thanksgiving and the voice of them that make merry: [r]and I will multiply them, and they shall not be few; I will also glorify them, and they shall not be small.

20 Their children also shall be [s]as aforetime, and their congregation shall be established before me, and I will punish all that oppress them.

21 And their nobles shall be of themselves, [t]and their governor shall proceed from the midst of them; and I will [u]cause him to draw near, and he shall approach unto me: for who *is* this that engaged his heart to approach unto me? saith the LORD.

22 And ye shall be [v]my people, and I will be your God.

23 Behold, the [w]whirlwind of the LORD goeth forth with fury, a [z]continuing whirlwind: it shall [a]fall with pain upon the head of the wicked.

24 The fierce anger of the LORD shall not return, until he have done *it*, and until he have performed the intents of his heart: [x]in the latter days ye shall consider it.

31

AT [y]THE same time, saith the LORD, [z]will I be the God of all the families of Israel, and they shall be my people.

2 Thus saith the LORD, The people *which were* left of the sword found grace in the wilderness; *even* Israel, when [a]I went to cause him to rest.

3 The LORD hath appeared [b]of old unto me, *saying,* Yea, [b]I have loved thee with [c]an everlasting love: therefore [c]with lovingkindness have I [d]drawn thee.

4 Again [e]I will build thee, and thou shalt be built, O virgin of Israel: thou shalt again be adorned with thy [f]tabrets,[d] and shalt go forth in the dances of them that make merry.

5 [g]Thou shalt yet plant vines upon the mountains of Samaria: the planters shall plant, and shall [h]eat[e] *them* as common things.

6 For there shall be a day, *that* the watchmen upon the mount Ephraim shall cry, [i]Arise ye, and let us go up to Zion unto the LORD our God.

7 For thus saith the LORD; [j]Sing with gladness for Jacob, and shout among the chief of the nations: publish ye, praise ye, and say, O LORD, save thy people, the remnant of Israel. Dan 2:20–23

8 Behold, I will bring them [k]from the north country, and [l]gather them from the coasts of the earth, *and* with them the blind and the lame, the woman with child and her that travaileth with child together: a great company shall return thither.

9 [m]They shall come with weeping, and with [n]supplications[f] will I lead them: I will cause them to walk [o]by the rivers of waters in a straight way, wherein they shall not stumble: for I am a father to Israel, and Ephraim *is* my [p]firstborn.

10 ¶ Hear the word of the LORD, O ye nations, and declare *it* in the isles afar off, and say, He that scattered Israel [q]will gather him, and keep him, as a shepherd *doth* his flock.

11 For [r]the LORD hath redeemed Jacob, and ransomed him [s]from the hand of *him that was* stronger than he.

12 Therefore they shall come and

30:18 [p]Ps. 102:13 **30:19** [q]Is. 51:11 [r]Zech. 10:8 **30:20** [s]Is. 1:26 **30:21** [t]Gen. 49:10 [u]Num. 16:5 **30:22** [v]ch. 31:1,33 **30:23** [w]ch. 23:19 & 25:32 **30:24** [x]Gen. 49:1 **31:1** [y]ch. 30:24 [z]ch. 30:22 **31:2** [a]Num. 10:33 Deut. 1:33 Ps. 95:11 Is. 63:14 **31:3** [b]Mal. 1:2 [c]Rom. 11:28 [d]Hos. 11:4 **31:4** [e]ch. 33:7 [f]Ex. 15:20 Judg. 11:34 Ps. 149:3 **31:5** [g]Is. 65:21 Amos 9:14 [h]Deut. 20:6 **31:6** [i]Is. 2:3 Mic. 4:2 **31:7** [j]Is. 12:5,6 **31:8** [k]ch. 3:12,18 & 23:8 [l]Ezek. 20:34,41 & 34:13 **31:9** [m]ch. 50:4 [n]Zech. 12:10 [o]Is. 35:8 & 43:19 & 49:10,11 [p]Ex. 4:22 **31:10** [q]Is. 40:11 Ezek. 34:12-14 **31:11** [r]Is. 44:23 & 48:20 [s]Is. 49:24

[y] Or, *little hill* [z] Heb. *cutting* [a] Or, *remain* [b] Heb. *from afar* [c] Or, *have I extended lovingkindness unto thee* [d] Or, *timbrels* [e] Heb. *profane* them [f] Or, *favours*

30:21 THEIR GOVERNOR. Jesus Christ is ultimately the new ruler who will lead the people to God. He will have intimate access to God; thus He will have a priestly ministry, resulting in the nation's restoration to the spiritual vitality and worship that God had always intended. But before this happens, the wrath of God will judge evil among the nations (vv. 23–24).

31:1–40 AT THE SAME TIME. This chapter concerns the restoration of Israel generally (vv. 2–22), and Judah specifically (vv. 23–26), to the promised land. God's people would again dwell together under His blessing (vv. 27–30). After assuring them of this regathering, Jeremiah reveals that God would make a new and better covenant with His people that would include spiritual power to obey His commandments.

31:2 THE PEOPLE. These people are the remnant from all the families of Israel who would return from captivity. Many were carried away by the Assyrians in 722 B.C., others by the Babylonians in 605, 597, and 586 B.C. God would bring them back because of His everlasting love for His people (v. 3) and His commitment to the covenant He made with Abraham (see Gen. 15:7–21) and with Israel (Ex. 19:3–8; Deut. 28:1—30:10). Israel would have renewed joy, peace, prosperity, and fellowship in the Lord.

sing in [t]the height of Zion, and shall
flow together to [u]the goodness of the
LORD, for wheat, and for wine, and for
oil, and for the young of the flock and
of the herd: and their soul shall be as
a [v]watered garden; [w]and they shall
not sorrow any more at all.
13 Then shall the virgin rejoice in
the dance, both young men and old to-
gether: for I will turn their mourning
into joy, and will comfort them, and
make them rejoice from their sorrow.
14 And I will satiate the soul of the
priests with fatness, and my people
shall be satisfied with my goodness,
saith the LORD.
15 ¶ Thus saith the LORD; [x]A voice
was heard in [y]Ramah, lamentation,
and bitter weeping; Rahel weeping for
her children refused to be comforted
for her children, because [z]they *were*
not.
16 Thus saith the LORD; Refrain thy
voice from weeping, and thine eyes
from tears: for thy work shall be re-
warded, saith the LORD; and [a]they
shall come again from the land of the
enemy.
17 And there is hope in thine end,
saith the LORD, that thy children shall
come again to their own border.
18 ¶ I have surely heard Ephraim
bemoaning himself *thus;* Thou hast
chastised me, and I was chastised, as
a bullock unaccustomed *to the yoke:*
[b]turn thou me, and I shall be turned;
for thou *art* the LORD my God.
19 Surely [c]after that I was turned,
I repented; and after that I was in-
structed, I smote upon *my* thigh: I was
ashamed, yea, even confounded, be-
cause I did bear the reproach of my
youth.
20 *Is* Ephraim my dear son? *is he* a
pleasant child? for since I spake
against him, I do earnestly remember
him still: [d]therefore my bowels [g]are
troubled for him; [e]I will surely have
mercy upon him, saith the LORD.

31:12 [t]Ezek. 17:23 [u]Hos. 3:5 [v]Is. 58:11 [w]Is. 35:10 & 65:19 Rev. 21:4
31:15 [x]Mat. 2:17,18 [y]Josh. 18:25 [z]Gen. 42:13
31:16 [a]ver. 4,5 Ezra 1:5 Hos. 1:11
31:18 [b]Lam. 5:21
31:19 [c]Deut. 30:2
31:20 [d]Deut. 32:36 Is. 63:15 Hos. 11:8 [e]Is. 57:18 Hos. 14:4
31:21 [f]ch. 50:5
31:22 [g]ch. 2:18,23,36 [h]ch. 3:6,8,11,12, 14,22
31:23 [i]Ps. 122:5-8 Is. 1:26 [j]Zech. 8:3
31:24 [k]ch. 33:12
31:27 [l]Ezek. 36:9-11
31:28 [m]ch. 44:27 [n]ch. 1:10 & 18:7 [o]ch. 24:6
31:29 [p]Ezek. 18:2,3
31:30 [q]Gal. 6:5,7
31:31 [r]ch. 32:40 & 33:14 Ezek. 37:26 Heb. 8:8-12 & 10:16,17

21 Set thee up waymarks, make
thee high heaps: [f]set thine heart to-
ward the highway, *even* the way *which*
thou wentest: turn again, O virgin of
Israel, turn again to these thy cities.
22 ¶ How long wilt thou [g]go about,
O thou [h]backsliding daughter? for the
LORD hath created a new thing in the
earth, A woman shall compass a man.
23 Thus saith the LORD of hosts, the
God of Israel; As yet they shall use this
speech in the land of Judah and in the
cities thereof, when I shall bring again
their captivity; [i]The LORD bless thee,
O habitation of justice, *and* [j]mountain
of holiness.
24 And there shall dwell in Judah it-
self, and [k]in all the cities thereof to-
gether, husbandmen, and they *that* go
forth with flocks.
25 For I have satiated the weary
soul, and I have replenished every sor-
rowful soul.
26 Upon this I awaked, and beheld;
and my sleep was sweet unto me.
27 ¶ Behold, the days come, saith
the LORD, that [l]I will sow the house of
Israel and the house of Judah with the
seed of man, and with the seed of
beast.
28 And it shall come to pass, *that*
like as I have [m]watched over them,
[n]to pluck up, and to break down, and
to throw down, and to destroy, and to
afflict; so will I watch over them, [o]to
build, and to plant, saith the LORD.
29 [p]In those days they shall say no
more, The fathers have eaten a sour
grape, and the children's teeth are set
on edge.
30 [q]But every one shall die for his
own iniquity: every man that eateth the
sour grape, his teeth shall be set on
edge.
31 ¶ Behold, the [r]days come, saith
the LORD, that I will make a new cov-

[g] Heb. *sound*

31:15 A VOICE WAS HEARD IN RAMAH . . . RACHEL WEEPING. Ramah was a town about five miles north of Jerusalem, probably the place where the captives were held before deportation to Babylon (cf. 40:1–3). Rachel was one of the wives of Jacob, the mother of Joseph and Benjamin. She represents Israel weeping for those who were being deported into exile. God states that she did not need to weep any more, for the people would return (vv. 16–20). Matthew sees this passage as having a prophetic application to the time when Herod killed the children of Bethelem after the birth of Jesus (Mat. 2:16–18).

31:18 EPHRAIM BEMOANING. "Ephraim," a synonym for Israel (the northern kingdom), expressed grief for its sins and a willingness to repent.

31:23–30 JUDAH. Jeremiah prophesies that Judah, the southern kingdom, would be restored and the nation united through God's grace and blessing.

31:31–34 A NEW COVENANT. This is the only

enant with the house of Israel, and
with the house of Judah:
32 Not according to the covenant
that I made with their fathers in the
day *that* [s]I took them by the hand to
bring them out of the land of Egypt;
which my covenant they brake, [h]al-
though I was an husband unto them,
saith the LORD:
33 [t]But this *shall be* the covenant
that I will make with the house of Isra-
el; After those days, saith the LORD, [u]I
will put my law in their inward parts,
and write it in their hearts; [v]and will
be their God, and they shall be my peo-
ple.
34 And they shall teach no more ev-
ery man his neighbour, and every man
his brother, saying, Know the LORD: for
[w]they shall all know me, from the
least of them unto the greatest of
them, saith the LORD: for [x]I will for-
give their iniquity, and I will remember
their sin no more.
35 ¶ Thus saith the LORD, [y]which
giveth the sun for a light by day, *and*
the ordinances of the moon and of the
stars for a light by night, which di-
videth [z]the sea when the waves there-
of roar; [a]The LORD of hosts *is* his
name:
36 [b]If those ordinances depart
from before me, saith the LORD, *then* the
seed of Israel also shall cease from be-
ing a nation before me for ever.
37 Thus saith the LORD; [c]If heaven
above can be measured, and the foun-
dations of the earth searched out be-
neath, I will also cast off all the seed
of Israel for all that they have done,
saith the LORD.
38 ¶ Behold, the days come, saith
the LORD, that the city shall be built to
the LORD [d]from the tower of Hananeel
unto the gate of the corner.
39 And [e]the measuring line shall
yet go forth over against it upon the hill
Gareb, and shall compass about to
Goath.
40 And the whole valley of the dead
bodies, and of the ashes, and all the

31:32 [s]Deut. 1:31 **31:33** [t]ch. 32:40 [u]Ps. 40:8 Ezek. 11:19 & 36:26,27 [v]ch. 24:7 & 30:22 & 32:38 **31:34** [w]Is. 54:13 John 6:45 1 Cor. 2:10 1 John 2:20 [x]ch. 33:8 & 50:20 Mic. 7:18 Acts 10:43 & 13:39 Rom. 11:27 **31:35** [y]Gen. 1:16 Ps. 72:5,17 & 89:2,36 & 119:91 [z]Is. 51:15 [a]ch. 10:16 **31:36** [b]Ps. 148:6 Is. 54:9,10 ch. 33:20 **31:37** [c]ch. 33:22 **31:38** [d]Neh. 3:1 Zech. 14:10 **31:39** [e]Ezek. 40:8 Zech. 2:1

[h] Or, *should I have continued an husband unto them?*

explicit statement referring to the "new covenant" in the O.T. (1) These verses are quoted in Heb. 8:8–12, revealing that N.T. believers saw the fulfillment of Jeremiah's words in the new covenant instituted by Jesus Christ for all who repent of their sins and believe in Him (see article on THE OLD COVENANT AND THE NEW COVENANT, p. 1954). (2) However, the N.T. also teaches that Jeremiah's words will not be completely fulfilled until the last days of this age when a good portion of national Israel turns to the Lord Jesus as their true Messiah and Savior (Rom. 11:25–27; cf. Ezek. 36:24–28; Zech. 12:10—13:1; see article on ISRAEL IN GOD'S PLAN OF SALVATION, p. 1748).

31:31 WITH THE HOUSE OF ISRAEL . . . JUDAH. God promises to make a new covenant with all His people, both Israel and Judah, accomplished by Jesus Christ through His death and resurrection (Mat. 26:28; Mark 14:24; 1 Cor. 11:25; Heb. 9:14–15; 10:29; 12:24) and the outpouring of the Holy Spirit upon His followers (John 20:22; Acts 2:4). Furthermore, the N.T. makes it clear that Gentiles (i.e., all non-Jews) can participate in the new covenant if they believe in Jesus as God's Messiah and commit themselves to Him as their Lord and Savior. Through faith in Christ, they become children of Abraham (Gal. 3:7–9,29).

31:32 COVENANT THAT I MADE WITH THEIR FATHERS. The new covenant was necessary because the old covenant was inadequate. Whereas the old covenant had been written in stone, Jeremiah prophesied the new covenant would be written on the hearts of God's people (v. 33; cf. 2 Cor. 3). Because of the indwelling of the Holy Spirit, the new covenant would be accompanied by sufficient power and grace for all the people to live righteously before God.

31:33 I WILL PUT MY LAW IN THEIR INWARD PARTS. A distinctive feature of the new covenant is God's gift of a new heart and nature to all who believe in Christ so that they may spontaneously love and obey the Lord (Ezek. 11:19–20; Heb. 8:10); the ability to respond to the Lord comes from the Holy Spirit dwelling within the believer and the regeneration or new birth that results (see Ezek. 36:24–28; see article on REGENERATION, p. 1597). One sure way to know that we are saved people who participate in the new covenant is whether we possess a sincere desire to please God and to live by His righteous law and standards (cf. Rom. 8:2–4).

31:34 FOR THEY SHALL ALL KNOW ME. In the age of the new covenant, every person who believes in Christ will personally know the Lord and have intimate fellowship with Him. All will have direct access to God, and the Lord's presence will be imparted to believers through the Holy Spirit.

31:34 I WILL FORGIVE THEIR INIQUITY. Forgiveness of sins and the resulting reconciliation with God are foundational in the new covenant; they are based on the atoning sacrifice of Christ on the cross (cf. Is. 53:4–6; Mat. 26:27–28; Luke 22:20).

31:38 THE CITY. Jeremiah foresaw that Jerusalem would be rebuilt and never again be destroyed (v. 40). This prophetic promise will have its ultimate fulfillment during Christ's reign on earth (Rev. 19—22).

fields unto the brook of Kidron, [f]unto
the corner of the horse gate toward the
east, [g]*shall be* holy unto the LORD; it
shall not be plucked up, nor thrown
down any more for ever.

Jeremiah buys a field

32 THE WORD that came to Jere-
miah from the LORD [h]in the
tenth year of Zedekiah king of Judah,
which *was* the eighteenth year of Nebu-
chadrezzar.
2 For then the king of Babylon's
army besieged Jerusalem: and Jeremi-
ah the prophet was shut up [i]in the
court of the prison, which *was* in the
king of Judah's house.
3 For Zedekiah king of Judah had
shut him up, saying, Wherefore dost
thou prophesy, and say, Thus saith the
LORD, [j]Behold, I will give this city into
the hand of the king of Babylon, and he
shall take it;
4 And Zedekiah king of Judah
[k]shall not escape out of the hand of
the Chaldeans, but shall surely be de-
livered into the hand of the king of Bab-
ylon, and shall speak with him mouth
to mouth, and his eyes shall behold his
eyes;
5 And he shall lead Zedekiah to
Babylon, and there shall he be [l]until
I visit him, saith the LORD: [m]though ye
fight with the Chaldeans, ye shall not
prosper.
6 ¶ And Jeremiah said, The word of
the LORD came unto me, saying,
7 Behold, Hanameel the son of
Shallum thine uncle shall come unto
thee, saying, Buy thee my field that *is*
in Anathoth: for the [n]right of redemp-
tion *is* thine to buy *it.*
8 So Hanameel mine uncle's son
came to me in the court of the prison
according to the word of the LORD, and

31:40 [f]2 Chr. 23:15 Neh. 3:28 [g]Joel 3:17
32:1 [h]2 Ki. 25:1 ch. 39:1
32:2 [i]Neh. 3:25 ch. 33:1 & 37:21 & 39:14
32:3 [j]ch. 34:2
32:4 [k]ch. 34:3 & 38:18,23 & 39:5 & 52:9
32:5 [l]ch. 27:22 [m]ch. 21:4 & 33:5
32:7 [n]Lev. 25:24,25,32 Ruth 4:4
32:9 [o]Gen. 23:16 Zech. 11:12
32:12 [p]ch. 36:4 [q]See Is. 8:2
32:15 [r]ver. 37,43

said unto me, Buy my field, I pray thee,
that *is* in Anathoth, which *is* in the
country of Benjamin: for the right of
inheritance *is* thine, and the redemp-
tion *is* thine; buy *it* for thyself. Then I
knew that this *was* the word of the
LORD.
9 And I bought the field of Hana-
meel my uncle's son, that *was* in Ana-
thoth, and [o]weighed him the money,
even [i]seventeen shekels of silver.
10 And I [j]subscribed the evidence,
and sealed *it*, and took witnesses, and
weighed *him* the money in the bal-
ances.
11 So I took the evidence of the pur-
chase, *both* that which was sealed *ac-
cording* to the law and custom, and that
which was open:
12 And I gave the evidence of the
purchase unto [p]Baruch the son of Ne-
riah, the son of Maaseiah, in the sight
of Hanameel mine uncle's *son,* and in
the presence of the [q]witnesses that
subscribed the book of the purchase,
before all the Jews that sat in the court
of the prison.
13 ¶ And I charged Baruch before
them, saying,
14 Thus saith the LORD of hosts, the
God of Israel; Take these evidences,
this evidence of the purchase, both
which is sealed, and this evidence
which is open; and put them in an
earthen vessel, that they may continue
many days.
15 For thus saith the LORD of hosts,
the God of Israel; Houses and fields
and vineyards [r]shall be possessed
again in this land.
16 ¶ Now when I had delivered the
evidence of the purchase unto Baruch

i Or, *seven shekels and ten pieces of silver*
j Heb. *wrote in the book*

32:2 BABYLON'S ARMY BESIEGED JERUSALEM. The siege occurred in 587 B.C. A year later, the city fell. Jeremiah's prophecies were coming true.

32:2 JEREMIAH . . . PRISON. King Zedekiah had put Jeremiah in prison for persistently advising surrender to the Babylonian army (vv. 3–5; cf. 37:11–21). As far as the king was concerned, his preaching was having a demoralizing effect on the people and their will to resist. But Jeremiah knew that what he was proclaiming was the word of God.

32:6–15 BUY THEE MY FIELD. During his confinement (v. 2), Jeremiah was instructed by the Lord to buy a field in his hometown village of Anathoth, a place already controlled by the forces of Babylon; it must have seemed foolish to buy land that was already in enemy hands. (1) By purchasing the land, Jeremiah demonstrated faith in God's promise that God's remnant would return to the land and again buy land and build houses (v. 15). It was a prophetic sign of hope, despite Judah's present desperate situation. (2) In a similar manner, our situations may at times seem hopeless and desperate; yet if we belong to God, we have the promise and hope of a better future (Rom. 8:28).

32:12 BARUCH. Baruch was Jeremiah's trusted friend and secretary (36:4–8). After the fall of Jerusalem, he was taken to Egypt along with Jeremiah (43:6).

the son of Neriah, I prayed unto the LORD, saying,

17 Ah Lord GOD! behold, [s]thou hast made the heaven and the earth by thy great power and stretched out arm, *and* [t]there is nothing [k]too hard for thee:

18 Thou showest [u]lovingkindness unto thousands, and recompensest the iniquity of the fathers into the bosom of their children after them: the Great, [v]the Mighty God, [w]the LORD of hosts, *is* his name,

19 [x]Great in counsel, and mighty in [l]work: for thine [y]eyes *are* open upon all the ways of the sons of men: [z]to give every one according to his ways, and according to the fruit of his doings:

20 Which hast set signs and wonders in the land of Egypt, *even* unto this day, and in Israel, and among *other* men; and hast made thee [a]a name, as at this day;

21 And [b]hast brought forth thy people Israel out of the land of Egypt with signs, and with wonders, and with a strong hand, and with a stretched out arm, and with great terror;

22 And hast given them this land, which thou didst swear to their fathers to give them, [c]a land flowing with milk and honey;

23 And they came in, and possessed it; but [d]they obeyed not thy voice, neither walked in thy law; they have done nothing of all that thou commandedst them to do: therefore thou hast caused all this evil to come upon them:

24 Behold the [e]mounts,[m] they are come unto the city to take it; and the city [f]is given into the hand of the Chaldeans, that fight against it, because of [g]the sword, and of the famine, and of the pestilence: and what thou hast spoken is come to pass; and, behold, thou seest *it*.

25 And thou hast said unto me, O Lord GOD, Buy thee the field for money, and take witnesses; [n]for [h]the city is given into the hand of the Chaldeans.

32:17 [s]2 Ki. 19:15 [t]ver. 27 Gen. 18:14 Luke 1:37
32:18 [u]Ex. 20:6 & 34:7 Deut. 5:9,10 [v]Is. 9:6 [w]ch. 10:16
32:19 [x]Is. 28:29 [y]Job 34:21 Ps. 33:13 Prov. 5:21 ch. 16:17 [z]ch. 17:10
32:20 [a]Ex. 9:16 1 Chr. 17:21 Is. 63:12 Dan. 9:15
32:21 [b]Ex. 6:6 2 Sam. 7:23 1 Chr. 17:21 Ps. 136:11,12
32:22 [c]Ex. 3:8,17 ch. 11:5
32:23 [d]Neh. 9:26 ch. 11:8 Dan. 9:10-14
32:24 [e]ch. 33:4 [f]ver. 25,36 [g]ch. 14:12
32:25 [h]ver. 24
32:27 [i]Num. 16:22 [j]ver. 17
32:28 [k]ver. 3
32:29 [l]ch. 21:10 & 37:8,10 & 52:13 [m]ch. 19:13
32:30 [n]ch. 2:7 & 3:25 & 7:22-26 Ezek. 20:28
32:31 [o]2 Ki. 24:3
32:32 [p]Is. 1:4,6 Dan. 9:8
32:33 [q]ch. 2:27 & 7:24 [r]ch. 7:13
32:34 [s]ch. 23:11 Ezek. 8:5,6
32:35 [t]ch. 7:31 & 19:5 [u]Lev. 18:21 1 Ki. 11:33 [v]ch. 7:31

26 ¶ Then came the word of the LORD unto Jeremiah, saying,

27 Behold, I *am* the LORD, the [i]God of all flesh: [j]is there any thing too hard for me?

28 Therefore thus saith the LORD; Behold, [k]I will give this city into the hand of the Chaldeans, and into the hand of Nebuchadrezzar king of Babylon, and he shall take it:

29 And the Chaldeans, that fight against this city, shall come and [l]set fire on this city, and burn it with the houses, [m]upon whose roofs they have offered incense unto Baal, and poured out drink offerings unto other gods, to provoke me to anger.

30 For the children of Israel and the children of Judah [n]have only done evil before me from their youth: for the children of Israel have only provoked me to anger with the work of their hands, saith the LORD.

31 For this city hath been to me *as* [o]a provocation of mine anger and of my fury from the day that they built it even unto this day; [o]that I should remove it from before my face,

32 Because of all the evil of the children of Israel and of the children of Judah, which they have done to provoke me to anger, [p]they, their kings, their princes, their priests, and their prophets, and the men of Judah, and the inhabitants of Jerusalem.

33 And they have turned unto me the [q]back,[p] and not the face: though I taught them, [r]rising up early and teaching *them*, yet they have not hearkened to receive instruction.

34 But they [s]set their abominations in the house, which is called by my name, to defile it.

35 And they built the high places of Baal, which *are* in the valley of the son of Hinnom, to [t]cause their sons and their daughters to pass through *the fire* unto [u]Molech; [v]which I commanded them not, neither came it into my mind,

[k] Or, *hid from thee* [l] Heb. *doing* [m] Or, *engines of shot* [n] Or, *though* [o] Heb. *for my anger* [p] Heb. *neck*

32:25 THOU HAST SAID TO ME. Jeremiah was puzzled by God's instruction to buy land just when Jerusalem was about to fall. Thus he prayed (v. 16) to God for understanding, while maintaining faith in His word.

32:27 IS THERE ANYTHING TOO HARD FOR ME. With the Babylonians at the city walls, the future looked bleak; yet God assured Jeremiah that through His power the people would be restored to the land. God's word promises a blessed future for all believers in Christ. We can depend on His word even though we may not know the specific manner in which it will be accomplished.

that they should do this abomination,
to cause Judah to sin.
36 ¶ And now therefore thus saith
the LORD, the God of Israel, concerning
this city, whereof ye say, [w]It shall be
delivered into the hand of the king of
Babylon by the sword, and by the fam-
ine, and by the pestilence;
37 Behold, I will [x]gather them out
of all countries, whither I have driven
them in mine anger, and in my fury,
and in great wrath; and I will bring
them again unto this place, and I will
cause them [y]to dwell safely:
38 And they shall be [z]my people,
and I will be their God:
39 And I will [a]give them one heart,
and one way, that they may fear me
[q]for ever, for the good of them, and of
their children after them:
40 And [b]I will make an everlasting
covenant with them, that I will not turn
away [r]from them, to do them good;
but [c]I will put my fear in their hearts,
that they shall not depart from me.
41 Yea, [d]I will rejoice over them to
do them good, and [e]I will plant them
in this land [s]assuredly with my whole
heart and with my whole soul.
42 For thus saith the LORD; [f]Like
as I have brought all this great evil
upon this people, so will I bring upon
them all the good that I have promised
them.
43 And [g]fields shall be bought in
this land, [h]whereof ye say, *It is* deso-
late without man or beast; it is given
into the hand of the Chaldeans.
44 Men shall buy fields for money,
and subscribe evidences, and seal
them, and take witnesses in [i]the land
of Benjamin, and in the places about
Jerusalem, and in the cities of Judah,
and in the cities of the mountains, and
in the cities of the valley, and in the
cities of the south: for [j]I will cause
their captivity to return, saith the LORD.

Promise of restoration

33 MOREOVER THE word of the
LORD came unto Jeremiah the
second time, while he was yet [k]shut
up in the court of the prison, saying,
2 Thus saith the LORD the [l]maker
thereof, the LORD that formed it, to es-
tablish it; [m]the[t] LORD *is* his name;
3 [n]Call unto me, and I will answer
thee, and show thee great and
[o]mighty[u] things, which thou know-
est not.
4 For thus saith the LORD, the God of
Israel, concerning the houses of this
city, and concerning the houses of the
kings of Judah, which are thrown down
by [p]the mounts, and by the sword;
5 [q]They come to fight with the
Chaldeans, but *it is* to fill them with the
dead bodies of men, whom I have slain
in mine anger and in my fury, and for
all whose wickedness I have hid my
face from this city.
6 Behold, [r]I will bring it health and
cure, and I will cure them, and will re-
veal unto them the abundance of peace
and truth.
7 And [s]I will cause the captivity of
Judah and the captivity of Israel to re-
turn, and will build them, [t]as at the
first.
8 And I will [u]cleanse them from all
their iniquity, whereby they have
sinned against me; and I will [v]pardon
all their iniquities, whereby they have
sinned, and whereby they have trans-
gressed against me.
9 ¶ [w]And it shall be to me a name
of joy, a praise and an honour before all
the nations of the earth, which shall
hear all the good that I do unto them:
and they shall [x]fear and tremble for
all the goodness and for all the pros-
perity that I procure unto it.
10 Thus saith the LORD; Again there
shall be heard in this place, [y]which ye
say *shall be* desolate without man and
without beast, *even* in the cities of Ju-
dah, and in the streets of Jerusalem,
that are desolate, without man, and

32:36 [w]ver. 24
32:37 [x]Deut. 30:3 ch. 23:3 & 29:14 Ezek. 37:21 [y]ch. 33:16
32:38 [z]ch. 24:7 & 30:22 & 31:33
32:39 [a]ch. 24:7 Ezek. 11:19
32:40 [b]Is. 55:3 ch. 31:31 [c]ch. 31:33
32:41 [d]Deut. 30:9 Zeph. 3:17 [e]ch. 24:6 & 31:28 Amos 9:15
32:42 [f]ch. 31:28
32:43 [g]ver. 15 [h]ch. 33:10
32:44 [i]ch. 17:26 [j]ch. 33:7,11
33:1 [k]ch. 32:2,3
33:2 [l]Is. 37:26 [m]Ex. 15:3 Amos 5:8 & 9:6
33:3 [n]Ps. 91:15 ch. 29:12 [o]Is. 48:6
33:4 [p]ch. 32:24
33:5 [q]ch. 32:5
33:6 [r]ch. 30:17
33:7 [s]ch. 30:3 & 32:44 [t]Is. 1:26 ch. 24:6 & 30:20 & 31:4,28 & 42:10
33:8 [u]Ezek. 36:25 Zech. 13:1 Heb. 9:13,14 [v]ch. 31:34 Mic. 7:18
33:9 [w]Is. 62:7 ch. 13:11 [x]Is. 60:5
33:10 [y]ch. 32:43

[q] Heb. *all days* [r] Heb. *from after them*
[s] Heb. *in truth,* or, *stability* [t] Or, *JEHOVAH*
[u] Or, *hidden*

32:37–44 I WILL GATHER THEM OUT OF ALL COUNTRIES. Once again God told Jeremiah that the people would be restored to the land and to a right relationship with Him (v. 38); thereafter God would make an everlasting covenant with them (see 31:31–34, notes).

33:1–26 THE SECOND TIME. This chapter speaks again of Israel's and Judah's restoration to peace, prosperity, and spiritual wholeness. Jeremiah's prophecy goes beyond the return of the exiles from Babylon; he foresees the days when Jesus the Messiah will establish His kingdom on earth.

33:6 THE ABUNDANCE OF PEACE. In contrast to the false prophets who had been proclaiming a false peace (see 6:14, note; 23:17, note), Jeremiah offered the hope of true peace in the Lord. For more on peace, see article on THE PEACE OF GOD, p. 1122.

without inhabitant, and without beast,
11 The [z]voice of joy, and the voice
of gladness, the voice of the bride-
groom, and the voice of the bride, the
voice of them that shall say, [a]Praise
the LORD of hosts: for the LORD *is* good;
for his mercy *endureth* for ever: *and* of
them that shall bring [b]the sacrifice of
praise into the house of the LORD. For
[c]I will cause to return the captivity of
the land, as at the first, saith the LORD.
12 Thus saith the LORD of hosts;
[d]Again in this place, which is desolate
without man and without beast, and in
all the cities thereof, shall be an habi-
tation of shepherds causing *their* flocks
to lie down.
13 [e]In the cities of the mountains,
in the cities of the vale, and in the cit-
ies of the south, and in the land of Ben-
jamin, and in the places about Jerusa-
lem, and in the cities of Judah, shall the
flocks [f]pass again under the hands of
him that telleth *them,* saith the LORD.
14 [g]Behold, the days come, saith
the LORD, that [h]I will perform that
good thing which I have promised unto
the house of Israel and to the house of
Judah.
15 ¶ In those days, and at that time,
will I cause the [i]Branch of righteous-
ness to grow up unto David; and he
shall execute judgment and righteous-
ness in the land.
16 In those days shall Judah be
saved, and Jerusalem shall dwell safe-
ly: and this *is the name* wherewith she
shall be called, [v]The LORD our righ-
teousness.
17 ¶ For thus saith the LORD; [w]Da-
vid shall never [j]want a man to sit
upon the throne of the house of Israel;
18 Neither shall the priests the Le-
vites want a man before me to [k]offer
burnt offerings, and to kindle meat of-
ferings, and to do sacrifice continually.
19 ¶ And the word of the LORD came
unto Jeremiah, saying,
20 Thus saith the LORD; [l]if ye can
break my covenant of the day, and my
covenant of the night, and that there
should not be day and night in their
season;
21 *Then* may also [m]my covenant be
broken with David my servant, that he
should not have a son to reign upon his
throne; and with the Levites the
priests, my ministers.
22 As [n]the host of heaven cannot
be numbered, neither the sand of the
sea measured: so will I multiply the
seed of David my servant, and the Le-
vites that minister unto me.
23 Moreover the word of the LORD
came to Jeremiah, saying,
24 Considerest thou not what this
people have spoken, saying, [o]The two
families which the LORD hath chosen,
he hath even cast them off ? thus they
have despised my people, that they
should be no more a nation before
them.
25 Thus saith the LORD; If [p]my cov-
enant *be* not with day and night, *and if*
I have not [q]appointed the ordinances
of heaven and earth;
26 [r]Then will I cast away the seed
of Jacob, and David my servant, *so* that
I will not take *any* of his seed *to be* rul-
ers over the seed of Abraham, Isaac,
and Jacob: for [s]I will cause their cap-
tivity to return, and have mercy on
them.

33:11 [z]ch. 7:34 & 16:9 & 25:10 Rev. 18:23 [a]1 Chr. 16:8 2 Chr. 5:13 Ezra 3:11 Ps. 136:1 Is. 12:4 [b]Lev. 7:12 Ps. 107:22 & 116:17 [c]ver. 7
33:12 [d]Is. 65:10 ch. 31:24 & 50:19
33:13 [e]ch. 17:26 & 32:44 [f]Lev. 27:32
33:14 [g]ch. 23:5 & 31:27,31 [h]ch. 29:10
33:15 [i]Is. 4:2 & 11:1 ch. 23:5
33:17 [j]2 Sam. 7:16 1 Ki. 2:4 Ps. 89:29 Luke 1:32
33:18 [k]Rom. 12:1 & 15:16 1 Pet. 2:5,9 Rev. 1:6
33:20 [l]ver. 25 Ps. 89:37 Is. 54:9 ch. 31:36
33:21 [m]Ps. 89:34
33:22 [n]Gen. 15:5
33:24 [o]ver. 21,22
33:25 [p]ver. 20 Gen. 8:22 [q]Ps. 74:16 & 104:19 ch. 31:35,36
33:26 [r]ch. 31:37 [s]ver. 7,11 Ezra 2:1

[v] Heb. *Jehovah-tsidkenu* [w] Heb. *There shall not be cut off from David*

33:15 THE BRANCH OF RIGHTEOUSNESS. This "Branch" refers to Jesus Christ, who would come from the ancestral line of David (see next note). The initial fulfillment of this prophecy occurred at His first coming to earth. Through His death and resurrection He became King of all of God's people on earth. The final fulfillment will occur when He returns a second time to "execute judgment and righteousness" throughout the earth (cf. Rev. 19; see Jer. 23:5–6, note).

33:17 THE THRONE OF THE HOUSE OF ISRAEL. Through an unbroken line of descendants from David would come the righteous Branch, who would reign as King over God's people (cf. Luke 1:31–33). Jesus Christ fulfilled this promise; His *legal* lineage can be traced through Joseph to David (Mat. 1:1–16), and His *physical* line through Mary back to David (Luke 3:23–31). The reign of Christ will last throughout eternity.

33:18 PRIESTS AND LEVITES. Jeremiah foresees an eternal priesthood through whom God's people would enjoy access and communion with Him (cf. Num. 25:13). This prophecy is fulfilled in Jesus Christ, who as "a priest for ever . . . is able also to save them to the uttermost that come unto God by him" (Heb. 7:21–25; cf. Ps. 110:4; Heb. 5:6–10; 6:19–20; 7:11–28).

33:22 AS THE HOST OF HEAVEN. Jeremiah envisions an innumerable host in the royal family of David and the priestly line of Levi. This will be fulfilled in those who will reign with Christ in His future kingdom (Rom. 8:17; 1 Cor. 6:3; 2 Tim. 2:12; Rev. 3:21; 5:10; 19:6–16; 20:5–6; 22:5) and in those who have in Christ been made "an holy priesthood, to offer up spiritual sacrifices" (1 Pet. 2:5,9; cf. Rev. 5:10).

Zedekiah's broken promise

34 THE WORD which came unto
Jeremiah from the LORD,
[t]when Nebuchadnezzar king of Bab-
ylon, and all his army, and [u]all the
kingdoms of the earth [x]of his domin-
ion, and all the people, fought against
Jerusalem, and against all the cities
thereof, saying,
2 Thus saith the LORD, the God of
Israel; Go and speak to Zedekiah king
of Judah, and tell him, Thus saith the
LORD; Behold, [v]I will give this city into
the hand of the king of Babylon, and
[w]he shall burn it with fire:
3 And [x]thou shalt not escape out of
his hand, but shalt surely be taken, and
delivered into his hand; and thine eyes
shall behold the eyes of the king of
Babylon, and [y]he shall speak with
thee mouth to mouth, and thou shalt go
to Babylon.
4 Yet hear the word of the LORD, O
Zedekiah king of Judah; Thus saith the
LORD of thee, Thou shalt not die by the
sword:
5 *But* thou shalt die in peace: and
with [y]the burnings of thy fathers, the
former kings which were before thee,
[z]so shall they burn *odours* for thee;
and [a]they will lament thee, *saying,* Ah
lord! for I have pronounced the word,
saith the LORD.
6 Then Jeremiah the prophet spake
all these words unto Zedekiah king of
Judah in Jerusalem,
7 When the king of Babylon's army
fought against Jerusalem, and against
all the cities of Judah that were left,
against Lachish, and against Azekah:
for [b]these defenced cities remained of
the cities of Judah.
8 ¶ *This is* the word that came unto
Jeremiah from the LORD, after that the
king Zedekiah had made a covenant
with all the people which *were* at Jeru-
salem, to proclaim [c]liberty unto them;
9 [d]That every man should let his

34:1 [t]2 Ki. 25:1 ch. 39:1 & 52:4 [u]ch. 1:15 **34:2** [v]ch. 21:10 & 32:3,28 [w]ver. 22 ch. 32:29 **34:3** [x]ch. 32:4 **34:5** [y]2 Chr. 16:14 & 21:19 [z]Dan. 2:46 [a]See ch. 22:18 **34:7** [b]2 Ki. 18:13 & 19:8 2 Chr. 11:5,9 **34:8** [c]ver. 14 Ex. 21:2 Lev. 25:10 **34:9** [d]Neh. 5:11 [e]Lev. 25:39-46 **34:11** [f]See ver. 21 ch. 37:5 **34:14** [g]Ex. 21:2 & 23:10 Deut. 15:12 **34:15** [h]2 Ki. 23:3 Neh. 10:29 [i]ch. 7:10 **34:16** [j]Ex. 20:7 Lev. 19:12

manservant, and every man his maid-
servant, *being* an Hebrew or an He-
brewess, go free; [e]that none should
serve himself of them, *to wit,* of a Jew
his brother.
10 Now when all the princes, and all
the people, which had entered into the
covenant, heard that every one should
let his manservant, and every one his
maidservant, go free, that none should
serve themselves of them any more,
then they obeyed, and let *them* go.
11 But [f]afterward they turned,
and caused the servants and the hand-
maids, whom they had let go free, to
return, and brought them into subjec-
tion for servants and for handmaids.

Jeremiah warns of punishment

12 ¶ Therefore the word of the LORD
came to Jeremiah from the LORD, say-
ing,
13 Thus saith the LORD, the God of
Israel; I made a covenant with your fa-
thers in the day that I brought them
forth out of the land of Egypt, out of the
house of bondmen, saying,
14 At the end of [g]seven years let ye
go every man his brother an Hebrew,
which [z]hath been sold unto thee; and
when he hath served thee six years,
thou shalt let him go free from thee:
but your fathers hearkened not unto
me, neither inclined their ear.
15 And ye were [a]now turned, and
had done right in my sight, in proclaim-
ing liberty every man to his neighbour;
and ye had [h]made a covenant before
me [i]in the house [b]which is called by
my name:
16 But ye turned and [j]polluted my
name, and caused every man his ser-
vant, and every man his handmaid,
whom ye had set at liberty at their

[x] Heb. *the dominion of his hand* [y] Heb. *his mouth shall speak to thy mouth* [z] Or, *hath sold himself* [a] Heb. *today* [b] Heb. *whereupon my name is called*

34:8 TO PROCLAIM LIBERTY UNTO THEM. "Them" refers to Hebrew slaves. The law of Moses stated that all Hebrew men or women sold into slavery because of debts were to be freed after six years (Ex. 21:2–11; Deut. 15:12–18). The king urged all the rulers and the people to obey this law by setting their slaves free. In this way he hoped to gain God's blessing; furthermore, the freed slaves would be more willing to help defend Jerusalem.

34:11 BROUGHT THEM INTO SUBJECTION. When the Babylonian siege of Jerusalem was temporarily interrupted by an Egyptian challenge to the Babylonian army (cf. vv. 21–22), the Jews forced their slaves back into bondage. This action showed that the previous freeing of the slaves (v. 8) had not been motivated by a concern for justice and God's law, but by selfishness. About these flagrant violaters of His law, God states: "Their dead bodies shall be for meat unto the fowls of the heaven" (v. 20).

pleasure, to return, and brought them
into subjection, to be unto you for ser-
vants and for handmaids.
17 Therefore thus saith the LORD;
Ye have not hearkened unto me, in pro-
claiming liberty, every one to his broth-
er, and every man to his neighbour:
[k]behold, I proclaim a liberty for you,
saith the LORD, [l]to the sword, to the
pestilence, and to the famine; and I will
make you [c]to be [m]removed into all
the kingdoms of the earth.
18 And I will give the men that have
transgressed my covenant, which
have not performed the words of the
covenant which they had made be-
fore me, when [n]they cut the calf in
twain, and passed between the parts
thereof,
19 The princes of Judah, and the
princes of Jerusalem, the eunuchs, and
the priests, and all the people of the
land, which passed between the parts
of the calf;
20 I will even give them into the
hand of their enemies, and into the
hand of them that seek their life: and
their [o]dead bodies shall be for meat
unto the fowls of the heaven, and to the
beasts of the earth.
21 And Zedekiah king of Judah and
his princes will I give into the hand of
their enemies, and into the hand of
them that seek their life, and into the
hand of the king of Babylon's army,
[p]which are gone up from you.
22 [q]Behold, I will command, saith
the LORD, and cause them to return to
this city; and they shall fight against it,
[r]and take it, and burn it with fire: and
[s]I will make the cities of Judah a deso-
lation without an inhabitant.

34:17 [k]Mat. 7:2 Gal. 6:7 Jas. 2:13 [l]ch. 32:24,36 [m]Deut. 28:25,64 ch. 29:18
34:18 [n]See Gen. 15:10, 17
34:20 [o]ch. 7:33 & 16:4 & 19:7
34:21 [p]See ch. 37:5,11
34:22 [q]ch. 37:8,10 [r]ch. 38:3 & 39:1,2,8 & 52:7,13 [s]ch. 9:11 & 44:2,6
35:2 [t]2 Ki. 10:15 1 Chr. 2:55 [u]1 Ki. 6:5
35:4 [v]2 Ki. 12:9 & 25:18 1 Chr. 9:18,19
35:6 [w]2 Ki. 10:15
35:7 [x]Ex. 20:12 Eph. 6:2,3

The Rechabites

35 THE WORD which came unto
Jeremiah from the LORD in the
days of Jehoiakim the son of Josiah
king of Judah, saying,
2 Go unto the house of the [t]Rech-
abites, and speak unto them, and bring
them into the house of the LORD, into
one of [u]the chambers, and give them
wine to drink.
3 Then I took Jaazaniah the son of
Jeremiah, the son of Habaziniah, and
his brethren, and all his sons, and the
whole house of the Rechabites;
4 And I brought them into the house
of the LORD, into the chamber of the
sons of Hanan, the son of Igdaliah, a
man of God, which *was* by the chamber
of the princes, which *was* above the
chamber of Maaseiah the son of Shal-
lum, [v]the keeper of the [d]door:
5 And I set before the sons of the
house of the Rechabites pots full of
wine, and cups, and I said unto them,
Drink ye wine.
6 But they said, We will drink no
wine: for [w]Jonadab the son of Rechab
our father commanded us, saying, Ye
shall drink no wine, *neither* ye, nor your
sons for ever:
7 Neither shall ye build house, nor
sow seed, nor plant vineyard, nor have
any: but all your days ye shall dwell in
tents; [x]that ye may live many days in
the land where ye *be* strangers.
8 Thus have we obeyed the voice of
Jonadab the son of Rechab our father
in all that he hath charged us, to drink

[c] Heb. *for a removing* [d] Heb. *threshold,* or, *vessel*

34:18 CUT THE CALF IN TWAIN. Those involved in making a covenant would walk between two halves of a slain calf; this act may have signified that they deserved to be cut to pieces if they broke the covenant (cf. Gen. 15:10).

35:2 RECHABITES. These people were a nomadic tribe related to the Kenites and to Jethro, Moses' father-in-law (cf. Judg. 1:16; 1 Chr. 2:55). Their forefather, Jonadab (cf. 2 Ki. 10:15–27), had commanded his sons more than two hundred years before not to drink any type of wine, not to live in permanent houses, and not to plant crops. Instead, they were to live as nomads tending livestock. God instructed Jeremiah to test the Rechabites in order to highlight their faithfulness to their forefather in contrast to the unfaithfulness of the nation of Judah to their God.

35:6–11 WE WILL DRINK NO WINE. The Rechabites remained true to their convictions, refusing to disobey the rules of their forefather (see previous note). (1) Jonadab had given these rules so that his descendants might live lives of simplicity, stay separate from the Canaanites, and avoid conforming to the Israelites and their persistent apostasy. Abstinence from wine helped them escape the immorality and idolatry of Baal worship, which was often accompanied by drunkenness and carousing. The other prohibitions helped them sustain their simple nomadic lifestyle and remain untouched by the influences of spiritual, moral, and social decay in their own nation.

(2) Although some of the rules of the Rechabites need not be followed by believers today, their goal to remain separated from evil must always be the goal of true followers of Christ. Like Jonadab, all parents should have standards for their children that help them remain faithful to God and His Word.

no wine all our days, we, our wives, our
sons, nor our daughters;
9 Nor to build houses for us to dwell
in: neither have we vineyard, nor field,
nor seed:
10 But we have dwelt in tents, and
have obeyed, and done according to all
that Jonadab our father command-
ed us.
11 But it came to pass, when Nebu-
chadrezzar king of Babylon came up
into the land, that we said, Come, and
let us go to Jerusalem for fear of the
army of the Chaldeans, and for fear of
the army of the Syrians: so we dwell at
Jerusalem.
12 ¶ Then came the word of the
LORD unto Jeremiah, saying,
13 Thus saith the LORD of hosts, the
God of Israel; Go and tell the men of
Judah and the inhabitants of Jerusa-
lem, Will ye not [y]receive instruction
to hearken to my words? saith the
LORD.
14 The words of Jonadab the son of
Rechab, that he commanded his sons
not to drink wine, are performed; for
unto this day they drink none, but obey
their father's commandment: [z]not-
withstanding I have spoken unto you,
[a]rising early and speaking; but ye
hearkened not unto me.
15 I have sent also unto you all my
servants the prophets, rising up early
and sending *them,* saying, [b]Return ye
now every man from his evil way, and
amend your doings, and go not after
other gods to serve them, and ye shall
dwell in the land which I have given to
you and to your fathers: but ye have
not inclined your ear, nor hearkened
unto me.
16 Because the sons of Jonadab the
son of Rechab have performed the
commandment of their father, which
he commanded them; but this people
hath not hearkened unto me:
17 Therefore thus saith the LORD
God of hosts, the God of Israel; Behold,

35:13 [y]ch. 32:33
35:14 [z]2 Chr. 36:15 [a]ch. 7:13 & 25:3
35:15 [b]ch. 18:11 & 25:5,6
35:17 [c]Prov. 1:24 Is. 65:12 & 66:4 ch. 7:13
35:19 [d]ch. 15:19
36:2 [e]Is. 8:1 Ezek. 2:9 Zech. 5:1 [f]ch. 30:2 [g]ch. 25:15 [h]ch. 25:3
36:3 [i]ver. 7 ch. 26:3 [j]ch. 18:8 Jonah 3:8
36:4 [k]ch. 32:12 [l]See ch. 45:1

I will bring upon Judah and upon all the
inhabitants of Jerusalem all the evil
that I have pronounced against them:
[c]because I have spoken unto them,
but they have not heard; and I have
called unto them, but they have not an-
swered.
18 ¶ And Jeremiah said unto the
house of the Rechabites, Thus saith
the LORD of hosts, the God of Israel;
Because ye have obeyed the command-
ment of Jonadab your father, and kept
all his precepts, and done according
unto all that he hath commanded you:
19 Therefore thus saith the LORD of
hosts, the God of Israel; •Jonadab the
son of Rechab shall not want a man to
[d]stand before me for ever.

The reading of the roll

36 AND IT came to pass in the
fourth year of Jehoiakim the
son of Josiah king of Judah, *that* this
word came unto Jeremiah from the
LORD, saying,
2 Take thee a [e]roll of a book, and
[f]write therein all the words that I
have spoken unto thee against Israel,
and against Judah, and against [g]all
the nations, from the day I spake unto
thee, from the days of [h]Josiah, even
unto this day.
3 [i]It may be that the house of Ju-
dah will hear all the evil which I pur-
pose to do unto them; that they may
[j]return every man from his evil way;
that I may forgive their iniquity and
their sin.
4 Then Jeremiah [k]called Baruch
the son of Neriah: and [l]Baruch wrote
from the mouth of Jeremiah all the
words of the LORD, which he had spo-
ken unto him, upon a roll of a book.
5 And Jeremiah commanded Bar-
uch, saying, I *am* shut up; I cannot go
into the house of the LORD:

• Heb. *There shall not a man be cut off from Jonadab the son of Rechab to stand*

35:19 SHALL NOT WANT A MAN TO STAND BEFORE ME FOR EVER. The faithfulness of the Rechabites to their forefather would be rewarded. They would always have descendants who would serve the Lord. All believers who have godly convictions and remain true to them out of honor for God, church, and parents will receive the blessing and rewards of God.

36:1 FOURTH YEAR OF JEHOIAKIM. The incident described in ch. 36 occurred in 605 B.C., after Nebuchadnezzar's army had defeated the Egyptians at Carchemish and was again advancing toward Jerusalem (cf. 25:1–38).

36:2 WRITE THEREIN ALL THE WORDS. This is the first time that Jeremiah's prophecies were compiled into one book. Initially, all the prophecies were recorded so that they could be read aloud to the people. God intended that the nation of Judah would respond to the written word by turning from their wicked way and receiving forgiveness, thus avoiding His wrath against them for their wickedness (vv. 3,6–7).

6 Therefore go thou, and read in the roll, which thou hast written from my mouth, the words of the LORD in the ears of the people in the LORD's house upon [m]the fasting day: and also thou shalt read them in the ears of all Judah that come out of their cities.

7 [n]It may be [f]they will present their supplication before the LORD, and will return every one from his evil way: for great *is* the anger and the fury that the LORD hath pronounced against this people.

8 And Baruch the son of Neriah did according to all that Jeremiah the prophet commanded him, reading in the book the words of the LORD in the LORD's house.

9 And it came to pass in the fifth year of Jehoiakim the son of Josiah king of Judah, in the ninth month, *that* they proclaimed a fast before the LORD to all the people in Jerusalem, and to all the people that came from the cities of Judah unto Jerusalem.

10 Then read Baruch in the book the words of Jeremiah in the house of the LORD, in the chamber of Gemariah the son of Shaphan the scribe, in the higher court, at the [o]entry[g] of the new gate of the LORD's house, in the ears of all the people.

11 ¶ When Michaiah the son of Gemariah, the son of Shaphan, had heard out of the book all the words of the LORD,

12 Then he went down into the king's house, into the scribe's chamber: and, lo, all the princes sat there, *even* Elishama the scribe, and Delaiah the son of Shemaiah, and Elnathan the son of Achbor, and Gemariah the son of Shaphan, and Zedekiah the son of Hananiah, and all the princes.

13 Then Michaiah declared unto them all the words that he had heard, when Baruch read the book in the ears of the people.

14 Therefore all the princes sent Jehudi the son of Nethaniah, the son of Shelemiah, the son of Cushi, unto Baruch, saying, Take in thine hand the roll wherein thou hast read in the ears of the people, and come. So Baruch the son of Neriah took the roll in his hand, and came unto them.

15 And they said unto him, Sit down now, and read it in our ears. So Baruch read *it* in their ears.

16 Now it came to pass, when they had heard all the words, they were afraid both one and other, and said unto Baruch, We will surely tell the king of all these words.

17 And they asked Baruch, saying, Tell us now, How didst thou write all these words at his mouth?

18 Then Baruch answered them, He pronounced all these words unto me with his mouth, and I wrote *them* with ink in the book.

19 Then said the princes unto Baruch, Go, hide thee, thou and Jeremiah; and let no man know where ye be.

20 ¶ And they went in to the king into the court, but they laid up the roll in the chamber of Elishama the scribe, and told all the words in the ears of the king.

21 So the king sent Jehudi to fetch the roll: and he took it out of Elishama the scribe's chamber. And Jehudi read it in the ears of the king, and in the ears of all the princes which stood beside the king.

22 Now the king sat in [p]the winterhouse in the ninth month: and *there was a fire* on the hearth burning before him.

23 And it came to pass, *that* when Jehudi had read three or four leaves, he cut it with the penknife, and cast *it* into the fire that *was* on the hearth, until all the roll was consumed in the fire that *was* on the hearth.

24 Yet they were not afraid, nor [q]rent their garments, *neither* the king, nor any of his servants that heard all these words.

36:6 [m]Lev. 16:29 & 23:27-32 Acts 27:9
36:7 [n]ver. 3
36:10 [o]ch. 26:10
36:22 [p]See Amos 3:15
36:24 [q]2 Ki. 22:11 Is. 36:22 & 37:1

[f]Heb. *their supplications shall fall* [g]Or, *door*

36:16 WHEN THEY HAD HEARD . . . THEY WERE AFRAID. Evidently the officials believed the prophecies and knew they had to be read to the king. However, knowing the king's opposition to truth and righteousness, they suggested that Baruch and Jeremiah go into hiding.

36:23 HE CUT IT . . . CAST *IT* INTO THE FIRE. As the king began destroying the scroll, he was revealing not only his open hostility to Jeremiah's warnings and pleas for repentance, but also his contempt for God's written Word and for the Lord Himself. It is essential to our spiritual lives that we strive to maintain a love and respect for God's written revelation. Even though we may not attempt to destroy it as did King Jehoiakim, we may still find ourselves casting the Word behind our backs by neglecting to read, study, and meditate on its inspired truths, and by faililng to live by its precepts.

25 Nevertheless Elnathan and Delaiah and Gemariah had made intercession to the king that he would not burn the roll: but he would not hear them.

26 But the king commanded Jerahmeel the son [h]of Hammelech, and Seraiah the son of Azriel, and Shelemiah the son of Abdeel, to take Baruch the scribe and Jeremiah the prophet: but the LORD hid them.

27 ¶ Then the word of the LORD came to Jeremiah, after that the king had burned the roll, and the words which Baruch wrote at the mouth of Jeremiah, saying,

28 Take thee again another roll, and write in it all the former words that were in the first roll, which Jehoiakim the king of Judah hath burned.

29 And thou shalt say to Jehoiakim king of Judah, Thus saith the LORD; Thou hast burned this roll, saying, Why hast thou written therein, saying, The king of Babylon shall certainly come and destroy this land, and shall cause to cease from thence man and beast?

30 Therefore thus saith the LORD of Jehoiakim king of Judah; [r]He shall have none to sit upon the throne of David: and his dead body shall be [s]cast out in the day to the heat, and in the night to the frost.

31 And I will [t]punish[i] him and his seed and his servants for their iniquity; and I will bring upon them, and upon the inhabitants of Jerusalem, and upon the men of Judah, all the evil that I have pronounced against them; but they hearkened not.

32 ¶ Then took Jeremiah another roll, and gave it to Baruch the scribe, the son of Neriah; who wrote therein from the mouth of Jeremiah all the words of the book which Jehoiakim king of Judah had burned in the fire: and there were added besides unto them many [j]like words.

Jeremiah's imprisonment

37 AND KING [u]Zedekiah the son of Josiah reigned instead of Coniah the son of Jehoiakim, whom Nebuchadrezzar king of Babylon made king in the land of Judah.

2 [v]But neither he, nor his servants, nor the people of the land, did hearken unto the words of the LORD, which he spake [k]by the prophet Jeremiah.

3 And Zedekiah the king sent Jehucal the son of Shelemiah and [w]Zephaniah the son of Maaseiah the priest to the prophet Jeremiah, saying, Pray now unto the LORD our God for us.

4 Now Jeremiah came in and went out among the people: for they had not put him into prison.

5 Then [x]Pharaoh's army was come forth out of Egypt: [y]and when the Chaldeans that besieged Jerusalem heard tidings of them, they departed from Jerusalem.

6 ¶ Then came the word of the LORD unto the prophet Jeremiah, saying,

7 Thus saith the LORD, the God of Israel; Thus shall ye say to the king of Judah, [z]that sent you unto me to inquire of me; Behold, Pharaoh's army, which is come forth to help you, shall return to Egypt into their own land.

8 [a]And the Chaldeans shall come again, and fight against this city, and take it, and burn it with fire.

9 Thus saith the LORD; Deceive not

36:30 [r]ch. 22:30 [s]ch. 22:19 **36:31** [t]ch. 23:34
37:1 [u]2 Ki. 24:17 2 Chr. 36:10 ch. 22:24 **37:2** [v]2 Chr. 36:12,14 **37:3** [w]ch. 21:1,2 & 29:25 & 52:24 **37:5** [x]See 2 Ki. 24:7 Ezek. 17:15 [y]ver. 11 ch. 34:21 **37:7** [z]ch. 21:2 **37:8** [a]ch. 34:22

[h] Or, *of the king* [i] Heb. *visit upon* [j] Heb. *as they* [k] Heb. *by the hand of the prophet*

36:30 NONE TO SIT UPON THE THRONE. Jehoiakim's son Jehoiachin (2 Ki. 24:6,8) assumed the throne for only three months before he was carried away to Babylon in 597 B.C. No other descendant of Jehoiakim ascended the throne of David.

36:32 ANOTHER ROLL. Jeremiah and Baruch prepared another scroll with some additions. As time passed, more was added, thus completing the book of Jeremiah as we know it today, a part of the inspired Scriptures.

37:1 ZEDEKIAH. Nebuchadnezzar placed Zedekiah on the throne in Jerusalem as a vassal of Babylon; previously King Jehoiachin had reigned for only three months before being deported to Babylon (see 36:30, note).

37:3 PRAY . . . FOR US. Though Zedekiah refused to "hearken unto the words of the LORD" (v. 2), he still wanted Jeremiah to pray for Judah, hoping in some way to gain the Lord's blessing. Zedekiah was like many today who want God's help, yet at the same time want to enjoy the sinful pleasures of the world. Such people are superficial religionists who have no real relationship with God and yet believe that when trouble comes, they can call upon Him and receive His help. Like Zedekiah, they will be disappointed (vv. 6–9).

37:9 THUS SAITH THE LORD. Jeremiah stood before the king and unwaveringly proclaimed God's word. He did not hesitate to announce the unpopular word that the city would be destroyed (vv. 8,10). Beatings, imprisonment, and the threat of death did not cause him to waver from faithfulness to the Lord and to what God

[l]yourselves, saying, The Chaldeans
shall surely depart from us: for they
shall not depart.
10 [b]For though ye had smitten the
whole army of the Chaldeans that fight
against you, and there remained *but*
[m]wounded men among them, *yet*
should they rise up every man in his
tent, and burn this city with fire.
11 ¶ [c]And it came to pass, that
when the army of the Chaldeans was
[n]broken up from Jerusalem for fear of
Pharaoh's army,
12 Then Jeremiah went forth out of
Jerusalem to go into the land of Benja-
min, [o]to separate himself thence in
the midst of the people.
13 And when he was in the gate of
Benjamin, a captain of the ward *was*
there, whose name *was* Irijah, the son
of Shelemiah, the son of Hananiah; and
he took Jeremiah the prophet, saying,
Thou fallest away to the Chaldeans.
14 Then said Jeremiah, *It is* [p]false;
I fall not away to the Chaldeans. But he
hearkened not to him: so Irijah took
Jeremiah, and brought him to the
princes.
15 Wherefore the princes were
wroth with Jeremiah, and smote him,
[d]and put him in prison in the house of
Jonathan the scribe: for they had made
that the prison.
16 ¶ When Jeremiah was entered
into [e]the dungeon, and into the [q]cab-
ins, and Jeremiah had remained there
many days;
17 Then Zedekiah the king sent,
and took him out: and the king asked
him secretly in his house, and said, Is
there *any* word from the LORD? And Jer-
emiah said, There is: for, said he, thou
shalt be delivered into the hand of the
king of Babylon.
18 Moreover Jeremiah said unto
king Zedekiah, What have I offended
against thee, or against thy servants,
or against this people, that ye have put
me in prison?

37:10 [b]ch. 21:4,5
37:11 [c]ver. 5
37:15 [d]ch. 38:26
37:16 [e]ch. 38:6
37:21 [f]ch. 32:2 & 38:13,28 [g]ch. 38:9 & 52:6
38:1 [h]ch. 37:3 [i]ch. 21:1 [j]ch. 21:8
38:2 [k]ch. 21:9
38:3 [l]ch. 21:10 & 32:3
38:4 [m]See ch. 26:11

19 Where *are* now your prophets
which prophesied unto you, saying,
The king of Babylon shall not come
against you, nor against this land?
20 Therefore hear now, I pray thee,
O my lord the king: [r]let my supplica-
tion, I pray thee, be accepted before
thee; that thou cause me not to return
to the house of Jonathan the scribe,
lest I die there.
21 Then Zedekiah the king com-
manded that they should commit Jere-
miah [f]into the court of the prison, and
that they should give him daily a piece
of bread out of the bakers' street, [g]un-
til all the bread in the city were spent.
Thus Jeremiah remained in the court of
the prison.

The miry dungeon

38 THEN SHEPHATIAH the son
of Mattan, and Gedaliah the
son of Pashur, and [h]Jucal the son of
Shelemiah, and [i]Pashur the son of
Malchiah, [j]heard the words that Jere-
miah had spoken unto all the people,
saying,
2 Thus saith the LORD, [k]He that re-
maineth in this city shall die by the
sword, by the famine, and by the pesti-
lence: but he that goeth forth to the
Chaldeans shall live; for he shall have
his life for a prey, and shall live.
3 Thus saith the LORD, [l]This city
shall surely be given into the hand of
the king of Babylon's army, which
shall take it.
4 Therefore the princes said unto
the king, We beseech thee, [m]let this
man be put to death: for thus he weak-
eneth the hands of the men of war that
remain in this city, and the hands of all
the people, in speaking such words
unto them: for this man seeketh not

[l] Heb. *souls* [m] Heb. *thrust through* [n] Heb. *made to ascend* [o] Or, *to slip away from thence in the midst of the people* [p] Heb. *falsehood,* or, *a lie* [q] Or, *cells* [r] Heb. *let my supplication fall*

---

wanted him to say (vv. 11–17).

37:15 PUT HIM IN PRISON. Some officials in the Judean army were hostile to Jeremiah because he had urged the people to surrender to the Babylonians (21:9; 38:2). Thus they confined him to an underground dungeon (v. 16). He would likely have died in that dark and dangerous cell if he had remained there much longer (v. 20).

37:17 *ANY* WORD FROM THE LORD. Knowing Jeremiah was a true prophet of the Lord, Zedekiah hoped for a more encouraging word from God. But Jeremiah's word remained the same—Jerusalem would fall and Zedekiah would be taken by the king of Babylon. The prophet would not compromise the truth even in such desperate circumstances.

38:2 HE THAT REMAINETH IN THE CITY SHALL DIE. Jeremiah's message was demoralizing the soldiers and weakening their will to resist the Babylonians. Because of this, the officials wanted to put him to death (v. 4; see 32:2, note).

the [s]welfare of this people, but the hurt.

5 Then Zedekiah the king said, Behold, he *is* in your hand: for the king *is* not *he that* can do *any* thing against you.

6 [n]Then took they Jeremiah, and cast him into the dungeon of Malchiah the son [t]of Hammelech, that *was* in the court of the prison: and they let down Jeremiah with cords. And in the dungeon *there was* no water, but mire: so Jeremiah sunk in the mire.

7 ¶ [o]Now when Ebed-melech the Ethiopian, one of the eunuchs which was in the king's house, heard that they had put Jeremiah in the dungeon; the king then sitting in the gate of Benjamin;

8 Ebed-melech went forth out of the king's house, and spake to the king, saying,

9 My lord the king, these men have done evil in all that they have done to Jeremiah the prophet, whom they have cast into the dungeon; and [u]he is like to die for hunger in the place where he is: for *there is* no more bread in the city.

10 Then the king commanded Ebed-melech the Ethiopian, saying, Take from hence thirty men [v]with thee, and take up Jeremiah the prophet out of the dungeon, before he die.

11 So Ebed-melech took the men with him, and went into the house of the king under the treasury, and took thence old cast clouts and old rotten rags, and let them down by cords into the dungeon to Jeremiah.

12 And Ebed-melech the Ethiopian said unto Jeremiah, Put now *these* old cast clouts and rotten rags under thine armholes under the cords. And Jeremiah did so.

13 [p]So they drew up Jeremiah with cords, and took him up out of the dungeon: and Jeremiah remained [q]in the court of the prison.

38:6 [n]ch. 37:21 **38:7** [o]ch. 39:16 **38:13** [p]ver. 6 [q]ch. 37:21 **38:16** [r]Is. 57:16 **38:17** [s]2 Ki. 24:12 [t]ch. 39:3 **38:18** [u]ver. 23 ch. 32:4 & 34:3 **38:19** [v]1 Sam. 31:4

Jeremiah's advice to Zedekiah

14 ¶ Then Zedekiah the king sent, and took Jeremiah the prophet unto him into the [w]third entry that *is* in the house of the LORD: and the king said unto Jeremiah, I will ask thee a thing; hide nothing from me.

15 Then Jeremiah said unto Zedekiah, If I declare *it* unto thee, wilt thou not surely put me to death? and if I give thee counsel, wilt thou not hearken unto me?

16 So Zedekiah the king sware secretly unto Jeremiah, saying, *As* the LORD liveth, [r]that made us this soul, I will not put thee to death, neither will I give thee into the hand of these men that seek thy life.

17 Then said Jeremiah unto Zedekiah, Thus saith the LORD, the God of hosts, the God of Israel; If thou wilt assuredly [s]go forth [t]unto the king of Babylon's princes, then thy soul shall live, and this city shall not be burned with fire; and thou shalt live, and thine house:

18 But if thou wilt not go forth to the king of Babylon's princes, then shall this city be given into the hand of the Chaldeans, and they shall burn it with fire, and [u]thou shalt not escape out of their hand.

19 And Zedekiah the king said unto Jeremiah, I am afraid of the Jews that are fallen to the Chaldeans, lest they deliver me into their hand, and they [v]mock me.

20 But Jeremiah said, They shall

[s] Heb. *peace* [t] Or, *of the king* [u] Heb. *he will die* [v] Heb. *in thine hand* [w] Or, *principal*

38:5 HE IS IN YOUR HAND. King Zedekiah turned Jeremiah over to the officials because he feared their power and influence. His weakness and lack of moral fiber were evident throughout his reign.

38:6 CAST HIM INTO THE DUNGEON. The dungeon was a cistern used to catch rainwater during the winter and store it for summer use. It was shaped like a bell with the opening at the top approximately three feet wide. The officials knew Jeremiah would not live long confined to the cistern. Jeremiah suffered greatly for maintaining his faithfulness to God and His word. For those faithful to God's revelation and righteousness, opposition can be expected in this world. Persecution for righteousness' sake will come from the world, and at times even from those within the church (see Mat. 5:10, note).

38:7 EBED-MELECH. Acting on Jeremiah's behalf, this Ethiopian sought to rescue him by appealing to the king. He showed both compassion for Jeremiah and courage in opposing the prophet's enemies. Believers should always try to help those who are being mistreated, even if it means standing against the majority. Because of his kindness to Jeremiah, Ebed-melech's life was spared when Jerusalem fell; God did not forget this true servant (39:15–18).

38:20 OBEY . . . THE VOICE OF THE LORD. Zedekiah believed Jeremiah's message, but his

not deliver *thee.* Obey, I beseech thee,
the voice of the LORD, which I speak
unto thee: so it shall be well unto thee,
and thy soul shall live.
21 But if thou refuse to go forth,
this *is* the word that the LORD hath
shown me:
22 And, behold, all the women that
are left in the king of Judah's house
shall be brought forth to the king of
Babylon's princes, and those *women*
shall say, [x]Thy friends have set thee
on, and have prevailed against thee:
thy feet are sunk in the mire, *and* they
are turned away back.
23 So they shall bring out all thy
wives and [w]thy children to the Chalde-
ans: and thou shalt not escape out of
their hand, but shalt be taken by the
hand of the king of Babylon: and
[y]thou shalt cause this city to be
burned with fire.
24 ¶ Then said Zedekiah unto Jere-
miah, Let no man know of these words,
and thou shalt not die.
25 But if the princes hear that I
have talked with thee, and they come
unto thee, and say unto thee, Declare
unto us now what thou hast said unto
the king, hide it not from us, and we
will not put thee to death; also what
the king said unto thee:
26 Then thou shalt say unto them,
[x]I presented my supplication before
the king, that he would not cause me
to return [y]to Jonathan's house, to die
there.
27 Then came all the princes unto
Jeremiah, and asked him: and he told
them according to all these words that
the king had commanded. So [z]they
left off speaking with him; for the mat-
ter was not perceived.

38:23 [w]ch. 39:6 & 41:10
38:26 [x]ch. 37:20 [y]ch. 37:15
38:28 [z]ch. 37:21 & 39:14
39:1 [a]2 Ki. 25:1-4
39:3 [b]ch. 38:17
39:4 [c]2 Ki. 25:4 ch. 52:7
39:5 [d]ch. 32:4 & 38:18,23 [e]2 Ki. 23:33

28 So [z]Jeremiah abode in the court
of the prison until the day that Jerusa-
lem was taken: and he was *there* when
Jerusalem was taken.

The fall of Jerusalem

39:1–10pp — 2 Ki. 25:1–12; Jer. 52:4–16

39 IN THE [a]ninth year of Zedeki-
ah king of Judah, in the tenth
month, came Nebuchadrezzar king of
Babylon and all his army against Jeru-
salem, and they besieged it.
2 *And* in the eleventh year of Zede-
kiah, in the fourth month, the ninth *day*
of the month, the city was broken up.
3 [b]And all the princes of the king
of Babylon came in, and sat in the mid-
dle gate, *even* Nergal-sharezer, Sam-
gar-nebo, Sarsechim, Rabsaris, Ner-
gal-sharezer, Rab-mag, with all the
residue of the princes of the king of
Babylon.
4 ¶ [c]And it came to pass, *that* when
Zedekiah the king of Judah saw them,
and all the men of war, then they fled,
and went forth out of the city by night,
by the way of the king's garden, by the
gate betwixt the two walls: and he
went out the way of the plain.
5 But the Chaldeans' army pursued
after them, and [d]overtook Zedekiah in
the plains of Jericho: and when they
had taken him, they brought him up to
Nebuchadnezzar king of Babylon to
[e]Riblah in the land of Hamath, where
he [a]gave judgment upon him.
6 Then the king of Babylon slew the
sons of Zedekiah in Riblah before his
eyes: also the king of Babylon slew all
the nobles of Judah.

[x] Heb. *Men of thy peace* [y] Heb. *thou shalt burn* [z] Heb. *they were silent from him* [a] Heb. *spake with him judgments*

fear of others (v. 19), his weak character, and his lack of faith in God kept him from firmly resolving to obey God. As a result, Zedekiah brought shame upon himself and ruin upon the nation. He was like many today who refuse to do right even though they know their actions will bring the judgment of God on them and calamity to others.

39:1 NINTH YEAR OF ZEDEKIAH . . . THE TENTH MONTH. The siege against Jerusalem lasted about eighteen months, during which time the city was cut off from all outside help and supplies. After some time, severe famine set in. The fall of Jerusalem is described in great detail in ch. 52 (cf. 2 Ki. 25; 2 Chr. 36); its defeat fulfilled Jeremiah's prophecies of God's judgment on an apostate people.

39:5–7 OVERTOOK ZEDEKIAH. Zedekiah suffered much because he refused to listen to God and obey His word (cf. 38:20–23). Grief and suffering will be the lot of all who persist in going their own sinful way while ignoring the voice of God, who seeks to save all who are perishing (Luke 19:10; John 3:16). If people could only understand that sin brings unhappiness and death, they might turn to God for mercy and grace. (Rom. 6:16,23). However, Satan has so blinded the eyes of unbelievers that they cannot see their present condition or the awful fate that awaits them (2 Cor. 4:4). Only through prayer, the proclamation of God's word, and the convicting work of the Holy Spirit (see John 16:8, note) will the unsaved recognize their true spiritual condition and the danger facing them.

7 Moreover [f]he put out Zedekiah's
eyes, and bound him [b]with chains, to
carry him to Babylon.
8 ¶ [g]And the Chaldeans burned the
king's house, and the houses of the
people, with fire, and brake down
the walls of Jerusalem.
9 [h]Then Nebuzar-adan the [c]cap-
tain of the guard carried away captive
into Babylon the remnant of the people
that remained in the city, and those
that fell away, that fell to him, with the
rest of the people that remained.
10 But Nebuzar-adan the captain of
the guard left of the poor of the people,
which had nothing, in the land of Ju-
dah, and gave them vineyards and
fields [d]at the same time.
11 ¶ Now Nebuchadrezzar king of
Babylon gave charge concerning Jere-
miah [e]to Nebuzar-adan the captain of
the guard, saying,
12 Take him, and [f]look well to
him, and do him no harm; but do unto
him even as he shall say unto thee.
13 So Nebuzar-adan the captain of
the guard sent, and Nebushasban, Rab-
saris, and Nergal-sharezer, Rab-mag,
and all the king of Babylon's princes;
14 Even they sent, [i]and took Jere-
miah out of the court of the prison, and
committed him [j]unto Gedaliah the
son of [k]Ahikam the son of Shaphan,
that he should carry him home: so he
dwelt among the people.
15 ¶ Now the word of the LORD came
unto Jeremiah, while he was shut up in
the court of the prison, saying,
16 Go and speak to [l]Ebed-melech
the Ethiopian, saying, Thus saith the
LORD of hosts, the God of Israel; Be-
hold, [m]I will bring my words upon this
city for evil, and not for good; and they
shall be *accomplished* in that day before
thee.
17 But I will deliver thee in that
day, saith the LORD: and thou shalt not
be given into the hand of the men of
whom thou *art* afraid.
18 For I will surely deliver thee, and
thou shalt not fall by the sword, but
[n]thy life shall be for a prey unto thee:
[o]because thou hast put thy trust in
me, saith the LORD.

39:7 [f]Ezek. 12:13, compared with ch. 32:4
39:8 [g]2 Ki. 25:9 ch. 38:18 & 52:13
39:9 [h]2 Ki. 25:11
39:14 [i]ch. 38:28 [j]ch. 40:5 [k]ch. 26:24
39:16 [l]ch. 38:7,12 [m]Dan. 9:12
39:18 [n]ch. 21:9 & 45:5 [o]1 Chr. 5:20 Ps. 37:40
40:1 [p]ch. 39:14
40:2 [q]ch 50:7
40:3 [r]Deut. 29:24,25 Dan. 9:11
40:4 [s]ch. 39:12 [t]Gen. 20:15
40:5 [u]See ch. 41:10
40:6 [v]ch. 39:14

Jeremiah released

40 THE WORD that came to Jere-
miah from the LORD, [p]after that
Nebuzar-adan the captain of the guard
had let him go from Ramah, when he
had taken him being bound in [g]chains
among all that were carried away cap-
tive of Jerusalem and Judah, which
were carried away captive unto Bab-
ylon.
2 And the captain of the guard took
Jeremiah, and [q]said unto him, The
LORD thy God hath pronounced this evil
upon this place.
3 Now the LORD hath brought *it*, and
done according as he hath said: [r]be-
cause ye have sinned against the LORD,
and have not obeyed his voice, there-
fore this thing is come upon you.
4 And now, behold, I loose thee this
day from the chains which [h]*were* upon
thine hand. [s]If it seem good unto thee
to come with me into Babylon, come;
and [i]I will look well unto thee: but if
it seem ill unto thee to come with me
into Babylon, forbear: behold, [t]all the
land *is* before thee: whither it seemeth
good and convenient for thee to go,
thither go.
5 Now while he was not yet gone
back, *he said*, Go back also to Gedaliah
the son of Ahikam the son of Shaphan,
[u]whom the king of Babylon hath made
governor over the cities of Judah, and
dwell with him among the people: or go
wheresoever it seemeth convenient
unto thee to go. So the captain of the
guard gave him victuals and a reward,
and let him go.
6 [v]Then went Jeremiah unto Geda-

[b] Heb. *with two brasen chains*, or, *fetters* [c] Or, *chief marshal* [d] Heb. *in that day* [e] Heb. *by the hand of* [f] Heb. *set thine eyes upon him* [g] Or, *manacles* [h] Or, are *upon thine hand* [i] Heb. *I will set mine eye upon thee*

39:11 JEREMIAH. Nebuchadnezzar had undoubtedly heard of Jeremiah's advice to submit to Babylon, and the Babylonians treated him kindly when they captured Jerusalem. He was put under the protection of Gedaliah, the appointed governor. After being freed, Jeremiah was apparently again arrested by mistake and put in chains, awaiting transport to Babylon; once again he was set free (40:1–6).

39:16 EBED-MELECH. See 38:7, note.

40:1—44:30 CARRIED AWAY CAPTIVE. These chapters deal with events that occurred in Judah after the fall of Jerusalem. Many of the people were carried off to Babylon, while a few of them were left behind. What happened after the fall of the city demonstrates that the people still refused to trust in God.

40:1 JEREMIAH . . . BOUND IN CHAINS. See 39:11, note.

liah the son of Ahikam to [w]Mizpah; and dwelt with him among the people that were left in the land.

Gedaliah slain by Ishmael

40:7–9; 41:1–3pp — 2 Ki. 25:22–26

7 ¶ [x]Now when all the captains of the forces which *were* in the fields, *even* they and their men, heard that the king of Babylon had made Gedaliah the son of Ahikam governor in the land, and had committed unto him men, and women, and children, and of [y]the poor of the land, of them that were not carried away captive to Babylon;

8 Then they came to Gedaliah to Mizpah, [z]even Ishmael the son of Nethaniah, and Johanan and Jonathan the sons of Kareah, and Seraiah the son of Tanhumeth, and the sons of Ephai the Netophathite, and Jezaniah the son of a Maachathite, they and their men.

9 And Gedaliah the son of Ahikam the son of Shaphan sware unto them and to their men, saying, Fear not to serve the Chaldeans: dwell in the land, and serve the king of Babylon, and it shall be well with you.

10 As for me, behold, I will dwell at Mizpah to serve the Chaldeans, which will come unto us: but ye, gather ye wine, and summer fruits, and oil, and put *them* in your vessels, and dwell in your cities that ye have taken.

11 Likewise when all the Jews that *were* in Moab, and among the Ammonites, and in Edom, and that *were* in all the countries, heard that the king of Babylon had left a remnant of Judah, and that he had set over them Gedaliah the son of Ahikam the son of Shaphan;

12 Even all the Jews returned out of all places whither they were driven, and came to the land of Judah, to Gedaliah, unto Mizpah, and gathered wine and summer fruits very much.

13 ¶ Moreover Johanan the son of Kareah, and all the captains of the forces that *were* in the fields, came to Gedaliah to Mizpah,

14 And said unto him, Dost thou certainly know that [a]Baalis the king of the Ammonites hath sent Ishmael the son of Nethaniah [j]to slay thee? But Gedaliah the son of Ahikam believed them not.

15 Then Johanan the son of Kareah spake to Gedaliah in Mizpah secretly, saying, Let me go, I pray thee, and I will slay Ishmael the son of Nethaniah, and no man shall know *it:* wherefore should he slay thee, that all the Jews which are gathered unto thee should be scattered, and the remnant in Judah perish?

16 But Gedaliah the son of Ahikam said unto Johanan the son of Kareah, Thou shalt not do this thing: for thou speakest falsely of Ishmael.

41 NOW IT came to pass in the seventh month, [b]*that* Ishmael the son of Nethaniah the son of Elishama, of the seed royal, and the princes of the king, even ten men with him, came unto Gedaliah the son of Ahikam to Mizpah; and there they did eat bread together in Mizpah.

2 Then arose Ishmael the son of Nethaniah, and the ten men that were with him, and [c]smote Gedaliah the son of Ahikam the son of Shaphan with the sword, and slew him, whom the king of Babylon had made governor over the land.

3 Ishmael also slew all the Jews that were with him, *even* with Gedaliah, at Mizpah, and the Chaldeans that were found there, *and* the men of war.

4 And it came to pass the second day after he had slain Gedaliah, and no man knew *it,*

5 That there came certain from Shechem, from Shiloh, and from Samaria, *even* fourscore men, [d]having their beards shaven, and their clothes rent, and having cut themselves, with offerings and incense in their hand, to bring *them* to [e]the house of the LORD.

6 And Ishmael the son of Nethaniah went forth from Mizpah to meet them, [k]weeping all along as he went: and it came to pass, as he met them, he said

40:6 [w]Judg. 20:1
40:7 [x]2 Ki. 25:23 [y]ch. 39:10
40:8 [z]ch. 41:1
40:14 [a]See ch. 41:10
41:1 [b]2 Ki. 25:25 ch. 40:6,8
41:2 [c]2 Ki. 25:25
41:5 [d]Lev. 19:27,28 Deut. 14:1 Is. 15:2 [e]See 1 Sam. 1:7 2 Ki. 25:9

[j] Heb. *to strike thee in soul?* [k] Heb. *in going and weeping*

40:7–16 GEDALIAH . . . GOVERNOR IN THE LAND. Gedaliah, a good ruler, helped restore order and peace to the land; he served approximately five years before being assassinated by Ishmael, who wanted to continue opposition to Babylon. Gedaliah trusted Ishmael too much, even after being warned of an assassination plot.

41:2 SMOTE GEDALIAH. Because he was violently anti-Babylon, Ishmael killed Gedaliah, the governor appointed by Nebuchadnezzar. He may have believed that Gedaliah had supported the cruelty inflicted on Zedekiah (39:6–7).

unto them, Come to Gedaliah the son of
Ahikam.
7 And it was *so,* when they came
into the midst of the city, that Ishmael
the son of Nethaniah slew them, *and*
cast them into the midst of the pit, he,
and the men that *were* with him.
8 But ten men were found among
them that said unto Ishmael, Slay us
not: for we have treasures in the field,
of wheat, and of barley, and of oil, and
of honey. So he forbare, and slew them
not among their brethren.
9 Now the pit wherein Ishmael had
cast all the dead bodies of the men,
whom he had slain [1][m]because of
Gedaliah, *was* it [f]which Asa the king
had made for fear of Baasha king of
Israel: *and* Ishmael the son of Nethani-
ah filled it with *them that were* slain.
10 Then Ishmael carried away cap-
tive all the residue of the people that
were in Mizpah, [g]*even* the king's
daughters, and all the people that re-
mained in Mizpah, [h]whom Nebuzar-
adan the captain of the guard had com-
mitted to Gedaliah the son of Ahikam:
and Ishmael the son of Nethaniah car-
ried them away captive, and departed
to go over to [i]the Ammonites.
11 ¶ But when Johanan the son of
Kareah, and all [j]the captains of the
forces that *were* with him, heard of all
the evil that Ishmael the son of Netha-
niah had done,
12 Then they took all the men, and
went to fight with Ishmael the son of
Nethaniah, and found him by [k]the
great waters that *are* in Gibeon.
13 Now it came to pass, *that* when
all the people which *were* with Ishmael
saw Johanan the son of Kareah, and all
the captains of the forces that *were*
with him, then they were glad.
14 So all the people that Ishmael
had carried away captive from Mizpah
cast about and returned, and went unto
Johanan the son of Kareah.
15 But Ishmael the son of Nethani-
ah escaped from Johanan with eight
men, and went to the Ammonites.
16 Then took Johanan the son of
Kareah, and all the captains of the
forces that *were* with him, all the rem-
nant of the people whom he had recov-
ered from Ishmael the son of Nethani-
ah, from Mizpah, after *that* he had slain
Gedaliah the son of Ahikam, *even*
mighty men of war, and the women,
and the children, and the eunuchs,
whom he had brought again from Gib-
eon:
17 And they departed, and dwelt in
the habitation of [l]Chimham, which is
by Bethlehem, to go to enter into
Egypt,
18 Because of the Chaldeans: for
they were afraid of them, because Ish-
mael the son of Nethaniah had slain
Gedaliah the son of Ahikam, [m]whom
the king of Babylon made governor in
the land.

The flight to Egypt

42 THEN ALL the captains of the
forces, [n]and Johanan the son
of Kareah, and Jezaniah the son of Ho-
shaiah, and all the people from the
least even unto the greatest, came
near,
2 And said unto Jeremiah the proph-
et, [n]Let, we beseech thee, our suppli-
cation be accepted before thee, and
[o]pray for us unto the LORD thy God,
even for all this remnant; (for we are
left *but* [p]a few of many, as thine eyes
do behold us:)
3 That the LORD thy God may show
us [q]the way wherein we may walk,
and the thing that we may do.
4 Then Jeremiah the prophet said
unto them, I have heard *you;* behold, I
will pray unto the LORD your God ac-
cording to your words; and it shall
come to pass, *that* [r]whatsoever thing
the LORD shall answer you, I will de-
clare *it* unto you; I will [s]keep nothing
back from you.
5 Then they said to Jeremiah, [t]The
LORD be a true and faithful witness be-

41:9 [f]1 Ki. 15:22; 2 Chr. 16:6
41:10 [g]ch. 43:6 [h]ch. 40:7 [i]ch. 40:14
41:11 [j]ch. 40:7,8,13
41:12 [k]2 Sam. 2:13
41:17 [l]2 Sam. 19:37,38
41:18 [m]ch. 40:5
42:1 [n]ch. 40:8,13 & 41:11
42:2 [o]1 Sam. 7:8 & 12:19; Is. 37:4; Jas. 5:16 [p]Lev. 26:22
42:3 [q]Ezra 8:21
42:4 [r]1 Ki. 22:14 [s]1 Sam. 3:18; Acts 20:20
42:5 [t]Gen. 31:50

[1] Or, *near Gedaliah* [m] Heb. *by the hand,* or, *by the side of Gedaliah* [n] Or, *Let our supplication fall before thee*

41:7 SLEW THEM. Ishmael slaughtered seventy of eighty pilgrims, evidently to get their supplies and money (cf. v. 8). He did not fear God or desire to do what was right; he failed to recognize that the Lord would one day judge his actions and punish him accordingly.

42:1–22 ALL THE PEOPLE ... CAME NEAR. After Gedaliah was murdered, the people feared the wrath of Babylon, and so they sought God's will from Jeremiah. However, having already made up their minds to flee to Egypt, they only wanted to hear God's word if it confirmed their intentions. God's answer was to "abide in this land" (v. 10). The leaders rejected God's word and went to Egypt anyway, taking Jeremiah along against his will (43:1–7).

tween us, if we do not even according
to all things for the which the LORD thy
God shall send thee to us.
6 Whether *it be* good, or whether *it*
be evil, we will obey the voice of the
LORD our God, to whom we send thee;
[u]that it may be well with us, when we
obey the voice of the LORD our God.
7 ¶ And it came to pass after ten
days, that the word of the LORD came
unto Jeremiah.
8 Then called he Johanan the son of
Kareah, and all the captains of the
forces which *were* with him, and all the
people from the least even to the great-
est,
9 And said unto them, Thus saith
the LORD, the God of Israel, unto whom
ye sent me to present your supplication
before him;
10 If ye will still abide in this land,
then [v]will I build you, and not pull *you*
down, and I will plant you, and not
pluck *you* up: for I [w]repent me of the
evil that I have done unto you.
11 Be not afraid of the king of Bab-
ylon, of whom ye are afraid; be not
afraid of him, saith the LORD: [x]for I *am*
with you to save you, and to deliver you
from his hand.
12 And [y]I will show mercies unto
you, that he may have mercy upon you,
and cause you to return to your own
land.
13 ¶ But if [z]ye say, We will not
dwell in this land, neither obey the
voice of the LORD your God,
14 Saying, No; but we will go into
the land of Egypt, where we shall see
no war, nor hear the sound of the trum-
pet, nor have hunger of bread; and
there will we dwell:
15 And now therefore hear the word
of the LORD, ye remnant of Judah; Thus
saith the LORD of hosts, the God of Isra-
el; If ye [a]wholly set [b]your faces to
enter into Egypt, and go to sojourn
there;
16 Then it shall come to pass, *that*
the sword, which ye feared, shall over-
take you there in the land of Egypt, and
the famine, whereof ye were afraid,
[o]shall follow close after you there in
Egypt; and there ye shall die.

42:6 [u]Deut. 6:3 ch. 7:23
42:10 [v]ch. 24:6 & 31:28 & 33:7 [w]Deut. 32:36 ch. 18:8
42:11 [x]Is. 43:5 Rom. 8:31
42:12 [y]Ps. 106:45,46
42:13 [z]ch. 44:16
42:15 [a]Deut. 17:16 ch. 44:12-14 [b]Luke 9:51
42:17 [c]ver. 22 ch. 24:10 [d]See ch. 44:14,28
42:18 [e]ch. 7:20 [f]ch. 18:16 & 24:9 & 26:6 & 29:18,22 & 44:12 Zech. 8:13
42:19 [g]Deut. 17:16
42:22 [h]ver. 17 Ezek. 6:11
43:2 [i]ch. 42:1

17 [p]So shall it be with all the men
that set their faces to go into Egypt to
sojourn there; they shall die [c]by the
sword, by the famine, and by the pesti-
lence: and [d]none of them shall remain
or escape from the evil that I will bring
upon them.
18 For thus saith the LORD of hosts,
the God of Israel; As mine anger and
my fury hath been [e]poured forth upon
the inhabitants of Jerusalem; so shall
my fury be poured forth upon you,
when ye shall enter into Egypt: and
[f]ye shall be an execration, and an as-
tonishment, and a curse, and a re-
proach; and ye shall see this place no
more.
19 ¶ The LORD hath said concerning
you, O ye remnant of Judah; [g]Go ye
not into Egypt: know certainly that I
have [q]admonished you this day.
20 For [r]ye dissembled in your
hearts, when ye sent me unto the LORD
your God, saying, Pray for us unto the
LORD our God; and according unto all
that the LORD our God shall say, so de-
clare unto us, and we will do *it*.
21 And *now* I have this day declared
it to you; but ye have not obeyed the
voice of the LORD your God, nor any
thing for the which he hath sent me
unto you.
22 Now therefore know certainly
that [h]ye shall die by the sword, by the
famine, and by the pestilence, in the
place whither ye desire [s]to go *and* to
sojourn.

43

AND IT came to pass, *that*
when Jeremiah had made an
end of speaking unto all the people all
the words of the LORD their God, for
which the LORD their God had sent him
to them, *even* all these words,
2 [i]Then spake Azariah the son of
Hoshaiah, and Johanan the son of Ka-
reah, and all the proud men, saying
unto Jeremiah, Thou speakest falsely:
the LORD our God hath not sent thee to
say, Go not into Egypt to sojourn there:
3 But Baruch the son of Neriah

[o] Heb. *shall cleave after you* [p] Heb. *So shall all the men be* [q] Heb. *testified against you*
[r] Or, *ye have used deceit against your souls*
[s] Or, *to go to sojourn*

43:2 THOU SPEAKEST FALSELY. The people only pretended to want to follow God's will. Because of this folly, their punishment would include the sword, famine, and plagues (42:22). It is a fatal mistake to attend church, pray, and partake of the Lord's Supper without sincerely desiring to follow the Lord (see 42:20). Such persons will experience God's wrath and judgment (see 1 Cor. 11:27, note).

setteth thee on against us, for to deliver us into the hand of the Chaldeans, that they might put us to death, and carry us away captives into Babylon.

4 So Johanan the son of Kareah, and all the captains of the forces, and all the people, obeyed not the voice of the LORD, to dwell in the land of Judah.

5 But Johanan the son of Kareah, and all the captains of the forces, took [j]all the remnant of Judah, that were returned from all nations, whither they had been driven, to dwell in the land of Judah;

6 *Even* men, and women, and children, [k]and the king's daughters, [l]and every person that Nebuzar-adan the captain of the guard had left with Gedaliah the son of Ahikam the son of Shaphan, and Jeremiah the prophet, and Baruch the son of Neriah.

7 So they came into the land of Egypt: for they obeyed not the voice of the LORD: thus came they *even* to [m]Tahpanhes.

8 ¶ Then came the word of the LORD unto Jeremiah in Tahpanhes, saying,

9 Take great stones in thine hand, and hide them in the clay in the brickkiln, which *is* at the entry of Pharaoh's house in Tahpanhes, in the sight of the men of Judah;

10 And say unto them, Thus saith the LORD of hosts, the God of Israel; Behold, I will send and take Nebuchadrezzar the king of Babylon, [n]my servant, and will set his throne upon these stones that I have hid; and he shall spread his royal pavilion over them.

11 [o]And when he cometh, he shall smite the land of Egypt, *and deliver* [p]such *as are* for death to death; and such *as are* for captivity to captivity; and such *as are* for the sword to the sword.

12 And I will kindle a fire in the houses of [q]the gods of Egypt; and he shall burn them, and carry them away captives: and he shall array himself with the land of Egypt, as a shepherd putteth on his garment; and he shall go forth from thence in peace.

13 He shall break also the [t]images of [u]Beth-shemesh, that *is* in the land of Egypt; and the houses of the gods of the Egyptians shall he burn with fire.

43:5 [j]ch. 40:11,12
43:6 [k]ch. 41:10 [l]ch. 39:10 & 40:7
43:7 [m]ch. 2:16 & 44:1 called *Hanes*, Is. 30:4
43:10 [n]ch. 25:9 & 27:6 See Ezek. 29:18, 20
43:11 [o]ch. 44:13 & 46:13 [p]ch. 15:2 Zech. 11:9
43:12 [q]ch. 46:25

The refugees rebuked

44 THE WORD that came to Jeremiah concerning all the Jews which dwell in the land of Egypt, which dwell at [r]Migdol, and at [s]Tahpanhes, and at [t]Noph, and in the country of Pathros, saying,

2 Thus saith the LORD of hosts, the God of Israel; Ye have seen all the evil that I have brought upon Jerusalem, and upon all the cities of Judah; and, behold, this day they *are* [u]a desolation, and no man dwelleth therein,

3 Because of their wickedness which they have committed to provoke me to anger, in that they went [v]to burn incense, *and* to [w]serve other gods, whom they knew not, *neither* they, ye, nor your fathers.

4 Howbeit [x]I sent unto you all my servants the prophets, rising early and sending *them*, saying, Oh, do not this abominable thing that I hate.

5 But they hearkened not, nor inclined their ear to turn from their wickedness, to burn no incense unto other gods.

6 Wherefore my fury and mine anger was poured forth, and was kindled in the cities of Judah and in the streets of Jerusalem; and they are wasted *and* desolate, as at this day.

7 Therefore now thus saith the LORD, the God of hosts, the God of Israel; Wherefore commit ye *this* great evil

44:1 [r]Ex. 14:2 ch. 46:14 [s]ch. 43:7 [t]Is. 19:13
44:2 [u]ch. 9:11 & 34:22
44:3 [v]ch. 19:4 [w]Deut. 13:6 & 32:17
44:4 [x]2 Chr. 36:15 ch. 7:25 & 25:4 & 26:5 & 29:19

[t] Heb. *statues*, or, *standing images* [u] Or, *The house of the sun*

43:7 THEY CAME INTO THE LAND OF EGYPT. The people disobeyed the Lord's command (v. 4) and went to Egypt, taking Jeremiah with them (v. 6). Perhaps they thought the presence of Jeremiah would guarantee God's protection. But this was not to be, for Jeremiah prophesied that God would send Nebuchadnezzar's army against Egypt and destroy its armies and all its gods (vv. 10–13). The country in which they sought security would be defeated. There is never divine security or protection outside of God's will.

44:1 ALL THE JEWS . . . EGYPT. Jeremiah delivered his last message to the unrepentant Jews in Egypt. God's judgment upon them was certain (vv. 11–14) because of their persistent rejection of the Lord God and their idolatry.

44:5 THEY HEARKENED NOT. Judah sinned in failing to listen to God's word and to take seriously what He said. Many people continue to sin and to live selfishly because they ignore God's word or treat it lightly. They simply do not believe God means what He says. Even the church has members who are not afraid of God's warnings and do not respect His commands (see v. 11, note).

[y]against your souls, to cut off from
you man and woman, child and suck-
ling, [v]out of Judah, to leave you none
to remain;
8 In that ye [z]provoke me unto
wrath with the works of your hands,
burning incense unto other gods in the
land of Egypt, whither ye be gone to
dwell, that ye might cut yourselves off,
and that ye might be [a]a curse and a
reproach among all the nations of the
earth?
9 Have ye forgotten the [w]wicked-
ness of your fathers, and the wicked-
ness of the kings of Judah, and the
wickedness of their wives, and your
own wickedness, and the wickedness
of your wives, which they have commit-
ted in the land of Judah, and in the
streets of Jerusalem?
10 They are not [x]humbled *even*
unto this day, neither have they
[b]feared, nor walked in my law, nor in
my statutes, that I set before you and
before your fathers.
11 ¶ Therefore thus saith the LORD
of hosts, the God of Israel; Behold, [c]I
will set my face against you for evil,
and to cut off all Judah.
12 And I will take the remnant of
Judah, that have set their faces to go
into the land of Egypt to sojourn there,
and [d]they shall all be consumed, *and*
fall in the land of Egypt; they shall *even*
be consumed by the sword *and* by the
famine: they shall die, from the least
even unto the greatest, by the sword
and by the famine: and [e]they shall be
an execration, *and* an astonishment,
and a curse, and a reproach.
13 [f]For I will punish them that
dwell in the land of Egypt, as I have
punished Jerusalem, by the sword, by
the famine, and by the pestilence:
14 So that none of the remnant of
Judah, which are gone into the land of
Egypt to sojourn there, shall escape or
remain, that they should return into
the land of Judah, to the which they
[y]have a desire to return to dwell
there: for [g]none shall return but such
as shall escape.
15 ¶ Then all the men which knew
that their wives had burned incense
unto other gods, and all the women
that stood by, a great multitude, even
all the people that dwelt in the land of
Egypt, in Pathros, answered Jeremiah,
saying,
16 *As for* the word that thou hast
spoken unto us in the name of the
LORD, [h]we will not hearken unto thee.
17 But we will certainly do [i]what-
soever thing goeth forth out of our own
mouth, to burn incense unto the
[j]queen[z] of heaven, and to pour out
drink offerings unto her, as we have
done, we, and our fathers, our kings,
and our princes, in the cities of Judah,
and in the streets of Jerusalem: for *then*
had we plenty of [a]victuals, and were
well, and saw no evil.
18 But since we left off to burn in-
cense to the queen of heaven, and to
pour out drink offerings unto her, we
have wanted all *things,* and have been
consumed by the sword and by the fam-
ine.
19 [k]And when we burned incense
to the queen of heaven, and poured out
drink offerings unto her, did we make
her cakes to worship her, and pour out
drink offerings unto her, without our
[b]men?
20 ¶ Then Jeremiah said unto all the
people, to the men, and to the women,

44:7 [y]Num. 16:38 ch. 7:19 **44:8** [z]ch. 25:6,7 [a]ver. 12 ch. 42:18 **44:10** [b]Prov. 28:14 **44:11** [c]Lev. 17:10 & 20:5,6 ch. 21:10 Amos 9:4 **44:12** [d]ch. 42:15-17,22 [e]ch. 42:18 **44:13** [f]ch. 43:11 **44:14** [g]ver. 28 **44:16** [h]ch. 6:16 **44:17** [i]See ver. 25 Num. 30:12 Deut. 23:23 Judg. 11:36 [j]ch. 7:18 **44:19** [k]ch. 7:18

[v]Heb. *out of the midst of Judah* [w]Heb. *wickednesses,* or, *punishments* [x]Heb. *contrite;* see Ps. 51:17 [y]Heb. *lift up their soul* [z]Or, *frame of heaven* [a]Heb. *bread* [b]Or, *husbands?*

44:8 BURNING INCENSE UNTO OTHER GODS. The exiles in Egypt spurned their covenant with their God and turned to the gods of Egypt in hope of gaining the prosperity and protection they wanted. Jeremiah pleaded with them to turn back to the Lord and renew the covenant (vv. 7–10). Fundamental to Jeremiah's theology and practice is the truth that a person can only serve God by giving Him total allegiance and devotion and by seeking to obey His revealed word.

44:11 I WILL SET MY FACE AGAINST YOU. By their apostasy and disobedience, the Jews in Egypt forfeited God's promises of help and restoration. Therefore, Jeremiah prophesied that God's judgment upon them would be complete; they would all perish. Those who stubbornly determine to reject God's way and have their own way give Him no other choice than to bring calamity upon them.

44:17 QUEEN OF HEAVEN. See 7:18, note.

44:18 SINCE WE LEFT OFF TO BURN INCENSE. The people attributed their latest problems to stopping the worship of the queen of heaven at the time of Josiah's reform. They felt idolatry had done more for them than the Lord God of Israel, and they were planning to continue their idolatrous worship (v. 23). Thus they would perish in Egypt (v. 27).

and to all the people which had given
him *that* answer, saying,
21 The incense that ye burned in
the cities of Judah, and in the streets
of Jerusalem, ye, and your fathers, your
kings, and your princes, and the people
of the land, did not the LORD remember
them, and came it *not* into his mind?
22 So that the LORD could no longer
bear, because of the evil of your doings,
and because of the abominations which
ye have committed; therefore is your
land [l]a desolation, and an astonish-
ment, and a curse, without an inhabi-
tant, [m]as at this day.
23 Because ye have burned incense,
and because ye have sinned against
the LORD, and have not obeyed the
voice of the LORD, nor walked in his
law, nor in his statutes, nor in his tes-
timonies; [n]therefore this evil is hap-
pened unto you, as at this day.
24 Moreover Jeremiah said unto all
the people, and to all the women, Hear
the word of the LORD, all Judah [o]that
are in the land of Egypt:
25 Thus saith the LORD of hosts, the
God of Israel, saying; [p]Ye and your
wives have both spoken with your
mouths, and fulfilled with your hand,
saying, We will surely perform our
vows that we have vowed, to burn in-
cense to the queen of heaven, and to
pour out drink offerings unto her: ye
will surely accomplish your vows, and
surely perform your vows.
26 Therefore hear ye the word of
the LORD, all Judah that dwell in the
land of Egypt; Behold, [q]I have sworn
by my great name, saith the LORD, that
[r]my name shall no more be named in
the mouth of any man of Judah in all
the land of Egypt, saying, The Lord GOD
liveth.
27 [s]Behold, I will watch over them
for evil, and not for good: and all the
men of Judah that *are* in the land of
Egypt [t]shall be consumed by the
sword and by the famine, until there be
an end of them.
28 Yet [u]a small number that es-
cape the sword shall return out of the
land of Egypt into the land of Judah,
and all the remnant of Judah, that are
gone into the land of Egypt to sojourn
there, shall know whose [v]words shall
stand, **[c]**mine, or theirs.
29 ¶ And this *shall be* a sign unto
you, saith the LORD, that I will punish
you in this place, that ye may know
that my words shall surely stand
against you for evil:
30 Thus saith the LORD; Behold, [w]I
will give Pharaoh-hophra king of Egypt
into the hand of his enemies, and into
the hand of them that seek his life; as
I gave [x]Zedekiah king of Judah into
the hand of Nebuchadrezzar king of
Babylon, his enemy, and that sought
his life.

Encouragement to Baruch

45 THE [y]WORD that Jeremiah
the prophet spake unto Baruch
the son of Neriah, when he had written
these words in a book at the mouth of
Jeremiah, in the fourth year of Jehoia-
kim the son of Josiah king of Judah,
saying,
2 Thus saith the LORD, the God of
Israel, unto thee, O Baruch;
3 Thou didst say, Woe is me now!
for the LORD hath added grief to my sor-
row; I fainted in my sighing, and I find
no rest.
4 ¶ Thus shalt thou say unto him,
The LORD saith thus; Behold, [z]*that*
which I have built will I break down,
and that which I have planted I will
pluck up, even this whole land.
5 And seekest thou great things for
thyself? seek *them* not: for, behold, [a]I
will bring evil upon all flesh, saith the
LORD: but thy life will I give unto thee
[b]for a prey in all places whither thou
goest.

The prophecy about Egypt

46 THE WORD of the LORD which
came to Jeremiah the prophet
against [c]the Gentiles;
2 Against Egypt, [d]against the

44:22 [l]ch. 25:11,18,38 [m]ver. 6
44:23 [n]Dan. 9:11,12
44:24 [o]ver. 15 ch. 43:7
44:25 [p]ver. 15
44:26 [q]Gen. 22:16 [r]Ezek. 20:39
44:27 [s]ch. 1:10 & 31:28 Ezek. 7:6 [t]ver. 12
44:28 [u]ver. 14 Is. 27:13 [v]ver. 17,25,26
44:30 [w]ch. 46:25,26 Ezek. 29:3 & 30:21 [x]ch. 39:5
45:1 [y]ch. 36:1,4,32
45:4 [z]Is. 5:5
45:5 [a]ch. 25:26 [b]ch. 21:9 & 38:2 & 39:18
46:1 [c]ch. 25:15
46:2 [d]2 Ki. 23:29 2 Chr. 35:20 Fulfilled presently

c Heb. *from me, or them*

45:1–5 BARUCH. Chronologically, this chapter goes back to the fourth year of King Jehoiakim's reign in Jerusalem. Its message was intended to strengthen the faith of Jeremiah's secretary Baruch, who had become discouraged because of the apparent failure of Jeremiah's ministry and the impending judgment upon Judah (cf. ch. 36). God instructed him not to seek power or position for himself (cf. Mat. 20:26–28). Because of his faithfulness to Jeremiah and to God's message, he would survive the destruction of Jerusalem.

46:1–51:64 AGAINST THE GENTILES. These chapters contain prophecies of divine judgment against foreign nations. Jeremiah was ordained not only a prophet to Judah but also "a prophet unto the nations" (1:5).

army of Pharaoh-necho king of Egypt, which was by the river Euphrates in Carchemish, which Nebuchadrezzar king of Babylon smote in the fourth year of Jehoiakim the son of Josiah king of Judah.

3 [e]Order ye the buckler and shield, and draw near to battle.

4 Harness the horses; and get up, ye horsemen, and stand forth with *your* helmets; furbish the spears, *and* put on the brigandines.

5 Wherefore have I seen them dismayed *and* turned away back? and their mighty ones are [d]beaten down, and are [e]fled apace, and look not back: *for* [f]fear *was* round about, saith the LORD.

6 Let not the swift flee away, nor the mighty man escape; they shall [g]stumble, and fall toward the north by the river Euphrates.

7 Who *is* this *that* cometh up [h]as a flood, whose waters are moved as the rivers?

8 Egypt riseth up like a flood, and *his* waters are moved like the rivers; and he saith, I will go up, *and* will cover the earth; I will destroy the city and the inhabitants thereof.

9 Come up, ye horses; and rage, ye chariots; and let the mighty men come forth; [f]the Ethiopians and [g]the Libyans, that handle the shield; and the Lydians, [i]that handle *and* bend the bow.

10 For this *is* [j]the day of the Lord GOD of hosts, a day of vengeance, that he may avenge him of his adversaries: and [k]the sword shall devour, and it shall be satiate and made drunk with their blood: for the Lord GOD of hosts [l]hath a sacrifice in the north country by the river Euphrates.

11 [m]Go up into Gilead, and take balm, [n]O virgin, the daughter of Egypt: in vain shalt thou use many medicines; *for* [o]thou[h] shalt not be cured.

12 The nations have heard of thy shame, and thy cry hath filled the land: for the mighty man hath stumbled against the mighty, *and* they are fallen both together.

13 ¶ The word that the LORD spake to Jeremiah the prophet, how Nebuchadrezzar king of Babylon should come *and* [p]smite the land of Egypt.

14 Declare ye in Egypt, and publish in Migdol, and publish in Noph and in Tahpanhes: say ye, [q]Stand fast, and prepare thee; for [r]the sword shall devour round about thee.

15 Why are thy valiant *men* swept away? they stood not, because the LORD did drive them.

16 He [i]made many to fall, yea, [s]one fell upon another: and they said, Arise, and let us go again to our own people, and to the land of our nativity, from the oppressing sword.

17 They did cry there, Pharaoh king of Egypt *is but* a noise; he hath passed the time appointed.

18 *As* I live, saith the King, [t]whose name *is* the LORD of hosts, Surely as Tabor *is* among the mountains, and as Carmel by the sea, *so* shall he come.

19 O [u]thou daughter dwelling in Egypt, [j]furnish thyself [v]to go into captivity: for Noph shall be waste and desolate without an inhabitant.

20 Egypt *is like* a very fair [w]heifer, *but* destruction cometh; it cometh [x]out of the north.

21 Also her hired men *are* in the midst of her like [k]fatted bullocks; for they also are turned back, *and* are fled away together: they did not stand, because [y]the day of their calamity was come upon them, *and* the time of their visitation.

22 [z]The voice thereof shall go like a serpent; for they shall march with an army, and come against her with axes, as hewers of wood.

23 They shall [a]cut down her for-

46:3 [e]ch. 51:11,12 Nah. 2:1 & 3:14
46:5 [f]ch. 49:29
46:6 [g]Dan. 11:19
46:7 [h]Is. 8:7,8 ch. 47:2
46:9 [i]Is. 66:19
46:10 [j]Is. 13:6 Joel 1:15 [k]Deut. 32:42 Is. 34:6 [l]Is. 34:6 Zeph. 1:7 See Ezek. 39:17
46:11 [m]ch. 8:22 [n]Is. 47:1 [o]Ezek. 30:21
46:13 [p]Is. 19:1 Ezek. 29 & 30 & 32
46:14 [q]ver. 3,4 [r]ver. 10
46:16 [s]Lev. 26:37
46:18 [t]Is. 47:4 ch. 48:15
46:19 [u]ch. 48:18 [v]Is. 20:4
46:20 [w]Hos. 10:11 [x]ch. 1:14
46:21 [y]Ps. 37:13 ch. 50:27
46:22 [z]Is. 29:4
46:23 [a]Is. 10:34

[d] Heb. *broken in pieces* [e] Heb. *fled a flight* [f] Heb. *Cush* [g] Heb. *Put* [h] Heb. *no cure shall be unto thee* [i] Heb. *multiplied the faller* [j] Heb. *make thee instruments of captivity* [k] Heb. *bullocks of the stall*

46:2 EGYPT . . . CARCHEMISH. Carchemish, located in northern Syria some 300 miles north of Jerusalem, was the place where the Babylonians defeated the Egyptians in 605 B.C. At that time Babylon became the dominant power of the world.

46:10 THE DAY OF THE LORD. Egypt's defeat was God's doing. It was "a day of vengeance" because of Egypt's oppression of Judah (e.g., 2 Ki. 23:29,33–35). Ultimately, God will punish all nations that have rejected His gospel and righteous commands.

46:13 SMITE THE LAND OF EGYPT. Jeremiah prophesied that not only would the Babylonians defeat Egypt at Carchemish, but they would also defeat the Egyptian armies on their own land (568–567 B.C.). God would make it abundantly clear that the gods of Egypt could not deliver them from defeat (vv. 25–26).

est, saith the LORD, though it cannot be
searched; because they are more than
the [b]grasshoppers, and *are* innumera-
ble.
24 The daughter of Egypt shall be
confounded; she shall be delivered into
the hand of [c]the people of the north.
25 The LORD of hosts, the God of Is-
rael, saith; Behold, I will punish the
[1] [m]multitude of [d]No, and Pharaoh,
and Egypt, [e]with their gods, and their
kings: even Pharaoh, and *all* them that
trust in him:
26 [f]And I will deliver them into the
hand of those that seek their lives, and
into the hand of Nebuchadrezzar king
of Babylon, and into the hand of his
servants: and [g]afterward it shall be
inhabited, as in the days of old, saith
the LORD.
27 ¶ [h]But fear not thou, O my ser-
vant Jacob, and be not dismayed, O Is-
rael: for, behold, I will save thee from
afar off, and thy seed from the land of
their captivity; and Jacob shall return,
and be in rest and at ease, and none
shall make *him* afraid.
28 Fear thou not, O Jacob my ser-
vant, saith the LORD: for I *am* with thee;
for I will make a full end of all the na-
tions whither I have driven thee: but I
will not make [i]a full end of thee, but
correct thee in measure; yet will I
[n]not leave thee wholly unpunished.

Prophecy about the Philistines

47 THE WORD of the LORD that
came to Jeremiah the prophet
[j]against the Philistines, [k]before that
Pharaoh smote [o]Gaza.
2 Thus saith the LORD; Behold,
[l]waters rise up [m]out of the north, and
shall be an overflowing flood, and shall
overflow the land, and [p]all that is
therein; the city, and them that dwell
therein: then the men shall cry, and all
the inhabitants of the land shall howl.
3 At the [n]noise of the stamping of
the hoofs of his strong *horses,* at the
rushing of his chariots, *and at* the rum-
bling of his wheels, the fathers shall
not look back to *their* children for fee-
bleness of hands;
4 Because of the day that cometh to
spoil all the Philistines, *and* to cut off
from [o]Tyrus and Zidon every helper
that remaineth: for the LORD will spoil
the Philistines, [p]the remnant of [q]the
country of [q]Caphtor.
5 [r]Baldness is come upon Gaza;
[s]Ashkelon is cut off *with* the remnant
of their valley: how long wilt thou cut
thyself?
6 O thou [t]sword of the LORD, how
long *will it be* ere thou be quiet? [r]put
up thyself into thy scabbard, rest, and
be still.
7 [s]How can it be quiet, seeing the
LORD hath [u]given it a charge against
Ashkelon, and against the sea shore?
there hath he [v]appointed it.

The prophecy against Moab

48:29–36pp — Is. 16:6–12

48 AGAINST [w]MOAB thus saith
the LORD of hosts, the God of Is-
rael; Woe unto [x]Nebo! for it is spoiled:
[y]Kiriathaim is confounded *and* taken:
[t]Misgab is confounded and dismayed.
2 [z]*There shall be* no more praise of
Moab: in [a]Heshbon they have devised
evil against it; come, and let us cut it
off from *being* a nation. Also thou shalt

46:23 [b]Judg. 6:5 **46:24** [c]ch. 1:15 **46:25** [d]Ezek. 30:14 [e]ch. 43:12 **46:26** [f]Ezek. 32:11 [g]Ezek. 29:11,13, 14 **46:27** [h]Is. 41:13 **46:28** [i]ch. 10:24 **47:1** [j]Zeph. 2:4 [k]Amos 1:6 **47:2** [l]Is. 8:7 [m]ch. 1:14

47:3 [n]ch. 8:16 **47:4** [o]ch. 25:22 [p]Ezek. 25:16 [q]Gen. 10:14 **47:5** [r]Mic. 1:16 [s]ch. 25:20 **47:6** [t]Ezek. 21:3 **47:7** [u]Ezek. 14:17 [v]Mic. 6:9 **48:1** [w]Is. 15 & 16 [x]Is. 15:2 [y]Num. 32:37 **48:2** [z]Is. 16:14 [a]Is. 15:4

[1] Or, *nourisher* [m] Heb. *Amon* [n] Or, *not utterly cut thee off* [o] Heb. *Azzah* [p] Heb. *the fulness thereof* [q] Heb. *the isle* [r] Heb. *gather thyself* [s] Heb. *How canst thou* [t] Or, *The high place*

46:26 AFTERWARD IT SHALL BE INHABITED. The destruction of Egypt would not be forever. It would be restored in the future and in the Messianic Age (cf. Is. 19:23–25; Ezek. 29:8–14).

46:27–28 FEAR NOT ... ISRAEL. Israel must not fear complete destruction. She would be punished for her sins, but a remnant would survive and be brought back to the promised land and to God's blessing (cf. 30:10–11; 31:1–6).

47:1–7 PHILISTINES. The Philistines occupied the coastal region of Judah. Hostility often existed between them and God's people. Other prophecies against the Philistines are found in Is. 14:28–31; Ezek. 25:15–17; Amos 1:6–8; Zeph. 2:4–7.

48:1 AGAINST MOAB. The country of Moab was on the eastern shore of the Dead Sea. The Moabites were descendants of Lot, Abraham's nephew (Gen. 19:30–37), and were often in conflict with Israel. During Jeremiah's time bands of Moabites attacked parts of Judah after Nebuchadnezzar invaded Palestine (2 Ki. 24:2). Jeremiah identified many of the Moabite cities that would be overthrown. They were conquered by the Babylonians and consequently disappeared as a nation (but see v. 47, note). Other prophecies against Moab are found in Is. 15—16; Jer 9:25–26; 25:14–21; 27:2–3; Ezek. 25:8–11; Amos 2:1–3; Zeph. 2:8–11.

[u]be cut down, O Madmen; the sword shall [v]pursue thee.

3 A voice of crying *shall be* from Horonaim, spoiling and great destruction.

4 Moab is destroyed; her little ones have caused a cry to be heard.

5 [b]For in the going up of Luhith [w]continual weeping shall go up; for in the going down of Horonaim the enemies have heard a cry of destruction.

6 Flee, save your lives, and be like [x]the [c]heath in the wilderness.

7 ¶ For because thou hast trusted in thy works and in thy treasures, thou shalt also be taken: and [d]Chemosh shall go forth into captivity *with* his [e]priests and his princes together.

8 And [f]the spoiler shall come upon every city, and no city shall escape: the valley also shall perish, and the plain shall be destroyed, as the LORD hath spoken.

9 [g]Give wings unto Moab, that it may flee and get away: for the cities thereof shall be desolate, without any to dwell therein.

10 [h]Cursed *be* he that doeth the work of the LORD [y]deceitfully, and cursed *be* he that keepeth back his sword from blood.

11 ¶ Moab hath been at ease from his youth, and he [i]hath settled on his lees, and hath not been emptied from vessel to vessel, neither hath he gone into captivity: therefore his taste [z]remained in him, and his scent is not changed.

12 Therefore, behold, the days come, saith the LORD, that I will send unto him wanderers, that shall cause him to wander, and shall empty his vessels, and break their bottles.

13 And Moab shall be ashamed of [j]Chemosh, as the house of Israel [k]was ashamed of [l]Beth-el their confidence.

14 ¶ How say ye, [m]We *are* mighty and strong men for the war?

15 [n]Moab is spoiled, and gone up *out of* her cities, and [a]his chosen young men are [o]gone down to the slaughter, saith [p]the King, whose name *is* the LORD of hosts.

16 The calamity of Moab *is* near to come, and his affliction hasteth fast.

17 All ye that are about him, bemoan him; and all ye that know his name, say, [q]How is the strong staff broken, *and* the beautiful rod!

18 [r]Thou daughter that dost inhabit [s]Dibon, come down from *thy* glory, and sit in thirst; for [t]the spoiler of Moab shall come upon thee, *and* he shall destroy thy strong holds.

19 O [b]inhabitant of [u]Aroer, [v]stand by the way, and espy; ask him that fleeth, and her that escapeth, *and* say, What is done?

20 Moab is confounded; for it is broken down: [w]howl and cry; tell ye it in [x]Arnon, that Moab is spoiled,

21 And judgment is come upon [y]the plain country; upon Holon, and upon Jahazah, and upon Mephaath,

22 And upon Dibon, and upon Nebo, and upon Beth-diblathaim,

23 And upon Kiriathaim, and upon Beth-gamul, and upon Beth-meon,

24 And upon [z]Kerioth, and upon Bozrah, and upon all the cities of the land of Moab, far or near.

25 [a]The horn of Moab is cut off, and his [b]arm is broken, saith the LORD.

26 ¶ [c]Make ye him drunken: for he magnified *himself* against the LORD: Moab also shall wallow in his vomit, and he also shall be in derision.

27 For [d]was not Israel a derision unto thee? [e]was he found among thieves? for since thou spakest of him, thou [c]skippedst for joy.

28 O ye that dwell in Moab, leave the cities, and [f]dwell in the rock, and be like [g]the dove *that* maketh her nest in the sides of the hole's mouth.

29 We have heard the [h]pride of Moab, (he is exceeding proud) his lofti-

48:5 [b]Is. 15:5 **48:6** [c]ch. 17:6 **48:7** [d]Num. 21:29 Judg. 11:24 Is. 46:1,2 [e]ch. 49:3 **48:8** [f]ch. 6:26 **48:9** [g]Ps. 55:6 **48:10** [h]Judg. 5:23 1 Sam. 15:3 1 Ki. 20:42 **48:11** [i]Zeph. 1:12 **48:13** [j]1 Ki. 11:7 [k]Hos. 10:6 [l]1 Ki. 12:29 **48:14** [m]Is. 16:6 **48:15** [n]ver. 8,9,18 [o]ch. 50:27 [p]ch. 46:18 **48:17** [q]Is. 9:4 & 14:4,5 **48:18** [r]Is. 47:1 [s]Num. 21:30 Is. 15:2 [t]ver. 8 **48:19** [u]Deut. 2:36 [v]1 Sam. 4:13 **48:20** [w]Is. 16:7 [x]Num. 21:13 **48:21** [y]ver. 8 **48:24** [z]Amos 2:2 **48:25** [a]Ps. 75:10 [b]Ezek. 30:21 **48:26** [c]ch. 25:15 **48:27** [d]Zeph. 2:8 [e]ch. 2:26 **48:28** [f]Ps. 55:6,7 [g]Sol. 2:14 **48:29** [h]Is. 16:6

[u] Or, *be brought to silence;* see Is. 15:1 [v] Heb. *go after thee* [w] Heb. *weeping with weeping* [x] Or, *a naked tree* [y] Or, *negligently* [z] Heb. *stood* [a] Heb. *the choice of* [b] Heb. *inhabitress* [c] Or, *movedst thyself*

48:7 TRUSTED IN THY WORKS ... TREASURES. The tendency of all the nations of the world is to trust in their technology, military might, accomplishments, and wealth; this misguided trust, along with ungodly behavior by their people, will cause their downfall. Just as God destroyed Moab, a day is coming when He will bring down all the nations of the world—a day called "the day of the Lord" (see 1 Thes. 5:2–4, notes).

48:7 CHEMOSH. This is the chief god of the Moabites (see 1 Ki. 11:7,33; 2 Ki. 23:13).

48:10 CURSED. This verse is addressed to those who were assigned to destroy Moab.

ness, and his arrogancy, and his pride, and the haughtiness of his heart.

30 I know his wrath, saith the LORD; but *it shall* not *be* so; [i]his[d] lies shall not so effect *it*.

31 Therefore [j]will I howl for Moab, and I will cry out for all Moab; *mine heart* shall mourn for the men of Kir-heres.

32 [k]O vine of Sibmah, I will weep for thee with the weeping of Jazer: thy plants are gone over the sea, they reach *even* to the sea of Jazer: the spoiler is fallen upon thy summer fruits and upon thy vintage.

33 And [l]joy and gladness is taken from the plentiful field, and from the land of Moab; and I have caused wine to fail from the winepresses: none shall tread with shouting; *their* shouting *shall be* no shouting.

34 [m]From the cry of Heshbon *even* unto Elealeh, *and even* unto Jahaz, have they uttered their voice, [n]from Zoar *even* unto Horonaim, *as* an heifer of three years old: for the waters also of Nimrim shall be [e]desolate.

35 Moreover I will cause to cease in Moab, saith the LORD, [o]him that offereth in the high places, and him that burneth incense to his gods.

36 Therefore [p]mine heart shall sound for Moab like pipes, and mine heart shall sound like pipes for the men of Kir-heres: because [q]the riches *that* he hath gotten are perished.

37 For [r]every head *shall be* bald, and every beard [f]clipped: upon all the hands *shall be* cuttings, and [s]upon the loins sackcloth.

38 *There shall be* lamentation generally upon all the housetops of Moab, and in the streets thereof: for I have broken Moab like [t]a vessel wherein *is* no pleasure, saith the LORD.

39 They shall howl, *saying,* How is it broken down! how hath Moab turned the [g]back with shame! so shall Moab be a derision and a dismaying to all them about him.

40 For thus saith the LORD; Behold, [u]he shall fly as an eagle, and shall [v]spread his wings over Moab.

41 [w]Kerioth[h] is taken, and the strong holds are surprised, and [x]the mighty men's hearts in Moab at that day shall be as the heart of a woman in her pangs.

42 And Moab shall be destroyed [y]from *being* a people, because he hath magnified *himself* against the LORD.

43 [z]Fear, and the pit, and the snare, *shall be* upon thee, O inhabitant of Moab, saith the LORD.

44 He that fleeth from the fear shall fall into the pit; and he that getteth up out of the pit shall be taken in the snare: for [a]I will bring upon it, *even* upon Moab, the year of their visitation, saith the LORD.

45 They that fled stood under the shadow of Heshbon because of the force: but [b]a fire shall come forth out of Heshbon, and a flame from the midst of Sihon, and [c]shall devour the corner of Moab, and the crown of the head of the [i]tumultuous ones.

46 [d]Woe be unto thee, O Moab! the people of Chemosh perisheth: for thy sons are taken [j]captives, and thy daughters captives.

47 ¶ Yet will I bring again the captivity of Moab [e]in the latter days, saith the LORD. Thus far *is* the judgment of Moab.

The prophecy against Ammon

49 CONCERNING[k] [f]THE Ammonites, thus saith the LORD; Hath Israel no sons? hath he no heir? why *then* doth [l]their king inherit [g]Gad, and his people dwell in his cities?

2 Therefore, behold, the days come, saith the LORD, that I will cause an alarm of war to be heard in [h]Rabbah of the Ammonites; and it shall be a desolate heap, and her daughters shall be burned with fire: then shall Israel be heir unto them that were his heirs, saith the LORD.

3 Howl, O Heshbon, for Ai is spoiled: cry, ye daughters of Rabbah,

48:30 [i]Is. 16:6 ch. 50:36 **48:31** [j]Is. 15:5 **48:32** [k]Is. 16:8,9 **48:33** [l]Is. 16:10 Joel 1:12 **48:34** [m]Is. 15:4-6 [n]Is. 15:5,6 **48:35** [o]Is. 15:2 & 16:12 **48:36** [p]Is. 15:5 & 16:11 [q]Is. 15:7 **48:37** [r]Is. 15:2,3 [s]Gen. 37:34 **48:38** [t]ch. 22:28 **48:40** [u]Deut. 28:49 Hab. 1:8 [v]Is. 8:8 **48:41** [w]ver. 24

[x]Is. 13:8 & 21:3 Mic. 4:9 **48:42** [y]Ps. 83:4 **48:43** [z]Is. 24:17 **48:44** [a]ch. 11:23 **48:45** [b]Num. 21:28 [c]Num. 24:17 **48:46** [d]Num 21:29 **48:47** [e]ch. 49:6 **49:1** [f]Ezek. 21:28 & 25:2 Amos 1:13 Zeph. 2:8,9 [g]Amos 1:13 **49:2** [h]Ezek. 25:5 Amos 1:14

[d] Or, *those on whom he stayeth* (Heb. *his bars*) *do not right* [e] Heb. *desolations* [f] Heb. *diminished* [g] Heb. *neck* [h] Or, *The cities*
[i] Heb. *children of noise* [j] Heb. *in captivity* [k] Or, *Against* [l] Or, *Melcom*

48:47 MOAB IN THE LATTER DAYS. Not all Moabites would be destroyed; a remnant would survive. The phrase "in the latter days" indicates that this restoration will occur in the Messianic age, i.e., when Christ reigns over the nations.

49:1 AMMONITES. These were descendants of Lot, Abraham's nephew (Gen. 19:30–38), who lived east of the Jordan River and north of Moab. Their sins were idolatry, pride, trust in riches (vv. 3–4), and hostility toward Israel (v. 1).

[i]gird you with sackcloth; lament, and run to and fro by the hedges; for [m]their king shall go into captivity, *and* his [j]priests and his princes together.

4 Wherefore gloriest thou in the valleys, [n]thy flowing valley, O [k]backsliding daughter? that trusted in her treasures, [l]*saying,* Who shall come unto me?

5 Behold, I will bring a fear upon thee, saith the Lord GOD of hosts, from all those that be about thee; and ye shall be driven out every man right forth; and none shall gather up him that wandereth.

6 And [m]afterward I will bring again the captivity of the children of Ammon, saith the LORD.

The prophecy against Edom

49:9–10pp — Obad. 5–6
49:14–16pp — Obad. 1–4

7 ¶ [n]Concerning Edom, thus saith the LORD of hosts; [o]*Is* wisdom no more in Teman? [p]is counsel perished from the prudent? is their wisdom vanished?

8 [q]Flee ye, [o]turn back, dwell deep, O inhabitants of [r]Dedan; for I will bring the calamity of Esau upon him, the time *that* I will visit him.

9 If [s]grapegatherers come to thee, would they not leave *some* gleaning grapes? if thieves by night, they will destroy [p]till they have enough.

10 [t]But I have made Esau bare, I have uncovered his secret places, and he shall not be able to hide himself: his seed is spoiled, and his brethren, and his neighbours, and [u]he *is* not.

11 Leave thy fatherless children, I will preserve *them* alive; and let thy widows trust in me.

12 For thus saith the LORD; Behold, [v]they whose judgment *was* not to drink of the cup have assuredly drunken; and *art* thou he *that* shall altogether go unpunished? thou shalt not go unpunished, but thou shalt surely drink *of it.*

13 For [w]I have sworn by myself, saith the LORD, that [x]Bozrah shall become a desolation, a reproach, a waste, and a curse; and all the cities thereof shall be perpetual wastes.

14 I have heard a [y]rumour from the LORD, and an ambassador is sent unto the heathen, *saying,* Gather ye together, and come against her, and rise up to the battle.

15 For, lo, I will make thee small among the heathen, *and* despised among men.

16 Thy terribleness hath deceived thee, *and* the pride of thine heart, O thou that dwellest in the clefts of the rock, that holdest the height of the hill: [z]though thou shouldest make thy [a]nest as high as the eagle, [b]I will bring thee down from thence, saith the LORD.

17 Also Edom shall be a desolation: [c]every one that goeth by it shall be astonished, and shall hiss at all the plagues thereof.

18 [d]As in the overthrow of Sodom and Gomorrah and the neighbour *cities* thereof, saith the LORD, no man shall abide there, neither shall a son of man dwell in it.

19 [e]Behold, he shall come up like a lion from [f]the swelling of Jordan against the habitation of the strong: but I will suddenly make him run away from her: and who *is* a chosen *man, that* I may appoint over her? for [g]who *is* like me? and who will [q]appoint me the time? and [h]who *is* that shepherd that will stand before me?

20 [i]Therefore hear the counsel of the LORD, that he hath taken against Edom; and his purposes, that he hath purposed against the inhabitants of Teman: Surely the least of the flock shall draw them out: surely he shall make their habitations desolate with them.

21 [j]The earth is moved at the noise of their fall, at the cry the noise thereof was heard in the [r]Red sea.

22 Behold, [k]he shall come up and fly as the eagle, and spread his wings

49:3 [i]Is. 32:11 [j]ch. 48:7 **49:4** [k]ch. 3:14 [l]ch. 21:13 **49:6** [m]ver. 39 ch. 48:47 **49:7** [n]Ezek. 25:12 [o]Obad. 8 [p]Is. 19:11 **49:8** [q]ver. 30 [r]ch. 25:23 **49:9** [s]Obad. 5 **49:10** [t]Mal. 1:3 [u]Is. 17:14 **49:12** [v]ch. 25:29 Obad. 16 **49:13** [w]Gen. 22:16 Is. 45:23 Amos 6:8 [x]Is. 34:6 & 63:1 **49:14** [y]Obad. 1-3 **49:16** [z]Obad. 4 [a]Job 39:27 [b]Amos 9:2 **49:17** [c]ch. 18:16 & 50:13 **49:18** [d]Gen. 19:25 Deut. 29:23 ch. 50:40 **49:19** [e]ch. 50:44 [f]ch. 12:5 [g]Ex. 15:11 [h]Job 41:10 **49:20** [i]ch. 50:45 **49:21** [j]ch. 50:46 **49:22** [k]ch. 48:40,41

[m] Or, *Melcom;* see 1 Ki. 11:5 [n] Or, *thy valley floweth away* [o] Or, *they are turned back* [p] Heb. *their sufficiency* [q] Or, *summon me in judgment* [r] Heb. *Weedy sea*

49:7 EDOM. The Edomites were descendants of Jacob's twin brother, Esau (Gen. 36:1). Living in the mountainous region south of the Dead Sea, they had a history of enmity and conflict with Israel. Edom's great sins were its pride (v. 16) and fervent hatred of Israel (cf. Obad. 3,10–14).

49:16 THE PRIDE OF THINE HEART. The downfall of the Edomites was their pride, which had made them overly confident. They thought that because of their strong fortifications, they could never be defeated. Pride, overconfidence, and material wealth can also deceive us into thinking we do not need to rely continually on God for His help and grace.

over Bozrah: and at that day shall the
heart of the mighty men of Edom be as
the heart of a woman in her pangs.
23 ¶ [l]Concerning Damascus. Ha-
math is confounded, and Arpad: for
they have heard evil tidings: they are
[s]fainthearted; [m]*there is* sorrow [t]on
the sea; it cannot be quiet.
24 Damascus is waxed feeble, *and*
turneth herself to flee, and fear hath
seized on *her*: [n]anguish and sorrows
have taken her, as a woman in travail.
25 How is [o]the city of praise not
left, the city of my joy!
26 [p]Therefore her young men shall
fall in her streets, and all the men of
war shall be cut off in that day, saith
the LORD of hosts.
27 And I will kindle a [q]fire in the
wall of Damascus, and it shall con-
sume the palaces of Ben-hadad.

The prophecy against Kedar

28 ¶ [r]Concerning Kedar, and con-
cerning the kingdoms of Hazor, which
Nebuchadrezzar king of Babylon shall
smite, thus saith the LORD; Arise ye, go
up to Kedar, and spoil [s]the men of the
east.
29 Their [t]tents and their flocks
shall they take away: they shall take to
themselves their curtains, and all their
vessels, and their camels; and they
shall cry unto them, [u]Fear *is* on every
side.
30 ¶ [v]Flee, [u]get you far off, dwell
deep, O ye inhabitants of Hazor, saith
the LORD; for Nebuchadrezzar king of
Babylon hath taken counsel against
you, and hath conceived a purpose
against you.
31 Arise, get you up unto [w]the
[v]wealthy nation, that dwelleth with-
out care, saith the LORD, which have
neither gates nor bars, *which* [x]dwell
alone.
32 And their camels shall be a
booty, and the multitude of their cattle
a spoil: and I will scatter into all winds
them *that are* [w]in the utmost corners;
and I will bring their calamity from all
sides thereof, saith the LORD.
33 And Hazor [y]shall be a dwelling
for dragons, *and* a desolation for ever:
[z]there shall no man abide there, nor
any son of man dwell in it.

The prophecy against Elam

34 ¶ The word of the LORD that came
to Jeremiah the prophet against
[a]Elam in the beginning of the reign of
Zedekiah king of Judah, saying,
35 Thus saith the LORD of hosts; Be-
hold, I will break [b]the bow of Elam,
the chief of their might.
36 And upon Elam will I bring the
four winds from the four quarters of
heaven, and [c]will scatter them toward
all those winds; and there shall be no
nation whither the outcasts of Elam
shall not come.
37 For I will cause Elam to be dis-
mayed before their enemies, and before
them that seek their life: and I will
bring evil upon them, *even* my fierce an-
ger, saith the LORD; [d]and I will send
the sword after them, till I have con-
sumed them:
38 And I will [e]set my throne in
Elam, and will destroy from thence the
king and the princes, saith the LORD.
39 ¶ But it shall come to pass [f]in
the latter days, *that* I will bring again
the captivity of Elam, saith the LORD.

The prophecy against Babylon

51:15–19pp — Jer. 10:12–16

50 THE WORD that the LORD
spake [g]against Babylon *and*

49:23 [l]Is. 17:1 & 37:13 Amos 1:3 Zech. 9:1,2 [m]Is. 57:20 **49:24** [n]Is. 13:8 ch. 4:31 & 6:24 & 48:41 **49:25** [o]ch. 33:9 **49:26** [p]ch. 50:30 **49:27** [q]Amos 1:4 **49:28** [r]Is. 21:13 [s]Judg. 6:3 Job 1:3 **49:29** [t]Ps. 120:5 [u]ch. 46:5 **49:30** [v]ver. 8 **49:31** [w]Ezek. 38:11 [x]Num. 23:9 Deut. 33:28 Mic. 7:14 **49:33** [y]ch. 9:11 & 10:22 Mal. 1:3 [z]ver. 18 **49:34** [a]ch. 25:25 **49:35** [b]Is. 22:6 **49:36** [c]ver. 32 **49:37** [d]ch. 9:16 **49:38** [e]ch. 43:10 **49:39** [f]ch. 48:47 **50:1** [g]Is. 13:1 & 47:1

[s]Heb. *melted* [t]Or, *as on the sea* [u]Heb. *flit greatly* [v]Or, *that is at ease* [w]Heb. *cut off into corners,* or, *that have the corners* of their hair *polled*

49:23–26 DAMASCUS. Damascus was the major city of Syria and was located in the southern part of that country. Amos also prophesied against the people of Damascus because of their cruelty (Amos 1:3–5).

49:28–33 KEDER . . . HAZOR. This section is a prophecy against Arab tribes. The people of Keder were descendants of Ishmael, Abraham's son by Hagar (Gen. 25:13; cf. Is. 21:13,16).

49:34–39 ELAM. Elam was located 200 miles east of Babylon in what is now the country of Iran. After experiencing the judgment of God, Elam would be restored. Several Elamites were in Jerusalem when the Holy Spirit was poured out on the disciples on the day of Pentecost (Acts 2:5–9).

50:1 BABYLON. Jeremiah also prophesied concerning the fall of Babylon, an event that played an important part in the history of redemption. (1) When the prophet spoke these words, God's people were in exile in Babylon and in danger of being assimilated by another people and culture. Were that to occur, salvation through Abraham's descendants would be impossible. Babylon's grip on Israel had to be broken and God's people freed in order for God to work His will and prepare for the coming of the Messiah. Even though Babylon

against the land of the Chaldeans [x]by Jeremiah the prophet.

2 Declare ye among the nations, and publish, and [y]set up a standard; publish, *and* conceal not: say, Babylon is taken, [h]Bel is confounded, Merodach is broken in pieces; [i]her idols are confounded, her images are broken in pieces.

3 [j]For out of the north there cometh up [k]a nation against her, which shall make her land desolate, and none shall dwell therein: they shall remove, they shall depart, both man and beast.

4 ¶ In those days, and in that time, saith the LORD, the children of Israel shall come, [l]they and the children of Judah together, [m]going and weeping: they shall go, [n]and seek the LORD their God.

5 They shall ask the way to Zion with their faces thitherward, *saying,* Come, and let us join ourselves to the LORD in [o]a perpetual covenant *that* shall not be forgotten.

6 My people hath been [p]lost sheep: their shepherds have caused them to go astray, they have turned them away *on* [q]the mountains: they have gone from mountain to hill, they have forgotten their [z]restingplace.

7 All that found them have [r]devoured them: and [s]their adversaries said, [t]We offend not, because they have sinned against the LORD, [u]the habitation of justice, even the LORD, [v]the hope of their fathers.

8 [w]Remove out of the midst of Babylon, and go forth out of the land of the Chaldeans, and be as the he goats before the flocks.

9 ¶ [x]For, lo, I will raise and cause to come up against Babylon an assembly of great nations from the north country: and they shall set themselves in array against her; from thence she shall be taken: their arrows *shall be* as of a mighty [a]expert man; [y]none shall return in vain.

10 And Chaldea shall be a spoil: [z]all that spoil her shall be satisfied, saith the LORD.

11 [a]Because ye were glad, because ye rejoiced, O ye destroyers of mine heritage, because ye are grown [b]fat [b]as the heifer at grass, and [c]bellow as bulls;

12 Your mother shall be sore confounded; she that bare you shall be ashamed: behold, the hindermost of the nations *shall be* a wilderness, a dry land, and a desert.

13 Because of the wrath of the LORD it shall not be inhabited, [c]but it shall be wholly desolate: [d]every one that goeth by Babylon shall be astonished, and hiss at all her plagues.

14 [e]Put yourselves in array against Babylon round about: all ye [f]that bend the bow, shoot at her, spare no arrows: for she hath sinned against the LORD.

15 Shout against her round about: she hath [g]given her hand: her foundations are fallen, [h]her walls are thrown down: for [i]it *is* the vengeance of the LORD: take vengeance upon her; as she hath done, do unto her.

16 Cut off the sower from Babylon, and him that handleth the [d]sickle in the time of harvest: for fear of the oppressing sword [j]they shall turn every one to his people, and they shall flee every one to his own land.

17 ¶ Israel *is* [k]a scattered sheep; [l]the lions have driven *him* away: first

50:2 [h]Is. 46:1 ch. 51:44 [i]See ch. 43:12,13
50:3 [j]ch. 51:48 [k]Is. 13:17,18,20
50:4 [l]Hos. 1:11 [m]Ezra 3:12 ch. 31:9 Zech. 12:10 [n]Hos. 3:5
50:5 [o]ch. 31:31
50:6 [p]Is. 53:6 1 Pet. 2:25 [q]ch. 2:20 & 3:6,23
50:7 [r]Ps. 79:7 [s]ch. 40:2,3 Zech. 11:5 [t]See ch. 2:3 Dan 9:16 [u]Ps. 90:1 & 91:1 [v]Ps. 22:4
50:8 [w]Is. 48:20 ch. 51:6,45 Zech. 2:6,7 Rev. 18:4
50:9 [x]ch. 15:14 & 51:27 [y]2 Sam. 1:22
50:10 [z]Rev. 17:16
50:11 [a]Is. 47:6 [b]Hos. 10:11
50:13 [c]ch. 25:12 [d]ch. 49:17
50:14 [e]ch. 51:2 [f]ver. 29
50:15 [g]1 Chr. 29:24 2 Chr. 30:8 Lam. 5:6 Ezek. 17:18 [h]ch. 51:58 [i]ch. 51:6,11
50:16 [j]Is. 13:14
50:17 [k]ver. 6 [l]ch. 2:15

[x] Heb. *by the hand of Jeremiah* [y] Heb. *lift up* [z] Heb. *place to lie down in* [a] Or, *destroyer* [b] Heb. *big,* or, *corpulent* [c] Or, *neigh as steeds* [d] Or, *scythe*

was the undisputed world power at this time, Jeremiah predicted its downfall five years before Jerusalem was taken (51:59–60).

(2) Jeremiah's prophecy, however, goes beyond Babylon's future defeat by Cyrus (see next note). It predicts a destruction of Babylon that will cause Israel and Judah to make an everlasting covenant with God that will never be broken (vv. 4–5). This destruction will occur at the end of the tribulation period (see Rev. 17:1, note).

50:3 MAKE HER LAND DESOLATE. Jeremiah foresaw that Babylon would experience a great destruction. In his day the nation from the north was the Medo-Persian coalition. Babylon fell in 539 B.C. at the hands of an army led by Cyrus of Persia.

50:4–5 IN THOSE DAYS. This passage speaks of the Jews' repentance and return to God in the last days (cf. 31:31; 32:40). They will turn to God and remain faithful to Him forever (cf. vv. 19–20; see Rev. 12:6, note).

50:9 AN ASSEMBLY OF GREAT NATIONS. These nations are named in 51:27–28.

50:11 BECAUSE YOU WERE GLAD. God would bring defeat upon the Babylonians because they had rejoiced over their defeat of Judah and Jerusalem. What Babylon had done to others would now happen to her (v. 29).

50:17 ISRAEL *IS* A SCATTERED SHEEP. Assyria destroyed Israel, the northern kingdom, in 722 B.C. (2 Ki. 17:1–6), and Babylon destroyed Ju-

[m]the king of Assyria hath devoured him; and last this [n]Nebuchadrezzar king of Babylon hath broken his bones.

18 Therefore thus saith the LORD of hosts, the God of Israel; Behold, I will punish the king of Babylon and his land, as I have punished the king of Assyria.

19 [o]And I will bring Israel again to his habitation, and he shall feed on Carmel and Bashan, and his soul shall be satisfied upon mount Ephraim and Gilead.

20 In those days, and in that time, saith the LORD, [p]the iniquity of Israel shall be sought for, and *there shall be* none; and the sins of Judah, and they shall not be found: for I will pardon them [q]whom I reserve.

21 ¶ Go up against the land [e]of Merathaim, *even* against it, and against the inhabitants of [r]Pekod:[f] waste and utterly destroy after them, saith the LORD, and do [s]according to all that I have commanded thee.

22 [t]A sound of battle *is* in the land, and of great destruction.

23 How is [u]the hammer of the whole earth cut asunder and broken! how is Babylon become a desolation among the nations!

24 I have laid a snare for thee, and thou art also taken, O Babylon, [v]and thou wast not aware: thou art found, and also caught, because thou hast striven against the LORD.

25 The LORD hath opened his armoury, and hath brought forth [w]the weapons of his indignation: for this *is* the work of the Lord GOD of hosts in the land of the Chaldeans.

26 Come against her [g]from the utmost border, open her storehouses: [h]cast her up as heaps, and destroy her utterly: let nothing of her be left.

27 Slay all her [x]bullocks; let them go down to the slaughter: woe unto them! for their day is come, the time of [y]their visitation.

28 The voice of them that flee and escape out of the land of Babylon, [z]to declare in Zion the vengeance of the LORD our God, the vengeance of his temple.

29 Call together the archers against Babylon: [a]all ye that bend the bow, camp against it round about; let none thereof escape: [b]recompense her according to her work; according to all that she hath done, do unto her: [c]for she hath been proud against the LORD, against the Holy One of Israel.

30 [d]Therefore shall her young men fall in the streets, and all her men of war shall be cut off in that day, saith the LORD.

31 Behold, I *am* against thee, *O thou* [i]most proud, saith the Lord GOD of hosts: for [e]thy day is come, the time *that* I will visit thee.

32 And [i]the most proud shall stumble and fall, and none shall raise him up: and [f]I will kindle a fire in his cities, and it shall devour all round about him.

33 ¶ Thus saith the LORD of hosts; The children of Israel and the children of Judah *were* oppressed together: and all that took them captives held them fast; they refused to let them go.

34 [g]Their Redeemer *is* strong; [h]the LORD of hosts *is* his name: he shall thoroughly plead their cause, that he may give rest to the land, and disquiet the inhabitants of Babylon.

35 ¶ A sword *is* upon the Chaldeans, saith the LORD, and upon the inhabitants of Babylon, and [i]upon her princes, and upon [j]her wise *men*.

36 A sword *is* [k]upon the [j,k]liars; and they shall dote: a sword *is* upon her mighty men; and they shall be dismayed.

37 A sword *is* upon their horses, and upon their chariots, and upon all [l]the mingled people that *are* in the midst of her; and [m]they shall become as women: a sword *is* upon her treasures; and they shall be robbed.

38 [n]A drought *is* upon her waters; and they shall be dried up: for it *is* the

50:17 [m]2 Ki. 17:6 [n]2 Ki. 24:10,14
50:19 [o]Is. 65:10 ch. 33:12 Ezek. 34:13
50:20 [p]ch. 31:34 [q]Is. 1:9
50:21 [r]Ezek. 23:23 [s]See 2 Sam. 16:11 2 Ki. 18:25 2 Chr. 36:23 Is. 10:6 & 44:28 & 48:14
50:22 [t]ch. 51:54
50:23 [u]Is. 14:6 ch. 51:20
50:24 [v]ch. 51:8,31 Dan. 5:30
50:25 [w]Is. 13:5
50:27 [x]Ps. 22:12 Is. 34:7 ch. 46:21 [y]ch. 48:44
50:28 [z]ch. 51:10
50:29 [a]ver. 14 [b]ver. 15 ch. 51:56 Rev. 18:6 [c]Is. 47:10
50:30 [d]ch. 49:26 & 51:4
50:31 [e]ver. 27
50:32 [f]ch. 21:14
50:34 [g]Rev. 18:8 [h]Is. 47:4
50:35 [i]Dan. 5:30 [j]Is. 47:13
50:36 [k]Is. 44:25 ch. 48:30
50:37 [l]ch. 25:20 Ezek. 30:5 [m]ch. 51:30 Nah. 3:13
50:38 [n]Is. 44:27 ch. 51:36 Rev. 16:12

[e] Or, *of the rebels* [f] Or, *Visitation* [g] Heb. *from the end* [h] Or, *tread her* [i] Heb. *pride* [j] Or, *chief stays* [k] Heb. *bars*

dah, the southern kingdom, in 586 B.C. (2 Ki. 24). Both nations took captives from among God's people and settled them far away from their homeland.

50:32 THE MOST PROUD. Babylon defied the Lord and lived in pride. For this she would be brought low. Nothing is more odious than the pride of nations and people who live as they please while scorning the laws and righteous standards set forth in God's Word. What happened to ancient Babylon will happen to all the ungodly in the last days (see Rev. 18:2–21, notes).

land of [o]graven images, and they are mad upon *their* idols.

39 [p]Therefore the wild beasts of the desert with the wild beasts of the islands shall dwell *there,* and the owls shall dwell therein: [q]and it shall be no more inhabited for ever; neither shall it be dwelt in from generation to generation.

40 [r]As God overthrew Sodom and Gomorrah and the neighbour *cities* thereof, saith the LORD; *so* shall no man abide there, neither shall any son of man dwell therein.

41 [s]Behold, a people shall come from the north, and a great nation, and many kings shall be raised up from the coasts of the earth.

42 [t]They shall hold the bow and the lance: [u]they *are* cruel, and will not show mercy: [v]their voice shall roar like the sea, and they shall ride upon horses, *every one* put in array, like a man to the battle, against thee, O daughter of Babylon.

43 The king of Babylon hath heard the report of them, and his hands waxed feeble: anguish took hold of him, *and* pangs as of a woman in travail.

44 [w]Behold, he shall come up like a lion from the swelling of Jordan unto the habitation of the strong: but I will make them suddenly run away from her: and who *is* a chosen *man, that* I may appoint over her? for who *is* like me? and who will [1]appoint me the time? and [x]who *is* that shepherd that will stand before me?

45 Therefore hear ye [y]the counsel of the LORD, that he hath taken against Babylon; and his purposes, that he hath purposed against the land of the Chaldeans: Surely the least of the flock shall draw them out: surely he shall make *their* habitation desolate with them.

46 [z]At the noise of the taking of Babylon the earth is moved, and the cry is heard among the nations.

50:38 [o]ver. 2
50:39 [p]Is. 13:21,22 & 34:14 ch. 51:37 Rev. 18:2 [q]Is. 13:20 ch. 25:12
50:40 [r]Gen. 19:25 Is. 13:19 ch. 51:26
50:41 [s]ver. 9 ch. 6:22 & 25:14 & 51:27 Rev. 17:16
50:42 [t]ch. 6:23 [u]Is. 13:18 [v]Is. 5:30
50:44 [w]ch. 49:19 [x]Job 41:10 ch. 49:19
50:45 [y]Is. 14:24 ch. 51:11
50:46 [z]Rev. 18:9
51:1 [a]2 Ki. 19:7 ch. 4:11
51:2 [b]ch. 15:7 [c]ch. 50:14
51:3 [d]ch. 50:14 [e]ch. 50:21
51:4 [f]ch. 49:26 & 50:30,37
51:6 [g]ch. 50:8 Rev. 18:4 [h]ch. 50:15 [i]ch. 25:14
51:7 [j]Rev. 17:4 [k]Rev. 14:8 [l]ch. 25:16
51:8 [m]Is. 21:9 Rev. 14:8 & 18:2 [n]ch. 48:20 Rev. 18:9,11,19 [o]ch. 46:11
51:9 [p]Is. 13:14 ch. 50:16 [q]Rev. 18:5
51:10 [r]Ps. 37:6 [s]ch. 50:28
51:11 [t]ch. 46:4 [u]ver. 28 Is. 13:17

51 THUS SAITH the LORD; Behold, I will raise up against Babylon, and against them that dwell in the [m]midst of them that rise up against me, [a]a destroying wind;

2 And will send unto Babylon [b]fanners, that shall fan her, and shall empty her land: [c]for in the day of trouble they shall be against her round about.

3 Against *him that* bendeth [d]let the archer bend his bow, and against *him that* lifteth himself up in his brigandine: and spare ye not her young men; [e]destroy ye utterly all her host.

4 Thus the slain shall fall in the land of the Chaldeans, [f]and *they that are* thrust through in her streets.

5 For Israel *hath* not *been* forsaken, nor Judah of his God, of the LORD of hosts; though their land was filled with sin against the Holy One of Israel.

6 [g]Flee out of the midst of Babylon, and deliver every man his soul: be not cut off in her iniquity; for [h]this *is* the time of the LORD's vengeance; [i]he will render unto her a recompence.

7 [j]Babylon *hath been* a golden cup in the LORD's hand, that made all the earth drunken: [k]the nations have drunken of her wine; therefore the nations [l]are mad.

8 Babylon is suddenly [m]fallen and destroyed: [n]howl for her; [o]take balm for her pain, if so be she may be healed.

9 We would have healed Babylon, but she is not healed: forsake her, and [p]let us go every one into his own country: [q]for her judgment reacheth unto heaven, and is lifted up *even* to the skies.

10 The LORD hath [r]brought forth our righteousness: come, and let us [s]declare in Zion the work of the LORD our God.

11 [t]Make [n]bright the arrows; gather the shields: [u]the LORD hath raised up the spirit of the kings of the

[1] Or, *summon me to plead?* [m] Heb. *heart*
[n] Heb. *pure*

51:1–64 AGAINST BABYLON. A second chapter concerning Babylon's doom prophesies that the Lord would bring about the complete overthrow of Babylon in order to deliver His people from oppression. In the last days of this age, Christ will overthrow the whole world system, symbolically called "Babylon the great" (Rev. 18:2), with all its sin and immorality; this destruction will be God's righteous judgment on a world dominated by Satan and evil (see Rev. 17:1, note).

51:6 FLEE OUT OF THE MIDST OF BABYLON. God calls on His people to flee from Babylon before its final destruction. Similarly, the N.T. exhorts believers to come out of the end-time Babylon (i.e., the ungodly world system), lest they participate in her sins and receive her judgment (see Rev. 18:4, note; see article on SPIRITUAL SEPARATION FOR BELIEVERS, p. 1814).

51:11 THE MEDES. The Medes, together with the Persians, overthrew Babylon in 539 B.C.

Medes: [v]for his device *is* against Bab-
ylon, to destroy it; because it *is* [w]the
vengeance of the LORD, the vengeance
of his temple.
12 [x]Set up the standard upon the
walls of Babylon, make the watch
strong, set up the watchmen, prepare
the [o]ambushes: for the LORD hath both
devised and done that which he spake
against the inhabitants of Babylon.
13 [y]O thou that dwellest upon
many waters, abundant in treasures,
thine end is come, *and* the measure of
thy covetousness.
14 [z]The LORD of hosts hath sworn
[p]by himself, *saying,* Surely I will fill
thee with men, [a]as with caterpillars;
and they shall [q]lift [b]up a shout
against thee.
15 [c]He hath made the earth by his
power, he hath established the world
by his wisdom, and [d]hath stretched
out the heaven by his understanding.
16 When he uttereth *his* voice, *there*
is a [r]multitude of waters in the heav-
ens; and [e]he causeth the vapours to
ascend from the ends of the earth: he
maketh lightnings with rain, and
bringeth forth the wind out of his trea-
sures.
17 [f]Every man [s]is brutish by *his*
knowledge; every founder is confound-
ed by the graven image: [g]for his mol-
ten image *is* falsehood, and *there is* no
breath in them.
18 [h]They *are* vanity, the work of er-
rors: in the time of their visitation they
shall perish.
19 [i]The portion of Jacob *is* not like
them; for he *is* the former of all things:
and *Israel is* the rod of his inheritance:
the LORD of hosts *is* his name.
20 [j]Thou *art* my battle axe *and*
weapons of war: for [t]with thee will I
break in pieces the nations, and with
thee will I destroy kingdoms;
21 And with thee will I break in
pieces the horse and his rider; and with
thee will I break in pieces the chariot
and his rider;
22 With thee also will I break in
pieces man and woman; and with thee
will I break in pieces [k]old and young;
and with thee will I break in pieces the
young man and the maid;
23 I will also break in pieces with
thee the shepherd and his flock; and
with thee will I break in pieces the hus-
bandman and his yoke of oxen; and
with thee will I break in pieces cap-
tains and rulers.
24 [l]And I will render unto Babylon
and to all the inhabitants of Chaldea all
their evil that they have done in Zion in
your sight, saith the LORD.
25 Behold, I *am* against thee, [m]O
destroying mountain, saith the LORD,
which destroyest all the earth: and I
will stretch out mine hand upon thee,
and roll thee down from the rocks,
[n]and will make thee a burnt moun-
tain.
26 And they shall not take of thee a
stone for a corner, nor a stone for foun-
dations; [o]but thou shalt be [u]desolate
for ever, saith the LORD.
27 [p]Set ye up a standard in the
land, blow the trumpet among the na-
tions, [q]prepare the nations against
her, call together against her [r]the
kingdoms of Ararat, Minni, and Ash-
chenaz; appoint a captain against her;
cause the horses to come up as the
rough caterpillars.
28 Prepare against her the nations
with [s]the kings of the Medes, the cap-
tains thereof, and all the rulers there-
of, and all the land of his dominion.
29 And the land shall tremble and
sorrow: for every purpose of the LORD
shall be performed against Babylon,
[t]to make the land of Babylon a deso-
lation without an inhabitant.
30 The mighty men of Babylon have
forborne to fight, they have remained
in *their* holds: their might hath failed;
[u]they became as women: they have
burned her dwellingplaces; [v]her bars
are broken.
31 [w]One post shall run to meet an-
other, and one messenger to meet an-
other, to show the king of Babylon that
his city is taken at *one* end,
32 And that [x]the passages are
stopped, and the reeds they have
burned with fire, and the men of war
are affrighted.
33 For thus saith the LORD of hosts,

51:11 [v]ch. 50:45 [w]ch. 50:28
51:12 [x]Nah. 2:1 & 3:14
51:13 [y]Rev. 17:1,15
51:14 [z]ch. 49:13 Amos 6:8 [a]Nah. 3:15 [b]ch. 50:15
51:15 [c]Gen. 1:1,6 ch. 10:12 [d]Job 9:8 Ps. 104:2 Is. 40:22
51:16 [e]Ps. 135:7
51:17 [f]ch. 10:14 [g]ch. 50:2
51:18 [h]ch. 10:15
51:19 [i]ch. 10:16
51:20 [j]Is. 10:5,15 ch. 50:23
51:22 [k]2 Chr. 36:17
51:24 [l]ch. 50:15
51:25 [m]Is. 13:2 Zech. 4:7 [n]Rev. 8:8
51:26 [o]ch. 50:40
51:27 [p]Is. 13:2 [q]ch. 25:14 [r]ch. 50:41
51:28 [s]ver. 11
51:29 [t]ver. 43 ch. 50:13
51:30 [u]Is. 19:16 ch. 48:41 & 50:37 [v]Lam. 2:9 Amos 1:5 Nah. 3:13
51:31 [w]ch. 50:24
51:32 [x]ch. 50:38

o Heb. *liers in wait* p Heb. *by his soul* q Heb. *utter* r Or, *noise* s Or, *is more brutish than to know* t Or, *in thee,* or, *by thee* u Heb. *everlasting desolations*

51:27 ARARAT. The people of Ararat were conquered by the Medes in the sixth century B.C. They joined with the Medes in overthrowing Babylon.

51:33 THE TIME OF HER HARVEST SHALL COME. Babylon had sown seeds of cruelty, idolatry, and immorality; now she would reap the har-

the God of Israel; The daughter of Babylon *is* [y]like a threshingfloor, [z]*it*[v] *is* time to thresh her: yet a little while, [a]and the time of her harvest shall come.

34 Nebuchadrezzar the king of Babylon hath [b]devoured me, he hath crushed me, he hath made me an empty vessel, he hath swallowed me up like a dragon, he hath filled his belly with my delicates, he hath cast me out.

35 [w]The violence done to me and to my [x]flesh *be* upon Babylon, shall the [y]inhabitant of Zion say; and my blood upon the inhabitants of Chaldea, shall Jerusalem say.

36 Therefore thus saith the LORD; Behold, [c]I will plead thy cause, and take vengeance for thee; [d]and I will dry up her sea, and make her springs dry.

37 [e]And Babylon shall become heaps, a dwellingplace for dragons, [f]an astonishment, and an hissing, without an inhabitant.

38 They shall roar together like lions: they shall [z]yell as lions' whelps.

39 In their heat I will make their feasts, and [g]I will make them drunken, that they may rejoice, and sleep a perpetual sleep, and not wake, saith the LORD.

40 I will bring them down like lambs to the slaughter, like rams with he goats.

41 How is [h]Sheshach taken! and how is [i]the praise of the whole earth surprised! how is Babylon become an astonishment among the nations!

42 [j]The sea is come up upon Babylon: she is covered with the multitude of the waves thereof.

43 [k]Her cities are a desolation, a dry land, and a wilderness, a land wherein no man dwelleth, neither doth *any* son of man pass thereby.

44 [l]And I will punish Bel in Babylon, and I will bring forth out of his mouth that which he hath swallowed up: and the nations shall not flow together any more unto him: yea, [m]the wall of Babylon shall fall.

45 [n]My people, go ye out of the midst of her, and deliver ye every man his soul from the fierce anger of the LORD.

46 And [a]lest your heart faint, and ye fear [o]for the rumour that shall be heard in the land; a rumour shall both come *one* year, and after that in *another* year *shall come* a rumour, and violence in the land, ruler against ruler.

47 Therefore, behold, the days come, that [p]I will [b]do judgment upon the graven images of Babylon: and her whole land shall be confounded, and all her slain shall fall in the midst of her.

48 Then [q]the heaven and the earth, and all that *is* therein, shall sing for Babylon: [r]for the spoilers shall come unto her from the north, saith the LORD.

49 [c]As Babylon *hath caused* the slain of Israel to fall, so at Babylon shall fall the slain of all [d]the earth.

50 [s]Ye that have escaped the sword, go away, stand not still: remember the LORD afar off, and let Jerusalem come into your mind.

51 [t]We are confounded, because we have heard reproach: shame hath covered our faces: for strangers are come into the sanctuaries of the LORD's house.

52 Wherefore, behold, the days come, saith the LORD, [u]that I will do judgment upon her graven images: and through all her land the wounded shall groan.

53 [v]Though Babylon should mount up to heaven, and though she should fortify the height of her strength, *yet* from me shall spoilers come unto her, saith the LORD.

54 [w]A sound of a cry *cometh* from Babylon, and great destruction from the land of the Chaldeans:

55 Because the LORD hath spoiled Babylon, and destroyed out of her the great voice; when her waves do roar like great waters, a noise of their voice is uttered:

51:33 [y]Is. 21:10 Amos 1:3 Mic. 4:13 [z]Is. 41:15 Hab. 3:12 [a]Is. 17:5 Hos. 6:11 Joel 3:13 Rev. 14:15
51:34 [b]ch. 50:17
51:36 [c]ch. 50:34 [d]ch. 50:38
51:37 [e]Is. 13:22 ch. 50:39 Rev. 18:2 [f]ch. 25:9,18
51:39 [g]ver. 57
51:41 [h]ch. 25:26 [i]Is. 13:19
51:42 [j]See Is. 8:7
51:43 [k]ver. 29 ch. 50:39
51:44 [l]Is. 46:1 [m]ver. 58
51:45 [n]ver. 6 ch. 50:8 Rev. 18:4
51:46 [o]2 Ki. 19:7
51:47 [p]ver. 52
51:48 [q]Is. 44:23 [r]ch. 50:3,41
51:50 [s]ch. 44:28
51:51 [t]Ps. 44:15 & 79:4
51:52 [u]ver. 47
51:53 [v]ch. 49:16 Amos 9:2 Obad. 4
51:54 [w]ch. 50:22

[v] Or, *in the time that he thresheth her* [w] Heb. *My violence* [x] Or, *remainder* [y] Heb. *inhabitress* [z] Or, *shake themselves* [a] Or, *let not* [b] Heb. *visit upon* [c] Or, *Both Babylon is to fall, O ye slain of Israel, and with Babylon* [d] Or, *the country*

vest of God's judgment. We must remember that sins are seeds from which a large and terrible harvest will eventually spring. "Be not deceived; God is not mocked: for whatsoever a man soweth, that shall he also reap" (Gal. 6:7).

51:50 JERUSALEM. Having escaped from the danger of Babylon's fall, the exiles had to consider that now was the time to return to Jerusalem and serve the Lord.

56 Because the spoiler is come
upon her, *even* upon Babylon, and her
mighty men are taken, every one of
their bows is broken: [x]for the LORD
God of recompences shall surely re-
quite.
57 [y]And I will make drunk her
princes, and her wise *men*, her cap-
tains, and her rulers, and her mighty
men: and they shall sleep a perpetual
sleep, and not wake, saith [z]the King,
whose name *is* the LORD of hosts.
58 Thus saith the LORD of hosts;
[a]The[e] broad walls of Babylon shall
be utterly [f]broken, and her high gates
shall be burned with fire; and [b]the
people shall labour in vain, and the folk
in the fire, and they shall be weary.
59 ¶ The word which Jeremiah the
prophet commanded Seraiah the son of
Neriah, the son of Maaseiah, when he
went [g]with Zedekiah the king of Ju-
dah into Babylon in the fourth year of
his reign. And *this* Seraiah *was* a [h]qui-
et prince.
60 So Jeremiah wrote in a book all
the evil that should come upon Bab-
ylon, *even* all these words that are writ-
ten against Babylon.
61 And Jeremiah said to Seraiah,
When thou comest to Babylon, and
shalt see, and shalt read all these
words;
62 Then shalt thou say, O LORD,
thou hast spoken against this place, to
cut it off, that [c]none shall remain in
it, neither man nor beast, but that it
shall be [i]desolate for ever.
63 And it shall be, when thou hast
made an end of reading this book,
[d]*that* thou shalt bind a stone to it, and
cast it into the midst of Euphrates:
64 And thou shalt say, Thus shall
Babylon sink, and shall not rise from
the evil that I will bring upon her:
[e]and they shall be weary. Thus far *are*
the words of Jeremiah.

51:56 [x]ver. 24 Ps. 94:1 ch. 50:29
51:57 [y]ver. 39 [z]ch. 46:18 & 48:15
51:58 [a]ver. 44 [b]Hab. 2:13
51:62 [c]ver. 29 ch. 50:3,39
51:63 [d]See Rev. 18:21
51:64 [e]ver. 58
52:1 [f]2 Ki. 24:18

Downfall of Jerusalem

52:1–3pp — 2 Ki. 24:18–20; 2 Chr. 36:11–16
52:4–16pp — Jer. 39:1–10
52:4–21pp — 2 Ki. 25:1–21; 2 Chr. 36:17–20

52 ZEDEKIAH *WAS* [f]one and
twenty years old when he [j]be-
gan to reign, and he reigned eleven
years in Jerusalem. And his mother's
name *was* Hamutal the daughter of Jer-
emiah of Libnah.
2 And he did *that which was* evil in
the eyes of the LORD, according to all
that Jehoiakim had done.
3 For through the anger of the LORD
it came to pass in Jerusalem and Judah,
till he had cast them out from his pres-
ence, that Zedekiah rebelled against
the king of Babylon.
4 ¶ And it came to pass in the
[g]ninth year of his reign, in the tenth
month, in the tenth *day* of the month,
that Nebuchadrezzar king of Babylon
came, he and all his army, against Jeru-
salem, and pitched against it, and built
forts against it round about.
5 So the city was besieged unto the
eleventh year of king Zedekiah.
6 And in the fourth month, in the
ninth *day* of the month, the famine was
sore in the city, so that there was no
bread for the people of the land.
7 Then the city was broken up, and
all the men of war fled, and went forth
out of the city by night by the way of
the gate between the two walls, which
was by the king's garden; (now the
Chaldeans *were* by the city round
about:) and they went by the way of the
plain.
8 ¶ But the army of the Chaldeans
pursued after the king, and overtook
Zedekiah in the plains of Jericho; and
all his army was scattered from him.
9 [h]Then they took the king, and
carried him up unto the king of Bab-
ylon to Riblah in the land of Hamath;
where he gave judgment upon him.
10 [i]And the king of Babylon slew
the sons of Zedekiah before his eyes:
he slew also all the princes of Judah in
Riblah.
11 Then he [k]put out the eyes of
Zedekiah; and the king of Babylon
bound him in [l]chains, and carried him
to Babylon, and put him in [m]prison till
the day of his death.
12 ¶ [j]Now in the fifth month, in the
tenth *day* of the month, [k]which *was*

52:4 [g]2 Ki. 25:1-27 ch. 39:1 Zech. 8:19
52:9 [h]ch. 32:4
52:10 [i]Ezek. 12:13
52:12 [j]Zech. 7:5 & 8:19 [k]See ver. 29

[e] Or, *The walls of broad Babylon* [f] Or, *made naked* [g] Or, *on the behalf of Menucha*, or, *chief chamberlain* [h] Or, *prince of Menucha* [i] Heb. *desolations* [j] Heb. *reigned* [k] Heb. *blinded* [l] Or, *fetters* [m] Heb. *house of the wards*

52:1–34 ZEDEKIAH. Jeremiah's last chapter shows that the prophet truly spoke God's word and that the doom he foretold had become a reality. This chapter is almost identical to 2 Ki. 24:18—25:30; cf. also Jer. 39:1–10.

the nineteenth year of Nebuchadrezzar king of Babylon, [l]came Nebuzar-adan, [n]captain of the guard, *which* [o]served the king of Babylon, into Jerusalem,

13 And burned the house of the LORD, and the king's house; and all the houses of Jerusalem, and all the houses of the great *men,* burned he with fire:

14 And all the army of the Chaldeans, that *were* with the captain of the guard, brake down all the walls of Jerusalem round about.

15 [m]Then Nebuzar-adan the captain of the guard carried away captive *certain* of the poor of the people, and the residue of the people that remained in the city, and those that fell away, that fell to the king of Babylon, and the rest of the multitude.

16 But Nebuzar-adan the captain of the guard left *certain* of the poor of the land for vinedressers and for husbandmen.

17 [n]Also the [o]pillars of brass that *were* in the house of the LORD, and the bases, and the brasen sea that *was* in the house of the LORD, the Chaldeans brake, and carried all the brass of them to Babylon.

18 [p]The caldrons also, and the [p]shovels, and the snuffers, and the [q]bowls, and the spoons, and all the vessels of brass wherewith they ministered, took they away.

19 And the basins, and the [r]firepans, and the bowls, and the caldrons, and the candlesticks, and the spoons, and the cups; *that* which *was* of gold *in* gold, and *that* which *was* of silver *in* silver, took the captain of the guard away.

20 The two pillars, one sea, and twelve brasen bulls that *were* under the bases, which king Solomon had made in the house of the LORD: [q]the[s] brass of all these vessels was without weight.

21 And *concerning* the [r]pillars, the height of one pillar *was* eighteen cubits; and a [t]fillet of twelve cubits did compass it; and the thickness thereof *was* four fingers: *it was* hollow.

22 And a chapiter of brass *was* upon it; and the height of one chapiter *was* five cubits, with network and pomegranates upon the chapiters round about, all *of* brass. The second pillar also and the pomegranates *were* like unto these.

23 And there were ninety and six pomegranates on a side; *and* [s]all the pomegranates upon the network *were* an hundred round about.

24 ¶ And [t]the captain of the guard took Seraiah the chief priest, [u]and Zephaniah the second priest, and the three keepers of the [u]door:

25 He took also out of the city an eunuch, which had the charge of the men of war; and seven men of them that [v]were near the king's person, which were found in the city; and the [w]principal scribe of the host, who mustered the people of the land; and threescore men of the people of the land, that were found in the midst of the city.

26 So Nebuzar-adan the captain of the guard took them, and brought them to the king of Babylon to Riblah.

27 And the king of Babylon smote them, and put them to death in Riblah in the land of Hamath. Thus Judah was carried away captive out of his own land.

28 [v]This *is* the people whom Nebuchadrezzar carried away captive: in the [w]seventh year [x]three thousand Jews and three and twenty:

29 [y]In the eighteenth year of Nebuchadrezzar he carried away captive from Jerusalem eight hundred thirty and two [x]persons:

30 In the three and twentieth year of Nebuchadrezzar Nebuzar-adan the captain of the guard carried away captive of the Jews seven hundred forty and five persons: all the persons *were* four thousand and six hundred.

52:12 [l]ch. 39:9
52:15 [m]ch. 39:9
52:17 [n]ch. 27:19 [o]See 1 Ki. 7:15, 23,27,50
52:18 [p]Ex. 27:3 2 Ki. 25:14-16
52:20 [q]1 Ki. 7:47
52:21 [r]1 Ki. 7:15 2 Ki. 25:17 2 Chr. 3:15
52:23 [s]See 1 Ki. 7:20
52:24 [t]2 Ki. 25:18 [u]ch. 21:1 & 29:5
52:28 [v]2 Ki. 24:2 [w]See 2 Ki. 24:12 [x]See 2 Ki. 24:14
52:29 [y]See ver. 12 ch. 39:9

[n] Or, *chief marshal* [o] Heb. *stood before* [p] Or, *instruments to remove the ashes* [q] Or, *basins* [r] Or, *censers* [s] Heb. *their brass* [t] Heb. *thread* [u] Heb. *threshold* [v] Heb. *saw the face of the king* [w] Or, *scribe of the captain of the host* [x] Heb. *souls*

52:28–30 CARRIED AWAY. The three deportations to Babylon mentioned here occurred in 597 B.C., in 586 B.C., and in 581 B.C. The number of Jews taken captive may refer to adult males only. The total number of exiles was probably much higher (see 2 Ki. 24:14, 16).

The honour given Jehoiachin

52:31–34pp — 2 Ki. 25:27–30

31 ¶ [z]And it came to pass in the
seven and thirtieth year of the captivity
of Jehoiachin king of Judah, in the
twelfth month, in the five and twenti-
eth *day* of the month, *that* Evil-mero-
dach king of Babylon in the *first* year of
his reign [a]lifted up the head of Jehoia-
chin king of Judah, and brought him
forth out of prison,
32 And spake [y]kindly unto him,
and set his throne above the throne of
the kings that *were* with him in Bab-
ylon,
33 And changed his prison gar-
ments: [b]and he did continually eat
bread before him all the days of his life.
34 And *for* his diet, there was a con-
tinual diet given him of the king of Bab-
ylon, [z]every day a portion until the
day of his death, all the days of his life.

52:31 [z] 2 Ki. 25:27-30 [a] Gen. 40:13,20
52:33 [b] 2 Sam. 9:13

[y] Heb. *good things with him* [z] Heb. *the matter of the day in his day*

LAMENTATIONS

Outline

I. Jerusalem's Devastation (1:1–22)
   A. Description of the Destroyed City (1:1–7)
   B. The Cause of the Destruction (1:8–11)
   C. The Agony of the People (1:12–22)
II. God's Anger and Jerusalem's Sorrow (2:1–22)
   A. God's Anger Against Zion (2:1–9)
   B. The People's Anguish (2:10–17)
   C. The Prophet's Appeal for Mercy (2:18–22)
III. God's Afflicted People and Their Hope (3:1–66)
   A. The Cry of Despair (3:1–18)
   B. The Confession of Hope (3:19–39)
   C. A Call to Repentance (3:40–42)
   D. The Prophet's Suffering (3:43–54)
   E. The Prophet's Prayer (3:55–66)
IV. Zion's Past, Present, and Future (4:1–22)
   A. Zion's Past and Present Contrasted (4:1–12)
   B. The Cause of Zion's Devastation (4:13–20)
   C. Punishment for Edom and Restoration for Judah (4:21–22)
V. Prayer for Restoration (5:1–22)
   A. The Need for Mercy (5:1–15)
   B. The Confession of Sin (5:16–18)
   C. The Appeal for Restoration (5:19–22)

Author: Jeremiah

Theme: Present Sorrow and Future Hope

Date of Writing: 586–585 B.C.

Background

The title of this book is derived from the subtitle in the Greek and Latin versions of the O.T.—"The Lamentations of Jeremiah." The Hebrew O.T. includes the book as one of the five scrolls (with Ruth, Esther, Ecclesiastes, and the Song of Solomon) of the third part of the Hebrew Bible, the *Hagiographa* ("Holy Writings"); each of these five books was traditionally read at a set time in the Jewish liturgical year. This one was assigned to be read on the ninth day of the month Ab (about mid-July), when the Jews commemorated the destruction of Jerusalem. The Septuagint placed Lamentations immediately after the prophet Jeremiah, where it is located in most Bibles today.

That Jeremiah was the author of Lamentations has long been the consensus of both Jewish and Christian traditions. Among the various evidences that support this conclusion are the following: (1) From 2 Chr. 35:25 we know that Jeremiah was familiar with making lamentation. Furthermore, the prophetic book of Jeremiah contains frequent references to his weeping about the coming devastation of Jerusalem (see Jer. 7:29; 8:21; 9:1,10,20). (2) The vivid portrayal in Lamentations of that catastrophic event suggests an eyewitness

account; Jeremiah is the only known O.T. writer to have witnessed firsthand Jerusalem's tragedy in 586 B.C. (3) There are various thematic and linguistic parallels between the book of Jeremiah and Lamentations. For example, both books attribute Judah's suffering and Jerusalem's destruction to her persistent sin and rebellion against God. In both books Jeremiah calls God's people His "virgin daughter" (Jer. 14:17; 18:13; Lam. 1:15; 2:13). These facts, along with similarities between the two books in their poetic style, point to the same human author.

The desolation of Jerusalem is depicted in Lamentations so vividly and clearly that it indicates that it was experienced by the author as a recent event. Jeremiah himself was in his fifties when the city fell, fully experienced its trauma, and was forced against his will to go to Egypt in 585 B.C. (see Jer. 41—44), where he died (perhaps as a martyr) in the decade thereafter. Thus the book was most likely written immediately after the destruction of Jerusalem (c. 586–585 B.C.).

Purpose

Jeremiah wrote a series of five lamentations to express his intense sorrow and emotional pain over Jerusalem's tragic devastation, involving (1) the humiliating downfall of the Davidic monarchy and kingdom, (2) the utter destruction of the city walls, the temple, the king's palace, and the city generally, and (3) the pitiful deportation of most survivors far away to Babylon. "Jeremiah sat weeping and lamented with this lamentation over Jerusalem," says a superscription to the book in the Septuagint and the Latin Vulgate. In the book, the prophet's grief gushes forth like the grief of a mourner at a funeral of a close relative who died tragically. The laments acknowledge that the tragedy was God's judgment on Judah for long centuries of rebellion against Him by its rulers and people. The day of reckoning had come and it was terrible indeed. In Lamentations, Jeremiah not only acknowledged that God was righteous and just in all His ways, but also that He is merciful and compassionate to those who hope in Him (3:22–23,32). Thus Lamentations enabled the people to have hope in the midst of their despair and to look beyond the judgment of the moment to God's restoration of His people in the future.

Survey

The book is a series of five laments, each one complete in itself. The first one (ch. 1) describes the devastation of Jerusalem and the prophet's lament over it as he cries out to God in anguish of soul. Sometimes his lament is personified as that of Jerusalem (1:12–22). In his second lament (ch. 2), Jeremiah describes the cause of this devastation as God's wrath toward a rebellious people who refused to repent. Judah's enemy was God's instrument of judgment. The next poem (ch. 3) urges the nation to remember that God is indeed merciful and faithful, and that He is good to those who hope in Him. The fourth one (ch. 4) reiterates the themes of the previous three. In the final poem (ch. 5), after a confession of Judah's sin and need for mercy, Jeremiah petitions God to restore His people to His favor.

The book's five laments, which correspond to its five chapters, each have twenty-two verses (except for ch. 3, which has twenty-two times three or sixty-six verses); the number twenty-two is the number of letters in the Hebrew alphabet. The first four poems are alphabetic acrostics, i.e., each verse (or in ch. 3, each set of three verses) begins with a different letter of the Hebrew alphabet in succession from Aleph to Taw. This alphabetizing structure, in addition to being an aid to memory, accomplishes two things. (1) It conveys the idea that the lamentations are complete, covering everything from A to Z (Heb. *Aleph* to *Taw*). (2) By keeping the lamentations within this structure, the prophet is inhibited from going on and on with endless weeping and groaning. There is an end to the lament, just as there would someday be an end to the exile and a rebuilding of Jerusalem.

Special Features

Five major features or emphases characterize the book of Lamentations. (1) Although songs of individual and community lament occur in the psalms and in the prophetic books, only this Bible book is composed exclusively of grief-filled poems. (2) Its literary structure

is entirely poetic, with four of the book's five poetic laments being acrostic (see the last paragraph under "Survey"). In keeping with the book's poetic structure, the fifth poem also has twenty-two verses. (3) While 2 Ki. 25 and Jer. 52 describe the historical event of Jerusalem's destruction, only this book vividly portrays the emotions and feelings of those who actually experienced the catastrophe. (4) At the very heart of the book is one of the most powerful statements about God's faithfulness and salvation found in the Bible (3:21–26). Though Lamentations begins with a lament (1:1–2), it fittingly ends on a note of repentance and hope for restoration (5:16–22). (5) There are no quotations of this book in the N.T. and only a few possible allusions (cf. Lam. 1:15 with Rev. 14:19; Lam. 2:1 with Mat. 5:35; Lam. 3:30 with Mat. 5:39; Lam. 3:45 with 1 Cor. 4:13).

New Testament Fulfillment

Though Lamentations is nowhere quoted in the N.T., it does have direct relevance for those who believe in Christ. Like Rom. 1:18—3:20, these five chapters call believers to reflect on the seriousness of sin and the certainty of divine judgment. At the same time, they remind us that because of the compassion and mercy of the Lord, salvation is available for those who repent of their sins and turn to Him. Furthermore, the tears of the prophet call to mind the tears of Jesus Christ, who wept over the sins of the city of Jerusalem as He foresaw its coming destruction at the hands of the Romans (Mat. 23:37–38; Luke 13:34–35; 19:41–44).

Reading Lamentations

In order to read the entire Old Testament in one year, the book of Lamentations should be read in 2 days, according to the following schedule: ☐ 1–2 ☐ 3–5

NOTES

Jerusalem's desolation

1 HOW DOTH the city sit solitary,
that was full of people! [a]*how* is she
become as a widow! she *that was* great
among the nations, *and* princess
among the provinces, *how* is she be-
come tributary!
2 She [b]weepeth sore in the
[c]night, and her tears *are* on her
cheeks: among all her lovers she hath
none to comfort *her:* all her friends
have dealt treacherously with her, they
are become her enemies.
3 Judah is gone into captivity be-
cause of affliction, and [a]because of
great servitude: [d]she dwelleth among
the heathen, she findeth no rest: all her
persecutors overtook her between the
straits.
4 The ways of Zion do mourn, be-
cause none come to the solemn feasts:
all her gates are desolate: her priests
sigh, her virgins are afflicted, and she
is in bitterness.
5 Her adversaries [e]are the chief,
her enemies prosper; for the LORD hath
afflicted her [f]for the multitude of her
transgressions: her [g]children are
gone into captivity before the enemy.
6 And from the daughter of Zion all
her beauty is departed: her princes are
become like harts *that* find no pasture,
and they are gone without strength be-
fore the pursuer.
7 Jerusalem remembered in the
days of her affliction and of her miser-
ies all her [b]pleasant things that she
had in the days of old, when her people
fell into the hand of the enemy, and
none did help her: the adversaries saw
her, *and* did mock at her sabbaths.
8 [h]Jerusalem hath grievously
sinned; therefore she [c]is removed: all
that honoured her despise her, because
[i]they have seen her nakedness: yea,
she sigheth, and turneth backward.
9 Her filthiness *is* in her skirts; she
[j]remembereth not her last end; there-
fore she came down wonderfully: [k]she
had no comforter. O LORD, behold my
affliction: for the enemy hath magni-
fied *himself.*
10 The adversary hath spread out
his hand upon [l]all her [b]pleasant
things: for she hath seen *that* [m]the
heathen entered into her sanctuary,
whom thou didst command *that* [n]they
should not enter into thy congregation.
11 All her people sigh, [o]they seek
bread; they have given their pleasant
things for meat [d]to relieve the soul:
see, O LORD, and consider; for I am be-
come vile.
12 ¶ [e]*Is it* nothing to you, all ye
that [f]pass by? behold, and see [p]if
there be any sorrow like unto my sor-
row, which is done unto me, wherewith
the LORD hath afflicted *me* in the day of
his fierce anger.
13 From above hath he sent fire into
my bones, and it prevaileth against
them: he hath [q]spread a net for my
feet, he hath turned me back: he hath
made me desolate *and* faint all the day.
14 [r]The yoke of my transgressions
is bound by his hand: they are
wreathed, *and* come up upon my neck:
he hath made my strength to fall, the
Lord hath delivered me into *their*
hands, *from whom* I am not able to
rise up.

1:1 [a]Is. 47:7,8 **1:2** [b]Jer. 13:17 [c]Job 7:3 **1:3** [d]ch. 2:9 **1:5** [e]Deut. 28:43 [f]Jer. 30:14 Dan. 9:7 [g]Jer. 52:28 **1:8** [h]1 Ki. 8:46 [i]Jer. 13:22 Ezek. 16:37 Hos. 2:10 **1:9** [j]Deut. 32:29 Is. 47:7 [k]ver. 2,17,21 **1:10** [l]ver. 7 [m]Jer. 51:51 [n]Deut. 23:3 Neh. 13:1 **1:11** [o]Jer. 38:9 & 52:6 **1:12** [p]Dan. 9:12 **1:13** [q]Ezek. 12:13 **1:14** [r]Deut. 28:48

[a] Heb. *for the greatness of servitude* [b] Or, *desirable* [c] Heb. *is become a removing,* or, *wandering* [d] Or, *to make the soul to come again* [e] Or, It is *nothing* [f] Heb. *pass by the way?*

1:1 HOW DOTH THE CITY SIT SOLITARY. Jeremiah expresses his deep sorrow because of Jerusalem's fall and the tragic circumstances that brought it about. The holy city is personified as a deserted widow who has lost her children and been betrayed by her friends; she is left completely alone with no one to comfort her.

1:5 AFFLICTED HER FOR . . . HER TRANSGRESSIONS. The catastrophe of suffering, devastation, and loss is attributed to the peoples' sin (cf. vv. 8–9,14,18,20,22). It is they who have brought judgment upon themselves. Continuing in sin always results in punishment from God (Rom. 6:23).

1:7 NONE DID HELP HER. Those who go their own way and ignore the conviction of the Holy Spirit in their hearts may find in their hour of need that there is no one to help them. Individuals can reach a point in rebellion against God where He will ordain calamity rather than good for them. Such awful consequences can be avoided only by maintaining a holy fear of God and His judgment.

1:12 MY SORROW. In the first eleven verses Jeremiah is the one lamenting; in vv. 12–22 Jerusalem is personified as the one lamenting.

1:12 THE DAY OF HIS FIERCE ANGER. Some believers emphasize God's love and forgiveness and ignore His fierce anger against all who refuse to heed His call to righteousness. The view that Christ tolerates sin and immorality because of His love finds no support in Scripture (see Rev. 19:15–17, notes). In order to gain insight into the coming wrath of God, be sure to read and study the book of Revelation.

15 The Lord hath trodden under
foot all my mighty *men* in the midst of
me: he hath called an assembly against
me to crush my young men: [s]the Lord
hath trodden [g]the virgin, the daugh-
ter of Judah, *as* in a winepress.
16 For these *things* I weep; [t]mine
eye, mine eye runneth down with wa-
ter, because [u]the comforter that
should [h]relieve my soul is far from
me: my children are desolate, because
the enemy prevailed.
17 [v]Zion spreadeth forth her
hands, *and* [w]*there is* none to comfort
her: the LORD hath commanded con-
cerning Jacob, *that* his adversaries
should be round about him: Jerusalem
is as a menstruous woman among
them.
18 ¶ The LORD is [x]righteous; for I
have [y]rebelled against his [i]com-
mandment: hear, I pray you, all people,
and behold my sorrow: my virgins and
my young men are gone into captivity.
19 I called for my lovers, *but* [z]they
deceived me: my priests and mine el-
ders gave up the ghost in the city,
[a]while they sought their meat to re-
lieve their souls.
20 Behold, O LORD; for I *am* in dis-
tress: my [b]bowels are troubled; mine
heart is turned within me; for I have
grievously rebelled: [c]abroad the
sword bereaveth, at home *there is* as
death.
21 They have heard that I sigh:
[d]*there is* none to comfort me: all mine
enemies have heard of my trouble; they
are glad that thou hast done *it:* thou
wilt bring [e]the day *that* thou hast
[j]called, and they shall be like
unto me.
22 [f]Let all their wickedness come
before thee; and do unto them, as thou
hast done unto me for all my transgres-
sions: for my sighs *are* many, and [g]my
heart *is* faint.

1:15 [s]Is. 63:3 Rev. 14:19 **1:16** [t]Jer. 13:17 ch. 2:18 [u]ver. 2,9 **1:17** [v]Jer. 4:31 [w]ver. 2,9 **1:18** [x]Neh. 9:33 Dan. 9:7,14 [y]1 Sam. 12:14 **1:19** [z]ver. 2 Jer. 30:14 [a]ver. 11 **1:20** [b]Job 30:27 Is. 16:11 Jer. 4:19 Hos. 11:8 [c]Deut. 32:25 Ezek. 7:15 **1:21** [d]ver. 2 [e]Is. 13 Jer. 46 **1:22** [f]Ps. 109:15 [g]ch. 5:17

The judgment of the LORD

2 HOW HATH the Lord covered the
daughter of Zion with a cloud in his
anger, [h]*and* cast down from heaven
unto the earth [i]the beauty of Israel,
and remembered not [j]his footstool in
the day of his anger!
2 The Lord hath swallowed up all
the habitations of Jacob, and hath not
pitied: he hath thrown down in his
wrath the strong holds of the daughter
of Judah; he hath [k]brought *them* down
to the ground: [k]he hath polluted the
kingdom and the princes thereof.
3 He hath cut off in *his* fierce anger
all the horn of Israel: [l]he hath drawn
back his right hand from before the en-
emy, [m]and he burned against Jacob
like a flaming fire, *which* devoureth
round about.
4 [n]He hath bent his bow like an en-
emy: he stood with his right hand as an
adversary, and slew [o]all[l] *that were*
pleasant to the eye in the tabernacle of
the daughter of Zion: he poured out his
fury like fire.
5 [p]The Lord was as an enemy: he
hath swallowed up Israel, [q]he hath
swallowed up all her palaces: he hath
destroyed his strong holds, and
hath increased in the daughter of
Judah mourning and lamentation.
6 And he hath violently [r]taken
away his [m]tabernacle, [s]as *if it were of*
a garden: he hath destroyed his places
of the assembly: [t]the LORD hath
caused the solemn feasts and sabbaths
to be forgotten in Zion, and hath de-
spised in the indignation of his anger
the king and the priest.
7 The Lord hath cast off his altar,
he hath abhorred his sanctuary, he

2:1 [h]Mat. 11:23 [i]2 Sam. 1:19 [j]1 Chr. 28:2 Ps. 99:5 **2:2** [k]Ps. 89:39 **2:3** [l]Ps. 74:11 [m]Ps. 89:46 **2:4** [n]Is. 63:10 [o]Ezek. 24:25 **2:5** [p]Jer. 30:14 [q]2 Ki. 25:9 Jer. 52:13 **2:6** [r]Ps. 80:12 & 89:40 Is. 5:5 [s]Is. 1:8 [t]ch. 1:4

[g] Or, *the winepress of the virgin* [h] Heb. *bring back* [i] Heb. *mouth* [j] Or, *proclaimed* [k] Heb. *made to touch* [l] Heb. *all the desirable of the eye* [m] Or, *hedge*

1:18 BEHOLD MY SORROW. This verse expresses the main theme of the book of Lamentations: sin brings sorrow. A person may enjoy the pleasures of sin and immorality for a time, but eventually slavery to Satan and the consequences of one's sinful desires will become evident (John 8:34; Rom. 1:26–32). Distress, despair, and destruction will come to all those who do not turn to God in repentance.

1:22 WICKEDNESS CAME BEFORE THEE. Prayer for God's judgment on evil nations and all who oppose God's work is appropriate if we are concerned about God's glory, the gospel, and His righteous cause on earth.

2:5 THE LORD WAS AS AN ENEMY. To have once known the Lord and then turned from Him to the pleasures of sin is to make God an enemy; Israel and Judah did so, and they suffered greatly as a result. Believers cannot forsake the Lord and His word and expect that God will do nothing. A time will come when God will pour out His wrath on all who have unrepentant hearts (cf. Rom. 2:8–9; Rev. 2:16,22–23).

2:7 INTO THE HAND OF THE ENEMY. The Lord turned His apostate people over to their enemies for destruction. Likewise, under the new cov-

hath [n]given up into the hand of the
enemy the walls of her palaces; [u]they
have made a noise in the house of
the LORD, as in the day of a solemn
feast.
8 The LORD hath purposed to de-
stroy the wall of the daughter of Zion:
[v]he hath stretched out a line, he hath
not withdrawn his hand from [o]de-
stroying: therefore he made the ram-
part and the wall to lament; they lan-
guished together.
9 Her gates are sunk into the
ground; he hath destroyed and [w]bro-
ken her bars: [x]her king and her
princes *are* among the Gentiles: [y]the
law *is* no *more;* her [z]prophets also find
no vision from the LORD.
10 The elders of the daughter of
Zion [a]sit upon the ground, *and* keep
silence: they have [b]cast up dust upon
their heads; they have [c]girded them-
selves with sackcloth: the virgins of Je-
rusalem hang down their heads to the
ground.
11 [d]Mine eyes do fail with tears,
[e]my bowels are troubled, [f]my liver is
poured upon the earth, for the destruc-
tion of the daughter of my people; be-
cause [g]the children and the sucklings
[p]swoon in the streets of the city.
12 They say to their mothers,
Where *is* corn and wine? when they
swooned as the wounded in the streets
of the city, when their soul was poured
out into their mothers' bosom.
13 What thing shall I take to wit-
ness for thee? [h]what thing shall I lik-
en to thee, O daughter of Jerusalem?
what shall I equal to thee, that I may
comfort thee, O virgin daughter of
Zion? for thy breach *is* great like the
sea: who can heal thee?
14 Thy [i]prophets have seen vain
and foolish things for thee: and they
have not [j]discovered thine iniquity, to
turn away thy captivity; but have seen
for thee false burdens and causes of
banishment.
15 All that pass [q]by [k]clap *their*
hands at thee; they hiss [l]and wag
their head at the daughter of Jerusa-
lem, *saying, Is* this the city that *men*
call [m]The perfection of beauty, The joy
of the whole earth?
16 [n]All thine enemies have opened
their mouth against thee: they hiss and
gnash the teeth: they say, [o]We have
swallowed *her* up: certainly this *is* the
day that we looked for; we have found,
[p]we have seen *it.*
17 The LORD hath done *that* which
he had [q]devised; he hath fulfilled his
word that he had commanded in the
days of old: he hath thrown down, and
hath not pitied: and he hath caused

2:7 [u]Ps. 74:4 **2:8** [v]2 Ki. 21:13 Is. 34:11 **2:9** [w]Jer. 51:30 [x]Deut. 28:36 2 Ki. 24:15 [y]2 Chr. 15:3 [z]Ps. 74:9 Ezek. 7:26 **2:10** [a]Job 2:13 Is. 3:26 [b]Job 2:12 [c]Is. 15:3 **2:11** [d]ch. 3:48 [e]ch. 1:20 [f]Job 16:13 Ps. 22:14 [g]ch. 4:4 **2:13** [h]ch. 1:12 Dan. 9:12 **2:14** [i]Jer. 2:8 Ezek. 13:2 [j]Is. 58:1 **2:15** [k]Ezek. 25:6 [l]2 Ki. 19:21 Ps. 44:14 [m]Ps. 48:2 **2:16** [n]Job 16:9 ch. 3:46 [o]Ps. 56:2 [p]Ps. 35:21 **2:17** [q]Lev. 26:16 Deut. 28:15

[n] Heb. *shut up* [o] Heb. *swallowing up* [p] Or, *faint* [q] Heb. *by the way*

enant, both churches and individuals who turn to lives of sin and persist in worldliness will be handed over to Satan (1 Cor. 5:7). The sinful ways and values of ungodly society will bring destruction and retribution to all who forsake the Lord (see Mat. 5:13, note).

2:9 FIND NO VISION FROM THE LORD. God was no longer communicating directly with His people, for sin had caused Him to withdraw prophecies and visions. Likewise, under the new covenant, the Holy Spirit may cease to manifest His gifts and miraculous powers through believers (cf. 1 Cor. 12—14) because of sin among God's leaders and people. This kind of judgment is a sure indication that God's people have departed from a lifestyle of seeking first God's kingdom and righteousness. The only remedy is to turn from all compromise with sin, to seek God earnestly, and to pray for the restoration of His favor and kingdom power (see article on SPIRITUAL GIFTS FOR BELIEVERS, p. 1790).

2:11 MINE EYES DO FAIL WITH TEARS. Jeremiah weeps because of the tragic sorrow and suffering brought about by the people's rejection of their God. Jesus Christ Himself wept for the people of Israel who would soon suffer terrible judgment for rejecting God's salvation (Luke 19:41–44), and the apostle Paul expressed deep sorrow and ceaseless concern over fellow Jews who did not accept Christ (Rom. 9:1–3; 10:1). We who have experienced redemption and life in Christ should be heartbroken over the terrible suffering of people enslaved to sin and Satan. We should be grieved because of the moral breakdown in society, knowing the tragic pain and suffering that will result.

2:12 WHERE *IS* CORN AND WINE. Infants and small children were crying out in famished distress to their mothers for basic physical nourishment. Here wine (Heb. *yayin*) undoubtedly means nourishing grape juice rather than an intoxicating beverage (see article on WINE IN THE OLD TESTAMENT, p. 220).

2:14 THEY HAVE NOT DISCOVERED THINE INIQUITY. One mark of a false prophet was that his words and visions did not expose sin among the people (see article on THE PROPHET IN THE OLD TESTAMENT, p. 1002). Those in the church who do not rebuke sin, thereby releasing the convicting work of the Holy Spirit (John 16:8–11), prove that they are false ministers. Conversely, those who live holy lives and sincerely cry out against worldliness and sin in the congregation, just as Christ did (see Rev. 2—3), prove themselves to be faithful ministers of their Lord.

thine enemy to [r]rejoice over thee, he hath set up the horn of thine adversaries.

18 Their heart cried unto the Lord, O wall of the daughter of Zion, [s]let tears run down like a river day and night: give thyself no rest: let not the apple of thine eye cease.

19 Arise, [t]cry out in the night: in the beginning of the watches [u]pour out thine heart like water before the face of the Lord: lift up thy hands toward him for the life of thy young children, that faint for hunger [v]in the top of every street.

20 ¶ Behold, O LORD, and consider to whom thou hast done this. [w]Shall the women eat their fruit, *and* children [r]of a span long? [x]shall the priest and the prophet be slain in the sanctuary of the Lord?

21 [y]The young and the old lie on the ground in the streets: my virgins and my young men are fallen by the sword; thou hast slain *them* in the day of thine anger; [z]thou hast killed, *and* not pitied.

22 Thou hast called as in a solemn day [a]my terrors round about, so that in the day of the LORD's anger none escaped nor remained: [b]those that I have swaddled and brought up hath mine enemy consumed.

Lament and hope

3 I *AM* the man *that* hath seen affliction by the rod of his wrath.

2 He hath led me, and brought *me* *into* darkness, but not *into* light.

3 Surely against me is he turned; he turneth his hand *against me* all the day.

4 [c]My flesh and my skin hath he made old; he hath [d]broken my bones.

5 He hath builded against me, and compassed *me* with gall and travail.

6 [e]He hath set me in dark places, as *they that be* dead of old.

7 [f]He hath hedged me about, that I cannot get out: he hath made my chain heavy.

8 Also [g]when I cry and shout, he shutteth out my prayer.

9 He hath inclosed my ways with hewn stone, he hath made my paths crooked.

10 [h]He *was* unto me *as* a bear lying in wait, *and as* a lion in secret places.

11 He hath turned aside my ways, and [i]pulled me in pieces: he hath made me desolate.

12 He hath bent his bow, and [j]set me as a mark for the arrow.

13 He hath caused [k]the [s]arrows of his quiver to enter into my reins.

14 I was a [l]derision to all my people; *and* [m]their song all the day.

15 [n]He hath filled me with [t]bitterness, he hath made me drunken with wormwood.

16 He hath also broken my teeth [o]with gravel stones, he hath [u]covered me with ashes.

17 And thou hast removed my soul far off from peace: I forgat [v]prosperity.

18 [p]And I said, My strength and my hope is perished from the LORD:

19 [w]Remembering mine affliction and my misery, [q]the wormwood and the gall.

20 My soul hath *them* still in remembrance, and is [x]humbled in me.

21 This I [y]recall to my mind, therefore have I hope.

22 ¶ [r]*It is of* the LORD's mercies

[r] Or, *swaddled with their hands?* [s] Heb. *sons*
[t] Heb. *bitternesses* [u] Or, *rolled me in the ashes*
[v] Heb. *good* [w] Or, *Remember* [x] Heb. *bowed*
[y] Heb. *make to return to my heart*

2:17 [r]Ps. 38:16
2:18 [s]Jer. 14:17
2:19 [t]Ps. 119:147 [u]Ps. 62:8 [v]Is. 51:20 Nah. 3:10
2:20 [w]Lev. 26:29 Deut. 28:53 Jer. 19:9 ch. 4:10 [x]ch. 4:13,16
2:21 [y]2 Chr. 36:17 [z]ch. 3:43
2:22 [a]Ps. 31:13 Jer. 6:25 & 46:5 [b]Hos. 9:12
3:4 [c]Job 16:8 [d]Ps. 51:8 Is. 38:13
3:6 [e]Ps. 88:5,6
3:7 [f]Hos. 2:6
3:8 [g]Job 30:20
3:10 [h]Is. 38:13 Hos. 5:14
3:11 [i]Hos. 6:1
3:12 [j]Job 7:20 Ps. 38:2
3:13 [k]Job 6:4
3:14 [l]Jer. 20:7 [m]Job 30:9 Ps. 69:12
3:15 [n]Jer. 9:15
3:16 [o]Prov. 20:17
3:18 [p]Ps. 31:22
3:19 [q]Jer. 9:15
3:22 [r]Mal. 3:6

2:18 LET TEARS RUN DOWN. Jeremiah calls the people to prayer, weeping, and repentance, with the hope that God would hear the intercessory cry of the remnant (cf. v. 19).

3:1 I *AM* THE MAN. In ch. 3 the afflicted people of Israel are portrayed as a human being who is under the punishment of God, yet who has the hope of restoration. Such a person claims the truth that God's love and help will come to those who repent and continue to wait upon the Lord (vv. 22–27).

3:8 HE SHUTTETH OUT MY PRAYER. For the ungodly, one of the terrible consequences of living in sin and immorality is that God refuses to hear their prayers (cf. v. 44; Ps. 18:41; Prov. 1:28; Jer. 7:16; see article on EFFECTIVE PRAYING, p. 540).

3:21–33 THEREFORE HAVE I HOPE. Jeremiah wants the people to know that all is not lost. They may have hope for the following reasons: (1) The Lord's anger lasts only a brief time, but His lovingkindness never ceases (v. 22). God had not rejected Judah as His covenant people, and He still had a purpose for them. (2) The Lord is good and merciful to those who wait upon Him in humility and repentance (vv. 24–27). (3) The Lord desires to have compassion on sufferers when His chastisement has accomplished its purpose (vv. 28–33; see next note).

that we are not consumed, because his
compassions fail not.
23 *They are* new [s]every morning:
great *is* thy faithfulness.
24 The LORD *is* my [t]portion, saith
my soul; therefore will I hope in him.
25 The LORD *is* good unto them that
[u]wait for him, to the soul *that* seeketh
him.
26 *It is* good that *a man* should both
hope [v]and quietly wait for the salva-
tion of the LORD.
27 [w]*It is* good for a man that he
bear the yoke in his youth.
28 [x]He sitteth alone and keepeth
silence, because he hath borne *it* upon
him.
29 [y]He putteth his mouth in the
dust; if so be there may be hope.
30 [z]He giveth *his* cheek to him that
smiteth him: he is filled full with re-
proach.
31 [a]For the Lord will not cast off
for ever:
32 But though he cause grief, yet
will he have compassion according to
the multitude of his mercies.
33 For [b]he doth not afflict [z]will-
ingly nor grieve the children of men.
34 To crush under his feet all the
prisoners of the earth,
35 To turn aside the right of a man
before the face of [a]the most High,
36 To subvert a man in his cause,
[c]the Lord [b]approveth not.
37 ¶ Who *is* he [d]*that* saith, and it
cometh to pass, *when* the Lord com-
mandeth *it* not?
38 Out of the mouth of the most
High proceedeth not [e]evil and good?
39 [f]Wherefore doth a living man
[c]complain, [g]a man for the punish-
ment of his sins?
40 Let us search and try our ways,
and turn again to the LORD.
41 [h]Let us lift up our heart with *our*
hands unto God in the heavens.
42 [i]We have transgressed and
have rebelled: thou hast not pardoned.
43 Thou hast covered with anger,
and persecuted us: thou hast slain,
thou hast not pitied.
44 Thou hast covered thyself with a
cloud, [j]that *our* prayer should not
pass through.
45 Thou hast made us *as* the [k]off-
scouring and refuse in the midst of the
people.
46 [l]All our enemies have opened
their mouths against us.
47 [m]Fear and a snare is come upon
us, [n]desolation and destruction.
48 [o]Mine eye runneth down with
rivers of water for the destruction of
the daughter of my people.
49 [p]Mine eye trickleth down, and
ceaseth not, without any intermission,
50 Till the LORD [q]look down, and
behold from heaven.
51 Mine eye affecteth [d]mine heart
[e]because of all the daughters of my
city.
52 Mine enemies chased me sore,
like a bird, [r]without cause.
53 They have cut off my life [s]in the
dungeon, and [t]cast a stone upon me.
54 [u]Waters flowed over mine head;
then [v]I said, I am cut off.
55 ¶ [w]I called upon thy name,
O LORD, out of the low dungeon.
56 [x]Thou hast heard my voice:
hide not thine ear at my breathing, at
my cry.
57 Thou [y]drewest near in the day
that I called upon thee: thou saidst,
Fear not.
58 O Lord, thou hast [z]pleaded the
causes of my soul; [a]thou hast re-
deemed my life.
59 O LORD, thou hast seen my
wrong: [b]judge thou my cause.
60 Thou hast seen all their ven-
geance *and* all their [c]imaginations
against me.
61 Thou hast heard their reproach,

3:23 [s]Is. 33:2
3:24 [t]Ps. 16:5
3:25 [u]Is. 30:18 Mic. 7:7
3:26 [v]Ps. 37:7
3:27 [w]Ps. 94:12
3:28 [x]Jer. 15:17
3:29 [y]Job 42:6
3:30 [z]Is. 50:6 Mat. 5:39
3:31 [a]Ps. 94:14
3:33 [b]Ezek. 33:11
3:36 [c]Hab. 1:13
3:37 [d]Ps. 33:9
3:38 [e]Job 2:10 Amos 3:6
3:39 [f]Prov. 19:3 [g]Mic. 7:9
3:41 [h]Ps. 86:4
3:42 [i]Dan. 9:5
3:44 [j]ver. 8
3:45 [k]1 Cor. 4:13
3:46 [l]ch. 2:16
3:47 [m]Is. 24:17 [n]Is. 51:19
3:48 [o]Jer. 4:19
3:49 [p]Ps. 77:2
3:50 [q]Is. 63:15
3:52 [r]Ps. 35:7
3:53 [s]Jer. 37:16 [t]Dan. 6:17
3:54 [u]Ps. 69:2 [v]Is. 38:10
3:55 [w]Ps. 130:1
3:56 [x]Ps. 3:4
3:57 [y]Jas. 4:8
3:58 [z]Ps. 35:1 Jer. 51:36 [a]Ps. 71:23
3:59 [b]Ps. 9:4
3:60 [c]Jer. 11:19

[z] Heb. *from his heart* [a] Or, *a superior* [b] Or, *seeth not* [c] Or, *murmur* [d] Heb. *my soul* [e] Or, *more than all*

3:27–33 BEAR THE YOKE. God sometimes sends afflictions to those who have rebelled against Him in order to accomplish a beneficial and purifying work in their lives. Those undergoing such trials should confess their sin, plead for pardon, and trust the Lord for forgiveness and restoration.

3:33 DOTH NOT AFFLICT WILLINGLY. God does not delight in punishing people for their sins; rather, He does so because He has to maintain moral order in the world. God's ultimate hope is that His affliction will turn people back to Him (see Ezek. 18:23,32; Hos. 11:8; 2 Pet. 3:9).

3:40–41 LET US . . . TURN AGAIN TO THE LORD. The prophet identifies himself with the people in a spiritual examination that would lead them to turn to the Lord, obey His Word, and exhibit a sincere change in their hearts. If they do this, God will hear them and redeem them (vv. 55–58).

O LORD, *and* all their imaginations
against me;
62 The lips of those that rose up
against me, and their device against
me all the day.
63 Behold their [d]sitting down, and
their rising up; I *am* their music.
64 ¶ [e]Render unto them a recom-
pence, O LORD, according to the work
of their hands.
65 Give them [f]sorrow of heart, thy
curse unto them.
66 Persecute and destroy them in
anger [f]from under the [g]heavens of
the LORD.

The punishment of Zion

4 HOW IS the gold become dim! *how*
is the most fine gold changed! the
stones of the sanctuary are poured out
[h]in the top of every street.
2 The precious sons of Zion, com-
parable to fine gold, how are they es-
teemed [i]as earthen pitchers, the
work of the hands of the potter!
3 Even the [g]sea monsters draw out
the breast, they give suck to their
young ones: the daughter of my people
is become cruel, [j]like the ostriches in
the wilderness.
4 [k]The tongue of the sucking child
cleaveth to the roof of his mouth for
thirst: [l]the young children ask bread,
and no man breaketh *it* unto them.
5 They that did feed delicately are
desolate in the streets: they that were
brought up in scarlet [m]embrace dung-
hills.
6 For the [h]punishment of the iniq-
uity of the daughter of my people is
greater than the punishment of the sin
of Sodom, that was [n]overthrown as in
a moment, and no hands stayed on her.
7 Her Nazarites were purer than
snow, they were whiter than milk, they
were more ruddy in body than rubies,
their polishing *was* of sapphire:
8 Their visage is [o]blacker[i] than a
coal; they are not known in the streets:
[p]their skin cleaveth to their bones; it
is withered, it is become like a stick.
9 *They that be* slain with the sword
are better than *they that be* slain with
hunger: for these [j]pine away, strick-
en through for *want of* the fruits of the
field.
10 [q]The hands of the [r]pitiful
women have sodden their own chil-
dren: they were their [s]meat in the de-
struction of the daughter of my people.
11 The LORD hath accomplished his
fury; [t]he hath poured out his fierce
anger, and [u]hath kindled a fire in
Zion, and it hath devoured the founda-
tions thereof.
12 The kings of the earth, and all
the inhabitants of the world, would not
have believed that the adversary and
the enemy should have entered into the
gates of Jerusalem.
13 ¶ [v]For the sins of her prophets,
and the iniquities of her priests, [w]that
have shed the blood of the just in the
midst of her,
14 They have wandered *as* blind
men in the streets, [x]they have polluted
themselves with blood, [y]so[k] that
men could not touch their garments.
15 They cried unto them, Depart ye;
[l]*It is* [z]unclean; depart, depart, touch
not: when they fled away and wan-
dered, they said among the heathen,
They shall no more sojourn *there.*
16 The [m]anger of the LORD hath di-
vided them; he will no more regard
them: [a]they respected not the persons
of the priests, they favoured not the el-
ders.
17 As for us, [b]our eyes as yet failed
for our vain help: in our watching we
have watched for a nation *that* could
not save *us.*
18 [c]They hunt our steps, that we
cannot go in our streets: our end is
near, our days are fulfilled; for [d]our
end is come.
19 Our persecutors are [e]swifter
than the eagles of the heaven: they
pursued us upon the mountains, they
laid wait for us in the wilderness.
20 The [f]breath of our nostrils, the
anointed of the LORD, [g]was taken in

3:63 [d]Ps. 139:2
3:64 [e]Ps. 28:4 Jer. 11:20
3:66 [f]Deut. 25:19 Jer. 10:11 [g]Ps. 8:3
4:1 [h]ch. 2:19
4:2 [i]Is. 30:14 Jer. 19:11
4:3 [j]Job 39:14
4:4 [k]Ps. 22:15 [l]See ch. 2:11,12
4:5 [m]Job 24:8
4:6 [n]Gen. 19:25
4:8 [o]ch. 5:10 Joel 2:6 Nah. 2:10 [p]Ps. 102:5
4:10 [q]ch. 2:20 [r]Is. 49:15 [s]Deut. 28:57
4:11 [t]Jer. 7:20 [u]Deut. 32:22
4:13 [v]Jer. 6:13 Ezek. 22:26 [w]Mat. 23:31
4:14 [x]Jer. 2:34 [y]Num. 19:16
4:15 [z]Lev. 13:45
4:16 [a]ch. 5:12
4:17 [b]2 Ki. 24:7 Is. 20:5 Jer. 37:7
4:18 [c]2 Ki. 25:4 [d]Ezek 7:2,3
4:19 [e]Deut. 28:49
4:20 [f]Gen. 2:7 [g]Jer. 52:9 Ezek. 12:13

[f] Or, *obstinacy of heart* [g] Or, *sea calves* [h] Or, *iniquity* [i] Heb. *darker than blackness* [j] Heb. *flow out* [k] Or, *in that they could not but touch* [l] Or, *ye polluted* [m] Or, *face*

4:1–12 GOLD BECOME DIM! Jeremiah compares the glories of Jerusalem before the siege with the present devastation of the people brought on as a result of God's punishment.

4:13 THE SINS OF HER PROPHETS. Judah's tragic condition was brought on by her own sins, of which Jeremiah lists two key categories: (1) the corruption of those who claimed to be spiritual leaders (see Jer. 26:7–11,16; Ezek. 22:26,28), and (2) the people's trust in human and political alliances rather than in God (v. 17).

their pits, of whom we said, Under his
shadow we shall live among the hea-
then.
21 ¶ Rejoice and be glad, O daugh-
ter of Edom, that dwellest in the land
of Uz; [h]the cup also shall pass
through unto thee: thou shalt be
drunken, and shalt make thyself na-
ked.
22 ¶ [i]The[n] punishment of thine
iniquity is accomplished, O daughter of
Zion; he will no more carry thee away
into captivity: [j]he will visit thine iniq-
uity, O daughter of Edom; he will [o]dis-
cover thy sins.

A prayer for mercy

5 REMEMBER,[k] O LORD, what is
come upon us: consider, and be-
hold [l]our reproach.
2 [m]Our inheritance is turned to
strangers, our houses to aliens.
3 We are orphans and fatherless,
our mothers *are* as widows.
4 We have drunken our water for
money; our wood [p]is sold unto us.
5 [n]Our[q] necks *are* under persecu-
tion: we labour, *and* have no rest.
6 [o]We have given the hand [p]*to* the
Egyptians, *and to* the Assyrians, to be
satisfied with bread.
7 [q]Our fathers have sinned, *and are*
not; and we have borne their iniquities.
8 Servants have ruled over us: *there*
is none that doth deliver *us* out of their
hand.
9 We gat our bread with *the peril of*
our lives because of the sword of the
wilderness.
10 Our skin was black like an oven
because of the [r]terrible famine.
11 They ravished the women in
Zion, *and* the maids in the cities of Ju-
dah.
12 Princes are hanged up by their
hand: the faces of elders were not hon-
oured.
13 They took the young men to
grind, and the children fell under the
wood.
14 The elders have ceased from the
gate, the young men from their music.
15 The joy of our heart is ceased;
our dance is turned into mourning.
16 [r]The[s] crown is fallen *from* our
head: woe unto us, that we have
sinned!
17 For this our heart is faint; [s]for
these *things* our eyes are dim.
18 Because of the mountain of Zion,
which is desolate, the foxes walk
upon it.
19 Thou, O LORD, [t]remainest for
ever; [u]thy throne from generation to
generation.
20 [v]Wherefore dost thou forget us
for ever, *and* forsake us [t]so long time?
21 Turn thou us unto thee, O LORD,
and we shall be turned; renew our days
as of old.
22 [u]But thou hast utterly rejected
us; thou art very wroth against us.

4:21 [h]Jer. 25:15 Obad. 10
4:22 [i]Is. 40:2 [j]Ps. 137:7
5:1 [k]Ps. 89:50 [l]Ps. 79:4 ch. 2:15
5:2 [m]Ps. 79:1
5:5 [n]Jer. 28:14
5:6 [o]Gen. 24:2 [p]Hos. 12:1
5:7 [q]Jer. 31:29
5:16 [r]Ps. 89:39
5:17 [s]Ps. 6:7
5:19 [t]Ps. 9:7 [u]Ps. 45:6
5:20 [v]Ps. 13:1

[n] Or, *Thine iniquity* [o] Or, *carry* thee *captive for thy sins* [p] Heb. *cometh for price* [q] Heb. *On our necks are we persecuted* [r] Or, *terrors,* or, *storms* [s] Heb. *The crown of our head is fallen* [t] Heb. *for length of days?* [u] Or, *For wilt thou utterly reject us?*

4:22 THE PUNISHMENT ... IS ACCOMPLISHED. Jeremiah prophesies that Judah's captivity would come to an end when God's purpose for her affliction was achieved.

5:1–22 REMEMBER, O LORD. The last chapter of Lamentations is an intercessory prayer in which Jeremiah acknowledges that even though God is responsible for Jerusalem's judgment and calamity, He will yet listen to their cry, accept their sincere confession of sin, and respond in mercy and favor.

5:2–18 INHERITANCE IS TURNED TO STRANGERS. The author vividly describes the desperate physical and emotional condition of the exiles. Persecution and fear were common experiences for them.

5:21–22 TURN THOU US UNTO THEE. The book of Lamentations ends in a prayer that expresses hope for God's mercy. It teaches us to call upon God in the worst of circumstances, even when we are under His chastising hand.

EZEKIEL

Outline

I. Ezekiel's Call and Commissioning (1:1—3:27)
  A. Envisioned by the Glory of God (1:1–28)
  B. Commissioned for the Prophetic Word (2:1—3:27)
II. The Prophetic Message of Judgment for Judah and Jerusalem (4:1—24:27)
  A. Prophetic Signs of Coming Judgment (4:1—5:17)
    1. A Clay Tablet (4:1–3)
    2. Ezekiel Lies on His Side (4:4–8)
    3. The Bread of Scarcity (4:9–17)
    4. The Divine Razor (5:1–17)
  B. Prophetic Messages of Coming Judgment (6:1—7:27)
  C. Prophetic Visions of Coming Judgment (8:1—11:25)
    1. Vision of Abominations in the Temple (8:1–18)
    2. Vision of Jerusalem's Destruction (9:1–11)
    3. Vision of God's Departing Glory (10:1–22)
    4. Vision of Wicked Rulers and Departed Glory (11:1–25)
  D. Prophetic Signs, Messages, and Parables of Coming Judgment (12:1—24:27)
    1. Signs of Jerusalem's Exile (12:1–28)
    2. Message Against False Prophets (13:1–23)
    3. Message Against Idolatrous Elders (14:1–23)
    4. Parables of the Fruitless Vine (15:1–8), Adulterous Women (16:1–23), and Two Eagles (17:1–24)
    5. A Lesson (18:1–32) and a Lamentation (19:1–14)
    6. Further Messages and Signs of the Judgment of Jerusalem (20:1—24:27)
III. The Prophetic Message of Judgment for Foreign Nations (25:1—32:32)
  A. Ammon (25:1–7)
  B. Moab (25:8–11)
  C. Edom (25:12–14)
  D. Philistia (25:15–17)
  E. Tyre (26:1—28:19)
  F. Sidon (28:20–26)
  G. Egypt (29:1—32:32)
IV. The Prophetic Message of Restoration (33:1—48:35)
  A. The Watchman of Restoration (33:1–33)
  B. The Promises of Restoration (34:1—39:28)
  C. The Vision of Restoration (40:1—48:35)

Author: Ezekiel

Theme: God's Judgment and Glory

Date of Writing: 590–570 B.C.

Background

The historical setting for the book of Ezekiel is Babylon during the early years of the Babylonian exile (593–571 B.C.). Nebuchadnezzar took Jewish captives from Jerusalem to Babylon in three stages: (1) In 605 B.C., select Jewish youth were deported to Babylon, among whom were Daniel and his three friends; (2) in 597 B.C., 10,000 captives were taken to Babylon, among whom was Ezekiel; and (3) in 586 B.C., Nebuchadnezzar's forces totally destroyed both the city and the temple, with most of its surviving inhabitants carried off to Babylon. Ezekiel's prophetic ministry occurred during the darkest hour of O.T. history: the seven years preceding the 586 B.C. destruction (593–586 B.C.) and the fifteen years following it (586–571 B.C.). The book was probably completed c. 570 B.C.

Ezekiel, whose name means "God strengthens," was from a priestly family (1:3) and spent his first twenty-five years in Jerusalem. He was in priestly training for service in the temple when he was taken captive to Babylon in 597 B.C. About five years later, at age thirty (1:2–3), Ezekiel received his prophetic call and divine commissioning, after which he faithfully ministered for at least twenty-two years (29:17). Ezekiel was about age seventeen when Daniel was deported, making the two men virtually the same age. Both Ezekiel and Daniel were younger contemporaries of Jeremiah and most likely were influenced considerably by the older Jerusalem prophet (cf. Dan. 9:2). By the time Ezekiel arrived in Babylon, Daniel was already well-known as a man of extraordinary prophetic wisdom; Ezekiel refers to him three times in his book (14:14,20; 28:3). Unlike Daniel, Ezekiel was married (24:15–18) and lived as a private citizen among the Jewish exiles along the river Chebar (1:1; 3:15,24; cf. Ps. 137:1).

The book clearly attributes its prophecies to Ezekiel by name (1:3; 24:24). The use of the personal pronoun "I" throughout the book, along with the book's unity in style and language, point to sole authorship by Ezekiel. His prophecies can be dated with precision because of his orderly method of dating (cf. 1:1–2; 8:1; 20:1; 24:1; 26:1; 29:1,17; 30:20; 31:1; 32:1,17; 33:21; 40:1). His ministry began in July, 593 B.C. and continued at least until the last recorded prophecy in April, 571 B.C.

Purpose

The purpose of Ezekiel's prophecies was primarily twofold: (1) to deliver God's message of judgment to apostate Judah and Jerusalem (chs. 1—24) and to seven foreign nations around her (chs. 25—32); and (2) to sustain the faith of God's remnant in exile concerning the restoration of His covenant people and the final glory of God's kingdom (chs. 33—48). The prophet also emphasized the personal responsbility of each individual before God, rather than passing off the exilic judgment as simply the result of their ancestors' sins (18:1–32; 33:10–20).

Survey

Ezekiel's book is well-organized, and its forty-eight chapters divide naturally into four major sections. (1) The introductory section (chs. 1—3) describes Ezekiel's powerful vision of God's glory and throne (ch. 1) and the prophet's subsequent divine commissioning for the prophetic ministry (chs. 2—3); note Moses' experience at the burning bush (Ex. 3—4) and Isaiah's vision in the temple (Is. 6) as similar momentous revelations of God at the outset of their prophetic mission.

(2) The second section (chs. 4—24) records Ezekiel's hard-hitting and hope-crushing message of Judah's and Jerusalem's inescapable approaching judgment because of their persistent rebellion and apostasy. During Jerusalem's last seven years (593–586 B.C.), Ezekiel warned the Jews in Jerusalem and the captives in Babylon against any false hope that Jerusalem would survive judgment. Jerusalem's past and present sins made her present doom certain. Ezekiel thunders this prophetic message of doom through various visions, parables, and symbolic actions. Chs. 8—11 describe God's transporting Ezekiel to

Jerusalem in a vision where he delivers prophecies to the city. In ch. 24, the death of Ezekiel's own beloved wife served as a parable and a sign of Jerusalem's end.

(3) The third section (chs. 25—32) contains prophecies of judgment against seven foreign nations that were rejoicing over Judah's calamity. In the exceptionally long prophecy against Tyre appears a veiled description of Satan (28:11–19) as the real power behind the king of Tyre.

(4) The book's final section (chs. 33—48) marks a transition in the prophet's message from gloomy judgment to comfort and future hope (cf. Is. 40—66). After the fall of Jerusalem, Ezekiel prophesies about future revival and restoration, when God would be the true shepherd of His people (ch. 34) and give them a "new heart" and a "new spirit" (ch. 36). In this context occurs Ezekiel's famous vision of a whole army of dead bones being prophetically resurrected to life (ch. 37). The book concludes by describing the eschatological restoration of the holy temple, holy city, and holy land (chs. 40—48).

Special Features

Seven major features or emphases characterize the book of Ezekiel. (1) It abounds in mysterious visions, daring parables, and weird symbolic actions as media for God's prophetic revelation. (2) Its contents are carefully arranged and dated; it contains more dates than any other O.T. prophetic book. (3) Two distinctive phrases occur throughout the book: (a)"Then they shall know that I am the LORD" (sixty-five occurrences with its variations) and (b) "the glory of the LORD" (nineteen occurrences with its variations). (4) Ezekiel is characteristically addressed by God as "son of man" or "watchman." (5) This book records two extraordinary visions of the temple: one as desecrated and awaiting destruction (chs. 8—11), and the other as purified and perfectly restored (chs. 40—48). (6) More than any other prophet, Ezekiel was required by God to identify himself personally with the prophetic word by acting it out in prophetic symbolism. (7) Ezekiel emphasizes the individual's personal responsibility and accountability to God.

New Testament Fulfillment

The message of chs. 33—48 essentially concerns God's future redemptive work as revealed in the N.T. It speaks not only of Israel's physical restoration to their land, but also of a final future restoration that involves the full realization of God's destiny for spiritual Israel in relation to God's glory and power in the temple (worship), and God's destiny for the nations as a result of missions. Important prophecies in Ezekiel about the N.T. Messiah are 17:22–24; 21:26–27; 34:23–24; 36:16–38; and 37:1–28.

Reading Ezekiel

In order to read the entire Old Testament in one year, the book of Ezekiel should be read in 22 days, according to the following schedule: ☐ 1–2 ☐ 3–4 ☐ 5–7 ☐ 8–10 ☐ 11–12 ☐ 13–15 ☐ 16 ☐ 17–19 ☐ 20–21 ☐ 22–23 ☐ 24–26 ☐ 27–28 ☐ 29–30 ☐ 31–32 ☐ 33–34 ☐ 35–36 ☐ 37–38 ☐ 39–40 ☐ 41–42 ☐ 43–44 ☐ 45–46 ☐ 47–48

NOTES

The vision of the four creatures

1 NOW IT came to pass in the thirti-
eth year, in the fourth *month,* in the
fifth *day* of the month, as I *was* among
the [a]captives [a]by the river of Chebar,
that [b]the heavens were opened, and I
saw [c]visions of God.
2 In the fifth *day* of the month,
which *was* the fifth year of [d]king Jehoi-
achin's captivity,
3 The word of the LORD came ex-
pressly unto [b]Ezekiel the priest, the
son of Buzi, in the land of the Chalde-
ans by the river Chebar; and [e]the hand
of the LORD was there upon him.
4 ¶ And I looked, and, behold, [f]a
whirlwind came [g]out of the north, a
great cloud, and a fire [c]infolding it-
self, and a brightness *was* about it,
and out of the midst thereof as the
colour of amber, out of the midst of
the fire.
5 [h]Also out of the midst thereof
came the likeness of four living crea-
tures. And [i]this *was* their appear-
ance; they had [j]the likeness of a man.
6 And every one had four faces, and
every one had four wings.
7 And their feet *were* [d]straight
feet; and the sole of their feet *was* like
the sole of a calf's foot: and they spar-
kled [k]like the colour of burnished
brass.
8 [l]And *they had* the hands of a man
under their wings on their four sides;
and they four had their faces and their
wings.
9 [m]Their wings *were* joined one to
another; [n]they turned not when they
went; they went every one straight for-
ward.
10 As for [o]the likeness of their
faces, they four [p]had the face of a
man, [q]and the face of a lion, on the
right side: [r]and they four had the face
of an ox on the left side; [s]they four
also had the face of an eagle.
11 Thus *were* their faces: and their
wings *were* [e]stretched upward; two
wings of every one *were* joined one to
another, and [t]two covered their bod-
ies.
12 And [u]they went every one
straight forward: [v]whither the spirit
was to go, they went; *and* they turned
not when they went.
13 As for the likeness of the living
creatures, their appearance *was* like
burning coals of fire, [w]*and* like the ap-
pearance of lamps: it went up and
down among the living creatures; and
the fire was bright, and out of the fire
went forth lightning.
14 And the living creatures ran and
returned [x]as the appearance of a flash
of lightning.

1:1 [a]ch. 3:15,23 [b]Mat. 3:16 Acts 7:56 [c]ch. 8:3
1:2 [d]2 Ki. 24:12
1:3 [e]1 Ki. 18:46 ch. 3:14
1:4 [f]Jer. 23:19 & 25:32 [g]Jer. 1:14
1:5 [h]Rev. 4:6 [i]ch. 10:8 [j]ch. 10:14
1:7 [k]Dan. 10:6 Rev. 1:15
1:8 [l]ch. 10:8
1:9 [m]ver. 11 [n]ver. 12
1:10 [o]Rev. 4:7 [p]Num. 2:10 [q]Num. 2:3 [r]Num. 2:18 [s]Num. 2:25
1:11 [t]Is. 6:2
1:12 [u]ch. 10:22 [v]ver. 20
1:13 [w]Rev. 4:5
1:14 [x]Mat. 24:27

[a] Heb. *captivity* [b] Heb. *Jehezkel* [c] Heb. *catching itself* [d] Heb. *a straight foot* [e] Or, *divided above*

1:1 THE THIRTIETH YEAR. This designation most likely refers to Ezekiel's age. At that time he was living among the exiles in Babylon, having been brought there in 597 B.C., nine years after Daniel had arrived and eleven years before Jerusalem was destroyed. Ezekiel was called to be a prophet during the captivity, proclaiming God's message to the exiles at the same time that Jeremiah was preaching in Jerusalem. Ezekiel ministered for at least twenty-seven years; the Babylonian captivity of Judah lasted approximately seventy years (from 605 to 538 B.C.).

1:3 THE WORD OF THE LORD CAME ... UNTO EZEKIEL. Ezekiel the priest received his prophetic calling in 593 B.C., four years after his arrival in Babylon. He evidently had settled by the Chebar River, possibly a ship canal on the Euphrates about fifty miles southeast of Babylon. His mission was to explain the reason for the captivity, foretell the fall of Jerusalem, bring the exiled people back to God, and give them hope through God's promise of restoration.

1:4 I LOOKED. Ezekiel is given a vision of the glory and holiness of God (see v. 28, note). Visions were essential for his ministry to the exiles.

1:5 FOUR LIVING CREATURES. These creatures are later identified as cherubim (10:20). Cherubim are angelic beings who manifest the holiness and glory of God to humans (cf. 1 Chr. 28:18; Ps. 18:10; see article on ANGELS AND THE ANGEL OF THE LORD, p. 368). They may accompany God at times of judgment or blessing. They guarded the garden of Eden after the fall (Gen. 3:22–24), and images of cherubim appeared on the mercy seat of the ark (Ex. 25:18–22). In Ezekiel's vision the cherubim were manifesting God's glory and holiness to the exiles.

1:10 LIKENESS OF THEIR FACES. The faces of a man, a lion, an ox, and an eagle represent God's living creation (cf. Rev. 4:7). In the new heavens and new earth all of God's creation, having been fully redeemed from the curse of sin, will manifest His glory.

1:12 THE SPIRIT. The cherubim are directed by "the spirit," which most likely refers to the Spirit of God (cf. v. 20).

1:13 BURNING COALS OF FIRE. These coals point to the holiness of God (cf. Ex. 3:1–5) and to His judgment that punishes sin (cf. Rev. 20:14–15). The fire moving back and forth symbolizes the energy and power of the Spirit, who is always active and never rests.

The vision of the four wheels

15 ¶ Now as I beheld the living creatures, behold [y]one wheel upon the earth by the living creatures, with his four faces.

16 [z]The appearance of the wheels and their work *was* [a]like unto the colour of a beryl: and they four had one likeness: and their appearance and their work *was* as it were a wheel in the middle of a wheel.

17 When they went, they went upon their four sides: [b]*and* they turned not when they went.

18 As for their rings, they were so high that they were dreadful; and their [f]rings *were* [c]full of eyes round about them four.

19 And [d]when the living creatures went, the wheels went by them: and when the living creatures were lifted up from the earth, the wheels were lifted up.

20 [e]Whithersoever the spirit was to go, they went, thither *was their* spirit to go; and the wheels were lifted up over against them: [f]for the spirit [g]of the living creature *was* in the wheels.

21 [g]When those went, *these* went; and when those stood, *these* stood; and when those were lifted up from the earth, the wheels were lifted up over against them: for the spirit [g]of the living creature *was* in the wheels.

22 [h]And the likeness of the firmament upon the heads of the living creature *was* as the colour of the terrible crystal, stretched forth over their heads above.

23 And under the firmament *were* their wings straight, the one toward the other: every one had two, which covered on this side, and every one had two, which covered on that side, their bodies.

24 [i]And when they went, I heard the noise of their wings, [j]like the noise of great waters, as [k]the voice of the Almighty, the voice of speech, as the noise of an host: when they stood, they let down their wings.

25 And there was a voice from the firmament that *was* over their heads, when they stood, *and* had let down their wings.

26 ¶ [l]And above the firmament that *was* over their heads *was* the likeness of a throne, [m]as the appearance of a sapphire stone: and upon the likeness of the throne *was* the likeness as the appearance of a man above upon it.

27 [n]And I saw as the colour of amber, as the appearance of fire round about within it, from the appearance of his loins even upward, and from the appearance of his loins even downward, I saw as it were the appearance of fire, and it had brightness round about.

28 [o]As the appearance of the bow that is in the cloud in the day of rain, so *was* the appearance of the brightness round about. [p]This *was* the appearance of the likeness of the glory of the LORD. And when I saw *it,* [q]I fell upon my face, and I heard a voice of one that spake.

Ezekiel's commission

2 AND HE said unto me, Son of man, [r]stand upon thy feet, and I will speak unto thee.

1:15 [y]ch. 10:9 **1:16** [z]ch. 10:9,10 [a]Dan. 10:6 **1:17** [b]ver. 12 **1:18** [c]ch. 10:12 Zech. 4:10 **1:19** [d]ch. 10:16,17 **1:20** [e]ver. 12 [f]ch. 10:17 **1:21** [g]ver. 19,20 ch. 10:17 **1:22** [h]ch. 10:1 **1:24** [i]ch. 10:5 [j]ch. 43:2 Dan. 10:6 Rev. 1:15 [k]Job 37:4,5 Ps. 29:3,4 & 68:33 **1:26** [l]ch. 10:1 [m]Ex. 24:10 **1:27** [n]ch. 8:2 **1:28** [o]Rev. 4:3 & 10:1 [p]ch. 3:23 & 8:4 [q]ch. 3:23 Dan. 8:17 Acts 9:4 Rev. 1:17 **2:1** [r]Dan. 10:11

[f] Or, *strakes* [g] Or, *of life*

1:16–25 THE APPEARANCE OF THE WHEELS. Ezekiel sees a supernatural throne-chariot in constant motion. God is pictured on an ever-moving mobile throne that goes wherever the Spirit commands. The imagery symbolizes both God's sovereignty over all things and His presence throughout His creation. He is present with the exiles by the Chebar River.

1:26 THE LIKENESS AS THE APPEARANCE OF A MAN. Ezekiel sees God sitting upon the throne in the likeness of a man. This vision points to the fact that when God chose to reveal Himself fully, He did so in human form—through Jesus Christ (cf. Phil. 2:5–7; Col. 2:9).

1:28 THE GLORY OF THE LORD. This verse gives the significance of the entire vision: it was a vision of God's glory (see article on THE GLORY OF GOD, p. 1186). (1) God revealed His glory and might to Ezekiel to prepare him for the work to which He was calling him. The Lord would continue to appear to Ezekiel throughout his life in order to sustain him in that ministry (3:12,23–24; 8:2–4; 9:3; 10:1–22; 11:22–23; 43:2–4). (2) The appearance of God's glory to Ezekiel indicated that it had left the temple in Jerusalem (cf. 1 Ki. 8:11; Ps. 26:8; 63:2) and was now being manifested to the exiles. Ezekiel later prophesied that the glory of God would return to Canaan and Jerusalem (see 43:2–3,7). (3) Just as Ezekiel needed a vision of God's glory to prepare him to serve the Lord, so we too must experience the power of God's glory and holiness before we can actively enter into His work (cf. Is. 6). We receive an understanding of God in all His glory through Jesus Christ (cf. John 1:14), through the Holy Spirit (1 Pet. 4:14), and through the Word of God (2 Cor. 3:7–11; see Acts 1:8, notes).

2:1 SON OF MAN. God refers to Ezekiel more

2 And [s]the spirit entered into me
when he spake unto me, and set me
upon my feet, that I heard him that
spake unto me.
3 And he said unto me, Son of man,
I send thee to the children of Israel, to
a rebellious [h]nation that hath rebelled
against me: [t]they and their fathers
have transgressed against me, *even*
unto this very day.
4 [u]For *they are* [i]impudent chil-
dren and stiffhearted. I do send thee
unto them; and thou shalt say unto
them, Thus saith the Lord GOD.
5 [v]And they, whether they will
hear, or whether they will forbear, (for
they *are* a rebellious house,) yet [w]shall
know that there hath been a prophet
among them.
6 ¶ And thou, son of man, [x]be not
afraid of them, neither be afraid of their
words, though [y]briers[j] and thorns *be*
with thee, and thou dost dwell among
scorpions: [z]be not afraid of their
words, nor be dismayed at their
looks, [a]though they *be* a rebellious
house.
7 [b]And thou shalt speak my words
unto them, [c]whether they will hear, or
whether they will forbear: for they *are*
[k]most rebellious.
8 But thou, son of man, hear what I
say unto thee; Be not thou rebellious
like that rebellious house: open thy
mouth, and [d]eat that I give thee.
9 ¶ And when I looked, behold, [e]an
hand *was* sent unto me; and, lo, [f]a roll
of a book *was* therein;
10 And he spread it before me; and
it *was* written within and without: and
there was written therein lamentations,
and mourning, and woe.

3 MOREOVER HE said unto me, Son
of man, eat that thou findest; [g]eat
this roll, and go speak unto the house
of Israel.
2 So I opened my mouth, and he
caused me to eat that roll.
3 And he said unto me, Son of man,
cause thy belly to eat, and fill thy bow-
els with this roll that I give thee. Then
did I [h]eat *it;* and it was in my mouth
[i]as honey for sweetness.
4 ¶ And he said unto me, Son of
man, go, get thee unto the house of Is-
rael, and speak with my words unto
them.
5 For thou *art* not sent to a people
[l]of a strange speech and of an hard
language, *but* to the house of Israel;
6 Not to many people [m]of a strange
speech and of an hard language, whose
words thou canst not understand.
[n]Surely, [j]had I sent thee to them,
they would have hearkened unto thee.
7 But the house of Israel will not
hearken unto thee; [k]for they will not

2:2 [s]ch. 3:24
2:3 [t]Jer. 3:25; ch. 20:18,21,30
2:4 [u]ch. 3:7
2:5 [v]ch. 3:11,26,27 [w]ch. 33:33
2:6 [x]Jer. 1:8,17; Luke 12:4 [y]Is. 9:18; Jer. 6:28; Mic. 7:4 [z]ch. 3:9; 1 Pet. 3:14 [a]ch. 3:9,26,27
2:7 [b]Jer. 1:7,17 [c]ver. 5
2:8 [d]Rev. 10:9
2:9 [e]Jer. 1:9; ch. 8:3 [f]ch. 3:1
3:1 [g]ch. 2:8,9
3:3 [h]Rev. 10:9; See Jer. 15:16 [i]Ps. 19:10 & 119:103
3:6 [j]Mat. 11:21
3:7 [k]John 15:20

[h] Heb. *nations* [i] Heb. *hard of face* [j] Or, *rebels* [k] Heb. *rebellion* [l] Heb. *deep of lip, and heavy of tongue* [m] Heb. *deep of lip, and heavy of language* [n] Or, *If I had sent thee, &c., would they not have hearkened unto thee?*

than ninety times as "son of man." This title emphasized the prophet's humanity and weakness and reminded him that he was dependent on the Spirit's enabling power to fulfill his ministry. Jesus also used this title to refer to Himself (Mat. 8:20; 9:6; 11:19; Mark 2:28; 8:31,38; 9:9; Luke 5:24; John 3:13), emphasizing His relationship with humankind and His dependence on the Holy Spirit (cf. Dan. 8:17).

2:2 THE SPIRIT ENTERED INTO ME. Ezekiel is empowered by the Spirit of God in order to proclaim God's message. Then and now, God requires that His people be empowered by the Holy Spirit in order to preach the gospel effectively to all nations (see Acts 1:8, 2:4).

2:5 THERE HATH BEEN A PROPHET AMONG THEM. God wants genuine and faithful servants to proclaim His word to the people. They must speak all that God wants them to speak without fear or compromise. Their message must not be determined by the people's response, but rather spoken out of an absolute loyalty to God and His truth (v. 7). If some in their audience are determined to resist God and His law, so be it; the prophets must continue to speak God's words, rebuke sin and rebellion, and call the people to faithfulness to the Lord.

2:10 LAMENTATIONS. Ezekiel's initial message was to be one of judgment, which would produce lamentation in the people who heard.

3:1 EAT THIS SCROLL. On the scroll were the words and judgments of God for His people. Ezekiel's eating the scroll symbolized that he had to receive God's message and commit himself to it before proclaiming it.

3:3 IN MY MOUTH AS HONEY. Although Ezekiel was to bring a message of destruction and lamentation, God caused it to be as sweet as honey to the prophet himself. The word of God, simply because it is His word, will be loved and valued by all who are committed to God and His cause.

3:7 WILL NOT HEARKEN UNTO THEE. The people would not believe Ezekiel's prophetic message of judgment upon Jerusalem, for they were still hardened to the truth. To enable Ezekiel to face that coming rejection, God promised to give him courage and the determination to proclaim God's prophetic word under all circumstances (vv. 8–9).

hearken unto me: [l]for all the house of Israel *are* [o]impudent and hardhearted.

8 Behold, I have made thy face strong against their faces, and thy forehead strong against their foreheads.

9 [m]As an adamant harder than flint have I made thy forehead: [n]fear them not, neither be dismayed at their looks, though they *be* a rebellious house.

10 Moreover he said unto me, Son of man, all my words that I shall speak unto thee receive in thine heart, and hear with thine ears.

11 And go, get thee to them of the captivity, unto the children of thy people, and speak unto them, and tell them, [o]Thus saith the Lord GOD; whether they will hear, or whether they will forbear.

Ezek. 33:7-11

12 Then [p]the spirit took me up, and I heard behind me a voice of a great rushing, *saying,* Blessed *be* the glory of the LORD from his place.

13 *I heard* also the noise of the wings of the living creatures that [p]touched one another, and the noise of the wheels over against them, and a noise of a great rushing.

14 So [q]the spirit lifted me up, and took me away, and I went [q]in bitterness, in the [r]heat of my spirit; but [r]the hand of the LORD was strong upon me.

15 ¶ Then I came to them of the captivity at Tel-abib, that dwelt by the river of Chebar, and [s]I sat where they sat, and remained there astonished among them seven days.

Warning to Israel

16 And it came to pass at the end of seven days, that the word of the LORD came unto me, saying,

17 [t]Son of man, I have made thee [u]a watchman unto the house of Israel: therefore hear the word at my mouth, and give them warning from me.

18 When I say unto the wicked, Thou shalt surely die; and thou givest him not warning, nor speakest to warn the wicked from his wicked way, to save his life; the same wicked *man* [v]shall die in his iniquity; but his blood will I require at thine hand.

19 Yet if thou warn the wicked, and he turn not from his wickedness, nor from his wicked way, he shall die in his iniquity; [w]but thou hast delivered thy soul.

20 Again, When a [x]righteous *man* doth turn from his [s]righteousness, and commit iniquity, and I lay a stumblingblock before him, he shall die: because thou hast not given him warning, he shall die in his sin, and his righteousness which he hath done shall not be remembered; but his blood will I require at thine hand.

21 Nevertheless if thou warn the righteous *man,* that the righteous sin not, and he doth not sin, he shall surely live, because he is warned; also thou hast delivered thy soul.

Ezek 18:21-23

22 ¶ [y]And the hand of the LORD was there upon me; and he said unto me, Arise, go forth [z]into the plain, and I will there talk with thee.

23 Then I arose, and went forth into the plain: and, behold, [a]the glory of the LORD stood there, as the glory

3:7 [l]ch. 2:4
3:9 [m]Is. 50:7 Jer. 1:18 Mic. 3:8 [n]Jer. 1:8,17 ch. 2:6
3:11 [o]ch. 2:5,7
3:12 [p]ch. 8:3 1 Ki. 18:12 Acts 8:39
3:14 [q]ver. 12 ch. 8:3 [r]2 Ki. 3:15 ch. 1:3 & 8:1
3:15 [s]Job 2:13 Ps. 137:1
3:17 [t]ch. 33:7-9 [u]Is. 52:8 & 56:10 Jer. 6:17
3:18 [v]ch. 33:6 John 8:21
3:19 [w]Is. 49:4,5 Acts 20:26
3:20 [x]ch. 18:24 & 33:12,13
3:22 [y]ch. 1:3 [z]ch. 8:4
3:23 [a]ch. 1:28

[o] Heb. *stiff of forehead and hard of heart*
[p] Heb. *kissed* [q] Heb. *bitter* [r] Heb. *hot anger*
[s] Heb. *righteousnesses*

3:14 I WENT IN BITTERNESS. Ezekiel shows great sadness because of the impending calamities God had commissioned him to announce. Though deeply disturbed, he remained faithful to his calling. One sure sign that we are in a right relationship to God is that we begin to love righteousness and hate iniquity to the same extent that God does (see Heb. 1:9, note).

3:18 THE WICKED, THOU SHALT SURELY DIE. Ezekiel was to be a watchman, warning his countrymen that those who persisted in sin and rejection of God would be punished with death. If Ezekiel failed to warn the wicked, he would be held accountable for their death. (1) Under the new covenant, the faithful minister of God must likewise warn those in his congregation who are living unrighteous lives that they will be excluded from the kingdom of God and salvation if they do not repent (see 1 Cor. 6:9, note; Gal 5:21, note; Eph. 5:5, note). Those who teach that believers may live immoral and unrighteous lives without jeopardizing their eternal salvation will themselves face the severe judgment of God.

(2) We must always remember that God has given us the commission to go into all the world and proclaim the gospel (Mat. 28:18–20; Acts 1:8), which includes the warning of eternal death for all who refuse to repent and believe in Christ (cf. Acts 17:22–31). God has thus made the church a watchman (see Mat. 18:15, note).

3:20 HE SHALL DIE. A righteous person who turns from God, begins to live wickedly, and refuses to repent will experience God's judgment and die. Note the words of the apostle Paul: "If ye live after the flesh, ye shall die," i.e., receive eternal death (Rom. 8:13).

which I [b]saw by the river of Chebar:
[c]and I fell on my face.
24 Then [d]the spirit entered into
me, and set me upon my feet, and
spake with me, and said unto me, Go,
shut thyself within thine house.
25 But thou, O son of man, behold,
[e]they shall put bands upon thee, and
shall bind thee with them, and thou
shalt not go out among them:
26 And [f]I will make thy tongue
cleave to the roof of thy mouth, that
thou shalt be dumb, and shalt not be to
them [t]a reprover: [g]for they *are* a re-
bellious house.
27 [h]But when I speak with thee, I
will open thy mouth, and thou shalt say
unto them, [i]Thus saith the Lord GOD;
He that heareth, let him hear; and he
that forbeareth, let him forbear: for
they *are* a rebellious house.

Symbol of the siege and exile

4 THOU ALSO, son of man, take
thee a tile, and lay it before thee,
and portray upon it the city, *even* Jeru-
salem:
2 And lay siege against it, and build
a fort against it, and cast a mount
against it; set the camp also against it,
and set [u]*battering* rams against it
round about.
3 Moreover take thou unto thee
[v]an iron pan, and set it *for* a wall of
iron between thee and the city: and set
thy face against it, and it shall be be-
sieged, and thou shalt lay siege against
it. [j]This *shall be* a sign to the house of
Israel.
4 Lie thou also upon thy left side,
and lay the iniquity of the house of Is-
rael upon it: *according* to the number of
the days that thou shalt lie upon it thou
shalt bear their iniquity.
5 For I have laid upon thee the
years of their iniquity, according to the
number of the days, three hundred and
ninety days: [k]so shalt thou bear the
iniquity of the house of Israel.
6 And when thou hast accomplished
them, lie again on thy right side, and
thou shalt bear the iniquity of the
house of Judah forty days: I have ap-
pointed thee [w]each day for a year.
7 Therefore thou shalt set thy face
toward the siege of Jerusalem, and
thine arm *shall be* uncovered, and thou
shalt prophesy against it.
8 [l]And, behold, I will lay bands
upon thee, and thou shalt not turn thee
[x]from one side to another, till thou
hast ended the days of thy siege.
9 ¶ Take thou also unto thee wheat,
and barley, and beans, and lentils, and
millet, and [y]fitches, and put them in
one vessel, and make thee bread there-
of, *according* to the number of the days
that thou shalt lie upon thy side, three
hundred and ninety days shalt thou eat
thereof.
10 And thy meat which thou shalt
eat *shall be* by weight, twenty shekels
a day: from time to time shalt thou
eat it.
11 Thou shalt drink also water by

3:23 [b]ch. 1:1 [c]ch. 1:28
3:24 [d]ch. 2:2
3:25 [e]ch. 4:8
3:26 [f]ch. 24:27 Luke 1:20 [g]ch. 2:5-7
3:27 [h]ch. 24:27 & 33:22 [i]ver. 11
4:3 [j]ch. 12:6,11 & 24:24,27
4:5 [k]Num. 14:34
4:8 [l]ch. 3:25

[t]Heb. *a man reproving* [u]Or, *chief leaders;* see ch. 21:22 [v]Or, *a flat plate,* or, *slice*
[w]Heb. *a day for a year, a day for a year*
[x]Heb. *from thy side to thy side* [y]Or, *spelt*

3:26 THOU SHALT BE DUMB. Ezekiel was restrained from speaking to the people except when he received a direct message from the Lord. Because the people had refused to hear and obey what the prophets were saying, God deprived them of His word by imposing silence on Ezekiel. Denying His people the divine oracle was a powerful manifestation of God's judgment on them for their persistent wickedness (see Amos 8:11, note). Ezekiel's muteness lasted approximately seven and one-half years, until the fall of Jerusalem (24:27; 33:22).

4:1 TAKE THEE A TILE. Ezekiel was commanded to symbolize the siege of Jerusalem and the resulting exile by specific actions. He portrayed these events by making a small model of the siege. The iron plate (v. 3) may represent the unbreakable strength of the Babylonians. Through this action, Ezekiel impressed on the people that God Himself would bring the Babylonians against Jerusalem.

4:4 LIE THOU ALSO UPON THY LEFT SIDE. God instructed Ezekiel to bear, in a symbolic way, the punishment God intended for Israel's and Judah's sin (see next note). Each day that Ezekiel lay on his side represented one year of their sin. He did not lie on his side all day long, however, for he had other duties to perform (vv. 9–17).

4:5 THREE HUNDRED AND NINETY DAYS. The number of days assigned to Ezekiel for lying on his side corresponded to the years of Israel's and Judah's sin. The 390 years appear to encompass the period of the monarchy from Solomon to the fall of Jerusalem. The forty additional years that were applied to Judah (v. 6) may represent the exceedingly wicked reign of Manasseh, which influenced Judah for the rest of its history (2 Ki. 21:11–15).

4:9–11 MAKE THEE BREAD. The purpose of the meager food and water was to symbolize the scarcity of provisions in Jerusalem during the siege (vv. 16–17). Famine would be severe.

measure, the sixth part of an hin: from
time to time shalt thou drink.
12 And thou shalt eat it *as* barley
cakes, and thou shalt bake it with dung
that cometh out of man, in their sight.
13 And the LORD said, Even thus
[m]shall the children of Israel eat their
defiled bread among the Gentiles,
whither I will drive them.
14 Then said I, [n]Ah Lord GOD! be-
hold, my soul hath not been polluted:
for from my youth up even till now have
I not eaten of [o]that which dieth of it-
self, or is torn in pieces; neither came
there [p]abominable flesh into my
mouth.
15 Then he said unto me, Lo, I have
given thee cow's dung for man's dung,
and thou shalt prepare thy bread there-
with.
16 Moreover he said unto me, Son
of man, behold, I will break the [q]staff
of bread in Jerusalem: and they shall
[r]eat bread by weight, and with care;
and they shall [s]drink water by mea-
sure, and with astonishment:
17 That they may want bread and
water, and be astonied one with anoth-
er, and [t]consume away for their iniq-
uity.

5 AND THOU, son of man, take thee
a sharp knife, take thee a barber's
razor, [u]and cause *it* to pass upon thine
head and upon thy beard: then take
thee balances to weigh, and divide the
hair.
2 [v]Thou shalt burn with fire a third
part in the midst of [w]the city, when
[x]the days of the siege are fulfilled:
and thou shalt take a third part, *and*
smite about it with a knife: and a third
part thou shalt scatter in the wind; and
I will draw out a sword after them.
3 [y]Thou shalt also take thereof a
few in number, and bind them in thy
[z]skirts.
4 Then take of them again, and
[z]cast them into the midst of the fire,
and burn them in the fire; *for* thereof
shall a fire come forth into all the
house of Israel.
5 ¶ Thus saith the Lord GOD; This *is*
Jerusalem: I have set it in the midst of
the nations and countries *that are*
round about her.
6 And she hath changed my judg-
ments into wickedness more than the
nations, and my statutes more than the
countries that *are* round about her: for
they have refused my judgments and
my statutes, they have not walked in
them.
7 Therefore thus saith the Lord
GOD; Because ye multiplied more than
the nations that *are* round about you,
and have not walked in my statutes,
neither have kept my judgments, [a]nei-
ther have done according to the judg-
ments of the nations that *are* round
about you;
8 Therefore thus saith the Lord
GOD; Behold, I, even I, *am* against thee,
and will execute judgments in the
midst of thee in the sight of the na-
tions.
9 [b]And I will do in thee that which
I have not done, and whereunto I will
not do any more the like, because of all
thine abominations.
10 Therefore the fathers [c]shall eat
the sons in the midst of thee, and the
sons shall eat their fathers; and I will
execute judgments in thee, and the
whole remnant of thee will I [d]scatter
into all the winds.
11 Wherefore, *as* I live, saith the
Lord GOD; Surely, because thou hast
[e]defiled my sanctuary with all thy
[f]detestable things, and with all thine
abominations, therefore will I also di-
minish *thee;* [g]neither shall mine eye
spare, neither will I have any pity.
12 ¶ [h]A third part of thee shall die
with the pestilence, and with famine

4:13 [m]Hos. 9:3 **4:14** [n]Acts 10:14 [o]Ex. 22:31 Lev. 11:40 & 17:15 [p]Deut. 14:3 Is. 65:4 **4:16** [q]Lev. 26:26 Ps. 105:16 Is. 3:1 ch. 5:16 & 14:13 [r]ver. 10 ch. 12:19 [s]ver. 11 **4:17** [t]Lev. 26:39 ch. 24:23 **5:1** [u]See Lev. 21:5 Is. 7:20 ch. 44:20 **5:2** [v]ver. 12 [w]ch. 4:1 [x]ch. 4:8,9 **5:3** [y]Jer. 40:6 & 52:16 **5:4** [z]Jer. 41:1,2 & 44:14 **5:7** [a]Jer. 2:10,11 ch. 16:47 **5:9** [b]Lam. 4:6 Dan. 9:12 Amos 3:2 **5:10** [c]Lev. 26:29 Deut. 28:53 2 Ki. 6:29 Jer. 19:9 Lam. 2:20 & 4:10 [d]Lev. 26:33 Deut. 28:64 ch. 12:14 Zech. 2:6 **5:11** [e]2 Chr. 36:14 ch. 7:20 [f]ch. 11:21 [g]ch. 7:4,9 **5:12** [h]Jer. 15:2 & 21:9 ch. 6:12

[z] Heb. *wings*

5:1–2 TAKE THEE A SHARP KNIFE. Ezekiel's shaved hair and beard, divided into three portions, symbolized the fate of the inhabitants of Jerusalem. The third that was set on fire represented those who would die by plague or by famine; another third would die by the sword, and the final third would be scattered in exile (v. 12).

5:3 A FEW IN NUMBER. The few hairs put in Ezekiel's garment represented a remnant of the people whom God would preserve. Even some of these, however, would be burned and experience God's judgment (v. 4).

5:11 BECAUSE THOU HAST DEFILED MY SANCTUARY. One of the major reasons God's anger was directed against Jerusalem was her defilement of the temple through idol worship (see chs. 8–11). The N.T. warns believers against this same terrible sin. The apostle Paul states that "if any man defile the temple of God, him shall God destroy" (1 Cor. 3:17); in this passage, the temple refers to a local church or group of churches. People defile the church of God by participating in its worship while living in sin and immorality, or by promoting unbiblical doctrines.

shall they be consumed in the midst of thee: and a third part shall fall by the sword round about thee; and [i]I will scatter a third part into all the winds, and [j]I will draw out a sword after them.

13 Thus shall mine anger [k]be accomplished, and I will [l]cause my fury to rest upon them, [m]and I will be comforted: [n]and they shall know that I the LORD have spoken *it* in my zeal, when I have accomplished my fury in them.

14 Moreover [o]I will make thee waste, and a reproach among the nations that *are* round about thee, in the sight of all that pass by.

15 So it shall be a [p]reproach and a taunt, an instruction and an astonishment unto the nations that *are* round about thee, when I shall execute judgments in thee in anger and in fury and in [q]furious rebukes. I the LORD have spoken *it.*

16 When I shall [r]send upon them the evil arrows of famine, which shall be for *their* destruction, *and* which I will send to destroy you: and I will increase the famine upon you, and will break your [s]staff of bread:

17 So will I send upon you famine and [t]evil beasts, and they shall bereave thee; and [u]pestilence and blood shall pass through thee; and I will bring the sword upon thee. I the LORD have spoken *it.*

The high places to be destroyed

6 AND THE word of the LORD came unto me, saying,

2 Son of man, [v]set thy face toward the [w]mountains of Israel, and prophesy against them,

3 And say, Ye mountains of Israel, hear the word of the Lord GOD; Thus saith the Lord GOD to the mountains, and to the hills, to the rivers, and to the valleys; Behold, I, *even* I, will bring a sword upon you, and [x]I will destroy your high places.

4 And your altars shall be desolate, and your [a]images shall be broken: and [y]I will cast down your slain *men* before your idols.

5 And I will [b]lay the dead carcases of the children of Israel before their idols; and I will scatter your bones round about your altars.

6 In all your dwellingplaces the cities shall be laid waste, and the high places shall be desolate; that your altars may be laid waste and made desolate, and your idols may be broken and cease, and your images may be cut down, and your works may be abolished.

7 And the slain shall fall in the midst of you, and [z]ye shall know that I *am* the LORD.

8 ¶ [a]Yet will I leave a remnant, that ye may have *some* that shall escape the sword among the nations, when ye shall be scattered through the countries.

9 And they that escape of you shall remember me among the nations whither they shall be carried captives, because [b]I am broken with their whorish heart, which hath departed from me, and [c]with their eyes, which go a whoring after their idols: and [d]they shall loathe themselves for the evils which they have committed in all their abominations.

10 And they shall know that I *am* the LORD, *and that* I have not said in

[a] Or, *sun images* [b] Heb. *give*

5:12 [i]Jer. 9:16 [j]ver. 2 Lev. 26:33 ch. 12:14
5:13 [k]Lam. 4:11 ch. 6:12 & 7:8 [l]ch. 21:17 [m]Deut. 32:36 Is. 1:24 [n]ch. 36:6 & 38:19
5:14 [o]Lev. 26:31 Neh. 2:17
5:15 [p]Deut. 28:37 1 Ki. 9:7 Ps. 79:4 Jer. 24:9 Lam. 2:15 [q]ch. 25:17
5:16 [r]Deut. 32:23 [s]Lev. 26:26 ch. 4:16 & 14:13
5:17 [t]Lev. 26:22 Deut. 32:24 ch. 14:21 & 33:27 & 34:25 [u]ch. 38:22
6:2 [v]ch. 20:46 & 21:2 & 25:2 [w]ch. 36:1
6:3 [x]Lev. 26:30
6:4 [y]Lev. 26:30
6:7 [z]ver. 13 ch. 7:4,9
6:8 [a]Jer. 44:28 ch. 5:2,12 & 12:16 & 14:22
6:9 [b]Ps. 78:40 Is. 7:13 & 43:24 [c]Num. 15:39 ch. 20:7,24 [d]Lev. 26:39 Job 42:6 ch. 20:43 & 36:31

5:17 I THE LORD HAVE SPOKEN *IT*. Statements about God's determination to execute His judgment against Judah occur some sixty times in the book of Ezekiel. We must not make God out to be One who is unwilling to punish those who defile His church (see previous note) or reject His ways. God keeps His word, and His threats of judgment will be fulfilled. For a more complete understanding of the outpouring of God's wrath in the future, see the book of Revelation.

6:4 YOUR IDOLS. The Israelites' chief sin against the Lord was their idolatry. They repeatedly spurned the goodness of God and gave their worship and allegiance to other gods. Today people become guilty of idolatry whenever they seek satisfaction, pleasure, meaning, or help in the sinful and secular things of this world (see Mat. 6:19–24; Col. 3:5) rather than place their trust in God alone as the hope of their lives. For more on idolatry, see article on THE NATURE OF IDOLATRY, p. 428.

6:9 I AM BROKEN. God was genuinely grieved and hurt by the spiritual adultery (i.e., idolatry) of His people (see Eph. 4:30, note). Their unfaithfulness broke His heart.

6:9 THEY SHALL LOATHE THEMSELVES. God's punishment would cause some to recognize the seriousness of their sin, to experience true sorrow for their transgression, and consequently to return to God. Note that repentance is not merely a change of mind, but also a change of feeling. It is a godly sorrow and regret because of personal sin (Ps. 51:17; 2 Cor. 7:9–10).

vain that I would do this evil unto them.

11 ¶ Thus saith the Lord GOD; Smite [e]with thine hand, and stamp with thy foot, and say, Alas for all the evil abominations of the house of Israel! [f]for they shall fall by the sword, by the famine, and by the pestilence.

12 He that is far off shall die of the pestilence; and he that is near shall fall by the sword; and he that remaineth and is besieged shall die by the famine: [g]thus will I accomplish my fury upon them.

13 Then [h]shall ye know that I *am* the LORD, when their slain *men* shall be among their idols round about their altars, [i]upon every high hill, [j]in all the tops of the mountains, and [k]under every green tree, and under every thick oak, the place where they did offer sweet savour to all their idols.

14 So will I [l]stretch out my hand upon them, and make the land desolate, yea, [c]more desolate than the wilderness toward [m]Diblath, in all their habitations: and they shall know that I *am* the LORD.

An end is come

7 MOREOVER THE word of the LORD came unto me, saying,

2 Also, thou son of man, thus saith the Lord GOD unto the land of Israel; [n]An end, the end is come upon the four corners of the land.

3 Now *is* the end *come* upon thee, and I will send mine anger upon thee, and will judge thee according to thy ways, and will [d]recompense upon thee all thine abominations.

4 And [o]mine eye shall not spare thee, neither will I have pity: but I will recompense thy ways upon thee, and thine abominations shall be in the midst of thee: [p]and ye shall know that I *am* the LORD.

5 Thus saith the Lord GOD; An evil, an only evil, behold, is come.

6 An end is come, the end is come: it [e]watcheth for thee; behold, it is come.

7 [q]The morning is come unto thee, O thou that dwellest in the land: [r]the time is come, the day of trouble *is* near, and not the [f]sounding again of the mountains.

8 Now will I shortly [s]pour out my fury upon thee, and accomplish mine anger upon thee: and I will judge thee according to thy ways, and will recompense thee for all thine abominations.

9 And mine eye shall not spare, neither will I have pity: I will recompense [g]thee according to thy ways and thine abominations *that* are in the midst of thee; and ye shall know that I *am* the LORD that smiteth.

10 Behold the day, behold, it is come: [t]the morning is gone forth; the rod hath blossomed, pride hath budded.

11 [u]Violence is risen up into a rod of wickedness: none of them *shall remain,* nor of their [h]multitude, nor of any of [i]theirs: [v]neither *shall there be* wailing for them.

12 The time is come, the day draweth near: let not the buyer rejoice, nor the seller mourn: for wrath *is* upon all the multitude thereof.

13 For the seller shall not return to that which is sold, [j]although they were yet alive: for the vision *is* touching the whole multitude thereof, *which* shall not return; neither shall any strengthen himself [k]in [l]the iniquity of his life.

14 They have blown the trumpet, even to make all ready; but none goeth to the battle: for my wrath *is* upon all the multitude thereof.

15 [w]The sword *is* without, and the pestilence and the famine within: he

6:11 [e]ch. 21:14 [f]ch. 5:12
6:12 [g]ch. 5:13
6:13 [h]ver. 7 [i]Jer. 2:20 [j]Hos. 4:13 [k]Is. 57:5
6:14 [l]Is. 5:25 [m]Num. 33:46 Jer. 48:22
7:2 [n]Amos 8:2 Mat. 24:6,13,14
7:4 [o]ch. 5:11 [p]ch. 12:20
7:7 [q]ver. 10 [r]Zeph. 1:14,15
7:8 [s]ch. 20:8,21
7:10 [t]ver. 7
7:11 [u]Jer. 6:7 [v]Jer. 16:5,6 ch. 24:16,22
7:15 [w]Deut. 32:25 Lam. 1:20

[c] Or, *desolate from the wilderness* [d] Heb. *give* [e] Heb. *awaketh against thee* [f] Or, *echo* [g] Heb. *upon thee* [h] Or, *tumult* [i] Or, *their tumultuous persons* [j] Heb. *though their life were yet among the living* [k] Or, *whose life is in his iniquity* [l] Heb. *his iniquity*

6:11 SMITE WITH THINE HAND. Those loyal to God and dedicated to serving Him would feel grief and sorrow because of the sinful practices occurring in the world, even among those who professed the name of the Lord (see 9:4, note).

7:7 THE DAY OF TROUBLE *IS* NEAR. The day of wrath and destruction was soon to come for the Israelites. Their rebellion against God would come to an abrupt end (vv. 2–3,6) when He punished them for their abominations; few would survive. Today, it may seem that God is ignoring the evil and immorality of the nations. Nevertheless, the Bible assures us over and over again that the day of the Lord is coming (cf. Amos 5:18–20), a day of great judgment bringing destruction and God's wrath on the entire world (see 1 Pet. 4:7,17). Just as the day of God's wrath finally came on Judah, so it will come on all the wicked, immoral, and arrogant of this world (see 1 Thes. 5:2, note).

that *is* in the field shall die with the
sword; and he that *is* in the city, famine
and pestilence shall devour him.
16 ¶ But they that escape of them
shall escape, and shall be on the moun-
tains like doves of the valleys, all of
them mourning, every one for his iniq-
uity.
17 All [x]hands shall be feeble, and
all knees shall [m]be weak *as* water.
18 They shall also [y]gird *themselves*
with sackcloth, and horror shall cover
them; and shame *shall be* upon all
faces, and baldness upon all their
heads.
19 They shall cast their silver in the
streets, and their gold shall be [n]re-
moved: their [z]silver and their gold
shall not be able to deliver them in the
day of the wrath of the LORD: they shall
not satisfy their souls, neither fill their
bowels: [o]because it is the stumbling-
block of their iniquity.
20 ¶ As for the beauty of his orna-
ment, he set it in majesty: [a]but they
made the images of their abominations
and of their detestable things therein:
therefore have I [p]set it far from them.
21 And I will give it into the hands
of the strangers for a prey, and to the
wicked of the earth for a spoil; and they
shall pollute it.
22 My face will I turn also from
them, and they shall pollute my secret
place: for the [q]robbers shall enter into
it, and defile it.
23 ¶ Make a chain: for [b]the land is
full of bloody crimes, and the city is full
of violence.
24 Wherefore I will bring the worst
of the heathen, and they shall possess
their houses: I will also make the pomp
of the strong to cease; and [r]their holy
places shall be defiled.
25 [s]Destruction cometh; and they
shall seek peace, and *there shall be*
none.
26 [c]Mischief shall come upon mis-
chief, and rumour shall be upon ru-
mour; [d]then shall they seek a vision of
the prophet; but the law shall perish
from the priest, and counsel from the
ancients.
27 The king shall mourn, and the
prince shall be clothed with desolation,
and the hands of the people of the land
shall be troubled: I will do unto them
after their way, and [t]according to
their deserts will I judge them; and
they shall know that I *am* the LORD.

An end is come

8 AND IT came to pass in the sixth
year, in the sixth *month,* in the fifth
day of the month, *as* I sat in mine
house, and [e]the elders of Judah sat
before me, that [f]the hand of the Lord
GOD fell there upon me.
2 [g]Then I beheld, and lo a likeness
as the appearance of fire: from the ap-
pearance of his loins even downward,
fire; and from his loins even upward, as
the appearance of brightness, [h]as the
colour of amber.
3 And he [i]put forth the form of an
hand, and took me by a lock of mine
head; and [j]the spirit lifted me up be-
tween the earth and the heaven, and
[k]brought me in the visions of God to

7:17 [x]Is. 13:7; Jer. 6:24 **7:18** [y]Is. 3:24; Amos 8:10 **7:19** [z]Prov. 11:4; Zeph. 1:18 **7:20** [a]Jer. 7:30 **7:23** [b]2 Ki. 21:16 **7:26** [c]Deut. 32:23; Jer. 4:20 [d]Ps. 74:9; ch. 20:1,3 **8:1** [e]ch. 14:1 & 20:1 & 33:31 [f]ch. 1:3 & 3:22 **8:2** [g]ch. 1:26,27 [h]ch. 1:4 **8:3** [i]Dan. 5:5 [j]ch. 3:14 [k]ch. 11:1,24 & 40:2

[m] Heb. *go into water* [n] Heb. *for a separation,* or, *uncleanness* [o] Or, *because their iniquity is their stumblingblock* [p] Or, *made it unto them an unclean thing* [q] Or, *burglars* [r] Or, *they shall inherit their holy places* [s] Heb. *Cutting off* [t] Heb. *with their judgments*

7:19 THEIR SILVER . . . AND THEIR GOLD. When God's coming wrath falls upon this world, the wealth and the abundant possessions of the unrighteous will not be able to deliver them. God's people must be careful not to strive selfishly for excessive material gain. If we do, we will find that worldly goods do not satisfy (cf. Eccl. 2) and we will become subject to the severe judgment of God.

7:25 DESTRUCTION COMETH. At first sin may seem pleasant and pleasurable; when it has run its course, however, it brings destruction, anguish, and despair. The only hope for deliverance is to turn to God in repentance and faith and to trust in the atoning death of Jesus Christ.

8:1 THE HAND OF THE LORD GOD. Ezekiel experienced an awesome visitation of God's presence and power as he was transported "in the visions of God to Jerusalem" (v. 3; cf. 2 Cor. 12:1–4). N.T. believers likewise experienced the presence and power of God when they were filled with the Holy Spirit (Acts 4:29–31) and received visions and dreams (Acts 2:16–18). Believers today should ask, seek, and knock for the Holy Spirit to come upon them in power (Luke 11:5–13) and to bestow on them His spiritual gifts, so that they may witness for Christ (Acts 1:8; 2:4,16–18). In this way, the word of God will go forth to God's house and to the world in boldness, with miraculous power, and with full conviction (Acts 2:1–12,37–41; 1 Thes. 1:5; Heb. 2:4).

8:3 BROUGHT ME ... TO JERUSALEM. Ezekiel was transported to the temple in Jerusalem in order to see the abominations that the people were committing. This revelation disclosed clearly why God would judge the holy city.

Jerusalem, to the door of the inner gate
that looketh toward the north; [l]where
was the seat of the image of jealousy,
which [m]provoketh to jealousy.
4 And, behold, the glory of the God
of Israel *was* there, according to the vi-
sion that I [n]saw in the plain.

Zech. 7:12

5 ¶ Then said he unto me, Son of
man, lift up thine eyes now the way to-
ward the north. So I lifted up mine eyes
the way toward the north, and behold
northward at the gate of the altar this
image of jealousy in the entry.
6 He said furthermore unto me, Son
of man, seest thou what they do? *even*
the great abominations that the house
of Israel committeth here, that I
should go far off from my sanctuary?
but turn thee yet again, *and* thou shalt
see greater abominations.
7 ¶ And he brought me to the door
of the court; and when I looked, behold
a hole in the wall.
8 Then said he unto me, Son of man,
dig now in the wall: and when I had
digged in the wall, behold a door.
9 And he said unto me, Go in, and
behold the wicked abominations that
they do here.
10 So I went in and saw; and behold
every form of creeping things, and
abominable beasts, and all the idols of
the house of Israel, portrayed upon the
wall round about.
11 And there stood before them sev-
enty men of the ancients of the house
of Israel, and in the midst of them
stood Jaazaniah the son of Shaphan,
with every man his censer in his hand;
and a thick cloud of incense went up.
12 Then said he unto me, Son of
man, hast thou seen what the ancients
of the house of Israel do in the dark,
every man in the chambers of his imag-
ery? for they say, [o]The LORD seeth us
not; the LORD hath forsaken the earth.
13 ¶ He said also unto me, Turn
thee yet again, *and* thou shalt see
greater abominations that they do.
14 Then he brought me to the door
of the gate of the LORD's house which
was toward the north; and, behold,
there sat women weeping for Tammuz.
15 ¶ Then said he unto me, Hast
thou seen *this,* O son of man? turn thee
yet again, *and* thou shalt see greater
abominations than these.
16 And he brought me into the inner
court of the LORD's house, and, behold,
at the door of the temple of the LORD,
[p]between the porch and the altar,
[q]*were* about five and twenty men,
[r]with their backs toward the temple
of the LORD, and their faces toward the
east; and they worshipped [s]the sun
toward the east.
17 ¶ Then he said unto me, Hast
thou seen *this,* O son of man? [u]Is it a
light thing to the house of Judah that
they commit the abominations which
they commit here? for they have
[t]filled the land with violence, and
have returned to provoke me to anger:
and, lo, they put the branch to their
nose.
18 [u]Therefore will I also deal in
fury: mine [v]eye shall not spare, nei-
ther will I have pity: and though they
[w]cry in mine ears with a loud voice, *yet*
will I not hear them.

The slaughter of the idolaters

9 HE CRIED also in mine ears with
a loud voice, saying, Cause them
that have charge over the city to draw
near, even every man *with* his destroy-
ing weapon in his hand.
2 And, behold, six men came from
the way of the higher gate, [v]which
lieth toward the north, and every man
[w]a slaughter weapon in his hand;

8:3 [l]Jer. 7:30 & 32:34 ch. 5:11 [m]Deut. 32:16,21
8:4 [n]ch. 1:28 & 3:22,23
8:12 [o]ch. 9:9
8:16 [p]Joel 2:17 [q]ch. 11:1 [r]Jer. 2:27 & 32:33 [s]Deut. 4:19 2 Ki. 23:5,11 Job 31:26 Jer. 44:17
8:17 [t]ch. 9:9
8:18 [u]ch. 5:13 & 16:42 & 24:13 [v]ch. 5:11 & 7:4,9 & 9:5,10 [w]Prov. 1:28 Is. 1:15 Jer. 11:11 & 14:12 Mic. 3:4 Zech. 7:13

[u] Or, *Is there any thing lighter than to commit*
[v] Heb. *which is turned* [w] Heb. *a weapon of his breaking in pieces*

8:6 THAT I SHOULD GO FAR OFF FROM MY SANCTUARY? God revealed to Ezekiel that He would not dwell in the temple if idolatry and sin were tolerated. Jesus likewise stated that churches that compromise with the world, forsake apostolic teaching, or tolerate immorality will lose His presence and their place in the kingdom of God (see Rev. 2—3).

8:14 TAMMUZ. Tammuz was the Babylonian god of vegetation. When plant life died in the fall, the people mourned what they thought was his death. Judah's women had forsaken the Lord God, turning to gods such as these for help and blessing.

8:17 PUT THE BRANCH TO THEIR NOSE. This act may have been a ritual of the worship of the sun or of nature.

9:2 SIX MEN. The six men are six angels assigned by God to carry out His judgment against the city. They were each carrying a weapon (v. 1) by which to kill all the wicked. With them appeared a seventh angel clothed in white linen, with a writing case in his girdle. His task was to place a mark on the foreheads of those who remained faithful to God (cf. Rev. 7:3; 9:4; 14:1; 22:4; see next note).

[x]and one man among them *was* clothed with linen, with a writer's inkhorn [x]by his side: and they went in, and stood beside the brasen altar.

3 And [y]the glory of the God of Israel was gone up from the cherub, whereupon he was, to the threshold of the house. And he called to the man clothed with linen, which *had* the writer's inkhorn by his side;

4 And the LORD said unto him, Go through the midst of the city, through the midst of Jerusalem, and [y]set [z]a mark upon the foreheads of the men [a]that sigh and that cry for all the abominations that be done in the midst thereof.

5 ¶ And to the others he said in [z]mine hearing, Go ye after him through the city, and smite: [b]let not your eye spare, neither have ye pity:

6 [c]Slay [a]utterly old *and* young, both maids, and little children, and women: but [d]come not near any man upon whom *is* the mark; and [e]begin at my sanctuary. [f]Then they began at the ancient men which *were* before the house.

7 And he said unto them, Defile the house, and fill the courts with the slain: go ye forth. And they went forth, and slew in the city.

8 ¶ And it came to pass, while they were slaying them, and I was left, that I [g]fell upon my face, and cried, and said, [h]Ah Lord GOD! wilt thou destroy all the residue of Israel in thy pouring out of thy fury upon Jerusalem?

9 Then said he unto me, The iniquity of the house of Israel and Judah *is* exceeding great, and [i]the land is [b]full of blood, and the city full of [c]perverseness: for they say, [j]The LORD hath forsaken the earth, and [k]the LORD seeth not.

10 And as for me also, mine [l]eye shall not spare, neither will I have pity, *but* [m]I will recompense their way upon their head.

11 And, behold, the man clothed with linen, which *had* the inkhorn by his side, [d]reported the matter, saying, I have done as thou hast commanded me.

The glory of the LORD

10 THEN I looked, and, behold, in the [n]firmament that was above the head of the cherubims there appeared over them as it were a sapphire stone, as the appearance of the likeness of a throne.

2 [o]And he spake unto the man clothed with linen, and said, Go in between the wheels, *even* under the cherub, and fill [e]thine hand with [p]coals of fire from between the cherubims, and [q]scatter *them* over the city. And he went in in my sight.

3 Now the cherubims stood on the right side of the house, when the man went in; and the cloud filled the inner court.

4 [r]Then the glory of the LORD [f]went up from the cherub, *and stood*

9:2 [x]Lev. 16:4 ch. 10:2,6,7 Rev. 15:6
9:3 [y]See ch. 3:23 & 8:4 & 10:4,18 & 11:22,23
9:4 [z]Ex. 12:7 Rev. 7:3 & 9:4 & 13:16,17 & 20:4 [a]Ps. 119:53,136 Jer. 13:17 2 Cor. 12:21 2 Pet. 2:8
9:5 [b]ver. 10 ch. 5:11
9:6 [c]2 Chr. 36:17 [d]Rev. 9:4 [e]Jer. 25:29 1 Pet. 4:17 [f]ch. 8:11,12,16
9:8 [g]Num. 14:5 & 16:4,22,45 Josh. 7:6 [h]ch. 11:13
9:9 [i]2 Ki. 21:16 ch. 8:17 [j]ch. 8:12 [k]Ps. 10:11 Is. 29:15
9:10 [l]ch. 5:11 & 7:4 & 8:18 [m]ch. 11:21
10:1 [n]ch. 1:2,26
10:2 [o]ch. 9:2,3 [p]ch. 1:13 [q]See Rev. 8:5
10:4 [r]See ver. 18 ch. 1:28 & 9:3

[x] Heb. *upon his loins* [y] Heb. *mark a mark* [z] Heb. *mine ears* [a] Heb. *to destruction* [b] Heb. *filled with* [c] Or, *wresting* of judgment [d] Heb. *returned the word* [e] Heb. *the hollow of thine hand* [f] Heb. *was lifted up*

9:4 THAT CRY FOR ALL THE ABOMINATIONS. God commanded that only those who remained faithful to Him and His word were to be spared the coming judgment. (1) Their loyalty to God was determined by their love for righteousness and their grief and hatred over the sins committed around them. They were to receive a special mark of identification from God—the Hebrew letter *taw* (the final letter of the Hebrew alphabet, which took the form of a cross). (2) Grief over sin is evidence of true saving faith. Those who genuinely belong to the Lord will grieve just as He does when they see sin and immorality in the world and in the church (see Heb. 1:9, note).

9:6 BEGIN AT MY SANCTUARY . . . THE ANCIENT MEN. God's wrath and judgment begin with His own people (see 1 Pet. 4:17), especially with the spiritual leaders of His congregations. Leaders and overseers in the church are particularly accountable to God for their faithfulness to His Word and for their perseverance in righteous and holy living (Jas. 3:1). If they fail to be good examples, they will lead many away from God and His word.

10:2 COALS OF FIRE. The burning coals scattered over the city symbolized judgment and destruction. The Babylonians destroyed Jerusalem by fire shortly after this vision (2 Chr. 36:19; 2 Ki. 25:8–9).

10:4 THE GLORY OF THE LORD WENT UP. The focus of chs. 10—11 is the departure of God's glory and presence from the temple and the city (see article on THE GLORY OF GOD, p. 1186). God's glory first left the most holy place and moved to the entrance of the temple (v. 4). The glory then departed from the temple and rested on the cherubim throne-chariot (v. 18). The cherubim moved the glory of God to the east gate of the temple (v. 19), and then it departed from the temple area altogether. Finally, the divine glory left the city of Jerusalem and rested on the Mount of Olives (11:23). (1) The glory of God left the temple because

THE GLORY OF GOD

***Ezek. 10:4** "Then the glory of the* L*ORD went up from the cherub,* and stood *over the threshold of the house; and the house was filled with the cloud, and the court was full of the brightness of the* L*ORD's glory."*

THE GLORY OF GOD DEFINED. The phrase "the glory of God" is used several ways in the Bible. (1) Sometimes it describes the splendor and majesty of God (cf. 1 Chr. 29:11; Hab. 3:3–5), a glory so great that no human being can look upon it and live (see Ex. 33:18–23). At best one can see only an "appearance of the likeness of the glory of the LORD" (cf. Ezekiel's vision of the throne of God, Ezek. 1:26–28). In this sense, the glory of God designates His uniqueness, His holiness (cf. Is. 6:1–3), and His transcendence (cf. Rom. 11:36; Heb. 13:21). Peter uses the term "the excellent glory" as a name for God (2 Pet. 1:17).

(2) The glory of God also refers to the visible presence of God among His people, sometimes called the "*Shekinah*" glory by later rabbis. "*Shekinah*" is a Hebrew word meaning "dwelling [of God]," employed to describe a visible manifestation of God's presence and glory. Moses saw God's *Shekinah* glory in a pillar of cloud and fire (Ex. 13:21); in Ex. 29:43 it is called "my glory" (cf. Is. 60:2). It covered Sinai when God gave the law (see Ex. 24:16–17, note), filled the tabernacle (Ex. 40:34), guided Israel in the wilderness (Ex. 40:36–38), and later filled Solomon's temple (2 Chr. 7:1; 1 Ki. 8:11–13). More specifically, God dwelt between the two cherubim in the Most Holy Place (1 Sam. 4:4; 2 Sam. 6:2; Ps. 80:1). Ezekiel saw the glory of the Lord in the temple of God (Ezek. 10:4) rise and depart from the temple because of rampant idolatry there (Ezek. 10:18–19). The N.T. equivalent of the *Shekinah* is Jesus Christ, who as the glory of God in human flesh came to dwell among us (John 1:14). The shepherds of Bethlehem saw the glory of the Lord at Jesus' birth (Luke 2:9), the disciples saw it at Christ's transfiguration (Mat. 17:2; 2 Pet. 1:16–18), and Stephen saw it at the time of his martyrdom (Acts 7:55).

(3) A third aspect of the "glory of God" is His spiritual presence and power. Even though the heavens declare the glory of God (Ps. 19:1; cf. Rom. 1:19–20) and the whole earth is full of His glory (Is. 6:3; cf. Hab. 2:14), the brightness of God's majesty is not now visibly evident and often goes unnoticed. However, believers experience God's glory and presence in His nearness, love, righteousness, and manifestations through the power of the Holy Spirit (see 2 Cor. 3:18, note; Eph. 3:16–19, note; 1 Pet. 4:14, note).

(4) Finally, the O.T. warns that any kind of idolatry encroaches on God's glory and brings reproach to God's name. Whenever God manifests Himself as our Redeemer, then His name is glorified (see Ps. 79:9; Jer. 14:21). The entire ministry of Christ on earth brought glory to the name of our God (John 14:13; 17:1,4–5).

THE GLORY OF GOD REVEALED IN JESUS CHRIST. When Isaiah spoke about the coming of Jesus Christ, he prophesied that in Him the glory of God would be revealed for all flesh to see (Is. 40:5). Both John (John 1:14) and the writer to the Hebrews (Heb. 1:3) testify that Jesus Christ fulfilled this prophecy. Christ's glory was the same glory that He had with His Father before the world began (John 1:14; 17:5). The glory of His ministry far surpassed the glory of the O.T.'s ministry (2 Cor. 3:7–11). Both Paul and James call Jesus "the Lord of glory" (1 Cor. 2:8; Jas. 2:1).

Repeatedly the N.T. refers to the relationship between Jesus Christ and the glory of God. His miracles manifested His glory (John 2:11; 11:40–44). Christ was transfigured in a "bright cloud" (Mat. 17:5) and "in glory" (Luke 9:31; cf. 2 Pet. 1:16–19). The hour of His death was the hour of His glorification (John 12:23–24; cf. 17:2–5). He ascended into heaven in a cloud of glory (cf. Acts 1:9; 1 Tim. 3:16), is now exalted in glory (Rev. 5:12–13), and will someday return "in the clouds . . . with power and great glory" (Mat. 24:30; cf. 25:31; Mark 14:62; 1 Thes. 4:17).

THE GLORY OF GOD EXPERIENCED IN THE LIVES OF BELIEVERS. How does the glory of God apply to believers personally? (1) Regarding God's majestic heavenly glory, it is still true that no one can see that glory of God and live. We know it is there, but we do not see it. Because God dwells in unapproachable light and glory, no mortal man can behold Him face to face (1 Tim. 6:16).

(2) God's *Shekinah* glory, however, was experienced by God's people in Bible times. Throughout history to the present time there have been believers who have had visions of God similar to those of Isaiah (Is. 6) and Ezekiel (Ezek. 1), though this was not common then or now. The experience of God's glory, however, is something that all believers will have at the consummation, when we behold Jesus face to face. We will be brought into the presence of God's glory (Heb. 2:10; 1 Pet. 5:10; Jude 24), share in Christ's glory (Rom. 8:17–18), and be given a crown of glory (1 Pet. 5:4). Even our resurrection bodies will bear the glory of the risen Christ (1 Cor. 15:42–43; Phil. 3:21).

(3) On a more immediate basis, sincere believers experience the spiritual presence of God. The Holy Spirit brings the presence of God and the Lord Jesus near to us (2 Cor. 3:17; 1 Pet. 4:14). When the Spirit becomes powerfully active in the church through His supernatural manifestations (1 Cor. 12:1–12), believers experience the glory of God in their midst, i.e., an awesome feeling of the presence of God, similar to what the shepherds felt in the fields of Bethlehem (Luke 2:8–20).

(4) Believers who forsake sin and shun idolatry may be filled with both Christ's glory (see John 17:22, note) and the Spirit of glory (1 Pet. 4:14); indeed, one reason Jesus came into the world was to fill believers with glory (Luke 2:29–32). As believers, we must conduct our entire lives to the glory of God, so that He is glorified in us (John 17:10; 1 Cor. 10:31; 2 Cor. 3:18).

over the threshold of the house; and
[s]the house was filled with the cloud,
and the court was full of the brightness
of the LORD's glory.
5 And the [t]sound of the cheru-
bims' wings was heard *even* to the out-
er court, as [u]the voice of the Almighty
God when he speaketh.
6 And it came to pass, *that* when he
had commanded the man clothed with
linen, saying, Take fire from between
the wheels, from between the cheru-
bims; then he went in, and stood beside
the wheels.
7 And *one* cherub [g]stretched forth
his hand from between the cherubims
unto the fire that *was* between the
cherubims, and took *thereof,* and put *it*
into the hands of *him that was* clothed
with linen: who took *it,* and went out.
8 ¶ [v]And there appeared in the
cherubims the form of a man's hand
under their wings.
9 [w]And when I looked, behold the
four wheels by the cherubims, one
wheel by one cherub, and another
wheel by another cherub: and the ap-
pearance of the wheels *was* as the col-
our of a [x]beryl stone.
10 And *as for* their appearances,
they four had one likeness, as if a
wheel had been in the midst of a wheel.
11 [y]When they went, they went
upon their four sides; they turned not
as they went, but to the place whither
the head looked they followed it; they
turned not as they went.
12 And their whole [h]body, and
their backs, and their hands, and their
wings, and the wheels, *were* full of eyes
round about, *even* the wheels that they
four had.
13 As for the wheels, [i]it was cried
unto them in my hearing, O wheel.
14 [z]And every one had four faces:
the first face *was* the face of a cherub,
and the second face *was* the face of a
man, and the third the face of a lion,
and the fourth the face of an eagle.
15 And the cherubims were lifted
up. This *is* [a]the living creature that I
saw by the river of Chebar.
16 [b]And when the cherubims went,
the wheels went by them: and when the
cherubims lifted up their wings to
mount up from the earth, the same
wheels also turned not from beside
them.
17 [c]When they stood, *these* stood;
and when they were lifted up, *these* lift-
ed up themselves *also:* for the spirit
[j]of the living creature *was* in them.
18 Then [d]the glory of the LORD
[e]departed from off the threshold of
the house, and stood over the cheru-
bims.
19 And [f]the cherubims lifted up
their wings, and mounted up from the
earth in my sight: when they went out,
the wheels also *were* beside them, and
every one stood at the door of the east
gate of the LORD's house; and the glory
of the God of Israel *was* over them
above.
20 [g]This *is* the living creature that
I saw under the God of Israel [h]by the
river of Chebar; and I knew that they
were the cherubims.
21 [i]Every one had four faces
apiece, and every one four wings; and
the likeness of the hands of a man *was*
under their wings.
22 And [j]the likeness of their faces
was the same faces which I saw by the
river of Chebar, their appearances and
themselves: [k]they went every one
straight forward.

Ungodly rulers to be punished

11 MOREOVER [l]THE spirit lift-
ed me up, and brought me unto
[m]the east gate of the LORD's house,
which looketh eastward: and behold
[n]at the door of the gate five and twen-
ty men; among whom I saw Jaazaniah
the son of Azur, and Pelatiah the son
of Benaiah, princes of the people.
2 Then said he unto me, Son of man,

10:4 [s]1 Ki. 8:10 ch. 43:5
10:5 [t]ch. 1:24 [u]Ps. 29:3
10:8 [v]ver. 21
10:9 [w]ch. 1:15 [x]ch. 1:16
10:11 [y]ch. 1:17
10:14 [z]ch. 1:6,10
10:15 [a]ch. 1:5
10:16 [b]ch. 1:19
10:17 [c]ch. 1:12,20,21
10:18 [d]ver. 4 [e]Hos. 9:12
10:19 [f]ch. 11:22
10:20 [g]ver. 15 ch. 1:22 [h]ch. 1:1
10:21 [i]ch. 1:6
10:22 [j]ch. 1:10 [k]ch. 1:12
11:1 [l]ver. 24 ch. 3:12,14 [m]ch. 10:19 [n]See ch. 8:16

[g]Heb. *sent forth* [h]Heb. *flesh* [i]Or, *they were called in my hearing, wheel* [j]Or, *of life*

of the people's sin and idolatry. God left His house reluctantly and gradually, but because of His holiness, He knew He had to separate Himself from the idolatry in the temple.

(2) What happened to Israel and the temple can also happen to churches. If leaders permit sin, Satan, and worldliness to gain a foothold, then God's glory and presence will depart from that congregation; as a result, the church will become an empty shell and the manifestations of the Spirit will be absent (see 1 Cor. 14).

(3) We must fervently desire God's glory and presence and at the same time intensely hate sin and immorality (see Heb. 1:9, note). Any other attitude will lead to spiritual compromise and the judgment of God (see Rev. 2—3; cf. Deut. 31:17; 1 Sam. 4:21; Hos. 9:12).

these *are* the men that devise mischief,
and give wicked counsel in this city:
3 Which say, [k]*It is* not [o]near; let
us build houses: [p]this *city is* the cal-
dron, and we *be* the flesh.
4 ¶ Therefore prophesy against
them, prophesy, O son of man.
5 And [q]the spirit of the LORD fell
upon me, and said unto me, Speak;
Thus saith the LORD; Thus have ye said,
O house of Israel: for I know the things
that come into your mind, *every one of*
them.
6 [r]Ye have multiplied your slain in
this city, and ye have filled the streets
thereof with the slain.
7 Therefore thus saith the Lord
GOD; [s]Your slain whom ye have laid in
the midst of it, they *are* the flesh, and
this *city is* the caldron: [t]but I will
bring you forth out of the midst of it.
8 Ye have feared the sword; and I
will bring a sword upon you, saith the
Lord GOD.
9 And I will bring you out of the
midst thereof, and deliver you into the
hands of strangers, and [u]will execute
judgments among you.
10 [v]Ye shall fall by the sword; I
will judge you in [w]the border of Israel;
[x]and ye shall know that I *am* the LORD.
11 [y]This *city* shall not be your cal-
dron, neither shall ye be the flesh in
the midst thereof; *but* I will judge you
in the border of Israel:
12 And [z]ye shall know that I *am*
the LORD: [l]for ye have not walked in
my statutes, neither executed my judg-
ments, but [a]have done after the man-
ners of the heathen that *are* round
about you.

Hope for the remnant of Israel

13 ¶ And it came to pass, when I
prophesied, that [b]Pelatiah the son of
Benaiah died. Then [c]fell I down upon
my face, and cried with a loud voice,
and said, Ah Lord GOD! wilt thou make
a full end of the remnant of Israel?
14 Again the word of the LORD came
unto me, saying,
15 Son of man, thy brethren, *even*
thy brethren, the men of thy kindred,
and all the house of Israel wholly, *are*
they unto whom the inhabitants of Je-
rusalem have said, Get you far from the
LORD: unto us is this land given in pos-
session.
16 Therefore say, Thus saith the
Lord GOD; Although I have cast them
far off among the heathen, and al-
though I have scattered them among
the countries, [d]yet will I be to them as
a little sanctuary in the countries
where they shall come.
17 Therefore say, Thus saith the
Lord GOD; [e]I will even gather you from
the people, and assemble you out of the
countries where ye have been scat-
tered, and I will give you the land of
Israel.
18 And they shall come thither, and
[f]they shall take away all the detest-
able things thereof and all the abomi-
nations thereof from thence.
19 And [g]I will give them one heart,

11:3 [o]ch. 12:22,27; 2 Pet. 3:4 [p]See Jer. 1:13; ch. 24:3
11:5 [q]ch. 2:2 & 3:24
11:6 [r]ch. 7:23
11:7 [s]ch. 24:3,6; Mic. 3:3 [t]ver. 9
11:9 [u]ch. 5:8
11:10 [v]2 Ki. 25:19-21; Jer. 39:6 & 52:10 [w]1 Ki. 8:65; 2 Ki. 14:25 [x]Ps. 9:16; ch. 6:7 & 13:9,14,21,23
11:11 [y]See ver. 3
11:12 [z]ver. 10 [a]Lev. 18:3,24; Deut. 12:30,31; ch. 8:10,14,16
11:13 [b]Acts 5:5 [c]ch. 9:8
11:16 [d]Ps. 90:1 & 91:9; Is. 8:14
11:17 [e]Jer. 24:5; ch. 38:25 & 34:13
11:18 [f]ch. 37:23
11:19 [g]Jer. 32:39; ch. 36:26; See Zeph. 3:9

[k] Or, It is *not* for us *to build houses near*
[l] Or, *which have not walked*

11:3 LET US BUILD HOUSES. Those who remained in Jerusalem after the Babylonian invasion of 597 B.C. felt that they were secure and favored by God. They thought of themselves as choice portions of meat in a caldron (Jerusalem), while the exiles were the bones. They refused to believe the prophet's message that because of their sins God would destroy them as well.

11:7 I WILL BRING YOU FORTH. God threatened to pour the people out of the pot (Jerusalem) and allow them to be destroyed by Babylon (vv. 8–11).

11:12 HAVE DONE AFTER THE MANNERS OF THE HEATHEN. Just as the nation of Judah adopted the religious practices of the surrounding nations, so God's people are constantly tempted to conform to the ways of the evil societies around them. We must firmly resist the desire to copy the ways and customs of the wicked. Since we belong to God, He calls us to be a holy people separated from our evil generation (see Rom. 12:1–2, notes; see articles on SPIRITUAL SEPARATION FOR BELIEVERS, p. 1814, and THE CHRISTIAN'S RELATIONSHIP TO THE WORLD, p. 2004). The determination to resist the spirit of the world must be accompanied by a bold proclamation of the eternal truth and righteous standards of the gospel.

11:16 A LITTLE SANCTUARY. God answers Ezekiel's question about the remnant of Israel (v. 13) by stating that He still cared for the exiles; he would be a sanctuary for them and would regather them to the promised land (vv. 16–20).

11:17–21 I WILL GIVE YOU THE LAND. This was partially fulfilled when a remnant returned after the Babylonian captivity (beginning in 538 B.C.). Furthermore, these verses point to a future gathering of Israel at the end of this age (see Rev. 12:6, note).

11:19 A NEW SPIRIT WITHIN YOU. This was initially fulfilled at the time of the resurrection of Christ (see article on THE REGENERATION OF THE DISCIPLES, p. 1638) and the outpouring of

and I will put [h]a new spirit within you; and I will take [i]the stony heart out of their flesh, and will give them an heart of flesh:

20 [j]That they may walk in my statutes, and keep mine ordinances, and do them: [k]and they shall be my people, and I will be their God.

Ezek. 36:26-27

21 But *as for them* whose heart walketh after the heart of their detestable things and their abominations, [l]I will recompense their way upon their own heads, saith the Lord GOD.

22 ¶ Then did the cherubims [m]lift up their wings, and the wheels beside them; and the glory of the God of Israel *was* over them above.

23 And [n]the glory of the LORD went up from the midst of the city, and stood [o]upon the mountain [p]which *is* on the east side of the city.

24 ¶ Afterwards [q]the spirit took me up, and brought me in a vision by the spirit of God into Chaldea, to them of the captivity. So the vision that I had seen went up from me.

25 Then I spake unto them of the captivity all the things that the LORD had shown me.

Captivity symbolized

12 THE WORD of the LORD also came unto me, saying,

2 Son of man, thou dwellest in the midst of [r]a rebellious house, which [s]have eyes to see, and see not; they have ears to hear, and hear not: [t]for they *are* a rebellious house.

11:19 [h]Ps. 51:10 Jer. 31:33 ch. 18:31 [i]Zech. 7:12
11:20 [j]Ps. 105:45 [k]Jer. 24:7 ch. 14:11 & 36:28 & 37:27
11:21 [l]ch. 9:10 & 22:31
11:22 [m]ch. 1:19 & 10:19
11:23 [n]ch. 8:4 & 9:3 & 10:4,18 & 43:4 [o]See Zech. 14:4 [p]ch. 43:2
11:24 [q]ch. 8:3
12:2 [r]ch. 2:3,6-8 & 3:26,27 [s]Is. 6:9 & 42:20 Jer. 5:21 Mat. 13:13,14 [t]ch. 2:5
12:6 [u]ver. 11 Is. 8:18 ch. 4:3 & 24:24
12:9 [v]ch. 2:5 [w]ch. 17:12 & 24:19
12:10 [x]Mal. 1:1

3 Therefore, thou son of man, prepare thee [m]stuff for removing, and remove by day in their sight; and thou shalt remove from thy place to another place in their sight: it may be they will consider, though they *be* a rebellious house.

4 Then shalt thou bring forth thy stuff by day in their sight, as stuff for removing: and thou shalt go forth at even in their sight, [n]as they that go forth into captivity.

5 [o]Dig thou through the wall in their sight, and carry out thereby.

6 In their sight shalt thou bear *it* upon *thy* shoulders, *and* carry *it* forth in the twilight: thou shalt cover thy face, that thou see not the ground: [u]for I have set thee *for* a sign unto the house of Israel.

7 And I did so as I was commanded: I brought forth my stuff by day, as stuff for captivity, and in the even I [p]digged through the wall with mine hand; I brought *it* forth in the twilight, *and* I bare *it* upon *my* shoulder in their sight.

8 ¶ And in the morning came the word of the LORD unto me, saying,

9 Son of man, hath not the house of Israel, [v]the rebellious house, said unto thee, [w]What doest thou?

10 Say thou unto them, Thus saith the Lord GOD; This [x]burden *concerneth* the prince in Jerusalem, and all the house of Israel that *are* among them.

[m] Or, *instruments* [n] Heb. *as the goings forth of captivity* [o] Heb. *Dig for thee* [p] Heb. *digged for me*

---

the Holy Spirit on Pentecost (see Acts 2:4, note; cf. Joel 2:28–29). Ezekiel prophesied that the people would be empowered by the Holy Spirit to live according to the will and law of God. God's Holy Spirit, with all His gifts and activity, is available today to all who place their faith in Jesus Christ.

11:23 THE GLORY OF THE LORD WENT UP. God's glory departed from Jerusalem and stopped at the Mount of Olives (see 10:4, note). Later, Ezekiel had a vision of His glory returning at a time when the Lord sets up His eternal kingdom (43:1–4).

12:2 A REBELLIOUS HOUSE. Judah refused to believe God would destroy Jerusalem and eliminate the Davidic king. Because they were God's chosen people, they felt the Lord would protect them regardless of their sinful actions. Thus the Lord appointed Ezekiel to be a sign to the nation (v. 6), portraying in symbolic actions what the people would experience as a result of their rebellion; here Ezekiel gives two further dramatic demonstrations (vv. 3–7 and vv. 17–20) of God's coming judgment on the people of Judah.

12:3–7 PREPARE THEE STUFF FOR REMOVING. Ezekiel was to play out the role of a captive heading to another place while leaving everything behind except the absolute essentials needed for the journey. This action portrayed that another wave of exiles from Jerusalem would be brought to Babylon; it also discouraged the exiles from unrealistically expecting to return soon to Jerusalem.

12:5 DIG THOU THROUGH THE WALL. This action illustrated the Jews' desperate attempt to escape captivity.

12:6 COVER THY FACE. This action probably refers to the disgrace and grief that would be experienced by the captives.

12:10–13 THE PRINCE IN JERUSALEM. "The prince" is Judah's last king, Zedekiah, a resident of Jerusalem. Ezekiel prophesied that God had destined him for judgment. He would be taken captive to Babylon; yet he would never see it (v. 13), for he would be blinded by his captors (see 2 Ki. 25:7; Jer. 39:6–7).

11 Say, [y]I *am* your sign: like as I
have done, so shall it be done unto
them: [z]they[q] shall remove *and* go
into captivity.
12 And [a]the prince that *is* among
them shall bear upon *his* shoulder in
the twilight, and shall go forth: they
shall dig through the wall to carry
out thereby: he shall cover his face,
that he see not the ground with *his*
eyes.
13 My [b]net also will I spread upon
him, and he shall be taken in my snare:
and [c]I will bring him to Babylon *to* the
land of the Chaldeans; yet shall he not
see it, though he shall die there.
14 And [d]I will scatter toward every
wind all that *are* about him to help him,
and all his bands; and [e]I will draw out
the sword after them.
15 [f]And they shall know that I *am*
the LORD, when I shall scatter them
among the nations, and disperse them
in the countries.
16 [g]But I will leave [r]a few men of
them from the sword, from the famine,
and from the pestilence; that they may
declare all their abominations among
the heathen whither they come; and
they shall know that I *am* the LORD.
17 ¶ Moreover the word of the LORD
came to me, saying,
18 Son of man, [h]eat thy bread with
quaking, and drink thy water with
trembling and with carefulness;
19 And say unto the people of the
land, Thus saith the Lord GOD of the
inhabitants of Jerusalem, *and* of
the land of Israel; They shall eat their
bread with carefulness, and drink their
water with astonishment, that her land
may [i]be desolate from [s]all that is
therein, [j]because of the violence of all
them that dwell therein.
20 And the cities that are inhabited
shall be laid waste, and the land shall
be desolate; and ye shall know that I
am the LORD.
21 ¶ And the word of the LORD came
unto me, saying,
22 Son of man, what *is* that proverb
that ye have in the land of Israel, saying,
[k]The days are prolonged, and every vision faileth?
23 Tell them therefore, Thus saith
the Lord GOD; I will make this proverb
to cease, and they shall no more use it
as a proverb in Israel; but say unto
them, [l]The days are at hand, and the
effect of every vision.
24 For [m]there shall be no more any
[n]vain vision nor flattering divination
within the house of Israel.
25 For I *am* the LORD: I will speak,
and [o]the word that I shall speak shall
come to pass; it shall be no more prolonged: for in your days, O rebellious
house, will I say the word, and will perform it, saith the Lord GOD.
26 ¶ Again the word of the LORD
came to me, saying,
27 [p]Son of man, behold, *they of* the
house of Israel say, The vision that he
seeth *is* for many days *to come,* and he
prophesieth of the times *that are* far off.
28 [q]Therefore say unto them, Thus
saith the Lord GOD; There shall none of
my words be prolonged any more, but
the word which I have spoken shall be
done, saith the Lord GOD.

Prophecy against false prophets

13 AND THE word of the LORD
came unto me, saying,
2 Son of man, prophesy against the
prophets of Israel that prophesy, and
say thou unto [r]them[t] that prophesy
out of their own [s]hearts, Hear ye the
word of the LORD;
3 Thus saith the Lord GOD; Woe
unto the foolish prophets, that [u]follow their own spirit, [v]and have seen
nothing!
4 O Israel, thy prophets are [t]like
the foxes in the deserts.
5 Ye [u]have not gone up into the
[w]gaps, neither [x]made up the hedge
for the house of Israel to stand in the
battle in the day of the LORD.

12:11 [y]ver:6 [z]2 Ki. 25:4,5,7 **12:12** [a]Jer. 39:4 **12:13** [b]Job 19:6 Jer. 52:9 Lam. 1:13 ch. 17:20 [c]2 Ki. 25:7 Jer. 52:11 ch. 17:16 **12:14** [d]2 Ki. 25:4 ch. 5:10 [e]ch. 5:2,12 **12:15** [f]ver. 16,20 Ps. 9:16 ch. 6:7,14 & 11:10 **12:16** [g]ch. 6:8-10 **12:18** [h]ch. 4:16 **12:19** [i]Zech. 7:14 [j]Ps. 107:34 **12:22** [k]ver. 27 ch. 11:3 Amos 6:3 2 Pet. 3:4 **12:23** [l]Joel 2:1 Zeph. 1:14 **12:24** [m]ch. 13:23 [n]Lam. 2:14 **12:25** [o]ver. 28 Is. 55:11 Dan. 9:12 Luke 21:33 **12:27** [p]ver. 22 **12:28** [q]ver. 23,25 **13:2** [r]ver. 17 [s]Jer. 14:14 & 23:16,26 **13:4** [t]Sol. 2:15 **13:5** [u]Ps. 106:23,30 ch. 22:30

[q] Heb. *by removing go into captivity* [r] Heb. *men of number* [s] Heb. *the fulness thereof* [t] Heb. *them that are prophets out of their own hearts* [u] Heb. *walk after* [v] Or, *and things which they have not seen* [w] Or, *breaches* [x] Heb. *hedged the hedge*

12:21–28 THE DAYS ARE PROLONGED. The Jewish exiles refused to believe that Ezekiel's messages were true. So far nothing had happened, and thus they continued to expect that a time of peace was at hand. God declared, however, that judgment was imminent.

13:2–23 THEM THAT PROPHESY OUT OF THEIR OWN HEARTS. God condemns the false prophets of Israel who were proclaiming that there would be no coming judgment. They were falsely predicting the people were secure even though they were living in sin and idolatry (see Jer. 6:14, note; 23:17, note). God was against such prophets (v. 8).

6 [v]They have seen vanity and lying divination, saying, The LORD saith: and the LORD hath not sent them: and they have made *others* to hope that they would confirm the word.

7 Have ye not seen a vain vision, and have ye not spoken a lying divination, whereas ye say, The LORD saith *it;* albeit I have not spoken?

8 Therefore thus saith the Lord GOD; Because ye have spoken vanity, and seen lies, therefore, behold, I *am* against you, saith the Lord GOD.

9 And mine hand shall be upon the prophets that see vanity, and that divine lies: they shall not be in the [y]assembly of my people, [w]neither shall they be written in the writing of the house of Israel, [x]neither shall they enter into the land of Israel; [y]and ye shall know that I *am* the Lord GOD.

10 ¶ Because, even because they have seduced my people, saying, [z]Peace; and *there was* no peace; and one built up [z]a wall, and, lo, others [a]daubed it with untempered *mortar:*

11 Say unto them which daub *it* with untempered *mortar,* that it shall fall: [b]there shall be an overflowing shower; and ye, O great hailstones, shall fall; and a stormy wind shall rend *it.*

12 Lo, when the wall is fallen, shall it not be said unto you, Where *is* the daubing wherewith ye have daubed *it?*

13 Therefore thus saith the Lord GOD; I will even rend *it* with a stormy wind in my fury; and there shall be an overflowing shower in mine anger, and great hailstones in *my* fury to consume *it.*

14 So will I break down the wall that ye have daubed with untempered *mortar,* and bring it down to the ground, so that the foundation thereof shall be discovered, and it shall fall, and ye shall be consumed in the midst thereof: [c]and ye shall know that I *am* the LORD.

15 Thus will I accomplish my wrath upon the wall, and upon them that have daubed it with untempered *mortar,* and will say unto you, The wall *is* no *more,* neither they that daubed it;

16 *To wit,* the prophets of Israel which prophesy concerning Jerusalem, and which [d]see visions of peace for her, and *there is* no peace, saith the Lord GOD.

17 ¶ Likewise, thou son of man, [e]set thy face against the daughters of thy people, [f]which prophesy out of their own heart; and prophesy thou against them,

18 And say, Thus saith the Lord GOD; Woe to the *women* that sew pillows to all [a]armholes, and make kerchiefs upon the head of every stature to hunt souls! Will ye [g]hunt the souls of my people, and will ye save the souls alive *that come* unto you?

19 And will ye pollute me among my people [h]for handfuls of barley and for pieces of bread, to slay the souls that should not die, and to save the souls alive that should not live, by your lying to my people that hear *your* lies?

20 Wherefore thus saith the Lord GOD; Behold, I *am* against your pillows, wherewith ye there hunt the souls [b]to make *them* fly, and I will tear them from your arms, and will let the souls go, *even* the souls that ye hunt to make *them* fly.

21 Your kerchiefs also will I tear, and deliver my people out of your hand, and they shall be no more in your hand to be hunted; [i]and ye shall know that I *am* the LORD.

22 Because with lies ye have made the heart of the righteous sad, whom I have not made sad; and [j]strength-

13:6 [v]ver. 23 ch. 12:24 & 22:28 **13:9** [w]Ezra 2:59,62 Neh. 7:5 Ps. 69:28 [x]ch. 20:38 [y]ch. 11:10,12 **13:10** [z]Jer. 6:14 & 8:11 [a]ch. 22:28 **13:11** [b]ch. 38:22 **13:14** [c]ver. 9,21,23 ch. 14:8 **13:16** [d]Jer. 6:14 & 28:9 **13:17** [e]ch. 20:46 & 21:2 [f]ver. 2 **13:18** [g]2 Pet. 2:14 **13:19** [h]See Prov. 28:21 Mic. 3:5 **13:21** [i]ver. 9 **13:22** [j]Jer. 23:14

[y] Or, *secret,* or, *council* [z] Or, *a slight wall*
[a] Or, *elbows* [b] Or, *into gardens*

13:10 SEDUCED MY PEOPLE, SAYING, PEACE. The false prophets seduced the people into a false sense of security by pronouncing God's peace and salvation to them while they continued in rebellion against His laws. For this God would cut them off from the nation of Israel and from His salvation (see previous note). (1) Today, there are false prophets in the church who teach that a person can be a genuine believer and possess eternal life in Christ, yet at the same time participate in and enjoy the sins of immorality, greed, homosexuality, sorcery, or any other kind of abominable evil. (2) The apostle Paul states that believers must not be deceived by such lying words (Eph. 5:6), for those who do such things will have no inheritance in the kingdom of God (see 1 Cor. 6:9, note; Gal. 5:21, note; Eph. 5:5, note).

13:18 WOE TO THE *WOMEN*. These women were involved in sorcery, spiritism, and black magic. They were even using the powers of evil to bring death to certain individuals (v. 19). These false prophetesses would tie cloth to their wrists to serve as magic charms and place veils over their heads.

ened the hands of the wicked, that he
should not return from his wicked way,
[c] [d]by promising him life:
23 Therefore [k]ye shall see no more
vanity, nor divine divinations: for I will
deliver my people out of your hand: and
ye shall know that I *am* the LORD.

Call to turn from idols

14 THEN [l]CAME certain of the
elders of Israel unto me, and
sat before me.
2 And the word of the LORD came
unto me, saying,
3 Son of man, these men have set up
their idols in their heart, and put [m]the
stumblingblock of their iniquity before
their face: [n]should I be inquired of at
all by them?
4 Therefore speak unto them, and
say unto them, Thus saith the Lord
GOD; Every man of the house of Israel
that setteth up his idols in his heart,
and putteth the stumblingblock of his
iniquity before his face, and cometh to
the prophet; I the LORD will answer him
that cometh according to the multitude
of his idols;
5 That I may take the house of Isra-
el in their own heart, because they are
all estranged from me through their
idols.
6 ¶ Therefore say unto the house of
Israel, Thus saith the Lord GOD; Re-
pent, and turn [e]*yourselves* from your
idols; and turn away your faces from
all your abominations.
7 For every one of the house of Isra-
el, or of the stranger that sojourneth in
Israel, which separateth himself from
me, and setteth up his idols in his
heart, and putteth the stumblingblock
of his iniquity before his face, and com-

13:23 [k]ver. 6 ch. 12:24 Mic. 3:6
14:1 [l]ch. 8:1 & 20:1 & 33:31
14:3 [m]ver. 4,7 ch. 7:19 [n]2 Ki. 3:13
14:8 [o]Lev. 17:10 & 20:3,5,6 Jer. 44:11 ch. 15:7 [p]Num. 26:10 Deut. 28:37 ch. 5:15 [q]ch. 6:7
14:9 [r]1 Ki. 22:23 Job 12:16 Jer. 4:10 2 Thes. 2:11
14:11 [s]2 Pet. 2:15 [t]ch. 11:20 & 37:27
14:13 [u]Lev. 26:26 Is. 3:1 ch. 4:16 & 5:16
14:14 [v]ver. 16,18,20 Jer. 15:1 See Jer. 7:16 & 11:14 & 14:11 [w]Prov. 11:4
14:15 [x]Lev. 26:22 ch. 5:17

eth to a prophet to inquire of him con-
cerning me; I the LORD will answer him
by myself:
8 And [o]I will set my face against
that man, and will make him a [p]sign
and a proverb, and I will cut him off
from the midst of my people; [q]and ye
shall know that I *am* the LORD.
9 And if the prophet be deceived
when he hath spoken a thing, I the
LORD [r]have deceived that prophet, and
I will stretch out my hand upon him,
and will destroy him from the midst of
my people Israel.
10 And they shall bear the punish-
ment of their iniquity: the punishment
of the prophet shall be even as the pun-
ishment of him that seeketh *unto him;*
11 That the house of Israel may
[s]go no more astray from me, neither
be polluted any more with all their
transgressions; [t]but that they may be
my people, and I may be their God,
saith the Lord GOD.

Deliverance through righteousness

12 ¶ The word of the LORD came
again to me, saying,
13 Son of man, when the land sin-
neth against me by trespassing griev-
ously, then will I stretch out mine hand
upon it, and will break the [u]staff of the
bread thereof, and will send famine
upon it, and will cut off man and beast
from it:
14 [v]Though these three men,
Noah, Daniel, and Job, were in it, they
should deliver *but* their own souls [w]by
their righteousness, saith the Lord
GOD.
15 ¶ If I cause [x]noisome beasts to

[c] Or, *that I should save his life* [d] Heb. *by quickening him* [e] Or, others

14:3 IDOLS IN THEIR HEART. The elders of Israel (v. 1) were guilty of idolatry in their heart, i.e., they were not loyal to God and His word. They spurned God's will and desired an ungodly way of life. Therefore, God refused to guide them by answering their prayers. In a similar manner, those today who look for guidance from God will find no help from His Spirit if their hearts are filled with ungodly desires for the sinful things of the world (see article on THE NATURE OF IDOLATRY, p. 428).

14:7 WHICH SEPARATETH HIMSELF FROM ME. Believers who forsake God to pursue sinful and immoral lives, while continuing to seek religious comfort, assurance, and guidance from Him, make God their enemy (v. 8). He will judge and punish such people. They should either repent of and forsake their sinful ways or leave the fellowship of believers (see 1 Cor. 5:5, note; 11:27, note).

14:9–10 THE PROPHET . . . DESTROY HIM. God would destroy any prophet who tolerated, supported, or encouraged the idolatry of the Israelites. Likewise, ministers of the church who tolerate immoral members and refuse to condemn their persistent wickedness by expelling them from the congregation (see previous note) will be considered as guilty as the hypocritical members themselves.

14:14 NOAH, DANIEL, AND JOB. The judgment coming upon Jerusalem was so certain that even these three men of God known for their righteousness (Gen. 6:9; Job 1:1,8; 2:3; Dan. 6:4–5,22) could not deliver anyone by their prayers of intercession.

pass through the land, and they [f]spoil
it, so that it be desolate, that no man
may pass through because of the
beasts:
16 [y]*Though* these three men *were*
[g]in it, *as* I live, saith the Lord GOD,
they shall deliver neither sons nor
daughters; they only shall be deliv-
ered, but the land shall be desolate.
17 ¶ Or *if* [z]I bring a sword upon
that land, and say, Sword, go through
the land; so that I [a]cut off man and
beast from it:
18 [b]Though these three men *were*
in it, *as* I live, saith the Lord GOD, they
shall deliver neither sons nor daugh-
ters, but they only shall be delivered
themselves.
19 ¶ Or *if* I send [c]a pestilence into
that land, and [d]pour out my fury upon
it in blood, to cut off from it man and
beast:
20 [e]Though Noah, Daniel, and Job,
were in it, *as* I live, saith the Lord GOD,
they shall deliver neither son nor
daughter; they shall *but* deliver their
own souls by their righteousness.
21 For thus saith the Lord GOD;
[h]How much more when [f]I send my
four sore judgments upon Jerusalem,
the sword, and the famine, and the noi-
some beast, and the pestilence, to cut
off from it man and beast?
22 ¶ [g]Yet, behold, therein shall be
left a remnant that shall be brought
forth, *both* sons and daughters: behold,
they shall come forth unto you, and
[h]ye shall see their way and their do-
ings: and ye shall be comforted con-
cerning the evil that I have brought
upon Jerusalem, *even* concerning all
that I have brought upon it.
23 And they shall comfort you,
when ye see their ways and their do-
ings: and ye shall know that I have not
done [i]without cause all that I have
done in it, saith the Lord GOD.

The parable of the vine

15 AND THE word of the LORD
came unto me, saying,
2 Son of man, What is the vine tree
more than any tree, *or than* a branch
which is among the trees of the forest?
3 Shall wood be taken thereof to do
any work? or will *men* take a pin of it
to hang any vessel thereon?
4 Behold, [j]it is cast into the fire for
fuel; the fire devoureth both the ends
of it, and the midst of it is burned. [i]Is
it meet for *any* work?
5 Behold, when it was whole, it was
[j]meet for no work: how much less
shall it be meet yet for *any* work, when
the fire hath devoured it, and it is
burned?
6 ¶ Therefore thus saith the Lord
GOD; As the vine tree among the trees
of the forest, which I have given to the
fire for fuel, so will I give the inhabi-
tants of Jerusalem.
7 And [k]I will set my face against
them; [l]they shall go out from *one* fire,
and *another* fire shall devour them;
[m]and ye shall know that I *am* the LORD,
when I set my face against them.
8 And I will make the land desolate,
because they have [k]committed a tres-
pass, saith the Lord GOD.

The judgment upon Israel

16 AGAIN THE word of the LORD
came unto me, saying,
2 Son of man, [n]cause Jerusalem to
know her abominations,
3 And say, Thus saith the Lord GOD

14:16 [y]ver. 14,18,20
14:17 [z]Lev. 26:25 ch. 5:12 & 21:3,4 & 29:8 & 38:21 [a]ch. 25:13 Zeph. 1:3
14:18 [b]ver. 14
14:19 [c]2 Sam. 24:15 ch. 38:22 [d]ch. 7:8
14:20 [e]ver. 14
14:21 [f]ch. 5:17 & 33:27
14:22 [g]ch. 6:8 [h]ch. 20:43
14:23 [i]Jer. 22:8,9
15:4 [j]John 15:6
15:7 [k]Lev. 17:10 ch. 14:8 [l]Is. 24:18 [m]ch. 7:4
16:2 [n]ch. 20:4 & 22:2

[f] Or, *bereave* [g] Heb. *in the midst of it* [h] Or, *Also when* [i] Heb. *Will it prosper?* [j] Heb. *made fit* [k] Heb. *trespassed a trespass*

14:16 DELIVER NEITHER SONS OR DAUGHTERS. Judah's moral climate had become so sinful that the righteous prayers of Noah, Daniel, and Job would not be sufficient to save even their own children. Believers must be very careful about the social and educational environment in which they place their children. It may become so ungodly that neither our righteous living nor our fervent prayers will be enough to bring them to accept Christ as their Lord and Savior.

15:2–8 THE VINE. The people of Jerusalem are compared to a vine that does not bear fruit and is therefore useless. The fruit of righteousness and faithfulness to the Lord could not be found in them (v. 8). Thus they would be burned in the fire (v. 6). Jesus likewise taught that all believers who fail to abide faithfully in Him and to bear fruit will be cut off and cast into the fire (see John 15:1–7, notes).

16:1–63 JERUSALEM. This chapter portrays Jerusalem as a wife and God as her husband (see Hos. 1:2, note). In the beginning Jerusalem had no natural endowments that would entitle her to be God's chosen city. But God in love lifted her up, took care of her, and made her into a city of beauty and splendor. Yet she was ungrateful to her husband, became unfaithful, and began committing adultery with anyone who passed by. Because of her harlotry, she would be put to death.

16:3 LAND OF CANAAN. Jerusalem was originally founded not by Hebrews but by the heathen

unto Jerusalem; Thy [l]birth [o]and thy nativity *is* of the land of Canaan; [p]thy father *was* an Amorite, and thy mother an Hittite.

4 And *as for* thy nativity, [q]in the day thou wast born thy navel was not cut, neither wast thou washed in water [m]to supple *thee;* thou wast not salted at all, nor swaddled at all.

5 None eye pitied thee, to do any of these unto thee, to have compassion upon thee; but thou wast cast out in the open field, to the loathing of thy person, in the day that thou wast born.

6 ¶ And when I passed by thee, and saw thee [n]polluted in thine own blood, I said unto thee *when thou wast* in thy blood, Live; yea, I said unto thee *when thou wast* in thy blood, Live.

7 [r]I have [o]caused thee to multiply as the bud of the field, and thou hast increased and waxen great, and thou art come to [p]excellent ornaments: *thy* breasts are fashioned, and thine hair is grown, whereas thou *wast* naked and bare.

8 Now when I passed by thee, and looked upon thee, behold, thy time *was* the time of love; [s]and I spread my skirt over thee, and covered thy nakedness: yea, I sware unto thee, and entered into a covenant with thee, saith the Lord GOD, and [t]thou becamest mine.

9 Then washed I thee with water; yea, I thoroughly washed away thy [q]blood from thee, and I anointed thee with oil.

10 I clothed thee also with broidered work, and shod thee with badgers' skin, and I girded thee about with fine linen, and I covered thee with silk.

11 I decked thee also with ornaments, and I [u]put bracelets upon thy hands, [v]and a chain on thy neck.

12 And I put a jewel on thy [r]forehead, and earrings in thine ears, and a beautiful crown upon thine head.

13 Thus wast thou decked with gold and silver; and thy raiment *was of* fine linen, and silk, and broidered work; [w]thou didst eat fine flour, and honey, and oil: and thou wast exceeding [x]beautiful, and thou didst prosper into a kingdom.

14 And [y]thy renown went forth among the heathen for thy beauty: for it *was* perfect through my comeliness, which I had put upon thee, saith the Lord GOD.

15 ¶ [z]But thou didst trust in thine own beauty, [a]and playedst the harlot because of thy renown, and pouredst out thy fornications on every one that passed by; his it was.

16 [b]And of thy garments thou didst take, and deckedst thy high places with divers colours, and playedst the harlot thereupon: *the like things* shall not come, neither shall it be *so.*

17 Thou hast also taken thy fair jewels of my gold and of my silver, which I had given thee, and madest to thyself images [s]of men, and didst commit whoredom with them,

18 And tookest thy broidered garments, and coveredst them: and thou hast set mine oil and mine incense before them.

19 [c]My meat also which I gave thee, fine flour, and oil, and honey, *wherewith* I fed thee, thou hast even set it before them for [t]a sweet savour: and *thus* it was, saith the Lord GOD.

16:3 [o]ch. 21:30 [p]ver. 45
16:4 [q]Hos. 2:3
16:7 [r]Ex. 1:7
16:8 [s]Ruth 3:9 [t]Ex. 19:5 Jer. 2:2
16:11 [u]Gen. 24:22 [v]Prov. 1:9
16:13 [w]Deut. 32:13,14 [x]Ps. 48:2
16:14 [y]Lam. 2:15
16:15 [z]Deut. 32:15 Jer. 7:4 Mic. 3:11 [a]Is. 1:21 & 57:8 Jer. 2:20 & 3:2,6,20 ch. 23:3,8
16:16 [b]2 Ki. 23:7 ch. 7:20 Hos. 2:8
16:19 [c]Hos. 2:8

[l] Heb. *cutting out,* or, *habitation* [m] Or, *when I looked* upon thee [n] Or, *trodden under foot* [o] Heb. *made thee a million* [p] Heb. *ornament of ornaments* [q] Heb. *bloods* [r] Heb. *nose* [s] Heb. *of a male* [t] Heb. *a savour of rest*

people of Canaan (cf. Gen. 14:18; Josh. 15:63).

16:6 LIVE. God gave Jerusalem life, choosing it to be the holy city and inspiring David to capture it from the Jebusites (2 Sam. 5:6–10).

16:8–14 ENTERED INTO A COVENANT. As chosen by God, Jerusalem received blessings and gifts from the Lord. Under His care she grew to full maturity, and the Lord gave her great beauty and claimed her for Himself. After the marriage her fame spread throughout the ancient world (especially during the reigns of David and Solomon).

16:8 SPREAD MY SKIRT OVER THEE. This metaphor is symbolic of protection and of entering into a marriage contract (see Ruth 3:9, note).

16:15 PLAYEDST THE HARLOT. Jerusalem began to trust in her beauty and riches (cf. Deut. 6:10–12) rather than in God. She became a prostitute in the sense of spiritually becoming unfaithful to and forsaking the Lord. She entered into alliances with other nations (cf. 1 Ki. 11:1–13) and began to worship their gods. Today spiritual adultery is committed by those churches or individuals who turn from the Lord and give themselves to sinful pleasures and worldly values rather than to God and His kingdom.

16:17 COMMIT WHOREDOM. The people of Jerusalem not only committed spiritual harlotry, but they also participated in physical sexual immorality in the fertility rites of the Canaanite religions.

20 [d]Moreover thou hast taken thy sons and thy daughters, whom thou hast borne unto me, and these hast thou sacrificed unto them [u]to be devoured. *Is this* of thy whoredoms a small matter,

21 That thou hast slain my children, and delivered them to cause them to pass through *the fire* for them?

22 And in all thine abominations and thy whoredoms thou hast not remembered the days of thy [e]youth, [f]when thou wast naked and bare, *and* wast polluted in thy blood.

23 And it came to pass after all thy wickedness, (woe, woe unto thee! saith the Lord GOD;)

24 *That* [g]thou hast also built unto thee an [v]eminent place, and [h]hast made thee an high place in every street.

25 Thou hast built thy high place [i]at every head of the way, and hast made thy beauty to be abhorred, and hast opened thy feet to every one that passed by, and multiplied thy whoredoms.

26 Thou hast also committed fornication with [j]the Egyptians thy neighbours, great of flesh; and hast increased thy whoredoms, to provoke me to anger.

27 Behold, therefore I have stretched out my hand over thee, and have diminished thine ordinary *food,* and delivered thee unto the will of them that hate thee, [k]the [w]daughters of the Philistines, which are ashamed of thy lewd way.

28 Thou hast played the whore also with the Assyrians, because thou wast unsatiable; yea, thou hast played the harlot with them, and yet couldest not be satisfied.

29 Thou hast moreover multiplied thy fornication in the land of Canaan [l]unto Chaldea; and yet thou wast not satisfied herewith.

30 How weak is thine heart, saith the Lord GOD, seeing thou doest all these *things,* the work of an imperious whorish woman;

31 [x]In that [m]thou buildest thine eminent place in the head of every way, and makest thine high place in every street; and hast not been as an harlot, in that thou scornest hire;

32 *But as* a wife that committeth adultery, *which* taketh strangers instead of her husband!

33 They give gifts to all whores: but [n]thou givest thy gifts to all thy lovers, and [y]hirest them, that they may come unto thee on every side for thy whoredom.

34 And the contrary is in thee from *other* women in thy whoredoms, whereas none followeth thee to commit whoredoms: and in that thou givest a reward, and no reward is given unto thee, therefore thou art contrary.

35 ¶ Wherefore, O harlot, hear the word of the LORD:

36 Thus saith the Lord GOD; Because thy filthiness was poured out, and thy nakedness discovered through thy whoredoms with thy lovers, and with all the idols of thy abominations, and by [o]the blood of thy children, which thou didst give unto them;

37 Behold, therefore [p]I will gather all thy lovers, with whom thou hast taken pleasure, and all *them* that thou hast loved, with all *them* that thou hast hated; I will even gather them round about against thee, and will discover thy nakedness unto them, that they may see all thy nakedness.

38 And I will judge thee, [z]as [q]women that break wedlock and [r]shed blood are judged; and I will give thee blood in fury and jealousy.

39 And I will also give thee into their hand, and they shall throw down [s]thine eminent place, and shall break down thy high places: [t]they shall strip thee also of thy clothes, and shall take [a]thy fair jewels, and leave thee naked and bare.

40 [u]They shall also bring up a company against thee, [v]and they shall

16:20 [d]2 Ki. 16:3 Ps. 106:37 Is. 57:5 Jer. 7:31 ch. 20:26
16:22 [e]ver. 43,60 Jer. 2:2 Hos. 11:1 [f]ver. 4,5,6
16:24 [g]ver. 31 [h]Is. 57:5,7 Jer. 2:20 & 3:2
16:25 [i]Prov. 9:14
16:26 [j]ch. 8:10,14
16:27 [k]ver. 57 2 Chr. 28:18
16:29 [l]ch. 23:14
16:31 [m]ver. 24,39
16:33 [n]Is. 30:6 Hos. 8:9
16:36 [o]ver. 20 Jer. 2:34
16:37 [p]Jer. 13:22,26 Lam. 1:8 ch. 23:9,10,22,29 Hos. 2:10 & 8:10 Nah. 3:5
16:38 [q]Lev. 20:10 Deut. 22:22 ch. 23:45 [r]See ver. 20,36 Gen. 9:6 Ex. 21:12
16:39 [s]ver. 24,31 [t]ch. 23:26 Hos. 2:3
16:40 [u]ch. 23:46 [v]John 8:5,7

[u] Heb. *to devour* [v] Or, *brothel house* [w] Or, *cities* [x] Or, *In thy daughters is thine* [y] Heb. *bribest* [z] Heb. *with judgments of* [a] Heb. *instruments of thine ornament*

16:20 SONS ... DAUGHTERS ... SACRIFICED. Ultimately the apostasy of Jerusalem resulted in their participation in child sacrifice (cf. 2 Ki. 16:3; 21:6) and all kinds of religious abominations of the pagans (vv. 21–25).

16:37–42 THEREFORE I WILL GATHER ALL THY LOVERS. Jerusalem had engaged in spiritual adultery with other nations and their gods (see v. 15, note). Now God would use those very nations to punish her. They would bring such devastating destruction that there would be no need of further punishment.

stone thee with stones, and thrust thee
through with their swords.
41 And they shall [w]burn thine
houses with fire, and [x]execute judg-
ments upon thee in the sight of many
women: and I will cause thee to
[y]cease from playing the harlot, and
thou also shalt give no hire any more.
42 So [z]will I make my fury toward
thee to rest, and my jealousy shall de-
part from thee, and I will be quiet, and
will be no more angry.
43 Because [a]thou hast not remem-
bered the days of thy youth, but hast
fretted me in all these *things;* behold,
therefore [b]I also will recompense thy
way upon *thine* head, saith the Lord
GOD: and thou shalt not commit this
lewdness above all thine abomina-
tions.
44 ¶ Behold, every one that useth
proverbs shall use *this* proverb against
thee, saying, As *is* the mother, *so is* her
daughter.
45 Thou *art* thy mother's daughter,
that loatheth her husband and her chil-
dren; and thou *art* the sister of thy sis-
ters, which loathed their husbands and
their children: [c]your mother *was* an
Hittite, and your father an Amorite.
46 And thine elder sister *is* Samar-
ia, she and her daughters that dwell at
thy left hand: and [d]thy[b] younger sis-
ter, that dwelleth at thy right hand, *is*
Sodom and her daughters.
47 Yet hast thou not walked after
their ways, nor done after their abomi-
nations: but, [c]as *if that were* a very
little *thing,* [e]thou wast corrupted
more than they in all thy ways.
48 *As* I live, saith the Lord GOD,
[f]Sodom thy sister hath not done, she
nor her daughters, as thou hast done,
thou and thy daughters.
49 Behold, this was the iniquity of
thy sister Sodom, pride, [g]fulness of
bread, and abundance of idleness was
in her and in her daughters, neither did
she strengthen the hand of the poor
and needy.
50 And they were haughty, and
[h]committed abomination before me:
therefore [i]I took them away as I saw
good.
51 Neither hath Samaria committed
half of thy sins; but thou hast multi-
plied thine abominations more than
they, and [j]hast justified thy sisters in
all thine abominations which thou hast
done.
52 Thou also, which hast judged thy
sisters, bear thine own shame for thy
sins that thou hast committed more
abominable than they: they are more
righteous than thou: yea, be thou con-
founded also, and bear thy shame, in
that thou hast justified thy sisters.
53 [k]When I shall bring again their
captivity, [l]the captivity of Sodom and
her daughters, and the captivity of Sa-
maria and her daughters, then *will I*
bring again the captivity of thy captives
in the midst of them:
54 That thou mayest bear thine own
shame, and mayest be confounded in
all that thou hast done, in that thou art
[m]a comfort unto them.
55 When thy sisters, Sodom and her
daughters, shall return to their former
estate, and Samaria and her daughters
shall return to their former estate,
then thou and thy daughters shall re-
turn to your former estate.
56 For thy sister Sodom was not
[d]mentioned by thy mouth in the day of
thy [e]pride,
57 Before thy wickedness was dis-
covered, as at the time of *thy* [n]re-
proach of the daughters of [f]Syria, and
all *that are* round about her, [o]the
daughters of the Philistines, which
[g]despise thee round about.
58 [p]Thou hast [h]borne thy lewd-
ness and thine abominations, saith the
LORD.
59 For thus saith the Lord GOD; I
will even deal with thee as thou hast
done, which hast [q]despised [r]the oath
in breaking the covenant.
60 ¶ Nevertheless I will [s]remem-

16:41 [w]Deut. 13:16 2 Ki. 25:9 Jer. 39:8 & 52:13 [x]ch. 5:8 & 23:10,48 [y]ch. 23:27 **16:42** [z]ch. 5:13 **16:43** [a]ver. 22 Ps. 78:42 [b]ch. 9:10 & 11:21 & 22:31 **16:45** [c]ver. 3 **16:46** [d]Deut. 32:32 Is. 1:10 **16:47** [e]ver. 48,51 2 Ki. 21:9 ch. 5:6,7 **16:48** [f]Mat. 10:15 & 11:24 **16:49** [g]Gen. 13:10 **16:50** [h]Gen. 13:13 & 18:20 & 19:5 [i]Gen. 19:24 **16:51** [j]Jer. 3:11 Mat. 12:41 **16:53** [k]See Is. 1:9 & ver. 60 [l]Jer. 20:16 **16:54** [m]ch. 14:22 **16:57** [n]2 Ki. 16:5 2 Chr. 28:18 Is. 7:1 & 14:28 [o]ver. 27 **16:58** [p]ch. 23:49 **16:59** [q]ch. 17:13 [r]Deut. 29:12 **16:60** [s]Ps. 106:45

[b] Heb. *lesser than thou* [c] Or, *that was loathed as a small* thing [d] Heb. *for a report,* or, *hearing* [e] Heb. *prides,* or, *excellencies* [f] Heb. *Aram* [g] Or, *spoil* [h] Heb. *borne them*

16:43 THOU HAST NOT REMEMBERED . . . THY YOUTH. In her formative days, Jerusalem had been dependent on the Lord and on His blessings. But she had forgotten those days and was now seeking after other gods. This same tragic error is committed by churches or denominations when they no longer hunger for God's presence or seek first His kingdom in the righteousness, peace, joy, and power in the Holy Spirit (cf. Rom. 14:17). Instead, they tolerate worldly practices and the absence of genuine spiritual life and the Spirit's manifestation.

16:60 I WILL REMEMBER MY COVENANT WITH THEE. After God's judgment upon Jerusa-

ber my covenant with thee in the days of thy youth, and I will establish unto thee [t]an everlasting covenant.

61 Then [u]thou shalt remember thy ways, and be ashamed, when thou shalt receive thy sisters, thine elder and thy younger: and I will give them unto thee for [v]daughters, [w]but not by thy covenant.

62 [x]And I will establish my covenant with thee; and thou shalt know that I *am* the LORD:

63 That thou mayest remember, and be confounded, [y]and never open thy mouth any more because of thy shame, when I am pacified toward thee for all that thou hast done, saith the Lord GOD.

The eagles and the cedar

17 AND THE word of the LORD came unto me, saying,

2 Son of man, put forth a riddle, and speak a parable unto the house of Israel;

3 And say, Thus saith the Lord GOD; [z]A great eagle with great wings, longwinged, full of feathers, which had [i]divers colours, came unto Lebanon, and [a]took the highest branch of the cedar:

4 He cropped off the top of his young twigs, and carried it into a land of traffic; he set it in a city of merchants.

5 He took also of the seed of the land, and [j]planted it in [b]a fruitful field; he placed *it* by great waters, *and* set it [c]*as* a willow tree.

6 And it grew, and became a spreading vine [d]of low stature, whose branches turned toward him, and the roots thereof were under him: so it became a vine, and brought forth branches, and shot forth sprigs.

7 There was also another great eagle with great wings and many feathers: and, behold, [e]this vine did bend her roots toward him, and shot forth her branches toward him, that he might water it by the furrows of her plantation.

8 It was planted in a good [k]soil by great waters, that it might bring forth branches, and that it might bear fruit, that it might be a goodly vine.

9 Say thou, Thus saith the Lord GOD; Shall it prosper? [f]shall he not pull up the roots thereof, and cut off the fruit thereof, that it wither? it shall wither in all the leaves of her spring, even without great power or many people to pluck it up by the roots thereof.

10 Yea, behold, *being* planted, shall it prosper? [g]shall it not utterly wither, when the east wind toucheth it? it shall wither in the furrows where it grew.

11 ¶ Moreover the word of the LORD came unto me, saying,

12 Say now to [h]the rebellious house, Know ye not what these *things mean?* tell *them,* Behold, [i]the king of Babylon is come to Jerusalem, and hath taken the king thereof, and the princes thereof, and led them with him to Babylon;

13 [j]And hath taken of the king's seed, and made a covenant with him, [k]and hath [l]taken an oath of him: he hath also taken the mighty of the land:

14 That the kingdom might be [l]base, that it might not lift itself up, [m]*but* that by keeping of his covenant it might stand.

15 But [m]he rebelled against him in sending his ambassadors into Egypt, [n]that they might give him horses and much people. [o]Shall he prosper? shall

16:60 [t]Jer. 32:40 & 50:5
16:61 [u]ch. 20:43 & 36:31 [v]Is. 54:1 & 60:4 Gal. 4:26 [w]Jer. 31:31
16:62 [x]Hos. 2:19
16:63 [y]Rom 3:19
17:3 [z]See ver. 12 [a]2 Ki. 24:12
17:5 [b]Deut. 8:7 [c]Is. 44:4
17:6 [d]ver. 14
17:7 [e]ver. 15
17:9 [f]2 Ki. 25:7
17:10 [g]ch. 19:12 Hos. 13:15
17:12 [h]ch. 2:5 & 12:9 [i]ver. 3 2 Ki. 24:11-16
17:13 [j]2 Ki. 24:17 [k]2 Chr. 36:13
17:14 [l]ver. 6 ch. 29:14
17:15 [m]2 Ki. 24:20 2 Chr. 36:13 [n]Deut. 17:16 Is. 31:1,3 & 36:6,9 [o]ver. 9

[i] Heb. *embroidering* [j] Heb. *put it in a field of seed* [k] Heb. *field* [l] Heb. *brought him to an oath* [m] Heb. *to keep his covenant, to stand to it*

lem and the whole house of Israel, He would remember His promise to Abraham (cf. Gen. 17:7–8; Lev. 26:42; see article on GOD'S COVENANT WITH ABRAHAM, ISAAC, AND JACOB, p. 48) and restore them to the land of Canaan and to fellowship with Him. This "new covenant" spoken of by Jeremiah (Jer. 31:31–34) and Ezekiel (Ezek. 11:18–20; 36:26–28; 37:26–28) would involve the atoning sacrifice and death of Jesus Christ on the cross.

17:3 A GREAT EAGLE. Ezekiel expresses God's message in a parable. The great eagle refers to Nebuchadnezzar, king of Babylon (see v. 12); "Lebanon" refers to Jerusalem (see v. 12).

17:4 TOP OF HIS YOUNG TWIGS. This designation refers to Jehoiachin, king of Judah, who was carried away into Babylon (see 2 Ki. 24:11–16).

17:7 ANOTHER GREAT EAGLE. This eagle represents the pharaoh of Egypt. King Zedekiah of Judah rebelled against Nebuchadnezzar and turned to Egypt for military aid (2 Ki. 24:20).

17:10 THE EAST WIND. "The east wind" refers to the Babylonian army. Because Judah's last king, Zedekiah, broke the oath of allegiance that he had made in the Lord's name with Nebuchadnezzar, he would be carried away captive to Babylon and would die there (vv. 16–21; see 2 Ki. 25:7).

he escape that doeth such *things?* or shall he break the covenant, and be delivered?

16 *As* I live, saith the Lord GOD, surely [p]in the place *where* the king *dwelleth* that made him king, whose oath he despised, and whose covenant he brake, *even* with him in the midst of Babylon he shall die.

17 [q]Neither shall Pharaoh with *his* mighty army and great company make for him in the war, [r]by casting up mounts, and building forts, to cut off many persons:

18 Seeing he despised the oath by breaking the covenant, when, lo, he had [s]given his hand, and hath done all these *things,* he shall not escape.

19 Therefore thus saith the Lord GOD; *As* I live, surely mine oath that he hath despised, and my covenant that he hath broken, even it will I recompense upon his own head.

20 And I will [t]spread my net upon him, and he shall be taken in my snare, and I will bring him to Babylon, and [u]will plead with him there for his trespass that he hath trespassed against me.

21 And [v]all his fugitives with all his bands shall fall by the sword, and they that remain shall be scattered toward all winds: and ye shall know that I the LORD have spoken *it.*

22 ¶ Thus saith the Lord GOD; I will also take of the highest [w]branch of the high cedar, and will set *it;* I will crop off from the top of his young twigs [x]a tender one, and will [y]plant *it* upon an high mountain and eminent:

23 [z]In the mountain of the height of Israel will I plant it: and it shall bring forth boughs, and bear fruit, and be a goodly cedar: and [a]under it shall dwell all fowl of every wing; in the shadow of the branches thereof shall they dwell.

24 And all the trees of the field shall know that I the LORD [b]have brought down the high tree, have exalted the low tree, have dried up the green tree, and have made the dry tree to flourish: [c]I the LORD have spoken and have done *it.* Hos. 6:1-3

The soul that sinneth shall die

18 THE WORD of the LORD came unto me again, saying,

2 What mean ye, that ye use this proverb concerning the land of Israel, saying, The [d]fathers have eaten sour grapes, and the children's teeth are set on edge?

3 *As* I live, saith the Lord GOD, ye shall not have *occasion* any more to use this proverb in Israel.

4 Behold, all souls are mine; as the soul of the father, so also the soul of the son is mine: [e]the soul that sinneth, it shall die.

5 ¶ But if a man be just, and do [n]that which is lawful and right,

6 [f]*And* hath not eaten upon the mountains, neither hath lifted up his eyes to the idols of the house of Israel, neither hath [g]defiled his neighbour's wife, neither hath come near to [h]a menstruous woman,

7 And hath not [i]oppressed any, *but* hath restored to the debtor his [j]pledge, hath spoiled none by violence, hath [k]given his bread to the

[n] Heb. *judgment and justice*

17:16 [p]Jer. 32:5 & 34:3 ch. 12:13
17:17 [q]Jer. 37:7 [r]Jer. 52:4
17:18 [s]1 Chr. 29:24 Lam. 5:6
17:20 [t]ch. 12:13 [u]ch. 20:36
17:21 [v]ch. 12:14
17:22 [w]Is. 11:1 Jer. 23:5 Zech. 3:8 [x]Is. 53:2 [y]Ps. 2:6
17:23 [z]Is. 2:2,3 [a]See ch. 31:6 Dan. 4:12
17:24 [b]Luke 1:52 [c]ch. 22:14
18:2 [d]Jer. 31:29 Lam. 5:7
18:4 [e]Rom. 6:23
18:6 [f]ch. 22:9 [g]Lev. 18:20 & 20:10 [h]Lev. 18:19 & 20:18
18:7 [i]Ex. 22:21 Lev. 19:15 & 25:14 [j]Ex. 22:26 Deut. 24:12 [k]Deut. 15:7 Is. 58:7 Mat. 25:35

17:22 THE HIGHEST BRANCH. God Himself would plant a branch, the Messiah, Jesus Christ; His kingdom would be established throughout the whole earth (see 34:23, note; Is. 11:1, note; Jer. 23:5–6, note).

18:1–32 WHAT MEAN YE. Apparently many Jews believed that they were being punished for the sins of their forefathers and that therefore God was unjust. They failed to recognize that their own sins were even worse than those of their fathers. This chapter teaches the basic truths that each person is accountable to God for his or her own life and that each person who persists in sin will die spiritually and experience eternal judgment.

18:2–4 THIS PROVERB. This proverb was probably based on Ex. 20:5 and Deut. 5:9, both of which teach that children are affected by the sins of their parents. However, Ezekiel makes it clear that these passages were not intended to teach that children were to be punished for their fathers' sins. All are accountable for their own sins and their own unwillingness to trust in Christ as Savior and to live righteous lives (see v. 4). The apostle Paul restates the principle with these words: "For the wages of sin *is* death; but the gift of God *is* eternal life through Jesus Christ our Lord" (Rom. 6:23).

18:5–9 IF A MAN BE JUST. These verses describe a person who has a right relationship with the Lord and manifests that commitment to God by loving righteousness and justice. It is this individual who will live eternally in communion and favor with the Lord. Paul emphasized this same truth when he referred "to them who by patient continuance in well doing seek for glory and honour and immortality, [receive] eternal life" (Rom. 2:7); this lifestyle is now made possible by grace through faith in Christ (Eph. 2:8–10).

hungry, and hath covered the naked
with a garment;
8 He *that* hath not given forth upon
[l]usury, neither hath taken any in-
crease, *that* hath withdrawn his hand
from iniquity, [m]hath executed true
judgment between man and man,
9 Hath walked in my statutes, and
hath kept my judgments, to deal truly;
he *is* just, he shall surely [n]live, saith
the Lord GOD.
10 ¶ If he beget a son *that is* a [o]rob-
ber, [o]a shedder of blood, and [p]*that*
doeth the like to *any* one of these
things,
11 And that doeth not any of those
duties, but even hath eaten upon the
mountains, and defiled his neighbour's
wife,
12 Hath oppressed the poor and
needy, hath spoiled by violence, hath
not restored the pledge, and hath lifted
up his eyes to the idols, hath [p]commit-
ted abomination,
13 Hath given forth upon usury, and
hath taken increase: shall he then live?
he shall not live: he hath done all these
abominations; he shall surely die; [q]his
[q]blood shall be upon him.
14 ¶ Now, lo, *if* he beget a son, that
seeth all his father's sins which he
hath done, and considereth, and doeth
not such like,
15 [r]*That* hath not eaten upon the
mountains, neither hath lifted up his
eyes to the idols of the house of Israel,
hath not defiled his neighbour's wife,
16 Neither hath oppressed any,
[r]hath not withholden the pledge, nei-
ther hath spoiled by violence, *but* hath
given his bread to the hungry, and hath
covered the naked with a garment,
17 *That* hath taken off his hand
from the poor, *that* hath not received
usury nor increase, hath executed my
judgments, hath walked in my stat-
utes; he shall not die for the iniquity of
his father, he shall surely live.
18 *As for* his father, because he cru-
elly oppressed, spoiled his brother by
violence, and did *that* which *is* not good
among his people, lo, even [s]he shall
die in his iniquity.
19 ¶ Yet say ye, Why? [t]doth not
the son bear the iniquity of the father?
When the son hath done that which is
lawful and right, *and* hath kept all my
statutes, and hath done them, he shall
surely live.
20 [u]The soul that sinneth, it shall
die. [v]The son shall not bear the iniqui-
ty of the father, neither shall the father
bear the iniquity of the son: [w]the righ-
teousness of the righteous shall be
upon him, [x]and the wickedness of the
wicked shall be upon him.
21 But [y]if the wicked will turn
from all his sins that he hath commit-
ted, and keep all my statutes, and do
that which is lawful and right, he shall
surely live, he shall not die.
22 [z]All his transgressions that he
hath committed, they shall not be men-
tioned unto him: in his righteousness
that he hath done he shall live.
23 [a]Have I any pleasure at all that
the wicked should die? saith the Lord
GOD: *and* not that he should return from
his ways, and live?
24 ¶ But [b]when the righteous
turneth away from his righteousness,
and committeth iniquity, *and* doeth ac-
cording to all the abominations that
the wicked *man* doeth, shall he live?
[c]All his righteousness that he hath
done shall not be mentioned: in his
trespass that he hath trespassed, and
in his sin that he hath sinned, in them
shall he die.
25 ¶ Yet ye say, [d]The way of the
Lord is not equal. Hear now, O house
of Israel; Is not my way equal? are not
your ways unequal?
26 [e]When a righteous *man* turneth

Eze 33:16

18:8 [l]Ex. 22:25 Lev. 25:36 Deut. 23:19 Neh. 5:7 Ps. 15:5 [m]Deut. 1:16 Zech. 8:16 **18:9** [n]ch. 20:11 Amos 5:4 **18:10** [o]Gen. 9:6 Ex. 21:12 Num. 35:31 **18:12** [p]ch. 8:6,17 **18:13** [q]Lev. 20:9,11-13, 16,27 ch. 3:18 Acts 18:6 **18:15** [r]ver. 6 **18:18** [s]ch. 3:18 **18:19** [t]Ex. 20:5 Deut. 5:9 2 Ki. 23:26 & 24:3,4 **18:20** [u]ver. 4 [v]Deut. 24:16 2 Ki. 14:6 2 Chr. 25:4 Jer. 31:29,30 [w]Is. 3:10,11 [x]Rom. 2:9 **18:21** [y]ver. 27 ch. 33:12,19 **18:22** [z]ch. 33:16 **18:23** [a]ver. 32 ch. 33:11 1 Tim. 2:4 2 Pet. 3:9 **18:24** [b]ch. 3:20 & 33:12,13,18 [c]2 Pet. 2:20 **18:25** [d]ver. 29 ch. 33:17,20 **18:26** [e]ver. 24

[o] Or, *breaker up of an house* [p] Or, *that doeth to his brother besides any of these* [q] Heb. *bloods* [r] Heb. *hath not pledged the pledge,* or, *taken to pledge*

18:10–13 A SON *THAT IS* A ROBBER. The unrighteous children of a godly father will be held accountable for their own sins. As a result of their refusal to repent and turn to God, they will experience spiritual and eternal death (see Rom. 2:8).

18:21–23 IF THE WICKED WILL TURN. God promises salvation to any of the wicked who choose to forsake their sins and turn to God. No one is forced to follow the sins of his or her family. God desires to bring each sinner into fellowship with Himself and is never pleased when a wicked person dies in sin (cf. 1 Tim. 2:4).

18:24 WHEN THE RIGHTEOUS TURNETH. The righteous who trust in God and follow His way must not think they are eternally secure if they later become unfaithful and rebellious against God. Such people also will die, just like the one who has always lived in sin. Paul warns believers: "If ye live after the flesh, ye shall die" (Rom. 8:13; see also Heb. 2:3; 3:6; 2 Pet. 2:20–22; see article on PERSONAL APOSTASY, p. 1946).

away from his righteousness, and com-
mitteth iniquity, and dieth in them; for
his iniquity that he hath done shall he
die.
27 Again, [f]when the wicked *man*
turneth away from his wickedness that
he hath committed, and doeth that
which is lawful and right, he shall save
his soul alive.
28 Because he [g]considereth, and
turneth away from all his transgres-
sions that he hath committed, he shall
surely live, he shall not die.
29 [h]Yet saith the house of Israel,
The way of the Lord is not equal.
O house of Israel, are not my ways
equal? are not your ways unequal?
30 [i]Therefore I will judge you,
O house of Israel, every one according
to his ways, saith the Lord GOD. [j]Re-
pent, and turn [s]*yourselves* from all
your transgressions; so iniquity shall
not be your ruin.
31 ¶ [k]Cast away from you all your
transgressions, whereby ye have
transgressed; and make you a [l]new
heart and a new spirit: for why will ye
die, O house of Israel?
32 For [m]I have no pleasure in the
death of him that dieth, saith the Lord
GOD: wherefore turn [s]*yourselves,* and
live ye.

Lament for Israel's princes

19 MOREOVER [n]TAKE thou up a
lamentation for the princes of
Israel,
2 And say, What *is* thy mother? A
lioness: she lay down among lions, she
nourished her whelps among young li-
ons.
3 And she brought up one of her
whelps: [o]it became a young lion, and
it learned to catch the prey; it devoured
men.
4 The nations also heard of him; he
was taken in their pit, and they
brought him with chains unto the land
of [p]Egypt.
5 Now when she saw that she had
waited, *and* her hope was lost, then she
took [q]another of her whelps, *and*
made him a young lion.
6 [r]And he went up and down
among the lions, [s]he became a young
lion, and learned to catch the prey, *and*
devoured men.
7 And he knew [t]their desolate pal-
aces, and he laid waste their cities; and
the land was desolate, and the fulness
thereof, by the noise of his roaring.
8 [t]Then the nations set against
him on every side from the provinces,
and spread their net over him: [u]he
was taken in their pit.
9 [v]And they put him in ward [u]in
chains, and brought him to the king of
Babylon: they brought him into holds,
that his voice should no more be heard
upon [w]the mountains of Israel.
10 ¶ Thy mother *is* [x]like a vine [v]in
thy blood, planted by the waters: she
was [y]fruitful and full of branches by
reason of many waters.
11 And she had strong rods for the
sceptres of them that bare rule, and
her [z]stature was exalted among the
thick branches, and she appeared in
her height with the multitude of her
branches.
12 But she was plucked up in fury,
she was cast down to the ground, and
the [a]east wind dried up her fruit: her
strong rods were broken and withered;
the fire consumed them.
13 And now she *is* planted in the
wilderness, in a dry and thirsty ground.
14 [b]And fire is gone out of a rod of
her branches, *which* hath devoured her
fruit, so that she hath no strong rod *to*
be a sceptre to rule. [c]This *is* a lamen-
tation, and shall be for a lamentation.

Israel's apostasy

20 AND IT came to pass in the sev-
enth year, in the fifth *month,*

[s] Or, others [t] Or, *their widows* [u] Or, *in hooks* [v] Or, *in thy quietness,* or, *in thy likeness*

18:27 [f]ver. 21
18:28 [g]ver. 14
18:29 [h]ver. 25
18:30 [i]ch. 7:3 & 33:20 [j]Mat. 3:2 Rev. 2:5
18:31 [k]Eph. 4:22,23 [l]Jer. 32:39 ch. 11:19 & 36:26
18:32 [m]ver. 23 Lam. 3:33 ch. 33:11 2 Pet. 3:9
19:1 [n]ch. 26:17 & 27:2
19:3 [o]ver. 6 2 Ki. 23:31,32
19:4 [p]2 Ki. 23:33 2 Chr. 36:4 Jer. 22:11,12
19:5 [q]2 Ki. 23:34
19:6 [r]Jer. 22:13-17 [s]ver. 3
19:8 [t]2 Ki. 24:2 [u]ver. 4
19:9 [v]2 Chr. 36:6 Jer. 22:18 [w]ch. 6:2
19:10 [x]ch. 17:6 [y]Deut. 8:7-9
19:11 [z]ch. 31:3 Dan. 4:11
19:12 [a]ch. 17:10 Hos. 13:15
19:14 [b]Judg. 9:15 2 Ki. 24:20 ch. 17:18 [c]Lam. 4:20

19:1–14 A LAMENTATION. The lamentation in this chapter compares Judah's last king to a caged lion and the nation to a ruined vine.

19:3–4 A YOUNG LION. Young King Jehoahaz (see 2 Ki. 23:31–34) reigned for three months; then he was taken captive to Egypt, where he eventually died.

19:5–9 ANOTHER OF HER WHELPS. This designation refers either to Jehoiachin or to Zedekiah. Both were carried away captive to Babylon (see 2 Ki. 24:8—25:7).

19:10–14 THY MOTHER. The lioness (Israel, see vv. 1–2) is here pictured as a fruitful vine that was uprooted and its branches burned. What was left of the vine was planted in a desert (i.e., the Babylonian captivity).

20:1–49 CERTAIN OF THE ELDERS. This chapter expresses the sad truth that the history of Israel had been one of continual idol worship and moral failure. Ezekiel told the elders of his day

the tenth *day* of the month, *that* [d]certain of the elders of Israel came to inquire of the LORD, and sat before me.

2 Then came the word of the LORD unto me, saying,

3 Son of man, speak unto the elders of Israel, and say unto them, Thus saith the Lord GOD; Are ye come to inquire of me? *As* I live, saith the Lord GOD, [e]I will not be inquired of by you.

4 Wilt thou [f]judge[w] them, son of man, wilt thou judge *them?* [g]cause them to know the abominations of their fathers:

5 ¶ And say unto them, Thus saith the Lord GOD; In the day when [h]I chose Israel, and [x]lifted up mine hand unto the seed of the house of Jacob, and made myself [i]known unto them in the land of Egypt, when I lifted up mine hand unto them, saying, [j]I *am* the LORD your God;

6 In the day *that* I lifted up mine hand unto them, [k]to bring them forth of the land of Egypt into a land that I had espied for them, flowing with milk and honey, [l]which *is* the glory of all lands:

7 Then said I unto them, [m]Cast ye away every man [n]the abominations of his eyes, and defile not yourselves with [o]the idols of Egypt: I *am* the LORD your God.

8 But they rebelled against me, and would not hearken unto me: they did not every man cast away the abominations of their eyes, neither did they forsake the idols of Egypt: then I said, I will [p]pour out my fury upon them, to accomplish my anger against them in the midst of the land of Egypt.

9 [q]But I wrought for my name's sake, that it should not be polluted before the heathen, among whom they *were,* in whose sight I made myself known unto them, in bringing them forth out of the land of Egypt.

10 ¶ Wherefore I [r]caused them to go forth out of the land of Egypt, and brought them into the wilderness.

11 [s]And I gave them my statutes, and [y]showed them my judgments, [t]which *if* a man do, he shall even live in them.

12 Moreover also I gave them my [u]sabbaths, to be a sign between me and them, that they might know that I *am* the LORD that sanctify them.

13 But the house of Israel [v]rebelled against me in the wilderness: they walked not in my statutes, and they [w]despised my judgments, which *if* a man do, he shall even live in them; and my sabbaths they greatly [x]polluted: then I said, I would pour out my fury upon them in the [y]wilderness, to consume them.

14 [z]But I wrought for my name's sake, that it should not be polluted before the heathen, in whose sight I brought them out.

15 Yet also [a]I lifted up my hand unto them in the wilderness, that I would not bring them into the land which I had given *them,* flowing with milk and honey, [b]which *is* the glory of all lands;

16 [c]Because they despised my judgments, and walked not in my statutes, but polluted my sabbaths: for [d]their heart went after their idols.

17 [e]Nevertheless mine eye spared them from destroying them, neither did I make an end of them in the wilderness.

18 But I said unto their children in the wilderness, Walk ye not in the statutes of your fathers, neither observe their judgments, nor defile yourselves with their idols:

19 I *am* the LORD your God; [f]walk in my statutes, and keep my judgments, and do them;

20 [g]And hallow my sabbaths; and they shall be a sign between me and you, that ye may know that I *am* the LORD your God.

21 Notwithstanding [h]the children rebelled against me: they walked not in my statutes, neither kept my judgments to do them, [i]which *if* a man do,

20:1 [d]ch. 8:1
20:3 [e]ch. 14:3
20:4 [f]ch. 22:2 [g]ch. 16:2
20:5 [h]Ex. 6:7 Deut. 7:6 [i]Ex. 3:8 & 4:31 Deut. 4:34 [j]Ex. 20:2
20:6 [k]Ex. 3:8,17 Deut. 8:7-9 Jer. 32:22 [l]ver. 15 Ps. 48:2 Dan. 8:9 Zech. 7:14
20:7 [m]ch. 18:31 [n]2 Chr. 15:8 [o]Lev. 18:3 Deut. 29:16 Josh. 24:14
20:8 [p]ch. 7:8
20:9 [q]Num. 14:13 ch. 36:21,22
20:10 [r]Ex. 13:18
20:11 [s]Deut. 4:8 Neh. 9:13 Ps. 147:19 [t]Lev. 18:5 Rom. 10:5 Gal. 3:12
20:12 [u]Ex. 20:8 Deut. 5:12 Neh. 9:14
20:13 [v]Num. 14:22 Ps. 78:40 & 95:8-10 [w]Prov. 1:25 [x]Ex. 16:27 [y]Num. 14:29 Ps. 106:23
20:14 [z]ver. 9,22
20:15 [a]Num. 14:28 Ps. 95:11 & 106:26 [b]ver. 6
20:16 [c]ver. 13,24 [d]Num. 15:39 Ps. 78:37 Amos 5:25 Acts 7:42
20:17 [e]Ps. 78:38
20:19 [f]Deut. 5:32 & chs. 6,7,8,10, 11,12
20:20 [g]Jer. 17:22
20:21 [h]Num. 25:1 Deut. 9:23 [i]ver. 11,13

[w] Or, *plead for them* [x] Or, *sware* [y] Heb. *made them to know*

that they themselves had not yet removed their love for idols from their hearts. Thus they too were guilty before God.

20:9 FOR MY NAME'S SAKE. God did not totally destroy the Israelites in the desert after the exodus because He wanted to uphold the honor of His name. He made Himself known to them by bringing them out of Egypt, so that he could fulfill His promise of universal blessing through His chosen people (see Gen. 12:1–3).

20:12 MY SABBATHS. Israel's observance of the weekly and annual Sabbaths was intended to remind her that she had been set apart as a holy nation in order to manifest God's righteousness and glory before the world (see Ex. 31:13–17; Lev. 23:32).

he shall even live in them; they polluted my sabbaths: then I said, [j]I would pour out my fury upon them, to accomplish my anger against them in the wilderness.

22 [k]Nevertheless I withdrew mine hand, and [l]wrought for my name's sake, that it should not be polluted in the sight of the heathen, in whose sight I brought them forth.

23 I lifted up mine hand unto them also in the wilderness, that [m]I would scatter them among the heathen, and disperse them through the countries;

24 [n]Because they had not executed my judgments, but had despised my statutes, and had polluted my sabbaths, and [o]their eyes were after their fathers' idols.

25 Wherefore [p]I gave them also statutes *that were* not good, and judgments whereby they should not live;

26 And I polluted them in their own gifts, in that they caused to pass [q]through *the fire* all that openeth the womb, that I might make them desolate, to the end that they [r]might know that I *am* the LORD.

27 ¶ Therefore, son of man, speak unto the house of Israel, and say unto them, Thus saith the Lord GOD; Yet in this your fathers have [s]blasphemed me, in that they have [z]committed a trespass against me.

28 *For* when I had brought them into the land, *for* the which I lifted up mine hand to give it to them, then [t]they saw every high hill, and all the thick trees, and they offered there their sacrifices, and there they presented the provocation of their offering: there also they made their [u]sweet savour, and poured out there their drink offerings.

29 Then [a]I said unto them, What *is* the high place whereunto ye go? And the name thereof is called Bamah unto this day.

30 Wherefore say unto the house of Israel, Thus saith the Lord GOD; Are ye polluted after the manner of your fathers? and commit ye whoredom after their abominations?

31 For when ye offer [v]your gifts, when ye make your sons to pass through the fire, ye pollute yourselves with all your idols, even unto this day: and shall I be inquired of by you, O house of Israel? *As* I live, saith the Lord GOD, I will not be inquired of by you.

Israel purged and accepted

32 And that [w]which cometh into your mind shall not be at all, that ye say, We will be as the heathen, as the families of the countries, to serve wood and stone.

33 ¶ *As* I live, saith the Lord GOD, surely with a mighty hand, and [x]with a stretched out arm, and with fury poured out, will I rule over you:

34 And I will bring you out from the people, and will gather you out of the countries wherein ye are scattered, with a mighty hand, and with a stretched out arm, and with fury poured out.

35 And I will bring you into the wilderness of the people, and there [y]will I plead with you face to face.

36 [z]Like as I pleaded with your fathers in the wilderness of the land of Egypt, so will I plead with you, saith the Lord GOD.

37 And I will cause you to [a]pass under the rod, and I will bring you into [b]the bond of the covenant:

38 And [b]I will purge out from among you the rebels, and them that

20:21 [j]ver. 8,13 **20:22** [k]ver. 17 [l]ver. 9,14 **20:23** [m]Lev. 26:33 Deut. 28:64 Ps. 106:27 Jer. 15:4 **20:24** [n]ver. 13,16 [o]See ch. 6:9 **20:25** [p]See Ps. 81:12 Rom. 1:24 2 Thes. 2:11 **20:26** [q]2 Ki. 17:17 & 21:6 2 Chr. 28:3 & 33:6 Jer. 32:35 ch. 16:20 [r]ch. 6:7 **20:27** [s]Rom. 2:24 **20:28** [t]Is. 57:5 ch. 6:13 [u]ch. 16:19 **20:31** [v]ver. 26 **20:32** [w]ch. 11:5 **20:33** [x]Jer. 21:5 **20:35** [y]Jer. 2:9,35 ch. 17:20 **20:36** [z]Num. 14:21-23, 28 **20:37** [a]Lev. 27:32 Jer. 33:13 **20:38** [b]ch. 34:17 Mat. 25:32

[z] Heb. *trespassed a trespass* [a] Or, *I told them what the high place* was, or, *Bamah* [b] Or, *a delivering*

20:30 ARE YE POLLUTED. The crucial question of this chapter is: "Will you Israelites continue to pollute yourselves?" Believers today face daily decisions on whether to surrender to the sinful desires of their human nature or to yield themselves to the Holy Spirit and serve the cause of Christ (Rom. 6:11–14; Gal. 5:16–25).

20:32 WE WILL BE AS THE HEATHEN. God's people are constantly tempted to conform to the customs and ways of the world and thereby cease being God's special people. We must always ask ourselves two basic questions: (1) Do I give in to peer pressure at school, on the job, or among friends? (2) Am I different in my ways and actions or do I instead conform to the ways and expectations of the ungodly (see Rom. 12:1–2, notes)?

20:34–44 I WILL BRING YOU OUT. God promised to bring Israel back from their captivity after He had purged out the rebels and evildoers (cf. 11:17,21; Mal. 3:2–5). A faithful remnant would return to the land (cf. Is. 10:21–23) and would no longer profane the name of God by disobedience or idol worship (v. 39). They would ultimately enjoy the blessings of the "new covenant" (see Jer. 31:31–34; Heb. 8:1—10:18).

transgress against me: I will bring them forth out of the country where they sojourn, and [c]they shall not enter into the land of Israel: and ye shall know that I *am* the LORD.

39 As for you, O house of Israel, thus saith the Lord GOD; [d]Go ye, serve ye every one his idols, and hereafter *also,* if ye will not hearken unto me: [e]but pollute ye my holy name no more with your gifts, and with your idols.

40 For [f]in mine holy mountain, in the mountain of the height of Israel, saith the Lord GOD, there shall all the house of Israel, all of them in the land, serve me: there [g]will I accept them, and there will I require your offerings, and the [c]firstfruits of your oblations, with all your holy things.

41 I will accept you with your [h]sweet[d] savour, when I bring you out from the people, and gather you out of the countries wherein ye have been scattered; and I will be sanctified in you before the heathen.

42 [i]And ye shall know that I *am* the LORD, [j]when I shall bring you into the land of Israel, into the country *for* the which I lifted up mine hand to give it to your fathers.

43 And [k]there shall ye remember your ways, and all your doings, wherein ye have been defiled; and [l]ye shall loathe yourselves in your own sight for all your evils that ye have committed.

44 [m]And ye shall know that I *am* the LORD, when I have wrought with you [n]for my name's sake, not according to your wicked ways, nor according to your corrupt doings, O ye house of Israel, saith the Lord GOD.

Dan. 9:4-6

The prophecy against the south

45 ¶ Moreover the word of the LORD came unto me, saying,

46 [o]Son of man, set thy face toward the south, and drop *thy word* toward the south, and prophesy against the forest of the south field;

47 And say to the forest of the south, Hear the word of the LORD; Thus saith the Lord GOD; Behold, [p]I will kindle a fire in thee, and it shall devour [q]every green tree in thee, and every dry tree: the flaming flame shall not be quenched, and all faces [r]from the south to the north shall be burned therein.

48 And all flesh shall see that I the LORD have kindled it: it shall not be quenched.

49 Then said I, Ah Lord GOD! they say of me, Doth he not speak parables?

The LORD's sword

21 AND THE word of the LORD came unto me, saying,

2 [s]Son of man, set thy face toward Jerusalem, and [t]drop *thy word* toward the holy places, and prophesy against the land of Israel,

3 And say to the land of Israel, Thus saith the LORD; Behold, I *am* against thee, and will draw forth my sword out of his sheath, and will cut off from thee [u]the righteous and the wicked.

4 Seeing then that I will cut off from thee the righteous and the wicked, therefore shall my sword go forth out of his sheath against all flesh [v]from the south to the north:

5 That all flesh may know that I the LORD have drawn forth my sword out of his sheath: it [w]shall not return any more.

6 [x]Sigh therefore, thou son of man, with the breaking of *thy* loins; and with bitterness sigh before their eyes.

7 And it shall be, when they say unto thee, Wherefore sighest thou? that thou shalt answer, For the tidings; because it cometh: and every heart shall melt, and [y]all hands shall be feeble, and every spirit shall faint, and all knees [e]shall be weak *as* water: behold, it cometh, and shall be brought to pass, saith the Lord GOD.

8 ¶ Again the word of the LORD came unto me, saying,

9 Son of man, prophesy, and say, Thus saith the LORD; Say, [z]A sword, a sword is sharpened, and also furbished:

10 It is sharpened to make a sore slaughter; it is furbished that it may glitter: should we then make mirth?

20:38 [c]Jer. 44:14 **20:39** [d]Judg. 10:14 Ps. 81:12 Amos 4:4 [e]Is. 1:13 ch. 23:38 **20:40** [f]Is. 2:2,3 ch. 17:23 Mic. 4:1 [g]Is. 56:7 & 60:7 Zech. 8:20 Mal. 3:4 Rom. 12:1 **20:41** [h]Eph. 5:2 Phil. 4:18 **20:42** [i]ver. 38,44 ch. 36:23 & 38:23 [j]ch. 11:17 & 34:13 & 36:24 **20:43** [k]ch. 16:61 [l]Lev. 26:39 ch. 6:9 Hos. 5:15 **20:44** [m]ver. 38 ch. 24:24 [n]ch. 36:22 **20:46** [o]ch. 21:2 **20:47** [p]Jer. 21:14 [q]Luke 23:31 [r]ch. 21:4 **21:2** [s]ch. 20:46 [t]Amos 7:16 **21:3** [u]Job 9:22 **21:4** [v]ch. 20:47 **21:5** [w]Is. 45:23 & 55:11 **21:6** [x]Is. 22:4 **21:7** [y]ch. 7:17 **21:9** [z]ver. 15,28 Deut. 32:41

[c] Or, *chief* [d] Heb. *savour of rest* [e] Heb. *shall go into water*

21:3–32 MY SWORD. The judgment against Jerusalem and the nation of Judah would come by the sword (i.e., by the Babylonian army) that God was going to use to destroy them.

21:3 THE RIGHTEOUS AND THE WICKED. In natural catastrophies or national disasters, the righteous and the wicked often suffer alike. Note, however, that Ezekiel had earlier made it clear that the righteous would not experience the eternal judgment of the wicked (see 18:1–24).

[f]it contemneth the rod of my son, *as*
every tree.
11 And he hath given it to be furb-
ished, that it may be handled: this
sword is sharpened, and it is furbished,
to give it into the hand of [a]the slayer.
12 Cry and howl, son of man: for it
shall be upon my people, it *shall be*
upon all the princes of Israel: [g]terrors
by reason of the sword shall be upon
my people: [b]smite therefore upon *thy*
thigh.
13 [h]Because *it is* [c]a trial, and
what if *the sword* contemn even the
rod? [d]it shall be no *more,* saith the
Lord GOD.
14 Thou therefore, son of man,
prophesy, and [e]smite *thine* [i]hands
together, and let the sword be doubled
the third time, the sword of the slain:
it *is* the sword of the great *men that are*
slain, which entereth into their [f]privy
chambers.
15 I have set the [j]point of the
sword against all their gates, that *their*
heart may faint, and *their* ruins be mul-
tiplied: ah! [g]*it is* made bright, *it is*
[k]wrapped up for the slaughter.
16 [h]Go thee one way or other, *ei-
ther* on the right hand, [l]*or* on the left,
whithersoever thy face *is* set.
17 I will also [i]smite mine hands
together, and [j]I will cause my fury to
rest: I the LORD have said *it.*
18 ¶ The word of the LORD came
unto me again, saying,
19 Also, thou son of man, appoint
thee two ways, that the sword of the
king of Babylon may come: both twain
shall come forth out of one land: and
choose thou a place, choose *it* at the
head of the way to the city.
20 Appoint a way, that the sword
may come to [k]Rabbath of the Ammon-
ites, and to Judah in Jerusalem the de-
fenced.
21 For the king of Babylon stood at
the [m]parting of the way, at the head of
the two ways, to use divination: he
made *his* [n]arrows bright, he consulted
with [o]images, he looked in the liver.
22 At his right hand was the divina-
tion for Jerusalem, to appoint [p]cap-
tains, to open the mouth in the slaugh-
ter, to [l]lift up the voice with shouting,
[m]to appoint *battering* rams against the
gates, to cast a mount, *and* to build a
fort.
23 And it shall be unto them as a
false divination in their sight, [q]to
them that [n]have sworn oaths: but he
will call to remembrance the iniquity,
that they may be taken.
24 Therefore thus saith the Lord
GOD; Because ye have made your iniq-
uity to be remembered, in that your
transgressions are discovered, so that
in all your doings your sins do appear;
because, *I say,* that ye are come to re-
membrance, ye shall be taken with the
hand.
25 ¶ And thou, [o]profane wicked
prince of Israel, [p]whose day is come,
when iniquity *shall have* an end,
26 Thus saith the Lord GOD; Re-
move the diadem, and take off the
crown: this *shall* not *be* the same: [q]ex-
alt *him that is* low, and abase *him that
is* high.
27 [r]I will overturn, overturn, over-
turn, it: [r]and it shall be no *more,* until
he come whose right it is; and I will
give it *him.*
28 ¶ And thou, son of man, prophe-
sy and say, Thus saith the Lord GOD
[s]concerning the Ammonites, and con-
cerning their reproach; even say thou,
The sword, the sword *is* drawn: for the
slaughter *it is* furbished, to consume
because of the glittering:

21:11 [a]ver. 19
21:12 [b]Jer. 31:19
21:13 [c]Job 9:23; 2 Cor. 8:2; [d]ver. 27
21:14 [e]Num. 24:10; [f]1 Ki. 20:30
21:15 [g]ver. 10,28
21:16 [h]ch. 14:17
21:17 [i]ver. 14; ch. 22:13; [j]ch. 5:13
21:20 [k]Jer. 49:2; Amos 1:14
21:22 [l]Jer. 51:14; [m]ch. 4:2
21:23 [n]ch. 17:13
21:25 [o]Jer. 52:2; [p]ver. 29
21:26 [q]Luke 1:52
21:27 [r]Gen. 49:10; Luke 1:32
21:28 [s]ch. 25:2,3

[f] Or, it is *the rod of my son, it despiseth every tree* [g] Or, *they are thrust down to the sword with my people* [h] Or, *When the trial* hath been, *what then? shall they not also belong to the despising rod?* [i] Heb. *hand to hand* [j] Or, *glittering,* or, *fear* [k] Or, *sharpened* [l] Heb. *set thyself, take the left hand* [m] Heb. *mother of the way* [n] Or, *knives* [o] Heb. *teraphim* [p] Or, battering *rams;* see ch. 4:2 [q] Or, *for the oaths made unto them* [r] Heb. *Perverted, perverted, perverted, will I make it*

21:12 TERRORS . . . UPON MY PEOPLE. Because God's people had not accepted His chastising correction, God had no choice but to deliver them to the sword. To remain stubborn and self-willed while being chastened by the Lord results in being condemned along with the world (see Heb. 12:5, note).

21:19–23 THE KING OF BABYLON. Spiritists believed they could tell the future by examining the livers of slain animals (v. 21). Ezekiel insists, however, that God controlled the pagan practices of King Nebuchadnezzar in order to accomplish His will (cf. Jer. 27:6).

21:27 UNTIL HE COMES. Ezekiel prophesies that though the Davidic line would continue, the Davidic throne would not be reinstituted until the Messianic King came to establish His rule (cf. Gen. 49:10; Zech. 9:9; Mat. 21:1–11; Rev. 19:11–16; 20:4). Jesus Christ, the Messiah, will yet rule over Israel.

29 Whiles they [t]see vanity unto thee, whiles they divine a lie unto thee, to bring thee upon the necks of *them that are* slain, of the wicked, [u]whose day is come, when their iniquity *shall have* an end.

30 [v]Shall[s] I cause *it* to return into his sheath? [w]I will judge thee in the place where thou wast created, [x]in the land of thy nativity.

31 And I will [y]pour out mine indignation upon thee, I will [z]blow against thee in the fire of my wrath, and deliver thee into the hand of [t]brutish men, *and* skilful to destroy.

32 Thou shalt be for fuel to the fire; thy blood shall be in the midst of the land; [a]thou shalt be no *more* remembered: for I the LORD have spoken *it.*

The indictment of Jerusalem

22 MOREOVER THE word of the LORD came unto me, saying,

2 Now, thou son of man, [b]wilt thou [u]judge, wilt thou judge [c]the [v]bloody city? yea, thou shalt [w]show her all her abominations.

3 Then say thou, Thus saith the Lord GOD, The city sheddeth blood in the midst of it, that her time may come, and maketh idols against herself to defile herself.

4 Thou art become guilty in thy blood that thou hast [d]shed; and hast defiled thyself in thine idols which thou hast made; and thou hast caused thy days to draw near, and art come *even* unto thy years: [e]therefore have I made thee a reproach unto the heathen, and a mocking to all countries.

5 *Those that be* near, and *those that be* far from thee, shall mock thee, *which art* [x]infamous *and* much vexed.

6 Behold, [f]the princes of Israel, every one were in thee to their [y]power to shed blood.

7 In thee have they [g]set light by father and mother: in the midst of thee have they [h]dealt by [z]oppression with the stranger: in thee have they vexed the fatherless and the widow.

8 Thou hast despised mine holy things, and hast [i]profaned my sabbaths.

9 In thee are [j]men[a] that carry tales to shed blood: [k]and in thee they eat upon the mountains: in the midst of thee they commit lewdness.

10 In thee have they [l]discovered their fathers' nakedness: in thee have they humbled her that was [m]set apart for pollution.

11 And [b]one hath committed abomination [n]with his neighbour's wife; and [b]another [o]hath [c]lewdly defiled his daughter-in-law; and another in thee hath humbled his [p]sister, his father's daughter.

12 In thee [q]have they taken gifts to shed blood; [r]thou hast taken usury and increase, and thou hast greedily gained of thy neighbours by extortion, and [s]hast forgotten me, saith the Lord GOD.

13 ¶ Behold, therefore I have [t]smitten mine hand at thy dishonest gain which thou hast made, and at thy blood which hath been in the midst of thee.

14 [u]Can thine heart endure, or can thine hands be strong, in the days that I shall deal with thee? [v]I the LORD have spoken *it*, and will do *it.*

15 And [w]I will scatter thee among the heathen, and disperse thee in the countries, and [x]will consume thy filthiness out of thee.

16 And thou [d]shalt take thine inheritance in thyself in the sight of the heathen, and [y]thou shalt know that I *am* the LORD.

17 And the word of the LORD came unto me, saying,

18 Son of man, [z]the house of Israel is to me become dross: all they *are* brass, and tin, and iron, and lead, in

21:29 [t]ch. 12:24 [u]Job 18:20 Ps. 37:13
21:30 [v]Jer. 47:6,7 [w]Gen. 15:14 [x]ch. 16:3
21:31 [y]ch. 7:8 [z]ch. 22:20
21:32 [a]ch. 25:10
22:2 [b]ch. 20:4 [c]Nah. 3:1
22:4 [d]2 Ki. 21:16 [e]Deut. 28:37 Dan. 9:16
22:6 [f]Is. 1:23
22:7 [g]Deut. 27:16 [h]Ex. 22:21
22:8 [i]Lev. 19:30
22:9 [j]Lev. 19:16 [k]ch. 18:6,11
22:10 [l]Lev. 18:7,8 [m]Lev. 18:19
22:11 [n]Lev. 18:20 [o]Lev. 18:15 [p]Lev. 18:9
22:12 [q]Ex. 23:8 Deut. 16:19 [r]Ex. 22:25 [s]Jer. 3:21
22:13 [t]ch. 21:17
22:14 [u]ch. 21:7 [v]ch. 17:24
22:15 [w]Deut. 4:27 [x]ch. 23:27
22:16 [y]Ps. 9:16
22:18 [z]Ps. 119:119 Is. 1:22 Jer. 6:28

[s] Or, *Cause* it *to return* [t] Or, *burning* [u] Or, *plead for* [v] Heb. *city of bloods?* [w] Heb. *make her know* [x] Heb. *polluted of name, much in vexation* [y] Heb. *arm* [z] Or, *deceit*
[a] Heb. *men of slanders* [b] Or, *every one*
[c] Or, *by lewdness* [d] Or, *shalt be profaned*

22:2–12 THE CITY SHEDDETH BLOOD. Jerusalem had become a city of violence and all sorts of wickedness. There was no longer any respect for holy things, family, or the poor and needy. Sexual immorality was rampant, and cheating and bribery were commonplace. All this occurred because the people had turned from God and His word. Therefore, God was giving the city over to severe judgment and destruction. Today the social and spiritual condition of cities throughout the world is similar to that of ancient Jerusalem. Unless these cities repent, they will perish just as Jerusalem did. Nations, cities, and people cannot despise God and His ways without ultimately reaping the consequences.

the midst of the furnace; they are *even*
the [e]dross of silver.
19 Therefore thus saith the Lord
GOD; Because ye are all become dross,
behold, therefore I will gather you into
the midst of Jerusalem.
20 [f]*As* they gather silver, and
brass, and iron, and lead, and tin, into
the midst of the furnace, to blow the
fire upon it, to melt *it;* so will I gather
you in mine anger and in my fury, and
I will leave *you there,* and melt you.
21 Yea, I will gather you, and blow
upon you in the fire of my wrath, and
ye shall be melted in the midst thereof.
22 As silver is melted in the midst
of the furnace, so shall ye be melted in
the midst thereof; and ye shall know
that I the LORD have [a]poured out my
fury upon you.
23 ¶ And the word of the LORD came
unto me, saying,
24 Son of man, say unto her, Thou
art the land that is not cleansed, nor
rained upon in the day of indignation.
25 [b]*There is* a conspiracy of her
prophets in the midst thereof, like a
roaring lion ravening the prey; they
[c]have devoured souls; [d]they have
taken the treasure and precious
things; they have made her many wid-
ows in the midst thereof.
26 [e]Her priests have [g]violated my
law, and have [f]profaned mine holy
things: they have put no [g]difference
between the holy and profane, neither
have they shown *difference* between the
unclean and the clean, and have hid
their eyes from my sabbaths, and I am
profaned among them.
27 Her [h]princes in the midst there-
of *are* like wolves ravening the prey, to
shed blood, *and* to destroy souls, to get
dishonest gain.
28 And [i]her prophets have daubed
them with untempered *mortar,* [j]see-
ing vanity, and divining lies unto them,
saying, Thus saith the Lord GOD, when
the LORD hath not spoken.
29 The people of the land have used
[h]oppression, and exercised robbery,
and have vexed the poor and needy:
yea, they have [k]oppressed the strang-
er [i]wrongfully.
30 [l]And I sought for a man among
them, that should [m]make up the
hedge, and [n]stand in the gap before
me for the land, that I should not de-
stroy it: but I found none.
31 Therefore have I [o]poured out
mine indignation upon them; I have
consumed them with the fire of my
wrath: [p]their own way have I recom-
pensed upon their heads, saith the
Lord GOD.

22:22 [a]ch. 20:8,33 **22:25** [b]Hos. 6:9 [c]Mat. 23:14 [d]Mic. 3:11 **22:26** [e]Mal. 2:8 [f]1 Sam. 2:29 [g]Lev. 10:10 **22:27** [h]Is. 1:23 ch. 22:6 **22:28** [i]ch. 13:10 [j]ch. 13:6,7 **22:29** [k]Ex. 23:9 Lev. 19:33 **22:30** [l]Jer. 5:1 [m]ch. 13:5 [n]Ps. 106:23 **22:31** [o]ver. 22 [p]ch. 9:10 **23:2** [q]Jer. 3:7,8

Two adulterous sisters

23 THE WORD of the LORD came
again unto me, saying,
2 Son of man, there were [q]two
women, the daughters of one mother:

[e] Heb. *drosses* [f] Heb. According *to the gathering* [g] Heb. *offered violence to* [h] Or, *deceit* [i] Heb. *without right*

22:25–28 HER PROPHETS. Instead of being loyal to God and to their holy calling, the spiritual leaders of the people used their offices for personal financial gain and gave themselves to sinful gratification. Some so-called Christian leaders today are guilty of the same sins, bringing incalculable harm to the church.

22:28 HER PROPHETS . . . LIES. The prophets of Jerusalem were whitewashing the situation; as a result, the people did not fear God or His judgment as they persisted in sin. Today some ministers comfort people in their sins, assuring them that: (1) everyone sins that way; (2) we live in an age when it is impossible to live above sin and immorality because of a tidal wave of evil; (3) we are only human and cannot expect to live up to God's holy standards; (4) God loves us just the way we are, no matter what we do, so that there is no reason to fear Him or His judgment; and (5) God does not see our sin if we are believers, since He sees only Christ's righteousness.

22:30 I SOUGHT FOR A MAN. Corruption among leaders (vv. 25–28) and the people (v. 29) was so widespread in Judah that God could not find even one person who would attempt to lead the people back to God. It is a tragedy when some churches are so gripped by worldliness and spiritual compromise that God can find no one in the congregation who is willing to intercede by building "the hedge" and standing "in the gap" of the collapsing situation, no one to cry out against spiritual and moral decay, no one to lead the way in humble prayer, true repentance, and an earnest seeking of God for revival (cf. 2 Chr. 7:14). All too often many good people remain silent out of a spirit of fear or compromise, rather than risking becoming fervent intercessors for revival and for averting God's wrath and judgment.

23:2 TWO WOMEN. God's people are pictured as two sisters—Samaria (representing the northern kingdom of Israel) and Jerusalem (representing the southern kingdom of Judah). Ezekiel describes them as those who are unfaithful to God and who have committed spiritual adultery by prostituting themselves to other nations. Prostitution here represents Israel's and Judah's seeking alliances with ungodly nations instead of trusting in God alone as their source

3 And [r]they committed whoredoms in Egypt; they committed whoredoms in [s]their youth: there were their breasts pressed, and there they bruised the teats of their virginity.

4 And the names of them *were* Aholah the elder, and Aholibah her sister: and [t]they were mine, and they bare sons and daughters. Thus *were* their names; Samaria *is* [j]Aholah, and Jerusalem [k]Aholibah.

5 And Aholah played the harlot when she was mine; and she doted on her lovers, on [u]the Assyrians *her* neighbours,

6 *Which were* clothed with blue, captains and rulers, all of them desirable young men, horsemen riding upon horses.

7 Thus she [l]committed her whoredoms with them, with all them *that were* [m]the chosen men of Assyria, and with all on whom she doted: with all their idols she defiled herself.

8 Neither left she her whoredoms *brought* [v]from Egypt: for in her youth they lay with her, and they bruised the breasts of her virginity, and poured their whoredom upon her.

9 Wherefore I have delivered her into the hand of her lovers, into the hand of the [w]Assyrians, upon whom she doted.

10 These discovered her nakedness: they took her sons and her daughters, and slew her with the sword: and she became [n]famous among women; for they had executed judgment upon her.

11 And [x]when her sister Aholibah saw *this,* [y]she[o] was more corrupt in her inordinate love than she, and in her whoredoms [p]more than her sister in *her* whoredoms.

12 She doted upon the [z]Assyrians *her* neighbours, [a]captains and rulers clothed most gorgeously, horsemen riding upon horses, all of them desirable young men.

13 Then I saw that she was defiled, *that* they *took* both one way,

14 And *that* she increased her whoredoms: for when she saw men portrayed upon the wall, the images of the Chaldeans portrayed with vermilion,

15 Girded with girdles upon their loins, exceeding in dyed attire upon their heads, all of them princes to look to, after the manner of the Babylonians of Chaldea, the land of their nativity:

16 [b]And [q]as soon as she saw them with her eyes, she doted upon them, and sent messengers unto them into Chaldea.

17 And the [r]Babylonians came to her into the bed of love, and they defiled her with their whoredom, and she was polluted with them, and [c]her mind was [s]alienated from them.

18 So she discovered her whoredoms, and discovered her nakedness: then [d]my mind was alienated from her, like as my mind was alienated from her sister.

19 Yet she multiplied her whoredoms, in calling to remembrance the days of her youth, [e]wherein she had played the harlot in the land of Egypt.

20 For she doted upon their paramours, whose flesh *is as* the flesh of asses, and whose issue *is like* the issue of horses.

21 Thus thou calledst to remembrance the lewdness of thy youth, in bruising thy teats by the Egyptians for the paps of thy youth.

22 ¶ Therefore, O Aholibah, thus saith the Lord GOD; [f]Behold, I will raise up thy lovers against thee, from whom thy mind is alienated, and I will bring them against thee on every side;

23 The Babylonians, and all the Chaldeans, [g]Pekod, and Shoa, and Koa, *and* all the Assyrians with them: [h]all of them desirable young men, captains and rulers, great lords and renowned, all of them riding upon horses.

24 And they shall come against thee with chariots, wagons, and

23:3 [r]Lev. 17:7 Josh. 24:14 [s]ch. 16:22 **23:4** [t]ch. 16:8,20 **23:5** [u]Hos. 8:9 **23:8** [v]ver. 3 **23:9** [w]2 Ki. 17:3 **23:11** [x]Jer. 3:8 [y]Jer. 3:11 **23:12** [z]2 Ki. 16:7 [a]ver. 6,23 **23:16** [b]2 Ki. 24:1 **23:17** [c]ver. 22,28 **23:18** [d]Jer. 6:8 **23:19** [e]ver. 3 **23:22** [f]ver. 28 ch. 16:37 **23:23** [g]Jer. 50:21 [h]ver. 12

[j]i.e. *His tent,* or, *tabernacle* [k]i.e. *My tabernacle in her* [l]Heb. *bestowed her whoredoms upon them* [m]Heb. *the choice of the children of Asshur* [n]Heb. *a name* [o]Heb. *she corrupted her inordinate love more than* [p]Heb. *more than the whoredoms of her sister* [q]Heb. *at the sight of her eyes* [r]Heb. *children of Babel* [s]Heb. *loosed,* or, *disjointed*

of strength and protection.

23:5–9 PLAYED THE HARLOT. Israel entered into alliances first with Assyria (2 Ki. 15:19–29) and then with Egypt (2 Ki. 17:3–6). Eventually they began conforming to the pagan practices and idolatry of these nations. The younger sister, Judah, later did the same thing (cf. 2 Ki. 24:1; Is. 7:1–25; 30—31).

wheels, and with an assembly of peo-
ple, *which* shall set against thee buck-
ler and shield and helmet round about:
and I will set judgment before them,
and they shall judge thee according to
their judgments.
25 And I will set my jealousy
against thee, and they shall deal furi-
ously with thee: they shall take away
thy nose and thine ears; and thy rem-
nant shall fall by the sword: they shall
take thy sons and thy daughters; and
thy residue shall be devoured by the
fire.
26 [i]They shall also strip thee out
of thy clothes, and take away thy [t]fair
jewels.
27 Thus [j]will I make thy lewdness
to cease from thee, and thy [k]whore-
dom *brought* from the land of Egypt: so
that thou shalt not lift up thine eyes
unto them, nor remember Egypt any
more.
28 For thus saith the Lord GOD; Be-
hold, I will deliver thee into the hand
of them [l]whom thou hatest, into the
hand *of them* [m]from whom thy mind is
alienated:
29 And they shall deal with thee
hatefully, and shall take away all thy
labour, and [n]shall leave thee naked
and bare: and the nakedness of thy
whoredoms shall be discovered, both
thy lewdness and thy whoredoms.
30 I will do these *things* unto thee,
because thou hast [o]gone awhoring af-
ter the heathen, *and* because thou art
polluted with their idols.
31 Thou hast walked in the way of
thy sister; therefore will I give her
[p]cup into thine hand.
32 Thus saith the Lord GOD; Thou
shalt drink of thy sister's cup deep and
large: [q]thou shalt be laughed to scorn
and had in derision; it containeth
much.
33 Thou shalt be filled with drunk-
enness and sorrow, with the cup of as-
tonishment and desolation, with the
cup of thy sister Samaria.
34 Thou shalt [r]even drink it and
suck *it* out, and thou shalt break the
sherds thereof, and pluck off thine own
breasts: for I have spoken *it,* saith the
Lord GOD.
35 Therefore thus saith the Lord
GOD; Because thou [s]hast forgotten
me, and [t]cast me behind thy back,
therefore bear thou also thy lewdness
and thy whoredoms.
36 ¶ The LORD said moreover unto
me; Son of man, wilt thou [u]judge[u]
Aholah and Aholibah? yea, [v]declare
unto them their abominations;
37 That they have committed adul-
tery, and [w]blood *is* in their hands, and
with their idols have they committed
adultery, and have also caused their
sons, [x]whom they bare unto me, to
pass for them through *the fire,* to de-
vour *them.*
38 Moreover this they have done
unto me: they have defiled my sanctu-
ary in the same day, and [y]have pro-
faned my sabbaths.
39 For when they had slain their
children to their idols, then they came
the same day into my sanctuary to pro-
fane it; and, lo, [z]thus have they done
in the midst of mine house.
40 And furthermore, that ye have
sent for men [v]to come from far,
[a]unto whom a messenger *was* sent;
and, lo, they came: for whom thou didst
[b]wash thyself, [c]paintedst thy eyes,
and deckedst thyself with ornaments,
41 And satest upon a [w]stately
[d]bed, and a table prepared before it,
[e]whereupon thou hast set mine in-
cense and mine oil.
42 And a voice of a multitude being
at ease *was* with her: and with the men
[x]of the common sort *were* brought
[y]Sabeans from the wilderness, which
put bracelets upon their hands, and
beautiful crowns upon their heads.
43 Then said I unto *her that was* old
in adulteries, Will they now commit
[z]whoredoms with her, and she *with
them?*
44 Yet they went in unto her, as
they go in unto a woman that playeth
the harlot: so went they in unto Aholah

23:26 [i]ch. 16:39
23:27 [j]ch. 16:41 & 22:15 [k]ver. 3,19
23:28 [l]ch. 16:37 [m]ver. 17
23:29 [n]ver. 26 ch. 16:39
23:30 [o]ch. 6:9
23:31 [p]Jer. 25:15
23:32 [q]ch. 22:4,5
23:34 [r]Ps. 75:8 Is. 51:17
23:35 [s]Jer. 2:32 & 3:21 & 13:25 ch. 22:12 [t]1 Ki. 14:9 Neh. 9:26
23:36 [u]ch. 20:4 & 22:2 [v]Is. 58:1
23:37 [w]ver. 45 ch. 16:38 [x]ch. 16:20,21,36, 45 & 20:26,31
23:38 [y]ch. 22:8
23:39 [z]2 Ki. 21:4
23:40 [a]Is. 57:9 [b]Ruth 3:3 [c]2 Ki. 9:30 Jer. 4:30
23:41 [d]Esth. 1:6 Is. 57:7 Amos 2:8 & 6:4 [e]Prov. 7:17 ch. 16:18,19 Hos. 2:8

[t]Heb. *instruments of thy decking* [u]Or, *plead for* [v]Heb. *coming* [w]Heb. *honourable* [x]Heb. *of the multitude of men* [y]Or, *drunkards* [z]Heb. *her whoredoms*

23:35 CAST ME BEHIND THY BACK. To revert to the ungodly ways and values of the world after having experienced God's salvation and deliverance is equivalent to despising the Lord and throwing Him away as though He were useless (cf. Heb. 6:1–8). Believers must never abandon the Lord; instead, we must show love and gratitude to Him who has redeemed us by the death of His Son Jesus.

and unto Aholibah, the lewd women.
45 ¶ And the righteous men, they
shall [f]judge them after the manner of
adulteresses, and after the manner of
women that shed blood; because they
are adulteresses, and [g]blood *is* in their
hands.
46 For thus saith the Lord GOD; [h]I
will bring up a company upon them,
and will give them [a]to be removed and
spoiled.
47 [i]And the company shall stone
them with stones, and [b]dispatch them
with their swords; [j]they shall slay
their sons and their daughters, and
burn up their houses with fire.
48 Thus [k]will I cause lewdness to
cease out of the land, [l]that all women
may be taught not to do after your
lewdness.
49 And they shall recompense your
lewdness upon you, and ye shall [m]bear
the sins of your idols: [n]and ye shall
know that I *am* the Lord GOD.

The parable of the boiling pot

24 AGAIN IN the ninth year, in the
tenth month, in the tenth *day* of
the month, the word of the LORD came
unto me, saying,
2 Son of man, write thee the name
of the day, *even* of this same day: the
king of Babylon set himself against Je-
rusalem [o]this same day.
3 [p]And utter a parable unto the re-
bellious house, and say unto them,
Thus saith the Lord GOD; [q]Set on a
pot, set *it* on, and also pour water
into it:
4 Gather the pieces thereof into it,
even every good piece, the thigh, and
the shoulder; fill *it* with the choice
bones.
5 Take the choice of the flock, and
[c]burn also the bones under it, *and*
make it boil well, and let them seethe
the bones of it therein.
6 ¶ Wherefore thus saith the Lord
GOD; Woe to [r]the bloody city, to the
pot whose scum *is* therein, and whose
scum is not gone out of it! bring it out
piece by piece; let no [s]lot fall upon it.
7 For her blood is in the midst of
her; she set it upon the top of a rock;
[t]she poured it not upon the ground, to
cover it with dust;
8 That it might cause fury to come
up to take vengeance; [u]I have set her
blood upon the top of a rock, that it
should not be covered.
9 Therefore thus saith the Lord
GOD; [v]Woe to the bloody city! I will
even make the pile for fire great.
10 Heap on wood, kindle the fire,
consume the flesh, and spice it well,
and let the bones be burned.
11 Then set it empty upon the coals
thereof, that the brass of it may be hot,
and may burn, and *that* [w]the filthiness
of it may be molten in it, *that* the scum
of it may be consumed.
12 She hath wearied *herself* with
lies, and her great scum went not forth
out of her: her scum *shall be* in the fire.
13 In thy filthiness *is* lewdness: be-
cause I have purged thee, and thou
wast not purged, thou shalt not be
purged from thy filthiness any more,
[x]till I have caused my fury to rest
upon thee.
14 [y]I the LORD have spoken *it:* it
shall come to pass, and I will do *it;* I
will not go back, [z]neither will I spare,
neither will I repent; according to thy
ways, and according to thy doings,
shall they judge thee, saith the Lord
GOD.

The death of Ezekiel's wife

15 ¶ Also the word of the LORD came
unto me, saying,
16 Son of man, behold, I take away
from thee the desire of thine eyes with

23:45 [f]ch. 16:38 [g]ver. 37
23:46 [h]ch. 16:40
23:47 [i]ch. 16:40 [j]2 Chr. 36:17,19 ch. 24:21
23:48 [k]ch. 22:15 [l]Deut. 13:11 2 Pet. 2:6
23:49 [m]ver. 35 [n]ch. 20:38,42,44 & 25:5
24:2 [o]2 Ki. 25:1 Jer. 39:1 & 52:4
24:3 [p]ch. 17:12 [q]See Jer. 1:13 ch. 11:3
24:6 [r]ch. 22:3 [s]See 2 Sam. 8:2 Joel 3:3 Obad. 11 Nah. 3:10
24:7 [t]Lev. 17:13 Deut. 12:16
24:8 [u]Mat. 7:2
24:9 [v]ver. 6 Hab. 2:12
24:11 [w]ch. 22:15
24:13 [x]ch. 8:18
24:14 [y]1 Sam. 15:29 [z]ch. 5:11

[a] Heb. *for a removing and spoil* [b] Or, *single them out* [c] Or, *heap*

24:2 WRITE THEE THE NAME OF THE DAY. This date was Jan. 15, 588 B.C. Ezekiel received his message on the same day that the Babylonian siege of Jerusalem began. The attack lasted nearly two years and brought total destruction to Jerusalem.

24:3–12 SET ON A POT. God gives Ezekiel a parable to speak to His rebellious people. Jerusalem would be like a cooking pot and its inhabitants like pieces of meat and choice bones. The meat and bones would be consumed by the Babylonians. After the contents of the pot were emptied, the pot would be further purified by the fire of judgment until its bronze glowed, its filthiness melted, and its rust was consumed (v. 11).

24:13 THOU SHALT NOT BE PURGED . . . TILL. Because Jerusalem refused to let God cleanse her from her impurity, she had to face His furious wrath. Likewise, all the nations will face the wrath of God at the end of time. Only by God's righteous judgment will the world be cleansed of sin (Rev. 5—22).

24:16 THE DESIRE OF THINE EYES. God told Ezekiel that he would lose his wife whom he

a stroke: yet neither shalt thou mourn nor weep, neither shall thy tears [d]run down.

17 [e]Forbear to cry, [a]make no mourning for the dead, [b]bind the tire of thine head upon thee, and [c]put on thy shoes upon thy feet, and [d]cover not *thy* [e]lips,[f] and eat not the bread of men.

18 So I spake unto the people in the morning: and at even my wife died; and I did in the morning as I was commanded.

19 ¶ And the people said unto me, [f]Wilt thou not tell us what these *things are* to us, that thou doest *so?*

20 Then I answered them, The word of the LORD came unto me, saying,

21 Speak unto the house of Israel, Thus saith the Lord GOD; Behold, [g]I will profane my sanctuary, the excellency of your strength, the desire of your eyes, and [g]that which your soul pitieth; [h]and your sons and your daughters whom ye have left shall fall by the sword.

22 And ye shall do as I have done: [i]ye shall not cover *your* lips, nor eat the bread of men.

23 And your tires *shall be* upon your heads, and your shoes upon your feet: [j]ye shall not mourn nor weep; but [k]ye shall pine away for your iniquities, and mourn one toward another.

24 Thus [l]Ezekiel is unto you a sign: according to all that he hath done shall ye do: [m]and when this cometh, [n]ye shall know that I *am* the Lord GOD.

25 Also, thou son of man, *shall it* not *be* in the day when I take from them [o]their strength, the joy of their glory, the desire of their eyes, and [h]that whereupon they set their minds, their sons and their daughters,

26 *That* [p]he that escapeth in that day shall come unto thee, to cause *thee* to hear *it* with *thine* ears?

27 [q]In that day shall thy mouth be opened to him which is escaped, and thou shalt speak, and be no more dumb: and thou shalt be a sign unto them; and they shall know that I *am* the LORD.

24:17 [a]Jer. 16:5 [b]See Lev. 10:6 & 21:10 [c]2 Sam. 15:30 [d]Mic. 3:7 [e]ver. 22 Lev. 13:45
24:19 [f]ch. 12:9 & 37:18
24:21 [g]Jer. 7:14 ch. 7:20 [h]ch. 23:47
24:22 [i]ver. 17 Jer. 16:6,7
24:23 [j]Job 27:15 Ps. 78:64 [k]Lev. 26:39
24:24 [l]Is. 20:3 ch. 4:3 & 12:6,11 [m]Jer. 17:15 John 13:19 & 14:29 [n]ch. 6:7 & 25:5
24:25 [o]ver. 21
24:26 [p]ch. 33:21
24:27 [q]ch. 3:26
25:2 [r]ch. 35:2 [s]Jer. 49:1 ch. 21:28 Zeph. 2:9
25:3 [t]Prov. 17:5 ch. 26:2
25:5 [u]ch. 21:20 [v]Is. 17:2 [w]ch. 24:24
25:6 [x]Job 27:23 Lam. 2:15 Zeph. 2:15

Prophecy against Ammon

25 THE WORD of the LORD came again unto me, saying,

2 Son of man, [r]set thy face [s]against the Ammonites, and prophesy against them;

3 And say unto the Ammonites, Hear the word of the Lord GOD; Thus saith the Lord GOD; [t]Because thou saidst, Aha, against my sanctuary, when it was profaned; and against the land of Israel, when it was desolate; and against the house of Judah, when they went into captivity;

4 Behold, therefore I will deliver thee to the [i]men of the east for a possession, and they shall set their palaces in thee, and make their dwellings in thee: they shall eat thy fruit, and they shall drink thy milk.

5 And I will make [u]Rabbah [v]a stable for camels, and the Ammonites a couching place for flocks: [w]and ye shall know that I *am* the LORD.

6 For thus saith the Lord GOD; Because thou [x]hast clapped *thine*

[d] Heb. *go* [e] Heb. *Be silent* [f] Heb. *upper lip* [g] Heb. *the pity of your soul* [h] Heb. *the lifting up of their soul* [i] Heb. *children*

loved dearly, yet he was not to bewail her death publicly or to engage in the usual customs of mourning. By this command, however, God did not forbid Ezekiel the right to grieve privately over the loss of his wife. Ezekiel's refusal to show any outward expression of grief was intended as a sign to the exiles that the fall of Jerusalem and the temple would be so devastating that the people would be unable to make the usual expressions of sorrow.

24:18 I DID ... AS I WAS COMMANDED. Ezekiel's obedience in this situation must have been one of his most difficult tasks as a prophet. Though experiencing great sorrow over the loss of his wife, he still had to keep on prophesying day after day to a rebellious people. He was sharing in God's sufferings, for God Himself was about to lose His people, His city, and His temple, just as the faithful prophet had lost his precious wife. Being faithful to God can be very costly. In a similar manner, N.T. believers are called upon to share the sufferings of Christ (see 2 Cor. 1:7; 4:10–11).

25:1—32:32 SET THY FACE AGAINST. These chapters contain prophecies against seven nations that were hostile to God, His commandments, and His people. Ezekiel reveals in these eight chapters that all nations are ultimately answerable to God and that worldly powers will never destroy his plan of salvation. Though at times the ungodly forces of the world seem victorious, the day is coming when God will bring all evil into judgment, the wicked nations will perish, and His faithful people will receive full salvation.

25:2–3 AMMONITES. The Ammonites were a people living east of Israel whom God chastised for taking great delight in the fall of Jerusalem and the devastation of the temple.

25:4 MEN OF THE EAST. These people are most likely the Babylonian army.

[j]hands, and stamped with the [k]feet, and [y]rejoiced in [l]heart with all thy despite against the land of Israel;

7 Behold, therefore I will [z]stretch out mine hand upon thee, and will deliver thee for [m]a spoil to the heathen; and I will cut thee off from the people, and I will cause thee to perish out of the countries: I will destroy thee; and thou shalt know that I *am* the LORD.

Prophecy against Moab

8 ¶ Thus saith the Lord GOD; Because that [a]Moab and [b]Seir do say, Behold, the house of Judah *is* like unto all the heathen;

9 Therefore, behold, I will open the [n]side of Moab from the cities, from his cities *which are* on his frontiers, the glory of the country, Beth-jeshimoth, Baal-meon, and Kiriathaim,

10 [c]Unto the men of the east [o]with the Ammonites, and will give them in possession, that the Ammonites [d]may not be remembered among the nations.

11 And I will execute judgments upon Moab; and they shall know that I *am* the LORD.

Prophecy against Edom

12 ¶ Thus saith the Lord GOD; [e]Because that Edom hath dealt against the house of Judah [p]by taking vengeance, and hath greatly offended, and revenged himself upon them;

13 Therefore thus saith the Lord GOD; I will also stretch out mine hand upon Edom, and will cut off man and beast from it; and I will make it desolate from Teman; and [q]they of Dedan shall fall by the sword.

14 And [f]I will lay my vengeance upon Edom by the hand of my people Israel: and they shall do in Edom according to mine anger and according to my fury; and they shall know my vengeance, saith the Lord GOD.

Prophecy against Philistia

15 ¶ Thus saith the Lord GOD; [g]Because [h]the Philistines have dealt by revenge, and have taken vengeance with a despiteful heart, to destroy *it* [r]for the old hatred;

16 Therefore thus saith the Lord GOD; Behold, [i]I will stretch out mine hand upon the Philistines, and I will cut off the [j]Cherethims, [k]and destroy the remnant of the [s]sea coast.

17 And I will [l]execute great [t]vengeance upon them with furious rebukes; [m]and they shall know that I *am* the LORD, when I shall lay my vengeance upon them.

Prophecy against Tyrus

26 AND IT came to pass in the eleventh year, in the first *day* of the month, *that* the word of the LORD came unto me, saying,

2 Son of man, [n]because that Tyrus hath said against Jerusalem, [o]Aha, she is broken *that was* the gates of the people: she is turned unto me: I shall be replenished, *now* she is laid waste:

3 Therefore thus saith the Lord GOD; Behold, I *am* against thee, O Tyrus, and will cause many nations to come up against thee, as the sea causeth his waves to come up.

4 And they shall destroy the walls of Tyrus, and break down her towers: I will also scrape her dust from her, and [p]make her like the top of a rock.

5 It shall be *a place for* the spreading of nets [q]in the midst of the sea: for I have spoken *it,* saith the Lord GOD: and it shall become a spoil to the nations.

6 And her daughters which *are* in the field shall be slain by the sword;

[j] Heb. *hand* [k] Heb. *foot* [l] Heb. *soul* [m] Or, *meat* [n] Heb. *shoulder of Moab* [o] Or, *against the children of Ammon* [p] Heb. *by revenging revengement* [q] Or, *they shall fall by the sword unto Dedan* [r] Or, *with perpetual hatred* [s] Or, *haven of the sea* [t] Heb. *vengeances*

25:6 [y]ch. 36:5
25:7 [z]ch. 35:3
25:8 [a]Is. 15 & 16 Jer. 48:1 Amos 2:1 [b]ch. 35:2,5
25:10 [c]ver. 4 [d]ch. 21:32
25:12 [e]2 Chr. 28:17 Ps. 137:7 Jer. 49:7,8 Amos 1:11 Obad. 10
25:14 [f]Is. 11:14
25:15 [g]Jer. 25:20 Amos 1:6 [h]2 Chr. 28:18
25:16 [i]Zeph. 2:4 [j]1 Sam. 30:14 [k]Jer. 47:4
25:17 [l]ch. 5:15 [m]Ps. 9:16
26:2 [n]Is. 23 Jer. 25:22 Amos 1:9 Zech. 9:2 [o]ch. 25:3
26:4 [p]ver. 14
26:5 [q]ch. 27:32

25:8 JUDAH *IS* LIKE . . . THE HEATHEN. Ezekiel prophesies that Moab would be punished because they believed that Israel's God was no greater than the gods of other nations (cf. v. 11).
25:12 VENGEANCE. The Edomites would be punished for their intense hatred of Israel.
26:2 TYRUS. Tyre, the capital of Phoenicia, was located sixty miles northwest of Nazareth on the Mediterranean coast. Part of the city was an island and part was coastland at the foot of the Lebanon mountains. Tyre rejoiced over the fall of Jerusalem because its citizens believed they would gain financially from trade advantages now that Judah was out of the picture. Tyre's desire for wealth with no thought of the suffering it caused others brought God's judgment (see also Is. 23). The city was subjugated by "many nations" (v. 3), i.e., the Babylonians, next the Persians, and then the Greeks, led by Alexander the Great (332 B.C.).

[r]and they shall know that I *am* the
LORD.
7 ¶ For thus saith the Lord GOD; Be-
hold, I will bring upon Tyrus Nebu-
chadrezzar king of Babylon, [s]a king of
kings, from the north, with horses, and
with chariots, and with horsemen, and
companies, and much people.
8 He shall slay with the sword thy
daughters in the field: and he shall
[t]make a fort against thee, and [u]cast
a mount against thee, and lift up the
buckler against thee.
9 And he shall set engines of war
against thy walls, and with his axes he
shall break down thy towers.
10 By reason of the abundance of
his horses their dust shall cover thee:
thy walls shall shake at the noise of
the horsemen, and of the wheels, and
of the chariots, when he shall enter
into thy gates, [v]as men enter into a
city wherein is made a breach.
11 With the hoofs of his horses
shall he tread down all thy streets: he
shall slay thy people by the sword, and
thy strong garrisons shall go down to
the ground.
12 And they shall make a spoil of
thy riches, and make a prey of thy mer-
chandise: and they shall break down
thy walls, and destroy [w]thy pleasant
houses: and they shall lay thy stones
and thy timber and thy dust in the
midst of the water.
13 [u]And I will cause the noise of
[v]thy songs to cease; and the sound of
thy harps shall be no more heard.
14 And [w]I will make thee like the
top of a rock: thou shalt be *a place* to
spread nets upon; thou shalt be built
no more: for I the LORD have spoken *it*,
saith the Lord GOD.
15 ¶ Thus saith the Lord GOD to
Tyrus; Shall not the isles [x]shake at
the sound of thy fall, when the wound-
ed cry, when the slaughter is made in
the midst of thee?
16 Then all the [y]princes of the sea
shall [z]come down from their thrones,
and lay away their robes, and put off
their broidered garments: they shall
clothe themselves with [x]trembling;
[a]they shall sit upon the ground, and
[b]shall tremble at *every* moment, and
[c]be astonished at thee.
17 And they shall take up a [d]lam-
entation for thee, and say to thee, How
art thou destroyed, *that wast* inhabited
[y]of seafaring men, the renowned city,
which wast [e]strong in the sea, she
and her inhabitants, which cause their
terror *to be* on all that haunt it!
18 Now shall [f]the isles tremble in
the day of thy fall; yea, the isles that
are in the sea shall be troubled at thy
departure.
19 For thus saith the Lord GOD;
When I shall make thee a desolate city,
like the cities that are not inhabited;
when I shall bring up the deep upon
thee, and great waters shall cover
thee;
20 When I shall bring thee down
[g]with them that descend into the pit,
with the people of old time, and shall
set thee in the low parts of the earth,
in places desolate of old, with them
that go down to the pit, that thou be not
inhabited; and I shall set glory [h]in the
land of the living;
21 [i]I will make thee [z]a terror,
and thou *shalt be* no *more:* [j]though
thou be sought for, yet shalt thou never
be found again, saith the Lord GOD.

The lament for Tyrus

27 THE WORD of the LORD came
again unto me, saying,
2 Now, thou son of man, [k]take up
a lamentation for Tyrus;
3 And say unto Tyrus, [l]O thou that
art situate at the entry of the sea, *which
art* [m]a merchant of the people for many
isles, Thus saith the Lord GOD; O
Tyrus, thou hast said, [n]I *am* [a]of per-
fect beauty.
4 Thy borders *are* in the [b]midst of
the seas, thy builders have perfected
thy beauty.
5 They have [c]made all thy *ship*
boards of fir trees of [o]Senir: they have

26:6 [r]ch. 25:5 **26:7** [s]Ezra 7:12 Dan. 2:37 **26:8** [t]ch. 21:22 **26:13** [u]Is. 14:11 & 24:8 Jer. 7:34 & 25:10 [v]Is. 23:16 ch. 28:13 Rev. 18:22 **26:14** [w]ver. 4,5 **26:15** [x]ver. 18 Jer. 49:21 ch. 27:28 **26:16** [y]Is. 23:8 [z]Jonah 3:6 [a]Job 2:13 [b]ch. 32:10 [c]ch. 27:35 **26:17** [d]ch. 27:32 Rev. 18:9 [e]Is. 23:4 **26:18** [f]ver. 15 **26:20** [g]ch. 32:18 [h]ch. 32:23 **26:21** [i]ch. 28:19 [j]Ps. 37:36 **27:2** [k]ch. 26:17 **27:3** [l]ch. 28:2 [m]Is. 23:3 [n]ch. 28:12 **27:5** [o]Deut. 3:9

[u] Or, *pour out the engine of shot* [v] Heb. *according to the enterings of a city broken up* [w] Heb. *houses of thy desire* [x] Heb. *tremblings* [y] Heb. *of the seas* [z] Heb. *terrors* [a] Heb. *perfect of beauty* [b] Heb. *heart* [c] Heb. *built*

27:1–36 LAMENTATION FOR TYRUS. Tyre had a great fleet of merchant ships. This chapter pictures her as a great and beautiful ship bringing merchandise and treasures to many nations. Yet God in His judgment would break the ship to pieces, and many would lament its destruction. Compare this chapter with Rev. 18, where God destroys the commercial center of the world (see Rev. 18:2–9, notes).

taken cedars from Lebanon to make masts for thee.

6 *Of* the oaks of Bashan have they made thine oars; [d] [e]the company of the Ashurites have made thy benches *of* ivory, *brought* out of [p]the isles of Chittim.

7 Fine linen with broidered work from Egypt was that which thou spreadest forth to be thy sail; [f]blue and purple from the isles of Elishah was that which covered thee.

8 The inhabitants of Zidon and Arvad were thy mariners: thy wise *men,* O Tyrus, *that* were in thee, were thy pilots.

9 The ancients of [q]Gebal and the wise *men* thereof were in thee thy [g] [h]calkers: all the ships of the sea with their mariners were in thee to occupy thy merchandise.

10 They of Persia and of Lud and of Phut were in thine army, thy men of war: they hanged the shield and helmet in thee; they set forth thy comeliness.

11 The men of Arvad with thine army *were* upon thy walls round about, and the Gammadims were in thy towers: they hanged their shields upon thy walls round about; they have made [r]thy beauty perfect.

12 [s]Tarshish *was* thy merchant by reason of the multitude of all *kind of* riches; with silver, iron, tin, and lead, they traded in thy fairs.

13 [t]Javan, Tubal, and Meshech, they *were* thy merchants: they traded [u]the persons of men and vessels of brass in thy [i]market.

14 They of the house of [v]Togarmah traded in thy fairs with horses and horsemen and mules.

15 The men of [w]Dedan *were* thy merchants; many isles *were* the merchandise of thine hand: they brought thee *for* a present horns of ivory and ebony.

16 Syria *was* thy merchant by reason of the multitude of [j]the wares of thy making: they occupied in thy fairs with emeralds, purple, and broidered work, and fine linen, and coral, and [k]agate.

17 Judah, and the land of Israel, they *were* thy merchants: they traded in thy market wheat of [x]Minnith, and Pannag, and honey, and oil, and [y]balm.[l]

18 Damascus *was* thy merchant in the multitude of the wares of thy making, for the multitude of all riches; in the wine of Helbon, and white wool.

19 Dan also and Javan [m]going to and fro occupied in thy fairs: bright iron, cassia, and calamus, were in thy market.

20 [z]Dedan *was* thy merchant in [n]precious clothes for chariots.

21 Arabia, and all the princes of [a]Kedar, [o]they occupied with thee in lambs, and rams, and goats: in these *were they* thy merchants.

22 The merchants of [b]Sheba and Raamah, they *were* thy merchants: they occupied in thy fairs with chief of all spices, and with all precious stones, and gold.

23 [c]Haran, and Canneh, and Eden, the merchants of [d]Sheba, Asshur, *and* Chilmad, *were* thy merchants.

24 These *were* thy merchants in [p]all sorts *of things,* in blue [q]clothes, and broidered work, and in chests of rich apparel, bound with cords, and made of cedar, among thy merchandise.

25 [e]The ships of Tarshish did sing of thee in thy market: and thou wast replenished, and made very glorious [f]in the midst of the seas.

26 ¶ Thy rowers have brought thee into great waters: [g]the east wind hath broken thee in the [r]midst of the seas.

27 Thy [h]riches, and thy fairs, thy merchandise, thy mariners, and thy pilots, thy calkers, and the occupiers of thy merchandise, and all thy men of war, that *are* in thee, [s]and in all thy company which *is* in the midst of thee, shall fall into the [r]midst of the seas in the day of thy ruin.

28 The [t]suburbs[i] shall shake at the sound of the cry of thy pilots.

29 And [j]all that handle the oar, the mariners, *and* all the pilots of the sea, shall come down from their ships, they shall stand upon the land;

30 And shall cause their voice to be heard against thee, and shall cry bitterly, and shall [k]cast up dust upon

27:6 [p]Jer. 2:10
27:9 [q]1 Ki. 5:18 Ps. 83:7
27:11 [r]ver. 3
27:12 [s]Gen. 10:4 2 Chr. 20:36
27:13 [t]Gen. 10:2 [u]Rev. 18:13
27:14 [v]ch. 38:6
27:15 [w]Gen. 10:7
27:17 [x]Judg. 11:33 [y]Jer. 8:22
27:20 [z]Gen. 25:3
27:21 [a]Gen. 25:13 Is. 60:7
27:22 [b]Gen. 10:7 1 Ki. 10:1,2 Ps. 72:10 Is. 60:6
27:23 [c]Gen. 11:31 2 Ki. 19:12 [d]Gen. 25:3
27:25 [e]Ps. 48:7 Is. 2:16 [f]ver. 4
27:26 [g]Ps. 48:7
27:27 [h]Prov. 11:4
27:28 [i]ch. 26:15
27:29 [j]Rev. 18:17
27:30 [k]Job 2:12 Rev. 18:19

[d] Or, *they have made thy hatches of ivory well trodden* [e] Heb. *the daughter* [f] Or, *purple and scarlet* [g] Or, *stoppers of chinks* [h] Heb. *strengtheners* [i] Or, *merchandise* [j] Heb. *thy works* [k] Heb. *chrysoprase* [l] Or, *rosin* [m] Or, *Meuzal* [n] Heb. *clothes of freedom* [o] Heb. *they were the merchants of thy hand* [p] Or, *excellent things* [q] Heb. *foldings* [r] Heb. *heart* [s] Or, *even with all* [t] Or, *waves*

their heads, they [l]shall wallow them-
selves in the ashes:
31 And they shall [m]make them-
selves utterly bald for thee, and gird
them with sackcloth, and they shall
weep for thee with bitterness of heart
and bitter wailing.
32 And in their wailing they shall
[n]take up a lamentation for thee, and
lament over thee, *saying,* [o]What *city is*
like Tyrus, like the destroyed in the
midst of the sea?
33 [p]When thy wares went forth out
of the seas, thou filledst many people;
thou didst enrich the kings of the earth
with the multitude of thy riches and of
thy merchandise.
34 In the time *when* [q]thou shalt be
broken by the seas in the depths of the
waters [r]thy merchandise and all thy
company in the midst of thee shall fall.
35 [s]All the inhabitants of the isles
shall be astonished at thee, and their
kings shall be sore afraid, they shall be
troubled in *their* countenance.
36 The merchants among the peo-
ple [t]shall hiss at thee; [u]thou shalt be
[u]a terror, and [v]never *shalt be* any
more.

Tyrus' pride and ruin

28 THE WORD of the LORD came
again unto me, saying,
2 Son of man, say unto the prince of
Tyrus, Thus saith the Lord GOD; Be-
cause thine heart *is* lifted up, and
[v]thou hast said, I *am* a God, I sit *in* the
seat of God, [w]in the [w]midst of the
seas; [x]yet thou *art* a man, and not
God, though thou set thine heart as the
heart of God:
3 Behold, [y]thou *art* wiser than
Daniel; there is no secret that they can
hide from thee:
4 With thy wisdom and with thine
understanding thou hast gotten thee
riches, and hast gotten gold and silver
into thy treasures:
5 [z]By[x] thy great wisdom *and* by
thy traffic hast thou increased thy
riches, and thine heart is lifted up be-
cause of thy riches:
6 Therefore thus saith the Lord
GOD; Because thou hast set thine heart
as the heart of God;
7 Behold, therefore I will bring
strangers upon thee, [a]the terrible of
the nations: and they shall draw their
swords against the beauty of thy wis-
dom, and they shall defile thy bright-
ness.
8 They shall bring thee down to the
pit, and thou shalt die the deaths of
them that are slain in the midst of the
seas.
9 Wilt thou yet [b]say before him
that slayeth thee, I *am* God? but thou
shalt be a man, and no God, in the hand
of him that [y]slayeth thee.
10 Thou shalt die the deaths of
[c]the uncircumcised by the hand of
strangers: for I have spoken *it,* saith
the Lord GOD.
11 ¶ Moreover the word of the LORD
came unto me, saying,
12 Son of man, [d]take up a lamenta-
tion upon the king of Tyrus, and say
unto him, Thus saith the Lord GOD;
[e]Thou sealest up the sum, full of wis-
dom, and perfect in beauty.
13 Thou hast been in [f]Eden the
garden of God; every precious stone
was thy covering, the [z]sardius, topaz,
and the diamond, the [a]beryl, the onyx,
and the jasper, the sapphire, the [b]em-
erald, and the carbuncle, and gold: the
workmanship of [g]thy tabrets and of
thy pipes was prepared in thee in the
day that thou wast created.
14 Thou *art* the anointed [h]cherub
that covereth; and I have set thee *so:*
thou wast upon [i]the holy mountain of
God; thou hast walked up and down in
the midst of the stones of fire.
15 Thou *wast* perfect in thy ways

27:30 [l]Esth. 4:1,3 Jer. 6:26 **27:31** [m]Jer. 16:6 **27:32** [n]ch. 26:17 [o]Rev. 18:18 **27:33** [p]Rev. 18:19 **27:34** [q]ch. 26:19 [r]ver. 27 **27:35** [s]ch. 26:15 **27:36** [t]Jer. 18:16 [u]ch. 26:21 **28:2** [v]ver. 9 [w]ch. 27:3,4 [x]Is. 31:3 **28:3** [y]Zech. 9:2 **28:5** [z]Ps. 62:10 Zech. 9:3 **28:7** [a]ch. 30:11 & 31:12 & 32:12 **28:9** [b]ver. 2 **28:10** [c]ch. 31:18 & 32:19,21,25,27 **28:12** [d]ch. 27:2 [e]ver. 3 ch. 27:3 **28:13** [f]ch. 31:8,9 [g]ch. 26:13 **28:14** [h]ver. 16 See Ex. 25:20 [i]ch. 20:40

[u]Heb. *terrors* [v]Heb. shalt *not* be *for ever* [w]Heb. *heart* [x]Heb. *By the greatness of thy wisdom* [y]Or, *woundeth* [z]Or, *ruby* [a]Or, *chrysolite* [b]Or, *chrysoprase*

28:1–10 PRINCE OF TYRUS. The king of Tyre's fundamental sin was pride, which led him to exalt himself as a deity. For this he would face the judgment of the Lord God and be brought down to the pit like all mortals (v. 8). Many today, especially those caught up in New Age thinking, actually believe that we are gods or at least are becoming gods. Such deceivers and their victims will receive the same condemnation as the ruler of Tyre.

28:12 KING OF TYRUS. In its context, Ezekiel's prophecy against the ruler of Tyre appears to contain a veiled description of Satan as the true ruler of Tyre and as the god of this world (cf. 1 John 5:19). The king is described as having been a visitor to the garden of Eden (v. 13), an "anointed cherub," or angel (v. 14), and a perfect creature in all his ways until unrighteousness was found in him (v. 15). Because of his sinful pride (v. 17), he was cast down from the mountain of God (vv. 16–17; cf. Is. 14:13–15).

from the day that thou wast created,
till iniquity was found in thee.
16 By the multitude of thy merchan-
dise they have filled the midst of thee
with violence, and thou hast sinned:
therefore I will cast thee as profane out
of the mountain of God: and I will de-
stroy thee, [j]O covering cherub, from
the midst of the stones of fire.
17 [k]Thine heart was lifted up be-
cause of thy beauty, thou hast corrupt-
ed thy wisdom by reason of thy bright-
ness: I will cast thee to the ground, I
will lay thee before kings, that they
may behold thee.
18 Thou hast defiled thy sanctuar-
ies by the multitude of thine iniquities,
by the iniquity of thy traffic; therefore
will I bring forth a fire from the midst
of thee, it shall devour thee, and I will
bring thee to ashes upon the earth in
the sight of all them that behold thee.
19 All they that know thee among
the people shall be astonished at thee:
[l]thou shalt be [c]a terror, and never
shalt thou *be* any more.

Zidon to perish

20 ¶ Again the word of the LORD
came unto me, saying,
21 Son of man, [m]set thy face
[n]against Zidon, and prophesy
against it,
22 And say, Thus saith the Lord
GOD; [o]Behold, I *am* against thee, O Zi-
don; and I will be glorified in the midst
of thee: and [p]they shall know that I
am the LORD, when I shall have execut-
ed judgments in her, and shall be
[q]sanctified in her.
23 [r]For I will send into her pesti-
lence, and blood into her streets; and
the wounded shall be judged in the
midst of her by the sword upon her on
every side; and they shall know that I
am the LORD.
24 ¶ And there shall be no more [s]a
pricking brier unto the house of Israel,
nor *any* grieving thorn of all *that are*
round about them, that despised them;
and they shall know that I *am* the Lord
GOD.

28:16 [j]ver. 14 **28:17** [k]ver. 2,5 **28:19** [l]ch. 26:21 & 27:36 **28:21** [m]ch. 6:2 & 25:2 & 29:2 [n]Is. 23:4,12 Jer. 25:22 & 27:3 ch. 32:30 **28:22** [o]Ex. 14:4,17 ch. 39:13 [p]Ps. 9:16 [q]ver. 25 ch. 20:41 & 36:23 **28:23** [r]ch. 38:22 **28:24** [s]Num. 33:55 Josh. 23:13

28:25 [t]Is. 11:12 ch. 11:17 & 20:41 & 34:13 & 37:21 [u]ver. 22 **28:26** [v]Jer. 23:6 ch. 36:28 [w]Is. 65:21 Amos 9:14 [x]Jer. 31:5 **29:2** [y]ch. 28:21 [z]Is. 19:1 Jer. 25:19 & 46:2,25 **29:3** [a]ver. 10 Jer. 44:30 ch. 28:22 [b]Ps. 74:13,14 Is. 27:1 & 51:9 ch. 32:2 [c]See ch. 28:2 **29:4** [d]Is. 37:29 ch. 38:4 **29:5** [e]Jer. 8:2 & 16:4 & 25:33 [f]Jer. 7:33 & 34:20 **29:6** [g]2 Ki. 18:21 Is. 36:6

25 Thus saith the Lord GOD; When I
shall have [t]gathered the house of Is-
rael from the people among whom they
are scattered, and shall be [u]sanctified
in them in the sight of the heathen,
then shall they dwell in their land that
I have given to my servant Jacob.
26 And they shall [v]dwell [d]safely
therein, and shall [w]build houses, and
[x]plant vineyards; yea, they shall dwell
with confidence, when I have executed
judgments upon all those that [e]de-
spise them round about them; and they
shall know that I *am* the LORD their
God.

Egypt's pride and desolation

29 IN THE tenth year, in the tenth
month, in the twelfth *day* of the
month, the word of the LORD came unto
me, saying,
2 Son of man, [y]set thy face against
Pharaoh king of Egypt, and prophesy
against him, and [z]against all Egypt:
3 Speak, and say, Thus saith the
Lord GOD; [a]Behold, I *am* against thee,
Pharaoh king of Egypt, the great
[b]dragon that lieth in the midst of his
rivers, [c]which hath said, My river *is*
mine own, and I have made *it* for my-
self.
4 But [d]I will put hooks in thy jaws,
and I will cause the fish of thy rivers
to stick unto thy scales, and I will bring
thee up out of the midst of thy rivers,
and all the fish of thy rivers shall stick
unto thy scales.
5 And I will leave thee *thrown* into
the wilderness, thee and all the fish of
thy rivers: thou shalt fall upon the
[f]open fields; [e]thou shalt not be
brought together, nor gathered: [f]I
have given thee for meat to the beasts
of the field and to the fowls of the
heaven.
6 And all the inhabitants of Egypt
shall know that I *am* the LORD, because
they have been a [g]staff of reed to the
house of Israel.

[c] Heb. *terrors* [d] Or, *with confidence* [e] Or, *spoil* [f] Heb. *face of the field*

28:25 GATHERED THE HOUSE OF ISRAEL. Ezekiel frequently emphasizes the promise to restore Israel (11:17; 20:34,41–42; 34:13; 36:24; 37:21; 38:8; 39:27). This restoration will not fully take place until God executes judgment upon all the nations in the end times. By regathering Israel to serve Him in righteousness, God will demonstrate that He is indeed a holy God who will accomplish all His purposes in this world (Gen. 12:7; 26:3; 35:12).

29:1—32:32 EGYPT. These chapters give seven prophecies of judgment against Egypt. Egypt was judged because it was a world power that worshiped many gods and arrogantly boasted of its might.

7 [h]When they took hold of thee by thy hand, thou didst break, and rend all their shoulder: and when they leaned upon thee, thou brakest, and madest all their loins to be at a stand.

8 ¶ Therefore thus saith the Lord GOD; Behold, I will bring [i]a sword upon thee, and cut off man and beast out of thee.

9 And the land of Egypt shall be desolate and waste; and they shall know that I *am* the LORD: because he hath said, The river *is* mine, and I have made *it*.

10 Behold, therefore I *am* against thee, and against thy rivers, [j]and I will make the land of Egypt [g]utterly waste *and* desolate, [k]from[h] the tower of [i]Syene even unto the border of Ethiopia.

11 [l]No foot of man shall pass through it, nor foot of beast shall pass through it, neither shall it be inhabited forty years.

12 [m]And I will make the land of Egypt desolate in the midst of the countries *that are* desolate, and her cities among the cities *that are* laid waste shall be desolate forty years: and I will scatter the Egyptians among the nations, and will disperse them through the countries.

13 ¶ Yet thus saith the Lord GOD; At the [n]end of forty years will I gather the Egyptians from the people whither they were scattered:

14 And I will bring again the captivity of Egypt, and will cause them to return *into* the land of Pathros, into the land of their [j]habitation; and they shall be there a [o]base[k] kingdom.

15 It shall be the basest of the kingdoms; neither shall it exalt itself any more above the nations: for I will diminish them, that they shall no more rule over the nations.

16 And it shall be no more [p]the confidence of the house of Israel, which bringeth *their* iniquity to remembrance, when they shall look after them: but they shall know that I *am* the Lord GOD.

17 ¶ And it came to pass in the seven and twentieth year, in the first *month*, in the first *day* of the month, the word of the LORD came unto me, saying,

18 Son of man, [q]Nebuchadrezzar king of Babylon caused his army to serve a great service against Tyrus: every head *was* made bald, and every shoulder *was* peeled: yet had he no wages, nor his army, for Tyrus, for the service that he had served against it:

19 Therefore thus saith the Lord GOD; Behold, I will give the land of Egypt unto Nebuchadrezzar king of Babylon; and he shall take her multitude, and [l]take her spoil, and take her prey; and it shall be the wages for his army.

20 I have given him the land of Egypt [m]*for* his labour wherewith he [r]served against it, because they wrought for me, saith the Lord GOD.

21 ¶ In that day [s]will I cause the horn of the house of Israel to bud forth, and I will give thee [t]the opening of the mouth in the midst of them; and they shall know that I *am* the LORD.

A lament for Egypt

30 THE WORD of the LORD came again unto me, saying,

2 Son of man, prophesy and say, Thus saith the Lord GOD; [u]Howl ye, Woe worth the day!

3 For [v]the day *is* near, even the day of the LORD *is* near, a cloudy day; it shall be the time of the heathen.

4 And the sword shall come upon Egypt, and great [n]pain shall be in Ethiopia, when the slain shall fall in Egypt, and they [w]shall take away her multitude, and [x]her foundations shall be broken down.

5 Ethiopia, and [o]Libya, and Lydia, and [y]all the mingled people, and Chub, and the [p]men of the land that is in league, shall fall with them by the sword.

6 Thus saith the LORD; They also that uphold Egypt shall fall; and the

29:7 [h]Jer. 37:5,7,11 ch. 17:17 **29:8** [i]ch. 14:17 & 32:11-13 **29:10** [j]ch. 30:12 [k]ch. 30:6 **29:11** [l]ch. 32:13 **29:12** [m]ch. 30:7,26 **29:13** [n]Is. 19:23 Jer. 46:26 **29:14** [o]ch. 17:6,14 **29:16** [p]Is. 30:2,3 & 36:4,6

29:18 [q]Jer. 27:6 ch. 26:7,8 **29:20** [r]Jer. 25:9 **29:21** [s]Ps. 132:17 [t]ch. 24:27 **30:2** [u]Is. 13:6 **30:3** [v]ch. 7:7,12 Joel 2:1 Zeph. 1:7 **30:4** [w]ch. 29:19 [x]Jer. 50:15 **30:5** [y]Jer. 25:20,24

[g] Heb. *wastes of waste* [h] Or, *from Migdol to Syene;* see Ex. 14:2; Jer. 44:1 [i] Heb. *Seveneh* [j] Or, *birth* [k] Heb. *low* [l] Heb. *spoil her spoil, and prey her prey* [m] Or, for *his hire* [n] Or, *fear* [o] Heb. *Phut;* see ch. 27:10 [p] Heb. *children*

29:8 I WILL BRING A SWORD UPON THEE. God would send Nebuchadnezzar, the Babylonian king, against Egypt and reduce it to "the basest of the kingdoms" (v. 15; cf. vv. 19–20). Babylon attacked Egypt in 572 and 568 B.C.

30:3 THE DAY OF THE LORD. Egypt's doom foreshadows the coming "day of the LORD," when God will bring judgment upon all the ungodly nations of the world (see 1 Thes. 5:2,4, notes).

pride of her power shall come down: [z]from[q] the tower of Syene shall they fall in it by the sword, saith the Lord GOD.

7 [a]And they shall be desolate in the midst of the countries *that are* desolate, and her cities shall be in the midst of the cities *that are* wasted.

8 And they shall know that I *am* the LORD, when I have set a fire in Egypt, and *when* all her helpers shall be [r]destroyed.

9 In that day [b]shall messengers go forth from me in ships to make the careless Ethiopians afraid, and great pain shall come upon them, as in the day of Egypt: for, lo, it cometh.

10 Thus saith the Lord GOD; [c]I will also make the multitude of Egypt to cease by the hand of Nebuchadrezzar king of Babylon.

11 He and his people with him, [d]the terrible of the nations, shall be brought to destroy the land: and they shall draw their swords against Egypt, and fill the land with the slain.

12 And [e]I will make the rivers [s]dry, and [f]sell the land into the hand of the wicked: and I will make the land waste, and [t]all that is therein, by the hand of strangers: I the LORD have spoken *it*.

13 Thus saith the Lord GOD; I will also [g]destroy the idols, and I will cause *their* images to cease out of Noph; [h]and there shall be no more a prince of the land of Egypt: [i]and I will put a fear in the land of Egypt.

14 And I will make [j]Pathros desolate, and will set fire in [k]Zoan,[u] [l]and will execute judgments in No.

15 And I will pour my fury upon [v]Sin, the strength of Egypt; and [m]I will cut off the multitude of No.

16 And I will [n]set fire in Egypt: Sin shall have great pain, and No shall be rent asunder, and Noph *shall have* distresses daily.

17 The young men of [w]Aven and of [x]Pi-beseth shall fall by the sword: and these *cities* shall go into captivity.

18 [o]At Tehaphnehes also the day shall be [y]darkened, when I shall break there the yokes of Egypt: and the pomp of her strength shall cease in her: as for her, a cloud shall cover her, and her daughters shall go into captivity.

19 Thus will I execute judgments in Egypt: and they shall know that I *am* the LORD.

20 ¶ And it came to pass in the eleventh year, in the first *month,* in the seventh *day* of the month, *that* the word of the LORD came unto me, saying,

21 Son of man, I have [p]broken the arm of Pharaoh king of Egypt; and, lo, [q]it shall not be bound up to be healed, to put a roller to bind it, to make it strong to hold the sword.

22 Therefore thus saith the Lord GOD; Behold, I *am* against Pharaoh king of Egypt, and will [r]break his arms, the strong, and that which was broken; and I will cause the sword to fall out of his hand.

23 [s]And I will scatter the Egyptians among the nations, and will disperse them through the countries.

24 And I will strengthen the arms of the king of Babylon, and put my sword in his hand: but I will break Pharaoh's arms, and he shall groan before him with the groanings of a deadly wounded *man.*

25 But I will strengthen the arms of the king of Babylon, and the arms of Pharaoh shall fall down; and [t]they shall know that I *am* the LORD, when I shall put my sword into the hand of the king of Babylon, and he shall stretch it out upon the land of Egypt.

26 [u]And I will scatter the Egyptians among the nations, and disperse them among the countries; and they shall know that I *am* the LORD.

Parable of the cedar of Lebanon

31 AND IT came to pass in the eleventh year, in the third *month,* in the first *day* of the month, *that* the word of the LORD came unto me, saying,

2 Son of man, speak unto Pharaoh king of Egypt, and to his multitude; [v]Whom art thou like in thy greatness?

3 ¶ [w]Behold, the Assyrian *was* a ce-

30:6 [z]ch. 29:10 **30:7** [a]ch. 29:12 **30:9** [b]Is. 18:1,2 **30:10** [c]ch. 29:19 **30:11** [d]ch. 28:7 **30:12** [e]Is. 19:5,6 [f]Is. 19:4 **30:13** [g]Is. 19:1 Jer. 43:12 & 46:25 Zech. 13:2 [h]Zech. 10:11 [i]Is. 19:16 **30:14** [j]ch. 29:14 [k]Ps. 78:12,43 [l]Nah. 3:8-10 **30:15** [m]Jer. 46:25 **30:16** [n]ver. 8 **30:18** [o]Jer. 2:16 **30:21** [p]Jer. 48:25 [q]Jer. 46:11 **30:22** [r]Ps. 37:17 **30:23** [s]ver. 26 ch. 29:12 **30:25** [t]Ps. 9:16 **30:26** [u]ver. 23 ch. 29:12 **31:2** [v]ver. 18 **31:3** [w]Dan. 4:10

[q] Or, *from Migdol to Syene* [r] Heb. *broken*
[s] Heb. *drought* [t] Heb. *the fulness thereof*
[u] Or, *Tanis* [v] Or, *Pelusium* [w] Or, *Heliopolis*
[x] Or, *Pubastum* [y] Or, *restrained*

31:3 THE ASSYRIAN. Ezekiel compares Egypt's situation to Assyria's days of glory and to its fall. Once a world power, Assyria had been destroyed by Babylon, the same nation that would defeat Egypt.

dar in Lebanon [z]with fair branches, and with a shadowing shroud, and of an high stature; and his top was among the thick boughs.

4 [x]The waters [a]made him great, the deep [b]set him up on high with her rivers running round about his plants, and sent out her [c]little rivers unto all the trees of the field.

5 Therefore [y]his height was exalted above all the trees of the field, and his boughs were multiplied, and his branches became long because of the multitude of waters, [d]when he shot forth.

6 All the [z]fowls of heaven made their nests in his boughs, and under his branches did all the beasts of the field bring forth their young, and under his shadow dwelt all great nations.

7 Thus was he fair in his greatness, in the length of his branches: for his root was by great waters.

8 The cedars in the [a]garden of God could not hide him: the fir trees were not like his boughs, and the chestnut trees were not like his branches; nor any tree in the garden of God was like unto him in his beauty.

9 I have made him fair by the multitude of his branches: so that all the trees of Eden, that *were* in the garden of God, envied him.

10 ¶ Therefore thus saith the Lord GOD; Because thou hast lifted up thyself in height, and he hath shot up his top among the thick boughs, and [b]his heart is lifted up in his height;

11 I have therefore delivered him into the hand of the mighty one of the heathen; [e]he shall surely deal with him: I have driven him out for his wickedness.

12 And strangers, [c]the terrible of the nations, have cut him off, and have left him: [d]upon the mountains and in all the valleys his branches are fallen, and his boughs are broken by all the rivers of the land; and all the people of the earth are gone down from his shadow, and have left him.

13 [e]Upon his ruin shall all the fowls of the heaven remain, and all the beasts of the field shall be upon his branches:

14 To the end that none of all the trees by the waters exalt themselves for their height, neither shoot up their top among the thick boughs, neither their trees [f]stand up in their height, all that drink water: for [f]they are all delivered unto death, [g]to the nether parts of the earth, in the midst of the children of men, with them that go down to the pit.

15 Thus saith the Lord GOD; In the day when he went down to the grave I caused a mourning: I covered the deep for him, and I restrained the floods thereof, and the great waters were stayed: and I caused Lebanon [g]to mourn for him, and all the trees of the field fainted for him.

16 I made the nations to [h]shake at the sound of his fall, when I [i]cast him down to hell with them that descend into the pit: and [j]all the trees of Eden, the choice and best of Lebanon, all that drink water, [k]shall be comforted in the nether parts of the earth.

17 They also went down into hell with him unto *them that be* slain with the sword; and *they that were* his arm, *that* [l]dwelt under his shadow in the midst of the heathen.

18 ¶ [m]To whom art thou thus like in glory and in greatness among the trees of Eden? yet shalt thou be brought down with the trees of Eden unto the nether parts of the earth: [n]thou shalt lie in the midst of the uncircumcised with *them that be* slain by the sword. This *is* Pharaoh and all his multitude, saith the Lord GOD.

The lament for Pharaoh

32 AND IT came to pass in the twelfth year, in the twelfth month, in the first *day* of the month, *that* the word of the LORD came unto me, saying,

2 Son of man, [o]take up a lamentation

31:4 [x]Jer. 51:36
31:5 [y]Dan. 4:11
31:6 [z]ch. 17:23 Dan. 4:12
31:8 [a]Gen. 2:8 & 13:10 ch. 28:13
31:10 [b]Dan. 5:20
31:12 [c]ch. 28:7 [d]ch. 32:5 & 35:8
31:13 [e]Is. 18:6 ch. 32:4
31:14 [f]Ps. 82:7 [g]ch. 32:18
31:16 [h]ch. 26:15 [i]Is. 14:15 [j]Is. 14:8 [k]ch. 32:31
31:17 [l]Lam. 4:20
31:18 [m]ver. 2 ch. 32:19 [n]ch. 28:10 & 32:19,21,24
32:2 [o]ver. 16 ch. 27:2

[z] Heb. *fair of branches* [a] Or, *nourished* [b] Or, *brought him up* [c] Or, *conduits* [d] Or, *when it sent them forth* [e] Heb. *in doing he shall do unto him* [f] Or, *stand upon themselves for their height* [g] Heb. *to be black*

31:11 FOR HIS WICKEDNESS. God's judgments are not arbitrary; they are always in accordance with the wickedness of individuals or nations. At the present time, God desires not to exercise judgment but to offer forgiveness to all those who turn to Him through His Son Jesus Christ.

32:2 LAMENTATION FOR PHARAOH. This lament mocks Pharaoh, who believed that he was as strong as a lion or a great sea monster. Howev-

tion for Pharaoh king of Egypt, and say
unto him, [p]Thou art like a young lion
of the nations, [q]and thou *art* as a
[h]whale in the seas: and thou camest
forth with thy rivers, and troubledst
the waters with thy feet, and [r]fouledst
their rivers.
3 Thus saith the Lord GOD; I will
therefore [s]spread out my net over
thee with a company of many people;
and they shall bring thee up in my net.
4 Then [t]will I leave thee upon the
land, I will cast thee forth upon
the open field, and [u]will cause all the
fowls of the heaven to remain upon
thee, and I will fill the beasts of the
whole earth with thee.
5 And I will lay thy flesh [v]upon the
mountains, and fill the valleys with thy
height.
6 I will also water with thy blood
[i]the land wherein thou swimmest,
even to the mountains; and the rivers
shall be full of thee.
7 And when I shall [j]put thee out,
[w]I will cover the heaven, and make the
stars thereof dark; I will cover the sun
with a cloud, and the moon shall not
give her light.
8 All the [k]bright lights of heaven
will I make [l]dark over thee, and set
darkness upon thy land, saith the Lord
GOD.
9 I will also [m]vex the hearts of
many people, when I shall bring thy de-
struction among the nations, into the
countries which thou hast not known.
10 Yea, I will make many people
amazed at thee, and their kings shall
be horribly afraid for thee, when I shall
brandish my sword before them; and
[x]they shall tremble at *every* moment,
every man for his own life, in the day
of thy fall.
11 ¶ [y]For thus saith the Lord GOD;
The sword of the king of Babylon shall
come upon thee.
12 By the swords of the mighty will
I cause thy multitude to fall, [z]the ter-
rible of the nations, all of them: and
[a]they shall spoil the pomp of Egypt,
and all the multitude thereof shall be
destroyed.
13 I will destroy also all the beasts
thereof from beside the great waters;
[b]neither shall the foot of man trouble
them any more, nor the hoofs of beasts
trouble them.
14 Then will I make their waters
deep, and cause their rivers to run like
oil, saith the Lord GOD.
15 When I shall make the land of
Egypt desolate, and the country shall
be [n]destitute of that whereof it was
full, when I shall smite all them that
dwell therein, [c]then shall they know
that I *am* the LORD.
16 This *is* the [d]lamentation where-
with they shall lament her: the daugh-
ters of the nations shall lament her:
they shall lament for her, *even* for
Egypt, and for all her multitude, saith
the Lord GOD.
17 ¶ It came to pass also in the
twelfth year, in the fifteenth *day* of the
month, *that* the word of the LORD came
unto me, saying,
18 Son of man, wail for the multi-
tude of Egypt, and [e]cast them down,
even her, and the daughters of the fa-
mous nations, unto the nether parts of
the earth, with them that go down into
the pit.
19 [f]Whom dost thou pass in beau-
ty? [g]go down, and be thou laid with
the uncircumcised.
20 They shall fall in the midst of
them that are slain by the sword: [o]she
is delivered to the sword: draw her and
all her multitudes.
21 [h]The strong among the mighty
shall speak to him out of the midst of
hell with them that help him: they are
[i]gone down, they lie uncircumcised,
slain by the sword.
22 Asshur *is* there and all her com-
pany: his graves *are* about him: all of
them slain, fallen by the sword:
23 [j]Whose graves are set in the
sides of the pit, and her company is
round about her grave: all of them
slain, fallen by the sword, which
[k]caused [p]terror in the land of the liv-
ing.

32:2 [p]ch. 19:3,6 & 38:13 [q]ch. 29:3 [r]ch. 34:18 **32:3** [s]ch. 12:13 & 17:20 Hos. 7:12 **32:4** [t]ch. 29:5 [u]ch. 31:13 **32:5** [v]ch. 31:12 **32:7** [w]Is. 13:10 Joel 2:31 & 3:15 Amos 8:9 Mat. 24:29 Rev. 6:12,13 **32:10** [x]ch. 26:16 **32:11** [y]Jer. 46:26 ch. 30:4 **32:12** [z]ch. 28:7 [a]ch. 29:19

32:13 [b]ch. 29:11 **32:15** [c]Ex. 7:5 & 14:4,18 Ps. 9:16 ch. 6:7 **32:16** [d]ver. 2 2 Sam. 1:17 2 Chr. 35:25 ch. 26:17 **32:18** [e]ch. 26:20 & 31:14 **32:19** [f]ch. 31:2,18 [g]ver. 21,24 ch. 28:10 **32:21** [h]ver. 27 Is. 1:31 & 14:9,10 [i]ver. 19,25 **32:23** [j]Is. 14:15 [k]ver. 24-27,32

[h] Or, *dragon* [i] Or, *the land of thy swimming* [j] Or, *extinguish* [k] Heb. *lights of the light in heaven* [l] Heb. *them dark* [m] Heb. *provoke to anger,* or, *grief* [n] Heb. *desolate from the fulness thereof* [o] Or, *the sword is laid* [p] Or, *dismaying*

er, he would have to answer to the Lord God, as all world leaders will eventually have to do.

32:18–31 THE NETHER PARTS OF THE EARTH. Egypt is pictured as joining other nations in the underworld which had been punished for their cruelty and injustice (v. 27). Other mighty leaders who had died would speak to Egypt there (v. 21).

24 There *is* [l]Elam and all her multitude round about her grave, all of them slain, fallen by the sword, which are [m]gone down uncircumcised into the nether parts of the earth, [n]which caused their terror in the land of the living; yet have they borne their shame with them that go down to the pit.

25 They have set her a bed in the midst of the slain with all her multitude: her graves *are* round about him: all of them uncircumcised, slain by the sword: though their terror was caused in the land of the living, yet have they borne their shame with them that go down to the pit: he is put in the midst of *them that be* slain.

26 There *is* [o]Meshech, Tubal, and all her multitude: her graves *are* round about him: all of them [p]uncircumcised, slain by the sword, though they caused their terror in the land of the living.

27 [q]And they shall not lie with the mighty *that are* fallen of the uncircumcised, which are gone down to hell [q]with their weapons of war: and they have laid their swords under their heads, but their iniquities shall be upon their bones, though *they were* the terror of the mighty in the land of the living.

28 Yea, thou shalt be broken in the midst of the uncircumcised, and shalt lie with *them that are* slain with the sword.

29 There *is* [r]Edom, her kings, and all her princes, which with their might are [r]laid by *them that were* slain by the sword: they shall lie with the uncircumcised, and with them that go down to the pit.

30 [s]There *be* the princes of the north, all of them, and all the [t]Zidonians, which are gone down with the slain; with their terror they are ashamed of their might; and they lie uncircumcised with *them that be* slain by the sword, and bear their shame with them that go down to the pit.

31 Pharaoh shall see them, and shall be [u]comforted over all his multitude, *even* Pharaoh and all his army slain by the sword, saith the Lord GOD.

32 For I have caused my terror in the land of the living: and he shall be laid in the midst of the uncircumcised with *them that are* slain with the sword, *even* Pharaoh and all his multitude, saith the Lord GOD.

Ezekiel as Israel's watchman

33 AGAIN THE word of the LORD came unto me, saying,

2 Son of man, speak to [v]the children of thy people, and say unto them, [w]When[s] I bring the sword upon a land, if the people of the land take a man of their coasts, and set him for their [x]watchman:

3 If when he seeth the sword come upon the land, he blow the trumpet, and warn the people;

4 Then [t]whosoever heareth the sound of the trumpet, and taketh not warning; if the sword come, and take him away, [y]his blood shall be upon his own head.

5 He heard the sound of the trumpet, and took not warning; his blood shall be upon him. But he that taketh warning shall deliver his soul.

6 But if the watchman see the sword come, and blow not the trumpet, and the people be not warned; if the sword come, and take *any* person from among them, [z]he is taken away in his iniquity; but his blood will I require at the watchman's hand.

7 ¶ [a]So thou, O son of man, I have set thee a watchman unto the house of

32:24 [l]Jer. 49:34 [m]ver. 21 [n]ver. 23
32:26 [o]Gen. 10:2 ch. 27:13 [p]ver. 19,20
32:27 [q]ver. 21 Is. 14:18,19
32:29 [r]ch. 25:12
32:30 [s]ch. 38:6,15 & 39:2 [t]ch. 28:21
32:31 [u]ch. 31:16
33:2 [v]ch. 3:11 [w]ch. 14:17 [x]ver. 7 2 Sam. 18:24,25 2 Ki. 9:17 Hos. 9:8
33:4 [y]ch. 18:13
33:6 [z]ver. 8
33:7 [a]ch. 3:17

[q] Heb. *with weapons of their war* [r] Heb. *given,* or, *put upon her* [s] Heb. *A land when I bring a sword upon her* [t] Heb. *he that hearing heareth*

32:31 SHALL BE COMFORTED. The pharaoh would be somewhat "comforted" upon discovering that he was not the only one in the underworld, reflecting the truths that misery loves company and that the judged do not want to suffer alone.

33:6 HIS BLOOD I WILL REQUIRE AT THE WATCHMAN'S HAND. The watchman who saw destruction coming and did not warn the people would be held responsible for their blood. (1) Likewise, in the kingdom of God, a prophet or preacher who does not warn a lukewarm church of coming judgment will be held responsible for the people's blood. (2) To a great extent all believers have the responsibility to witness to the lost and to help fulfill the mission task given to the church by Jesus (see Mat. 28:19, note). We will have to give an account to God if we refuse to obey Jesus' Great Commission (see Acts 20:26, note).

33:7 I HAVE SET THEE A WATCHMAN. God emphasizes again that Ezekiel was to be a faithful prophet to his people, warning them to turn from sin and to accept God's salvation. Today the church and its ministers must witness to all nations about salvation in Jesus Christ (see 3:18, note).

Israel; therefore thou shalt hear the word at my mouth, and warn them from me.

8 When I say unto the wicked, O wicked *man,* thou shalt surely die; if thou dost not speak to warn the wicked from his way, that wicked *man* shall die in his iniquity; but his blood will I require at thine hand.

9 Nevertheless, if thou warn the wicked of his way to turn from it; if he do not turn from his way, he shall die in his iniquity; but thou hast delivered thy soul.

10 Therefore, O thou son of man, speak unto the house of Israel; Thus ye speak, saying, If our transgressions and our sins *be* upon us, and we [b]pine away in them, [c]how should we then live?

11 Say unto them, *As* I live, saith the Lord GOD, [d]I have no pleasure in the death of the wicked; but that the wicked turn from his way and live: turn ye, turn ye from your evil ways; for [e]why will ye die, O house of Israel?

Amos 7:14-15

12 Therefore, thou son of man, say unto the children of thy people, The [f]righteousness of the righteous shall not deliver him in the day of his transgression: as for the wickedness of the wicked, [g]he shall not fall thereby in the day that he turneth from his wickedness; neither shall the righteous be able to live for his *righteousness* in the day that he sinneth.

13 When I shall say to the righteous, *that* he shall surely live; [h]if he trust to his own righteousness, and commit iniquity, all his righteousnesses shall not be remembered; but for his iniquity that he hath committed, he shall die for it.

14 Again, [i]when I say unto the wicked, Thou shalt surely die; if he turn from his sin, and do [u]that which is lawful and right;

15 *If* the wicked [j]restore the pledge, [k]give again that he had robbed, walk in [l]the statutes of life, without committing iniquity; he shall surely live, he shall not die.

16 [m]None of his sins that he hath committed shall be mentioned unto him: he hath done that which is lawful and right; he shall surely live.

Joel 2:32

17 ¶ [n]Yet the children of thy people say, The way of the Lord is not equal: but as for them, their way is not equal.

18 [o]When the righteous turneth from his righteousness, and committeth iniquity, he shall even die thereby.

19 But if the wicked turn from his wickedness, and do that which is lawful and right, he shall live thereby.

20 ¶ Yet ye say, [p]The way of the Lord is not equal. O ye house of Israel, I will judge you every one after his ways.

Jerusalem's fall

21 ¶ And it came to pass in the twelfth year [q]of our captivity, in the tenth *month,* in the fifth *day* of the month, [r]*that* one that had escaped out of Jerusalem came unto me, saying, [s]The city is smitten.

22 Now [t]the hand of the LORD was upon me in the evening, afore he that was escaped came; and had opened my mouth, until he came to me in the morning; [u]and my mouth was opened, and I was no more dumb.

23 Then the word of the LORD came unto me, saying,

33:10 [b]ch. 24:23 [c]Is. 49:14
33:11 [d]2 Sam. 14:14 2 Pet. 3:9 [e]ch. 18:31
33:12 [f]ch. 3:20 & 18:24,26 [g]2 Chr. 7:14
33:13 [h]ch. 3:20 & 18:24
33:14 [i]ch. 3:18,19 & 18:27
33:15 [j]ch. 18:7 [k]Ex. 22:1,4 Lev. 6:2,4,5 [l]Lev. 18:5 ch. 20:11,13,21
33:16 [m]ch. 18:22
33:17 [n]ver. 20 ch. 18:25,29
33:18 [o]ch. 18:26
33:20 [p]ver. 17 ch. 18:25
33:21 [q]ch. 1:2 [r]ch. 24:26 [s]2 Ki. 25:4
33:22 [t]ch. 1:3 [u]ch. 24:27

[u] Heb. *judgment and justice*

33:11 I HAVE NO PLEASURE IN THE DEATH OF THE WICKED. God wants everyone to turn to Him for salvation so that they will not die in their sins (see 2 Pet. 3:9, note). Believers should share God's desire for the repentance of the wicked.

33:12–20 IN THE DAY OF HIS TRANSGRESSION. God judges everyone righteously and justly. (1) The righteous who turn away from God and back to sin will be held accountable for their sins and will die in them if they do not repent. They cannot count on their past deeds of righteousness to save them (vv. 12–13). (2) On the other hand, the wicked who turn to God and away from sin will be saved, and none of their sins will be remembered against them (vv. 14–16); they will receive the gift of eternal life. (3) This passage, therefore, emphasizes the importance of our present relationship with God. To turn away from God and His word while assuming that our past faith and good works will save us is spiritually fatal. Conversely, if we turn to God in sincere repentance and true faith, He will accept us, regardless of our past sins (see 18:21–24, notes).

33:21 THE CITY IS SMITTEN. News came to Ezekiel and the exiles in Babylon that Jerusalem had fallen, fulfilling his prophecies and vindicating his message to the people. His ministry changed at this point, for he now began to prophesy redemption and restoration for Judah at some future time.

24 Son of man, [v]they that inhabit those [w]wastes of the land of Israel speak, saying, [x]Abraham was one, and he inherited the land: [y]but we *are* many; the land is given us for inheritance.

25 Wherefore say unto them, Thus saith the Lord GOD; [z]Ye eat with the blood, and [a]lift up your eyes toward your idols, and [b]shed blood: and shall ye possess the land?

26 Ye stand upon your sword, ye work abomination, and ye [c]defile every one his neighbour's wife: and shall ye possess the land?

27 Say thou thus unto them, Thus saith the Lord GOD; *As* I live, surely [d]they that *are* in the wastes shall fall by the sword, and him that *is* in the open field [e]will I give to the beasts [v]to be devoured, and they that *be* in the forts and [f]in the caves shall die of the pestilence.

28 [g]For I will lay the land [w]most desolate, and the [h]pomp of her strength shall cease; and [i]the mountains of Israel shall be desolate, that none shall pass through.

29 Then shall they know that I *am* the LORD, when I have laid the land most desolate because of all their abominations which they have committed.

30 ¶ Also, thou son of man, the children of thy people still are talking [x]against thee by the walls and in the doors of the houses, and [j]speak one to another, every one to his brother, saying, Come, I pray you, and hear what is the word that cometh forth from the LORD.

31 And [k]they come unto thee [y]as the people cometh, and [z]they [l]sit before thee *as* my people, and they hear thy words, but they will not do them: [m]for with their mouth [a]they shew much love, *but* [n]their heart goeth after their covetousness.

32 And, lo, thou *art* unto them as [b]a very lovely song of one that hath a pleasant voice, and can play well on an instrument: for they hear thy words, but they do them not.

33 [o]And when this cometh to pass, (lo, it will come,) then [p]shall they know that a prophet hath been among them.

Israel's shepherds

34 AND THE word of the LORD came unto me, saying,

2 Son of man, prophesy against the shepherds of Israel, prophesy, and say unto them, Thus saith the Lord GOD unto the shepherds; [q]Woe *be* to the shepherds of Israel that do feed themselves! should not the shepherds feed the flocks?

3 [r]Ye eat the fat, and ye clothe you with the wool, ye kill them that are fed: *but* ye feed not the flock.

4 [s]The diseased have ye not strengthened, neither have ye healed that which was sick, neither have ye bound up *that which was* broken, neither have ye brought again that which was driven away, neither have ye [t]sought that which was lost; but with [u]force and with cruelty have ye ruled them.

5 [v]And they were [w]scattered, [x]because[c] *there is* no shepherd: [y]and they became meat to all the beasts of the field, when they were scattered.

6 My sheep wandered through all

33:24 [v]ch. 34:2 [w]ver. 27 ch. 36:4 [x]Is. 51:2 Acts 7:5 [y]Mic. 3:11 Mat. 3:9 John 8:39 **33:25** [z]Gen. 9:4 Lev. 3:17 & 7:26 & 17:10 & 19:26 Deut. 12:16 [a]ch. 18:6 [b]ch. 22:6,9 **33:26** [c]ch. 18:6 & 22:11 **33:27** [d]ver. 24 [e]ch. 39:4 [f]Judg. 6:2 1 Sam. 13:6 **33:28** [g]Jer. 44:2,6,22 ch. 36:34,35 [h]ch. 7:24 & 24:21 & 30:6,7 [i]ch. 6:2,3,6 **33:30** [j]Is. 29:13 **33:31** [k]ch. 14:1 & 20:1 [l]ch. 8:1 [m]Ps. 78:36,37 Is. 29:13 [n]Mat. 13:22 **33:33** [o]1 Sam. 3:20 [p]ch. 2:5 **34:2** [q]Jer. 23:1 Zech. 11:17 **34:3** [r]Is. 56:11 Zech. 11:16 **34:4** [s]Zech. 11:16 [t]Luke 15:4 [u]1 Pet. 5:3 **34:5** [v]ch. 33:21 [w]1 Ki. 22:17 Mat. 9:36 [x]ver. 8 [y]Is. 56:9 Jer. 12:9

[v] Heb. *to devour him* [w] Heb. *desolation and desolation* [x] Or, *of thee* [y] Heb. *according to the coming of the people* [z] Or, *my people sit before thee* [a] Heb. *they make loves,* or, *jests* [b] Heb. *a song of loves* [c] Or, *without a shepherd*

33:31 THEY SIT BEFORE THEE. The people were listening to Ezekiel, but they were not obeying God's word. Their hearts were still far from the Lord. They viewed Ezekiel as a performer on stage and God's message as entertainment (v. 32). N.T. believers must be careful not to turn worship services into performances staged for entertainment. God and His word are not honored by such activity, and the Holy Spirit will not manifest His presence in such worship (see article on WORSHIP, p. 730). Believers must be not only hearers but also doers of God's word (see Jas. 1:22).

34:1–31 THE SHEPHERDS OF ISRAEL. Ezekiel prophesies against the leaders of Israel, i.e., its kings, priests, and prophets. By greed, corruption, and selfishness, they had failed to lead God's people in the way He wanted. They were exploiting the people (v. 3) and using them for personal gain instead of helping them spiritually (v. 4). Thus, they were responsible for Judah's captivity, and God would bring them into judgment. In contrast to the faithless shepherds, Ezekiel went on to prophesy a day when God would send a Shepherd after His own heart (i.e., the Messiah), who would truly care for the people. Rather than being exploited and manipulated, the flock would then receive "showers of blessing" (v. 26).

the mountains, and upon every high hill: yea, my flock was scattered upon all the face of the earth, and none did search or seek *after them*.

7 ¶ Therefore, ye shepherds, hear the word of the LORD;

8 *As* I live, saith the Lord GOD, surely because my flock became a prey, and my flock [z]became meat to every beast of the field, because *there was* no shepherd, neither did my shepherds search for my flock, [a]but the shepherds fed themselves, and fed not my flock;

9 Therefore, O ye shepherds, hear the word of the LORD;

10 Thus saith the Lord GOD; Behold, I *am* against the shepherds; and [b]I will require my flock at their hand, and cause them to cease from feeding the flock; neither shall the shepherds [c]feed themselves any more; for I will deliver my flock from their mouth, that they may not be meat for them.

The LORD God is a shepherd

11 ¶ For thus saith the Lord GOD; Behold, I, *even* I, will both search my sheep, and seek them out.

12 [d]As a shepherd seeketh out his flock in the day that he is among his sheep *that are* scattered; so will I seek out my sheep, and will deliver them out of all places where they have been scattered in [d]the cloudy and dark day.

13 And [e]I will bring them out from the people, and gather them from the countries, and will bring them to their own land, and feed them upon the mountains of Israel by the rivers, and in all the inhabited places of the country.

14 [f]I will feed them in a good pasture, and upon the high mountains of Israel shall their fold be: [g]there shall they lie in a good fold, and *in* a fat pasture shall they feed upon the mountains of Israel.

34:8 [z]ver. 5,6 [a]ver. 2,10
34:10 [b]ch. 3:18 Heb. 13:17 [c]ver. 2,8
34:12 [d]ch. 30:3
34:13 [e]Is. 65:9,10 Jer. 23:3
34:14 [f]Ps. 23:2 [g]Jer. 33:12
34:16 [h]Is. 40:11 Mic. 4:6 Mat. 18:11 Luke 5:32 [i]Is. 10:16 Amos 4:1 [j]Jer. 10:24
34:17 [k]ch. 20:37 Mat. 25:32
34:20 [l]ver. 17
34:23 [m]Is. 40:11 John 10:11 Heb. 13:20 1 Pet. 2:25 [n]Jer. 30:9 Hos. 3:5
34:24 [o]Ex. 29:45 [p]ch. 37:22
34:25 [q]ch. 37:26 [r]Lev. 26:6 Is. 11:6-9 Hos. 2:18

15 I will feed my flock, and I will cause them to lie down, saith the Lord GOD.

16 [h]I will seek that which was lost, and bring again that which was driven away, and will bind up *that which was* broken, and will strengthen that which was sick: but I will destroy [i]the fat and the strong; I will feed them [j]with judgment.

17 And *as for* you, O my flock, thus saith the Lord GOD; [k]Behold, I judge between [e]cattle and cattle, between the rams and the [f]he goats.

18 *Seemeth it* a small thing unto you to have eaten up the good pasture, but ye must tread down with your feet the residue of your pastures? and to have drunk of the deep waters, but ye must foul the residue with your feet?

19 And *as for* my flock, they eat that which ye have trodden with your feet; and they drink that which ye have fouled with your feet.

20 ¶ Therefore thus saith the Lord GOD unto them; [l]Behold, I, *even* I, will judge between the fat cattle and between the lean cattle.

21 Because ye have thrust with side and with shoulder, and pushed all the diseased with your horns, till ye have scattered them abroad;

22 Therefore will I save my flock, and they shall no more be a prey; and I will judge between cattle and cattle.

23 And I will set up one [m]shepherd over them, and he shall feed them, [n]*even* my servant David; he shall feed them, and he shall be their shepherd.

24 And [o]I the LORD will be their God, and my servant David [p]a prince among them; I the LORD have spoken *it*.

25 And [q]I will make with them a covenant of peace, and [r]will cause the

[d] Heb. *According to the seeking* [e] Heb. *small cattle of lambs and kids* [f] Heb. *great he goats*

34:11 I WILL BOTH SEARCH MY SHEEP, AND SEEK THEM OUT. Because of the failure of the leaders of Israel, the Lord Himself would take charge of His people. He would care for His flock (vv. 11–16), judge between the sheep, rams, and goats (vv. 17–24), and establish a covenant of peace (vv. 25–31).

34:23 I WILL SET UP ONE SHEPHERD. This shepherd is Jesus the Messiah, who came from the lineage of David (cf. Ps. 89:4,20,29; Jer. 23:5–6). He shepherded God's people as a righteous priest, prophet, and king. He is "the good shepherd" (John 10:14), who laid down His life for the sheep (John 10:1–18; 1 John 3:16; cf. 1 Pet. 2:25; 5:4). In the future, when God's people are restored to their land, the Messiah will set up His kingdom of peace and justice (see next note).

34:25 A COVENANT OF PEACE. The Messiah-Shepherd will restore the peace and perfection that characterized life before sin entered the world (Gen. 1—3). This covenant, also called the "new covenant" (see Jer. 31:31–34), will reach its full realization only when God's kingdom is forever established in the new heaven and earth (Rev. 21—22). Then there will be "showers of blessing" for the redeemed (v. 26) and the full presence of

evil beasts to cease out of the land: and
they [s]shall dwell safely in the wilder-
ness, and sleep in the woods.
26 And I will make them and the
places round about [t]my hill [u]a bless-
ing; and I will [v]cause the shower to
come down in his season; there shall
be [w]showers of blessing.
27 And [x]the tree of the field shall
yield her fruit, and the earth shall yield
her increase, and they shall be safe in
their land, and shall know that I *am* the
LORD, when I have [y]broken the bands
of their yoke, and delivered them out of
the hand of those that [z]served them-
selves of them.
28 And they shall no more be a prey
to the heathen, neither shall the beast
of the land devour them; but [a]they
shall dwell safely, and none shall make
them afraid.
29 And I will raise up for them a
[b]plant [g]of renown, and they shall be
no more [h]consumed with hunger in
the land, [c]neither bear the shame of
the heathen any more.
30 Thus shall they know that [d]I
the LORD their God *am* with them, and
that they, *even* the house of Israel, *are*
my people, saith the Lord GOD.
31 And ye my [e]flock, the flock of
my pasture, *are* men, *and* I *am* your
God, saith the Lord GOD.

Prophecy against mount Seir

35 MOREOVER THE word of the
LORD came unto me, saying,
2 Son of man, set thy face against
[f]mount Seir, and [g]prophesy
against it,
3 And say unto it, Thus saith the
Lord GOD; Behold, O mount Seir, I *am*
against thee, and [h]I will stretch out
mine hand against thee, and I will
make thee [i]most desolate.
4 I will lay thy cities waste, and
thou shalt be desolate, and thou shalt
know that I *am* the LORD.
5 [i]Because thou hast had a [j]per-
petual hatred, and hast [k]shed *the*
blood of the children of Israel by the
[l]force of the sword in the time of their
calamity, [j]in the time *that their* iniqui-
ty *had* an end:
6 Therefore, *as* I live, saith the Lord
GOD, I will prepare thee unto blood, and
blood shall pursue thee: [k]since thou
hast not hated blood, even blood shall
pursue thee.
7 Thus will I make mount Seir
[i]most desolate, and cut off from it
[l]him that passeth out and him that
returneth.
8 And I will fill his mountains with
his slain *men:* in thy hills, and in thy
valleys, and in all thy rivers, shall they
fall that are slain with the sword.
9 [m]I will make thee perpetual deso-
lations, and thy cities shall not return:
[n]and ye shall know that I *am* the LORD.
10 Because thou hast said, These
two nations and these two countries
shall be mine, and we will [o]possess it;
[m]whereas [p]the LORD was there:
11 Therefore, *as* I live, saith the
Lord GOD, I will even do [q]according to
thine anger, and according to thine
envy which thou hast used out of thy
hatred against them; and I will make
myself known among them, when I
have judged thee.
12 [r]And thou shalt know that I *am*
the LORD, *and that* I have heard all thy
blasphemies which thou hast spoken
against the mountains of Israel, say-
ing, They are laid desolate, they are
given us [n]to consume.
13 Thus [s]with your mouth ye have
[o]boasted against me, and have multi-
plied your words against me: I have
heard *them*.
14 Thus saith the Lord GOD; [t]When
the whole earth rejoiceth, I will make
thee desolate.
15 [u]As thou didst rejoice at the in-
heritance of the house of Israel, be-
cause it was desolate, so will I do unto
thee: thou shalt be desolate, O mount

34:25 [s]Jer. 23:6 **34:26** [t]Is. 56:7 [u]Gen. 12:2 Is. 19:24 Zech. 8:13 [v]Lev. 26:4 [w]Ps. 68:9 **34:27** [x]Lev. 26:4 Ps. 85:12 Is. 4:2 [y]Jer. 2:20 [z]Jer. 25:14 **34:28** [a]Jer. 30:10 **34:29** [b]Is. 11:1 [c]ch. 36:3,6 **34:30** [d]ver. 24 **34:31** [e]Ps. 100:3 John 10:11 **35:2** [f]Deut. 2:5 [g]Amos 1:11 **35:3** [h]ch. 6:14 **35:5** [i]ch. 25:12 [j]Ps. 137:7 Dan. 9:24 **35:6** [k]Ps. 109:17 **35:7** [l]Judg. 5:6 **35:9** [m]Jer. 49:17 [n]ch. 36:11 **35:10** [o]Ps. 83:4,12 [p]Ps. 48:1,3 ch. 48:35 **35:11** [q]Mat. 7:2 Jas. 2:13 **35:12** [r]Ps. 9:16 **35:13** [s]1 Sam. 2:3 **35:14** [t]Is. 65:13 **35:15** [u]Obad. 12,15

g Or, *for renown* **h** Heb. *taken away* **i** Heb. *desolation and desolation* **j** Or, *hatred of old* **k** Heb. *poured out the children* **l** Heb. *hands* **m** Or, *though the LORD was there* **n** Heb. *to devour* **o** Heb. *magnified*

God among His people (v. 30).

35:2 SET THY FACE AGAINST MOUNT SEIR. Ezekiel prophesies against Idumea or Edom (Mount Seir, cf. v. 15), the descendants of Esau. They had been perpetual enemies of Israel (v. 5); after the fall of Israel and Judah, they hoped to possess the promised land (v. 10). But all their attempts to gain the land would fail, for God would bring them to ruin (vv. 10–15). They would not be able to prevent God from carrying out His plan to restore Israel.

35:10 THESE TWO NATIONS. This designation refers to Israel and Judah.

Seir, and all Idumea, *even* all of it: and they shall know that I *am* the LORD.

A prophecy to Israel

36 ALSO, THOU son of man, prophesy unto the [v]mountains of Israel, and say, Ye mountains of Israel, hear the word of the LORD:

2 Thus saith the Lord GOD; Because [w]the enemy hath said against you, Aha, [x]even the ancient high places [y]are ours in possession:

3 Therefore prophesy and say, Thus saith the Lord GOD; [p]Because they have made *you* desolate, and swallowed you up on every side, that ye might be a possession unto the residue of the heathen, [z]and [q]ye are taken up in the lips of talkers, and *are* an infamy of the people:

4 Therefore, ye mountains of Israel, hear the word of the Lord GOD; Thus saith the Lord GOD to the mountains, and to the hills, to the [r]rivers, and to the valleys, to the desolate wastes, and to the cities that are forsaken, which [a]became a prey and [b]derision to the residue of the heathen that *are* round about;

5 Therefore thus saith the Lord GOD; [c]Surely in the fire of my jealousy have I spoken against the residue of the heathen, and against all Idumea, [d]which have appointed my land into their possession with the joy of all *their* heart, with despiteful minds, to cast it out for a prey.

6 Prophesy therefore concerning the land of Israel, and say unto the mountains, and to the hills, to the rivers, and to the valleys, Thus saith the Lord GOD; Behold, I have spoken in my jealousy and in my fury, because ye have [e]borne the shame of the heathen:

7 Therefore thus saith the Lord GOD; I have [f]lifted up mine hand, Surely the heathen that *are* about you, they shall bear their shame.

8 ¶ But ye, O mountains of Israel, ye shall shoot forth your branches, and yield your fruit to my people of Israel; for they are at hand to come.

9 For, behold, I *am* for you, and I will turn unto you, and ye shall be tilled and sown:

10 And I will multiply men upon you, all the house of Israel, *even* all of it: and the cities shall be inhabited, and [g]the wastes shall be builded:

11 And [h]I will multiply upon you man and beast; and they shall increase and bring fruit: and I will settle you after your old estates, and will do better *unto you* than at your beginnings: [i]and ye shall know that I *am* the LORD.

12 Yea, I will cause men to walk upon you, *even* my people Israel; [j]and they shall possess thee, and thou shalt be their inheritance, and thou shalt no more henceforth [k]bereave them *of men*.

13 Thus saith the Lord GOD; Because they say unto you, [l]Thou *land* devourest up men, and hast bereaved thy nations;

14 Therefore thou shalt devour men no more, neither [s]bereave thy nations any more, saith the Lord GOD.

15 [m]Neither will I cause *men* to hear in thee the shame of the heathen any more, neither shalt thou bear the reproach of the people any more, neither shalt thou cause thy nations to fall any more, saith the Lord GOD.

16 ¶ Moreover the word of the LORD came unto me, saying,

17 Son of man, when the house of Israel dwelt in their own land, [n]they defiled it by their own way and by their doings: their way was before me as [o]the uncleanness of a removed woman.

18 Wherefore I poured my fury upon them [p]for the blood that they had shed upon the land, and for their idols *wherewith* they had polluted it:

19 And I scattered them among the heathen, and they were dispersed through the countries: [q]according to their way and according to their doings I judged them.

36:1 [v]ch. 6:2,3
36:2 [w]ch. 25:3 [x]Deut. 32:13 [y]ch. 35:10
36:3 [z]Deut. 28:37
36:4 [a]ch. 34:28 [b]Ps. 79:4
36:5 [c]Deut. 4:24 ch. 38:19 [d]ch. 35:10,12
36:6 [e]ver. 15 Ps. 123:3,4 ch. 34:29
36:7 [f]ch. 20:5
36:10 [g]ver. 33 Is. 58:12 & 61:4 Amos 9:14
36:11 [h]Jer. 31:27 & 33:12 [i]ch. 35:9 & 37:6,13
36:12 [j]Obad. 17 [k]See Jer. 15:7
36:13 [l]Num. 13:32
36:15 [m]ch. 34:29
36:17 [n]Lev. 18:25,27,28 Jer. 2:7 [o]Lev. 15:19
36:18 [p]ch. 16:36,38 & 23:37
36:19 [q]ch. 7:3 & 18:30 & 39:24

[p] Heb. *Because for because* [q] Or, *ye are made to come upon the lip of the tongue* [r] Or, *bottoms,* or, *dales* [s] Or, *cause to fall*

36:2–7 THE ENEMY. The enemies of Israel would be punished for their slander (v. 3), their plunder of Israel (vv. 4–5), and their attempt to take over the promised land (v. 2).

36:8–15 O MOUNTAINS OF ISRAEL. In these verses, God personifies the promised land and speaks directly to it. He promises to restore the devoured land as a place of blessing (vv. 13–14). This prophecy will be most fully realized when Israel possesses the land of Palestine during the millennial reign of Christ.

20 And when they entered unto the heathen, whither they went, they [r]profaned my holy name, when they said to them, These *are* the people of the LORD, and are gone forth out of his land.

21 ¶ But I had pity [s]for mine holy name, which the house of Israel had profaned among the heathen, whither they went.

22 Therefore say unto the house of Israel, Thus saith the Lord GOD; I do not *this* for your sakes, O house of Israel, [t]but for mine holy name's sake, which ye have profaned among the heathen, whither ye went.

23 And I will sanctify my great name, which was profaned among the heathen, which ye have profaned in the midst of them; and the heathen shall know that I *am* the LORD, saith the Lord GOD, when I shall be [u]sanctified in you before [†]their eyes.

24 For [v]I will take you from among the heathen, and gather you out of all countries, and will bring you into your own land.

25 ¶ [w]Then will I sprinkle clean water upon you, and ye shall be clean: [x]from all your filthiness, and from all your idols, will I cleanse you.

26 A [y]new heart also will I give you, and a new spirit will I put within you: and I will take away the stony heart out of your flesh, and I will give you an heart of flesh.

27 And I will put my [z]spirit within you, and cause you to walk in my statutes, and ye shall keep my judgments, and do *them*.

Ezek. 37:14

28 [a]And ye shall dwell in the land that I gave to your fathers; [b]and ye shall be my people, and I will be your God.

29 I will also [c]save you from all your uncleannesses: and [d]I will call for the corn, and will increase it, and [e]lay no famine upon you.

30 [f]And I will multiply the fruit of the tree, and the increase of the field, that ye shall receive no more reproach of famine among the heathen.

31 Then [g]shall ye remember your own evil ways, and your doings that *were* not good, and [h]shall loathe yourselves in your own sight for your iniquities and for your abominations.

32 [i]Not for your sakes do I *this*, saith the Lord GOD, be it known unto you: be ashamed and confounded for your own ways, O house of Israel.

33 Thus saith the Lord GOD; In the day that I shall have cleansed you from all your iniquities I will also cause *you* to dwell in the cities, [j]and the wastes shall be builded.

34 And the desolate land shall be tilled, whereas it lay desolate in the sight of all that passed by.

35 And they shall say, This land that was desolate is become like the garden of [k]Eden; and the waste and desolate and ruined cities *are become* fenced, *and* are inhabited.

36 Then the heathen that are left round about you shall know that I the LORD build the ruined *places, and* plant that that was desolate: [l]I the LORD have spoken *it*, and I will do *it*.

37 Thus saith the Lord GOD; [m]I will yet *for* this be inquired of by the house of Israel, to do *it* for them; I will [n]increase them with men like a flock.

38 As the [‡]holy flock, as the flock of Jerusalem in her solemn feasts; so shall the waste cities be filled with flocks of men: and they shall know that I *am* the LORD.

36:20 [r]Is. 52:5 Rom. 2:24
36:21 [s]ch. 20:9,14
36:22 [t]Ps. 106:8
36:23 [u]ch. 20:41 & 28:22
36:24 [v]ch. 34:13 & 37:21
36:25 [w]Is. 52:15 Heb. 10:22 [x]Jer. 33:8
36:26 [y]Jer. 32:39 ch. 11:19
36:27 [z]ch. 11:19 & 37:14
36:28 [a]ch. 28:25 & 37:25 [b]Jer. 30:22 ch. 11:20 & 37:27
36:29 [c]Mat. 1:21 Rom. 11:26 [d]See Ps. 105:16 [e]ch. 34:29
36:30 [f]ch. 34:27
36:31 [g]ch. 16:61,63 [h]Lev. 26:39 ch. 6:9 & 20:43
36:32 [i]ver. 22 Deut. 9:5
36:33 [j]ver. 10
36:35 [k]Is. 51:3 ch. 28:13 Joel 2:3
36:36 [l]ch. 17:24 & 22:14 & 37:14
36:37 [m]See ch. 14:3 & 20:3,31 [n]ver. 10

† Or, *your* ‡ Heb. *flock of holy things*

36:20–22 THEY PROFANED MY HOLY NAME. Israel had profaned the name of God through their iniquity, and they were destroyed. As a result, the nations viewed that defeat as a sign of the Lord's weakness. God therefore intended to restore Israel to the land, not primarily for their sake, but to vindicate the holiness of His great name. When that time came, all nations would know that the Lord God of Israel is the only true God (v. 23; cf. 1 Ki. 18:20–39).

36:26–27 A NEW HEART. God promises to restore Israel not only physically, but also spiritually; this restoration involves giving them a new heart that is as tender as flesh so that they will respond to God's word. Also, God will put His Holy Spirit within them (cf. 11:19–20; Ps. 51:7–11; see Rom. 11:26, note; see article on ISRAEL IN GOD'S PLAN OF SALVATION, p. 1748). This work of God encompasses the new covenant established by Christ (see Jer. 31:31–34).

36:27 MY SPIRIT WITHIN YOU. Apart from the indwelling of the Holy Spirit, it is impossible for a person to have true life and to follow God's ways. It is essential that we remain open to the voice and guidance of the Holy Spirit (see articles on BAPTISM IN THE HOLY SPIRIT, p. 1652, and THE DOCTRINE OF THE HOLY SPIRIT, p. 1668).

Vision of dry bones in the valley

37 THE [o]HAND of the LORD was
upon me, and carried me out
[p]in the spirit of the LORD, and set me
down in the midst of the valley which
was full of bones,
2 And caused me to pass by them
round about: and, behold, *there were*
very many in the open [v]valley; and, lo,
they were very dry.
3 And he said unto me, Son of man,
can these bones live? And I answered,
O Lord GOD, [q]thou knowest.
4 Again he said unto me, Prophesy
upon these bones, and say unto them,
O ye dry bones, hear the word of the
LORD.
5 Thus saith the Lord GOD unto
these bones; Behold, I will [r]cause
breath to enter into you, and ye shall
live:
6 And I will lay sinews upon you,
and will bring up flesh upon you, and
cover you with skin, and put breath in
you, and ye shall live; [s]and ye shall
know that I *am* the LORD.
7 So I prophesied as I was com-
manded: and as I prophesied, there
was a noise, and behold a shaking, and
the bones came together, bone to his
bone.
8 And when I beheld, lo, the sinews
and the flesh came up upon them, and
the skin covered them above: but *there*
was no breath in them.
9 Then said he unto me, Prophesy
unto the [w]wind, prophesy, son of man,
and say to the wind, Thus saith the
Lord GOD; [t]Come from the four winds,
O breath, and breathe upon these slain,
that they may live.
10 So I prophesied as he command-
ed me, [u]and the breath came into
them, and they lived, and stood up
upon their feet, an exceeding great
army.
11 ¶ Then he said unto me, Son of
man, these bones are the whole house
of Israel: behold, they say, [v]Our bones
are dried, and our hope is lost: we are
cut off for our parts.
12 Therefore prophesy and say unto
them, Thus saith the Lord GOD; Behold,
[w]O my people, I will open your graves,
and cause you to come up out of your
graves, and [x]bring you into the land of
Israel.
13 And ye shall know that I *am* the
LORD, when I have opened your graves,
O my people, and brought you up out of
your graves,
14 And [y]shall put my spirit in you,
and ye shall live, and I shall place you
in your own land: then shall ye know
that I the LORD have spoken *it*, and per-
formed *it*, saith the LORD.

Ezek. 39:29

The parable of the two sticks

15 ¶ The word of the LORD came
again unto me, saying,
16 Moreover, thou son of man,
[z]take thee one stick, and write upon
it, For Judah, and for [a]the children of
Israel his companions: then take an-
other stick, and write upon it, For Jo-

37:1 [o]ch. 1:3 [p]ch. 3:14 & 8:3 & 11:24 Luke 4:1 **37:3** [q]Deut. 32:39 1 Sam. 2:6 John 5:21 Rom. 4:17 2 Cor. 1:9 **37:5** [r]ver. 9 Ps. 104:30 **37:6** [s]ch. 6:7 & 35:12 Joel 2:27 & 3:17 **37:9** [t]ver. 5 Ps. 104:30 **37:10** [u]Rev. 11:11 **37:11** [v]Ps. 141:7 Is. 49:14 **37:12** [w]Is. 26:19 Hos. 13:14 [x]ver. 25 ch. 36:24 **37:14** [y]ch. 36:27 **37:16** [z]See Num. 17:2 [a]2 Chr. 11:12,13, 16 & 15:9 & 30:11,18

[v]Or, *champaign* [w]Or, *breath*

37:1–14 THE HAND OF THE LORD ... BONES. By the Holy Spirit Ezekiel sees in a vision a valley full of bones. The bones represent "the whole house of Israel" (v. 11), i.e., both Israel and Judah in exile, whose hope had died when they were dispersed among the heathen. God instructed Ezekiel to prophesy upon the bones (vv. 4–6). The bones were then raised to life in two stages: (1) a political restoration to the land (vv. 7–8), and (2) a spiritual restoration to faith (vv. 9–10). This vision was given to assure the exiles that they would be restored by the power of God and again become a living community in the promised land, in spite of their seemingly hopeless circumstances (vv. 11–14). The time between these two stages is not given.

37:10 BREATH CAME ... AND THEY LIVED. Israel's restoration to life reminds us of the creation of man as recorded in Gen. 2:7. Adam was first formed physically, after which God gave him "the breath of life." In like manner, dead Israel would first be restored physically, and then God would give them His breath of life (i.e., pour out His Spirit on them).

37:12–14 THE LAND OF ISRAEL. The vision of the revived bones would be fulfilled at the time of Israel's restoration, not only physically but also spiritually. This restoration was initially fulfilled in the time of Cyrus (cf. Ezra 1), but it will be fully realized only when God gathers the Israelites to their land in the end time and a great spiritual awakening occurs. Many Jews will believe in and accept Jesus Christ as their Messiah before He returns to establish His kingdom (cf. Rom. 11:15, 25–26; see article on ISRAEL IN GOD'S PLAN OF SALVATION, p. 1748).

37:16–23 TAKE THEE ONE STICK. After the death of Solomon, God's people were divided into two kingdoms (see 1 Ki. 12) — one was called Judah, the other Israel (or sometimes Ephraim). God now promises that the two kingdoms will be reunited as one kingdom, with one King to rule over them.

seph, the stick of Ephraim, and *for* all the house of Israel his companions:

17 And [b]join them one to another into one stick; and they shall become one in thine hand.

18 ¶ And when the children of thy people shall speak unto thee, saying, [c]Wilt thou not show us what thou *meanest* by these?

19 [d]Say unto them, Thus saith the Lord GOD; Behold, I will take [e]the stick of Joseph, which *is* in the hand of Ephraim, and the tribes of Israel his fellows, and will put them with him, *even* with the stick of Judah, and make them one stick, and they shall be one in mine hand.

20 ¶ And the sticks whereon thou writest shall be in thine hand [f]before their eyes.

21 And say unto them, Thus saith the Lord GOD; Behold, [g]I will take the children of Israel from among the heathen, whither they be gone, and will gather them on every side, and bring them into their own land:

22 And [h]I will make them one nation in the land upon the mountains of Israel; and [i]one king shall be king to them all: and they shall be no more two nations, neither shall they be divided into two kingdoms any more at all:

23 [j]Neither shall they defile themselves any more with their idols, nor with their detestable things, nor with any of their transgressions: but [k]I will save them out of all their dwellingplaces, wherein they have sinned, and will cleanse them: so shall they be my people, and I will be their God.

24 And [l]David my servant *shall be* king over them; and [m]they all shall have one shepherd: [n]they shall also walk in my judgments, and observe my statutes, and do them.

25 [o]And they shall dwell in the land that I have given unto Jacob my servant, wherein your fathers have dwelt; and they shall dwell therein, *even* they, and their children, and their children's children [p]for ever: and [q]my servant David *shall be* their prince for ever.

26 Moreover I will make a [r]covenant of peace with them; it shall be an everlasting covenant with them: and I will place them, and [s]multiply them, and will set my [t]sanctuary in the midst of them for evermore.

27 [u]My tabernacle also shall be with them: yea, I will be [v]their God, and they shall be my people.

28 [w]And the heathen shall know that I the LORD do [x]sanctify Israel, when my sanctuary shall be in the midst of them for evermore.

Prophecy against Gog

38 AND THE word of the LORD came unto me, saying,

2 [y]Son of man, [z]set thy face against [a]Gog, the land of Magog, [x]the chief prince of [b]Meshech and Tubal, and prophesy against him,

3 And say, Thus saith the Lord GOD; Behold, I *am* against thee, O Gog, the chief prince of Meshech and Tubal:

4 And [c]I will turn thee back, and put hooks into thy jaws, and I will bring thee forth, and all thine army, horses and horsemen, [d]all of them clothed with all sorts *of armour, even* a great company *with* bucklers and shields, all of them handling swords:

5 Persia, Ethiopia, and [y]Libya with

37:17 [b]See ver. 22,24 **37:18** [c]ch. 12:9 & 24:19 **37:19** [d]Zech. 10:6 [e]ver. 16,17 **37:20** [f]ch. 12:3 **37:21** [g]ch. 36:24 **37:22** [h]Is. 11:13 Jer. 3:18 Hos. 1:11 [i]ch. 34:23 John 10:16 **37:23** [j]ch. 36:25 [k]ch. 36:28 **37:24** [l]Is. 40:11 Jer. 23:5 Luke 1:32 [m]John 10:16 [n]ch. 36:27 **37:25** [o]ch. 36:28 [p]Is. 60:21 Joel 3:20 Amos 9:15 [q]John 12:34 **37:26** [r]Ps. 89:3 Is. 55:3 Jer. 32:40 [s]ch. 36:10 [t]2 Cor. 6:16 **37:27** [u]Lev. 26:11 John 1:14 [v]ch. 11:20 **37:28** [w]ch. 36:23 [x]ch. 20:12 **38:2** [y]ch. 39:1 [z]ch. 35:2,3 [a]Rev. 20:8 [b]ch. 32:26 **38:4** [c]2 Ki. 19:28 ch. 29:4 [d]ch. 23:12

[x] Or, *prince of the chief* [y] Or, *Phut;* see ch. 27:10

37:24 DAVID MY SERVANT. The coming Messiah is called "David" because He would be *the* descendant of David and the fulfillment of the Davidic covenant (cf. 2 Sam. 7:16; see article on GOD'S COVENANT WITH DAVID, p. 470). He would cleanse Israel from her sin, and the people would receive forgiveness and keep God's law. These benefits would become effective through His death on the cross and the ministry of the Holy Spirit (cf. 36:16–32; Jer. 31:31–34).

38:1–23 GOG . . . MAGOG. In this chapter, Ezekiel describes a coalition of nations that will make a final assault on Israel after the people's restoration to their homeland, attempting to destroy the nation and possess the land. The leader of these nations is named Gog. In the end, however, the invading nations will not succeed; they will be defeated by God Himself.

38:2 GOG. Gog was king of the land of Magog and chief ruler over Rosh, Meshech, and Tubal. In Gen. 10:2, Magog, Meshech, and Tubal are the names of the sons of Japheth. Thus the future battle described here will be led by a descendant of Japheth. Gog may also be a name symbolizing evil and opposition to God (see Rev. 20:7–9). These countries are probably located to the far north of Israel (vv. 6,15; 39:2). They will be joined by armies from the east and south (v. 5). The time of this battle is difficult to establish, but most likely it is not identical with the battle of Gog and Magog in Rev. 20:7–9, which will occur at the end of the millennium.

them; all of them with shield and hel-
met:
6 [e]Gomer, and all his bands; the
house of [f]Togarmah of the north
quarters, and all his bands: *and* many
people with thee.
7 [g]Be thou prepared, and prepare
for thyself, thou, and all thy company
that are assembled unto thee, and be
thou a guard unto them.
8 ¶ [h]After many days [i]thou shalt
be visited: in the latter years thou shalt
come into the land *that is* brought back
from the sword, [j]*and is* gathered out
of many people, against [k]the moun-
tains of Israel, which have been always
waste: but it is brought forth out of the
nations, and they shall [l]dwell safely
all of them.
9 Thou shalt ascend and come
[m]like a storm, thou shalt be [n]like a
cloud to cover the land, thou, and all
thy bands, and many people with thee.
10 Thus saith the Lord GOD; It shall
also come to pass, *that* at the same
time shall things come into thy mind,
and thou shalt [z]think an evil thought:
11 And thou shalt say, I will go up
to the land of unwalled villages; I will
[o]go to them that are at rest, [p]that
dwell [a]safely, all of them dwelling
without walls, and having neither bars
nor gates,
12 [q]To[b] take a spoil, and to take
a prey; to turn thine hand upon the des-
olate places *that are now* inhabited,
[r]and upon the people *that are* gath-
ered out of the nations, which have got-
ten cattle and goods, that dwell in the
[c]midst of the land.
13 [s]Sheba, and [t]Dedan, and the
merchants [u]of Tarshish, with all [v]the
young lions thereof, shall say unto
thee, Art thou come to take a spoil?
hast thou gathered thy company to
take a prey? to carry away silver and
gold, to take away cattle and goods, to
take a great spoil?
14 ¶ Therefore, son of man, prophe-
sy and say unto Gog, Thus saith the
Lord GOD; [w]In that day when my peo-
ple of Israel [x]dwelleth safely, shalt
thou not know *it?*
15 [y]And thou shalt come from thy
place out of the north parts, thou,
[z]and many people with thee, all of
them riding upon horses, a great com-
pany, and a mighty army:
16 [a]And thou shalt come up
against my people of Israel, as a cloud
to cover the land; [b]it shall be in the
latter days, and I will bring thee
against my land, that the heathen may
know me, when I shall be sanctified in
thee, O Gog, before their eyes.
17 Thus saith the Lord GOD; *Art*
thou he of whom I have spoken in old
time [d]by my servants the prophets of
Israel, which prophesied in those days
many years that I would bring thee
against them?
18 And it shall come to pass at the
same time when Gog shall come
against the land of Israel, saith the
Lord GOD, *that* my fury shall come up in
my face.
19 For [c]in my jealousy [d]*and* in the
fire of my wrath have I spoken, [e]Sure-
ly in that day there shall be a great
shaking in the land of Israel;
20 So that [f]the fishes of the sea,
and the fowls of the heaven, and the
beasts of the field, and all creeping
things that creep upon the earth, and
all the men that *are* upon the face of the
earth, shall shake at my presence,
[g]and the mountains shall be thrown
down, and the [e]steep places shall fall,
and every wall shall fall to the ground.
21 And I will [h]call for [i]a sword
against him throughout all my moun-
tains, saith the Lord GOD: [j]every
man's sword shall be against his
brother.
22 And I will [k]plead against him
with [l]pestilence and with blood; and
[m]I will rain upon him, and upon his
bands, and upon the many people that
are with him, an overflowing rain, and
[n]great hailstones, fire, and brimstone.
23 Thus will I magnify myself, and
[o]sanctify myself; [p]and I will be
known in the eyes of many nations, and
they shall know that I *am* the LORD.

39

THEREFORE, [q]THOU son of
man, prophesy against Gog,

38:6 [e]Gen. 10:2 [f]ch. 27:14 **38:7** [g]Is. 8:9,10 Jer. 46:3,4 **38:8** [h]ver. 16 Deut. 4:30 [i]Is. 29:6 [j]ch. 34:13 [k]ch. 36:1,4 [l]Jer. 23:6 **38:9** [m]Is. 28:2 [n]Jer. 4:13 **38:11** [o]Jer. 49:31 [p]ver. 8 **38:12** [q]ch. 29:19 [r]ver. 8 **38:13** [s]ch. 27:22 [t]ch. 27:15 [u]ch. 27:12 [v]ch. 19:3,5 **38:14** [w]Is. 4:1 [x]ver. 8 **38:15** [y]ch. 39:2 [z]ver. 6 **38:16** [a]ver. 9 [b]ver. 8 **38:19** [c]ch. 36:5,6 [d]Ps. 89:46 [e]Hag. 2:6,7 Rev. 16:18 **38:20** [f]Hos. 4:3 [g]Jer. 4:24 **38:21** [h]Ps. 105:16 [i]ch. 14:17 [j]Judg. 7:22 1 Sam. 14:20 **38:22** [k]Is. 66:16 Jer. 25:31 [l]ch. 5:17 [m]Ps. 11:6 Is. 30:30 [n]Rev. 16:21 **38:23** [o]ch. 36:23 [p]ch. 37:28 **39:1** [q]ch. 38:2,3

[z] Or, *conceive a mischievous purpose* [a] Or, *confidently* [b] Heb. *To spoil the spoil, and to prey the prey* [c] Heb. *navel;* see Judg. 9:37 [d] Heb. *by the hands* [e] Or, *towers,* or, *stairs*

38:21–22 EVERY MAN'S SWORD. God will confuse the invading army so that some nations will turn against their allies. He will also directly destroy the armies by earthquakes, disease, and other catastrophic events.

39:1–29 PROPHESY AGAINST GOG. This chapter reiterates God's judgment against Gog and portrays the total annihilation of Israel's ene-

and say, Thus saith the Lord GOD; Behold, I *am* against thee, O Gog, the chief prince of Meshech and Tubal:

2 And I will turn thee back, and leave but the sixth part of thee, [r]and will cause thee to come up from [f]the north parts, and will bring thee upon the mountains of Israel:

3 And I will smite thy bow out of thy left hand, and will cause thine arrows to fall out of thy right hand.

4 [s]Thou shalt fall upon the mountains of Israel, thou, and all thy bands, and the people that *is* with thee: [t]I will give thee unto the ravenous birds of every [g]sort, and *to* the beasts of the field [h]to be devoured.

5 Thou shalt fall upon [i]the open field: for I have spoken *it,* saith the Lord GOD.

6 [u]And I will send a fire on Magog, and among them that dwell [j]carelessly in [v]the isles: and they shall know that I *am* the LORD.

7 [w]So will I make my holy name known in the midst of my people Israel; and I will not *let them* [x]pollute my holy name any more: [y]and the heathen shall know that I *am* the LORD, the Holy One in Israel.

8 ¶ [z]Behold, it is come, and it is done, saith the Lord GOD; this *is* the day [a]whereof I have spoken.

9 And they that dwell in the cities of Israel shall go forth, and shall set on fire and burn the weapons, both the shields and the bucklers, the bows and the arrows, and the [k]handstaves, and the spears, and they shall [l]burn them with fire seven years:

10 So that they shall take no wood out of the field, neither cut down *any* out of the forests; for they shall burn the weapons with fire: [b]and they shall spoil those that spoiled them, and rob those that robbed them, saith the Lord GOD.

11 ¶ And it shall come to pass in that day, *that* I will give unto Gog a place there of graves in Israel, the valley of the passengers on the east of the sea: and it shall stop the [m]*noses* of the passengers: and there shall they bury Gog and all his multitude: and they shall call *it* The valley of [n]Hamon-gog.

12 And seven months shall the house of Israel be burying of them, [c]that they may cleanse the land.

13 Yea, all the people of the land shall bury *them;* and it shall be to them a renown the day that [d]I shall be glorified, saith the Lord GOD.

14 And they shall sever out [o]men of continual employment, passing through the land to bury with the passengers those that remain upon the face of the earth, [e]to cleanse it: after the end of seven months shall they search.

15 And the passengers *that* pass through the land, when *any* seeth a man's bone, then shall he [p]set up a sign by it, till the buriers have buried it in the valley of Hamon-gog.

16 And also the name of the city *shall be* [q]Hamonah. Thus shall they [f]cleanse the land.

17 ¶ And, thou son of man, thus saith the Lord GOD; [g]Speak [r]unto every feathered fowl, and to every beast of the field, [h]Assemble yourselves, and come; gather yourselves on every side to my [s]sacrifice that I do sacrifice for you, *even* a great sacrifice [i]upon the mountains of Israel, that ye may eat flesh, and drink blood.

18 [j]Ye shall eat the flesh of the mighty, and drink the blood of the princes of the earth, of rams, of lambs, and of [t]goats, of bullocks, all of them [k]fatlings of Bashan.

19 And ye shall eat fat till ye be full, and drink blood till ye be drunken, of my sacrifice which I have sacrificed for you.

20 [l]Thus ye shall be filled at my

39:2 [r]ch. 38:15
39:4 [s]ch. 38:21 [t]ch. 33:27
39:6 [u]Amos 1:4 [v]Ps. 72:10
39:7 [w]ver. 22 [x]Lev. 18:21 [y]ch. 38:16
39:8 [z]Rev. 16:17 & 21:6 [a]ch. 38:17
39:10 [b]Is. 14:2
39:12 [c]Deut. 21:23
39:13 [d]ch. 28:22
39:14 [e]ver. 12
39:16 [f]ver. 12
39:17 [g]Rev. 19:7 [h]Is. 18:6 Zeph. 1:7 [i]ver. 4
39:18 [j]Rev. 19:18 [k]Deut. 32:14 Ps. 22:12
39:20 [l]Ps. 76:6 ch. 38:4

[f]Heb. *the sides of the north* [g]Heb. *wing* [h]Heb. *to devour* [i]Heb. *the face of the field* [j]Or, *confidently* [k]Or, *javelins* [l]Or, *make a fire of them* [m]Or, mouths [n]i.e., *The multitude of Gog* [o]Heb. *men of continuance* [p]Heb. *build* [q]i.e. *The multitude* [r]Heb. *to the fowl of every wing* [s]Or, *slaughter* [t]Heb. *great goats*

my. It emphasizes the miraculous intervention of God on behalf of His people.

39:6 THEY SHALL KNOW THAT I *AM* THE LORD. By destroying the armies of the invading evil nations, the Lord will manifest His glory so that everyone will know that He alone is Lord.

39:9 SEVEN YEARS. The "seven years" (see also v. 12) may mean a literal seven years, or it may be a symbolic number signifying the completeness of the enemies' destruction. In either case, the message of this chapter is clear: God's people will ultimately be victorious, and all evil and suffering will be abolished.

table with horses and chariots, [m]with mighty men, and with all men of war, saith the Lord GOD.

21 [n]And I will set my glory among the heathen, and all the heathen shall see my judgment that I have executed, and [o]my hand that I have laid upon them.

22 [p]So the house of Israel shall know that I *am* the LORD their God from that day and forward.

23 ¶ [q]And the heathen shall know that the house of Israel went into captivity for their iniquity: because they trespassed against me, therefore [r]hid I my face from them, and [s]gave them into the hand of their enemies: so fell they all by the sword.

24 [t]According to their uncleanness and according to their transgressions have I done unto them, and hid my face from them.

25 Therefore thus saith the Lord GOD; [u]Now will I bring again the captivity of Jacob, and have mercy upon the [v]whole house of Israel, and will be jealous for my holy name;

26 [w]After that they have borne their shame, and all their trespasses whereby they have trespassed against me, when they [x]dwelt safely in their land, and none made *them* afraid.

27 [y]When I have brought them again from the people, and gathered them out of their enemies' lands, and [z]am sanctified in them in the sight of many nations;

28 [a]Then shall they know that I *am* the LORD their God, [u]which caused them to be led into captivity among the heathen: but I have gathered them unto their own land, and have left none of them any more there.

29 [b]Neither will I hide my face any more from them: for I have [c]poured out my spirit upon the house of Israel, saith the Lord GOD.

Joel 2:28-2

The new temple arrangements

40 IN THE five and twentieth year of our captivity, in the beginning of the year, in the tenth *day* of the month, in the fourteenth year after that [d]the city was smitten, in the selfsame day [e]the hand of the LORD was upon me, and brought me thither.

2 [f]In the visions of God brought he me into the land of Israel, and [g]set me upon a very high mountain, [v]by which *was* as the frame of a city on the south.

3 And he brought me thither, and, behold, *there was* a man, whose appearance *was* [h]like the appearance of brass, [i]with a line of flax in his hand, [j]and a measuring reed; and he stood in the gate.

4 And the man said unto me, [k]Son of man, behold with thine eyes, and hear with thine ears, and set thine heart upon all that I shall show thee; for to the intent that I might show *them* unto thee *art* thou brought hither: [l]declare all that thou seest to the house of Israel.

5 And behold [m]a wall on the outside of the house round about, and in the man's hand a measuring reed of six cubits *long* by the cubit and an handbreadth: so he measured the breadth of the building, one reed; and the height, one reed.

6 ¶ Then came he unto the gate [w]which looketh toward the east, and went up the stairs thereof, and measured the threshold of the gate, *which was* one reed broad; and the other

39:20 [m]Rev. 19:18
39:21 [n]ch. 38:16,23 [o]Ex. 7:4
39:22 [p]ver. 7,28
39:23 [q]ch. 36:18-20,23 [r]Deut. 31:17 Is. 59:2 [s]Lev. 26:25
39:24 [t]ch. 36:19
39:25 [u]Jer. 30:3,18 ch. 34:13 & 36:24 [v]ch. 20:40 Hos. 1:11
39:26 [w]Dan. 9:16 [x]Lev. 26:5,6
39:27 [y]ch. 28:25,26 [z]ch. 36:23,24 & 38:16
39:28 [a]ver. 22 ch. 34:30
39:29 [b]Is. 54:8 [c]Joel 2:28 Zech. 12:10 Acts 2:17
40:1 [d]ch. 33:21 [e]ch. 1:3
40:2 [f]ch. 8:3 [g]Rev. 21:10
40:3 [h]ch. 1:7 Dan. 10:6 [i]ch. 47:3 [j]Rev. 11:1 & 21:15
40:4 [k]ch. 44:5 [l]ch. 43:10
40:5 [m]ch. 42:20

[u] Heb. *by my causing of them* [v] Or, *upon which* [w] Heb. *whose face* was *the way toward the east*

40:1—43:27 THE VISIONS OF GOD. The vision of the temple came to Ezekiel in 573 B.C., twenty-five years after his exile had begun. Its purpose was to encourage the people that there would be a full restoration of God's glory in the future, resulting in an anointing and blessing that would endure forever.

40:5 THE HOUSE. This house refers to the temple, the house of God. There are three main interpretations of Ezekiel's vision of the temple: (1) a symbolic temple picturing the eternal state described in Rev. 21—22; (2) a symbolic temple describing the blessings of the millennial kingdom; or (3) a future literal temple that will be built during the millennial kingdom. Regardless of which interpretation is adopted, the main teachings are (1) that someday God's presence and His glory will be restored to His people forever (43:7), and (2) that the blessings of Christ will flow forth in an ever-deepening stream (47:1–12).

40:5 A WALL ON THE OUTSIDE OF THE HOUSE. This wall would mark the temple area and set it apart from the rest of the city. Believers, whose bodies are now the living temples of the Holy Spirit (1 Cor. 6:19), must keep themselves separated from the sinful society around them and set apart for God and His holy purposes (see article on SPIRITUAL SEPARATION FOR BELIEVERS, p. 1814).

threshold *of the gate, which was* one reed broad.

7 And *every* little chamber *was* one reed long, and one reed broad; and between the little chambers *were* five cubits; and the threshold of the gate by the porch of the gate within *was* one reed.

8 He measured also the porch of the gate within, one reed.

9 Then measured he the porch of the gate, eight cubits; and the posts thereof, two cubits; and the porch of the gate *was* inward.

10 And the little chambers of the gate eastward *were* three on this side, and three on that side; they three *were* of one measure: and the posts had one measure on this side and on that side.

11 And he measured the breadth of the entry of the gate, ten cubits; *and* the length of the gate, thirteen cubits.

12 The [x]space also before the little chambers *was* one cubit *on this side,* and the space *was* one cubit on that side: and the little chambers *were* six cubits on this side, and six cubits on that side.

13 He measured then the gate from the roof of *one* little chamber to the roof of another: the breadth *was* five and twenty cubits, door against door.

14 He made also posts of threescore cubits, even unto the post of the court round about the gate.

15 And from the face of the gate of the entrance unto the face of the porch of the inner gate *were* fifty cubits.

16 And *there were* [n]narrow[y] windows to the little chambers, and to their posts within the gate round about, and likewise to the [z]arches: and windows *were* round about [a]inward: and upon *each* post *were* palm trees.

17 Then brought he me into [o]the outward court, and, lo, *there were* [p]chambers, and a pavement made for the court round about: [q]thirty chambers *were* upon the pavement.

18 And the pavement by the side of the gates over against the length of the gates *was* the lower pavement.

19 Then he measured the breadth from the forefront of the lower gate unto the forefront of the inner court [b]without, an hundred cubits eastward and northward.

40:16
[n] 1 Ki. 6:4
40:17
[o] Rev. 11:2
[p] 1 Ki. 6:5
[q] ch. 45:5

Location and size of gates

20 ¶ And the gate of the outward court [c]that looked toward the north, he measured the length thereof, and the breadth thereof.

21 And the little chambers thereof *were* three on this side and three on that side; and the posts thereof and the [z]arches thereof were after the measure of the first gate: the length thereof *was* fifty cubits, and the breadth five and twenty cubits.

22 And their windows, and their arches, and their palm trees, *were* after the measure of the gate that looketh toward the east; and they went up unto it by seven steps; and the arches thereof *were* before them.

23 And the gate of the inner court *was* over against the gate toward the north, and toward the east; and he measured from gate to gate an hundred cubits.

24 ¶ After that he brought me toward the south, and behold a gate toward the south: and he measured the posts thereof and the arches thereof according to these measures.

25 And *there were* windows in it and in the arches thereof round about, like those windows: the length *was* fifty cubits, and the breadth five and twenty cubits.

26 And *there were* seven steps to go up to it, and the arches thereof *were* before them: and it had palm trees, one on this side, and another on that side, upon the posts thereof.

27 And *there was* a gate in the inner court toward the south: and he measured from gate to gate toward the south an hundred cubits.

28 And he brought me to the inner court by the south gate: and he measured the south gate according to these measures;

29 And the little chambers thereof, and the posts thereof, and the arches thereof, according to these measures: and *there were* windows in it and in the arches thereof round about: *it was* fifty cubits long, and five and twenty cubits broad.

30 And the arches round about *were*

[x] Heb. *limit,* or, *bound* [y] Heb. *closed* [z] Or, *galleries,* or, *porches* [a] Or, *within* [b] Or, *from without* [c] Heb. *whose face* was

[r]five and twenty cubits long, and five
cubits [d]broad.
31 And the arches thereof *were* toward the utter court; and palm trees *were* upon the posts thereof: and the going up to it *had* eight steps.
32 ¶ And he brought me into the inner court toward the east: and he measured the gate according to these measures.
33 And the little chambers thereof, and the posts thereof, and the arches thereof, *were* according to these measures: and *there were* windows therein and in the arches thereof round about: *it was* fifty cubits long, and five and twenty cubits broad.
34 And the arches thereof *were* toward the outward court; and palm trees *were* upon the posts thereof, on this side, and on that side: and the going up to it *had* eight steps.
35 ¶ And he brought me to the north gate, and measured *it* according to these measures;
36 The little chambers thereof, the posts thereof, and the arches thereof, and the windows to it round about: the length *was* fifty cubits, and the breadth five and twenty cubits.
37 And the posts thereof *were* toward the utter court; and palm trees *were* upon the posts thereof, on this side, and on that side: and the going up to it *had* eight steps.

The porch and its furnishings

38 And the chambers and the entries thereof *were* by the posts of the gates, where they washed the burnt offering.
39 ¶ And in the porch of the gate *were* two tables on this side, and two tables on that side, to slay thereon the burnt offering and [s]the sin offering and [t]the trespass offering.
40 And at the side without, [e]as one goeth up to the entry of the north gate, *were* two tables; and on the other side, which *was* at the porch of the gate, *were* two tables.
41 Four tables *were* on this side, and four tables on that side, by the side of the gate; eight tables, whereupon they slew *their sacrifices.*

40:30 [r]See ver. 21,25, 33,36
40:39 [s]Lev. 4:2,3 [t]Lev. 5:6 & 6:6 & 7:1
40:44 [u]1 Chr. 6:31
40:45 [v]Lev. 8:35 Num. 3:27,28,32, 38 & 18:5 1 Chr. 9:23 2 Chr. 13:11 Ps. 134:1
40:46 [w]Num. 18:5 ch. 44:15 [x]1 Ki. 2:35 ch. 43:19 & 44:15,16
40:49 [y]1 Ki. 6:3 [z]1 Ki. 7:21

42 And the four tables *were* of hewn stone for the burnt offering, of a cubit and an half long, and a cubit and an half broad, and one cubit high: whereupon also they laid the instruments wherewith they slew the burnt offering and the sacrifice.
43 And within *were* [f]hooks, an hand broad, fastened round about: and upon the tables *was* the flesh of the offering.
44 ¶ And without the inner gate *were* the chambers of [u]the singers in the inner court, which *was* at the side of the north gate; and their prospect *was* toward the south: one at the side of the east gate *having* the prospect toward the north.
45 And he said unto me, This chamber, whose prospect *is* toward the south, *is* for the priests, [v]the keepers of the [g]charge of the house.
46 And the chamber whose prospect *is* toward the north *is* for the priests, [w]the keepers of the charge of the altar: these *are* the sons of [x]Zadok among the sons of Levi, which come near to the LORD to minister unto him.
47 So he measured the court, an hundred cubits long, and an hundred cubits broad, foursquare; and the altar *that was* before the house.
48 ¶ And he brought me to the porch of the house, and measured *each* post of the porch, five cubits on this side, and five cubits on that side: and the breadth of the gate *was* three cubits on this side, and three cubits on that side.
49 [y]The length of the porch *was* twenty cubits, and the breadth eleven cubits; and *he brought me* by the steps whereby they went up to it: and *there were* [z]pillars by the posts, one on this side, and another on that side.

The temple and its walls

41 AFTERWARD HE brought me to the temple, and measured the posts, six cubits broad on the one side, and six cubits broad on the other

[d]Heb. *breadth* [e]Or, *at the step* [f]Or, *endirons,* or, *the two hearthstones* [g]Or, *ward,* or, *ordinance*

40:38 BURNT OFFERING. See 43:18–27, note.
41:1 THE TEMPLE. The temple Ezekiel saw is somewhat different from Solomon's temple. Nothing is said about the altar of incense, the lampstand, or the ark of the covenant. The reason for the difference is not explained.

side, *which was* the breadth of the tabernacle.

2 And the breadth of the [h]door *was* ten cubits; and the sides of the door *were* five cubits on the one side, and five cubits on the other side: and he measured the length thereof, forty cubits: and the breadth, twenty cubits.

3 Then went he inward, and measured the post of the door, two cubits; and the door, six cubits; and the breadth of the door, seven cubits.

4 So [a]he measured the length thereof, twenty cubits; and the breadth, twenty cubits, before the temple: and he said unto me, This *is* the most holy *place.*

5 After he measured the wall of the house, six cubits; and the breadth of *every* side chamber, four cubits, round about the house on every side.

6 [b]And the side chambers *were* three, [i]one over another, and [j]thirty in order; and they entered into the wall which *was* of the house for the side chambers round about, that they might [k]have hold, but they had not hold in the wall of the house.

7 And [c]*there*[l] *was* an enlarging, and a winding about still upward to the side chambers: for the winding about of the house went still upward round about the house: therefore the breadth of the house *was still* upward, and so increased *from* the lowest *chamber* to the highest by the midst.

8 I saw also the height of the house round about: the foundations of the side chambers *were* [d]a full reed of six great cubits.

9 The thickness of the wall, which *was* for the side chamber without, *was* five cubits: and *that* which *was* left *was* the place of the side chambers that *were* within.

10 And between the chambers *was* the wideness of twenty cubits round about the house on every side.

11 And the doors of the side chambers *were* toward *the place that was* left, one door toward the north, and another door toward the south: and the breadth of the place that was left *was* five cubits round about.

12 Now the building that *was* before the separate place at the end toward the west *was* seventy cubits broad; and the wall of the building *was* five cubits thick round about, and the length thereof ninety cubits.

41:4 [a]1 Ki. 6:20 2 Chr. 3:8
41:6 [b]1 Ki. 6:5,6
41:7 [c]1 Ki. 6:8
41:8 [d]ch. 40:5

41:16 [e]ver. 26 ch. 40:16
41:18 [f]1 Ki. 6:29
41:19 [g]See ch. 1:10
41:22 [h]Ex. 30:1 [i]ch. 44:16 Mal. 1:7,12 [j]Ex. 30:8
41:23 [k]1 Ki. 6:31-35

13 So he measured the house, an hundred cubits long; and the separate place, and the building, with the walls thereof, an hundred cubits long;

14 Also the breadth of the face of the house, and of the separate place toward the east, an hundred cubits.

15 And he measured the length of the building over against the separate place which *was* behind it, and the [m]galleries thereof on the one side and on the other side, an hundred cubits, with the inner temple, and the porches of the court;

16 The door posts, and [e]the narrow windows, and the galleries round about on their three stories, over against the door, [n]ceiled with wood round about, [o]and from the ground up to the windows, and the windows *were* covered;

17 To that above the door, even unto the inner house, and without, and by all the wall round about within and without, by [p]measure.

18 And *it was* made [f]with cherubims and palm trees, so that a palm tree *was* between a cherub and a cherub; and *every* cherub had two faces;

19 [g]So that the face of a man *was* toward the palm tree on the one side, and the face of a young lion toward the palm tree on the other side: *it was* made through all the house round about.

20 From the ground unto above the door *were* cherubims and palm trees made, and *on* the wall of the temple.

21 The [q]posts of the temple *were* squared, *and* the face of the sanctuary; the appearance *of the one* as the appearance *of the other.*

22 [h]The altar of wood *was* three cubits high, and the length thereof two cubits; and the corners thereof, and the length thereof, and the walls thereof, *were* of wood: and he said unto me, This *is* [i]the table that *is* [j]before the LORD.

23 [k]And the temple and the sanctuary had two doors.

24 And the doors had two leaves *apiece,* two turning leaves; two *leaves*

[h] Or, *entrance* [i] Heb. *side chamber over side chamber* [j] Or, *three and thirty times,* or, *foot* [k] Heb. *be holden* [l] Heb. it was *made broader, and went round* [m] Or, *several walks,* or, *walks with pillars* [n] Heb. *ceiling of wood* [o] Or, *and the ground unto the windows* [p] Heb. *measures* [q] Heb. *post*

for the one door, and two leaves for the other *door.*

25 And *there were* made on them, on the doors of the temple, cherubims and palm trees, like as *were* made upon the walls; and *there were* thick planks upon the face of the porch without.

26 And *there were* [l]narrow windows and palm trees on the one side and on the other side, on the sides of the porch, and *upon* the side chambers of the house, and thick planks.

The priests' chambers

42 THEN HE brought me forth into the utter court, the way toward the north: and he brought me into [m]the chamber that *was* over against the separate place, and which *was* before the building toward the north.

2 Before the length of an hundred cubits *was* the north door, and the breadth *was* fifty cubits.

3 Over against the twenty *cubits* which *were* for the inner court, and over against the pavement which *was* for the utter court, *was* [n]gallery against gallery in three *stories.*

4 And before the chambers *was* a walk of ten cubits breadth inward, a way of one cubit; and their doors toward the north.

5 Now the upper chambers *were* shorter: for the galleries [r]were higher than these, [s]than the lower, and than the middlemost of the building.

6 For they *were* in three *stories,* but had not pillars as the pillars of the courts: therefore *the building* was straitened more than the lowest and the middlemost from the ground.

7 And the wall that *was* without over against the chambers, toward the utter court on the forepart of the chambers, the length thereof *was* fifty cubits.

8 For the length of the chambers that *were* in the utter court *was* fifty cubits: and, lo, before the temple *were* an hundred cubits.

9 And [t]from under these chambers *was* [u]the entry on the east side, [v]as one goeth into them from the utter court.

10 The chambers *were* in the thickness of the wall of the court toward the east, over against the separate place, and over against the building.

11 And [o]the way before them *was* like the appearance of the chambers which *were* toward the north, as long as they, *and* as broad as they: and all their goings out *were* both according to their fashions, and according to their doors.

12 And according to the doors of the chambers that *were* toward the south *was* a door in the head of the way, *even* the way directly before the wall toward the east, as one entereth into them.

13 ¶ Then said he unto me, The north chambers *and* the south chambers, which *are* before the separate place, they *be* holy chambers, where the priests that approach unto the LORD [p]shall eat the most holy things: there shall they lay the most holy things, and [q]the meat offering, and the sin offering, and the trespass offering; for the place *is* holy.

14 [r]When the priests enter therein, then shall they not go out of the holy *place* into the utter court, but there they shall lay their garments wherein they minister; for they *are* holy; and shall put on other garments, and shall approach to *those things* which *are* for the people.

15 Now when he had made an end of measuring the inner house, he brought me forth toward the gate whose prospect *is* toward the east, and measured it round about.

16 He measured the east [w]side with the measuring reed, five hundred reeds, with the measuring reed round about.

17 He measured the north side, five hundred reeds, with the measuring reed round about.

18 He measured the south side, five hundred reeds, with the measuring reed.

19 ¶ He turned about to the west side, *and* measured five hundred reeds with the measuring reed.

20 He measured it by the four sides: [s]it had a wall round about, [t]five hundred *reeds* long, and five hundred broad, to make a separation between the sanctuary and the profane place.

The LORD's glory fills the temple

43 AFTERWARD HE brought me to the gate, *even* the gate [u]that looketh toward the east:

41:26 [l]ver. 16 ch. 40:16
42:1 [m]ch. 41:12,15
42:3 [n]ch. 41:16
42:11 [o]ver. 4
42:13 [p]Lev. 6:16,26 & 24:9 [q]Lev. 2:3,10 & 6:14,17,25,29
42:14 [r]ch. 44:19
42:20 [s]ch. 40:5 [t]ch. 45:2
43:1 [u]ch. 10:19 & 46:1

[r] Or, *did eat of these* [s] Or, and *the building consisted of the lower and the middlemost*
[t] Or, *from the place* [u] Or, *he that brought me*
[v] Or, *as he came* [w] Heb. *wind*

2 [v]And, behold, the glory of the God of Israel came from the way of the east: and [w]his voice *was* like a noise of many waters: [x]and the earth shined with his glory.

3 And *it was* [y]according to the appearance of the vision which I saw, *even* according to the vision that I saw [z]when[x] I came [a]to destroy the city: and the visions *were* like the vision that I saw [b]by the river Chebar; and I fell upon my face.

4 [c]And the glory of the LORD came into the house by the way of the gate whose prospect *is* toward the east.

5 [d]So the spirit took me up, and brought me into the inner court; and, behold, [e]the glory of the LORD filled the house.

6 And I heard *him* speaking unto me out of the house; and [f]the man stood by me.

7 ¶ And he said unto me, Son of man, [g]the place of my throne, and [h]the place of the soles of my feet, [i]where I will dwell in the midst of the children of Israel for ever, and my holy name, shall the house of Israel [j]no more defile, *neither* they, nor their kings, by their whoredom, nor by [k]the carcases of their kings in their high places.

8 [l]In their setting of their threshold by my thresholds, and their post by my posts, [y]and the wall between me and them, they have even defiled my holy name by their abominations that they have committed: wherefore I have consumed them in mine anger.

9 Now let them put away their whoredom, and [m]the carcases of their kings, far from me, [n]and I will dwell in the midst of them for ever.

10 ¶ Thou son of man, [o]show the house to the house of Israel, that they may be ashamed of their iniquities: and let them measure the [z]pattern.

11 And if they be ashamed of all that they have done, show them the form of the house, and the fashion thereof, and the goings out thereof, and the comings in thereof, and all the forms thereof, and all the ordinances thereof, and all the forms thereof, and all the laws thereof: and write *it* in their sight, that they may keep the whole form thereof, and all the ordinances thereof, and do them.

12 This *is* the law of the house; Upon [p]the top of the mountain the whole limit thereof round about *shall be* most holy. Behold, this *is* the law of the house.

The size and use of the altar

13 ¶ And these *are* the measures of the altar after the cubits: [q]The cubit *is* a cubit and an handbreadth; even the [a]bottom *shall be* a cubit, and the breadth a cubit, and the border thereof by the [b]edge thereof round about *shall be* a span: and this *shall be* the higher place of the altar.

14 And from the bottom *upon* the ground *even* to the lower settle *shall be* two cubits, and the breadth one cubit; and from the lesser settle *even* to the greater settle *shall be* four cubits, and the breadth *one* cubit.

15 So [c]the altar *shall be* four cubits; and from [d]the altar and upward *shall be* four horns.

16 And the altar *shall be* twelve *cubits* long, twelve broad, square in the four squares thereof.

43:2 [v]ch. 11:23 [w]ch. 1:24 Rev. 1:15 & 14:2 [x]ch. 10:4 Rev. 18:1 **43:3** [y]ch. 1:4,28 [z]See ch. 9:1 [a]Jer. 1:10 [b]ch. 3:23 **43:4** [c]ch. 10:19 **43:5** [d]ch:3:12,14 & 8:3 [e]1 Ki. 8:10,11 **43:6** [f]ch. 40:3 **43:7** [g]Ps. 99:1 [h]1 Chr. 28:2 Ps. 99:5 [i]Ex. 29:45 Ps. 68:16 & 132:14 Joel 3:17 John 1:14 2 Cor. 6:16 [j]ch. 39:7 [k]Lev. 26:30 Jer. 16:18 **43:8** [l]See 2 Ki. 16:14 & 21:4,5,7 ch. 8:3 & 23:39 & 44:7 **43:9** [m]ver. 7 [n]ver. 7 **43:10** [o]ch. 40:4 **43:12** [p]ch. 40:2 **43:13** [q]ch. 41:8

[x] Or, *when I came to* prophesy *that the city should be destroyed* [y] Or, *for* there was but *a wall between me and them* [z] Or, *sum,* or, *number* [a] Heb. *bosom* [b] Heb. *lip* [c] Heb. *Harel,* i.e. *the mountain of God* [d] Heb. *Ariel,* i.e. *the lion of God*

43:5 THE GLORY OF THE LORD FILLED THE HOUSE. The book of Ezekiel began with an awe-inspiring vision of God's glory. Chs. 8–11 described how God's glory progressively departed from the temple and the city because of the sins of the people. Ezekiel concludes with another awe-inspiring vision: God's glory, power, and love filling the temple again. We should desire above all else to see God's glory manifested within the church through the operation of the Holy Spirit (see article on THE GLORY OF GOD, p. 1186). The absence of such holy and burning desire is evidence of spiritual decline among God's people.

43:7 I WILL DWELL IN THE MIDST OF . . . ISRAEL. God's eternal plan is to dwell in a caring fellowship with His people forever. The blessing and joy He has in store for us will be far beyond what we can perceive (cf. 1 Cor. 2:9; Rev. 21—22).

43:12 THE LAW OF THE HOUSE. The fundamental law of God's temple is holiness, which requires separation from all sin and evil. Similarly, believers, as the temple of the Holy Spirit (1 Cor. 6:19), must live in accordance with the Spirit of holiness (Rom. 1:4) and remain cleansed from all sin (1 Cor. 6:18–20; see article on SPIRITUAL SEPARATION FOR BELIEVERS, p. 1814).

17 And the settle *shall be* fourteen *cubits* long and fourteen broad in the four squares thereof; and the border about it *shall be* half a cubit; and the bottom thereof *shall be* a cubit about; and [r]his stairs shall look toward the east.

18 ¶ And he said unto me, Son of man, thus saith the Lord GOD; These *are* the ordinances of the altar in the day when they shall make it, to offer burnt offerings thereon, and to [s]sprinkle blood thereon.

19 And thou shalt give to [t]the priests the Levites that be of the seed of Zadok, which approach unto me, to minister unto me, saith the Lord GOD, [u]a young bullock for a sin offering.

20 And thou shalt take of the blood thereof, and put *it* on the four horns of it, and on the four corners of the settle, and upon the border round about: thus shalt thou cleanse and purge it.

21 Thou shalt take the bullock also of the sin offering, and he [v]shall burn it in the appointed place of the house, [w]without the sanctuary.

22 And on the second day thou shalt offer a kid of the goats without blemish for a sin offering; and they shall cleanse the altar, as they did cleanse *it* with the bullock.

23 When thou hast made an end of cleansing *it,* thou shalt offer a young bullock without blemish, and a ram out of the flock without blemish.

24 And thou shalt offer them before the LORD, [x]and the priests shall cast salt upon them, and they shall offer them up *for* a burnt offering unto the LORD.

25 [y]Seven days shalt thou prepare every day a goat *for* a sin offering: they shall also prepare a young bullock, and a ram out of the flock, without blemish.

26 Seven days shall they purge the altar and purify it; and they shall [e]consecrate themselves.

27 [z]And when these days are expired, it shall be, *that* upon the eighth day, and *so* forward, the priests shall make your burnt offerings upon the altar, and your [f]peace offerings; and I will [a]accept you, saith the Lord GOD.

The use of the temple

44 THEN HE brought me back the way of the gate of the outward sanctuary [b]which looketh toward the east; and it *was* shut.

2 Then said the LORD unto me; This gate shall be shut, it shall not be opened, and no man shall enter in by it; [c]because the LORD, the God of Israel, hath entered in by it, therefore it shall be shut.

3 *It is* for the prince; the prince, he shall sit in it to [d]eat bread before the LORD; [e]he shall enter by the way of the porch of *that* gate, and shall go out by the way of the same.

4 ¶ Then brought he me the way of the north gate before the house: and I looked, and, [f]behold, the glory of the LORD filled the house of the LORD: [g]and I fell upon my face.

5 And the LORD said unto me, [h]Son of man, [g]mark well, and behold with thine eyes, and hear with thine ears all that I say unto thee concerning all the ordinances of the house of the LORD, and all the laws thereof; and mark well the entering in of the house, with every going forth of the sanctuary.

6 And thou shalt say to the [i]rebellious, *even* to the house of Israel, Thus saith the Lord GOD; O ye house of Israel, [j]let it suffice you of all your abominations,

7 [k]In that ye have brought *into my sanctuary* [l]strangers,[h] [m]uncircumcised in heart, and uncircumcised in flesh, to be in my sanctuary, to pollute it, *even* my house, when ye offer [n]my bread, [o]the fat and the blood, and they have broken my covenant because of all your abominations.

8 And ye have not [p]kept the charge

43:17 [r]See Ex. 20:26 **43:18** [s]Lev. 1:5 **43:19** [t]ch. 44:15 [u]Ex. 29:10 Lev. 8:14 ch. 45:18 **43:21** [v]Ex. 29:14 [w]Heb. 13:11 **43:24** [x]Lev. 2:13 **43:25** [y]Ex. 29:35 Lev. 8:33 **43:27** [z]Lev. 9:1 [a]ch. 20:40,41 Rom. 12:1 1 Pet. 2:5 **44:1** [b]ch. 43:1 **44:2** [c]ch. 43:4 **44:3** [d]Gen. 31:54 1 Cor. 10:18 [e]ch. 46:2,8 **44:4** [f]ch. 3:23 [g]ch. 1:28 **44:5** [h]ch. 40:4 **44:6** [i]ch. 2:5 [j]ch. 45:9 1 Pet. 4:3 **44:7** [k]ver. 9 ch. 43:8 Acts 21:28 [l]Lev. 22:25 [m]Lev. 26:41 Acts 7:51 [n]Lev. 21:17 [o]Lev. 3:16 **44:8** [p]Lev. 22:2

[e] Heb. *fill their hands* [f] Or, *thank offerings* [g] Heb. *set thine heart* [h] Heb. *children of a stranger*

43:18–27 OFFER BURNT OFFERINGS. The issue of resuming animal sacrifices after the final and ultimate sacrifice of Christ has perplexed interpreters. Some insist that Ezekiel's temple with its sacrifices cannot be literal because Jesus' atoning sacrifice fulfilled and made obsolete O.T. sacrifices (see Heb. 9:10–15; 10:1–4,8). Perhaps Ezekiel was describing in O.T. terms the benefits of Christ's atoning sacrifice, which avails for all time. Some believe that the sacrifices will be literal, offered as memorials of the sacrifice of Christ on the cross.

44:3 THE PRINCE. Only the prince is allowed to enter the eastern gate. His function seems to be to lead the people in worship (45:17). The identity of the prince is unknown, though he cannot be the Messiah because he makes a sin offering for himself (45:22) and has biological children (46:16).

of mine holy things: but ye have set
keepers of my [i]charge in my sanctu-
ary for yourselves.
9 ¶ Thus saith the Lord GOD; [q]No
stranger, uncircumcised in heart, nor
uncircumcised in flesh, shall enter into
my sanctuary, of any stranger that *is*
among the children of Israel.
10 [r]And the Levites that are gone
away far from me, when Israel went
astray, which went astray away from
me after their idols; they shall even
bear their iniquity.
11 Yet they shall be ministers in my
sanctuary, [s]*having* charge at the
gates of the house, and ministering to
the house: [t]they shall slay the burnt
offering and the sacrifice for the peo-
ple, and [u]they shall stand before them
to minister unto them.
12 Because they ministered unto
them before their idols, and
[v]caused[j] the house of Israel to fall
into iniquity; therefore have I [w]lifted
up mine hand against them, saith the
Lord GOD, and they shall bear their in-
iquity.
13 [x]And they shall not come near
unto me, to do the office of a priest
unto me, nor to come near to any of my
holy things, in the most holy *place:* but
they shall [y]bear their shame, and
their abominations which they have
committed.
14 But I will make them [z]keepers
of the charge of the house, for all the
service thereof, and for all that shall be
done therein.
15 ¶ [a]But the priests the Levites,
[b]the sons of Zadok, that kept the
charge of my sanctuary [c]when the
children of Israel went astray from me,
they shall come near to me to minister
unto me, and they [d]shall stand before
me to offer unto me [e]the fat and the
blood, saith the Lord GOD:
16 They shall enter into my sanctu-
ary, and they shall come near to [f]my
table, to minister unto me, and they
shall keep my charge.
17 ¶ And it shall come to pass, *that*
when they enter in at the gates of the
inner court, [g]they shall be clothed
with linen garments; and no wool shall
come upon them, whiles they minister
in the gates of the inner court, and
within.
18 [h]They shall have linen bonnets
upon their heads, and shall have linen
breeches upon their loins; they shall
not gird *themselves* [k] [l]with any thing
that causeth sweat.
19 And when they go forth into the
utter court, *even* into the utter court to
the people, [i]they shall put off their
garments wherein they ministered,
and lay them in the holy chambers, and
they shall put on other garments; and
they shall [j]not sanctify the people
with their garments.
20 [k]Neither shall they shave their
heads, nor suffer their locks to grow
long; they shall only poll their
heads.
21 [l]Neither shall any priest drink
wine, when they enter into the inner
court.
22 Neither shall they take for their
wives a [m]widow, nor her that is [m]put
away: but they shall take maidens of
the seed of the house of Israel, or a
widow [n]that had a priest before.
23 And [n]they shall teach my peo-
ple *the difference* between the holy and
profane, and cause them to discern be-
tween the unclean and the clean.
24 And [o]in controversy they shall
stand in judgment; *and* they shall judge
it according to my judgments: and they
shall keep my laws and my statutes in
all mine assemblies; [p]and they shall
hallow my sabbaths.
25 And they shall come at no dead
person to defile themselves: but for fa-
ther, or for mother, or for son, or for
daughter, for brother, or for sister that
hath had no husband, they may defile
themselves.

44:9 [q]ver. 7 **44:10** [r]2 Ki. 23:8 ch. 48:11 **44:11** [s]1 Chr. 26:1 [t]2 Chr. 29:34 [u]Num. 16:9 **44:12** [v]Is. 9:16 Mal. 2:8 [w]Ps. 106:26 **44:13** [x]Num. 18:3 2 Ki. 23:9 [y]ch. 32:30 **44:14** [z]Num. 18:4 1 Chr. 23:28 **44:15** [a]ch. 40:46 [b]1 Sam. 2:35 [c]ver. 10 [d]Deut. 10:8 [e]ver. 7 **44:16** [f]ch. 41:22 **44:17** [g]Ex. 28:39 **44:18** [h]Ex. 28:40 & 39:28 **44:19** [i]ch. 42:14 [j]ch. 46:20 Ex. 30:29 Lev. 6:27 Mat. 23:17 **44:20** [k]Lev. 21:5 **44:21** [l]Lev. 10:9 **44:22** [m]Lev. 21:7 **44:23** [n]ch. 22:26 Mal. 2:7 **44:24** [o]Deut. 17:8 2 Chr. 19:8 [p]See ch. 22:26

i Or, *ward,* or, *ordinance* j Heb. *were for a stumblingblock of iniquity unto;* see ch. 14:3,4 k Or, *in sweating* places l Heb. *in,* or, *with sweat* m Heb. *thrust forth* n Heb. *from a priest*

44:15 THE LEVITES, THE SONS OF ZADOK. Zadok had remained faithful to God when other Levites had abandoned God's way (1 Ki. 1). Because of his loyalty, he and his descendants were granted the privilege of ministering before the Lord in the future temple. This honor reveals that the extent of our faithfulness to God during our earthly lives will determine our place in the eternal kingdom of God (see article on THE JUDGMENT OF BELIEVERS, p. 1811).

44:17–31 WHERE THEY ENTER IN AT THE GATES. This regulation for the priests indicates that God must be worshiped with holy reverence.

26 And [q]after he is cleansed, they shall reckon unto him seven days.

27 And in the day that he goeth into the sanctuary, [r]unto the inner court, to minister in the sanctuary, [s]he shall offer his sin offering, saith the Lord GOD.

28 And it shall be unto them for an inheritance: I [t]*am* their inheritance: and ye shall give them no possession in Israel: I *am* their possession.

29 [u]They shall eat the meat offering, and the sin offering, and the trespass offering; and [v]every [o]dedicated thing in Israel shall be theirs.

30 And the [w]first[p] of all the firstfruits of all *things*, and every oblation of all, of every *sort* of your oblations, shall be the priest's: ye [x]shall also give unto the priest the first of your dough, [y]that he may cause the blessing to rest in thine house.

31 The priests shall not eat of any thing that is [z]dead of itself, or torn, whether it be fowl or beast.

Division of the land

45 MOREOVER, [q]WHEN ye shall [a]divide by lot the land for inheritance, ye shall [b]offer an oblation unto the LORD, [r]an holy portion of the land: the length *shall be* the length of five and twenty thousand *reeds*, and the breadth *shall be* ten thousand. This *shall be* holy in all the borders thereof round about.

2 Of this there shall be for the sanctuary five hundred *in length*, with five hundred *in breadth*, square round about; and fifty cubits round about for the [s]suburbs thereof.

3 And of this measure shalt thou measure the length of five and twenty thousand, and the breadth of ten thousand: [c]and in it shall be the sanctuary *and* the most holy *place*.

4 [d]The holy *portion* of the land shall be for the priests the ministers of the sanctuary, which shall come near to minister unto the LORD: and it shall be a place for their houses, and an holy place for the sanctuary.

5 [e]And the five and twenty thousand of length, and the ten thousand of breadth, shall also the Levites, the ministers of the house, have for themselves, for a possession for [f]twenty chambers.

6 ¶ [g]And ye shall appoint the possession of the city five thousand broad, and five and twenty thousand long, over against the oblation of the holy *portion:* it shall be for the whole house of Israel.

7 ¶ [h]And *a portion shall be* for the prince on the one side and on the other side of the oblation of the holy *portion,* and of the possession of the city, before the oblation of the holy *portion,* and before the possession of the city, from the west side westward, and from the east side eastward: and the length *shall be* over against one of the portions, from the west border unto the east border.

8 In the land shall be his possession in Israel: and [i]my princes shall no more oppress my people; and *the rest of* the land shall they give to the house of Israel according to their tribes.

9 ¶ Thus saith the Lord GOD; [j]Let it suffice you, O princes of Israel: [k]remove violence and spoil, and execute judgment and justice, take away your [t]exactions from my people, saith the Lord GOD.

Laws about weights and offerings

10 Ye shall have just [l]balances, and a just ephah, and a just bath.

11 The ephah and the bath shall be of one measure, that the bath may contain the tenth part of an homer, and the ephah the tenth part of an homer: the measure thereof shall be after the homer.

12 And the [m]shekel *shall be* twenty gerahs: twenty shekels, five and twenty shekels, fifteen shekels, shall be your maneh.

13 This *is* the oblation that ye shall offer; the sixth part of an ephah of an homer of wheat, and ye shall give the sixth part of an ephah of an homer of barley:

14 Concerning the ordinance of oil,

44:26 [q]Num. 6:10 & 19:11
44:27 [r]ver. 17 [s]Lev. 4:3
44:28 [t]Num. 18:20 Deut. 10:9 & 18:1,2 Josh. 13:14
44:29 [u]Lev. 7:6 [v]Lev. 27:21,28, compared with Num. 18:14
44:30 [w]Ex. 13:2 & 22:29 & 23:19 Num. 3:13 & 18:12 [x]Num. 15:20 Neh. 10:37 [y]Prov. 3:9 Mal. 3:10
44:31 [z]Ex. 22:31 Lev. 22:8
45:1 [a]ch. 47:22 [b]ch. 48:8
45:3 [c]ch. 48:10
45:4 [d]ver. 1 ch. 48:10
45:5 [e]ch. 48:13 [f]See ch. 40:17
45:6 [g]ch. 48:15
45:7 [h]ch. 48:21
45:8 [i]See Jer. 22:17 ch. 22:27 & 46:18
45:9 [j]ch. 44:6 [k]Jer. 22:3
45:10 [l]Lev. 19:35,36 Prov. 11:1
45:12 [m]Ex. 30:13 Lev. 27:25 Num. 3:47

[o] Or, *devoted* [p] Or, *chief* [q] Heb. *when ye cause the land to fall* [r] Heb. *holiness* [s] Or, *void places* [t] Heb. *expulsions*

45:1–8 THE LAND FOR INHERITANCE. These verses speak of the land that was to be set apart as the inheritance for the priests who minister before the Lord in His holy temple. These ministers will no longer exploit the people financially, but will be satisfied with their "holy *portion*" (v. 4).

45:9–12 REMOVE VIOLENCE AND SPOIL. Ezekiel exhorts the leaders to cease their oppression and violence, and instead to practice justice and honesty.

the bath of oil, *ye shall offer* the tenth
part of a bath out of the cor, *which is*
an homer of ten baths; for ten baths *are*
an homer:
15 And one [u]lamb out of the flock,
out of two hundred, out of the fat pas-
tures of Israel; for a meat offering, and
for a burnt offering, and for [v]peace of-
ferings, [n]to make reconciliation for
them, saith the Lord GOD.
16 All the people of the land [w]shall
give this oblation [x]for the prince in
Israel.
17 And it shall be the prince's part
to give burnt offerings, and meat offer-
ings, and drink offerings, in the feasts,
and in the new moons, and in the sab-
baths, in all solemnities of the house of
Israel: he shall prepare the sin offer-
ing, and the meat offering, and the
burnt offering, and the [v]peace offer-
ings, to make reconciliation for the
house of Israel.
18 Thus saith the Lord GOD; In the
first *month,* in the first *day* of the
month, thou shalt take a young bullock
without blemish, and [o]cleanse the
sanctuary:
19 [p]And the priest shall take of the
blood of the sin offering, and put *it*
upon the posts of the house, and upon
the four corners of the settle of the al-
tar, and upon the posts of the gate of
the inner court.
20 And so thou shalt do the seventh
day of the month [q]for every one that
erreth, and for *him that is* simple: so
shall ye reconcile the house.
21 [r]In the first *month,* in the four-
teenth day of the month, ye shall have
the passover, a feast of seven days; un-
leavened bread shall be eaten.
22 And upon that day shall the
prince prepare for himself and for all
the people of the land [s]a bullock *for* a
sin offering.
23 And [t]seven days of the feast he
shall prepare a burnt offering to the
LORD, seven bullocks and seven rams
without blemish daily the seven days;
[u]and a kid of the goats daily *for* a sin
offering.
24 [v]And he shall prepare a meat
offering of an ephah for a bullock, and

45:15 [n]Lev. 1:4
45:18 [o]Lev. 16:16
45:19 [p]ch. 43:20
45:20 [q]Lev. 4:27
45:21 [r]Ex. 12:18 Lev. 23:5,6 Num. 9:2,3 & 28:16,17 Deut. 16:1
45:22 [s]Lev. 4:14
45:23 [t]Lev. 23:8 [u]See Num. 28:15, 22,30 & 29:5,11,16,19
45:24 [v]ch. 46:5,7

45:25 [w]Lev. 23:34 Num. 29:12 Deut. 16:13
46:2 [x]ver. 8 ch. 44:3
46:4 [y]ch. 45:17
46:5 [z]ver. 7,11 ch. 45:24 [a]Deut. 16:17
46:8 [b]ver. 2
46:9 [c]Ex. 23:14-17 Deut. 16:16

an ephah for a ram, and an hin of oil for
an ephah.
25 In the seventh *month,* in the fif-
teenth day of the month, shall he do
the like in the [w]feast of the seven
days, according to the sin offering, ac-
cording to the burnt offering, and
according to the meat offering,
and according to the oil.

46 THUS SAITH the Lord GOD;
The gate of the inner court that
looketh toward the east shall be shut
the six working days; but on the sab-
bath it shall be opened, and in the day
of the new moon it shall be opened.
2 [x]And the prince shall enter by
the way of the porch of *that* gate with-
out, and shall stand by the post of the
gate, and the priests shall prepare his
burnt offering and his peace offerings,
and he shall worship at the threshold
of the gate: then he shall go forth; but
the gate shall not be shut until the eve-
ning.
3 Likewise the people of the land
shall worship at the door of this gate
before the LORD in the sabbaths and in
the new moons.
4 And the burnt offering that [y]the
prince shall offer unto the LORD in the
sabbath day *shall be* six lambs without
blemish, and a ram without blemish.
5 [z]And the meat offering *shall be*
an ephah for a ram, and the meat offer-
ing for the lambs [a]as[y] he shall be
able to give, and an hin of oil to an
ephah.
6 And in the day of the new moon *it*
shall be a young bullock without blem-
ish, and six lambs, and a ram: they
shall be without blemish.
7 And he shall prepare a meat offer-
ing, an ephah for a bullock, and an
ephah for a ram, and for the lambs ac-
cording as his hand shall attain unto,
and an hin of oil to an ephah.
8 [b]And when the prince shall en-
ter, he shall go in by the way of the
porch of *that* gate, and he shall go forth
by the way thereof.
9 ¶ But when the people of the land
[c]shall come before the LORD in the sol-

[u] Or, *kid* [v] Or, *thank offerings* [w] Heb. *shall be for* [x] Or, *with* [y] Heb. *the gift of his hand*

45:21 THE PASSOVER. The seven-day Passover feast commemorated Israel's deliverance from slavery in Egypt (see article on THE PASSOVER, p. 110). The exodus was the most significant O.T. event involving Israel's redemption.

46:1–24 THE SABBATH . . . THE NEW MOON. This chapter deals with offerings and worship on the Sabbath day, the day of the new moon (vv. 1–8), the appointed feasts (vv. 9–12), and the daily offerings (vv. 13–15).

emn feasts, he that entereth in by the
way of the north gate to worship shall
go out by the way of the south gate;
and he that entereth by the way of the
south gate shall go forth by the way of
the north gate: he shall not return by
the way of the gate whereby he came
in, but shall go forth over against it.
10 And the prince in the midst of
them, when they go in, shall go in; and
when they go forth, shall go forth.
11 And in the feasts and in the
solemnities [d]the meat offering shall
be an ephah to a bullock, and an ephah
to a ram, and to the lambs as he is able
to give, and an hin of oil to an ephah.
12 Now when the prince shall prepare
a voluntary burnt offering or
peace offerings voluntarily unto the
LORD, [e]*one* shall then open him the
gate that looketh toward the east, and
he shall prepare his burnt offering and
his peace offerings, as he did on the
sabbath day: then he shall go forth;
and after his going forth *one* shall shut
the gate.
13 [f]Thou shalt daily prepare a
burnt offering unto the LORD *of* a lamb
[z]of the first year without blemish:
thou shalt prepare it [a]every morning.
14 And thou shalt prepare a meat
offering for it every morning, the sixth
part of an ephah, and the third part of
an hin of oil, to temper with the fine
flour; a meat offering continually by a
perpetual ordinance unto the LORD.
15 Thus shall they prepare the
lamb, and the meat offering, and the
oil, every morning *for* a continual burnt
offering.
16 ¶ Thus saith the Lord GOD; If the
prince give a gift unto any of his sons,
the inheritance thereof shall be his
sons'; it *shall be* their possession by inheritance.
17 But if he give a gift of his inheritance
to one of his servants, then it
shall be his to [g]the year of liberty; after
it shall return to the prince: but his
inheritance shall be his sons' for them.

46:11 [d]ver. 5
46:12 [e]ver. 2 ch. 44:3
46:13 [f]Ex. 29:38 Num. 28:3
46:17 [g]Lev. 25:10
46:18 [h]ch. 45:8
46:20 [i]2 Chr. 35:13 [j]Lev. 2:4,5,7 [k]ch. 44:19
46:24 [l]See ver. 20
47:1 [m]Joel 3:18 Zech. 13:1 & 14:8 Rev. 22:1

18 Moreover [h]the prince shall not
take of the people's inheritance by oppression,
to thrust them out of their
possession; *but* he shall give his sons
inheritance out of his own possession:
that my people be not scattered every
man from his possession.
19 ¶ After he brought me through
the entry, which *was* at the side of the
gate, into the holy chambers of
the priests, which looked toward the
north: and, behold, there *was* a place
on the two sides westward.
20 Then said he unto me, This *is* the
place where the priests shall [i]boil the
trespass offering and the sin offering,
where they shall [j]bake the meat offering;
that they bear *them* not out into the
utter court, [k]to sanctify the people.
21 Then he brought me forth into
the utter court, and caused me to pass
by the four corners of the court; and,
behold, [b]in every corner of the court
there was a court.
22 In the four corners of the court
there were courts [c]joined of forty *cubits*
long and thirty broad: these four [d]corners
were of one measure.
23 And *there was* a row *of building*
round about in them, round about them
four, and *it was* made with boiling
places under the rows round about.
24 Then said he unto me, These *are*
the places of them that boil, where the
ministers of the house shall [l]boil the
sacrifice of the people.

The river from the temple

47 AFTERWARD HE brought me
again unto the door of the
house; and, behold, [m]waters issued
out from under the threshold of the
house eastward: for the forefront of the
house *stood toward* the east, and the
waters came down from under from the

[z] Heb. *a son of his year* [a] Heb. *morning by morning* [b] Heb. *a court in a corner of a court and a court in a corner of a court* [c] Or, *made with chimneys* [d] Heb. *cornered*

47:1–12 WATERS ISSUED OUT FROM ... THE HOUSE. In his vision, Ezekiel sees a life-giving river coming from the temple. As it flows, it grows in depth and width (vv. 2–5), giving life and fruitfulness to everything it touches (vv. 9–12). The river flows into the Dead Sea area and rids it of death (vv. 8–9). The purpose of the river is to bring abundant life and healing from God to the land and people (v. 12). (1) This river is similar to the river flowing from the Garden of Eden (Gen. 2:8–10) and the river of life in the new Jerusalem (Rev. 22:1–2; cf. Zech. 14:8), which flows from the throne of God.

(2) This river also is similar to the one mentioned by Jesus: "He that believeth on me, as the scripture hath said, out of his belly shall flow rivers of living water" (John 7:38). The "living water" is the Holy Spirit and the blessings of life He has come to bring.

right side of the house, at the south
side of the altar.
2 Then brought he me out of the
way of the gate northward, and led me
about the way without unto the utter
gate by the way that looketh eastward;
and, behold, there ran out waters on
the right side.
3 And when [n]the man that had the
line in his hand went forth eastward,
he measured a thousand cubits, and he
brought me through the waters; the
[e]waters *were* to the ankles.
4 Again he measured a thousand,
and brought me through the waters;
the waters *were* to the knees. Again he
measured a thousand, and brought me
through; the waters *were* to the loins.
5 Afterward he measured a thou-
sand; *and it was* a river that I could not
pass over: for the waters were risen,
[f]waters to swim in, a river that could
not be passed over.
6 ¶ And he said unto me, Son of
man, hast thou seen *this?* Then he
brought me, and caused me to return to
the brink of the river.
7 Now when I had returned, behold,
at the [g]bank of the river *were* very
many [o]trees on the one side and on
the other.
8 Then said he unto me, These wa-
ters issue out toward the east country,
and go down into the [h]desert, and go
into the sea: *which being* brought forth
into the sea, the waters shall be
healed.
9 And it shall come to pass, *that* ev-
ery thing that liveth, which moveth,
whithersoever the [i]rivers shall come,
shall live: and there shall be a very
great multitude of fish, because these
waters shall come thither: for they
shall be healed; and every thing shall
live whither the river cometh.
10 And it shall come to pass, *that*
the fishers shall stand upon it from En-
gedi even unto En-eglaim; they shall be
a *place* to spread forth nets; their fish
shall be according to their kinds, as the
fish [p]of the great sea, exceeding
many.
11 But the miry places thereof and
the marshes thereof [j]shall not be
healed; they shall be given to salt.
12 And [q]by the river upon the bank
thereof, on this side and on that side,
[k]shall grow all trees for meat,
[r]whose leaf shall not fade, neither
shall the fruit thereof be consumed: it
shall bring forth [l]new fruit according
to his months, because their waters
they issued out of the sanctuary: and
the fruit thereof shall be for meat, and
the leaf thereof [m]for [s]medicine. Hos. 11:3-4

The borders of the land

13 ¶ Thus saith the Lord GOD; This
shall be the border, whereby ye shall
inherit the land according to the twelve
tribes of Israel: [t]Joseph *shall have two*
portions.
14 And ye shall inherit it, one as
well as another: *concerning* the which I
[u]lifted[n] up mine hand to give it unto
your fathers: and this land shall [v]fall
unto you for inheritance.
15 And this *shall be* the border of the
land toward the north side, from the
great sea, [w]the way of Hethlon, as
men go to [x]Zedad;
16 [y]Hamath, [z]Berothah, Sibraim,
which *is* between the border of Damas-
cus and the border of Hamath; [o]Ha-
zar-hatticon, which *is* by the coast of
Hauran.
17 And the border from the sea
shall be [a]Hazar-enan, the border of
Damascus, and the north northward,
and the border of Hamath. And *this is*
the north side.
18 And the east side ye shall mea-
sure [p]from Hauran, and from Damas-
cus, and from Gilead, and from the land
of Israel *by* Jordan, from the border
unto the east sea. And *this is* the east
side.
19 And the south side southward,
from Tamar *even* to [b]the waters of
[q]strife *in* Kadesh, the [r]river to the
great sea. And *this is* [s]the south side
southward.
20 The west side also *shall be* the
great sea from the border, till a man
come over against Hamath. This *is* the
west side.
21 So shall ye divide this land unto

47:3 [n]ch. 40:3
47:7 [o]ver. 12; Rev. 22:2
47:10 [p]Num. 34:3; Josh. 23:4; ch. 48:28
47:12 [q]ver. 7; [r]Job 8:16; Ps. 1:3; Jer. 17:8; [s]Rev. 22:2
47:13 [t]Gen. 48:5; 1 Chr. 5:1; ch. 48:4,5
47:14 [u]Gen. 12:7 & 13:15 & 15:7 & 17:8 & 26:3 & 28:13; ch. 20:5,6,28,42; [v]ch. 48:29
47:15 [w]ch. 48:1; [x]Num. 34:8
47:16 [y]Num. 34:8; [z]2 Sam. 8:8
47:17 [a]Num. 34:9; ch. 48:1
47:19 [b]Num. 20:13; Deut. 32:51; Ps. 81:7; ch. 48:28

[e] Heb. *waters of the ankles* [f] Heb. *waters of swimming* [g] Heb. *lip* [h] Or, *plain;* see Deut. 3:17 & 4:49; Josh. 3:16 [i] Heb. *two rivers* [j] Or, *and that which shall not be healed* [k] Heb. *shall come up* [l] Or, *principal* [m] Or, *for bruises and sores* [n] Or, *swore* [o] Or, *the middle village* [p] Heb. *from between* [q] Or, *Meribah* [r] Or, *valley* [s] Or, *toward Teman*

47:21–23 AN INHERITANCE UNTO YOU, AND TO THE STRANGERS THAT SOJOURN AMONG YOU. Though the land is redivided in east-west strips among the tribes of Israel, God's

you according to the tribes of Israel.

22 ¶ And it shall come to pass, *that* ye shall divide it by lot for an inheritance unto you, [c]and to the strangers that sojourn among you, which shall beget children among you: [d]and they shall be unto you as born in the country among the children of Israel; they shall have inheritance with you among the tribes of Israel.

23 And it shall come to pass, *that* in what tribe the stranger sojourneth, there shall ye give *him* his inheritance, saith the Lord GOD.

The division of the land

48 NOW THESE *are* the names of the tribes. [e]From the north end to the coast of the way of Hethlon, as one goeth to Hamath, Hazar-enan, the border of Damascus northward, to the coast of Hamath; for these are his sides east *and* west; [t]a *portion for* Dan.

2 And by the border of Dan, from the east side unto the west side, a *portion for* Asher.

3 And by the border of Asher, from the east side even unto the west side, a *portion for* Naphtali.

4 And by the border of Naphtali, from the east side unto the west side, a *portion for* Manasseh.

5 And by the border of Manasseh, from the east side unto the west side, a *portion for* Ephraim.

6 And by the border of Ephraim, from the east side even unto the west side, a *portion for* Reuben.

7 And by the border of Reuben, from the east side unto the west side, a *portion for* Judah.

8 ¶ And by the border of Judah, from the east side unto the west side, shall be [f]the offering which ye shall offer of five and twenty thousand *reeds in* breadth, and *in* length as one of the other parts, from the east side unto the west side: and the sanctuary shall be in the midst of it.

9 The oblation that ye shall offer unto the LORD *shall be* of five and twenty thousand in length, and of ten thousand in breadth.

10 And for them, *even* for the priests, shall be *this* holy oblation; toward the north five and twenty thousand *in length,* and toward the west ten thousand in breadth, and toward the east ten thousand in breadth, and toward the south five and twenty thousand in length: and the sanctuary of the LORD shall be in the midst thereof.

11 [g]*It*[u] *shall be* for the priests that are sanctified of the sons of Zadok; which have kept my [v]charge, which went not astray when the children of Israel went astray, [h]as the Levites went astray.

12 And *this* oblation of the land that is offered shall be unto them a thing most holy by the border of the Levites.

13 And over against the border of the priests the Levites *shall have* five and twenty thousand in length, and ten thousand in breadth: all the length *shall be* five and twenty thousand, and the breadth ten thousand.

14 [i]And they shall not sell of it, neither exchange, nor alienate the firstfruits of the land: for *it is* holy unto the LORD.

15 ¶ [j]And the five thousand, that are left in the breadth over against the five and twenty thousand, shall be [k]a profane *place* for the city, for dwelling, and for suburbs: and the city shall be in the midst thereof.

16 And these *shall be* the measures thereof; the north side four thousand and five hundred, and the south side four thousand and five hundred, and on the east side four thousand and five

47:22 [c]See Eph. 3:6 Rev. 7:9,10 [d]Rom. 10:12 Gal. 3:28 Col. 3:11 **48:1** [e]ch. 47:15 **48:8** [f]ch. 45:1-6

48:11 [g]ch. 44:15 [h]ch. 44:10 **48:14** [i]Ex. 22:29 Lev. 27:10,28,33 **48:15** [j]ch. 45:6 [k]ch. 42:20

[t] Heb. *one* portion [u] Or, *The sanctified portion shall be for the priests* [v] Or, *ward,* or, *ordinance*

purpose is not to build up again the "middle wall of partition" (Eph. 2:14) between Jews and Gentiles. Resident aliens will also be given an inheritance among the tribes. Some believe that the children mentioned here are spiritual children, and that those Gentiles who have had a ministry among the people of Israel will share in their inheritance in the restored millennial land.

48:1–29 THE BORDER. This final chapter of Ezekiel continues designating the boundaries of the restored land and the location of the tribes (47:13 – 48:29).

48:11–12 WHICH WENT NOT ASTRAY. Once again God emphasizes that those who remain faithful to His will and righteous standards while on earth will be rewarded in the future kingdom. Here the gift for the Zadokites is the privilege of dwelling near God's sanctuary (see 44:15, note). It is eternally important to endeavor with all our heart to remain faithful to God and to spurn the influences of this evil generation.

hundred, and the west side four thousand and five hundred.

17 And the suburbs of the city shall be toward the north two hundred and fifty, and toward the south two hundred and fifty, and toward the east two hundred and fifty, and toward the west two hundred and fifty.

18 And the residue in length over against the oblation of the holy *portion shall be* ten thousand eastward, and ten thousand westward: and it shall be over against the oblation of the holy *portion;* and the increase thereof shall be for food unto them that serve the city.

19 [l]And they that serve the city shall serve it out of all the tribes of Israel.

20 All the oblation *shall be* five and twenty thousand by five and twenty thousand: ye shall offer the holy oblation foursquare, with the possession of the city.

21 ¶ [m]And the residue *shall be* for the prince, on the one side and on the other of the holy oblation, and of the possession of the city, over against the five and twenty thousand of the oblation toward the east border, and westward over against the five and twenty thousand toward the west border, over against the portions for the prince: and it shall be the holy oblation; [n]and the sanctuary of the house *shall be* in the midst thereof.

22 Moreover from the possession of the Levites, and from the possession of the city, *being* in the midst *of that* which is the prince's, between the border of Judah and the border of Benjamin, shall be for the prince.

23 As for the rest of the tribes, from the east side unto the west side, Benjamin *shall have* [w]a *portion.*

24 And by the border of Benjamin, from the east side unto the west side, Simeon *shall have* a *portion.*

48:19 [l]ch. 45:6
48:21 [m]ch. 45:7 [n]ver. 8,10
48:28 [o]ch. 47:19
48:29 [p]ch. 47:14,21,22
48:31 [q]Rev. 21:12
48:35 [r]Jer. 33:16 [s]Jer. 3:17 Joel 3:21 Zech. 2:10 Rev. 21:3 & 22:3

25 And by the border of Simeon, from the east side unto the west side, Issachar a *portion.*

26 And by the border of Issachar, from the east side unto the west side, Zebulun a *portion.*

27 And by the border of Zebulun, from the east side unto the west side, Gad a *portion.*

28 And by the border of Gad, at the south side southward, the border shall be even from Tamar *unto* [o]the waters of [x]strife *in* Kadesh, *and* to the river toward the great sea.

29 [p]This *is* the land which ye shall divide by lot unto the tribes of Israel for inheritance, and these *are* their portions, saith the Lord GOD.

The name of the city

30 ¶ And these *are* the goings out of the city on the north side, four thousand and five hundred measures.

31 [q]And the gates of the city *shall be* after the names of the tribes of Israel: three gates northward; one gate of Reuben, one gate of Judah, one gate of Levi.

32 And at the east side four thousand and five hundred: and three gates; and one gate of Joseph, one gate of Benjamin, one gate of Dan.

33 And at the south side four thousand and five hundred measures: and three gates; one gate of Simeon, one gate of Issachar, one gate of Zebulun.

34 At the west side four thousand and five hundred, *with* their three gates; one gate of Gad, one gate of Asher, one gate of Naphtali.

35 *It was* round about eighteen thousand *measures:* [r]and the name of the city from *that* day *shall be,* [s]The[y] LORD *is* there.

[w]Heb. *one* portion [x]Heb. *Meribah-kadesh*
[y]Heb. *Jehovah-shammah*

48:35 THE LORD *IS* THERE. The book of Ezekiel ends with the great promise that one day God will dwell eternally with His people, a promise that is repeated in Rev. 21:3: "Behold, the tabernacle of God *is* with men, and he will dwell with them." The greatest blessing for us as God's people is to have God in our midst; this is the essence of joy and happiness. As a result of God's enduring presence, we will never again experience the sorrows, disappointments, and troubles of our former life (Rev. 21:4). This is our ultimate vision and hope as we look for the day of the appearing of our Lord and Savior, Jesus Christ.

DANIEL

Outline

I. The Historical Setting of Daniel (1:1–21)
   A. Daniel and His Friends Deported to Babylon (1:1–7)
   B. The Faithfulness of Daniel and His Friends in Babylon (1:8–16)
   C. The Promotion of Daniel and His Friends in the King's Court (1:17–21)

II. Daniel's Message Concerning God's Sovereignty Over the Nations (2:1—7:28)
   A. Nebuchadnezzar's Prophetic Dream and Daniel's Revelation About It (2:1–49)
   B. The Image of Gold and the Furnace of Fire (3:1–30)
   C. The Prophetic Dream of Nebuchadnezzar's Insanity and Its Fulfillment (4:1–37)
   D. Belshazzar's Feast and Babylon's Downfall (5:1–31)
   E. Darius's Decree and Daniel's Deliverance (6:1–28)
   F. Daniel's Prophetic Dream of Four World Empires and the Ancient of Days (7:1–28)

III. Daniel's Visions Concerning the Nation of Israel (8:1—12:13)
   A. Daniel's Vision of a Ram, a Male Goat, and a Little Horn (8:1–27)
   B. Daniel's Intercession for Restoration and His Vision of the Seventy "Sevens" (9:1–27)
   C. Daniel's Vision of Israel's Future (10:1—12:13)
      1. Daniel's Revelation and Angelic Visitation (10:1—11:1)
      2. Prophetic Revelation About Persia and Greece (11:2–4), Egypt and Syria (11:5–35), and the Coming Antichrist (11:36–45)
      3. Prophetic Revelation About Other End-Time Events (12:1–13)

Author: Daniel

Theme: God's Sovereignty in History

Date of Writing: c. 536–530 B.C.

Background

Daniel, whose name means "God is my Judge," is both the chief character and the author of the book that bears his name. Authorship by Daniel is not only explicitly stated in 12:4, but also implied by the numerous autobiographical references in chs. 7—12. Jesus attributes the book to "Daniel the prophet" (Mat. 24:15) when quoting from 9:27.

The book records events from Nebuchadnezzar's first invasion of Jerusalem (605 B.C.) to the third year of Cyrus (536 B.C.). Thus the historical setting for the book is Babylon during the seventy-year Babylonian captivity prophesied by Jeremiah (cf. Jer. 25:11). Daniel would have been a teenager when the events of ch. 1 began and in his late eighties when receiving his visions in chs. 9—12. He may have lived until c. 530 B.C., completing the book as an old man during the last decade of his life (cf. John and the apocalyptic book of Revelation). Modern critics who regard the book of Daniel as a second century B.C. pseudepigraphon are guided by their philosophical presuppositions rather than by facts.

Our knowledge of the prophet Daniel comes almost entirely from this book (cf. Ezek. 14:14,20). Perhaps Daniel was a descendant of King Hezekiah (cf. 2 Ki. 20:17–18; Is.

39:6–7); certainly he was from an upper-class educated family in Jerusalem (1:3–6), for Nebuchadnezzar would not have selected young foreigners from a lower class for his royal court (1:4,17). Daniel may have been made a eunuch in Babylon, as was common in those days when a male served in a royal court (cf. 1:3; 2 Ki. 20:18; Mat. 19:12). Daniel's success in Babylon is attributed to his integrity of character, prophetic gifts, and the interventions of God that resulted in his rapid advancement to places of prominence and responsibility (2:46–49; 6:1–3).

Chronologically, Daniel is one of the last O.T. prophets. Only Haggai, Zechariah, and Malachi come after him in the prophetic stream of O.T. history. He was a younger contemporary of Jeremiah and probably the same age as Ezekiel.

Purpose

There is a twofold purpose for the writing of Daniel: (1) to reassure the O.T. covenant people that their judgment of captivity under Gentile nations was not to be their permanent fate; and (2) to bequeath to God's people throughout history the prophetic visions of God's sovereignty over nations and the final triumph of His kingdom in the earth. This twofold purpose is demonstrated throughout the book in the lives of Daniel and his three friends and illustrated in Daniel's prophetic message and ministry. The book affirms that God's promises to preserve and restore His covenant people are as sure as the coming Messianic kingdom that will last forever.

Survey

The content of Daniel is a blend of autobiography, history, and prophecy. Its literary form is apocalyptic literature, meaning that its prophetic message unveils God's revelation (1) through visions and dreams and symbolism, (2) for the purpose of encouraging God's people during a crisis period of history, and (3) for the envisioning of Israel's hope concerning the eventual triumph of God's kingdom and righteousness in the earth (see the introduction to the book of Revelation).

The book divides naturally into three major parts. (1) Ch. 1 is written in Hebrew and introduces the historical setting for the book. (2) Chs. 2—7, beginning at 2:4, were written in Aramaic, describing the rise and fall of four mighty successive world kingdoms and followed by the establishment of God's kingdom as an everlasting one (especially chs. 2; 7). These chapters emphasize God's sovereignty over and intervention in the affairs of humans and nations by describing: (a) Daniel's rise to prominence in Nebuchadnezzar's court (ch. 2); (b) the Son of God in the fiery furnace with Daniel's three friends (ch. 3); (c) Nebuchadnezzar's temporary insanity as God's judgment (ch. 4); (d) Daniel's role at Belshazzar's feast, declaring the end of the Babylonian kingdom (ch. 5); (e) Daniel's miraculous deliverance from the lions' den (ch. 6); and (f) the vision of the four successive world kingdoms being judged by the "Ancient of days" (ch. 7). (3) In chs. 8—12, Daniel once again writes in Hebrew and describes unusual revelations and angelic visitations from God concerning (a) the Jewish people under future Gentile domination (chs. 8—11), (b) the period of seventy "sevens" as the time set by God for the accomplishment of the Messiah's mission on their behalf (ch. 9), and (c) their ultimate deliverance from all tribulation at the end of time (ch. 12).

Daniel's prophetic messages involve two dimensions: (1) the close-at-hand future and (2) the far-distant future, though these two dimensions often blend together. For example, in chs. 8 and 11, Daniel prophesies about the "antichrist"-type figure of Antiochus IV Epiphanes, who desecrated the Jerusalem temple in 168 B.C., while he also prophesied about the antichrist of the end time (8:23–26; 11:36–45; cf. Rev. 13:1–10). This interplay between these two futures characterizes Biblical prophecy generally and Daniel specifically. God reveals to Daniel that the far-distant prophecy is a concealed message until "the time of the end" (12:4,9), at which time insight will be given to God's people who in purity and wisdom seek Him for understanding just as Daniel did (12:3,10).

Special Features

Eight special features or emphases characterize the book of Daniel. (1) It is the shortest of the four major prophetic books and the most read and studied of all the O.T. prophets. (2) In prophetic passages of the N.T., Daniel is quoted or alluded to more often than any other O.T. book. (3) It is "the Apocalypse" of the O.T., as the book of Revelation is of the N.T., revealing great themes of prophecy that are vitally important to the end-time church. (4) It contains the most detailed prophetic summary of history in the O.T. It is the only O.T. prophecy to set the time of the Messiah's first advent (9:24–27). (5) It discloses more about its author than any other O.T. prophetic writing (with the possible exception of Jeremiah). Note especially that Daniel was a man characterized by great integrity of character, prophetic wisdom, and diligence in prayer and fasting. (6) It contains the Bible's foremost model of intercession for the restoration of God's people, based on the inspired promises of God's word (see ch. 9, inspired by Jer. 25:11–16; 29:7,10–14). (7) The stories about Daniel and his friends are among the best-loved stories in the Bible (especially chs. 3; 6). (8) The drama of "the handwriting on the wall" at Belshazzar's feast has made that phrase a proverbial part of our language to this day.

New Testament Fulfillment

The influence of Daniel on the N.T. goes far beyond the five or six times the book is directly quoted. Much of Daniel's history and prophecy reappears in prophetic passages in the Gospels, epistles, and Revelation. Daniel's prophecy about the coming Messiah includes a description of Him as (1) the "great stone," who would crush earthly kingdoms (2:34–35,45), (2) the Son of man, who would be given dominion, glory, and a kingdom by the Ancient of days (7:13–14), and (3) "the Messiah and Prince," who would come and then be cut off (9:25–26). Some interpreters believe that Daniel's vision in 10:5–9 is a preincarnate appearance of Christ (cf. Rev. 1:12–16).

Daniel contains numerous prophetic themes that are more fully developed in the N.T.: e.g., the great tribulation and the antichrist, the second advent of our Lord, the triumph of God's kingdom, the resurrection of the righteous and the wicked, and the day of judgment. The lives of Daniel and his three friends demonstrate the N.T. teaching about personal separation from sin and the world, i.e., living in the unbelieving world but not partaking of its spirit and ways (1:8; 3:12; 6:10; cf. John 17:6,15–16,18; 2 Cor. 6:14—7:1).

Reading Daniel

In order to read the entire Old Testament in one year, the book of Daniel should be read in 6 days, according to the following schedule: ☐ 1–2 ☐ 3–4 ☐ 5–6 ☐ 7–8 ☐ 9–10 ☐ 11–12

NOTES

The test of Daniel and his friends

1 IN THE third year of the reign of
Jehoiakim king of Judah [a]came
Nebuchadnezzar king of Babylon unto
Jerusalem, and besieged it.
2 And the Lord gave Jehoiakim king
of Judah into his hand, with [b]part of
the vessels of the house of God: which
he carried [c]into the land of Shinar to
the house of his god; [d]and he brought
the vessels into the treasure house of
his god.
3 ¶ And the king spake unto Ashpe-
naz the master of his eunuchs, that he
should bring [a]*certain* of the children of
Israel, and of the king's seed, and of
the princes;
4 Children [e]in whom *was* no blem-
ish, but wellfavoured, and skilful in all
wisdom, and cunning in knowledge,
and understanding science, and such
as *had* ability in them to stand in the
king's palace, and [f]whom they might
teach the learning and the tongue of
the Chaldeans.
5 And the king appointed them a
daily provision of the king's meat, and
of [b]the wine which he drank: so nour-
ishing them three years, that at the end
thereof they might [g]stand before the
king.
6 Now among these were of the chil-
dren of Judah, Daniel, Hananiah, Mish-
ael, and Azariah:
7 [h]Unto whom the prince of the eu-
nuchs gave names: [i]for he gave unto
Daniel *the name* of Belteshazzar; and to
Hananiah, of Shadrach; and to Misha-
el, of Meshach; and to Azariah, of
Abed-nego.
8 ¶ But Daniel purposed in his heart
that he would not defile himself [j]with
the portion of the king's meat, nor with
the wine which he drank: therefore he
requested of the prince of the eunuchs
that he might not defile himself.
9 Now [k]God had brought Daniel
into favour and tender love with the
prince of the eunuchs.
10 And the prince of the eunuchs
said unto Daniel, I fear my lord the
king, who hath appointed your meat
and your drink: for why should he see
your faces [c]worse liking than the chil-
dren which *are* of your [d]sort? then
shall ye make *me* endanger my head to
the king.
11 Then said Daniel to [e]Melzar,
whom the prince of the eunuchs had

1:1 [a]2 Ki. 24:1; 2 Chr. 36:6 **1:2** [b]Jer. 27:19 [c]Gen. 10:10; Zech. 5:11 [d]2 Chr. 36:7 **1:4** [e]See Lev. 24:19, 20 [f]Acts 7:22 **1:5** [g]ver. 19; Gen. 41:46; 1 Ki. 10:8 **1:7** [h]Gen. 41:45; 2 Ki. 24:17 [i]ch. 4:8 & 5:12 **1:8** [j]Deut. 32:38; Ezek. 4:13; Hos. 9:3 **1:9** [k]See Gen. 39:21; Ps. 106:46; Prov. 16:7

[a] Foretold in 2 Ki. 20:17,18; Is. 39:7 [b] Heb. *the wine of his drink* [c] Heb. *sadder* [d] Or, *term*, or, *continuance?* [e] Or, *The steward*

1:4 SUCH AS *HAD* ABILITY TO STAND IN THE KING'S PALACE. When God gave Nebuchadnezzar the victory over Jehoiakim in 605 B.C., the Babylonian monarch took some of the vessels of the temple and also some of the choice princes. Since the destruction of Nineveh seven years earlier, the Babylonian empire had grown so fast that they did not have enough of their own educated men needed to run the government. So Nebuchadnezzar took good-looking, healthy, well-educated young men to Babylon in order to teach them the culture and language of the Chaldeans (i.e, the Babylonians) and thus to make them useful in the king's royal service. Among them were Daniel and his three friends.

1:7 THE PRINCE OF THE EUNUCHS GAVE NAMES. In order for Daniel and his friends to enter the king's service, they needed to have Babylonian citizenship. This was accomplished by giving them Babylonian names. The young prince Daniel ("God is my Judge") was named Belteshazzar ("Bel [chief god of Babylon] protect his life"); Hananiah ("The LORD has been gracious") was named Shadrach ("Servant of Aku", i.e., the moon god); Mishael ("Who is equal to God?") was named Meshach ("The shadow of the prince" or "Who is this?"); Azariah ("The LORD has helped") was named Abednego ("Servant of Nego", i.e., the god of wisdom, or the morning star). As citizens of Babylon, they now carried official responsibilities. Despite having these new names, these Jewish men resolved that they would remain loyal to the one true God (see next note).

1:8 DANIEL PURPOSED IN HIS HEART THAT HE WOULD NOT DEFILE HIMSELF. Babylon's moral climate was totally heathen. We can be sure that what Daniel and his friends were being taught often contradicted God's law and righteous principles. The same food and wine served to King Nebuchadnezzar was served to them — food and wine that may have been offered to idols. To eat such food would have disobeyed God's laws; to drink such wine would have dulled their minds because of its intoxicating effect. (1) Daniel made up his mind from the start not to defile himself. He would not compromise his convictions even if it meant death. Note that Daniel no longer had his parents around to guide him in his decisions; his love for God and his law had been so instilled into him as a child that he desired to serve the Lord from the heart (see Deut. 6:7, note; see article on PARENTS AND CHILDREN, p. 1880).

(2) Those who are determined to remain faithful to God when confronted with temptation will be given the strength to stand firm for God. Conversely, those who have not previously decided to remain true to God and His word will find it difficult to resist sin or avoid conforming to the ways of the world.

set over Daniel, Hananiah, Mishael,
and Azariah,
12 Prove thy servants, I beseech
thee, ten days; and let them give us
[f]pulse [g]to eat, and water to drink.
13 Then let our countenances be
looked upon before thee, and the coun-
tenance of the children that eat of the
portion of the king's meat: and as thou
seest, deal with thy servants.
14 So he consented to them in this
matter, and proved them ten days.
15 And at the end of ten days their
countenances appeared fairer and fat-
ter in flesh than all the children which
did eat the portion of the king's meat.
16 Thus Melzar took away the por-
tion of their meat, and the wine that
they should drink; and gave them
pulse.
17 ¶ As for these four children,
[l]God gave them [m]knowledge and
skill in all learning and wisdom: and
[h]Daniel had [n]understanding in all vi-
sions and dreams.
18 Now at the end of the days that
the king had said he should bring them
in, then the prince of the eunuchs
brought them in before Nebuchadnez-
zar.
19 And the king communed with
them; and among them all was found
none like Daniel, Hananiah, Mishael,
and Azariah: therefore [o]stood they be-
fore the king.
20 [p]And in all matters of [i]wisdom
and understanding, that the king in-
quired of them, he found them ten
times better than all the magicians *and*
astrologers that *were* in all his realm.
21 [q]And Daniel continued *even*
unto the first year of king Cyrus.

Nebuchadnezzar's dream

2 AND IN the second year of the
reign of Nebuchadnezzar, Nebu-
chadnezzar dreamed dreams, [r]where-
with his spirit was troubled, and [s]his
sleep brake from him.
2 [t]Then the king commanded to
call the magicians, and the astrolo-
gers, and the sorcerers, and the Chal-
deans, for to show the king his dreams.
So they came and stood before the
king.
3 And the king said unto them, I
have dreamed a dream, and my spirit
was troubled to know the dream.
4 Then spake the Chaldeans to the
king in Syriac, [u]O king, live for ever:
tell thy servants the dream, and we will
show the interpretation.
5 The king answered and said to the
Chaldeans, The thing is gone from me:
if ye will not make known unto me the
dream, with the interpretation thereof,

1:17 [l]1 Ki. 3:12 Jas. 1:5,17 [m]Acts 7:22 [n]Num. 12:6 2 Chr. 26:5 ch. 5:11,12,14 & 10:1
1:19 [o]ver:5 Gen. 41:46
1:20 [p]1 Ki. 10:1
1:21 [q]ch. 6:28 & 10:1
2:1 [r]Gen. 41:8 ch. 4:5 [s]Esth. 6:1 ch. 6:18
2:2 [t]Gen. 41:8 Ex. 7:11 ch. 5:7
2:4 [u]1 Ki. 1:31 ch. 3:9 & 5:10 & 6:6,21

[f] Heb. *of pulse* [g] Heb. *that we may eat* [h] Or, *he made Daniel understand* [i] Heb. *wisdom of understanding*

1:12 PROVE THY SERVANTS . . . TEN DAYS. Because Daniel and his friends were objects of the king's special attention, the king's wrath could fall on the official if he agreed to Daniel's request. Thus he refused (v. 10). Daniel did not argue; instead, with grace and dignity he went to "the Melzar" (v. 11, i.e., the steward who actually served their food) and proposed an experimental ten-day diet.

1:17 GOD GAVE THEM KNOWLEDGE AND SKILL IN ALL LEARNING AND WISDOM. Because the four young men were committed to God, God committed Himself to help them. If you are endeavoring to be faithful to God and His ways, rest assured that He will remain with you and give you the help and grace needed to accomplish His will.

1:20 IN ALL MATTERS OF WISDOM . . . THE KING . . . FOUND THEM TEN TIMES BETTER THAN ALL. At the final examination, Daniel and his friends stood healthy and unafraid before the king. They had remained faithful to the Lord, and by their demonstration of wisdom and knowledge they gave testimony to the power of God.

1:21 FIRST YEAR OF KING CYRUS. This date (539 B.C.) was sixty-six years after Daniel was deported to Babylon. He lived to see the first exiles return to Judah from the Babylonian captivity in 538 B.C., since he was still alive in 537 B.C. (cf. 10:1).

2:1 NEBUCHADNEZZAR DREAMED. The king was greatly troubled about his dream and undoubtedly believed that the gods were trying to communicate something to him. Thus he called for the diviners to tell him the dream and its meaning.

2:4 IN SYRIAC. Up to this point, the book of Daniel is written in Hebrew. Here it changes to Syriac (i.e., Aramaic), which was the language of trade and of government communication at that time. The use of Aramaic in Daniel continues through ch. 7. Chs. 8—12 are again in Hebrew.

2:5 THE THING IS GONE FROM ME. This phrase can also be translated: "This is what I have decided," i.e., the decision had gone out from him and would not be changed. The king sensed the importance of his dream and wanted to put the Babylonian wise men to the test. If they could tell him the dream (which he probably remembered very well), then he would know they could give him the correct interpretation. If they could not give him both, then he would destroy them.

ye shall be [v]cut[j] in pieces, and your houses shall be made a dunghill.

6 [w]But if ye show the dream, and the interpretation thereof, ye shall receive of me gifts and [x]rewards[k] and great honour: therefore show me the dream, and the interpretation thereof.

7 They answered again and said, Let the king tell his servants the dream, and we will show the interpretation of it.

8 The king answered and said, I know of certainty that ye would gain the time, because ye see the thing is gone from me.

9 But if ye will not make known unto me the dream, *there is but* one decree for you: for ye have prepared lying and corrupt words to speak before me, till the time be changed: therefore tell me the dream, and I shall know that ye can show me the interpretation thereof.

10 ¶ The Chaldeans answered before the king, and said, There is not a man upon the earth that can show the king's matter: therefore *there is* no king, lord, nor ruler, *that* asked such things at any magician, or astrologer, or Chaldean.

11 And *it is* a rare thing that the king requireth, and there is none other that can show it before the king, [y]except the gods, whose dwelling is not with flesh.

12 For this cause the king was angry and very furious, and commanded to destroy all the wise *men* of Babylon.

13 And the decree went forth that the wise *men* should be slain; and they sought Daniel and his fellows to be slain.

14 ¶ Then Daniel [l]answered with counsel and wisdom to Arioch the [m,n]captain of the king's guard, which was gone forth to slay the wise *men* of Babylon:

15 He answered and said to Arioch the king's captain, Why *is* the decree *so* hasty from the king? Then Arioch made the thing known to Daniel.

16 Then Daniel went in, and desired of the king that he would give him time, and that he would show the king the interpretation.

17 Then Daniel went to his house, and made the thing known to Hananiah, Mishael, and Azariah, his companions:

18 [z]That they would desire mercies [o]of the God of heaven concerning this secret; [p]that Daniel and his fellows should not perish with the rest of the wise *men* of Babylon.

19 ¶ Then was the secret revealed unto Daniel [a]in a night vision. Then Daniel blessed the God of heaven.

20 Daniel answered and said, [b]Blessed be the name of God for ever and ever: [c]for wisdom and might are his:

21 And he changeth [d]the times and the seasons: [e]he removeth kings, and setteth up kings: [f]he giveth wisdom unto the wise, and knowledge to them that know understanding:

22 [g]He revealeth the deep and secret things: [h]he knoweth what *is* in the darkness, and [i]the light dwelleth with him.

23 I thank thee, and praise thee, O thou God of my fathers, who hast given me wisdom and might, and hast made known unto me now what we [j]desired of thee: for thou hast *now* made known unto us the king's matter.

Joel 2:23-27

Daniel interprets the dream

24 ¶ Therefore Daniel went in unto Arioch, whom the king had ordained to destroy the wise *men* of Babylon: he went and said thus unto him; Destroy not the wise *men* of Babylon: bring me in before the king, and I will show unto the king the interpretation.

25 Then Arioch brought in Daniel before the king in haste, and said thus unto him, [q]I have found a man of the

2:5 [v]2 Ki. 10:27 Ezra 6:11 ch. 3:29
2:6 [w]ch. 5:16 [x]ver. 48 ch. 5:17
2:11 [y]ch. 5:11
2:18 [z]Mat. 18:19
2:19 [a]Num. 12:6 Job 33:15
2:20 [b]Ps. 113:2 [c]Jer. 32:19
2:21 [d]Esth. 1:13 [e]Job 12:18 Ps. 75:6,7 Jer. 27:5 [f]Jas. 1:5
2:22 [g]Job 12:22 Ps. 25:14 [h]Ps. 139:11 Heb. 4:13 [i]ch. 5:11,14
2:23 [j]ver. 18

j Chald. *made pieces* k Or, *fee* l Chald. *returned* m Or, *chief marshal* n Chald. *chief of the executioners,* or, *slaughtermen* o Chald. *from before God* p Or, *that they should not destroy Daniel* q Chald. *That I have found*

2:16 DANIEL . . . DESIRED OF THE KING THAT HE WOULD GIVE HIM TIME. Being recent graduates, Daniel and his three friends were not called in before the king with the rest of the wise men, but the decree to kill all of them included those four as well. Daniel then approached the king and asked for time to interpret the dream. He needed time to pray and to receive God's assistance. So the four Hebrew men sought the Lord earnestly in prayer and waited for His revelation.

2:19–23 DANIEL BLESSED THE GOD OF HEAVEN. Daniel's first thought after God revealed the dream and its interpretation was to praise the Lord for His goodness and power. Spontaneous expressions of praise to God are characteristic of those who truly love and serve Him.

[r]captives of Judah, that will make known unto the king the interpretation.

26 The king answered and said to Daniel, whose name *was* Belteshazzar, Art thou able to make known unto me the dream which I have seen, and the interpretation thereof?

27 Daniel answered in the presence of the king, and said, The secret which the king hath demanded cannot the wise *men*, the astrologers, the magicians, the soothsayers, show unto the king;

28 [k]But there is a God in heaven that revealeth secrets, and [s]maketh known to the king Nebuchadnezzar [l]what shall be in the latter days. Thy dream, and the visions of thy head upon thy bed, are these;

29 As for thee, O king, thy thoughts [t]came *into thy mind* upon thy bed, what should come to pass hereafter: [m]and he that revealeth secrets maketh known to thee what shall come to pass.

30 [n]But as for me, this secret is not revealed to me for *any* wisdom that I have more than any living, [u]but for *their* sakes that shall make known the interpretation to the king, [o]and that thou mightest know the thoughts of thy heart.

31 ¶ Thou, O king, [v]sawest, and behold a great image. This great image, whose brightness *was* excellent, stood before thee; and the form thereof *was* terrible.

32 [p]This image's head *was* of fine gold, his breast and his arms of silver, his belly and his [w]thighs of brass,

33 His legs of iron, his feet part of iron and part of clay.

34 Thou sawest till that a stone was cut out [q]without hands, which smote the image upon his feet *that were* of iron and clay, and brake them to pieces.

35 Then was the iron, the clay, the brass, the silver, and the gold, broken to pieces together, and became [r]like the chaff of the summer threshingfloors; and the wind carried them away, that [s]no place was found for them: and the stone that smote the image [t]became a great mountain, [u]and filled the whole earth.

36 ¶ This *is* the dream; and we will tell the interpretation thereof before the king.

37 [v]Thou, O king, *art* a king of kings: [w]for the God of heaven hath given thee a kingdom, power, and strength, and glory.

38 [x]And wheresoever the children of men dwell, the beasts of the field and the fowls of the heaven hath he given into thine hand, and hath made thee ruler over them all. [y]Thou *art* this head of gold.

39 And after thee shall arise [z]another kingdom [a]inferior to thee, and another third kingdom of brass, which shall bear rule over all the earth.

40 And [b]the fourth kingdom shall be strong as iron: forasmuch as iron breaketh in pieces and subdueth all *things:* and as iron that breaketh all these, shall it break in pieces and bruise.

41 And whereas thou sawest the feet and toes, part of potters' clay, and part of iron, the kingdom shall be divided; but there shall be in it of the strength of the iron, forasmuch as thou sawest the iron mixed with miry clay.

42 And *as* the toes of the feet *were* part of iron, and part of clay, *so* the kingdom shall be partly strong, and partly [x]broken.

2:28 [k]Gen. 40:8 Amos 4:13 [l]Gen. 49:1
2:29 [m]ver. 22,28
2:30 [n]Acts 3:12 [o]ver. 47
2:32 [p]See ver. 38
2:34 [q]Zech. 4:6 2 Cor. 5:1 Heb. 9:24
2:35 [r]Hos. 13:3 [s]Ps. 37:10,36 [t]Is. 2:2,3 [u]Ps. 80:9
2:37 [v]Ezra 7:12 Is. 47:5 Jer. 27:6,7 Ezek. 26:7 Hos. 8:10 [w]Ezra 1:2
2:38 [x]ch. 4:21,22 Jer. 27:6 [y]ver. 32
2:39 [z]ch. 5:28,31 [a]ver. 32
2:40 [b]ch. 7:7,23

[r] Chald. *children of the captivity of Judah* [s] Chald. *hath made known* [t] Chald. *came up* [u] Or, *but for the intent that the interpretation may be made known to the king* [v] Chald. *wast seeing* [w] Or, *sides* [x] Or, *brittle*

2:28–30 THERE IS A GOD IN HEAVEN THAT REVEALETH SECRETS. Daniel took no personal credit for making the dream and its interpretation known to the king. We must be careful never to take credit and glory for what God does through us (cf. Deut. 8:11–20). Because Daniel was humble, straightforward, and honest about God, Nebuchadnezzar was able to make a proper response of acknowledging Daniel's God (v. 47).

2:37–38 THOU *ART* THIS HEAD OF GOLD. Nebuchadnezzar was the head of gold, representing the Neo-Babylonian empire (605–539 B.C.). After he died, the empire soon began to disintegrate.

2:39 KINGDOM INFERIOR TO THEE. Nebuchadnezzar's kingdom would be followed by an inferior kingdom, represented by the silver chest and arms (v. 32); this kingdom would be the Medo-Persian empire established by Cyrus (539 B.C.). A third kingdom, symbolized by the brass belly and thighs, represented the Greek empire established by Alexander the Great (330 B.C.).

2:40 THE FOURTH KINGDOM SHALL BE STRONG AS IRON. The iron kingdom (v. 33) represents the Roman empire, which began about 67 B.C. and subdued the world to a degree that no empire had done previously.

43 And whereas thou sawest iron mixed with miry clay, they shall mingle themselves with the seed of men: but they shall not cleave [y]one to another, even as iron is not mixed with clay.

44 And in [z]the days of these kings [c]shall the God of heaven set up a kingdom, [d]which shall never be destroyed: and the [a]kingdom shall not be left to other people, [e]*but* it shall break in pieces and consume all these kingdoms, and it shall stand for ever.

45 [f]Forasmuch as thou sawest that the stone was cut out of the mountain [b]without hands, and that it brake in pieces the iron, the brass, the clay, the silver, and the gold; the great God hath made known to the king what shall come to pass [c]hereafter: and the dream *is* certain, and the interpretation thereof sure.

46 ¶ [g]Then the king Nebuchadnezzar fell upon his face, and worshipped Daniel, and commanded that they should offer an oblation [h]and sweet odours unto him.

47 The king answered unto Daniel, and said, Of a truth *it is*, that your God *is* a God of gods, and a Lord of kings, and a revealer of secrets, seeing thou couldest reveal this secret.

48 Then the king made Daniel a great man, [i]and gave him many great gifts, and made him ruler over the whole province of Babylon, and [j]chief of the governors over all the wise *men* of Babylon.

49 Then Daniel requested of the king, [k]and he set Shadrach, Meshach, and Abed-nego, over the affairs of the province of Babylon: but Daniel [l]*sat* in the gate of the king.

2:44 [c]ver. 28 [d]ch. 4:3,34 & 6:26 & 7:14,27 Mic. 4:7 Luke 1:32,33 [e]Ps. 2:9 Is. 60:12 1 Cor. 15:24 **2:45** [f]ver. 35 Is. 28:16 **2:46** [g]See Acts 10:25 & 14:13 & 28:6 [h]Ezra 6:10 **2:48** [i]ver. 6 [j]ch. 4:9 & 5:11 **2:49** [k]ch. 3:12 [l]Esth. 2:19,21 & 3:2

The fiery furnace

3 NEBUCHADNEZZAR THE king made an image of gold, whose height *was* threescore cubits, *and* the breadth thereof six cubits: he set it up in the plain of Dura, in the province of Babylon.

2 Then Nebuchadnezzar the king sent to gather together the princes, the governors, and the captains, the judges, the treasurers, the counsellors, the sheriffs, and all the rulers of the provinces, to come to the dedication of the image which Nebuchadnezzar the king had set up.

3 Then the princes, the governors, and captains, the judges, the treasurers, the counsellors, the sheriffs, and all the rulers of the provinces, were gathered together unto the dedication of the image that Nebuchadnezzar the

[y]Chald. *this with this* [z]Chald. *their days* [a]Chald. *kingdom thereof* [b]Or, *which* was *not in hand* [c]Chald. *after this*

2:41–43 IRON, AND ... CLAY ... PARTLY STRONG, AND PARTLY BROKEN. The feet of iron and clay probably represent the nationalistic states that have existed in the area of the Roman empire since that empire fell. Some of them have been strong and lasted a long time; others are brittle, breaking up again and again.

2:44–45 A KINGDOM, WHICH SHALL NEVER BE DESTROYED. In the dream, a stone cut out of the mountain without hands, (i.e., supernaturally) hit the image in the feet. Not only were the feet destroyed, but the gold, silver, copper, iron, and clay all turned to powder and were blown away. (1) When Babylon gave way to Medo-Persia, the latter coalition remained part of the same image. The same was true of Greece and Rome, and is still true of the modern nationalistic states. All are part of the same world system. Furthermore, we still have around us Babylonian astrology, Medo-Persian ethics, Greek art and philosophy, and both Roman law and the Roman idea that peace can be obtained by military might. According to Nebuchadnezzar's dream, the world order with its philosophy and values must be completely destroyed in order that Christ's kingdom may be fully established.

(2) The stone became a kingdom that filled the whole earth (v. 35). This fifth kingdom is the kingdom of God established by Jesus the Messiah. It will fill the whole earth and extend to the new heavens and earth (cf. Rev. 21:1). We can be sure that the present world order will not last forever, but that God's kingdom will last forever (cf. 2 Pet. 3:10–13).

3:1 THE KING MADE AN IMAGE OF GOLD. Nebuchadnezzar may have carried out this proud act because, as had been revealed through Daniel (2:37–38), he was the head of gold on the statue in his dream. Nebuchadnezzar's empire had just risen to power, and he was undoubtedly trying to use religion to consolidate the many provinces he had added to his empire. He demanded worship of the image as a means of promoting loyalty to himself. He was not the first, nor will he be the last, world leader to try to use religion for political purposes or for self-exaltation.

3:2 THE DEDICATION OF THE IMAGE. At Daniel's request, his three friends were appointed by the king to positions of responsibility in the administration of Babylon, while Daniel served in the king's court (2:49). Daniel may not have been present among the officials commanded to bow before the gold image; he could have been traveling in the provinces at the time on a business trip for the king, or his responsibilities may have differed from those mentioned in this verse.

king had set up; and they stood before the image that Nebuchadnezzar had set up.

4 Then an herald cried [d]aloud, To you [e]it is commanded, [m]O people, nations, and languages,

5 *That* at what time ye hear the sound of the cornet, flute, harp, sackbut, psaltery, [f] [g]dulcimer, and all kinds of music, ye fall down and worship the golden image that Nebuchadnezzar the king hath set up:

6 And whoso falleth not down and worshippeth shall the same hour [n]be cast into the midst of a burning fiery furnace.

7 Therefore at that time, when all the people heard the sound of the cornet, flute, harp, sackbut, psaltery, and all kinds of music, all the people, the nations, and the languages, fell down *and* worshipped the golden image that Nebuchadnezzar the king had set up.

8 ¶ Wherefore at that time certain Chaldeans [o]came near, and accused the Jews.

9 They spake and said to the king Nebuchadnezzar, [p]O king, live for ever.

10 Thou, O king, hast made a decree, that every man that shall hear the sound of the cornet, flute, harp, sackbut, psaltery, and dulcimer, and all kinds of music, shall fall down and worship the golden image:

11 And whoso falleth not down and worshippeth, *that* he should be cast into the midst of a burning fiery furnace.

12 [q]There are certain Jews whom thou hast set over the affairs of the province of Babylon, Shadrach, Meshach, and Abed-nego; these men, O king, [h]have not regarded thee: they serve not thy gods, nor worship the golden image which thou hast set up.

13 ¶ Then Nebuchadnezzar in *his* rage and fury commanded to bring Shadrach, Meshach, and Abed-nego. Then they brought these men before the king.

14 Nebuchadnezzar spake and said unto them, *Is it* [i]true, O Shadrach, Meshach, and Abed-nego, do not ye serve my gods, nor worship the golden image which I have set up?

15 Now if ye be ready that at what time ye hear the sound of the cornet, flute, harp, sackbut, psaltery, and dulcimer, and all kinds of music, ye fall down and worship the image which I have made; [r]*well:* but if ye worship not, ye shall be cast the same hour into the midst of a burning fiery furnace; [s]and who *is* that God that shall deliver you out of my hands?

16 Shadrach, Meshach, and Abed-nego, answered and said to the king, O Nebuchadnezzar, [t]we *are* not careful to answer thee in this matter.

17 If it be *so*, our God whom we serve is able to deliver us from the burning fiery furnace, and he will deliver *us* out of thine hand, O king.

18 But if not, be it known unto thee, O king, that we will not serve thy gods, nor worship the golden image which thou hast set up.

19 ¶ Then was Nebuchadnezzar [j]full of fury, and the form of his visage was changed against Shadrach, Meshach, and Abed-nego: *therefore* he spake, and commanded that they should heat the furnace one seven times more than it was wont to be heated.

3:4 [m]ch. 4:1 & 6:25
3:6 [n]Jer. 29:22 Rev. 13:15
3:8 [o]ch. 6:12
3:9 [p]ch. 2:4 & 5:10 & 6:6,21
3:12 [q]ch. 2:49
3:15 [r]As Ex. 32:32 Luke 13:9 [s]Ex. 5:2 2 Ki. 18:35
3:16 [t]Mat. 10:19

[d] Chald. *with might* [e] Chald. *they command* [f] Or, *singing* [g] Chald. *symphony* [h] Chald. *have set no regard upon thee* [i] Or, *of purpose* [j] Chald. *filled*

3:12 THEY SERVE NOT THY GODS. Though the Bible teaches us to obey, honor, and pray for those who rule over us (Rom. 13:1–7; 1 Tim. 2:1–2; 1 Pet. 2:13–17), our first duty is to God Himself. If we obey the first and greatest commandment—to love the one true God with all our hearts, souls, minds, and strength (Deut. 6:5; Mat. 22:37–38)—we cannot worship or bestow divine honor upon any false god or any image representing a god.

3:17–18 OUR GOD . . . IS ABLE TO DELIVER US . . . BUT IF NOT. Neither the jealous insinuations of the Chaldeans nor the ugly threats of King Nebuchadnezzar frightened these three young men into compromising their personal convictions. Instead, they gave bold and unhesitating witness to their allegiance to the one true God. They had a hope and a faith that were fixed on Him who was their refuge and strength (Ps. 46:1; 56:4). They also knew that the wrath of God against sin and disobedience was far worse than human wrath (cf. Lev. 26; Deut. 28). Thus, as an expression of unconditional faith, complete trust, and total loyalty to God, they said, "But if not." They possessed a faith that trusted and obeyed God regardless of the consequences. Obedience and persevering trust in God, and not necessarily the experience of deliverance, give true evidence of Biblical faith. Like many of the great saints of the Bible, these three friends had their faith greatly tested.

20 And he commanded the [k]most
mighty men that *were* in his army to
bind Shadrach, Meshach, and Abed-
nego, *and* to cast *them* into the burning
fiery furnace.
21 Then these men were bound in
their [l]coats, their hosen, and their
[m]hats, and their *other* garments, and
were cast into the midst of the burning
fiery furnace.
22 Therefore because the king's
[n]commandment was urgent, and the
furnace exceeding hot, the [o]flame of
the fire slew those men that took up
Shadrach, Meshach, and Abed-nego.
23 And these three men, Shadrach,
Meshach, and Abed-nego, fell down
bound into the midst of the burning fi-
ery furnace.
24 Then Nebuchadnezzar the king
was astonied, and rose up in haste, *and*
spake, and said unto his [p]counsellors,
Did not we cast three men bound into
the midst of the fire? They answered
and said unto the king, True, O king.
25 He answered and said, Lo, I see
four men loose, [u]walking in the midst
of the fire, and [q]they have no hurt;
and the form of the fourth is like [v]the
Son of God.
26 ¶ Then Nebuchadnezzar came
near to the [r]mouth of the burning fi-
ery furnace, *and* spake, and said, Sha-
drach, Meshach, and Abed-nego, ye
servants of the most high God, come
forth, and come *hither*. Then Shadrach,
Meshach, and Abed-nego, came forth
of the midst of the fire.
27 And the princes, governors, and
captains, and the king's counsellors,
being gathered together, saw these
men, [w]upon whose bodies the fire had
no power, nor was an hair of their head
singed, neither were their coats
changed, nor the smell of fire had Dan.
passed on them. 6:1-23
28 *Then* Nebuchadnezzar spake,
and said, Blessed *be* the God of Sha-
drach, Meshach, and Abed-nego, who
hath sent his angel, and delivered his
servants that [x]trusted in him, and
have changed the king's word, and
yielded their bodies, that they might
not serve nor worship any god, except
their own God.
29 [y]Therefore [s]I make a decree,
That every people, nation, and lan-
guage, which speak [t]any thing amiss
against the God of Shadrach, Meshach,
and Abed-nego, shall be [z]cut[u] in
pieces, and their houses shall be made
a dunghill: [a]because there is no other
God that can deliver after this sort.
30 Then the king [v]promoted Sha-
drach, Meshach, and Abed-nego, in the
province of Babylon.

The king's dream

4 NEBUCHADNEZZAR THE king,
[b]unto all people, nations, and lan-
guages, that dwell in all the earth;
Peace be multiplied unto you.
2 [w]I thought it good to show the
signs and wonders [c]that the high God
hath wrought toward me.
3 [d]How great *are* his signs! and
how mighty *are* his wonders! his king-
dom *is* [e]an everlasting kingdom, and
his dominion *is* from generation to gen-
eration.

3:25 [u]Is. 43:2 [v]ver. 28 Job 1:6 & 38:7 Ps. 34:7 **3:27** [w]Heb. 11:34 **3:28** [x]Ps. 34:7,8 Jer. 17:7 ch. 6:22,23 **3:29** [y]ch. 6:26 [z]ch. 2:5 [a]ch. 6:27 **4:1** [b]ch. 3:4 & 6:25 **4:2** [c]ch. 3:26 **4:3** [d]ch. 6:27 [e]ver. 34 ch. 2:44 & 6:26

[k] Chald. *mighty of strength* [l] Or, *mantles* [m] Or, *turbans* [n] Chald. *word* [o] Or, *spark* [p] Or, *governors* [q] Chald. *there is no hurt in them* [r] Chald. *door* [s] Chald. *a decree is made by me* [t] Chald. *error* [u] Chald. *made pieces* [v] Chald. *made to prosper* [w] Chald. *It was seemly before me*

3:24–25 I SEE FOUR MEN LOOSE . . . THE FOURTH IS LIKE THE SON OF GOD. The king's reference to the fourth man walking about freely in the fire could be translated either "the Son of God," or "a son of the gods," i.e., a supernatural being. Since Nebuchadnezzar was still a worshiper of many gods, the latter translation seems more probable. The fourth man could have been an angel or a preincarnate manifestation of Christ sent to protect the three friends of Daniel and be with them in their time of great trial. Note that the meaning of the three youths' Hebrew names correspond to the deliverance God gave them. "The LORD was gracious" (Hananiah) to them and "the LORD helped" (Azariah) them. The form of the fourth man in the fire was as one "who was equal to God" (Mishael; see 1:7, note).

3:30 SHADRACH, MESHACH, AND ABED-NEGO. These three men who remained true to God even at the possible cost of their lives serve to condemn the spiritual and moral compromise of those who use contemporary influences and customs as an excuse for their worldly actions. God does not accept the reasoning that we may do something simply because "everyone is doing it." We should diligently ask God to put a firm determination within our hearts to remain true to Him and His Word, regardless of the consequences.

4:1–3 THE SIGNS AND WONDERS. Nebuchadnezzar testifies to the greatness and power of God. He came to this conviction after his humbling experience of insanity described in this chapter.

THE NEO-BABYLONIAN EMPIRE 626-539 B.C.

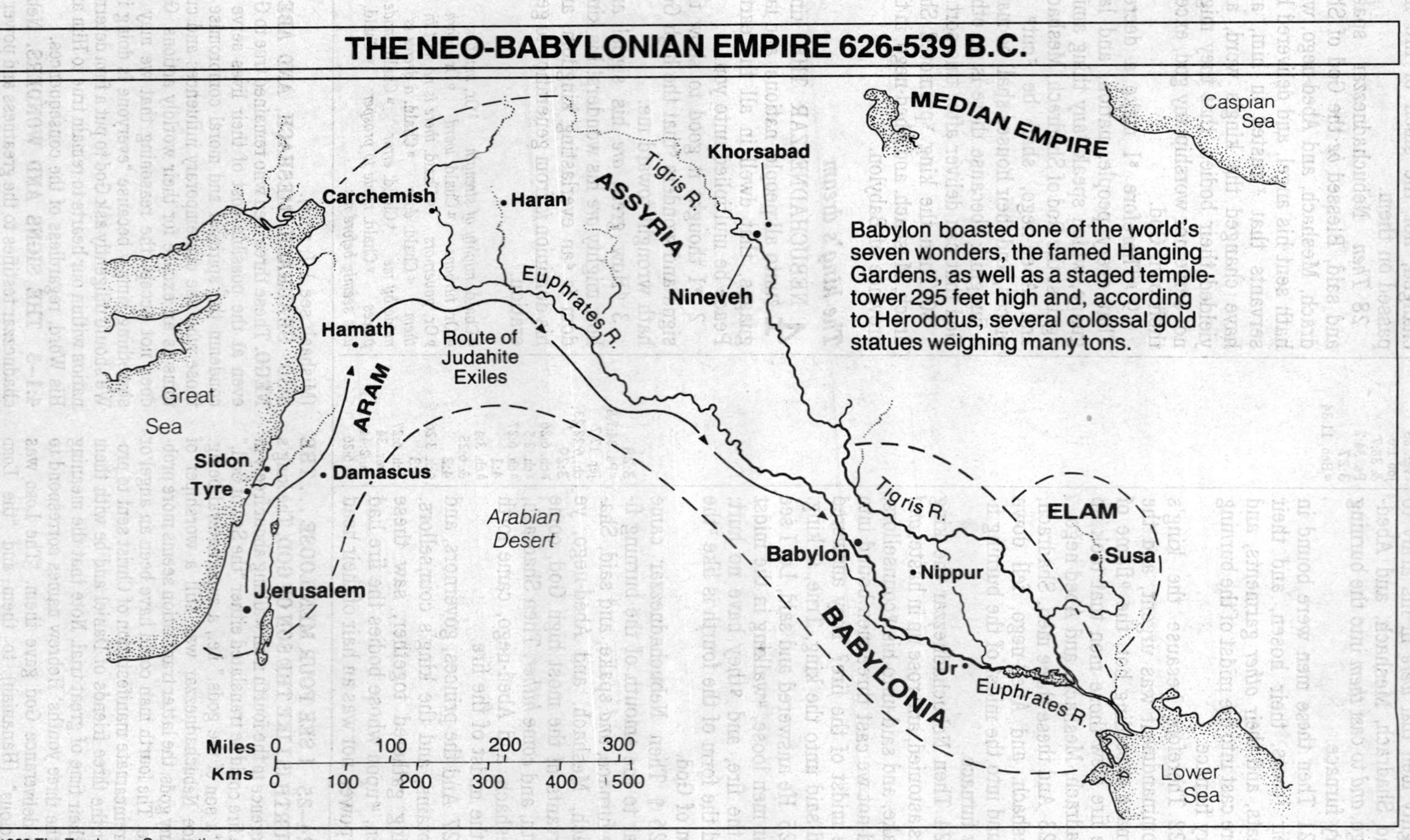

4 ¶ I Nebuchadnezzar was at rest in mine house, and flourishing in my palace:

5 I saw a dream which made me afraid, [f]and the thoughts upon my bed and the visions of my head [g]troubled me.

6 Therefore made I a decree to bring in all the wise *men* of Babylon before me, that they might make known unto me the interpretation of the dream.

7 [h]Then came in the magicians, the astrologers, the Chaldeans, and the soothsayers: and I told the dream before them; but they did not make known unto me the interpretation thereof.

8 ¶ But at the last Daniel came in before me, [i]whose name *was* Belteshazzar, according to the name of my god, [j]and in whom *is* the spirit of the holy gods: and before him I told the dream, *saying*,

9 O Belteshazzar, [k]master of the magicians, because I know that the spirit of the holy gods *is* in thee, and no secret troubleth thee, tell me the visions of my dream that I have seen, and the interpretation thereof.

10 Thus *were* the visions of mine head in my bed; [x]I saw, and behold [l]a tree in the midst of the earth, and the height thereof *was* great.

11 The tree grew, and was strong, and the height thereof reached unto heaven, and the sight thereof to the end of all the earth:

12 The leaves thereof *were* fair, and the fruit thereof much, and in it *was* meat for all: [m]the beasts of the field had shadow under it, and the fowls of the heaven dwelt in the boughs thereof, and all flesh was fed of it.

13 I saw in the visions of my head upon my bed, and, behold, [n]a watcher and [o]an holy one came down from heaven;

14 He cried [y]aloud, and said thus, [p]Hew down the tree, and cut off his branches, shake off his leaves, and scatter his fruit: [q]let the beasts get away from under it, and the fowls from his branches:

15 Nevertheless leave the stump of his roots in the earth, even with a band of iron and brass, in the tender grass of the field; and let it be wet with the dew of heaven, and *let* his portion *be* with the beasts in the grass of the earth:

16 Let his heart be changed from man's, and let a beast's heart be given unto him; and let seven [r]times pass over him.

17 This matter *is* by the decree of the watchers, and the demand by the word of the holy ones: to the intent [s]that the living may know [t]that the most High ruleth in the kingdom of men, and giveth it to whomsoever he will, and setteth up over it the basest of men.

18 This dream I king Nebuchadnezzar have seen. Now thou, O Belteshazzar, declare the interpretation thereof, [u]forasmuch as all the wise *men* of my kingdom are not able to make known unto me the interpretation: but thou *art* able; [v]for the spirit of the holy gods *is* in thee.

The interpretation and warning

19 ¶ Then Daniel, [w]whose name *was* Belteshazzar, was astonied for one hour, and his thoughts troubled him. The king spake, and said, Belteshazzar, let not the dream, or the interpretation thereof, trouble thee. Belteshazzar answered and said, My lord, [x]the

4:5 [f]ch. 2:28,29 [g]ch. 2:1
4:7 [h]ch. 2:2
4:8 [i]ch. 1:7 [j]ver. 18 Is. 63:11 ch. 2:11 & 5:11,14
4:9 [k]ch. 2:48 & 5:11
4:10 [l]ver. 20 Ezek. 31:3
4:12 [m]Ezek. 17:23 & 31:6 See Lam. 4:20
4:13 [n]ver. 17,23 [o]Deut. 33:2 ch. 8:13 Zech. 14:5 Jude 14
4:14 [p]Mat. 3:10 [q]Ezek. 31:12
4:16 [r]ch. 11:13 & 12:7
4:17 [s]Ps. 9:16 [t]ver. 25,32 ch. 2:21 & 5:21
4:18 [u]Gen. 41:8,15 ch. 5:8,15 [v]ver. 8
4:19 [w]ver. 8 [x]See 2 Sam. 18:32 Jer. 29:7

x Chald. *I was seeing* y Chald. *with might*

4:9 MASTER OF THE MAGICIANS. "Magicians" (Aramaic, *hartumaya*) actually refers to the learned scribes who copied and understood the most ancient cuneiform writings. Some of these people did make use of magic formulas. However, the king recognized that Daniel's knowledge and ability were supernaturally given and not derived from the things he may have read in ancient heathen lore.

4:10 A TREE. See v. 22 for the symbolism that Daniel saw in this tree.

4:16 LET A BEAST'S HEART BE GIVEN UNTO HIM; AND LET SEVEN TIMES PASS OVER HIM. At this point the picture changes from that of a felled tree to that of a living being. This being was to lose his own heart, (i.e., his mind or reasoning powers) and be given the heart and mind of an animal. This loss of reason was to last "seven times," which probably means seven seasons (i.e., three and one-half years, since there were essentially only two seasons, a wet season and a dry one).

4:17 THE MOST HIGH RULETH IN THE KINGDOM OF MEN. The king needed to learn that the Lord God is all-powerful and can place whomever He wants over the kingdoms of the world.

dream *be* to them that hate thee, and the interpretation thereof to thine enemies.

20 [y]The tree that thou sawest, which grew, and was strong, whose height reached unto the heaven, and the sight thereof to all the earth;

21 Whose leaves *were* fair, and the fruit thereof much, and in it *was* meat for all; under which the beasts of the field dwelt, and upon whose branches the fowls of the heaven had their habitation:

22 [z]It *is* thou, O king, that art grown and become strong: for thy greatness is grown, and reacheth unto heaven, [a]and thy dominion to the end of the earth.

23 [b]And whereas the king saw a watcher and an holy one coming down from heaven, and saying, Hew the tree down, and destroy it; yet leave the stump of the roots thereof in the earth, even with a band of iron and brass, in the tender grass of the field; and let it be wet with the dew of heaven, [c]and *let* his portion *be* with the beasts of the field, till seven times pass over him;

24 This *is* the interpretation, O king, and this *is* the decree of the most High, which is come upon my lord the king:

25 That they shall [d]drive thee from men, and thy dwelling shall be with the beasts of the field, and they shall make thee [e]to eat grass as oxen, and they shall wet thee with the dew of heaven, and seven times shall pass over thee, [f]till thou know that the most High ruleth in the kingdom of men, and [g]giveth it to whomsoever he will.

26 And whereas they commanded to leave the stump of the tree roots; thy kingdom shall be sure unto thee, after that thou shalt have known that the [h]heavens do rule.

27 Wherefore, O king, let my counsel be acceptable unto thee, and [i]break off thy sins by righteousness, and thine iniquities by showing mercy to the poor; [j]if it may be [k]a[z] lengthening of thy tranquillity.

4:20 [y]ver. 10,11,12
4:22 [z]ch. 2:38 [a]Jer. 27:6-8
4:23 [b]ver. 13 [c]ch. 5:21
4:25 [d]ver. 32 ch. 5:21 [e]Ps. 106:20 [f]ver. 17,32 Ps. 83:18 [g]Jer. 27:5
4:26 [h]Mat. 21:25 Luke 15:18
4:27 [i]1 Pet. 4:8 [j]Ps. 41:1 [k]1 Ki. 21:29
4:30 [l]Prov. 16:18 ch. 5:20
4:31 [m]ch. 5:5 Luke 12:20 [n]ver. 24
4:32 [o]ver. 25
4:34 [p]ver. 26 [q]ch. 12:7 Rev. 4:10 [r]Ps. 10:16 ch. 2:44 Mic. 4:7 Luke 1:33
4:35 [s]Is. 40:15 [t]Ps. 115:3 & 135:6 [u]Job 34:29 [v]Job 9:12 Is. 45:9 Rom. 9:20
4:36 [w]ver. 26

The dream is fulfilled

28 ¶ All this came upon the king Nebuchadnezzar.

29 At the end of twelve months he walked [a]in the palace of the kingdom of Babylon.

30 The king [l]spake, and said, Is not this great Babylon, that I have built for the house of the kingdom by the might of my power, and for the honour of my majesty?

31 [m]While the word *was* in the king's mouth, there fell [n]a voice from heaven, *saying,* O king Nebuchadnezzar, to thee it is spoken; The kingdom is departed from thee.

32 And [o]they shall drive thee from men, and thy dwelling *shall be* with the beasts of the field: they shall make thee to eat grass as oxen, and seven times shall pass over thee, until thou know that the most High ruleth in the kingdom of men, and giveth it to whomsoever he will.

33 The same hour was the thing fulfilled upon Nebuchadnezzar: and he was driven from men, and did eat grass as oxen, and his body was wet with the dew of heaven, till his hairs were grown like eagles' *feathers,* and his nails like birds' *claws.*

34 And [p]at the end of the days I Nebuchadnezzar lifted up mine eyes unto heaven, and mine understanding returned unto me, and I blessed the most High, and I praised and honoured him [q]that liveth for ever, whose dominion *is* [r]an everlasting dominion, and his kingdom *is* from generation to generation:

35 And [s]all the inhabitants of the earth *are* reputed as nothing: and [t]he doeth according to his will in the army of heaven, and *among* the inhabitants of the earth: and [u]none can stay his hand, or say unto him, [v]What doest thou?

36 At the same time my reason returned unto me; [w]and for the glory of

[z] Or, *an healing of thine error* [a] Or, *upon*

4:27 BREAK OFF THY SINS BY RIGHTEOUSNESS. The very fact that Daniel called for the king to repent indicates that God's terrible judgment could be avoided. If Nebuchadnezzar would forsake his sins and turn to a righteous lifestyle, showing mercy to the poor and downtrodden whom he had oppressed, God would not carry out what He had revealed in the dream.

4:34–37 MINE UNDERSTANDING RETURNED UNTO ME, AND I BLESSED THE MOST HIGH. Seven is a number of completion, so at the end of the seven seasons, Nebuchadnezzar's understanding returned. He not only understood what had happened to him, but also recognized the power, greatness, and sovereignty of Daniel's God, the Lord God of Israel.

my kingdom, mine honour and bright-
ness returned unto me; and my coun-
sellors and my lords sought unto me;
and I was established in my kingdom,
and excellent majesty was [x]added
unto me.
37 Now I Nebuchadnezzar praise
and extol and honour the King of heav-
en, [y]all whose works *are* truth, and his
ways judgment: [z]and those that walk
in pride he is able to abase.

The handwriting on the wall

5 BELSHAZZAR THE king [a]made a
great feast to a thousand of his
lords, and drank wine before the thou-
sand.
2 Belshazzar, whiles he tasted the
wine, commanded to bring the golden
and silver vessels [b]which his [b]father
Nebuchadnezzar had [c]taken out of
the temple which *was* in Jerusalem;
that the king, and his princes, his
wives, and his concubines, might drink
therein.
3 Then they brought the golden ves-
sels that were taken out of the temple
of the house of God which *was* at Jeru-
salem; and the king, and his princes,
his wives, and his concubines, drank in
them.
4 They drank wine, [c]and praised
the gods of gold, and of silver, of brass,
of iron, of wood, and of stone.
5 ¶ [d]In the same hour came forth
fingers of a man's hand, and wrote over
against the candlestick upon the plas-
ter of the wall of the king's palace: and
the king saw the part of the hand that
wrote.
6 Then the king's countenance was
changed, and his thoughts troubled
him, so that the [e][d]joints of his loins
were loosed, and his [f]knees smote
one against another.
7 [g]The king cried [e]aloud to bring
in [h]the astrologers, the Chaldeans,
and the soothsayers. *And* the king
spake, and said to the wise *men* of Bab-
ylon, Whosoever shall read this writ-
ing, and show me the interpretation
thereof, shall be clothed with [f]scar-
let, and *have* a chain of gold about his
neck, [i]and shall be the third ruler in
the kingdom.
8 Then came in all the king's wise
men: [j]but they could not read the writ-
ing, nor make known to the king the
interpretation thereof.
9 Then was king Belshazzar greatly
[k]troubled, and his [g]countenance was
changed in him, and his lords were as-
tonied.
10 ¶ *Now* the queen, by reason of
the words of the king and his lords,
came into the banquet house: *and* the
queen spake and said, O king, live for
ever: let not thy thoughts trouble thee,
nor let thy countenance be changed:
11 [l]There is a man in thy kingdom,
in whom *is* the spirit of the holy gods;
and in the days of thy [b]father light
and understanding and wisdom, like
the wisdom of the gods, was found in
him; whom the king Nebuchadnezzar
thy [h]father, the king, *I say,* thy father,
made [m]master of the magicians, as-
trologers, Chaldeans, *and* soothsayers;
12 [n]Forasmuch as an excellent
spirit, and knowledge, and understand-
ing, [i]interpreting of dreams, and
showing of hard sentences, and [j]dis-
solving of [k]doubts, were found in the
same Daniel, [o]whom the king named
Belteshazzar: now let Daniel be called,
and he will show the interpretation.
13 Then was Daniel brought in be-
fore the king. *And* the king spake and
said unto Daniel, *Art* thou that Daniel,
which *art* of the children of the captivi-
ty of Judah, whom the king my [b]father
brought out of Jewry?
14 I have even heard of thee, that
[p]the spirit of the gods *is* in thee, and
that light and understanding and excel-
lent wisdom is found in thee.

4:36 [x]Job 42:12 Prov. 22:4 Mat. 6:33
4:37 [y]Ps. 33:4 Rev. 15:3 [z]Ex. 18:11 ch. 5:20
5:1 [a]Esth. 1:3
5:2 [b]ch. 1:2 Jer. 52:19
5:4 [c]Rev. 9:20
5:5 [d]ch. 4:31
5:6 [e]Is. 5:27 [f]Nah. 2:10
5:7 [g]ch. 4:6 [h]Is. 47:13 [i]ch. 6:2
5:8 [j]ch. 2:27
5:9 [k]ch. 2:1
5:11 [l]ch. 2:48 & 4:8,9,18 [m]ch. 4:9
5:12 [n]ch. 6:3 [o]ch. 1:7
5:14 [p]ver. 11,12

[b] Or, *grandfather* [c] Chald. *brought forth* [d] Or, *girdles* [e] Chald. *with might* [f] Or, *purple* [g] Chald. *brightnesses* [h] Or, *grandfather;* ver. 2 [i] Or, *of an interpreter* [j] Or, *of a dissolver* [k] Chald. *knots*

5:1 BELSHAZZAR ... MADE A GREAT FEAST. Nebuchadnezzar's brilliant reign lasted forty-four years. After his death, Babylon's glory began to decline. Though the empire lasted another twenty-two years, revolutions and assassinations weakened it. The last Babylonian kings were Nabonidus and his eldest son Belshazzar, who served together as co-regents.

5:2 HIS FATHER NEBUCHADNEZZAR. "Father" is used here in the general sense of an ancestor or predecessor, not one's biological parent.

5:3 THEY BROUGHT THE GOLDEN VESSELS ... TAKEN OUT OF ... THE HOUSE OF GOD. By drinking from the Lord's sacred vessels in honor of the pagan gods of Babylon, Belshazzar and his lords dishonored the one true God and brought final judgment upon themselves (vv. 22–24).

15 And now [q]the wise *men,* the astrologers, have been brought in before me, that they should read this writing, and make known unto me the interpretation thereof: but they could not show the interpretation of the thing:

16 And I have heard of thee, that thou canst [1]make interpretations, and dissolve doubts: [r]now if thou canst read the writing, and make known to me the interpretation thereof, thou shalt be clothed with scarlet, and *have* a chain of gold about thy neck, and shalt be the third ruler in the kingdom.

17 ¶ Then Daniel answered and said before the king, Let thy gifts be to thyself, and give thy [s]rewards[m] to another; yet I will read the writing unto the king, and make known to him the interpretation.

18 O thou king, [t]the most high God gave Nebuchadnezzar thy father a kingdom, and majesty, and glory, and honour:

19 And for the majesty that he gave him, [u]all people, nations, and languages, trembled and feared before him: whom he would he slew; and whom he would he kept alive; and whom he would he set up; and whom he would he put down.

20 [v]But when his heart was lifted up, and his mind hardened in pride, he was [n]deposed from his kingly throne, and they took his glory from him:

21 And he was [w]driven from the sons of men; and [o]his heart was made like the beasts, and his dwelling *was* with the wild asses: they fed him with grass like oxen, and his body was wet with the dew of heaven; [x]till he knew that the most high God ruled in the kingdom of men, and *that* he appointeth over it whomsoever he will.

22 And thou his son, O Belshazzar, [y]hast not humbled thine heart, though thou knewest all this;

23 [z]But hast lifted up thyself against the Lord of heaven; and they have brought the vessels of his house before thee, and thou, and thy lords, thy wives, and thy concubines, have drunk wine in them; and thou hast praised the gods of silver, and gold, of brass, iron, wood, and stone, [a]which see not, nor hear, nor know: and the God in whose hand thy breath *is,* [b]and whose *are* all thy ways, hast thou not glorified:

24 Then was the part of the hand sent from him; and this writing was written.

25 ¶ And this *is* the writing that was written, MENE, MENE, TEKEL, UPHARSIN.

26 This *is* the interpretation of the thing: MENE; God hath numbered thy kingdom, and finished it.

27 TEKEL; [c]Thou art weighed in the balances, and art found wanting.

28 PERES; Thy kingdom is divided, and given to the [d]Medes and [e]Persians.

29 Then commanded Belshazzar, and they clothed Daniel with scarlet, and *put* a chain of gold about his neck, and made a proclamation concerning him, [f]that he should be the third ruler in the kingdom.

30 ¶ [g]In that night was Belshazzar the king of the Chaldeans slain.

5:15 [q]ver. 7,8
5:16 [r]ver. 7
5:17 [s]ch. 2:6
5:18 [t]ch. 2:37,38 & 4:17,22,25
5:19 [u]Jer. 27:7 ch. 3:4
5:20 [v]ch. 4:30,37
5:21 [w]ch. 4:32 [x]ch. 4:17,25
5:22 [y]2 Chr. 33:23 & 36:12
5:23 [z]ver. 3,4 [a]Ps. 115:5,6 [b]Jer. 10:23
5:27 [c]Job 31:6 Ps. 62:9 Jer. 6:30
5:28 [d]Foretold Is. 21:2 ver. 31 ch. 9:1 [e]ch. 6:28
5:29 [f]ver. 7
5:30 [g]Jer. 51:31,39,57

[1]Chald. *interpret* [m]Or, *fee* [n]Chald. *made to come down* [o]Or, *he made his heart equal*

5:22 THOU . . . HAST NOT HUMBLED THINE HEART, THOUGH THOU KNEWEST ALL THIS. Daniel reminded Belshazzar of how God had humbled Nebuchadnezzar. Though Belshazzar surely had heard about this tragic event, he refused to learn anything from it. His desecration of the Lord's holy vessels was a deliberate act of defiance toward the living God. Few people learn the lessons of history. Allegiance to the things of this world—the lust of the eyes, the lust of the flesh, and the pride of life (see 1 John 2:15–17; see article on THE CHRISTIAN'S RELATIONSHIP TO THE WORLD, p. 2004)—lead them along the same broad road to destruction that others before them have taken (cf. Mat. 7:13–14).

5:26 MENE; GOD HATH NUMBERED THY KINGDOM, AND FINISHED IT. "Mene" was written twice by the hand, for it had a twofold meaning: "numbered" and "tested." Daniel's interpretation was surprisingly simple: God had tested the kingdom of Babylon, found it to be wanting, and therefore numbered its days.

5:27 TEKEL; THOU ART WEIGHED . . . AND ART FOUND WANTING. The term "wanting" here means "defective" or "of poor quality." Belshazzar had been weighed on heaven's scales and was found seriously defective according to God's standard of measurement.

5:28 PERES; THY KINGDOM IS DIVIDED, AND GIVEN TO THE MEDES AND THE PERSIANS. Note that v. 25 has "upharsin." "U" is Aramaic for "and"; "pharsin" is the Aramaic plural of "peres," which has two meanings: "division" and "Persia." It signified the division of the kingdom of Babylon and its conquest by the Persians and the Medes.

31 [h]And Darius the Median took
the kingdom, [p]*being* [q]about three-
score and two years old.

Daniel in the den of lions

6 IT PLEASED Darius to set over
the kingdom an hundred and twen-
ty princes, which should be over the
whole kingdom;
2 And over these three presidents;
of whom Daniel *was* first: that the
princes might give accounts unto
them, and the king should have no
damage.
3 Then this Daniel was preferred
above the presidents and princes, [i]be-
cause an excellent spirit *was* in him;
and the king thought to set him over
the whole realm.
4 ¶ [j]Then the presidents and
princes sought to find occasion against
Daniel concerning the kingdom; but
they could find none occasion nor fault;
forasmuch as he *was* faithful, neither
was there any error or fault found in
him.
5 Then said these men, We shall not
find any occasion against this Daniel,
except we find *it* against him concern-
ing the law of his God.
6 Then these presidents and
princes [r]assembled together to the
king, and said thus unto him, [k]King
Darius, live for ever.
7 All the presidents of the kingdom,
the governors, and the princes, the
counsellors, and the captains, have
consulted together to establish a royal
statute, and to make a firm [s]decree,
that whosoever shall ask a petition of
any God or man for thirty days, save of
thee, O king, he shall be cast into the
den of lions.
8 Now, O king, establish the de-
cree, and sign the writing, that it be not
changed, according to the [l]law of the
Medes and Persians, which [t]altereth
not.
9 Wherefore king Darius signed the
writing and the decree.
10 ¶ Now when Daniel knew that
the writing was signed, he went into
his house; and his windows being open

5:31 [h]ch. 9:1
6:3 [i]ch. 5:12
6:4 [j]Eccl. 4:4
6:6 [k]ver. 21 Neh. 2:3 ch. 2:4
6:8 [l]ver. 12,15 Esth. 1:19 & 8:8

[p] Chald. he as *the son of* [q] Or, *now* [r] Or, *came tumultuously* [s] Or, *interdict* [t] Chald. *passeth not*

5:30 IN THAT NIGHT WAS BELSHAZZAR . . . SLAIN. Both Babylonian and Persian records indicate that when the Medo-Persian army approached Babylon, the people swung open the gates to admit his army without resistance. Belshazzar may have been the only one killed. A little later Cyrus entered the city and was hailed as the deliverer from the tyranny of Nabonidus and Belshazzar.

5:31 DARIUS THE MEDIAN TOOK THE KINGDOM. It is possible that "Darius" was a title Cyrus adopted when he took over Babylon; alternatively, it may have been another name for Gubaru, whom Cyrus appointed as his subordinate and who continued to rule in Babylon for some time after Cyrus died.

6:3 THE KING THOUGHT TO SET HIM OVER THE WHOLE REALM. Daniel was the foremost of three presidents or administrators who assisted Darius in ruling the empire. Because of an "excellent spirit" in Daniel, which included an extraordinary intelligence, the king planned to give him a new position above all the other administrators and princes or satraps. It was due to God's goodness that at eighty years of age his mind was still sharp and his abilities undiminished (cf. Moses, Caleb, and Joshua at age eighty—Ex. 7:7; Deut. 34:7; Josh. 14:10–11; 24:29).

6:5 NO OCCASION AGAINST THIS DANIEL . . . EXCEPT. Daniel's enemies had no hope of accusing him of wrongdoing. Their only hope of condemning him would be to require something that had official government sanction and conflicted with Daniel's loyalty to God and His word. This same strategy will be used by Satan against God's faithful people during the rule of the antichrist at the end of time. In order to find any ground on which to accuse God's people, he will create a situation where there is conflict between God's laws and official government requirements. Thus the antichrist will set up his image and command that it be worshiped as deity (cf. 3:1–6; see 2 Thes. 2:1–12; see article on THE AGE OF THE ANTICHRIST, p. 1896).

6:7 ALL THE PRESIDENTS . . . HAVE CONSULTED TOGETHER. Jealous because of Daniel's promotion, those under him plotted to make an issue of Daniel's faithfulness to the law of his God. They agreed together to get Darius to make a decree that they knew Daniel would not obey; his act of disobedience would force the king to command the death penalty. Daniel's uncompromising loyalty to God and His word is a good example for all believers. We should demonstrate integrity and do superior work even in the most difficult situations without compromising our Biblical convictions. In this way God will be honored.

6:10 DANIEL . . . PRAYED, AND GAVE THANKS . . . AS HE DID AFORETIME. The king's decree did not cause Daniel to become timid and change his habit of praying. His windows remained open toward Jerusalem where the temple once stood (cf. 2 Chr. 6:21). Though he knew of the danger, he did not let anything keep him from presenting his petitions before God (cf. Phil. 4:6). Likewise, we must not allow anything to cause us to neglect our daily prayer and devotion to God.

in his chamber [m]toward Jerusalem, he kneeled upon his knees [n]three times a day, and prayed, and gave thanks before his God, as he did aforetime.

11 Then these men assembled, and found Daniel praying and making supplication before his God.

12 [o]Then they came near, and spake before the king concerning the king's decree; Hast thou not signed a decree, that every man that shall ask *a petition* of any God or man within thirty days, save of thee, O king, shall be cast into the den of lions? The king answered and said, The thing *is* true, [p]according to the law of the Medes and Persians, which altereth not.

13 Then answered they and said before the king, That Daniel, [q]which *is* of the children of the captivity of Judah, [r]regardeth not thee, O king, nor the decree that thou hast signed, but maketh his petition three times a day.

14 Then the king, when he heard *these* words, [s]was sore displeased with himself, and set *his* heart on Daniel to deliver him: and he laboured till the going down of the sun to deliver him.

15 Then these men assembled unto the king, and said unto the king, Know, O king, that [t]the law of the Medes and Persians *is,* That no decree nor statute which the king establisheth may be changed.

16 Then the king commanded, and they brought Daniel, and cast *him* into the den of lions. *Now* the king spake and said unto Daniel, Thy God whom thou servest continually, he will deliver thee.

17 [u]And a stone was brought, and laid upon the mouth of the den; [v]and the king sealed it with his own signet, and with the signet of his lords; that the purpose might not be changed concerning Daniel.

18 ¶ Then the king went to his palace, and passed the night fasting: neither were [u]instruments of music brought before him: [w]and his sleep went from him.

19 Then the king arose very early in the morning, and went in haste unto the den of lions.

20 And when he came to the den, he cried with a lamentable voice unto Daniel: *and* the king spake and said to Daniel, O Daniel, servant of the living God, [x]is thy God, whom thou servest continually, able to deliver thee from the lions?

21 Then said Daniel unto the king, [y]O king, live for ever.

22 [z]My God hath sent his angel, and hath [a]shut the lions' mouths, that they have not hurt me: forasmuch as before him innocency was found in me; and also before thee, O king, have I done no hurt.

23 Then was the king exceeding glad for him, and commanded that they should take Daniel up out of the den. So Daniel was taken up out of the den, and no manner of hurt was found upon him, [b]because he believed in his God. Hab. 3:17-19

24 ¶ And the king commanded, [c]and they brought those men which had accused Daniel, and they cast *them* into the den of lions, them, [d]their children, and their wives; and the lions had the mastery of them, and brake all their bones in pieces or ever they came at the bottom of the den.

25 ¶ [e]Then king Darius wrote unto all people, nations, and languages, that dwell in all the earth; Peace be multiplied unto you.

6:10 [m]1 Ki. 8:44,48 Ps. 5:7 Jonah 2:4 [n]Ps. 55:17 Acts 2:1,2,15 & 3:1 & 10:9
6:12 [o]ch. 3:8 [p]ver. 8
6:13 [q]ch. 1:6 & 5:13 [r]ch. 3:12
6:14 [s]Mark 6:26
6:15 [t]ver. 8
6:17 [u]Lam. 3:53 [v]Mat. 27:66
6:18 [w]ch. 2:1
6:20 [x]ch. 3:15
6:21 [y]ch. 2:4
6:22 [z]ch. 3:28 [a]Heb. 11:33
6:23 [b]Heb. 11:33
6:24 [c]Deut. 19:19 [d]Esth. 9:10 See Deut. 24:16 2 Ki. 14:6
6:25 [e]ch. 4:1

[u] Or, *table*

6:17 A STONE WAS . . . LAID ON THE MOUTH OF THE DEN; AND THE KING SEALED IT. The den of lions was underground, with an opening at the top. A large flat stone was laid over the opening, and the king's seal meant it could not be opened without his authorization. Because of Daniel's integrity (v. 4) and his "excellent spirit" (v. 3), the king had come to admire Daniel and to respect Daniel's God. Thus, as the king dutifully fulfilled the letter of his decree, he expressed the hope that God would deliver Daniel (v. 16). Perhaps he had heard accounts of God's deliverance of Daniel's three friends from the fiery furnace (ch. 3).

6:23 NO MANNER OF HURT WAS FOUND UPON HIM, BECAUSE HE BELIEVED IN GOD. Though the king tried to encourage Daniel to believe in his God (v. 16), his voice the next morning did not express expectation that Daniel had been delivered (v. 20). But God's angel had shut the lions' mouths before the faithful prophet, and he was alive and well. This deliverance prompted Darius to testify to the power of a God who is greater than the power of lions (vv. 26–27). Note also that Daniel's name, meaning "God is my Judge," had been shown to be true in his own experience. He was vindicated by the Lord and judged to be right with respect to his choosing the purity of God's law (ch. 1) and to his faithfulness in prayer (ch. 6).

26 [f]I make a decree, That in every dominion of my kingdom men [g]tremble and fear before the God of Daniel: [h]for he *is* the living God, and stedfast for ever, and his kingdom *that* which shall not be [i]destroyed, and his dominion *shall be even* unto the end.

27 He delivereth and rescueth, [j]and he worketh signs and wonders in heaven and in earth, who hath delivered Daniel from the [v]power of the lions.

28 So this Daniel prospered in the reign of Darius, [k]and in the reign of [l]Cyrus the Persian.

Daniel's dream of four beasts

7 IN THE first year of Belshazzar king of Babylon [m]Daniel [w]had a dream and [n]visions of his head upon his bed: then he wrote the dream, *and* told the sum of the [x]matters.

2 Daniel spake and said, I saw in my vision by night, and, behold, the four winds of the heaven strove upon the great sea.

3 And four great beasts [o]came up from the sea, diverse one from another.

4 The first *was* [p]like a lion, and had eagle's wings: I beheld till the wings thereof were plucked, [y]and it was lifted up from the earth, and made stand upon the feet as a man, and a man's heart was given to it.

5 [q]And behold another beast, a second, like to a bear, and [z]it raised up itself on one side, and *it had* three ribs in the mouth of it between the teeth of it: and they said thus unto it, Arise, devour much flesh.

6 After this I beheld, and lo another, like a leopard, which had upon the back of it four wings of a fowl; the beast had also [r]four heads; and dominion was given to it.

7 After this I saw in the night visions, and behold [s]a fourth beast, dreadful and terrible, and strong exceedingly; and it had great iron teeth: it devoured and brake in pieces, and stamped the residue with the feet of it: and it *was* diverse from all the beasts that *were* before it; [t]and it had ten horns.

8 I considered the horns, and, behold, [u]there came up among them another little horn, before whom there were three of the first horns plucked up by the roots: and, behold, in this horn *were* eyes like the eyes [v]of man, [w]and a mouth speaking great things.

9 ¶ [x]I beheld till the thrones were cast down, and [y]the Ancient of days did sit, [z]whose garment *was* white as

6:26 [f]ch. 3:29 [g]Ps. 99:1 [h]ch. 4:34 [i]ch. 2:44 & 4:3,34 Luke 1:33 **6:27** [j]ch. 4:3 **6:28** [k]ch. 1:21 [l]Ezra 1:1,2 **7:1** [m]Num. 12:6 Amos 3:7 [n]ch. 2:28 **7:3** [o]Rev. 13:1 **7:4** [p]Deut. 28:49 2 Sam. 1:23 Jer. 48:40 Ezek. 17:3 Hab. 1:8 **7:5** [q]ch. 2:39 **7:6** [r]ch. 8:8,22 **7:7** [s]ch. 2:40 [t]ch. 2:41 Rev. 13:1 **7:8** [u]ch. 8:9 [v]Rev. 9:7 [w]Ps. 12:3 Rev. 13:5 **7:9** [x]Rev. 20:4 [y]Ps. 90:2 [z]Ps. 104:2 Rev. 1:14

[v] Heb. *hand* [w] Chald. *saw* [x] Or, *words* [y] Or, *wherewith* [z] Or, *it raised up one dominion*

7:1 DANIEL HAD A DREAM AND VISIONS. The words "dream" and "vision" are sometimes used interchangeably in the Bible. Daniel interpreted the prophetic dreams of others; God also gave Daniel himself unusual dreams and visions. He was probably close to seventy years old by this time. Prophetic dreams and visions are also among the manifestations that will characterize God's people in the last days when the Holy Spirit's ministry and activity are fully manifested in believers (cf. Joel 2:28; Acts 2:16, note; see article on SPIRITUAL GIFTS FOR BELIEVERS, p. 1790).

7:3 FOUR GREAT BEASTS CAME UP FROM THE SEA. Some modern writers take these beasts to represent nations existing in the end times. Most Bible expositors, however, take this vision to parallel Nebuchadnezzar's dream in ch. 2 (see 2:37–43, notes) but to reveal the bestial, i.e., the inner characteristics of the kingdoms. (1) The lion, a symbol of royal power, represents the Neo-Babylonian empire. The eagle, the king of birds, may specifically represent King Nebuchadnezzar's power, and the plucking of the wings represents what happened in ch. 4.

(2) The bear, raised up on one side, represents Medo-Persia, with Persia dominating Media. The three ribs in its mouth may represent its conquests of Babylon, Lydia, and Egypt.

(3) The leopard, a powerful and swift animal, with its four wings, represents Alexander's Greek empire and his rapid conquests. The four heads are the four kingdoms that came out of his empire when he died, for it was divided among his generals: Lysimachus (who took Thrace and Bithynia), Cassander (who took Greece and Macedonia), Seleucus (who took Babylonia and Syria), and Ptolemy (who took Palestine, Egypt, and Arabia).

(4) The fourth beast, dreadful and terrible, and with iron teeth, represents Rome, as does the remainder of the image, including the ten toes.

7:8 LITTLE HORN. The little horn symbolizes the last great ruler in the world—the antichrist (1 John 2:18), the man of sin (2 Thes. 2:3,8), the beast who puts down three of the ten kings (vv. 11,24; Rev. 13:7; 19:19–20). He will make war with God's saints, overpower them (vv.21–22,25), and speak words against God (v. 25). When Jesus Christ comes (v. 9), the saints will possess the kingdom (vv.22,27; cf. Rev. 11:15–18; 20:4–6); the antichrist will be destroyed (vv. 11,26) and consigned to the burning fire (Rev. 19:20). See also 7:13, note.

7:9 THE ANCIENT OF DAYS DID SIT. "Ancient of days" is another way of recognizing God as the Eternal One, the One Abraham acknowl-

snow, and the hair of his head like the
pure wool: his throne *was like* the fiery
flame, [a]*and* his wheels *as* burning fire.
10 [b]A fiery stream issued and
came forth from before him: [c]thou-
sand thousands ministered unto him,
and ten thousand times ten thousand
stood before him: [d]the judgment was
set, and the books were opened.
11 I beheld then because of the
voice of the great words which the horn
spake: [e]I beheld *even* till the beast
was slain, and his body destroyed, and
given to the burning flame.
12 As concerning the rest of the
beasts, they had their dominion taken
away: yet [a]their lives were prolonged
for a season and time.
13 I saw in the night visions, and,
behold, [f]*one* like the Son of man came
with the clouds of heaven, and came to
the Ancient of days, and they brought
him near before him.
14 [g]And there was given him do-
minion, and glory, and a kingdom, that
all [h]people, nations, and languages,
should serve him: his dominion *is* [i]an
everlasting dominion, which shall not
pass away, and his kingdom *that* which
shall not be destroyed.

The dream explained

15 ¶ I Daniel was grieved in my
spirit in the midst of *my* [b]body, and
the visions of my head troubled me.
16 I came near unto one of them
that stood by, and asked him the truth
of all this. So he told me, and made me
know the interpretation of the things.
17 These great beasts, which are
four, *are* four kings, *which* shall arise
out of the earth.
18 But [j]the saints of the [c]most
High shall take the kingdom, and pos-
sess the kingdom for ever, even for
ever and ever.
19 Then I would know the truth of
the fourth beast, which was diverse
[d]from all the others, exceeding dread-
ful, whose teeth *were of* iron, and his
nails *of* brass; *which* devoured, brake in
pieces, and stamped the residue with
his feet;
20 And of the ten horns that *were* in
his head, and *of* the other which came
up, and before whom three fell; even *of*
that horn that had eyes, and a mouth
that spake very great things, whose
look *was* more stout than his fellows.
21 I beheld, [k]and the same horn
made war with the saints, and pre-
vailed against them;
22 Until the Ancient of days came,
[l]and judgment was given to the saints
of the most High; and the time came
that the saints possessed the kingdom.
23 Thus he said, The fourth beast
shall be [m]the fourth kingdom upon
earth, which shall be diverse from all
kingdoms, and shall devour the whole
earth, and shall tread it down, and
break it in pieces.
24 [n]And the ten horns out of this

7:9 [a]Ezek. 1:15 **7:10** [b]Ps. 50:3 Is. 30:33 & 66:15 [c]1 Ki. 22:19 Ps. 68:17 Rev. 5:11 [d]Rev. 20:4 **7:11** [e]Rev. 19:20 **7:13** [f]Ezek. 1:26 Mat. 24:30 Rev. 1:7 **7:14** [g]Ps. 2:6-8 Mat. 28:18 John 3:35 1 Cor. 15:27 Eph. 1:22 [h]ch. 3:4 [i]Ps. 145:13 Mic. 4:7 Luke 1:33 John 12:34 Heb. 12:28

7:18 [j]Is. 60:12 2 Tim. 2:11 Rev. 2:26 **7:21** [k]Rev. 17:14 **7:22** [l]Rev. 1:6 **7:23** [m]ch. 2:40 **7:24** [n]Rev. 17:12

[a] Chald. *a prolonging in life was given them*
[b] Chald. *sheath* [c] Chald. *high ones,* i.e. *things,* or, *places* [d] Chald. *from all those*

edged as "the Judge of all the earth" (Gen. 18:25). He is pictured as judging all people and all kingdoms at the end of time. The description of God in this verse also reveals His holiness ("whose garment *was* white as snow"), majesty ("the hair of his head like the pure wool"), and fiery justice ("his throne *was like* the fiery flame, *and* his wheels *as* burning fire").

7:13 *ONE* LIKE THE SON OF MAN CAME. This majestic being is presented before God the Father as a person separate and distinct from Him, in order to receive an eternal kingdom that will never be given to others (as were the preceding kingdoms). The clouds of heaven are probably clouds of glory (cf. Ex. 40:34,38; Acts 1:9,11; 1 Thes. 4:17; Rev. 1:7), indicating that He is the divine Son (Mat. 26:64), our Lord Jesus Christ (cf. Luke 21:27; John 1:51).

7:17 FOUR KINGS . . . OUT OF THE EARTH. "Out of the earth" does not contradict "up from the sea" (v. 3), since in the Bible the sea is symbolic of the peoples or nations of the earth (cf. Rev. 13:1).

7:18 SAINTS. . . TAKE THE KINGDOM. The Aramaic is better translated, "holy ones . . . receive the kingdom" (cf. Mat. 5:3,10). The kingdom belongs to the Son of man (vv. 13–14), but the saints (who here probably include the saints of all ages) share in His rule (cf. Rev. 3:21). Saints are those who are holy (1) because in their relationship to the holy God, they are sanctified by His holy presence, and (2) because they have separated themselves from sin and the corrupt world and consecrated themselves instead to the service and worship of God.

7:22 JUDGMENT WAS GIVEN TO THE SAINTS. During the tribulation, the saints will be persecuted by the antichrist. As an answer to their prayers (Rev. 6:10; 8:3–4), God will terminate the authority of the antichrist and grant to his people the power to rule with Him.

7:24–25 ANOTHER SHALL RISE. The little horn (see v. 8, note) will appear after the ten horns (ten kingdoms or nations), i.e., at the end of this present age in the area of the old Roman empire. The little horn here is different from the little horn

kingdom *are* ten kings *that* shall arise:
and another shall rise after them; and
he shall be diverse from the first, and
he shall subdue three kings.
25 [o]And he shall speak *great*
words against the most High, and shall
[p]wear out the saints of the most High,
and [q]think to change times and laws:
and [r]they shall be given into his hand
[s]until a time and times and the divid-
ing of time.
26 [t]But the judgment shall sit, and
they shall take away his dominion, to
consume and to destroy *it* unto the end.
27 And the [u]kingdom and domin-
ion, and the greatness of the kingdom
under the whole heaven, shall be given
to the people of the saints of the most
High, [v]whose kingdom *is* an everlast-
ing kingdom, [w]and all [e]dominions
shall serve and obey him.
28 Hitherto *is* the end of the matter.
As for me Daniel, [x]my cogitations
much troubled me, and my counte-
nance changed in me: but I [y]kept the
matter in my heart.

Vision of the ram, goat and horn

8 IN THE third year of the reign of
king Belshazzar a vision appeared
unto me, *even unto* me Daniel, after
that which appeared unto me [z]at the
first.
2 And I saw in a vision; and it came
to pass, when I saw, that I *was* at
[a]Shushan *in* the palace, which *is* in
the province of Elam; and I saw in a
vision, and I was by the river of Ulai.
3 Then I lifted up mine eyes, and
saw, and, behold, there stood before
the river a ram which had *two* horns:
and the *two* horns *were* high; but one
was higher than [f]the other, and the
higher came up last.
4 I saw the ram pushing westward,
and northward, and southward; so that
no beasts might stand before him, nei-
ther *was there any* that could deliver
out of his hand; [b]but he did according
to his will, and became great.
5 And as I was considering, behold,
an he goat came from the west on the
face of the whole earth, and [g]touched
not the ground: and the goat *had* [h]a
notable horn between his eyes.
6 And he came to the ram that had
two horns, which I had seen standing
before the river, and ran unto him in
the fury of his power.
7 And I saw him come close unto
the ram, and he was moved with choler
against him, and smote the ram, and
brake his two horns: and there was no
power in the ram to stand before him,
but he cast him down to the ground,
and stamped upon him: and there was
none that could deliver the ram out of
his hand.
8 Therefore the he goat waxed very
great: and when he was strong, the
great horn was broken; and for it came
up [c]four notable ones toward the four
winds of heaven.
9 [d]And out of one of them came
forth a little horn, which waxed ex-
ceeding great, [e]toward the south, and
toward the east, and toward the
[f]pleasant *land*.
10 [g]And it waxed great, *even* [i]to
[h]the host of heaven; and [i]it cast

7:25 [o]Is. 37:23 [p]Rev. 17:6 [q]ch. 2:21 [r]Rev. 13:7 [s]Rev. 12:14
7:26 [t]ver. 10,22
7:27 [u]ver. 14,18 [v]Luke 1:33 John 12:34 Rev. 11:15 [w]Is. 60:12
7:28 [x]ch. 8:27 [y]Luke 2:19
8:1 [z]ch. 7:1
8:2 [a]Esth. 1:2
8:4 [b]ch. 5:19
8:8 [c]ver. 22
8:9 [d]ch. 11:21 [e]ch. 11:25 [f]Ps. 48:2
8:10 [g]ch. 11:28 [h]Is. 14:13 [i]Rev. 12:4

[e] Or, *rulers* [f] Heb. *the second* [g] Or, *none touched* him *in the earth* [h] Heb. *a horn of sight* [i] Or, *against the host*

of 8:9, who comes out of the Greek kingdom and represents Antiochus Epiphanes, a type of the antichrist. This little horn comes out of the Roman beast and takes control of three kingdoms by force; the remaining kingdoms seem to delegate their powers to him. He speaks great words of blasphemy against the Most High, i.e., the Ancient of days, God the Father (cf. 2 Thes. 2:4). He will "wear out the saints" by persecution as he tries to change "times" (seasons for special religious worship) and the laws of God. He will continue to persecute the saints for a period of three and one-half years until he is destroyed (cf. 9:27; Rev. 11:2–3; 12:11; 13:5). All this serves to identify the little horn with the first beast of the book of Revelation (see Rev. 13), the one who is usually called the antichrist (see articles on THE GREAT TRIBULATION, p. 1456, and THE AGE OF THE ANTICHRIST, p. 1896).

8:1 THE THIRD YEAR. The third year is 551 B.C. The remainder of the book of Daniel is written in Hebrew (cf. 2:4, note).

8:3 A RAM WHICH HAD *TWO* HORNS. This ram represents the Medo-Persian empire (see v. 20).

8:5 AN HE GOAT. The goat from the west is the Greek empire and its great horn represents Alexander the Great (see vv. 21–22), who died prematurely at the height of his power. Subsequently, his empire was divided among his four generals (see 7:3, note).

8:9 A LITTLE HORN. Out of one of the horns came a little horn; it refers to Antiochus Epiphanes, who in 168 B.C. set up an image of the Greek god Zeus in the temple and sacrificed a pig on the altar (see vv. 23–25). Judas Maccabeus later recaptured Jerusalem and reconsecrated the temple and altar (165 B.C.).

down *some* of the host and of the stars
to the ground, and stamped upon them.
11 Yea, [j]he magnified *himself* even
[j]to [k]the prince of the host, [l]and
[k]by him [m]the daily *sacrifice* was taken
away, and the place of his sanctuary
was cast down.
12 And [n]an[l] host was given *him*
against the daily *sacrifice* by reason of
transgression, and it cast down [o]the
truth to the ground; and it [p]practised,
and prospered.
13 ¶ Then I heard [q]one saint
speaking, and another saint said unto
[m] [n]that certain *saint* which spake,
How long *shall be* the vision *concerning*
the daily *sacrifice,* and the transgres-
sion [r]of[o] desolation, to give both the
sanctuary and the host to be trodden
under foot?
14 And he said unto me, Unto
two thousand and three hundred
[p]days; then shall the sanctuary be
[q]cleansed.

Gabriel explains the vision

15 ¶ And it came to pass, when I,
even I Daniel, had seen the vision, and
[s]sought for the meaning, then, be-
hold, there stood before me [t]as the
appearance of a man.
16 And I heard a man's voice [u]be-
tween *the banks of* Ulai, which called,
and said, [v]Gabriel, make this *man* to
understand the vision.
17 So he came near where I stood:
and when he came, I was afraid, and
[w]fell upon my face: but he said unto
me, Understand, O son of man: for at
the time of the end *shall be* the vision.
18 [x]Now as he was speaking with
me, I was in a deep sleep on my face
toward the ground: [y]but he touched
me, and [r]set me upright.
19 And he said, Behold, I will make
thee know what shall be in the last end
of the indignation: [z]for at the time ap-
pointed the end *shall be.*
20 The ram which thou sawest hav-
ing *two* horns *are* the kings of Media
and Persia.
21 And the rough goat *is* the king of
Grecia: and the great horn that *is* be-
tween his eyes [a]*is* the first king.
22 [b]Now that being broken,
whereas four stood up for it, four king-
doms shall stand up out of the nation,
but not in his power.
23 And in the latter time of their
kingdom, when the transgressors
[s]are come to the full, a king [c]of
fierce countenance, and understanding
dark sentences, shall stand up.
24 And his power shall be mighty,
[d]but not by his own power: and he
shall destroy wonderfully, [e]and shall
prosper, and practise, [f]and shall de-
stroy the mighty and the [t]holy people.
25 And [g]through his policy also he
shall cause craft to prosper in his
hand; [h]and he shall magnify *himself* in
his heart, and by [u]peace shall destroy
many: [i]he shall also stand up against
the Prince of princes; but he shall be
[j]broken without hand.
26 And the vision of the evening
and the morning which was told *is* true:
[k]wherefore shut thou up the vision;
for it *shall be* for many days.
27 [l]And I Daniel fainted, and was
sick *certain* days; afterward I rose up,
and did the king's business; and I was
astonished at the vision, but none un-
derstood *it.*

8:11 [j]ch. 11:36 [k]Josh. 5:14 [l]ch. 11:31 [m]Ex. 29:38
8:12 [n]ch. 11:31 [o]Ps. 119:43 Is. 59:14 [p]ver. 4
8:13 [q]ch. 4:13 1 Pet. 1:12 [r]ch. 11:31
8:15 [s]1 Pet. 1:10 [t]Ezek. 1:26
8:16 [u]ch. 12:6,7 [v]Luke 1:19
8:17 [w]Ezek. 1:28 Rev. 1:17
8:18 [x]Luke 9:32 [y]Ezek. 2:2
8:19 [z]Hab. 2:3
8:21 [a]ch. 11:3
8:22 [b]ch. 11:4
8:23 [c]Deut. 28:50
8:24 [d]Rev. 17:13 [e]ch. 11:36 [f]ch. 7:25
8:25 [g]ch. 11:21 [h]ch. 11:36 [i]ch. 11:36 [j]Job 34:20 Lam. 4:6
8:26 [k]Ezek. 12:27 Rev. 22:10
8:27 [l]ch. 7:28

[j] Or, *against* [k] Or, *from him* [l] Or, *the host was given over for the transgression against the daily* sacrifice [m] Or, *the numberer of secrets,* or, *the wonderful numberer* [n] Heb. *Palmoni* [o] Or, *making desolate* [p] Heb. *evening morning* [q] Heb. *justified* [r] Heb. *made me stand upon my standing* [s] Heb. *are accomplished* [t] Heb. *people of the holy ones* [u] Or, *prosperity*

8:14 THEN SHALL THE SANCTUARY BE CLEANSED. The cleansing of the sanctuary took place three years and two months after the Lord's altar had been removed by Antiochus. "Days" is literally "evenings and mornings" (see v. 26 for a reference to this same period of time). Thus the time elapsed was actually 1,150 days.

8:16 GABRIEL, MAKE THIS *MAN* TO UNDERSTAND. Gabriel (literally, "Mighty one of God" or "God has shown Himself mighty") is a leading angel who also appears to Daniel in 9:21, to Zacharias in Luke 1:19, and to the virgin Mary in Luke 1:26 (see article on ANGELS AND THE ANGEL OF THE LORD, p. 368).

8:23 A KING OF FIERCE COUNTENANCE. Because of the mention of "the latter time," some believe Gabriel is speaking here of the antichrist. However, the reference is more likely to the latter time of the four kingdoms that came out of Alexander's kingdom (see v. 5, note). Thus, the king of fierce countenance is Antiochus Epiphanes, who is a type of the antichrist. The reference to "the evening and the morning" (v. 26; see v. 14, note; the singular here is collective) indicates that the time is still that of Antiochus.

Daniel's prayer for the people

9 IN THE first year [m]of Darius the son of Ahasuerus, of the seed of the Medes, [v]which was made king over the realm of the Chaldeans;

2 In the first year of his reign I Daniel understood by books the number of the years, whereof the word of the LORD came to [n]Jeremiah the prophet, that he would accomplish seventy years in the desolations of Jerusalem.

3 ¶ [o]And I set my face unto the Lord God, to seek by prayer and supplications, with fasting, and sackcloth, and ashes:

4 And I prayed unto the LORD my God, and made my confession, and said, O [p]Lord, the great and dreadful God, keeping the covenant and mercy to them that love him, and to them that keep his commandments;

5 [q]We have sinned, and have committed iniquity, and have done wickedly, and have rebelled, even by departing from thy precepts and from thy judgments:

6 [r]Neither have we hearkened unto thy servants the prophets, which spake in thy name to our kings, our princes, and our fathers, and to all the people of the land. Mic. 6:8

7 O Lord, [s]righteousness [w]*belongeth* unto thee, but unto us confusion of faces, as at this day; to the men of Judah, and to the inhabitants of Jerusalem, and unto all Israel, *that are* near, and *that are* far off, through all the countries whither thou hast driven them, because of their trespass that they have trespassed against thee.

8 O Lord, to us *belongeth* confusion of face, to our kings, to our princes, and to our fathers, because we have sinned against thee.

9 [t]To the Lord our God *belong* mercies and forgivenesses, though we have rebelled against him;

10 Neither have we obeyed the voice of the LORD our God, to walk in his laws, which he set before us by his servants the prophets.

11 Yea, [u]all Israel have transgressed thy law, even by departing, that they might not obey thy voice; therefore the curse is poured upon us, and the oath that *is* written in the [v]law of Moses the servant of God, because we have sinned against him.

12 And he hath [w]confirmed his words, which he spake against us, and against our judges that judged us, by bringing upon us a great evil: [x]for under the whole heaven hath not been done as hath been done upon Jerusalem.

13 [y]As *it is* written in the law of Moses, all this evil is come upon us: [z]yet [x]made we not our prayer before the LORD our God, that we might turn from our iniquities, and understand thy truth.

14 Therefore hath the LORD [a]watched upon the evil, and brought it upon us: for [b]the LORD our God *is* righteous in all his works which he doeth: for we obeyed not his voice.

15 And now, O Lord our God, [c]that hast brought thy people forth out of the land of Egypt with a mighty hand, and hast [y]gotten thee [d]renown, as at this day; we have sinned, we have done wickedly.

16 ¶ O Lord, [e]according to all thy righteousness, I beseech thee, let thine anger and thy fury be turned away from thy city Jerusalem, [f]thy holy moun-

9:1 [m]ch. 1:21
9:2 [n]2 Chr. 36:21 Jer. 25:11
9:3 [o]Neh. 1:4 Jer. 29:12 ch. 6:10
9:4 [p]Ex. 20:6 Deut. 7:9
9:5 [q]1 Ki. 8:47 Ps. 106:6 Jer. 14:7
9:6 [r]2 Chr. 36:15
9:7 [s]Neh. 9:33
9:9 [t]Ps. 130:4,7
9:11 [u]Is. 1:4-6 [v]Lev. 26:14 Deut. 27:15 Lam. 2:17
9:12 [w]Zech. 1:6 [x]Lam. 1:12 Ezek. 5:9 Amos 3:2
9:13 [y]Deut. 28:15 Lam. 2:17 [z]Is. 9:13 Jer. 2:30 Hos. 7:7
9:14 [a]Jer. 31:28 [b]Neh. 9:33
9:15 [c]Ex. 32:11 1 Ki. 8:51 Neh. 1:10 [d]Ex. 14:18 Neh. 9:10 Jer. 32:20
9:16 [e]1 Sam. 12:7 Ps. 31:1 Mic. 6:4,5 [f]Zech. 8:3

[v] Or, *in which he* [w] Or, *thou* hast [x] Heb. *entreated we not the face of the* [y] Heb. *made thee a name*

9:2 SEVENTY YEARS. Jeremiah had prophesied that restoration would begin for Jerusalem in seventy years (Jer. 25:11–12; 29:10–14). The seventy years were just about up, and still there was no indication of the promised return and restoration; thus Daniel was severely troubled. From this verse, it is clear that Daniel expected a literal fulfillment of Jeremiah's prophecy. In general, prophecies should be interpreted literally unless there is something in the context to show that a prophecy or vision is symbolic. Even then, the symbols represent literal historical realities (cf. 7:3, note; 8:3,-5, notes).

9:5 WE HAVE SINNED. Daniel did not sit back and passively wait for the promised restoration to come about (see previous note). Instead, he began to intercede earnestly with prayer and fasting (v. 3) for the fulfillment of God's word. Daniel began his intercessory prayer by recognizing the awe-inspiring greatness of God, His faithful love, and His covenant mercy shown to those who love and obey Him. Then he made his confession, identifying himself with the people of Israel who had sinned and rebelled against God. He asked for Jerusalem's restoration not because of any righteousness on the part of Daniel or of Israel, but "for the Lord's sake" (9:17–18). When God responded, He demonstrated His great mercy and loving compassion as a God who fulfills His promises.

INTERCESSION

Dan. 9:3 "And I set my face unto the Lord God, to seek by prayer and supplications, with fasting, and sackcloth, and ashes."

Intercession may be defined as holy, believing, persevering prayer whereby someone pleads with God on behalf of another or others who desperately need God's intervention. Daniel's prayer in Dan. 9 is an intercessory prayer, as he prays earnestly for the restoration of Jerusalem and for the entire nation. The Bible records the intercession of Christ and the Holy Spirit, and of numerous godly men and women under both the old and new covenants.

THE INTERCESSION OF CHRIST AND THE HOLY SPIRIT. (1) During His earthly ministry, Jesus prayed for the multitudes whom He came to seek and to save (Luke 19:10). He wept in brokenness over the city of Jerusalem (Luke 19:41). He prayed for his disciples, both individually (see Luke 22:32) and as a group (John 17:6–26). He even prayed for His enemies while He was hanging on the cross (Luke 23:34).

(2) A present aspect of Christ's ministry is to intercede on our behalf before the throne of God (Rom. 8:34; Heb. 7:25; 9:24; see 7:25, note). For this reason, John calls Jesus our "advocate" with the Father, i.e., one who pleads our case (see 1 John 2:1, note). Christ's intercession is essential to our salvation (cf. Is. 53:12); without His grace, mercy, and help mediated to us through His intercession, we would fall away from God and once again become enslaved to sin.

(3) The Holy Spirit is also involved in intercession. Paul states, "We know not what we should pray for as we ought: but the Spirit itself maketh intercession for us with groanings which cannot be uttered" (Rom. 8:26, see note). The Holy Spirit through the human spirit of the believer intercedes "according to *the will of* God" (Rom. 8:27). Thus, Christ intercedes for the believer in heaven; the Spirit intercedes within the believer on earth.

THE INTERCESSION OF THE BELIEVER. The Bible often refers to the intercessory prayers of believers and records numerous examples of remarkable, powerful prayers. (1) In the O.T., the leaders of God's people, such as kings (1 Chr. 21:17; 2 Chr. 6:14–42), prophets (1 Ki. 18:41–45; Dan. 9), and priests (Ezra 9:5–15; Joel 1:13; 2:17–18), were to lead the way in intercessory prayer for the nation. Superb examples of O.T. intercession include Abraham's prayers for Ishmael (Gen. 17:18) and for Sodom and Gomorrah (Gen. 18:23–32), David's prayers for a son (2 Sam. 12:16; 1 Chr. 29:19), and Job's for his children (Job 1:5). In Moses' life, we see the supreme O.T. example of the power of intercessory prayer. On several occasions, he prayed intensely to God to change His declared will, even when God had told Moses His course of action. For example, after the Israelites rebelled against the Lord and refused to go into Canaan, God told Moses that He would destroy them and make a greater nation of Moses (Num. 14:1–12). Moses then took the matter to the Lord in prayer and pleaded for them (Num. 14:13–19). At the conclusion of his prayer God said, "I have pardoned according to thy word" (Num. 14:20; see also Ex. 32:11–14; Num. 11:2; 12:13; 21:7; 27:5; see article on EFFECTIVE PRAYING, p. 540). Other powerful O.T. intercessors include Elijah (1 Ki. 18:21–46; Jas. 5:16–18), Daniel (Dan. 9:2–23), and Nehemiah (Neh. 1:3–11).

(2) The N.T. presents even more examples of intercessory prayers. The Gospels record how parents and others interceded with Jesus on behalf of loved ones. Parents pleaded with Jesus to heal their sick children (Mark 5:22–43; John 4:47–53); a group of mothers asked Jesus to bless their children (Mark 10:13); a man pleaded for his servant to be healed (Mat. 8:6–13); and the mother of James and John interceded with Jesus on their behalf (Mat. 20:20–21).

(3) The N.T. church frequently interceded on behalf of various individuals. For example, the church in Jerusalem gathered together to pray for Peter's release from prison (Acts 12:5,12). The church in Antioch prayed for the success of the ministry of Barnabas and Paul (Acts 13:3). James specifically instructs the elders of the church to pray for the sick (Jas. 5:14) and for all Christians to "pray one for another" (Jas. 5:16; cf. Heb. 13:18–19). Paul goes one step further and asks that prayers be offered for *everyone* (1 Tim. 2:1–3).

(4) The apostle Paul deserves special mention. In many of his letters he tells of his own prayers on behalf of various churches or individuals (e.g., Rom. 1:9–10; 2 Cor. 13:7; Phil. 1:4–11; Col. 1:3,9–12; 1 Thes. 1:2–3; 2 Thes. 1:11–12; 2 Tim. 1:3; Philem. 4–6). On occasion he records his prayers (e.g., Eph. 1:15–19; 3:14–19; 1 Thes. 3:11–13). At the same time, Paul frequently requests the churches to pray for him, knowing that only through their prayers will his ministry have its fullest effect (Rom. 15:30–32; 2 Cor. 1:11; Eph. 6:18–20; Phil. 1:19; Col. 4:3–4; 1 Thes. 5:25; 2 Thes. 3:1–2).

PURPOSES OF INTERCESSORY PRAYERS. In the numerous intercessory prayers in the Scriptures, God-fearing saints pleaded with God to turn aside His judgment (Gen. 18:23–32; Num. 14:13–19; Joel 2:17), to restore His people (Neh. 1; Dan. 9), to deliver individuals from danger (Acts 12:5,12; Rom. 15:31), and to bless His people (Num. 6:24–26; 1 Ki. 18:41–45; Ps. 122:6–8). Intercessors also prayed for the Holy Spirit's power to come (Acts 8:15–17; Eph. 3:14–17), for someone to be healed (1 Ki. 17:20–21; Acts 28:8; Jas. 5:14–16), for the forgiveness of sins (Ezra 9:5–15; Dan. 9; Acts 7:60), for the ability of people in authority to rule well (1 Chr. 29:19; 1 Tim. 2:1–2), for Christian growth (Phil. 1:9–11; Col. 1:10–11), for effective pastors (2 Tim. 1:3–7), for effective mission work (Mat. 9:38; Eph. 6:19–20), for the salvation of others (Rom. 10:1), and for people to praise God (Ps. 67:3–5). Anything that the Bible reveals as God's perfect will for His people (see article on THE WILL OF GOD, p. 1060) can appropriately be the focus of intercessory prayer.

tain: because for our sins, [g]and for the
iniquities of our fathers, [h]Jerusalem
and thy people [i]*are become* a reproach
to all *that are* about us.
17 Now therefore, O our God, hear
the prayer of thy servant, and his sup-
plications, [j]and cause thy face to
shine upon thy sanctuary [k]that is des-
olate, [l]for the Lord's sake.
18 [m]O my God, incline thine ear,
and hear; open thine eyes, [n]and be-
hold our desolations, and the city
[o]which[z] is called by thy name: for we
do not [a]present our supplications be-
fore thee for our righteousnesses, but
for thy great mercies.
19 O Lord, hear; O Lord, forgive;
O Lord, hearken and do; defer not,
for thine own sake, O my God: for
thy city and thy people are called by
thy name.

The meaning of the seventy weeks

20 ¶ And whiles I *was* speaking, and
praying, and confessing my sin and the
sin of my people Israel, and presenting
my supplication before the LORD my
God for the holy mountain of my God;
21 Yea, whiles I *was* speaking in
prayer, even the man [p]Gabriel, whom
I had seen in the vision at the begin-
ning, being caused to fly [b]swiftly,
touched me about the time of the eve-
ning oblation.

9:16 [g]Ex. 20:5 [h]Lam. 2:16 [i]Ps. 79:4 **9:17** [j]Num. 6:25 [k]Lam. 5:18 [l]John 16:24 **9:18** [m]Is. 37:17 [n]Ex. 3:7 [o]Jer. 25:29 **9:21** [p]ch. 8:16 **9:23** [q]Mat. 24:15 **9:24** [r]Is. 53:10 [s]Rev. 14:6 [t]Ps. 45:7 **9:25** [u]John 1:41 [v]Is. 55:4

22 And he informed *me,* and talked
with me, and said, O Daniel, I am now
come forth [c]to give thee skill and un-
derstanding.
23 At the beginning of thy supplica-
tions the [d]commandment came forth,
and I am come to show *thee;* for thou
art [e]greatly beloved: therefore [q]un-
derstand the matter, and consider the
vision.
24 Seventy weeks are determined
upon thy people and upon thy holy
city, [f]to finish the transgression, and
[g]to make an end of sins, [r]and to
make reconciliation for iniquity,
[s]and to bring in everlasting righteous-
ness, and to seal up the vision and
[h]prophecy, [t]and to anoint the most
Holy.
25 Know therefore and understand,
that from the going forth of the com-
mandment to restore and to build Jeru-
salem unto [u]the Messiah [v]the Prince
shall be seven weeks, and threescore
and two weeks: the street shall be built
again, and the wall, even in troublous
times.
26 And after threescore and two

[z] Heb. *whereupon thy name is called* [a] Heb. *cause to fall* [b] Heb. *with weariness,* or, *flight* [c] Heb. *to make thee skilful of understanding* [d] Heb. *word* [e] Heb. a man *of desires* [f] Or, *to restrain* [g] Or, *to seal up* [h] Heb. *prophet*

9:24 SEVENTY WEEKS. Daniel's prophecy here concerning Israel and the holy city is crucial for the last days of this age. The word translated "weeks" here means a unit of seven years. Hence, "seventy weeks" is a period of 490 years. Six specific things would be accomplished for Israel during the 490 years. (1) An atonement for iniquity will be made, accomplished in the atoning death of Jesus.

(2) There will be "an end of sins." All Israel (i.e., the remnant) will return to God in righteousness (see Rom. 11:26, note; see article on ISRAEL IN GOD'S PLAN OF SALVATION, p. 1748).

(3) The "transgression" will be finished; i.e., the national transgression of unbelief will cease (cf. Jer. 33:7–8; Ezek. 37:21–23).

(4) A rule of "everlasting righteousness" will be brought in (cf. Is. 59:2–21; Jer. 31:31–34).

(5) Prophecy will be fulfilled and completed.

(6) Jesus Christ will be anointed as King (cf. Ezek. 21:26–27).

9:25 SEVEN WEEKS, AND THREESCORE AND TWO WEEKS. God revealed to Daniel that sixty-nine periods of sevens, i.e., 483 years, would occur between the time of the commandment to rebuild Jerusalem and the coming of the Messiah, the Anointed One. There are differences of opinion as to the exact time when the 483 years began. Some say 538 B.C., when the decree of Cyrus was given; that decree, however, was for the rebuilding of the temple, not the city. Most likely it began in 457 B.C., when Ezra returned and began rebuilding the city (Ezra 4:12–13,16; see 4:11,23, notes); that would make the 483 years end in A.D. 27, about the time Jesus began his ministry.

9:26 MESSIAH BE CUT OFF. After the "seven weeks" (v. 25) and after "the sixty-two weeks," i.e., a total of sixty-nine weeks (483 years), two things would happen: (1) The Messiah would be "cut off," or crucified (cf. Is. 53:8). (2) The "people of the prince that shall come" would destroy Jerusalem and the temple. The "people" are the Roman army, which destroyed Jerusalem in A.D. 70 (see Luke 21:20, note). The "prince" refers to the end-time antichrist. (3) Note that the destruction of Jerusalem did not follow immediately after the crucifixion of Christ. Thus, the conclusion of the sixty-nine weeks are separated from the beginning seventieth week by an interval of time. Many interpreters say that the church age is the interval between the sixty-ninth and seventieth sevens.

weeks [w]shall Messiah be cut off,
[x]but[i] not for himself: [j]and [y]the
people of the prince that shall come
[z]shall destroy the city and the sanctu-
ary; and the end thereof *shall be* with a
flood, and unto the end of the war deso-
lations are determined.
27 And he shall confirm [a]the[k]
covenant with [b]many for one week:
and in the midst of the week he shall
cause the sacrifice and the oblation to
cease, and for the overspreading of
abominations he shall make *it* deso-
late, [c]even until the consummation,
and that determined shall be poured
upon the desolate.

9:26 [w]Is. 53:8 [x]1 Pet. 2:21 [y]Mat. 22:7 [z]Luke 19:44
9:27 [a]Is. 42:6 [b]Mat. 26:28 [c]ch. 11:36

Daniel's vision of an angel

10 IN THE third year of Cyrus king
of Persia a thing was revealed
unto Daniel, whose name was called
Belteshazzar; and the thing *was* true,
but the time appointed *was* [l]long: and
he understood the thing, and had un-
derstanding of the vision.
2 In those days I Daniel was mourn-
ing three [m]full weeks.
3 I ate no [n]pleasant bread, neither
came flesh nor wine in my mouth, nei-
ther did I anoint myself at all, till three
whole weeks were fulfilled.
4 And in the four and twentieth day
of the first month, as I was by the side
of the great river, which *is* Hiddekel;
5 Then I lifted up mine eyes, and
looked, and behold [o]a certain man
clothed in linen, whose loins *were*
[d]girded with fine gold of Uphaz:
6 His body also *was* like the beryl,
and his face as the appearance of light-
ning, and his eyes as lamps of fire, and
his arms and his feet like in colour to
polished brass, [e]and the voice of his
words like the voice of a multitude.
7 And I Daniel alone saw the vision:
for the men that were with me saw not
the vision; but a great quaking fell
upon them, so that they fled to hide
themselves.
8 Therefore I was left alone, and
saw this great vision, and there re-
mained no strength in me: for my

10:5 [d]Rev. 1:13
10:6 [e]Rev. 1:15

[i] Or, *and shall have nothing* [j] Or, *and [the Jews* they shall be no more his people, ch. 11:17, or, *and the prince's [Messiah's,* ver. 25 *future people* [k] Or, *a* [l] Heb. *great* [m] Heb. *weeks of days* [n] Heb. *bread of desires* [o] Heb. *one man*

9:27 HE SHALL CONFIRM THE COVENANT . . . FOR ONE WEEK. The making of a covenant between "the prince that shall come" (v. 26) and Israel will signal the beginning of the seventieth week, the final seven years of this age. Concerning this event, the Bible teaches the following: (1) The prince who will make the covenant with Israel is the antichrist, but he will be unrevealed at the time (cf. 2 Thes. 2:3–10; 1 John 2:18). Evidently a peace treaty will be negotiated by the antichrist between Israel and its enemies concerning a land dispute (11:39).

(2) In the middle of the seven years (i.e., after three and one-half years), the prince will break his covenant with Israel, declare himself to be God, take over the temple in Jerusalem, forbid the worship of the Lord (cf. 2 Thes. 2:4), and devastate Palestine. He will reign for three and one-half years (Rev. 11:1–2; 13:4–6; see article on THE AGE OF THE ANTICHRIST, p. 1896).

(3) The prophetic significance of "the abomination" of desolation will be known only to the faithful of God (12:10–11). Jesus said that believers must take heed concerning this pivotal sign, for it will bring the final three and one-half year countdown to His coming to earth in glory (see Mat. 24:15). By taking heed, believers in the tribulation will know Christ's coming is near, even at the door (Mat. 24:33; see article on THE GREAT TRIBULATION, p. 1456). The coming of the Messiah (2 Thes. 2:8; Rev. 19:11–20) will occur at the end of the seven years or the second three and one-half years. Revelation confirms the time by stating twice that the antichrist (i.e., "the beast") will have power for only forty-two months (Rev. 11:1–2; 13:4–6). Daniel later states again that it will be three and one-half years ("a time, times, and an half") from the time of great distress to the end (12:7).

(4) In the three and one-half years allotted to the antichrist, Jerusalem will continue to be trodden down by the Gentiles (Rev. 11:2).

(5) The "abomination that maketh desolate" is the unmistakable sign that the great tribulation has begun (12:11; Mat. 24:15–21; cf. Deut. 4:30–31; Jer. 30:5–7; Zech. 13:8–9).

(6) The tribulation and the rule of the antichrist will end with the coming of Christ in power to judge the wicked (Mat. 25:31–46), to destroy the antichrist, and to begin His millennial reign (Jer. 23:5–6; Mat. 24:27,30).

9:27 ABOMINATIONS HE SHALL MAKE *IT* DESOLATE. Christ referred to Daniel's vision when he said: "when ye therefore shall see the abomination of desolation, spoken of by Daniel the prophet" (Mat. 24:15). Jesus' remark may refer to the future desecration of the temple in Jerusalem by the antichrist (cf. 2 Thes. 2:3–4; Rev. 13:14–15; see article on THE AGE OF THE ANTICHRIST, p. 1896).

10:5 A CERTAIN MAN CLOTHED IN LINEN. Daniel was visited by a heavenly being, probably an angel, for the messenger spoke of being hindered by the prince of Persia (i.e., a demon) and of needing the help of Michael (see v. 13, note).

[p]comeliness was turned in me into corruption, and I retained no strength.

9 Yet heard I the voice of his words: and when I heard the voice of his words, then was I in a deep sleep on my face, and my face toward the ground.

10 ¶ [f]And, behold, an hand touched me, which [q]set me upon my knees and *upon* the palms of my hands.

11 And he said unto me, O Daniel, [g]a[r] man greatly beloved, understand the words that I speak unto thee, and [s]stand upright: for unto thee am I now sent. And when he had spoken this word unto me, I stood trembling.

Mat. 4:1-11

12 Then said he unto me, [h]Fear not, Daniel: for from the first day that thou didst set thine heart to understand, and to chasten thyself before thy God, [i]thy words were heard, and I am come for thy words.

13 [j]But the prince of the kingdom of Persia withstood me one and twenty days: but, lo, [k]Michael, [t]one of the chief princes, came to help me; and I remained there with the kings of Persia.

14 Now I am come to make thee understand what shall befall thy people [l]in the latter days: [m]for yet the vision *is* for *many* days.

15 And when he had spoken such words unto me, [n]I set my face toward the ground, and I became dumb.

16 And, behold, [o]*one* like the similitude of the sons of men [p]touched my lips: then I opened my mouth, and spake, and said unto him that stood before me, O my lord, by the vision [q]my sorrows are turned upon me, and I have retained no strength.

17 For how can [u]the servant of this my lord talk with this my lord? for as for me, straightway there remained no strength in me, neither is there breath left in me.

18 Then there came again and touched me *one* like the appearance of a man, and he strengthened me,

19 [r]And said, O man greatly beloved, [s]fear not: peace *be* unto thee, be strong, yea, be strong. And when he had spoken unto me, I was strengthened, and said, Let my lord speak; for thou hast strengthened me.

20 Then said he, Knowest thou wherefore I come unto thee? and now will I return to fight [t]with the prince of Persia: and when I am gone forth, lo, the prince of Grecia shall come.

21 But I will show thee that which is noted in the scripture of truth: and *there is* none that [v]holdeth with me in these things, [u]but Michael your prince.

11 ALSO I [v]in the first year of [w]Darius the Mede, *even* I, stood to confirm and to strengthen him.

Conflict between north and south

2 And now will I show thee the

10:10 [f]ch. 9:21 **10:11** [g]ch. 9:23 **10:12** [h]Rev. 1:17 [i]ch. 9:3,4,22,23 Acts 10:4 **10:13** [j]ver. 20 [k]ver. 21 ch. 12:1 Jude 9 Rev. 12:7 **10:14** [l]Gen. 49:1 ch. 2:28 [m]ver. 1 ch. 8:26 Hab. 2:3 **10:15** [n]ver. 9 ch. 8:18 **10:16** [o]ch. 8:15 [p]ver. 10 Jer. 1:9 [q]ver. 8 **10:19** [r]ver. 11 [s]Judg. 6:23 **10:20** [t]ver. 13 **10:21** [u]ver. 13 Jude 9 Rev. 12:7 **11:1** [v]ch. 9:1 [w]ch. 5:31

[p] Or, *vigour* [q] Heb. *moved* [r] Heb. *a man of desires* [s] Heb. *stand upon thy standing* [t] Or, *the first* [u] Or, *this servant of my lord* [v] Heb. *strengtheneth himself*

10:11 A MAN GREATLY BELOVED. The glory and awe of the vision drained Daniel's strength. Then the hand of an angel touched him and raised him to his hands and knees. Daniel was encouraged as this angel called him "a man greatly beloved" and told him, "Fear not" (v. 12). God loves the world (John 3:16), but He responds in a special way to the love and faithfulness of people who, like Daniel, are His true servants. God's faithful people never need to be afraid when God speaks to them.

10:13 THE PRINCE OF THE KINGDOM OF PERSIA WITHSTOOD ME. While Daniel was fasting and praying, a spiritual battle of great magnitude was occurring. (1) The prince of Persia prevented Daniel from receiving God's message from the angel. Because of this conflict, he had to wait twenty-one days for the revelation. This prince of Persia was not a human king, but a demon from Satan's kingdom. He was defeated only when Michael, Israel's prince (v. 21), came to help the angel. Though satanic forces wished to hinder the reception of this vision about Israel, Israel's angelic prince (12:1) proved stronger (cf. Rev. 12:7–12).

(2) This incident gives us a glimpse of the unseen battles going on in the spiritual realm on our behalf. Note that God had responded to Daniel's prayer, but the answer was delayed for twenty-one days by satanic forces. Since we know Satan always desires to hinder our prayers (2 Cor. 2:11), we must persevere in prayer (cf. Luke 18:1–8), in spite of the spiritual forces of the evil one assailed against us (see Eph. 6:11–12, notes; see article on POWER OVER SATAN AND DEMONS, p. 1486).

10:20 PRINCE OF PERSIA . . . GRECIA. The nations of the world have powerful demons assigned to them to oppose the forces of God and to promote evil and ungodliness among the people.

11:2 NOW I WILL SHOW THEE THE TRUTH. The "truth" is a prophecy that outlined the key events leading to the rise of Antiochus Epiphanes, the Greek ruler who profaned the temple (vv. 2–35). Persia would have three more kings, Cambyses (530–522 B.C.), Pseudo-Smerdis or Gaumata (522 B.C.), and Darius I (522–486 B.C.). Then a fourth king, Xerxes (486–465 B.C.), would fight

truth. Behold, there shall stand up yet
three kings in Persia; and the fourth
shall be far richer than *they* all: and by
his strength through his riches he shall
stir up all against the realm of Grecia.
3 And [x]a mighty king shall stand
up, that shall rule with great dominion,
and [y]do according to his will.
4 And when he shall stand up, [z]his
kingdom shall be broken, and shall be
divided toward the four winds of heav-
en; and not to his posterity, [a]nor ac-
cording to his dominion which he
ruled: for his kingdom shall be plucked
up, even for others beside those.
5 ¶ And the king of the south shall
be strong, and *one* of his princes; and
he shall be strong above him, and have
dominion; his dominion *shall be* a great
dominion.
6 And in the end of years they
[w]shall join themselves together; for
the king's daughter of the south shall
come to the king of the north to make
[x]an agreement: but she shall not re-
tain the power of the arm; neither shall
he stand, nor his arm: but she shall be
given up, and they that brought her,
and [y]he that begat her, and he that
strengthened her in *these* times.
7 But out of a branch of her roots
shall *one* stand up [b]in[z] his estate,
which shall come with an army, and
shall enter into the fortress of the king
of the north, and shall deal against
them, and shall prevail:
8 And shall also carry captives into
Egypt their gods, with their princes,
and with [a]their precious vessels of sil-
ver and of gold; and he shall continue

11:3 [x]ch. 7:6 & 8:5 [y]ver. 16,36 ch. 8:4 **11:4** [z]ch. 8:8 [a]ch. 8:22 **11:7** [b]ver. 20

11:10 [c]Is. 8:8 ch. 9:26 [d]ver. 7

more years than the king of the north.
9 So the king of the south shall
come into *his* kingdom, and shall re-
turn into his own land.
10 But his sons [b]shall be stirred
up, and shall assemble a multitude of
great forces: and *one* shall certainly
come, [c]and overflow, and pass
through: [c]then shall he return, and be
stirred up, [d]*even* to his fortress.
11 And the king of the south shall
be moved with choler, and shall come
forth and fight with him, *even* with the
king of the north: and he shall set forth
a great multitude; but the multitude
shall be given into his hand.
12 *And* when he hath taken away
the multitude, his heart shall be lifted
up; and he shall cast down *many* ten
thousands: but he shall not be
strengthened *by it.*
13 For the king of the north shall
return, and shall set forth a multitude
greater than the former, and shall cer-
tainly come [d]after certain years with
a great army and with much riches.
14 And in those times there shall
many stand up against the king of the
south: also [e]the robbers of thy people
shall exalt themselves to establish the
vision; but they shall fall.
15 So the king of the north shall
come, and cast up a mount, and take

[w] Heb. *shall associate themselves* [x] Heb. *rights* [y] Or, *whom she brought forth* [z] Or, *in his place,* or, *office* [a] Heb. *vessels of their desire* [b] Or, *shall war* [c] Or, *then shall he be stirred up again* [d] Heb. *at the end of times, even years;* see ch. 4:16 & 12:7 [e] Heb. *the children of robbers*

against Greece. With the mention of Greece (the next kingdom), no more is said about Persia, though Persia continued for a time.

11:3 A MIGHTY KING. The mighty king who would rise up was Alexander the Great (336–323 B.C.), who died at the height of his power. Instead of his kingdom going to his heirs, it was divided among his four generals (v. 4; see 7:3, note).

11:5 THE KING OF THE SOUTH. This first king of the south is Ptolemy I Soter of Egypt (323–285 B.C.). The commander referred to is Seleucus I Nicator (311–280 B.C.).

11:6 THE KING'S DAUGHTER OF THE SOUTH. After several years, Berenice, the daughter of Ptolemy II Philadelphus of Egypt (285–246 B.C.), married Antiochus II Theos (261–246 B.C.), the king of the north, who had divorced Laodice to marry Berenice. In 246 B.C. Ptolemy II died; about the same time Laodice murdered Berenice and Antiochus and their son.

11:7–9 A BRANCH. . . SHALL PREVAIL. The "branch" is Berenice's brother, Ptolemy III Euergetes of Egypt (246–221 B.C.). He won a victory over the king of the north, Seleucus II Callinicus (246–226 B.C.). Ptolemy III entered the "fortress" (probably Syrian Antioch) and took to Egypt both Syrian images and the Egyptian images that had been taken by the Persian King Cambyses when he conquered Egypt in 525 B.C. Ptolemy III returned to Egypt with much booty, but he refrained from any further attacks on Seleucus. After a time Seleucus attempted to invade Egypt to recoup his losses, but he failed and was forced to go back to his own land.

11:10–12 HIS SONS SHALL BE STIRRED UP. The two sons of Seleucus II were Seleucus III Ceraunus (226–223 B.C.) and Antiochus III the Great (223–187 B.C.). Antiochus III was defeated by Ptolemy IV Philopater (221–203 B.C.), with the loss of nearly 10,000 Syrian soldiers at the fortress of Raphia in southern Palestine.

[f]the most fenced cities: and the arms
of the south shall not withstand, nei-
ther [g]his chosen people, neither *shall*
there be any strength to withstand.
16 But he that cometh against him
[e]shall do according to his own will,
and [f]none shall stand before him: and
he shall stand in [h]the [i]glorious land,
which by his hand shall be consumed.
17 He shall also [g]set his face to en-
ter with the strength of his whole king-
dom, and [j]upright ones with him;
thus shall he do: and he shall give him
the daughter of women, [k]corrupting
her: but she shall not stand *on his side,*
[h]neither be for him.
18 After this shall he turn his face
unto the isles, and shall take many: but
a prince [l]for his own behalf shall
cause [m]the reproach offered by him to
cease; without his own reproach he
shall cause *it* to turn upon him.
19 Then he shall turn his face to-
ward the fort of his own land: but he
shall stumble and fall, [i]and not be
found.
20 Then shall stand up [n]in his es-
tate [o]a raiser of taxes *in* the glory of
the kingdom: but within few days he
shall be destroyed, neither in [p]anger,
nor in battle.
21 And [n]in his estate [j]shall stand
up a vile person, to whom they shall
not give the honour of the kingdom: but
he shall come in peaceably, and obtain
the kingdom by flatteries.
22 And with the arms of a flood
shall they be overflown from before
him, and shall be broken; [k]yea, also
the prince of the covenant.
23 And after the league *made* with
him [l]he shall work deceitfully: for he
shall come up, and shall become strong
with a small people.
24 He shall enter [q]peaceably even
upon the fattest places of the province;
and he shall do *that* which his fathers
have not done, nor his fathers' fathers;
he shall scatter among them the prey,
and spoil, and riches: *yea,* and he shall
[r]forecast his devices against the
strong holds, even for a time.
25 And he shall stir up his power
and his courage against the king of the
south with a great army; and the king
of the south shall be stirred up to battle
with a very great and mighty army; but
he shall not stand: for they shall fore-
cast devices against him.
26 Yea, they that feed of the portion
of his meat shall destroy him, and his
army shall overflow: and many shall
fall down slain.
27 And both these kings' [s]hearts
shall be to do mischief, and they shall
speak lies at one table; but it shall not
prosper: for yet the end *shall be* at the
time appointed.
28 Then shall he return into his

11:16 [e]ch. 8:4,7 [f]Josh. 1:5
11:17 [g]2 Chr. 20:3 [h]ch. 9:26
11:19 [i]Ps. 37:36
11:21 [j]ch. 7:8
11:22 [k]ch. 8:10,11
11:23 [l]ch. 8:25

[f]Heb. *the city of munitions* [g]Heb. *the people of his choices* [h]Heb. *the land of ornament* [i]Or, *goodly* [j]Or, *much uprightness:* or, *equal conditions* [k]Heb. *to corrupt* [l]Heb. *for him* [m]Heb. *his* [n]Or, *in his place* [o]Heb. *one that causeth an exacter to pass over* [p]Heb. *angers* [q]Or, *into the peaceable and fat* [r]Heb. *think his thoughts* [s]Heb. *their hearts*

11:16 THE GLORIOUS LAND. Antiochus III attacked Egypt in 200 B.C., but was crushed by the king of the south, Ptolemy V Epiphanes (203–181 B.C.); Antiochus then gained new strength and conquered "the most fenced cities" (v. 15; i.e., the well-fortified city of Sidon). By 197 B.C., Antiochus had taken control of the glorious land, Palestine.

11:19 HE SHALL STUMBLE AND FALL. After several years Antiochus III made a peace treaty with Egypt (194 B.C.) and gave his daughter Cleopatra I as wife to Ptolemy V. Then Antiochus III moved north but was defeated at Magnesia in Asia Minor in 190 B.C. Later (187 B.C.) he attempted to plunder a heathen temple in the province of Elymais, and he died in the attempt.

11:20 HE SHALL BE DESTROYED. The murder of Seleucus IV Philopater (187–175 B.C.) was arranged by his finance minister, Heliodorus.

11:21 A VILE PERSON. This chapter has been leading up to the coming of the "vile person," Antiochus IV Epiphanes (175–164 B.C.), the brother of Seleucus IV. He took the throne that really belonged to Demetrius, the young son of Seleucus IV. Antiochus (the "little horn" of 8:9–14,23–25) made several campaigns against Egypt. He murdered the "prince of the covenant" (a prophecy of the murder of the high priest Onias in 170 B.C., v. 22). His treaties with other nations were full of intrigue and deceit. He supported Ptolemy Philometor against Ptolemy Euergetes for selfish reasons. He made unexpected attacks on rich cities in times of peace (v. 24). His attacks on Egypt were successful because those who should have helped Egypt did not, and Antiochus was able to return home with great wealth (vv. 25–28).

11:28 HIS HEART *SHALL BE* AGAINST THE HOLY COVENANT. Antiochus developed a hatred of the Jews and their holy covenant law. He was persuaded that Greek culture and language were superior to any other culture and language, and he hated the Jews because their religion was exclusivistic. About 168 B.C. he invaded Egypt again, but the ships of Chittim (v. 30; i.e., Cyprus) headed by the Roman consul Laenas defeated him, and he withdrew to his own land. There he took out his frustration against the Jews, though some Jews

land with great riches; and his heart
shall be against the holy covenant; and
he shall do *exploits,* and return to his
own land.
29 At the time appointed he shall
return, and come toward the south; but
it shall not be as the former, or as the
latter.
30 ¶ [m]For the ships of Chittim shall
come against him: therefore he shall be
grieved, and return, and have indigna-
tion against the holy covenant: so shall
he do; he shall even return, and have
intelligence with them that forsake the
holy covenant.
31 And arms shall stand on his part,
[n]and they shall pollute the sanctuary
of strength, and shall take away the
daily *sacrifice,* and they shall place the
abomination that [t]maketh desolate.
32 And such as do wickedly against
the covenant shall he [u]corrupt by flat-
teries: but the people that do know
their God shall be strong, and do *ex-
ploits.*
33 And they that understand among
the people shall instruct many: yet
they shall fall by the sword, and by
flame, by captivity, and by spoil, *many*
days.
34 Now when they shall fall, they
shall be helped with a little help: but
many shall cleave to them with flatter-
ies.
35 And *some* of them of understand-
ing shall fall, [o]to try [v]them, and to
purge, and to make *them* white, *even* to
the time of the end: because *it is* yet for
a time appointed.

The power of the northern king

36 And the king shall do according
to his will; and he shall [p]exalt himself,
and magnify himself above every god,
and shall speak marvellous things
against the God of gods, and shall
prosper till the indignation be accom-
plished: for that that is determined
shall be done.
37 Neither shall he regard the God
of his fathers, nor the desire of women,
[q]nor regard any god: for he shall mag-
nify himself above all.
38 But [w]in his [x]estate shall he
honour the God of [y][z]forces: and a
god whom his fathers knew not shall
he honour with gold, and silver, and
with precious stones, and [a]pleasant
things.
39 Thus shall he do in the [b]most
strong holds with a strange god, whom
he shall acknowledge *and* increase
with glory: and he shall cause them to

11:30 [m]Jer. 2:10
11:31 [n]ch. 8:11
11:35 [o]ch. 12:10
11:36 [p]ch. 7:8,25
11:37 [q]Is. 14:13

[t] Or, *astonisheth* [u] Or, *cause to dissemble*
[v] Or, *by them* [w] Heb. *as for the almighty God, in his seat he shall honour, yea, he shall honour a god, whom* [x] Or, *stead* [y] Or, *munitions*
[z] Heb. *Mauzzim,* or, *God's protectors* [a] Heb. *things desired* [b] Heb. *fortresses of munitions*

forsook the holy covenant and joined him. These apostate Jews invited Antiochus to bring in Greek culture and religion (v. 30). Thus Antiochus marched to Jerusalem, offered a pig on the altar in the temple, stopped the daily sacrifices required by God's law, and set up in the holy place an image of the Greek god Zeus; this altar to Zeus is "the abomination that maketh desolate" (v. 31), prefiguring another abomination that Jesus prophesied will occur in the last days of this age (see article on THE GREAT TRIBULATION, p. 1456).

11:32 THE PEOPLE THAT DO KNOW THEIR GOD SHALL BE STRONG. Flattery corrupted some Jews and caused them to join Antiochus, but God always had a faithful remnant among the Jews in O.T. times (see 1 Ki. 19:18; see Isa 6:13, note; 8:16, note; 10:20, note). In this situation too, there were Jews who knew God and remained loyal to Him. Though the persecution by Antiochus continued, the faithful Jews under the leadership of Judas Maccabeus of the Hasmonean priestly family offered strong resistance and carried on a guerrilla-type warfare that eventually wore down Antiochus and caused him to take his armies home. Thereupon the temple was cleansed and the lamps relit, an event still celebrated by the Jews as the Feast of Hanukkah. God has not yet completed His dealings with the Jews, however (see v. 35). A purging process will continue to the time of the end.

11:36–45 THE KING SHALL MAGNIFY HIMSELF. The prophecies in these verses do not fit Antiochus. The mention of "the time of the end" (vv. 35,40) indicates that this prophecy is jumping ahead to the end of the age and to the one of whom Antiochus was the type, i.e., the antichrist (see 7:8, note; 9:27, note). The antichrist will be a dictatorial ruler who will present himself as greater than any god and will speak "marvellous things" (blasphemies) against the true God; he will be allowed to prosper for a time, thus bringing the fulfillment of this prophecy. He will not regard "the God [or the gods] of his fathers" (v. 37; Heb. *'elohim*, which can mean either "God" or "gods"); neither will he regard what is desired by women (some take this to be Tammuz-adonis, a Babylonian fertility god; see Ezek. 8:14). The only god he will honor will be "the God of forces" (v. 38; Heb. *ma'uzim*, "fortresses"), which may refer to his own ability to make war. He will also redivide territories he conquers in order to promote his own gain (v. 39).

rule over many, and shall divide the land for [c]gain.

40 And at the time of the end shall the king of the south push at him: and the king of the north shall come against him [r]like a whirlwind, with chariots, [s]and with horsemen, and with many ships; and he shall enter into the countries, and shall overflow and pass over.

41 He shall enter also into the [d] [e]glorious land, and many *countries* shall be overthrown: but these shall escape out of his hand, [t]*even* Edom, and Moab, and the chief of the children of Ammon.

42 He shall [f]stretch forth his hand also upon the countries: and the land of Egypt shall not escape.

43 But he shall have power over the treasures of gold and of silver, and over all the precious things of Egypt: and the Libyans and the Ethiopians *shall be* [u]at his steps.

44 But tidings out of the east and out of the north shall trouble him: therefore he shall go forth with great fury to destroy, and utterly to make away many.

45 And he shall plant the tabernacles of his palace between the seas in [v]the [g,h]glorious holy mountain; [w]yet he shall come to his end, and none shall help him.

The time of great trouble

12 AND AT that time shall Michael stand up, the great prince which standeth for the children of thy people: [x]and there shall be a time of trouble, such as never was since there was a nation *even* to that same time: and at that time thy people [y]shall be delivered, every one that shall be found [z]written in the book.

2 And many of them that sleep in the dust of the earth shall awake, [a]some to everlasting life, and some to shame [b]*and* everlasting contempt.

3 And they that be [i]wise shall [c]shine as the brightness of the firmament; [d]and they that turn many to righteousness [e]as the stars for ever and ever.

4 But thou, O Daniel, [f]shut up the words, and seal the book, *even* to the time of the end: many shall run to and fro, and knowledge shall be increased.

5 ¶ Then I Daniel looked, and, behold, there stood other two, the one on this side of the [j]bank of the river, and the other on that side of the bank [g]of the river.

6 And *one* said to the man clothed in linen, which *was* [k]upon the waters of the river, [h]How long *shall it be to* the end of these wonders?

7 And I heard the man clothed in linen, which *was* upon the waters of the river, when he [i]held up his right hand and his left hand unto heaven, and sware by him [j]that liveth for ever [k]that *it shall be* for a time, times, and [l]an half; [l]and when he shall have accomplished to scatter the power of

11:40 [r]Is. 21:1 [s]Ezek. 38:4 Rev. 9:16
11:41 [t]Is. 11:14
11:43 [u]Ex. 11:8
11:45 [v]Ps. 48:2 [w]Rev. 19:20
12:1 [x]Is. 26:20 Jer. 30:7 Rev. 16:18 [y]Rom. 11:26 [z]Ex. 32:32 Ps. 56:8
12:2 [a]Mat. 25:46 John 5:28 Acts 24:15 [b]Is. 66:24 Rom. 9:21
12:3 [c]Mat. 13:43 [d]Jas. 5:20 [e]1 Cor. 15:41
12:4 [f]Rev. 22:10
12:5 [g]ch. 10:4
12:6 [h]ch. 8:13
12:7 [i]Deut. 32:40 [j]ch. 4:34 [k]ch. 7:25 [l]Luke 21:24

[c] Heb. *a price* [d] Or, *goodly land* [e] Heb. *land of delight,* or, *ornament* [f] Heb. *send forth* [g] Or, *goodly* [h] Heb. *mountain of delight of holiness* [i] Or, *teachers* [j] Heb. *lip* [k] Or, *from above* [l] Or, *part*

11:45 HE SHALL COME TO HIS END. Though the antichrist will prosper for a time, there will be further battles with another king of the north and another king of the south, culminating in the battle of Armageddon, where the antichrist will be finally defeated by the sword of Christ's mouth (i.e., by His word) and be cast into the lake of fire (Rev. 19:20).

12:1 A TIME OF TROUBLE. Since the word "nation" in this verse refers to Israel, Daniel prophesies a time of trouble for Israel, fulfilling Jer. 30:7 (see also Mat. 24:15,21; Rev. 6:17), but God's purpose is still to deliver those of Daniel's people whose names are written "in the book" (i.e., "the book of life," see Phil. 4:3; Rev. 3:5; 21:27). They will have finally placed their faith in Jesus as their Messiah, Savior, and Lord.

12:2 MANY . . . SHALL AWAKE. This verse contains the clearest O.T. reference to the resurrection of the righteous and the wicked (cf. Job 19:25–26; Ps. 16:10; Is. 26:19), revealing that there are two, and only two, destinies for all humankind. Jesus indicates that there are two distinct resurrections (John 5:28–29).

12:3 WISE SHALL SHINE. The wise, as described in the O.T., are the godly. They show their wisdom not only by how they live but by the effect of their lives and testimony, for they lead many to a righteous way of life. Their shining means they will be transformed and the glory of God will be reflected in and through them.

12:4 SEAL THE BOOK. Daniel is told to seal the book. The prophecies are not merely for his own time, but for the time of the end, to encourage those who will be alive at the end of the age. Then Daniel observes two angels, one on each side of the (Tigris) river, asking how long it would be until the time of the end. The man clothed in white linen (cf. 10:5–6) swore by God that the time would be three and one-half years, probably referring to the last half of the seventieth period of seven years (see 9:27, note).

[m]the holy people, all these *things* shall
be finished.
8 And I heard, but I understood not:
then said I, O my Lord, what *shall be*
the end of these *things?*
9 And he said, Go thy way, Daniel:
for the words *are* closed up and sealed
till the time of the end.
10 [n]Many shall be purified, and
made white, and tried; [o]but the wick-
ed shall do wickedly: and none of the
wicked shall understand; but [p]the
wise shall understand.
11 And from the time *that* the daily
sacrifice shall be taken away, and [m]the
abomination that [n]maketh desolate
set up, *there shall be* a thousand two
hundred and ninety days.
12 Blessed *is* he that waiteth, and
cometh to the thousand three hundred
and five and thirty days.
13 But go thou thy way till the end
be: [q]for[o] thou shalt rest, [r]and stand
in thy lot at the end of the days.

12:7 [m]ch. 8:24
12:10 [n]Zech. 13:9 [o]Hos. 14:9 [p]John 8:47
12:13 [q]Rev. 14:13 [r]Ps. 1:5

[m] Heb. *to set up the abomination* [n] Or, *astonisheth* [o] Or, *and thou*

12:10 THE WISE SHALL UNDERSTAND. Daniel is told that the full understanding of his prophecy will not come until the time of the end. At that time, some will be purified through testing; these will be the wise who understand. No wicked or rebellious person will be among them. Furthermore, there will be an "abomination that maketh desolate" (cf. Mat. 24:15; see article on THE GREAT TRIBULATION, p. 1456), which will be followed by a period of 1,290 days, corresponding to the last three and one-half years of the tribulation plus forty-five days. A special blessing will also be pronounced on those who come through the 1,335 days. The significance of these days is not explained to Daniel, but this vision does let us know that there will be a period of time between the battle of Armageddon and the full establishment of the millennial kingdom. The important thing for us is that the wise, the godly, will understand. Even if they do not understand everything, they will understand enough about end-time events to cause them to believe in Jesus and His kingdom and to enter into its final form.

HOSEA

Outline

Title (1:1)

I. Hosea's Marriage Illustrates Israel's Unfaithfulness, Rejection, and Restoration (1:2—3:5)
   A. Marriage to Gomer (1:2)
   B. Birth of Their Three Children (1:3–9)
   C. A Prophecy of Restoration (1:10—2:1)
   D. Gomer as a Symbol of Israel (2:2–23)
      1. Israel's Adultery (2:2–5)
      2. God's Judgment (2:6–13)
      3. God's Promised Restoration of Israel (2:14–23)
   E. Hosea's Redemption of Gomer (3:1–5)

II. Hosea's Message Describes Israel's Unfaithfulness, Rejection, and Restoration (4:1—14:9)
   A. Israel's Spiritual Adultery (4:1–19)
   B. God's Judgment Against Israel (5:1–14)
   C. Israel's Insincere Repentance (5:15—6:3)
   D. Record of Israel's Sins (6:4—8:6)
      1. Breaking the Covenant (6:4–10)
      2. Refusal to Trust and Obey God (6:11—7:16)
      3. Going after False Gods (8:1–6)
   E. Israel's Judgment Predicted (8:7—10:15)
      1. To Be Swallowed Up by the Nations (8:7–14)
      2. Prosperity to Evaporate (9:1–9)
      3. The Womb to Become Barren (9:10–17)
      4. Nation to Be Destroyed (10:1–15)
   F. God's Persistent Love for Israel (11:1–11)
   G. Israel's Sins Repeated (11:12—12:14)
   H. God's Past Care and Present Anger (13:1–16)
      1. Israel's Idolatry (13:1–3)
      2. God's Care in the Exodus (13:4–6)
      3. God's Plan to Destroy Israel (13:7–13)
      4. God's Plan for Israel's Ultimate Restoration (13:14)
      5. Israel's Coming Destruction Reemphasized (13:15–16)
   I. God's Promise to Restore Israel (14:1–9)
      1. Call to Repentance (14:1–3)
      2. Abundant Blessings Promised (14:4–9)

Author: Hosea

Theme: God's Judgment and Redeeming Love

Date of Writing: 715–710 B.C.

Background

Hosea, whose name means "salvation," is identified as the son of Beeri (1:1). Nothing else is known about the prophet apart from the autobiographical glimpses in the book itself. That Hosea was a native of Israel, not Judah, who prophesied to his own nation is apparent from (1) his numerous references to "Israel" and "Ephraim" (the two foremost designations for the northern kingdom) and to "Samaria" (the capital of the northern kingdom), (2) his reference to Israel's king at Samaria as "our king" (7:5), and (3) his intense concern about Israel's spiritual, moral, political, and social corruption. Hosea's ministry to the northern kingdom followed closely on the heels of Amos's ministry (a prophet from Judah who prophesied to Israel). Amos and Hosea are the only two O.T. prophets whose prophetic books addressed entirely the northern kingdom and its coming destruction.

Hosea was called by God to prophesy to the crumbling kingdom of Israel during her last thirty-plus years, just as Jeremiah was later required to do in Judah. When Hosea began his ministry during the latter years of Jeroboam II, Israel was enjoying a temporary period of economic prosperity and political peace that produced a false sense of security. Immediately after Jeroboam II died (753 B.C.), however, the nation began to deteriorate rapidly and ran swiftly to its destruction in 722 B.C. Within fifteen years following his death, four of Israel's kings were assassinated; in fifteen more years Samaria was a smoking ruin and the Israelites were deported to Assyria and later dispersed among the nations. Hosea's tragic marriage and prophetic word combined together as God's message to Israel during these final chaotic years of her slide to destruction.

God commanded Hosea to take "a wife of whoredoms" (1:2) to illustrate Israel's spiritual infidelity to God. Although some have interpreted Hosea's marriage as a fictitious allegory, most conservative Bible scholars view it as literal. It seems unlikely, however, that God would command a godly prophet to marry a whore in order to illustrate His message to Israel. It seems more likely that Hosea married Gomer when she was chaste, and she became a harlot afterwards. Thus the command to take a "wife of whoredoms" was in prophetic anticipation of what was to be.

The historical setting of Hosea's ministry is identified as the reigns of Jeroboam II of Israel and four kings of Judah (Uzziah, Jotham, Ahaz, and Hezekiah; see 1:1)—i.e., about 755–715 B.C. This not only makes him a younger contemporary of Amos, but also of Isaiah and Micah. The fact that Hosea dates much of his ministry by referring to four kings in Judah, rather than the brief reigns of Israel's last six kings, may indicate that he fled from the northern kingdom to live in the land of Judah shortly before Samaria was destroyed by Assyria (722 B.C.). There he compiled his prophecies into the book that now bears his name.

Purpose

The prophecy of Hosea was God's last attempt to call Israel to repent of her persistent idolatry and wickedness before giving her over to the full judgment of her sins. The book was written to reveal (1) that God maintained His love for His covenant people and intensely desired to redeem them from their iniquity, and (2) that tragic consequences follow when a people persist in disobeying God and in rejecting His redeeming love. The infidelity of Hosea's wife is recorded as an illustration of Israel's unfaithfulness to God. Gomer runs after other men, while Israel runs after other gods; Gomer commits physical harlotry, while Israel commits spiritual harlotry.

Survey

Chs. 1—3 describe Hosea's marriage to Gomer. The names of their three children are prophetic signs to Israel : Jezreel ("God-Scatters"), Lo-ruhamah ("Not-Pitied"), and Lo-ammi ("Not My People"). Hosea's persevering love for his adulterous wife symbolizes God's steadfast love for Israel.

Chs. 4—14 contain a series of prophecies by Hosea that parallel Israel's unfaithfulness to that of his wife. Gomer's desertion of Hosea for other lovers (ch. 1) represents Israel's

departure from God (chs. 4—7). Gomer's degradation (ch. 2) represents Israel's shame and judgment (chs. 8—10). Hosea's redemption of Gomer from the slave market (ch. 3) represents God's desire and intention to restore Israel in the future (chs. 11—14). The book emphasizes that since Israel has spurned God's love and call to repentance, judgment can no longer be delayed.

Special Features

Seven major features or emphases characterize the book of Hosea. (1) It stands first in that part of the O.T. called "The Book of the Twelve," also known as the "Minor Prophets" ("minor" because of their brevity when compared with Isaiah, Jeremiah, and Ezekiel). (2) Hosea is one of only two prophets from the north with a prophetic book in the O.T. (the other is Jonah). (3) As with Jeremiah and Ezekiel, Hosea's personal experiences illustrated his prophetic message. (4) It contains about 150 statements concerning Israel's sins, more than half of which relate to idolatry. (5) More than any other O.T. prophet, Hosea reminded the Israelites that the Lord had been longsuffering and faithful in His love for them. (6) There is no discernible order among Hosea's prophecies in the main body of the book (chs. 4–14). It is difficult to tell where one prophecy ends and another begins. (7) Its prophecies are filled with vivid figures of speech, many of them taken from the rural scene.

New Testament Fulfillment

Hosea contains several verses which the N.T. quotes as being fulfilled in Jesus Christ: (1) the call of God's Son out of Egypt (11:1; cf. Mat. 2:15); (2) Christ's victory over death (13:14; cf. 1 Cor. 15:55); (3) God's desire for mercy and not sacrifice (6:6; cf. Mat. 9:13; 12:7); and (4) the Gentiles, who were not God's people, now becoming His people (1:6,9–10; 2:23; cf. Rom. 9:25–26; 1 Pet. 1:10). In addition to specific passages, the N.T. expands the book's theme of God being the husband of His people, in that Christ is the bridegroom/husband of His redeemed bride, the church (see 1 Cor. 11:2; Eph. 5:22–32; Rev. 19:6–9; 21:1–2,9–10). Hosea emphasizes the N.T. message of truly knowing God in order to enter into life (2:20; 4:6; 5:15; 6:3,6; cf. John 17:1–3). Coupled with this message, Hosea shows clearly the direct relationship between persistent sin and inescapable judgment. The two main emphases in Hosea are summed up by Paul in Rom. 6:23: "For the wages of sin *is* death; but the gift of God *is* eternal life through Jesus Christ our Lord."

Reading Hosea

In order to read the entire Old Testament in one year, the book of Hosea should be read in 4 days, according to the following schedule: ☐ 1–2 ☐ 3–6 ☐ 7–10 ☐ 11–14

NOTES

1 THE [a]WORD of the LORD that
came unto Hosea, the son of Beeri,
in the days of Uzziah, Jotham, Ahaz,
and Hezekiah, kings of Judah, and in
the days of Jeroboam the son of Joash,
king of Israel.

Hosea's wife and children

2 The beginning of the word of the
LORD by Hosea. And the LORD said to
Hosea, [b]Go, take unto thee a wife of
whoredoms and children of whore-
doms: for [c]the land hath committed
great whoredom, *departing* from the
LORD.
3 So he went and took Gomer the
daughter of Diblaim; which conceived,
and bare him a son.
4 And the LORD said unto him, Call
his name Jezreel; for yet a little *while,*
[d]and I will [a]avenge the blood of Jez-
reel upon the house of Jehu, [e]and will
cause to cease the kingdom of the
house of Israel.
5 [f]And it shall come to pass at that
day, that I will break the bow of Israel
in the valley of Jezreel.
6 ¶ And she conceived again, and
bare a daughter. And *God* said unto
him, Call her name [b]Lo-ruhamah:
[g]for [c]I will no more have mercy upon
the house of Israel; [d]but I will utterly
take them away.
7 [h]But I will have mercy upon the
house of Judah, and will save them by
the LORD their God, and [i]will not save
them by bow, nor by sword, nor by bat-
tle, by horses, nor by horsemen.
8 ¶ Now when she had weaned Lo-
ruhamah, she conceived, and bare a
son.
9 Then said *God,* Call his name
[e]Lo-ammi: for ye *are* not my people,
and I will not be your *God.*
10 ¶ Yet [j]the number of the chil-
dren of Israel shall be as the sand of
the sea, which cannot be measured nor
numbered; [k]and it shall come to pass,
that [f]in the place where it was said
unto them, Ye *are* not my people, *there*
it shall be said unto them, *Ye are* [l]the
sons of the living God.
11 [m]Then shall the children of Ju-
dah and the children of Israel be gath-

1:1 [a]2 Pet. 1:21
1:2 [b]ch. 3:1 [c]Deut. 31:16 Ps. 73:27 Jer. 2:13 Ezek. 23:3
1:4 [d]2 Ki. 10:11 [e]2 Ki. 15:10
1:5 [f]2 Ki. 15:29
1:6 [g]2 Ki. 17:6
1:7 [h]2 Ki. 19:35 [i]Zech. 4:6
1:10 [j]Gen. 32:12 [k]1 Pet. 2:10 [l]John 1:12
1:11 [m]Is. 11:12

[a] Heb. *visit* [b] i.e. *Not having obtained mercy* [c] Heb. *I will not add any more to* [d] Or, *that I should altogether pardon them* [e] i.e. *Not my people* [f] Or, *instead of that*

1:2 GO, TAKE UNTO THEE A WIFE OF WHOREDOMS. God's relationship with Israel is frequently compared to a marriage contract (e.g., Is. 54:5; Jer. 3:14; cf. Eph. 5:22–32); Israel's "*departing* from the LORD" in order to worship idols was treated by God as spiritual infidelity or prostitution. Hosea's marriage was to be an object lesson for the unfaithful northern kingdom. Gomer was likely not a prostitute at the time of her marriage, but she would later turn to physical adultery and immorality, perhaps as a prostitute in the temple of Baal. Her departure from the Lord led not only to false worship, but also to lower moral standards. The same pattern of immoral living can be seen today wherever God's people turn away from true commitment to Him (see Prov. 5:3, note).

1:4 I WILL AVENGE THE BLOOD OF JEZREEL. This verse most likely refers back to the killing of the seventy sons of Ahab by Jehu (2 Ki. 10:1–8). Though Jehu was commended for bringing God's just judgment on the family of Ahab, Jehu was too severe (2 Ki. 10:30–31).

1:4 WILL CAUSE TO CEASE THE KINGDOM OF ISRAEL. God would soon bring judgment and destruction upon the northern kingdom of Israel. Hosea probably lived to see this prophecy fulfilled in 722 B.C., when the Assyrians took Samaria, carried off about ten percent of the people, and made the remaining people part of a province of the Assyrian empire.

1:6 I WILL NO MORE HAVE MERCY. The name "Lo-ruhamah" (literally, "she is not pitied" or "she does not receive compassion and love") means that God in His holiness had said it was time for His longsuffering to come to an end. Judgment must eventually come to a sinful and rebellious people.

1:7 I . . . WILL SAVE THEM. The southern kingdom (Judah) would not come to an end at the same time as the northern kingdom (Israel). Because King Hezekiah was leading his nation in faith and repentance, the Lord saved them from Samaria's fate at that time (2 Ki. 19:32–36; Is. 37:36). Judah's kingdom lasted for another 136 years.

1:9 YE *ARE* NOT MY PEOPLE. Gomer's third child, a boy named "Lo-ammi" (meaning "not my people"), is not thought to be Hosea's. The child's name symbolized the breaking of the covenant relationship through ongoing rebellion against God and through idolatry; the people of the northern kingdom could no longer expect God to bless them and deliver their nation. Hosea was learning through his own anguish how God's heart was broken over the sins of His people.

1:10–11 ISRAEL SHALL BE AS THE SAND OF THE SEA. God's rejection of northern kingdom as a separate nation did not mean God would forget His promise to Abraham, Isaac, and Jacob concerning the land and the nation. In spite of Israel's sin, God would find a way to restore them to sonship. He would bring all twelve tribes together into one nation and under one leader. This promise of reuniting points to the coming Messiah.

1:11 GREAT *SHALL BE* THE DAY OF JEZREEL. Jezreel means "God scatters," and it is used

ered together, and appoint themselves
one head, and they shall come up out
of the land: for great *shall be* the day of
Jezreel.

2 SAY YE unto your brethren,
[g]Ammi; and to your sisters,
[h]Ruhamah.

Gomer punished and restored

2 Plead with your mother, plead: for
[n]she *is* not my wife, neither *am* I her
husband: let her therefore put away
her [o]whoredoms out of her sight, and
her adulteries from between her
breasts;
3 Lest [p]I strip her naked, and set
her as in the day that she was [q]born,
and make her as a wilderness, and set
her like a dry land, and slay her with
[r]thirst.
4 And I will not have mercy upon
her children; for they *be* the [s]children
of whoredoms.
5 For their mother hath played the
harlot: she that conceived them hath
done shamefully: for she said, I will go
after my lovers, [t]that give *me* my
bread and my water, my wool and my
flax, mine oil and my [i]drink.
6 ¶ Therefore, behold, [u]I will
hedge up thy way with thorns, and
[j]make a wall, that she shall not find
her paths.
7 And she shall follow after her lov-
ers, but she shall not overtake them;
and she shall seek them, but shall not
find *them:* then shall she say, [v]I will go
and return to my [w]first husband; for
then *was it* better with me than now.
8 For she did not [x]know that I gave
her corn, and [k]wine, and oil, and mul-
tiplied her silver and gold, [l]*which*
they prepared for Baal.
9 Therefore will I return, and take
away my corn in the time thereof, and
my wine in the season thereof, and will
[m]recover my wool and my flax *given* to
cover her nakedness.
10 And now [y]will I discover her
[n]lewdness in the sight of her lovers,
and none shall deliver her out of mine
hand.
11 [z]I will also cause all her mirth
to cease, her feast days, her new
moons, and her sabbaths, and all her
solemn feasts.
12 And I will [o]destroy her vines
and her fig trees, whereof she hath
said, These *are* my rewards that my
lovers have given me: and I will make
them a forest, and the beasts of the
field shall eat them.
13 And I will visit upon her the days
of Baalim, wherein she burned incense
to them, and she decked herself with
her earrings and her jewels, and she
went after her lovers, and forgat me,
saith the LORD.
14 ¶ Therefore, behold, I will allure

2:2 [n]Is. 50:1 [o]Ezek. 16:25
2:3 [p]Jer. 13:22 [q]Ezek. 16:4 [r]Amos 8:11
2:4 [s]John 8:41
2:5 [t]ver. 8,12
2:6 [u]Lam. 3:7,9
2:7 [v]Luke 15:18 [w]Ezek. 16:8
2:8 [x]Is. 1:3
2:10 [y]Ezek. 16:37
2:11 [z]Amos 8:10

[g]i.e. *My people* [h]i.e. *Having obtained mercy* [i]Heb. *drinks* [j]Heb. *wall a wall* [k]Heb. *new wine* [l]Or, wherewith *they made Baal* [m]Or, *take away* [n]Heb. *folly,* or, *villany* [o]Heb. *make desolate*

in a slightly different sense here from v. 4. God would scatter His people (v. 4), but later He would bring them out of the lands where they were scattered and would sow them in their own land again, as a farmer scatters seeds.

2:2–7 PLEAD WITH YOUR MOTHER. Hosea returns again to warnings of judgment. "Plead" is a legal term used for presenting a case against someone with complaints, rebukes, and reproaches. The nation is the wife and mother; the individual Israelites are the children who have turned to idolatry. They must repent and turn from their "lovers" (2:5), i.e., from the various Canaanite gods.

2:6 THEREFORE . . . I WILL HEDGE UP THY WAY. God promised to put obstacles in the way of the Israelites—not to destroy them, but to make them realize it would be better for them to return to God. It is always appropriate to pray that God will bring difficulties into the lives of our unsaved loved ones, so that they will learn that it is far better to turn to the Lord and His goodness than to remain in the sorrow of sin.

2:8 HE DID NOT KNOW. Israel attributed their good harvest to the Baals (Canaanite gods), when in reality it was God's mercy and grace that brought good things to them. We must be careful always to acknowledge God's grace and the blessings that He gives us, and to thank Him with grateful hearts. To fail to do so is to take a first step away from Him.

2:11 I WILL . . . CAUSE ALL HER MIRTH TO CEASE. God intended Israel's holy days and holy feasts to be times for rejoicing in His blessings; yet their rejoicing had turned to mere mirth and the hollow laughter of people trying to have a good time. The feasts God commanded were no longer His feasts; rather, they had become "her" (i.e., Israel's) feasts, mere social gatherings celebrated with empty ritual.

2:13 I WILL VISIT UPON HER THE DAYS OF BAALIM. God would "visit" His people. In the O.T., such visitation meant that God would enter into the situation and do something about it. Sometimes He would bless, but in this case He would bring judgment upon them for their sin and idolatry.

2:14 THEREFORE . . . I WILL ALLURE HER.

her, and bring her into the wilderness, and speak [p] [q]comfortably unto her.

15 And I will give her her vineyards from thence, and [a]the valley of Achor for a door of hope: and she shall sing there, as in [b]the days of her youth, and [c]as in the day when she came up out of the land of Egypt.

16 And it shall be at that day, saith the LORD, *that* thou shalt call me [r]Ishi; and shalt call me no more [s]Baali.

17 For [d]I will take away the names of Baalim out of her mouth, and they shall no more be remembered by their name.

18 And in that day will I make a [e]covenant for them with the beasts of the field, and with the fowls of heaven, and *with* the creeping things of the ground: and [f]I will break the bow and the sword and the battle out of the earth, and will make them to [g]lie down safely.

19 And I will betroth thee unto me for ever; yea, I will betroth thee unto me in righteousness, and in judgment, and in lovingkindness, and in mercies.

20 I will even betroth thee unto me in faithfulness: and [h]thou shalt know the LORD.

21 And it shall come to pass in that day, [i]I will hear, saith the LORD, I will hear the heavens, and they shall hear the earth;

22 And the earth shall hear the corn, and the wine, and the oil; and they shall hear Jezreel.

23 And [j]I will sow her unto me in the earth; [k]and I will have mercy upon her that had not obtained mercy; and I [l]will say to *them which were* not my people, Thou *art* my people; and they shall say, *Thou art* my God.

2:15 [a]Josh. 7:26 [b]Jer. 2:2 Ezek. 16:8 [c]Ex. 15:1
2:17 [d]Ex. 23:13 Ps. 16:4
2:18 [e]Job 5:23 [f]Is. 2:4 [g]Lev. 26:5 Jer. 23:6
2:20 [h]Jer. 31:33 John 17:3
2:21 [i]Zech. 8:12
2:23 [j]Jer. 31:27 [k]ch. 1:6 [l]ch. 1:10
3:1 [m]ch. 1:2 [n]Jer. 3:20
3:3 [o]Deut. 21:13
3:4 [p]ch. 10:3 [q]Ex. 28:6 [r]Judg. 17:5

Israel will return to God

3 THEN SAID the LORD unto me, [m]Go yet, love a woman beloved of *her* [n]friend, yet an adulteress, according to the love of the LORD toward the children of Israel, who look to other gods, and love flagons [t]of wine.

2 So I bought her to me for fifteen *pieces* of silver, and *for* an homer of barley, and an [u]half homer of barley:

3 And I said unto her, Thou shalt [o]abide for me many days; thou shalt not play the harlot, and thou shalt not be for *another* man: so *will* I also *be* for thee.

4 For the children of Israel shall abide many days [p]without a king, and without a prince, and without a sacrifice, and without [v]an image, and without an [q]ephod, and *without* [r]teraphim:

5 Afterward shall the children of Is-

[p] Or, *friendly* [q] Heb. *to her heart* [r] i.e. *My husband* [s] i.e. *My lord* [t] Heb. *of grapes* [u] Heb. *lethech* [v] Heb. *a standing,* or, *statue,* or, *pillar*

Hosea alternates between warnings of judgment and promises of hope and restoration. The two preceding "therefores" (vv. 6,9) spoke of judgment. Now God reveals a great and marvelous contrast. In His grace He would still call Israel to return. As in the exodus when God brought His people out of Egypt into the wilderness to give them His law and to lead them to the promised land, so He would again bring them out of the Egypt of their sin into a new wilderness, where He would guide, teach, and restore them.

2:20 I WILL BETROTH THEE UNTO ME IN FAITHFULNESS. In Bible times, betrothal was a covenant commitment as binding as marriage itself. God here promised to restore Israel to a covenant relationship by His redeeming love and to cause them to know Him in a real, personal way. In return, God was looking for righteousness, justice, steadfast love, kindness, and faithfulness in His people. Likewise, He wants us to manifest faithfulness to Him and sincere love and compassion for others.

2:23 I WILL SOW HER UNTO ME IN THE EARTH. God's purpose for His people in bringing them out of Egypt was to establish a covenant relationship with them (Ex. 19:4). That has always been His purpose with humankind. The N.T. applies the latter part of this verse to the inclusion of Gentiles into the church as His new Israel (Rom. 9:25–26; 1 Pet. 2:10).

3:1 YET, GO LOVE A WOMAN . . . AN ADULTERESS. Hosea must now illustrate God's love for Israel in a new way. Gomer had apparently deserted her husband in order to continue her immoral Baal worship. But Hosea had never given up his love for her, even though his heart was broken. He must go and express his love and care for her again, just as God would do for Israel, even though they have broken His heart by turning to other gods and loving "flagons of wine" (i.e., "sacred raisin cakes").

3:2 I BOUGHT HER TO ME. Gomer was most likely now in debt and about to be sold as a slave, as the laws allowed. But Hosea came and bought her back at a great cost to himself. This response of Hosea illustrates God's redeeming love for sinners, who have no way to redeem, deliver, or save themselves; our only hope is His grace.

3:5 AFTERWARD SHALL . . . ISRAEL RETURN. After many days without a king or prince and without the sacrifices, Israel would return to God and to their Davidic King, i.e., the Mes-

rael return, and [s]seek the LORD their
God, and [t]David their king; and shall
fear the LORD and his goodness in the
[u]latter days.

Israel's immorality

4 HEAR THE word of the LORD, ye
children of Israel: for the LORD
hath a [v]controversy with the inhabi-
tants of the land, because *there is* no
truth, nor mercy, nor [w]knowledge of
God in the land.
2 By swearing, and lying, and kill-
ing, and stealing, and committing adul-
tery, they break out, and [w]blood
toucheth blood.
3 Therefore [x]shall the land mourn,
and [y]every one that dwelleth therein
shall languish, with the beasts of the
field, and with the fowls of heaven; yea,
the fishes of the sea also shall be taken
away.
4 Yet let no man strive, nor reprove
another: for thy people *are* as they
[z]that strive with the priest.
5 Therefore shalt thou fall [a]in the
day, and the prophet also shall fall
with thee in the night, and I will [x]de-
stroy thy mother.
6 ¶ [b]My people are [x]destroyed for
lack of knowledge: because thou hast
rejected knowledge, I will also reject
thee, that thou shalt be no priest to me:
seeing thou hast forgotten the law of
thy God, I will also forget thy children.
7 As they were increased, so they
sinned against me: [c]*therefore* will I
change their glory into shame.

3:5 [s]ch. 5:6 [t]Jer. 30:9 Ezek. 34:23,24 [u]Is. 2:2 Jer. 30:24 Ezek. 38:8
4:1 [v]Is. 1:18 [w]Jer. 4:22
4:3 [x]Amos 5:16 [y]Zeph. 1:3
4:4 [z]Deut. 17:12
4:5 [a]Jer. 15:8
4:6 [b]Is. 5:13
4:7 [c]1 Sam. 2:30 Mal. 2:9
4:9 [d]Is. 24:2 Jer. 5:31
4:10 [e]Lev. 26:26 Mic. 6:14
4:11 [f]Is. 28:7
4:12 [g]Jer. 2:27 [h]Is. 44:20
4:13 [i]Is. 1:29 Ezek. 6:13 [j]Amos 7:17 Rom. 1:28

8 They eat up the sin of my people,
and they [y]set their heart on their iniq-
uity.
9 And there shall be, [d]like people,
like priest: and I will [z]punish them for
their ways, and [a]reward them their
doings.
10 For [e]they shall eat, and not
have enough: they shall commit whore-
dom, and shall not increase: because
they have left off to take heed to the
LORD.
11 Whoredom and wine and new
wine [f]take away the heart.
12 ¶ My people ask counsel at their
[g]stocks, and their staff declareth unto
them: for [h]the spirit of whoredoms
hath caused *them* to err, and they have
gone a-whoring from under their God.
13 [i]They sacrifice upon the tops of
the mountains, and burn incense upon
the hills, under oaks and poplars and
elms, because the shadow thereof *is*
good: [j]therefore your daughters shall
commit whoredom, and your spouses
shall commit adultery.
14 [b]I will not punish your daugh-
ters when they commit whoredom, nor
your spouses when they commit adul-
tery: for themselves are separated with
whores, and they sacrifice with har-
lots: therefore the people *that* doth not
understand shall [c]fall.
15 ¶ Though thou, Israel, play the

[w] Heb. *bloods* [x] Heb. *cut off* [y] Heb. *lift up their soul to their iniquity* [z] Heb. *visit upon* [a] Heb. *cause to return* [b] Or, *Shall I not* [c] Or, *be punished*

---

siah. They would humble themselves, come with godly sorrow (2 Cor. 7:10), and recognize their need for the Savior, Jesus.

4:1 THE LORD HATH A CONTROVERSY. This chapter begins a section dealing in great detail with Israel's sin, the root of which was a lack of knowledge of God and the Scriptures (see next note). Crime and violence had reached a critical point; fear and misery prevailed in the land (v. 2). An increase in crimes of violence always follows when a nation does not acknowledge God and His Word as its ultimate authority.

4:6 THOU HAST REJECTED KNOWLEDGE. Lack of personal knowledge of God was destroying the people, but not because knowledge was not available. The people were willfully rejecting the truth God had given them through the prophets and His written Word. Even today within the church, some are being destroyed by the sinful ways of the world because they do not know God and His inspired Word.

4:9 LIKE PEOPLE, LIKE PRIEST. Instead of leading the people into paths of truth and righteousness, the priests were following the people, telling them what they wanted to hear and no longer rebuking their sins. God would therefore punish both the spiritual leaders and the people for their wickedness.

4:11 WINE AND NEW WINE. The spirit of harlotry, whether associated with old wine or new wine, was destroying sound judgment and the discernment of God's ways. By itself, new, unfermented wine (i.e., *tirosh*) is a blessing (see Is. 65:8, note), but it ceases to be a blessing when it is associated with evil practices such as harlotry and idolatry (v. 12; see article on WINE IN THE OLD TESTAMENT, p. 220).

4:15 NOR SWEAR, THE LORD LIVETH. The priests were using religious and pious language to deceive the people and turn them away from the pure worship of the Lord. False teachers know how to use Biblical language to communicate unscriptural teachings. We must listen carefully to what is preached in order to evaluate whether the ideas being expressed are a proper exposition of the written Word of God (see article on FALSE

harlot, *yet* let not Judah offend; [k]and come not ye unto Gilgal, neither go ye up to [l]Beth-aven, [m]nor swear, The LORD liveth.

16 For Israel [n]slideth back as a backsliding heifer: now the LORD will feed them as a lamb in a large place.

17 Ephraim *is* joined to idols: [o]let him alone.

18 Their drink [d]is sour: they have committed whoredom continually: [p]her rulers *with* shame do love, Give ye.

19 [q]The wind hath bound her up in her wings, and [r]they shall be ashamed because of their sacrifices.

God's severity toward Israel

5 HEAR YE this, O priests; and hearken, ye house of Israel; and give ye ear, O house of the king; for judgment *is* toward you, because [s]ye have been a snare on Mizpah, and a net spread upon Tabor.

2 And the revolters are [t]profound to make slaughter, [e]though I *have been* [f]a rebuker of them all.

3 [u]I know Ephraim, and Israel is not hid from me: for now, O Ephraim, [v]thou committest whoredom, *and* Israel is defiled.

4 [g]They will not frame their doings to turn unto their God: for [w]the spirit of whoredoms *is* in the midst of them, and they have not known the LORD.

5 And the pride of Israel doth testify to his face: therefore shall Israel and Ephraim fall in their iniquity; Judah also shall fall with them.

6 [x]They shall go with their flocks and with their herds to seek the LORD; but they shall not find *him;* he hath withdrawn himself from them.

7 They have [y]dealt treacherously against the LORD: for they have begotten strange children: now shall a month devour them with their portions.

8 [z]Blow ye the cornet in Gibeah, *and* the trumpet in Ramah: [a]cry aloud *at* [b]Beth-aven, after thee, O Benjamin.

9 Ephraim shall be desolate in the day of rebuke: among the tribes of Israel have I made known that which shall surely be.

10 The princes of Judah were like them that [c]remove the bound: *therefore* I will pour out my wrath upon them like water.

11 Ephraim *is* [d]oppressed *and* broken in judgment, because he willingly walked after [e]the commandment.

12 Therefore *will* I *be* unto Ephraim as a moth, and to the house of Judah [f]as [h]rottenness.

13 When Ephraim saw his sickness, and Judah *saw* his [g]wound, then went Ephraim [h]to the Assyrian, and sent [i]to king Jareb: yet could he not heal you, nor cure you of your wound.

14 For [i]I *will be* unto Ephraim as a lion, and as a young lion to the house of Judah: [j]I, *even* I, will tear and go away; I will take away, and none shall rescue *him.*

15 ¶ I will go *and* return to my place, [j]till they acknowledge their offence, and seek my face: in their affliction they will seek me early.

6 COME, AND let us return unto the LORD: for [k]he hath torn, and [l]he

4:15 [k]ch. 9:15 [l]1 Ki. 12:29 [m]Amos 8:14 **4:16** [n]Jer. 3:6 **4:17** [o]Mat. 15:14 **4:18** [p]Mic. 3:11 **4:19** [q]Jer. 51:1 [r]Is. 1:29 **5:1** [s]ch. 6:9 **5:2** [t]Is. 29:15 **5:3** [u]Amos 3:2 [v]ch. 4:17 **5:4** [w]ch. 4:12 **5:6** [x]Prov. 1:28 **5:7** [y]Jer. 3:20 **5:8** [z]Joel 2:1 [a]Is. 10:30 [b]Josh. 7:2 **5:10** [c]Deut. 19:14 **5:11** [d]Deut. 28:33 [e]Mic. 6:16 **5:12** [f]Prov. 12:4 **5:13** [g]Jer. 30:12 [h]2 Ki. 15:19 **5:14** [i]Lam. 3:10 [j]Ps. 50:22 **6:1** [k]Deut. 32:39 [l]Jer. 30:17

[d] Heb. *is gone* [e] Or, *and* [f] Heb. *a correction* [g] Or, *Their doings will not suffer* them [h] Or, *a worm* [i] Or, *to the king of Jareb,* or, *to the king* that *should plead* [j] Heb. *till they be guilty*

TEACHERS, p. 1508).

5:1 YE HAVE BEEN A SNARE. The people were snared, or trapped, into idolatry by the same religious and political leaders who should have been drawing them to the Lord.

5:6 HE HATH WITHDRAWN HIMSELF. The Israelites were coming with their flocks and herds to offer sacrifices and to seek the Lord, but they would not find Him. He had withdrawn Himself from them because their deeds were evil. There was no love, no faith, no faithfulness, and no real repentance; their hearts had been given over to sinful pleasures. Sometimes when people seek help from the Lord, they do not find it because they keep holding on to the immoral and sinful attractions of the world (cf. Jas. 4:1–4; see article on EFFECTIVE PRAYING, p. 540).

5:10 THEM THAT REMOVE THE BOUND. To "remove the bound" is to move the boundary stones of one's neighbor's property (Deut. 19:14; 27:17); the effect of this action was to steal a strip of his land.

5:12 AS A MOTH . . . AS ROTTENNESS. Because of their rebellion, God would give His people sickness and disease. Ephraim (the northern Israel) and Judah would decay. Sin brings God's judgment. There is only one cure for sin, the cure God has provided—the blood of Jesus.

5:15 I WILL GO *AND* RETURN TO MY PLACE. God would not hear Israel's prayer for help until they admitted their guilt, bore their punishment, and genuinely sought His help. The next chapter records the prophetic words that a future repentant generation would pray (6:1–3).

6:1 HE WILL HEAL US. In yet another call to repentance, Hosea gives assurance that though

will heal us; he hath smitten, and he will bind us up.

2 [m]After two days will he revive us: in the third day he will raise us up, and we shall live in his sight.

3 [n]Then shall we know, *if* we follow on to know the LORD: his going forth is prepared [o]as the morning; and [p]he shall come unto us [q]as the rain, as the latter *and* former rain unto the earth.

Hos. 14:4-8

Israel's unfaithfulness

4 ¶ O Ephraim, what shall I do unto thee? O Judah, what shall I do unto thee? for your [k]goodness *is* as a morning cloud, and as the early dew it goeth away.

5 Therefore have I hewed *them* by the prophets; I have slain them by [r]the words of my mouth: [l]and thy judgments *are as* the light *that* goeth forth.

6 For I desired [s]mercy, and [t]not sacrifice; and the [u]knowledge of God more than burnt offerings.

7 But they [m]like men have transgressed the covenant: there have they dealt treacherously against me.

8 Gilead *is* a city of them that work iniquity, *and is* [n]polluted with blood.

9 And as troops of robbers wait for a man, *so* the company of priests murder in the way [o]by consent: for they commit [p]lewdness.

10 I have seen an horrible thing in the house of Israel: there *is* the whoredom of Ephraim, Israel is defiled.

11 Also, O Judah, he hath set an harvest for thee, when I returned the captivity of my people.

6:2 [m]1 Cor. 15:4
6:3 [n]Is. 54:13 [o]2 Sam. 23:4 [p]Ps. 72:6 [q]Job 29:23
6:5 [r]Jer. 23:29
6:6 [s]Mat. 9:13 [t]Is. 1:11 [u]John 17:3
7:1 [v]ch. 5:1
7:2 [w]Jer. 17:1
7:3 [x]Rom. 1:32
7:4 [y]Jer. 9:2

7 WHEN I would have healed Israel, then the iniquity of Ephraim was discovered, and the [q]wickedness of Samaria: for [v]they commit falsehood; and the thief cometh in, *and* the troop of robbers [r]spoileth without.

2 And they [s]consider not in their hearts *that* I [w]remember all their wickedness: now their own doings have beset them about; they are before my face.

3 They make the king glad with their wickedness, and the princes [x]with their lies.

4 [y]They *are* all adulterers, as an oven heated by the baker, [t]*who* ceaseth [u]from raising after he hath kneaded the dough, until it be leavened.

5 In the day of our king the princes have made *him* sick [v]with bottles of wine; he stretched out his hand with scorners.

6 For they have [w]made ready their heart like an oven, whiles they lie in wait: their baker sleepeth all the night; in the morning it burneth as a flaming fire.

7 They are all hot as an oven, and have devoured their judges; all their

[k] Or, *mercy,* or, *kindness* [l] Or, *that thy judgments might be* [m] Or, *like Adam;* see Job 31:33 [n] Or, *cunning for blood* [o] Heb. *with* one *shoulder,* or, *to Shechem* [p] Or, *enormity* [q] Heb. *evils* [r] Heb. *strippeth* [s] Heb. *say not to* [t] Or, *the raiser will cease* [u] Or, *from waking* [v] Or, *with heat through wine* [w] Or, *applied*

God must judge sin, He always desires to heal and restore.

6:2–3 AFTER TWO DAYS WILL HE REVIVE US. Genuine repentance by God's people would bring renewed spiritual life. Then as they began to know the Lord better, He would come like the rain, bringing further spiritual life and blessing. Water is often used as a symbol or type of the Holy Spirit (see John 7:37–39; see Ps. 1:3, note). The former rain is the rain that comes in the time of plowing and planting; it symbolizes the Holy Spirit's work in O.T. times (see article on THE SPIRIT IN THE OLD TESTAMENT, p. 1302). The latter rain is the rain that comes in the time of harvest; it symbolizes the Holy Spirit's work in the age of the church.

6:4 YOUR GOODNESS *IS* AS A MORNING CLOUD. "Goodness" (Heb. *hesed*) refers to a covenant love that is holy, steadfast, and loyal. Israel claimed to have a deep love for God. But just as the morning clouds and the early dew vanish in the heat of the day, so did that love, for it was superficial and selfish. We must always test our love for God by our loyalty to Jesus Christ and our commitment to His righteous law and to His purposes on earth.

6:6 I DESIRED MERCY . . . AND THE KNOWLEDGE OF GOD. What God really wanted from His people was "mercy" (Heb. *hesed*, cf. previous note), i.e., a steadfast and loyal love that responded to His love; He also wanted a personal acknowledgement of Him as Lord of their lives. God wants the same from us.

7:2 ALL THEIR WICKEDNESS . . . BEFORE MY FACE. We must remember that God observes all our thoughts and actions and records them in His book. A keen awareness of His presence will keep us from evil. Satan's goal, on the other hand, is to make us forget that God is always there watching us.

kings are fallen: [z]*there is* none among
them that calleth unto me.
8 Ephraim, he [a]hath mixed himself
among the people; Ephraim is a cake
not turned.
9 [b]Strangers have devoured his
strength, and he knoweth *it* not: yea,
gray hairs are [x]here and there upon
him, yet he knoweth not.
10 And the [c]pride of Israel testi-
fieth to his face: and [d]they do not re-
turn to the LORD their God, nor seek
him for all this.
11 ¶ [e]Ephraim also is like a silly
dove without heart: [f]they call to
Egypt, they go to Assyria.
12 When they shall go, I will spread
my net upon them; I will bring them
down as the fowls of the heaven; I will
chastise them, [g]as their congregation
hath heard.
13 Woe unto them! for they have
fled from me: [y]destruction unto them!
because they have transgressed
against me: though [h]I have redeemed
them, yet they have spoken lies
against me.
14 [i]And they have not cried unto
me with their heart, when they howled
upon their beds: they assemble them-
selves for corn and wine, *and* they rebel
against me.
15 Though I [z]have bound *and*
strengthened their arms, yet do they
imagine mischief against me.
16 They return, *but* not to the most
High: [j]they are like a deceitful bow:
their princes shall fall by the sword for
the [k]rage of their tongue: this *shall be*
their derision [l]in the land of Egypt.

7:7 [z]Is. 64:7
7:8 [a]Ps. 106:35
7:9 [b]ch. 8:7
7:10 [c]ch. 5:5 [d]Is. 9:13
7:11 [e]ch. 11:11 [f]ch. 5:13
7:12 [g]Lev. 26:14 Deut. 28:15 2 Ki. 17:13
7:13 [h]Mic. 6:4
7:14 [i]Job 35:9 Jer. 3:10 Zech. 7:5
7:16 [j]Ps. 78:57 [k]Ps. 73:9 [l]ch. 9:3,6
8:1 [m]Deut. 28:49 Jer. 4:13
8:2 [n]Ps. 78:34 [o]Tit. 1:16
8:4 [p]2 Ki. 15:13,17,25 Shallum, Menahem, Pekahiah
8:5 [q]Jer. 13:27
8:7 [r]Prov. 22:8
8:8 [s]2 Ki. 17:6 [t]Jer. 22:28
8:9 [u]Jer. 2:24 [v]Ezek. 16:33,34
8:10 [w]Ezek. 16:37

God's sentence

8 *SET* THE trumpet to [a]thy mouth.
He shall come [m]as an eagle against
the house of the LORD, because they
have transgressed my covenant, and
trespassed against my law.
2 [n]Israel shall cry unto me, My
God, [o]we know thee.
3 Israel hath cast off *the thing that*
is good: the enemy shall pursue him.
4 [p]They have set up kings, but not
by me: they have made princes, and I
knew *it* not: of their silver and their
gold have they made them idols, that
they may be cut off.
5 ¶ Thy calf, O Samaria, hath cast
thee off; mine anger is kindled against
them: [q]how long *will it be* ere they at-
tain to innocency?
6 For from Israel *was* it also: the
workman made it; therefore it *is* not
God: but the calf of Samaria shall be
broken in pieces.
7 For [r]they have sown the wind,
and they shall reap the whirlwind: it
hath no [b]stalk: the bud shall yield no
meal: if so be it yield, the strangers
shall swallow it up.
8 [s]Israel is swallowed up: now
shall they be among the Gentiles [t]as
a vessel wherein *is* no pleasure.
9 For they are gone up to Assyria,
[u]a wild ass alone by himself: Ephraim
[v]hath hired [c]lovers.
10 Yea, though they have hired
among the nations, now [w]will I gather

[x] Heb. *sprinkled* [y] Heb. *spoil* [z] Or, *chastened* [a] Heb. *the roof of thy mouth* [b] Or, *standing corn* [c] Heb. *loves*

7:8 MIXED HIMSELF AMONG THE PEOPLE. The Israelites had entered into close fellowship with unbelievers, adopting many of their ways; as a result, they were now as worthless as a half-cooked piece of bread. It is true that God calls us to witness to the lost and help them as we are able, but we must not enter into close fellowship with the world, for we run the risk of adopting their ways and attitudes and hence turning to sin and away from God (cf. Jude 23; see articles on SPIRITUAL SEPARATION FOR BELIEVERS, p. 1814, and THE CHRISTIAN'S RELATIONSHIP TO THE WORLD, p. 2004).

7:13–16 THEY HAVE FLED FROM ME. Israel rebelled against God by refusing to turn to Him as the One who could help them. They felt that Egypt and Assyria offered more security than the Lord God (v. 11). People commit the same sort of sin today when they seek personal fulfillment in possessions, activities, or sinful pleasures rather than in the will and word of God.

8:2–3 ISRAEL SHALL CRY UNTO ME. Israel would keep calling on God and claiming to serve Him, but their profession would do them no good. Their worship of God was corrupted by their worldly and sinful lives. They were praising God while at the same time rejecting His righteous ways.

8:4 THEY HAVE SET UP KINGS, BUT NOT BY ME. The people were choosing leaders who did not meet with God's approval. The apostle Paul warns of a time when churches will choose pastors who are not qualified according to God's righteous standards (see 2 Tim. 4:3–4, note; see article on MORAL QUALIFICATIONS FOR OVERSEERS, p. 1908).

8:7 SOWN THE WIND ... REAP THE WHIRLWIND. Israel had sown the wind of sin and idolatry; now they would reap the whirlwind of the Assyrian attack. We must remember that sinful actions and attitudes sow seeds that will yield evil fruit in our lives (see Job 4:8; Gal. 6:7; cf. Ps. 126:5–6; Prov. 11:18; 2 Cor. 9:6; Gal. 6:7).

them, and they shall [d]sorrow a little for the burden of [x]the king of princes.

11 Because Ephraim hath made many altars to sin, altars shall be unto him to sin.

12 I have written to him [y]the great things of my law, *but* they were counted as a strange thing.

13 [z]They[e] sacrifice flesh *for* the sacrifices of mine offerings, and eat *it;* [a]*but* the LORD accepteth them not; now will he remember their iniquity, and visit their sins: they shall return to Egypt.

14 [b]For Israel hath forgotten [c]his Maker, and buildeth temples; and Judah hath multiplied fenced cities: but [d]I will send a fire upon his cities, and it shall devour the palaces thereof.

Israel's punishment

9 REJOICE NOT, O Israel, for joy, as *other* people: for thou hast gone a-whoring from thy God, thou hast loved a [e]reward [f]upon every cornfloor.

2 The floor and the [g]winepress shall not feed them, and the new wine shall fail in her.

3 They shall not dwell in [f]the LORD's land; [g]but Ephraim shall return to Egypt, and [h]they shall eat unclean *things* in Assyria.

4 They shall not offer wine *offerings* to the LORD, [i]neither shall they be pleasing unto him: their sacrifices *shall be* unto them as the bread of mourners; all that eat thereof shall be polluted: for their bread for their soul shall not come into the house of the LORD.

5 What will ye do in the solemn day, and in the day of the feast of the LORD?

6 For, lo, they are gone because of [h]destruction: Egypt shall gather them up, Memphis shall bury them: [i] [j]the pleasant *places* for their silver, nettles shall possess them: thorns *shall be* in their tabernacles.

7 The days of visitation are come, the days of recompence are come; Israel shall know *it:* the prophet *is* a fool, [j]the [k]spiritual man *is* mad, for the multitude of thine iniquity, and the great hatred.

8 The watchman of Ephraim *was* with my God: *but* the prophet *is* a snare of a fowler in all his ways, *and* hatred [l]in the house of his God.

9 [k]They have deeply corrupted *themselves,* as in the days of [l]Gibeah: *therefore* he will remember their iniquity, he will visit their sins.

10 I found Israel like grapes in the wilderness; I saw your fathers as the firstripe in the fig tree at her first time: *but* they went to [m]Baal-peor, and separated themselves unto *that* shame; [n]and *their* abominations were according as they loved.

11 *As for* Ephraim, their glory shall fly away like a bird, from the birth, and from the womb, and from the conception.

12 Though they bring up their children, yet will I bereave them, *that there shall* not *be* a man *left:* yea, [o]woe also to them when I depart from them!

13 Ephraim, [p]as I saw Tyrus, *is* planted in a pleasant place: but Ephraim shall bring forth his children to the murderer.

14 Give them, O LORD: what wilt

8:10 [x]Is. 10:8 Ezek. 26:7 Dan. 2:37
8:12 [y]Deut. 4:6,8 Ps. 119:18
8:13 [z]Zech. 7:6 [a]Jer. 14:10
8:14 [b]Deut. 32:18 [c]Is. 29:23 [d]Jer. 17:27
9:1 [e]Jer. 44:17
9:3 [f]Lev. 25:23 Jer. 2:7 [g]ch. 8:13 [h]Ezek. 4:13
9:4 [i]Jer. 6:20
9:7 [j]Mic. 2:11
9:9 [k]ch. 10:9 [l]Judg. 19:22
9:10 [m]Num. 25:3 Ps. 106:28 [n]Ps. 81:12
9:12 [o]Deut. 31:17
9:13 [p]Ezek. 26 & 27 & 28

[d] Or, *begin* [e] Or, *In the sacrifices of mine offerings they* [f] Or, *in* [g] Or, *winevat* [h] Heb. *spoil* [i] Or, *their silver shall be desired, the nettle* [j] Heb. *the desire* [k] Heb. *man of the spirit* [l] Or, *against*

8:11 ALTARS TO SIN. The altars Israel built in the north were not commanded by God. Their sacrifices thus expressed their selfish ambitions and desires. Our worship of the Lord must be based on the teachings of Scripture and follow the practices of the N.T. church. False worship may appear beautiful to our senses and may entertain us, but it is still sinful, for it substitutes worldly ways of worship for true worship in the Spirit of God (cf. John 4:23–24; see article on WORSHIP, p. 730).

8:12 MY LAW . . . COUNTED AS A STRANGE THING. Long before Hosea's day, God had given the Israelites His laws and commandments. But the people were treating God's word as a strange or foreign thing. Many people in the church today rarely read their Bibles or cherish God's laws. The commandments of His Word do not suit them because they want to continue in their sin.

9:3 EPHRAIM SHALL RETURN TO EGYPT. Hosea prophesies that Ephraim (i.e., the northern kingdom) would go into exile. Egypt symbolized the slavery and oppression they once endured; the Egypt they were now about to go to was Assyria (see 11:5, note).

9:7 THE PROPHET *IS* A FOOL. Many Israelites regarded God's prophets as foolish and insane (cf. 2 Ki. 9:103,11. They were hostile toward any prophet who preached against their sins and warned them of the coming judgment of God. Frequently today those ministers who challenge the lifestyles of church members and confront them with their conformity to the world will find themselves ridiculed by some within the church.

thou give? give them [q]a [m]miscarrying
womb and dry breasts.
15 All their wickedness *is* in Gilgal:
for there I hated them: for the wicked-
ness of their doings I will drive them
out of mine house, I will love them no
more: [r]all their princes *are* revolters.
16 Ephraim is smitten, their root is
dried up, they shall bear no fruit: yea,
though they bring forth, yet will I slay
even [s]the[n] beloved *fruit* of their
womb.
17 My God will cast them away, be-
cause they did not hearken unto him:
and they shall be wanderers among the
nations.

10 ISRAEL *IS* [t]an[o] empty vine,
he bringeth forth fruit unto
himself: according to the multitude of
his fruit [u]he hath increased the altars;
according to the goodness of his land
they have made goodly [p]images.
2 [q]Their heart is [v]divided; now
shall they be found faulty: he shall
[r]break down their altars, he shall
spoil their images.
3 For now they shall say, We have
no king, because we feared not the
LORD; what then should a king do
to us?
4 They have spoken words, swear-
ing falsely in making a covenant: thus
judgment springeth up [w]as hemlock in
the furrows of the field.
5 The inhabitants of Samaria shall
fear because of the calves of Beth-
aven: for the people thereof shall
mourn over it, and [x]the[s] priests
thereof *that* rejoiced on it, for the glory
thereof, because it is departed from it.
6 It shall be also carried unto As-
syria *for* a present to king Jareb: Ephra-
im shall receive shame, and Israel
shall be ashamed of his own counsel.
7 *As for* Samaria, her king is cut off
as the foam upon [t]the water.
8 The high places also of Aven,
[y]the sin of Israel, shall be destroyed:
the thorn and the thistle shall come up
on their altars; [z]and they shall say to
the mountains, Cover us; and to the
hills, Fall on us.
9 O Israel, thou hast sinned from
the days of Gibeah: there they stood:
the battle in Gibeah against the chil-
dren of iniquity did not overtake them.
10 *It is* in my desire that I should
chastise them; and [a]the people shall
be gathered against them, [u]when they
shall bind themselves in their two fur-
rows.
11 And Ephraim *is as* [b]an heifer
that is taught, *and* loveth to tread out
the corn; but I passed over upon [v]her
fair neck: I will make Ephraim to ride;
Judah shall plow, *and* Jacob shall break
his clods.
12 Sow to yourselves in righteous-
ness, reap in mercy; [c]break up your
fallow ground: for *it is* time to seek the
LORD, till he come and rain righteous-
ness upon you.
13 [d]Ye have plowed wickedness,
ye have reaped iniquity; ye have eaten

9:14 [q]Luke 23:29
9:15 [r]Is. 1:23
9:16 [s]Ezek. 24:21
10:1 [t]Nah. 2:2 [u]ch. 8:11
10:2 [v]1 Ki. 18:21 Mat. 6:24
10:4 [w]Amos 5:7
10:5 [x]2 Ki. 23:5
10:8 [y]Deut. 9:21 [z]Is. 2:19 Luke 23:30
10:10 [a]Jer. 16:16
10:11 [b]Mic. 4:13
10:12 [c]Jer. 4:3
10:13 [d]Prov. 22:8 Gal. 6:7,8

[m] Heb. *that casteth the fruit* [n] Heb. *the desires*
[o] Or, *a vine emptying the fruit which it giveth*
[p] Heb. *statues,* or, *standing images* [q] Or, *he hath divided their heart* [r] Heb. *behead*
[s] Or, *Chemarim* [t] Heb. *the face of the water*
[u] Or, *when I shall bind them for their two transgressions,* or, *in their two habitations*
[v] Heb. *the beauty of her neck*

9:15 I WILL LOVE THEM NO MORE. God's love is not unconditional for those who repeatedly reject His grace and word. The teaching that God will love us forever no matter what evil we do is contrary to Biblical revelation.

9:17 THEY SHALL BE WANDERERS. In fulfillment of Deut. 28:65–66, Israel was to become a disbanded nation of homeless vagabonds because they had not listened to the warnings of God's word through the prophets.

10:1 ACCORDING TO THE MULTITUDE OF HIS FRUIT. The more Israel's land had prospered and brought forth fruit, the more the Israelites engaged in idolatry. Great prosperity is not necessarily a blessing. The more money some people have, the more they spend on themselves. They forget God and the needs of His kingdom, becoming self-centered rather than God-centered.

10:8 THEY SHALL SAY TO THE MOUNTAINS, COVER US. Those who had trusted in false gods and adopted sensual pagan lifestyles would call on the mountains and hills to fall on them and hide them from God's wrath, once His judgment began. Backsliders and the enemies of God and His people will do the same when the present world system collapses and they see the wrath of God poured out on this world (see Luke 23:30; Rev. 6:16; see article on THE GREAT TRIBULATION, p. 1456).

10:12 BREAK UP YOUR FALLOW GROUND. Fallow ground is soil that has been so neglected and hardened that it cannot receive seed. The peoples' hearts had become like that spiritually (v. 13). They needed to break up their own hearts and minds by sorrow for sin and a repentance that would open them to the word and will of God. They had to begin sowing seeds of righteousness by earnestly seeking God, until they once again experienced His faithful love and mercy.

the fruit of lies: because thou didst trust in thy way, in the multitude of thy mighty men.

14 Therefore shall a tumult arise among thy people, and all thy fortresses shall be spoiled, as Shalman spoiled Beth-arbel in the day of battle: the mother was dashed in pieces upon *her* children.

15 So shall Beth-el do unto you because of [w]your great wickedness: in a morning shall the king of Israel utterly be cut off.

God's compassion toward Israel

11 WHEN ISRAEL *was* a child, then I loved him, and [e]called my [f]son out of Egypt.

2 *As* they called them, so they went from them: they sacrificed unto Baalim, and burned incense to graven images.

3 [g]I taught Ephraim also to go, taking them by their arms; but they knew not that [h]I healed them.

Mat. 4:23-24 4 I drew them with cords of a man, with bands of love: and [i]I was to them as they that [x]take off the yoke on their jaws, and [j]I laid meat unto them.

5 ¶ He shall not return into the land of Egypt, but the Assyrian shall be his king, because they refused to return.

6 And the sword shall abide on his cities, and shall consume his branches, and devour *them*, because of their own counsels.

7 And my people are bent to [k]backsliding from me: though they called them to the most High, [y]none at all would exalt *him*.

8 [l]How shall I give thee up, Ephraim? *how* shall I deliver thee, Israel? how shall I make thee as [m]Admah? *how* shall I set thee as Zeboim? mine heart is turned within me, my repentings are kindled together.

9 I will not execute the fierceness of mine anger, I will not return to destroy Ephraim: [n]for I *am* God, and not man; the Holy One in the midst of thee: and I will not enter into the city.

10 They shall walk after the LORD: [o]he shall roar like a lion: when he shall roar, then the children shall tremble from the west.

11 They shall tremble as a bird out of Egypt, [p]and as a dove out of the land of Assyria: [q]and I will place them in their houses, saith the LORD.

Israel's sin

12 Ephraim compasseth me about

11:1 [e]Mat. 2:15 [f]Ex. 4:22
11:3 [g]Deut. 1:31 [h]Ex. 15:26
11:4 [i]Lev. 26:13 [j]Ps. 78:25
11:7 [k]Jer. 3:6
11:8 [l]Jer. 9:7 [m]Gen. 14:8
11:9 [n]Num. 23:19
11:10 [o]Joel 3:16
11:11 [p]Is. 60:8 [q]Ezek. 28:25,26

[w] Heb. *the evil of your evil* [x] Heb. *lift up* [y] Heb. *together they exalted not*

10:14 SHALMAN. This name probably refers to Shalmaneser (2 Ki. 17:3), who took Samaria in 722 B.C. and made the northern kingdom of Israel an Assyrian province. His son Sargon later claimed that victory, but he may simply have been present with his father.

11:1 I LOVED HIM AND CALLED MY SON OUT OF EGYPT. God points to Israel's history when they were brought out of Egypt to become an independent nation. He calls them His "son" (cf. Ex. 4:22), yet they soon became a wayward and disobedient child (v. 2). Mat. 2:14–15 applies this verse to Jesus, who was taken by Joseph and Mary to Egypt and was then called back to Palestine after Herod's death.

11:4 THE BANDS OF LOVE. God's care was seen in the way He drew His people with cords of kindness and with bands of His divine love and compassion. He as Father and Physician was always caring for, healing, and guiding them; yet they did not acknowledge His love and blessing. We ought always to be thankful for God's love demonstrated to us in our salvation and in many other ways, both in the past and in the present. We must work hard at developing grateful hearts that love Him in response.

11:5 THE ASSYRIAN SHALL BE HIS KING. "Egypt" represents the place of slavery (see 9:3, note). The Egypt to which northern Israel would go because of its idolatry would be Assyria. This exile took place when Samaria was destroyed in 722 B.C. Northern Israel was never restored as a separate nation, though a remnant did return (Ezra 8:35; Ezek. 47:13). Note that in the N.T., Anna was of the tribe of Asher (Luke 2:36), one of the northern tribes. Thus, the idea of "ten lost tribes" is fictitious; they were never lost. Some members of the northern kingdom rejected Israel's idolatry and joined the nation of Judah, both before and after Samaria's fall (cf. 2 Chr. 15:9; 34:9; see 2 Ki. 17:18, note), while others intermarried with people from other nations and became the Samaritans (see 2 Ki. 17:24, note).

11:8 HOW SHALL I GIVE THEE UP, EPHRAIM? This is one of the Bible's most powerful verses that shows the intense love, compassion, and grief experienced by the Lord for the plight of sinners. It demonstrates so clearly that His love and compassion are like that of a caring Father (Jer. 31:9). He does not want to give up His wayward people, and it grieves Him to be forced to punish them.

11:9 I WILL NOT EXECUTE . . . MINE ANGER. Israel would not experience God's full anger. They would not be completely destroyed when He punished them; rather, He would save a remnant by which He would rebuild the nation.

with lies, and the house of Israel with deceit: but Judah yet ruleth with God, and is faithful [z]with the saints.

12 EPHRAIM FEEDETH on wind, and followeth after the east wind: he daily increaseth lies and desolation; [r]and they do make a covenant with the Assyrians, and [s]oil is carried into Egypt.

2 [t]The LORD hath also a controversy with Judah, and will [a]punish Jacob according to his ways; according to his doings will he recompense him.

3 ¶ He took his brother [u]by the heel in the womb, and by his strength he [v]had[b] power with God:

4 Yea, he had power over the angel, and prevailed: he wept, and made supplication unto him: he found him *in* [w]Beth-el, and there he spake with us;

5 Even the LORD God of hosts; the LORD *is* his [x]memorial.

6 [y]Therefore turn thou to thy God: keep mercy and judgment, and wait on thy God continually.

7 ¶ *He is* [c]a merchant, [z]the balances of deceit *are* in his hand: he loveth to [d]oppress.

8 And Ephraim said, [a]Yet I am become rich, I have found me out substance: [e]*in* all my labours they shall find none iniquity in me [f]that *were* sin.

9 And I *that am* the LORD thy God from the land of Egypt [b]will yet make thee to dwell in tabernacles, as in the days of the solemn feast.

10 [c]I have also spoken by the prophets, and I have multiplied visions, and used similitudes, [g]by the ministry of the prophets.

11 *Is there* iniquity *in* Gilead? surely they are vanity: they sacrifice bullocks in Gilgal; yea, their altars *are* as heaps in the furrows of the fields.

12 And Jacob [d]fled into the country of Syria, and Israel served for a wife, and for a wife he kept *sheep*.

13 [e]And by a prophet the LORD brought Israel out of Egypt, and by a prophet was he preserved.

14 Ephraim provoked *him* to anger [h]most bitterly: therefore shall he leave his [i]blood upon him, [f]and his reproach shall his Lord return unto him.

12:1 [r]2 Ki. 17:4 [s]Is. 30:6
12:2 [t]Mic. 6:2
12:3 [u]Gen. 25:26 [v]Gen. 32:28
12:4 [w]Gen. 28:12
12:5 [x]Ex. 3:15
12:6 [y]Mic. 6:8
12:7 [z]Amos 8:5
12:8 [a]Rev. 3:17
12:9 [b]Lev. 23:42
12:10 [c]2 Ki. 17:13
12:12 [d]Gen. 28:5
12:13 [e]Ex. 12:50
12:14 [f]Dan. 11:18

Ephraim's doom

13 WHEN EPHRAIM spake trembling, he exalted himself in Israel; but when he offended in Baal, he died.

2 And now [j]they sin more and more, and have made them molten images of their silver, *and* idols according to their own understanding, all of it the work of the craftsmen: they say of them, Let [k]the men that sacrifice kiss the calves.

3 Therefore they shall be as the

[z] Or, *with the most holy* [a] Heb. *visit upon*
[b] Heb. *was a prince*, or, *behaved himself princely*
[c] Or, *Canaan* [d] Or, *deceive* [e] Or, *all my labours suffice me not:* he shall have *punishment of iniquity in whom* is *sin* [f] Heb. *which*
[g] Heb. *by the hand* [h] Heb. *with bitternesses*
[i] Heb. *bloods* [j] Heb. *they add to sin* [k] Or, *the sacrificers of men*

12:1 EPHRAIM FEEDETH ON WIND. Feeding on or pursuing the wind symbolized Israel's foreign alliances with Egypt and Assyria. This foreign policy would be worthless in gaining protection from their enemies.

12:6 TURN THOU TO THY GOD. Though God's people were unfaithful, He kept reminding them that they must return to Him, manifest love and justice, and keep waiting on Him. Returning to the Lord and repenting of sin mean more than merely being sorry for sin. We must earnestly follow the Lord in love and righteousness according to the Scriptures and persistently seek His face in prayer.

12:7 *HE IS* A MERCHANT. Hosea implies that the Israelites were using Canaanite business practices that were contrary to the honesty God required. At the same time the merchants felt that they would not be called into account for their dishonesty. God's people must always be told that He will judge them if they follow sinful practices and worldly ways.

12:10 I HAVE ALSO SPOKEN BY THE PROPHETS. God had been faithful in sending numerous prophets to speak His message in a variety of ways and to drive home the truth of His word. The people could therefore not plead ignorance of His requirements. They were rejecting divine revelation, and God would repay them for the contempt they were showing to His messengers. Those who have heard God's word have no excuse if they fail to obey what He has said.

13:2 THEY SIN MORE AND MORE. The Israelites suffered spiritual death when they turned to Baal worship; they in turn engaged in ever-increasing sin and idolatry. Kissing the golden calves was a picture of the false worship of the Lord that they had mixed with their worship of idols. The threefold picture of dew, chaff, and smoke (v. 3) emphasized that God's judgment would soon come and the people would disappear. Those who try to pervert the worship of the Lord by allegiance to the ways of the world make their worship worthless, and they cannot expect God to help them.

morning cloud, and as the early dew
that passeth away, [g]as the chaff *that*
is driven with the whirlwind out of the
floor, and as the smoke out of the chim-
ney.
4 Yet [h]I *am* the LORD thy God from
the land of Egypt, and thou shalt know
no god but me: for [i]*there is* no saviour
beside me.
5 ¶ [j]I did know thee in the wilder-
ness, [k]in the land of [1]great drought.
6 [l]According to their pasture, so
were they filled; they were filled, and
their heart was exalted; therefore have
they forgotten me.
7 Therefore [m]I will be unto them as
a lion: as [n]a leopard by the way will
I observe *them:*
8 I will meet them [o]as a bear *that*
is bereaved *of her whelps,* and will rend
the caul of their heart, and there will
I devour them like a lion: [m]the wild
beast shall tear them.
9 ¶ O Israel, thou hast destroyed
thyself; but in me [n]*is* thine help.
10 [o]I will be thy king: [p]where *is*
any other that may save thee in all thy
cities? and thy judges of whom [q]thou
saidst, Give me a king and princes?
11 [r]I gave thee a king in mine an-
ger, and took *him* away in my wrath.
12 [s]The iniquity of Ephraim *is*
bound up; his sin *is* hid.
13 [t]The sorrows of a travailing
woman shall come upon him: he *is* an
unwise son; for he should not stay
[p]long in *the place of* the breaking forth
of children.
14 I will ransom them from [q]the
power of the grave; I will redeem them

13:3 [g]Dan. 2:35
13:4 [h]Is. 43:11 [i]Is. 43:11
13:5 [j]Deut. 2:7 [k]Deut. 8:15
13:6 [l]Deut. 8:12
13:7 [m]Lam. 3:10 [n]Jer. 5:6
13:8 [o]2 Sam. 17:8
13:10 [p]Deut. 32:38 [q]1 Sam. 8:5
13:11 [r]1 Sam. 8:7
13:12 [s]Deut. 32:34
13:13 [t]Is. 13:8
13:14 [u]1 Cor. 15:54 [v]Jer. 15:6
13:15 [w]Jer. 4:11
13:16 [x]2 Ki. 8:12
14:1 [y]Joel 2:13
14:2 [z]Heb. 13:15
14:3 [a]Ps. 33:17 [b]Ps. 10:14

from death: [u]O death, I will be thy
plagues; O grave, I will be thy destruc-
tion: [v]repentance shall be hid from
mine eyes.
15 ¶ Though he be fruitful among
his brethren, [w]an east wind shall
come, the wind of the LORD shall come
up from the wilderness, and his spring
shall become dry, and his fountain
shall be dried up: he shall spoil the
treasure of all [r]pleasant vessels.
16 Samaria shall become desolate;
for she hath rebelled against her God:
[x]they shall fall by the sword: their in-
fants shall be dashed in pieces, and
their women with child shall be
ripped up.

The call to repent

14 O ISRAEL, [y]return unto the
LORD thy God; for thou hast fall-
en by thine iniquity.
2 Take with you words, and turn to
the LORD: say unto him, Take away all
iniquity, and [s]receive *us* graciously:
so will we render the [z]calves of our
lips.
3 Asshur shall not save us; [a]we
will not ride upon horses: neither will
we say any more to the work of our
hands, *Ye are* our gods: [b]for in thee the
fatherless findeth mercy.
4 ¶ I will heal their backsliding, I
will love them freely: for mine anger is
turned away from him.

[1] Heb. *droughts* [m] Heb. *the beast of the field* [n] Heb. *in thy help* [o] Rather, *Where is thy king?* King Hoshea being then in prison; see 2 Ki. 17:4 [p] Heb. *a time* [q] Heb. *the hand* [r] Heb. *vessels of desire* [s] Or, *give good*

13:6 THEIR HEART WAS EXALTED. God had blessed the land, and the people had prospered. Because of their wealth and success, they had become satisfied and self-sufficient, thinking that they did not need God or His word. Likewise, when we have an abundance of blessings, we are often tempted to feel that we do not need to seek God and His help. Our hearts and minds are prone to turn to earthly matters (cf. Deut. 6:10–15; 8:11–20). The Lord will punish us as He did the Israelites if we forget Him in our pride.

13:14 I WILL REDEEM THEM FROM DEATH. God's promise to redeem the nation from death means that a remnant would be saved (see 11:5, note). God's purpose has not changed. He is the Redeemer from death, the grave, and hell, and He stands ready to deliver now. The ultimate deliverance will be on the day of resurrection. Death and the grave are cruel tyrants, but they cannot frustrate God's purpose for His people. The N.T. points to Christ's resurrection as the guarantee of God's victory (1 Cor. 15:54–55; see article on THE RESURRECTION OF THE BODY, p. 1799).

14:1 RETURN UNTO THE LORD. Though their sins were their downfall, the Israelites still had opportunity to repent and return to the Lord. But God wanted more than the meaningless sacrifices they had been offering. He wanted them to offer words that came from their hearts—words of submission, words of praise, words showing a changed attitude of heart, words of complete trust in the Lord. Words such as these would lead to deeds that would please the Lord.

14:4–7 I WILL LOVE THEM FREELY. After the people bore their punishment, God would heal and restore them, caring for them as a father cares for his children. Their lifestyle would be beautiful and pure like the lily; like the cedars of Lebanon the people would be strong, highly prized, and deeply rooted in God's word. All the figures of speech in these verses show how precious God's restored people will be to Him.

5 I will be as [c]the dew unto Israel:
he shall [t]grow as the lily, and [u]cast
forth his roots as Lebanon.
6 His branches [v]shall spread, and
[d]his beauty shall be as the olive tree,
and [e]his smell as Lebanon.
7 [f]They that dwell under his shadow shall return; they shall revive *as* the
corn, and [t]grow as the vine: the
[w]scent thereof *shall be* as the wine of
Lebanon.
8 Ephraim *shall say,* What have I to
do any more with idols? I have heard
him, and observed him: I *am* like a
green fir tree. From me is thy fruit
found.
9 Who *is* wise, and he shall understand these *things?* prudent, and he
shall know them? for [g]the ways of the
LORD *are* right, and the just shall walk
in them: but the transgressors shall
fall therein.

14:5 [c]Prov. 19:12
14:6 [d]Ps. 52:8 [e]Gen. 27:27
14:7 [f]Ps. 91:1
14:9 [g]Prov. 10:29

Mat. 7:16-20

[t] Or, *blossom* [u] Heb. *strike* [v] Heb. *shall go* [w] Or, *memorial*

14:9 WHO *IS* WISE? True wisdom involves understanding God and His ways; it is expressed through a lifestyle in accordance with His standards of righteousness (Deut. 4:3–9; Ps. 111:10; Prov. 1:7; 8:10,32–36). Wisdom in the Bible is never merely the possession of intellectual skill; it is always practical and includes a right relationship with the Lord (see Prov. 1:2, note).

JOEL

Outline

Introduction (1:1)
- I. Judah's Present Calamity (1:2–20)
  - A. A Devastating Plague of Locusts (1:2–12)
  - B. The Prophet's Call to National Repentance (1:13–14)
  - C. Judah's Desperate Situation (1:15–20)
- II. The Imminence of Even Greater Judgment (2:1–17)
  - A. A Foreboding Army Prepared to March Against Judah (2:1–11)
  - B. The Prophet's Call to National Repentance (2:12–17)
- III. The Future Day of the Lord (2:18—3:21)
  - A. Prophetic Promise of Restoration (2:18–27)
  - B. Prophetic Promise of the Outpouring of the Holy Spirit (2:28–32)
  - C. Prophetic Promise of Judgment and Salvation (3:1–21)
    1. For the Nations (3:1–15)
    2. For Zion (3:16–21)

Author: Joel

Theme: The Great and Awesome Day of the Lord

Date of Writing: 835–830 B.C.(?)

Background

Joel, whose name means "The LORD is God", identifies himself as "the son of Pethuel" (1:1). His numerous references throughout the book to Zion and the ministry of the temple indicate that he was a prophet to Judah and Jerusalem. His familiarity with the priests has caused some to think he was a "priestly" prophet (cf. Jer. 28:1,5) who spoke the true word of the Lord.

Since Joel mentions no king or datable historical events, the time of his prophetic message and ministry is uncertain. Some believe Joel's ministry occurred after the Jewish exiles returned to Jerusalem and rebuilt the temple (c. 510–400 B.C.). At this time there was no king in Judah and the most prominent spiritual leaders were priests. Others believe Joel's message occurred during the early days of young King Joash (835–830 B.C.), who ascended Judah's throne at age seven (2 Ki. 11:21) and remained under the regency of the high priest Jehoiada while a minor; that situation would account for the priests' prominence in Joel and the absence of any reference to the king. Joel's prophetic theme and literary style are closer to those of the eighth-century prophets Amos, Micah, and Isaiah than to the post-exilic prophets Haggai, Zechariah, and Malachi. These and other facts favor a ninth-century setting for the book.

The immediate occasion for the book was an invasion of locusts and a severe drought, the combination of which devastated the people of Judah at nearly every level of society. The ability of a large locust plague to strip bare everything green over many square miles is well-documented as occurring in that part of the world in both ancient and modern times.

Purpose

Joel spoke and wrote because of two recent natural disasters and the imminence of a foreign military invasion of Judah. His purpose was threefold: (1) to bring the people together before the Lord in a great solemn assembly (1:14; 2:15–16); (2) to exhort the people to repent and humbly return to the Lord God with fasting, weeping, mourning, and intercession for God's mercy (2:12–17); and (3) to record God's prophetic word to His people on the occasion of their sincere repentance (2:18—3:21).

Survey

The book's contents divide into three sections. (1) Section one (1:2–20) describes the devastation of Judah when a large invasion of locusts stripped the foliage from vineyards, trees, and fields (1:7,10), thereby reducing the people to great hardship. In the midst of this disaster, the prophet Joel called Judah's spiritual leaders to lead the people in national repentance (1:13–14).

(2) Section two (2:1–17) records the imminence of an even greater judgment of God from the north (1:1–11), either in the form of (a) another locust plague described metaphorically as an army of destroyers, or (b) an actual foreign military invasion. Again the prophet sounded a spiritual alarm in Zion (2:1,15), calling for a great solemn assembly in which the priests and all the people would earnestly seek God's mercy in repentance, fasting, intercession, and true brokenness before Him (2:12–17).

(3) The final section (2:18—3:21) begins by declaring that God had pity on His people when He saw their sincere repentance (the Hebrew verbs in 2:18–19a indicate completed action and should be translated in past tense). Judah's humble repentance and God's great mercy became the occasion for Joel's prophecies about the future, encompassing promises of restoration (2:19b-27), the outpouring of the Holy Spirit on all humankind (2:28–31), and God's end-time judgments and salvation (3:1–21).

Special Features

Five major features or emphases characterize the book of Joel. (1) It is one of the most polished literary masterpieces in the O.T. (2) It contains the most profound prophecy in the O.T. about the Pentecostal outpouring of the Holy Spirit on all humankind. (3) It records numerous national disasters—locust plagues, drought and famine, raging fires, foreign military invasions, celestial calamities—as God's judgments for spiritual and moral disintegration. (4) It emphasizes that God sometimes sovereignly works in history through such natural disasters and military invasions in order to bring about repentance, revival, and redemption. (5) It models a prophetic preacher who, because of his close communion with God and his spiritual stature, is able to call God's people decisively to repent as a nation at a critical hour in their history and to achieve positive results through that repentance.

New Testament Fulfillment

Several verses of Joel contributed powerfully to the N.T. message. (1) The prophecy about the coming of the Holy Spirit (2:28–32) is specifically quoted by Peter in his message at Pentecost (Acts 2:16–21), after the Holy Spirit had descended from heaven with power on the 120 charter members of the early church with them the spiritual manifestations of speaking in tongues, prophesying, and praising God (Acts 2:4,6–8,11,17–18). (2) Moreover, Peter's invitation to the multitudes at that Jewish feast concerning their need to call upon the name of the Lord and be saved was inspired (in part) by what Joel had said (2:32a; 3:14; see Acts 2:21,37–41); Paul also quotes this same verse from Joel (see Rom. 10:13). (3) The apocalyptic signs in the heavens which Joel prophesied would occur at the end of time (2:30–31) are not only quoted by Peter (Acts 2:19–20) but also referred to by Jesus (e.g., Mat. 24:29) and by John on Patmos (Rev. 6:12–14). (4) Finally, Joel's prophecy about God judging the nations in the valley of Jehoshaphat (3:2,12–14) is further developed in the last book of the Bible (Rev. 14:18–20; 16:12–16; 19:19–21: 20:7–9).

There are both present and future dimensions to all these N.T. applications of Joel. The gifts of the Spirit that began to flow through God's people at Pentecost are still available today to believers (cf. 1 Cor. 12:1—14:40). Also, the verses immediately preceding Joel's prophecy about the Holy Spirit (i.e., the harvest analogy of the former and latter rain, 2:23–27) and those immediately following (i.e., the end-time celestial signs, 2:30–32) indicate that the prophecy about the outpouring of the Holy Spirit (2:28–29) includes not only the initial rain of the Holy Spirit at Pentecost, but also a final climactic outpouring of the Spirit on all humankind at the end of the age.

Reading Joel

In order to read the entire Old Testament in one year, the book of Joel should be read in 1 day: ☐ Joel

NOTES

1 THE WORD of the LORD that came
to Joel the son of Pethuel.

The plague of insects

2 Hear this, ye old men, and give
ear, all ye inhabitants of the land.
[a]Hath this been in your days, or even
in the days of your fathers?
3 [b]Tell ye your children of it, and
let your children *tell* their children, and
their children another generation.
4 [c]That[a] which the palmerworm
hath left hath the locust eaten; and
that which the locust hath left hath the
cankerworm eaten; and that which the
cankerworm hath left hath the cater-
pillar eaten.
5 Awake, ye drunkards, and weep;
and howl, all ye drinkers of wine, be-
cause of the new wine; [d]for it is cut off
from your mouth.
6 For [e]a nation is come up upon my
land, strong, and without number,
[f]whose teeth *are* the teeth of a lion,
and he hath the cheek teeth of a great
lion.
7 He hath [g]laid my vine waste, and
[b]barked my fig tree: he hath made it
clean bare, and cast *it* away; the
branches thereof are made white.
8 ¶ [h]Lament like a virgin girded
with sackcloth for [i]the husband of her
youth.
9 [j]The meat offering and the drink
offering is cut off from the house of the
LORD; the priests, the LORD's ministers,
mourn.
10 The field is wasted, [k]the land
mourneth; for the corn is wasted: [l]the
new wine is [c]dried up, the oil lan-
guisheth.
11 [m]Be ye ashamed, O ye husband-
men; howl, O ye vinedressers, for the
wheat and for the barley; because the
harvest of the field is perished.
12 [n]The vine is dried up, and the
fig tree languisheth; the pomegranate
tree, the palm tree also, and the apple
tree, *even* all the trees of the field, are
withered: because [o]joy is withered
away from the sons of men.
13 [p]Gird yourselves, and lament,
ye priests: howl, ye ministers of the al-
tar: come, lie all night in sackcloth, ye
ministers of my God: for the meat offer-
ing and the drink offering is withhold-
en from the house of your God.
14 ¶ [q]Sanctify ye a fast, call [r]a
[d]solemn assembly, gather the elders
and [s]all the inhabitants of the land
into the house of the LORD your God,
and cry unto the LORD.
15 [t]Alas for the day! for [u]the day
of the LORD *is* at hand, and as a destruc-

1:2 [a]ch. 2:2
1:3 [b]Ps. 78:4
1:4 [c]Deut. 28:38
1:5 [d]Is. 32:10
1:6 [e]Prov. 30:23 [f]Rev. 9:8
1:7 [g]Is. 5:6
1:8 [h]Is. 22:12 [i]Prov. 2:17 Jer. 3:4
1:9 [j]ch. 2:14
1:10 [k]Jer. 12:11 [l]Is. 24:7
1:11 [m]Jer. 14:3,4
1:12 [n]ver. 10 [o]Is. 24:11 Jer. 48:33
1:13 [p]Jer. 4:8
1:14 [q]2 Chr. 20:3 [r]Lev. 23:36 [s]2 Chr. 20:13
1:15 [t]Jer. 30:7 [u]Is. 13:6,9

[a] Heb. *The residue of the palmerworm* [b] Heb. laid *my fig tree for a barking* [c] Or, *ashamed* [d] Or, day of *restraint*

1:1 THE WORD OF THE LORD. The prophet indicates that his message is the very word he received from the Lord. Thus it has relevance for all generations of believers.

1:2 HEAR THIS, YE OLD MEN. The people of God had been overwhelmed by a terrible catastrophe. To Joel, this crisis was sent by God, and the elders and people needed to turn to the Lord and cry out for His help.

1:4 THE PALMERWORM. The nature of the crisis was a severe locust plague that had swept over the land. The countryside and all vegetation were destroyed, and the people were facing a severe famine. The precise meaning of the four words used for locusts here is uncertain; they may represent the successive stages in the growth of the locust.

1:5 AWAKE YE DRUNKARDS. Drunkenness is the only specific sin mentioned in Joel. Perhaps its inclusion indicates that the people's moral sensitivity to sin and evil was so dulled that they could not recognize when they were offending the holiness of God. The church must be careful that it does not slowly accept the ways of the world and become oblivious to that which grieves the Holy Spirit (see Eph. 4:30, note; see article on SPIRITUAL SEPARATION FOR BELIEVERS, p. 1814).

1:6 A NATION. The locusts are compared to the powerful army of a great nation, with its innumerable soldiers.

1:14 SANCTIFY YE A FAST . . . CRY UNTO THE LORD. Because of the serious desolation of the land and distress among God's people, Joel calls on them to intensify their mourning, to intercede with God through fasting and prayer night and day, and to repent of all sin. Today God's people may not experience literal locust plagues, but they may find their congregations plagued by overwhelming trouble, sin, and sickness that devastate family after family (cf. 1 Cor. 11:30–32). The Biblical pattern for resolving such situations is for ministers and laypeople alike to recognize that God's help, power, and blessing are severely lacking. They must turn to Him with the kind of sincerity, intensity, repentance, and intercession described by Joel (vv. 13–14; 2:12–17).

1:15 THE DAY OF THE LORD. This "day" is the major theme in the book of Joel (cf. 2:1,11,31; 3:14). It can refer (1) to a present judgment of God on His people or on foreign nations; or (2) to God's final judgment on all evil at the end of this age, which will include the seven-year tribulation and the return of Christ to reign upon the earth (see 1 Thes. 5:2, note). At this point in Joel, it refers primarily to God's present judgment, though it is a reminder of that coming day as well. Joel speaks

Zech. 8:3-15 tion from the Almighty shall it come.

16 Is not the meat cut off before our eyes, *yea,* [v]joy and gladness from the house of our God?

17 The [e]seed is rotten under their clods, the garners are laid desolate, the barns are broken down; for the corn is withered.

18 How do [w]the beasts groan! the herds of cattle are perplexed, because they have no pasture; yea, the flocks of sheep are made desolate.

19 O LORD, [x]to thee will I cry: for [y]the fire hath devoured the [f]pastures of the wilderness, and the flame hath burned all the trees of the field.

20 The beasts of the field [z]cry also unto thee: for [a]the rivers of waters are dried up, and the fire hath devoured the pastures of the wilderness.

The coming day of the LORD

2 BLOW[b] YE the [g]trumpet in Zion, and [c]sound an alarm in my holy mountain: let all the inhabitants of the land tremble: for [d]the day of the LORD cometh, for *it is* nigh at hand;

2 [e]A day of darkness and of gloominess, a day of clouds and of thick darkness, as the morning spread upon the mountains: [f]a great people and a strong; [g]there hath not been ever the like, neither shall be any more after it, *even* to the years [h]of many generations.

3 A fire devoureth before them; and behind them a flame burneth: the land *is* as [h]the garden of Eden before them, [i]and behind them a desolate wilderness; yea, and nothing shall escape them.

4 [j]The appearance of them *is* as the appearance of horses; and as horsemen, so shall they run.

5 [k]Like the noise of chariots on the tops of mountains shall they leap, like the noise of a flame of fire that devoureth the stubble, as a strong people set in battle array.

6 Before their face the people shall be much pained: [l]all faces shall gather [i]blackness.

7 They shall run like mighty men; they shall climb the wall like men of war; and they shall march every one on his ways, and they shall not break their ranks:

8 Neither shall one thrust another; they shall walk every one in his path: and *when* they fall upon the [j]sword, they shall not be wounded.

9 They shall run to and fro in the city; they shall run upon the wall, they shall climb up upon the houses; they shall [m]enter in at the windows [n]like a thief.

10 [o]The earth shall quake before them; the heavens shall tremble: [p]the sun and the moon shall be dark, and the stars shall withdraw their shining:

11 [q]And the LORD shall utter his voice before his army: for his camp *is* very great: [r]for *he is* strong that executeth his word: for the [s]day of the LORD *is* great and very terrible; and [t]who can abide it?

The call to repentance

12 ¶ Therefore also now, saith the LORD, [u]turn ye *even* to me with all your heart, and with fasting, and with weeping, and with mourning:

13 And [v]rend your heart, and not [w]your garments, and turn unto the LORD your God: for he *is* [x]gracious and merciful, slow to anger, and of great kindness, and repenteth him of the evil.

14 [y]Who knoweth *if* he will return and repent, and leave [z]a blessing behind him; *even* [a]a meat offering and a drink offering unto the LORD your God?

15 ¶ [b]Blow the trumpet in Zion, [c]sanctify a fast, call a solemn assembly:

16 Gather the people, [d]sanctify the congregation, assemble the elders, gather the children, and those that suck the breasts: [e]let the bridegroom go forth of his chamber, and the bride out of her closet.

1:16 [v]See Deut. 12:6,7
1:18 [w]Hos. 4:3
1:19 [x]Ps. 50:15 [y]Jer. 9:10
1:20 [z]Job 38:41 Ps. 104:21 [a]1 Ki. 17:7
2:1 [b]Jer. 4:5 [c]Num. 10:5 [d]Obad. 15 Zeph. 1:14
2:2 [e]Amos 5:18 [f]ch. 1:6 [g]Ex. 10:14
2:3 [h]Gen. 2:8 Is. 51:3 [i]Zech. 7:14
2:4 [j]Rev. 9:7
2:5 [k]Rev. 9:9
2:6 [l]Jer. 8:21 Lam. 4:8 Nah. 2:10
2:9 [m]Jer. 9:21 [n]John 10:1
2:10 [o]Ps. 18:7 [p]Is. 13:10 Mat. 24:29
2:11 [q]Jer. 25:30 [r]Jer. 50:34 Rev. 18:8 [s]Jer. 30:7 Amos 5:18 Zeph. 1:15 [t]Mal. 3:2
2:12 [u]Jer. 4:1 Hos. 12:6
2:13 [v]Ps. 34:18 [w]Gen. 37:34 2 Sam. 1:11 Job 1:20 [x]Ex. 34:6
2:14 [y]Josh. 14:12 2 Ki. 19:4 [z]Hag. 2:19 [a]ch. 1:9,13
2:15 [b]Num. 10:3 [c]ch. 1:14
2:16 [d]Ex. 19:10 [e]1 Cor. 7:5

[e] Heb. *grains* [f] Or, *habitations* [g] Or, *cornet* [h] Heb. *of generation and generation* [i] Heb. *pot* [j] Or, *dart*

more of the final day of the Lord in the next two chapters.

2:1–2 BLOW YE THE TRUMPET. Joel intensifies his warning by referring to "darkness" and "gloominess," symbols of judgment and destruction. The appropriate response to God's day of judgment is fear and trembling.

2:13 REND YOUR HEARTS. The prophet calls for broken and contrite hearts (Ps. 51:17). If the people would turn from their sins to God, He would have pity on them. It is God's character to show mercy and compassion to His people if they sincerely repent (see article on THE ATTRIBUTES OF GOD, p. 912).

17 Let the priests, the ministers of the LORD, weep [f]between the porch and the altar, and let them say, [g]Spare thy people, O LORD, and give not thine heritage to reproach, that the heathen should [k]rule over them: [h]wherefore should they say among the people, Where *is* their God?

Deliverance to follow repentance

18 ¶ Then will the LORD [i]be jealous for his land, [j]and pity his people.

19 Yea, the LORD will answer and say unto his people, Behold, I will send you [k]corn, and wine, and oil, and ye shall be satisfied therewith: and I will no more make you a reproach among the heathen:

20 But [l]I will remove far off from you [m]the northern *army*, and will drive him into a land barren and desolate, with his face toward the east sea, and his hinder part [n]toward the utmost sea, and his stink shall come up, and his ill savour shall come up, because [l]he hath done great things.

21 ¶ Fear not, O land; be glad and rejoice: for the LORD will do great things.

22 Be not afraid, ye beasts of the field: for [o]the pastures of the wilderness do spring, for the tree beareth her fruit, the fig tree and the vine do yield their strength.

23 Be glad then, ye children of Zion, and [p]rejoice in the LORD your God: for he hath given you [m]the former rain [n]moderately, and he [q]will cause to come down for you the rain, the former rain, and the latter rain in the first *month*.

24 And the floors shall be full of wheat, and the vats shall overflow with wine and oil.

25 And I will restore to you the years [r]that the locust hath eaten, the cankerworm, and the caterpillar, and the palmerworm, my great army which I sent among you.

26 And ye shall [s]eat in plenty, and be satisfied, and praise the name of the LORD your God, that hath dealt wondrously with you: and my people shall never be ashamed.

27 And ye shall know that I *am* [t]in the midst of Israel, and *that* [u]I *am* the LORD your God, and none else: and my people shall never be ashamed. Hab. 3:3

Promised outpouring of the Spirit

28 ¶ [v]And it shall come to pass afterward, *that* I [w]will pour out my spirit upon all flesh; [x]and your sons and

2:17 [f]Ezek. 8:16 Mat. 23:35 [g]Ex. 32:11,12 [h]Ps. 42:10 **2:18** [i]Zech. 1:14 [j]Is. 60:10 **2:19** [k]ch. 1:10 Mal. 3:10 **2:20** [l]Ex. 10:19 [m]Jer. 1:14 [n]Deut. 11:24 **2:22** [o]ch. 1:19 **2:23** [p]Is. 41:16 Hab. 3:18 Zech. 10:7 [q]Lev. 26:4 Deut. 11:14 **2:25** [r]ch. 1:4 **2:26** [s]Lev. 26:5 **2:27** [t]Lev. 26:11 [u]Is. 45:5 **2:28** [v]Ezek. 39:29 [w]Zech. 12:10 [x]Is. 54:13

[k] Or, *use a byword against them* [l] Heb. *he hath magnified to do* [m] Or, *a teacher of righteousness* [n] Heb. *according to righteousness*

2:17 THE MINISTERS OF THE LORD. When ministers and church leaders see hurt and devastation among God's people, they are the ones who should lead the way in turning to God with a broken heart, with weeping, and with intense prayer. God expects them to intercede earnestly for Him to spare His people from physical and spiritual calamity; He wants them to plead night and day for the outpouring of His favor and Spirit upon them (vv. 18–29). Only then will the people be restored and renewed in their love for and dedication to God.

2:18 THEN WILL THE LORD . . . PITY HIS PEOPLE. When God's people humble themselves, seek His face in prayer, and turn from their wicked ways (see 2 Chr. 7:14, notes), God hears from heaven, reverses His temporal judgment, renews the land, and pours out His blessing (vv. 18–20). In other words, God answers the humble prayers of His people that come from repentant hearts. Furthermore, persistent and sincere prayer for revival will result in the outpouring of God's Spirit upon His people (see vv. 28–32).

2:26 MY PEOPLE SHALL NEVER BE ASHAMED. This promise is contingent on God's people remaining humble and faithful to Him. If they become arrogant and return to the paths of sin, God's blessings will be withheld and judgment will follow.

2:28–29 I WILL POUR OUT MY SPIRIT. Joel predicts a day when God would pour out His Spirit on all those who "call on the name of the LORD" (v. 32). This outpouring will result in a charismatic flow of the Spirit of prophecy among God's people. Peter quoted this passage on the day of Pentecost, explaining that the outpouring of the Holy Spirit on that day was the beginning of the fulfillment of Joel's prophecy (Acts 2:14–21). This prophecy is an ongoing promise to all who accept Christ as Lord, for all believers can and should be filled with the Holy Spirit (cf. Acts 2:38–39; 10:44–48; 11:15–18; see article on BAPTISM IN THE HOLY SPIRIT, p. 1652). For more on the Holy Spirit, see articles on THE SPIRIT IN THE OLD TESTAMENT, p. 1302, and THE DOCTRINE OF THE HOLY SPIRIT, p. 1668.

2:28 YOUR SONS AND YOUR DAUGHTERS SHALL PROPHESY. Joel envisions that one of the primary results of the outpouring of the Holy Spirit will be the impartation and release of prophetic gifts. The manifestation of the Spirit through His gifts makes known the presence of God among His people. The apostle Paul declared that if the church prophesies, an unbelieving visitor will be compelled to "report that God is in you of a truth" (1 Cor. 14:24–25).

[y]your daughters shall prophesy, your old men shall dream dreams, your young men shall see visions:

29 And also upon [z]the servants and upon the handmaids in those days will I pour out my spirit.

Mic. 3:8

30 And [a]I will show wonders in the heavens and in the earth, blood, and fire, and pillars of smoke.

31 [b]The sun shall be turned into darkness, and the moon into blood, [c]before the great and the terrible day of the LORD come.

32 And it shall come to pass, *that* [d]whosoever shall call on the name of the LORD shall be delivered: for [e]in mount Zion and in Jerusalem shall be deliverance, as the LORD hath said, and in [f]the remnant whom the LORD shall call.

Mic. 7:7

Judgment of Judah's enemies

3 FOR, BEHOLD, [g]in those days, and in that time, when I shall bring again the captivity of Judah and Jerusalem,

2 [h]I will also gather all nations, and will bring them down into the valley of Jehoshaphat, and [i]will plead with them there for my people and *for* my heritage Israel, whom they have scattered among the nations, and parted my land.

3 And they have [j]cast lots for my people; and have given a boy for an harlot, and sold a girl for wine, that they might drink.

4 Yea, and what have ye to do with me, [k]O Tyre, and Zidon, and all the coasts of Palestine? will ye render me a recompense? and if ye recompense me, swiftly *and* speedily will I return your recompense upon your own head;

5 Because ye have taken my silver and my gold, and have carried into your temples my goodly [l]pleasant[o] things:

6 The children also of Judah and the children of Jerusalem have ye sold unto [p]the Grecians, that ye might remove them far from their border.

7 Behold, [m]I will raise them out of the place whither ye have sold them, and will return your recompense upon your own head:

8 And I will sell your sons and your daughters into the hand of the children of Judah, and they shall sell them to the [n]Sabeans, to a people [o]far off: for the LORD hath spoken *it*.

9 ¶ [p]Proclaim ye this among the Gentiles; [q]Prepare war, wake up the mighty men, let all the men of war draw near; let them come up:

10 [q]Beat your plowshares into swords, and your [r]pruning hooks into spears: [r]let the weak say, I *am* strong.

11 Assemble yourselves, and come, all ye heathen, and gather yourselves together round about: thither [s]cause

2:28 [y]Acts 21:9 **2:29** [z]Gal. 3:28 **2:30** [a]Mat. 24:29 Mark 13:24 Luke 21:11 **2:31** [b]Is. 13:9,10 [c]Mal. 4:5 **2:32** [d]Rom. 10:13 [e]Is. 46:13 Rom. 11:26 [f]Is. 11:11 Jer. 31:7 Mic. 4:7 Rom. 9:27 **3:1** [g]Jer. 30:3 Ezek. 38:14 **3:2** [h]Zech. 14:2 [i]Is. 66:16 Ezek. 38:22 **3:3** [j]Obad. 11 Nah. 3:10 **3:4** [k]Amos 1:6 **3:5** [l]Dan. 11:38 **3:7** [m]Is. 43:5,6 Jer. 23:8 **3:8** [n]Ezek. 23:42 [o]Jer. 6:20 **3:9** [p]Ezek. 38:7 **3:10** [q]Is. 2:4 Mic. 4:3 [r]Zech. 12:8

[o] Heb. *desirable* [p] Heb. *the sons of the Grecians* [q] Heb. *Sanctify* [r] Or, *scythes* [s] Or, *the LORD shall bring down*

2:30–31 WONDERS IN THE HEAVENS. The full realization of this outpouring of the Spirit and the offer of salvation to all people will someday be followed by the end-time cosmic signs and the "day of the LORD" (cf. Mat. 24:29–31). At that time, God's enemies will experience His wrath (cf. Rev. 6:12–17). When examined in the light of Scriptural prophecy, worldwide conditions indicate that the time for these future events is near (see article on THE AGE OF THE ANTICHRIST, p. 1896).

3:1–21 IN THOSE DAYS. This chapter deals with Israel's future restoration and God's judgment on all the nations of the world; this judgment will include the great battle of Armageddon that precedes Christ's reign over all the earth (see Rev. 16:16, note).

3:2 THE VALLEY OF JEHOSHAPHAT. The Valley of Jehoshaphat, meaning "valley where the LORD judges," is also called "the valley of decision" (v. 14); it may be the valley of Megiddo in north-central Palestine. More important than its physical location, however, is the message that God will one day destroy all evil and will vindicate and rescue His faithful people.

3:3 CAST LOTS FOR MY PEOPLE. God will judge the nations for their cruelty and for treating people as if they were possessions to be traded for money and pleasure. We must be careful how we treat other people, for God will hold us accountable on the day of His judgment for mistreating another person (see Col. 3:25, note).

3:4–8 TYRE AND ZIDON. The Lord addresses cities and a region that had been especially cruel to Israel. The prophecy of judgment was at least partly fulfilled in the fourth century when they were subjugated by Alexander the Great and later by Antiochus III (see also Is. 23; Ezek. 26—28; Amos 1:9–10).

3:9–16 PREPARE WAR. The nations are told to prepare for war, for the Lord will come against them with a great destruction. Those who stand against God and His word will be called to account for their sins (see Rev. 14:19, note; 16:16, note; cf. Rev. 19:11–21). Believers must remember that ungodliness, lawlessness, and evil will prevail only for a limited time; God's people will ultimately inherit the earth (cf. Ps. 37:11; Mat. 5:5).

[s]thy mighty ones to come down,
O LORD.
12 Let the heathen be wakened, and
come up to the valley of Jehoshaphat:
for there will I sit to [t]judge all the
heathen round about.
13 [u]Put ye in the sickle, for [v]the
harvest is ripe: come, get you down; for
the [w]press is full, the vats overflow;
for their wickedness *is* great.
14 Multitudes, multitudes in the
valley of [t]decision: for [x]the day of
the LORD *is* near in the valley of deci-
sion.
15 The sun and the moon shall be
darkened, and the stars shall withdraw
their shining.
16 The LORD also shall roar out of
Zion, and utter his voice from Jerusa-
lem; and the heavens and the earth
shall shake: [y]but the LORD *will be* the
[u]hope of his people, and the strength
of the children of Israel.

Eternal blessing for God's people

17 So shall ye know that I *am* the
LORD your God dwelling in Zion, my
holy mountain: then shall Jerusalem be
[v]holy, and there shall no strangers
pass through her any more.
18 ¶ And it shall come to pass in
that day, *that* the mountains shall drop
down new wine, and the hills shall flow
with milk, and all the rivers of Judah
shall [w]flow with waters, and a foun-
tain shall come forth of the house of
the LORD, and shall water the valley of
Shittim.
19 Egypt shall be a desolation, and
Edom shall be a desolate wilderness,
for the violence *against* the children of
Judah, because they have shed inno-
cent blood in their land.
20 But Judah shall [x]dwell for ever,
and Jerusalem from generation to gen-
eration.
21 For I will [z]cleanse their blood
that I have not cleansed: [y]for the LORD
dwelleth in Zion.

3:11 [s]Ps. 103:20 Is. 13:3
3:12 [t]Ps. 96:13 Is. 2:4
3:13 [u]Mat. 13:39 Rev. 14:15 [v]Jer. 51:33 [w]Is. 63:3 Rev. 14:19
3:14 [x]ch. 2:1
3:16 [y]Is. 51:5,6
3:21 [z]Is. 4:4

[t] Or, *concision,* or, *threshing* [u] Heb. *place of repair,* or, *harbour* [v] Heb. *holiness* [w] Heb. *go* [x] Or, *abide* [y] Or, *even I the LORD that dwelleth in Zion*

3:13 THE HARVEST IS RIPE. The harvest of God's judgment on the nations is about to occur, for "their wickedness *is* great." When sin reaches a certain fullness, judgment is unavoidable (cf. Gen. 15:16).

3:17–21 GOD DWELLING IN ZION. The book of Joel ends with a promise that Jerusalem will someday be delivered from her enemies and God's blessing will be showered upon His people. This blessing consists first of all in God Himself dwelling among His people and showing them His love and care. With the destruction of the ungodly in all nations, God's kingdom will prevail. Joel's conclusion shows Israel that those who remain unrepentant will face God's wrath, while those who repent and seek the Lord will experience His blessings and have a glorious future for all eternity.

THE SPIRIT IN THE OLD TESTAMENT

***Joel 2:28–29** "And it shall come to pass afterward, that I will pour out my spirit upon all flesh; and your sons and your daughters shall prophesy, your old men shall dream dreams, your young men shall see visions: And also upon the servants and upon the handmaids in those days will I pour out my spirit."*

The Holy Spirit is one of the three persons of the eternal triune God (see Mark 1:11, note; see article on THE DOCTRINE OF THE HOLY SPIRIT, p. 1668). Although His full power was not revealed to God's people until the ministry of Jesus (see article on JESUS AND THE HOLY SPIRIT, p. 1550) and, later, at Pentecost (see Acts 2), there are O.T. passages that refer to Him and His work. This article examines the O.T. teaching about the Holy Spirit.

TERM USED. The Hebrew word for "Spirit" is *ruah*, a word that is sometimes translated as "wind" and "breath." Thus, the references in the O.T. to the breath of God or a wind from God (e.g., Gen. 2:7; Ezek. 37:9–10,14) can also refer to the work of the Spirit of God.

THE WORK OF THE HOLY SPIRIT IN THE OLD TESTAMENT. The Bible describes various activities of the Holy Spirit during O.T. times. (1) The Holy Spirit had an active role in creation. The second verse of the Bible says that "the spirit of God moved upon the face of the waters" (Gen. 1:2), preparing for the creative word of God to shape the world. Both the Word of God (i.e., the second person of the Trinity) and the Spirit of God were agents in creation (see Job 26:13; Ps. 33:6; see article on CREATION, p. 6). The Spirit is also the author of life. When God created Adam, it was undoubtedly His Spirit that breathed into him the breath of life (Gen. 2:7; cf. Job 27:3), and the Holy Spirit continues to be involved in giving life to God's creatures (Job 33:4; Ps. 104:30).

(2) The Spirit was active in communicating God's message to His people. For example, it was the Spirit who instructed the Israelites in the wilderness (Neh. 9:20). When the psalmists of Israel sang their songs, they did so by the Spirit of the Lord (2 Sam. 23:2; cf. Acts 1:16,20). Similarly, the prophets were inspired by the Spirit of God to declare God's word to the people (Num. 11:29; 1 Sam. 10:5–6,10; 2 Chr. 20:14; 24:19–20; Neh. 9:30; Is. 61:1–3; Mic. 3:8; Zech. 7:12; cf. 2 Pet. 1:20–21). According to Ezekiel, one clue to detecting false prophets is that they "follow their own spirit" rather than the Spirit of God (Ezek. 13:2–3); note, though, that it was possible for God's Spirit to come upon someone who was not in a right relationship with Him in order to speak a true message regarding God's people (see Num. 24:2, note).

(3) The leadership of God's people in the O.T. was energized by the Spirit of the Lord. Moses, for example, was one with the Spirit of God to such an extent that he shared the very feelings of God, suffering when He suffered and grieving when He grieved at sin (see Ex. 33:11, note; cf. Ex. 32:19). When Moses obediently chose seventy elders to help him lead the Israelites, God took the Spirit that was on Moses and put it on them (Num. 11:16–17; see 11:12, note). Similarly, when Joshua was commissioned to succeed Moses as leader, God indicated that "the spirit" (i.e., the Holy Spirit) was in him (Num. 27:18, see note). The same Spirit came upon Gideon (Judg. 6:34), David (1 Sam. 16:13), and Zerubbabel (Zech. 4:6). In other words, in the O.T. the greatest qualification needed for leadership was the presence of the Spirit of God.

(4) The Spirit of God could also come upon individuals to equip them for special service. A notable example in the O.T. was Joseph, who was given the Spirit to enable him to function effectively in Pharaoh's cabinet (Gen. 41:38). Also note Bazaleel and Aholiab, whom God filled with His Spirit in order to do the artistic work needed for the

construction of the tabernacle and to teach others also (see Ex. 31:1–11; 35:30–35). The idea of "being filled with the Holy Spirit" here is not precisely the same as the baptism in the Holy Spirit in the N.T. (see article on BAPTISM IN THE HOLY SPIRIT, p. 1652). In the O.T., in other words, the Holy Spirit came upon and empowered only a few select individuals chosen for special service to God (see Ex. 31:3, note). The Spirit of the Lord came upon many of the judges, such as Othniel (Judg. 3:9–10), Gideon (Judg. 6:34), Jephthah (Judg. 11:29), and Samson (Judg. 14:5–6; 15:14–16). These examples reveal God's enduring principle that when He chooses to use people greatly, the Spirit of the Lord comes upon them.

(5) There was also an awareness in the O.T. that the Spirit desired to lead a person along the paths of righteous living. David testified to this in some of his psalms (Ps. 51:10–13; 143:10). God's people who followed their own way instead of listening to God were really refusing to follow the way of the Spirit (see Gen. 16:2, note). Those who failed to live by the Spirit of God inevitably experienced some form of God's judgment (see Num. 14:29, note; Deut. 1:26, note).

(6) It should be noted that in O.T. times the Holy Spirit came upon or filled only a few people, empowering them for service or prophecy. There was no general outpouring of the Holy Spirit on all Israel (cf. Joel 2:28–29; Acts 2:4,16–18). The outpouring of the Spirit in this larger sense did not begin until the great day of Pentecost (Acts 2).

THE PROMISE OF THE FULL POWER OF THE SPIRIT. The O.T. looks forward to the coming age of the Spirit, i.e., the N.T. age. (1) On several occasions, the prophets prophesied about the role that the Spirit would play in the life of the coming Messiah. Isaiah especially characterized the coming King and Servant of the Lord as one on whom the Spirit of God would rest in a special way (see Is. 11:1–2; 42:1; 61:1–3). When Jesus read the words from Is. 61 in His hometown synagogue at Nazareth, He ended with: "This day is this scripture fulfilled in your ears" (Luke 4:21).

(2) Other O.T. prophecies looked forward to the time when there would be a general outpouring of the Holy Spirit on all God's people. Most prominent among these passages is Joel 2:28–29, a text quoted on the day of Pentecost by Peter (Acts 2:17–18). But the same message can also be found in Is. 32:15–17; 44:3–5; 59:20–21; Ezek. 11:19–20; 36:26–27; 37:14; 39:29. God promised that when the life and power of His Spirit would come upon His people, they would be enabled to prophesy, see visions, have prophetic dreams, live a life of obedience, holiness, and righteousness, and witness with great power. Thus, the O.T. prophets foresaw and prophesied about the age of the Messiah when the outpouring and filling of the Holy Spirit among all humanity would take place. It finally did happen on Pentecost Sunday (ten days after Jesus ascended into heaven), with a subsequent great harvest of salvation (cf. Joel 2:28,32; Acts 2:41; 4:4; 13:44,48–49).

AMOS

Outline

Introduction (1:1–2)
- I. Eight Oracles of Judgment for Nations (1:3—2:16)
  - A. Damascus (1:3–5)
  - B. Gaza (Philistia) (1:6–8)
  - C. Tyre (Phoenicia) (1:9–10)
  - D. Edom (1:11–12)
  - E. Ammon (1:13–15)
  - F. Moab (2:1–3)
  - G. Judah (2:4–5)
  - H. Israel (2:6–16)
- II. Three Prophetic Messages for Israel (3:1—6:14)
  - A. Israel's Sin Assures Her of Coming Judgment (3:1–15)
  - B. Israel's Corruption Is at Every Level (4:1–13)
  - C. Israel's Just Judgment Will Be Destruction and Exile (5:1—6:14)
    1. The Death Dirge (5:1–3)
    2. Israel's Refusal to Seek the Lord (5:4–17)
    3. Israel's Perverted Religion (5:18–27)
    4. Israel's Reprimand and Woe (6:1–14)
- III. Five Visions of Coming Retribution for Sin (7:1—9:10)
  - A. Vision of Devouring Locusts (7:1–3)
  - B. Vision of a Consuming Fire (7:4–6)
  - C. Vision of a Plumb Line (7:7–9)
  - D. Historical Parenthesis: Amaziah and His Punishment (7:10–17)
  - E. Vision of a Basket of Ripe Fruit (8:1–14)
  - F. Vision of the Lord Judging (9:1–10)

Epilogue: Future Restoration of Israel (9:11–15)

Author: Amos

Theme: Justice, Righteousness, and Divine Retribution for Sin

Date of Writing: c. 760–755 B.C.

Background

Amos was an eighth-century B.C. prophet, a contemporary of Jonah and Hosea in Israel. He reveals four important facts about himself in 1:1. (1) He was a shepherd (7:14 adds, "and a gatherer of sycamore fruit") from Tekoa, a village in Judah about twelve miles south of Jerusalem. (2) He "saw" his message (i.e., he had prophetic visions; cf. 7:1,4,7; 8:1–2; 9:1) concerning Israel, the northern kingdom. Though he was a layman and did not have the official status of a prophet, God nevertheless gave him a prophetic burden and ministry for rebellious Israel (cf. 7:14–15). His name means "burdened" or "burden-bearer." (3) Amos's ministry to Israel occurred during the days when Uzziah was king of Judah and Jeroboam II was king of Israel. The reign of these two kings overlapped during the years 767–753 B.C. Most likely his ministry was c. 760–755 B.C. (4) Amos prophesied during the two years

before "the earthquake." Archaeologists have found evidence of a major destructive earthquake from this time period at sites in Israel, including its capital, Samaria. Zechariah mentioned the same earthquake (Zech. 14:5) more than 200 years later, further indicating that it was a massive quake. The reference to it by Amos suggests that he saw it as a confirmation of his prophetic message and ministry to Israel (cf. 9:1).

When Amos prophesied to the northern kingdom in the mid-eighth century B.C., the nation outwardly was at its zenith in territorial expansion, political peace, and national prosperity. But inwardly it was rotten. Hypocrisy and idolatrous religion were popular, society extravagantly indulgent, immorality rampant, the judicial system corrupt, and the oppression of the poor commonplace. In response to God's call, Amos went to Bethel, the residential home of King Jeroboam II and a religious center crowded with worshipers. There Amos courageously proclaimed his message of justice, righteousness, and divine retribution for sin to a people who did not want to hear what the Lord had to say to them.

Purpose

Israel's prosperity served only to deepen her corruption. When God mercifully sent Amos to Bethel to proclaim the message "repent or perish," the prophet was expelled from the city and commanded not to prophesy there again (cf. Nineveh's contrasting response to Jonah's message). Then, or soon afterwards, Amos apparently returned to his home in Judah and committed his message to writing. His purpose in doing so was (1) to deliver a written copy of his prophetic warning to King Jeroboam II, and (2) to disseminate the message widely in Israel (and Judah) about the certainty of God's approaching judgment on Israel and the nations around her, unless they repented of their idolatry, immorality, and injustice. Israel's destruction occurred only three decades later.

Survey

The book divides naturally into three major sections. (1) In section one (1:3—2:16), Amos first addresses his message of judgment to seven nations surrounding the land of Israel, including Judah. Having drawn Israel at the outset into pleasant agreement concerning God's judgment of other nations (1:3—2:5), Amos then vividly describes Israel's sins and God's judgment against her (2:6–16). This section sets the tone for the book's message of judgment, resulting in national destruction and exile.

(2) Section two (3:1—6:14) records three bold messages, each beginning with the phrase "Hear this word" (3:1; 4:1; 5:1). In the first, God indicts Israel as a privileged people whom He delivered from Egypt: "You only have I known of all the families of the earth; therefore I will punish you for all your iniquities" (3:2). The second message begins by addressing Israel's affluent women at Samaria as "ye kine [[cows]] of Bashan . . . which oppress the poor, which crush the needy, which say to their masters, Bring, and let us drink" (4:1). Amos prophesied that they would be led into captivity with meat and fish hooks as their just judgment from God (4:2–3). Amos had similar words for dishonest merchants, corrupt rulers, opportunistic lawyers and judges, and compromising priests and prophets. The third message (chs. 5—6) lists Israel's abhorrent sins, and Amos called the people to repent. "Woe to them *that are* at ease in Zion" (6:1); terrible ruin and retribution for sin were coming.

(3) The final major section (7:1—9:10) records five prophetic visions of Amos about God's approaching judgment. The fourth vision graphically describes Israel as a basket of overripe summer fruit, soon to be exposed as rotten in the heat of God's judgment (8:1–14). The last vision sees God standing beside the altar, ready to smite the capital city of Samaria and the decadent kingdom (9:1–10). The book closes with a brief but powerful promise of future restoration for the surviving remnant (9:11–15).

Special Features

Six major features or emphases characterize the book of Amos. (1) It is primarily a prophetic cry for justice and righteousness, based on the character of God. Whereas Hosea was crushed by Israel's unfaithfulness to God, Amos is outraged at Israel's violation of God's

standards of justice and righteousness for His people. (2) It vividly illustrates how abhorrent religion is to God when divorced from righteous conduct in daily living. (3) It is thoroughly and vigorously confrontational. Amos's confrontation with the priest Amaziah (7:10–17) is a classic scene in Hebrew prophecy. (4) Its bold and vigorous style reflects the prophet's strong, unbending loyalty to God and to His righteous standards for the covenant people. (5) It demonstrates God's willingness and readiness to use God-fearing people without formal ministerial credentials to proclaim His message in an age of professionalism. (6) It has numerous well-known passages, some of which are 3:3,7; 4:6–12; 5:14–15, 21–24; 6:1a; 7:8; 8:11; 9:13.

New Testament Fulfillment

The message of Amos is most clearly seen in the teaching of Jesus and in the N.T. book of James. Jesus and James both applied Amos's message that true worship of God is not the formal observance of religious ritual, but "hearing" and "doing" the will of God, demonstrated in a just and righteous treatment of one's fellow human beings (e.g., Mat. 7:15–27; 23; Jas. 2). Also, both Amos and James emphasize the principle that "true religion demands righteous behavior." Finally, James quoted 9:11–12 at the Council in Jerusalem (see Acts 15:16–18) in regards to the inclusion of the Gentiles into the church.

Reading Amos

In order to read the entire Old Testament in one year, the book of Amos should be read in 2 days, according to the following schedule: ☐ 1–4 ☐ 5–9

NOTES

1 THE WORDS of Amos, who was among the herdmen of [a]Tekoa, which he saw concerning Israel in the days of Uzziah king of Judah, and in the days of [b]Jeroboam the son of Joash king of Israel, two years before the [c]earthquake.

2 And he said, the LORD will [d]roar from Zion, and utter his voice from Jerusalem; and the habitations of the shepherds shall mourn, and the top of [e]Carmel shall wither.

Judgment on the nations

3 Thus saith the LORD; For three transgressions of [f]Damascus, [a]and for four, I will not [b]turn away *the punishment* thereof; because they have threshed Gilead with threshing instruments of iron:

4 [g]But I will send a fire into the house of Hazael, which shall devour the palaces of Ben-hadad.

5 I will break also the [h]bar of Damascus, and cut off the inhabitant from [c]the plain of Aven, and him that holdeth the sceptre from [d]the house of Eden: and the people of Syria shall go into captivity unto Kir, saith the LORD.

6 ¶ Thus saith the LORD; For three transgressions of [i]Gaza, and for four, I will not turn away *the punishment* thereof; because they [e]carried away captive the whole captivity, to deliver *them* up to Edom:

7 [j]But I will send a fire on the wall of Gaza, which shall devour the palaces thereof:

8 And I will cut off the inhabitant [k]from Ashdod, and him that holdeth the sceptre from Ashkelon, and I will [l]turn mine hand against Ekron: and [m]the remnant of the Philistines shall perish, saith the Lord GOD.

9 ¶ Thus saith the LORD; For three transgressions of [n]Tyrus, and for four, I will not turn away *the punishment* thereof; because they delivered up the whole captivity to Edom, and remembered not [o]the[f] brotherly covenant:

10 But I will send a fire on the wall of Tyrus, which shall devour the palaces thereof.

11 ¶ Thus saith the LORD; For three transgressions of [p]Edom, and for four, I will not turn away *the punishment* thereof; because he did pursue his brother with the sword, and [g]did cast off all pity, and his anger did tear perpetually, and he kept his wrath for ever:

12 But [q]I will send a fire upon Teman, which shall devour the palaces of Bozrah.

13 ¶ Thus saith the LORD; For three transgressions of [r]the children of Ammon, and for four, I will not turn away *the punishment* thereof; because they have [h]ripped up the women with child of Gilead, that they might enlarge their border:

14 But I will kindle a fire in the wall of [s]Rabbah, and it shall devour the palaces thereof, [t]with shouting in the day of battle, with a tempest in the day of the whirlwind:

15 And [u]their king shall go into captivity, he and his princes together, saith the LORD.

1:1 [a]2 Sam. 14:2 [b]ch. 7:10 [c]Zech. 14:5 **1:2** [d]Joel 3:16 [e]1 Sam. 25:2 Is. 33:9 **1:3** [f]Is. 8:4 **1:4** [g]Jer. 17:27 **1:5** [h]Jer. 51:30 **1:6** [i]Jer. 47:4,5 **1:7** [j]Jer. 47:1 **1:8** [k]Zeph. 2:4 [l]Ps. 81:14 [m]Ezek. 25:16 **1:9** [n]Is. 23:1 [o]1 Ki. 5:1 **1:11** [p]Is. 21:11 Jer. 49:8 **1:12** [q]Obad. 9,10 **1:13** [r]Jer. 49:1 Ezek. 25:2 **1:14** [s]Deut. 3:11 [t]ch. 2:2 **1:15** [u]Jer. 49:3

[a] Or, *yea, for four* [b] Or, *convert it,* or, *let it be quiet* [c] Or, *Bikath-aven* [d] Or, *Beth-eden* [e] Or, *carried them away with an entire captivity* [f] Heb. *the covenant of brethren* [g] Heb. *corrupted his compassions* [h] Or, *divided the mountains*

1:1 AMOS. Amos was a prophet whose home was in Judah, the southern kingdom, yet whose message was to Israel, the northern kingdom. He was a godly layman who earned his living as a herdsman and grower of sycamore figs (cf. 7:14). God called this faithful man to deliver a message of judgment to Israel and to give them a final warning. His ministry took place most likely in the years 760–750 B.C. Other prophets who probably ministered during this time were Jonah and Hosea.

1:3–2:5 FOR THREE TRANSGRESSIONS . . . AND FOR FOUR. Amos begins by pronouncing judgment on the seven neighboring nations of Israel. He lists each nation's particular sins, even Judah's, placing all of them under the same formula, "For three transgressions . . . and for four" (i.e., for their many sins, and especially the one named).

1:4 I WILL A SEND FIRE. This phrase (used also in vv. 7,10,12,14; 2:2,5) alludes to God's judgment by the fiery destruction carried out by an invading army. Major cities would be burned to the ground.

1:6 BECAUSE THEY CARRIED AWAY CAPTIVE. The majority of the sins listed are sins of brutality and cruelty (see vv. 6,9,11,13). God especially hates sins of mistreating other human beings and will severely judge violent and inhumane acts, void of all compassion (cf. Rom. 1:18–32). In the light of God's hatred of cruelty, it is essential that God's people endeavor always to treat others with fairness, justice, and love.

2 THUS SAITH the LORD; For three transgressions of Moab, and for four, I will not turn away *the punishment* thereof; because he [v]burned the bones of the king of Edom into lime:

2 But I will send a fire upon Moab, and it shall devour the palaces of [w]Kirioth: and Moab shall die with tumult, with shouting, *and* with the sound of the trumpet:

3 And I will cut off [x]the judge from the midst thereof, and will slay all the princes thereof with him, saith the LORD.

4 ¶ Thus saith the LORD; For three transgressions of Judah, and for four, I will not turn away *the punishment* thereof; [y]because they have despised the law of the LORD, and have not kept his commandments, and [z]their lies caused them to err, [a]after the which their fathers have walked:

5 [b]But I will send a fire upon Judah, and it shall devour the palaces of Jerusalem.

Prophecy against Israel

6 ¶ Thus saith the LORD; For three transgressions of Israel, and for four, I will not turn away *the punishment* thereof; because [c]they sold the righteous for silver, and the poor for a pair of shoes;

7 That pant after the dust of the earth on the head of the poor, and [d]turn aside the way of the meek: [e]and a man and his father will go in unto the *same* [i]maid, [f]to profane my holy name:

8 And they lay *themselves* down upon clothes [g]laid to pledge [h]by every altar, and they drink the wine of [j]the condemned *in* the house of their god.

9 ¶ Yet destroyed I the [i]Amorite before them, whose height *was* like the height of the cedars, and he *was* strong as the oaks; yet I [j]destroyed his fruit from above, and his roots from beneath.

10 Also [k]I brought you up from the land of Egypt, and [l]led you forty years through the wilderness, to possess the land of the Amorite.

11 And I raised up of your sons for prophets, and of your young men for [m]Nazarites. *Is it* not even thus, O ye children of Israel? saith the LORD.

12 But ye gave the Nazarites wine to drink; and commanded the prophets, [n]saying, Prophesy not.

13 [o]Behold, [k]I am pressed under you, as a cart is pressed *that is* full of sheaves.

14 [p]Therefore the flight shall perish from the swift, and the strong shall

2:1 [v]2 Ki. 3:27 **2:2** [w]Jer. 48:41 **2:3** [x]Num. 24:17 Jer. 48:7 **2:4** [y]Lev. 26:14 [z]Is. 28:15 Jer. 16:19 [a]Ezek. 20:13,16, 18 **2:5** [b]Jer. 17:27 Hos. 8:14 **2:6** [c]Is. 29:21 **2:7** [d]ch. 5:12 [e]Ezek. 22:11 [f]Lev. 20:3 **2:8** [g]Ex. 22:26 [h]1 Cor. 8:10 **2:9** [i]Num. 21:24 Deut. 2:31 [j]Is. 5:24 Mal. 4:1 **2:10** [k]Ex. 12:51 [l]Deut. 2:7 **2:11** [m]Num. 6:2 Judg. 13:5 **2:12** [n]Is. 30:10 Jer. 11:21 Mic. 2:6 **2:13** [o]Is. 1:14 **2:14** [p]Jer. 9:23

[i] Or, *young woman* [j] Or, *such as have fined,* or, *mulcted* [k] Or, *I will press your place, as a cart full of sheaves presseth*

2:4 TRANSGRESSIONS OF JUDAH. The nations of Judah and Israel were God's chosen people, but they too would come under His judgment for their sins. Judah's sins centered in their rejection of God's law and their refusal to keep His word. They had been led astray into idolatry, i.e., the worship of the false gods of other nations. God's people always face the temptation of being led astray by the customs and beliefs of the surrounding society.

2:6 TRANSGRESSIONS OF ISRAEL. Having addressed the sins of Israel's neighbors, Amos now reaches his climax and focuses on the sins and coming judgment of Israel, the northern kingdom. Instead of following the word of God, they were mistreating the poor (vv. 6–7), living immorally (v. 7), and corrupting the worship of God (vv. 7–8). Elsewhere it is made clear that they opposed the ministry of God's true prophets (cf. 7:10–17).

2:10 I BROUGHT YOU UP. Despite having received God's covenant love and blessings, the Israelites turned their backs on the covenant and forgot all that He had done for them; this rejection made their sin worse and their guilt greater. Likewise, we as N.T. believers should never forget God's love for us through Christ. Remembering His blessings should lead us to remain faithful to Him throughout our lives.

2:12 GAVE THE NAZARITES WINE TO DRINK. God had consecrated the Nazarites to be the highest examples of dedication and righteousness in Israel (see Num. 6:2, note). Part of their consecration was to abstain from all types of wine (see article on WINE IN THE OLD TESTAMENT, p. 220). Many Israelites loved intoxicating drink (6:6); they subverted the faithfulness of the Nazarites by making them abandon their pledge of abstinence. Because they placed this temptation before the Nazarites, God would bring judgment on them (2:12–16). Those who influence others to a life of sin, including the sin of drinking intoxicating beverages, should listen to God's warning in these verses.

2:13–16 PRESSED. Because of Israel's sin, God's wrath would come upon that wicked nation. Those who thought themselves strong, independent, and brave would collapse in fear and be crushed. Likewise, when God's judgment comes upon the earth at the end of time, all the ungodly who thought they were strong and tough will cringe in fear as they see their coming destruction.

not strengthen his force, [q]neither
shall the mighty deliver [l]himself:
15 Neither shall he stand that han-
dleth the bow; and *he that is* swift of
foot shall not deliver *himself*: neither
shall he that rideth the horse deliver
himself.
16 And *he that is* [m]courageous
among the mighty shall flee away na-
ked in that day, saith the LORD.

The relation of Israel to God

3 HEAR THIS word that the LORD
hath spoken against you, O chil-
dren of Israel, against the whole family
which I brought up from the land of
Egypt, saying,
2 [r]You only have I known of all the
families of the earth: [s]therefore I will
[n]punish you for all your iniquities.
3 Can two walk together, except
they be agreed?
4 Will a lion roar in the forest, when
he hath no prey? will a young lion [o]cry
out of his den, if he have taken noth-
ing?
5 Can a bird fall in a snare upon the
earth, where no gin *is* for him? shall *one*
take up a snare from the earth, and
have taken nothing at all?
6 Shall a trumpet be blown in the
city, and the people [p]not be afraid?
[t]shall there be evil in a city, [q]and the
LORD hath not done *it?*
7 Surely the Lord GOD will do noth-
ing, but [u]he revealeth his secret unto
his servants the prophets.
8 The lion hath roared, who will not
fear? the Lord GOD hath spoken, [v]who
can but prophesy?
9 ¶ Publish in the palaces at Ash-
dod, and in the palaces in the land of
Egypt, and say, Assemble yourselves
upon the mountains of Samaria, and
behold the great tumults in the midst
thereof, and the [r]oppressed in the
midst thereof.
10 For they [w]know not to do right,
saith the LORD, who store up violence
and [s]robbery in their palaces.
11 Therefore thus saith the Lord
GOD; An adversary *there shall be* even
round about the land; and he shall
bring down thy strength from thee, and
thy palaces shall be spoiled.
12 Thus saith the LORD; As the
shepherd [t]taketh out of the mouth of
the lion two legs, or a piece of an ear;
so shall the children of Israel be taken
out that dwell in Samaria in the corner
of a bed, and [u]in Damascus *in* a couch.
13 Hear ye, and testify in the house
of Jacob, saith the Lord GOD, the God of
hosts,
14 That in the day that I shall [v]vis-
it the transgressions of Israel upon
him I will also visit the altars of Beth-
el: and the horns of the altar shall be
cut off, and fall to ground.
15 And I will smite [x]the winter

2:14 [q]Ps. 33:16
3:2 [r]Deut. 7:6 Ps. 147:19 [s]Mat. 11:22 Rom. 2:9
3:6 [t]Is. 45:7
3:7 [u]Gen. 6:13 John 15:15
3:8 [v]Acts 4:20
3:10 [w]Jer. 4:22
3:15 [x]Jer. 36:22

[l] Heb. *his soul,* or *life* [m] Heb. *strong of his heart* [n] Heb. *visit upon* [o] Heb. *give forth his voice* [p] Or, *not run together?* [q] Or, *and shall not the LORD do* somewhat? [r] Or, *oppressions* [s] Or, *spoil* [t] Heb. *delivereth* [u] Or, *on the bed's feet* [v] Or, *punish Israel for*

3:1 THE WHOLE FAMILY. Both Israel and Judah are in mind here. They were God's chosen people who had to be brought to accountability.

3:2 YOU ONLY HAVE I KNOWN. The word "known" here refers to God's choosing of His people. The Israelites were objecting to Amos's message, for they believed God would not punish them; they were, after all, His elect whom He had called and redeemed. They felt that God's past salvation meant their present security, even if they turned from God and His ways. They had forgotten that election established a relationship with God that brought with it the responsibility to remain faithful in their obedience to God (see articles on GOD'S COVENANT WITH THE ISRAELITES, p. 314, and ELECTION AND PREDESTINATION, p. 1846). The punishment that Israel would receive was the result of her failure to fulfill her part in election.

3:3–8 CAN TWO WALK TOGETHER, EXCEPT. The examples in these verses show that a second event happens only when it is preceded by a first event. Thus, as surely as God had spoken, Amos had to pronounce divine judgment; he was not simply speaking his own opinions (vv. 7–8).

3:3 CAN TWO WALK TOGETHER? No real fellowship can exist between two people unless they agree on fundamental truths. Thus we can have no genuine relationship with God unless we accept His Word and agree with it. It is impossible to call yourself a believer and at the same time not believe God's Word.

3:7–8 HE REVEALETH HIS SECRET. The Lord did nothing with regard to His people Israel without first revealing His plans to the prophets. When God did so, they were compelled to prophesy and to warn the people of God's threatened judgments.

3:9–15 ASSEMBLE YOURSELVES. Amos called on Israel's neighbors to witness the guilt, sin, and judgment of Israel. They would recognize that this judgment was well-deserved.

3:11–12 AN ADVERSARY *THERE SHALL BE.* The adversary was Assyria, the nation God used to destroy Israel. Only a small remnant in Israel would survive to tell the story of God's judgment (v. 12).

house with [y]the summer house; and [z]the houses of ivory shall perish, and the great houses shall have an end, saith the LORD.

4 HEAR THIS word, ye [a]kine of Bashan, that *are* in the mountain of Samaria, which oppress the poor, which crush the needy, which say to their masters, Bring, and let us drink.

2 [b]The Lord GOD hath sworn by his holiness, that, lo, the days shall come upon you, that he will take you away [c]with hooks, and your posterity with fishhooks.

3 And [d]ye shall go out at the breaches, every *cow at that which is* before her; and [w]ye shall cast *them* into the palace, saith the LORD.

Israel's failure to return to God

4 ¶ [e]Come to Beth-el, and transgress; at [f]Gilgal multiply transgression; and [g]bring your sacrifices every morning, [h]*and* your tithes after [x]three years:

5 [i]And [y]offer a sacrifice of thanksgiving with leaven, and proclaim *and* publish [j]the free offerings: for [z]this liketh you, O ye children of Israel, saith the Lord GOD.

6 ¶ And I also have given you cleanness of teeth in all your cities, and want of bread in all your places: [k]yet have ye not returned unto me, saith the LORD.

7 And also I have withholden the rain from you, when *there were* yet three months to the harvest: and I caused it to rain upon one city, and caused it not to rain upon another city: one piece was rained upon, and the piece whereupon it rained not withered.

8 So two *or* three cities wandered unto one city, to drink water; but they were not satisfied: yet have ye not returned unto me, saith the LORD.

9 [l]I have smitten you with blasting and mildew: [a]when your gardens and your vineyards and your fig trees and your olive trees increased, [m]the palmerworm devoured *them:* yet have ye not returned unto me, saith the LORD.

10 I have sent among you the pestilence [n]after[b] the manner of Egypt: your young men have I slain with the sword, [o]and[c] have taken away your horses; and I have made the stink of your camps to come up unto your nostrils: yet have ye not returned unto me, saith the LORD.

11 I have overthrown *some* of you, as God overthrew [p]Sodom and Gomorrah, and ye were as a firebrand plucked out of the burning: yet have ye not returned unto me, saith the LORD.

12 Therefore thus will I do unto thee, O Israel: *and* because I will do this unto thee, [q]prepare to meet thy God, O Israel.

13 For, lo, he that formeth the mountains, and createth the [d]wind, [r]and declareth unto man what *is* his thought, that maketh the morning darkness, [s]and treadeth upon the high places of the earth, [t]The LORD, The God of hosts, *is* his name.

5 HEAR YE this word which I [u]take up against you, *even* a lamentation, O house of Israel.

3:15 [y]Judg. 3:20 [z]1 Ki. 22:39
4:1 [a]Ps. 22:12 Ezek. 39:18
4:2 [b]Ps. 89:35 [c]Jer. 16:16 Hab. 1:15
4:3 [d]Ezek. 12:5
4:4 [e]Ezek. 20:39 [f]Hos. 4:15 [g]Num. 28:3 [h]Deut. 14:28
4:5 [i]Lev. 7:13 [j]Lev. 22:18 Deut. 12:6
4:6 [k]Is. 26:11 Jer. 5:3 Hag. 2:17
4:9 [l]Deut. 28:22 Hag. 2:17 [m]Joel 1:4
4:10 [n]Ex. 9:3,6 Deut. 28:27 Ps. 78:50 [o]2 Ki. 13:7
4:11 [p]Gen. 19:24 Is. 13:19
4:12 [q]Ezek. 13:5
4:13 [r]Ps. 139:2 Dan. 2:28 [s]Mic. 1:3 [t]Is. 47:4 Jer. 10:16
5:1 [u]Jer. 7:29

[w] Or, *ye shall cast away the things of the palace* [x] Heb. *three years of days* [y] Heb. *offer by burning* [z] Heb. *so ye love* [a] Or, *the multitude of your gardens, &c. did the palmerworm* [b] Or, *in the way* [c] Heb. *with the captivity of your horses* [d] Or, *spirit*

4:1 YE KINE OF BASHAN. The upper-class women are called "kine [cows] of Bashan" (i.e. the highly bred and well-fed cattle of Canaan, cf. Ps. 22:12). As these women drank their wine, they would urge their husbands to gain even more money by oppressing the poor so that they could drink all the more and bask in luxury.

4:2 TAKE YOU AWAY WITH HOOKS. Assyrian pictures engraved on stone portray prisoners being led away with ropes tied to hooks in their nose or lips. The wealthy women of Israel's capital would be led away in judgment like cattle.

4:4–5 MULTIPLY TRANSGRESSION. Many Israelites were adding to their sins by going to worship and offering sacrifices and tithes while continuing to live in sin. Those who profess to be saved and to worship the Lord and give offerings while loving the sinful pleasures of the world, are an abomination before the Lord. God accepts only the worship and devotion of those who love Him and are committed to His ways and word.

4:6–11 YET HAVE YE NOT RETURNED UNTO ME. God had sent disaster after disaster on the people in order to urge them to repent and return to Him. However, nothing availed to bring the people out of their corrupt lifestyle. For this they would face the ultimate judgment of God (v. 12).

4:12 PREPARE TO MEET THY GOD. Israel would meet God's judgment at the hands of the Assyrians, an ultimate judgment that would be terrible. This passage reminds us that all God's people will one day be judged for their deeds (see John 5:29, notes; see article on THE JUDGMENT OF BELIEVERS, p. 1811).

5:1–27 A LAMENTATION. In this lamenta-

2 The virgin of Israel is fallen; she shall no more rise: she is forsaken upon her land; *there is* none to raise her up.

3 For thus saith the Lord GOD; The city that went out *by* a thousand shall leave an hundred, and that which went forth *by* an hundred shall leave ten, to the house of Israel.

The call to repentance

4 ¶ For thus saith the LORD unto the house of Israel, [v]Seek ye me, [w]and ye shall live:

5 But seek not [x]Beth-el, nor enter into Gilgal, and pass not to [y]Beer-sheba: for Gilgal shall surely go into captivity, and [z]Beth-el shall come to nought.

6 Seek the LORD, and ye shall live; lest he break out like fire in the house of Joseph, and devour *it*, and *there be* none to quench *it* in Beth-el.

7 Ye who [a]turn judgment to wormwood, and leave off righteousness in the earth,

8 *Seek him* that maketh the [b]seven stars and Orion, and turneth the shadow of death into the morning, [c]and maketh the day dark with night: that [d]calleth for the waters of the sea, and poureth them out upon the face of the earth: [e]The LORD *is* his name:

9 That strengtheneth the [e]spoiled against the strong, so that the spoiled shall come against the fortress.

10 [f]They hate him that rebuketh in the gate, and they [g]abhor him that speaketh uprightly.

11 Forasmuch therefore as your treading *is* upon the poor, and ye take from him burdens of wheat: [h]ye have built houses of hewn stone, but ye shall not dwell in them; ye have planted [f]pleasant vineyards, but ye shall not drink wine of them.

12 For I know your manifold transgressions and your mighty sins: [i]they afflict the just, they take [g]a bribe, and they [j]turn aside the poor in the gate *from their right.*

13 Therefore [k]the prudent shall keep silence in that time; for it *is* an evil time.

14 Seek good, and not evil, that ye may live: and so the LORD, the God of hosts, shall be with you, [l]as ye have spoken.

15 [m]Hate the evil, and love the good, and establish judgment in the gate: [n]it may be that the LORD God of hosts will be gracious unto the remnant of Joseph.

16 Therefore the LORD, the God of hosts, the Lord, saith thus; Wailing *shall be* in all streets; and they shall say in all the highways, Alas! alas! and they shall call the husbandman to mourning, and [o]such as are skilful of lamentation to Wailing.

17 And in all vineyards *shall be* wailing: for [p]I will pass through thee, saith the LORD.

The day of the LORD

18 [q]Woe unto you that desire the day of the LORD! to what end *is* it for

5:4 [v]Jer. 29:13 [w]Is. 55:3
5:5 [x]ch. 4:4 [y]ch. 8:14 [z]Hos. 4:15
5:7 [a]ch. 6:12
5:8 [b]Job 9:9 [c]Ps. 104:20 [d]Job 38:34 [e]ch. 4:13
5:10 [f]Is. 29:21 [g]1 Ki. 22:8
5:11 [h]Mic. 6:15
5:12 [i]ch. 2:6 [j]Is. 29:21
5:13 [k]ch. 6:10
5:14 [l]Mic. 3:11
5:15 [m]Rom. 12:9 [n]Joel 2:14
5:16 [o]Jer. 9:17
5:17 [p]Ex. 12:12
5:18 [q]Is. 5:19 Jer. 17:15

[e] Heb. *spoil* [f] Heb. *vineyards of desire* [g] Or, *a ransom*

tion, Amos communicates the Lord's sorrow because of Israel's sins. The song maintains that their doom was certain, speaking as if it had already taken place. Yet Amos appeals to the people to turn to God so that at least a "remnant" might be saved (v. 15).

5:4 SEEK YE ME, AND YE SHALL LIVE. If the people would seek the Lord, a remnant could be spared the doom of which Amos spoke (see v. 15). In this life, seeking the Lord daily is essential to receiving His grace and mercy. You should be alarmed if you find yourself neglecting prayer and meditation on God's Word.

5:7 LEAVE OFF RIGHTEOUSNESS. True spirituality does not exist where there is no desire for righteousness. We all must have an intense concern for righteousness in our own lives and in the society in which we live (cf. Mat. 6:33). Righteousness comes to expression by following the direction of the Holy Spirit, by hating evil, and by loving the good (see v. 15, note).

5:12 THEY AFFLICT THE JUST. Of all the sins that Amos pointed out, prominent were the social sins of the people—the rich taking advantage of the poor and exploiting them. It is God's will that we have a special love and compassion for the needy (see article on THE CARE OF THE POOR AND NEEDY, p. 1312).

5:15 HATE THE EVIL, AND LOVE THE GOOD. If God's people would only hate evil and love what was good, God would have mercy on the remnant, i.e., those who survived the coming judgment. A sure sign that we have committed ourselves to God is a sincere hatred of all sin and a deep love for God's righteous standards (see Heb. 1:9, note).

5:18 DAY OF THE LORD. The Israelites believed that "the day of the LORD" would be a day when God would judge all their enemies and they themselves would be exalted. Amos shocked them by insisting that when that day came, it would mean judgment for the sinful nation of

THE CARE OF THE POOR AND NEEDY

***Amos 5:12–14** "For I know your manifold transgressions and your mighty sins: they afflict the just, they take a bribe, and they turn aside the poor in the gate* from their right. *Therefore the prudent shall keep silence in that time; for it* is *an evil time. Seek good, and not evil, that ye may live: and so the* L*ORD, the God of hosts, shall be with you, as ye have spoken."*

In this world where there are both rich and poor, haves and have-nots, frequently those who have material wealth take advantage of those who have little, often gaining more at the expense of the exploited poor (see Ps. 10:2,9–10; Isa 3:14–15; Jer. 2:34; Amos 2:6–7; 5:12–13; Jas. 2:6). The Bible says much about how believers are to treat the poor and needy.

GOD'S CONCERN FOR THE POOR AND NEEDY. In various ways God has revealed His great concern for the poor, the needy, and the oppressed. (1) The Lord God is the champion of the poor and the needy. He reveals Himself as their refuge (Ps. 14:6; Is. 25:4), their helper (Ps. 40:17; 70:5), their deliverer (1 Sam. 2:8; Ps. 12:5; 34:6; 35:10; 113:7; cf. Luke 1:52–53), and their provider (Ps. 10:14; 68:10; 132:15).

(2) When God revealed His law to the Israelites, He provided a number of ways to eliminate poverty among them (see Deut. 15:7–11, note). He stated His overall goal for them as follows: "there shall be no poor among you; for the LORD shall greatly bless thee in the land which the LORD thy God giveth *thee* for an inheritance to possess it" (Deut. 15:4). Thus, God forbade in His law the charging of interest on loans to the poor (Ex. 22:25; Lev. 25:35–36). If the poor gave something as a security ("a pledge") against a loan (such as his garment), the person loaning the money had to return that pledge by sunset. If a poor person was hired to work for a rich man, he was to receive his pay every day so that he could buy food for himself and his family (Deut. 24:14–15). During the harvest season, grain that dropped was to be left so that the poor could glean it for themselves (Lev. 19:10; Deut. 24:19–21); in fact, the corners of the field were specifically to be left unharvested for gleaning (Lev. 19:9). Even more striking was God's command that every seven years, all debts of poor Israelites were to be cancelled (Deut. 15:1–6); neither could a man with means refuse to loan a poor person something simply because it was too close to that seventh year (Deut. 15:7–11). In addition to providing the year for cancelling debts, God provided a year for return of property—the Year of Jubilee (every fifty years), when He commanded that all land that had traded hands since the previous Year of Jubilee was to be returned to its original family owner (see Lev. 25:8–55). And most important of all, justice was to be impartial; neither the rich nor the poor were to receive any favoritism in the law courts (Ex. 23:2–3,6; Deut. 1:17; cf. Prov. 31:9). Thus, God sought to protect the poor from being exploited by those with material means and to ensure justice for them (see Deut. 24:14, note).

(3) Unfortunately, the Israelites did not always keep these laws of God. Instead, many of the rich took advantage of the poor and increased their misery. For such actions the Lord through the prophets pronounced severe words of judgment upon the wealthy Israelites (see Is. 1:21–25; Jer. 17:11; Amos 4:1–3; 5:11–13; Mic. 2:1–5; Hab. 2:6–8; Zech. 7:8–14).

THE NEW TESTAMENT BELIEVER'S RESPONSIBILITY TO THE POOR AND NEEDY. In the N.T., God also instructed His people to manifest a deep concern for the poor and needy, especially for those within the Christian church. (1) Much of Jesus' ministry was to the poor and disadvantaged in Jewish society whom no one else seemed to care about—such as the afflicted and downtrodden (Luke 4:18–19), Samaritans (Luke 17:11–19; John 4:1–42), lepers (Mat. 8:2–4; Luke 17:11–19), widows (Luke 7:11–15;

20:45–47), and the like. He had harsh words of judgment for those who clung tightly to worldly possessions and ignored the poor (Mark 10:17–25; Luke 6:24–25; 12:16–20; 16:13–15,19–31; see article on RICHES AND POVERTY, p. 1568).

(2) Jesus assumed and expected that His people would give alms for the poor and needy (see Mat. 6:1–4). Jesus Himself practiced what He preached, keeping a money bag from which He and His disciples would give to the poor (see John 12:5–6; 13:29). On more than one occasion He instructed those who wanted to be His followers to care about the poor, to help them, and to give them money (Mat. 19:21; Luke 12:33; 14:12–14,16–24; 18:22). Such giving was not regarded as optional by Jesus. In fact, one of His requirements for entrance into His eternal kingdom is whether we have been kind to our brothers and sisters who are hungry, thirsty, and naked (Mat. 25:31–46).

(3) The apostle Paul and the early church likewise demonstrated deep concern for those in need. Very early in Paul's ministry, he and Barnabas, representing the church at Antioch of Syria, brought an offering to Jerusalem for the needy Christians in Judea (Acts 11:28–30). When the council met at Jerusalem, the leaders there refused to declare that circumcision was necessary for salvation, but they did suggest that Paul and his associates "remember the poor; the same which I also was forward to do" (Gal. 2:10). One of his goals on his third missionary journey was to gather money for "the poor saints . . . at Jerusalem" (Rom. 15:26). He instructed his churches both in Galatia and in Corinth to give for this cause (1 Cor. 16:1–4). When the church in Corinth did not give as he thought they should, he exhorted them at great length about helping the poor and needy (2 Cor. 8—9). He praised the churches in Macedonia who had voluntarily and eagerly begged Paul to let them participate in this collection (2 Cor. 8:1–4; 9:2). Regarding giving, Paul goes so far in the book of Romans as to state that one of the gifts that the Holy Spirit gives to Christians is the ability to give freely to the needs of God's work or people (see Rom. 12:8, note; cf. 1 Tim. 6:17–19).

(4) Our first priority in the care of the poor and needy is those who are brothers and sisters in Christ. Jesus equated gifts given to our fellow believers with gifts given to Him (Mat. 25:40,45). The early church established a caring community that shared their possessions to help meet each other's needs (Acts 2:44–45; 4:34–37). When the increased size of the church made it impossible for the apostles to care for the needy in a fair and equitable manner, seven men full of the Holy Spirit were chosen for that task (Acts 6:1–6). Paul states the principle of a caring community explicitly: "As we have therefore opportunity, let us do good unto all *men*, especially unto them who are of the household of faith" (Gal. 6:10). God wants those with abundance to share with those who have needs, so that there may be no lack or inequities among God's people (2 Cor. 8:14–15; cf. Eph. 4:28; Titus 3:14). In summary, then, the Scriptures give us no choice but to be sensitive to the material needs of those around us, especially our brothers and sisters in Christ.

you? [r]the day of the LORD *is* darkness, and not light.

19 [s]As if a man did flee from a lion, and a bear met him; or went into the house, and leaned his hand on the wall, and a serpent bit him.

20 *Shall* not the day of the LORD *be* darkness, and not light? even very dark, and no brightness in it?

21 ¶ [t]I hate, I despise your feast days, and [u]I will not [h]smell in your solemn assemblies.

22 [v]Though ye offer me burnt offerings and your meat offerings, I will not accept *them:* neither will I regard the [i]peace offerings of your fat beasts.

23 Take thou away from me the noise of thy songs; for I will not hear the melody of thy viols.

24 [w]But let judgment [j]run down as waters, and righteousness as a mighty stream.

25 [x]Have ye offered unto me sacrifices and offerings in the wilderness forty years, O house of Israel?

26 But ye have borne [k]the tabernacle [y]of your Moloch and Chiun your images, the star of your god, which ye made to yourselves.

27 Therefore will I cause you to go into captivity [z]beyond Damascus, saith the LORD, [a]whose name *is* The God of hosts.

Captivity inevitable

6 WOE [b]TO them *that* [l]*are* at ease in Zion, and trust in the mountain of Samaria, *which are* named [c]chief[m] of the nations, to whom the house of Israel came!

2 [d]Pass ye unto [e]Calneh, and see; and from thence go ye to [f]Hamath the great: then go down to Gath of the Philistines: [g]*be they* better than these kingdoms? or their border greater than your border?

3 Ye that [h]put far away the [i]evil day, [j]and cause [k]the [n]seat of violence to come near;

4 That lie upon beds of ivory, and [o]stretch themselves upon their couches, and eat the lambs out of the flock, and the calves out of the midst of the stall;

5 [l]That [p]chant to the sound of the viol, *and* invent to themselves instruments of music, [m]like David;

6 That drink [q]wine in bowls, and anoint themselves with the chief ointments: [n]but they are not grieved for the [r]affliction of Joseph.

7 ¶ Therefore now shall they go captive with the first that go captive, and the banquet of them that stretched themselves shall be removed.

8 [o]The Lord GOD hath sworn by himself, saith the LORD the God of hosts, I abhor [p]the excellency of Jacob, and hate his palaces: therefore will I deliver up the city with all [s]that is therein.

Oppression and desolation

9 And it shall come to pass, if there remain ten men in one house, that they shall die.

10 And a man's uncle shall take

5:18 [r]Joel 2:2 **5:19** [s]Jer. 48:44 **5:21** [t]Is. 1:11-16 [u]Lev. 26:31 **5:22** [v]Is. 66:3 Mic. 6:6,7 **5:24** [w]Hos. 6:6 Mic. 6:8 **5:25** [x]Deut. 32:17 Josh. 24:14 Is. 43:23 **5:26** [y]1 Ki. 11:33 **5:27** [z]2 Ki. 17:6 [a]ch. 4:13 **6:1** [b]Luke 6:24 [c]Ex. 19:5 **6:2** [d]Jer. 2:10 [e]Is. 10:9 [f]2 Ki. 18:34 [g]Nah. 3:8 **6:3** [h]Ezek. 12:27 [i]ch. 5:18 [j]ch. 5:12 [k]Ps. 94:20 **6:5** [l]Is. 5:12 [m]1 Chr. 23:5 **6:6** [n]Gen. 37:25 **6:8** [o]Jer. 51:14 [p]Ps. 47:4 Ezek. 24:21

[h] Or, *smell your holy days* [i] Or, *thank offerings* [j] Heb. *roll* [k] Or, *Siccuth your king* [l] Or, *are secure* [m] Or, *firstfruits* [n] Or, *habitation* [o] Or, *abound with superfluities* [p] Or, *quaver* [q] Or, *in bowls of wine* [r] Heb. *breach* [s] Heb. *the fulness thereof*

Israel (see Joel 1:15, note).

5:21–27 I DESPISE YOUR FEAST DAYS. God hates worship rituals, church attendance, and songs of praise by those who profess to be believers while they seek the sinful pleasures of the world. (1) God desires worship and praise only from those whose hearts are turned toward Him in sincere love and adoration and who seek to live godly lives (see article on WORSHIP, p. 730). (2) Religious hypocrisy is an abomination to God and will bring special condemnation upon those who are guilty of it (see 1 Cor. 11:27, note).

6:1–7 WOE TO THEM *THAT ARE* AT EASE IN ZION. God's people in both Israel (Samaria) and Judah (Zion) are addressed here. (1) They possessed power and prosperity, but had become complacent about their sins. They believed that their material success proved that they were living under God's blessing. They felt confident that God's judgment would never come. (2) Likewise, prosperity and a comfortable lifestyle can cause us to drift into a worldly lifestyle where a deep and abiding hunger for God no longer exists (see article on RICHES AND POVERTY, p. 1568).

6:6 THEY ARE NOT GRIEVED. Rather than happily living in material luxury, the Israelites should have been grieving over the sins of the nation and its impending doom. Those who experience sorrow for the sins of the people will escape God's judgment (see Ezek. 9:4) and experience His blessing instead (Mat. 5:4).

6:8 THEREFORE WILL I DELIVER UP THE CITY. Because the people had refused to return to the Lord, their cities would be destroyed. Their doom was certain, for God Almighty had declared it by a solemn oath.

6:10 HOLD THY TONGUE. When the day of the Lord came, the place of disaster would be filled

him up, and he that burneth him, to
bring out the bones out of the house,
and shall say unto him that *is* by the
sides of the house, *Is there* yet *any* with
thee? and he shall say, No. Then shall
he say, [q]Hold thy tongue: [r]for [t]we
may not make mention of the name of
the LORD.
11 For, behold, [s]the LORD com-
mandeth, [t]and he will smite the great
house with [u]breaches, and the little
house with clefts.
12 ¶ Shall horses run upon the
rock? will *one* plow *there* with oxen? for
[u]ye have turned judgment into gall,
and the fruit of righteousness into
hemlock:
13 Ye which rejoice in a thing of
nought, which say, Have we not taken
to us horns by our own strength?
14 But, behold, [v]I will raise up
against you a nation, O house of Israel,
saith the LORD the God of hosts; and
they shall afflict you from the [w]enter-
ing in of Hemath unto the [v]river of the
wilderness.

Two plagues

7 THUS HATH the Lord GOD shown
unto me; and, behold, he formed
[w]grasshoppers in the beginning of the
shooting up of the latter growth; and,
lo, *it was* the latter growth after the
king's mowings.
2 And it came to pass, *that* when
they had made an end of eating the
grass of the land, then I said, O Lord
GOD, forgive, I beseech thee: [x]by[x]
whom shall Jacob arise? for he *is* small.
3 [y]The LORD repented for this: It
shall not be, saith the LORD.
4 ¶ Thus hath the Lord GOD shown
unto me: and, behold, the Lord GOD
called to contend by fire, and it de-
voured the great deep, and did eat up
a part.
5 Then said I, O Lord GOD, cease, I
beseech thee: [z]by whom shall Jacob
arise? for he *is* small.
6 The LORD repented for this: This
also shall not be, saith the Lord GOD.

The vision of the plumbline

7 ¶ Thus he showed me: and, be-
hold, the Lord stood upon a wall *made*
by a plumbline, with a plumbline in his
hand.
8 And the LORD said unto me, Amos,
what seest thou? And I said, A plumb-
line. Then said the Lord, Behold, [a]I
will set a plumbline in the midst of my
people Israel: [b]I will not again pass by
them any more:
9 [c]And the high places of Isaac
shall be desolate, and the sanctuaries
of Israel shall be laid waste; and [d]I
will rise against the house of Jeroboam
with the sword.
10 ¶ Then Amaziah [e]the priest of
Beth-el sent to [f]Jeroboam king of Is-
rael, saying, Amos hath conspired
against thee in the midst of the house
of Israel: the land is not able to bear all
his words.
11 For thus Amos saith, Jeroboam
shall die by the sword, and Israel shall
surely be led away captive out of their
own land.
12 Also Amaziah said unto Amos, O
thou seer, go, flee thee away into the
land of Judah, and there eat bread, and
prophesy there:
13 But [g]prophesy not again any
more at Beth-el: [h]for it *is* the king's
[y]chapel, and it *is* the [z]king's court.

6:10 [q]ch. 5:13 [r]ch. 8:3
6:11 [s]Is. 55:11 [t]ch. 3:15
6:12 [u]Hos. 10:4
6:14 [v]Jer. 5:15 [w]1 Ki. 8:65
7:2 [x]Is. 51:19
7:3 [y]Deut. 32:36 Jonah 3:10 Jas. 5:16
7:5 [z]ver. 2,3
7:8 [a]See 2 Ki. 21:13 Is. 28:17 Lam. 2:8 [b]Mic. 7:18
7:9 [c]Beer-sheba Gen. 26:23 & 46:1 ch. 5:5 & 8:14 [d]Fulfilled 2 Ki. 15:10
7:10 [e]1 Ki. 12:32 [f]2 Ki. 14:23
7:13 [g]ch. 2:12 [h]1 Ki. 12:32

[t] Or, *they will not,* or, *have not* [u] Or, *droppings* [v] Or, *valley* [w] Or, *green worms* [x] Or, *who* of (or, for) *Jacob shall stand?* [y] Or, *sanctuary* [z] Heb. *house of the kingdom*

with the fear of God. People would not even dare to mention His name, lest it bring further destruction and death on them.

7:1–6 THUS HATH THE LORD GOD SHOWN UNTO ME. Amos was given two visions of God's imminent judgment on Israel. It would come in the form of grasshoppers (v. 1) and intense heat (v. 4), causing the land to be devoured and mass starvation to result. The prophet interceded for the people, and the Lord delayed His judgment (vv. 3,6). God does not desire the death of sinners (1 Tim. 2:4; 2 Pet. 3:9), and He promises to respond to the prayers of a righteous person (Jas. 5:16).

7:7–9 A PLUMBLINE. Amos's third vision revealed God measuring Israel with a plumbline. A plumbline was a string with a weight tied on the end by which builders ascertained the straightness of a wall. Israel was found to be out of plumb and in danger of collapsing because they had rejected God's word (vv. 12–17); therefore, God's judgment would certainly come.

7:12–17 O THOU SEER, GO, FLEE. These verses reveal one of the main reasons God would spare the people no longer. Amaziah the priest, representing the people and especially their leaders, openly rejected God's prophet and his message. Those who consciously reject God's word are dooming themselves to eternal death. A time will come when intercession will do no good.

14 ¶ Then answered Amos, and said to Amaziah, I *was* no prophet, neither *was* I [i]a prophet's son; [j]but I *was* an herdman, and a gatherer of [a]sycamore fruit:

15 And the LORD took me [b]as I followed the flock, and the LORD said unto me, Go, prophesy unto my people Israel.

Jonah 1:1-2

16 ¶ Now therefore hear thou the word of the LORD: Thou sayest, Prophesy not against Israel, and [k]drop not *thy word* against the house of Isaac.

17 [l]Therefore thus saith the LORD; [m]Thy wife shall be an harlot in the city, and thy sons and thy daughters shall fall by the sword, and thy land shall be divided by line; and thou shalt die in a polluted land: and Israel shall surely go into captivity forth of his land.

The vision of Israel's ruin

8 THUS HATH the Lord GOD shown unto me: and behold a basket of summer fruit.

2 And he said, Amos, what seest thou? And I said, A basket of summer fruit. Then said the LORD unto me, [n]The end is come upon my people of Israel; [o]I will not again pass by them any more.

3 And [p]the songs of the temple [c]shall be howlings in that day, saith the Lord GOD: *there shall be* many dead bodies in every place; [q]they shall cast *them* forth [d]with silence.

4 ¶ Hear this, O ye that [r]swallow up the needy, even to make the poor of the land to fail,

5 Saying, When will the [e]new moon be gone, that we may sell corn? and [s]the sabbath, that we may [f]set forth wheat, [t]making the ephah small, and the shekel great, and [g]falsifying the balances by deceit?

6 That we may buy the poor for [u]silver, and the needy for a pair of shoes; *yea,* and sell the refuse of the wheat?

7 The LORD hath sworn by [v]the excellency of Jacob, Surely [w]I will never forget any of their works.

8 [x]Shall not the land tremble for this, and every one mourn that dwelleth therein? and it shall rise up wholly as a flood; and it shall be cast out and drowned, [y]as *by* the flood of Egypt.

9 And it shall come to pass in that day, saith the Lord GOD, [z]that I will cause the sun to go down at noon, and I will darken the earth in the clear day:

10 And I will turn your feasts into mourning, and all your songs into lamentation; [a]and I will bring up sackcloth upon all loins, and baldness upon every head; [b]and I will make it as the mourning of an only *son,* and the end thereof as a bitter day.

11 ¶ Behold, the days come, saith the Lord GOD, that I will send a famine in the land, not a famine of bread, nor a thirst for water, but [c]of hearing the words of the LORD:

12 And they shall wander from sea to sea, and from the north even to the east, they shall run to and fro to seek the word of the LORD, and shall not find *it.*

13 In that day shall the fair virgins and young men faint for thirst.

14 They that [d]swear by [e]the sin of Samaria, and say, Thy god, O Dan, liveth; and, The [h]manner of [f]Beersheba liveth; even they shall fall, and never rise up again.

7:14 [i]1 Ki. 20:35 2 Ki. 2:5 [j]Zech. 13:5 **7:16** [k]Ezek. 21:2 Mic. 2:6 **7:17** [l]Jer. 28:12 & 29:21,32 [m]Is. 13:16 Lam. 5:11 Hos. 4:13 Zech. 14:2 **8:2** [n]Ezek. 7:2 [o]ch. 7:8 **8:3** [p]ch. 5:23 [q]ch. 6:9,10 **8:4** [r]Ps. 14:4 Prov. 30:14 **8:5** [s]Neh. 13:15 [t]Mic. 6:10

8:6 [u]ch. 2:6 **8:7** [v]ch. 6:8 [w]Hos. 8:13 **8:8** [x]Hos. 4:3 [y]ch. 9:5 **8:9** [z]Job 5:14 Is. 13:10 & 59:9,10 Jer. 15:9 Mic. 3:6 **8:10** [a]Is. 15:2,3 Jer. 48:37 Ezek. 27:31 [b]Jer. 6:26 Zech. 12:10 **8:11** [c]1 Sam. 3:1 Ps. 74:9 Ezek. 7:26 **8:14** [d]Hos. 4:15 [e]Deut. 9:21 [f]ch. 5:5

[a] Or, *wild figs* [b] Heb. *from behind* [c] Heb. *shall howl* [d] Heb. *be silent* [e] Or, *month* [f] Heb. *open* [g] Heb. *perverting the balances of deceit* [h] Heb. *way*

8:1 A BASKET OF SUMMER FRUIT. The ripe fruit signifies that the people were ripe for judgment; their end was at hand.

8:5 THE SABBATH. The merchants were so materialistic that they were anxious for the Sabbath to be over so they might resume selling their products. We must ask ourselves: Am I so caught up in making money that I have little or no concern for God's word and the advancement of His kingdom? According to the Lord Jesus Himself, we cannot serve both God and money at the same time (see Mat. 6:24, note).

8:11 A FAMINE ... OF HEARING THE WORDS OF THE LORD. Israel had repeatedly rejected the word of God spoken to them (2:11–12; 7:10–13,16); now they would receive what they desired. (1) God would send no prophet to them, and no word of God would come to them. In other words, whenever they might seek God's guidance during the coming calamity, they would find only silence. (2) No judgment is worse than God giving a person over to his or her own sinful desires. Such a person will plunge into degradation and perversion and end up becoming a slave to the demonic (Rom. 1:21–32; see Rom. 1:24, note).

The destruction of the sanctuary

9 I SAW the Lord standing upon the altar: and he said, Smite the [i]lintel of the door, that the posts may shake: and [g]cut[j] them in the head, all of them; and I will slay the last of them with the sword: [h]he that fleeth of them shall not flee away, and he that escapeth of them shall not be delivered.

2 [i]Though they dig into hell, thence shall mine hand take them; [j]though they climb up to heaven, thence will I bring them down:

3 And though they hide themselves in the top of Carmel, I will search and take them out thence; and though they be hid from my sight in the bottom of the sea, thence will I command the serpent, and he shall bite them:

4 And though they go into captivity before their enemies, [k]thence will I command the sword, and it shall slay them: and [l]I will set mine eyes upon them for evil, and not for good.

5 And the Lord GOD of hosts *is* he that toucheth the land, and it shall [m]melt, [n]and all that dwell therein shall mourn: and it shall rise up wholly like a flood; and shall be drowned, as *by* the flood of Egypt.

6 *It is* he that buildeth his [o]stories[k l] in the heaven, and hath founded his [m]troop in the earth; he that [p]calleth for the waters of the sea, and poureth them out upon the face of the earth: [q]The LORD *is* his name.

7 *Are* ye not as children of the Ethiopians unto me, O children of Israel? saith the LORD. Have not I brought up Israel out of the land of Egypt? and the [r]Philistines from [s]Caphtor, and the Syrians from [t]Kir?

8 Behold, [u]the eyes of the Lord GOD *are* upon the sinful kingdom, and I [v]will destroy it from off the face of the earth; saving that I will not utterly destroy the house of Jacob, saith the LORD.

9 For, lo, I will command, and I will [n]sift the house of Israel among all nations, like as *corn* is sifted in a sieve, yet shall not the least [o]grain fall upon the earth.

10 All the sinners of my people shall die by the sword, [w]which say, The evil shall not overtake nor prevent us.

Israel's fortunes to be restored

11 ¶ [x]In that day will I raise up the tabernacle of David that is fallen, and [p]close up the breaches thereof; and I will raise up his ruins, and I will build it as in the days of old:

12 [y]That they may possess the remnant of [z]Edom, and of all the heathen, [q]which are called by my name, saith the LORD that doeth this.

13 Behold, [a]the days come, saith the LORD, that the plowman shall overtake the reaper, and the treader of grapes him that [r]soweth seed; [b]and the mountains shall drop [s]sweet

9:1 [g]Ps. 68:21 Hab. 3:13 [h]ch. 2:14
9:2 [i]Ps. 139:8 [j]Jer. 51:53
9:4 [k]Lev. 26:33 [l]Lev. 17:10
9:5 [m]Mic. 1:4 [n]ch. 8:8
9:6 [o]Ps. 104:3 [p]ch. 5:8 [q]ch. 4:13
9:7 [r]Jer. 47:4 [s]Deut. 2:23 Jer. 47:4 [t]ch. 1:5
9:8 [u]ver. 4 [v]Jer. 30:11 Obad. 16,17
9:10 [w]ch. 6:3
9:11 [x]Acts 15:16
9:12 [y]Obad. 19 [z]Num. 24:18
9:13 [a]Lev. 26:5 [b]Joel 3:18

[i] Or, *chapiter,* or, *knob* [j] Or, *wound them*
[k] Or, *spheres* [l] Heb. *ascensions*
[m] Or, *bundle* [n] Heb. *cause to move*
[o] Heb. *stone* [p] Heb. *hedge,* or, *wall*
[q] Heb. *upon whom my name is called*
[r] Heb. *draweth forth* [s] Or, *new wine*

9:1–10 I SAW THE LORD. In his fifth vision, Amos saw the Lord beside the altar in His sanctuary, ready to destroy all the worshipers by bringing the sanctuary down upon their heads. Those who escaped would be killed by the sword; all the sinners among His people would die (v. 10). Likewise, when Christ returns, He will severely judge all within His churches who are living a sinful lifestyle; none of them will escape God's wrath.

9:11–15 IN THAT DAY. The book of Amos ends with a promise that Israel would not be totally destroyed (cf. v. 8). The prophet envisions a day when the nation would be restored to its land and would bless all the nations of the earth. The Lord will be their God (v. 15). This day refers to the Messianic kingdom when Christ reigns over all the earth. James quotes vv. 11–12 to show that God's plan of salvation was designed to include non-Jews in His kingdom (see Acts 15:16, note).

9:11 THE TABERNACLE OF DAVID. This phrase refers to all twelve tribes of Israel living under the rule of the Messiah.

9:12 ALL OF THE HEATHEN. The Messiah will reign over all nations, and Israel will be a blessing to them. This is the ultimate fulfillment of God's covenant with Abraham and with David (see articles on GOD'S COVENANT WITH ABRAHAM, ISAAC, AND JACOB, p. 48, and GOD'S COVENANT WITH DAVID, p. 470).

9:13–15 THE PLOWMAN SHALL OVERTAKE THE REAPER. Amos prophesies a transformed and glorious earth where God's people can continually plant and reap at the same time. The land will be abundantly productive, and the blessings of God will never end. Israel will finally be restored to the Lord and will never again abandon Him. They will be secure in the land.

wine, and all the hills shall melt.
14 [c]And I will bring again the captivity of my people of Israel, and [d]they shall build the waste cities, and inhabit *them;* and they shall plant vineyards, and drink the wine thereof; they shall also make gardens, and eat the fruit of them.
15 And I will plant them upon their land, and [e]they shall no more be pulled up out of their land which I have given them, saith the LORD thy God.

9:14 [c]Jer. 30:3 [d]Is. 61:4
9:15 [e]Ezek. 34:28

OBADIAH

Outline

I. The Judgment of Edom (1–14)
   A. Destruction to Come on Edom (1–4)
   B. Devastation Will Be Complete (5–9)
   C. Reason: Their Joy at Judah's Troubles (10–14)
II. The Day of the Lord (15–21)
   A. Judgment on Edom and Other Nations (15–16)
   B. Israel's Place in "The Day of the LORD" (17–21)
      1. Salvation for Israel (17–18a)
      2. Destruction for Edom (18b)
      3. Israel's Borders Enlarged As Part of God's Kingdom (19–21)

Author: Obadiah

Theme: Judgment of Edom

Date of Writing: c. 840 B.C.

Background

The author of this short book is a prophet named Obadiah. In the book, neither ancestry nor any other details about his life are given. The name "Obadiah" is rather common, meaning "servant of the LORD"; twelve or thirteen people are mentioned in the Bible with that name (e.g., 1 Ki. 18:3–16; 2 Chr. 17:7; 34:12–13).

Whether the Obadiah who wrote this book is mentioned elsewhere in the O.T. depends on the date of this prophecy. Since no king is mentioned, we do not know for certain the date of its origin. The only historical allusion in the text is to a time when the Edomites rejoiced at an invasion in Jerusalem and even participated in its plunder (vv. 11–14). However, it is not clear what invasion of Jerusalem Obadiah had in mind. There were five significant ones during O.T. times: (1) by Shishak, king of Egypt, in 926 B.C., during Rehoboam's reign (1 Ki. 14:25–26); (2) by the Philistines and Arabians during the reign of Jehoram c. 848–841 B.C. (see 2 Chr. 21:16–17); (3) by King Jehoash of Israel during the reign of Amaziah c. 790 B.C. (2 Ki. 14:13–14); (4) by Sennacherib, king of Assyria, during the reign of Hezekiah, in 701 B.C. (2 Ki. 18:13); and (5) by the Babylonians during the years 605–586 B.C. (2 Ki. 24—25). Most scholars believe Obadiah prophesied in connection with either (2) or (5). The destruction of Jerusalem by Nebuchadnezzar seems the less likely of the two, since there is no hint of the complete destruction of Jerusalem or the deportation of its people into exile. Other prophets who refer to Jerusalem's destruction always identify the enemy as Nebuchadnezzar and Babylon, not just "strangers" and "foreigners" (v. 11). Thus the occasion for Obadiah's prophecy is more likely the second one, when the Philistines and Arabians pillaged the city. Just prior to that event, the Edomites (who had been under the control of Jerusalem) had managed to free themselves (2 Chr. 21:8–10). Their rejoicing at Jerusalem's downfall shortly thereafter is quite understandable. Since the dates for Jehoram's reign are 848–841 B.C., and since the pillaging of Jerusalem had already occurred when Obadiah wrote, 840 B.C. is a likely date for this book.

Part of the background of this prophecy recalls Gen. 25:19–34; 27:1—28:9, i.e., the long-standing rivalry between Esau (the father of the Edomites) and Jacob (the father of the twelve tribes of Israel). Though we read in Genesis about the reconciliation of these two brothers (Gen. 33), the hatred between their descendants often erupted into war throughout Biblical history (cf. Num. 20:14–21; 1 Sam. 14:47; 2 Sam. 8:14; 1 Ki. 11:14–22). In keeping with their history of hostility, the Edomites rejoiced at Jerusalem's troubles.

Purpose

This prophetic book was written (1) to reveal God's intense anger at Edom for their rejoicing at Judah's suffering, and (2) to deliver the word of God's coming judgment against Edom. Obadiah prophesies the end result of God's dealings: for the Edomites—destruction; for God's people Israel—deliverance in a coming day of the Lord.

Survey

The book of Obadiah has two main sections. In the first (vv. 1–14), God expresses through the prophet His hot displeasure with Edom and calls them to accountability for their sins, especially the sin of pride (because of their geographical security) and the sin of rejoicing at Judah's downfall. The foreboding judgment of God is coming upon them, and the prophet offers no hope of reprieve based on an invitation to repent and turn to the Lord. They will be cut off forever (v. 10). The second section (vv. 15–21) refers prophetically to a coming day of the Lord when Edom and all God's enemies will be destroyed, while God's people will be saved and His kingdom triumph.

Special Features

Four major features or emphases characterize the prophecy of Obadiah. (1) This is the shortest book in the O.T. (2) Obadiah is one of three prophets who were called by God to direct their written message almost exclusively to a nation other than Israel or Judah (the other two are Jonah and Nahum). (3) There are many similarities between the book of Obadiah and Jer. 49:7–22. (4) This book is neither quoted nor alluded to in the N.T.

New Testament Fulfillment

Although the N.T. does not refer to Obadiah directly, the feud between Esau and Jacob underlying this book is also played out in the N.T. Paul refers to the Esau-Jacob rivalry in Rom. 9:10–13, but goes on to remind us of God's message of hope: all who repent of their sins, both Jews and Gentiles, and call on the name of the Lord will be saved (Rom. 10:9–13; 15:7–12).

Reading Obadiah

In order to read the entire Old Testament in one year, the book of Obadiah should be read in 1 day: ☐ Obadiah

NOTES

Edom's destruction

1–4pp — Jer. 49:14–16
5–6pp — Jer. 49:9–10

1 THE VISION of Obadiah. Thus
saith the Lord GOD [a]concerning Edom;
We [b]have heard a rumour from the
LORD, and an ambassador is sent
among the heathen, Arise ye, and let
us rise up against her in battle.
2 Behold, I have made thee small
among the heathen: thou art greatly
despised.
3 ¶ The pride of thine heart hath deceived thee, thou that dwellest in the
clefts of the rock, whose habitation *is*
high; [c]that saith in his heart, Who
shall bring me down to the ground?
4 [d]Though thou exalt *thyself* as the
eagle, and though thou [e]set thy nest
among the stars, thence will I bring
thee down, saith the LORD.
5 If [f]thieves came to thee, if robbers by night, (how art thou cut off!)
would they not have stolen till they had
enough? if the grapegatherers came to
thee, [g]would they not leave [a]*some*
grapes?
6 How are *the things* of Esau
searched out! *how* are his hidden
things sought up!
7 All the men of thy confederacy
have brought thee *even* to the border:
[h]the[b] men that were at peace with
thee have deceived thee, *and* prevailed
against thee; [c]*they that eat* thy bread
have laid a wound under thee: [i]*there
is* none understanding [d]in him.
8 [j]Shall I not in that day, saith the
LORD, even destroy the wise *men* out of
Edom, and understanding out of the
mount of Esau?
9 And thy [k]mighty *men*, O [l]Teman, shall be dismayed, to the end that
every one of the mount of Esau may be
cut off by slaughter.
10 ¶ For *thy* [m]violence against thy
brother Jacob shame shall cover thee,
and [n]thou shalt be cut off for ever.
11 In the day that thou stoodest on
the other side, in the day that the
strangers [e]carried away captive his
forces, and foreigners entered into his
gates, and [o]cast lots upon Jerusalem,
even thou *wast* as one of them.
12 But [f]thou shouldest not have
[p]looked on the day of thy brother in
the day that he became a stranger; neither shouldest thou have [q]rejoiced
over the children of Judah in the day of
their destruction; neither shouldest
thou have [g]spoken proudly in the day
of distress.
13 Thou shouldest not have entered
into the gate of my people in the day of
their calamity; yea, thou shouldest not
have looked on their affliction in the
day of their calamity, nor have laid
hands on their [h]substance in the day
of their calamity;
14 Neither shouldest thou have

1:1 [a]Is. 21:11 Ezek. 25:12 Joel 3:19 Mal. 1:3 [b]Jer. 49:14 **1:3** [c]Is. 14:13-15 Rev. 18:7 **1:4** [d]Job 20:6 [e]Hab. 2:9 **1:5** [f]Jer. 49:9 [g]Deut. 24:21 **1:7** [h]Jer. 38:22 [i]Is. 19:11 **1:8** [j]Job 5:12 Is. 29:14 **1:9** [k]Ps. 76:5 [l]Jer. 49:7 **1:10** [m]Gen. 27:41 [n]Ezek. 35:9 **1:11** [o]Nah. 3:10 **1:12** [p]Mic. 4:11 [q]Prov. 17:5

[a] Or, *gleanings?* [b] Heb. *the men of thy peace* [c] Heb. the men *of thy bread* [d] Or, *of it* [e] Or, *carried away his substance* [f] Or, *do not behold* [g] Heb. *magnified thy mouth* [h] Or, *forces*

1 OBADIAH. Obadiah was a prophet to Judah who prophesied about God's judgment against Edom (see the introduction).

1 CONCERNING EDOM. The Edomites, Judah's southern neighbors, were descendants of Esau (v. 6), Jacob's brother; thus, they were related to Israel (v. 10). However, that nation had become a perpetual enemy of God's people, often giving aid to heathen armies attacking Israel. Because of Edom's long hostility toward and hatred of the Israelites, the wrath of God would come upon them.

3 THE PRIDE OF THINE HEART. (1) The Edomites lived in a rocky range of mountains. They arrogantly regarded their homeland as secure and were proud of their self-sufficiency and power. Yet God would bring them down. (2) The Bible teaches that pride and haughtiness lead to self-deception, go before a fall (v. 4; Prov. 16:18), and cause God to become one's enemy (v. 8; Jas. 4:6; 1 Pet. 5:5).

5–6 IF THIEVES CAME TO THEE. The Edomites had made it a practice to plunder other people, robbing and killing them. Now they would experience the same thing, for God would bring another nation against them.

10 CUT OFF FOR EVER. Obadiah prophesies that the Edomites would be completely destroyed because of their violence and cruelty (cf. vv. 16, 18), whereas Judah would be restored and God's kingdom would prevail (vv. 17,19,21). In 582 B.C., four years after Jerusalem was destroyed, the Edomite people were nearly destroyed by the Babylonians and forced to live in southern Judah. In A.D. 70, after the destruction of Jerusalem by Rome, they were never heard of again.

11–14 THOU STOODEST ON THE OTHER SIDE. (1) Edom refused to help Israel, its neighbor and relative, when they were in trouble. For this God would judge them. (2) God is concerned that His people who have received His help and mercy show mercy to others in their time of need. Indifference and self-centeredness demonstrate that God's love and grace do not abide in us (1 John 3:15–17; see article on THE CARE OF THE POOR AND NEEDY, p. 1312).

stood in the crossway, to cut off those
of his that did escape; neither should-
est thou have [i]delivered up those of
his that did remain in the day of dis-
tress.

Judgment upon the nations

15 [r]For the day of the LORD *is* near
upon all the heathen: [s]as thou hast
done, it shall be done unto thee: thy
reward shall return upon thine own
head.
16 [t]For as ye have drunk upon my
holy mountain, *so* shall all the heathen
drink continually, yea, they shall
drink, and they shall [j]swallow down,
and they shall be as though they had
not been.

Deliverance in Zion

17 ¶ But upon mount Zion [u]shall
be [k]deliverance, and [l]there shall be
holiness; and the house of Jacob shall
possess their possessions.
18 And the house of Jacob [v]shall
be a fire, and the house of Joseph a
flame, and the house of Esau for stub-
ble, and they shall kindle in them, and
devour them; and there shall not be *any*
remaining of the house of Esau; for the
LORD hath spoken *it.*
19 And *they of* the south shall pos-
sess the mount of Esau; [w]and *they of*
the plain the Philistines: and they shall
possess the fields of Ephraim, and the
fields of Samaria: and Benjamin *shall
possess* Gilead.
20 And the captivity of this host of
the children of Israel *shall possess* that
of the Canaanites, *even* [x]unto Zare-
phath; and the captivity of Jerusalem,
[m]which *is* in Sepharad, [y]shall pos-
sess the cities of the south.
21 And [z]saviours shall come up on
mount Zion to judge the mount of
Esau; and the [a]kingdom shall be the
LORD'S.

1:15 [r]Ezek. 30:3 [s]Hab. 2:8 **1:16** [t]Joel 3:17 **1:17** [u]Amos 9:8 **1:18** [v]Zech. 12:6 **1:19** [w]Zeph. 2:7 **1:20** [x]1 Ki. 17:9 [y]Jer. 32:44 **1:21** [z]Jas. 5:20 [a]Rev. 11:15

[i] Or, *shut up;* see Ps. 31:8 [j] Or, *sup up*
[k] Or, *they that escape* [l] Or, *it shall be holy*
[m] Or, shall possess *that which is in Sepharad*

15 IT SHALL BE DONE UNTO THEE. Obadiah prophesies that God would recompense Edom and all other nations according to their treatment of others. This same principle applies to N.T. believers (see Col. 3:25, note).

17–21 UPON MOUNT ZION SHALL BE DELIVERANCE. Mount Zion represents Jerusalem under the old covenant and the heavenly abode of the church under the new covenant (Heb. 12:22–24; see article on THE CITY OF JERUSALEM, p. 622). The Bible prophesies that Israel and all of God's faithful people will be delivered from their enemies, inherit the earth, and reign with Christ. This fulfillment awaits the return of Jesus the Messiah to earth, at which time evil will be defeated; then "the kingdom shall be the LORD'S" (v. 21).

JONAH

Outline

I. God's First Call to Jonah (1:1—2:10)
   A. Jonah's Call: "Go to Nineveh" (1:1–2)
   B. Jonah's Disobedience (1:3)
   C. Consequences of Jonah's Disobedience (1:4–17)
      1. To Others (1:4–11)
      2. To Himself (1:12–17)
   D. Jonah's Prayer Amidst Calamity (2:1–9)
   E. Jonah's Deliverance (2:10)
II. God's Second Call to Jonah (3:1—4:11)
   A. Jonah's Call: "Go to Nineveh" (3:1–2)
   B. Jonah's Obedient Mission (3:3–4)
   C. Consequences of Jonah's Obedience (3:5–10)
      1. The Ninevites Repent (3:5–9)
      2. The Ninevites Spared God's Judgment (3:10)
   D. Jonah's Complaint (4:1–3)
   E. Jonah's Rebuke and Lesson (4:4–11)

Author: Jonah

Theme: The Breadth of God's Saving Mercy

Date of Writing: c. 760 B.C.

Background

Jonah, whose name means "dove," is introduced as the son of Amittai (1:1). He is mentioned in 2 Ki. 14:25 as (1) a prophet to the northern kingdom of Israel during the reign of Jeroboam II (793–753 B.C.), and (2) from Gath-hepher, two to three miles north of Nazareth in Galilee. Thus the Pharisees were mistaken when they suggested that no prophet ever came from Galilee (John 7:52). Jonah's prophetic ministry occurred shortly after that of Elisha (cf. 2 Ki. 13:14–19), overlapped that of Amos (cf. Amos 1:1), and was followed by that of Hosea (cf. Hos. 1:1). Though the book makes no claim as to its author, most likely the author was Jonah himself.

Nineveh's repentance in response to Jonah's preaching most likely occurred during the reign of one of two Assyrian monarchs: (1)Adad-nirari III (810–783 B.C.), whose reign was marked by a swing toward monotheism, or (2) Ashurdan III (733–755 B.C.), whose reign experienced two major plagues (765 and 759 B.C.) and an eclipse of the sun (763 B.C.), both of which may have been interpreted as signs of divine judgment and thus prepared Assyria's capital city for Jonah's prophetic message. Nineveh was about 500 miles northeast of Galilee.

Purpose

This book appears to have been written for a threefold purpose: (1) to demonstrate to Israel and the nations the magnitude and breadth of God's saving mercy and activity through the preaching of repentance; (2) to show through Jonah's experience how far Israel had fallen

from her original missionary calling to be a light of redemption to those who dwell in darkness (Gen. 12:1–3; Is. 42:6–7; 49:6); and (3) to remind backslidden Israel that God in love and mercy had sent her not just one prophet but many faithful prophets, who delivered His message of repentance so as to avert inevitable judgment for sin. Yet unlike Nineveh, Israel had rejected God's prophets and His offer to repent and receive mercy.

Survey

The book of Jonah tells the story of the prophet's call to go to Nineveh and of his reactions. Ch. 1 describes Jonah's initial disobedience and God's subsequent judgment. Instead of going northeast to Nineveh, Jonah boarded a west-bound ship going to Tarshish (in Spain), the farthest destination possible in the opposite direction from God's will. Jonah soon faced God's countermeasure of a severe storm on the Mediterranean Sea, with the disgrace of being found out by the sailors and thrown overboard. God providentially had "a great fish" ready to spare his life. Ch. 2 recounts Jonah's prayer from his unique chamber inside the fish, in which he thanked God for sparing his life, vowed to obey God's call, and was then vomited by the fish onto dry land. Ch. 3 records Jonah's second chance to go to Nineveh and his preaching of God's message to that city's inhabitants. In one of the most remarkable city-wide spiritual awakenings in all of history, the king called the entire city to fasting and repentance, through which they were spared God's judgment. Ch. 4 contains Jonah's complaint against God for sparing this enemy city of Israel. Using a plant, a worm, and an east wind, God taught his angry prophet that He delights in making His grace available to everyone, not just to Israel and Judah.

Special Features

Four major features or emphases characterize the book of Jonah. (1) It is one of only two O.T. prophetic books written by a prophet born and raised in the northern kingdom of Israel (Hosea is the other one). (2) It is a masterpiece of condensed prose narrative; only Jonah's prayer of thanksgiving (2:2–9) is in poetry. (3) It is full of God's supernatural activity: besides the providential timing of the storm and the great fish, there are the gourd, the worm, the east wind, and (greatest of all) the repentance of the entire city of Nineveh. (4) It contains the clearest message in the O.T. that God's saving grace is for Gentiles as well as for Jews.

New Testament Fulfillment

Jesus likened Himself to Jonah as follows: "An evil and adulterous generation seeketh after a sign; and there shall no sign be given to it, but the sign of the prophet Jonas: For as Jonas was three days and three nights in the whale's belly; so shall the Son of man be three days and three nights in the heart of the earth. The men of Nineveh shall rise in judgment with this generation, and shall condemn it: because they repented at the preaching of Jonas; and, behold, a greater than Jonas *is* here" (Mat. 12:39–41).

Historical Reliability

Liberal theologians and unbelievers regard this book as a fictional story coming out of the fifth to the third century B.C., designed to counter the narrow Jewish nationalism of post-exilic Judaism. According to this view, the book of Jonah does not represent actual historical events. However, the O.T. elsewhere mentions Jonah as an accredited prophet from the eighth century B.C. (2 Ki. 14:25). In the N.T., Jesus Himself refers to Jonah (1) as being the foremost O.T. prophetic sign of His three days in the grave and His subsequent resurrection (Mat. 12:39–40; Luke 11:29), (2) as having historically preached repentance to the Ninevites who repented (Mat. 12:41; Luke 11:30,32), and (3) as being as much a part of O.T. history as Solomon and his visit from the Queen of Sheba (Mat. 12:42; Luke 11:31). Jesus clearly regarded the book as historically reliable. To view the book otherwise not only implies that we have a fallible Bible, but also a fallible Savior.

Reading Jonah

In order to read the entire Old Testament in one year, the book of Jonah should be read in 1 day: ☐ Jonah

NOTES

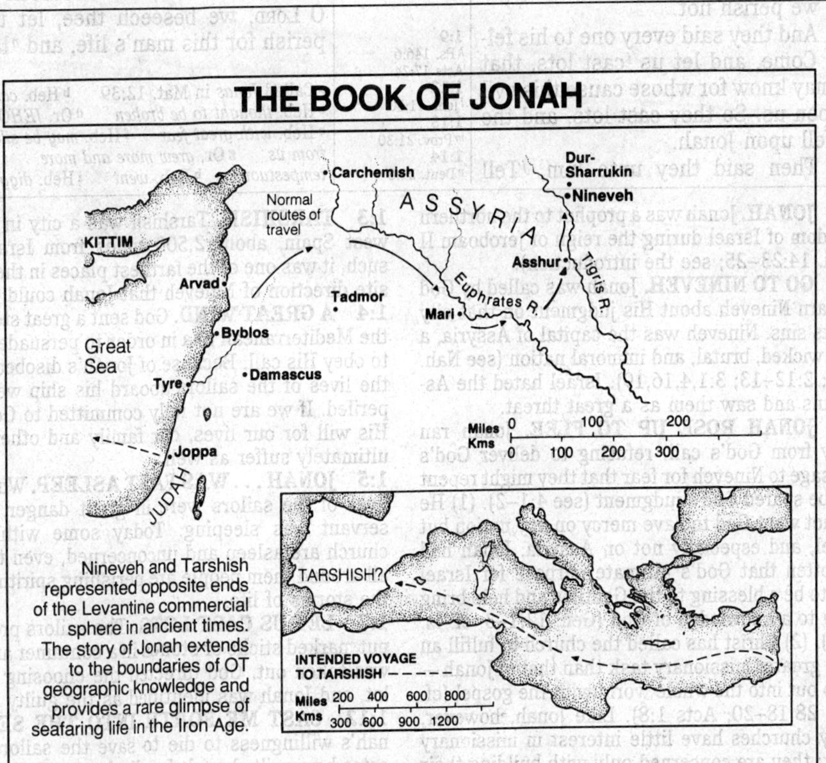

Nineveh and Tarshish represented opposite ends of the Levantine commercial sphere in ancient times. The story of Jonah extends to the boundaries of OT geographic knowledge and provides a rare glimpse of seafaring life in the Iron Age.

Jonah flees to Tarshish

1 NOW THE word of the LORD came
unto [a]Jonah the son of Amittai,
saying,
2 Arise, go to Nineveh, that [a]great
city, and cry against it; for [b]their
wickedness is come up before me.
3 But Jonah rose up to flee unto Tar-
shish from the presence of the LORD,
and went down to [c]Joppa; and he
found a ship going to Tarshish: so he
paid the fare thereof, and went down
into it, to go with them unto Tarshish
[d]from the presence of the LORD.
4 ¶ But [e]the LORD [b]sent out a
great wind into the sea, and there was
a mighty tempest in the sea, so that the
ship was [c]like to be broken.
5 Then the mariners were afraid,
and cried every man unto his god, and
cast forth the wares that *were* in the
ship into the sea, to lighten *it* of them.
But Jonah was gone down [f]into the
sides of the ship; and he lay, and was
fast asleep.
6 So the shipmaster came to him,
and said unto him, What meanest thou,
O sleeper? arise, [g]call upon thy God,
[h]if so be that God will think upon us,
that we perish not.
7 And they said every one to his fel-
low, Come, and let us [i]cast lots, that
we may know for whose cause this evil
is upon us. So they cast lots, and the
lot fell upon Jonah.
8 Then said they unto him, [j]Tell
us, we pray thee, for whose cause this
evil *is* upon us; What *is* thine occupa-
tion? and whence comest thou? what *is*
thy country? and of what people *art*
thou?
9 And he said unto them, I *am* an
Hebrew; and I fear [d]the LORD, the God
of heaven, [k]which hath made the sea
and the dry *land.*
10 Then were the men [e]exceeding-
ly afraid, and said unto him, Why hast
thou done this? For the men knew that
he fled from the presence of the LORD,
because he had told them.
11 ¶ Then said they unto him, What
shall we do unto thee, that the sea
[f]may be calm unto us? for the sea
[g] [h]wrought, and was tempestuous.
12 And he said unto them, [l]Take
me up, and cast me forth into the sea;
so shall the sea be calm unto you: for
I know that for my sake this great tem-
pest *is* upon you.
13 Nevertheless the men [i]rowed
hard to bring *it* to the land; [m]but they
could not: for the sea wrought, and was
tempestuous against them.
14 Wherefore they cried unto the
LORD, and said, We beseech thee,
O LORD, we beseech thee, let us not
perish for this man's life, and [n]lay not

Jonah 3:1-5

1:2 [a]Gen. 10:11 [b]Gen. 18:20
1:3 [c]Josh. 19:46 [d]Gen. 4:16
1:4 [e]Ps. 107:25
1:5 [f]1 Sam. 24:3
1:6 [g]Ps. 107:28 [h]Joel 2:14
1:7 [i]Josh. 7:14 1 Sam. 14:41
1:8 [j]Josh. 7:19
1:9 [k]Ps. 146:6 Acts 17:24
1:12 [l]John 11:50
1:13 [m]Prov. 21:30
1:14 [n]Deut. 21:8

[a] Called *Jonas* in Mat. 12:39 [b] Heb. *cast forth* [c] Heb. *thought to be broken* [d] Or, *JEHOVAH* [e] Heb. *with great fear* [f] Heb. *may be silent from us* [g] Or, *grew more and more tempestuous* [h] Heb. *went* [i] Heb. *digged*

1:1 JONAH. Jonah was a prophet to the northern kingdom of Israel during the reign of Jeroboam II (2 Ki. 14:23–25; see the introduction).

1:2 GO TO NINEVEH. Jonah was called by God to warn Nineveh about His judgment on that city for its sins. Nineveh was the capital of Assyria, a very wicked, brutal, and immoral nation (see Nah. 1:11; 2:12–13; 3:1,4,16,19). Israel hated the Assyrians and saw them as a great threat.

1:3 JONAH ROSE UP TO FLEE. Jonah ran away from God's call, refusing to deliver God's message to Nineveh for fear that they might repent and be spared God's judgment (see 4:1–2). (1) He did not want God to have mercy on any nation but Israel, and especially not on Assyria. Jonah had forgotten that God's ultimate purpose for Israel was to be a blessing to the Gentiles and help bring them to a knowledge of God (Gen. 12:1–3; cf. Is. 49:3). (2) Christ has called the church to fulfill an even greater missionary task than that of Jonah—to go out into the whole world with the gospel (cf. Mat. 28:18–20; Acts 1:8). Like Jonah, however, many churches have little interest in missionary work; they are concerned only with building their own kingdom at home.

1:3 TARSHISH. Tarshish was a city in southwest Spain, about 2,500 miles from Israel. As such, it was one of the farthest places in the opposite direction of Nineveh that Jonah could go.

1:4 A GREAT WIND. God sent a great storm on the Mediterranean Sea in order to persuade Jonah to obey His call. Because of Jonah's disobedience, the lives of the sailors aboard his ship were imperiled. If we are not fully committed to God and His will for our lives, our family and others will ultimately suffer as well.

1:5 JONAH . . . WAS FAST ASLEEP. While the lives of the sailors were in great danger, God's servant was sleeping. Today some within the church are asleep and unconcerned, even though all around them people are perishing spiritually in the storms of life.

1:7 LET US CAST LOTS. The sailors probably put marked sticks or stones in a container and one was taken out. God directed the choosing of the lot, and Jonah was identified as the guilty one.

1:12 CAST ME FORTH INTO THE SEA. Jonah's willingness to die to save the sailors indicates how guilty he felt for disobeying God and for putting their lives in peril.

upon us innocent blood: for thou,
O LORD, [o]hast done as it pleased thee.
15 So they took up Jonah, and cast
him forth into the sea: [p]and the sea
[j]ceased from her raging.
16 Then the men [q]feared the LORD
exceedingly, and [k]offered a sacrifice
unto the LORD, and made vows.
17 ¶ Now the LORD had prepared a
great fish to swallow up Jonah. And
[r]Jonah was in the [l]belly of the fish
three days and three nights.

Prayer and deliverance of Jonah

2 THEN JONAH prayed unto the
LORD his God out of the fish's belly,
2 And said, I [s]cried [m]by reason of
mine affliction unto the LORD, [t]and he
heard me; out of the belly of [u]hell[n]
cried I, *and* thou heardest my voice.
3 [v]For thou hadst cast me into the
deep, in the [o]midst of the seas; and
the floods compassed me about: [w]all
thy billows and thy waves passed
over me.
4 [x]Then I said, I am cast out of thy
sight; yet I will look again [y]toward thy
holy temple.
5 The [z]waters compassed me
about, *even* to the soul: the depth
closed me round about, the weeds were
wrapped about my head.
6 I went down to the [p]bottoms of
the mountains; the earth with her bars
was about me for ever: yet hast thou
brought up my life [a]from [q]corrup-
tion, O LORD my God.
7 When my soul fainted within me I
remembered the LORD: [b]and my prayer
came in unto thee, into thine holy tem-
ple.
8 They that observe [c]lying vanities
forsake their own mercy.
9 But I will [d]sacrifice unto thee
with the voice of thanksgiving; I will
pay *that* that I have vowed. [e]Salvation
is of the LORD.
10 ¶ And the LORD spake unto the
fish, and it vomited out Jonah upon the
dry *land*.

Jonah preaches at Nineveh

3 AND THE word of the LORD came
unto Jonah the second time, say-
ing,
2 Arise, go unto Nineveh, that great

1:14 [o]Ps. 115:3
1:15 [p]Ps. 89:9 Luke 8:24
1:16 [q]Mark 4:41 Acts 5:11
1:17 [r]Mat. 12:40 Luke 11:30
2:2 [s]Ps. 120:1 Lam. 3:55 [t]Ps. 65:2 [u]Is. 14:9
2:3 [v]Ps. 88:6 [w]Ps. 42:7
2:4 [x]Ps. 31:22 [y]1 Ki. 8:38
2:5 [z]Ps. 69:1 Lam. 3:54
2:6 [a]Ps. 16:10
2:7 [b]Ps. 18:6
2:8 [c]2 Ki. 17:15 Jer. 10:8
2:9 [d]Ps. 50:14 Hos. 14:2 [e]Ps. 3:8

[j] Heb. *stood* [k] Heb. *sacrificed a sacrifice unto the LORD, and vowed vows* [l] Heb. *bowels* [m] Or, *out of mine affliction* [n] Or, *the grave* [o] Heb. *heart* [p] Heb. *cuttings off* [q] Or, *the pit*

1:17 PREPARED A GREAT FISH TO SWALLOW JONAH. God provided a great fish, perhaps a large whale, to save Jonah's life. God miraculously kept Jonah alive for three days in the stomach of the fish. (1) Unbelievers in the world and false teachers in the church have rejected this miracle, calling it fiction. Jesus, however, regarded it as historical fact. He used the incident of Jonah and the whale to illustrate His own death, burial, and resurrection (see Mat. 12:39–41). (2) In other words, Jesus put Jonah's experience with the great fish in the same category as His death and resurrection. Jesus accepted it as a miracle of God occurring according to His purpose in redemptive history. For all true believers, that should settle the question of its authenticity (see also the introduction to this book).

2:1–10 JONAH PRAYED. This is Jonah's prayer for deliverance from death and his subsequent thanksgiving. (1) Inside the whale, he found himself still alive and cried out to the Lord. Although he thought himself as good as dead (v. 6), the Lord heard his prayer and spared his life. (2) Believers should never give up hope in seemingly impossible situations. Like Jonah, we must cry out to God for mercy and help and entrust our lives to His hands.

2:3 THOU HADST CAST ME. Jonah knew he had been disobedient and recognized that it was God who threw him into the sea. His greatest sorrow and fear was to be banished forever from God's presence (v. 4).

2:7 I REMEMBERED THE LORD. To "remember" the Lord means that God becomes such a living presence within us and around us that we can call out to Him at any time in faith, hope, and love (cf. Deut. 8:18).

2:7 MY PRAYER CAME IN UNTO THEE. When we pray, we must believe that our prayers go to the very presence of God in heaven.

2:9 SACRIFICE . . . THANKSGIVING. At the very moment when Jonah was offering up to God a sincere sacrifice of thanksgiving and praise (v. 9), God intervened on his behalf (v. 10).

2:10 IT VOMITED OUT JONAH. So far in the narrative of Jonah seven miracles have occurred: God (1) caused a great storm (1:4); (2) directed the lot to implicate Jonah (1:7); (3) calmed the sea (1:15); (4) arranged for a great fish to swallow Jonah (1:17); (5) kept him alive inside the fish for three days (v. 6; 1:17); (6) caused the fish to transport him to land; and (7) made the fish throw up Jonah onto dry land.

3:2 THE PREACHING THAT I BID THEE. (1) Jonah was called a second time to preach doom and judgment (see v. 4). It was his responsibility to deliver that message whether the Ninevites received it or not. (2) Preachers of the gospel are similarly called to proclaim the whole counsel of God (Acts 20:27; 2 Tim. 4:2). They must preach both God's mercy and God's wrath, both forgiveness and condemnation; they must be careful not

city, and preach unto it the preaching
that I bid thee.
3 So Jonah arose, and went unto
Nineveh, according to the word of the
LORD. Now Nineveh was an exceeding
great city of three days' journey.
4 And Jonah began to enter into the
city a day's journey, and [f]he cried,
and said, Yet forty days, and Nineveh
shall be overthrown.
5 ¶ So the people of Nineveh [g]be-
lieved God, and proclaimed a fast, and
Zech. 8:20-23 put on sackcloth, from the greatest of
them even to the least of them.
6 For word came unto the king of
Nineveh, and he arose from his throne,
and he laid his robe from him, and cov-
ered *him* with sackcloth, [h]and sat in
ashes.
7 [i]And he caused *it* to be pro-
claimed and [r]published through Nine-
veh by the decree of the king and his
[s]nobles, saying, Let neither man nor
beast, herd nor flock, taste any thing:
let them not feed, nor drink water:
8 But let man and beast be covered
with sackcloth, and cry mightily unto
God: yea, [j]let them turn every one
from his evil way, and from [k]the vio-
lence that *is* in their hands.
9 [l]Who can tell *if* God will turn and
repent, and turn away from his fierce
anger, that we perish not?

3:4 [f]Deut. 18:22
3:5 [g]Mat. 12:41 Luke 11:32
3:6 [h]Job 2:8
3:7 [i]2 Chr. 20:3 Joel 2:15
3:8 [j]Is. 58:6 [k]Is. 59:6
3:9 [l]2 Sam. 12:22 Joel 2:14

3:10 [m]Jer. 18:8 Amos 7:3,6
4:2 [n]ch. 1:3 [o]Ex. 34:6 Ps. 86:5 Joel 2:13
4:3 [p]1 Ki. 19:4 [q]ver. 8

Sparing of the city angers Jonah

10 ¶ [m]And God saw their works,
that they turned from their evil way;
and God repented of the evil, that he
had said that he would do unto them;
and he did *it* not.

4 BUT IT displeased Jonah exceed-
ingly, and he was very angry.
2 And he prayed unto the LORD, and
said, I pray thee, O LORD, *was* not this
my saying, when I was yet in my coun-
try? Therefore I [n]fled before unto Tar-
shish: for I knew that thou *art* a [o]gra-
cious God, and merciful, slow to anger,
and of great kindness, and repentest
thee of the evil.
3 [p]Therefore now, O LORD, take, I
beseech thee, my life from me; for [q]*it*
is better for me to die than to live.
4 ¶ Then said the LORD, [t]Doest
thou well to be angry?
5 So Jonah went out of the city, and
sat on the east side of the city, and
there made him a booth, and sat under
it in the shadow, till he might see what
would become of the city.

The unlimited mercy of God

6 And the LORD God prepared a

[r] Heb. *said* [s] Heb. *great men* [t] Or, *Art thou greatly angry?*

to water down the gospel so as to avoid the difficult doctrines and ethics of God's Word. They must preach in such a way that people turn from their sins (see Acts 14:15).

3:3 EXCEEDING GREAT CITY. The city of Nineveh had more than 120,000 inhabitants (see 4:11).

3:5 THE PEOPLE OF NINEVEH BELIEVED GOD. (1) The Ninevites accepted Jonah's message, believing that they were doomed unless they repented. As an outward expression of their true repentance and humility, they fasted (cf. 1 Sam. 7:6; 2 Sam. 1:12) and put on sackcloth (a coarse cloth, usually made of goats' hair; cf. 2 Sam. 3:31; 2 Ki. 19:1–2). (2) Jesus stated that Nineveh would stand up at the judgment to condemn Israel for their failure to repent and believe in Him (Mat. 12:41).

3:10 GOD REPENTED OF THE EVIL. Because the people repented, God canceled His plan of judgment. (1) God's primary desire is to have mercy, not to execute His threatened punishment. The Lord is a God who is moved with compassion for sinners who sincerely repent. (2) This book illustrates the Biblical truth that God does not desire anyone to perish, but all people to come to repentance, forgiveness, and eternal life (see 2 Pet. 3:9).

4:1 DISPLEASED JONAH EXCEEDINGLY. Jonah was angry that God had decided to forgive the Ninevites; he did not want God to spare this enemy of Israel. (1) Jonah's fundamental problem was that he was not dedicated first and foremost to God's will. He was more concerned about Israel's physical security. (2) People today can be committed to the "success" of the church, yet not really be committed to God's will, purposes, and holy standards as revealed in the Bible.

4:2 A GRACIOUS GOD. God is "gracious" (i.e., He longs to help others); "merciful" (i.e., He is moved to compassion); "slow to anger" (i.e., He does not desire to punish the wicked); "of great kindness" (i.e., He is sympathetic and forbearing); "and repentest thee of the evil" (i.e., He delights in canceling His plans of judgment when people repent). These characteristics of God are revealed throughout the Bible (see Ps. 103:8; 111:4; 112:4; 145:8; see article on THE ATTRIBUTES OF GOD, p. 912).

4:3 *IT IS* BETTER FOR ME TO DIE. Jonah was so disappointed and emotionally distraught that he preferred to die. In some way he felt God had turned against him and His people by sparing the Ninevites.

4:6 GOD PREPARED A GOURD. Rather than rejecting Jonah because of his wrong response, God compassionately attempted to convince him, by the use of a fast-growing vine, that He was con-

[u,v]gourd, and made *it* to come up
over Jonah, that it might be a shadow
over his head, to deliver him from his
grief. So Jonah [w]was exceeding glad
of the gourd.
7 But God prepared a worm when
the morning rose the next day, and it
smote the gourd that it withered.
8 And it came to pass, when the sun
did arise, that God prepared a [x]vehe-
ment east wind; and the sun beat upon
the head of Jonah, that he fainted,
and wished in himself to die, and
said, [r]*It is* better for me to die than
to live.
9 And God said to Jonah, [y]Doest
thou well to be angry for the gourd?
And he said, [z]I do well to be angry,
even unto death.
10 Then said the LORD, Thou hast
[a]had pity on the gourd, for the which
thou hast not laboured, neither madest
it grow; which [b]came up in a night,
and perished in a night:
11 And should not I spare Nineveh,
[s]that great city, wherein are more
than sixscore thousand persons [t]that
cannot discern between their right
hand and their left hand; and *also* much
[u]cattle?

4:8 [r]ver. 3
4:11 [s]ch. 1:2 & 3:2,3 [t]Deut. 1:39 [u]Ps. 36:6 & 145:9

[u] Or, *palmcrist* [v] Heb. *Kikajon* [w] Heb. *rejoiced with great joy* [x] Or, *silent* [y] Or, *Art thou greatly angry?* [z] Or, *I am greatly angry* [a] Or, *spared* [b] Heb. *was the son of the night*

cerned for both Israel and other nations.

4:9 DOEST THOU WELL TO BE ANGRY. God's action with the vine and the hot east wind (vv. 6–9) was intended to show Jonah's selfish concern for his own physical welfare in contrast to his lack of concern for the Ninevites. Jonah cared more for his own physical comfort than he did for God's will for this lost nation.

4:11 SHOULD I NOT SPARE NINEVEH. God expresses His love for Nineveh. (1) It is the love of the Creator for His creatures even though they have lived in sin and rebellion against His laws. It is a love that goes far beyond any human love (cf. Rom. 5:8). (2) God's love for humankind extends beyond His own people to lost people everywhere. This truth was fully seen (a) when God sent His Son Jesus to die for all people (John 3:16), and (b) when Jesus sent forth His disciples into all the world to preach the gospel and make disciples of all nations (Mat. 28:18–20).

MICAH

Outline

- I. Judgment Against Israel and Judah (1:1—3:12)
  - A. Introduction (1:1)
  - B. Destruction Predicted for Samaria (1:2–7)
  - C. Destruction Predicted for Judah (1:8–16)
  - D. Specific Sins Among God's People Requiring Judgment (2:1–11)
    - 1. Greed and Pride (2:1–5)
    - 2. False Prophets (2:6–11)
  - E. First Glimpse of Promised Deliverance (2:12–13)
  - F. Specific Sins Among the Leaders of God's People (3:1–12)
    - 1. Injustice and Oppression (3:1–4)
    - 2. False Prophecy (3:5–7)
    - 3. Micah As a True Prophet (3:8)
    - 4. Summary of the Sins of the Leaders (3:9–12)
- II. Prophetic Message of Hope (4:1—5:15)
  - A. The Promise of the Coming Kingdom (4:1–8)
  - B. Defeat of Israel's Enemies (4:9–13)
  - C. The Coming King from Bethlehem (5:1–5)
  - D. The Nature of the New Kingdom (5:6–15)
- III. God's Lawsuit Against Israel and His Final Mercy (6:1—7:20)
  - A. God's Case Against His People (6:1–8)
  - B. Israel's Guilt and God's Judgment (6:9–16)
  - C. The Prophet's Painful Lament (7:1–6)
  - D. The Prophet's Personal Hope (7:7)
  - E. Israel Will Rise Again (7:8–13)
  - F. God's Final Blessings for His People (7:14–20)

Author: Micah

Theme: Judgment and Messianic Salvation

Date of Writing: c. 740–710 B.C.

Background

The prophet Micah was from the small town of Moresheth-gath (1:14) in southern Judah, a productive agricultural area about twenty-five miles southwest of Jerusalem. Like Amos, he was from the countryside and probably came from a family of humble standing. While Isaiah, his contemporary in Jerusalem, addressed the king and international situations, Micah was a country prophet who condemned Judah's corrupt rulers, false prophets, ungodly priests, dishonest merchants, and bribed judges. He preached against the sins of injustice, oppression of the peasants and villagers, greed, avarice, immorality, and idolatry, and he warned of severe consequences if the people and their leaders persisted in their evil ways. He predicted the fall of Israel and its capital, Samaria (1:6–7), as well as that of Judah and its capital, Jerusalem (1:9–16; 3:9–12).

Micah's prophetic ministry occurred during the reign of three kings of Judah: Jotham (751–736 B.C.), Ahaz (736–716), and Hezekiah (716–687). Though some of Micah's prophecies were spoken during the time of King Hezekiah (cf. Jer. 26:18), most of them reflect Judah's condition during the reigns of Jotham and Ahaz prior to Hezekiah's religious reforms. Undoubtedly his ministry, along with that of Isaiah, helped to bring about the revival and reforms under the righteous King Hezekiah.

Purpose

Micah wrote to warn his nation of the certainty of divine judgment, to specify the sins that were provoking God's anger, and to summarize God's prophetic word to Samaria and Jerusalem (1:1). He accurately predicted Israel's downfall before it happened in 722 B.C.; he prophesied that a similar destruction would come to Judah and Jerusalem because of their flagrant sin and rebellion. This book thus preserves Micah's serious prophetic message for Judah's last generations before the Babylonians came against the nation; it also makes an important contribution to the total O.T. revelation about the coming Messiah.

Survey

The book of Micah consists of a three-part message: (1) it indicts Israel (Samaria) and Judah (Jerusalem) for specific sins including idolatry, pride, oppression of the poor, bribery among leaders, covetousness and greed, immorality, and empty religion; (2) it warns that God's judgment is coming because of these sins; and (3) it promises that true peace, righteousness, and justice will prevail in the future when the Messiah reigns. Amost equal attention is given to these three themes throughout the book.

Viewed another way, chs. 1—3 record the Lord's denunciation of Israel's and Judah's sins, their corrupt leaders, and the impending doom awaiting these nations and their capitals. Chs. 4—5 offer hope and comfort to the remnant concerning days to come when God's house will be established in peace and righteousness, and idolatry and oppression will be purged from the land. Chs. 6—7 describe God's grievance with His people in terms of a great court scene: God presents His case against Israel; this is followed by Israel's confession of guilt and a prophetic prayer and promise. Micah concludes with a wordplay on the meaning of his own name: "Who *is* a God like unto thee?" (7:18). Answer: He alone is merciful and can render the final verdict of "pardoned" (7:18–20).

Special Features

Five major features or emphases characterize the book of Micah. (1) It champions the cause of the humble peasants who face exploitation by the arrogant wealthy, similar to James's message in the N.T. (cf. 6:6–8 and Jas. 1:27). In this connection, Micah gives his most memorable exhortation of the Lord's requirement for His people: "to do justly, and to love mercy, and to walk humbly with thy God" (6:8). (2) Some of Micah's language is rugged and direct; other times it is eloquently poetic, with intricate use of wordplays (as in 1:10–15). (3) Like the prophet Isaiah (cf. Is. 48:16; 59:21), Micah expresses a keen awareness of God's call and his prophetic anointing by the Holy Spirit: "Truly I am full of power by the spirit of the LORD, and of judgment, and of might, to declare unto Jacob his transgression, and to Israel his sin" (3:8). (4) The book contains one of the grandest expressions in the Bible about God's mercy and forgiving grace (7:18–20). (5) It has three important prophecies quoted elsewhere in the Bible: one which saved Jeremiah's life (3:12; Jer. 26:18), one concerning the Messiah's birthplace (5:2; Mat. 2:5–6), and one used by Jesus Himself (7:6; Mat. 10:35–36).

New Testament Fulfillment

Like other O.T. prophets, Micah saw beyond God's judgment of Israel and Judah to the coming Messiah and His righteous reign on earth. Seven hundred years before the incarnation of Christ, Micah prophesied that He would be born in Bethlehem (5:2). Mat. 2:4–6 records that the priests and scribes quoted this verse in reply to Herod's inquiry about the birthplace of the Messiah. Micah also revealed that the Messianic kingdom would

be a kingdom of peace (5:5; cf. Eph. 2:14–18), and that the Messiah would shepherd God's people justly (5:4; cf. John 10:1–16; Heb. 13:20). Micah's frequent references to future redemption reveal that God's enduring desire and purpose for His people is salvation, not judgment; this truth is magnified in the N.T. (e.g., John 3:16).

Reading Micah

In order to read the entire Old Testament in one year, the book of Micah should be read in 3 days, according to the following schedule: □ 1–3 □ 4–5 □ 6–7

NOTES

1 THE WORD of the LORD that came to [a]Micah the Morasthite in the days of Jotham, Ahaz, *and* Hezekiah, kings of Judah, which he saw concerning Samaria and Jerusalem.

Samaria and Judah

2 [a]Hear, all ye people; hearken, O earth, and all that therein is: and let the Lord GOD be witness against you, the Lord from [b]his holy temple.

3 For, behold, the LORD cometh forth out of his place, and will come down, and tread upon the high places of the earth.

4 And [c]the mountains shall be molten under him, and the valleys shall be cleft, as wax before the fire, *and* as the waters *that are* poured down [b]a steep place.

5 For the transgression of Jacob *is* all this, and for the sins of the house of Israel. What *is* the transgression of Jacob? *is it* not Samaria? and what *are* the high places of Judah? *are they* not Jerusalem?

6 Therefore I will make Samaria [d]as an heap of the field, *and* as plantings of a vineyard: and I will pour down the stones thereof into the valley, and I will [e]discover the foundations thereof.

7 And all the graven images thereof shall be beaten to pieces, and all the [f]hires thereof shall be burned with the fire, and all the idols thereof will I lay desolate: for she gathered *it* of the hire of an harlot, and they shall return to the hire of an harlot.

The lament of the prophet

8 Therefore I will wail and howl, I will go stripped and naked: [g]I will make a wailing like the dragons, and mourning as the [c]owls.

9 For [d]her wound *is* incurable; for [h]it is come unto Judah; he is come unto the gate of my people, *even* to Jerusalem.

10 ¶ [i]Declare ye *it* not at Gath, weep ye not at all: in the house of [e]Aphrah roll thyself in the dust.

11 Pass ye away, [f]thou [g]inhabitant of Saphir, having thy shame naked: the inhabitant of [h]Zaanan came not forth in the mourning of [i]Beth-ezel; he shall receive of you his standing.

12 For the inhabitant of Maroth [j]waited carefully for good: but [j]evil came down from the LORD unto the gate of Jerusalem.

13 O thou inhabitant of [k]Lachish, bind the chariot to the swift beast: she *is* the beginning of the sin to the daughter of Zion: for the transgressions of Israel were found in thee.

14 Therefore shalt thou [l]give presents [k]to Moresheth-gath: the houses of [m]Achzib[l] *shall be* a lie to the kings of Israel.

15 Yet will I bring an heir unto thee, O inhabitant of [n]Mareshah: [m]he shall come unto [o]Adullam the glory of Israel.

16 Make thee [p]bald, and poll thee for thy [q]delicate children; enlarge thy

1:1 [a]Jer. 26:18
1:2 [b]Ps. 11:4
1:4 [c]Amos 9:5
1:6 [d]2 Ki. 19:25 [e]Ezek. 13:14
1:7 [f]Hos. 2:5
1:8 [g]Ps. 102:6
1:9 [h]2 Ki. 18:13
1:10 [i]2 Sam. 1:20
1:12 [j]Amos 3:6
1:13 [k]2 Ki. 18:14
1:14 [l]2 Sam. 8:2 2 Ki. 18:14 [m]Josh. 15:44
1:15 [n]Josh. 15:44 [o]2 Chr. 11:7
1:16 [p]Job 1:20 Is. 15:2 Jer. 7:29 [q]Lam. 4:5

[a] Heb. *Hear, ye people, all of them* [b] Heb. *a descent* [c] Heb. *daughters of the owl* [d] Or, *she is grievously sick of her wounds* [e] i.e. *Dust* [f] Or, *thou that dwellest fairly* [g] Heb. *inhabitress* [h] Or, *the country of flocks* [i] Or, *a place near* [j] Or, *was grieved* [k] Or, *for* [l] i.e. *a lie* [m] Or, *the glory of Israel shall come*

1:1 MICAH. Micah, from southern Judah, prophesied sometime between 750–687 B.C. He was a contemporary of Isaiah (cf. Is. 1:1) and Hosea (cf. Hos. 1:1; see the introduction to Micah). His message was directed mainly to Judah (the southern kingdom), though he also had revelation concerning Israel (the northern kingdom). While Micah's predominant theme was judgment, he also stressed the restoration of God's people.

1:1 SAMARIA AND JERUSALEM. Samaria was the capital of Israel; Jerusalem was Judah's capital. Both represented apostate nations that would be judged by God (vv. 5–7).

1:5 TRANSGRESSION . . . SINS. The people would be judged because of their sins, especially idolatry (v. 7), immorality (v. 7), crime, and injustice (2:1–2). The sins prevalent in the capital cities were typical of the sins being committed throughout the nations.

1:6 SAMARIA AS AN HEAP. This prophecy was fulfilled in 722 B.C., when the Assyrians completely destroyed the city (see 2 Ki. 17:1–5). The fulfillment came shortly after Micah prophesied it.

1:8–9 THEREFORE I WILL WAIL AND HOWL. Micah mourned the fall of Samaria (Israel; cf. v. 6). He was heartsick that they had rejected God and had to be punished. Do we experience regret and grief when people persist in sinning against God and are heading toward their own destruction and doom?

1:9 IT IS COME UNTO JUDAH. Judah was equally guilty of transgression and rebellion against God. Thus, Micah called on certain towns in Judah (vv. 10–16) to mourn for the destruction that was coming upon them. Micah's prophecy was fulfilled when Sennacherib took walled cities of Judah (2 Ki. 18:13); according to Assyrian records, he took forty-six of them.

baldness as the eagle; for they are gone into captivity from thee.

Wicked deeds of the rich

2 WOE TO them that devise iniquity, and work evil upon their beds! when the morning is light, they practice it, because it is in the power of their hand.

2 And they covet fields, and take *them* by violence; and houses, and take *them* away: so they [n]oppress a man and his house, even a man and his heritage.

3 Therefore thus saith the LORD; Behold, against this family do I devise an evil, from which ye shall not remove your necks; neither shall ye go haughtily: for this time *is* evil.

4 ¶ In that day shall *one* take up a parable against you, and [r]lament[o] with a doleful lamentation, *and* say, We be utterly spoiled: he hath changed the portion of my people: how hath he removed *it* from me! [p]turning away he hath divided our fields.

5 Therefore thou shalt have none that shall cast a cord by lot in the congregation of the LORD.

6 [q]Prophesy ye not, *say they to them that* prophesy: they shall not prophesy to them, *that* they shall not take shame.

7 ¶ O *thou that art* named the house of Jacob, is the spirit of the LORD [r]straitened? *are* these his doings? do not my words do good to him that walketh [s]uprightly?

8 Even [t]of late my people is risen up as an enemy: ye pull off the robe [u]with the garment from them that pass by securely as men averse from war.

9 The [v]women of my people have ye cast out from their pleasant houses; from their children have ye taken away my glory for ever.

10 Arise ye, and depart; for this *is* not *your* [s]rest: because it is [t]polluted, it shall destroy *you*, even with a sore destruction.

11 If a man [w]walking in the spirit and falsehood do lie, *saying*, I will prophesy unto thee of wine and of strong drink; he shall even be the prophet of this people.

The remnant regathered

12 ¶ [u]I will surely assemble, O Jacob, all of thee; I will surely gather

2:4 [r]2 Sam. 1:17
2:10 [s]Deut. 12:9 [t]Lev. 18:25 Jer. 3:2
2:12 [u]ch. 4:6,7

[n] Or, *defraud* [o] Heb. *with a lamentation of lamentations* [p] Or, *instead of restoring* [q] Or, *Prophesy not* as *they prophesy* [r] Or, *shortened?* [s] Heb. *upright?* [t] Heb. *yesterday* [u] Heb. *over against a garment* [v] Or, *wives* [w] Or, *walk with the wind, and lie falsely*

1:16 MAKE THEE BALD. Shaving one's hair was an external sign of sorrow. Thus Micah called on God's people to anticipate intense mourning. (1) Judgment would be severe; their children would be taken from them and carried away into captivity. Micah emphasized that God's people could not turn from Him without suffering terrible consequences. (2) Those who leave God and His Word to align themselves with the world and its sinful activities will find that God is against them and may bring disaster into their lives.

2:1–5 WOE TO THEM THAT DEVISE INIQUITY. Micah pronounces doom on certain people who were powerful enough to exploit others in order to achieve their own selfish aims. (1) They were land barons, who either bought or stole farm after farm. They did not hesitate to defraud others in order to gain more property. Having devoted their hearts to greed, they did not care about the suffering they inflicted on others. (2) God had a plan for them; they would reap what they sowed. God would send Assyria to take their land away from them and to carry them into captivity. (3) We must be careful that we do not become greedy and mistreat others to gain money or possessions (see article on RICHES AND POVERTY, p. 1568).

2:6 PROPHESY YE NOT. Judah's false prophets were condemning Micah for bringing a message of judgment (cf. Is. 30:10). (1) They rejected his prophecy of gloom and doom, insisting that shame and disgrace would not overtake the people, for God was a God of love and forgiveness, not anger. (2) Their optimistic message allowed the people to continue in their sinful ways of disregarding God's righteous demands. (3) Sometimes the church manifests this same insistence on the positive message of God's love, mercy, and forgiveness, while ignoring His righteous standards and His call for holy living. A church that tolerates any kind of sin among its people should listen again to the clear message of both the O.T. prophets and the N.T. apostles (cf. 1 Cor. 5–6).

2:11 WINE AND STRONG DRINK. Micah sarcastically declares that if Judah's false prophets were prophesying prosperity and plenty of intoxicating drink for everyone who wanted it, the people would eagerly accept such a prophet. Today there are still pastors who refuse to warn God's people about the consequences of adopting the drinking customs of the society in which they live (see article on WINE IN THE OLD TESTAMENT, p. 220).

2:12–13 THE REMNANT OF ISRAEL. Micah adds a word of hope by proclaiming that God would spare a remnant of Israel and Judah, who would return to the promised land (see Is. 6:13, note; 10:20, note; 17:7, note). The land would again be filled with the hustle and bustle of

the remnant of Israel; I will put them
together [v]as the sheep of Bozrah, as
the flock in the midst of their fold:
[w]they shall make great noise by rea-
son of *the multitude of* men.
13 The breaker is come up before
them: they have broken up, and have
passed through the gate, and are gone
out by it: and [x]their king shall pass
before them, [y]and the LORD on the
head of them.

Israel's sins denounced

3 AND I said, Hear, I pray you, O
heads of Jacob, and ye princes of
the house of Israel; [z]*Is it* not for you
to know judgment?
2 Who hate the good, and love the
evil; who pluck off their skin from off
them, and their flesh from off their
bones;
3 Who also [a]eat the flesh of my
people, and flay their skin from off
them; and they break their bones, and
chop them in pieces, as for the pot, and
[b]as flesh within the caldron.
4 Then [c]shall they cry unto the
LORD, but he will not hear them: he will
even hide his face from them at that
time, as they have behaved themselves
ill in their doings.
5 ¶ Thus saith the LORD [d]concern-
ing the prophets that make my people
err, that [e]bite with their teeth, and
cry, Peace; and [f]he that putteth not
into their mouths, they even prepare
war against him.
6 [g]Therefore night *shall be* unto
you, [x]that ye shall not have a vision;
and it shall be dark unto you, [y]that ye
shall not divine; [h]and the sun shall go
down over the prophets, and the day
shall be dark over them.
7 Then shall the seers be ashamed,
and the diviners confounded: yea, they
shall all cover their [z]lips; [i]for *there
is* no answer of God.
8 ¶ But truly I am full of power by
the spirit of the LORD, and of judgment,
and of might, [j]to declare unto Jacob
his transgression, and to Israel his
sin. Zech. 4:6

Destruction of Jerusalem foretold

9 Hear this, I pray you, ye heads of
the house of Jacob, and princes of the
house of Israel, that abhor judgment,
and pervert all equity.
10 [k]They build up Zion with
[l]blood,[a] and Jerusalem with iniq-
uity.
11 [m]The heads thereof judge for re-
ward, and [n]the priests thereof teach
for hire, and the prophets thereof di-
vine for money: [o]yet will they lean
upon the LORD, [b]and say, *Is* not the
LORD among us? none evil can come
upon us.
12 Therefore shall Zion for your
sake be [p]plowed *as* a field, [q]and Jeru-
salem shall become heaps, and [r]the
mountain of the house as the high
places of the forest.

2:12 [v]Jer. 31:10 [w]Ezek. 36:37 **2:13** [x]Hos. 3:5 [y]Is. 52:12 **3:1** [z]Jer. 5:4,5 **3:3** [a]Ps. 14:4 [b]Ezek. 11:3 **3:4** [c]Ps. 18:41 Prov. 1:28 Is. 1:15 **3:5** [d]Is. 56:10,11 Ezek. 13:10 [e]Mat. 7:15 [f]Ezek. 13:18 **3:6** [g]Is. 8:20 Ezek. 13:23 [h]Amos 8:9 **3:7** [i]Amos 8:11 **3:8** [j]Is. 58:1 **3:10** [k]Jer. 22:13 [l]Ezek. 22:27 Zeph. 3:3 **3:11** [m]Is. 1:23 Ezek. 22:12 [n]Jer. 6:13 [o]Is. 48:2 Jer. 7:4 **3:12** [p]Jer. 26:18 [q]Ps. 79:1 [r]ch. 4:2

[x] Heb. *from a vision* [y] Heb. *from divining* [z] Heb. *upper lip* [a] Heb. *bloods* [b] Heb. *saying*

people coming and going.

3:1–12 O HEADS OF JACOB. This passage prophesies against the cruelty of the ruling classes (vv. 1–4), the deceit of false prophets (vv. 5–7), and the perversion of Judah's apostate leaders, priests, and prophets (vv. 9–12). God would judge all of them accordingly.

3:2 HATE THE GOOD, AND LOVE THE EVIL. The leaders of the nation had abandoned the godly standards of the past and substituted their own legal codes. They purposely loved evil and injustice in their pursuit of material gain. God calls us to do the opposite: to love righteousness and hate evil (see Amos 5:15; Rom. 12:9; Heb. 1:9).

3:3 EAT THE FLESH OF MY PEOPLE. This vivid expression describes the severe oppression and exploitation of the common folk.

3:4 HE WILL NOT HEAR THEM. Because of the evil and cruel behavior of the leaders, God would refuse to hear their prayers, and they themselves would come to a God-forsaken end.

3:5–7 CONCERNING THE PROPHETS. God longed to lead His people back to the paths of righteousness and truth, yet the false prophets cared for none of this. They made the people feel comfortable in their sinful lifestyles by proclaiming a false hope and security. Instead of taking an uncompromising stand against sin among God's people, they actually encouraged it. Because of their refusal to lead the people back to God's ways, the false prophets would be abandoned by God.

3:8 I AM FULL OF POWER BY THE SPIRIT. Micah had been called to be a spokesman for God. (1) He spoke by the power and inspiration of the Holy Spirit (cf. Jer. 20:9; Eph. 3:7). The Spirit moved him to condemn sin in the house of God. It was his task to reflect the heart of God, to encourage right, and to discourage wrong. (2) Pastors and prophets today have the same task. They must not bend to pressures within the church to conform to the ways of the world. Instead, they must be God's voice for truth, godliness, and righteousness (see article on THE CHRISTIAN'S RELATIONSHIP TO THE WORLD, p. 2004).

The coming of law and peace

4:1–3pp — Is. 2:1–4

4 BUT [s]IN the last days it shall
come to pass, *that* the mountain of
the house of the LORD shall be estab-
lished in the top of the mountains, and
it shall be exalted above the hills; and
people shall flow unto it.
2 And many nations shall come, and
say, Come, and let us go up to the
mountain of the LORD, and to the house
of the God of Jacob; and he will teach
us of his ways, and we will walk in his
paths: for the law shall go forth of Zion,
and the word of the LORD from Jerusa-
lem.
3 ¶ And he shall judge among many
people, and rebuke strong nations afar
off; and they shall beat their swords
into [t]plowshares, and their spears
into [c]pruninghooks: nation shall not
lift up a sword against nation, [u]nei-
ther shall they learn war any more.
4 [v]But they shall sit every man un-
der his vine and under his fig tree; and
none shall make *them* afraid: for the
mouth of the LORD of hosts hath spoken
it.
5 For all people will walk every one
in the name of his god, and [w]we will
walk in the name of the LORD our God
for ever and ever.

The LORD reigns in Zion

6 In that day, saith the LORD, [x]will
I assemble her that halteth, [y]and I
will gather her that is driven out, and
her that I have afflicted;
7 And I will make her that halted a
[z]remnant, and her that was cast far
off a strong nation: and the LORD
[a]shall reign over them in mount Zion
from henceforth, even for ever.
8 ¶ And thou, O tower of [d]the
flock, the strong hold of the daughter
of Zion, unto thee shall it come, even
the first dominion; the kingdom shall
come to the daughter of Jerusalem.
9 Now why dost thou cry out aloud?
[b]*is there* no king in thee? is thy coun-
sellor perished? for [c]pangs have tak-
en thee as a woman in travail.
10 Be in pain, and labour to bring
forth, O daughter of Zion, like a woman
in travail: for now shalt thou go forth
out of the city, and thou shalt dwell in
the field, and thou shalt go *even* to Bab-
ylon; there shalt thou be delivered;
there the LORD shall redeem thee from
the hand of thine enemies.
11 ¶ [d]Now also many nations are
gathered against thee, that say, Let
her be defiled, and let our eye [e]look
upon Zion.
12 But they know not [f]the
thoughts of the LORD, neither under-
stand they his counsel: for he shall
gather them [g]as the sheaves into the
floor.
13 [h]Arise and thresh, O daughter
of Zion: for I will make thine horn iron,
and I will make thy hoofs brass: and
thou shalt [i]beat in pieces many peo-
ple: [j]and I will consecrate their gain
unto the LORD, and their substance
unto [k]the Lord of the whole earth.

The coming ruler and his reign

5 NOW GATHER thyself in troops, O
daughter of troops: he hath laid
siege against us: they shall [l]smite the
judge of Israel with a rod upon the
cheek.
2 But thou, [m]Bethlehem Ephratah,
though thou be little [n]among the
[o]thousands of Judah, *yet* out of thee
shall he come forth unto me *that is* to

4:1 [s]Ezek. 17:22
4:3 [t]Is. 2:4 Joel 3:10 [u]Ps. 72:7
4:4 [v]1 Ki. 4:25 Zech. 3:10
4:5 [w]Zech. 10:12
4:6 [x]Ezek. 34:16 [y]Ps. 147:2 Ezek. 34:13
4:7 [z]ch. 2:12 [a]Is. 9:6 Dan. 7:14 Luke 1:33 Rev. 11:15
4:9 [b]Jer. 8:19 [c]Is. 13:8 Jer. 30:6
4:11 [d]Lam. 2:16 [e]Obad. 12
4:12 [f]Is. 55:8 [g]Is. 21:10
4:13 [h]Jer. 51:33 [i]Dan. 2:44 [j]Is. 18:7 [k]Zech. 4:14
5:1 [l]Lam. 3:30
5:2 [m]Mat. 2:6 John 7:42 [n]1 Sam. 23:23 [o]Ex. 18:25

[c] Or, *scythes* [d] Or, *Edar;* see Gen. 35:21

4:1 IN THE LAST DAYS. Micah prophesies a time when God will rule over the entire world. (1) It will be a time of peace, happiness, and godliness. God will be honored and worshiped not only by Israel, but also by all the nations of the world. (2) The "mountain of the house of the LORD" (i.e., Jerusalem) will be the center of God's government. This future kingdom of God will begin when Christ returns to destroy all evil and to establish His righteous reign on earth (see Rev. 20:4, note).

4:5 WE WILL WALK IN THE NAME OF THE LORD. How should we live while we wait for God's kingdom to come to the earth in all its fullness? We must live for God, walk in His righteous ways, and witness to all the nations (cf. 2 Pet. 3:11–12).

4:9–13 WHY DOST THOU CRY OUT. The prophet returns to the doom of the present Jerusalem, stating that the people would be carried away to Babylon. He spoke this prophecy one hundred years before the Babylonian empire became the dominant world power (the Babylonians destroyed Jerusalem in 586 B.C.). Micah also foresaw the restoration of Judah from Babylon (v. 10).

5:2 BUT THOU, BETHLEHEM. Micah prophesies that a ruler would come out of Bethlehem, who would fulfill God's promises to His people. This verse refers to Jesus the Messiah (see Mat. 2:1,3–6), whose origin is "from everlasting" (i.e., from eternity; see John 1:1; Col. 1:17; Rev. 1:8); yet He would be born as a human (v. 3; see John 1:14; Phil. 2:7–8).

be [p]ruler in Israel; [q]whose goings
forth *have been* from of old, from
[e]everlasting.
3 Therefore will he give them up,
until the time *that* [r]she which tra-
vaileth hath brought forth: then [s]the
remnant of his brethren shall return
unto the children of Israel.
4 ¶ And he shall stand and [t]feed[f]
in the strength of the LORD, in the maj-
esty of the name of the LORD his God;
and they shall abide: for now [u]shall he
be great unto the ends of the earth.
5 And this *man* [v]shall be the peace,
when the Assyrian shall come into our
land: and when he shall tread in our
palaces, then shall we raise against
him seven shepherds, and eight [g]prin-
cipal men.
6 And they shall [h]waste the land of
Assyria with the sword, and the land of
[w]Nimrod [i]in the entrances thereof:
thus shall he [x]deliver *us* from the As-
syrian, when he cometh into our land,
and when he treadeth within our bor-
ders.
7 And [y]the remnant of Jacob shall
be in the midst of many people [z]as a
dew from the LORD, as the showers
upon the grass, that tarrieth not for
man, nor waiteth for the sons of men.
8 ¶ And the remnant of Jacob shall
be among the Gentiles in the midst of
many people as a lion among the
beasts of the forest, as a young lion
among the flocks of [j]sheep: who, if he
go through, both treadeth down, and
teareth in pieces, and none can de-
liver.
9 Thine hand shall be lifted up upon
thine adversaries, and all thine ene-
mies shall be cut off.

Idols and weapons destroyed

10 [a]And it shall come to pass in
that day, saith the LORD, that I will cut
off thy horses out of the midst of thee,
and I will destroy thy chariots:
11 And I will cut off the cities of thy
land, and throw down all thy strong
holds:
12 And I will cut off witchcrafts out
of thine hand; and thou shalt have no
more [b]soothsayers:
13 [c]Thy graven images also will I
cut off, and thy [k]standing images out
of the midst of thee; and thou shalt
[d]no more worship the work of thine
hands.
14 And I will pluck up thy groves
out of the midst of thee: so will I de-
stroy thy [l]cities.
15 And I will [e]execute vengeance
in anger and fury upon the heathen,
such as they have not heard.

God's complaint

6 HEAR YE now what the LORD
saith; Arise, contend thou [m]be-
fore the mountains, and let the hills
hear thy voice.
2 [f]Hear ye, O mountains, [g]the
LORD's controversy, and ye strong foun-
dations of the earth: for [h]the LORD
hath a controversy with his people, and
he will plead with Israel.

5:2 [p]Gen. 49:10 Is. 9:6 [q]Ps. 90:2 John 1:1 **5:3** [r]ch. 4:10 [s]ch. 4:7 **5:4** [t]Is. 40:11 Ezek. 34:23 [u]Ps. 72:8 Is. 52:13 Zech. 9:10 **5:5** [v]Ps. 72:7 Is. 9:6 **5:6** [w]Gen. 10:8 [x]Luke 1:71 **5:7** [y]ver. 3 [z]Deut. 32:2 Ps. 72:6 **5:10** [a]Zech. 9:10 **5:12** [b]Is. 2:6 **5:13** [c]Zech. 13:2 [d]Is. 2:8 **5:15** [e]2 Thes. 1:8 **6:2** [f]Ps. 50:1,4 [g]Hos. 12:2 [h]Is. 1:18

[e] Heb. *the days of eternity* [f] Or, *rule* [g] Heb. *princes of men* [h] Heb. *eat up* [i] Or, *with her own naked swords* [j] Or, *goats* [k] Or, *statues* [l] Or, *enemies* [m] Or, *with*

5:3 THEREFORE WILL HE GIVE THEM UP. Israel would be abandoned by God until the birth of the Messiah. "She which travaileth" refers physically to the virgin Mary, the mother of Jesus, and spiritually to the godly remnant. All hope for Israel, indeed for all nations, lies with the birth, life, death, and resurrection of Jesus the Messiah. "The remnant of his brethren" refers to the northern tribes and shows that the Messiah would be for all of the twelve tribes of Israel.

5:4 UNTO THE ENDS OF THE EARTH. Like Isaiah (see Is. 9:6–7; 61:1–2), Micah did not distinguish between the first and second advents of Jesus Christ. When Christ returns to destroy all evil, Israel will live securely and Christ will reign over all the world.

5:5 THIS *MAN* SHALL BE THE PEACE. Only Jesus the Messiah will bring everlasting peace to Israel. Even with His first coming, He gives peace with God, forgiveness of sin, and the assurance of eternal life to those who repent and receive Him by faith (see Rom. 5:1–11). True believers will not face condemnation because they believe in His atoning death (see John 14:27; Eph. 2:14).

5:5 ASSYRIAN. Assyria represents all God's enemies. The Messiah will one day deliver His people from those who oppose them and their worship of God.

5:10–14 I WILL DESTROY THY CHARIOTS. When the Messiah returns to judge the world's evil, He will also purge Israel of her military power (vv. 10–11) and her sin, witchcraft, and idolatry (vv. 12–14). All those in Israel not loyal to God and His ways will be destroyed.

6:1–5 HEAR YE NOW WHAT THE LORD SAITH. The Lord had an accusation against His people, so He summoned them to listen to His complaint and to justify their evil actions if they could. What right did they have to reject their covenant God and to disobey His laws? The charges against the people are given in vv. 9–16.

3 O my people, [i]what have I done
unto thee? and wherein have I wearied
thee? testify against me.
4 [j]For I brought thee up out of the
land of Egypt, and redeemed thee out
of the house of servants; and I sent be-
fore thee Moses, Aaron, and Miriam.
5 O my people, remember now what
[k]Balak king of Moab consulted, and
what Balaam the son of Beor answered
him from [l]Shittim unto Gilgal; that ye
may know [m]the righteousness of the
LORD.
6 ¶ Wherewith shall I come before
the LORD, *and* bow myself before the
high God? shall I come before him with
burnt offerings, with calves [n]of a year
old?
7 [n]Will the LORD be pleased with
thousands of rams, *or* with ten thou-
sands of [o]rivers of oil? [p]shall I give
my firstborn *for* my transgression, the
fruit of my [o]body *for* the sin of my
soul?
8 He hath [q]shown thee, O man,
what *is* good; and what doth the LORD
require of thee, but [r]to do justly, and
to love mercy, and to [p]walk humbly
Mal. 2:5-6 with thy God?

The corruption of Israel

9 The LORD's voice crieth unto the
city, and [q]*the man of* wisdom shall see
thy name: hear ye the rod, and who
hath appointed it.
10 ¶ [r]Are there yet the treasures
of wickedness in the house of the wick-
ed, and the [s]scant[s] measure *that is*
abominable?
11 [t]Shall I count *them* pure with
[t]the wicked balances, and with the
bag of deceitful weights?
12 For the rich men thereof are full
of violence, and the inhabitants thereof
have spoken lies, and [u]their tongue *is*
deceitful in their mouth.
13 Therefore also will I [v]make *thee*
sick in smiting thee, in making *thee*
desolate because of thy sins.
14 [w]Thou shalt eat, but not be sat-
isfied; and thy casting down *shall be* in
the midst of thee; and thou shalt take
hold, but shalt not deliver; and *that*
which thou deliverest will I give up to
the sword.
15 Thou shalt [x]sow, but thou shalt
not reap; thou shalt tread the olives,
but thou shalt not anoint thee with oil;
and sweet wine, but shalt not drink
wine.
16 ¶ For [u]the statutes of [y]Omri
are [z]kept, and all the works of the
house of Ahab, and ye walk in their
counsels; that I should make thee a
[v]desolation, and the inhabitants
thereof an hissing: therefore ye shall
bear the [a]reproach of my people.

The counsel of despair

7 WOE IS me! for I am as [w]when
they have gathered the summer
fruits, as [b]the grapegleanings of the

6:3 [i]Jer. 2:5,31
6:4 [j]Deut. 4:20
6:5 [k]Num. 22:5 Josh. 24:9 [l]Num. 25:1 [m]Judg. 5:11
6:7 [n]Ps. 50:9 Is. 1:11 [o]Job 29:6 [p]2 Ki. 16:3 Ezek. 23:37
6:8 [q]Deut. 10:12 1 Sam. 15:22 [r]Gen. 18:19 Is. 1:17
6:10 [s]Amos 8:5
6:11 [t]Hos. 12:7
6:12 [u]Jer. 9:3,5
6:13 [v]Lev. 26:16 Ps. 107:17
6:14 [w]Lev. 26:26
6:15 [x]Amos 5:11
6:16 [y]1 Ki. 16:25 [z]Hos. 5:11 [a]Is. 25:8
7:1 [b]Is. 17:6

[n] Heb. *sons of a year?* [o] Heb. *belly* [p] Heb. *humble thyself to walk* [q] Or, *thy name shall see that which is* [r] Or, Is there *yet unto every man an house of the wicked* [s] Heb. *measure of leanness* [t] Or, *Shall I be pure with* [u] Or, *he doth much keep the* [v] Or, *astonishment* [w] Heb. *the gatherings of summer*

6:3–5 WHAT HAVE I DONE UNTO THEE. God asks His people if He had failed them in some way. (1) Could it be His fault that they had disobeyed His word? Had He neglected the people or failed to love them sufficiently? The answer is obvious. Israel had no excuse; God had treated His people with goodness and patience throughout their history. (2) Today God could ask the very same questions of all those who turn their backs on Him. If we become disloyal to Him and His righteous standards and accept the ungodly ways of the world, it will not be because God has been unfaithful to us. Rather, it will be due to our own selfish desires and our ingratitude for His grace and love.

6:8 WHAT DOTH THE LORD REQUIRE OF THEE. Micah gives a threefold definition of what God's standard of goodness and our commitment to Him involve: (1) we must act justly, i.e., be fair and honest in our dealings with others (cf. Mat. 7:12); (2) we must love mercy, i.e., show genuine compassion and mercy to individuals in need; (3) we must walk humbly with our God, i.e., humble ourselves daily before Him in godly fear and reverence for His will (cf. Jas. 4:6–10; 1 Pet. 5:5–6). Public worship is only a small part of our total commitment to Christ. A genuine love for the Lord must manifest itself in an abiding concern for people in need (see article on THE CARE OF THE POOR AND NEEDY, p. 1312).

6:9–16 THE LORD'S VOICE CRIETH. The Lord lists some of Israel's sins and announces the judgment they had to face.

7:1–7 WOE IS ME! Micah laments the corruption of the society in which he lived. Violence, dishonesty, and immorality were rampant in Israel. Few people were really godly (v. 2), and family love had nearly disappeared (v. 6). If we are truly committed to the Lord and His ways, we will also mourn over the evil that is so prevalent around us. We will intensify our intercession and pray for the intervention of the God of our salvation (vv. 7–9).

vintage: *there is* no cluster to eat: [c]my soul desired the firstripe fruit.

2 The [d]good[x] *man* is perished out of the earth: and *there is* none upright among men: they all lie in wait for blood; [e]they hunt every man his brother with a net.

3 ¶ That they may do evil with both hands earnestly, the prince asketh, and the judge *asketh* for a reward; and the great *man,* he uttereth [y]his mischievous desire: so they wrap it up.

4 The best of them [f]*is* as a brier: the most upright *is sharper* than a thorn hedge: the day of thy watchmen *and* thy visitation cometh; now shall be their perplexity.

5 ¶ Trust ye not in a friend, put ye not confidence in a guide: keep the doors of thy mouth from her that lieth in thy bosom.

6 For [g]the son dishonoureth the father, the daughter riseth up against her mother, the daughter-in-law against her mother-in-law; a man's enemies *are* the men of his own house.

Trust in God's salvation

(✝ Mat. 1:21) 7 Therefore I will look unto the LORD; I will wait for the God of my salvation: my God will hear me.

8 ¶ [h]Rejoice not against me, O mine enemy: [i]when I fall, I shall arise; when I sit in darkness, the LORD *shall be* a light unto me.

9 [j]I will bear the indignation of the LORD, because I have sinned against him, until he plead my cause, and execute judgment for me: he will bring me forth to the light, *and* I shall behold his righteousness.

10 [z]Then *she that is* mine enemy shall see *it,* and [k]shame shall cover her which said unto me, [l]Where is the LORD thy God? mine eyes shall behold her: now [a]shall she be trodden down as the mire of the streets.

11 *In* the day that thy walls are to be built, *in* that day shall the decree be far removed.

12 *In* that day *also* [m]he shall come even to thee from Assyria, [b]and *from* the fortified cities, and from the fortress even to the river, and from sea to sea, and *from* mountain to mountain.

13 [c]Notwithstanding the land shall be desolate because of them that dwell therein, [n]for the fruit of their doings.

14 ¶ [o]Feed[d] thy people with thy rod, the flock of thine heritage, which dwell solitarily *in* [p]the wood, in the midst of Carmel: let them feed *in* Bashan and Gilead, as in the days of old.

God's pardon and love

15 [q]According to the days of thy coming out of the land of Egypt will I show unto him marvellous *things.*

16 ¶ The nations [r]shall see and be confounded at all their might: [s]they shall lay *their* hand upon *their* mouth, their ears shall be deaf.

17 They shall lick the [t]dust like a serpent, [u]they shall move out of their holes like [e]worms of the earth: they shall be afraid of the LORD our God, and shall fear because of thee.

18 [v]Who *is* a God like unto thee, that [w]pardoneth iniquity, and passeth

7:1 [c]Is. 28:4 **7:2** [d]Ps. 12:1 Is. 57:1 [e]Hab. 1:15 **7:4** [f]Ezek. 2:6 Is. 55:13 **7:6** [g]Mat. 10:21 **7:8** [h]Prov. 24:17 [i]Ps. 37:24 Prov. 24:16 **7:9** [j]Lam. 3:39 **7:10** [k]Ps. 35:26 [l]Ps. 42:3

7:12 [m]Is. 11:16 **7:13** [n]Jer. 21:14 **7:14** [o]Ps. 28:9 [p]Is. 37:24 **7:15** [q]Ps. 68:22 **7:16** [r]Is. 26:11 [s]Job 21:5 **7:17** [t]Ps. 72:9 Is. 49:23 [u]Ps. 18:45 **7:18** [v]Ex. 15:11 [w]Ex. 34:6 Jer. 50:20

[x] Or, *godly,* or, *merciful* [y] Heb. *the mischief of his soul* [z] Or, *And thou wilt see her that is mine enemy, and cover her with shame* [a] Heb. *she shall be for a treading down* [b] Or, *even to* [c] Or, *After that it hath been* [d] Or, *Rule* [e] Or, *creeping things*

7:7 THEREFORE I WILL LOOK UNTO THE LORD. In the midst of a morally sick society, Micah put his faith in God and His promises. He knew that God would sustain him, execute justice one day against all evil, and cause righteousness to reign (v. 9). (1) God calls believers in Christ to live "in the midst of a crooked and perverse nation" and to "shine as lights in the world" (Phil. 2:15). (2) Although evil may increase and society disintegrate, we can offer God's gift of salvation to all those who will listen, while we pray and look for the day when He will set things right (cf. vv. 15–20).

7:8–13 I SHALL ARISE. The righteous remnant of Judah was facing dark days ahead because of God's judgment for the nation's sins. However, Micah trumpeted words of faith on their behalf and looked beyond the temporary triumph of their enemies to the glorious day of their restoration by God. "I shall arise" is an affirmation of faith comparable to Job's (see Job 19:25–27, notes).

7:14–20 FEED THY PEOPLE. These verses are a prayer of supplication, beseeching God to fulfill the words of vv. 8–13. Micah's chief concern was that God would once again care for Israel as a shepherd cares for his sheep.

by the transgression of [x]the remnant
of his heritage? [y]he retaineth not his
anger for ever, because he delighteth
in mercy.
19 He will turn again, he will have
compassion upon us; he will subdue
our iniquities; and thou wilt cast all
their sins into the depths of the sea.
20 [z]Thou wilt perform the truth to
Jacob, *and* the mercy to Abraham,
[a]which thou hast sworn unto our fathers from the days of old.

7:18 [x]ch. 4:7 [y]Ps. 103:9 Is. 57:16

7:20 [z]Luke 1:72 [a]Ps. 105:9

NAHUM

Outline

Title (1:1)

I. The Nature of God and His Judgment (1:2–15)
   A. Characteristics of God's Administration of Justice (1:2–7)
   B. The Impending Doom of Nineveh (1:8–11,14)
   C. Comfort for Judah (1:12–13,15)

II. Oracle Concerning the Fall of Nineveh (2:1–13)
   A. Introduction (2:1–2)
   B. The Soldiers Clash (2:3–5)
   C. The City Breached and Devastated (2:6–12)
   D. The Voice of the Lord (2:13)

III. Reasons for Nineveh's Fall (3:1–19)
   A. Nineveh's Sins of Cruelty (3:1–4)
   B. The Just Recompense of God (3:5–19)

Author: Nahum

Theme: Nineveh's Approaching Destruction

Date of Writing: c. 630–620 B.C.

Background

This brief prophetic book about Nineveh's coming destruction was written by a prophet whose name means "comfort." Nothing is known about Nahum except that he came from Elkosh (1:1), a town whose location is uncertain. Jerome believed it to be near Ramah in Galilee, some have suggested the vicinity of Capernaum, and still others believe it was in southern Judah. Most likely Nahum was a prophet in Judah, since the northern kingdom (Israel) had already been dissolved at the time of this book.

Nahum uttered his prophecy before the fall of Nineveh in 612 B.C. He refers in 3:8–10 to the fall of "No" or "No-amon" (i.e., the Egyptian city of Thebes) as a past event (this occurred in 663 B.C.). Thus Nahum's prophecy occurred sometime between 663 and 612, more likely nearer the later date, during the time of King Josiah and his reform movement (c. 630–620 B.C.).

The Assyrians were known in the ancient world for their extreme cruelty to people whom they conquered. After attacking a city, they would ruthlessly slaughter hundreds of people and deport the remaining population to other parts of their empire; many more would die as a result of the brutal marches into exile (cf. 3:3). Leaders of conquered cities and nations were tortured without mercy and finally executed. A century earlier, Jonah had been sent to preach to Assyria's capital city of Nineveh. For a brief time the Assyrians repented of their sins, but sometime thereafter returned to their wicked ways. God used the wicked Assyrians as His instrument of judgment to destroy Israel's capital city of Samaria and to deport the northern kingdom into exile. Now the day for Assyria's own judgment was fast approaching.

Purpose

Nahum had a twofold purpose in this prophetic book. (1) God used him to pronounce the impending destruction of the wicked and cruel Assyrian capital of Nineveh. No nation as wicked as the Assyrians could expect to go unpunished by God. (2) At the same time, Nahum delivered a message of comfort for God's own people. The comfort derives not from seeing the bloodshed of their enemies, but from knowing that God was upholding justice in the world and would someday establish His kingdom of peace.

Survey

The book of Nahum is a series of three separate oracles against Assyria, especially the capital city of Nineveh. The three oracles correspond to the book's three chapters. Ch. 1 contains a clear and bold description of God's nature—especially His wrath, justice, and power, which make inevitable the judgment of the wicked generally and the doom of Nineveh specifically. Ch. 2 predicts Nineveh's approaching judgment and describes in vivid language what it would be like. Ch. 3 lists briefly the sins of Nineveh, declares that God is just in His judgment, and concludes by envisioning the completed judgment.

Special Features

Three major features or emphases characterize the book of Nahum. (1) Nahum is one of three O.T. prophetic books whose message is almost exclusively addressed to a foreign nation (the other two are Obadiah and Jonah). (2) Its prophetic content and poetic imagery is punctuated with some of the most graphic metaphors, vivid word pictures, and blunt language found anywhere in the Bible. (3) There is a conspicuous absence of any prophetic message to Judah concerning her sins or idolatry, perhaps because it was written during the time of King Josiah's reforms (2 Ki. 22:8—23:5). It does contain a few words of hope and comfort for Judah (e.g., 1:12–13,15).

New Testament Fulfillment

The N.T. makes no direct use of this book. The only verse that may appear in the N.T. is 1:15, a verse that Nahum himself borrowed from Is. 52:7. Paul used its imagery of "beautiful feet" to emphasize that just as a messenger in the O.T. was joyfully received by God's people when bearing the good news of peace and deliverance from their enemies Assyria (1:15) and Babylon (Is. 52:7), so new covenant preachers bear the good news of deliverance from sin's bondage and Satan's power through Jesus Christ (Rom. 10:15). The book of Nahum also underscores the N.T. message that God will not allow guilty sinners to go unpunished (1:3).

Reading Nahum

In order to read the entire Old Testament in one year, the book of Nahum should be read in 1 day: ☐ Nahum

NOTES

God's vengeance and goodness

1 THE BURDEN [a]of Nineveh. The book of the vision of Nahum the Elkoshite.

2 [a]God *is* [b]jealous, and the LORD revengeth; the LORD revengeth, and [b]*is* furious; the LORD will take vengeance on his adversaries, and he reserveth *wrath* for his enemies.

3 The LORD *is* [c]slow to anger, and [d]great in power, and will not at all acquit *the wicked:* [e]the LORD *hath* his way in the whirlwind and in the storm, and the clouds *are* the dust of his feet.

4 [f]He rebuketh the sea, and maketh it dry, and drieth up all the rivers: [g]Bashan languisheth, and Carmel, and the flower of Lebanon languisheth.

5 The mountains quake at him, and the hills melt, and the earth is burned at his presence, yea, the world, and all that dwell therein.

6 Who can stand before his indignation? and [h]who can [c]abide in the fierceness of his anger? his fury is poured out like fire, and the rocks are thrown down by him.

7 [i]The LORD *is* good, a [d]strong hold in the day of trouble; and he knoweth them that trust in him.

8 But with an overrunning flood he will make an utter end of the place thereof, and darkness shall pursue his enemies.

9 [j]What do ye imagine against the LORD? [k]he will make an utter end: affliction shall not rise up the second time.

1:1 [a]Zeph. 2:13
1:2 [b]Ex. 20:5 Deut. 4:24 Josh. 24:19
1:3 [c]Ex. 34:6,7 Neh. 9:17 [d]Job 9:4 [e]Ps. 18:7
1:4 [f]Mat. 8:26 [g]Is. 33:9
1:6 [h]Mal. 3:2
1:7 [i]Jer. 33:11
1:9 [j]Ps. 2:1 [k]1 Sam. 3:12
1:10 [l]2 Sam. 23:6 [m]ch. 3:11 [n]Mal. 4:1

10 For while *they be* folden together [l]*as* thorns, [m]and while they are drunken *as* drunkards, [n]they shall be devoured as stubble fully dry.

11 There is *one* come out of thee, that imagineth evil against the LORD, [e]a wicked counsellor.

12 Thus saith the LORD; [f]Though *they be* quiet, and likewise many, yet thus shall they be [g]cut down, when he shall pass through. Though I have afflicted thee, I will afflict thee no more.

13 For now will I break his yoke from off thee, and will burst thy bonds in sunder.

14 And the LORD hath given a commandment concerning thee, *that* no more of thy name be sown: out of the house of thy gods will I cut off the graven image and the molten image: I will make thy grave; for thou art vile.

15 Behold upon the mountains the feet of him that bringeth good tidings, that publisheth peace! O Judah, [h]keep thy solemn feasts, perform thy vows: for [i]the wicked shall no more pass through thee; he is utterly cut off.

The siege of Nineveh

2 HE [j]THAT dasheth in pieces is come up before thy face: keep the munition, watch the way, make *thy*

[a] Or, *The LORD is a jealous God, and a revenger* [b] Heb. *that hath fury* [c] Heb. *stand up* [d] Or, *strength* [e] Heb. *a counsellor of Belial* [f] Or, *If* they would have been *at peace, so* should they have been *many, and so should they have been shorn, and he should have passed away* [g] Heb. *shorn* [h] Heb. *feast* [i] Heb. *Belial* [j] Or, *The disperser,* or, *hammer*

1:1 NINEVEH. Prophesying sometime between 663–612 B.C., Nahum predicts the downfall of Assyria's capital city, Nineveh (see the introduction). Nineveh had repented under the preaching of Jonah more than one hundred years earlier, but the people had returned to their idolatry, cruelty, and oppression. The Assyrians had conquered the northern kingdom of Israel and were now plundering parts of Judah. Nahum comforts God's people by telling them that God would destroy the Assyrians. Nineveh's fall occurred in 612 B.C., when it was conquered by a coalition of the Babylonians, Medes, and Scythians.

1:2 GOD *IS* JEALOUS . . . REVENGETH. "Jealous" is used here in the sense of the Lord's zeal for the protection of His people (cf. Deut. 4:24; 5:9). He would take vengeance on those who opposed His word and kingdom by justly repaying them for their hostility and sins (see Deut. 32:35, 41).

1:3 THE LORD *IS* SLOW TO ANGER. God desires to give sinners time to repent (2 Pet. 3:9), but there is a limit to His kindness and patience. Those who persist in wickedness will eventually encounter His wrath (cf. Rom. 11:22).

1:9 IMAGINE AGAINST THE LORD. The Assyrians were plotting ways to destroy Jerusalem and Judah, but God would not allow their plans to be carried out.

1:15 GOOD TIDINGS. This passage parallels Is. 52:7 (see note there). (1) The good news for Judah was that the Assyrians would be completely destroyed so they could no longer attack their cities. (2) Likewise, N.T. preachers bear the good news of deliverance from sin's bondage and Satan's power through faith in the Lord Jesus Christ (Rom. 10:15). At an appointed time in the future, sickness, sorrow, the ungodly world, and Satan himself will be completely destroyed (see Rev. 19—21).

2:1–13 HE THAT DASHETH IN PIECES. This chapter gives a detailed prediction of the attack on and the destruction of Nineveh by the Babylonian coalition in 612 B.C.

loins strong, fortify *thy* power mightily.

2 For the LORD hath turned away [k]the excellency of Jacob, as the excellency of Israel: for the emptiers have emptied them out, and marred their vine branches.

3 The shield of his mighty men is made red, the valiant men *are* [l]in scarlet: the chariots *shall be* with [m]flaming torches in the day of his preparation, and the fir trees shall be terribly shaken.

4 The chariots shall rage in the streets, they shall justle one against another in the broad ways: [n]they shall seem like torches, they shall run like the lightnings.

5 He shall recount his [o]worthies: they shall stumble in their walk; they shall make haste to the wall thereof, and the [p]defence shall be prepared.

6 The gates of the rivers shall be opened, and the palace shall be [q]dissolved.

7 And [r]Huzzab shall be [s]led away captive, she shall be brought up, and her maids shall lead *her* as with the voice of doves, tabering upon their breasts.

8 But Nineveh *is* [t]of old like a pool of water: yet they shall flee away. Stand, stand, *shall they cry;* but none shall [u]look back.

9 Take ye the spoil of silver, take the spoil of gold: [v]for *there is* none end of the store *and* glory out of all the [w]pleasant furniture.

10 She is empty, and void, and waste: and the heart melteth, and the knees smite together, and much pain *is* in all loins, and the faces of them all gather blackness.

11 Where *is* the dwelling of the lions, and the feedingplace of the young lions, where the lion, *even* the old lion, walked, *and* the lion's whelp, and none made *them* afraid?

12 The lion did tear in pieces enough for his whelps, and strangled for his lionesses, and filled his holes with prey, and his dens with ravin.

13 Behold, I *am* against thee, saith the LORD of hosts, and I will burn her chariots in the smoke, and the sword shall devour thy young lions: and I will cut off thy prey from the earth, and the voice of thy messengers shall no more be heard.

The sure destruction

3 WOE TO the [x]bloody city! it *is* all full of lies *and* robbery; the prey departeth not;

2 The noise of a whip, and the noise of the rattling of the wheels, and of the prancing horses, and of the jumping chariots.

3 The horseman lifteth up both [y]the bright sword and the glittering spear: and *there is* a multitude of slain, and a great number of carcases; and *there is* none end of *their* corpses; they stumble upon their corpses:

4 Because of the multitude of the whoredoms of the wellfavoured harlot,

[k] Or, *the pride of Jacob as the pride of Israel*
[l] Or, *dyed* [m] Or, *fiery* [n] Heb. *their show*
[o] Or, *gallants* [p] Heb. *covering,* or, *coverer*
[q] Or, *molten* [r] Or, *that which was established,* or, *there was a stand made* [s] Or, *discovered*
[t] Or, *from the days* that *she* hath been [u] Or, *cause* them *to turn* [v] Or, *and* their *infinite store* [w] Heb. *vessels of desire* [x] Heb. *city of bloods* [y] Heb. *the flame of the sword, and the lightning of the spear*

2:3 THE SHIELD OF HIS MIGHTY MEN. The appearance of the attackers would be fearsome.

2:5 HE SHALL RECOUNT. "He" is probably the Assyrian king, summoning his soldiers to resist the attackers.

2:6 THE GATES OF THE RIVERS. These "gates" are apparently the flood gates or dams that controlled the Khoser River, which ran through the city. They may have been closed to gather a large body of water and then released by the attackers to damage the walls of the city.

2:8 THEY SHALL FLEE AWAY. Many people would flee from the city, like water flowing from a pool.

2:11–12 THE DWELLING OF THE LIONS. The Assyrians had mercilessly plundered other nations as a lion kills its prey. They had had no compassion or mercy for other people. Now they themselves would be plundered and killed (v. 10). Jesus articulates this principle when He said, "All they that take the sword shall perish with the sword" (Mat. 26:52; cf. Rev. 13:10).

2:13 I *AM* AGAINST THEE. God Himself stood against Nineveh. Their brutality, cruelty, and inhumane atrocities had been so great that the almighty God of the universe declared war against them. The time for their repentance was past; they would now receive the torture and grief they deserved (cf. Rev. 18:6–8).

3:1 THE BLOODY CITY. Nineveh is called "bloody" because she had cruelly massacred large numbers of people.

3:4 WHOREDOMS . . . WITCHCRAFT. Sin never exists in isolation. Not only were the Assyrians brutally cruel, but they were also extremely immoral. (1) Externally Nineveh appeared attractive, but internally she was full of cult prostitution, degrading immorality, and sensual activity. The

[o]the mistress of witchcrafts, that
selleth nations through her whore-
doms, and families through her witch-
crafts.
5 [p]Behold, I *am* against thee, saith
the LORD of hosts; and [q]I will discover
thy skirts upon thy face, and I will
show the nations thy nakedness, and
the kingdoms thy shame.
6 And I will cast abominable filth
upon thee, and make thee vile, and will
set thee as [r]a gazingstock.
7 And it shall come to pass, *that* all
they that look upon thee [s]shall flee
from thee, and say, Nineveh is laid
waste: [t]who will bemoan her? whence
shall I seek comforters for thee?
8 [u]Art thou better than [z] [a]popu-
lous [v]No, that was situate among the
rivers, *that had* the waters round about
it, whose rampart *was* the sea, *and* her
wall *was* from the sea?
9 Ethiopia and Egypt *were* her
strength, and *it was* infinite; Put and
Lubim were [b]thy helpers.
10 Yet *was* she carried away, she
went into captivity: [w]her young chil-
dren also were dashed in pieces [x]at
the top of all the streets: and they
[y]cast lots for her honourable men, and
all her great men were bound in chains.
11 Thou also shalt be [z]drunken:
thou shalt be hid, thou also shalt seek
strength because of the enemy.
12 All thy strong holds *shall be like*
[a]fig trees with the firstripe figs: if they
be shaken, they shall even fall into the
mouth of the eater.
13 Behold, [b]thy people in the
midst of thee *are* women: the gates of
thy land shall be set wide open unto
thine enemies: the fire shall devour thy
[c]bars.
14 Draw thee waters for the siege,
[d]fortify thy strong holds: go into clay,
and tread the mortar, make strong the
brickkiln.
15 There shall the fire devour thee;
the sword shall cut thee off, it shall eat
thee up like [e]the cankerworm: make
thyself many as the cankerworm,
make thyself many as the locusts.
16 Thou hast multiplied thy mer-
chants above the stars of heaven: the
cankerworm [c]spoileth, and flieth
away.
17 [f]Thy crowned *are* as the lo-
custs, and thy captains as the great
grasshoppers, which camp in the
hedges in the cold day, *but* when the
sun ariseth they flee away, and their
place is not known where they *are*.
18 [g]Thy shepherds slumber, O
[h]king of Assyria: thy [d]nobles shall
dwell *in the dust:* thy people is [i]scat-
tered upon the mountains, and no man
gathereth *them*.
19 *There is* no [e]healing of thy
bruise; [j]thy wound is grievous: [k]all
that hear the bruit of thee shall clap
the hands over thee: for upon whom
hath not thy wickedness passed con-
tinually?

3:4 [o]Is. 47:9,12
3:5 [p]ch. 2:13 [q]Is. 47:2,3
3:6 [r]Heb. 10:33
3:7 [s]Rev. 18:10 [t]Jer. 15:5
3:8 [u]Amos 6:2 [v]Jer. 46:25
3:10 [w]Ps. 137:9 Is. 13:16 Hos. 13:16 [x]Lam. 2:19 [y]Joel 3:3 Obad. 11
3:11 [z]Jer. 25:17 ch. 1:10
3:12 [a]Rev. 6:13
3:13 [b]Jer. 50:37 [c]Ps. 147:13 Jer. 51:30
3:14 [d]ch. 2:1
3:15 [e]Joel 1:4
3:17 [f]Rev. 9:7
3:18 [g]Ex. 15:16 Ps. 76:6 [h]Jer. 50:18 Ezek. 31:3 [i]1 Ki. 22:17
3:19 [j]Mic. 1:9 [k]Lam. 2:15 Zeph. 2:15

[z] Or, *nourishing* [a] Heb. *No Amon* [b] Heb. *in thy help* [c] Or, *spreadeth himself* [d] Or, *valiant ones* [e] Heb. *wrinkling*

city was also given over to witchcraft, black magic, and spiritism; demons and evil spirits controlled the lives of the people. (2) The relationship between these two elements is clear. Those who give themselves over to sin and immorality are opening up their lives to being controlled by demonic spirits.

3:5 I *AM* AGAINST YOU. Because of Nineveh's great sin, God Himself would personally expose the depravity of its residents and destroy them. No power on earth can protect a nation that God has determined to oppose. When sin reaches a certain level in any society, God will expose the people to shame by bringing down all their means of security; such a society will collapse.

3:8 ART THOU BETTER THAN POPULOUS NO? If Nineveh thought it was invincible, it should remember how God had brought down other great cities, such as the city of Thebes (No Amon) in Egypt, conquered by the Assyrians in 663 B.C.

3:19 *THERE IS* NO HEALING. Nineveh would be destroyed and never again rebuilt. After the city fell in 612 B.C., it became a wilderness area for animals and birds (see Zeph. 2:13–15).

HABAKKUK

Outline

Introduction (1:1)

I. The Questions of Habakkuk (1:2—2:20)
   - A. Question 1: How Can God Allow Wicked Judah To Go Unpunished? (1:2–4)
   - B. Answer 1: God Will Use Babylon to Punish Judah (1:5–11)
   - C. Question 2: How Can God Use a More Wicked Nation Than Judah As the Instrument of His Judgment? (1:12—2:1)
   - D. Answer 2: God Will Also Judge Babylon (2:2–20)
     1. Introduction of the Answer (2:2–3)
     2. Sins of Babylon (2:4–5)
     3. Series of Five Woes on Babylon (2:6–19)
     4. The Lord of the Whole Earth (2:20)

II. The Song of Habakkuk (3:1–19)
   - A. Habakkuk's Prayer for Mercy (3:1–2)
   - B. The Power of the Lord (3:3–7)
   - C. The Saving Acts of the Lord (3:8–15)
   - D. Habakkuk's Unwavering Faith (3:16–19)

Author: Habakkuk

Theme: Living By Faith

Date of Writing: c. 606 B.C.

Background

The author of this book identifies himself as "Habakkuk the prophet" (1:1; 3:1). Otherwise he gives no personal or family background, nor does his name (which means "embrace") appear elsewhere in the Scriptures. Habakkuk's reference to "the chief singer on my stringed instruments" (3:19) suggests that he may have also been a Levite and a musician in Jerusalem.

Unlike other O.T. prophets, Habakkuk does not date his prophecy by referring to contemporary kings. However, the fact that he was perplexed about God using the Babylonians (the "Chaldeans" of 1:6) as an instrument of His judgment against Judah suggests a time when Babylon was already a world power and an invasion of Judah was imminent (c. 608–598 B.C.). Nebuchadnezzar defeated the Egyptians at the battle of Carchemish (605 B.C.), as the last strong nation to oppose Babylonian expansion. If the description of the Babylonian army in 1:6–11 refers to the Babylonian march towards Carchemish, as many interpret it, then the date for Habakkuk's prophecy is c. 606–605 B.C., during the early years of Judah's King Jehoiakim.

The results of Babylon's rise to world power were devastating for apostate Judah (see 2 Ki. 24—25). As Nebuchadnezzar was returning from Egypt, he invaded Judah and took a significant number of captives to Babylon, among whom were Daniel and his three friends (605 B.C.). In 597 B.C. the Babylonian forces again invaded Jerusalem, ransacked the temple, and took 10,000 captives back to Babylon, among whom was the prophet Ezekiel. When King Zedekiah tried to free Judah from Babylonian control eleven years later (586 B.C.), Nebuchadnezzar angrily laid siege to Jerusalem, burned the temple, totally destroyed the

city, and brought back to Babylon as captives most of the surviving inhabitants. Habakkuk probably lived through most or all of this time of Judah's judgment.

Purpose

Unlike his contemporary, Jeremiah, Habakkuk does not prophesy to backslidden Judah. He writes instead to help the godly remnant in Judah comprehend God's ways with regard to their sinful nation and its approaching judgment. Having himself wrestled with the profoundly disturbing problem of God using a deplorably wicked people like the Chaldeans to swallow up His people in judgment (1:6–13), Habakkuk assures fellow believers that God will deal with all wickedness at the appointed time. In the meantime, "the just shall live by his faith" (2:4) and not by his understanding, and shall "rejoice . . . in the God of [his] salvation" (3:18).

Survey

Chs. 1—2 constitute Habakkuk's perplexing questions concerning God's ways and the answers that God gave to him. Having seen so much wickedness and idolatry in Judah, his first question was how God could allow His rebellious people to get away with so much sin without being punished. God answered by showing the prophet that He would soon be using the Babylonians to punish the nation of Judah. Habakkuk's second question followed immediately: how could God allow a nation even more wicked and cruel than Judah to punish her? God answered this by assuring the prophet that a day of reckoning would also come for the Babylonians. Throughout the entire book, Habakkuk expresses his faith in the sovereignty of God and in the certainty that God is just in all His ways. The revelation of God's love for the righteous and His purpose to destroy wicked Babylon evoked a prophetic hymn of praise and promise concerning salvation in Zion (ch. 3).

Special Features

Five major features or emphases characterize the prophecy of Habakkuk. (1) Rather than prophesying to apostate Judah, it records from the prophet's personal "journal" his conversations with God and subsequent prophetic revelation. (2) It contains at least three distinct literary forms: "dialogue" between the prophet and God (1:2—2:5), classic "prophetic woes" (2:6–20), and a prophetic song (ch. 3)—all with vigorous diction and graphic metaphors. (3) The prophet manifests three characteristics in the midst of adverse times: honest inquiry of the Lord (ch. 1), unshakable faith (2:4; 3:18–19), and concern for revival (3:2). (4) The prophet's vision of God in ch. 3 is one of the most lofty in the Bible, reminiscent of the theophany to the Israelites at Mount Sinai; other memorable passages in Habakkuk are 1:5; 2:3–4,20; 3:2,17–19. (5) No prophet in the O.T. is more eloquent on the issue of faith than Habakkuk—not only in his declaration that "the just shall live by his faith" (2:4), but also in his personal testimony (3:17–19).

New Testament Fulfillment

Habakkuk's declaration that the righteous will live by faith (2:4) is the key O.T. text used by Paul in his theology of justification by faith. The apostle of faith quotes this verse both in Rom. 1:17 and Gal. 3:11 (cf. also Heb. 10:37–38).

Reading Habakkuk

In order to read the entire Old Testament in one year, the book of Habakkuk should be read in 1 day: ☐ Habakkuk

NOTES

Wrong judgment prevails

1 THE BURDEN which Habakkuk the prophet did see.

2 O LORD, how long shall I cry, [a]and thou wilt not hear! *even* cry out unto thee *of* violence, and thou wilt not save!

3 Why dost thou show me iniquity, and cause *me* to behold grievance? for spoiling and violence *are* before me: and there are *that* raise up strife and contention.

4 Therefore the law is slacked, and judgment doth never go forth: for the [b]wicked doth compass about the righteous; therefore [a]wrong judgment proceedeth.

Punishment by the Chaldeans

5 ¶ [c]Behold ye among the heathen, and regard, and wonder marvellously: for *I* will work a work in your days, *which* ye will not believe, though it be told *you.*

6 For, lo, [b]I raise up the Chaldeans, *that* bitter and hasty nation, which shall march through the [c]breadth of the land, to possess the dwellingplaces *that are* not theirs.

7 They *are* terrible and dreadful: [d]their judgment and their dignity shall proceed of themselves.

8 Their horses also are swifter than the leopards, and are more [e]fierce than the evening wolves: and their horsemen shall spread themselves, and their horsemen shall come from far; they shall fly as the eagle *that* hasteth to eat.

9 They shall come all for violence: [f] [g]their faces shall sup up *as* the east wind, and they shall gather the captivity as the sand.

10 And they shall scoff at the kings, and the princes shall be a scorn unto them: they shall deride every strong hold; for they shall heap dust, and take it.

11 Then shall *his* mind change, and he shall pass over, and offend, [d]*imputing* this his power unto his god.

The wicked destroy the righteous

12 ¶ *Art* thou not from everlasting, O LORD my God, mine Holy One? we shall not die. O LORD, [e]thou hast ordained them for judgment; and, O [h]mighty God, thou hast [i]established them for correction.

13 *Thou art* of purer eyes than to behold evil, and canst not look on [j]iniquity: wherefore lookest thou upon them that deal treacherously, *and* hold-

1:2 [a]Lam. 3:8
1:4 [b]Jer. 12:1
1:5 [c]Is. 29:14
1:11 [d]Dan. 5:4
1:12 [e]Is. 10:5-7

[a] Or, *wrested* [b] Fulfilled in 2 Chr. 36:6 [c] Heb. *breadths* [d] Or, *from them shall proceed the judgment of these, and the captivity of these* [e] Heb. *sharp* [f] Or, *the supping up of their faces,* or, *their faces shall look toward the east* [g] Heb. *the opposition of their faces toward the east* [h] Heb. *rock* [i] Heb. *founded* [j] Or, *grievance*

1:1 HABAKKUK. Habakkuk prophesied to Judah between the defeat of the Assyrians at Nineveh and the invasion of Jerusalem by the Babylonians (605–597 B.C.; see the introduction). (1) The book is unique in that it is not a prophecy addressed directly to Israel, but rather a dialogue between the prophet and God. Habakkuk asked the question: "Why doesn't God do something about the evil so dominant in Judah?" God responded by stating that He was sending the Babylonians to punish Judah. (2) This answer only confused the prophet more, and he wanted to know, "Why does God punish His people with a nation more wicked than they?" In the end, Habakkuk learned to trust God and to live by faith in God's way, regardless of the circumstances.

1:2–4 HOW LONG SHALL I CRY. Habakkuk had been praying to God to stop the wrong he saw among the covenant people. Yet God seemed to be doing nothing but tolerating violence, injustice, and the destruction of the righteous. His questions dealt with the age-old theme: "Why does God wait so long to punish evil?" and "Why are our prayers generally not answered quickly?" Note, however, that these complaints came out of a heart of faith in a righteous God.

1:5–11 *I* WILL WORK A WORK. God answered Habakkuk by telling him He already had plans to chastise Judah for its sins. He would use the ruthless and pagan Babylonians to correct Judah. That God would use such a wicked, pagan people to punish Judah was astonishing to the prophet and unbelievable to God's people (see next note).

1:12 *ART* THOU NOT FROM EVERLASTING. Habakkuk was appalled that God would use such a wicked nation to attack Judah, yet he was confident that God would not allow them to annihilate His own people and by that destruction cancel His redemptive purpose for the human race.

1:13 CANST NOT LOOK ON INIQUITY. This phrase does not mean that God does not see evil, for He observes everything; He is omniscient (see article on THE ATTRIBUTES OF GOD, p. 912). Rather, the statement means that God never looks on evil to condone or tolerate it. What perplexed Habakkuk was this: God's use of the wicked Babylonians made it seem like He was tolerating *their* sin while punishing Judah, who, in spite of all their evil, was still a more righteous nation than the Babylonians.

est thy tongue when the wicked devoureth *the man that is* more righteous than he?

14 And makest men as the fishes of the sea, as the [k]creeping things, *that have* no ruler over them?

15 They take up all of them with the angle, they catch them in their net, and gather them in their [l]drag: therefore they rejoice and are glad.

16 Therefore [f]they sacrifice unto their net, and burn incense unto their drag; because by them their portion *is* fat, and their meat [m] [n]plenteous.

17 Shall they therefore empty their net, and not spare continually to slay the nations?

Life to the just

2 I WILL [g]stand upon my watch, and set me upon the [o]tower, and will watch to see what he will say [p]unto me, and what I shall answer [q] [r]when I am reproved.

2 And the LORD answered me, and said, [h]Write the vision, and make *it* plain upon tables, that he may run that readeth it.

3 For [i]the vision *is* yet for an appointed time, but at the end it shall speak, and not lie: though it tarry, wait for it; because it will [j]surely come, it will not tarry.

4 Behold, his soul *which* is lifted up is not upright in him: but the [k]just shall live by his faith.

5 ¶ [s]Yea also, because he transgresseth by wine, *he is* a proud man, neither keepeth at home, who enlargeth his desire as hell, and *is* as death, and cannot be satisfied, but gathereth unto him all nations, and heapeth unto him all people:

Woe to the unrighteous

6 Shall not all these take up a parable against him, and a taunting proverb against him, and say, [t]Woe to him that increaseth *that which is* not his! how long? and to him that ladeth himself with thick clay!

7 Shall they not rise up suddenly that shall bite thee, and awake that shall vex thee, and thou shalt be for booties unto them?

8 [l]Because thou hast spoiled many nations, all the remnant of the people shall spoil thee; because of men's [u]blood, and *for* the violence of the land, of the city, and of all that dwell therein.

9 ¶ Woe to him that [v]coveteth an evil covetousness to his house, that he may [m]set his nest on high, that he may be delivered from the [w]power of evil!

10 Thou hast consulted shame to thy house by cutting off many people, and hast sinned *against* thy soul.

11 For the stone shall cry out of the wall, and the [x]beam out of the timber shall [y]answer it.

12 ¶ Woe to him that buildeth a

1:16 [f]Deut. 8:17
2:1 [g]Is. 21:8,11
2:2 [h]Is. 8:1
2:3 [i]Dan. 10:14 [j]Heb. 10:37
2:4 [k]John 3:36
2:8 [l]Is. 33:1
2:9 [m]Obad. 4

[k] Or, *moving* [l] Or, *flue net* [m] Or, *dainty* [n] Heb. *fat* [o] Heb. *fenced place* [p] Or, *in me* [q] Or, *when I am argued with* [r] Heb. *upon my reproof,* or, *arguing* [s] Or, *How much more* [t] Or, *Ho, he* [u] Heb. *bloods* [v] Or, *gaineth an evil gain* [w] Heb. *palm of the hand* [x] Or, *piece,* or, *fastening* [y] Or, *witness against it*

2:2–20 WRITE THE VISION. In ch. 2 God gave Habakkuk an answer to his questions concerning the dominance of evil in the world and the possible annihilation of the righteous. The Lord stated that a time was coming when all the wicked would be destroyed and the only people not shaken would be the righteous, those who are related to God by their faith (see v. 4, note).

2:3 THE VISION . . . FOR AN APPOINTED TIME. The final solution to Habakkuk's problem would come only in the future, at God's "appointed time." (1) There would be a termination point to wickedness in the world. The faithful people of God had to "wait for it," even though it seemed to take such a long time. (2) Like Habakkuk, we must wait for the Lord's righteous intervention at the end of this age. Ultimately, Christ will take away the righteous from the earth and bring destruction on all evil (see 1 Thes. 4:16–17; see article on THE RAPTURE, p. 1889).

2:4 THE JUST SHALL LIVE BY HIS FAITH. It is "the just," i.e., the righteous, who at the end will emerge victorious. (1) The righteous are contrasted with the proud and the ungodly, whose lives are not upright. The hearts of the righteous are turned to God, and they desire to be His children, to have close fellowship with Him, and to obey His will. (2) The righteous must live in this world by faith in God. Here "faith" means a steadfast trust in God that His ways are right, a personal loyalty to Him as Savior and Lord, and a moral steadfastness to follow His ways. Paul develops this theme in Rom. 1:17 and Gal. 3:11 (cf. Heb. 10:38; see article on FAITH AND GRACE, p. 1738).

2:6–20 WOE TO HIM. These verses pronounce woes of judgment on anyone whose "soul . . . is not upright in him" (v. 4). Such people will be judged because of their aggression (vv. 6–8), injustice (vv. 9–11), violence and crime (vv. 12–14), immorality (vv. 15–17), and idolatry (vv. 18–20).

town with [z]blood, and stablisheth a
city by iniquity!
13 Behold, *is it* not of the LORD of
hosts that the people shall labour in
the very fire, and the people shall wea-
ry themselves [a]for very vanity?
14 For the earth shall be filled
[b]with the knowledge of the glory of
the LORD, as the waters cover the sea.
15 ¶ Woe unto him that giveth his
neighbour drink, that puttest thy
[n]bottle to *him,* and makest *him* drunk-
en also, that thou mayest look on their
nakedness!
16 Thou art filled [c]with shame for
glory: drink thou also, and let thy fore-
skin be uncovered: the cup of the
LORD'S right hand shall be turned unto
thee, and shameful spewing *shall be* on
thy glory.
17 For the violence of Lebanon
shall cover thee, and the spoil of
beasts, *which* made them afraid, be-
cause of men's blood, and for the vio-
lence of the land, of the city, and of all
that dwell therein.
18 ¶ What profiteth the graven im-
age that the maker thereof hath graven
it; the molten image, and a teacher of
lies, that [d]the maker of his work
trusteth therein, to make dumb idols?
19 Woe unto him that saith to the
wood, Awake; to the dumb stone,
Arise, it shall teach! Behold, it *is* laid
over with gold and silver, and *there is*
no breath at all in the midst of it.
20 But the LORD *is* in his holy tem-
ple: [e]let all the earth keep silence be-
fore him.

Habakkuk's prayer

3 A PRAYER of Habakkuk the
prophet [f]upon Shigionoth.
2 O LORD, I have heard [g]thy
speech, *and* was afraid: O LORD, [h]re-
vive thy work in the midst of the years,
in the midst of the years make known;
in wrath remember mercy.
3 God came from [i]Teman, and the
Holy One from mount Paran. Selah.
His glory covered the heavens, and the
earth was full of his praise.
4 And *his* brightness was as the
light; he had [j]horns *coming* out of his
hand: and there *was* the hiding of his
power.
5 Before him went the pestilence,
and [k]burning coals went forth at his
feet.
6 He stood, and measured the
earth: he beheld, and drove asunder
the nations; [o]and the everlasting
mountains were scattered, the per-
petual hills did bow: his ways *are* ever-
lasting.
7 I saw the tents of [l]Cushan [m]in
affliction: *and* the curtains of the land
of Midian did tremble.
8 Was the LORD displeased against
the rivers? *was* thine anger against the
rivers? *was* thy wrath against the sea,
that thou didst ride upon thine horses
and [n]thy chariots of salvation?
9 Thy bow was made quite naked,
according to the oaths of the tribes,
even thy word. Selah. [o]Thou didst
cleave the earth with rivers.
10 The mountains saw thee, *and*
they trembled: the overflowing of the
water passed by: the deep uttered his

2:15 [n] Hos. 7:5
3:6 [o] Nah. 1:5
Zeph 3:19-20

[z] Heb. *bloods* [a] Or, *in vain?* [b] Or, *by knowing the glory of the LORD* [c] Or, *more with shame than with glory* [d] Heb. *the fashioner of his fashion* [e] Heb. *be silent all the earth before him* [f] Or, *according to variable songs,* or, *tunes,* called in Hebrew, *Shigionoth* [g] Heb. *thy report,* or, *thy hearing* [h] Or, *preserve alive* [i] Or, *the south* [j] Or, *bright beams out of his side* [k] Or, *burning diseases* [l] Or, *Ethiopia* [m] Or, *under affliction,* or, *vanity* [n] Or, *thy chariots were salvation?* [o] Or, *Thou didst cleave the rivers of the earth*

3:1–19 A PRAYER. This chapter is Habakkuk's response to God's answer of ch. 2. In the midst of the world's sin and God's judgment, he has learned to live by faith in God and to trust in the wisdom of His ways.

3:2 REVIVE THY WORK IN THE MIDST OF THE YEARS. Habakkuk knew God's people had sinned and would experience His judgment. In this situation he made two petitions. (1) He prayed for God to come among His people with a fresh manifestation of His power. Habakkuk knew that God's people would not survive if the Lord did not intervene in their lives with an outpouring of His grace and Spirit. Only then would there be true spiritual life among them. (2) Habakkuk prayed that in times of distress and trouble for the Lord's people, God would remember to be merciful. Without mercy His people would not be sustained. As the foundation of the church is being shaken today and trouble seems to be on every hand, we too need to plead with the Lord to manifest Himself, His mercy, and His power anew, in order that life and revival might come to His people.

3:3–16 GOD CAME. In these verses Habakkuk refers to the time God delivered His people from Egypt (see Ex. 14). The same God who came with salvation in the past would come again in all His glory. All who were waiting for that coming would live and see His triumph over empires and nations.

voice, *and* [p]lifted up his hands on
high.
11 The sun *and* moon stood still in
their habitation: [p]at the light of thine
arrows they went, *and* at the shining of
thy glittering spear.
12 Thou didst march through the
land in indignation, thou didst thresh
the heathen in anger.
13 Thou wentest forth for the salva-
tion of thy people, *even* for salvation
with thine anointed; thou woundedst
the head out of the house of the wick-
ed, [q]by discovering the foundation
unto the neck. Selah.
14 Thou didst strike through with
his staves the head of his villages: they
[r]came out as a whirlwind to scatter
me: their rejoicing *was* as to devour the
poor secretly.
15 [q]Thou didst walk through the
sea with thine horses, *through* the
[s]heap of great waters.
16 When I heard, [r]my belly trem-
bled; my lips quivered at the voice: rot-
tenness entered into my bones, and I
trembled in myself, that I might rest in
the day of trouble: when he cometh up
unto the people, he will [t]invade them
with his troops.
17 ¶ Although the fig tree shall not
blossom, neither *shall* fruit *be* in the
vines; the labour of the olive shall
[u]fail, and the fields shall yield no
meat; the flock shall be cut off from the
fold, and *there shall be* no herd in the
stalls:
18 Yet I will rejoice in the LORD, I
will joy in the God of my salvation.
19 The LORD God *is* my strength,
and he will make my feet like [s]hinds'
feet, and he will make me to [t]walk
upon mine high places. To the chief
singer on my [v]stringed instruments. Mat. 8:10

3:10 [p]Ex. 14:22
3:15 [q]Ps. 77:19
3:16 [r]Ps. 119:120
3:19 [s]2 Sam. 22:34 [t]Deut. 32:13

[p] Or, *thine arrows walked in the light* [q] Heb. *making naked* [r] Heb. *were tempestuous* [s] Or, *mud* [t] Or, *cut them in pieces* [u] Heb. *lie* [v] Heb. *Neginoth;* see Ps. 4, title

3:18–19 I WILL REJOICE IN THE LORD. Habakkuk testifies that he served God not for what He gave, but because He was God. Even in the midst of God's judgment on Judah (v. 16), Habakkuk chose to rejoice in the Lord; God would be his salvation and an unfailing source of strength. He knew beyond a doubt that a righteous remnant would survive the Babylonian invasion, and he proclaimed with confidence the ultimate victory of all who live by faith in God (cf. 2:4).

ZEPHANIAH

Outline

Introduction (1:1)
- I. Judgment and the Day of the Lord (1:2 — 3:8)
  - A. Judgment on the Whole Earth (1:2–3)
  - B. Judgment Against the People of Judah (1:4–18)
    - 1. Description of Judah's Sins (1:4–9)
    - 2. Warning to Jerusalem (1:10–13)
    - 3. The Great Day of the Lord (1:14–18)
  - C. Call to Repentance (2:1–3)
  - D. Judgment Against the Nations (2:4–15)
    - 1. The Philistines (2:4–7)
    - 2. The Ammonites and Moabites (2:8–11)
    - 3. The Ethiopians (2:12)
    - 4. The Assyrians (2:13–15)
  - E. Judgment Against Jerusalem (3:1–7)
    - 1. Sins of Jerusalem (3:1–4)
    - 2. God's Justice Against Jerusalem (3:5–7)
  - F. Judgment on the Whole Earth (3:8)
- II. Salvation and the Day of the Lord (3:9–20)
  - A. The Remnant Restored and Jerusalem Purified (3:9–13)
  - B. The Jubilant People with God in Their Midst (3:14–17)
  - C. Final Promises Concerning Restoration (3:18–20)

Author: Zephaniah

Theme: The Day of the Lord

Date of Writing: c. 630 B.C.

Background

Zephaniah, whose name means "the LORD hides," was a great-great-grandson of King Hizkiah (Hezekiah) and prophesied during the reign of Josiah (639–609 B.C.), Judah's last godly ruler (1:1). His reference to Jerusalem as "this place" (1:4), as well as his precise description of its topography and sins, indicates that he resided in the capital. Being a descendant of royalty and related to King Josiah means he had access to the royal palace. Understandably, his prophecies focused on the word of the Lord for Judah and the nations.

The sins that Zephaniah charged against Jerusalem and Judah (1:4–13; 3:1–7) indicate that he prophesied before Josiah's revival and reform, at a time when the terrible sins of Josiah's wicked predecessors (Manasseh and Amon) were still rampant in society. It was not until the twelfth year of Josiah's reign (i.e., 627 B.C.) that the king set about to purge the nation of idolatry and to reinstitute the true worship of the Lord; eight years later he ordered the repair and purification of Solomon's temple, during which time a copy of the law of the Lord was discovered (cf. 2 Ki. 22:1–10). The description that Zephaniah gave of Judah's pathetic spiritual and moral condition must have been written about 630 B.C.. Most likely Zephaniah's prophetic preaching had a direct influence on the king and helped to inspire his reforms. A date of 630 B.C. is further indicated by Zephaniah's total lack of reference to Babylon as a power to be reckoned with on the international scene; Babylon

began its rise to prominence with the ascendancy of Nabopolassar in 625 B.C.. However, Zephaniah did prophesy the destruction of mighty Assyria, an event that occurred in 612 B.C. with Nineveh's downfall. Jeremiah was a younger contemporary of Zephaniah.

Purpose

Zephaniah prophesied and wrote to warn Judah and Jerusalem of the impending ominous judgment of God called "the great day of the LORD" (1:14). The imminent application of this prophetic word was that apostate Judah would receive just retribution for her wickedness, as would the heathen nations around her, whom he listed by name. The far-distant dimension of the prophecy applies to the church and the world at the end of history. Zephaniah also wrote to encourage the godly that God would one day restore His people; then Judah would sing the praises of their just God, who was dwelling in their midst.

Survey

For the most part, the book is a sober warning about the coming day of God's judgment for sin. Zephaniah saw a worldwide judgment coming for the sins of all humanity (1:2; 3:8), but he especially focused on the judgment coming on Judah for her sins (1:4–18; 3:1–7). Zephaniah made a prophetic appeal for the nation to repent and to seek the Lord in humility before the decree took effect (2:1–3); this national repentance happened in part during Josiah's revival (627–609 B.C.).

Zephaniah also prophesied coming judgment on five foreign nations: Philistia, Ammon, Moab, Ethiopia, and Assyria (2:4–15). After addressing again the sins of Jerusalem (3:1–7), the prophet predicted a time when God would regather, redeem, and restore His people; they would shout for joy as true worshipers of the Lord God; He would be in their midst as a victorious warrior (3:9–20).

Special Features

Five major features or emphases characterize the book of Zephaniah. (1) Zephaniah is the only prophet to give an extended list of his ancestry, going back four generations to King Hezekiah. (2) It has the most extensive revelation in the O.T. about the future "day of the LORD." (3) It demonstrates that God's people need to be confronted by God's warnings as well as comforted by His promises. (4) It contains a rather well-developed teaching about the faithful remnant that would be restored in the day of the Lord's visitation (3:9–20). (5) Zephaniah's revelation about the coming day of God's wrath for the wicked and the great day of salvation for His people contributed to the N.T. revelation about the end of time.

New Testament Fulfillment

Jesus may have alluded to Zephaniah twice (1:2–3, cf. Mat. 13:40–42; 1:15, cf. Mat. 24:29); both references are associated with His second coming. N.T. writers understood Zephaniah's message about the "day of the LORD" as a description of the eschatological events that begin with the Great Tribulation and conclude with Jesus' return to judge the living and the dead (compare 1:14 with Rev. 6:17; 3:8 with Rev. 16:1). Frequently the N.T. refers to Christ's second coming and the day of judgment as "the Day" (e.g., 1 Cor. 3:13; cf. 2 Tim. 1:12,18; 4:8).

Reading Zephaniah

In order to read the entire Old Testament in one year, the book of Zephaniah should be read in 1 day: □ Zephaniah

NOTES

1 THE WORD of the LORD which
came unto Zephaniah the son of
Cushi, the son of Gedaliah, the son of
Amariah, the son of Hizkiah, in the
days of Josiah the son of Amon, king of
Judah.

Judgment upon Jerusalem

2 [a]I will utterly consume all *things*
from off [b]the land, saith the LORD.
3 [a]I will consume man and beast;
I will consume the fowls of the heaven,
and the fishes of the sea, and the
[c]stumblingblocks with the wicked;
and I will cut off man from off the land,
saith the LORD.
4 I will also stretch out mine hand
upon Judah, and upon all the inhabi-
tants of Jerusalem; and I will cut off
the remnant of Baal from this place,
and the name of [b]the Chemarims with
the priests;
5 And them [c]that worship the host
of heaven upon the housetops; and
them that worship *and* that swear [d]by
the LORD, and that swear [d]by Mal-
cham;
6 And [e]them that are turned back
from the LORD; and *those* that [f]have
not sought the LORD, nor inquired for
him.

1:3 [a]Hos. 4:3
1:4 [b]Hos. 10:5
1:5 [c]2 Ki. 23:12 [d]Josh. 23:7
1:6 [e]Is. 1:4 Jer. 2:13 [f]Hos. 7:7
1:7 [g]Hab. 2:20 Zech. 2:13 [h]Is. 13:6 [i]Is. 34:6 Jer. 46:10
1:8 [j]Jer. 39:6
1:10 [k]2 Chr. 33:14
1:11 [l]Jas. 5:1
1:12 [m]Jer. 48:11 [n]Ps. 94:7

7 [g]Hold thy peace at the presence
of the Lord GOD: [h]for the day of the
LORD *is* at hand: for [i]the LORD hath pre-
pared a sacrifice, he hath [e]bid his
guests.
8 And it shall come to pass in the
day of the LORD's sacrifice, that I will
[f]punish [j]the princes, and the king's
children, and all such as are clothed
with strange apparel.
9 In the same day also will I punish
all those that leap on the threshold,
which fill their masters' houses with
violence and deceit.
10 And it shall come to pass in that
day, saith the LORD, *that there shall be*
the noise of a cry from [k]the fish gate,
and an howling from the second, and a
great crashing from the hills.
11 [l]Howl, ye inhabitants of Mak-
tesh, for all the merchant people are
cut down; all they that bear silver are
cut off.
12 And it shall come to pass at that
time, *that* I will search Jerusalem with
candles, and punish the men that are
[m]settled[g] on their lees: [n]that say in

[a] Heb. *By taking away I will make an end* [b] Heb. *the face of the land* [c] Or, *idols* [d] Or, *to the LORD* [e] Heb. *sanctified*, or, *prepared* [f] Heb. *visit upon* [g] Heb. *curded*, or, *thickened*

1:1 ZEPHANIAH. Zephaniah prophesied during the reign of Josiah, king of Judah (640–609 B.C.). The nation was entangled in violence and idolatry, and was scornfully indifferent toward the Lord God. His message to the nation was probably given before the reform movement led by Josiah and may have been a motivating force encouraging the king to call for renewed obedience to God and His law (see the introduction).

1:2–3 UTTERLY CONSUME ALL *THINGS*. Zephaniah begins by announcing God's coming judgment on the entire world. Because the majority of humankind will refuse to turn from their sins to the Lord, God has appointed a day when He will destroy all the wicked as well as the world itself. It will be a time of distress, anguish, trouble, and ruin (v. 15; see article on THE GREAT TRIBULATION, p. 1456).

1:4 UPON JUDAH. Judah, God's people of Zephaniah's day, would soon experience God's wrath for turning from the Lord, worshiping other gods, and engaging in violence, corruption, and deceit (vv. 4–9).

1:5 WORSHIP THE HOST OF HEAVEN. This form of idolatry is prevalent among us today in those who seek comfort or direction for their lives by astrological signs and horoscope readings (cf. Deut. 4:19).

1:5 THEM . . . THAT SWEAR BY THE LORD. Many in Judah were participating in other forms of religion while at the same time worshiping the Lord God. This mixture was both idolatrous and flagrantly evil. God will not tolerate those who claim to be His followers, and yet at the same time participate in idolatrous, sinful, and immoral activity. Condemnation awaits all who fail to separate themselves as holy unto the Lord (see article on SPIRITUAL SEPARATION FOR BELIEVERS, p. 1814).

1:7 THE DAY OF THE LORD. This prophecy applies first of all to the destruction of Judah by the Babylonians in 605 B.C., and secondly to God's worldwide judgment on all the nations at the end of time (cf. Is. 2:12; 13:6,9; Jer. 46:10; Ezek. 13:5; Joel 1:15; 2:1; see Joel 1:15, note; Amos 5:18, note). The latter day of wrath is yet to come (Rom. 2:5), associated with the final return of Jesus Christ (Mat. 24:29–33; see 1 Thes. 5:2, note).

1:12 THE LORD WILL NOT DO GOOD, NEITHER . . . EVIL. Some in Judah had a deistic view of God (i.e., the view that God is not actively involved in the everyday affairs of people's lives); they believed that God would not punish sin among His people. (1) Those who had this attitude would fearfully discover on the day of judgment that God did indeed hold them accountable for those sins that they refused to abandon. (2) We too need to know that God is not distant from or uninvolved in the affairs of humans. He will reward those who seek Him and judge those who turn from Him and do evil (see Rom. 2:5–11).

their heart, The LORD will not do good, neither will he do evil.

13 Therefore their goods shall become a booty, and their houses a desolation: they shall also build houses, but [o]not inhabit *them;* and they shall plant vineyards, but [p]not drink the wine thereof.

The day of wrath

14 [q]The great day of the LORD *is* near, *it is* near, and hasteth greatly, *even* the voice of the day of the LORD: the mighty man shall cry there bitterly.

15 [r]That day *is* a day of wrath, a day of trouble and distress, a day of wasteness and desolation, a day of darkness and gloominess, a day of clouds and thick darkness,

16 A day of [s]the trumpet and alarm against the fenced cities, and against the high towers.

17 And I will bring distress upon men, that they shall [t]walk like blind men, because they have sinned against the LORD: and [u]their blood shall be poured out as dust, and their flesh [v]as the dung.

18 [w]Neither their silver nor their gold shall be able to deliver them in the day of the LORD's wrath; but the whole land shall be [x]devoured by the fire of his jealousy: for [y]he shall make even a speedy riddance of all them that dwell in the land.

The call to repentance

2 GATHER[z] YOURSELVES together, yea, gather together, O nation [h]not desired;

2 Before the decree bring forth, *before* the day pass [a]as the chaff, before [b]the fierce anger of the LORD come upon you, before the day of the LORD's anger come upon you.

3 [c]Seek ye the LORD, [d]all ye meek of the earth, which have wrought his judgment; seek righteousness, seek meekness: [e]it may be ye shall be hid in the day of the LORD's anger.

4 ¶ For [f]Gaza shall be forsaken, and Ashkelon a desolation: they shall drive out Ashdod [g]at the noon day, and Ekron shall be rooted up.

The woe upon the nations

5 Woe unto the inhabitants of [h]the sea coast, the nation of the Cherethites! the word of the LORD *is* against you; O [i]Canaan, the land of the Philistines, I will even destroy thee, that there shall be no inhabitant.

6 And the sea coast shall be dwellings *and* cottages for shepherds, [j]and folds for flocks.

7 And the coast shall be for [k]the remnant of the house of Judah; they shall feed thereupon: in the houses of Ashkelon shall they lie down in the evening: [i]for the LORD their God shall [l]visit them, and [m]turn away their captivity.

8 ¶ [n]I have heard the reproach of Moab, and [o]the revilings of the children of Ammon, whereby they have reproached my people, and [p]magnified *themselves* against their border.

9 Therefore *as* I live, saith the LORD of hosts, the God of Israel, Surely [q]Moab shall be as Sodom, and [r]the children of Ammon as Gomorrah, [s]*even* the breeding of nettles, and salt-

1:13 [o]Amos 5:11 [p]Mic. 6:15
1:14 [q]Joel 2:1,11
1:15 [r]Is. 22:5 Jer. 30:7
1:16 [s]Jer. 4:19
1:17 [t]Deut. 28:29 [u]Ps. 79:3 [v]Jer. 9:22
1:18 [w]Ezek. 7:19 [x]ch. 3:8 [y]ver. 2,3
2:1 [z]Joel 2:16
2:2 [a]Job 21:18 Is. 17:13 [b]2 Ki. 23:26
2:3 [c]Amos 5:6 [d]Ps. 76:9 [e]Amos 5:15
2:4 [f]Zech. 9:5,6 [g]Jer. 6:4
2:5 [h]Ezek. 25:16 [i]Josh. 13:3
2:6 [j]Is. 17:2
2:7 [k]Mic. 5:7,8 [l]Luke 1:68 [m]Jer. 29:14
2:8 [n]Jer. 48:27 [o]Ezek. 25:3 [p]Jer. 49:1
2:9 [q]Is. 15 [r]Amos 1:13 [s]Deut. 29:23

h Or, *not desirous* i Or, *when*

2:1–3 GATHER YOURSELVES TOGETHER . . . O NATION. Zephaniah had declared the coming day of God's wrath upon Judah, a day that would not be canceled. The time and certainty of judgment had been set, and the nation had to be punished for its apostasy and sin. Nevertheless, God offered hope for those who repented before that day; the truly righteous would be protected by the Lord on the day of His fierce anger (see next note).

2:3 SEEK YE THE LORD . . . SEEK RIGHTEOUSNESS, SEEK MEEKNESS. The prophet offers hope to those who had already turned to the Lord. He exhorted them to deepen their commitment to God and His ways; perhaps God would protect them when He came to punish His people. They had to seek three things if they hoped to experience revival and renewed blessing from the Lord, three things equally essential today for N.T. believers. (1) First, they had to seek God Himself. Their hearts were to be turned toward Him with a deep desire to know and love Him as their covenant Lord and protector (cf. Jer. 29:13). (2) They had to seek righteousness according to God's Word as their way of life (cf. Is. 1:21; Amos 5:24; Mat. 6:33). (3) They had to seek humility, realizing their helplessness and their need to submit in obedience to God (cf. Num. 12:3; Ps. 45:4; Prov. 15:33).

2:4–15 GAZA SHALL BE FORSAKEN. After warning Judah, Zephaniah prophesies that God's judgment would also come on their sinful and idolatrous neighbors.

pits, and a perpetual desolation: [t]the
residue of my people shall spoil them,
and the remnant of my people shall
possess them.
10 This shall they have [u]for their
pride, because they have reproached
and magnified *themselves* against the
people of the LORD of hosts.
11 The LORD *will be* terrible unto
them: for he will [j]famish all the gods
of the earth; [v]and *men* shall worship
him, every one from his place, *even* all
[w]the isles of the heathen.
12 ¶ [x]Ye Ethiopians also, ye *shall*
be slain by [y]my sword.
13 And he will stretch out his hand
against the north, and [z]destroy Assyr-
ia; and will make Nineveh a desolation,
and dry like a wilderness.
14 And [a]flocks shall lie down in
the midst of her, all [b]the beasts of the
nations: both the [c]cormorant[k] and
the bittern shall lodge in the [l]upper
lintels of it; *their* voice shall sing in the
windows; desolation *shall be* in the
thresholds: [m]for he shall uncover
the [d]cedar work.
15 This *is* the rejoicing city [e]that
dwelt carelessly, [f]that said in her
heart, I *am*, and *there is* none beside
me: how is she become a desolation, a
place for beasts to lie down in! every
one that passeth by her [g]shall hiss,
and [h]wag his hand.

2:9 [t]ver. 7
2:10 [u]Is. 16:6; Jer. 48:29
2:11 [v]Mal. 1:11; John 4:21 [w]Gen. 10:5
2:12 [x]Is. 18:1; Jer. 46:9 [y]Ps. 17:13
2:13 [z]Is. 10:12; Nah. 1:1
2:14 [a]ver. 6 [b]Is. 13:21 [c]Is. 34:11 [d]Jer. 22:14
2:15 [e]Is. 47:8 [f]Rev. 18:7 [g]Lam. 2:15 [h]Nah. 3:19
3:2 [i]Jer. 22:21 [j]Jer. 5:3
3:3 [k]Ezek. 22:27; Mic. 3:9 [l]Hab. 1:8
3:4 [m]Hos. 9:7 [n]Ezek. 22:26
3:5 [o]Deut. 32:4 [p]Mic. 3:11 [q]Jer. 3:3
3:7 [r]Jer. 8:6

The future of Jerusalem

3 WOE TO [n,o]her that is filthy and
polluted, to the oppressing city!
2 She [i]obeyed not the voice; she
[j]received not [p]correction; she trust-
ed not in the LORD; she drew not near
to her God.
3 [k]Her princes within her *are* roar-
ing lions; her judges *are* [l]evening
wolves; they gnaw not the bones till
the morrow.
4 Her [m]prophets *are* light *and*
treacherous persons: her priests have
polluted the sanctuary, they have done
[n]violence to the law.
5 [o]The just LORD [p]*is* in the midst
thereof; he will not do iniquity: [q]every
morning doth he bring his judgment to
light, he faileth not; but [q]the unjust
knoweth no shame.
6 I have cut off the nations: their
[r]towers are desolate; I made their
streets waste, that none passeth by:
their cities are destroyed, so that there
is no man, that there is none inhabi-
tant.
7 [r]I said, Surely thou wilt fear me,
thou wilt receive instruction; so their
dwelling should not be cut off, howso-

[j] Heb. *make lean* [k] Or, *pelican* [l] Or, *knobs*, or, *chapiters* [m] Or, *when he hath uncovered* [n] Or, *gluttonous* [o] Heb. *craw* [p] Or, *instruction* [q] Heb. *morning by morning* [r] Or, *corners*

2:10 REPROACHED AND MAGNIFIED *THEMSELVES* AGAINST THE PEOPLE OF THE LORD. The unbelieving world insults and mocks God's people, those who are committed to the righteous and holy standards of His Word. (1) This kind of treatment is unavoidable in a world under the control of Satan and dominated by people whose minds are darkened (cf. 2 Cor. 4:4; Eph. 2:2–3; 4:18). Jesus Himself experienced mocking and reproach while on earth (see Mat. 27:39–44; cf. Ps. 69:10). (2) The persecution of the righteous will not last forever. God has appointed a day when He will vindicate those who have remained loyal to His ways and will bring just punishment on those who have mocked the faithful.

3:1–7 WOE . . . TO THE OPPRESSING CITY. After condemning the other nations, Zephaniah turned again to the sins of Jerusalem and God's people. They had become a people who were opposed to God and His law. Moral decay had penetrated every stratum of society, and they were refusing to listen to God's true prophets.

3:3–4 HER PRINCES . . . JUDGES . . . PROPHETS . . . PRIESTS. These were the four main categories of leadership in Judah. God condemned these spiritual leaders for failing to be holy and righteous. (1) The officials and judges perverted the law and unjustly used their positions to gain money and property for themselves. (2) The prophets altered God's message so as to gain popularity and the approval. (3) The priests profaned the house of God by violating His precepts and living immoral lives. (4) We must resist leaders who tolerate or promote worldliness and immorality in God's name and replace them with leaders and laypeople who insist that God's holy standards be followed. God's standards must never be lowered to accommodate the sins of some leaders (see article on MORAL QUALIFICATIONS FOR OVERSEERS, p. 1908).

3:5 THE JUST LORD . . . WILL NOT DO INIQUITY. Though humans fail and fall into sin, God Himself will remain righteous and never do wrong. That truth is inherent in His very nature (see article on THE ATTRIBUTES OF GOD, p. 912). (1) The Lord God is truthful, righteous, and just in all His ways (cf. Deut. 32:4). We must maintain faith in His never-failing righteousness. (2) Although things may happen to us that we cannot understand (see article on THE SUFFERING OF THE RIGHTEOUS, p. 764), we must remain convinced that His love and faithfulness to us will never cease. Every day He will work in our lives that which is right; He cannot fail.

ever I punished them: but they rose early, *and* [s]corrupted all their doings.

8 ¶ Therefore [t]wait ye upon me, saith the LORD, until the day that I rise up to the prey: for my determination *is* to [u]gather the nations, that I may assemble the kingdoms, to pour upon them mine indignation, *even* all my fierce anger: for all the earth [v]shall be devoured with the fire of my jealousy.

9 For then will I turn to the people [w]a pure [s]language, that they may all call upon the name of the LORD, to serve him with one [t]consent.

10 [x]From beyond the rivers of Ethiopia my suppliants, *even* the daughter of my dispersed, shall bring mine offering.

11 In that day shalt thou not be ashamed for all thy doings, wherein thou hast transgressed against me: for then I will take away out of the midst of thee them that [y]rejoice in thy pride, and thou shalt no more be haughty [u]because of my holy mountain.

12 I will also leave in the midst of thee [z]an afflicted and poor people, and they shall trust in the name of the LORD.

13 [a]The remnant of Israel [b]shall not do iniquity, [c]nor speak lies; neither shall a deceitful tongue be found in their mouth: for [d]they shall feed and lie down, and none shall make *them* afraid.

14 ¶ [e]Sing, O daughter of Zion; shout, O Israel; be glad and rejoice with all the heart, O daughter of Jerusalem.

15 The LORD hath taken away thy judgments, he hath cast out thine enemy: [f]the king of Israel, *even* the LORD, [g]*is* in the midst of thee: thou shalt not see evil any more.

16 In that day [h]it shall be said to Jerusalem, Fear thou not: *and to* Zion, [i]Let not thine hands be [v]slack.

17 The LORD thy God [j]in the midst of thee *is* mighty; he will save, [k]he will rejoice over thee with joy; [w]he will rest in his love, he will joy over thee with singing.

18 I will gather *them that* [l]*are* sorrowful for the solemn assembly, *who* are of thee, *to whom* [x]the reproach of it *was* a burden.

19 Behold, at that time I will undo all that afflict thee: and I will save her that [m]halteth, and gather her that was driven out; and [y]I will get them praise and fame in every land [z]where they have been put to shame.

20 At that time [n]will I bring you *again*, even in the time that I gather you: for I will make you a name and a praise among all people of the earth, when I turn back your captivity before your eyes, saith the LORD.

Mat. 9:8

3:7 [s]Gen. 6:12
3:8 [t]Prov. 20:22 [u]Joel 3:2 [v]ch. 1:18
3:9 [w]Is. 19:18
3:10 [x]Ps. 68:31 Acts 8:27
3:11 [y]Mat. 3:9
3:12 [z]Is. 14:32
3:13 [a]Mic. 4:7 [b]Is. 60:21 [c]Rev. 14:5 [d]Ezek. 34:28
3:14 [e]Is. 12:6
3:15 [f]John 1:49 [g]Ezek. 48:35 Rev. 7:15
3:16 [h]Is. 35:3,4 [i]Heb. 12:12
3:17 [j]ver. 15 [k]Is. 62:5 Jer. 32:41
3:18 [l]Lam. 2:6
3:19 [m]Ezek. 34:16 Mic. 4:6,7
3:20 [n]Is. 11:12 Ezek. 28:25

[s]Heb. *lip* [t]Heb. *shoulder* [u]Heb. *in my holy* [v]Or, *faint* [w]Heb. *he will be silent* [x]Heb. *the burden upon it* was *reproach* [y]Heb. *I will set them for a praise* [z]Heb. *of their shame*

3:9–20 THEY MAY ALL CALL UPON THE NAME OF THE LORD. Zephaniah now turns to God's plan to redeem the nations after they have been purified by judgment. The nations will someday be reconciled to God, will call upon Him, and will serve Him. These promises will be fulfilled during the millennium, when Christ rules over the entire world (see Rev. 20:4, note).

3:10 BEYOND THE RIVERS OF ETHIOPIA. Ethiopia represents one of the most distant lands known at that time. The nations will bring offerings to God in Jerusalem (cf. Is. 66:18,20).

3:11 IN THAT DAY. When God brings the nations to a true knowledge of Him, He will restore the fortunes of His own people (v. 20).

3:14–17 BE GLAD AND REJOICE. God's people must rejoice over their salvation. Joy in one's heart is not a natural response; it is a supernatural response resulting from God's redemptive activity in our lives. Note that joy comes to us because: (1) we are forgiven and no longer punished for our sins (v. 15); (2) our enemy has been defeated, i.e., we are set free from the bondage of Satan and sin (v. 15); (3) God is with us, giving us His fellowship, grace, and help throughout our lives (v. 15–17; cf. Heb. 4:16); and (4) we are objects of God's great love and delight (v. 17). These conditions for joy exist now for those who have a full knowledge of what God has done for us in His Son (see Eph. 1:17–18; 3:16–20). Our joy will reach its pinnacle in that day when God manifests His full glory and majesty on the earth (cf. Is. 35:1–10).

HAGGAI

Outline

I. The First Message: Finish Building the Temple (1:1–15)
   A. Date: 1 Elul (Aug. 29), 520 B.C. (1:1)
   B. The Prophet's Rebuke for the Unfinished Temple (1:2–11)
   C. The People's Response (1:12–15)
II. The Second Message: The Promise of Greater Glory (2:1–9)
   A. Date: 21 Tishri (Oct. 17), 520 B.C. (2:1)
   B. The Latter Temple Compared with the Former (2:2–4)
   C. The Glory of the Latter Temple to Be Greater (2:5–9)
III. The Third Message: The Call to Holiness with Blessing (2:10–19)
   A. Date: 24 Kislev (Dec. 18), 520 B.C. (2:10)
   B. The Corrupting Effect of Sin (2:11–14)
   C. The Blessing of Obedience (2:15–19)
IV. The Fourth Message: A Prophetic Promise (2:20–23)
   A. Date: 24 Kislev (Dec. 18), 520 B.C. (2:20)
   B. The Future Overthrow of Nations (2:21–22)
   C. The Prophetic Significance of Zerubbabel (2:23)

Author: Haggai

Theme: Rebuilding the Temple

Date of Writing: 520 B.C.

Background

Haggai is the first of three post-exilic prophetic books in the O.T. (Haggai, Zechariah, and Malachi). Haggai is mentioned by name twice in Ezra (5:1; 6:14) and nine times in this book. He is called "the prophet" (1:1; 2:1,10; Ezra 6:14) and "the LORD's messenger" (1:13). He may have been one of a small handful of exiles who, upon returning to resettle Jerusalem, could remember Solomon's temple before it was destroyed by Nebuchadnezzar's army in 586 B.C. (2:3). If so, Haggai would have been in his seventies or eighties at the time of this writing. The book is dated precisely: the second year of King Darius of Persia (520 B.C.; 1:1).

The historical setting of the book is important for understanding its message. In 538 B.C., Cyrus king of Persia issued a decree permitting the Jewish exiles to return to their homeland to rebuild Jerusalem and the temple in fulfillment of Isaiah's and Jeremiah's prophecies (Isa. 45:1–3; Jer. 25:11–12; 29:10–14) and Daniel's intercession (Dan. 9). The first company of Jews to return to Jerusalem laid the foundation for a new temple in 536 B.C. amid great excitement and expectation (Ezra 3:8–10). However, soon afterwards the Samaritans and other neighbors physically opposed the building project and discouraged the workers so that work on the temple stopped in 534 B.C. Spiritual lethargy set in, and the people turned to rebuilding their own houses. In 520 B.C., Haggai, accompanied by the younger prophet Zechariah (see the introduction to Zechariah), began urging Zerubbabel and the people to resume building God's house. Four years later the temple was completed and dedicated (cf. Ezra 4—6).

Purpose

During a four-month period in 520 B.C., Haggai delivered the four terse messages recorded in this book (see the outline). These messages had a twofold purpose: (1) to exhort Zerubbabel (the governor) and Joshua (the high priest) to mobilize the people to rebuild the temple, and (2) to motivate the people to reorder their lives and priorities so as to resume the work in a dedicated way with God's blessing.

Survey

The book contains four messages, each of which is introduced by the phrase, "the word of the LORD" (1:1; 2:1; 2:10; 2:20). (1) Haggai first rebuked the former exiles for being preoccupied with their own paneled houses while God's house remained desolate (1:4). The prophet twice exhorted them to "consider" their ways (1:5,7), revealing that God had withdrawn His blessing from them because of their ways (1:6,9–11). In response to Haggai's words, Zerubbabel, Joshua, and all the people showed reverence to God and began the work (1:12–15).

(2) A few weeks later, the evaluation of some returned exiles discouraged the people, i.e., persons who had seen the glory of the former temple and regarded the present efforts at rebuilding as nothing in comparison with it (2:3). Haggai exhorted the leaders to take courage because (a) their efforts were part of a larger prophetic picture (2:4–7) and (b) "the glory of this latter house shall be greater than of the former" (2:9).

(3) Haggai's third message, which called the people to lives of holy obedience (2:10–19), and his (4) fourth message (2:20–23) were both delivered on the same day. The latter message prophesied that Zerubbabel represented the continuation of the Messianic lineage and promise (2:23).

Special Features

Four major features or emphases characterize the book of Haggai. (1) It was the first clear prophetic word heard in Judah after the Babylonian exile. (2) It is the second shortest book in the O.T. (a total of thirty-eight verses); Obadiah is the shortest. (3) The phrase "thus saith the LORD" (and its variations) occurs twenty-nine times and underscores the urgency of its message for the returned remnant in Jerusalem. (4) It contains one of the boldest prophecies in the O.T. about God's future visitation (2:6–9).

New Testament Fulfillment

Several verses in ch. 2 speak of the coming of the Messiah (vv. 6–9,21–23). The future shaking of the heavens and the earth and of nations and kingdoms is referred to by the author of Hebrews (Heb. 12:26–28). Also, Haggai prophesies that Zerubbabel will be like a "signet" or official seal; in the two N.T. genealogies of Jesus Christ (Mat. 1:12–13; Luke 3:27), Zerubbabel is the center that ties the two branches of the Messianic line together: from Solomon (son of David) to Zerubbabel to Joseph, and from Nathan (son of David) to Zerubbabel to Mary.

Reading Haggai

In order to read the entire Old Testament in one year, the book of Haggai should be read in 1 day: ☐ Haggai

NOTES

The call to rebuild the temple

1 IN [a]THE second year of Darius
the king, in the sixth month, in the
first day of the month, came the word
of the LORD [a]by Haggai the prophet
unto [b]Zerubbabel the son of Shealtiel,
[b]governor of Judah, and to [c]Joshua
the son of [d]Josedech, the high priest,
saying,
2 Thus speaketh the LORD of hosts,
saying, This people say, The time is
not come, the time that the LORD's
house should be built.
3 Then came the word of the LORD
[e]by Haggai the prophet, saying,
4 [f]*Is it* time for you, O ye, to dwell
in your ceiled houses, and this house
lie waste?
5 Now therefore thus saith the LORD
of hosts; [g]Consider[c] your ways.
6 Ye have [h]sown much, and bring
in little; ye eat, but ye have not enough;
ye drink, but ye are not filled with
drink; ye clothe you, but there is none
warm; and [i]he that earneth wages
earneth wages *to put it* into a bag
[d]with holes.
7 ¶ Thus saith the LORD of hosts;
Consider your ways.
8 Go up to the mountain, and bring
wood, and build the house; and I will
take pleasure in it, and I will be glori-
fied, saith the LORD.
9 [j]Ye looked for much, and, lo, *it*
came to little; and when ye brought *it*
home, [k]I did [e]blow upon it. Why?
saith the LORD of hosts. Because of
mine house that *is* waste, and ye run
every man unto his own house.
10 Therefore [l]the heaven over you
is stayed from dew, and the earth is
stayed *from* her fruit.
11 And I [m]called for a drought
upon the land, and upon the moun-
tains, and upon the corn, and upon the
new wine, and upon the oil, and upon
that which the ground bringeth forth,
and upon men, and upon cattle, and
[n]upon all the labour of the hands.
12 ¶ [o]Then Zerubbabel the son of
Shealtiel, and Joshua the son of Jose-
dech, the high priest, with all the rem-
nant of the people, obeyed the voice of
the LORD their God, and the words of
Haggai the prophet, as the LORD their
God had sent him, and the people did
fear before the LORD.
13 Then spake Haggai the LORD's
messenger in the LORD's message unto
the people, saying, [p]I *am* with you,
saith the LORD.
14 And [q]the LORD stirred up the
spirit of Zerubbabel the son of Shealti-
el, [r]governor of Judah, and the spirit
of Joshua the son of Josedech, the high
priest, and the spirit of all the remnant
of the people; [s]and they came and did
work in the house of the LORD of hosts,
their God,
15 In the four and twentieth day of
the sixth month, in the second year of
Darius the king.

1:1 [a]Ezra 4:24 [b]1 Chr. 3:17 [c]Ezra 5:2 [d]1 Chr. 6:15
1:3 [e]Ezra 5:1
1:4 [f]2 Sam. 7:2
1:5 [g]Lam. 3:40
1:6 [h]Deut. 28:38 [i]Zech. 8:10
1:9 [j]ch. 2:16 [k]ch. 2:17
1:10 [l]Lev. 26:19 Deut. 28:23 1 Ki. 8:35
1:11 [m]1 Ki. 17:1 2 Ki. 8:1 [n]ch. 2:17
1:12 [o]Ezra 5:2
1:13 [p]Mat. 28:20 Rom. 8:31
1:14 [q]2 Chr. 36:22 Ezra 1:1 [r]ch. 2:21 [s]Ezra 5:2,8

[a] Heb. *by the hand of Haggai* [b] Or, *captain* [c] Heb. *Set your heart on your ways* [d] Heb. *pierced through* [e] Or, *blow it away*

1:1 CAME THE WORD OF THE LORD BY HAGGAI. Cyrus, king of Persia, permitted 50,000 exiled Jews to return to Jerusalem under the leadership of Zerubbabel as governor and Joshua the high priest (see Ezra 1:2–4; 2:64–65; 3:2; 5:1). During the second year of the return (536/535 B.C.), the foundation of the temple was laid (see Ezra 3:8–10). However, Samaritan opposition halted work on the temple (see Ezra 4:1–5,24), after which the Jewish people became spiritually apathetic and stopped building the temple for sixteen years. Then God sent the prophets Haggai and Zechariah to encourage His people to resume work on the temple (see the introduction to Haggai).

1:4 CEILED HOUSES. Having become so busy with their own interests, the returned Jews were neglecting the construction of God's house. Their own houses were paneled with beautiful cedar, while the temple remained in ruins. Haggai insisted that God and His work had to come first. Likewise for us, God's kingdom and righteous concerns must be the first and highest priority in our lives (Mat. 6:33). Note how zealous the Lord Jesus was for God's house and work (John 2:17; 4:34; 6:38; 9:4). What we set as a priority indicates the love we have for our Lord.

1:6–11 SOWN MUCH, AND BRING IN LITTLE. God's people had lost His blessing because they were living self-seeking lives; they showed minimal interest in His goals and purposes. We too can expect God's blessing and help in our lives to decline if we are not vitally concerned for His work, both at home and among the nations.

1:12 THE PEOPLE OBEYED. The leaders and the people responded to Haggai's message by obeying and fearing the Lord; they took God's word seriously and committed themselves to resuming work on God's house.

1:13 I *AM* WITH YOU. God responded to His obedient people by promising to be with them. He strengthened their resolve and helped them accomplish the work (cf. Zech. 4:6). To be "with you" is the greatest commitment the Lord can make to any believer (see Gen. 26:24; 28:15; 39:2–3, 21,23; Ex. 3:12; Mat. 28:20).

Comfort and hope from God

2 IN THE seventh *month,* in the one
and twentieth *day* of the month,
came the word of the LORD [f]by the
prophet Haggai, saying,
2 Speak now to Zerubbabel the son
of Shealtiel, governor of Judah, and to
Joshua the son of Josedech, the high
priest, and to the residue of the people,
saying,
3 [t]Who *is* left among you that saw
this house in her first glory? and how
do ye see it now? [u]*is it* not in your eyes
in comparison of it as nothing?
4 Yet now [v]be strong, O Zerubba-
bel, saith the LORD; and be strong, O
Joshua, son of Josedech, the high
priest; and be strong, all ye people of
the land, saith the LORD, and work: for
I *am* with you, saith the LORD of hosts:
5 [w]*According to* the word that I cov-
enanted with you when ye came out of
Egypt, so [x]my spirit remaineth among
you: fear ye not.
6 For thus saith the LORD of hosts;
[y]Yet once, it *is* a little while, and [z]I
will shake the heavens, and the earth,
and the sea, and the dry *land;*
7 And I will shake all nations, [a]and
the desire of all nations shall come:
and I will fill this house with glory,
saith the LORD of hosts.
8 The silver *is* mine, and the gold *is*
mine, saith the LORD of hosts.
9 [b]The glory of this latter house
shall be greater than of the former,
saith the LORD of hosts: and in this
place will I give [c]peace, saith the LORD
of hosts.

Holiness and uncleanness

10 ¶ In the four and twentieth *day* of
the ninth *month,* in the second year of
Darius, came the word of the LORD by
Haggai the prophet, saying,
11 Thus saith the LORD of hosts;
[d]Ask now the priests *concerning* the
law, saying,
12 If one bear holy flesh in the skirt
of his garment, and with his skirt do
touch bread, or pottage, or wine, or oil,
or any meat, shall it be holy? And the
priests answered and said, No.
13 Then said Haggai, If *one that is*
[e]unclean by a dead body touch any of
these, shall it be unclean? And the
priests answered and said, It shall be
unclean.
14 Then answered Haggai, and
said, [f]So *is* this people, and so *is* this
nation before me, saith the LORD; and
so *is* every work of their hands; and
that which they offer there *is* unclean.
15 And now, I pray you, [g]consider
from this day and upward, from before
a stone was laid upon a stone in the
temple of the LORD:
16 Since those *days* were, [h]when
one came to an heap of twenty *mea-
sures,* there were *but* ten: when *one*

2:3 [t]Ezra 3:12 [u]Zech. 4:10 **2:4** [v]Zech. 8:9 **2:5** [w]Ex. 29:45,46 [x]Neh. 9:20 Is. 63:11 **2:6** [y]ver. 21 Heb. 12:26 [z]Joel 3:16 **2:7** [a]Gen. 49:10 Mal. 3:1 **2:9** [b]John 1:14 [c]Ps. 85:8,9 Luke 2:14 Eph. 2:14 **2:11** [d]Lev. 10:10,11 Deut. 33:10 Mal. 2:7 **2:13** [e]Num. 19:11 **2:14** [f]Tit. 1:15 **2:15** [g]ch. 1:5 **2:16** [h]ch. 1:6,9 Zech. 8:10

[f] Heb. *by the hand of*

2:3 THIS HOUSE IN HER FIRST GLORY. When the post-exilic temple was completed, some people were discouraged and disillusioned because they viewed the present temple as "nothing" in comparison with the magnificence of the first temple built by Solomon. Thus God encouraged the people with three promises: (1) God Himself would be with them to fulfill all His covenant promises (v. 4; see previous note), (2) God's Spirit would remain among the people (v. 5), and (3) the latter glory of God's house would be greater than the former because of the great demonstration of His power there (v. 9; cf. the ministry of Jesus and the apostles as recorded in the Gospels and Acts).

It is not the beauty of church structures that will ultimately yield fruit for the kingdom of God. The one essential thing in our congregations is the presence of God manifested through the Holy Spirit and His gifts, ministries, and power (see article on SPIRITUAL GIFTS FOR BELIEVERS, p. 1790). We must ask ourselves: Is the Holy Spirit manifested greatly in our gatherings, or is there little or no evidence of His presence and power among us?

2:6–9 I WILL SHAKE THE HEAVENS, AND THE EARTH. These verses refer to God's judgment on the world preceding and accompanying the return of Jesus Christ to earth (cf. Heb. 12:26–27): "The heavens and the earth shall shake" (Joel 3:16; cf. Mat. 24:29–30). God's glory will then fill the temple more than ever before and He will dwell among His people in peace as the glorious Savior.

2:10–14 ASK NOW THE PRIESTS. God explains to the people that whereas holiness could not be transmitted by contact, the corrupting influence of sin could. In other words, living in the holy land would not make them holy, but sin in their lives would defile everything they did, including their worship.

2:15–19 CONSIDER FROM THIS DAY AND UPWARD. God asked the people to consider why they had not been blessed by Him in the past; it was because of their disobedience (see 1:9–11). Now, however, because of their willingness to build the temple, God would cause all that they did to succeed. This principle is expressed also in the N.T.: God's favor, love, and fellowship come to us only as we continue to seek Him and follow His commandments (see John 14:21–23).

came to the pressvat for to draw out
fifty *vessels* out of the press, there were
but twenty.
17 [i]I smote you with blasting and
with mildew and with hail [j]in all the
labours of your hands; [k]yet ye *turned*
not to me, saith the LORD.
18 Consider now from this day and
upward, from the four and twentieth
day of the ninth *month, even* from [l]the
day that the foundation of the LORD's
temple was laid, consider *it.*
19 [m]Is the seed yet in the barn?
yea, as yet the vine, and the fig tree,
and the pomegranate, and the olive
tree, hath not brought forth: from this
day will I bless *you.*

Zerubbabel chosen by the LORD

20 ¶ And again the word of the
LORD came unto Haggai in the four and
twentieth *day* of the month, saying,
21 Speak to Zerubbabel, [n]governor
of Judah, saying, [o]I will shake the
heavens and the earth;
22 And [p]I will overthrow the
throne of kingdoms, and I will destroy
the strength of the kingdoms of the
heathen; and [q]I will overthrow the
chariots, and those that ride in them;
and the horses and their riders shall
come down, every one by the sword of
his brother.
23 In that day, saith the LORD of
hosts, will I take thee, O Zerubbabel,
my servant, the son of Shealtiel, saith
the LORD, [r]and will make thee as a signet:
for [s]I have chosen thee, saith the
LORD of hosts.

2:17 [i]Deut. 28:22 1 Ki. 8:37 Amos 4:9 ch. 1:9 [j]ch. 1:11 [k]Jer. 5:3 Amos 4:6,8-11
2:18 [l]Zech. 8:9
2:19 [m]Zech. 8:12
2:21 [n]ch. 1:14 [o]ver. 6,7
2:22 [p]Dan. 2:44 [q]Mic. 5:10 Zech. 9:10
2:23 [r]Sol. 8:6 Jer. 22:24 [s]Is. 42:1 & 43:10

2:21 I WILL SHAKE THE HEAVENS AND EARTH. The prophet encouraged Zerubbabel, the governor of God's people, by saying that one day God would destroy the power of kingdoms and nations throughout the earth; that day is the time Jesus Christ will reign over all the inhabitants of the world (see Rev. 19:11–21).

2:23 ZERUBBABEL . . . AS A SIGNET. When the time came for God to shake the heavens and earth, He would make Zerubbabel like a signet ring. This ring was the official mark of supreme authority and a pledge of favor towards God's people. Haggai may have been prophesying that Jesus Christ, a descendant of Zerubbabel (see Mat. 1:12–13), would "in that day" be the supreme ruler who would have absolute and universal reign.

ZECHARIAH

Outline

I. Part One: Prophetic Words in the Context of Rebuilding the Temple (520–518 B.C.) (1:1—8:23)
   A. Introduction (1:1–6)
   B. A Series of Eight Night Visions (1:7—6:8)
      1. Vision of the Horseman Among the Myrtle Trees (1:7–17)
      2. Vision of the Four Horns and Four Craftsmen (1:18–21)
      3. Vision of a Man Measuring Jerusalem (2:1–13)
      4. Vision of the Cleansing of Joshua, the High Priest (3:1–10)
      5. Vision of the Gold Lampstand and Two Olive Trees (4:1–14)
      6. Vision of the Flying Scroll (5:1–4)
      7. Vision of the Woman in a Basket (5:5–11)
      8. Vision of the Four Chariots (6:1–8)
   C. The Crowning of Joshua as High Priest and Its Prophetic Significance (6:9–15)
   D. Two Messages (7:1—8:23)
      1. Fasting and Social Justice (7:1–14)
      2. The Restoration of Zion (8:1–23)

II. Part Two: Prophetic Words Concerning Israel and the Coming Messiah (undated) (9:1—14:21)
   A. First Burden of the Lord (9:1—11:17)
      1. The Triumphant Intervention of the Lord (9:1–10)
      2. Announcement of Messianic Salvation (9:11—10:12)
      3. Rejection of the Messiah (11:1–17)
   B. Second Burden of the Lord (12:1—14:21)
      1. The Mourning and Conversion of Israel (12:1—13:9)
      2. The Enthronement of the Messiah-King (14:1–21)

Author: Zechariah

Theme: Finishing the Temple and Messianic Promises

Date of Writing: 520–470 B.C.

Background

The opening verse identifies the prophet Zechariah, the son of Berechiah and grandson of Iddo (1:1), as the book's author. The book of Nehemiah further states that Zechariah was the head of the priestly family of Iddo (Neh. 12:16), indicating he was from the tribe of Levi and served in Jerusalem after the exile as both a priest and a prophet.

Zechariah was a younger contemporary of the prophet Haggai. Ezra 5:1 states that both were prophets who stirred up the Jews in Judah and Jerusalem to resume rebuilding the temple in the days of Zerubbabel (the governor) and Joshua (the high priest). Thus the historical setting for chs. 1–8 (dated 520–518 B.C.) is identical to that of Haggai (see the introduction to Haggai). As a result of Zechariah's and Haggai's prophetic ministry, the temple was completed and dedicated in 516/515 B.C.

Whereas Zechariah was a young man (cf. 2:4) when he prophesied alongside of Haggai, he apparently was an old man when he wrote chs. 9—14 (dated by most scholars between 480–470 B.C.). All of Zechariah's prophecy occurred in Jerusalem for the 50,000 Jewish exiles who had returned to Judah in the first stage of the restoration. The N.T. indicates that in the end, Zechariah the son of Berechiah was "murdered between the temple and the altar" (i.e., the place of intercession) by hostile temple officials (Mat. 23:35), in a manner similar to the death of an earlier man of God by the same name (see 2 Chr. 24:20–21).

Purpose

Zechariah's twofold purpose in writing corresponds to the two major parts of the book. (1) Chs. 1–8 were given to encourage the Jewish remnant in Judah to resume building the temple and to stick with it until the task was completed. (2) Chs. 9–14 were given to encourage the same people who, having completed the temple, were disheartened when the Messiah did not appear immediately, and to reveal what it will mean when the Messiah does come.

Survey

The book divides into two major parts. (1) Part one (chs. 1—8) begins by exhorting the Jews to return to the Lord that He might return to them (1:1–6). While encouraging the people to finish rebuilding the temple, the prophet Zechariah received a series of eight visions (1:7—6:8), which assured the Jewish community in Judah and Jerusalem that God cared for His people and ruled over their future destiny. The first five visions conveyed hope and consolation; the last three visions involved judgment. The fourth vision contains an important Messianic prophecy (3:8–9). The coronation scene in 6:9–15 is a classic O.T. Messianic prophecy. Two messages (chs. 7—8) provided both present and future perspectives for the original readers.

(2) Part two (chs. 9—14) contains two blocks of apocalyptic prophecy, each of which is introduced with the phrase, "the burden of the word of the LORD" (9:1; 12:1). The first "burden" (9:1—11:17) included promises of Messianic salvation for Israel, revealing that the future Messiah-Shepherd, who would accomplish this salvation, would first be rejected and smitten (11:4–17; cf. 13:7). The second "burden" (12:1—14:21) focused on the restoration and conversion of Israel. In an amazing prophecy, God predicted Israel would mourn over God Himself "whom they have pierced" (12:10). In that day a fountain for cleansing from sin would be opened for the house of David (13:1); Israel would say, "The LORD *is* my God" (13:9), and the Messiah would reign as King over Jerusalem (ch. 14).

Special Features

Six special features or emphases characterize the book of Zechariah. (1) It is the most Messianic of all the O.T. books in that its many clear references to the Messiah occur in fourteen chapters. Only Isaiah (in sixty-six chapters) contains more prophecies about the Messiah than Zechariah. (2) Among the minor prophets, it contains the most specific and comprehensive prophecies concerning end-time events. (3) It represents the most successful merger of the priestly and the prophetic roles in Israel's history. (4) More than any other O.T. book, its visions and highly symbolic language resemble the apocalyptic books of Daniel and Revelation. (5) It records a bold example of divine sarcasm in the prophecy about the Messiah's betrayal for thirty pieces of silver, referring to it as the "goodly [magnificent] price that I was prised at of [appraised by] them" (11:13). (6) Zechariah's prophecy of the Messiah in ch. 14 as the great Warrior-King reigning over Jerusalem is one of the awe-inspiring prophecies in the O.T.

New Testament Fulfillment

There is profound N.T. application from Zechariah. The merger in Zechariah's personal life of the priestly and the prophetic may have contributed to the N.T. understanding of Christ as both priest and prophet. Also, Zechariah prophesied about the atoning death of Jesus at the hands of the Jews, which at the end of time will cause Israel to mourn, repent, and be

saved (12:10—13:9; Rom. 11:25–27). But Zechariah's most obvious contribution relates to his numerous prophecies about the Messiah, which the N.T. writers cite as being fulfilled in Jesus Christ. Among these are: (1) He will come in a humble and lowly fashion (9:9; 13:7; Mat. 21:5; 26:31,56); (2) He will restore Israel by the blood of His covenant (9:11; Mark 14:24); (3) He will be a Shepherd to God's scattered and wandering sheep (10:2; Mat. 9:36); (4) He will be betrayed and rejected (11:12–13; Mat. 26:15; 27:9–10); (5) He will be pierced and struck down (12:10; 13:7; Mat. 26:31,56; Jn 19:37); (6) He will return in glory to deliver Israel from her enemies (14:1–6; Mat. 24:30–31; Rev. 19:15); (7) He will rule as King in peace and righteousness (9:9–10; 14:9,16; Rom 14:17; Rev. 11:15); and (8) He will establish His glorious kingdom forever over all the nations (14:6–19; Rev. 11:15; 21:24–26; 22:1–5).

Reading Zechariah

In order to read the entire Old Testament in one year, the book of Zechariah should be read in 5 days, according to the following schedule: □ 1–3 □ 4–6 □ 7–8 □ 9–11 □ 12–14

NOTES

Call for national repentance

1 IN THE eighth month, [a]in the sec-
ond year of Darius, came the word
of the LORD [b]unto Zechariah, the son
of Berechiah, the son of Iddo the
prophet, saying,
2 The LORD hath been [a]sore dis-
pleased with your fathers.
3 Therefore say thou unto them,
Thus saith the LORD of hosts; Turn [c]ye
unto me, saith the LORD of hosts, and
I will turn unto you, saith the LORD of
hosts.
4 Be ye not as your fathers, [d]unto
whom the former prophets have cried,
saying, Thus saith the LORD of hosts;
[e]Turn ye now from your evil ways, and
from your evil doings: but they did not
hear, nor hearken unto me, saith the
LORD.
5 Your fathers, where *are* they?
and the prophets, do they live for
ever?
6 But [f]my words and my statutes,
which I commanded my servants
the prophets, did they not [b]take
hold of your fathers? and they re-
turned and said, [g]Like as the LORD
of hosts thought to do unto us, ac-
cording to our ways, and according
to our doings, so hath he dealt with
us.

1:1 [a]Ezra 4:24 Hag. 1:1 [b]Ezra 5:1 Mat. 23:35
1:3 [c]Jer. 25:5 & 35:15 Mic. 7:19 Mal. 3:7 Luke 15:20 Jas. 4:8
1:4 [d]2 Chr. 36:15,16 [e]Is. 31:6 Jer 3:12 & 18:11 Ezek. 18:30 Hos. 14:1
1:6 [f]Is. 55:1 [g]Lam. 1:18 & 2:17
1:8 [h]Josh. 5:13 Rev. 6:4 [i]ch. 6:2-7
1:10 [j]Heb. 1:14
1:11 [k]Ps. 103:20,21

The horsemen among the myrtles

7 ¶ Upon the four and twentieth day
of the eleventh month, which *is* the
month Sebat, in the second year of Da-
rius, came the word of the LORD unto
Zechariah, the son of Berechiah, the
son of Iddo the prophet, saying,
8 I saw by night, and behold [h]a
man riding upon a red horse, and he
stood among the myrtle trees that *were*
in the bottom; and behind him *were*
there [i]red horses, [c]speckled, and
white.
9 Then said I, O my lord, what *are*
these? And the angel that talked with
me said unto me, I will show thee what
these *be*.
10 And the man that stood among
the myrtle trees answered and said,
[j]These *are they* whom the LORD hath
sent to walk to and fro through the
earth.
11 [k]And they answered the angel
of the LORD that stood among the myr-
tle trees, and said, We have walked to
and fro through the earth, and, behold,
all the earth sitteth still, and is at rest.
12 ¶ Then the angel of the LORD an-
swered and said, O LORD of hosts, how
long wilt thou not have mercy on Jeru-

[a] Heb. *with displeasure* [b] Or, *overtake* [c] Or, *bay*

1:1 IN THE EIGHTH MONTH . . . CAME THE WORD OF THE LORD UNTO ZECHARIAH. In November of 520 B.C., about a month after Haggai's second prophecy (see Hag. 2:1), God raised up Zechariah, a younger man, to help Haggai encourage the people to rebuild the temple. The first six chapters contain a series of eight night visions given during the first two years of the rebuilding. These visions encouraged the people to look at what they were doing in the light of God's plan to bring a greater restoration, a spiritual one, in the future. Both the first and second coming of Christ come into view in these prophecies.

1:3 TURN YE UNTO ME . . . AND I WILL TURN UNTO YOU. God's message through Zechariah begins with a call for the people to turn to God, i.e., to repent. God was waiting for them to obey, and He in turn promised to bless and protect them.

1:4 BE YE NOT AS YOUR FATHERS. God reminds the people of how he had given the same call to their fathers through the earlier prophets, but they had not repented. (1) Because they had not turned from their evil ways, the fathers missed their opportunities and suffered the consequences; the warnings of Deut. 28 were fulfilled. (2) Likewise, if we live for the sinful pleasures of the present world system, we too will miss God's plan for our lives and be forever denied the ultimate blessings and good that He intends for us.

1:8–11 I SAW BY NIGHT. In February of 519 B.C., God gave Zechariah a vision of a man on a red horse among myrtle trees, with various other horses behind him. Some believe this man was a manifestation of Christ as the angel of the Lord (cf. v. 12; see article on ANGELS AND THE ANGEL OF THE LORD, p. 368). An interpreting angel explained that these horses had patrolled the whole earth and found it at rest and peace (v. 11). Yet God's people in Judah were still oppressed and insecure. The Lord would change the world situation by restoring and blessing Jerusalem and the cities of Judah.

1:9 THE ANGEL THAT TALKED WITH ME. The interpreting angel continued to explain things to Zechariah (vv. 3–14,19; 2:3; 4:1,4–5; 5:5,10; 6:4–5); this angel is not, however, the same as the angel of the Lord (see previous note).

1:12 THE ANGEL OF THE LORD . . . SAID. The rider on the red horse is now identified as the angel of the Lord, interceding on behalf of Israel and Jerusalem to bring an end to the seventy years of God's judgment on Jerusalem and the temple, which were destroyed in 586 B.C.; the rebuilding of the temple was finished in 516 B.C., seventy years later. The angel of the Lord is probably Christ (see vv. 8–11, note; cf. Ex. 23:20–21; Is. 63:9), who is still our "advocate with the Father" (1 John 2:1).

salem and on the cities of Judah, against which thou hast had indignation [l]these threescore and ten years?

13 And the LORD answered the angel that talked with me *with* [m]good words *and* comfortable words.

14 So the angel that communed with me said unto me, Cry thou, saying, Thus saith the LORD of hosts; I am [n]jealous for Jerusalem and for Zion with a great jealousy.

15 And I am very sore displeased with the heathen *that are* at ease: for [o]I was but a little displeased, and they helped forward the affliction.

16 Therefore thus saith the LORD; [p]I am returned to Jerusalem with mercies: my house shall be built in it, saith the LORD of hosts, and [q]a line shall be stretched forth upon Jerusalem.

17 Cry yet, saying, Thus saith the LORD of hosts; My cities through [d]prosperity shall yet be spread abroad; [r]and the LORD shall yet comfort Zion, and [s]shall yet choose Jerusalem.

Four horns and four carpenters

18 ¶ Then lifted I up mine eyes, and saw, and behold four horns.

19 And I said unto the angel that talked with me, What *be* these? And he answered me, [t]These *are* the horns which have scattered Judah, Israel, and Jerusalem.

20 And the LORD showed me four carpenters.

21 Then said I, What come these to do? And he spake, saying, These *are* the horns which have scattered Judah, so that no man did lift up his head: but these are come to fray them, to cast out the horns of the Gentiles, which [u]lifted up *their* horn over the land of Judah to scatter it.

The measuring line of Jerusalem

2 I LIFTED up mine eyes again, and looked, and behold [v]a man with a measuring line in his hand.

2 Then said I, Whither goest thou? And he said unto me, [w]To measure Jerusalem, to see what *is* the breadth thereof, and what *is* the length thereof.

3 And, behold, the angel that talked with me went forth, and another angel went out to meet him,

4 And said unto him, Run, speak to this young man, saying, [x]Jerusalem shall be inhabited *as* towns without walls for the multitude of men and cattle therein:

5 For I, saith the LORD, will be unto her [y]a wall of fire round about, [z]and will be the glory in the midst of her.

6 ¶ Ho, ho, *come forth,* and flee

1:12 [l]Jer. 25:11,12 Dan. 9:2 ch. 7:5
1:13 [m]Jer. 29:10
1:14 [n]Joel 2:18 ch. 8:2
1:15 [o]Is. 47:6
1:16 [p]Is. 12:1 & 54:8 ch. 2:10 & 8:3 [q]ch. 2:1,2
1:17 [r]Is. 51:3 [s]Is. 14:1 ch. 2:12 & 3:2
1:19 [t]Ezra 4:1,4,7 & 5:3
1:21 [u]Ps. 75:4,5
2:1 [v]Ezek. 40:3
2:2 [w]Rev. 11:1
2:4 [x]Jer. 31:27 Ezek. 36:10
2:5 [y]Is. 26:1 [z]Is. 60:19

[d] Heb. *good*

1:14 I AM JEALOUS FOR JERUSALEM. God's love was behind His choice of Jerusalem and the nation of Israel. That love, however, was not meant to stay just with the Israelites; it was intended to reach out to all people. God desired to bless all the families of the earth through Abraham and his descendants (see Gen. 12:3, note).

1:15 HEATHEN ... HELPED FORWARD THE AFFLICTION. God used heathen nations to bring His judgment on Jerusalem (Is. 10:5–6; Hab. 1:6). In their greed for wealth and power, however, these nations went too far. Now they would be judged by God for their proud self-sufficiency.

1:18–19 THESE *ARE* THE HORNS THAT HAVE SCATTERED JUDAH, ISRAEL, AND JERUSALEM. The animal horns represent Assyria, Egypt, Babylon, and Medo-Persia.

1:20–21 FOUR CARPENTERS. These carpenters are probably four empires that brought God's judgment on the horns (v. 18). All the oppressors of God's people must eventually come under His judgment (cf. Ps. 2:5,9).

2:1 A MAN WITH A MEASURING LINE. Jerusalem was still in pitiful condition at the end of the Babylonian exile. The number of the returnees was comparatively small. God encouraged them by telling them that He was not through with Jerusalem; it would become the most glorious place on earth. This third vision looks ahead to the millennial kingdom, when the city will have no walls and will overflow with a great crowd of people (see next note).

2:5 THE LORD WILL BE UNTO HER A WALL OF FIRE . . . AND . . . GLORY IN THE MIDST. In the millennial kingdom, the city will not need walls, for the Lord Himself will be a wall of fire around it (cf. Is. 4:5). Even more important, God's glory in the midst of the people will make the whole city a temple filled with His presence (cf. Ezek. 43:1–7). Even now, the presence and glory of God in the midst of His people is something the church must desire and seek above all else (see article on THE GLORY OF GOD, p. 1186).

2:6 FLEE FROM THE LAND OF THE NORTH. This instruction of Zechariah can be interpreted on several different levels. (1) The rebuilding of the temple was a signal for more of the exiled Jews to return from Babylon (v. 7). (2) The O.T. prophets also saw a future return of Jews at the end of the age that will climax in the millennial kingdom (vv. 7–9). (3) We can apply this in our own day as a call to flee from the idolatry, immorality, wickedness, occult practices, and sinful ways of today's world system.

[a]from the land of the north, saith the
LORD: for I have [b]spread you abroad as
the four winds of the heaven, saith the
LORD.
7 [c]Deliver thyself, O Zion, that
dwellest *with* the daughter of Babylon.
8 For thus saith the LORD of hosts;
After the glory hath he sent me unto
the nations which spoiled you: for he
that [d]toucheth you toucheth the apple
of his eye.
9 For, behold, I will [e]shake mine
hand upon them, and they shall be a
spoil to their servants: and [f]ye shall
know that the LORD of hosts hath
sent me.
10 ¶ [g]Sing and rejoice, O daughter
of Zion: for, lo, I come, and I [h]will
dwell in the midst of thee, saith the
LORD.
11 [i]And many nations shall be
joined to the LORD [j]in that day, and
shall be [k]my people: and I will dwell
in the midst of thee, and [l]thou shalt
know that the LORD of hosts hath sent
me unto thee.
12 And the LORD shall [m]inherit Judah his portion in the holy land, and
[n]shall choose Jerusalem again.
13 [o]Be silent, O all flesh, before
the LORD: for he is raised up [p]out of
[e]his holy habitation.

2:6 [a]Is. 48:20 [b]Deut. 28:64 Ezek. 17:21
2:7 [c]Rev. 18:4
2:8 [d]Deut. 32:10
2:9 [e]Is. 19:16 [f]ch. 4:9
2:10 [g]Is. 12:6 [h]Lev. 26:12
2:11 [i]Is. 2:2,3 [j]ch. 3:10 [k]Ex. 12:49 [l]Ezek. 33:33
2:12 [m]Deut. 32:9 [n]ch. 1:17
2:13 [o]Hab. 2:20 [p]Ps. 68:5 Is. 57:15
3:1 [q]Hag. 1:1 [r]Ps. 109:6
3:2 [s]Jude 9 [t]Rom. 8:33 [u]Amos 4:11 Rom. 11:5
3:3 [v]Is. 64:6
3:4 [w]Is. 61:10 Luke 15:22
3:5 [x]Ex. 29:6
3:7 [y]Lev. 8:35 Ezek. 44:16

Joshua cleansed and reclothed

3 AND HE showed me [q]Joshua the
high priest standing before the angel of the LORD, and [r]Satan[f] standing
at his right hand [g]to resist him.
2 And the LORD said unto Satan,
[s]The LORD rebuke thee, O Satan; even
the LORD that [t]hath chosen Jerusalem
rebuke thee: [u]*is* not this a brand
plucked out of the fire?
3 Now Joshua was clothed with
[v]filthy garments, and stood before the
angel.
4 And he answered and spake unto
those that stood before him, saying,
Take away the filthy garments from
him. And unto him he said, Behold, I
have caused thine iniquity to pass from
thee, [w]and I will clothe thee with
change of raiment.
5 And I said, Let them set a fair
[x]mitre upon his head. So they set a
fair mitre upon his head, and clothed
him with garments. And the angel of
the LORD stood by.
6 And the angel of the LORD protested unto Joshua, saying,
7 Thus saith the LORD of hosts; If
thou wilt walk in my ways, and if thou
wilt [y]keep my [h]charge, then thou

[e] Heb. *the habitation of his holiness* [f] i.e. *an adversary* [g] Heb. *to be his adversary* [h] Or, *ordinance*

2:8 HE THAT TOUCHETH YOU TOUCHETH THE APPLE OF HIS EYE. Zion (v. 7) represents the godly remnant of Israel; they are the apple (pupil) of God's eye, precious and important to Him (see Ps. 17:8, note). Believers today are as important and loved as were God's people of O.T. times; we are under His protective care and concern.

2:10–12 MANY NATIONS SHALL BE JOINED TO THE LORD IN THAT DAY. "That day" refers to the time when Jesus Christ will reign on earth. Then Zion, the godly remnant of Israel, along with the Gentiles, will all be God's people. They will have the blessing of God's presence in their midst as well as the blessings of God's choice of Jerusalem as His holy city.

3:1 JOSHUA . . . AND SATAN STANDING AT HIS RIGHT HAND TO RESIST HIM. Joshua was representing the nation of Israel before God. Satan, "the adversary" (see Mat. 4:10, note), stood to oppose him, signifying that the hindrances and opposition to the rebuilding of the temple were really coming from Satan. He is still our adversary, the "accuser of our brethren" (Rev. 12:10), who seeks to take advantage of us.

3:2 THE LORD REBUKE THEE, O SATAN. As Israel's representative, Joshua could not resist Satan, for the high priest was clothed in smelly, filthy garments (i.e., sin). (1) God Himself resisted Satan and rebuked him, for He had chosen Israel to carry out His purposes. (2) Israel was a "brand plucked out of the fire." The fire represents Israel's sufferings in the Babylonian exile. God had brought Israel through these sufferings, not to destroy them, but to discipline them and prepare them for greater things.

3:4 I WILL CLOTHE THEE WITH CHANGE OF RAIMENT. God had Joshua's filthy garments removed, symbolizing the removal of his (and Israel's) sin. He was then clothed with costly festive robes and had a clean mitre or turban placed on his head, indicating full restoration to priestly office. Israel's sin was cleansed and they were clothed with divine righteousness. This same cleansing is available to us through Christ (Eph. 1:7; Rom. 1:16–17; 3:22,25–26).

3:7 IF THOU WILT WALK IN MY WAYS. God's personal word to Joshua strongly encouraged him to follow the Lord and keep His word. If Joshua did so, he would govern in the temple, have charge of God's courts on earth, and have free access to God's throne-room in heaven, where the angels minister. We too can have free access to heaven's courts through prayer if we walk in God's ways.

shalt also [z]judge my house, and shalt
also keep my courts, and I will give
thee [i]places to walk among these
that [a]stand by.
8 Hear now, O Joshua the high
priest, thou, and thy fellows that sit be-
fore thee: for they *are* [b]men[j] won-
dered at: for, behold, I will bring forth
[c]my servant the [d]BRANCH.
9 For behold the stone that I have
laid before Joshua; [e]upon one stone
shall be [f]seven eyes: behold, I will en-
grave the graving thereof, saith the
LORD of hosts, and [g]I will remove the
iniquity of that land in one day.
10 [h]In that day, saith the LORD of
hosts, shall ye call every man his
neighbour [i]under the vine and under
the fig tree.

The candlestick and two olive trees

4 AND [j]THE angel that talked with
me came again, and waked me,
[k]as a man that is wakened out of his
sleep,
2 And said unto me, What seest
thou? And I said, I have looked, and
behold [l]a candlestick all *of* gold,
[k]with a bowl upon the top of it, [m]and
his seven lamps thereon, and [l]seven
pipes to the seven lamps, which *are*
upon the top thereof:
3 [n]And two olive trees by it, one
upon the right *side* of the bowl, and the
other upon the left *side* thereof.
4 So I answered and spake to the
angel that talked with me, saying,
What *are* these, my lord?
5 Then the angel that talked with
me answered and said unto me, Know-
est thou not what these be? And I said,
No, my lord.
6 Then he answered and spake unto
me, saying, This *is* the word of the LORD
unto Zerubbabel, saying, [o]Not by
[m]might, nor by power, but by my spir- Mat.
it, saith the LORD of hosts. 3:11
7 Who *art* thou, [p]O great moun-
tain? before Zerubbabel *thou shalt be-
come* a plain: and he shall bring forth
[q]the headstone *thereof* [r]*with* shout-
ings, *crying,* Grace, grace unto it.
8 Moreover the word of the LORD
came unto me, saying,
9 The hands of Zerubbabel [s]have
laid the foundation of this house; his
hands [t]shall also finish it; and [u]thou

3:7 [z]Deut. 17:9 [a]ch. 4:14 **3:8** [b]Ps. 71:7 Is. 8:18 [c]Is. 42:1 Ezek. 34:23 [d]Is. 11:1 ch. 6:12 **3:9** [e]Ps. 118:22 Is. 28:16 [f]Rev. 5:6 [g]Jer. 31:34 Mic. 7:18 **3:10** [h]ch. 2:11 [i]Is. 36:16 Mic. 4:4 **4:1** [j]ch. 2:3 [k]Dan. 8:18 **4:2** [l]Rev. 1:12 [m]Rev. 4:5 **4:3** [n]Rev. 11:4 **4:6** [o]Hos. 1:7 **4:7** [p]Jer. 51:25 Mat. 21:21 [q]Ps. 118:22 [r]Ezra 3:11,13 **4:9** [s]Ezra 3:10 [t]Ezra 6:15 [u]ch. 2:9,11 & 6:15

[i] Heb. *walks* [j] Heb. *men of wonder,* or, *sign* [k] Heb. *with her bowl* [l] Or, *seven several pipes to the lamps* [m] Or, *army*

3:8 MY SERVANT THE BRANCH. Joshua and the other priests were prophetic types, pointing to the work of God's Servant, the Branch (see Is. 4:2, note; 11:1, note; Jer. 23:5, note). The angel of the Lord (i.e., Christ), standing by during Joshua's cleansing and restoration (v. 5), is now identified as the Branch, the new shoot who would bear our sins as a sin offering and accomplish our redemption (cf. Is. 53:1–6). He would defeat Satan by taking the filthy garments of the sins of the world upon Himself and by dying in our place.

3:9 UPON ONE STONE *SHALL BE* SEVEN EYES. The stone is another figure for the Messiah (cf. Is. 28:16; 1 Pet. 2:6). The seven eyes represent a fullness of insight, omniscience, and divine intelligence (cf. Rev. 5:6). Christ would remove sin in a single day, i.e., on the day He atoned for sin on the cross.

4:2 A CANDLESTICK ALL OF GOLD. This candlestick is an olive oil lampstand. (1) It had seven lamps all on the same level, arranged under a reservoir bowl. Oil flowed from the bowl to keep the lamps full. The bowl of oil symbolized the inexhaustible and abundant power of God through the Holy Spirit. (2) Each lamp had seven pipes or lips with a wick, thus giving forty-nine lights in all. These lamps represent God's people giving fullness of light to the world because of the abundant flow of the Holy Spirit.

4:3 TWO OLIVE TREES. The two olive trees represent the royal and priestly ministries of Zerubbabel and Joshua (see Hag. 1:1, note). (1) The trees symbolize a continual source of oil; the two leaders were to lead the people into a life made possible by the power of the Spirit (v. 12). (2) Thus the trees represent the kingly and priestly ministries of Jesus Christ Himself. He is the One who baptizes in the Holy Spirit, and all further fillings come from Christ.

4:6 NOT BY MIGHT, NOR BY POWER, BUT BY MY SPIRIT. Though this message was spoken to Zerubbabel, it applies to all believers (cf. 2 Tim. 3:16). Military might, political power, or human strength cannot accomplish the work of God. We can only do His work if we are enabled by the Holy Spirit (cf. Judg. 6:34; Is. 31:3). Jesus entered His ministry in the power of the Spirit (Luke 4:1,18), and the church was empowered by the Holy Spirit at Pentecost (Acts 1:8; 2:4; see article on BAPTISM IN THE HOLY SPIRIT, p. 1652). Only if the Spirit continues to govern and empower our lives will we accomplish God's will for us. This is why Jesus baptizes His followers in the Holy Spirit (see Luke 3:16, note).

4:7 O GREAT MOUNTAIN. Difficulties that seem as large as a mountain can be overcome by the power of the Spirit working through us. Conversely, when the manifestations of the Spirit are not present among God's people, opposition to His work and spiritual problems will overwhelm them (see article on SPIRITUAL GIFTS FOR BELIEVERS, p. 1790).

shalt know that the [v]LORD of hosts hath sent me unto you.

10 For who hath despised the day of [w]small things? [n]for they shall rejoice, and shall see the [o]plummet in the hand of Zerubbabel *with* those seven; [x]they *are* the eyes of the LORD, which run to and fro through the whole earth.

11 ¶ Then answered I, and said unto him, What *are* these [y]two olive trees upon the right *side* of the candlestick and upon the left *side* thereof?

12 And I answered again, and said unto him, What *be these* two olive branches which [p]through the two golden pipes [q]empty [r]the golden *oil* out of themselves?

13 And he answered me and said, Knowest thou not what these *be?* And I said, No, my lord.

14 Then said he, [z]These *are* the two [s]anointed ones, [a]that stand by [b]the Lord of the whole earth.

The flying roll

5 THEN I turned, and lifted up mine eyes, and looked, and behold a flying [c]roll.

2 And he said unto me, What seest thou? And I answered, I see a flying roll; the length thereof *is* twenty cubits, and the breadth thereof ten cubits.

3 Then said he unto me, This *is* the [d]curse that goeth forth over the face of the whole earth: for [t]every one that stealeth shall be cut off *as* on this side according to it; and every one that sweareth shall be cut off *as* on that side according to it.

4 I will bring it forth, saith the LORD of hosts, and it shall enter into the house of the thief, and into the house of [e]him that sweareth falsely by my name: and it shall remain in the midst of his house, and [f]shall consume it with the timber thereof and the stones thereof.

The ephah of iniquity

5 ¶ Then the angel that talked with me went forth, and said unto me, Lift up now thine eyes, and see what *is* this that goeth forth.

6 And I said, What *is* it? And he said, This *is* an ephah that goeth forth. He said moreover, This *is* their resemblance through all the earth.

7 And, behold, there was lifted up a [u]talent of lead: and this *is* a woman that sitteth in the midst of the ephah.

8 And he said, This *is* wickedness. And he cast it into the midst of the ephah; and he cast the weight of lead upon the mouth thereof.

9 Then lifted I up mine eyes, and looked, and, behold, there came out two women, and the wind *was* in their wings; for they had wings like the wings of a stork: and they lifted up the ephah between the earth and the heaven.

10 Then said I to the angel that talked with me, Whither do these bear the ephah?

11 And he said unto me, To [g]build it an house in [h]the land of Shinar: and it shall be established, and set there upon her own base.

Four chariots of divine judgment

6 AND I turned, and lifted up mine eyes, and looked, and, behold,

4:9 [v]Is. 48:16 ch. 2:8
4:10 [w]Hag. 2:3 [x]2 Chr. 16:9 Prov. 15:3 ch. 3:9
4:11 [y]ver. 3
4:14 [z]Rev. 11:4 [a]ch. 3:7 [b]See Josh. 3:11, 13 ch. 6:5
5:1 [c]Ezek. 2:9
5:3 [d]Mal. 4:6
5:4 [e]Lev. 19:12 ch. 8:17 Mal. 3:5 [f]See Lev. 14:45
5:11 [g]Jer. 29:5,28 [h]Gen. 10:10

[n] Or, *since the seven eyes of the LORD shall rejoice* [o] Heb. *stone of tin* [p] Heb. *by the hand* [q] Or, *empty out of themselves* oil into *the gold* [r] Heb. *the gold* [s] Heb. *sons of oil* [t] Or, *every one of this* people *that stealeth holdeth* himself *guiltless, as it* doth [u] Or, *weighty piece*

4:10 WHO HATH DESPISED THE DAY OF SMALL THINGS? What the people were doing seemed unimportant to some. However, no work done in the power and with the blessing of God's Spirit is ever insignificant, but has eternal value and importance.

5:1–4 A FLYING ROLL. This flying roll represented the curse or judgment of God against sinners in the land of Israel. Though God is merciful and longsuffering (see 2 Pet. 3:9), a time for judgment is coming that will quickly consume the wicked. The age of grace will someday come to an end. Judgment's ultimate fulfillment will come during the great tribulation.

5:5–11 AN EPHAH. The ephah or measuring basket represents the sin and immorality of the people of the land. (1) The woman represents idolatry and all kinds of wickedness. She was imprisoned in the basket by a heavy lead cover and was then taken to Shinar (i.e., Babylon), which represents the godless world system dominated by Satan (see Rev. 17:1, note). The wicked among God's people not only had to be punished, but also removed from the land. (2) Sin and wickedness must be removed from our churches or God will remove His Spirit from us (see Rev. 2–3). In the end time God will remove sin from the whole earth, and Jesus Christ will reign in glory with His people (Rev. 19—22).

6:1–5 THESE *ARE* THE FOUR SPIRITS OF

there came four chariots out from be-
tween two mountains; and the moun-
tains *were* mountains of brass.
2 In the first chariot *were* [i]red
horses; and in the second chariot
[j]black horses;
3 And in the third chariot white
horses; and in the fourth chariot
grisled and [v]bay horses.
4 Then I answered [k]and said unto
the angel that talked with me, What *are*
these, my lord?
5 And the angel answered and said
unto me, [l]These *are* the four [w]spirits
of the heavens, which go forth from
[m]standing before the Lord of all the
earth.
6 The black horses which *are* there-
in go forth into [n]the north country;
and the white go forth after them; and
the grisled go forth toward the south
country.
7 And the bay went forth, and
sought to go that they might [o]walk to
and fro through the earth: and he said,
Get you hence, walk to and fro through
the earth. So they walked to and fro
through the earth.
8 Then cried he upon me, and spake
unto me, saying, Behold, these that go
toward the north country have quieted
my [p]spirit in the north country.

The crowning of Joshua

9 ¶ And the word of the LORD came
unto me, saying,
10 Take of *them of* the captivity,
even of Heldai, of Tobijah, and of Jeda-

6:2 [i]ch. 1:8 [j]Rev. 6:5
6:4 [k]ch. 5:10
6:5 [l]Ps. 104:4 Heb. 1:7,14 [m]1 Ki. 22:19 Dan. 7:10 ch. 4:14 Luke 1:19
6:6 [n]Jer. 1:14
6:7 [o]Gen. 13:17 ch. 1:10
6:8 [p]Eccl. 10:4
6:11 [q]Ex. 29:6
6:12 [r]Luke 1:78 John 1:45 [s]ch. 3:8 [t]Mat. 16:18 Eph. 2:20 Heb. 3:3
6:13 [u]Is. 22:24 [v]Ps. 110:4 Heb. 3:1
6:14 [w]Ex. 12:14 Mark 14:9
6:15 [x]Is. 57:19 Eph. 2:13

iah, which are come from Babylon, and
come thou the same day, and go into
the house of Josiah the son of Zepha-
niah;
11 Then take silver and gold, and
make [q]crowns, and set *them* upon the
head of Joshua the son of Josedech, the
high priest;
12 And speak unto him, saying,
Thus speaketh the LORD of hosts, say-
ing, Behold [r]the man whose name *is*
The [s]BRANCH; and he shall [x]grow
up out of his place, [t]and he shall build
the temple of the LORD:
13 Even he shall build the temple of
the LORD; and he [u]shall bear the glory,
and shall sit and rule upon his throne;
and [v]he shall be a priest upon his
throne: and the counsel of peace shall
be between them both.
14 And the crowns shall be to He-
lem, and to Tobijah, and to Jedaiah,
and to Hen the son of Zephaniah, [w]for
a memorial in the temple of the LORD.
15 And [x]they *that are* far off shall
come and build in the temple of the
LORD, and ye shall know that the LORD
of hosts hath sent me unto you. And
this shall come to pass, if ye will dili-
gently obey the voice of the LORD your
God.

Hearts of stone

7 AND IT came to pass in the fourth
year of king Darius, *that* the word

[v] Or, *strong* [w] Or, *winds* [x] Or, *branch up from under him*

THE HEAVENS. In his eighth vision, Zechariah saw four war chariots between two copper or bronze mountains. (1) The colors of the horses pulling the chariots were red (signifying war), black (signifying famine and death), white (signifying victory), and grisled (dappled or spotted, signifying pestilence; cf. Rev. 6:2–8). Most interpreters believe the chariot drawn by the white horses represents the glorious victory of God's agents of judgment. (2) The four spirits are actually angelic beings (cf. Ps. 104:4; Rev. 7:1–3). (3) Both the war chariots and the bronze mountains speak of judgment against God's enemies. The riders and chariots go toward the north and the south, i.e., toward Babylon and Egypt; these nations also represent the northern and southern powers at the end of time, which God will destroy.

6:8 THESE . . . HAVE QUIETED MY SPIRIT. By bringing God's judgment, these angelic beings had satisfied His justice and caused His anger to cease. God would see to it that His purposes were carried out in His own time.

6:13 HE SHALL BE A PRIEST UPON HIS THRONE. The Lord commanded Zechariah to make crowns of silver and gold and set them on the head of Joshua the high priest. (1) The crowning of Joshua foreshadows the crowning and reign of Jesus, who is the "Branch," the Messiah (Is. 11:1; Jer. 33:15; cf. Is. 53:2; see Zech. 3:8, note). Jesus would be both priest and king; He would first do his priestly work, and then reign (cf. Is. 53:10; Luke 24:26). (2) At the present time, Jesus is our peace (Eph. 2:14–15), and in Him we find the kingdom of God, which exists in righteousness, peace, and joy in the Holy Spirit (Rom. 14:17). The ultimate fulfillment of Christ's reign begins in the millennium, when He will rule on earth in a reign of peace (cf. Is. 9:6).

6:15 THEY *THAT ARE* FAR OFF. This phrase refers to the Gentiles (cf. Eph. 2:11–13).

7:1–5 DID YE AT ALL FAST UNTO ME. The law of God called for only one fast day each year, the Day of Atonement in the seventh month. The Jews at this time had added a fast in the fifth month to commemorate the destruction of the temple by Nebuchadnezzar's armies (2 Ki.

of the LORD came unto Zechariah in the
fourth *day* of the ninth month, *even* in
Chisleu;
2 When they had sent unto the
house of God Sherezer and Regem-me-
lech, and their men, [y]to[y] pray before
the LORD,
3 *And* to [z]speak unto the priests
which *were* in the house of the LORD of
hosts, and to the prophets, saying,
Should I weep in [a]the fifth month,
separating myself, as I have done
these so many years?
4 ¶ Then came the word of the LORD
of hosts unto me, saying,
5 Speak unto all the people of the
land, and to the priests, saying, When
ye [b]fasted and mourned in the fifth
[c]and seventh *month,* [d]even those
seventy years, did ye at all fast [e]unto
me, *even* to me?
6 And when ye did eat, and when ye
did drink, [z]did not ye eat *for your-*
selves, and drink *for yourselves?*
7 [a]*Should ye* not *hear* the words
which the LORD hath cried [b]by the for-
mer prophets, when Jerusalem was in-
habited and in prosperity, and the cit-
ies thereof round about her, when *men*
inhabited [f]the south and the plain?
8 ¶ And the word of the LORD came
unto Zechariah, saying,
9 Thus speaketh the LORD of hosts,
saying, [g]Execute[c] true judgment,
and show mercy and compassions ev-
ery man to his brother:
10 And [h]oppress not the widow,
nor the fatherless, the stranger, nor
the poor; [i]and let none of you imagine
evil against his brother in your heart.
11 But they refused to hearken, and
[j]pulled[d] away the shoulder, and
[k]stopped[e] their ears, that they
should not hear.
12 Yea, they made their [l]hearts *as*
an adamant stone, [m]lest they should
hear the law, and the words which the
LORD of hosts hath sent in his spirit
[b]by the former prophets: [n]therefore
came a great wrath from the LORD of
hosts.
13 Therefore it is come to pass, *that*
as he cried, and they would not hear;
so [o]they cried, and I would not hear,
saith the LORD of hosts:
14 But [p]I scattered them with a
whirlwind among all the nations whom
they knew not. Thus the land was des-
olate after them, that no man passed
through nor returned: for they laid the
[f]pleasant land desolate.

God's intent to restore Jerusalem

8 AGAIN THE word of the LORD of
hosts came *to me,* saying,
2 Thus saith the LORD of hosts; [q]I
was jealous for Zion with great jealou-
sy, and I was jealous for her with great
fury.
3 Thus saith the LORD; I am re-
turned unto Zion, and will dwell in the
midst of Jerusalem: and Jerusalem
[r]shall be called a city of truth; and
[s]the mountain of the LORD of hosts
[t]the holy mountain.
4 Thus saith the LORD of hosts;
[u]There shall yet old men and old wom-
en dwell in the streets of Jerusalem,

Mar 16:18

7:2 [y]1 Sam. 13:12 **7:3** [z]Deut. 17:9 Mal. 2:7 [a]ch. 8:19 **7:5** [b]Is. 58:5 [c]Jer. 41:1 [d]ch. 1:12 [e]Rom. 14:6 **7:7** [f]Jer. 17:26 **7:9** [g]Is. 58:6,7 Jer. 7:23 **7:10** [h]Ex. 22:21 Is. 1:17 Jer. 5:28 [i]Ps. 36:4 Mic. 2:1 **7:11** [j]Neh. 9:29 [k]Acts 7:57 **7:12** [l]Ezek. 11:19 [m]Neh. 9:29 [n]2 Chr. 36:16 Dan. 9:11 **7:13** [o]Prov. 1:24 Is. 1:15 Mic. 3:4 **7:14** [p]Deut. 28:64 **8:2** [q]Nah. 1:2 **8:3** [r]Is. 1:21 [s]Is. 2:2,3 [t]Jer. 31:23 **8:4** [u]1 Sam. 2:31 Is. 65:20

[y]Heb. *to entreat the face of the LORD* [z]Or, be *not ye they that* [a]Or, Are not these *the words* [b]Heb. *by the hand of* [c]Heb. *Judge judgment of truth* [d]Heb. *they gave a backsliding shoulder* [e]Heb. *made heavy* [f]Heb. *land of desire*

25:8–9). Now that the temple was being rebuilt (518 B.C.), they wanted to know if they had to continue observing that fast day. (1) The word of the Lord was that they were not fasting in the right way (see Mat. 6:16, note); their fasting was mere formalism, empty of real hunger and thirst for God and His righteousness. (2) The people needed to pay attention to prophets such as Isaiah (cf. Is. 58:3–5), and to respond by fasting and by praying for grace to live holy and just lives before God and others (vv. 8–10).

7:12 THEY MADE THEIR HEARTS *AS* AN ADAMANT STONE. "Adamant" can also be translated as "diamond" (see Jer. 17:1); it is the hardest substance known in nature. (1) God's call by His Spirit through earlier prophets was for justice, mercy, and compassion, but the people stubbornly refused to obey. Then when judgment came, it was too late to repent. (2) What God expects of His people has not changed, for He desires that we show love and compassion to those who experience various needs (see article on THE CARE OF THE POOR AND NEEDY, p. 1312).

8:3 I AM RETURNED UNTO ZION. The key to Israel's full restoration is God's return to Zion, pointing to the time when Christ returns in glory and begins His earthly reign over the nations. At that time God's presence will make Jerusalem a city of truth and faithfulness, and the mountain of the Lord will be holy, i.e., separated to His worship. This chapter gives ten blessings that will accompany that earthly reign, each one beginning with the phrase, "Thus saith the LORD."

8:4–5 OLD MEN . . . OLD WOMEN . . . BOYS AND GIRLS. These verses picture the peace, prosperity, and happiness in the future millennial Jerusalem.

and every man with his staff in his hand [g]for very age.

5 And the streets of the city shall be full of boys and girls playing in the streets thereof.

6 Thus saith the LORD of hosts; If it be [h]marvellous in the eyes of the remnant of this people in these days, [v]should it also be marvellous in mine eyes? saith the LORD of hosts.

7 Thus saith the LORD of hosts; Behold, [w]I will save my people from the east country, and from [x]the[i] west country;

8 And I will bring them, and they shall dwell in the midst of Jerusalem: [y]and they shall be my people, and I will be their God, [z]in truth and in righteousness.

9 ¶ Thus saith the LORD of hosts; [a]Let your hands be strong, ye that hear in these days these words by the mouth of [b]the prophets, which *were* in [c]the day *that* the foundation of the house of the LORD of hosts was laid, that the temple might be built.

10 For before these days [j]there was no [d]hire for man, nor any hire for beast; neither *was there any* peace to him that went out or came in because of the affliction: for I set all men every one against his neighbour.

11 But now I *will* not *be* unto the residue of this people as in the former days, saith the LORD of hosts.

12 [e]For the seed *shall be* [k]prosperous; the vine shall give her fruit, and [f]the ground shall give her increase, and [g]the heavens shall give their dew; and I will cause the remnant of this people to possess all these *things.*

13 And it shall come to pass, *that* as ye were [h]a curse among the heathen, O house of Judah, and house of Israel; so will I save you, and [i]ye shall be a blessing: fear not, *but* let your hands be strong.

14 For thus saith the LORD of hosts; [j]As I thought to punish you, when your fathers provoked me to wrath, saith the LORD of hosts, [k]and I repented not:

15 So again have I thought in these days to do well unto Jerusalem and to the house of Judah: fear ye not. Zech. 9:10

16 ¶ These *are* the things that ye shall do; [l]Speak ye every man the truth to his neighbour; [l]execute the judgment of truth and peace in your gates:

17 [m]And let none of you imagine evil in your hearts against his neighbour; and love no false oath: for all these *are things* that I hate, saith the LORD.

18 ¶ And the word of the LORD of hosts came unto me, saying,

19 Thus saith the LORD of hosts; [n]The fast of the fourth *month,* [o]and the fast of the fifth, [p]and the fast of the seventh, [q]and the fast of the tenth, shall be to the house of Judah [r]joy and gladness, and cheerful [m]feasts; [s]therefore love the truth and peace.

20 Thus saith the LORD of hosts; *It shall* yet *come to pass,* that there shall come people, and the inhabitants of many cities:

21 And the inhabitants of one *city* shall go to another, saying, [t]Let us go [n,o]speedily [p]to pray before the LORD, and to seek the LORD of hosts: I will go also.

22 Yea, [u]many people and strong

8:6 [v]Gen. 18:14 Luke 1:37 **8:7** [w]Is. 11:11 Ezek. 37:21 [x]See Ps. 50:1 **8:8** [y]Jer. 31:1,33 [z]Jer. 4:2 **8:9** [a]Hag. 2:4 [b]Ezra 5:1,2 [c]Hag. 2:18 **8:10** [d]Hag. 1:6,9 **8:12** [e]Joel 2:22 [f]Ps. 67:6 [g]Hag. 1:10 **8:13** [h]Jer. 42:18 [i]Gen. 12:2 Ruth 4:11

8:14 [j]Jer. 31:28 [k]2 Chr. 36:16 **8:16** [l]Eph. 4:25 **8:17** [m]Prov. 3:29 **8:19** [n]Jer. 52:6 [o]Jer. 52:12 [p]2 Ki. 25:25 Jer. 41:1,2 [q]Jer. 52:4 [r]Esth. 8:17 [s]ver. 16 **8:21** [t]Is. 2:3 Mic. 4:1,2 **8:22** [u]Is. 60:3

[g] Heb. *for multitude of days* [h] Or, *hard,* or, *difficult* [i] Heb. *the country of the going down of the sun* [j] Or, *the hire of man became nothing* [k] Heb. *of peace* [l] Heb. *judge truth, and the judgment of peace* [m] Or, *solemn,* or, *set times* [n] Or, *continually* [o] Heb. *going* [p] Heb. *to entreat the face of the LORD*

8:7–8 I WILL SAVE MY PEOPLE. The restoration after the Babylonian exile was only from the east. Thus, this section refers to a future restoration from the east and west, i.e., from the whole earth (cf. Is. 43:5–6). God will truly become the God of His people, and they will partake of His righteousness through Christ.

8:16–17 THESE *ARE* THE THINGS THAT YE SHALL DO. In view of God's return to His people and of the hope contained within these millennial prophecies, the people of Zechariah's day were to respond with conduct worthy of the Lord they served (cf. 7:9–10). Prophecy has never been given merely to satisfy our curiosity. God expects our hope for the future to cause us to seek Him and His kingdom with greater intensity and commitment (cf. Jas. 1:22; 1 John 3:2–3).

8:22 MANY PEOPLE . . . SHALL COME TO SEEK THE LORD. Incomparable joy will come as many Gentiles join the Jews in seeking the Lord in Jerusalem, for the Lord will be there (see Ezek. 48:35). This pictures the final fulfillment of the promise in the Abrahamic covenant that the Gentiles would be brought to the Lord (Gen. 12:3; Gal. 3:8,26–29; see article on GOD'S COVENANT WITH ABRAHAM, ISAAC, AND JACOB, p. 48).

nations shall come to seek the LORD of
hosts in Jerusalem, and to pray before
the LORD.
23 Thus saith the LORD of hosts; In
those days *it shall come to pass,* that ten
men shall [v]take hold out of all lan-
guages of the nations, even shall take
hold of the skirt of him that is a Jew,
Mat. 10:18-20 saying, We will go with you: for we
have heard [w]*that* God *is* with you.

The coming of the king

9 THE [x]BURDEN of the word of the
LORD in the land of Hadrach, and
[y]Damascus *shall be* the rest thereof:
when [z]the eyes of man, as of all the
tribes of Israel, *shall be* toward the
LORD.
2 And [a]Hamath also shall border
thereby; [b]Tyrus, and [c]Zidon, though
it be very [d]wise.
3 And Tyrus did build herself a
strong hold, and heaped up silver as
the dust, and fine gold as the mire of
the streets.
4 Behold, [e]the Lord will cast her
out, and he will smite [f]her power in
the sea; and she shall be devoured with
fire.
5 Ashkelon shall see *it,* and fear;
Gaza also *shall see it,* and be very sor-
rowful, and Ekron; for her expectation
shall be ashamed; and the king shall
perish from Gaza, and Ashkelon shall
not be inhabited.
6 And a bastard shall dwell [g]in
Ashdod, and I will cut off the pride of
the Philistines.
7 And I will take away his [q]blood
out of his mouth, and his abominations
from between his teeth: but he that re-
maineth, even he, *shall be* for our God,
and he shall be as a governor in Judah,
and Ekron as a Jebusite.
8 And [h]I will encamp about mine
house because of the army, because of
him that passeth by, and because of
him that returneth: and no oppressor
shall pass through them any more: for
now have I seen with mine eyes.
9 ¶ [i]Rejoice greatly, O daughter of
Zion; shout, O daughter of Jerusalem:
behold, [j]thy King cometh unto thee:
he *is* just, and [r]having salvation; low-
ly, and riding upon an ass, and upon a
colt the foal of an ass.
10 And I [k]will cut off the chariot
from Ephraim, and the horse from Jeru-
salem, and the battle bow shall be cut
off: and he shall speak peace unto the
heathen: and his dominion *shall be* from
sea *even* to sea, and from the river *even*
to the ends of the earth. Zech 14:3
11 As for thee also, [l]by[s] the
blood of thy covenant I have sent forth
thy [m]prisoners out of the pit wherein
is no water.
12 ¶ Turn you to the strong hold,
[n]ye prisoners of hope: even today do
I declare *that* I will render double unto
thee;
13 When I have bent Judah for me,
filled the bow with Ephraim, and raised
up thy sons, O Zion, against thy sons,

8:23 [v]Is. 3:6 [w]1 Cor. 14:25
9:1 [x]Jer. 23:33 [y]Amos 1:3 [z]2 Chr. 20:12 Ps. 145:15
9:2 [a]Jer. 49:23 [b]Is. 23 Ezek. 26 [c]1 Ki. 17:9 [d]Ezek. 28:3
9:4 [e]Is. 23:1 [f]Ezek. 26:17
9:6 [g]Amos 1:8
9:8 [h]Ps. 34:7
9:9 [i]ch. 2:10 [j]Jer. 23:5 Luke 19:38
9:10 [k]Hos. 1:7 Mic. 5:10
9:11 [l]Ex. 24:8 [m]Is. 42:7
9:12 [n]Is. 49:9

[q] Heb. *bloods* [r] Or, *saving himself* [s] Or, *whose covenant* is *by blood*

9:1 THE EYES OF MAN, AS OF . . . ISRAEL, *SHALL BE* TOWARD THE LORD. Because of God's promises, Israel would turn to the Lord for deliverance, as would many others. The result would be judgment on the various nations around Israel who had caused them so much suffering in the past. Alexander the Great brought a partial fulfillment of this prophecy in 332 B.C.

9:8 NO OPPRESSOR SHALL PASS THROUGH. Ultimate peace will come to earthly Jerusalem during the millennial reign of the Messiah. God will not allow His people to be totally destroyed. The same assurance is given to the church, for the gates of hell will never prevail against it (see Mat. 16:18, note).

9:9 BEHOLD, THY KING COMETH . . . HAVING SALVATION; LOWLY. A still greater cause for rejoicing is the coming of the King, not in royal splendor but in humility (cf. Phil. 2:5–8), riding on an ass. Zechariah's prophecy foresees the triumphal entry of Jesus into Jerusalem (Mat. 21:1–5). By riding into the holy city in this way, Jesus declared Himself to be the Messiah and Savior, ready to go to the cross.

9:10 HE SHALL SPEAK PEACE . . . AND HIS DOMINION . . . TO THE ENDS OF THE EARTH. Without referring to the period of time between Christ's resurrection and His second coming, Zechariah jumps ahead to His second coming at the end of the age. After Christ's triumph over the antichrist and his armies, there will be no more need for battle chariots, war horses, or any instruments of war. His dominion will cover the entire earth.

9:12 TURN YOU TO THE STRONG HOLD, YE PRISONERS OF HOPE. The future of the scattered Israelites is not hopeless; God promises to restore them with His double blessing because of all they had suffered.

9:13 GREECE. Greece came into prominence in 480–479 B.C., when the Greeks defeated Xerxes. Fulfillment of the prophecy in this verse came in the defeat of Antiochus Epiphanes about 168 B.C.

O Greece, and made thee as the sword of a mighty man.

14 And the LORD shall be seen over them, and [o]his arrow shall go forth as the lightning: and the Lord GOD shall blow the trumpet, and shall go [p]with whirlwinds of the south.

15 The LORD of hosts shall defend them; and they shall devour, and [t]subdue with sling stones; and they shall drink, *and* make a noise as through wine; and they [u]shall be filled like bowls, *and* as the corners of the altar.

16 And the LORD their God shall save them in that day as the flock of his people: for [q]*they shall be as* the stones of a crown, [r]lifted up as an ensign upon his land.

17 For [s]how great *is* his goodness, and how great *is* his beauty! [t]corn shall make the young men [v]cheerful, and new wine the maids.

The redemption of God's people

10 ASK YE [u]of the LORD [v]rain [w]in the time of the latter rain; *so* the LORD shall make [w]bright clouds, and give them showers of rain, to every one grass in the field.

2 For the [x]idols[x] have spoken vanity, and the diviners have seen a lie, and have told false dreams; they [y]comfort in vain: therefore they went their way as a flock, they [y]were troubled, [z]because *there was* no shepherd.

3 Mine anger was kindled against the shepherds, [a]and I [z]punished the goats: for the LORD of hosts [b]hath visited his flock the house of Judah, and [c]hath made them as his goodly horse in the battle.

9:14 [o]Ps. 18:14 [p]Is. 21:1 **9:16** [q]Is. 62:3 Mal. 3:17 [r]Is. 11:12 **9:17** [s]Ps. 31:19 [t]Joel 3:18 **10:1** [u]Jer. 14:22 [v]Deut. 11:14 [w]Joel 2:23 **10:2** [x]Jer. 10:8 Hab. 2:18 [y]Job 13:4 [z]Ezek. 34:5 **10:3** [a]Ezek. 34:17 [b]Luke 1:68 [c]Sol. 1:9

10:4 [d]Is. 28:16 [e]Is. 22:23 **10:5** [f]Ps. 18:42 **10:6** [g]Jer. 3:18 Ezek. 37:21 [h]Hos. 1:7 [i]ch. 13:9 **10:7** [j]Ps. 104:15 **10:8** [k]Is. 5:26 [l]Is. 49:19 Ezek. 36:37 **10:9** [m]Hos. 2:23 [n]Deut. 30:1 **10:10** [o]Is. 11:11 Hos. 11:11 [p]Is. 49:20 **10:11** [q]Is. 11:15

4 Out of him came forth [d]the corner, out of him [e]the nail, out of him the battle bow, out of him every oppressor together.

5 ¶ And they shall be as mighty *men*, which [f]tread down *their enemies* in the mire of the streets in the battle: and they shall fight, because the LORD *is* with them, and [a]the riders on horses shall be confounded.

6 And I will strengthen the house of Judah, and I will save the house of Joseph, and [g]I will bring them again to place them; for I [h]have mercy upon them: and they shall be as though I had not cast them off: for I *am* the LORD their God, and [i]will hear them.

7 And *they of* Ephraim shall be like a mighty *man*, and their [j]heart shall rejoice as through wine: yea, their children shall see *it*, and be glad; their heart shall rejoice in the LORD.

8 I will [k]hiss for them, and gather them; for I have redeemed them: [l]and they shall increase as they have increased.

9 And [m]I will sow them among the people: and they shall [n]remember me in far countries; and they shall live with their children, and turn again.

10 [o]I will bring them again also out of the land of Egypt, and gather them out of Assyria; and I will bring them into the land of Gilead and Lebanon; and [p]*place* shall not be found for them.

11 [q]And he shall pass through the

[t] Or, *subdue the stones of the sling* [u] Or, *shall fill both the bowls* [v] Or, *grow*, or, *speak* [w] Or, *lightnings* [x] Heb. *teraphims;* see Judg. 17:5 [y] Or, *answered that* [z] Heb. *visited upon* [a] Or, *they shall make the riders on horses ashamed*

9:16–17 THEIR GOD SHALL SAVE THEM. God's salvation will reach a climax when He makes Israel His flock. Their salvation will be a crowning work, lifted up for the rest of the world to see. This result is guaranteed by the great goodness and beauty of the Lord. All that the Lord does for His people reflects His goodness and the beauty of His holiness.

10:1 ASK YE OF THE LORD RAIN IN THE TIME OF THE LATTER RAIN. The latter rain was the spring rain, so essential to ripen the harvest. There is a sense in which the work of the Spirit in O.T. times was like former rain, a time of preparation and planting (see Hos. 6:2–3, note). The latter rain began at Pentecost, and with it the harvest of souls began. We can look for a continued "latter rain" outpouring of the Holy Spirit until the end of this age.

10:2 THE DIVINERS HAVE SEEN A LIE. Because the people had no true shepherd to lead them in the right paths, i.e., the paths of trust in God, they had turned to reliance on idols, fortune tellers, and other occult practices. Pastors and teachers who destroy faith and confidence in the Bible by denying its divine inspiration and infallibility indirectly influence people to turn to such practices today.

10:4 OUT OF HIM CAME FORTH THE CORNER. Out of the tribe of Judah came the cornerstone (Ps. 118:22; Is. 28:16), Jesus the Messiah, who would be like the nail, indicating security (cf. Is. 22:22–23); He would be the victorious King (cf. Rev. 19:11–16).

10:6–8 JUDAH . . . JOSEPH. God's purpose was to redeem and save all twelve tribes of Israel. Judah represents the southern two tribes and Joseph the northern ten tribes.

10:11 ASSYRIA . . . EGYPT. Assyria repre-

sea with affliction, and shall smite the
waves in the sea, and all the deeps of
the river shall dry up: and [r]the pride
of Assyria shall be brought down, and
[s]the sceptre of Egypt shall depart
away.
12 And I will strengthen them in the
LORD; and [t]they shall walk up and
down in his name, saith the LORD.

The rejection of the king

11 OPEN [u]THY doors, O Lebanon, that the fire may devour
thy cedars.
2 Howl, fir tree; for the cedar is fallen; because the [b]mighty are spoiled:
howl, O ye oaks of Bashan; [v]for [c]the
forest of the vintage is come down.
3 ¶ *There is* a voice of the howling of
the shepherds; for their glory is
spoiled: a voice of the roaring of young
lions; for the pride of Jordan is spoiled.
4 Thus saith the LORD my God; Feed
the flock of the slaughter;
5 Whose possessors slay them, and
[w]hold themselves not guilty: and they
that sell them [x]say, Blessed *be* the
LORD; for I am rich: and their own shepherds pity them not.
6 For I will no more pity the inhabitants of the land, saith the LORD: but,
lo, I will [d]deliver the men every one
into his neighbour's hand, and into the
hand of his king: and they shall smite
the land, and out of their hand I will not
deliver *them*.
7 And I will feed the flock of slaughter, [e]*even* you, [y]O poor of the flock.
And I took unto me two staves; the one

10:11 [r]Is. 14:25 [s]Ezek. 30:13
10:12 [t]Mic. 4:5
11:1 [u]ch. 10:10
11:2 [v]Is. 32:19
11:5 [w]Jer. 2:3 & 50:7 [x]Deut. 29:19 Hos. 12:8
11:7 [y]Zeph. 3:12 Mat. 11:5
11:8 [z]Hos. 5:7
11:9 [a]Jer. 15:2
11:11 [b]Zeph. 3:12
11:12 [c]Mat. 26:15 Ex. 21:32
11:13 [d]Mat. 27:9

I called Beauty, and the other I called
[f]Bands; and I fed the flock.
8 Three shepherds also I cut off [z]in
one month; and my soul [g]loathed
them, and their soul also abhorred me.
9 Then said I, I will not feed you:
[a]that that dieth, let it die; and that
that is to be cut off, let it be cut off; and
let the rest eat every one the flesh [h]of
another.
10 ¶ And I took my staff, *even* Beauty, and cut it asunder, that I might
break my covenant which I had made
with all the people.
11 And it was broken in that day:
and [i]so [b]the poor of the flock that
waited upon me knew that it *was* the
word of the LORD.
12 And I said unto them, [j]If ye
think good, give *me* my price; and if
not, forbear. So they [c]weighed for my
price thirty *pieces* of silver.
13 And the LORD said unto me, Cast
it unto the [d]potter: a goodly price that
I was prised at of them. And I took the
thirty *pieces* of silver, and cast them to
the potter in the house of the LORD.
14 Then I cut asunder mine other
staff, *even* [f]Bands, that I might break
the brotherhood between Judah and Israel.

The false shepherd described

15 ¶ And the LORD said unto me,

[b] Or, *gallants* [c] Or, *the defenced forest*
[d] Heb. *make to be found* [e] Or, *verily the poor*
[f] Or, *Binders* [g] Heb. *was straitened for them*
[h] Heb. *of his fellow,* or, *neighbour* [i] Or, *the poor of the flock, &c. certainly knew* [j] Heb. *If it be good in your eyes*

sented Israel's enemies to the north and east, while Egypt represented the enemies to the south. God promised to remove all opposition to Israel's restoration.

11:4–17 FEED THE FLOCK. Zechariah was instructed to represent God's appointed Shepherd of Israel, the Messiah (vv. 4–14). Next, he was to portray Israel's wicked shepherd (vv. 15–17), which may prefigure the end-time antichrist.

11:4 THE FLOCK OF THE SLAUGHTER. The flock is Israel, marked for punishment because they would reject the Messiah. The slaughter would be carried out by the Romans in A.D. 70.

11:7 TWO STAVES. Zechariah, representing the Messiah, uses two staffs to protect his flock; the staffs represent God's favor toward Israel and His plan to unite Israel and Judah as a single nation. These blessings would become reality if the people would follow the Messiah.

11:9 I WILL NOT FEED YOU. Because the flock hated the Shepherd-Messiah, He would turn from His role as Shepherd and give the people over to their doom.

11:10 BREAK MY COVENANT. God had made a covenant to restrain the nations from attacking Israel. Zechariah describes God removing that protection and Israel being destroyed and dispersed; this occurred in 70 A.D., when the Romans destroyed Jerusalem.

11:12 MY PRICE THIRTY *PIECES* OF SILVER. Zechariah, still representing the Messiah, asked the leaders to pay him what they thought his services were worth. They insulted him by offering him the price of a slave (Ex. 21:32); thirty pieces of silver was also the price paid to Judas for betraying Jesus (Mat. 27:3–10).

11:14 THAT I MIGHT BREAK THE BROTHERHOOD BETWEEN JUDAH AND ISRAEL. Part of God's judgment was the destruction of the unity of Israel; the covenant nation would break up into hostile factions.

11:15–16 A FOOLISH SHEPHERD. Zechariah was now to take the equipment of a shepherd and impersonate a godless shepherd, who used

[e]Take unto thee yet the instruments
of a foolish shepherd.
16 For, lo, I will raise up a shepherd
in the land, *which* shall not visit those
that be [k]cut off, neither shall seek the
young one, nor heal that that is broken,
nor [l]feed that that standeth still: but
he shall eat the flesh of the fat, and
tear their claws in pieces.
17 [f]Woe to the idol shepherd that
leaveth the flock! the sword *shall be*
upon his arm, and upon his right eye:
his arm shall be clean dried up, and his
right eye shall be utterly darkened.

12 THE BURDEN of the word of
the LORD for Israel, saith the
LORD, [g]which stretcheth forth the
heavens, and layeth the foundation of
the earth, and [h]formeth the spirit of
man within him.
2 Behold, I will make Jerusalem [i]a
cup of [m]trembling unto all the people
round about, [n]when they shall be in
the siege both against Judah *and*
against Jerusalem.
3 ¶ [j]And in that day will I make
Jerusalem [k]a burdensome stone for all
people: all that burden themselves
with it shall be cut in pieces, though all
the people of the earth be gathered to-
gether against it.
4 In that day, saith the LORD, [l]I will
smite every horse with astonishment,
and his rider with madness: and I will
open mine eyes upon the house of Ju-
dah, and will smite every horse of the
people with blindness.
5 And the governors of Judah shall
say in their heart, [o]The inhabitants of
Jerusalem *shall be* my strength in the
LORD of hosts their God.
6 ¶ In that day will I make the gov-
ernors of Judah [m]like an hearth of fire
among the wood, and like a torch of fire
in a sheaf; and they shall devour all the
people round about, on the right hand
and on the left: and Jerusalem shall be
inhabited again in her own place, *even*
in Jerusalem.
7 The LORD also shall save the tents
of Judah first, that the glory of the
house of David and the glory of the in-
habitants of Jerusalem do not magnify
themselves against Judah.
8 In that day shall the LORD defend
the inhabitants of Jerusalem; and he
that is [p,q]feeble among them at that
day shall be as David; and the house of
David *shall be* as God, as the angel of
the LORD before them.
9 ¶ And it shall come to pass in that
day, *that* I will seek to [n]destroy all the
nations that come against Jerusalem.

The compassion of Jerusalem

10 [o]And I will pour upon the house
of David, and upon the inhabitants of
Jerusalem, the spirit of grace and of
supplications: and they shall [p]look
upon me whom they have pierced, and
they shall mourn for him, [q]as one
mourneth for *his* only *son,* and shall be
in bitterness for him, as one that is in
bitterness for *his* firstborn.
11 In that day shall there be a great
[r]mourning in Jerusalem, [s]as the
mourning of Hadadrimmon in the val-
ley of Megiddon.
12 [t]And the land shall mourn,
[r]every family apart; the family of the
house of David apart, and their wives

11:15 [e]Ezek. 34:2
11:17 [f]Jer. 23:1 Ezek. 34:2 John 10:12
12:1 [g]Is. 42:5 & 44:24 [h]Num. 16:22 Eccl. 12:7 Is. 57:16
12:2 [i]Is. 51:17
12:3 [j]ver. 4,6,8 & ch. 13:1 [k]Mat. 21:44
12:4 [l]Ps. 76:6 Ezek. 38:4
12:6 [m]Obad. 18
12:9 [n]Hag. 2:22
12:10 [o]Jer. 31:9 & 50:4 Ezek. 39:29 Joel 2:28 [p]John 19:34 Rev. 1:7 [q]Jer. 6:26 Amos 8:10
12:11 [r]Acts 2:37 [s]2 Ki. 23:29
12:12 [t]Rev. 1:7

[k] Or, *hidden* [l] Or, *bear* [m] Or, *slumber,* or, *poison* [n] Or, *and also against Judah* shall he *be which shall be in siege against Jerusalem* [o] Or, There is *strength to me* and *to the inhabitants* [p] Or, *abject* [q] Heb. *fallen* [r] Heb. *families, families*

that equipment to hurt the sheep rather than help them (see vv. 4–17, note). The foolish shepherd will have its final fulfillment in the antichrist (cf. Ezek. 34:2–4; Dan. 11:36–39; John 5:43; 2 Thes. 2:3–10; Rev. 13:1–8).

12:3–9 ALL THE PEOPLE OF THE EARTH BE GATHERED TOGETHER AGAINST IT. At the end of time, many nations will gather against Jerusalem and Israel. God will intervene and destroy her enemies, and the world powers will be overthrown at the battle called Armageddon (see Rev. 16:16, note; 19:19).

12:10–14 THE SPIRIT OF GRACE. These verses speak of the conversion of individual Jews who, in danger of being defeated by their enemies, come to believe in Jesus as the true Messiah.

12:10 THEY SHALL MOURN FOR HIM. In the midst of danger on that day of battle, the people will cry out to God for His help. God will pour out His Holy Spirit to bring His grace and to answer their prayers. (1) The repentant people will then recognize that they were guilty for the Roman sword which pierced the side of Jesus the Messiah (cf. Ps. 22:16; Is. 53:5; John 19:34) and for His death. (2) Their mourning will be bitter. Each family will mourn separately, as will husbands and wives. Thus, each individual will have to repent personally of his or her sin and rejection of Jesus Christ (cf. Rom. 3:23; 6:23; Acts 16:31; 1 Pet. 2:24).

apart; the family of the house of [u]Nathan apart, and their wives apart;

13 The family of the house of Levi apart, and their wives apart; the family [s]of Shimei apart, and their wives apart;

14 All the families that remain, every family apart, and their wives apart.

13 IN THAT day there shall be [v]a fountain opened to the house of David and to the inhabitants of Jerusalem for sin and for [t]uncleanness.

2 ¶ And it shall come to pass in that day, saith the LORD of hosts, *that* I will [w]cut off the names of the idols out of the land, and they shall no more be remembered: and also I will cause [x]the prophets and the unclean spirit to pass out of the land.

3 And it shall come to pass, *that* when any shall yet prophesy, then his father and his mother that begat him shall say unto him, Thou shalt not live; for thou speakest lies in the name of the LORD: and his father and his mother that begat him [y]shall thrust him through when he prophesieth.

4 And it shall come to pass in that day, *that* [z]the prophets shall be ashamed every one of his vision, when he hath prophesied; neither shall they wear [a]a[u] rough garment [v]to deceive:

5 [b]But he shall say, I *am* no prophet, I *am* an husbandman; for man taught me to keep cattle from my youth.

6 And *one* shall say unto him, What *are* these wounds in thine hands? Then he shall answer, *Those* with which I was wounded *in* the house of my friends.

12:12 [u]Luke 3:31
13:1 [v]Heb. 9:14
13:2 [w]Ex. 23:13 [x]2 Pet. 2:1
13:3 [y]Deut. 18:20
13:4 [z]Mic. 3:6,7 [a]2 Ki. 1:8
13:5 [b]Amos 7:14
13:7 [c]Is. 40:11 [d]John 10:30 [e]Mat. 26:31 [f]Luke 12:32
13:8 [g]Rom. 11:5
13:9 [h]Is. 48:10 [i]1 Pet. 1:6 [j]Ps. 50:15 [k]Jer. 30:22
14:1 [l]Is. 13:9
14:2 [m]Joel 3:2

Israel chastened

7 ¶ Awake, O sword, against [c]my shepherd, and against the man [d]*that is* my fellow, saith the LORD of hosts: [e]smite the shepherd, and the sheep shall be scattered: and I will turn mine hand upon [f]the little ones.

8 And it shall come to pass, *that* in all the land, saith the LORD, two parts therein shall be cut off *and* die; [g]but the third shall be left therein.

9 And I will bring the third part [h]through the fire, and will [i]refine them as silver is refined, and will try them as gold is tried: [j]they shall call on my name, and I will hear them: [k]I will say, It *is* my people: and they shall say, The LORD *is* my God.

Judah's king supreme

14 BEHOLD, [l]THE day of the LORD cometh, and thy spoil shall be divided in the midst of thee.

2 For [m]I will gather all nations against Jerusalem to battle; and the city shall be taken, and the houses rifled, and the women ravished; and half of the city shall go forth into captivity, and the residue of the people shall not be cut off from the city.

[s] Or, *of Simeon,* as LXX [t] Heb. *separation for uncleanness* [u] Heb. *a garment of hair* [v] Heb. *to lie*

13:1–6 A FOUNTAIN OPENED TO THE HOUSE OF DAVID. This fountain pictures the cleansing from sin brought about by Christ's death on the cross. The Jewish people will be cleansed from sin in the same way that all believers in Christ are (cf. 1 John 1:7,9).

13:4 THE PROPHETS SHALL BE ASHAMED. In those days God will expose all false prophets, who will be so afraid and ashamed that each will say, "I am not a prophet, just a simple farmer." Until that time we must recognize that there will be many false prophets among the churches; in that light, God calls us to test the spirits (1 John 4:1, note; see article on FALSE TEACHERS, p. 1508).

13:6 WOUNDS IN THINE HANDS. These wounds are probably self-inflicted wounds associated with idol worship (vv. 2–5).

13:7 SWORD . . . SMITE THE SHEPHERD. In this prophetic view of the future, the shepherd is the Messiah. (1) God calls the shepherd a mighty man who is "my fellow" (i.e., my equal, my associate), and thus, a divine Messiah. (2) The Shepherd-Messiah would be smitten, i.e., crucified. His disciples would then scatter like sheep (see Mat. 26:31,56; Mark 14:27); this prophecy may also foreshadow the scattering of the Jewish nation in A.D. 70.

13:8–9 I WILL BRING THE THIRD PART THROUGH THE FIRE. These verses probably refer to the tribulation period at the end of time (see article on THE GREAT TRIBULATION, p. 1456). The unbelieving Jews (two-thirds) will be killed (v. 8); only one-third will be left. These people are the ones who will "look upon [him] whom they have pierced" (12:10–14). Thus, only a remnant of Israel will be saved (Rev. 11 — 18).

14:1 THE DAY OF THE LORD COMETH. "The day of the LORD" is a time of both judgment and restoration. Here it refers to the time when Christ will return to judge the nations and establish His earthly reign.

14:2 I WILL GATHER ALL NATIONS AGAINST JERUSALEM. The nations will appear to gain a military victory, but they will ultimately be destroyed (see 12:3–9, note).

3 Then shall the LORD go forth, and
fight against those nations, as when he
fought in the day of battle.
4 ¶ And his feet shall stand in that
day [n]upon the mount of Olives, which
is before Jerusalem on the east, and the
mount of Olives shall cleave in the
midst thereof toward the east and to-
ward the west, [o]*and there shall be* a
very great valley; and half of the moun-
tain shall remove toward the north,
and half of it toward the south.
5 And ye shall flee *to* the valley of
[w]the mountains; [x]for the valley of
the mountains shall reach unto Azal:
yea, ye shall flee, like as ye fled from
before the [p]earthquake in the days of
Uzziah king of Judah: [q]and the LORD
my God shall come, *and* [r]all the saints
with thee.
6 And it shall come to pass in that
day, [y]*that* the light shall not be
[z]clear, *nor* [a]dark:
7 But [b]it shall be one day [s]which
shall be known to the LORD, not day,
nor night: but it shall come to pass,
that at [t]evening time it shall be light.
8 And it shall be in that day, *that*
living [u]waters shall go out from Jeru-
salem; half of them toward the [c]for-
mer sea, and half of them toward the
hinder sea: in summer and in winter
shall it be.
9 And the LORD shall be [v]king over
all the earth: in that day shall there be
Mal. 4:2-3 [w]one LORD, and his name one.
10 All the land shall be [d]turned as
a plain from Geba to Rimmon south of
Jerusalem: and it shall be lifted up, and
[x]inhabited[e] in her place, from Benja-
min's gate unto the place of the first
gate, unto the corner gate, [y]and *from*
the tower of Hananeel unto the king's
winepresses.
11 And *men* shall dwell in it, and
there shall be [z]no more utter destruc-
tion; [a]but Jerusalem [e]shall be safely
inhabited.
12 ¶ And this shall be the plague
wherewith the LORD will smite all the
people that have fought against Jerusa-
lem; Their flesh shall consume away
while they stand upon their feet, and
their eyes shall consume away in their
holes, and their tongue shall consume
away in their mouth.
13 And it shall come to pass in that
day, *that* [b]a great tumult from the
LORD shall be among them; and they
shall lay hold every one on the hand of
his neighbour, and [c]his hand shall
rise up against the hand of his neigh-
bour.
14 And [f]Judah also shall fight [g]at
Jerusalem; [d]and the wealth of all the
heathen round about shall be gathered
together, gold, and silver, and apparel,
in great abundance.
15 And [e]so shall be the plague of
the horse, of the mule, of the camel,
and of the ass, and of all the beasts
that shall be in these tents, as this
plague.
16 ¶ And it shall come to pass, *that*

14:4 [n]Ezek. 11:23 [o]Joel 3:12
14:5 [p]Amos 1:1 [q]Mat. 24:30 [r]Joel 3:11
14:7 [s]Mat. 24:36 [t]Is. 30:26
14:8 [u]Ezek. 47:1
14:9 [v]Rev. 11:15 [w]Eph. 4:5,6
14:10 [x]ch. 12:6 [y]Neh. 3:1
14:11 [z]Jer. 31:40 [a]Jer. 23:6
14:13 [b]1 Sam. 14:15,20 [c]Judg. 7:22 2 Chr. 20:23 Ezek. 38:21
14:14 [d]Ezek. 39:10,17
14:15 [e]ver. 12

[w]Or, *my mountains* [x]Or, *when he shall touch the valley of the mountains to the place he separated* [y]*i.e.* it shall not be clear in some places, and dark in other places of the world [z]Heb. *precious* [a]Heb. *thickness* [b]Or, *the day shall be one* [c]Or, *eastern;* see Joel 2:20 [d]Or, *compassed* [e]Or, *shall abide* [f]Or, *thou also, O Judah, shalt* [g]Or, *against*

14:3 THEN SHALL THE LORD GO FORTH. The Lord will intervene in the battle and defeat the nations.

14:4 HIS FEET SHALL STAND IN THAT DAY UPON THE MOUNT OF OLIVES. This prophecy will be fulfilled by Jesus Christ at His final coming, when He returns to the place from which He left (Luke 24:50–51; Acts 1:9–12). The topography of that area will be dramatically changed as the mountain splits in two, half moving north, half south, leaving a valley between.

14:8 LIVING WATERS SHALL GO OUT FROM JERUSALEM. Living waters (in contrast to stagnant waters) will flow out of Jerusalem (cf. Ps. 46:4; Ezek. 47:1–12; Joel 3:18). Instead of drying up in summer, as most Palestinian streams do, its flow will be constant to the Mediterranean Sea and to the Dead Sea. This passage envisions God's blessings flowing from the millennial Jerusalem (Rev. 22:1).

14:9 THE LORD SHALL BE KING OVER ALL THE EARTH. When Christ establishes His kingdom, He will be worshiped by all people of the earth (cf. 4:14; 6:5; Mic. 4:13; Rev. 17:14; 19:16).

14:10 ALL THE LAND SHALL BE TURNED AS A PLAIN. As a result of our Lord's return, the land around Jerusalem will be flattened, even though Jerusalem itself will be a plateau, elevated a little above the surrounding area so that it stands out.

14:12–15 THE LORD WILL SMITE. These verses give more details of the judgment on the nations (see v. 3, note).

14:16 EVERYONE THAT IS LEFT . . . SHALL . . . WORSHIP THE KING. After the return of Christ and the destruction of the antichrist and his armies (cf. Rev. 19), those left of the nations will come annually to Jerusalem at the Feast of Tabernacles to worship the Messianic King, the Lord Jesus. The survivors are most likely civilian per-

every one that is left of all the nations
which came against Jerusalem shall
even [f]go up from year to year to wor-
ship the King, the LORD of hosts, and to
keep [g]the feast of tabernacles.
17 [h]And it shall be, *that* whoso will
not come up of *all* the families of the
earth unto Jerusalem to worship the
King, the LORD of hosts, even upon
them shall be no rain.
18 And if the family of Egypt go not
up, and come not, [i]that[h] *have* no
rain; there shall be the plague, where-
with the LORD will smite the heathen
that come not up to keep the feast of
tabernacles.
19 This shall be the [i]punishment
of Egypt, and the punishment of all na-
tions that come not up to keep the
feast of tabernacles.
20 ¶ In that day shall there be upon
the [j]bells of the horses, [j]HOLINESS
UNTO THE LORD; and the pots in the
LORD's house shall be like the bowls be-
fore the altar.
21 Yea, every pot in Jerusalem and
in Judah shall be holiness unto the
LORD of hosts: and all they that sacri-
fice shall come and take of them, and
seethe therein: and in that day there
shall be no more the [k]Canaanite in
[l]the house of the LORD of hosts.

14:16 [f]Is. 60:6 & 66:23 [g]Lev. 23:34 Neh. 8:14 Hos. 12:9 John 7:2 **14:17** [h]Is. 60:12 **14:18** [i]Deut. 11:10 **14:20** [j]Is. 23:18 **14:21** [k]Is. 35:8 Joel 3:17 Rev. 21:27 & 22:15 [l]Eph. 2:19-22

[h] Heb. *upon whom* there is *not* [i] Or, *sin*
[j] Or, *bridles*

sonnel who had remained in their homeland and who accepted Christ as Lord.

14:17 NO RAIN. A total absence of rain will be the punishment of nations that do not come up to worship the Lord and keep the Feast of Tabernacles. But Egypt has practically no rain anyway, so a plague will be its punishment instead (v. 18).

14:20 HOLINESS UNTO THE LORD. No longer will there be separation between the holy and the common. Everything and everyone will be holy, consecrated, and dedicated to the worship and service of the Lord.

14:21 NO MORE THE CANAANITE IN THE HOUSE OF THE LORD. The term "Canaanite" was synonymous with immorality and wickedness. God will establish holiness and righteousness as the prevailing and all-pervasive characteristics of His kingdom.

MALACHI

Outline

Introduction (1:1)

I. The Burden of the Lord and Israel's Questions (1:2—3:18)

A. First Burden: God Has Loved Israel (1:2–5)

Israel's Question: "Wherein hast thou loved us?" (1:2)

B. Second Burden: Israel Has Dishonored the Lord (1:6—2:9)

Israel's Questions: "Wherein have we despised thy name?" (1:6); "Wherein have we polluted thee?" (1:7)

C. Third Burden: God Does Not Accept Israel's Offerings (2:10–16)

Israel's Question: "Wherefore?" (2:14)

D. Fourth Burden: The Lord Will Come Suddenly (2:17—3:6)

Israel's Questions: "Wherein have we wearied *him*?"; "Where *is* the God of judgment?" (2:17)

E. Fifth Burden: Return to the Lord (3:7–12)

Israel's Questions: "Wherein shall we return?" (3:7); "Wherein have we robbed thee?" (3:8)

F. Sixth Burden: Israel's Unwarranted Assertions Against God (3:13–18)

Israel's Questions: "What have we spoken *so much* against thee?" (3:13); "What profit *is it* that we have kept his ordinance?" (3:14)

II. The Day of the Lord (4:1–6)

A. Will Be a Day of Judgment for the Arrogant and Evildoer (4:1)

B. Will Be a Day of Triumph for the Righteous (4:2–3)

C. Will Be Preceded by a Supernatural Restoration of Father/Child Relationships Among God's People (4:4–6)

Author: Malachi

Theme: God's Indictments Against Post-Exilic Judaism

Date of Writing: c. 430–420 B.C.

Background

The name Malachi means "my messenger"; it may be an abbreviation of "Malachiah," which means "the messenger of the LORD." The view that "Malachi" in 1:1 is a descriptive title rather than a personal name is highly unlikely. Though we are told nothing about the prophet elsewhere in the O.T., his personality is quite visible in this book. He was a devout Jew in post-exilic Judah, a contemporary of Nehemiah, and most likely a priestly prophet. His staunch convictions in favor of faithfulness to the covenant (2:4,5,8,10) and against hypocritical and perfunctory worship (1:7—2:9), idolatry (2:10–12), divorce (2:13–16), and robbing God of tithes and offerings (3:8–10) all speak of a man of strict integrity and intense devotion to God.

The content of the book indicates that (1) the temple had been rebuilt (516/515 B.C.) and the sacrifices and feasts reinstituted, (2) a general knowledge of the law had been reintroduced by Ezra (c. 457–455 B.C.; see Ezra 7:10,14,25–26), and (3) a subsequent backsliding had occurred among the priests and the people (c. 433 B.C.). In addition, the

spiritual climate and neglect which Malachi addressed closely resembles the situation which Nehemiah found when he returned from a stay in Persia (c. 433–425 B.C.) to serve as governor a second time in Jerusalem (cf. Neh. 13:4–30). At that time, (a) the priests had become corrupt (1:6—2:9; Neh. 13:1–9), (b) tithes and offerings were being neglected (3:7–12; Neh. 13:10–13), and (c) the marriage covenant was being violated as men divorced their Hebrew wives to marry (probably younger and prettier) pagan women (2:10–16; Neh. 13:23–28). It is likely, therefore, that Malachi proclaimed his message sometime between 430–420 B.C.

Purpose

When Malachi wrote, the post-exilic Jews in Palestine were again experiencing adversity and spiritual decline. The people had become cynical, doubting God's love and promises, questioning His justice, and disbelieving there was any profit in obeying His commandments. As their faith dimmed, they became mechanical and insensitive in their observances of worship, indifferent to the requirements of the law, and guilty of all kinds of trespasses against the covenant. Malachi confronted both the priests and the people with the prophetic summons (1) to repent of their sins and religious hypocrisy before God suddenly came in judgment, (2) to remove the obstacles of disobedience that were blocking the flow of God's favor and blessing, and (3) to return to the Lord and His covenant with sincere and obedient hearts.

Survey

The book consists of a sixfold "burden of the word of the LORD to Israel by Malachi" (1:1), intermingled with a series of ten rhetorical, sarcastic questions by Israel and God's response through the prophet. Though the use of debate-like questions and answers is not unique to Malachi among the O.T. prophets, his use of this style is distinctive in that it is central to the book's literary structure (see the outline).

The Lord's "burden" through Malachi is as follows. (1) First, God affirmed His covenant love for Israel (1:2–5). (2) The second burden indicted the priests for being unfaithful guardians of the covenant relationship between God and Israel (1:6—2:9). (3) The third rebuked the people for breaking the covenant of their fathers (2:10–16). (4) The fourth reminded Israel of the certainty of God's judgment for sinning against the covenant (2:17—3:6). (5) The fifth called the entire post-exilic Jewish community in Palestine to repent and return to the Lord, in order that they might once again be blessed by Him (3:7–12). (6) The final burden refers to God's "book of remembrance" concerning those who fear Him and esteem His name (3:13–18). Malachi concludes with a prophetic warning and promise concerning the coming "day of the LORD" (4:1–6).

Special Features

Five special features or emphases characterize the book of Malachi. (1) In a simple, direct, and forceful manner, it vividly pictures an encounter between God and His people, largely using the first person. (2) It features a question-and-answer method of presenting the prophetic word, with no fewer than twenty-three questions asked back and forth between God and the people. One scholar suggests Malachi's "method" of writing may have originated because of questioning by hecklers when Malachi first delivered his prophetic message on the streets of Jerusalem or in the temple courts. (3) Malachi, the last of the O.T. prophets, is followed by 400 years without a major prophetic voice in Israel. The long absence of a major prophet of the Lord finally ended when John the Baptist appeared, whom Malachi foresaw and prophesied would precede the Messiah (3:1). (4) The phrase "the LORD of hosts" occurs twenty times in this brief book. (5) Significantly, the final prophecy (which concludes the O.T. prophetic message) predicted that God would someday send the spirit of Elijah to restore strong godly fathers in Zion, contrary to prevailing societal trends toward family disintegration (4:5–6).

New Testament Fulfillment

Three specific passages from Malachi are quoted in the N.T. (1) The phrases "I loved Jacob" and "I hated Esau" (1:2–3) are quoted by Paul in his discourse on election (Rom. 9:13; see article on ELECTION AND PREDESTINATION, p. 1846). (2) Malachi's prophecy about "the messenger" who "shall prepare the way before me" (3:1; cf. Is. 40:3) is quoted by Jesus as referring to John the Baptist and his ministry (Mat. 11:7–15). (3) Likewise, Jesus understood that Malachi's prophecy about God sending "Elijah the prophet before the coming . . . day of the LORD" (4:5) applied to John the Baptist (Mat. 11:14; 17:10–13; Mark 9:11–13). The last book of the Bible adds that the spirit of Elijah will appear again before the second coming of Christ (Rev. 11:3–6).

In addition to these three clear N.T. references to Malachi, the prophet's condemnation of unjust divorce (2:14–16) anticipates the strict N.T. teaching on this topic (Mat. 5:31–32; 19:3–10; Mark 10:2–12; Rom. 7:1–3; 1 Cor. 7:10–16,39). Malachi's prophecy about the appearance of the future Messiah (3:1–6; 4:1–3) encompasses both the first and second comings of Christ.

Reading Malachi

In order to read the entire Old Testament in one year, the book of Malachi should be read in 2 days, according to the following schedule: ☐ 1–2 ☐ 3–4

NOTES

Fall of Edom shows God's love

1 THE BURDEN of the word of the
LORD to Israel [a]by Malachi.
2 [a]I have loved you, saith the LORD.
Yet ye say, Wherein hast thou loved
us? *Was* not Esau Jacob's brother?
saith the LORD: yet [b]I loved Jacob,
3 And I hated Esau, and [c]laid his
mountains and his heritage waste for
the dragons of the wilderness.
4 Whereas Edom saith, We are im-
poverished, but we will return and
build the desolate places; thus saith
the LORD of hosts, They shall build, but
I will throw down; and they shall call
them, The border of wickedness, and,
The people against whom the LORD
hath indignation for ever.
5 And your eyes shall see, and ye
shall say, [d]The LORD will be magnified
[b,c]from the border of Israel.

The sins of the priesthood

6 ¶ A son [e]honoureth *his* father,
and a servant his master: [f]if then I *be*
a father, where *is* mine honour? and if
I *be* a master, where *is* my fear? saith
the LORD of hosts unto you, O priests,
that despise my name. [g]And ye say,
Wherein have we despised thy name?
7 [d]Ye offer [h]polluted bread upon
mine altar; and ye say, Wherein have
we polluted thee? In that ye say, [i]The
table of the LORD *is* contemptible.
8 And [j]if ye offer the blind [e]for
sacrifice, *is it* not evil? and if ye offer
the lame and sick, *is it* not evil? offer
it now unto thy governor; will he be
pleased with thee, or [k]accept thy per-
son? saith the LORD of hosts.
9 And now, I pray you, beseech
[f]God that he will be gracious unto us:
[l]this hath been [g]by your means: will
he regard your persons? saith the LORD
of hosts.
10 Who *is there* even among you that
would shut the doors *for nought?* [m]nei-
ther do ye kindle *fire* on mine altar for
nought. I have no pleasure in you, saith
the LORD of hosts, [n]neither will I ac-
cept an offering at your hand.
11 For [o]from the rising of the sun
even unto the going down of the same
my name *shall be* great [p]among the
Gentiles; [q]and in every place [r]in-
cense *shall be* offered unto my name,
and a pure offering: [s]for my name
shall be great among the heathen, saith
the LORD of hosts.
12 ¶ But ye have profaned it, in that
ye say, [t]The table of the LORD *is* pol-
luted; and the fruit thereof, *even* his
meat, *is* contemptible.
13 Ye said also, Behold, what a
weariness *is it!* [h]and ye have snuffed

1:2 [a]Deut. 7:8 & 10:15 [b]Rom. 9:13
1:3 [c]Jer. 49:18 Ezek. 35:3 Obad. 10
1:5 [d]Ps. 35:27
1:6 [e]Ex. 20:12 [f]Luke 6:46 [g]ch. 2:14
1:7 [h]Deut. 15:21 [i]Ezek. 41:22
1:8 [j]Lev. 22:22 [k]Job 42:8
1:9 [l]Hos. 13:9
1:10 [m]1 Cor. 9:13 [n]Is. 1:11
1:11 [o]Is. 59:19 [p]Is. 60:3,5 [q]1 Tim. 2:8 [r]Rev. 8:3 [s]Is. 66:19
1:12 [t]ver. 7

[a] Heb. *by the hand of Malachi* [b] Or, *upon* [c] Heb. *from upon* [d] Or, *Bring unto* [e] Heb. *to sacrifice* [f] Heb. *the face of God* [g] Heb. *from your hand* [h] Or, *whereas ye might have blown it away*

1:1 MALACHI. Malachi prophesied about one hundred years after the first exiles had returned from Babylon to their homeland. Although the people had initially responded to their restoration with a zeal for God, their commitment to Him diminished as the years went by. About 430 B.C., Malachi confronted the people with their lack of trust in God, their insincere worship, and their refusal to obey God's law.

1:2 I HAVE LOVED YOU. The people were doubting that God really loved them; having experienced trouble, they accused God of being unfaithful to His covenant promises. The Lord insisted that He had cared for them over the years in a special way; in reality, it was Israel who had failed to love and honor God by their disobedience to His law (vv. 6–8).

1:3 I HATED ESAU. The term "hated" means only that God chose Esau's brother Jacob, and not Esau himself, to inherit the covenant promises and to be one of the forefathers of the chosen people from whom the Messiah would come. God's rejection of Esau and his descendants as the progenitors of the Messiah had nothing to do with their eternal destiny. God's desire was that Esau and his people would serve Him and thus also receive His blessing (see Gen. 25:23, note; Rom. 9:13, note).

1:6–8 O PRIESTS, THAT DESPISE MY NAME. Malachi brings an accusation against the priests of the land. (1) They were showing contempt for God by offering to Him animals that were crippled or sick, contrary to the law of God (Lev. 22:22). (2) As believers in Christ we must give to God the best we have. Our whole life should be a living sacrifice to Him (Rom. 12:1). The time we spend in prayer and Bible study should be at the choice time of the day, not when we are too tired to do anything else. (3) "The table of the LORD" was the table used for slaughtering the sacrifices.

1:11 MY NAME *SHALL BE* GREAT AMONG THE GENTILES. Malachi predicts a time when people from the nations of the world would worship God in sincerity and truth (cf. Is. 45:22–25; 49:5–7; 59:19). The God of the Scriptures would be known around the world. This prophecy is being partially fulfilled now as churches send forth missionaries into all the world to preach the gospel. One way to demonstrate the genuineness of our faith is by assisting in God's worldwide missionary outreach.

at it, saith the LORD of hosts; and ye
brought *that which was* torn, and the
lame, and the sick; thus ye brought an
offering: [u]should I accept this of your
hand? saith the LORD.
14 But cursed *be* [v]the deceiver,
[i]which hath in his flock a male, and
voweth, and sacrificeth unto the Lord
a corrupt thing: for [w]I *am* a great King,
saith the LORD of hosts, and my name
is dreadful among the heathen.

The warning to the priesthood

2 AND NOW, O ye priests, this commandment *is* for you.
2 [x]If ye will not hear, and if ye will
not lay *it* to heart, to give glory unto my
name, saith the LORD of hosts, I will
even send a curse upon you, and I will
curse your blessings: yea, I have
cursed them already, because ye do not
lay *it* to heart.
3 Behold, I will [j]corrupt your seed,
and [k]spread dung upon your faces,
even the dung of your solemn feasts;
and [l]*one* shall [y]take you away
with it.
4 And ye shall know that I have
sent this commandment unto you, that
my covenant might be with Levi, saith
the LORD of hosts.
5 [z]My covenant was with him of
life and peace; and I gave them to him
[a]*for* the fear wherewith he feared me,
and was afraid before my name.
6 [b]The law of truth was in his
mouth, and iniquity was not found in
his lips: he walked with me in peace
Mat. 7:21-23 and equity, and did [c]turn many away
from iniquity.

1:13 [u]Lev. 22:20
1:14 [v]ver. 8 [w]Ps. 47:2 1 Tim. 6:15
2:2 [x]Deut. 28:15
2:3 [y]1 Ki. 14:10
2:5 [z]Num. 25:12 Ezek. 34:25 [a]Deut. 33:9
2:6 [b]Deut. 33:10 [c]Jer. 23:22 Jas. 5:20
2:7 [d]Deut. 17:9 [e]Gal. 4:14
2:8 [f]Jer. 18:15 [g]Neh. 13:29
2:9 [h]1 Sam. 2:30
2:10 [i]1 Cor. 8:6 [j]Job 31:15
2:11 [k]Ezra 9:1 Neh. 13:23
2:12 [l]Neh. 13:29

7 [d]For the priest's lips should keep
knowledge, and they should seek the
law at his mouth: [e]for he *is* the messenger of the LORD of hosts.
8 But ye are departed out of the
way; ye [f]have caused many to
[m]stumble at the law; [g]ye have corrupted the covenant of Levi, saith the
LORD of hosts.
9 Therefore [h]have I also made you
contemptible and base before all the
people, according as ye have not kept
my ways, but [n,o]have been partial in
the law.

The warning to the unfaithful

10 [i]Have we not all one father?
[j]hath not one God created us? why do
we deal treacherously every man
against his brother, by profaning the
covenant of our fathers?
11 ¶ Judah hath dealt treacherously, and an abomination is committed in
Israel and in Jerusalem; for Judah hath
profaned the holiness of the LORD
which he [p]loved, [k]and hath married
the daughter of a strange god.
12 The LORD will cut off the man
that doeth this, [q]the master and the
scholar, out of the tabernacles of Jacob, [l]and him that offereth an offering
unto the LORD of hosts.
13 And this have ye done again,
covering the altar of the LORD with

[i] Or, *in whose flock is* [j] Or, *reprove* [k] Heb. *scatter* [l] Or, *it shall take you away to it* [m] Or, *fall in the law* [n] Or, *lifted up the face against* [o] Heb. *accepted faces* [p] Or, *ought to love* [q] Or, *him that waketh, and him that answereth*

2:1–4 O YE PRIESTS. The priests had corrupted the ministry to which God had called them. They did not fear Him or revere His name. They failed to proclaim His word and to live a good and righteous life. For this God would send terrible punishment upon them; He would curse them and their ministry.

2:4–6 MY COVENANT MIGHT BE WITH LEVI. The priests were to be chosen from the tribe of Levi. Here God used Levi and his faithful descendants as examples of what ministers should be. Ministers today must have the same qualities mentioned in these verses. They must show love and respect for God, live honestly and righteously, preach the truth, and by their example and word turn many from sin (see article on MORAL QUALIFICATIONS FOR OVERSEERS, p. 1908).

2:9 BEEN PARTIAL IN THE LAW. The priests were showing partiality to the rich and influential, allowing them to continue in their unjust and sinful ways and failing to confront them with God's word of warning. Pastoral leaders must preach the whole counsel of God (see Acts 20:27), proclaiming His righteous demands to all the people. To preach the blessings of the Lord God and omit His righteous requirements for us is an abomination to Him.

2:11–16 AN ABOMINATION IS COMMITTED. Malachi rebukes the people for a double transgression of God's law: divorcing their wives and marrying pagan women (see next two notes).

2:11 MARRIED THE DAUGHTER OF A STRANGE GOD. The men were marrying pagan women who served other gods, a practice forbidden in the law of Moses (see Ex. 34:15–16; Deut. 7:3–4; 1 Ki. 11:1–6). The N.T. states that believers are to marry only believers (see 1 Cor. 7:39). For a Christian to marry someone not committed to the Lord opens him or her to the possibility of being influenced to depart from the Lord and their children influenced against commitment to Him.

tears, with weeping, and with crying out, insomuch that he regardeth not the offering any more, or receiveth *it* with good will at your hand.

14 ¶ Yet ye say, Wherefore? Because the LORD hath been witness between thee and [m]the wife of thy youth, against whom thou hast dealt treacherously: [n]yet *is* she thy companion, and the wife of thy covenant.

15 And [o]did not he make one? Yet had he the [r]residue of the spirit. And wherefore one? That he might seek [p]a[s] godly seed. Therefore take heed to your spirit, and let none deal [t]treacherously against the wife of his youth.

16 For [q]the LORD, the God of Israel, saith [u]that he hateth [v]putting away: for *one* covereth violence with his garment, saith the LORD of hosts: therefore take heed to your spirit, that ye deal not treacherously.

The sending of the Messiah

17 ¶ [r]Ye have wearied the LORD with your words. Yet ye say, Wherein have we wearied *him?* When ye say, Every one that doeth evil *is* good in the sight of the LORD, and he delighteth in them; or, Where *is* the God of judgment?

3 BEHOLD, [s]I will send my messenger, and he shall [t]prepare the way before me: and the Lord, whom ye seek, shall suddenly come to his temple, [u]even the messenger of the covenant, whom ye delight in: behold, [v]he shall come, saith the LORD of hosts.

2 But who may abide [w]the day of his coming? and [x]who shall stand when he appeareth? for [y]he *is* like a refiner's fire, and like fullers' soap:

3 And [z]he shall sit *as* a refiner and purifier of silver: and he shall purify the sons of Levi, and purge them as gold and silver, that they may [a]offer unto the LORD an offering in righteousness.

4 Then [b]shall the offering of Judah and Jerusalem be pleasant unto the LORD, as in the days of old, and as in [w]former years.

5 And I will come near to you to judgment; and I will be a swift witness against the sorcerers, and against the adulterers, [c]and against false swearers, and against those that [x]oppress the hireling in *his* wages, the widow, and the fatherless, and that turn aside the stranger *from his right,* and fear not me, saith the LORD of hosts.

The sins of the people

6 For I *am* the LORD, [d]I change not; [e]therefore ye sons of Jacob are not consumed.

7 ¶ Even from the days of [f]your fathers ye are gone away from mine ordinances, and have not kept *them.* [g]Return unto me, and I will return unto you, saith the LORD of hosts. [h]But ye said, Wherein shall we return?

8 ¶ Will a man rob God? Yet ye have

2:14 [m]Prov. 5:18 [n]Prov. 2:17
2:15 [o]Mat. 19:4 [p]Ezra 9:2 1 Cor. 7:14
2:16 [q]Deut. 24:1 Mat. 5:32
2:17 [r]Is. 43:24
3:1 [s]Mat. 11:10 Luke 1:76 [t]Is. 40:3 [u]Is. 63:9 [v]Hag. 2:7
3:2 [w]ch. 4:1 [x]Rev. 6:17 [y]Is. 4:4 Mat. 3:10
3:3 [z]Is. 1:25 [a]1 Pet. 2:5
3:4 [b]ch. 1:11
3:5 [c]Zech. 5:4 Jas. 5:4
3:6 [d]Num. 23:19 Rom. 11:29 Jas. 1:17 [e]Lam. 3:22
3:7 [f]Acts 7:51 [g]Zech. 1:3 [h]ch. 1:6

[r] Or, *excellency* [s] Heb. *a seed of God* [t] Or, *unfaithfully* [u] Or, *if he hate* her, *put* her *away* [v] Heb. *to put away* [w] Or, *ancient* [x] Or, *defraud*

2:14 THE WIFE OF THY YOUTH. Many men were being unfaithful to the wives whom they had married when they were young; they were seeking to divorce them, only because they wanted to marry someone else. The Lord detested this kind of selfish action, stating that He had made a husband and his wife one (v. 15). Because of their sin, God had turned His back on the transgressors and refused to hear their prayers (vv. 13–14).

2:16 HE HATETH PUTTING AWAY. God hates divorce that is initiated for selfish purposes; this kind of divorce is like one covering "violence with his garment," indicating that unjust divorce is equal in God's sight to gross injustice, cruelty, and murder (see Mat. 19:9, note on the N.T. teaching on divorce).

3:1 I WILL SEND MY MESSENGER. In answer to the people's skepticism, Malachi emphasizes the certainty of the Messiah's coming. Before the Messiah came, He would send a messenger to prepare the way. This prophecy was fulfilled when John the Baptist came as the forerunner of Jesus Christ (see Mat. 11:10; Mark 1:2; Luke 1:76; 7:27).

3:1–5 THE MESSENGER OF THE COVENANT. This "messenger" is Jesus the Messiah. The first and second comings of Christ are united in this passage.

3:2 THE DAY OF HIS COMING. The ultimate fulfillment of this verse will be at the second coming of Christ, when He will purify (v. 3) and judge (v. 5) Israel. He will purge out all the wicked in the land; only the righteous will remain (cf. Is. 1:25; Ezek. 22:17–22).

3:8 WILL A MAN ROB GOD? The people were robbing God by failing to bring to Him their tithes (one-tenth of their income). Tithing was required of the people in the law of Moses (Lev. 27:30). (1) God threatened to curse those who selfishly refused to give (vv. 8–9) and to bless those who supported His work (vv. 10–12; see next note). (2) N.T. believers are obligated to give in order to support the work of the Lord both at home and on the mission field (see 2 Cor. 8:2, note).

robbed me. But ye say, Wherein have
we robbed thee? [i]In tithes and offer-
ings.
9 Ye *are* cursed with a curse: for ye
have robbed me, *even* this whole na-
tion.
10 [j]Bring ye all the tithes into
[k]the storehouse, that there may be
meat in mine house, and prove me now
herewith, saith the LORD of hosts, if I
will not open you the [l]windows of
heaven, and [m]pour[y] you out a bless-
ing, that *there shall* not *be room* enough
to receive it.
11 And I will rebuke [n]the devourer
for your sakes, and he shall not [z]de-
stroy the fruits of your ground; neither
shall your vine cast her fruit before the
time in the field, saith the LORD of
hosts.
12 And all nations shall call you
blessed: for ye shall be [o]a delight-
some land, saith the LORD of hosts.
13 ¶ [p]Your words have been stout
against me, saith the LORD. Yet ye say,
What have we spoken *so much* against
thee?
14 [q]Ye have said, It *is* vain to serve
God: and what profit *is it* that we have
kept [a]his ordinance, and that we have
walked [b]mournfully before the LORD
of hosts?
15 And now [r]we call the proud
happy; yea, they that work wickedness
[c]are set up; yea, *they that* [s]tempt God
are even delivered.
16 ¶ Then they [t]that feared the
LORD [u]spake often one to another: and
the LORD hearkened, and heard *it,* and
[v]a book of remembrance was written
before him for them that feared the
LORD, and that thought upon his name.
17 And [w]they shall be mine, saith
the LORD of hosts, in that day when I
make up my [x]jewels;[d] and [y]I will
spare them, as a man spareth his own
son that serveth him.
18 [z]Then shall ye return, and dis-
cern between the righteous and the
wicked, between him that serveth God
and him that serveth him not.

The coming day of the LORD

4 FOR, BEHOLD, [a]the day cometh,
that shall burn as an oven; and all
[b]the proud, yea, and all that do wick-
edly, shall be [c]stubble: and the day
that cometh shall burn them up, saith
the LORD of hosts, that it shall [d]leave
them neither root nor branch.
2 ¶ But unto you that [e]fear my
name shall the [f]Sun of righteousness
arise with healing in his wings; and ye
shall go forth, and grow up as calves of
the stall.
3 [g]And ye shall tread down the
wicked; for they shall be ashes under
the soles of your feet in the day that I Mat. 16:27-28
shall do *this,* saith the LORD of hosts.
4 ¶ Remember ye the [h]law of Mo-
ses my servant, which I commanded

3:8 [i]Neh. 13:10 **3:10** [j]Prov. 3:9 [k]1 Chr. 26:20 2 Chr. 31:11 Neh. 10:38 [l]Gen. 7:11 2 Ki. 7:2 [m]2 Chr. 31:10 **3:11** [n]Amos 4:9 **3:12** [o]Dan. 8:9 **3:13** [p]ch. 2:17 **3:14** [q]Job 21:14 **3:15** [r]Ps. 73:12 [s]Ps. 95:9 **3:16** [t]Ps. 66:16 [u]Heb. 3:13 [v]Ps. 56:8 Is. 65:6 Rev. 20:12 **3:17** [w]Ex. 19:5 Deut. 7:6 Ps. 135:4 [x]Is. 62:3 [y]Ps. 103:13 **3:18** [z]Ps. 58:11 **4:1** [a]Joel 2:31 2 Pet. 3:7 [b]ch. 3:18 [c]Obad. 18 [d]Amos 2:9 **4:2** [e]ch. 3:16 [f]Luke 1:78 Eph. 5:14 Rev. 2:28 **4:3** [g]Mic. 7:10 **4:4** [h]Ex. 20:3

[y] Heb. *empty out* [z] Heb. *corrupt* [a] Heb. *his observation* [b] Heb. *in black* [c] Heb. *are built* [d] Or, *special treasure*

3:10 POUR YOU OUT A BLESSING. If the people would repent, return to God, and, as a sign of their repentance, begin to support God's work and ministers with their tithes and offerings, God would abundantly bless them. God expects His people to demonstrate their love for and devotion to Him and His work by giving tithes and offerings to further His kingdom (see article on TITHES AND OFFERINGS, p. 1388). The blessings that accompany faithfulness in financial giving will come both in this life and in the hereafter.

3:14 IT *IS* VAIN TO SERVE GOD. The people believed that mere external worship of God was enough to gain His blessing, but it was not. Thus they felt it was useless to serve Him. They failed to see that their hearts were not right before Him (see article on WORSHIP, p. 730).

3:16 THEY THAT FEARED THE LORD. In contrast to the majority, there were still a few who honored God. (1) The Lord promises to keep in heaven a permanent record of those who honor and fear Him by living faithfully before Him. They will not be forgotten. (2) This passage assures us that God observes and records our faithfulness to and love for Him. When we stand before Him in heaven, He will remember our devoted commitment and will treat us accordingly.

4:1 THE DAY COMETH. "The day" refers both to Christ's first coming and to His second coming. The prophet speaks as though the two comings would occur as a single event; this blending is seen often in O.T. prophecy (see Zech. 9:9–10, notes). Those committed to pride and wrongdoing will be excluded from God's kingdom (cf. 3:2–3; Is. 66:15; Zeph. 1:18; 3:8; 1 Cor. 6:9–11).

4:2 BUT UNTO YOU THAT FEAR MY NAME. The day of the Lord will also mean salvation and deliverance for all who love and serve Him. In His kingdom God's glory and righteousness will shine like the sun, bringing to His faithful people the ultimate in goodness, blessing, salvation, and healing. Everything will be made right, and God's people will leap for joy like calves released from the stall.

4:4 REMEMBER YE THE LAW OF MOSES. Malachi tells the people of God that to survive the day of the Lord, they must observe His laws. Faith in God always includes an attitude of obedience to

TITHES AND OFFERINGS

Mal. 3:10 "Bring ye all the tithes into the storehouse, that there may be meat in mine house, and prove me now herewith, saith the LORD *of hosts, if I will not open you the windows of heaven, and pour you out a blessing, that* there shall *not* be room *enough* to receive it."

DEFINITION OF TITHES AND OFFERINGS. The Hebrew word for "tithe" (*ma'ser*) literally means "a tenth part." (1) In the law of God, the Israelites were required to give one-tenth of the production of the land, the livestock, and their income as a recognition that God had blessed them (see Lev. 27:30–32; Num. 18:21,26; Deut. 14:22–29; see Lev. 27:30, note); the tithe was used primarily for the expenses of the worship of the Lord and for the support of the priests. God held His people responsible to manage the resources He had given them in the promised land (cf. Mat. 25:15, note; Luke 19:13, note).

(2) At the heart of tithing was the notion that God owns everything (Ex. 19:5; Ps. 24:1; 50:10–12; Hag. 2:8). Humans are created by Him, and they owe to Him every breath they take (Gen. 1:26–27; Acts 17:28). Thus, no one has anything that he or she has not first of all received from the Lord (Job 1:21; John 3:27; 1 Cor. 4:7). In the laws about tithing, God was simply commanding them to return to Him what He had first given to them.

(3) In addition to tithes, the Israelites were required to bring numerous offerings to the Lord, mostly in the form of sacrifices. The book of Leviticus describes various ritual offerings: the burnt offering (Lev. 1; 6:8–13), the meat offering (Lev. 2; 6:14–23), the peace offering (Lev. 3; 7:11–21), the sin offering (Lev. 4:1—5:13; 6:24–30), and the guilt or trespass offering (Lev. 5:14—6:7; 7:1–10).

(4) In addition to these prescribed offerings, the Israelites could offer freewill offerings to the Lord. Some of these were repeated (see Lev. 22:18–23; Num. 15:3; Deut. 12:6,17), while others were one-time occasions. For example, when the Israelites undertook the building of the tabernacle at Mount Sinai, the people gave freely for this tent and its furnishings (see Ex. 35:20–29); they were so excited about this project that Moses had to tell them to stop giving to it (Ex. 36:3–7). In the time of Joash, the high priest Jehoiada made a chest in which people could put freewill offerings to finance needed repairs on the temple, and they gave generously (2 Ki. 12:9–10). Similarly, in the time of Hezekiah, people gave freely for the reconstruction work required on the temple (2 Chr. 31:5–19).

(5) There were also numerous times in O.T. history that God's people selfishly held on to their money rather than give it to the Lord in regular tithes and offerings. During the building of the second temple, the Jews seemed to be more interested in building up their own property, while leaving the house of God in ruins. As a result, said Haggai, many of them were suffering financial reverses (Hag. 1:3–6). A similar thing was happening in the time of the prophet Malachi, and once again God was judging His people for refusing to bring in the tithe (Mal. 3:9–12).

STEWARDSHIP OF OUR MONEY. These O.T. examples of tithes and offerings contain important principles about the stewardship of money that are valid for N.T. believers. (1) We must remember that everything we have belongs to the Lord, so that what we do possess is not our own but what God has entrusted to us; we have no rightful ownership of our possessions.

(2) We must decide within our hearts to serve God and not money (Mat. 6:19–24; cf. 2 Cor. 8:1–5). The Bible makes it plain that any greed is a form of idolatry (Col. 3:5).

(3) Our giving must be to advance the kingdom of God, especially the work of the local church and of the spread of the gospel throughout the world (1 Cor. 9:4–14; Phil. 4:15–18; 1 Tim. 5:17–18), to help those who are in need (Prov. 19:17; Gal. 2:10; 2 Cor. 8:14; see article on THE CARE OF THE POOR AND NEEDY, p. 1312), to lay up treasures in heaven (Mat. 6:20), and to learn to fear the Lord (Deut. 14:22–23).

(4) Our giving should always be in proportion to our income. In the O.T. the tithe amounted to one-tenth. Giving less than that was disobedience to the law of God and was in effect robbing God (Mal. 3:8–10). Similarly, the N.T. requires that our giving be in proportion to what God has given us (1 Cor. 16:2; 2 Cor. 8:3,12; see 2 Cor. 8:2, note).

(5) Our giving should be voluntary and generous; this practice is taught in both the O.T. (see Ex. 25:1–2; 2 Chr. 24:8–11) and in the N.T. (see 2 Cor. 8:1–5,11–12). We should not hesitate to give sacrificially (2 Cor. 8:3), for that is the spirit in which the Lord Jesus gave Himself for us (see 2 Cor. 8:9, note). Far more important to God than the monetary value of the gift is the sacrifice involved (see Luke 21:1–4, note).

(6) Our giving should be cheerful (2 Cor. 9:7). Both the example of the Israelites in the O.T. (Ex. 35:21–29; 2 Chr. 24:10) and the Macedonian Christians in the N.T. (2 Cor. 8:1–5) serve as models for us.

(7) God has promised to reward us according to how we have given to Him (see Deut. 15:4; Mal. 3:10–12; Mat. 19:21; 1 Tim. 6:18–19; see 2 Cor. 9:6, note).

unto him [i]in Horeb for all Israel, *with*
[j]the statutes and judgments.
5 ¶ Behold, I will send you [k]Elijah
the prophet [l]before the coming of the
great and dreadful day of the LORD:
6 And he shall turn the heart of the
fathers to the children, and the heart of
the children to their fathers, lest I
come and [m]smite the earth with [n]a
curse.

4:4 [i]Deut. 4:10 [j]Ps. 147:19
4:5 [k]Mat. 11:14 Luke 1:17 [l]Joel 2:31
4:6 [m]Zech. 14:12 [n]Zech. 5:3

the Lord from the heart. Believers in Christ are still required to follow the moral demands of the O.T. law as well as the commandments of Christ (see Mat. 5:17, note; see article on THE OLD TESTAMENT LAW, p. 124).

4:5 I WILL SEND YOU ELIJAH THE PROPHET. Malachi prophesies that Elijah would come and minister before the coming of the day of the Lord. The N.T. reveals that this prophecy refers to John the Baptist (Mat. 11:7–14), who, "in the spirit and power of Elias" (see Luke 1:17, note), prepared the way for the Messiah. Some also believe that Elijah will again come during the tribulation period and will be one of the two witnesses mentioned in Revelation (see Rev. 11:3, note).

4:6 TURN THE HEART OF THE FATHERS TO THE CHILDREN. The future ministry of the coming prophet is described in terms of putting families right with God and each other. John the Baptist preached to this end (see Luke 1:17). (1) There can be no blessing from God or abundant life in the Spirit if God's people do not make family authority, love, and faithfulness absolute priorities in the church. The purity and righteousness of the home must be maintained or our congregations will fail.

(2) The one most responsible for accomplishing this task is the father of the family. Fathers must love their children by praying for them (see John 17:1, note), spending time with them, pointing out the ungodly ways of the world, and diligently teaching them God's Word and righteous standards (see article on PARENTS AND CHILDREN, p. 1880).

(3) Pastors must also make this goal of John the Baptist their own purpose for their ministry, thus preparing the church for the Lord's coming (see Luke 1:17, note).

FROM MALACHI TO CHRIST

THE PERSIAN PERIOD 450-330 B.C.

For about 100 years after Nehemiah's time the Persians controlled Judah, but the Jews were allowed to carry on their religious observances and were not interfered with. During this time Judah was ruled by high priests who were responsible to the Jewish government.

Rule of Alexander the Great

THE HELLENISTIC PERIOD 330-166 B.C.

In 333 B.C. the Persian armies stationed in Macedonia were defeated by Alexander the Great. He was convinced that Greek culture was the one force that could unify the world. Alexander permitted the Jews to observe their laws and even granted them exemption from tribute or tax during their sabbath years. The Greek conquest prepared the way for the translation of the OT into Greek (Septuagint version) c. 250 B.C.

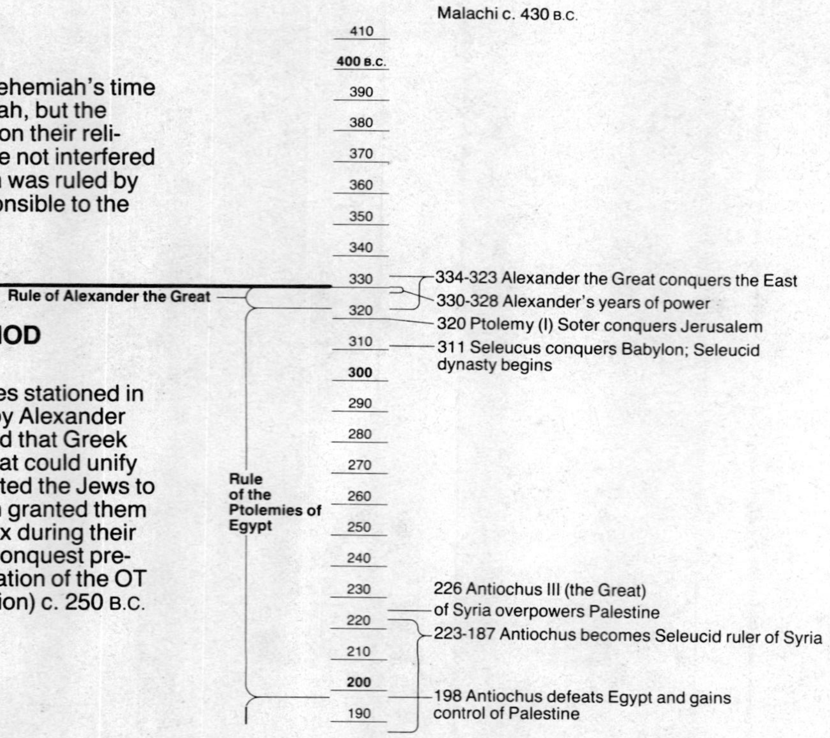

Rule of the Ptolemies of Egypt

	Malachi c. 430 B.C.
410	
400 B.C.	
390	
380	
370	
360	
350	
340	
330	334-323 Alexander the Great conquers the East; 330-328 Alexander's years of power
320	320 Ptolemy (I) Soter conquers Jerusalem
310	311 Seleucus conquers Babylon; Seleucid dynasty begins
300	
290	
280	
270	
260	
250	
240	
230	226 Antiochus III (the Great) of Syria overpowers Palestine
220	223-187 Antiochus becomes Seleucid ruler of Syria
210	
200	198 Antiochus defeats Egypt and gains control of Palestine
190	

THE HASMONEAN PERIOD 166-63 B.C.

When this historical period began, the Jews were being greatly oppressed. The Ptolemies had been tolerant of the Jews and their religious practices but the Seleucid rulers were determined to force Hellenism on them. Copies of the Scriptures were ordered destroyed and laws were enforced with extreme cruelty. The oppressed Jews revolted, led by Judas the Maccabee.

THE ROMAN PERIOD 63 B.C. . . .

In the year 63 B.C. Pompey, the Roman general, captured Jerusalem, and the provinces of Palestine became subject to Rome. The local government was entrusted part of the time to princes and the rest of the time to procurators who were appointed by the emperors. Herod the Great was ruler of all Palestine at the time of Christ's birth.

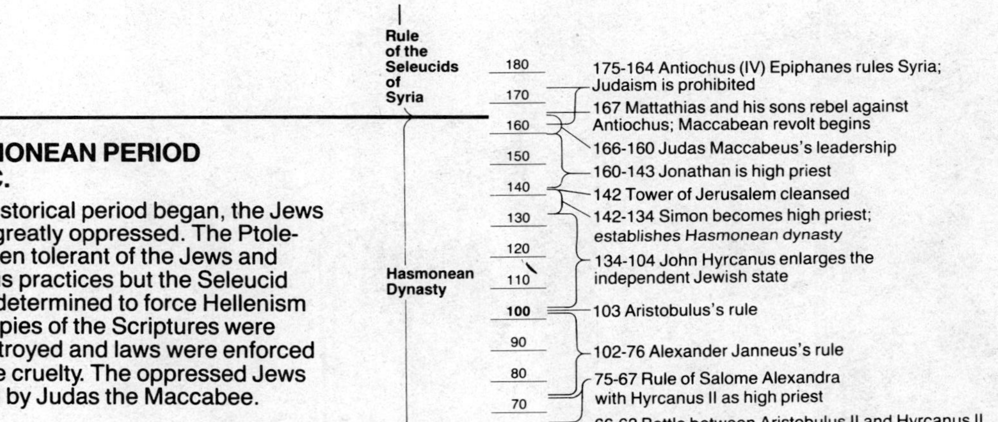

THE NEW TESTAMENT

ST. MATTHEW

Outline

I. Introduction to the Messiah (1:1—4:11)
   A. The Jewish Lineage of Jesus (1:1–17)
   B. His Birth and Flight to Egypt (1:18—2:23)
   C. Prophetic Forerunner to the Messiah (3:1–12)
   D. Baptism of the Messiah (3:13–17)
   E. Temptation of the Messiah (4:1–11)

II. Jesus' Messianic Ministry in and around Galilee (4:12—18:35)
   A. Summary of His Early Galilean Ministry (4:12–25)
   B. Discourse about Discipleship in the Kingdom (5:1—7:29)
   C. Narrative I: Mighty Deeds of the Kingdom (8:1—9:38)
   D. Discourse about the Proclamation of the Kingdom (10:1–42)
   E. Narrative II: The Presence of the Kingdom (11:1—12:50)
   F. Discourse about the Mystery of the Kingdom (13:1–58)
   G. Narrative III: Crisis of the Kingdom (14:1—17:27)
   H. Discourse about Membership in the Kingdom (18:1–35)

III. The Climax of Jesus' Messianic Mission in Judea/Perea and Jerusalem (19:1—26:46)
   A. Jesus' Journey to Jerusalem (19:1—20:34)
   B. Jesus' Last Week at Jerusalem (21:1—26:46)
      1. Triumphal Entry and Cleansing the Temple (21:1–22)
      2. Controversies with the Jews (21:23—22:46)
      3. Denunciations of the Scribes and Pharisees (23:1–39)
      4. Olivet Discourse about the Future of the Kingdom (24:1—25:46)
      5. The Plot to Betray Jesus (26:1–16)
      6. The Last Supper (26:17–30)
      7. Gethsemane (26:31–46)

IV. Jesus' Arrest, Trial, and Crucifixion (26:47—27:66)
   A. The Arrest (26:47–56)
   B. The Trial (26:57—27:26)
   C. The Crucifixion (27:27–56)
   D. The Burial (27:57–66)

V. The Resurrection (28:1–20)
   A. The Women's Glorious Discovery (28:1–10)
   B. False Witnesses (28:11–15)
   C. The Risen Lord's Commission (28:16–20)

Author: Matthew

Theme: Jesus, the Messianic King

Date of Writing: A.D. 60s

Background

This Gospel is appropriately placed first as an introduction to the N.T. and to "the Christ, the Son of the living God" (16:16). Although the author is not identified by name in the Biblical text, the unanimous testimony of all early church fathers (beginning c. A.D. 130) is that this Gospel was written by Matthew, one of Jesus' twelve disciples.

Whereas Mark's Gospel was written for the Romans (see Introduction to Mark) and Luke's Gospel for Theophilus and for all Gentile believers (see Introduction to Luke), Matthew's Gospel was written for Jewish believers. The Jewish background of this Gospel is evident in many ways, including (1) its reliance on O.T. revelation, promises, and prophecy to prove that Jesus was the long-awaited Messiah; (2) its tracing of Jesus' lineage, starting from Abraham (1:1–17); (3) its repeated declaration that Jesus is the "Son of David" (1:1; 9:27; 12:23; 15:22; 20:30–31; 21:9,15; 22:41–45); (4) its use of preferred Jewish terminology such as "kingdom of heaven" (a synonym for "kingdom of God") because of the Jews' reverential reluctance to say the name of God directly; and (5) its reference to Jewish customs without any explanation (unlike the other Gospels).

However, this Gospel is not exclusively Jewish. Like the message of Jesus Himself, Matthew's Gospel was intended ultimately for the whole church, faithfully revealing the universal scope of the gospel (e.g., 2:1–12; 8:11–12; 13:38; 21:43; 28:18–20).

The date and location of its origin are uncertain. However, there are good reasons for believing that Matthew wrote prior to A.D. 70 while in Palestine or Syrian Antioch. Some Bible scholars believe Matthew was the first of the four Gospels to be written; others ascribe that place to the Gospel of Mark.

Purpose

Matthew wrote this Gospel (1) to provide his readers with an eyewitness account of Jesus' life, (2) to assure his readers that Jesus was God's Son and the long-awaited Messiah foretold by the O.T. prophets, and (3) to show that God's kingdom was manifested in and through Jesus in an unprecedented way. Matthew is concerned that his readers understand (1) that Israel for the most part rejected Jesus and His kingdom, refusing to believe because He came as a spiritual rather than as a political Messiah, and (2) that only at the end of the age will Jesus come in glory as the King of kings to judge and rule the nations.

Survey

Matthew presents Jesus as the fulfillment of Israel's prophetic hope. He fulfills O.T. prophecy in His birth (1:22–23), birthplace (2:5–6), return from Egypt (2:15), and residence in Nazareth (2:23); as the One for whom the Messianic forerunner was sent (3:1–3); in the primary location of His public ministry (4:14–16), His healing ministry (8:17), His role as God's servant (12:17–21), His teaching in parables (13:34–35), His triumphal entry into Jerusalem (21:4–5), and His arrest (26:50).

Chs. 5–25 record five major discourses by Jesus and five major narratives about His mighty deeds as Messiah. The five major discourses are: (1) Sermon on the Mount (chs. 5–7), (2) instruction for itinerant proclaimers of the kingdom (ch. 10), (3) parables about the kingdom (ch. 13), (4) the character of true disciples (ch. 18), and (5) the Olivet discourse about the end of the age (chs. 24–25). The five major narratives in this Gospel are: (1) Jesus performs mighty deeds and miracles which testify concerning the reality of the kingdom (chs. 8–9); (2) Jesus further demonstrates the presence of the kingdom (chs. 11–12); (3) proclamation of the kingdom provokes various crises (chs. 14–17); (4) Jesus journeys to Jerusalem and spends his last week there (19:1—26:46); (5) Jesus is arrested, tried, crucified, and raised from the dead (26:47—28:20). The last three verses of the Gospel record Jesus' "Great Commission."

Special Features

Seven major features or emphases characterize this Gospel. (1) It is the most Jewish of the N.T. Gospels. (2) It contains the most systematic arrangement of Jesus' teaching and ministry of healing and deliverance. This led the church in the second century to rely

heavily on it for instructing new converts. (3) The five major discourses contain the most extensive blocks of material in the Gospels on Jesus' teaching (a) during His Galilean ministry, and (b) on the subject of eschatology (the last things). (4) This Gospel specifically identifies events in Jesus' life as fulfilling the O.T. far more often than any other N.T. book. (5) It mentions the kingdom of heaven/kingdom of God twice as often as any other Gospel. (6) Matthew emphasizes (a) the righteous standards of the kingdom (chs. 5–7); (b) the present power of the kingdom over sin, sickness, demons, and even death; and (c) the future triumph of the kingdom in that final victory at the end of the age. (7) It is the only Gospel to mention or predict the church as a future entity belonging to Jesus (16:18; 18:17).

Reading Matthew

In order to read the entire New Testament in one year, the book of Matthew should be read in 44 days, according to the following schedule:
☐ 1 ☐ 2 ☐ 3 ☐ 4 ☐ 5:1–20 ☐ 5:21–48 ☐ 6:1–18 ☐ 6:19—7:6 ☐ 7:7–29 ☐ 8:1–27 ☐ 8:28—9:17 ☐ 9:18–38 ☐ 10:1–23 ☐ 10:24–42 ☐ 11 ☐ 12:1–21 ☐ 12:22–50 ☐ 13:1–23 ☐ 13:24–43 ☐ 13:44—14:12 ☐ 14:13–36 ☐ 15:1–28 ☐ 15:29—16:12 ☐ 16:13—17:13 ☐ 17:14—18:14 ☐ 18:15–35 ☐ 19:1–15 ☐ 19:16—20:16 ☐ 20:17–34 ☐ 21:1–32 ☐ 21:33—22:14 ☐ 22:15–46 ☐ 23 ☐ 24:1–35 ☐ 24:36–51 ☐ 25:1–30 ☐ 25:31–46 ☐ 26:1–30 ☐ 26:31–56 ☐ 26:57–75 ☐ 27:1–26 ☐ 27:26–44 ☐ 27:45–66 ☐ 28

NOTES

The genealogy of Jesus

1:1–17pp — Luke 3:23–38
1:3–6pp — Ruth 4:18–22
1:7–11pp — 1 Chr. 3:10–17

1 THE BOOK of the [a]generation of Jesus Christ, [b]the son of David, [c]the son of Abraham.

2 [d]Abraham begat Isaac; and [e]Isaac begat Jacob; and [f]Jacob begat Judas and his brethren;

3 And [g]Judas begat Phares and Zara of Thamar; and [h]Phares begat Esrom; and Esrom begat Aram;

4 And Aram begat Aminadab; and Aminadab begat Naasson; and Naasson begat Salmon;

5 And Salmon begat Booz of Rachab; and Booz begat Obed of Ruth; and Obed begat Jesse;

6 And [i]Jesse begat David the king; and [j]David the king begat Solomon of her *that had been the wife* of Urias;

7 And [k]Solomon begat Roboam; and Roboam begat Abia; and Abia begat Asa;

8 And Asa begat Josaphat; and Josaphat begat Joram; and Joram begat Ozias;

9 And Ozias begat Joatham; and Joatham begat Achaz; and Achaz begat Ezekias;

10 And [l]Ezekias begat Manasses; and Manasses begat Amon; and Amon begat Josias;

11 And [m]Josias[a] begat Jechonias and his brethren, about the time they were [n]carried away to Babylon:

12 And after they were brought to Babylon, [o]Jechonias begat Salathiel; and Salathiel begat [p]Zorobabel;

13 And Zorobabel begat Abiud; and Abiud begat Eliakim; and Eliakim begat Azor;

14 And Azor begat Sadoc; and Sadoc begat Achim; and Achim begat Eliud;

15 And Eliud begat Eleazar; and Eleazar begat Matthan; and Matthan begat Jacob;

16 And Jacob begat Joseph the husband of Mary, of whom was born Jesus, who is called Christ.

17 So all the generations from Abraham to David *are* fourteen generations; and from David until the carrying away into Babylon *are* fourteen generations; and from the carrying away into Babylon unto Christ *are* fourteen generations.

The birth of Jesus

18 ¶ Now the [q]birth of Jesus Christ was on this wise: When as his mother Mary was espoused to Joseph, before they came together, she was found with child [r]of the Holy Ghost.

19 Then Joseph her husband, being a just *man,* and not willing [s]to make her a public example, was minded to put her away privily.

20 But while he thought on these things, behold, the angel of the Lord appeared unto him in a dream, saying, Joseph, thou son of David, fear not to take unto thee Mary thy wife: [t]for

1:1 [a]Luke 3:23 [b]Ps. 132:11 Is. 11:1 Jer. 23:5 ch. 22:42 John 7:42 Acts 2:30 Rom. 1:3 [c]Gen. 12:3
1:2 [d]Gen. 21:2 [e]Gen. 25:26 [f]Gen. 29:35
1:3 [g]Gen. 38:27 [h]Ruth 4:18 1 Chr. 2:5
1:6 [i]1 Sam. 16:1 & 17:12 [j]2 Sam. 12:24
1:7 [k]1 Chr. 3:10
1:10 [l]2 Ki. 20:21 1 Chr. 3:13
1:11 [m]See 1 Chr. 3:15, 16 [n]2 Ki. 24:14-16 & 25:11 2 Chr. 36:10 Jer. 27:20 & 52:11,15 Dan. 1:2
1:12 [o]1 Chr. 3:17 [p]Ezra 3:2 Neh. 12:1 Hag. 1:1
1:18 [q]Luke 1:27 [r]Luke 1:35
1:19 [s]Deut. 24:1
1:20 [t]Luke 1:35

[a] Some read *Josias begat Jakim, and Jakim begat Jechonias*

1:1 GENERATION OF JESUS CHRIST. Matthew's Gospel opens with this genealogy which traces Jesus' legal and ancestral lineage through the paternal line (the line of Joseph), as was customary with the Jews (v. 16). Although Joseph was not Jesus' biological father (v. 20), he was His legal father. Since God had promised that the Messiah would be a descendant of Abraham (Gen. 12:3; 22:18; Gal. 3:16) and David (2 Sam. 7:12–19; Jer. 23:5), Matthew traces Jesus' legal lineage back to these two men in order to demonstrate for the Jews that Jesus had the proper genealogy.

1:1 CHRIST. The word "Christ" (Gk. *christos*) signifies "anointed"; it is the Greek equivalent of the Hebrew term "Messiah" (Dan. 9:25–26). (1) From the beginning Matthew affirms that Jesus is God's Anointed One, anointed with the Holy Spirit (cf. Is. 61:1; Luke 4:18; John 3:34; Acts 10:38). (2) He was anointed as Prophet to bring knowledge and truth (Deut. 18:15); as Priest to offer the sacrifice and cancel the guilt (Ps. 110:4; Heb. 10:10–14); as King to rule, guide, and establish the kingdom of righteousness (Zech. 9:9).

1:1 SON OF DAVID. (1) Matthew establishes that Jesus was a legal descendant of David by tracing the genealogy of Joseph, who was of the house of David. Although Jesus was conceived by the Holy Spirit, He was still formally registered as Joseph's son and, legally, a son of David. (2) Luke's genealogy traces the lineage of Jesus through the males in Mary's line. Luke stresses that Jesus is of the flesh and blood (i.e., offspring) of Mary and therefore one of us (cf. Rom. 1:3). Thus, the Gospel writers assert both Jesus' legal and biological right to the Messiahship.

1:16 MARY ... JESUS. The virgin birth of Jesus is safeguarded in the genealogy. Notice the word "begat" is used of all the names down to Joseph, but then the statement is altered. It is not said that Joseph begat Jesus, but rather Joseph is the husband of Mary, "of whom was born Jesus" (see v. 23, note).

that which is [b]conceived in her is of
the Holy Ghost.
21 [u]And she shall bring forth a
son, and thou shalt call his name
[c]JESUS: for [v]he shall save his people
from their sins.
22 Now all this was done, that it
might be fulfilled which was spoken of
the Lord by the prophet, saying,
23 [w]Behold, a virgin shall be with
child, and shall bring forth a son, and
[d]they shall call his name Emmanuel,
which being interpreted is, God
with us.
24 Then Joseph being raised from
sleep did as the angel of the Lord had
bidden him, and took unto him his wife:
25 And knew her not till she had
brought forth [x]her firstborn son: and
he called his name JESUS.

1:21 [u]Luke 1:31 [v]Acts. 4:12 & 5:31 & 13:23,38
1:23 [w]Is. 7:14
1:25 [x]Ex:13:2 Luke 2:7,21
2:1 [y]Luke 2:4,6 [z]Gen. 25:6 1 Ki. 4:30
2:2 [a]Luke 2:11 [b]Num. 24:17 Is. 60:3
2:4 [c]2 Chr. 36:14 [d]2 Chr. 34:13 [e]Mal. 2:7

The coming of the wise men

2 NOW WHEN [y]Jesus was born in
Bethlehem of Judaea in the days of
Herod the king, behold, there came
wise men [z]from the east to Jerusalem,
2 Saying, [a]Where is he that is born
King of the Jews? for we have seen
[b]his star in the east, and are come to
worship him.
3 When Herod the king had heard
these things, he was troubled, and all
Jerusalem with him.
4 And when he had gathered all
[c]the chief priests and [d]scribes of the
people together, [e]he demanded of
them where Christ should be born.
5 And they said unto him, In Bethle-

[b] Gk. *begotten* [c] i.e. *Saviour*
[d] Or, *his name shall be called*

1:21 JESUS. Jesus is the Greek form of the Hebrew word *yeshua* (Joshua), meaning "The Lord is salvation" (see Josh. 1:1, note). This describes the future task of Mary's son and is the initial promise of the gospel. Jesus as Savior "shall save his people from their sins." Sin is the greatest enemy of the human race, destroying one's soul and life. Through the atoning death of Jesus and the sanctifying power of the Holy Spirit, those who turn to Jesus will be set free from the guilt and slavery of sin (see John 8:31–36; Acts 26:18; Rom. 6; 8:1–16).

1:23 VIRGIN . . . BRING FORTH A SON. Both Matthew and Luke agree unequivocally that Jesus Christ was conceived by the Holy Spirit (v. 18; Luke 1:34–35) and born of a virgin mother without the intervention of a human father. The doctrine of Jesus' virgin birth has been opposed by liberal theologians for years. However, it is undeniable that the prophet Isaiah promised a virgin-born child who would be called "Immanuel," a Hebrew term meaning "God with us" (Is. 7:14). This prediction was made 700 years before the birth of Christ.

(1) The word "virgin" in Mat. 1:23 is the correct translation of the Greek *parthenos* found in the Septuagint in Is. 7:14. The Hebrew word for virgin (*almah*) used by Isaiah means a virgin of marriageable age and is never used in the O.T. for any state other than virginity (cf. Gen. 24:43; Sol. 1:3; 6:8). Hence, Isaiah in the O.T. and both Matthew and Luke in the N.T. ascribed virginity to the mother of Jesus (see Is. 7:14, note).

(2) The importance of the virgin birth cannot be overemphasized. In order for our Redeemer to qualify to pay for our sins and bring salvation, He must be, in one person, fully human, sinless, and fully divine (Heb. 7:25–26). The virgin birth satisfies all three of these requirements. (a) The only way He could be born a human being was to be born of a woman. (b) The only way He could be sinless man was to be conceived by the Holy Spirit (1:20; cf. Heb. 4:15). (c) The only way He could have been deity was to have God as His Father. As a result, His conception was not by natural but by supernatural means: "the holy thing which shall be born of thee shall be called the Son of God" (Luke 1:35). Jesus Christ is therefore revealed to us as one divine person with two natures—divine and sinless human.

(3) In living and suffering as a human person, Jesus sympathizes with our weaknesses (Heb. 4:15–16). As the divine Son of God He has the power to deliver us from the bondage of sin and the power of Satan (Acts 26:18; Col. 2:15; Heb. 2:14; 7:25). As both divine and sinless man, He qualifies to serve as a sacrifice for the sins of every person and as a high priest to intercede for all who come to God (Heb. 2:9–18; 5:1–9; 7:24–28; 10:4–12).

1:25 KNEW HER NOT TILL. The word "till" draws attention to the fact that after Christ's birth, Joseph and Mary entered into the full physical union commonly associated with marriage. We are told that Jesus had brothers and sisters (12:46–47; Mark 3:31–32; 6:3; Luke 8:19,20).

2:1 WISE MEN. These men were probably members of a learned religious class from the region that is now called Iran. They specialized in astrology, medicine, and natural science. Their visit occurred when Jesus was between 40 days (v. 22) and 2 years old (cf. v. 16). The importance of this story is that (1) Jesus is worthy of royal honor from all humanity, and (2) Gentiles as well as Jews are included in God's redemptive plan (cf. 8:11; 28:19; Rom. 10:12).

2:4 CHIEF PRIESTS AND SCRIBES. Chief priests were the temple ministers in charge of worship; scribes were copyists of Scripture in O.T. times. They became the teachers of the Law and consequently were called lawyers (22:35). Together the scribes and the chief priests constituted the Sanhedrin, or the Jewish Senate and Supreme Court. This was composed of approximately seventy/seventy-one men who had charge of the civil and religious affairs of the Jews and were given considerable authority under the Romans.

hem of Judaea: for thus it is written by
the prophet,
6 [f]And thou Bethlehem, *in* the
land of Judah, art not the least among
the princes of Judah: for out of thee
shall come a Governor, [g]that shall
[e]rule my people Israel.
7 Then Herod, when he had privily
called the wise men, inquired of them
diligently what time the star appeared.
8 And he sent them to Bethlehem,
and said, Go and search diligently for
the young child; and when ye have
found *him,* bring me word again, that I
may come and worship him also.
9 When they had heard the king,
they departed; and, lo, the star, which
they saw in the east, went before them,
till it came and stood over where the
young child was.
10 When they saw the star, they re-
joiced with exceeding great joy.
11 ¶ And when they were come into
the house, they saw the young child
with Mary his mother, and fell down,
and worshipped him: and when they
had opened their treasures, [h]they
[f]presented unto him gifts; gold, and
frankincense, and myrrh.
12 And being warned of God [i]in a
dream that they should not return to
Herod, they departed into their own
country another way.

The flight into Egypt

13 And when they were departed,
behold, the angel of the Lord appeareth
to Joseph in a dream, saying, Arise,
and take the young child and his moth-
er, and flee into Egypt, and be thou
there until I bring thee word: for Herod
will seek the young child to destroy
him.
14 When he arose, he took the
young child and his mother by night,
and departed into Egypt:
15 And was there until the death of
Herod: that it might be fulfilled which
was spoken of the Lord by the prophet,
saying, [j]Out of Egypt have I called my
son.
16 ¶ Then Herod, when he saw that
he was mocked of the wise men, was
exceeding wroth, and sent forth, and
slew all the children that were in Beth-
lehem, and in all the coasts thereof,
from two years old and under, accord-
ing to the time which he had diligently
inquired of the wise men.
17 Then was fulfilled that which
was spoken by [k]Jeremy the prophet,
saying,
18 In Rama was there a voice
heard, lamentation, and weeping, and
great mourning, Rachel weeping *for*
her children, and would not be comfort-
ed, because they are not.

From Egypt to Nazareth

19 ¶ But when Herod was dead, be-
hold, an angel of the Lord appeareth in
a dream to Joseph in Egypt,
20 Saying, Arise, and take the
young child and his mother, and go into
the land of Israel: for they are dead
which sought the young child's life.
21 And he arose, and took the
young child and his mother, and came
into the land of Israel.
22 But when he heard that Arche-
laus did reign in Judaea in the room
of his father Herod, he was afraid

2:6 [f]John 7:42 [g]Rev. 2:27
2:11 [h]Ps. 72:10 Is. 60:6
2:12 [i]ch. 1:20
2:15 [j]Hos. 11:1
2:17 [k]Jer. 31:15

[e] Or, *feed* [f] Or, *offered*

2:13 FLEE INTO EGYPT. Herod's attempt to kill Jesus and God's way of protecting the child reveal several truths about God's method of guiding and protecting His people. (1) God did not protect Joseph and Mary and their child without their cooperation (vv. 13,19–20,22). Protection required obedience to God's guidance, which in this case involved fleeing the country (v. 14).

(2) God may allow some things that are hard to understand to enter our lives in order to accomplish His will (see article on THE SUFFERING OF THE RIGHTEOUS, p. 764). In a real sense Christ began life as a refugee and stranger in another country (vv. 14–15). To our limited understanding, it would seem easier if God had removed Herod immediately, thus avoiding the flight to Egypt and all the trials involved in that circumstance.

(3) Even after a particular trial is resolved, there may be other problems to face (vv. 19–23). God's protection and providential care will always be needed, for the believer's enemy never ceases his attack upon the faithful (Eph. 6:10–18; 1 Pet. 5:8; see article on THE PROVIDENCE OF GOD, p. 80).

2:16 SLEW ALL THE CHILDREN. Bethlehem and its vicinity were not large. It most likely contained between one and two thousand inhabitants; in this case the number of children (i.e., male children) slain would be around twenty.

2:22 WARNED OF GOD. From the two warnings of God (vv. 12,22) we learn that God watches over those whom He loves, and that He knows best how to frustrate the plans of the wicked and how to deliver His faithful out of the hands of those who would harm them.

to go thither: notwithstanding, being
warned of God in a dream, he turned
aside [l]into the parts of Galilee:
23 And he came and dwelt in a city
called [m]Nazareth: that it might be ful-
filled [n]which was spoken by the
prophets, He shall be called a Naza-
rene.

John the Baptist

3:1–12pp — Mark 1:3–8; Luke 3:2–17

3 IN THOSE days came [o]John the
Baptist, preaching [p]in the wilder-
ness of Judaea,
2 And saying, Repent ye: for [q]the
kingdom of heaven is at hand.
3 For this is he that was spoken of
by the prophet Esaias, saying, [r]The
voice of one crying in the wilderness,
[s]Prepare ye the way of the Lord, make
his paths straight.
4 And [t]the same John [u]had his
raiment of camel's hair, and a leathern
girdle about his loins; and his meat
was [v]locusts and [w]wild honey.
5 [x]Then went out to him Jerusa-
lem, and all Judaea, and all the region
round about Jordan,
6 [y]And were baptized of him in Jor-
dan, confessing their sins.
7 ¶ But when he saw many of the
Pharisees and Sadducees come to his
baptism, he said unto them, [z]O gener-
ation of vipers, who hath warned you to
flee from [a]the wrath to come?
8 Bring forth therefore fruits
[g]meet for repentance:
9 And think not to say within your-
selves, [b]We have Abraham to *our* fa-
ther: for I say unto you, that God is
able of these stones to raise up chil-
dren unto Abraham.
10 And now also the axe is laid unto
the root of the trees: [c]therefore every
tree which bringeth not forth good fruit
is hewn down, and cast into the fire.
11 [d]I indeed baptize you with wa-
ter unto repentance: but he that com-

2:22 [l]ch. 3:13 Luke 2:39 **2:23** [m]John 1:45 [n]Judg. 13:5 1 Sam. 1:11 **3:1** [o]Mark. 1:4,15 Luke 3:2,3 John 1:28 [p]Josh. 14:10 **3:2** [q]Dan. 2:44 ch. 4:17 & 10:7 **3:3** [r]Is. 40:3 Mark 1:3 Luke 3:4 John 1:23 [s]Luke 1:76 **3:4** [t]Mark 1:6 [u]2 Ki. 1:8 Zech. 13:4 [v]Lev. 11:22 [w]1 Sam. 14:25,26 **3:5** [x]Mark 1:5 Luke 3:7 **3:6** [y]Acts 19:4,18 **3:7** [z]ch. 12:34 & 23:33 Luke 3:7-9 [a]Rom. 5:9 1 Thes. 1:10

3:9 [b]John 8:33,39; Acts 13:26; Rom. 4:1,11,16 **3:10** [c]ch. 7:19; Luke 13:7,9; John 15:6 **3:11** [d]Mark 1:8; Luke 3:16; John 1:15,26,33; Acts 1:5 & 11:16 & 19:4

[g] Or, *answerable to amendment of life*

3:2 REPENT. The basic meaning of repentance (Gk. *metanoeō*) is "to turn around." It is a turning from evil ways and a turning to Christ, and through Him to God (John 14:1,6; Acts 8:22; 26:18; 1 Pet. 2:25). (1) The decision to turn from sin and to salvation in Christ involves accepting Christ not only as Savior from the penalty of sin, but also as Lord of one's life. Thus, repentance involves a change of lords—from the lordship of Satan (Eph. 2:2) to the Lordship of Christ and His Word (Acts 26:18).

(2) Repentance is a free decision on the part of the sinner, made possible by the enabling grace given to him as he hears and believes the gospel (Acts 11:21; see article on FAITH AND GRACE, p. 1738).

(3) The definition of saving faith as mere "trust" in Christ as Savior is wholly inadequate in the light of Christ's demand for repentance. To define saving faith in a way which does not necessarily involve a radical break with sin is to dangerously distort the Biblical view of redemption. Faith which includes repentance is ever a condition for salvation (cf. Mark 1:15; Luke 13:3,5; Acts 2:38; 3:19; 11:21).

(4) Repentance was a basic message in the preaching of O.T. prophets (Jer. 7:3; Ezek. 18:30; Joel 2:12–14; Mal. 3:7), John the Baptist (Mat. 3:2), Jesus Christ (Mat. 4:17; 18:3; Luke 5:32), and N.T. Christians (Acts 2:38; 8:22; 11:18; 2 Pet. 3:9). The preaching of repentance must always accompany the gospel message (Luke 24:47).

3:7 PHARISEES . . . SADDUCEES. Two of the most prominent religious groups in Judaism were the Pharisees and Sadducees. (1) Pharisees were a Jewish religious group who adhered to both the entire O.T. and their human interpretations of it. They especially emphasized that salvation came by obeying the letter of God's law and their own interpretations. They taught that the coming Messiah would be an earthly ruler who would help Israel dominate the nations and force all people to obey God's law. However, their religion was outward in form with no inward godliness of heart (23:25), and they refused to recognize the depravity of their own nature. By and large they opposed Jesus and His message that religion is a matter of the heart and spirit, and not simply a legalistic obedience to the commandments of Scripture (cf. 9:14; 23:2–4; Luke 18:9–14).

(2) The Sadducees were the theological liberals and anti-supernaturalists of their day. While appearing to hold to the law of God, they really denied many of its teachings. They rejected the doctrines of the resurrection, angels, miracles, immortality, and the judgment to come. Their lives were morally lax and worldly. They, too, were persecutors of Jesus Christ (16:1–4).

3:8 FRUITS MEET FOR REPENTANCE. Genuine repentance will be accompanied by the fruit of righteousness (cf. 23:23; Luke 3:10–14; Acts 26:20). True saving faith and conversion must become evident through lives that forsake sin and bear godly fruit (see John 15:16, note). Those who say they believe in Christ and are God's children, yet do not live lives that produce good fruit, will be like trees that are cut down and thrown into the fire (vv. 8–10,12).

3:11 BAPTIZE YOU WITH THE HOLY GHOST. John teaches that the work of the coming Messiah will involve baptizing His followers in the Holy Spirit and fire—a baptism which gives great power to live and witness for Him (see Luke 3:16,

Mark 1:7-8 eth after me is mightier than I, whose shoes I am not worthy to bear: [e]he shall baptize you with the Holy Ghost, and *with* fire:

12 [f]Whose fan *is* in his hand, and he will thoroughly purge his floor, and gather his wheat into the garner; but he will [g]burn up the chaff with unquenchable fire.

The baptism of Jesus

3:13–17pp — Mark 1:9–11; Luke 3:21–22; John 1:31–34

13 ¶ [h]Then cometh Jesus [i]from Galilee to Jordan unto John, to be baptized of him.

14 But John forbad him, saying, I have need to be baptized of thee, and comest thou to me?

15 And Jesus answering said unto him, Suffer *it to be so* now: for thus it becometh us to fulfil all righteousness. Then he suffered him.

16 [j]And Jesus, when he was baptized, went up straightway out of the water: and, lo, the heavens were opened unto him, and he saw [k]the Spirit of God descending like a dove, and lighting upon him:

17 [l]And lo a voice from heaven, saying, [m]This is my beloved Son, in whom I am well pleased.

3:11 [e]Is 4:4 & 44:3 Mal. 3:2 Acts 2:3,4 1 Cor. 12:13
3:12 [f]Mal. 3:3 [g]Mal. 4:1 ch. 13:30
3:13 [h]Mark 1:9 Luke 3:21 [i]ch. 2:22
3:16 [j]Mark 1:10 [k]Is. 11:2 & 42:1 Luke 3:22 John 1:32
3:17 [l]John 12:28 [m]Ps. 2:7 Is. 42:1 ch. 17:5 Mark 1:11 Luke 9:35 Eph. 1:6 Col. 1:13 2 Pet. 1:17

The temptation in the wilderness

4:1–11pp — Mark 1:12–13; Luke 4:1–13

4 THEN WAS [n]Jesus led up of [o]the Spirit into the wilderness to be tempted of the devil.

2 And when he had fasted forty days

4:1 [n]Mark 1:12; Luke 4:1 [o]See 1 Ki. 18:12; Ezek. 3:14 & 8:3 & 11:1,24 & 40:2; & 43:5; Acts 8:39

note on the baptism in the Holy Spirit).

3:13 JESUS . . . BAPTIZED. Jesus was baptized by John for the following reasons: (1) "To fulfil all righteousness" (v. 15; cf. Lev. 16:4; Gal. 4:4–5). Christ, through baptism, publicly consecrated Himself to God and His kingdom and thus fulfilled God's righteous requirement. (2) To identify Himself with sinners—although Jesus Himself did not need to repent of sin (2 Cor. 5:21; 1 Pet. 2:24). (3) To associate Himself with the new movement of God that was calling everyone to repentance; note the message of John the Baptist as the forerunner of the Messiah (John 1:23,32–33).

3:16 SPIRIT . . . UPON HIM. Everything Jesus did—His preaching, His healing, His suffering, His victory over sin—He did by the power of the Holy Spirit. If Jesus could do nothing apart from the working of the Holy Spirit, how much more do we need the Spirit's enablement (cf. Luke 4:1,14,18; John 3:34; Acts 1:2; 10:38). The Spirit came upon Jesus to equip Him with power for His work of redemption (see Luke 3:22, note). Jesus Himself would later baptize His followers in the Holy Spirit so that they too might have the Spirit's enablement (see Mat. 3:11, note; Acts 1:5,8; 2:4).

3:17 THE TRINITY IN EXAMPLE. The baptism of Jesus is a striking manifestation of the fact of the Trinity. (1) Jesus Christ, declared to be equal with God (John 10:30), is baptized in the Jordan River. (2) The Holy Spirit, who is also equal with the Father (Acts 5:3–4), descends upon Jesus in the form of a dove. (3) The Father declares that He is well pleased with Jesus. Thus, we have three equal divine persons; it is contrary to the entire Scripture to explain this event consistently in any other manner. The trinitarian understanding of God teaches that these three divine Persons exist in such unity that they are one God (see Mark 1:11, note on Trinity; cf. Mat. 28:19; John 15:26; 1 Cor. 12:4–13; Eph. 2:18; 1 Pet. 1:2).

4:1–11 JESUS . . . TEMPTED. The temptation of Jesus by Satan was an attempt to entice Him from the pathway of perfect obedience to the will of God. Notice that in each temptation, Jesus submitted Himself to the authority of the Word of God rather than to the desires of Satan (vv. 4,7,10). What can we learn from the temptation of Christ? (1) Satan is our greatest enemy. As Christians, we must be aware that we are engaged in a spiritual warfare with unseen but very real powers of evil (see Eph. 6:12, note).

(2) Without the Holy Spirit and the proper use of God's Word, the Christian cannot overcome sin and temptation. The following are suggestions on how to use God's Word in overcoming temptation: (a) Realize that through the Word you have the power to resist any appeal Satan can make (John 15:3,7). (b) Engraft (i.e., memorize) the Word of God into your soul and mind (see Jas. 1:21, note). (c) Meditate day and night on the verses you have memorized (see Deut. 6:6, note; Ps. 1:2, notes; 119:47–48, note). (d) Say the memorized passage to yourself and God the instant you are tempted (vv. 4,7,10). (e) Recognize and obey the prompting of the Holy Spirit to obey God's Word (Rom. 8:12–14; Gal. 5:18). (f) Surround all these steps with prayer (Eph. 6:18).

Some passages to memorize in facing temptation: General (Rom. 6 and 8); Specific: concerning immorality (Rom. 13:14), lying (John 8:44; Col. 3:9), gossiping (Jas. 4:11), disobeying parents (Heb. 13:17), discouragement (Gal. 6:9), fear of the future (2 Tim. 1:7), lust (Mat. 5:28; 2 Tim. 2:22), desire for revenge (Mat. 6:15), neglect of God's Word (Mat. 4:4), worry over finances (Mat. 6:24–34; Phil. 4:6).

4:2 FASTED FORTY DAYS. After fasting "forty days and forty nights," Jesus "was afterward an hungered" and was tempted by Satan to eat. This seems to indicate that Christ abstained from food, but not from water (see Luke 4:2). To abstain from water for forty days would have required a miracle. Christ, insofar as He had to encounter temptation as our human representative (cf. Heb. 2:17; 4:15),

and forty nights, he was afterward an
hungered.
3 And when the tempter came to
him, he said, If thou be the Son of God,
command that these stones be made
bread.
4 But he answered and said, It
is written, [p]Man shall not live by
bread alone, but by every word
that proceedeth out of the mouth
of God.
5 Then the devil taketh him up
[q]into the holy city, and setteth him on
a pinnacle of the temple,
6 And saith unto him, If thou be the
Son of God, cast thyself down: for it is
written, [r]He shall give his angels
charge concerning thee: and in *their*
hands they shall bear thee up, lest at
any time thou dash thy foot against a
stone.
7 Jesus said unto him, It is written
again, [s]Thou shalt not tempt the Lord
thy God.
8 Again, the devil taketh him up
into an exceeding high mountain, and
showeth him all the kingdoms of the
world, and the glory of them;
9 And saith unto him, All these
things will I give thee, if thou wilt fall
down and worship me.
10 Then saith Jesus unto him, Get
thee hence, Satan: for it is written,
[t]Thou shalt worship the Lord thy
God, and him only shalt thou serve.
11 Then the devil leaveth him, and,
behold, [u]angels came and ministered
unto him.

Mat. 8:28-33

The beginning of Jesus' ministry

12 ¶ [v]Now when Jesus had heard
that John was [h]cast into prison, he de-
parted into Galilee;
13 And leaving Nazareth, he came
and dwelt in Capernaum, which is upon
the sea coast, in the borders of Zabulon
and Nephthalim:
14 That it might be fulfilled which
was spoken by Esaias the prophet, say-
ing,
15 [w]The land of Zabulon, and the

4:4 [p]Deut. 8:3
4:5 [q]Neh. 11:1 Is. 48:2 & 52:1 ch. 27:53 Rev. 11:2
4:6 [r]Ps. 91:11,12
4:7 [s]Deut. 6:16
4:10 [t]Deut. 6:13 & 10:20 Josh. 24:14 1 Sam. 7:3
4:11 [u]Heb. 1:14
4:12 [v]Mark 1:14 Luke 3:20 & 4:14,31 John 4:43
4:15 [w]Is. 9:1,2

[h] Or, *delivered up*

could not have used any other means than is available to the Spirit-filled believer (see Ex. 34:28, note; 1 Ki. 19:8, note; Mat. 6:16, note). During the forty-day fast it is reasonable to assume that He was preparing Himself by means of prayer and meditation on God's Word for the work the Father had sent Him to do.

4:6 IT IS WRITTEN. Satan used the Word of God to tempt Christ to sin. At times worldly people will use Scripture in an attempt to persuade a believer to do something he knows is wrong or unwise. Some Scripture, when taken out of context or not compared with other passages of God's Word, may even appear to condone sinful behavior (see, e.g., 1 Cor. 6:12). Believers must know God's Word thoroughly and beware of those who pervert the Scriptures in order to fulfill the desires of the sinful human nature. The apostle Peter speaks of those who distort the Scriptures to their own destruction (2 Pet. 3:16).

4:8 ALL THE KINGDOMS OF THE WORLD. See Luke 4:5, note.

4:10 SATAN. Satan (Heb. word meaning "an adversary") was a great angel created perfect and good. He was appointed to be a minister at the throne of God; yet sometime before the world began, he rebelled and became the chief antagonist of God and man (Ezek. 28:12–15).

(1) In his rebellion against God, Satan drew with him a great multitude of lesser angels (Rev. 12:4), who are probably to be identified, after their fall, with demons or evil spirits (see article on POWER OVER SATAN AND DEMONS, p. 1486). Satan and many of these lesser angels were exiled to the earth and the atmosphere around it and operate within this sphere under the permissive will of God.

(2) Satan, also called "the serpent," caused the fall of the human race (Gen. 3:1–6; see 1 John 5:19, note).

(3) Satan's kingdom (12:26) is a highly systematized empire of evil which has authority over the lower heavenly realm (Eph. 2:2), fallen angels (25:41; Rev. 12:7), unregenerate humanity (vv. 8–9; John 12:31; Eph. 2:2), and the world (Luke 4:5–6; 2 Cor. 4:4; see 1 John 5:19, note). He is not omnipresent, omnipotent, or omniscient; hence, most of his activity is delegated to demons (8:28; Rev. 16:13–14; see Job 1:12, note).

(4) Jesus came to earth to destroy the works of Satan (1 John 3:8), establish the kingdom of God, and deliver us from Satan's dominion (12:28; Luke 4:18; 13:16; Acts 26:18). By His death and resurrection, Christ initiated the defeat of Satan and thereby ensured God's ultimate victory over him (Heb. 2:14).

(5) At the end of the age Satan is to be confined to the abyss for a thousand years (Rev. 20:1–3). After his release he will make a final attempt to overthrow God; this will result in Satan's final defeat and his being cast into the lake of fire (Rev. 20:7–10).

(6) Satan presently wars against God and His people (Job 1–2; Eph. 6:11–18), seeking to draw them away from loyalty to Christ (2 Cor. 11:3), and into sin and this present world system (cf. 2 Cor. 11:3; 1 Tim. 5:15; 1 John 5:16). The believer is to pray constantly for deliverance from Satan (Mat. 6:13), to be on the alert concerning his schemes and temptations (Eph. 6:11), and to resist him by spiritual warfare while remaining firm in the faith (Eph. 6:10–18; 1 Pet. 5:8–9).

land of Nephthalim, *by* the way of the
sea, beyond Jordan, Galilee of the Gen-
tiles;
16 [x]The people which sat in dark-
ness saw great light; and to them
which sat in the region and shadow of
death light is sprung up.
17 ¶ [y]From that time Jesus began
to preach, and to say, [z]Repent: for the
kingdom of heaven is at hand.

Jesus calls four disciples

4:18–22pp — Mark 1:16–20; Luke 5:2–11; John 1:35–42

18 ¶ [a]And Jesus, walking by the
sea of Galilee, saw two brethren, Si-
mon [b]called Peter, and Andrew his
brother, casting a net into the sea: for
they were fishers.
19 And he saith unto them, Follow
me, and [c]I will make you fishers of
men.
20 [d]And they straightway left *their*
nets, and followed him.
21 [e]And going on from thence, he
saw other two brethren, James *the son*
of Zebedee, and John his brother, in a
ship with Zebedee their father, mend-
ing their nets; and he called them.
22 And they immediately left the
ship and their father, and followed him.

Jesus heals the sick

23 ¶ And Jesus went about all Gali-
lee, [f]teaching in their synagogues,
and preaching [g]the gospel of the king-
dom, [h]and healing all manner of sick-
ness and all manner of disease among
the people.
24 And his fame went throughout
all Syria: and they brought unto him all
sick people that were taken with divers
diseases and torments, and those
which were possessed with devils, and
those which were lunatic, and those
that had the palsy; and he healed them. Mat 8:16 17
25 [i]And there followed him great
multitudes of people from Galilee, and
from Decapolis, and *from* Jerusalem,
and *from* Judaea, and *from* beyond Jor-
dan.

4:16 [x]Is. 42:7; Luke 2:32
4:17 [y]Mark 1:14; [z]ch. 3:2 & 10:7
4:18 [a]Mark 1:16-18; Luke 5:2; [b]John 1:42
4:19 [c]Luke 5:10
4:20 [d]Mark 10:28; Luke 18:28
4:21 [e]Mark 1:19; Luke 5:10
4:23 [f]ch. 9:35; Mark 1:21,39; Luke 4:15,44; [g]ch. 24:14; Mark 1:14; [h]Mark 1:34
4:25 [i]Mark 3:7
5:1 [j]Mark 3:13
5:3 [k]Luke 6:20; See Ps. 51:17; Prov. 16:19 & 29:23; Is. 57:15 & 66:2
5:4 [l]Is. 61:2,3; Luke 6:21; John 16:20; 2 Cor. 1:7; Rev. 21:4
5:5 [m]Ps. 37:11; [n]Rom. 4:13

The Beatitudes

5:3–12pp — Luke 6:20–23

5 AND SEEING the multitudes, [j]he
went up into a mountain: and when
he was set, his disciples came unto
him:
2 And he opened his mouth, and
taught them, saying,
3 [k]Blessed *are* the poor in spirit:
for theirs is the kingdom of heaven.
4 [l]Blessed *are* they that mourn: for
they shall be comforted.
5 [m]Blessed *are* the meek: for [n]they
shall inherit the earth.
6 Blessed *are* they which do hunger

4:19 FISHERS OF MEN. One may be a pastor, evangelist, missionary, writer, teacher, deacon, or layman, but if he or she is not actually seeking and endeavoring to bring others to Christ, they are not fulfilling their work for God (see 28:19; Luke 5:10; John 15:16; Acts 1:8; 1 Cor. 9:19).

4:23 THE KINGDOM, AND HEALING. In the Gospels, the kingdom of God is closely associated with healing, miracles, and casting out demons (4:23–24; 9:35; 10:7–8; 12:28; Luke 9:1–2; cf. Acts 8:6–7,12). The kingdom includes blessings for the body as well as for the soul (see article on DIVINE HEALING, p. 1418).

5–7 SERMON ON THE MOUNT. In chs. 5–7 we have what is commonly called Christ's Sermon on the Mount. It contains a revelation of God's principles of righteousness by which all Christians are to live through faith in the Son of God (Gal. 2:20) and through the power of the indwelling Spirit (cf. Rom. 8:2–14; Gal. 5:16–25). All of us belonging to the kingdom of God are to have an intense hunger and thirst for the righteousness taught in Christ's sermon (see Mat. 5:6, note).

5:3 BLESSED . . . POOR IN SPIRIT. The word "blessed" refers to the well-being of those who, because of their relationship to Christ and His Word, receive God's kingdom, including His love, care, salvation, and daily presence (see 14:19, note; Luke 24:50, note). There are certain requirements if we wish to receive the blessings of God's kingdom; we must be guided by God's ways and values revealed in Scripture and not by the ways and values of the world. The first of these requirements is to be "poor in spirit." That is, we must recognize that we are not spiritually self-sufficient; we need the Holy Spirit's life, power, and sustaining grace to inherit the kingdom of God.

5:4 THEY THAT MOURN. To "mourn" is to grieve over our own weakness in relation to God's standard of righteousness and kingdom power (v. 6; 6:3). It is also to "mourn" over the things that grieve God, to have our feelings in sympathy with the feelings of God, and to be afflicted in our spirit over the sin, immorality, and cruelty manifested in the world (see Luke 19:41, note; Acts 20:19; 2 Pet. 2:8, note). Those who mourn are comforted by receiving from the Father "righteousness and peace, and joy in the Holy Ghost" (Rom. 14:17).

5:5 THE MEEK. The "meek" are those who are humble and submissive before God. They find their refuge in Him and commit their way entirely to Him. They are more concerned about God's work and God's people than about what might happen to them personally (cf. Ps. 37:11). The meek, rather than the aggressors, ultimately inherit the earth.

and thirst after righteousness: [o]for
they shall be filled.
7 Blessed *are* the merciful: [p]for
they shall obtain mercy.
8 [q]Blessed *are* the pure in heart:
for [r]they shall see God.
9 Blessed *are* the peacemakers: for
they shall be called the children of
God.
10 [s]Blessed *are* they which are
persecuted for righteousness' sake: for
theirs is the kingdom of heaven.
11 [t]Blessed are ye, when *men* shall
revile you, and persecute *you,* and
shall say all manner of [u]evil against
you [i]falsely, for my sake.
12 [v]Rejoice, and be exceeding
glad: for great *is* your reward in heav-
en: for [w]so persecuted they the proph-
ets which were before you.

Teaching about salt and light

13 ¶ Ye are the salt of the earth:
[x]but if the salt have lost his savour,
wherewith shall it be salted? it is
thenceforth good for nothing, but to be
cast out, and to be trodden under foot
of men.
14 [y]Ye are the light of the world. A

5:6 [o]Is. 55:1 & 65:13
5:7 [p]Ps. 41:1 Mark 11:25
5:8 [q]Ps. 15:2 Heb. 12:14 [r]1 Cor. 13:12
5:10 [s]2 Cor. 4:17 1 Pet. 3:14
5:11 [t]Luke 6:22 [u]1 Pet. 4:14
5:12 [v]Luke 6:23 Acts 5:41 1 Pet. 4:13 [w]Neh. 9:26 Acts 7:52
5:13 [x]Mark 9:50 Luke 14:34
5:14 [y]Prov. 4:18; Phil. 2:15

[i] Gk. *lying*

5:6 HUNGER AND THIRST AFTER RIGHTEOUSNESS. This is one of the most important verses in the Sermon on the Mount. (1) The foundational requirement for all godly living is to "hunger and thirst after righteousness" (cf. 6:33). Such hunger is seen in Moses (Ex. 33:13,18), the psalmist (Ps. 42:2,6, notes; 63:1–11, note), and the apostlePaul (Phil. 3:10). The spiritual condition of Christians all throughout their lives will depend on their hunger and thirst for (a) the presence of God (Deut. 4:29), (b) the Word of God (Ps. 119), (c) the communion of Christ (Phil. 3:8–10), (d) the fellowship of the Spirit (John 7:37–39; 2 Cor. 13:14), (e) righteousness (5:6), (f) kingdom power (6:33), and (g) the return of the Lord (2 Tim. 4:8).

(2) The Christian's hunger for the things of God is destroyed by worldly anxiety, deceitfulness of riches (13:22), desire for things (Mark 4:19) and worldly pleasures (Luke 8:14), and failure to abide in Christ (see John 15:4, note). When the hunger of believers for God and His righteousness is destroyed, they will die spiritually. For this reason it is essential that we be sensitive to the Holy Spirit's convicting work in our lives (see John 16:8–13; Rom. 8:5–16). Those who consistently hunger and thirst after righteousness "shall be filled."

5:7 THE MERCIFUL. The "merciful" are full of compassion and pity toward those who are suffering either from sin or sorrow. The merciful sincerely desire to make such suffering less by bringing those people to the grace and help of God through Jesus Christ (cf. 18:23–35; Luke 10:30–37; Heb. 2:17). In showing mercy to others we "shall obtain mercy."

5:8 THE PURE IN HEART. The "pure in heart" are those who have been delivered from the power of sin by the grace of God and now strive without deceit to please and glorify God and to be like Him. (1) They seek to have the same attitude of heart that God has—a love for righteousness and a hatred for evil (see Heb. 1:9, note). Their heart (which includes mind, will, and emotions; see article on THE HEART, p. 932) is in tune with the heart of God (1 Sam. 13:14; Mat. 22:37; 1 Tim. 1:5). (2) Only the pure in heart "shall see God." To see God means to be His child and to dwell in His presence, both now and in the future kingdom (Ex. 33:11; Rev. 21:7; 22:4).

5:9 THE PEACEMAKERS. The "peacemakers" are those who have been reconciled to God. They have peace with Him through the cross (Rom. 5:1; Eph. 2:14–16; see article on THE PEACE OF GOD, p. 1122). They now strive by their witness and life to bring others, including their enemies, to peace with God.

5:10 PERSECUTED FOR RIGHTEOUSNESS' SAKE. Persecution will be the lot of all those who seek to live in harmony with God's Word for the sake of righteousness. (1) Those who uphold God's standards of truth, justice, and purity, and who at the same time refuse to compromise with the present evil society or the lifestyle of lukewarm believers (Rev. 2; 3:1–4,14–22), will undergo unpopularity, rejection, and criticism. Persecution and opposition will come from the world (10:22; 24:9; John 15:19) and at times from those within the professing church (Acts 20:28–31; 2 Cor. 11:3–15; 2 Tim. 1:15; 3:8–14; 4:16). When they experience this suffering, Christians are to rejoice (v. 12), for to those who suffer most God imparts the highest blessing (2 Cor. 1:5; 2 Tim. 2:12; 1 Pet. 1:7; 4:13). (2) Christians must beware of the temptation to compromise God's will in order to avoid shame, ridicule, embarrassment, or loss (10:33; Mark 8:38; Luke 9:26; 2 Tim. 2:12). The principles of God's kingdom never change: ". . . all that will live godly in Christ Jesus shall suffer persecution" (2 Tim. 3:12). Those who suffer and endure persecution for righteousness' sake are promised the kingdom and heavenly rewards.

5:13 SALT OF THE EARTH. Salt is valuable to give flavor and to preserve from corruption. Hence, the believer and the church are to be godly examples in the world and to resist moral decay and corruption evident in society. (1) Churches that become lukewarm, quench the power of the Holy Spirit, and cease to resist the prevailing spirit in the world, will be "cast out" by God (see Rev. 3:15–16, note). (2) They consequently will be "trodden under foot of men" (v. 13), i.e., those who are lukewarm, together with their families, will be destroyed by the ways and values of ungodly society (cf. Deut. 28:13,43,48; Judg. 2:20–22).

city that is set on an hill cannot be hid.
15 Neither do men [z]light a candle,
and put it under [j]a bushel, but on a
candlestick; and it giveth light unto all
that are in the house.
16 Let your light so shine before
men, [a]that they may see your good
Mat. 6:19-24 works, and [b]glorify your Father which
is in heaven.

The higher righteousness

17 ¶ [c]Think not that I am come to
destroy the law, or the prophets: I am
not come to destroy, but to fulfil.
18 For verily I say unto you, [d]Till
heaven and earth pass, one jot or one
tittle shall in no wise pass from the
law, till all be fulfilled.
19 [e]Whosoever therefore shall
break one of these least command-
ments, and shall teach men so, he shall
be called the least in the kingdom of
heaven: but whosoever shall do and
teach *them,* the same shall be called
great in the kingdom of heaven.
20 For I say unto you, That except
your righteousness shall exceed [f]*the
righteousness* of the scribes and Phari-
sees, ye shall in no case enter into the
kingdom of heaven.

Anger and reconciliation

5:25–26pp — Luke 12:58–59

21 ¶ Ye have heard that it was said
[k]by them of old time, [g]Thou shalt not
kill; and whosoever shall kill shall be
in danger of the judgment:
22 But I say unto you, That [h]who-
soever is angry with his brother with-
out a cause shall be in danger of the
judgment: and whosoever shall say to
his brother, [i]Raca,[l] shall be in dan-
ger of the council: but whosoever shall

5:15 [z]Mark 4:21 Luke 8:16
5:16 [a]1 Pet. 2:12 [b]John 15:8 1 Cor. 14:25
5:17 [c]Rom. 10:4
5:18 [d]Luke 16:17
5:19 [e]Jas. 2:10
5:20 [f]Rom. 10:3
5:21 [g]Ex. 20:13
5:22 [h]1 John 3:15 [i]Jas. 2:20

[j] The word in the original signifieth *a measure containing about a pint less than a peck* [k] Or, *to them* [l] i.e. *Vain fellow*

5:17 THE LAW . . . TO FULFIL. It is Christ's intention that the spiritual requirement of God's law be fulfilled in the lives of His followers (Rom. 3:31; 8:4). The believer's relation to the law of God involves the following:

(1) The law that the believer is obliged to keep consists of the ethical and moral principles of the O.T. (7:12; 22:36–40; Rom. 3:31; Gal. 5:14; see article on THE OLD TESTAMENT LAW, p. 124) as well as the teachings of Christ and the apostles (28:20; 1 Cor. 7:19; 9:21; Gal. 6:2). These laws reveal the nature and will of God for all people and still apply today. O.T. laws which applied directly to the nation of Israel, such as the sacrificial, ceremonial, social, or civil laws, are no longer binding (Heb. 10:1–4; e.g., Lev. 1:2–3; 24:10).

(2) The believer must not view the law as a system of legal commandments by which to obtain merit for forgiveness and salvation (Gal. 2:16,19). Rather, the law must be seen as a moral code for those who are already in a saved relationship with God and who, by obeying it, express the life of Christ within themselves (Rom. 6:15–22).

(3) Faith in Christ is the point of departure for the fulfilling of the law. Through faith in Him, God becomes our Father (cf. John 1:12). Hence, our obedience as believers is done not only out of a relationship to God as sovereign Law-giver, but also out of a relationship of children to their Father (Gal. 4:6).

(4) Through faith in Christ, believers, by the grace of God (Rom. 5:21) and the indwelling Holy Spirit (Gal. 3:5,14; Rom. 8:13), are given an inner compulsion and power to fulfill God's law (Rom. 16:25–26; Heb. 10:16). We fulfill it by walking after the Spirit (Rom. 8:4–14). The Spirit helps us put to death the sinful deeds of the body and to fulfill the will of God (Rom. 8:13; see Mat. 7:21, note). Thus, external conformity to God's law must be accompanied by the inner transformation of our hearts and spirits (cf. vv. 21–28).

(5) Having been freed from the power of sin and now enslaved to God (Rom. 6:18–22), believers follow the principle of "faith" by being "under the law to Christ" (1 Cor. 9:21). In so doing we fulfill "the law of Christ" (Gal. 6:2) and are thus faithful in ourselves to the requirement of the law (see Rom. 8:4, note; Gal. 2:19, note; 3:19, note; 5:16–25).

(6) Jesus emphatically taught that doing the will of His heavenly Father is an ongoing condition of entering the kingdom of heaven (see 7:21, note).

5:19 GREAT IN THE KINGDOM. The position of believers in the kingdom of heaven will be determined by our attitude toward God's law and by our teaching and practice of it. Our degree of faithfulness in this respect will determine our degree of glory in heaven (see article on THE JUDGMENT OF BELIEVERS, p. 1811).

5:20 EXCEPT YOUR RIGHTEOUSNESS. The righteousness of the scribes and Pharisees was external only. They kept many rules, prayed, praised, fasted, read God's Word, and attended worship services. However, they substituted the outward act for the correct inner attitudes. Jesus said the righteousness that God requires of the believer is more. The heart and spirit, not only the outward deeds, must conform to God's will in faith and love (see Mark 7:6, note on legalism.)

5:22 ANGRY . . . RACA . . . FOOL. Jesus is not speaking of a righteous anger at those who are wicked and unjust (cf. John 2:13–17), but is condemning the vindictive anger that would unjustly desire the death of another. "Raca" is a term of contempt and probably means "empty-headed fool." To call a person a "godless fool" in anger and contempt may indicate a heart attitude that places one "in danger of hell fire."

say, Thou fool, shall be in danger of
hell fire.
23 Therefore [j]if thou bring thy gift
to the altar, and there rememberest
that thy brother hath aught against
thee;
24 [k]Leave there thy gift before the
altar, and go thy way; first be recon-
ciled to thy brother, and then come and
offer thy gift.
25 [l]Agree with thine adversary
quickly, [m]whiles thou art in the way
with him; lest at any time the adver-
sary deliver thee to the judge, and the
judge deliver thee to the officer, and
thou be cast into prison.
26 Verily I say unto thee, Thou
shalt by no means come out thence,
till thou hast paid the uttermost
farthing.

Adultery

27 ¶ Ye have heard that it was said
by them of old time, [n]Thou shalt not
commit adultery:
28 But I say unto you, That whoso-
ever [o]looketh on a woman to lust after
her hath committed adultery with her
already in his heart.
29 [p]And if thy right eye [m]offend
thee, [q]pluck it out, and cast *it* from
thee: for it is profitable for thee that
one of thy members should perish, and
not *that* thy whole body should be cast
into hell.
30 And if thy right hand offend thee,
cut it off, and cast *it* from thee: for it
is profitable for thee that one of thy
members should perish, and not *that*
thy whole body should be cast into
hell.

5:23 [j]ch. 8:4
5:24 [k]Job 42:8 1 Tim. 2:8 1 Pet. 3:7
5:25 [l]Prov. 25:8 Luke 12:58 [m]Ps. 32:6 Is. 55:6
5:27 [n]Ex. 20:14 Deut. 5:18
5:28 [o]Job. 31:1 Prov. 6:25
5:29 [p]Mark 9:43 [q]Col. 3:5
5:31 [r]Deut. 24:1 Jer. 3:1 Mark 10:2
5:32 [s]Luke 16:18 Rom. 7:3
5:33 [t]ch. 23:16 [u]Ex. 20:7 Lev. 19:12 [v]Deut. 23:23
5:34 [w]ch. 23:16 Jas. 5:12 [x]Is. 66:1
5:35 [y]Ps. 48:2
5:37 [z]Col. 4:6 Jas. 5:12
5:38 [a]Ex. 21:24 Lev. 24:20 Deut. 19:21
5:39 [b]Prov. 20:22 Luke 6:29 Rom. 12:17 1 Cor. 6:7 1 Pet. 3:9 [c]Is. 50:6 Lam. 3:30

Divorce

31 It hath been said, [r]Whosoever
shall put away his wife, let him give her
a writing of divorcement:
32 But I say unto you, That [s]who-
soever shall put away his wife, saving
for the cause of fornication, causeth
her to commit adultery: and whosoever
shall marry her that is divorced com-
mitteth adultery.

Oaths and retaliation

33 ¶ Again, ye have heard that [t]it
hath been said by them of old time,
[u]Thou shalt not forswear thyself, but
[v]shalt perform unto the Lord thine
oaths:
34 But I say unto you, [w]Swear not
at all; neither by heaven; for it is
[x]God's throne:
35 Nor by the earth; for it is his foot-
stool: neither by Jerusalem; for it is
[y]the city of the great King.
36 Neither shalt thou swear by thy
head, because thou canst not make one
hair white or black.
37 [z]But let your communication
be, Yea, yea; Nay, nay: for whatsoever
is more than these cometh of evil.
38 ¶ Ye have heard that it hath been
said, [a]An eye for an eye, and a tooth
for a tooth:
39 But I say unto you, [b]That ye re-
sist not evil: but [c]whosoever shall
smite thee on thy right cheek, turn to
him the other also.
40 And if any man will sue thee at
the law, and take away thy coat, let
him have *thy* cloak also.

[m] Or, *do cause thee to offend*

5:28 LOOKETH . . . TO LUST. What Christ condemns is not the sudden thought which Satan may place in a person's mind or an improper desire that arises suddenly. Rather it is a wrong thought or desire that is accompanied with the approval of our will. It is having an immoral desire which would seek fulfillment if the opportunity arose. The inner desire for illicit sexual pleasure, if contemplated and not resisted, is sin (see article on STANDARDS OF SEXUAL MORALITY, p. 1964).

(1) The Christian must be particularly careful to abstain from taking pleasure in scenes of immorality such as those shown in films or pornographic literature (cf. 1 Cor. 6:15,18; Gal. 5:19,21; Eph. 5:5; Col. 3:5; 2 Tim. 2:22; Tit. 2:12; Heb. 13:4; Jas. 1:14; 1 Pet. 2:11; 2 Pet. 3:3; 1 John 2:16).

(2) In the area of maintaining sexual purity, the woman as well as the man has a responsibility. The Christian woman must be careful not to dress in a way that attracts attention to her body, thereby creating temptation for men and encouraging lust. Dressing immodestly or sensually is sin (1 Tim. 2:9; 1 Pet. 3:2–3).

5:29 HELL. See Mark 9:43, note.

5:32 SAVING FOR . . . FORNICATION. See 19:9, note.

5:39 RESIST NOT EVIL. Jesus is not speaking against the administration of proper justice toward those who are evil (cf. Rom. 13:1–4). The verses that follow (vv. 43–48) indicate that He is referring to loving one's enemies (v. 44; Luke 6:27). We are not to react to the wrong done toward us in a spirit of hate, but in a way that shows we have values that are centered in Christ and His kingdom. Our actions toward those who are unkind to us should be such that it might lead them to accept Christ as their Savior. As examples of this spirit, compare Gen. 13:1–13 with Gen. 14:14, and Gen. 50:19–21 with Gen. 37:18–28; see also 1 Sam. 24 and 26; Luke 23:34; Acts 7:60.

41 And whosoever [d]shall compel thee to go a mile, go with him twain.

42 Give to him that asketh thee, and [e]from him that would borrow of thee turn not thou away.

Love for enemies

43 ¶ Ye have heard that it hath been said, [f]Thou shalt love thy neighbour, [g]and hate thine enemy.

44 But I say unto you, [h]Love your enemies, bless them that curse you, do good to them that hate you, and pray [i]for them which despitefully use you, and persecute you;

45 That ye may be the children of your Father which is in heaven: for [j]he maketh his sun to rise on the evil and on the good, and sendeth rain on the just and on the unjust.

46 [k]For if ye love them which love you, what reward have ye? do not even the publicans the same?

47 And if ye salute your brethren only, what do ye more *than others?* do not even the publicans so?

48 [l]Be ye therefore perfect, even [m]as your Father which is in heaven is perfect.

Giving to the needy

6 TAKE HEED that ye do not your [n]alms before men, to be seen of them: otherwise ye have no reward [o]of your Father which is in heaven.

2 Therefore [n]when thou doest *thine* alms, [p]do not sound a trumpet before thee, as the hypocrites do in the synagogues and in the streets, that they may have glory of men. Verily I say unto you, They have their reward.

3 But when thou doest alms, let not thy left hand know what thy right hand doeth:

4 That thine alms may be in secret: and thy Father which seeth in secret himself [o]shall reward thee openly.

Prayer

6:9–13pp — Luke 11:2–4

5 ¶ And when thou prayest, thou shalt not be as the hypocrites *are:* for they love to pray standing in the synagogues and in the corners of the streets, that they may be seen of men. Verily I say unto you, They have their reward.

6 But thou, when thou prayest, [p]enter into thy closet, and when thou hast shut thy door, pray to thy Father which is in secret; and thy Father which seeth in secret shall reward thee openly.

7 But when ye pray, [q]use not vain repetitions, as the heathen *do:* [r]for they think that they shall be heard for their much speaking.

8 Be not ye therefore like unto them: for your Father knoweth what things ye have need of, before ye ask him.

9 After this manner therefore pray

5:41 [d]ch. 27:32
5:42 [e]Deut. 15:8 Luke 6:30
5:43 [f]Lev. 19:18 [g]Deut. 23:6 Ps. 41:10
5:44 [h]Luke 6:27 Rom. 12:14 [i]Luke 23:34 Acts 7:60 1 Cor. 4:12 1 Pet. 2:23
5:45 [j]Job 25:3
5:46 [k]Luke 6:32
5:48 [l]Gen. 17:1 Lev. 11:44 & 19:2 Luke 6:36 Col. 1:28 & 4:12 Jas. 1:4 1 Pet. 1:15 [m]Eph. 5:1
6:2 [n]Rom. 12:8
6:4 [o]Luke 14:14
6:6 [p]2 Ki. 4:33
6:7 [q]Eccl. 5:2 [r]1 Ki. 18:26

[n] Or, *righteousness;* Deut. 24:13; Ps. 112:9; Dan. 4:27; 2 Cor. 9:9 [o] Or, *with* [p] Or, *cause not a trumpet to be sounded*

6:1 ALMS BEFORE MEN. The principle stated here concerns the Christian's motive for doing righteousness. (1) If any believer, whether layman or minister, does good for the admiration of others or for selfish reasons, he will lose his reward and praise from God. Instead he will stand exposed as a hypocrite who, under the guise of giving glory to God, is really seeking glory for himself. (2) Jesus speaks of acts of righteousness in three areas: giving (vv. 2–4), prayer (vv. 5–8), and fasting (vv. 16–18). His condemnation of doing righteousness to be seen by others challenges much of contemporary Christian activity, including competition for bigness, advertising one's success, performance and entertainment in the church, and the desire to be first (see 1 Cor. 3:13–15; 4:5).

6:6 PRAY . . . IN SECRET. Every child of God should have some place to be alone with God. Unless such a place exists, secret prayer will not be long or consistently maintained. Jesus had His secret places (14:23; Mark 1:35; Luke 4:42; 5:16; 6:12). Secret prayer is especially important: (1) in the morning to commit our day to Him; (2) in the evening to render thanks for His mercies; (3) in times when the Holy Spirit prompts us to pray. Our Father promises to reward us openly—with answered prayer, with His intimate presence, and with true honor for eternity (see 6:9, note on God as Father).

6:9 AFTER THIS MANNER . . . PRAY. With this model prayer, Christ indicates areas of concern that should occupy a Christian's prayer. The prayer contains six petitions: three concerned with the holiness and will of God; three concerned with our personal needs. The brevity of the prayer does not mean we should pray only briefly about our concerns. At times Christ prayed all night long (Luke 6:12).

6:9 OUR FATHER . . . IN HEAVEN. Prayer involves worship of the heavenly Father. (1) As Father, God loves us, cares for us, and welcomes our fellowship and intimacy; through Christ we have access to Him at any time to worship Him and communicate our needs to Him (vv. 25–34). (2) God as Father does not mean that He is like an earthly father who tolerates evil in his children or fails to

ye: [s]Our Father which art in heaven,
Hallowed be thy name.
10 Thy kingdom come. [t]Thy will
be done in earth, [u]as *it is* in heaven.
11 Give us this day our [v]daily
bread.
12 And [w]forgive us our debts, as
we forgive our debtors.
13 [x]And lead us not into temptation,
but [y]deliver us from evil: [z]For
thine is the kingdom, and the power,
and the glory, for ever. Amen.
14 [a]For if ye forgive men their trespasses,
your heavenly Father will also
forgive you:
15 But [b]if ye forgive not men their
trespasses, neither will your Father
forgive your trespasses.

Fasting

16 ¶ Moreover [c]when ye fast, be
not, as the hypocrites, of a sad countenance:
for they disfigure their faces,
that they may appear unto men to fast.

6:9 [s]Luke 11:2 **6:10** [t]ch. 26:39 Acts 21:14 [u]Ps. 103:20 **6:11** [v]See Job 23:12 Prov. 30:8 **6:12** [w]ch. 18:21 **6:13** [x]ch. 26:41 1 Cor. 10:13 2 Pet. 2:9 Rev. 3:10 [y]John 17:15 [z]1 Chr. 29:11

6:14 [a]Mark 11:25; Eph. 4:32; Col 3:13 **6:15** [b]ch. 18:35; Jas. 2:13 **6:16** [c]Is. 58:5

discipline them correctly. God is a Father of holiness who must oppose sin. He will not tolerate evil, even in those who name Him as Father. His name must be "hallowed." (3) Hence, as a heavenly Father He can punish as well as bless, withhold as well as give, act with justice as well as mercy. How He responds to His children depends upon our faith and obedience to Him.

6:9 HALLOWED BE THY NAME. The greatest concern in our prayers and life should be the hallowing of the name of God. It is of utmost importance that God Himself be reverenced, honored, glorified, and exalted (cf. Ps. 34:3). In our prayer and daily walk we must be intensely concerned with the reputation of God, His church, His gospel, and His kingdom. To do something that brings scandal upon the name and character of the Lord is a hideous sin that puts Him to open shame.

6:10 THY KINGDOM COME. Prayer must be concerned with the kingdom of God on earth now and with its ultimate fulfillment in the future. (1) We must pray for the return of Christ and the establishment of God's eternal kingdom in the new heaven and the new earth (Rev. 21:1; cf. 2 Pet. 3:10–12; Rev. 20:11; 22:20). (2) We must pray for the spiritual presence and manifestation of the kingdom of God now. This includes asserting God's power among His people in order to destroy the works of Satan, heal the sick, save the lost, promote righteousness, and pour out the Holy Spirit upon His people (see article on THE KINGDOM OF GOD, p. 1428).

6:10 THY WILL BE DONE. To pray "thy will be done" means that we sincerely desire God's will and purpose to be fulfilled in our lives and the lives of our family, according to His eternal plan. We can determine what God's will is primarily in His revealed will, the Bible, and through the Holy Spirit's leading in our hearts (cf. Rom. 8:4–14; see article on THE WILL OF GOD, p. 1060). God's will is accomplished when we pray for "the kingdom of God, and his righteousness" to come among us (v. 33; see article on THE KINGDOM OF GOD, p. 1428).

6:11 DAILY BREAD. Prayer should contain requests concerned with the individual's daily needs (Phil. 4:19; see Luke 11:3, note).

6:12 FORGIVE . . . AS WE FORGIVE. Prayer must be concerned with transgressions and a willingness to forgive those who have harmed us (vv. 14–15; Heb. 9:14; 1 John 1:9).

6:13 DELIVER US FROM EVIL. All believers are the special object of Satan's enmity and evil purpose. For this reason, we must never forget to pray for deliverance from his power and schemes (see Luke 11:26, note; 18:1, note; 22:31; John 17:15; 2 Cor. 2:11; see article on POWER OVER SATAN AND DEMONS, p. 1486).

6:15 IF YE FORGIVE NOT. Jesus here emphasizes that the Christian must be ready and willing to forgive the offenses of others. If he does not forgive a repenting offender, God will not forgive him, and his prayers will be to no avail. This is an important principle by which God forgives (18:35; Mark 11:26; Luke 11:4.)

6:16 WHEN YE FAST. In the Bible fasting refers to the discipline of abstaining from food for spiritual purposes. Although it was often linked with prayer, it should be considered a spiritual exercise all its own. In fact, fasting can be called "prayer without words."

(1) There are three main forms of fasting presented in the Bible. (a) The normal fast: abstaining from all food, solid or liquid, but not from water (see 4:2, note). (b) The absolute fast: abstaining from both food and water (Esth. 4:16; Acts 9:9). Normally this kind of fast should not be for more than three days, for the body then begins to dehydrate. Moses and Elijah undertook the absolute fast for 40 days, but only under supernatural conditions (Ex. 34:28; Deut. 9:9,18; 1 Ki. 19:8). (c) The partial fast: a restriction of diet rather than complete abstention (Dan. 10:3).

(2) Christ Himself practiced this discipline and taught that it was to be a part of Christian devotion and an act of preparation for His return (see 9:15, note). The N.T. church practiced fasting (Acts 13:2–3; 14:23; 27:33).

(3) Fasting with prayer has several purposes: (a) to honor God (vv. 16–18; Zech. 7:5; Luke 2:37; Acts 13:2); (b) to humble one's soul before God (Ezra 8:21; Ps. 69:10; Is. 58:3) in order to receive more grace (1 Pet. 5:5) and God's close presence (Is. 57:15; 58:6–9); (c) to mourn over personal sin and failure (1 Sam. 7:6; Neh. 9:1–2); (d) to mourn over the sins of the church, nation, and world (1 Sam. 7:6; Neh. 9:1–2); (e) to seek grace for a new task and to reaffirm our consecration to God (4:2); (f) to seek God by drawing near to Him and prevailing in prayer against opposing spiritual forces (Judg. 20:26; Ezra 8:21,23,31; Jer. 29:12–14; Joel 2:12; Luke 18:3; Acts 9:10–19);

Verily I say unto you, They have their reward.

17 But thou, when thou fastest, [d]anoint thine head, and wash thy face;

18 That thou appear not unto men to fast, but unto thy Father which is in secret: and thy Father, which seeth in secret, shall reward thee openly.

Treasures in heaven

6:22–23pp — Luke 11:34–36

19 ¶ [e]Lay not up for yourselves treasures upon earth, where moth and rust doth corrupt, and where thieves break through and steal:

20 [f]But lay up for yourselves treasures in heaven, where neither moth nor rust doth corrupt, and where thieves do not break through nor steal:

21 For where your treasure is, there will your heart be also.

22 [g]The light of the body is the eye: if therefore thine eye be single, thy whole body shall be full of light.

23 But if thine eye be evil, thy whole body shall be full of darkness. If therefore the light that is in thee be darkness, how great *is* that darkness!

24 ¶ [h]No man can serve two masters: for either he will hate the one, and love the other; or else he will hold to the one, and despise the other. [i]Ye cannot serve God and mammon.

John 15:18-20

6:17 [d]Ruth 3:3 Dan. 10:3
6:19 [e]Prov. 23:4 1 Tim. 6:17 Heb. 13:5 Jas. 5:1
6:20 [f]ch. 19:21 Luke 12:33 & 18:22 1 Tim. 6:19 1 Pet. 1:4
6:22 [g]Luke 11:34
6:24 [h]Luke 16:13 [i]Gal. 1:10 1 Tim. 6:17 Jas. 4:4 1 John 2:15
6:25 [j]Ps. 55:22 Luke 12:22 Phil. 4:6 1 Pet. 5:7
6:26 [k]Job 38:41 Ps. 147:9 Luke 12:24
6:33 [l]See 1 Ki. 3:13 Ps. 37:25 Mark 10:30 Luke 12:31 1 Tim. 4:8

Do not worry

6:25–33pp — Luke 12:22–31

25 Therefore I say unto you, [j]Take no thought for your life, what ye shall eat, or what ye shall drink; nor yet for your body, what ye shall put on. Is not the life more than meat, and the body than raiment?

26 [k]Behold the fowls of the air: for they sow not, neither do they reap, nor gather into barns; yet your heavenly Father feedeth them. Are ye not much better than they?

27 Which of you by taking thought can add one cubit unto his stature?

28 And why take ye thought for raiment? Consider the lilies of the field, how they grow; they toil not, neither do they spin:

29 And yet I say unto you, That even Solomon in all his glory was not arrayed like one of these.

30 Wherefore, if God so clothe the grass of the field, which today is, and tomorrow is cast into the oven, *shall he* not much more *clothe* you, O ye of little faith?

31 Therefore take no thought, saying, What shall we eat? or, What shall we drink? or, Wherewithal shall we be clothed?

32 (For after all these things do the Gentiles seek:) for your heavenly Father knoweth that ye have need of all these things.

33 But [l]seek ye first the kingdom

(g) to show repentance and so make a way for God to change His declared intentions of judgment (2 Sam. 12:16,22; 1 Ki. 21:27–29; Jer. 18:7–8; Joel 2:12–14; Jonah 3:5,10); (h) to save souls from the bondage of evil (Is. 58:6; Mat. 17:14–21; Luke 4:18); (i) to gain revelation, wisdom, and understanding concerning the will of God (Is. 58:5–6,11; Dan. 9:3,21–22; Acts 13:2–3); (j) to open the way for the outpouring of the Spirit and Christ's return to earth for His people (see 9:15, note).

6:24 MAMMON. "Mammon" means money or valuable possessions. Jesus states unequivocally that one cannot at the same time serve God and money. (1) To serve money is to place such a high value on it that we (a) place our trust and faith in it, (b) look to it for our ultimate security and happiness, (c) expect it to guarantee our future, and (d) desire it more than we desire God's righteousness and kingdom. (2) The accumulation of wealth soon dominates one's mind and life so that God's glory will no longer be first (see Luke 16:13, note; see article on RICHES AND POVERTY, p. 1568).

6:25 TAKE NO THOUGHT. Jesus does not mean that it is wrong to make provisions for future physical needs (cf. 2 Cor. 12:14; 1 Tim. 5:8). What He does forbid is anxiety or worry which shows a lack of faith in God's fatherly care and love (Ezek. 34:12; 1 Pet. 5:7; see next note).

6:30 IF GOD SO CLOTHE. These words contain God's promise to all of His children in this age of trouble and uncertainty. God has promised to provide for our food, clothing, and necessities. We need not worry; if we seek to let God reign in our life (v. 33), we can be sure that He will assume full responsibility for the life wholly yielded to Him (Phil. 4:6; 1 Pet. 5:7; see article on THE PROVIDENCE OF GOD, p. 80).

6:33 SEEK ... KINGDOM ... RIGHTEOUSNESS. Those who follow Christ are urged to seek above all else God's kingdom and His righteousness. The verb "seek" implies being continually absorbed in a search for something, or making a strenuous and diligent effort to obtain something (cf. 13:45). Christ refers to two objects of our seeking: (1) "The kingdom of God" — we must seek earnestly to have the rule and power of God demonstrated in our lives and assemblies. We must pray that God's kingdom will come in the mighty power of the Holy Spirit to save sinners, to destroy the

of God, and his righteousness; and all these things shall be added unto you.

34 Take therefore no thought for the morrow: for the morrow shall take thought for the things of itself. Sufficient unto the day *is* the evil thereof.

Judging and hypocrisy

7:3–5pp — Luke 6:41–42

7 JUDGE[m] NOT, that ye be not judged.

2 For with what judgment ye judge, ye shall be judged: [n]and with what measure ye mete, it shall be measured to you again.

3 [o]And why beholdest thou the mote that is in thy brother's eye, but considerest not the beam that is in thine own eye?

4 Or how wilt thou say to thy brother, Let me pull out the mote out of thine eye; and, behold, a beam *is* in thine own eye?

5 Thou hypocrite, first cast out the beam out of thine own eye; and then shalt thou see clearly to cast out the mote out of thy brother's eye.

6 ¶ [p]Give not that which is holy unto the dogs, neither cast ye your pearls before swine, lest they trample them under their feet, and turn again and rend you.

Prayer and the Golden Rule

7:7–11pp — Luke 11:9–13

7 ¶ [q]Ask, and it shall be given you; seek, and ye shall find; knock, and it shall be opened unto you:

8 For [r]every one that asketh receiveth; and he that seeketh findeth; and to him that knocketh it shall be opened.

9 [s]Or what man is there of you, whom if his son ask bread, will he give him a stone?

10 Or if he ask a fish, will he give him a serpent?

11 If ye then, [t]being evil, know how to give good gifts unto your children, how much more shall your Father which is in heaven give good things to them that ask him?

12 Therefore all things [u]whatsoever ye would that men should do to you, do ye even so to them: for [v]this is the law and the prophets.

The strait and wide gates

13 ¶ [w]Enter ye in at the strait gate: for wide *is* the gate, and broad *is* the way, that leadeth to destruction, and many there be which go in thereat:

14 [⁋]Because strait *is* the gate, and

[⁋] Or, *How*

7:1 [m]Luke 6:37 Rom. 14:3 1 Cor. 4:3 Jas. 4:11
7:2 [n]Mark 4:24 Luke 6:38
7:3 [o]Luke 6:41
7:6 [p]Prov. 9:7,8 & 23:9 Acts 13:45
7:7 [q]ch. 21:22 Mark 11:24 Luke 11:9 & 18:1 John 14:13 & 15:7 & 16:23,24 Jas. 1:5,6 1 John 3:22 & 5:14,15
7:8 [r]Prov. 8:17 Jer. 29:12
7:9 [s]Luke 11:11
7:11 [t]Gen. 6:5 & 8:21
7:12 [u]Luke 6:31 [v]Lev. 19:18 ch. 22:40 Rom. 13:8 Gal. 5:14 1 Tim. 1:5
7:13 [w]Luke 13:24

---

demonic, to heal the sick, and to magnify the name of the Lord Jesus (see article on THE KINGDOM OF GOD, p. 1428). (2) "His righteousness"—through the Holy Spirit we must seek to obey the commands of Christ, possess His righteousness, remain separated from the world, and manifest His love toward everyone (cf. Phil. 2:12–13).

7:1 JUDGE NOT. Jesus condemns the habit of criticizing others while ignoring one's own faults. A believer must first submit himself to God's righteous standard before attempting to examine and influence the conduct of other Christians (vv. 3–5). Judging in an unjust manner also includes condemning a wrongdoer without desiring to see the offender return to God and His ways (Luke 6:36–37).

(1) Christ is not denying the necessity of exercising a certain degree of discernment or of making value judgments with respect to sin in others. Elsewhere we are commanded to identify false ministers within the church (v. 15) and to evaluate the character of individuals (v. 6; cf. John 7:24; 1 Cor. 5:12; 1 John 4:1; see Gal. 1:9, note; 1 Tim. 4:1, note).

(2) This verse must not be used as an excuse for laxity in exercising church discipline (see 18:15, note).

7:7–8 ASK . . . SEEK . . . KNOCK. Jesus encourages perseverance in prayer. The tense of the Greek verbs in v. 8 designates continuous action. This means we must keep on asking, seeking, and knocking. Asking implies consciousness of need and the belief that God hears our prayer. Seeking implies earnest petitioning along with obedience to God's will. Knocking implies perseverance in coming to God when He does not respond quickly. Christ's assurance that those who ask will receive what they ask is based on: (1) seeking first the kingdom of God (see 6:33, note); (2) recognizing God's fatherly goodness and love (6:8; 7:11; John 15:16; 16:23, 26f; Col. 1:9–12); (3) praying in accordance with His will (Mark 11:24; John 21:22; 1 John 5:14); (4) maintaining fellowship with Christ (John 15:7); and (5) obeying Christ (1 John 3:22; see article on EFFECTIVE PRAYING, p. 540).

7:11 YOUR FATHER . . . GIVE GOOD THINGS. Christ promises that the Father in heaven will not disappoint His children. He loves us even more than a good earthly father and wants us to ask Him for whatever we need, promising to give us what is good. He desires to provide solutions for our problems and bread for our daily need. And most of all, He gives the Holy Spirit to His children as their Helper (Luke 11:13; John 14:16–18).

7:14 STRAIT *IS* THE GATE . . . AND FEW THERE BE. Christ taught that we are not to ex-

narrow *is* the way, which leadeth unto life, and few there be that find it.

The test of false prophets

15 ¶ [x]Beware of false prophets, [y]which come to you in sheep's clothing, but inwardly they are [z]ravening wolves.

16 [a]Ye shall know them by their fruits. [b]Do men gather grapes of thorns, or figs of thistles?

17 Even so [c]every good tree bringeth forth good fruit; but a corrupt tree bringeth forth evil fruit.

18 A good tree cannot bring forth evil fruit, neither *can* a corrupt tree bring forth good fruit.

19 [d]Every tree that bringeth not forth good fruit is hewn down, and cast into the fire.

20 Wherefore by their fruits ye shall know them. Mat. 12:3

The saved do God's will

21 ¶ Not every one that saith unto me, [e]Lord, Lord, shall enter into the kingdom of heaven; but he that doeth the will of my Father which is in heaven.

22 Many will say to me in that day, Lord, Lord, have we [f]not prophesied in thy name? and in thy name have cast

7:15 [x]Deut. 13:3 Jer. 23:16 ch. 24:4,5 Mark 13:22 Rom. 16:17 Eph. 5:6 Col. 2:8 2 Pet. 2:1 1 John 4:1 [y]Mic. 3:5 2 Tim. 3:5 [z]Acts 20:29 **7:16** [a]ver. 20 [b]Luke 6:43 **7:17** [c]Jer. 11:19 ch. 12:33 **7:19** [d]ch. 3:10 Luke 3:9 John 15:2 **7:21** [e]Hos. 8:2 ch. 25:11 Luke 6:46 & 13:25; Acts 19:13; Rom. 2:13; Jas. 1:22 **7:22** [f]Num. 24:4; John 11:51; 1 Cor. 13:2

pect the majority to follow Him on the road that leads to life. (1) Comparatively few will enter the humble gate of true repentance and thereafter deny themselves to follow Jesus, sincerely endeavor to obey His commandments, earnestly seek His kingdom and His righteousness, and persevere until the end in true faith, purity, and love.

(2) Jesus in His Sermon on the Mount describes the great blessings that accompany discipleship in His kingdom (5:3–12), but He also insists that His disciples will not escape persecution (5:10–12). Furthermore, contrary to some evangelists who preach that "getting saved" is one of the easiest things in the world, Jesus taught that following Him involves heavy obligations concerning righteousness, acceptance of persecution, love for enemies, and self-denial.

7:15 BEWARE OF FALSE PROPHETS. See article on FALSE TEACHERS, p. 1508.

7:16 KNOW THEM BY THEIR FRUITS. False teachers who outwardly appear righteous but "inwardly . . . are ravening wolves" (v. 15) can, at times, be identified by their "fruits." The "fruit" of a false teacher will be unwholesome characteristics evident in the lives of his followers (see 1 John 4:5–6), such as those listed below. (1) They will be professing Christians whose loyalty is more to personalities than to the Word of God (v. 21). They worship the creature more than the Creator (cf. Rom. 1:25).

(2) They will be more concerned with their own desires than with the glory and honor of God. Their doctrine will be man-centered rather than God-centered (vv. 21–23; see 2 Tim. 4:3, note).

(3) They will accept human teachings and traditions even when those teachings contradict the Word of God (vv. 24–27; 1 John 4:6).

(4) They will seek after and respond to religious experiences and supernatural manifestations as their final authority in validating truth (vv. 22–23), rather than grounding themselves in the whole counsel of God's Word.

(5) They will not endure sound doctrine, but will seek teachers who offer salvation with the "broad way" of unrighteousness (vv. 13–14,23; see 2 Tim. 4:3, note).

7:21 DOETH THE WILL OF MY FATHER. Jesus emphatically taught that carrying out the will of His heavenly Father was a condition of entering the kingdom of heaven (cf. vv. 22–27; 19:16–26; 25:31–46). However, this does not mean that we can gain or merit salvation by our own efforts or works alone. This is true for the following reasons: (1) The forgiveness of God comes to us through faith and repentance made possible by the grace and sacrificial death of Christ (see 26:28, note; Luke 15:11–32; 18:9–14).

(2) The obedience to the will of God demanded by Christ is indeed an ongoing condition for salvation, but Christ also declares that it is a grace belonging to the salvation of the kingdom. As such we must continually pray for it, receive it, and put it into effect by a sincere faith and earnest endeavor. Note the Lord's Prayer (6:9–13) and the many admonitions directed toward believers to put sin to death and to present ourselves to God as living sacrifices (cf. Rom. 6:1–23; 8:1–17; 12:1–2; see Mat. 5:6, note on hungering and thirsting for righteousness; see article on THE WILL OF GOD, p. 1060).

(3) We are capable of doing God's will and living a righteous life by virtue of this gift, i.e., God's grace, power, and spiritual life continually given to us through Christ (Eph. 2:5). Scripture declares that "by grace are ye saved through faith; and that not of yourselves: it is the gift of God . . . for we are his workmanship" (Eph. 2:8–10).

(4) Thus, God always makes available the obedience He demands of us. It is ascribed to God's redemptive action. "For it is God which worketh in you both to will and to do of *his* good pleasure" (see Phil. 2:13, note). Yet God's gift of grace does not annul human responsibility or action. We must respond positively to God's gift of obedience (Eph. 4:22–32; Jude 20–21,24; see Phil. 2:12, note), for we remain free to reject God's grace, to refuse to draw near to God through Christ (see Heb. 7:25, note), and to refuse to pray for and accept the life of obedience (see 5:6, note; see article on FAITH AND GRACE, p. 1738).

7:22 MANY WILL SAY . . . LORD, LORD. In vv. 22–23 Jesus emphatically states that there will

out devils? and in thy name done many
wonderful works?
23 And [g]then will I profess unto
them, I never knew you: [h]depart from
me, ye that work iniquity.

The wise and foolish builders

7:24–27pp — Luke 6:47–49

24 ¶ Therefore [i]whosoever hear-
eth these sayings of mine, and doeth
them, I will liken him unto a wise man,
which built his house upon a rock:
25 And the rain descended, and the
floods came, and the winds blew, and
beat upon that house; and it fell not:
for it was founded upon a rock.
26 And every one that heareth
these sayings of mine, and doeth them
not, shall be likened unto a foolish
man, which built his house upon the
sand:
27 And the rain descended, and the
floods came, and the winds blew, and
beat upon that house; and it fell: and
great was the fall of it.
28 And it came to pass, when Jesus
had ended these sayings, [j]the people
were astonished at his doctrine:
29 [k]For he taught them as *one* hav-
ing authority, and not as the scribes.

The leper cleansed

8:2–4pp — Mark 1:40–44; Luke 5:12–14

8 WHEN HE was come down from
the mountain, great multitudes
followed him.
2 [l]And, behold, there came a leper
and worshipped him, saying, Lord, if
thou wilt, thou canst make me clean.
3 And Jesus put forth *his* hand, and
touched him, saying, I will; be thou
clean. And immediately his leprosy
was cleansed.
4 And Jesus saith unto him, [m]See
thou tell no man; but go thy way, show
thyself to the priest, and offer the gift
that [n]Moses commanded, for a testi-
mony unto them.

The centurion's servant healed

8:5–13pp — Luke 7:1–10

5 ¶ [o]And when Jesus was entered
into Capernaum, there came unto him
a centurion, beseeching him,
6 And saying, Lord, my servant
lieth at home sick of the palsy, griev-
ously tormented.
7 And Jesus saith unto him, I will
come and heal him.
8 The centurion answered and said,
Lord, [p]I am not worthy that thou
shouldest come under my roof: but
[q]speak the word only, and my servant
shall be healed.
9 For I am a man under authority,
having soldiers under me: and I say to
this *man*, Go, and he goeth; and to an-
other, Come, and he cometh; and to my
servant, Do this, and he doeth *it*.
10 When Jesus heard *it*, he mar-
velled, and said to them that followed,
Verily I say unto you, I have not found
so great faith, no, not in Israel. Mat. 9:2

7:23 [g]ch. 25:12 Luke 13:25 2 Tim. 2:19 [h]Ps. 5:5 & 6:8 ch. 25:41 **7:24** [i]Luke 6:47 **7:28** [j]ch. 13:54 Mark 1:22 & 6:2 Luke 4:32 **7:29** [k]John 7:46 **8:2** [l]Mark 1:40 Luke 5:12 **8:4** [m]ch. 9:30 Mark 5:43 [n]Lev. 14:3,4,10 Luke 5:14 **8:5** [o]Luke 7:1 **8:8** [p]Luke 15:19,21 [q]Ps. 107:20

be "many" within the church who will minister in His name and believe they are His servants, yet in reality He never knew them (v. 23). To escape the deceit of the last days, a church leader (or any disciple) must be totally committed to the truth and righteousness revealed in God's Word (see Rev. 22:19, note) and not consider "ministerial success" as the standard by which to judge his relation to Christ.

7:23 I NEVER KNEW YOU. These words of Christ make it unmistakably clear that a preacher may proclaim the gospel in the name of Christ, cast out demons, and perform miracles while he himself has no genuine saving faith in Christ. (1) Scripture teaches that fervent gospel preaching, an apparent zeal for righteousness, and the occurrence of miracles can be performed in this age under the influence and power of Satan. Paul warns that "Satan himself is transformed into an angel of light. Therefore *it is* no great thing if his ministers also be transformed as the ministers of righteousness" (2 Cor. 11:14–15; cf. Mat. 24:24). Paul makes it clear that an apparent powerful anointing can be "the working of Satan" (see 2 Thes. 2:9–10; Rev. 13:3,12; see aarticle on FALSE TEACHERS, p. 1508).

(2) Many times God overrides the activity of Satan in false preachers in order to bring salvation or healing to those who sincerely respond to God's Word (see Phil. 1:15–18). It is always God's desire that those who proclaim the gospel be righteous (see 1 Tim. 3:1–7); yet when an evil or immoral person preaches His Word, God can still work in the hearts of those who receive His Word with commitment to Christ. God does not endorse any unrighteous preacher of the gospel, but He will endorse Biblical truth and those who accept it in faith.

8:10 GREAT FAITH. The centurion's faith surpassed anything that Jesus found among the Jews, for it combined a loving concern for another person with great trust in Christ. This story, along with Christ's application to the unbelieving Jews (vv. 11–12), warns us that we may be excluded from what God is doing by adhering to human traditions or by failing to believe in the power of His kingdom.

11 And I say unto you, That [r]many shall come from the east and west, and shall sit down with Abraham, and Isaac, and Jacob, in the kingdom of heaven.

12 But [s]the children of the kingdom [t]shall be cast out into outer darkness: there shall be weeping and gnashing of teeth.

13 And Jesus said unto the centurion, Go thy way; and as thou hast believed, *so* be it done unto thee. And his servant was healed in the selfsame hour.

Peter's mother-in-law healed

8:14–16pp — Mark 1:29–34; Luke 4:38–41

14 ¶ [u]And when Jesus was come into Peter's house, he saw [v]his wife's mother laid, and sick of a fever.

15 And he touched her hand, and the fever left her: and she arose, and ministered unto them.

16 ¶ [w]When the even was come, they brought unto him many that were possessed with devils: and he cast out the spirits with *his* word, and healed all that were sick:

17 That it might be fulfilled which was spoken by Esaias the prophet, saying, [x]Himself took our infirmities, and bare *our* sicknesses. Mat. 10:1

Cost of following Jesus

8:19–22pp — Luke 9:57–60

18 ¶ Now when Jesus saw great multitudes about him, he gave commandment to depart unto the other side.

19 [y]And a certain scribe came, and said unto him, Master, I will follow thee whithersoever thou goest.

20 And Jesus saith unto him, The foxes have holes, and the birds of the air *have* nests; but the Son of man hath not where to lay *his* head.

21 [z]And another of his disciples said unto him, Lord, [a]suffer me first to go and bury my father.

22 But Jesus said unto him, Follow me; and let the dead bury their dead.

8:11 [r]Gen. 12:3 Is. 2:2,3 & 11:10 Mal. 1:11 Luke 13:29 Acts 10:45 & 11:18 & 14:27 Rom. 15:9 Eph. 3:6
8:12 [s]ch. 21:43 [t]ch. 13:42,50 & 22:13 & 24:51 & 25:30 Luke 13:28 2 Pet. 2:17 Jude 13
8:14 [u]Mark 1:29-31 Luke 4:38,39 [v]1 Cor. 9:5
8:16 [w]Mark 1:32 Luke 4:40,41
8:17 [x]Is. 53:4 1 Pet. 2:24
8:19 [y]Luke 9:57,58
8:21 [z]Luke 9:59,60 [a]See 1 Ki. 19:20
8:24 [b]Mark 4:37 Luke 8:23
8:26 [c]Ps. 65:7 & 89:9 & 107:29
8:28 [d]Mark 5:1 Luke 8:26
8:34 [e]See Deut. 5:25 1 Ki. 17:18 Luke 5:8 Acts 16:39

The storm stilled

8:23–27pp — Mark 4:36–41; Luke 8:22–25
8:23–27Ref — Mat. 14:22–33

23 ¶ And when he was entered into a ship, his disciples followed him.

24 [b]And, behold, there arose a great tempest in the sea, insomuch that the ship was covered with the waves: but he was asleep.

25 And his disciples came to *him*, and awoke him, saying, Lord, save us: we perish.

26 And he saith unto them, Why are ye fearful, O ye of little faith? Then [c]he arose, and rebuked the winds and the sea; and there was a great calm.

27 But the men marvelled, saying, What manner of man is this, that even the winds and the sea obey him!

Devils cast out

8:28–34pp — Mark 5:1–17; Luke 8:26–37

28 ¶ [d]And when he was come to the other side into the country of the Gergesenes, there met him two possessed with devils, coming out of the tombs, exceeding fierce, so that no man might pass by that way.

29 And, behold, they cried out, saying, What have we to do with thee, Jesus, thou Son of God? art thou come hither to torment us before the time?

30 And there was a good way off from them an herd of many swine feeding.

31 So the devils besought him, saying, If thou cast us out, suffer us to go away into the herd of swine.

32 And he said unto them, Go. And when they were come out, they went into the herd of swine: and, behold, the whole herd of swine ran violently down a steep place into the sea, and perished in the waters.

33 And they that kept them fled, and went their ways into the city, and told every thing, and what was befallen to the possessed of the devils. Mat. 17:14-18

34 And, behold, the whole city came out to meet Jesus: and when they saw him, [e]they besought *him* that he would depart out of their coasts.

8:16–17 HEALED ALL THAT WERE SICK. See article on DIVINE HEALING, p. 1418.

8:22 LET THE DEAD BURY THEIR DEAD. Christ's saying means, "Let the spiritually dead bury the physically dead." The disciple of v. 21 probably wanted to stay with his elderly father until he died.

8:28 POSSESSED WITH DEVILS. See 17:17, note; see article on POWER OVER SATAN AND DEMONS, p. 1486.

Jesus heals a paralytic

9:2–8pp — Mark 2:3–12; Luke 5:18–26

9 AND HE entered into a ship, and
passed over, [f]and came into his
own city.
2 [g]And, behold, they brought to
him a man sick of the palsy, lying on
a bed: [h]and Jesus seeing their faith
said unto the sick of the palsy; Son, be
of good cheer; thy sins be forgiven
thee.
3 And, behold, certain of the scribes
said within themselves, This *man* blas-
phemeth.
4 And Jesus [i]knowing their
thoughts said, Wherefore think ye evil
in your hearts?
5 For whether is easier, to say, *Thy
sins be forgiven thee;* or to say, Arise,
and walk?
6 But that ye may know that the
Son of man hath power on earth to for-
give sins, (then saith he to the sick of
the palsy,) Arise, take up thy bed, and
go unto thine house.
7 And he arose, and departed to his
house.
8 But when the multitudes saw *it,*
they marvelled, and glorified God,
which had given such power unto men.

Matthew called

9:9–13pp — Mark 2:14–17; Luke 5:27–32

9 ¶ [j]And as Jesus passed forth
from thence, he saw a man, named
Matthew, sitting at the receipt of cus-
tom: and he saith unto him, Follow me.
And he arose, and followed him.
10 ¶ [k]And it came to pass, as Jesus
sat at meat in the house, behold, many
publicans and sinners came and sat
down with him and his disciples.
11 And when the Pharisees saw *it,*
they said unto his disciples, Why
eateth your Master with [l]publicans
and [m]sinners?
12 But when Jesus heard *that,* he
said unto them, They that be whole
need not a physician, but they that are
sick.
13 But go ye and learn what *that*
meaneth, [n]I will have mercy, and not
sacrifice: for I am not come to call the
righteous, [o]but sinners to repentance.

The question about fasting

9:14–17pp — Mark 2:18–22; Luke 5:33–39

14 ¶ Then came to him the disciples
of John, saying, [p]Why do we and the
Pharisees fast oft, but thy disciples
fast not?
15 And Jesus said unto them, Can
[q]the children of the bridechamber
mourn, as long as the bridegroom is
with them? but the days will come,
when the bridegroom shall be taken
from them, and [r]then shall they fast.
16 No man putteth a piece of [1]new
cloth unto an old garment, for that
which is put in to fill it up taketh from
the garment, and the rent is made
worse.
17 Neither do men put new wine
into old bottles: else the bottles break,
and the wine runneth out, and the bot-

9:1 [f]ch. 4:13
9:2 [g]Mark 2:3 Luke 5:18 [h]ch. 8:10
9:4 [i]Ps. 139:2 ch. 12:25 Mark 12:15 Luke 5:22 & 6:8 & 9:47 & 11:17
9:9 [j]Mark 2:14 Luke 5:27
9:10 [k]Mark 2:15 Luke 5:29
9:11 [l]ch. 11:19 Luke 5:30 & 15:2 [m]Gal. 2:15
9:13 [n]Hos. 6:6 Mic. 6:6-8 ch. 12:7 [o]1 Tim. 1:15
9:14 [p]Mark 2:18 Luke 5:33 & 18:12
9:15 [q]John 3:29 [r]Acts 13:2,3 & 14:23 1 Cor. 7:5

[1] Or, *raw,* or, *unwrought cloth*

9:11 EATETH . . . WITH . . . SINNERS. In vv. 11–13 Jesus gives the rule to guide us in our contact with nonbelievers: It should not be for pleasure or intimate friendship, but in order to do good to them and to show them the way of salvation (v. 12; Ps. 1:1). At no time should a believer date or marry a nonbeliever (see 1 Cor. 7:39; see article on SPIRITUAL SEPARATION FOR BELIEVERS, p. 1814).

9:15 THEN SHALL THEY FAST. It is clear that Jesus expected believers to fast after He was gone. The days of the "bridegroom's" absence is the period of this age, from the time of His ascension until His return. The church awaits this return of the bridegroom (25:6; see John 14:3, note). Therefore, fasting in this age is (1) a sign of the believer's longing for the return of his Lord, (2) a preparation for His coming, (3) a mourning of His absence, and (4) a sign of sorrow for the sin and decay of the world (see 6:16, note).

9:17 NEW WINE INTO OLD BOTTLES. This verse has been interpreted in various ways by commentators. Two views are: (1) The "new wine" was fresh grape juice. As it began to ferment, the new bottles (wineskins) would stretch and not break, whereas the old skins would break. The "new wine" represented the gospel as fermenting change which the old forms of Judaism could not contain. This view is questionable, however, because those familiar with the process of fermentation state that even the newest and strongest of wineskins, if sealed, would burst from the violent action of fermentation (see Job 32:19).

(2) A second interpretation sees the parable as emphasizing the importance of preserving both the "new wine" and the fresh wineskins (v. 17). (a) The "new wine" was fresh unfermented grape juice, representing the original saving message of Jesus Christ and the power of the Holy Spirit thrust forth at Pentecost. Jesus' overriding concern was that the original gospel and redemptive power of the Holy Spirit be preserved from all change, corruption, or loss. This interpretation is supported by Christ's concern that the gospel (new

DIVINE HEALING

Mat. 8:16–17 "When the even was come, they brought unto him many that were possessed with devils: and he cast out the spirits with his word, and healed all that were sick; That it might be fulfilled which was spoken by Esaias the prophet, saying, Himself took our infirmities, and bare our sicknesses."

GOD'S REDEMPTIVE PROVISION. (1) The problem of sickness and disease is intertwined with the problem of sin and death — i.e., the consequences of the fall. Whereas medical science views the causes of sickness and disease in physiological or psychosomatic terms, the Bible presents spiritual causes as the underlying or basic problem. These are twofold: (a) *sin*, which has affected our spiritual and physical makeup (e.g., John 5:5,14), and (b) *Satan* (e.g., Acts 10:38; cf. Mark 9:17,20,25; Luke 13:11; Acts 19:11–12).

(2) God's provision in redemption is as extensive as the consequences of the fall. For sin, God provides forgiveness; for death, God provides eternal and resurrection life; and for sickness, God provides healing (cf. Ps. 103:1–5; Luke 4:18; 5:17–26; Jas. 5:14–15). Thus, during Jesus' earthly life, His threefold ministry was *teaching* God's Word, *preaching* repentance (the sin problem) and the blessings of God's kingdom (life), and *healing* every kind of sickness, disease, and infirmity among the people (Mat. 4:23–24).

REVELATION CONCERNING GOD'S WILL. God's will concerning healing is revealed in four main ways in Scripture. (1) *God's own pronouncement.* In Ex. 15:26 God promised health and healing for His people if they remained faithful to His covenant and commandments (see Ex. 15:26, note). His pronouncement was twofold: (a) "I will put none of these diseases upon thee [as judgment] which I have brought upon the Egyptians"; and (b) "I am the Lord that healeth thee [as Redeemer]." God continued to be the doctor or healer of His people throughout the O.T. whenever they gave earnest heed to seek His face and obey His Word (cf. 2 Ki. 20:5; Ps. 103:3).

(2) *Jesus' ministry.* Jesus as the incarnate Son of God was and is the exact representation of God's nature and character (Heb. 1:3; cf. Col. 1:15; 2:9). In His earthly ministry (Mat. 4:23–24; 8:14–16; 9:35; 15:28; Mark 1:32–34,40–41; Luke 4:40; Acts 10:38), Jesus revealed God's will in action (John 6:38; 14:10), proving that it is in the heart, nature, and purpose of God to heal all who are sick and oppressed by the devil.

(3) *The provision of Christ's atonement* (Is. 53:4–5; Mat. 8:16–17; 1 Pet. 2:24). Jesus' atoning death was complete and adequate for redeeming the whole person—spirit, soul, and body. As sin and sickness have become the twin giants designed by Satan to destroy us, so forgiveness and healing are joined as twin blessings designed by God to redeem us and make us whole (cf. Ps. 103:3; Jas. 5:14–16). The believer should press on in humility and faith to possess the full provision of Christ's atonement, including the healing of the body.

(4) *The ongoing ministry of the church.* Jesus commissioned His twelve disciples to heal the sick as part of their proclamation of the kingdom of God (Luke 9:1–2,6). Later, He commissioned seventy disciples to do the same (Luke 10:1,8–9,19). After Pentecost, the early church carried on Jesus' healing ministry as part of preaching the gospel (Acts 3:1–10,4:30; 5:16; 8:7; 9:34; 14:8–10,19:11–12; cf. Mark 16:18; 1 Cor. 12:9,28,30; Jas. 5:14–16). The N.T. records three ways that God's healing power and faith were imparted through the church: (a) the laying on of hands (Mark 16:15–18; Acts 9:17), (b) confession of known sin, followed by anointing the sick with oil and the prayer of faith by the

elders (Jas. 5:14–16), and (c) spiritual gifts of healings given to the church (1 Cor. 12:9). Note that it is the elders who are to pray the prayer of faith.

HINDRANCES TO HEALING. Sometimes there are hindrances to receiving divine healing; for example, (1) unconfessed sin (Jas. 5:16), (2) demonic oppression or bondage (Luke 13:11–13), (3) fear or acute anxiety (Prov. 3:5–8; Phil. 4:6–7), (4) past disappointments which undermine faith in the present (Mark 5:26; John 5:5–7), (5) people (Mark 10:48), (6) unbiblical teaching (Mark 3:1–5; 7:13), (7) failure of the elders to pray the prayer of faith (Mark 11:22–24; Jas. 5:14–16), (8) failure of the church to seek and obtain the gifts of miracles and healings as God intended (Acts 4:29–30; 6:8; 8:5–6; 1 Cor. 12:9–10,29–31; Heb. 2:4), (9) unbelief (Mark 6:3–6; 9:19,23–24), and (10) carnal behavior (1 Cor. 11:29–30). At other times, the reason for the persistence of physical affliction in godly people is not readily apparent (e.g., Gal. 4:13; 1 Tim. 5:23; 2 Tim. 4:20). In still other instances, God chooses to take His beloved saints to heaven during an illness (cf. 2 Ki. 13:14).

STEPS TO TAKE. What can you do when praying and seeking for God's healing of your body? (1) Be certain you are in a right relationship with God and others (Mat. 6:33; see John 15:7, note; 1 Cor. 11:27–30; James 5:16).

(2) Seek the presence of Jesus in your life, for it is He who will impart to your heart the faith you need (Rom. 12:3; 1 Cor. 12:9; Phil. 2:13; see Mat. 17:20, note on true faith).

(3) Saturate your life with the Word of God (John 15:7; Rom. 10:17).

(4) If you are not finding healing, continue to abide in Him (John 15:1–7). Examine your life to see what changes God may desire to work in you.

(5) Call for the prayers of the elders of the church with the anointing of oil as well as the prayers of family and friends (Jas. 5:14–16).

(6) Attend a service where a person with a respected healing ministry is present (cf. Acts 5:15–16; 8:5–7).

(7) Expect a miracle—trust in the power of Christ (Mat. 7:8; 19:26).

(8) Rejoice if healing comes this day. Rejoice if it does not come in the present hour (Phil. 4:4,11–13).

(9) Know that God's delays in answering prayers are not necessarily denials of those requests. Sometimes God has a larger purpose in mind which, when realized, results in greater glory of God (e.g., John 9:3; 11:4,14–15,45; 2 Cor. 12:7–10) and in good for us (Rom. 8:28).

(10) Realize that if you are a committed Christian, God will never forsake you or forget you. He loves you so much that he has engraved you on the palms of His hands (Is. 49:15–16).

Note: The Bible acknowledges the proper use of medical care (Mat. 9:12; Luke 10:34; Col. 4:14).

tles perish: but they put new wine into new bottles, and both are preserved.

A ruler's daughter raised

9:18–26pp — Mark 5:22–43; Luke 8:41–56

18 ¶ [s]While he spake these things unto them, behold, there came a certain ruler, and worshipped him, saying, My daughter is even now dead: but come and lay thy hand upon her, and she shall live.

19 And Jesus arose, and followed him, and *so did* his disciples.

20 ¶ [t]And, behold, a woman, which was diseased with an issue of blood twelve years, came behind *him*, and touched the hem of his garment:

21 For she said within herself, If I may but touch his garment, I shall be whole.

22 But Jesus turned him about, and when he saw her, he said, Daughter, be of good comfort; [u]thy faith hath made thee whole. And the woman was made whole from that hour.

23 [v]And when Jesus came into the ruler's house, and saw [w]the minstrels and the people making a noise,

24 He said unto them, [x]Give place: for the maid is not dead, but sleepeth. And they laughed him to scorn.

25 But when the people were put forth, he went in, and took her by the hand, and the maid arose.

26 And [s]the fame hereof went abroad into all that land.

Jesus heals the blind and mute

27 ¶ And when Jesus departed thence, two blind men followed him, crying, and saying, [y]*Thou* Son of David, have mercy on us.

9:18 [s]Mark 5:22 Luke 8:41
9:20 [t]Mark 5:25 Luke 8:43
9:22 [u]Luke 7:50 & 8:48 & 17:19 & 18:42
9:23 [v]Mark 5:38 Luke 8:51 [w]See 2 Chr. 35:25
9:24 [x]Acts 20:10
9:27 [y]ch. 15:22 Mark 10:47 Luke 18:38

9:30 [z]ch. 8:4 Luke 5:14
9:31 [a]Mark 7:36
9:32 [b]ch. 12:22 Luke 11:14
9:34 [c]ch. 12:24 Luke 11:15
9:35 [d]ch. 4:23
9:36 [e]Mark 6:34 [f]Num. 27:17 1 Ki. 22:17
9:37 [g]Luke 10:2 John 4:35
9:38 [h]2 Thes. 3:1

28 And when he was come into the house, the blind men came to him: and Jesus saith unto them, Believe ye that I am able to do this? They said unto him, Yea, Lord.

29 Then touched he their eyes, saying, According to your faith be it unto you.

30 And their eyes were opened; and Jesus straitly charged them, saying, [z]See *that* no man know *it*. Mat. 17:20

31 [a]But they, when they were departed, spread abroad his fame in all that country.

32 ¶ [b]As they went out, behold, they brought to him a dumb man possessed with a devil.

33 And when the devil was cast out, the dumb spake: and the multitudes marvelled, saying, It was never so seen in Israel.

34 But the Pharisees said, [c]He casteth out devils through the prince of the devils.

The need for labourers

35 And Jesus went about all the cities and villages, [d]teaching in their synagogues, and preaching the gospel of the kingdom, and healing every sickness and every disease among the people.

36 ¶ [e]But when he saw the multitudes, he was moved with compassion on them, because they [t]fainted, and were scattered abroad, [f]as sheep having no shepherd.

37 Then saith he unto his disciples, [g]The harvest truly *is* plenteous, but the labourers *are* few;

38 [h]Pray ye therefore the Lord of

[s] Or, *this fame* [t] Or, *were tired and lay down*

wine) not be altered by the teachings (leaven) of the Pharisees and Judaism (leaven being a fermenting/altering agent, cf. 16:6,12; Ex. 12:19; 1 Cor. 5:7).

(b) In ancient times, in order to preserve the sweetness of the juice for an adequate period of time, people would strain or boil the juice, bottle it, and place it in a cool area (see articles on WINE IN NEW TESTAMENT TIMES (1) and (2), p. 1538 and p. 1594). Fresh wineskins were required because they would be free from all residual fermenting matter such as mature yeast cells. If placed in old wineskins, new wine would more easily begin to ferment because of the yeast cells which remained in the old wineskins. The subsequent fermentation would then cause the loss of both the new wine and the wineskins (which would burst from pressure). Columella, the great Roman authority on agriculture in the first century A.D., wrote that in order to keep new wine "always sweet" it must be put into a new sealed container (*On Agriculture*, 12.29).

9:17 NEW WINE . . . PRESERVED. Christ's emphasis here is on preserving the new wine for as long a time as possible (see previous note). For the various methods used in Bible times of keeping wine in a sweet and unfermented state, see articles on WINE IN NEW TESTAMENT TIMES (1) and (2), p. 1538 and p. 1594.

9:37 THE HARVEST TRULY *IS* PLENTEOUS. Jesus admonishes all believers to be constantly aware that the lost have an invaluable, everlasting soul and must spend eternity in heaven or in hell, and that many of them can be saved if only someone presents the gospel to them (see 10:28, note).

the harvest, that he will send forth la-
bourers into his harvest.

The mission of the Twelve

10:2–4pp — Mark 3:16–19; Luke 6:14–16; Acts 1:13
10:9–15pp — Mark 6:8–11; Luke 9:3–5; 10:4–12

10 AND [i]WHEN he had called
unto *him* his twelve disciples,
he gave them power [u]*against* unclean
spirits, to cast them out, and to heal all
manner of sickness and all manner of
disease.
2 Now the names of the twelve
apostles are these; The first, Simon,
[j]who is called Peter, and Andrew his
brother; James *the son* of Zebedee, and
John his brother;
3 Philip, and Bartholomew; Thom-
as, and Matthew the publican; James
the son of Alphaeus, and Lebbaeus,
whose surname was Thaddaeus;
4 [k]Simon the Canaanite, and Judas
[l]Iscariot, who also betrayed him.
5 These twelve Jesus sent forth,
and commanded them, saying, [m]Go
not into the way of the Gentiles, and
into *any* city of [n]the Samaritans enter
ye not:
6 [o]But go rather to the [p]lost
sheep of the house of Israel.
7 [q]And as ye go, preach, saying,
[r]The kingdom of heaven is at hand.
8 Heal the sick, cleanse the lepers,
raise the dead, cast out devils: [s]freely
ye have received, freely give.
9 [t]Provide[v] neither gold, nor sil-
ver, nor [u]brass in your purses,
10 Nor scrip for *your* journey, nei-
ther two coats, neither shoes, nor yet
[w]staves: [v]for the workman is worthy
of his meat.
11 [w]And into whatsoever city or
town ye shall enter, inquire who in it is
worthy; and there abide till ye go
thence.
12 And when ye come into an
house, salute it.
13 [x]And if the house be worthy, let
your peace come upon it: [y]but if it be
not worthy, let your peace return to
you.
14 [z]And whosoever shall not re-
ceive you, nor hear your words, when
ye depart out of that house or city,
[a]shake off the dust of your feet.
15 Verily I say unto you, [b]It shall
be more tolerable for the land of Sodom
and Gomorrha in the day of judgment,
than for that city.
16 ¶ [c]Behold, I send you forth as
sheep in the midst of wolves: [d]be ye
therefore wise as serpents, and
[e]harmless[x] as doves.

Discipleship and suffering

10:19–22pp — Mark 13:11–13; Luke 21:12–17

17 But beware of men: for [f]they
will deliver you up to the councils, and
[g]they will scourge you in their syna-
gogues;
18 And [h]ye shall be brought before
governors and kings for my sake, for a
testimony against them and the Gen-
tiles.
19 [i]But when they deliver you up,
take no thought how or what ye shall
speak: for [j]it shall be given you in

10:1 [i]Mark 3:13 Luke 6:13 **10:2** [j]John 1:42 **10:4** [k]Luke 6:15 Acts 1:13 [l]John 13:26 **10:5** [m]ch. 4:15 [n]2 Ki. 17:24 John 4:9 **10:6** [o]ch. 15:24 Acts 13:46 [p]Is. 53:6 Jer. 50:6 Ezek. 34:5 1 Pet. 2:25 **10:7** [q]Luke 9:2 [r]ch. 3:2 Luke 10:9 **10:8** [s]Acts 8:18 **10:9** [t]1 Sam. 9:7 Mark 6:8 Luke 9:3 & 10:4 [u]Mark 6:8 **10:10** [v]Luke 10:7 1 Cor. 9:7 1 Tim. 5:18 **10:11** [w]Luke 10:8 **10:13** [x]Luke 10:5 [y]Ps. 35:13 **10:14** [z]Mark 6:11 Luke 9:5 & 10:10,11 [a]Neh. 5:13 Acts 13:51 **10:15** [b]ch. 11:22 **10:16** [c]Luke 10:3 [d]Rom. 16:19 Eph. 5:15 [e]Phil. 2:15 **10:17** [f]Mark 13:9 Luke 12:11 [g]Acts 5:40 **10:18** [h]Acts 12:1 & 25:7,23 2 Tim. 4:16 **10:19** [i]Luke 21:14 [j]Ex. 4:12; Jer. 1:7

[u] Or, over [v] Or, *Get* [w] Gk. *a staff* [x] Or, *simple*

9:38 PRAY . . . THAT HE WILL SEND. This verse expresses one of God's own spiritual principles. Before He acts, He usually calls His people to prayer. Only after His people have prayed does God accomplish that work. In other words, God has limited Himself to the prayers of His people. It is clear from the context (9:35—10:1,8) that the kind of workers Jesus desires in His kingdom are those who (1) teach and preach the gospel of the kingdom (9:35), (2) heal the sick (9:35; 10:1,8), and (3) cast out unclean spirits (10:1,8).

10:1 POWER *AGAINST* UNCLEAN SPIRITS. Jesus wants His followers to wage war against the forces of evil by driving out evil spirits and healing the sick. This demonstration of authority in spiritual confrontation is considered a continuing manifestation of the kingdom of God on earth (see article on THE KINGDOM OF GOD, p. 1428).

10:7 PREACH . . . THE KINGDOM. The context (vv. 1,8) makes clear that the preaching of the kingdom of heaven is to be accompanied by God asserting His power against the forces of sin, sickness, and Satan (see article on THE KINGDOM OF GOD, p. 1428). It is Christ's purpose that the kingdom of heaven and its power be "at hand" to bring salvation, grace, and healing to God's people. When the "kingdom of heaven" is not being manifested among God's people, they should turn from the spirit of the world and all that is not pleasing to Him, "seek . . . first the kingdom of God, and his righteousness" (6:33), and pray "Thy kingdom come. Thy will be done" (6:10; cf. Mark 9:29).

10:19 GIVEN . . . WHAT YE SHALL SPEAK. This promise of Christ is seen in operation in Acts 4:8–12,19–20; 21:39—22:21; 23:1,6; 24:10–21; 26:1–29. After Pentecost the Spirit was poured out in all His fullness to give power to witness (Acts 1:8).

that same hour what ye shall speak.
20 [k]For it is not ye that speak, but
Mat. 24:14 the Spirit of your Father which
speaketh in you.
21 [l]And the brother shall deliver
up the brother to death, and the father
the child: and the children shall rise up
against *their* parents, and cause them
to be put to death.
22 And [m]ye shall be hated of all
men for my name's sake: [n]but he that
endureth to the end shall be saved.
23 But [o]when they persecute you
in this city, flee ye into another: for
verily I say unto you, Ye shall not
[y]have gone over the cities of Israel,
[p]till the Son of man be come.
24 [q]The disciple is not above *his*
master, nor the servant above his
lord.
25 It is enough for the disciple that
he be as his master, and the servant as
his lord. If [r]they have called the master
of the house [z]Beelzebub, how
much more *shall they call* them of his
household?

10:20 [k]2 Sam. 23:2; 2 Tim. 4:17 **10:21** [l]Mic. 7:6; Luke 21:16 **10:22** [m]Luke 21:17 [n]Dan. 12:12; Mark 13:13 **10:23** [o]ch. 2:13; Acts 8:1 [p]ch. 16:28 **10:24** [q]Luke 6:40; John 15:20 **10:25** [r]Mark 3:22; John 8:48 **10:26** [s]Mark 4:22; Luke 8:17 & 12:2,3 **10:28** [t]Is. 8:12,13; Luke 12:4; 1 Pet. 3:14 **10:30** [u]1 Sam. 14:45; Luke 21:18; Acts 27:34

The worth of a disciple

10:26–33pp — Luke 12:2–9
10:34–35pp — Luke 12:51–53

26 Fear them not therefore: [s]for
there is nothing covered, that shall not
be revealed; and hid, that shall not be
known.
27 What I tell you in darkness, *that*
speak ye in light: and what ye hear in
the ear, *that* preach ye upon the
housetops.
28 [t]And fear not them which kill
the body, but are not able to kill the
soul: but rather fear him which is able
to destroy both soul and body in hell.
29 Are not two sparrows sold for a
[a]farthing? and one of them shall not
fall on the ground without your Father.
30 [u]But the very hairs of your head
are all numbered.
31 Fear ye not therefore, ye are of
more value than many sparrows.

[y] Or, *end*, or, *finish* [z] Gk. *Beelzebul* [a] A farthing is a small amount of money, worth approximately one cent.

10:23 CITIES OF ISRAEL. Christ may have been telling His disciples that the gospel would continue to be proclaimed to the Jews until His return.

10:26 FEAR THEM NOT. The disciples' work for Christ and their battle against Satan will expose them to Satan's counterattack (vv. 16–25); yet they do not need to be afraid, because the Holy Spirit and the Father will sustain them (vv. 20, 29–31). They must remain faithful to the Word of Christ, preaching openly, frankly, and courageously.

10:28 HELL. The word translated "hell" (Gk. *gehenna*; see Jer. 7:31, note) in this passage refers to a place of eternal torment reserved for the ungodly (cf. Mark 9:43,48). The Bible teaches that one's existence does not end at death but continues on forever, either in the presence of God or in a place of punishment. Concerning the state of the lost, we should note the following:

(1) Jesus teaches that there is a place of eternal punishment for those condemned before God (see 5:22,29–30; 18:9; 23:15,33; Mark 9:43,45,47; Luke 10:15; 12:5). It is the terrifying reality of continuous punishment, the place of a "fire that never shall be quenched" (Mark 9:43), of "everlasting fire, prepared for the devil and his angels" (25:41), of "wailing and gnashing of teeth" (13:42, 50), of binding and outer darkness (22:13), and of torment and anguish and separation from heaven (Luke 16:23).

(2) The teaching of the epistles is essentially the same. The apostles speak of a coming judgment of God to inflict vengeance on those who disobey the gospel (2 Thes. 1:5–9), of a separation from the presence and glory of the Lord (2 Thes. 1:9), and of the destruction of God's enemies (Phil. 3:18–19; see also Rom. 9:22; 1 Cor. 16:22; Gal. 1:9; 2 Tim. 2:12; Heb. 10:27; 2 Pet. 2:4; Jude 1:7; Rev. 14:10; 19:20; 20:10,14).

(3) The Bible teaches that judgment on evildoers is certain. The main idea is condemnation, suffering, and separation from God with no time limit. Christians may find this doctrine unpleasant or hard to understand. Yet we must submit to the authority of God's Word and trust God's decision and justice.

(4) We must keep foremost in our thinking that God sent His Son to die in order that no one need perish (John 3:16). It is not God's intention or desire to send anyone to hell (2 Pet. 3:9). Those who enter hell do so by resisting the salvation provided by God (Rom. 1:16—2:10). The fact and reality of hell should cause all of God's people to hate sin fervently, to seek continually the salvation of the lost, and to warn everyone of the future righteous judgment of God (see Rev. 20:14, note).

10:31 YE ARE OF MORE VALUE. Jesus teaches that God's faithful children are of great worth to their heavenly Father. (1) God values you and your personal needs; He desires your love and fellowship so much that He sent Jesus to die on the cross for you (see John 3:16, note). You are never away from His presence, care, and concern. He knows all your needs, trials, and sorrows (6:8). (2) You are so important to God that He treasures your faithfulness, love, and loyalty to Himself above all earthly things. Your unwavering faith in Christ, proved genuine in the midst of trials and trouble, is His glory and honor. Read the assurances found in Ps. 91:14–16; 116:15; Is. 49:16; Mat. 11:28–29; Luke 12:32; John 13:1; 14:3; 17:24; Rom. 8:28; 1 John 4:19.

the Son, but the Father; [h]neither
knoweth any man the Father, save the
Son, and *he* to whomsoever the Son
will reveal *him*.

28 ¶ Come unto me, all *ye* that la-
bour and are heavy laden, and I will
give you rest.

29 Take my yoke upon you, [i]and
learn of me; for I am meek and [j]lowly
in heart: [k]and ye shall find rest unto
your souls.

30 [l]For my yoke *is* easy, and my
burden is light.

Jesus the Lord of the Sabbath

12:1–8pp — Mark 2:23–28; Luke 6:1–5
12:9–14pp — Mark 3:1–6; Luke 6:6–11

12 AT THAT time [m]Jesus went on
the sabbath day through the
corn; and his disciples were an hun-
gered, and began to pluck the ears of
corn, and to eat.

2 But when the Pharisees saw *it*,
they said unto him, Behold, thy disci-
ples do that which is not lawful to do
upon the sabbath day.

3 But he said unto them, Have ye
not read [n]what David did, when he
was an hungered, and they that were
with him;

4 How he entered into the house of
God, and did eat [o]the showbread,
which was not lawful for him to eat,
neither for them which were with him,
[p]but only for the priests?

5 Or have ye not read in the [q]law,
how that on the sabbath days the
priests in the temple profane the sab-
bath, and are blameless?

6 But I say unto you, That in this
place is [r]*one* greater than the temple.

7 But if ye had known what *this*
meaneth, [s]I will have mercy, and not
sacrifice, ye would not have con-
demned the guiltless.

8 For the Son of man is Lord even
of the sabbath day.

9 [t]And when he was departed
thence, he went into their synagogue:

10 ¶ And, behold, there was a man
which had *his* hand withered. And they
asked him, saying, [u]Is it lawful to heal
on the sabbath days? that they might
accuse him.

11 And he said unto them, What
man shall there be among you, that

11:27 [h]John 1:18 & 6:46 & 10:15
11:29 [i]John 13:15 Phil. 2:5 1 Pet. 2:21 1 John 2:6 [j]Zech. 9:9 Phil. 2:7,8 [k]Jer. 6:16
11:30 [l]1 John 5:3
12:1 [m]Deut. 23:25 Mark 2:23 Luke 6:1
12:3 [n]1 Sam. 21:6
12:4 [o]Ex. 25:30 Lev. 24:5 [p]Ex. 29:32 Lev. 8:31 & 24:9
12:5 [q]Num. 28:9 John 7:22
12:6 [r]2 Chr. 6:18 Mal. 3:1
12:7 [s]Hos. 6:6 Mic. 6:6-8 ch. 9:13
12:9 [t]Mark 3:1 Luke 6:6
12:10 [u]Luke 13:14 & 14:3 John 9:16

11:28 COME UNTO ME. Jesus' gracious invitation comes to all "that labour and are heavy laden" with the troubles of life and the sins of their own human nature. By coming to Jesus, becoming His servant, and obeying His direction, Jesus will free you from your insurmountable burdens and give you rest, peace, and His Holy Spirit to lead you through life. What trials and cares you carry will be borne with His help and grace (see Heb. 4:16).

12:1 SABBATH. The weekly Sabbath (Gk. *sabbaton*, meaning rest, ceasing) was the seventh day of the week set apart by the Law of Moses as a day for ceasing from normal work and for giving of oneself to rest and to the worship of the Lord (Ex. 20:10; Deut. 5:14; see Ex. 20:8, note). There are strong reasons to believe that the principles of the Sabbath have permanent validity for Christians and that we should still set aside one day in seven as a day of rest and of worship to God.

(1) The concept of a sacred day of rest was instituted before the Jewish Law: "God blessed the seventh day, and sanctified it" (see Gen 2:3, note; cf. Ex. 20:11). This indicates that from the time of creation God wanted one day in seven to be a source of blessing for everyone, not just for the Jewish race.

(2) Jesus never abrogated the principle of a day of rest, only the misuse of it by Jewish leaders (vv. 1–8; Luke 13:10–17; 14:1–6). He stated that the day of rest was given for our spiritual and physical well-being (Mark 2:27). Nowhere does the Bible indicate that this principle has been done away with.

(3) The spiritual purpose of a seventh day of rest benefits the Christian. In the O.T. it was used as a day to rest from labor and to dedicate oneself to God—a special time to get to know God, to worship Him, and to concentrate in private and in public on the things of God (Lev. 24:8; Num. 28:9). Today it provides us an opportunity to reaffirm that our trust and delight are in the Lord and not in the world, our own selfish way, material goods, or pleasure (cf. Ex. 20:10; 34:21; Is. 38:13). We can use this day to renew our initial commitment to Christ and our oneness with other believers, and to acknowledge that our entire lives, not just one-seventh, belong to God (see Heb. 4:9–10).

(4) As the Sabbath was a covenant sign that the Israelites were the people of God (Ex. 31:16–17), so the Christian day of worship (Sunday) can be seen as a sign to the world that we belong to Christ and that He is our Lord. Christians in the N.T. set aside the first day of the week to worship God and to commemorate the resurrection of Christ (Acts 20:7; 1 Cor. 16:2).

(5) The Sabbath was set apart by God as a holy day (Gen. 2:3; Ex. 16:23; 20:11; 31:14; Is. 58:13). Thus the believer who sets aside one day in seven as holy is reminded that he himself is set apart by God to live a life of holiness in the midst of a perverse generation (cf. Ex. 31:13; 1 Pet. 2:9).

(6) Finally, the Sabbath can be seen as God's commitment to believers that He will carry out His will for them and that He is constantly available to act in behalf of their needs. He is always open to their prayers and devoted to their interest (cf. Ex. 31:13; Ezek. 20:12).

shall have one sheep, and if [v]it fall into a pit on the sabbath day, will he not lay hold on it, and lift *it* out?

12 How much then is a man better than a sheep? Wherefore it is lawful to do well on the sabbath days.

13 Then saith he to the man, Stretch forth thine hand. And he stretched *it* forth; and it was restored whole, like as the other.

14 ¶ Then [w]the Pharisees went out, and [c]held a council against him, how they might destroy him.

Jesus heals many

15 But when Jesus knew *it*, [x]he withdrew himself from thence: [y]and great multitudes followed him, and he healed them all;

16 And [z]charged them that they should not make him known:

17 That it might be fulfilled which was spoken by Esaias the prophet, saying,

18 [a]Behold my servant, whom I have chosen; my beloved, [b]in whom my soul is well pleased: I will put my spirit upon him, and he shall show judgment to the Gentiles.

19 He shall not strive, nor cry; neither shall any man hear his voice in the streets.

20 A bruised reed shall he not break, and smoking flax shall he not quench, till he send forth judgment unto victory.

21 And in his name shall the Gentiles trust.

Jesus versus Satan

12:25–27pp — Mark 3:23–26; Luke 11:17–19

22 ¶ [c]Then was brought unto him one possessed with a devil, blind, and dumb: and he healed him, insomuch that the blind and dumb both spake and saw.

23 And all the people were amazed, and said, Is not this the son of David?

24 [d]But when the Pharisees heard *it*, they said, This *fellow* doth not cast out devils, but by [d]Beelzebub the prince of the devils.

25 And Jesus [e]knew their thoughts, and said unto them, Every kingdom divided against itself is brought to desolation; and every city or house divided against itself shall not stand:

26 And if Satan cast out Satan, he is divided against himself; how shall then his kingdom stand?

27 And if I by Beelzebub cast out devils, by whom do your children cast *them* out? therefore they shall be your judges.

Kingdom power overcomes Satan

12:28–29pp — Mark 3:27; Luke 11:20–22

28 But if I cast out devils by the Spirit of God, then [f]the kingdom of God is come unto you.

29 [g]Or else how can one enter into a strong man's house, and spoil his goods, except he first bind the strong man? and then he will spoil his house.

30 He that is not with me is against me; and he that gathereth not with me scattereth abroad.

31 ¶ Wherefore I say unto you, [h]All manner of sin and blasphemy shall be forgiven unto men: [i]but the blasphemy *against* the *Holy* Ghost shall not be forgiven unto men.

32 And whosoever [j]speaketh a word against the Son of man, [k]it shall be forgiven him: but whosoever

12:11 [v]See Ex. 23:4,5 Deut. 22:4 **12:14** [w]ch. 27:1 Mark 3:6 Luke 6:11 John 5:18 & 10:39 & 11:53 **12:15** [x]See ch. 10:23 Mark 3:7 [y]ch. 19:2 **12:16** [z]ch. 9:30 **12:18** [a]Is. 42:1 [b]ch. 3:17 & 17:5 **12:22** [c]See ch. 9:32 Mark 3:11 Luke 11:14 **12:24** [d]ch. 9:34 Mark 3:22 Luke 11:15 **12:25** [e]ch. 9:4 John 2:25 Rev. 2:23 **12:28** [f]Dan. 2:44 & 7:14 Luke 1:33 & 11:20 & 17:20,21 **12:29** [g]Is. 49:24 Luke 11:21-23 **12:31** [h]Mark 3:28 Luke 12:10 Heb. 6:4 & 10:26,29 1 John 5:16 [i]Acts 7:51 **12:32** [j]ch. 11:19 & 13:55 John 7:12,52 [k]1 Tim. 1:13

[c] Or, *took counsel* [d] Gk. *Beelzebul;* also ver. 27

12:28 THE KINGDOM OF GOD. See article on THE KINGDOM OF GOD, p. 1428.

12:29 BIND THE STRONG MAN. See article on POWER OVER SATAN AND DEMONS, p. 1486.

12:31 BLASPHEMY *AGAINST* THE *HOLY* GHOST. Blasphemy against the Holy Spirit is the continual and deliberate rejection of the Holy Spirit's witness to Christ, to His Word, and to His convicting work against sin (cf. John 16:7–11). He who rejects and opposes the voice of the Spirit removes himself from the only force that can lead him to forgiveness. The process leading to blasphemy against the Spirit is as follows: (1) Grieving the Spirit (Eph. 4:30), if continued, leads to resisting the Spirit (Acts 7:51); (2) Resisting the Spirit leads to quenching the Spirit (1 Thes. 5:19); (3) Quenching the Spirit leads to hardening of the heart (Heb. 3:8–13); (4) Hardening of the heart leads to a depraved mind and to a labeling of good as evil and evil as good (Is. 5:20; Rom. 1:28). When this hardening of the heart reaches a certain fullness of development, determined only by God, theSpirit will no longer strive to lead that person to repentance (cf. Gen. 6:3; see Deut. 29:18–21, note; 1 Sam. 2:25, note; Prov. 29:1, note). For those who are worried about having committed the unpardonable sin, the very fact of wanting to be forgiven and the willingness to repent of sin is evidence that one has not committed the unpardonable sin (see article on PERSONAL APOSTASY, p. 1946).

speaketh against the Holy Ghost, it shall not be forgiven him, neither in this world, neither in the *world* to come.

33 Either make the tree good, and [l]his fruit good; or else make the tree corrupt, and his fruit corrupt: for the tree is known by *his* fruit.

34 O [m]generation of vipers, how can ye, being evil, speak good things? [n]for out of the abundance of the heart the mouth speaketh.

35 A good man out of the good treasure of the heart bringeth forth good things: and an evil man out of the evil treasure bringeth forth evil things.

36 But I say unto you, That every idle word that men shall speak, they shall give account thereof in the day of judgment.

37 For by thy words thou shalt be justified, and by thy words thou shalt be condemned.

The sign of Jonah

12:39–42pp — Luke 11:29–32
12:43–45pp — Luke 11:24–26

38 ¶ [o]Then certain of the scribes and of the Pharisees answered, saying, Master, we would see a sign from thee.

39 But he answered and said unto them, An evil and [p]adulterous generation seeketh after a sign; and there shall no sign be given to it, but the sign of the prophet Jonas:

40 [q]For as Jonas was three days and three nights in the whale's belly; so shall the Son of man be three days and three nights in the heart of the earth.

41 [r]The men of Nineveh shall rise in judgment with this generation, and [s]shall condemn it: [t]because they repented at the preaching of Jonas; and, behold, a greater than Jonas *is* here.

42 [u]The queen of the south shall rise up in the judgment with this generation, and shall condemn it: for she came from the uttermost parts of the earth to hear the wisdom of Solomon; and, behold, a greater than Solomon *is* here.

43 [v]When the unclean spirit is gone out of a man, [w]he walketh through dry places, seeking rest, and findeth none.

44 Then he saith, I will return into my house from whence I came out; and when he is come, he findeth *it* empty, swept, and garnished.

45 Then goeth he, and taketh with himself seven other spirits more wicked than himself, and they enter in and dwell there: [x]and the last *state* of that man is worse than the first. Even so shall it be also unto this wicked generation.

Jesus' true family

12:46–50pp — Mark 3:31–35; Luke 8:19–21

46 ¶ While he yet talked to the people, [y]behold, *his* mother and [z]his brethren stood without, desiring to speak with him.

47 Then one said unto him, Behold, thy mother and thy brethren stand without, desiring to speak with thee.

48 But he answered and said unto him that told him, Who is my mother? and who are my brethren?

49 And he stretched forth his hand toward his disciples, and said, Behold my mother and my brethren!

50 For [a]whosoever shall do the will of my Father which is in heaven, the same is my brother, and sister, and mother.

Parable of the sower

13:1–15pp — Mark 4:1–12; Luke 8:4–10
13:16–17pp — Luke 10:23–24
13:18–23pp — Mark 4:13–20; Luke 8:11–15

13 THE SAME day went Jesus out of the house, [b]and sat by the sea side.

2 [c]And great multitudes were gathered together unto him, so that [d]he went into a ship, and sat; and the whole multitude stood on the shore.

3 And he spake many things unto

12:33 [l]ch. 7:17 Luke 6:43
12:34 [m]ch. 3:7 & 23:33 [n]Luke 6:45
12:38 [o]ch. 16:1 Mark 8:11 Luke 11:16 John 2:18 1 Cor. 1:22
12:39 [p]Is. 57:3 ch. 16:4 Mark 8:38 John 4:48
12:40 [q]Jonah 1:17
12:41 [r]Luke 11:32 [s]See Jer. 3:11 Ezek. 16:51 Rom. 2:27 [t]Jonah 3:5
12:42 [u]1 Ki. 10:1 2 Chr. 9:1 Luke 11:31
12:43 [v]Luke 11:24 [w]Job 1:7 1 Pet. 5:8
12:45 [x]Heb. 6:4 & 10:26 2 Pet. 2:20-22
12:46 [y]Mark 3:31 Luke 8:19-21 [z]ch. 13:55 Mark 6:3 John 2:12 & 7:3,5 Acts 1:14 1 Cor. 9:5 Gal. 1:19
12:50 [a]See John 15:14 Gal. 5:6 & 6:15 Col. 3:11 Heb. 2:11
13:1 [b]Mark 4:1
13:2 [c]Luke 8:4 [d]Luke 5:3

12:36 THE DAY OF JUDGMENT. See article on THE JUDGMENT OF BELIEVERS, p. 1811.

12:37 BY THY WORDS . . . JUSTIFIED. See Luke 13:34, note.

12:40 JONAS. It is clear that Jesus accepted the O.T. account of Jonah as historical fact (see Jonah 1:17, note). The modern skeptics who deny the possibility of O.T. miracles must reckon with the words of Jesus.

12:43 THE UNCLEAN SPIRIT. Vv. 43–45 teach three important truths concerning demon possession. (1) Unclean spirits desire to return to one formerly possessed (v. 44). (2) Unclean spirits cannot return if that person's heart is occupied by the Holy Spirit (v. 44; cf. 1 Cor. 6:19; 2 Cor. 6:15–16, note). (3) A whole nation or society may seek the pleasure of evil to such an extent that the society itself can become demon possessed (v. 45; cf. Rev. 16:14).

13:3 PARABLES OF THE KINGDOM. In ch.

THE KINGDOM OF GOD

Mat. 12:28 "But if I cast out devils by the Spirit of God, then the kingdom of God is come unto you."

THE NATURE OF THE KINGDOM. The kingdom of God (or heaven) carries the idea of God coming into the world to assert His power, glory, and rights against the dominion of Satan and the present course of this world. It is more than salvation or the church; it is God expressing Himself with power in all His works.

(1) The kingdom is primarily an assertion of divine power in action. God has begun His spiritual rule on earth in the hearts and in the midst of His people (John 14:23; 20:22). His kingdom is now present in the world with power (Is. 64:1; Mark 9:1; 1 Cor. 4:20). We must not conceive of this power as material or political but as spiritual. That is, the kingdom is not a religio-political theocracy; it is not a matter of social or political dominion over the nations or kingdoms of this world (John 18:36). God does not intend at this time to redeem and reform the world through social or political activism, force, or violent action (Mat. 26:52; see John 18:36, note). The world throughout this age will remain an enemy of God and His people (John 15:19; Rom. 12:1–2; Jas. 4:4; 1 John 2:15–17; 4:4). The rule of God by direct judgment will occur only at the end of this age (Rev. 19:11–21).

(2) Because God asserts Himself with power, the world enters into a crisis. This power fills the devil's empire with alarm (Mat. 4:3ff; 12:29; Mark 1:24), and everyone is confronted with the decision whether to submit to God's rule or not (Mat. 3:1–2; 4:17; Mark 1:14–15). The necessary and fundamental condition of entry into the kingdom of God is, "repent ye, and believe the gospel" (Mark 1:15).

(3) God's breaking into our world with power involves: (a) spiritual power over Satan's rule and dominion (Mat. 12:28; John 18:36)—the coming of the kingdom is the beginning of the destruction of Satan's rule (John 12:31; 16:11) and of the deliverance of mankind from the demonic (Mark 1:34,39; 3:14–15; Acts 26:18) and from sin (Rom. 6); (b) power to work miracles and to heal the sick (Mat. 4:23; 9:35; Acts 4:30; 8:7; see article on DIVINE HEALING, p. 1418); (c) the preaching of the gospel, bringing conviction of sin, righteousness, and judgment (Mat. 11:5; John 16:8–11; Acts 4:33); (d) the salvation and sanctification of those who repent and believe the gospel (see John 3:3; 17:17; Acts 2:38–40; 2 Cor. 6:14–18; see article on SPIRITUAL SEPARATION FOR BELIEVERS, p. 1814); and (e) the baptism in the Holy Spirit with power to witness for Christ (see Acts 1:8, notes; 2:4, notes).

(4) An essential evidence that one is experiencing the kingdom of God is a life of "righteousness, and peace, and joy in the Holy Ghost" (Rom. 14:17).

(5) This kingdom has both a present and a future aspect. It is a present reality in the world today (Mark 1:15; Luke 18:16–17; Col. 1:13; Heb. 12:28), yet God's rule and power are not completely realized. The work and influence of Satan and evil men will continue until the end of the age (1 Tim. 4:1; 2 Tim. 3:1–5; Rev. 19:19–20:10). The future manifestation of God's glory, power, and kingdom will occur when Jesus returns to judge the world (Mat. 24:30; Luke 21:27; Rev. 19:11–20; 20:1–15). The ultimate fulfillment of the kingdom comes when Christ finally triumphs over all evil and opposition and delivers up the kingdom to God the Father (1 Cor. 15:24–28; Rev. 20:7—21:8; see also Mark 1:15, note concerning the various manifestations of the kingdom in redemptive history.)

THE BELIEVER'S ROLE IN THE KINGDOM. The N.T. also has much to say about the role of the believer in the kingdom of God.

(1) It is the believer's responsibility to seek unceasingly the kingdom of God in all its manifestations, hungering and thirsting for God's presence and power both in his life and in the midst of the Christian community (see Mat. 5:10, note; 6:33, note).

(2) In Mat. 11:12 Jesus gives additional information on the nature of kingdom people. There He indicates that the kingdom of heaven is taken hold of only by forceful people who are committed to breaking away from the sinful and immoral practices of the human race and who turn to Christ, His Word, and His righteous ways. No matter what may be the cost to themselves, such people vigorously seek the kingdom in all its power. In other words, experiencing the kingdom of heaven and all its blessings requires earnest endeavor and constant exertion—a fight of faith, accompanied by a strong will to resist Satan, sin, and one's perverse society.

(3) The kingdom of God is not for those who seldom pray, compromise with the world, neglect the Word, and have little spiritual hunger. It is for men like Joseph (Gen. 39:9), Nathan (2 Sam. 12:7), Elijah (1 Ki. 18:21), Daniel and his three friends (Dan. 1:8, 3:16–18), Mordecai (Esth. 3:4–5), Peter and John (Acts 4:19–20), Stephen (Acts 6:8, 7:51), and Paul (Phil. 3:13–14); and it is for women like Deborah (Judg. 4:9), Ruth (Ruth 1:16–18), Esther (Esth. 4:16), Mary (Luke 1:26–35), Anna (Luke 2:36–38), and Lydia (Acts 16:14–15,40).

JEWISH SECTS

PHARISEES

Their roots can be traced to the second century B.C. — to the Hasidim.

1. Along with the Torah, they accepted as equally inspired and authoritative, all material contained within the oral tradition.
2. On free will and determination, they held to a mediating view that made it impossible for either free will or the sovereignty of God to cancel out the other.
3. They accepted a rather developed hierarchy of angels and demons.
4. They taught that there was a future for the dead.
5. They believed in the immortality of the soul and in reward and retribution after death.
6. They were champions of human equality.
7. The emphasis of their teaching was ethical rather than theological.

SADDUCEES

They probably had their beginning during the Hasmonean period (166-63 B.C.). Their demise occurred C. A.D. 70 with the fall of Jerusalem.

1. They denied that the oral law was authoritative and binding.
2. They interpreted Mosaic law more literally than did the Pharisees.
3. They were very exacting in Levitical purity.
4. They attributed all to free will.
5. They argued there is neither resurrection of the dead nor a future life.
6. They rejected a belief in angels and demons.
7. They rejected the idea of a spiritual world.
8. Only the books of Moses were canonical Scripture.

them in parables, saying, Behold, a [e]sower went forth to sow;

4 And when he sowed, some *seeds* fell by the way side, and the fowls came and devoured them up:

5 Some fell upon stony places, where they had not much earth: and forthwith they sprung up, because they had no deepness of earth:

6 And when the sun was up, they were scorched; and because they had no root, they withered away.

7 And some fell among thorns; and the thorns sprung up, and choked them:

8 But other fell into good ground, and brought forth fruit, some [f]an hundredfold, some sixtyfold, some thirtyfold.

9 [g]Who hath ears to hear, let him hear.

10 And the disciples came, and said unto him, Why speakest thou unto them in parables?

11 He answered and said unto them, Because [h]it is given unto you to know the mysteries of the kingdom of heaven, but to them it is not given.

12 [i]For whosoever hath, to him shall be given, and he shall have more abundance: but whosoever hath not, from him shall be taken away even that he hath.

13 Therefore speak I to them in parables: because they seeing see not; and hearing they hear not, neither do they understand.

14 And in them is fulfilled the prophecy of Esaias, which saith, [j]By hearing ye shall hear, and shall not understand; and seeing ye shall see, and shall not perceive:

15 For this people's heart is waxed gross, and *their* ears [k]are dull of hearing, and their eyes they have closed; lest at any time they should see with *their* eyes, and hear with *their* ears, and should understand with *their* heart, and should be converted, and I should heal them.

16 But [l]blessed *are* your eyes, for they see: and your ears, for they hear.

17 For verily I say unto you, [m]That many prophets and righteous *men* have desired to see *those things* which ye see, and have not seen *them;* and to hear *those things* which ye hear, and have not heard *them*.

18 ¶ [n]Hear ye therefore the parable of the sower.

19 When any one heareth the word [o]of the kingdom, and understandeth *it* not, then cometh the wicked *one,* and catcheth away that which was sown in his heart. This is he which received seed by the way side.

20 But he that received the seed into stony places, the same is he that heareth the word, and anon [p]with joy receiveth it;

21 Yet hath he not root in himself, but dureth for a while: for when tribulation or persecution ariseth because of the word, by and by [q]he is offended.

22 [r]He also that received seed [s]among the thorns is he that heareth the word; and the care of this world, and the deceitfulness of riches, choke the word, and he becometh unfruitful.

23 But he that received seed into the good ground is he that heareth the word, and understandeth *it;* which also beareth fruit, and bringeth forth, some an hundredfold, some sixty, some thirty.

13:3 [e]Luke 8:5
13:8 [f]Gen. 26:12
13:9 [g]ch. 11:15 Mark 4:9
13:11 [h]ch. 11:25 & 16:17 Mark 4:11 1 Cor. 2:10 1 John 2:27
13:12 [i]ch. 25:29 Mark 4:25 Luke 8:18 & 19:26
13:14 [j]Is. 6:9 Ezek. 12:2 Mark 4:12 Luke 8:10 John 12:40 Acts 28:26,27 Rom. 11:8 2 Cor. 3:14,15
13:15 [k]Heb. 5:11
13:16 [l]ch. 16:17 Luke 10:23,24 John 20:29
13:17 [m]Heb. 11:13 1 Pet. 1:10,11
13:18 [n]Mark 4:14 Luke 8:11
13:19 [o]ch. 4:23
13:20 [p]Is. 58:2 Ezek. 33:31,32 John 5:35
13:21 [q]ch. 11:6 2 Tim. 1:15
13:22 [r]ch. 19:23 Mark 10:23 Luke 18:24 1 Tim. 6:9 2 Tim. 4:10 [s]Jer. 4:3

---

13 we have the parables of the kingdom of heaven, describing both the results of preaching the gospel and the spiritual conditions that will prevail on earth within the visible manifestation of the kingdom of heaven (i.e., the churches) until the end of the age.

(1) In most of these parables, Christ teaches that there will be good and evil in His visible kingdom throughout the entire age. Among those who profess His name, there will be apostasy and worldliness as well as faithfulness and godliness. At the end of the age the evil will be destroyed (vv. 41,49); "then shall the righteous shine forth as the sun in the kingdom of their Father" (v. 43).

(2) Christ speaks these parables in order to alert His true disciples to expect evil within the kingdom and to teach them how to overcome the influence and opposition of Satan and his followers. The only way to do so is through wholehearted devotion to Christ (vv. 44,46) and a life committed to righteousness (v. 43; see Rev. 2–3 for examples of good and evil within the churches of the kingdom).

(3) Parables are stories from everyday life that relate and illustrate certain spiritual truths. Their uniqueness is found in revealing truth to the spiritual while at the same time concealing it from the unbeliever (v. 11). Parables may at times demand a decision (e.g., Luke 10:30–37).

13:3 SOWER WENT FORTH TO SOW. See Mark 4:3, note.

13:12 WHOSOEVER HATH . . . SHALL HAVE MORE. See 25:29, note; Mark 4:25, note.

13:19 WICKED *ONE* . . . CATCHETH AWAY. See Mark 4:15, note.

Parable of the tares

24 ¶ Another parable put he forth unto them, saying, The kingdom of heaven is likened unto a man which sowed good seed in his field:

25 But while men slept, his enemy came and sowed tares among the wheat, and went his way.

26 But when the blade was sprung up, and brought forth fruit, then appeared the tares also.

27 So the servants of the householder came and said unto him, Sir, didst not thou sow good seed in thy field? from whence then hath it tares?

28 He said unto them, An enemy hath done this. The servants said unto him, Wilt thou then that we go and gather them up?

29 But he said, Nay; lest while ye gather up the tares, ye root up also the wheat with them.

30 Let both grow together until the harvest: and in the time of harvest I will say to the reapers, Gather ye together first the tares, and bind them in bundles to burn them: but [t]gather the wheat into my barn.

Parable of the mustard seed

13:31–32pp — Mark 4:30–32; Luke 11:18–19

31 ¶ Another parable put he forth unto them, saying, [u]The kingdom of heaven is like to a grain of mustard seed, which a man took, and sowed in his field:

32 Which indeed is the least of all seeds: but when it is grown, it is the greatest among herbs, and becometh a tree, so that the birds of the air come and lodge in the branches thereof.

Parable of the leaven

13:33pp — Luke 13:20–21

33 ¶ [v]Another parable spake he unto them; The kingdom of heaven is like unto leaven, which a woman took, and hid in three [e]measures of meal, till the whole was leavened.

34 [w]All these things spake Jesus unto the multitude in parables; and without a parable spake he not unto them:

35 That it might be fulfilled which was spoken by the prophet, saying, [x]I will open my mouth in parables; [y]I will utter things which have been kept secret from the foundation of the world.

Parable of the tares explained

36 Then Jesus sent the multitude away, and went into the house: and his disciples came unto him, saying, De-

13:30 [t]ch. 3:12
13:31 [u]Is. 2:2,3 Mic. 4:1 Mark 4:30 Luke 13:18
13:33 [v]Luke 13:20
13:34 [w]Mark 4:33
13:35 [x]Ps. 78:2 [y]Rom. 16:25,26 1 Cor. 2:7 Eph. 3:9 Col. 1:26

[e] The word in the Greek is *a measure containing about a peck and a half, wanting a little more than a pint*

13:24–25 GOOD SEED . . . TARES. The parable of the wheat and tares emphasizes that Satan will sow alongside those who sow the Word of God. The "field" is the world, and the "good seed" are the faithful of the kingdom (v. 38). (1) The gospel and true believers will be planted throughout the world (v. 38). Satan also will plant his followers, "the children of the wicked *one*" (v. 38), among God's people to counteract God's truth (vv. 25, 38–39).

(2) The principal work of Satan's emissaries within the visible kingdom of heaven will be undermining the authority of God's Word (see Gen. 3:4) and promoting unrighteousness and false doctrine (cf. Acts 20:29–30; 2 Thes. 2:7,12). Christ later spoke of a great deception among His people because of these professed Christians who are really false teachers (see 24:11, note; see article on THE GREAT TRIBULATION, p. 1456).

(3) This condition of Satan's people existing among God's people will terminate with God's final destruction of all the wicked at the end of the age (vv. 38–43). For other parables emphasizing the mixed condition of believers with unbelievers, see 22:11–14; 25:1–13,14–30; Luke 18:10–14; see article on CHRIST'S MESSAGE TO THE SEVEN CHURCHES, p. 2036.

13:30 LET BOTH GROW TOGETHER. Concerning the growing together of Christ's true followers and the children of Satan who masquerade as believers (v. 38; cf. 2 Cor. 11:13–15), three points should be noted. (1) Throughout the age of the gospel such coexistence will occur. God will not command His angels to destroy the sons of the evil one until the end of the age (vv. 30,38–41).

(2) The above parable does not contradict the Biblical instructions found elsewhere that command believers to discipline sinning members and expel unrepentant and false members from its fellowship (see 18:15, note; 1 Cor. 5:1, note; see article on OVERSEERS AND THEIR DUTIES, p. 1706). However, it must be understood that church discipline at its best will be only a partial solution to evil individuals in the kingdom. God and His angels will make the final separation.

(3) Faithful believers must always be alert to the subversive elements and individuals that Satan is planting within all parts of God's work. They will in many ways appear like true children of God (see 2 Cor. 11:13, note; see article on FALSE TEACHERS, p. 1508).

13:31 MUSTARD SEED. See Luke 13:19, note.

13:33 LEAVEN. See Luke 13:21, note.

clare unto us the parable of the tares of the field.

37 He answered and said unto them, He that soweth the good seed is the Son of man;

38 [z]The field is the world; the good seed are the children of the kingdom; but the tares are [a]the children of the wicked *one;*

39 The enemy that sowed them is the devil; [b]the harvest is the end of the world; and the reapers are the angels.

40 As therefore the tares are gathered and burned in the fire; so shall it be in the end of this world.

41 The Son of man shall send forth his angels, [c]and they shall gather out of his kingdom all [f]things that offend, and them which do iniquity;

42 [d]And shall cast them into a furnace of fire: [e]there shall be wailing and gnashing of teeth.

43 [f]Then shall the righteous shine forth as the sun in the kingdom of their Father. [g]Who hath ears to hear, let him hear.

Parable of the hidden treasure

44 ¶ Again, the kingdom of heaven is like unto treasure hid in a field; the which when a man hath found, he hideth, and for joy thereof goeth and [h]selleth all that he hath, and [i]buyeth that field.

45 ¶ Again, the kingdom of heaven is like unto a merchant man, seeking goodly pearls:

46 Who, when he had found [j]one pearl of great price, went and sold all that he had, and bought it.

Parable of the net

47 ¶ Again, the kingdom of heaven is like unto a net, that was cast into the sea, and [k]gathered of every kind:

48 Which, when it was full, they drew to shore, and sat down, and gathered the good into vessels, but cast the bad away.

49 So shall it be at the end of the world: the angels shall come forth, and [l]sever the wicked from among the just,

50 And shall cast them into the furnace of fire: there shall be wailing and gnashing of teeth.

51 Jesus saith unto them, Have ye understood all these things? They say unto him, Yea, Lord.

52 Then said he unto them, Therefore every scribe *which is* instructed unto the kingdom of heaven is like unto a man *that is* an householder,

13:38 [z]ch. 24:14 & 28:19 Mark 16:15 Luke 24:47 Rom. 10:18 Col. 1:6 [a]Gen. 3:15 John 8:44 Acts 13:10 1 John 3:8
13:39 [b]Joel 3:13 Rev. 14:15
13:41 [c]ch. 18:7 2 Pet. 2:1,2
13:42 [d]ch. 3:12 Rev. 19:20 & 20:10 [e]ver. 50 ch. 8:12
13:43 [f]Dan. 12:3 1 Cor. 15:42,43,58 [g]ver. 9
13:44 [h]Phil. 3:7,8 [i]Is. 55:1 Rev. 3:18
13:46 [j]Prov. 2:4 & 3:14,15 & 8:10,19
13:47 [k]ch. 22:10
13:49 [l]ch. 25:32

[f] Or, *scandals*

13:41 GATHER OUT . . . THINGS THAT OFFEND. At the return of Christ to earth after the tribulation and at the end of the age (Rev. 19:11–21), there will be a time of harvest of both the wicked and the righteous living upon the earth (vv. 30,40–42; see article on THE GREAT TRIBULATION, p. 1456). (1) The wicked are first gathered and taken out from among the righteous (vv. 30,41,49). (2) The righteous are gathered next (vv. 30b,41–43,49); this gathering will be from "out of his kingdom" (v. 41). (3) After the harvest and the destruction of the wicked, "then shall the righteous shine forth as the sun in the kingdom of their Father" (v. 43; cf. 25:31–34; see Rev. 20:4, notes).

13:42 A FURNACE OF FIRE. Jesus describes what will happen to all who cause sin and do evil (v. 41). They will be tormented with fire and experience great suffering (cf. Rev. 14:9–11; 20:10). No one accepting the Bible as the Word of God can reject this doctrine. The wicked are not annihilated, but are cast into "a furnace of fire" (see 10:28, note).

13:44–46 KINGDOM . . . TREASURE. The parables of the treasure and pearl teach two truths: (1) The kingdom is a priceless treasure which is to be desired above all else. (2) The kingdom is to be acquired by giving up everything that would prevent our being part of it. "Selling all" means that one must transfer his whole heart from other interests to the one supreme interest, Christ (Rom. 12:1).

13:47 KINGDOM . . . A NET. The parable of the fishing net reveals once again the truth Christ has so greatly emphasized, i.e., that not all who are in the visible kingdom are truly children of God. Churches and Christian organizations are not synonymous with the true people of God, who consist of all believers living in true faith and righteousness (cf. 24:11,24; Gal. 5:19–21; see Luke 13:21, note).

13:49 SEVER THE WICKED FROM . . . THE JUST. In the parable of the dragnet, the gathering of the wicked and the righteous at the end of the age is in the same order as that given in the parable of the tares and wheat (vv. 30,41,43): the wicked are gathered first and the just are gathered second (cf. Rev. 19:11—20:4). This order clearly shows that the gathering occurs at the end of the tribulation (24:29–31; Rev. 19:11—20:4) and not at the rapture, at which time the faithful of Christ's churches are gathered from among the wicked (see 1 Thes. 4:13–18; Rev. 3:10). In this parable Christ again stresses that among God's people there will be many who are not truly loyal to Him and His Word.

which bringeth forth out of his treasure [m]*things* new and old.

Jesus rejected at Nazareth

13:54–58pp — Mark 6:1–6

53 ¶ And it came to pass, *that* when Jesus had finished these parables, he departed thence.

54 [n]And when he was come into his own country, he taught them in their synagogue, insomuch that they were astonished, and said, Whence hath this *man* this wisdom, and *these* mighty works?

55 [o]Is not this the carpenter's son? is not his mother called Mary? and [p]his brethren, [q]James, and Joses, and Simon, and Judas?

56 And his sisters, are they not all with us? Whence then hath this *man* all these things?

57 And they [r]were offended in him. But Jesus said unto them, [s]A prophet is not without honour, save in his own country, and in his own house.

58 And [t]he did not many mighty works there because of their unbelief.

Death of John the Baptist

14:1–12pp — Mark 6:14–29

14 AT THAT time [u]Herod the tetrarch heard of the fame of Jesus,

2 And said unto his servants, This is John the Baptist; he is risen from the dead; and therefore mighty works [g]do show forth themselves in him.

3 ¶ [v]For Herod had laid hold on John, and bound him, and put *him* in prison for Herodias' sake, his brother Philip's wife.

4 For John said unto him, [w]It is not lawful for thee to have her.

5 And when he would have put him to death, he feared the multitude, [x]because they counted him as a prophet.

6 But when Herod's birthday was kept, the daughter of Herodias danced [h]before them, and pleased Herod.

7 Whereupon he promised with an oath to give her whatsoever she would ask.

8 And she, being before instructed of her mother, said, Give me here John Baptist's head in a charger.

9 And the king was sorry: nevertheless for the oath's sake, and them which sat with him at meat, he commanded *it* to be given *her*.

10 And he sent, and beheaded John in the prison.

11 And his head was brought in a charger, and given to the damsel: and she brought *it* to her mother.

12 And his disciples came, and took up the body, and buried it, and went and told Jesus.

The five thousand fed

14:13–21pp — Mark 6:32–44; Luke 9:10–17; John 6:1–13
14:13–21Ref — Mat. 15:32–38

13 ¶ [y]When Jesus heard *of it,* he departed thence by ship into a desert place apart: and when the people had heard *thereof,* they followed him on foot out of the cities.

14 And Jesus went forth, and saw a great multitude, and [z]was moved with compassion toward them, and he healed their sick.

15 ¶ [a]And when it was evening, his disciples came to him, saying, This is a desert place, and the time is now past; send the multitude away, that they may go into the villages, and buy themselves victuals.

16 But Jesus said unto them, They need not depart; give ye them to eat.

17 And they say unto him, We have here but five loaves, and two fishes.

18 He said, Bring them hither to me.

19 And he commanded the multi-

13:52 [m]Sol. 7:13
13:54 [n]ch. 2:23; Mark 6:1; Luke 4:16
13:55 [o]Is. 49:7; Mark 6:3; Luke 3:23; John 6:42; [p]ch. 12:46; [q]Mark 15:40
13:57 [r]ch. 11:6; Mark 6:3,4; [s]Luke 4:24; John 4:44
13:58 [t]Mark 6:5,6
14:1 [u]Mark 6:14; Luke 9:7
14:3 [v]Mark 6:17; Luke 3:19,20
14:4 [w]Lev. 18:16 & 20:21
14:5 [x]ch. 21:26; Luke 20:6
14:13 [y]ch. 10:23 & 12:15; Mark 6:32; Luke 9:10; John 6:1,2
14:14 [z]ch. 9:36; Mark 6:34
14:15 [a]Mark 6:35; Luke 9:12; John 6:5

[g] Or, *are wrought by him* [h] Gk. *in the midst*

14:6 DANCED BEFORE THEM. The public dancing of an ungodly girl before men led to the death of one of the holiest of men. (1) Worldly parties, dancing, and ungodly films lead to a forgetfulness of God, an inciting of passion, and a hardening of one's ability to discern sin, righteousness, or judgment. In these things the true children of God will not participate (see article on THE CHRISTIAN'S RELATIONSHIP TO THE WORLD, p. 2004).

(2) According to Scripture spontaneous dancing by Hebrew women and girls was done on exceptionally joyful occasions (cf. Jer. 31:4), and especially after victory in battle as they sang to the Lord (Ex. 15:19–21). There is no Scriptural record, however, that Jewish men danced with women, nor is there any indication that Jewish women ever danced publicly before men or an audience. The dancing of the daughter of Herodias before men was a pagan practice.

14:19 LOAVES, AND . . . FISHES. The miracle of the feeding of the five thousand is recorded in

tude to sit down on the grass, and took the five loaves, and the two fishes, and looking up to heaven, [b]he blessed, and brake, and gave the loaves to *his* disciples, and the disciples to the multitude.

20 And they did all eat, and were filled: and they took up of the fragments that remained twelve baskets full.

21 And they that had eaten were about five thousand men, beside women and children.

Jesus walks on the sea

14:22–33pp — Mark 6:45–51; John 6:15–21
14:34–36pp — Mark 6:53–56

22 ¶ And straightway Jesus constrained his disciples to get into a ship, and to go before him unto the other side, while he sent the multitudes away.

23 [c]And when he had sent the multitudes away, he went up into a mountain apart to pray: [d]and when the evening was come, he was there alone.

24 But the ship was now in the midst of the sea, tossed with waves: for the wind was contrary.

25 And in the fourth watch of the night Jesus went unto them, walking on the sea.

26 And when the disciples saw him [e]walking on the sea, they were troubled, saying, It is a spirit; and they cried out for fear.

27 But straightway Jesus spake unto them, saying, Be of good cheer; it is I; be not afraid.

28 And Peter answered him and said, Lord, if it be thou, bid me come unto thee on the water.

29 And he said, Come. And when Peter was come down out of the ship, he walked on the water, to go to Jesus.

30 But when he saw the wind [i]boisterous, he was afraid; and beginning to sink, he cried, saying, Lord, save me.

31 And immediately Jesus stretched forth *his* hand, and caught him, and said unto him, O thou of little faith, wherefore didst thou doubt?

32 And when they were come into the ship, the wind ceased.

33 Then they that were in the ship came and worshipped him, saying, Of a truth [f]thou art the Son of God.

34 ¶ [g]And when they were gone over, they came into the land of Gennesaret.

35 And when the men of that place had knowledge of him, they sent out into all that country round about, and brought unto him all that were diseased;

36 And besought him that they might only touch the hem of his garment: and [h]as many as touched were made perfectly whole.

Tradition versus God's commandments

15:1–9pp — Mark 7:1–8

15 THEN [i]CAME to Jesus scribes and Pharisees, which were of Jerusalem, saying,

2 [j]Why do thy disciples transgress the tradition of the elders? for they wash not their hands when they eat bread.

3 But he answered and said unto them, Why do ye also transgress the

14:19 [b]ch. 15:36
14:23 [c]Mark 6:46 [d]John 6:16
14:26 [e]Job 9:8
14:33 [f]Ps. 2:7 ch. 16:16 & 26:63 Mark 1:1 Luke 4:41 John 1:49 & 6:69 & 11:27 Acts 8:37 Rom. 1:4
14:34 [g]Mark 6:53
14:36 [h]ch. 9:20 Mark 3:10 Luke 6:19 Acts 19:12
15:1 [i]Mark 7:1
15:2 [j]Mark 7:5

[i] Or, *strong*

---

all four Gospels (Mark 6:34–44; Luke 9:10–17; John 6:1–14). The significance of the miracle includes the following. (1) It points to Jesus as the Bread of Life (cf. John 6), the one who provides for both body and soul. (2) It is proof of the Lord's power to perform miracles. (3) It is an example of His compassion for needy people (v. 14; cf. Ex. 34:6; Mic. 7:18). (4) It teaches that the little we have can be made into much if put into the Lord's hands and blessed.

14:23 PRAY . . . ALONE. While on earth, Jesus often sought time to be alone with God (cf. Mark 1:35; 6:46; Luke 5:16; 6:12; 9:18; 22:41–42; Heb. 5:7). Time alone with God is essential to the spiritual well-being of every believer. We must continually remember that the lack of desire for solitary prayer to our heavenly Father is an unmistakable sign that the spiritual life within us is in a process of decline. If this is happening, we must turn from all that offends the Lord and renew our commitment to persevere in seeking God and His saving grace (see Luke 18:1, note).

14:27 BE NOT AFRAID. In this life there are many things to fear, yet Jesus wants us to look to Him and not be afraid. His words of encouragement are founded upon His limitless power and intense personal love for all who truly belong to Him. Often in Scripture, God or Jesus Christ encourages His people, "be not afraid" (see, for example, Josh. 1:9; 11:6; 2 Ki. 19:6; 2 Chr. 20:15; 32:7; Neh. 4:14; Ps. 49:16; 91:5; Is. 10:24; 37:6; 44:8; Mat. 17:7; 28:10; Mark 5:36; Luke 12:4; John 14:1,27; Acts 18:9; 1 Pet. 3:14).

commandment of God by your tradition?

4 For God commanded, saying, [k]Honour thy father and mother: and, [l]He that curseth father or mother, let him die the death.

5 But ye say, Whosoever shall say to *his* father or *his* mother, [m]*It is* a gift, by whatsoever thou mightest be profited by me;

6 And honour not his father or his mother, *he shall be free*. Thus have ye made the commandment of God of none effect by your tradition.

7 *Ye* [n]hypocrites, well did Esaias prophesy of you, saying,

8 [o]This people draweth nigh unto me with their mouth, and honoureth me with *their* lips; but their heart is far from me.

9 But in vain they do worship me, [p]teaching *for* doctrines the commandments of men.

What defiles a man

15:10–20pp — Mark 7:9–23

10 ¶ [q]And he called the multitude, and said unto them, Hear, and understand:

11 [r]Not that which goeth into the mouth defileth a man; but that which cometh out of the mouth, this defileth a man.

12 Then came his disciples, and said unto him, Knowest thou that the Pharisees were offended, after they heard this saying?

13 But he answered and said, [s]Every plant, which my heavenly Father hath not planted, shall be rooted up.

14 Let them alone: [t]they be blind leaders of the blind. And if the blind lead the blind, both shall fall into the ditch.

15 [u]Then answered Peter and said unto him, Declare unto us this parable.

16 And Jesus said, [v]Are ye also yet without understanding?

17 Do not ye yet understand, that [w]whatsoever entereth in at the mouth goeth into the belly, and is cast out into the draught?

18 But [x]those things which proceed out of the mouth come forth from the heart; and they defile the man.

19 [y]For out of the heart proceed evil thoughts, murders, adulteries, fornications, thefts, false witness, blasphemies:

20 These are *the things* which defile a man: but to eat with unwashen hands defileth not a man.

The faith of a Canaanite woman

15:21–28pp — Mark 7:24–30

21 ¶ [z]Then Jesus went thence, and departed into the coasts of Tyre and Sidon.

22 And, behold, a woman of Canaan came out of the same coasts, and cried unto him, saying, Have mercy on me, O Lord, *thou* Son of David; my daughter is grievously vexed with a devil.

23 But he answered her not a word. And his disciples came and besought him, saying, Send her away; for she crieth after us.

24 But he answered and said, [a]I am not sent but unto the lost sheep of the house of Israel.

25 Then came she and worshipped him, saying, Lord, help me.

26 But he answered and said, It is not meet to take the children's bread, and to cast *it* to [b]dogs.

27 And she said, Truth, Lord: yet the dogs eat of the crumbs which fall from their masters' table.

28 Then Jesus answered and said unto her, O woman, great *is* thy faith: be it unto thee even as thou wilt. And her daughter was made whole from that very hour.

The four thousand fed

15:29–31pp — Mark 7:31–37
15:32–39pp — Mark 8:1–10
15:32–39Ref — Mat. 14:13–21

29 [c]And Jesus departed from thence, and came nigh [d]unto the sea

15:4 [k]Ex. 20:12 Lev. 19:3 Deut. 5:16 Prov. 23:22 Eph. 6:2 [l]Ex. 21:17 Lev. 20:9 Deut. 27:16 Prov. 20:20 & 30:17
15:5 [m]Mark 7:11,12
15:7 [n]Mark 7:6
15:8 [o]Is. 29:13 Ezek. 33:31
15:9 [p]Is. 29:13 Col. 2:18-22 Tit. 1:14
15:10 [q]Mark 7:14
15:11 [r]Acts 10:15 Rom. 14:14,17,20 1 Tim. 4:4 Tit. 1:15
15:13 [s]John 15:2 1 Cor. 3:12
15:14 [t]Is 9:16 Mal. 2:8 ch. 23:16 Luke 6:39
15:15 [u]Mark 7:17
15:16 [v]ch. 16:9 Mark 7:18
15:17 [w]1 Cor. 6:13
15:18 [x]Jas. 3:6
15:19 [y]Gen. 6:5 & 8:21 Prov. 6:14 Jer. 17:9 Mark 7:21
15:21 [z]Mark 7:24
15:24 [a]ch. 10:5,6
15:26 [b]ch. 7:6 Phil. 3:2
15:29 [c]Mark 7:31 [d]ch. 4:18

15:6 BY YOUR TRADITION. Some Pharisees invalidated the commandments of God for the sake of their traditions and the ideas of people. Believers today must be on the alert that they do not nullify the Word of God because of tradition, popular ideas, or present-day cultural norms. To do so is to fall into this sin of the Pharisees and Jewish leaders (see Mark 7:8, note).

15:8 THEIR HEART IS FAR FROM ME. See Mark 7:6, note.

15:11 THIS DEFILETH A MAN. See Mark 7:18, note.

15:19 OUT OF THE HEART. See Mark 7:21, note.

15:28 GREAT *IS* THY FAITH. To persevere in true faith is to trust God in all circumstances and remain true to Him, even when you are in great trouble and He does not seem to answer or to care. This is "the test of faith" (Luke 18:1–7; 1 Pet. 1:7; see Mark 7:27, note).

of Galilee; and went up into a mountain, and sat down there.

30 [e]And great multitudes came unto him, having with them *those that were* lame, blind, dumb, maimed, and many others, and cast them down at Jesus' feet; and he healed them:

31 Insomuch that the multitude wondered, when they saw the dumb to speak, the maimed to be whole, the lame to walk, and the blind to see: and they glorified the God of Israel.

Mark 2:3-12

32 ¶ [f]Then Jesus called his disciples *unto him*, and said, I have compassion on the multitude, because they continue with me now three days, and have nothing to eat: and I will not send them away fasting, lest they faint in the way.

33 [g]And his disciples say unto him, Whence should we have so much bread in the wilderness, as to fill so great a multitude?

34 And Jesus saith unto them, How many loaves have ye? And they said, Seven, and a few little fishes.

35 And he commanded the multitude to sit down on the ground.

36 And [h]he took the seven loaves and the fishes, and [i]gave thanks, and brake *them*, and gave to his disciples, and the disciples to the multitude.

37 And they did all eat, and were filled: and they took up of the broken *meat* that was left seven baskets full.

38 And they that did eat were four thousand men, beside women and children.

39 [j]And he sent away the multitude, and took ship, and came into the coasts of Magdala.

Pharisees ask for a sign

16:1–4pp — Mark 8:11–13

16 THE [k]PHARISEES also with the Sadducees came, and tempting desired him that he would show them a sign from heaven.

2 He answered and said unto them, When it is evening, ye say, *It will be* fair weather: for the sky is red.

3 And in the morning, *It will be* foul weather today: for the sky is red and lowering. O *ye* hypocrites, ye can discern the face of the sky; but can ye not *discern* the signs of the times?

4 [l]A wicked and adulterous generation seeketh after a sign; and there shall no sign be given unto it, but the sign of the prophet Jonas. And he left them, and departed.

The leaven of the Pharisees

16:5–12pp — Mark 8:14–21

5 And [m]when his disciples were come to the other side, they had forgotten to take bread.

6 ¶ Then Jesus said unto them, [n]Take heed and beware of the leaven of the Pharisees and of the Sadducees.

7 And they reasoned among themselves, saying, *It is* because we have taken no bread.

8 *Which* when Jesus perceived, he said unto them, O ye of little faith, why reason ye among yourselves, because ye have brought no bread?

9 [o]Do ye not yet understand, neither remember the five loaves of the five thousand, and how many baskets ye took up?

10 [p]Neither the seven loaves of the four thousand, and how many baskets ye took up?

11 How is it that ye do not understand that I spake *it* not to you concerning bread, that ye should beware of the leaven of the Pharisees and of the Sadducees?

12 Then understood they how that he bade *them* not beware of the leaven of bread, but of the doctrine of the Pharisees and of the Sadducees.

Peter's confession of faith

16:13–16pp — Mark 8:27–29; Luke 9:18–20

13 ¶ When Jesus came into the coasts of Caesarea Philippi, he asked his disciples, saying, [q]Whom do men say that I the Son of man am?

14 And they said, [r]Some *say that thou art* John the Baptist: some, Elias; and others, Jeremias, or one of the prophets.

15 He saith unto them, But whom say ye that I am?

16 And Simon Peter answered and said, [s]Thou art the Christ, the Son of the living God.

15:30 [e]Is. 35:5,6 ch. 11:5 Luke 7:22
15:32 [f]Mark 8:1
15:33 [g]2 Ki. 4:43
15:36 [h]ch. 14:19 [i]1 Sam. 9:13 Luke 22:19
15:39 [j]Mark 8:10
16:1 [k]ch. 12:38 Mark 8:11 Luke 11:16 & 12:54-56 1 Cor. 1:22
16:4 [l]ch. 12:39
16:5 [m]Mark 8:14
16:6 [n]Luke 12:1
16:9 [o]ch. 14:17 John 6:9
16:10 [p]ch. 15:34
16:13 [q]Mark 8:27 Luke 9:18
16:14 [r]ch. 14:2 Luke 9:7-9
16:16 [s]ch. 14:33 Mark 8:29 Luke 9:20 John 6:69 & 11:27 Acts 8:37 & 9:20 Heb. 1:2,5 1 John 4:15

16:6 LEAVEN. Here "leaven," a symbol of evil and corruption, refers to the teachings of the Pharisees and Sadducees. Christ calls their teaching "leaven" (yeast) because even a small amount can penetrate and influence a large group of people to believe the wrong thing (see Mark 8:15, note).

17 And Jesus answered and said
unto him, Blessed art thou, Simon Bar-
jona: [t]for flesh and blood hath not re-
vealed *it* unto thee, but [u]my Father
which is in heaven.
18 And I say also unto thee, That
[v]thou art Peter, and [w]upon this rock
I will build my church; and [x]the gates
of hell shall not prevail against it.
19 [y]And I will give unto thee the
keys of the kingdom of heaven: and
whatsoever thou shalt bind on earth
shall be bound in heaven: and whatso-
ever thou shalt loose on earth shall be
loosed in heaven.
20 [z]Then charged he his disciples
that they should tell no man that he
was Jesus the Christ.

Jesus foretells his death

16:21–23pp — Mark 8:31–33; Luke 9:22

21 ¶ From that time forth began
Jesus [a]to show unto his disciples, how
that he must go unto Jerusalem, and
suffer many things of the elders and
chief priests and scribes, and be killed,
and be raised again the third day.
22 Then Peter took him, and began
to rebuke him, saying, [j]Be it far from
thee, Lord: this shall not be unto thee.
23 But he turned, and said unto Pe-
ter, Get thee behind me, [b]Satan:
[c]thou art an offence unto me: for thou
savourest not the things that be of
God, but those that be of men.

Following Jesus and self-denial

16:24–28pp — Mark 8:34—9:1; Luke 9:23–27

24 ¶ [d]Then said Jesus unto his dis-
ciples, If any *man* will come after me,
let him deny himself, and take up his
cross, and follow me.
25 For [e]whosoever will save his
life shall lose it: and whosoever will
lose his life for my sake shall find it.
26 For what is a man profited, if he
shall gain the whole world, and lose his

16:17 [t]Eph. 2:8 [u]1 Cor. 2:10 Gal. 1:16
16:18 [v]John 1:42 [w]Eph. 2:20 Rev. 21:14 [x]Job 38:17 Ps. 9:13 & 107:18 Is. 38:10
16:19 [y]ch. 18:18 John 20:23
16:20 [z]ch. 17:9 Luke 9:21
16:21 [a]ch. 20:17 Mark 8:31 & 9:31 & 10:33 Luke 9:22 & 18:31 & 24:6,7
16:23 [b]See 2 Sam. 19:22 [c]Rom. 8:7
16:24 [d]Mark 8:34 Luke 9:23 & 14:27 Acts 14:22 1 Thes. 3:3 2 Tim. 3:12
16:25 [e]Luke 17:33; John 12:25

j Gk. *Pity thyself*

16:18 PETER ... ROCK ... CHURCH. In these words Christ promises to build His church on the truth of Peter's and the other disciples' confession that Jesus is the Christ, the Son of the living God (v. 16; cf. Acts 2:14–26). Jesus uses a play on words here. He calls His disciple "Peter" (Gk. *Petros*, meaning a small stone), but goes on to say, "upon this rock [Gk. *Petra*, meaning a massive rock or a rocky cliff] I will build my church," i.e., He will build His church on Peter's solid confession.

(1) It is Jesus Christ who is the Rock, the first and great foundation of the church (1 Cor. 3:11). Peter states in his first letter that Jesus is the "living stone, . . . a chief corner stone . . . the stone which the builders disallowed" (1 Pet. 2:4,6–7). At the same time, Peter and all other Christians are living stones who become part of the structure of the spiritual house which God is building (1 Pet. 2:5).

(2) Nowhere in Scripture is it stated that Peter would be the supreme and infallible authority above all other disciples (cf. Acts 15; Gal. 2:11). Nor is it stated that Peter should have infallible successors who would represent Christ and function as the official head of the church.

For a discussion of the doctrine of the church as seen here and elsewhere in Scripture, see article on THE CHURCH, p. 1438.

16:18 THE GATES OF HELL SHALL NOT PREVAIL. The "gates of hell" represent Satan and all the evil in the world striving to destroy the church of Jesus Christ. (1) This passage does not mean that any particular believer, local church, fellowship of churches, or denomination will never fall into immorality, doctrinal error, or apostasy. Jesus Himself predicted that many will fall from the faith, and He warns churches that are abandoning the N.T. faith to turn from their sins or face removal from His kingdom (Mat. 24:10–11; Rev. 2:5,12–29; 3:1–6,14–16; see 1 Tim. 4:1, note; see article on PERSONAL APOSTASY, p. 1946). The promise of v. 18 does not apply to those who deny the faith or to lukewarm churches.

(2) What Christ means is that in spite of Satan doing his worst, apostasy occurring among believers, churches becoming lukewarm, and false teachers infiltrating God's kingdom, the church will not be destroyed. By His sovereign grace, wisdom, and power, God will always have a remnant of believers and churches throughout redemptive history who will remain faithful to the original gospel of Christ and the apostles and who experience His fellowship, the Lordship of Christ, and the power of the Holy Spirit. As God's true people, they will demonstrate the kingdom power of the Holy Spirit against Satan, sin, disease, the world, and the demonic. It is this church that Satan and all his host cannot destroy or resist.

16:19 KEYS OF THE KINGDOM. The "keys" represent God's delegated authority to Peter and the church. By these keys they (1) rebuke sin and carry out church discipline (18:15–18); (2) pray effectively for God's cause on earth (18:19–20); (3) bind the demonic and loose the captives (see article on POWER OVER SATAN AND DEMONS, p. 1486); (4) announce the guilt of sin, God's standard of righteousness, and the judgment to come (Acts 2:23; 5:3,9); (5) proclaim salvation and the forgiveness of sin for all who repent and believe in Christ (John 20:23; Acts 2:37–40; 15:7–9).

16:24 TAKE UP HIS CROSS. See Mark 8:34, note.

THE CHURCH

***Mat. 16:18** "And I say also unto thee, That thou art Peter, and upon this rock I will build my church; and the gates of hell shall not prevail against it."*

The Greek word *ekklēsia* (church) refers to a meeting of a people called out (Gk. *ekkaleō*) and summoned together. In the N.T. it designates primarily the congregation of God's people in Christ, who come together as citizens of God's kingdom (Eph. 2:19) for the purpose of worshiping God. The word "church" can refer to a local church (Mat. 18:17; Acts 15:4) or the universal church (Mat. 16:18; Acts 20:28; cf. Eph. 2:21–22).

(1) The church is presented as the people of God (1 Cor. 1:2; 10:32; 1 Pet. 2:4–10), the company of redeemed believers made possible by the death of Christ (1 Pet. 1:18–19). It is a pilgrim people no longer belonging to this earth (Heb. 13:12–14), whose first function is to stand as a community in a living, personal relationship with God (1 Pet. 2:5; see Heb. 11:6, note).

(2) The church has been called out of the world and into the kingdom of God. Separation from the world is inherent to the nature of the church and is rewarded by having the Lord as one's God and Father (2 Cor. 6:16–18; see article on SPIRITUAL SEPARATION FOR BELIEVERS, p. 1814).

(3) The church is the temple of God and of the Holy Spirit (see 1 Cor. 3:16, note; 2 Cor. 6:14—7:1; Eph. 2:11–22; 1 Pet. 2:4–10). This truth about the church demands separation from unrighteousness and from worldly, pagan immorality.

(4) The church is the body of Christ (1 Cor. 6:15–16; 10:16–17; 12:12–27). This indicates that no true church exists apart from vital union of the members with Christ. The head of the body is Christ (Col. 1:18; Eph. 1:22; 4:15; 5:23).

(5) The church is the bride of Christ (2 Cor. 11:2; Eph. 5:21–27; Rev. 19:7–9). This nuptial concept emphasizes both the loyalty, devotion, and faithfulness of the church to Christ, and Christ's love for and intimacy with His church.

(6) The church is a spiritual fellowship (Gk. *koinōnia*) (2 Cor. 13:14; Phil. 2:1). This involves the indwelling of the Holy Spirit (Luke 11:13; John 7:37–39; 20:22), the unity of the Spirit (Eph. 4:4), and the baptism in the Spirit (Acts 1:5; 2:4; 8:14–17; 10:44; 19:1–7). This fellowship is to demonstrate observable love and care one to another (John 13:34–35).

(7) The church is a spiritual ministry (Gk. *diakonia*). It ministers by gifts (Gk. *charismata*) bestowed by the Holy Spirit (Rom. 12:6; 1 Cor. 1:7; 12:4–11,20–31; Eph. 4:11).

(8) The church is an army involved in spiritual conflict, fighting by the sword and power of the Spirit (Eph. 6:17) in a spiritual struggle against Satan and sin (see article on THE KINGDOM OF GOD, p. 1428). The Spirit with which the church is filled is like a warrior wielding the living Word of God, delivering people from the dominion of Satan, and conquering every power of darkness (Acts 26:18; Eph. 6:10–18; Heb. 4:12; Rev. 1:16; 2:16; 19:15,21).

(9) The church is the pillar and ground of the truth (1 Tim. 3:15), supporting the truth that God has revealed just as a foundation supports a building. The church must uphold the truth and keep it safe, defending it against distorters and false teachers (see Phil. 1:17, note; Jude 3, note).

(10) The church is a people with a future hope. This hope centers in the return of Christ for His people (see John 14:3, note; 1 Tim. 6:14; 2 Tim. 4:8; Tit. 2:13; Heb. 9:28; see article on THE RAPTURE, p. 1889).

(11) The church is both invisible and visible. (a) The church invisible is the body of true believers united by their living faith in Christ (see article on FAITH AND GRACE, p. 1738). (b) The visible church consists of local congregations containing faithful overcomers (Rev. 2:11,17,26; see 2:7, note) as well as those professed Christians who are false (2:2), "fallen" (2:5), spiritually "dead" (3:1), and "lukewarm" (Rev. 3:16; see Mat. 13:24–25, note; Acts 12:5, note on essential characteristics of a N.T. church).

own soul? or [f]what shall a man give
in exchange for his soul?
27 For [g]the Son of man shall come
in the glory of his Father [h]with his an-
gels; [i]and then he shall reward every
man according to his works.
28 Verily I say unto you, [j]There be
some standing here, which shall not
taste of death, till they see the Son of
man coming in his kingdom.

Mat. 24:15-

The transfiguration

17:1–8pp — Luke 9:28–36
17:1–13pp — Mark 9:2–13

17 AND [k]AFTER six days Jesus
taketh Peter, James, and John
his brother, and bringeth them up into
an high mountain apart,
2 And was transfigured before
them: and his face did shine as the sun,
and his raiment was white as the light.
3 And, behold, there appeared unto
them Moses and Elias talking with
him.
4 Then answered Peter, and said
unto Jesus, Lord, it is good for us to be
here: if thou wilt, let us make here
three tabernacles; one for thee, and
one for Moses, and one for Elias.
5 [l]While he yet spake, behold, a
bright cloud overshadowed them: and
behold a voice out of the cloud, which
said, [m]This is my beloved Son, [n]in
whom I am well pleased; [o]hear ye
him.
6 [p]And when the disciples heard *it*,
they fell on their face, and were sore
afraid.
7 And Jesus came and [q]touched
them, and said, Arise, and be not
afraid.
8 And when they had lifted up their
eyes, they saw no man, save Jesus
only.

16:26 [f]Ps. 49:7,8
16:27 [g]ch. 26:64 Mark 8:38 Luke 9:26 [h]Dan. 7:10 Zech. 14:5 ch. 25:31 Jude 14 [i]Job 34:11 Ps. 62:12 Prov. 24:12 Jer. 17:10 & 32:19 Rom. 2:6 1 Cor. 3:8 2 Cor. 5:10 1 Pet. 1:17 Rev. 2:23 & 22:12
16:28 [j]Mark 9:1 Luke 9:27
17:1 [k]Mark 9:2 Luke 9:28
17:5 [l]2 Pet. 1:17 [m]ch. 3:17 Mark 1:11 Luke 3:22 [n]Is. 42:1 [o]Deut. 18:15,19 Acts 3:22,23
17:6 [p]2 Pet. 1:18
17:7 [q]Dan. 8:18 & 9:21 & 10:10,18
17:9 [r]ch. 16:20 Mark 8:30 & 9:9
17:10 [s]Mal. 4:5 ch. 11:14 Mark 9:11
17:11 [t]Mal. 4:6 Luke 1:16,17 Acts 3:21
17:12 [u]ch. 11:14 Mark 9:12,13 [v]ch. 14:3,10 [w]ch. 16:21
17:13 [x]ch. 11:14
17:14 [y]Mark 9:14 Luke 9:37

9 And as they came down from the
mountain, [r]Jesus charged them, say-
ing, Tell the vision to no man, until the
Son of man be risen again from the
dead.
10 And his disciples asked him,
saying, [s]Why then say the scribes that
Elias must first come?
11 And Jesus answered and said
unto them, Elias truly shall first come,
and [t]restore all things.
12 [u]But I say unto you, That Elias
is come already, and they knew him
not, but [v]have done unto him whatso-
ever they listed. Likewise [w]shall also
the Son of man suffer of them.
13 [x]Then the disciples understood
that he spake unto them of John the
Baptist.

A demoniac boy healed

17:14–19pp — Mark 9:14–28; Luke 9:37–42

14 ¶ [y]And when they were come to
the multitude, there came to him a *cer-*
tain man, kneeling down to him, and
saying,
15 Lord, have mercy on my son: for
he is lunatic, and sore vexed: for oft-
times he falleth into the fire, and oft
into the water.
16 And I brought him to thy disci-
ples, and they could not cure him.
17 Then Jesus answered and said, O
faithless and perverse generation, how
long shall I be with you? how long shall
I suffer you? bring him hither to me.
18 And Jesus rebuked the devil; and
he departed out of him: and the child Mark 1:23-28
was cured from that very hour.
19 Then came the disciples to Jesus
apart, and said, Why could not we cast
him out?
20 And Jesus said unto them, Be-
cause of your unbelief: for verily I say

16:28 COMING IN HIS KINGDOM. The "Son of man coming in his kingdom" probably refers to the event of Pentecost when Christ baptized His followers in the Holy Spirit and great power (cf. Mark 9:1; Acts 1:8; 2:4).

17:2 WAS TRANSFIGURED. See Luke 9:29, note.

17:17 FAITHLESS AND PERVERSE. This text reflects Jesus' estimation of disciples and churches who fail to minister to others in the real power of God's kingdom (see article on THE KINGDOM OF GOD, p. 1428). (1) Failure to deliver those oppressed by Satan or demons (vv. 15–21) demonstrates a lack of faith, understanding, and spiritual dedication (vv. 17,20–21; Mark 9:29). (2) The Holy Spirit's purpose in recording the narratives in vv. 14–21 emphasizes not only that Jesus cast out demons, but also that He desires His disciples to do the same thing through faith, prayer, and fasting (vv. 20–21; see article on POWER OVER SATAN AND DEMONS, p. 1486). Jesus is intensely disappointed and pained when His people fail to share His ministry against the forces of Satan (see 10:1, note; 10:8; Mark 9:28–29; Luke 9:1; John 14:12, note).

17:20 FAITH ... NOTHING SHALL BE IMPOSSIBLE. Jesus frequently comments on the nature of true faith. He speaks of a faith that can move mountains, cause miracles and healing, and accomplish great things for God. Just what is this faith that Jesus speaks of? (1) True faith is an effective faith that produces results: "it

unto you, [z]If ye have faith as a grain
of mustard seed, ye shall say unto this
mountain, Remove hence to yonder
Mat. 21:21-22 place; and it shall remove; and nothing
shall be impossible unto you.
21 Howbeit this kind goeth not out
but by prayer and fasting.
22 ¶ [a]And while they abode in Gali-
lee, Jesus said unto them, The Son of
man shall be betrayed into the hands of
men:
23 And they shall kill him, and the
third day he shall be raised again. And
they were exceeding sorry.

The money in the fish's mouth

24 ¶ And [b]when they were come to
Capernaum, they that received [c]trib-
ute[k] *money* came to Peter, and said,
Doth not your master pay tribute?
25 He saith, Yes. And when he was
come into the house, Jesus prevented
him, saying, What thinkest thou, Si-
mon? of whom do the kings of the earth
take custom or tribute? of their own
children, or of strangers?
26 Peter saith unto him, Of strang-
ers. Jesus saith unto him, Then are the
children free.
27 Notwithstanding, lest we should
offend them, go thou to the sea, and
cast an hook, and take up the fish that
first cometh up; and when thou hast
opened his mouth, thou shalt find [l]a
piece of money: that take, and give
unto them for me and thee.

17:20 [z]ch. 21:21 Mark 11:23 Luke 17:6 1 Cor. 12:9 & 13:2
17:22 [a]ch. 16:21 & 20:17 Mark 8:31 & 9:30,31 & 10:33 Luke 9:22,44 & 18:31 & 24:6,7
17:24 [b]Mark 9:33 [c]Ex. 30:13 & 38:26
18:1 [d]Mark 9:33 Luke 9:46 & 22:24
18:3 [e]Ps. 131:2 ch. 19:14 Mark 10:14 Luke 18:16 1 Cor. 14:20 1 Pet. 2:2
18:4 [f]ch. 20:27 & 23:11
18:5 [g]ch. 10:42 Luke 9:48
18:6 [h]Mark 9:42 Luke 17:1,2

The greatest in the kingdom

18:1–5pp — Mark 9:33–37; Luke 9:46–48

18 AT [d]THE same time came the
disciples unto Jesus, saying,
Who is the greatest in the kingdom of
heaven?
2 And Jesus called a little child unto
him, and set him in the midst of them,
3 And said, Verily I say unto you,
[e]Except ye be converted, and become
as little children, ye shall not enter into
the kingdom of heaven.
4 [f]Whosoever therefore shall hum-
ble himself as this little child, the same
is greatest in the kingdom of heaven.
5 And [g]whoso shall receive one
such little child in my name re-
ceiveth me.
6 [h]But whoso shall offend one of

[k] Called in the original, *didrachma,* worth about 32 cents or 2 days' wages for a laborer

[l] Or, *a stater,* worth about 64 cents or 4 days' wages for a laborer

shall remove" mountains.

(2) True faith is not a belief in "faith" as a force or power, but it is a "faith in God" (Mark 11:22).

(3) True faith is a work of God within the Christian's heart (Mark 9:24; Phil. 2:13). It involves an awareness divinely imparted to our hearts that our prayers are answered (Mark 11:23). It is created within us by the Holy Spirit; we cannot produce it in our own minds (Rom. 12:3; 1 Cor. 12:9; see article on FAITH AND GRACE, p. 1738).

(4) Since true faith is a gift imparted to us by Christ, it is important to draw near to Christ and His Word and to deepen our commitment to, and confidence in, Him (Rom. 10:17; Phil. 3:8–15). We are dependent upon Him for everything; "for without me ye can do nothing" (John 15:5; see also John 3:27; Heb. 4:16; 7:25). In other words, we must seek Christ as the author and finisher of our faith (Heb. 12:2). His close presence and our obedience to His Word are the source and the secret of faith (9:21; John 15:7).

(5) Furthermore, true faith is also under God's control. Faith is given on the basis of His love, wisdom, grace, and kingdom purpose in order to accomplish the will of God and to express His love for us. It is not to be used for our own selfish interest (Jas. 4:3).

18:1 WHO IS THE GREATEST. See Luke 22:24–30, note.

18:3 BE CONVERTED. The change required by Jesus in conversion begins with becoming like little children—i.e., in being humble, unpretentious, dependent, weak, and ready to be molded by the heavenly Father. Theologically, after the initial childlike step of humility, the conversion or change required by Jesus consists of two parts: radically turning away from everything that is ungodly, and turning to God and doing the works of righteousness (i.e., producing fruits worthy of repentance; see 3:8, note). (1) Conversion does not denote merely a single act of sorrow or penitence but an all-embracing attitude of life (see 2 Cor. 7:10, note). This is necessary because by nature we follow a way of life that leads away from God and towards eternal death (Rom. 1:18–32; Eph. 2:2–3). Conversion is the human response to God's gift of salvation, accomplished by the grace and power of the Holy Spirit received through faith (Acts 11:18).

(2) Because of our new relation to God, conversion involves changes in the areas of relationships, habits, commitments, pleasures, and our whole view of life. Conversion is a part of genuine saving faith and a basic requirement of salvation and sanctification (Acts 26:18).

18:6 MILLSTONE ... ABOUT HIS NECK. This verse means that whoever spiritually destroys a child or a childlike believer will incur the greatest wrath of Christ. (1) Pastors, teachers, and especially parents should give special attention to these words of Christ. The parents' responsibility is to instruct their children in the ways of God (see Deut. 6:1–9; Luke 1:17, note; Eph. 6:4; 1 Tim. 4:16; see article on PARENTS AND CHIL-

these little ones which believe in me, it
were better for him that a millstone
were hanged about his neck, and *that*
he were drowned in the depth of the
sea.
7 ¶ Woe unto the world because of
offences! for [i]it must needs be that
offences come; but [j]woe to that man
by whom the offence cometh!
8 [k]Wherefore if thy hand or thy
foot offend thee, cut them off, and cast
them from thee: it is better for thee to
enter into life halt or maimed, rather
than having two hands or two feet to be
cast into everlasting fire.
9 And if thine eye offend thee, pluck
it out, and cast *it* from thee: it is better
for thee to enter into life with one eye,
rather than having two eyes to be cast
into hell fire.

Parable of the lost sheep

18:12–14pp — Luke 15:4–7

10 Take heed that ye despise not
one of these little ones; for I say unto
you, That in heaven [l]their angels do
always [m]behold the face of my Father
which is in heaven.
11 [n]For the Son of man is come to
save that which was lost.
12 [o]How think ye? if a man have an
hundred sheep, and one of them be
gone astray, doth he not leave the nine-
ty and nine, and goeth into the moun-
tains, and seeketh that which is gone
astray?
13 And if so be that he find it, verily
I say unto you, he rejoiceth more of
that *sheep,* than of the ninety and nine
which went not astray.
14 Even so it is not the will of your
Father which is in heaven, that one of
these little ones should perish.

Sin and forgiveness

15 ¶ Moreover [p]if thy brother shall
trespass against thee, go and tell him
his fault between thee and him alone:

18:7 [i]Luke 17:1; 1 Cor. 11:19 [j]ch. 26:24 **18:8** [k]ch. 5:29,30; Mark 9:43,45 **18:10** [l]Ps. 34:7; Zech. 13:7; Heb. 1:14 [m]Esth. 1:14; Luke 1:19 **18:11** [n]Luke 9:56 & 19:10; John 3:17 & 12:47 **18:12** [o]Luke 15:4 **18:15** [p]Lev. 19:17; Luke 17:3

DREN, p. 1880) and to protect them from the influence of the world and Satan (Tit. 1:10–11; 2:11–12; 1 John 2:15–17). (2) Christian parents must not allow their children to be influenced by ungodly friends. They must be especially careful about what they allow the world to put into their children's minds and hearts by means of public education or the entertainment media (cf. Ps. 101:3; Eph. 6:4; Col. 3:21).

18:7 WOE TO THAT MAN. Jesus warns that those who are instrumental in placing sinful things before others and especially before children will receive the ultimate condemnation (vv. 2,5–7). (1) To place "offences" in the path of others — such as worldly entertainment, humanistic teaching, immoral films, pornographic literature, drugs, alcoholic beverages, wicked examples, false teaching, and unrighteous companions — is to join oneself with Satan who is the great tempter (cf. 4:1; Gen. 3:1–6; John 8:44; Jas. 1:12). (2) The godly way of the faithful is to remove from the lives of our family, our homes, our churches, and our own selves any and all things which might lead others into temptation and sin (vv. 7–9).

18:10 ANGELS. Scripture teaches that God often takes care of His faithful by means of angels. These angels carry a sincere interest and love for God's children (cf. Ps. 34:7; 91:11; Luke 15:10; 16:22; Heb. 1:14; Rev. 5:11–12; see article on ANGELS AND THE ANGEL OF THE LORD, p. 368).

18:15 IF THY BROTHER SHALL TRESPASS. In vv. 15–17 Jesus sets forth the method of restoring or disciplining a professing Christian who sins against another member of the church in a private manner. To neglect Christ's instruction will bring spiritual compromise and ultimate destruction to the church as a holy people of God (cf. 1 Pet. 2:9; see Mat. 5:13, note).

(1) The purpose of church discipline is to protect God's reputation (6:9; Rom. 2:23–24), to guard the moral purity and doctrinal integrity of the church (1 Cor. 5:6–7; 2 John 7–11), and to attempt to save the soul of the wayward member and restore him to full Christlikeness (1 Cor. 5:5; Jas. 5:19–20).

(2) The offender must first be dealt with and reproved in private. If he listens, he must be forgiven (v. 15). If the offender refuses to respond to his Christian brother (vv. 15–16), after that to one or two members (v. 16), and finally to the local church, he must be considered "as an heathen man," i.e., as one outside the kingdom of God, severed from Christ and fallen from grace (v. 17; cf. Gal. 5:4). He has no right to church membership and must be removed from the fellowship of the church.

(3) This practice of the purity of the church is to operate not only in areas of sin and immorality, but also in cases of doctrinal heresy and unfaithfulness to the original and fundamental N.T. faith (see Gal. 1:9, note; Jude 3, note; see articles on FALSE TEACHERS, p. 1508, and OVERSEERS AND THEIR DUTIES, p. 1706).

(4) Church discipline must be carried out in a spirit of humility, love, regret, and self-examination (see 22:37, note; 2 Cor. 2:6–7; Gal. 6:1).

(5) Sins within the church involving sexual immorality must be dealt with according to 1 Cor. 5:1–5 and 2 Cor. 2:6–11. These types of grave sins require regret and mourning by the whole congregation (1 Cor. 5:2), "sufficient . . . punishment" for the transgressor (2 Cor. 2:6), and expulsion from the church (1 Cor. 5:2,13). Later, after a period of evident repentance, the individual may be forgiven, receive a reaffirmation of love, and be restored

if he shall hear thee, [q]thou hast
gained thy brother.
16 But if he will not hear *thee, then*
take with thee one or two more, that in
[r]the mouth of two or three witnesses
every word may be established.
17 And if he shall neglect to hear
them, tell *it* unto the church: but if he
neglect to hear the church, let him be
unto thee as an [s]heathen man and a
publican.
18 Verily I say unto you, [t]Whatso-
ever ye shall bind on earth shall be
bound in heaven: and whatsoever ye
shall loose on earth shall be loosed in
heaven.
19 [u]Again I say unto you, That if
two of you shall agree on earth as
touching any thing that they shall ask,
[v]it shall be done for them of my Father
which is in heaven.
20 For where two or three are gath-
ered together in my name, there am I
in the midst of them.
21 ¶ Then came Peter to him, and
said, Lord, how oft shall my brother sin
against me, and I forgive him? [w]till
seven times?
22 Jesus saith unto him, I say not
unto thee, Until seven times: [x]but, Un-
til seventy times seven.

Parable of the unforgiving servant

23 ¶ Therefore is the kingdom of
heaven likened unto a certain king,
which would take account of his ser-
vants.
24 And when he had begun to reck-
on, one was brought unto him, which
owed him ten thousand [m]talents.
25 But forasmuch as he had not to
pay, his lord commanded him [y]to be
sold, and his wife, and children, and all

18:15 [q]Jas. 5:20; 1 Pet. 3:1
18:16 [r]Deut. 17:6 & 19:15; John 8:17; 2 Cor. 13:1; Heb. 10:28
18:17 [s]Rom. 16:17; 1 Cor. 5:9; 2 Thes. 3:6,14; 2 John 10
18:18 [t]ch. 16:19; John 20:23; 1 Cor. 5:4
18:19 [u]ch. 5:24; [v]1 John 3:22 & 5:14
18:21 [w]Luke 17:4
18:22 [x]ch. 6:14; Mark 11:25; Col. 3:13
18:25 [y]2 Ki. 4:1; Neh. 5:8
18:35 [z]Prov. 21:13; ch. 6:12; Mark 11:26; Jas. 2:13

that he had, and payment to be made.
26 The servant therefore fell down,
and [n]worshipped him, saying, Lord,
have patience with me, and I will pay
thee all.
27 Then the lord of that servant was
moved with compassion, and loosed
him, and forgave him the debt.
28 But the same servant went out,
and found one of his fellowservants,
which owed him an hundred [o]pence:
and he laid hands on him, and took *him*
by the throat, saying, Pay me that thou
owest.
29 And his fellowservant fell down
at his feet, and besought him, saying,
Have patience with me, and I will pay
thee all.
30 And he would not: but went and
cast him into prison, till he should pay
the debt.
31 So when his fellowservants saw
what was done, they were very sorry,
and came and told unto their lord all
that was done.
32 Then his lord, after that he had
called him, said unto him, O thou wick-
ed servant, I forgave thee all that debt,
because thou desiredst me:
33 Shouldest not thou also have
had compassion on thy fellowservant,
even as I had pity on thee?
34 And his lord was wroth, and de-
livered him to the tormentors, till he
should pay all that was due unto him.
35 [z]So likewise shall my heavenly
Father do also unto you, if ye from your

[m] Ten thousand talents are equivalent to several million dollars [n] Or, *besought him*
[o] A hundred pence are equivalent to a few dollars

to fellowship (2 Cor. 2:6–8).

(6) Sins of an elder, after being dealt with privately, must also involve public exposure and discipline, i.e., "rebuke before all, that others also may fear" (Gal. 2:11–18; 1 Tim. 5:19–20, note; see article on MORAL QUALIFICATIONS FOR OVERSEERS, p. 1908).

(7) Leaders within the church and pastors of local congregations do well to remember that they are charged to "take heed . . . to all the flock" (see article on OVERSEERS AND THEIR DUTIES, p. 1706). The Lord will require of them a personal accounting of "the blood of all men" (Acts 20:26) who are lost because the leaders failed to restore, discipline, or expel according to the will and purpose of God (cf. Ezek. 3:20–21; Acts 20:26–27; see Ezek. 3:18, note).

18:19 IF TWO . . . SHALL AGREE. There is great authority in corporate and agreeing prayer. The reason is that where two or three are gathered together in faith and commitment to Christ, He is in their midst (v. 20). His presence will impart faith, strength, direction, grace, and consolation (cf. Ps. 46:5; Is. 12:6).

18:35 IF YE . . . FORGIVE NOT. In this parable, Jesus teaches that the forgiveness of God, though freely given to repentant sinners, nevertheless remains conditional, according to the individual's willingness to forgive his fellow humans. In other words, one may forfeit the forgiveness of God by maintaining a bitter and unforgiving heart (see 6:14–15; Heb. 12:15; Jas. 3:11,14; note especially Eph. 4:31–32 where Paul maintains that bitterness, resentment, and animosity are totally incompatible with the Christian profession and must be done away with).

Go ye also into the vineyard; and whatsoever is right, *that* shall ye receive.

8 So when even was come, the lord of the vineyard saith unto his steward, Call the labourers, and give them *their* hire, beginning from the last unto the first.

9 And when they came that *were hired* about the eleventh hour, they received every man a penny.

10 But when the first came, they supposed that they should have received more; and they likewise received every man a penny.

11 And when they had received *it,* they murmured against the goodman of the house,

12 Saying, These last [q]have wrought *but* one hour, and thou hast made them equal unto us, which have borne the burden and heat of the day.

13 But he answered one of them, and said, Friend, I do thee no wrong: didst not thou agree with me for a penny?

14 Take *that* thine *is,* and go thy way: I will give unto this last, even as unto thee.

15 [y]Is it not lawful for me to do what I will with mine own? [z]Is thine eye evil, because I am good?

16 [a]So the last shall be first, and the first last: [b]for many be called, but few chosen.

Jesus again foretells his death

20:17–19pp — Mark 10:32–34; Luke 18:31–33

17 ¶ [c]And Jesus going up to Jerusalem took the twelve disciples apart in the way, and said unto them,

18 [d]Behold, we go up to Jerusalem; and the Son of man shall be betrayed unto the chief priests and unto the scribes, and they shall condemn him to death,

19 [e]And shall deliver him to the Gentiles to mock, and to scourge, and to crucify *him:* and the third day he shall rise again.

20:15
[y]Rom. 9:21
[z]Deut. 15:9
Prov. 23:6
ch. 6:23
20:16
[a]ch. 19:30
[b]ch. 22:14
20:17
[c]Mark 10:32
Luke 18:31
John 12:12
20:18
[d]ch. 16:21
20:19
[e]ch. 27:2
Mark 15:1,16
Luke 23:1
John 18:28
Acts 3:13
20:20
[f]Mark 10:35
[g]ch. 4:21
20:21
[h]ch. 19:28
20:22
[i]ch. 26:39,42
Mark 14:36
Luke 22:42
John 18:11
[j]Luke 12:50
20:23
[k]Acts 12:2
Rom. 8:17
2 Cor. 1:7
Rev. 1:9
[l]ch. 25:34
20:24
[m]Mark 10:41
Luke 22:24,25
20:26
[n]1 Pet. 5:3
[o]ch. 23:11
Mark 9:35
& 10:43
20:27
[p]ch. 18:4
20:28
[q]John 13:4
[r]Phil. 2:7
[s]Luke 22:27
John 13:14
[t]Is. 53:10,11
Dan. 9:24,26
John 11:51,52
1 Tim. 2:6
Tit. 2:14
1 Pet. 1:19
[u]ch. 26:28
Rom. 5:15,19
Heb. 9:28
20:29
[v]Mark 10:46
Luke 18:35

The ambition of James and John

20:20–28pp — Mark 10:35–45

20 ¶ [f]Then came to him the mother of [g]Zebedee's children with her sons, worshipping *him,* and desiring a certain thing of him.

21 And he said unto her, What wilt thou? She saith unto him, Grant that these my two sons [h]may sit, the one on thy right hand, and the other on the left, in thy kingdom.

22 But Jesus answered and said, Ye know not what ye ask. Are ye able to drink of [i]the cup that I shall drink of, and to be baptized with [j]the baptism that I am baptized with? They say unto him, We are able.

23 And he saith unto them, [k]Ye shall drink indeed of my cup, and be baptized with the baptism that I am baptized with: but to sit on my right hand, and on my left, is not mine to [l]give, but *it shall be given to them* for whom it is prepared of my Father.

24 [m]And when the ten heard *it,* they were moved with indignation against the two brethren.

25 But Jesus called them *unto him,* and said, Ye know that the princes of the Gentiles exercise dominion over them, and they that are great exercise authority upon them.

26 But [n]it shall not be so among you: but [o]whosoever will be great among you, let him be your minister;

27 [p]And whosoever will be chief among you, let him be your servant:

28 [q]Even as the [r]Son of man came not to be ministered unto, [s]but to minister, and [t]to give his life a ransom [u]for many.

Jesus' compassion for two blind men

20:29–34pp — Mark 10:46–52; Luke 18:35–43

29 [v]And as they departed from Jer-

[q] Or, *have continued one hour only*

20:26 SHALL NOT BE SO AMONG YOU. In this world those who "exercise dominion" and "authority" are considered great men and women. Jesus says that in the kingdom of God greatness will not be measured by dominion over others, but by giving of one's self in service to others. The believer must not try to reach the top in order to exert his authority or rule. Rather he must give his life in helping others, and especially in laboring for the spiritual good of all people (v. 28; cf. John 13:34; 1 Cor. 13; Col. 3:14; 1 John 3:14; 4:8).

20:28 RANSOM FOR MANY. Ransom conveys the meaning of a price paid to obtain the freedom of others. In the redemptive work of Christ, His death is the price paid for the release of men and women from sin's dominion (see article on BIBLICAL WORDS FOR SALVATION, p. 1726). The release is from condemnation (Rom. 3:25–26), sin (Eph. 1:7), and death (Rom. 8:2). "Many" is used in the sense of "all people" (1 Tim. 2:5–6; see Rom. 3:25, note on the meaning of the cross of Christ).

icho, a great multitude followed him.

30 ¶ And, behold, [w]two blind men sitting by the way side, when they heard that Jesus passed by, cried out, saying, Have mercy on us, O Lord, *thou* Son of David.

31 And the multitude rebuked them, because they should hold their peace: but they cried the more, saying, Have mercy on us, O Lord, *thou* Son of David.

32 And Jesus stood still, and called them, and said, What will ye that I shall do unto you?

33 They say unto him, Lord, that our eyes may be opened.

34 So Jesus had compassion *on them,* and touched their eyes: and immediately their eyes received sight, and they followed him.

The triumphal entry

21:1–9pp — Mark 11:1–10; Luke 19:29–38
21:4–9pp — John 12:12–15

21 AND [x]WHEN they drew nigh unto Jerusalem, and were come to Bethphage, unto [y]the mount of Olives, then sent Jesus two disciples,

2 Saying unto them, Go into the village over against you, and straightway ye shall find an ass tied, and a colt with her: loose *them,* and bring *them* unto me.

3 And if any *man* say aught unto you, ye shall say, The Lord hath need of them; and straightway he will send them.

4 All this was done, that it might be fulfilled which was spoken by the prophet, saying,

5 [z]Tell ye the daughter of Zion, Behold, thy King cometh unto thee, meek, and sitting upon an ass, and a colt the foal of an ass.

6 [a]And the disciples went, and did as Jesus commanded them,

7 And brought the ass, and the colt, and [b]put on them their clothes, and they set *him* thereon.

8 And a very great multitude spread their garments in the way; [c]others cut down branches from the trees, and strawed *them* in the way.

9 And the multitudes that went before, and that followed, cried, saying, [d]Hosanna to the son of David: [e]Blessed *is* he that cometh in the name of the Lord; Hosanna in the highest.

10 [f]And when he was come into Jerusalem, all the city was moved, saying, Who is this?

11 And the multitude said, This is Jesus [g]the prophet of Nazareth of Galilee.

Cleansing of the temple

21:12–16pp — Mark 11:15–18; Luke 19:45–47

12 ¶ [h]And Jesus went into the temple of God, and cast out all them that sold and bought in the temple, and overthrew the tables of the [i]moneychangers, and the seats of them that sold doves,

13 And said unto them, It is written, [j]My house shall be called the house of prayer; [k]but ye have made it a den of thieves.

14 And the blind and the lame came to him in the temple; and he healed them.

15 And when the chief priests and scribes saw the wonderful things that he did, and the children crying in the temple, and saying, Hosanna to the son of David; they were sore displeased,

16 And said unto him, Hearest thou what these say? And Jesus saith unto them, Yea; have ye never read, [l]Out of the mouth of babes and sucklings thou hast perfected praise?

Luke 1:42-47

17 ¶ And he left them, and went out of the city into [m]Bethany; and he lodged there.

The barren fig tree

21:18–22pp — Mark 11:12–14,20–24

18 [n]Now in the morning as he returned into the city, he hungered.

19 [o]And when he saw [r]a fig tree in the way, he came to it, and found

20:30 [w]ch. 9:27 **21:1** [x]Mark 11:1 Luke 19:29 [y]Zech. 14:4 **21:5** [z]Is. 62:11 Zech. 9:9 John 12:15 **21:6** [a]Mark 11:4 **21:7** [b]2 Ki. 9:13 **21:8** [c]See Lev. 23:40 John 12:13 **21:9** [d]Ps. 118:25 [e]Ps. 118:26 ch. 23:39 **21:10** [f]Mark 11:15 Luke 19:45 John 2:13,15 **21:11** [g]ch. 2:23 Luke 7:16 John 6:14 & 7:40 & 9:17 **21:12** [h]Mark 11:11 Luke 19:45 John 2:15 [i]Deut. 14:25 **21:13** [j]Is. 56:7 [k]Jer. 7:11 Mark 11:17 Luke 19:46 **21:16** [l]Ps. 8:2 **21:17** [m]Mark 11:11 John 11:18 **21:18** [n]Mark 11:12 **21:19** [o]Mark 11:13

[r] Gk. *one fig tree*

21:12 JESUS ... OVERTHREW THE TABLES. This is the second time that Jesus entered the temple and cleansed it from unrighteousness (for the temple cleansing at the beginning of His ministry, see John 2:15). Those who bear Christ's name must know that hypocrisy, greed, self-serving interest, immorality, and irreverence in the house of God will bring God's judgment and righteous indignation. Christ is Lord of His church and demands that it be a "house of prayer" (v. 13; see Luke 19:45, note).

21:13 THE HOUSE OF PRAYER. See Mark 11:17, note.

nothing thereon, but leaves only, and
said unto it, Let no fruit grow on thee
henceforward for ever. And presently
the fig tree withered away.
20 [p]And when the disciples saw *it,*
they marvelled, saying, How soon is
the fig tree withered away!
21 Jesus answered and said unto
them, Verily I say unto you, [q]If ye
have faith, and [r]doubt not, ye shall
not only do this *which is done* to the fig
tree, [s]but also if ye shall say unto this
mountain, Be thou removed, and be
thou cast into the sea; it shall be done.
22 And [t]all things, whatsoever ye
shall ask in prayer, believing, ye shall
receive.

Jesus' authority challenged

21:23–27pp — Mark 11:27–33; Luke 20:1–8

23 ¶ [u]And when he was come into
the temple, the chief priests and the
elders of the people came unto him as
he was teaching, and [v]said, By what
authority doest thou these things? and
who gave thee this authority?
24 And Jesus answered and said
unto them, I also will ask you one
thing, which if ye tell me, I in like wise
will tell you by what authority I do
these things.
25 The baptism of John, whence
was it? from heaven, or of men? And
they reasoned with themselves, say-
ing, If we shall say, From heaven; he
will say unto us, Why did ye not then
believe him?
26 But if we shall say, Of men; we
fear the people; [w]for all hold John as
a prophet.
27 And they answered Jesus, and
said, We cannot tell. And he said unto
them, Neither tell I you by what author-
ity I do these things.

Parable of the two sons

28 ¶ But what think ye? A *certain*
man had two sons; and he came to the
first, and said, Son, go work today in
my vineyard.
29 He answered and said, I will not:
but afterward he repented, and went.
30 And he came to the second, and
said likewise. And he answered and
said, I *go,* sir: and went not.
31 Whether of them twain did the
will of *his* father? They say unto him,
The first. Jesus saith unto them,
[x]Verily I say unto you, That the publi-
cans and the harlots go into the king-
dom of God before you.
32 For [y]John came unto you in the
way of righteousness, and ye believed
him not: [z]but the publicans and the
harlots believed him: and ye, when ye
had seen *it,* repented not afterward,
that ye might believe him.

Parable of the tenants

21:33–46pp — Mark 12:1–12; Luke 20:9–19

33 ¶ Hear another parable: There
was a certain householder, [a]which
planted a vineyard, and hedged it
round about, and digged a winepress in
it, and built a tower, and let it out to
husbandmen, and [b]went into a far
country:
34 And when the time of the fruit
drew near, he sent his servants to the
husbandmen, [c]that they might receive
the fruits of it.
35 [d]And the husbandmen took his
servants, and beat one, and killed an-
other, and stoned another.
36 Again, he sent other servants
more than the first: and they did unto
them likewise.
37 But last of all he sent unto them
his son, saying, They will reverence my
son.
38 But when the husbandmen saw
the son, they said among themselves,
[e]This is the heir; [f]come, let us kill
him, and let us seize on his inheri-
tance.
39 [g]And they caught him, and cast
him out of the vineyard, and slew *him.*
40 When the lord therefore of the
vineyard cometh, what will he do unto
those husbandmen?
41 [h]They say unto him, [i]He will
miserably destroy those wicked men,
[j]and will let out *his* vineyard unto oth-
er husbandmen, which shall render
him the fruits in their seasons.
42 Jesus saith unto them, [k]Did ye

21:20 [p]Mark 11:20
21:21 [q]ch. 17:20 [r]Jas. 1:6 [s]1 Cor. 13:2
21:22 [t]ch. 7:7 Mark 11:24 Luke 11:9 Jas. 5:16 1 John 3:22 & 5:14
21:23 [u]Mark 11:27 Luke 20:1 [v]Ex. 2:14 Acts 4:7 & 7:27
21:26 [w]ch. 14:5 Mark 6:20 Luke 20:6
21:31 [x]Luke 7:29,50
21:32 [y]ch. 3:1 [z]Luke 3:12,13
21:33 [a]Ps. 80:9 Sol. 8:11 Is. 5:1 Jer. 2:21 Mark 12:1 Luke 20:9 [b]ch. 25:14
21:34 [c]Sol. 8:11,12
21:35 [d]2 Chr. 24:21 & 36:16 Neh. 9:26 ch. 5:12 & 23:34,37 Acts 7:52 1 Thes. 2:15 Heb. 11:36,37
21:38 [e]Ps. 2:8 Heb. 1:2 [f]Ps. 2:2 ch. 26:3 & 27:1 John 11:53 Acts 4:27
21:39 [g]ch. 26:50 Mark 14:46 Luke 22:54 John 18:12 Acts 2:23
21:41 [h]Luke 20:16 [i]Luke 21:24 Heb. 2:3 [j]Acts 13:46 & 15:7 & 18:6 & 28:28 Rom. 9 & 10 & 11
21:42 [k]Ps. 118:22 Is. 28:16 Mark 12:10 Luke 20:17 Acts 4:11 Eph. 2:20 1 Pet. 2:6,7

21:21 IF YE HAVE FAITH. Jesus speaks of faith and prayer (v. 22), stating that answers to prayer are related to our faith. Everything that is in harmony with God's will is possible to perform or receive for those who do not doubt (see 17:20, note; Mark 11:24, note; cf. 1 Ki. 17:1,7; 18:42–45; Luke 17:5–6; see article on EFFECTIVE PRAYING, p. 540).

21:33–44 THE WICKED HUSBANDMEN. This parable pictures Israel's rejection of God's beloved Son (cf. Mark 12:1, note; Luke 20:9).

never read in the scriptures, The stone which the builders rejected, the same is become the head of the corner: this is the Lord's doing, and it is marvellous in our eyes?

43 Therefore say I unto you, [l]The kingdom of God shall be taken from you, and given to a nation bringing forth the fruits thereof.

44 And whosoever [m]shall fall on this stone shall be broken: but on whomsoever it shall fall, [n]it will grind him to powder.

45 And when the chief priests and Pharisees had heard his parables, they perceived that he spake of them.

46 But when they sought to lay hands on him, they feared the multitude, because [o]they took him for a prophet.

The wedding dinner

22:2–14Ref — Luke 14:16–24

22 AND JESUS answered [p]and spake unto them again by parables, and said,

2 The kingdom of heaven is like unto a certain king, which made a marriage for his son,

3 And sent forth his servants to call them that were bidden to the wedding: and they would not come.

4 Again, he sent forth other servants, saying, Tell them which are bidden, Behold, I have prepared my dinner: [q]my oxen and *my* fatlings *are* killed, and all things *are* ready: come unto the marriage.

5 But they made light of *it,* and went their ways, one to his farm, another to his merchandise:

6 And the remnant took his servants, and entreated *them* spitefully, and slew *them.*

21:43 [l]ch. 8:12
21:44 [m]Is. 8:14,15 Zech. 12:3 Luke 20:18 Rom. 9:33 1 Pet. 2:8 [n]Is. 60:12 Dan. 2:44
21:46 [o]ver. 11 Luke 7:16 John 7:40
22:1 [p]Luke 14:16 Rev. 19:7,9
22:4 [q]Prov. 9:2
22:7 [r]Dan. 9:26 Luke 19:27
22:8 [s]ch. 10:11 Acts 13:46
22:10 [t]ch. 13:38
22:11 [u]2 Cor. 5:3 Eph. 4:24 Col. 3:10,12 Rev. 3:4 & 16:15 & 19:8
22:13 [v]ch. 8:12
22:14 [w]ch. 20:16
22:15 [x]Mark 12:13 Luke 20:20

7 But when the king heard *thereof,* he was wroth: and he sent forth [r]his armies, and destroyed those murderers, and burned up their city.

8 Then saith he to his servants, The wedding is ready, but they which were bidden were not [s]worthy.

9 Go ye therefore into the highways, and as many as ye shall find, bid to the marriage.

10 So those servants went out into the highways, and [t]gathered together all as many as they found, both bad and good: and the wedding was furnished with guests.

11 ¶ And when the king came in to see the guests, he saw there a man [u]which had not on a wedding garment:

12 And he saith unto him, Friend, how camest thou in hither not having a wedding garment? And he was speechless.

13 Then said the king to the servants, Bind him hand and foot, and take him away, and cast *him* [v]into outer darkness; there shall be weeping and gnashing of teeth.

14 [w]For many are called, but few *are* chosen.

Paying taxes to Caesar

22:15–22pp — Mark 12:13–17; Luke 20:20–26

15 ¶ [x]Then went the Pharisees, and took counsel how they might entangle him in *his* talk.

16 And they sent out unto him their disciples with the Herodians, saying, Master, we know that thou art true, and teachest the way of God in truth, neither carest thou for any *man:* for thou regardest not the person of men.

17 Tell us therefore, What thinkest

21:43 KINGDOM . . . TAKEN FROM YOU. Israel rejects the Messiah and His kingdom. As a result, the kingdom of God and its power are given to others, to those who respond to the gospel, whether they be Jew or Gentile (1 Pet. 2:9). This principle is still in operation. The kingdom and its power will be taken from those who fail to remain faithful to Christ, rejecting His righteous ways (Rom. 11:19–22); instead, it will be given to a people who separate from the world and seek first the kingdom of God and His righteousness (see 5:6; 6:33).

21:44 SHALL BE BROKEN. See Luke 20:18, note.

22:11 WEDDING GARMENT. Many within the visible manifestation of the kingdom of heaven will not be wearing a wedding garment and hence are not of the chosen (v. 14). The "wedding garment" symbolizes a condition of readiness—present possession of true faith in Christ and continued obedience made possible through the grace of Christ (cf. 24:44; 25:21). Christ refers to the man who was not wearing wedding clothes in order to make all of us examine ourselves and ask, "Lord, is it I?"

22:14 FEW *ARE* CHOSEN. The call to salvation goes out to the many. However, the few who are chosen to inherit the kingdom of heaven are only those who respond to God's call, repent of their sins, and believe in Christ. Responding to God's grace by the free exercise of our will brings us into the chosen people of God (see article on ELECTION AND PREDESTINATION, p. 1846).

thou? Is it lawful to give tribute unto
Caesar, or not?
18 But Jesus perceived their wick-
edness, and said, Why tempt ye me, *ye*
hypocrites?
19 Show me the tribute money. And
they brought unto him a [s]penny.
20 And he saith unto them, Whose
is this image and [t]superscription?
21 They say unto him, Caesar's.
Then saith he unto them, [y]Render
therefore unto Caesar the things which
are Caesar's; and unto God the things
that are God's.
22 When they had heard *these*
words, they marvelled, and left him,
and went their way.

Marriage and heaven

22:23–33pp — Mark 12:18–27; Luke 20:27–40

23 ¶ [z]The same day came to him
the Sadducees, [a]which say that there
is no resurrection, and asked him,
24 Saying, Master, [b]Moses said, If
a man die, having no children, his
brother shall marry his wife, and raise
up seed unto his brother.
25 Now there were with us seven
brethren: and the first, when he had
married a wife, deceased, and having
no issue, left his wife unto his brother:
26 Likewise the second also, and
the third, unto the [u]seventh.
27 And last of all the woman died
also.
28 Therefore in the resurrection
whose wife shall she be of the seven?
for they all had her.
29 Jesus answered and said unto
them, Ye do err, [c]not knowing the
scriptures, nor the power of God.
30 For in the resurrection they nei-
ther marry, nor are given in marriage,
but [d]are as the angels of God in
heaven.
31 But as touching the resurrection
of the dead, have ye not read that
which was spoken unto you by God,
saying,
32 [e]I am the God of Abraham, and
the God of Isaac, and the God of Jacob?
God is not the God of the dead, but of
the living.
33 And when the multitude heard
this, [f]they were astonished at his doc-
trine.

The greatest commandment

22:34–40pp — Mark 12:28–31

34 ¶ [g]But when the Pharisees had
heard that he had put the Sadducees to
silence, they were gathered together.
35 Then one of them, *which was* [h]a
lawyer, asked *him a question,* tempting
him, and saying,
36 Master, which *is* the great com-
mandment in the law?
37 Jesus said unto him, [i]Thou
shalt love the Lord thy God with all thy
heart, and with all thy soul, and with
all thy mind.
38 This is the first and great com-
mandment.
39 And the second *is* like unto it,

22:21 [y]ch. 17:25 Rom. 13:7
22:23 [z]Mark 12:18 Luke 20:27 [a]Acts 23:8
22:24 [b]Deut. 25:5
22:29 [c]John 20:9
22:30 [d]1 John 3:2
22:32 [e]Ex. 3:6,16 Mark 12:26 Luke 20:37 Acts 7:32 Heb. 11:16
22:33 [f]ch. 7:28
22:34 [g]Mark 12:28
22:35 [h]Luke 10:25
22:37 [i]Deut. 6:5 & 10:12 & 30:6 Luke 10:27

[s] The penny, worth about 16 cents, was the usual day's wage for a laborer [t] Or, *inscription?* [u] Gk. *seven*

22:30 THEY NEITHER MARRY. See Mark 12:25, note.

22:35 A LAWYER. A "lawyer" (Gk. *nomikos*) was an interpreter and teacher of the law of Moses.

22:37 LOVE THE LORD THY GOD. What God asks of all those who believe in Christ and receive His salvation is devoted love (cf. Deut. 6:5; Rom. 13:9–10; 1 Cor. 13). (1) This love requires an attitude of heart where God is so valued and esteemed that we truly long for His fellowship, strive to obey Him, and sincerely care for His honor and will on earth. Those who truly love God will desire to share His suffering (Phil. 3:10), promote His kingdom (1 Cor. 9:23), and live for His honor and righteous standards on earth (6:9–10,33).

(2) One's love to God must be a wholehearted and dominating love, a love inspired by His love to us whereby He gave His Son for our sake (see John 3:16, note; Rom. 8:32). Our love is to be identical to the love expressed in Rom. 12:1–2; 1 Cor. 6:20; 10:31; 2 Cor. 9:15; Eph. 4:30; 5:1–2; Col. 3:12–17.

(3) Love to God includes: (a) a personal attachment of allegiance and loyalty to Him; (b) faith as a firm, unswerving adherence to the One to whom we are united by sonship; (c) faithfulness to our pledge and commitment to Him; (d) heartfelt devotion, expressed in our dedication to God's righteous standards in the midst of a God-rejecting world; and (e) a desire for God's presence and fellowship.

22:39 LOVE THY NEIGHBOUR. The child of God is required to love all people (Gal. 6:10; 1 Thes. 3:12), including his enemies (5:44). He is also commanded to love all true born-again Christians in a special way (see John 13:34, note; Gal. 6:10; cf. 1 Thes. 3:12; 1 John 3:11). (1) The believer's love to his Christian brother, his neighbor, and his enemy must be subordinated to, and controlled and directed by, his love and devotion to God. (2) Love to God is the "first and great commandment" (vv. 37–38). Hence, the holiness of God, His desire for purity, and His will and standard as revealed

[j]Thou shalt love thy neighbour as thy-
self.
40 [k]On these two commandments
hang all the law and the prophets.

Whose Son is the Christ?

22:41–46pp — Mark 12:35–37; Luke 20:41–44

41 ¶ [l]While the Pharisees were
gathered together, Jesus asked them,
42 Saying, What think ye of Christ?
whose son is he? They say unto him,
The son of David.
43 He saith unto them, How then
doth David in spirit call him Lord, say-
ing,
44 [m]The LORD said unto my Lord,
Sit thou on my right hand, till I make
thine enemies thy footstool?
45 If David then call him Lord, how
is he his son?
46 [n]And no man was able to an-
swer him a word, [o]neither durst any
man from that day forth ask him any
more *questions.*

The sins of the Pharisees

23:1–7pp — Mark 12:38–39; Luke 20:45–46

23 THEN SPAKE Jesus to the mul-
titude, and to his disciples,
2 Saying, [p]The scribes and the
Pharisees sit in Moses' seat:
3 All therefore whatsoever they bid
you observe, *that* observe and do; but
do not ye after their works: for [q]they
say, and do not.

22:39 [j]Lev. 19:18 ch. 19:19 Mark 12:31 Luke 10:27 Rom. 13:9 Gal. 5:14 Jas. 2:8
22:40 [k]ch. 7:12 1 Tim. 1:5
22:41 [l]Mark 12:35 Luke 20:41
22:44 [m]Ps. 110:1 Acts 2:34 1 Cor. 15:25 Heb. 1:13 & 10:12,13
22:46 [n]Luke 14:6 [o]Mark 12:34 Luke 20:40
23:2 [p]Neh. 8:4,8 Mal. 2:7 Mark 12:38 Luke 20:45
23:3 [q]Rom. 2:19
23:4 [r]Luke 11:46 Acts 15:10 Gal. 6:13
23:5 [s]ch. 6:1,2,5,16 [t]Num. 15:38 Deut. 6:8 & 22:12 Prov. 3:3
23:6 [u]Mark 12:38,39 Luke 11:43 & 20:46 3 John 9
23:8 [v]Jas. 3:1 See 2 Cor. 1:24 1 Pet. 5:3
23:9 [w]Mal. 1:6
23:11 [x]ch. 20:26,27

4 [r]For they bind heavy burdens
and grievous to be borne, and lay *them*
on men's shoulders; but they *them-
selves* will not move them with one of
their fingers.
5 But [s]all their works they do for
to be seen of men: [t]they make broad
their phylacteries, and enlarge the bor-
ders of their garments,
6 [u]And love the uppermost rooms
at feasts, and the chief seats in the syn-
agogues,
7 And greetings in the markets, and
to be called of men, Rabbi, Rabbi.
8 [v]But be not ye called Rabbi: for
one is your Master, *even* Christ; and all
ye are brethren.
9 And call no *man* your father upon
the earth: [w]for one is your Father,
which is in heaven.
10 Neither be ye called masters: for
one is your Master, *even* Christ.
11 But [x]he that is greatest among
you shall be your servant.
12 [y]And whosoever shall exalt
himself shall be abased; and he that
shall humble himself shall be exalted.

The woes upon the Pharisees

13 ¶ But [z]woe unto you, scribes
and Pharisees, hypocrites! for ye shut
up the kingdom of heaven against men:
for ye neither go in *yourselves,* neither

23:12 [y]Job 22:29; Prov. 15:33 & 29:23; Luke 14:11 & 18:14; Jas. 4:6; 1 Pet. 5:5 **23:13** [z]Luke 11:52

---

in Scripture must never be compromised in our practice of love to all people.

23:13 WOE UNTO YOU . . . PHARISEES. Jesus' words in ch. 23 constitute His most severe denunciation. They were directed against religious leaders and false teachers who had rejected at least a part of the revealed Word of God and replaced it with their own ideas and interpretations (vv. 23,28; 15:3,6–9; Mark 7:6–9). (1) The spirit of Jesus should be noted. It is not the tolerant, permissive, and accommodative spirit of someone who is unconcerned about faithfulness to God and His Word. Christ was not a weak preacher, tolerating sin. He was true enough to His calling to be angry with evil (cf. 21:12–17; John 2:13–16) and to denounce sin and corruption in high places (vv. 23, 25).

(2) Christ's love for the inspired Scriptures of His Father, as well as His concern for those who were being destroyed by its distortion (see 15:2–3; 18:6–7; 23:13,15), was so great that it caused Him to use words like "hypocrites" (v. 15), "child of hell" (v. 15), "blind guides" (v. 16), "fools" (v. 17), "extortion and excess" (v. 25), "whited sepulchres . . . unclean" (v. 27), "full of . . . iniquity" (v. 28), "serpents," "generation of vipers" (v. 33), and murderers (v. 34). These words, though severe and condemning, were spoken with a broken heart (v. 37) by One who died for those to whom they were addressed (cf. John 3:16; Rom. 5:6,8).

(3) Jesus describes the character of false teachers and preachers as those ministers who seek to be popular, important, and noticed by others (v. 5), who love honor (v. 6) and titles (v. 7), and who keep people out of heaven by their distorted gospel (v. 13; see article on FALSE TEACHERS, p. 1508). They are professional religionists who appear spiritual and godly, but are really unrighteous (vv. 14, 25–27). They speak well of godly spiritual leaders of the past, but do not follow their practices or their commitment to God and His Word and righteousness (vv. 29–30).

(4) The Bible commands believers to beware of such false religious leaders (7:15; 24:11), consider them to be unbelievers (see Gal. 1:9, note), and refuse to support their ministry or have fellowship with them (2 John 9–11).

(5) Those of the church who, in the name of love, toleration, or unity, refuse to share Jesus' spirit and attitude towards those who distort the original teaching of Christ and the Scriptures (7:15; Gal. 1:6–7; 2 John 9), are participating in the evil

suffer ye them that are entering to go in.

14 Woe unto you, scribes and Pharisees, hypocrites! [a]for ye devour widows' houses, and for a pretence make long prayer: therefore ye shall receive the greater damnation.

15 Woe unto you, scribes and Pharisees, hypocrites! for ye compass sea and land to make one proselyte, and when he is made, ye make him twofold more the child of hell than yourselves.

16 Woe unto you, [b]*ye* blind guides, which say, [c]Whosoever shall swear by the temple, it is nothing; but whosoever shall swear by the gold of the temple, he is a debtor!

17 *Ye* fools and blind: for whether is greater, the gold, [d]or the temple that sanctifieth the gold?

18 And, Whosoever shall swear by the altar, it is nothing; but whosoever sweareth by the gift that is upon it, he is [v]guilty.

19 *Ye* fools and blind: for whether *is* greater, the gift, or [e]the altar that sanctifieth the gift?

20 Whoso therefore shall swear by the altar, sweareth by it, and by all things thereon.

21 And whoso shall swear by the temple, sweareth by it, and by [f]him that dwelleth therein.

22 And he that shall swear by heaven, sweareth by [g]the throne of God, and by him that sitteth thereon.

23 Woe unto you, scribes and Pharisees, hypocrites! [h]for ye pay tithe of mint and [w]anise and cummin, and [i]have omitted the weightier *matters* of the law, judgment, mercy, and faith: these ought ye to have done, and not to leave the other undone.

24 *Ye* blind guides, which strain at a gnat, and swallow a camel.

25 Woe unto you, scribes and Pharisees, hypocrites! [j]for ye make clean the outside of the cup and of the platter, but within they are full of extortion and excess.

26 *Thou* blind Pharisee, cleanse first that *which is* within the cup and platter, that the outside of them may be clean also.

27 Woe unto you, scribes and Pharisees, hypocrites! [k]for ye are like unto whited sepulchres, which indeed appear beautiful outward, but are within full of dead *men's* bones, and of all uncleanness.

28 Even so ye also outwardly appear righteous unto men, but within ye are full of hypocrisy and iniquity.

29 [l]Woe unto you, scribes and Pharisees, hypocrites! because ye build the tombs of the prophets, and garnish the sepulchres of the righteous,

30 And say, If we had been in the days of our fathers, we would not have been partakers with them in the blood of the prophets.

31 Wherefore ye be witnesses unto yourselves, that [m]ye are the children of them which killed the prophets.

32 [n]Fill ye up then the measure of your fathers.

33 *Ye* serpents, *ye* [o]generation of vipers, how can ye escape the damnation of hell?

34 ¶ [p]Wherefore, behold, I send unto you prophets, and wise men, and scribes: and [q]*some* of them ye shall kill and crucify; and [r]*some* of them shall ye scourge in your synagogues, and persecute *them* from city to city:

35 [s]That upon you may come all the righteous blood shed upon the earth, [t]from the blood of righteous Abel unto [u]the blood of Zacharias son of Barachias, whom ye slew between the temple and the altar.

36 Verily I say unto you, All these things shall come upon this generation.

Jesus' lament over Jerusalem

23:37–39pp — Luke 13:34–35

37 [v]O Jerusalem, Jerusalem, *thou* that killest the prophets, [w]and stonest them which are sent unto thee, how often would [x]I have gathered thy chil-

23:14 [a]Mark 12:40 Luke 20:47 2 Tim. 3:6 Tit. 1:11
23:16 [b]ver. 24 ch. 15:14 [c]ch. 5:33,34
23:17 [d]Ex. 30:29
23:19 [e]Ex. 29:37
23:21 [f]1 Ki. 8:13 2 Chr. 6:2 Ps. 26:8 & 132:14
23:22 [g]Ps. 11:4 ch. 5:34 Acts 7:49
23:23 [h]Luke 11:42 [i]1 Sam. 15:22 Hos. 6:6 Mic. 6:8 ch. 9:13 & 12:7
23:25 [j]Mark 7:4 Luke 11:39
23:27 [k]Luke 11:44 Acts 23:3
23:29 [l]Luke 11:47
23:31 [m]Acts 7:51,52 1 Thes. 2:15
23:32 [n]Gen. 15:16 1 Thes. 2:16
23:33 [o]ch. 3:7 & 12:34
23:34 [p]ch. 21:34,35 Luke 11:49 [q]Acts 5:40 & 7:58,59 & 22:19 [r]ch. 10:17 2 Cor. 11:24,25
23:35 [s]Rev. 18:24 [t]Gen. 4:8 1 John 3:12 [u]2 Chr. 24:20,21
23:37 [v]Luke 13:34 [w]2 Chr. 24:21 [x]Deut. 32:11,12

[v]Or, *debtor,* or, *bound* [w]Or, *dill*

deeds of false prophets and teachers (2 John 10–11).

23:28 OUTWARDLY APPEAR RIGHTEOUS. Jesus continues His speech about religious leaders and ministers of His day whose public conduct appeared righteous, but whose hearts were full of hypocrisy, pride, lust, and iniquity. They were like painted sepulchers, beautiful and attractive on the outside, yet with foulness and corruption hidden inside. For more on what the Bible has to say about false teachers, see article on FALSE TEACHERS, p. 1508.

23:37 O JERUSALEM, JERUSALEM. See Luke 13:34, note; 19:41, note.

dren together, even as a hen gathereth
her chickens [y]under *her* wings, and ye
would not!
38 Behold, your house is left unto
you desolate.
39 For I say unto you, Ye shall not
see me henceforth, till ye shall say,
[z]Blessed *is* he that cometh in the
name of the Lord.

Prophecy about the end of this age

24:1–14pp — Mark 13:1–13; Luke 21:5–19

24 AND [a]JESUS went out, and de-
parted from the temple: and his
disciples came to *him* for to show him
the buildings of the temple.

23:37 [y]Ps. 17:8 & 91:4
23:39 [z]Ps. 118:26 ch. 21:9
24:1 [a]Mark 13:1 Luke 21:5
24:2 [b]1 Ki. 9:7 Jer. 26:18 Mic. 3:12 Luke 19:44
24:3 [c]Mark 13:3 [d]1 Thes. 5:1
24:4 [e]Eph. 5:6 Col. 2:8,18 2 Thes. 2:3 1 John 4:1
24:5 [f]ver. 24 Jer. 14:14 & 23:21,25; John 5:43

2 And Jesus said unto them, See ye
not all these things? verily I say unto
you, [b]There shall not be left here one
stone upon another, that shall not be
thrown down.
3 ¶ And as he sat upon the mount of
Olives, [c]the disciples came unto him
privately, saying, [d]Tell us, when shall
these things be? and what *shall be* the
sign of thy coming, and of the end of
the world?
4 And Jesus answered and said unto
them, [e]Take heed that no man deceive
you.
5 For [f]many shall come in my

23:39 YE SHALL NOT SEE ME . . . TILL. The city of Jerusalem had repeatedly rejected Jesus' message. Therefore, in sorrow (vv. 37–38) Christ must withdraw and would not be seen by Israel again until they acknowledge their offense and call for the Messiah to come as their Deliverer. (1) This will occur only when Israel (i.e., a remnant, see Is. 6:13, note; 10:20, note; 17:7, note) experiences the dreadful days of the tribulation and are in their greatest peril (Hos. 5:15—6:3; see article on THE GREAT TRIBULATION, p. 1456).

(2) When Israel experiences intense tribulation at the end of the age (Amos 9:9), the nations of the world will gather against Jerusalem (Zech. 12:1–4) and two-thirds of Israel will be killed (Zech. 13:8–9). At the point when Israel is nearly destroyed, the remnant will turn in repentance and mourning (Is. 26:16–17; 64:1,6; Hos. 5:15; Zech. 12:4–5,10; Rom. 11:26; see Rev. 11:2, note; 12:6, note; see article on ISRAEL IN GOD'S PLAN OF SALVATION, p. 1748).

24:3—25:46 THE OLIVET DISCOURSE. Jesus' Olivet prophecy was primarily a reply to the disciples' question: "What shall be the sign of Thy coming, and of the end of the world?" Jesus gave them: (1) general signs of the course of the age leading up to the last days (24:4–14); (2) special signs to indicate the final days of the age, the great tribulation (24:15–28); (3) spectacular signs to occur at His triumphant coming with power and great glory (24:29–31); (4) admonition to tribulation saints to be alert to the signs leading up to Christ's expected coming immediately after the tribulation (24:32–35); (5) admonition to believers living before the tribulation to be spiritually ready for the unexpected and unknown time of Christ's coming for His faithful (24:36–51; 25:1–30; see John 14:3, note; see article on THE RAPTURE, p. 1889); (6) a description of the judgment of nations after His return to earth (25:31–46).

It should be observed that many details of Christ's coming are not disclosed in Mat. 24. Furthermore, no one has so far deciphered all the prophecies concerning the end time with complete certainty. There remains in Jesus' discourse an element of mystery requiring humility and a heart fixed on the Lord Jesus Himself. We can expect additional unfolding of revelatory understanding at the time of the end (cf. Dan. 12:9).

24:4–51 JESUS . . . SAID UNTO THEM. Jesus' words in the Olivet discourse are addressed to His disciples and to all of God's faithful people until the end of the age and His triumphant return to earth to begin His millennial reign. (1) Concerning believers living before the tribulation period, Christ tells them they cannot calculate or even estimate the time of His return for them (vv. 42–44). Therefore they must be ready at any time, for He shall return to take them to heaven (i.e., His "Father's house," see John 14:2–3, notes) at a time when they do not think He will (see v. 44, note; see article on THE RAPTURE, p. 1889).

(2) For those who converted to Christ during the great tribulation, they can know the time of His coming for them with a high degree of certainty, for Christ gives them signs by which to expect and know that His return is very near (vv. 15–29). When they see these signs they will "know that it is near, *even* at the doors" (see v. 33, note).

24:4 SIGNS OF THE END OF THIS AGE. In vv. 4–14 Jesus gives the signs (cf. v. 3) which will characterize the whole course of the last days and which will intensify as the end draws nearer. (1) False prophets and religious compromisers within the visible church will increase and deceive many (vv. 4–5,11). (2) The increase of wars, famines, and earthquakes (vv. 6–7) will be "the beginning of sorrows" (v. 8) of the new Messianic age. (3) As the end draws nearer, the persecution of God's people will become more severe (v. 9), and many will forsake their loyalty to Christ (vv. 9–10). (4) Disregard for God's law, violence, and crime will increase rapidly, and natural love and family affection will decrease (v. 12; cf. Mark 13:12; 2 Tim. 3:3). (5) In spite of this intensification of trouble, the gospel will be preached in the whole world (v. 14). (6) The saved will be those who stand firm in their faith through all the end-time distress (v. 13). (7) The faithful, as they see the intensification of these signs, will know that the day of the Lord's return for them is "approaching" (Heb. 10:25; see John 14:3, note).

name, saying, I am Christ; [g]and shall
deceive many.
6 And ye shall hear of wars and ru-
mours of wars: see that ye be not trou-
bled: for all *these things* must come to
pass, but the end is not yet.
7 For [h]nation shall rise against na-
tion, and kingdom against kingdom:
and there shall be famines, and pesti-
lences, and earthquakes, in divers
places.
8 All these *are* the beginning of sor-
rows.
9 [i]Then shall they deliver you up
to be afflicted, and shall kill you: and
ye shall be hated of all nations for my
name's sake.

24:5 [g]ver. 11
24:7 [h]2 Chr. 15:6 Is. 19:2 Hag. 2:22 Zech. 14:13
24:9 [i]ch. 10:17 Luke 21:12 John 16:2 Acts 4:2,3
24:10 [j]2 Tim. 1:15 & 4:10,16
24:11 [k]Acts 20:29 2 Pet. 2:1 [l]1 Tim. 4:1
24:13 [m]ch. 10:22 Mark 13:13 Rev. 2:10
24:14 [n]ch. 4:23

10 And then shall many [j]be offend-
ed, and shall betray one another, and
shall hate one another.
11 And [k]many false prophets shall
rise, and [l]shall deceive many.
12 And because iniquity shall
abound, the love of many shall wax
cold.
13 [m]But he that shall endure unto
the end, the same shall be saved.
14 And this [n]gospel of the king-
dom [o]shall be preached in all the
world for a witness unto all nations;
and then shall the end come.

Mat. 28:18-20

[o]Rom. 10:18; Col. 1:6,23

24:5 MANY SHALL ... DECEIVE MANY. This first major sign has special importance. Toward the end of this age, religious deception will be rampant on the earth. Christ is so concerned that His followers be aware of the coming worldwide spiritual deception to occur just before the end that He repeats His warning twice more in the Olivet discourse (see v. 11, note; v. 24; see article on THE AGE OF THE ANTICHRIST, p. 1896).

24:9 YE SHALL BE HATED. All believers in Christ may expect tribulation during their pilgrimage on earth. Suffering for Christ because of our loyalty to Him and His Word is an intrinsic part of the Christian faith (cf. John 15:20; 16:33; Acts 14:22; Rom. 5:3; see Mat. 5:10, note; 2 Tim. 3:12, note).

24:11 MANY FALSE PROPHETS SHALL RISE. As the last days begin to close, false teachers and preachers will be exceedingly prevalent (see article on FALSE TEACHERS, p. 1508). Much of Christendom will be in an apostate condition. Loyalty and total commitment to the truth of God's Word and Biblical righteousness will be in the minority.

(1) Professing believers will accept "new revelation" even though it conflicts with the revealed Word of God. This will lead to opposition to Biblical truth within the churches (see 1 Tim. 4:1, note; 2 Tim. 3:8; 4:3, note). Those who preach a distorted gospel may even gain strategic leadership positions in denominations and theological schools of Christendom (see 7:22, note), enabling them to deceive and mislead many within the church (see Gal. 1:9, note; 2 Tim. 4:3, note; 2 Pet. 3:3–4).

(2) Throughout the world millions will be involved in the occult, astrology, witchcraft, spiritism, and Satanism. The influence of demons and evil spirits will multiply greatly (see 1 Tim. 4:1, note).

(3) Protection against being deceived is found in an enduring faith and love for Christ, in a commitment to the absolute authority of His Word (vv. 4,11,13,25), and in a thorough knowledge of that Word (see 1 Tim. 4:16, note).

24:12 INIQUITY SHALL ABOUND. An unbelievable increase in immorality, shamelessness, rebellion against God, and a casting off of moral restraint will characterize the last days. Sexual perversion, fornication, adultery, pornography, drugs, ungodly music, and lustful entertainment will abound. It will be "as the days of Noe" (v. 37), when the very imaginations of human hearts were evil continually (see Gen. 6:5). It will be as "in the days of Lot" (Luke 17:28,30), when homosexuality, lesbianism, and all kinds of sexual perversion permeated society (see Gen. 19:5, note; 1 Tim. 4:1, note; 2 Tim. 3:1–8, notes). Jesus goes on to indicate that true love will be in short supply.

24:14 THIS GOSPEL OF THE KINGDOM ... THE END. The end shall come only after the "gospel of the kingdom" has been adequately preached in the whole world. (1) This "gospel of the kingdom" refers to the gospel preached in the power and righteousness of the Holy Spirit and accompanied by the major signs of the gospel (see article on THE KINGDOM OF GOD, p. 1428).

(2) Only God will know when this task is accomplished according to His purpose. The believer's task is to faithfully and continually press on to "all nations" till the Lord returns to take His church to heaven (see 28:19–20, notes; John 14:3, note; 1 Thes. 4:13, note).

(3) Many interpreters believe "the end" refers to the time when "the dead in Christ shall rise" and the faithful of Christ's churches "shall be caught up together with them in the clouds to meet the Lord in the air" (1 Thes. 4:16–17; see article on THE RAPTURE, p. 1889). Christ gives more details about His unexpected appearance for the faithful church in vv. 37–44.

24:14 THEN SHALL THE END COME. Christ speaks to the disciples as though everything He predicts could be fulfilled within their generation. This, therefore, was the hope of the N.T. church. It must also be the hope of all who believe in Jesus Christ throughout the ages. We are to hope that the Lord will return and that the end of the age will occur in our generation (see 1 Cor. 15:51, note). We must live in a tension between the imminency of Christ's coming and the fact that Christ has commanded us to keep on spreading the gospel.

The great tribulation

24:15–28pp — Mark 13:14–23; Luke 21:20–26

15 [p]When ye therefore shall see the abomination of desolation, spoken of by [q]Daniel the prophet, stand in the holy place, ([r]whoso readeth, let him understand:)

16 Then let them which be in Judaea flee into the mountains:

17 Let him which is on the housetop not come down to take any thing out of his house:

18 Neither let him which is in the field return back to take his clothes.

19 And [s]woe unto them that are with child, and to them that give suck in those days!

20 But pray ye that your flight be not in the winter, neither on the sabbath day:

21 For [t]then shall be great tribulation, such as was not since the beginning of the world to this time, no, nor ever shall be.

22 And except those days should be shortened, there should no flesh be saved: [u]but for the elect's sake those days shall be shortened.

23 [v]Then if any man shall say unto you, Lo, here *is* Christ, or there; believe *it* not.

24 For [w]there shall arise false Christs, and false prophets, and shall show great signs and wonders; insomuch that, [x]if *it were* possible, they shall deceive the very elect.

25 Behold, I have told you before.

24:15 [p]Mark 13:14 Luke 21:20 [q]Dan. 9:27 & 12:11 [r]Dan. 9:23
24:19 [s]Luke 23:29
24:21 [t]Dan. 9:26 Joel 2:2
24:22 [u]Is. 65:8,9 Zech. 14:2
24:23 [v]Mark 13:21 Luke 17:23 & 21:8
24:24 [w]Deut. 13:1 2 Thes. 2:9 Rev. 13:13 [x]John 6:37 & 10:28,29 Rom. 8:28 2 Tim. 2:19
24:27 [y]Luke 17:24
24:28 [z]Job 39:30 Luke 17:37
24:29 [a]Dan. 7:11 [b]Ezek. 32:7 Joel 2:10 Amos 8:9 Mark 13:24 Acts 2:20
24:30 [c]Dan. 7:13 [d]Zech. 12:12 [e]Mark 13:26 Rev. 1:7
24:31 [f]1 Cor. 15:52 1 Thes. 4:16
24:32 [g]Luke 21:29

26 Wherefore if they shall say unto you, Behold, he is in the desert; go not forth: behold, *he is* in the secret chambers; believe *it* not.

27 [y]For as the lightning cometh out of the east, and shineth even unto the west; so shall also the coming of the Son of man be.

28 [z]For wheresoever the carcase is, there will the eagles be gathered together.

Christ's coming after the tribulation

24:29–35pp — Mark 13:24–31; Luke 21:27–33

29 ¶ [a]Immediately after the tribulation of those days [b]shall the sun be darkened, and the moon shall not give her light, and the stars shall fall from heaven, and the powers of the heavens shall be shaken:

30 [c]And then shall appear the sign of the Son of man in heaven: [d]and then shall all the tribes of the earth mourn, [e]and they shall see the Son of man coming in the clouds of heaven with power and great glory.

31 [f]And he shall send his angels [x]with a great sound of a trumpet, and they shall gather together his elect from the four winds, from one end of heaven to the other.

32 Now learn [g]a parable of the fig tree; When his branch is yet tender,

[x] Or, *with a trumpet, and a great voice*

24:15–28 THE GREAT TRIBULATION. This entire section deals with the great tribulation. For a study of this material, see article on THE GREAT TRIBULATION, p. 1456.

24:29 SHALL THE SUN BE DARKENED. Immediately after the tribulation, there will occur spectacular cosmic signs that will precede the appearing of Christ and give clear warning of His immediate return (v. 30). Christ's return to earth with power and great glory will not take by surprise any tribulation believer who heeds God's Word and observes the cosmic signs related to the sun, moon, stars, and the shaking of the powers of the heavens (cf. see Is. 13:6–13, note).

24:30 SON OF MAN COMING. This verse portrays Christ's appearing in the sky after the tribulation and the cosmic signs. He will come to judge the wicked (Rev. 19:11—20:3), to deliver His faithful people, and to establish righteousness on earth (Rev. 20:4). All Christians, both the living and the dead who had been taken from the earth at the rapture (see John 14:3, note; see article on THE RAPTURE, p. 1889), will return with Christ at His coming with power and great glory (see Rev. 19:14, note). The "sign" is probably Christ Himself coming on the clouds of glory, surrounded by brilliant light.

24:31 GATHER . . . HIS ELECT. When Jesus Christ returns to earth after the tribulation, the following events will take place. (1) God's judgment falls on the wicked (v. 30; Rev. 19:11–21), the antichrist (Rev. 19:20), and Satan (Rev. 20:1–3). (2) The judgment and the separation of people on earth alive at His coming occur (see 13:41, note; 25:32, note). (3) The saints of all ages are gathered together, including the saints already in heaven (cf. Mark 13:27; see John 14:3, note; Rev. 19:14, note; 20:4,6) and those alive on earth at Christ's advent (see 13:40). (4) The thousand-year reign of Christ on earth begins (see Rev. 20:4, notes).

24:32 THE FIG TREE. The putting forth of the leaves of the fig tree (cf. Luke 21:29–31) refers to events occurring during the tribulation (vv. 15–29). Some interpret "the fig tree" to represent the restoration of Israel as a political state (cf. Hos. 9:10; Luke 13:6–9).

and putteth forth leaves, ye know that
summer *is* nigh:
33 So likewise ye, when ye shall see
all these things, know [h]that [y]it is
near, *even* at the doors.
34 Verily I say unto you, [i]This
generation shall not pass, till all these
things be fulfilled.
35 [j]Heaven and earth shall pass
away, but my words shall not pass
away.

The unexpected coming of Christ

24:37–44pp — Mark 13:32–37; Luke 17:26–27

36 ¶ [k]But of that day and hour
knoweth no *man,* no, not the angels of
heaven, [l]but my Father only.
37 But as the days of Noe *were,* so
shall also the coming of the Son of
man be.
38 [m]For as in the days that were
before the flood they were eating and
drinking, marrying and giving in mar-
riage, until the day that Noe entered
into the ark,
39 And knew not until the flood
came, and took them all away; so shall
also the coming of the Son of man be.
40 [n]Then shall two be in the field;
the one shall be taken, and the other
left.
41 Two *women shall be* grinding at
the mill; the one shall be taken, and the
other left.
42 ¶ [o]Watch therefore: for ye know

24:33 [h]Jas. 5:9
24:34 [i]ch. 16:28 Mark 13:30 Luke 21:32
24:35 [j]Ps. 102:26 Is. 51:6 Jer. 31:35 Mark 13:31 Luke 21:33
24:36 [k]Mark 13:32 Acts 1:7 1 Thes. 5:2 2 Pet. 3:10 [l]Zech. 14:7
24:38 [m]Gen. 6:3-5 Luke 17:26 1 Pet. 3:20
24:40 [n]Luke 17:34
24:42 [o]ch. 25:13 Luke 21:36

[y]Or, *he*

24:33 ALL THESE THINGS. This refers to all the signs that will occur during the great tribulation (vv. 15–29), the pivotal sign being the "abomination of desolation" (v. 15; see article on THE GREAT TRIBULATION, p. 1456). As the prophetic events unfold, the tribulation faithful who search the Scriptures will "see all these things" and know that the Lord's return "is near, *even* at the doors."

24:34 THIS GENERATION. "This generation" may refer to the generation that begins to see the intensification of the general signs of the age (vv. 4–14) which consummate with the signs of the tribulation (see v. 5, note); or it may refer to the Jewish people as a race.

24:36 MY FATHER ONLY. This verse speaks of only the Father knowing the time of Christ's return. We must understand this as referring to the time when Christ was on earth. Certainly now Jesus, who has returned to His former glory (John 17:5), has future knowledge of His return. Tribulation saints can also know the time of His final return by observing the signs of the tribulation which Christ described (see article on THE GREAT TRIBULATION, p. 1456).

24:37 THE COMING OF THE SON OF MAN. Jesus' statements concerning "the coming of the Son of man" have a double reference: to the first stage of His return at an unknown and unexpected time (i.e., the rapture of the church saints; see v. 42, notes; John 14:3, note; Rev. 3:10, note; see article on THE RAPTURE, p. 1889), and to the second stage of His coming after the tribulation, when He will destroy the wicked and gather all the righteous into His kingdom (Rev. 19:11—20:4). We encounter this double reference when Christ describes three different categories of people in His illustration of "the days of Noe" (vv. 37–44). These three categories and their relation to Christ's coming are as follows:

(1) The tribulation unbelievers, represented by the flood victims of Noah's day. They do not know the time of Christ's return, are unprepared, and are thus destroyed at the end time (vv. 38–39,43; cf. Luke 17:26–28). This is the second stage of His return, the one occurring after the tribulation.

(2) The tribulation believers, represented by Noah. Because of the signs of the end time, tribulation saints know almost the precise time of the Lord's return and are prepared and saved. Christ returns for them at the expected time (v. 27; cf. Gen. 7:4; see article on THE GREAT TRIBULATION, p. 1456). This too refers to the second stage of Christ's return.

(3) Present-day believers or church saints living before the tribulation, represented by Jesus' disciples. They will not know the time of Christ's return to take them to heaven (vv. 42,44; see John 14:3, note; cf. 1 Thes. 4:14). There will be no definite signs preceding the Lord's return for them, for Christ states that it will occur unexpectedly (vv. 42,44). Notice that Jesus likens the disciples (i.e., church saints) not to Noah (i.e., tribulation believers) but to the flood victims (compare they "knew not," v. 39 with "ye know not," v. 42). That is, the church saints will be like the flood victims in one sense: they will not know the time of Christ's return for them and will be surprised when He comes, just as the flood victims did not know the time of the flood and were surprised when it came. Hence, church saints must be ready at any time (v. 44).

24:40 ONE ... TAKEN ... THE OTHER LEFT. Christ's statement that "one shall be taken, and the other left" comes before His exhortation to church saints (vv. 42–44). Therefore, these words likely refer to church saints who are taken out from among the wicked when Christ calls the faithful to Himself at the rapture (see John 14:3, note; see article on THE RAPTURE, p. 1889). He emphasizes the surprise element for the church believers (see v. 37, note).

24:42 WATCH THEREFORE. "Watch" (G *grēgoreō*) is a present imperative, indicating a c stant vigil at the present time. The reason for vigil today instead of only in the future is present-day believers do not know when the will come for them (see John 14:3, note).

THE GREAT TRIBULATION

Mat. 24:21 "For then shall be great tribulation, such as was not since the beginning of the world to this time, no, nor ever shall be."

Beginning with Mat. 24:15, Jesus speaks about special signs that will occur during the great tribulation, signs to indicate that the end of the age is very near (Mat. 24:15–28). These signs will lead up to and signal the return of Christ to earth after the tribulation (24:29–31; cf. Rev. 19:11 – 20:4).

The major sign is "the abomination of desolation" (Mat. 24:15), a specific observable event which tells the faithful living during the tribulation that Christ's coming to earth at the end of the age will occur very shortly. This visible sign-event refers primarily to the future desecration of the Jewish temple in Jerusalem by the antichrist (see Dan. 9:27, note; see article on THE AGE OF THE ANTICHRIST, p. 1896). The antichrist or man of sin will set up an image of himself in the temple of God, declaring himself to be God (2 Thes. 2:3–4; Rev. 13:14–15). The following are important facts concerning this pivotal event.

(1) The "abomination of desolation" will mark the beginning of the final stage of the tribulation, which culminates in the return of Christ to earth and His judgment upon the ungodly at Armageddon (Mat. 24:21,29–30; see Dan. 9:27; Rev. 19:11–21).

(2) By noting the time of this event ("when ye therefore shall see," Mat. 24:15), tribulation saints can know with a high degree of certainty when the tribulation will end and Christ will come to reign on earth (see Mat. 24:33, note). The time span between this event and the end is given four times in Scripture as three and one half years or 1260 days (see Dan. 9:25–27, note; Rev. 11:1–2; 12:6; 13:5–7).

(3) Because of the strong expectancy on the part of the tribulation saints for Christ's coming (Mat. 24:33), the faithful must be aware that any report that Christ has returned is false (24:23–27). The "coming of the Son of man" after the tribulation will be observable and known to all who are in the world (24:27–30).

Another sign to occur during the great tribulation, and even before, will be false prophets who, as ministers of Satan, will do "great signs and wonders" (Mat. 24:24). (1) Jesus admonishes all believers to be especially alert for these professed Christian prophets, teachers, and preachers who are false, yet perform miracles, healings, signs, and wonders, and who appear to have great success in their ministries. At the same time, they will distort and reject the truth found in God's Word (see Mat. 7:22, note; Gal. 1:9, note; see article on THE AGE OF THE ANTICHRIST, p. 1896).

(2) Elsewhere Scripture admonishes believers to continually test the spirit energizing all teachers, leaders, and preachers (see 1 John 4:1, note). God allows deception accompanied with miracles in order to test believers as to their love for Him and their loyalty to the truth of Holy Scripture (see Deut. 13:3). This will not be easy, for Jesus states in Mat. 24:24 that during the last days religious deceit will be so widespread that it will be difficult even for "the very elect" (i.e., committed Christians) to discern truth from error (see 1 Tim. 4:16, note; Jas. 1:21, note; see article on ELECTION AND PREDESTINATION, p. 1846).

(3) Those among God's people who do not love the truth will be deceived. They will be given no further opportunity to believe the truth of the gospel after the coming of the antichrist (see 2 Thes. 2:11, note).

Finally, the "great tribulation" will be a specific period of terrible suffering and tribulation for all the people in the world. Observe:

(1) It will be worldwide (see Rev. 3:10, note). (2) It will be the worst time of affliction and distress ever to occur in the history of humanity (Dan. 12:1; Mat. 24:21). (3) It will be a terrible time of suffering for the Jews (Jer. 30:5–7). (4) The period will be dominated by the "man of sin" (1 Thes. 2:3; i.e., antichrist; cf. Dan. 9:27; Rev. 13:12; see article on THE AGE OF THE ANTICHRIST, p. 1896). (5) The faithful of Christ's churches are promised deliverance and "escape" from the tribulation time (see Luke 21:36, note; 1 Thes. 5:8–10; Rev. 3:10, note). (6) During this time, among both Jews and Gentiles will be those who believe in Jesus Christ and are saved (Deut. 4:30–31; Hos. 5:15; Rev. 7:9–17; 14:6–7). (7) It will be a time of great suffering and dreadful persecution for all who remain faithful to God (Rev. 12:17; 13:15). (8) It will be a time of God's wrath and judgment upon the ungodly (1 Thes. 5:1–11; Rev. 6:16–17). (9) The statement of Jesus that those days will be shortened (Mat. 24:22) must not be understood to imply that there will be any reduction of the predicted three and a half years or 1260 days. Rather, it seems to refer to the fact that the period is so awful that if it were not confined to a limited period of time, the whole human race would be destroyed. (10) The great tribulation will end with the coming of Jesus Christ in glory with His bride (Rev. 19:7–8,14) to bring deliverance to the remaining faithful, and judgment and destruction to the wicked (Mat. 24:29–31; Luke 19:11–27; Rev. 19:11–21). (11) We must not confuse this coming at the end of the great tribulation with Jesus' reference to his unexpected descent from heaven in Mat. 24:42,44 (see notes on those verses, which demonstrate that Jesus' coming there refers to the rapture of believers, occurring at a time earlier than that of His final return at the end of the tribulation). (12) The major passage in Scripture describing the whole seven-year tribulation is in the book of Revelation, chs. 6–18.

not what hour your Lord doth come.
43 [p]But know this, that if the good-
man of the house had known in what
watch the thief would come, he would
have watched, and would not have suf-
fered his house to be broken up.
44 [q]Therefore be ye also ready: for
in such an hour as ye think not the Son
of man cometh.

The wise and faithful servant

24:45–51pp — Luke 12:42–46

45 [r]Who then is a faithful and wise
servant, whom his lord hath made rul-
er over his household, to give them
meat in due season?
46 [s]Blessed *is* that servant, whom
his lord when he cometh shall find so
doing.
47 Verily I say unto you, That [t]he
shall make him ruler over all his
goods.
48 But and if that evil servant shall
say in his heart, My lord delayeth his
coming;
49 And shall begin to smite *his* fel-
lowservants, and to eat and drink with
the drunken;
50 The lord of that servant shall
come in a day when he looketh not for
him, and in an hour that he is not
aware of,
51 And shall [z]cut him asunder,
and appoint *him* his portion with the
hypocrites: [u]there shall be weeping
and gnashing of teeth.

Ma 25: 46

24:43 [p]Luke 12:39 1 Thes. 5:2 Rev. 3:3
24:44 [q]1 Thes. 5:6
24:45 [r]Luke 12:42 Acts 20:28
24:46 [s]Rev. 16:15
24:47 [t]ch. 25:21,23 Luke 22:29
24:51 [u]ch. 8:12 & 25:30

[z] Or, *cut him off*

will be no warning signs, and they may never assume that He cannot come today. In other words, they must be committed to the historical possibility of Christ returning at any time (see v. 44, note; cf. Mark 13:33–37). His return for the church is possible any day, impossible no day.

24:42 YE KNOW NOT WHAT HOUR. Christ's warning in this verse that His disciples must always be ready for His coming must be understood as referring to His return from heaven to take church saints out of the world, i.e., the rapture (see John 14:3, note; see article on THE RAPTURE, p. 1889). (1) Jesus explicitly states that His coming for the saints living before the tribulation will be at an unexpected time and without warning. He declares that they not only "know not" the time, but that He will return at a time when they "think not the Son of Man cometh" (v. 44). This clearly points to an element of surprise, amazement, and unexpectedness for the faithful at this particular return of Christ's. This is sometimes referred to as the first stage of Christ's second coming.

(2) With regard to Christ's coming with power and glory to judge the world after the tribulation (v. 30; Rev. 19:11–21), His coming will be expected, anticipated, and foreseen (see v. 33, note; Luke 21:28; see article on THE GREAT TRIBULATION, p. 1456). The events and signs during the tribulation will create an attitude of certainty and expectancy for tribulation saints, and not the attitude of surprise that the present-day church saints will have at the time of the rapture (see v. 44, note; John 14:3, note). Christ's coming after the tribulation is sometimes regarded as the second stage of Christ's second coming.

24:43 THE THIEF. Christ's coming at an unknown time is to be as unexpected as that of a thief who breaks into a house. Thus the devoted disciple must be ready at any time for the appearance of the Lord (v. 44).

24:44 AN HOUR AS YE THINK NOT. Once again Christ refers to His return for the faithful of His churches at an unexpected and unknown time. (1) This warning is not for tribulation saints (see article on THE GREAT TRIBULATION, p. 1456). The only way to harmonize Christ's teaching about His unexpected coming (vv. 42,44) with His statement concerning His expected coming (v. 33), is to assume two phases to His second coming. The first stage involves Christ's return to catch up believers from earth at an unexpected time (see John 14:3, note; 1 Thes. 4:17; Rev. 3:10, note; see article on THE RAPTURE, p. 1889), and the second stage is His coming at the end of the age, at an expected time (i.e., after the tribulation and cosmic signs, vv. 29–30) to destroy the wicked and begin His reign on earth (see v. 42, notes; Rev. 19:11–21; 20:4).

(2) This second coming of Christ as one event consisting of two phases parallels Christ's coming predicted in the O.T.; that is, the O.T. speaks of one coming of the Messiah, but in its fulfillment this divides into two phases: His coming to die for sin and His coming to reign (see Is. 9:2–7; 40:3–5; compare Is. 61:1–3 with Luke 4:18–19; see Is. 9:7, note).

(3) Christ's urgent warning to be always spiritually ready for His unexpected coming (i.e., the rapture) applies to all generations of Christians before the tribulation (vv. 15–29). It is a motive for perseverance in the faith.

24:48 MY LORD DELAYETH. Concerning those within the church who are unfaithful to the Lord, Christ's unexpected return cannot possibly be a motive for present vigilance, if they believe it is impossible for Christ to come now. (1) Any professed believer living in sin who believes that Christ will delay His coming for a few years can be compared to the unjust steward. He will feel no impending threat that the return of the Lord will overtake him (see v. 44, note; Luke 12:45–46, notes). (2) It is significant that Jesus associates unfaithfulness and hypocrisy with the belief and desire that Christ will delay His return.

Parable of the ten virgins

25 THEN SHALL the kingdom of heaven be likened unto ten virgins, which took their lamps, and went forth to meet [v]the bridegroom.

2 [w]And five of them were wise, and five *were* foolish.

3 They that *were* foolish took their lamps, and took no oil with them:

4 But the wise took oil in their vessels with their lamps.

5 While the bridegroom tarried, [x]they all slumbered and slept.

6 And at midnight [y]there was a cry made, Behold, the bridegroom cometh; go ye out to meet him.

7 Then all those virgins arose, and [z]trimmed their lamps.

8 And the foolish said unto the wise, Give us of your oil; for our lamps are [a]gone out.

9 But the wise answered, saying, *Not so;* lest there be not enough for us and you: but go ye rather to them that sell, and buy for yourselves.

10 And while they went to buy, the bridegroom came; and they that were ready went in with him to the marriage: and [a]the door was shut.

11 Afterward came also the other virgins, saying, [b]Lord, Lord, open to us.

12 But he answered and said, Verily I say unto you, [c]I know you not.

13 [d]Watch therefore, for ye know neither the day nor the hour wherein the Son of man cometh.

Parable of the talents

25:14–30Ref — Luke 19:12–27

14 ¶ [e]For *the kingdom of heaven is* [f]as a man travelling into a far country, *who* called his own servants, and delivered unto them his goods.

15 And unto one he gave five [b]talents, to another two, and to another one; [g]to every man according to his several ability; and straightway took his journey.

16 Then he that had received the five talents went and traded with the same, and made *them* other five talents.

17 And likewise he that *had received* two, he also gained other two.

18 But he that had received one went and digged in the earth, and hid his lord's money.

19 After a long time the lord of those servants cometh, and reckoneth with them.

20 And so he that had received five talents came and brought other five talents, saying, Lord, thou deliveredst unto me five talents: behold, I have gained beside them five talents more.

21 His lord said unto him, Well done, *thou* good and faithful servant:

25:1 [v]Eph. 5:29,30 Rev. 19:7 & 21:2,9
25:2 [w]ch. 13:47 & 22:10
25:5 [x]1 Thes. 5:6
25:6 [y]ch. 24:31 1 Thes. 4:16
25:7 [z]Luke 12:35
25:10 [a]Luke 13:25
25:11 [b]ch. 7:21-23
25:12 [c]Ps. 5:5 Hab. 1:13 John 9:31
25:13 [d]ch. 24:42,44 Mark 13:33,35 Luke 21:36
25:14 [e]Luke 19:12 [f]ch. 21:33
25:15 [g]Rom. 12:6 1 Cor. 12:7,11,29 Eph. 4:11

[a] Or, *going out* [b] The talent was worth more than a thousand dollars

25:1 PARABLE OF THE TEN VIRGINS. The parable of the ten virgins emphasizes that all believers must constantly look to their own spiritual condition in light of Christ's coming at an unknown and unexpected time. They must persevere in faith so that when the day and hour arrive they will be received by the returning Lord (v. 10). Failure to be in a personal relationship with the Lord at His return means being excluded from His presence and kingdom.

(1) What differentiates the foolish from the wise is the failure of the foolish to recognize that the returning Lord (see John 14:3, note) will come at an unexpected time, a time not preceded with unmistakable and specific observable signs (v. 13; see 24:36,44, notes).

(2) Christ indicates here and elsewhere (Luke 18:8) that a large portion of the church will be unprepared at the time of His return (vv. 8–13). Thus Christ makes it clear He will not wait until all churches are prepared for His coming.

(3) It should be noticed that all the virgins (both faithful and unfaithful) were taken by surprise at the bridegroom's coming (vv. 5–7). This suggests that the parable of the ten virgins applies to believers living before the tribulation and not to those living during the tribulation, who will have adequate signs preceding Christ's return at the end of the tribulation (see article on THE GREAT TRIBULATION, p. 1456).

25:4 OIL. Jesus, in a series of illustrations (ch. 25), stresses the requirement of faithfulness and watchfulness until He returns. The parable of the ten virgins stresses the urgent necessity of perseverance in the faith because of the danger of Christ's coming at an unforeseeable date (see Luke 21:19, note). The oil in the parable represents true faith, righteousness, and the abiding presence of the Holy Spirit. Five other parables which teach the lesson of perseverance are the sower (Luke 8:4–15), the goodman (Luke 12:35–40), the steward (Luke 12:42–48), the tower builder (Luke 14:28–30), and the savorless salt (Luke 14:34–35).

25:15 TALENTS. The parable of the talents warns us that our place and service in heaven will depend on the faithfulness of our lives and service here (cf. v. 29). A talent represents our abilities, time, resources, and opportunities to serve God while on earth. These things are considered by God as a trust that we are responsible to administer in the wisest possible way.

thou hast been faithful over a few things, [h]I will make thee ruler over many things: enter thou into [i]the joy of thy lord.

22 He also that had received two talents came and said, Lord, thou deliveredst unto me two talents: behold, I have gained two other talents beside them.

23 His lord said unto him, [j]Well done, good and faithful servant; thou hast been faithful over a few things, I will make thee ruler over many things: enter thou into the joy of thy lord.

24 Then he which had received the one talent came and said, Lord, I knew thee that thou art an hard man, reaping where thou hast not sown, and gathering where thou hast not strawed:

25 And I was afraid, and went and hid thy talent in the earth: lo, *there* thou hast *that is* thine.

26 His lord answered and said unto him, *Thou* wicked and slothful servant, thou knewest that I reap where I sowed not, and gather where I have not strawed:

27 Thou oughtest therefore to have put my money to the exchangers, and *then* at my coming I should have received mine own with usury.

28 Take therefore the talent from him, and give *it* unto him which hath ten talents.

29 [k]For unto every one that hath shall be given, and he shall have abundance: but from him that hath not shall be taken away even that which he hath.

30 And cast ye the unprofitable servant [l]into outer darkness: there shall be weeping and gnashing of teeth.

25:21 [h]ver. 34,46 ch. 24:47 Luke 12:44 & 22:29,30 [i]2 Tim. 2:12 Heb. 12:2 1 Pet. 1:8
25:23 [j]ver. 21
25:29 [k]ch. 13:12 Mark 4:25 Luke 8:18 & 19:26 John 15:2
25:30 [l]ch. 8:12 & 24:51
25:31 [m]Zech. 14:5 ch. 16:27 & 19:28 Mark 8:38 Acts 1:11 1 Thes. 4:16 2 Thes. 1:7 Jude 14 Rev. 1:7
25:32 [n]Rom. 14:10 2 Cor. 5:10 Rev. 20:12 [o]Ezek. 20:38
25:34 [p]Rom. 8:17 1 Pet. 1:4,9 & 3:9 Rev. 21:7 [q]ch. 20:23 Mark 10:40 1 Cor. 2:9 Heb. 11:16
25:35 [r]Is. 58:7 Ezek. 18:7 Jas. 1:27 [s]Heb. 13:2 3 John 5
25:36 [t]Jas. 2:15,16 [u]2 Tim. 1:16
25:40 [v]Prov. 14:31 & 19:17 ch. 10:42 Mark 9:41 Heb. 6:10
25:41 [w]Ps. 6:8 ch. 7:23 Luke 13:27 [x]ch. 13:40,42

The judgment of the nations

31 ¶ [m]When the Son of man shall come in his glory, and all the holy angels with him, then shall he sit upon the throne of his glory:

32 And [n]before him shall be gathered all nations: and [o]he shall separate them one from another, as a shepherd divideth *his* sheep from the goats:

33 And he shall set the sheep on his right hand, but the goats on the left.

34 Then shall the King say unto them on his right hand, Come, ye blessed of my Father, [p]inherit the kingdom [q]prepared for you from the foundation of the world:

35 [r]For I was an hungered, and ye gave me meat: I was thirsty, and ye gave me drink: [s]I was a stranger, and ye took me in:

36 [t]Naked, and ye clothed me: I was sick, and ye visited me: [u]I was in prison, and ye came unto me.

37 Then shall the righteous answer him, saying, Lord, when saw we thee an hungered, and fed *thee?* or thirsty, and gave *thee* drink?

38 When saw we thee a stranger, and took *thee* in? or naked, and clothed *thee?*

39 Or when saw we thee sick, or in prison, and came unto thee?

40 And the King shall answer and say unto them, Verily I say unto you, [v]Inasmuch as ye have done *it* unto one of the least of these my brethren, ye have done *it* unto me.

41 Then shall he say also unto them on the left hand, [w]Depart from me, ye cursed, [x]into everlasting fire, pre-

---

25:29 EVERY ONE THAT HATH. Jesus gives an important principle with regard to the believer's reward and state in heaven. What each believer receives in the future kingdom of God will depend on what he possesses of it now. His position and inheritance in heaven will be in proportion to his present dedication and commitment to God's ways and kingdom (see Luke 22:24–30, note).

25:32 SHEEP FROM THE GOATS. The sheep and goat judgment occurs after the tribulation and Christ's return to earth but before the beginning of His earthly reign (cf. Rev. 5:10; 19:11—20:4; cf. Dan. 7:9–14). (1) At the time of Christ's coming the saved and the lost who are living on earth and who survived the tribulation are still mingled together. (2) The judgment involves the separation of the wicked from the righteous (vv. 32–33; see 13:41, note). (3) It will be based on outward works of love and kindness to those belonging to Christ and who are suffering. The presence of love and compassion is taken as an inherent part of true faith and salvation (vv. 35–46). (4) The wicked will not be allowed to enter Christ's kingdom, but will go into eternal punishment (vv. 41,46; Rev. 14:11). (5) The righteous will inherit eternal life (v. 46) and the kingdom of God (v. 34; see Rev. 20:4, notes).

25:41 DEVIL AND HIS ANGELS. Satan's initial rebellion against God (see 4:10, note) drew with him a third of the heavenly angels (Rev. 12:4). A part of these are bound in hell (2 Pet. 2:4; Jude 6), while the rest are free and exist under Satan's dominion and control (12:24; 25:41; Eph. 2:2; Rev. 12:7). These free angels are his highly organized emissaries (Eph. 6:11–12) and are probably identical with the demons referred to in the Bible (see article on POWER OVER SATAN AND DEMONS, p. 1486).

pared for [y]the devil and his angels:
42 For I was an hungered, and ye
gave me no meat; I was thirsty, and ye
gave me no drink:
43 I was a stranger, and ye took me
not in: naked, and ye clothed me not:
sick, and in prison, and ye visited me
not.
44 Then shall they also answer him,
saying, Lord, when saw we thee an
hungered, or athirst, or a stranger, or
naked, or sick, or in prison, and did not
minister unto thee?
45 Then shall he answer them, say-
ing, Verily I say unto you, [z]Inasmuch
as ye did *it* not to one of the least of
these, ye did *it* not to me.
46 And [a]these shall go away into
everlasting punishment: but the righ-
teous into life eternal.

The plot to kill Jesus

26:2–5pp — Mark 14:1–2; Luke 22:1–2

26 AND IT came to pass, when
Jesus had finished all these
sayings, he said unto his disciples,
2 [b]Ye know that after two days is
the feast of the passover, and the Son of
man is betrayed to be crucified.
3 [c]Then assembled together the
chief priests, and the scribes, and the
elders of the people, unto the palace of
the high priest, who was called Caia-
phas,
4 And consulted that they might
take Jesus by subtlety, and kill *him*.
5 But they said, Not on the feast
day, lest there be an uproar among the
people.

Anointing of Jesus at Bethany

26:6–13pp — Mark 14:3–9
26:6–13Ref — Luke 7:37–38; John 12:1–8

6 ¶ [d]Now when Jesus was in
[e]Bethany, in the house of Simon the
leper,
7 There came unto him a woman
having an alabaster box of very pre-
cious ointment, and poured it on his
head, as he sat *at meat*.
8 [f]But when his disciples saw *it*,
they had indignation, saying, To what
purpose *is* this waste?
9 For this ointment might have been
sold for much, and given to the poor.
10 When Jesus understood *it*, he
said unto them, Why trouble ye the
woman? for she hath wrought a good
work upon me.
11 [g]For ye have the poor always
with you; but [h]me ye have not always.
12 For in that she hath poured this
ointment on my body, she did *it* for my
burial.
13 Verily I say unto you, Whereso-
ever this gospel shall be preached in
the whole world, *there* shall also this,
that this woman hath done, be told for
a memorial of her.

Judas agrees to betray Jesus

26:14–16pp — Mark 14:10–11; Luke 22:3–6

14 ¶ [i]Then one of the twelve,
called [j]Judas Iscariot, went unto the
chief priests,
15 And said *unto them*, [k]What will
ye give me, and I will deliver him unto
you? And they covenanted with him for
thirty pieces of silver.
16 And from that time he sought op-
portunity to betray him.

The last supper

26:17–19pp — Mark 14:12–16; Luke 22:7–13
26:20–24pp — Mark 14:17–21

17 ¶ [l]Now the first *day* of the *feast*
of unleavened bread the disciples came
to Jesus, saying unto him, Where wilt
thou that we prepare for thee to eat the
passover?
18 And he said, Go into the city to
such a man, and say unto him, The
Master saith, My time is at hand; I will
keep the passover at thy house with
my disciples.
19 And the disciples did as Jesus

25:41 [y]2 Pet. 2:4 Jude 6
25:45 [z]Prov. 14:31 & 17:5 Zech. 2:8 Acts 9:5
25:46 [a]Dan 12:2 John 5:29 Rom. 2:7
26:2 [b]Mark 14:1 Luke 22:1 John 13:1
26:3 [c]Ps. 2:2 John 11:47 Acts 4:25
26:6 [d]Mark 14:3 John 11:1,2 & 12:3 [e]ch. 21:17
26:8 [f]John 12:4
26:11 [g]Deut. 15:11 John 12:8 [h]See ch. 18:20 & 28:20 John 13:33 & 14:19 & 16:5,28 & 17:11
26:14 [i]Mark 14:10 Luke 22:3 John 13:2,30 [j]ch. 10:4
26:15 [k]Zech. 11:12 ch. 27:3
26:17 [l]Ex. 12:6,18 Mark 14:12 Luke 22:7

26:2 PASSOVER. The Passover (Gk. *pascha*) was a spring festival associated with the historical episode of Israel's departure from Egypt. It celebrated the "passing over" of the Hebrews' houses by the death angel because of the blood of the lamb which had been put upon the doorposts and frames of the houses (see Ex. 12:7; see article on THE PASSOVER, p. 110). Christ's crucifixion occurred on the day of "the preparation of the passover" (John 19:14). He is "our passover . . . sacrificed for us" (1 Cor. 5:7).

26:13 FOR A MEMORIAL OF HER. The Lord has ordained that this story of Mary anointing Him (vv. 6–13) should always accompany the preaching of the gospel. This is because she exemplifies better than anyone else the dedication that all followers of Christ should have. Her act was the expression of her deep devotion and profound love for the Master. The Christian faith is more than working for Jesus. It is first of all a personal ministering unto Him. We learn here that our heartfelt attachment and love to Jesus is the most valuable aspect of our relationship to Him (see John 21:15, note).

had appointed them; and they made
ready the passover.
20 [m]Now when the even was come,
he sat down with the twelve.
21 And as they did eat, he said,
Verily I say unto you, that one of you
shall betray me.
22 And they were exceeding sor-
rowful, and began every one of them to
say unto him, Lord, is it I?
23 And he answered and said, [n]He
that dippeth *his* hand with me in the
dish, the same shall betray me.
24 The Son of man goeth [o]as it is
written of him: but [p]woe unto that
man by whom the Son of man is be-
trayed! it had been good for that man
if he had not been born.
25 Then Judas, which betrayed him,
answered and said, Master, is it I? He
said unto him, Thou hast said.

The institution of the Lord's Supper

26:26–29pp — Mark 14:22–25; Luke 22:17–20; 1 Cor. 11:23–25

26 ¶ [q]And as they were eating,
[r]Jesus took bread, and [c]blessed *it,*
and brake *it,* and gave *it* to the disci-
ples, and said, Take, eat; [s]this is my
body.
27 And he took the cup, and gave
thanks, and gave *it* to them, saying,
[t]Drink ye all of it;
28 For [u]this is my blood [v]of the
new testament, which is shed [w]for
many for the remission of sins.
29 But [x]I say unto you, I will not
drink henceforth of this fruit of the
vine, [y]until that day when I drink it

26:20 [m]Mark 14:17-21 Luke 22:14 John 13:21
26:23 [n]Ps. 41:9 Luke 22:21 John 13:18
26:24 [o]Ps. 22 Is. 53 Dan. 9:26 Mark 9:12 Luke 24:25,26,46 Acts 17:2,3 & 26:22,23 1 Cor. 15:3 [p]John 17:12
26:26 [q]Mark 14:22 Luke 22:19 [r]1 Cor. 11:23 [s]1 Cor. 10:16
26:27 [t]Mark 14:23
26:28 [u]See Ex. 24:8 Lev. 17:11 [v]Jer. 31:31 [w]ch. 20:28 Rom. 5:15 Heb. 9:22
26:29 [x]Mark 14:25 Luke 22:18 [y]Acts 10:41
26:30 [z]Mark 14:26
26:31 [a]Mark 14:27 John 16:32 [b]ch. 11:6 [c]Zech. 13:7
26:32 [d]ch. 28:7,10 Mark 14:28 & 16:7
26:34 [e]Mark 14:30 Luke 22:34 John 13:38
26:36 [f]Mark 14:32-35 Luke 22:39 John 18:1
26:37 [g]ch. 4:21
26:38 [h]John 12:27

new with you in my Father's kingdom.
30 [z]And when they had sung an
[d]hymn, they went out into the mount
of Olives.

Jesus predicts Peter's denial

26:31–35pp — Mark 14:27–31; Luke 22:31–34

31 Then saith Jesus unto them,
[a]All ye shall [b]be offended because of
me this night: for it is written, [c]I will
smite the shepherd, and the sheep of
the flock shall be scattered abroad.
32 But after I am risen again, [d]I
will go before you into Galilee.
33 Peter answered and said unto
him, Though all *men* shall be offended
because of thee, *yet* will I never be of-
fended.
34 Jesus said unto him, [e]Verily I
say unto thee, That this night, before
the cock crow, thou shalt deny me
thrice.
35 Peter said unto him, Though I
should die with thee, yet will I not deny
thee. Likewise also said all the disci-
ples.

Jesus' agony in Gethsemane

26:36–46pp — Mark 14:32–42; Luke 22:40–46

36 ¶ [f]Then cometh Jesus with
them unto a place called Gethsemane,
and saith unto the disciples, Sit ye
here, while I go and pray yonder.
37 And he took with him Peter and
[g]the two sons of Zebedee, and began
to be sorrowful and very heavy.
38 Then saith he unto them, [h]My

c Many Greek copies have, *gave thanks;* see Mark 6:41   d Or, *psalm*

26:26 TAKE, EAT; THIS IS MY BODY. See 1 Cor. 11:24–25, note on the Lord's Supper.

26:28 THE NEW TESTAMENT. See article on THE OLD COVENANT AND THE NEW COVENANT, p. 1954.

26:28 REMISSION OF SINS. Forgiveness is necessary because we have sinned, destroyed our relationship with God, and become subject to condemnation (Rom. 1:18–32). Forgiveness is the means by which this relationship is restored (Eph. 1:7; Col. 2:13).

(1) The Hebrew and Greek words for forgiveness denote the ideas of "to cover," "to pardon," "to cancel," "to send away." God's forgiveness involves making of no account the sin that has been committed (Mark 2:5; John 8:11), saving sinners from eternal punishment (Rom. 5:9; 1 Thes. 1:10), accepting them (Luke 15:20ff), delivering them from the dominion of sin and transferring them into Christ's kingdom (Col. 1:13), and renewing the whole person and promising eternal life (Luke 23:43; John 14:19b).

(2) In order for us to receive forgiveness, there must be repentance, faith, and confession of sin (Luke 17:3–4; Acts 2:38; 5:31; 20:21; 1 John 1:9). For God to be able to extend forgiveness, the shedding of blood was required (Heb. 9:22). Thus, forgiveness is based on Jesus' death on the cross (v. 28; John 1:29; 3:16; Rom. 8:32). Divine forgiveness is an ongoing need for believers, so that we might maintain our saving relationship with God (6:12,14–15; 1 John 1:9).

26:37 HE . . . BEGAN TO BE SORROWFUL. The sufferings of Christ, stage one. The physical and spiritual suffering of Christ begins in Gethsemane. "His sweat was as it were great drops of blood" (Luke 22:44). Under great stress, the small capillaries in the sweat glands can break and mix blood with sweat (see next note for further insights into this stage of Christ's suffering). (For the second stage of Christ's sufferings, see v. 67, note.)

soul is exceeding sorrowful, even unto
death: tarry ye here, and watch
with me.
39 And he went a little farther, and
fell on his face, and [i]prayed, saying,
[j]O my Father, if it be possible, [k]let
this cup pass from me: nevertheless
[l]not as I will, but as thou *wilt.*
40 And he cometh unto the disci-
ples, and findeth them asleep, and
saith unto Peter, What, could ye not
watch with me one hour?
41 [m]Watch and pray, that ye enter
not into temptation: the spirit indeed *is*
willing, but the flesh *is* weak.
42 He went away again the second
time, and prayed, saying, O my Father,
if this cup may not pass away from me,
except I drink it, thy will be done.
43 And he came and found them
asleep again: for their eyes were
heavy.
44 And he left them, and went away
again, and prayed the third time, say-
ing the same words.
45 Then cometh he to his disciples,
and saith unto them, Sleep on now, and
take *your* rest: behold, the hour is at
hand, and the Son of man is betrayed
into the hands of sinners.
46 Rise, let us be going: behold, he
is at hand that doth betray me.

Jesus' betrayal and arrest

26:47–56pp — Mark 14:43–50; Luke 22:47–53

47 ¶ And [n]while he yet spake, lo,
Judas, one of the twelve, came, and
with him a great multitude with swords
and staves, from the chief priests and
elders of the people.
48 Now he that betrayed him gave

26:39 [i]Mark 14:36 Luke 22:42 Heb. 5:7 [j]John 12:27 [k]ch. 20:22 [l]John 5:30 & 6:38 Phil. 2:8
26:41 [m]Mark 13:33 & 14:38 Luke 22:40,46 Eph. 6:18
26:47 [n]Mark 14:43 Luke 22:47 John 18:3 Acts 1:16
26:49 [o]2 Sam. 20:9
26:50 [p]Ps. 41:9 & 55:13
26:51 [q]John 18:10
26:52 [r]Gen. 9:6 Rev. 13:10
26:53 [s]2 Ki. 6:17 Dan. 7:10
26:54 [t]ver. 24 Is. 53:7 Luke 24:25,44,46
26:56 [u]Lam. 4:20 [v]See John 18:15
26:57 [w]Mark 14:53 Luke 22:54 John 18:12,13,24

them a sign, saying, Whomsoever I
shall kiss, that same is he: hold him
fast.
49 And forthwith he came to Jesus,
and said, Hail, master; [o]and kissed
him.
50 And Jesus said unto him,
[p]Friend, wherefore art thou come?
Then came they, and laid hands on
Jesus, and took him.
51 And, behold, [q]one of them
which were with Jesus stretched out
his hand, and drew his sword, and
struck a servant of the high priest's,
and smote off his ear.
52 Then said Jesus unto him, Put up
again thy sword into his place: [r]for all
they that take the sword shall perish
with the sword.
53 Thinkest thou that I cannot now
pray to my Father, and he shall pre-
sently give me [s]more than twelve le-
gions of angels?
54 But how then shall the scrip-
tures be fulfilled, [t]that thus it
must be?
55 In that same hour said Jesus to
the multitudes, Are ye come out as
against a thief with swords and staves
for to take me? I sat daily with you
teaching in the temple, and ye laid no
hold on me.
56 But all this was done, that the
[u]scriptures of the prophets might be
fulfilled. Then [v]all the disciples for-
sook him, and fled.

Jesus before Caiaphas

26:57–68pp — Mark 14:53–65; John 18:12–13,19–24

57 ¶ [w]And they that had laid hold

26:39 LET THIS CUP PASS. What Christ meant by "this cup" has been the subject of much discussion. (1) It is doubtful that Christ was praying to be saved from physical death, for He had resolutely set Himself to die for the sin of mankind (cf. Mark 10:33–34; Luke 9:51; John 12:24,27; Heb. 10:5–9).

(2) It is more probable that He was praying to be delivered from the punishment of separation from God, the ultimate penalty for sin. Christ prayed that His physical death might be accepted as full payment for the sin of sinners. However, He prayed, "nevertheless, not as I will, but as thou wilt." He then committed Himself to undergo both physical death and spiritual separation from His heavenly Father in order to achieve our salvation (cf. 27:46). His prayer was "heard," for He was strengthened by His Father to drink the appointed cup (see Heb. 5:7).

26:57 LAID HOLD ON JESUS. A study of the events from Christ's arrest to His crucifixion can be very rewarding. The order is as follows: (1) the arrest (26:47–56; Mark 14:43–52; Luke 22:47–53; John 18:2–12); (2) the religious trial before Annas (John 18:12–14,19–24) and before Caiaphas (26:57,59–68; Mark 14:53,55–65; Luke 22:54,63–65; John 18:24); (3) the denial by Peter (26:58,69–75; Mark 14:54,66–72; Luke 22:54–62; John 18:15–18,25–27); (4) the condemnation by the Sanhedrin (27:1; Mark 15:1; Luke 22:66–71); (5) the death of Judas (27:3–10); (6) the civil trial before Pilate (27:2,11–14; Mark 15:2–5; Luke 23:1–5; John 18:28–38); (7) the trial before Herod (Luke 23:6–12), who sent Him back to Pilate (27:11–26; Mark 15:6–15; Luke 23:11–25; John 18:28—19:1,4–16); (8) the mockery (27:27–30; Mark 15:16–19; John 19:2–3), after which He was beaten and then led away to be crucified (27:31); (9) the procession to Calvary (27:31–34; Mark 15:20–23; Luke 23:26–33);

on Jesus led *him* away to Caiaphas the
high priest, where the scribes and the
elders were assembled.
58 But Peter followed him afar off
unto the high priest's palace, and went
in, and sat with the servants, to see the
end.
59 Now the chief priests, and el-
ders, and all the council, sought false
witness against Jesus, to put him to
death;
60 But found none: yea, though
[x]many false witnesses came, *yet*
found they none. At the last came
[y]two false witnesses,
61 And said, This *fellow* said, [z]I am
able to destroy the temple of God, and
to build it in three days.
62 [a]And the high priest arose, and
said unto him, Answerest thou noth-
ing? what *is it which* these witness
against thee?
63 But [b]Jesus held his peace. And
the high priest answered and said unto
him, [c]I adjure thee by the living God,
that thou tell us whether thou be the
Christ, the Son of God.
64 Jesus saith unto him, Thou hast
said: nevertheless I say unto you,
[d]Hereafter shall ye see the Son
Mark 13:1-37 of man [e]sitting on the right hand of
power, and coming in the clouds
of heaven.
65 [f]Then the high priest rent his
clothes, saying, He hath spoken blas-
phemy; what further need have we of
witnesses? behold, now ye have heard
his blasphemy.
66 What think ye? They answered
and said, [g]He is guilty of death.
67 [h]Then did they spit in his
face, and buffeted him; and [i]others
smote *him* with [e]the palms of their
hands,
68 Saying, [j]Prophesy unto us,
thou Christ, Who is he that smote
thee?

26:60 [x]Ps. 27:12 & 35:11 Mark 14:55 Acts 6:13 [y]Deut. 19:15
26:61 [z]ch. 27:40 John 2:19
26:62 [a]Mark 14:60
26:63 [b]Is. 53:7 ch. 27:12 [c]Lev. 5:1 1 Sam. 14:24,26
26:64 [d]Dan. 7:13 ch. 16:27 & 24:30 & 25:31 Luke 21:27 John 1:51 Rom. 14:10 1 Thes. 4:16 Rev. 1:7 [e]Ps. 110:1 Acts 7:55
26:65 [f]2 Ki. 18:37
26:66 [g]Lev. 24:16 John 19:7
26:67 [h]Is. 50:6 & 53:3 ch. 27:30 [i]Luke 22:63
26:68 [j]Mark 14:65 Luke 22:64
26:69 [k]Mark 14:66 Luke 22:55 John 18:16,17,25
26:73 [l]Luke 22:59
26:74 [m]Mark 14:71
26:75 [n]ver. 34 Luke 22:61 John 13:38
27:1 [o]Ps. 2:2 Mark 15:1 Luke 22:66 & 23:1 John 18:28
27:2 [p]ch. 20:19 Acts 3:13
27:3 [q]ch. 26:14

Peter's denial of Jesus

26:69–75pp — Mark 14:66–72; Luke 22:55–62; John 18:16–18,25–27

69 ¶ [k]Now Peter sat without in the
palace: and a damsel came unto him,
saying, Thou also wast with Jesus of
Galilee.
70 But he denied before *them* all,
saying, I know not what thou sayest.
71 And when he was gone out into
the porch, another *maid* saw him, and
said unto them that were there, This
fellow was also with Jesus of Nazareth.
72 And again he denied with an
oath, I do not know the man.
73 And after a while came unto *him*
they that stood by, and said to Peter,
Surely thou also art *one* of them; for thy
[l]speech betrayeth thee.
74 Then [m]began he to curse and to
swear, *saying,* I know not the man. And
immediately the cock crew.
75 And Peter remembered the word
of Jesus, which said unto him, [n]Before
the cock crow, thou shalt deny me
thrice. And he went out, and wept bit-
terly.

The death of Judas Iscariot

27 WHEN THE morning was
come, [o]all the chief priests
and elders of the people took counsel
against Jesus to put him to death:
2 And when they had bound him,
they led *him* away, and [p]delivered him
to Pontius Pilate the governor.
3 ¶ [q]Then Judas, which had be-
trayed him, when he saw that he was
condemned, repented himself, and
brought again the thirty pieces of silver
to the chief priests and elders,
4 Saying, I have sinned in that I
have betrayed the innocent blood. And
they said, What *is that* to us? see thou
to that.

[e] Or, *rods*

(10) the crucifixion (27:35, note).

26:67 THEY . . . SPIT . . . BUFFETED . . . SMOTE. The sufferings of Christ, stage two. After the arrest at night and abandonment by His disciples (vv. 55–57), Jesus is brought before Caiaphas and the Jewish Council. He is blindfolded, mocked repeatedly, spat on, and struck in the face. (For the third stage of Christ's sufferings, see 27:2, note.)

27:2 DELIVERED HIM TO . . . PILATE. The sufferings of Christ, stage three. In the morning, Jesus, battered and exhausted, is taken across Jerusalem to be interrogated by Pilate. Barabbas is released (v. 21), and Jesus is scourged and delivered over to be crucified (v. 26). (For the fourth stage of Christ's sufferings, see v. 26, note.)

27:3 JUDAS . . . REPENTED. Judas learned that his sinful actions would lead to the death of Jesus. Likewise, our actions inevitably affect others for good or for evil. Many things we set in motion cannot be stopped, and their evil and destructive results will be experienced by us and others. It is of utmost importance to avoid all actions and plans that may have potentially harmful consequences.

5 And he cast down the pieces of silver in the temple, [r]and departed, and went and hanged himself.

6 And the chief priests took the silver pieces, and said, It is not lawful for to put them into the treasury, because it is the price of blood.

7 And they took counsel, and bought with them the potter's field, to bury strangers in.

8 Wherefore that field was called, [s]The field of blood, unto this day.

9 Then was fulfilled that which was spoken by Jeremy the prophet, saying, [t]And they took the thirty pieces of silver, the price of him that was valued, [f]whom they of the children of Israel did value;

10 And gave them for the potter's field, as the Lord appointed me.

Jesus before Pontius Pilate

27:11–23pp — Mark 15:2–14; Luke 23:2–3,18–23; John 18:29—19:15

11 And Jesus stood before the governor: [u]and the governor asked him, saying, Art thou the King of the Jews? And Jesus said unto him, [v]Thou sayest.

12 And when he was accused of the chief priests and elders, [w]he answered nothing.

13 Then said Pilate unto him, [x]Hearest thou not how many things they witness against thee?

14 And he answered him to never a word; insomuch that the governor marvelled greatly.

15 [y]Now at *that* feast the governor was wont to release unto the people a prisoner, whom they would.

16 And they had then a notable prisoner, called Barabbas.

17 Therefore when they were gathered together, Pilate said unto them, Whom will ye that I release unto you? Barabbas, or Jesus which is called Christ?

18 For he knew that for envy they had delivered him.

19 ¶ When he was set down on the judgment seat, his wife sent unto him, saying, Have thou nothing to do with that just man: for I have suffered many things this day in a dream because of him.

20 [z]But the chief priests and elders persuaded the multitude that they should ask Barabbas, and destroy Jesus.

21 The governor answered and said unto them, Whether of the twain will ye that I release unto you? They said, Barabbas.

22 Pilate saith unto them, What shall I do then with Jesus which is called Christ? *They* all say unto him, Let him be crucified.

23 And the governor said, Why, what evil hath he done? But they cried out the more, saying, Let him be crucified.

Jesus delivered for crucifixion

27:24–26pp — Mark 15:15; Luke 23:24–25; John 19:16

24 ¶ When Pilate saw that he could prevail nothing, but *that* rather a tumult was made, he [a]took water, and washed *his* hands before the multitude, saying, I am innocent of the blood of this just person: see ye *to it.*

25 Then answered all the people, and said, [b]His blood *be* on us, and on our children.

26 ¶ Then released he Barabbas unto them: and when [c]he had

27:5 [r]2 Sam. 17:23 Acts. 1:18
27:8 [s]Acts 1:19
27:9 [t]Zech. 11:12
27:11 [u]Mark 15:2 Luke 23:3 John 18:33 [v]John 18:37 1 Tim. 6:13
27:12 [w]ch. 26:63 John 19:9
27:13 [x]ch. 26:62 John 19:10
27:15 [y]Mark 15:6 Luke 23:17 John 18:39
27:20 [z]Mark 15:11 Luke 23:18 John 18:40 Acts 3:14
27:24 [a]Deut. 21:6
27:25 [b]Deut. 19:10 Josh. 2:19 2 Sam. 1:16 1 Ki. 2:32 Acts 5:28
27:26 [c]Is. 53:5 Mark 15:15 Luke 23:16,24,25 John 19:1,16

[f] Or, *whom they bought of the children of Israel*

27:5 HANGED HIMSELF. Matthew states that Judas "hanged himself"; Acts 1:18 records that he died by falling. What Judas probably did was to throw himself on a sharpened stake. Hanging in those days was done by crucifixion or impalement.

27:9 JEREMY THE PROPHET. Matthew here combines and summarizes elements of prophetic symbolism, one from Jeremiah (Jer. 32:6–9) and one from Zechariah (Zech. 11:12–13). Then he mentions the older and more prominent prophet as the source, a custom frequently used in alluding to passages from the prophets.

27:24 PILATE. Pilate's greatest sin was compromising what he knew to be true and right for the sake of position, status, and personal gain. Pilate knew Christ was innocent, and declared this so on several occasions (v. 18; John 19:4,6).

27:26 SCOURGED JESUS. The sufferings of Christ, stage four. (1) The Roman scourge consisted of the victim being stripped and stretched against a pillar or bent over a low post, his hands being tied. The instrument of torture was a short wooden handle to which several leather thongs were attached, with bits of iron or bone tied to the thongs. The blows were laid on the victim's back by two men, one lashing the victim from one side, one from the other side. This resulted in the flesh being cut to such an extent that veins, arteries, sometimes even inner organs were exposed. Often the victim died during the flogging.

(2) Scourging was hideous torture. The inability of Jesus to bear His own cross is no doubt due to

scourged Jesus, he delivered *him* to be crucified.

The soldiers mock Jesus

27:27–31pp — Mark 15:16–20

27 [d]Then the soldiers of the governor took Jesus into the [g]common hall, and gathered unto him the whole band *of soldiers.*

28 And they stripped him, and [e]put on him a scarlet robe.

29 ¶ [f]And when they had plaited a crown of thorns, they put *it* upon his head, and a reed in his right hand: and they bowed the knee before him, and mocked him, saying, Hail, King of the Jews!

30 And [g]they spit upon him, and took the reed, and smote him on the head.

31 And after that they had mocked him, they took the robe off from him, and put his own raiment on him, [h]and led him away to crucify *him.*

Jesus crucified

27:33–44pp — Mark 15:22–32; Luke 23:33–43; John 19:17–24

32 [i]And as they came out, [j]they found a man of Cyrene, Simon by name: him they compelled to bear his cross.

33 [k]And when they were come unto a place called Golgotha, that is to say, a place of a skull,

34 ¶ [l]They gave him vinegar to drink mingled with gall: and when he had tasted *thereof,* he would not drink.

35 [m]And they crucified him, and parted his garments, casting lots: that it might be fulfilled which was spoken by the prophet, [n]They parted my garments among them, and upon my vesture did they cast lots.

36 [o]And sitting down they watched him there;

37 And [p]set up over his head his accusation written, THIS IS JESUS THE KING OF THE JEWS.

38 [q]Then were there two thieves crucified with him, one on the right hand, and another on the left.

39 ¶ And [r]they that passed by reviled him, wagging their heads,

40 And saying, [s]Thou that destroyest the temple, and buildest *it* in three days, save thyself. [t]If thou be the Son of God, come down from the cross.

41 Likewise also the chief priests mocking *him,* with the scribes and elders, said,

42 He saved others; himself he cannot save. If he be the King of Israel, let him now come down from the cross, and we will believe him.

43 [u]He trusted in God; let him deliver him now, if he will have him: for he said, I am the Son of God.

27:27 [d]Mark 15:16 John 19:2
27:28 [e]Luke 23:11
27:29 [f]Ps. 69:19 Is. 53:3
27:30 [g]Is. 50:6 ch. 26:67
27:31 [h]Is. 53:7
27:32 [i]Num. 15:35 1 Ki. 21:13 Acts 7:58 Heb. 13:12 [j]Mark 15:21 Luke 23:26
27:33 [k]Mark 15:22 Luke 23:33 John 19:17
27:34 [l]See ver. 48 Ps. 69:21
27:35 [m]Mark 15:24 Luke 23:34 John 19:24 [n]Ps. 22:18
27:36 [o]ver. 54
27:37 [p]Mark 15:26 Luke 23:38 John 19:19
27:38 [q]Is. 53:12 Mark 15:27 Luke 23:32,33 John 19:18
27:39 [r]Ps. 22:7 & 109:25 Mark 15:29 Luke 23:35
27:40 [s]ch. 26:61 John 2:19 [t]ch. 26:63
27:43 [u]Ps. 22:8

[g] Or, *governor's house*

this severe infliction (v. 32; Luke 23:26). "But he *was* wounded for our transgressions, *he was* bruised for our iniquities: the chastisement of our peace *was* upon him; and with his stripes we are healed" (Is. 53:5; 1 Pet. 2:24). (For the fifth stage of the sufferings of Christ, see vv. 28–29, note.)

27:28–29 A SCARLET ROBE . . . A CROWN OF THORNS. The sufferings of Christ, stage five. Jesus is untied and placed in the middle of the Roman battalion (v. 27). The soldiers put a robe across His shoulders, place a stick in His hand, and press a circle of branches covered with long thorns on his head. The soldiers mock and strike Him across the face and head, driving the thorns deeper into His scalp (vv. 30–31). (For the sixth stage of the sufferings of Christ, see v. 31, note.)

27:31 LED HIM AWAY TO CRUCIFY *HIM*. The sufferings of Christ, stage six. The heavy beam of the cross is tied to Christ's shoulder. He begins the slow journey to Golgotha. The weight of the wooden beam, together with sheer physical exhaustion, causes Him to fall. He tries to rise, but cannot. Simon is then pressed into service to bear His cross. (For the seventh stage of the sufferings of Christ, see v. 35, note.)

27:35 THEY CRUCIFIED HIM. The sufferings of Christ, stage seven. At Golgotha the cross beam is placed on the ground and Jesus is laid on it. His arms are stretched along the beams and a heavy, square, wrought-iron nail is driven through His hand (or wrist), first into the right, then into the left hand, and deep into the wood. Next Christ is lifted up by means of ropes or ladders, the cross beam is bound or nailed to the upright beam, and a support for the body fastened on it. Lastly, His feet are extended and a larger piece of iron is driven through the two. (For the eighth stage of the sufferings of Christ, see v. 39, note.)

27:39 REVILED HIM. The sufferings of Christ, stage eight. Jesus is now a pathetic spectacle, blood-streaked, covered with wounds, and exposed to the view of the people. He experiences hours of pain in his entire body, fatigue in His arms, great waves of cramps in the muscles, and skin torn from His back. Then another agony begins—a crushing pain deep in the chest as fluid begins to compress the heart. He feels an intense thirst (John 19:28) and is aware of the abuse and ridicule of those who pass by the cross (vv. 39–44). (For the ninth stage of the sufferings of Christ, see v. 46, note.)

44 [v]The thieves also, which were
crucified with him, cast the same in his
teeth.

The death of Jesus

27:45–56pp — Mark 15:33–41; Luke 23:44–49

45 [w]Now from the sixth hour there
was darkness over all the land unto the
ninth hour.
46 And about the ninth hour
[x]Jesus cried with a loud voice, saying,
Eli, Eli, lama sabachthani? that is to
say, [y]My God, my God, why hast thou
forsaken me?
47 Some of them that stood there,
when they heard *that,* said, This *man*
calleth for Elias.
48 And straightway one of them
ran, and took a sponge, [z]and filled *it*
with vinegar, and put *it* on a reed, and
gave him to drink.
49 The rest said, Let be, let us see
whether Elias will come to save him.
50 ¶ [a]Jesus, when he had cried
again with a loud voice, yielded up the
ghost.
51 And, behold, the [b]veil of the
temple was rent in twain from the top
to the bottom; and the earth did quake,
and the rocks rent;
52 And the graves were opened;
and many bodies of the saints which
slept arose,
53 And came out of the graves after
his resurrection, and went into the holy
city, and appeared unto many.
54 [c]Now when the centurion, and
they that were with him, watching
Jesus, saw the earthquake, and those
things that were done, they feared
greatly, saying, Truly this was the Son
of God.
55 And many women were there be-
holding afar off, [d]which followed
Jesus from Galilee, ministering unto
him:
56 [e]Among which was Mary Mag-
dalene, and Mary the mother of James
and Joses, and the mother of Zebedee's
children.

The burial of Jesus

27:57–61pp — Mark 15:42–47; Luke 23:50–56; John 19:38–42

57 [f]When the even was come,
there came a rich man of Arimathaea,
named Joseph, who also himself was
Jesus' disciple:
58 He went to Pilate, and begged
the body of Jesus. Then Pilate com-
manded the body to be delivered.
59 And when Joseph had taken the
body, he wrapped it in a clean linen
cloth,
60 And [g]laid it in his own new
tomb, which he had hewn out in the
rock: and he rolled a great stone to the
door of the sepulchre, and departed.
61 And there was Mary Magdalene,
and the other Mary, sitting over
against the sepulchre.

The sepulchre guarded

62 ¶ Now the next day, that fol-
lowed the day of the preparation, the
chief priests and Pharisees came to-
gether unto Pilate,
63 Saying, Sir, we remember that
that deceiver said, while he was yet

27:44 [v]Mark 15:32 Luke 23:39
27:45 [w]Amos 8:9 Mark 15:33 Luke 23:44
27:46 [x]Heb. 5:7 [y]Ps. 22:1
27:48 [z]Ps. 69:21 Mark 15:36 Luke 23:36 John 19:29
27:50 [a]Mark 15:37 Luke 23:46
27:51 [b]Ex. 26:31 2 Chr. 3:14 Mark 15:38 Luke 23:45
27:54 [c]ver. 36 Mark 15:39 Luke 23:47
27:55 [d]Luke 8:2,3
27:56 [e]Mark 15:40
27:57 [f]Mark 15:42 Luke 23:50 John 19:38
27:60 [g]Is. 53:9

27:46 WHY HAST THOU FORSAKEN ME? The sufferings of Christ, stage nine. These words mark the climax of the sufferings of Christ for a lost world. His cry in Aramaic, "My God, my God, why hast thou forsaken me," testifies that He experiences separation from God as the sinner's substitute. Here the sorrow, grief, and pain are at their worst. He is wounded for our transgressions (Is. 53:5) and gives Himself a "ransom for many" (20:28; 1 Tim. 2:6). Him who knew no sin God makes "to be sin for us" (2 Cor. 5:21); He dies forsaken, that we might never be forsaken (cf. Ps. 22). Thus we are redeemed by the sufferings of Christ (1 Pet. 1:19). (For the tenth stage of the sufferings of Christ, see v. 50, note.)

27:50 JESUS . . . CRIED AGAIN. The sufferings of Christ, stage ten. Christ utters His final words with a loud voice, "It is finished" (John 19:30). This cry signifies the end of His sufferings and the completion of the work of redemption. The debt for our sin has been paid in full, and the plan of salvation established. Only then does He offer a final prayer, "Father, into Thy hands I commend my spirit" (Luke 23:46). (For the first stage of Christ's sufferings, see 26:37, note.)

27:51 THE VEIL . . . WAS RENT. The tearing of the "veil of the temple" (see Ex. 26:33, note) signified that a way was open into the presence of God. The curtain separating the holy place from the most holy place barred the way into the presence of God. Through the death of Christ, the curtain was removed and the way into the most holy place (i.e., God's presence) was open for all who believe in Christ and His saving word (cf. Heb. 9:1–14; 10:19–22).

27:52 THE SAINTS . . . AROSE. The significance of this event is the prophetic indication that Christ's death and resurrection guarantees our glorious resurrection at His return. His resurrection was the defeat of death (see 1 Cor. 15:50–58; 1 Thes. 4:14).

alive, [h]After three days I will rise
again.
64 Command therefore that the sep-
ulchre be made sure until the third day,
lest his disciples come by night, and
steal him away, and say unto the peo-
ple, He is risen from the dead: so the
last error shall be worse than the first.
65 Pilate said unto them, Ye have a
watch: go your way, make *it* as sure as
ye can.
66 So they went, and made the sep-
ulchre sure, [i]sealing the stone, and
setting a watch.

The resurrection of Jesus

28:1–8pp — Mark 16:1–8; Luke 24:1–10

28 IN THE [j]end of the sabbath,
as it began to dawn toward the
first *day* of the week, came Mary Mag-
dalene [k]and the other Mary to see the
sepulchre.
2 And, behold, there [h]was a great
earthquake: for [l]the angel of the Lord
descended from heaven, and came and
rolled back the stone from the door,
and sat upon it.
3 [m]His countenance was like light-
ning, and his raiment white as snow:
4 And for fear of him the keepers
did shake, and became as dead *men.*
5 And the angel answered and said
unto the women, Fear not ye: for I
know that ye seek Jesus, which was
crucified.
6 He is not here: for he is risen, [n]as
he said. Come, see the place where the
Lord lay.
7 And go quickly, and tell his disci-
ples that he is risen from the dead; and,
behold, [o]he goeth before you into Gali-
lee; there shall ye see him: lo, I have
told you.
8 And they departed quickly from
the sepulchre with fear and great joy;
and did run to bring his disciples word.
9 ¶ And as they went to tell his dis-
ciples, behold, [p]Jesus met them, say-
ing, All hail. And they came and held
him by the feet, and worshipped him.
10 Then said Jesus unto them, Be
not afraid: go tell [q]my brethren that
they go into Galilee, and there shall
they see me.

The bribing of the soldiers

11 ¶ Now when they were going, be-
hold, some of the watch came into the
city, and showed unto the chief priests
all the things that were done.
12 And when they were assembled
with the elders, and had taken counsel,
they gave large money unto the sol-
diers,
13 Saying, Say ye, His disciples
came by night, and stole him *away*
while we slept.
14 And if this come to the gover-

27:63 [h]ch. 16:21 & 17:23 & 20:19 & 26:61 Mark 8:31 & 10:34 Luke 9:22 & 18:33 & 24:6,7 John 2:19
27:66 [i]Dan. 6:17
28:1 [j]Mark 16:1 Luke 24:1 John 20:1 [k]ch. 27:56
28:2 [l]See Mark 16:5 Luke 24:4 John 20:12
28:3 [m]Dan. 10:6
28:6 [n]ch. 12:40 & 16:21 & 17:23 & 20:19
28:7 [o]ch. 26:32 Mark 16:7
28:9 [p]See Mark 16:9 John 20:14
28:10 [q]See John 20:17 Rom. 8:29 Heb. 2:11

h Or, *had been*

28:6 HE IS RISEN. The resurrection of Jesus is one of the central truths of the gospel (1 Cor. 15:1–8). What is the importance of Christ's resurrection to those who believe in Him? (1) It proves He is the Son of God (John 10:17–18; Rom. 1:4). (2) It guarantees the efficacy of His redemptive death (Rom. 6:4; 1 Cor. 15:17). (3) It verifies the truth of Scripture (Ps. 16:10; Luke 24:44–47; Acts 2:31). (4) It is proof of future judgment upon the wicked (Acts 17:30–31). (5) It is the foundation for Christ's giving the Holy Spirit and spiritual life to His people (John 20:22; Rom. 5:10; 1 Cor. 15:45) and for His heavenly ministry of intercession for the believer (Heb. 7:23–28). (6) It assures the believer of his future heavenly inheritance (1 Pet. 1:3–4) and of his resurrection or translation when the Lord returns (see John 14:3, note; 1 Thes. 4:14ff). (7) It makes available the presence of Christ and His power over sin in our everyday experience (Gal. 2:20; Eph. 1:18–20).

28:9 JESUS MET THEM. The resurrection is well verified historically. After His resurrection, Christ remained on earth for forty days, appearing and talking to the apostles and many of His followers. The resurrection appearances are as follows: (1) Mary Magdalene (John 20:11–18); (2) the women returning from the tomb (vv. 9–10); (3) Peter (Luke 24:34); (4) two people on the Emmaus road (Luke 24:13–32); (5) all the disciples except Thomas, and others with them (Luke 24:36–43; John 20:19–23); (6) all the disciples on Sunday night one week later (John 20:26–31); (7) seven disciples beside the Sea of Galilee (John 21:1–25); (8) five hundred people in Galilee (compare vv. 16–20 with 1 Cor. 15:6); (9) James (1 Cor. 15:7); (10) the disciples receiving the Great Commission (vv. 16–20); (11) the apostles at the ascension (Acts 1:3–11); and (12) the apostle Paul (1 Cor. 15:8).

28:10 BE NOT AFRAID. Why were these women not to be afraid? The angel's response gives us the answer: "for I know that ye seek Jesus" (v. 5). The women had remained loyal friends of Jesus when the world despised and crucified Him. At Christ's return for His faithful, they will have no reason to fear if they also have remained loyal to Him in the midst of a world that rejects His love, salvation, and holy Word. John expresses this truth in 1 John 2:28: "And now, little children, abide in him; that, when he shall appear, we may have confidence, and not be ashamed before him at his coming."

nor's ears, we will persuade him, and
secure you.
15 So they took the money, and did
as they were taught: and this saying is
commonly reported among the Jews
until this day.

The Great Commission

28:18–20pp — Mark 16:15–16; Luke 24:47

16 ¶ Then the eleven disciples went
away into Galilee, into a mountain
[r]where Jesus had appointed them.
17 And when they saw him, they
worshipped him: but some doubted.
18 And Jesus came and spake unto
them, saying, [s]All power is given unto
me in heaven and in earth.
19 ¶ [t]Go ye therefore, and
[u]teach[i] all nations, baptizing them
in the name of the Father, and of the
Son, and of the Holy Ghost:
20 [v]Teaching them to observe all
things whatsoever I have commanded
you: and, lo, I am with you always, *even*
unto the end of the world. Amen.

Mark 16:15-16

28:16 [r]ver. 7 ch. 26:32

28:18 [s]Dan. 7:13,14 ch. 11:27 & 16:28 Luke 1:32 & 10:22 John 3:35 & 5:22 & 13:3 & 17:2 Acts 2:36 Rom. 14:9 1 Cor. 15:27 Eph. 1:10,21 Phil. 2:9,10 Heb. 1:2 & 2:8 1 Pet. 3:22 Rev. 17:14

28:19 [t]Mark 16:15 [u]Is. 52:10; Luke 24:47; Acts 2:38,39; Rom. 10:18; Col. 1:23 **28:20** [v]Acts 2:42

[i] Or, *make disciples,* or, *Christians of all nations*

28:18 ALL POWER. God's people are promised authority and power to proclaim the gospel throughout the world (vv. 19–20). But first they must obey Jesus' command to wait for the promise of the Father, which is the power of the Holy Spirit at Pentecost. We cannot expect the power of Acts 1:8 to accompany our going to the nations without first following the pattern of Acts 1:4 (see Luke 24:47–49; Acts 1:8; 2:4).

28:19 GO ... TEACH ... BAPTIZING. These words are Christ's Great Commission to all His followers of every generation. They state the goal, responsibility, and commissioning of the church's missionary task. (1) The church is to go into all the world and preach the gospel to all people according to the N.T. revelation of Christ and the apostles (see Eph. 2:20, note). This task includes the primary responsibility of sending forth missionaries into every nation (Acts 13:1–4).

(2) The preaching of the gospel is centered on "repentance and remission [forgiveness] of sins" (Luke 24:47), the promise of receiving "the gift of the Holy Ghost" (Acts 2:38), and the exhortation to separate from this wicked generation (Acts 2:40) while waiting for the return of Jesus from heaven (Acts 3:19–20; 1 Thes. 1:10).

(3) The purpose is to make disciples who will observe Christ's commandments. This is the only direct imperative in this passage. Christ does not intend that evangelism and missionary witness result only in conversion decisions. Spiritual energies must not be concentrated in merely enlarging church membership, but in making disciples who separate themselves from the world, observe the commandments of Christ, and follow Him with all their heart, mind, and will (cf. John 8:31).

(4) Furthermore, it should be noted that Christ commands us to concentrate on reaching lost men and women, not on Christianizing society or taking over the world. Those who believe must come out of the current evil world system and be separated from its immorality (Rom. 13:12; 2 Cor. 6:14; see article on SPIRITUAL SEPARATION FOR BELIEVERS, p. 1814), while exposing its evil by word and deed (Eph. 5:11).

(5) Those who believe in Christ and the gospel are to be "baptized" in water. This represents their covenant pledge to renounce immorality, the world, and their own sinful nature, and to unreservedly commit themselves to Christ and His kingdom purposes (see Acts 22:16, note on water baptism).

(6) Christ will be with His obedient followers in the presence and power of the Holy Spirit (cf. v. 20; 1:23; 18:20). They are to go to all nations and witness only after they are "endued with power from on high" (Luke 24:49; see Acts 1:8, notes).

28:20 I AM WITH YOU. This promise is Christ's assurance to those involved in winning the lost and teaching them to observe His righteous standards. Jesus arose, is now alive, and is personally interested in each one of His children. He is with them in the person of the Holy Spirit (John 14:16,26) and through His Word (John 14:23). No matter what your condition is—weak, poor, humble, apparently unimportant—He cares for you, watches with concern every detail of life's trials and struggles, and gives both the grace that is sufficient (2 Cor. 12:9) and His presence to guide you home (18:20; Acts 18:10). This is the Christian's answer to every fear, every doubt, every trouble, every heartache, and every discouragement.

THE KINGDOM OF GOD VERSUS THE KINGDOM OF SATAN

A. The Nature of the Kingdoms

Item	Kingdom of God: Description	Kingdom of God: Reference	Kingdom of Satan: Description	Kingdom of Satan: Reference
1. Rulership	a. Rule by God—Theocracy	2 Chr. 20:6; Ps. 95:3; Dan. 4:17,32; 1 Tim. 1:17	a. Rule by Satan—the god of this age	John 12:31; 14:30; 2 Cor. 4:4; Eph. 2:2; 1 John 5:19
	b. God's rule through His Son	Ps. 110:1; Is. 9:6–7; Dan. 7:13–14; Mat. 28:18; Luke 1:32–33; Eph. 1:20–22; Heb. 1:3–8; Rev. 1:5; 19:13–16	b. Satan assisted by principalities, powers, and rulers of this dark world	Eph. 1:21; 6:12; Col. 1:16; 2:15; cf. Dan. 10:13
2. Character	a. Righteousness, peace, and joy in the Holy Spirit	Mat. 6:33; John 18:36; Rom. 14:17	a. Centered in the things of this world	1 John 2:15–17; 5:19; Rev. 2:9,13
	b. Divine power	Luke 11:20–22; 1 Cor. 2:4; 4:20; 1 Thes. 1:5	b. Disease, sickness, slavery	Mat. 10:1; Luke 9:1
	c. Truth	John 8:31–32; 14:6,16–17; 15:26; 16:13; 17:17	c. Deception	Gen. 3:4–5,13; John 8:44; Rom. 1:25; 2 Cor. 4:4; 2 Thes. 2:10–12
	d. Holiness	1 Cor. 1:2,30; 2 Cor. 6:17—7:1; Eph. 4:24; Heb. 12:10,14; 1 Pet. 1:15–16	d. Sin and evil	Rom. 1:28–32; 1 Cor. 6:9–10; Eph. 2:1–3; 1 John 3:7–10,12
	e. Light	John 1:4–9; 3:19; Acts 26:18; Col. 1:12–13; 1 Tim. 6:16; 1 John 1:5,7	e. Darkness	Luke 22:53; Acts 26:18; Eph. 6:12; Col. 1:13; 1 John 1:6; cf. 2 Cor. 11:14
	f. Eternal life	John 1:4; 3:16; Rom. 5:17; 6:4,12; 8:2; 1 John 5:12; Rev. 1:18	f. Eternal death	Rom. 5:12,14; 6:23; Eph. 2:1; Rev. 20:14–15; 21:8
3. Manifestation	a. Salvation	Mark 1:15; Acts 8:12; 1 Cor. 5:10–11	a. Destruction	John 10:10; 1 Pet. 5:8

	Kingdom of God		Kingdom of Satan	
Item	Description	Reference	Description	Reference
3. Manifestation (cont.)	b. Baptism in the Holy Spirit	Mat. 3:2,11–12; Acts 1:3–8	b. Filled with the spirit of the world	1 Cor. 2:12; Jas. 4:4; 1 John 2:15
	c. Miracles and casting out demons	Mat. 4:23–24; 10:7–8; 12:28; Luke 9:1–2,11; 11:20–22; 13:11–16	c. By counterfeit miracles and demon possession	Mat. 4:24; 8:28; 24:24; 2 Thes. 2:9; Rev. 13:13–14
	d. The presence of Jesus	Mat. 3:1–3; 4:17; Mark 1:14–15	d. The presence of evil spirits	Mat. 8:28; 12:22–29; Mark 5:2–5,9; 6:7; Acts 19:16; Rev. 18:2
	e. Gifts of the Spirit	Rom. 12:6–8; 1 Cor. 12:1–31	e. Sorcery, witchcraft, drugs, occult activity	Acts 16:16; 19:18–19; 1 Cor. 10:20; Gal. 5:20; Rev. 2:24
	f. Fruit of the Spirit	Gal. 5:22–23	f. Works of the flesh	Gal. 5:19–21

B. The People of the Kingdoms

	Kingdom of God		Kingdom of Satan	
Item	Description	Reference	Description	Reference
1. Entrance	a. Repentance and forgiveness	Mark 1:15; Acts 2:37–38; 1 John 1:9	a. All unregenerate humanity	Rom. 3:23; 5:12; Eph. 2:2–3; Col. 1:13
	b. Humility	Mat. 18:3; Mark 10:15	b. Pride, independence	Ps. 2:1–2; Prov. 16:18; Ezek. 16:40–50; Dan. 4:30; Obad. 3; Rom. 1:30; 2 Tim. 3:2; Jude 16
	c. Confession and faith	Rom. 10:8–13; Heb. 4:2	c. Rebellion and unbelief	Rom. 1:18–32; Heb. 3:19; 12:25
	d. New birth	John 3:3,5	d. Spiritual death	Rom. 5:12,17; 6:23; Eph. 2:1; Col. 2:13
	e. Union with Christ	Rom. 6:3–8	e. Separation from God	Eph. 2:12

Item	Kingdom of God: Description	Kingdom of God: Reference	Kingdom of Satan: Description	Kingdom of Satan: Reference
2. Characteristics of Members	a. Children of God	John 1:12–13; 3:3–5; Rom. 8:15; Gal. 4:5; Eph. 1:5	a. Children of Satan	John 8:44; 1 John 3:8–10
	b. Faith and obedience	Mat. 6:25–32; John 14:21; Rom. 1:5; 16:26; Heb. 11:6	b. Unbelief and rebellion	Mat. 17:17; Luke 12:46; 2 Thes. 3:2; Tit. 1:15; Rev. 21:8
	c. Eternal life	John 3:16,36; 5:24; 6:40; 1 John 2:25; 5:11; Rev. 2:7	c. Eternal death	John 3:18,36; Rom. 5:12; 6:23; Jas. 1:15; 1 John 5:12; Rev. 20:14–15; 21:8
	d. Walk in the light	Rom. 13:13; Eph. 5:8; Phil. 2:15; 1 Thes. 5:5,8	d. Walk in darkness	John 3:19; Rom. 13:12–13; Eph. 5:11–12; 1 John 1:6; 2:9,11
	e. Devoted to the truth	2 Thes. 2:13; 1 Tim. 3:15; 3 John 3–5	e. Speak lies and oppose truth	John 8:44; Rom. 1:18,25; 2 Tim. 2:18; 3:8; 4:4
	f. Strangers in the world	Heb. 11:13; 1 Pet. 2:11	f. Love things of the world	1 Cor. 6:9; 2 Tim. 3:4; 2 Pet. 2:3; Jude 11; Rev. 3:17–19
	g. Live by the Spirit	Rom. 8:9–11; 1 Cor. 2:10–13; Gal. 5:16–26	g. Live by the sinful nature	Rom. 8:5–6; Gal. 5:16–26
	h. Humble and childlike, living righteously	Mat. 5:6,20; 6:33; 18:1–4; Luke 18:16–17; 1 Thes. 2:12; Eph. 4:24	h. Wicked, disobedient, and immoral	Gal. 5:19–21; Eph. 2:2–3; 5:5–6; Jas. 1:14–15; 1 John 2:15–17; 3:8
	i. Meekness and submission	Prov. 16:19; Mat. 5:5; Eph. 5:21–22; Jas. 3:17; 1 Pet. 2:13—3:9	i. Arrogance and self-assertion	2 Tim. 3:2; Jas. 4:6
	j. Freedom in Christ	Rom. 6:6,18,22; 1 Pet. 2:16	j. Bondage to sin and Satan	Rom. 7:14–24
	k. Honesty	Ex. 20:15–16; Eph. 4:25,28	k. Deceit	Prov. 12:5,20a; Rom. 1:29; Eph. 4:22; Rev. 21:8

	Kingdom of God		Kingdom of Satan	
Item	Description	Reference	Description	Reference
2. Characteristics of Members (cont.)	l. Love	Mat. 5:43–48; 7:12; 1 Cor. 13; Eph. 5:2	l. Hatred and hostility	Luke 21:17; John 15:18–19; 18:14; Rom. 1:30; Tit. 3:3; Jas. 4:4
	m. Forgiveness	Mat. 5:14–15; Eph. 4:32	m. Bitterness	Rom. 3:14; Eph. 4:31
	n. Godly influence	Mat. 5:13–16; Tit. 2:12; 1 Pet. 2:12; 2 Pet. 3:11	n. Corrupting influence	Gen. 19:1–38; Prov. 2:12–22; 1 Cor. 15:33
	o. Sexual purity, and marital faithfulness	Eph. 5:3; 1 Thes. 4:3–8	o. Lust and immorality	Rom. 1:24–27; 1 Cor. 6:9–10; Gal. 5:19; Eph. 5:5–6
	p. Generosity	Luke 12:33–34; 6:38; 2 Cor. 8:2–5	p. Greed and covetousness	Luke 12:15–21; Col. 3:5; 2 Pet. 2:14
	q. Holy	Mat. 5:8; 1 Pet. 1:15–16; Rev. 22:11	q. Unholy	2 Tim. 3:2; 2 Pet. 2:5–6; Jude 15; Rev. 22:11
	r. Upright speech	Ex. 20:16; Prov. 10:19–21; Eccl. 5:2,6–7; Eph. 4:29; 5:4; Jas. 1:26; 3:1–2	r. Corrupt speech	Prov. 10:18; 15:28; Rom. 3:13–14
	s. Inherit the kingdom	Mat. 25:34–40; John 3:3–5; 1 Cor. 6:11; Rev. 21:7	s. Do not inherit the kingdom	1 Cor. 6:9–11; Gal. 5:21; Eph. 5:5
3. Duties	a. Worship only God	Ex. 20:2–6; Mat. 4:10; John 4:23–24; 1 Thes. 1:9	a. Idolatry; living for self; ultimately worship Satan & antichrist	Dan. 11:30–33; 2 Thes. 2:4; Rev. 13:4,8,12,15
	b. Hate sin and Satan	Ps. 139:21; Rom. 12:9; Heb. 1:9; 1 John 2:15	b. Hate and persecute believers; hate righteousness and Christ	John 15:19; 16:3; 17:14; 2 Tim. 3:12; Rev. 12:13,17
	c. Seek to advance God's kingdom and His righteousness	Mat. 6:31–33; 11:12; 28:19–20; Acts 1:6–8; 19:8; 28:23,31; Col. 4:11	c. Promote evil and corrupt God's kingdom and righteousness	Mat. 7:15; 13:24–28,36–43; 24:23–24; Luke 21:8; Acts 20:29–30; Gal. 1:8–9; 1 John 2:18–19; 2 John 7–11

	Kingdom of God		Kingdom of Satan	
Item	**Description**	**Reference**	**Description**	**Reference**
3. Duties (cont.)	d. Love not the world	Mat. 6:19–24; John 17:15–16; Rom. 12:1–2; 1 Cor. 10:21–22; 2 Cor. 6:14–18; 2 Tim. 3:1–5; Jas. 4:4; 1 John 2:15–17	d. Love the world	Ps. 17:14; Mark 8:36; Phil. 3:19; 2 Tim. 4:10; 1 John 2:15–16
	e. Wait for Christ's return from heaven	1 Thes. 1:10; 4:13–18; 1 Tim. 4:8; Tit. 2:13	e. Do not watch for Christ's return	Mat. 24:45–51; Luke 12:42–46; 1 Thes. 5:4–6
4. Power and dominion	a. Personal level	Luke 10:17; John 16:33; Rom. 6:12,14	a. Personal level	John 8:23; Eph. 2:1; 1 John 3:8
	b. Family level	Deut. 6:1–9; 1 Cor. 11:3; Eph. 5:22—6:4	b. Family level	Luke 16:27–31; 21:16; 2 Tim. 3:2–3,6
	c. Church level	Mat. 5:13–20; 18:15–20	c. Organizational level	John 12:31; Eph. 6:12; Rev. 13:1–11; 17—18
	d. Business level	Luke 16:1–13; Col. 3:23–25	d. Business level	Acts 16:16–21; 19:23–28; Rev. 18:3,11–24

C. The Warfare of the Kingdoms

	Kingdom of God		Kingdom of Satan	
Item	**Description**	**Reference**	**Description**	**Reference**
1. Christ's Warfare with Satan	a. Christ came to destroy Satan's kingdom	Luke 4:18–21; John 12:31; Acts 26:15–18; 1 John 3:8	a. Satan intent on destroying Christ's kingdom	Mat. 4:1–11; 16:22–23
	b. Christ overcame temptation	Mat. 4:1–11; Luke 4:1–11; Heb. 4:15	b. Satan tempted Christ to sin	Mat. 4:1–11; Luke 4:1–11; Heb. 4:15
	c. Christ cast out demons	Mark 1:25–26,32–34,39; 3:12; 5:12–15; 7:24–30; 9:14–29; Luke 11:20–22	c. Demons challenged Christ	Mark 1:24,34; 3:11; 5:7

Item	Kingdom of God: Description	Kingdom of God: Reference	Kingdom of Satan: Description	Kingdom of Satan: Reference
1. Christ's Warfare with Satan (cont.)	d. All power belongs eternally to Christ	Mat. 28:18; 1 John 4:4	d. Satan has only temporary and limited power	Job 1:6–12; 2:1–6; Luke 22:53; Rev. 20:7–9
	e. Deliverance from sin and disease provided in the cross	Is. 53; 1 Pet. 2:24	e. Satan cannot withstand the power of the cross	2 Cor. 4:10; Rev. 12:10–11
	f. Final victory belongs to Christ	2 Thes. 2:7–8; 2 Pet. 3:10–13; Rev. 17:14; 19:11–21	f. Satan will be finally defeated and destroyed	Mat. 25:41,46; John 16:11; Rev. 20:10,14–15
2. Believers' warfare with Satan	a. Believers hate sin and seek to destroy the works of the devil	Mat. 12:29–30; Mark 3:27; Luke 11:21–23	a. Satan hates and persecutes believers	John 15:19; 17:14; Rev. 12:13,17
	b. The weapons of believers are spiritual and not carnal	Mat. 26:52; 2 Cor. 10:4–5; Eph. 6:10–17	b. Satan uses the world, flesh, and the demonic against believers	2 Cor. 11:3,14–15; Gal. 5:17–21; Eph. 6:11–12; 1 Pet. 2:11; 5:8; Rev. 12:13,17; 13:15–18
	c. Believers are given authority to cast out demons	Mark 3:14–15; 6:7; 16:17; Luke 9:1–2; 10:17; Acts 5:16; 8:7; 16:18; 19:12	c. Demons try to destroy believers spiritually	Mark 9:17–18; Acts 8:7; 16:16–17;1 Pet. 5:8
	d. Believers must overcome the world	Gal. 6:14; 1 John 2:13–14; 4:4; 5:4; Rev. 2:7,11,17,26: 3:5,12,21; 12:11; 21:7,11	d. Satan seeks to overcome believers	Jer. 1:19; Luke 10:19; Rom. 12:21; 1 Tim. 5:11; 2 Pet. 2:20
	e. By the cross believers are dead to the world	Gal. 6:14; Heb. 11:25–26	e. Satan entices to sinful pleasures of the world	Phil. 3:19; 2 Tim. 3:4; 1 John 2:16–17

ST. MARK

Outline

I. Preparation for Jesus' Ministry (1:1–13)
   A. The Ministry of John the Baptist (1:2–8)
   B. The Baptism of Jesus (1:9–11)
   C. The Temptation of Jesus (1:12–13)
II. Early Galilean Ministry (1:14—3:6)
   A. The First Four Disciples (1:14–20)
   B. A Sabbath in Capernaum (1:21–34)
   C. First Preaching Tour (1:35–45)
   D. Conflicts with the Pharisees (2:1—3:6)
III. Later Galilean Ministry (3:7—7:23)
   A. Withdrawal to the Seaside (3:7–12)
   B. Appointment of the Twelve Disciples (3:13–19)
   C. Friends and Foes (3:20–35)
   D. Teaching in Parables (4:1–34)
   E. Teaching Through Mighty Works (4:35—5:43)
   F. Jesus at Nazareth (6:1–6)
   G. The Mission of the Twelve (6:7–13)
   H. Herod and John the Baptist (6:14–29)
   I. Miracles and Teaching Around the Sea of Galilee (6:30–56)
   J. Conflict with Tradition (7:1–23)
IV. Ministry Beyond Galilee (7:24–9:29)
   A. Two Gentiles' Healings (7:24–37)
   B. More Miracles (8:1–26)
   C. The Caesarea Philippi Episode (8:27—9:1)
   D. The Transfiguration Episode (9:2–29)
V. The Road Toward Jerusalem (9:30—10:52)
   A. En Route Through Galilee (9:30–50)
   B. Ministry in Perea (10:1–52)
VI. Passion Week (11:1—15:47)
   A. Sunday: Triumphal Entry to Jerusalem (11:1–11)
   B. Monday: 1. Cursing the Fig Tree (11:12–14)
      2. Cleansing the Temple (11:15–19)
   C. Tuesday: 1. Faith and Fear (11:20–33)
      2. Parable and Controversy (12:1–44)
      3. The Olivet Discourse (13:1–37)
      4. The Anointing at Bethany (14:1–11)
   D. Thursday: The Last Supper (14:12–25)
   E. Friday: 1. Jesus in Gethsemane (14:26–52)
      2. The Jewish Trial (14:53–72)
      3. The Roman Trial (15:1–20)
      4. The Crucifixion and Burial (15:21–47)
VII. The Resurrection (16:1–20)
   A. The Resurrection Discovery (16:1–8)
   B. Post-Resurrection Appearances (16:9–18)
   C. Ascension and Apostolic Mission (16:19–20)

Author: Mark

Theme: Jesus, the Servant-Son

Date of Writing: A.D. 55–65

Background

Among the four Gospels, Mark is the most concise account of "the beginning of the gospel of Jesus Christ, the Son of God" (1:1). Although the author is not identified by name in the book itself (true of all the Gospels), the early and unanimous testimony of the church is that John Mark was responsible for its writing. This man grew up as a youth in Jerusalem and was among the first generation Christians (Acts 12:12). He had the unique opportunity of being associated in ministry with three N.T. apostles: Paul (Acts 13:1–13; Col. 4:10; Philem. 24), Barnabas (Acts 15:39), and Peter (1 Pet. 5:13). According to Papias (c. A.D. 130) and other second-century church fathers, Mark derived the content of his Gospel from his association with Peter, wrote it in Rome, and designed it for Roman believers. Although the specific date for the writing of Mark's Gospel is uncertain, most scholars place it in the late 50s or the 60s; it is possibly the first of the four Gospels to be written.

Purpose

In the 60s of the first century A.D., believers in Rome were treated cruelly by the populace, and many were tortured and put to death by the Roman emperor Nero. According to tradition, among the Christian martyrs in Rome during this decade were the apostles Peter and Paul. As one of the church leaders in Rome, John Mark was moved by the Holy Spirit to write this Gospel as a prophetic anticipation of, or a pastoral response to, this time of persecution. His intention was to strengthen the foundations of faith in Roman believers and, if need be, to inspire them to suffer faithfully for the gospel, placing before them the life, suffering, death, and resurrection of Jesus their Lord.

Survey

In a fast-moving narrative, Mark presents Jesus as the Son of God and the suffering servant Messiah. The watershed of the book is the episode in Caesarea Philippi, followed by the transfiguration (8:27—9:10), where both the identity of Jesus and His mission of suffering are fully disclosed to His twelve disciples. The first half of Mark focuses primarily both on Jesus' mighty miracles and on His authority over sickness and demons as signs that the kingdom of God is at hand. At Caesarea Philippi, however, Jesus tells His disciples openly that He "must suffer many things and be rejected of the elders, and *of* the chief priests, and scribes, and be killed, and after three days rise again" (8:31). There are numerous references throughout Mark to suffering as the cost of discipleship (e.g., 3:21–22,30; 8:34–38; 10:30,33–34,45; 13:8,11–13). God's vindication, however, will follow righteous suffering, as demonstrated in Jesus' resurrection.

Special Features

Four features characterize Mark's Gospel: (1) It is a Gospel of action, emphasizing what Jesus did rather than what He said. Thus Mark records eighteen miracles but only four parables (not including parabolic statements). (2) It is distinctively a Gospel for the Romans—explaining Jewish customs, omitting all Jewish genealogies and birth narratives, translating Aramaic words, and using Latin terms. (3) The Gospel begins abruptly and proceeds rapidly from one episode to another with the frequent use of the Greek adverb for "immediately" (42 times). (4) Mark describes the events of Jesus' life succinctly and vividly, and with the picturesque skill of a literary artist.

Reading Mark

In order to read the entire New Testament in one year, the book of Mark should be read in 29 days, according to the following schedule:
☐ 1:1–20 ☐ 1:21–45 ☐ 2:1–22 ☐ 2:23–3:12 ☐ 3:13–35 ☐ 4:1–20 ☐ 4:21–41 ☐ 5:1–20 ☐ 5:21–43 ☐ 6:1–29 ☐ 6:30–56 ☐ 7:1–23 ☐ 7:24–8:13 ☐ 8:14–26 ☐ 8:27–9:13 ☐ 9:14–32 ☐ 9:33–50 ☐ 10:1–31 ☐ 10:32–52 ☐ 11:1–26 ☐ 11:27–12:17 ☐ 12:18–44 ☐ 13 ☐ 14:1–26 ☐ 14:27–52 ☐ 14:53–72 ☐ 15:1–20 ☐ 15:21–47 ☐ 16

NOTES

John the Baptist

1:2–6pp — Mat. 3:1–10; Luke 3:2–15

1 THE BEGINNING of the gospel of Jesus Christ, [a]the Son of God;

2 As it is written in the prophets, [b]Behold, I send my messenger before thy face, which shall prepare thy way before thee.

3 [c]The voice of one crying in the wilderness, Prepare ye the way of the Lord, make his paths straight.

4 [d]John did baptize in the wilderness, and preach the baptism of repentance [a]for the remission of sins.

5 [e]And there went out unto him all the land of Judaea, and they of Jerusalem, and were all baptized of him in the river of Jordan, confessing their sins.

6 And John was [f]clothed with camel's hair, and with a girdle of a skin about his loins; and he did eat locusts and wild honey;

Jesus will baptize us with the Spirit

1:7–8pp — Mat. 3:11; Luke 3:16

7 And preached, saying, [g]There cometh one mightier than I after me, the latchet of whose shoes I am not worthy to stoop down and unloose.

8 [h]I indeed have baptized you with water: but he shall baptize you [i]with the Holy Ghost.

Baptism and temptation of Jesus

1:9–11pp — Mat. 3:13–17; Luke 3:21–22
1:12–13pp — Mat. 4:1–11; Luke 4:1–13

9 [j]And it came to pass in those days, that Jesus came from Nazareth of Galilee, and was baptized of John in Jordan.

10 [k]And straightway coming up out of the water, he saw the heavens [b]opened, and the Spirit like a dove descending upon him:

11 And there came a voice from heaven, *saying,* [l]Thou art my beloved Son, in whom I am well pleased.

12 [m]And immediately the Spirit driveth him into the wilderness.

13 And he was there in the wilderness forty days, tempted of Satan; and was with the wild beasts; [n]and the angels ministered unto him.

14 [o]Now after that John was put in prison, Jesus came into Galilee, [p]preaching the gospel of the kingdom of God,

15 And saying, [q]The time is ful-

1:1 [a]Mat. 14:33 Luke 1:35 John 1:34 **1:2** [b]Mal. 3:1 Mat. 11:10 Luke 7:27 **1:3** [c]Is. 40:3 Mat. 3:3 Luke 3:4 John 1:15,23 **1:4** [d]Mat. 3:1 Luke 3:3 John 3:23 **1:5** [e]Mat. 3:5 **1:6** [f]Mat. 3:4 **1:7** [g]Mat. 3:11 John 1:27 Acts 13:25 **1:8** [h]Acts 1:5 & 11:16 & 19:4 [i]Is. 44:3 Joel 2:28 Acts 2:4 & 10:45 & 11:15,16 1 Cor. 12:13 Luke 1:15 **1:9** [j]Mat. 3:13 Luke 3:21 **1:10** [k]Mat. 3:16 John 1:32 **1:11** [l]Ps. 2:7 Mat. 3:17 ch. 9:7 **1:12** [m]Mat. 4:1 Luke 4:1

1:13 [n]Mat. 4:11 **1:14** [o]Mat. 4:12 [p]Mat. 4:23 **1:15** [q]Dan. 9:25; Gal. 4:4; Eph. 1:10

[a] Or, *unto* [b] Or, *cloven,* or, *rent*

1:4 REPENTANCE. See Mat. 3:2, note.

1:5 ALL THE LAND OF JUDEA. There was a general spiritual awakening in Judea and Galilee that accompanied the ministry of John the Baptist. The spiritual climate of Israel changed among the common people as a result, helping prepare the way for the full revelation of God in His incarnate Son, Jesus Christ.

1:7–8 BAPTIZE YOU WITH THE HOLY GHOST. John the Baptist was the first one who preached the good news concerning Jesus; his preaching is condensed by Mark into one single theme: the proclamation of Jesus Christ, who would come and baptize His followers in the Holy Spirit. All those who accept Christ as Lord and Savior should proclaim that Jesus is still the One who baptizes in the Holy Spirit (see Acts 1:8; 2:4, 38–39; see Mat. 3:11, note on the promised baptism in the Holy Spirit).

1:9 JESUS . . . BAPTIZED. See Mat. 3:13, note.

1:10 THE SPIRIT . . . DESCENDING UPON HIM. See Mat. 3:16, note.

1:11 MY BELOVED SON. All three persons of the Trinity are involved in Jesus' baptism (see Mat. 3:17, note). Here and elsewhere in Scripture God is revealed as one essence existing in three distinct persons who share a common divine nature: Father, Son, and Holy Spirit (cf. Mat. 3:16–17; 28:19; 2 Cor. 13:14; Eph. 4:4–6; 1 Pet. 1:2; Jude 20–21). Thus God is singular (i.e., a unity) in one sense and plural (i.e., three) in another (see article on THE ATTRIBUTES OF GOD, p. 912. (1) Scripture declares that God is one Being—a perfect unity of one nature, substance, and essence (Deut. 6:4; Mark 12:29; Gal. 3:20). Of the persons in the Godhead none is God without the others and each with the others is God.

(2) The one God exists in a plurality of three identifiable, distinct, though not separate, persons. The three are not three gods or three parts or expressions of God, but are three persons so completely united that they form the one true and eternal God. Both the Son and the Holy Spirit possess attributes which can only be true of God (see Gen. 1:2; Is. 61:1; John 1:1,14, note; 5:18, note; 14:16; 16:8,13; 20:28, note; Acts 5:3–4; Rom. 8:2, 26–27; 1 Cor. 2:10–11; 2 Thes. 2:13; Heb. 9:14). None of the three persons was ever made or created, but each exists equal in essential being, attributes, power, and glory.

(3) This one God existing in three persons made possible from all eternity reciprocal love, fellowship, the exercise of divine attributes, mutual communion in knowledge, and interrelationship within the Godhead (cf. John 10:15; 11:27; 17:24; 1 Cor. 2:10).

1:13 TEMPTED OF SATAN. See Mat. 4:1, note.

1:14 THE GOSPEL. See 14:9, note.

1:15 KINGDOM OF GOD. Christ came to pro-

filled, and [r]the kingdom of God is at hand: repent ye, and believe the gospel.

Jesus calls four disciples

1:16–20pp — Mat. 4:18–22; Luke 5:2–11; John 1:35–42

16 [s]Now as he walked by the sea of Galilee, he saw Simon and Andrew his brother casting a net into the sea: for they were fishers.

17 And Jesus said unto them, Come ye after me, and I will make you to become fishers of men.

18 And straightway [t]they forsook their nets, and followed him.

19 [u]And when he had gone a little farther thence, he saw James the *son* of Zebedee, and John his brother, who also were in the ship mending their nets.

20 And straightway he called them: and they left their father Zebedee in the ship with the hired servants, and went after him.

The unclean spirit cast out

1:21–28pp — Luke 4:31–37

21 [v]And they went into Capernaum; and straightway on the sabbath day he entered into the synagogue, and taught.

22 [w]And they were astonished at his doctrine: for he taught them as one that had authority, and not as the scribes.

23 And there was in their synagogue a man with an unclean spirit; and he cried out,

24 Saying, Let *us* alone; [x]what have we to do with thee, thou Jesus of Nazareth? art thou come to destroy us? I know thee who thou art, the Holy One of God.

25 And Jesus [y]rebuked him, saying, Hold thy peace, and come out of him.

26 And when the unclean spirit [z]had torn him, and cried with a loud voice, he came out of him.

27 And they were all amazed, insomuch that they questioned among themselves, saying, What thing is this? what new doctrine *is* this? for with authority commandeth he even the unclean spirits, and they do obey him.

28 And immediately his fame spread abroad throughout all the region round about Galilee.

Mark 3:10-15

The sick healed; devils cast out

1:29–31pp — Mat. 8:14–15; Luke 4:38–39
1:32–34pp — Mat. 8:16–17; Luke 4:40–41

29 [a]And forthwith, when they were come out of the synagogue, they entered into the house of Simon and Andrew, with James and John.

30 But Simon's wife's mother lay

1:15 [r]Mat. 3:2 & 4:17 **1:16** [s]Mat. 4:18 Luke 5:4 **1:18** [t]Mat. 19:27 Luke 5:11 **1:19** [u]Mat. 4:21 **1:21** [v]Mat. 4:13 Luke 4:31 **1:22** [w]Mat. 7:28 **1:24** [x]Mat. 8:29 **1:25** [y]ver. 34 **1:26** [z]ch. 9:20 **1:29** [a]Mat. 8:14 Luke 4:38

claim and bring to completion the kingdom of God. This was the theme of His earthly message (Mat. 4:17). Concerning the form of its appearing, we should be aware of several aspects of the kingdom:

(1) The kingdom in Israel. The kingdom in the O.T. was God's redemptive action within Israel in order to prepare the way for the salvation of the human race (see article on GOD'S COVENANT WITH ABRAHAM, ISAAC, AND JACOB, p. 48). Because Israel rejected Jesus, the Messiah, the kingdom was taken away from them (see Mat. 21:43, note).

(2) The kingdom in Christ. The kingdom and its power were present in the person and work of Jesus the King (Luke 11:20).

(3) The kingdom in the church. This involves the present manifestation of God's power and rule in the hearts and lives of all who repent and believe the gospel (John 3:3,5; Rom. 14:17; Col. 1:13). Its presence comes with great spiritual power, asserting itself against the dominion of Satan, sin, and evil. It is not a political or material kingdom, but a powerful and forceful presence and activity of God among His people (see 1:27; 9:1; see article on THE KINGDOM OF GOD, p. 1428, for a detailed description of the kingdom of God in the church age).

(4) The kingdom in the consummation. This is the Messianic kingdom foretold by the prophets (Ps. 89:36–37; Is. 11:1–9; Dan. 7:13–14). Christ will reign on earth for a thousand years (Rev. 20:4–6), and the church will reign with Him over the nations (1 Cor. 6:2–3; 2 Tim. 2:12; Rev. 2:26–27; see 20:4, notes).

(5) The kingdom in eternity. The Messianic kingdom will terminate after a thousand years and God's eternal kingdom will be established in the new heaven and new earth (Rev. 21:1–4). The center of the new earth is the holy city, the New Jerusalem (Rev. 21:9–11). Its inhabitants are the redeemed from the O.T. (Rev. 21:12) and the N.T. (Rev. 21:14). Their greatest blessing is, "They shall see his face" (Rev. 22:4; see 21:1, note).

1:17 COME YE AFTER ME. The first calling of the disciples is to follow Jesus and to personally know Him (Phil. 3:8–10). As a result of this relationship, they must then lead others to a saving knowledge of Jesus (cf. Prov. 11:30; Dan. 12:3; 1 Cor. 9:22).

1:27 UNCLEAN SPIRITS . . . OBEY HIM. See article on POWER OVER SATAN AND DEMONS, p. 1486, for comments on this text.

sick of a fever, and anon they tell him
of her.
31 And he came and took her by the
hand, and lifted her up; and immediate-
ly the fever left her, and she ministered
unto them.
32 [b]And at even, when the sun did
set, they brought unto him all that
were diseased, and them that were
possessed with devils.
33 And all the city was gathered to-
gether at the door.
34 And he healed many that were
sick of divers diseases, and cast out
many devils; and [c]suffered not the
devils [c]to speak, because they knew
him.

Jesus preaches in Galilee

1:35–38pp — Luke 4:42–43

35 And [d]in the morning, rising up
a great while before day, he went out,
and departed into a solitary place, and
there prayed.
36 And Simon and they that were
with him followed after him.
37 And when they had found him,
they said unto him, All *men* seek for
thee.
38 And he said unto them, [e]Let us
go into the next towns, that I may
preach there also: for [f]therefore came
I forth.
39 [g]And he preached in their syna-
gogues throughout all Galilee, and cast
out devils.

The leper cleansed

1:40–44pp — Mat. 8:2–4; Luke 5:12–14

40 [h]And there came a leper to him,
beseeching him, and kneeling down to
him, and saying unto him, If thou wilt,
thou canst make me clean.
41 And Jesus, moved with compas-
sion, put forth *his* hand, and touched
him, and saith unto him, I will; be thou
clean.
42 And as soon as he had spoken,
immediately the leprosy departed from
him, and he was cleansed.
43 And he straitly charged him, and
forthwith sent him away;
44 And saith unto him, See thou say
nothing to any man: but go thy way,
show thyself to the priest, and offer for

1:32 [b]Mat. 8:16 Luke 4:40
1:34 [c]ch. 3:12 Luke 4:41 See Acts 16:17,18
1:35 [d]Luke 4:42
1:38 [e]Luke 4:43 [f]Is. 61:1 John 16:28 & 17:4
1:39 [g]Mat. 4:23 Luke 4:44
1:40 [h]Mat. 8:2 Luke 5:12
1:44 [i]Lev. 14:3,4,10
1:45 [j]Luke 5:15 [k]ch. 2:13
2:1 [l]Mat. 9:1
2:7 [m]Job 14:4 Is. 43:25
2:9 [n]Mat. 9:5

thy cleansing those things [i]which
Moses commanded, for a testimony
unto them.
45 [j]But he went out, and began to
publish *it* much, and to blaze abroad
the matter, insomuch that Jesus could
no more openly enter into the city, but
was without in desert places: [k]and
they came to him from every quarter.

Jesus heals a paralytic

2:3–12pp — Mat. 9:2–8; Luke 5:18–26

2 AND AGAIN [l]he entered into Ca-
pernaum after *some* days; and it
was noised that he was in the house.
2 And straightway many were gath-
ered together, insomuch that there
was no room to receive *them*, no, not so
much as about the door: and he
preached the word unto them.
3 And they come unto him, bringing
one sick of the palsy, which was borne
of four.
4 And when they could not come
nigh unto him for the press, they un-
covered the roof where he was: and
when they had broken *it* up, they let
down the bed wherein the sick of the
palsy lay.
5 When Jesus saw their faith, he
said unto the sick of the palsy, Son, thy
sins be forgiven thee.
6 But there were certain of the
scribes sitting there, and reasoning in
their hearts,
7 Why doth this *man* thus speak
blasphemies? [m]who can forgive sins
but God only?
8 And immediately when Jesus per-
ceived in his spirit that they so rea-
soned within themselves, he said unto
them, Why reason ye these things in
your hearts?
9 [n]Whether is it easier to say to the
sick of the palsy, *Thy* sins be forgiven
thee; or to say, Arise, and take up thy
bed, and walk?
10 But that ye may know that the
Son of man hath power on earth to for-
give sins, (he saith to the sick of the
palsy,)
11 I say unto thee, Arise, and take

[c] Or, *to say that they knew him*

1:34 CAST OUT MANY DEVILS. See article on POWER OVER SATAN AND DEMONS, p. 1486.
2:10 SON OF MAN. See Luke 5:24, note.
2:11 HEALING THE PARALYZED MAN. It was never God's intention that people should live with sickness, disease, and death. These things are the results of the sinfulness of the human race and the activity of Satan in the world. Consequent-

up thy bed, and go thy way into thine house.

12 And immediately he arose, took up the bed, and went forth before them all; insomuch that they were all amazed, and glorified God, saying, We never saw it on this fashion.

Mark 5:25-34

Matthew called

2:14–17pp — Mat. 9:9–13; Luke 5:27–32

13 [o]And he went forth again by the sea side; and all the multitude resorted unto him, and he taught them.

14 [p]And as he passed by, he saw Levi the *son* of Alphaeus sitting [d]at the receipt of custom, and said unto him, Follow me. And he arose and followed him.

15 [q]And it came to pass, that, as Jesus sat at meat in his house, many publicans and sinners sat also together with Jesus and his disciples: for there were many, and they followed him.

16 And when the scribes and Pharisees saw him eat with publicans and sinners, they said unto his disciples, How is it that he eateth and drinketh with publicans and sinners?

17 When Jesus heard *it*, he saith unto them, [r]They that are whole have no need of the physician, but they that are sick: I came not to call the righteous, but sinners to repentance.

The question about fasting

2:18–22pp — Mat. 9:14–17; Luke 5:33–38

18 [s]And the disciples of John and of the Pharisees used to fast: and they come and say unto him, Why do the disciples of John and of the Pharisees fast, but thy disciples fast not?

19 And Jesus said unto them, Can the children of the bridechamber fast, while the bridegroom is with them? as long as they have the bridegroom with them, they cannot fast.

20 But the days will come, when the bridegroom shall be taken away from them, and then shall they fast in those days.

21 No man also seweth a piece of [e]new cloth on an old garment: else the new piece that filled it up taketh away from the old, and the rent is made worse.

22 And no man putteth new wine into old bottles: else the new wine doth burst the bottles, and the wine is spilled, and the bottles will be marred: but new wine must be put into new bottles.

Jesus the Lord of the Sabbath

2:23–28pp — Mat. 12:1–8; Luke 6:1–5
3:1–6pp — Mat. 12:9–14; Luke 6:6–11

23 [t]And it came to pass, that he went through the corn fields on the sabbath day; and his disciples began, as they went, [u]to pluck the ears of corn.

24 And the Pharisees said unto him, Behold, why do they on the sabbath day that which is not lawful?

25 And he said unto them, Have ye never read [v]what David did, when he had need, and was an hungered, he, and they that were with him?

26 How he went into the house of God in the days of Abiathar the high priest, and did eat the showbread, [w]which is not lawful to eat but for the priests, and gave also to them which were with him?

27 And he said unto them, The sabbath was made for man, and not man for the sabbath:

28 Therefore [x]the Son of man is Lord also of the sabbath.

3 AND [y]HE entered again into the synagogue; and there was a man there which had a withered hand.

2 And they watched him, whether he would heal him on the sabbath day; that they might accuse him.

3 And he saith unto the man

2:13 [o]Mat. 9:9
2:14 [p]Mat. 9:9; Luke 5:27
2:15 [q]Mat. 9:10
2:17 [r]Mat. 9:12,13 & 18:11; Luke 5:31,32 & 19:10; 1 Tim. 1:15
2:18 [s]Mat. 9:14; Luke 5:33
2:23 [t]Mat. 12:1; Luke 6:1; [u]Deut. 23:25
2:25 [v]1 Sam. 21:6
2:26 [w]Ex. 29:32,33; Lev. 24:9
2:28 [x]Mat. 12:8
3:1 [y]Mat. 12:9; Luke 6:6

[d] Or, *at the place where the custom was received*
[e] Or, *raw*, or, *unwrought*

ly, every healing through Christ involves God invading and driving back death and the realm of Satan (see article on DIVINE HEALING, p. 1418).

2:17 SINNERS TO REPENTANCE. See Mat. 9:11, note.

2:20 THEN SHALL THEY FAST. See Mat. 9:15, note.

2:22 NEW WINE INTO OLD BOTTLES. See Mat. 9:17, note.

2:23 SABBATH DAY. See Mat. 12:1, note.

2:27 THE SABBATH WAS MADE FOR MAN. The Sabbath was instituted by God as a blessing for humans (see Ex. 20:8, note). On this day we must refrain from our daily work. Instead we must worship God and seek fellowship with Him, in order to keep ourselves physically healthy and spiritually strong and refreshed (Is. 58:13–14). Those who ignore the principle of the Sabbath do so to their own ruin (see Mat. 12:1, note).

which had the withered hand, [f]Stand
forth.
4 And he saith unto them, Is it law-
ful to do good on the sabbath days, or
to do evil? to save life, or to kill? But
they held their peace.
5 And when he had looked round
about on them with anger, being
grieved for the [g]hardness of their
hearts, he saith unto the man, Stretch
forth thine hand. And he stretched *it*
out: and his hand was restored whole
as the other.
6 [z]And the Pharisees went forth,
and straightway took counsel with
[a]the Herodians against him, how they
might destroy him.

Jesus heals many by the sea

3:7–12pp — Mat. 12:15–16; Luke 6:17–19

7 But Jesus withdrew himself with
his disciples to the sea: and a great
multitude from Galilee followed him,
[b]and from Judaea,
8 And from Jerusalem, and from
Idumaea, and *from* beyond Jordan; and
they about Tyre and Sidon, a great
multitude, when they had heard what
great things he did, came unto him.
9 And he spake to his disciples, that
a small ship should wait on him be-
cause of the multitude, lest they
should throng him.
10 For he had healed many; in-
somuch that they [h]pressed upon him
for to touch him, as many as had
plagues.
11 [c]And unclean spirits, when
they saw him, fell down before him,
and cried, saying, [d]Thou art the Son
of God.

3:6 [z]Mat. 12:14 [a]Mat. 22:16
3:7 [b]Luke 6:17
3:11 [c]ch. 1:23,24 Luke 4:41 [d]Mat. 14:33 ch. 1:1
3:12 [e]Mat. 12:16 ch. 1:25,34
3:13 [f]Mat. 10:1 Luke 6:12 & 9:1
3:16 [g]John 1:42
3:20 [h]ch. 6:31
3:21 [i]John 7:5 & 10:20

12 And [e]he straitly charged them
that they should not make him known.

The Twelve appointed

3:16–19pp — Mat. 10:2–4; Luke 6:14–16; Acts 1:13

13 [f]And he goeth up into a moun-
tain, and calleth *unto him* whom he
would: and they came unto him.
14 And he ordained twelve, that
they should be with him, and that he
might send them forth to preach,
15 And to have power to heal sick- Mark 3:20-27
nesses, and to cast out devils:
16 And Simon [g]he surnamed Pe-
ter;
17 And James the *son* of Zebedee,
and John the brother of James; and he
surnamed them Boanerges, which is,
The sons of thunder:
18 And Andrew, and Philip, and
Bartholomew, and Matthew, and
Thomas, and James the *son* of Alphae-
us, and Thaddaeus, and Simon the Ca-
naanite,
19 And Judas Iscariot, which also
betrayed him: and they went [i]into an
house.

Jesus and Satan

3:23–27pp — Mat. 12:25–29; Luke 11:17–22

20 And the multitude cometh to-
gether again, [h]so that they could not
so much as eat bread.
21 And when his [j]friends heard *of*
it, they went out to lay hold on him:
[i]for they said, He is beside himself.
22 ¶ And the scribes which came

[f] Gk. *Arise,* stand forth *in the midst* [g] Or, *blindness* [h] Or, *rushed* [i] Or, *home* [j] Or, *kinsmen*

3:5 LOOKED . . . WITH ANGER. The anger of Jesus indicates His hatred and disapproval of all unrighteousness and injustice (see Heb. 1:9, note). Though the Christian must resist unrighteous anger (Gal. 5:20; Col. 3:8), it is thoroughly Christlike to be angry at evil (Ex. 32:19; 1 Sam. 11:6; 2 Sam. 12:5; Neh. 5:6). Indignation at the sins of one's generation is evidence of the believer placing himself on the side of God against evil (Ex. 32:19; 1 Sam. 11:6; Ps. 94:16; Jer. 6:11; Acts 17:16).

3:10 HEALED MANY. See article on DIVINE HEALING, p. 1418.

3:15 POWER . . . TO CAST OUT DEVILS. In coming to earth, Jesus' purpose was to destroy the works of the devil (1:27; 1 John 3:8) and set at liberty those who were oppressed by Satan and sin (Luke 4:18; see article on POWER OVER SATAN AND DEMONS, p. 1486). Inherent in this purpose was the power and authority He gave His followers to continue His battle against the forces of darkness. This truth is verified by the following observations.

(1) It is recorded that after Jesus appointed the twelve disciples, He gave them "power . . . to cast out devils" (vv. 14–15; cf. Mat. 10:1). After He appointed the seventy, He gave them "power . . . over all the power of the enemy" (Luke 10:1, 17–19; cf. Mat. 10:1–8; Mark 6:7,13).

(2) The disciples were not only to "go forth and preach" (v. 14; Mat. 10:7), but also to manifest the kingdom's rule, power, and authority by doing battle against Satan, casting out demons, and healing every kind of disease and every kind of sickness (Mat. 10:1,7–8, notes).

(3) Mark teaches that Jesus, after His resurrection, reemphasized to His followers their task of preaching the gospel and their authority over Satan and his demons (see article on SIGNS OF BELIEVERS, p. 1516).

down from Jerusalem said, [j]He hath Beelzebub, and by the prince of the devils casteth he out devils.

23 [k]And he called them *unto him*, and said unto them in parables, How can Satan cast out Satan?

24 And if a kingdom be divided against itself, that kingdom cannot stand.

25 And if a house be divided against itself, that house cannot stand.

26 And if Satan rise up against himself, and be divided, he cannot stand, but hath an end.

27 [l]No man can enter into a strong man's house, and spoil his goods, except he will first bind the strong man; and then he will spoil his house.

Mark 5:1-16

Blasphemy against the Holy Spirit

3:28–29pp — Mat. 12:31–32; Luke 12:10

28 [m]Verily I say unto you, All sins shall be forgiven unto the sons of men, and blasphemies wherewith soever they shall blaspheme:

29 But he that shall blaspheme against the Holy Ghost hath never forgiveness, but is in danger of eternal damnation:

30 Because they said, He hath an unclean spirit.

Jesus' true family

3:31–35pp — Mat. 12:46–50; Luke 8:19–21

31 ¶ [n]There came then his brethren and his mother, and, standing without, sent unto him, calling him.

32 And the multitude sat about him, and they said unto him, Behold, thy mother and thy brethren without seek for thee.

33 And he answered them, saying, Who is my mother, or my brethren?

34 And he looked round about on them which sat about him, and said, Behold my mother and my brethren!

35 For whosoever shall do the will of God, the same is my brother, and my sister, and mother.

Parable of the sower

4:1–12pp — Mat. 13:1–15; Luke 8:4–10
4:13–20pp — Mat. 13:18–23; Luke 8:11–15

4 AND [o]HE began again to teach by the sea side: and there was gathered unto him a great multitude, so that he entered into a ship, and sat in the sea; and the whole multitude was by the sea on the land.

2 And he taught them many things by parables, [p]and said unto them in his doctrine,

3 Hearken; Behold, there went out a sower to sow:

4 And it came to pass, as he sowed, some fell by the way side, and the fowls of the air came and devoured it up.

5 And some fell on stony ground, where it had not much earth; and immediately it sprang up, because it had no depth of earth:

6 But when the sun was up, it was scorched; and because it had no root, it withered away.

7 And some fell among thorns, and the thorns grew up, and choked it, and it yielded no fruit.

8 And other fell on good ground, [q]and did yield fruit that sprang up and increased; and brought forth, some thirty, and some sixty, and some an hundred.

9 And he said unto them, He that hath ears to hear, let him hear.

10 [r]And when he was alone, they that were about him with the twelve asked of him the parable.

11 And he said unto them, Unto you it is given to know the mystery of the kingdom of God: but unto [s]them that are without, all *these* things are done in parables:

12 [t]That seeing they may see, and not perceive; and hearing they may hear, and not understand; lest at any

3:22 [j]Mat. 9:34 & 10:25 Luke 11:15 John 7:20 & 8:48,52 & 10:20
3:23 [k]Mat. 12:25
3:27 [l]Is. 49:24 Mat. 12:29
3:28 [m]Mat. 12:31 Luke 12:10 1 John 5:16
3:31 [n]Mat. 12:46 Luke 8:19
4:1 [o]Mat. 13:1 Luke 8:4
4:2 [p]ch. 12:38
4:8 [q]John 15:5 Col. 1:6
4:10 [r]Mat. 13:10 Luke 8:9
4:11 [s]1 Cor. 5:12 Col. 4:5 1 Thes. 4:12 1 Tim. 3:7
4:12 [t]Is. 6:9 Mat. 13:14 Luke 8:10 John 12:40 Acts. 28:26 Rom. 11:8

3:27 BIND THE STRONG MAN. See article on POWER OVER SATAN AND DEMONS, p. 1486.

3:29 BLASPHEME AGAINST THE HOLY GHOST. See Mat. 12:31, note.

4:2 PARABLES. Jesus often taught in parables. A parable is a simple story from everyday life that reveals truth to those whose hearts are prepared to hear, and conceals truth from those whose hearts are unprepared (cf. Is. 6:9–10; see Mat. 13:3, note).

4:3 THERE WENT OUT A SOWER. Jesus uses this parable to tell how the gospel will be received in the world. Three truths may be learned: (1) Conversion and fruitfulness depend on how one responds to God's Word (v. 14; cf. John 15:1–10). (2) There will be a mixed reaction to the gospel by the world. Some who hear will not understand (v. 15); others will believe unto salvation, but will later fall away (vv. 16–19); still others will persevere and bear fruit in varying degrees (v. 20). (3) The enemies of God's Word are Satan, worldly concerns, riches, and pleasures (vv. 15,19).

time they should be converted, and *their* sins should be forgiven them.

13 And he said unto them, Know ye not this parable? and how then will ye know all parables?

14 ¶ [u]The sower soweth the word.

15 And these are they by the way side, where the word is sown; but when they have heard, Satan cometh immediately, and taketh away the word that was sown in their hearts.

16 And these are they likewise which are sown on stony ground; who, when they have heard the word, immediately receive it with gladness;

17 And have no root in themselves, and so endure but for a time: afterward, when affliction or persecution ariseth for the word's sake, immediately they are offended.

18 And these are they which are sown among thorns; such as hear the word,

19 And the cares of this world, [v]and the deceitfulness of riches, and the lusts of other things entering in, choke the word, and it becometh unfruitful.

20 And these are they which are sown on good ground; such as hear the word, and receive *it*, and bring forth fruit, some thirtyfold, some sixty, and some an hundred.

A lamp on a stand

21 ¶ [w]And he said unto them, Is a candle brought to be put under a [k]bushel, or under a bed? and not to be set on a candlestick?

22 [x]For there is nothing hid, which shall not be manifested; neither was any thing kept secret, but that it should come abroad.

23 [y]If any man have ears to hear, let him hear.

24 And he said unto them, Take heed what ye hear: [z]with what measure ye mete, it shall be measured to you: and unto you that hear shall more be given.

25 [a]For he that hath, to him shall be given: and he that hath not, from him shall be taken even that which he hath.

Parable of the growing grain

26 ¶ And he said, [b]So is the kingdom of God, as if a man should cast seed into the ground;

27 And should sleep, and rise night and day, and the seed should spring and grow up, he knoweth not how.

28 For the earth bringeth forth fruit of herself; first the blade, then the ear, after that the full corn in the ear.

29 But when the fruit is [l]brought forth, immediately [c]he putteth in the sickle, because the harvest is come.

Parable of the mustard seed

4:30–32pp — Mat. 13:31–32; Luke 13:18–19

30 ¶ And he said, [d]Whereunto shall we liken the kingdom of God? or with what comparison shall we compare it?

31 *It is* like a grain of mustard seed, which, when it is sown in the earth, is less than all the seeds that be in the earth:

32 But when it is sown, it groweth

4:14 [u]Mat. 13:19
4:19 [v]1 Tim. 6:9,17
4:21 [w]Mat. 5:15 Luke 8:16 & 11:33
4:22 [x]Mat. 10:26
4:23 [y]ver. 9 Mat. 11:15
4:24 [z]Mat. 7:2 Luke 6:38
4:25 [a]Mat. 13:12 & 25:29 Luke 8:18 & 19:26
4:26 [b]Mat. 13:24
4:29 [c]Rev. 14:15
4:30 [d]Mat. 13:31 Luke 13:18 Acts 2:41 & 4:4 & 5:14 & 19:20

[k] The word in the original signifies a less measure; see Mat. 5:15 [l] Or, *ripe*

4:15 TAKETH AWAY THE WORD. Christ speaks here about an incomplete conversion—one in which an individual seeks forgiveness of his sins but falls short of actual regeneration by the Holy Spirit (see article on REGENERATION, p. 1597). He does not receive salvation and the new birth and never enters into fellowship with believers; or if he does become a church member, he fails to show real commitment to Christ and separation from the world.

Halfway conversions result from the following: (1) The church deals with a seeker quickly without communicating to him a proper understanding of the gospel and its demands. (2) The church fails to deal with the demonic bondage of the seeker (Mat. 10:1,8; 12:22–29; Mark 16:15–17). (3) The seeker believes in Christ only with his mind, not his whole heart (i.e., his innermost being, his whole personality; cf. Acts 2:37; 2 Cor. 4:6). (4) The seeker fails to repent in true sincerity or to turn from sin (cf. Mat. 3:2; Acts 8:18–23). (5) The seeker wants to accept Christ as Savior, but not as Lord (Mat. 13:20–21). (6) The seeker's faith is based on the persuasiveness of human words rather than on the demonstration of the Spirit and the power of God (1 Cor. 2:4–5).

4:25 TAKEN EVEN THAT WHICH HE HATH. Jesus states a principle of His kingdom here. Believers must continue to acquire truth and grace or they will lose even what they have. Growth in grace or spiritual decline may be hardly perceptible in the lives of many. Nevertheless, it is a fact that a Christian either grows or degenerates (2 Pet. 3:17–18). The peril of final apostasy increases in proportion as one declines spiritually (Heb. 3:12–15; 4:11; 6:11–12; 10:23–39; 12:15; see article on PERSONAL APOSTASY, p. 1946).

4:31 MUSTARD SEED. See Luke 13:19, note.

POWER OVER SATAN AND DEMONS

***Mark 3:27** "No man can enter into a strong man's house, and spoil his goods, except he will first bind the strong man; then he will spoil his house."*

One of the primary emphases in Mark's Gospel is Jesus' overriding concern to defeat Satan and his demonic powers; in 3:27, this is phrased as "binding the strong man" (i.e., Satan) and "spoiling his house" (i.e., setting at liberty those who are enslaved to Satan). This power over Satan is especially evident in the casting out of demons (Gk. *daimonion*) or evil spirits.

DEMONS. (1) The N.T. frequently refers to those who are suffering from Satan's oppression or influence because of the indwelling of an evil spirit, and to Jesus' conflict with demons. In the Gospel of Mark, for example, numerous such encounters are described: 1:23–28,32–34,39; 3:10–12,14–15; 5:1–20; 6:7,13; 7:24–30; 9:14–29; 16:17.

(2) Demons are spirit beings who have personality and intelligence. As members of Satan's kingdom and enemies of God and humans (Mat. 12:43–45), they are evil, malicious, and under Satan's authority (see Mat. 4:10, note).

(3) Demons are the power behind idol gods, so that the worship of false gods is essentially the worship of demons (see 1 Cor. 10:20, note; see article on THE NATURE OF IDOLATRY, p. 428).

(4) The N.T. presents the world as estranged from God and seized by Satan (see John 12:31, note; 2 Cor. 4:4; Eph. 6:10–12; see article on THE CHRISTIAN'S RELATIONSHIP TO THE WORLD, p. 2004). Demons are the rulers of this age, and Christians must wage continual warfare with them (see Eph. 6:12, note).

(5) Demons can, and often do, dwell in the bodies of unbelievers (see Mark 5:15; Luke 4:41; 8:27–28; Acts 16:18) and use their voices to talk. They enslave such individuals and influence them toward evil, immorality, and destruction.

(6) Demons can cause physical illness in the human body (Mat. 9:32–33; 12:22; 17:14–18; Luke 13:11,16), although not all sickness and disease are the result of evil spirits (Mat. 4:24; Luke 5:12–13).

(7) Those involved in spiritism and magic (i.e., sorcery) are dealing with evil spirits; this practice can easily lead to demonic bondage (cf. Acts 13:8–10; 19:19; Gal. 5:20; Rev. 9:20).

(8) Evil spirits will be especially active in the last days of this age, promoting the occult, immorality, violence, and cruelty; they will assault the Word of God and sound doctrine (Mat. 24:24; 2 Cor. 11:14–15; 1 Tim. 4:1). The ultimate occurrence of demonic activity will be in the antichrist and his followers (2 Thes. 2:9; Rev. 13:2–8; 16:13–14).

JESUS AND DEMONS. (1) In His miracles, Jesus often attacks the power of Satan and the demonic (e.g., Mark 1:25–26,34,39; 3:10–11; 5:1–20; 9:17–29; cf. Luke 13:16). One of His clearly stated purposes in coming to the earth was to bind Satan and set at liberty those enslaved by him (Mat. 12:29; Mark 1:27; Luke 4:18).

(2) Jesus' binding of Satan, accomplished in part through His casting out of demons and more completely in His death and resurrection (John 12:31–33), shatters the power of Satan's realm and restores the power of the kingdom of God (see article on THE KINGDOM OF GOD, p. 30).

(3) Hell (Gk. *Gehenna*), the place of torment, has been prepared by our Lord for the devil and his demons (Mat. 8:29; 25:41).

BELIEVERS AND DEMONS. (1) The Scriptures teach that no true believer who is indwelt by the Holy Spirit, can be demon possessed; that is, the Spirit and demons can never dwell in the same body (see 2 Cor. 6:15–16, note). Demons may, however, influence the thoughts, emotions, and actions of Christians who fail to follow the leading of the Holy Spirit (Mat. 16:23; 2 Cor. 11:3,14).

(2) Jesus promised true believers authority over the power of Satan and his cohorts. As we confront them, we must break the power they want to exert over us and others by waging intense spiritual warfare through the power of the Holy Spirit (see Luke 4:14–19). In this way we can be set free from the powers of darkness.

(3) According to the parable in Mark 3:27, spiritual conflict against Satan involves three separate aspects: (a) declaring war against Satan according to the purpose of God (see Luke 4:14–19); (b) entering Satan's house (any place where he has a stronghold), attacking and overpowering him by prayer and proclamation of the Word, and destroying his weapons of demonic deception and temptation (cf. Luke 11:20–22); (c) carrying off his possessions, i.e., delivering those who have been held captive by Satan's power and giving them over to God so that they may receive forgiveness and sanctification by faith in Christ (Luke 11:22; Acts 26:18).

(4) The following are the individual steps we must use in this process: (a) Recognize that we are not in a conflict against flesh and blood but against spiritual forces and powers of evil (Eph. 6:12). (b) Live a life before God, fervently committed to His truth and righteousness (Rom. 12:1–2; Eph. 6:14). (c) Have faith that Satan's power can be broken in any specific area of his domain (Acts 26:18; Eph. 6:16; 1 Thes. 5:8), and realize that the believer has powerful spiritual weapons which God has given for the destruction of Satan's strongholds (2 Cor. 10:4–5). (d) Proclaim the gospel of the kingdom in the fullness of the Holy Spirit (Mat. 4:23; Luke 1:15–17; Acts 1:8; 2:4; 8:12; Rom. 1:16; Eph. 6:15). (e) Challenge Satan and his power directly by believing in Jesus' name (Acts 16:16–18), by using the Word of God (Eph. 6:17), by praying in the Spirit (Acts 6:4; Eph. 6:18), by fasting (see Mat. 6:16, note; Mark 9:29), and by casting out demons (see Mat. 10:1, note; 12:28; 17:17–21; Mark 16:17; Luke 10:17; Acts 5:16; 8:7; 16:18; 19:12; see article on SIGNS OF BELIEVERS, p. 1516). (f) Pray especially for the Holy Spirit to produce conviction within the lost concerning sin, righteousness, and the coming judgment (John 16:7–11). (g) Pray for and eagerly desire the manifestation of the Spirit through gifts of healing, tongues, miracles, signs, and wonders (Acts 4:29–33; 10:38; 1 Cor. 12:7–11).

up, and becometh greater than all herbs, and shooteth out great branches; so that the fowls of the air may lodge under the shadow of it.

33 [e]And with many such parables spake he the word unto them, as they were able to hear *it*.

34 But without a parable spake he not unto them: and when they were alone, he expounded all things to his disciples.

The storm stilled

4:35–41pp — Mat. 8:18,23–27; Luke 8:22–25

35 [f]And the same day, when the even was come, he saith unto them, Let us pass over unto the other side.

36 And when they had sent away the multitude, they took him even as he was in the ship. And there were also with him other little ships.

37 And there arose a great storm of wind, and the waves beat into the ship, so that it was now full.

38 And he was in the hinder part of the ship, asleep on a pillow: and they awake him, and say unto him, Master, carest thou not that we perish?

39 And he arose, and rebuked the wind, and said unto the sea, Peace, be still. And the wind ceased, and there was a great calm.

Mark 9:23-24

40 And he said unto them, Why are ye so fearful? how is it that ye have no faith?

41 And they feared exceedingly, and said one to another, What manner of man is this, that even the wind and the sea obey him?

Devils cast out

5:1–17pp — Mat. 8:28–34; Luke 8:26–37
5:18–20pp — Luke 8:38–39

5 AND [g]THEY came over unto the other side of the sea, into the country of the Gadarenes.

2 And when he was come out of the ship, immediately there met him out of the tombs a man with an unclean spirit,

3 Who had *his* dwelling among the tombs; and no man could bind him, no, not with chains:

4 Because that he had been often bound with fetters and chains, and the chains had been plucked asunder by him, and the fetters broken in pieces: neither could any *man* tame him.

5 And always, night and day, he was in the mountains, and in the tombs, crying, and cutting himself with stones.

6 But when he saw Jesus afar off, he ran and worshipped him,

7 And cried with a loud voice, and said, What have I to do with thee, Jesus, *thou* Son of the most high God? I adjure thee by God, that thou torment me not.

8 For he said unto him, Come out of the man, *thou* unclean spirit.

9 And he asked him, What *is* thy name? And he answered, saying, My name *is* Legion: for we are many.

10 And he besought him much that he would not send them away out of the country.

11 Now there was there nigh unto the mountains a great herd of swine feeding.

12 And all the devils besought him, saying, Send us into the [h]swine, that we may enter into them.

13 And forthwith Jesus gave them leave. And the unclean spirits went out, and entered into the swine: and the herd ran violently down a steep place into the sea, (they were about two thousand;) and were choked in the sea.

14 And they that fed the swine fled, and told *it* in the city, and in the country. And they went out to see what it was that was done.

15 And they come to Jesus, and see him that was possessed with the devil, and had the legion, sitting, and clothed, and in his right mind: and they were afraid.

16 And they that saw *it* told them how it befell to him that was possessed with the devil, and *also* concerning the swine. Luke 4:2-13

17 And [i]they began to pray him to depart out of their coasts.

18 And when he was come into the ship, [j]he that had been possessed

4:33 [e]Mat. 13:34; John 16:12
4:35 [f]Mat. 8:18,23; Luke 8:22
5:1 [g]Mat. 8:28; Luke 8:26
5:12 [h]Lev. 11:7; Deut. 14:8; Is. 65:4; Luke 15:15
5:17 [i]Mat. 8:34; Acts 16:39
5:18 [j]Luke 8:38

5:2 A MAN WITH AN UNCLEAN SPIRIT. A demon-possessed person is one who suffers from satanic oppression (Acts 10:38) or influence (Mat. 12:45; Acts 16:16–18) because an evil spirit dwells within him (see Luke 13:11, note). The Scriptures record many occasions in which Jesus cast out demons (for a full discussion on demons and the Christian's power over them, see article on POWER OVER SATAN AND DEMONS, p. 1486).

with the devil prayed him that he might be with him.

19 Howbeit Jesus suffered him not, but saith unto him, Go home to thy friends, and tell them how great things the Lord hath done for thee, and hath had compassion on thee.

20 And he departed, and began to publish in Decapolis how great things Jesus had done for him: and all *men* did marvel.

Jairus' daughter raised

5:22–43pp — Mat. 9:18–26; Luke 8:41–56

21 [k]And when Jesus was passed over again by ship unto the other side, much people gathered unto him: and he was nigh unto the sea.

22 [l]And, behold, there cometh one of the rulers of the synagogue, Jairus by name; and when he saw him, he fell at his feet,

23 And besought him greatly, saying, My little daughter lieth at the point of death: *I pray thee,* come and lay thy hands on her, that she may be healed; and she shall live.

24 And *Jesus* went with him; and much people followed him, and thronged him.

25 And a certain woman, [m]which had an issue of blood twelve years,

26 And had suffered many things of many physicians, and had spent all that she had, and was nothing bettered, but rather grew worse,

27 When she had heard of Jesus, came in the press behind, and touched his garment.

28 For she said, If I may touch but his clothes, I shall be whole.

29 And straightway the fountain of her blood was dried up; and she felt in *her* body that she was healed of that plague.

30 And Jesus, immediately knowing in himself that [n]virtue had gone out of him, turned him about in the press, and said, Who touched my clothes?

31 And his disciples said unto him, Thou seest the multitude thronging thee, and sayest thou, Who touched me?

32 And he looked round about to see her that had done this thing.

33 But the woman fearing and trembling, knowing what was done in her, came and fell down before him, and told him all the truth.

34 And he said unto her, Daughter, [o]thy faith hath made thee whole; go in peace, and be whole of thy plague. Mark 6:13

35 [p]While he yet spake, there came from the ruler of the synagogue's *house certain* which said, Thy daughter is dead: why troublest thou the Master any further?

36 As soon as Jesus heard the word that was spoken, he saith unto the ruler of the synagogue, Be not afraid, only believe.

37 And he suffered no man to follow him, save Peter, and James, and John the brother of James.

38 And he cometh to the house of the ruler of the synagogue, and seeth the tumult, and them that wept and wailed greatly.

39 And when he was come in, he saith unto them, Why make ye this ado, and weep? the damsel is not dead, but [q]sleepeth.

40 And they laughed him to scorn. [r]But when he had put them all out, he taketh the father and the mother of the damsel, and them that were with him, and entereth in where the damsel was lying.

41 And he took the damsel by the hand, and said unto her, Talitha cumi; which is, being interpreted, Damsel, I say unto thee, arise.

5:21 [k]Mat. 9:1 Luke 8:40
5:22 [l]Mat. 9:18 Luke 8:41
5:25 [m]Lev. 15:25 Mat. 9:20
5:30 [n]Luke 6:19 & 8:46
5:34 [o]Mat. 9:22 ch. 10:52 Acts 14:9
5:35 [p]Luke 8:49
5:39 [q]John 11:11
5:40 [r]Acts 9:40

5:28 TOUCH BUT HIS CLOTHES. The Gospels often speak of the sick touching Jesus (3:10; 5:27–34; 6:56) or of Jesus touching the sick (1:41–42; 7:33–35; Mat. 8:3,15; 9:29–30; 20:34; Luke 5:13; 7:14–15; 22:51). It was the contact and presence of Jesus that mattered. His touch has healing power because He sympathizes with our infirmities and is the source of life and grace (Heb. 4:16). Our responsibility in seeking healing is to draw near to Jesus and to abide in His presence (see Mat. 17:20, note on true faith).

5:36 ONLY BELIEVE. The daughter of the synagogue ruler had died (v. 35). Jesus' response was to encourage his faith even in this seemingly hopeless situation. Throughout redemptive history, believers placed their trust in God when it seemed as if all was lost. In such times, God gave the necessary faith and delivered His people according to His will and purpose (cf. Ps. 22:4; Is. 26:3–4; 43:2). This was true for Abraham (Gen. 22:2; Jas. 2:21–22), Moses (Ex. 14:10–22; 32:10–14), David (1 Sam. 17:44–47), Jehoshaphat (2 Chr. 20:1–2,12), and Jairus (vv. 21–23,35–42).

42 And straightway the damsel
arose, and walked; for she was *of the
age* of twelve years. And they were
astonished with a great astonish-
ment.
43 And [s]he charged them straitly
that no man should know it; and com-
manded that something should be giv-
en her to eat.

Jesus rejected at Nazareth

6:1–6pp — Mat. 13:54–58

6 AND [t]HE went out from thence,
and came into his own country;
and his disciples follow him.
2 And when the sabbath day was
come, he began to teach in the syna-
gogue: and many hearing *him* were as-
tonished, saying, [u]From whence hath
this *man* these things? and what wis-
dom *is* this which is given unto him,
that even such mighty works are
wrought by his hands?
3 Is not this the carpenter, the son
of Mary, [v]the brother of James, and
Joses, and of Judah, and Simon? and
are not his sisters here with us?
And they [w]were offended at him.
4 But Jesus said unto them, [x]A
prophet is not without honour, but in
his own country, and among his own
kin, and in his own house.
5 [y]And he could there do no mighty
work, save that he laid his hands upon
a few sick folk, and healed *them*.
6 And [z]he marvelled because of
their unbelief. [a]And he went round
about the villages, teaching.

5:43 [s]Mat. 8:4 & 9:30 & 12:16 & 17:19 ch. 3:12 Luke 5:14
6:1 [t]Mat. 13:54 Luke 4:16
6:2 [u]John 6:42
6:3 [v]See Mat. 12:46 Gal. 1:19 [w]Mat. 11:6
6:4 [x]Mat. 13:57 John 4:44
6:5 [y]See Gen. 19:22 & 32:25 Mat. 13:58 ch. 9:23
6:6 [z]Is. 59:16 [a]Mat. 9:35 Luke 13:22
6:7 [b]Mat. 10:1 ch. 3:13,14 Luke 9:1
6:9 [c]Acts 12:8
6:10 [d]Mat. 10:11 Luke 9:4 & 10:7,8
6:11 [e]Mat. 10:14 Luke 10:10 [f]Acts 13:51 & 18:6
6:13 [g]Jas. 5:14
6:14 [h]Mat. 14:1 Luke 9:7

The Twelve sent to cast out demons

6:7–11pp — Mat. 10:1,9–14; Luke 9:1,3–5

7 ¶ [b]And he called *unto him* the
twelve, and began to send them forth
by two and two; and gave them power
over unclean spirits;
8 And commanded them that they
should take nothing for *their* journey,
save a staff only; no scrip, no bread, no
[m]money in *their* purse:
9 But [c]*be* shod with sandals; and
not put on two coats.
10 [d]And he said unto them, In
what place soever ye enter into an
house, there abide till ye depart from
that place.
11 [e]And whosoever shall not re-
ceive you, nor hear you, when ye de-
part thence, [f]shake off the dust under
your feet for a testimony against them.
Verily I say unto you, It shall be more
tolerable for Sodom [n]and Gomorrha in
the day of judgment, than for that city.
12 And they went out, and preached
that men should repent.
13 And they cast out many devils, Mark
[g]and anointed with oil many that were 7:32-
sick, and healed *them*. 37

Death of John the Baptist

6:14–29pp — Mat. 14:1–12
6:14–16pp — Luke 9:7–9

14 [h]And king Herod heard *of him;*

[m] The word signifies *a piece of brass money,* worth about one cent, Mat. 10:9: but here it is taken in general for *money,* Luke 9:3
[n] Gk. *or*

6:4 JESUS . . . A PROPHET. Jesus is portrayed in the Gospels as a prophet (vv. 4,15; Mat. 21:11; Luke 4:24; cf. Acts 3:20–23), in keeping with the calling of a prophet in the O.T. (see article on THE PROPHET IN THE OLD TESTAMENT, p. 1002). The following characteristics identify Him as a prophet: (1) He was a man of the Spirit and the Word (Mat. 21:42; 22:29; Luke 4:1,18; 24:27; John 3:34). (2) He was in intimate communion with God (see Luke 5:16, note). (3) He gave prophetic predictions (Mat. 24; Luke 19:43–44). (4) He performed symbolic actions that expressed a zeal for God's honor (Mat. 21:12–13; John 2:13–17). (5) He exposed the hypocrisy of the religious leaders and criticized their adherence to traditions rather than God's Word (7:7–9,13). (6) He shared the pathos and suffering of God over the lost condition of those who refused to repent (Luke 13:34; 19:41). (7) He emphasized the ethical teaching of God's Word (holiness, justice, righteousness, love, mercy) in contrast to ceremonial observance (12:38–40; Mat. 23:1–36). (8) He proclaimed the impending reign and judgment of God on all evil (Mat. 11:22,24; 10:15; Luke 10:12,14). (9) He was a preacher of repentance, calling people to turn from sin and the world to God (v. 12; Mat. 4:17).

6:6 UNBELIEF. As lack of faith hindered the working of miracles in Jesus' hometown, so unbelief in the church still hinders the working of His power. Failure to believe Biblical truth, denial of the possibility of the gifts of the Spirit for today, or rejection of God's righteous standards will prevent our Lord from manifesting His kingdom power among His people. Believers must maintain a hunger for the Word and pray, "Lord, Increase our faith" (Luke 17:5).

6:7 UNCLEAN SPIRITS. See 3:15, note.

6:13 ANOINTED WITH OIL. Healing by anointing with oil is mentioned only here and in Jas. 5:14. The oil was probably used as a symbol of the presence and power of the Holy Spirit (see Zech. 4:3–6, notes) and as a point of contact to encourage faith.

(for his name was spread abroad:) and
he said, That John the Baptist was ris-
en from the dead, and therefore mighty
works do show forth themselves in
him.
15 [i]Others said, That it is Elias.
And others said, That it is a prophet,
or as one of the prophets.
16 [j]But when Herod heard *thereof*,
he said, It is John, whom I beheaded:
he is risen from the dead.
17 For Herod himself had sent forth
and laid hold upon John, and bound him
in prison for Herodias' sake, his broth-
er Philip's wife: for he had married her.
18 For John had said unto Herod,
[k]It is not lawful for thee to have thy
brother's wife.
19 Therefore Herodias had [o]a
quarrel against him, and would have
killed him; but she could not:
20 For Herod [l]feared John, know-
ing that he was a just man and an holy,
and [p]observed him; and when he
heard him, he did many things, and
heard him gladly.
21 [m]And when a convenient day
was come, that Herod [n]on his birthday
made a supper to his lords, high cap-
tains, and chief *estates* of Galilee;
22 And when the daughter of the
said Herodias came in, and danced,
and pleased Herod and them that sat
with him, the king said unto the dam-
sel, Ask of me whatsoever thou wilt,
and I will give *it* thee.
23 And he sware unto her, [o]What-
soever thou shalt ask of me, I will give
it thee, unto the half of my kingdom.
24 And she went forth, and said
unto her mother, What shall I ask? And
she said, The head of John the Baptist.
25 And she came in straightway
with haste unto the king, and asked,
saying, I will that thou give me by and
by in a charger the head of John the
Baptist.
26 [p]And the king was exceeding
sorry; *yet* for his oath's sake, and for
their sakes which sat with him, he
would not reject her.
27 And immediately the king sent
[q]an executioner, and commanded his
head to be brought: and he went and
beheaded him in the prison,
28 And brought his head in a
charger, and gave it to the damsel: and
the damsel gave it to her mother.
29 And when his disciples heard *of*
it, they came and took up his corpse,
and laid it in a tomb.

The five thousand fed

6:32–44pp — Mat. 14:13–21; Luke 9:10–17; John 6:5–13
6:32–44Ref — Mark 8:2–9

30 [q]And the apostles gathered
themselves together unto Jesus, and
told him all things, both what they had
done, and what they had taught.
31 [r]And he said unto them, Come
ye yourselves apart into a desert place,
and rest a while: for [s]there were many
coming and going, and they had no lei-
sure so much as to eat.
32 [t]And they departed into a
desert place by ship privately.
33 And the people saw them depart-
ing, and many knew him, and ran afoot
thither out of all cities, and outwent
them, and came together unto him.
34 [u]And Jesus, when he came out,
saw much people, and was moved with
compassion toward them, because
they were as sheep not having a shep-
herd: and [v]he began to teach them
many things.
35 [w]And when the day was now far
spent, his disciples came unto him, and
said, This is a desert place, and now
the time *is* far passed:
36 Send them away, that they may
go into the country round about, and
into the villages, and buy themselves
bread: for they have nothing to eat.
37 He answered and said unto
them, Give ye them to eat. And they
say unto him, [x]Shall we go and buy
two hundred [r]pennyworth of bread,
and give them to eat?
38 He saith unto them, How many

[o] Or, *an inward grudge* [p] Or, *kept him*, or *saved him* [q] Or, *one of his guard* [r] The penny, worth about 16 cents, was the usual day's wage for a laborer

6:15 [i]Mat. 16:14 ch. 8:28
6:16 [j]Mat. 14:2 Luke 3:19
6:18 [k]Lev. 18:16 & 20:21
6:20 [l]Mat. 14:5 & 21:26
6:21 [m]Mat. 14:6 [n]Gen. 40:20
6:23 [o]Esth. 5:3,6 & 7:2
6:26 [p]Mat. 14:9
6:30 [q]Luke 9:10
6:31 [r]Mat. 14:13 [s]ch. 3:20
6:32 [t]Mat. 14:13
6:34 [u]Mat. 9:36 & 14:14 [v]Luke 9:11
6:35 [w]Mat. 14:15 Luke 9:12
6:37 [x]Num. 11:13,22 2 Ki. 4:43

6:17 JOHN ... IN PRISON. See Mat. 11:7, note.

6:22 DANCED. See Mat. 14:6, note.

6:34 COMPASSION. Compassion is an emotion which moves one to the very depth of his being. It involves a sorrow felt for another's suffering and misfortune, accompanied by an intense desire to help. It is a characteristic both of God (Deut. 30:3; 2 Ki. 13:23; Ps. 78:38; 111:4) and of His Son Jesus (1:41; 8:2, note; Mat. 9:36; 14:14; 15:32; Luke 7:13). In this present age of indifference to the suffering of others, Jesus expects this attitude to characterize His followers (Mat. 18:33; Luke 10:33).

loaves have ye? go and see. And when they knew, they say, [y]Five, and two fishes.

39 And he commanded them to make all sit down by companies upon the green grass.

40 And they sat down in ranks, by hundreds, and by fifties.

41 And when he had taken the five loaves and the two fishes, he looked up to heaven, [z]and blessed, and brake the loaves, and gave *them* to his disciples to set before them; and the two fishes divided he among them all.

42 And they did all eat, and were filled.

43 And they took up twelve baskets full of the fragments, and of the fishes.

44 And they that did eat of the loaves were about five thousand men.

Jesus walks on the sea

6:45–51pp — Mat. 14:22–32; John 6:15–21

45 [a]And straightway he constrained his disciples to get into the ship, and to go to the other side before [s]unto Bethsaida, while he sent away the people.

46 And when he had sent them away, he departed into a mountain to pray.

47 [b]And when even was come, the ship was in the midst of the sea, and he alone on the land.

48 And he saw them toiling in rowing; for the wind was contrary unto them: and about the fourth watch of the night he cometh unto them, walking upon the sea, and [c]would have passed by them.

49 But when they saw him walking upon the sea, they supposed it had been a spirit, and cried out:

50 For they all saw him, and were troubled. And immediately he talked with them, and saith unto them, Be of good cheer: it is I; be not afraid.

51 And he went up unto them into the ship; and the wind ceased: and they were sore amazed in themselves beyond measure, and wondered.

52 For [d]they considered not *the miracle* of the loaves: for their [e]heart was hardened.

The miracles at Gennesaret

6:53–56pp — Mat. 14:34–36

53 [f]And when they had passed over, they came into the land of Gennesaret, and drew to the shore.

54 And when they were come out of the ship, straightway they knew him,

55 And ran through that whole region round about, and began to carry about in beds those that were sick, where they heard he was.

56 And whithersoever he entered, into villages, or cities, or country, they laid the sick in the streets, and besought him that [g]they might touch if it were but the border of his garment: and as many as touched [t]him were made whole.

What defiles a man

7:1–23pp — Mat. 15:1–20

7 THEN [h]CAME together unto him the Pharisees, and certain of the scribes, which came from Jerusalem.

2 And when they saw some of his disciples eat bread with [u]defiled, that is to say, with unwashen, hands, they found fault.

3 For the Pharisees, and all the Jews, except they wash *their* hands [v]oft, eat not, holding the tradition of the elders.

4 And *when they come* from the market, except they wash, they eat not. And many other things there be, which they have received to hold, *as* the washing of cups, and [w]pots, brasen vessels, and of [x]tables.

5 [i]Then the Pharisees and scribes asked him, Why walk not thy disciples according to the tradition of the elders, but eat bread with unwashen hands?

6 He answered and said unto them, Well hath Esaias prophesied of you

6:38 [y]Mat. 14:17 Luke 9:13 John 6:9 See Mat. 15:34 ch:8:5
6:41 [z]1 Sam. 9:13 Mat. 26:26
6:45 [a]Mat. 14:22 John 6:17
6:47 [b]Mat. 14:23 John 6:16,17
6:48 [c]See Luke 24:28
6:52 [d]ch. 8:17,18
[e]ch. 3:5 & 16:14
6:53 [f]Mat. 14:34
6:56 [g]Mat. 9:20 ch. 5:27,28 Acts 19:12
7:1 [h]Mat. 15:1
7:5 [i]Mat. 15:2

[s] Or, *over against Bethsaida* [t] Or, *it* [u] Or, *common* [v] Or, *diligently:* in the original, *with the fist* Theophylact, *up to the elbow* [w] Sextarius is about a pint and a half [x] Or, *beds*

6:41 FIVE LOAVES . . . TWO FISHES. See Mat. 14:19, note.

6:41 THANKSGIVING AT MEALTIMES. Before eating, Christ gave thanks to His heavenly Father for the food. Believers ought to follow His example and give thanks at every meal. To eat with thanksgiving unto God is to recognize His care and provision for us. Every meal should be an act of worship, done to the glory of God. On giving thanks or saying grace before meals, see 1 Sam. 9:13; Mat. 14:19; 15:36; 26:26; Rom. 14:6; 1 Cor. 10:31; 1 Tim. 4:4–5.

7:6 THEIR HEART IS FAR FROM ME. The Pharisees and the scribes were guilty of the sin of

DECAPOLIS AND LANDS BEYOND THE JORDAN

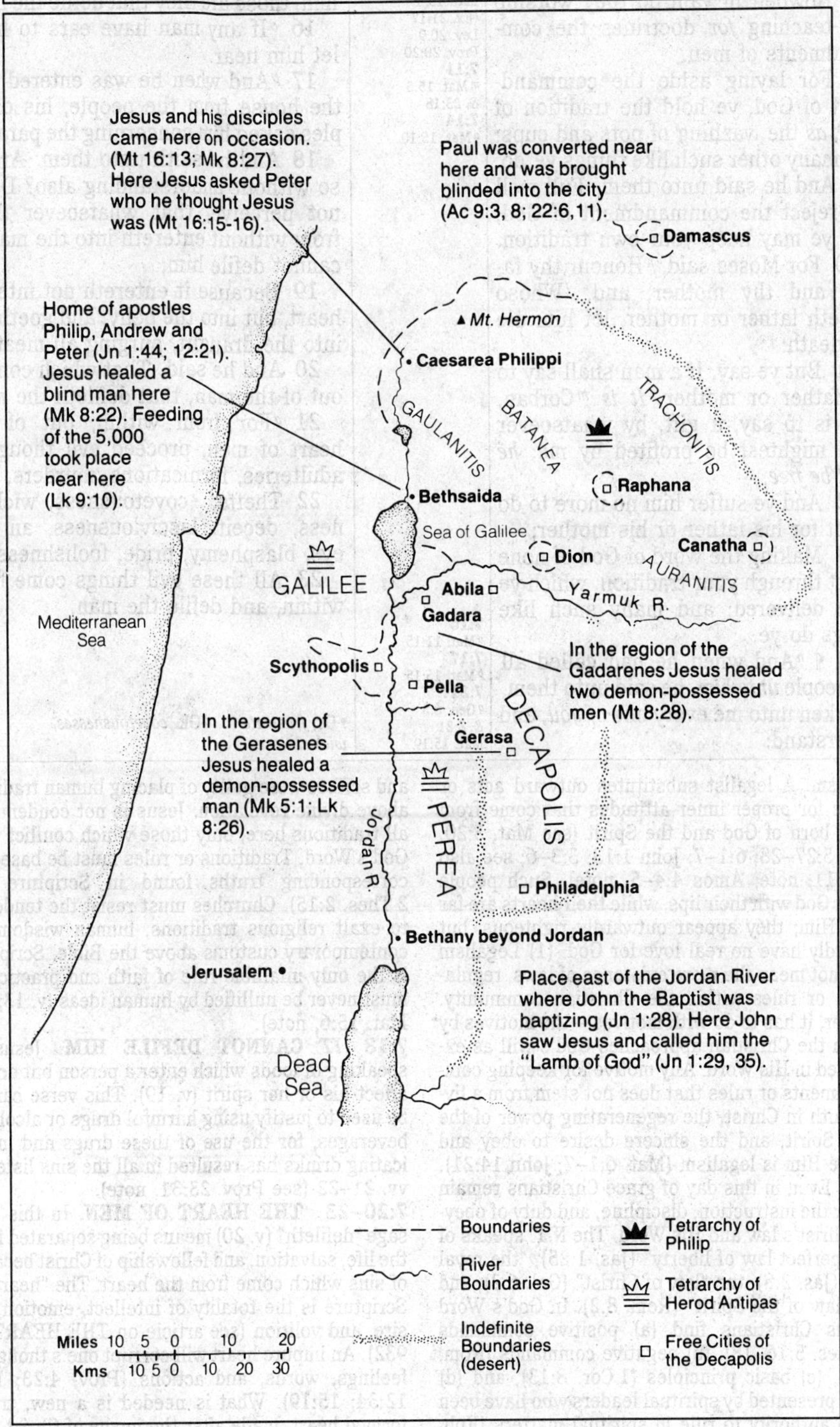

hypocrites, as it is written, [j]This peo-
ple honoureth me with *their* lips, but
their heart is far from me.
7 Howbeit in vain do they worship
me, teaching *for* doctrines the com-
mandments of men.
8 For laying aside the command-
ment of God, ye hold the tradition of
men, *as* the washing of pots and cups:
and many other such like things ye do.
9 And he said unto them, Full well
ye [y]reject the commandment of God,
that ye may keep your own tradition.
10 For Moses said, [k]Honour thy fa-
ther and thy mother; and, [l]Whoso
curseth father or mother, let him die
the death:
11 But ye say, If a man shall say to
his father or mother, *It is* [m]Corban,
that is to say, a gift, by whatsoever
thou mightest be profited by me; *he
shall be free*.
12 And ye suffer him no more to do
aught for his father or his mother;
13 Making the word of God of none
effect through your tradition, which ye
have delivered: and many such like
things do ye.
14 ¶ [n]And when he had called all
the people *unto him*, he said unto them,
Hearken unto me every one *of you*, and
understand:

7:6
[j]Is. 29:13
7:10
[k]Ex. 20:12
Deut. 5:16
Mat. 15:4
[l]Ex. 21:17
Lev. 20:9
Prov. 20:20
7:11
[m]Mat. 15:5
& 23:18
7:14
[n]Mat. 15:10
7:16
[o]Mat. 11:15
7:17
[p]Mat. 15:15
7:21
[q]Gen. 6:5
& 8:21
Mat. 15:19

15 There is nothing from without a
man, that entering into him can defile
him: but the things which come out of
him, those are they that defile the man.
16 [o]If any man have ears to hear,
let him hear.
17 [p]And when he was entered into
the house from the people, his disci-
ples asked him concerning the parable.
18 And he saith unto them, Are ye
so without understanding also? Do ye
not perceive, that whatsoever thing
from without entereth into the man, *it*
cannot defile him;
19 Because it entereth not into his
heart, but into the belly, and goeth out
into the draught, purging all meats?
20 And he said, That which cometh
out of the man, that defileth the man.
21 [q]For from within, out of the
heart of men, proceed evil thoughts,
adulteries, fornications, murders,
22 Thefts, [z]covetousness, wicked-
ness, deceit, lasciviousness, an evil
eye, blasphemy, pride, foolishness:
23 All these evil things come from
within, and defile the man.

[y] Or, *frustrate* [z] Gk. *covetousnesses, wickednesses*

legalism. A legalist substitutes outward acts or words for proper inner attitudes that come from being born of God and the Spirit (see Mat. 5:20, note; 5:27–28; 6:1–7; John 1:13; 3:3–6; see also Is. 1:11, note; Amos 4:4–5, note). Such people honor God with their lips, while their hearts are far from Him; they appear outwardly righteous, but inwardly have no real love for God. (1) Legalism does not mean the mere existence of laws, regulations, or rules within the Christian community. Rather, it has to do with motives—the motives by which the Christian approaches God's will as expressed in His Word. Any motive for keeping commandments or rules that does not stem from a living faith in Christ, the regenerating power of the Holy Spirit, and the sincere desire to obey and please Him is legalism (Mat. 6:1–7; John 14:21).

(2) Even in this day of grace Christians remain under the instruction, discipline, and duty of obeying Christ's law and His Word. The N.T. speaks of the "perfect law of liberty" (Jas. 1:25), "the royal law" (Jas. 2:8), the "law of Christ" (Gal. 6:2), and the "law of the Spirit" (Rom. 8:2). In God's Word we as Christians find (a) positive commands (1 Thes. 5:16–18), (b) negative commands (Rom. 12:2), (c) basic principles (1 Cor. 8:13), and (d) rules presented by spiritual leaders who have been given authority to rule in spiritual matters (Eph. 4:11–12; 1 Tim. 3:5; Heb. 13:7,17).

7:8 THE TRADITION OF MEN. The Pharisees and scribes were guilty of placing human tradition above divine revelation. Jesus is not condemning all traditions here, only those which conflict with God's Word. Traditions or rules must be based on corresponding truths found in Scripture (cf. 2 Thes. 2:15). Churches must resist the tendency to exalt religious traditions, human wisdom, or contemporary customs above the Bible. Scripture is the only infallible rule of faith and practice; it must never be nullified by human ideas (v. 13; see Mat. 15:6, note).

7:18 *IT* CANNOT DEFILE HIM. Jesus is speaking of foods which enter a person but do not affect his or her spirit (v. 19). This verse cannot be used to justify using harmful drugs or alcoholic beverages, for the use of these drugs and intoxicating drinks has resulted in all the sins listed in vv. 21–22 (see Prov. 23:31, note).

7:20–23 THE HEART OF MEN. In this passage "defileth" (v. 20) means being separated from the life, salvation, and fellowship of Christ because of sins which come from the heart. The "heart" in Scripture is the totality of intellect, emotion, desire, and volition (see article on THE HEART, p. 932). An impure heart will corrupt one's thoughts, feelings, words, and actions (Prov. 4:23; Mat. 12:34; 15:19). What is needed is a new, transformed heart, made after the image of Christ (see Luke 6:45; see article on REGENERATION, p. 1597).

A Greek woman's faith

7:24–30pp — Mat. 15:21–28

24 ¶ [r]And from thence he arose, and went into the borders of Tyre and Sidon, and entered into an house, and would have no man know *it:* but he could not be hid.

25 For a *certain* woman, whose young daughter had an unclean spirit, heard of him, and came and fell at his feet:

26 The woman was a [a]Greek, a Syrophenician by nation; and she besought him that he would cast forth the devil out of her daughter.

27 But Jesus said unto her, Let the children first be filled: for it is not meet to take the children's bread, and to cast *it* unto the dogs.

28 And she answered and said unto him, Yes, Lord: yet the dogs under the table eat of the children's crumbs.

29 And he said unto her, For this saying go thy way; the devil is gone out of thy daughter.

30 And when she was come to her house, she found the devil gone out, and her daughter laid upon the bed.

A deaf mute healed

7:31–37pp — Mat. 15:29–31

31 ¶ [s]And again, departing from the coasts of Tyre and Sidon, he came unto the sea of Galilee, through the midst of the coasts of Decapolis.

32 And [t]they bring unto him one that was deaf, and had an impediment in his speech; and they beseech him to put his hand upon him.

33 And he took him aside from the multitude, and put his fingers into his ears, and [u]he spit, and touched his tongue;

34 And [v]looking up to heaven, [w]he sighed, and saith unto him, Ephphatha, that is, Be opened.

35 [x]And straightway his ears were opened, and the string of his tongue was loosed, and he spake plain.

36 And [y]he charged them that they should tell no man: but the more he charged them, so much the more a great deal they published *it;*

37 And were beyond measure astonished, saying, He hath done all things well: he maketh both the deaf to hear, and the dumb to speak.

Luke 6:17-19

7:24 [r]Mat. 15:21 **7:31** [s]Mat. 15:29 **7:32** [t]Mat. 9:32 Luke 11:14 **7:33** [u]ch. 8:23 John 9:6 **7:34** [v]ch. 6:41 John 11:41 & 17:1 [w]John 11:33,38 **7:35** [x]Is. 35:5,6

The four thousand fed

8:1–9pp — Mat. 15:32–39
8:1–9Ref — Mark 6:32–44

8 IN THOSE days [z]the multitude being very great, and having nothing to eat, Jesus called his disciples *unto him*, and saith unto them,

2 I have compassion on the multitude, because they have now been with me three days, and have nothing to eat:

3 And if I send them away fasting to their own houses, they will faint by the way: for divers of them came from far.

4 And his disciples answered him, From whence can a man satisfy these *men* with bread here in the wilderness?

5 [a]And he asked them, How many loaves have ye? And they said, Seven.

6 And he commanded the people to sit down on the ground: and he took the seven loaves, and gave thanks, and brake, and gave to his disciples to set before *them;* and they did set *them* before the people.

7 And they had a few small fishes: and [b]he blessed, and commanded to set them also before *them*.

8 So they did eat, and were filled: and they took up of the broken *meat* that was left seven baskets.

9 And they that had eaten were about four thousand: and he sent them away.

10 ¶ And [c]straightway he entered into a ship with his disciples, and came into the parts of Dalmanutha.

7:36 [y]ch. 5:43 **8:1** [z]Mat. 15:32 **8:5** [a]Mat. 15:34 See ch. 6:38 **8:7** [b]Mat. 14:19 ch. 6:41 **8:10** [c]Mat. 15:39

[a] Or, *Gentile*

7:27 CHILDREN'S BREAD. The word "children" refers to Israel. Jesus expresses the thought that the gospel must be taken first to Israel. The woman understands this, yet responds to Christ in wisdom, perseverance, and faith. She argues that it is God's purpose for Gentiles to receive blessings indirectly when He blesses Israel. Christ rewards her according to her diligent faith, for He heals her child (vv. 28–30). The believer, while in prayer for himself or others, must persevere in prayer, and occasionally even reason with God (see Mat. 15:28, note).

8:2 I HAVE COMPASSION. Jesus was touched with compassion and pity for the needs and suffering of humanity (see 1:41). Jesus is the same today. He is moved with a deep and earnest sympathy by the needs and hurts of each child of God. This assures us that in our troubles we can draw near to Him in prayer in order to receive grace, mercy, and help (Mat. 6:31–32; Heb. 4:14–16; 7:25).

Pharisees ask for a sign

8:11–21pp — Mat. 16:1–12

11 [d]And the Pharisees came forth, and began to question with him, seeking of him a sign from heaven, tempting him.

12 And he sighed deeply in his spirit, and saith, Why doth this generation seek after a sign? verily I say unto you, There shall no sign be given unto this generation.

13 And he left them, and entering into the ship again departed to the other side.

14 ¶ [e]Now *the disciples* had forgotten to take bread, neither had they in the ship with them more than one loaf.

15 [f]And he charged them, saying, Take heed, beware of the leaven of the Pharisees, and *of* the leaven of Herod.

16 And they reasoned among themselves, saying, *It is* because we have no bread.

17 And when Jesus knew *it*, he saith unto them, Why reason ye, because ye have no bread? [g]perceive ye not yet, neither understand? have ye your heart yet hardened?

18 Having eyes, see ye not? and having ears, hear ye not? and do ye not remember?

19 [h]When I brake the five loaves among five thousand, how many baskets full of fragments took ye up? They say unto him, Twelve.

20 And [i]when the seven among four thousand, how many baskets full of fragments took ye up? And they said, Seven.

21 And he said unto them, How is it that [j]ye do not understand?

A blind man healed

22 ¶ And he cometh to Bethsaida; and they bring a blind man unto him, and besought him to touch him.

23 And he took the blind man by the hand, and led him out of the town; and when [k]he had spit on his eyes, and put his hands upon him, he asked him if he saw aught.

24 And he looked up, and said, I see men as trees, walking.

25 After that he put *his* hands again upon his eyes, and made him look up: and he was restored, and saw every man clearly.

26 And he sent him away to his house, saying, Neither go into the town, [l]nor tell *it* to any in the town.

Peter's confession of faith

8:27–29pp — Mat. 16:13–16; Luke 9:18–20

27 ¶ [m]And Jesus went out, and his disciples, into the towns of Caesarea Philippi: and by the way he asked his disciples, saying unto them, Whom do men say that I am?

28 And they answered, [n]John the Baptist: but some *say,* Elias; and others, One of the prophets.

29 And he saith unto them, But whom say ye that I am? And Peter answereth and saith unto him, [o]Thou art the Christ.

Jesus foretells his death

8:31–33pp — Mat. 16:21–23; Luke 9:22

30 [p]And he charged them that they should tell no man of him.

31 And [q]he began to teach them, that the Son of man must suffer many things, and be rejected of the elders, and *of* the chief priests, and scribes, and be killed, and after three days rise again.

32 And he spake that saying openly. And Peter took him, and began to rebuke him.

33 But when he had turned about and looked on his disciples, he rebuked Peter, saying, Get thee behind me, Satan: for thou savourest not the things that be of God, but the things that be of men.

8:11 [d]Mat. 12:38 & 16:1 John 6:30
8:14 [e]Mat. 16:5
8:15 [f]Mat. 16:6 Luke 12:1
8:17 [g]ch. 6:52
8:19 [h]Mat. 14:20 ch. 6:43 Luke 9:17 John 6:13
8:20 [i]ver. 8 Mat. 15:37
8:21 [j]ver. 17 ch. 6:52
8:23 [k]ch. 7:33
8:26 [l]Mat. 8:4 ch. 5:43
8:27 [m]Mat. 16:13 Luke 9:18
8:28 [n]Mat. 14:2
8:29 [o]Mat. 16:16 John 6:69 & 11:27
8:30 [p]Mat. 16:20
8:31 [q]Mat. 16:21 & 17:22 Luke 9:22

8:15 LEAVEN. In the N.T. "leaven" (yeast) is usually a symbol for evil or corruption (see Ex. 13:7, note; Mat. 13:33; 16:6,11; Luke 12:1; 1 Cor. 5:6–8; Gal. 5:9). A small amount of leaven will ferment and affect the whole. (1) The "leaven" of the Pharisees refers to their religious traditions by which they set aside the righteous commandments of God and invalidated portions of His word and will (7:5–8, notes). (2) The "leaven" of Herod is identical with that of the Sadducees; it refers to a spirit of secularism and worldliness (see Mat. 3:7, note). Followers of Christ must always guard against accepting the views of those who preach human ideas, unbiblical traditions, or a secular, humanistic type of gospel. To accept the "leaven of Herod" will cause the church to turn against Christ and His Word.

8:25 HE WAS RESTORED. This healing in Bethsaida is the only instance of a gradual cure by Jesus. It teaches that not every healing has to be instantaneous, for in some cases the victory of divine power over sickness will be gradual.

The cost of discipleship

8:34–9:1pp — Mat. 16:24–28; Luke 9:23–27

34 ¶ And when he had called the
people *unto him* with his disciples also,
he said unto them, [r]Whosoever will
come after me, let him deny himself,
and take up his cross, and follow me.
35 For [s]whosoever will save his
life shall lose it; but whosoever shall
lose his life for my sake and the gos-
pel's, the same shall save it.
36 For what shall it profit a man, if
he shall gain the whole world, and lose
his own soul?
37 Or what shall a man give in ex-
change for his soul?
38 [t]Whosoever therefore [u]shall
be ashamed of me and of my words in
this adulterous and sinful generation;
of him also shall the Son of man be
ashamed, when he cometh in the glory
of his Father with the holy angels.
9 AND HE said unto them, [v]Verily
I say unto you, That there be some
of them that stand here, which shall
not taste of death, till they have seen
[w]the kingdom of God come with
power.

The transfiguration

9:2–8pp — Luke 9:28–36
9:2–13pp — Mat. 17:1–13

2 ¶ [x]And after six days Jesus
taketh *with him* Peter, and James, and
John, and leadeth them up into an high
mountain apart by themselves: and he
was transfigured before them.
3 And his raiment became shining,
exceeding [y]white as snow; so as no
fuller on earth can white them.
4 And there appeared unto them
Elias with Moses: and they were talk-
ing with Jesus.
5 And Peter answered and said to
Jesus, Master, it is good for us to be
here: and let us make three taberna-
cles; one for thee, and one for Moses,
and one for Elias.
6 For he wist not what to say; for
they were sore afraid.
7 And there was a cloud that over-
shadowed them: and a voice came out
of the cloud, saying, This is my beloved
Son: hear him.
8 And suddenly, when they had
looked round about, they saw no man
any more, save Jesus only with them-
selves.
9 [z]And as they came down from
the mountain, he charged them that
they should tell no man what things
they had seen, till the Son of man were
risen from the dead.
10 And they kept that saying with
themselves, questioning one with an-
other what the rising from the dead
should mean.
11 ¶ And they asked him, saying,
Why say the scribes [a]that Elias must
first come?
12 And he answered and told them,
Elias verily cometh first, and restoreth
all things; and [b]how it is written of the
Son of man, that he must suffer many
things, and [c]be set at nought.
13 But I say unto you, That [d]Elias
is indeed come, and they have done

8:34 [r]Mat. 10:38 & 16:24 Luke 9:23 & 14:27
8:35 [s]John 12:25
8:38 [t]Mat. 10:33 Luke 9:26 & 12:9 [u]See Rom. 1:16 2 Tim. 1:8 & 2:12
9:1 [v]Mat. 16:28 Luke 9:27 [w]Mat. 24:30
9:2 [x]Mat. 17:1 Luke 9:28
9:3 [y]Dan. 7:9
9:9 [z]Mat. 17:9
9:11 [a]Mal. 4:5 Mat. 17:10
9:12 [b]Ps. 22:6 Is. 53:2 Dan. 9:26 [c]Luke 23:11 Phil. 2:7
9:13 [d]Mat. 11:14 & 17:12 Luke 1:17

8:34 TAKE UP HIS CROSS. The cross of Christ is a symbol of suffering (1 Pet. 2:21; 4:13), death (Acts 10:39), shame (Heb. 12:2), ridicule (Mat. 27:39), rejection (1 Pet. 2:4), and self-denial (Mat. 16:24). When we as believers take up our cross and follow Christ, we deny our own selves (Luke 14:26–27) and commit ourselves to three areas of struggle and suffering:

(1) We suffer in a lifelong battle against sin (Rom. 6; 1 Pet. 4:1–2) by crucifying our own fleshly desires (Rom. 6; 8:13; Gal. 2:20; 6:14; Tit. 2:12; 1 Pet. 2:11,21–24).

(2) We suffer in a war against Satan and the powers of darkness as we advance the kingdom of God (2 Cor. 10:4–5; 6:7; Eph. 6:12; 1 Tim. 6:12). We experience both the hostility of the adversary with his demonic host (2 Cor. 6:3–7; 11:23–29; 1 Pet. 5:8–10) and the persecution which comes from standing against false teachers who distort the true gospel (Mat. 23:1–36; Gal. 1:9; Phil. 1:15–17).

(3) We suffer the reproach, hatred, and ridicule of the world (John 15:18–25; Heb. 11:25–26) by testifying in love that its deeds are evil (John 7:7), by separating ourselves from it both morally and spiritually (see article on SPIRITUAL SEPARATION FOR BELIEVERS, p. 1814), and by refusing to accept its standards or philosophy as our own (1 Cor. 1:21–27).

(4) Like Jesus, we may also suffer ridicule and persecution from the religious world (v. 31; see v. 15, note).

8:38 ASHAMED OF ME AND OF MY WORDS. Jesus sees the world and society in which we live as an "adulterous and sinful generation." All those who seek to be popular in or accepted by their present evil generation rather than follow Christ and His righteous standards, will be rejected by Christ at His return (cf. Mat. 7:23; 25:41–46; Luke 9:26, note; 13:27).

9:1 KINGDOM OF GOD . . . WITH POWER. See Mat. 16:28, note.

9:2 HE WAS TRANSFIGURED. See Luke 9:29, note.

unto him whatsoever they listed, as it is written of him.

The demoniac boy cured

9:14–28,30–32pp — Mat. 17:14–19,22–23; Luke 9:37–45

14 ¶ [e]And when he came to *his* disciples, he saw a great multitude about them, and the scribes questioning with them.

15 And straightway all the people, when they beheld him, were greatly amazed, and running to *him* saluted him.

16 And he asked the scribes, What question ye [b]with them?

17 And [f]one of the multitude answered and said, Master, I have brought unto thee my son, which hath a dumb spirit;

18 And wheresoever he taketh him, he [c]teareth him: and he foameth, and gnasheth with his teeth, and pineth away: and I spake to thy disciples that they should cast him out; and they could not.

19 He answereth him, and saith, O faithless generation, how long shall I be with you? how long shall I suffer you? bring him unto me.

20 And they brought him unto him: and [g]when he saw him, straightway the spirit tare him; and he fell on the ground, and wallowed foaming.

21 And he asked his father, How long is it ago since this came unto him? And he said, Of a child.

22 And ofttimes it hath cast him into the fire, and into the waters, to destroy him: but if thou canst do any thing, have compassion on us, and help us.

23 Jesus said unto him, [h]If thou canst believe, all things *are* possible to him that believeth.

24 And straightway the father of the child cried out, and said with tears, Lord, I believe; help thou mine unbelief.

25 When Jesus saw that the people came running together, he rebuked the foul spirit, saying unto him, *Thou* dumb and deaf spirit, I charge thee, come out of him, and enter no more into him.

26 And *the spirit* cried, and rent him sore, and came out of him: and he was as one dead; insomuch that many said, He is dead.

27 But Jesus took him by the hand, and lifted him up; and he arose.

28 [i]And when he was come into the house, his disciples asked him privately, Why could not we cast him out?

29 And he said unto them, This kind can come forth by nothing, but by prayer and fasting.

30 ¶ And they departed thence, and passed through Galilee; and he would not that any man should know *it*.

31 [j]For he taught his disciples, and said unto them, The Son of man is delivered into the hands of men, and they shall kill him; and after that he is killed, he shall rise the third day.

32 But they understood not that saying, and were afraid to ask him.

True discipleship

9:33–37pp — Mat. 18:1–5; Luke 9:46–48
9:38–40pp — Luke 9:49–50

33 ¶ [k]And he came to Capernaum: and being in the house he asked them, What was it that ye disputed among yourselves by the way?

34 But they held their peace: for by

9:14 [e]Mat. 17:14 Luke 9:37
9:17 [f]Mat. 17:14 Luke 9:38
9:20 [g]ch. 1:26 Luke 9:42
9:23 [h]Mat. 17:20 ch. 11:23 Luke 17:6 John 11:40
9:28 [i]Mat. 17:19
9:31 [j]Mat. 17:22 Luke 9:44
9:33 [k]Mat. 18:1 Luke 9:46 & 22:24

[b] Or, *among yourselves?* [c] Or, *dasheth him*

9:19 FAITHLESS GENERATION. Failure to wage effective warfare against demons is seen as a spiritual weakness on the part of Christ's disciples (see Mat. 17:17, note).

9:23 ALL THINGS *ARE* POSSIBLE. This statement of Jesus must not be taken as an unqualified promise. (1) The "all things" does not mean everything we can think of. The prayer of faith must be based on the will of God; it never asks for anything foolish or wrong (Jas. 4:3). (2) The faith required here must be received as a gift of God. He implants it in the heart of a sincere seeker who lives faithfully according to God's will (see Mat. 17:20, note).

9:24 HELP THOU MINE UNBELIEF. In this life our faith is often mixed with doubt. This weakness does not mean, however, that Christ will not respond to our petitions, for He understands and sympathizes with our weaknesses (Heb. 4:15). We should confess our lack of faith to Him and pray that He would give us the faith that is needed (see Mat. 17:20, note).

9:29 PRAYER AND FASTING. Jesus does not mean that a time of prayer and fasting was necessary before this kind of evil spirit could be cast out. Rather a principle is implied here: where there is little faith, there is little prayer and fasting. Where there is much prayer and fasting, founded on true commitment to God and His Word, there is much faith. Had the disciples been maintaining, as Jesus, a life of prayer and fasting, they could have dealt successfully with this case.

9:34 THE GREATEST. See Luke 22:24–30, note.

the way they had disputed among themselves, who *should be* the greatest.

35 And he sat down, and called the twelve, and saith unto them, [l]If any man desire to be first, *the same* shall be last of all, and servant of all.

36 And [m]he took a child, and set him in the midst of them: and when he had taken him in his arms, he said unto them,

37 Whosoever shall receive one of such children in my name, receiveth me: and [n]whosoever shall receive me, receiveth not me, but him that sent me.

38 ¶ [o]And John answered him, saying, Master, we saw one casting out devils in thy name, and he followeth not us: and we forbad him, because he followeth not us.

39 But Jesus said, Forbid him not: [p]for there is no man which shall do a miracle in my name, that can lightly speak evil of me.

40 For [q]he that is not against us is on our part.

41 [r]For whosoever shall give you a cup of water to drink in my name, because ye belong to Christ, verily I say unto you, he shall not lose his reward.

Sin sends one to hell

42 [s]And whosoever shall offend one of *these* little ones that believe in me, it is better for him that a millstone were hanged about his neck, and he were cast into the sea.

43 [t]And if thy hand [d]offend thee, cut it off: it is better for thee to enter into life maimed, than having two hands to go into hell, into the fire that never shall be quenched:

44 [u]Where their worm dieth not, and the fire is not quenched.

45 And if thy foot offend thee, cut it off: it is better for thee to enter halt into life, than having two feet to be cast into hell, into the fire that never shall be quenched:

46 Where their worm dieth not, and the fire is not quenched.

47 And if thine eye offend thee, pluck it out: it is better for thee to enter into the kingdom of God with one eye, than having two eyes to be cast into hell fire:

48 Where their worm dieth not, and the fire is not quenched. Luke 6:46-49

49 For every one shall be salted with fire, [v]and every sacrifice shall be salted with salt.

50 [w]Salt *is* good: but if the salt have lost his saltness, wherewith will ye season it? [x]Have salt in yourselves, and [y]have peace one with another.

Marriage and divorce

10:1–12pp — Mat. 19:1–9

10 AND [z]HE arose from thence, and cometh into the coasts of Judaea by the farther side of Jordan: and the people resort unto him again; and, as he was wont, he taught them again.

2 ¶ [a]And the Pharisees came to him, and asked him, Is it lawful for a man to put away *his* wife? tempting him.

3 And he answered and said unto them, What did Moses command you?

4 And they said, [b]Moses suffered to write a bill of divorcement, and to put *her* away.

5 And Jesus answered and said unto them, For the hardness of your heart he wrote you this precept.

6 But from the beginning of the creation [c]God made them male and female.

7 [d]For this cause shall a man leave

9:35 [l]Mat. 20:26,27 ch. 10:43
9:36 [m]Mat. 18:2 ch. 10:16
9:37 [n]Mat. 10:40 Luke 9:48
9:38 [o]Num. 11:28 Luke 9:49
9:39 [p]1 Cor. 12:3
9:40 [q]See Mat. 12:30
9:41 [r]Mat. 10:42
9:42 [s]Mat. 18:6 Luke 17:1
9:43 [t]Deut. 13:6 Mat. 5:29 & 18:8
9:44 [u]Is. 66:24
9:49 [v]Lev. 2:13 Ezek. 43:24
9:50 [w]Mat. 5:13 Luke 14:34 [x]Eph. 4:29 Col. 4:6 [y]Rom. 12:18 & 14:19 2 Cor. 13:11 Heb. 12:14
10:1 [z]Mat. 19:1 John 10:40 & 11:7
10:2 [a]Mat. 19:3
10:4 [b]Deut. 24:1 Mat. 5:31 & 19:7
10:6 [c]Gen. 1:27 & 5:2
10:7 [d]Gen. 2:24 1 Cor. 6:16 Eph. 5:31

[d] Or, *cause thee to offend;* also ver. 45,47

9:42 OFFEND . . . LITTLE ONES. One of the highest priorities for believers is to set a holy example for their children by life and teaching. In doing so, they demonstrate a sincere love for them. Christian parents must likewise diligently do their best to keep their children from the ungodly influences of the world (see Mat. 18:6, note). To fail in this responsibility can bring eternal disaster.

9:43 HELL. "Hell," the place of unquenchable fire, is so terrible that every influence of sin must be opposed and rejected, whatever the cost. Sin must be put to death (Col. 3:5); we must never stop waging war against it through the Spirit (Rom. 8:13; Eph. 6:10).

9:49 SALTED WITH FIRE. Everyone will be salted with fire in one of two ways: (1) either by fiery tribulation in this life that comes to those who genuinely follow Jesus Christ (John 15:18–21; Luke 14:33–34), or (2) by the fire of hell in the next life that comes to those who reject Jesus in this life (cf. vv. 47–48). (Rom. 12:1–2).

9:50 SALT. See Mat. 5:13, note.

his father and mother, and cleave to his wife;

8 And they twain shall be one flesh: so then they are no more twain, but one flesh.

9 What therefore God hath joined together, let not man put asunder.

10 And in the house his disciples asked him again of the same *matter.*

11 And he saith unto them, [e]Whosoever shall put away his wife, and marry another, committeth adultery against her.

12 And if a woman shall put away her husband, and be married to another, she committeth adultery.

Jesus blesses the little children

10:13–16pp — Mat. 19:13–15; Luke 18:15–17

13 ¶ [f]And they brought young children to him, that he should touch them: and *his* disciples rebuked those that brought *them.*

14 But when Jesus saw *it,* he was much displeased, and said unto them, Suffer the little children to come unto me, and forbid them not: for [g]of such is the kingdom of God.

15 Verily I say unto you, [h]Whosoever shall not receive the kingdom of God as a little child, he shall not enter therein.

16 And he took them up in his arms, put *his* hands upon them, and blessed them.

The rich young ruler

10:17–22pp — Mat. 19:16–22; Luke 18:18–22

17 ¶ [i]And when he was gone forth into the way, there came one running, and kneeled to him, and asked him, Good Master, what shall I do that I may inherit eternal life?

18 And Jesus said unto him, Why callest thou me good? *there is* none good but one, *that is,* God.

19 Thou knowest the commandments, [j]Do not commit adultery, Do not kill, Do not steal, Do not bear false witness, Defraud not, Honour thy father and mother.

20 And he answered and said unto him, Master, all these have I observed from my youth.

21 Then Jesus beholding him loved him, and said unto him, One thing thou lackest: go thy way, sell whatsoever thou hast, and give to the poor, and thou shalt have [k]treasure in heaven: and come, take up the cross, and follow me.

22 And he was sad at that saying, and went away grieved: for he had great possessions.

The perils of riches

10:23–27pp — Mat. 19:23–26; Luke 18:23–27

23 ¶ [l]And Jesus looked round about, and saith unto his disciples, How hardly shall they that have riches enter into the kingdom of God!

24 And the disciples were astonished at his words. But Jesus answereth again, and saith unto them, Children, how hard is it for them [m]that trust in riches to enter into the kingdom of God!

25 It is easier for a camel to go through the eye of a needle, than for a rich man to enter into the kingdom of God.

26 And they were astonished out of measure, saying among themselves, Who then can be saved?

27 And Jesus looking upon them saith, With men *it is* impossible, but not with God: for [n]with God all things are possible.

10:11 [e]Mat. 5:32 & 19:9 Luke 16:18 Rom. 7:3 1 Cor. 7:10,11
10:13 [f]Mat. 19:13 Luke 18:15
10:14 [g]1 Cor. 14:20 1 Pet. 2:2
10:15 [h]Mat. 18:3
10:17 [i]Mat. 19:16 Luke 18:18
10:19 [j]Ex. 20 Rom. 13:9
10:21 [k]Mat. 6:19,20 & 19:21 Luke 12:33 & 16:9
10:23 [l]Mat. 19:23 Luke 18:24
10:24 [m]Job 31:24 Ps. 52:7 & 62:10 1 Tim. 6:17
10:27 [n]Jer. 32:17 Mat. 19:26 Luke 1:37

10:11 COMMITTETH ADULTERY. Anyone who divorces for other than Biblical reasons and marries again sins against God by committing adultery (see Mal. 2:14, note; Mat. 19:9, note; 1 Cor. 7:15). In other words, divorce is not necessarily recognized as right or legitimate by God merely because the state (or any human institution) legalizes it.

10:14 KINGDOM OF GOD. Mark uses the term "kingdom of God" while Matthew generally uses "kingdom of heaven." The meaning, however, is the same; compare the following parallel passages: Mat. 4:17 with Mark 1:15; Mat. 5:3 with Luke 6:20; Mat. 11:11 with Luke 7:28; Mat. 10:7 with Luke 10:9 (see article on THE KINGDOM OF GOD, p. 1428).

10:15 AS A LITTLE CHILD. Receiving the kingdom of God like a child means accepting it in such a simple, humble, trustful, and wholehearted manner that you turn from sin and receive Christ as your Lord and Savior, and God as your heavenly Father (see Mat. 18:3, note).

10:16 AND BLESSED THEM. Christ is deeply concerned about the salvation and the spiritual upbringing of children. Christian parents should use every means of grace available to bring their children to Christ, for He longs to receive them, love them, and bless them (vv. 13–16; see article on PARENTS AND CHILDREN, p. 1880).

10:23 THEY THAT HAVE RICHES. See article on RICHES AND POVERTY, p. 1568.

The reward of sacrifice

10:28–31pp — Mat. 19:27–30; Luke 18:28–30

28 ¶ [o]Then Peter began to say
unto him, Lo, we have left all, and have
followed thee.
29 And Jesus answered and said,
Verily I say unto you, There is no man
that hath left house, or brethren, or sis-
ters, or father, or mother, or wife, or
children, or lands, for my sake, and the
gospel's,
30 [p]But he shall receive an hun-
dredfold now in this time, houses, and
brethren, and sisters, and mothers,
and children, and lands, with persecu-
tions; and in the world to come eternal
life.
31 [q]But many *that are* first shall be
last; and the last first.

Jesus again foretells his death

10:32–34pp — Mat. 20:17–19; Luke 18:31–33

32 ¶ [r]And they were in the way go-
ing up to Jerusalem; and Jesus went be-
fore them: and they were amazed; and
as they followed, they were afraid.
[s]And he took again the twelve, and
began to tell them what things should
happen unto him,
33 *Saying,* Behold, we go up to Jeru-
salem; and the Son of man shall be de-
livered unto the chief priests, and unto
the scribes; and they shall condemn
him to death, and shall deliver him to
the Gentiles:
34 And they shall mock him, and
shall scourge him, and shall spit upon
him, and shall kill him: and the third
day he shall rise again.

The ambition of James and John

10:35–45pp — Mat. 20:20–28

35 ¶ [t]And James and John, the
sons of Zebedee, come unto him, say-
ing, Master, we would that thou
shouldest do for us whatsoever we
shall desire.
36 And he said unto them, What
would ye that I should do for you?
37 They said unto him, Grant unto
us that we may sit, one on thy right
hand, and the other on thy left hand, in
thy glory.
38 But Jesus said unto them, Ye
know not what ye ask: can ye drink of
the cup that I drink of? and be baptized
with the baptism that I am baptized
with?
39 And they said unto him, We can.
And Jesus said unto them, Ye shall in-
deed drink of the cup that I drink of;
and with the baptism that I am bap-
tized withal shall ye be baptized:
40 But to sit on my right hand and
on my left hand is not mine to give; but
it shall be given to them for whom it is
prepared.
41 [u]And when the ten heard *it,*
they began to be much displeased with
James and John.
42 But Jesus called them *to him,* and
saith unto them, [v]Ye know that they
which [e]are accounted to rule over the
Gentiles exercise lordship over them;
and their great ones exercise authority
upon them.
43 [w]But so shall it not be among
you: but whosoever will be great
among you, shall be your minister:
44 And whosoever of you will be the
chiefest, shall be servant of all.
45 For even [x]the Son of man came
not to be ministered unto, but to minis-
ter, and [y]to give his life a ransom for
many.

Bartimaeus receives his sight

10:46–52pp — Mat. 20:29–34; Luke 18:35–43

46 ¶ [z]And they came to Jericho:
and as he went out of Jericho with his
disciples and a great number of people,
blind Bartimaeus, the son of Timaeus,
sat by the highway side begging.
47 And when he heard that it was

10:28 [o]Mat. 19:27 Luke 18:28
10:30 [p]2 Chr. 25:9 Luke 18:30
10:31 [q]Mat. 19:30 & 20:16 Luke 13:30
10:32 [r]Mat. 20:17 Luke 18:31 [s]ch. 8:31 & 9:31 Luke 9:22 & 18:31
10:35 [t]Mat. 20:20
10:41 [u]Mat. 20:24
10:42 [v]Luke 22:25
10:43 [w]Mat. 20:26,28 ch. 9:35 Luke 9:48
10:45 [x]John 13:14 Phil. 2:7 [y]Mat. 20:28 1 Tim. 2:6 Tit. 2:14
10:46 [z]Mat. 20:29 Luke 18:35

[e] Or, *think good*

10:30 RECEIVE AN HUNDREDFOLD. The rewards promised in this verse are not to be understood in a literal way. Rather, the blessings and joy inherent in the relationships listed here will be experienced by the true disciple who sacrifices for Christ's sake.

10:31 FIRST SHALL BE LAST. See Mat. 19:30, note.

10:43 WHOSOEVER WILL BE GREAT. True greatness is not a matter of leadership, authority, or high personal achievement (v. 42), but an attitude of the heart that sincerely desires to live for God and others. We must be so committed to God that we identify with His will and purposes on earth without desiring glory, position, or material rewards. Accomplishing God's will, bringing others to salvation in Christ, and pleasing Him are the rewards of the truly great (see Luke 22:24–30, note on greatness).

10:45 A RANSOM. See Mat. 20:28, note; Rom. 3:25, note on the meaning of Christ's death for humankind.

Jesus of Nazareth, he began to cry out, and say, Jesus, *thou* son of David, have mercy on me.

48 And many charged him that he should hold his peace: but he cried the more a great deal, *Thou* son of David, have mercy on me.

49 And Jesus stood still, and commanded him to be called. And they call the blind man, saying unto him, Be of good comfort, rise; he calleth thee.

50 And he, casting away his garment, rose, and came to Jesus.

51 And Jesus answered and said unto him, What wilt thou that I should do unto thee? The blind man said unto him, Lord, that I might receive my sight.

52 And Jesus said unto him, Go thy way; [a]thy faith hath [f]made thee whole. And immediately he received his sight, and followed Jesus in the way.

Mark 11:22-24

The triumphal entry

11:1–10pp — Mat. 21:1–9; Luke 19:29–38
11:7–10pp — John 12:12–15

11 AND [b]WHEN they came nigh to Jerusalem, unto Bethphage and Bethany, at the mount of Olives, he sendeth forth two of his disciples,

2 And saith unto them, Go your way into the village over against you: and as soon as ye be entered into it, ye shall find a colt tied, whereon never man sat; loose him, and bring *him*.

3 And if any man say unto you, Why do ye this? say ye that the Lord hath need of him; and straightway he will send him hither.

4 And they went their way, and found the colt tied by the door without in a place where two ways met; and they loose him.

5 And certain of them that stood there said unto them, What do ye, loosing the colt?

6 And they said unto them even as Jesus had commanded: and they let them go.

10:52 [a]Mat. 9:22 ch. 5:34
11:1 [b]Mat. 21:1 Luke 19:29 John 12:14

11:8 [c]Mat. 21:8
11:9 [d]Ps. 118:26
11:10 [e]Ps. 148:1
11:11 [f]Mat. 21:12
11:12 [g]Mat. 21:18
11:13 [h]Mat. 21:19
11:15 [i]Mat. 21:12 Luke 19:45 John 2:14

7 And they brought the colt to Jesus, and cast their garments on him; and he sat upon him.

8 [c]And many spread their garments in the way: and others cut down branches off the trees, and strawed *them* in the way.

9 And they that went before, and they that followed, cried, saying, [d]Hosanna; Blessed *is* he that cometh in the name of the Lord:

10 Blessed *be* the kingdom of our father David, that cometh in the name of the Lord: [e]Hosanna in the highest.

11 [f]And Jesus entered into Jerusalem, and into the temple: and when he had looked round about upon all things, and now the eventide was come, he went out unto Bethany with the twelve.

The cleansing of the temple

11:12–14pp — Mat. 21:18–22
11:15–18pp — Mat. 21:12–16; Luke 19:45–47; John 2:13–16

12 ¶ [g]And on the morrow, when they were come from Bethany, he was hungry:

13 [h]And seeing a fig tree afar off having leaves, he came, if haply he might find any thing thereon: and when he came to it, he found nothing but leaves; for the time of figs was not *yet*.

14 And Jesus answered and said unto it, No man eat fruit of thee hereafter for ever. And his disciples heard *it*.

15 ¶ [i]And they come to Jerusalem: and Jesus went into the temple, and began to cast out them that sold and bought in the temple, and overthrew the tables of the moneychangers, and the seats of them that sold doves;

16 And would not suffer that any man should carry *any* vessel through the temple.

17 And he taught, saying unto

[f] Or, *saved thee*

11:1 PASSION WEEK. At this point in the Gospel of Mark, the events of Passion Week begin (chs. 11–15), followed by the resurrection (ch. 16).

11:9 BLESSED *IS* HE THAT COMETH. The crowd believed that the Messiah would restore Israel nationally and rule the nations politically. They had failed to understand the purpose that Jesus expressed regarding His coming into the world. Later the crowd shouted, "Crucify him," when they saw He was not the Messiah they desired (15:13).

11:15 JESUS WENT INTO THE TEMPLE. Christ's casting out of those who were buying and selling in the temple manifests His zeal for true holiness among those who claim to worship God (see Luke 19:45, note).

11:17 THE HOUSE OF PRAYER. Jesus makes clear that God's house was meant to be a "house of prayer," a place where God's people could meet

them, Is it not written, [j]My house shall be called [g]of all nations the house of prayer? but [k]ye have made it a den of thieves.

18 And [l]the scribes and chief priests heard *it*, and sought how they might destroy him: for they feared him, because [m]all the people was astonished at his doctrine.

19 And when even was come, he went out of the city.

The power of faith

11:20–24pp — Mat. 21:19–22

20 ¶ [n]And in the morning, as they passed by, they saw the fig tree dried up from the roots.

21 And Peter calling to remembrance saith unto him, Master, behold, the fig tree which thou cursedst is withered away.

22 And Jesus answering saith unto them, [h]Have faith in God.

23 For [o]verily I say unto you, That whosoever shall say unto this mountain, Be thou removed, and be thou cast into the sea; and shall not doubt in his heart, but shall believe that those things which he saith shall come to pass; he shall have whatsoever he saith.

24 Therefore I say unto you, [p]What things soever ye desire, when ye pray, believe that ye receive *them*, and ye shall have *them*.

Luke 7:50

25 And when ye stand praying, [q]forgive, if ye have aught against any: that your Father also which is in heaven may forgive you your trespasses.

26 But [r]if ye do not forgive, neither will your Father which is in heaven forgive your trespasses.

11:17 [j]Is. 56:7 [k]Jer. 7:11 **11:18** [l]Mat. 21:45,46 Luke 19:47 [m]Mat. 7:28 ch. 1,22 Luke 4:32 **11:20** [n]Mat. 21:19 **11:23** [o]Mat. 17:20 & 21:21 Luke 17:6 **11:24** [p]Mat. 7:7 Luke 11:9 John 14:13 & 15:7 & 16:24 Jas. 1:5,6 **11:25** [q]Mat. 6:14 Col. 3:13 **11:26** [r]Mat. 18:35

11:27 [s]Mat. 21:23 Luke 20:1 **11:32** [t]Mat. 3:5 & 14:5 ch. 6:20 **12:1** [u]Mat. 21:33 Luke 20:9

Jesus' authority challenged

11:27–33pp — Mat. 21:23–27; Luke 20:1–8

27 ¶ And they come again to Jerusalem: [s]and as he was walking in the temple, there come to him the chief priests, and the scribes, and the elders,

28 And say unto him, By what authority doest thou these things? and who gave thee this authority to do these things?

29 And Jesus answered and said unto them, I will also ask of you one [i]question, and answer me, and I will tell you by what authority I do these things.

30 The baptism of John, was *it* from heaven, or of men? answer me.

31 And they reasoned with themselves, saying, If we shall say, From heaven; he will say, Why then did ye not believe him?

32 But if we shall say, Of men; they feared the people: for [t]all *men* counted John, that he was a prophet indeed.

33 And they answered and said unto Jesus, We cannot tell. And Jesus answering saith unto them, Neither do I tell you by what authority I do these things.

Parable of the tenants

12:1–12pp — Mat. 21:33–46; Luke 20:9–19

12 AND [u]HE began to speak unto them by parables. A *certain* man planted a vineyard, and set an hedge about *it*, and digged *a place for* the winevat, and built a tower, and let it out to husbandmen, and went into a far country.

2 And at the season he sent to the husbandmen a servant, that he might

[g]Or, *an house of prayer for all nations?* [h]Or, *Have the faith of God* [i]Or, *thing*

with Him in spiritual devotion, prayer, and worship (see Is. 56:7, note; Luke 19:45, note). It must not therefore be profaned by making it the means of social advancement, monetary gain, entertainment, or showmanship. Whenever God's house is so used by worldly-minded people, it once again becomes "a den of thieves."

11:24 BELIEVE . . . YE SHALL HAVE. Believing that receives is not something humanly produced; rather, it is a believing faith imparted to the believer's heart by God Himself (see 9:23, note). Sometimes the fulfillment which true faith desires is granted immediately; at other times it is not. Yet God gives the faith that the prayer has been heard and the request will be granted. The uncertainty concerns the time of the fulfillment, not the granting of the request (see Mat. 17:20, note; 21:21, note).

11:25 WHEN YE STAND PRAYING, FORGIVE. Let no Christian delude himself that he has faith sufficient for answered prayer if he is secretly holding animosity or bitterness in his heart against anyone (see Mat. 18:35, note).

12:1 PARABLE OF THE WICKED HUSBANDMEN. This parable points out the guilt of the Jewish nation. They turned God's kingdom into a private possession, showed contempt for His Word, and refused to obey His Son, Jesus Christ. Churches today show the same attitude as the wicked husbandmen whenever they reject Christ's Word and His true messengers, and create a church after their own ideas.

receive from the husbandmen of the fruit of the vineyard.

3 And they caught *him,* and beat him, and sent *him* away empty.

4 And again he sent unto them another servant; and at him they cast stones, and wounded *him* in the head, and sent *him* away shamefully handled.

5 And again he sent another; and him they killed, and many others; beating some, and killing some.

6 Having yet therefore one son, his wellbeloved, he sent him also last unto them, saying, They will reverence my son.

7 But those husbandmen said among themselves, This is the heir; come, let us kill him, and the inheritance shall be ours.

8 And they took him, and killed *him,* and cast *him* out of the vineyard.

9 What shall therefore the lord of the vineyard do? he will come and destroy the husbandmen, and will give the vineyard unto others.

10 And have ye not read this scripture; [v]The stone which the builders rejected is become the head of the corner:

11 This was the Lord's doing, and it is marvellous in our eyes?

12 [w]And they sought to lay hold on him, but feared the people: for they knew that he had spoken the parable against them: and they left him, and went their way.

Paying taxes to Caesar

12:13–17pp — Mat. 22:15–22; Luke 20:20–26

13 ¶ [x]And they send unto him certain of the Pharisees and of the Herodians, to catch him in *his* words.

14 And when they were come, they say unto him, Master, we know that thou art true, and carest for no man: for thou regardest not the person of men, but teachest the way of God in truth: Is it lawful to give tribute to Caesar, or not?

15 Shall we give, or shall we not give? But he, knowing their hypocrisy, said unto them, Why tempt ye me?

12:10
[v]Ps. 118:22
12:12
[w]Mat. 21:45,46
ch. 11:18
John 7:25,30,44
12:13
[x]Mat. 22:15
Luke 20:20

bring me a [j]penny, that I may see *it.*

16 And they brought *it.* And he saith unto them, Whose *is* this image and superscription? And they said unto him, Caesar's.

17 And Jesus answering said unto them, Render to Caesar the things that are Caesar's, and to God the things that are God's. And they marvelled at him.

Marriage and heaven

12:18–27pp — Mat. 22:23–33; Luke 20:27–38

18 ¶ [y]Then come unto him the Sadducees, [z]which say there is no resurrection; and they asked him, saying,

19 Master, [a]Moses wrote unto us, If a man's brother die, and leave *his* wife *behind him,* and leave no children, that his brother should take his wife, and raise up seed unto his brother.

20 Now there were seven brethren: and the first took a wife, and dying left no seed.

21 And the second took her, and died, neither left he any seed: and the third likewise.

22 And the seven had her, and left no seed: last of all the woman died also.

23 In the resurrection therefore, when they shall rise, whose wife shall she be of them? for the seven had her to wife.

24 And Jesus answering said unto them, Do ye not therefore err, because ye know not the scriptures, neither the power of God?

25 For when they shall rise from the dead, they neither marry, nor are given in marriage; but [b]are as the angels which are in heaven.

26 And as touching the dead, that they rise: have ye not read in the book of Moses, how in the bush God spake

12:18
[y]Mat. 22:23
Luke 20:27
[z]Acts 23:8
12:19
[a]Deut. 25:5
12:25
[b]1 Cor. 15:42,49, 52

[j]The penny, worth about 16 cents, was the usual day's wage for a laborer

12:10 THE STONE ... OF THE CORNER. Christ is the "rejected" stone, thrown away by Israel but about to become the cornerstone of God's new people, the church (Acts 4:11–12; see Ps. 118:22, note). He is the most important stone in this new structure that God is building.

12:25 THEY NEITHER MARRY. Jesus' teaching does not mean that a husband or wife will lose their particular identity and thus not recognize each other. Rather, the relationship with our earthly partners will be a deeper, spiritual one, though it will no longer be governed by the marriage union as on earth.

unto him, saying, [c]I *am* the God of Abraham, and the God of Isaac, and the God of Jacob?

27 He is not the God of the dead, but the God of the living: ye therefore do greatly err.

The greatest commandment

12:28–34pp — Mat. 22:34–40

28 ¶ [d]And one of the scribes came, and having heard them reasoning together, and perceiving that he had answered them well, asked him, Which is the first commandment of all?

29 And Jesus answered him, The first of all the commandments *is*, [e]Hear, O Israel; The Lord our God is one Lord:

30 And thou shalt love the Lord thy God with all thy heart, and with all thy soul, and with all thy mind, and with all thy strength: this *is* the first commandment.

31 And the second *is* like, *namely* this, [f]Thou shalt love thy neighbour as thyself. There is none other commandment greater than these.

32 And the scribe said unto him, Well, Master, thou hast said the truth: for there is one God; [g]and there is none other but he:

33 And to love him with all the heart, and with all the understanding, and with all the soul, and with all the strength, and to love *his* neighbour as himself, [h]is more than all whole burnt offerings and sacrifices.

34 And when Jesus saw that he answered discreetly, he said unto him, Thou art not far from the kingdom of God. [i]And no man after that durst ask him *any question*.

12:26
[c]Ex. 3:6
12:28
[d]Mat. 22:35
12:29
[e]Deut. 6:4
Luke 10:27
12:31
[f]Lev. 19:18
Mat. 22:39
Rom. 13:9
Gal. 5:14
Jas. 2:8
12:32
[g]Deut. 4:39
Is. 45:6,14
& 46:9
12:33
[h]1 Sam. 15:22
Hos. 6:6
Mic. 6:6-8
12:34
[i]Mat. 22:46
12:35
[j]Mat. 22:41
Luke 20:41
12:36
[k]2 Sam. 23:2
[l]Ps. 110:1
12:38
[m]ch. 4:2
[n]Mat. 23:1
Luke 20:46
[o]Luke 11:43
12:40
[p]Mat. 23:14
12:41
[q]Luke 21:1
[r]2 Ki. 12:9
12:43
[s]2 Cor. 8:12

Whose Son is the Christ?

12:35–37pp — Mat. 22:41–46; Luke 20:41–44
12:38–40pp — Mat. 23:1–7; Luke 20:45–47

35 ¶ [j]And Jesus answered and said, while he taught in the temple, How say the scribes that Christ is the son of David?

36 For David himself said [k]by the Holy Ghost, [l]The LORD said to my Lord, Sit thou on my right hand, till I make thine enemies thy footstool.

37 David therefore himself calleth him Lord; and whence is he *then* his son? And the common people heard him gladly.

38 ¶ And [m]he said unto them in his doctrine, [n]Beware of the scribes, which love to go in long clothing, and [o]*love* salutations in the marketplaces,

39 And the chief seats in the synagogues, and the uppermost rooms at feasts:

40 [p]Which devour widows' houses, and for a pretence make long prayers: these shall receive greater damnation.

The widow's mite

12:41–44pp — Luke 21:1–4

41 ¶ [q]And Jesus sat over against the treasury, and beheld how the people cast [k]money [r]into the treasury: and many that were rich cast in much.

42 And there came a certain poor widow, and she threw in two [l]mites, which make a farthing.

43 And he called *unto him* his disciples, and saith unto them, Verily I say unto you, That [s]this poor widow hath

[k]*A piece of brass money,* worth about one cent; see Mark 6:8 [l]Two mites were worth only a fraction of a cent

12:30 THOU SHALT LOVE THE LORD. See Mat. 22:37, note.

12:31 LOVE THY NEIGHBOUR. See Mat. 22:39, note.

12:38–39 LOVE . . . THE CHIEF SEATS. Jesus warns His followers to be on guard for religious leaders who seek recognition and honor from others. He calls them hypocrites (Mat. 23:13–15,23,25,29) and describes them as frauds and deceivers in the area of observable righteousness (cf. Mat. 23:25–28). Such persons do not possess the indwelling Holy Spirit with His regenerating grace (cf. Rom. 8:5–14). While remaining in this condition, they cannot "escape the damnation of hell" (Mat. 23:33; see 23:13, note; see article on FALSE TEACHERS, p. 1508).

12:40 DEVOUR WIDOWS' HOUSES. Some of the Jewish religious leaders took advantage of unsuspecting and lonely widows. They would seek and receive exorbitant offerings from them, exploiting their willingness to help those whom the widows believed to be men of God. By deceit and fraud they persuaded the widows to give more than they could afford, then lived in luxury on these misguided offerings. This same pattern has occurred throughout the history of the church, right up to today; each age has its experts in the art of religious extortion.

12:42 POOR WIDOW. See Luke 7:13, note on God's special care and love for women who are alone, abandoned, or widowed.

12:42 TWO MITES. God measures giving not by the amount, but by the love, devotion, and sacrifice represented in the gift (see Luke 21:1–4, note).

cast more in, than all they which have cast into the treasury:

44 For all *they* did cast in of their abundance; but she of her want did cast in all that she had, [t]*even* all her living.

Signs of the end of this age

13:1–13pp — Mat. 24:1–14; Luke 21:5–19

13 AND [u]AS he went out of the temple, one of his disciples saith unto him, Master, see what manner of stones and what buildings *are here!*

2 And Jesus answering said unto him, Seest thou these great buildings? [v]there shall not be left one stone upon another, that shall not be thrown down.

3 And as he sat upon the mount of Olives over against the temple, Peter and James and John and Andrew asked him privately,

4 [w]Tell us, when shall these things be? and what *shall be* the sign when all these things shall be fulfilled?

5 And Jesus answering them began to say, [x]Take heed lest any *man* deceive you:

6 For many shall come in my name, saying, I am *Christ;* and shall deceive many.

7 And when ye shall hear of wars and rumours of wars, be ye not troubled: for *such things* must needs be; but the end *shall* not *be* yet.

8 For nation shall rise against nation, and kingdom against kingdom: and there shall be earthquakes in divers places, and there shall be famines and troubles: [y]these *are* the beginnings of [m]sorrows.

9 ¶ But [z]take heed to yourselves: for they shall deliver you up to councils; and in the synagogues ye shall be beaten: and ye shall be brought before rulers and kings for my sake, for a testimony against them.

10 And [a]the gospel must first be published among all nations.

11 [b]But when they shall lead *you,* and deliver you up, take no thought beforehand what ye shall speak, neither do ye premeditate: but whatsoever shall be given you in that hour, that speak ye: for it is not ye that speak, [c]but the Holy Ghost.

12 Now [d]the brother shall betray the brother to death, and the father the son; and children shall rise up against *their* parents, and shall cause them to be put to death.

13 [e]And ye shall be hated of all *men* for my name's sake: but [f]he that shall endure unto the end, the same shall be saved.

The great tribulation

13:14–23pp — Mat. 24:15–28; Luke 21:20–26

14 ¶ [g]But when ye shall see the abomination of desolation, [h]spoken of by Daniel the prophet, standing where it ought not, (let him that readeth un-

[m] The word in the original importeth *the pains of a woman in travail*

12:44 [t]Deut. 24:6; 1 John 3:17
13:1 [u]Mat. 24:1; Luke 21:5
13:2 [v]Luke 19:44
13:4 [w]Mat. 24:3; Luke 21:7
13:5 [x]Jer. 29:8; Eph. 5:6; 1 Thes. 2:3
13:8 [y]Mat. 24:8
13:9 [z]Mat. 10:17,18 & 24:9; Rev. 2:10
13:10 [a]Mat. 24:14
13:11 [b]Mat. 10:19; Luke 12:11 & 21:14; [c]Acts 2:4 & 4:8,31
13:12 [d]Mic. 7:6; Mat. 10:21 & 24:10; Luke 21:16
13:13 [e]Mat. 24:9; Luke 21:17; [f]Dan. 12:12; Mat. 10:22 & 24:13; Rev. 2:10
13:14 [g]Mat. 24:15; [h]Dan. 9:27

13:5 TAKE HEED. The Olivet discourse of Jesus contains repeated warnings that as the end draws near, His people must be on constant alert to the danger of religious deception. Jesus admonishes, "take heed" (v. 5), "take heed to yourselves" (v. 9), "but take ye heed" (v. 23), "take ye heed, watch" (v. 33), "watch ye therefore" (v. 35), and "watch" (v. 37). These warnings indicate that many unbiblical teachings will be prominent among the churches. The believer, more than ever, must know and adhere only to the Word of God (see Mat. 24:5, note).

13:6 MANY . . . SHALL DECEIVE MANY. See Mat. 24:11, note.

13:10 GOSPEL ... PUBLISHED AMONG ALL NATIONS. See Mat. 24:14, notes.

13:13 ENDURE UNTO THE END. Perseverance in the faith and endurance in our loyalty to Christ is a Scriptural condition for final salvation (cf. Heb. 3:14; 6:11–12; 10:36). The glory of final salvation is described in Rev. 2:7,17,26–28; 3:5, 12,20–21; 7:9–17; 14:13; 21:1–7.

13:14 ABOMINATION OF DESOLATION. The abomination that causes desolation refers to that which defames or pollutes what is holy (see Dan. 9:25–27). (1) Christ's statement may prophetically refer both to the Roman invasion of Jerusalem when the temple was destroyed (A.D. 70), and to the placing of the image of the antichrist in Jerusalem just before Christ returns to judge the wicked (see 2 Thes. 2:2–3; Rev. 13:14–15; 19:11–21).

(2) This is sometimes called "prophetic foreshadowing," a term used when two or more events are viewed as if they are one. Examples would be the combining of Christ's first coming to preach the gospel with His second coming to bring judgment in Is. 11:1–4; 61:1–2; and Zech. 9:9–10 (see notes on those passages; see Mat. 24:44, note). Likewise, the Pentecostal outpouring of the Spirit and "the great and the terrible day of the LORD" are combined and spoken of as one event in Joel 2:28–31. What Christ does here is to describe Jerusalem's destruction as a type of the great tribulation that occurs at the end of the age (see article on THE GREAT TRIBULATION, p. 1456).

derstand,) then [i]let them that be in
Judaea flee to the mountains:
15 And let him that is on the
housetop not go down into the house,
neither enter *therein,* to take any thing
out of his house:
16 And let him that is in the field
not turn back again for to take up his
garment.
17 [j]But woe to them that are with
child, and to them that give suck in
those days!
18 And pray ye that your flight be
not in the winter.
19 [k]For *in* those days shall be af-
fliction, such as was not from the be-
ginning of the creation which God cre-
ated unto this time, neither shall be.
20 And except that the Lord had
shortened those days, no flesh should
be saved: but for the elect's sake,
whom he hath chosen, he hath short-
ened the days.
21 [l]And then if any man shall say
to you, Lo, here *is* Christ; or, lo, *he is*
there; believe *him* not:
22 For false Christs and false
prophets shall rise, and shall show
signs and wonders, to seduce, if *it were*
possible, even the elect.
23 But [m]take ye heed: behold, I
have foretold you all things.

Christ's coming after the tribulation

13:24–31pp — Mat. 24:29–35; Luke 21:27–33

24 ¶ [n]But in those days, after that
tribulation, the sun shall be darkened,
and the moon shall not give her light,
25 And the stars of heaven shall
fall, and the powers that are in heaven
shall be shaken.
26 [o]And then shall they see the
Son of man coming in the clouds with
great power and glory.
27 And then shall he send his an-
gels, and shall gather together his
elect from the four winds, from the ut-
termost part of the earth to the utter-
most part of heaven.
28 [p]Now learn a parable of the fig
tree; When her branch is yet tender,
and putteth forth leaves, ye know that
summer is near:
29 So ye in like manner, when ye
shall see these things come to pass,
know that it is nigh, *even* at the doors.
30 Verily I say unto you, that this
generation shall not pass, till all these
things be done.
31 Heaven and earth shall pass
away: but [q]my words shall not pass
away.

Christ's unexpected coming

13:32–34pp — Mat. 24:36,42

32 ¶ But of that day and *that* hour
knoweth no man, no, not the angels
which are in heaven, neither the Son,
but the Father.
33 [r]Take ye heed, watch and pray:
for ye know not when the time is.
34 [s]*For the Son of man is* as a man
taking a far journey, who left his
house, and gave authority to his ser-
vants, and to every man his work, and
commanded the porter to watch.

Christ's coming at any time

13:35–37pp — Mat. 24:43–44

35 [t]Watch ye therefore: for ye
know not when the master of the house
cometh, at even, or at midnight, or at
the cockcrowing, or in the morning:
36 Lest coming suddenly he find
you sleeping.

13:14 [i]Luke 21:21
13:17 [j]Luke 21:23
13:19 [k]Dan. 9:26 & 12:1 Joel 2:2 Mat. 24:21
13:21 [l]Mat. 24:23 Luke 17:23 & 21:8
13:23 [m]2 Pet. 3:17
13:24 [n]Dan. 7:10 Zeph. 1:15 Mat. 24:29
13:26 [o]Dan. 7:13,14 Mat. 16:27 & 24:30 ch. 14:62 Acts 1:11 1 Thes. 4:16 2 Thes. 1:7,10 Rev. 1:7
13:28 [p]Mat. 24:32 Luke 21:29
13:31 [q]Is. 40:8
13:33 [r]Mat. 24:42 & 25:13 Luke 12:40 & 21:34 Rom. 13:11 1 Thes. 5:6
13:34 [s]Mat. 24:45 & 25:14
13:35 [t]Mat. 24:42,44

13:19–22 AFFLICTION. See article on THE GREAT TRIBULATION, p. 1456, for the interpretation of these verses.

13:22 FALSE PROPHETS. See article on FALSE TEACHERS, p. 1508.

13:24 THE SUN . . . DARKENED. See Mat. 24:29, note.

13:26 SON OF MAN COMING. See Mat. 24:30, note.

13:27 GATHER TOGETHER HIS ELECT. See Mat. 24:31, note.

13:28 THE FIG TREE. See Mat. 24:32, note.

13:29 THESE THINGS. See Mat. 24:33, note.

13:30 THIS GENERATION. See Mat. 24:34, note.

13:32 *THAT* HOUR KNOWETH NO MAN. See Mat. 24:36, note.

13:33 WATCH AND PRAY. See Mat. 24:42, notes.

13:35 AT EVEN . . . MIDNIGHT . . . MORNING. Christ affirms that His return for the faithful of His churches could occur at four possible times during the night or early morning. This points to the fact that his coming for them could be at anytime and emphasizes the unexpectedness and hiddenness of the time of the first stage of His coming, when the faithful will be caught up from the earth (i.e., the rapture; see article on THE RAPTURE, p. 1889). Since it is imminent and unexpected, all believers must be spiritually alert and faithful (see Mat. 24:42, notes; 24:44, note; cf. Luke 12:35–36,38–40,46; 21:34–36).

FALSE TEACHERS

***Mark 13:22** "For false Christs and false prophets shall rise, and shall show signs and wonders, to seduce, if* it were *possible, even the elect."*

DESCRIPTION. Believers today must be aware that within the churches there may be preachers, pastors, and ministers of God's Word who are of the same spirit and life as the corrupt teachers of God's law in Jesus' day (Mat. 24:11,24). Jesus warns that not everyone who professes Christ is a true believer, nor are all Christian writers, missionaries, pastors, evangelists, teachers, deacons, and workers what they claim to be.

(1) These ministers will "outwardly appear righteous unto men" (Mat. 23:28). They come "in sheep's clothing" (Mat. 7:15). They may base their message solidly on God's Word, proclaiming high righteous standards. They may appear sincerely concerned for God's work and kingdom and show great interest in the salvation of the lost, professing love for all people. They may appear to be great ministers of God, commendable spiritual leaders, anointed by His Holy Spirit. They may perform great miracles and have great success, and multitudes may follow them (see Mat. 7:21–23; 24:11,24; 2 Cor. 11:13–15).

(2) Nevertheless, these people find their spiritual ancestors in the false prophets of the O.T. (see Deut. 13:3, note; 1 Ki. 18:40, note; Neh. 6:12, note; Jer. 14:14, note; Hos. 4:15, note; see article on THE PROPHET IN THE OLD TESTAMENT, p. 1002) and in the Pharisees of the N.T. Away from the crowds and in their private lives, the Pharisees were given over to "extortion and excess" (Mat. 23:25), "full of dead men's bones, and of all uncleanness" (Mat. 23:27), "full of hypocrisy and iniquity" (Mat. 23:28). Their lives behind closed doors involved such things as lust, immorality, adultery, greed, and self-centered indulgence.

(3) These imposters attain a place of influence in the church in two ways. (a) Some false teachers/preachers begin their ministry in sincerity, truth, purity, and genuine faith in Christ. Then because of their pride and their own immoral desires, personal commitment and love to Christ gradually die. Consequently, they are severed from the kingdom of God (1 Cor. 6:9–10; Gal. 5:19–21; Eph. 5:5–6) and become instruments of Satan while disguising themselves as ministers of righteousness (see 2 Cor. 11:15). (b) Other false teachers/preachers are never genuine believers in Christ. Satan has planted them within the church from the very beginning of their ministry (Mat. 13:24–28,36–43), using their ability and charisma and aiding in their success. His strategy is to place them in influential positions so that they can undermine the genuine work of Christ. If they are discovered or exposed, Satan knows that great damage will come to the gospel and that the name of Christ will be put to open shame.

TESTING. Jesus warned His disciples thirteen times in the Gospels to be aware of leaders who would mislead (Mat. 7:15; 16:6,11; 24:4,24; Mark 4:24; 8:15; 12:38–40; 13:5; Luke 12:1; 17:23; 20:46; 21:8). Elsewhere believers are exhorted to examine teachers, preachers, and leaders in the church (1 Thes. 5:21; 1 John 4:1). The following steps can be taken in testing false teachers or false prophets:

(1) Discern the person's character. Does he have a diligent prayer life and manifest a sincere and pure devotion to God? Does he manifest the fruit of the Spirit (Gal. 5:22–23), love sinners (John 3:16), hate evil and love righteousness (Heb. 1:9, note), and cry out against sin (Mat. 23; Luke 3:18–20)?

(2) Discern the person's motives. True Christian leaders will seek to do four things: (a) honor Christ (2 Cor. 8:23; Phil. 1:20); (b) lead the church into sanctification (Acts 26:18; 2 Cor. 6:16–18); (c) save the lost (1 Cor. 9:19–22); and (d) proclaim and defend the gospel of Christ and the apostles (see Phil. 1:17, note; Jude 3, note).

(3) Test the fruit of a person's life and message. The fruit of false preachers will often consist in converts not totally committed to all of God's Word (see Mat. 7:16, note).

(4) Discern the person's level of reliance on Scripture. This is a key issue. Does he believe and teach that the original writings of both the O.T. and N.T. are fully inspired by God, and that we are to submit to all their teachings (see 2 John 9–11; see article on THE INSPIRATION AND AUTHORITY OF SCRIPTURE, p. 1924)? If not, we can be assured that the teacher and his message are not of God.

(5) Finally, test his integrity with respect to the Lord's money. Does he refuse large amounts for himself, handle all finances with integrity and responsibility, and seek to promote the work of God in ways consistent with the N.T. standards for leaders (1 Tim. 3:3; 6:9–10)?

It must be understood that in spite of all that a faithful believer can do in evaluating a person's life and message, there will still be false teachers within the churches who, with the help of Satan, remain undetected until God determines to expose those persons for what they are.

Luke 17:22-37 37 And what I say unto you I say
unto all, Watch.

Anointing of Jesus at Bethany

14:1–11pp — Mat. 26:2–16
14:1–2,10–11pp — Luke 22:1–6
14:3–8Ref — John 12:1–8

14 AFTER [u]TWO days was *the*
feast of the passover, and of un-
leavened bread: and the chief priests
and the scribes sought how they might
take him by craft, and put *him* to death.

2 But they said, Not on the feast
day, lest there be an uproar of the peo-
ple.

3 ¶ [v]And being in Bethany in the
house of Simon the leper, as he sat at
meat, there came a woman having an
alabaster box of ointment of [n]spike-
nard very precious; and she brake the
box, and poured *it* on his head.

4 And there were some that had in-
dignation within themselves, and said,
Why was this waste of the ointment
made?

5 For it might have been sold for
more than three hundred [w]pence, and
have been given to the poor. And they
murmured against her.

6 And Jesus said, Let her alone;
why trouble ye her? she hath wrought
a good work on me.

7 For ye have the poor with you al-
ways, and whensoever ye will ye may
do them good: but me ye have not al-
ways.

8 She hath done what she could:
she is come aforehand to anoint my
body to the burying.

9 Verily I say unto you, Wheresoev-
er this gospel shall be preached
throughout the whole world, *this* also
that she hath done shall be spoken of
for a memorial of her.

10 ¶ [x]And Judas Iscariot, one of
the twelve, went unto the chief priests,
to betray him unto them.

11 And when they heard *it,* they
were glad, and promised to give him
money. And he sought how he might
conveniently betray him.

The last supper

14:12–21pp — Mat. 26:17–25; Luke 22:7–13

12 ¶ [y]And the first day of unleav-
ened bread, when they [o]killed the
passover, his disciples said unto him,
Where wilt thou that we go and prepare
that thou mayest eat the passover?

13 And he sendeth forth two of his
disciples, and saith unto them, Go ye
into the city, and there shall meet you
a man bearing a pitcher of water: fol-
low him.

14 And wheresoever he shall go in,
say ye to the goodman of the house,
The Master saith, Where is the guest-
chamber, where I shall eat the pass-
over with my disciples?

15 And he will show you a large up-
per room furnished *and* prepared: there
make ready for us.

16 And his disciples went forth, and
came into the city, and found as he had
said unto them: and they made ready
the passover.

17 [z]And in the evening he cometh
with the twelve.

18 And as they sat and did eat,
Jesus said, Verily I say unto you, One
of you which eateth with me shall be-
tray me.

19 And they began to be sorrowful,
and to say unto him one by one, *Is* it I?
and another *said, Is* it I?

20 And he answered and said unto
them, *It is* one of the twelve, that
dippeth with me in the dish.

21 [a]The Son of man indeed goeth,

14:1 [u]Mat. 26:2 Luke 22:1 John 11:55 & 13:1
14:3 [v]Mat. 26:6 John 12:1,3 See Luke 7:37
14:5 [w]Mat. 18:28 ch. 12:15
14:10 [x]Mat. 26:14 Luke 22:3,4
14:12 [y]Mat. 26:17 Luke 22:7
14:17 [z]Mat. 26:20
14:21 [a]Mat. 26:24 Luke 22:22

[n] Or, *pure nard,* or, *liquid nard* [o] Or, *sacrificed*

14:9 THIS GOSPEL. Gospel (Gk. *euangelion*) means good news—the good news that God has acted to save the perishing human race through the incarnation, death, and resurrection of Jesus Christ (Luke 4:18–21; 7:22; John 3:16). Wherever this is proclaimed in the power of the Spirit (1 Cor. 2:4; Gal. 1:11), it comes with authority (Mat. 28:18–20); it reveals God's righteousness (Rom. 1:16–17); it creates faith (Rom. 10:17; Phil. 1:27); it brings salvation, life, and the gift of the Holy Spirit (Acts 2:33,38–39; Rom. 1:16; 1 Cor. 15:22; 1 Pet. 1:23); it delivers from the dominion of sin and Satan (Mat. 12:28; Acts 26:18; Rom. 6); it brings hope (Col. 1:5,23), peace (Eph. 2:17; 6:15), and immortality (2 Tim. 1:10); it warns of judgment (Rom. 2:16); and it brings condemnation and eternal death when refused (John 3:18).

14:9 FOR A MEMORIAL OF HER. See Mat. 26:13, note.

14:14 PASSOVER. See Mat. 26:2, note.

14:21 HAD NEVER BEEN BORN. Jesus always judges and evaluates life from a spiritual and eternal viewpoint. He affirms that it would be better that a person never be born than to come into this world, fail to accept Jesus as his Lord and Savior, and consequently perish eternally in hell (see John 6:64, note).

as it is written of him: but woe to that man by whom the Son of man is betrayed! good were it for that man if he had never been born.

The institution of the Lord's Supper

14:22–25pp — Mat. 26:26–29; Luke 22:13–21; 1 Cr. 11:23–25

22 ¶ [b]And as they did eat, Jesus took bread, and blessed, and brake *it*, and gave to them, and said, Take, eat: this is my body.

23 And he took the cup, and when he had given thanks, he gave *it* to them: and they all drank of it.

24 And he said unto them, This is my blood of the new testament, which is shed for many.

25 Verily I say unto you, I will drink no more of the fruit of the vine, until that day that I drink it new in the kingdom of God.

Peter's denial foretold

14:26pp — Mat. 26:30
14:27–31pp — Mat. 26:31–35

26 ¶ [c]And when they had sung an [p]hymn, they went out into the mount of Olives.

27 [d]And Jesus saith unto them, All ye shall be offended because of me this night: for it is written, [e]I will smite the shepherd, and the sheep shall be scattered.

28 But [f]after that I am risen, I will go before you into Galilee.

29 [g]But Peter said unto him, Although all shall be offended, yet *will* not I.

30 And Jesus saith unto him, Verily I say unto thee, That this day, *even* in this night, before the cock crow twice, thou shalt deny me thrice.

31 But he spake the more vehemently, If I should die with thee, I will not deny thee in any wise. Likewise also said they all.

14:22 [b]Mat. 26:26 Luke 22:19 1 Cor. 11:23
14:26 [c]Mat. 26:30
14:27 [d]Mat. 26:31 [e]Zech. 13:7
14:28 [f]ch. 16:7
14:29 [g]Mat. 26:33,34 Luke 22:33,34 John 13:37,38

Jesus' agony in Gethsemane

14:32–42pp — Mat. 26:36–46; Luke 22:40–46

32 [h]And they came to a place which was named Gethsemane: and he saith to his disciples, Sit ye here, while I shall pray.

33 And he taketh with him Peter and James and John, and began to be sore amazed, and to be very heavy;

34 And saith unto them, [i]My soul is exceeding sorrowful unto death: tarry ye here, and watch.

35 And he went forward a little, and fell on the ground, and prayed that, if it were possible, the hour might pass from him.

36 And he said, [j]Abba, Father, [k]all things *are* possible unto thee; take away this cup from me: [l]nevertheless not what I will, but what thou wilt.

37 And he cometh, and findeth them sleeping, and saith unto Peter, Simon, sleepest thou? couldest not thou watch one hour?

38 Watch ye and pray, lest ye enter into temptation. [m]The spirit truly *is* ready, but the flesh *is* weak.

39 And again he went away, and prayed, and spake the same words.

40 And when he returned, he found them asleep again, (for their eyes were heavy,) neither wist they what to answer him.

14:32 [h]Mat. 26:36 Luke 22:39 John 18:1
14:34 [i]John 12:27
14:36 [j]Rom. 8:15 Gal. 4:6 [k]Heb. 5:7 [l]John 5:30 & 6:38
14:38 [m]Rom. 7:23 Gal. 5:17

[p] Or, *psalm*

14:22 BREAD . . . MY BODY. See Luke 22:20, notes; 1 Cor. 11:24–25,27 notes.

14:24 BLOOD OF THE NEW TESTAMENT. Christ's blood was shed for us in order to bring us forgiveness of sins and salvation. His death on the cross established a new covenant between God and all who receive Christ as Lord and Savior (see Jer. 31:31–34, notes). Those who repent of their sins and turn to God through faith in Christ will be forgiven, be delivered from the power of Satan, receive new spiritual life, be made children of God, be baptized in the Holy Spirit, and have access to God at any time in order to receive mercy, grace, strength, and help (see Mat. 26:28, note; Heb. 4:16; 7:25).

14:32 GETHSEMANE . . . PRAY. Jesus' action is an example of what believers ought to do in times of great distress or grief. (1) Turn to God in prayer (vv. 32,35–36,39). (2) Seek the support of friends (vv. 33–34,42). (3) Affirm in your heart that God is your heavenly Father who cares for you (v. 36). (4) Trust God and commit yourself to His will (v. 36). See Mat. 26:37ff, notes on the ten stages of the sufferings of Christ.

14:35 HOUR MIGHT PASS FROM HIM. See Mat. 26:39, note.

14:37 WATCH ONE HOUR. Peter and the disciples neglected to watch and pray, the only thing which could have saved them from failure at this time of testing (v. 50). Failure in our Christian life is absolutely certain without prayer (see Acts 10:9, note on the commitment to pray for one hour).

41 And he cometh the third time,
and saith unto them, Sleep on now, and
take *your* rest: it is enough, [n]the hour
is come; behold, the Son of man is be-
trayed into the hands of sinners.
42 [o]Rise up, let us go; lo, he that
betrayeth me is at hand.

Jesus' betrayal and arrest

14:43–50pp — Mat. 26:47–56; Luke 22:47–50; John 18:3–11

43 ¶ [p]And immediately, while he
yet spake, cometh Judas, one of the
twelve, and with him a great multitude
with swords and staves, from the chief
priests and the scribes and the elders.
44 And he that betrayed him had
given them a token, saying, Whomso-
ever I shall kiss, that same is he; take
him, and lead *him* away safely.
45 And as soon as he was come, he
goeth straightway to him, and saith,
Master, master; and kissed him.
46 ¶ And they laid their hands on
him, and took him.
47 And one of them that stood by
drew a sword, and smote a servant of
the high priest, and cut off his ear.
48 [q]And Jesus answered and said
unto them, Are ye come out, as against
a thief, with swords and *with* staves to
take me?
49 I was daily with you in the tem-
ple teaching, and ye took me not: but
[r]the scriptures must be fulfilled.
50 [s]And they all forsook him, and
fled.
51 And there followed him a certain
young man, having a linen cloth cast
about *his* naked *body;* and the young
men laid hold on him:
52 And he left the linen cloth, and
fled from them naked.

14:41 [n]John 13:1
14:42 [o]Mat. 26:46 John 18:1,2
14:43 [p]Mat. 26:47 Luke 22:47 John 18:3
14:48 [q]Mat. 26:55 Luke 22:52
14:49 [r]Ps. 22:6 Is. 53:7 Luke 22:37 & 24:44
14:50 [s]ver. 27 Ps. 88:8
14:53 [t]Mat. 26:57 Luke 22:54 John 18:13
14:55 [u]Mat. 26:59
14:58 [v]ch. 15:29 John 2:19
14:60 [w]Mat. 26:62
14:61 [x]Is. 53:7 [y]Mat. 26:63
14:62 [z]Mat. 24:30 & 26:64 Luke 22:69

Jesus before Caiaphas

14:53–65pp — Mat. 26:57–68; John 18:12–13,19–24
14:61–63pp — Luke 22:67–71

53 ¶ [t]And they led Jesus away to
the high priest: and with him were as-
sembled all the chief priests and the
elders and the scribes.
54 And Peter followed him afar off,
even into the palace of the high priest:
and he sat with the servants, and
warmed himself at the fire.
55 [u]And the chief priests and all
the council sought for witness against
Jesus to put him to death; and found
none.
56 For many bare false witness
against him, but their witness agreed
not together.
57 And there arose certain, and
bare false witness against him, say-
ing,
58 We heard him say, [v]I will de-
stroy this temple that is made with
hands, and within three days I will
build another made without hands.
59 But neither so did their witness
agree together.
60 [w]And the high priest stood up in
the midst, and asked Jesus, saying, An-
swerest thou nothing? what *is it which*
these witness against thee?
61 But [x]he held his peace, and an-
swered nothing. [y]Again the high
priest asked him, and said unto him,
Art thou the Christ, the Son of the
Blessed?
62 And Jesus said, I am: [z]and ye
shall see the Son of man sitting on the
right hand of power, and coming in the
clouds of heaven.
63 Then the high priest rent his

14:46 THEY . . . TOOK HIM. See Mat. 26:57, note, for the order of events from Christ's arrest to His crucifixion.

14:50 THEY ALL FORSOOK HIM. We should never compare the failure of Peter and the other disciples at Jesus' arrest to the spiritual and moral failure of pastors or overseers after the death and resurrection of Christ. This is so for the following reasons: (1) Peter and the disciples at the time of their failure were not yet under the new covenant. The new covenant did not go into effect until Christ shed His blood upon the cross (Heb. 9:15–20).

(2) Peter and the disciples had not yet experienced the new birth or regeneration by the Holy Spirit in the full N.T. sense. The Holy Spirit was not imparted to them in His indwelling and sanctifying presence until the day of Christ's resurrection when He "breathed on *them*" and said to them, "Receive ye the Holy Ghost" (John 20:22). The disciples' failure was an act of weakness rather than wickedness.

(3) When Peter and the disciples forsook Christ, they did not possess the advantage of those who are conscious of the moral implications of Christ's sacrificial death on the cross (see Rom. 6), nor did they have a sustaining faith inspired by His resurrection from the dead.

In other words, this passage should not be used to justify restoring a leader to ministry who, because of his own sins and moral laxity, has voluntarily cast aside in his personal and spiritual life the qualifications necessary for the office of overseer (see article on MORAL QUALIFICATIONS FOR OVERSEERS, p. 1908).

clothes, and saith, What need we any further witnesses?

64 Ye have heard the blasphemy: what think ye? And they all condemned him to be guilty of death.

65 And some began to spit on him, and to cover his face, and to buffet him, and to say unto him, Prophesy: and the servants did strike him with the palms of their hands.

Peter's denial of Jesus

14:66–72pp — Mat. 26:69–75; Luke 22:56–62; John 18:16–18,25–27

66 ¶ [a]And as Peter was beneath in the palace, there cometh one of the maids of the high priest:

67 And when she saw Peter warming himself, she looked upon him, and said, And thou also wast with Jesus of Nazareth.

68 But he denied, saying, I know not, neither understand I what thou sayest. And he went out into the porch; and the cock crew.

69 [b]And a maid saw him again, and began to say to them that stood by, This is *one* of them.

70 And he denied it again. [c]And a little after, they that stood by said again to Peter, Surely thou art *one* of them: [d]for thou art a Galilaean, and thy speech agreeth *thereto.*

71 But he began to curse and to swear, *saying,* I know not this man of whom ye speak.

72 [e]And the second time the cock crew. And Peter called to mind the word that Jesus said unto him, Before the cock crow twice, thou shalt deny me thrice. And ¶when he thought thereon, he wept.

Jesus before Pontius Pilate

15:2–5pp — Mat. 27:11–14; Luke 23:2–3; John 18:29—19:11

15 AND [f]STRAIGHTWAY in the morning the chief priests held a consultation with the elders and scribes and the whole council, and bound Jesus, and carried *him* away, and delivered *him* to Pilate.

2 [g]And Pilate asked him, Art thou the King of the Jews? And he answering said unto him, Thou sayest *it.*

3 And the chief priests accused him of many things: but he answered nothing.

4 [h]And Pilate asked him again, saying, Answerest thou nothing? behold how many things they witness against thee.

5 [i]But Jesus yet answered nothing; so that Pilate marvelled.

Jesus delivered to be crucified

15:6–15pp — Mat. 27:15–26; Luke 23:18–25; John 19:12–16

6 Now [j]at *that* feast he released unto them one prisoner, whomsoever they desired.

7 And there was *one* named Barabbas, *which lay* bound with them that had made insurrection with him, who had committed murder in the insurrection.

8 And the multitude crying aloud began to desire *him to do* as he had ever done unto them.

9 But Pilate answered them, saying, Will ye that I release unto you the King of the Jews?

10 For he knew that the chief priests had delivered him for envy.

11 But [k]the chief priests moved the people, that he should rather release Barabbas unto them.

12 And Pilate answered and said again unto them, What will ye then that I shall do *unto him* whom ye call the King of the Jews?

13 And they cried out again, Crucify him.

14 Then Pilate said unto them, Why, what evil hath he done? And they cried out the more exceedingly, Crucify him.

15 ¶ [l]And *so* Pilate, willing to content the people, released Barabbas unto them, and delivered Jesus, when he had scourged *him,* to be crucified.

The soldiers mock Jesus

15:16–20pp — Mat. 27:27–31

16 [m]And the soldiers led him away

14:66 [a]Mat. 26:58,69 Luke 22:55 John 18:16
14:69 [b]Mat. 26:71 Luke 22:58 John 18:25
14:70 [c]Mat. 26:73 Luke 22:59 John 18:26 [d]Acts 2:7
14:72 [e]Mat. 26:75
15:1 [f]Ps. 2:2 Mat. 27:1 Luke 22:66 & 23:1 John 18:28 Acts 3:13 & 4:26
15:2 [g]Mat. 27:11
15:4 [h]Mat. 27:13
15:5 [i]Is. 53:7 John 19:9
15:6 [j]Mat. 27:15 Luke 23:17 John 18:39
15:11 [k]Mat. 27:20 Acts 3:14
15:15 [l]Mat. 27:26 John 19:1,16
15:16 [m]Mat. 27:27

¶ Or, *he wept abundantly,* or, *he began to weep*

14:65 TO BUFFET HIM. See Mat. 26:67, note.

14:71 TO CURSE AND TO SWEAR. The passage does not mean that Peter used profanity; rather, he affirmed what he was saying with an oath and called the curse of God down on himself if his statements should prove to be false.

15:1 DELIVERED *HIM* TO PILATE. See Mat. 27:2, note.

15:15 SCOURGED *HIM*. See Mat. 27:26, note.

into the hall, called Praetorium; and they call together the whole band.

17 And they clothed him with purple, and plaited a crown of thorns, and put it about his *head,*

18 And began to salute him, Hail, King of the Jews!

19 And they smote him on the head with a reed, and did spit upon him, and bowing *their* knees worshipped him.

20 And when they had mocked him, they took off the purple from him, and put his own clothes on him, and led him out to crucify him.

Jesus crucified

15:22–32pp — Mat. 27:33–44; Luke 23:33–43; John 19:17–24

21 [n]And they compel one Simon a Cyrenian, who passed by, coming out of the country, the father of Alexander and Rufus, to bear his cross.

22 [o]And they bring him unto the place Golgotha, which is, being interpreted, The place of a skull.

23 [p]And they gave him to drink wine mingled with myrrh: but he received *it* not.

24 And when they had crucified him, [q]they parted his garments, casting lots upon them, what every man should take.

25 And [r]it was the third hour, and they crucified him.

26 And [s]the superscription of his accusation was written over, THE KING OF THE JEWS.

27 And [t]with him they crucify two thieves; the one on his right hand, and the other on his left.

28 And the scripture was fulfilled, which saith, [u]And he was numbered with the transgressors.

29 And [v]they that passed by railed on him, wagging their heads, and saying, Ah, [w]thou that destroyest the temple, and buildest *it* in three days,

30 Save thyself, and come down from the cross.

31 Likewise also the chief priests mocking said among themselves with the scribes, He saved others; himself he cannot save.

15:21 [n]Mat. 27:32 Luke 23:26
15:22 [o]Mat. 27:33 Luke 23:33 John 19:17
15:23 [p]Mat. 27:34
15:24 [q]Ps. 22:18 Luke 23:34 John 19:23
15:25 [r]See Mat. 27:45 Luke 23:44 John 19:14
15:26 [s]Mat. 27:37 John 19:19
15:27 [t]Mat. 27:38
15:28 [u]Is. 53:12 Luke 22:37
15:29 [v]Ps. 22:7 [w]ch. 14:58 John 2:19
15:32 [x]Mat. 27:44 Luke 23:39
15:33 [y]Mat. 27:45 Luke 23:44
15:34 [z]Ps. 22:1 Mat. 27:46
15:36 [a]Mat. 27:48 John 19:29 [b]Ps. 69:21
15:37 [c]Mat. 27:50 Luke 23:46 John 19:30
15:38 [d]Mat. 27:51 Luke 23:45
15:39 [e]Mat. 27:54 Luke 23:47
15:40 [f]Mat. 27:55 Luke 23:49 [g]Ps. 38:11
15:41 [h]Luke 8:2,3
15:42 [i]Mat. 27:57 Luke 23:50 John 19:38
15:43 [j]Luke 2:25,38

32 Let Christ the King of Israel descend now from the cross, that we may see and believe. And [x]they that were crucified with him reviled him.

The death of Jesus

15:33–41pp — Mat. 27:45–56; Luke 23:44–49

33 And [y]when the sixth hour was come, there was darkness over the whole land until the ninth hour.

34 And at the ninth hour Jesus cried with a loud voice, saying, [z]Eloi, Eloi, lama sabachthani? which is, being interpreted, My God, my God, why hast thou forsaken me?

35 And some of them that stood by, when they heard *it,* said, Behold, he calleth Elias.

36 And [a]one ran and filled a sponge full of vinegar, and put *it* on a reed, and [b]gave him to drink, saying, Let alone; let us see whether Elias will come to take him down.

37 [c]And Jesus cried with a loud voice, and gave up the ghost.

38 And [d]the veil of the temple was rent in twain from the top to the bottom.

39 ¶ And [e]when the centurion, which stood over against him, saw that he so cried out, and gave up the ghost, he said, Truly this man was the Son of God.

40 [f]There were also women looking on [g]afar off: among whom was Mary Magdalene, and Mary the mother of James the less and of Joses, and Salome;

41 (Who also, when he was in Galilee, [h]followed him, and ministered unto him;) and many other women which came up with him unto Jerusalem.

Jesus laid in the tomb

15:42–47pp — Mat. 27:57–61; Luke 23:50–56; John 19:38–42

42 ¶ [i]And now when the even was come, because it was the preparation, that is, the day before the sabbath,

43 Joseph of Arimathaea, an honourable counsellor, which also [j]waited for the kingdom of God, came, and

---

15:17 CROWN OF THORNS. See Mat. 27:28–29, note.

15:20 LED HIM OUT TO CRUCIFY HIM. See Mat. 27:31, note.

15:24 THEY . . . CRUCIFIED HIM. See Mat. 27:35, note.

15:29 RAILED ON HIM. See Mat. 27:39, note.

15:34 WHY HAST THOU FORSAKEN ME? See Mat. 27:46, note.

15:37 GAVE UP THE GHOST. See Mat. 27:50, note.

went in boldly unto Pilate, and craved the body of Jesus.

44 And Pilate marvelled if he were already dead: and calling *unto him* the centurion, he asked him whether he had been any while dead.

45 And when he knew *it* of the centurion, he gave the body to Joseph.

46 [k]And he bought fine linen, and took him down, and wrapped him in the linen, and laid him in a sepulchre which was hewn out of a rock, and rolled a stone unto the door of the sepulchre.

47 And Mary Magdalene and Mary *the mother* of Joses beheld where he was laid.

The resurrection of Jesus

16:1–8pp — Mat. 28:1–8; Luke 24:1–8

16 AND [l]WHEN the sabbath was past, Mary Magdalene, and Mary the *mother* of James, and Salome, [m]had bought sweet spices, that they might come and anoint him.

2 [n]And very early in the morning the first *day* of the week, they came unto the sepulchre at the rising of the sun.

3 And they said among themselves, Who shall roll us away the stone from the door of the sepulchre?

4 And when they looked, they saw that the stone was rolled away: for it was very great.

5 [o]And entering into the sepulchre, they saw a young man sitting on the right side, clothed in a long white garment; and they were affrighted.

6 [p]And he saith unto them, Be not affrighted: Ye seek Jesus of Nazareth, which was crucified: he is risen; he is not here: behold the place where they laid him.

7 But go your way, tell his disciples and Peter that he goeth before you into Galilee: there shall ye see him, [q]as he said unto you.

8 And they went out quickly, and fled from the sepulchre; for they trembled and were amazed: [r]neither said they any thing to any *man;* for they were afraid.

Resurrection appearances of Jesus

16:9–14pp — Luke 24:9–39

9 ¶ Now when *Jesus* was risen early the first *day* of the week, he appeared first to Mary Magdalene, [s]out of whom he had cast seven devils.

10 [t]*And* she went and told them that had been with him, as they mourned and wept.

11 [u]And they, when they had heard that he was alive, and had been seen of her, believed not.

12 ¶ After that he appeared in another form [v]unto two of them, as they walked, and went into the country.

13 And they went and told *it* unto the residue: neither believed they them.

The Great Commission

16:15–16pp — Mat. 28:19; Luke 24:47–48

14 ¶ [w]Afterward he appeared unto the eleven as they sat [r]at meat, and upbraided them with their unbelief and hardness of heart, because they believed not them which had seen him after he was risen.

15 [x]And he said unto them, Go ye into all the world, [y]and preach the gospel to every creature.

16 [z]He that believeth and is baptized shall be saved; [a]but he that believeth not shall be damned. Luke 24:47-48

Signs following those who believe

17 And these signs shall follow them that believe; [b]In my name shall they cast out devils; [c]they shall speak with new tongues;

18 [d]They shall take up serpents; and if they drink any deadly thing, it shall not hurt them; [e]they shall lay

[r] Or, *together*

15:46 [k]Mat. 27:59,60 Luke 23:53 John 19:40
16:1 [l]Mat. 28:1 Luke 24:1 John 20:1 [m]Luke 23:56
16:2 [n]Luke 24:1 John 20:1
16:5 [o]Luke 24:3 John 20:11
16:6 [p]Mat. 28:5
16:7 [q]Mat. 26:32 ch. 14:28
16:8 [r]Mat. 28:8 Luke 24:9
16:9 [s]Luke 8:2
16:10 [t]Luke 24:10 John 20:18
16:11 [u]Luke 24:11
16:12 [v]Luke 24:13
16:14 [w]Luke 24:36 John 20:19 1 Cor. 15:5
16:15 [x]Mat. 28:19 John 15:16 [y]Col. 1:23
16:16 [z]John 3:18 Acts 2:38 & 16:30-32 Rom. 10:9 1 Pet. 3:21 [a]John 12:48
16:17 [b]Luke 10:17 Acts 5:16 [c]Acts 2:4 1 Cor. 12:10
16:18 [d]Luke 10:19 Acts 28:5 [e]Acts 5:15 Jas. 5:14

16:6 HE IS RISEN. See Mat. 28:6, note.

16:9–20 APPEARANCES OF JESUS AFTER HIS RESURRECTION. Although vv. 9–20 are omitted from two of the oldest Greek manuscripts, they do appear in other old manuscripts, as well as in the vast majority of Greek manuscripts from all over the ancient world. It is reasonable to conclude, therefore, that any reading overwhelmingly attested to by the majority of ancient manuscripts is likely to be the original writing of the Biblical author. In other words, vv. 9–20 should be considered as part of the inspired Word of God.

16:17 THESE SIGNS SHALL FOLLOW. See article on SIGNS OF BELIEVERS, p. 1516.

16:18 TAKE UP SERPENTS. Picking up snakes or drinking poison is not to be ritualized and made into a "trial by ordeal" in order to prove one's spirituality. These are promises given to believers who encounter such dangers in their normal work for Christ. It is a sin to "test" God by initiating unnecessary danger or trials (Mat. 4:5–7; 10:23; 24:16–18).

SIGNS OF BELIEVERS

***Mark 16:17–18** "And these signs shall follow them that believe; In my name shall they cast out devils; they shall speak with new tongues; They shall take up serpents; and if they drink any deadly thing, it shall not hurt them; they shall lay hands on the sick, and they shall recover."*

The Scriptures clearly teach that it is the desire of Christ for His followers to perform miraculous deeds as they announce the gospel of the kingdom of God (see Mat. 10:1; Mark 3:14–15; Luke 9:2, note; 10:17; John 14:12, note).

(1) These signs (Gk. *sēmeion*), performed by true disciples, confirm that the gospel message is genuine, that the kingdom of God has come to earth in power (see article on THE KINGDOM OF GOD, p. 1428), and that the living and risen Jesus is present with His people and working through them (see John 10:25; Acts 10:38).

(2) Every one of these signs (except for drinking poison) occurred in the recorded history of the early church: (a) speaking with new tongues (see Acts 2:4; 10:46; 19:6; 1 Cor. 12:30; 14; see article on SPEAKING IN TONGUES, p. 1656); (b) expelling demons (Acts 5:15–16; 16:18; 19:11–12); (c) escaping death from snakebites (Acts 28:3–5); and (d) healing the sick (Acts 3:1–7; 8:7; 9:33–34; 14:8–10; 28:7–8).

(3) These spiritual manifestations are intended to continue within Christ's churches until Jesus returns. The Scriptures never suggest that these signs were restricted to the period immediately following Jesus' ascension (see 1 Cor. 1:7, note; 12:28; Gal. 3:5).

(4) It is clear that the followers of Christ were not only to preach the gospel of the kingdom and bring salvation to those who believe (Mat. 28:19–20; Mark 16:15–16; Luke 24:47), but were also to bring in that kingdom, just as Jesus did (Acts 10:38), by casting out demons and healing diseases and sicknesses (see article on THE KINGDOM OF GOD, p. 1428).

(5) Jesus indicates in Mark 16:15–20 that these signs are not special gifts for a few, but were to be given to *all* believers who, in obedience to Christ, witness to the gospel and claim His promises.

(6) The failure of these "signs" to occur in the church today is not the failure of Christ to keep His promises. Failure, Jesus states, lies within the hearts of His followers (see Mat. 17:17, note).

(7) Christ has promised that His authority, power, and presence will accompany us as we battle the kingdom of Satan (Mat. 28:18–20; Luke 24:47–49). We must liberate people from their captivity by the preaching of the gospel, by living a righteous life (Mat. 6:33; Rom. 6:13; 14:17), and by performing signs and miracles through the power of the Holy Spirit (see Mat. 10:1, note; Mark 16:16–20; Acts 4:31–33; see article on POWER OVER SATAN AND DEMONS, p. 1486).

hands on the sick, and they shall re-
cover.

19 ¶ So then [f]after the Lord had
spoken unto them, he was [g]received
up into heaven, and [h]sat on the right
hand of God.

20 And they went forth, and
preached every where, the Lord work-
ing with *them,* [i]and confirming the
word with signs following. Amen.

16:19
[f]Acts 1:2,3
[g]Luke 24:51
[h]Ps. 110:1
Acts 7:55

16:20
[i]Acts 5:12
1 Cor. 2:4,5; Heb. 2:4

ST. LUKE

Outline

I. Preface to Luke's Gospel (1:1–4)
II. The Coming of the Savior (1:5—2:52)
  A. Announcement of John's Coming Birth (1:5–25)
  B. Announcement of Jesus' Coming Birth (1:26–56)
  C. Birth of John the Baptist (1:57–80)
  D. Birth of Jesus (2:1–20)
  E. Jesus at the Temple as an Infant (2:21–39)
  F. Jesus' Visit to the Temple as a Boy (2:40–52)
III. Preparation for the Savior's Ministry (3:1—4:13)
  A. Preaching of John the Baptist (3:1–20)
  B. Baptism of Jesus (3:21–22)
  C. Genealogy of Jesus (3:23–38)
  D. Temptation of Jesus (4:1–13)
IV. Ministry in Galilee (4:14—9:50)
  A. Beginning of Jesus' Ministry and Rejection at Nazareth (4:14–30)
  B. Capernaum: Jesus' Divine Authority Manifested (4:31–44)
  C. Miraculous Catch of Fishes (5:1–11)
  D. Healing the Leper (5:12–16)
  E. Jesus' Authority Is Challenged (5:17–26)
  F. The Savior of Sinners (5:27–32)
  G. Inauguration of the New Order (5:33—6:49)
  H. Demonstration of Divine Power (7:1—8:56)
  I. Jesus Gives Power to His Disciples (9:1–6)
  J. Herod and John the Baptist (9:7–9)
  K. Feeding of the Five Thousand (9:10–17)
  L. Peter's Confession and Jesus' Response (9:18–27)
  M. The Savior's Glory Revealed (9:28–50)
V. Ministry During the Final Journey Toward Jerusalem (9:51—19:28)
  A. The Savior's Mission of Redemption (9:51—10:37)
  B. Jesus' Special Instruction on Service and Prayer (10:38—11:13)
  C. Jesus' Warnings to Both Enemies and Followers (11:14—14:35)
  D. Parables About Lost and Found (15:1–32)
  E. Christ's Commands to His Followers (16:1—17:10)
  F. Ingratitude of Nine Lepers Who Were Healed (17:11–19)
  G. Suddenness of His Return Predicted (17:20—18:14)
  H. The Savior, Little Children, and the Rich Young Man (18:15–30)
  I. Toward the End of the Journey (18:31—19:28)
VI. Passion Week (19:29—23:56)
  A. Jesus Enters Jerusalem (19:29–48)
  B. Jesus Teaches Daily in the Temple (20:1—21:4)
  C. Jesus Foretells the Destruction of the Temple and His Return (21:5–38)
  D. Final Preparations and the Last Supper (22:1–38)
  E. Gethsemane and the Betrayal (22:39–53)
  F. The Jewish Trial (22:54–71)

- G. The Roman Trial (23:1–25)
- H. The Crucifixion (23:26–49)
- I. The Burial (23:50–56)

VII. Resurrection to Ascension (24:1–53)
- A. The Resurrection Morning (24:1–12)
- B. The Risen Lord's Appearances (24:13–43)
- C. The Farewell Instructions (24:44–53)

Author: Luke

Theme: Jesus, the Divine-Human Savior

Date of Writing: A.D. 60–63

Background

Luke's Gospel is the first of two books addressed to a man named Theophilus (1:3; Acts 1:1). Although the author is not identified by name in either book, the unanimous testimony of early Christianity and the corroborating internal evidence of the two books point to common authorship by Luke.

Apparently Luke was a Gentile convert, the only non-Jewish author of a Bible book. The Holy Spirit prompted him to write to Theophilus (whose name means "one who loves God") in order to fill a need in the Gentile church for a full account of the beginnings of Christianity. This included two parts: (1) Jesus' birth, life and ministry, death, resurrection, and ascension (Luke's Gospel), and (2) the outpouring of the Spirit at Jerusalem and the subsequent development of the early church (book of Acts). These two books comprise more than one-fourth of the N.T.

From Paul's letters we learn that Luke was a "beloved physician" (Col. 4:14) and a loyal co-worker with Paul (2 Tim. 4:11; Philem. 24; cf. "we" passages in Acts, see Introduction to Acts). From Luke's own writings we know he was well-educated, a skilled writer, a careful historian, and an inspired theologian. When he wrote his Gospel, the Gentile church apparently had no complete or widely circulated Gospel about Jesus. Matthew wrote initially for the Jews, and Mark wrote a concise Gospel for the church in Rome. The Greek-speaking Gentile world did have oral accounts about Jesus by eyewitnesses, as well as short written digests, but no complete and orderly Gospel (see 1:1–4). Thus Luke set about to investigate everything carefully "from the very first" (1:3), probably doing research in Palestine while Paul was in prison at Caesarea (Acts 21:17; 23:23—26:32) and completing his Gospel toward the end of that time or soon after arriving in Rome with Paul (Acts 28:16).

Purpose

Luke wrote this Gospel to the Gentiles to provide a full and accurate record "of all that Jesus began both to do and teach, Until the day in which he was taken up" (Acts 1:1b-2a). Writing under the inspiration of the Holy Spirit, he intended Theophilus and other Gentile inquirers and converts to know with certainty the exact truth about which they had been orally instructed (1:3–4). This purpose is apparent throughout the Gospel; for example, he traces Jesus' human genealogy back *to Adam* (3:23–38) and not just *to Abraham* as did Matthew (cf. Mat. 1:1–17). In Luke, Jesus is clearly seen as the divine-human Savior who came as God's provision of salvation for all of Adam's descendants.

Survey

Luke's Gospel begins with the most complete infancy narratives (1:5—2:40) and gives the only glimpse in the Gospels of Jesus' boyhood (2:41–52). After describing John the Baptist's ministry and giving the genealogy of Jesus, Luke divides Jesus' ministry into three major sections: (1) His ministry in and around Galilee (4:14—9:50), (2) His ministry during the final journey to Jerusalem (9:51—19:27), and (3) His last week in Jerusalem (19:28—24:43).

While Jesus' miracles are prominent in Luke's record of His Galilean ministry, the main focus in this Gospel is on Jesus' teaching and parables during His extended ministry on the way to Jerusalem (9:51—19:27). This section comprises the greatest block of material unique to Luke, and includes many well-loved stories and parables. The pivotal verse (9:51) and the key verse (19:10) of the Gospel occur at the beginning and toward the end of this special Lukan material.

Special Features

Eight major features or emphases characterize Luke's Gospel: (1) It is the most comprehensive Gospel, recording events in Jesus' life from pre-birth to His ascension, and is the longest book in the N.T. (2) It is the most literary of the Gospels, demonstrating exceptional style and content, a rich vocabulary, and an excellent command of Greek. (3) It emphasizes the universal scope of the gospel, that Jesus came to bring salvation for Jews and Gentiles alike. (4) It stresses Jesus' concern for the underprivileged, including women, children, the poor, and social outcasts. (5) It emphasizes Jesus' prayer life and His teaching about prayer. (6) The prominent title for Jesus in this Gospel is "Son of Man." (7) The response of joy characterizes those who accept Jesus and His message. (8) The Holy Spirit is given a place of prominence and importance in the life of Jesus and of His people (e.g., 1:15,41,67; 2:25–27; 4:1,14,18; 10:21; 12:12; 24:49).

Reading Luke

In order to read the entire New Testament in one year, the book of Luke should be read in 49 days, according to the following schedule:

☐ 1:1–25 ☐ 1:26–56 ☐ 1:57–80 ☐ 2:1–20 ☐ 2:21–52 ☐ 3 ☐ 4:1–13 ☐ 4:14–44 ☐ 5:1–16 ☐ 5:17–39 ☐ 6:1–16 ☐ 6:17–49 ☐ 7:1–35 ☐ 7:36–50 ☐ 8:1–21 ☐ 8:22–39 ☐ 8:40–56 ☐ 9:1–17 ☐ 9:18–36 ☐ 9:37–62 ☐ 10:1–24 ☐ 10:25–42 ☐ 11:1–13 ☐ 11:14–36 ☐ 11:37–54 ☐ 12:1–21 ☐ 12:22–48 ☐ 12:49–59 ☐ 13:1–21 ☐ 13:22–53 ☐ 14:1–24 ☐ 14:25—15:10 ☐ 15:11–32 ☐ 16 ☐ 17:1–19 ☐ 17:20—18:14 ☐ 18:15–43 ☐ 19:1–27 ☐ 19:28–48 ☐ 20:1–19 ☐ 20:20—21:4 ☐ 21:5–38 ☐ 22:1–38 ☐ 22:39–65 ☐ 22:66—23:25 ☐ 23:26–49 ☐ 23:50—24:12 ☐ 24:13–35 ☐ 24:36–53

NOTES

Introduction

1:1–4Ref — Acts 1:1

1 FORASMUCH AS many have taken in hand to set forth in order a declaration of those things which are most surely believed among us,

2 [a]Even as they delivered them unto us, which [b]from the beginning were eyewitnesses, and ministers of the word;

3 [c]It seemed good to me also, having had perfect understanding of all things from the very first, to write unto thee [d]in order, [e]most excellent Theophilus,

4 [f]That thou mightest know the certainty of those things, wherein thou hast been instructed.

Birth of John foretold

5 ¶ There was [g]in the days of Herod, the king of Judaea, a certain priest named Zacharias, [h]of the course of Abia: and his wife *was* of the daughters of Aaron, and her name *was* Elisabeth.

6 And they were both [i]righteous before God, walking in all the commandments and ordinances of the Lord blameless.

7 And they had no child, because that Elisabeth was barren, and they both were *now* well stricken in years.

8 And it came to pass, that while he executed the priest's office before God [j]in the order of his course,

9 According to the custom of the priest's office, his lot was [k]to burn incense when he went into the temple of the Lord.

10 [l]And the whole multitude of the people were praying without at the time of incense.

11 And there appeared unto him an angel of the Lord standing on the right side of [m]the altar of incense.

12 And when Zacharias saw *him*, [n]he was troubled, and fear fell upon him.

13 But the angel said unto him, Fear not, Zacharias: for thy prayer is heard; and thy wife Elisabeth shall bear thee a son, and [o]thou shalt call his name John.

14 And thou shalt have joy and gladness; and [p]many shall rejoice at his birth.

15 For he shall be great in the sight of the Lord, and [q]shall drink neither wine nor strong drink; and he shall be filled with the Holy Ghost, [r]even from his mother's womb. Luke 1:41

16 [s]And many of the children of Israel shall he turn to the Lord their God.

17 [t]And he shall go before him in the spirit and power of Elias, to turn

1:2 [a]Heb. 2:3 1 Pet. 5:1 2 Pet. 1:16 [b]Mark 1:1 John 15:27
1:3 [c]Acts 15:19 1 Cor. 7:40 [d]Acts 11:4 [e]Acts 1:1
1:4 [f]John 20:31
1:5 [g]Mat. 2:1 [h]1 Chr. 24:10 Neh. 12:4
1:6 [i]Gen. 7:1 1 Ki. 9:4 2 Ki. 20:3
1:8 [j]1 Chr. 24:19 2 Chr. 8:14
1:9 [k]Ex. 30:7,8 1 Chr. 23:13 2 Chr. 29:11
1:10 [l]Lev. 16:17
1:11 [m]Ex. 30:1
1:12 [n]Judg. 6:22 & 13:22 Dan. 10:8 ch. 2:9 Acts 10:4 Rev. 1:17
1:13 [o]ver. 60,63
1:14 [p]ver. 58
1:15 [q]Num. 6:3 Judg. 13:4 ch. 7:33 [r]Jer. 1:5 Gal. 1:15
1:16 [s]Mal. 4:5,6
1:17 [t]Mal. 4:5; Mat. 11:14; Mark 9:12

1:6 RIGHTEOUS BEFORE GOD. See Luke 2:25, note.

1:15 FILLED WITH THE HOLY GHOST. Notice the outcome of John's Spirit-filled life and ministry. Through the power of the Holy Spirit, (1) he convicts people of their sins, brings them to repentance, and turns them back to God (vv. 15–17; see John 16:8, note); (2) he preaches in the spirit and power of Elijah (v. 17; see Acts 1:8, notes); (3) he reconciles families and turns many to a life of righteousness (v. 17).

1:15 WINE . . . STRONG DRINK. The Greek word used for "strong drink" is *sikera*. Its exact meaning has not been determined, but it undoubtedly corresponds to the O.T. word *shekar* (see articles on WINE IN THE OLD TESTAMENT, p. 220, and WINE IN NEW TESTAMENT TIMES (1), p. 1538).

1:17 SPIRIT AND POWER OF ELIAS. In many ways John will be like the fearless prophet Elijah (see Mal. 4:5, note). Because he is filled with the Holy Spirit (v. 15), John will be a preacher of moral righteousness (3:7–14; Mat. 3:1–10). He will demonstrate the Holy Spirit's ministry by preaching about sin, righteousness, and judgment (see John 16:8, note). He will turn the hearts of "the disobedient to the wisdom of the just" (v. 17; see Mat. 11:7, note). He will not compromise his conscience or bend Biblical principles for the sake of status or security (3:19–20; Mat. 14:1–11). He will obey God and remain loyal to all truth. In short, John will be a "man of God."

1:17 THE FATHERS TO THE CHILDREN. One of the greatest sins of God's people in the O.T. had been the failure of the fathers to love their sons and daughters enough to teach them the ways and commandments of God (see Mal. 4:6, note). With the coming of John and the gospel of Christ, the hearts of the fathers will return to their children.

(1) This is a clear statement that one of the foremost goals of the gospel is to reestablish God's will for the family in a correct relation between fathers and children. Through the preaching of repentance and the Lordship of Christ, fathers will become dedicated to their children in an attitude of righteousness.

(2) If the church today fails to become what God wants it to be, one factor may be because once again the fathers' hearts have forsaken their children by failing to love them, spend time with them, and teach them diligently God's Word and righteous standards. As a result, the children will reject God's ways (Mal. 4:6).

(3) The following are important passages related to fathers and children: (a) teaching children

the hearts of the fathers to the children, and the disobedient [a]to the wisdom of the just; to make ready a people prepared for the Lord.

18 And Zacharias said unto the angel, [u]Whereby shall I know this? for I am an old man, and my wife well stricken in years.

19 And the angel answering said unto him, I am [v]Gabriel, that stand in the presence of God; and am sent to speak unto thee, and to show thee these glad tidings.

20 And, behold, [w]thou shalt be dumb, and not able to speak, until the day that these things shall be performed, because thou believest not my words, which shall be fulfilled in their season.

21 And the people waited for Zacharias, and marvelled that he tarried so long in the temple.

22 And when he came out, he could not speak unto them: and they perceived that he had seen a vision in the temple: for he beckoned unto them, and remained speechless.

23 And it came to pass, that as soon as [x]the days of his ministration were accomplished, he departed to his own house.

24 And after those days his wife Elisabeth conceived, and hid herself five months, saying,

25 Thus hath the Lord dealt with me in the days wherein he looked on *me,* to [y]take away my reproach among men.

The birth of Jesus foretold

26 And in the sixth month the angel Gabriel was sent from God unto a city of Galilee, named Nazareth,

27 To a virgin [z]espoused to a man whose name was Joseph, of the house of David; and the virgin's name *was* Mary.

28 And the angel came in unto her, and said, [a]Hail, *thou that art* [b]highly favoured, [b]the Lord *is* with thee: blessed *art* thou among women.

29 And when she saw *him,* [c]she was troubled at his saying, and cast in her mind what manner of salutation this should be.

30 And the angel said unto her, Fear not, Mary: for thou hast found favour with God.

31 [d]And, behold, thou shalt conceive in thy womb, and bring forth a son, and [e]shalt call his name JESUS.

32 He shall be great, [f]and shall be called the Son of the Highest: and [g]the Lord God shall give unto him the throne of his father David:

33 [h]And he shall reign over the house of Jacob for ever; and of his kingdom there shall be no end.

Mary will conceive miraculously

34 Then said Mary unto the angel, How shall this be, seeing I know not a man?

35 And the angel answered and said unto her, [i]The Holy Ghost shall come upon thee, and the power of the Highest shall overshadow thee: therefore also that holy thing which shall be born of thee shall be called [j]the Son of God.

1:18 [u]Gen. 17:17
1:19 [v]Dan. 8:16 & 9:21-23 Mat. 18:10 Heb. 1:14
1:20 [w]Ezek. 3:26 & 24:27
1:23 [x]2 Ki. 11:5 1 Chr. 9:25
1:25 [y]Gen. 30:23 Is. 4:1 & 54:1,4
1:27 [z]Mat. 1:18 ch. 2:4,5
1:28 [a]Dan. 9:23 & 10:19 [b]Judg. 6:12
1:29 [c]ver. 12
1:31 [d]Is. 7:14 Mat. 1:21 [e]ch. 2:21
1:32 [f]Mark 5:7 [g]2 Sam. 7:11 Ps. 132:11 Is. 9:6,7 & 16:5 Jer. 23:5 Rev. 3:7
1:33 [h]Dan. 2:44 & 7:14,27 Obad. 21 Mic. 4:7 John 12:34 Heb. 1:8
1:35 [i]Mat. 1:20 [j]Mat. 14:33 & 26:63,64 Mark 1:1 John 1:34 & 20:31 Acts 8:37 Rom. 1:4

[a] Or, *by* [b] Or, *graciously accepted,* or, *much graced;* see ver. 30

faithfulness to God's ways: Ex. 10:2; 13:8; Deut. 4:9–10; 6:6–25; 11:18–21; Ps. 78:5–8; Is. 38:19; Joel 1:3; Eph. 6:4; 1 Thes. 2:11; (b) loving and correcting children: Ps. 103:13; Prov. 3:12; 13:24; 23:13–14; Mal. 4:6; Luke 11:11–13; 2 Cor. 12:14; Eph. 6:4; Col. 3:21; 1 Thes. 2:11; 1 Tim. 3:4–5,12; 5:8; Tit. 2:4; Heb. 12:7; (c) fathers praying for their children: Gen. 17:18; 2 Sam. 12:16; 1 Chr. 22:11–12; 29:19; Job 1:5; Eph. 3:14–19. See John 17:1, note on a model prayer of a father for his children; see also article on PARENTS AND CHILDREN, p. 1880.

1:28 *THOU THAT ART* HIGHLY FAVOURED. Mary was favored above all women in being chosen as the mother of Jesus. The N.T. writers never indicate, however, that she is to be worshiped, prayed to, or given special titles. Mary merits our respect, but only her Son merits our worship. (1) Note that Mary was chosen because she found favor with God (cf. Gen. 6:8). Her humble and godly life pleased God to such an extent that He chose her for this most important task (cf. 2 Tim. 2:21). (2) Mary's blessing not only brought her great joy, but also much suffering and pain (see 2:35), for her Son would be rejected and crucified. In this world God's calling will always involve blessing and suffering, joy and sadness, successes and disappointments.

1:35 THAT HOLY THING. Both Matthew and Luke state explicitly that Jesus was born of a virgin (v. 27; Mat. 1:18,23, note). The Holy Spirit would come upon Mary and the child would be conceived solely by a miraculous deed of God. As a result, Jesus would be "holy" (i.e., free from all taint of sin). For more on this, see article on JESUS AND THE HOLY SPIRIT, p. 1550.

36 And, behold, thy cousin Elisabeth, she hath also conceived a son in her old age: and this is the sixth month with her, who was called barren.

37 For [k]with God nothing shall be impossible.

38 And Mary said, Behold the handmaid of the Lord; be it unto me according to thy word. And the angel departed from her.

Mary visits Elisabeth

39 And Mary arose in those days, and went into the hill country with haste, [l]into a city of Judah;

40 And entered into the house of Zacharias, and saluted Elisabeth.

41 And it came to pass, that, when Elisabeth heard the salutation of Mary, the babe leaped in her womb; and Elisabeth was filled with the Holy Ghost:

Luke 1:67

42 And she spake out with a loud voice, and said, [m]Blessed *art* thou among women, and blessed *is* the fruit of thy womb.

43 And whence *is* this to me, that the mother of my Lord should come to me?

44 For, lo, as soon as the voice of thy salutation sounded in mine ears, the babe leaped in my womb for joy.

45 And blessed *is* she [c]that believed: for there shall be a performance of those things which were told her from the Lord.

The song of Mary

1:46–53pp — 1 Sam. 2:1–10

46 And Mary said, [n]My soul doth magnify the Lord,

47 And my spirit hath rejoiced in God my Saviour.

Luke 2:13-14

48 For [o]he hath regarded the low estate of his handmaiden: for, behold, from henceforth [p]all generations shall call me blessed.

49 For he that is mighty [q]hath done to me great things; and [r]holy *is* his name.

50 And [s]his mercy *is* on them that fear him from generation to generation.

51 [t]He hath shown strength with his arm; [u]he hath scattered the proud in the imagination of their hearts.

52 [v]He hath put down the mighty from *their* seats, and exalted them of low degree.

53 [w]He hath filled the hungry with good things; and the rich he hath sent empty away.

54 He hath helped his servant Israel, [x]in remembrance of *his* mercy;

55 [y]As he spake to our fathers, to Abraham, and to his seed for ever.

56 And Mary abode with her about three months, and returned to her own house.

The birth of John the Baptist

57 Now Elisabeth's full time came that she should be delivered; and she brought forth a son.

58 And her neighbours and her cousins heard how the Lord had shown great mercy upon her; and they rejoiced with her.

59 And it came to pass, that [z]on the eighth day they came to circumcise the child; and they called him Zacharias, after the name of his father.

60 And his mother answered and said, [a]Not *so;* but he shall be called John.

61 And they said unto her, There is none of thy kindred that is called by this name.

62 And they made signs to his father, how he would have him called.

63 And he asked for a writing table, and wrote, saying, His name is John. And they marvelled all.

64 And his mouth was opened immediately, and his tongue *loosed,* and he spake, and praised God.

65 And fear came on all that dwelt round about them: and all these [d]sayings were noised abroad throughout all the hill country of Judaea.

66 And all they that heard *them* [b]laid *them* up in their hearts, saying, What manner of child shall this be!

1:37 [k]Gen. 18:14 Jer. 32:17 Zech. 8:6 Mat. 19:26 Mark 10:27 ch. 18:27 Rom. 4:21
1:39 [l]Josh. 21:9
1:42 [m]Judg. 5:24
1:46 [n]1 Sam. 2:1 Ps. 34:2,3 Hab. 3:18
1:48 [o]1 Sam. 1:11 Ps. 138:6 [p]ch. 11:27
1:49 [q]Ps. 71:19 & 126:2,3 [r]Ps. 111:9
1:50 [s]Gen. 17:7 Ex. 20:6 Ps. 103:17
1:51 [t]Ps. 98:1 & 118:15 Is. 40:10 [u]Ps. 33:10 1 Pet. 5:5
1:52 [v]1 Sam. 2:6 Job 5:11 Ps. 113:6
1:53 [w]1 Sam. 2:5 Ps. 34:10
1:54 [x]Ps. 98:3 Jer. 31:3
1:55 [y]Gen. 17:19 Ps. 132:11 Gal. 3:16
1:59 [z]Gen. 17:12 Lev. 12:3
1:60 [a]ver. 13
1:66 [b]ch. 2:19

[c] Or, *which believed that there* [d] Or, *things*

1:38 ACCORDING TO THY WORD. Mary submitted herself completely to God's will and trusted His message. She willingly accepted the honor and the reproach that being the mother of the holy child would bring. Young women in the church should follow the example of Mary in purity, chastity, love for God, faith in His Word, and a willingness to obey the Holy Spirit.

1:47 GOD MY SAVIOUR. In these words Mary recognizes her own need of salvation. She was a sinner who needed Christ as "Saviour." The idea that Mary was immaculately conceived and lived without sin is taught nowhere in Scripture (cf. Rom. 3:9,23).

And [c]the hand of the Lord was with
him.

The song of Zacharias

Luke 3:16
67 And his father Zacharias [d]was
filled with the Holy Ghost, and prophe-
sied, saying,
68 [e]Blessed *be* the Lord God of Is-
rael; for [f]he hath visited and re-
deemed his people,
69 [g]And hath raised up an horn of
salvation for us in the house of his ser-
vant David;
70 [h]As he spake by the mouth of
his holy prophets, which have been
since the world began:
71 That we should be saved from
our enemies, and from the hand of all
that hate us;
72 [i]To perform the mercy *promised*
to our fathers, and to remember his
holy covenant;
73 [j]The oath which he sware to
our father Abraham,
74 That he would grant unto us,
that we being delivered out of the hand
of our enemies might [k]serve him with-
out fear,
75 [l]In holiness and righteousness
before him, all the days of our life.
76 And thou, child, shalt be called
the prophet of the Highest: for [m]thou
shalt go before the face of the Lord to
prepare his ways;
77 To give knowledge of salvation
unto his people [n]by[e] the remission of
their sins,
78 Through the [f]tender mercy of
our God; whereby the [g]dayspring
from on high hath visited us,
79 [o]To give light to them that sit in
darkness and *in* the shadow of death,
Luke 19:10
to guide our feet into the way of peace.
80 And [p]the child grew, and waxed
strong in spirit, and [q]was in the

1:66 [c]Gen. 39:2 Ps. 80:17 Acts 11:21
1:67 [d]Joel 2:28
1:68 [e]1 Ki. 1:48 Ps. 41:13 [f]Ex. 3:16 Ps. 111:9 ch. 7:16
1:69 [g]Ps. 132:17
1:70 [h]Jer. 23:5 Dan. 9:24
1:72 [i]Lev. 26:42 Ezek. 16:60
1:73 [j]Gen. 12:3 Heb. 6:13
1:74 [k]Rom. 6:18 Heb. 9:14
1:75 [l]Jer. 32:39 Eph. 4:24 2 Thes. 2:13
1:76 [m]Is. 40:3 Mal. 3:1 Mat. 11:10
1:77 [n]Mark 1:4
1:79 [o]Is. 9:2 Mat. 4:16
1:80 [p]ch. 2:40 [q]Mat. 3:1
2:2 [r]Acts 5:37
2:4 [s]1 Sam. 16:1 John 7:42 [t]Mat. 1:16
2:5 [u]Mat. 1:18
2:7 [v]Mat. 1:25
2:9 [w]ch. 1:12
2:10 [x]Gen. 12:3 Mat. 28:19 Mark 1:15 Col. 1:23
2:11 [y]Is. 9:6

deserts till the day of his showing unto
Israel.

The birth of Jesus

2 AND IT came to pass in those
days, that there went out a decree
from Caesar Augustus, that all the
world should be [h]taxed.
2 ([r]*And* this taxing was first made
when Cyrenius was governor of Syria.)
3 And all went to be taxed, every
one into his own city.
4 And Joseph also went up from
Galilee, out of the city of Nazareth, into
Judaea, unto [s]the city of David, which
is called Bethlehem; ([t]because he
was of the house and lineage of David:)
5 To be taxed with Mary [u]his es-
poused wife, being great with child.
6 And so it was, that, while they
were there, the days were accom-
plished that she should be delivered.
7 And [v]she brought forth her first-
born son, and wrapped him in swad-
dling clothes, and laid him in a manger;
because there was no room for them in
the inn.

The angels and the shepherds

8 And there were in the same coun-
try shepherds abiding in the field,
keeping [i]watch over their flock by
night.
9 And, lo, the angel of the Lord
came upon them, and the glory of the
Lord shone round about them: [w]and
they were sore afraid.
10 And the angel said unto them,
Fear not: for, behold, I bring you good
tidings of great joy, [x]which shall be to
all people.
11 [y]For unto you is born this day in

[e] Or, *for* [f] Or, *bowels of the mercy* [g] Or, *sunrising,* or, *branch;* Num. 24:17; Is. 11:1
[h] Or, *enrolled* [i] Or, *the night watches*

1:67 FILLED WITH THE HOLY GHOST. Luke records how the Holy Spirit empowered many of the important people associated with the birth of Christ (vv. 15,35,41,67; 2:25). After Christ's ascension, the way was made for all believers to be filled with the Holy Spirit (Acts 1–2).

1:75 HOLINESS AND RIGHTEOUSNESS. The ultimate aim of our redemption is to be delivered out of the kingdom of Satan (Acts 26:18) in order to serve God "in holiness and righteousness before him, all the days of our life" (cf. Eph. 1:4). Every child of God must aim at a life of holiness and righteousness in the midst of an evil world. This holy life is "before him," i.e., in His presence.

2:7 A MANGER. Christ was born in a stable, a place where animals were kept. The stable was probably a cave and the manger a feeding trough for animals. The birth of the Savior, the greatest event in all history, occurred in the most humble of circumstances. Jesus was the King of kings, but He was neither born nor did He live like a king in this life. God's people are kings and priests, but in this life we must be as He was—humble and simple.

2:11 A SAVIOUR . . . CHRIST THE LORD. At His birth, Jesus is called "a Saviour." (1) As Savior, He has come to deliver us from sin, Satan's domain, the ungodly world, fear, death, and the condemnation of our transgressions (see Mat. 1:21, note). (2) The Savior is also "Christ the Lord." He

the city of David [z]a Saviour, [a]which
is Christ the Lord.
12 And this *shall be* a sign unto you;
Ye shall find the babe wrapped in
swaddling clothes, lying in a manger.
13 [b]And suddenly there was with
the angel a multitude of the heavenly
host praising God, and saying,
14 [c]Glory to God in the highest,
ke and on earth [d]peace, [e]good will to-
20 ward men.
15 And it came to pass, as the an-
gels were gone away from them into
heaven, [j]the shepherds said one to
another, Let us now go even unto Beth-
lehem, and see this thing which is
come to pass, which the Lord hath
made known unto us.
16 And they came with haste, and
found Mary, and Joseph, and the babe
lying in a manger.
17 And when they had seen *it*,
they made known abroad the saying
which was told them concerning this
child.
18 And all they that heard *it* won-
dered at those things which were told
them by the shepherds.
19 [f]But Mary kept all these
things, and pondered *them* in her
heart.
20 And the shepherds returned, glo-
rifying and praising God for all the
uke things that they had heard and seen, as
18:43 it was told unto them.

2:11 [z]Mat. 1:21 [a]Mat. 1:16 & 16:16 Acts 2:36 Phil. 2:11
2:13 [b]Gen. 28:12 Ps. 103:20 & 148:2 Dan. 7:10 Heb. 1:14 Rev. 5:11
2:14 [c]ch. 19:38 Eph. 1:6 [d]Is. 57:19 Rom. 5:1 Eph. 2:17 Col. 1:20 [e]John 3:16 Eph. 2:4,7 2 Thes. 2:16 1 John 4:9
2:19 [f]Gen. 37:11 ch. 1:66
2:21 [g]Gen. 17:12 Lev. 12:3 ch. 1:59 [h]Mat. 1:21,25 ch. 1:31
2:22 [i]Lev. 12:2
2:23 [j]Ex. 13:2 & 22:29 Num. 3:13
2:24 [k]Lev. 12:2
2:25 [l]ver. 38 Is. 40:1 Mark 15:43
2:26 [m]Ps. 89:48 Heb. 11:5
2:27 [n]Mat. 4:1

Jesus presented in the temple

21 [g]And when eight days were ac-
complished for the circumcising of the
child, his name was called [h]JESUS,
which was so named of the angel be-
fore he was conceived in the womb.
22 And when [i]the days of her puri-
fication according to the law of Moses
were accomplished, they brought him
to Jerusalem, to present *him* to the
Lord;
23 (As it is written in the law of the
Lord, [j]Every male that openeth the
womb shall be called holy to the Lord;)
24 And to offer a sacrifice according
to [k]that which is said in the law of the
Lord, A pair of turtledoves, or two
young pigeons.
25 And, behold, there was a man in
Jerusalem, whose name *was* Simeon;
and the same man *was* just and devout,
[l]waiting for the consolation of Israel:
and the Holy Ghost was upon him.
26 And it was revealed unto him by
the Holy Ghost, that he should not
[m]see death, before he had seen the
Lord's Christ.
27 And he came [n]by the Spirit into
the temple: and when the parents
brought in the child Jesus, to do for him
after the custom of the law,

j Gk. *the men the shepherds*

has been anointed as the Messiah of God and the Lord who rules over His people (see Mat. 1:1, note on the name of Christ). No person can have Jesus as Savior while turning from His Lordship.

2:22 PRESENT *HIM* TO THE LORD. As Joseph and Mary presented Jesus to the Lord, so all parents should sincerely consecrate their children to the Lord. They should pray constantly that from the beginning to the end of each child's life, he or she will be found in the Lord's will, serving and glorifying God with complete devotion.

2:24 A PAIR OF TURTLEDOVES. The offering of a pair of turtledoves indicates that Joseph and Mary were poor (Lev. 12:8). From the very beginning Christ was identified with the underprivileged (9:58; Mat. 8:20; see Rev. 2:9, note).

2:25 JUST AND DEVOUT. "Just" or "righteous" (cf. 1:6) translates the Greek word *dikaios* (Heb. *yasher*), meaning "straight" or "upright." In the O.T. this word did not mean mere conformity to the commandments, but indicated a person was right with God both in heart and in action (see Ps. 32:2, note). (1) The righteousness that God sought in the O.T. was one that came from the heart, based on true faith, love, and fear of God (Deut. 4:10,29; 5:29). This condition of the heart was seen in the parents of John the Baptist, who walked "in all the commandments and ordinances of the Lord blameless" (1:6; see Gen. 7:1, Noah; 17:1, Abraham; 1 Ki. 9:4, where the term includes "integrity of heart"). Simeon manifested the same characteristic in his life. (2) The O.T. righteous man was not perfect. When sin entered his life he obtained forgiveness by presenting an animal sacrifice unto God in an attitude of sincere repentance and faith (Lev. 4:27–35; see article on THE DAY OF ATONEMENT, p. 188).

2:25 WAITING FOR THE CONSOLATION. In a time of deplorable spiritual conditions righteous Simeon was devoted to God and filled with the Holy Spirit, waiting in faith, patience, and great longing for the coming of the Messiah. Likewise, in the last days of this present age, when many abandon the N.T. apostolic faith and the blessed hope for the coming of Christ (Tit. 2:13), there will always be the faithful Simeons. Others may place their hope in this life and this world, but the faithful will be like the loyal slave who keeps watch through the long, dark night, waiting for the return of his Master (Mat. 24:45–47). Our greatest blessing is to see face to face "the Lord's Christ" (v. 26; cf. Rev. 22:4), to be ready when He comes, and to dwell forever in His presence (Rev. 21–22).

The praise of Simeon and Anna

28 Then took he him up in his arms,
and blessed God, and said,
29 Lord, [o]now lettest thou thy ser-
vant depart in peace, according to thy
word:
30 For mine eyes [p]have seen thy
salvation,
31 Which thou hast prepared before
the face of all people;
32 [q]A light to lighten the Gentiles,
and the glory of thy people Israel.
33 And Joseph and his mother mar-
velled at those things which were spo-
ken of him.
34 And Simeon blessed them, and
said unto Mary his mother, Behold,
this *child* is set for the [r]fall and rising
again of many in Israel; and for [s]a
sign which shall be spoken against;
35 (Yea, [t]a sword shall pierce
through thy own soul also,) that the
thoughts of many hearts may be re-
vealed.
36 And there was one Anna, a
prophetess, the daughter of Phanuel,
of the tribe of Aser: she was of a great
age, and had lived with an husband
seven years from her virginity;
37 And she *was* a widow of about
fourscore and four years, which de-
parted not from the temple, but served
God with fastings and prayers [u]night
and day.
38 And she coming in that instant
gave thanks likewise unto the Lord,
and spake of him to all them that
[v]looked for redemption in [k]Jerusa-
lem.
39 And when they had performed
all things according to the law of the
Lord, they returned into Galilee, to
their own city Nazareth.
40 [w]And the child grew, and waxed
strong in spirit, filled with wisdom: and
the grace of God was upon him.

2:29 [o]Gen. 46:30 Phil. 1:23 **2:30** [p]Is. 52:10 **2:32** [q]Is. 9:2 & 42:6 & 49:6 & 60:1-3 Mat. 4:16 Acts 13:47 & 28:28 **2:34** [r]Is. 8:14 Hos. 14:9 Mat. 21:44 Rom. 9:32 1 Cor. 1:23 2 Cor. 2:16 1 Pet. 2:7,8 [s]Acts 28:22 **2:35** [t]Ps. 42:10 John 19:25 **2:37** [u]Acts 26:7 1 Tim. 5:5 **2:38** [v]ver. 25 Mark 15:43 ch. 24:21 **2:40** [w]ver. 52 ch. 1:80 **2:41** [x]Ex. 23:15,17 & 34:23 Deut. 16:1,16 **2:47** [y]Mat. 7:28 Mark 1:22 ch. 4:22,32 John 7:15,46 **2:49** [z]John 2:16 **2:50** [a]ch. 9:45 & 18:34 **2:51** [b]ver. 19 Dan. 7:28 **2:52** [c]ver. 40 1 Sam. 2:26

The boy Jesus in the temple

41 Now his parents went to Jerusa-
lem [x]every year at the feast of the
passover.
42 And when he was twelve years
old, they went up to Jerusalem after
the custom of the feast.
43 And when they had fulfilled the
days, as they returned, the child Jesus
tarried behind in Jerusalem; and Jo-
seph and his mother knew not *of it.*
44 But they, supposing him to have
been in the company, went a day's jour-
ney; and they sought him among *their*
kinsfolk and acquaintance.
45 And when they found him not,
they turned back again to Jerusalem,
seeking him.
46 And it came to pass, that after
three days they found him in the tem-
ple, sitting in the midst of the doctors,
both hearing them, and asking them
questions.
47 And [y]all that heard him were
astonished at his understanding and
answers.
48 And when they saw him, they
were amazed: and his mother said unto
him, Son, why hast thou thus dealt
with us? behold, thy father and I have
sought thee sorrowing.
49 And he said unto them, How is it
that ye sought me? wist ye not that I
must be about [z]my Father's business?
50 And [a]they understood not the
saying which he spake unto them.
51 And he went down with them,
and came to Nazareth, and was subject
unto them: but his mother [b]kept all
these sayings in her heart.
52 And Jesus [c]increased in wis-
dom and [l]stature, and in favour with
God and man.

[k] Or, *Israel* [l] Or, *age*

2:36–37 ANNA . . . SERVED *GOD*. Anna was a prophetess who earnestly hoped for the coming of Christ. She remained a widow for many years, never remarrying, but devoting herself to the Lord "with fastings and prayers night and day." The Bible teaches that the unmarried state can be a greater blessing than the married. Paul states that the unmarried have greater opportunity to be concerned about the things of the Lord, how to please Him and how to give undistracted devotion to Him (see 1 Cor. 7:32–35).

2:40 THE CHILD GREW. As a true human child, Jesus experienced the process of physical and spiritual development. He kept increasing in wisdom as the grace of God was upon Him. He was perfect in His human nature, developing perfectly as God desired.

2:52 JESUS INCREASED IN WISDOM. Between 2:52 and 3:1, approximately eighteen years of Jesus' life passed without comment. What was His life like during those years? From Mat. 13:55 and Mark 6:3, we learn that He grew up in a large family, that His father was a carpenter, and that Jesus learned the trade. It seems likely that Joseph died before Jesus began His public ministry and that Jesus provided for His mother and younger brothers and sisters. The carpenter's trade included household repairs, furniture making, and con-

devil. And [e]in those days he did eat nothing: and when they were ended, he afterward hungered.

3 And the devil said unto him, If thou be the Son of God, command this stone that it be made bread.

4 And Jesus answered him, saying, [f]It is written, That man shall not live by bread alone, but by every word of God.

5 And the devil, taking him up into an high mountain, showed unto him all the kingdoms of the world in a moment of time.

6 And the devil said unto him, All this power will I give thee, and the glory of them: for [g]that is delivered unto me; and to whomsoever I will I give it.

7 If thou therefore wilt [r]worship me, all shall be thine.

8 And Jesus answered and said unto him, Get thee behind me, Satan: for [h]it is written, Thou shalt worship the Lord thy God, and him only shalt thou serve.

9 [i]And he brought him to Jerusalem, and set him on a pinnacle of the temple, and said unto him, If thou be the Son of God, cast thyself down from hence:

10 For [j]it is written, He shall give his angels charge over thee, to keep thee:

4:2 [e]Ex. 34:28 1 Ki. 19:8
4:4 [f]Deut. 8:3
4:6 [g]John 12:31 & 14:30 Rev. 13:2,7
4:8 [h]Deut. 6:13 & 10:20
4:9 [i]Mat. 4:5
4:10 [j]Ps. 91:11
4:12 [k]Deut. 6:16
4:13 [l]John 14:30 Heb. 4:15
4:14 [m]Mat. 4:12 John 4:43 [n]ver. 1 [o]Acts 10:37
4:16 [p]Mat. 2:23 & 13:54 Mark 6:1 [q]Acts 13:14 & 17:2
4:18 [r]Is. 61:1

11 And in *their* hands they shall bear thee up, lest at any time thou dash thy foot against a stone.

12 And Jesus answering said unto him, [k]It is said, Thou shalt not tempt the Lord thy God.

13 And when the devil had ended all the temptation, he departed from him [l]for a season. Luke 4:33-36

Jesus and the power of the Spirit

14 ¶ [m]And Jesus returned [n]in the power of the Spirit into [o]Galilee: and there went out a fame of him through all the region round about.

15 And he taught in their synagogues, being glorified of all.

Jesus rejected at Nazareth

16 ¶ And he came to [p]Nazareth, where he had been brought up: and, as his custom was, [q]he went into the synagogue on the sabbath day, and stood up for to read.

17 And there was delivered unto him the book of the prophet Esaias. And when he had opened the book, he found the place where it was written,

18 [r]The Spirit of the Lord *is* upon me, because he hath anointed me to

[r] Or, *fall down before me*

---

ing, position, and ability for their own self-interest, to establish their own glory and kingdom, and to please people rather than God. Those who selfishly compromise with Satan have in reality surrendered to the lordship of Satan.

4:2 HE DID EAT NOTHING. See Mat. 4:2, note on fasting.

4:4 NOT LIVE BY BREAD ALONE. Jesus quotes the O.T. (Deut. 8:3) in meeting Satan's temptation. (1) He is saying that everything important in life depends on God and His will (John 4:34). To strive for success, happiness, or material things apart from God's way and purpose will lead to bitter disappointment and end in failure. (2) Jesus emphasizes this truth when He teaches we must seek first the kingdom of God (i.e., God's rule, activity, and power in our lives); only then will other necessary things be given according to His will and way (see Mat. 5:6, note; 6:33, note).

4:5 THE KINGDOMS OF THE WORLD. Jesus rejects Satan's offer of dominion over all the kingdoms of the world. (1) Jesus' kingdom in this age is *not* a kingdom of this world (John 18:36–37). He refuses to seek a kingdom for Himself by the worldly methods of compromise, earthly power, political maneuvering, external violence, human rule, popularity, honor, and glory. (2) Jesus' kingdom is a spiritual kingdom, ruling in the hearts of His people who have been taken out of the kingdoms of the world. As a heavenly kingdom: (a) it is gained through suffering, self-denial, humility, and meekness; (b) it requires giving our bodies as a living and holy sacrifice (Rom. 12:1), in complete devotion and obedience to God; (c) it involves struggling with spiritual weapons against sin, temptation, and Satan (Eph. 6:10–20); (d) it means resisting being conformed to this world (Rom. 12:2). See article on THE KINGDOM OF GOD, p. 1428.

4:8 SATAN. See Mat. 4:10, note on Satan.

4:10 SATAN'S USE OF SCRIPTURE. See Mat. 4:6, note.

4:18 THE SPIRIT . . . UPON ME. See article on JESUS AND THE HOLY SPIRIT, p. 1550.

4:18 HE HATH ANOINTED ME. Here Jesus gives the purpose of His Spirit-anointed ministry. (1) It is to preach the gospel to the poor, the destitute, the afflicted, the humble, those crushed in spirit, the brokenhearted, and those who tremble at His Word (see Is. 61:1–3, note; 66:2, note). (2) It is to heal those who are bruised and oppressed. This healing involves the total person, both physical and spiritual. (3) It is to open the spiritual eyes of those blinded by the world and Satan in order that they might see the truth of God's good news (cf. John 9:39). (4) It is to proclaim the time of true freedom and salvation from Satan's domain, sin, fear, and guilt (cf. John 8:36; Acts 26:18).

All those who are filled with the Spirit are called to share Jesus' ministry in these ways. To do so we

preach the gospel to the poor; he hath
sent me to heal the brokenhearted, to
preach deliverance to the captives, and
recovering of sight to the blind, to set
at liberty them that are bruised,
19 To preach the acceptable year of
the Lord.
20 And he closed the book, and he
gave *it* again to the minister, and sat
down. And the eyes of all them that
were in the synagogue were fastened
on him.
21 And he began to say unto them,
This day is this scripture fulfilled in
your ears.
22 And all bare him witness, and
[s]wondered at the gracious words
which proceeded out of his mouth. And
they said, [t]Is not this Joseph's son?
23 And he said unto them, Ye will
surely say unto me this proverb, Physi-
cian, heal thyself: whatsoever we have
heard done in [u]Capernaum, do also
here in [v]thy country.
24 And he said, Verily I say unto
you, No [w]prophet is accepted in his
own country.
25 But I tell you of a truth, [x]many
widows were in Israel in the days of
Elias, when the heaven was shut up
three years and six months, when
great famine was throughout all the
land;
26 But unto none of them was Elias
sent, save unto Sarepta, *a city* of Sidon,
unto a woman *that was* a widow.
27 [y]And many lepers were in Isra-
el in the time of Eliseus the prophet;
and none of them was cleansed, saving
Naaman the Syrian.
28 And all they in the synagogue,
when they heard these things, were
filled with wrath,
29 And rose up, and thrust him out
of the city, and led him unto the [s]brow
of the hill whereon their city was built,
that they might cast him down head-
long.

4:22 [s]Ps. 45:2 Mat. 13:54 Mark 6:2 ch. 2:47 [t]John 6:42
4:23 [u]Mat. 4:13 & 11:23 [v]Mat. 13:54 Mark 6:1
4:24 [w]Mat. 13:57 Mark 6:4 John 4:44
4:25 [x]1 Ki. 17:9 & 18:1 Jas. 5:17
4:27 [y]2 Ki. 5:14
4:30 [z]John 8:59 & 10:39
4:31 [a]Mat. 4:13 Mark 1:21
4:32 [b]Mat. 7:28,29
4:33 [c]Mark 1:23
4:34 [d]ver. 41 [e]Ps. 16:10 Dan. 9:24 ch. 1:35
4:38 [f]Mat. 8:14 Mark 1:29
4:40 [g]Mat. 8:16 Mark 1:32

30 But he [z]passing through the
midst of them went his way,

The unclean spirit cast out

4:31–37pp — Mark 1:21–28

31 And [a]came down to Caperna-
um, a city of Galilee, and taught them
on the sabbath days.
32 And they were astonished at his
doctrine: [b]for his word was with
power.
33 ¶ [c]And in the synagogue there
was a man, which had a spirit of an
unclean devil, and cried out with a loud
voice,
34 Saying, [t]Let *us* alone; what
have we to do with thee, *thou* Jesus of
Nazareth? art thou come to destroy us?
[d]I know thee who thou art; [e]the Holy
One of God.
35 And Jesus rebuked him, saying,
Hold thy peace, and come out of him.
And when the devil had thrown him in
the midst, he came out of him, and hurt
him not.
36 And they were all amazed, and
spake among themselves, saying,
What a word *is* this! for with authority
and power he commandeth the unclean
spirits, and they come out.
37 And the fame of him went out
into every place of the country round
about.

Luke 10:19

The sick healed; devils cast out

4:38–41pp — Mat. 8:14–17
4:38–43pp — Mark 1:29–38

38 ¶ [f]And he arose out of the syna-
gogue, and entered into Simon's
house. And Simon's wife's mother was
taken with a great fever; and they be-
sought him for her.
39 And he stood over her, and re-
buked the fever; and it left her: and im-
mediately she arose and ministered
unto them.
40 ¶ [g]Now when the sun was set-

[s] Or, *edge* [t] Or, *Away*

must gain a deep realization of the terrible need and misery of the human race that has resulted from sin and the power of Satan—a condition of enslavement to evil, brokenheartedness, bondage, spiritual blindness, and physical distress.

4:33 UNCLEAN DEVIL. Luke records that one of Jesus' first acts after announcing His Messiahship was to enter into direct conflict with the demonic. (1) Jesus' foremost concern in His ministry was to destroy the works of the devil (1 John 3:8). There can be no realization of the kingdom of God without confronting the kingdom of Satan (see Mat. 12:28; see article on THE KINGDOM OF GOD, p. 1428). (2) One unmistakable sign that the kingdom has ceased to be manifested among God's people is the failure to confront directly the power of evil by setting sinners free from the bondage of sin and the demonic (see article on POWER OVER SATAN AND DEMONS, p. 1486).

4:40 HEALED THEM. See Mat. 4:23, note; see article on DIVINE HEALING, p. 1418.

ting, all they that had any sick with di-
vers diseases brought them unto him;
and he laid his hands on every one of
them, and healed them.
41 [h]And devils also came out of
many, crying out, and saying, Thou art
Christ the Son of God. And [i]he rebuk-
ing *them* suffered them not [u]to speak:
for they knew that he was Christ.
42 [j]And when it was day, he de-
parted and went into a desert place:
and the people sought him, and came
unto him, and stayed him, that he
should not depart from them.
43 And he said unto them, I must
preach the kingdom of God to other cit-
ies also: for therefore am I sent.
44 [k]And he preached in the syna-
gogues of Galilee.

The call of the first disciples

5:1–11pp — Mat. 4:18–22; Mark 1:16–20; John 1:40–42

5 AND [l]IT came to pass, that, as
the people pressed upon him to
hear the word of God, he stood by the
lake of Gennesaret,
2 And saw two ships standing by
the lake: but the fishermen were gone
out of them, and were washing *their*
nets.
3 And he entered into one of the
ships, which was Simon's, and prayed
him that he would thrust out a little
from the land. And he sat down, and
taught the people out of the ship.
4 Now when he had left speaking,
he said unto Simon, [m]Launch out into
the deep, and let down your nets for a
draught.
5 And Simon answering said unto
him, Master, we have toiled all the
night, and have taken nothing: never-
theless at thy word I will let down the
net.
6 And when they had this done, they
inclosed a great multitude of fishes:
and their net brake.
7 And they beckoned unto *their*
partners, which were in the other ship,
that they should come and help them.
And they came, and filled both the
ships, so that they began to sink.
8 When Simon Peter saw *it,* he fell
down at Jesus' knees, saying, [n]Depart
from me; for I am a sinful man, O Lord.
9 For he was astonished, and all
that were with him, at the draught of
the fishes which they had taken:
10 And so *was* also James, and John,
the sons of Zebedee, which were part-
ners with Simon. And Jesus said unto
Simon, Fear not; [o]from henceforth
thou shalt catch men.
11 And when they had brought their
ships to land, [p]they forsook all, and
followed him.

The leper cleansed

5:12–14pp — Mat. 8:2–4; Mark 1:40–44

12 ¶ [q]And it came to pass, when he
was in a certain city, behold a man full
of leprosy: who seeing Jesus fell on *his*
face, and besought him, saying, Lord,
if thou wilt, thou canst make me clean.
13 And he put forth *his* hand, and
touched him, saying, I will: be thou
clean. And immediately the leprosy de-
parted from him.
14 [r]And he charged him to tell no
man: but go, and show thyself to the
priest, and offer for thy cleansing,
[s]according as Moses commanded, for
a testimony unto them.
15 But so much the more went
there a fame abroad of him: [t]and
great multitudes came together to
hear, and to be healed by him of their
infirmities.
16 ¶ [u]And he withdrew himself
into the wilderness, and prayed.

[u] Or, *to say that they knew him to be Christ*

4:41 [h]Mark 1:34 & 3:11 [i]ver. 34,35 Mark 1:25,34 **4:42** [j]Mark 1:35 **4:44** [k]Mark 1:39 **5:1** [l]Mat. 4:18 Mark 1:16 **5:4** [m]John 21:6 **5:8** [n]2 Sam. 6:9 1 Ki. 17:8 **5:10** [o]Mat. 4:19 Mark 1:17 **5:11** [p]Mat. 4:20 & 19:27 Mark 1:18 ch. 18:28 **5:12** [q]Mat. 8:2 Mark 1:40 **5:14** [r]Mat. 8:4 [s]Lev. 14:4,10,21, 22 **5:15** [t]Mat. 4:25 Mark 3:7 John 6:2 **5:16** [u]Mat. 14:23 Mark 6:46

5:10 THOU SHALT CATCH MEN. See Mat. 4:19, note.

5:16 PRAYERS OF JESUS. Luke stresses more than the other Gospels the place of prayer in the life and work of Jesus. When the Holy Spirit descended upon Jesus at the Jordan, He was "praying" (3:21); at times He withdrew from the multitudes "and prayed" (5:16); and He "continued all night in prayer" before choosing the twelve disciples (6:12). He was "alone praying" before He asked His disciples an important question (9:18); at His transfiguration He climbed the mountain "to pray" (9:28); the actual transfiguration occurred while "he prayed" (9:29); and He "was praying" just before He taught the disciples the Lord's Prayer (11:1). In Gethsemane He "prayed more earnestly" (22:44); on the cross He prayed for others (23:34); and His last words uttered before His death were a prayer (23:46). Luke also mentions that He prayed after His resurrection (24:30).

In examining the life of Jesus in the other Gospels, we note that He prayed before extending the invitation, "Come unto me, all *ye* that labour. . ." (Mat. 11:25–28); He prayed at Lazarus's tomb (John 11:41–42), for Peter (Luke 22:32), and during the institution of the Lord's

A paralytic healed

5:18–26pp — Mat. 9:2–8; Mark 2:3–12

17 And it came to pass on a certain
day, as he was teaching, that there
were Pharisees and doctors of the law
sitting by, which were come out of ev-
ery town of Galilee, and Judaea, and
Jerusalem: and the power of the Lord
was *present* to heal them.
18 ¶ [v]And, behold, men brought in
a bed a man which was taken with a
palsy: and they sought *means* to bring
him in, and to lay *him* before him.
19 And when they could not find by
what *way* they might bring him in be-
cause of the multitude, they went upon
the housetop, and let him down
through the tiling with *his* couch into
the midst before Jesus.
20 And when he saw their faith, he
said unto him, Man, thy sins are forgiv-
en thee.
21 [w]And the scribes and the Phari-
sees began to reason, saying, Who is
this which speaketh blasphemies?
[x]Who can forgive sins, but God alone?
22 But when Jesus perceived their
thoughts, he answering said unto
them, What reason ye in your hearts?
23 Whether is easier, to say, Thy
sins be forgiven thee; or to say, Rise up
and walk?
24 But that ye may know that the
Son of man hath power upon earth to
forgive sins, (he said unto the sick of
the palsy,) I say unto thee, Arise, and
take up thy couch, and go into thine
house.
25 And immediately he rose up be-
fore them, and took up that whereon he
lay, and departed to his own house,
glorifying God.
26 And they were all amazed, and
they glorified God, and were filled with
fear, saying, We have seen strange
things today.

The call of Levi

5:27–32pp — Mat. 9:9–13; Mark 2:14–17

27 ¶ [y]And after these things he
went forth, and saw a publican, named
Levi, sitting at the receipt of custom:
and he said unto him, Follow me.
28 And he left all, rose up, and fol-
lowed him.
29 [z]And Levi made him a great
feast in his own house: and [a]there
was a great company of publicans and
of others that sat down with them.
30 But their scribes and Pharisees
murmured against his disciples, say-
ing, Why do ye eat and drink with pub-
licans and sinners?
31 And Jesus answering said unto
them, They that are whole need not a
physician; but they that are sick.
32 [b]I came not to call the righ-
teous, but sinners to repentance.

The question about fasting

5:33–39pp — Mat. 9:14–17; Mark 2:18–22

33 ¶ And they said unto him, [c]Why
do the disciples of John fast often, and
make prayers, and likewise *the disci-
ples* of the Pharisees; but thine eat and
drink?
34 And he said unto them, Can ye
make the children of the bridechamber
fast, while the bridegroom is with
them?
35 But the days will come, when the

5:18 [v]Mat. 9:2 Mark 2:3 **5:21** [w]Mat. 9:3 Mark 2:6,7 [x]Ps. 32:5 Is. 43:25 **5:27** [y]Mat. 9:9 Mark 2:13,14 **5:29** [z]Mat. 9:10 Mark 2:15 [a]ch. 15:1 **5:32** [b]Mat. 9:13 1 Tim. 1:15 **5:33** [c]Mat. 9:14 Mark 2:18

Supper (John 17). For more on prayer in Jesus' life, see Mat. 14:23, note.

5:18 BROUGHT IN A BED A MAN. The friends of the paralyzed man had strong faith that Jesus could heal him, for they were determined to present him to Jesus. We too must have faith that Christ can meet the needs of those we know, using every opportunity to bring them to Jesus. God's Spirit will open up such opportunities for us if we desire to lead others to Christ.

5:22 JESUS PERCEIVED THEIR THOUGHTS. Every believer must be made aware that God knows and is constantly evaluating his every thought, desire, and imagination (see Ps. 139; Mat. 17:25; John 1:48; 2:25; 21:17; Heb. 4:13).

5:24 SON OF MAN. The "Son of man" is Jesus' favorite expression by which He refers to Himself. Dan. 7:13 seems to be the background for Jesus' use of the expression. Daniel used the title to describe a person he saw in a vision, one "like the Son of man" coming with the clouds of heaven, who is given an everlasting kingdom (see Dan. 7:13, note). Thus Jesus expresses the truth that He is the predicted Messiah, sent by God. Jesus uses the term: (1) as a substitute for "I" (Mat. 11:19); (2) when making important claims (Mat. 20:28; Mark 10:45); (3) when foretelling His death on the cross (9:44; Mat. 17:22; Mark 8:31); (4) when speaking about His resurrection (Mat. 17:9); (5) when referring to His glorious return to earth (Mat. 24:27; Mark 13:26; 14:62); (6) when speaking of His role in judgment (Mat. 13:41).

5:30 EAT AND DRINK WITH . . . SINNERS. See Mat. 9:11, note.

5:35 THEN SHALL THEY FAST. See Mat. 9:15, note.

bridegroom shall be taken away from them, and then shall they fast in those days.

36 ¶ [d]And he spake also a parable unto them; No man putteth a piece of a new garment upon an old; if otherwise, then both the new maketh a rent, and the piece that was *taken* out of the new agreeth not with the old.

37 And no man putteth new wine into old bottles; else the new wine will burst the bottles, and be spilled, and the bottles shall perish.

38 But new wine must be put into new bottles; and both are preserved.

39 No man also having drunk old *wine* straightway desireth new: for he saith, The old is better.

Jesus the Lord of the sabbath

6:1–11pp — Mat. 12:1–14; Mark 2:23—3:6

6 AND [e]IT came to pass on the second sabbath after the first, that he went through the corn fields; and his disciples plucked the ears of corn, and did eat, rubbing *them* in *their* hands.

2 And certain of the Pharisees said unto them, Why do ye that [f]which is not lawful to do on the sabbath days?

3 And Jesus answering them said, Have ye not read so much as this, [g]what David did, when himself was an hungered, and they which were with him;

4 How he went into the house of God, and did take and eat the showbread, and gave also to them that were with him; [h]which it is not lawful to eat but for the priests alone?

5 And he said unto them, That the Son of man is Lord also of the sabbath.

6 [i]And it came to pass also on another sabbath, that he entered into the synagogue and taught: and there was a man whose right hand was withered.

7 And the scribes and Pharisees watched him, whether he would heal on the sabbath day; that they might find an accusation against him.

8 But he knew their thoughts, and said to the man which had the withered hand, Rise up, and stand forth in the midst. And he arose and stood forth.

9 Then said Jesus unto them, I will ask you one thing; Is it lawful on the sabbath days to do good, or to do evil? to save life, or to destroy *it?*

10 And looking round about upon them all, he said unto the man, Stretch forth thy hand. And he did so: and his hand was restored whole as the other.

11 And they were filled with madness; and communed one with another what they might do to Jesus.

The choosing of the twelve

6:13–16pp — Mat. 10:2–4; Mark 3:16–19; Acts 1:13

12 And it came to pass in those days, that he went out into a mountain

5:36 [d]Mat. 9:16,17 Mark 2:21,22
6:1 [e]Mat. 12:1 Mark 2:23
6:2 [f]Ex. 20:10
6:3 [g]1 Sam. 21:6
6:4 [h]Lev. 24:9
6:6 [i]Mat. 12:9 Mark 3:1 See ch. 13:14 & 14:3 John 9:16

5:37 NEW WINE INTO OLD BOTTLES. See Mat. 9:17, notes.

5:39 THE OLD IS BETTER. V. 39 is probably an ironic comment about the Jews who rejected the "new wine" of the gospel and held that the "old wine" (first century Judaism) was good enough. Christ suggests here that those who are accustomed to drinking fermented wine acquire a desire for it and do not want unfermented wine (see articles on WINE IN THE OLD TESTAMENT, p. 220, and WINE IN NEW TESTAMENT TIMES (1), p. 1538). He recognizes the habit-forming, addictive effect of alcoholic beverages. It is not Jesus, but the one who drinks the old wine, who thinks "the old is better."

(1) We may not interpret this verse to state that the old wine (i.e., Judaism) is better than new wine (i.e., Christ's gospel), for this would invert the parable's meaning. What Jesus is stating is that the Pharisees and their followers will not even recognize the merits of the new; they feel that "the old" is good enough. The Pharisees prefer the rabbinical interpretation of the law to the pure, new, sweet wine of the gospel of Christ.

(2) The Pharisees have no desire for the best wine. They refuse to accept the fresh natural revelation of God, and instead seek only what humans have altered (i.e., fermented). Yet for those who receive Jesus, the fresh new juice of the grape (gospel) is preferable to old fermented wine (Pharisaic religion).

6:1 SABBATH. See Mat. 12:1, note on Sabbath.

6:2–10 LORD . . . OF THE SABBATH. Though the Pharisees accuse Jesus of breaking the Sabbath, in reality He broke only their extreme interpretation of it. Jesus states that Sabbath observance must not degenerate into a ritual to be kept at the cost of the essential needs of man. Christ is the Lord of the Sabbath (v. 5), and it should be used to disengage ourselves from our daily work and the pursuit of material gain and turn to God as a pledge that He is Lord over all of life. Furthermore, Jesus' words and actions (vv. 6–10) teach us that the Lord's Day should be an opportunity to seek out and help those in need, spiritually as well as physically.

6:12 ALL NIGHT IN PRAYER. Again and again, Jesus sought to be alone with His Father in prayer, especially at times of momentous decisions (see 5:16, note). (1) His entire night of earnest prayer gave tremendous results (see Jas. 5:16, note). Following this night of prayer, Jesus

to pray, and continued all night in
prayer to God.
13 ¶ And when it was day, he called
unto him his disciples: [j]and of them he
chose twelve, whom also he named
apostles;
14 Simon, ([k]whom he also named
Peter,) and Andrew his brother, James
and John, Philip and Bartholomew,
15 Matthew and Thomas, James the
son of Alphaeus, and Simon called
Zelotes,
16 And Judas [l]*the brother* of James,
and Judas Iscariot, which also was the
traitor.

Beatitudes and woes

6:20–23pp — Mat. 5:3–12

17 ¶ And he came down with them,
and stood in the plain, and the compa-
ny of his disciples, [m]and a great multi-
tude of people out of all Judaea and Je-
rusalem, and from the sea coast of
Tyre and Sidon, which came to hear
him, and to be healed of their diseases;
18 And they that were vexed with
unclean spirits: and they were healed.
19 And the whole multitude
[n]sought to touch him: for [o]there
went virtue out of him, and healed *them*
all.
20 ¶ And he lifted up his eyes on his
disciples, and said, [p]Blessed *be ye*
poor: for yours is the kingdom of God.
21 [q]Blessed *are ye* that hunger
now: for ye shall be filled. [r]Blessed
are ye that weep now: for ye shall
laugh.
22 [s]Blessed are ye, when men
shall hate you, and when they [t]shall
separate you *from their company,* and
shall reproach *you,* and cast out your
name as evil, for the Son of man's
sake.
23 [u]Rejoice ye in that day, and
leap for joy: for, behold, your reward *is*
great in heaven: for [v]in the like man-
ner did their fathers unto the prophets.
24 [w]But woe unto you [x]that are
rich! for [y]ye have received your conso-
lation.
25 [z]Woe unto you that are full! for
ye shall hunger. [a]Woe unto you that
laugh now! for ye shall mourn and
weep.
26 [b]Woe unto you, when all men

6:13 [j]Mat. 10:1
6:14 [k]John 1:42
6:16 [l]Jude 1
6:17 [m]Mat. 4:25 Mark 3:7
6:19 [n]Mat. 14:36 [o]Mark 5:30 ch. 8:46
6:20 [p]Mat. 5:3 & 11:5 Jas. 2:5
6:21 [q]Is. 55:1 & 65:13 Mat. 5:6 [r]Is. 61:3 Mat. 5:4
6:22 [s]Mat. 5:11 1 Pet. 2:19 & 3:14 & 4:14 [t]John 16:2
6:23 [u]Mat. 5:12 Acts 5:41 Col. 1:24 Jas. 1:2 [v]Acts 7:51
6:24 [w]Amos 6:1 Jas. 5:1 [x]ch. 12:21 [y]Mat. 6:2,5,16 ch. 16:25
6:25 [z]Is. 65:13 [a]Prov. 14:13
6:26 [b]John 15:19; 1 John 4:5

Luke 9:1-6

chose the twelve to become His apostles (vv. 13–16), healed many who were sick (vv. 17–19), and preached His most quoted sermon (vv. 20–49). (2) If Jesus, the perfect Son of God, spent a whole night in prayer to the Father in order to make an important decision, how much more do we, with all our weaknesses and failings, need to spend nights in prayer and in close communion with our heavenly Father.

6:17 SERMON ON THE PLAIN. See Mat. 5–7, note on the Sermon on the Mount.

6:20 BLESSED. See Mat. 5:3, note.

6:20 YE POOR. See article on RICHES AND POVERTY, p. 1568, for comments on this verse.

6:21 YE THAT WEEP. See Mat. 5:4, note.

6:22 WHEN MEN SHALL HATE YOU. Followers of Jesus should rejoice and "leap for joy" (v. 23) when, because of faithfulness to Christ and His godly standards, they are criticized and scorned. Persecution from others because of righteousness is proof that they are in true fellowship with the Lord, since Jesus was also hated by the world and ill-treated (John 15:18–21; see Mat. 5:10, note).

6:23 LIKE MANNER . . . UNTO THE PROPHETS. In the O.T., the people of Israel rejected the prophets' messages many times (1 Ki. 19:10; Mat. 5:12; 23:31,37; Acts 7:51–52). (1) Churches today should bear in mind that God sends to them prophets (1 Cor. 12:28; Eph. 4:11) for the purpose of calling both leaders and people to a life of righteousness, faithfulness to all Scripture, and separation from the world (see Rev. 2–3).

(2) Churches can do the same thing as Israel of old by rejecting the words of their prophets and losing the blessing and salvation of God. On the other hand, churches can accept God's message, draw back from sin, deepen their loyalty to God and His Word, and continue as God's people. Those churches that reject God's true prophets will ultimately be rejected by God Himself (13:34–35; Rev. 2–3).

(3) It should be also recognized that Satan will deliberately send false prophets into the churches (Mat. 13:24–30,36–43), prophets who reject the absolute authority of God's Word, claim to have authority equal to God's Word, and maintain that their revelation is infallible and that their words may not be judged by the churches (see article on FALSE TEACHERS, p. 1508). These prophets must be firmly rejected.

6:24 WOE UNTO YOU THAT ARE RICH. Jesus is speaking of those who center their lives, purpose, happiness, or goals primarily in material things or in the pursuit of great wealth (see article on RICHES AND POVERTY, p. 1568).

6:26 WOE UNTO YOU, WHEN ALL MEN SHALL SPEAK WELL. When a large portion of the unbelieving world speaks well of a believer or a professed minister of God, it may be evidence that he is not a true follower of Christ, for false prophets are often popular with those who are not loyal to Christ. The prophet or minister who serves God will have the same thing happen to him as happened to Christ; his life and message will come into collision with the sins of the ungodly and will consequently be rejected by them.

shall speak well of you! for so did their
fathers to the false prophets.

Kingdom principles

6:29–30pp — Mat. 5:39–42
6:37–38pp — Mat. 7:1–2

27 ¶ [c]But I say unto you which
hear, Love your enemies, do good to
them which hate you,
28 Bless them that curse you, and
[d]pray for them which despitefully use
you.
29 [e]And unto him that smiteth
thee on the *one* cheek offer also the
other; [f]and him that taketh away thy
cloak forbid not *to take thy* coat also.
30 [g]Give to every man that asketh
of thee; and of him that taketh away
thy goods ask *them* not again.
31 [h]And as ye would that men
should do to you, do ye also to them
likewise.
32 [i]For if ye love them which love
you, what thank have ye? for sinners
also love those that love them.
33 And if ye do good to them which
do good to you, what thank have ye?
for sinners also do even the same.
34 [j]And if ye lend *to them* of whom
ye hope to receive, what thank have
ye? for sinners also lend to sinners, to
receive as much again.
35 But [k]love ye your enemies, and
do good, and [l]lend, hoping for nothing
again; and your reward shall be great,
and [m]ye shall be the children of the
Highest: for he is kind unto the un-
thankful and *to* the evil.
36 [n]Be ye therefore merciful, as
your Father also is merciful.
37 [o]Judge not, and ye shall not be
judged: condemn not, and ye shall not
be condemned: forgive, and ye shall be
forgiven:

6:27 [c]ver. 35 Ex. 23:4 Prov. 25:21 Mat. 5:44 Rom. 12:20 **6:28** [d]ch. 23:34 Acts 7:60 **6:29** [e]Mat. 5:39 [f]1 Cor. 6:7 **6:30** [g]Deut. 15:7,8,10 Prov. 21:26 Mat. 5:42 **6:31** [h]Mat. 7:12 **6:32** [i]Mat. 5:46 **6:34** [j]Mat. 5:42 **6:35** [k]ver. 27 [l]ver. 30 Ps. 37:26 [m]Mat. 5:45 **6:36** [n]Mat. 5:48 **6:37** [o]Mat. 7:1 **6:38** [p]Prov. 19:17 [q]Ps. 79:12 [r]Mat. 7:2 Mark 4:24 Jas. 2:13 **6:39** [s]Mat. 15:14 **6:40** [t]Mat. 10:24 John 13:16 & 15:20 **6:41** [u]Mat. 7:3 **6:43** [v]Mat. 7:16,17 **6:44** [w]Mat. 12:33 **6:45** [x]Mat. 12:35

38 [p]Give, and it shall be given unto
you; good measure, pressed down, and
shaken together, and running over,
shall men give into your [q]bosom. For
[r]with the same measure that ye mete
withal it shall be measured to you
again.

The blind leading the blind

6:41–42pp — Mat. 7:3–5

39 And he spake a parable unto
them, [s]Can the blind lead the blind?
shall they not both fall into the ditch?
40 [t]The disciple is not above his
master: but every one [v]that is perfect
shall be as his master.
41 [u]And why beholdest thou the
mote that is in thy brother's eye, but
perceivest not the beam that is in thine
own eye?
42 Either how canst thou say to thy
brother, Brother, let me pull out the
mote that is in thine eye, when thou
thyself beholdest not the beam that is
in thine own eye? Thou hypocrite, cast
out first the beam out of thine own eye,
and then shalt thou see clearly to pull
out the mote that is in thy brother's
eye.

A tree and its fruit

6:43–44pp — Mat. 7:16,18,20

43 [v]For a good tree bringeth not
forth corrupt fruit; neither doth a cor-
rupt tree bring forth good fruit.
44 For [w]every tree is known by his
own fruit. For of thorns men do not
gather figs, nor of a bramble bush gath-
er they [w]grapes.
45 [x]A good man out of the good
treasure of his heart bringeth forth

John 15:1-8

[v] Or, *shall be perfected as his master* [w] Gk. *a grape*

6:27 LOVE YOUR ENEMIES. In vv. 27–42, Jesus tells us how we are to live with other persons. As members of the new covenant, we are obligated to follow the demands He sets forth here.

(1) Loving our enemies does not mean an emotional love, such as liking our enemies, but rather a genuine concern for their good and their eternal salvation. Since we know the terrible fate that awaits those who are hostile toward God and His people, we must pray for them and attempt, by returning good for evil, to bring them to Christ and the faith of the gospel.

(2) Loving our enemies does not mean standing by idly while evildoers continue their wicked deeds. When it is necessary for the honor of God, the good or safety of others, or the ultimate good of the wicked, severe action must be taken to stop evil (see Mark 11:15; John 2:13–17).

6:29 FORBID NOT *TO TAKE THY* COAT. See Mat. 5:39, note.

6:37 JUDGE NOT. See Mat. 7:1, note.

6:38 GIVE. In conformity with the principle of love, we must give to those in need (see 2 Cor. 8:2, note; see article on THE CARE OF THE POOR AND NEEDY, p. 1312). God Himself will measure our giving and in return will give to us. The measure of blessing and reward we receive will be in proportion to our concern for and help given to others (see 2 Cor. 9:6).

6:45 THE HEART. The heart, the center of our being, determines our outward behavior and deeds and must be changed or converted (see Mark

that which is good; and an evil man out of the evil treasure of his heart bringeth forth that which is evil: for [y]of the abundance of the heart his mouth speaketh.

The wise and foolish builders

6:47–49pp — Mat. 7:24–27

46 ¶ [z]And why call ye me, Lord, Lord, and do not the things which I say?

47 [a]Whosoever cometh to me, and heareth my sayings, and doeth them, I will show you to whom he is like:

48 He is like a man which built an house, and digged deep, and laid the foundation on a rock: and when the flood arose, the stream beat vehemently upon that house, and could not shake it: for it was founded upon a rock.

49 But he that heareth, and doeth not, is like a man that without a foundation built an house upon the earth; against which the stream did beat vehemently, and immediately it fell; and the ruin of that house was great.

Luke 10:25-37

The centurion's servant healed

7:1–10pp — Mat. 8:5–13

7 NOW WHEN he had ended all his sayings in the audience of the people, [b]he entered into Capernaum.

2 And a certain centurion's servant, who was dear unto him, was sick, and ready to die.

3 And when he heard of Jesus, he sent unto him the elders of the Jews, beseeching him that he would come and heal his servant.

4 And when they came to Jesus, they besought him instantly, saying, That he was worthy for whom he should do this:

6:45 [y]Mat. 12:34
6:46 [z]Mal. 1:6 Mat. 7:21 & 25:11 ch. 13:25
6:47 [a]Mat. 7:24
7:1 [b]Mat. 8:5

5 For he loveth our nation, and he hath built us a synagogue.

6 Then Jesus went with them. And when he was now not far from the house, the centurion sent friends to him, saying unto him, Lord, trouble not thyself: for I am not worthy that thou shouldest enter under my roof:

7 Wherefore neither thought I myself worthy to come unto thee: but say in a word, and my servant shall be healed.

8 For I also am a man set under authority, having under me soldiers, and I say unto [x]one, Go, and he goeth; and to another, Come, and he cometh; and to my servant, Do this, and he doeth *it.*

9 When Jesus heard these things, he marvelled at him, and turned him about, and said unto the people that followed him, I say unto you, I have not found so great faith, no, not in Israel.

10 And they that were sent, returning to the house, found the servant whole that had been sick.

The raising of the widow's son

7:11–16Ref — 1 Ki. 17:17–24; 2 Ki. 4:32–37; Mark 5:21–24,35–43; John 11:1–44

11 ¶ And it came to pass the day after, that he went into a city called Nain; and many of his disciples went with him, and much people.

12 Now when he came nigh to the gate of the city, behold, there was a dead man carried out, the only son of his mother, and she was a widow: and much people of the city was with her.

13 And when the Lord saw her, he had compassion on her, and said unto her, Weep not.

[x] Gk. *this man*

7:20–23, note; see articles on THE HEART, p. 932, and REGENERATION, p. 1597). Without that inward change, no one can do God's will (cf. Jer. 24:7; 31:33; 32:39; Ezek. 36:23,27; Mat. 7:16–20; 12:33–35; 15:18–19; 21:43; Luke 1:17; Rom. 6:17).

6:46 DO NOT THE THINGS WHICH I SAY. See Mat. 7:21, note.

7:9 SO GREAT FAITH. See Mat. 8:10, note.

7:13 HE HAD COMPASSION ON HER. Jesus' compassion for this widow shows that God has a special love and care for widows or for any person left alone in the world. Concerning God's feeling of sympathy for such women, the Scriptures teach the following: (1) God is a Father of the fatherless and a defender of widows (see Ps. 68:5, note). They are under His special care and protection (Ex. 22:22–23; Deut. 10:18; Ps. 146:9; Prov. 15:25). (2) By means of the tithe and the abundance of His people, God provides for them (Deut. 14:28–29; 24:19–21; 26:12–13). (3) He blesses those who help and honor them (Is. 1:17,19; Jer. 7:6–7; 22:3–4). (4) He is against those who take advantage of or hurt them (Ex. 22:22–24; Deut. 24:17; 27:19; Job 24:3; Ps. 94:6,16; Zech. 7:10). (5) They are recipients of God's tender love and compassion (Mark 12:42–43; Luke 7:11–17; 18:2–8; 21:2–4). (6) The early church made it a priority to care for them (Acts 6:1–6). (7) James states that one aspect of true faith in Christ is to look after the fatherless and widows in their affliction (Jas. 1:27; cf. 1 Tim. 5:3–8).

14 And he came and touched the
[y]bier: and they that bare *him* stood
still. And he said, Young man, I say
unto thee, [c]Arise.
15 And he that was dead sat up, and
began to speak. And he delivered him
to his mother.
16 [d]And there came a fear on all:
and they glorified God, saying, [e]That
a great prophet is risen up among us;
and, [f]That God hath visited his peo-
ple.
17 And this rumour of him went
forth throughout all Judaea, and
throughout all the region round about.

Tribute to John the Baptist

7:18–35pp — Mat. 11:2–19

18 [g]And the disciples of John
showed him of all these things.
19 ¶ And John calling *unto him* two
of his disciples sent *them* to Jesus, say-
ing, Art thou he that should come? or
look we for another?
20 When the men were come unto
him, they said, John Baptist hath sent
us unto thee, saying, Art thou he that
should come? or look we for another?
21 And in that same hour he cured
many of *their* infirmities and plagues,
and of evil spirits; and unto many *that*
were blind he gave sight.
22 [h]Then Jesus answering said
unto them, Go your way, and tell John
what things ye have seen and heard;
[i]how that the blind see, the lame
walk, the lepers are cleansed, the deaf
hear, the dead are raised, [j]to the poor
the gospel is preached.
23 And blessed is *he,* whosoever
shall not be offended in me.
24 ¶ [k]And when the messengers of
John were departed, he began to speak
unto the people concerning John, What
went ye out into the wilderness for to
see? A reed shaken with the wind?

7:14 [c]ch. 8:54 John 11:43 Acts 9:40 Rom. 4:17 **7:16** [d]ch. 1:65 [e]ch. 24:19 John 4:19 & 6:14 & 9:17 [f]ch. 1:68 **7:18** [g]Mat. 11:2 **7:22** [h]Mat. 11:4 [i]Is. 35:5 [j]ch. 4:18 **7:24** [k]Mat. 11:7 **7:27** [l]Mal. 3:1 **7:29** [m]Mat. 3:5 ch. 3:12 **7:30** [n]Acts 20:27 **7:31** [o]Mat. 11:16 **7:33** [p]Mat. 3:4 Mark 1:6 ch. 1:15 **7:35** [q]Mat. 11:19

25 But what went ye out for to see?
A man clothed in soft raiment? Behold,
they which are gorgeously apparelled,
and live delicately, are in kings' courts.
26 But what went ye out for to see?
A prophet? Yea, I say unto you, and
much more than a prophet.
27 This is *he,* of whom it is written,
[l]Behold, I send my messenger before
thy face, which shall prepare thy way
before thee.
28 For I say unto you, Among those
that are born of women there is not a
greater prophet than John the Baptist:
but he that is least in the kingdom of
God is greater than he.
29 And all the people that heard
him, and the publicans, justified God,
[m]being baptized with the baptism of
John.
30 But the Pharisees and lawyers
[z]rejected [n]the counsel of God
[a]against themselves, being not bap-
tized of him.
31 ¶ And the Lord said, [o]Where-
unto then shall I liken the men of this
generation? and to what are they
like?
32 They are like unto children sit-
ting in the marketplace, and calling
one to another, and saying, We have
piped unto you, and ye have not
danced; we have mourned to you, and
ye have not wept.
33 For [p]John the Baptist came nei-
ther eating bread nor drinking wine;
and ye say, He hath a devil.
34 The Son of man is come eating
and drinking; and ye say, Behold a
gluttonous man, and a winebibber, a
friend of publicans and sinners!
35 But [q]wisdom is justified of all
her children.

[y] Or, *coffin* [z] Or, *frustrated* [a] Or, *within themselves*

7:24 A REED SHAKEN. See Mat. 11:7, note.

7:28 JOHN THE BAPTIST. See Mat. 11:11, note.

7:33 WINE. For an examination of Biblical words for wine and for its use in N.T. times, see 1:15, note; see articles on WINE IN NEW TESTAMENT TIMES (1) and (2), p. 1538 and p. 1594.

7:34 GLUTTONOUS . . . WINEBIBBER. Wine (Gk. *oinos*) in the N.T. referred to all kinds of wine, both unfermented and fermented (see article on WINE IN NEW TESTAMENT TIMES (1), p. 1538). Jesus' statement indicates that He drank some types of wine, whereas John did not. However, it cannot be determined from this passage what types of wine He drank, for the allegation of the Pharisees concerning Jesus' character is clearly false. They accuse Jesus of being a glutton and a drunkard or of drinking with sinners, but these were characteristically slanderous lies designed to destroy His influence as a teacher of righteousness (see Mat. 12:24; John 7:20; 8:48). Jesus Himself implies that those who "eat and drink with the drunken" are evil servants (Mat. 24:48–49). Therefore, it can in no way be proven from this passage that Jesus drank intoxicating wine. For a discussion on the kind of wine Jesus used, see articles on WINE IN NEW TESTAMENT TIMES (1) and (2), p. 1538 and p. 1594; cf. Prov. 23:31.

WINE IN NEW TESTAMENT TIMES (1)

***Luke 7:33–34** "For John the Baptist came neither eating bread nor drinking wine; and ye say, He hath a devil. The Son of man is come eating and drinking; and ye say, Behold a gluttonous man, and a winebibber, a friend of publicans and sinners."*

WINE: FERMENTED OR UNFERMENTED? The following is an examination of the most common Biblical word for wine. The Greek word for "wine" in Luke 7:33 is *oinos*. *Oinos* can refer to two distinctly different types of juice of the grape: (1) unfermented juice, and (2) fermented or intoxicating wine. This interpretation is supported by the following data.

(1) The Greek word *oinos* was used by secular and religious authors in pre-Christian and early church times to refer to fresh grape juice (see Aristotle, *Metereologica*, 387.b.9–13). (a) Anacreon (c. 500 B.C.) writes, "Squeeze the grape, let out the wine [*oinos*]" (Ode 5). (b) Nicander (second century B.C.) writes of squeezing grapes and refers to the produced juice as *oinos* (*Georgica*, fragment 86). (c) Papias (A.D. 60–130), an early church father, mentions that when grapes are crushed they yield "jars of wine [*oinos*]" (cited by Irenaeus, *Against Heresies*, 5.33.3–4). (d) A Greek papyrus letter (P. Oxy. 729; A.D. 137) speaks of "fresh wine [*oinos*] from the treading vat" (see Moulton and Milligan, *The Vocabulary of the Greek Testament*, p. 10). (e) Athenaeus (A.D. 200) speaks of a "sweet wine [*oinos*]" that "does not make the head heavy" (Athenaeus, *Banquet*, 1.54). In another place, he writes of a man gathering grapes who "went about, and took wine [*oinos*] from the field" (1.54). For more detailed discussions on use of *oinos* by ancient writers, see Robert P. Teachout, "The Use of 'Wine' in the Old Testament" (Th.D. dissertation, Dallas Theological Seminary, 1979).

(2) The Jewish scholars who translated the O.T. into Greek about 200 B.C. used *oinos* when translating several Hebrew words for wine (see article on WINE IN THE OLD TESTAMENT, p. 220). In other words, the writers of the N.T. knew that *oinos* could either be fermented or unfermented juice from the grape.

(3) As in secular Greek and the O.T., an examination of N.T. passages reveals that *oinos* may mean either fermented or unfermented wine. In Eph. 5:18 the command, "be not drunk with wine [*oinos*]," refers to alcoholic wine. On the other hand, in Rev. 19:15 Christ is described as treading out the winepress. The Greek text reads: "He treads the winepress of the wine [*oinos*]"; the *oinos* that comes forth from the winepress would be grape juice (see Is. 66:10, note; Jer. 48:32–37, note). In Rev. 6:6 *oinos* refers to grapes on the vine as a crop not to be destroyed. Thus, for believers in N.T. times, "wine" (*oinos*) was a general word that could be used for two distinctly different grape beverages, fermented and unfermented wine.

(4) Finally, ancient Roman writers have explained in detail various processes used in dealing with freshly squeezed grape juice, especially ways to preserve it from fermenting. (a) Columella (*On Agriculture*, 12.29), knowing that grape juice would not ferment if kept cool (under 50 degrees) and oxygen free, writes as follows: "That your grape juice may be always as sweet as when it is new, thus proceed. After you apply the press to the grapes, take the newest must [i.e., fresh juice], put it in a new container (*amphora*), bung it up, and cover it up very carefully with pitch lest any water should enter; then sink it in a cistern or pond of cold water and allow no part of the amphora to remain above the surface. After forty days take it out. It will remain sweet for a year" (see also Columella, *Agriculture and Trees*; Cato, *On Agriculture*). The Roman writer Pliny (first century A.D.) writes: "as soon as the must [grape juice] is taken from the vat and put into casks, they plunge the casks in water till midwinter passes and regular cold weather sets in" (Pliny, *Natural History*, 14.11.83). Israel would have had no problem in applying the above method (see Deut. 8:7; 11:11–12; Ps. 65:9–13).

(b) Another method to keep grapes from fermenting was to boil them into a syrup (for more details, see article on WINE IN NEW TESTAMENT TIMES (2), p. 1594). Ancient historians actually referred to this product as wine (*oinos*). Canon Farrar (*Smith's Bible Dictionary*, p. 747) states that "the wines of antiquity were more like syrups; many of them were not intoxicant." Also, *The New Bible Dictionary* (p. 1332) notes that "there were means of keeping wine sweet all year round."

USE OF WINE IN LORD'S SUPPER. Did Jesus use fermented or unfermented grape drink when He instituted the Lord's Supper (Mat. 26:26–29; Mark 14:22–25; Luke 22:17–20; 1 Cor. 11:23–26)? The following data support the conclusion that what Jesus and His disciples drank was unfermented grape juice.

(1) Neither Luke nor any other Biblical writer uses the word "wine" (Gk. *oinos*) in regard to the Lord's Supper. The first three Gospel writers use "fruit of the vine" (Mat. 26:29; Mark 14:25; Luke 22:18). Unfermented wine is the only true natural "fruit of the vine," containing approximately 20 percent sugar and no alcohol. Fermentation destroys much of the sugar and alters what the vine produced. Fermented wine is not the product of the vine.

(2) The Lord's Supper was instituted when Jesus and His disciples were eating the Passover. The Passover law in Ex. 12:14–20 prohibited, during Passover week, the presence and use of *seor* (Ex. 12:15), a word referring to leaven, yeast, or any agent of fermentation. *Seor* in the ancient world was often obtained from the thick scum on top of fermenting wine. Furthermore, all *hametz* (i.e., anything containing any fermentation) was forbidden (Ex. 12:19; 13:7; see 13:7, note). God had given these laws because fermentation symbolized corruption and sin (cf. Mat. 16:6,12; 1 Cor. 5:7–8). Jesus, the Son of God, fulfilled the law in every requirement (Mat. 5:17). Thus, He would have followed God's law for the Passover and not used fermented wine.

(3) A rather lively debate has taken place over the centuries among Jewish rabbis and scholars as to whether fermented products of the vine were allowed in the Passover. Those who held to a stricter and more literal interpretation of the Hebrew Scriptures, especially Ex. 13:7, insisted that no fermented wine was to be used on this occasion.

(4) Some Jewish sources affirm that the use of unfermented wine at the Passover was common in N.T. times. For example, "According to the synoptic Gospels, it would appear that on the Thursday evening of the last week of his life Jesus with his disciples entered Jerusalem in order to eat the Passover meal with them in the sacred city; if so, the wafer and the wine of . . . the communion service then instituted by him as a memorial would be the unleavened bread and the unfermented wine of the Seder service" (see "Jesus," *The Jewish Encyclopedia*, 1904 edition, V.165).

(5) In the O.T. fermented drink was never to be used in the house of God, nor were the priests allowed to draw near to God in worship while drinking intoxicating beverages (see Lev. 10:9, note). Jesus Christ was God's High Priest of the new covenant, drawing nigh to God for the sake of His people (Heb. 3:1; 5:1–10).

(6) The value of a symbol is determined by its capacity to conceptualize the spiritual reality. Therefore, just as the bread represented the pure body of Christ and had to be unleavened (i.e., uncorrupted with fermentation), the fruit of the vine, representing the incorruptible blood of Christ, would have been best represented by juice that was unfermented (cf. 1 Pet. 1:18–19). Since Scripture states explicitly that the process of corruption was not allowed to work in either the body or blood of Christ (Ps. 16:10; Acts 2:27; 13:37), both of these are properly symbolized by that which is uncorrupted and unfermented.

(7) Paul instructed the Corinthians to put away spiritual yeast, i.e., the fermenting agent of "malice and wickedness," because Christ is our Passover (1 Cor. 5:6–8). It would be inconsistent with the goal and spiritual requirement of the Lord's Supper to use something which was a symbol of evil, i.e., something with leaven or yeast.

For more on wine in N.T. times, see article on WINE IN NEW TESTAMENT TIMES (2), p. 1594.

Jesus anointed by a sinful woman

7:37–39Ref — Mat. 26:6–13; Mark 14:3–9; John 12:1–8
7:41–42Ref — Mat. 18:23–34

36 ¶ [r]And one of the Pharisees desired him that he would eat with him. And he went into the Pharisee's house, and sat down to meat.

37 And, behold, a woman in the city, which was a sinner, when she knew that *Jesus* sat at meat in the Pharisee's house, brought an alabaster box of ointment,

38 And stood at his feet behind *him* weeping, and began to wash his feet with tears, and did wipe *them* with the hairs of her head, and kissed his feet, and anointed *them* with the ointment.

39 Now when the Pharisee which had bidden him saw *it,* he spake within himself, saying, [s]This man, if he were a prophet, would have known who and what manner of woman *this is* that toucheth him: for she is a sinner.

40 And Jesus answering said unto him, Simon, I have somewhat to say unto thee. And he saith, Master, say on.

41 There was a certain creditor which had two debtors: the one owed five hundred [b]pence, and the other fifty.

42 And when they had nothing to pay, he frankly forgave them both. Tell me therefore, which of them will love him most?

43 Simon answered and said, I suppose that *he,* to whom he forgave most. And he said unto him, Thou hast rightly judged.

7:36 [r]Mat. 26:6 Mark 14:3 John 11:2
7:39 [s]ch. 15:2
7:46 [t]Ps. 23:5
7:47 [u]1 Tim. 1:14
7:48 [v]Mat. 9:2 Mark 2:5
7:49 [w]Mat. 9:3 Mark 2:7
7:50 [x]Mat. 9:22 Mark 5:34 & 10:52 ch. 8:48 & 18:42
8:2 [y]Mat. 27:55,56 [z]Mark 16:9

Jesus saves the woman

44 And he turned to the woman, and said unto Simon, Seest thou this woman? I entered into thine house, thou gavest me no water for my feet: but she hath washed my feet with tears, and wiped *them* with the hairs of her head.

45 Thou gavest me no kiss: but this woman since the time I came in hath not ceased to kiss my feet.

46 [t]My head with oil thou didst not anoint: but this woman hath anointed my feet with ointment.

47 [u]Wherefore I say unto thee, Her sins, which are many, are forgiven; for she loved much: but to whom little is forgiven, *the same* loveth little.

48 And he said unto her, [v]Thy sins are forgiven.

49 And they that sat at meat with him began to say within themselves, [w]Who is this that forgiveth sins also?

50 And he said to the woman, [x]Thy faith hath saved thee; go in peace. Luke 8:48

Certain women minister to Jesus

8 AND IT came to pass afterward, that he went throughout every city and village, preaching and showing the glad tidings of the kingdom of God: and the twelve *were* with him,

2 And [y]certain women, which had been healed of evil spirits and infirmities, Mary called Magdalene, [z]out of whom went seven devils,

3 And Joanna the wife of Chuza Herod's steward, and Susanna, and many others, which ministered unto him of their substance.

[b] See Mat. 20:2

7:38 WEEPING. Because of her love and devotion for Jesus, this woman wets the feet of Christ with her tears. Weeping can be an expression of sorrow and grief or of grateful love toward Christ.

(1) By weeping in prayer and faith, the believer expresses to God what is in his heart; such tears are valued as an offering and service unto Him (vv. 37–50; Ps. 126:5–6; Jer. 9:1; 14:17; 31:15–16; Acts 20:19,31; 2 Cor. 2:4; see Neh. 8:9, note). In this manner the believer also participates in the sufferings of Christ (2 Cor. 1:5; Phil. 3:10; 1 Pet. 4:13).

(2) Christ Himself wept while praying and was heard (Heb. 5:7); likewise, the apostle Paul served the Lord with many tears (Acts 20:19; 2 Cor. 2:4). Even today those who weep in Christ are considered blessed (6:21). In Christ's future kingdom God will wipe away all tears from the eyes of His people (Rev. 7:17; 21:4; concerning prayer and tears, read 2 Ki. 20:5; Ps. 39:12; see 56:8, note).

7:47 SHE LOVED MUCH. Real love and devotion toward Jesus must come from a deep consciousness of the sinfulness of our past condition, the love He had for us when He gave Himself on Calvary, and the inner assurance that we are now forgiven and cared for. Faith that is not based on these foundations will not endure.

8:3 MINISTERED UNTO HIM. These women, who had received healing and special care from Jesus, honored Him by faithfully contributing to the support of Jesus and His disciples. Their service and devotion to Him continue to be an example for every woman who believes in Him. To the extent that you minister unto Him, the words of Mat. 25:34–40 apply to you.

Parable of the sower

8:4–10pp — Mat. 13:2–13; Mark 4:1–12

4 ¶ [a]And when much people were gathered together, and were come to him out of every city, he spake by a parable:

5 A sower went out to sow his seed: and as he sowed, some fell by the way side; and it was trodden down, and the fowls of the air devoured it.

6 And some fell upon a rock; and as soon as it was sprung up, it withered away, because it lacked moisture.

7 And some fell among thorns; and the thorns sprang up with it, and choked it.

8 And other fell on good ground, and sprang up, and bare fruit an hundredfold. And when he had said these things, he cried, He that hath ears to hear, let him hear.

9 [b]And his disciples asked him, saying, What might this parable be?

10 And he said, Unto you it is given to know the mysteries of the kingdom of God: but to others in parables; [c]that seeing they might not see, and hearing they might not understand.

The parable explained

8:11–15pp — Mat. 13:18–23; Mark 4:13–20

11 [d]Now the parable is this: The seed is the word of God.

12 Those by the way side are they that hear; then cometh the devil, and taketh away the word out of their hearts, lest they should believe and be saved.

13 They on the rock *are they,* which, when they hear, receive the word with joy; and these have no root, which for a while believe, and in time of temptation fall away.

14 And that which fell among thorns are they, which, when they have heard, go forth, and are choked with cares and riches and pleasures of *this* life, and bring no fruit to perfection.

15 But that on the good ground are they, which in an honest and good heart, having heard the word, keep *it,* and bring forth fruit with patience.

A lamp on a stand

8:16–18pp — Mat. 5:15; Mark 4:21–23

16 ¶ [e]No man, when he hath lighted a candle, covereth it with a vessel, or putteth *it* under a bed; but setteth *it* on a candlestick, that they which enter in may see the light.

17 [f]For nothing is secret, that shall not be made manifest; neither *any thing* hid, that shall not be known and come abroad.

18 Take heed therefore how ye hear: [g]for whosoever hath, to him shall be given; and whosoever hath not, from him shall be taken even that which he [c]seemeth to have.

Jesus' true family

8:19–21pp — Mat. 12:46–50; Mark 3:31–35

19 ¶ [h]Then came to him *his* mother and his brethren, and could not come at him for the press.

20 And it was told him *by certain* which said, Thy mother and thy brethren stand without, desiring to see thee.

21 And he answered and said unto them, My mother and my brethren are

8:4 [a]Mat. 13:2 Mark 4:1
8:9 [b]Mat. 13:10 Mark 4:10
8:10 [c]Is. 6:9 Mark 4:12
8:11 [d]Mat. 13:18 Mark 4:14
8:16 [e]Mat. 5:15 Mark 4:21 ch. 11:33
8:17 [f]Mat. 10:26 ch. 12:2
8:18 [g]Mat. 13:12 & 25:29 ch. 19:26
8:19 [h]Mat. 12:46 Mark 3:31

[c] Or, *thinketh that he hath*

8:4 PARABLE. See Mat. 13:3, note.

8:5 A SOWER WENT OUT TO SOW. See Mark 4:3, note.

8:12 TAKETH AWAY THE WORD. See Mark 4:15, note on halfway conversions.

8:13 FOR A WHILE BELIEVE ... FALL AWAY. In Christ's interpretation of this parable, He explicitly affirms the possibility of a person "believing" (i.e., making a sincere beginning in the life of faith), but subsequently falling away because of a failure to resist temptation. In contrast are those who, "having heard the word, keep *it,* and bring forth fruit" with perseverance (v. 15). Jesus teaches that it is essential that those who receive the Word unto salvation "keep it" (11:28; John 8:51; 1 Cor. 15:1–2; Col. 1:21–23; 1 Tim. 4:1, 16; 2 Tim. 3:13–15; 1 John 2:24–25; see John 15:6, note on abiding in Christ).

8:14 CHOKED WITH CARES AND RICHES. We who have believed in Jesus must ever be on the alert that worldly responsibilities, abundance, or pleasures do not absorb our thoughts or goals until our spiritual life is altogether destroyed. These kinds of thorns/weeds can slowly but surely choke the Word from our lives. Let us ask ourselves: What is happening in my life? Am I being caught up more and more in the temporal things of life? Or are the Word of God and heavenly things becoming more important as time goes by?

8:18 TO HIM SHALL BE GIVEN. See Mat. 25:29, note.

8:21 MY MOTHER AND MY BRETHREN. Only those who hear and obey the Word of God are personally related to Jesus and a part of God's family. Faith without obedience does not exist in the spiritual family of God.

these which hear the word of God, and do it.

The storm stilled

8:22–25pp — Mat. 8:23–27; Mark 4:36–41
8:22–25Ref — Mark 6:47–52; John 6:16–21

22 ¶ [i]Now it came to pass on a certain day, that he went into a ship with his disciples: and he said unto them, Let us go over unto the other side of the lake. And they launched forth.

23 But as they sailed he fell asleep: and there came down a storm of wind on the lake; and they were filled *with water,* and were in jeopardy.

24 And they came to him, and awoke him, saying, Master, master, we perish. Then he arose, and rebuked the wind and the raging of the water: and they ceased, and there was a calm.

25 And he said unto them, Where is your faith? And they being afraid wondered, saying one to another, What manner of man is this! for he commandeth even the winds and water, and they obey him.

Devils cast out

8:26–37pp — Mat. 8:28–34
8:26–39pp — Mark 5:1–20

26 ¶ [j]And they arrived at the country of the Gadarenes, which is over against Galilee.

27 And when he went forth to land, there met him out of the city a certain man, which had devils long time, and ware no clothes, neither abode in *any* house, but in the tombs.

28 When he saw Jesus, he cried out, and fell down before him, and with a loud voice said, What have I to do with thee, Jesus, *thou* Son of God most high? I beseech thee, torment me not.

29 (For he had commanded the unclean spirit to come out of the man. For oftentimes it had caught him: and he was kept bound with chains and in fetters; and he brake the bands, and was driven of the devil into the wilderness.)

30 And Jesus asked him, saying, What is thy name? And he said, Legion: because many devils were entered into him.

31 And they besought him that he would not command them to go out [k]into the deep.

32 And there was there an herd of many swine feeding on the mountain: and they besought him that he would suffer them to enter into them. And [l]he suffered them.

33 Then went the devils out of the man, and entered into the swine: and the herd ran violently down a steep place into the lake, and were choked.

34 When they that fed *them* saw what was done, they fled, and went and told *it* in the city and in the country.

35 Then they went out to see what was done; and came to Jesus, and found the man, out of whom the devils were departed, sitting at the feet of Jesus, clothed, and in his right mind: and they were afraid.

36 They also which saw *it* told them by what means he that was possessed of the devils was healed.

37 ¶ [m]Then the whole multitude of the country of the Gadarenes round about [n]besought him to depart from them; for they were taken with great fear: and he went up into the ship, and returned back again.

38 Now [o]the man out of whom the devils were departed besought him that he might be with him: but Jesus sent him away, saying,

39 Return to thine own house, and show how great things God hath done unto thee. And he went his way, and published throughout the whole city how great things Jesus had done unto him.

A ruler's daughter raised

8:40–56pp — Mat. 9:18–26; Mark 5:22–43

40 And it came to pass, that, when Jesus was returned, the people *gladly* received him: for they were all waiting for him.

41 ¶ [p]And, behold, there came a man named Jairus, and he was a ruler of the synagogue: and he fell down at Jesus' feet, and besought him that he would come into his house:

42 For he had one only daughter, about twelve years of age, and she lay a dying. But as he went the people thronged him.

8:22 [i]Mat. 8:23; Mark 4:35
8:26 [j]Mat. 8:28; Mark 5:1
8:31 [k]Rev. 20:3
8:32 [l]Job 1:12 & 12:16; Rev. 20:7
8:37 [m]Mat. 8:34; [n]Acts 16:39
8:38 [o]Mark 5:18
8:41 [p]Mat. 9:18; Mark 5:22

8:27–33 A CERTAIN MAN, WHICH HAD DEVILS. Demon possession (or the indwelling of demons within a human personality) is one of the means used by Satan and the kingdom of evil in their struggle against the kingdom of God. For more on this subject, see article on POWER OVER SATAN AND DEMONS, p. 1486.

43 ¶ [q]And a woman having an is-
sue of blood twelve years, which had
spent all her living upon physicians,
neither could be healed of any,
44 Came behind *him,* and touched
the border of his garment: and immedi-
ately her issue of blood stanched.
45 And Jesus said, Who touched
me? When all denied, Peter and they
that were with him said, Master, the
multitude throng thee and press *thee,*
and sayest thou, Who touched me?
46 And Jesus said, Somebody hath
touched me: for I perceive that [r]virtue
is gone out of me.
47 And when the woman saw that
she was not hid, she came trembling,
and falling down before him, she de-
clared unto him before all the people
for what cause she had touched him,
and how she was healed immediately.
48 And he said unto her, Daughter,
Luke be of good comfort: thy faith hath made
2:28 thee whole; go in peace.
49 ¶ [s]While he yet spake, there
cometh one from the ruler of the syna-
gogue's *house,* saying to him, Thy
daughter is dead; trouble not the Mas-
ter.
50 But when Jesus heard *it,* he an-
swered him, saying, Fear not: believe
only, and she shall be made whole.
51 And when he came into the
house, he suffered no man to go in,
save Peter, and James, and John, and
the father and the mother of the
maiden.
52 And all wept, and bewailed her:
but he said, Weep not; she is not dead,
[t]but sleepeth.

8:43 [q]Mat. 9:20
8:46 [r]Mark 5:30; ch. 6:19
8:49 [s]Mark 5:35
8:52 [t]John 11:11,13
8:54 [u]ch. 7:14; John 11:43
8:56 [v]Mat. 8:4 & 9:30; Mark 5:43
9:1 [w]Mat. 10:1; Mark 3:13 & 6:7
9:2 [x]Mat. 10:7,8; Mark 6:12; ch. 10:1,9
9:3 [y]Mat. 10:9; Mark 6:8; ch. 10:4 & 22:35
9:4 [z]Mat. 10:11; Mark 6:10
9:5 [a]Mat. 10:14; [b]Acts 13:51
9:6 [c]Mark 6:12
9:7 [d]Mark 14:1; Mark 6:14

53 And they laughed him to scorn,
knowing that she was dead.
54 And he put them all out, and
took her by the hand, and called, say-
ing, Maid, [u]arise.
55 And her spirit came again, and
she arose straightway: and he com-
manded to give her meat.
56 And her parents were aston-
ished: but [v]he charged them that they
should tell no man what was done.

The mission of the Twelve

9:3–5pp — Mat. 10:9–15; Mark 6:8–11
9:7–9pp — Mat. 14:1–2; Mark 6:14–16

9 THEN [w]HE called his twelve dis-
ciples together, and gave them
power and authority over all devils,
and to cure diseases.
2 And [x]he sent them to preach the
kingdom of God, and to heal the sick.
3 [y]And he said unto them, Take
nothing for *your* journey, neither
staves, nor scrip, neither bread, nei-
ther money; neither have two coats
apiece.
4 [z]And whatsoever house ye enter
into, there abide, and thence depart.
5 [a]And whosoever will not receive
you, when ye go out of that city,
[b]shake off the very dust from your
feet for a testimony against them.
6 [c]And they departed, and went
through the towns, preaching the gos- Luke
pel, and healing every where. 10:9
7 ¶ [d]Now Herod the tetrarch heard
of all that was done by him: and he was
perplexed, because that it was said of
some, that John was risen from the
dead;
8 And of some, that Elias had ap-

8:44 TOUCHED . . . HIS GARMENT. See Mark 5:28, note.

8:50 FEAR NOT: BELIEVE ONLY. See Mark 5:36, note.

9:1 AUTHORITY OVER ALL DEVILS. See Mat. 10:1, note.

9:2 PREACH THE KINGDOM . . . HEAL THE SICK. (1) This is the first time Jesus sent out the twelve disciples to represent Him by word and deed. The instruction given to the twelve, according to the parallel passage in Matthew, was to go to "the lost sheep of the house of Israel" (Mat. 10:6). After His resurrection, however, Jesus changed the scope to encompass all nations, in a commission that is to continue "to the end of the world" (Mat. 28:18–20; Mark 16:15–20).

(2) The Gospel writers make it clear that Jesus' command to preach the kingdom of God (see article on THE KINGDOM OF GOD, p. 1428) was seldom given apart from the command to heal the sick and to cast out demons (Mat. 9:35–38; 10:7–8; Mark 3:14–15; 6:7–13; 16:15,17; Luke 9:2,6; 10:1,9; cf. 4:17–19). The presentation of the gospel today must be accompanied by the same demonstration of the Spirit and of power (Mat. 10:1, note; Mark 16:15–18; Acts 1:8; Rom. 15:18–19; 1 Cor. 2:4–5; 4:20; see article on SIGNS OF BELIEVERS, p. 1516) in order to meet Satan's challenge in these last days (1 Tim. 4:1; 2 Tim. 3:1–5). That is, we must call people to repentance and faith in Jesus Christ as the Lord and Savior who baptizes them in the Holy Spirit and saves them from sin, and we must continue His works of mercy.

(3) Churches today should not compare themselves with other churches, but with this N.T. message and pattern. Are we seeing and experiencing the kingdom of God as did the early Christians? Is the kingdom of God nigh unto us? If not, why not?

peared; and of others, that one of the old prophets was risen again.

9 And Herod said, John have I beheaded: but who is this, of whom I hear such things? [e]And he desired to see him.

The five thousand fed

9:10–17pp — Mat. 14:13–21; Mark 6:32–44; John 6:5–13
9:13–17Ref — 2 Ki. 4:42–44

10 ¶ [f]And the apostles, when they were returned, told him all that they had done. [g]And he took them, and went aside privately into a desert place belonging to the city called Bethsaida.

11 And the people, when they knew *it,* followed him: and he received them, and spake unto them of the kingdom of God, and healed them that had need of healing.

12 [h]And when the day began to wear away, then came the twelve, and said unto him, Send the multitude away, that they may go into the towns and country round about, and lodge, and get victuals: for we are here in a desert place.

13 But he said unto them, Give ye them to eat. And they said, We have no more but five loaves and two fishes; except we should go and buy meat for all this people.

14 For they were about five thousand men. And he said to his disciples, Make them sit down by fifties in a company.

15 And they did so, and made them all sit down.

16 Then he took the five loaves and the two fishes, and looking up to heaven, he blessed them, and brake, and gave to the disciples to set before the multitude.

17 And they did eat, and were all filled: and there was taken up of fragments that remained to them twelve baskets.

Peter's confession of faith

9:18–20pp — Mat. 16:13–16; Mark 8:27–29
9:22–27pp — Mat. 16:21–28; Mark 8:31 – 9:1

18 ¶ [i]And it came to pass, as he was alone praying, his disciples were with him: and he asked them, saying, Whom say the people that I am?

19 They answering said, [j]John the Baptist; but some *say,* Elias; and others *say,* that one of the old prophets is risen again.

20 He said unto them, But whom say ye that I am? [k]Peter answering said, The Christ of God.

21 [l]And he straitly charged them, and commanded *them* to tell no man that thing;

22 Saying, [m]The Son of man must suffer many things, and be rejected of the elders and chief priests and scribes, and be slain, and be raised the third day.

23 ¶ [n]And he said to *them* all, If any *man* will come after me, let him deny himself, and take up his cross daily, and follow me.

24 For whosoever will save his life shall lose it: but whosoever will lose his life for my sake, the same shall save it.

25 [o]For what is a man advantaged, if he gain the whole world, and lose himself, or be cast away?

26 [p]For whosoever shall be ashamed of me and of my words, of him shall the Son of man be ashamed, when he shall come in his own glory, and *in his* Father's, and of the holy angels.

27 [q]But I tell you of a truth, there be some standing here, which shall not taste of death, till they see the kingdom of God.

9:9 [e]ch. 23:8
9:10 [f]Mark 6:30 [g]Mat. 14:13
9:12 [h]Mat. 14:15 Mark 6:35 John 6:1,5
9:18 [i]Mat. 16:13 Mark 8:27
9:19 [j]ver. 7,8 Mat. 14:2
9:20 [k]Mat. 16:16 John 6:69
9:21 [l]Mat. 16:20
9:22 [m]Mat. 16:21 & 17:22
9:23 [n]Mat. 10:38 & 16:24 Mark 8:34 ch. 14:27
9:25 [o]Mat. 16:26 Mark 8:36
9:26 [p]Mat. 10:33 Mark 8:38 2 Tim. 2:12
9:27 [q]Mat. 16:28 Mark 9:1

9:12–17 ABOUT FIVE THOUSAND MEN. See Mat. 14:19, note.

9:23 TAKE UP HIS CROSS DAILY. Accepting Jesus as Lord and Savior demands not only believing the truth of the gospel, but also committing ourselves to sacrificially follow Him (see Mark 8:34, note). The choice between denying ourselves or living for our own selfish desires must be made daily. That choice determines our eternal destiny.

9:24 WHOSOEVER WILL LOSE HIS LIFE. Making the achievement of happiness and pleasure our goal in life instead of living in God's will and by His principles will end in disappointment and loss. To renounce our own ways and live in fellowship with Jesus, basing our lives on the teachings of His Word, is to find true life and joy, here and hereafter.

9:26 ASHAMED OF ME. To be ashamed of Jesus means to feel shame or embarrassment before the world when we identify with the ways, values, and goals that Jesus taught. It is to be ashamed of His Word, ashamed to claim its full divine inspiration, ashamed to live by it and defend it. Such people Christ will reject and condemn (Mat. 10:33; Mark 8:34, note; Rom. 1:16; 2 Tim. 1:8,12,16; Rev. 3:14–16).

9:27 SEE THE KINGDOM OF GOD. See Mat. 16:28, note.

The transfiguration

9:28–36pp — Mat. 17:1–8; Mark 9:2–8

28 ¶ [r]And it came to pass about an eight days after these [d]sayings, he took Peter and John and James, and went up into a mountain to pray.

29 And as he prayed, the fashion of his countenance was altered, and his raiment *was* white *and* glistering.

30 And, behold, there talked with him two men, which were Moses and Elias:

31 Who appeared in glory, and spake of his decease which he should accomplish at Jerusalem.

32 But Peter and they that were with him [s]were heavy with sleep: and when they were awake, they saw his glory, and the two men that stood with him.

33 And it came to pass, as they departed from him, Peter said unto Jesus, Master, it is good for us to be here: and let us make three tabernacles; one for thee, and one for Moses, and one for Elias: not knowing what he said.

34 While he thus spake, there came a cloud, and overshadowed them: and they feared as they entered into the cloud.

35 And there came a voice out of the cloud, saying, [t]This is my beloved Son: [u]hear him.

36 And when the voice was past, Jesus was found alone. [v]And they kept *it* close, and told no man in those days any of those things which they had seen.

A demon possessed boy healed

9:37–45pp — Mat. 17:14–18,22–23; Mark 9:14–27,30–32

37 ¶ [w]And it came to pass, that on the next day, when they were come down from the hill, much people met him.

38 And, behold, a man of the company cried out, saying, Master, I beseech thee, look upon my son: for he is mine only child.

39 And, lo, a spirit taketh him, and he suddenly crieth out; and it teareth him that he foameth again, and bruising him hardly departeth from him.

40 And I besought thy disciples to cast him out; and they could not.

41 And Jesus answering said, O faithless and perverse generation, how long shall I be with you, and suffer you? Bring thy son hither.

42 And as he was yet a-coming, the devil threw him down, and tare *him*. And Jesus rebuked the unclean spirit, and healed the child, and delivered him again to his father.

43 ¶ And they were all amazed at the mighty power of God. But while they wondered every one at all things which Jesus did, he said unto his disciples,

44 [x]Let these sayings sink down into your ears: for the Son of man shall be delivered into the hands of men.

45 [y]But they understood not this saying, and it was hid from them, that they perceived it not: and they feared to ask him of that saying.

True discipleship

9:46–48pp — Mat. 18:1–5
9:46–50pp — Mark 9:33–40

46 ¶ [z]Then there arose a reasoning among them, which of them should be greatest.

47 And Jesus, perceiving the thought of their heart, took a child, and set him by him,

48 And said unto them, [a]Whosoever shall receive this child in my name receiveth me: and whosoever shall receive me receiveth him that sent me: [b]for he that is least among you all, the same shall be great.

49 ¶ [c]And John answered and said, Master, we saw one casting out devils in thy name; and we forbad him, because he followeth not with us.

50 And Jesus said unto him, Forbid *him* not: for [d]he that is not against us is for us.

James and John rebuked

51 ¶ And it came to pass, when the time was come that [e]he should be re-

9:28 [r]Mat. 17:1 Mark 9:2
9:32 [s]Dan. 8:18 & 10:9
9:35 [t]Mat. 3:17 [u]Acts 3:22
9:36 [v]Mat. 17:9
9:37 [w]Mat. 17:14 Mark 9:14,17
9:44 [x]Mat. 17:22
9:45 [y]Mark 9:32 ch. 2:50 & 18:34
9:46 [z]Mat. 18:1 Mark 9:34
9:48 [a]Mat. 10:40 & 18:5 Mark 9:37 John 12:44 & 13:20 [b]Mat. 23:11,12
9:49 [c]Mark 9:38 See Num. 11:28
9:50 [d]See Mat. 12:30 ch. 11:23
9:51 [e]Mark 16:19 Acts 1:2

[d] Or, *things*

9:29 WAS ALTERED. In His transfiguration, Jesus was transformed in the presence of three disciples, and they beheld His heavenly glory as He really was, God in human flesh. The experience of the transfiguration was: (1) an encouragement to Jesus as He faced death on the cross (cf. Mat. 16:21); (2) an announcement to the disciples that Jesus had to suffer on the cross (v. 31); (3) an endorsement by God that Jesus was His true Son, qualified to redeem the human race (v. 35).

9:41 FAITHLESS . . . GENERATION. See Mat. 17:17, note.

ceived up, he stedfastly set his face to
go to Jerusalem,
52 And sent messengers before his
face: and they went, and entered into
a village of the Samaritans, to make
ready for him.
53 And [f]they did not receive him,
because his face was as though he
would go to Jerusalem.
54 And when his disciples James
and John saw *this,* they said, Lord, wilt
thou that we command fire to come
down from heaven, and consume them,
even as [g]Elias did?
55 But he turned, and rebuked
them, and said, Ye know not what man-
ner of spirit ye are of.
56 For [h]the Son of man is not come
to destroy men's lives, but to save
them. And they went to another village.

The cost of following Jesus

9:57–60pp — Mat. 8:19–22

57 ¶ [i]And it came to pass, that, as
they went in the way, a certain *man*
said unto him, Lord, I will follow thee
whithersoever thou goest.
58 And Jesus said unto him, Foxes
have holes, and birds of the air *have*
nests; but the Son of man hath not
where to lay *his* head.
59 [j]And he said unto another, Fol-
low me. But he said, Lord, suffer me
first to go and bury my father.
60 Jesus said unto him, Let the dead
bury their dead: but go thou and preach
the kingdom of God.
61 And another also said, Lord, [k]I
will follow thee; but let me first go bid
them farewell, which are at home at my
house.
62 And Jesus said unto him, No
man, having put his hand to the
plough, and looking back, is fit for the
kingdom of God.

9:53 [f]John 4:4,9
9:54 [g]2 Ki. 1:10,12
9:56 [h]John 3:17 & 12:47
9:57 [i]Mat. 8:19
9:59 [j]Mat. 8:21
9:61 [k]See 1 Ki. 19:20

10:1 [l]Mat. 10:1 Mark 6:7
10:2 [m]Mat. 9:37 John 4:35 [n]2 Thes. 3:1
10:3 [o]Mat. 10:16
10:4 [p]Mat. 10:9 Mark 6:8 ch. 9:3 [q]2 Ki. 4:29
10:5 [r]Mat. 10:12
10:7 [s]Mat. 10:11 [t]1 Cor. 10:27 [u]Mat. 10:10 1 Cor. 9:4 1 Tim. 5:18
10:9 [v]ch. 9:2 [w]ver. 11 Mat. 3:2 & 4:17 & 10:7
10:11 [x]Mat. 10:14 ch. 9:5 Acts 13:51 & 18:6
10:12 [y]Mat. 10:15 Mark 6:11

The mission of the seventy

10:2pp — Mat. 9:37–38
10:4–7pp — Mat. 10:5–10; Luke 9:3–5

10 AFTER THESE things the Lord
appointed other seventy also,
and [l]sent them two and two before his
face into every city and place, whither
he himself would come.
2 Therefore said he unto them,
[m]The harvest truly *is* great, but the la-
bourers *are* few: [n]pray ye therefore
the Lord of the harvest, that he would
send forth labourers into his harvest.
3 Go your ways: [o]behold, I send
you forth as lambs among wolves.
4 [p]Carry neither purse, nor scrip,
nor shoes: and [q]salute no man by the
way.
5 [r]And into whatsoever house ye
enter, first say, Peace *be* to this house.
6 And if the son of peace be there,
your peace shall rest upon it: if not, it
shall turn to you again.
7 [s]And in the same house remain,
[t]eating and drinking such things as
they give: for [u]the labourer is worthy
of his hire. Go not from house to house.

Authority to heal

10:13–15,21–22pp — Mat. 11:21–23,25–27

8 And into whatsoever city ye enter,
and they receive you, eat such things
as are set before you:
9 [v]And heal the sick that are there- Luke
in, and say unto them, [w]The kingdom 13:10
of God is come nigh unto you. 17
10 But into whatsoever city ye en-
ter, and they receive you not, go your
ways out into the streets of the same,
and say,
11 [x]Even the very dust of your city,
which cleaveth on us, we do wipe off
against you: notwithstanding be ye
sure of this, that the kingdom of God
is come nigh unto you.
12 But I say unto you, that [y]it shall

9:55 WHAT . . . SPIRIT YE ARE OF. We must be careful that our outward loyalty and zeal for Christ do not conceal a spirit of revenge or violence against the unsaved who live in darkness and sin.

10:1 SENT THEM TWO AND TWO. The principle of sending out workers two by two is very important in the work of the Lord, for it provides each one with double faith and wisdom; in addition, a companion helps bolster courage. Other passages dealing with the two by two principle are: Eccl. 4:9–12; Mat. 18:16; Mark 6:7; 14:13; Luke 7:19; John 1:35–41; 8:17; Acts 9:38; 10:7; 15:36–41; 19:22; 2 Cor. 13:1; 1 Tim. 5:19; Heb. 10:28; Rev. 11:3–6,10–12.

10:2 THE HARVEST TRULY *IS* GREAT. See Mat. 9:37, note.

10:3 LAMBS AMONG WOLVES. The believer who faithfully follows the will of God will be threatened by many dangers. He or she will be like a defenseless lamb among wolves. We must pray for God's presence, protection, and provision.

10:9 HEAL THE SICK . . . THE KINGDOM OF GOD. Jesus once again emphasizes that the "kingdom of God" is associated with healing the sick. For more on this, see 9:2, note.

be more tolerable in that day for Sod-
om, than for that city.
13 [z]Woe unto thee, Chorazin! woe
unto thee, Bethsaida! [a]for if the
mighty works had been done in Tyre
and Sidon, which have been done in
you, they had a great while ago repent-
ed, sitting in sackcloth and ashes.
14 But it shall be more tolerable for
Tyre and Sidon at the judgment, than
for you.
15 [b]And thou, Capernaum, which
art [c]exalted to heaven, [d]shalt be
thrust down to hell.
16 [e]He that heareth you heareth
me; and [f]he that despiseth you de-
spiseth me; [g]and he that despiseth me
despiseth him that sent me.

Authority over demons

10:23–24pp — Mat. 13:16–17

17 ¶ And [h]the seventy returned
again with joy, saying, Lord, even the
devils are subject unto us through thy
name.
18 And he said unto them, [i]I be-
held Satan as lightning fall from
heaven.
19 Behold, [j]I give unto you power
to tread on serpents and scorpions,
and over all the power of the enemy:
uke 1:20-26 and nothing shall by any means hurt
you.
20 Notwithstanding in this rejoice
not, that the spirits are subject unto
you; but rather rejoice, because [k]your
names are written in heaven.
21 ¶ [l]In that hour Jesus rejoiced in
spirit, and said, I thank thee, O Father,
Lord of heaven and earth, that thou
hast hid these things from the wise and
prudent, and hast revealed them unto
babes: even so, Father; for so it seemed
good in thy sight.
22 [m]All[e] things are delivered to
me of my Father: and [n]no man
knoweth who the Son is, but the Fa-
ther; and who the Father is, but the
Son, and *he* to whom the Son will re-
veal *him.*
23 ¶ And he turned him unto *his* dis-
ciples, and said privately, [o]Blessed
are the eyes which see the things that
ye see:
24 For I tell you, [p]that many
prophets and kings have desired to see
those things which ye see, and have
not seen *them;* and to hear those things
which ye hear, and have not heard
them.

The good Samaritan

10:25–28pp — Mat. 22:34–40; Mark 12:28–31

25 ¶ And, behold, a certain lawyer
stood up, and tempted him, saying,
[q]Master, what shall I do to inherit
eternal life?
26 He said unto him, What is writ-
ten in the law? how readest thou?
27 And he answering said, [r]Thou
shalt love the Lord thy God with all thy
heart, and with all thy soul, and with
all thy strength, and with all thy mind;
and [s]thy neighbour as thyself.
28 And he said unto him, Thou hast
answered right: this do, and [t]thou
shalt live.
29 But he, willing to [u]justify him-
self, said unto Jesus, And who is my
neighbour?
30 And Jesus answering said, A cer-
tain *man* went down from Jerusalem to

10:13 [z]Mat. 11:21 [a]Ezek. 3:6
10:15 [b]Mat. 11:23 [c]See Gen. 11:4 Deut. 1:28 Is. 14:13 Jer. 51:53 [d]See Ezek. 26:20 & 32:18
10:16 [e]Mat. 10:40 Mark 9:37 John 13:20 [f]1 Thes. 4:8 [g]John 5:23
10:17 [h]ver. 1
10:18 [i]John 12:31 & 16:11 Rev. 9:1 & 12:8,9
10:19 [j]Mark 16:18 Acts 28:5
10:20 [k]Ex. 32:32 Ps. 69:28 Is. 4:3 Dan. 12:1 Phil. 4:3 Heb. 12:23 Rev. 13:8 & 20:12
10:21 [l]Mat. 11:25
10:22 [m]Mat. 28:18 John 3:35 & 5:27 & 17:2 [n]John 1:18 & 6:44,46
10:23 [o]Mat. 13:16
10:24 [p]1 Pet. 1:10
10:25 [q]Mat. 19:16 & 22:35
10:27 [r]Deut. 6:5 [s]Lev. 19:18
10:28 [t]Lev. 18:5 Neh. 9:29 Ezek. 20:11,13,21 Rom. 10:5
10:29 [u]ch. 16:15

e Many ancient copies add these words, *And turning to his disciples, he said*

10:19 SERPENTS AND SCORPIONS. "Serpents and scorpions" are terms representing the most dangerous forces of spiritual evil. Christians have dominion over evil spirits because Christ has given to us His power and authority over Satan (see article on POWER OVER SATAN AND DEMONS, p. 1486).

10:20 IN THIS REJOICE NOT. Christ warns the disciples that they must not make power over demons or success in ministry a fundamental source of their joy. Their rejoicing must come from the fact that they are redeemed from sin and destined for heaven (see Mat. 7:22–23, notes).

10:21 THE WISE . . . AND . . . BABES. Jesus rejoices that His heavenly Father has given the understanding of spiritual truths not to those who are intellectually wise in their own eyes, but to those who accept in childlike humility the truth revealed in His Word. Those who believe themselves wise enough to question the teachings of Scripture by their own "superior" knowledge and use that as a basis for accepting or rejecting God's Word, are excluded from the fellowship and knowledge of the Son (v. 22).

10:27 LOVE THE LORD THY GOD . . . AND THY NEIGHBOUR. See Mat. 22:37,39, notes.

10:30 THE PARABLE OF THE GOOD SAMARITAN. This parable emphasizes that inherent in true saving faith and obedience to Christ are compassion and care for those in genuine need. The call to love God is a call to love others. (1) The new life and grace that Christ gives to those who accept Him will produce love, mercy, and compassion for those who are distressed and afflicted. It is the believer's responsibility to act upon the Holy Spirit's love within him and not to harden his

Jericho, and fell among thieves, which stripped him of his raiment, and wounded *him,* and departed, leaving *him* half dead.

31 And by chance there came down a certain priest that way: and when he saw him, [v]he passed by on the other side.

32 And likewise a Levite, when he was at the place, came and looked *on him,* and passed by on the other side.

33 But a certain [w]Samaritan, as he journeyed, came where he was: and when he saw him, he had compassion *on him,*

34 And went to *him,* and bound up his wounds, pouring in oil and wine, and set him on his own beast, and brought him to an inn, and took care of him.

35 And on the morrow when he departed, he took out two [f]pence, and gave *them* to the host, and said unto him, Take care of him; and whatsoever thou spendest more, when I come again, I will repay thee.

36 Which now of these three, thinkest thou, was neighbour unto him that fell among the thieves?

37 And he said, He that showed mercy on him. Then said Jesus unto him, Go, and do thou likewise.

Luke 12:42-48

Jesus visits Mary and Martha

38 ¶ Now it came to pass, as they went, that he entered into a certain village: and a certain woman named [x]Martha received him into her house.

39 And she had a sister called Mary, [y]which also [z]sat at Jesus' feet, and heard his word.

40 But Martha was cumbered about much serving, and came to him, and said, Lord, dost thou not care that my sister hath left me to serve alone? bid her therefore that she help me.

41 And Jesus answered and said unto her, Martha, Martha, thou art careful and troubled about many things:

42 But [a]one thing is needful: and Mary hath chosen that good part, which shall not be taken away from her.

Jesus' teaching on prayer

11:2–4pp — Mat. 6:9–13
11:9–13pp — Mat. 7:7–11

11 AND IT came to pass, that, as he was praying in a certain place, when he ceased, one of his disciples said unto him, Lord, teach us to pray, as John also taught his disciples.

2 And he said unto them, When ye pray, say, [b]Our Father which art in heaven, Hallowed be thy name. Thy kingdom come. Thy will be done, as in heaven, so in earth.

3 Give us [g]day by day our daily bread.

4 And forgive us our sins; for we also forgive every one that is indebted to us. And lead us not into temptation; but deliver us from evil.

5 And he said unto them, Which of you shall have a friend, and shall go unto him at midnight, and say unto him, Friend, lend me three loaves;

6 For a friend of mine [h]in his journey is come to me, and I have nothing to set before him?

7 And he from within shall answer and say, Trouble me not: the door is now shut, and my children are with me in bed; I cannot rise and give thee.

8 I say unto you, [c]Though he will not rise and give him, because he is his friend, yet because of his importunity he will rise and give him as many as he needeth.

10:31 [v]Ps. 38:11 **10:33** [w]John 4:9 **10:38** [x]John 11:1 & 12:2,3 **10:39** [y]1 Cor. 7:32 [z]ch. 8:35 Acts 22:3 **10:42** [a]Ps. 27:4 **11:2** [b]Mat. 6:9 **11:8** [c]ch. 18:1

[f] See Mat. 20:2 [g] Or, *for the day* [h] Or, *out of his way*

heart. (2) Those who are professed Christians, yet whose hearts are insensitive to the suffering and needs of others, give sure evidence that they do not have eternal life abiding in them (vv. 25–28,31–37; cf. Mat. 25:41–46).

10:42 ONE THING IS NEEDFUL. Although active and practical service to God is essential and good, our first and most important task is a love and devotion that expresses itself in quiet worship, prayer, and fellowship with the Lord (see Mat. 26:13, note). Are we so busy doing the work of the Lord, attending church services, and performing good works that we forget spiritual communion with our Savior?

11:2–4 WHEN YE PRAY, SAY. See Mat. 6:9–15, notes on the Lord's Prayer.

11:3 OUR DAILY BREAD. The believer should learn to pray for life's necessary provisions (cf. Mat. 6:11) based on four principles. (1) We must pray such petitions according to God's will and for His glory (Mat. 6:10,33; 1 Cor. 10:31; 1 John 5:14–15). (2) We must want God to demonstrate His fatherly love for us (Mat. 6:9,25–34). (3) The provisions prayed for must supply our basic needs and give us the ability to perform Christian service (2 Cor. 9:8; 1 Tim. 6:8; Heb. 13:5). (4) We may ask for things only after we have faithfully given to God and others (2 Cor. 9:6; see 8:2, note).

9 [d]And I say unto you, Ask, and it
shall be given you; seek, and ye shall
find; knock, and it shall be opened unto
you.
10 For every one that asketh re-
ceiveth; and he that seeketh findeth;
and to him that knocketh it shall be
opened.
11 [e]If a son shall ask bread of any
of you that is a father, will he give him
a stone? or if *he ask* a fish, will he for
a fish give him a serpent?
12 Or if he shall ask an egg, will he
[i]offer him a scorpion?
13 If ye then, being evil, know how
to give good gifts unto your children:
how much more shall *your* heavenly
Father give the Holy Spirit to them that
ask him?

The Pharisees' slander

11:14–15,17–19pp — Mat. 12:22,24–27; Mark 3:23–26

14 ¶ [f]And he was casting out a
devil, and it was dumb. And it came to
pass, when the devil was gone out, the
dumb spake; and the people wondered.
15 But some of them said, [g]He
casteth out devils through [j]Beelze-
bub the chief of the devils.
16 And others, tempting *him,*
[h]sought of him a sign from heaven.
17 [i]But [j]he, knowing their
thoughts, said unto them, Every king-
dom divided against itself is brought to
desolation; and a house *divided* against
a house falleth.

11:9 [d]Mat. 7:7 & 21:22 Mark 11:24 John 15:7 Jas. 1:6 1 John 3:22
11:11 [e]Mat. 7:9
11:14 [f]Mat. 9:32 & 12:22
11:15 [g]Mat. 9:34 & 12:24
11:16 [h]Mat. 12:38 & 16:1
11:17 [i]Mat. 12:25 Mark 3:24 [j]John 2:25
11:20 [k]Ex. 8:19
11:21 [l]Mat. 12:29 Mark 3:27
11:22 [m]Is. 53:12 Col. 2:15
11:23 [n]Mat. 12:30
11:24 [o]Mat. 12:43

18 If Satan also be divided against
himself, how shall his kingdom stand?
because ye say that I cast out devils
through Beelzebub.
19 And if I by Beelzebub cast out
devils, by whom do your sons cast *them*
out? therefore shall they be your
judges.

The kingdom's power over Satan

11:20–22pp — Mat. 12:28–29; Mark 3:27
11:24–26pp — Mat. 12:43–45

20 But if I [k]with the finger of God
cast out devils, no doubt the kingdom
of God is come upon you.
21 [l]When a strong man armed
keepeth his palace, his goods are in
peace:
22 But [m]when a stronger than he
shall come upon him, and overcome
him, he taketh from him all his armour
wherein he trusted, and divideth his
spoils.
23 [n]He that is not with me is
against me: and he that gathereth not
with me scattereth.
24 [o]When the unclean spirit is
gone out of a man, he walketh through
dry places, seeking rest; and finding
none, he saith, I will return unto my
house whence I came out.
25 And when he cometh, he findeth
it swept and garnished.
26 Then goeth he, and taketh *to him*
seven other spirits more wicked than

[i] Gk. *give* [j] Gk. *Beelzebul;* also ver. 18,19

11:9 ASK . . . SEEK . . . KNOCK. See Mat. 7:7, note.

11:11 WILL HE GIVE HIM A STONE? See Mat. 7:11, note on God's care for His children.

11:13 GIVE THE HOLY SPIRIT TO THEM THAT ASK. This verse does not refer to the impartation of the Spirit at the new birth (John 3:3), because at conversion all believers are automatically given the indwelling presence of the Holy Spirit (Rom. 8:9–10; 1 Cor. 6:19–20; see article on THE REGENERATION OF THE DISCIPLES, p. 1638). Rather, the verse refers to the baptism in the Holy Spirit that Christ promised to His followers (see article on JESUS AND THE HOLY SPIRIT, p. 1550).

11:20 DEVILS . . . THE KINGDOM OF GOD. This passage reveals three things: (1) The success of the kingdom of God on earth is in direct proportion to the destruction of Satan and the deliverance of sinners from their bondage to sin and the demonic; (2) Satan will resist the coming of Christ's kingdom on earth (vv. 24–26; cf. Mat. 13:18–30; Rev. 12:12); (3) Jesus is stronger than Satan and He came to destroy him (vv. 20–22). For more on this, see articles on THE KINGDOM OF GOD, p. 1428, and POWER OVER SATAN AND DEMONS, p. 1486.

11:23 HE THAT IS NOT WITH ME IS AGAINST ME. Jesus states it is impossible to remain neutral in the spiritual conflict between His kingdom and the power of evil. (1) The one who does not, along with Christ, oppose Satan and the evil of the world has in reality set himself against Jesus Christ. Every person is fighting either on the side of Christ and righteousness, or on the side of Satan and the ungodly. (2) Jesus' words condemn any attempt at compromise with unrighteousness or any partial obedience.

11:26 SEVEN OTHER SPIRITS . . . DWELL THERE. The point of this passage is made clear in the corresponding one in Mat. 12:43–45 (see note), which speaks of the house left unoccupied. (1) In conversion and salvation (John 3:3) the believer must not only be delivered from sin, but also commit himself to radical obedience to Christ, prayer, righteousness, the Word, and being filled with the Holy Spirit (see Acts 2:4; Rom. 8).

(2) After conversion Satan's power does not

JESUS AND THE HOLY SPIRIT

Luke 11:13 "If ye then, being evil, know how to give good gifts unto your children: how much more shall your heavenly Father give the Holy Spirit to them that ask him?"

Jesus had a special relationship with the Holy Spirit, a relationship that is important for our own personal lives. This article explores that relationship and its practical implications.

OLD TESTAMENT PROPHECY. Several prophecies of the O.T. concerning the coming Messiah, predicted specifically that He would be empowered by the Holy Spirit (see Is. 11:2, note; 61:1–3, note). When Jesus read from Is. 61:1–2 in the synagogue at Nazareth, he stated "This day is this scripture fulfilled in your ears" (Luke 4:18–21).

JESUS' BIRTH. Both Matthew and Luke state explicitly and unmistakably that Jesus came into this world as a result of a miraculous deed of God. He was conceived by the Holy Spirit and born of a virgin, Mary (Mat. 1:18,23; Luke 1:27). Because of this miraculous conception, Jesus was "holy" (Luke 1:35), that is, free from all taint of sin. This made Him worthy to take the guilt of our sin on Himself and to make atonement for it (see Mat. 1:23, note). Without a perfect, sinless Savior, we could not experience redemption.

JESUS' BAPTISM. When He was baptized by John the Baptist, Jesus, who would later baptize His disciples in the Spirit at Pentecost and throughout the church age (see Luke 3:16; Acts 1:4–5; 2:33,38–39), was Himself personally anointed by the Spirit (Mat. 3:16–17; Luke 3:21–22). The Spirit came upon Him in the form of a dove, equipping Him with great power to perform His ministry, including His work of redemption. When our Lord departed into the wilderness after His baptism, He was "full of the Holy Ghost" (Luke 4:1). In the same manner as our Lord, all those who have experienced a supernatural rebirth by the Holy Spirit ought to experience the baptism in the Holy Spirit to give them power in their lives and for their ministry (see Acts 1:8, notes).

JESUS' TEMPTATION BY SATAN. Immediately after His baptism, Jesus was led by the Spirit into the wilderness, where He was tempted by the devil for forty days (Luke 4:1–2). Being full of the Holy Spirit (4:1), He was able to face Satan squarely and resist the temptations that came His way. Likewise, it is God's intention that we never face the spiritual forces of evil and sin without the power of the Spirit. We must be equipped with His fullness and follow His leading in order to be victorious against Satan. In God's sight we are not "normal" children of His unless we are filled with the Spirit and live by His power.

JESUS' MINISTRY. In Jesus' reference to the fulfillment of Isaiah's prophecy about the Spirit coming upon Him, He used the same passage to outline the nature of His ministry as a preaching, healing, and liberating one (Is. 61:1–2; Luke 4:16–19). (1) The Spirit anointed Jesus and empowered Him for His mission. Jesus was God (John 1:1), but He was also man (1 Tim. 2:5). As a human being He had to rely on the help and power of the Holy Spirit to fulfill His responsibilities before God (cf. Mat. 12:28; Luke 4:1,14; Rom. 8:11; Heb. 9:14). (2) It was only as a Spirit-anointed man that Jesus could live, serve, and proclaim the gospel (Acts 10:38). In this He is a perfect example for the Christian; each believer should receive the fullness of the Holy Spirit (see Acts 1:8, notes; 2:4, notes).

JESUS' PROMISE REGARDING THE HOLY SPIRIT. John the Baptist had prophesied that Jesus would baptize His followers in the Holy Spirit (Mat. 3:11; Mark 1:8; Luke 3:16, see note; John 1:33), a prophecy that Jesus Himself reiterated (Acts 1:5; 11:16). In Luke 11:13, Jesus promised to give the Holy Spirit to *all* those who ask (see note on

that verse). All of these verses refer to the fullness of the Spirit which Christ promises to give to those who are already children of the heavenly Father—a promise that was first fulfilled at Pentecost (see Acts 2:4, note), and remains a promise for all those who have become His disciples and ask for the baptism in the Holy Spirit (see Acts 1:5; 2:39, note).

JESUS' RESURRECTION. Through the power of the Holy Spirit, Jesus was raised from the grave and thereby vindicated as the true Messiah and Son of God. In Rom. 1:3–4, we read that through the Spirit of holiness (i.e., the Holy Spirit) Christ Jesus was declared with power to be the Son of God, and in Rom. 8:11, that "the Spirit . . . raised up Jesus from the dead." As Jesus depended on the Holy Spirit for His resurrection from the dead, so believers depend on the Spirit for spiritual life now and bodily resurrection in the future (Rom. 8:10–11).

JESUS' ASCENSION INTO HEAVEN. After Jesus' resurrection He ascended into heaven and sat down at the right hand of His Father as co-ruler of God's kingdom (Mark 16:19; Luke 24:51; Acts 1:9–11; Eph. 4:8–10). In this exalted position He received the Holy Spirit from His Father and sent Him forth upon His people at Pentecost (Acts 2:33; cf. John 16:5–14), thereby proclaiming His Lordship as king, priest, and prophet. This outpouring of the Holy Spirit at Pentecost and throughout this present age testifies to the continual presence and authority of the exalted Savior.

JESUS' NEARNESS TO HIS PEOPLE. As one of His present tasks, the Holy Spirit takes that which is Christ's and reveals it to believers (John 16:14–15). That is, the redemptive benefits of salvation in Christ are mediated to us through the Holy Spirit (cf. Rom. 8:14–16; Gal. 4:6). Most important is Jesus' nearness to us (John 14:18). The Spirit makes us aware of the personal presence of Jesus, His love, blessing, help, forgiveness, healing, and all that is ours through faith. Likewise, the Spirit draws our hearts to seek the Lord in love, prayer, devotion, and worship (see John 4:23–24; 16:14, note).

JESUS' RETURN FOR HIS PEOPLE. Jesus has promised to return and receive His faithful people to Himself so that we may be with Him always (see John 14:3, note; 1 Thes. 4:13–18). This second coming of Christ is the blessed hope of all believers (Tit. 2:13), the event that we pray for and long for (2 Tim. 4:8). Scripture reveals that the Holy Spirit directs our hearts to cry out to God for the return of our Lord. It is the Spirit who testifies that our redemption remains incomplete until Christ returns (cf. Rom. 8:23). At the very close of the Bible, the Holy Spirit inspired the words, "come, Lord Jesus" (Rev. 22:20).

himself; and they enter in, and dwell
Acts 5:3-5 there: and [p]the last *state* of that man
is worse than the first.
27 ¶ And it came to pass, as he
spake these things, a certain woman of
the company lifted up her voice, and
said unto him, [q]Blessed *is* the womb
that bare thee, and the paps which
thou hast sucked.
28 But he said, Yea [r]rather,
blessed *are* they that hear the word of
God, and keep it.

Warning against seeking signs

11:29–32pp — Mat. 12:39–42

29 ¶ [s]And when the people were
gathered thick together, he began to
say, This is an evil generation: they
seek a sign; and there shall no sign be
given it, but the sign of Jonas the
prophet.
30 For as [t]Jonas was a sign unto
the Ninevites, so shall also the Son of
man be to this generation.
31 [u]The queen of the south shall
rise up in the judgment with the men
of this generation, and condemn them:
for she came from the utmost parts of
the earth to hear the wisdom of Solo-
mon; and, behold, a greater than Solo-
mon *is* here.
32 The men of Nineve shall rise up
in the judgment with this generation,
and shall condemn it: for [v]they re-
pented at the preaching of Jonas; and,
behold, a greater than Jonas *is* here.

Parable of the lighted candle

11:34–35pp — Mat. 6:22–23

33 [w]No man, when he hath lighted
a candle, putteth *it* in a secret place,
neither under a [k]bushel, but on a
candlestick, that they which come in
may see the light.
34 [x]The light of the body is the
eye: therefore when thine eye is single,
thy whole body also is full of light; but
when *thine eye* is evil, thy body also *is*
full of darkness.
35 Take heed therefore that the
light which is in thee be not darkness.
36 If thy whole body therefore *be*
full of light, having no part dark, the
whole shall be full of light, as when
[l]the bright shining of a candle doth
give thee light.

The warning against Pharisaism

37 ¶ And as he spake, a certain
Pharisee besought him to dine with
him: and he went in, and sat down to
meat.
38 And [y]when the Pharisee saw *it*,
he marvelled that he had not first
washed before dinner.
39 [z]And the Lord said unto him,
Now do ye Pharisees make clean the
outside of the cup and the platter; but
[a]your inward part is full of ravening
and wickedness.
40 *Ye* fools, did not he that made
that which is without make that which
is within also?
41 [b]But rather give alms [m]of such
things as ye have; and, behold, all
things are clean unto you.
42 [c]But woe unto you, Pharisees!
for ye tithe the mint and rue and all man-

11:26 [p]John 5:14 Heb. 6:4 & 10:26 2 Pet. 2:20
11:27 [q]ch. 1:28,48
11:28 [r]Mat. 7:21 ch. 8:21 Jas. 1:25
11:29 [s]Mat. 12:38,39
11:30 [t]Jonah 1:17 & 2:10
11:31 [u]1 Ki. 10:1
11:32 [v]Jonah 3:5
11:33 [w]Mat. 5:15 Mark 4:21 ch. 8:16
11:34 [x]Mat. 6:22
11:38 [y]Mark 7:3
11:39 [z]Mat. 23:25 [a]Tit. 1:15
11:41 [b]Is. 58:7 Dan. 4:27 ch. 12:33
11:42 [c]Mat. 23:23

[k]See Mat. 5:15 [l]Gk. *a candle by its bright shining* [m]Or, *as you are able*

---

end, but continues as a never-ceasing menace (22:31; see Mat. 6:13, note). There is safety from sin and Satan only by full commitment to Christ and by using all the means of grace available through Christ (see Eph. 6:11, note).

(3) The believer who is delivered from the demonic but has still not completely renounced sin or opened his life to the Spirit of God is inviting the evil spirit to come back with renewed power to dwell in that person.

11:34 THE LIGHT OF THE BODY IS THE EYE. The eye is the body's means of receiving light. If the eye is healthy, then one can fully receive and use light. If the eye is defective, then darkness prevails and one cannot see in order to walk or work.

(1) Likewise when a person's spiritual eye, i.e., when his attitudes, motives, and desires are directed toward the will of God, then the light of His Word enters into his spirit to produce blessings, fruit, and salvation (Gal. 5:22–23). But if his desires are not focused on the things of God, then God's revelation and truth will have no effect.

(2) We must examine our lives to make sure that our spiritual eyes are such that the gospel can really sanctify us and renew our inward lives. Do we respond to the teaching or reading of Scripture with a spirit that loves God, Christ, and the Word more and more; or, in spite of all the gospel messages and Bible teaching we have received, is there deadness in our souls and are we in bondage to sin? If the latter is the case, then our spiritual eyes are still evil and our bodies full of darkness. We must then confess our sins, repent of them, and separate ourselves from all compromise that leads to darkness.

11:42 WOE UNTO YOU. See Mat. 23:13, note on Christ's denunciation of the sins of the Pharisees.

ner of herbs, and pass over judgment
and the love of God: these ought ye to
have done, and not to leave the other
undone.
43 [d]Woe unto you, Pharisees! for
ye love the uppermost seats in the syn-
agogues, and greetings in the markets.
44 [e]Woe unto you, scribes and
Pharisees, hypocrites! [f]for ye are as
graves which appear not, and the men
that walk over *them* are not aware *of
them.*
45 ¶ Then answered one of the law-
yers, and said unto him, Master, thus
saying thou reproachest us also.
46 And he said, Woe unto you also,
ye lawyers! [g]for ye lade men with bur-
dens grievous to be borne, and ye your-
selves touch not the burdens with one
of your fingers.
47 [h]Woe unto you! for ye build the
sepulchres of the prophets, and your
fathers killed them.
48 Truly ye bear witness that ye al-
low the deeds of your fathers: for they
indeed killed them, and ye build their
sepulchres.
49 Therefore also said the wisdom
of God, [i]I will send them prophets and
apostles, and *some* of them they shall
slay and persecute:
50 That the blood of all the proph-
ets, which was shed from the founda-
tion of the world, may be required of
this generation;
51 [j]From the blood of Abel unto
[k]the blood of Zacharias, which per-
ished between the altar and the tem-
ple: verily I say unto you, It shall be
required of this generation.
52 [l]Woe unto you, lawyers! for ye
have taken away the key of knowledge:
ye entered not in yourselves, and them
that were entering in ye [n]hindered.
53 And as he said these things unto
them, the scribes and the Pharisees be-
gan to urge *him* vehemently, and to
provoke him to speak of many things:
54 Laying wait for him, and [m]seek-
ing to catch something out of his
mouth, that they might accuse him.

The leaven of hypocrisy

12:2–9pp — Mat. 10:26–33

12 IN [n]THE mean time, when
there were gathered together
an innumerable multitude of people, in-
somuch that they trode one upon an-
other, he began to say unto his disci-
ples first of all, [o]Beware ye of the
leaven of the Pharisees, which is hy-
pocrisy.
2 [p]For there is nothing covered,
that shall not be revealed; neither hid,
that shall not be known.
3 Therefore whatsoever ye have
spoken in darkness shall be heard in
the light; and that which ye have spo-
ken in the ear in closets shall be pro-
claimed upon the housetops.
4 [q]And I say unto you [r]my
friends, Be not afraid of them that kill
the body, and after that have no more
that they can do.
5 But I will forewarn you whom ye
shall fear: Fear him, which after he
hath killed hath power to cast into hell;
yea, I say unto you, Fear him.
6 Are not five sparrows sold for two
[o]farthings, and not one of them is for-
gotten before God?
7 But even the very hairs of your
head are all numbered. Fear not there-
fore: ye are of more value than many
sparrows.
8 [s]Also I say unto you, Whosoever
shall confess me before men, him shall

11:43 [d]Mat. 23:6 Mark 12:38,39
11:44 [e]Mat. 23:27 [f]Ps. 5:9
11:46 [g]Mat. 23:4
11:47 [h]Mat. 23:29
11:49 [i]Mat. 23:34
11:51 [j]Gen. 4:8 [k]2 Chr. 24:20,21
11:52 [l]Mat. 23:13
11:54 [m]Mark 12:13
12:1 [n]Mat 16:6 Mark 8:15 [o]Mat. 16:12
12:2 [p]Mat. 10:26 Mark 4:22 ch. 8:17
12:4 [q]Is. 51:7,8,12,13 Jer. 1:8 Mat. 10:28 [r]John 15:14,15
12:8 [s]Mat. 10:32 Mark 8:38 2 Tim. 2:12 1 John 2:23

[n] Or, *forbad* [o] See Mat. 10:29

12:1 HYPOCRISY. Jesus condemns the hypocrisy of the Pharisees, warning His disciples to be careful that this sin does not enter into their own lives and ministry. (1) Hypocrisy means acting as if you are what you are not—for example, acting publicly as a godly and faithful believer, when in reality you harbor hidden sin, immorality, greed, lust, or other unrighteousness. The hypocrite is a deceiver in the area of observable righteousness (see article on FALSE TEACHERS, p. 1508).

(2) Since hypocrisy involves living a lie, it makes one a co-worker and ally with Satan, the father of lies (John 8:44).

(3) Jesus warns His disciples that all hypocrisy and hidden sin will be exposed, if not in this life, certainly on the day of judgment (see Rom. 2:16; 1 Cor. 3:13; 4:5; Rev. 20:12). What is done secretly behind closed doors, will be at some point revealed openly (vv. 2–3).

(4) Hypocrisy is a sign that one does not fear God (v. 5) and does not possess the Holy Spirit with His regenerating grace (see Rom. 8:5–14; 1 Cor. 6:9–10; Gal. 5:19–21; Eph. 5:5). While remaining in this condition, one cannot "escape the damnation of hell" (Mat. 23:33).

12:5 FEAR HIM. The disciples of Jesus must stand in awe of the majesty and holiness of God, and of His wrath against sin (cf. Is. 6:1–5).

12:8 CONFESS ME BEFORE MEN. See Mat. 10:32, note.

the Son of man also confess before the angels of God:

9 But he that denieth me before men shall be denied before the angels of God.

10 And [t]whosoever shall speak a word against the Son of man, it shall be forgiven him: but unto him that blasphemeth against the Holy Ghost it shall not be forgiven.

11 [u]And when they bring you unto the synagogues, and *unto* magistrates, and powers, take ye no thought how or what thing ye shall answer, or what ye shall say:

12 For the Holy Ghost shall teach you in the same hour what ye ought to say.

The parable of the rich fool

13 ¶ And one of the company said unto him, Master, speak to my brother, that he divide the inheritance with me.

14 And he said unto him, [v]Man, who made me a judge or a divider over you?

15 And he said unto them, [w]Take heed, and beware of covetousness: for a man's life consisteth not in the abundance of the things which he possesseth.

16 And he spake a parable unto them, saying, The ground of a certain rich man brought forth plentifully:

17 And he thought within himself, saying, What shall I do, because I have no room where to bestow my fruits?

18 And he said, This will I do: I will pull down my barns, and build greater; and there will I bestow all my fruits and my goods.

19 And I will say to my soul, [x]Soul, thou hast much goods laid up for many years; take thine ease, eat, drink, *and* be merry.

20 But God said unto him, *Thou* fool, this night [y]thy[p] soul shall be required of thee: [z]then whose shall those things be, which thou hast provided?

21 So *is* he that layeth up treasure for himself, [a]and is not rich toward God.

The teaching about anxiety

12:22–31pp — Mat. 6:25–33

22 ¶ And he said unto his disciples, Therefore I say unto you, [b]Take no thought for your life, what ye shall eat; neither for the body, what ye shall put on.

23 The life is more than meat, and the body *is more* than raiment.

24 Consider the ravens: for they neither sow nor reap; which neither have storehouse nor barn; and [c]God feedeth them: how much more are ye better than the fowls?

25 And which of you with taking thought can add to his stature one cubit?

26 If ye then be not able to do that thing which is least, why take ye thought for the rest?

27 Consider the lilies how they grow: they toil not, they spin not; and yet I say unto you, that Solomon in all his glory was not arrayed like one of these.

28 If then God so clothe the grass, which is today in the field, and tomorrow is cast into the oven; how much more *will he clothe* you, O ye of little faith? Luke 17:5-6

29 And seek not ye what ye shall eat, or what ye shall drink, [q]neither be ye of doubtful mind.

30 For all these things do the nations of the world seek after: and your Father knoweth that ye have need of these things.

[p] Or, *do they require thy soul* [q] Or, *live not in careful suspense*

12:10 [t]Mat. 12:31,32 Mark 3:28 1 John 5:16
12:11 [u]Mat. 10:19 Mark 13:11
12:14 [v]John 18:36
12:15 [w]1 Tim. 6:7
12:19 [x]Eccl. 11:9 1 Cor. 15:32 Jas. 5:5
12:20 [y]Job 20:22 & 27:8 Ps. 52:7 Jas. 4:14
[z]Ps. 39:6 Jer. 17:11
12:21 [a]ver. 33 Mat. 6:20 1 Tim. 6:18,19 Jas. 2:5
12:22 [b]Mat. 6:25
12:24 [c]Job 38:41 Ps. 147:9

12:9 HE THAT DENIETH ME. To deny Christ is (1) to fail to acknowledge before the ungodly that we are followers of Jesus, and (2) to refuse to stand by the gospel and Christ's principles of righteousness in the face of society's non-Christian values.

12:10 BLASPHEMETH AGAINST THE HOLY GHOST. See Mat. 12:31, note.

12:15 BEWARE OF COVETOUSNESS. To make earthly gain or riches the desire of one's life is a fatal error that leads to eternal loss (vv. 20–21). (1) The Greek word for greed (*pleonexia*) literally signifies the thirst for having more. (2) Covetousness does not refer to providing for one's own needs and those of one's family (cf. Prov. 6:6). While we labor for our needs, however, we must be rich toward God by seeking first His kingdom and His righteousness (v. 31; cf. Mat. 6:33, note). (3) Each one of us should heed Jesus' warning and examine whether selfishness and greed exist in our own hearts. For more on this subject, see article on RICHES AND POVERTY, p. 1568.

12:22 TAKE NO THOUGHT FOR YOUR LIFE. See Mat. 6:25, note.

12:24 HOW MUCH MORE ARE YE BETTER. See Mat. 6:25,30, notes.

certain *man* had a fig tree planted in his
vineyard; and he came and sought fruit
thereon, and found none.
7 Then said he unto the dresser of
his vineyard, Behold, these three years
I come seeking fruit on this fig tree,
and find none: cut it down; why cum-
bereth it the ground?
8 And he answering said unto him,
Lord, let it alone this year also, till I
shall dig about it, and dung *it:*
9 And if it bear fruit, *well:* and if not,
then after that thou shalt cut it down.

A woman healed on the Sabbath

10 And he was teaching in one of
the synagogues on the sabbath.
11 ¶ And, behold, there was a wom-
an which had a spirit of infirmity eigh-
teen years, and was bowed together,
and could in no wise lift up *herself.*
12 And when Jesus saw her, he
called *her to him,* and said unto her,
Woman, thou art loosed from thine in-
firmity.
13 [a]And he laid *his* hands on her:
and immediately she was made
straight, and glorified God.
14 And the ruler of the synagogue
answered with indignation, because
that Jesus had healed on the sabbath
day, and said unto the people, [b]There
are six days in which men ought to
work: in them therefore come and be
healed, and [c]not on the sabbath day.
15 The Lord then answered him,
and said, *Thou* hypocrite, [d]doth not
each one of you on the sabbath loose
his ox or *his* ass from the stall, and lead
him away to watering?
16 And ought not this woman, [e]be-
ing a daughter of Abraham, whom Sa-
tan hath bound, lo, these eighteen
years, be loosed from this bond on the
sabbath day?
17 And when he had said these
things, all his adversaries were
ashamed: and all the people rejoiced
for all the glorious things that were Luke 17:12-19
done by him.

Parables of the mustard seed and the yeast

13:18–19pp — Mark 4:30–32
13:18–21pp — Mat. 13:31–33

18 ¶ [f]Then said he, Unto what is
the kingdom of God like? and where-
unto shall I resemble it?
19 It is like a grain of mustard seed,
which a man took, and cast into his
garden; and it grew, and waxed a great
tree; and the fowls of the air lodged in
the branches of it.
20 And again he said, Whereunto
shall I liken the kingdom of God?
21 It is like leaven, which a woman

13:13 [a]Mark 16:18 Acts 9:17 **13:14** [b]Ex. 20:9 [c]Mat. 12:10 Mark 3:2 ch. 6:7 & 14:3 **13:15** [d]ch. 14:5 **13:16** [e]ch. 19:9 **13:18** [f]Mat. 13:31 Mark 4:30

also to all individuals who profess to believe in Jesus, yet fail to turn from sin. While God gives everyone sufficient opportunity to repent, He will not tolerate sin and immorality forever. A time will come when God's grace and mercy will be withdrawn and the unrepentant be punished without mercy (cf. 20:16; 21:20–24).

13:11 A SPIRIT OF INFIRMITY. Jesus sees some physical sickness as the direct result of demonic activity or oppression. This crippled lady was afflicted by "a spirit of infirmity" (i.e., a representative of Satan; see 13:16; cf. Mat. 9:32–33; 12:22; Mark 5:1–5; 9:17–18; Acts 10:38).

13:16 THIS WOMAN ... SATAN HATH BOUND. It is a detestable sin in the eyes of Christ when a person no longer hears the sighs of suffering humanity (vv. 11–14). Jesus teaches that people are imprisoned by sin, sickness, and death, and are in distress and great need (vv. 11,16; Mat. 4:23; Acts 26:18). Today we are in great danger of becoming insensitive to the world's misery and suffering because of the entertainment media that major in the showing of immorality and violence for the sake of pleasure. The true disciple will be like his Master, able to see the distresses of life and hear the groaning of creation (10:33–37; Rom. 8:22; see article on THE CARE OF THE POOR AND NEEDY, p. 1312).

13:19 MUSTARD SEED. The parables of the mustard seed and of the leaven form a pair. They speak of the growth of evil within the visible kingdom.

The parable of the mustard seed illustrates the small beginning of the kingdom and its subsequent development through the ages. It began only with Jesus and a group of committed disciples (see John 20:22; Acts 2:4). However, the visible manifestation of the kingdom grows until it becomes large, organized, and powerful. It will then accept in its "branches" (fellowship) "the fowls of the air," i.e., evil imposters who take away the seed of truth. Note that in Mat. 13:4,19, fowls are agents of evil in Christ's parable, and in Rev. 18:2, Babylon the great (representing the apostate church) becomes a dwelling place of demons and "a cage of every unclean and hateful bird" (see Rev. 2–3 for Christ's description of how spiritual decay had permeated the majority of the seven churches; Rev. 18:4, note on the false church).

13:21 LEAVEN. Leaven or yeast is normally regarded in the O.T. as a symbol of the presence of evil or impurity; it ferments, disintegrates, or corrupts (see Ex. 12:19; 13:6–8; Lev. 2:11; 6:17; Deut. 16:3–4; Amos 4:4–5; see Ex. 13:7, note). In the N.T. leaven represents the false teaching and evil doctrines of the Pharisees, Sadducees (16:12), and Herodians (see Mark 8:15, note). In 1 Cor. 5:6–8 leaven is regarded by Paul as representing

took and hid in three [v]measures of meal, till the whole was leavened.

The strait gate

22 [g]And he went through the cities and villages, teaching, and journeying toward Jerusalem.

23 Then said one unto him, Lord, are there few that be saved? And he said unto them,

24 ¶ [h]Strive to enter in at the strait gate: for [i]many, I say unto you, will seek to enter in, and shall not be able.

25 [j]When once the master of the house is risen up, and [k]hath shut to the door, and ye begin to stand without, and to knock at the door, saying, [l]Lord, Lord, open unto us; and he shall answer and say unto you, [m]I know you not whence ye are:

26 Then shall ye begin to say, We have eaten and drunk in thy presence, and thou hast taught in our streets.

27 [n]But he shall say, I tell you, I know you not whence ye are; [o]depart from me, all *ye* workers of iniquity.

28 [p]There shall be weeping and gnashing of teeth, [q]when ye shall see Abraham, and Isaac, and Jacob, and all the prophets, in the kingdom of God, and you *yourselves* thrust out.

29 And they shall come from the east, and *from* the west, and from the north, and *from* the south, and shall sit down in the kingdom of God.

30 [r]And, behold, there are last which shall be first, and there are first which shall be last.

13:22 [g]Mat. 9:35 Mark 6:6 **13:24** [h]Mat. 7:13 [i]See John 7:34 & 8:21 & 13:33 Rom. 9:31 **13:25** [j]Ps. 32:6 Is. 55:6 [k]Mat. 25:10 [l]ch. 6:46 [m]Mat. 7:23 & 25:12 **13:27** [n]ver. 25 Mat. 7:23 & 25:41 [o]Ps. 6:8 Mat. 25:41 **13:28** [p]Mat. 8:12 & 13:42 & 24:51 [q]Mat. 8:11 **13:30** [r]Mat. 19:30 & 20:16 Mark 10:31

The lament over Jerusalem

13:34–35pp — Mat. 23:37–39
13:34–35Ref — Luke 19:41

31 ¶ The same day there came certain of the Pharisees, saying unto him, Get thee out, and depart hence: for Herod will kill thee.

32 And he said unto them, Go ye, and tell that fox, Behold, I cast out devils, and I do cures today and tomorrow, and the third *day* [s]I shall be perfected.

33 Nevertheless I must walk today, and tomorrow, and the *day* following: for it cannot be that a prophet perish out of Jerusalem.

34 [t]O Jerusalem, Jerusalem, which killest the prophets, and stonest them that are sent unto thee; how often would I have gathered thy children together, as a hen *doth gather* her brood under *her* wings, and ye would not!

35 Behold, [u]your house is left unto you desolate: and verily I say unto you, Ye shall not see me, until *the time* come when ye shall say, [v]Blessed *is* he that cometh in the name of the Lord.

13:32 [s]Heb. 2:10 **13:34** [t]Mat. 23:37 **13:35** [u]Lev. 26:31,32 Ps. 69:25 Is. 1:7 Dan. 9:27 Mic. 3:12 [v]Ps. 118:26 Mat. 21:9 Mark 11:10 ch. 19:38 John 12:13

Jesus heals on the Sabbath

14 AND IT came to pass, as he went into the house of one of

[v]See Mat. 13:33

"malice and wickedness," while the absence of leaven represents "sincerity and truth" (cf. Gal. 5:9). Hence, many understand this parable to indicate evil, false doctrine, and unrighteousness existing and spreading within the visible kingdom of God.

(1) This leaven of evil will spread throughout all parts of God's work. It is in: (a) modernism, liberalism, and liberation theology, which exalt human ideas over the authority of Scripture (cf. Mat. 22:23,29); (b) worldliness and immorality within the churches and permitted by their leaders (cf. 1 Cor. 5:1–2; Rev. 2–3); (c) the seeking of position or power within the church by those who are concerned more for their own ambition than for God's honor (cf. Mat. 23); (d) false doctrines (cf. Gal. 1:9); (e) false teachers (cf. Mat. 24:11,24); (f) professing Christians who appear righteous, but are not really born again (cf. Mat. 23; Jude 12–19). Toward the end of this present age these evils will infiltrate God's work in Christian churches, denominations, colleges, and seminaries until the N.T. apostolic gospel and righteous living will be seldom found (see 18:8; Mat. 24:10–12; Gal. 1:9, note; 2 Thes. 2:3; 1 Tim. 4:1, note; Rev. 2–3; see articles on THE GREAT TRIBULATION, p. 1456, and OVERSEERS AND THEIR DUTIES, p. 1706).

(2) Every Christian must be careful that the yeast of evil does not affect his own life. The secret of victory lies in keeping our eyes fixed on Jesus in faith (Tit. 2:13; Heb. 12:2,15), despising the things of the world (Jas. 1:27; 1 John 2:15–17), abiding in God's Word (John 15:7; Jas. 1:21), looking forward to Christ's return (12:35–40), continually listening to the voice of the Holy Spirit (Rom. 8:12–14; Gal. 5:16–18), being willing to suffer (1 Pet. 4:1–2), fighting against all evil (1 Cor. 10:6; 1 Thes. 5:15; 1 Pet. 3:11), defending the gospel (Phil. 1:17), and putting on the full armor of God (Eph. 6:11–18).

13:24 THE STRAIT GATE. See Mat. 7:14, note.

13:30 LAST . . . SHALL BE FIRST. See Mat. 19:30, note.

13:34 O JERUSALEM. The sorrow and tears (cf. 19:41) of our Lord over the stubbornness of Jerusalem bear witness to the freedom of the human will to resist the grace and will of God (see 19:41, note; Acts 7:51; Rom. 1:18–32; 2:5).

the chief Pharisees to eat bread on the
sabbath day, that they watched him.

2 And, behold, there was a certain
man before him which had the dropsy.

3 And Jesus answering spake unto
the lawyers and Pharisees, saying,
[w]Is it lawful to heal on the sabbath
day?

4 And they held their peace. And he
took *him,* and healed him, and let
him go;

5 And answered them, saying,
[x]Which of you shall have an ass or an
ox fallen into a pit, and will not
straightway pull him out on the sab-
bath day?

6 And they could not answer him
again to these things.

The honoured place

14:8–10Ref — Prov. 25:6–7

7 ¶ And he put forth a parable to
those which were bidden, when he
marked how they chose out the chief
rooms; saying unto them,

8 When thou art bidden of any *man*
to a wedding, sit not down in the high-
est room; lest a more honourable man
than thou be bidden of him;

9 And he that bade thee and him
come and say to thee, Give this man
place; and thou begin with shame to
take the lowest room.

10 [y]But when thou art bidden, go
and sit down in the lowest room; that
when he that bade thee cometh, he may
say unto thee, Friend, go up higher:
then shalt thou have worship in the
presence of them that sit at meat with
thee.

11 [z]For whosoever exalteth him-
self shall be abased; and he that hum-
bleth himself shall be exalted.

14:3
[w]Mat. 12:10
14:5
[x]Ex. 23:5
Deut. 22:4
ch. 13:15
14:10
[y]Prov. 25:6,7
14:11
[z]Job 22:29
Ps. 18:27
Prov. 29:23
Mat. 23:12
ch. 18:14
Jas. 4:6
1 Pet. 5:5

14:13
[a]Neh. 8:10,12
14:15
[b]Rev. 19:9
14:16
[c]Mat. 22:2
14:17
[d]Prov. 9:2,5

12 ¶ Then said he also to him that
bade him, When thou makest a dinner
or a supper, call not thy friends, nor
thy brethren, neither thy kinsmen, nor
thy rich neighbours; lest they also bid
thee again, and a recompence be made
thee.

13 But when thou makest a feast,
call [a]the poor, the maimed, the lame,
the blind:

14 And thou shalt be blessed; for
they cannot recompense thee: for thou
shalt be recompensed at the resurrec-
tion of the just.

The parable of the great supper

14:16–24Ref — Mat. 22:2–14

15 ¶ And when one of them that sat
at meat with him heard these things,
he said unto him, [b]Blessed *is* he that
shall eat bread in the kingdom of God.

16 [c]Then said he unto him, A cer-
tain man made a great supper, and
bade many:

17 And [d]sent his servant at supper
time to say to them that were bidden,
Come; for all things are now ready.

18 And they all with one *consent* be-
gan to make excuse. The first said unto
him, I have bought a piece of ground,
and I must needs go and see it: I pray
thee have me excused.

19 And another said, I have bought
five yoke of oxen, and I go to prove
them: I pray thee have me excused.

20 And another said, I have married
a wife, and therefore I cannot come.

21 So that servant came, and
showed his lord these things. Then the
master of the house being angry said to
his servant, Go out quickly into the
streets and lanes of the city, and bring

14:11 EXALTED ... ABASED. The Savior warns that those who exalt themselves in this life will be put to shame in the future kingdom of heaven. Important is our place of honor before God. Such honor cannot be secured by self-assertiveness, for it comes only through humility and servanthood (vv. 12–14), and by seeking "the honour that *cometh* from God only" (John 5:44).

14:15–24 A GREAT SUPPER. Although this parable originally applied to Israel and its rejection of the gospel, it is also applicable to the churches and every professed believer today. (1) The subject of this parable is the day of resurrection in its future heavenly glory (vv. 14–15; cf. 22:18), i.e., the return of Christ to bring His people into the heavenly kingdom.

(2) Those who initially accepted the invitation but then refused to come represent those who have accepted or appear to accept the invitation of Jesus to salvation, yet their love for Him and the heavenly kingdom has grown cold (vv. 17–20).

(3) Such people have ceased to set their goals on heavenly things (vv. 18–20). They have rejected the Biblical admonition to set their "affection on things above, not on things on the earth," while waiting for the appearing of Christ (Col. 3:1–4). Their hope and life are centered on the things of this world, and they no longer "desire a better country, that is, an heavenly" (Heb. 11:16).

(4) Vv. 21–23 indicate that there will also be those whose hearts are with Christ in heaven and not fixed on their prospects in this world. They pray with the Spirit and the bride: "Even so, come, Lord Jesus" (Rev. 22:20).

in hither the poor, and the maimed, and
the halt, and the blind.
22 And the servant said, Lord, it is
done as thou hast commanded, and yet
there is room.
23 And the lord said unto the ser-
vant, Go out unto the highways and
hedges, and compel *them* to come in,
that my house may be filled.
24 For I say unto you, [e]That none
of those men which were bidden shall
taste of my supper.

The cost of discipleship

25 ¶ And there went great multi-
tudes with him: and he turned, and
said unto them,
26 [f]If any *man* come to me, [g]and
hate not his father, and mother, and
wife, and children, and brethren,
and sisters, [h]yea, and his own life
also, he cannot be my disciple.
27 And [i]whosoever doth not bear
his cross, and come after me, cannot be
my disciple.
28 For [j]which of you, intending to
build a tower, sitteth not down first,
and counteth the cost, whether he have
sufficient to finish *it?*
29 Lest haply, after he hath laid the
foundation, and is not able to finish *it,*
all that behold *it* begin to mock him,
30 Saying, This man began to build,
and was not able to finish.
31 Or what king, going to make war
against another king, sitteth not down
first, and consulteth whether he be
able with ten thousand to meet him
that cometh against him with twenty
thousand?
32 Or else, while the other is yet a
great way off, he sendeth an ambas-

14:24 [e]Mat. 21:43 & 22:8 Acts 13:46
14:26 [f]Deut. 13:6 & 33:9 Mat. 10:37 [g]Rom. 9:13 [h]Rev. 12:11
14:27 [i]Mat. 16:24 Mark 8:34 ch. 9:23 2 Tim. 3:12
14:28 [j]Prov. 24:27
14:34 [k]Mat. 5:13 Mark 9:50
15:1 [l]Mat. 9:10
15:2 [m]Acts 11:3 Gal. 2:12
15:4 [n]Mat. 18:12
15:6 [o]1 Pet. 2:10,25
15:7 [p]ch. 5:32

sage, and desireth conditions of peace.
33 So likewise, whosoever he be of
you that forsaketh not all that he hath,
he cannot be my disciple.
34 ¶ [k]Salt *is* good: but if the salt
have lost his savour, wherewith shall it
be seasoned?
35 It is neither fit for the land, nor
yet for the dunghill; *but* men cast it out.
He that hath ears to hear, let him hear.

Parable of the lost sheep

15:4–7pp — Mat. 18:12–14

15 THEN [l]DREW near unto him
all the publicans and sinners
for to hear him.
2 And the Pharisees and scribes
murmured, saying, This man receiveth
sinners, [m]and eateth with them.
3 ¶ And he spake this parable unto
them, saying,
4 [n]What man of you, having an
hundred sheep, if he lose one of them,
doth not leave the ninety and nine in
the wilderness, and go after that which
is lost, until he find it?
5 And when he hath found *it,* he
layeth *it* on his shoulders, rejoicing.
6 And when he cometh home, he
calleth together *his* friends and neigh-
bours, saying unto them, Rejoice with
me; for I have found my sheep [o]which
was lost.
7 I say unto you, that likewise joy
shall be in heaven over one sinner that
repenteth, [p]more than over ninety and
nine just persons, which need no re-
pentance.

Parable of the lost coin

8 ¶ Either what woman having ten

14:26 HATE NOT HIS FATHER. The word "hate" in this passage means "love less" (compare this text with Mat. 10:37; see Gen. 29:31, note; Mal. 1:3, note). Jesus demands that our loyalty and love to Him be greater than every other attachment, even to our own families.

14:27 BEAR HIS CROSS. See 9:23, note; Mark 8:34, note.

14:28–33 COUNTETH THE COST. Jesus teaches that whoever desires to follow Him and be His disciple should first decide whether he or she is prepared to pay the cost. The cost of real discipleship is to give up all relationships and possessions, i.e., all that we have: material things, family, our own lives, desires, plans, and interests (v. 33). This does not mean that we must reject all we have, but that all that we have must be placed at the service of Christ and under His guidance (see 13:24; Mat. 7:14; cf. John 16:33; 2 Tim. 3:12).

15:4 THAT WHICH IS LOST. The three parables in ch. 15 reveal God as One who, in His love, seeks the lost to save them for time and eternity. We learn that (1) seeking lost sinners to bring them to redemption is of utmost importance to the heart of God (vv. 4,8,20,24); (2) both God and heaven rejoice when even one sinner repents (vv. 7,10); and (3) no amount of trouble, sacrifice, or suffering is too great in seeking the lost and bringing them to Jesus (vv. 4,8).

15:7 JOY . . . IN HEAVEN. God and the angels in heaven have such love, pity, and grief for those who have fallen into sin and spiritual death that when one sinner repents, they openly rejoice. On God's love and concern for sinners, see Is. 62:5; Jer. 32:41; Ezek. 18:23,32; Hos. 11:8; John 3:16; Rom. 5:6–11; 2 Pet. 3:9.

15:8 SEEK DILIGENTLY TILL SHE FIND. We should pray that the Holy Spirit might fill our

[w]pieces of silver, if she lose one piece,
doth not light a candle, and sweep the
house, and seek diligently till she find
it?

9 And when she hath found *it,* she
calleth *her* friends and *her* neighbours
together, saying, Rejoice with me; for
I have found the piece which I had lost.

10 Likewise, I say unto you, there is
joy in the presence of the angels of God
over one sinner that repenteth.

Parable of the lost son

11 ¶ And he said, A certain man had
two sons:

12 And the younger of them said to
his father, Father, give me the portion
of goods that falleth *to me.* And he di-
vided unto them [q]*his* living.

13 And not many days after the
younger son gathered all together, and
took his journey into a far country, and
there wasted his substance with riot-
ous living.

14 And when he had spent all, there
arose a mighty famine in that land; and
he began to be in want.

15 And he went and joined himself
to a citizen of that country; and he sent
him into his fields to feed swine.

16 And he would fain have filled his
belly with the husks that the swine did
eat: and no man gave unto him.

17 And when he came to himself, he
said, How many hired servants of my
father's have bread enough and to
spare, and I perish with hunger!

18 I will arise and go to my father,
and will say unto him, Father, I have
sinned against heaven, and before
thee,

19 And am no more worthy to be
called thy son: make me as one of thy
hired servants.

20 And he arose, and came to his
father. But [r]when he was yet a great
way off, his father saw him, and had
compassion, and ran, and fell on his
neck, and kissed him.

21 And the son said unto him, Fa-
ther, I have sinned against heaven,
[s]and in thy sight, and am no more
worthy to be called thy son.

22 But the father said to his ser-
vants, Bring forth the best robe, and
put *it* on him; and put a ring on his
hand, and shoes on *his* feet:

23 And bring hither the fatted calf,
and kill *it;* and let us eat, and be merry:

24 [t]For this my son was dead, and
is alive again; he was lost, and is
found. And they began to be merry.

25 Now his elder son was in the
field: and as he came and drew nigh to
the house, he heard music and danc-
ing.

26 And he called one of the ser-
vants, and asked what these things
meant.

27 And he said unto him, Thy broth-
er is come; and thy father hath killed

15:12 [q]Mark 12:44
15:20 [r]Acts 2:39 Eph. 2:13,17
15:21 [s]Ps. 51:4
15:24 [t]ver. 32

[w]*Drachma,* here translated ***a piece of silver,*** was the usual day's wage for a laborer

hearts with concern to bring sinners to salvation.

15:13 JOURNEY INTO A FAR COUNTRY. In this parable the Lord teaches that a life of sin and selfishness, in its deepest sense, is a separation from God's love, fellowship, and authority. The sinner or backslider is like the young son who, pursuing the pleasures of sin, wastes the physical, intellectual, and spiritual gifts given to him by God. Such waste results in disillusionment and sorrow, sometimes degrading personal conditions, and always the lack of a true and real life that can be found only in a right relationship with God.

15:17 HE CAME TO HIMSELF. Before a lost person can come to God, he must see his true state of slavery to sin and separation from God (vv. 14–17). He must humbly return to the Father, confess his sin, and be willing to do whatever the Father requires (vv. 17–19). To bring the lost to this realization is the work of the Holy Spirit (John 16:7–11).

15:20 WHEN HE WAS YET A GREAT WAY OFF. Every Christian father and mother must understand that God loves their prodigal child and desires his salvation as much as they do. Pray and trust God to seek that child until he or she returns to the heavenly Father.

15:20–24 HIS FATHER SAW HIM, AND HAD COMPASSION. Jesus' description of the father's response to the son's return teaches several important truths: (1) God has compassion for the lost because of their sorrowful condition. (2) God's love for them is so great that He never ceases to grieve over them and to wait for their return. (3) When a sinner sincerely turns to God, God is more than ready to receive him with forgiveness, love, compassion, grace, and the full rights of sonship (cf. John 1:12). The benefits of Christ's death, the influence of the Holy Spirit, and God's grace are all made available to those who seek God. (4) God's joy over the return of sinners is immeasurable (vv. 6–7,10,22–24; see v. 7, note).

15:24 MY SON WAS DEAD . . . LOST. "Lost" is used in the sense of being lost to God, like "sheep going astray" (1 Pet. 2:25; cf. Is. 53:6). Life away from God's fellowship is spiritual death (Eph. 2:1; 1 John 3:14). Returning to God brings true life (John 11:26).

the fatted calf, because he hath received him safe and sound.

28 And he was angry, and would not go in: therefore came his father out, and entreated him.

29 And he answering said to *his* father, Lo, these many years do I serve thee, neither transgressed I at any time thy commandment: and yet thou never gavest me a kid, that I might make merry with my friends:

30 But as soon as this thy son was come, which hath devoured thy living with harlots, thou hast killed for him the fatted calf.

31 And he said unto him, Son, thou art ever with me, and all that I have is thine.

32 It was meet that we should make merry, and be glad: [u]for this thy brother was dead, and is alive again; and was lost, and is found.

The shrewd steward

16 AND HE said also unto his disciples, There was a certain rich man, which had a steward; and the same was accused unto him that he had wasted his goods.

2 And he called him, and said unto him, How is it that I hear this of thee? give an [v]account of thy stewardship; for thou mayest be no longer steward.

3 Then the steward said within himself, What shall I do? for my lord taketh away from me the stewardship: I cannot dig; to beg I am ashamed.

4 I am resolved what to do, that, when I am put out of the stewardship, they may receive me into their houses.

5 So he called every one of his lord's debtors *unto him*, and said unto the first, How much owest thou unto my lord?

15:32 [u]ver. 24
16:2 [v]Eccl. 11:9,10 Rom. 14:12 2 Cor. 5:10 1 Pet. 4:5
16:8 [w]John 12:36 Eph. 5:8 1 Thes. 5:5
16:9 [x]Dan. 4:27 Mat. 6:19 & 19:21 ch. 11:41 1 Tim. 6:17-19
16:10 [y]Mat. 25:21 ch. 19:17
16:13 [z]Mat. 6:24
16:14 [a]Mat. 23:14

6 And he said, An hundred [x]measures of oil. And he said unto him, Take thy bill, and sit down quickly, and write fifty.

7 Then said he to another, And how much owest thou? And he said, An hundred [y]measures of wheat. And he said unto him, Take thy bill, and write fourscore.

8 And the lord commended the unjust steward, because he had done wisely: for the children of this world are in their generation wiser than [w]the children of light.

9 And I say unto you, [x]Make to yourselves friends of the [z]mammon of unrighteousness; that, when ye fail, they may receive you into everlasting habitations.

10 [y]He that is faithful in that which is least is faithful also in much: and he that is unjust in the least is unjust also in much.

11 If therefore ye have not been faithful in the unrighteous [z]mammon, who will commit to your trust the true *riches*?

12 And if ye have not been faithful in that which is another man's, who shall give you that which is your own?

13 ¶ [z]No servant can serve two masters: for either he will hate the one, and love the other; or else he will hold to the one, and despise the other. Ye cannot serve God and mammon.

Christ warns the Pharisees

14 And the Pharisees also, [a]who were covetous, heard all these things: and they derided him.

[x] The word *Batus* in the original contains nine gallons three quarts [y] The word here interpreted *a measure* in the original contains about fourteen bushels. [z] Or, *riches*

15:28 HE WAS ANGRY. The "elder son" represents those who have a form of religion and outwardly keep the commandments of God, but inwardly they are separated from Him and His purposes for the kingdom (vv. 28–30).

16:8 COMMENDED THE UNJUST STEWARD. The point of Jesus' illustration is that the worldly are earthly-minded enough to promote their own interest and welfare. In contrast, believers often are not heavenly-minded enough to use their earthly possessions to promote their spiritual and heavenly interest.

16:9 MAMMON OF UNRIGHTEOUSNESS. Mammon means wealth, riches, or material possessions. Jesus calls it unrighteous because injustice, greed, and worldly power are often involved in its accumulation and use (see article on RICHES AND POVERTY, p. 1568). We must use possessions and money in a way that promotes God's interests and the salvation of others.

16:11 IF . . . YE HAVE NOT BEEN FAITHFUL. Those who are dishonest, unjust, or otherwise untrustworthy in their acquisition and use of worldly goods (the least things) will be the same with spiritual things. This is why believers, and especially church leaders, must be free from the love of money (1 Tim. 3:1–3).

16:13 YE CANNOT SERVE GOD AND MAMMON. The world's riches (i.e., mammon) make it very difficult to keep God at the center of our lives. For more on this subject, see article on RICHES AND POVERTY, p. 1568.

15 And he said unto them, Ye are
they which [b]justify yourselves before
men; but [c]God knoweth your hearts:
for [d]that which is highly esteemed
among men is abomination in the sight
of God.

16 [e]The law and the prophets *were*
until John: since that time the kingdom
of God is preached, and every man
presseth into it.

17 [f]And it is easier for heaven and
earth to pass, than one tittle of the law
to fail.

18 [g]Whosoever putteth away his
wife, and marrieth another, com-
mitteth adultery: and whosoever mar-
rieth her that is put away from *her* hus-
band committeth adultery.

The rich man and Lazarus

19 ¶ There was a certain rich man,
which was clothed in purple and fine
linen, and fared sumptuously every
day:

20 And there was a certain beggar
named Lazarus, which was laid at his
gate, full of sores,

21 And desiring to be fed with the
crumbs which fell from the rich man's
table: moreover the dogs came and
licked his sores.

22 And it came to pass, that the
beggar died, and was carried by the an-
gels into Abraham's bosom: the rich
man also died, and was buried;

23 And in hell he lift up his eyes,
being in torments, and seeth Abraham
afar off, and Lazarus in his bosom.

24 And he cried and said, Father
Abraham, have mercy on me, and send
Lazarus, that he may dip the tip of his
finger in water, and [h]cool my tongue;
for I [i]am tormented in this flame.

25 But Abraham said, Son, [j]re-
member that thou in thy lifetime re-
ceivedst thy good things, and likewise
Lazarus evil things: but now he is com-
forted, and thou art tormented.

26 And beside all this, between us
and you there is a great gulf fixed: so
that they which would pass from hence
to you cannot; neither can they pass to
us, that *would come* from thence.

27 Then he said, I pray thee there-
fore, father, that thou wouldest send
him to my father's house:

28 For I have five brethren; that he
may testify unto them, lest they also
come into this place of torment.

29 Abraham saith unto him, [k]They
have Moses and the prophets; let them
hear them.

30 And he said, Nay, father Abra-
ham: but if one went unto them from
the dead, they will repent.

31 And he said unto him, If they
hear not Moses and the prophets,
[l]neither will they be persuaded,
though one rose from the dead.

Faith and forgiveness

17 THEN SAID he unto the disci-
ples, [m]It is impossible but that

16:15 [b]ch. 10:29 [c]Ps. 7:9 [d]1 Sam. 16:7
16:16 [e]Mat. 4:17 & 11:12,13 ch. 7:29
16:17 [f]Ps. 102:26,27 Is. 40:8 & 51:6 Mat. 5:18 1 Pet. 1:25
16:18 [g]Mat. 5:32 & 19:9 Mark 10:11 1 Cor. 7:10,11
16:24 [h]Zech. 14:12 [i]Is. 66:24 Mark 9:44
16:25 [j]Job 21:13 ch. 6:24
16:29 [k]Is. 8:20 & 34:16 John 5:39,45 Acts 15:21 & 17:11
16:31 [l]John 12:10,11
17:1 [m]Mat. 18:6,7 Mark 9:42 1 Cor. 11:19

16:14 PHARISEES . . . COVETOUS. The Pharisees loved money and regarded riches as a blessing from God for their faithful observance of the law. They "derided" Jesus who was poor, for they regarded His poverty as a sign that God had not honored Him (see article on RICHES AND POVERTY, p. 1568).

16:18 COMMITTETH ADULTERY. Anyone who divorces (or deserts) his or her marriage partner for unscriptural reasons (see Mat. 19:9, note) and then remarries, "committeth adultery." "Committeth adultery" in Greek is a present active indicative, denoting continuing action; that is, as long as the innocent and divorced spouse desires and seeks reconciliation, the guilty party who enters into another marriage relationship is living in an adulterous union. Since God does not regard the former marriage as annulled, any other union is sexual adultery.

(1) The primary moral issue in this case is whether or not the remarriage of the guilty partner involves disregarding the covenant obligations and parental responsibilities of the first marriage, which are still capable of fulfillment. If there is a desire for reconciliation by the innocent partner, the issue is decisive. The guilty party is living in adultery if he/she marries another (cf. Mark 10:11–12).

(2) However, if the offending party (a) does not have the possibility of returning to the first marriage, (b) has already entered into the adulterous type of marriage relationship described by Jesus, and (c) sincerely repents before God and makes the commitment to build the present relationship on godly principles, then the present marriage relationship may become legitimate (i.e., accepted by God).

16:19–31 RICH MAN . . . LAZARUS. The rich man's life was consumed in self-centered living. He made the wrong choice and suffered eternally (vv. 22–23). Lazarus lived all his life in poverty, but his heart was right with God. His name means "God is my help," and he never gave up his faith in God. He died and was immediately taken to Paradise with Abraham (v. 22; see 23:43; Acts 7:59; 2 Cor. 5:8; Phil. 1:23). The destinies of both men were irreversible at death (vv. 24–26).

offences will come: but woe *unto him,*
through whom they come!
2 It were better for him that a mill-
stone were hanged about his neck, and
he cast into the sea, than that he
should offend one of these little ones.
3 ¶ Take heed to yourselves: [n]If
thy brother trespass against thee, [o]re-
buke him; and if he repent, forgive him.
4 And if he trespass against thee
seven times in a day, and seven times
in a day turn again to thee, saying, I
repent; thou shalt forgive him.
5 And the apostles said unto the
Lord, Increase our faith.
6 [p]And the Lord said, If ye had
faith as a grain of mustard seed, ye
might say unto this sycamine tree, Be
thou plucked up by the root, and be
thou planted in the sea; and it should
obey you. (John 14:12)
7 But which of you, having a ser-
vant plowing or feeding cattle, will say
unto him by and by, when he is come
from the field, Go and sit down to
meat?
8 And will not rather say unto him,
Make ready wherewith I may sup, and
gird thyself, [q]and serve me, till I have
eaten and drunken; and afterward thou
shalt eat and drink?
9 Doth he thank that servant be-
cause he did the things that were com-
manded him? I trow not.
10 So likewise ye, when ye shall
have done all those things which are
commanded you, say, We are [r]unprof-
itable servants: we have done that
which was our duty to do.

The healing of the ten lepers

11 ¶ And it came to pass, [s]as he
went to Jerusalem, that he passed
through the midst of Samaria and Gali-
lee.
12 And as he entered into a certain
village, there met him ten men that
were lepers, [t]which stood afar off:
13 And they lifted up *their* voices,
and said, Jesus, Master, have mercy
on us.
14 And when he saw *them,* he said
unto them, [u]Go show yourselves unto
the priests. And it came to pass, that,
as they went, they were cleansed.
15 And one of them, when he saw
that he was healed, turned back, and
with a loud voice glorified God,
16 And fell down on *his* face at his
feet, giving him thanks: and he was a
Samaritan.
17 And Jesus answering said, Were
there not ten cleansed? but where *are*
the nine?
18 There are not found that re-
turned to give glory to God, save this
stranger.
19 [v]And he said unto him, Arise,
go thy way: thy faith hath made thee
whole. (John 4:46-53)

The coming of the kingdom

17:26–27pp — Mat. 24:37–39

20 ¶ And when he was demanded of
the Pharisees, when the kingdom of
God should come, he answered them
and said, The kingdom of God cometh
not [a]with observation:
21 [w]Neither shall they say, Lo
here! or, lo there! for, behold, [x]the
kingdom of God is [b]within you.

[a] Or, *with outward show* [b] Or, *among you;* cf. John 1:26

17:3 [n]Mat. 18:15,21 [o]Lev. 19:17 Prov. 17:10 Jas. 5:19 **17:6** [p]Mat. 17:20 & 21:21 Mark 9:23 & 11:23 **17:8** [q]ch. 12:37 **17:10** [r]Job 22:3 & 35:7 Ps. 16:2 Mat. 25:30 Rom. 3:12 & 11:35 1 Cor. 9:16,17 Philem. 11 **17:11** [s]ch. 9:51,52 John 4:4 **17:12** [t]Lev. 13:46 **17:14** [u]Lev. 13:2 & 14:2 Mat. 8:4 ch. 5:14 **17:19** [v]Mat. 9:22 Mark 5:34 & 10:52 ch. 7:50 & 8:48 & 18:42 **17:21** [w]ver. 23 [x]Rom. 14:17

17:2 MILLSTONE . . . ABOUT HIS NECK. Causing someone to sin because of our example, attitude, or neglect will bring such severe punishment that death before committing this sin would be preferable (see Mat. 18:6, note).

17:3–4 IF HE REPENT, FORGIVE. Concerning Jesus' statement about forgiving others, observe the following: (1) Jesus is concerned that we possess an attitude that desires to forgive and help those who offend us, rather than a spirit of revenge or hate.

(2) Forgiveness and reconciliation should not be given until the offending person acknowledges his wrong action and sincerely repents. Furthermore, Jesus was not referring to the same offense constantly repeated.

(3) We should be willing to persevere in forgiveness if the offender sincerely repents (v. 4). Jesus' statement concerning forgiving "seven times in a day" is not meant to encourage and condone habitual sin. Nor is He saying that the believer must allow someone to severely mistreat or abuse him or her indefinitely. Instead, He teaches that we must maintain an attitude that is always ready to help and forgive the offender.

17:6 FAITH. See Mat. 17:20, note; 21:21, note; Mark 11:24, note; see article on FAITH AND GRACE, p. 1738.

17:16 GIVING HIM THANKS. We who have received from God love, grace, salvation, and all His spiritual blessings must not forget to give thanks to Him. What He has done for us should cause us to draw near to Him with a grateful heart. "We love him, because he first loved us" (1 John 4:19).

17:21 THE KINGDOM OF GOD IS WITHIN YOU. According to Jesus, the present nature of the kingdom is spiritual, not material or political. The "kingdom of God cometh not with observation" (v.

22 And he said unto the disciples,
[y]The days will come, when ye shall
desire to see one of the days of the Son
of man, and ye shall not see *it.*
23 [z]And they shall say to you, See
here; or, see there: go not after *them,*
nor follow *them.*
24 [a]For as the lightning, that light-eneth out of the one *part* under heaven, shineth unto the other *part* under heaven; so shall also the Son of man be in his day.
25 [b]But first must he suffer many
things, and be rejected of this generation.
26 [c]And as it was in the days of
Noe, so shall it be also in the days of
the Son of man.
27 They did eat, they drank, they
married wives, they were given in marriage, until the day that Noe entered into the ark, and the flood came, and destroyed them all.
28 [d]Likewise also as it was in the
days of Lot; they did eat, they drank,
they bought, they sold, they planted,
they builded;
29 But [e]the same day that Lot
went out of Sodom it rained fire and
brimstone from heaven, and destroyed
them all.
30 Even thus shall it be in the day
when the Son of man [f]is revealed.
31 In that day, he [g]which shall be
upon the housetop, and his stuff in the
house, let him not come down to take
it away: and he that is in the field, let
him likewise not return back.
32 [h]Remember Lot's wife.
33 [i]Whosoever shall seek to save
his life shall lose it; and whosoever
shall lose his life shall preserve it.
34 [j]I tell you, in that night there
shall be two *men* in one bed; the one
shall be taken, and the other shall be
left.
35 Two *women* shall be grinding together; the one shall be taken, and the other left.
36 [c]Two *men* shall be in the field;
the one shall be taken, and the other
left.
37 And they answered and said
unto him, [k]Where, Lord? And he said
unto them, Wheresoever the body *is,*
thither will the eagles be gathered together.

John 14:3

17:22 [y]See Mat. 9:15 John 17:12
17:23 [z]Mat. 24:23 Mark 13:21 ch. 21:8
17:24 [a]Mat. 24:27
17:25 [b]Mark 8:31 & 9:31 & 10:33 ch. 9:22
17:26 [c]Gen. 7 Mat. 24:37
17:28 [d]Gen. 19
17:29 [e]Gen. 19:16,24
17:30 [f]2 Thes. 1:7
17:31 [g]Mat. 24:17 Mark 13:15
17:32 [h]Gen. 19:26
17:33 [i]Mat. 10:39 & 16:25 Mark 8:35 ch. 9:24 John 12:25
17:34 [j]Mat. 24:40,41 1 Thes. 4:17
17:37 [k]Job 39:30 Mat. 24:28
18:1 [l]ch. 11:5 & 21:36 Rom. 12:12 Eph. 6:18 Col. 4:2 1 Thes. 5:17

The persistent widow

18 AND HE spake a parable unto
them *to this end,* that men ought
[l]always to pray, and not to faint;
2 Saying, There was [d]in a city a
judge, which feared not God, neither
regarded man:
3 And there was a widow in that
city; and she came unto him, saying,
Avenge me of mine adversary.

[c] This 36th verse is wanting in most of the Greek copies [d] Gk. *in a certain city*

20), i.e., it does not come as an earthly political power. Instead it is within the hearts and in the midst of His people, consisting of "righteousness, and peace, and joy in the Holy Ghost" (Rom. 14:17). We manifest it by conquering, through the power of the Holy Spirit, the forces of sin, sickness, and Satan, not by conquering kings and nations (see article on THE KINGDOM OF GOD, p. 1428). When Jesus comes to earth the second time, then the kingdom will be seen in its full power and glory (v. 24; cf. Mat. 24:30) as it triumphs over kings and nations (Rev. 11:15–18; 19:11–21).

17:26 THE DAYS OF NOE. See Mat. 24:37, note.

17:31 IN THAT DAY. See Mark 13:14, note on the abomination of desolation; see article on THE GREAT TRIBULATION, p. 1456.

17:32 REMEMBER LOT'S WIFE. The tragic error of Lot's wife was placing her affections on an earthly society rather than on a heavenly one (cf. Heb. 11:10). She turned back because her heart was still in Sodom (Gen. 19:17,26; see 19:26, note). Every believer should ask: Is my heart more attached to earthly things than to Jesus and the hope of His return?

17:37 THE BODY ... THE EAGLES. This verse suggests the certainty of judgment and destruction on those who are spiritually dead (cf. Mat. 24:28; Rev. 19:17–18). Just as surely as eagles (i.e., vultures) come where the carrion is, so also judgment will come on the wicked when Christ returns.

18:1 MEN OUGHT ALWAYS TO PRAY. Jesus was frequently concerned that His followers pray continually in order to accomplish God's will for their lives (see article on EFFECTIVE PRAYING, p. 540). From this parable of the widow who persevered we learn several things: (1) We must persevere in prayer with regard to all matters until Jesus returns (vv. 7–8; Rom. 12:12; Eph. 6:18; Col. 4:2; 1 Thes. 5:17). (2) In this life we have an adversary (v. 3), Satan (1 Pet. 5:8). Prayer can protect us from the evil one (Mat. 6:13). (3) In our prayers, we should cry out against sin and for justice (v. 7). (4) Persistent prayer is counted as faith (v. 8). (5) In the final days before the return of Christ, there will be increased diabolic opposition to the prayers of the faithful (1 Tim. 4:1). Because of Satan and the pleasures of the world, many will cease having a persistent prayer life (8:14; Mat. 13:22; Mark 4:19).

4 And he would not for a while: but
afterward he said within himself,
Though I fear not God, nor regard man;
5 [m]Yet because this widow trou-
bleth me, I will avenge her, lest by her
continual coming she weary me.
6 And the Lord said, Hear what the
unjust judge saith.
7 And [n]shall not God avenge his
own elect, which cry day and night
unto him, though he bear long with
them?
8 I tell you [o]that he will avenge
them speedily. Nevertheless when the
Son of man cometh, shall he find faith
on the earth?

The Pharisee and the publican

9 And he spake this parable unto
certain [p]which trusted in themselves
[e]that they were righteous, and de-
spised others:
10 Two men went up into the tem-
ple to pray; the one a Pharisee, and the
other a publican.
11 The Pharisee [q]stood and
prayed thus with himself, [r]God, I
thank thee, that I am not as other men
are, extortioners, unjust, adulterers, or
even as this publican.
12 I fast twice in the week, I give
tithes of all that I possess.
13 And the publican, standing afar
off, would not lift up so much as *his*
eyes unto heaven, but smote upon his
breast, saying, God be merciful to me
a sinner.
14 I tell you, this man went down to
his house justified *rather* than the oth-
er: [s]for every one that exalteth him-
self shall be abased; and he that hum-
bleth himself shall be exalted.

Jesus and the little children

18:15–17pp — Mat. 19:13–15; Mark 10:13–16

15 [t]And they brought unto him
also infants, that he would touch them:
but when *his* disciples saw *it,* they re-
buked them.
16 But Jesus called them *unto him,*
and said, Suffer little children to come
unto me, and forbid them not: for [u]of
such is the kingdom of God.
17 [v]Verily I say unto you, Whoso-
ever shall not receive the kingdom of
God as a little child shall in no wise
enter therein.

The rich young ruler

18:18–30pp — Mat. 19:16–29; Mark 10:17–30

18 [w]And a certain ruler asked him,
saying, Good Master, what shall I do to
inherit eternal life?
19 And Jesus said unto him, Why
callest thou me good? none *is* good,
save one, *that is,* God.
20 Thou knowest the command-
ments, [x]Do not commit adultery, Do
not kill, Do not steal, Do not bear false

18:5 [m]ch. 11:8
18:7 [n]Rev. 6:10
18:8 [o]Heb. 10:37 2 Pet. 3:8,9
18:9 [p]ch. 10:29 & 16:15
18:11 [q]Ps. 135:2 [r]Is. 1:15 & 58:2 Rev. 3:17
18:14 [s]Job 22:29 Mat. 23:12 ch. 14:11 Jas. 4:6 1 Pet. 5:5
18:15 [t]Mat. 19:13 Mark 10:13
18:16 [u]1 Cor. 14:20 1 Pet. 2:2
18:17 [v]Mark 10:15
18:18 [w]Mat. 19:16 Mark 10:17
18:20 [x]Ex. 20:12,16 Deut. 5:16-20 Rom. 13:9

[e] Or, *as being righteous*

18:7 ELECT . . . CRY DAY AND NIGHT. God's true elect (i.e., those persevering in faith and holiness) will never cease crying out to God for Christ's return to earth to destroy the power of Satan and the present evil world system. They will persevere in prayer for God to "avenge them speedily" (v. 8) and for Christ to reign in righteousness, knowing that His coming is the only real hope for this world (cf. John 14:2; 1 Thes. 5:2–3; 2 Thes. 2:8; Rev. 19:11–21).

18:8 HE WILL AVENGE THEM. When Jesus returns for those who cry unto Him day and night (v. 7), He will put an end to their distress, suffering, and persecution received at the hands of a hostile and evil world, and He will take them to Himself (John 14:2–3, notes). At His coming, the faithful of His churches will be "caught up [or snatched away] . . . in the clouds, to meet the Lord in the air" (1 Thes. 4:17). Then God will administer His justice and wrath on the wicked (1 Thes. 5:2–3,9).

18:8 SHALL HE FIND FAITH. Jesus' question in this verse probably indicates that as the time for His return draws near, evil will become so dominant that many in the church will fall away from genuine faith (Mat. 24:11–13,24; 1 Tim. 4:1; see articles on THE GREAT TRIBULATION, p. 1456, THE AGE OF THE ANTICHRIST, p. 1896, and PERSONAL APOSTASY, p. 1946). As we approach history's end, the question for each believer is: Am I persevering in faith, continuing steadfast in prayer, and calling on God that justice may be done and His righteous cause triumph completely and forever? Or am I so preoccupied with this life that I am not looking forward to Christ's return and His eternal kingdom (Rev. 19–22)?

18:9–14 A PHARISEE . . . A PUBLICAN. (1) The Pharisee was self-righteous. A self-righteous person thinks that he is righteous because of his own efforts; he is not conscious of the sinful nature within him, his own unworthiness, and his constant need for God's help, mercy, and grace. Because of his exceptional acts of piety and outward goodness, he feels that he does not need the grace of God.

(2) The publican, on the other hand, was deeply conscious of his sin and guilt, and in true repentance turned from sin to God for forgiveness and mercy. He typifies the true child of God.

witness, [y]Honour thy father and thy mother.

21 And he said, All these have I kept from my youth up.

22 Now when Jesus heard these things, he said unto him, Yet lackest thou one thing: [z]sell all that thou hast, and distribute unto the poor, and thou shalt have treasure in heaven: and come, follow me.

23 And when he heard this, he was very sorrowful: for he was very rich.

24 And when Jesus saw that he was very sorrowful, he said, [a]How hardly shall they that have riches enter into the kingdom of God!

25 For it is easier for a camel to go through a needle's eye, than for a rich man to enter into the kingdom of God.

26 And they that heard *it* said, Who then can be saved?

27 And he said, [b]The things which are impossible with men are possible with God.

28 [c]Then Peter said, Lo, we have left all, and followed thee.

29 And he said unto them, Verily I say unto you, [d]There is no man that hath left house, or parents, or brethren, or wife, or children, for the kingdom of God's sake,

30 [e]Who shall not receive manifold more in this present time, and in the world to come life everlasting.

Jesus again foretells his death

18:31–33pp — Mat. 20:17–19; Mark 10:32–34

31 ¶ [f]Then he took *unto him* the twelve, and said unto them, Behold, we go up to Jerusalem, and all things [g]that are written by the prophets concerning the Son of man shall be accomplished.

32 For [h]he shall be delivered unto the Gentiles, and shall be mocked, and spitefully entreated, and spitted on:

33 And they shall scourge *him,* and put him to death: and the third day he shall rise again.

34 [i]And they understood none of these things: and this saying was hid from them, neither knew they the things which were spoken.

A blind man healed

18:35–43pp — Mat. 20:29–34; Mark 10:46–52

35 ¶ [j]And it came to pass, that as he was come nigh unto Jericho, a certain blind man sat by the way side begging:

36 And hearing the multitude pass by, he asked what it meant.

37 And they told him, that Jesus of Nazareth passeth by.

38 And he cried, saying, Jesus, *thou* son of David, have mercy on me.

39 And they which went before rebuked him, that he should hold his peace: but he cried so much the more, *Thou* son of David, have mercy on me.

40 And Jesus stood, and commanded him to be brought unto him: and when he was come near, he asked him,

41 Saying, What wilt thou that I shall do unto thee? And he said, Lord, that I may receive my sight.

42 And Jesus said unto him, Receive thy sight: [k]thy faith hath saved thee.

43 And immediately he received his sight, and followed him, [l]glorifying God: and all the people, when they saw *it,* gave praise unto God. ♪ Luke 19:36-40

The conversion of Zacchaeus

19 AND *JESUS* entered and passed through Jericho.

2 And, behold, *there was* a man named Zacchaeus, which was the chief among the publicans, and he was rich.

3 And he sought to see Jesus who he was; and could not for the press, because he was little of stature.

4 And he ran before, and climbed up into a sycamore tree to see him: for he was to pass that *way.*

5 And when Jesus came to the place, he looked up, and saw him, and said unto him, Zacchaeus, make haste,

18:20 [y]Eph. 6:2 Col. 3:20
18:22 [z]Mat. 6:19,20 & 19:21 1 Tim. 6:19
18:24 [a]Prov. 11:28 Mat. 19:23 Mark 10:23
18:27 [b]Jer. 32:17 Zech. 8:6 Mat. 19:26 ch. 1:37
18:28 [c]Mat. 19:27
18:29 [d]Deut. 33:9
18:30 [e]Job 42:10
18:31 [f]Mat. 16:21 & 17:22 & 20:17 Mark 10:32 [g]Ps. 22 Is. 53
18:32 [h]Mat. 27:2 ch. 23:1 John 18:28 Acts 3:13
18:34 [i]Mark 9:32 ch. 2:50 & 9:45 John 10:6 & 12:16
18:35 [j]Mat. 20:29 Mark 10:46
18:42 [k]ch. 17:19
18:43 [l]ch. 5:26 Acts 4:21 & 11:18

18:22 SELL ALL THAT THOU HAST. See Mat. 19:21, note.

18:25 A RICH MAN . . . THE KINGDOM. The disciples, holding the view generally held by the Jews, were amazed at these declarations of Christ concerning the rich (vv. 24–26). For more on this topic, see RICHES AND POVERTY, p. 1568.

18:30 RECEIVE MANIFOLD MORE. See Mark 10:30, note.

19:1–10 ZACCHAEUS. Jesus was still seeking to save the lost (v. 10) only a few days before His crucifixion; this was the purpose of His coming (cf. 15:3–7; Ezek. 34:16). Zacchaeus, a publican or tax collector, earned his living by collecting more than he should from the people. For this reason, publicans were despised by the people. Jesus' concern for Zacchaeus admonishes us to bring the gospel to the socially undesirables of society, for all people are lost and in need of Christ.

RICHES AND POVERTY

***Luke 18:24–25** "And when Jesus saw that he was very sorrowful, he said, How hardly shall they that have riches enter into the kingdom of God! For it is easier for a camel to go through a needle's eye, than for a rich man to enter into the kingdom of God."*

One of the most shocking statements made by our Lord is that it is virtually impossible for a rich person to enter into the kingdom of God. Yet this is but one of many statements that He made on the subject of riches and poverty, giving a perspective that is repeated by the apostles in several of the N.T. letters.

RICHES. (1) The prevailing view among the Jews in N.T. times was that wealth was a sign of God's special favor and that poverty was a sign of faithlessness and God's displeasure (cf. Prov. 10:15, note). The Pharisees, for example, thought this way and derided Jesus for His poverty (Luke 16:14). Although this false idea reoccurs at times in the history of the Christian church, it is soundly rejected by Christ (see Luke 6:20; 16:13; 18:24–25).

(2) The Bible identifies the pursuit of wealth or covetousness with idolatry, which is demonic (cf. 1 Cor. 10:19–20; Col. 3:5; see article on THE NATURE OF IDOLATRY, p. 428). Because of the demonic power associated with possessions, the desire for wealth and the pursuit of it often bring enslavement (cf. Mat. 6:24).

(3) Riches are, in Jesus' perspective, an obstacle both to salvation and to discipleship (Mat. 19:24; 13:22). They give a false sense of security (Luke 12:15ff), they deceive (Mat. 13:22), and they demand the total loyalty of one's heart (Mat. 6:21). The rich often show that they have no need of God. By searching for riches, their spiritual life is choked (Luke 8:14) and they are led into temptation and harmful desires (1 Tim. 6:9), resulting in the abandonment of saving faith (1 Tim. 6:10). All too often those who are rich take advantage of the poor (Jas. 2:5–6). Thus, no Christian ought to desire to get rich (1 Tim. 6:9–11).

(4) Selfish amassing of material possessions is an indication that life is no longer seen from the vantage point of eternity (Col. 3:1). A selfish, greedy person no longer has his goal and fulfillment in God, but rather in himself and his possessions. The tragedy of Lot's wife, for example, was her placing all her affections on an earthly city rather than a heavenly one (Gen. 19:16–17,26; Luke 17:28–33; Heb. 11:8–10). In other words, striving after wealth has in it the seed of total alienation from God (1 Tim. 6:10).

(5) True riches for a Christian consist in faith and love that express themselves in self-denial and following Jesus (1 Cor. 13:4–7; Phil. 2:3–5). Those who have true riches have gained freedom from the things of the world through confidence that God is their Father and that He will not forsake them (2 Cor. 9:8; Phil. 4:19; Heb. 13:5–6).

(6) With regard to the proper attitude toward, and use of, our possessions, the righteous are under the obligation of faithfulness (Luke 16:11). Christians must regard them not as personal wealth or security; rather, they must relinquish their wealth and place their resources in the hands of the Lord for use in His kingdom, for the furtherance of Christ's cause on earth, and for the salvation and need of others (see article on TITHES AND OFFERINGS, p. 1388). Thus, believers with wealth and possessions must see themselves as no longer rich, but merely as stewards of that which is God's (Luke 12:31–48). They must be generous, ready to share, and rich in good works (Eph. 4:28; 1 Tim. 6:17–19).

(7) Every Christian should examine his or her own heart and desires: Am I a greedy person? Am I a selfish person? Do I yearn for abundance? Do I have a great desire for the honor, prestige, power, and position that often come from obtaining great wealth?

POVERTY. One of the tasks that Jesus saw as His Spirit-directed mission was "to preach the gospel to the poor" (Luke 4:18; cf. Is. 61:1). In other words, the gospel of Christ can be defined as a gospel of the poor (Mat. 5:3; 11:5; Luke 7:22; Jas. 2:5).

(1) The "poor" (Gk. *ptōchos*) are the humble and afflicted within the world who turn to God in great need and seek His help. At the same time, they are faithful to God and look forward to God's redemption of His people from the sin, suffering, hunger, and hatred that are in the world. They do not seek their wealth and life in earthly things (see Ps. 18:27; 22:26; 25:9; 37:11; 72:2,12–13; 74:19; 147:6; Is. 11:4; 29:19; Luke 6:20; 16:25; John 14:3, note).

(2) Deliverance from suffering, oppression, injustice, and poverty will most certainly come to God's poor (Luke 6:20–23; 18:1–8). Their relief must come in part from alms given by those among God's people who are blessed with material possessions (see article on THE CARE OF THE POOR AND NEEDY, p. 1312).

(3) God sees His people in poverty and declares that they "are rich" (Rev. 2:9). In no way can they be seen as spiritually or morally inferior (see Rev. 2:9, note).

JESUS IN GALILEE

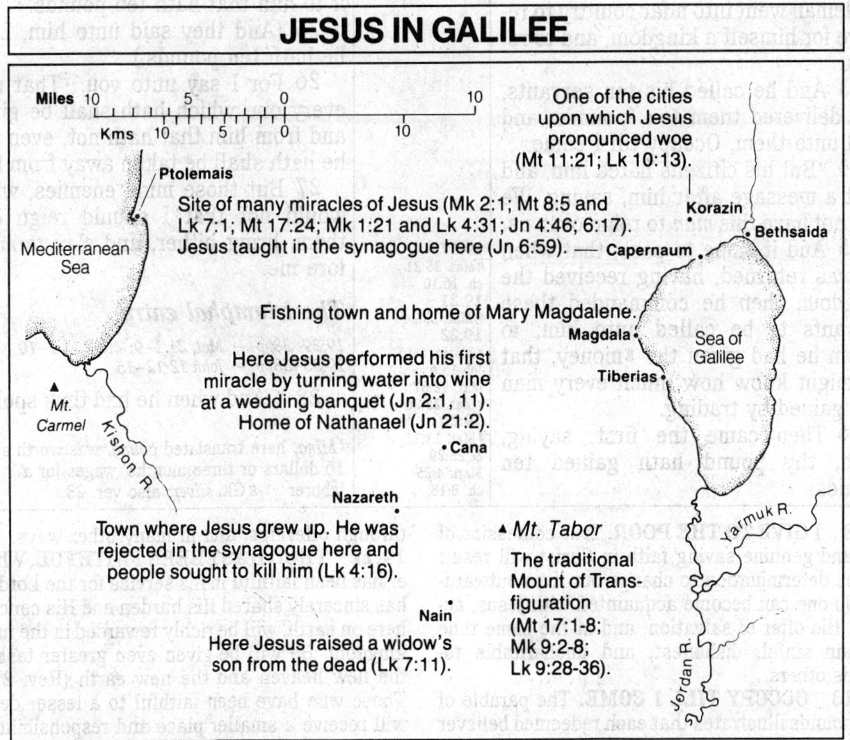

and come down; for today I must abide at thy house.

6 And he made haste, and came down, and received him joyfully.

7 And when they saw *it,* they all murmured, saying, [m]That he was gone to be guest with a man that is a sinner.

8 And Zacchaeus stood, and said unto the Lord; Behold, Lord, the half of my goods I give to the poor; and if I have taken any thing from any man by [n]false accusation, [o]I restore *him* fourfold.

9 And Jesus said unto him, This day is salvation come to this house, forsomuch as [p]he also is [q]a son of Abraham.

✝ John 1:12

10 [r]For the Son of man is come to seek and to save that which was lost.

Parable of the pounds

19:12–27Ref — Mat. 25:14–30

11 And as they heard these things, he added and spake a parable, because he was nigh to Jerusalem, and because [s]they thought that the kingdom of God should immediately appear.

12 [t]He said therefore, A certain nobleman went into a far country to receive for himself a kingdom, and to return.

13 And he called his ten servants, and delivered them ten [f]pounds, and said unto them, Occupy till I come.

14 [u]But his citizens hated him, and sent a message after him, saying, We will not have this *man* to reign over us.

15 And it came to pass, that when he was returned, having received the kingdom, then he commanded these servants to be called unto him, to whom he had given the [g]money, that he might know how much every man had gained by trading.

16 Then came the first, saying, Lord, thy pound hath gained ten pounds.

17 And he said unto him, Well, thou good servant: because thou hast been [v]faithful in a very little, have thou authority over ten cities.

18 And the second came, saying, Lord, thy pound hath gained five pounds.

19 And he said likewise to him, Be thou also over five cities.

20 And another came, saying, Lord, behold, *here is* thy pound, which I have kept laid up in a napkin:

21 [w]For I feared thee, because thou art an austere man: thou takest up that thou layedst not down, and reapest that thou didst not sow.

22 And he saith unto him, [x]Out of thine own mouth will I judge thee, *thou* wicked servant. [y]Thou knewest that I was an austere man, taking up that I laid not down, and reaping that I did not sow:

23 Wherefore then gavest not thou my money into the bank, that at my coming I might have required mine own with usury?

24 And he said unto them that stood by, Take from him the pound, and give *it* to him that hath ten pounds.

25 (And they said unto him, Lord, he hath ten pounds.)

26 For I say unto you, [z]That unto every one which hath shall be given; and from him that hath not, even that he hath shall be taken away from him.

27 But those mine enemies, which would not that I should reign over them, bring hither, and slay *them* before me.

The triumphal entry

19:29–38pp — Mat. 21:1–9; Mark 11:1–10
19:35–38pp — John 12:12–15

28 ¶ And when he had thus spoken,

19:7 [m]Mat. 9:11 ch. 5:30
19:8 [n]ch. 3:14 [o]Ex. 22:1 1 Sam. 12:3 2 Sam. 12:6
19:9 [p]Rom. 4:11,12,16 Gal. 3:7 [q]ch. 13:16
19:10 [r]Mat. 18:11 See Mat. 10:6 & 15:24
19:11 [s]Acts 1:6
19:12 [t]Mat. 25:14 Mark 13:34
19:14 [u]John 1:11
19:17 [v]Mat. 25:21 ch. 16:10
19:21 [w]Mat. 25:24
19:22 [x]2 Sam. 1:16 Job 15:6 Mat. 12:37 [y]Mat. 25:26
19:26 [z]Mat. 13:12 & 25:29 Mark 4:25 ch. 8:18

[f] *Mina,* here translated *pound,* was worth about 16 dollars or three months' wages for a laborer [g] Gk. *silver;* also ver. 23

19:8 I GIVE TO THE POOR. True confession of sin and genuine saving faith in Christ will result in the determination to change our lives outwardly. No one can become acquainted with Jesus, accept His offer of salvation, and at the same time remain sinful, dishonest, and uncharitable towards others.

19:13 OCCUPY TILL I COME. The parable of the pounds illustrates that each redeemed believer has the responsibility to use faithfully what God has given him. Each one of us has been given the chance, the time, and the means to live for Christ by word and deed, by acts of kindness, in prayer, through offerings, and in many other ways.

19:17 THOU HAST BEEN FAITHFUL. Whoever has been faithful in his service for the Lord and has sincerely shared His burden and His concerns here on earth, will be richly rewarded in the future kingdom. He will be given even greater tasks in the new heaven and the new earth (Rev. 21:1). Those who have been faithful to a lesser degree will receive a smaller place and responsibility.

19:26 THAT HE HATH SHALL BE TAKEN. See Mat. 25:29, note.

19:28 ASCENDING UP TO JERUSALEM. By His entry into Jerusalem on a donkey, Jesus public-

[a]he went before, ascending up to Jerusalem.

29 [b]And it came to pass, when he was come nigh to Bethphage and Bethany, at the mount called *the mount* of Olives, he sent two of his disciples,

30 Saying, Go ye into the village over against *you;* in the which at your entering ye shall find a colt tied, whereon yet never man sat: loose him, and bring *him hither.*

31 And if any man ask you, Why do ye loose *him?* thus shall ye say unto him, Because the Lord hath need of him.

32 And they that were sent went their way, and found even as he had said unto them.

33 And as they were loosing the colt, the owners thereof said unto them, Why loose ye the colt?

34 And they said, The Lord hath need of him.

35 And they brought him to Jesus: [c]and they cast their garments upon the colt, and they set Jesus thereon.

36 And as he went, they spread their clothes in the way.

37 And when he was come nigh, even now at the descent of the mount of Olives, the whole multitude of the disciples began to rejoice and praise God with a loud voice for all the mighty works that they had seen;

19:28 [a]Mark 10:32
19:29 [b]Mat. 21:1 Mark 11:1
19:35 [c]2 Ki. 9:13 Mat. 21:7 Mark 11:7 John 12:14
19:38 [d]Ps. 118:26 ch. 13:35 [e]ch. 2:14 Eph. 2:14
19:40 [f]Hab. 2:11
19:41 [g]John 11:35
19:43 [h]Is. 29:3,4 Jer. 6:3,6 ch. 21:20
19:44 [i]1 Ki. 9:7,8 Mic. 3:12 [j]Mat. 24:2 Mark 13:2 ch. 21:6 [k]Dan. 9:24 ch. 1:68,78 1 Pet. 2:12
19:45 [l]Mat. 21:12 Mark 11:11,15 John 2:14,15

38 Saying, [d]Blessed *be* the King that cometh in the name of the Lord: [e]peace in heaven, and glory in the highest.

39 And some of the Pharisees from among the multitude said unto him, Master, rebuke thy disciples.

40 And he answered and said unto them, I tell you that, if these should hold their peace, [f]the stones would immediately cry out. Acts 2:46-47

Jesus weeps over Jerusalem

41 ¶ And when he was come near, he beheld the city, and [g]wept over it,

42 Saying, If thou hadst known, even thou, at least in this thy day, the things *which belong* unto thy peace! but now they are hid from thine eyes.

43 For the days shall come upon thee, that thine enemies shall [h]cast a trench about thee, and compass thee round, and keep thee in on every side,

44 And [i]shall lay thee even with the ground, and thy children within thee; and [j]they shall not leave in thee one stone upon another; [k]because thou knewest not the time of thy visitation.

The cleansing of the temple

19:45–46pp — Mat. 21:12–16; Mark 11:15–18; John 2:13–16

45 [l]And he went into the temple,

---

ly testifies that He is Israel's predicted King and Messiah (see Zech. 9:9, note). (1) This entry into Jerusalem was predicted by the prophet Zechariah. (2) Jesus' humble entry is a deliberate symbolic action intended to show that His kingdom is not of this world and that He did not come to rule the world with force or violence. His refusal to take action as a military conqueror proves that His kingdom is spiritual.

19:41 HE BEHELD THE CITY, AND WEPT. Jesus, knowing that the people and their leaders expect a political Messiah and will ultimately reject Him as God's promised Messiah, weeps in pity for the people who will soon suffer terrible judgment. The word "wept" in Greek means more than shedding tears. It suggests rather a lamentation, a wailing, a heaving of the bosom, the sob and the cry of a soul in agony. Jesus, as God, reveals not only His own feelings, but also the broken heart of God over the lostness of the human race and their refusal to repent and accept salvation (see Mark 11:9, note).

19:43 THINE ENEMIES . . . COMPASS THEE ROUND. Jesus' prediction was fulfilled forty years later (A.D. 70) when Jerusalem was destroyed by the Roman army and hundreds of thousands of Jews were killed.

19:45 CAST OUT THEM THAT SOLD THEREIN. The cleansing of the temple was the first great public act of Jesus' ministry (John 2:13–22) and the last great public act of His ministry (cf. Mat. 21:12–17; Mark 11:15–17). In blazing anger, He drove from God's house the ungodly, the greedy, and those who were destroying its true spiritual purpose. Jesus' double cleansing of the temple during His three-year ministry indicates how important the spiritual lessons to be learned from these two incidents are. Those truths include the following:

(1) Christ's greatest concern is for holiness, sanctification, and godly sincerity within His church (cf. John 17:17,19). He died that He "might sanctify and cleanse it . . . that it should be holy and without blemish" (Eph. 5:25–27).

(2) Worship within the church must be in spirit and in truth (John 4:24). The church must be a place of prayer and communion with God (cf. Mat. 21:13).

(3) Christ will condemn all who use the church, the gospel, or His kingdom for personal gain, glory, or self-promotion.

(4) Sincere love for God and for His redemptive purpose among mankind will result in a consuming "zeal" for the righteousness of God's house and kingdom (John 2:17). That is, true Christlikeness includes intolerance towards unrighteousness

and began to cast out them that sold therein, and them that bought;

46 Saying unto them, [m]It is written, My house is the house of prayer: but [n]ye have made it a den of thieves.

47 And he taught daily in the temple. But [o]the chief priests and the scribes and the chief of the people sought to destroy him,

48 And could not find what they might do: for all the people were very attentive to hear him.

Jesus' authority challenged

20:1–8pp — Mat. 21:23–27; Mark 11:27–33

20 AND [p]IT came to pass, *that* on one of those days, as he taught the people in the temple, and preached the gospel, the chief priests and the scribes came upon *him* with the elders,

2 And spake unto him, saying, Tell us, [q]by what authority doest thou these things? or who is he that gave thee this authority?

3 And he answered and said unto them, I will also ask you one thing; and answer me:

4 The baptism of John, was it from heaven, or of men?

5 And they reasoned with themselves, saying, If we shall say, From heaven; he will say, Why then believed ye him not?

6 But and if we say, Of men; all the people will stone us: [r]for they be persuaded that John was a prophet.

7 And they answered, that they could not tell whence *it was.*

8 And Jesus said unto them, Neither tell I you by what authority I do these things.

19:46 [m]Is. 56:7 [n]Jer. 7:11
19:47 [o]Mark 11:18 John 7:19 & 8:37
20:1 [p]Mat. 21:23
20:2 [q]Acts 4:7 & 7:27
20:6 [r]Mat. 14:5 & 21:26 ch. 7:29
20:9 [s]Mat. 21:33 Mark 12:1
20:17 [t]Ps. 118:22 Mat. 21:42
20:18 [u]Dan. 2:34,35 Mat. 21:44

Parable of the tenants

20:9–19pp — Mat. 21:33–46; Mark 12:1–12

9 Then began he to speak to the people this parable; [s]A certain man planted a vineyard, and let it forth to husbandmen, and went into a far country for a long time.

10 And at the season he sent a servant to the husbandmen, that they should give him of the fruit of the vineyard: but the husbandmen beat him, and sent *him* away empty.

11 And again he sent another servant: and they beat him also, and entreated *him* shamefully, and sent *him* away empty.

12 And again he sent a third: and they wounded him also, and cast *him* out.

13 Then said the lord of the vineyard, What shall I do? I will send my beloved son: it may be they will reverence *him* when they see him.

14 But when the husbandmen saw him, they reasoned among themselves, saying, This is the heir: come, let us kill him, that the inheritance may be ours.

15 So they cast him out of the vineyard, and killed *him.* What therefore shall the lord of the vineyard do unto them?

16 He shall come and destroy these husbandmen, and shall give the vineyard to others. And when they heard *it,* they said, God forbid.

17 And he beheld them, and said, What is this then that is written, [t]The stone which the builders rejected, the same is become the head of the corner?

18 Whosoever shall fall upon that stone shall be broken; but [u]on whom-

within the church (cf. Rev. 2–3).

(5) Essential to all true Christian ministry is protest against those who profane and degrade the kingdom of God (cf. Rom. 14:17; 1 Cor. 6:9–11; Gal. 1:6–10; Rev. 2–3).

(6) Either we will allow Christ into our assemblies to purge out deceit, immorality, secularization, and desecration (see Rev. 2–3) or later at His second coming, He, in divine judgment, will cleanse His churches with finality (see Mal. 3:2).

19:46 HOUSE OF PRAYER. See Mark 11:17, note.

20:2 BY WHAT AUTHORITY? The religious leaders questioned Jesus' authority to cleanse the temple or to teach the people (19:45–48). They were offended and angered because Jesus condemned the evil practices within God's house, while they themselves condoned, tolerated, and participated in those practices. Such actions demonstrate how unfit they were to be ministers and spiritual leaders. Jesus, as a true spiritual leader, used His authority for the sake of truth and righteousness, even though it cost Him His life.

20:9–16 THE PARABLE OF THE HUSBANDMEN. See Mat. 21:33, note.

20:16 GIVE THE VINEYARD TO OTHERS. See Mat. 21:43, note on the kingdom of God taken from Israel.

20:18 THAT STONE. Those who do not accept Jesus will be broken, and those who fall under His judgment will be completely pulverized. See Is. 8:14 and Luke 2:34, where Christ is presented as a stone of stumbling and a rock of offense; also Dan. 2:34–35,44–45, where the Messiah is a rock who crushes the kingdoms of the world.

soever it shall fall, it will grind him to powder.

19 ¶ And the chief priests and the scribes the same hour sought to lay hands on him; and they feared the people: for they perceived that he had spoken this parable against them.

Paying taxes to Caesar

20:20–26pp — Mat. 22:15–22; Mark 12:13–17

20 [v]And they watched *him,* and sent forth spies, which should feign themselves just men, that they might take hold of his words, that so they might deliver him unto the power and authority of the governor.

21 And they asked him, saying, [w]Master, we know that thou sayest and teachest rightly, neither acceptest thou the person *of any,* but teachest the way of God [h]truly:

22 Is it lawful for us to give tribute unto Caesar, or no?

23 But he perceived their craftiness, and said unto them, Why tempt ye me?

24 Show me a [i]penny. Whose image and superscription hath it? They answered and said, Caesar's.

25 And he said unto them, Render therefore unto Caesar the things which be Caesar's, and unto God the things which be God's.

26 And they could not take hold of his words before the people: and they marvelled at his answer, and held their peace.

Marriage in heaven

20:27–40pp — Mat. 22:23–33; Mark 12:18–27

27 ¶ [x]Then came to *him* certain of the Sadducees, [y]which deny that there is any resurrection; and they asked him,

28 Saying, Master, Moses wrote unto us, If any man's brother die, having a wife, and he die without children, that his brother should take his wife, and raise up seed unto his brother.

20:20 [v]Mat. 22:15
20:21 [w]Mat. 22:16 Mark 12:14
20:27 [x]Mat. 22:23 Mark 12:18 [y]Acts 23:6,8

20:36 [z]1 Cor. 15:42,49, 52 1 John 3:2 [a]Rom. 8:23
20:37 [b]Ex. 3:6
20:38 [c]Rom. 6:10,11
20:41 [d]Mat. 22:42 Mark 12:35
20:42 [e]Ps. 110:1 Acts 2:34
20:45 [f]Mat. 23:1 Mark 12:38

29 There were therefore seven brethren: and the first took a wife, and died without children.

30 And the second took her to wife, and he died childless.

31 And the third took her; and in like manner the seven also: and they left no children, and died.

32 Last of all the woman died also.

33 Therefore in the resurrection whose wife of them is she? for seven had her to wife.

34 And Jesus answering said unto them, The children of this world marry, and are given in marriage:

35 But they which shall be accounted worthy to obtain that world, and the resurrection from the dead, neither marry, nor are given in marriage:

36 Neither can they die any more: for [z]they are equal unto the angels; and are the children of God, [a]being the children of the resurrection.

37 Now that the dead are raised, [b]even Moses showed at the bush, when he calleth the Lord the God of Abraham, and the God of Isaac, and the God of Jacob.

38 For he is not a God of the dead, but of the living: for [c]all live unto him.

39 ¶ Then certain of the scribes answering said, Master, thou hast well said.

40 And after that they durst not ask him any *question at all.*

Whose Son is the Christ?

20:41–47pp — Mat. 22:41–23:7; Mark 12:35–40

41 And he said unto them, [d]How say they that Christ is David's son?

42 And David himself saith in the book of Psalms, [e]The LORD said unto my Lord, Sit thou on my right hand,

43 Till I make thine enemies thy footstool.

44 David therefore calleth him Lord, how is he then his son?

45 ¶ [f]Then in the audience of all

[h] Or, *of a truth* [i] See Mat. 20:2

20:25 RENDER THEREFORE UNTO CAESAR. Believers under normal circumstances must pay taxes and submit to governmental authority (see Rom. 13:1–7), even though our highest loyalty is to God. We must obey secular government except when it conflicts with the law of God; we must *never* disobey Jesus' command to "render . . . unto Caesar the things which be Caesar's."

20:36 EQUAL UNTO THE ANGELS. About the believer's life in the next age, Jesus reveals that it begins with a resurrection from the dead, involves having a glorified body that can never die, but no longer includes earthly relationships such as marriage. The fact that earthly relationships will be different does not mean we will not recognize each other. Jesus, after His resurrection, was recognized by His disciples (24:31,39; Mat. 28:9).

20:44 DAVID . . . CALLETH HIM LORD. The Jews thought that the Messiah would merely be a descendant of David and therefore only a human

the people he said unto his disciples,
46 [g]Beware of the scribes, which
desire to walk in long robes, and [h]love
greetings in the markets, and the high-
est seats in the synagogues, and the
chief rooms at feasts;
47 [i]Which devour widows' houses,
and for a show make long prayers: the
same shall receive greater damnation.

The widow's offering

21:1–4pp — Mark 12:41–44

21 AND HE looked up, [j]and saw
the rich men casting their gifts
into the treasury.
2 And he saw also a certain poor
widow casting in thither two [j]mites.
3 And he said, Of a truth I say unto
you, [k]that this poor widow hath cast
in more than they all:
4 For all these have of their abun-
dance cast in unto the offerings of God:
but she of her penury hath cast in all
the living that she had.

Signs occurring before Christ's coming

21:5–12pp — Mat. 24:1–9; Mark 13:1–9
21:12–17pp — Mat. 10:17–22; Mark 13:11

5 ¶ [l]And as some spake of the tem-
ple, how it was adorned with goodly
stones and gifts, he said,
6 *As for* these things which ye be-
hold, the days will come, in the which
[m]there shall not be left one stone upon
another, that shall not be thrown
down.
7 And they asked him, saying, Mas-
ter, but when shall these things be?
and what sign *will there be* when these
things shall come to pass?
8 And he said, [n]Take heed that ye
be not deceived: for many shall come in
my name, saying, I am *Christ;* [k]and
the time draweth near: go ye not there-
fore after them.
9 But when ye shall hear of wars
and commotions, be not terrified: for
these things must first come to pass;
but the end *is* not by and by.
10 [o]Then said he unto them, Na-
tion shall rise against nation, and king-
dom against kingdom:
11 And great earthquakes shall be
in divers places, and famines, and pes-
tilences; and fearful sights and great
signs shall there be from heaven.
12 [p]But before all these, they shall
lay their hands on you, and persecute
you, delivering *you* up to the syna-
gogues, and [q]into prisons, [r]being
brought before kings and rulers [s]for
my name's sake.
13 And [t]it shall turn to you for a
testimony.
14 [u]Settle *it* therefore in your
hearts, not to meditate before what ye
shall answer:
15 For I will give you a mouth and
wisdom, [v]which all your adversaries
shall not be able to gainsay nor resist.
16 [w]And ye shall be betrayed both
by parents, and brethren, and kins-

20:46 [g]Mat. 23:5 [h]ch. 11:43
20:47 [i]Mat. 23:14
21:1 [j]Mark 12:41
21:3 [k]2 Cor. 8:12
21:5 [l]Mat. 24:1 Mark 13:1
21:6 [m]ch. 19:44
21:8 [n]Mat. 24:4 Mark 13:5 Eph. 5:6 2 Thes. 2:3
21:10 [o]Mat. 24:7
21:12 [p]Mark 13:9 Rev. 2:10 [q]Acts 4:3 & 5:18 & 12:4 & 16:24 [r]Acts 25:23 [s]1 Pet. 2:13
21:13 [t]Phil. 1:28 2 Thes. 1:5
21:14 [u]Mat. 10:19 Mark 13:11 ch. 12:11
21:15 [v]Acts 6:10
21:16 [w]Mic. 7:6 Mark 13:12

j See Mark 12:42 k Or, *and, The time;* see Mat. 3:2 & 4:17

ruler. Jesus shows that David's statement in Ps. 110:1, where he refers to his son as "Lord," indicates that the Messiah is more than a human ruler; He is also the divine Son of God (see Ps. 110:1–7, note).

20:46 BEWARE OF THE SCRIBES. See Mat. 23:13, note; see article on FALSE TEACHERS, p. 1508.

21:1–4 A CERTAIN POOR WIDOW. Jesus gives a lesson on how God evaluates giving. (1) A person's gift is determined, not by the amount he gives, but by the amount of sacrifice involved in the giving. The rich at times give only from their abundance—it costs them no sacrifice. The gift of the widow cost her everything. She gave as much as she possibly could. (2) This principle can be applied to all our service for Jesus. He judges our work and ministry for Him, not by its size or influence or success, but by the amount of sincere dedication, sacrifice, faith, and love involved (see 22:24–30, note; Mat. 20:26, note).

21:6 NOT BE LEFT ONE STONE UPON ANOTHER. The fulfillment of this prediction of the destruction of the temple occurred in A.D. 70, when the Roman general Titus and his army destroyed Jerusalem and burned the temple after a siege of 134 days. The temple was destroyed as a judgment upon Israel for their rejection of God's Son and His redemption.

21:7–19 WHEN SHALL THESE THINGS BE? Jesus' response to the disciples' question links the destruction of Jerusalem so closely with His return to earth after the tribulation that it is difficult to distinguish between the portions referring only to Jerusalem and those referring to His second coming. Jesus probably meant the destruction of Jerusalem as a type of His coming to judge the world.

21:8 TAKE HEED . . . BE NOT DECEIVED. See Mat. 24:5, note.

21:9 WARS AND COMMOTIONS. See Mat. 24:4, note.

21:16 YOU SHALL . . . BE PUT TO DEATH. Ancient writers state that all the apostles (except John) died as martyrs at the hands of persecutors. Many believers were tortured and killed in the early days of Christianity (see Mat. 24:9, note).

PASSION WEEK

Event	Day	References
1. ARRIVAL IN BETHANY	FRIDAY	Jn 12:1

Jesus arrived in Bethany six days before the Passover to spend some time with his friends, Mary, Martha and Lazarus. While here, Mary anointed his feet with costly perfume as an act of humility. This tender expression indicated Mary's devotion to Jesus and her willingness to serve him.

2. SABBATH — DAY OF REST	SATURDAY	Not mentioned in the Gospels

Since this day was the Sabbath, the Lord spent the day in traditional fashion with his friends.

3. THE TRIUMPHAL ENTRY	SUNDAY	Mt 21:1-11; Mk 11:1-11; Lk 19:28-44; Jn 12:12-19

On the first day of the week Jesus rode into Jerusalem on a donkey, fulfilling an ancient prophecy (Zec 9:9). The crowd welcomed him with "Hosanna" and the words of Ps 118:25-26, thus ascribing to him a Messianic title as the agent of the Lord, the coming King of Israel.

4. CLEARING OF THE TEMPLE	MONDAY	Mt 21:10-17; Mk 11:15-18; Lk 19:45-48

On this day he returned to the temple and found the court of the Gentiles full of traders and money changers making a large profit as they gave out Jewish coins in exchange for "pagan" money. Jesus drove them out and overturned their tables.

5. DAY OF CONTROVERSY AND PARABLES	TUESDAY	Mt 21:23–24:51; Mk 11:27–13:37; Lk 20:1–21:36

In Jerusalem - Jesus evaded the traps set by the priests.
On the Mount of Olives Overlooking Jerusalem - He taught in parables and warned the people against the Pharisees. He predicted the destruction of Herod's great temple and told his disciples about future events, including his own return.

6. DAY OF REST	WEDNESDAY	Not mentioned in the Gospels

The Scriptures do not mention this day, but the counting of the days (Mk 14:1; Jn 12:1) seems to indicate that there was another day concerning which the Gospels record nothing.

7. PASSOVER LAST SUPPER	THURSDAY	Mt 26:17-30; Mk 14:12-26; Lk 22:7-23; Jn 13:1-30

In an upper room Jesus prepared both himself and his disciples for his death. He gave the Passover meal a new meaning. The loaf of bread and cup of wine represented his body soon to be sacrificed and his blood soon to be shed. And so he instituted the "Lord's Supper." After singing a hymn they went to the Garden of Gethsemane, where Jesus prayed in agony, knowing what lay ahead for him.

8. CRUCIFIXION	FRIDAY	Mt 27:1-66; Mk 15:1-47; Lk 22:66–23:56; Jn 18:28–19:37

Following betrayal, arrest, desertion, false trials, denial, condemnation, beatings and mockery, Jesus was required to carry his cross to "The Place of the Skull," where he was crucified with two other prisoners.

9. IN THE TOMB	FRIDAY	Mt 27:57-61; Mk 15:42-47; Lk 23:50-56; Jn 19:38-42

Jesus' body was placed in the tomb before 6:00 P.M. Friday night, when the Sabbath began and all work stopped, and it lay in the tomb throughout the Sabbath.

10. RESURRECTION	SUNDAY	Mt 28:1-13; Mk 16:1-20; Lk 24:1-49; Jn 20:1-31

Early in the morning, women went to the tomb and found that the stone closing the tomb's entrance had been rolled back. An angel told them Jesus was alive and gave them a message. Jesus appeared to Mary Magdalene in the garden, to Peter, to two disciples on the road to Emmaus, and later that day to all the disciples but Thomas. His resurrection was established as a fact.

folks, and friends; and [x]*some* of you
shall they cause to be put to death.
17 And [y]ye shall be hated of all
men for my name's sake.
18 [z]But there shall not an hair of
your head perish.
19 In your patience possess ye your
souls.

The destruction of Jerusalem

21:20–24pp — Mat. 24:15–25; Mark 13:14–23

20 [a]And when ye shall see Jerusa-
lem compassed with armies, then
know that the desolation thereof is
nigh.
21 Then let them which are in Ju-
daea flee to the mountains; and let
them which are in the midst of it depart
out; and let not them that are in the
countries enter thereinto.
22 For these be the days of ven-
geance, that [b]all things which are
written may be fulfilled.
23 [c]But woe unto them that are
with child, and to them that give suck,
in those days! for there shall be great
distress in the land, and wrath upon
this people.
24 And they shall fall by the edge of
the sword, and shall be led away cap-
tive into all nations: and Jerusalem
shall be trodden down of the Gentiles,

21:16 [x]Acts 7:59 & 12:2
21:17 [y]Mat. 10:22
21:18 [z]Mat. 10:30
21:20 [a]Mat. 24:15 Mark 13:14
21:22 [b]Dan. 9:26,27 Zech. 11:1
21:23 [c]Mat. 24:19
21:24 [d]Dan. 9:27 & 12:7 Rom. 11:25
21:25 [e]Mat. 24:29 Mark 13:24 2 Pet. 3:10,12
21:26 [f]Mat. 24:29
21:27 [g]Mat. 24:30 Rev. 1:7 & 14:14
21:28 [h]Rom. 8:19,23
21:29 [i]Mat. 24:32 Mark 13:28

[d]until the times of the Gentiles be ful-
filled.

The coming of Christ

21:25–28pp — Mat. 24:26–31; Mark 13:24–27
21:29–33pp — Mat. 24:32–35; Mark 13:28–31

25 ¶ [e]And there shall be signs in
the sun, and in the moon, and in the
stars; and upon the earth distress of
nations, with perplexity; the sea and
the waves roaring;
26 Men's hearts failing them for
fear, and for looking after those things
which are coming on the earth: [f]for
the powers of heaven shall be shaken.
27 And then shall they see the Son
of man [g]coming in a cloud with power
and great glory.
28 And when these things begin to
come to pass, then look up, and lift up
your heads; for [h]your redemption
draweth nigh.
29 [i]And he spake to them a para-
ble; Behold the fig tree, and all the
trees;
30 When they now shoot forth, ye
see and know of your own selves that
summer is now nigh at hand.
31 So likewise ye, when ye see
these things come to pass, know ye
that the kingdom of God is nigh at
hand.
32 Verily I say unto you, This gener-

21:18 SHALL NOT . . . PERISH. This promise guarantees spiritual security, not physical preservation (cf. death referred to in v. 16). If believers remain faithful, nothing can happen to them out of God's will (cf. Rom. 8:28) or separate them from His love (Rom. 8:35–39).

21:19 IN YOUR PATIENCE. The word "patience" in Greek means perseverance or standing firm. We must engage ourselves in the most intense and concentrated devotion to Christ through the means of grace, i.e., prayer, witness, study of the Word, worship, Christian fellowship, and daily resistance to sin (see John 15:6, note). By persevering in true faith, believers gain eternal life and are victorious in all circumstances.

21:20 JERUSALEM COMPASSED WITH ARMIES. Once again Christ refers to the events of A.D. 70 (see note on v. 6). Those events fulfilled Christ's prophecy that divine justice and wrath would "come upon this generation" (Mat. 23:36; cf. Luke 23:27–30) for their rejection of the Messiah and refusal to turn from their sins. Jesus warns His followers to flee the city when they first see the armies (v. 21).

21:24 THE TIMES OF THE GENTILES. "The times of the Gentiles" refers to the time Israel would be under the domination or oppression of non-Jews. It began when a part of Israel was taken to Babylon in 586 B.C. (2 Chr. 36:1–21; Dan. 1:1–2). It will not end until the times of the nations are fulfilled, which probably means when Christ comes in glory and power to establish His rule over all the nations (1:32–33; Jer. 23:5–6; Zech. 6:13; 9:10; Rom. 11:25–26; Rev. 20:4).

21:25 SIGNS IN THE SUN . . . MOON . . . STARS. Cosmic signs will precede Jesus' coming, and the world will be in utmost distress because of the great tribulation (see Mat. 24:29, note; article on THE GREAT TRIBULATION, p. 1456). The impenitent will be in great terror and despair.

21:27 THE SON OF MAN COMING. "Son of man" is the term Jesus often used to refer to Himself (see 5:24, note; Mat. 24:30, note on Christ's coming after the tribulation).

21:31 WHEN YE SEE THESE THINGS COME TO PASS. One can tell that the time of Jesus' glorious appearing to establish His kingdom is close by watching the signs (see Mat. 24:33, note). On the other hand, Christ's return for the faithful believers of His churches at an unknown and unexpected time (i.e., the rapture or snatching away of all true believers, cf. John 14:1–4; 1 Thes. 4:13–18) is probably referred to in vv. 34–36 (see Mat. 24:44, note).

21:31 KINGDOM OF GOD IS NIGH. See Mat. 24:33, note.

21:32 THIS GENERATION. See Mat. 24:34, note.

ation shall not pass away, till all be fulfilled.

33 [j]Heaven and earth shall pass away: but my words shall not pass away.

Watch and pray

34 ¶ And [k]take heed to yourselves, lest at any time your hearts be overcharged with surfeiting, and drunkenness, and cares of this life, and *so* that day come upon you unawares.

35 For [l]as a snare shall it come on all them that dwell on the face of the whole earth.

36 [m]Watch ye therefore, and [n]pray always, that ye may be accounted worthy to escape all these things that shall come to pass, and [o]to stand before the Son of man.

37 [p]And in the day time he was teaching in the temple; and [q]at night he went out, and abode in the mount that is called *the mount* of Olives.

38 And all the people came early in the morning to him in the temple, for to hear him.

The plot to kill Jesus

22:1–2pp — Mat. 26:2–5; Mark 14:1–2,10–11

22 NOW [r]THE feast of unleavened bread drew nigh, which is called the Passover.

2 And [s]the chief priests and scribes sought how they might kill him; for they feared the people.

3 ¶ [t]Then entered Satan into Judas surnamed Iscariot, being of the number of the twelve.

4 And he went his way, and communed with the chief priests and captains, how he might betray him unto them.

5 And they were glad, and [u]covenanted to give him money.

6 And he promised, and sought opportunity to betray him unto them [1]in the absence of the multitude.

The last supper

22:7–13pp — Mat. 26:17–19; Mark 14:12–16

7 ¶ [v]Then came the day of unleavened bread, when the passover must be killed.

8 And he sent Peter and John, saying, Go and prepare us the passover, that we may eat.

9 And they said unto him, Where wilt thou that we prepare?

10 And he said unto them, Behold, when ye are entered into the city, there shall a man meet you, bearing a pitcher of water; follow him into the house where he entereth in.

11 And ye shall say unto the goodman of the house, The Master saith unto thee, Where is the guestchamber, where I shall eat the passover with my disciples?

12 And he shall show you a large upper room furnished: there make ready.

13 And they went, and found as he had said unto them: and they made ready the passover.

14 [w]And when the hour was come,

[1] Or, *without tumult*

21:33 [j]Mat. 24:35
21:34 [k]Rom. 13:13; 1 Thes. 5:6; 1 Pet. 4:7
21:35 [l]1 Thes. 5:2; 2 Pet. 3:10; Rev. 3:3 & 16:15
21:36 [m]Mat. 24:42 & 25:13; Mark 13:33; [n]ch. 18:1; [o]Ps. 1:5; Eph. 6:13
21:37 [p]John 8:1,2; [q]ch. 22:39
22:1 [r]Mat. 26:2; Mark 14:1
22:2 [s]Ps. 2:2; John 11:47; Acts 4:27
22:3 [t]Mat. 26:14; Mark 14:10; John 13:2,27
22:5 [u]Zech. 11:12
22:7 [v]Mat. 26:17; Mark 14:12
22:14 [w]Mat. 26:20; Mark 14:17

21:34 DAY COME UPON YOU UNAWARES. Jesus concludes His prophetic message by admonishing His followers not to be so preoccupied with the pleasures and cares of the world that they fail to be prepared for His coming. (1) These words are meant for all God's people of all ages, not just those living during the final days of tribulation. The demand for spiritual faithfulness is critical in the light of Jesus' teaching that He will return for the faithful believers at an unexpected time. Since the time of His coming for the church cannot be determined, believers must always be ready (see Mat. 24:40,42, notes; John 14:3, note). (2) Christ's rapture of the faithful in His churches (1 Thes. 4:16–17) delivers us from the "wrath to come" (1 Thes. 1:10), in order that we might "escape all these things that shall come to pass" upon the earth (vv. 35–36; cf. vv. 25–26; see Rev. 3:10, note; see next note).

21:36 ESCAPE ALL THESE THINGS. Followers of Christ must guard against sin and pray that their love toward Christ will not diminish, in order that they might receive grace and strength to persevere in faith and righteousness in Jesus Christ. Only by such perseverance will they be able to "escape" all the terrible things coming upon the world in the last days (see 1 Thes. 1:10, note; Rev. 3:10, note; see article on THE GREAT TRIBULATION, p. 1456). Many believe that the means of "escape" for those who faithfully keep on praying is the rapture (see John 14:3, note; see article on THE RAPTURE, p. 1889).

22:1 PASSOVER. See Mat. 26:2, note.

22:3 ENTERED SATAN INTO JUDAS. The tragic story of Judas, who at one time was in intimate fellowship with Jesus (Ps. 41:9; cf. John 13:18) but then forsook his Lord by betraying Him (see John 6:64, note), serves as a warning to all who follow Christ. In this life there is always the possibility that we might grow cold toward Christ, allow Satan little by little to lead us into compromise with sin and the world, and then in the end betray the Lord and His cause.

he sat down, and the twelve apostles with him.

15 And he said unto them, [m]With desire I have desired to eat this passover with you before I suffer:

16 For I say unto you, I will not any more eat thereof, [x]until it be fulfilled in the kingdom of God.

The institution of the Lord's Supper

22:17–20pp — Mat. 26:26–29; Mark 14:22–25; 1 Cor. 11:23–25
22:21–23pp — Mat. 26:21–24; Mark 14:18–21; John 13:21–30
22:25–27pp — Mat. 20:25–28; Mark 10:42–45

17 And he took the cup, and gave thanks, and said, Take this, and divide *it* among yourselves:

18 For [y]I say unto you, I will not drink of the fruit of the vine, until the kingdom of God shall come.

19 ¶ [z]And he took bread, and gave thanks, and brake *it*, and gave unto them, saying, This is my body which is given for you: [a]this do in remembrance of me.

20 Likewise also the cup after supper, saying, [b]This cup *is* the new testament in my blood, which is shed for you.

21 ¶ [c]But, behold, the hand of him that betrayeth me *is* with me on the table.

22 [d]And truly the Son of man goeth, [e]as it was determined: but woe unto that man by whom he is betrayed!

23 [f]And they began to inquire among themselves, which of them it was that should do this thing.

24 ¶ [g]And there was also a strife among them, which of them should be accounted the greatest.

25 [h]And he said unto them, The kings of the Gentiles exercise lordship over them; and they that exercise authority upon them are called benefactors.

26 [i]But ye *shall* not *be* so: [j]but he that is greatest among you, let him be as the younger; and he that is chief, as he that doth serve.

27 [k]For whether *is* greater, he that sitteth at meat, or he that serveth? *is* not he that sitteth at meat? but [l]I am among you as he that serveth.

22:16 [x]ch. 14:15 Acts 10:41 Rev. 19:9
22:18 [y]Mat. 26:29 Mark 14:25
22:19 [z]Mat. 26:26 Mark 14:22 [a]1 Cor. 11:24
22:20 [b]1 Cor. 10:16
22:21 [c]Ps. 41:9 Mat. 26:21,23 Mark 14:18 John 13:21,26
22:22 [d]Mat. 26:24 [e]Acts 2:23 & 4:28
22:23 [f]Mat. 26:22 John 13:22,25
22:24 [g]Mark 9:34 ch. 9:46
22:25 [h]Mat. 20:25 Mark 10:42
22:26 [i]Mat. 20:26 1 Pet. 5:3 [j]ch. 9:48
22:27 [k]ch. 12:37 [l]Mat. 20:28 John 13:13,14 Phil. 2:7

[m] Or, *I have heartily desired*

22:18 THE LORD'S SUPPER. See 1 Cor. 11:24–25, note.

22:18 THE FRUIT OF THE VINE. What Jesus and the disciples drank at the Passover supper is called "a cup" or "the cup of blessing" (22:17; Mat. 26:27; Mark 14:23; 1 Cor. 10:16; 11:25) and "the fruit of the vine" (22:18; Mat. 26:29; Mark 14:25). Scriptural evidence supports the view that the juice of the vine was unfermented at the Lord's Supper (see article on WINE IN NEW TESTAMENT TIMES (1), p. 1538).

22:20 THE NEW TESTAMENT IN MY BLOOD. With the words "the new testament in my blood," Jesus announces the inauguration of the new testament or covenant, based on His sacrificial death (cf. Mat. 26:28; 1 Cor. 11:25; see Jer. 31:31, note). Scripture teaches that the new covenant could only become valid by the death of Christ (Heb. 9:15–18). The disciples entered into this new covenant when they were regenerated and indwelt by the Holy Spirit on the evening of Jesus' resurrection (see article on THE REGENERATION OF THE DISCIPLES, p. 1638). They later were baptized in the Holy Spirit on the day of Pentecost (see Acts 2:4, note; see article on BAPTISM IN THE HOLY SPIRIT, p. 1652).

22:20 MY BLOOD, WHICH IS SHED FOR YOU. See Mat. 26:28, note.

22:24–30 ACCOUNTED THE GREATEST. True greatness is a matter of inward spirit and heart. It is seen in the person who expresses his faith and love to Christ in sincere humility (Phil. 2:3), in a desire to serve both God and man, and in a willingness to be seen as the least important in God's kingdom.

(1) We must understand that greatness is not position, office, leadership, power, influence, academic degrees, fame, ability, great accomplishments, or success. It is not so much what we *do* for God as what we *are* in spirit before Him (vv. 25–27; Mat. 18:3–4; 20:25–28).

(2) True greatness requires that we become great in the right areas. We need to learn to be great in faith, godly character, wisdom, self-control, patience, and love (Gal. 5:22–23). It is to have the greatness of Christ who "loved righteousness and hated iniquity" (Heb. 1:9).

(3) True greatness is a matter of heartfelt love, commitment, and dedication to God. What is important is to be consecrated and faithful where God chooses to place us. Therefore, in God's sight, the greatest in His kingdom are those with the greatest love, loyalty, and commitment to Him and to His revealed Word (21:3; Rom. 12:1–2).

(4) Consecration will improve your results in God's work, but only in that area in which God has placed you and in the context of the gifts that He has given you (Rom. 12:3–8; 1 Cor. 12).

22:27 HE THAT SERVETH. Concerning those who are chosen to lead in the church (1 Tim. 3:1–7), Christ says that they must lead as servants, helping those under them to fulfill God's will for their lives. They must never misuse or betray their position by seeking fame, power, wealth, or special privilege.

28 Ye are they which have continued with me in [m]my temptations.

29 And [n]I appoint unto you a kingdom, as my Father hath appointed unto me;

30 That [o]ye may eat and drink at my table in my kingdom, [p]and sit on thrones judging the twelve tribes of Israel.

Jesus foretells Peter's denial

22:33–34pp — Mat. 26:33–35; Mark 14:29–31; John 13:37–38

31 ¶ And the Lord said, Simon, Simon, behold, [q]Satan hath desired *to have* you, that he may [r]sift *you* as wheat:

32 But [s]I have prayed for thee, that thy faith fail not: and when thou art converted, strengthen thy brethren.

33 And he said unto him, Lord, I am ready to go with thee, both into prison, and to death.

34 [t]And he said, I tell thee, Peter, the cock shall not crow this day, before that thou shalt thrice deny that thou knowest me.

35 [u]And he said unto them, When I sent you without purse, and scrip, and shoes, lacked ye any thing? And they said, Nothing.

36 Then said he unto them, But now, he that hath a purse, let him take *it,* and likewise *his* scrip: and he that hath no sword, let him sell his garment, and buy one.

37 For I say unto you, that this that is written must yet be accomplished in me, [v]And he was reckoned among the transgressors: for the things concerning me have an end.

22:28 [m]Heb. 4:15
22:29 [n]Mat. 24:47; ch. 12:32
22:30 [o]Mat. 8:11; ch. 14:15; Rev. 19:9; [p]Ps. 49:14; Mat. 19:28; 1 Cor. 6:2; Rev. 3:21
22:31 [q]1 Pet. 5:8; [r]Amos 9:9
22:32 [s]John 17:9,11,15
22:34 [t]Mat. 26:34; Mark 14:30; John 13:38
22:35 [u]Mat. 10:9; ch. 9:3 & 10:4
22:37 [v]Is. 53:12; Mark 15:28
22:39 [w]Mat. 26:36; Mark 14:32; John 18:1; [x]ch. 21:37
22:40 [y]ver. 46; Mat. 6:13 & 26:41; Mark 14:38
22:41 [z]Mat. 26:39; Mark 14:35
22:42 [a]John 5:30 & 6:38
22:43 [b]Mat. 4:11
22:44 [c]John 12:27; Heb. 5:7
22:46 [d]ver. 40
22:47 [e]Mat. 26:47; Mark 14:43; John 18:3

38 And they said, Lord, behold, here *are* two swords. And he said unto them, It is enough.

Jesus' agony in Gethsemane

22:40–46pp — Mat. 26:36–46; Mark 14:32–42

39 ¶ [w]And he came out, and [x]went, as he was wont, to the mount of Olives; and his disciples also followed him.

40 [y]And when he was at the place, he said unto them, Pray that ye enter not into temptation.

41 [z]And he was withdrawn from them about a stone's cast, and kneeled down, and prayed,

42 Saying, Father, if thou be [n]willing, remove this cup from me: nevertheless [a]not my will, but thine, be done.

43 And there appeared [b]an angel unto him from heaven, strengthening him.

44 [c]And being in an agony he prayed more earnestly: and his sweat was as it were great drops of blood falling down to the ground.

45 And when he rose up from prayer, and was come to his disciples, he found them sleeping for sorrow,

46 And said unto them, Why sleep ye? rise and [d]pray, lest ye enter into temptation.

Jesus' betrayal and arrest

22:47–53pp — Mat. 26:47–56; Mark 14:43–50; John 18:3–11

47 ¶ And while he yet spake, [e]behold a multitude, and he that was

[n] Gk. *willing to remove*

22:28 CONTINUED WITH ME. Jesus acknowledges to His disciples that He is grateful for their faithfulness to Him during His life and the trying circumstances that surrounded it. Our greatest concern should also be to stand by Him in a world that is hostile and indifferent to His cause and righteous standards.

22:29 APPOINT UNTO YOU A KINGDOM. Jesus provides "a kingdom" for His faithful followers. This future kingdom is established by Himself (v. 30). The disciples must not expect earthly glory and worldly power in this age.

22:31–32 SATAN . . . SIFT *YOU* AS WHEAT. Jesus' statement concerning Peter reveals two important truths. (1) God allows Satan to tempt us only within certain limits and according to His permission (see Job 1:10,12, notes). The devil is not free to do what he wants with God's people. (2) Jesus prays that the faith of His people may not fail. As our heavenly intercessor, He prays for everyone who "comes unto God by him, seeing he ever liveth to make intercession for them" (Heb. 7:25). God is faithful in all our temptations to make a way of escape (1 Cor. 10:13). However, the prayers of Jesus are not absolute. If a person rejects the grace of God, Christ's intercession is then of no effect (see 19:41, note).

22:36 SWORD . . . BUY ONE. Jesus' statement that His disciples buy a sword could have been irony. After all, up to this point He has been challenging them to live the life of the cross that He had taught, rather than choose the way of the world. Jesus then goes on to state (v. 37) His commitment to God's way of suffering and to the cross. V. 38 indicates that the disciples did not understand what Jesus meant.

22:42 THIS CUP. See Mat. 26:39, note.

22:44 SWEAT . . . DROPS OF BLOOD. For the ten stages of Christ's redemptive suffering, see notes on Mat. 26:37ff.

called Judas, one of the twelve, went before them, and drew near unto Jesus to kiss him.

48 But Jesus said unto him, Judas, betrayest thou the Son of man with a kiss?

49 When they which were about him saw what would follow, they said unto him, Lord, shall we smite with the sword?

50 ¶ And [f]one of them smote the servant of the high priest, and cut off his right ear.

51 And Jesus answered and said, Suffer ye thus far. And he touched his ear, and healed him.

52 [g]Then Jesus said unto the chief priests, and captains of the temple, and the elders, which were come to him, Be ye come out, as against a thief, with swords and staves?

53 When I was daily with you in the temple, ye stretched forth no hands against me: [h]but this is your hour, and the power of darkness.

Peter's denial of Jesus

22:55–62pp — Mat. 26:69–75; Mark 14:66–72; John 18:16–18,25–27
22:63–65pp — Mat. 26:67–68; Mark 14:65; John 18:22–23

54 ¶ [i]Then took they him, and led *him,* and brought him into the high priest's house. [j]And Peter followed afar off.

55 [k]And when they had kindled a fire in the midst of the hall, and were set down together, Peter sat down among them.

56 But a certain maid beheld him as he sat by the fire, and earnestly looked upon him, and said, This man was also with him.

57 And he denied him, saying, Woman, I know him not.

58 And [l]after a little while another saw him, and said, Thou art also of them. And Peter said, Man, I am not.

59 [m]And about the space of one hour after another confidently affirmed, saying, Of a truth this *fellow* also was with him: for he is a Galilaean.

60 And Peter said, Man, I know not what thou sayest. And immediately, while he yet spake, the cock crew.

61 And the Lord turned, and looked upon Peter. [n]And Peter remembered the word of the Lord, how he had said unto him, [o]Before the cock crow, thou shalt deny me thrice.

62 And Peter went out, and wept bitterly.

63 ¶ [p]And the men that held Jesus mocked him, and smote *him.*

64 And when they had blindfolded him, they struck him on the face, and asked him, saying, Prophesy, who is it that smote thee?

65 And many other things blasphemously spake they against him.

Jesus before Pontius Pilate

22:67–71pp — Mat. 26:63–66; Mark 14:61–63; John 18:19–21
23:2–3pp — Mat. 27:11–14; Mark 15:2–5; John 18:29–37

66 ¶ [q]And as soon as it was day, [r]the elders of the people and the chief priests and the scribes came together, and led him into their council, saying,

67 [s]Art thou the Christ? tell us. And he said unto them, If I tell you, ye will not believe:

68 And if I also ask *you,* ye will not answer me, nor let *me* go.

69 [t]Hereafter shall the Son of man sit on the right hand of the power of God.

70 Then said they all, Art thou then the Son of God? And he said unto them, [u]Ye say that I am.

71 [v]And they said, What need we any further witness? for we ourselves have heard of his own mouth.

23 AND [w]THE whole multitude of them arose, and led him unto Pilate.

22:50 [f]Mat. 26:51 Mark 14:47
22:52 [g]Mat. 26:55 Mark 14:48
22:53 [h]John 12:27
22:54 [i]Mat. 26:57 [j]Mat. 26:58 John 18:15
22:55 [k]Mat. 26:69 Mark 14:66 John 18:17,18
22:58 [l]Mat. 26:71 Mark 14:69 John 18:25
22:59 [m]Mat. 26:73 Mark 14:70 John 18:26
22:61 [n]Mat. 26:75 Mark 14:72 [o]Mat. 26:34,75 John 13:38
22:63 [p]Mat. 26:67,68 Mark 14:65
22:66 [q]Mat. 27:1 [r]Acts 4:26 See Acts 22:5
22:67 [s]Mat. 26:63 Mark 14:61
22:69 [t]Mat 26:64 Mark 14:62 Heb. 1:3 & 8:1
22:70 [u]Mat. 26:64 Mark 14:62
22:71 [v]Mat. 26:65 Mark 14:63
23:1 [w]Mat. 27:2 Mark 15:1 John 18:28

22:54 THEN TOOK THEY HIM. For the order of events from Christ's arrest to His crucifixion, see Mat. 26:57, note.

22:62 PETER . . . WEPT BITTERLY. Peter denied the Lord out of weakness, not out of wickedness, for he never ceased to love his Master and to believe in Him. Peter was spiritually weak and incapable of resisting great temptation since he had not yet, along with the other disciples, received the Holy Spirit and His regenerating grace in the full new covenant sense. They received the Holy Spirit's indwelling presence only on the resurrection day (see Mark 14:50, note; see article on THE REGENERATION OF THE DISCIPLES, p. 1638).

22:63 MOCKED HIM. See Mat. 26:67, note.

23:1 PILATE. Pilate was the Roman governor in Jerusalem at the time of the Passover. Jesus was brought to him because under Roman law the Jews could not legally carry out the death penalty on anyone. Pilate has become a symbol of those who make religious decisions based on political expedi-

2 And they began to accuse him, saying, We found this *fellow* [x]perverting the nation, and [y]forbidding to give tribute to Caesar, saying [z]that he himself is Christ a King.

3 [a]And Pilate asked him, saying, Art thou the King of the Jews? And he answered him and said, Thou sayest *it.*

4 Then said Pilate to the chief priests and *to* the people, [b]I find no fault in this man.

5 And they were the more fierce, saying, He stirreth up the people, teaching throughout all Jewry, beginning from Galilee to this place.

Jesus before Herod

6 When Pilate heard of Galilee, he asked whether the man were a Galilaean.

7 And as soon as he knew that he belonged unto [c]Herod's jurisdiction, he sent him to Herod, who himself also was at Jerusalem at that time.

8 ¶ And when Herod saw Jesus, he was exceeding glad: for [d]he was desirous to see him of a long *season,* because [e]he had heard many things of him; and he hoped to have seen some miracle done by him.

9 Then he questioned with him in many words; but he answered him nothing.

10 And the chief priests and scribes stood and vehemently accused him.

11 [f]And Herod with his men of war set him at nought, and mocked *him,* and arrayed him in a gorgeous robe, and sent him again to Pilate.

12 ¶ And the same day [g]Pilate and Herod were made friends together: for before they were at enmity between themselves.

Pilate delivers Jesus to be crucified

23:18–25pp — Mat. 27:15–26; Mark 15:6–15; John 18:39—19:16

13 ¶ [h]And Pilate, when he had called together the chief priests and the rulers and the people,

14 Said unto them, [i]Ye have brought this man unto me, as one that perverteth the people: and, behold, [j]I, having examined *him* before you, have found no fault in this man touching those things whereof ye accuse him:

15 No, nor yet Herod: for I sent you to him; and, lo, nothing worthy of death is done unto him.

16 [k]I will therefore chastise him, and release *him.*

17 [l](For of necessity he must release one unto them at the feast.)

18 And [m]they cried out all at once, saying, Away with this *man,* and release unto us Barabbas:

19 (Who for a certain sedition made in the city, and for murder, was cast into prison.)

20 Pilate therefore, willing to release Jesus, spake again to them.

21 But they cried, saying, Crucify *him,* crucify him.

22 And he said unto them the third time, Why, what evil hath he done? I have found no cause of death in him: I will therefore chastise him, and let *him* go.

23 And they were instant with loud voices, requiring that he might be crucified. And the voices of them and of the chief priests prevailed.

24 And [n]Pilate [o]gave[o] sentence that it should be as they required.

25 And he released unto them him that for sedition and murder was cast into prison, whom they had desired; but he delivered Jesus to their will.

[o] Or, *assented*

23:2 [x]Acts 17:7 [y]See Mat. 17:27 & 22:21 Mark 12:17 [z]John 19:12
23:3 [a]Mat. 27:11 1 Tim. 6:13
23:4 [b]1 Pet. 2:22
23:7 [c]ch. 3:1
23:8 [d]ch. 9:9 [e]Mat. 14:1 Mark 6:14
23:11 [f]Is 53:3
23:12 [g]Acts 4:27
23:13 [h]Mat. 27:23 Mark 15:14 John 18:38 & 19:4
23:14 [i]ver. 1,2 [j]ver. 4
23:16 [k]Mat. 27:26 John 19:1
23:17 [l]Mat. 27:15 Mark 15:6 John 18:39
23:18 [m]Acts 3:14
23:24 [n]Mat:27:26 Mark 15:15 John 19:16 [o]Ex. 23:2

---

ency rather than truth and justice. Every believer must be careful not to compromise the Word of God because of political, career, or self-serving interests; he should always stand for what is right.

23:3 ART THOU THE KING OF THE JEWS? See Mat. 27:2, note.

23:8–11 HEROD. This is the same Herod who had John the Baptist beheaded. Because Herod's heart is so hardened, Jesus refuses to speak a word to him. In anger Herod and his men mock His claim of being the king of the Jews.

23:11 MOCKED HIM . . . GORGEOUS ROBE. See Mat. 27:28–29, note.

23:14 NO FAULT IN THIS MAN. Jesus was accused of treason against Rome. Pilate, in talking to Jesus, comes to the conclusion that He is innocent of any rebellion against the Roman government. Jesus declares to Pilate that His kingdom is not a political kingdom of this world, but a spiritual kingdom (see John 18:36).

23:22 CHASTISE HIM. See Mat. 27:26, note.

23:25 HE DELIVERED JESUS TO THEIR WILL. It is because of political expediency that Pilate delivers Jesus over to the Jewish authorities (see 23:1, note).

Jesus crucified

23:33–43pp — Mat. 27:33–44; Mark 15:22–32; John 19:17–24

26 [p]And as they led him away, they laid hold upon one Simon, a Cyrenian, coming out of the country, and on him they laid the cross, that he might bear *it* after Jesus.

27 ¶ And there followed him a great company of people, and of women, which also bewailed and lamented him.

28 But Jesus turning unto them said, Daughters of Jerusalem, weep not for me, but weep for yourselves, and for your children.

29 [q]For, behold, the days are coming, in the which they shall say, Blessed *are* the barren, and the wombs that never bare, and the paps which never gave suck.

30 [r]Then shall they begin to say to the mountains, Fall on us; and to the hills, Cover us.

31 [s]For if they do these things in a green tree, what shall be done in the dry?

32 [t]And there were also two other, malefactors, led with him to be put to death.

33 And [u]when they were come to the place, which is called [p]Calvary, there they crucified him, and the malefactors, one on the right hand, and the other on the left.

34 ¶ Then said Jesus, Father, [v]forgive them; for [w]they know not what they do. And [x]they parted his raiment, and cast lots.

35 And [y]the people stood beholding. And the [z]rulers also with them derided *him*, saying, He saved others; let him save himself, if he be Christ, the chosen of God.

36 And the soldiers also mocked him, coming to him, and offering him vinegar,

37 And saying, If thou be the king of the Jews, save thyself.

38 [a]And a superscription also was written over him in letters of Greek, and Latin, and Hebrew, THIS IS THE KING OF THE JEWS.

39 ¶ [b]And one of the malefactors which were hanged railed on him, saying, If thou be Christ, save thyself and us.

40 But the other answering rebuked him, saying, Dost not thou fear God, seeing thou art in the same condemnation?

41 And we indeed justly; for we receive the due reward of our deeds: but this man hath done nothing amiss.

42 And he said unto Jesus, Lord, re-

23:26
[p]Mat. 27:32
Mark 15:21
See John 19:17
23:29
[q]Mat. 24:19
ch. 21:23
23:30
[r]Is. 2:19
Hos. 10:8
Rev. 6:16
& 9:6
23:31
[s]Prov. 11:31
Jer. 25:29
Ezek. 20:47
& 21:3,4
1 Pet. 4:17
23:32
[t]Is. 53:12
Mat. 27:38
23:33
[u]Mat. 27:33
Mark 15:22
John 19:17,18
23:34
[v]Mat. 5:44
Acts 7:60
1 Cor. 4:12
[w]Acts 3:17
[x]Mat. 27:35
Mark 15:24
John 19:23
23:35
[y]Ps. 22:17
Zech. 12:10
[z]Mat. 27:39
Mark 15:29
23:38
[a]Mat. 27:37
Mark 15:26
John 19:19
23:39
[b]Mat. 27:44
Mark 15:32

p Or, *The place of a skull*

23:31 A GREEN TREE ... DRY. If the innocent Jesus meets with such a fate, what will be the fate of guilty Jerusalem?

23:33 THEY CRUCIFIED HIM. The crucifixion and death of Jesus are the core and foundation of God's plan of redemption (1 Cor. 1:23–24). Jesus, who had never sinned, died in the place of sinful humanity. By His crucifixion the penalty for sin was paid and the work of Satan undone (cf. Rom. 3:25, note). Now all people may turn to God in repentance and faith in Christ and receive forgiveness, salvation from sin, and eternal life.

23:34 SEVEN LAST SAYINGS OF CHRIST. In all probability, this is the first of the seven last sayings of Christ on the cross. The seven sayings were spoken in the following order:

(1) From 9 o'clock until noon: (a) The word of forgiveness: "Father, forgive them" (v. 34). (b) The word of salvation: "Today shalt thou be with me in paradise" (v. 43). (c) The word of love: "Woman, behold thy son! . . . Behold thy mother!" (John 19:26–27).

(2) The three hours of darkness: from noon until 3 o'clock, no words reported.

(3) About 3 o'clock: (a) The word of spiritual suffering: "My God, my God, why hast thou forsaken me?" (Mark 15:34). (b) The word of physical suffering: "I thirst" (John 19:28). (c) The word of triumph: "It is finished" (John 19:30). (d) The word of committal: "Father, into thy hands I commend my spirit" (v. 46).

23:35 THE PEOPLE STOOD BEHOLDING. One of the surest proofs of the depravity of the human heart is the fact that people take pleasure in violence, blood, and death. (1) We see this attitude in the Roman and Greek arenas, where the spectators enjoyed watching men fight and kill each other. We see this in the casual onlookers who came by and watched Christ die a horrible death (vv. 35–37). We see this in the history of the persecution of believers.

(2) We see this same attitude in our modern society as millions of adults and children find pleasure and entertainment on television and other entertainment media as they watch human suffering, blood, violence, and death (see Rom. 1:32, note).

(3) Jesus died to change this attitude and to bring love and care. He wants us to see the impact of sin on human life and to hear the groaning of suffering humanity (see 13:16, note).

(4) It is the responsibility of parents to guard themselves and their families against all influences that would desensitize them to human pain and tragedy (see Mat. 18:6, note).

23:35 DERIDED *HIM*. See Mat. 27:39, note.

member me when thou comest into thy
kingdom.
43 And Jesus said unto him, Verily
I say unto thee, Today shalt thou be
with me in paradise.

The death of Jesus

23:44–49pp — Mat. 27:45–56; Mark 15:33–41

44 [c]And it was about the sixth
hour, and there was a darkness over all
the [q]earth until the ninth hour.
45 And the sun was darkened, and
[d]the veil of the temple was rent in the
midst.
46 ¶ And when Jesus had cried with
a loud voice, he said, [e]Father, into thy
hands I commend my spirit: [f]and having
said thus, he gave up the ghost.
47 [g]Now when the centurion saw
what was done, he glorified God, saying,
Certainly this was a righteous
man.
48 And all the people that came together
to that sight, beholding the
things which were done, smote their
breasts, and returned.
49 [h]And all his acquaintance, and
the women that followed him from Galilee,
stood afar off, beholding these
things.

The burial of Jesus

23:50–56pp — Mat. 27:57–61; Mark 15:42–47; John 19:38–42

50 ¶ [i]And, behold, *there was* a man
named Joseph, a counsellor; *and he was*
a good man, and a just:
51 (The same had not consented to
the counsel and deed of them;) *he was*
of Arimathaea, a city of the Jews:
[j]who also himself waited for the kingdom
of God.

23:44 [c]Mat. 27:45 Mark 15:33
23:45 [d]Mat. 27:51 Mark 15:38
23:46 [e]Ps. 31:5 1 Pet. 2:23 [f]Mat. 27:50 Mark 15:37 John 19:30
23:47 [g]Mat. 27:54 Mark 15:39
23:49 [h]Ps. 38:11 Mat. 27:55 Mark 15:40 See John 19:25
23:50 [i]Mat. 27:57 Mark 15:42 John 19:38
23:51 [j]Mark 15:43 ch. 2:25,38
23:53 [k]Mat. 27:59 Mark 15:46
23:54 [l]Mat. 27:62
23:55 [m]ch. 8:2 [n]Mark 15:47
23:56 [o]Mark 16:1 [p]Ex. 20:10
24:1 [q]Mat. 28:1 Mark 16:1 John 20:1 [r]ch. 23:56
24:2 [s]Mat. 28:2 Mark 16:4
24:3 [t]ver. 23 Mark 16:5
24:4 [u]John 20:12 Acts 1:10
24:6 [v]Mat. 16:21 & 17:23 Mark 8:31 & 9:31 ch. 9:22

52 This *man* went unto Pilate, and
begged the body of Jesus.
53 [k]And he took it down, and
wrapped it in linen, and laid it in a sepulchre
that was hewn in stone, wherein
never man before was laid.
54 And that day was [l]the preparation,
and the sabbath drew on.
55 And the women also, [m]which
came with him from Galilee, followed
after, and [n]beheld the sepulchre, and
how his body was laid.
56 And they returned, and [o]prepared
spices and ointments: and rested
the sabbath day [p]according to the
commandment.

The resurrection of Jesus

24:1–10pp — Mat. 28:1–8; Mark 16:1–8; John 20:1–8

24 NOW [q]UPON the first *day* of
the week, very early in the
morning, they came unto the sepulchre,
[r]bringing the spices which they
had prepared, and certain *others* with
them.
2 [s]And they found the stone rolled
away from the sepulchre.
3 [t]And they entered in, and found
not the body of the Lord Jesus.
4 And it came to pass, as they were
much perplexed thereabout, [u]behold,
two men stood by them in shining garments:
5 And as they were afraid, and
bowed down *their* faces to the earth,
they said unto them, Why seek ye
[r]the living among the dead?
6 He is not here, but is risen: [v]remember
how he spake unto you when
he was yet in Galilee,

[q] Or, *land* [r] Or, *him that liveth*

23:43 PARADISE. The term "paradise" is used to indicate heaven or the presence of God (that "heaven" and "paradise" indicate the same place is clear from 2 Cor. 12:2,4). Jesus' words clearly teach that after death, the saved go immediately into the presence of Jesus in heaven.

23:45 VEIL OF THE TEMPLE WAS RENT. See Mat. 27:51, note.

23:46 FATHER, INTO THY HANDS. Jesus voluntarily gave His life over to death. At that moment He went in spirit to His Father in heaven (see Ps. 31:5, note).

23:46 I COMMEND MY SPIRIT. See Mat. 27:50, note.

24:6 HE . . . IS RISEN. The resurrection of Christ Jesus (see Mat. 28:6, note) is confirmed by the following facts. (1) The empty tomb. If the enemies of Jesus had taken His body, they would have shown it to prove He had not risen. If the disciples had taken His body, they would have never sacrificed their lives and possessions for what they knew to be a lie. The empty tomb reveals that Jesus did arise and truly was the Son of God.

(2) The existence, power, joy, and devotion of the early church. If Jesus had not risen and appeared to them, they would have never changed from despondency to unheard-of joy, courage, and hope (vv. 52–53).

(3) The writing of the New Testament. The New Testament was written by men giving their lives for the truth and righteousness taught by Jesus. They would never have taken the trouble to write about a Messiah and His teaching if His ministry had ended in death and disillusionment (see 1 Cor. 15:12–19).

(4) The baptism in the Holy Spirit and His ac-

7 Saying, The Son of man must be delivered into the hands of sinful men, and be crucified, and the third day rise again.

8 And [w]they remembered his words,

9 [x]And returned from the sepulchre, and told all these things unto the eleven, and to all the rest.

10 It was Mary Magdalene, and [y]Joanna, and Mary *the mother* of James, and other *women that were* with them, which told these things unto the apostles.

11 [z]And their words seemed to them as idle tales, and they believed them not.

12 [a]Then arose Peter, and ran unto the sepulchre; and stooping down, he beheld the linen clothes laid by themselves, and departed, wondering in himself at that which was come to pass.

The walk to Emmaus

13 ¶ [b]And, behold, two of them went that same day to a village called Emmaus, which was from Jerusalem *about* threescore furlongs.

14 And they talked together of all these things which had happened.

15 And it came to pass, that, while they communed *together* and reasoned, [c]Jesus himself drew near, and went with them.

16 But [d]their eyes were holden that they should not know him.

17 And he said unto them, What manner of communications *are* these that ye have one to another, as ye walk, and are sad?

18 And the one of them, [e]whose name was Cleopas, answering said unto him, Art thou only a stranger in Jerusalem, and hast not known the things which are come to pass there in these days?

19 And he said unto them, What things? And they said unto him, Concerning Jesus of Nazareth, [f]which was a prophet [g]mighty in deed and word before God and all the people:

20 [h]And how the chief priests and our rulers delivered him to be condemned to death, and have crucified him.

21 But we trusted [i]that it had been he which should have redeemed Israel: and beside all this, today is the third day since these things were done.

22 Yea, and [j]certain women also of our company made us astonished, which were early at the sepulchre;

23 And when they found not his body, they came, saying, that they had also seen a vision of angels, which said that he was alive.

24 And [k]certain of them which were with us went to the sepulchre, and found *it* even so as the women had said: but him they saw not.

25 Then he said unto them, O fools, and slow of heart to believe all that the prophets have spoken:

26 [l]Ought not Christ to have suffered these things, and to enter into his glory?

27 [m]And beginning at [n]Moses and [o]all the prophets, he expounded unto them in all the scriptures the things concerning himself.

28 And they drew nigh unto the village, whither they went: and [p]he made as though he would have gone further.

29 But [q]they constrained him, saying, Abide with us: for it is toward evening, and the day is far spent. And he went in to tarry with them.

24:8 [w]John 2:22 **24:9** [x]Mat. 28:8 Mark 16:10 **24:10** [y]ch. 8:3 **24:11** [z]ver. 25 **24:12** [a]John 20:3 **24:13** [b]Mark 16:12 **24:15** [c]Mat. 18:20 **24:16** [d]John 20:14 & 21:4 **24:18** [e]John 19:25 **24:19** [f]Mat. 21:11 ch. 7:16 John 3:2 & 4:19 & 6:14 Acts 2:22 [g]Acts 7:22 **24:20** [h]ch. 23:1 Acts 13:27 **24:21** [i]ch. 1:68 & 2:38 Acts 1:6 **24:22** [j]ver. 9,10 Mat. 28:8 Mark 16:10 John 20:18 **24:24** [k]ver. 12 **24:26** [l]Acts 17:3 1 Pet. 1:11 **24:27** [m]ver. 45 [n]Gen. 3:15 & 22:18 & 26:4 & 49:10 Num. 21:9 Deut. 18:15 [o]Ps. 16:9,10 & 22 & 132:11 Is. 7:14 & 9:6 & 40:10,11 & 50:6 Jer. 23:5 & 33:14,15 Ezek. 34:23 & 37:25 Dan. 9:24 Mic. 7:20 Mal. 3:1 & 4:2 See John 1:45

24:28 [p]Gen. 32:26 & 42:7; Mark 6:48 **24:29** [q]Gen. 19:3; Acts 16:15

companying manifestations within the church. That the Holy Spirit was poured forth at Pentecost as an experiential reality is proof that Jesus had risen and was exalted at the right hand of God (cf. Acts 1:3–5; 2:33). If Christ had not risen, there would have been no experiential baptism in the Holy Spirit (cf. John 16:7).

(5) The millions of people throughout the last 2,000 years who have experienced in their own hearts and lives the presence of Jesus and the witness of the Holy Spirit.

24:15 JESUS HIMSELF DREW NEAR. For the post-resurrection appearances of Christ, see Mat. 28:9, note.

24:19 JESUS . . . A PROPHET. The Gospel writers understood Jesus as "the prophet" sent from God (cf. Deut. 18:15–16,19; Mark 6:4; Acts 3:22; see Luke 6:23, note).

24:27 HE EXPOUNDED . . . THE SCRIPTURES. The Messiah and His redemptive work through suffering is a central theme in the O.T. Christ may have cited such passages as Gen. 3:15; 22:18; 49:10; Num. 24:17; Ps. 22:1,18; 110:1; Is. 25:8; 52:14; 53; Jer. 23:5; Dan. 2:24,35,44; Mic. 5:2; Zech. 3:8; 9:9; 13:7; Mal. 3:1 (see article on CHRIST IN THE OLD TESTAMENT, p. 562).

30 And it came to pass, as he sat at
meat with them, [r]he took bread, and
blessed *it,* and brake, and gave to
them.
31 And their eyes were opened, and
they knew him; and he [8]vanished out
of their sight.
32 And they said one to another,
Did not our heart burn within us, while
he talked with us by the way, and while
he opened to us the scriptures?
33 And they rose up the same hour,
and returned to Jerusalem, and found
the eleven gathered together, and
them that were with them,
34 Saying, The Lord is risen indeed,
and [s]hath appeared to Simon.
35 And they told what things *were*
done in the way, and how he was
known of them in breaking of bread.

Jesus appears to the ten

36 ¶ [t]And as they thus spake,
Jesus himself stood in the midst of
them, and saith unto them, Peace *be*
unto you.
37 But they were terrified and af-
frighted, and supposed that they had
seen [u]a spirit.
38 And he said unto them, Why are
ye troubled? and why do thoughts arise
in your hearts?
39 Behold my hands and my feet,
that it is I myself: [v]handle me, and
see; for a spirit hath not flesh and
bones, as ye see me have.
40 And when he had thus spoken,
he showed them *his* hands and *his* feet.

24:30 [r]Mat. 14:19
24:34 [s]1 Cor. 15:5
24:36 [t]Mark 16:14 John 20:19 1 Cor. 15:5
24:37 [u]Mark 6:49
24:39 [v]John 20:20
24:41 [w]Gen. 45:26 [x]John 21:5
24:43 [y]Acts 10:41
24:44 [z]ver. 6 Mat. 16:21 & 17:22 & 20:18 Mark 8:31 ch. 9:22 & 18:31
24:45 [a]Acts 16:14
24:46 [b]Ps. 22 Acts 17:3
24:47 [c]Dan. 9:24 Acts 13:38 [d]Ps. 22:27 Jer. 31:34 Mic. 4:2
24:48 [e]Acts 1:8
24:49 [f]Is. 44:3 Joel 2:28
24:50 [g]Acts 1:12

41 And while they yet believed not
[w]for joy, and wondered, he said unto
them, [x]Have ye here any meat?
42 And they gave him a piece of a
broiled fish, and of an honeycomb.
43 [y]And he took *it,* and did eat be-
fore them.
44 And he said unto them, [z]These
are the words which I spake unto you,
while I was yet with you, that all things
must be fulfilled, which were written in
the law of Moses, and *in* the prophets,
and *in* the psalms, concerning me.
45 Then [a]opened he their under-
standing, that they might understand
the scriptures,

Evangelize with power from on high

46 And said unto them, [b]Thus it is
written, and thus it behooved Christ to
suffer, and to rise from the dead the
third day:
47 And that repentance and [c]re-
mission of sins should be preached in
his name [d]among all nations, begin-
ning at Jerusalem.
48 And [e]ye are witnesses of these
things. John 1:7
49 ¶ [f]And, behold, I send the
promise of my Father upon you: but
tarry ye in the city of Jerusalem, until
ye be endued with power from on high. John 1:32-33

Jesus' ascension

50 ¶ And he led them out [g]as far as

[8] Or, *ceased to be seen of them*

24:39 A SPIRIT HATH NOT FLESH. Christ's statement that "a spirit hath not flesh and bones" does not imply that a spirit has no form or body, but only that they do not have bodies as humans do. Jesus has a glorified, spiritual body (Phil. 3:20–21), as do the saints in heaven (1 Cor. 15:40).

24:46 TO RISE FROM THE DEAD. See Mat. 28:6, note.

24:47 REPENTANCE AND REMISSION OF SINS. The disciples were not to preach forgiveness of sins without the demand of repentance. The preacher who offers salvation on the basis of an easy faith or by a mere acceptance of free salvation devoid of a commitment to obey Christ and His Word, preaches a false gospel. Repentance involves forsaking sin; this has always been an essential element in the true gospel of the N.T. (see Mat. 3:2, note on repentance).

24:47 SHOULD BE PREACHED. For comments on the Great Commission, see Mat. 28:19, note.

24:47 AMONG ALL NATIONS. Christ Himself institutes Christian missions as a holy and mandatory task of the church. Missions is a main theme in both the O.T. (Gen. 22:18; 1 Ki. 8:41–43; Ps. 72:8–11; Is. 2:3; 45:22–25) and the N.T. (Mat. 28:19; Acts 1:8; 28:28; Eph. 2:14–18).

24:49 THE PROMISE OF MY FATHER. The "promise of my Father" that will bring "power from on high" refers to the outpouring of the Holy Spirit that began at Pentecost (see 2:4, note; see article on BAPTISM IN THE HOLY SPIRIT, p. 1652); we find this promise recorded in the O.T. (Is. 32:15; 44:3; Ezek. 39:29; Joel 2:28) and in the N.T. (John 14:16–17,26; 15:26; 16:7; Acts 1:4–8; 2:33, 38–39). The disciples waited for this promise in praise to God and in devoted prayer (Acts 1:14, note). The believer today seeking the baptism in the Holy Spirit should do the same.

24:50 HE . . . BLESSED THEM. The blessing of God on the lives of His followers is essential. Concerning God's blessing, Scripture teaches several things.

(1) The word "blessing" (Gk. *eulogia*) has the meaning of: (a) a divine gift causing our work to

to Bethany, and he lifted up his hands, and blessed them.

51 [h]And it came to pass, while he blessed them, he was parted from them, and carried up into heaven.

24:51 [h]Mark 16:19
24:52 [i]Mat. 28:9
24:53 [j]Acts 2:46

52 [i]And they worshipped him, and returned to Jerusalem with great joy:

53 And were continually [j]in the temple, praising and blessing God. Amen.

succeed (Deut. 28:12); (b) God's presence with us (Gen. 26:3); (c) God giving us strength, power, and help (Eph. 3:16; Col. 1:11); and (d) God working in and through us to produce good (Phil. 2:13).

(2) In the O.T., words related to "blessing" occur more than 400 times. The first thing God did in relation to humanity was to bless them (Gen. 1:28). God also sustains His work by His blessing (Ezek. 34:26). The life and history of God's people are under the operation of blessing and cursing (Deut. 11:26ff).

(3) In the N.T. the whole work of Christ can be summed up by the statement that God has "sent him to bless you" (Acts 3:26). We see His blessing given to children (Mark 10:13–16) and to His followers during His departure from earth (vv. 50–51). Blessing is likewise deeply involved in the ministry of the apostles (Rom. 15:29).

(4) The blessing of God is conditional. God's people must make a choice: either blessing by obedience or cursing by disobedience (Deut. 30:15–18; Jer. 17:5,7).

(5) How do we receive the Lord's blessing? Three things are required: (a) We must always look to Jesus for His blessing on our ministry, work, lives, and family (Heb. 12:2). (b) We must believe in, love, and obey Him (cf. Mat. 5:3–11; 24:45–46; Rev. 1:3; 16:15; 22:7). (c) We must remove everything from our lives that would hinder the blessing (Rom. 13:12; Eph. 4:22; Heb. 12:1).

(6) God's "blessing" may not be equated with personal material gain or the absence of suffering in our lives (see Heb. 11:37–39; Rev. 2:8–10).

ST. JOHN

Outline

The Logos Prologue (1:1–18)
- I. Introduction of the Christ to Israel (1:19–51)
  - A. By John the Baptist (1:19–36)
  - B. To the First Disciples (1:37–51)
- II. Christ's Signs and Discourses to Israel and His Rejection (2:1—12:50)
  - A. Christ's Revelation to Israel (2:1—11:46)
    1. First Sign: The Water into Wine (2:1–11)
       Interlude (2:12)
    2. Initial Witness to the Jews in Jerusalem (2:13–25)
       Feast in Jerusalem (Passover) (2:23–25)
    3. First Discourse: New Birth and New Life (3:1–21)
       Interlude: About John the Baptist and Jesus (3:22—4:3)
    4. Second Discourse: The Water of Life (4:4–42)
       Interlude in Galilee (4:43–45)
    5. Second Sign: Healing the Nobleman's Son (4:46–54)
       Feast in Jerusalem (5:1)
    6. Third Sign: Healing the Paralytic at Bethesda on the Sabbath (5:2–18)
    7. Third Discourse: The Divine Sonship of Christ (5:19–47)
    8. Fourth Sign: Feeding the Five Thousand (6:1–15)
    9. Fifth Sign: Walking on the Water (6:16–21)
    10. Fourth Discourse: The Bread of Life (6:22–59)
    11. Sifting of the Disciples (6:60–71)
        Interlude (7:1)
    12. Feast in Jerusalem (Tabernacles) (7:2–36)
    13. Fifth Discourse: The Life-Giving Spirit (7:37–52)
        [Woman Taken in Adultery (7:53—8:11)]
    14. Sixth Discourse: The Light of the World (8:12–30)
    15. Debate with the Jews (8:31–59)
    16. Sixth Sign: Healing the Man Born Blind (9:1–41)
    17. Seventh Discourse: The Good Shepherd (10:1–21)
        Feast in Jerusalem (Dedication) 10:22–42
    18. Seventh Sign: The Raising of Lazarus (11:1–46)
  - B. Christ's Rejection by Israel (11:47—12:50)
- III. Christ and the Inception of the New Covenant People (13:1—20:31)
  - A. The Last Supper (13:1—14:31)
    1. Washing the Disciples' Feet and Subsequent Conversation (13:1–38)
    2. Jesus the Way to the Father (14:1–31)
  - B. Discourse on the True Vine and the Consequences of Union with Christ (15:1—16:33)
  - C. Prayer of Consecration for Himself and the New Covenant People (17:1–26)
  - D. The Suffering Servant (18:1—19:42)
    1. The Arrest (18:1–12)
    2. The Jewish Trial (18:13–27)
    3. The Roman Trial (18:28—19:16)

4. Crucifixion (19:17–37)
5. Burial (19:38–42)

E. The Risen Lord (20:1–29)
1. Discovery of the Empty Tomb (20:1–10)
2. Appearances of the Risen Lord (20:11–29)

The Author's Statement of Purpose (20:30–31)
The Epilogue (21:1–25)

Author: John

Theme: Jesus, the Son of God

Date of Writing: A.D. 80–95

Background

John's Gospel is unique among the four Gospels. It records much about Jesus' ministry in Judea and Jerusalem that the Synoptics omit, and reveals more fully the mystery of His personhood. The author is identified indirectly as "the disciple, whom Jesus loved" (13:23; 19:26; 20:2; 21:7,20). The testimony of ancient Christianity and the internal evidence of the Gospel itself point to authorship by John the son of Zebedee, one of the twelve original apostles and a member of Jesus' inner circle (Peter, James, and John).

According to several ancient sources, the elderly apostle John, while residing at Ephesus, was requested by the elders of Asia to write this "spiritual Gospel" in order to counteract and refute a dangerous heresy about the nature, person, and deity of Jesus led by a persuasive Jew named Cerinthus. John's Gospel continues to serve the church as a profound theological statement about "the truth" as it is incarnate in Jesus Christ.

Purpose

John states his purpose for writing in 20:31, namely, "that ye might believe that Jesus is the Christ, the Son of God; and that believing ye might have life through his name." Ancient Greek manuscripts of John have one of two tenses for the word "believe" (20:31): the aorist subjunctive ("that you might begin believing") and the present subjunctive ("that you might go on believing"). If John intended the former, he wrote to convince unbelievers to believe on the Lord Jesus Christ and be saved. If the latter, John wrote to strengthen the foundations of faith so that believers might go on believing in spite of false teaching, and so enter fully into fellowship with the Father and the Son (cf. 17:3). While both of these purposes find support in John, the content of the Gospel as a whole favors the latter emphasis as the overriding purpose.

Survey

The fourth Gospel presents carefully selected evidence that Jesus was Israel's Messiah and God's incarnate (not adopted) Son. The supporting evidence includes (1) seven signs (2:1–11; 4:46–54; 5:2–18; 6:1–15; 6:16–21; 9:1–41; 11:1–46) and seven discourses (3:1–21; 4:4–42; 5:19–47; 6:22–59; 7:37–44; 8:12–30; 10:1–21) by which Jesus disclosed clearly His true identity; (2) seven "I am" statements (6:35; 8:12; 10:7; 10:11; 11:25; 14:6; 15:1) by which Jesus revealed figuratively what He is redemptively for the human race; and (3) the bodily resurrection of Jesus as the ultimate sign and the climactic proof that He is "the Christ, the Son of God" (20:31).

John has two major divisions. (1) Chs. 1–12 present the incarnation and public ministry of Jesus. In spite of Jesus' seven convincing signs, seven profound discourses, and seven astounding "I am" claims, the Jews rejected Him as their Messiah. (2) Having been rejected by the old covenant Israel, Jesus then (chs. 13–21) focused on His disciples as the nucleus of the new covenant people (i.e., the church which He founded). These chapters include Jesus' last supper (ch. 13), His last discourses (chs. 14–16), and His final prayer with His disciples (ch. 17). The new covenant was then initiated and established by His death (chs. 18–19) and resurrection (chs. 20–21).

Special Features

Eight major features and emphases characterize John's Gospel. (1) It emphasizes the deity of Jesus as "the Son of God". From John's prologue with its grand declaration, "we beheld his glory" (1:14), to the conclusion of Thomas' confession, "my Lord and my God" (20:28), Jesus is God the Son come in the flesh. (2) The word "believe" occurs 98 times, is the equivalent of receiving Christ (1:12), and involves a heart (not just a mental) response that results in an ongoing commitment of one's whole life to Him. (3) "Eternal life" is a key Johannine concept and refers not so much to endless existence as to a changed quality of life now that comes through a saving union with Christ, resulting in freedom from slavery to sin and demons, and a growing knowledge and fellowship with God. (4) Personal encounters with Jesus are featured throughout the Gospel (no less than twenty-seven). (5) The ministry of the Holy Spirit enables believers to experience Jesus' life and power in an ongoing way after His death and resurrection. (6) It emphasizes "Truth"—Jesus is the truth, the Holy Spirit is the Spirit of truth, and God's Word is truth. Truth sets people free (8:32), cleanses them (15:3), and is the antithesis of Satan's nature and activity (8:44–47,51). (7) The number seven is prominent: seven signs, seven discourses, and seven "I AM" claims testify to who Jesus is (cf. the prominence of the number "seven" in the book of Revelation by the same author). (8) Other prominent Johannine words and concepts are: "light," "word," "flesh," "love," "witness," "know," "darkness," and "world."

Reading John

In order to read the entire New Testament in one year, the book of John should be read in 37 days, according to the following schedule:
☐ 1:1–18 ☐ 1:19–51 ☐ 2 ☐ 3:1–21 ☐ 3:22–36 ☐ 4:1–26 ☐ 4:27–54 ☐ 5:1–30 ☐ 5:31–47 ☐ 6:1–24 ☐ 6:25–59 ☐ 6:60–71 ☐ 7:1–24 ☐ 7:25—8:11 ☐ 8:12–30 ☐ 8:31–47 ☐ 8:48–59 ☐ 9 ☐ 10:1–21 ☐ 10:22–42 ☐ 11:1–16 ☐ 11:17–57 ☐ 12:1–19 ☐ 12:20–50 ☐ 13:1–30 ☐ 13:31—14:14 ☐ 14:15–31 ☐ 15:1–17 ☐ 15:18—16:16 ☐ 16:17–33 ☐ 17 ☐ 18:1–27 ☐ 18:28—19:16 ☐ 19:17–42 ☐ 20:1–18 ☐ 20:19–31 ☐ 21

NOTES

Jesus the eternal God

1 IN THE beginning [a]was the Word,
and the Word was [b]with God,
[c]and the Word was God.
2 [d]The same was in the beginning
with God.
3 [e]All things were made by him;
and without him was not any thing
made that was made.
4 [f]In him was life; and [g]the life
was the light of men.
5 And [h]the light shineth in dark-
ness; and the darkness comprehended
it not.

John the forerunner of Christ

6 ¶ [i]There was a man sent from
God, whose name *was* John.
7 [j]The same came for a witness, to
bear witness of the Light, that all *men*
through him might believe.
8 He was not that Light, but *was*
sent to bear witness of that Light.

Christ rejected

9 [k]*That* was the true Light, which
lighteth every man that cometh into
the world.
10 He was in the world, and [l]the
world was made by him, and the world
knew him not.
11 [m]He came unto his own, and his
own received him not.

Christ accepted

12 But [n]as many as received him,

1:1 [a]Prov. 8:22; 1 John 1:1 [b]Prov. 8:30; ch. 17:5 [c]1 John 5:7 **1:2** [d]Gen. 1:1 **1:3** [e]Ps. 33:6; Eph. 3:9; Col. 1:16 **1:4** [f]1 John 5:11 [g]ch. 8:12 **1:5** [h]ch. 3:19 **1:6** [i]Mal. 3:1; Mat. 3:1; Luke 3:2 **1:7** [j]Acts 19:4 **1:9** [k]Is. 49:6 **1:10** [l]Heb. 1:2 **1:11** [m]Luke 19:14 **1:12** [n]Gal. 3:26

1:1 THE WORD. John begins his Gospel by calling Jesus "the Word" (Gk. *logos*). In using this designation for Christ, John presents Him as the personal Word of God and indicates that in these last days God has spoken to us by His Son (cf. Heb. 1:1–3). The Scriptures declare that Jesus Christ is the manifold wisdom of God (1 Cor. 1:30; Eph. 3:10–11; Col. 2:2–3) and the perfect revelation of the nature and person of God (John 1:3–5,14,18; Col. 2:9). Just as a person's words reveal his heart and mind, Christ as "the Word" reveals the heart and mind of God (14:9; see article on THE WORD OF GOD, p. 1064). John gives us three main characteristics of Jesus Christ as "the Word."

(1) The Word's relation to the Father. (a) Christ was preexistent "with God" before the creation of the world (cf. Col. 1:15). He was a person existing from eternity, distinct from but in eternal fellowship with God the Father. (b) Christ was divine ("the Word was God"), having the same nature and essence as the Father (Col. 2:9; see Mark 1:11, note).

(2) The Word's relation to the world. It was through Christ that God the Father created and now sustains the world (v. 3; Col. 1:16; Heb. 1:2).

(3) The Word's relation to humanity. "The Word was made flesh" (v. 14). In Jesus, God became a human being, having the same nature as man but without sin. This is the basic statement of the incarnation: Christ left heaven and entered the condition of human life through the gateway of human birth (see Mat. 1:23, note).

1:2 IN THE BEGINNING WITH GOD. Christ was not created; He is eternal, and He has always been in loving fellowship with the Father and the Holy Spirit (see Mark 1:11, note on the Trinity).

1:4 LIFE . . . THE LIGHT OF MEN. True and genuine life is embodied in Christ (cf. 14:6; 17:3). His life was the light for everyone, i.e., God's truth, nature, purpose, and power are made available to all people through Him (8:12; 12:35–36,46).

1:5 LIGHT SHINETH IN DARKNESS. The light of Christ shines in an evil and sinful world, controlled by Satan. The majority of the world has not accepted His life or light, but the darkness has not "comprehended it" (i.e., mastered it, won over it).

1:9 LIGHTETH EVERY MAN. Christ illumines every person who hears His gospel by imparting a measure of grace and understanding in order that the person may freely choose to accept or reject that message. Apart from this light of Christ, there is no other light by which we may see the truth and be saved.

1:10 THE WORLD KNEW HIM NOT. The "world" refers to the whole of society organized and operating independently of God, His Word, and His rule. The world will never know Christ; it will remain indifferent to or an enemy of Christ and His gospel until the end of the age (see Jas. 4:4). For John the world is the great opponent of the Savior in salvation history (cf. Jas. 4:4; 1 John 2:15–17; 4:5).

1:12 RECEIVED . . . BELIEVE. This verse depicts clearly how saving faith is both the act of a single instant and an attitude of a life. (1) To become a child of God, one must "receive" (Gk. *elabon*, from *lambanō*) Christ. The past tense here denotes a definite act of faith. (2) Following the act of faith, there must be a continual action of believing. The verb "believe" (Gk. *pisteuousin*, from *pisteuō*) is a present active participle, indicating the need of perseverance in believing. In order for one to be finally saved, true faith must continue after the initial act of accepting Christ (Mat. 10:22; 24:12–13; Col. 1:21–23; Heb. 3:6,12–15).

1:12 SONS OF GOD. People have the power (i.e., the right) to become the adopted children of God only if they are believing in the name of Christ. When they receive Him, they are born again and become God's children (3:1–21). Not all people are "sons of God."

1:12 BELIEVE. It is important to note that John never uses the noun "belief" (Gk. *pistis*). Yet he uses the verb "believe" (*pisteuō*) 98 times. For John, saving faith is an activity, something that people do. True faith is not a static belief and trust in Jesus and His redeeming work, but a loving,

to them gave he [a]power to become the sons of God, *even* to them that believe on his name:

13 [o]Which were born, not of blood, nor of the will of the flesh, nor of the will of man, but of God.

The incarnation of Christ

14 [p]And the Word [q]was made [r]flesh, and dwelt among us, (and [s]we beheld his glory, the glory as of the only begotten of the Father,) [t]full of grace and truth.

15 ¶ [u]John bare witness of him, and cried, saying, This was he of whom I spake, [v]He that cometh after me is preferred before me: [w]for he was before me.

16 And of his [x]fulness have all we received, and grace for grace.

17 For [y]the law was given by Moses, *but* [z]grace and [a]truth came by Jesus Christ.

18 [b]No man hath seen God at any time; [c]the only begotten Son, which is in the bosom of the Father, he hath declared *him*.

John's witness to himself

19 ¶ And this is [d]the record of John, when the Jews sent priests and Levites from Jerusalem to ask him, Who art thou?

20 And [e]he confessed, and denied not; but confessed, I am not the Christ.

21 And they asked him, What then? Art thou [f]Elias? And he saith, I am not. Art thou [g]that[b] prophet? And he answered, No.

22 Then said they unto him, Who art thou? that we may give an answer to them that sent us. What sayest thou of thyself?

23 [h]He said, I *am* the voice of one crying in the wilderness, Make straight the way of the Lord, as [i]said the prophet Esaias.

24 And they which were sent were of the Pharisees.

25 And they asked him, and said unto him, Why baptizest thou then, if thou be not that Christ, nor Elias, neither that prophet?

26 John answered them, saying, [j]I baptize with water: [k]but there standeth one among you, whom ye know not;

27 [l]He it is, who coming after me is preferred before me, whose shoe's latchet I am not worthy to unloose.

28 These things were done [m]in Bethabara beyond Jordan, where John was baptizing.

Jesus the Lamb of God

29 ¶ The next day John seeth Jesus coming unto him, and saith, Behold [n]the Lamb of God, [o]which [c]taketh away the sin of the world.

30 [p]This is he of whom I said, After me cometh a man which is preferred before me: for he was before me.

31 And I knew him not: but that he should be made manifest to Israel,

1:13 [o]1 Pet. 1:23 **1:14** [p]Mat. 1:16 Luke 1:31 [q]Gal. 4:4 [r]Heb. 2:11 [s]Is. 40:5 [t]Col. 1:19 **1:15** [u]ch. 3:32 [v]Mat. 3:11 Mark 1:7 Luke 3:16 [w]Col. 1:17 **1:16** [x]Col. 1:19 **1:17** [y]Ex. 20:1 [z]Rom. 5:21 [a]ch. 8:32 **1:18** [b]Ex. 33:20 Mat. 11:27 1 Tim. 6:16 [c]1 John 4:9 **1:19** [d]ch. 5:33 **1:20** [e]Luke 3:15 Acts 13:25 **1:21** [f]Mal. 4:5 [g]Deut. 18:15 **1:23** [h]Mat. 3:3 [i]Is. 40:3 **1:26** [j]Mat. 3:11 [k]Mal. 3:1 **1:27** [l]Act. 19:4 **1:28** [m]Judg. 7:24 ch. 10:40 **1:29** [n]Ex. 12:3 Is. 53:7 Acts 8:32 1 Pet. 1:19 Rev. 5:6 [o]Is. 53:11 1 Cor. 15:3 Gal. 1:4 Heb. 1:3 & 2:17 & 9:28 1 Pet. 2:24 & 3:18 1 John 2:2; & 3:5; Rev. 1:5 **1:30** [p]ver. 15,27

[a] Or, *the right*, or, *privilege* [b] Or, *a prophet?* [c] Or, *beareth*

self-abandoning commitment that constantly draws near to Him as Lord and Savior (cf. Heb. 7:25).

1:13 BORN, NOT OF . . . THE WILL OF MAN. God was under no constraint to offer us salvation through the death of Christ, other than the constraint of His own love and compassion. The initiative to bring salvation is with God.

1:14 THE WORD WAS MADE FLESH. Christ, the eternal God, became a human being (Phil. 2:5–9). Humanity and deity were united together in Him. In a humble way He entered human life and environment with all the limitations of human experiences (cf. 3:17; 6:38–42; 7:29; 9:5; 10:36).

1:14 THE ONLY BEGOTTEN. The term "the only begotten" does not mean Christ was created sometime in the past. Rather, the statement refers to His unique relationship with the Father, i.e., to the fact that he is the one and only Son of God from all eternity. His trinitarian sonship is in view here (1:1,18; 3:16,18; see Mark 1:11, note).

1:17 GRACE AND TRUTH. For those under the O.T. law there was a measure of grace as seen in the faith of the few (Gen. 5:24; 7:1; 15:6) and in the promises of forgiveness (Ex. 34:6–7; Lev. 5:17–18). Now through Christ, grace and truth are available to the fullest extent (Rom. 5:17–21). Truth is no longer veiled through the types (such as the sacrifices). "Grace for grace" (v. 16) means that a constant impartation of grace and power is given to those who believe and respond to the grace given them. Grace is the power, presence, and blessing of God experienced by those who receive Christ (see article on FAITH AND GRACE, p. 1738). Salvation does not come by our efforts to keep the law, but by the Holy Spirit and Christ's grace coming into our lives to generate our spirits and to re-create us after the image of Christ.

1:29 LAMB OF GOD. Jesus is the Lamb provided by God to be sacrificed in the place of sinners (cf. Ex. 12:3–17; Is. 53:7; see article on THE PASSOVER, p. 110). By His death, Jesus made provision for the removal of the guilt and power of sin and opened the way to God for all in the world.

[q]therefore am I come baptizing with water.

Jesus will baptize with the Holy Spirit

32 [r]And John bare record, saying, I saw the Spirit descending from heaven like a dove, and it abode upon him.

33 And I knew him not: but he that sent me to baptize with water, the same said unto me, Upon whom thou shalt see the Spirit descending, and remaining on him, [s]the same is he which baptizeth with the Holy Ghost.

John 7:38-39

34 And I saw, and bare record that this is the Son of God.

Andrew and Peter follow Jesus

1:40–42pp — Mat. 4:18–22; Mark 1:16–20; Luke 5:2–11

35 ¶ Again the next day after John stood, and two of his disciples;

36 And looking upon Jesus as he walked, he saith, [t]Behold the Lamb of God!

37 And the two disciples heard him speak, and they followed Jesus.

38 Then Jesus turned, and saw them following, and saith unto them, What seek ye? They said unto him, Rabbi, (which is to say, being interpreted, Master,) where [d]dwellest thou?

39 He saith unto them, Come and see. They came and saw where he dwelt, and abode with him that day: for it was [e]about the tenth hour.

40 One of the two which heard John *speak,* and followed him, was Andrew, Simon Peter's brother.

41 He first findeth his own brother Simon, and saith unto him, We have found the Messias, which is, being interpreted, [f]the Christ.

42 And he brought him to Jesus. And when Jesus beheld him, he said, Thou art Simon the son of Jona: [u]thou shalt be called Cephas, which is by interpretation, [g]A stone.

Philip and Nathanael follow Jesus

43 ¶ The day following Jesus would go forth into Galilee, and findeth Philip, and saith unto him, Follow me.

44 Now [v]Philip was of Bethsaida, the city of Andrew and Peter.

45 Philip findeth [w]Nathanael, and saith unto him, We have found him, of whom [x]Moses in the law, and the [y]prophets, did write, Jesus [z]of Nazareth, the son of Joseph.

46 And Nathanael said unto him, [a]Can there any good thing come out of Nazareth? Philip saith unto him, Come and see.

47 Jesus saw Nathanael coming to him, and saith of him, Behold [b]an Israelite indeed, in whom is no guile!

48 Nathanael saith unto him, Whence knowest thou me? Jesus answered and said unto him, Before that Philip called thee, when thou wast under the fig tree, I saw thee.

49 Nathanael answered and saith unto him, Rabbi, [c]thou art the Son of God; thou art [d]the King of Israel.

50 Jesus answered and said unto him, Because I said unto thee, I saw thee under the fig tree, believest thou? thou shalt see greater things than these.

51 And he saith unto him, Verily, verily, I say unto you, [e]Hereafter ye shall see heaven open, and the angels of God ascending and descending upon the Son of man.

Water made into wine

2 AND THE third day there was a marriage in [f]Cana of Galilee; and the mother of Jesus was there:

2 And both Jesus was called, and his disciples, to the marriage.

3 And when they wanted wine, the

1:31 [q]Mal. 3:1 Mat. 3:6 Luke 1:17,76,77 & 3:3,4
1:32 [r]Mat. 3:16 Mark. 1:10 ch. 5:32
1:33 [s]Mat. 3:11 Acts 2:4 & 10:44
1:36 [t]ver. 29
1:42 [u]Mat. 16:18
1:44 [v]ch. 12:21
1:45 [w]ch. 21:2 [x]Gen. 3:15 & 49:10 Deut. 18:18 See Luke 24:27 [y]Is. 4:2 & 7:14 & 9:6 Mic. 5:2 Zech. 6:12 See more on Luke 24:27 [z]Mat. 2:23 Luke 2:4
1:46 [a]ch. 7:41,42
1:47 [b]Ps. 32:2 & 73:1 ch. 8:39 Rom. 2:28 & 9:6
1:49 [c]Mat. 14:33 [d]Mat. 21:5 ch. 18:37
1:51 [e]Gen. 28:12 Mat. 4:11 Luke 2:9,13 & 22:43 Acts 1:10
2:1 [f]See Josh. 19:28

[d] Or, *abidest* [e] *That was two hours before night* [f] Or, *the Anointed* [g] Or, *Peter*

1:33 BAPTIZETH WITH THE HOLY GHOST. The word "with" is a translation of the Greek preposition *en* and can be rendered "by," "with," or "in." Hence, an alternate translation would be "he which baptizeth in the Holy Ghost," just as "baptize with water" may be rendered "baptize in water."

All the Gospels emphasize that Jesus is "he which baptizeth with [in] the Holy Ghost" (Mat. 3:11; Mark 1:8; Luke 3:16; John 1:33). This baptism was to be the sign and dynamic mark of the followers of Jesus. The Holy Spirit would be poured out on them in order that they might carry on His saving work in all the world (cf. Acts 1:8). Jesus' task of baptizing in the Spirit is His ongoing purpose throughout this age (see Mat. 3:11, note; Acts 2:39, note).

1:51 YE SHALL SEE HEAVEN OPEN. Jesus represents Himself as the ladder by which God's revelation comes to the world (cf. Gen. 28:12; see also Luke 5:24, note on the term "Son of man").

2:3 WINE. The word "wine" (Gk. *oinos*) in the N.T. is a generic term and can refer to either fermented wine or unfermented wine (see articles on

mother of Jesus saith unto him, They
have no wine.
4 Jesus saith unto her, [g]Woman,
[h]what have I to do with thee? [i]mine
hour is not yet come.
5 His mother saith unto the ser-
vants, Whatsoever he saith unto you,
do *it*.
6 And there were set there six wa-
terpots of stone, [j]after the manner of
the purifying of the Jews, containing
two or three firkins apiece.
7 Jesus saith unto them, Fill the wa-
terpots with water. And they filled
them up to the brim.
8 And he saith unto them, Draw out
now, and bear unto the governor of the
feast. And they bare *it*.
9 When the ruler of the feast had
tasted [k]the water that was made
wine, and knew not whence it was: (but
the servants which drew the water

2:4 [g]ch. 19:26 [h]2 Sam. 16:10 [i]ch. 7:6
2:6 [j]Mark 7:3
2:9 [k]ch. 4:46
2:11 [l]ch. 1:14
2:12 [m]Mat. 12:46
2:13 [n]Ex. 12:14 Deut. 16:1 ch. 5:1

knew;) the governor of the feast called
the bridegroom,
10 And saith unto him, Every man
at the beginning doth set forth good
wine; and when men have well drunk,
then that which is worse: *but* thou hast
kept the good wine until now.
11 This beginning of miracles did
Jesus in Cana of Galilee, [l]and mani-
fested forth his glory; and his disciples
believed on him.
12 ¶ After this he went down to Ca-
pernaum, he, and his mother, and [m]his
brethren, and his disciples: and they
continued there not many days.

The cleansing of the temple

2:14–16pp — Mat. 21:12–13; Mark 11:15–17; Luke 19:45–46

13 ¶ [n]And the Jews' passover was
at hand, and Jesus went up to Jerusa-
lem,

WINE IN NEW TESTAMENT TIMES (1) and (2), p. 1538 and p. 1594). The nature of *oinos* must be determined by context and moral likelihood.

2:3 THEY HAVE NO WINE. In contrast to the position taken here, some believe that both the wine provided at the wedding and the wine made by Jesus were intoxicants, consumed in great quantity. If this thesis were accepted, then the following implications must be acknowledged and reckoned with: (1) The guests at the wedding would likely be drunk. (2) Mary, the mother of Jesus, would be regretting that the intoxicating drink had run out and would be asking Jesus to furnish the already drunken festivity with more fermented wine. (3) Jesus would be making, in order to oblige the wishes of His mother (v. 3), 120–180 gallons of intoxicating wine (vv. 6–9), more than a sufficient amount to keep all the guests totally drunk. (4) Jesus would be making this intoxicating wine as His very first "miracle" in order to "manifest his glory" (v. 11) and to persuade people to believe on Him as the holy and righteous Son of God.

The above implications of the thesis in question cannot be avoided. To allege that Christ made and used alcoholic wine is not only beyond the warrant of exegetical requirement, but leads us into conflict with moral principles that are embedded in the total witness of Scripture. Clearly in light of God's nature, Christ's righteousness, His loving concern for humanity, and Mary's good character, the implications of the view that the wine at Cana was fermented are blasphemous. An interpretation that involves such assertions and contradictions cannot be adopted. The only plausible and credible explanation is that the wine made by Jesus to manifest His glory was the nonintoxicating pure juice of the grape. Furthermore, the initial inferior wine furnished by the one in charge of the wedding was most likely nonintoxicating as well. For further discussion of this issue, see article on WINE IN NEW TESTAMENT TIMES (2), p. 1594.

2:10 GOOD WINE. According to various ancient writers, the "good" (or best) wine was the sweetest wine—one that could be drunk freely and in large quantities without harm (i.e., wine that had not had its sugar content destroyed through fermentation). The "worse" wine was that which had been diluted with too much water.

(1) The Roman writer Pliny affirms this. He expressly states that "good wine," called *sapa*, was not fermented. *Sapa* was grape juice boiled down to one-third of its bulk to increase its sweet flavor (IV.13). He writes elsewhere that "wines are most beneficial when all their potency has been removed by the strainer" (Pliny, *Natural History*, XIV.23–24). Pliny, Plutarch, and Horace all suggest that the best wine was the type that was "harmless and innocent."

(2) Rabbinical witnesses affirm that some rabbis recommended boiled wine. The Mishna says: "Rabbi Yehuda permits it [boiled wine as heave-offering], because it improves it."

(3) It is significant that the Greek adjective translated "good" is not *agathos* but *kalos*, meaning "morally excellent or befitting."

2:10 WHEN MEN HAVE WELL DRUNK. This phrase is from the Greek word *methuskō*, a word that has two meanings: (1) to be or become drunk, and (2) to be filled or satisfied (without reference to intoxication). We ought to understand *methuskō* in 2:10 in the second of these two meanings. (1) Regardless of how one translates this text, it cannot be used to defend the thesis that fermented wine was drunk at this wedding. The master of ceremonies was merely stating a general policy, a policy that covered any wedding celebration regardless of the type of drink that was served. (2) In no way ought we to imply that Jesus participated in and contributed to a drunken party (see v. 3, note; also see article on WINE IN NEW TESTAMENT TIMES (2), p. 1594).

WINE IN NEW TESTAMENT TIMES (2)

John 2:11 "This beginning of miracles did Jesus in Cana of Galilee, and manifested forth his glory; and his disciples believed on him."

In conjunction with this article, be sure to read WINE IN NEW TESTAMENT TIMES (1), p. 1538.

WINE: MIXED OR FULL STRENGTH? Historical data concerning the making and use of wine by the Jews and other nations in the Biblical world indicate that it was (a) often unfermented and (b) normally mixed with water. The previous article on WINE IN NEW TESTAMENT TIMES (p. 1538) discusses one of the processes used in keeping freshly squeezed grape juice in a sweet and unfermented state. This article discusses two other processes of dealing with grapes, preparatory to mixing them with water.

(1) One method was to dehydrate the grapes to a proper point, sprinkle them with olive oil to keep them moist, and store them in earthenware jars (*Zondervan Pictorial Encyclopedia of the Bible*, V.882; see also Columella, *On Agriculture*, 12.44.1–8). A very sweet grape beverage could be made from these stored grapes at any time by later adding water and steeping or boiling them. Polybius indicated that the Roman women were allowed to drink this kind of grape beverage, but were forbidden to drink fermented wine (see Polybius, *Fragments*, 6.4; cf. Pliny, 14.11.81).

(2) Another method was to boil freshly squeezed grape juice until it became a thick paste or syrup (grape honey); this process made it storable, removed any intoxicating quality because of the high concentration of sugar, and preserved its sweetness (see Columella, *On Agriculture*, 12.19.1–6 and 20.1–8; Pliny, *Natural History*, 14.11.80). This was then stored in large jars or skins. The paste could be used as a jam for their bread or dissolved in water to make grape juice once again (*Zondervan Pictorial Encyclopedia of the Bible*, V.882–884). "It is probable that the grape was largely cultivated as a source of sugar: the juice expressed in the 'wine press' was reduced by boiling to a liquid . . . known as 'grape honey'" (*The International Standard Bible Encyclopedia*, V.3050). References to honey in the Bible frequently refer to grape honey (called *debash* by the Jews) rather than to the honey of the bee.

(3) Water, then, could be mixed with dehydrated grapes and with grape syrup, as well as with fermented wine. Greek and Roman authors gave various ratios that were used. Homer (*Odyssey*. IX.208f) mentions a ratio of twenty parts water to one part wine. Plutarch (*Sumposiacs*, III.ix) states, "We call a mixture 'wine,' although the larger of the component parts is water." Pliny (*Natural History*, XIV.6.54) mentions a ratio of eight parts water to one part wine.

(4) Among Jewish people in Bible times, social and religious customs mandated never serving unmixed wine, especially if it was fermented. The Talmud (a Jewish work that describes the traditions of Judaism from about 200 B.C. to A.D. 200) discusses in several tractates the mixture of water and wine (e.g., Shabbath 77a; Pesahim 1086). Some Jewish rabbis insisted that unless fermented wine was mixed with three parts water, it could not be blessed and would defile the drinker. Others demanded that ten parts of water must be mixed with one part of fermented wine before it could be acceptable.

(5) An interesting passage emerges in the book of Revelation: when speaking of "the wine of the wrath of God," an angel declares that it will be "without mixture," i.e., full strength (Rev. 14:10; see Jer. 25:15, note). It was stated in this way because the readers normally would expect all grape beverages to be mixed with water (see John 2:3, notes).

In summary, then, the normal uses of wine by the Jews in Biblical days were not the same as today. It was (a) grape juice freshly squeezed, (b) grape juice preserved, (c) juice from dried grapes, (d) grape wine made from grape syrup and water, and (e) unfermented or fermented stored wine diluted with water at a ratio as high as 20 to 1.

If the wine was fermented and served unmixed, it was considered barbaric, defiling, and incapable of being blessed by the rabbis. In the light of these facts, it is impossible to defend the modern-day practice of drinking alcoholic beverages on the basis of the Jews' use of "wine" in Biblical times. They are clearly not the same. Furthermore, Christians of Biblical days exercised a more careful attitude towards the various kinds of wines than did the Jews (see Rom. 14:21, note; 1 Thes. 5:6, note; 1 Tim. 3:3, note; Tit. 2:2, note).

JESUS' GLORY MANIFESTED THROUGH WINE. In his second chapter, John records that Jesus made "wine" out of water at a wedding at Cana. The question is, "What kind of wine?" As we have seen, it could be fermented or unfermented, full strength or diluted. We must determine our answer to this question by contextual implication and moral likelihood. The position of this study Bible is that Jesus made wine (*oinos*) that was pure unfermented grape juice. The following data support this conclusion and give strong reasons for rejecting the opinion that Jesus made intoxicating wine.

(1) The primary object of this miracle was to "manifest forth his glory" (John 2:11) in such a way as to induce personal faith and confidence in Him as the holy and righteous Son of God who came to save people from their sin (2:11; cf. Mat. 1:21). To suggest that Christ showed forth His deity as the One and Only Son of the Father (John 1:14) by miraculously creating gallons of intoxicating wine for a drunken party (note 2:10, which implies that the people had already drunk freely), and that this was immensely important to His Messianic mission, requires an irreverence few are willing to display. It would testify more to the honor of God, and the honor and glory of Christ, to believe that He supernaturally created the same juices of the grape that God makes annually through the process of His natural created order (see John 2:3, note). This miracle, therefore, points to Christ's sovereignty over the natural world and becomes a symbol of His power to transform sinful people spiritually into children of God (John 3:1–15). Because of this miracle "we beheld his glory, the glory as of the only begotten of the Father, full of grace and truth" (John 1:14; cf. 2:11).

(2) It is contrary to Scriptural revelation concerning the perfect obedience of Christ to His heavenly Father (cf. 2 Cor. 5:21; Heb. 4:15; 1 Pet. 2:22) to suppose that He disobeyed the Father's moral command, "look not thou upon the wine when it is red . . . when it moveth itself aright," i.e., when it is fermented (see Prov. 23:31, note). Indeed, Christ came to fulfill the law (Mat. 5:17) and would have supported the Biblical passage which condemns intoxicating wine as "a mocker" and "raging" (see Prov. 20:1, note) and the words of Hab. 2:15: "Woe unto him that giveth his neighbour drink . . . and makest *him* drunken" (cf. Lev. 10:8–11; Num. 6:1–5; Deut. 21:20; Prov. 31:4–7; Is. 28:7; Amos 2:8,12; 4:1; 6:6; Rom. 14:13,21).

(3) Furthermore, note the following modern medical evidence. (a) Current leading medical experts on human birth defects have found unmistakable evidence that moderate alcoholic consumption is damaging to the reproductive systems of women of child-bearing age, causing miscarriages and births of babies with incurable mental and physical defects. World authorities on early embryology maintain that women who drink even moderate amounts of alcohol around the time of conception (a 48-hour time period) risk damaging the chromosomes of an egg preparing to leave the ovary and hence, causing disastrous results to the mental and physical development of the infant. (b) It would be theologically absurd to maintain that Jesus served and encouraged the use of alcoholic beverages at a wedding which included many women as well as the young bride with the possibility of her immediate conception. To maintain that He did not know of the potential terrible effects of intoxicating drink on unborn children is to call into question His deity, wisdom, and discernment of good and evil. To maintain that He knew of the potential harm and disfiguring results of alcohol, and yet promoted and encouraged its use, is to call into question His goodness, compassion, and love.

The only sound conclusion rationally, Biblically, and theologically is that the wine which Christ made at the wedding in order to manifest His glory was pure, sweet, unfermented fruit of the vine.

14 [o]And found in the temple those that sold oxen and sheep and doves, and the changers of money sitting:

15 And when he had made a scourge of small cords, he drove them all out of the temple, and the sheep, and the oxen; and poured out the changers' money, and overthrew the tables;

16 And said unto them that sold doves, Take these things hence; make not [p]my Father's house an house of merchandise.

17 And his disciples remembered that it was written, [q]The zeal of thine house hath eaten me up.

18 ¶ Then answered the Jews and said unto him, [r]What sign showest thou unto us, seeing that thou doest these things?

19 Jesus answered and said unto them, [s]Destroy this temple, and in three days I will raise it up.

20 Then said the Jews, Forty and six years was this temple in building, and wilt thou rear it up in three days?

21 But he spake [t]of the temple of his body.

22 When therefore he was risen from the dead, [u]his disciples remembered that he had said this unto them; and they believed the scripture, and the word which Jesus had said.

23 ¶ Now when he was in Jerusalem at the passover, in the feast *day,* many believed in his name, when they saw the miracles which he did.

24 But Jesus did not commit himself unto them, because he knew all *men,*

25 And needed not that any should testify of man: for [v]he knew what was in man.

Jesus' teaching about new birth

3 THERE WAS a man of the Pharisees, named Nicodemus, a ruler of the Jews:

2 [w]The same came to Jesus by night, and said unto him, Rabbi, we know that thou art a teacher come from God: for [x]no man can do these miracles that thou doest, except [y]God be with him.

3 Jesus answered and said unto him, Verily, verily, I say unto thee, [z]Except a man be born [h]again, he cannot see the kingdom of God.

4 Nicodemus saith unto him, How can a man be born when he is old? can he enter the second time into his mother's womb, and be born?

5 Jesus answered, Verily, verily, I say unto thee, [a]Except a man be born of water and *of* the Spirit, he cannot enter into the kingdom of God.

6 That which is born of the flesh is flesh; and that which is born of the Spirit is spirit.

7 Marvel not that I said unto thee, Ye must be born [h]again.

8 [b]The wind bloweth where it listeth, and thou hearest the sound thereof, but canst not tell whence it cometh, and whither it goeth: so is every one that is born of the Spirit.

9 Nicodemus answered and said unto him, [c]How can these things be?

10 Jesus answered and said unto him, Art thou a master of Israel, and knowest not these things?

11 [d]Verily, verily, I say unto thee, We speak that we do know, and testify that we have seen; and [e]ye receive not our witness.

12 If I have told you earthly things, and ye believe not, how shall ye believe, if I tell you *of* heavenly things?

13 And [f]no man hath ascended up to heaven, but he that came down from heaven, *even* the Son of man which is in heaven.

14 ¶ [g]And as Moses lifted up the serpent in the wilderness, even so [h]must the Son of man be lifted up:

15 That whosoever believeth in him should not perish, but [i]have eternal life.

The Son given for the world

16 ¶ [j]For God so loved the world,

2:14 [o]Mat. 21:12 Mark 11:15 Luke 19:45
2:16 [p]Luke 2:49
2:17 [q]Ps. 69:9
2:18 [r]Mat. 12:38 ch. 6:30
2:19 [s]Mat. 26:61 & 27:40 Mark 14:58 & 15:29
2:21 [t]Col. 2:9 Heb. 8:2 1 Cor. 3:16 & 6:19 2 Cor. 6:16
2:22 [u]Luke 24:8
2:25 [v]1 Sam. 16:7 1 Chr. 28:9 Mat. 9:4 Mark 2:8 ch. 6:64 & 16:30 Acts 1:24 Rev. 2:23
3:2 [w]ch. 7:50 & 19:39 [x]ch. 9:16,33 Acts 2:22 [y]Acts 10:38
3:3 [z]ch. 1:13 Gal. 6:15 Tit. 3:5 Jas. 1:18 1 Pet. 1:23 1 John 3:9
3:5 [a]Mark 16:16 Acts 2:38
3:8 [b]Eccl. 11:5 1 Cor. 2:11
3:9 [c]ch. 6:52,60
3:11 [d]Mat. 11:27 ch. 1:18 & 7:16 & 8:28 [e]ver. 32
3:13 [f]Prov. 30:4 ch. 6:33,38 Acts 2:34 1 Cor. 15:47 Eph. 4:9
3:14 [g]Num. 21:9 [h]ch. 8:28 & 12:32
3:15 [i]ver. 36 ch. 6:47
3:16 [j]Rom. 5:8 1 John 4:9

[h] Or, *from above*

2:15 HE DROVE THEM ALL OUT OF THE TEMPLE. See Luke 19:45, note.

2:19 THE TEMPLE. See article on THE TEMPLE, p. 654.

3:3 BORN AGAIN. For a discussion of the Biblical doctrine of regeneration (being born again), see article on REGENERATION, p. 1597.

3:5 BORN OF WATER. Jesus was probably referring to the cleansing work of the Holy Spirit in the new birth. In Tit. 3:5 Paul speaks of "the washing of regeneration, and renewing of the Holy Ghost."

3:8 THE WIND . . . THE SPIRIT. As the wind, though unseen, is identified by its activity and sound, so also the Holy Spirit is observed by His activity in and effect on those who are born again.

3:16 GOD SO LOVED THE WORLD. This verse reveals the heart and purpose of God. (1) God's

REGENERATION

John 3:3 "Jesus answered and said unto him, Verily, verily, I say unto thee, Except a man be born again, he cannot see the kingdom of God."

In John 3:1–8, Jesus discusses one of the fundamental doctrines of the Christian faith: regeneration (Tit. 3:5) or spiritual birth. Without the new birth one cannot see the kingdom of God, i.e., receive eternal life and salvation through Jesus Christ. The following are important facts concerning the new birth.

(1) Regeneration is a re-creating and transformation of the person (Rom. 12:2; Eph. 4:23) by God the Holy Spirit (John 3:6; Tit. 3:5; see article on THE REGENERATION OF THE DISCIPLES, p. 1638). Through this process eternal life from God Himself is imparted to the believer (John 3:16; 2 Pet. 1:4; 1 John 5:11), and he becomes a child of God (John 1:12; Rom. 8:16–17; Gal. 3:26) and a new person (2 Cor. 5:17; Col. 3:9–10). He no longer conforms to this world (Rom. 12:2), but is now created after God "in righteousness and true holiness" (Eph. 4:24).

(2) Regeneration is necessary because apart from Christ, all people, by their inherent natures, are sinners, incapable of obeying and pleasing God (Ps. 51:5; Jer. 17:9; Rom. 8:7–8; 1 Cor. 2:14; Eph. 2:3).

(3) Regeneration comes to those who repent of their sin, turn to God (Mat. 3:2), and place personal faith in Jesus Christ as Lord and Savior (see John 1:12, note).

(4) Regeneration involves a transition from an old life of sin to a new life of obedience to Jesus Christ (2 Cor. 5:17; Gal. 6:15; Eph. 4:23–24; Col. 3:10). The one who is truly born again is set free from the bondage of sin (see John 8:36, note; Rom. 6:14–23) and receives a spiritual desire and disposition to obey God and follow the leading of the Spirit (Rom. 8:13–14). Those born again live righteous lives (1 John 2:29), love other believers (1 John 4:7), avoid a life of sin (1 John 3:9; 5:18), and do not love the world (1 John 2:15–16).

(5) One born of God cannot make sin a habitual practice in his life (see 1 John 3:9, note). That is, one cannot remain a child of God without a sincere desire and victorious endeavor to please Him and to avoid evil (1 John 1:5–7). This is accomplished only through the grace given to the believer by Christ (1 John 2:3–11,15–17,24–29; 3:6–24; 4:7–8,20; 5:1), through a sustained relationship with Christ (see John 15:4, note), and through a dependence on the Holy Spirit (Rom. 8:2–14).

(6) Those who do live in immorality and follow the world's ways, whatever they profess, demonstrate that they are still unregenerated and children of Satan (1 John 3:6–10).

(7) Just as one can be born of the Spirit by receiving the life of God, he can also extinguish that life by ungodly choices and unrighteous living, and hence, die spiritually. Scripture affirms, "if ye live after the flesh, ye shall die" (Rom. 8:13). Thus, sin and the refusal to follow the Holy Spirit extinguish the life of God in the soul of the believer and causes spiritual death and exclusion from the kingdom of God (cf. Mat. 12:31–32; 1 Cor. 6:9–10; Gal. 5:19–21; Heb. 6:4–6; 1 John 5:16).

(8) The new birth cannot be equated with physical birth, for the relationship of God with the believer is a matter of spirit rather than flesh (John 3:6). Hence, while the physical tie of a father and son can never be annulled, the father and son relationship which God desires with us is voluntary and not indissoluble during our probationary time on earth (see Rom. 8:13, note). Our membership in God's family remains conditional on our faith in Christ throughout our earthly existence, demonstrated by a life of sincere obedience and love (Rom. 8:12–14; 2 Tim. 2:12).

that he gave his only begotten Son, that whosoever believeth in him should not perish, but have everlasting life.

17 [k]For God sent not his Son into the world to condemn the world; but that the world through him might be saved.

John 11:25-26

18 ¶ [l]He that believeth on him is not condemned: but he that believeth not is condemned already, because he hath not believed in the name of the only begotton Son of God.

19 And this is the condemnation, [m]that light is come into the world, and men loved darkness rather than light, because their deeds were evil.

20 For [n]every one that doeth evil hateth the light, neither cometh to the light, lest his deeds should be [i]reproved.

21 But he that doeth truth cometh to the light, that his deeds may be made manifest, that they are wrought in God.

22 ¶ After these things came Jesus and his disciples into the land of Judaea; and there he tarried with them, [o]and baptized.

23 ¶ And John also was baptizing in Aenon near to [p]Salim, because there was much water there: [q]and they came, and were baptized.

24 For [r]John was not yet cast into prison.

John's testimony to Jesus

25 ¶ Then there arose a question between *some* of John's disciples and the Jews about purifying.

26 And they came unto John, and said unto him, Rabbi, he that was with thee beyond Jordan, [s]to whom thou barest witness, behold, the same baptizeth, and all *men* come to him.

27 John answered and said, [t]A man can [j]receive nothing, except it be given him from heaven.

28 Ye yourselves bear me witness, that I said, [u]I am not the Christ, but [v]that I am sent before him.

29 [w]He that hath the bride is the bridegroom: but [x]the friend of the bridegroom, which standeth and heareth him, rejoiceth greatly because of the bridegroom's voice: this my joy therefore is fulfilled.

30 He must increase, but I *must* decrease.

31 [y]He that cometh from above [z]is above all: [a]he that is of the earth is earthly, and speaketh of the earth: [b]he that cometh from heaven is above all.

32 And [c]what he hath seen and heard, that he testifieth; and no man receiveth his testimony.

33 He that hath received his testimony [d]hath set to his seal that God is true.

34 [e]For he whom God hath sent speaketh the words of God: for God giveth not the Spirit [f]by measure *unto him.*

35 [g]The Father loveth the Son, and hath given all things into his hand.

3:17 [k]Luke 9:56 ch. 5:45 & 8:15 & 12:47 1 John 4:14 **3:18** [l]ch. 5:24 & 6:40,47 & 20:31 **3:19** [m]ch. 1:4,9-11 & 8:12 **3:20** [n]Job 24:13 Eph. 5:13 **3:22** [o]ch. 4:2 **3:23** [p]1 Sam. 9:4 [q]Mat. 3:5,6 **3:24** [r]Mat. 14:3 **3:26** [s]ch. 1:7,15,27,34 **3:27** [t]1 Cor. 4:7 Heb. 5:4 Jas. 1:17 **3:28** [u]ch. 1:20,27 [v]Mal. 3:1 Mark 1:2 Luke 1:17 **3:29** [w]Mat. 22:2 2 Cor. 11:2 Eph. 5:25,27 Rev. 21:9 [x]Sol. 5:1 **3:31** [y]ver. 13 ch. 8:23 [z]Mat. 28:18 ch. 1:15,27 Rom. 9:5 [a]1 Cor. 15:47 [b]ch. 6:33 1 Cor. 15:47 Eph. 1:21 Phil. 2:9 **3:32** [c]ver. 11 ch. 8:26 & 15:15 **3:33** [d]Rom. 3:4 1 John 5:10 **3:34** [e]ch. 7:16 [f]ch. 1:16

3:35 [g]Mat. 11:27 & 28:18; Luke 10:22; ch. 5:20,22 & 13:3 & 17:2; Heb. 2:8

i Or, *discovered* j Or, *take unto himself*

love is wide enough to embrace all persons, i.e., "the world" (cf. 1 Tim. 2:4).

(2) God "gave" His Son as an offering for sin on the cross. The atonement proceeds from the loving heart of God. It was not something forced upon Him (Rom. 8:32; 1 John 4:10).

(3) To believe (Gk. *pisteuō*) includes three main elements: (a) a sure conviction that Christ is God's Son and the only Savior for lost humanity; (b) a self-surrendering fellowship with and obedience to Christ (cf. 15:1–10; see 14:21, note; 15:4, note); (c) a fully assured trust in Christ that He is both able and willing to bring you to final salvation and to fellowship with God in heaven (see article on FAITH AND GRACE, p. 1738).

(4) "Perish" is often the forgotten word of John 3:16. It points to the dreadful reality of eternal punishment (Mat. 10:28, note).

(5) "Eternal life" is the gift God bestows on us when we are born again (see article on REGENERATION, p. 1597). "Eternal" not only expresses perpetuity but also the quality of life—a divine type of life, a life that frees us from the power of sin and Satan and removes us from what is merely earthly in order to know God (cf. 8:34–36; see 17:3, note).

3:19 LOVED DARKNESS RATHER THAN LIGHT. A fundamental characteristic of the wicked is that they love darkness, i.e., they find their pleasure in sin and immorality (Rom. 1:18–32; Phil. 3:19; 2 Tim. 3:2–5; 2 Pet. 2:12–15). The truly born-again person, in contrast, loves righteousness and hates iniquity (see Heb. 1:9, note), and is grieved when he sees the unrighteous deeds of depraved people (1 Cor. 13:6). He takes no pleasure in the sensual entertainment or the expression of sinful conduct manifested so openly in present society (Ps. 97:10; Prov. 8:13; Rom. 12:9; see 2 Pet. 2:8, note; Rev. 2:6, note).

3:34 GIVETH NOT THE SPIRIT BY MEASURE. See Mat. 3:16 and Luke 3:22, notes on Jesus' anointing with the Holy Spirit; see article on JESUS AND THE HOLY SPIRIT, p. 1550.

36 [h]He that believeth on the Son hath everlasting life: and he that believeth not the Son shall not see life; but the wrath of God abideth on him.

The woman of Samaria

4 WHEN THEREFORE the Lord knew how the Pharisees had heard that Jesus made and [i]baptized more disciples than John,

2 (Though Jesus himself baptized not, but his disciples,)

3 He left Judaea, and departed again into Galilee.

4 And he must needs go through Samaria.

5 Then cometh he to a city of Samaria, which is called Sychar, near to the parcel of ground [j]that Jacob gave to his son Joseph.

6 Now Jacob's well was there. Jesus therefore, being wearied with *his* journey, sat thus on the well: *and* it was about the sixth hour.

7 There cometh a woman of Samaria to draw water: Jesus saith unto her, Give me to drink.

8 (For his disciples were gone away unto the city to buy meat.)

9 Then saith the woman of Samaria unto him, How is it that thou, being a Jew, askest drink of me, which am a woman of Samaria? for [k]the Jews have no dealings with the Samaritans.

10 Jesus answered and said unto her, If thou knewest the gift of God, and who it is that saith to thee, Give me to drink; thou wouldest have asked of him, and he would have given thee [l]living water.

11 The woman saith unto him, Sir, thou hast nothing to draw with, and the well is deep: from whence then hast thou that living water?

12 Art thou greater than our father Jacob, which gave us the well, and drank thereof himself, and his children, and his cattle?

13 Jesus answered and said unto her, Whosoever drinketh of this water shall thirst again:

14 But [m]whosoever drinketh of the water that I shall give him shall never thirst; but the water that I shall give him [n]shall be in him a well of water springing up into everlasting life.

15 [o]The woman saith unto him, Sir, give me this water, that I thirst not, neither come hither to draw.

16 Jesus saith unto her, Go, call thy husband, and come hither.

17 The woman answered and said, I have no husband. Jesus said unto her, Thou hast well said, I have no husband:

18 For thou hast had five husbands; and he whom thou now hast is not thy husband: in that saidst thou truly. John 15:26-27

19 The woman saith unto him, Sir, [p]I perceive that thou art a prophet.

20 Our fathers worshipped in [q]this mountain; and ye say, that in [r]Jerusalem is the place where men ought to worship.

21 Jesus saith unto her, Woman, believe me, the hour cometh, [s]when ye shall neither in this mountain, nor yet at Jerusalem, worship the Father.

22 Ye worship [t]ye know not what: we know what we worship: for [u]salvation is of the Jews.

23 But the hour cometh, and now is,

3:36 [h]ver. 15,16 ch. 1:12 & 6:47 Rom. 1:17 1 John 5:10
4:1 [i]ch. 3:22,26
4:5 [j]Gen. 33:19 & 48:22 Josh. 24:32
4:9 [k]2 Ki. 17:24 Luke 9:52,53 Acts 10:28
4:10 [l]Is. 12:3 & 44:3 Jer. 2:13 Zech. 13:1 & 14:8
4:14 [m]ch. 6:35,58 [n]ch. 7:38
4:15 [o]ch. 6:34 & 17:2,3 Rom. 6:23 1 John 5:20
4:19 [p]Luke 7:16 & 24:19 ch. 6:14
4:20 [q]Judg. 9:7 [r]Deut. 12:5,11 1 Ki. 9:3 2 Chr. 7:12
4:21 [s]Mal. 1:11 1 Tim. 2:8
4:22 [t]2 Ki. 17:29 [u]Is. 2:3 Luke 24:47 Rom. 9:4,5

3:36 HE THAT BELIEVETH NOT. The Greek for "believeth not" is *apeitheō* and means to "disobey" or "be not subject to"; it is contrasted to "he that believeth" (Gk. *pisteuō*) at the beginning of the verse. For John unbelief means to "not obey the Son." Faith and obedience belong together and can often be used interchangeably (compare Rom. 1:8 with 16:19; 1 Thes. 1:8; also see Rom. 15:18). The gospel comes to us as a free gift (Rom. 5:15–16; 6:23), but once accepted it does not leave us free to do as we please. It requires that we enter into the way of salvation ordained by God and subject ourselves to the righteousness of God (Rom. 10:3; see 1:5, note; see article on FAITH AND GRACE, p. 1738).

4:7 WOMAN OF SAMARIA. Jesus' conversation with the woman of Samaria reveals His commitment to the purpose of His heavenly Father and His own inner desire to bring this person to eternal life. Jesus' consuming passion was to save the lost (see Luke 15; cf. Prov. 11:30; Dan. 12:3; Jas. 5:20), a goal infinitely more important to Him than food and drink (v. 34). We must follow Jesus' example. All around us are people ready to hear God's Word. We must speak to them of their spiritual need and of Jesus, who can meet that need.

4:13–14 DRINKS THIS WATER . . . EVERLASTING LIFE. The "water" given by Christ means spiritual life (cf. Is. 12:3). To partake of this living water, one must "drink" (see 7:37). This act of drinking is not a momentary, single act, but rather a progressive or repeated drinking. Drinking the water of life requires regular communion with the source of the living water, Jesus Christ Himself. No one can continue to drink of the water of life if he becomes severed from its source. Such people will become, as Peter describes, "springs without water" (2 Pet. 2:17).

when the true worshippers shall worship the Father in [v]spirit [w]and in truth: for the Father seeketh such to worship him.

24 [x]God *is* a Spirit: and they that worship him must worship *him* in spirit and in truth.

25 The woman saith unto him, I know that Messias cometh, which is called Christ: when he is come, [y]he will tell us all things.

26 Jesus saith unto her, [z]I that speak unto thee am *he.*

The disciples rejoin Jesus

27 ¶ And upon this came his disciples, and marvelled that he talked with the woman: yet no man said, What seekest thou? or, Why talkest thou with her?

28 The woman then left her waterpot, and went her way into the city, and saith to the men,

29 Come, see a man, [a]which told me all things that ever I did: is not this the Christ?

John 15:26-27

30 Then they went out of the city, and came unto him.

31 ¶ In the mean while his disciples prayed him, saying, Master, eat.

32 But he said unto them, I have meat to eat that ye know not of.

33 Therefore said the disciples one to another, Hath any man brought him *aught* to eat?

34 Jesus saith unto them, [b]My meat is to do the will of him that sent me, and to finish his work.

35 Say not ye, There are yet four months, and *then* cometh harvest? behold, I say unto you, Lift up your eyes, and look on the fields; [c]for they are white already to harvest.

36 [d]And he that reapeth receiveth wages, and gathereth fruit unto life eternal: that both he that soweth and he that reapeth may rejoice together.

37 And herein is that saying true, One soweth, and another reapeth.

38 I sent you to reap that whereon ye bestowed no labour: other men laboured, and ye are entered into their labours.

The conversion of Samaritans

39 ¶ And many of the Samaritans of that city believed on him [e]for the saying of the woman, which testified, He told me all that ever I did.

40 So when the Samaritans were come unto him, they besought him that he would tarry with them: and he abode there two days.

41 And many more believed because of his own word;

42 And said unto the woman, Now we believe, not because of thy saying: for [f]we have heard *him* ourselves, and know that this is indeed the Christ, the Saviour of the world.

43 ¶ Now after two days he departed thence, and went into Galilee.

44 For [g]Jesus himself testified, that a prophet hath no honour in his own country.

45 Then when he was come into Galilee, the Galilaeans received him, [h]having seen all the things that he did at Jerusalem at the feast: [i]for they also went unto the feast.

4:23 [v]Phil. 3:3 [w]ch. 1:17
4:24 [x]2 Cor. 3:17
4:25 [y]ver. 29,39
4:26 [z]Mat. 26:63,64 Mark 14:61,62
4:29 [a]ver. 25
4:34 [b]Job 23:12 ch. 6:38 & 17:4 & 19:30
4:35 [c]Mat. 9:37 Luke 10:2
4:36 [d]Dan. 12:3
4:39 [e]ver. 29
4:42 [f]ch. 17:8 1 John 4:14
4:44 [g]Mat. 13:57
4:45 [h]ch. 2:23 & 3:2 [i]Deut. 16:16

4:23 WORSHIP ... IN SPIRIT AND IN TRUTH. Jesus teaches several things in this verse. (1) "In spirit" points to the level at which true worship occurs. One must come to God in complete sincerity and with a spirit that is directed by the life and activity of the Holy Spirit. (2) "Truth" (Gk. *alētheia*) is characteristic of God (Ps. 31:5; Rom. 1:25; 3:7; 15:8), incarnate in Christ (14:6; 2 Cor. 11:10; Eph. 4:21), intrinsic to the Holy Spirit (14:17; 15:26; 16:13), and at the heart of the gospel (8:32; Gal. 2:5; Eph. 1:13). Therefore, worship must take place according to the truth of the Father that is revealed in the Son and received through the Spirit. Those who advocate a worship that sets aside the truth and doctrines of the Word of God have in reality set aside the only foundation for true worship (see article on WORSHIP, p. 730).

4:24 TRUTH. Because Christ is the truth (1:14; 5:31; 14:6; Luke 4:25; 9:27; 12:44), to live in union with Christ requires speaking the truth (1 Cor. 5:8; Eph. 4:25). To claim to have fellowship with Christ and to possess salvation, yet not to live and speak according to the truth, is to be deceived (1 John 1:6). Untruth reveals the basic condition of one's heart (8:44; Acts 5:3), that one is still in fundamental opposition to God and is thus unregenerated and outside of the kingdom of heaven (Rev. 21:8,27; 22:15; cf. Rev. 14:5). A liar is of "the synagogue of Satan" (Rev. 3:9).

4:35 LOOK ON THE FIELDS. See Mat. 9:37, note.

4:36 FRUIT UNTO LIFE ETERNAL. The person who brings others to saving faith in Jesus Christ is doing something of eternal consequence. He will one day rejoice in heaven over those who were saved because of his diligence, prayers, and witness. At the same time, he must understand that his work is an entering into the labors of others (v. 38). All that we do for God is in large part the result of the sacrificial labor of Christ and others.

The healing of the nobleman's son

46 So Jesus came again into Cana of Galilee, [j]where he made the water wine. And there was a certain [k]nobleman, whose son was sick at Capernaum.

47 When he heard that Jesus was come out of Judaea into Galilee, he went unto him, and besought him that he would come down, and heal his son: for he was at the point of death.

48 Then said Jesus unto him, [k]Except ye see signs and wonders, ye will not believe.

49 The nobleman saith unto him, Sir, come down ere my child die.

50 Jesus saith unto him, Go thy way; thy son liveth. And the man believed the word that Jesus had spoken unto him, and he went his way.

51 And as he was now going down, his servants met him, and told *him,* saying, Thy son liveth.

52 Then inquired he of them the hour when he began to amend. And they said unto him, Yesterday at the seventh hour the fever left him.

53 So the father knew that *it was* at the same hour, in the which Jesus said unto him, Thy son liveth: and himself
John 5:5-15 believed, and his whole house.

54 This *is* again the second miracle *that* Jesus did, when he was come out of Judaea into Galilee.

The healing at the pool

5 AFTER [l]THIS there was a feast of the Jews; and Jesus went up to Jerusalem.

2 Now there is at Jerusalem [m]by the sheep [1]*market* a pool, which is called in the Hebrew tongue Bethesda, having five porches.

3 In these lay a great multitude of impotent folk, of blind, halt, withered, waiting for the moving of the water.

4 For an angel went down at a certain season into the pool, and troubled the water: whosoever then first after the troubling of the water stepped in was made whole of whatsoever disease he had.

5 And a certain man was there, which had an infirmity thirty and eight years.

6 When Jesus saw him lie, and knew that he had been now a long time *in that case,* he saith unto him, Wilt thou be made whole?

7 The impotent man answered him, Sir, I have no man, when the water is troubled, to put me into the pool: but while I am coming, another steppeth down before me.

8 Jesus saith unto him, [n]Rise, take up thy bed, and walk.

9 And immediately the man was made whole, and took up his bed, and walked: and [o]on the same day was the sabbath.

10 ¶ The Jews therefore said unto him that was cured, It is the sabbath day: [p]it is not lawful for thee to carry *thy* bed.

11 He answered them, He that made me whole, the same said unto me, Take up thy bed, and walk.

12 Then asked they him, What man is that which said unto thee, Take up thy bed, and walk?

13 And he that was healed wist not who it was: for Jesus had conveyed

4:46 [j]ch. 2:1,11
4:48 [k]1 Cor. 1:22
5:1 [l]Lev. 23:2; Deut. 16:1; ch. 2:13
5:2 [m]Neh. 3:1 & 12:39
5:8 [n]Mat. 9:6; Mark 2:11; Luke 5:24
5:9 [o]ch. 9:14
5:10 [p]Ex. 20:10; Neh. 13:19; Jer. 17:21; Mat. 12:2; Mark 2:24; Luke 6:2

[k] Or, *courtier,* or, *ruler* [1] Or, *gate*

4:48 SIGNS AND WONDERS. Although signs and wonders are an authentic work of the kingdom of God, our faith must not be centered on them (see article on THE KINGDOM OF GOD, p. 1428). Rather, we must believe in Jesus Christ because of who He is, God's Son, our Lord and Savior. Jesus must be worshiped and esteemed because of His love, mercy, holiness, and righteous character, not just for what He can do for us in a physical or material way. Signs, miracles, and wonders must lead us to a deep attachment to the Lord and to a stronger faith in Him, as the miracle performed here did for the nobleman (vv. 50–53).

5:5 THIRTY AND EIGHT YEARS. This man's infirmity had lasted 38 years. He had experienced prolonged disappointment at not being healed, while repeatedly looking unto God in expectation. Yet healing did finally come. It was largely because of the length of this man's suffering that Jesus, in compassion, chose to help him. We must never give up hope that the time for God to move directly on our behalf may come soon.

5:9 THE MAN WAS MADE WHOLE. Jesus often healed as a response to the faith of individuals. Here, however, He required no faith at all; the man was made whole merely at the word of Jesus. Even today people may be healed according to God's purpose even though they do not demonstrate faith in Christ. The Bible teaches that there are three contacts for healing faith: (1) the faith of the one being healed (Mat. 9:27–29); (2) the faith of others on behalf of the afflicted (Mat. 8:5–10; cf. 17:15–20; Jas. 5:14–16); (3) the faith of one who is anointed to heal (1 Cor. 12:9).

himself away, [m]a multitude being in *that* place.

14 Afterward Jesus findeth him in the temple, and said unto him, Behold, thou art made whole: [q]sin no more, lest a worse thing come unto thee.

15 The man departed, and told the Jews that it was Jesus, which had made him whole.

John 9:1-12

16 And therefore did the Jews persecute Jesus, and sought to slay him, because he had done these things on the sabbath day.

Jesus claims equality with God

17 ¶ But Jesus answered them, [r]My Father worketh hitherto, and I work.

18 Therefore the Jews [s]sought the more to kill him, because he not only had broken the sabbath, but said also that God was his Father, [t]making himself equal with God.

19 Then answered Jesus and said unto them, Verily, verily, I say unto you, [u]The Son can do nothing of himself, but what he seeth the Father do: for what things soever he doeth, these also doeth the Son likewise.

20 For [v]the Father loveth the Son, and showeth him all things that himself doeth: and he will show him greater works than these, that ye may marvel.

21 For as the Father raiseth up the dead, and quickeneth *them;* [w]even so the Son quickeneth whom he will.

22 For the Father judgeth no man, but [x]hath committed all judgment unto the Son:

23 That all *men* should honour the Son, even as they honour the Father. [y]He that honoureth not the Son honoureth not the Father which hath sent him.

24 Verily, verily, I say unto you, [z]He that heareth my word, and believeth on him that sent me, hath everlasting life, and shall not come into condemnation; [a]but is passed from death unto life.

Resurrection to life or judgment

25 Verily, verily, I say unto you, The hour is coming, and now is, when [b]the dead shall hear the voice of the Son of God: and they that hear shall live.

26 For as the Father hath life in himself; so hath he given to the Son to have life in himself;

27 And [c]hath given him authority to execute judgment also, [d]because he is the Son of man.

28 Marvel not at this: for the hour is coming, in the which all that are in the graves shall hear his voice,

5:14 [q]Mat. 12:45 ch. 8:11
5:17 [r]ch. 9:4 & 14:10
5:18 [s]ch. 7:19 [t]ch. 10:30 Phil. 2:6
5:19 [u]ver. 30 ch. 8:28 & 9:4
5:20 [v]Mat. 3:17 ch. 3:35
5:21 [w]Luke 7:14 & 8:54 ch. 11:25
5:22 [x]Mat. 11:27 & 28:18 ch. 3:35 & 17:2 Acts 17:31 1 Pet. 4:5
5:23 [y]1 John 2:23
5:24 [z]ch. 3:16,18 & 6:40,47 & 8:51 [a]1 John 3:14
5:25 [b]Eph. 2:1,5 & 5:14 Col 2:13
5:27 [c]Acts 10:42 & 17:31 [d]Dan. 7:13

[m] Or, *from the multitude that was*

5:14 SIN NO MORE. Jesus demands that all who profess faith in His name are to stop sinning; those truly saved will stop. Although not perfect or above occasional transgression, the true believer will commit his life to Christ so that, through the power of the Holy Spirit, sin will no longer be the characteristic of his life (1 Pet. 1:5; 1 John 3:6,9). Jesus' expectation for the born-again life contrasts sharply with those who emphasize that the believer will continue to sin daily in thought, word, and deed.

5:16 SOUGHT TO SLAY HIM. At this point in his Gospel, John begins to show that in spite of Jesus' miracles, and even because of them, the religious leaders intensely opposed Him and sought to put Him to death.

5:18–24 MAKING HIMSELF EQUAL WITH GOD. Jesus makes several astounding claims here: (1) God is His Father in a unique and special way; (2) He maintains unity, communion, and authority with God (vv. 19–20); (3) He has the power to give life and raise the dead (v. 21); (4) He has the right to judge all people (v. 22); (5) He has the right to divine honor (v. 23); and (6) He has the power to give everlasting life (v. 24).

5:24 HEARETH . . . BELIEVETH. Jesus describes those who have eternal life and will not come into condemnation: those who are "hearing" and "believing." The hearing (Gk. *akouōn*, from *akouō*) and believing (Gk. *pisteuōn*, from *pisteuō*) are present participles, emphasizing continuous action (i.e., "He who is hearing and is believing"). Thus, the "hearing" and "believing" are not acts of a single moment, but actions that must continue. Christ affirms that our present possession of eternal life is conditional on a present living faith rather than on a momentary decision of faith sometime in the past (see 1:12, note; 4:14, note).

5:24 NOT COME INTO CONDEMNATION. "Condemnation" (Gk. *krisis*) is used in the sense of condemnation to eternal death. The believer will not be condemned with the world (1 Cor. 11:32). This does not refer to a Christian's future accountability and judgment concerning his faithfulness to the grace of God given to him while on earth (see article on THE JUDGMENT OF BELIEVERS, p. 1811).

5:26 HATH . . . GIVEN TO THE SON TO HAVE LIFE IN HIMSELF. Christ's own nature is a source of eternal life; it is inherent within Him. God, however, has not given the believer the power to have eternal life inherent in himself. We have life only as we have fellowship with Christ, i.e., Christ living within us through a living faith relationship (see 15:4,6, notes; Gal. 2:20).

29 [e]And shall come forth; [f]they
that have done good, unto the resurrec-
tion of life; and they that have done
evil, unto the resurrection of damna-
tion.

Testimonies about Jesus

30 [g]I can of mine own self do noth-
ing: as I hear, I judge: and my judg-
ment is just; because [h]I seek not mine
own will, but the will of the Father
which hath sent me.
31 [i]If I bear witness of myself, my
witness is not true.
32 ¶ [j]There is another that
beareth witness of me; and I know that
the witness which he witnesseth of me
is true.
33 Ye sent unto John, [k]and he bare
witness unto the truth.
34 But I receive not testimony from
man: but these things I say, that ye
might be saved.
35 He was a burning and [l]a shin-
ing light: and [m]ye were willing for a
season to rejoice in his light.
36 ¶ But [n]I have greater witness
than *that* of John: for [o]the works
which the Father hath given me to fin-
ish, the same works that I do, bear wit-
ness of me, that the Father hath
sent me.
37 And the Father himself, which
hath sent me, [p]hath borne witness of
me. Ye have neither heard his voice at
any time, [q]nor seen his shape.
38 And ye have not his word abiding
in you: for whom he hath sent, him ye
believe not.
39 ¶ [r]Search the scriptures; for in
them ye think ye have eternal life: and
[s]they are they which testify of me.
40 [t]And ye will not come to me,
that ye might have life.
41 [u]I receive not honour from men.
42 But I know you, that ye have not
the love of God in you.
43 I am come in my Father's name,
and ye receive me not: if another shall
come in his own name, him ye will re-
ceive.
44 [v]How can ye believe, which re-
ceive honour one of another, and seek
not [w]the honour that *cometh* from God
only?
45 Do not think that I will accuse
you to the Father: [x]there is *one* that
accuseth you, *even* Moses, in whom ye
trust.
46 For had ye believed Moses, ye
would have believed me: [y]for he wrote
of me.
47 But if ye believe not his writings,
how shall ye believe my words?

5:29 [e]Is. 26:19 1 Cor. 15:52 [f]Dan. 12:2 Mat. 25:32,33,46 **5:30** [g]ver. 19 [h]Mat. 26:39 ch. 4:34 & 6:38 **5:31** [i]ch. 8:14 Rev. 3:14 **5:32** [j]Mat. 3:17 & 17:5 ch. 8:18 1 John 5:6 **5:33** [k]ch. 1:15,19,27,32 **5:35** [l]2 Pet. 1:19 [m]Mat. 13:20 Mark 6:20 **5:36** [n]1 John 5:9 [o]ch. 3:2 & 10:25 & 15:24 **5:37** [p]Mat. 3:17 & 17:5 ch. 6:27 & 8:18 [q]Deut. 4:12 ch. 1:18 1 Tim. 1:17 1 John 4:12 **5:39** [r]ver. 46 Is. 8:20 & 34:16 Luke 16:29 Acts 17:11 [s]Deut. 18:15,18 Luke 24:27 **5:40** [t]ch. 1:11 & 3:19 **5:41** [u]ver. 34

1 Thes. 2:6 **5:44** [v]ch. 12:43 [w]Rom. 2:29 **5:45** [x]Rom. 2:12 **5:46** [y]Gen. 3:15 & 12:3 & 18:18 & 22:18 & 49:10; Deut. 18:15,18; ch. 1:45; Acts 26:22

5:29 THEY THAT HAVE DONE GOOD. According to Scripture, judgment is always on the basis of works, because one's works are a manifestation of his faith and inner condition. This means that we will be judged not by our profession of faith in Christ, but by the life we have lived (Mat. 12:36–37; 16:27; Rom. 2:6–10; 14:12; 1 Cor. 3:13–15; 2 Cor. 5:10; Eph. 6:8; Col. 3:25; Rev. 2:23; 20:12; 22:12).

5:29 RESURRECTION OF LIFE. The N.T. does not teach a single general simultaneous resurrection for all the dead. (1) It speaks of a resurrection of many "saints" occurring immediately after Christ's resurrection (Mat. 27:52–53), of a resurrection occurring at the time of the rapture or catching up of the church by Christ (1 Cor. 15:51–52; see article on THE RAPTURE, p. 1889), of a "first resurrection" (see Rev. 20:6, note), and of a resurrection occurring one thousand years after the "first resurrection" of Rev. 20:6 (i.e., after the millennial reign of Christ on earth, Rev. 20:4). (2) It is possible that "the first resurrection" includes the resurrection of *all* believers before the thousand-year reign of Christ (Rev. 20:4–6). Hence, the resurrection of Rev. 20:4–6 would complete the first resurrection.

5:29 THEY THAT HAVE DONE EVIL. Those who teach, contrary to Christ and the apostles, that one may have everlasting life while at the same time be out of fellowship with Christ and live an evil life of immorality, lust, drunkenness, or other grave sins of the flesh, are teaching the ultimate deception. It leads them and their followers to trust in a false doctrine of eternal security (see 1 Cor. 6:9–10; Gal. 5:19–21; Eph. 5:5–6). The words of Jesus must be heeded: those who have done evil will come forth "unto the resurrection of damnation."

5:44 RECEIVE HONOUR ONE OF ANOTHER. Those who have true saving faith will not be motivated by the love of praise, honor, esteem, or glory from other people. They will set before themselves the goal of pleasing the Father. Those who establish a habit of receiving glory from others make idols of themselves and place themselves outside the kingdom of God. To care for the praise of men more than the praise of God is to disbelieve the gospel of Christ and make genuine faith impossible (cf. Rom. 2:29).

5:47 IF YE BELIEVE NOT HIS WRITINGS. This passage is important in establishing Christ's view of the O.T. He indeed believed that Moses wrote the Pentateuch. The lesson the Jews needed, and one that we need today, is this: if one does not believe in the inspiration and truthfulness of the O.T. writings, he will not believe or submit to

The five thousand fed

6:1–13pp — Mat. 14:13–21; Mark 6:32–44; Luke 9:10–17

6 AFTER [z]THESE things Jesus
went over the sea of Galilee, which
is *the sea* of Tiberias.
2 And a great multitude followed
him, because they saw his miracles
which he did on them that were dis-
eased.
3 And Jesus went up into a moun-
tain, and there he sat with his disci-
ples.
4 [a]And the passover, a feast of the
Jews, was nigh.
5 ¶ [b]When Jesus then lifted up *his*
eyes, and saw a great company come
unto him, he saith unto Philip, Whence
shall we buy bread, that these may eat?
6 And this he said to prove him: for
he himself knew what he would do.
7 Philip answered him, [c]Two hun-
dred pennyworth of bread is not suffi-
cient for them, that every one of them
may take a little.
8 One of his disciples, Andrew, Si-
mon Peter's brother, saith unto him,
9 There is a lad here, which hath
five barley loaves, and two small
fishes: [d]but what are they among so
many?
10 And Jesus said, Make the men
sit down. Now there was much grass in
the place. So the men sat down, in
number about five thousand.
11 And Jesus took the loaves; and
when he had given thanks, he distrib-
uted to the disciples, and the disciples
to them that were set down; and like-
wise of the fishes as much as they
would.
12 When they were filled, he said
unto his disciples, Gather up the frag-
ments that remain, that nothing be
lost.
13 Therefore they gathered *them* to-
gether, and filled twelve baskets with
the fragments of the five barley loaves,
which remained over and above unto
them that had eaten.
14 Then those men, when they had
seen the miracle that Jesus did, said,
This is of a truth [e]that prophet that
should come into the world.

Jesus walks on the sea

6:16–21pp — Mat. 14:22–33; Mark 6:47–51

15 ¶ When Jesus therefore per-
ceived that they would come and take
him by force, to make him a king, he
departed again into a mountain himself
alone.
16 [f]And when even was *now* come,
his disciples went down unto the sea,
17 And entered into a ship, and
went over the sea toward Capernaum.
And it was now dark, and Jesus was
not come to them.
18 And the sea arose by reason of a
great wind that blew.

6:1 [z]Mat. 14:15 Mark 6:35 Luke 9:10,12
6:4 [a]Lev. 23:5,7 Deut. 16:1 ch. 2:13 & 5:1
6:5 [b]Mat. 14:14 Mark 6:35 Luke 9:12
6:7 [c]See Num. 11:21, 22
6:9 [d]2 Ki. 4:43
6:14 [e]Gen. 49:10 Deut. 18:15,18 Mat. 11:3 ch. 1:21 & 4:19,25 & 7:40
6:16 [f]Mat. 14:23 Mark 6:47

---

the authority of Jesus' words and the N.T. writings which bear witness to Him (see Acts 24:14, note on Paul's view of the O.T.; see article on THE INSPIRATION AND AUTHORITY OF SCRIPTURE, p. 1924).

6:2 MIRACLES. (1) What are miracles? (a) They are works of a supernatural origin and power (Gk. *dunamis*; see Acts 8:13; 19:11). (b) They function as a sign or mark (Gk. *semeion*) of divine authority (Luke 23:8; Acts 4:16,30,33). The central and greatest miracle of the N.T. faith is the resurrection of Christ (1 Cor. 15).

(2) Miracles serve at least three purposes in the kingdom of God. (a) They give witness to Jesus Christ, authenticating the truth of His message and proving His identity as the Christ of God (2:23; 5:1–21; 10:25; 11:42). (b) They express Christ's compassionate love (Mark 8:2; Luke 7:12–15; Acts 10:38). (c) They signify the age of salvation (Mat. 11:2ff), the coming of the kingdom of God (see article on THE KINGDOM OF GOD, p. 1428), and God's invasion into the realm of Satan (see article on POWER OVER SATAN AND DEMONS, p. 1486).

(3) The Scriptures maintain that miracles are to be operative throughout the entire church age. (a) Jesus sent out His followers to preach and perform miracles (Mat. 10:7–8; Mark 3:14–15; see Luke 9:2, note). (b) Jesus declared that those who believed in Him through the preaching of the gospel were to do the works that He did, and would do even greater works (14:12; Mark 16:15–20). (c) The book of Acts speaks of miracle-working in the lives of the believers (Acts 3:1ff; 5:12; 6:8; 8:6ff; 9:32ff; 15:12; 20:7ff); elsewhere in the N.T. these are called "signs" by which the proclamation of the gospel was confirmed (Acts 4:29–30; 14:3; Rom. 15:18–19; 2 Cor. 12:12; Heb. 2:3–4). (d) The Spirit desires to give these signs to the church throughout this present age (1 Cor. 12:8–12,28; Jas. 5:14–15; see article on SIGNS OF BELIEVERS, p. 1516).

(4) Note should also be taken that the N.T. teaches that signs and wonders will be performed by false teachers and preachers, especially by the antichrist (see articles on THE GREAT TRIBULATION, p. 1456, and FALSE TEACHERS, p. 1508).

6:5–14 ABOUT FIVE THOUSAND. See Mat. 14:19, note.

6:15 JESUS PRAYS ALONE. See Mat. 14:23, note.

19 So when they had rowed about
five and twenty or thirty furlongs, they
see Jesus walking on the sea, and
drawing nigh unto the ship: and they
were afraid.
20 But he saith unto them, It is I; be
not afraid.
21 Then they willingly received him
into the ship: and immediately the ship
was at the land whither they went.

Jesus the bread of life

22 ¶ The day following, when the
people which stood on the other side of
the sea saw that there was none other
boat there, save that one whereinto his
disciples were entered, and that Jesus
went not with his disciples into the
boat, but *that* his disciples were gone
away alone;
23 (Howbeit there came other boats
from Tiberias nigh unto the place
where they did eat bread, after that the
Lord had given thanks:)
24 When the people therefore saw
that Jesus was not there, neither his
disciples, they also took shipping, and
came to Capernaum, seeking for Jesus.
25 And when they had found him on
the other side of the sea, they said unto
him, Rabbi, when camest thou hither?
26 Jesus answered them and said,
Verily, verily, I say unto you, Ye seek
me, not because ye saw the miracles,
but because ye did eat of the loaves,
and were filled.
27 [n]Labour not for the meat which
perisheth, but [g]for that meat which en-
dureth unto everlasting life, which
the Son of man shall give unto you:
[h]for him hath God the Father sealed.

6:27
[g]ch. 4:14
[h]Mat. 3:17
& 17:5
Mark 1:11
& 9:7
Luke 3:22
& 9:35
ch. 5:37
Acts 2:22
2 Pet. 1:17

6:29
[i]1 John 3:23
6:30
[j]Mat. 12:38
& 16:1
Mark 8:11
1 Cor. 1:22
6:31
[k]Ex. 16:15
Num. 11:7
Neh. 9:15
1 Cor. 10:3
[l]Ps. 78:24
6:34
[m]See ch. 4:15
6:35
[n]ver. 48,58
[o]ch. 4:14
& 7:37
6:36
[p]ver. 26,64
6:37
[q]ver. 45
[r]Mat. 24:24
ch. 10:28,29
2 Tim. 2:19
1 John 2:19
6:38
[s]Mat. 26:39
ch. 5:30
[t]ch. 4:34
6:39
[u]ch. 10:28
& 17:12
& 18:9

28 Then said they unto him, What
shall we do, that we might work the
works of God?
29 Jesus answered and said unto
them, [i]This is the work of God, that
ye believe on him whom he hath sent.
30 They said therefore unto him,
[j]What sign showest thou then, that
we may see, and believe thee? what
dost thou work?
31 [k]Our fathers did eat manna in
the desert; as it is written, [l]He gave
them bread from heaven to eat.
32 Then Jesus said unto them, Veri-
ly, verily, I say unto you, Moses gave
you not that bread from heaven; but my
Father giveth you the true bread from
heaven.
33 For the bread of God is he which
cometh down from heaven, and giveth
life unto the world.
34 [m]Then said they unto him, Lord,
evermore give us this bread.

The Jews reject Jesus' claim

35 And Jesus said unto them, [n]I
am the bread of life: [o]he that cometh
to me shall never hunger; and he that
believeth on me shall never thirst.
36 [p]But I said unto you, That ye
also have seen me, and believe not.
37 [q]All that the Father giveth me
shall come to me; and [r]him that com-
eth to me I will in no wise cast out.
38 For I came down from heaven,
[s]not to do mine own will, [t]but the
will of him that sent me.
39 And this is the Father's will
which hath sent me, [u]that of all which

[n] Or, *Work not*

6:20 BE NOT AFRAID. See Mat. 14:27, note.

6:35 I AM THE BREAD OF LIFE. "I am the bread of life" is the first of the seven "I am" statements recorded in the Gospel of John, each one emphasizing an important aspect of the personal ministry of Jesus. This statement tells us that Christ is the sustenance that nourishes spiritual life (see 6:53). The other "I am" statements are: "the light of the world" (8:12), "the door" (10:9), "the good shepherd" (10:11,14), "the resurrection, and the life" (11:25), "the way, the truth, and the life" (14:6), and "the true vine" (15:1,5).

6:37 I WILL IN NO WISE CAST OUT. Jesus promises to welcome all who come to Him in repentance and faith. Those who come to Jesus come in response to the grace of God given to them (see article on FAITH AND GRACE, p. 1738).

6:39 THE FATHER'S WILL. It is important to understand the relationship of the Father's will to human responsibility. (1) It is not God's will that any believer fall from grace (cf. Gal. 5:4) and subsequently be separated from God. Neither is it His will that any individual in the world should perish (2 Pet. 3:9) or fail to come to the truth and be saved (1 Tim. 2:4).

(2) However, there is a great difference between God's perfect will and His permissive will (see article on THE WILL OF GOD, p. 1060). He does not abrogate the human responsibility to repent and believe, even if it means His perfect will is not done (see Luke 19:41, note on Jesus weeping over Jerusalem).

(3) God's desire that all believers might be saved on the last day does not relieve them of the responsibility of obeying His voice and following Him (10:27; 14:21). Jesus in sorrow prayed on the night of His betrayal that "those that thou gavest me I have kept, and none of them is lost, but the son of perdition," i.e., the one headed for eternal destruction (17:12).

he hath given me I should lose nothing,
but should raise it up again at the last
day.
40 And this is the will of him that
sent me, [v]that every one which seeth
the Son, and believeth on him, may
have everlasting life: and I will raise
him up at the last day.
41 The Jews then murmured at him,
because he said, I am the bread which
came down from heaven.
42 And they said, [w]Is not this
Jesus, the son of Joseph, whose father
and mother we know? how is it then
that he saith, I came down from
heaven?
43 Jesus therefore answered and
said unto them, Murmur not among
yourselves.
44 [x]No man can come to me, ex-
cept the Father which hath sent me
draw him: and I will raise him up at the
last day.
45 [y]It is written in the prophets,
And they shall be all taught of God.
[z]Every man therefore that hath heard,
and hath learned of the Father, cometh
unto me.
46 [a]Not that any man hath seen
the Father, [b]save he which is of God,
he hath seen the Father.
47 Verily, verily, I say unto you,
[c]He that believeth on me hath ever-
lasting life.
48 [d]I am that bread of life.
49 [e]Your fathers did eat manna in
the wilderness, and are dead.
50 [f]This is the bread which com-
eth down from heaven, that a man may
eat thereof, and not die.
51 I am the living bread [g]which
came down from heaven: if any man eat

6:40 [v]ver. 27,47,54 ch. 3:15,16 & 4:14
6:42 [w]Mat. 13:55 Mark 6:3 Luke 4:22
6:44 [x]ver. 65 Sol. 1:4
6:45 [y]Is. 54:13 Jer. 31:34 Mic. 4:2 Heb. 8:10 [z]ver. 37
6:46 [a]ch. 1:18 [b]Mat. 11:27 Luke 10:22 ch. 7:29
6:47 [c]ch. 3:16,18
6:48 [d]ver. 33,35
6:49 [e]ver. 31
6:50 [f]ver. 51,58
6:51 [g]ch. 3:13 [h]Heb. 10:5
6:52 [i]ch. 7:43 & 9:16 & 10:19
6:53 [j]Mat. 26:16
6:54 [k]ver. 27,40 ch. 4:14
6:56 [l]1 John 3:24 & 4:15,16
6:58 [m]ver. 49-51
6:60 [n]ver. 66 Mat. 11:6
6:62 [o]Mark 16:19 ch. 3:13 Acts 1:9 Eph. 4:8
6:63 [p]2 Cor. 3:6

of this bread, he shall live for ever: and
[h]the bread that I will give is my flesh,
which I will give for the life of the
world.
52 The Jews therefore [i]strove
among themselves, saying, How can
this man give us *his* flesh to eat?
53 Then Jesus said unto them, Veri-
ly, verily, I say unto you, Except [j]ye
eat the flesh of the Son of man, and
drink his blood, ye have no life in you.
54 [k]Whoso eateth my flesh, and
drinketh my blood, hath eternal life;
and I will raise him up at the last day.
55 For my flesh is meat indeed, and
my blood is drink indeed.
56 He that eateth my flesh, and
drinketh my blood, [l]dwelleth in me,
and I in him.
57 As the living Father hath sent
me, and I live by the Father: so he that
eateth me, even he shall live by me.
58 [m]This is that bread which came
down from heaven: not as your fathers
did eat manna, and are dead: he that
eateth of this bread shall live for ever.
59 These things said he in the syna-
gogue, as he taught in Capernaum.

Many disciples desert Jesus

60 [n]Many therefore of his disci-
ples, when they had heard *this*, said,
This is an hard saying; who can
hear it?
61 When Jesus knew in himself that
his disciples murmured at it, he said
unto them, Doth this offend you?
62 [o]*What* and if ye shall see the
Son of man ascend up where he was
before?
63 [p]It is the spirit that quickeneth;
the flesh profiteth nothing: the words

6:44 THE FATHER . . . DRAW HIM. The Father gives people to Jesus by drawing them to His Son through the Holy Spirit. His work of "drawing" covers all people, as Jesus says: "I . . . will draw all *men*" (12:32). But this drawing is not irresistible, since it can be rejected (see Mat. 23:37, "and ye would not").

6:54 EATETH MY FLESH, AND DRINKETH MY BLOOD. One receives spiritual life by believing in Christ and sharing in the redemptive benefits of His death on the cross (Rom. 3:24–25; 1 John 1:7). We continue to have spiritual life as we abide in fellowship with Christ and His Word. Compare v. 53 with v. 63, where He says, "The words that I speak unto you, *they* are spirit, and *they* are life." Thus, we partake of Christ as we continue to have faith in Him and prayerfully receive His Word.

(1) Jesus is the living Word (1:1–5); the Bible is the written Word (2 Tim. 3:16; 2 Pet. 1:21). Jesus calls Himself here the "bread of life" (v. 35), and elsewhere He relates this bread to the Word of God: "Man shall not live by bread alone, but by every word that proceedeth out of the mouth of God" (Mat. 4:4). Hence, we "eat his flesh" by abiding in Him and by receiving and obeying the Word of God (v. 63).

(2) We are saved by God's grace and regenerating power of the Holy Spirit when we first hear and receive the Word (1:12; Acts 2:41). We continue to be saved and receive grace by remaining in union with Christ and partaking of the Word of God continually through reading, obeying, and absorbing its truths into our spirits (1 Tim. 4:13–16; Jas. 1:21). It is fatal to withdraw from fellowship with Christ or to neglect His Word.

that I speak unto you, *they* are spirit,
and *they* are life.
64 But [q]there are some of you that
believe not. For [r]Jesus knew from the
beginning who they were that believed
not, and who should betray him.
65 And he said, Therefore [s]said I
unto you, that no man can come unto
me, except it were given unto him of
my Father.
66 ¶ [t]From that *time* many of his
disciples went back, and walked no
more with him.

Peter's great confession

67 Then said Jesus unto the twelve,
Will ye also go away?
68 Then Simon Peter answered
him, Lord, to whom shall we go? thou
hast [u]the words of eternal life.
69 [v]And we believe and are sure
that thou art that Christ, the Son of the
living God.
70 Jesus answered them, [w]Have
not I chosen you twelve, [x]and one of
you is a devil?
71 He spake of Judas Iscariot *the
son* of Simon: for he it was that should
betray him, being one of the twelve.

Jesus at the feast of tabernacles

7 AFTER THESE things Jesus
walked in Galilee: for he would not
walk in Jewry, [y]because the Jews
sought to kill him.
2 [z]Now the Jews' feast of taberna-
cles was at hand.
3 [a]His brethren therefore said unto
him, Depart hence, and go into Judaea,
that thy disciples also may see the
works that thou doest.
4 For *there is* no man *that* doeth any
thing in secret, and he himself seeketh
to be known openly. If thou do these
things, show thyself to the world.
5 For [b]neither did his brethren be-
lieve in him.
6 Then Jesus said unto them, [c]My
time is not yet come: but your time is
always ready.
7 [d]The world cannot hate you; but
me it hateth, [e]because I testify of it,
that the works thereof are evil.
8 Go ye up unto this feast: I go not
up yet unto this feast; [f]for my time is
not yet full come.
9 When he had said these words
unto them, he abode *still* in Galilee.
10 ¶ But when his brethren were
gone up, then went he also up unto the
feast, not openly, but as it were in se-
cret.
11 Then [g]the Jews sought him at
the feast, and said, Where is he?
12 And [h]there was much murmur-
ing among the people concerning him:
for [i]some said, He is a good man: oth-
ers said, Nay; but he deceiveth the peo-
ple.
13 Howbeit no man spake openly of
him [j]for fear of the Jews.

Jesus teaches in the temple

14 ¶ Now about the midst of the
feast Jesus went up into the temple,
and taught.
15 [k]And the Jews marvelled, say-
ing, How knoweth this man °letters,
having never learned?
16 Jesus answered them, and said,
[l]My doctrine is not mine, but his that
sent me.
17 [m]If any man will do his will, he
shall know of the doctrine, whether it

6:64 [q]ver. 36 [r]ch. 2:24,25 & 13:11 **6:65** [s]ver. 44,45 **6:66** [t]ver. 60 **6:68** [u]Acts 5:20 **6:69** [v]Mat. 16:16 Mark 8:29 Luke 9:20 ch. 1:49 & 11:27 **6:70** [w]Luke 6:13 [x]ch. 13:27 **7:1** [y]ch. 5:16,18 **7:2** [z]Lev. 23:34 **7:3** [a]Mat. 12:46 Mark 3:31 Acts 1:14 **7:5** [b]Mark 3:21 **7:6** [c]ch. 2:4 & 8:20 **7:7** [d]ch. 15:19 [e]ch. 3:19 **7:8** [f]ch. 8:20 **7:11** [g]ch. 11:56 **7:12** [h]ch. 9:16 & 10:19 [i]ver. 40 Mat. 21:46 Luke 7:16 ch. 6:14 **7:13** [j]ch. 9:22 & 12:42 & 19:38 **7:15** [k]Mat. 13:54 Mark 6:2 Luke 4:22 Acts 2:7 **7:16** [l]ch. 3:11 & 8:28 & 12:49 & 14:10,24 **7:17** [m]ch. 8:43

° Or, *learning*

6:64 JESUS KNEW FROM THE BEGINNING. This may mean that Jesus knew when Judas began to drift from his original faith and formed plans to betray Him. Judas had the same choice as the other eleven disciples. He was a believer and a trusted familiar friend of Jesus (13:18; Ps. 41:9), as shown by Christ's commitment of Himself to Judas (2:23–24; Mat. 10:1–15). Judas later turned aside of his own choice (Acts 1:25); he did not have to betray Jesus. In other words, the betrayal of Jesus was prophesied as to its occurrence only. The specific person to betray Christ was not predestined from all eternity. Judas's defection to the enemy and consequent tragedy should warn every follower of Christ not to reject the Spirit's warning about friendship with the world and treachery to Christ (Heb. 10:29; 12:25; Jas. 4:4).

7:2 FEAST OF TABERNACLES. The "feast of tabernacles" commemorated the post-exodus journeys of Israel and the time when they wandered in the wilderness, living in tabernacles (or tents) under God's care (see Lev. 23:34–43, note; Zech. 14:16–19).

7:7 THE WORLD . . . HATETH. Jesus was hated by the world because He proclaimed that all people separated from God are depraved, sinful, and inherently selfish and evil (cf. 2:14–16; 3:19–20; 5:30–47). Throughout His ministry Jesus faithfully denounced injustice, cruelty, and immorality. This unfailing and forthright testimony to human sinfulness contradicts those ministers who self-righteously claim to preach a "positive gospel," i.e., one void of the prophetic demand for repentance and righteousness.

7:17 IF ANY MAN WILL DO HIS WILL. True saving faith and an experiential knowledge of His

be of God, or *whether* I speak of myself.
18 [n]He that speaketh of himself
seeketh his own glory: but he that
seeketh his glory that sent him, the
same is true, and no unrighteousness
is in him.
19 [o]Did not Moses give you the
law, and *yet* none of you keepeth the
law? [p]Why go ye about to kill me?
20 The people answered and said,
[q]Thou hast a devil: who goeth about
to kill thee?
21 Jesus answered and said unto
them, I have done one work, and ye all
marvel.
22 [r]Moses therefore gave unto you
circumcision; (not because it is of Mo-
ses, [s]but of the fathers;) and ye on the
sabbath day circumcise a man.
23 If a man on the sabbath day re-
ceive circumcision, [p]that the law of
Moses should not be broken; are ye an-
gry at me, because [t]I have made a
man every whit whole on the sabbath
day?
24 [u]Judge not according to the ap-
pearance, but judge righteous judg-
ment.

Jesus sent from the Father

25 Then said some of them of Jeru-
salem, Is not this he, whom they seek
to kill?
26 But, lo, he speaketh boldly, and
they say nothing unto him. [v]Do the
rulers know indeed that this is the very
Christ?
27 [w]Howbeit we know this man
whence he is: but when Christ cometh,
no man knoweth whence he is.
28 Then cried Jesus in the temple as
he taught, saying, [x]Ye both know me,
and ye know whence I am: and [y]I am
not come of myself, but he that sent me
[z]is true, [a]whom ye know not.
29 But [b]I know him: for I am from
him, and he hath sent me.
30 Then [c]they sought to take him:
but [d]no man laid hands on him, be-
cause his hour was not yet come.
31 And [e]many of the people be-
lieved on him, and said, When Christ
cometh, will he do more miracles than
these which this *man* hath done?
32 ¶ The Pharisees heard that the
people murmured such things concern-
ing him; and the Pharisees and the
chief priests sent officers to take him.
33 Then said Jesus unto them,
[f]Yet a little while am I with you, and
then I go unto him that sent me.
34 Ye [g]shall seek me, and shall not
find *me:* and where I am, *thither* ye can-
not come.
35 Then said the Jews among them-
selves, Whither will he go, that we
shall not find him? will he go unto
[h]the dispersed among the [q]Gentiles,
and teach the Gentiles?
36 What *manner of* saying is this
that he said, Ye shall seek me, and
shall not find *me:* and where I am,
thither ye cannot come?

The Spirit as living water

37 [i]In the last day, that great *day*
of the feast, Jesus stood and cried, say-
ing, [j]If any man thirst, let him come
unto me, and drink.
38 [k]He that believeth on me, as the

7:18 [n]ch. 5:41 & 8:50 **7:19** [o]Ex. 24:3 Deut. 33:4 ch. 1:17 Acts 7:38 [p]Mat. 12:14 Mark 3:6 ch. 5:16,18 & 10:31,39 & 11:53 **7:20** [q]ch. 8:48,52 & 10:20 **7:22** [r]Lev. 12:3 [s]Gen. 17:10 **7:23** [t]ch. 5:8,9,16 **7:24** [u]Deut. 1:16 Prov. 24:23 ch. 8:15 Jas. 2:1 **7:26** [v]ver. 48 **7:27** [w]Mat. 13:55 Mark 6:3 Luke 4:22 **7:28** [x]ch. 8:14 [y]ch. 5:43 & 8:42 [z]ch. 5:32 & 8:26 Rom. 3:4 [a]ch. 1:18 & 8:55 **7:29** [b]Mat. 11:27 ch. 10:15 **7:30** [c]Mark 11:18 Luke 19:47 & 20:19 ch. 8:37 [d]ver. 44 **7:31** [e]Mat. 12:23 ch. 3:2 & 8:30 **7:33** [f]ch. 13:33 & 16:16 **7:34** [g]Hos. 5:6 ch. 8:21 & 13:33 **7:35** [h]Is. 11:12 Jas. 1:1 1 Pet. 1:1

7:37 [i]Lev. 23:36 [j]Is. 55:1; ch. 6:35; Rev. 22:17 **7:38** [k]Deut. 18:15

[p] Or, *without breaking the law of Moses* [q] Or, *Greeks*

---

teachings require a sincere desire to do the will of God. To believe is to obey (see article on FAITH AND GRACE, p. 1738).

7:18 SEEKETH HIS OWN GLORY. Jesus emphasizes an all-important criterion for testing whether or not a religious speaker is of God: Does he seek his own glory or advancement? In evaluating a minister, ask whether his preaching magnifies himself or Christ.

7:38 AS THE SCRIPTURE HATH SAID. Jesus referred to the "Scripture" because it was the very Word of His Father and, therefore, the supreme authority of His life and teaching. Scripture is also the supreme authority for the Christian, for God alone has the right to determine our beliefs and standards of conduct. He has chosen to exercise this authority by making His truth known in Scripture. The Bible, as the revelation of God, carries the same authority as if God Himself were speaking to us directly (see article on THE INSPIRATION AND AUTHORITY OF SCRIPTURE, p. 1924).

(1) The inspired Scriptures are the believer's ultimate authority. Ecclesiastical traditions, prophecies, supposed new revelations, doctrines, or human ideas must be tested against Scripture and should never be elevated to a place of equal authority with the Bible (cf. Mark 7:13; Col. 2:8; 1 Pet. 1:18–19).

(2) To profess equal or greater allegiance to any other authority than to God and His inspired Word is to withdraw oneself from the Christian faith and the Lordship of Christ. To say that any person, institution, creed, or church possesses equal or higher authority than God's inspired revelation is tantamount to idolatry. Thus, if any person is not

scripture hath said, [l]out of his belly shall flow rivers of living water.

39 ([m]But this spake he of the Spirit, which they that believe on him should receive: for the Holy Ghost was not yet *given;* because that Jesus was not yet [n]glorified.)

Israel is divided over Christ

40 ¶ Many of the people therefore, when they heard this saying, said, Of a truth this is [o]the Prophet.

41 Others said, [p]This is the Christ. But some said, Shall Christ come [q]out of Galilee?

42 [r]Hath not the scripture said, That Christ cometh of the seed of David, and out of the town of Bethlehem, [s]where David was?

43 So [t]there was a division among the people because of him.

44 And [u]some of them would have taken him; but no man laid hands on him.

45 ¶ Then came the officers to the chief priests and Pharisees; and they said unto them, Why have ye not brought him?

46 The officers answered, Never man spake like this man.

47 Then answered them the Pharisees, Are ye also deceived?

48 [v]Have any of the rulers or of the Pharisees believed on him?

49 But this people who knoweth not the law are cursed.

50 Nicodemus saith unto them, ([w]he that came [r]to Jesus by night, being one of them,)

51 [x]Doth our law judge *any* man, before it hear him, and know what he doeth?

52 They answered and said unto him, Art thou also of Galilee? Search, and look: for [y]out of Galilee ariseth no prophet.

53 And every man went unto his own house.

The woman caught in adultery

8 JESUS WENT unto the mount of Olives.

2 And early in the morning he came again into the temple, and all the people came unto him; and he sat down, and taught them.

3 And the scribes and Pharisees brought unto him a woman taken in adultery; and when they had set her in the midst,

4 They say unto him, Master, this woman was taken in adultery, in the very act.

5 [z]Now Moses in the law commanded us, that such should be stoned: but what sayest thou?

6 This they said, tempting him, that they might have to accuse him. But Jesus stooped down, and with *his* finger wrote on the ground, *as though he heard them not.*

7 So when they continued asking him, he lifted up himself, and said unto them, [a]He that is without sin among you, let him first cast a stone at her.

8 And again he stooped down, and wrote on the ground.

9 And they which heard *it,* [b]being convicted by *their own* conscience, went out one by one, beginning at the eldest, *even* unto the last: and Jesus was left alone, and the woman standing in the midst.

10 When Jesus had lifted up him-

r Gk. *to him*

7:38 [l]Prov. 18:4 Is. 12:3 & 44:3 ch. 4:14
7:39 [m]Is. 44:3 Joel 2:28 ch. 16:7 Acts 2:17,33,38 [n]ch. 12:16 & 16:7
7:40 [o]Deut. 18:15 ch. 1:21 & 6:14
7:41 [p]ch. 4:42 & 6:69 [q]ver. 52 ch. 1:46
7:42 [r]Ps. 132:11 Jer. 23:5 Mic. 5:2 Mat. 2:5 Luke 2:4 [s]1 Sam. 16:1,4
7:43 [t]ver. 12 ch. 9:16 & 10:19
7:44 [u]ver. 30
7:48 [v]ch. 12:42 Acts 6:7 1 Cor. 1:20,26 & 2:8
7:50 [w]ch. 3:2
7:51 [x]Deut 1:17 & 17:8 & 19:15
7:52 [y]ver. 41 Is. 9:1,2 Mat. 4:15 ch. 1:46
8:5 [z]Lev. 20:10 Deut. 22:22
8:7 [a]Deut. 17:7 Rom. 2:1
8:9 [b]Rom. 2:22

willing to submit his belief and doctrine to the scrutiny and authority of the N.T., he has placed himself outside of Biblical Christianity and salvation in Christ.

7:38 RIVERS OF LIVING WATER. The analogy of rivers of living water teaches us that when the gift of the Spirit is given to believers, they will experience His overflowing life. Then this living water will "flow" out to others with the healing message of Christ (10:10; 14:12; 15:5; see also Ps. 1:3; 46:4; Is. 32:15; 44:3; 58:11; Jer. 31:12; Ezek. 47:1–12; Joel 3:18; Zech. 14:8).

7:39 JESUS WAS NOT YET GLORIFIED. This refers to Christ's glory on the cross and His resurrection (see 12:23–24). The Spirit cannot be fully given until sin is dealt with. The "Spirit" refers to all the work of the Holy Spirit in the believer, both regeneration (20:22) and the baptism in the Spirit (Acts 2:4).

8:7 HE THAT IS WITHOUT SIN. These words must not be taken as justification for refusing to condemn sin within the church, or for treating lightly the moral failure of professed Christians. To do so distorts the Scriptural attitude toward sin among God's people. (1) The church's conduct toward sinners outside the church who have had little chance to respond to God's grace in Christ, and its conduct towards those within the church who sin and do not obey Christ, are two different situations. (2) Scripture teaches that sins committed by those within the church must not be tolerated (Rev. 2:20), but ought to be sharply rebuked and reproved (Luke 17:3; 1 Cor. 5:1–13; 2 Cor. 2:6–8; Eph. 5:11; 2 Tim. 4:2; Tit. 1:13; 2:15; Rev. 3:19; see Mat. 13:30, note on church discipline).

self, and saw none but the woman, he said unto her, Woman, where are those thine accusers? hath no man condemned thee?

11 She said, No man, Lord. And Jesus said unto her, [c]Neither do I condemn thee: go, and [d]sin no more.

Jesus the light of the world

12 ¶ Then spake Jesus again unto them, saying, [e]I am the light of the world: he that followeth me shall not walk in darkness, but shall have the light of life.

13 The Pharisees therefore said unto him, [f]Thou bearest record of thyself; thy record is not true.

14 Jesus answered and said unto them, Though I bear record of myself, *yet* my record is true: for I know whence I came, and whither I go; but [g]ye cannot tell whence I come, and whither I go.

15 [h]Ye judge after the flesh; [i]I judge no man.

16 And yet if I judge, my judgment is true: for [j]I am not alone, but I and the Father that sent me.

17 [k]It is also written in your law, that the testimony of two men is true.

18 I am one that bear witness of myself, and [l]the Father that sent me beareth witness of me.

19 Then said they unto him, Where is thy Father? Jesus answered, [m]Ye neither know me, nor my Father: [n]if ye had known me, ye should have known my Father also.

20 These words spake Jesus in [o]the treasury, as he taught in the temple: and [p]no man laid hands on him; for [q]his hour was not yet come.

8:11 [c]Luke 9:56 & 12:14 ch. 3:17 [d]ch. 5:14
8:12 [e]ch. 1:4,5,9 & 3:19 & 9:5 & 12:35,36,46
8:13 [f]ch. 5:31
8:14 [g]ch. 7:28 & 9:29
8:15 [h]ch. 7:24 [i]ch. 3:17 & 12:47 & 18:36
8:16 [j]ch. 16:32
8:17 [k]Deut. 17:6 & 19:15 Mat. 18:16 2 Cor. 13:1 Heb. 10:28
8:18 [l]ch. 5:37
8:19 [m]ch. 16:3 [n]ch. 14:7
8:20 [o]Mark 12:41 [p]ch. 7:30 [q]ch. 7:8
8:21 [r]ch. 7:34 & 13:33 [s]ver. 24
8:23 [t]ch. 3:31 [u]ch. 15:19 & 17:16 1 John 4:5
8:24 [v]ver. 21 [w]Mark 16:16
8:26 [x]ch. 7:28 [y]ch. 3:32 & 15:15
8:28 [z]ch. 3:14 & 12:32 [a]Rom. 1:4 [b]ch. 5:19,30 [c]ch. 3:11
8:29 [d]ch. 14:10 [e]ver. 16 [f]ch. 4:34 & 5:30 & 6:38

Jesus warns against unbelief

21 Then said Jesus again unto them, I go my way, and [r]ye shall seek me, and [s]shall die in your sins: whither I go, ye cannot come.

22 Then said the Jews, Will he kill himself? because he saith, Whither I go, ye cannot come.

23 And he said unto them, [t]Ye are from beneath; I am from above: [u]ye are of this world; I am not of this world.

24 [v]I said therefore unto you, that ye shall die in your sins: [w]for if ye believe not that I am *he,* ye shall die in your sins.

25 Then said they unto him, Who art thou? And Jesus saith unto them, Even *the same* that I said unto you from the beginning.

26 I have many things to say and to judge of you: but [x]he that sent me is true; and [y]I speak to the world those things which I have heard of him.

27 They understood not that he spake to them of the Father.

28 Then said Jesus unto them, When ye have [z]lifted up the Son of man, [a]then shall ye know that I am *he,* and [b]*that* I do nothing of myself; but [c]as my Father hath taught me, I speak these things.

29 And [d]he that sent me is with me: [e]the Father hath not left me alone; [f]for I do always those things that please him.

30 As he spake these words, [g]many believed on him.

The true children of Abraham

31 Then said Jesus to those Jews

8:30 [g]ch. 7:31 & 10:42 & 11:45

8:11 NEITHER DO I CONDEMN THEE. Jesus' attitude toward the woman reflects His redemptive purpose for the human race (3:16). He does not condemn her as unfit for forgiveness, but treats her with kindness, forbearance, and patience in order to lead her to repentance. For her there is salvation if she "sins no more," i.e., ceases to live in adultery and returns to her own husband (cf. Luke 7:47). (1) However, it would be blasphemous to use these words of Christ to suggest that He looks casually upon the sin of adultery and the untold heartbreak and misery it causes for both adults and children. (2) What Christ offers this woman is salvation and a way out of her life of sin. The condemnation and wrath of Christ awaits her if she refuses to repent and enter the kingdom of God (Rom. 2:1–10).

8:12 THE LIGHT OF THE WORLD. Jesus is the true light (1:9); as such, He removes darkness and deception by illuminating the right way to God and to salvation. (1) All those who follow Jesus are delivered from the darkness of sin, the world, and Satan. Those who still walk in darkness do not follow Him (cf. 1 John 1:6–7). (2) "He that followeth me" is a present participle and has the idea of a continuous following. Jesus recognized only persevering discipleship (see next note).

8:31 IF YE CONTINUE IN MY WORD. Jesus never encouraged his disciples to place confidence in the mere fact of past faith or experience. It is only as we continue in His word that confidence in salvation is warranted. Genuine disciples of Christ continue to obey the words of Christ (see 15:6, note; Luke 21:19).

which believed on him, If ye continue
in my word, *then* are ye my disciples
indeed;
32 And ye shall know the truth, and
[h]the truth shall make you free.
33 ¶ They answered him, [i]We be
Abraham's seed, and were never in
bondage to any man: how sayest thou,
Ye shall be made free?
34 Jesus answered them, Verily,
verily, I say unto you, [j]Whosoever
committeth sin is the servant of sin.
35 And [k]the servant abideth not in
the house for ever: *but* the Son abideth
ever.
36 [l]If the Son therefore shall
make you free, ye shall be free indeed.
37 I know that ye are Abraham's
seed; but [m]ye seek to kill me, because
my word hath no place in you.
38 [n]I speak that which I have seen
with my Father: and ye do that which
ye have seen with your father.
39 They answered and said unto
him, [o]Abraham is our father. Jesus
saith unto them, [p]If ye were Abra-
ham's children, ye would do the works
of Abraham.
40 [q]But now ye seek to kill me, a
man that hath told you the truth,
[r]which I have heard of God: this did
not Abraham.
41 Ye do the deeds of your father.
Then said they to him, We be not born
of fornication; [s]we have one Father,
even God.
42 Jesus said unto them, [t]If God
were your Father, ye would love me:
[u]for I proceeded forth and came from
God; [v]neither came I of myself, but he
sent me.
43 [w]Why do ye not understand my
speech? *even* because ye cannot hear
my word.
44 [x]Ye are of *your* father the devil,

8:32 [h]Rom. 6:14,18,22 Jas. 1:25 & 2:12
8:33 [i]Lev. 25:42 Mat. 3:9
8:34 [j]Rom 6:16 2 Pet. 2:19
8:35 [k]Gal. 4:30
8:36 [l]Rom. 8:2 Gal. 5:1
8:37 [m]ch. 7:19
8:38 [n]ch. 3:32 & 5:19,30 & 14:10,24
8:39 [o]Mat. 3:9 [p]Rom. 2:28 & 9:7 Gal. 3:7,29
8:40 [q]ver. 37 [r]ver. 26
8:41 [s]Is. 63:16 & 64:8 Mal. 1:6
8:42 [t]1 John 5:1 [u]ch. 16:27 & 17:8,25 [v]ch. 5:43 & 7:28,29 **8:43** [w]ch. 7:17 **8:44** [x]Mat. 13:38; 1 John 3:8

8:32 THE TRUTH SHALL MAKE YOU FREE. In the context of human existence and knowledge, many things are true. Yet there is only one truth that will set people free from sin, destruction, and Satan's dominion—the truth of Jesus Christ found in God's Word. Some observations about truth are as follows: (1) The Scriptures, especially the original revelation of Christ and the N.T. apostles, testify to the truth which frees one from sin, the world, and the demonic (see Eph. 2:20, note). (2) Further revelation of "truth" is not needed to complete or make more adequate the gospel of Christ. (3) Saving truth is revealed only from God "by his Spirit" (1 Cor. 2:10) and does not originate from any person or from human wisdom (1 Cor. 2:12–13).

8:34 WHOSOEVER COMMITTETH SIN. The N.T. clearly teaches that the Lord Jesus Christ breaks the power and dominion of sin in the lives of those who are His true followers (vv. 31–32,36). Individuals who habitually sin are still slaves to sin and unrighteousness and therefore the property of Satan (cf. 1 John 3:6–10). The union of sincere believers with Christ in His death and resurrection will result in freedom from sin (cf. Rom. 6; see v. 36, note).

8:36 YE SHALL BE FREE INDEED. The unsaved person is a slave to sin, impurity, and lawlessness (v. 34; Rom. 6:17–20). Enslaved to sin and Satan, he must live according to the lusts of the flesh and desires of Satan (Eph. 2:1–3). (1) A true believer, who possesses salvation in Christ with the accompanying grace of the indwelling Holy Spirit, is set free from the power of sin and immorality (Rom. 6:17–22; 8:1–17). When he faces temptation to sin, he now has the power to act according to God's will. He is free to be enslaved to God and righteousness (Rom. 6:18,22).

(2) Freedom from the slavery of sin is one sure criterion by which all professing believers may test and prove whether they have eternal life with its regenerating and sanctifying grace dwelling in them. Anyone presently in a state of bondage to immorality either has never experienced spiritual rebirth by the Holy Spirit or, having experienced spiritual regeneration, has yielded to sin and once more entered into the spiritual death that brings slavery to sin (Rom. 6:16,21,23; 8:12–13; see 1 John 3:15, note).

(3) This is not to say, however, that believers are free from spiritual warfare against sin. Throughout our lives, we will have to constantly fight against the pressures of the world, the flesh, and the devil (see Gal. 5:17, note; Eph. 6:11–12, notes). Full freedom from temptation and the pull of sin will come only with complete redemption at death or at the return of Christ for His faithful. What Christ offers us now is the sanctifying power of His life, whereby those who follow the Spirit are set free from the desires and passions of the flesh (Gal. 5:16–24) and enabled to live holy and blameless before Him in love (Eph. 1:4).

8:42 IF GOD WERE YOUR FATHER. Here Jesus states a fundamental principle of salvation, namely, that the evidence of being a true child of God (i.e., born again of God) lies in one's attitude of love toward Jesus. For this reason, one must manifest an attitude of sincere loyalty, faith, and obedience toward Christ. Otherwise, the claim to be a child of God is illegitimate (vv. 31,42; 10:2–5,14,27–28; 14:15,21).

8:44 HE IS A LIAR, AND THE FATHER OF IT. Lying is specifically mentioned as a characteristic of the devil; he is the source of all falsehood (Gen. 3:1–6; Acts 5:3; 2 Thes. 2:9–11; Rev. 12:9). It is a sin wholly opposite to the mind of God, who is truth (Rev. 19:11). An indifference to the sin of lying is one of the most unmistakable symptoms

and the lusts of your father ye will do. He was a murderer from the beginning, and [y]abode not in the truth, because there is no truth in him. When he speaketh a lie, he speaketh of his own: for he is a liar, and the father of it.

45 And because I tell *you* the truth, ye believe me not.

46 Which of you convinceth me of sin? And if I say the truth, why do ye not believe me?

47 [z]He that is of God heareth God's words: ye therefore hear *them* not, because ye are not of God.

Controversy with the Jews

48 Then answered the Jews, and said unto him, Say we not well that thou art a Samaritan, and [a]hast a devil?

49 Jesus answered, I have not a devil; but I honour my Father, and ye do dishonour me.

50 And [b]I seek not mine own glory: there is one that seeketh and judgeth.

51 Verily, verily, I say unto you, [c]If a man keep my saying, he shall never see death.

52 Then said the Jews unto him, Now we know that thou hast a devil. [d]Abraham is dead, and the prophets; and thou sayest, If a man keep my saying, he shall never taste of death.

53 Art thou greater than our father Abraham, which is dead? and the prophets are dead: whom makest thou thyself ?

54 Jesus answered, If I honour myself, my honour is nothing: [e]it is my Father that honoureth me; of whom ye say, that he is your God:

55 Yet [f]ye have not known him; but I know him: and if I should say, I know him not, I shall be a liar like unto you: but I know him, and keep his saying.

56 Your father Abraham [g]rejoiced to see my day: [h]and he saw *it*, and was glad.

57 Then said the Jews unto him, Thou art not yet fifty years old, and hast thou seen Abraham?

58 Jesus said unto them, Verily, verily, I say unto you, Before Abraham was, [i]I am.

59 Then [j]took they up stones to cast at him: but Jesus hid himself, and went out of the temple, [k]going through the midst of them, and so passed by.

Jesus heals the man born blind

9 AND AS *Jesus* passed by, he saw a man which was blind from *his* birth.

2 And his disciples asked him, saying, Master, [l]who did sin, this man, or his parents, that he was born blind?

3 Jesus answered, Neither hath this man sinned, nor his parents: [m]but that the works of God should be made manifest in him.

4 [n]I must work the works of him that sent me, while it is day: the night cometh, when no man can work.

5 As long as I am in the world, [o]I am the light of the world.

6 When he had thus spoken, [p]he spat on the ground, and made clay of the spittle, and he [*]anointed the eyes of the blind man with the clay,

7 And said unto him, Go, wash [q]in the pool of Siloam, (which is by interpretation, Sent.) [r]He went his way therefore, and washed, and came seeing.

8 ¶ The neighbours therefore, and they which before had seen him that he was blind, said, Is not this he that sat and begged?

9 Some said, This is he: others *said*, He is like him: *but* he said, I am *he*.

10 Therefore said they unto him, How were thine eyes opened?

11 He answered and said, [s]A man that is called Jesus made clay, and anointed mine eyes, and said unto me, Go to the pool of Siloam, and wash: and

[*] Or, *spread the clay upon the eyes of the blind man*

8:44 [y]Jude 6
8:47 [z]ch. 10:26; 1 John 4:6
8:48 [a]ver. 52; ch. 7:20 & 10:20
8:50 [b]ch. 5:41 & 7:18
8:51 [c]ch. 5:24 & 11:26
8:52 [d]Zech. 1:5; Heb. 11:13
8:54 [e]ch. 5:41 & 16:14 & 17:1; Acts 3:13
8:55 [f]ch. 7:28,29
8:56 [g]Luke 10:24 [h]Heb. 11:13
8:58 [i]Ex. 3:14; Is. 43:13; ch. 17:5,24; Col. 1:17; Rev. 1:8
8:59 [j]ch. 10:31,39 & 11:8 [k]Luke 4:30
9:2 [l]ver. 34
9:3 [m]ch. 11:4
9:4 [n]ch. 4:34 & 5:19,36 & 11:9 & 12:35 & 17:4
9:5 [o]ch. 1:5,9 & 3:19 & 8:12 & 12:35,46
9:6 [p]Mark 7:33 & 8:23
9:7 [q]Neh. 3:15 [r]See 2 Ki. 5:14
9:11 [s]ver. 6,7

of an ungodly condition, an indication that one is not born of the Spirit (3:6), but is presently under the influence of Satan as his spiritual father (see 4:24, note; Rev. 22:15, note).

9:3 WORKS OF GOD . . . BE MADE MANIFEST. Jesus corrects the disciples' erroneous belief that every serious affliction or calamity is the result of some sin. At times sickness does result from a serious sin (5:14), but not always. Sometimes affliction is permitted because of a divine purpose, i.e., to show forth God's mercy, love, and power. Often in the world the innocent suffer when the wicked do not (cf. Ps. 73:1–14; see article on THE SUFFERING OF THE RIGHTEOUS, p. 764).

9:4 THE NIGHT COMETH. The term "day" refers to life, while "night" refers to death. We go through this world only once; what we do or do not do now will have eternal consequences.

I went and washed, and I received sight.

12 Then said they unto him, Where is he? He said, I know not.

Pharisees question the healed man

13 ¶ They brought to the Pharisees him that aforetime was blind.

14 And it was the sabbath day when Jesus made the clay, and opened his eyes.

15 Then again the Pharisees also asked him how he had received his sight. He said unto them, He put clay upon mine eyes, and I washed, and do see.

16 Therefore said some of the Pharisees, This man is not of God, because he keepeth not the sabbath day. Others said, [t]How can a man that is a sinner do such miracles? And [u]there was a division among them.

17 They say unto the blind man again, What sayest thou of him, that he hath opened thine eyes? He said, [v]He is a prophet.

18 But the Jews did not believe concerning him, that he had been blind, and received his sight, until they called the parents of him that had received his sight.

19 And they asked them, saying, Is this your son, who ye say was born blind? how then doth he now see?

20 His parents answered them and said, We know that this is our son, and that he was born blind:

21 But by what means he now seeth, we know not; or who hath opened his eyes, we know not: he is of age; ask him: he shall speak for himself.

22 These *words* spake his parents, because [w]they feared the Jews: for the Jews had agreed already, that if any man did confess that he was Christ, he [x]should be put out of the synagogue.

23 Therefore said his parents, He is of age; ask him.

24 Then again called they the man that was blind, and said unto him, [y]Give God the praise: [z]we know that this man is a sinner.

25 He answered and said, Whether he be a sinner *or no,* I know not: one thing I know, that, whereas I was blind, now I see.

26 Then said they to him again, What did he to thee? how opened he thine eyes?

27 He answered them, I have told you already, and ye did not hear: wherefore would ye hear *it* again? will ye also be his disciples?

28 Then they reviled him, and said, Thou art his disciple; but we are Moses' disciples.

29 We know that God spake unto Moses: *as for* this *fellow,* [a]we know not from whence he is.

30 The man answered and said unto them, [b]Why herein is a marvellous thing, that ye know not from whence he is, and *yet* he hath opened mine eyes.

31 Now we know that [c]God heareth not sinners: but if any man be a worshipper of God, and doeth his will, him he heareth.

32 Since the world began was it not heard that any man opened the eyes of one that was born blind.

33 [d]If this man were not of God, he could do nothing.

34 They answered and said unto him, [e]Thou wast altogether born in sins, and dost thou teach us? And they [†]cast him out.

Jesus talks to the healed man

35 Jesus heard that they had cast him out; and when he had found him, he said unto him, Dost thou believe on [f]the Son of God?

36 He answered and said, Who is he, Lord, that I might believe on him?

37 And Jesus said unto him, Thou hast both seen him, and [g]it is he that talketh with thee.

9:16 [t]ver. 33 ch. 3:2 [u]ch. 7:12,43 & 10:19 **9:17** [v]ch. 4:19 & 6:14 **9:22** [w]ch. 7:13 & 12:42 & 19:38 Acts 5:13 [x]ver. 34 ch. 16:2 **9:24** [y]Josh. 7:19 1 Sam. 6:5 [z]ver. 16 **9:29** [a]ch. 8:14 **9:30** [b]ch. 3:10 **9:31** [c]Job 27:9 & 35:12 Ps. 18:41 & 34:15 & 66:18 Prov. 1:28 & 15:29 & 28:9 Is. 1:15 Jer. 11:11 & 14:12 Ezek. 8:18 Mic. 3:4 Zech. 7:13 **9:33** [d]ver. 16 **9:34** [e]ver. 2 **9:35** [f]Mat. 14:33 & 16:16 Mark 1:1 ch. 10:36 1 John 5:13 **9:37** [g]ch. 4:26

† Or, *excommunicated him;* see ver. 22

9:34 THEY CAST HIM OUT. One of the best things that happened to the man born blind was excommunication from his former religion. If he had been allowed to stay in the synagogue, he would have been in danger of drifting back to the traditional ways of Judaism and gradually be alienated from Christ and the gospel. Today the same thing can happen to those finding salvation in Christ who are in lukewarm churches or non-Biblical religious organizations. If they remain in that church or system, they may lose their hunger for true Biblical Christianity and return to embrace the false ways of their former religion. The best thing is to be separated from what is not of God, so that Christ may come near to us in the fullest sense (vv. 35–38).

38 And he said, Lord, I believe. And he worshipped him.

39 ¶ And Jesus said, [h]For judgment I am come into this world, [i]that they which see not might see; and that they which see might be made blind.

40 And *some* of the Pharisees which were with him heard these words, [j]and said unto him, Are we blind also?

41 Jesus said unto them, [k]If ye were blind, ye should have no sin: but now ye say, We see; therefore your sin remaineth.

9:39 [h]ch. 5:22,27 See ch. 3:17 & 12:47 [i]Mat. 13:13
9:40 [j]Rom. 2:19
9:41 [k]ch. 15:22,24

Jesus the good shepherd

10 VERILY, VERILY, I say unto you, He that entereth not by the door into the sheepfold, but climbeth up some other way, the same is a thief and a robber.

2 But he that entereth in by the door is the shepherd of the sheep.

3 To him the porter openeth; and the sheep hear his voice: and he calleth his own sheep by name, and leadeth them out.

4 And when he putteth forth his own sheep, he goeth before them, and the sheep follow him: for they know his voice.

5 And a stranger will they not follow, but will flee from him: for they know not the voice of strangers.

6 This parable spake Jesus unto them: but they understood not what things they were which he spake unto them.

7 Then said Jesus unto them again, Verily, verily, I say unto you, I am the door of the sheep.

8 All that ever came before me are thieves and robbers: but the sheep did not hear them.

9 [l]I am the door: by me if any man enter in, he shall be saved, and shall go in and out, and find pasture.

10 The thief cometh not, but for to steal, and to kill, and to destroy: I am come that they might have life, and that they might have *it* more abundantly.

11 [m]I am the good shepherd: the good shepherd giveth his life for the sheep.

12 But he that is an hireling, and not the shepherd, whose own the sheep are not, seeth the wolf coming, and [n]leaveth the sheep, and fleeth: and the wolf catcheth them, and scattereth the sheep.

13 The hireling fleeth, because he is an hireling, and careth not for the sheep.

14 I am the good shepherd, and [o]know my *sheep,* and am known of mine.

15 [p]As the Father knoweth me, even so know I the Father: [q]and I lay down my life for the sheep.

16 And [r]other sheep I have, which are not of this fold: them also I must bring, and they shall hear my voice; [s]and there shall be one fold, *and* one shepherd.

17 Therefore doth my Father love me, [t]because I lay down my life, that I might take it again.

10:9 [l]ch. 14:6 Eph. 2:18
10:11 [m]Is. 40:11 Ezek. 34:12,23 & 37:24 Heb. 13:20 1 Pet. 2:25 & 5:4
10:12 [n]Zech. 11:16,17
10:14 [o]2 Tim. 2:19
10:15 [p]Mat. 11:27 [q]ch. 15:13
10:16 [r]Is. 56:8 [s]Ezek. 37:22 Eph. 2:14 1 Pet. 2:25
10:17 [t]Is. 53:7,8,12 Heb. 2:9

10:1 JESUS THE GOOD SHEPHERD. The discourse about the good shepherd (vv. 1–30) sets forth Jesus as the true shepherd and ruler of His people in contrast to all false shepherds. To better understand this chapter, O.T. passages condemning false shepherds should be read: Is. 56:9–12; Jer. 23:1–4; Ezek. 34; Zech. 11. In vv. 7–18, Jesus applies vv. 1–5 to Himself.

10:9 I AM THE DOOR. Jesus is the door for the sheep. Those who enter through Him will be "saved," i.e., will have abundant eternal life (v. 10) and have all they need to be delivered from sin, guilt, and condemnation. Jesus is the *only* door for salvation; none other exists (Acts 4:12).

10:11 I AM THE GOOD SHEPHERD. Jesus declares Himself to be the promised good shepherd (see Ps. 23:1, note; Is. 40:11, note; Ezek. 34:23, note; 37:24). (1) This metaphor illustrates Jesus' tender and devoted care for His people. It is as if He is saying, "I am toward all who believe in me, as a good shepherd is toward his sheep—caring, watchful, and loving."

(2) The distinguishing mark of Christ as the good shepherd is His willingness to die for His sheep. This emphasizes the uniqueness of Christ the shepherd: His death on the cross saves His sheep (Is. 53:12; Mat. 20:28; Mark 10:45). Christ is called the "good shepherd" here, the "great shepherd" in Heb. 13:20, and the "chief Shepherd" in 1 Pet. 5:4.

(3) Be sure to note that the minister who serves merely to earn a living or to obtain honor is the "hireling" of vv. 12–13. The true pastor cares for his sheep, while the false pastor's first thought is for himself and his position before others.

10:14 I . . . KNOW MY *SHEEP*. God's knowledge of and love for His children involves personal affection, faithfulness, and constant providential care. The believer is graven in the palms of His hands (Is. 49:14–17, note). He is never out of God's mind, for God's eye continually watches over him for his good (cf. Ex. 33:17; Jer. 1:5; see Mat. 10:31, note; Rom. 8:28, note; see article on THE PROVIDENCE OF GOD, p. 80).

18 No man taketh it from me, but I
lay it down of myself. I have power to
lay it down, and I [u]have power to take
it again. [v]This commandment have I
received of my Father.
19 ¶ [w]There was a division there-
fore again among the Jews for these
sayings.
20 And many of them said, [x]He
hath a devil, and is mad; why hear ye
him?
21 Others said, These are not the
words of him that hath a devil. [y]Can
a devil [z]open the eyes of the blind?

The Jews try to arrest Jesus

22 ¶ And it was at Jerusalem the
feast of the dedication, and it was win-
ter.
23 And Jesus walked in the temple
[a]in Solomon's porch.
24 Then came the Jews round about
him, and said unto him, How long dost
thou [u]make us to doubt? If thou be the
Christ, tell us plainly.
25 Jesus answered them, I told you,
and ye believed not: [b]the works that
I do in my Father's name, they bear
witness of me.
26 But [c]ye believe not, because ye
are not of my sheep, as I said unto you.
27 [d]My sheep hear my voice, and I
know them, and they follow me:
28 And I give unto them eternal life;
and they shall never perish, neither
shall any *man* pluck them out of my
hand.
29 [e]My Father, [f]which gave *them*
me, is greater than all; and no *man* is
able to pluck *them* out of my Father's
hand.
30 [g]I and *my* Father are one.

10:18 [u]ch. 2:19 [v]ch. 6:38 & 15:10 Acts 2:24,32
10:19 [w]ch. 7:43 & 9:16
10:20 [x]ch. 7:20 & 8:48,52
10:21 [y]Ex. 4:11 Ps. 94:9 & 146:8 [z]ch. 9:6,7,32,33
10:23 [a]Acts 3:11 & 5:12
10:25 [b]ver. 38 ch. 3:2 & 5:36
10:26 [c]ch. 8:47
10:27 [d]ver. 4,14
10:29 [e]ch. 14:28 [f]ch. 17:2,6
10:30 [g]ch. 17:11,22
10:31 [h]ch. 8:59
10:33 [i]ch. 5:18
10:34 [j]Ps. 82:6
10:35 [k]Rom. 13:1
10:36 [l]ch. 6:27 [m]ch. 3:17 & 5:36,37 & 8:42 [n]ver. 30 ch. 5:17,18 [o]Luke 1:35 ch. 9:35,37
10:37 [p]ch. 15:24
10:38 [q]ch. 5:36 & 14:10,11 [r]ch. 14:10,11 & 17:21
10:39 [s]ch. 7:30,44 & 8:59
10:40 [t]ch. 1:28
10:41 [u]ch. 3:30
10:42 [v]ch. 8:30 & 11:45

31 Then [h]the Jews took up stones
again to stone him.
32 Jesus answered them, Many
good works have I shown you from my
Father; for which of those works do ye
stone me?
33 The Jews answered him, saying,
For a good work we stone thee not; but
for blasphemy; and because that thou,
being a man, [i]makest thyself God.
34 Jesus answered them, [j]Is it not
written in your law, I said, Ye are gods?
35 If he called them gods, [k]unto
whom the word of God came, and the
scripture cannot be broken;
36 Say ye of him, [l]whom the Fa-
ther hath sanctified, and [m]sent into
the world, Thou blasphemest; [n]be-
cause I said, I am [o]the Son of God?
37 [p]If I do not the works of my Fa-
ther, believe me not.
38 But if I do, though ye believe not
me, [q]believe the works: that ye may
know, and believe, [r]that the Father *is*
in me, and I in him.
39 [s]Therefore they sought again to
take him: but he escaped out of their
hand,
40 And went away again beyond
Jordan into the place [t]where John at
first baptized; and there he abode.
41 And many resorted unto him,
and said, John did no miracle: [u]but all
things that John spake of this man
were true.
42 [v]And many believed on him
there.

Jesus hears of Lazarus' death

11 NOW A certain *man* was sick,
named Lazarus, of Bethany, the

[u] Or, *hold us in suspense?*

10:27 MY SHEEP HEAR MY VOICE. Those who are true sheep of Christ obey His voice and follow Him; they are in constant fellowship with the shepherd. "Hear" and "follow" are in the present tense and denote habitual activity. To those who are following, the shepherd gives eternal life. Those sheep who stray from the shepherd and refuse to hear and follow His voice, prove that they are not His sheep (15:1–6).

10:28 THEY SHALL NEVER PERISH. Here is a precious promise given to all who are Christ's sheep. They will never perish (i.e., be banished forever from the presence of God), nor will any power or circumstance on earth take them from the shepherd. There is indeed safety and security for even the weakest sheep who follow and listen to the good shepherd (see previous note).

10:34 YE ARE GODS? In no way does this statement of Jesus teach that believers are to consider themselves gods. Those who declare themselves to be gods will fall under the condemnation of God, for He declares, "The gods that have not made the heavens and the earth, *even* they shall perish from the earth, and from under these heavens" (Jer. 10:11). (1) The term "ye are gods" was spoken by God to corrupt rulers of Israel who judged unjustly, were partial to the wicked, and were cruel to children (Ps. 82:1–4). These rulers, who thought they were gods, were to suffer the judgment of God and die (Ps. 82:7; see 82:6, note). (2) To declare oneself a god is the sin of the antichrist (see 2 Thes. 2:4,11; see article on THE AGE OF THE ANTICHRIST, p. 1896).

town of [w]Mary and her sister Martha.
2 ([x]It was *that* Mary which anointed the Lord with ointment, and wiped his feet with her hair, whose brother Lazarus was sick.)
3 Therefore his sisters sent unto him, saying, Lord, behold, he whom thou lovest is sick.
4 When Jesus heard *that*, he said, This sickness is not unto death, [y]but for the glory of God, that the Son of God might be glorified thereby.
5 Now Jesus loved Martha, and her sister, and Lazarus.
6 When he had heard therefore that he was sick, [z]he abode two days still in the same place where he was.
7 Then after that saith he to *his* disciples, Let us go into Judaea again.
8 *His* disciples say unto him, Master, [a]the Jews of late sought to stone thee; and goest thou thither again?
9 Jesus answered, Are there not twelve hours in the day? [b]If any man walk in the day, he stumbleth not, because he seeth the light of this world.
10 But [c]if a man walk in the night, he stumbleth, because there is no light in him.
11 These things said he: and after that he saith unto them, Our friend Lazarus [d]sleepeth; but I go, that I may awake him out of sleep.
12 Then said his disciples, Lord, if he sleep, he shall do well.
13 Howbeit Jesus spake of his death: but they thought that he had spoken of taking of rest in sleep.

11:1 [w]Luke 10:38,39
11:2 [x]Mat. 26:7 Mark 14:3 ch. 12:3
11:4 [y]ver. 40 ch. 9:3
11:6 [z]ch. 10:40
11:8 [a]ch. 10:31
11:9 [b]ch. 9:4
11:10 [c]ch. 12:35
11:11 [d]Deut. 31:16 Dan. 12:2 Mat. 9:24 Acts 7:60 1 Cor. 15:18,51
11:22 [e]ch. 9:31
11:24 [f]Luke 14:14 ch. 5:29
11:25 [g]ch. 5:21 & 6:39,40,44

14 Then said Jesus unto them plainly, Lazarus is dead.
15 And I am glad for your sakes that I was not there, to the intent ye may believe; nevertheless let us go unto him.
16 Then said Thomas, which is called Didymus, unto his fellowdisciples, Let us also go, that we may die with him.

Jesus the resurrection and the life

17 Then when Jesus came, he found that he had *lain* in the grave four days already.
18 Now Bethany was nigh unto Jerusalem, [v]about fifteen furlongs off:
19 And many of the Jews came to Martha and Mary, to comfort them concerning their brother.
20 Then Martha, as soon as she heard that Jesus was coming, went and met him: but Mary sat *still* in the house.
21 Then said Martha unto Jesus, Lord, if thou hadst been here, my brother had not died.
22 But I know, that even now, [e]whatsoever thou wilt ask of God, God will give *it* thee.
23 Jesus saith unto her, Thy brother shall rise again.
24 Martha saith unto him, [f]I know that he shall rise again in the resurrection at the last day.
25 Jesus said unto her, I am [g]the 

[v]i.e. *about two* miles

11:4 SICKNESS ... FOR THE GLORY OF GOD. Sickness among God's people will never result in death as the final outcome. Death ultimately will be destroyed by the resurrection (vv. 25–26). The final truth is that those who believe in Christ "shall never die" (v. 26; see article on DEATH, p. 782).

11:5 JESUS LOVED MARTHA, AND HER SISTER, AND LAZARUS. Here is a family that had a genuine and strong devotion to Jesus (v. 2), enjoyed intimate fellowship with Him (Luke 10:38–42), and was especially loved by Him (vv. 3–5). Nevertheless, they experienced sorrow, distress, sickness, and death. Today these afflictions can and will happen to God's faithful and chosen believers (see article on THE SUFFERING OF THE RIGHTEOUS, p. 764). Churches will have people like Mary persevering in loving devotion to the Lord, like Martha being faithful in good works, and like Lazarus suffering and dying. Families like this may cry out, "How long wilt thou forget me, O Lord?" (Ps. 13:1; cf. Mat. 27:46; Rev. 6:10). Jesus states that His delay is not for lack of love, mercy, or compassion, but for the glory of God (v. 4) and His kingdom and for the ultimate eternal good of the sufferers (vv. 15,23–26,40–44).

11:6 HE ABODE TWO DAYS STILL. Jesus delayed going to the family He loved (v. 5) in order to strengthen the faith of that family and the disciples, and to perform for them a greater good. Initially, Jesus' actions appeared to indicate that He was unconcerned and untouched by their suffering. This was not the case, however, since John repeatedly emphasizes that Jesus loved the family and shared their sorrow (vv. 3,5,35). The timing and purpose of Jesus was different from what they wanted. God's timing and will, in the midst of our trials or troubles, may be different from what we desire. God answers us according to His wisdom and love.

11:25–26 I AM THE RESURRECTION. For the person who believes in Jesus, physical death is not a tragic end. It is instead the gateway to abundant eternal life and fellowship with God. "Yet shall he live" refers to the resurrection; the "shall never die" of v. 26 means that the resurrect-

JESUS IN JUDEA AND SAMARIA

Ptolemais

Mediterranean Sea

Capernaum

Sea of Galilee

GALILEE

Tiberias

Cana

Yarmuk R.

Nazareth

Mt. Tabor

Nain

Jordan R.

Scythopolis

Caesarea

The most important port in Judea in NT times.

Pella

Salim

Aenon

John the Baptist baptized here (Jn 3:23). It was also the probable location of John's ministry.

SAMARIA

Here Jesus talked with a Samaritan woman, at Jacob's well (Jn 4:5).

Samaria

Sychar

Mt. Gerizim

Jabbok R.

The mountain referred to by the Samaritan woman at the well as the worship center for the Samaritans (Jn 4:20-23).

Jordan R.

PEREA

JUDEA

Most important Biblical city. Jesus was crucified here as predicted (Mt 16:21; Mk 10:33; Lk 18:31).

The resurrected Jesus appeared to two people walking to Emmaus and he ate with them there (Lk 24:13).

Jericho

Jesus healed a blind man here (Mt 20:29), and called Zacchaeus down from a tree (Lk 19:1). The Good Samaritan helped a traveler en route here (Lk 10:30).

Emmaus

Jerusalem

Bethany

Jesus raised Lazarus from the dead (Jn 11:43-44). Here Jesus was anointed in the house of Simon the Leper (Mt 26:6). It was also the scene of the ascension (Lk 24:50-51).

Bethlehem

The birthplace of Jesus (Mt 2:1; Lk 2:4).

Dead Sea

Machaerus

Arnon R.

Miles 5 0 10 20

Kms 5 0 10 20 30

resurrection, and the life: [h]he that be-
lieveth in me, though he were dead, yet
shall he live:
26 And whosoever liveth and be-
lieveth in me shall never die. Believest
John 20:31 thou this?
27 She saith unto him, Yea, Lord:
[i]I believe that thou art the Christ, the
Son of God, which should come into the
world.
28 And when she had so said, she
went her way, and called Mary her sis-
ter secretly, saying, The Master is
come, and calleth for thee.
29 As soon as she heard *that,* she
arose quickly, and came unto him.
30 Now Jesus was not yet come into
the town, but was in that place where
Martha met him.
31 [j]The Jews then which were
with her in the house, and comforted
her, when they saw Mary, that she rose
up hastily and went out, followed her,
saying, She goeth unto the grave to
weep there.
32 Then when Mary was come
where Jesus was, and saw him, she fell
down at his feet, saying unto him,
[k]Lord, if thou hadst been here, my
brother had not died.
33 When Jesus therefore saw her
weeping, and the Jews also weeping
which came with her, he groaned in the
spirit, and [w]was troubled,
34 And said, Where have ye laid
him? They said unto him, Lord, come
and see.
35 [l]Jesus wept.
36 Then said the Jews, Behold how
he loved him!
37 And some of them said, Could
not this man, [m]which opened the eyes
of the blind, have caused that even this
man should not have died?

Jesus raises Lazarus

38 Jesus therefore again groaning
in himself cometh to the grave. It was
a cave, and a stone lay upon it.
39 Jesus said, Take ye away the
stone. Martha, the sister of him that
was dead, saith unto him, Lord, by this
time he stinketh: for he hath been *dead*
four days.
40 Jesus saith unto her, Said I not
unto thee, that, if thou wouldest be-
lieve, thou shouldest [n]see the glory of
God?
41 Then they took away the stone
from the place where the dead was laid.
And Jesus lifted up *his* eyes, and said,
Father, I thank thee that thou hast
heard me.
42 And I knew that thou hearest me
always: but [o]because of the people
which stand by I said *it,* that they may
believe that thou hast sent me.
43 And when he thus had spoken,
he cried with a loud voice, Lazarus,
come forth.
44 And he that was dead came
forth, bound hand and foot with grave-

11:25 [h]ch. 3:36; 1 John 5:10 **11:27** [i]Mat. 16:16; ch. 4:42 & 6:14,69 **11:31** [j]ver. 19 **11:32** [k]ver. 21 **11:35** [l]Luke 19:41 **11:37** [m]ch. 9:6 **11:40** [n]ver. 4,23 **11:42** [o]ch. 12:30

[w] Gk. *he troubled himself*

ed believer will never die. He will have a new body, immortal and incorruptible (1 Cor. 15;42,54), one that cannot die or deteriorate (cf. Rom. 8:10; 2 Cor. 4:16; see article on THE RESURRECTION OF THE BODY, p. 1799).

11:33 HE GROANED IN THE SPIRIT. This passage reveals the heart and feelings of Jesus as He faces the heartbreak and suffering caused by all the evil in the world. (1) The verb rendered "groaned" (Gk. *embrimaomai*) denotes profound emotion involving anger. It signifies that Jesus was moved to deep grief and anger by all the misery resulting from sin, Satan, and death. His soul is filled not with cold unconcern, but with rage toward evil, as He fights for the salvation of the human race (see 11:35, note; Mat. 23:13, note; also Mat. 21:12–13; Mark 11:15,17; Luke 19:45–46; John 2:14–16).

(2) Likewise for us as believers, one of the surest signs of the work of God in our lives is that we begin to notice how much misery, sorrow, and suffering sin has caused in the world (cf. Gen. 3:16–19; Rom. 5:12). As we do so, a compassion for the suffering and a hatred for sin will arise in our hearts . In no way can we experience pleasure in sin (see Rom. 1:32, note; 2 Thes. 2:12, note; Heb. 1:9, note).

11:35 JESUS WEPT. This shortest verse of the Bible reveals the deep sympathy God feels for the sorrow of His people. The verb "wept" (Gk. *dakruō*) indicates He burst into tears, then wept silently. Let this be a comfort to all who experience sorrow. Christ feels the same sympathy for you that He felt for the relatives of Lazarus. He loves you that much. Note that this verse occurs in the book which stresses His deity more than any other book. This was Jesus, the God/man, deity Himself weeping. God does have a deep, emotional, and sympathetic love for you and others (Luke 19:41).

11:44 HE THAT WAS DEAD CAME FORTH. The miracle of Lazarus's resurrection was a sign pointing to Jesus as the resurrection and the life. It was a demonstration of what God will do for all believers who have died, for they too will be raised from the dead (14:3; 1 Thes. 4:13–18). This miracle was also the final issue that caused the Jewish leaders to resolve that Jesus must be put to death (vv. 45–53).

clothes: and [p]his face was bound about with a napkin. Jesus saith unto them, Loose him, and let him go.

Pharisees plot to kill Jesus

45 Then many of the Jews which came to Mary, [q]and had seen the things which Jesus did, believed on him.

46 But some of them went their ways to the Pharisees, and told them what things Jesus had done.

47 ¶ [r]Then gathered the chief priests and the Pharisees a council, and said, [s]What do we? for this man doeth many miracles.

48 If we let him thus alone, all *men* will believe on him: and the Romans shall come and take away both our place and nation.

49 And one of them, *named* [t]Caiaphas, being the high priest that same year, said unto them, Ye know nothing at all,

50 [u]Nor consider that it is expedient for us, that one man should die for the people, and that the whole nation perish not.

51 And this spake he not of himself: but being high priest that year, he prophesied that Jesus should die for that nation;

52 And [v]not for that nation only, [w]but that also he should gather together in one the children of God that were scattered abroad.

53 Then from that day forth they took counsel together for to put him to death.

54 Jesus [x]therefore walked no more openly among the Jews; but went thence unto a country near to the wilderness, into a city called [y]Ephraim, and there continued with his disciples.

55 ¶ [z]And the Jews' passover was nigh at hand: and many went out of the country up to Jerusalem before the passover, to purify themselves.

56 [a]Then sought they for Jesus, and spake among themselves, as they stood in the temple, What think ye, that he will not come to the feast?

57 Now both the chief priests and the Pharisees had given a commandment, that, if any man knew where he were, he should show *it*, that they might take him.

11:44 [p]ch. 20:7
11:45 [q]ch. 2:23 & 10:42 & 12:11,18
11:47 [r]Ps. 2:2 Mat. 26:3 Mark 14:1 Luke 22:2 [s]ch. 12:19 Acts 4:16
11:49 [t]Luke 3:2 ch. 18:14 Acts 4:6
11:50 [u]ch. 18:14
11:52 [v]Is. 49:6 1 John 2:2 [w]ch. 10:16 Eph. 2:14-17
11:54 [x]ch. 4:1,3 & 7:1 [y]See 2 Chr. 13:19
11:55 [z]ch. 2:13 & 5:1 & 6:4
11:56 [a]ch. 7:11
12:1 [b]ch. 11:1,43
12:2 [c]Mat. 26:6 Mark 14:3
12:3 [d]Luke 10:38,39 ch. 11:2
12:6 [e]ch. 13:29
12:8 [f]Mat. 26:11 Mark 14:7
12:9 [g]ch. 11:43,44
12:10 [h]Luke 16:31
12:11 [i]ver. 18 ch. 11:45
12:12 [j]Mat. 21:8 Mark 11:8 Luke 19:35,36

Mary anoints Jesus

12:1–8Ref — Mat. 26:6–13; Mark 14:3–9; Luke 7:37–39

12 THEN JESUS six days before the passover came to Bethany, [b]where Lazarus was which had been dead, whom he raised from the dead.

2 [c]There they made him a supper; and Martha served: but Lazarus was one of them that sat at the table with him.

3 Then took [d]Mary a pound of ointment of spikenard, very costly, and anointed the feet of Jesus, and wiped his feet with her hair: and the house was filled with the odour of the ointment.

4 Then saith one of his disciples, Judas Iscariot, Simon's *son*, which should betray him,

5 Why was not this ointment sold for three hundred pence, and given to the poor?

6 This he said, not that he cared for the poor; but because he was a thief, and [e]had the bag, and bare what was put therein.

7 Then said Jesus, Let her alone: against the day of my burying hath she kept this.

8 For [f]the poor always ye have with you; but me ye have not always.

9 Much people of the Jews therefore knew that he was there: and they came not for Jesus' sake only, but that they might see Lazarus also, [g]whom he had raised from the dead.

10 ¶ [h]But the chief priests consulted that they might put Lazarus also to death;

11 [i]Because that by reason of him many of the Jews went away, and believed on Jesus.

The triumphal entry

12:12–15pp — Mat. 21:4–9; Mark 11:7–10; Luke 19:35–38

12 ¶ [j]On the next day much people

12:3 MARY . . . ANOINTED THE FEET OF JESUS. Since the perfume was very expensive, Mary's anointing of Jesus was an act of great sacrifice and loving devotion. She knew that her opportunity to express devotion to Jesus would soon be over, so she took the opportunity she had. Her faith in and devotion to the Lord is the highest example of what God desires in believers. For this reason Jesus stated that her act of love would be told wherever the gospel is preached (see Mat. 26:13, note).

12:12 COMING TO JERUSALEM. See Mark

that were come to the feast, when they
heard that Jesus was coming to Jerusa-
lem,
13 Took branches of palm trees,
and went forth to meet him, and cried,
[k]Hosanna: Blessed *is* the King of Isra-
el that cometh in the name of the Lord.
14 [l]And Jesus, when he had found
a young ass, sat thereon; as it is writ-
ten,
15 [m]Fear not, daughter of Zion: be-
hold, thy King cometh, sitting on an
ass's colt.
16 These things [n]understood not
his disciples at the first: [o]but when
Jesus was glorified, [p]then remem-
bered they that these things were writ-
ten of him, and *that* they had done
these things unto him.
17 The people therefore that was
with him when he called Lazarus out of
his grave, and raised him from the
dead, bare record.
18 [q]For this cause the people also
met him, for that they heard that he
had done this miracle.
19 The Pharisees therefore said
among themselves, [r]Perceive ye how
ye prevail nothing? behold, the world is
gone after him.

Jesus sought by the Gentiles

20 ¶ And there [s]were certain
Greeks among them [t]that came up to
worship at the feast:
21 The same came therefore to
Philip, [u]which was of Bethsaida of
Galilee, and desired him, saying, Sir,
we would see Jesus.
22 Philip cometh and telleth An-
drew: and again Andrew and Philip tell
Jesus.
23 ¶ And Jesus answered them, say-
ing, [v]The hour is come, that the Son
of man should be glorified.
24 Verily, verily, I say unto you,
[w]Except a corn of wheat fall into
the ground and die, it abideth alone:
but if it die, it bringeth forth much
fruit.
25 [x]He that loveth his life shall
lose it; and he that hateth his life in
this world shall keep it unto life eter-
nal.
26 If any man serve me, let him fol-
low me; and [y]where I am, there shall
also my servant be: if any man serve
me, him will *my* Father honour.
27 [z]Now is my soul troubled; and
what shall I say? Father, save me from
this hour: [a]but for this cause came I
unto this hour.
28 Father, glorify thy name. [b]Then
came there a voice from heaven, *say-
ing*, I have both glorified *it*, and will
glorify *it* again.
29 The people therefore, that stood
by, and heard *it*, said that it thundered:
others said, An angel spake to him.
30 Jesus answered and said, [c]This
voice came not because of me, but for
your sakes.
31 Now is the judgment of this
world: now shall [d]the prince of this
world be cast out.
32 And I, [e]if I be lifted up from the
earth, will draw [f]all *men* unto me.
33 [g]This he said, signifying what
death he should die.

12:13 [k]Ps. 118:25,26
12:14 [l]Mat. 21:7
12:15 [m]Zech. 9:9
12:16 [n]Luke 18:34 [o]ch. 7:39 [p]ch. 14:26
12:18 [q]ver. 11
12:19 [r]ch. 11:47,48
12:20 [s]Acts 17:4 [t]1 Ki. 8:41,42 Acts 8:27
12:21 [u]ch. 1:44
12:23 [v]ch. 13:32 & 17:1
12:24 [w]1 Cor. 15:36
12:25 [x]Mat. 10:39 & 16:25 Mark 8:35 Luke 9:24 & 17:33
12:26 [y]ch. 14:3 & 17:24 1 Thes. 4:17
12:27 [z]Mat. 26:38,39 Luke 12:50 ch. 13:21 [a]Luke 22:53 ch. 18:37
12:28 [b]Mat. 3:17
12:30 [c]ch. 11:42
12:31 [d]Mat. 12:29 Luke 10:18 ch. 14:30 & 16:11 Acts 26:18 2 Cor. 4:4 Eph. 2:2 & 6:12
12:32 [e]ch. 3:14 & 8:28 [f]Rom. 5:18 Heb. 2:9
12:33 [g]ch. 18:32

11:9, note; Luke 19:28, note.

12:23 SON OF MAN . . . GLORIFIED. Jesus speaks of His death on the cross as a glorification rather than a tragedy. He tells His disciples that the way to fruitfulness is through suffering and death (v. 24).

12:25 HATETH HIS LIFE IN THIS WORLD. Hating one's own life points to the attitude that values heavenly and spiritual interests far above those of this earth. The believer places little importance in the pleasures, philosophies, successes, values, goals, or ways of the world. This type of person will gain "life eternal," for he counts nothing in this world so dear that he will not give it up for the sake of the Lord (Mat. 16:24–25; Mark 8:34–35).

12:26 IF ANY MAN SERVE ME. Faith in Jesus involves a personal commitment to follow Him, keep His teaching, and be where He is. Following Christ includes self-denial and taking up one's cross (see Mark 8:34, note on the meaning of taking up one's cross).

12:31 PRINCE OF THIS WORLD BE CAST OUT. Through the cross and resurrection of Christ the defeat of Satan and all he stands for has begun. His final defeat will occur when he is cast forever into the lake of fire (Rev. 20:10). At this present time, however, Satan is still active as the ruler or "god of this world" (14:30; 16:11; 2 Cor. 4:4; cf. Eph. 2:2). Satan has power and authority in the world and uses the things of the world against Christ and the church. This is why "friendship of the world is enmity with God" (Jas. 4:4; see also 1 John 2:15–16).

12:32 DRAW ALL *MEN* UNTO ME. The grace of God is not exclusive, i.e., for some people, but not for others. However, some, because of their love for sin, nullify the grace of God by their decisions and actions (see Mat. 23:37).

34 The people answered him, [h]We have heard out of the law that Christ abideth for ever: and how sayest thou, The Son of man must be lifted up? who is this Son of man?

35 Then Jesus said unto them, Yet a little while [i]is the light with you. [j]Walk while ye have the light, lest darkness come upon you: for [k]he that walketh in darkness knoweth not whither he goeth.

36 While ye have light, believe in the light, that ye may be [l]the children of light. These things spake Jesus, and departed, and [m]did hide himself from them.

The Jews continue in unbelief

37 ¶ But though he had done so many miracles before them, yet they believed not on him:

38 That the saying of Esaias the prophet might be fulfilled, which he spake, [n]Lord, who hath believed our report? and to whom hath the arm of the Lord been revealed?

39 Therefore they could not believe, because that Esaias said again,

40 [o]He hath blinded their eyes, and hardened their heart; that they should not see with *their* eyes, nor understand with *their* heart, and be converted, and I should heal them.

41 [p]These things said Esaias, when he saw his glory, and spake of him.

42 ¶ Nevertheless among the chief rulers also many believed on him; but [q]because of the Pharisees they did not confess *him,* lest they should be put out of the synagogue:

43 [r]For they loved the praise of men more than the praise of God.

A summary of Jesus' claims

44 ¶ Jesus cried and said, [s]He that believeth on me, believeth not on me, but on him that sent me.

45 And [t]he that seeth me seeth him that sent me.

46 [u]I am come a light into the world, that whosoever believeth on me should not abide in darkness.

47 And if any man hear my words, and believe not, [v]I judge him not: for [w]I came not to judge the world, but to save the world.

48 [x]He that rejecteth me, and receiveth not my words, hath one that judgeth him: [y]the word that I have spoken, the same shall judge him in the last day.

49 For [z]I have not spoken of myself; but the Father which sent me, he gave me a commandment, [a]what I should say, and what I should speak.

50 And I know that his commandment is life everlasting: whatsoever I speak therefore, even as the Father said unto me, so I speak.

Jesus in the upper room

13 NOW [b]BEFORE the feast of the passover, when Jesus knew that [c]his hour was come that he should depart out of this world unto the Father, having loved his own which were in the world, he loved them unto the end.

2 And supper being ended, [d]the devil having now put into the heart of Judas Iscariot, Simon's *son,* to betray him;

3 Jesus knowing [e]that the Father had given all things into his hands, and that he was come from God, and went to God;

Washing the disciples' feet

4 [f]He riseth from supper, and laid

12:34 [h]Ps. 89:36,37 & 110:4 Is. 9:7 & 53:8 Ezek. 37:25 Dan. 2:44 & 7:14,27 Mic. 4:7
12:35 [i]ch. 1:9 & 8:12 & 9:5 [j]Jer. 13:16 Eph. 5:8 [k]ch. 11:10 1 John 2:11
12:36 [l]Luke 16:8 Eph. 5:8 1 Thes. 5:5 1 John 2:9-11 [m]ch. 8:59 & 11:54
12:38 [n]Is. 53:1 Rom. 10:16
12:40 [o]Is. 6:9,10 Mat. 13:14
12:41 [p]Is. 6:1
12:42 [q]ch. 7:13 & 9:22
12:43 [r]ch. 5:44
12:44 [s]Mark 9:37 1 Pet. 1:21
12:45 [t]ch. 14:9
12:46 [u]ver. 35,36 ch. 3:19 & 9:5,39
12:47 [v]ch. 5:45 & 8:15,26 [w]ch. 3:17
12:48 [x]Luke 10:16 [y]Deut. 18:19 Mark 16:16
12:49 [z]ch. 8:38 & 14:10 [a]Deut. 18:18
13:1 [b]Mat. 26:2 [c]ch. 12:23 & 17:1,11
13:2 [d]Luke 22:3
13:3 [e]Mat. 11:27 & 28:18 ch. 3:35 & 17:2 Acts 2:36 1 Cor. 15:27 Heb. 2:8
13:4 [f]Luke 22:27; Phil. 2:7,8

12:39 THEY COULD NOT BELIEVE. The people could not believe because their decisions about Jesus brought God's action of hardening. The gospel never leaves unchanged the person who refuses to listen, repent, and believe. The apostle Paul says that Israel was broken off because of their unbelief (Rom. 11:20; cf. Ps. 95:8; Heb. 3:8). Yet the hardening was not permanent for every individual in that nation. Anyone who believed would receive everlasting life (vv. 44–50). In fact, many in Israel did believe after Pentecost (Acts 2:41).

12:43 LOVED THE PRAISE OF MEN. Because they love the approval of their fellow human beings, many sacrifice faith and conviction and act contrary to their consciences. They are ready to join the majority (cf. Dan. 11:32,34) and seek the favorable opinion of the powerful or the crowd. What is the secret of gaining victory over the fear of others and the desire for their praise? It is our faith (1 John 5:4), the faith that sees God, Christ, heaven, hell, the judgment, and eternity as ultimate realities (Rom. 1:20; Eph. 3:16–19; Heb. 11). Professing to follow Christ while loving human glory above the glory of God is blatant hypocrisy.

12:50 LIFE EVERLASTING. See 17:3, note.

aside his garments; and took a towel,
and girded himself.
5 After that he poureth water into a
basin, and began to wash the disciples'
feet, and to wipe *them* with the towel
wherewith he was girded.
6 Then cometh he to Simon Peter:
and [x]Peter saith unto him, Lord,
[g]dost thou wash my feet?
7 Jesus answered and said unto
him, What I do thou knowest not now;
[h]but thou shalt know hereafter.
8 Peter saith unto him, Thou shalt
never wash my feet. Jesus answered
him, [i]If I wash thee not, thou hast no
part with me.
9 Simon Peter saith unto him, Lord,
not my feet only, but also *my* hands and
my head.
10 Jesus saith to him, He that is
washed needeth not save to wash *his*
feet, but is clean every whit: and [j]ye
are clean, but not all.
11 For [k]he knew who should be-
tray him; therefore said he, Ye are not
all clean.
12 So after he had washed their
feet, and had taken his garments, and
was set down again, he said unto them,
Know ye what I have done to you?
13 [l]Ye call me Master and Lord:
and ye say well; for *so* I am.
14 [m]If I then, *your* Lord and Mas-
ter, have washed your feet; [n]ye also
ought to wash one another's feet.
15 For [o]I have given you an exam-
ple, that ye should do as I have done
to you.
16 [p]Verily, verily, I say unto you,
The servant is not greater than his
lord; neither he that is sent greater
than he that sent him.
17 [q]If ye know these things, happy
are ye if ye do them.
18 ¶ I speak not of you all: I know
whom I have chosen: but that the scrip-
ture may be fulfilled, [r]He that eateth
bread with me hath lifted up his heel
against me.
19 [s]Now[y] I tell you before it
come, that, when it is come to pass, ye
may believe that I am *he.*
20 [t]Verily, verily, I say unto you,
He that receiveth whomsoever I send
receiveth me; and he that receiveth me
receiveth him that sent me.

Judas Iscariot the traitor

21 [u]When Jesus had thus said,
[v]he was troubled in spirit, and testi-
fied, and said, Verily, verily, I say unto
you, that [w]one of you shall betray me.
22 Then the disciples looked one on
another, doubting of whom he spake.
23 Now [x]there was leaning on
Jesus' bosom one of his disciples,
whom Jesus loved.
24 Simon Peter therefore beckoned
to him, that he should ask who it
should be of whom he spake.
25 He then lying on Jesus' breast
saith unto him, Lord, who is it?
26 Jesus answered, He it is, to
whom I shall give a [z]sop, when I have
dipped *it.* And when he had dipped the
sop, he gave *it* to Judas Iscariot, *the son*
of Simon.
27 [y]And after the sop Satan en-

13:6 [g]Mat. 3:14 **13:7** [h]ver. 12 **13:8** [i]ch. 3:5 1 Cor. 6:11 Eph. 5:26 Tit. 3:5 Heb. 10:22 **13:10** [j]ch. 15:3 **13:11** [k]ch. 6:64 **13:13** [l]Mat. 23:8 Luke 6:46 1 Cor. 8:6 & 12:3 Phil. 2:11 **13:14** [m]Luke 22:27 [n]Rom. 12:10 Gal. 6:1,2 1 Pet. 5:5 **13:15** [o]Mat. 11:29 Phil. 2:5 1 Pet. 2:21 1 John 2:6 **13:16** [p]Mat. 10:24 Luke 6:40 ch. 15:20 **13:17** [q]Jas. 1:25 **13:18** [r]ver. 21 Ps. 41:9 Mat. 26:23 **13:19** [s]ch. 14:29 & 16:4 **13:20** [t]Mat. 10:40 & 25:40 Luke 10:16 **13:21** [u]Mat. 26:21 Mark 14:18 Luke 22:21 [v]ch. 12:27 [w]Acts 1:17 1 John 2:19 **13:23** [x]ch. 19:26 & 20:2 & 21:7,20 **13:27** [y]Luke 22:3 ch. 6:70

[x] Gk. *he* [y] Or, *From henceforth* [z] Or, *morsel*

13:5 WASH THE DISCIPLES' FEET. This dramatic act of foot washing occurred on the last night of Jesus' life on earth. Jesus did it (1) to demonstrate to His disciples how much He loved them; (2) to foreshadow His self-sacrifice on the cross; and (3) to convey to His disciples the truth that He was calling them to serve one another in humility. The passion to be great had continually plagued the disciples (Mat. 18:1–4; 20:20–27; Mark 9:33–37; Luke 9:46–48). Christ wanted them to see that the desire to be first — to be superior, honored, and glorified above our fellow Christians — is contrary to the spirit of Christ (see 13:12–17; Luke 22:24–30, note; 1 Pet. 5:5).

13:8 IF I WASH THEE NOT. These words point to a spiritual washing from sin through the cross. Apart from this no one can belong to Christ (1 John 1:7).

13:14 WASH ONE ANOTHER'S FEET. The early church appears to have followed Jesus' example and literally obeyed His admonition to humbly wash one another's feet in love and devotion. For example, in 1 Tim. 5:10 Paul states that widows should be cared for by the church if they qualified according to certain standards. One of those qualifications was, "if she have washed the saints' feet."

13:22 DOUBTING OF WHOM HE SPAKE. It is important to note that at no time did the disciples discern the duplicity of Judas. He had covered his hypocrisy very well. Even today there will be those in the church who outwardly appear righteous, yet inwardly have no real faith in and devotion to Christ (see article on FALSE TEACHERS, p. 1508).

13:26 SOP. The "sop" was a small piece of bread or meat. Jesus' giving the sop to Judas was probably a final appeal to persuade him to turn from his sin. Judas, however, refused to change his mind, and Satan took control (v. 27; see Luke 22:3, note).

tered into him. Then said Jesus unto
him, That thou doest, do quickly.
28 Now no man at the table knew
for what intent he spake this unto him.
29 For some *of them* thought, be-
cause [z]Judas had the bag, that Jesus
had said unto him, Buy *those things*
that we have need of against the feast;
or, that he should give something to
the poor.
30 He then having received the sop
went immediately out: and it was
night.

Jesus' time has come

31 ¶ Therefore, when he was gone
out, Jesus said, [a]Now is the Son of
man glorified, and [b]God is glorified in
him.
32 If God be glorified in him, God
shall also glorify him in himself, and
[c]shall straightway glorify him.
33 Little children, yet a little while
I am with you. Ye shall seek me: [d]and
as I said unto the Jews, Whither I go,
ye cannot come; so now I say to you.
34 [e]A new commandment I give
unto you, That ye love one another; as
I have loved you, that ye also love one
another.
35 [f]By this shall all *men* know that
ye are my disciples, if ye have love one
to another.

Peter's denial foretold

13:37–38pp — Mat. 26:33–35; Mark 14:29–31; Luke 22:33–34

36 ¶ Simon Peter said unto him,
Lord, whither goest thou? Jesus an-
swered him, Whither I go, thou canst
not follow me now; but [g]thou shalt fol-
low me afterwards.
37 Peter said unto him, Lord, why
cannot I follow thee now? I will [h]lay
down my life for thy sake.
38 Jesus answered him, Wilt thou
lay down thy life for my sake? Verily,
verily, I say unto thee, The cock shall
not crow, till thou hast denied me
thrice.

Jesus promises to return

14 LET [i]NOT your heart be trou-
bled: ye believe in God, believe
also in me.
2 In my Father's house are many
mansions: if *it were* not *so,* I would have
told you. [j]I go to prepare a place for
you.
3 And if I go and prepare a place for

13:29 [z]ch. 12:6
13:31 [a]ch. 12:23 [b]ch. 14:13 1 Pet. 4:11
13:32 [c]ch. 12:23
13:33 [d]ch. 8:21
13:34 [e]Lev. 19:18 ch. 15:12,17 Eph. 5:2 1 Thes. 4:9 Jas. 2:8 1 Pet. 1:22 1 John 2:7 & 3:11,23
13:35 [f]1 John 2:5 & 4:20
13:36 [g]ch. 21:18 2 Pet. 1:14
13:37 [h]Mat. 26:33 Mark 14:29 Luke 22:33
14:1 [i]ver. 27
14:2 [j]ch. 13:33

13:34 LOVE ONE ANOTHER. The Christian is commanded to love, in a greater and special way, all true Christians, whether or not they are members of one's own church or of one's particular theological persuasion. (1) Believers must distinguish true Christians from those whose profession is false, on the basis of their love and obedience to Jesus Christ and their loyalty to God's holy Scripture (5:24; 8:31; 10:27; Mat. 7:21; Gal. 1:9, note).

(2) Any person who possesses a living faith in Jesus Christ and remains loyal to God's inspired and inerrant Word as he sincerely understands it, while standing against the prevailing popular spirit of our day, is my brother or sister in Christ and one who deserves my special love, honor, and support.

(3) Loving all true Christians, including those who are not of our church, does not mean that we must compromise or accommodate our particular Biblical beliefs or doctrinal differences. Nor does it mean we must necessarily seek organizational unity.

(4) The Christian, as he practices love towards everyone and especially towards all true believers, must never compromise the holiness of God. It is essential that love for God and His will as revealed in His Word control and direct our love for others. Love for God must always be first (see next note; Mat. 22:37,39, notes).

13:35 KNOW THAT YE ARE MY DISCIPLES. Love (Gk. *agapē*) must be the distinguishing mark of Christ's followers (1 John 3:23; 4:7–21). This agape love is basically a self-giving and sacrificial love which seeks the good of another (1 John 4:9–10). Thus, the relationship between all believers must be characterized by a devoted purposeful concern which sacrificially seeks to promote the highest good of our brothers and sisters in Christ. Christians must befriend each other in trials, be careful of each other's feelings and reputation, and deny themselves to promote each other's welfare (cf. 1 Cor. 13; Gal. 6:2; 1 Thes. 4:9; 2 Thes. 1:3; 1 Pet. 1:22; 2 Pet. 1:7; 1 John 3:23).

14:2 MY FATHER'S HOUSE. This phrase clearly refers to heaven, for Jesus must "go" there in order to prepare a place for us (Mat. 6:9; cf. Ps. 33:13–14; Is. 63:15). God has a home where there are many rooms and to which the "household of God" now on earth (Eph. 2:19) will be transferred; "here we have no continuing city" (Heb. 13:14).

14:3 I WILL COME AGAIN. (1) As certain as Christ went to heaven, so He will return from His Father's presence and take His followers to be with Him in heaven (see previous note; cf. 17:24), to the place prepared for them. This is the hope of all believers. The ultimate purpose of the Lord's return is that believers may forever be with Him (see articles on THE RESURRECTION OF THE BODY, p. 1799, and THE RAPTURE, p. 1889).

(2) The words "receive you unto myself" refer to the rapture, when all living believers "shall be caught up together . . . in the clouds, to meet the Lord in the air: and so shall we ever

Acts 1:11
you, [k]I will come again, and receive
you unto myself; that [l]where I am,
there ye may be also.
4 And whither I go ye know, and the
way ye know.
5 Thomas saith unto him, Lord, we
know not whither thou goest; and how
can we know the way?

The way, the truth, and the life

6 Jesus saith unto him, I am [m]the
way, [n]the truth, and [o]the life: [p]no
man cometh unto the Father, but
by me.
7 [q]If ye had known me, ye should
have known my Father also: and from
henceforth ye know him, and have seen
him.
8 Philip saith unto him, Lord, show
us the Father, and it sufficeth us.
9 Jesus saith unto him, Have I been
so long time with you, and yet hast
thou not known me, Philip? [r]he that
hath seen me hath seen the Father;
and how sayest thou *then*, Show us the
Father?
10 Believest thou not that [s]I am in
the Father, and the Father in me? the
words that I speak unto you [t]I speak
not of myself: but the Father that
dwelleth in me, he doeth the works.
11 Believe me that I *am* in the Fa-
ther, and the Father in me: [u]or else
believe me for the very works' sake.

The promise of miracles

12 [v]Verily, verily, I say unto you,
He that believeth on me, the works
that I do shall he do also; and greater
works than these shall he do; because
I go unto my Father. Acts 3:1
13 [w]And whatsoever ye shall ask
in my name, that will I do, that the Fa-
ther may be glorified in the Son.
14 If ye shall ask any thing in my
name, I will do *it*.

The promise of the Spirit

15 ¶ [x]If ye love me, keep my com-
mandments.
16 And I will pray the Father, and
[y]he shall give you another Comforter,
that he may abide with you for ever;
17 *Even* [z]the Spirit of truth;

14:3 [k]Acts 1:11 [l]ch. 12:26 & 17:24 1 Thes. 4:17 **14:6** [m]Heb. 9:8 [n]ch. 8:32 [o]ch. 11:25 [p]ch. 10:9 **14:7** [q]ch. 8:19 **14:9** [r]ch. 12:45 Col. 1:15 Heb. 1:3 **14:10** [s]ch. 10:38 & 17:21,23 [t]ch. 5:19 & 8:28 **14:11** [u]ch. 10:38 **14:12** [v]Mat. 21:21 Mark 16:17 Luke 10:17 **14:13** [w]Mat. 7:7 & 21:22 Mark 11:24 Luke 11:9 ch. 15:7,16 & 16:23,24 Jas. 1:5 1 John 3:22 & 5:14 **14:15** [x]ver. 21,23 ch. 15:10 1 John 5:3 **14:16** [y]ch. 15:26 & 16:7; Rom. 8:15 **14:17** [z]ch. 15:26 & 16:13; 1 John 4:6

be with the Lord" (1 Thes. 4:17).

(3) Christ's coming for His faithful will enable them to escape the future hour of testing that will come upon the world (see Luke 21:36, note; 1 Thes. 1:10, note; 5:9; Rev. 3:10, note).

(4) This glorious and eternal reunion is a doctrine of comfort for all followers of Jesus who desire to "ever be with the Lord. Wherefore comfort one another with these words" (1 Thes. 4:17–18).

14:12 GREATER *WORKS*. It is Jesus' purpose and desire that His followers do the works that He did. (1) The "greater works" include both the work of converting people to Christ and the performing of miracles. This is shown in the narratives of Acts (Acts 2:41,43; 4:33; 5:12) and in Jesus' declaration in Mark 16:17–18 (see article on SIGNS OF BELIEVERS, p. 1516). (2) The reason for the "greater works" of the disciples is that Jesus will go to His Father, send forth the power of the Holy Spirit (see v. 16; 16:7; Acts 1:8; 2:4), and answer prayer in His name (v. 14). The disciples' works will be "greater" in number and scope.

14:13 ASK IN MY NAME. Prayer in the name of Jesus involves at least two things: (1) praying in harmony with His person, character, and will; (2) praying with faith in Him and His authority, and with the desire to glorify both the Father and the Son (Acts 3:16). Praying in the name of Jesus, therefore, means that Jesus will honor any prayer that He would have prayed Himself. There is no limit to the power of prayer when addressed to Jesus or the Father in faith according to His desire (see Mat. 17:20, note; see article on EFFECTIVE PRAYING, p. 540).

14:16 I WILL PRAY THE FATHER. Jesus will pray that the Father will give the Comforter only to those who are serious about their love for Him and their devotion to His Word. Jesus uses the present tense in v. 15 ("If ye love me"), thus emphasizing a continuing attitude of love and obedience.

14:16 COMFORTER. Jesus calls the Holy Spirit "another Comforter." "Comforter" translates the Greek *paraklētos*, meaning literally "one called alongside to help." This is a rich word, meaning Comforter, Strengthener, Counselor, Helper, Adviser, Advocate, Ally, and Friend. The Greek word for "another" is *allon*, meaning "another of the same kind," rather than *heteros*, meaning another of a different kind. In other words, the Holy Spirit continues what Christ Himself did while on earth.

(1) Jesus promises to send *another* Comforter. The Holy Spirit will do for the disciples what Christ did for them while He was with them. The Spirit will be by their side to help and strengthen them (cf. Mat. 14:30–31), to teach the true course for their lives (v. 26), to comfort in difficult situations (v. 18), to intercede in prayer for them (Rom. 8:26–27; cf. 8:34), to be a friend to further their best interest (v. 17), and to remain with them forever.

(2) The word *paraklētos* is applied to the Lord Jesus in 1 John 2:1. Therefore Jesus is our helper and intercessor in heaven (cf. Heb. 7:25), while the Holy Spirit is our indwelling helper and intercessor on earth (Rom. 8:9,26; 1 Cor. 3:16; 6:19; 2 Cor. 6:16; 2 Tim. 1:14).

14:17 THE SPIRIT OF TRUTH. The Holy Spir-

[a]whom the world cannot receive, be-
cause it seeth him not, neither
knoweth him: but ye know him; for he
dwelleth with you, [b]and shall be in
you.
18 [c]I will not leave you [a]comfort-
less: [d]I will come to you.
19 Yet a little while, and the world
seeth me no more; but [e]ye see me:
[f]because I live, ye shall live also.
20 At that day ye shall know that
[g]I *am* in my Father, and ye in me, and
I in you.
21 [h]He that hath my command-
ments, and keepeth them, he it is that
loveth me: and he that loveth me shall
be loved of my Father, and I will
love him, and will manifest myself
to him.
22 [i]Judas saith unto him, not Is-
cariot, Lord, how is it that thou wilt
manifest thyself unto us, and not unto
the world?
23 Jesus answered and said unto
him, If a man love me, he will keep my
words: and my Father will love him,
[j]and we will come unto him, and
make our abode with him.
24 He that loveth me not keepeth
not my sayings: and [k]the word which
ye hear is not mine, but the Father's
which sent me. Acts 10:34-35
25 These things have I spoken unto
you, being *yet* present with you.
26 But [l]the Comforter, *which is* the
Holy Ghost, whom the Father will send
in my name, [m]he shall teach you all
things, and bring all things to your re-
membrance, whatsoever I have said
unto you.

The promise of comfort

27 [n]Peace I leave with you, my
peace I give unto you: not as the world
giveth, give I unto you. Let not your
heart be troubled, neither let it be
afraid.
28 Ye have heard how [o]I said unto
you, I go away, and come *again* unto
you. If ye loved me, ye would rejoice,

14:17 [a]1 Cor. 2:14 [b]1 John 2:27
14:18 [c]Mat. 28:20 [d]ver. 3,28
14:19 [e]ch. 16:16 [f]1 Cor. 15:20
14:20 [g]ch. 10:38
14:21 [h]1 John 2:5 & 5:3
14:22 [i]Luke 6:16
14:23 [j]1 John 2:24 Rev. 3:20
14:24 [k]ch. 5:19
14:26 [l]Luke 24:49 ch. 15:26 [m]ch. 2:22 & 12:16 1 John 2:20
14:27 [n]Phil. 4:7 Col. 3:15
14:28 [o]ver. 3,18

[a] Or, *orphans*

it is called "the Spirit of truth" (15:26; 16:13; cf. 1 John 4:6; 5:6), because He is the Spirit of Jesus who is the truth. As such, He bears witness to the truth (18:37), enlightens concerning the truth, exposes untruth (16:8), and guides the believer into all truth (16:13). Those who support the sacrifice of truth for the sake of unity, love, or any other reason deny the Spirit of truth whom they claim to have dwelling in them. The church which abandons the truth abandons itself. The Holy Spirit will not be the Comforter of those who are indifferent to the faith or halfhearted in their commitment to the truth. He comes only to those who worship the Lord "in spirit and in truth" (4:24).

14:17 WITH YOU, AND SHALL BE IN YOU. The Holy Spirit now abides with the disciples, and Christ promises them that in the future He shall "be in you." This promise of the indwelling of the Holy Spirit was fulfilled after Christ's resurrection when He breathed on them and said to them, "Receive ye the Holy Ghost" (20:22). For a discussion of the role of the Holy Spirit in regeneration, see article on THE REGENERATION OF THE DISCIPLES, p. 1638.

14:18 I WILL COME TO YOU. Jesus reveals Himself to the obedient believer through the Holy Spirit, who makes known the personal presence of Jesus in and with the one who loves Him (v. 21). The Spirit makes us aware of the nearness of Jesus, the reality of His love, His blessing, and His help. This is one of His primary tasks. Christ's coming to us by the Spirit should result in a response of love, worship, and devotion.

14:21 HE THAT HATH MY COMMANDMENTS. Keeping the commandments of Christ is not optional for those who would have eternal life (3:36; 14:21,23; 15:8–10,13–14; Luke 6:46–49; Jas. 1:22; 2 Pet. 1:5–11; 1 John 2:3–6). (1) Obedience to Christ, though never perfect, must nevertheless be real. It is an essential aspect of saving faith, springing from our love for Him (vv. 15,21, 23–24; see Mat. 7:21, note). Without love for Christ, trying to keep His commandments becomes legalism. (2) To the person who loves Christ and strives to keep His commandments consistently, Christ promises a special love, grace, favor, and His deepest inward presence (cf. v. 23).

14:23 WE WILL ... MAKE OUR ABODE WITH HIM. Those who truly love Jesus and obey His words will experience the immediate presence and love of the Father and the Son. The Father and the Son come to believers by means of the Holy Spirit (see v. 18, note). It should be noted that the Father's love is conditioned on our loving Jesus and being loyal to His Word.

14:24 HE THAT LOVETH ME NOT. The person who does not keep the teachings of Christ does not have a personal love for Him, and without love for Jesus true saving faith does not exist (1 John 2:3–4). To say that a person remains saved even though he ceases to love Christ and begins to live a life of immorality, blasphemy, cruelty, murder, drunkenness, sorcery, etc., directly contradicts these and other words of Jesus concerning love, obedience, and the indwelling of the Holy Spirit.

14:26 HOLY GHOST. The Comforter is identified here as the "Holy Ghost." For the N.T. Christian the most important thing about the Spirit is not His power (Acts 1:8), but that He is "Holy." His holy character, along with the manifestation of that holy character in the lives of believers, is what matters most (cf. Rom. 1:4; Gal. 5:22–26).

because I said, [p]I go unto the Father:
for [q]my Father is greater than I.
29 And [r]now I have told you before
it come to pass, that, when it is come
to pass, ye might believe.
30 Hereafter I will not talk much
with you: [s]for the prince of this
world cometh, and hath nothing
in me.
31 But that the world may know
that I love the Father; and [t]as the Fa-
ther gave me commandment, even so I
do. Arise, let us go hence.

The relationship of believers to Christ

15 I AM the true vine, and my Fa-
ther is the husbandman.
2 [u]Every branch in me that beareth
not fruit he taketh away: and every
branch that beareth fruit, he purgeth it,
that it may bring forth more fruit.
3 [v]Now ye are clean through the
word which I have spoken unto you.
4 [w]Abide in me, and I in you. As the
branch cannot bear fruit of itself, ex-
cept it abide in the vine; no more can
ye, except ye abide in me.
5 I am the vine, ye *are* the branches:
He that abideth in me, and I in him, the
same bringeth forth much [x]fruit: for
[b]without me ye can do nothing.
6 If a man abide not in me, [y]he is
cast forth as a branch, and is withered;
and men gather them, and cast *them*
into the fire, and they are burned.
7 If ye abide in me, and my words

14:28 [p]ch. 16:16 & 20:17 [q]ch. 5:18 & 10:30 Phil. 2:6
14:29 [r]ch. 13:19 & 16:4
14:30 [s]ch. 12:31 & 16:11
14:31 [t]ch. 10:18 Phil. 2:8 Heb. 5:8
15:2 [u]Mat. 15:13
15:3 [v]ch. 13:10 Eph. 5:26 1 Pet. 1:22
15:4 [w]Col. 1:23 1 John 2:6
15:5 [x]Hos. 14:8 Phil. 1:11 & 4:13
15:6 [y]Mat. 3:10 & 7:19

[b] Or, *severed from me;* see Acts 4:12

15:1 I AM THE TRUE VINE. In this parable or allegory, Jesus describes Himself as "the true vine" and those who have become His disciples as "the branches." By remaining attached to Him as the Source of life, they produce fruit. God is the gardener who takes care of the branches in order that they may bear fruit (vv. 2,8). God expects all of us to bear fruit (see next note).

15:2 EVERY BRANCH. Jesus speaks of two categories of branches: fruitless and fruitful. (1) The branches that cease to bear fruit are those who no longer have the life in them that comes from enduring faith in and love for Christ. These branches the Father takes away, i.e., He separates them from vital union with Christ (cf. Mat. 3:10). When they stop abiding in Christ, God then judges and rejects them (v. 6).

(2) The branches that bear fruit are those who have life in them because of their enduring faith in and love for Christ (see article on THE WORKS OF THE FLESH AND THE FRUIT OF THE SPIRIT, p. 1840). These branches the Father prunes in order that they might become more fruitful. That is, He removes from their lives anything that diverts or hinders the vital life-flow of Christ into them. The fruit is the quality of Christian character that brings glory to God through life and witness (see Mat. 3:8; 7:20; Rom. 6:22; Gal. 5:22–23; Eph. 5:9; Phil. 1:11).

15:4 ABIDE IN ME. After a person believes in Christ and is forgiven, he receives eternal life and the power to abide in Christ. Given that power, the believer must then accept that responsibility in salvation and abide in Christ. The Greek word *menō* means to continue, remain, abide, or dwell. Just as the branch has life only as long as the life of the vine flows into it, so the believer has Christ's life only as long as Christ's life flows into him through his abiding in Christ. The conditions by which we abide in Christ are: (1) keeping God's Word continually before our memories and minds and making it the guide of our actions (v. 7); (2) maintaining the habit of constant close communion with Christ in order to draw strength and grace from Him (v. 7); (3) obeying His commandments, abiding in His love (v. 10), and loving one another (vv. 12,17); (4) keeping our lives clean through the Word, resisting all sin, and yielding to the direction of the Holy Spirit (v. 3; 17:17; Rom. 8:14; Gal. 5:16–25; Eph. 5:26; 1 Pet. 1:22).

15:6 HE IS CAST FORTH AS A BRANCH. The parable of the vine and branches makes it unmistakably clear that Christ did not believe "once in the vine, always in the vine." Rather, in this parable Jesus gave His disciples a solemn but loving warning that it is indeed possible for true believers to ultimately abandon faith, turn their backs on Jesus, fail to abide in Him, and thus to be cast into the everlasting fire of hell (v. 6).

(1) We have here the foundational principle governing the saving relationship of Christ and the believer, namely, that it is never a static relationship based solely on a past decision or experience. Rather, it is a progressive relationship as Christ dwells in the believer and shares with him His divine life (see 17:3, note; Col. 3:4; 1 John 5:11–13).

(2) In summary, three important truths are taught in this parable. (a) The responsibility of abiding in Christ is placed upon the disciples (see v. 4, note). This is our response to God's prior gift of divine life and power given at conversion. (b) Abiding in Christ results in Jesus' continued indwelling (v. 4a), fruitfulness of the disciple (v. 5), success in prayer (v. 7), and fullness of joy (v. 11). (c) The consequences of failure to abide in Christ are fruitlessness (vv. 4–5), removal from Christ, and destruction (vv. 2a,6).

15:7 ASK WHAT YE WILL. The secret of answered prayer is abiding in Christ. The nearer we live to Christ through meditation and study of the Scriptures and communion with Him, the more our prayers will be in line with the nature and words of Christ, and hence, the more effectual our prayers will be (see 14:13, note; 15:4, note; Ps. 66:18, note; see article on EFFECTIVE PRAYING, p. 540).

abide in you, [z]ye shall ask what ye will, and it shall be done unto you.

8 [a]Herein is my Father glorified, that ye bear much fruit; [b]so shall ye be my disciples.

ts
52

9 As the Father hath loved me, so have I loved you: continue ye in my love.

10 [c]If ye keep my commandments, ye shall abide in my love; even as I have kept my Father's commandments, and abide in his love.

11 These things have I spoken unto you, that my joy might remain in you, and [d]*that* your joy might be full.

Love one another

12 [e]This is my commandment, That ye love one another, as I have loved you.

13 [f]Greater love hath no man than this, that a man lay down his life for his friends.

14 [g]Ye are my friends, if ye do whatsoever I command you.

15 Henceforth I call you not servants; for the servant knoweth not what his lord doeth: but I have called you friends; [h]for all things that I have heard of my Father I have made known unto you.

16 [i]Ye have not chosen me, but I have chosen you, and [j]ordained you, that ye should go and bring forth fruit, and *that* your fruit should remain: that [k]whatsoever ye shall ask of the Father in my name, he may give it you.

17 These things I command you, that ye love one another.

The world hates Christ's disciples

18 [l]If the world hate you, ye know that it hated me before *it hated* you.

15:7 [z]ch. 16:23
15:8 [a]Mat. 5:16 Phil. 1:11 [b]ch. 8:31
15:10 [c]ch. 14:15
15:11 [d]ch. 16:24 & 17:13 1 John 1:4
15:12 [e]ch. 13:34 1 Thes. 4:9 1 Pet. 4:8 1 John 3:11
15:13 [f]ch. 10:11 Rom. 5:7,8 Eph. 5:2 1 John 3:16
15:14 [g]Mat. 12:50 ch. 14:15
15:15 [h]Gen. 18:17 ch. 17:26
15:16 [i]ch. 6:70 & 13:18 1 John 4:10 [j]Mat. 28:19 Mark 16:15 Col. 1:6 [k]ver. 7
15:18 [l]1 John 3:13
15:19 [m]1 John 4:5 [n]ch. 17:14
15:20 [o]Mat. 10:24 Luke 6:40 [p]Ezek. 3:7
15:21 [q]Mat. 10:22 & 24:9
15:22 [r]ch. 9:41 [s]Rom. 1:20 Jas. 4:17
15:23 [t]1 John 2:23
15:24 [u]ch. 3:2
15:25 [v]Ps. 35:19 & 69:4
15:26 [w]Luke 24:49 ch. 14:17 Acts 2:33 [x]1 John 5:6
15:27 [y]Luke 24:48

19 [m]If ye were of the world, the world would love his own: but [n]because ye are not of the world, but I have chosen you out of the world, therefore the world hateth you.

20 Remember the word that I said unto you, [o]The servant is not greater than his lord. If they have persecuted me, they will also persecute you; [p]if they have kept my saying, they will keep yours also. John 16:33

21 But [q]all these things will they do unto you for my name's sake, because they know not him that sent me.

22 [r]If I had not come and spoken unto them, they had not had sin: [s]but now they have no [c]cloak for their sin.

23 [t]He that hateth me hateth my Father also.

24 If I had not done among them [u]the works which none other man did, they had not had sin: but now have they both seen and hated both me and my Father.

25 But *this cometh to pass,* that the word might be fulfilled that is written in their law, [v]They hated me without a cause.

The Spirit and the witness

26 [w]But when the Comforter is come, whom I will send unto you from the Father, *even* the Spirit of truth, which proceedeth from the Father, [x]he shall testify of me:

27 And [y]ye also shall bear witness, because [z]ye have been with me from the beginning. Acts 1:8

Acts 1:21 & 2:32 & 3:15 & 4:20,33 & 5:32 & 10:39 & 13:31; 1 Pet. 5:1; 2 Pet. 1:16 [z]Luke 1:2; 1 John 1:1

[c]Or, *excuse*

15:9–10 CONTINUE YE IN MY LOVE. The believer must live in the atmosphere of the love of Christ. Jesus goes on to state that this is done by keeping His commandments.

15:16 GO AND BRING FORTH FRUIT. All Christians are chosen "out of the world" (v. 19) to "bear fruit" (vv. 2,4–5,8). This fruit-bearing refers to (1) spiritual virtues, such as the fruit of the Spirit mentioned in Gal. 5:22–23—love, joy, peace, patience, kindness, goodness, faithfulness, gentleness, self-control (cf. Eph. 5:9; Col. 1:6; Heb. 12:11; Jas. 3:18); and (2) conversion of others to Christ (4:36; 12:24).

15:20 THEY WILL ALSO PERSECUTE YOU. While Christ's followers are in this world they will be hated, persecuted, maligned, and rejected for His sake. The world is the great opponent of Christ and His people throughout history. (1) The true believer must understand that the world—including false religious organizations and churches—will always oppose God and the principles of His kingdom; thus the world will remain an enemy and persecutor of faithful believers until the end (Jas. 4:4; see Mat. 5:10, note). (2) The reason why believers suffer at the hands of the world is because they are fundamentally different; they are "not of the world" and have come "out of the world" (v. 19). The values, standards, and direction of the faithful are in conflict with the unrighteous ways of their perverse society. They refuse to compromise with its ungodly standards, and instead set their "affection on things above, not on things on the earth" (Col. 3:2).

16 THESE THINGS have I spoken
unto you, that ye [a]should not
be offended.
2 [b]They shall put you out of the
synagogues: yea, the time cometh,
[c]that whosoever killeth you will think
that he doeth God service.
3 And [d]these things will they do
unto you, because they have not known
the Father, nor me.
4 But [e]these things have I told
you, that when the time shall come, ye
may remember that I told you of them.
And these things I said not unto you at
the beginning, because I was with you.

The work of the Holy Spirit

5 But now [f]I go my way to him that
sent me; and none of you asketh me,
Whither goest thou?
6 But because I have said these
things unto you, sorrow hath filled
your heart.
7 Nevertheless I tell you the truth;
It is expedient for you that I go away:
for if I go not away, [g]the Comforter
will not come unto you; but [h]if I de-
part, I will send him unto you.
8 And when he is come, he will [d]re-
prove the world of sin, and of righ-
teousness, and of judgment:
9 [i]Of sin, because they believe not
on me;
10 [j]Of righteousness, [k]because I
go to my Father, and ye see me no
more;
11 [l]Of judgment, because [m]the
prince of this world is judged.
12 I have yet many things to say
unto you, [n]but ye cannot bear them
now.
13 Howbeit when he, [o]the Spirit of

16:1 [a]Mat. 11:6 & 24:10 & 26:31 **16:2** [b]ch. 9:22 [c]Acts 8:1 & 9:1 & 26:9,10 **16:3** [d]ch. 15:21 Rom. 10:2 1 Cor. 2:8 1 Tim. 1:13 **16:4** [e]ch. 13:19 & 14:29 **16:5** [f]ch. 7:33 & 14:28 **16:7** [g]ch. 7:39 & 14:16,26 & 15:26 [h]Acts 2:33 Eph. 4:8 **16:9** [i]Acts 2:22 **16:10** [j]Acts 2:32 [k]ch. 5:32 **16:11** [l]Acts 26:18 [m]Luke 10:18 Eph. 2:2; Col. 2:15; Heb. 2:14 **16:12** [n]Mark 4:33; 1 Cor. 3:2; Heb. 5:12 **16:13** [o]ch. 14:17

d Or, *convince*

16:2 PUT YOU OUT OF THE SYNAGOGUES. Jesus does not speak here of persecution coming from pagans, but of opposition and hostility from religious authorities and congregations. His reference earlier to the world hating believers (15:18–19) must include these religious people. (1) All professed believers or churches that do not adhere to Jesus' teaching and apostolic revelation, or that do not seek to remain separated from the corrupt world and system of society, belong to the world (cf. 1 John 4:5–6). (2) These so-called professed believers have values so different from the true N.T. gospel that when they persecute or kill true followers of Christ, they think they are serving God.

16:7 IF I DEPART, I WILL SEND HIM. The Pentecostal outpouring of the Holy Spirit will occur only after Christ goes away (cf. Acts 2:33; see article on THE REGENERATION OF THE DISCIPLES, p. 1638). This outpouring at Pentecost fully ushered in the age of the Spirit.

16:8 REPROVE THE WORLD. When the Holy Spirit comes at Pentecost (see previous note; Acts 2:4), His principal work in relation to witnessing and proclaiming the gospel will be that of "reproving" (v. 8). The term reprove (Gk. *elenchō*) means to convict, expose, refute, and convince.

(1) The Spirit's ministry of convicting operates in three areas. (a) Sin. The Holy Spirit will expose and reprove sin and unbelief in order to awaken a consciousness of guilt and the need of forgiveness. Conviction also makes clear the fearful results if the guilty persist in their wrongdoing. After conviction, a choice must be made. This will often lead to true repentance and a turning to Jesus as Lord and Savior (Acts 2:37–38). (b) Righteousness. The Spirit convinces people that Jesus is the righteous Son of God, resurrected, vindicated, and now the Lord of all. He makes them aware of God's standard of righteousness in Christ, shows them what is sin, and gives them power to overcome the world (Acts 3:12–16; 7:51–60; 17:31; 1 Pet. 3:18). (c) Judgment. The Spirit convinces people of Satan's defeat at the cross (12:31; 16:11), God's present judgment of the world (Rom. 1:18–32), and the future judgment of the entire human race (Mat. 16:27; Acts 17:31; 24:25; Rom. 14:10; 1 Cor. 6:2; 2 Cor. 5:10; Jude 14).

(2) The Spirit's work of convicting people of sin, righteousness, and judgment will be manifested in all who are baptized in the Holy Spirit and are truly Spirit-filled believers. Christ, filled with the Spirit (Luke 4:1), testified to the world that its "works . . . are evil" (see 7:7; 15:18) and called people to repent (Mat. 4:17). John the Baptist, "filled with the Holy Ghost" from birth (see Luke 1:15, note), exposed the sin of the Jewish people and commanded them to change their ways (see Mat. 11:7, note; Luke 3:1–20); Peter, "filled with the Holy Ghost" (Acts 2:4), convicted the hearts of 3,000 sinners and called them to repent and receive forgiveness (Acts 2:37–41).

(3) It is obvious from this passage that any preacher or church that does not publicly reprove sin, expose its accountability, and call for repentance and Biblical righteousness is not of the Holy Spirit. 1 Cor. 14:24–25 explicitly states that God's presence in the congregation is recognized by the exposure of the unbeliever's sin (i.e., secrets of his heart), his consequent conviction and salvation.

16:13 HE WILL GUIDE YOU INTO ALL TRUTH. The convicting work of the Holy Spirit is not only directed toward the unsaved (vv. 7–8), but also operates in believers and the church in order to instruct, teach, correct, and guide them into truth (Mat. 18:15; 1 Tim. 5:20; Rev. 3:19).

(1) The Holy Spirit will speak to believers concerning sin, the righteousness of Christ, and the judgment of evil in order to (a) conform them to Christ and His standard of righteousness (cf.

truth, is come, [p]he will guide you into
all truth: for he shall not speak of him-
self; but whatsoever he shall hear, *that*
shall he speak: and he will show you
things to come.
14 He shall glorify me: for he shall
receive of mine, and shall show *it* unto
you.
15 [q]All things that the Father hath
are mine: therefore said I, that he shall
take of mine, and shall show *it* unto
you.

Jesus' farewell to his disciples

16 A little while, and ye shall not
see me: and again, a little while, and ye
shall see me, [r]because I go to the Fa-
ther.
17 Then said *some* of his disciples
among themselves, What is this that
he saith unto us, A little while, and ye
shall not see me: and again, a little
while, and ye shall see me: and, Be-
cause I go to the Father?
18 They said therefore, What is this
that he saith, A little while? we cannot
tell what he saith.
19 Now Jesus knew that they were
desirous to ask him, and said unto
them, Do ye inquire among yourselves
of that I said, A little while, and ye
shall not see me: and again, a little
while, and ye shall see me?
20 Verily, verily, I say unto you,
That ye shall weep and lament, but the
world shall rejoice: and ye shall be sor-
rowful, but your sorrow shall be turned
into joy.
21 [s]A woman when she is in tra-
vail hath sorrow, because her hour is
come: but as soon as she is delivered
of the child, she remembereth no more
the anguish, for joy that a man is born
into the world.
22 And ye now therefore have sor-
row: but I will see you again, and
[t]your heart shall rejoice, and your joy
no man taketh from you.
23 And in that day ye shall ask me
nothing. [u]Verily, verily, I say unto
you, Whatsoever ye shall ask the Fa-
ther in my name, he will give *it* you.
24 Hitherto have ye asked nothing
in my name: ask, and ye shall receive,
[v]that your joy may be full.
25 These things have I spoken unto
you in [e]proverbs: but the time com-
eth, when I shall no more speak unto
you in proverbs, but I shall show you
plainly of the Father.
26 At that day ye shall ask in my
name: and I say not unto you, that I
will pray the Father for you:
27 [w]For the Father himself loveth
you, because ye have loved me, and
[x]have believed that I came out from
God.
28 [y]I came forth from the Father,
and am come into the world: again, I
leave the world, and go to the Father.
29 His disciples said unto him, Lo,

16:13 [p]ch. 14:26 1 John 2:20 **16:15** [q]Mat. 11:27 ch. 3:35 **16:16** [r]ch. 13:3 **16:21** [s]Is. 26:17 **16:22** [t]Luke 24:41 ch. 14:1,27 & 20:20 Acts 2:46 & 13:52 1 Pet. 1:8 **16:23** [u]Mat. 7:7 ch. 14:13 & 15:16 **16:24** [v]ch. 15:11 **16:27** [w]ch. 14:21 [x]ch. 3:13 **16:28** [y]ch. 13:3

[e] Or, *parables*

2 Cor. 3:18), (b) lead them into all truth, and (c) glorify Christ (v. 14). Thus, the Holy Spirit works within believers to reproduce Christ's holy life in their lives.

(2) If Spirit-filled believers resist or reject the Spirit's guidance and His reproving work and righteous standards, and if they do not "through the Spirit" mortify "the deeds of the body" (Rom. 8:13), then they will enter into condemnation. Only those who receive the truth and are "led by the Spirit of God" are "sons of God" (Rom. 8:14) and are therefore able to continue in the Spirit's fullness (see Eph. 5:18, note). Sin destroys both the life and fullness of the Holy Spirit within the believer (Rom. 6:23; 8:13; Gal. 5:17; cf. Eph. 5:18; 1 Thes. 5:19).

16:13 HE SHALL NOT SPEAK OF HIMSELF. The translation "he shall not speak of himself" does not correctly communicate the truth of John 16:13–14. A more accurate rendering of the Greek text would be: "He will not speak on His own initiative." The Holy Spirit receives His message and instructions from Christ; believers ought to talk about and rejoice in the work of the Holy Spirit.

16:14 HE SHALL RECEIVE OF MINE. The Spirit takes that which is of Christ and reveals it to the believer. That is, He takes the presence, love, forgiveness, redemption, sanctification, life, power, spiritual gifts, healing, and all that is ours through our faith relationship with Christ, and makes it experientially real in our lives. Through the Spirit Jesus returns to us to disclose His love, grace, and personal fellowship (cf. 14:16–23). The Spirit works within us to do what is necessary to awaken and deepen our awareness of Jesus' presence in our lives, drawing our hearts toward Him in faith, love, obedience, communion, worship, and praise (see article on JESUS AND THE HOLY SPIRIT, p. 1550).

16:27 THE FATHER HIMSELF LOVETH YOU. The Father loves all people (3:16). But it is also true that He has a special family love for those who through Jesus are reconciled to Him, love Him, and remain loyal to Him while experiencing tribulation in this world (v. 33). Our affection for Jesus brings forth the Father's affection toward us. Love responds to love.

now speakest thou plainly, and speakest no [f]proverb.

30 Now are we sure that [z]thou knowest all things, and needest not that any man should ask thee: by this [a]we believe that thou camest forth from God.

31 Jesus answered them, Do ye now believe?

32 [b]Behold, the hour cometh, yea, is now come, that ye shall be scattered, [c]every man to [g]his own, and shall leave me alone: and [d]yet I am not alone, because the Father is with me.

John 17:14-18

33 These things I have spoken unto you, that [e]in me ye might have peace. [f]In the world ye shall have tribulation: but be of good cheer; [g]I have overcome the world.

Christ's prayer to be glorified

17 THESE WORDS spake Jesus, and lifted up his eyes to heaven, and said, Father, [h]the hour is come; glorify thy Son, that thy Son also may glorify thee:

2 [i]As thou hast given him power over all flesh, that he should give eternal life to as many [j]as thou hast given him.

3 And [k]this is life eternal, that they might know thee [l]the only true God, and Jesus Christ, [m]whom thou hast sent.

4 [n]I have glorified thee on the earth: [o]I have finished the work [p]which thou gavest me to do.

5 And now, O Father, glorify thou me with thine own self with the glory [q]which I had with thee before the world was.

Christ's prayer for the disciples

6 [r]I have manifested thy name unto the men [s]which thou gavest me out of the world: thine they were, and thou gavest them me; and they have kept thy word.

7 Now they have known that all things whatsoever thou hast given me are of thee.

8 For I have given unto them the words [t]which thou gavest me; and they have received *them,* [u]and have known surely that I came out from thee, and they have believed that thou didst send me.

9 I pray for them: [v]I pray not for the world, but for them which thou hast given me; for they are thine.

10 And all mine are thine, and [w]thine are mine; and I am glorified in them.

11 [x]And now I am no more in the world, but these are in the world, and I come to thee. Holy Father, [y]keep through thine own name those whom thou hast given me, that they may be one, [z]as we *are.*

12 While I was with them in the world, [a]I kept them in thy name: those that thou gavest me I have kept,

16:30 [z]ch. 21:17 [a]ch. 17:8
16:32 [b]Mat. 26:31 Mark 14:27 [c]ch. 20:10 [d]ch. 8:29
16:33 [e]Is. 9:6 Rom. 5:1 Eph. 2:14 [f]2 Tim. 3:12 [g]Rom. 8:37 1 John 4:4
17:1 [h]ch. 12:23
17:2 [i]Dan. 7:14 Mat. 11:27 ch. 3:35 Phil. 2:10 Heb. 2:8 [j]ver. 6,9,24 ch. 6:37
17:3 [k]Is. 53:11 Jer. 9:24 [l]1 Cor. 8:4 1 Thes. 1:9 [m]ch. 3:34
17:4 [n]ch. 13:31 [o]ch. 4:34 [p]ch. 14:31
17:5 [q]Phil. 2:6 Col. 1:15 Heb. 1:3
17:6 [r]Ps. 22:22 [s]ch. 6:37
17:8 [t]ch. 8:28 [u]ch. 16:27
17:9 [v]1 John 5:19
17:10 [w]ch. 16:15
17:11 [x]ch. 13:1 [y]1 Pet. 1:5 Jude 1 [z]ch. 10:30
17:12 [a]Heb. 2:13

f Or, *parable* g Or, *his own home*

17:1 CHRIST'S PRAYER FOR ALL BELIEVERS. Jesus' final prayer for His disciples in this chapter shows us our Lord's deepest desires and longings for His followers, both then and now. It is also a Spirit-inspired example of how every pastor should pray for his people, and how Christian parents should pray for their children. In praying for those under our care, our greatest concerns should be: (1) that they may know Jesus Christ and His Word intimately (vv. 2–3,17,19; see v. 3, note); (2) that God will keep them from the world, from falling away, from Satan, evil, and false teachings (vv. 6,11,14–17); (3) that they may constantly possess the joy of Christ (v. 13); (4) that they may be holy in thought, deed, and character (see v. 17, note); (5) that they may be one (vv. 11,21–22; see v. 21, note); (6) that they may lead others to Christ (vv. 21,23); (7) that they may persevere in the faith and finally be with Christ in heaven (v. 24); and (8) that they may constantly abide in the love and presence of God (v. 26).

17:3 LIFE ETERNAL. Eternal life is more than endless existence. It is a special quality of life that we as believers receive when we partake of the essential life of God through Christ; this allows us to know God in an ever-growing knowledge and fellowship with the Father, Son, and Holy Spirit. In the N.T. eternal life is described as:

(1) A present reality (5:24; 10:27–28). The present possession of eternal life requires a living faith. Eternal life is not secured and maintained merely by an act of repentance and faith occurring in the past (see 5:24, note). It involves also a present living union and fellowship with Christ (1 John 5:12); there is no eternal life apart from Him (10:27–28; 11:25–26; 1 John 5:11–13).

(2) A future hope. Eternal life is associated with the coming of Christ for His faithful (see 14:3, note; cf. Mark 10:30; 2 Tim. 1:1,10; Tit. 1:2; 3:7) and is contingent upon living by the Spirit (Rom. 8:12–17; Gal. 6:8).

17:6 THEY HAVE KEPT THY WORD. Christ's prayer for protection, joy, sanctification, love, and unity applies only to a particular people, that is, to those who belong to God, believe in Christ (v. 8), are separated from the world (vv. 14–16), and keep the Word of Christ and accept His teachings (vv. 6,8).

and [b]none of them is lost, [c]but the son of perdition; [d]that the scripture might be fulfilled.

13 And now come I to thee; and these things I speak in the world, that they might have my joy fulfilled in themselves.

14 I have given them thy word; [e]and the world hath hated them, because they are not of the world, [f]even as I am not of the world.

15 I pray not that thou shouldest take them out of the world, but [g]that thou shouldest keep them from the evil.

16 They are not of the world, even as I am not of the world.

17 [h]Sanctify them through thy truth: [i]thy word is truth.

18 [j]As thou hast sent me into the world, even so have I also sent them into the world.

19 And [k]for their sakes I sanctify myself, that they also might be [h]sanctified through the truth.

Christ's prayer for future believers

20 Neither pray I for these alone, but for them also which shall believe on me through their word;

21 [l]That they all may be one; as [m]thou, Father, *art* in me, and I in thee, that they also may be one in us: that the world may believe that thou hast sent me.

22 And the glory which thou gavest me I have given them; [n]that they may be one, even as we are one:

23 I in them, and thou in me, [o]that they may be made perfect in one; and that the world may know that thou hast sent me, and hast loved them, as thou hast loved me.

24 [p]Father, I will that they also, whom thou hast given me, be with me where I am; that they may behold my glory, which thou hast given me: [q]for thou lovedst me before the foundation of the world.

25 O righteous Father, [r]the world hath not known thee: but [s]I have known thee, and [t]these have known that thou hast sent me.

26 [u]And I have declared unto them thy name, and will declare *it:* that the love [v]wherewith thou hast loved me may be in them, and I in them.

17:12 [b]1 John 2:19 [c]ch. 6:70 [d]Ps. 109:8 Acts 1:20
17:14 [e]1 John 3:13 [f]ch. 8:23
17:15 [g]Mat. 6:13 Gal. 1:4 1 John 5:18
17:17 [h]Acts 15:9 Eph. 5:26 1 Pet. 1:22 [i]Ps. 119:142,151
17:18 [j]ch. 20:21
17:19 [k]1 Cor. 1:2 1 Thes. 4:7 Heb. 10:10
17:21 [l]ch. 10:16 Rom. 12:5 Gal. 3:28 [m]ch. 10:38
17:22 [n]ch. 14:20 1 John 1:3
17:23 [o]Col. 3:14
17:24 [p]ch. 12:26 1 Thes. 4:17 [q]ver. 5
17:25 [r]ch. 15:21 & 16:3 [s]ch. 7:29 & 8:55 & 10:15 [t]ver. 8 ch. 16:27
17:26 [u]ver. 6 ch. 15:15 [v]ch. 15:9

[h] Or, *truly sanctified*

17:17 SANCTIFY THEM THROUGH THY TRUTH. Sanctify means to make holy, to separate. Jesus prays the evening before His crucifixion that His disciples will be a holy people, separated from the world and sin for the purpose of worshiping and serving God. They must be set apart in order to be near God, to live for Him, and to be like Him. This sanctification is accomplished by their devotion to the truth, revealed to them by the Spirit of truth (cf. 14:17; 16:13). The truth is both the living Word of God (see 1:1) and the revelation of God's written Word (see article on SANCTIFICATION, p. 1982).

17:19 I SANCTIFY MYSELF. Jesus "sanctifies" Himself by setting Himself apart to do the will of God, i.e., to die on the cross. Jesus suffered on Calvary in order that His followers might be separated from the world and set apart for God (see Heb. 13:12).

17:21 THAT THEY ALL MAY BE ONE. The unity that Jesus prayed for was not an organizational unity, but rather a spiritual unity based on: (1) abiding in Christ (v. 23); (2) love for Christ (v. 26); (3) separation from the world (vv. 14–16); (4) sanctification in truth (vv. 17,19); (5) receiving and believing the truth of the Word (vv. 6,8,17); (6) obedience to the Word (v. 6); and (7) the desire to bring salvation to the lost (vv. 21,23). When any one of these factors is missing, the true unity that Jesus prayed for cannot exist.

(1) Jesus does not pray for His followers to "become" one, but rather that they "may be one." This is a present subjunctive and means "continually be one," a oneness based on their common relationship to the Father and the Son, and on all of them having the same basic attitude toward the world, the Word, righteous standards, and the lost (cf. 1 John 1:7).

(2) To attempt to create an artificial unity by meetings, seminars, conferences, or complex organization can result in a betrayal of the very unity for which Jesus prayed. What Jesus had in mind is much more than cosmetic "unity meetings." It is a spiritual unity of heart, purpose, mind, and will in those who are fully devoted to Christ, the Word, and holiness (see Eph. 4:3, note).

17:22 THE GLORY WHICH THOU GAVEST ME. The "glory" of Christ was His life of self-denying service and His dying on the cross in order to redeem the human race. Likewise, the "glory" of the believer is the path of humble service and bearing his cross (cf. Luke 9:23, note). Humility, self-denial, service, and the willingness to suffer for Christ will insure the true unity of believers and will lead to true glory (see article on THE GLORY OF GOD, p. 1186).

Jesus' betrayal and arrest

18:3–11pp — Mat. 26:47–56; Mark 14:43–50; Luke 22:47–53

18 WHEN JESUS had spoken these words, [w]he went forth with his disciples over [x]the brook Cedron, where was a garden, into the which he entered, and his disciples.

2 And Judas also, which betrayed him, knew the place: [y]for Jesus ofttimes resorted thither with his disciples.

3 [z]Judas then, having received a band *of men* and officers from the chief priests and Pharisees, cometh thither with lanterns and torches and weapons.

4 Jesus therefore, knowing all things that should come upon him, went forth, and said unto them, Whom seek ye?

5 They answered him, Jesus of Nazareth. Jesus saith unto them, I am *he.* And Judas also, which betrayed him, stood with them.

6 As soon then as he had said unto them, I am *he,* they went backward, and fell to the ground.

7 Then asked he them again, Whom seek ye? And they said, Jesus of Nazareth.

8 Jesus answered, I have told you that I am *he:* if therefore ye seek me, let these go their way:

9 That the saying might be fulfilled, which he spake, [a]Of them which thou gavest me have I lost none.

10 [b]Then Simon Peter having a sword drew it, and smote the high priest's servant, and cut off his right ear. The servant's name was Malchus.

11 Then said Jesus unto Peter, Put up thy sword into the sheath: [c]the cup which my Father hath given me, shall I not drink it?

Jesus taken to Annas

18:12–13pp — Mat. 26:57

12 Then the band and the captain and officers of the Jews took Jesus, and bound him,

13 And [d]led him away to [e]Annas first; for he was father-in-law to Caiaphas, which was the high priest that same year.

18:1
[w]Mat. 26:36
Mark 14:32
Luke 22:39
[x]2 Sam. 15:23
18:2
[y]Luke 21:37
& 22:39
18:3
[z]Mat. 26:47
Mark 14:43
Luke 22:47
Acts 1:16
18:9
[a]ch. 17:12
18:10
[b]Mat. 26:51
Mark 14:47
Luke 22:49,50
18:11
[c]Mat. 20:22
& 26:39,42
18:13
[d]See Mat. 26:57
[e]Luke 3:2

18:14
[f]ch. 11:50
18:15
[g]Mat. 26:58
Mark 14:54
Luke 22:54
18:16
[h]Mat. 26:69
Mark 14:66
Luke 22:54
18:20
[i]Mat. 26:55
Luke 4:15
ch. 7:14,26,28
& 8:2
18:22
[j]Jer. 20:2
Acts 23:2
18:24
[k]Mat. 26:57

14 [f]Now Caiaphas was he, which gave counsel to the Jews, that it was expedient that one man should die for the people.

Peter's first denial

18:16–18pp — Mat. 26:69–70; Mark 14:66–68; Luke 22:55–57

15 ¶ [g]And Simon Peter followed Jesus, and *so did* another disciple: that disciple was known unto the high priest, and went in with Jesus into the palace of the high priest.

16 [h]But Peter stood at the door without. Then went out that other disciple, which was known unto the high priest, and spake unto her that kept the door, and brought in Peter.

17 Then saith the damsel that kept the door unto Peter, Art not thou also *one* of this man's disciples? He saith, I am not.

18 And the servants and officers stood there, who had made a fire of coals; for it was cold: and they warmed themselves: and Peter stood with them, and warmed himself.

The high priest questions Jesus

18:19–24pp — Mat. 26:59–68; Mark 14:55–65; Luke 22:63–71

19 ¶ The high priest then asked Jesus of his disciples, and of his doctrine.

20 Jesus answered him, [i]I spake openly to the world; I ever taught in the synagogue, and in the temple, whither the Jews always resort; and in secret have I said nothing.

21 Why askest thou me? ask them which heard me, what I have said unto them: behold, they know what I said.

22 And when he had thus spoken, one of the officers which stood by [j]struck Jesus [i]with the palm of his hand, saying, Answerest thou the high priest so?

23 Jesus answered him, If I have spoken evil, bear witness of the evil: but if well, why smitest thou me?

24 [k]Now Annas had sent him bound unto Caiaphas the high priest.

[i] Or, *with a rod*

18:11 THE CUP. See Mat. 26:39, note on Christ's cup of sorrow.

18:12 TOOK JESUS, AND BOUND HIM. See Mat. 26:57, note on the order of the events from Christ's arrest to His crucifixion.

18:15–27 PETER'S DENIAL. See Mark 14:50, note; 14:71, note; Luke 22:62, note.

Peter's second and third denials

18:25–27pp — Mat. 26:71–75; Mark 14:69–72; Luke 22:58–62

25 And Simon Peter stood and warmed himself. [l]They said therefore unto him, Art not thou also *one* of his disciples? He denied *it,* and said, I am not.

26 One of the servants of the high priest, being *his* kinsman whose ear Peter cut off, saith, Did not I see thee in the garden with him?

27 Peter then denied again: and [m]immediately the cock crew.

Jesus before Pontius Pilate

18:29–40pp — Mat. 27:11–18,20–23; Mark 15:2–15; Luke 23:2–3

28 ¶ [n]Then led they Jesus from Caiaphas unto [o]the[j] hall of judgment: and it was early; [p]and they themselves went not into the judgment hall, lest they should be defiled; but that they might eat the passover.

29 Pilate then went out unto them, and said, What accusation bring ye against this man?

30 They answered and said unto him, If he were not a malefactor, we would not have delivered him up unto thee.

31 Then said Pilate unto them, Take ye him, and judge him according to your law. The Jews therefore said unto him, It is not lawful for us to put any man to death:

32 [q]That the saying of Jesus might be fulfilled, which he spake, signifying what death he should die.

33 [r]Then Pilate entered into the judgment hall again, and called Jesus, and said unto him, Art thou the King of the Jews?

34 Jesus answered him, Sayest thou this thing of thyself, or did others tell it thee of me?

35 Pilate answered, Am I a Jew? Thine own nation and the chief priests have delivered thee unto me: what hast thou done?

36 [s]Jesus answered, [t]My kingdom is not of this world: if my kingdom were of this world, then would my servants fight, that I should not be delivered to the Jews: but now is my kingdom not from hence.

37 Pilate therefore said unto him,

18:25 [l]Mat. 26:69,71 Mark 14:69 Luke 22:58
18:27 [m]Mat. 26:74 Mark 14:72 Luke 22:60 ch. 13:38
18:28 [n]Mat. 27:2 Mark 15:1 Luke 23:1 Acts 3:13 [o]Mat. 27:27 [p]Acts 10:28 & 11:3
18:32 [q]Mat. 20:19 ch. 12:32,33
18:33 [r]Mat. 27:11
18:36 [s]1 Tim. 6:13 [t]Dan. 2:44 & 7:14 Luke 12:14 ch. 6:15 & 8:15

[j] Or, *Pilate's house*

18:28 JESUS BEFORE PILATE. See Mat. 27:2, note; Luke 23:1, note.

18:36 MY KINGDOM IS NOT OF THIS WORLD. Concerning the true nature of Christ's kingdom and its redemptive purpose, three points should be observed: (1) What Jesus' kingdom is not. It is "not of this world." It did not originate in this world nor does it seek to take over the world's system. Jesus did not come to establish a religio-political theocracy or aspire to world dominion. Jesus states that if He had come to establish a political kingdom on earth, then would His "servants fight." Since this is not the nature of the kingdom, they do not resort to war or revolution to promote Christ's purpose on earth (cf. Mat. 26:51–52). They do not ally themselves with political parties, social pressure groups, or any secular organizations in order to establish God's kingdom. They refuse to turn the cross into a boastful attempt to rule society. Rather than using carnal weapons (2 Cor. 10:4), Jesus' followers are armed only with spiritual weapons (Eph. 6:10–18). However, this does not mean that Jesus' disciples are indifferent to God's demand for just government, justice, peace, or curtailing lawlessness. Christians must bring a "prophetic word" to the state concerning its moral responsibilities under God.

(2) What Jesus' kingdom is. Christ's kingdom, i.e., the kingdom of God, involves His rule, Lordship, power, and spiritual activity in the lives and hearts of all those who receive Him and obey His word of truth (v. 37). The kingdom of God is "righteousness, and peace, and joy in the Holy Ghost" (Rom. 14:17). It confronts the spiritual forces of Satan with spiritual weapons (see Mat. 12:28; Luke 11:20; Acts 26:18; Eph. 6:12). The church's role is that of a bondservant of Jesus Christ, not that of a ruler of this present world. Her strength is not in worldly power but in the cross; her suffering and rejection at the hands of the world are her glory (2 Cor. 3:7–18). Only in renouncing worldly power did the N.T. church find God's power. The church today faces this same choice: only by losing her life in the world will she find herself in God (see article on THE KINGDOM OF GOD, p. 1428).

(3) What Jesus' kingdom will be. In the future, Christ's kingdom and rule will be ultimately over the new heaven and earth. This will occur after His coming to earth in judgment to judge the nations, destroy the antichrist, rule on earth for a thousand years, and then bring Satan to a final end in the lake of fire (Rev. 19:11—20:15).

18:37 BEAR WITNESS UNTO THE TRUTH. Jesus affirms that an essential part of His earthly mission was to bear witness to the truth and to point people to the truth. This refers to His incarnate witness to the Father and to the revealed truth of His gospel now recorded in the Scriptures. How strange that some ministers today compromise truth and sound doctrine, obscure the clear meaning of Scripture, and promote unity at the cost of sacrificing Biblical faith. Such ministers err in tolerating false doctrine and refusing to draw distinctions between right and wrong, truth and

Art thou a king then? Jesus answered, Thou sayest that I am a king. To this end was I born, and for this cause came I into the world, that I should bear witness unto the truth. Every one that [u]is of the truth heareth my voice.

Rom. 12:1-2

38 Pilate saith unto him, What is truth? And when he had said this, he went out again unto the Jews, and saith unto them, [v]I find in him no fault *at all.*

39 [w]But ye have a custom, that I should release unto you one at the passover: will ye therefore that I release unto you the King of the Jews?

40 [x]Then cried they all again, saying, Not this man, but Barabbas. [y]Now Barabbas was a robber.

Jesus scourged and mocked

19:1–11pp — Mat. 27:27–31; Mark 15:16–20

19 THEN [z]PILATE therefore took Jesus, and scourged *him.*

2 And the soldiers plaited a crown of thorns, and put *it* on his head, and they put on him a purple robe,

3 And said, Hail, King of the Jews! and they smote him with their hands.

4 Pilate therefore went forth again, and saith unto them, Behold, I bring him forth to you, [a]that ye may know that I find no fault in him.

5 Then came Jesus forth, wearing the crown of thorns, and the purple robe. And *Pilate* saith unto them, Behold the man!

6 [b]When the chief priests therefore and officers saw him, they cried out, saying, Crucify *him,* crucify *him.* Pilate saith unto them, Take ye him, and crucify *him:* for I find no fault in him.

7 The Jews answered him, [c]We have a law, and by our law he ought to die, because [d]he made himself the Son of God.

8 ¶ When Pilate therefore heard that saying, he was the more afraid;

9 And went again into the judgment hall, and saith unto Jesus, Whence art thou? [e]But Jesus gave him no answer.

10 Then saith Pilate unto him, Speakest thou not unto me? knowest thou not that I have power to crucify thee, and have power to release thee?

11 Jesus answered, [f]Thou couldest have no power *at all* against me, except it were given thee from above: therefore he that delivered me unto thee hath the greater sin.

Pilate delivers Jesus to be crucified

19:12–16pp — Mat. 27:22–26; Mark 15:12–15; Luke 23:20–25

12 And from thenceforth Pilate sought to release him: but the Jews cried out, saying, [g]If thou let this man go, thou art not Caesar's friend: [h]whosoever maketh himself a king speaketh against Caesar.

13 ¶ When Pilate therefore heard that saying, he brought Jesus forth, and sat down in the judgment seat in a place that is called the Pavement, but in the Hebrew, Gabbatha.

14 And [i]it was the preparation of the passover, and about the sixth hour: and he saith unto the Jews, Behold your King!

15 But they cried out, Away with *him,* away with *him,* crucify him. Pilate saith unto them, Shall I crucify your King? The chief priests answered, [j]We have no king but Caesar.

16 [k]Then delivered he him therefore unto them to be crucified. And they took Jesus, and led *him* away.

Jesus crucified

19:17–24pp — Mat. 27:33–44; Mark 15:22–32; Luke 23:33–43

17 [l]And he bearing his cross

18:37 [u]ch. 8:47 1 John 3:19 & 4:6
18:38 [v]Mat. 27:24 Luke 23:4 ch. 19:4,6
18:39 [w]Mat. 27:15 Mark 15:6 Luke 23:17
18:40 [x]Acts 3:14 [y]Luke 23:19
19:1 [z]Mat. 20:19 & 27:26 Mark 15:15 Luke 18:33
19:4 [a]ver. 6 ch. 18:38
19:6 [b]Acts 3:13
19:7 [c]Lev. 24:16 [d]Mat. 26:65 ch. 5:18 & 10:33
19:9 [e]Is. 53:7 Mat. 27:12,14
19:11 [f]Luke 22:53 ch. 7:30
19:12 [g]Luke 23:2 [h]Acts 17:7
19:14 [i]Mat. 27:62
19:15 [j]Gen. 49:10
19:16 [k]Mat. 27:26,31 Mark 15:15 Luke 23:24
19:17 [l]Mat. 27:31,33 Mark 15:21,22 Luke 23:26,33

error. In the name of love and broad-mindedness, they reject this purpose of His coming. Truth is one thing that churches must never sacrifice (cf. 17:8,17; 2 Thes. 2:10).

19:1 SCOURGED *HIM*. For details concerning the method of Roman scourgings, see Mat. 27:26, note.

19:4 I FIND NO FAULT IN HIM. See Luke 23:14, note.

19:11 POWER ... GIVEN THEE FROM ABOVE. Jesus says that all earthly power and authority exist only as God permits it (cf. Dan. 4:34–35; Rom. 13:1). Pilate's sin was yielding to the crowd because of political expediency. Israel's sin was greater—they were rejecting their Messiah.

19:14 THE SIXTH HOUR. John states that Jesus' trial neared completion "about the sixth hour." Mark, however, says that Jesus was crucified at "the third hour" (Mark 15:25). This problem is resolved if we understand that John used the Roman method of computing time, while Mark used the Palestinian method. The Roman day began at midnight, the Palestinian began at sunrise.

19:16 DELIVERED HE HIM ... TO BE CRUCIFIED. See Luke 23:25, note.

19:17 HE BEARING HIS CROSS. See Mat. 27:31, note.

[m]went forth into a place called *the place* of a skull, which is called in the Hebrew Golgotha:

18 Where they crucified him, and two other with him, on either side one, and Jesus in the midst.

19 ¶ [n]And Pilate wrote a title, and put *it* on the cross. And the writing was, JESUS OF NAZARETH THE KING OF THE JEWS.

20 This title then read many of the Jews: for the place where Jesus was crucified was nigh to the city: and it was written in Hebrew, *and* Greek, *and* Latin.

21 Then said the chief priests of the Jews to Pilate, Write not, The King of the Jews; but that he said, I am King of the Jews.

22 Pilate answered, What I have written I have written.

23 ¶ [o]Then the soldiers, when they had crucified Jesus, took his garments, and made four parts, to every soldier a part; and also *his* coat: now the coat was without seam, [k]woven from the top throughout.

24 They said therefore among themselves, Let us not rend it, but cast lots for it, whose it shall be: that the scripture might be fulfilled, which saith, [p]They parted my raiment among them, and for my vesture they did cast lots. These things therefore the soldiers did.

25 ¶ [q]Now there stood by the cross of Jesus his mother, and his mother's sister, Mary the *wife* of [r]Cleophas,[1] and Mary Magdalene.

26 When Jesus therefore saw his mother, and [s]the disciple standing by, whom he loved, he saith unto his mother, [t]Woman, behold thy son!

27 Then saith he to the disciple, Behold thy mother! And from that hour that disciple took her [u]unto his own *home*.

19:17 [m]Num. 15:36 Heb. 13:12
19:19 [n]Mat. 27:37 Mark 15:26 Luke 23:38
19:23 [o]Mat. 27:35 Mark 15:24 Luke 23:34
19:24 [p]Ps. 22:18
19:25 [q]Mat. 27:55 Mark 15:40 Luke 23:49 [r]Luke 24:18
19:26 [s]ch. 13:23 & 20:2 & 21:7,20,24 [t]ch. 2:4
19:27 [u]ch. 1:11 & 16:32
19:28 [v]Ps. 69:21
19:29 [w]Mat. 27:48
19:30 [x]ch. 17:4
19:31 [y]ver. 42 Mark 15:42 [z]Deut. 21:23
19:34 [a]1 John 5:6,8
19:36 [b]Ex. 12:46 Num. 9:12 Ps. 34:20
19:37 [c]Ps. 22:16,17 Zech. 12:10 Rev. 1:7
19:38 [d]Mat. 27:57 Mark 15:42 Luke 23:50 [e]ch. 9:22 & 12:42

The death of Jesus

19:29–30pp — Mat. 27:48,50; Mark 15:36–37; Luke 23:36

28 ¶ After this, Jesus knowing that all things were now accomplished, [v]that the scripture might be fulfilled, saith, I thirst.

29 Now there was set a vessel full of vinegar: and [w]they filled a sponge with vinegar, and put *it* upon hyssop, and put *it* to his mouth.

30 When Jesus therefore had received the vinegar, he said, [x]It is finished: and he bowed his head, and gave up the ghost.

31 The Jews therefore, [y]because it was the preparation, [z]that the bodies should not remain upon the cross on the sabbath day, (for that sabbath day was an high day,) besought Pilate that their legs might be broken, and *that* they might be taken away.

32 Then came the soldiers, and brake the legs of the first, and of the other which was crucified with him.

33 But when they came to Jesus, and saw that he was dead already, they brake not his legs:

34 But one of the soldiers with a spear pierced his side, and forthwith [a]came there out blood and water.

35 And he that saw *it* bare record, and his record is true: and he knoweth that he saith true, that ye might believe.

36 For these things were done, [b]that the scripture should be fulfilled, A bone of him shall not be broken.

37 And again another scripture saith, [c]They shall look on him whom they pierced.

Jesus laid in the sepulchre

19:38–42pp — Mat. 27:57–61; Mark 15:42–47; Luke 23:50–56

38 ¶ [d]And after this Joseph of Arimathaea, being a disciple of Jesus, but secretly [e]for fear of the Jews, be-

[k]Or, *wrought* [1]Or, *Clopas*

19:18 THEY CRUCIFIED HIM. For commentary on the crucifixion, see Mat. 27:35, note.

19:26 WOMAN, BEHOLD THY SON! Even in the agony of His death, Jesus is concerned about the welfare of His mother. He appoints "the disciple whom he loved" (probably John) to take care of and provide for her. To assist needy family members is a responsibility we have until death. The emphasis here is on the responsibility of children toward their parents.

19:29 VINEGAR. Christ's tasting of the vinegar was a fulfillment of the prophecy of Ps. 69:21, "in my thirst they gave me vinegar to drink."

19:30 IT IS FINISHED. Jesus' sufferings and the agonies in providing redemption for fallen humanity were over and His work of redemption stood completed. He had borne the punishment for our sins and opened the way of salvation for all (see Mat. 27:50, note; Luke 23:46, note).

sought Pilate that he might take away
the body of Jesus: and Pilate gave *him*
leave. He came therefore, and took the
body of Jesus.
39 And there came also [f]Nicode-
mus, which at the first came to Jesus
by night, and brought a mixture of
myrrh and aloes, about an hundred
pound *weight.*
40 Then took they the body of
Jesus, and [g]wound it in linen clothes
with the spices, as the manner of the
Jews is to bury.
41 Now in the place where he was
crucified there was a garden; and in
the garden a new sepulchre, wherein
was never man yet laid.
42 [h]There laid they Jesus therefore
[i]because of the Jews' preparation *day;*
for the sepulchre was nigh at hand.

The resurrection of Jesus

20:1–8pp — Mat. 28:1–8; Mark 16:1–8; Luke 24:1–10

20 THE [j]FIRST *day* of the week
cometh Mary Magdalene early,
when it was yet dark, unto the sepul-
chre, and seeth the stone taken away
from the sepulchre.
2 Then she runneth, and cometh to
Simon Peter, and to the [k]other disci-
ple, whom Jesus loved, and saith unto
them, They have taken away the Lord
out of the sepulchre, and we know not
where they have laid him.
3 [l]Peter therefore went forth, and
that other disciple, and came to the
sepulchre.
4 So they ran both together: and the
other disciple did outrun Peter, and
came first to the sepulchre.
5 And he stooping down, *and look-
ing in,* saw [m]the linen clothes lying;
yet went he not in.
6 Then cometh Simon Peter follow-
ing him, and went into the sepulchre,
and seeth the linen clothes lie,

19:39 [f]ch. 3:1,2 & 7:50
19:40 [g]Acts 5:6
19:42 [h]Is. 53:9 [i]ver. 31
20:1 [j]Mat. 28:1 Mark 16:1 Luke 24:1
20:2 [k]ch. 13:23 & 19:26 & 21:7,20,24
20:3 [l]Luke 24:12
20:5 [m]ch. 19:40
20:7 [n]ch. 11:44
20:9 [o]Ps. 16:10 Acts 2:25-31 & 13:34,35
20:11 [p]Mark 16:5
20:14 [q]Mat. 28:9 Mark 16:9 [r]Luke 24:16,31 ch. 21:4
20:17 [s]Ps. 22:22 Mat. 28:10 Rom. 8:29 Heb. 2:11 [t]ch. 16:28 [u]Eph. 1:17
20:18 [v]Mat. 28:10 Luke 24:10

7 And [n]the napkin, that was about
his head, not lying with the linen
clothes, but wrapped together in a
place by itself.
8 Then went in also that other disci-
ple, which came first to the sepulchre,
and he saw, and believed.
9 For as yet they knew not the
[o]scripture, that he must rise again
from the dead.
10 Then the disciples went away
again unto their own home.

Jesus appears to Mary Magdalene

11 ¶ [p]But Mary stood without at
the sepulchre weeping: and as she
wept, she stooped down, *and looked*
into the sepulchre,
12 And seeth two angels in white
sitting, the one at the head, and the
other at the feet, where the body of
Jesus had lain.
13 And they say unto her, Woman,
why weepest thou? She saith unto
them, Because they have taken away
my Lord, and I know not where they
have laid him.
14 [q]And when she had thus said,
she turned herself back, and saw Jesus
standing, and [r]knew not that it was
Jesus.
15 Jesus saith unto her, Woman,
why weepest thou? whom seekest
thou? She, supposing him to be the gar-
dener, saith unto him, Sir, if thou have
borne him hence, tell me where thou
hast laid him, and I will take him away.
16 Jesus saith unto her, Mary. She
turned herself, and saith unto him,
Rabboni; which is to say, Master.
17 Jesus saith unto her, Touch me
not; for I am not yet ascended to my
Father: but go to [s]my brethren, and
say unto them, [t]I ascend unto my Fa-
ther, and your Father; and *to* [u]my God,
and your God.
18 [v]Mary Magdalene came and

19:41 A NEW SEPULCHRE. The sepulchre had been hewn out of solid rock (Mark 15:46). It was probably large enough to walk into, but with a low entrance (John 20:11). After placing the body of Jesus in the tomb, Joseph rolled a great stone in front of its entrance (Mat. 27:60).

20:9 HE MUST RISE AGAIN. See Mat. 28:6, note on the importance of Christ's resurrection, and Luke 24:6, note on the confirmation of Christ's resurrection.

20:16 JESUS SAITH UNTO HER, MARY. The first person to whom Jesus appears after His resurrection is Mary. She was not a particularly prominent person in the Gospels. Yet Jesus appears first to her rather than to any of the outstanding leaders among the disciples. Throughout the ages, Jesus manifests His presence and love especially to those who are "least." God's special people are the unknown, those who, like Mary in her grief, maintain a steadfast love for and devotion to their Lord.

20:17 TOUCH ME NOT. This verse probably means, "Do not continue to cling to Me; I am not yet going to ascend unto My Father. You will still have an opportunity to see Me again." In the meantime He has something for her to do.

told the disciples that she had seen the Lord, and *that* he had spoken these things unto her.

Jesus appears to the disciples

19 ¶ [w]Then the same day at evening, being the first *day* of the week, when the doors were shut where the disciples were assembled for fear of the Jews, came Jesus and stood in the midst, and saith unto them, Peace *be* unto you.

20 And when he had so said, he showed unto them *his* hands and his side. [x]Then were the disciples glad, when they saw the Lord.

21 Then said Jesus to them again, Peace *be* unto you: [y]as *my* Father hath sent me, even so send I you.

The disciples receive the Holy Spirit

22 And when he had said this, he breathed on *them*, and saith unto them, Receive ye the Holy Ghost:

23 [z]Whosesoever sins ye remit, they are remitted unto them; *and* whosesoever *sins* ye retain, they are retained.

Thomas' doubt and belief

24 ¶ But Thomas, one of the twelve, [a]called Didymus, was not with them when Jesus came.

25 The other disciples therefore said unto him, We have seen the Lord. But he said unto them, Except I shall see in his hands the print of the nails, and put my finger into the print of the nails, and thrust my hand into his side, I will not believe.

26 ¶ And after eight days again his disciples were within, and Thomas with them: *then* came Jesus, the doors being shut, and stood in the midst, and said, Peace *be* unto you.

27 Then saith he to Thomas, Reach hither thy finger, and behold my hands; and [b]reach hither thy hand, and thrust *it* into my side: and be not faithless, but believing.

28 And Thomas answered and said unto him, My Lord and my God.

29 Jesus saith unto him, Thomas, because thou hast seen me, thou hast believed: [c]blessed *are* they that have not seen, and *yet* have believed.

30 ¶ [d]And many other signs truly did Jesus in the presence of his disciples, which are not written in this book:

31 [e]But these are written, that ye might believe that Jesus is the Christ, the Son of God; [f]and that believing ye might have life through his name. † Acts 4:12

20:19 [w]Mark 16:14 Luke 24:36 1 Cor. 15:5
20:20 [x]ch. 16:22
20:21 [y]Mat. 28:18 ch. 17:18,19 2 Tim. 2:2 Heb. 3:1
20:23 [z]Mat. 16:10 & 18:18
20:24 [a]ch. 11:16
20:27 [b]1 John 1:1
20:29 [c]2 Cor. 5:7 1 Pet 1:8
20:30 [d]ch. 21:25
20:31 [e]Luke 1:4 [f]ch. 3:15,16 & 5:24 1 Pet. 1:8,9

20:22 RECEIVE YE THE HOLY GHOST. For an extensive discussion of this important verse and how it relates to our regeneration and baptism in the Holy Spirit, see article on THE REGENERATION OF THE DISCIPLES, p. 1638.

20:23 WHOSESOEVER SINS YE REMIT. See Mat. 16:19, note.

20:28 MY LORD AND MY GOD. The Scriptures declare that Jesus is God. This is the foundation of the Christian faith and is of utmost importance for our salvation. Without Christ being divine, He could not have made atonement for the sins of the world. The deity of Jesus Christ is shown by the following:

(1) Divine names are given to Him in the Scriptures: (a) God (20:28; Is. 9:6; Rom. 9:5; Tit. 2:13; Heb. 1:8); (b) the Son of God (5:25; Mat. 16:16–17; 8:29; 27:40,43; Mark 14:61–62; Luke 22:70); (c) the first and the last (Is. 41:4; Rev. 1:11,17; 22:13); (d) the Holy One (Hos. 11:9; Acts 3:14); (e) the Lord (Luke 2:11; Acts 4:33; 9:17; 16:31); (f) Lord of all and Lord of glory (Ps. 24:8–10; Acts 10:36; 1 Cor. 2:8).

(2) Divine worship is rendered to Christ (5:23; 13:13; 20:28; Mat. 14:33; Luke 5:8), and prayers are addressed to Him (Acts 7:59; 1 Cor. 1:2; 2 Cor. 12:8–9).

(3) Divine offices are assigned to Christ: (a) creator of the universe (1:3; Col. 1:16; Heb. 1:8,10; Rev. 3:14); (b) preserver of all things (Col. 1:17; Heb. 1:3); (c) forgiver of sins (Mark 2:5,10; Luke 7:48–50); (d) bestower of resurrection life (5:28–29; 6:39–44); (e) judge of all people (5:21–23; Mat. 25:31–46; Acts 17:31; 2 Tim. 4:1); (f) giver of salvation (5:24–26; 6:47; 10:28; 17:2).

(4) The N.T. attributes to Christ many O.T. statements concerning the Lord. Compare Ps. 23:1 with John 10:11; Ps. 102:24–27 with Heb. 1:10–12; Is. 8:13–14 with 1 Pet. 2:7–8; Jer. 17:10 with Rev. 2:23; Ezek. 34:11–12 with Luke 19:10.

(5) The name of Jesus Christ is associated with that of God the Father (14:1,23; Mat. 28:19; Rom. 1:7; 2 Cor. 13:14; Col. 2:2; 1 Thes. 3:11; Jas. 1:1; Rev. 5:13; 7:10).

(6) His sinlessness and holiness testify to His deity (Luke 1:35; 2 Cor. 5:21; Heb. 4:15).

(7) He was declared to be the Son of God by His resurrection (Rom. 1:4).

These conclusive proofs of Christ's deity mean that the believer must act toward Christ in exactly the same manner as he must act toward God the Father. He must believe in Him, reverence and worship Him, pray to Him, serve Him, and love Him (see also 1:1, note; Mark 1:11, note on Trinity).

THE REGENERATION OF THE DISCIPLES

John 20:22 "And when he had said this, he breathed on them, and saith unto them, Receive ye the Holy Ghost."

The impartation of the Holy Spirit by Jesus to His disciples on resurrection day was not the baptism in the Spirit as experienced by them at Pentecost (Acts 1:5; 2:4). It was rather an infusing of the disciples for the first time with the regenerating presence of the Holy Spirit and with new life from the risen Christ.

(1) During the last discourse that Jesus had with His disciples before His trial and crucifixion, He promised them that they would receive the Holy Spirit as the One who would regenerate them: "he dwelleth with you, and shall be in you"(John 14:17, see note). Jesus now fulfills that promise.

(2) That John 20:22 refers to regeneration can be inferred from the phrase, "he breathed on *them*." The Greek word for "breathed" (*emphusaō*) is the same verb used in the Septuagint (the Greek translation of the O.T.) at Gen. 2:7, where God "breathed into his [Adam's] nostrils the breath of life; and man became a living soul." It is the same verb that is found in Ezek. 37:9, "Breathe upon these slain, that they may live." John's use of this verb in 20:22 indicates that Jesus was giving the Spirit in order to bring forth life and a new creation. That is, just as God breathed into physical man the breath of life and he became a new creation (Gen. 2:7), so Jesus now breathed into the disciples spiritual life and they became a new creation (see article on REGENERATION, p. 1597). Through His resurrection, Jesus became a "quickening [life-giving] spirit" (1 Cor. 15:45).

(3) The words "receive ye the Holy Ghost" establishes that the Spirit, *at that historical moment*, entered and began to dwell in the disciples. The verb form for "receive" is aorist imperative (Gk. *labete*, from the word *lambanō*), denoting a single act of reception. The Holy Spirit was given to regenerate them, to make them new creatures in Christ (cf. 2 Cor. 5:17). This "receiving" of life from the Holy Spirit preceded both their receiving the authority of Jesus (John 20:23) and their baptism in the Holy Spirit on the day of Pentecost (Acts 2:4).

(4) Prior to this time, the disciples were technically true believers and followers of Jesus and were saved according to the old covenant provisions. Yet they were not regenerated in the full new covenant sense. Not until this point did the disciples enter into the new covenant provisions based on Jesus' death and resurrection (see Mat. 26:28; Luke 22:20; 1 Cor. 11:25; Eph. 2:15–16; Heb. 9:15–17; see article on REGENERATION, p. 1597). It was also technically at this time and not at Pentecost that the church was born. The spiritual birth of the first disciples and the birth of the church are one and the same.

(5) This passage is crucial in understanding the Holy Spirit's ministry to the people of God. These two statements are true: (a) the disciples received the Holy Spirit (i.e., were indwelt and regenerated by the Holy Spirit) before the day of Pentecost; and (b) the outpouring of the Holy Spirit upon them in Acts 2:4 was an experience occurring after their regeneration by the Holy Spirit. Their baptism in the Spirit at Pentecost was, therefore, a second and distinct work of the Spirit in them.

(6) These two separate and distinct works of the Holy Spirit in the lives of Jesus' disciples are normative for all Christians. That is, all believers receive the Holy Spirit at the time of their regeneration, and afterwards must experience the baptism in the Holy Spirit for power to be His witnesses (Acts 1:5,8; 2:4; see 2:39, note).

(7) There is no Scriptural foundation to suggest that Jesus' bestowal of the Holy Spirit in John 20:22 was simply symbolical prophecy of the coming of the Holy Spirit at Pentecost. The use of the aorist imperative for "receive" (see above) denotes reception at that moment and in that place. What occurred was a historical reality in space and time, and John records it as such.

The appearance beside the sea

21 AFTER THESE things Jesus showed himself again to the disciples at the sea of Tiberias; and on this wise showed he *himself.*

2 There were together Simon Peter, and Thomas called Didymus, and [g]Nathanael of Cana in Galilee, and [h]the *sons* of Zebedee, and two other of his disciples.

3 Simon Peter saith unto them, I go a-fishing. They say unto him, We also go with thee. They went forth, and entered into a ship immediately; and that night they caught nothing.

4 But when the morning was now come, Jesus stood on the shore: but the disciples [i]knew not that it was Jesus.

5 Then [j]Jesus saith unto them, [m]Children, have ye any meat? They answered him, No.

6 And he said unto them, [k]Cast the net on the right side of the ship, and ye shall find. They cast therefore, and now they were not able to draw it for the multitude of fishes.

7 Therefore [l]that disciple whom Jesus loved saith unto Peter, It is the Lord. Now when Simon Peter heard that it was the Lord, he girt *his* fisher's coat *unto him,* (for he was naked,) and did cast himself into the sea.

8 And the other disciples came in a little ship; (for they were not far from land, but as it were two hundred cubits,) dragging the net with fishes.

21:2 [g]ch. 1:45 [h]Mat. 4:21
21:4 [i]ch. 20:14
21:5 [j]Luke 24:41
21:6 [k]Luke 5:4,6,7
21:7 [l]ch. 13:23 & 20:2
21:12 [m]Acts 10:41
21:14 [n]See ch. 20:19,26
21:16 [o]Acts 20:28 Heb. 13:20 1 Pet. 2:25 & 5:2,4

9 As soon then as they were come to land, they saw a fire of coals there, and fish laid thereon, and bread.

10 Jesus saith unto them, Bring of the fish which ye have now caught.

11 Simon Peter went up, and drew the net to land full of great fishes, an hundred and fifty and three: and for all there were so many, yet was not the net broken.

12 Jesus saith unto them, [m]Come *and* dine. And none of the disciples durst ask him, Who art thou? knowing that it was the Lord.

13 Jesus then cometh, and taketh bread, and giveth them, and fish likewise.

14 This is now [n]the third time that Jesus showed himself to his disciples, after that he was risen from the dead.

Jesus' conversation with Peter

15 ¶ So when they had dined, Jesus saith to Simon Peter, Simon, *son* of Jonas, lovest thou me more than these? He saith unto him, Yea, Lord; thou knowest that I love thee. He saith unto him, Feed my lambs.

16 He saith to him again the second time, Simon, *son* of Jonas, lovest thou me? He saith unto him, Yea, Lord; thou knowest that I love thee. [o]He saith unto him, Feed my sheep.

17 He saith unto him the third time,

[m] Or, *Sirs*

21:1 JESUS SHOWED HIMSELF AGAIN. See Mat. 28:9, note on Christ's resurrection appearances.

21:3 I GO A-FISHING. The disciples' plan to go fishing does not mean they were forsaking their commitment to Christ and their calling to preach the gospel. They knew that Jesus had risen from the grave, yet they did not know what to do at that time. They had not yet received the instruction to wait in Jerusalem until the Holy Spirit came upon them in mighty power (Acts 1:4–5). To go fishing was a necessity, for these men still had to gain a living for themselves and their families.

21:6 CAST THE NET ON THE RIGHT SIDE. It is crucial to receive guidance from the Lord in all our work. If we live and expend our lives without the presence, blessing, and guiding hand of Christ, then all we do becomes empty failure and wasted effort.

21:7 HE GIRT *HIS* FISHER'S COAT. The "fisher's coat" was an outer garment. The expression "for he was naked" probably means "dressed in underclothes," i.e., a loincloth or sleeveless tunic.

21:15 LOVEST THOU ME. The most important question that Peter ever faced was whether he possessed a devoted love for his Lord. (1) Two Greek words for "love" are used here. The first, *agapaō*, means an intelligent and purposeful love, primarily of mind and will. The second, *phileō*, involves warm natural affection of the emotions, thus a more personal and feeling love. Through these two words, Jesus indicates that Peter's love must be not only of the will, but also of the heart, a love springing from both purpose and personal attachment. (2) Jesus' question to Peter is the great question for all believers. We must all have a personal heartfelt love for and devotion to Jesus (14:15; 16:27; Mat. 10:37; Luke 7:47; 1 Cor. 16:22; 2 Cor. 5:14; Gal. 5:6; Eph. 6:24; Jas. 1:12; 1 Pet. 1:8; Rev. 2:4).

21:16 FEED MY SHEEP. Jesus' description of believers as lambs (v. 15) and sheep (v. 16) implies three things. (1) We need continual pastoral care. (2) We need to feed constantly upon the Word. (3) Since sheep are prone to wander into danger, we need repeated guidance, protection, and correction.

21:17 LOVEST THOU ME? . . . FEED MY SHEEP. Jesus considers love for Him as the basic

Simon, *son* of Jonas, lovest thou me?
Peter was grieved because he said
unto him the third time, Lovest thou
me? And he said unto him, Lord,
[p]thou knowest all things; thou know-
est that I love thee. Jesus saith unto
him, Feed my sheep.
18 [q]Verily, verily, I say unto thee,
When thou wast young, thou girdedst
thyself, and walkedst whither thou
wouldest: but when thou shalt be old,
thou shalt stretch forth thy hands, and
another shall gird thee, and carry *thee*
whither thou wouldest not.
19 This spake he, signifying [r]by
what death he should glorify God. And
when he had spoken this, he saith unto
him, Follow me.
20 Then Peter, turning about, seeth
the disciple [s]whom Jesus loved fol-
lowing; which also leaned on his breast
at supper, and said, Lord, which is he
that betrayeth thee?

21:17 [p]ch. 2:24,25 & 16:30
21:18 [q]ch. 13:36 Acts 12:3,4
21:19 [r]2 Pet. 1:14
21:20 [s]ch. 13:23,25 & 20:2
21:22 [t]Mat. 16:27,28 & 25:31 1 Cor. 4:5 & 11:26 Rev. 2:25 & 3:11 & 22:7,20
21:24 [u]ch. 19:35 3 John 12
21:25 [v]ch. 20:30 [w]Amos 7:10

21 Peter seeing him saith to Jesus,
Lord, and what *shall* this man *do?*
22 Jesus saith unto him, If I will
that he tarry [t]till I come, what *is that*
to thee? follow thou me.
23 Then went this saying abroad
among the brethren, that that disciple
should not die: yet Jesus said not unto
him, He shall not die; but, If I will that
he tarry till I come, what *is that* to
thee?

Jesus' witness and testimony

24 This is the disciple which testi-
fieth of these things, and wrote these
things: and [u]we know that his testi-
mony is true.
25 [v]And there are also many other
things which Jesus did, the which, if
they should be written every one, [w]I
suppose that even the world itself
could not contain the books that
should be written. Amen.

---

qualification for Christian service. Other qualifications are needed (1 Tim. 3:1–13), but love for Christ and for others is indispensable (cf. 1 Cor. 13:1–3).

21:18 THOU SHALT STRETCH FORTH THY HANDS. These words refer to the kind of death by which Peter would glorify God. Tradition records that Peter was crucified in Rome under Nero at about the same time that Paul was martyred (c. A.D. 67/68), and that at his own request he was crucified head downward because he considered himself unworthy to be crucified in the same manner as his Lord.

THE MINISTRY OF JESUS

THE YEAR OF INAUGURATION

Event	Place	Matthew	Mark	Luke	John
Jesus baptized	Jordan River	3:13–17	1:9–11	3:21–23	1:29–39
Jesus tempted by Satan	Wilderness	4:1–11	1:12–13	4:1–13	
Jesus' first miracle	Cana				2:1–11
Jesus and Nicodemus	Judea				3:1–21
Jesus talks to a Samaritan woman	Samaria				4:5–42
Jesus heals a nobleman's son	Cana				4:46–54
The people of Nazareth try to kill Jesus	Nazareth			4:16–31	

THE YEAR OF POPULARITY

Event	Place	Matthew	Mark	Luke	John
Jesus calls four fishermen	Sea of Galilee	4:18–22	1:16–20	5:1–11	
Jesus heals Peter's mother-in-law	Capernaum	8:14–17	1:29–34	4:38–41	
Jesus begins preaching in Galilee	Galilee	4:23–25	1:35–39	4:42–4	
Matthew decides to follow Jesus	Capernaum	9:9–13	2:13–17	5:27–32	
Jesus chooses twelve disciples	Galilee	10:2–4	3:13–19	6:12–15	
Jesus preaches the Sermon on the Mount	Galilee	5:1–7:29		6:20–49	
A sinful woman anoints Jesus	Capernaum			7:36–50	
Jesus travels again through Galilee	Galilee			8:1–3	
Jesus tells kingdom parables	Galilee	13:1–52	4:1–34	8:4–18	
Jesus quiets the storm	Sea of Galilee	8:23–27	4:35–41	8:22–25	
Jairus's daughter raised to life	Capernaum	9:18–26	5:21–43	8:40–56	
Jesus sends out the twelve	Galilee	9:35—11:1	6:6–13	9:1–6	

THE YEAR OF OPPOSITION

Event	Place	Matthew	Mark	Luke	John
John the Baptist killed by Herod	Machaerus in Judea	14:1–12	6:14–29	9:7–9	
Jesus feeds the 5000	Bethsaida	14:13–21	6:30–44	9:10–17	6:1–14
Jesus walks on water	Sea of Galilee	14:22–23	6:45–52		6:16–21
Jesus feeds the 4000	Sea of Galilee	15:32–39	8:1–9		
Peter confesses Jesus as the Son of God	Caesarea Philippi	16:13–20	8:27–30	9:18–21	
Jesus predicts his death	Caesarea Philippi	16:21–26	8:31–37	9:22–25	
Jesus is transfigured	Mount Hermon	17:1–13	9:2–13	9:28–36	

THE MINISTRY OF JESUS

THE YEAR OF OPPOSITION (cont.)

Event	Place	Matthew	Mark	Luke	John
Jesus pays his temple taxes	Capernaum	17:24–27			
Jesus attends the Feast of Tabernacles	Jerusalem				7:11–52
Jesus heals a man born blind	Jerusalem				9:1–41
Jesus visits Mary and Martha	Bethany			10:38–42	
Jesus raises Lazarus	Bethany				11:1–44
Jesus begins his last trip to Jerusalem	Border road			17:11	
Jesus blesses the little children	Transjordan	19:13–15	10:13–16	18:15–17	
Jesus talks to the rich young man	Transjordan	19:16–30	10:17–31	18:18–30	
Jesus again predicts his death	Near the Jordan	20:17–19	10:32–34	18:31–34	
Jesus heals blind Bartimaeus	Jericho	20:29–34	10:46–52	18:35–43	
Jesus talks to Zacchaeus	Jericho			19:1–10	
Jesus visits Mary and Martha again	Bethany				11:55–12:1

THE LAST WEEK

Event	Place	Day of Week	Matthew	Mark	Luke	John
The triumphal entry	Jerusalem	Sunday	21:1–11	11:1–10	19:29–44	12:12–19
Jesus curses the fig tree	Jerusalem	Monday	21:18–19	11:12–14		
Jesus cleanses the temple	Jerusalem	Monday	21:12–13	11:15–18	19:45–48	
The authority of Jesus questioned	Jerusalem	Tuesday	21:23–27	11:27–33	20:1–8	
Jesus teaches in the temple	Jerusalem	Tuesday	21:28–23:29	12:1–44	20:9–21:4	
Jesus' feet anointed	Bethany	Tuesday	26:6–13	14:3–9		12:2–11
The plot against Jesus	Jerusalem	Wednesday	26:14–16	14:10–11	22:3–6	
The Last Supper	Jerusalem	Thursday	26:17–29	14:12–25	22:7–20	13:1–38
Jesus comforts his disciples	Jerusalem	Thursday				14:1–16:33
Jesus' high priestly prayer	Jerusalem	Thursday				17:1–26
Gethsemane	Jerusalem	Thursday	26:36–46	14:32–42	22:40–46	
Jesus' arrest and trial	Jerusalem	Friday	26:47–27:26	14:43–15:15	22:47–23:25	18:2–19:16
Jesus' crucifixion and death	Golgotha	Friday	27:27–56	15:16–41	23:26–49	19:17–30
The burial of Jesus	Garden tomb	Friday	27:57–66	15:42–47	23:50–56	19:31–42

RESURRECTION APPEARANCES

Event	Place	Day of week	Matthew	Mark	Luke	John	Acts	1 Corinthians
The empty tomb	Jerusalem	Resurrection Sunday	28:1–8	16:1–8	24:1–12	20:1–10		
To Mary Magdalene in the garden	Jerusalem	Resurrection Sunday		16:9–11		20:11–18		
To other women	Jerusalem	Resurrection Sunday	28:9–10					
To two people going to Emmaus	Road to Emmaus	Resurrection Sunday		16:12–13	24:13–32			
To Peter	Jerusalem	Resurrection Sunday			24:34			15:5
To the ten disciples in the upper room	Jerusalem	Resurrection Sunday		16:14	24:36–43	20:19–25		
To the eleven disciples in the upper room	Jerusalem	Following Sunday				20:26–31		15:5
To seven disciples fishing	Sea of Galilee	Some time later				21:1–25		
To the eleven disciples on a mountain	Galilee	Some time later	28:16–20	16:15–18				
To more than five hundred	Unknown	Some time later						15:6
To James	Unknown	Some time later						15:7
To his disciples at his ascension	Mount of Olives	Forty days after Jesus' Resurrection			24:44–51		1:3–9	15:7
To Paul	Damascus	Several years later					9:1–19; 22:3–16; 26:9–18	9:1; 15:8

THE PARABLES OF JESUS

Parable	Matthew	Mark	Luke
Light under a bushel	5:14–15	4:21–22	8:16; 11:33
Wise and foolish builders	7:24–27		6:47–49
New cloth on an old garment	9:16	2:21	5:36
New wine in old wineskins	9:17	2:22	5:37–38
Sower and the soils	13:3–8, 18–23	4:3–8, 14–20	8:5–8, 11–15
Tares	13:24–30, 36–43		
Mustard seed	13:31–32	4:30–32	13:18–19
Leaven	13:33		13:20–21
Hidden treasure	13:44		
Valuable pearl	13:45–46		
Net	13:47–50		
Owner of a house	13:52		
Lost sheep	18:12–14		15:4–7
Unmerciful servant	18:23–34		
Labourers in the vineyard	20:1–16		
Two sons	21:28–32		
Husbandmen	21:33–44	12:1–11	20:9–18
Wedding banquet	22:2–14		
Fig tree	24:32–35	13:28–29	21:29–31
Faithful and wise servant	24:45–51		12:42–48
Ten virgins	25:1–13		
Talents (pounds)	25:14–30		19:12–27
Sheep and goats	25:31–46		
Growing seed		4:26–29	
Watchful servants		13:35–37	12:35–40
Moneylender			7:41–43
Good Samaritan			10:30–37
Friend in need			11:5–8
Rich fool			12:16–21
Unfruitful fig tree			13:6–9
Lowest seat at the feast			14:7–14
Great banquet			14:16–24
Cost of discipleship			14:28–33
Lost coin			15:8–10
Prodigal son			15:11–32
Shrewd steward			16:1–8

THE PARABLES OF JESUS (cont.)

Parable	Matthew	Mark	Luke
Rich man and Lazarus			16:19–31
Master and his servant			17:7–10
Persistent widow			18:2–8

THE MIRACLES OF JESUS

	Matthew	Mark	Luke	John
Healing Miracles				
Man with leprosy	8:2–4	1:40–42	5:12–13	
Roman centurion's servant	8:5–13		7:1–10	
Peter's mother-in-law	8:14–15	1:30–31	4:38–39	
Two men from Gadara	8:28–34	5:1–15	8:27–35	
Man with palsy	9:2–7	2:3–12	5:18–25	
Woman with bleeding	9:20–22	5:25–29	8:43–48	
Two blind men	9:27–31			
Mute, demon-possessed man	9:32–33			
Man with a withered hand	12:10–13	3:1–5	6:6–10	
Blind, mute, demon-possessed man	12:22		11:14	
Canaanite woman's daughter	15:21–28	7:24–30		
Boy with a demon	17:14–18	9:17–29	9:38–43	
Two blind men (including Bartimaeus)	20:29–34	10:46–52	18:35–43	
Deaf mute		7:31–37		
Possessed man in synagogue		1:23–26	4:33–35	
Blind man at Bethsaida		8:22–26		
Crippled woman			13:11–13	
Man with dropsy			14:1–4	
Ten men with leprosy			17:11–19	
The high priest's servant			22:50–51	
Nobleman's son at Capernaum				4:46–54
Sick man at pool of Bethesda				5:1–9
Man born blind				9:1–7
Miracles showing power over nature				
Calming the storm	8:23–27	4:37–41	8:22–25	
Walking on water	14:25	6:48–51		6:19–21
Feeding of the 5000	14:15–21	6:35–44	9:12–17	6:5–13
Feeding of the 4000	15:32–38	8:1–9		
Coin in fish	17:24–27			
Fig tree withered	21:18–22	11:12–14, 20–25		

THE MIRACLES OF JESUS (cont.)

	Matthew	Mark	Luke	John
Miracles showing power over nature				
Large catch of fish			5:4–11	
Water turned into wine				2:1– 11
Another large catch of fish				21:1–11
Miracles of raising the dead				
Jairus's daughter	9:18–19, 23–25	5:22–24, 38–42	8:41–42, 49–56	
Widow's son at Nain			7:11–15	
Lazarus				11:1–44

MIRACLES OF THE APOSTLES

Miracle	Acts
Lame man cured (by Peter)	3:6–9
Death of Ananias and Sapphira	5:1–10
Saul's sight restored	9:17–18
Healing of Aeneas	9:33–35
Raising of Dorcas	9:36–41
Elymas blinded	13:8–11
Lame man cured (by Paul)	14:8–10
Demon cast out of a girl	16:16–18
Raising of Eutychus	20:9–10
Paul unharmed by viper	28:3–5
Healing of Publius's father	28:7–9

ACTS

Outline

Introduction (1:1–11)

I. The Outpouring of the Holy Spirit (1:12—2:41)
   A. Preparing for the Promise (1:12–26)
   B. The Day of Pentecost (2:1–41)

II. Early Days of the Church in Jerusalem (2:42—8:1a)
   A. Characteristics of the Apostolic Church Immediately After the Outpouring of the Spirit (2:42–47)
   B. A Remarkable Miracle and its Effects (3:1—4:31)
   C. The Continuing Experiment in Community Sharing (4:32—5:11)
   D. Further Healings and Resistance from the Religious Establishment (5:12–42)
   E. The Selection of Seven Deacons (6:1–7)
   F. Stephen: The First-Known Christian Martyr (6:8—8:1a)

III. Persecution Leads to Expansion (8:1b—9:31)
   A. Christians Scattered Throughout Judea and Samaria (8:1b-4)
   B. Philip: The Ministry of an Evangelist (8:5–40)
   C. Saul of Tarsus: The Conversion of a Persecutor (9:1–31)

IV. Christianity Began Spreading to the Gentiles (9:32—12:25)
   A. Peter's Ministry at Lydda and Joppa (9:32–43)
   B. Peter's Mission to the Gentiles at Caesarea (10:1–48)
   C. Peter's Report to the Jerusalem Church and His Action Approved (11:1–18)
   D. Antioch: The First Gentile Church (11:19–30)
   E. Persecution Under Herod Agrippa I (12:1–23)
   F. Summary of the Church's Progress (12:24–25)

V. Paul's First Missionary Journey (13:1—14:28)
   A. Paul and Barnabas Commissioned by the Local Church at Antioch (13:1–3)
   B. The Territory Evangelized (13:4—14:28)

VI. The Jerusalem Conference (15:1–35)

VII. Paul's Second Missionary Journey (15:36—18:22)
   A. Disagreement Between Paul and Barnabas (15:36–40)
   B. Old Territory Revisited (15:41—16:5)
   C. New Territory Evangelized (16:6—18:21)
   D. Return to Syrian Antioch (18:22)

VIII. Paul's Third Missionary Journey (18:23—21:16)
   A. En Route to Ephesus (18:23)
      Parenthesis: The Ministry of Apollos (18:24–28)
   B. A Lengthy Ministry at Ephesus (19:1–41)
   C. To Macedonia, Greece, and Back to Macedonia (20:1–5)
   D. Return Trip to Jerusalem (20:6—21:16)

IX. Paul's Arrest and Ministry During Imprisonment (21:17—28:31)
   A. In Jerusalem (21:17—23:35)
   B. In Caesarea (24:1—26:32)
   C. En Route to Rome (27:1—28:15)
   D. In Rome (28:16–31)

Author: Luke

Theme: The Triumphant Spread of the Gospel through the Power of the Holy Spirit

Date of Writing: c. A.D. 63

Background

The book of Acts, like the Gospel of Luke, is addressed to a man named "Theophilus" (1:1). Although the author is not identified by name in either book, the unanimous testimony of early Christianity and the corroborating internal evidence of the two books point to common authorship by Luke, "the beloved physician" (Col. 4:14).

The Holy Spirit prompted Luke to write to Theophilus in order to fill a need in the Gentile church for a full account of the beginnings of Christianity—(1) the "former treatise" being his Gospel about Jesus' life, and (2) the latter being his account in Acts about the outpouring of the Spirit at Jerusalem and the subsequent development of the early church. It is apparent that Luke was a skilled writer, a careful historian, and an inspired theologian.

Acts selectively covers the first thirty years of the church's history. As a church historian, Luke traces the spread of the gospel from Jerusalem to Rome, mentioning in Acts no fewer than 32 countries, 54 cities, 9 Mediterranean islands, 95 different persons by name, and a variety of governmental officials and administrators by their precise titles. Archaeology continues to confirm Luke's amazing accuracy in all his details. As a theologian, Luke astutely describes the significance of various experiences and events in the church's early years.

In its first stages, the N.T. Scriptures comprised two collections: (1) the four Gospels, and (2) the epistles of Paul. Acts played an indispensable role as the connecting link between the two collections and rightly belongs in its present canonical order. Chs. 13–28 provide the historical background necessary for understanding more fully Paul's ministry and letters. Luke's "we" passages in Acts (16:10–17; 20:5—21:18; 27:1—28:16) reveal his personal participation in Paul's travels.

Purpose

Luke has at least two purposes in recounting the church's beginnings. (1) He shows that the gospel moved triumphantly from the narrow borders of Judaism into the Gentile world in spite of opposition and persecution. (2) He reveals the role of the Holy Spirit in the church's life and mission, emphasizing the baptism in the Holy Spirit as God's provision for empowering the church to proclaim the gospel and to continue Jesus' ministry. Luke explicitly records three times that the baptism in the Holy Spirit was accompanied by speaking in tongues (2:4ff; 10:45–46; 19:1–7). The context of these passages indicate that this was normative in early Christianity and is God's enduring pattern for the church.

Survey

Whereas Luke's Gospel records "all that Jesus began both to do and teach" (Acts 1:1), Acts describes what Jesus continued to do and teach after His ascension, by the power of the Holy Spirit working in and through His disciples and the early church. When Jesus ascended into heaven (1:9–11), His last instruction to His disciples was to wait in Jerusalem until they were baptized in the Holy Spirit (1:4–5). The key verse of Acts (1:8) contains a theological and geographical capsule summary of the book: Jesus promises the disciples they will receive power when the Holy Spirit comes upon them, power to be His witnesses (1) "in Jerusalem" (chs. 1–7), (2) "in all Judaea and in Samaria" (chs. 8–12), and (3) "unto the uttermost part of the earth" (chs. 13–28).

Acts contains an intermingling of divine and human action. The entire church, not just the apostles, "went every where preaching the word" (8:4). Deacons like Stephen and Philip (6:1–6) became mighty in the Holy Spirit and faith, performing "great wonders and miracles" (6:8) and even shaking entire cities with the gospel (8:5–13). Godly men prayed

fervently, saw angels, had visions, witnessed mighty signs and wonders, cast out demons, healed the sick, and proclaimed the gospel with great boldness and authority. In spite of problems within the church, such as the Jewish-Gentile tension (ch. 15), and in spite of persistent persecution from outside the church by religious and civil authorities, the name of the Lord Jesus was magnified in word and deed from one city to the next.

In chs. 1–12 the main center of the church's outreach is Jerusalem; the foremost human vessel whom God used to spread the gospel in these chapters is Peter. In chs. 13–28 the main center of the church's mission is Antioch in Syria; the foremost human vessel whom God used to spread the gospel to the Gentiles is Paul. Acts ends abruptly with Paul in Rome still awaiting his trial before Caesar. Though the outcome of the trial is left hanging, the book ends on a triumphant note with Paul, though yet a prisoner, "preaching the kingdom of God, and teaching those things which concern the Lord Jesus Christ with all confidence, no man forbidding him" (28:31).

Special Features

Nine major features or emphases characterize Acts: (1) The church: Acts reveals the source of power of the church and the true nature of its mission, along with principles that should govern the church in every generation. (2) The Holy Spirit: the third person of the Trinity is mentioned specifically fifty times; the baptism in and ministry of the Holy Spirit imparts power (1:8), boldness (4:31), holy fear of God (5:3,5,11), wisdom (6:3,10), guidance (16:6–10), and spiritual gifts (19:6). (3) Early church messages: Luke skillfully recounts inspired speeches by Peter, Stephen, Paul, James, and others, providing insight into the early church that is not found elsewhere in the N.T. (4) Prayer: the early Christians devoted themselves to regular and fervent prayer, sometimes lasting all night and producing great results. (5) Signs, wonders, and miracles: these manifestations accompanied the proclamation of the gospel in the power of the Holy Spirit. (6) Persecution: proclaiming the gospel with power consistently stirred up religious and/or secular opposition. (7) Jew/Gentile sequence: throughout Acts the gospel goes first to the Jews, then to the Gentiles. (8) Women: special mention is made of women involved in the ongoing work of the church. (9) Triumph: no barriers (national, religious, cultural, or racial) and no opposition or persecution could thwart the advance of the gospel.

Hermeneutical Principle

Some interpreters view Acts as if it were under another N.T. covenant, rather than seeing it as God's standard for the church and its witness during the entire period of time which the N.T. calls "the last days" (cf. 2:17, note). Acts is not just a history book of the early church, it is a handbook for the Christian life and for a Spirit-filled church. Believers ought to desire, seek, and expect today as the norm for the church, all elements in the N.T. church's ministry and experience (except the writing of N.T. Scripture); these are attainable when the church moves in the full power of the Holy Spirit. Nothing in Acts or the N.T. indicates that signs, wonders, miracles, spiritual gifts, or the apostolic standard for the church's life and ministry generally were to cease suddenly or permanently at the end of the apostolic age. Rather, Acts records what the church must be and do in any generation as it continues Jesus' ministry in the Pentecostal power of the Holy Spirit (cf. 7:44, note).

Reading Acts

In order to read the entire New Testament in one year, the book of Acts should be read in 46 days, according to the following schedule:
☐ 1 ☐ 2:1–36 ☐ 2:37–47 ☐ 3 ☐ 4:1–31 ☐ 4:32—5:11 ☐ 5:12–42 ☐ 6 ☐ 7:1–53 ☐ 7:54—8:8 ☐ 8:9–40 ☐ 9:1–31 ☐ 9:32–43 ☐ 10:1–23 ☐ 10:24–48 ☐ 11:1–18 ☐ 11:19–30 ☐ 12 ☐ 13:1–12 ☐ 13:13–52 ☐ 14 ☐ 15:1–21 ☐ 15:22–35 ☐ 15:36—16:15 ☐ 16:16–40 ☐ 17:1–15 ☐ 17:16–34 ☐ 18:1–23 ☐ 18:24—19:7 ☐ 19:8–41 ☐ 20:1–26 ☐ 20:27–38 ☐ 21:1–16 ☐ 21:17–36 ☐ 21:37—22:21 ☐ 22:22—23:11 ☐ 23:12–35 ☐ 24 ☐ 25:1–12 ☐ 25:13—26:1 ☐ 26:2–18 ☐ 26:19–32 ☐ 27:1–26 ☐ 27:27–44 ☐ 28:1–16 ☐ 28:17–31

NOTES

The promised baptism in the Holy Spirit

1 THE FORMER treatise have I
made, O [a]Theophilus, of all that
Jesus began both to do and teach,
2 [b]Until the day in which he was
taken up, after that he through the
Holy Ghost [c]had given command-
ments unto the apostles whom he had
chosen:
3 [d]To whom also he showed him-
self alive after his passion by many in-
fallible proofs, being seen of them forty
days, and speaking of the things per-
taining to the kingdom of God:
4 [e]And, [a]being assembled togeth-
er with *them*, commanded them that
they should not depart from Jerusalem,
but wait for the promise of the Father,
[f]which, *saith he*, ye have heard of me.
5 [g]For John truly baptized with wa-
ter; [h]but ye shall be baptized with the
Holy Ghost not many days hence.
6 When they therefore were come
together, they asked of him, saying,
[i]Lord, wilt thou at this time [j]restore
again the kingdom to Israel?
7 And he said unto them, [k]It is not
for you to know the times or the sea-
sons, which the Father hath put in his
own power.
8 [l]But ye shall receive [b]power,

1:1 [a]Luke 1:3 **1:2** [b]Mark 16:19 1 Tim. 3:16 [c]Mat. 28:19 John 20:21 **1:3** [d]Mark 16:14 **1:4** [e]Luke 24:43 [f]Luke 24:49 John 14:16 **1:5** [g]Mat. 3:11 [h]Joel 3:18 **1:6** [i]Mat. 24:3 [j]Is. 1:26 **1:7** [k]1 Thes. 5:1 **1:8** [l]ch. 2:1,4

Acts 2:4-13

[a] Or, *eating together with them* [b] Or, *the power of the Holy Ghost coming upon you*

1:1 THE FORMER TREATISE. In Luke's former book, the Gospel of Luke (and in the other Gospels), we have the account of all Jesus began to do and teach in the power of the Holy Spirit (Luke 4:1,18). In the book of Acts we have the continuing story of how Jesus' followers, in the same power of the Holy Spirit, proclaimed the same gospel, worked the same kind of miracles, and lived the same kind of life. The Holy Spirit reproducing the life and ministry of Jesus through the church is the theological keynote of Acts. The book could well be called "The Acts of the Holy Spirit." Observe the following concerning the Holy Spirit's inspired record in the book of Acts:

(1) All Scripture, including the historical narratives in Acts, has didactic (i.e., teaching) and theological significance. This is confirmed by two facts. (a) The Biblical declaration that "all scripture *is* given by inspiration of God, and *is* profitable for doctrine, for reproof, for correction, for instruction in righteousness" (2 Tim. 3:16). (b) Paul's statement that the O.T. historical narratives have a teaching and instructional purpose (1 Cor. 10:11). He maintains that these stories are examples with practical and theological relevance for the believer (Rom. 15:4). What is true for historical narrative in the O.T. is also true for Acts.

(2) In writing his inspired history of the early church, Luke provides: (a) a definitive pattern of the activity of the Holy Spirit to be followed during the entire church age, (b) data for developing a doctrine of the Holy Spirit, and (c) revelation concerning how the ministry of the Holy Spirit must relate to the lives of believers in Christ. Note specifically two elements in this book that are theologically and practically normative: (a) the baptism in or a filling with the Holy Spirit as God's promise for all believers (see 2:39, note; cf. 1:5,8; 2:4; 4:8,31; 8:15–17; 9:17; 10:44–46; 13:9,52; 15:8; 19:1–6); (b) the numerous activities of the Holy Spirit that provided the church with the standards of righteousness, witness, and power that God desires for His people in the last days (i.e., the church age).

1:3 SHOWED HIMSELF ALIVE. See Mat. 28:9, note on the resurrection appearances of Christ.

1:4 THE PROMISE OF THE FATHER. The gift that the Father promised (Joel 2:28–29; Mat. 3:11) is the baptism in the Holy Spirit (see v. 5, note). The fulfillment of that promise, however, is described as being "filled with the Holy Ghost" (2:4). Thus, "baptized in the Spirit" and "filled with the Spirit" are at times used interchangeably in Acts.

This baptism in the Holy Spirit should not be identified with receiving the Holy Spirit at regeneration (see article on REGENERATION, p. 1597). These are two distinct works of the Spirit, often separated by a period of time (see article on THE REGENERATION OF THE DISCIPLES, p. 1638).

1:5 WITH [IN] THE HOLY GHOST. The preposition "with" is the translation of the Greek word *en* and is often translated as "in." Hence, many prefer the rendering "ye shall be baptized in the Holy Ghost." Likewise, "baptized with water" may be translated "baptized in water." Jesus Himself is the one who baptizes His believers in the Holy Spirit (see John 1:33, note).

1:8 YE SHALL RECEIVE POWER. This is the key verse in the book of Acts. The primary purpose of the baptism in the Spirit is the receiving of power to witness for Christ, in order to win the lost to Him and to teach them to observe all that Christ commanded. The end result is that Christ may be known, loved, honored, praised, and made Lord of God's chosen people (cf. Mat. 28:18–20; Luke 24:49; John 5:23; 15:26–27).

(1) "Power" (Gk. *dunamis*) means more than strength or ability; it designates especially power in action. Luke (in his Gospel and in Acts) emphasizes that the Holy Spirit's power included the authority to drive out evil spirits and the anointing to heal the sick as the two essential signs accompanying the proclamation of the kingdom of God (e.g., 6:8; 8:4–8.12–13, 10:38; 14:3; 19:8–12; Luke 4;14,18,36; 5:17; 6:19; 9;1–2). The baptism in the Holy Spirit is God's provision for releasing the power of the Holy Spirit into the believer's life (see article on BAPTISM IN THE HOLY SPIRIT, p. 1652).

(2) Note that in this verse Luke does not relate

BAPTISM IN THE HOLY SPIRIT

Acts 1:5 "For John truly baptized with water; but ye shall be baptized with the Holy Ghost not many days hence."

One of the cardinal doctrines of Scripture is the baptism in the Holy Spirit (see Acts 1:4, note on reading "baptism *in*" rather than "baptism with" the Holy Spirit). Concerning the baptism in the Holy Spirit, the Word of God teaches the following.

(1) The baptism in the Spirit is intended for all who profess faith in Christ, have been born again, and have received the indwelling of the Holy Spirit (see article on THE REGENERATION OF THE DISCIPLES, p. 1638).

(2) One of Christ's key goals in His mission on earth was to baptize His people in the Holy Spirit (Mat. 3:11; Mark 1:8; Luke 3:16; John 1:33). He instructed His disciples not to begin witnessing until they were baptized in the Holy Spirit and endued with power from on high (Luke 24:49; Acts 1:4–5,8). Jesus Christ Himself did not enter His ministry until He had been "anointed . . . with the Holy Ghost and with power" (Acts 10:38; cf. Luke 4:1,18).

(3) The baptism in the Holy Spirit is an operation of the Holy Spirit distinct and separate from His work of regeneration. Just as the sanctifying work of the Spirit is a distinct work complementing the regenerating work of the Spirit, so the baptism in the Spirit complements the regenerating and sanctifying work of the Spirit. On the day of Christ's resurrection He breathed on His disciples and said, "Receive ye the Holy Ghost" (John 20:22), indicating that regeneration and new life were being given to them (see article on THE REGENERATION OF THE DISCIPLES, p. 1638). Then later He told them they must also be "endued with power" by the Holy Spirit (Luke 24:49; cf. Acts 1:5,8). For the disciples it was clearly a post-regeneration experience (see Acts 11:17, note). One can be regenerated and indwelt by the Holy Spirit, but still not be baptized in the Holy Spirit (see Acts 19:6, note).

(4) To be baptized in the Spirit means to be filled with the Spirit (compare Acts 1:5; 2:4). However, this baptism occurred only at and after Pentecost. Concerning those filled with the Holy Spirit before Pentecost (e.g. Luke 1:15,67), Luke does not use the term baptized in the Holy Spirit. This experience occurred only after Christ's ascension (Luke 24:49–51; John 16:7–14; Acts 1:4).

(5) In the book of Acts, speaking with tongues as the Spirit gives utterance is the initial outward sign accompanying the baptism in the Holy Spirit (Acts 2:4; 10:45–46; 19:6). Baptism in the Holy Spirit is linked so closely with the external manifestation of speaking in tongues that this should be considered the norm when receiving that baptism (see article on SPEAKING IN TONGUES, p. 1656).

(6) The baptism in the Holy Spirit will bring the personal boldness and power of the Holy Spirit into the believer's life in order to accomplish mighty works in Christ's name and to make the believer's witness and proclamation effective (cf. Acts 1:8; 2:14–41; 4:31; 6:8; Rom. 15:18–19; 1 Cor. 2:4). This power is not some impersonal force, but is a manifestation of the Holy Spirit by which the presence, glory, and works of Jesus are present with His people (John 14:16–18; 16:14; 1 Cor. 12:7).

(7) Other results of a genuine baptism in the Holy Spirit are: (a) prophetic utterances and praise (Acts 2:4,17; 10:46; 1 Cor. 14:2); (b) enhanced sensitivity to sin that grieves the Holy Spirit, a greater seeking after righteousness which conforms to Christ, and a deeper awareness of the judgment of God against all ungodliness (see John 16:8, note; Acts 1:8, note); (c) a life which glorifies Jesus Christ (John 16:13–14; Acts 4:33); (d) new visions (Acts 2:17); (e) a manifestation of the various gifts of the Holy Spirit (1 Cor.

12:4–11); (f) a greater desire to pray and intercede (Acts 2:41–42; 3:1; 4:23–31; 6:4; 10:9; Rom. 8:26); (g) a deeper love and understanding of the Word of God (John 16:13; Acts 2:42); and (h) an increasing awareness of God as one's Father (Acts 1:4; Rom. 8:15; Gal. 4:6).

(8) The Word of God cites several conditions by which the baptism in the Holy Spirit is given. (a) We must accept by faith Jesus Christ as Lord and Savior and turn from sin and the world (Acts 2:38–40; 8:12–17). This response involves surrendering our wills to God ("to them that obey him," Acts 5:32). We must turn from that which offends God before we can become "a vessel unto honour, sanctified, and meet for the master's use" (2 Tim. 2:21). (b) We must desire to be filled. Christians should have a deep hunger and thirst for the baptism in the Holy Spirit (John 7:37–39; cf. Is. 44:3; Mat. 5:6; 6:33). (c) We often receive it in answer to definite prayer (Luke 11:13; Acts 1:14; 2:1–4; 4:31; 8:15,17). (d) We should expect that God will baptize us in the Holy Spirit (Mark 11:24; Acts 1:4–5).

(9) The baptism in the Holy Spirit is sustained in the believer's life by prayer (Acts 4:31), witness (4:31,33), worship in the Spirit (Eph. 5:18–19), and a sanctified life (see Eph. 5:18, notes). However powerful the initial coming of the Holy Spirit upon the believer may be, if this does not find expression in a life of prayer, witness, and holiness, the experience will soon become a fading glory.

(10) The baptism in the Holy Spirit occurs only once in a believer's life and points to the consecration of the believer unto God's work of witnessing in power and righteousness. The Bible teaches that there may be new fillings with the Holy Spirit after the believer has been baptized in the Holy Spirit (see Acts 4:31, note; cf. 2:4; 4:8,31; 13:9; Eph. 5:18). Thus, the baptism in the Spirit brings the believer into a relationship with the Spirit that is to be renewed (Acts 4:31) and maintained (Eph. 5:18).

[m]after that the Holy Ghost is come
upon you: and [n]ye shall be wit-
nesses unto me both in Jerusalem,
and in all Judaea, and in Samaria,
and unto the uttermost part of the
Acts 2:32 earth.

Jesus taken up into heaven

9 [o]And when he had spoken these
things, while they beheld, [p]he was
taken up; and a cloud received him out
of their sight.
10 And while they looked stedfastly
toward heaven as he went up, behold,
two men stood by them [q]in white ap-
parel;
11 Which also said, [r]Ye men of
Galilee, why stand ye gazing up into
heaven? this same Jesus, which is tak-
en up from you into heaven, [s]shall so
come in like manner as ye have seen
him go into heaven.

Praying for the Spirit

12 [t]Then returned they unto Jeru-
salem from the mount called Olivet,
which is from Jerusalem a sabbath
day's journey.
13 And when they were come in,
they went up [u]into an upper room,
where abode both [v]Peter, and James,
and John, and Andrew, Philip, and
Thomas, Bartholomew, and Matthew,
James *the son* of Alphaeus, and [w]Si-
mon Zelotes, and [x]Judas *the brother* of
James.
14 [y]These all continued with one
accord in prayer and supplication, with

1:8 [m]Luke 24:49 [n]Luke 24:48 **1:9** [o]Luke 24:51 [p]ver. 2 **1:10** [q]Mat. 28:3 Mark 16:5 Luke 24:4 John 20:12 ch. 10:3,30 **1:11** [r]ch. 2:7 & 13:31 [s]Dan. 7:13 Mat. 24:30 Mark 13:26 Luke 21:27 John 14:3 1 Thes. 1:10 & 4:16 2 Thes. 1:10 Rev. 1:7 **1:12** [t]Luke 24:52 **1:13** [u]ch. 9:37,39 & 20:8 [v]Mat. 10:2-4 [w]Luke 6:15 [x]Jude 1 **1:14** [y]ch. 2:1,46

the baptism in the Holy Spirit to personal salvation and regeneration, but to the power within the believer to witness with great effect (see article on THE REGENERATION OF THE DISCIPLES, p. 1638).

(3) The Holy Spirit's principal work in witnessing and proclamation concerns the saving work of Christ and His resurrection, and His coming upon believers with power (cf. 2:14–42). See next note for an examination of how the Spirit witnesses and what that means in our personal lives.

1:8 YE SHALL BE WITNESSES. The baptism in the Holy Spirit not only imparts power to preach Jesus as Lord and Savior (see previous note), but also increases the effectiveness of that witness because of a strengthening and deepening relationship with the Father, Son, and Holy Spirit that comes from being filled with the Spirit (cf. John 14:26; 15:26–27).

(1) The Holy Spirit discloses and makes more real to us the personal presence of Jesus (John 14:16–18). Any witness to an intimate fellowship with Jesus Christ Himself will result in an ever-growing desire on our part to love, honor, and please our Savior (see article on THE DOCTRINE OF THE HOLY SPIRIT, p. 1668).

(2) The Holy Spirit witnesses to "righteousness" (John 16:8,10) and "truth" (John 16:13) which "glorify" Christ (John 16:14), not only with words, but also in life and deeds. Thus, we who have received the witness of the Holy Spirit to the redemptive work of Jesus Christ will necessarily manifest Christlikeness, love, truth, and righteousness in our lives (cf. 1 Cor. 13).

(3) The baptism in the Holy Spirit is the initiation point whereby Spirit-filled believers receive the power to witness for Christ and to bring conviction of sin, righteousness, and judgment upon the lost (see John 16:8, note).The effects of such conviction will be evident both in those who sincerely proclaim the message and in those who receive it (2:37–40).

(4) The baptism in the Holy Spirit can be given only to those whose hearts are turned toward God in repentance from their wicked ways (2:38; 3:26). It is maintained by the same sincere commitment to Christ (see 5:32, note).

(5) The baptism in the Holy Spirit is a baptism into the Spirit who is holy (cf. "spirit of holiness," Rom. 1:4). Thus, if the Holy Spirit is truly at work in us in all His fullness, we will live in greater conformity to Christ's holiness.

In light of these Scriptural truths, therefore, we who have been baptized in the Holy Spirit will have an intense desire to please Christ in whatever way we can. That is, the fullness of the Spirit complements (i.e., completes, fills up) the saving and sanctifying work of the Holy Spirit in our lives. Those who claim the fullness of the Holy Spirit, yet live a life contrary to the Spirit of holiness are misled, deceived, and untruthful. Those who display spiritual gifts, miracles, spectacular signs, or inspiring oratory, yet lack a life of true faith, love, and righteousness, are operating not by the Holy Spirit, but by an unholy spirit not of God (Mat. 7:21–23; cf. Mat. 24:24; 2 Cor. 11:13–15; see also article on TESTING FOR GENUINE BAPTISM IN THE SPIRIT, p. 1682). For further comments on witnessing for Christ, see 13:31, note.

1:14 CONTINUED . . . IN PRAYER AND SUPPLICATION. The experience of Pentecost always involves human responsibility. Those needing the Spirit's outpouring for power to do God's work should make themselves available to the Holy Spirit through commitment to the will of God and through prayer (v. 4; 2:38; 9:11–17; cf. Is. 40:29–31; Luke 11:5–13; 24:49). Notice the parallels between the Spirit coming upon Jesus and the Spirit coming upon the disciples. (1) The Spirit descended upon them after they had prayed (Luke 3:21–22; Acts 1:14; 2:4). (2) There were observable manifestations of the Spirit (Luke 3:22; Acts 2:2–4). (3) The ministries of both Jesus and the disciples began after the Spirit came upon them (compare Mat. 3:16 with 4:17; Luke 3:21–23 with 4:14–19; cf. Acts 2:14–47).

[z]the women, and Mary the mother of Jesus, and with [a]his brethren.

Matthias chosen to replace Judas

15 ¶ And in those days Peter stood up in the midst of the disciples, and said, (the number [b]of names together were about an hundred and twenty,)

16 Men *and* brethren, this scripture must needs have been fulfilled, [c]which the Holy Ghost by the mouth of David spake before concerning Judas, [d]which was guide to them that took Jesus.

17 For [e]he was numbered with us, and had obtained part of [f]this ministry.

18 [g]Now this man purchased a field with [h]the reward of iniquity; and falling headlong, he burst asunder in the midst, and all his bowels gushed out.

19 And it was known unto all the dwellers at Jerusalem; insomuch as that field is called in their proper tongue, Aceldama, that is to say, The field of blood.

20 For it is written in the book of Psalms, [i]Let his habitation be desolate, and let no man dwell therein: and [j]his [c]bishopric let another take.

21 Wherefore of these men which have companied with us all the time that the Lord Jesus went in and out among us,

22 Beginning from the baptism of John, unto that same day that [k]he was taken up from us, must one be ordained [l]to be a witness with us of his resurrection.

23 And they appointed two, Joseph called [m]Barsabas, who was surnamed Justus, and Matthias.

24 And they prayed, and said, Thou, Lord, [n]which knowest the hearts of all *men,* show whether of these two thou hast chosen,

25 [o]That he may take part of this ministry and apostleship, from which Judas by transgression fell, that he might go to his own place.

26 And they gave forth their lots; and the lot fell upon Matthias; and he was numbered with the eleven apostles.

The Holy Spirit comes at Pentecost

2 AND WHEN [p]the day of Pentecost was fully come, [q]they were all with one accord in one place.

2 And suddenly there came a sound from heaven as of a rushing mighty wind, and [r]it filled all the house where they were sitting.

3 And there appeared unto them cloven tongues like as of fire, and it sat upon each of them.

Speaking with other tongues

4 And [s]they were all filled with the Holy Ghost, and began [t]to speak with

1:14 [z]Luke 23:49,55 [a]Mat. 13:55
1:15 [b]Rev. 3:4
1:16 [c]Ps. 41:9 John 13:18 [d]Luke 22:47 John 18:3
1:17 [e]Mat. 10:4 Luke 6:16 [f]ver. 25 ch. 12:25 & 20:24 & 21:19
1:18 [g]Mat. 27:5,7,8 [h]Mat. 26:15 2 Pet. 2:15
1:20 [i]Ps. 69:25 [j]Ps. 109:8
1:22 [k]ver. 9 [l]ver. 8 John 15:27 ch. 4:33
1:23 [m]ch. 15:22
1:24 [n]1 Sam. 16:7 1 Chr. 28:9 & 29:17 Jer. 11:20 & 17:10 ch. 15:8 Rev. 2:23
1:25 [o]ver. 17
2:1 [p]Lev. 23:15 Deut. 16:9 ch. 20:16 [q]ch. 1:14
2:2 [r]ch. 4:31
2:4 [s]ch. 1:5 [t]Mark 16:17 ch. 10:46 & 19:6 1 Cor. 12:10,28,30 & 13:1 & 14:2

[c] Or, *office,* or, *charge*

2:1 PENTECOST. Pentecost was the second great festival of the Jewish year. It was a harvest festival when the firstfruits of the grain harvest were presented to God (cf. Lev. 23:17). In like manner Pentecost symbolizes, for the church, the beginning of God's harvest for souls in the world.

2:2–3 A RUSHING MIGHTY WIND . . . AND . . . CLOVEN TONGUES LIKE AS OF FIRE. The external manifestations of a sound like a powerful wind and of tongues of fire demonstrated that God was present and active in a powerful way (cf. Ex. 3:1–6; 1 Ki. 18:38–39). The "fire" may symbolize consecrating and separating believers unto God for the work of glorifying Christ (John 16:13–14) and of witnessing for Him (1:8). These two manifestations preceded the baptism in the Holy Spirit and were not repeated elsewhere in Acts.

2:4 FILLED WITH THE HOLY GHOST. What is the significance of the filling of the Holy Spirit at Pentecost? (1) It meant the beginning of the fulfillment of God's promise in Joel 2:28–29 to pour out His Spirit upon all His people in the end times (cf. 1:4–5; Mat. 3:11; Luke 24:49; John 1:33; see Joel 2:28–29, notes).

(2) Since the last days of this age had begun (v. 17; cf. Heb. 1:2; 1 Pet. 1:20), everyone must now be confronted with the decision to repent and believe in Christ (3:19; Mat. 3:2; Luke 13:3; see Acts 2:17, notes).

(3) The disciples were "endued with power from on high" (Luke 24:49; cf. Acts 1:8), enabling them to witness for Christ, to be people through whom the Holy Spirit could bring great conviction to the lost in relation to sin, righteousness, and the judgment of God, and to turn them from sin to salvation in Christ (cf. 1:8, notes; 4:13,33; 6:8; Rom. 15:19; see John 16:8, note).

(4) The Holy Spirit revealed His nature as a Spirit who longs for and strives after the salvation of people of every nation, and those who received the baptism in the Holy Spirit were filled with the same longing for the salvation of the human race (vv. 38–40; 4:12,33; Rom. 9:1–3; 10:1). Thus Pentecost is the beginning of world missions.

(5) The disciples became ministers of the Spirit. They not only preached Jesus crucified and resurrected, leading others to repentance and faith in Christ, but also influenced converts to receive the

SPEAKING IN TONGUES

Acts 2:4 "And they were all filled with the Holy Ghost, and began to speak with other tongues, as the Spirit gave them utterance."

Speaking in tongues or glossalalia (from Gk. *glōssais lalō*) was considered by N.T. Christians as a God-given sign accompanying the baptism in the Holy Spirit (see Acts 2:4; 10:45–47; 19:6). This Biblical pattern for the Spirit-filled life is still valid for us today.

TRUE SPEAKING IN TONGUES. (1) Tongues as a manifestation of the Spirit. Speaking in tongues is a supernatural manifestation of the Holy Spirit, i.e., a Spirit-inspired utterance whereby the believer speaks in a language (Gk. *glōssa*) he has never learned (Acts 2:4; 1 Cor. 14:14–15). It may be in existing spoken human languages (Acts 2:6) or in languages unknown on earth (cf. 1 Cor. 13:1). It is not "ecstatic speech," as rendered in some translations, for the Bible never uses the term "ecstatic utterance" to refer to speaking in tongues.

(2) Tongues as the initial outward sign of the baptism in the Holy Spirit. Speaking in tongues is an inspired utterance whereby the spirit of the believer and the Holy Spirit join in verbal praise and/or prophecy. God linked speaking in tongues with the baptism in the Holy Spirit from the very beginning (Acts 2:4), so that the 120 believers at Pentecost, and believers thereafter, would have an experiential sign or confirmation that they have indeed received the baptism in the Holy Spirit (cf. Acts 10:45–46). Thus, this experience could be objectively validated as to place and time of reception. Throughout the history of the church, whenever tongues as a confirming sign has been denied or lost from view, the truth and experience of Pentecost has declined, been distorted, or been ignored entirely.

(3) Tongues as a gift. Speaking in tongues is also described as a gift given by the Holy Spirit to the believer (1 Cor. 12:4–10). This gift has two main purposes: (a) Speaking in tongues accompanied by interpretation is used in public worship services to communicate the content of the utterance to the congregation, in order that all may enter into the Spirit-directed worship, praise, or prophecy (1 Cor. 14:5–6,13–17). (b) Speaking in tongues is used by the believer to speak to God in his or her personal devotions and thus to build up one's spiritual life (1 Cor. 14:4). It means speaking at the level of the spirit (14:2,14) for the purpose of praying (14:2,14,15,28), giving thanks (14:16–17), or singing (14:15; see 1 Cor. 14, notes; see article on SPIRITUAL GIFTS FOR BELIEVERS, p. 1790).

FALSE SPEAKING IN TONGUES. It must be recognized that the mere occurrence of speaking with "other tongues," or any other supernatural manifestation, is not absolute or uncontestable evidence of the work and presence of the Holy Spirit. Speaking in tongues can be counterfeited by human initiative or demonic activity. The Bible cautions us not to believe every spirit, but examine whether the spiritual experiences we have really do come from God (see 1 John 4:1, note).

(1) Speaking in tongues, in order to be valid, must be "as the Spirit [gives] utterance" (Acts 2:4). To follow the norm in the book of Acts, speaking in tongues must be the *spontaneous* result of the initial filling of the Holy Spirit. It is not a learned phenomenon, nor can it be taught by instructing believers to speak incoherent syllables.

(2) The Holy Spirit explicitly warns that in the last days of this age there will be, within the church, hypocrisy (1 Tim. 4:1–2), signs and wonders from satanic powers (Mat. 7:22–23; cf. 2 Thes. 2:9), and deceitful workers disguising themselves as servants of God (2 Cor. 11:13–15). We must heed these warnings from the Holy Spirit as they relate to counterfeit spiritual manifestations and signs (Mat. 7:22–23; 2 Thes. 2:8–10).

(3) In order to discern whether our speaking in tongues is genuine, that is, truly of the Holy Spirit, we must look for the Biblically defined results of the baptism in the Holy Spirit (see article on TESTING FOR GENUINE BAPTISM IN THE SPIRIT, p. 1682). If someone claiming to speak in tongues is not committed to Jesus Christ and the authority of the Scriptures, and is not attempting to obey the Word of God, whatever manifestations he or she may have are not of the Holy Spirit (1 John 3:6–10; 4:1–3; cf. Mat. 24:11,24; John 8:31; Gal. 1:9, note).

other tongues, as the Spirit gave them utterance.

5 And there were dwelling at Jerusalem Jews, devout men, out of every nation under heaven.

6 Now [d]when this was noised abroad, the multitude came together, and were [e]confounded, because that every man heard them speak in his own language.

7 And they were all amazed and marvelled, saying one to another, Behold, are not all these which speak [u]Galilaeans?

8 And how hear we every man in our own tongue, wherein we were born?

9 Parthians, and Medes, and Elamites, and the dwellers in Mesopotamia, and in Judaea, and Cappadocia, in Pontus, and Asia,

10 Phrygia, and Pamphylia, in Egypt, and in the parts of Libya about Cyrene, and strangers of Rome, Jews and proselytes,

11 Cretes and Arabians, we do hear them speak in our tongues the wonderful works of God.

12 And they were all amazed, and were in doubt, saying one to another, What meaneth this?

13 Others mocking said, These men are full of new wine.

Peter explains the coming of the Spirit

14 ¶ But Peter, standing up with the eleven, lifted up his voice, and said unto them, Ye men of Judaea, and all *ye* that dwell at Jerusalem, be this known unto you, and hearken to my words:

15 For these are not drunken, as ye suppose, [v]seeing it is *but* the third hour of the day.

16 But this is that which was spoken by the prophet Joel;

17 [w]And it shall come to pass in the last days, saith God, [x]I will pour

2:7 [u]ch. 1:11
2:15 [v]1 Thes. 5:7
2:17 [w]Is. 44:3 Ezek. 11:19 Joel 2:28 Zech. 12:10 John 7:38 [x]ch. 10:45

[d] Gk. *when this voice was made* [e] Or, *troubled in mind*

"gift of the Holy Ghost" (vv. 38–39) which they themselves had received at Pentecost. This leading others into the baptism in the Holy Spirit is the key to the apostolic work in the N.T. (see 8:17; 9:17–18; 10:44–46; 19:6).

(6) Through this baptism in the Spirit, the followers of Christ became successors to His earthly ministry. They continued to do and to teach, in the power of the Holy Spirit, the same things which Jesus "began both to do and teach" (1:1; John 14:12, note; see article on SIGNS OF BELIEVERS, p. 1516).

2:4 BEGAN TO SPEAK WITH OTHER TONGUES. For a discussion of the meaning of speaking in tongues that occurred at Pentecost and elsewhere in the N.T. church, and of the possibility of false tongues, see article on SPEAKING IN TONGUES, p. 1656).

2:13 NEW WINE. "New wine" (Gk. *gleukos*) normally refers to sweet unfermented grape juice. Those mocking the disciples may have used this term rather than the common N.T. word for wine (*oinos*), because they believed that Jesus' disciples used only this type of wine. In this case, their mockery would have been spoken in sarcasm.

2:14–40 PETER'S PENTECOST SERMON. Peter's sermon on the day of Pentecost, along with his message in 3:11–26, contains a pattern for the proclamation of the gospel.

(1) Jesus is both Lord and Christ—crucified, resurrected, and exalted (vv. 22–36; 3:13–15).

(2) Being now at the right hand of His Father, Jesus Christ has received the authority to pour forth the Holy Spirit upon all believers (vv. 16–18,32–33; 3:19).

(3) Everyone must place his or her faith in Jesus as Lord, repent of sin, and be baptized in connection with forgiveness of sins (vv. 36–38; 3:19).

(4) Believers must expect the promised gift of or baptism in the Holy Spirit after faith and repentance (vv. 38–39).

(5) Those who hear in faith must separate themselves from the world and be saved from this perverse generation (v. 40; 3:26).

(6) Jesus Christ will return to restore God's kingdom completely (3:20–21).

2:16 SPOKEN BY THE PROPHET JOEL. The baptism in the Holy Spirit and the accompanying spiritual manifestations are a fulfillment of Joel 2:28–29 (see notes on that passage).

2:17 THE LAST DAYS. (1) In the O.T. "the last days" were considered the time when the Lord would act in a mighty way to judge evil and bring salvation to His people (cf. Is. 2:2–21; 3:18—4:6; 10:20–23; Hos. 1–2; Joel 1–3; Amos 8:9–11; 9:9–12).

(2) The N.T. reveals that the "last days" began with the first coming of Christ and the initial outpouring of the Spirit on God's people, and that the last days will end with the Lord's second coming (Mark 1:15; Luke 4:18–21; Heb. 1:1–2). This specific time is characterized as the age of judgment against evil, authority over demons, salvation unto the nations, and the presence of the kingdom of God.

(a) These "last days" will be carried on by the power of the Spirit (Mat. 12:28).

(b) The "last days" involve the invasion of God's power through Christ into the realm of Satan and sin. Yet the warfare has only begun; it is not yet consummated, since evil and satanic activity are still present in a mighty way (Eph. 6:10–18). Hence, only the second coming of Jesus will end the activity of evil forces and complete the "last days" (cf. 1 Pet. 1:3–5; Rev. 19).

(c) The "last days" constitute a time of prophetic

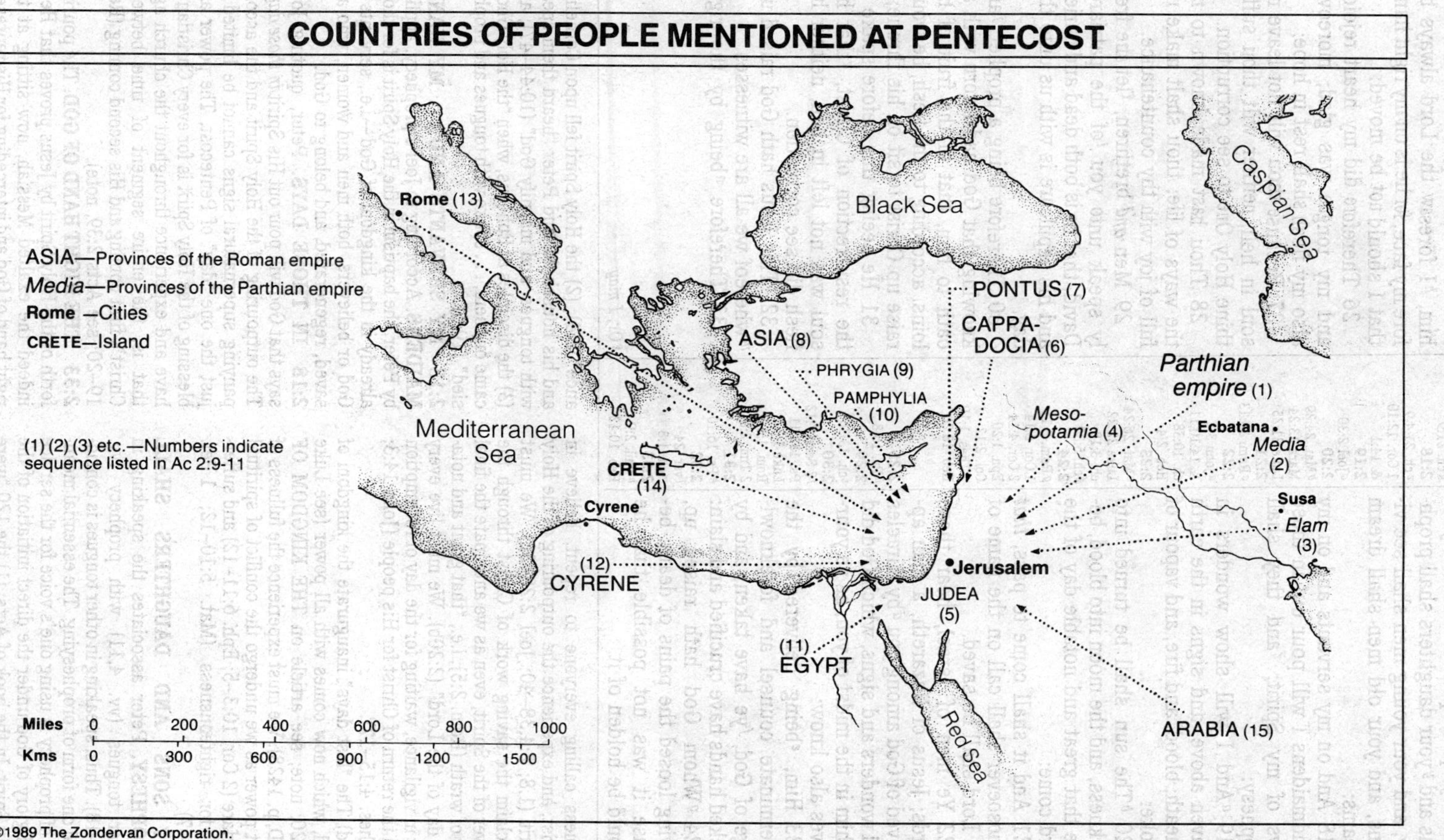
COUNTRIES OF PEOPLE MENTIONED AT PENTECOST
Caspian Sea
Black Sea
Mediterranean Sea
Red Sea
Rome (13)
ASIA (8)
PHRYGIA (9)
PAMPHYLIA (10)
PONTUS (7)
CAPPADOCIA (6)
Parthian empire (1)
Mesopotamia (4)
Ecbatana
Media (2)
Susa
Elam (3)
Jerusalem
JUDEA (5)
ARABIA (15)
EGYPT (11)
CYRENE (12)
Cyrene
CRETE (14)
ASIA—Provinces of the Roman empire
Media—Provinces of the Parthian empire
Rome —Cities
CRETE—Island
(1) (2) (3) etc.—Numbers indicate sequence listed in Ac 2:9-11
Miles 0 200 400 600 800 1000
Kms 0 300 600 900 1200 1500
©1989 The Zondervan Corporation.

out of my Spirit upon all flesh: and your
sons and [y]your daughters shall proph-
esy, and your young men shall see vi-
sions, and your old men shall dream
dreams:
18 And on my servants and on my
handmaidens I will pour out in those
days of my Spirit; [z]and they shall
prophesy:
19 [a]And I will show wonders in
heaven above, and signs in the earth
beneath; blood, and fire, and vapour of
smoke:
20 [b]The sun shall be turned into
darkness, and the moon into blood, be-
fore that great and notable day of the
Lord come:
21 And it shall come to pass, *that*
[c]whosoever shall call on the name of
the Lord shall be saved.
22 Ye men of Israel, hear these
words; Jesus of Nazareth, a man ap-
proved of God among you [d]by miracles
and wonders and signs, which God did
by him in the midst of you, as ye your-
selves also know:
23 Him, [e]being delivered by the
determinate counsel and foreknowl-
edge of God, [f]ye have taken, and by
wicked hands have crucified and slain:
24 [g]Whom God hath raised up,
having loosed the pains of death: be-
cause it was not possible that he
should be holden of it.

2:17 [y]ch. 21:9
2:18 [z]ch. 21:4,9 1 Cor. 12:10 & 14:1
2:19 [a]Joel 2:30
2:20 [b]Mat. 24:29 Mark 13:24 Luke 21:25
2:21 [c]Rom. 10:13
2:22 [d]John 3:2 & 14:10,11 ch. 10:38 Heb. 2:4
2:23 [e]Mat. 26:24 Luke 22:22 ch. 3:18 [f]ch. 5:30
2:24 [g]Rom. 8:11 1 Cor. 6:14 2 Cor. 4:14 Eph. 1:20 Col. 2:12 1 Thes. 1:10 Heb. 13:20
2:25 [h]Ps. 16:8
2:29 [i]ch. 13:36
2:30 [j]2 Sam. 7:12 Ps. 132:11 Luke 1:32 Rom. 1:3 2 Tim. 2:8
2:31 [k]Ps. 16:10
2:32 [l]ver. 24 [m]ch. 1:8
2:33 [n]Phil. 2:9 Heb. 10:12

25 For David speaketh concerning
him, [h]I foresaw the Lord always be-
fore my face, for he is on my right hand,
that I should not be moved:
26 Therefore did my heart rejoice,
and my tongue was glad; moreover
also my flesh shall rest in hope:
27 Because thou wilt not leave my
soul in hell, neither wilt thou suffer
thine Holy One to see corruption.
28 Thou hast made known to me
the ways of life; thou shalt make me
full of joy with thy countenance.
29 Men *and* brethren, [†]let me free-
ly speak unto you [i]of the patriarch
David, that he is both dead and buried,
and his sepulchre is with us unto this
day.
30 Therefore being a prophet, [j]and
knowing that God had sworn with an
oath to him, that of the fruit of his
loins, according to the flesh, he would
raise up Christ to sit on his throne;
31 He seeing this before spake of
the resurrection of Christ, [k]that his
soul was not left in hell, neither his
flesh did see corruption.
32 [l]This Jesus hath God raised up,
[m]whereof we all are witnesses. Acts 4:20
33 Therefore [n]being by the right

† Or, *I may*

witness calling everyone to repent, believe in Christ, and experience the outpouring of the Holy Spirit (1:8; 2:4,38–40; Joel 2:28–32). We must proclaim the saving work of Christ through the power of the Spirit, even as we anticipate the final day of wrath (Rom. 2:5), i.e., "that great and notable day of the Lord" (2:20b). We must live every day in vigilance, waiting for the day of redemption and the return of Christ for His people (John 14:3; 1 Thes. 4:15–17).

(d) The "last days" inaugurate the kingdom of God, which now comes with all power (see Luke 11:20, note; see article on THE KINGDOM OF GOD, p. 1428). We must experience the fullness of that power as we undergo the conflict of spiritual warfare (2 Cor. 10:3–5; Eph. 6:11–12) and suffering for righteousness (Mat. 5:10–12; 1 Pet. 1:6–7).

2:17 SONS AND DAUGHTERS SHALL PROPHESY. Peter associates the speaking in other tongues (vv. 4,11) with prophecy (vv. 17–18). Thus, speaking in other tongues is considered one form of prophesying. The essential meaning of prophecy is using one's voice for the service and glory of God under the direct initiation of the Holy Spirit. In the book of Acts: (1) the 120 "were all filled with the Holy Ghost, and began to speak with other tongues, as the Spirit gave them utterance" (2:4); (2) the Holy Spirit fell upon Cornelius and his household, and Peter "heard them speak with tongues, and magnify God" (10:44–47); and (3) the disciples at Ephesus, when "the Holy Ghost came on them, . . . spake with tongues and prophesied" (19:6).

2:18 MY SERVANTS AND . . . MY HANDMAIDENS. According to Joel's prophecy, applied by Peter, the baptism in the Holy Spirit is for those already in the kingdom of God—i.e., servants of God or believers, both men and women, who are saved, regenerated, and belong to God.

2:18 IN THOSE DAYS. Peter, quoting Joel, says that God will pour out His Spirit *in those days.* The outpouring of the Holy Spirit and the accompanying supernatural signs cannot be limited to just the one "day" of Pentecost. The power and blessing of the Holy Spirit is for every Christian to have and experience throughout the church age, that is, the entire segment of time between Christ's first coming and His second coming (Rev. 19–20; see Acts 2:39, note).

2:33 THE RIGHT HAND OF GOD. The pouring forth of the Holy Spirit by Jesus proves that He is indeed the exalted Messiah, now sitting at the right hand of God and interceding for His representatives on earth (Heb. 7:25). (1) From Jesus' baptism onward the Spirit was fully upon Him as the

hand of God exalted, and [o]having received of the Father the promise of the Holy Ghost, he [p]hath shed forth this, which ye now see and hear.

34 For David is not ascended into the heavens: but he saith himself, [q]The LORD said unto my Lord, Sit thou on my right hand,

35 Until I make thy foes thy footstool.

36 Therefore let all the house of Israel know assuredly, that God hath made that same Jesus, whom ye have crucified, both Lord and Christ.

The Holy Spirit for all

37 ¶ Now when they heard *this,* [r]they were pricked in their heart, and said unto Peter and to the rest of the apostles, Men *and* brethren, what shall we do?

38 Then Peter said unto them, [s]Repent, and be baptized every one of you in the name of Jesus Christ for the remission of sins, and ye shall receive the gift of the Holy Ghost.

39 For the promise is unto you, and [t]to your children, and [u]to all that are afar off, *even* as many as the Lord our God shall call.

2:33 [o]John 14:26 & 16:7,13 [p]ch. 10:45 Eph. 4:8
2:34 [q]Ps. 110:1 Mat. 22:44 1 Cor. 15:25 Eph. 1:20 Heb. 1:13
2:37 [r]Zech. 12:10 Luke 3:10 ch. 9:6
2:38 [s]Luke 24:47 ch. 3:19
2:39 [t]Joel 2:28 ch. 3:25 [u]ch. 11:15,18 Eph. 2:13
2:42 [v]ch. 1:14 Rom. 12:12 Eph. 6:18 Col. 4:2 Heb. 10:25
2:43 [w]Mark 16:17 ch. 5:12
2:44 [x]ch. 4:32,34
2:45 [y]Is. 58:7
2:46 [z]ch. 1:14 [a]Luke 24:53 [b]ch. 20:7

40 And with many other words did he testify and exhort, saying, Save yourselves from this untoward generation.

41 ¶ Then they that gladly received his word were baptized: and the same day there were added *unto them* about three thousand souls.

42 [v]And they continued stedfastly in the apostles' doctrine and fellowship, and in breaking of bread, and in prayers.

The Spirit working among believers

43 And fear came upon every soul: and [w]many wonders and signs were done by the apostles.

44 And all that believed were together, and [x]had all things common;

45 And sold their possessions and goods, and [y]parted them to all *men,* as every man had need.

46 [z]And they, continuing daily with one accord [a]in the temple, and [b]breaking bread [g]from house to house, did eat their meat with gladness and singleness of heart,

[g] Or, *at home*

Christ (i.e., the one anointed by the Spirit; cf. Luke 3:21–22; 4:1,14,18–19). Now at the right hand of God, He lives to pour forth the same Spirit upon those who believe in Him (see article on JESUS AND THE HOLY SPIRIT, p. 1550). (2) In pouring forth the Spirit, Jesus intends that the Spirit will mediate His presence to believers and empower them to continue to do all that He did while on earth.

2:38 REPENT, AND BE BAPTIZED. Repentance, forgiveness of sins, and baptism are the prior conditions for receiving the gift of the Holy Spirit. However, Peter's demand that his hearers be baptized in water before receiving the promise of the Father (cf. 1:4,8) must not be taken as an absolute requirement for the infilling with the Holy Spirit, nor is baptism in the Spirit an automatic consequence of water baptism.

(1) In this situation, Peter required water baptism prior to receiving the promise because in the mind of his Jewish listeners, the rite of baptism was taken for granted as being involved in any conversion decision. Water baptism did not precede the baptism in the Spirit, however, in the instances recorded in 9:17–18 (the apostle Paul) and 10:44–48 (those in the house of Cornelius).

(2) Each believer, after repenting of his or her sins and accepting Jesus Christ by faith, must "receive" (cf. Gal. 3:14) a personal baptism in the Spirit. The gift of the Spirit in the book of Acts was consciously desired, sought after, and appropriated (1:4,14; 4:31; 8:14–17; 19:2–6); the only possible exception to the rule in the N.T. was the case of Cornelius (10:44–48). Consequently, the baptism in the Spirit should not be considered as a gift that is automatically provided to the believer in Christ.

2:39 UNTO YOU . . . YOUR CHILDREN . . . TO ALL. The promise of the baptism in the Holy Spirit was not just for those present on the day of Pentecost (v. 4), but to all who would believe in Christ throughout this age: "unto you"—Peter's audience; "your children"—the next generation; "to all that are afar off"—the third and subsequent generations. (1) The baptism in the Holy Spirit with its accompanying power was not a once-for-all occurrence in the church's history. It did not cease with Pentecost (cf. v. 38; 8:15; 9:17; 10:44–46; 19:6), nor with the close of the apostolic age. (2) It is the birthright of every Christian to seek, expect, and experience the same baptism in the Spirit that was promised and given to the N.T. Christians (1:4,8; Joel 2:28; Mat. 3:11; Luke 24:49).

2:40 THIS UNTOWARD GENERATION. No one can be saved who does not turn away from the perversity and corruption of present society (cf. Luke 9:41; 11:29; 17:25; Phil. 2:15). All new Christians should be taught to break off from all evil companions, forsake the ungodly world, unite themselves to Christ and His people, and give themselves to the work of God (2 Cor. 6:14,17).

2:42 APOSTLES' DOCTRINE . . . FELLOWSHIP . . . BREAD . . . PRAYERS. See 12:5, note on the 15 characteristics of a N.T. church.

Rom. 15:5-11

47 Praising God, and [c]having favour with all the people. And [d]the Lord added to the church daily such as should be saved.

The healing of the lame man

3 NOW PETER and John went up together [e]into the temple at the hour of prayer, [f]*being* the ninth *hour.*

2 And [g]a certain man lame from his mother's womb was carried, whom they laid daily at the gate of the temple which is called Beautiful, [h]to ask alms of them that entered into the temple;

3 Who seeing Peter and John about to go into the temple asked an alms.

4 And Peter, fastening his eyes upon him with John, said, Look on us.

5 And he gave heed unto them, expecting to receive something of them.

6 Then Peter said, Silver and gold have I none; but such as I have give I thee: [i]In the name of Jesus Christ of Nazareth rise up and walk.

7 And he took him by the right hand, and lifted *him* up: and immediately his feet and ankle bones received strength.

8 And he [j]leaping up stood, and walked, and entered with them into the temple, walking, and leaping, and praising God.

9 [k]And all the people saw him walking and praising God:

10 And they knew that it was he which [l]sat for alms at the Beautiful gate of the temple: and they were filled with wonder and amazement at that which had happened unto him.

Acts 5:15-16

Peter speaks to the onlookers

11 And as the lame man which was healed held Peter and John, all the people ran together unto them in the porch [m]that is called Solomon's, greatly wondering.

12 ¶ And when Peter saw *it,* he answered unto the people, Ye men of Israel, why marvel ye at this? or why look ye so earnestly on us, as though by our own power or holiness we had made this man to walk?

13 [n]The God of Abraham, and of Isaac, and of Jacob, the God of our fathers, [o]hath glorified his Son Jesus; whom ye [p]delivered up, and [q]denied him in the presence of Pilate, when he was determined to let *him* go.

14 But ye denied [r]the Holy One [s]and the Just, and desired a murderer to be granted unto you;

15 And killed the [t]Prince[h] of life, [u]whom God hath raised from the dead; [v]whereof we are witnesses.

16 [w]And his name through faith in his name hath made this man strong, whom ye see and know: yea, the faith which is by him hath given him this perfect soundness in the presence of you all.

Acts 6:5

17 And now, brethren, I wot that [x]through ignorance ye did *it,* as *did* also your rulers.

18 But [y]those things, which God before had shown [z]by the mouth of all his prophets, that Christ should suffer, he hath so fulfilled.

19 ¶ [a]Repent ye therefore, and be

2:47 [c]ch. 4:33 Rom. 14:18 [d]ch. 5:14
3:1 [e]ch. 2:46 [f]Ps. 55:17
3:2 [g]ch. 14:8 [h]John 9:8
3:6 [i]ch. 4:10
3:8 [j]Is. 35:6
3:9 [k]ch. 4:16,21
3:10 [l]Like John 9:8
3:11 [m]John 10:23 ch. 5:12
3:13 [n]ch. 5:30 [o]John 7:39 & 12:16 & 17:1 [p]Mat. 27:2 [q]Mat 27:20 Mark 15:11 Luke 23:18 John 18:40 & 19:15 ch. 13:28
3:14 [r]Ps. 16:10 Mark 1:24 Luke 1:35 ch. 2:27 & 4:27 [s]ch. 7:52 & 22:14
3:15 [t]1 John 5:11 [u]ch. 2:24 [v]ch. 2:32
3:16 [w]Mat. 9:22 ch. 4:10 & 14:9
3:17 [x]Luke 23:34 John 16:3 ch. 13:27 1 Cor. 2:8 1 Tim. 1:13
3:18 [y]Luke 24:44 ch. 26:22 [z]Ps. 22 Is. 50:6 & 53:5 Dan. 9:26; 1 Pet. 1:10 **3:19** [a]ch. 2:38

[h] Or, *Author;* Heb. 2:10 & 5:9

3:6 IN THE NAME OF JESUS . . . WALK. The healing of the lame beggar was done by the power of Christ working through His apostles. Jesus said to His followers concerning those who would believe in Him: "In my name . . . they shall lay hands on the sick, and they shall recover" (Mark 16:17–18). The church continued Jesus' healing ministry in obedience to His will. The miracle was accomplished through faith "in the name of Jesus Christ" (v. 6) and "the gift of healing" operating through Peter (see 1 Cor. 12:1,9).

Peter stated that he had no silver or gold, but would give the lame beggar something much more valuable. Churches that possess a fair degree of material prosperity should ponder these words of Peter. Many churches today can no longer say "Silver and gold have I none," nor do they seem capable of saying, "In the name of Jesus Christ of Nazareth rise up and walk."

3:19 REPENT . . . AND BE CONVERTED. God has chosen to bless His people with the outpouring of the Holy Spirit only on the conditions of repentance, i.e., turning from sin and the unrighteous ways of their surrounding perverse generation, and conversion, i.e., turning to God, listening to everything that Christ, the prophet, tells them (vv. 22–23), and ever moving toward sincere obedience to Christ (cf. 2:38–41; 5:29–32).

3:19 TIMES OF REFRESHING. Throughout this present age and until the return of Christ, God will send "times of refreshing" (i.e., the outpouring of the Holy Spirit) to all who repent and are converted. Although perilous times will come toward the end of this age and a great falling away from the faith will occur (2 Thes. 2:3; 2 Tim. 3:1), God still promises to send revival and times of refreshing upon the faithful. The presence of Christ, spiritual blessings, miracles, and outpourings of the

converted, that your sins may be blot-
ted out, when the times of refreshing
shall come from the presence of the
Lord;
20 And he shall send Jesus Christ,
which before was preached unto you:
21 [b]Whom the heaven must re-
ceive until the times of [c]restitution of
all things, [d]which God hath spoken by
the mouth of all his holy prophets since
the world began.
22 For Moses truly said unto the fa-
thers, [e]A prophet shall the Lord your
God raise up unto you of your brethren,
like unto me; him shall ye hear in all
things whatsoever he shall say unto
you.
23 And it shall come to pass, *that*
every soul, which will not hear that
prophet, shall be destroyed from
among the people.
24 Yea, and all the prophets from
Samuel and those that follow after, as
many as have spoken, have likewise
foretold of these days.
25 [f]Ye are the children of the
prophets, and of the covenant which
God made with our fathers, saying
unto Abraham, [g]And in thy seed shall
all the kindreds of the earth be blessed.
26 [h]Unto you first God, having
raised up his Son Jesus, [i]sent him to
bless you, [j]in turning away every one
of you from his iniquities.

3:21 [b]ch. 1:11 [c]Mat. 17:11 [d]Luke 1:70 **3:22** [e]Deut. 18:15,18, 19 ch. 7:37 **3:25** [f]ch. 2:39 Rom. 9:4,8 & 15:8 Gal. 3:26 [g]Gen. 12:3 & 18:18 & 22:18 & 26:4 & 28:14 Gal. 3:8 **3:26** [h]Mat. 10:5 & 15:24 Luke 24:47 ch. 13:32,33,46 [i]ver. 22 [j]Mat. 1:21 **4:1** [k]Luke 22:4 ch. 5:24 **4:6** [l]Luke 3:2 John 11:49 & 18:13 **4:7** [m]Ex. 2:14 Mat. 21:23 ch. 7:27 **4:8** [n]Luke 12:11,12

Peter and John arrested

4 AND AS they spake unto the peo-
ple, the priests, and the [k]cap-
tain[i] of the temple, and the Saddu-
cees, came upon them,
2 Being grieved that they taught the
people, and preached through Jesus
the resurrection from the dead.
3 And they laid hands on them, and
put *them* in hold unto the next day: for
it was now eventide.
4 Howbeit many of them which
heard the word believed; and the num-
ber of the men was about five thou-
sand.

Peter before the Jewish council

5 ¶ And it came to pass on the mor-
row, that their rulers, and elders, and
scribes,
6 And [l]Annas the high priest, and
Caiaphas, and John, and Alexander,
and as many as were of the kindred of
the high priest, were gathered together
at Jerusalem.
7 And when they had set them in
the midst, they asked, [m]By what pow-
er, or by what name, have ye done this?

Peter speaks, filled with the Holy Spirit

8 [n]Then Peter, filled with the Holy

i Or, *ruler*

Holy Spirit will come upon the remnant who faithfully seek Him and overcome the world, the flesh, and the dominion of Satan (cf. 26:18).

3:21 TIMES OF RESTITUTION. "The times of restitution of all things" refers to the time of Christ's return from heaven to put down evil and establish the kingdom of God on earth free from all sin. Ultimately all things prophesied in the O.T. to be restored (cf. Zech. 12–14; Luke 1:32–33) will be restored. Christ will redeem or renovate all nature (Rom. 8:18–23) and reign personally on the earth (see Rev. 20–21). Note that not people on earth, but Christ and the armies from heaven will bring in the triumph of God and His kingdom (Rev. 19:11—20:9).

3:22 A PROPHET. Moses' prediction in Deut. 18:18–19 that "a prophet shall the Lord your God raise up . . . like unto me" was a prophecy concerning Jesus Christ. In what way was Jesus like Moses? (1) Moses was anointed by the Spirit (Num. 11:17); the Spirit of the Lord was upon Jesus to preach the gospel (Luke 4:18–19). (2) God used Moses to initiate the old covenant; Jesus brought in the new covenant. (3) Moses led Israel out of Egypt to Sinai and established the covenant relationship with God; Christ redeemed His people from sin and satanic bondage and established a new, living relationship with God whereby His people might enter into the very presence of God. (4) Moses in the O.T. laws referred to the sacrifice of a lamb to bring redemption; Christ Himself became the Lamb of God to furnish salvation for all who accept Him. (5) Moses faithfully pointed to the law and the obligation of God's people to obey its statutes in order to receive God's blessing; Christ pointed to Himself and the Holy Spirit as God's way of fulfilling His will and receiving God's blessing and eternal life.

3:26 TURNING . . . FROM HIS INIQUITIES. Peter once again emphasizes that believing in Christ and receiving the baptism in the Holy Spirit are conditioned by turning from sin and being separated from evil (see 2:38,40, notes; 3:19, note; 8:21, note). In the original apostolic message, there was no promised blessing without holiness.

4:8 PETER, FILLED WITH THE HOLY GHOST. Peter received a fresh filling with the Holy Spirit that brought a sudden inspiration, wisdom, and boldness by which to proclaim the truth of God. It is theologically significant that the filling with the Spirit was not a one-time experience, but a repetitive one. This episode is a fulfillment of Jesus' promise in Luke 12:11–12; other in-

Acts 4:31 Ghost, said unto them, Ye rulers of the
people, and elders of Israel,
9 If we this day be examined of the
good deed done to the impotent man,
by what means he is made whole;
10 Be it known unto you all, and to
all the people of Israel, [o]that by the
name of Jesus Christ of Nazareth,
whom ye crucified, [p]whom God raised
from the dead, *even* by him doth this
man stand here before you whole.
11 [q]This is the stone which was
set at nought of you builders, which is
become the head of the corner.
12 [r]Neither is there salvation in
any other: for there is none other name
Acts 13:38-39 under heaven given among men,
whereby we must be saved.

The release of Peter and John

13 ¶ Now when they saw the bold-
ness of Peter and John, [s]and per-
ceived that they were unlearned and ig-
norant men, they marvelled; and they
took knowledge of them, that they had
been with Jesus.
14 And beholding the man which
was healed [t]standing with them, they
could say nothing against it.
15 But when they had commanded
them to go aside out of the council,
they conferred among themselves,
16 Saying, [u]What shall we do to
these men? for that indeed a notable
miracle hath been done by them *is*
[v]manifest to all them that dwell in Je-
rusalem; and we cannot deny *it.*
17 But that it spread no further
among the people, let us straitly
threaten them, that they speak hence-
forth to no man in this name.
18 [w]And they called them, and
commanded them not to speak at all
nor teach in the name of Jesus.

4:10 [o]ch. 3:6,16 [p]ch. 2:24
4:11 [q]Ps. 118:22 Is. 28:16 Mat. 21:42
4:12 [r]Mat. 1:21 ch. 10:43 1 Tim. 2:5,6
4:13 [s]Mat. 11:25 1 Cor. 1:27
4:14 [t]ch. 3:11
4:16 [u]John 11:47 [v]ch. 3:9,10
4:18 [w]Again, ch. 5:40
4:19 [x]ch. 5:29
4:20 [y]ch. 1:8 & 2:32 [z]ch. 22:15 1 John 1:1,3
4:21 [a]Mat. 21:26 Luke 20:6,19 & 22:2 ch. 5:26 [b]ch. 3:7,8
4:23 [c]ch. 12:12
4:24 [d]2 Ki. 19:15
4:25 [e]Ps. 2:1
4:27 [f]Mat. 26:3 Luke 22:2 & 23:1,8 [g]Luke 1:35 [h]Luke 4:18 John 10:36
4:28 [i]ch. 2:23 & 3:18

19 But Peter and John answered
and said unto them, [x]Whether it be
right in the sight of God to hearken
unto you more than unto God,
judge ye.
20 [y]For we cannot but speak the
things which [z]we have seen and Acts 4:33
heard.
21 So when they had further threat-
ened them, they let them go, finding
nothing how they might punish them,
[a]because of the people: for all *men* glo-
rified God for [b]that which was done.
22 For the man was above forty
years old, on whom this miracle of
healing was shown.

Prayer for power and boldness

23 ¶ And being let go, [c]they went
to their own company, and reported all
that the chief priests and elders had
said unto them.
24 And when they heard that, they
lifted up their voice to God with one
accord, and said, Lord, [d]thou *art* God,
which hast made heaven, and earth,
and the sea, and all that in them is:
25 Who by the mouth of thy servant
David hast said, [e]Why did the heathen
rage, and the people imagine vain
things?
26 The kings of the earth stood up,
and the rulers were gathered together
against the Lord, and against his
Christ.
27 For [f]of a truth against [g]thy
holy child Jesus, [h]whom thou hast
anointed, both Herod, and Pontius Pi-
late, with the Gentiles, and the people
of Israel, were gathered together,
28 [i]For to do whatsoever thy hand
and thy counsel determined before to
be done.
29 And now, Lord, behold their

---

stances of renewed fillings can be found in Acts 7:55 and 13:9.

4:12 SALVATION IN ... NONE OTHER NAME. The disciples were convinced that the greatest need of every individual was salvation from sin and the wrath of God, and they preached that this need could be met by no one other than the person of Jesus Christ. This truth reveals the exclusive nature of the gospel and places upon the church the heavy responsibility of preaching the gospel to every person. If there were other ways of salvation, the church could be at ease. But according to Christ Himself (John 14:6), there is no hope for anyone apart from salvation through Christ (cf. 10:43; 1 Tim. 2:5–6). This is the basis for the missionary imperative.

4:20 WE CANNOT BUT SPEAK. The Holy Spirit given to the apostles created in them an overwhelming desire to proclaim the gospel. Throughout the book of Acts the Spirit impelled believers to carry the gospel to others (1:8; 2:14–41; 3:12–26; 8:25,35; 9:15; 10:44–48; 13:1–4).

4:29 GRANT UNTO THY SERVANTS ... BOLDNESS. The disciples needed their courage to witness and speak for Christ renewed. Throughout our Christian life, we too will need to approach God in prayer in order to overcome our fear of embarrassment, rejection, criticism, or persecution. God's grace, through fillings of the Holy Spirit, will help us speak about Jesus with boldness (cf. Mat. 10:32).

threatenings: and grant unto thy ser-
vants, [j]that with all boldness they
may speak thy word,
30 By stretching forth thine hand to
heal; [k]and that signs and wonders
may be done [l]by the name of [m]thy
holy child Jesus.

The Holy Spirit fills the believers

31 ¶ And when they had prayed,
[n]the place was shaken where they
were assembled together; and they
were all filled with the Holy Ghost,
[o]and they spake the word of God with
cts 3 boldness.
32 And the multitude of them that
believed [p]were of one heart and of one
soul: [q]neither said any *of them* that
aught of the things which he possessed
was his own; but they had all things
common.

Believers witness with great power

33 And with [r]great power gave the
apostles [s]witness of the resurrection
of the Lord Jesus: and [t]great grace
was upon them all. Acts 5:32
34 Neither was there any among
them that lacked: [u]for as many
as were possessors of lands or
houses sold them, and brought
the prices of the things that were
sold,
35 [v]And laid *them* down at the
apostles' feet: [w]and distribution was
made unto every man according as he
had need.
36 And Joses, who by the apostles
was surnamed Barnabas, (which is, be-
ing interpreted, The son of consola-
tion,) a Levite, *and* of the country of
Cyprus,
37 [x]Having land, sold *it*, and
brought the money, and laid *it* at the
apostles' feet.

4:29 [j]ver. 13,31 ch. 9:27 & 13:46 & 14:3 & 19:8 & 26:26 Eph. 6:19 **4:30** [k]ch. 2:43 & 5:12 [l]ch. 3:6,16 [m]ver. 27 **4:31** [n]ch. 2:2,4 & 16:26 [o]ver. 29 **4:32** [p]ch. 5:12 Rom. 15:5,6 2 Cor. 13:11 Phil. 1:27 & 2:2 1 Pet. 3:8 [q]ch. 2:44 **4:33** [r]ch. 1:8 [s]ch. 1:22 [t]ch. 2:45 **4:34** [u]ch. 2:45 **4:35** [v]ver. 37 ch. 5:2 [w]ch. 2:45 & 6:1 **4:37** [x]ver. 34,35; ch. 5:1,2

4:30 HEAL ... SIGNS AND WONDERS. Preaching and miracles belong together (3:1–10; 4:8–22,29–33; 5:12–16; 6:7–8; 8:6ff; 15:12; 20:7ff). Miracles are accompanying signs by which Christ confirms the word of the witnesses (14:3; cf. Mark 16:20). (1) "Signs" generally refer to miraculous deeds performed in order to certify the existence of a divine power, to give warning, or to encourage faith. (2) "Wonders" refer to unusual events that cause the beholder to marvel. Note that the church is *praying* that healings, signs, and wonders will take place. The church today as it faces the challenge of the last days needs to intercede earnestly in prayer that God will confirm the gospel with great power, miracles, and abundant grace (v. 33). Only when we proclaim the gospel in the power of the N.T. witness will we be able adequately to reach this lost generation for Christ.

4:31 SPAKE THE WORD OF GOD WITH BOLDNESS. The inner power of the Spirit and the reality of God's presence brought about by the filling of the Spirit frees the believer from fear of others and greatly increases the courage and motivation to speak forth for God.

4:31–33 THEY WERE ALL FILLED WITH THE HOLY GHOST. Several important truths stand out here. (1) The term "baptized with or in the Holy Spirit" (see 1:5, note) describes the consecrating work of the Holy Spirit in initiating the believer in the Holy Spirit's power for witness. The terms "filled," "clothed," and "empowered" describe His actual equipping them for ministry (2:4; 4:8,31; 9:17; 13:9,52). As need arises, the "filling" may be repeated.

(2) The terms "pouring out of the Spirit" (2:17–18; 10:45), "receiving of the gift of the Holy Spirit" (2:38; 8:15), "falling of the Spirit upon" (8:16; 10:44; 11:15), "coming of the Spirit upon" (19:6) are different expressions for the occasion when believers are "filled with the Holy Spirit" (2:4; 4:31; 9:17).

(3) All the believers, including the apostles who had been previously filled (2:4), are freshly filled to meet the continuing opposition of the Jews (v. 29). Fresh fillings with the Holy Spirit are part of God's will and provision for all who have received the baptism in the Holy Spirit (cf. v. 8, note; 13:52). We should expect and seek them.

(4) The Spirit here visits a whole congregation. Hence, to fulfill God's will for the church, not only must individuals be filled with the Spirit (v. 8; 9:17; 13:9), but entire congregations (2:4; 4:31; 13:53) should experience repeated visitations of the Holy Spirit when special needs and challenges are present.

(5) God's moving upon the entire congregation with a renewed filling of the Holy Spirit results in boldness and power in witness, love for one another, and the reception of abundant grace upon all.

4:33 WITH GREAT POWER. "Great power" is the distinguishing characteristic of apostolic preaching and witness (cf. 1:8) for three reasons: (1) Apostolic witness was based on God's Word (v. 29) and the conviction that it was given by the inspiration of the Holy Spirit (see article on THE INSPIRATION AND AUTHORITY OF SCRIPTURE, p. 1924). (2) The disciples were conscious that they had been sent and commissioned by Jesus Christ Himself, the resurrected Lord. (3) The Holy Spirit through the disciples brought great conviction upon those who heard the gospel concerning personal sin, the righteousness of Christ, and the judgment of God (see John 16:8, note).

Anianias and Sapphira punished

5 BUT A certain man named Anani-
as, with Sapphira his wife, sold a
possession,
2 And kept back *part* of the price,
his wife also being privy *to it,* and
brought a certain part, and laid *it* at the
apostles' feet.
3 [y]But Peter said, Ananias, why
hath [z]Satan filled thine heart [j]to lie
to the Holy Ghost, and to keep back
part of the price of the land?
4 Whiles it remained, was it not
thine own? and after it was sold, was
it not in thine own power? why hast
thou conceived this thing in thine
heart? thou hast not lied unto men, but
unto God.
5 And Ananias hearing these words
[a]fell down, and gave up the ghost: and
Acts 16:16-18 great fear came on all them that heard
these things.
6 And the young men arose,
[b]wound him up, and carried *him* out,
and buried *him.*
7 And it was about the space of
three hours after, when his wife, not
knowing what was done, came in.
8 And Peter answered unto her,
Tell me whether ye sold the land for so
much? And she said, Yea, for so much.
9 Then Peter said unto her, How is
it that ye have agreed together [c]to
tempt the Spirit of the Lord? behold,
the feet of them which have buried thy
husband *are* at the door, and shall car-
ry thee out.
10 [d]Then fell she down straight-
way at his feet, and yielded up the
ghost: and the young men came in, and
found her dead, and, carrying *her* forth,
buried *her* by her husband.
11 [e]And great fear came upon all
the church, and upon as many as heard
these things.

Many signs and wonders

12 ¶ And [f]by the hands of the
apostles were many signs and wonders
wrought among the people; ([g]and
they were all with one accord in Solo-
mon's porch.
13 And [h]of the rest durst no man
join himself to them: [i]but the people
magnified them.
14 And believers were the more
added to the Lord, multitudes both of
men and women.)
15 Insomuch that they brought
forth the sick [k]into the streets, and
laid *them* on beds and couches, [j]that
at the least the shadow of Peter pass-
ing by might overshadow some of
them.
16 There came also a multitude *out*

5:3 [y]Num. 30:2 Deut. 23:21 Eccl. 5:4 [z]Luke 22:3 **5:5** [a]ver. 10,11 **5:6** [b]John 19:40 **5:9** [c]ver. 3 Mat. 4:7 **5:10** [d]ver. 5 **5:11** [e]ver. 5 ch. 2:43 & 19:17 **5:12** [f]ch. 2:43 & 14:3 & 19:11 Rom. 15:19 2 Cor. 12:12 Heb. 2:4 [g]ch. 3:11 & 4:32 **5:13** [h]John 9:22 & 12:42 & 19:38 [i]ch. 2:47 & 4:21 **5:15** [j]Mat. 9:21 & 14:36 ch. 19:12

[j]Or, *to deceive* [k]Or, *in every street*

5:3 LIE TO THE HOLY GHOST. In order to gain glory and recognition, Ananias and Sapphira lied to the church about their giving. God considered this lie against the Holy Spirit a serious offense. The deaths of Ananias and Sapphira are intended to be standing examples of God's attitude toward any deceitful heart among those who profess to be born-again and Spirit-filled believers. Notice too that lying to the Holy Spirit is the same as lying to God (vv. 3–4; see Rev. 22:15, note; see article on THE DOCTRINE OF THE HOLY SPIRIT, p. 1668).

5:4 WHY HAST THOU CONCEIVED THIS THING? The root of the sin of Ananias and Sapphira was their love for money and the praise of others. This set them against the Holy Spirit (v. 9). Once the love of money and of human praise take possession of a person, his spirit becomes open to all kinds of satanic evil (1 Tim. 6:10). A person cannot be filled with a love of money and at the same time love and serve God (Mat. 6:24; John 5:41–44).

5:5 ANANIAS . . . GAVE UP THE GHOST. God harshly struck down Ananias and Sapphira (vv. 5,10) in order to reveal His hatred for all deceit, lying, and dishonesty in the kingdom of God. One of the most abominable sins in the church is to deceive God's people about your relationship with Christ, your work for Him, and the extent of your ministry. To engage in this type of hypocrisy means using the shed blood of Christ to exalt and glorify your own self before other people. This sin seriously disregards the very purpose for which Christ suffered and died (Eph. 1:4; Heb. 13:12), indicating an absence of the fear of the Lord (vv. 5,11) and of respect and honor for the Holy Spirit (v. 3), and merits God's righteous judgment.

5:11 GREAT FEAR CAME UPON ALL. God's judgment upon the sin of Ananias and Sapphira caused an increase in humility, awe, reverence, and fear of a holy God. Without a proper fear of the holy God and His wrath against sin, God's people will soon return to the ungodly ways of the world, cease to experience the outpouring of the Spirit and God's miraculous presence, and be cut off from the flow of God's grace. The fear of the Lord is an essential element in the N.T. faith and in Biblical Christianity today (see article on THE FEAR OF THE LORD, p. 282).

5:16 THEY WERE HEALED EVERY ONE. The apostles did as their Lord had done: they healed those who were afflicted with unclean spirits (see Mark 1:34). This was a paramount sign that the kingdom of God had come among the people with great power (see article on POWER OVER SATAN AND DEMONS, p. 1486). It is never wrong

of the cities round about unto Jerusa-
lem, bringing [k]sick folks, and them
which were vexed with unclean spirits:
and they were healed every one.

Acts 5-7

The apostles imprisoned

17 ¶ [l]Then the high priest rose up,
and all they that were with him, (which
is the sect of the Sadducees,) and were
filled with [1]indignation,
18 [m]And laid their hands on the
apostles, and put them in the common
prison.
19 But [n]the angel of the Lord by
night opened the prison doors, and
brought them forth, and said,
20 Go, stand and speak in the tem-
ple to the people [o]all the words of this
life.
21 And when they heard *that,* they
entered into the temple early in the
morning, and taught. [p]But the high
priest came, and they that were with
him, and called the council together,
and all the senate of the children of Is-
rael, and sent to the prison to have
them brought.
22 But when the officers came, and
found them not in the prison, they re-
turned, and told,
23 Saying, The prison truly found
we shut with all safety, and the keep-
ers standing without before the doors:
but when we had opened, we found no
man within.
24 Now when the high priest and
[q]the captain of the temple and the
chief priests heard these things, they
doubted of them whereunto this would
grow.
25 Then came one and told them,
saying, Behold, the men whom ye put
in prison are standing in the temple,
and teaching the people.
26 Then went the captain with the
officers, and brought them without vio-
lence: [r]for they feared the people, lest
they should have been stoned.
27 And when they had brought
them, they set *them* before the council:
and the high priest asked them,
28 Saying, [s]Did not we straitly
command you that ye should not teach
in this name? and, behold, ye have
filled Jerusalem with your doctrine,
[t]and intend to bring this man's
[u]blood upon us.
29 ¶ Then Peter and the *other* apos-
tles answered and said, [v]We ought to
obey God rather than men.
30 [w]The God of our fathers raised
up Jesus, whom ye slew and [x]hanged
on a tree.
31 [y]Him hath God exalted with his
right hand *to be* [z]a Prince and [a]a Sav-
iour, [b]for to give repentance to Israel,
and forgiveness of sins.
32 And [c]we are his witnesses of
these things; and *so is* also the Holy
Ghost, [d]whom God hath given to them
that obey him.

Acts 8:4

The counsel of Gamaliel

33 ¶ [e]When they heard *that,* they
were cut *to the heart,* and took counsel
to slay them.
34 Then stood there up one in the
council, a Pharisee, named [f]Gamaliel,
a doctor of the law, had in reputation
among all the people, and commanded
to put the apostles forth a little space;
35 And said unto them, Ye men of
Israel, take heed to yourselves what ye
intend to do as touching these men.
36 For before these days rose up
Theudas, boasting himself to be some-
body; to whom a number of men, about
four hundred, joined themselves: who
was slain; and all, as many as
[m]obeyed him, were scattered, and
brought to nought.
37 After this man rose up Judas of
Galilee in the days of the taxing, and
drew away much people after him: he
also perished; and all, *even* as many as
obeyed him, were dispersed.
38 And now I say unto you, Refrain

5:16 [k]Mark 16:17,18 John 14:12
5:17 [l]ch. 4:1,2,6
5:18 [m]Luke 21:12
5:19 [n]ch. 12:7 & 16:26
5:20 [o]John 6:68 & 17:3 1 John 5:11
5:21 [p]ch. 4:5,6
5:24 [q]Luke 22:4 ch. 4:1
5:26 [r]Mat. 21:26
5:28 [s]ch. 4:18 [t]ch. 2:23,36 & 3:15 & 7:52 [u]Mat. 23:35 & 27:25
5:29 [v]ch. 4:19
5:30 [w]ch. 3:13,15 & 22:14 [x]ch. 10:39 & 13:29 Gal. 3:13 1 Pet. 2:24
5:31 [y]ch. 2:33,36 Phil. 2:9 Heb. 2:10 & 12:2 [z]ch. 3:15 [a]Mat. 1:21 [b]Luke 24:47 ch. 3:26 & 13:38 Eph. 1:7 Col. 1:14
5:32 [c]John 15:26,27 [d]ch. 2:4 & 10:44
5:33 [e]ch. 2:37 & 7:54
5:34 [f]ch. 22:3

[1]Or, *envy* [m]Or, *believed*

---

to pray that through the Holy Spirit we might do good and heal those oppressed by sickness and Satan (4:30; see article on DIVINE HEALING, p. 1418).

5:29 OBEY GOD RATHER THAN MEN. The great question before every believer is not, "Is it expedient, safe, pleasurable, or popular among men?" but, "What is right in the sight of God?" (cf. Gal. 1:10).

5:32 HOLY GHOST ... TO THEM THAT OBEY HIM. If there is no real obedience to Christ or a sincere seeking for the righteousness of His kingdom (Mat. 6:33; Rom. 14:17), then any claim to possess the fullness of the Holy Spirit is invalid. Pentecost without the Lordship of Christ is impossible (cf. 2:38–42), for the Holy Spirit in all His power is given only to those living in "obedience to the faith" (Rom. 1:5; see article on TESTING FOR GENUINE BAPTISM IN THE SPIRIT, p. 1682).

THE DOCTRINE OF THE HOLY SPIRIT

***Acts 5:3–4** "But Peter said, Ananias, why hath Satan filled thine heart to lie to the Holy Ghost, and to keep back part of the price of the land? Whiles it remained, was it not thine own? and after it was sold, was it not in thine own power? why hast thou conceived this thing in thine heart? thou hast not lied unto men, but unto God."*

It is essential that believers recognize the importance of the Holy Spirit in God's redemptive purpose. Many Christians have no idea what difference it would make if there were no Holy Spirit in this world. Without the Holy Spirit there would be no creation, no universe, no human race (Gen. 1:2; Job 33:4). Without the Holy Spirit there would be no Bible (2 Pet. 1:21), no New Testament (John 14:26; 15:26–27; 1 Cor. 2:10–14), no power to proclaim the gospel (Acts 1:8). Without the Holy Spirit there would be no faith, no new birth, no holiness, and no Christians at all in the world. This article explores some of the basic teachings about the Holy Spirit.

THE PERSON OF THE HOLY SPIRIT. Throughout Scripture the Holy Spirit is revealed to us as a person with an individuality all His own (cf. 2 Cor. 3:17–18; Heb. 9:14; 1 Pet. 1:2). He is a divine Person like the Father and the Son (Acts 5:3–4). Thus, we must never think of the Holy Spirit as a mere influence or power. He has personal characteristics, for He thinks (Rom. 8:27), feels (Rom. 15:30), wills (1 Cor. 12:11), and has the capacity to love and enjoy fellowship. He was sent by the Father to bring believers into the intimate presence and fellowship of Jesus (John 14:16–18,26; see article on JESUS AND THE HOLY SPIRIT, p. 1550). In the light of these truths we should treat Him as a person and regard Him as the infinite living God within our hearts, worthy of our worship, love, and surrender (see Mark 1:11, note on the Trinity).

THE WORK OF THE HOLY SPIRIT. (1) Revelation about the Holy Spirit in the O.T. For a description of the work of the Spirit of God in the O.T., see article on THE SPIRIT IN THE OLD TESTAMENT, p. 1302.

(2) Revelation about the Holy Spirit in the N.T. (a) The Holy Spirit is the agent of salvation, convicting us of sin (John 16:7–8), revealing to us the truth about Jesus (John 14:16,26), giving us new birth (John 3:3–6), and incorporating us into the body of Christ (1 Cor. 12:13). At conversion we as believers receive the Holy Spirit (John 3:3–6; 20:22) and become partakers of the nature of God (2 Pet. 1:4; see article on THE REGENERATION OF THE DISCIPLES, p. 1638).

(b) The Holy Spirit is the agent of sanctification. At conversion believers are indwelt by the Holy Spirit and come under His sanctifying influence (Rom. 8:9; 1 Cor. 6:19). Notice some of the things the Holy Spirit does as He dwells in us. He sanctifies us, i.e., cleanses, leads, guides, and motivates us to pursue a holy life, delivering us from the bondage of sin (Rom. 8:2–4; Gal. 5:16–17; 2 Thes. 2:13). He tells us that we are children of God (Rom. 8:16), helps us in the worship of God (Acts 10:45–46) and in our prayer lives, and intercedes for us as we cry to God (Rom. 8:26–27). He produces Christlike graces of character which glorify Christ (Gal. 5:22–23; 1 Pet. 1:2). He is our divine teacher, guiding us into all truth (John 16:13; 14:26; 1 Cor. 2:9–16), disclosing Jesus to us and guiding us in close fellowship and oneness with Jesus (John 14:16–18; 16:14). He continually imparts God's love to us (Rom. 5:5) and gives us joy, comfort, and help (John 14:16; 1 Thes. 1:6).

(c) The Holy Spirit is the agent of service, empowering believers for service and witness. This work of the Holy Spirit is related to the baptism in the Spirit or the fullness of the Spirit (see article on BAPTISM IN THE HOLY SPIRIT, p. 1652). When we are baptized in the Spirit, we receive power to witness for Christ and work effectively within

the church and before the world (Acts 1:8). We receive the same divine anointing that descended upon Christ (John 1:32–33) and upon the disciples (Acts 2:4; see 1:5), enabling us to proclaim God's Word (Acts 1:8; 4:31) and work miracles (Acts 2:43; 3:2–8; 5:15; 6:8; 10:38). It is God's intended purpose that all Christians experience the baptism in the Holy Spirit throughout this age (2:39). In the area of service, the Holy Spirit gives spiritual gifts to the individual members of the church to edify or strengthen the church (1 Cor. 12–14). These gifts are a manifestation of the Spirit through individuals by which Christ's presence, love, truth, and righteous standards are made real to the fellowship of believers for the common good (1 Cor. 12:7–11).

(d) The Holy Spirit is the agent who incorporates believers into the one body of Christ (1 Cor. 12:13), abides in the church (1 Cor. 3:16), builds the church (Eph. 2:22), inspires her worship (Phil. 3:3), directs her mission (Acts 13:2,4), appoints her workers (Acts 20:28), gives gifts to the church (1 Cor. 12:1–11), anoints her preachers (Acts 2:4; 1 Cor 2:4), guards the gospel against error (2 Tim. 1:14), and promotes her righteousness (John 16:8; 1 Cor. 3:16; 6:18–20).

(3) The various activities of the Spirit are complementary and not contradictory. At the same time, these facets of the Holy Spirit's work are interlocked and cannot be fully separated. We cannot experience (a) the fullness of new life in Christ, (b) righteousness as a way of living, (c) the power to witness for our Lord, or (d) fellowship in His body without becoming involved in all four. For example, baptism in the Holy Spirit cannot be maintained independently of the Spirit's work of producing righteousness within us and leading us into the knowledge of and commitment to Biblical truth.

from these men, and let them alone:
[g]for if this counsel or this work be of
men, it will come to nought:
39 [h]But if it be of God, ye cannot
overthrow it; lest haply ye be found
even [i]to fight against God.

The apostles are beaten

40 And to him they agreed: and
when they had [j]called the apostles,
[k]and beaten *them,* they commanded
that they should not speak in the name
of Jesus, and let them go.
41 ¶ And they departed from the
presence of the council, [l]rejoicing
that they were counted worthy to suf-
fer shame for his name.
42 And daily [m]in the temple, and in
every house, [n]they ceased not to
teach and preach Jesus Christ.

The appointment of the seven

6 AND IN those days, [o]when the
number of the disciples was multi-
plied, there arose a murmuring of the
[p]Grecians against the Hebrews, be-
cause their widows were neglected
[q]in the daily ministration.
2 Then the twelve called the multi-
tude of the disciples *unto them,* and
said, [r]It is not reason that we should
leave the word of God, and serve ta-
bles.
3 Wherefore, brethren, [s]look ye
out among you seven men of honest re-
port, full of the Holy Ghost and wis-
dom, whom we may appoint over this
business. Acts 7:55
4 But we [t]will give ourselves con-
tinually to prayer, and to the ministry
of the word.
5 ¶ And the saying pleased the
whole multitude: and they chose Ste-
phen, [u]a man full of faith and of the
Holy Ghost, and [v]Philip, and Procho-
rus, and Nicanor, and Timon, and Par-
menas, and [w]Nicolas a proselyte of
Antioch: Acts 14:9 10
6 Whom they set before the apos-

5:38 [g]Prov. 21:30 Is. 8:10 Mat. 15:13 **5:39** [h]Luke 21:15 1 Cor. 1:25 [i]ch. 7:51 & 9:5 & 23:9 **5:40** [j]ch. 4:18 [k]Mat. 10:17 & 23:34 Mark 13:9 **5:41** [l]Mat. 5:12 Rom. 5:3 2 Cor. 12:10 Phil. 1:29 Heb. 10:34 Jas. 1:2 1 Pet. 4:13,16 **5:42** [m]ch. 2:46 [n]ch. 4:20,29 **6:1** [o]ch. 2:41 & 4:4 & 5:14 & ver. 7 [p]ch. 9:29 & 11:20 [q]ch. 4:35 **6:2** [r]Ex. 18:17 **6:3** [s]Deut. 1:13 ch. 1:21 & 16:2 1 Tim. 3:7 **6:4** [t]ch. 2:42 **6:5** [u]ch. 11:24 [v]ch. 8:5,26 & 21:8 [w]Rev. 2:6,15

6:3 FULL OF THE HOLY GHOST AND WISDOM. The apostles stipulated that the seven men should be men (1) "of honest report," (2) "full of the Holy Ghost," and (3) "full of wisdom." That is, they had to give evidence of having continued faithfully under the influence of the Holy Spirit. Apparently the apostles assumed that not all believers continued to be full of the Spirit. In other words, those who fail to walk faithfully according to the Spirit (Gal. 5:16–25) will cease to be full of the Spirit.

Concerning the terms "full of the Holy Ghost" and "filled with the Holy Ghost," the following should be noted. (1) The phrase "full of the Holy Ghost" (cf. 6:5; 11:24) expresses a continuing character, quality, or condition within believers that results from experiencing the Spirit's fullness and that enables them to minister in the power of the Holy Spirit, and to speak under prophetic inspiration as the Spirit gives utterance.

(2) The term "filled with the Holy Ghost" is used three ways: (a) to indicate the reception of the baptism in the Holy Spirit (1:5; 2:4; 9:17; 11:16); (b) to indicate the empowering of a believer or believers on a specific occasion to speak under the impulse of the Holy Spirit (4:8; 13:9; Luke 1:41–45,67–79); and (c) to indicate a general prophetic ministry under the inspiration or anointing of the Holy Spirit without specifying duration of that ministry (4:31–33; 13:52; Luke 1:15).

(3) After the initial reception of the baptism in the Spirit, individuals who faithfully walk in the Spirit, putting to death the sinful deeds of the body (Rom. 8:13–14), may be described as "full of the Holy Ghost," i.e., maintaining the abiding fullness of the Holy Spirit (e.g., the seven men, especially Stephen, vv. 3,5; 7:55; or Barnabas, 11:24). In addition, those who maintain the fullness of the Spirit may receive a fresh filling with the Spirit for a particular purpose or task, especially a divine enabling for them to speak under the impulse of the Holy Spirit.

6:4 GIVE OURSELVES . . . TO PRAYER. Baptism in the Holy Spirit alone is insufficient for effective Christian leadership. Church leaders must constantly devote themselves to prayer and to the preaching of the Word. The verb translated "give ourselves" (Gk. *proskartereō*) denotes a steadfast and single-minded fidelity and a giving of much time to a certain course of action. Hence, the apostles felt that prayer and the ministry of the Word were the proper and highest work of Christian leaders. Note the frequent references to "prayer" in Acts (see 1:14,24; 2:42; 4:24–31; 6:4,6; 9:40; 10:2,4,9,31; 11:5; 12:5; 13:3; 14:23; 16:25; 22:17; 28:8).

6:6 LAID *THEIR* HANDS ON THEM. In the N.T. the laying on of hands was used in five ways: (1) in connection with miracles of healing (28:8; Mat. 9:18; Mark 5:23; 6:5); (2) in blessing others (Mat. 19:13,15); (3) in connection with the baptism in the Spirit (8:17,19; 19:6); (4) in commissioning for a specific work (v. 6; 13:3); and (5) in imparting spiritual gifts by the elders (1 Tim. 4:14). As one of the means by which God mediates gifts and blessings to others, laying on of hands became a foundational doctrine in the early church (Heb. 6:2). It must not be disassociated from prayer, for prayer indicates that the gifts of grace, healing, or baptism in the Holy Spirit are from God, not from the person who is laying on the hands.

Consecrating or ordaining the seven men here

tles: and [x]when they had prayed, [y]they laid *their* hands on them.

7 And [z]the word of God increased; and the number of the disciples multiplied in Jerusalem greatly; and a great company [a]of the priests were obedient to the faith.

Stephen full of grace and power

acts 1:27-8

8 And Stephen, full of faith and power, did great wonders and miracles among the people.

9 ¶ Then there arose certain of the synagogue, which is called *the synagogue* of the Libertines, and Cyrenians, and Alexandrians, and of them of Cilicia and of Asia, disputing with Stephen.

10 And [b]they were not able to resist the wisdom and the spirit by which he spake.

11 [c]Then they suborned men, which said, We have heard him speak blasphemous words against Moses, and *against* God.

The arrest of Stephen

12 And they stirred up the people, and the elders, and the scribes, and came upon *him*, and caught him, and brought *him* to the council,

13 And set up false witnesses, which said, This man ceaseth not to speak blasphemous words against this holy place, and the law:

14 [d]For we have heard him say, that this Jesus of Nazareth shall [e]destroy this place, and shall change the [n]customs which Moses delivered us.

15 And all that sat in the council, looking stedfastly on him, saw his face as it had been the face of an angel.

6:6 [x]ch. 1:24 [y]ch. 8:17 & 9:17 & 13:3 1 Tim. 4:14 & 5:22 2 Tim. 1:6
6:7 [z]ch. 12:24 & 19:20 Col. 1:6 [a]John 12:42
6:10 [b]Luke 21:15 ch. 5:39 See Ex. 4:12 Is. 54:17
6:11 [c]1 Ki. 21:10,13 Mat. 26:59,60
6:14 [d]ch. 25:8 [e]Dan. 9:26
7:2 [f]ch. 22:1
7:3 [g]Gen. 12:1
7:4 [h]Gen. 11:31 & 12:4,5
7:5 [i]Gen. 12:7 & 13:15 & 15:3,18 & 17:8 & 26:3
7:6 [j]Gen. 15:13,16 [k]Ex. 12:40 Gal. 3:17
7:7 [l]Ex. 3:12
7:8 [m]Gen. 17:9-11 [n]Gen. 21:2-4 [o]Gen. 25:26 [p]Gen. 29:31 & 30:5 & 35:18,23
7:9 [q]Gen. 37:4,11,28 Ps. 105:17 [r]Gen. 39:2,21,23

The defence of Stephen

7 THEN SAID the high priest, Are these things so?

2 And he said, [f]Men, brethren, and fathers, hearken; The God of glory appeared unto our father Abraham, when he was in Mesopotamia, before he dwelt in Charran,

3 And said unto him, [g]Get thee out of thy country, and from thy kindred, and come into the land which I shall show thee.

4 Then [h]came he out of the land of the Chaldaeans, and dwelt in Charran: and from thence, when his father was dead, he removed him into this land, wherein ye now dwell.

5 And he gave him none inheritance in it, no, not *so much as* to set his foot on: [i]yet he promised that he would give it to him for a possession, and to his seed after him, when *as yet* he had no child.

6 And God spake on this wise, [j]That his seed should sojourn in a strange land; and that they should bring them into bondage, and entreat *them* evil [k]four hundred years.

7 And the nation to whom they shall be in bondage will I judge, said God: and after that shall they come forth, and [l]serve me in this place.

8 [m]And he gave him the covenant of circumcision: [n]and so *Abraham* begat Isaac, and circumcised him the eighth day; [o]and Isaac *begat* Jacob; and [p]Jacob *begat* the twelve patriarchs.

9 [q]And the patriarchs, moved with envy, sold Joseph into Egypt: [r]but God was with him,

10 And delivered him out of all his

[n] Or, *rites*

meant primarily two things. (1) It was a public witness by the church that these seven men had a history of perseverance in godliness and faithfulness to the Holy Spirit's leading (cf. 1 Tim. 3:1–10). (2) It was an act consecrating the men to the work of God and a testimony of their willingness to accept the responsibility of God's call.

6:8 STEPHEN . . . FAITH AND POWER. The Holy Spirit empowered Stephen to perform "great wonders and miracles among the people" and gave him great wisdom to preach the gospel in such a way that his opponents could not refute his arguments (v. 10; cf. Ex. 4:15; Luke 21:15).

7:1–53 MEN, BRETHREN, AND FATHERS, HEARKEN. Stephen's speech before the Sanhedrin is a defense of the faith as preached by Christ and the apostles. He is the forerunner of all who defend the Biblical faith against those who oppose or distort its teaching, and he is the first to die for that reason. Jesus vindicates Stephen's action by standing in honor of him before His Father in heaven (v. 55, note). Stephen's love of the truth and his willingness to give his life to safeguard that truth contrast sharply with those who show little concern to "contend for the faith once delivered unto the saints" (Jude 3) and who, in the name of love, peace, and tolerance, feel no need or desire to oppose false teachers and those who distort the pure gospel for which Christ died (see Gal. 1:9, note; see article on OVERSEERS AND THEIR DUTIES, p. 1706).

afflictions, [s]and gave him favour and wisdom in the sight of Pharaoh king of Egypt; and he made him governor over Egypt and all his house.

11 [t]Now there came a dearth over all the land of Egypt and Chanaan, and great affliction: and our fathers found no sustenance.

12 [u]But when Jacob heard that there was corn in Egypt, he sent out our fathers first.

13 [v]And at the second *time* Joseph was made known to his brethren; and Joseph's kindred was made known unto Pharaoh.

14 [w]Then sent Joseph, and called his father Jacob to *him,* and [x]all his kindred, threescore and fifteen souls.

15 [y]So Jacob went down into Egypt, [z]and died, he, and our fathers,

16 And [a]were carried over into Sychem, and laid in [b]the sepulchre that Abraham bought for a sum of money of the sons of Emmor *the father* of Sychem.

17 But when [c]the time of the promise drew nigh, which God had sworn to Abraham, [d]the people grew and multiplied in Egypt,

18 Till another king arose, which knew not Joseph.

19 The same dealt subtly with our kindred, and evil entreated our fathers, [e]so that they cast out their young children, to the end they might not live.

20 [f]In which time Moses was born, and [g]was [o]exceeding fair, and nourished up in his father's house three months:

21 And [h]when he was cast out, Pharaoh's daughter took him up, and nourished him for her own son.

22 And Moses was learned in all the wisdom of the Egyptians, and was [i]mighty in words and in deeds.

23 [j]And when he was full forty years old, it came into his heart to visit his brethren the children of Israel.

24 And seeing one *of them* suffer wrong, he defended *him,* and avenged him that was oppressed, and smote the Egyptian:

25 [p]For he supposed his brethren would have understood how that God by his hand would deliver them: but they understood not.

26 And the next day he showed himself unto them as they strove, and would have set them at one again, saying, Sirs, ye are brethren; why do ye wrong one to another?

27 But he that did his neighbour wrong thrust him away, saying, [k]Who made thee a ruler and a judge over us?

28 Wilt thou kill me, as thou diddest the Egyptian yesterday?

29 [l]Then fled Moses at this saying, and was a stranger in the land of Madian, where he begat two sons.

30 [m]And when forty years were expired, there appeared to him in the wilderness of mount Sina an angel of the Lord in a flame of fire in a bush.

31 When Moses saw *it,* he wondered at the sight: and as he drew near to behold *it,* the voice of the Lord came unto him,

32 *Saying,* [n]I *am* the God of thy fathers, the God of Abraham, and the God of Isaac, and the God of Jacob. Then Moses trembled, and durst not behold.

33 [o]Then said the Lord to him, Put off thy shoes from thy feet: for the place where thou standest is holy ground.

34 [p]I have seen, I have seen the affliction of my people which is in Egypt, and I have heard their groaning, and am come down to deliver them. And now come, I will send thee into Egypt.

35 This Moses whom they refused, saying, Who made thee a ruler and a judge? the same did God send *to be* a ruler and a deliverer [q]by the hand of the angel which appeared to him in the bush.

36 [r]He brought them out, after that he had [s]shown wonders and signs in the land of Egypt, [t]and in the Red sea, [u]and in the wilderness forty years.

37 ¶ This is that Moses, which said unto the children of Israel, [v]A prophet shall the Lord your God raise up unto you of your brethren, [q]like unto me; [w]him shall ye hear.

38 [x]This is he, that was in the church in the wilderness with [y]the an-

7:10 [s]Gen. 41:37 & 42:6 **7:11** [t]Gen. 41:54 **7:12** [u]Gen. 42:1 **7:13** [v]Gen. 45:4,16 **7:14** [w]Gen. 45:9,27 [x]Gen. 46:27 Deut. 10:22 **7:15** [y]Gen. 46:5 [z]Gen. 49:33 Ex. 1:6 **7:16** [a]Ex. 13:19 Josh. 24:32 [b]Gen. 23:16 & 33:19 **7:17** [c]ver. 6 Gen. 15:13 [d]Ex. 1:7-9 Ps. 105:24,25 **7:19** [e]Ex. 1:22 **7:20** [f]Ex. 2:2 [g]Heb. 11:23 **7:21** [h]Ex. 2:3-10 **7:22** [i]Luke 24:19 **7:23** [j]Ex. 2:11,12 **7:27** [k]See Luke 12:14 ch. 4:7 **7:29** [l]Ex. 2:15,22 & 4:20 & 18:3,4 **7:30** [m]Ex. 3:2 **7:32** [n]Mat. 22:32 Heb. 11:16 **7:33** [o]Ex. 3:5 Josh. 5:15 **7:34** [p]Ex. 3:7 **7:35** [q]Ex. 14:19 Num. 20:16 **7:36** [r]Ex. 12:41 & 33:1 [s]Ex. 7 & 8 & 9 & 10 Ps. 105:27 [t]Ex. 14:21 [u]Ex. 16:1 **7:37** [v]Deut. 18:15 [w]Mat. 17:5 **7:38** [x]Ex. 19:3 [y]Is. 63:9 Gal. 3:19 Heb. 2:2

[o] Or, *fair to God* [p] Or, *Now* [q] Or, *as myself*

7:38 THE CHURCH IN THE WILDERNESS. "The church in the wilderness" refers to Israel as the people of God. In Hebrew the word translated "church" is *qahal* and is rendered in the Septuagint (Greek translation of the O.T.) as *ekklēsia* (i.e., "assembly" or "church"). (1) Just as Moses led the

gel which spake to him in the mount
Sina, and *with* our fathers: [z]who re-
ceived the lively [a]oracles to give
unto us:
39 To whom our fathers would not
obey, but thrust *him* from them, and in
their hearts turned back again into
Egypt,
40 [b]Saying unto Aaron, Make us
gods to go before us: for *as for* this Mo-
ses, which brought us out of the land
of Egypt, we wot not what is become of
him.
41 [c]And they made a calf in those
days, and offered sacrifice unto the
idol, and rejoiced in the works of their
own hands.
42 Then [d]God turned, and gave
them up to worship [e]the host of heav-
en; as it is written in the book of the
prophets, [f]O ye house of Israel, have
ye offered to me slain beasts and sacri-
fices *by the space of* forty years in the
wilderness?
43 Yea, ye took up the tabernacle of
Moloch, and the star of your god Rem-
phan, figures which ye made to wor-
ship them: and I will carry you away
beyond Babylon.

7:38 [z]Ex. 21:1 Deut. 5:27 John 1:17 [a]Rom. 3:2
7:40 [b]Ex. 32:1
7:41 [c]Deut. 9:16 Ps. 106:19
7:42 [d]Ps. 81:12 2 Thes. 2:11 [e]Deut. 4:19 2 Ki. 21:3 [f]Amos 5:25
7:44 [g]Ex. 25:40 Heb. 8:5
7:45 [h]Josh. 3:14 [i]Neh. 9:24 Ps. 44:2
7:46 [j]2 Sam. 7:1 Ps. 89:19 [k]1 Chr. 22:7
7:47 [l]1 Ki. 8:20
7:48 [m]1 Ki. 8:27 2 Chr. 2:6
7:49 [n]Is. 66:1,2 Mat. 5:34
7:51 [o]Ex. 32:9 [p]Lev. 26:41 Deut. 10:16 Jer. 4:4

44 Our fathers had the tabernacle of
witness in the wilderness, as he had
appointed, [r]speaking unto Moses,
[g]that he should make it according to
the fashion that he had seen.
45 [h]Which also our fathers [s]that
came after brought in with Jesus into
the possession of the Gentiles, [i]whom
God drave out before the face of our
fathers, unto the days of David;
46 [j]Who found favour before God,
and [k]desired to find a tabernacle for
the God of Jacob.
47 [l]But Solomon built him an
house.
48 Howbeit [m]the most High
dwelleth not in temples made with
hands; as saith the prophet,
49 [n]Heaven *is* my throne, and
earth *is* my footstool: what house will
ye build me? saith the Lord: or what *is*
the place of my rest?
50 Hath not my hand made all these
things?
51 ¶ Ye [o]stiffnecked and [p]uncir-
cumcised in heart and ears, ye do al-

[r] Or, *who spake* [s] Or, *having received*

church of the O.T., Christ leads the church of the N.T. The N.T. church, designated "Abraham's seed" (Gal. 3:29; cf. Rom. 4:11–18) and the "Israel of God" (Gal. 6:16), stands in continuity with the church of the O.T. (2) Like the O.T. church, the church of the N.T. is "in the wilderness," i.e., it is a pilgrim church, far from the promised land (Heb. 11:6–16). For this reason we must never become too comfortable with life here on this earth.

7:42 GOD ... GAVE THEM UP. Stephen's words reflect a principle well established in Scripture and redemptive history. Those who persist in repudiating God are not only given up by God, but are also delivered over to the influence of evil, Satan, and immorality (cf. Rom. 1:24,28). Contrary to popular teaching, God does not continue to show love and forgiveness without any condition on our part. He forgives and communicates His love only to those who turn their hearts toward Him in sincere repentance and true obedience. For those who harden their hearts, resist the Holy Spirit, and refuse to accept God's salvation, there remains only His wrath (Rom. 2:4–6,8).

7:44 ACCORDING TO THE FASHION. God has always had a divine pattern to be followed by His people. (1) God had a pattern for Moses which served as the standard under the old covenant. (a) In Ex. 12, God gave Moses specific instructions for the original Passover in Egypt, which became a pattern for all subsequent generations of Israelites to follow. (b) In Ex. 20, God gave Moses the Ten Commandments as the pattern and moral standard for all subsequent generations. (c) In Ex. 25, God instructed Moses to erect a tabernacle in the midst of the camp of Israel as a copy and shadow of heavenly things and the redemption which God planned to accomplish in the Lord Jesus Christ on earth. Moses carefully made the tabernacle and all its furnishings "according to the pattern" which God had fashioned in wisdom (Ex. 25:9,40; cf. Heb. 8:1–5).

(2) Just as surely as God had a pattern for the tabernacle under the old covenant, He has a pattern for His church under the new. The N.T. apostles did not arbitrarily or haphazardly decide how the church was to be fashioned. It was the Father and the Son, through what the Holy Spirit recorded in the Gospels, Acts, the epistles, and the letters to the seven churches (Rev. 2–3), who established the apostolic pattern for the church.

(3) Tragically, after the apostolic age the church began to depart from divine revelation and to modify God's heavenly pattern by accommodating itself culturally and organizationally according to human, earthly ideas. This has resulted in a proliferation of man-made patterns for the church.

(4) If the church of Jesus Christ is to experience again the full plan, power, favor, and presence of God, she must turn from her own ways and once again embrace the N.T. apostolic pattern as God's timeless standard for His church.

7:51 ALWAYS RESIST THE HOLY GHOST. The history of Israel is the story of a people who repeatedly refused to obey their God and His revealed Word. Instead of submitting to the restraints of His law, their hearts turned toward the

ways resist the Holy Ghost: as your fathers *did,* so *do* ye.

52 [q]Which of the prophets have not your fathers persecuted? and they have slain them which showed before of the coming of [r]the Just One; of whom ye have been now the betrayers and murderers:

53 [s]Who have received the law by the disposition of angels, and have not kept *it.*

The stoning of Stephen

54 ¶ [t]When they heard these things, they were cut to the heart, and they gnashed on him with *their* teeth.

Acts 8:14-17

55 But he, [u]being full of the Holy Ghost, looked up stedfastly into heaven, and saw the glory of God, and Jesus standing on the right hand of God,

56 And said, Behold, [v]I see the heavens opened, and the [w]Son of man standing on the right hand of God.

57 Then they cried out with a loud voice, and stopped their ears, and ran upon him with one accord,

58 And [x]cast *him* out of the city, [y]and stoned *him:* and [z]the witnesses laid down their clothes at a young man's feet, whose name was Saul.

7:52 [q]2 Chr. 36:16 Mat. 21:35 1 Thes. 2:15 [r]ch. 3:14
7:53 [s]Ex. 20:1 Gal. 3:19
7:54 [t]ch. 5:33
7:55 [u]ch. 6:5
7:56 [v]Mat. 3:16 [w]Dan. 7:13
7:58 [x]Luke 4:29 Heb. 13:12 [y]Lev. 24:16 [z]Deut. 13:9
7:59 [a]ch. 9:14 [b]Ps. 31:5 Luke 23:46
7:60 [c]ch. 9:40 [d]Mat. 5:44 Luke 6:28
8:1 [e]ch. 7:58 [f]ch. 11:19
8:2 [g]Gen. 23:2 & 50:10 2 Sam. 3:31
8:3 [h]ch. 7:58 1 Cor. 15:9 Gal. 1:13 Phil. 3:6 1 Tim. 1:13
8:4 [i]Mat. 10:23
8:5 [j]ch. 6:5

59 And they stoned Stephen, [a]calling upon *God,* and saying, Lord Jesus, [b]receive my spirit.

60 And he [c]kneeled down, and cried with a loud voice, [d]Lord, lay not this sin to their charge. And when he had said this, he fell asleep.

The persecution of the church

8 AND [e]SAUL was consenting unto his death. And at that time there was a great persecution against the church which was at Jerusalem; and [f]they were all scattered abroad throughout the regions of Judaea and Samaria, except the apostles.

2 And devout men carried Stephen *to his burial,* and [g]made great lamentation over him.

3 As for Saul, [h]he made havoc of the church, entering into every house, and haling men and women committed *them* to prison.

Philip preaches at Samaria

4 Therefore [i]they that were scattered abroad went every where preaching the word. Acts 8:26-40

5 Then [j]Philip went down to the

---

ways and lifestyle of the ungodly nations around them. They killed the prophets who called them to repentance and who prophesied about the coming of Christ (vv. 52–53). This is what resisting the Holy Spirit means.

Likewise, the Israel of Christ under the new covenant must be aware of its tendency to live as did the Israel of God under the old. Christ's churches can turn from Him and His Word and refuse to heed the voice of the Holy Spirit. When this happens, they too will incur judgment from God: the kingdom will be taken from them (see Rom. 11:20–22; Rev. 2–3).

7:55 SAW . . . JESUS STANDING. The Bible normally speaks of Jesus as seated at the right hand of God (2:34; Mark 14:62; Luke 22:69; Col. 3:1). But here Jesus stood up in order to welcome His first martyr to Himself. Stephen had confessed Christ before men and defended the faith. Now Christ, in honor of His servant, confesses him before His heavenly Father. For all faithful believers near death, the Savior stands ready to receive you as your intercessor and advocate (cf. Mark 8:38; Luke 12:8; Rom. 8:34; 1 John 2:1).

8:1 A GREAT PERSECUTION. Saul seems to have been the leader of the church's first widespread persecution (vv. 1–3; 9:1); it was intense and severe. Men and women were put in prison (v. 3) and beaten (22:19), and many were put to death (22:20; 26:10–11). Yet God used this persecution to start the great missionary work of the church (v. 4).

8:5–24 PHILIP WENT DOWN TO . . . SAMARIA. Notice the sequence of events in this record of the outpouring of the Holy Spirit upon the Samaritan believers. (1) Philip preached the gospel of the kingdom and God confirmed the Word with signs and wonders (vv. 5–7).

(2) Many Samaritans received the Word of God (v. 14), believed on Jesus (v. 12), were healed and delivered from unclean spirits (v. 7), and were baptized in water (vv. 12–13). Thus, they experienced salvation, the regenerative work of the Holy Spirit, and the power of the kingdom of God (see v. 12, note).

(3) The Holy Spirit, however, had not "fallen upon" any of them after their conversion to Christ and water baptism (v. 16).

(4) After some days following the Samaritans' conversion, Peter and John came to Samaria and prayed that the Holy Spirit might fall upon the new believers (vv. 14–15). There was a definite interval between their conversion to Christ and their receiving the baptism in the Holy Spirit (vv. 16–17; cf. 2:4). The Samaritans' reception of the Holy Spirit, in other words, follows the pattern of the disciples' experience at Pentecost (see articles on THE REGENERATION OF THE DISCIPLES, p. 1638, and BAPTISM IN THE HOLY SPIRIT, p. 1652).

(5) Some external manifestation (undoubtedly tongues and prophecy) must have accompanied receiving the Holy Spirit (see v. 18, note).

city of Samaria, and preached Christ unto them.

6 And the people with one accord gave heed unto those things which Philip spake, hearing and seeing the miracles which he did.

7 For [k]unclean spirits, crying with loud voice, came out of many that were possessed *with them:* and many taken with palsies, and that were lame, were healed.

8 And there was great joy in that city.

Conversion of Simon the sorcerer

9 But there was a certain man, called Simon, which beforetime in the same city [l]used sorcery, and bewitched the people of Samaria, [m]giving out that himself was some great one:

10 To whom they all gave heed, from the least to the greatest, saying, This man is the great power of God.

11 And to him they had regard, because that of long time he had bewitched them with sorceries.

8:7 [k]Mark 16:17
8:9 [l]ch. 13:6 [m]ch. 5:36
8:12 [n]ch. 1:3
8:15 [o]ch. 2:38
8:16 [p]ch. 19:2 [q]Mat. 28:19 ch. 2:38 [r]ch. 10:48 & 19:5
8:17 [s]ch. 6:6 & 19:6 Heb. 6:2

Acts 19:11-12

Samaritans believe and are baptized

12 But when they believed Philip preaching the things [n]concerning the kingdom of God, and the name of Jesus Christ, they were baptized, both men and women.

13 Then Simon himself believed also: and when he was baptized, he continued with Philip, and wondered, beholding the [t]miracles and signs which were done.

Samaritans receive the Holy Spirit

14 Now when the apostles which were at Jerusalem heard that Samaria had received the word of God, they sent unto them Peter and John:

15 Who, when they were come down, prayed for them, [o]that they might receive the Holy Ghost:

16 (For [p]as yet he was fallen upon none of them: only [q]they were baptized in [r]the name of the Lord Jesus.)

17 Then [s]laid they *their* hands on

[t] Gk. *signs and great miracles*

8:6 THE MIRACLES WHICH HE DID. Christ's promise to use signs and miracles to confirm the preaching of the Word was not limited to the apostles (Mark 16:15–16; see article on SIGNS OF BELIEVERS, p. 1516). He promises that their converts ("them that believe" their word) will perform miracles in the name of Jesus, such as casting out demons (Mark 16:17) and healing the sick (Mark 16:18). This is exactly what Philip did.

8:12 THEY BELIEVED ... THE NAME OF JESUS CHRIST. The Samaritans fully met the conditions for salvation and were Christians before the Spirit came upon them. (1) They "believed" and were "baptized." Two facts make it clear that the faith of the Samaritans was genuine saving faith. (a) Both Philip (v. 12) and the apostles (v. 14) considered their faith to be valid. (b) The Samaritans publicly committed themselves to Christ by water baptism. Scripture affirms that "he that believeth and is baptized shall be saved" (Mark 16:16). Thus, they were regenerated and indwelt by the Holy Spirit (Rom. 8:9).

(2) Their receiving the Holy Spirit several days later (v. 17) was not for salvation. It was rather a receiving of the Holy Spirit as the disciples did at Pentecost, i.e., to equip them with power for service and witness (1:8; 2:4). Luke uses the term "receive the Spirit" primarily in an empowering sense (1:8; 2:38; 8:17; 10:47; 19:2), not in the sense of new birth or regeneration (see articles on REGENERATION, p. 1597, THE REGENERATION OF THE DISCIPLES, p. 1638, and BAPTISM IN THE HOLY SPIRIT, p. 1652).

(3) Some have taught that the faith of the Samaritans was not a saving and regenerating faith. However, it is unreasonable to believe that Philip, a man full of faith, wisdom, and the Holy Spirit (6:3–5), would baptize, heal, and cast demons out of people whose faith he considered was not genuine nor saving.

8:16 HE WAS FALLEN UPON NONE OF THEM. The Spirit had not yet fallen upon any of them in the same way He descended on the believers on the day of Pentecost (2:4). He had not yet come upon them as the Father had promised (1:4) and as Christ had foretold when He said, "Ye shall be baptized with the Holy Ghost" (1:5). Evidently they had not demonstrated the expected spiritual manifestations, especially divinely inspired utterances (see vv. 5–24, note; v. 18, note).

8:17 THEY RECEIVED THE HOLY GHOST. Through the laying on of the apostles' hands, the Samaritans received the Holy Spirit in the same sense as the baptism in the Spirit that occurred at Pentecost (1:8; 2:4).

The Samaritans' "two-stage" experience—i.e., first believing, and then afterwards being filled with the Spirit—shows that the "two-stage" experience of the believers at Pentecost was not abnormal. The experiences of both Paul in 9:5–17 and the Ephesian disciples in 19:1–6 were the same as the Samaritans. They accepted Christ as Lord and afterwards were filled with the Spirit. There need not be a long time lapse, however, between saving faith and baptism in the Spirit, as demonstrated by the Gentiles at Caesarea (ch. 10).

Acts 9:17 them, and they received the Holy Ghost.

Simon rebuked by Peter

18 And when Simon saw that through laying on of the apostles' hands the Holy Ghost was given, he offered them money,

19 Saying, Give me also this power, that on whomsoever I lay hands, he may receive the Holy Ghost.

20 But Peter said unto him, Thy money perish with thee, because [t]thou hast thought that [u]the gift of God may be purchased with money.

21 Thou hast neither part nor lot in this matter: for thy heart is not right in the sight of God.

22 Repent therefore of this thy wickedness, and pray God, [v]if perhaps the thought of thine heart may be forgiven thee.

23 For I perceive that thou art in [w]the gall of bitterness, and *in* the bond of iniquity.

24 Then answered Simon, and said, [x]Pray ye to the Lord for me, that none of these things which ye have spoken come upon me.

25 And they, when they had testified and preached the word of the Lord, returned to Jerusalem, and preached the gospel in many villages of the Samaritans.

Conversion of the Ethiopian

26 And the angel of the Lord spake unto Philip, saying, Arise, and go toward the south unto the way that goeth down from Jerusalem unto Gaza, which is desert.

27 And he arose and went: and, behold, [y]a man of Ethiopia, an eunuch of great authority under Candace queen of the Ethiopians, who had the charge of all her treasure, and [z]had come to Jerusalem for to worship,

28 Was returning, and sitting in his chariot read Esaias the prophet.

29 Then the Spirit said unto Philip, Go near, and join thyself to this chariot.

30 And Philip ran thither to *him*, and heard him read the prophet Esaias, and said, Understandest thou what thou readest?

31 And he said, How can I, except some man should guide me? And he desired Philip that he would come up and sit with him.

32 The place of the scripture which he read was this, [a]He was led as a sheep to the slaughter; and like a lamb dumb before his shearer, so opened he not his mouth:

33 In his humiliation his judgment was taken away: and who shall declare his generation? for his life is taken from the earth.

34 And the eunuch answered Philip, and said, I pray thee, of whom speaketh the prophet this? of himself, or of some other man?

35 Then Philip opened his mouth, [b]and began at the same scripture, and preached unto him Jesus.

8:20 [t]Mat. 10:8 See 2 Ki. 5:16 [u]ch. 2:38 & 10:45 & 11:17
8:22 [v]Dan. 4:27 2 Tim. 2:25
8:23 [w]Heb. 12:15
8:24 [x]Gen. 20:7,17 Ex. 8:8 Num. 21:7 1 Ki. 13:6 Job 42:8 Jas. 5:16
8:27 [y]Zeph. 3:10 [z]John 12:20
8:32 [a]Is. 53:7,8
8:35 [b]Luke 24:27 ch. 18:28

8:18 WHEN SIMON SAW. The Spirit's falling upon the Samaritans was accompanied by observable external manifestations apparent even to Simon the sorcerer. It is reasonable to conclude that the observable manifestations were like those which occurred after His coming upon the earliest disciples at Pentecost, i.e., speaking with other tongues (see 2:4; 10:45–46; 11:15, note; 19:6; see article on SPEAKING IN TONGUES, p. 1656). This manifestation gave both the Samaritans and the apostles a verifiable sign that the Holy Spirit had fallen upon the new believers.

8:21 THY HEART IS NOT RIGHT. The baptism in the Holy Spirit throughout the book of Acts occurs only in the context of committed discipleship to Jesus Christ. (1) Simon, who sought the power and gift of the Holy Spirit as well as the authority to impart the gift (v. 19), was rejected by God because he was still wicked, "in the bond of iniquity" (vv. 22–23), and not right in his heart with God. The genuine gift of the Holy Spirit will be poured out only on the one "that feareth him, and worketh righteousness" (10:35, cf. 10:44–48; see also 5:32).

(2) Before and after the day of Pentecost, the followers of Christ were devoted to the risen Lord (1:2–14; 2:32) and engaged in continual prayer (1:14; 6:4). They lived lives of separation from sin and the world (2:38–40) and obeyed the apostles' teaching (2:42; 6:4). Repeated or new outpourings of the Spirit were given only to believers who had turned from their sins and wicked ways to lives of obedience to Jesus Christ (cf. 2:42; 3:1,19,22–26; 4:8,19–35; 5:29–32; 6:4; 8:14–21; 9:1–19; 10:34–47; 19:1–6; 24:16). Walking by the Spirit and being led by Him are always conditions of being filled with the Spirit (see Gal. 5:16–25; Eph. 5:18).

(3) Any supernatural experience thought to be the baptism in the Spirit that occurs in one who continues to follow the sinful ways of the flesh is not of Christ (cf. 1 John 4:1–6). It is rather a counterfeit baptism in the Spirit and may be accompanied by demonic gifts and powers (Mat. 7:21–23; 2 Thes. 2:7–10; see article on TESTING FOR GENUINE BAPTISM IN THE SPIRIT, p. 1682).

36 And as they went on *their* way,
they came unto a certain water: and
the eunuch said, See, *here is* water;
[c]what doth hinder me to be baptized?
37 And Philip said, [d]If thou believ-
est with all thine heart, thou mayest.
And he answered and said, [e]I believe
that Jesus Christ is the Son of God.
38 And he commanded the chariot
to stand still: and they went down both
into the water, both Philip and the eu-
nuch; and he baptized him.
39 And when they were come up out
of the water, [f]the Spirit of the Lord
caught away Philip, that the eunuch
saw him no more: and he went on his
way rejoicing.
40 But Philip was found at Azotus:
and passing through he preached in all
the cities, till he came to Caesarea.

cts 6:29- 2

Conversion of Saul

9:1–16pp — Acts 22:3–11; 26:9–18

9 AND [g]SAUL, yet breathing out
threatenings and slaughter
against the disciples of the Lord, went
unto the high priest,
2 And desired of him letters to Da-
mascus to the synagogues, that if he
found any [h]of[u] this way, whether
they were men or women, he might
bring them bound unto Jerusalem.
3 And [i]as he journeyed, he came
near Damascus: and suddenly there
shined round about him a light from
heaven:
4 And he fell to the earth, and heard
a voice saying unto him, Saul, Saul,
[j]why persecutest thou me?

8:36 [c]ch. 10:47
8:37 [d]Mat. 28:19 Mark 16:16 [e]Mat. 16:16 John 6:69 & 9:35,38 & 11:27 ch. 9:20 1 John 4:15 & 5:5,13
8:39 [f]1 Ki. 18:12 2 Ki. 2:16 Ezek. 3:12,14
9:1 [g]ch. 8:3 Gal. 1:13 1 Tim. 1:13
9:2 [h]ch. 19:9,23
9:3 [i]ch. 22:6 & 26:12 1 Cor. 15:8
9:4 [j]Mat. 25:40
9:6 [k]Luke 3:10 ch 2:37 & 16:30
9:7 [l]Dan. 10:7 See ch. 22:9 & 26:13
9:10 [m]ch. 22:12
9:11 [n]ch. 21:39 & 22:3
9:13 [o]ver. 1

5 And he said, Who art thou, Lord?
And the Lord said, I am Jesus whom
thou persecutest: *it is* hard for thee to
kick against the pricks.
6 And he trembling and astonished
said, Lord, [k]what wilt thou have me to
do? And the Lord *said* unto him, Arise,
and go into the city, and it shall be told
thee what thou must do.
7 And [l]the men which journeyed
with him stood speechless, hearing a
voice, but seeing no man.
8 And Saul arose from the earth;
and when his eyes were opened, he
saw no man: but they led him by the
hand, and brought *him* into Damascus.
9 And he was three days without
sight, and neither did eat nor drink.
10 ¶ And there was a certain disci-
ple at Damascus, [m]named Ananias;
and to him said the Lord in a vision,
Ananias. And he said, Behold, I *am
here,* Lord.
11 And the Lord *said* unto him,
Arise, and go into the street which is
called Straight, and inquire in the
house of Judas for *one* called Saul, [n]of
Tarsus: for, behold, he prayeth,
12 And hath seen in a vision a man
named Ananias coming in, and putting
his hand on him, that he might receive
his sight.
13 Then Ananias answered, Lord, I
have heard by many of this man, [o]how
much evil he hath done to thy saints at
Jerusalem:
14 And here he hath authority from

[u]Gk. *of the way*

9:3–19 THE CONVERSION OF PAUL. Verses 3–9 record the conversion of Paul outside the city of Damascus (cf. 22:3–16; 26:9–18). That his conversion occurs here rather than later at the house of Judas (v. 11) is clear from the following: (1) Paul obeys Christ's instruction (v. 6; 22:10; 26:15–19), commits himself to be a "minister and a witness" of the gospel (26:16) and a missionary to the Gentiles (26:17–19), and gives himself to prayer (v. 11). (2) Paul is called "brother Saul" by Ananias (v. 17). Ananias already assumes Paul is a believer who has experienced the new birth (see John 3:3–6), is committed to Christ and God's mission, and needs no more than to be baptized, have his sight restored, and be filled with the Holy Spirit (vv. 17–18; see 9:17, note).

9:11 FOR, BEHOLD, HE PRAYETH. After Paul encounters Jesus and accepts Him as Lord and Messiah, he prays and fasts for guidance with an attitude of deep commitment to God. Saving faith and the consequent new birth will always result in the believer seeking communion with his new Lord and Savior.

9:13 SAINTS. Believers in the N.T. are called "saints" (cf. 26:10; Rom. 1:7; 1 Cor. 1:2; Rev. 13:7; 19:8). (1) The basic idea of the term "saint" (Gk. *hagios*) is separation from sin and unto God. Saints, in other words, are "God's separated ones" or "God's holy ones." This implies being led and sanctified by the Holy Spirit (Rom. 8:14; 1 Cor. 6:11; 2 Thes. 2:13; 1 Pet. 1:2), turning one's back on the world to follow Jesus (John 17:15–17; see article on SANCTIFICATION, p. 1982). However, the term "saint" does not mean that the believer is already perfect or incapable of sin (cf. 1 John 2:1).

(2) Calling believers "saved sinners" is not N.T. practice. As the common Biblical term for all believers, "saint" emphasizes (a) the Scriptural expectation that all believers conform to God's way of righteousness (Eph. 5:3), and (b) the necessity that holiness be an internal reality for all who belong to Christ (1 Cor. 1:30).

the chief priests to bind all [p]that call on thy name.

15 But the Lord said unto him, Go thy way: for [q]he is a chosen vessel unto me, to bear my name before [r]the Gentiles, and [s]kings, and the children of Israel:

16 For [t]I will show him how great things he must suffer for my name's sake.

Saul filled with the Holy Spirit

9:17–19pp — Acts 22:12–16

17 [u]And Ananias went his way, and entered into the house; and [v]putting his hands on him said, Brother Saul, the Lord, *even* Jesus, that appeared unto thee in the way as thou camest, hath sent me, that thou mightest receive thy sight, and [w]be filled with the Holy Ghost.

Acts 10:44-47

18 And immediately there fell from his eyes as it had been scales: and he received sight forthwith, and arose, and was baptized.

19 And when he had received meat, he was strengthened. [x]Then was Saul certain days with the disciples which were at Damascus.

Paul preaches at Damascus

20 And straightway he preached Christ in the synagogues, that he is the Son of God.

21 But all that heard *him* were amazed, and said; [y]Is not this he that destroyed them which called on this name in Jerusalem, and came hither for

9:14 [p]ver. 21 ch. 7:59 1 Cor. 1:2 2 Tim. 2:22
9:15 [q]ch. 13:2 & 22:21 Rom. 1:1 1 Cor. 15:10 Gal. 1:15 Eph. 3:7,8 1 Tim. 2:7 2 Tim. 1:11 [r]Rom. 1:5 & 11:13 Gal. 2:7,8 [s]ch. 25:22,23 & 26:1
9:16 [t]ch. 20:23 & 21:11 2 Cor. 11:23
9:17 [u]ch. 22:12,13 [v]ch. 8:17 [w]ch. 2:4 & 4:31 & 8:17 & 13:52
9:19 [x]ch. 26:20
9:21 [y]ver. 1 ch. 8:3 Gal. 1:13,23
9:22 [z]ch. 18:28
9:23 [a]ch. 23:12 2 Cor. 11:26
9:24 [b]2 Cor. 11:32
9:25 [c]Josh. 2:15 1 Sam. 19:12
9:26 [d]ch. 22:17 Gal. 1:17,18
9:27 [e]ch. 4:36 & 13:2 [f]ver. 20,22
9:28 [g]Gal. 1:18

that intent, that he might bring them bound unto the chief priests?

22 But Saul increased the more in strength, [z]and confounded the Jews which dwelt at Damascus, proving that this is very Christ.

Paul escapes to Jerusalem

23 ¶ And after that many days were fulfilled, [a]the Jews took counsel to kill him:

24 [b]But their laying await was known of Saul. And they watched the gates day and night to kill him.

25 Then the disciples took him by night, and [c]let *him* down by the wall in a basket.

26 And [d]when Saul was come to Jerusalem, he assayed to join himself to the disciples: but they were all afraid of him, and believed not that he was a disciple.

27 [e]But Barnabas took him, and brought *him* to the apostles, and declared unto them how he had seen the Lord in the way, and that he had spoken to him, [f]and how he had preached boldly at Damascus in the name of Jesus.

28 And [g]he was with them coming in and going out at Jerusalem.

29 And he spake boldly in the name of the Lord Jesus, and disputed against the [h]Grecians: [i]but they went about to slay him.

30 *Which* when the brethren knew,

9:29 [h]ch. 6:1 & 11:20 [i]ver. 23; 2 Cor. 11:26

9:16 SUFFER FOR MY NAME'S SAKE. Paul's conversion and salvation meant not only a commission to preach the gospel but also a call to suffer for Christ. Paul is told from the beginning that he must undergo much suffering for the cause of Christ. In Christ's kingdom, suffering for His sake is a sign of God's highest favor (14:22; Mat. 5:11–12; Rom. 8:17; 2 Tim. 2:12) and the means to a fruitful ministry (John 12:24; 2 Cor. 1:3–6); it results in abundant reward in heaven (Mat. 5:12; 2 Tim. 2:12). Death must work in believers in order that God's life might flow from them to others (Rom. 8:17–18, 36–37; 2 Cor. 4:10–12). For additional passages on the sufferings of Paul, see 20:23; 2 Cor. 4:8–18; 6:3–10; 11:23–27; Gal. 6:17; 2 Tim. 1:11–12; see also 2 Cor. 1:4, note; 11:23, note.

9:17 BROTHER SAUL. See note on vv. 3–19.

9:17 FILLED WITH THE HOLY GHOST. Three days after Paul's conversion he is filled with the Holy Spirit. Paul's experience parallels that of the disciples' at Pentecost (see article on BAPTISM IN THE HOLY SPIRIT, p. 1652). First, he experiences the new birth and is saved (see 9:3–19, note); then he is "filled with the Holy Ghost."

Although Luke does not specifically say that Paul spoke in tongues when he received the Pentecostal gift of the Holy Spirit, it is reasonable to assume that he did. (1) The N.T. norm indicates that one filled with the Holy Spirit begins to speak in tongues (2:4; 10:45–46; 19:6; see 11:15, note). (2) Paul himself testifies that he frequently spoke in tongues: "I thank my God, I speak with tongues more than ye all" (1 Cor. 14:18).

9:18 HE . . . WAS BAPTIZED. Luke's primary concern is the actual baptism in the Spirit, rather than whether Paul spoke in tongues. Seeking the Spirit's fullness should be centered on the Holy Spirit Himself and not on any external manifestation. On the other hand, all believers who desire the fullness of the Holy Spirit should expect the spiritual manifestations of His coming (2:4, 17).

they brought him down to Caesarea, and sent him forth to Tarsus.

31 [j]Then had the churches rest throughout all Judaea and Galilee and Samaria, and were edified; and walking in the fear of the Lord, and in the comfort of the Holy Ghost, were multiplied.

Peter heals Aeneas

32 ¶ And it came to pass, as Peter passed [k]throughout all *quarters*, he came down also to the saints which dwelt at Lydda.

33 And there he found a certain man named Aeneas, which had kept his bed eight years, and was sick of the palsy.

34 And Peter said unto him, Aeneas, [l]Jesus Christ maketh thee whole: arise, and make thy bed. And he arose immediately.

35 And all that dwelt at Lydda and [m]Saron saw him, and [n]turned to the Lord.

Peter raises Tabitha from the dead

36 ¶ Now there was at Joppa a certain disciple named Tabitha, which by interpretation is called [v]Dorcas: this woman was full [o]of good works and almsdeeds which she did.

37 And it came to pass in those days, that she was sick, and died: whom when they had washed, they laid *her* in [p]an upper chamber.

38 And forasmuch as Lydda was nigh to Joppa, and the disciples had heard that Peter was there, they sent unto him two men, desiring *him* that he would not [w]delay to come to them.

39 Then Peter arose and went with them. When he was come, they brought him into the upper chamber: and all the widows stood by him weeping, and showing the coats and garments which Dorcas made, while she was with them.

40 But Peter [q]put them all forth, and [r]kneeled down, and prayed; and turning *him* to the body [s]said, Tabitha, arise. And she opened her eyes: and when she saw Peter, she sat up.

41 And he gave her *his* hand, and lifted her up, and when he had called the saints and widows, presented her alive.

42 And it was known throughout all Joppa; [t]and many believed in the Lord.

43 And it came to pass, that he tarried many days in Joppa with one [u]Simon a tanner.

Cornelius's vision

10 THERE WAS a certain man in Caesarea called Cornelius, a centurion of the band called the Italian *band,*

2 [v]*A* devout *man,* and one that [w]feared God with all his house, which gave much alms to the people, and prayed to God always.

3 [x]He saw in a vision evidently about the ninth hour of the day an angel of God coming in to him, and saying unto him, Cornelius.

4 And when he looked on him, he was afraid, and said, What is it, Lord? And he said unto him, Thy prayers and thine alms are come up for a memorial before God.

5 And now send men to Joppa, and call for *one* Simon, whose surname is Peter:

6 He lodgeth with one [y]Simon a tanner, whose house is by the sea side: [z]he shall tell thee what thou oughtest to do.

7 And when the angel which spake unto Cornelius was departed, he called

9:31 [j]See ch. 8:1
9:32 [k]ch. 8:14
9:34 [l]ch. 3:6,16 & 4:10
9:35 [m]1 Chr. 5:16 [n]ch. 11:21
9:36 [o]1 Tim. 2:10 Tit. 3:8
9:37 [p]ch. 1:13
9:40 [q]Mat. 9:25 [r]ch. 7:60 [s]Mark 5:41,42 John 11:43
9:42 [t]John 11:45
9:43 [u]ch. 10:6
10:2 [v]ver. 22 ch. 8:2 & 22:12 [w]ver. 35
10:3 [x]ver. 30 ch. 11:13
10:6 [y]ch. 9:43 [z]ch. 11:14

[v] Or, *Doe,* or, *Roe* [w] Or, *be grieved*

9:31 THE FEAR OF THE LORD. Luke emphasizes the formula "to fear God," both in his Gospel (see Luke 1:50; 18:2; 23:40) and in Acts. It is the God-fearers (i.e., Gentile adherents to the Jewish faith) that form the starting point for the Gentile mission in ch. 10 (10:2,22,35; 13:16,26). The fear of the Lord produces trust and obedience, as well as the avoidance of evil (Job 28:28; Ps. 111:10; Prov. 1:7); this response in turn results in "the comfort of the Holy Ghost." For more on this, see article on THE FEAR OF THE LORD, p. 282.

9:36 DORCAS . . . FULL OF GOOD WORKS. As God worked through Peter to heal (vv. 33–35) and to raise the dead (v. 40), He also worked through Dorcas with her deeds of kindness and love. Acts of love that help those in need are as much a manifestation of the Holy Spirit as are miracles, signs, and wonders. Paul emphasized this truth in 1 Cor. 13 (cf. 1 Pet. 4:10–11).

10:4 THY PRAYERS . . . A MEMORIAL BEFORE GOD. God considers our prayers a sacrifice ascending to Him, reminding Him of our perseverance in calling upon Him in faith and devotion (see Ps. 141:2; Heb. 13:15–16).

two of his household servants, and a
devout soldier of them that waited on
him continually;
8 And when he had declared all
these things unto them, he sent them to
Joppa.

Peter's vision

10:9–32Ref — Acts 11:5–14

9 ¶ On the morrow, as they went on
their journey, and drew nigh unto the
city, [a]Peter went up upon the
housetop to pray about the sixth hour:
10 And he became very hungry, and
would have eaten: but while they made
ready, he fell into a trance,
11 And [b]saw heaven opened, and a
certain vessel descending unto him, as
it had been a great sheet knit at the
four corners, and let down to the earth:
12 Wherein were all manner of four-
footed beasts of the earth, and wild
beasts, and creeping things, and fowls
of the air.
13 And there came a voice to him,
Rise, Peter; kill, and eat.
14 But Peter said, Not so, Lord;
[c]for I have never eaten any thing that
is common or unclean.
15 And the voice *spake* unto him
again the second time, [d]What God
hath cleansed, *that* call not thou com-
mon.
16 This was done thrice: and the
vessel was received up again into
heaven.

Cornelius sends for Peter

17 Now while Peter doubted in him-
self what this vision which he had seen
should mean, behold, the men which
were sent from Cornelius had made in-
quiry for Simon's house, and stood be-
fore the gate,
18 And called, and asked whether
Simon, which was surnamed Peter,
were lodged there.
19 ¶ While Peter thought on the vi-
sion, [e]the Spirit said unto him, Be-
hold, three men seek thee.
20 [f]Arise therefore, and get thee
down, and go with them, doubting
nothing: for I have sent them.
21 Then Peter went down to the
men which were sent unto him from
Cornelius; and said, Behold, I am he
whom ye seek: what *is* the cause
wherefore ye are come?
22 And they said, Cornelius the cen-
turion, a just man, and one that feareth
God, and [g]of good report among all
the nation of the Jews, was warned

10:9 [a]ch. 11:5 **10:11** [b]ch. 7:56 Rev. 19:11 **10:14** [c]Lev. 11:4 & 20:25 Deut. 14:3,7 Ezek. 4:14 **10:15** [d]ver. 28 Mat. 15:11 Rom. 14:14,17,20 1 Cor. 10:25 1 Tim. 4:4 Tit. 1:15 **10:19** [e]ch. 11:12 **10:20** [f]ch. 15:7 **10:22** [g]ch. 22:12

10:9 PETER WENT UP UPON THE HOUSETOP TO PRAY. The Holy Spirit, the author of the Scriptures, has revealed that the N.T. Christians were a people devoted to much prayer. They understood that the kingdom of God could not be manifested in its full power with only a few minutes of prayer a day (1:14; 2:42; 3:1; 6:4; Eph. 6:18; Col. 4:2). (1) The pious Jew prayed two or three times a day (cf. Ps. 55:17; Dan. 6:10). It was the custom of the followers of Christ, especially the apostles (6:4), to pray with the same devotion. Peter and John went to the temple to observe "the hour of prayer" (3:1), while Luke and Paul did the same (16:16). Peter prayed regularly at noon or "the sixth hour"; God rewarded Cornelius for his faithfulness in keeping his hours of prayer (10:30ff).

(2) The Scriptures urge believers to continue steadfastly in prayer (Rom. 12:12), pray always (Luke 18:1), pray without ceasing (1 Thes. 5:17), pray everywhere (1 Tim. 2:8), pray always with all prayer (Eph. 6:18), persevere in prayer (Col. 4:2), and pray fervently (Jas. 5:16). These exhortations indicate there can be no real kingdom power in our battle against sin, Satan, and the world, or victory in our attempt to win the lost, without much daily prayer (see article on EFFECTIVE PRAYING, p. 540).

(3) Would it not be pleasing to God in the light of the Lord's plea that His disciples watch and pray at least "one hour" (Mat. 26:38–41), and in the light of the urgency of the end times in which we live, for every believer to commit at least one hour a day to prayer and the study of God's Word for the advancement of His kingdom on the earth and all that this involves for us (Mat. 6:10,33)?

(4) One hour of prayer might include the following: (a) praise, (b) singing to the Lord, (c) thanksgiving, (d) waiting on God, (e) reading the Word, (f) listening to the Holy Spirit, (g) praying the very words of Scripture, (h) confessing failings, (i) intercession for others, (j) petition for one's own needs, and (k) praying in tongues.

10:19 THE SPIRIT SAID UNTO HIM. The Holy Spirit desires the salvation of all people (Mat. 28:19; 2 Pet. 3:9). Since the apostles received the Spirit, they too desired the salvation of all people. Intellectually, however, they did not understand that salvation was no longer restricted to Israel, but was now for all nations (vv. 34–35). It was the Holy Spirit that brought the church to a broader vision. In Acts He is the power of the mission enterprise, directing the church into new areas of witness (8:29,39; 10:19; 11:11–12; 13:2,4; 16:6; 19:21). The outpouring of the Spirit and the compulsion to mission always belong together (cf. 1:8). Even today, many believers desire the salvation of those in their own community, yet have not understood fully the Holy Spirit's purpose for world missions (see Mat. 28:19, note; Luke 24:47, note).

from God by an holy angel to send for thee into his house, and to hear words of thee.

23 Then called he them in, and lodged *them*. And on the morrow Peter went away with them, [h]and certain brethren from Joppa accompanied him.

Peter visits Cornelius

24 And the morrow after they entered into Caesarea. And Cornelius waited for them, and had called together his kinsmen and near friends.

25 And as Peter was coming in, Cornelius met him, and fell down at his feet, and worshipped *him*.

26 But Peter took him up, saying, [i]Stand up; I myself also am a man.

27 And as he talked with him, he went in, and found many that were come together.

28 And he said unto them, Ye know how [j]that it is an unlawful thing for a man that is a Jew to keep company, or come unto one of another nation; but [k]God hath shown me that I should not call any man common or unclean.

29 Therefore came I *unto you* without gainsaying, as soon as I was sent for: I ask therefore for what intent ye have sent for me?

30 And Cornelius said, Four days ago I was fasting until this hour; and at the ninth hour I prayed in my house, and, behold, [l]a man stood before me [m]in bright clothing,

31 And said, Cornelius, [n]thy prayer is heard, [o]and thine alms are had in remembrance in the sight of God.

32 Send therefore to Joppa, and call hither Simon, whose surname is Peter; he is lodged in the house of *one* Simon a tanner by the sea side: who, when he cometh, shall speak unto thee.

33 Immediately therefore I sent to thee; and thou hast well done that thou art come. Now therefore are we all here present before God, to hear all things that are commanded thee of God.

34 ¶ Then Peter opened *his* mouth, and said, [p]Of a truth I perceive that God is no respecter of persons:

35 But [q]in every nation he that feareth him, and worketh righteousness, is accepted with him.

Rom. 6:1-14

36 The word which *God* sent unto the children of Israel, [r]preaching peace by Jesus Christ: ([s]he is Lord of all:)

37 That word, *I say*, ye know, which was published throughout all Judaea, and [t]began from Galilee, after the baptism which John preached;

38 How [u]God anointed Jesus of Nazareth with the Holy Ghost and with power: who went about doing good, and healing all that were oppressed of the devil; [v]for God was with him.

39 And [w]we are witnesses of all things which he did both in the land of the Jews, and in Jerusalem; [x]whom they slew and hanged on a tree:

40 Him [y]God raised up the third day, and showed him openly;

41 [z]Not to all the people, but unto witnesses chosen before of God, *even* to us, [a]who did eat and drink with him after he rose from the dead.

42 And [b]he commanded us to preach unto the people, and to testify [c]that it is he which was ordained of God *to be* the Judge [d]of quick and dead.

43 [e]To him give all the prophets witness, that through his name [f]whosoever believeth in him shall receive remission of sins.

Gentiles receive the Holy Spirit

44 ¶ While Peter yet spake these

10:23 [h]ch. 11:12 **10:26** [i]ch. 14:14 **10:28** [j]John 4:9 & 18:28 ch. 11:3 Gal. 2:12 [k]ch. 15:8,9 Eph. 3:6 **10:30** [l]ch. 1:10 [m]Mat. 28:3 Mark 16:5 Luke 24:4 **10:31** [n]Dan. 10:12 [o]Heb. 6:10 **10:34** [p]Deut. 10:17 2 Chr. 19:7 Job 34:19 Rom. 2:11 Gal. 2:6 Eph. 6:9 Col. 3:25 1 Pet. 1:17 **10:35** [q]ch. 15:9 Rom. 2:13 & 3:22 & 10:12,13 1 Cor. 12:13 Gal. 3:28 Eph. 2:13 **10:36** [r]Is. 57:19 Eph. 2:14 Col. 1:20 [s]Mat. 28:18 Rom. 10:12 1 Cor. 15:27 Eph. 1:20 1 Pet. 3:22 Rev. 17:14 **10:37** [t]Luke 4:14 **10:38** [u]Luke 4:18 Heb. 1:9 [v]John 3:2 **10:39** [w]ch. 2:32 [x]ch. 5:30 **10:40** [y]ch. 2:24 **10:41** [z]John 14:17,22 ch. 13:31 [a]Luke 24:30 John 21:13 **10:42** [b]Mat. 28:19 ch. 1:8 [c]John 5:22 ch. 17:31 [d]Rom. 14:9 2 Cor. 5:10 2 Tim. 4:1 1 Pet. 4:5

10:43 [e]Is. 53:11; Jer. 31:34; Dan. 9:24; Mic. 7:18; Zech. 13:1; Mal. 4:2 [f]ch. 26:18; Rom. 10:11; Gal. 3:22

10:34 GOD IS NO RESPECTER OF PERSONS. God has no favorite nation or race, nor does He favor any individual because of nationality, birth, or position in life (cf. Jas. 2:1). God favors and accepts those from every nation who turn from sin, believe in Christ, fear God, and live righteously (v. 35; cf. Rom. 2:6–11). All who continue in this manner of life will remain in God's love and favor (John 15:10).

10:38 HEALING ALL . . . OPPRESSED OF THE DEVIL. See article on POWER OVER SATAN AND DEMONS, p. 1486.

10:44 THE HOLY GHOST FELL ON ALL. The Gentile household of Cornelius listened and received the Word with saving faith (vv. 34–48; 11:14). (1) Because of their acceptance of Christ, God at once pours out the Holy Spirit upon them as His witness that they have believed and received the regenerating life of Christ (cf. 11:17; 15:8–9).

(2) The coming of the Holy Spirit upon Cornelius's household has the same purpose as the gift of the Spirit had for the disciples on the day of Pentecost (cf. 1:8; 2:4). This outpouring does not describe God's work of regeneration, but His falling upon them for power. Note Peter's words later

TESTING FOR GENUINE BAPTISM IN THE SPIRIT

***Acts 10:44–45** "While Peter yet spake these words, the Holy Ghost fell on all them which heard the word. And they of the circumcision which believed were astonished, as many as came with Peter, because that on the Gentiles also was poured out the gift of the Holy Ghost."*

The Scriptures declare that we as believers must examine and prove all things alleging to be of the Holy Spirit (1 Thes. 5:19–21; cf. 1 Cor. 14:29). "Believe not every spirit, but try the spirits whether they are of God" (1 John 4:1). The following are Biblical principles by which to prove or test whether or not an assumed or professed baptism in the Holy Spirit is of God.

(1) A genuine baptism in the Holy Spirit will cause us to love, magnify, and glorify God the Father and the Lord Jesus Christ more than before (see John 16:13–14; Acts 2:11,36; 4:12; cf. 7:55–56; 10:44–46). It is the Holy Spirit who causes love for God to grow in our hearts (Rom. 5:5). Conversely, any assumed baptism in the Spirit that draws our prayers, worship, and adoration toward anything or anyone other than God and the Lord Jesus is not of God.

(2) A genuine baptism in the Holy Spirit will increase our consciousness of living sons and daughters of the heavenly Father (Acts 1:4; Rom. 8:15–16), will lead to a greater awareness of the presence of Christ in our daily lives (John 14:16,23; 15:26), and will increase the heartfelt cry of "Abba, Father!" (Rom. 8:15; Gal. 4:6). Conversely, any assumed baptism in the Spirit that does not result in a greater fellowship with Christ and more intense communion with God as our Father is not of God.

(3) A genuine baptism in the Holy Spirit will cause a greater love for and appreciation of the Scriptures. The Spirit of truth (John 14:17), who inspired the Scriptures (2 Tim. 3:16; 2 Pet. 1:20–21), will deepen our love for the truth of the Word of God (John 16:13; Acts 2:42; 3:22; 1 John 4:6). Conversely, any assumed baptism in the Spirit that diminishes our hunger to read and abide in God's Word is not from God (cf. John 8:31; 15:4–7).

(4) A genuine baptism in the Holy Spirit will deepen our love and concern for other followers of Christ (Acts 2:42–47; 4:31–37). Christian fellowship and communion can take place only in the Spirit (2 Cor. 13:14). Conversely, any assumed baptism in the Spirit that decreases our love for all who seek to sincerely follow and obey Jesus Christ as Lord and Savior is not from God (compare Rom. 5:5 with 1 John 4:21).

(5) A genuine baptism in the Holy Spirit must be preceded by our turning from sin and faithfully obeying Christ (Acts 2:38; 8:15–24); it will be sustained only as long as we continue to be sanctified by the Holy Spirit (cf. Acts 2:40; 3:26; 5:29–32; 8:19–21; 26:18; Gal. 5:16–25), to "mortify the [evil] deeds of the body," and to be "led by the Spirit of God" (Rom. 8:13–14; cf. Gal. 5:24–25). Conversely, any assumed baptism in the Spirit of one who is not set free from sin and who walks according to the flesh, cannot be ascribed to the Holy Spirit as its source (Acts 2:38–40; 8:18–23; Rom. 6:22–23; 8:2–15). Rather, any anointing and power on that person are from another source, the deceptive activity of Satan (cf. Ps. 5:4–5; 2 Cor. 11:13–15; 2 Thes. 2:9–10).

(6) A genuine baptism in the Holy Spirit will intensify our displeasure with the sinful enjoyments and godless pleasures of the world, and will diminish the selfish pursuit of earthly riches and reputation (Acts 4:32–37; 8:14–24; 20:33; 1 John 2:15–17). Conversely, any assumed baptism in the Spirit that increases one's acceptance of the world's ways, standards, and philosophies is not from God, for we have received not the spirit of the world, but the Spirit who is of God (1 Cor. 2:12).

(7) A genuine baptism in the Holy Spirit will give us a greater desire and power to witness concerning the saving work of the Lord Jesus Christ (see Luke 4:18; Acts 1:4–8;

2:1–4,37–42; 4:8–33; Rom. 9:1–3; 10:1). Conversely, any assumed baptism in the Spirit that does not result in a more intense desire to see others enter into a saving relationship with Christ is not from God (see Acts 4:20, note).

(8) A genuine baptism in the Holy Spirit will cause us to be more receptive to the Spirit's operation within the kingdom of God and His gifts within our personal lives, particularly the gift of speaking in tongues, which is presented in Acts as the initial outward sign of the baptism in the Holy Spirit (Acts 2:4,16–18,43; 4:29–30; 5:12–16; 6:8; 8:5–7; 10:38,44–46; 1 Cor. 12–14; Gal. 3:5; see article on SPEAKING IN TONGUES, p. 1656). Conversely, any assumed baptism in the Spirit that does not result in the manifestations of the Spirit in our lives is an obvious departure from the experience of N.T. believers and the norm presented in the book of Acts (Acts 2:4,18; 10:45–46; 19:6).

(9) A genuine baptism in the Holy Spirit will cause us to be more conscious of the work, guidance, and presence of the Holy Spirit in our daily lives. After receiving the fullness of the Holy Spirit, believers in Acts were continually conscious of the Spirit's presence, power, and guidance (Acts 2:4,16–18; 4:31; 6:5; 9:31; 10:19; 13:2,4,52; 15:28; 16:6–7; 20:23). Conversely, any assumed baptism in the Spirit that does not increase our awareness of the presence of the Holy Spirit, strengthen our desire to obey His leadings, and reinforce our goal to live before Him in such a way as not to grieve or quench the Spirit, is not from God.

PHILIP'S AND PETER'S MISSIONARY JOURNEYS

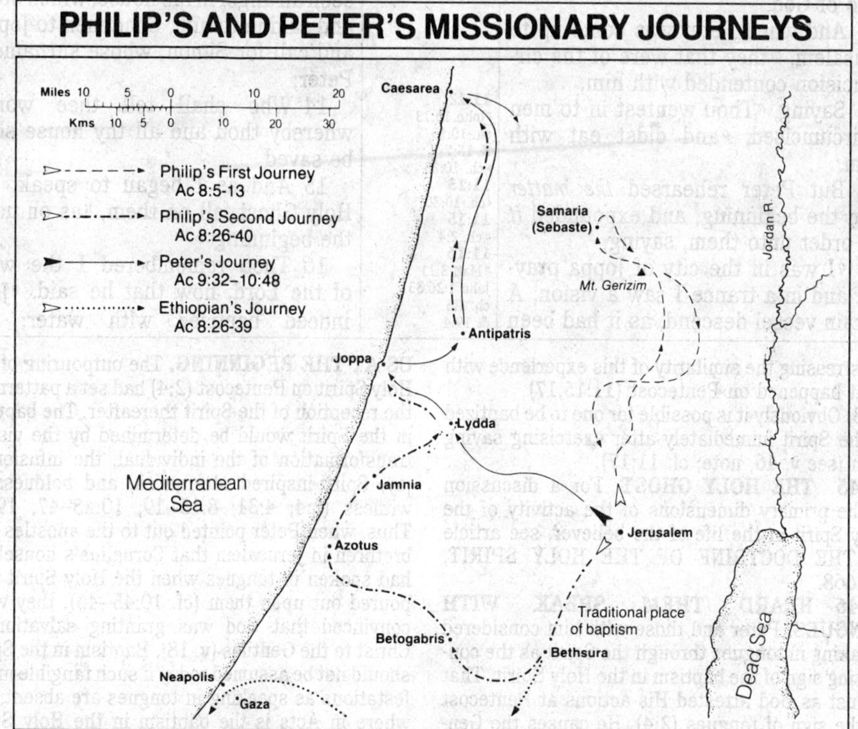

words, [g]the Holy Ghost fell on all
them which heard the word.
45 [h]And they of the circumcision
which believed were astonished, as
many as came with Peter, [i]because
that on the Gentiles also was poured
out the gift of the Holy Ghost.

Speaking in tongues as evidence of the Spirit's outpouring

46 For they heard them speak with
tongues, and magnify God. Then an-
swered Peter,
47 Can any man forbid water, that
these should not be baptized, which
Acts 11:15-17 have received the Holy Ghost [j]as well
as we?
48 [k]And he commanded them to be
baptized [l]in the name of the Lord.
Then prayed they him to tarry certain
days.

Peter defends the Gentiles' conversion

11 AND THE apostles and breth-
ren that were in Judaea heard
that the Gentiles had also received the
word of God.
2 And when Peter was come up to
Jerusalem, [m]they that were of the cir-
cumcision contended with him,
3 Saying, [n]Thou wentest in to men
uncircumcised, [o]and didst eat with
them.
4 But Peter rehearsed *the matter*
from the beginning, and expounded *it*
[p]by order unto them, saying,
5 [q]I was in the city of Joppa pray-
ing: and in a trance I saw a vision, A
certain vessel descend, as it had been

10:44 [g]ch. 4:31
10:45 [h]ver. 23 [i]ch. 11:18 Gal. 3:14
10:47 [j]ch. 11:17
10:48 [k]1 Cor. 1:17 [l]ch. 2:38 & 8:16
11:2 [m]ch. 10:45
11:3 [n]ch. 10:28 [o]Gal. 2:12
11:4 [p]Luke 1:3
11:5 [q]ch. 10:9
11:12 [r]John 16:13 ch. 10:19 & 15:7 [s]ch. 10:23
11:13 [t]ch. 10:30
11:15 [u]ch. 2:4
11:16 [v]Mat. 3:11 John 1:26,33 ch. 1:5 & 19:4

a great sheet, let down from heaven by
four corners; and it came even to me:
6 Upon the which when I had fas-
tened mine eyes, I considered, and saw
fourfooted beasts of the earth, and wild
beasts, and creeping things, and fowls
of the air.
7 And I heard a voice saying unto
me, Arise, Peter; slay and eat.
8 But I said, Not so, Lord: for noth-
ing common or unclean hath at any
time entered into my mouth.
9 But the voice answered me again
from heaven, What God hath cleansed,
that call not thou common.
10 And this was done three times:
and all were drawn up again into
heaven.
11 And, behold, immediately there
were three men already come unto the
house where I was, sent from Caesarea
unto me.
12 And [r]the Spirit bade me go with
them, nothing doubting. Moreover
[s]these six brethren accompanied me,
and we entered into the man's house:
13 [t]And he showed us how he had
seen an angel in his house, which stood
and said unto him, Send men to Joppa,
and call for Simon, whose surname is
Peter;
14 Who shall tell thee words,
whereby thou and all thy house shall
be saved.
15 And as I began to speak, the
Holy Ghost fell on them, [u]as on us at
the beginning.
16 Then remembered I the word
of the Lord, how that he said, [v]John
indeed baptized with water; but

---

on, stressing the similarity of this experience with what happened on Pentecost (11:15,17).

(3) Obviously it is possible for one to be baptized in the Spirit immediately after exercising saving faith (see v. 46, note; cf. 11:17).

10:45 THE HOLY GHOST. For a discussion of the primary dimensions of the activity of the Holy Spirit in the life of the believer, see article on THE DOCTRINE OF THE HOLY SPIRIT, p. 1668.

10:46 HEARD THEM SPEAK WITH TONGUES. Peter and those with him considered speaking in tongues through the Spirit as the convincing sign of the baptism in the Holy Spirit. That is, just as God attested His actions at Pentecost by the sign of tongues (2:4), He causes the Gentiles in Cornelius's house to speak in tongues as a convincing sign to Peter and the other Jewish believers (see article on SPEAKING IN TONGUES, p. 1656).

11:15 HOLY GHOST FELL ON THEM, AS ON US AT THE BEGINNING. The outpouring of the Holy Spirit on Pentecost (2:4) had set a pattern for the reception of the Spirit thereafter. The baptism in the Spirit would be determined by the visible transformation of the individual, the infusion of joy, Spirit-inspired utterances, and boldness in witness (2:4; 4:31; 8:15–19; 10:45–47; 19:6). Thus, when Peter pointed out to the apostles and brethren in Jerusalem that Cornelius's household had spoken in tongues when the Holy Spirit was poured out upon them (cf. 10:45–46), they were convinced that God was granting salvation in Christ to the Gentiles (v. 18). Baptism in the Spirit should not be assumed today if such tangible manifestations as speaking in tongues are absent; nowhere in Acts is the baptism in the Holy Spirit considered an experience to be known by faith-perception alone (see 8:12,16, notes; 19:6, note; see articles on SPEAKING IN TONGUES, p. 1656, and TESTING FOR GENUINE BAPTISM IN THE SPIRIT, p. 1682).

[w]ye shall be baptized with the Holy
Ghost.
17 [x]Forasmuch then as God gave
them the like gift as *he did* unto us, who
believed on the Lord Jesus Christ;
[y]what was I, that I could withstand
God?
18 When they heard these things,
they held their peace, and glorified
God, saying, [z]Then hath God also to
the Gentiles granted repentance unto
life.

The church at Antioch

19 ¶ [a]Now they which were scat-
tered abroad upon the persecution that
arose about Stephen travelled as far as
Phenice, and Cyprus, and Antioch,
preaching the word to none but unto
the Jews only.
20 And some of them were men of
Cyprus and Cyrene, which, when they
were come to Antioch, spake unto
[b]the Grecians, preaching the Lord
Jesus.
21 And [c]the hand of the Lord was
with them: and a great number be-
lieved, and [d]turned unto the Lord.

Barnabas, full of the Holy Spirit and faith

22 ¶ Then tidings of these things
came unto the ears of the church which
was in Jerusalem: and they sent forth
[e]Barnabas, that he should go as far as
Antioch.

11:16 [w]Is. 44:3 Joel 2:28 & 3:18
11:17 [x]ch. 15:8,9 [y]ch. 10:47
11:18 [z]Rom. 10:12,13 & 15:9,16
11:19 [a]ch. 8:1
11:20 [b]ch. 6:1 & 9:29
11:21 [c]Luke 1:66 ch. 2:47 [d]ch. 9:35
11:22 [e]ch. 9:27
11:23 [f]ch. 13:43 & 14:22
11:24 [g]ch. 6:5 [h]ver. 21 ch. 5:14
11:25 [i]ch. 9:30
11:27 [j]ch. 2:17 & 13:1 & 15:32 & 21:9 1 Cor. 12:28 Eph. 4:11
11:28 [k]ch. 21:10
11:29 [l]Rom. 15:26 1 Cor. 16:1 2 Cor. 9:1
11:30 [m]ch. 12:25

23 Who, when he came, and had
seen the grace of God, was glad, and
[f]exhorted them all, that with purpose
of heart they would cleave unto the
Lord.
24 For he was a good man, and
[g]full of the Holy Ghost and of faith:
[h]and much people was added unto the
Lord.
25 Then departed Barnabas to
[i]Tarsus, for to seek Saul:
26 And when he had found him, he
brought him unto Antioch. And it came
to pass, that a whole year they assem-
bled themselves [x]with the church,
and taught much people. And the disci-
ples were called Christians first in An-
tioch.
27 ¶ And in these days came
[j]prophets from Jerusalem unto Anti-
och.
28 And there stood up one of them
named [k]Agabus, and signified by the
Spirit that there should be great dearth
throughout all the world: which came
to pass in the days of Claudius Caesar. Acts 14:3
29 Then the disciples, every man
according to his ability, determined to
send [l]relief unto the brethren which
dwelt in Judaea:
30 [m]Which also they did, and sent
it to the elders by the hands of Barna-
bas and Saul.

[x] Or, *in the church*

11:17 US, WHO BELIEVED. The phrase "us, who believed" is a Greek aorist participle, normally describing action occurring before that of the main verb. Thus, a more exact translation would be "God gave to them the like gift as He did unto us also after believing." This agrees with the historical facts that the disciples had believed in Jesus and were regenerated by the Spirit before Pentecost (see article on THE REGENERATION OF THE DISCIPLES, p. 1638).

11:18 WHEN THEY HEARD THESE THINGS. The speech of Peter silenced all objections (vv. 4–18). God had baptized the Gentiles with the Holy Spirit (10:45), and accompanying this was the convincing evidence that they had spoken in other tongues (10:46). This was the only sign that was needed, and it was accepted without doubt.

11:23 CLEAVE UNTO THE LORD. The N.T. disciples did not assume that those who received "the grace of God" would automatically remain true to the Lord, for sin, the world, and Satan's temptations could persuade a new believer to turn from the way of salvation in Christ. Barnabas gives us an example of how new converts ought to be treated: our main interest should be to help and encourage them to continue in faith, love, and fellowship with Christ and His church (cf. 13:43; 14:22).

11:26 THE DISCIPLES WERE CALLED CHRISTIANS. The word "Christian" (Gk. *christianos*) occurs only three times in the N.T. (11:26; 26:28; 1 Pet. 4:16). It originally was a term denoting a servant and follower of Christ. Today it has become a general term devoid of the original N.T. meaning. For us who believe it should suggest the name of our Redeemer (Rom. 3:24), the idea of our intimate relation to Christ (Rom. 8:38–39), and the thought that we receive Him as our Lord (Rom. 5:1) and the author of our salvation (Heb. 5:9). To claim the name "Christian" means that Christ and His Word revealed in Scripture have become our supreme authority and our only source of future hope (Col. 1:5,27).

11:27 PROPHETS. The place of prophets in the church is recognized in the Pauline epistles (see article on THE MINISTRY GIFTS OF THE CHURCH, p. 1852).

James martyred and Peter imprisoned

12 NOW ABOUT that time Herod
the king [y]stretched forth *his*
hands to vex certain of the church.
2 And he killed James [n]the brother
of John with the sword.
3 And because he saw it pleased the
Jews, he proceeded further to take Pe-
ter also. (Then were [o]the days of un-
leavened bread.)
4 And [p]when he had apprehended
him, he put *him* in prison, and delivered
him to four quaternions of soldiers to
keep him; intending after Easter to
bring him forth to the people.
5 Peter therefore was kept in pris-
on: but [q]prayer[z] was made without
ceasing of the church unto God for him.

Peter delivered by an angel

6 And when Herod would have

12:2 [n]Mat. 4:21 & 20:23
12:3 [o]Ex. 12:14,15 & 23:15
12:4 [p]John 21:18
12:5 [q]2 Cor. 1:11 Eph. 6:18 1 Thes. 5:17

[y] Or, *began*   [z] Or, *instant and earnest prayer was made*

12:2 KILLED JAMES. God allowed James the brother of John (cf. Mat. 4:21) to die, yet He sent an angel to rescue Peter (vv. 3–17). That James should die while Peter lived for further ministry is the mysterious way of God with His people. James had the honor of being the first of the apostles to meet a martyr's death. He died as his Lord had done—for the cause of God (cf. Mark 10:36–39).

12:5 PRAYER . . . WITHOUT CEASING. The N.T. believers faced persecution with fervent prayer. The situation looked impossible; James had already died. Herod had Peter in the custody of sixteen men. Yet the early church lived by the conviction that "the effectual fervent prayer of a righteous man availeth much" (Jas. 5:16), and they prayed intensely and steadily over Peter's situation. Their prayer was soon answered (vv. 6–17).

The N.T. churches often engaged in prolonged corporate prayer (1:14; 2:42; 4:24–31; 12:5,12; 13:2). God intends His people to gather together for meaningful, enduring prayer; note Jesus' words, "My house shall be called the house of prayer" (Mat. 21:13). Churches claiming to base their theology, practice, and mission on the divine pattern set forth in the book of Acts and other N.T. writings should practice corporate prayer that fervently cries out to God as a vital element of their worship—and not just one or two minutes a service. In the early church the power and presence of God and prayer meetings went together. No amount of preaching, teaching, singing, music, or activity will bring forth the genuine power and presence of the Holy Spirit without N.T. prayer where believers "continue with one accord in prayer and supplication" (1:14).

12:5 THE CHURCH. From the book of Acts as well as other passages in the N.T., we gain insight into the norms or authoritative standards for a N.T. church. (1) First and foremost, a church will consist of people formed into local congregations and united by the Holy Spirit, diligently seeking a faithful and loyal personal relationship with God and Jesus Christ (13:2; 16:5; 20:7; Rom. 16:3–4; 1 Cor. 16:19; 2 Cor. 11:28; Heb. 11:6, note).

(2) Through its powerful witness, sinners will be saved, born again, baptized in water, and added to the church; they will partake of the Lord's Supper and wait for Christ's return (2:41–42; 4:33; 5:14; 11:24; 1 Cor. 11:26).

(3) The baptism in the Holy Spirit will be preached and communicated to new believers (see 2:39, note), and His presence and power manifested.

(4) The Holy Spirit's gifts will be in operation (Rom. 12:6–8; 1 Cor. 12:4–11; Eph. 4:11–12), including wonders, signs, and healings (2:18,43; 4:30; 5:12; 6:8; 14:10; 19:11; 28:8; Mark 16:18).

(5) God gives a fivefold leadership to the church in order to equip the saints for the work of ministry (Eph. 4:11–12; see article on THE MINISTRY GIFTS OF THE CHURCH, p. 1852).

(6) Believers will cast out demons (5:16; 8:7; 16:18; 19:12; Mark 16:17).

(7) There will be absolute loyalty to the gospel, i.e., the original teachings of Christ and the apostles (2:42; see Eph. 2:20, note). The people will devote themselves to studying and obeying the Word of God (6:4; 18:11; Rom. 15:18; Col. 3:16; 2 Tim. 2:15).

(8) On the first day of the week (20:7; 1 Cor. 16:2), the local congregation will meet together for worship and mutual edification through the written Word of God and the manifestations of the Spirit (1 Cor. 12:7–11; 14:26; 1 Tim. 5:17).

(9) The church will stand in humility, awe, and fear before the presence of a holy God (5:11). The people will be vitally concerned for the purity of the church, disciplining sinning members and teachers not loyal to the Biblical faith (20:28; 1 Cor. 5:1–13; see Mat. 18:15, note).

(10) Those who have persevered in the godly character and righteous standards set forth by the apostles will be ordained as elders to oversee local churches and maintain their spiritual life (Mat. 18:15, note; 1 Cor. 5:1–5; 1 Tim. 3:1–7; Tit. 1:5–9; see article on OVERSEERS AND THEIR DUTIES, p. 1706).

(11) Likewise, the church will have deacons responsible for the temporal and material affairs of the church (see 1 Tim. 3:8, note).

(12) There will be observable love and fellowship in the Spirit among the members (2:42, 44–46; see John 13:34, note), not only within the local congregation but also between other Bible-believing congregations (15:1–31; 2 Cor. 8:1–8).

(13) The church will be a praying and fasting church (1:14; 6:4; 12:5; 13:2; Rom. 12:12; Col. 4:2; Eph. 6:18).

(14) Believers will separate themselves from the prevailing world view and spirit of their surrounding culture (2:40; Rom. 12:2; 2 Cor. 6:17; Gal. 1:4; 1 John 2:15–16).

brought him forth, the same night Pe-
ter was sleeping between two soldiers,
bound with two chains: and the keep-
ers before the door kept the prison.
7 And, behold, [r]the angel of the
Lord came upon *him*, and a light shined
in the prison: and he smote Peter on
the side, and raised him up, saying,
Arise up quickly. And his chains fell off
from *his* hands.
8 And the angel said unto him, Gird
thyself, and bind on thy sandals. And
so he did. And he saith unto him, Cast
thy garment about thee, and fol-
low me.
9 And he went out, and followed
him; and [s]wist not that it was true
which was done by the angel; but
thought [t]he saw a vision.
10 When they were past the first
and the second ward, they came unto
the iron gate that leadeth unto the city;
[u]which opened to them of his own ac-
cord: and they went out, and passed on
through one street; and forthwith the
angel departed from him.
11 And when Peter was come to
himself, he said, Now I know of a sure-
ty, that [v]the Lord hath sent his angel,
and [w]hath delivered me out of the
hand of Herod, and *from* all the expec-
tation of the people of the Jews.

Peter at the prayer meeting

12 And when he had considered *the*
thing, [x]he came to the house of Mary
the mother of [y]John, whose surname
was Mark; where many were gathered
together [z]praying.
13 And as Peter knocked at the
door of the gate, a damsel came [a]to
hearken, named Rhoda.
14 And when she knew Peter's
voice, she opened not the gate for glad-
ness, but ran in, and told how Peter
stood before the gate.
15 And they said unto her, Thou art
mad. But she constantly affirmed that
it was even so. Then said they, [a]It is
his angel.
16 But Peter continued knocking:
and when they had opened *the door*,
and saw him, they were astonished.
17 But he, [b]beckoning unto them
with the hand to hold their peace, de-
clared unto them how the Lord had
brought him out of the prison. And he
said, Go show these things unto James,
and to the brethren. And he departed,
and went into another place.

The death of Herod

18 Now as soon as it was day, there
was no small stir among the soldiers,
what was become of Peter.
19 And when Herod had sought for
him, and found him not, he examined
the keepers, and commanded that *they*
should be put to death. And he went
down from Judaea to Caesarea, and
there abode.
20 ¶ And Herod [b]was highly dis-
pleased with them of Tyre and Sidon:
but they came with one accord to him,
and, having made Blastus [c]the king's
chamberlain their friend, desired
peace; because [c]their country was
nourished by the king's *country*.
21 And upon a set day Herod, ar-
rayed in royal apparel, sat upon his
throne, and made an oration unto
them.
22 And the people gave a shout,
saying, It is the voice of a god, and not
of a man.
23 And immediately the angel of the
Lord [d]smote him, because [e]he gave
not God the glory: and he was eaten of
worms, and gave up the ghost.
24 ¶ But [f]the word of God grew
and multiplied.
25 And Barnabas and Saul returned
from Jerusalem, when they had ful-
filled *their* [d]ministry, and [g]took with
them [h]John, whose surname was
Mark.

12:7 [r]ch. 5:19
12:9 [s]Ps. 126:1 [t]ch. 10:3,17 & 11:5
12:10 [u]ch. 16:26
12:11 [v]Ps. 34:7 Dan. 3:28 & 6:22 Heb. 1:14 [w]Job 5:19 Ps. 33:18,19 & 34:22 & 41:2 & 97:10 2 Cor. 1:10 2 Pet. 2:9
12:12 [x]ch. 4:23 [y]ch. 15:37 [z]ver. 5
12:15 [a]Gen. 48:16 Mat. 18:10
12:17 [b]ch. 13:16 & 19:33 & 21:40
12:20 [c]1 Ki. 5:9,11 Ezek. 27:17
12:23 [d]1 Sam. 25:38 2 Sam. 24:17 [e]Ps. 115:1
12:24 [f]Is. 55:11 ch. 6:7 & 19:20 Col. 1:6
12:25 [g]ch. 13:5,13 & 15:37 [h]ver. 12

[a] Or, *to ask who was there* [b] Or, *bare an hostile mind, intending war* [c] Gk. *that was over the king's bedchamber* [d] Or, *charge;* see ch. 11:29,30

(15) There will be suffering and affliction because of the world and its ways (4:1–3; 5:40; 9:16; 14:22).

(16) The church will actively help to send missionaries to other lands (2:39; 13:2–4).

No local church has the right to call itself a church after the N.T. norms unless these 16 characteristics are in operation among its people. See article on THE CHURCH, p. 1438, for further discussion on the Biblical doctrine of the church.

12:7 THE ANGEL. Angels are "ministering spirits, sent forth to minister for them who shall be heirs of salvation" (Heb. 1:14; see article on ANGELS AND THE ANGEL OF THE LORD, p. 368).

The Spirit calls Paul and Barnabas

13 NOW THERE were [i]in the
church that was at Antioch cer-
tain prophets and teachers; as [j]Bar-
nabas, and Simeon that was called Ni-
ger, and [k]Lucius of Cyrene, and
Manaen, [e]which had been brought up
with Herod the tetrarch, and Saul.
2 As they ministered to the Lord,
and fasted, the Holy Ghost said, [l]Sep-
arate me Barnabas and Saul for the
work [m]whereunto I have called them.
3 And [n]when they had fasted and
prayed, and laid *their* hands on them,
they sent *them* away.

Preaching on Cyprus

4 ¶ So they, being sent forth by the
Holy Ghost, departed unto Seleucia;
and from thence they sailed to [o]Cy-
prus.

13:1 [i]ch. 14:26 [j]ch. 11:22 [k]Rom. 16:21
13:2 [l]Num. 8:14 ch. 9:15 & 22:21 Rom. 1:1 Gal. 1:15 & 2:9 [m]Mat. 9:38 ch. 14:26 Rom. 10:15 Eph. 3:7,8 1 Tim. 2:7 2 Tim. 1:11 Heb. 5:4
13:3 [n]ch. 6:6
13:4 [o]ch. 4:36

[e] Or, *Herod's fosterbrother*

13:2 MINISTERED ... AND FASTED. Spirit-filled Christians are especially sensitive to the communication of the Holy Spirit during prayer and fasting (see Mat. 6:16, note). The communication from the Holy Spirit probably came through a prophetic utterance (cf. v. 1).

13:2 FOR THE WORK ... I HAVE CALLED THEM. Paul and Barnabas were called into missionary service and were commissioned by the church at Antioch. The nature of this work is described in 9:15; 13:5; 22:14–15,21; and 26:16–18.

(1) Paul and Barnabas were called to preach the gospel, bringing men and women into a saving relationship with Christ. Scripture nowhere indicates that the N.T. missionaries were sent out into the world to do social or political work, i.e., to propagate the gospel and establish churches by embarking on all sorts of organized social or political activities for the benefit of the people of the Roman Empire. Their goal was to bring people to Christ (16:31; 20:21), deliver them from the power of Satan (26:18), cause the Holy Spirit to come upon them (19:6), and establish them in churches. In these new Christians, the Holy Spirit came to live and manifest Himself through love; He gave spiritual gifts (1 Cor. 12–14) and transformed them from within so that their lives would bring glory to their living Savior.

(2) Missionaries of the gospel today ought to be devoted to the same kind of activity: to be ministers and witnesses to the gospel, bringing others to Christ by delivering them from the dominion of

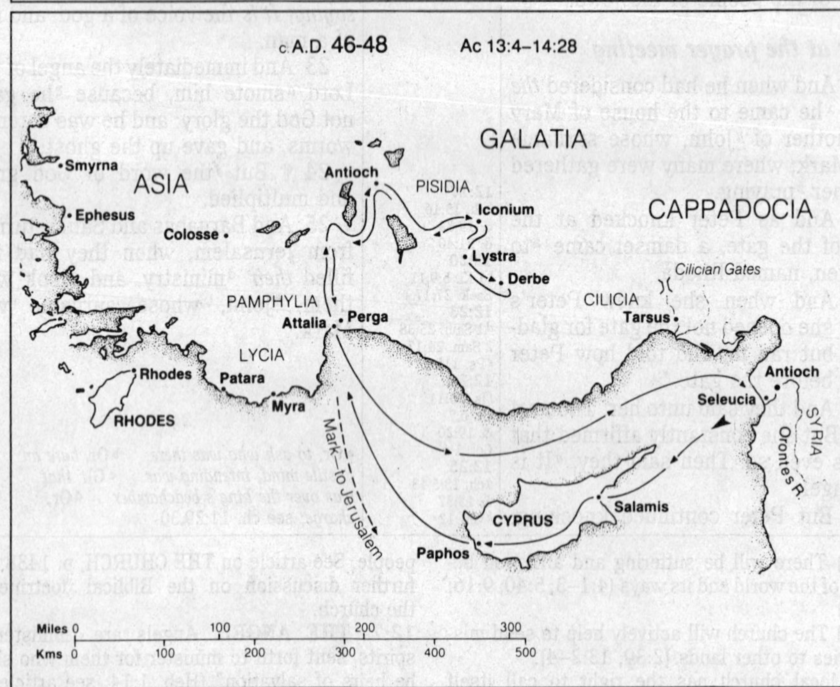

5 And when they were at Salamis, [p]they preached the word of God in the synagogues of the Jews: and they had also [q]John to *their* minister.

6 And when they had gone through the isle unto Paphos, they found [r]a certain sorcerer, a false prophet, a Jew, whose name *was* Bar-jesus:

7 Which was with the deputy of the country, Sergius Paulus, a prudent man; who called for Barnabas and Saul, and desired to hear the word of God.

8 But [s]Elymas the sorcerer (for so is his name by interpretation) withstood them, seeking to turn away the deputy from the faith.

cts 5:8

9 Then Saul, (who also *is called* Paul,) [t]filled with the Holy Ghost, set his eyes on him,

10 And said, O full of all subtlety and all mischief, [u]*thou* child of the devil, *thou* enemy of all righteousness, wilt thou not cease to pervert the right ways of the Lord?

13:5 [p]ver. 46 [q]ch. 12:25 & 15:37
13:6 [r]ch. 8:9
13:8 [s]Ex. 7:11 2 Tim. 3:8
13:9 [t]ch. 4:8
13:10 [u]Mat. 13:38 1 John 3:8
13:11 [v]1 Sam. 5:6
13:13 [w]ch. 15:38
13:14 [x]ch. 16:13
13:15 [y]Luke 4:16 [z]Heb. 13:22

11 And now, behold, [v]the hand of the Lord *is* upon thee, and thou shalt be blind, not seeing the sun for a season. And immediately there fell on him a mist and a darkness; and he went about seeking some to lead him by the hand.

12 Then the deputy, when he saw what was done, believed, being astonished at the doctrine of the Lord.

Preaching in Perga and Antioch

13 Now when Paul and his company loosed from Paphos, they came to Perga in Pamphylia: and [w]John departing from them returned to Jerusalem.

14 ¶ But when they departed from Perga, they came to Antioch in Pisidia, and [x]went into the synagogue on the sabbath day, and sat down.

15 And [y]after the reading of the law and the prophets the rulers of the synagogue sent unto them, saying, *Ye* men *and* brethren, if ye have [z]any

---

Satan (26:18), making them disciples, encouraging them to receive the Holy Spirit and His gifts (2:38; 8:17), and teaching them to observe all that Christ commanded (Mat. 28:19–20). Accompanying this should be signs and wonders, the healing of the sick, and deliverance for those oppressed by demons (2:43; 4:30; 8:7; 10:38; Mark 16:17–18). This supreme task of preaching the gospel, however, should also include personal acts of love, mercy, and kindness to those in need (cf. Gal. 2:10). In this way, all those called to bear witness to the gospel will model their ministry after Jesus (see Luke 9:2, note).

13:3 THEY SENT *THEM* AWAY. With this passage begins the great missionary movement "unto the uttermost part of the earth" (1:8). The missionary principles described in ch. 13 are a model for all missionary-sending churches.

(1) Missionary activity is initiated by the Holy Spirit through spiritual leaders who are deeply devoted to the Lord and His kingdom, seeking Him with prayer and fasting (v. 2).

(2) The church must be sensitive to the prophetic ministry and activity of the Holy Spirit and His guidance (v. 2).

(3) Missionaries who go out must do so under the specific call and will of the Holy Spirit (v. 2b).

(4) By prayer and fasting, constantly seeking to be aligned with the will of the Holy Spirit (vv. 3–4), the church confirms that God has called certain individuals to missionary work. The goal is that the church send out only those whom the Holy Spirit desires.

(5) Through the laying on of hands and the sending out of missionaries, the church indicates her commitment to the support and encouragement of those who go out. The responsibility of the sending church includes sending the missionaries on their way with love and in a manner worthy of God (3 John 6), praying for them (v. 3; Eph. 6:18–19), and giving them financial support (Luke 10:7; 3 John 6–8), including offerings of love for their needs (Phil. 4:10,14–18). Missionaries are considered an extension of the purpose, concern, and mission of the sending church. The church thus becomes a "fellow helper to the truth" (3 John 8; cf. Phil. 1:5).

(6) Those who go out as missionaries must be willing to "hazard their lives for the name of our Lord Jesus Christ" (15:26).

13:8 THE SORCERER. The sorcerer was probably a Jewish astrologer. Astrologers taught that the destiny of the individual was determined by celestial bodies. They believed they could foretell the future by examining the position of the stars and planets. All sorcery or astrology stands in opposition to the gospel of Christ because it involves Satan and the demonic (v. 10; see Deut. 18:9–11, notes).

13:9 SAUL ... FILLED WITH THE HOLY GHOST. One may be baptized in the Spirit as was Paul (9:17), yet in times of special need receive fresh fillings of the Spirit. Such repeated fillings are necessary (1) in confronting opposition to the gospel (4:8–12), (2) in advancing the gospel (4:8, 31), and (3) in directly challenging satanic activity (13:9,50–52). Repeated fillings of the Holy Spirit should be the norm for all believers who are baptized in the Holy Spirit.

13:11 THOU SHALT BE BLIND. Miracles in the N.T. were not always healings; some, such as God's anger against Elymas (vv. 8–11) and Herod (12:20–23), involved judgment on ungodly individuals. God's anger against Ananias and Sapphira (5:1–11) is an example of a miraculous judgment against sin within the church.

word of exhortation for the people,
say on.
16 Then Paul stood up, and beckon-
ing with *his* hand said, Men of Israel,
and [a]ye that fear God, give audience.
17 The God of this people of Israel
[b]chose our fathers, and exalted the
people [c]when they dwelt as strangers
in the land of Egypt, and with an high
arm brought he them out of it.
18 And [d]about the time of forty
years [f]suffered he their manners in
the wilderness.
19 And when he had destroyed sev-
en nations in the land of Chanaan, [e]he
divided their land to them by lot.
20 And after that [f]he gave *unto*
them judges about the space of four
hundred and fifty years, [g]until Samuel
the prophet.
21 [h]And afterward they desired a
king: and God gave unto them Saul the
son of Cis, a man of the tribe of Benja-
min, by the space of forty years.
22 And [i]when he had removed
him, [j]he raised up unto them David to
be their king; to whom also he gave
testimony, and said, [k]I have found Da-
vid the *son* of Jesse, [l]a man after mine
own heart, which shall fulfil all my will.
23 [m]Of this man's seed hath God
according [n]to *his* promise raised unto
Israel [o]a Saviour, Jesus:
24 [p]When John had first preached
before his coming the baptism of re-
pentance to all the people of Israel.
25 And as John fulfilled his course,
he said, [q]Whom think ye that I am? I
am not *he*. But, behold, there cometh
one after me, whose shoes of *his* feet I
am not worthy to loose.
26 Men *and* brethren, children of
the stock of Abraham, and whosoever

13:16 [a]ch. 10:35
13:17 [b]Deut. 7:6,7 [c]ch. 7:17
13:18 [d]Ex. 16:35
13:19 [e]Josh. 14:1
13:20 [f]Judg. 2:16 [g]1 Sam. 3:20
13:21 [h]1 Sam. 8:5
13:22 [i]1 Sam. 15:23 [j]1 Sam. 16:13 [k]Ps. 89:20 [l]1 Sam. 13:14
13:23 [m]Is. 11:1 [n]Ps. 132:11 [o]Mat. 1:21
13:24 [p]Mat. 3:1 Luke 3:3
13:25 [q]Mark 1:7
13:26 [r]Mat. 10:6
13:27 [s]Luke 23:34
13:28 [t]Mat. 27:22
13:29 [u]Luke 18:31 [v]Mat. 27:59
13:30 [w]Mat. 28:6
13:31 [x]Mat. 28:16
13:32 [y]Gen. 3:15
13:33 [z]Heb. 1:5
13:34 [a]Is. 55:3
13:35 [b]Ps. 16:10

among you feareth God, [r]to you is the
word of this salvation sent.
27 For they that dwell at Jerusalem,
and their rulers, [s]because they knew
him not, nor yet the voices of the
prophets which are read every sabbath
day, they have fulfilled *them* in con-
demning *him*.
28 [t]And though they found no
cause of death *in him*, yet desired they
Pilate that he should be slain.
29 [u]And when they had fulfilled all
that was written of him, [v]they took
him down from the tree, and laid *him* in
a sepulchre.
30 [w]But God raised him from the
dead:
31 And [x]he was seen many days of
them which came up with him from
Galilee to Jerusalem, who are his wit-
nesses unto the people.
32 And we declare unto you glad
tidings, how that [y]the promise which
was made unto the fathers,
33 God hath fulfilled the same unto
us their children, in that he hath raised
up Jesus again; as it is also written in
the second psalm, [z]Thou art my Son,
this day have I begotten thee.
34 And as concerning that he raised
him up from the dead, *now* no more to
return to corruption, he said on this
wise, [a]I will give you the sure [g]mer-
cies of David.
35 Wherefore he saith also in anoth-
er *psalm*, [b]Thou shalt not suffer thine
Holy One to see corruption.

[f] Gk. *bore*, or, *fed them, as a nurse beareth*, or, *feedeth her child*, Deut. 1:31; according to the LXX and so Chrysostom [g] Gk. *holy*, or, *just things:* which word the LXX both in the place of Is. 55:3, and in many others, use for that which is in the Hebrew, *mercies*

13:31 HIS WITNESSES UNTO THE PEOPLE. A witness (Gk. *martus*) is "one who testifies by act or word to the truth." Christian witnesses are those who confirm and testify to the saving work of Jesus Christ by word, deed, life, and if necessary, even death. It involves seven principles:

(1) Christian witnessing is the obligation of all believers (1:8; Mat. 4:19; 28:19–20).

(2) Christian witnesses must be missionary-minded, going to all the nations and bearing God's salvation unto the uttermost part of the earth (11:18; 13:2–4; 26:16–18; Mat. 28:19–20; Luke 24:47).

(3) Christian witnesses speak primarily about the meaning of Christ's life, death, resurrection, saving power, and promised Holy Spirit (2:32, 38–39; 3:15; 10:39–41,43; 18:5; 26:16; 1 Cor. 15:1–8).

(4) Christian witnesses must bring conviction concerning sin, righteousness, and judgment (2:37–40; 7:51–54; 24:24–25; see John 16:8, note). Through such witness people are brought to saving faith (2:41; 4:33; 6:7; 11:21).

(5) Christian witnesses at times will suffer (7:57–60; 22:20; 2 Cor. 11:23–29). The word "martyr" is derived from the Greek word for witness. Discipleship involves commitment, no matter what the cost.

(6) Christian witnessing must be accompanied by separation from the world (2:40), a life of righteousness (Rom. 14:17), and an utter reliance on the Holy Spirit (4:29–33) that results in the manifestation of God's Spirit and power (1 Cor. 2:4).

(7) Christian witnessing is prophetic (2:17), empowered (1:8) and inspired by the Spirit (2:4; 4:8).

36 For David, [h]after he had served his own generation by the will of God, [c]fell on sleep, and was laid unto his fathers, and saw corruption:

37 But he, whom God raised again, saw no corruption.

38 ¶ Be it known unto you therefore, men *and* brethren, that [d]through this man is preached unto you the forgiveness of sins:

39 And [e]by him all that believe are justified from all things, from which ye could not be justified by the law of Moses.

40 Beware therefore, lest that come upon you, which is spoken of in [f]the prophets;

41 Behold, ye despisers, and wonder, and perish: for I work a work in your days, a work which ye shall in no wise believe, though a man declare it unto you.

42 And when the Jews were gone out of the synagogue, the Gentiles besought that these words might be preached to them [i]the next sabbath.

43 Now when the congregation was broken up, many of the Jews and religious proselytes followed Paul and Barnabas: who, speaking to them, [g]persuaded them to continue in [h]the grace of God.

44 ¶ And the next sabbath day came almost the whole city together to hear the word of God.

45 But when the Jews saw the multitudes, they were filled with envy, and [i]spake against those things which were spoken by Paul, contradicting and blaspheming.

46 Then Paul and Barnabas waxed bold, and said, [j]It was necessary that the word of God should first have been spoken to you: but [k]seeing ye put it from you, and judge yourselves unworthy of everlasting life, lo, [l]we turn to the Gentiles.

47 For so hath the Lord commanded us, *saying,* [m]I have set thee to be a light of the Gentiles, that thou shouldest be for salvation unto the ends of the earth.

48 And when the Gentiles heard this, they were glad, and glorified the word of the Lord: [n]and as many as were ordained to eternal life believed.

49 And the word of the Lord was published throughout all the region.

50 But the Jews stirred up the devout and honourable women, and the chief men of the city, and [o]raised persecution against Paul and Barnabas, and expelled them out of their coasts.

51 [p]But they shook off the dust of their feet against them, and came unto Iconium.

52 And the disciples [q]were filled with joy, and with the Holy Ghost. Rom. 5:5

Preaching at Iconium

14 AND IT came to pass in Iconium, that they went both together into the synagogue of the Jews, and so spake, that a great multitude both of the Jews and also of the Greeks believed.

2 But the unbelieving Jews stirred up the Gentiles, and made their minds evil affected against the brethren.

God confirms the Word with miracles

3 Long time therefore abode they

13:36 [c]ch. 2:29 **13:38** [d]Jer. 31:34 **13:39** [e]Is. 53:11 **13:40** [f]Hab. 1:5 **13:43** [g]ch. 11:23 & 14:22 [h]Tit. 2:11 Heb. 12:15 1 Pet. 5:12 **13:45** [i]ch. 18:6 1 Pet. 4:4 Jude 10 **13:46** [j]ver. 26 Mat. 10:6 ch. 3:26 Rom. 1:16 [k]Ex. 32:10 Deut. 32:21 Is. 55:5 Mat. 21:43 Rom. 10:19 [l]ch. 18:6 & 28:28 **13:47** [m]Is. 42:6 & 49:6 Luke 2:32 **13:48** [n]ch. 2:47 **13:50** [o]2 Tim. 3:11 **13:51** [p]Mat. 10:14 Mark 6:11 Luke 9:5 ch. 18:6 **13:52** [q]Mat. 5:12 John 16:22 ch. 2:46

[h] Or, *after he had in his own age served the will of God;* see ver. 22 [i] Gk. *in the week between,* or, *in the sabbath between*

13:48 ORDAINED TO ETERNAL LIFE. Some have understood this verse as teaching arbitrary predestination. However, neither the context nor the word translated "ordained" (Gk. *tetagmenoi,* from *tassō*) warrant this interpretation. (1) V. 46 explicitly emphasizes human responsibility in accepting or rejecting eternal life. The best rendering of *tetagmenoi,* therefore, is "were disposed": "and as many as were disposed to eternal life believed." This rendering agrees completely with the affirmations of 1 Tim. 2:4; Tit. 2:11; 2 Pet. 3:9 (see article on ELECTION AND PREDESTINATION, p. 1846). (2) Furthermore, according to Paul no person is unconditionally appointed to eternal life (see Rom. 11:20–22).

13:52 FILLED . . . WITH THE HOLY GHOST. The Greek verb translated "filled" is in the imperfect tense, indicating continued action in past time. The disciples were being continually filled and empowered day by day. The Spirit's fullness is not merely a one-time initial experience, but a life of renewed fillings for God-given needs and tasks (cf. Eph. 5:18; see Acts 6:3, note).

14:3 SIGNS AND WONDERS. God intended that the preaching of the gospel be accompanied by miraculous signs to confirm the truth of the gospel (cf. Mark 16:20; see article on SIGNS OF BELIEVERS, p. 1516). In this way the Lord worked with His people and bore witness to the truth of the message. Such confirmation of God's grace with signs and wonders is no less needed today as we face the difficult times of the last days (1 Tim. 4:1; 2 Tim. 3:1–13).

speaking boldly in the Lord, [r]which gave testimony unto the word of his grace, and granted signs and wonders to be done by their hands.

Acts 15:32

4 But the multitude of the city was divided: and part held with the Jews, and part with the [s]apostles.

5 And when there was an assault made both of the Gentiles, and also of the Jews with their rulers, [t]to use *them* despitefully, and to stone them,

6 They were ware of *it,* and [u]fled unto Lystra and Derbe, cities of Lycaonia, and unto the region that lieth round about:

7 And there they preached the gospel.

Preaching at Lystra

8 ¶ [v]And there sat a certain man at Lystra, impotent in his feet, being a cripple from his mother's womb, who never had walked:

9 The same heard Paul speak: who stedfastly beholding him, and perceiving that he had faith to be healed,

10 Said with a loud voice, [w]Stand upright on thy feet. And he leaped and walked.

Acts 27:25

Paul and Barnabas thought to be gods

11 And when the people saw what Paul had done, they lifted up their voices, saying in the speech of Lycaonia, [x]The gods are come down to us in the likeness of men.

12 And they called Barnabas, Jupiter; and Paul, Mercurius, because he was the chief speaker.

13 Then the priest of Jupiter, which was before their city, brought oxen and garlands unto the gates, [y]and would have done sacrifice with the people.

14 *Which* when the apostles, Barnabas and Paul, heard *of,* [z]they rent their clothes, and ran in among the people, crying out,

15 And saying, Sirs, [a]why do ye these things? [b]We also are men of like passions with you, and preach unto you that ye should turn from [c]these vanities [d]unto the living God, [e]which made heaven, and earth, and the sea, and all things that are therein:

16 [f]Who in times past suffered all nations to walk in their own ways.

17 [g]Nevertheless he left not himself without witness, in that he did good, and [h]gave us rain from heaven, and fruitful seasons, filling our hearts with food and gladness.

Paul stoned

18 And with these sayings scarce restrained they the people, that they had not done sacrifice unto them.

19 ¶ [i]And there came thither *certain* Jews from Antioch and Iconium, who persuaded the people, [j]and, having stoned Paul, drew *him* out of the city, supposing he had been dead.

The return to Antioch

20 Howbeit, as the disciples stood round about him, he rose up, and came into the city: and the next day he departed with Barnabas to Derbe.

21 And when they had preached the gospel to that city, [k]and [j]had taught many, they returned again to Lystra, and *to* Iconium, and Antioch,

22 Confirming the souls of the disci-

14:3 [r]Mark 16:20 Heb. 2:4 **14:4** [s]ch. 13:2,3 **14:5** [t]2 Tim. 3:11 **14:6** [u]Mat. 10:23 **14:8** [v]ch. 3:2 **14:10** [w]Is. 35:6 **14:11** [x]ch. 8:10 & 28:6 **14:13** [y]Dan. 2:46 **14:14** [z]Mat. 26:65 **14:15** [a]ch. 10:26 [b]Jas. 5:17 Rev. 19:10 [c]1 Sam. 12:21 1 Ki. 16:13 Jer. 14:22 Amos 2:4 1 Cor. 8:4 [d]1 Thes. 1:9 [e]Gen. 1:1 Ps. 33:6 & 146:6 Rev. 14:7 **14:16** [f]Ps. 81:12 ch. 17:30 1 Pet. 4:3 **14:17** [g]ch. 17:27 Rom. 1:20 [h]Lev. 26:4 Deut. 11:14 & 28:12 Job 5:10 Ps. 65:10 & 68:9 & 147:8 Jer. 14:22 Mat. 5:45 **14:19** [i]ch. 13:45 [j]2 Cor. 11:25 2 Tim. 3:11 **14:21** [k]Mat. 28:19

j Gk. *had made many disciples*

14:4 APOSTLES. Both Paul and Barnabas are called apostles. As a more general term, "apostle" was applied to the first Christian missionaries who were sent out by the church to preach the N.T. message (vv. 4,14). "Apostle" in a more specialized sense is applied only to those who had received a direct commission by Christ to establish His original message and revelation (see Eph. 2:20, note). Paul was an apostle in this special sense.

14:9 PERCEIVING THAT HE HAD FAITH. Discerning the faith of the lame man most likely came through the Holy Spirit. Paul then encouraged this man's faith by commanding him to stand up. Believers should pray for spiritual insight to recognize the faith of individuals needing God's grace and healing.

14:19 STONED PAUL. In N.T. times God did not always protect His servants from harm. This truth is inherent in the gospel and valid today as well: the kingdom of God advances at great cost to God's servants. When Paul later described the suffering he endured for Christ's sake, he referred to this occasion by saying, "once was I stoned" (2 Cor. 11:25; Gal. 6:17; see Acts 9:16, note). When writing to the churches of Galatia, he said, "I bear in my body the marks of the Lord Jesus" (Gal. 6:17), most likely including this incident (see 2 Cor. 11:23, note on Paul's suffering).

14:22 THROUGH MUCH TRIBULATION. Those who commit themselves to the Lordship of Christ and who will finally enter into the kingdom of heaven must suffer "much tribulation" along the way. Living in the midst of a hostile world, they must engage in spiritual warfare against sin and the power of Satan (Eph. 6:12; cf. Rom. 8:17;

ples, *and* [l]exhorting them to continue
in the faith, and that [m]we must
through much tribulation enter into the
kingdom of God.
23 And when they had [n]ordained
them elders in every church, and had
prayed with fasting, they commended
them to the Lord, on whom they be-
lieved.
24 And after they had passed
throughout Pisidia, they came to Pam-
phylia.
25 And when they had preached the
word in Perga, they went down into At-
talia:
26 And thence sailed to Antioch,
[o]from whence they had been [p]recom-
mended to the grace of God for the
work which they fulfilled.
27 And when they were come, and
had gathered the church together,
[q]they rehearsed all that God had done
with them, and how he had [r]opened
the door of faith unto the Gentiles.
28 And there they abode long time
with the disciples.

The council at Jerusalem

15 AND [s]CERTAIN men which
came down from Judaea taught
the brethren, *and said,* [t]Except ye be
circumcised [u]after the manner of Mo-
ses, ye cannot be saved.
2 When therefore Paul and Barna-
bas had no small dissension and dispu-
tation with them, they determined that
[v]Paul and Barnabas, and certain oth-
er of them, should go up to Jerusalem
unto the apostles and elders about this
question.

14:22 [l]ch. 11:23 & 13:43 [m]Mat. 10:38 & 16:24 Luke 22:28 Rom. 8:17 2 Tim. 2:12 & 3:12
14:23 [n]Tit. 1:5
14:26 [o]ch. 13:1,3 [p]ch. 15:40
14:27 [q]ch. 15:4,12 & 21:19 [r]1 Cor. 16:9 2 Cor. 2:12 Col. 4:3 Rev. 3:8
15:1 [s]Gal. 2:12 [t]ver. 5 John 7:22 Gal. 5:2 Phil. 3:2 Col. 2:8,11,16 [u]Gen. 17:10 Lev. 12:3
15:2 [v]Gal. 2:1
15:3 [w]Rom. 15:24 1 Cor. 16:6,11 [x]ch. 14:27
15:4 [y]ver. 12 ch. 14:27
15:5 [z]ver. 1
15:7 [a]ch. 10:20 & 11:12
15:8 [b]1 Chr. 28:9 ch. 1:24 [c]ch. 10:44
15:9 [d]Rom. 10:12 [e]ch. 10:15,28 1 Cor. 1:2 1 Pet. 1:22
15:10 [f]Mat. 23:4 Gal. 5:1
15:11 [g]Rom. 3:24 Eph. 2:8 Tit. 2:11 & 3:4,5

3 And [w]being brought on their way
by the church, they passed through
Phenice and Samaria, [x]declaring the
conversion of the Gentiles: and they
caused great joy unto all the brethren.
4 And when they were come to Jeru-
salem, they were received of the
church, and *of* the apostles and elders,
and [y]they declared all things that God
had done with them.
5 But there [k]rose up certain of the
sect of the Pharisees which believed,
saying, [z]That it was needful to cir-
cumcise them, and to command *them* to
keep the law of Moses.
6 ¶ And the apostles and elders
came together for to consider of this
matter.
7 And when there had been much
disputing, Peter rose up, and said unto
them, [a]Men *and* brethren, ye know
how that a good while ago God made
choice among us, that the Gentiles by
my mouth should hear the word of the
gospel, and believe.
8 And God, [b]which knoweth the
hearts, bare them witness, [c]giving
them the Holy Ghost, even as *he did*
unto us; Acts 19:1-7
9 [d]And put no difference between
us and them, [e]purifying their hearts
by faith.
10 Now therefore why tempt ye
God, [f]to put a yoke upon the neck of
the disciples, which neither our fathers
nor we were able to bear?
11 But [g]we believe that through

[k] Or, *rose up,* said they, *certain*

2 Thes. 1:4–7; 2 Tim. 2:12).

(1) Those who are faithful to Christ, His Word, and righteous ways can expect trouble and distress in this world (John 16:33). Only the lukewarm or compromising "believer" will find peace and comfort from the world (cf. Rev. 3:14–17).

(2) The present evil world and false believers will remain adversaries to the gospel of Christ until the Lord overthrows the world's evil system at His coming (Rev. 19–20). Meanwhile the believer's hope is "laid up . . . in heaven" (Col. 1:5) and will be "revealed in the last time" (1 Pet. 1:5). His hope is not in this life, nor in this world, but in the appearance of his Savior to take him to Himself (John 14:1–3; 1 John 3:2–3; see article on BIBLICAL HOPE, p. 834).

14:23 ORDAINED THEM ELDERS. The appointing of elders (overseers or pastors) was done not only by seeking the Spirit's will through prayer and fasting, but also by examining the character, spiritual gifts, reputation, and history of blamelessness of the men under consideration (1 Tim. 3:1–10). If they were found to be beyond reproach, they were appointed to serve (see article on MORAL QUALIFICATIONS FOR OVERSEERS, p. 1908).

15:8 GOD, WHICH KNOWETH THE HEARTS. God's knowledge of the hearts of the Gentiles (i.e., Cornelius and his household) refers to His seeing saving faith within them. God testified (i.e., "bare witness") to the genuineness of their faith (1) by cleansing their hearts with the inward work of regeneration by the Holy Spirit (v. 9), and (2) by baptizing them in the Holy Spirit immediately afterwards, with the accompanying sign of speaking in tongues (10:44–46; 11:15–18).

15:11 THROUGH THE GRACE OF THE LORD JESUS CHRIST. The crucial question at the Jerusalem Conference was whether circumcision and obedience to the law of Moses were required for salvation in Christ. The representatives meeting there concluded that Gentiles were saved through

the grace of the Lord Jesus Christ we shall be saved, even as they.

12 ¶ Then all the multitude kept silence, and gave audience to Barnabas and Paul, declaring what miracles and wonders God had [h]wrought among the Gentiles by them.

13 ¶ And after they had held their peace, [i]James answered, saying, Men *and* brethren, hearken unto me:

14 [j]Simeon hath declared how God at the first did visit the Gentiles, to take out of them a people for his name.

15 And to this agree the words of the prophets; as it is written,

16 [k]After this I will return, and will build again the tabernacle of David, which is fallen down; and I will build again the ruins thereof, and I will set it up:

17 That the residue of men might seek after the Lord, and all the Gentiles, upon whom my name is called, saith the Lord, who doeth all these things.

18 Known unto God are all his works from the beginning of the world.

19 Wherefore [l]my sentence is, that we trouble not them, which from among the Gentiles [m]are turned to God:

20 But that we write unto them, that they abstain [n]from pollutions of idols, and [o]*from* fornication, and *from* things strangled, [p]and *from* blood.

21 For Moses of old time hath in every city them that preach him, [q]being read in the synagogues every sabbath day.

The decision of the council

22 Then pleased it the apostles and elders, with the whole church, to send chosen men of their own company to Antioch with Paul and Barnabas; *namely,* Judas surnamed [r]Barsabas, and Silas, chief men among the brethren:

23 And they wrote *letters* by them after this manner; The apostles and elders and brethren *send* greeting unto the brethren which are of the Gentiles in Antioch and Syria and Cilicia:

24 Forasmuch as we have heard, that [s]certain which went out from us have troubled you with words, subverting your souls, saying, *Ye must* be circumcised, and keep the law: to whom we gave no *such* commandment:

25 It seemed good unto us, being assembled with one accord, to send chosen men unto you with our beloved Barnabas and Paul,

26 [t]Men that have hazarded their lives for the name of our Lord Jesus Christ.

27 We have sent therefore Judas and Silas, who shall also tell *you* the same things by [1]mouth.

28 For it seemed good to the Holy Ghost, and to us, to lay upon you no greater burden than these necessary things;

29 [u]That ye abstain from meats of-

15:12 [h]ch. 14:27
15:13 [i]ch. 12:17
15:14 [j]ver. 7
15:16 [k]Amos 9:11
15:19 [l]See ver. 23 [m]1 Thes. 1:9
15:20 [n]Gen. 35:2 Ex. 20:3,23 Ezek. 20:30 1 Cor. 8:1 & 10:20,28 Rev. 2:14 [o]1 Cor. 6:9 Gal. 5:19 Eph. 5:3 Col. 3:5 1 Thes. 4:3 1 Pet. 4:3 [p]Gen. 9:4 Lev. 3:17 Deut. 12:16
15:21 [q]ch. 13:15,27
15:22 [r]ch. 1:23
15:24 [s]ver. 1 Gal. 2:4 & 5:12 Tit. 1:10,11
15:26 [t]ch. 13:50
15:29 [u]ver. 20 ch. 21:25 Rev. 2:14,20

[1]Gk. *word*

---

the grace of the Lord Jesus, who forgave them of sin and made them a new creation (see article on FAITH AND GRACE, p. 1738). Grace comes to a person when he repents of sin and believes in Christ as Lord and Savior (2:38–39). This response to God's grace enables him to receive power to become a child of God (John 1:12).

15:14 TO TAKE OUT OF THEM A PEOPLE. God's program for this age is to take out from among all the nations a people, separated unto Him for His name. This body of Christ, gathered out of the present world system, makes herself ready as the bride of Christ (Rev. 19:7–8).

15:16 THE TABERNACLE OF DAVID. James indicates that the redemptive mission of Christ includes both the Jew and the Gentile. The "tabernacle of David which is fallen" (see Amos 9:11–15, note) refers to a remnant of Israel that survives God's judgment. (1) Amos's prophecy states the following: (a) God will judge sinful Israel, yet not totally. (b) He will destroy all the unrighteous in the house of Jacob (Amos 9:10). (c) After the destruction of the ungodly Jews, God will "raise up the tabernacle of David that is fallen" (Amos 9:11). (2) The salvation of this purified Jewish remnant will result in the nations seeking the Lord (v. 17). Elsewhere Paul says the same thing when he refers to a blessing for the Gentiles that will come from the Jewish remnant's reconciliation to God (see Rom. 11:11–15,25–26).

15:28 IT SEEMED GOOD TO THE HOLY GHOST. The Jerusalem Conference was directed by the Holy Spirit. Jesus had promised that the Spirit would guide them into all truth (John 16:13). Decisions of the church must not be made by humans alone; they must seek the Spirit's guidance through prayer and fasting and commitment to the Word of God until His will is discerned clearly (cf. 13:2–4). The church, if it is to be the church of Christ, must hear what the Spirit says to the churches (cf. Rev. 2:7).

15:29 THAT YE ABSTAIN FROM. The Holy Spirit (v. 28) suggested certain restrictions for Gentiles that would enable Jewish Christians to

fered to idols, and [v]from blood, and from things strangled, and from fornication: from which if ye keep yourselves, ye shall do well. Fare ye well.

30 So when they were dismissed, they came to Antioch: and when they had gathered the multitude together, they delivered the epistle:

31 *Which* when they had read, they rejoiced for the [m]consolation.

32 And Judas and Silas, being prophets also themselves, [w]exhorted the brethren with many words, and confirmed *them.*

33 And after they had tarried *there* a space, they were let [x]go in peace from the brethren unto the apostles.

34 Notwithstanding it pleased Silas to abide there still.

35 [y]Paul also and Barnabas continued in Antioch, teaching and preaching the word of the Lord, with many others also.

Separation of Paul and Barnabas

36 ¶ And some days after Paul said unto Barnabas, Let us go again and visit our brethren [z]in every city where we have preached the word of the Lord, *and see* how they do.

37 And Barnabas determined to take with them [a]John, whose surname was Mark.

38 But Paul thought not good to take him with them, [b]who departed from them from Pamphylia, and went not with them to the work.

39 And the contention was so sharp between them, that they departed asunder one from the other: and so Barnabas took Mark, and sailed unto Cyprus;

40 And Paul chose Silas, and departed, [c]being recommended by the brethren unto the grace of God.

41 And he went through Syria and Cilicia, [d]confirming the churches.

The selection of Timothy

16 THEN CAME he to [e]Derbe and Lystra: and, behold, a certain disciple was there, [f]named Timotheus, [g]the son of a certain woman, which was a Jewess, and believed; but his father *was* a Greek:

2 Which [h]was well reported of by the brethren that were at Lystra and Iconium.

3 Him would Paul have to go forth with him; and [i]took and circumcised him because of the Jews which were in those quarters: for they knew all that his father was a Greek.

4 And as they went through the cities, they delivered them the decrees for to keep, [j]that were ordained of the apostles and elders which were at Jerusalem.

5 And [k]so were the churches established in the faith, and increased in number daily.

The Macedonian vision

6 Now when they had gone throughout Phrygia and the region of Galatia, and were forbidden of the Holy Ghost to preach the word in Asia,

7 After they were come to Mysia, they assayed to go into Bithynia: but the Spirit suffered them not.

8 And they passing by Mysia [l]came down to Troas.

9 And a vision appeared to Paul in the night; There stood a [m]man of Mac-

15:29 [v]Lev. 17:14
15:32 [w]ch. 14:22 & 18:23
15:33 [x]1 Cor. 16:11 Heb. 11:31
15:35 [y]ch. 13:1
15:36 [z]ch. 13:4,13,14,51 & 14:1,6,24,25
15:37 [a]ch. 12:12,25 & 13:5 Col. 4:10 2 Tim. 4:11 Philem. 24
15:38 [b]ch. 13:13
15:40 [c]ch. 14:26
15:41 [d]ch. 16:5
16:1 [e]ch. 14:6 [f]ch. 19:22 Rom. 16:21 1 Cor. 4:17 Phil. 2:19 1 Thes. 3:2 1 Tim. 1:2 2 Tim. 1:2 [g]2 Tim. 1:5
16:2 [h]ch. 6:3
16:3 [i]1 Cor. 9:20 Gal. 2:3 See Gal. 5:2
16:4 [j]ch. 15:28,29
16:5 [k]ch. 15:41
16:8 [l]2 Cor. 2:12 2 Tim. 4:13
16:9 [m]ch. 10:30

[m] Or, *exhortation*

live in harmony with their Gentile brothers. The Gentiles would be expected to abstain from activities which were offensive to Jews. One measure of mature Christians is their willingness to refrain from activities which some Christians think are right and others believe are wrong (see Paul's discussion in 1 Cor. 8:1–11).

15:39 THE CONTENTION. At times disagreements will occur among believers who love the Lord and one another. When these cannot be resolved, it is best to agree to disagree and let God work His will in the lives of all concerned. Differences in opinions that lead to a separation, as in the case of Paul and Barnabas, must never be accompanied by bitterness and hostility. Both Paul and Barnabas continued their work for God with His blessing and grace.

16:5 THE CHURCHES ESTABLISHED. For comments on the form that churches in the N.T. took, see note on 12:5.

16:6 FORBIDDEN OF THE HOLY GHOST. Every initiative in evangelism and missionary activity, especially in the missionary journeys recorded in Acts, is the result of the leading of the Holy Spirit (1:8; 2:14–41; 4:8–12,31; 8:26–29,39–40; 10:19–20; 13:2; 16:6–10; 20:22). The guidance may have taken the form of a prophetic revelation, inward prompting, external circumstances, or visions (vv. 6–9). Under the impulse of the Spirit they moved forward to take the gospel to the unsaved. When checked by the Spirit from going in one direction, they would go in another, trusting in the Holy Spirit to either approve or disapprove of their traveling plans.

edonia, and prayed him, saying, Come over into Macedonia, and help us.

10 And after he had seen the vision, immediately we endeavoured to go [n]into Macedonia, assuredly gathering that the Lord had called us for to preach the gospel unto them.

The conversion of Lydia

11 Therefore loosing from Troas, we came with a straight course to Samothracia, and the next *day* to Neapolis;

12 And from thence to [o]Philippi, which is [n]the chief city of that part of Macedonia, *and* a colony: and we were in that city abiding certain days.

13 And on the [o]sabbath we went out of the city by a river side, where prayer was wont to be made; and we sat down, and spake unto the women which resorted *thither.*

14 ¶ And a certain woman named Lydia, a seller of purple, of the city of Thyatira, which worshipped God, heard *us:* whose [p]heart the Lord opened, that she attended unto the things which were spoken of Paul.

15 And when she was baptized, and her household, she besought *us,* saying, If ye have judged me to be faithful to the Lord, come into my house, and abide *there.* And [q]she constrained us.

Paul and Silas in prison

16 ¶ And it came to pass, as we went to prayer, a certain damsel [r]possessed with a spirit [p]of divination met

16:10 [n]2 Cor. 2:13
16:12 [o]Phil. 1:1
16:14 [p]Luke 24:45
16:15 [q]Gen. 19:3 & 33:11 Judg. 19:21 Luke 24:29 Heb. 13:2
16:16 [r]1 Sam. 28:7

[n] Or, *the first* [o] Gk. *sabbath day* [p] Or, *of Python*

16:16 A SPIRIT OF DIVINATION. The slave girl was possessed by an evil spirit that was thought to have knowledge of the future. The demonic utterances were regarded as a voice of a god; hence, her services as a fortune-teller were much in demand. Through Paul, Christ showed His power over the world of evil (see article on POWER OVER SATAN AND DEMONS, p. 1486).

PAUL'S SECOND MISSIONARY JOURNEY

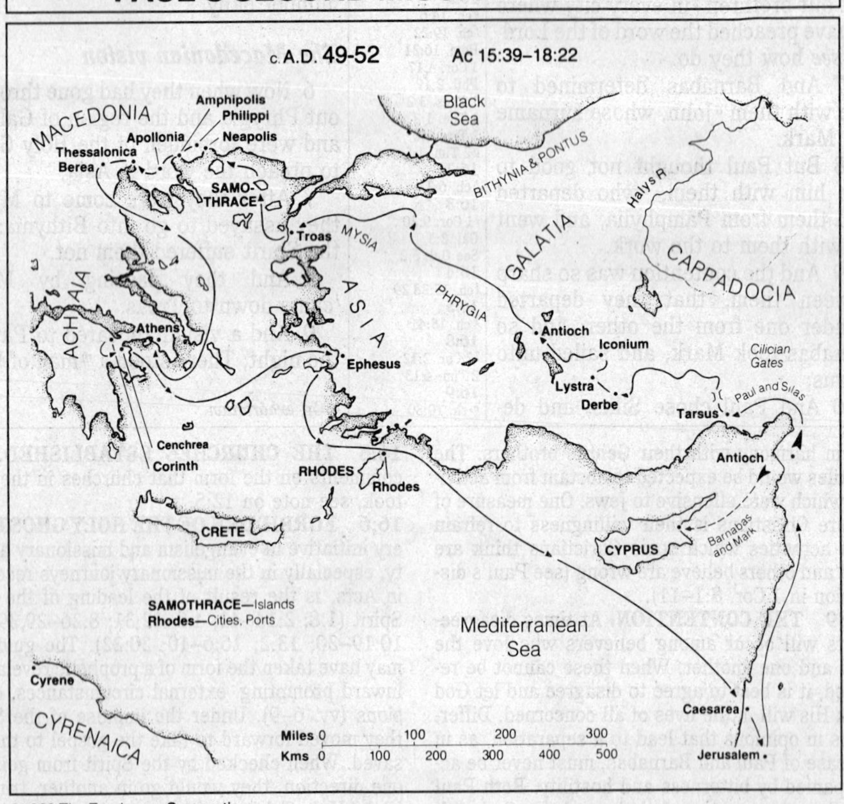

us, which brought her masters [s]much
gain by soothsaying:
17 The same followed Paul and us,
and cried, saying, These men are the
servants of the most high God, which
show unto us the way of salvation.
18 And this did she many days. But
Paul, [t]being grieved, turned and said
to the spirit, I command thee in the
name of Jesus Christ to come out of
her. [u]And he came out the same
hour.
19 ¶ And [v]when her masters saw
that the hope of their gains was gone,
they caught Paul and Silas, and [w]drew
them into the [q]marketplace unto the
rulers,
20 And brought them to the magis-
trates, saying, These men, being Jews,
[x]do exceedingly trouble our city,
21 And teach customs, which are
not lawful for us to receive, neither to
observe, being Romans.
22 And the multitude rose up to-
gether against them: and the magis-
trates rent off their clothes, [y]and com-
manded to beat *them*.
23 And when they had laid many
stripes upon them, they cast *them* into
prison, charging the jailer to keep
them safely:
24 Who, having received such a
charge, thrust them into the inner pris-
on, and made their feet fast in the
stocks.

cts 9:13-0

16:16 [s]ch. 19:24
16:18 [t]See Mark 1:25, 34 [u]Mark 16:17
16:19 [v]ch. 19:25,26 [w]Mat. 10:18
16:20 [x]1 Ki. 18:17 ch. 17:6
16:22 [y]2 Cor. 6:5 & 11:23,25 1 Thes. 2:2
16:26 [z]ch. 4:31 [a]ch. 5:19 & 12:7,10
16:30 [b]Luke 3:10 ch. 2:37 & 9:6
16:31 [c]John 3:16,36 & 6:47 1 John 5:10

The Philippian jailer converted

25 ¶ And at midnight Paul and Silas
prayed, and sang praises unto God:
and the prisoners heard them.
26 [z]And suddenly there was a
great earthquake, so that the founda-
tions of the prison were shaken: and
immediately [a]all the doors were
opened, and every one's bands were
loosed.
27 And the keeper of the prison
awaking out of his sleep, and seeing
the prison doors open, he drew out his
sword, and would have killed himself,
supposing that the prisoners had been
fled.
28 But Paul cried with a loud voice,
saying, Do thyself no harm: for we are
all here.
29 Then he called for a light, and
sprang in, and came trembling, and fell
down before Paul and Silas,
30 And brought them out, and said,
[b]Sirs, what must I do to be saved?
31 And they said, [c]Believe on the
Lord Jesus Christ, and thou shalt be
saved, and thy house.
32 And they spake unto him the
word of the Lord, and to all that were Acts 18:9-10
in his house.
33 And he took them the same hour
of the night, and washed *their* stripes;

[q] Or, *court*

16:23 LAID MANY STRIPES UPON THEM. The Jewish law concerning whippings was forty stripes minus one (2 Cor. 11:24). The Roman custom depended on the judge and could be terribly cruel. The beating was normally inflicted on the naked body.

16:25 PRAYED, AND SANG PRAISES. Paul and Silas had suffered the humiliation of imprisonment, their feet fastened in stocks and their backs lacerated with stripes. Yet in the midst of this suffering, they prayed and sang hymns of praise to God (cf. Mat. 5:10–12). From their missionary experience we learn: (1) that the believer's joy is within, not conditioned by outward circumstances; persecution cannot destroy our peace and joy (Jas. 1:2–4); (2) that the enemies of Christ cannot destroy the believer's faith in and love for God (Rom. 8:35–39); (3) that in the worst of circumstances God will furnish sufficient grace to those who are in His will and suffer for His name's sake (Mat. 5:10–12; 2 Cor. 12:9–10); (4) that "the Spirit of glory and of God resteth upon" those who suffer for the name of Christ (1 Pet. 4:14).

16:26 EVERY ONE'S BANDS WERE LOOSED. Throughout the book of Acts, Luke emphasizes that nothing can stop the gospel of Christ when carried by faithful believers. At Philippi God intervened, and Paul and Silas were delivered by an earthquake sent by Him. This resulted in further progress for the gospel, notably, the salvation of the jailer and his household.

16:30 WHAT MUST I DO TO BE SAVED? This is the most important question one can ask. The apostles' response is, "Believe on the Lord Jesus Christ" (v. 31). (1) To believe on the Lord Jesus is to focus our faith and commitment on the person of Christ. It means turning to Him as a living person who becomes our Redeemer from sin, our Savior from damnation, and the Lord of our lives. It means believing that He is the Son of God sent by the Father and that all He said is true and authoritative for our lives. It means believing that He forgives our sins, makes us His children, gives us the Holy Spirit, and is present with us always to help, guide, comfort, and lead us to heaven.

(2) Saving faith is much more than believing truths about Christ. It causes us to draw near to Him, remain with Him, and commit our troubled lives to Him with assurance that He, His Word, and the Holy Spirit will lead us through this life to the eternal presence of the Father (see article on FAITH AND GRACE, p. 1738).

and was baptized, he and all his, straightway.

34 And when he had brought them into his house, [d]he set meat before them, and rejoiced, believing in God with all his house.

Paul released from prison

35 And when it was day, the magistrates sent the sergeants, saying, Let those men go.

36 And the keeper of the prison told this saying to Paul, The magistrates have sent to let you go: now therefore depart, and go in peace.

37 But Paul said unto them, They have beaten us openly uncondemned, [e]being Romans, and have cast *us* into prison; and now do they thrust us out privily? nay verily; but let them come themselves and fetch us out.

38 And the sergeants told these words unto the magistrates: and they feared, when they heard that they were Romans.

39 And they came and besought them, and brought *them* out, and [f]desired *them* to depart out of the city.

40 And they went out of the prison, [g]and entered into *the house of* Lydia: and when they had seen the brethren, they comforted them, and departed.

Paul at Thessalonica

17 NOW WHEN they had passed through Amphipolis and Apollonia, they came to Thessalonica, where was a synagogue of the Jews:

2 And Paul, as his manner was, [h]went in unto them, and three sabbath days reasoned with them out of the scriptures,

3 Opening and alleging, [i]that Christ must needs have suffered, and risen again from the dead; and that this Jesus, [r]whom I preach unto you, is Christ.

4 [j]And some of them believed, and consorted with Paul and [k]Silas; and of the devout Greeks a great multitude, and of the chief women not a few.

5 ¶ But the Jews which believed not, moved with envy, took unto them certain lewd fellows of the baser sort, and gathered a company, and set all the city on an uproar, and assaulted the house of [l]Jason, and sought to bring them out to the people.

6 And when they found them not, they drew Jason and certain brethren unto the rulers of the city, crying, [m]These that have turned the world upside down are come hither also;

7 Whom Jason hath received: and these all do contrary to the decrees of Caesar, [n]saying that there is another king, *one* Jesus.

8 And they troubled the people and the rulers of the city, when they heard these things.

9 And when they had taken security of Jason, and of the other, they let them go.

Paul at Berea

10 ¶ And [o]the brethren immediately sent away Paul and Silas by night unto Berea: who coming *thither* went into the synagogue of the Jews.

11 These were more noble than those in Thessalonica, in that they received the word with all readiness of mind, and [p]searched the scriptures daily, whether those things were so.

12 Therefore many of them believed; also of honourable women which were Greeks, and of men, not a few.

13 But when the Jews of Thessalonica had knowledge that the word of God was preached of Paul at Berea, they came thither also, and stirred up the people.

14 [q]And then immediately the brethren sent away Paul to go as it were to the sea: but Silas and Timotheus abode there still.

15 And they that conducted Paul brought him unto Athens: and [r]receiving a commandment unto Silas and Timotheus for to come to him with all speed, they departed.

Paul at Athens

16 ¶ Now while Paul waited for

16:34 [d]Luke 5:29 & 19:6
16:37 [e]ch. 22:25
16:39 [f]Mat. 8:34
16:40 [g]ver. 14
17:2 [h]Luke 4:16 ch. 9:20 & 13:5,14 & 14:1 & 16:13 & 19:8
17:3 [i]Luke 24:26,46 ch. 18:28 Gal. 3:1
17:4 [j]ch. 28:24 [k]ch. 15:22,27,32, 40
17:5 [l]Rom. 16:21
17:6 [m]ch. 16:20
17:7 [n]Luke 23:2 John 19:12 1 Pet. 2:13
17:10 [o]ver. 14 ch. 9:25
17:11 [p]Is. 34:16 Luke 16:29 John 5:39
17:14 [q]Mat. 10:23
17:15 [r]ch. 18:5

[r] Or, *whom*, said he, *I preach*

17:11 SEARCHED THE SCRIPTURES DAILY. The action of those in Berea is a model for all who listen to preachers and teachers expound the Scriptures. No interpretation or doctrine ought to be accepted passively. Rather, it must be examined carefully by personal study of the Scriptures. The word translated "examine" (Gk. *anakrinō*) means "to sift up and down, make careful and exact research." Bible preaching should make Bible students out of the hearers. The truth of every doctrine should be examined according to the Word of God (see Eph. 2:20, note).

them at Athens, [s]his spirit was stirred in him, when he saw the city [s]wholly given to idolatry.

17 Therefore disputed he in the synagogue with the Jews, and with the devout persons, and in the market daily with them that met with him.

18 Then certain philosophers of the Epicureans, and of the Stoics, encountered him. And some said, What will this [t]babbler say? other some, He seemeth to be a setter forth of strange gods: because he preached unto them Jesus, and the resurrection.

19 And they took him, and brought him unto [u]Areopagus, saying, May we know what this new doctrine, whereof thou speakest, *is?*

20 For thou bringest certain strange things to our ears: we would know therefore what these things mean.

21 (For all the Athenians and strangers which were there spent their time in nothing else, but either to tell, or to hear some new thing.)

22 ¶ Then Paul stood in the midst of [v]Mars' hill, and said, *Ye* men of Athens, I perceive that in all things ye are too superstitious.

23 For as I passed by, and beheld your [w]devotions, I found an altar with this inscription, TO THE UNKNOWN GOD. Whom therefore ye ignorantly worship, him declare I unto you.

24 [t]God that made the world and all things therein, seeing that he is [u]Lord of heaven and earth, [v]dwelleth not in temples made with hands;

25 Neither is worshipped with men's hands, [w]as though he needed any thing, seeing [x]he giveth to all life, and breath, and all things;

26 And hath made of one blood all nations of men for to dwell on all the face of the earth, and hath determined the times before appointed, and [y]the bounds of their habitation;

27 [z]That they should seek the Lord, if haply they might feel after him, and find him, [a]though he be not far from every one of us:

28 For [b]in him we live, and move, and have our being; [c]as certain also of your own poets have said, For we are also his offspring.

29 Forasmuch then as we are the offspring of God, [d]we ought not to think that the Godhead is like unto gold, or silver, or stone, graven by art and man's device.

30 And [e]the times of this ignorance God winked at; but [f]now commandeth all men every where to repent:

31 Because he hath appointed a day, in the which [g]he will judge the world in righteousness by *that* man whom he hath ordained; *whereof* he hath [x]given assurance unto all *men,* in that [h]he hath raised him from the dead.

32 ¶ And when they heard of the resurrection of the dead, some mocked: and others said, We will hear thee again of this *matter.*

33 So Paul departed from among them.

34 Howbeit certain men clave unto him, and believed: among the which *was* Dionysius the Areopagite, and a woman named Damaris, and others with them.

17:16 [s]2 Pet. 2:8
17:24 [t]ch. 14:15 [u]Mat. 11:25 [v]ch. 7:48
17:25 [w]Ps. 50:8 [x]Gen. 2:7 Num. 16:22 Job 12:10 & 27:3 & 33:4 Is. 42:5 & 57:16 Zech. 12:1
17:26 [y]Deut. 32:8
17:27 [z]Rom. 1:20 [a]ch. 14:17
17:28 [b]Col. 1:17 Heb. 1:3 [c]Tit. 1:12
17:29 [d]Is. 40:18
17:30 [e]ch. 14:16 Rom. 3:25 [f]Luke 24:47 Tit. 2:11,12 1 Pet. 1:14 & 4:3
17:31 [g]ch. 10:42 Rom. 2:16 & 14:10 [h]ch. 2:24

[s] Or, *full of idols* [t] Or, *base fellow* [u] Or, *Mars hill.* It was the highest court in Athens [v] Or, *the court of the Areopagites* [w] Or, *gods that ye worship;* see 2 Thes. 2:4 [x] Or, *offered faith*

17:16 HIS SPIRIT WAS STIRRED. At the sight of idolatry and moral corruption, Paul became indignant and grief-stricken (see Heb. 1:9, note); his spirit stirred over people who were lost and needed salvation. Paul expressed the same attitude as Jesus did toward sin and its destructive work (see John 11:33, note). An attitude of holy anger toward sin and immorality should characterize all those who have the spirit of Christ. For the cause of Christ and the salvation of the lost, our spirits should rise in rebellion against sin denounced in Scripture, offensive to God, and destructive to the human race (cf. 1 Cor. 6:17).

17:30 COMMANDETH ALL . . . TO REPENT. In times past, before full knowledge of God came through Jesus Christ, God overlooked human ignorance of Himself and much of man's sin (cf. Rom. 3:25). Now that His full and perfect revelation has come with the coming of Christ, all are commanded to repent and believe in Jesus as Lord and Savior. There are no exceptions, for God will not overlook the sins of anyone. All must turn from sin or be condemned. Repentance, in other words, is essential for salvation (see Mat. 3:2, note).

17:31 JUDGE THE WORLD IN RIGHTEOUSNESS. For other Pauline references to the appointed day of judgment, see Rom. 2:5,16; 1 Cor. 1:8; Phil. 1:6,10; 1 Thes. 5:2,4; 2 Thes. 1:7–10; 2:2.

Paul at Corinth

18 AFTER THESE things Paul departed from Athens, and came to Corinth:

2 And found a certain Jew named [i]Aquila, born in Pontus, lately come from Italy, with his wife Priscilla; (because that Claudius had commanded all Jews to depart from Rome:) and came unto them.

3 And because he was of the same craft, he abode with them, [j]and wrought: for by their occupation they were tentmakers.

4 [k]And he reasoned in the synagogue every sabbath, and persuaded the Jews and the Greeks.

5 And [l]when Silas and Timotheus were come from Macedonia, Paul was [m]pressed in the spirit, and testified to the Jews *that* Jesus [y]*was* Christ.

6 And [n]when they opposed themselves, and blasphemed, [o]he shook *his* raiment, and said unto them, [p]Your blood *be* upon your own heads; [q]I *am* clean: [r]from henceforth I will go unto the Gentiles.

7 And he departed thence, and entered into a certain *man's* house, named Justus, *one* that worshipped God, whose house joined hard to the synagogue.

8 [s]And Crispus, the chief ruler of the synagogue, believed on the Lord with all his house; and many of the Corinthians hearing believed, and were baptized.

9 Then [t]spake the Lord to Paul in the night by a vision, Be not afraid, but speak, and hold not thy peace:

10 [u]For I am with thee, and no man shall set on thee to hurt thee: for I have much people in this city. Act 20:21

11 And he [z]continued *there* a year and six months, teaching the word of God among them.

12 ¶ And when Gallio was the deputy of Achaia, the Jews made insurrection with one accord against Paul, and brought him to the judgment seat,

13 Saying, This *fellow* persuadeth men to worship God contrary to the law.

14 And when Paul was now about to open *his* mouth, Gallio said unto the Jews, [v]If it were a matter of wrong or wicked lewdness, O *ye* Jews, reason would that I should bear with you:

15 But if it be a question of words and names, and *of* your law, look ye *to it;* for I will be no judge of such *matters.*

16 And he drave them from the judgment seat.

17 Then all the Greeks took [w]Sosthenes, the chief ruler of the syna-

18:2 [i]Rom. 16:3 1 Cor. 16:19 2 Tim. 4:19
18:3 [j]ch. 20:34 1 Cor. 4:12 1 Thes. 2:9 2 Thes. 3:8
18:4 [k]ch. 17:2
18:5 [l]ch. 17:14,15 [m]ver. 28 Job 32:18 ch. 17:3
18:6 [n]ch. 13:45 [o]Neh. 5:13 Mat. 10:14 ch. 13:51 [p]Lev. 20:9,11,12 2 Sam. 1:16 Ezek. 18:13 & 33:4 [q]Ezek. 3:18,19 & 33:9 ch. 20:26 [r]ch. 13:46 & 28:28
18:8 [s]1 Cor. 1:14
18:9 [t]ch. 23:11
18:10 [u]Jer. 1:18,19
18:14 [v]ch. 23:29 & 25:11,19
18:17 [w]1 Cor. 1:1

[y] Or, *is the Christ* [z] Gk. *sat* there

18:3 HE WAS OF THE SAME CRAFT. Paul practiced a trade as well as preached the gospel; he was a tentmaker, regularly earning his living in this way while traveling or staying in residence (20:34; 1 Thes. 2:9; 2 Thes. 3:8). From the example of Paul it is clear that ministers who must work in order to help support themselves and their families are not engaged in a second-class ministry. A dual-vocational ministry has Biblical and apostolic precedence.

18:9 BE NOT AFRAID. This passage reveals the inner, human feelings of the apostle. Evidently opposition and hatred toward Paul and the gospel were increasing, and Paul was becoming afraid and having doubts whether he should leave Corinth or become silent for a while (cf. 1 Cor. 2:3). These same feelings will occur at times in the hearts of all God's faithful, even as they did in such men as Elijah (1 Ki. 19:4) and Jeremiah (Jer. 15:15). In such circumstances God will minister to His saints and encourage their hearts. The promise of His presence (v. 10) is sufficient to deliver them from fear and to give the assurance and peace necessary to accomplish God's will for their lives (vv. 10–11).

18:10 FOR I AM WITH THEE. These words of Christ to Paul do not refer to His general presence everywhere, i.e., His omnipresence (cf. 17:26–28; Ps. 139; Jer. 23:23–24; Amos 9:2–4). Rather they refer to His special nearness to His faithful children. Christ's nearness means that He is personally here to communicate His will, love, and fellowship to us. He is present to act in every situation of our lives to bless, help, protect, and guide.

(1) We may learn something of the truth of "Christ with us" in the passages of the O.T. where God stated that He was with His faithful. When Moses was afraid to return to Egypt, God said: "I will be with thee" (Ex. 3:12). When Joshua assumed the leadership of Israel after Moses' death, God promised: "I will be with thee: I will not fail thee, nor forsake thee" (Josh. 1:5). And God encouraged Israel with the words: "When thou passeth through the water, I *will be* with thee .... Fear not: for I am with thee" (Is. 43:2,5).

(2) In the N.T. Matthew states that the purpose of Jesus' coming into the world was to achieve the nearness of God to His people. His name is "Emmanuel," meaning "God with us" (Mat. 1:23). Again, at the end of his Gospel Matthew records Jesus' promise to His disciples: "Lo, I am with you alway" (Mat. 28:20). Mark ends his Gospel with the words: "And they went forth, and preached every where, the Lord working with *them*" (Mark 16:20).

gogue, and beat *him* before the judg-
ment seat. And Gallio cared for none of
those things.

Paul returns to Antioch

18 ¶ And Paul *after this* tarried *there*
yet a good while, and then took his
leave of the brethren, and sailed
thence into Syria, and with him Priscil-
la and Aquila; having [x]shorn *his* head
in [y]Cenchrea: for he had a vow.
19 And he came to Ephesus, and
left them there: but he himself entered
into the synagogue, and reasoned with
the Jews.
20 When they desired *him* to tarry
longer time with them, he consented
not;
21 But bade them farewell, saying,
[z]I must by all means keep this feast
that cometh in Jerusalem: but I will re-
turn again unto you, [a]if God will. And
he sailed from Ephesus.
22 And when he had landed at Caes-
area, and gone up, and saluted the
church, he went down to Antioch.
23 And after he had spent some
time *there*, he departed, and went over
all the country of [b]Galatia and Phryg-
ia in order, [c]strengthening all the dis-
ciples.

Apollos's preaching at Ephesus

24 ¶ [d]And a certain Jew named
Apollos, born at Alexandria, an elo-
quent man, *and* mighty in the scrip-
tures, came to Ephesus.
25 This man was instructed in the
way of the Lord; and being [e]fervent in
the spirit, he spake and taught dili-
gently the things of the Lord, [f]know-
ing only the baptism of John.
26 And he began to speak boldly in
the synagogue: whom when Aquila and
Priscilla had heard, they took him unto
them, and expounded unto him the way
of God more perfectly.
27 And when he was disposed to
pass into Achaia, the brethren wrote,
exhorting the disciples to receive him:
who, when he was come, [g]helped
them much which had believed through
grace:
28 For he mightily convinced the
Jews, *and that* publicly, [h]showing by
the scriptures that Jesus [a]was Christ.

John's disciples receive the Holy Spirit

19 AND IT came to pass, that,
while [i]Apollos was at Corinth,
Paul having passed through the upper
coasts came to Ephesus: and finding
certain disciples,
2 He said unto them, Have ye re-
ceived the Holy Ghost since ye be-

18:18 [x]Num. 6:18 ch. 21:24 [y]Rom. 16:1 **18:21** [z]ch. 19:21 & 20:16 [a]1 Cor. 4:19 Heb. 6:3 Jas. 4:15 **18:23** [b]Gal. 1:2 & 4:14 [c]ch. 14:22 & 15:32,41 **18:24** [d]1 Cor. 1:12 & 3:5,6 & 4:6 Tit. 3:13 **18:25** [e]Rom. 12:11 [f]ch. 19:3 **18:27** [g]1 Cor. 3:6 **18:28** [h]ver. 5 ch. 9:22 & 17:3 **19:1** [i]1 Cor. 1:12 & 3:5,6

[a] Or, *is the Christ*

18:23 STRENGTHENING ALL THE DISCIPLES. This begins Paul's third missionary journey (18:23—21:15). He leaves to visit the churches established on his first (chs. 13–14) and second (15:36—18:22) journeys. Paul never won converts and then forgot them; he was equally concerned with following up new believers and strengthening them in the way of Christ. All new believers should be contacted immediately by established Christians, prayed with, instructed in the Christian way, and encouraged to meet with other believers for worship, prayer, the ministry of the Word, and the manifestations of the Holy Spirit for the common good (2:42; Mat. 28:19–20; 1 Cor. 12:7–11; 14).

18:25 KNOWING ONLY THE BAPTISM OF JOHN. At this time Apollos's understanding of the gospel was limited. He had accepted John's baptism and believed in Jesus as the crucified and resurrected Messiah. What he had not learned was that Jesus Himself was now baptizing all believers in the Holy Spirit. The Ephesian disciples were in much the same situation (19:2,6).

19:1 EPHESUS ... CERTAIN DISCIPLES. Were these twelve disciples at Ephesus Christians or disciples of John the Baptist? Either is a possibility. (1) Some believe they were Christians. (a) Luke calls them disciples, a word he commonly uses for Christians. Had Luke meant to indicate that they were disciples of only John the Baptist, not Christ, he most likely would have said so explicitly. (b) Paul speaks of them as already believing (v. 2). The verb "believe" is used about twenty times in Acts with no direct object. In every other case, the context indicates that believing in Christ for salvation is meant (see next note).

(2) Others maintain that the Ephesian disciples were "disciples" of John the Baptist who were still waiting for the Messiah. After they heard about Jesus from Paul, they believed in Him as the predicted Christ and were born again by the Spirit (vv. 4–5).

(3) Whatever the case might be, it is clear that their being filled with the Holy Spirit came after their faith, baptism, and the laying on of hands (vv. 5–6).

19:2 HAVE YE RECEIVED THE HOLY GHOST? Observe the following four facts concerning Paul's question to the disciples at Ephesus. (1) Paul's question strongly suggests that he regarded them as true converted Christians who had not yet been filled with the Holy Spirit.

(2) Paul's question here refers to the baptism in the Holy Spirit for power and ministry, the same as that which happened to the apostles at Pentecost (cf. 1:8; 2:4). It cannot refer to the Spirit's

lieved? And they said unto him, [j]We
have not so much as heard whether
there be any Holy Ghost.
3 And he said unto them, Unto what
then were ye baptized? And they said,
[k]Unto John's baptism.
4 Then said Paul, [l]John verily bap-
tized with the baptism of repentance,
saying unto the people, that they
should believe on him which should
come after him, that is, on Christ Jesus.
5 When they heard *this,* they were
baptized [m]in the name of the Lord
Jesus.
6 And when Paul had [n]laid *his*
hands upon them, the Holy Ghost came
on them; and [o]they spake with
tongues, and prophesied.
7 And all the men were about
Eph. 5:18 twelve.
8 [p]And he went into the syna-

19:2 [j]ch. 8:16 See 1 Sam. 3:7 **19:3** [k]ch. 18:25 **19:4** [l]Mat. 3:11 John 1:15,27,30 ch. 1:5 & 11:16 & 13:24,25 **19:5** [m]ch. 8:16 **19:6** [n]ch. 6:6 & 8:17 [o]ch. 2:4 & 10:46 **19:8** [p]ch. 17:2 & 18:4 [q]ch. 1:3 & 28:23 **19:9** [r]2 Tim. 1:15 2 Pet. 2:2 Jude 10 [s]ver. 23 See ch. 9:2 & 22:4 & 24:14

gogue, and spake boldly for the space
of three months, disputing and per-
suading the things [q]concerning the
kingdom of God.
9 But [r]when divers were hard-
ened, and believed not, but spake evil
[s]of that way before the multitude, he
departed from them, and separated the
disciples, disputing daily in the school
of one Tyrannus.
10 And [t]this continued by the
space of two years; so that all they
which dwelt in Asia heard the word of
the Lord Jesus, both Jews and Greeks.

Miracles at Ephesus

11 And [u]God wrought special mir-
acles by the hands of Paul:
12 [v]So that from his body were

19:10 [t]See ch. 20:31 **19:11** [u]Mark 16:20; ch. 14:3 **19:12** [v]See 2 Ki. 4:29; ch. 5:15

indwelling presence in the believer, for Paul clearly knew that all believers have the Spirit dwelling in them from the very moment of their belief, conversion, and regeneration (Rom. 8:9).

(3) The literal translation of Paul's question is, "Having believed, did you receive the Holy Spirit?" "Having believed" (Gk. *pisteusantes*, from *pisteuō*) is an aorist participle, which normally indicates action prior to the action of the main verb (in this case, "receive"). Hence we may render this: "Did you receive the Holy Spirit after you believed?" This translation agrees fully with the context of the passage, for this is exactly what did happen to the Ephesian believers. (a) They had already believed in Christ before Paul met them (vv. 1–2). (b) They then listened to Paul and further believed all he told them about Christ and the Holy Spirit (v. 4). (c) Paul then considered the Ephesians' belief in Christ to be genuine and adequate, for he baptized them in the name of the Lord Jesus (v. 5). (d) It was only then, after their belief and water baptism, that Paul laid his hands on them and the "Holy Ghost came on them" (v. 6). Thus, there was an interval of time between their belief in Christ and the coming of the Spirit in power.

Paul's question here indicates that he thought it quite possible to "believe" in Christ without experiencing the baptism in the Holy Spirit. This passage is decisive in showing that one may be a Christian without possessing the fullness of the Holy Spirit (see article on BAPTISM IN THE HOLY SPIRIT, p. 1652).

19:2 WE HAVE NOT . . . HEARD. The response of the Ephesian believers to Paul's question does not mean they had never heard of the Holy Spirit. They certainly were acquainted with the O.T. teaching about the Spirit, and they most assuredly had heard John's message concerning the baptism in the Holy Spirit which the Christ was to bring (Luke 3:16). They had not yet heard that the Spirit was being poured out upon believers (1:5,8).

19:5 THEY WERE BAPTIZED. Water baptism in "the name of the Lord Jesus" of these twelve men at Ephesus (v. 7) testifies that they had saving faith and were born again by the Spirit. This precedes their being filled with the Holy Spirit (v. 6).

19:6 THE HOLY GHOST CAME ON THEM. This event occurs some 25 years after the first Pentecost (2:4); yet, the pattern of these twelve men receiving the fullness of the Holy Spirit is consistent with the normal pattern already presented by Luke (see 8:5–24, note).

(1) They had believed in Jesus and were born again by the Spirit (see previous note).

(2) After they were baptized in water (v. 5), Paul laid his hands upon them and they were baptized in the Holy Spirit.

(3) As the Holy Spirit came upon them, they began speaking with tongues and prophesying. Luke never presents the outpouring of the Holy Spirit as something one could only perceive by faith. Rather he shows it to be a knowable and identifiable experience capable of being verified objectively; speaking in tongues was external and visible proof that the Holy Spirit had come upon these followers of Jesus (see article on SPEAKING IN TONGUES, p. 1656).

19:12 HANDKERCHIEFS OR APRONS. Paul's ministry at Ephesus was marked by extraordinary miracles of healing and deliverance from demons, accomplished directly or through handkerchiefs and aprons that had been in contact with his body (i.e., sweat cloths and aprons used in his leatherworking). Diseases disappeared and evil spirits left when the afflicted touched the cloth (cf. 5:15; Mark 5:27). Any minister today who attempts to gain money and support by advertising handkerchiefs for similar use is not acting according to the motive and spirit of Paul, for Paul did not offer these items for money. He simply multiplied the empowering that was on him through these tangible means, healing and delivering

brought unto the sick handkerchiefs or aprons, and the diseases departed from them, and the evil spirits went out of them.

13 ¶ [w]Then certain of the vagabond Jews, exorcists, [x]took upon them to call over them which had evil spirits the name of the Lord Jesus, saying, We adjure you by Jesus whom Paul preacheth.

14 And there were seven sons of *one* Sceva, a Jew, *and* chief of the priests, which did so.

15 And the evil spirit answered and said, Jesus I know, and Paul I know; but who are ye?

16 And the man in whom the evil spirit was leaped on them, and overcame them, and prevailed against them, so that they fled out of that house naked and wounded.

17 And this was known to all the Jews and Greeks also dwelling at Ephesus; and [y]fear fell on them all, and the name of the Lord Jesus was magnified.

18 And many that believed came, and [z]confessed, and showed their deeds.

19 Many of them also which used curious arts brought their books together, and burned them before all *men:* and they counted the price of them, and found *it* fifty thousand *pieces* of silver.

20 [a]So mightily grew the word of God and prevailed.

21 ¶ [b]After these things were ended, Paul [c]purposed in the spirit, when he had passed through Macedonia and Achaia, to go to Jerusalem, saying, After I have been there, [d]I must also see Rome.

22 So he sent into Macedonia two of them that ministered unto him, Timotheus and [e]Erastus; but he himself stayed in Asia for a season.

The riot at Ephesus

23 And [f]the same time there arose no small stir about [g]that way.

24 For a certain *man* named Demetrius, a silversmith, which made silver shrines for Diana, brought [h]no small gain unto the craftsmen;

25 Whom he called together with the workmen of like occupation, and said, Sirs, ye know that by this craft we have our wealth.

26 Moreover ye see and hear, that not alone at Ephesus, but almost throughout all Asia, this Paul hath persuaded and turned away much people, saying that [i]they be no gods, which are made with hands:

27 So that not only this our craft is in danger to be set at nought; but also that the temple of the great goddess Diana should be despised, and her magnificence should be destroyed, whom all Asia and the world worshippeth.

28 And when they heard *these sayings,* they were full of wrath, and cried out, saying, Great *is* Diana of the Ephesians.

29 And the whole city was filled with confusion: and having caught [j]Gaius and [k]Aristarchus, men of Macedonia, Paul's companions in travel, they rushed with one accord into the theatre.

30 And when Paul would have entered in unto the people, the disciples suffered him not.

31 And certain of the chief of Asia, which were his friends, sent unto him, desiring *him* that he would not adventure himself into the theatre.

32 Some therefore cried one thing, and some another: for the assembly was confused; and the more part knew not wherefore they were come together.

33 And they drew Alexander out of the multitude, the Jews putting him forward. And [l]Alexander [m]beckoned with the hand, and would have made his defence unto the people.

34 But when they knew that he was a Jew, all with one voice about the space of two hours cried out, Great *is* Diana of the Ephesians.

35 And when the townclerk had ap-

19:13 [w]Mat. 12:27 [x]See Mark 9:38 Luke 9:49
19:17 [y]Luke 1:65 & 7:16 ch. 2:43 & 5:5,11
19:18 [z]Mat. 3:6
19:20 [a]ch. 6:7 & 12:24
19:21 [b]Rom. 15:25 Gal. 2:1 [c]ch. 20:22 [d]ch. 18:21 & 23:11 Rom. 15:24-28
19:22 [e]Rom. 16:23 2 Tim. 4:20
19:23 [f]2 Cor. 1:8 [g]See ch. 9:2
19:24 [h]ch. 16:16,19
19:26 [i]Ps. 115:4 Is. 44:10-20 Jer. 10:3
19:29 [j]Rom. 16:23 1 Cor. 1:14 [k]ch. 20:4 & 27:2 Col. 4:10 Philem. 24
19:33 [l]1 Tim. 1:20 2 Tim. 4:14 [m]ch. 12:17

more people than he could personally lay hands on.

19:19 CURIOUS ARTS. This term refers to the practice of sorcery. The public burning of magical books shows that new believers in Christ were taught immediately to turn away from occult practices. Witchcraft, black magic, sorcery, spiritism, and other occult practices are satanic activities, completely incompatible with the Christian faith. One cannot be a true believer in Christ and at the same time deal with spirits or attempt to gain contact with the dead. God forbids and condemns all such activity as detestable (see Deut. 18:9–13, notes). Dabbling in the occult and spiritism will open one's life up to powerful satanic influence and demonic possession.

peased the people, he said, *Ye* men of
Ephesus, what man is there that
knoweth not how that the city of the
Ephesians is [b]a worshipper of the
great goddess Diana, and of the *image*
which fell down from Jupiter?
36 Seeing then that these things
cannot be spoken against, ye ought to
be quiet, and to do nothing rashly.
37 For ye have brought hither these
men, which are neither robbers of
churches, nor yet blasphemers of your
goddess.
38 Wherefore if Demetrius, and the
craftsmen which are with him, have a
matter against any man, [c]the law is
open, and there are deputies: let them
implead one another.
39 But if ye inquire any thing con-
cerning other matters, it shall be deter-
mined in a [d]lawful assembly.
40 For we are in danger to be called
in question for this day's uproar, there
being no cause whereby we may give
an account of this concourse.
41 And when he had thus spoken,
he dismissed the assembly.

Macedonia and Greece

20 AND AFTER the uproar was
ceased, Paul called unto *him*
the disciples, and embraced *them,* and
[n]departed for to go into Macedonia.
2 And when he had gone over those
parts, and had given them much exhor-
tation, he came into Greece,
3 And *there* abode three months.
And [o]when the Jews laid wait for him,
as he was about to sail into Syria, he
purposed to return through Macedo-
nia.
4 And there accompanied him into
Asia Sopater of Berea; and of the Thes-
salonians, [p]Aristarchus and Secun-
dus; and [q]Gaius of Derbe, and [r]Timo-
theus; and of Asia, [s]Tychicus and
[t]Trophimus.

From Philippi to Miletus

5 These going before tarried for us
at Troas.
6 And we sailed away from Philippi
after [u]the days of unleavened bread,
and came unto them [v]to Troas in five
days; where we abode seven days.
7 And upon [w]the first *day* of the
week, when the disciples came togeth-
er [x]to break bread, Paul preached
unto them, ready to depart on the mor-
row; and continued his speech until
midnight.
8 And there were many lights [y]in
the upper chamber, where they were
gathered together.
9 And there sat in a window a cer-
tain young man named Eutychus, be-
ing fallen into a deep sleep: and as
Paul was long preaching, he sunk
down with sleep, and fell down from
the third loft, and was taken up dead.
10 And Paul went down, and [z]fell
on him, and embracing *him* said,
[a]Trouble not yourselves; for his life is
in him.
11 When he therefore was come up
again, and had broken bread, and eat-
en, and talked a long while, even till
break of day, so he departed.
12 And they brought the young man
alive, and were not a little comforted.
13 ¶ And we went before to ship,
and sailed unto Assos, there intending
to take in Paul: for so had he appoint-
ed, minding himself to go afoot.
14 And when he met with us at As-
sos, we took him in, and came to Mity-
lene.
15 And we sailed thence, and came
the next *day* over against Chios; and
the next *day* we arrived at Samos, and
tarried at Trogyllium; and the next *day*
we came to Miletus.
16 For Paul had determined to sail
by Ephesus, because he would not
spend the time in Asia: for [b]he hasted,
if it were possible for him, [c]to be at
Jerusalem [d]the day of Pentecost.

Paul testimony to the Ephesian elders

17 ¶ And from Miletus he sent to
Ephesus, and called the elders of the
church.
18 And when they were come to
him, he said unto them, Ye know,
[e]from the first day that I came into
Asia, after what manner I have been
with you at all seasons,
19 Serving the Lord with all humili-

20:1 [n]1 Cor. 16:5 1 Tim. 1:3 **20:3** [o]ch. 9:23 & 23:12 & 25:3 2 Cor. 11:26 **20:4** [p]ch. 19:29 & 27:2 Col. 4:10 [q]ch. 19:29 [r]ch. 16:1 [s]Eph. 6:21 Col. 4:7 2 Tim. 4:12 Tit. 3:12 [t]ch. 21:29 2 Tim. 4:20 **20:6** [u]Ex. 12:14,15 & 23:15 [v]ch. 16:8 2 Cor. 2:12 2 Tim. 4:13 **20:7** [w]1 Cor. 16:2 Rev. 1:10

[x]ch. 2:42,46 1 Cor. 10:16 & 11:20 **20:8** [y]ch. 1:13 **20:10** [z]1 Ki. 17:21 2 Ki. 4:34 [a]Mat. 9:24 **20:16** [b]ch. 18:21 & 19:21 & 21:4,12 [c]ch. 24:17 [d]ch. 2:1 1 Cor. 16:8 **20:18** [e]ch. 18:19 & 19:1,10

b Gk. *the temple keeper* c Or, *the court days are kept* d Or, *ordinary*

20:19 WITH MANY TEARS. Paul on several occasions mentions his serving the Lord with "tears" (v. 31; 2 Cor. 2:4; Phil. 3:18). In this address to the Ephesian elders (vv. 17–38), he speaks of daily admonishing them with tears for a period of three years (v. 31). The tears were not

ty of mind, and with many tears, and
temptations, which befell me [f]by the
lying in wait of the Jews:
20 *And* how [g]I kept back nothing
that was profitable *unto you,* but have
shown you, and have taught you pub-
licly, and from house to house,
21 [h]Testifying both to the Jews,
and also to the Greeks, [i]repentance
toward God, and faith toward our Lord
Jesus Christ.
22 And now, behold, [j]I go bound in
the spirit unto Jerusalem, not knowing
the things that shall befall me there:
23 Save that [k]the Holy Ghost wit-
nesseth in every city, saying that
bonds and afflictions [e]abide me.
24 But [l]none of these things move
me, neither count I my life dear unto
myself, [m]so that I might finish my
course with joy, [n]and the ministry,
[o]which I have received of the Lord
Jesus, to testify the gospel of the grace
of God.
25 And now, behold, [p]I know that
ye all, among whom I have gone
preaching the kingdom of God, shall
see my face no more.
26 Wherefore I take you to record
this day, that I *am* [q]pure from the
blood of all *men.*
27 For [r]I have not shunned to de-
clare unto you all [s]the counsel of God.

cts
5:16-
7

20:19 [f]ver. 3 **20:20** [g]ver. 27 **20:21** [h]ch. 18:5 [i]Mark 1:15 Luke 24:27 ch. 2:38 **20:22** [j]ch. 19:21 **20:23** [k]ch. 21:4,11 1 Thes. 3:3 **20:24** [l]ch. 21:13 Rom. 8:35 2 Cor. 4:16 [m]2 Tim. 4:7 [n]ch. 1:17 2 Cor. 4:1 [o]Gal. 1:1 Tit. 1:3 **20:25** [p]ver. 38 Rom. 15:23 **20:26** [q]ch. 18:6 2 Cor. 7:2 **20:27** [r]ver. 20 [s]Luke 7:30 John 15:15 Eph. 1:11 **20:28** [t]1 Tim. 4:16 1 Pet. 5:2

Exhortation to guard the church

28 ¶ [t]Take heed therefore unto
yourselves, and to all the flock, over
the which the Holy Ghost [u]hath made
you overseers, to feed the church of
God, [v]which he hath purchased
[w]with his own blood.
29 For I know this, that after my
departing [x]shall grievous wolves

[u]1 Cor. 12:28 [v]Eph. 1:7,14; Col. 1:14; Heb. 9:12; 1 Pet. 1:19; Rev. 5:9 [w]See Heb. 9:14 **20:29** [x]Mat. 7:15; 2 Pet. 2:1

[e] Or, *wait for me*

---

the result of weakness; rather, Paul saw the lost condition of the human race, the evil of sin, the distortion of the gospel, and the peril of rejecting the Lord as such grave realities that his preaching was often accompanied by tears (cf. Mark 9:24; Luke 19:41).

20:20 I KEPT BACK NOTHING. Paul preached whatever he believed was useful or needful for the salvation of his hearers. A minister of the gospel must be faithful to declare the whole truth of God to his people. He must not seek to please their desires or gratify their tastes, nor to promote his own popularity. Even if he must speak words of reproof and rebuke, teach doctrines that run counter to natural prejudices, or preach Biblical standards that oppose the desires of the flesh, the faithful preacher will deliver the whole truth for the sake of the flock (e.g., Gal. 1:6–10; 2 Tim. 4:1–5).

20:22 BOUND IN THE SPIRIT. Paul's spirit, under the control of the Holy Spirit, felt compelled to go to Jerusalem. He knew that afflictions and suffering awaited him (v. 23), yet he committed his way to God, not knowing whether it would mean life or death (see 21:4, note).

20:23 THE HOLY GHOST WITNESSETH. The Holy Spirit's testimony to Paul that hardships and imprisonment awaited him probably came through the prophets or prophecy in the churches (cf. 1 Cor. 12:10).

20:24 NEITHER COUNT I MY LIFE DEAR. Paul's main concern was not preserving his own life. What counted most was that he might finish the ministry to which God had called him. Wherever it ended, even if in the sacrifice of his life, he would finish his course with joy and the prayer that "Christ shall be magnified in my body, whether it be by life, or by death" (Phil. 1:20). For Paul, life and service for Christ is represented as a course or race that one must run with absolute faithfulness to his Lord (cf. 13:25; 1 Cor. 9:24; 2 Tim. 4:7; Heb. 12:1).

20:26 I *AM* PURE FROM THE BLOOD OF ALL *MEN*. The word "blood" is used normally in the sense of bloodshed, i.e., the crime of causing someone's death (cf. 5:28; Mat. 23:35; 27:25). (1) Here it means that if any should die spiritually and be lost forever, Paul would not be blamed. (2) If overseers do not want to be held responsible for the perishing of those under their ministry, they must declare to them the whole will of God.

20:28 TAKE HEED . . . TO ALL THE FLOCK. For a discussion of this classic passage on overseers in the church, see article on OVERSEERS AND THEIR DUTIES, p. 1706.

20:29 GRIEVOUS WOLVES ENTER IN. Influenced by ambition to build their own kingdoms or by the love of money, power, or popularity (e.g., 1 Tim. 1:6–7; 2 Tim. 1:15; 4:3–4; 3 John 9), imposters in the church will "pervert" the original gospel as found in the N.T. (1) by repudiating or ignoring some of its fundamental truths; (2) by adding to it humanistic ideas, philosophies, wisdom, or psychology; (3) by mixing its doctrines and practices with such things as "new age" teaching or the occult and spiritism; (4) and by tolerating immoral lifestyles contrary to God's righteous standards (see 1 Tim. 4:1; Rev. 2—3; see article on FALSE TEACHERS, p. 1508). That such wolves did enter the flock and undermine apostolic doctrine and practice at Ephesus is evident from 1 Tim. 1:3–4,18–19; 4:1–3; 2 Tim. 1:15; 2:17–18; 3:1–8. The Pastoral Epistles reveal a general rejection of apostolic teaching beginning to gain momentum throughout the province of Asia.

OVERSEERS AND THEIR DUTIES

***Acts 20:28** "Take heed therefore unto yourselves, and to all the flock, over the which the Holy Ghost hath made you overseers, to feed the church of God, which he hath purchased with his own blood."*

No church can function without designated leaders. Thus, as Acts 14:23 indicates, certain individuals were appointed to the office of elder or overseer by Spirit-filled believers who sought the will of God through prayer and fasting, in accordance with the spiritual qualifications set down by the Holy Spirit in 1 Tim. 3:1–7; Tit. 1:5–9 (see article on MORAL QUALIFICATIONS FOR OVERSEERS, p. 1908). Ultimately, therefore, it is the Spirit who makes someone an overseer of the church. Paul's final address to the Ephesian elders (Acts 20:18–35) is a classic passage giving Scriptural principles on how to function as an overseer within the visible church. Their task is not unlike that of the prophet in the O.T. (see article on THE PROPHET IN THE OLD TESTAMENT, p. 1002).

PROMOTING THE FAITH. (1) The overseer or pastor is basically a shepherd of the church of God. One of his major duties is to feed the sheep by teaching God's Word. He must ever keep in mind that the flock which is given to him is no other than the congregation of God which He has purchased for Himself with the precious blood of His beloved Son (cf. Acts 20:28; 1 Cor. 6:20; 1 Pet. 1:19; 2:9; Rev. 5:9).

(2) In Acts 20:19–27, Paul describes how he served as a shepherd of the church in Ephesus; he has declared the whole will of God by faithfully warning and teaching the Ephesian Christians (Acts 20:27). Consequently, he is able to say, "I *am* pure from the blood of all *men*" (20:26; see note). Overseers today must likewise declare to their churches the whole will of God. They must "preach the word . . . reprove, rebuke, exhort, with all longsuffering and doctrine" (2 Tim. 4:2), and refuse to be preachers who seek only to please the people and say only what they want to hear (2 Tim. 4:3).

GUARDING THE FAITH. In addition to feeding the flock of God, the true pastor must diligently protect them from their enemies. Paul knows that in the church's future, Satan will raise up false teachers from within the church and infiltrate the flock of God from the outside with imposters who adhere to unbiblical doctrine, worldly thought, and pagan and humanistic ideas; their aim will be to destroy the faith of God's people (see article on FALSE TEACHERS, p. 1508). Paul calls them "grievous wolves," meaning that they are strong, difficult to handle, ravenous, and dangerous (see Acts 20:29, note; cf. Mat. 10:16). Such individuals will draw the people away from the teachings of Christ and toward themselves and their distorted gospel. Paul's urgent plea (Acts 20:25–31) places a solemn obligation upon all leaders within the church to guard the church and oppose all who would distort the original and fundamental revelation of N.T. faith.

(1) The true church consists of only those who by the grace of Christ and the fellowship of the Holy Spirit are faithful to the Lord Jesus Christ and the Word of God (see article on THE INSPIRATION AND AUTHORITY OF SCRIPTURE, p. 1924). Therefore, as a major aspect of guarding the church of God, church leaders must discipline, correct in love (Eph. 4:15), and firmly refute (2 Tim. 4:1–4; Tit. 1:9–11) all within the church who speak "perverse things," things not according to the Word of God and apostolic witness (Acts 20:30).

(2) Church leaders, pastors of local congregations, and administrative officials do well to remember that the Lord Jesus has made them responsible for the lives of all persons under their care (Acts 20:26–27; cf. Ezek. 3:20–21). If a leader fails to declare and perform the whole will of God for the church (Acts 20:27), especially in the area of guarding the flock (20:28), he will not be "pure from the blood of all men" (20:26, see

note; cf. Ezek. 34:1–10). Instead God will hold him guilty of the blood of all those who are lost because of his refusal to protect the flock from those who weaken and distort the Word (see also 2 Tim. 1:14, note; Rev. 2:2, note).

(3) Exercising discipline in regard to theological, doctrinal, and moral matters by and upon those responsible for the church's direction is especially important. Purity of doctrine and life must be carefully guarded in colleges, Bible schools, seminaries, publishing institutions, and all organizational structures of the church (2 Tim. 1:13–14).

(4) The main issue here is one's attitude toward the divinely inspired Scriptures, which Paul calls the "word of his grace" (Acts 20:32). The false teachers, pastors, and leaders will attempt to weaken the authority of the Bible by their subversive teachings and unbiblical principles. By rejecting the full authority of God's Word, they deny that the Bible is true and trustworthy in all that it teaches (Acts 20:28–31; see Gal. 1:6, note; 1 Tim. 4:1; 2 Tim. 3:8). These people, for the sake of the church of God, must be disciplined and removed from the fellowship (2 John 9–11, see Gal. 1:9, note).

(5) The church that fails to share the Holy Spirit's burning concern for church purity (Acts 20:18–35), refuses to maintain a firm stand for the truth, and refrains from disciplining those who undermine the authority of God's Word, will soon cease to exist as a church according to N.T. norms (see Acts 12:5, note; see article on THE CHURCH, p. 1438). It will become guilty of apostasy from the original revelation of Christ and the apostles, sliding further and further from the N.T. purpose, power, and life.

PAUL'S THIRD MISSIONARY JOURNEY

enter in among you, not sparing the flock.

30 Also [y]of your own selves shall men arise, speaking perverse things, to draw away disciples after them.

31 Therefore watch, and remember, that [z]by the space of three years I ceased not to warn every one night and day with tears.

32 And now, brethren, I commend you to God, and [a]to the word of his grace, which is able [b]to build you up, and to give you [c]an inheritance among all them which are sanctified.

33 [d]I have coveted no man's silver, or gold, or apparel.

34 Yea, ye yourselves know, [e]that these hands have ministered unto my necessities, and to them that were with me.

35 I have shown you all things, [f]how that so labouring ye ought to support the weak, and to remember the words of the Lord Jesus, how he said, It is more blessed to give than to receive.

36 ¶ And when he had thus spoken, he [g]kneeled down, and prayed with them all.

37 And they all wept sore, and [h]fell on Paul's neck, and kissed him,

38 Sorrowing most of all for the words [i]which he spake, that they should see his face no more. And they accompanied him unto the ship.

20:30 [y]1 Tim. 1:20; 1 John 2:19
20:31 [z]ch. 19:10
20:32 [a]Heb. 13:9 [b]ch. 9:31 [c]ch. 26:18 Eph. 1:18 Col. 1:12 & 3:24 Heb. 9:15 1 Pet. 1:4
20:33 [d]1 Sam. 12:3 1 Cor. 9:12 2 Cor. 7:2 & 11:9 & 12:17
20:34 [e]ch. 18:3 1 Cor. 4:12 1 Thes. 2:9 2 Thes. 3:8
20:35 [f]Rom. 15:1 1 Cor. 9:12 2 Cor. 11:9,12 & 12:13 Eph. 4:28 1 Thes. 4:11 & 5:14 2 Thes. 3:8
20:36 [g]ch. 7:60 & 21:5
20:37 [h]Gen. 45:14 & 46:29
20:38 [i]ver. 25
21:4 [j]ver. 12 ch. 20:23
21:5 [k]ch. 20:36
21:6 [l]John 1:11

Paul travels to Caesarea

21 AND IT came to pass, that after we were gotten from them, and had launched, we came with a straight course unto Coos, and the *day* following unto Rhodes, and from thence unto Patara:

2 And finding a ship sailing over unto Phenicia, we went aboard, and set forth.

3 Now when we had discovered Cyprus, we left it on the left hand, and sailed into Syria, and landed at Tyre: for there the ship was to unlade her burden.

4 And finding disciples, we tarried there seven days: [j]who said to Paul through the Spirit, that he should not go up to Jerusalem.

5 And when we had accomplished those days, we departed and went our way; and they all brought us on our way, with wives and children, till *we were* out of the city: and [k]we kneeled down on the shore, and prayed.

6 And when we had taken our leave one of another, we took ship; and they returned [l]home again.

7 And when we had finished *our* course from Tyre, we came to Ptolemais, and saluted the brethren, and abode with them one day.

8 And the next *day* we that were of Paul's company departed, and came unto Caesarea: and we entered into the

20:31 THEREFORE WATCH. "Watch" (literally "keep awake") means "be on your guard." Overseers of God's people must always be sensitive to and watch out for those within their congregations who are not earnestly loyal and committed to the original message of Christ and the apostles. They must be so united with the Holy Spirit that they are carefully and tearfully concerned for their people, never ceasing night and day to admonish the flock concerning the danger that faces them and ever pointing them to the only sure foundation — Christ and His Word.

20:33 I HAVE COVETED NO MAN'S SILVER. Paul sets an example for all of God's ministers. He never desires wealth or seeks to get rich from his work in the gospel (cf. 2 Cor. 12:14). Paul had great opportunity to amass wealth. He was an apostle, had influence over many believers, and could perform miracles of healing; furthermore, the early Christians were disposed to give money and property to prominent church leaders for distribution to those in need (see 4:34–35,37). If Paul had taken advantage of his gifts and position, and the liberality of the believers, he could have lived an affluent lifestyle. This he did not do because of the guidance of the Holy Spirit within him and because of his love for the gospel he preached (cf. 1 Cor. 9:4–18; 2 Cor. 11:7–12; 12:14–18; 1 Thes. 2:5–6).

20:37 THEY ALL WEPT SORE. This parting of Paul from the Ephesian brethren is a remarkable example of Christian fellowship and love. Paul had served them with unselfish care and concern, sharing their joys and their sorrows and ministering to them with tears and trials (vv. 19,31). They were heartbroken and wept aloud at the thought of not seeing his face again (v. 38). The devoted love shared between Paul and the Ephesian elders should characterize all those who are co-laborers in the faith.

21:4 THROUGH THE SPIRIT, THAT HE SHOULD NOT GO UP TO JERUSALEM. "Through the Spirit" means "on account of what the Spirit said." The Holy Spirit was not forbidding Paul to go to Jerusalem, for it was God's will that he go (see v. 14; 23:11). God, however, was giving Paul a warning that much suffering awaited him if he did go. Probably the Spirit had said the same thing at Tyre that He said at Caesarea (vv. 8–14). But Paul counted the cost and was willing even to die for the sake of the gospel (vv. 10–14).

house of Philip [m]the evangelist, [n]which was *one* of the seven; and abode with him.

9 And the same man had four daughters, virgins, [o]which did prophesy.

10 And as we tarried *there* many days, there came down from Judaea a certain prophet, named [p]Agabus.

11 And when he was come unto us, he took Paul's girdle, and bound his own hands and feet, and said, Thus saith the Holy Ghost, [q]So shall the Jews at Jerusalem bind the man that owneth this girdle, and shall deliver *him* into the hands of the Gentiles.

12 And when we heard these things, both we, and they of that place, besought him not to go up to Jerusalem.

13 Then Paul answered, [r]What mean ye to weep and to break mine heart? for I am ready not to be bound only, but also to die at Jerusalem for the name of the Lord Jesus.

14 And when he would not be persuaded, we ceased, saying, [s]The will of the Lord be done.

Paul in Jerusalem

15 And after those days we took up our carriages, and went up to Jerusalem.

16 There went with us also *certain* of the disciples of Caesarea, and brought with them one Mnason of Cyprus, an old disciple, with whom we should lodge.

17 [t]And when we were come to Jerusalem, the brethren received us gladly.

18 And the *day* following Paul went in with us unto [u]James; and all the elders were present.

19 And when he had saluted them, [v]he declared particularly what things God had wrought among the Gentiles [w]by his ministry.

20 And when they heard *it*, they glorified the Lord, and said unto him, Thou seest, brother, how many thousands of Jews there are which believe; and they are all [x]zealous of the law:

21 And they are informed of thee, that thou teachest all the Jews which are among the Gentiles to forsake Moses, saying that they ought not to circumcise *their* children, neither to walk after the customs.

22 What is it therefore? the multitude must needs come together: for they will hear that thou art come.

23 Do therefore this that we say to thee: We have four men which have a vow on them;

24 Them take, and purify thyself with them, and be at charges with them, that they may [y]shave *their*

21:8 [m]Eph. 4:11 2 Tim. 4:5 [n]ch. 6:5 & 8:26,40
21:9 [o]Joel 2:28 ch. 2:17
21:10 [p]ch. 11:28
21:11 [q]ver. 33 ch. 20:23
21:13 [r]ch. 20:24
21:14 [s]Mat. 6:10 & 26:42 Luke 11:2 & 22:42
21:17 [t]ch. 15:4
21:18 [u]ch. 15:13 Gal. 1:19 & 2:9
21:19 [v]ch. 15:4,12 Rom. 15:18,19 [w]ch. 1:17 & 20:24
21:20 [x]ch. 22:3 Rom. 10:2 Gal. 1:14
21:24 [y]Num. 6:2,13,18 ch. 18:18

21:10 A CERTAIN PROPHET, NAMED AGABUS. Agabus, one of the prophets who foretold the famine of A.D. 46 (11:27–28), now predicts Paul's arrest and imprisonment. The closer Paul got to Jerusalem, the clearer and more definite were the revelations (v. 11). Agabus's prophecy did not say Paul should not go to Jerusalem, only what awaited him if he did go.

Note that in no recorded incident of the N.T. was the gift of prophecy ever used to give personal guidance to individuals in matters that could be decided according to Scriptural principles. Decisions related to morality, buying or selling, marriage, home, and family must be made by applying and obeying the principles of God's Word and not on the mere basis of a "prophecy." In the N.T. prophetic utterances involved primarily edification, exhortation, consolation (1 Cor. 14:3), and, frequently, guidance in mission (see 16:6, note).

21:13 THEN PAUL ANSWERED. The will of the majority or even the unanimous wish of genuine caring believers is not necessarily the will of God. Paul was not indifferent to the pleas and tears of his friends; still, he could not change his resolute purpose to be willing to suffer imprisonment and even to die for the name of the Lord Jesus.

21:14 THE WILL OF THE LORD BE DONE. Many disciples (v. 4), as well as the prophet Agabus (v. 11), prophesied of the suffering that would happen to Paul if he went to Jerusalem. These Christians interpreted the prophetic word as a personal directive to Paul that he should not go to Jerusalem (vv. 4,12). Paul, although recognizing the truth of the revelation (v. 11), did not accept the disciples' sincere interpretation of the revealed prophecy (v. 13). He relied on the personal guidance of the Holy Spirit and God's Word personally to him for such an important decision (23:11; see 21:4, note). In regard to future ministry, one ought to wait on a personal word from God, not just the word of others.

21:20 BELIEVE . . . ZEALOUS OF THE LAW. James and Paul both knew that Jewish ceremonies would not bring one salvation (cf. 15:13–21; Gal. 2:15–21). But they did recognize that some of the law and Jewish customs could be followed as an expression of the believer's faith in and love for Christ. The Jewish believers had genuinely accepted Christ and been regenerated by and filled with the Spirit. Their zeal for the law and customs came not from an attitude of legalism, but from hearts dedicated to Christ and loyal to the ways of God (see Mat. 7:6).

heads: and all may know that those things, whereof they were informed concerning thee, are nothing; but *that* thou thyself also walkest orderly, and keepest the law.

25 As touching the Gentiles which believe, [z]we have written *and* concluded that they observe no such thing, save only that they keep themselves from *things* offered to idols, and from blood, and from strangled, and from fornication.

26 Then Paul took the men, and the next day purifying himself with them [a]entered into the temple, [b]to signify the accomplishment of the days of purification, until that an offering should be offered for every one of them.

Paul's arrest

27 And when the seven days were almost ended, [c]the Jews which were of Asia, when they saw him in the temple, stirred up all the people, and [d]laid hands on him,

28 Crying out, Men of Israel, help: This is the man, [e]that teacheth all *men* every where against the people, and the law, and this place: and further brought Greeks also into the temple, and hath polluted this holy place.

29 (For they had seen before with him in the city [f]Trophimus an Ephesian, whom they supposed that Paul had brought into the temple.)

30 And [g]all the city was moved, and the people ran together: and they took Paul, and drew him out of the temple: and forthwith the doors were shut.

31 And as they went about to kill him, tidings came unto the chief captain of the band, that all Jerusalem was in an uproar.

32 [h]Who immediately took soldiers and centurions, and ran down unto them: and when they saw the chief captain and the soldiers, they left beating of Paul.

33 Then the chief captain came near, and took him, and [i]commanded *him* to be bound with two chains; and demanded who he was, and what he had done.

34 And some cried one thing, some another, among the multitude: and when he could not know the certainty for the tumult, he commanded him to be carried into the castle.

35 And when he came upon the stairs, so it was, that he was borne of the soldiers for the violence of the people.

36 For the multitude of the people followed after, crying, [j]Away with him.

Paul's defence before the crowd

22:3–16pp — Acts 9:1–22; 26:9–18

37 And as Paul was to be led into the castle, he said unto the chief captain, May I speak unto thee? Who said, Canst thou speak Greek?

38 [k]Art not thou that Egyptian, which before these days madest an uproar, and leddest out into the wilderness four thousand men that were murderers?

39 But Paul said, [l]I am a man *which am* a Jew of Tarsus, *a city* in Cilicia, a citizen of no mean city: and, I beseech thee, suffer me to speak unto the people.

40 And when he had given him licence, Paul stood on the stairs, and [m]beckoned with the hand unto the people. And when there was made a great silence, he spake unto *them* in the Hebrew tongue, saying,

22 MEN, [n]BRETHREN, and fathers, hear ye my defence *which I make* now unto you.

2 (And when they heard that he spake in the Hebrew tongue to them, they kept the more silence: and he saith,)

3 [o]I am verily a man *which am* a Jew, born in Tarsus, *a city* in Cilicia, yet brought up in this city [p]at the feet of [q]Gamaliel, *and* taught [r]according to the perfect manner of the law of the fathers, and [s]was zealous toward God, [t]as ye all are this day.

4 [u]And I persecuted this way unto the death, binding and delivering into prisons both men and women.

5 As also the high priest doth bear me witness, and [v]all the estate of the elders: [w]from whom also I received letters unto the brethren, and went to Damascus, to bring them which were there bound unto Jerusalem, for to be punished.

6 And [x]it came to pass, that, as I made my journey, and was come nigh unto Damascus about noon, suddenly there shone from heaven a great light round about me.

7 And I fell unto the ground, and

21:25 [z]ch. 15:20,29
21:26 [a]ch. 24:18 [b]Num. 6:13
21:27 [c]ch. 24:18 [d]ch. 26:21
21:28 [e]ch. 24:5,6
21:29 [f]ch. 20:4
21:30 [g]ch. 26:21
21:32 [h]ch. 23:27 & 24:7
21:33 [i]ver. 11 ch. 20:23
21:36 [j]Luke 23:18 John 19:15 ch. 22:22
21:38 [k]See ch. 5:36
21:39 [l]ch. 9:11 & 22:3
21:40 [m]ch. 12:17
22:1 [n]ch. 7:2
22:3 [o]ch. 21:39 2 Cor. 11:22 Phil. 3:5 [p]Deut. 33:3 [q]ch. 5:34 [r]ch. 26:5 [s]ch. 21:20 Gal. 1:14 [t]Rom. 10:2
22:4 [u]ch. 8:3 & 26:9-11 Phil. 3:6 1 Tim. 1:13
22:5 [v]Luke 22:66 ch. 4:5 [w]ch. 9:2 & 26:10,12
22:6 [x]ch. 9:3 & 26:12,13

heard a voice saying unto me, Saul,
Saul, why persecutest thou me?
8 And I answered, Who art thou,
Lord? And he said unto me, I am Jesus
of Nazareth, whom thou persecutest.
9 And [y]they that were with me saw
indeed the light, and were afraid; but
they heard not the voice of him that
spake to me.
10 And I said, What shall I do,
Lord? And the Lord said unto me,
Arise, and go into Damascus; and
there it shall be told thee of all things
which are appointed for thee to do.
11 And when I could not see for the
glory of that light, being led by the
hand of them that were with me, I came
into Damascus.
12 And [z]one Ananias, a devout
man according to the law, [a]having a
good report of all the [b]Jews which
dwelt *there,*
13 Came unto me, and stood, and
said unto me, Brother Saul, receive thy
sight. And the same hour I looked up
upon him.
14 And he said, [c]The God of our
fathers [d]hath chosen thee, that thou
shouldest know his will, and [e]see
[f]that Just One, and [g]shouldest hear
the voice of his mouth.
15 [h]For thou shalt be his witness
unto all men of [i]what thou hast seen
and heard.
16 And now why tarriest thou?

22:9 [y]Dan. 10:7 ch. 9:7
22:12 [z]ch. 9:17 [a]ch. 10:22 [b]1 Tim. 3:7
22:14 [c]ch. 3:13 & 5:30 [d]ch. 9:15 & 26:16 [e]1 Cor. 9:1 & 15:8 [f]ch. 3:14 & 7:52 [g]1 Cor. 11:23 Gal. 1:12
22:15 [h]ch. 23:11 [i]ch. 4:20 & 26:16
22:16 [j]ch. 2:38 Heb. 10:22 [k]ch. 9:14 Rom. 10:13
22:17 [l]ch. 9:26 2 Cor. 12:2
22:18 [m]ver. 14 [n]Mat. 10:14
22:19 [o]ver. 4 ch. 8:3 [p]Mat. 10:17
22:20 [q]ch. 7:58 [r]Luke 11:48 ch. 8:1 Rom. 1:32
22:21 [s]ch. 9:15 & 13:2,46,47 & 18:6 & 26:17 Rom. 1:5 & 11:13 & 15:16 Gal. 1:15,16 & 2:7,8 Eph. 3:7,8 1 Tim. 2:7 2 Tim. 1:11
22:22 [t]ch. 21:36 [u]ch. 25:24

arise, and be baptized, [j]and wash
away thy sins, [k]calling on the name of
the Lord.
17 And [l]it came to pass, that,
when I was come again to Jerusalem,
even while I prayed in the temple, I
was in a trance;
18 And [m]saw him saying unto me,
[n]Make haste, and get thee quickly out
of Jerusalem: for they will not receive
thy testimony concerning me.
19 And I said, Lord, [o]they know
that I imprisoned and [p]beat in every
synagogue them that believed on thee:
20 [q]And when the blood of thy
martyr Stephen was shed, I also was
standing by, and [r]consenting unto his
death, and kept the raiment of them
that slew him.
21 And he said unto me, Depart:
[s]for I will send thee far hence unto the
Gentiles.

Paul with the centurion

22 And they gave him audience
unto this word, and *then* lifted up their
voices, and said, [t]Away with such a
fellow from the earth: for it is not fit
that [u]he should live.
23 And as they cried out, and cast
off *their* clothes, and threw dust into
the air,
24 The chief captain commanded
him to be brought into the castle, and

22:16 BE BAPTIZED. Water baptism accompanied the proclamation of the gospel from the beginning of the church's mission (2:38,41). It was a rite of Christian initiation used in the N.T. to indicate that a person was committing himself or herself fully to Jesus Christ. By going into the baptismal water in the name of the Trinity (Mat. 28:19) or of Christ (19:5), believers visibly demonstrated their faith before the Christian community.

(1) Water baptism "into Christ" (Gal. 3:27) or "in the name of Jesus Christ" (2:38; cf. Mat. 28:19) signifies that one now is the property of Christ and has a share in His life, His Spirit, and His Sonship to God (Rom. 8:14–17; Gal. 3:26—4:7).

(2) Water baptism is a response of the believer to what Christ has done for him. To be valid, it must be preceded by repentance (2:38) and a personal faith in Christ (Col. 2:12).

(3) Water baptism, when undertaken with a sincere heart of faith and commitment to Jesus as Lord and Savior, is a means of receiving grace from Christ (cf. 1 Pet. 3:21; see article on FAITH AND GRACE, p. 1738).

(4) Water baptism is an outward sign and testimony of our receiving Christ as Lord and Savior and of the washing away of our sins (cf. 2:38; Tit. 3:5; 1 Pet. 3:21).

(5) Water baptism portrays the union of the believer with Christ in His death, burial, and resurrection (Rom. 6:1–11; Col. 2:11–12). This signifies an end (i.e., "death") to a life of sin (Rom. 6:3–4,7,10,12; Col. 3:3–14) and the beginning of a new life in Christ (Rom. 6:4–5,11; Col. 2:12–13). Therefore, water baptism involves a commitment to a lifelong practice of turning one's back on the world and all that is evil and pledging oneself to live a new life in the Spirit that reflects God's standards of righteousness (Col. 2:1–17).

22:16 WASH AWAY THY SINS. Paul was converted and saved on the Damascus road (see 9:5, note). His baptism was his public testimony of forgiveness and commitment to forsake all sin and identify himself with the cause of Christ.

22:17 I WAS IN A TRANCE. The term "trance" here denotes a state of mind where one's attention is primarily aware of the realm of the Spirit rather than that of the natural. At such times one is especially receptive to revelation from God. It means being brought by the Spirit into a deeper and more intense communion with God (see Peter's trance in 10:10 and 11:5; cf. 2 Cor. 12:3–4).

bade that he should be examined by scourging; that he might know wherefore they cried so against him.

25 And as they bound him with thongs, Paul said unto the centurion that stood by, [v]Is it lawful for you to scourge a man that is a Roman, and uncondemned?

26 When the centurion heard *that,* he went and told the chief captain, saying, Take heed what thou doest: for this man is a Roman.

27 Then the chief captain came, and said unto him, Tell me, art thou a Roman? He said, Yea.

28 And the chief captain answered, With a great sum obtained I this freedom. And Paul said, But I was *free* born.

29 Then straightway they departed from him which should have [f]examined him: and the chief captain also was afraid, after he knew that he was a Roman, and because he had bound him.

Before the Sanhedrin

30 On the morrow, because he would have known the certainty wherefore he was accused of the Jews, he loosed him from *his* bands, and commanded the chief priests and all their council to appear, and brought Paul down, and set him before them.

23 AND PAUL, earnestly beholding the council, said, Men *and* brethren, [w]I have lived in all good conscience before God until this day.

2 And the high priest Ananias commanded them that stood by him [x]to smite him on the mouth.

3 Then said Paul unto him, God shall smite thee, *thou* whited wall: for sittest thou to judge me after the law, and [y]commandest me to be smitten contrary to the law?

4 And they that stood by said, Revilest thou God's high priest?

5 Then said Paul, [z]I wist not, brethren, that he was the high priest: for it is written, [a]Thou shalt not speak evil of the ruler of thy people.

6 But when Paul perceived that the one part were Sadducees, and the other Pharisees, he cried out in the council, Men *and* brethren, [b]I am a Pharisee, the son of a Pharisee: [c]of the hope and resurrection of the dead I am called in question.

7 And when he had so said, there arose a dissension between the Pharisees and the Sadducees: and the multitude was divided.

8 [d]For the Sadducees say that there is no resurrection, neither angel, nor spirit: but the Pharisees confess both.

9 And there arose a great cry: and the scribes *that were* of the Pharisees' part arose, and strove, saying, [e]We find no evil in this man: but [f]if a spirit or an angel hath spoken to him, [g]let us not fight against God.

10 And when there arose a great dissension, the chief captain, fearing lest Paul should have been pulled in pieces of them, commanded the soldiers to go down, and to take him by force from among them, and to bring *him* into the castle.

11 And [h]the night following the Lord stood by him, and said, Be of good cheer, Paul: for as thou hast testified of me in Jerusalem, so must thou bear witness also at Rome.

[f] Or, *tortured him*

22:25 [v]ch. 16:37
23:1 [w]ch. 24:16 1 Cor. 4:4 2 Cor. 1:12 & 4:2 2 Tim. 1:3 Heb. 13:18
23:2 [x]1 Ki. 22:24 Jer. 20:2 John 18:22
23:3 [y]Lev. 19:35 Deut. 25:1,2 John 7:51
23:5 [z]ch. 24:17 [a]Ex. 22:28 Eccl. 10:20 2 Pet. 2:10 Jude 8
23:6 [b]ch. 26:5 Phil. 3:5 [c]ch. 24:15,21 & 26:6 & 28:20
23:8 [d]Mat. 22:23 Mark 12:18 Luke 20:27
23:9 [e]ch. 25:25 & 26:31 [f]ch. 22:7,17,18 [g]ch. 5:39
23:11 [h]ch. 18:9 & 27:23,24

23:1 IN ALL GOOD CONSCIENCE BEFORE GOD. The conscience is an inner awareness that witnesses to our personality concerning the rightness or wrongness of our actions. A "good conscience before God" gives the verdict that we have not offended Him or His will. Paul's claim (probably referring to his public life before men) is sincere; note Phil. 3:6, where he states, "touching the righteousness which is in the law, blameless." Before his conversion, he even believed he was doing God's will in persecuting believers (26:9).

Paul's commitment to God, his intense resolve to please Him, and his "blameless" life even before his conversion to Christ, shame and condemn the lives of professed believers who excuse their unfaithfulness to Christ by claiming that everyone sins and that it is impossible to live before God with a good conscience.

23:11 THE LORD STOOD BY HIM. Paul is anxious and apprehensive about what will happen to him. It appears that he might be killed in Jerusalem and that his plans to carry the gospel to Rome and further west might never be realized. God appears to him at this critical time, encourages his heart, and assures him that he will witness for His cause in Rome. Scripture records that God appeared to Paul three times in order to reassure him (18:9–10; 22:17–18; 23:11; cf. 27:23–24; see 18:10, note).

The plot to kill Paul

12 And when it was day, [i]certain of the Jews banded together, and bound themselves [g]under a curse, saying that they would neither eat nor drink till they had killed Paul.

13 And they were more than forty which had made this conspiracy.

14 And they came to the chief priests and elders, and said, We have bound ourselves under a great curse, that we will eat nothing until we have slain Paul.

15 Now therefore ye with the council signify to the chief captain that he bring him down unto you tomorrow, as though ye would inquire something more perfectly concerning him: and we, or ever he come near, are ready to kill him.

16 And when Paul's sister's son heard of their lying in wait, he went and entered into the castle, and told Paul.

17 Then Paul called one of the centurions unto *him,* and said, Bring this young man unto the chief captain: for he hath a certain thing to tell him.

18 So he took him, and brought *him* to the chief captain, and said, Paul the prisoner called me unto *him,* and prayed me to bring this young man unto thee, who hath something to say unto thee.

19 Then the chief captain took him by the hand, and went *with him* aside privately, and asked *him,* What is that thou hast to tell me?

20 And he said, [j]The Jews have agreed to desire thee that thou wouldest bring down Paul tomorrow into the council, as though they would inquire somewhat of him more perfectly.

21 But do not thou yield unto them: for there lie in wait for him of them more than forty men, which have bound themselves with an oath, that they will neither eat nor drink till they have killed him: and now are they ready, looking for a promise from thee.

22 So the chief captain *then* let the young man depart, and charged *him, See thou* tell no man that thou hast shown these things to me.

Paul transferred to Caesarea

23 And he called unto *him* two centurions, saying, Make ready two hundred soldiers to go to Caesarea, and horsemen threescore and ten, and spearmen two hundred, at the third hour of the night;

24 And provide *them* beasts, that they may set Paul on, and bring *him* safe unto Felix the governor.

25 And he wrote a letter after this manner:

26 Claudius Lysias unto the most excellent governor Felix *sendeth* greeting.

27 [k]This man was taken of the Jews, and should have been killed of them: then came I with an army, and rescued him, having understood that he was a Roman.

28 [l]And when I would have known the cause wherefore they accused him, I brought him forth into their council:

29 Whom I perceived to be accused [m]of questions of their law, [n]but to have nothing laid to his charge worthy of death or of bonds.

30 And [o]when it was told me how that the Jews laid wait for the man, I sent straightway to thee, and [p]gave commandment to his accusers also to say before thee what *they had* against him. Farewell.

31 Then the soldiers, as it was commanded them, took Paul, and brought *him* by night to Antipatris.

32 On the morrow they left the horsemen to go with him, and returned to the castle:

33 Who, when they came to Caesarea, and delivered the epistle to the governor, presented Paul also before him.

34 And when the governor had read *the letter,* he asked of what province he was. And when he understood that *he was* of [q]Cilicia;

35 [r]I will hear thee, said he, when thine accusers are also come. And he commanded him to be kept in [s]Herod's judgment hall.

Paul tried before Felix

24 AND AFTER [t]five days [u]Ananias the high priest descended with the elders, and *with* a certain orator *named* Tertullus, who informed the governor against Paul.

2 And when he was called forth, Tertullus began to accuse *him,* saying, Seeing that by thee we enjoy great quietness, and that very worthy deeds are

23:12 [i]ver. 21,30 ch. 25:3
23:20 [j]ver. 12 ch. 20:3
23:27 [k]ch. 21:33 & 24:7
23:28 [l]ch. 22:30
23:29 [m]ch. 18:15 & 25:19 [n]ch. 26:31
23:30 [o]ver. 20 [p]ch. 24:8 & 25:6
23:34 [q]ch. 21:39
23:35 [r]ch. 24:1,10 & 25:16 [s]Mat. 27:27
24:1 [t]ch. 21:27 [u]ch. 23:2,30,35 & 25:2

[g] Or, *with an oath of execration*

done unto this nation by thy provi-
dence,
3 We accept *it* always, and in all
places, most noble Felix, with all
thankfulness.
4 Notwithstanding, that I be not fur-
ther tedious unto thee, I pray thee that
thou wouldest hear us of thy clemency
a few words.
5 [v]For we have found this man *a*
pestilent *fellow,* and a mover of sedi-
tion among all the Jews throughout the
world, and a ringleader of the sect of
the Nazarenes:
6 [w]Who also hath gone about to
profane the temple: whom we took,
and would [x]have judged according to
our law.
7 [y]But the chief captain Lysias
came *upon us,* and with great violence
took *him* away out of our hands,
8 [z]Commanding his accusers to
come unto thee: by examining of whom
thyself mayest take knowledge of all
these things, whereof we accuse him.
9 And the Jews also assented, say-
ing that these things were so.
10 Then Paul, after that the gover-
nor had beckoned unto him to speak,
answered, Forasmuch as I know that
thou hast been of many years a judge
unto this nation, I do the more cheer-
fully answer for myself:
11 Because that thou mayest un-
derstand, that there are yet but twelve
days since I went up to Jerusalem [a]for
to worship.
12 [b]And they neither found me in
the temple disputing with any man,
neither raising up the people, neither
in the synagogues, nor in the city:
13 Neither can they prove the
things whereof they now accuse me.
14 But this I confess unto thee, that
after [c]the way which they call heresy,
so worship I the [d]God of my fathers,
believing all things which are written
in [e]the law and in the prophets:
15 And [f]have hope toward God,
which they themselves also allow,
[g]that there shall be a resurrection of
the dead, both of the just and unjust.
16 And [h]herein do I exercise my-
self, to have always a conscience void
of offence toward God, and *toward* men.
17 Now after many years [i]I came
to bring alms to my nation, and offer-
ings.
18 [j]Whereupon certain Jews from
Asia found me purified in the temple,
neither with multitude, nor with tu-
mult.
19 [k]Who ought to have been here
before thee, and object, if they had
aught against me.
20 Or else let these same *here* say,
if they have found any evil doing in me,
while I stood before the council,
21 Except it be for this one voice,
that I cried standing among them,
[l]Touching the resurrection of the
dead I am called in question by you this
day.
22 And when Felix heard these

24:5 [v]Luke 23:2 ch. 6:13 & 16:20 & 17:6 & 21:28 1 Pet. 2:12,15
24:6 [w]ch. 21:28 [x]John 18:31
24:7 [y]ch. 21:33
24:8 [z]ch. 23:30
24:11 [a]ver. 17 ch. 21:26
24:12 [b]ch. 25:8 & 28:17
24:14 [c]See Amos 8:14 ch. 9:2 [d]2 Tim. 1:3 [e]ch. 26:22 & 28:23
24:15 [f]ch. 23:6 & 26:6,7 & 28:20 [g]Dan. 12:2 John 5:28,29
24:16 [h]ch. 23:1
24:17 [i]ch. 11:29,30 & 20:16 Rom. 15:25 2 Cor. 8:4 Gal. 2:10
24:18 [j]ch. 21:26,27 & 26:21
24:19 [k]ch. 23:30 & 25:16
24:21 [l]ch. 23:6 & 28:20

24:14 BELIEVING ALL THINGS WHICH ARE WRITTEN. Paul's faith in the holy Scriptures as inerrant, infallible, and trustworthy in all things lies in sharp contrast to many religious teachers of these last days who claim to believe only "some things" written in the law and the prophets (see article on THE INSPIRATION AND AUTHORITY OF SCRIPTURE, p. 1924). Those who are of the spirit and mind of Christ (Mat. 5:18) and of the apostles (2 Tim. 3:16) will believe and defend "all things" written in the Word of God. Those who are not of this heart and spirit will disagree with the words of the great apostle.

24:14 THE WAY. The salvation provided by Christ is called "the way" (cf 9:2; 16:17; 19:9,23; 24:14,22). The Greek word used here (*hodos*) denotes a path or road. The N.T. believer saw salvation in Christ not only as an experience to receive but also a road to walk in faith and fellowship with Jesus. We must walk that road until the end in order to enter into the final salvation of the age to come (see article on BIBLICAL WORDS FOR SALVATION, p. 1726).

24:15 RESURRECTION ... OF THE JUST AND UNJUST. The Bible teaches a resurrection of the unrighteous as well as the righteous dead. The righteous will be resurrected to live forever in their redeemed bodies with the Lord (1 Thes. 4:13–18), while the unrighteous will rise to be judged by God (for the two resurrections, see Dan. 12:2, note; John 5:29, notes; Rev. 20:6–14, notes). The fact that both resurrections are mentioned in the same verse does not necessarily mean that both occur simultaneously (see John 5:29, note).

24:16 A CONSCIENCE VOID OF OFFENCE. A blameless conscience is listed in Scripture as one of our essential weapons for a successful spiritual life and ministry (2 Cor. 1:12; 1 Tim. 1:19). (1) A good conscience involves an inner freedom of spirit that comes when we know that God is not offended by our thoughts and actions (see 23:1, note; Ps. 32:1; 1 Tim. 1:5; 1 Pet. 3:16; 1 John 3:21–22). (2) When a good conscience is defiled, one's faith, prayer life, communion with God, and life of good works are seriously damaged (Tit. 1:15–16); if one puts away a good conscience, that will result in the shipwreck of his faith (1 Tim. 1:19).

things, having more perfect knowledge of *that* way, he deferred them, and said, When [m]Lysias the chief captain shall come down, I will know the uttermost of your matter.

23 And he commanded a centurion to keep Paul, and to let *him* have liberty, and [n]that he should forbid none of his acquaintance to minister or come unto him.

24 And after certain days, when Felix came with his wife Drusilla, which was a Jewess, he sent for Paul, and heard him concerning the faith in Christ.

25 And as he reasoned of righteousness, temperance, and judgment to come, Felix trembled, and answered, Go thy way for this time; when I have a convenient season, I will call for thee.

26 He hoped also that [o]money should have been given him of Paul, that he might loose him: wherefore he sent for him the oftener, and communed with him.

27 But after two years Porcius Festus came into Felix' room: and Felix, [p]willing to show the Jews a pleasure, left Paul bound.

Paul tried before Festus

25 NOW WHEN Festus was come into the province, after three days he ascended from Caesarea to Jerusalem.

2 [q]Then the high priest and the chief of the Jews informed him against Paul, and besought him,

3 And desired favour against him, that he would send for him to Jerusalem, [r]laying wait in the way to kill him.

4 But Festus answered, that Paul should be kept at Caesarea, and that he himself would depart shortly *thither.*

5 Let them therefore, said he, which among you are able, go down with *me,* and accuse this man, [s]if there be any wickedness in him.

6 And when he had tarried among them [h]more than ten days, he went down unto Caesarea; and the next day sitting on the judgment seat commanded Paul to be brought.

7 And when he was come, the Jews which came down from Jerusalem stood round about, [t]and laid many and grievous complaints against Paul, which they could not prove.

8 While he answered for himself, [u]Neither against the law of the Jews, neither against the temple, nor yet against Caesar, have I offended any thing at all.

9 But Festus, [v]willing to do the Jews a pleasure, answered Paul, and said, [w]Wilt thou go up to Jerusalem, and there be judged of these things before me?

10 Then said Paul, I stand at Caesar's judgment seat, where I ought to be judged: to the Jews have I done no wrong, as thou very well knowest.

11 [x]For if I be an offender, or have committed any thing worthy of death, I refuse not to die: but if there be none of these things whereof these accuse me, no man may deliver me unto them. [y]I appeal unto Caesar.

12 Then Festus, when he had conferred with the council, answered, Hast thou appealed unto Caesar? unto Caesar shalt thou go.

Paul's case discussed

13 And after certain days king

[h] Or, as some copies read, *no more than eight or ten days*

24:22 [m]ver. 7
24:23 [n]ch. 27:3 & 28:16
24:26 [o]Ex. 23:8
24:27 [p]Ex. 23:2 ch. 12:3 & 25:9,14
25:2 [q]ver. 15 ch. 24:1
25:3 [r]ch. 23:12,15
25:5 [s]ver. 18 ch. 18:14
25:7 [t]Mark 15:3 Luke 23:2,10 ch. 24:5,13
25:8 [u]ch. 6:13 & 24:12 & 28:17
25:9 [v]ch. 24:27 [w]ver. 20
25:11 [x]ver. 25 ch. 18:14 & 23:29 & 26:31 [y]ch. 26:32 & 28:19

24:25 RIGHTEOUSNESS, TEMPERANCE, AND JUDGMENT TO COME. As Paul speaks before Felix concerning faith in Jesus Christ, preaching about "righteousness, temperance, and the judgment to come," Felix becomes frightened. This corresponds to the words of Jesus that when the Holy Spirit comes, He "will reprove the world of sin, and of righteousness, and of judgment" (John 16:8). The salvation of all people depends on the faithful proclamation of those solemn truths by which the Holy Spirit produces conviction in the sinner (see John 16:8, note).

25:8 NEITHER AGAINST THE LAW. Paul knows of no offense that he has committed against the Jews or the law. Paul indeed kept the moral law of the O.T. (cf. 21:24). He knew that the moral standards of the law never change, any more than God Himself does. To him, the law is holy, good, and spiritual (Rom. 7:12,14), expressing God's character and requirement for a righteous life (cf. Mat. 5:18–19). Yet Paul did not keep the law as a set of codes or standards by which to make himself righteous. A righteous life requires the work of the Holy Spirit in his heart and soul; only after we are regenerated through the grace of Christ can we successfully obey God's law as an expression of our desire to please Him. We are never without the law of God when we are under the law of Christ (1 Cor. 9:21; see Mat. 5:17, note; Rom. 3:21; 8:4).

Agrippa and Bernice came unto Caesarea to salute Festus.

14 And when they had been there many days, Festus declared Paul's cause unto the king, saying, [z]There is a certain man left in bonds by Felix:

15 [a]About whom, when I was at Jerusalem, the chief priests and the elders of the Jews informed *me,* desiring *to have* judgment against him.

16 [b]To whom I answered, It is not the manner of the Romans to deliver any man to die, before that he which is accused have the accusers face to face, and have licence to answer for himself concerning the crime laid against him.

17 Therefore, when they were come hither, [c]without any delay on the morrow I sat on the judgment seat, and commanded the man to be brought forth.

18 Against whom when the accusers stood up, they brought none accusation of such things as I supposed:

19 [d]But had certain questions against him of their own superstition, and of one Jesus, which was dead, whom Paul affirmed to be alive.

20 And because [i]I doubted of such manner of questions, I asked *him* whether he would go to Jerusalem, and there be judged of these matters.

21 But when Paul had appealed to be reserved unto the [j]hearing of Augustus, I commanded him to be kept till I might send him to Caesar.

22 Then [e]Agrippa said unto Festus, I would also hear the man myself. Tomorrow, said he, thou shalt hear him.

23 And on the morrow, when Agrippa was come, and Bernice, with great pomp, and was entered into the place of hearing, with the chief captains, and principal men of the city, at Festus' commandment Paul was brought forth.

24 And Festus said, King Agrippa, and all men which are here present with us, ye see this man, about whom [f]all the multitude of the Jews have dealt with me, both at Jerusalem, and *also* here, crying that he ought [g]not to live any longer.

25 But when I found that [h]he had committed nothing worthy of death, [i]and that he himself hath appealed to Augustus, I have determined to send him.

26 Of whom I have no certain thing to write unto my lord. Wherefore I have brought him forth before you, and specially before thee, O king Agrippa, that, after examination had, I might have somewhat to write.

27 For it seemeth to me unreasonable to send a prisoner, and not withal to signify the crimes *laid* against him.

Paul tried before Agrippa

26:12–18pp — Acts 9:3–8; 22:6–11

26 THEN AGRIPPA said unto Paul, Thou art permitted to speak for thyself. Then Paul stretched forth the hand, and answered for himself:

2 I think myself happy, king Agrippa, because I shall answer for myself this day before thee touching all the things whereof I am accused of the Jews:

3 Especially *because I know* thee to be expert in all customs and questions which are among the Jews: wherefore I beseech thee to hear me patiently.

4 My manner of life from my youth, which was at the first among mine own nation at Jerusalem, know all the Jews;

5 Which knew me from the beginning, if they would testify, that after [j]the most straitest sect of our religion I lived a Pharisee.

6 [k]And now I stand and am judged for the hope of [l]the promise made of God unto our fathers:

7 Unto which *promise* [m]our twelve tribes, instantly serving *God* [n]day[k] and night, [o]hope to come. For which hope's sake, king Agrippa, I am accused of the Jews.

8 Why should it be thought a thing incredible with you, that God should raise the dead?

9 [p]I verily thought with myself, that I ought to do many things contrary to the name of Jesus of Nazareth.

10 [q]Which thing I also did in Jerusalem: and many of the saints did I shut up in prison, having received authority [r]from the chief priests; and when they were put to death, I gave my voice against *them.*

11 [s]And I punished them oft in every synagogue, and compelled *them* to blaspheme; and being exceedingly mad against them, I persecuted *them* even unto strange cities.

12 [t]Whereupon as I went to Da-

25:14 [z]ch. 24:27
25:15 [a]ver. 2,3
25:16 [b]ver. 4,5
25:17 [c]ver. 6
25:19 [d]ch. 18:15 & 23:29
25:22 [e]See ch. 9:15
25:24 [f]ver. 2,3,7 [g]ch. 22:22
25:25 [h]ch. 23:9,29 & 26:31 [i]ver. 11,12
26:5 [j]ch. 22:3 & 23:6 & 24:15,21 Phil. 3:5
26:6 [k]ch. 23:6 [l]Gen. 3:15 & 22:18 & 26:4 & 49:10 Deut. 18:15 2 Sam. 7:12 Ps. 132:11 Is. 4:2 & 7:14 & 9:6 & 40:10 Jer. 23:5 & 33:14-16 Ezek. 34:23 & 37:24 Dan. 9:24 ch. 13:32 Rom. 15:8 Tit. 2:13
26:7 [m]Jas. 1:1 [n]Luke 2:37 1 Thes. 3:10 1 Tim. 5:5 [o]Phil. 3:11
26:9 [p]John 16:2 1 Tim. 1:13
26:10 [q]ch. 8:3 Gal. 1:13 [r]ch. 9:14,21 & 22:5
26:11 [s]ch. 22:19
26:12 [t]ch. 9:3 & 22:6

[i] Or, *I was doubtful how to inquire hereof* [j] Or, *judgment* [k] Gk. *night and day*

mascus with authority and commission from the chief priests,

13 At midday, O king, I saw in the way a light from heaven, above the brightness of the sun, shining round about me and them which journeyed with me.

14 And when we were all fallen to the earth, I heard a voice speaking unto me, and saying in the Hebrew tongue, Saul, Saul, why persecutest thou me? *it is* hard for thee to kick against the pricks.

15 And I said, Who art thou, Lord? And he said, I am Jesus whom thou persecutest.

16 But rise, and stand upon thy feet: for I have appeared unto thee for this purpose, [u]to make thee a minister and a witness both of these things which thou hast seen, and of those things in the which I will appear unto thee;

17 Delivering thee from the people, and *from* the Gentiles, [v]unto whom now I send thee,

18 [w]To open their eyes, *and* [x]to turn *them* from darkness to light, and *from* the power of Satan unto God, [y]that they may receive forgiveness of sins, and [z]inheritance among them which are [a]sanctified by faith that is in me.

19 Whereupon, O king Agrippa, I was not disobedient unto the heavenly vision:

20 But [b]showed first unto them of Damascus, and at Jerusalem, and throughout all the coasts of Judaea, and *then* to the Gentiles, that they should repent and turn to God, and do [c]works meet for repentance.

21 For these causes [d]the Jews caught me in the temple, and went about to kill *me*.

22 Having therefore obtained help of God, I continue unto this day, witnessing both to small and great, saying none other things than those [e]which the prophets and [f]Moses did say should come:

23 [g]That Christ should suffer, *and* [h]that he should be the first that should rise from the dead, and [i]should show light unto the people, and to the Gentiles.

24 And as he thus spake for himself, Festus said with a loud voice, Paul, [j]thou art beside thyself; much learning doth make thee mad.

25 But he said, I am not mad, most noble Festus; but speak forth the words of truth and soberness.

26 For the king knoweth of these things, before whom also I speak freely: for I am persuaded that none of these things are hidden from him; for this thing was not done in a corner.

27 King Agrippa, believest thou the prophets? I know that thou believest. Eph. 6:19

28 Then Agrippa said unto Paul, Almost thou persuadest me to be a Christian.

29 And Paul said, [k]I would to God, that not only thou, but also all that hear me this day, were both almost, and altogether such as I am, except these bonds.

30 And when he had thus spoken, the king rose up, and the governor, and

26:16 [u]ch. 22:15 **26:17** [v]ch. 22:21 **26:18** [w]Is. 35:5 & 42:7 Luke 1:79 John 8:12 2 Cor. 4:4 Eph. 1:18 1 Thes. 5:5 [x]2 Cor. 6:14 Eph. 4:18 & 5:8 Col. 1:13 1 Pet. 2:9 [y]Luke 1:77 [z]Eph. 1:11 Col. 1:12 [a]ch. 20:32 **26:20** [b]ch. 9:20,22 & 11:26 & chs. 13,14 & 16-21 [c]Mat. 3:8 **26:21** [d]ch. 21:30 **26:22** [e]Luke 24:27 ch. 24:14 & 28:23 Rom. 3:21 [f]John 5:46 **26:23** [g]Luke 24:26 [h]1 Cor. 15:20 Col. 1:18 Rev. 1:5 [i]Luke 2:32 **26:24** [j]2 Ki. 9:11 John 10:20 1 Cor. 1:23 & 2:13,14 & 4:10 **26:29** [k]1 Cor. 7:7

26:18 PAUL'S DIVINE COMMISSION. This verse is a classic statement by the Lord Jesus of what He desires from the preaching of the gospel to the lost.

(1) "Open their eyes." The lost are blinded by Satan to the reality of their lost and perishing condition and to the truth of the gospel (2 Cor. 4:4). Only preaching Christ Jesus in the power of the Holy Spirit will open their understanding (cf. 2 Cor. 4:5; Eph. 1:18).

(2) "Turn *them* from . . . the power of Satan unto God." Satan is the ruler of the world, and all those without Christ are under his control and enslaved to his power. Satan's spirit works in all sinners, i.e., "in the children of disobedience" (Eph. 2:2). The proclamation of the gospel in the power of the Spirit will deliver men and women from the power of Satan and to the kingdom of Christ (see Col. 1:13; 1 Pet. 2:9).

(3) "That they may receive forgiveness of sins." Forgiveness comes through faith in Christ that is based on His sacrificial death on the cross.

(4) "Sanctified by faith that is in me." The one who is forgiven, delivered from the dominion of sin and Satan, and indwelt by and baptized in the Holy Spirit, is set apart from the world and now lives unto God in fellowship with all those saved by faith in Christ.

26:19 I WAS NOT DISOBEDIENT. Paul's conversion to Christ occurred on his journey to Damascus. From that moment on he recognized Jesus as Lord and Savior and dedicated his life to obeying Him (cf. Rom. 1:5).

26:20 DO WORKS MEET FOR REPENTANCE. Paul did not preach, as some do, that salvation requires "only trusting in Christ and His atoning death." The N.T. apostles declare that no individuals will be saved in Christ unless they "repent and turn to God and do works meet for repentance" (see article on FAITH AND GRACE, p. 1738).

Bernice, and they that sat with them:

31 And when they were gone aside, they talked between themselves, saying, [l]This man doeth nothing worthy of death or of bonds.

32 Then said Agrippa unto Festus, This man might have been set at liberty, [m]if he had not appealed unto Caesar.

Paul sails for Rome

27 AND WHEN [n]it was determined that we should sail into Italy, they delivered Paul and certain other prisoners unto *one* named Julius, a centurion of Augustus' band.

2 And entering into a ship of Adramyttium, we launched, meaning to sail by the coasts of Asia; *one* [o]Aristarchus, a Macedonian of Thessalonica, being with us.

3 And the next *day* we touched at Sidon. And Julius [p]courteously entreated Paul, and gave *him* liberty to go unto his friends to refresh himself.

4 And when we had launched from thence, we sailed under Cyprus, because the winds were contrary.

5 And when we had sailed over the sea of Cilicia and Pamphylia, we came to Myra, *a city* of Lycia.

6 And there the centurion found a ship of Alexandria sailing into Italy; and he put us therein.

7 And when we had sailed slowly many days, and scarce were come over against Cnidus, the wind not suffering us, we sailed under [1]Crete, over against Salmone;

8 And, hardly passing it, came unto a place which is called The fair havens; nigh whereunto was the city *of* Lasea.

9 Now when much time was spent, and when sailing was now dangerous, [q]because the fast was now already past, Paul admonished *them*,

10 And said unto them, Sirs, I perceive that this voyage will be with [m]hurt and much damage, not only of the lading and ship, but also of our lives.

11 Nevertheless the centurion believed the master and the owner of the ship, more than those things which were spoken by Paul.

26:31 [l]ch. 23:9,29 & 25:25
26:32 [m]ch. 25:11
27:1 [n]ch. 25:12,25
27:2 [o]ch. 19:29
27:3 [p]ch. 24:23 & 28:16
27:9 [q]The fast was on the tenth day of the seventh month Lev. 23:27,29
27:19 [r]Jonah 1:5
27:23 [s]ch. 23:11 [t]Dan. 6:16 Rom. 1:9 2 Tim. 1:3

12 And because the haven was not commodious to winter in, the more part advised to depart thence also, if by any means they might attain to Phenice, *and there* to winter; *which is* an haven of Crete, and lieth toward the south west and north west.

The storm at sea

13 And when the south wind blew softly, supposing that they had obtained *their* purpose, loosing *thence,* they sailed close by Crete.

14 But not long after there [n]arose against it a tempestuous wind, called Euroclydon.

15 And when the ship was caught, and could not bear up into the wind, we let *her* drive.

16 And running under a certain island which is called Clauda, we had much work to come by the boat:

17 Which when they had taken up, they used helps, undergirding the ship; and, fearing lest they should fall into the quicksands, strake sail, and so were driven.

18 And we being exceedingly tossed with a tempest, the next *day* they lightened the ship;

19 And the third *day* [r]we cast out with our own hands the tackling of the ship.

20 And when neither sun nor stars in many days appeared, and no small tempest lay on *us,* all hope that we should be saved was then taken away.

21 But after long abstinence Paul stood forth in the midst of them, and said, Sirs, ye should have hearkened unto me, and not have loosed from Crete, and to have gained this harm and loss.

22 And now I exhort you to be of good cheer: for there shall be no loss of *any man's* life among you, but of the ship.

23 [s]For there stood by me this night the angel of God, whose I am, and [t]whom I serve,

24 Saying, Fear not, Paul; thou must be brought before Caesar: and, lo,

[1] Or, *Candy* [m] Or, *injury* [n] Or, *beat*

27:24 FEAR NOT, PAUL. As long as God has a place and purpose for one's life on earth and that person is seeking God and following the guidance of the Holy Spirit (cf. 23:11; 24:16), the Lord will protect him from death. All of God's faithful have the right to pray, "O Lord, I am thine; I serve thee; be thou my preserver" (cf. Ps. 16:1–2).

God hath given thee all them that sail with thee.

25 Wherefore, sirs, be of good cheer: [u]for I believe God, that it shall be even as it was told me.

26 Howbeit [v]we must be cast upon a certain island.

The shipwreck

27 But when the fourteenth night was come, as we were driven up and down in Adria, about midnight the shipmen deemed that they drew near to some country;

28 And sounded, and found *it* twenty fathoms: and when they had gone a little further, they sounded again, and found *it* fifteen fathoms.

29 Then fearing lest we should have fallen upon rocks, they cast four anchors out of the stern, and wished for the day.

30 And as the shipmen were about to flee out of the ship, when they had let down the boat into the sea, under colour as though they would have cast anchors out of the foreship,

31 Paul said to the centurion and to the soldiers, Except these abide in the ship, ye cannot be saved.

32 Then the soldiers cut off the ropes of the boat, and let her fall off.

33 And while the day was coming on, Paul besought *them* all to take meat, saying, This day is the fourteenth day that ye have tarried and continued fasting, having taken nothing.

34 Wherefore I pray you to take *some* meat: for this is for your health: for [w]there shall not an hair fall from the head of any of you.

35 And when he had thus spoken, he took bread, and [x]gave thanks to God in presence of them all: and when he had broken *it*, he began to eat.

36 Then were they all of good cheer, and they also took *some* meat.

37 And we were in all in the ship two hundred threescore and sixteen [y]souls.

38 And when they had eaten enough, they lightened the ship, and cast out the wheat into the sea.

39 And when it was day, they knew not the land: but they discovered a certain creek with a shore, into the which they were minded, if it were possible, to thrust in the ship.

40 And when they had [o]taken up the anchors, they committed *themselves* unto the sea, and loosed the rudder bands, and hoisted up the mainsail to the wind, and made toward shore.

41 And falling into a place where two seas met, [z]they ran the ship aground; and the forepart stuck fast, and remained unmoveable, but the hinderpart was broken with the violence of the waves.

42 And the soldiers' counsel was to kill the prisoners, lest any of them should swim out, and escape.

43 But the centurion, willing to save Paul, kept them from *their* purpose; and commanded that they which could swim should cast *themselves* first *into the sea*, and get to land:

44 And the rest, some on boards, and some on *broken pieces* of the ship. And so it came to pass, [a]that they escaped all safe to land.

The stopover at Melita

28 AND WHEN they were escaped, then they knew that [b]the island was called Melita.

2 And the [c]barbarous people showed us no little kindness: for they kindled a fire, and received us every one, because of the present rain, and because of the cold.

3 And when Paul had gathered a bundle of sticks, and laid *them* on the fire, there came a viper out of the heat, and fastened on his hand.

27:25 [u]Luke 1:45 Rom. 4:20,21 2 Tim. 1:12
27:26 [v]ch. 28:1
27:34 [w]1 Ki. 1:52 Mat. 10:30 Luke 12:7 & 21:18
27:35 [x]1 Sam. 9:13 Mat. 15:36 Mark 8:6 John 6:11 1 Tim. 4:3,4
27:37 [y]ch. 2:41 & 7:14 Rom. 13:1 1 Pet. 3:20
27:41 [z]2 Cor. 11:25
27:44 [a]ver:22
28:1 [b]ch. 27:26
28:2 [c]Rom. 1:14 1 Cor. 14:11 Col. 3:11

[o] Or, *cut the anchors, they left them in the sea*

27:25 BE OF GOOD CHEER. Paul is a prisoner in the ship; nevertheless, he is a free man in Christ, living free from fear in the presence of God, while those who sail with him are paralyzed with terror because of their danger at sea. In this life, only the sincere and faithful believer experiencing the nearness of God can face life's dangers with courage and assurance in Christ.

27:31 EXCEPT THESE ABIDE IN THE SHIP. Paul's statement here appears inconsistent with vv. 22,24. If God promised Paul that He will spare the lives of all those who are sailing with him (v. 24), and Paul reports the promise without qualification that "there shall be no loss of *any man's* life among you" (v. 22), how could the desertion of the sailors cause anyone's death among the passengers? The answer is in the Biblical truth that God's promises to His people are normally conditioned on their obedience to His will (see Gen. 1:26–31 and 6:5–7; Ex. 3:7–8 and Num. 14:28–34; 2 Sam. 7:12–16 and 1 Ki. 11:11–13; 12:16).

4 And when the barbarians saw the
venomous beast hang on his hand, they
said among themselves, No doubt this
man is a murderer, whom, though he
hath escaped the sea, yet vengeance
suffereth not to live.
5 And he shook off the beast into
the fire, and [d]felt no harm.
6 Howbeit they looked when he
should have swollen, or fallen down
dead suddenly: but after they had
looked a great while, and saw no harm
come to him, they changed their minds,
and [e]said that he was a god.
7 In the same quarters were posses-
sions of the chief man of the island,
whose name was Publius; who re-
ceived us, and lodged us three days
courteously.
8 And it came to pass, that the fa-
ther of Publius lay sick of a fever and
of a bloody flux: to whom Paul entered
in, and [f]prayed, and [g]laid his hands
on him, and healed him.
9 So when this was done, others
also, which had diseases in the island,
came, and were healed:

Jas. 5:14-16

10 Who also honoured us with many
[h]honours; and when we departed,
they laded *us* with such things as were
necessary.
11 And after three months we de-
parted in a ship of Alexandria, which
had wintered in the isle, whose sign
was Castor and Pollux.
12 And landing at Syracuse, we tar-
ried *there* three days.
13 And from thence we fetched a
compass, and came to Rhegium: and
after one day the south wind blew, and
we came the next day to Puteoli:
14 Where we found brethren, and
were desired to tarry with them seven
days: and so we went toward Rome.
15 And from thence, when the
brethren heard of us, they came to
meet us as far as Appiiforum, and The
three taverns: whom when Paul saw,
he thanked God, and took courage.
16 And when we came to Rome, the
centurion delivered the prisoners to
the captain of the guard: but [i]Paul
was suffered to dwell by himself with
a soldier that kept him.

The arrival at Rome

17 And it came to pass, that after
three days Paul called the chief of the
Jews together: and when they were
come together, he said unto them, Men
and brethren, [j]though I have commit-
ted nothing against the people, or cus-
toms of our fathers, yet [k]was I deliv-
ered prisoner from Jerusalem into the
hands of the Romans.
18 Who, [l]when they had examined
me, would have let *me* go, because
there was no cause of death in me.
19 But when the Jews spake against
it, [m]I was constrained to appeal unto
Caesar; not that I had aught to accuse
my nation of.
20 For this cause therefore have I
called for you, to see *you*, and to speak
with *you:* because that [n]for the hope
of Israel I am bound with [o]this chain.
21 And they said unto him, We nei-
ther received letters out of Judaea con-
cerning thee, neither any of the breth-
ren that came showed or spake any
harm of thee.
22 But we desire to hear of thee
what thou thinkest: for as concerning
this sect, we know that every where
[p]it is spoken against.
23 And when they had appointed
him a day, there came many to him into
his lodging; [q]to whom he expounded
and testified the kingdom of God, per-
suading them concerning Jesus, [r]both
out of the law of Moses, and *out of* the
prophets, from morning till evening.
24 And [s]some believed the things
which were spoken, and some believed
not.
25 And when they agreed not
among themselves, they departed, af-
ter that Paul had spoken one word,
Well spake the Holy Ghost by Esaias
the prophet unto our fathers,
26 Saying, [t]Go unto this people,
and say, Hearing ye shall hear, and
shall not understand; and seeing ye
shall see, and not perceive:

28:5 [d]Mark 16:18 Luke 10:19
28:6 [e]ch. 14:11
28:8 [f]Jas. 5:14,15 [g]Mark 6:5 & 7:32 & 16:18 Luke 4:40 ch. 19:11,12 1 Cor. 12:9,28
28:10 [h]Mat. 15:6 1 Tim. 5:17
28:16 [i]ch. 24:25 & 27:3
28:17 [j]ch. 24:12,13 [k]ch. 21:33
28:18 [l]ch. 22:24 & 24:10 & 25:8
28:19 [m]ch. 25:11
28:20 [n]ch. 26:6,7 [o]ch. 26:29 Eph. 3:1 & 4:1 & 6:20 2 Tim. 1:16 Philem. 10,13
28:22 [p]Luke 2:34 ch. 24:5,14 1 Pet. 2:12 & 4:14
28:23 [q]Luke 24:27 ch. 17:3 & 19:8 [r]See ch. 26:6,22
28:24 [s]ch. 14:4 & 19:9
28:26 [t]Is. 6:9 Jer. 5:21 Ezek. 12:2 Mat. 13:14 Mark 4:12 Luke 8:10 John 12:40 Rom. 11:8

28:5 HE . . . FELT NO HARM. The experience of Paul remarkably illustrates the promise of Jesus in Mark 16:18 (see note on that verse).

28:16 WE CAME TO ROME. It had been Paul's desire to preach the gospel in Rome (Rom. 15:22–29), and it was also God's will that he do so (23:11). Yet he arrived in Rome in chains and only after setbacks, storms, shipwreck, and many trials. Though Paul remained faithful, God did not make his way easy and trouble free. Likewise, we may be in God's will and entirely faithful to Him; nevertheless, He may direct us in unpleasant paths involving troubles. Through it all, however, we can know that "all things work together for good to them that love God" (Rom. 8:28).

27 For the heart of this people is
waxed gross, and their ears are dull of
hearing, and their eyes have they
closed; lest they should see with *their*
eyes, and hear with *their* ears, and understand with *their* heart, and should
be converted, and I should heal them.
28 Be it known therefore unto you,
that the salvation of God is sent [u]unto
the Gentiles, and *that* they will hear it.

28:28 [u]Mat. 21:41 ch. 13:46 & 18:6 & 26:17,18 Rom. 11:11

28:31 [v]ch. 4:31 Eph. 6:19

29 And when he had said these
words, the Jews departed, and had
great reasoning among themselves.
30 And Paul dwelt two whole years
in his own hired house, and received all
that came in unto him,
31 [v]Preaching the kingdom of
God, and teaching those things which
concern the Lord Jesus Christ, with all
confidence, no man forbidding him.

28:30 PAUL DWELT TWO WHOLE YEARS. Luke's history of the early church is brought to an end here. What happened to Paul afterwards is generally thought to be the following. Paul remained in confinement for two years. He was able to receive visitors and preach the gospel to them. During this time he wrote the Epistles to the Ephesians, Philippians, Colossians, and Philemon. In approximately A.D. 63, Paul was acquitted and released. For the next few years he continued his missionary endeavors, perhaps going to Spain as he had planned (Rom. 15:28). During this period he wrote 1 Timothy and Titus. Paul was again arrested, about A.D. 67, and was taken back to Rome. 2 Timothy was written during this second imprisonment at Rome. Paul's imprisonment ended by his being beheaded, suffering martyrdom under the Roman emperor Nero.

28:31 PREACHING THE KINGDOM OF GOD. The book of Acts breaks off suddenly, with no formal conclusion to what God did through the Holy Spirit and the N.T. apostles. God intends that the acts of the Holy Spirit and the preaching of the gospel continue in the lives of Christ's people until the end of the age (2:17–21; Mat. 28:18–20). Luke, under the inspiration of the Holy Spirit, has revealed God's pattern of what the church should be and do. He has given us examples of the faithfulness of believers, the triumph of the gospel against the opposition of the enemy, and the power of the Holy Spirit operating in the church and among men. This is God's pattern for present and future churches, and we must faithfully keep it, proclaim it, and live it (2 Tim. 1:14). All churches must measure themselves by what the Spirit said and did among the earliest believers. If the power, righteousness, joy, and faith found in our churches are not the same as what we read about in Acts, then we must ask God once more for a renewed faith in the resurrected Christ and for a fresh, new outpouring of His Holy Spirit.

ROMANS

Outline

Introduction (1:1–17)

I. Man's Desperate Need of Righteousness (1:18—3:20)
   A. The Gentiles' Need (1:18–32)
   B. The Jews' Need (2:1—3:8)
   C. The Universal Need (3:9–20)

II. God's Glorious Provision of Righteousness (3:21—5:21)
   A. Justification by Faith Summarized (3:21–31)
   B. Justification by Faith Illustrated in Abraham (4:1–25)
   C. The Blessings and Assurance Accompanying Justification (5:1–11)
   D. Adam and Christ Contrasted (5:12–21)
      1. Adam/Sin/Condemnation/Death
      2. Christ/Grace/Justification/Life

III. The Outworking of Righteousness Through Faith (6:1—8:39)
   A. Freedom from the Slavery of Sin (6:1–23)
      1. Dying with Christ to Sin (6:1–14)
      2. Living with Christ as Servants of Righteousness (6:15–23)
   B. Freedom from the Conflict under the Law (7:1–25)
   C. Freedom Through the Law of the Spirit of Life (8:1–39)

IV. Righteousness Through Faith As It Relates to Israel (9:1—11:36)
   A. The Problem of Israel's Rejection (9:1—10:21)
   B. The Triumph of God's Plan (11:1–36)

V. Practical Applications of Righteousness Through Faith (12:1—15:13)
   A. The Believer and Consecration (12:1–2)
   B. The Believer and Community (12:3–21)
   C. The Believer and the State (13:1–7)
   D. The Believer and the Law of Love (13:8—15:13)

Conclusion (15:14—16:27)

Author: Paul

Theme: The Righteousness of God is Revealed

Date of Writing: c. A.D. 57

Background

Romans is Paul's longest, most theological, and most influential epistle. Probably for these reasons it is placed first among his thirteen N.T. books. Paul wrote Romans in connection with his apostolic mission to the Gentile world. Contrary to some ecclesiastical traditions, the church in Rome was not founded by Peter or any other apostle. The Roman church may have been established by Paul's converts from Macedonia and Asia as well as by Jews and proselytes converted on the day of Pentecost (Acts 2:10). Paul did not regard Rome as the specific territory of another apostle (Rom. 15:20).

In the book of Romans Paul assures the believers at Rome that he has often planned to preach the gospel to them, but so far has been hindered from coming (1:13–15; 15:22). He affirms his earnest desire to come to them, and he communicates his plans for coming soon (15:23–32).

At the time of writing, toward the end of his third missionary journey (cf. 15:25–26; Acts 20:2–3; 1 Cor. 16:5–6), Paul was at Corinth as a guest in the home of Gaius (Rom. 16:23; 1 Cor. 1:14). As he penned Romans through his assistant Tertius (16:22), he was planning to return to Jerusalem for the day of Pentecost (Acts 20:16; probably spring A.D. 57 or 58) and to deliver personally a relief offering from the Gentile churches for the poverty-stricken saints in Jerusalem (15:25–27). Immediately afterwards, Paul hoped to go to Spain with the gospel, visiting the church in Rome on his way and receiving assistance from them as he headed further west (15:24,28).

Purpose

Paul wrote this letter to prepare the way for his anticipated ministry at Rome and his planned mission to Spain. His purpose was twofold. (1) Since the Romans apparently received distorted rumors about Paul's message and theology (e.g., 3:8; 6:1–2,15), he felt it necessary to put into writing the gospel he had been preaching for twenty-five years. (2) He sought to correct certain problems in the church occurring because of wrong attitudes of Jews toward Gentiles (e.g., 2:1–29; 3:1,9) and Gentiles toward Jews (e.g., 11:11–32).

Survey

The theme of Romans is presented in 1:16–17, namely that in the Lord Jesus the righteousness of God is revealed as the answer to His wrath against sin. Then Paul sets forth the foundational truths of the gospel. First, he emphasizes that the problem of sin and man's need of righteousness are universal (1:18—3:20). Since both Jews and Gentiles are under sin and thus under God's wrath, no person can be justified before God apart from the gift of righteousness through faith in Jesus Christ (3:21—4:25).

Having been justified freely by grace through faith and having been given assurance of salvation (ch. 5), God's gift of righteousness is demonstrated in the believer's death with Christ to sin (ch. 6), his deliverance from the struggle of law-righteousness (ch. 7), and his adoption as God's child and his new life according to the Spirit, leading to glorification (ch. 8). God is working out His plan of redemption in spite of the unbelief of Israel (chs. 9–11).

Finally, Paul declares that a transformed life in Christ results in the application of righteousness and love to all areas of behavior—social, civil, and moral (chs. 12–14). Paul concludes Romans with an explanation of his personal plans (ch. 15) and a long list of personal greetings, a final admonition, and a doxology (ch. 16).

Special Features

Seven major features and emphases characterize Romans. (1) Romans is Paul's most systematic epistle, the theological epistle *par excellence* in the N.T. (2) Paul writes in a question and answer or debating style (e.g., 3:1,4–6,9,31). (3) Paul uses the O.T. extensively as Scriptural authority for his presentation of the true nature of the gospel. (4) Paul presents "the righteousness of God" as the core revelation of the gospel (1:16–17): God set things right in and through Jesus Christ. (5) Paul focuses on the twofold nature of sin, along with God's provision in Christ for each aspect: (a) sin as personal transgression (1:1—5:11), and "the sin" (Gk. *hē hamartia*) principle, i.e., the inherent natural tendency to sin which dwells within the heart of every person since Adam's fall (5:12—8:39). (6) Ch. 8 is the most extensive chapter in the Bible on the role of the Holy Spirit in the life of the believer. (7) Romans contains the most powerful discussion in the Bible about the Jews' rejection of Christ (except for a remnant), and about God's plan for a full-circle redemption that ultimately comes back to Israel (chs. 9–11).

Reading Romans

In order to read the entire New Testament in one year, the book of Romans should be read in 21 days, according to the following schedule:

☐ 1:1–17 ☐ 1:18–32 ☐ 2 ☐ 3 ☐ 4 ☐ 5:1–11 ☐ 5:12–21 ☐ 6:1–14 ☐ 6:15—7:6 ☐ 7:7–25 ☐ 8:1–17 ☐ 8:18–39 ☐ 9:1–29 ☐ 9:30—10:21 ☐ 11:1–24 ☐ 11:25–36 ☐ 12:1–16 ☐ 12:17—13:14 ☐ 14:1—15:4 ☐ 15:5–33 ☐ 16

NOTES

1 PAUL, A servant of Jesus Christ,
[a]called *to be* an apostle, [b]sepa-
rated unto the gospel of God,
2 ([c]Which he had promised afore
[d]by his prophets in the holy scrip-
tures,)
3 Concerning his Son Jesus Christ
our Lord, which was [e]made of the
seed of David according to the flesh;
4 And [f]declared[a] *to be* the Son of
God with power, according [g]to the
spirit of holiness, by the resurrection
from the dead:
5 By whom [h]we have received
grace and apostleship, [b]for [i]obedi-
ence to the faith among all nations,
[j]for his name:
6 Among whom are ye also the
called of Jesus Christ:
7 To all that be in Rome, beloved of
God, [k]called *to be* saints: [l]Grace to
you and peace from God our Father,
and the Lord Jesus Christ.

Thanksgiving and prayers

8 First, [m]I thank my God through
Jesus Christ for you all, that [n]your
faith is spoken of throughout the whole
world.
9 For [o]God is my witness, [p]whom
I serve [c]with my spirit in the gospel
of his Son, that [q]without ceasing I
make mention of you always in my
prayers;
10 Making request, if by any means
now at length I might have a prosper-
ous journey by the will of God to come
unto you.
11 For I long to see you, that [r]I
may impart unto you some spiritual
gift, to the end ye may be established;
12 That is, that I may be comforted
together [d]with you by [s]the mutual
faith both of you and me.
13 Now I would not have you igno-
rant, brethren, that oftentimes I pur-
posed to come unto you, (but [t]was let
hitherto,) that I might have some
[u]fruit [d]among you also, even as
among other Gentiles.
14 I am debtor both to the Greeks,
and to the Barbarians; both to the wise,
and to the unwise.
15 So, as much as in me is, I am
ready to preach the gospel to you that
are at Rome also.
16 For [v]I am not ashamed of the
gospel of Christ: for [w]it is the power of
God unto salvation to every one that
believeth; [x]to the Jew first, and also to
the Greek.
17 For [y]therein is the righteous-
ness of God revealed from faith to
faith: as it is written, [z]The just shall
live by faith.

The Gentiles: guilty before God

18 [a]For the wrath of God is re-

Rom. 12:6-8

Rom. 3:21-26

1:1 [a]1 Tim. 1:11 [b]Acts 9:15 **1:2** [c]Acts 26:6 [d]Gal. 3:8 **1:3** [e]Gal. 4:4 **1:4** [f]Acts 13:33 [g]Heb. 9:14 **1:5** [h]Eph. 3:8 [i]Acts 6:7 [j]Acts 9:15 **1:7** [k]1 Cor. 1:2 [l]1 Cor. 1:3 **1:8** [m]1 Cor. 1:4 [n]ch. 16:19 **1:9** [o]ch. 9:1 [p]Acts 27:23 [q]1 Thes. 3:10 **1:11** [r]ch. 15:29 **1:12** [s]Tit. 1:4 **1:13** [t]1 Thes. 2:18 [u]Phil. 4:17 **1:16** [v]Ps. 40:9,10 Mark 8:38 [w]1 Cor. 1:18 [x]Luke 2:30 Acts 13:26 **1:17** [y]ch. 3:21 [z]Hab. 2:4 John 3:36 Gal. 3:11 **1:18** [a]Acts 17:30 Eph. 5:6

[a] Gk. *determined* [b] Or, *to the obedience of faith* [c] Or, *in my spirit* [d] Or, *in you*

1:4 THE SPIRIT OF HOLINESS. The "spirit of holiness" refers to the Holy Spirit, the third person in the divine Trinity. His holiness separates Him distinctly from the spirit of man, sin, and the world and describes both His preeminent characteristic and His work (cf. Gal. 5:16–24).

1:5 OBEDIENCE TO THE FAITH. Note that Paul, both at the beginning of the epistle to the Romans and at the end (16:26), defines faith in terms of "obedience." For Paul the nature of saving faith must be determined by its initial intention, namely, a joining of one's life to God through Jesus Christ in love, devotion, gratitude, and obedience (see Jas. 2:17, note; cf. John 15:10,14; Heb. 5:8–9; see article on FAITH AND GRACE, p. 1738).

1:7 CALLED *TO BE* SAINTS. The idea communicated by the word "saint" is "set apart to God" and "being holy" (cf. v. 1). Believers have been set apart from sin and the world, brought near to God, and consecrated for service (see Ex. 19:6, note; Lev. 11:44, note). With this action of consecration, the Spirit renews the character of the believer in true holiness (see Acts 9:13, note; cf. Eph. 4:23–24; see article on SANCTIFICATION, p. 1982).

1:16 SALVATION. For a discussion of the meaning of the word "salvation," as well as two other words the Bible uses for salvation, see article on BIBLICAL WORDS FOR SALVATION, p. 1726.

1:17 FAITH TO FAITH. "From faith to faith" means "faith from start to finish." The righteous person continues to live by faith, and in so doing, grows from one level of maturity to another. In this way the believer progresses along the path of righteousness to live a rich spiritual life (see 8:12–13; 14:13–23; Heb. 10:38, note; see article on FAITH AND GRACE, p. 1738).

1:18 THE WRATH OF GOD. The wrath (Gk. *orgē*) of God is an expression of His righteousness and love (see article on THE ATTRIBUTES OF GOD, p. 912). It is God's personal anger and unchanging reaction to all sin (Ezek. 7:8–9; Eph. 5:6; Rev. 19:15), provoked by the wicked behavior of individuals (Ex. 4:14; Num. 12:1–9; 2 Sam. 6:6–7) and nations (Is. 10:5; Jer. 50:13; Ezek. 30:15), and by the apostasy and unfaithfulness of His people (Num. 25:3; 32:10–13; Deut. 29:24–28).

(1) In the past God's anger and hatred towards sin was revealed by means of the flood (Gen. 6–8), famine and pestilence (Ezek. 6:11ff), annihilation

BIBLICAL WORDS FOR SALVATION

Rom. 1:16 "For I am not ashamed of the gospel of Christ: for it is the power of God unto salvation to every one that believeth; to the Jew first, and also to the Greek."

God freely offers us eternal life in Jesus Christ. But understanding the exact process used to make that available to us is sometimes difficult for us to grasp. Therefore, God presents various pictures in the Bible for salvation, each one with its own unique emphasis. This article examines three of those pictures: Salvation, Redemption, and Justification.

SALVATION. Salvation (Gk. *sōtēria*) means "deliverance," "bringing safely through," "keeping from harm"; already in the O.T. God revealed Himself as the one who saves His people (Ps. 27:1, 88:1; see Deut. 26:8, note; Ps. 61:2, note; Is. 25:6, note; 53:5, note). It is described in the N.T. as "the way" or road that leads through life to eternal fellowship with God in heaven (Mat. 7:14; Mark 12:14; John 14:6; Acts 16:17; cf. Acts 9:2; 22:4; Heb. 10:20; 2 Pet. 2:2,21). This road of salvation must be walked to the very end. We can describe salvation as *one* way with *two* sides and *three* stages:

(1) The one way of salvation. Christ is the way to the Father (John 14:6; Acts 4:12). Salvation is provided for us by God's grace which He gives in Christ Jesus (Rom. 3:24), based on His death (3:25; 5:8), resurrection (5:10), and continued intercession for believers (Heb. 7:25).

(2) The two sides of salvation. Salvation is received by grace, through faith in Christ (Rom. 3:22,24–25,28). That is, it comes as a result of God's grace (John 1:16) and the human response of faith (Acts 16:31; Rom. 1:17; Eph. 1:15; 2:8; see article on FAITH AND GRACE, p. 1738).

(3) The three stages of salvation. (a) The past stage of salvation includes the personal experience by which we as believers receive forgiveness of sins (Acts 10:43; Rom. 4:6–8) and pass from spiritual death to spiritual life (see article on REGENERATION, p. 1597; 1 John 3:14), from the power of sin to the power of the Lord (Rom. 6:17–23), from the dominion of Satan to the dominion of God (Acts 26:18). It brings us into a new personal relationship with God (John 1:12) and rescues us from the penalty of sin (Rom. 1:16; 6:23; 1 Cor. 1:18).

(b) The present stage of salvation saves us from the practice and dominion of sin, filling us with the Holy Spirit. It includes: (i) the privilege of a person-to-person relationship with God as our Father and Jesus as our Lord and Savior (Mat. 6:9; John 14:18–23; see Gal. 4:6, note); (ii) the call to reckon ourselves dead to sin (Rom. 6:1–14) and to submit to the leading of the Holy Spirit (Rom. 8:1–16) and the Word of God (John 8:31; 14:21; 2 Tim. 3:15–16); (iii) the invitation to be filled with the Holy Spirit and the command to keep being filled (see Acts 2:33–39; Eph. 5:18; see article on BAPTISM IN THE HOLY SPIRIT, p. 1652); (iv) the demand to separate ourselves from sin (Rom. 6:1–14) and the present perverse generation (Acts 2:40; 2 Cor. 6:17); and (v) the call to wage constant battle for God's kingdom against Satan and his demonic host (2 Cor. 10:4–5; Eph. 6:11,16; 1 Pet. 5:8).

(c) The future stage of salvation (Rom. 13:11–12; 1 Thes. 5:8–9; 1 Pet. 1:5) includes: (i) our deliverance from the coming wrath of God (Rom. 5:9; 1 Cor. 3:15; 5:5; 1 Thes. 1:10; 5:9); (ii) our sharing the divine glory (Rom. 8:29; 2 Thes. 2:13–14) and receiving a resurrected or transformed body (1 Cor. 15:49–52); and (iii) our receiving rewards as faithful overcomers (see Rev. 2:7, note). This future salvation is the goal toward which all Christians strive (1 Cor. 9:24–27; Phil. 3:8–14). All present warnings, discipline, and punishment have as their purpose that believers should not forfeit the final stage of salvation (1 Cor. 5:1–13; 9:24–27; Phil. 2:12,16; 2 Pet. 1:5–11; see Heb. 12:1, note).

REDEMPTION. The root meaning of "redemption" (Gk. *apolutrōsis*) is to ransom by the payment of a price. The expression denotes the means by which salvation is procured, namely by the payment of a ransom. The doctrine of redemption can be summarized as follows:

(1) The state of sin out of which we must be redeemed: The N.T. represents humans as alienated from God (Rom. 3:10–18), under the dominion of satanic powers (Acts 10:38; 26:18), slaves to sin (Rom. 6:6; 7:14), and in need of deliverance from its guilt, punishment, and power (Acts 26:18; Rom. 1:18; 6:1–18,23; Eph. 5:8; Col. 1:13; 1 Pet. 2:9).

(2) The price paid to free us from this bondage: Christ secured the ransom by shedding His blood and giving His life (Mat. 20:28; Mark 10:45; 1 Cor. 6:20; Eph. 1:7; Tit. 2:14; Heb. 9:12; 1 Pet. 1:18–19).

(3) The resultant state of the redeemed: Believers redeemed by Christ are now free from Satan's dominion and from the guilt and power of sin (Acts 26:18; Rom. 6:7,12,14,18; Col. 1:13). This freedom from sin, however, does not leave us free to do as we wish, for we become the property of God. Freedom from sin makes us willing slaves of God (Acts 26:18; Rom. 6:18,22; 1 Cor. 6:19–20; 7:22–23).

(4) The N.T. teaching of redemption was foreshadowed by redemption in the O.T. The great O.T. redemptive event was the exodus from Egypt (see Ex. 6:7; note, 12:26, note). Furthermore, through the sacrificial system, the blood of animals was used as the price paid for the atonement of sin (see Lev. 9:8, note; see article on THE DAY OF ATONEMENT, p. 188).

JUSTIFICATION. The word "justify" (Gk. *dikaioō*) means to be "just [or righteous] before God" (Rom. 2:13), "to be made righteous" (Rom. 5:18–19), "to establish as right," or "to set or put right." It denotes being in a right relationship with God rather than receiving a mere legal, judicial declaration. God forgives the repentant sinner, whom He had pronounced guilty through the law and condemned to eternal death, restores him to divine favor, and sets him in a right relationship (fellowship) with Himself and His will. The apostle Paul reveals several truths about justification and how it is accomplished:

(1) Being put right with God is a gift (Rom. 3:24; Eph. 2:8). No one can put himself right with God by keeping the law perfectly or by performing good works (Rom. 4:2–6; Eph. 2:8–9), "for all have sinned, and come short of the glory of God" (Rom. 3:23).

(2) Being put right with God happens "through the redemption that is in Christ Jesus" (Rom. 3:24). No one is justified who has not been redeemed by Christ from sin and its power.

(3) Being put right with God comes "by his grace" and is appropriated through faith in Jesus Christ as Lord and Savior (Rom. 3:22–24; cf. 4:3–5; see article on FAITH AND GRACE, p. 1738).

(4) Being put right with God is related to the forgiveness of our sins (Rom. 4:7). Sinners are declared guilty (Rom. 3:9–18,23), but are forgiven because of Christ's atoning death and resurrection (see Rom. 3:25, note; 4:5, note; 4:25; 5:6–11).

(5) When we are put right with God by faith in Christ, we are crucified with Christ and Christ comes to live in us (Gal. 2:16–21). Through this experience, we actually *become* righteous and begin living unto God (2:19–21). This transforming work of Christ in us through the Spirit (cf. 2 Thes. 2:13; 1 Pet. 1:2) cannot be separated from the redemptive work of Christ for us. The work of Christ and the Spirit are interdependent.

vealed from heaven against all ungodli-
ness and unrighteousness of men, who
hold the truth in unrighteousness;
19 Because [b]that which may be
known of God is manifest [e]in them;
for [c]God hath shown *it* unto them.
20 For [d]the invisible things of him
from the creation of the world are
clearly seen, being understood by the
things that are made, *even* his eternal
power and Godhead; [f]so that they are
without excuse:
21 Because that, when they knew
God, they glorified *him* not as God, nei-
ther were thankful; but [e]became vain
in their imaginations, and their foolish
heart was darkened.
22 [f]Professing themselves to be
wise, they became fools,
23 And changed the glory of the un-
corruptible [g]God into an image made
like to corruptible man, and to birds,
and fourfooted beasts, and creeping
things.

God's wrath against Gentiles

24 [h]Wherefore God also gave them
up to uncleanness through the lusts of
their own hearts, [i]to dishonour their
own bodies [j]between themselves:
25 Who changed [k]the truth of God

1:19 [b]Acts 14:17 [c]John 1:9
1:20 [d]Ps. 19:1 Acts 14:17
1:21 [e]2 Ki. 17:15 Jer. 2:5 Eph. 4:17
1:22 [f]Jer. 10:14
1:23 [g]Deut. 4:16 Ps. 106:20 Is. 40:18
1:24 [h]Ps. 81:12 Acts 7:42 Eph. 4:18 [i]1 Cor. 6:18 1 Thes. 4:4 [j]Lev. 18:22
1:25 [k]1 Thes. 1:9 1 John 5:20

[e] Or, *to them* [f] Or, *that they may be*

(Deut. 29:22–23), scattering (Lam. 4:16), and burning of the land (Is. 9:18–19).

(2) In the present God's anger is seen in His giving the wicked up to uncleanness and vile passions (see v. 24, note) and in bringing ruin and death to all who disobey God (1:18—3:20; 6:23; Ezek. 18:4; Eph. 2:3).

(3) In the future the wrath of God will include great tribulation upon the ungodly of this world (Mat. 24:21; Rev. 5–19) and a coming day of judgment for all people and nations (Ezek. 7:19; Dan. 8:19)—"a day of wasteness and desolation, a day of darkness and gloominess" (Zeph. 1:15), a day of reckoning for the unrighteous (2:5; Mat. 3:7; Luke 3:17; Eph. 5:6; Col. 3:6; Rev. 11:18; 14:8–10; 19:15). Ultimately it involves eternal punishment for the unrepentant (see Mat. 10:28, note).

(4) God's wrath is not His final word to humans, for He has provided a way of escape or salvation from His wrath. A person may repent of sin and turn in faith to Jesus Christ (5:8; John 3:36; 1 Thes. 1:10; 5:9; see article on BIBLICAL WORDS FOR SALVATION, p. 1726).

(5) Believers united to Christ must participate in God's anger against sin, not in the sense of vengeance, but in a sincere love for righteousness and hatred of evil (see Heb. 1:9, note). The N.T. recognizes a holy anger that hates what God hates, an anger evident above all in Jesus Himself (Mark 3:5; John 2:12–17; Heb. 1:9; see Luke 19:45, note), in Paul (Acts 17:16), and in righteous people (2 Pet. 2:7–8; Rev. 2:6, note).

1:21 THEY GLORIFIED *HIM* NOT. Although vv. 21–28 primarily address the downward course of depravity among the unregenerate, they also contain principles indicating why one of the major sins of fallen Christian leaders is immorality (see next note).

(1) When leaders in the church become proud and boastful (v. 22), they seek honor for themselves (v. 21) and exalt themselves (the creature) rather than the Creator (v. 25). A door is then opened within their lives to sexual impurity and shameful lust (vv. 24,26; see 2 Pet. 2:2,15, notes). If they do not turn and repent, they will ultimately be given over to a reprobate mind (v. 28).

(2) Such people may continue in shameful lust and sin while justifying their actions as common human weakness, persuading themselves that they are still in fellowship with the Holy Spirit and in possession of salvation. They blind themselves to the warning of Scripture that "no whoremonger, nor unclean [impure] person . . . hath any inheritance in the kingdom of Christ" (Eph. 5:5).

1:24 GOD ALSO GAVE THEM UP. A primary sign of God's abandonment of any society or people is that they become obsessed with sexual immorality and perversion. (1) The term "God also gave them up to uncleanness" means that God abandoned these persons to intensified and aggravated lusts. The term "lust" (Gk. *epithumia*) in v. 24 denotes a passionate desire for forbidden sexual pleasure (cf. 2 Cor. 12:21; Gal. 5:19; Eph. 5:3).

(2) The three stages of abandonment by God to impurity are: (a) God giving them over to lust for sinful sexual pleasures that degrade the body (v. 24); (b) God giving them over to shameful homosexual or lesbian passions (vv. 26–27); after this, (c) God giving them up to a reprobate mind, i.e., their minds justify their unrighteous actions and they become continually preoccupied with evil and the pleasures of sexual sin (v. 28). These three stages occur among all people who reject the truth of God's revelation and seek pleasure in ungodliness (v. 18; see v. 27, note).

(3) God has two purposes in abandoning the unrighteous to sin: (a) to allow sin and its consequences to accelerate as part of His judgment upon them (2:2), and (b) to make them realize their need for salvation (2:4).

1:25 A LIE. The "lie" is the word of Satan, the father of lies (John 8:44): "ye shall be as gods" (Gen. 3:5). (1) To believe the lie is to reject "the truth of God" and participate in idolatry (Gen. 3:5; Col. 3:5; 2 Thes. 2:11, note). (2) Man's propensity for self-worship is the reason the Bible incessantly warns against pride. "Because thine heart *is* lifted up [i.e., proud], and thou hast said, I *am* a God" (Ezek. 28:2; cf. Prov. 6:17; 8:13; 16:18; 1 Tim. 3:6; Jas. 4:6; 1 John 2:16).

[l]into a lie, and worshipped and served
the creature [g]more than the Creator,
who is blessed for ever. Amen.
26 For this cause God gave them up
unto [m]vile affections: for even their
women did change the natural use into
that which is against nature:
27 And likewise also the men, leav-
ing the natural use of the woman,
burned in their lust one toward anoth-
er; men with men working that which
is unseemly, and receiving in them-
selves that recompence of their error
which was meet.
28 And even as they did not like
[h]to retain God in *their* knowledge, God
gave them over to [i]a reprobate mind,
to do those things [n]which are not con-
venient;
29 Being filled with all unrighteous-
ness, fornication, wickedness, covet-
ousness, maliciousness; full of envy,
murder, debate, deceit, malignity;
whisperers,
30 Backbiters, haters of God, de-
spiteful, proud, boasters, inventors of
evil things, disobedient to parents,
31 Without understanding, cove-
nantbreakers, [j]without natural affec-
tion, implacable, unmerciful:
32 Who [o]knowing the judgment of
God, that they which commit such
things [p]are worthy of death, not only
do the same, but [q]have[k] pleasure in
them that do them.

The guilt of the Jews

2 THEREFORE THOU art [r]inex-
cusable, O man, whosoever thou
art that judgest: [s]for wherein thou
judgest another, thou condemnest thy-
self; for thou that judgest doest the
same things.
2 But we are sure that the judgment
of God is according to truth against
them which commit such things.
3 And thinkest thou this, O man,
that judgest them which do such
things, and doest the same, that thou
shalt escape the judgment of God?
4 Or despisest thou [t]the riches of
his goodness and [u]forbearance and
[v]longsuffering; [w]not knowing that
the goodness of God leadeth thee to re-
pentance?
5 But after thy hardness and im-
penitent heart [x]treasurest up unto
thyself wrath against the day of wrath
and revelation of the righteous judg-
ment of God;

1:25 [l]Is. 44:20 Jer. 10:14 **1:26** [m]Lev. 18:22 Eph. 5:12 **1:28** [n]Eph. 5:4 **1:32** [o]ch. 2:2 [p]ch. 6:21 [q]Ps. 50:18 Hos. 7:3 **2:1** [r]ch. 1:20 [s]2 Sam. 12:5 Mat. 7:1,2 John 8:9 **2:4** [t]Eph. 1:7 [u]ch. 3:25 [v]Ex. 34:6 [w]Is. 30:18 2 Pet. 3:9 **2:5** [x]Deut. 32:34 Jas. 5:3

[g] Or, *rather* [h] Or, *to acknowledge* [i] Or, *a mind void of judgment* [j] Or, *unsociable* [k] Or, *consent with them*

1:27 MEN WITH MEN. The apostle likely regarded the homosexual/lesbian abomination as the greatest evidence of human degeneracy resulting from immorality and abandonment by God (see Gen. 19:4–5; Lev. 18:22). Any nation that justifies homosexuality or lesbianism as an acceptable lifestyle is in its final stages of moral corruption (see v. 24, note). For more information about this horrible act read Gen. 19:4–9; Lev. 20:13; Deut. 23:17; 1 Ki. 14:24; 15:12; 22:46; Is. 3:9; 1 Cor. 6:9–10; 1 Tim. 1:10; 2 Pet. 2:6; Jude 7.

1:32 HAVE PLEASURE IN THEM THAT DO THEM. Paul's last word on general human sinfulness is God's condemnation of a condition even more damning than the practice itself, i.e., supporting, approving, and encouraging evil by taking pleasure in the immoral actions of others. This disposition is the ultimate in depravity—vicarious enjoyment of lust and evil. Sin becomes entertainment. (1) The word "have pleasure" (Gk. *suneudokeō*) means "are pleased with," "delight in," or "give approval to," and points to the casual enjoyment of the sins of others that prevails in human society.

(2) Today we know what great harm is produced by the portrayal of immorality that dominates the entertainment media; yet many consent to it and derive pleasure from it. Being entertained by watching other people sin and engage in ungodly actions, even while you yourself abstain, brings you under the same condemnation of God as those engaging in such evil practices. Iniquity is intensified in any society where sin meets with no inhibition from the disapproval of others and where people enjoy watching it.

(3) Hence, those (and especially those who profess faith in Christ) who use the immoral actions of others for entertainment and enjoyment are directly contributing to public opinion favorable to immorality and, therefore, to the corruption and eternal damnation of an indefinite number of other people. This sin is worthy of death and will be exposed and judged at the final day of judgment (2 Thes. 2:12).

2:1 THOU . . . DOEST THE SAME THINGS. In ch. 1 Paul explained that the Gentiles were given over to sin. Now, in ch. 2, he shows that the Jews practice the same things and likewise need salvation through Christ.

2:3 AND DOEST THE SAME. No one should attempt to direct others to do what is right while failing to correct his own evil conduct. Some churches attempt to persuade pagan society to follow Biblical law, while at the same time they are blind to the worldliness and immorality within their own membership (cf. Luke 6:42). Before the church seeks to influence the world to a better way, it must place its own life under the divine searchlight and reform itself accordingly.

God's principles of judgment

6 [y]Who will render to every man
according to his deeds:
7 To them who by patient continu-
ance in well doing seek for glory and
honour and immortality, eternal life:
8 But unto them that are conten-
tious, and [z]do not obey the truth, but
obey unrighteousness, indignation and
wrath,
9 Tribulation and anguish, upon ev-
ery soul of man that doeth evil, of the
Jew [a]first, and also of the [1]Gentile;
10 [b]But glory, honour, and peace,
to every man that worketh good, to the
Jew first, and also to the [1]Gentile:
11 For [c]there is no respect of per-
sons with God.
12 For as many as have sinned
without law shall also perish without
law: and as many as have sinned in the
law shall be judged by the law;
13 (For [d]not the hearers of the law
are just before God, but the doers of the
law shall be justified.
14 For when the Gentiles, which
have not the law, do by nature the
things contained in the law, these, hav-
ing not the law, are a law unto them-
selves:
15 Which show the work of the law
written in their hearts, [m]their con-
science also bearing witness, and *their*
thoughts [n]the mean while accusing or
else excusing one another;)
16 [e]In the day when God shall
judge the secrets of men [f]by Jesus
Christ [g]according to my gospel.

Jews do not obey the law

17 Behold, [h]thou art called a Jew,
and [i]restest in the law, [j]and makest
thy boast of God,
18 And [k]knowest *his* will, and
[l]approvest[o] the things that are more
excellent, being instructed out of the
law;
19 And [m]art confident that thou
thyself art a guide of the blind, a light
of them which are in darkness,
20 An instructor of the foolish, a
teacher of babes, [n]which hast the
form of knowledge and of the truth in
the law.
21 [o]Thou therefore which teachest
another, teachest thou not thyself?
thou that preachest a man should not
steal, dost thou steal?
22 Thou that sayest a man should
not commit adultery, dost thou commit
adultery? thou that abhorrest idols,
[p]dost thou commit sacrilege?
23 Thou that [q]makest thy boast of
the law, through breaking the law dis-
honourest thou God?
24 For the name of God is blas-

2:6 [y]Job 34:11 Ps. 62:12 Prov. 24:12 Jer. 17:10 2 Cor. 5:10 **2:8** [z]Job 24:13 2 Thes. 1:8 **2:9** [a]Amos 3:2 Luke 12:47 1 Pet. 4:17 **2:10** [b]1 Pet. 1:7 **2:11** [c]Deut. 10:17 Job 34:19 Acts 10:34 Eph. 6:9 **2:13** [d]Jas. 1:22 1 John 3:7 **2:16** [e]Eccl. 12:14 Mat. 25:31 Rev. 20:12 [f]John 5:22 Acts 10:42 [g]1 Tim. 1:11 **2:17** [h]Mat. 3:9 John 8:33 [i]Mic. 3:11 [j]Is. 48:2 **2:18** [k]Deut. 4:8 [l]Phil. 1:10 **2:19** [m]Mat. 15:14 John 9:34 **2:20** [n]2 Tim. 3:5 **2:21** [o]Ps. 50:16 Mat. 23:3 **2:22** [p]Mal. 3:8 **2:23** [q]ver. 17

[1]Gk. *Greek* [m]Or, *the conscience witnessing with them* [n]Or, *between themselves* [o]Or, *triest the things that differ*

2:7 GLORY AND HONOUR ... ETERNAL LIFE. In the very beginning of his treatise on salvation, Paul clarifies a fundamental truth concerning God's dealing with the entire human race: God punishes evildoers and rewards the righteous (see John 5:29, notes; Gal. 6:7–8). (1) The righteous are those who have been justified by faith (1:16–17; 3:24) and persevere in doing what is right according to God's standard (vv. 7,10; cf. Mat. 24:13; Col. 1:23; Heb. 3:14; Rev. 2:10). They value highly the glory that comes from God (1:23; 2:7; 5:2; 8:18), and they seek eternal life (8:23; 1 Cor. 15:51–57; 1 Pet. 1:4; Rev. 21:1—22:5).

(2) Those seeking immortality do so by grace through faith (3:24–25; Eph. 1:4–7; 2:8–10; 2 Tim. 2:1; see Phil 2:12–13, notes). The faithful enter into "honour and immortality, eternal life" by "patient continuance in well doing" (cf. Mat. 24:12–13), through the enabling grace given to them by Christ (see Mat. 7:21, note; see article on FAITH AND GRACE, p. 1738).

(3) Those who do evil are selfish, disobey the truth, and take pleasure in unrighteousness. They receive wrath, anger, and tribulation (1:28–32; 2:8–9).

2:12–15 SHALL ALSO PERISH. All those who continue in sin, even though they have no knowledge of God's law, will perish because they have a measure of knowledge of right and wrong (vv. 14–15). God will not automatically save those who do not hear the gospel, nor will He give them a second chance after death. The eternal consequence facing those who have not had an adequate chance to understand the gospel should cause us to make an unfailing effort to take the gospel to every person in every nation (see Mat. 4:19, note; 9:37, note).

2:13 THE DOERS OF THE LAW SHALL BE JUSTIFIED. Paul does not use the term "law" in the sense of a system of statutes that one may obey and earn his salvation without grace. "Law" here stands for the will of God made known to the human race. Merely hearing God's Word avails nothing apart from faith, submission, and obedience. There must be "obedience to the faith" (1:5; cf. 16:26), working through love (Gal. 5:6).

2:16 GOD SHALL JUDGE THE SECRETS. See article on THE JUDGMENT OF BELIEVERS, p. 1811.

2:24 THE NAME OF GOD IS BLASPHEMED. The sins of the Jews gave occasion for the Gentiles to blaspheme the name of God. Likewise today, the

phemed among the Gentiles through
you, as it is [r]written.
25 [s]For circumcision verily prof-
iteth, if thou keep the law: but if thou
be a breaker of the law, thy circumci-
sion is made uncircumcision.
26 Therefore [t]if the uncircumci-
sion keep the righteousness of the law,
shall not his uncircumcision be count-
ed for circumcision?
27 And shall not uncircumcision
which is by nature, if it fulfil the law,
[u]judge thee, who by the letter and cir-
cumcision dost transgress the law?
28 For [v]he is not a Jew, which is
one outwardly; neither *is that* circumci-
sion, which is outward in the flesh:
29 But he *is* a Jew, [w]which is one
inwardly; and [x]circumcision *is that* of
the heart, [y]in the spirit, *and* not in the
letter; [z]whose praise *is* not of men,
but of God.

Advantage of the Jews

3 WHAT ADVANTAGE then hath
the Jew? or what profit *is there* of
circumcision?
2 Much every way: chiefly, because
that [a]unto them were committed the
oracles of God.
3 For what if [b]some did not be-
lieve? [c]shall their unbelief make the
faith of God without effect?
4 [d]God forbid: yea, let [e]God be
true, but [f]every man a liar; as it is
written, [g]That thou mightest be justi-
fied in thy sayings, and mightest over-
come when thou art judged.
5 But if our unrighteousness com-
mend the righteousness of God, what
shall we say? *Is* God unrighteous who
taketh vengeance? ([h]I speak as a
man)
6 God forbid: for then [i]how shall
God judge the world?
7 For if the truth of God hath more
abounded through my lie unto his glo-
ry; why yet am I also judged as a sin-
ner?
8 And not *rather,* (as we be slander-
ously reported, and as some affirm that
we say,) [j]Let us do evil, that good
may come? whose damnation is just.

All are guilty before God

9 What then? are we better *than
they?* No, in no wise: for we have before
[p]proved both Jews and Gentiles, that
[k]they are all under sin;
10 As it is written, [l]There is none
righteous, no, not one:
11 There is none that under-
standeth, there is none that seeketh af-
ter God.
12 They are all gone out of the way,
they are together become unprofitable;
there is none that doeth good, no, not
one.
13 [m]Their throat *is* an open sepul-
chre; with their tongues they have
used deceit; [n]the poison of asps *is* un-
der their lips:
14 [o]Whose mouth *is* full of cursing
and bitterness:
15 [p]Their feet *are* swift to shed
blood:
16 Destruction and misery *are* in
their ways:
17 And the way of peace have they
not known:
18 [q]There is no fear of God before
their eyes.
19 Now we know that what things
soever [r]the law saith, it saith to them

2:24 [r]2 Sam. 12:14 Is. 52:5 Ezek. 36:20 **2:25** [s]Gal. 5:3 **2:26** [t]Acts 10:34 **2:27** [u]Mat. 12:41 **2:28** [v]Mat. 3:9 John 8:39 Gal. 6:15 **2:29** [w]1 Pet. 3:4 [x]Phil. 3:3 [y]ch. 7:6 [z]1 Cor. 4:5 2 Cor. 10:18 1 Thes. 2:4 **3:2** [a]Deut. 4:7 Ps. 147:19 **3:3** [b]Heb. 4:2 [c]Num. 23:19 2 Tim. 2:13 **3:4** [d]Job 40:8 [e]John 3:33 [f]Ps. 62:9 [g]Ps. 51:4 **3:5** [h]Gal. 3:15 **3:6** [i]Gen. 18:25 **3:8** [j]ch. 5:20 **3:9** [k]Gal. 3:22 **3:10** [l]Ps. 14:1-3 **3:13** [m]Ps. 5:9 Jer. 5:16 [n]Ps. 140:3 **3:14** [o]Ps. 10:7 **3:15** [p]Prov. 1:16 Is. 59:7,8 **3:18** [q]Ps. 36:1 **3:19** [r]John 10:34

[p] Gk. *charged*

sins of permissive churches or professed believers enable the ungodly to blaspheme the name of Christ.

2:29 CIRCUMCISION . . . OF THE HEART, IN THE SPIRIT. This refers to God's work of grace in the hearts of believers whereby they partake of the divine nature and become capable of living a pure life separated from sin for the glory of God (cf. Deut. 10:16; Jer. 4:4; 2 Pet. 1:4). Thus, holy living becomes the outward sign that we are under the new covenant.

3:9 THEY ARE ALL UNDER SIN. In chs. 1–2, Paul has shown that all people, both Gentiles and Jews, are under bondage to sin. In 3:9–18 he explains why and teaches that all people possess a sinful nature which draws them toward sin and evil (see next note). The result is that all are guilty and stand under the condemnation of God (v. 23). God's response to this tragic situation is to offer forgiveness, help, grace, righteousness, and salvation to all through the redemption which is in Christ Jesus (vv. 21–26).

3:10–18 NONE RIGHTEOUS. These verses portray a correct understanding of human nature. All people in their natural state are sinners. Their entire being is adversely affected by sin and inclines toward conformity to the world (see article on THE CHRISTIAN'S RELATIONSHIP TO THE WORLD, p. 2004), the devil (see Mat. 4:10, note), and the flesh (see article on THE WORKS OF THE FLESH AND THE FRUIT OF THE SPIRIT, p. 1840). All are guilty of turning aside from the way of godliness to the way of selfishness.

3:18 NO FEAR OF GOD. Why does the deplorable condition of mankind continue? Because "there is no fear of God before their eyes." If there

who are under the law: that [s]every
mouth may be stopped, and [t]all the
world may become [q]guilty before
God.
20 Therefore [u]by the deeds of the
law there shall no flesh be justified in
his sight: for [v]by the law *is* the knowl-
edge of sin.

Faith as the means of salvation

21 But now [w]the righteousness of
God without the law is manifested,
[x]being witnessed by the law [y]and the
prophets;
22 Even the righteousness of God
which is [z]by faith of Jesus Christ unto
all and upon all them that believe: for
[a]there is no difference:
23 For [b]all have sinned, and come
short of the glory of God;
24 Being justified freely [c]by his
grace [d]through the redemption that is
in Christ Jesus:
25 Whom God hath [r]set forth [e]*to
be* a propitiation through faith [f]in his
blood, to declare his righteousness for
the [s]remission of [g]sins that are past,
through the forbearance of God;
26 To declare, *I say,* at this time his
righteousness: that he might be just,
and the justifier of him which believeth Rom 10:4 13
in Jesus.
27 [h]Where *is* boasting then? It is
excluded. By what law? of works? Nay:
but by the law of faith.
28 Therefore we conclude [i]that a

3:19 [s]Job 5:16 Ps. 107:42 [t]ch. 2:2 **3:20** [u]Ps. 143:2 Acts 13:39 Gal. 2:16 [v]ch. 7:7 **3:21** [w]Acts 15:11 ch. 1:17 [x]John 5:46 [y]1 Pet. 1:10 **3:22** [z]ch. 4 [a]ch. 10:12 Gal. 3:28 Col. 3:11 **3:23** [b]ch. 11:32 Gal. 3:22 **3:24** [c]ch. 4:16 Eph. 2:8 Tit. 3:5,7 [d]Mat. 20:28 Eph. 1:7 Col. 1:14 1 Tim. 2:6 Heb. 9:12 1 Pet. 1:18 **3:25** [e]Lev. 16:15; 1 John 2:2 & 4:10 [f]Col. 1:20 [g]Acts 17:30; Heb. 9:15 **3:27** [h]ch. 2:17,23; 1 Cor. 1:29; Eph. 2:9 **3:28** [i]ver. 20-22; Gal. 2:16

[q] Or, *subject to the judgment of God* [r] Or, *foreordained* [s] Or, *passing over*

had been the "fear of God," they would have sought reconciliation and peace. "By the fear of the Lord men depart from evil" (Prov. 16:6; cf. Prov. 3:7; 8:13; 9:10; see Acts 5:11, note; see article on THE FEAR OF THE LORD, p. 282).

3:21 THE RIGHTEOUSNESS OF GOD. This phrase refers to God's redemptive activity in the sphere of human sin by which He, in a just way (v. 26), puts us in a right relationship with Himself and liberates us from the power of evil (vv. 21–22; note the O.T., where the working of salvation and the manifestation of righteousness are essentially the same thing—see Ps. 32:2, note; 98:1–2; Is. 46:13; 51:5–8; 56:1–2, note; 62:1). (1) This revelation of God's righteousness in the gospel is not something that occurred only in the past. As the power of God unto salvation that accompanies the believer, it is constantly fresh and relevant (see article on BIBLICAL WORDS FOR SALVATION, p. 1726). (2) This righteousness of God comes to us through faith in Jesus Christ (v. 22).

3:22 FAITH OF JESUS CHRIST. A better rendering of the phrase is "faith in Jesus Christ," for Jesus Christ is the object of our faith (cf. Mat. 1:21; John 3:16; 14:6; Acts 4:12). Faith in Jesus Christ is the only condition God requires for salvation. For a discussion of what saving faith is, see article on FAITH AND GRACE, p. 1738.

3:24 JUSTIFIED FREELY ... THROUGH THE REDEMPTION. This verse contains two of the most common words used by Paul to express salvation: "justified" and "redemption." For a discussion of these two concepts, see article on BIBLICAL WORDS FOR SALVATION, p. 1726.

3:25 HIS BLOOD. The N.T. emphasizes several truths concerning Christ's death for mankind. (1) It was a sacrifice, i.e., an offering of His blood, His life (1 Cor. 5:7; Eph. 5:2).

(2) It was vicarious, i.e., He died not for His own sake, but for the sake of others (5:8; 8:32; Mark 10:45; Eph. 5:2).

(3) It was substitutionary, i.e., Christ suffered death as the penalty for our sin, as our substitute (6:23; see article on THE DAY OF ATONEMENT, p. 188).

(4) It was propitiatory, i.e., Christ's death for sinners satisfied God's righteous nature and His moral order, thereby removing His wrath against the sinner. The integrity of God required that sin be punished and propitiation be made toward Him for our sake. Through propitiation in Christ's blood, God's holiness remained uncompromised and He was able to justly manifest His grace and love in salvation. It must be emphasized that God Himself set forth Christ as a propitiation. He did not need to be won over to show mercy and love, for "God was in Christ, reconciling the world unto himself" (2 Cor. 5:19; cf. John 3:16; Rom. 5:8; 8:3,32; 1 Cor. 8:6; Eph. 4:4–6).

(5) It was expiatory, i.e., a sacrifice to atone or make reparation for sin. As expiation, the sacrifice is directed towards annulling guilt. By Christ's death the guilt and power of sin that separate God and the believer were annulled.

(6) It was efficacious, i.e., His atoning death has within itself the power to produce the full desired effect of redemption when appropriated by faith.

(7) It was victorious, i.e., on the cross Christ fought against and was triumphant over the power of sin, of Satan, and of his demonic host that held people captive. His death was the initial victory over the spiritual enemies of both God and man (8:3; John 12:31–32; Col. 2:15). Hence, Christ's death is redemptive. By the ransom of His own life (1 Pet. 1:18–19), He liberated us from the enemies that hold the human race in bondage, i.e., sin (6:6), death (1 Cor. 15:54–57; 2 Tim. 1:10), and Satan (Acts 10:38), making us free to serve God (6:18; see article on BIBLICAL WORDS FOR SALVATION, p. 1726).

All the above results of Christ's sacrificial death occur potentially for all people but only actually for individuals who by faith accept Jesus Christ and His death for them.

man is justified by faith without the deeds of the law.

29 *Is he* the God of the Jews only? *is he* not also of the Gentiles? Yes, of the Gentiles also:

30 Seeing [j]*it is* one God, which shall justify the circumcision by faith, and uncircumcision through faith.

31 Do we then make void the law through faith? God forbid: yea, we establish the law.

Abraham's salvation apart from works

4 WHAT SHALL we say then that [k]Abraham our father, as pertaining to the flesh, hath found?

2 For if Abraham were [l]justified by works, he hath *whereof* to glory; but not before God.

3 For what saith the scripture? [m]Abraham believed God, and it was counted unto him for righteousness.

4 Now [n]to him that worketh is the reward not reckoned of grace, but of debt.

5 But to him that worketh not, but believeth on him that justifieth [o]the ungodly, his faith is counted for righteousness.

6 Even as David also describeth the blessedness of the man, unto whom God imputeth righteousness without works,

7 *Saying,* [p]Blessed *are* they whose iniquities are forgiven, and whose sins are covered.

8 Blessed *is* the man to whom the Lord will not impute sin.

Abraham's salvation apart from circumcision

9 *Cometh* this blessedness then upon the circumcision *only,* or upon the uncircumcision also? for we say that faith was reckoned to Abraham for righteousness.

10 How was it then reckoned? when he was in circumcision, or in uncircumcision? Not in circumcision, but in uncircumcision.

11 And [q]he received the sign of circumcision, a seal of the righteousness of the faith which *he had yet* being uncircumcised: that [r]he might be the father of all them that believe, though they be not circumcised; that righteousness might be imputed unto them also:

12 And the father of circumcision to them who are not of the circumcision only, but who also walk in the steps of

3:30
[j]ch. 10:12
Gal. 3:8,20
4:1
[k]Is. 51:2
Mat. 3:9
John 8:33
2 Cor. 11:22
4:2
[l]ch. 3:20,27
4:3
[m]Gen. 15:6
Gal. 3:6
Jas. 2:23
4:4
[n]ch. 11:6
4:5
[o]Josh. 24:2
4:7
[p]Ps. 32:1,2
4:11
[q]Gen. 17:10
[r]ver. 12,16
Luke 19:9
Gal. 3:7

3:31 WE ESTABLISH THE LAW. Salvation in Christ does not mean that the law has no value. In fact justification by faith establishes the law according to its right purpose and function. Through his reconciliation with God and through the regenerating work of the Holy Spirit, the believer becomes capable of honoring and obeying God's moral law (see 8:2–4).

4:3 ABRAHAM BELIEVED GOD. Salvation by faith, not by works (i.e., keeping the law), is not an exclusively N.T. doctrine; it is also characteristic of the O.T. Paul bypasses Moses and turns to Abraham as the example of faith. Abraham had faith in God, i.e., he maintained a loyal and devoted attachment to his God, believed in His promises (vv. 20–21; Gen. 12:1–3; 15:5–6), and responded in obedience (Gen. 12:1–4; 22:1–19; Heb. 11:8–19; Jas. 2:21–22; see article on THE CALL OF ABRAHAM, p. 25).

4:5 FAITH IS COUNTED FOR RIGHTEOUSNESS. Abraham's *faith* was "counted" for righteousness (vv. 3,5–12,22; see Gen. 15:6, note). "Count" means to put or credit to one's account, or to "impute" (v. 8). This means that the saving faith of the Christian is treated as equivalent to righteousness in regard to its effect.

(1) Paul speaks of "counting," "imputing," or "reckoning" something as "righteousness" to the believer six times in ch. 4, and in every instance Paul declares clearly that it is the believer's "faith" that is reckoned or counted as "righteousness" (vv. 3,5–6,9,11,22).

(2) The reckoning of the believer's faith as righteousness, however, is not solely the result of faith or commitment to Christ; it is above all an act of divine grace and mercy (v. 16).

(3) When God sees the believer's heart turned toward Christ in faith, He freely forgives his sins, counts his faith as righteousness, and accepts him as His child (vv. 5–8; see article on BIBLICAL WORDS FOR SALVATION, p. 1726). Along with this counting of faith as righteousness, God also bestows grace for sanctification (see v. 16; 5:2; Phil. 3:9; Tit. 3:5–7).

(4) The faith that is counted for righteousness and brings forgiveness is faith in Christ and His atoning death (3:24–26). Absolutely nothing else but Christ's sacrificial death on the cross is the ground for reconciliation to God (see 5:10, note).

4:7 THEY WHOSE INIQUITIES ARE FORGIVEN. This quotation from Ps. 32:1–2 shows that both David (see Ps. 32:2, note) and Paul understood that one's faith reckoned as righteousness includes pardon or forgiveness of sin and reconciliation to God. It is a gift based on God's mercy, made possible through the death of Christ on the cross (see v. 5, note; cf. 2 Cor. 5:19,21).

4:12 FAITH OF OUR FATHER ABRAHAM. The faith of Abraham was a true faith that endured, believed, trusted, obeyed, grew strong, and gave glory to God (vv. 16–21). This is the type of faith that makes us children of God.

that faith of our father Abraham, which
he had being *yet* uncircumcised.

Abraham's salvation apart from the law

13 For the promise, that he should
be the [s]heir of the world, *was* not to
Abraham, or to his seed, through the
law, but through the righteousness of
faith.
14 For [t]if they which are of the law
be heirs, faith is made void, and the
promise made of none effect:
15 Because [u]the law worketh
wrath: for where no law is, *there is* no
transgression.

Abraham's salvation was by faith

16 Therefore *it is* of faith, that *it*
might be [v]by grace; [w]to the end the
promise might be sure to all the seed;
not to that only which is of the law, but
to that also which is of the faith of
Abraham; [x]who is the father of us all,
17 (As it is written, [y]I have made
thee a father of many nations,) [†]be-
fore him whom he believed, *even* God,
[z]who quickeneth the dead, and
calleth those [a]things which be not as
though they were.
18 Who against hope believed in
hope, that he might become the father
of many nations, according to that
which was spoken, [b]So shall thy
seed be.
19 And being not weak in faith, [c]he
considered not his own body now dead,
when he was about an hundred years
old, neither yet the deadness of Sar-
ah's womb:
20 He staggered not at the promise
of God through unbelief; but was
strong in faith, giving glory to God;
21 And being fully persuaded that,
what he had promised, [d]he was able
also to perform. 1 Cor 13:2
22 And therefore it was imputed to
him for righteousness.
23 Now [e]it was not written for his
sake alone, that it was imputed to him;
24 But for us also, to whom it shall
be imputed, if we believe [f]on him that
raised up Jesus our Lord from the dead;
25 [g]Who was delivered for our of-
fences, and [h]was raised again for our
justification.

Results of salvation by faith

5 THEREFORE [i]BEING justified
by faith, we have [j]peace with God
through our Lord Jesus Christ:
2 [k]By whom also we have access

4:13 [s]Gen. 17:4 Gal. 3:29 **4:14** [t]Gal. 3:18 **4:15** [u]ch. 3:20 & 7:8,10,11 1 Cor. 15:56 2 Cor. 3:7,9 Gal. 3:10 1 John 3:4 **4:16** [v]ch. 3:24 [w]Gal. 3:22 [x]Is. 51:2 ch. 9:8 **4:17** [y]Gen. 17:5 [z]ch. 8:11 Eph. 2:1,5 [a]ch. 9:26 1 Cor. 1:28 1 Pet. 2:10 **4:18** [b]Gen. 15:5 **4:19** [c]Gen. 17:17 & 18:11 Heb. 11:11 **4:21** [d]Ps. 115:3 Luke 1:37 Heb. 11:19 **4:23** [e]ch. 15:4 1 Cor. 10:6 **4:24** [f]Acts 2:24 **4:25** [g]Is. 53:5,6 ch. 3:25 Gal. 1:4 Heb. 9:28 [h]1 Cor. 15:17 1 Pet. 1:21 **5:1** [i]Is. 32:17 John 16:33 [j]Eph. 2:14 **5:2** [k]John 10:9; Eph. 2:18

† Or, *like unto him*

4:16 ***IT IS* OF FAITH.** Believers are saved by faith alone through grace. But two Biblical truths about the nature of saving faith should be noted. (1) While one is saved by faith alone, the faith that saves is not alone. James states "faith without works is dead" (Jas. 2:14–26); Paul says it is "a faith which worketh by love" (Gal. 5:6). Saving faith is a faith so vital that it cannot avoid the expressions of love and obedience toward the Savior and of service toward others. Faith that merely trusts God to forgive our sins but does not include sincere repentance from sin and an active commitment to Christ as Lord falls short of N.T. saving faith (see article on FAITH AND GRACE, p. 1738).

(2) It is unbiblical to emphasize "faith" and ignore the broader picture of salvation and what it means. Salvation by faith includes not only being saved from condemnation but also being saved for fellowship with God, for holiness, and for good works (Eph. 2:10).

4:16 THAT *IT MIGHT BE* BY GRACE. If the salvation, justification, and righteousness that God provides came by perfect obedience to the law, no one would be saved because no one has obeyed it perfectly. But since it comes through faith by grace, then *all* may be saved who turn to God. God mercifully forgives our sins and imparts divine grace (i.e., His Spirit and power) to regenerate our lives and make us children of God (see article on FAITH AND GRACE, p. 1738).

4:22 IT WAS IMPUTED TO HIM FOR RIGHTEOUSNESS. In Paul's illustration of justification in ch. 4, nowhere does he state that the righteousness of God or of Christ is actually reckoned or transferred to the believer. We must be careful not to describe justification by stating that it comes by Christ's O.T. law-keeping transferred to the believer. If it did come by a transferred keeping of the law, then it is not the same kind of faith as Abraham had (v. 12), and that in turn nullifies the promise (v. 14) and makes salvation a result of merit rather than of grace (v. 16). Paul emphatically declares that justification and righteousness come "not . . . through the law" (v. 13), but by God's mercy, grace, love, and forgiveness (vv. 6–9), and that Abraham's *faith* (i.e., his believing, his attachment to God, his strong confidence and unwavering assurance in God and His promises) is counted as righteousness, by the mercy and grace of God (vv. 16–22).

4:25 RAISED AGAIN FOR OUR JUSTIFICATION. Justification does not exist without the life, presence, and grace of Jesus Christ operating in our lives. Justification is not a single judicial act in the past, but a "justification of life" (5:18) in fellowship with Jesus Christ our Lord.

5:1 THEREFORE BEING JUSTIFIED. Justification through faith brings the believer various re-

by faith into this grace [l]wherein we
stand, and [m]rejoice in hope of the glo-
ry of God.
3 And not only *so,* but [n]we glory in
tribulations also: [o]knowing that tribu-
lation worketh patience;
4 [p]And patience, experience; and
experience, hope:
5 [q]And hope maketh not ashamed;
[r]because the love of God is shed
abroad in our hearts by the Holy Ghost
which is given unto us.
6 For when we were yet without
strength, [u]in due time [s]Christ died
for the ungodly.
7 For scarcely for a righteous man
will one die: yet peradventure for a
good man some would even dare to die.
8 But [t]God commendeth his love
toward us, in that, while we were yet
sinners, Christ died for us.

5:2 [l]1 Cor. 15:1 [m]Heb. 3:6 **5:3** [n]Mat. 5:11 Acts 5:41 2 Cor. 12:10 Phil. 2:17 Jas. 1:2 [o]Jas. 1:3 **5:4** [p]Jas. 1:12 **5:5** [q]Phil. 1:20 [r]2 Cor. 1:22 Eph. 1:13 **5:6** [s]ch. 4:25 **5:8** [t]John 15:13 **5:9** [u]Eph. 2:13 1 John 1:7 [v]1 Thes. 1:10 **5:10** [w]ch. 8:32 [x]2 Cor. 5:18 Eph. 2:16 [y]John 14:19 **5:11** [z]Gal. 4:9

9 Much more then, being now justi-
fied [u]by his blood, we shall be saved
[v]from wrath through him.
10 For [w]if, when we were enemies,
[x]we were reconciled to God by the
death of his Son, much more, being rec-
onciled, we shall be saved [y]by his life.
11 And not only *so,* but we also
[z]joy in God through our Lord Jesus
Christ, by whom we have now received
the [v]atonement.

Death through Adam, life through Christ

12 Wherefore, as [a]by one man sin
entered into the world, and [b]death by

5:12 [a]Gen. 3:6; 1 Cor. 15:21 [b]Gen. 2:17

[u] Or, *according to the time* [v] Or, *reconciliation*

sults: peace with God (see article on THE PEACE OF GOD, p. 1122), grace, hope, assurance, tribulations, the love of God, the Holy Spirit, salvation from wrath, reconciliation to God, salvation by the life and presence of Jesus, and joy in God (vv. 1–11).

5:3 WE GLORY IN TRIBULATIONS. Paul lists "tribulations" as one of the blessings of our salvation in Christ. (1) The word "tribulation" refers to all kinds of trials which may press in upon us. This includes such things as financial or physical need, trying circumstances, the pressure of sorrow, sickness, persecution, mistreatment, or loneliness (see article on THE SUFFERING OF THE RIGHTEOUS, p. 764).

(2) In the midst of these afflictions God's grace enables us to seek His face more diligently and produces in us a persevering spirit and character that overcome the trials and troubles of life. Instead of driving us to despair and hopelessness, tribulation brings forth perseverance, perseverance brings forth proven character (v. 4), and proven character results in a mature hope that will not be disappointed (v. 5).

(3) God's grace enables us to look beyond our present problems to a fervent hope in God and a certain hope for the return of our Lord to establish righteousness and godliness in the new heaven and earth (1 Thes. 4:13; Rev. 19–22). In the meantime, while on this earth, we have the love of God shed abroad in our hearts by the Holy Spirit in order to comfort us in our trials and bring Christ's presence near (John 14:16–23).

5:5 THE LOVE OF GOD . . . IN OUR HEARTS. Christians experience the love of God (i.e., God's love for believers) in their hearts through the Holy Spirit, especially in times of affliction. The verb "shed abroad" is a present perfect tense, signifying that the Spirit continues to flood our hearts with love. It is this ever-present experience of God's love that sustains us in tribulation (v. 3) and assures us that our hope for future glory is not illusory (vv. 4–5). Christ's return for us is sure (cf. 8:17; John 14:3; see article on THE RAPTURE, p. 1889).

5:10 SAVED BY HIS LIFE. The believer's salvation lies in the blood of Christ and His resurrection life, whereby the believer is forgiven and reconciled to God. This experience is initial salvation (3:21–26; 4:5–9). The believer continues to be saved by a living faith and union with the living Christ (see article on BIBLICAL WORDS FOR SALVATION, p. 1726). If God loved us enough to send His Son to die for us while we were enemies, how much more, now that we are His children, will He make every provision to save us from the wrath to come through our present faith in His Son (4:22–5:2; 5:9–10; 1 Cor. 1:30; Phil. 2:12–16; Col. 3:3–4; 1 Thes. 1:10; 2 Tim. 2:12; Jas. 1:12; see Rev. 2:7, note).

5:12 BY ONE MAN SIN ENTERED. By the transgression and fall of Adam, sin as an active principle or power gained entrance into the human race (vv. 17,19; Gen. 3; 1 Cor. 15:21–22). (1) Two results followed: (a) Sin and corruption entered into Adam's heart and life. (b) Adam transmitted sin into the life-stream of the human race, corrupting all people thereafter. All humans are now born into the world with an impulse towards sin and evil (v. 19; 1:21; 7:24; Gen. 6:5,12; 8:21; Ps. 14:1–3; Jer. 17:9; Mark 7:21–22; 1 Cor. 2:14; Gal. 5:19–21; Eph. 2:1–3; Col. 1:21; 1 John 5:19).

(2) Paul does not explain how Adam's sin is transmitted to his descendants. Nor does he say that all people were present in Adam and participated in his sin, and therefore inherit the guilt of Adam. Nowhere does Paul say that Adam was the federal head of his descendants and that his sin was imputed to them. All are guilty before God because of their own personal sin, because "all have sinned." The only doctrine that finds Biblical support is that men and women inherit a moral corruption and an impulse toward sin and evil (see 6:1, note).

(3) Death entered the world through sin, and

sin; and so death passed upon all men,
[w]for that all have sinned:

13 (For until the law sin was in the
world: but [c]sin is not imputed when
there is no law.

14 Nevertheless death reigned from
Adam to Moses, even over them that
had not sinned after the similitude of
Adam's transgression, [d]who is the fig-
ure of him that was to come.

15 But not as the offence, so also *is*
the free gift. For if through the offence
of one many be dead, much more the
grace of God, and the gift by grace,
which is by one man, Jesus Christ, hath
abounded [e]unto many.

16 And not as *it was* by one that
sinned, *so is* the gift: for the judgment
was by one to condemnation, but the
free gift *is* of many offences unto justi-
fication.

17 For if [x]by one man's offence
death reigned by one; much more they
which receive abundance of grace and
of the gift of righteousness shall reign
in life by one, Jesus Christ.)

18 Therefore as [x]by the offence of
one *judgment came* upon all men to con-
demnation; even so [y]by the righteous-
ness of one *the free gift came* [f]upon all
men unto justification of life.

19 For as by one man's disobedi-
ence many were made sinners, so by
the obedience of one shall many be
made righteous.

20 Moreover [g]the law entered,
that the offence might abound. But
where sin abounded, grace did much
[h]more abound:

21 That as sin hath reigned unto
death, even so might grace reign
through righteousness unto eternal
life by Jesus Christ our Lord.

Believers dead to sin

6 WHAT SHALL we say then?
[i]Shall we continue in sin, that
grace may abound?

2 God forbid. How shall we, that are
[j]dead to sin, live any longer therein?

5:13 [c]1 John 3:4 **5:14** [d]1 Cor. 15:21 **5:15** [e]Is. 53:11 **5:18** [f]John 12:32 Heb. 2:9 **5:20** [g]John 15:22 Gal. 3:19 [h]Luke 7:47 **6:1** [i]ch. 3:8 **6:2** [j]Gal. 2:19 Col. 3:3

[w]Or, *in whom* [x]Or, *by one offence* [y]Or, *by one righteousness*

now all people are subject to death, "for that all have sinned" (vv. 12,14; cf. 3:23; Gen. 2:17; 3:19; see article on DEATH, p. 782).

5:14 DEATH REIGNED FROM ADAM TO MOSES. The human race experienced death, not because they transgressed the spoken law of God with its death penalty as did Adam (vv. 13–14), but because they were in fact sinners by action as well as by nature and transgressors of the law of conscience written in their hearts (2:14–15).

5:15 MUCH MORE THE GRACE OF GOD. In vv. 12–21 Paul stresses the supreme adequacy of the redemption provided by Jesus Christ to undo the effects of the fall. This is the real point of the passage: Adam brought sin and death; Christ brought grace and life (v. 17).

5:18 UPON ALL MEN . . . JUSTIFICATION OF LIFE. The condemnation on all people becomes actual for each person as he or she rejects God and His revelation written in the heart or revealed in His written Word (cf. 2:12–16). The "justification of life" for all people is potential; it becomes actualized in individuals as they believe in Christ and receive grace, life, and the gift of righteousness through Jesus Christ (v. 17).

5:21 GRACE. For a discussion of the meaning of the word "grace" in the Bible, see article on FAITH AND GRACE, p. 1738.

6:1 SHALL WE CONTINUE IN SIN? In ch. 6 Paul challenges the erroneous idea that believers may continue in sin, and yet remain secure from eternal condemnation because of the grace and mercy of God through Christ. Paul answers this antinomian distortion of the doctrine of grace by emphasizing one fundamental truth: a true believer is one who is identified by his death to sin. He has been translated from the realm of sin into another realm of life—with Christ (vv. 2–12). Since the true believer has made a definitive separation from sin, he or she will not continue to live in sin. Conversely, if one lives in sin, he or she is not a believer (cf. 1 John 3:4–10). Throughout this chapter Paul emphasizes that one cannot be a servant of sin and a servant of Christ at the same time (vv. 11–13,16–18). If one practices sin, the result will be condemnation and eternal death (vv. 16,23).

6:1 SIN. (1) The N.T. uses several Greek words to describe sin in its various aspects. The most important are: (a) *Hamartia*, which means "transgression," "wrongdoing," "sin against God" (John 9:41). (b) *Adikia*, which stands for "wrongdoing," "wickedness," or "injustice" (1:18; 1 John 5:17). It can be described as a lack of love, since all wrongdoing stems from a failure to love (Mat. 22:37–40; Luke 10:27–37). *Adikia* is also a personal power that can enslave and deceive (5:12; Heb. 3:13). (c) *Anomia*, which denotes "lawlessness," "iniquity," and "defiance of the law of God" (v. 19; 1 John 3:4). (d) *Apistia*, which indicates "disbelief" or "unfaithfulness" (3:3; Heb. 3:12).

(2) From these definitions we can conclude that the essence of sin is selfishness, i.e., a grasping of things or pleasures for ourselves, regardless of the welfare of others and the commandments of God. This leads to cruelty to others and to rebellion against God and His law. Ultimately sin becomes the refusal to be subject to God and His Word (1:18–25; 8:7). It is enmity against God (5:10; 8:7; Col. 1:21), disobedience, and unbelief (11:32; Gal. 3:22; Eph. 2:2; 5:6).

(3) Sin is also a moral corruption in humans that

3 Know ye not, that [k]so many of us
as [z]were baptized into Jesus Christ
[l]were baptized into his death?
4 Therefore we are [m]buried with
him by baptism into death: that [n]like
as Christ was raised up from the dead
by [o]the glory of the Father, [p]even so
we also should walk in newness of life.
5 [q]For if we have been planted to-
gether in the likeness of his death, we
shall be also *in the likeness* of *his* resur-
rection:
6 Knowing this, that [r]our old man
is crucified with *him,* that [s]the body of
sin might be destroyed, that hence-
forth we should not serve sin.
7 For [t]he that is dead is [a]freed
from sin.
8 Now [u]if we be dead with Christ,
we believe that we shall also live with
him:
9 Knowing that [v]Christ being
raised from the dead dieth no more;
death hath no more dominion over him.
10 For in that he died, [w]he died
unto sin once: but in that he liveth,
[x]he liveth unto God.

Alive in Christ

11 Likewise reckon ye also your-
selves to be [y]dead indeed unto sin, but
[z]alive unto God through Jesus Christ
our Lord.
12 [a]Let not sin therefore reign in
your mortal body, that ye should obey
it in the lusts thereof.
13 Neither yield ye your [b]members
as [b]instruments of unrighteousness
unto sin: but [c]yield yourselves unto
God, as those that are alive from the

6:3 [k]Gal. 3:27 [l]1 Cor. 15:29 **6:4** [m]Col. 2:12 [n]ch. 8:11 1 Cor. 6:14 [o]John 2:11 [p]Gal. 6:15 **6:5** [q]Phil. 3:10 **6:6** [r]Gal. 2:20 [s]Col. 2:11 **6:7** [t]1 Pet. 4:1 **6:8** [u]2 Tim. 2:11 **6:9** [v]Rev. 1:18 **6:10** [w]Heb. 9:27 [x]Luke 20:38 **6:11** [y]ver. 2 [z]Gal. 2:19 **6:12** [a]Ps. 19:13 **6:13** [b]ch. 7:5 Col. 3:5 Jas. 4:1 [c]ch. 12:1; 1 Pet. 2:24 & 4:2

[z] Or, *are* [a] Gk. *justified* [b] Gk. *arms,* or, *weapons*

opposes all better human intentions. It causes us both to commit unrighteousness with delight and to take pleasure in the evil actions of others (1:21–32; cf. Gen. 6:5). It is likewise a power that enslaves and corrupts as we give ourselves over to it (3:9; 6:12ff; 7:14; Gal. 3:22). Sin is rooted in human desire (Jas. 1:14; 4:1–2; see 1 Pet. 2:11, note).

(4) Sin was brought into the human race through Adam (5:12), affects everyone (5:12), results in divine judgment (1:18), brings physical and spiritual death (6:23; Gen. 2:17), and can be eliminated as a power only by faith in Christ and His redemptive work for mankind (5:8–11; Gal. 3:13; Eph. 4:20–24; 1 John 1:9; Rev. 1:5).

6:2 DEAD TO SIN. See v. 11, note.

6:4 BURIED WITH HIM BY BAPTISM. Baptism for the Christian is a symbol of the believer's burial and resurrection with Christ, but it is more. When accompanied by true faith, baptism is part of our rejection of sin and commitment to Christ, resulting in a continual flow of grace and divine life to us (see Acts 22:16, note on baptism). Baptism means identifying with Christ in His death and burial in order that we may live in union with his resurrected life (vv. 4–5). As surely as Christ rose from the dead, so surely we who exercise true saving faith in Him will walk in newness of life (v. 5).

6:6 OLD MAN ... BODY OF SIN. Paul uses two terms here: (1) The "old man": this refers to the believer's unregenerate self, the person he once was, the life he once lived in sin. This old self has been crucified (i.e., made powerless) with Christ on the cross in order that the believer might receive a new life in Christ and become a "new man" (cf. Gal. 2:20). (2) "Body of sin": this refers to the human body as controlled by sinful desires. Its slavery to sin has now been broken (cf. 2 Cor. 5:17; Eph. 4:22; Col. 3:9–10). Henceforth, the believer must not allow his old mode of existence again to dominate his life and body (2 Cor. 5:17; Eph. 4:22; Col. 3:9–10).

6:7 FREED FROM SIN. See John 8:36, note.

6:10 HE DIED UNTO SIN. Although Christ was sinless, He suffered from and was humiliated by the power of sin for our sake (5:21; cf. 2 Cor. 5:21). In His death, He died to the influence of sin; in His resurrection, He triumphed over its power. Likewise, those who are united with Him in His death are freed from the power of sin (vv. 2,11) to walk in newness of life (vv. 4–5,10).

6:11 RECKON ... YOURSELVES TO BE DEAD INDEED UNTO SIN. The fundamental premise in ch. 6 is the believer's union with Christ in both His death and life. Therefore, if you are a true believer, you have died to sin, and you need to reckon with this fact. You have died to sin in three different ways. (1) You died to sin in God's sight. You are considered by God to have died with Christ on the cross and to have been raised up in His resurrection (vv. 5–10). (2) You died to sin when you were born again by the Spirit (see article on REGENERATION, p. 1597). You have been given Christ's power to resist sin (vv. 14–18), to die to it daily by putting to death its evil desires (8:13), and to live a new life in obedience to God (vv. 5–14, 18, 22). (3) You died to sin in water baptism as you proclaimed your death to sin and committed yourself to reject it and to live unto Christ (vv. 3–5; see v. 4, note).

6:12 LET NOT SIN THEREFORE REIGN. Because sin has been dethroned, you must continually resist its effort to regain control. Since sin attempts to reign primarily through the desires of the body, these desires must be resisted by those with faith toward Christ (see next note). We can do so by denying the lusts of the body (v. 12), refusing to place our physical members at the disposal of sin (v. 13), and presenting our bodies and our whole personalities as slaves to God and righteousness (vv. 13–19).

FAITH AND GRACE

Rom. 5:21 "That as sin hath reigned unto death, even so might grace reign through righteousness unto eternal life by Jesus Christ our Lord."

Our salvation comes as a gift of God's *grace*, but it can only be appropriated by the human response of *faith*. To understand the process of salvation properly, we must understand these two words.

SAVING FAITH. Faith in Jesus Christ is the only condition God requires for salvation. Faith is not only a profession about Christ, but also an activity coming from the heart of the believer who seeks to follow Christ as Lord and Savior (cf. Mat. 4:19; 16:24; Luke 9:23–25; John 10:4,27; 12:26; Rev. 14:4).

(1) The N.T. conception of faith includes four main elements: (a) Faith means firmly believing and trusting in the crucified and risen Christ as our personal Lord and Savior (see Rom. 1:17, note). It involves believing from our hearts (Acts 8:37; Rom. 6:17; Eph. 6:6; Heb. 10:22), that is, yielding up our wills and committing our total selves to Jesus Christ as He is revealed in the N.T.

(b) Faith involves repentance, i.e., turning from sin with true sorrow (Acts 17:30; 2 Cor. 7:10) and turning to God through Christ. Saving faith is always a repentant faith (Acts 2:37–38; see Mat. 3:2, note on repentance).

(c) Faith includes obedience to Jesus Christ and His Word as a way of life inspired by our faith, by our gratitude to God, and by the regenerating work of the Holy Spirit (John 3:3–6; 14:15,21–24; Heb. 5:8–9). It is an "obedience of faith" (Rom. 16:26). Hence, faith and obedience belong inseparably together (cf. Rom. 1:5; 16:26). Saving faith without the commitment to sanctification is illegitimate and impossible.

(d) Faith includes a heartfelt personal devotion and attachment to Jesus Christ that expresses itself in trust, love, gratitude, and loyalty toward Him. Faith in an ultimate sense cannot properly be distinguished from love. It is a personal activity of sacrifice and self-giving directed toward Christ (cf. Mat. 22:37; John 21:15–17; Gal. 2:20; Eph. 6:6; 1 Pet. 1:8).

(2) Faith in Jesus as Lord and Savior is both the act of a single moment and a continuing attitude for life that must grow and be strengthened (see John 1:12, note). Because we have faith in a definite person who died for us (Rom. 4:25; 8:32; 1 Thes. 5:9–10), our faith should become greater (Rom. 4:20; 2 Thes. 1:3; 1 Pet. 1:3–9). Trust and obedience develop into loyalty and devotion (Rom. 14:8; 2 Cor. 5:15); loyalty and devotion develop into an intense feeling of personal attachment to and love for the Lord Jesus Christ (Phil. 1:21; 3:8–10; see John 15:4, note; 17:21; Gal. 2:20, note). This faith in Christ brings us into a new relationship with God and exempts us from His wrath (Rom. 1:18; 8:1); by it we become dead to sin (Rom. 6:1–12) and indwelt by the Holy Spirit (Gal. 3:5; 4:6).

GRACE. In the O.T., God revealed Himself as a God of grace and mercy, who manifested love to His people not because they deserved it but because of His own desire to be faithful to the promises made to Abraham, Isaac, and Jacob (see Ex. 6:9, note; see articles on THE PASSOVER, p. 110, and THE DAY OF ATONEMENT, p. 188). Grace in the N.T. continues this theme; it is God's presence and love through Christ Jesus, given to believers by the Holy Spirit and imparting to them mercy, forgiveness, and the desire and power to do God's will (John 3:16; 1 Cor. 15:10; Phil. 2:13; 1 Tim. 1:15–16). The whole movement of the Christian life from beginning to end is dependent on this grace.

(1) God gives a measure of grace as a gift (1 Cor. 1:4) to unbelievers in order that they may be able to believe on the Lord Jesus Christ (Eph. 2:8–9; Tit. 2:11; 3:4).

(2) God gives grace to believers to be "made free from sin" (Rom. 6:20,22), "to will and to do of his good pleasure" (Phil. 2:13; cf. Tit. 2:11–12; see Mat. 7:21, note on obedience as a gift of God's grace), to pray (Zech. 12:10), to grow in Christ (2 Pet. 3:18), and to witness for Christ (Acts 4:33; 11:23).

(3) God's grace must be diligently desired and sought after (Heb. 4:16). Some of the ways (i.e., means of grace) by which God's grace is received are: studying and obeying the Holy Scriptures (John 15:1–11; 20:31; 2 Tim. 3:15); hearing the proclamation of the gospel (Luke 24:47; Acts 1:8; Rom. 1:16; 1 Cor. 1:17–18); praying (Heb. 4:16; Jude 20); fasting (cf. Mat. 4:2; 6:16); worshiping Christ (Col. 3:16); being continually filled with the Holy Spirit (cf. Eph. 5:18); and participating in the Lord's Supper (cf. Acts 2:42; see Eph. 2:9, note on how grace works).

(4) God's grace can be resisted (Heb. 12:15), received in vain (2 Cor. 6:1), quenched (1 Thes. 5:19), nullified (Gal. 2:21), and abandoned by the believer (Gal. 5:4).

dead, and your members *as* instruments of righteousness unto God.

14 For [d]sin shall not have dominion over you: for ye are not under the law, but under grace.

Rom. 8:1-5

Slaves to righteousness

15 What then? shall we sin, [e]because we are not under the law, but under grace? God forbid.

16 Know ye not, that [f]to whom ye yield yourselves servants to obey, his servants ye are to whom ye obey; whether of sin unto death, or of obedience unto righteousness?

17 But God be thanked, that ye were the servants of sin, but ye have obeyed from the heart [g]that form of doctrine [c]which was delivered you.

18 Being then [h]made free from sin, ye became the servants of righteousness.

19 I speak after the manner of men because of the infirmity of your flesh: for as ye have yielded your members servants to uncleanness and to iniquity unto iniquity; even so now yield your members servants to righteousness unto holiness.

20 For when ye were [i]the servants of sin, ye were free [d]from righteousness.

21 [j]What fruit had ye then in those things whereof ye are now ashamed? for [k]the end of those things *is* death.

22 But now [l]being made free from sin, and become servants to God, ye have your fruit unto holiness, and the end everlasting life.

23 For [m]the wages of sin *is* death; but [n]the gift of God *is* eternal life through Jesus Christ our Lord.

Believers dead to the law

7 KNOW YE not, brethren, (for I speak to them that know the law,) how that the law hath dominion over a man as long as he liveth?

2 For [o]the woman which hath an husband is bound by the law to *her* husband so long as he liveth; but if the husband be dead, she is loosed from the law of *her* husband.

3 So then [p]if, while *her* husband liveth, she be married to another man, she shall be called an adulteress: but if her husband be dead, she is free from that law; so that she is no adulteress, though she be married to another man.

4 Wherefore, my brethren, ye also are become [q]dead to the law by the

6:14 [d]ch. 7:4,6 & 8:2 Gal. 5:18
6:15 [e]1 Cor. 9:21
6:16 [f]Mat. 6:24 John 8:34 2 Pet. 2:19
6:17 [g]2 Tim. 1:13
6:18 [h]John 8:32 1 Cor. 7:22 Gal. 5:1 1 Pet. 2:16
6:20 [i]John 8:34
6:21 [j]ch. 7:5 [k]ch. 1:32
6:22 [l]John 8:32
6:23 [m]Gen. 2:17 ch. 5:12 Jas. 1:15 [n]ch. 2:7 1 Pet. 1:4
7:2 [o]1 Cor. 7:39
7:3 [p]Mat. 5:32
7:4 [q]Gal. 2:19 & 5:18 Col. 2:14

[c] Gk. *whereto ye were delivered* [d] Gk. *to righteousness*

6:15 SHALL WE SIN? Some within the church in Paul's day thought that since grace pardons sin, the Christian does not need to be careful to resist sin. In answer to this, the apostle explains that every believer must continually reaffirm and implement his or her decision to resist sin and follow Christ (v. 19).

(1) After accepting Christ, believers must continue to choose whom they will serve (v. 16). (a) They may return to sin, cease to oppose its dominion in their personal lives, and become its slave once more, with death (spiritual and eternal) as the result (vv. 16,21,23); or (b) they may be freed from sin (v. 17) and may continue to present themselves as slaves of God and righteousness, with sanctification and eternal life as the result (vv. 19, 22).

(2) In the light of vv. 15–23, those not committed to the Lordship of Christ and not opposed to the dominion of sin in their personal lives have no right to speak of Christ as their Savior: "No man can serve two masters" (Mat. 6:24; see also Luke 6:46; 2 Cor. 6:14—7:1; Jas. 4:4; 1 John 2:15–17).

6:16 OBEY . . . SIN UNTO DEATH. Paul solemnly warns believers who think they may securely sin because they are under grace. If a believer gives himself to sin, he will in fact become a slave to sin (cf. Luke 16:13; John 8:34), resulting in "death" (cf. v. 23). "Death" here means "everlasting destruction from the presence of the Lord" (2 Thes. 1:9), the opposite of "eternal life" (cf. v. 23).

6:17 OBEYED . . . THAT FORM OF DOCTRINE. In the early church new believers were committed to certain defined standards of teaching and conduct, based on apostolic principles and the believer's relationship to Christ (cf. Mat. 5—7; Acts 2:42). (1) These standards were most likely a summary of Christian doctrine and ethics to which the convert subscribed when he accepted Christ as his new Master. It is the "sound doctrine" or "sound words" referred to in the Pastoral Epistles (see 1 Tim. 1:10; 2 Tim. 1:13; 4:3; Tit. 1:9; 2:1).

(2) The supposition that Christianity has no pattern of teaching that regulates thought and practice, or that it is legalism to have rules of conduct, is alien to Paul's concept of the Christian faith. Christianity demands obedience from the heart to godly standards (see Mark 7:6; note on legalism),

7:4 DEAD TO THE LAW. We no longer look to the O.,T. law and sacrifices for salvation and acceptance before God (see Gal. 3:23–25; 4:4–5; see article on THE OLD TESTAMENT LAW, p. 124). We have been separated from the old covenant of the law and united with Christ, and we now look to Christ for salvation. We must believe in Jesus (1 John 5:13), receive His Spirit and grace (see article on FAITH AND GRACE, p. 1738), and thereby receive forgiveness, be regenerated, and become

body of Christ; that ye should be married to another, *even* to him who is raised from the dead, that we should [r]bring forth fruit unto God.

5 For when we were in the flesh, the [e]motions of sins, which were by the law, [s]did work in our members [t]to bring forth fruit unto death.

6 But now we are delivered from the law, [f]that being dead wherein we were held; that we should serve [u]in newness of spirit, and not *in* the oldness of the letter.

Law cannot deliver from sin

7 What shall we say then? *Is* the law sin? God forbid. Nay, [v]I had not known sin, but by the law: for I had not known [g]lust, except the law had said, [w]Thou shalt not covet.

8 But [x]sin, taking occasion by the commandment, wrought in me all manner of concupiscence. For [y]without the law sin *was* dead.

9 For I was alive without the law once: but when the commandment came, sin revived, and I died.

10 And the commandment, [z]which *was ordained* to life, I found *to be* unto death.

11 For sin, taking occasion by the commandment, deceived me, and by it slew *me.*

12 Wherefore [a]the law *is* holy, and the commandment holy, and just, and good.

13 Was then that which is good made death unto me? God forbid. But sin, that it might appear sin, working death in me by that which is good; that sin by the commandment might become exceeding sinful.

14 For we know that the law is spiritual: but I am carnal, [b]sold under sin.

7:4 [r]Gal. 5:22
7:5 [s]ch. 6:13 [t]ch. 6:21 Gal. 5:19 Jas. 1:15
7:6 [u]ch. 2:29 2 Cor. 3:6
7:7 [v]ch. 3:20 [w]Ex. 20:17 Deut. 5:21 Acts 20:33
7:8 [x]ch. 4:15 [y]1 Cor. 15:56
7:10 [z]Lev. 18:5 Ezek. 20:11,13,21 2 Cor. 3:7
7:12 [a]Ps. 19:8 & 119:38 1 Tim. 1:8
7:14 [b]2 Ki. 17:17

[e] Gk. *passions* [f] Or, *being dead to that;* see ver. 4; ch. 6:2 [g] Or, *concupiscence*

able to "bring forth fruit unto God" (6:22–23; 8:3–4; Eph. 2:10; Galk. 5:22–23; Col. 1:5–6; see Mat. 5:17, note).

7:7–25 KNOWN SIN . . . BY THE LAW. This section describes the pre-conversion experience of Paul or anyone else who attempts to please God without depending on His grace, mercy, and strength (see 8:5; see article on FAITH AND GRACE, p. 1738). (1) In vv. 7–12, Paul describes a person's stage of innocence until he reaches an "age of accountability." He is "alive" (v. 9), i.e., without guilt and spiritual accountability, until he volitionally sins against God's law written externally or in his heart (cf. 2:14–15; 7:7,9–11).

(2) In vv. 13–20, Paul depicts a state of slavery to sin because the law, when it becomes known, brings unconscious sin into consciousness and makes a person an actual transgressor. Sin becomes his master, even though he endeavors to resist it.

(3) In vv. 21–25, Paul discloses a person's utter despair as the knowledge and power of sin reduces him to wretchedness.

7:9–11 I WAS ALIVE .. ONCE. Paul's statements that "I was alive" and that "sin slew *me*" (v. 11) support the view that a child is innocent until he wilfully sins against God's law from the heart (2;14–15; see previous note). The teaching that infants come into the world guilty and worthy of eternal damnation is not found in Scripture.

7:12 THE LAW *IS* HOLY. See Mat. 5:17, note; Gal. 3:19, note.

7:14 THE LAW. Remember that Paul in ch. 7 is analyzing the state of an unregenerate person who is under the O.T. law and accepts its truth, yet is conscious of his inability to live a life pleasing to God (cf. v. 1). He is describing a conflict between a person alone against the power of sin, showing that we cannot attain justification, holiness, goodness, and sanctification by our own endeavor to resist sin and keep God's law. The conflict of the Christian, on the other hand, is quite different: it is a conflict between a person in union with the Holy Spirit and the power of sin (cf. Gal. 5:16–18). In ch. 8 Paul describes the way to victory over sin through life in the Spirit.

7:14 I AM CARNAL, SOLD UNDER SIN. More than any other words in ch. 7, these clearly point to a pre-conversion period under the law. This is so for the following reasons: (1) In ch. 7 Paul is demonstrating the insufficiency of the law to redeem us apart from grace, not the insufficiency of the gospel of grace (cf. Gal. 5:24).

(2) In v. 5 Paul states that those who are "in the flesh" (i.e., carnal, sensual) are bringing "forth fruit unto death" (i.e., eternal death). And in 8:13 he maintains that "if ye live after the flesh, ye shall die" (cf. Gal. 5:19–21). Thus the type of person referred to in ch. 7 is spiritually dead.

(3) The expression "sold under sin" means slavery or bondage to the power of sin (cf. 1 Ki. 21:20, 25; 2 Ki. 17:17). This cannot apply to a believer in Christ since He, by the ransom of His blood (see Mat. 20:28, note), has redeemed us from the power of sin and declares that sin no longer has dominion over us (6:14). Christ Himself affirmed: "If the Son therefore shall make you free, ye shall be free indeed" (see John 8:36, note; cf. Rom. 8:2). In fact, the name Jesus means "he shall save his people from their sins" (Mat. 1:21).

(4) Nor does the indwelling presence of the Holy Spirit (ch. 8) leave believers "sold unto sin." Paul goes on to declare that "the law of the Spirit of life in Christ Jesus hath made me free from the law of sin" (8:2), and he includes himself with those "who walk not after the flesh, but after the Spirit" (8:4), because "we are debtors, not to the flesh" (8:12).

15 For that which I do I [h]allow not: for [c]what I would, that do I not; but what I hate, that do I.
16 If then I do that which I would not, I consent unto the law that *it is* good.
17 Now then it is no more I that do it, but sin that dwelleth in me.
18 For I know that [d]in me (that is, in my flesh,) dwelleth no good thing: for to will is present with me; but *how* to perform that which is good I find not.
19 For the good that I would I do not: but the evil which I would not, that I do.
20 Now if I do that I would not, it is no more I that do it, but sin that dwelleth in me.
21 I find then a law, that, when I would do good, evil is present with me.
22 For I [e]delight in the law of God after [f]the inward man:
23 But [g]I see another law in [h]my members, warring against the law of my mind, and bringing me into captivity to the law of sin which is in my members.

Jesus Christ delivers from sin

24 O wretched man that I am! who shall deliver me from [i]the body of this death?
25 [i]I thank God through Jesus Christ our Lord. So then with the mind I myself serve the law of God; but with the flesh the law of sin.

The Spirit delivers from the power of sin

8 *THERE IS* therefore now no condemnation to them which are in Christ Jesus, who [j]walk not after the flesh, but after the Spirit.
2 For [k]the law of [l]the Spirit of life in Christ Jesus hath made me free from [m]the law of sin and death.
3 For [n]what the law could not do, in that it was weak through the flesh, [o]God sending his own Son in the likeness of sinful flesh, and [j]for sin, condemned sin in the flesh:
4 That the righteousness of the law

7:15 [c]Gal. 5:17
7:18 [d]Gen. 6:5 & 8:21
7:22 [e]Ps. 1:2 [f]2 Cor. 4:16 Eph. 3:16 Col. 3:9,10
7:23 [g]Gal. 5:17 [h]ch. 6:13,19
7:25 [i]1 Cor. 15:57
8:1 [j]Gal. 5:16
8:2 [k]ch. 6:18,22 [l]1 Cor. 15:45 [m]ch. 7:24,25
8:3 [n]Acts 13:39 Heb. 7:18 [o]2 Cor. 5:21 Gal. 3:13

[h] Gk. *know;* see Ps. 1:6 [i] Or, *this body of death* [j] Or, *by a sacrifice for sin*

7:15 WHAT I WOULD, THAT DO I NOT. Those who attempt to obey God's commandments *without the saving grace of Christ* find themselves unable to accomplish the good intentions of their heart. They are not their own master; evil and sin rule within them. They are slaves to them (vv. 15–21) and are brought "into captivity to the law of sin" (v. 23). Only in Christ will God with every temptation "make a way to escape, that ye may be able to bear it" (1 Cor. 10:13).

7:22 I DELIGHT IN THE LAW OF GOD. Many under the O.T. law found that within the inward man (soul, reason), they delighted in the law and commandments of God (cf. Ps. 119; Is. 58:2). At the same time, however, as long as help was sought only from the law, sinful passions remained in control (v. 23). Likewise, there may be those in the church today who acknowledge the righteousness, purity, and excellence of the gospel of Christ, yet because they have not experienced the regenerating grace of Christ, find themselves in bondage and slavery to sin. As we attempt to live a life free from the bondage of sin and immorality, all our efforts will be useless if we are not truly born again, reconciled to God, redeemed from Satan's power, and made new creatures in Christ, living a renewed life in the Holy Spirit (ch. 8; John 3:3; 2 Cor. 5:17).

7:24 O WRETCHED MAN THAT I AM! The unregenerate person, after maintaining a losing conflict against sin, is at last taken captive (v. 23). Sin finally triumphs and the person is sold as a slave to sin. His state is miserable; who can deliver him? The answer is "through Jesus Christ our Lord" (v. 25). It is He alone who will set us free "from the law of sin and death" (8:2).

8:1 THEM WHICH ARE IN CHRIST JESUS. Paul has just shown that life without the grace of Christ is defeat, misery, and bondage to sin. Now in ch. 8, Paul tells us that spiritual life, freedom from condemnation, victory over sin, and fellowship with God come through union with Christ by the indwelling Holy Spirit. By receiving and following the Spirit, we are delivered from the power of sin and are led onward to final glorification in Christ. This experience is the normal Christian life under the full provision of the gospel.

8:2 THE LAW OF THE SPIRIT. This "law of the Spirit of life" is the regulating and activating power and life of the Holy Spirit operating in the heart of the believer. The Holy Spirit comes into a sinner and frees him or her from the power of sin (cf. 7:23). The law of the Spirit comes into full operation as believers commit themselves to obey the Holy Spirit (vv. 4–5,13–14). They find a new power operating within, a power that allows them to overcome sin. "The law of sin and death" in this verse is the controlling power of sin which places a person into bondage to sin (7:14), reducing him or her to wretchedness (7:24).

8:4 THE LAW MIGHT BE FULFILLED IN US. The Holy Spirit working within believers allows them to live a life of righteousness that is seen as the fulfillment of God's moral law. Thus, the operation of grace and obedience to the law of God are not in conflict (cf. 2:13; 3:31; 6:15; 7:12,14). They both point to righteousness and holiness.

might be fulfilled in us, [p]who walk
not after the flesh, but after the Spir-
it.
5 For [q]they that are after the flesh
do mind the things of the flesh; but
they that are after the Spirit [r]the
things of the Spirit.
6 For [s]to[k] be carnally minded *is*
death; but [l]to be spiritually minded *is*
life and peace.
7 Because [t]the[k] carnal mind *is*
enmity against God: for it is not subject
to the law of God, [u]neither indeed
can be.
8 So then they that are in the flesh
cannot please God.
9 But ye are not in the flesh, but in
the Spirit, if so be that the Spirit of God
dwell in you. Now if any man have not
[v]the Spirit of Christ, he is none of his.
10 And if Christ *be* in you, the body
is dead because of sin; but the Spirit *is*
life because of righteousness.
11 But if the Spirit of [w]him that
raised up Jesus from the dead dwell in
you, [x]he that raised up Christ from the
dead shall also quicken your mortal
bodies [m]by his Spirit that dwelleth in
you.

The Spirit gives sonship

12 [y]Therefore, brethren, we are
debtors, not to the flesh, to live after
the flesh.
13 For [z]if ye live after the flesh, ye
shall die: but if ye through the Spirit do
[a]mortify the deeds of the body, ye
shall live.
14 For [b]as many as are led by the

8:4 [p]ver. 1 **8:5** [q]John 3:6 [r]Gal. 5:22 **8:6** [s]Gal. 6:8 **8:7** [t]Jas. 4:4 [u]1 Cor. 2:14 **8:9** [v]John 3:34 Gal. 4:6 **8:11** [w]Acts 2:24 [x]1 Cor. 6:14 2 Cor. 4:14 **8:12** [y]ch. 6:7,14 **8:13** [z]Gal. 6:8 [a]Eph. 4:22 **8:14** [b]Gal. 5:18

[k] Gk. *the minding of the flesh* [l] Gk. *the minding of the Spirit* [m] Or, *because of his Spirit*

8:5–14 AFTER THE FLESH . . . AFTER THE SPIRIT. Paul describes two classes of people: those who live according to the flesh and those who live according to the Spirit. (1) To live "after the flesh" ("flesh" is the sinful element of human nature) is to desire, take pleasure in, be occupied with, and gratify the corrupt desires of sinful human nature. Such living includes not only fornication, adultery, hatred, selfish ambition, outburst of anger, etc. (see Gal. 5:19–21), but also obscenity, pornographic addiction, drug addiction, mental and emotional pleasure from sex scenes in plays, books, TV, or movies, and the like (see article on THE WORKS OF THE FLESH AND THE FRUIT OF THE SPIRIT, p. 1840).

(2) To live "after the Spirit" is to seek and submit to the Holy Spirit's direction and enablement, and to concentrate one's attention on the things of God (see article on THE WORKS OF THE FLESH AND THE FRUIT OF THE SPIRIT, p. 1840). It is to live consciously at all times in the presence of God, trusting Him to give us the help and grace we need to accomplish His will in and through us.

(3) It is impossible to follow the flesh and the Spirit at the same time (vv. 7–8; Gal. 5:17–18). If anyone fails to resist by the Holy Spirit his sinful desires and instead lives according to the flesh (v. 13), he becomes an enemy of God (v. 7; Jas. 4:4) and can expect spiritual and eternal death (v. 13). Those who make the things of God their chief love and concern can expect eternal life and communion with God (vv. 10–11,15–16).

8:9 IF . . . THE SPIRIT OF GOD DWELL IN YOU. Every believer from the moment he accepts Jesus Christ as Lord and Savior has the Holy Spirit dwelling within him (cf. 1 Cor. 3:16; 6:19–20; Eph. 1:13–14; see article on THE DOCTRINE OF THE HOLY SPIRIT, p. 1668).

8:10 THE BODY *IS* DEAD BECAUSE OF SIN. Because sin has invaded the physical aspect of our being, our bodies must die or be transformed (cf. 1 Cor. 15:50–54; 1 Thes. 4:13–17). Yet because Christ is in us, we now experience the life of the Spirit.

8:13 MORTIFY THE DEEDS OF THE BODY. Paul emphasizes the necessity for continual warfare against all that would limit the work of God in our lives (cf. 6:11–19), for sin is always striving to regain control over us. (1) This spiritual conflict, although directed against Satan and evil spiritual forces (Eph. 6:12), is primarily against the passions and desires of the "flesh," i.e., sinful human nature (Gal. 5:16–21; Jas. 4:1; 1 Pet. 2:11). We as believers must continually decide whether we will surrender to the inclinations of sinful human nature or to the demands of the divine nature of which we partake (Gal. 5:16,18; 2 Pet. 1:4).

(2) The result of failing to put to death the sinful deeds of the body is spiritual death (vv. 6,13) and the loss of inheritance in the kingdom of God (Gal. 5:19–21). The words "ye shall die" mean that a Christian can pass from spiritual life back into spiritual death. Thus, the life of God that we receive at our new birth (John 3:3–6) can be extinguished in the soul of a believer who refuses to put to death by the Spirit the sinful deeds of the body.

8:13–14 THEY ARE THE SONS OF GOD. Paul gives the basis for the assurance of salvation here. If one is consistently putting to death the sinful deeds of the body, then we are being led by the Spirit. Those led by the Spirit are the sons of God.

8:14 LED BY THE SPIRIT OF GOD. The Holy Spirit dwells within the child of God in order to lead him to think, speak, and act according to God's Word. (1) He leads primarily by promptings that (a) are inward urgings to do God's will and to put to death the sinful deeds of the body (v. 13; Phil. 2:13; Tit. 2:11–12); (b) are always in harmony with Scripture (1 Cor. 2:12–13; cf. 2 Pet. 1:20–21); (c) are intended to give direction in life (Luke 4:1; Acts 10:19–20; 16:6–7); (d) are opposed to the sinful desires of the believer's natural inclinations (Gal. 5:17–18; 1 Pet. 2:11); (e) are

Spirit of God, they are the sons of God.

15 For [c]ye have not received the spirit of bondage again [d]to fear; but ye have received the [e]Spirit of adoption, whereby we cry, [f]Abba, Father.

16 [g]The Spirit itself beareth witness with our spirit, that we are the children of God:

17 And if children, then heirs; [h]heirs of God, and joint-heirs with Christ; [i]if so be that we suffer with *him,* that we may be also glorified together.

The Spirit leads to future glory

18 For I reckon that [j]the sufferings of this present time *are* not worthy *to be compared* with the glory which shall be revealed in us.

19 For [k]the earnest expectation of the creature waiteth for the manifestation of the sons of God.

20 For [l]the creature was made subject to vanity, not willingly, but by reason of him who hath subjected *the same* in hope,

21 Because the creature itself also shall be delivered from the bondage of corruption into the glorious liberty of the children of God.

22 For we know that [n]the whole creation [m]groaneth and travaileth in pain together until now.

23 And not only *they,* but ourselves also, which have [n]the firstfruits of the Spirit, [o]even we ourselves groan within ourselves, [p]waiting for the adoption, *to wit,* the [q]redemption of our body.

24 For we are saved by hope: but [r]hope that is seen is not hope: for what a man seeth, why doth he yet hope for?

25 But if we hope for that we see not, *then* do we with patience wait for *it.*

8:15 [c]1 Cor. 2:12 Heb. 2:15 [d]2 Tim. 1:7 1 John 4:18 [e]Is. 56:5 [f]Mark 14:36 **8:16** [g]Eph. 1:13 **8:17** [h]Acts 26:18 [i]Phil. 1:29 **8:18** [j]2 Cor. 4:17 1 Pet. 1:6 **8:19** [k]2 Pet. 3:13 **8:20** [l]Gen. 3:19 **8:22** [m]Jer. 12:11 **8:23** [n]2 Cor. 5:5 Eph. 1:14 [o]2 Cor. 5:2 [p]Luke 20:36 [q]Luke 21:28 Eph. 4:30 **8:24** [r]2 Cor. 5:7 Heb. 11:1

[n] Or, *every creature*

concerned with the guilt of sin, Christ's standard of righteousness, and God's judgment against evil (John 16:8–11); (f) exhort the believer to persevere in the faith and warn him concerning falling away from a personal faith in Christ (v. 13; Heb. 3:7–14); (g) become weaker the longer the believer resists obeying the Spirit's prompting (1:28; Eph. 4:17–19,30–31; 1 Thes. 5:19); (h) result in spiritual death when rejected (vv. 6,13); (i) result in spiritual life and peace when obeyed (vv. 6, 10–11,13; Gal. 5:22–23).

(2) The Spirit's prompting comes by (a) reading God's Word (John 14:26; 15:7,26; 16:13; 2 Tim. 3:16–17); (b) praying fervently (8:26; Acts 13:2–3); (c) listening to godly preaching and teaching (2 Tim. 4:1–2; Heb. 13:7,17) (d) exercising the manifestations of the Spirit (see 1 Cor. 12:7–10; 14:6); and (e) heeding the counsel of Christian parents and trustworthy spiritual leaders (Eph. 6:1; Col. 3:20).

8:15 ABBA, FATHER. See Gal. 4:6, note.

8:16 THE SPIRIT . . . BEARETH WITNESS. The Holy Spirit imparts to us a confidence that, through Christ and with Christ, we are now God's children (v. 15). He makes real the truth that Christ loved us, still loves us, and lives for us in heaven as Mediator (cf. Heb. 7:25). The Spirit also shows us that the Father loves us as His adopted children, no less than He loves His only begotten Son (John 14:21,23; 17:23). Finally, the Spirit creates in us the love and confidence by which we cry unto Him, "Abba, Father" (v. 15).

8:17 IF . . . WE SUFFER WITH *HIM*. Paul reminds us that a victorious life in the Spirit is no easy path. Jesus suffered, and we who follow Him will also suffer. This suffering is considered a suffering with Him (cf. 2 Cor. 1:5; Phil. 3:10; Col. 1:24; 2 Tim. 2:11–12), and it is the consequence of our sonship to God, our identification with Christ, our witness for Him, and our refusal to conform to the world (cf. 12:1–2).

8:18 THE SUFFERINGS OF THIS PRESENT TIME. All the sufferings of this present age—sickness, pain, misery, disappointments, poverty, mistreatment, sorrow, persecution, and trouble of any kind—must be considered insignificant when compared with the blessing, experience, privileges, and glory that will be given to the faithful believer in the age to come (cf. 2 Cor. 4:17).

8:22 THE WHOLE CREATION GROANETH. In vv. 22–27 Paul speaks of a threefold groaning: of creation (v. 22), of believers (v. 23), and of the Holy Spirit (v. 26). The "creation" (i.e., animate and inanimate nature) has been subjected to suffering and physical catastrophies because of human sin (v. 20). Thus, God has purposed that nature itself will be redeemed and re-created. There will be a new heaven and a new earth, a restoration of all things according to God's will (cf. 2 Cor. 5:17; Gal. 6:15; Rev. 21:1,5), when God's faithful children receive their full inheritance (vv. 14,23).

8:23 WE OURSELVES GROAN. Although believers possess the Spirit and His blessings, they still groan inwardly, desiring their full redemption. This groaning is for two reasons. (1) Believers, living in a sinful world that grieves their spirits, still experience imperfection, pain, and sorrow. The groaning expresses the deep sorrow felt at these circumstances (cf. 2 Cor. 5:2–4). (2) They groan for complete redemption and the fullness of the Holy Spirit that will be bestowed at the resurrection. They groan for the glory to be revealed and for the privileges of full sonship (cf. 2 Cor. 5:4).

The Spirit helps in prayer

26 Likewise the Spirit also helpeth our infirmities: for [s]we know not what we should pray for as we ought: but [t]the Spirit itself maketh intercession for us with groanings which cannot be uttered.

27 And [u]he that searcheth the hearts knoweth what *is* the mind of the Spirit, [o]because he maketh intercession for the saints [v]according to *the will of* God.

28 And we know that all things work together for good to them that love God, to them [w]who are the called according to *his* purpose.

29 For whom [x]he did foreknow, [y]he also did predestinate [z]*to be* conformed to the image of his Son, [a]that he might be the firstborn among many brethren.

30 Moreover whom he did predestinate, them he also [b]called: and whom he called, them he also [c]justified: and whom he justified, them he also [d]glorified.

The Spirit communicates God's love

31 What shall we then say to these things? [e]If God *be* for us, who *can be* against us?

32 [f]He that spared not his own Son, but [g]delivered him up for us all, how shall he not with him also freely give us all things?

33 Who shall lay any thing to the charge of God's elect? [h]*It is* God that justifieth.

34 [i]Who *is* he that condemneth? *It is* Christ that died, yea rather, that is risen again, [j]who is even at the right hand of God, [k]who also maketh intercession for us.

35 Who shall separate us from the love of Christ? *shall* tribulation, or distress, or persecution, or famine, or nakedness, or peril, or sword?

36 As it is written, [l]For thy sake

8:26 [s]Mat. 20:22 Jas. 4:3 [t]Eph. 6:18 **8:27** [u]1 Chr. 28:9 Acts 1:24 [v]1 John 5:14 **8:28** [w]2 Tim. 1:9 **8:29** [x]2 Tim. 2:19 [y]Eph. 1:5 [z]2 Cor. 3:18 1 John 3:2 [a]Col. 1:15 Heb. 1:6 **8:30** [b]1 Pet. 2:9 [c]1 Cor. 6:11 [d]John 17:22 Eph. 2:6 **8:31** [e]Num. 14:9 Ps. 118:6 **8:32** [f]ch. 5:6,10 [g]ch. 4:25 **8:33** [h]Is. 50:8,9 Rev. 12:10 **8:34** [i]Job 34:29 [j]Mark 16:19 Col. 3:1 Heb. 1:3 [k]Heb. 7:25 & 9:24 1 John 2:1

8:36 [l]Ps. 44:22; 2 Cor. 4:11

[o] Or, *that*

8:26 SPIRIT . . . MAKETH INTERCESSION FOR US WITH GROANINGS. Concerning the Holy Spirit's activity in helping the believer in prayer, three observations are important: (1) The child of God has two divine intercessors. Christ intercedes for the believer in heaven (v. 34; see Heb. 7:25, note; 1 John 2:1) and the Holy Spirit intercedes within the believer on earth (see article on INTERCESSION, p. 1268).

(2) "With groanings" probably indicates that the Spirit intercedes with the groans uttered by the believer. These groanings occur in the hearts of believers.

(3) The spiritual desires and yearnings of believers find their source in the Holy Spirit, who dwells within our hearts. The Spirit Himself sighs, groans, and suffers within us, longing for the final day of redemption (vv. 23–25). He appeals to the Father on behalf of our needs "according to *the will of* God" (v. 27).

8:28 ALL THINGS WORK TOGETHER FOR GOOD. This passage greatly encourages the children of God when we must endure suffering in this life. (1) God will bring good out of all affliction, trials, persecution, and suffering; the good that God brings about is conforming us to the image of Christ and ultimately bringing about our glorification (v. 29; see articles on THE PROVIDENCE OF GOD, p. 80, and THE SUFFERING OF THE RIGHTEOUS, p. 764). (2) This promise is limited to those who love God and have submitted to Him by faith in Christ (cf. Ex. 20:6; Deut. 7:9; Ps. 37:17; Is. 56:4–7; 1 Cor. 2:9). (3) The "all things" do not include our sins and negligence (6:16,21,23; 8:6, 13; Gal. 6:8); no one can excuse sin by maintaining that God will work it out for good.

8:29 WHOM HE DID FOREKNOW. "Foreknow" in this verse is equivalent to "forelove" and is used in the sense of "to set loving regard upon," "to choose to bestow love upon from eternity" (cf. Gen. 18:19; Ex. 2:25; Ps. 1:6; Hos. 13:5; Mat. 7:23; 1 Cor. 8:3; Gal. 4:9; 1 John 3:1). (1) Foreknowledge means that God purposed from eternity to love and redeem the human race through Christ (5:8; John 3:16). The recipient of God's foreknowledge or forelove is stated in the plural and refers to the church. That is, God's forelove is primarily for the corporate body of Christ (Eph. 1:4; 2:4; 1 John 4:19) and includes individuals only as they identify themselves with this body through abiding faith and union with Christ (John 15:1–6; see article on ELECTION AND PREDESTINATION, p. 1846).

(2) The corporate body of Christ will attain to glorification (v. 30). The individual believer will fall short of such glorification if he separates himself from that foreloved body and fails to maintain his faith in Christ (vv. 12–14,17; Col. 1:21–23).

8:30 PREDESTINATE. For an explanation of what predestination is, see article on ELECTION AND PREDESTINATION, p. 1846.

8:34 MAKETH INTERCESSION FOR US. See Heb. 7:25, note on Christ's heavenly intercession for the believer; see article on INTERCESSION, p. 1268.

8:36 SHEEP FOR THE SLAUGHTER. The adversities listed by the apostle in vv. 35–36 have been the experience of the people of God in all generations (Acts 14:22; 2 Cor. 11:23–29; Heb. 11:35–38). No believer should think it strange if he experiences adversity, persecution, hunger, poverty, or peril. Trouble and calamity do not nec-

we are killed all the day long; we are accounted as sheep for the slaughter.

37 [m]Nay, in all these things we are more than conquerors through him that loved us.

38 For I am persuaded, that neither death, nor life, nor angels, nor [n]principalities, nor powers, nor things present, nor things to come,

39 Nor height, nor depth, nor any other creature, shall be able to separate us from the love of God, which is in Christ Jesus our Lord. 2 Cor. 11:12-15

Paul's concern for Israel

9 I [o]SAY the truth in Christ, I lie not, my conscience also bearing me witness in the Holy Ghost,

2 [p]That I have great heaviness and continual sorrow in my heart.

3 For [q]I could wish that myself were [p]accursed from Christ for my brethren, my kinsmen according to the flesh:

4 Who are Israelites; [r]to whom *pertaineth* the adoption, and [s]the glory, and [t]the [q]covenants, and [u]the giving of the law, and [v]the service *of God,* and [w]the promises;

5 [x]Whose *are* the fathers, and [y]of whom as concerning the flesh Christ *came,* [z]who is over all, God blessed for ever. Amen.

8:37 [m]1 Cor. 15:57; 1 John 4:4
8:38 [n]Eph. 1:21
9:1 [o]2 Cor. 1:23; Gal. 1:20; 1 Tim. 2:7
9:2 [p]ch. 10:1
9:3 [q]Ex. 32:32
9:4 [r]Ex. 4:22; Deut. 14:1; [s]1 Sam. 4:21; 1 Ki. 8:11; [t]Acts 3:25; [u]Ps. 147:19; [v]Heb. 9:1; [w]Acts 13:32; Eph. 2:12
9:5 [x]Deut. 10:15; [y]Luke 3:23; [z]Jer. 23:6; Heb. 1:8
9:6 [a]Num. 23:19; [b]John 8:39; Gal. 6:16
9:7 [c]Gal. 4:23; [d]Gen. 21:12
9:8 [e]Gal. 4:28
9:9 [f]Gen. 18:10
9:10 [g]Gen. 25:21
9:11 [h]ch. 4:17
9:12 [i]Gen. 25:23
9:13 [j]Mal. 1:2,3; Mat. 10:37

God's purpose of mercy and justice

6 [a]Not as though the word of God hath taken none effect. For [b]they *are* not all Israel, which are of Israel:

7 [c]Neither, because they are the seed of Abraham, *are they* all children: but, In [d]Isaac shall thy seed be called.

8 That is, They which are the children of the flesh, these *are* not the children of God: but [e]the children of the promise are counted for the seed.

9 For this *is* the word of promise, [f]At this time will I come, and Sarah shall have a son.

10 And not only *this;* but when [g]Rebecca also had conceived by one, *even* by our father Isaac;

11 (For *the children* being not yet born, neither having done any good or evil, that the purpose of God according to election might stand, not of works, but of [h]him that calleth;)

12 It was said unto her, [i]The [r]elder shall serve the [s]younger.

13 As it is written, [j]Jacob have I loved, but Esau have I hated.

14 What shall we say then? [k]*Is*

9:14 [k]Deut. 32:4; Job 8:3

[p] Or, *separated* [q] Or, *testaments* [r] Or, *greater* [s] Or, *lesser*

essarily mean that God has deserted us, nor that He has ceased to love us (v. 35). On the contrary, our suffering as believers will open up the means by which we experience more of God's love and comfort (2 Cor. 1:4–5). Paul assures us that in all these adversities we will overcome and be more than conquerors through Christ (vv. 37–39; cf. Mat. 5:10–12; Phil. 1:29).

8:39 THE LOVE OF GOD . . . IN CHRIST JESUS OUR LORD. If anyone fails in his spiritual life, it will not be from a lack of divine grace and love (vv. 31–34), nor from external force or overwhelming adversity (vv. 35–39), but from his own neglect to remain in Christ Jesus (see John 15:6, note). Only "in Christ Jesus" has God's love been manifest, and only in Him do we experience it. Only as we abide in Christ Jesus as "our Lord" can we have the certainty that we will never be separated from God's love.

9:1 I SAY THE TRUTH IN CHRIST. In chs. 9–11 Paul addresses the problem of Israel's past election (9:6–29), present rejection of the gospel (9:30–10:21), and future salvation (11:1–36). For an examination of his argument, see article on ISRAEL IN GOD'S PLAN OF SALVATION, p. 1748.

9:2 I HAVE . . . CONTINUAL SORROW IN MY HEART. Paul's ceaseless concern and sorrow over those without Christ (10:1; 11:14; 1 Cor. 9:22) should be the attitude of every Christian. This same attitude of grief and willingness to suffer for the salvation of others existed in Moses (Ex. 32:32) and Jesus (Mat. 23:37; Rom. 3:24–25).

9:6 THE WORD OF GOD . . . NONE EFFECT. With this verse, Paul begins an extended discussion of God's dealings with the nation of Israel and the reason for their present unbelief (see article on ISRAEL IN GOD'S PLAN OF SALVATION, p. 1748).

9:11 THE PURPOSE OF GOD. For comments on God's purpose fulfilled in Esau and Jacob, see articles on GOD'S COVENANT WITH ABRAHAM, ISAAC, AND JACOB, p. 48, and ISRAEL IN GOD'S PLAN OF SALVATION, p. 1748.

9:13 JACOB HAVE I LOVED . . . ESAU HAVE I HATED. This verse does not mean that Jacob and his descendants were elected to eternal salvation while Esau and his descendants were elected to eternal damnation. Rather, it was an election of Jacob's descendants to be the channel of God's revelation and blessing to the world (see Mal. 1:3, note). Observe that according to chs. 9–11, the majority of Jacob's descendants failed to carry out their calling and thus were finally rejected by God (vv. 27,30–33; 10:3; 11:20). Furthermore, those who were not "loved" (i.e., the Gentiles) obeyed God through faith and became "children of the living God" (vv. 25–26).

there unrighteousness with God? God
forbid.
15 For he saith to Moses, [l]I will
have mercy on whom I will have mercy,
and I will have compassion on whom I
will have compassion.
16 So then *it is* not of him that
willeth, nor of him that runneth, but of
God that showeth mercy.
17 For [m]the scripture saith unto
Pharaoh, [n]Even for this same purpose
have I raised thee up, that I might
show my power in thee, and that my
name might be declared throughout all
the earth.
18 Therefore hath he mercy on
whom he will *have mercy,* and whom he
will he hardeneth.

God's mercy and justice defended

19 Thou wilt say then unto me, Why
doth he yet find fault? For [o]who hath
resisted his will?
20 Nay but, O man, who art thou
that [t]repliest against God? [p]Shall
the thing formed say to him that
formed *it,* Why hast thou made me
thus?
21 Hath not the [q]potter power over
the clay, of the same lump to make
[r]one vessel unto honour, and another
unto dishonour?
22 *What* if God, willing to show *his*
wrath, and to make his power known,
endured with much longsuffering [s]the
vessels of wrath [t]fitted[u] to destruc-
tion:
23 And that he might make known
[u]the riches of his glory on the vessels
of mercy, which he had [v]afore pre-
pared unto glory,
24 Even us, whom he hath called,
[w]not of the Jews only, but also of the
Gentiles?
25 As he saith also in Osee, [x]I will
call them my people, which were not
my people; and her beloved, which was
not beloved.
26 [y]And it shall come to pass, *that*
in the place where it was said unto
them, Ye *are* not my people; there shall
they be called the children of the living
God.
27 Esaias also crieth concerning Is-
rael, [z]Though the number of the chil-
dren of Israel be as the sand of the sea,
[a]a remnant shall be saved:
28 For he will finish [v]the work,
and cut *it* short in righteousness: [b]be-
cause a short work will the Lord make
upon the earth.
29 And as Esaias said before, [c]Ex-
cept the Lord of Sabaoth had left us a
seed, [d]we had been as Sodoma, and
been made like unto Gomorrha.

The gospel rejected by the Jews

30 What shall we say then? [e]That

9:15 [l]Ex. 33:19 **9:17** [m]Gal. 3:8 [n]Ex. 9:16 **9:19** [o]2 Chr. 20:6 Dan. 4:35 **9:20** [p]Is. 29:16 **9:21** [q]Prov. 16:4 [r]2 Tim. 2:20 **9:22** [s]1 Thes. 5:9 [t]1 Pet. 2:8 **9:23** [u]Col. 1:27 [v]ch. 8:28-30 **9:24** [w]ch. 3:29 **9:25** [x]Hos. 2:23 **9:26** [y]Hos. 1:10 **9:27** [z]Is. 10:22 [a]ch. 11:5 **9:28** [b]Is. 28:22 **9:29** [c]Is. 1:9 Lam. 3:22 [d]Is. 13:19 Jer. 50:40 **9:30** [e]ch. 4:11

[t] Or, *answerest again,* or, *disputest with God?*
[u] Or, *made up* [v] Or, *the account*

9:15 I WILL HAVE MERCY. This verse emphasizes the freedom of God's mercy. His overflowing active compassion cannot be earned or controlled by humans (v. 16). He has willed to have mercy upon all (11:32).

9:18 ON WHOM HE WILL *HAVE MERCY.* God intends to show mercy upon those who repent and believe on Jesus as Lord and Savior, while He hardens all those who refuse to repent and choose to continue in their sins, thereby rejecting salvation in Christ. This purpose of God does not change for any person or nation (cf. 2:4–11).

9:18 WHOM HE WILL HE HARDENETH. The hardening of Pharaoh's heart is at times attributed to God (Ex. 4:21; 7:3,13; 9:12; 10:1; 11:10; 14:17) and at other times to Pharaoh himself (Ex. 7:22–23; 8:15,32). Pharaoh, whose heart was already in opposition to God, received God's appropriate judgment. When he resisted God's will, God responded by hardening him even more (see Ex. 7:3, note). Thus, God's hardening of Pharaoh's heart was not arbitrary; He acted according to His righteous principle of hardening all those who reject Him (cf. 1:21–32).

9:21 HATH NOT THE POTTER POWER OVER THE CLAY? Paul is arguing for God's right to use certain people to accomplish His redemptive purpose without having to answer to anyone. (1) We must not interpret this to mean that God has no moral principles inherent in His own holy character as He deals with individuals and nations. God is governed in His nature, not by human will, but by His love (John 3:16), mercy (Ps. 62:12), and moral integrity (Ps. 116:5). (2) Those who interpret vv. 6–29 to mean that God arbitrarily chooses some people for salvation and others for destruction have misconstrued the passage (see article on ELECTION AND PREDESTINATION, p. 1846).

9:22–23 VESSELS OF WRATH . . . VESSELS OF MERCY. The phrase "vessels of wrath" refers to those being made ready for eternal destruction. One becomes a vessel of wrath by his own sinful acts and rebellion toward God, as Paul stated earlier: "but after thy hardness and impenitent heart treasurest up unto thyself wrath" (2:5). However, vessels of wrath may still repent, turn to God, and receive His mercy. The phrase "vessels of mercy" refers to those, both Jew and Gentile, who believe and follow Jesus Christ (vv. 24–33).

ISRAEL IN GOD'S PLAN OF SALVATION

Rom. 9:6 "Not as though the word of God hath taken none effect. For they are not all Israel, which are of Israel."

INTRODUCTION. In Rom. 9–11, Paul addresses the problem of Israel's past election, present rejection of the gospel, and future salvation. These three chapters were written to answer the question Jewish believers were asking: how could God's promises to Abraham and the nation of Israel remain valid while the nation of Israel as a whole seems to have no part in the gospel? This article summarizes Paul's argument.

OVERVIEW. There are three separate elements to Paul's discussion of Israel in God's plan of salvation.

(1) The first (Rom. 9:6–29) is an examination of Israel's past election. (a) In 9:6–13, Paul maintains that God's promise to Israel has not failed, for the promise never included any except the faithful in the nation. It was meant only for true Israel, those who were faithful to the promise (see Gen. 12:1–3; 17:19). There is always an Israel within Israel who have received the promise. (b) In Rom. 9:14–29, Paul points out that God has the right to do as He pleases with individuals and nations. He has a right to reject Israel if they disobey and the right to show mercy to the Gentiles and offer them salvation if He chooses.

(2) The second major section (Rom. 9:30—10:21) analyzes Israel's present rejection of the gospel. Their failure to respond to Christ is not due to an unconditional decree of God, but to their own unbelief and disobedience (Rom. 10:3).

(3) Finally, Paul explains (Rom. 11) that the rejection of Israel is only partial and temporary. Israel will eventually accept God's salvation in Christ. There are several steps in his argument. (a) God has not rejected the true Israel, for He has remained faithful to the "remnant" that has remained faithful to Him by accepting Christ (11:1–6). (b) God's present hardening of the majority of Israel has come because they refused to believe in Christ (11:7–10; cf. 9:31—10:21). (c) God has turned Israel's transgression (i.e., the crucifixion of Christ) into an opportunity to proclaim salvation to all the world (11:11–12,15). (d) During this present time of Israel's national unbelief, the salvation of individuals, both Jew and Gentile (cf. 10:12–13) depends on faith in Jesus Christ (11:13–24). (e) Belief in Jesus Christ by a portion of national Israel will take place in the future (11:25–29). (f) God's sincere purpose is to have mercy on all, both Jew and Gentile, and to include in His kingdom all people who believe in Christ (11:30–36; cf. 10:12–13; 11:20–24).

PERSPECTIVE. Several things stand out prominently in these three chapters of the book of Romans.

(1) This discussion about Israel does not refer primarily to the eternal life and death of individuals after physical death. Rather, Paul is discussing God's dealing with nations and people historically, i.e., His right to use certain nations and people as He chooses. For example, the choice of the individual Jacob over his brother Esau (Rom. 9:11) was a choice for the purpose of founding and using the nations of Israel and Edom that came from them. It had nothing to do with their individual eternal destiny to salvation or condemnation. The point is that God has the right to call and place responsibility upon those individuals and nations that He chooses.

(2) Paul expresses ceaseless concern and intense sorrow over the Jewish nation (Rom. 9:1–3). The very fact that Paul prays for his countrymen to be saved indicates that he did not believe that form of predestination theology which teaches that all people are foreordained either to heaven or hell before they are born. Rather, Paul's heartfelt desire and prayer is a reflection of the desire of God for the Jewish people (cf. Rom. 10:21; see Luke 19:41, note on Jesus weeping over Israel's rejection of God's way of salvation). The N.T. nowhere teaches that some people have been predestined to hell before they come into the world (see article on ELECTION AND PREDESTINATION, p. 1846).

(3) The most significant element in this entire discussion is the issue of faith. The lost spiritual condition of the majority of Israel was not determined or fixed by an arbitrary decree of God, but came as a result of their own unwillingness to submit to God's plan of salvation through faith in Christ (Rom. 9:33; 10:3; 11:20). Many Gentiles, however, accepted God's way of faith and attained the righteousness which is by faith. They obeyed God through faith and became "children of the living God" (9:25–26). This underscores the importance of the obedience of faith (1:5; 16:26) in respect to God's call and election.

(4) Hope is still offered to the nation of Israel if she ceases to continue in her unbelief (Rom. 11:23). Similarly, the Gentile believers who now are a part of God's church are warned that they too face the same possibility of being cut off from salvation. Therefore, like the Israelites, they must be diligent to continue in the faith with fear (11:20–23). That warning is as valid today as it was at the time that Paul wrote it.

(5) The Scriptures are full of promises of the eventual restoration of Israel to God through their acceptance of the Messiah. This will occur at the end of the great tribulation, just before the return of Jesus (see Is. 11:10–16, note; 29:17–24, note; 49:22–26, note; Jer. 31:31–34, note; Ezek. 37:12–14, note; Rom. 11:26, note; Rev. 12:6, note).

the Gentiles, which followed not after
righteousness, have attained to righ-
teousness, [f]even the righteousness
which is of faith.
31 But Israel, [g]which followed af-
ter the law of righteousness, [h]hath
not attained to the law of righteous-
ness.
32 Wherefore? Because *they sought*
it not by faith, but as it were by the
works of the law. For [i]they stumbled
at that stumblingstone;
33 As it is written, [j]Behold, I lay in
Zion a stumblingstone and rock of of-
fence: and [k]whosoever believeth on
him shall not be [w]ashamed.

Israel's unbelief toward Christ

10 BRETHREN, MY heart's desire
and prayer to God for Israel is,
that they might be saved.
2 For I bear them record [l]that they
have a zeal of God, but not according
to knowledge.
3 For they being ignorant of [m]God's
righteousness, and going about to es-
tablish their own [n]righteousness,
have not submitted themselves unto
the righteousness of God.
 4 For [o]Christ *is* the end of the law
for righteousness to every one that be-
lieveth.
5 For Moses describeth the righ-
teousness which is of the law, [p]That
the man which doeth those things shall
live by them.
6 But the righteousness which is of
faith speaketh on this wise, [q]Say not
in thine heart, Who shall ascend into
heaven? (that is, to bring Christ down
from above:)
7 Or, Who shall descend into the
deep? (that is, to bring up Christ again
from the dead.)
8 But what saith it? [r]The word is
nigh thee, *even* in thy mouth, and in thy
heart: that is, the word of faith, which
we preach;
9 That [s]if thou shalt confess with
thy mouth the Lord Jesus, and shalt be-
lieve in thine heart that God hath
raised him from the dead, thou shalt be
saved.
10 For with the heart man believeth
unto righteousness; and with the
mouth confession is made unto salva-
tion.
11 For the scripture saith, [t]Who-

9:30 [f]ch. 1:17
9:31 [g]ch. 10:2 [h]Gal. 5:4
9:32 [i]Luke 2:34 1 Cor. 1:23
9:33 [j]Ps. 118:22 Is. 8:14 & 28:16 Mat. 21:42 1 Pet. 2:6-8 [k]ch. 10:11
10:2 [l]Acts 21:20 & 22:3 ch. 9:31 Gal. 1:14
10:3 [m]ch. 1:17 [n]Phil. 3:9
10:4 [o]Mat. 5:17 Gal. 3:24
10:5 [p]Lev. 18:5 Neh. 9:29 Ezek. 20:11 Gal. 3:12
10:6 [q]Deut. 30:12
10:8 [r]Deut. 30:14
10:9 [s]Mat. 10:32 Luke 12:8 Acts 8:37
10:11 [t]Is. 28:16 & 49:23 Jer. 17:7

[w] Or, *confounded*

9:32 *THEY SOUGHT IT* NOT BY FAITH. The spiritual condition of the majority of Israel was due to their being unwilling to submit to God's plan of salvation through faith in Christ (v. 33). Many Gentiles, however, accepted God's way of salvation and attained the righteousness which is by faith.

10:1 MY HEART'S DESIRE AND PRAYER TO GOD. For comments on how Paul's concern here demonstrates that he did not adhere to the doctrine of individuals being predestined or foreordained to heaven or hell, see article on ISRAEL IN GOD'S PLAN OF SALVATION, p. 1748.

10:3 NOT SUBMITTED THEMSELVES. For comments on how ch. 10 fits into Paul's argument in chs. 9–11, see article on ISRAEL IN GOD'S PLAN OF SALVATION, p. 1748.

10:9–10 CONFESS . . . BELIEVE IN THINE HEART. The essentials of salvation are summarized in this passage. They center on belief in the Lordship of Christ and His bodily resurrection. Faith must be in the heart, which includes the emotions, intellect, and will, and it takes hold of the whole person. Faith must also involve committing oneself publicly to Jesus as Lord, both in word and deed (see article on FAITH AND GRACE, p. 1738).

10:9 CONFESS . . . THE LORD JESUS. The earliest creed or confession of the N.T. church was not that Jesus is Savior, but that Jesus is Lord (cf. Acts 8:16; 19:5; 1 Cor. 12:3). Jesus Christ is specifically called Savior 16 times in the N.T. and Lord more than 450 times. (1) The current teaching in some evangelical circles that Jesus can be one's Savior without necessarily being one's Lord, is found nowhere in the N.T. No one can receive Jesus as Savior without receiving Him as Lord. This is an essential ingredient in apostolic preaching (Acts 2:36–40).

(2) "Lord" (Gk. *kyrios*) means having power, dominion, authority, and the right to master. To confess Jesus as Lord is to declare Him to be equal with God (v. 13; John 20:28; Acts 2:36; Heb. 1:10) and worthy of power (Rev. 5:12), worship (Phil. 2:10–11), trust (Heb. 2:13), obedience (Heb. 5:9), and prayer (Acts 7:59–60; 2 Cor. 12:8).

(3) When N.T. Christians called Jesus "Lord," this was not just an outward profession but an inward sincere attitude of the heart (cf. 1 Pet. 3:15) by which they made Christ and His Word Lord over all of life (Luke 6:46–49; John 15:14). Jesus must be Lord of spiritual matters at home and in the church, as well as Lord in intellectual, financial, educational, recreational, vocational, in fact, in *all* areas of life (12:1–2; 1 Cor. 10:31).

10:9 GOD HATH RAISED HIM FROM THE DEAD. Anyone denying the bodily resurrection of Jesus Christ cannot legitimately claim to be a Christian. He is still an unbeliever, for the death and resurrection of Christ is the central event in salvation (1:4; 4:25; 5:10,17; 6:4–10; 8:11,34).

soever believeth on him shall not be ashamed.

12 For [u]there is no difference between the Jew and the Greek: for [v]the same Lord over all [w]is rich unto all that call upon him.

13 [x]For whosoever shall call [y]upon the name of the Lord shall be saved.

14 How then shall they call on him in whom they have not believed? and how shall they believe in him of whom they have not heard? and how shall they hear [z]without a preacher?

15 And how shall they preach, except they be sent? as it is written, [a]How beautiful are the feet of them that preach the gospel of peace, and bring glad tidings of good things!

Unbelief toward the prophets

16 But they have not all obeyed the gospel. For Esaias saith, [b]Lord, who hath believed [x]our [y]report?

17 So then faith *cometh* by hearing, and hearing by the word of God.

18 But I say, Have they not heard? Yes verily, [c]their sound went into all the earth, [d]and their words unto the ends of the world.

19 But I say, Did not Israel know? First Moses saith, [e]I will provoke you to jealousy by *them that are* no people, *and* by a [f]foolish nation I will anger you.

20 But Esaias is very bold, and saith, [g]I was found of them that sought me not; I was made manifest unto them that asked not after me.

21 But to Israel he saith, [h]All day long I have stretched forth my hands unto a disobedient and gainsaying people.

A remnant of Israel believes

11 I SAY then, [i]Hath God cast away his people? God forbid.

10:12 [u]Acts 15:9 ch. 3:22 [v]Acts 10:36 1 Tim. 2:5 [w]Eph. 1:7 & 2:4,7
10:13 [x]Joel 2:32 Acts 2:21 [y]Acts 9:14
10:14 [z]Tit. 1:3
10:15 [a]Is. 52:7 Nah. 1:15
10:16 [b]Is. 53:1 John 12:38
10:18 [c]Ps. 19:4 Mat. 24:14 Mark 16:15 Col. 1:6,23 [d]1 Ki. 18:10 Mat. 4:8
10:19 [e]ch. 11:11 [f]Tit. 3:3
10:20 [g]Is. 65:1
10:21 [h]Is. 65:2
11:1 [i]1 Sam. 12:22 Jer. 31:37 [j]2 Cor. 11:22 Phil. 3:5
11:2 [k]ch. 8:29
11:3 [l]1 Ki. 19:10
11:4 [m]1 Ki. 19:18
11:5 [n]ch. 9:27
11:6 [o]ch. 4:4,5 Deut. 9:4,5 Gal. 5:4
11:7 [p]ch. 9:31
11:8 [q]Is. 29:10 [r]Deut. 29:4 Is. 6:9 Jer. 5:21 Ezek. 12:2 Mat. 13:14 John 12:40 Acts 28:26
11:9 [s]Ps. 69:22
11:10 [t]Ps. 69:23
11:11 [u]Acts 13:46 & 18:6 ch. 10:19

For [j]I also am an Israelite, of the seed of Abraham, *of* the tribe of Benjamin.

2 God hath not cast away his people which [k]he foreknew. Wot ye not what the scripture saith [z]of Elias? how he maketh intercession to God against Israel, saying,

3 [l]Lord, they have killed thy prophets, and digged down thine altars; and I am left alone, and they seek my life.

4 But what saith the answer of God unto him? [m]I have reserved to myself seven thousand men, who have not bowed the knee to *the image of* Baal.

5 [n]Even so then at this present time also there is a remnant according to the election of grace.

6 And [o]if by grace, then *is it* no more of works: otherwise grace is no more grace. But if *it be* of works, then is it no more grace: otherwise work is no more work.

7 What then? [p]Israel hath not obtained that which he seeketh for; but the election hath obtained it, and the rest were [a]blinded

8 (According as it is written, [q]God hath given them the spirit of [b]slumber, [r]eyes that they should not see, and ears that they should not hear;) unto this day.

9 And David saith, [s]Let their table be made a snare, and a trap, and a stumblingblock, and a recompence unto them:

10 [t]Let their eyes be darkened, that they may not see, and bow down their back always.

Consequences of Israel's failure

11 I say then, Have they stumbled that they should fall? God forbid: but *rather* [u]through their fall salvation *is*

[x] Gk. *the hearing of us* [y] Or, *preaching?* [z] Gk. *in Elias?* [a] Or, *hardened* [b] Or, *remorse*

11:1 HATH GOD CAST AWAY HIS PEOPLE? Paul now explains that God's rejection of Israel is only partial and temporary; Israel will eventually accept God's salvation in Christ. For an analysis of how this chapter fits into Paul's argument in chs. 9–11, see article on ISRAEL IN GOD'S PLAN OF SALVATION, p. 1748.

11:5 THE ELECTION OF GRACE. This phrase refers to God's gracious design in sending His Son into the world to save all those who believe in Him. Election proceeds from God's saving purpose "before the foundation of the world" (Eph. 1:4). Since the coming of the Savior and His death and resurrection, the election includes all who believe and obey Christ and the gospel. Thus, both God and man are active in election. The goal of the "election of grace" is to be holy and without blame before God (Eph. 1:4; cf. Rom. 3:22; 4:1–5,16; 11:11–24; 2 Cor. 5:19–20; Eph. 2:8–10; see article on ELECTION AND PREDESTINATION, p. 1846).

11:7 THE REST WERE BLINDED. See 9:18, note on the hardening of hearts.

11:11 SALVATION *IS COME* UNTO THE GENTILES. The transgression of Israel, i.e., their rejection and crucifixion of Jesus, has resulted in

come unto the Gentiles, for to provoke
them to jealousy.
12 Now if the fall of them *be* the
riches of the world, and the [c]dimin-
ishing of them the riches of the Gen-
tiles; how much more their fulness?
13 For I speak to you Gentiles, inas-
much as [v]I am the apostle of the Gen-
tiles, I magnify mine office:
14 If by any means I may provoke to
emulation *them which are* my flesh, and
[w]might save some of them.
15 For if the casting away of them
be the reconciling of the world, what
shall the receiving *of them be*, but life
from the dead?
16 For if [x]the firstfruit *be* holy, the
lump *is* also *holy:* and if the root *be*
holy, so *are* the branches.
17 And if [y]some of the branches be
broken off, [z]and thou, being a wild ol-
ive tree, wert grafted in [d]among them,
and with them partakest of the root
and fatness of the olive tree;
18 [a]Boast not against the
branches. But if thou boast, thou bear-
est not the root, but the root thee.
19 Thou wilt say then, The
branches were broken off, that I might
be grafted in.
20 Well; because of unbelief they
were broken off, and thou standest by
faith. [b]Be not highminded, but [c]fear:
21 For if God spared not the natural
branches, *take heed* lest he also spare
not thee.
22 Behold therefore the goodness
and severity of God: on them which
fell, severity; but toward thee, good-
ness, [d]if thou continue in *his* good-
ness: otherwise [e]thou also shalt be
cut off.
23 And they also, [f]if they abide not
still in unbelief, shall be grafted in: for
God is able to graft them in again.
24 For if thou wert cut out of the
olive tree which is wild by nature, and
wert grafted contrary to nature into a
good olive tree: how much more shall
these, which be the natural *branches*,
be grafted into their own olive tree?

11:13 [v]Acts 9:15 Gal. 1:16 Eph. 3:8 1 Tim. 2:7
11:14 [w]1 Cor. 9:22 1 Tim. 4:16 Jas. 5:20
11:16 [x]Lev. 23:10 Jas. 1:18
11:17 [y]Jer. 11:16 [z]Acts 2:39 Eph. 2:12
11:18 [a]1 Cor. 10:12
11:20 [b]ch. 12:16 [c]Prov. 28:14 Is. 66:2
11:22 [d]1 Cor. 15:2 Heb. 3:6 [e]John 15:2
11:23 [f]2 Cor. 3:16
11:25 [g]ch. 12:16 [h]2 Cor. 3:14 [i]Luke 21:24 Rev. 7:9
11:26 [j]Ps. 14:7 Is. 59:20

Israel's future salvation

25 For I would not, brethren, that
ye should be ignorant of this mystery,
lest ye should be [g]wise in your own
conceits; that [h]blindness[e] in part is
happened to Israel, [i]until the fulness
of the Gentiles be come in.
26 And so all Israel shall be saved:
as it is written, [j]There shall come out

c Or, *decay*, or, *loss* d Or, *for them* e Or, *hardness*

salvation coming to the whole world (see Is. 49:5–6, notes).

11:12 THEIR FULNESS. The fullness of Israel may refer to a time when many in Israel will believe in Jesus Christ as God's divine Son and Messiah (see v. 15), bringing even greater blessing to the world (see Is. 11:10–16, note; 29:7–24, note).

11:14 PROVOKE TO EMULATION. It should be the desire and prayer of all churches that God's power, favor, and blessing will rest upon them to such a degree that some in Israel will be moved to jealousy and turn to the Lord. Christ's salvation and the privileges of His kingdom worked out in our lives will create in Israel a desire for the same blessings.

11:20 BECAUSE OF UNBELIEF. The key to Israel's destiny is not an arbitrary decree of God, but her own unbelief and rejection of God's grace in Christ (see article on ISRAEL IN GOD'S PLAN OF SALVATION, p. 1748).

11:22 THOU ALSO SHALT BE CUT OFF. Paul directs a grave warning to all Gentile believers, i.e., to all Christian churches, denominations, or fellowships. (1) The terrible possibility exists that God will cast away or "cut off" any individual, ministry, church, or group of churches if they do not "continue in *his* goodness" and in the N.T. apostolic faith and standards of righteousness (v. 22).

(2) If God did not spare Israel, neither will He spare any particular church or fellowship (v. 21) if it rejects God's ways and conforms to the ways of this world (see 12:2, note). Therefore, all Christian churches are to "fear" (v. 20), keeping in mind both "the goodness and severity of God" and making every effort to continue in the apostolic faith and practice of the N.T. No Christian church or ministry may presume with confidence that it will never fall under the judgment of God. With churches as with individuals, "there is no respect of persons with God" (2:11; see also Rev. 2–3, notes).

11:25 FULNESS OF THE GENTILES. The "fulness of the Gentiles" means the completion of God's purpose in calling out a people from among the Gentiles (Acts 15:14). It may also be related to a time when their iniquity is full, i.e., when sin in the world reaches a full level of rebellion against God (cf. Gen. 15:16). At that time Christ will come again to judge the world (Luke 21:24,27; cf. Gen. 6:5–7,11–13; 18:20–33; 19:24–25; Luke 17:26–30).

11:26 ALL ISRAEL. The expression "all Israel" should be understood as the believers in Israel as a whole. (1) The number of Jews who believe in Christ will greatly increase during the dark days of the tribulation (Deut. 4:30–31; Hos. 5:14—6:3; Rev. 7:1–8). The tribulation will end when Christ brings deliverance to the believers in Israel and destroys the remaining unbelieving Jews (see Is. 10:20, note; Zech. 13:8–9, note). All "rebels" (i.e.,

of Zion the Deliverer, and shall turn
away ungodliness from Jacob:
27 [k]For this *is* my covenant unto
them, when I shall take away their
sins.
28 As concerning the gospel, *they*
are enemies for your sakes: but as
touching the election, *they are* [l]be-
loved for the fathers' sakes.
29 For the gifts and calling of God
are [m]without repentance.
30 For as ye [n]in times past have
not [f]believed God, yet have now ob-
tained mercy through their unbelief:
31 Even so have these also now not
[f]believed, that through your mercy
they also may obtain mercy.
32 For [o]God hath [g]concluded
them all in unbelief, that he might have
mercy upon all.
33 O the depth of the riches both of
the wisdom and knowledge of God!
[p]how unsearchable *are* his judgments,
and [q]his ways past finding out!
34 [r]For who hath known the mind
of the Lord? or [s]who hath been his
counsellor?
35 Or [t]who hath first given to him,
and it shall be recompensed unto him
again?
36 For [u]of him, and through him,
and to him, *are* all things: [v]to [h]whom
be glory for ever. Amen.

A call for consecration

12 I [w]BESEECH you therefore,
brethren, by the mercies of
God, [x]that ye [y]present your bodies
[z]a living sacrifice, holy, acceptable
unto God, *which is* your reasonable ser-
vice.
2 And [a]be not conformed to this
world: but [b]be ye transformed by the
renewing of your mind, that ye may
[c]prove what *is* that good, and accept-
able, and perfect, will of God. 1 Cor. 2:6-16
3 For I say, [d]through the grace giv-
en unto me, to every man that is among
you, [e]not to think *of himself* more
highly than he ought to think; but to
think [i]soberly, according as God hath
dealt [f]to every man the measure of
faith.
4 For [g]as we have many members
in one body, and all members have not
the same office:
5 So [h]we, *being* many, are one body

11:27 [k]Is. 27:9 Jer. 31:31 Heb. 8:8
11:28 [l]Deut. 7:8
11:29 [m]Num. 23:19
11:30 [n]Eph. 2:2 Col. 3:7
11:32 [o]ch. 3:9
11:33 [p]Ps. 36:6 [q]Job 11:7 Ps. 92:5
11:34 [r]Job 15:8 Is. 40:13 Jer. 23:18 [s]Job 36:22
11:35 [t]Job 35:7
11:36 [u]Col. 1:16 [v]Heb. 13:21 Rev. 1:6
12:1 [w]2 Cor. 10:1 [x]1 Pet. 2:5 [y]ch. 6 [z]Heb. 10:20
12:2 [a]1 John 2:15 [b]Eph. 4:23 Col. 3:10 [c]1 Thes. 4:3
12:3 [d]Gal. 2:9 [e]Prov. 25:27 [f]Eph. 4:7
12:4 [g]1 Cor. 12:12 Eph. 4:16
12:5 [h]1 Cor. 10:17; Eph. 1:23

[f] Or, *obeyed* [g] Or, *shut them all up together* [h] Gk. *him* [i] Gk. *to sobriety*

ungodly Jews) will be purged (see Ezek. 20:34–44, note). (2) The believing remnant of Israel (i.e., those who are the survivors at the end of the age) and the faithful in Israel of past generations constitute "all Israel" (see Ezek. 37:12–14, note).

11:29 GIFTS AND CALLING OF GOD. These words refer to the privileges of Israel mentioned in 9:4–5 and 11:26. The context clearly refers to Israel and God's purposes for her, not to the spiritual gifts or ministerial calling associated with the Holy Spirit's work within the church (cf. 12:6–8; 1 Cor. 12). The calling, placing, and maintaining of someone in the office of a bishop (i.e., pastor or overseer) must be according to the personal character qualifications and spiritual history of the individual (see article on MORAL QUALIFICATIONS FOR OVERSEERS, p. 1908).

12:1 PRESENT YOUR BODIES A LIVING SACRIFICE. Believers must possess a single-minded passion to please God in love, devotion, praise, and holiness, and to offer the members of their bodies for His service. (1) Our greatest desire and prayer should be to live a life of holiness and to be accepted by God. This requires separating ourselves from the world and drawing ever nearer to God (v. 2). We must live for God, worship Him, obey Him, take His side against sin, stand for righteousness, resist and hate evil, perform works of kindness for others, imitate Christ, follow Him, serve Him, walk after the Holy Spirit, and be filled with the Spirit. (2) We must present our bodies to God as dead to sin and as the temple of the Holy Spirit (see next note; cf. 1 Cor. 6:15,19).

12:2 BE NOT CONFORMED TO THIS WORLD: BUT BE YE TRANSFORMED. Paul implies several things in this verse. (1) We must realize that the present world system is evil (Acts 2:40; Gal. 1:4) and under the rule of Satan (John 12:31; 1 John 5:19; see article on THE CHRISTIAN'S RELATIONSHIP TO THE WORLD, p. 2004).

(2) We must stand against the prevailing and popular forms of the spirit of this world, proclaiming instead the eternal truths and righteous standards of God's Word for Christ's sake (1 Cor. 1:17–24).

(3) We must despise and abhor what is evil, love what is righteous (v. 9; 1 John 2:15–17; see Heb. 1:9, note), and refuse to yield to the various types of worldliness that constantly surround the church, such as greed, selfishness, humanistic thinking, political maneuvering for power, envy, hate, revenge, impurity, filthy language, ungodly entertainment, sensuality, immodesty, immorality, drugs, alcohol, and worldly companions.

(4) We must have our minds conformed to God's way of thinking (1 Cor. 2:16; Phil. 2:5) by reading and meditating on His Word (Ps. 119:11,148; John 8:31–32; 15:7). We must have our plans, goals, and ambitions determined by heavenly and eternal truths, not by this evil, temporal, and transient age.

in Christ, and every one members one of another.

6 [i]Having then gifts differing [j]according to the grace that is given to us, whether [k]prophecy, *let us prophesy* according to the proportion of faith;

7 Or ministry, *let us wait* on *our* ministering: or [l]he that teacheth, on teaching;

8 Or [m]he that exhorteth, on exhortation: [n]he that [j]giveth, *let him do it* [k]with simplicity; [o]he that ruleth, with diligence; he that showeth mercy,
Rom. 15:19 [p]with cheerfulness.

Exhortation to love

9 [q]*Let* love be without dissimulation. [r]Abhor that which is evil; cleave to that which is good.

10 [s]*Be* kindly affectioned one to another [l]with brotherly love; [t]in honour preferring one another;

11 Not slothful in business; fervent in spirit; serving the Lord;

12 [u]Rejoicing in hope; [v]patient in tribulation; [w]continuing instant in prayer;

13 [x]Distributing to the necessity of saints; [y]given to hospitality.

14 [z]Bless them which persecute you: bless, and curse not.

15 [a]Rejoice with them that do rejoice, and weep with them that weep.

16 [b]*Be* of the same mind one toward another. [c]Mind not high things, but [m]condescend to men of low estate. [d]Be not wise in your own conceits.

17 [e]Recompense to no man evil for evil. [f]Provide things honest in the sight of all men.

18 If it be possible, as much as lieth in you, [g]live peaceably with all men.

19 Dearly beloved, [h]avenge not yourselves, but *rather* give place unto wrath: for it is written, [i]Vengeance *is* mine; I will repay, saith the Lord.

20 [j]Therefore if thine enemy hunger, feed him; if he thirst, give him

12:6 [i]1 Cor. 12:4 [j]ver. 3 [k]Acts 11:27 **12:7** [l]Eph. 4:11 **12:8** [m]Acts 15:32 [n]Mat. 6:1-3 [o]Acts 20:28 [p]2 Cor. 9:7 **12:9** [q]1 Tim. 1:5 [r]Ps. 34:14 **12:10** [s]Heb. 13:1 [t]Phil. 2:3 **12:12** [u]Luke 10:20 [v]Luke 21:19 [w]Luke 18:1 **12:13** [x]1 Cor. 16:1 [y]1 Tim. 3:2 **12:14** [z]Mat. 5:44 **12:15** [a]1 Cor. 12:26 **12:16** [b]Phil. 2:2 [c]Jer. 45:5 [d]Prov. 3:7 **12:17** [e]Mat. 5:39 [f]2 Cor. 8:21 **12:18** [g]Heb. 12:14 **12:19** [h]Lev. 19:18 [i]Deut. 32:35 **12:20** [j]Mat. 5:44

[j] Or, *imparteth* [k] Or, *liberally* [l] Or, *in the love of the brethren* [m] Or, *be contented with mean things*

12:6 GIFTS DIFFERING ACCORDING TO THE GRACE. Paul lists what can be called the gifts of grace (Gk. *charismata*). They are inward desires as well as enablements or abilities (Phil. 2:13) given by the Holy Spirit to individuals in the congregation in order to build up the people of God and express God's love to others (see 1 Cor. 12:1, note; 14:12,26; 1 Pet. 4:10). Every believer has at least one such gift (1 Cor. 12:11; 1 Pet. 4:10). However, one's primary gift does not exclude the exercise of any other gifts as need may arise. Paul's list of seven grace gifts should be taken as representative rather than exhaustive (see 1 Cor. 12–14 for further explanation of spiritual gifts).

12:6 PROPHECY. For comments on the gift of prophecy, see articles on SPIRITUAL GIFTS FOR BELIEVERS, p. 1790, and THE MINISTRY GIFTS OF THE CHURCH, p. 1852.

12:7 MINISTRY . . . TEACHETH. "Ministry" or "serving" is the God-given desire, ability, and power to serve and render practical assistance to members and leaders of the church in order to help them fulfill their responsibilities to God (cf. Acts 6:2–3).

"Teaching" is the God-given desire, ability, and power to examine and study God's Word, and to clarify, expound, defend, and proclaim its truth in such a way that others grow in grace and godliness (1 Cor. 2:10–16; 1 Tim. 4:16; 6:3; 2 Tim. 4:1–2; see articles on THE MINISTRY GIFTS OF THE CHURCH, p. 1852, and BIBLE TRAINING FOR CHRISTIANS, p. 1920).

12:8 EXHORTETH . . . GIVETH . . . RULETH . . . MERCY. "Exhortation" is the God-given desire, ability, and power to proclaim God's Word in such a way that it touches the heart, conscience, and will of the hearers, stimulates faith, and produces a deeper dedication to Christ through separation from the world (see Acts 11:23; 14:22; 15:30–32; 16:40; 1 Cor. 14:3; 2 Cor. 6:14–7:1; 1 Thes. 5:14–22; Heb. 10:24–25).

"Giving" is the God-given desire, ability, and power, because one has resources above the basic needs of life, to contribute freely of one's personal possessions to the needs of God's work or people (2 Cor. 8:1–8; Eph. 4:28).

"Ruling" or "leading" is the God-given desire, ability, and power to pastor, guide, and oversee the various activities of the church for the spiritual good of all (Eph. 4:11–12; 1 Tim. 3:1–2; Heb. 13:7,17,24; see article on THE MINISTRY GIFTS OF THE CHURCH, p. 1852).

"Mercy" is the God-given desire, ability, and power to help and comfort those in need or distress (cf. Eph. 2:4).

12:9 ABHOR THAT WHICH IS EVIL. See Heb. 1:9, note.

12:10 *BE* KINDLY AFFECTIONED ONE TO ANOTHER. All those devoted in faith to Jesus Christ must be devoted to one another as brothers and sisters in Christ (1 Thes. 4:9–10) with a sincere, kind, and tender affection. We must be concerned for our brothers' and sisters' welfare, needs, and spiritual condition, sympathizing with them and helping them in their sorrows and troubles. We must prefer one another in honor, i.e., we should be eager to respect and honor the good qualities in other believers (see John 13:34–35, notes).

drink: for in so doing thou shalt heap
coals of fire on his head.
21 Be not overcome of evil, but
overcome evil with good.

Submission to the authorities

13 LET EVERY soul [k]be subject
unto the higher powers. For
[l]there is no power but of God: the
powers that be are [n]ordained of God.
2 Whosoever therefore resisteth
[m]the power, resisteth the ordinance of
God: and they that resist shall receive
to themselves damnation.
3 For rulers are not a terror to good
works, but to the evil. Wilt thou then
not be afraid of the power? [n]do that
which is good, and thou shalt have
praise of the same:
4 For he is the minister of God to
thee for good. But if thou do that which
is evil, be afraid; for he beareth not the
sword in vain: for he is the minister of
God, a revenger to *execute* wrath upon
him that doeth evil.
5 Wherefore [o]*ye* must needs be
subject, not only for wrath, [p]but also
for conscience sake.
6 For for this cause pay ye tribute
also: for they are God's ministers, at-

13:1 [k]1 Pet. 2:13 [l]Dan. 2:21
13:2 [m]Tit. 3:1
13:3 [n]1 Pet. 2:14
13:5 [o]Eccl. 8:2 [p]1 Pet. 2:19
13:7 [q]Mat. 22:21 Luke 20:25
13:8 [r]Gal. 5:14 1 Tim. 1:5
13:9 [s]Ex. 20:13 Mat. 19:18 [t]Lev. 19:18 Mark 12:31 Jas. 2:8
13:10 [u]Mat. 22:40
13:11 [v]1 Cor. 15:34 Eph. 5:14
13:12 [w]Eph. 5:11

tending continually upon this very
thing.
7 [q]Render therefore to all their
dues: tribute to whom tribute *is due;*
custom to whom custom; fear to whom
fear; honour to whom honour.

Responsibility toward others

8 Owe no man any thing, but to love
one another: for [r]he that loveth an-
other hath fulfilled the law.
9 For this, [s]Thou shalt not commit
adultery, Thou shalt not kill, Thou
shalt not steal, Thou shalt not bear
false witness, Thou shalt not covet;
and if *there be* any other command-
ment, it is briefly comprehended in this
saying, namely, [t]Thou shalt love thy
neighbour as thyself.
10 Love worketh no ill to his neigh-
bour: therefore [u]love *is* the fulfilling of
the law.
11 And that, knowing the time, that
now *it is* high time [v]to awake out of
sleep: for now *is* our salvation nearer
than when we believed.
12 The night is far spent, the day is
at hand: [w]let us therefore cast off the

[n] Or, *ordered*

13:1 SUBJECT UNTO THE HIGHER POWERS. The Christian is commanded by God to obey the state, for the state as an institution is ordained and established by God. God has instituted government because in this fallen world we need certain restraints and authority to protect us from the chaos and lawlessness that is a natural result of sin. (1) The civil government, as does all of life, stands under the law of God. (2) God has ordained the state to be an agent of justice, to restrain evil by punishing the wrongdoer, and to protect the good in society (vv. 3–4; 1 Pet. 2:13–17). (3) Paul describes government as it should be. When it abandons its proper function, it is no longer of God nor according to His purpose. For example, when the state requires something contrary to the Word of God, the Christian must obey God rather than man (Acts 5:29; cf. Dan. 3:16–18; 6:6–10). (4) It is the duty of all believers to pray for those in authority (1 Tim. 2:1–2).

13:4 THE SWORD. The sword is frequently associated with death as an instrument of execution (Mat. 26:52; Luke 21:24; Acts 12:2; 16:27; Heb. 11:34; Rev. 13:10). God has clearly commanded the execution of dangerous criminals who have committed vicious crimes (Gen. 9:6; Num. 35:31, 33).

13:8 OWE NO MAN ANY THING. Believers should have no unpaid debts. This does not mean that we are prohibited from borrowing from others in case of serious need (cf. Ex. 22:25; Ps. 37:26; Mat. 5:42; Luke 6:35). But it does speak against both contracting debts for unnecessary things and showing an attitude of indifference in repaying debts (cf. Ps. 37:21). The only debt from which there is no release is love to one another.

13:10 LOVE WORKETH NO ILL TO HIS NEIGHBOUR. "Love" is fulfilled not only by positive commands (12:9–21; 1 Cor. 13:4,6–7), but also by negative ones. All of the commandments mentioned here are negative in form (v. 9; cf. 1 Cor. 13:4–6). (1) Love is positive; yet it is also negative in that it takes into account the human propensity toward sin, selfishness, and cruelty. Eight of the Ten Commandments are negative because sin comes naturally, while goodness does not. The first evidence of Christian love is that we turn from sin and that which brings harm and sorrow to others. (2) The idea that Christian ethics must be only positive is a fallacy based on the ideas of a society which seeks to free itself from prohibitions that curb the unrestrained desires of the flesh (Gal. 5:19–21).

13:12 THE NIGHT IS FAR SPENT. Paul believed in the imminent return of the Lord to transfer the faithful of His churches to heaven (see John 14:3, note; see article on THE RAPTURE, p. 1889), an event that he believed could happen even in his generation. Christ warned that He would return at a time when the faithful were sure that He would not come (see Mat. 24:42,44 notes). For this reason, God's children must always be spiritually ready and "cast off the works of darkness" (see Luke 12:35, note).

works of darkness, and [x]let us put on
the armour of light.
13 [y]Let us walk [o]honestly, as in
the day; [z]not in rioting and drunken-
ness, [a]not in chambering and wanton-
ness, [b]not in strife and envying.
14 But [c]put ye on the Lord Jesus
Gal. 5:13-18 Christ, and [d]make not provision for
the flesh, to *fulfil* the lusts *thereof.*

The weak and the strong

14 HIM THAT [e]is weak in the
faith receive ye, *but* [p]not to
doubtful disputations.
2 For one believeth that he [f]may
eat all things: another, who is weak,
eateth herbs.
3 Let not him that eateth despise
him that eateth not; and [g]let not him
which eateth not judge him that eateth:
for God hath received him.
4 [h]Who art thou that judgest an-
other man's servant? to his own mas-
ter he standeth or falleth. Yea, he shall
be holden up: for God is able to make
him stand.
5 [i]One man esteemeth one day
above another: another esteemeth ev-
ery day *alike.* Let every man be [q]fully
persuaded in his own mind.
6 He that [j]regardeth[r] the day, re-
gardeth *it* unto the Lord; and he that
regardeth not the day, to the Lord he
doth not regard *it.* He that eateth,
eateth to the Lord, for [k]he giveth God
thanks; and he that eateth not, to the
Lord he eateth not, and giveth God
thanks.
7 For [l]none of us liveth to himself,
and no man dieth to himself.
8 For whether we live, we live unto
the Lord; and whether we die, we die
unto the Lord: whether we live there-
fore, or die, we are the Lord's.
9 For [m]to this end Christ both died,
and rose, and revived, that he might be
[n]Lord both of the dead and living.
10 But why dost thou judge thy
brother? or why dost thou set at
nought thy brother? for [o]we shall all
stand before the judgment seat of
Christ.
11 For it is written, [p]*As* I live, saith
the Lord, every knee shall bow to me,
and every tongue shall confess to God.
12 So then [q]every one of us shall
give account of himself to God.

Causing a brother to fall

13 Let us not therefore judge one
another any more: but judge this rath-
er, that [r]no man put a stumblingblock
or an occasion to fall in *his* brother's
way.
14 I know, and am persuaded by the
Lord Jesus, [s]that *there is* nothing
[s]unclean of itself: but [t]to him that
esteemeth any thing to be [s]unclean,
to him *it is* unclean.
15 But if thy brother be grieved with
thy meat, now walkest thou not
[t]charitably. [u]Destroy not him with
thy meat, for whom Christ died.
16 [v]Let not then your good be evil
spoken of:
17 [w]For the kingdom of God is not
meat and drink; but righteousness, and
peace, and joy in the Holy Ghost. Rom. 15:30

13:12 [x]Eph. 6:13 **13:13** [y]Phil. 4:8 [z]Prov. 23:20 [a]1 Cor. 6:9 [b]Jas. 3:14 **13:14** [c]Gal. 3:27 Eph. 4:24 [d]Gal. 5:16 **14:1** [e]1 Cor. 8:9 **14:2** [f]1 Cor. 10:25 Tit. 1:15 **14:3** [g]Col. 2:16 **14:4** [h]Jas. 4:12 **14:5** [i]Gal. 4:10 **14:6** [j]Gal. 4:10 [k]1 Cor. 10:31 1 Tim. 4:3 **14:7** [l]1 Cor. 6:19 Gal. 2:20 1 Thes. 5:10 1 Pet. 4:2 **14:9** [m]2 Cor. 5:15 [n]Acts 10:36 **14:10** [o]Mat. 25:31 2 Cor. 5:10 **14:11** [p]Is. 45:23 **14:12** [q]Mat. 12:36 Gal. 6:5 1 Pet. 4:5 **14:13** [r]1 Cor. 8:9 **14:14** [s]1 Cor. 10:25 [t]1 Cor. 8:7 **14:15** [u]1 Cor. 8:11 **14:16** [v]ch. 12:17 **14:17** [w]1 Cor. 8:8

[o] Or, *decently* [p] Or, *not to judge his doubtful thoughts* [q] Or, *fully assured* [r] Or, *observeth* [s] Gk. *common* [t] Gk. *according to charity*

13:14 PUT YE ON THE LORD JESUS CHRIST. We must be so united and identified with Him that we imitate His life as a pattern for our living, adopt His principles, obey His precepts, and become like Him. This calls for a complete rejection of immorality and the lusts of the flesh (cf. Gal. 5:19–21).

14:2 EAT ALL THINGS . . . EATETH HERBS. A number of believers in Rome were divided over an important issue: some were committed to eating only vegetables, while others were eating vegetables and all other foods including meat. Paul states that eating in itself is not a moral matter, but that one's personal attitude about what to eat could lead to unjustly condemning one another.

14:5 ESTEEMETH ONE DAY ABOVE ANOTHER. This probably refers to the special feast days of the O.T. ceremonial law. Some Christians apparently still regarded the holy days as having abiding usefulness, whereas many others were ignoring them. In his answer, Paul does not attempt to abrogate God's principle of setting aside one day in seven as a special day of rest and worship unto the Lord (see Mat. 12:1, note). God Himself set aside one day in seven to rest from daily work (Gen. 2:2–3; cf. Ex. 20:11; 31:17; Is. 58:13–14). In the N.T. the first day of the week is recognized as having a special significance because of Jesus' resurrection (Acts 20:7; 1 Cor. 16:2; Rev. 1:10).

14:13 LET US NOT . . . JUDGE ONE ANOTHER. Though we must refrain from judging one another in trivial matters, believers ought to consider how to encourage each other to true Christlikeness and holiness when it concerns faith, doctrine, and morals (Heb. 10:24). This involves sincerely evaluating (1 Thes. 5:21; 1 John 4:1), correcting, and rebuking one another in love and humility (Luke 17:3), and, when necessary, exercising church discipline (cf. 1 Cor. 5:12–13; 2 Thes. 3:6, 14; 1 Tim. 5:20–21; 2 Tim. 2:24–26; 4:2).

18 For he that in these things serveth Christ [x]*is* acceptable to God, and approved of men.

19 [y]Let us therefore follow after the things which make for peace, and things wherewith [z]one may edify another.

20 [a]For meat destroy not the work of God. [b]All things indeed *are* pure; [c]but *it is* evil for that man who eateth with offence.

21 *It is* good neither to eat [d]flesh, nor to drink wine, nor *any thing* whereby thy brother stumbleth, or is offended, or is made weak.

22 Hast thou faith? have *it* to thyself before God. [e]Happy *is* he that condemneth not himself in that thing which he alloweth.

23 And he that [u]doubteth is damned if he eat, because *he eateth* not of faith: for [f]whatsoever *is* not of faith is sin.

Self-denial on behalf of others

15 WE [g]THEN that are strong ought to bear the [h]infirmities of the weak, and not to please ourselves.

2 [i]Let every one of us please *his* neighbour for *his* good [j]to edification.

3 [k]For even Christ pleased not himself; but, as it is written, The [l]reproaches of them that reproached thee fell on me.

4 For [m]whatsoever things were written aforetime were written for our learning, that we through patience and comfort of the scriptures might have hope.

5 [n]Now the God of patience and consolation grant you to be likeminded one toward another [v]according to Christ Jesus:

6 That ye may [o]with one mind *and* one mouth glorify God, even the Father of our Lord Jesus Christ.

7 Wherefore [p]receive ye one another, [q]as Christ also received us to the glory of God.

8 Now I say that [r]Jesus Christ was a minister of the circumcision for the truth of God, [s]to confirm the promises *made* unto the fathers:

9 And [t]that the Gentiles might glorify God for *his* mercy; as it is written, [u]For this cause I will confess to thee among the Gentiles, and sing unto thy name.

10 And again he saith, [v]Rejoice, ye Gentiles, with his people.

11 And again, [w]Praise the Lord, all ye Gentiles; and laud him all ye people. Eph. 1:3-6

12 And again, Esaias saith, [x]There shall be a root of Jesse, and he that shall rise to reign over the Gentiles; in him shall the Gentiles trust.

13 Now the God of hope fill you with all [y]joy and peace in believing, that ye may abound in hope, through the power of the Holy Ghost.

Paul's reason for writing

14 And [z]I myself also am persuaded of you, my brethren, that ye also are full of goodness, [a]filled with all knowledge, able also to admonish one another.

15 Nevertheless, brethren, I have written the more boldly unto you in

14:18 [x]2 Cor. 8:21 **14:19** [y]ch. 12:18 [z]1 Cor. 14:12 1 Thes. 5:11 **14:20** [a]ver. 15 [b]Mat. 15:11 [c]1 Cor. 8:9 **14:21** [d]1 Cor. 8:13 **14:22** [e]1 John 3:21 **14:23** [f]Tit. 1:15 **15:1** [g]Gal. 6:1 [h]ch. 14:1 **15:2** [i]1 Cor. 10:33 [j]ch. 14:19 **15:3** [k]Mat. 26:39 [l]Ps. 69:9 **15:4** [m]1 Cor. 10:11 **15:5** [n]1 Cor. 1:10 **15:6** [o]Acts 4:24 **15:7** [p]ch. 14:1,3 [q]ch. 5:2 **15:8** [r]Mat. 15:24 John 1:11 Acts 3:25 [s]2 Cor. 1:20 **15:9** [t]John 10:16 [u]Ps. 18:49 **15:10** [v]Deut. 32:43 **15:11** [w]Ps. 117:1 **15:12** [x]Is. 11:1 Rev. 5:5 **15:13** [y]ch. 12:12 **15:14** [z]2 Pet. 1:12 1 John 2:21 [a]1 Cor. 8:1

[u] Or, *discerneth and putteth a difference between meats* [v] Or, *after the example of*

14:21 NOR TO DRINK WINE. The Bible gave the N.T. Christian two major laws regarding wine (Gk. *oinos*), which included both unfermented and fermented fruit of the vine (see article on WINE IN NEW TESTAMENT TIMES (1), p. 1538): (1) the law of abstinence from wine when it is fermented and intoxicating (see Prov. 23:31, note; 1 Thes. 5:6, note; Tit. 2:2, note); (2) the law of Christian love, which causes a person to abstain from what might lead others into harm (cf. 1 Cor. 8:13; 10:27–32). Paul affirms that in a pagan society (i.e., in a non-Jewish environment) where intoxicating beverages and drunkenness are prevalent, it is better to refuse to drink even the unfermented wines than to drink something that might cause another Christian to be led into sin. The use of nonintoxicating wines were technically safe for some believers, but they might influence weaker believers to partake of strongly fermented wine and thereby expose them to harm and drunkenness. Timothy carefully followed this law of Christian love (see 1 Tim. 5:23, note).

15:3 CHRIST PLEASED NOT HIMSELF. Disregarding the convictions of others in order to please ourselves destroys the work of God (14:15,20); living sacrificially so as to help others will strengthen the kingdom of God. Paul points to the example of Christ, who did not live for His own interest but for the interests of others.

15:4 WHATSOEVER THINGS WERE WRITTEN AFORETIME. The O.T. Scriptures are of utmost importance to the Christian's spiritual life. The wisdom and moral laws of God concerning every aspect of life, as well as His revelation concerning Himself, salvation, and the coming of Christ, have permanent value (2 Tim. 3:16; see Mat. 5:17, note; see article on THE OLD TESTAMENT LAW, p. 124).

some sort, as putting you in mind, [b]because of the grace that is given to me of God,

16 That [c]I should be the minister of Jesus Christ to the Gentiles, ministering the gospel of God, that the [d]offering[w] up of the Gentiles might be acceptable, being sanctified by the Holy Ghost.

17 I have therefore whereof I may glory through Jesus Christ [e]in those things which pertain to God.

18 For I will not dare to speak of any of those things [f]which Christ hath not wrought by me, [g]to make the Gentiles obedient, by word and deed,

19 [h]Through mighty signs and wonders, by the power of the Spirit of God; so that from Jerusalem, and round about unto Illyricum, I have fully preached the gospel of Christ.

1 Cor. 1:7

20 Yea, so have I strived to preach the gospel, not where Christ was named, [i]lest I should build upon another man's foundation:

21 But as it is written, [j]To whom he was not spoken of, they shall see: and they that have not heard shall understand.

Paul's future plans

22 For which cause also [k]I have been [x]much hindered from coming to you.

23 But now having no more place in these parts, and [l]having a great desire these many years to come unto you;

24 Whensoever I take my journey into Spain, I will come to you: for I trust to see you in my journey, [m]and to be brought on my way thitherward by you, if first I be somewhat filled [n]with[y] your *company*.

15:15 [b]ch. 1:5 & 12:3 Gal. 1:15 Eph. 3:7,8 **15:16** [c]ch. 11:13 Gal. 2:7-9 1 Tim. 2:7 2 Tim. 1:11 [d]Is. 66:20 Phil. 2:17 **15:17** [e]Heb. 5:1 **15:18** [f]Acts 21:19 Gal. 2:8 [g]ch. 1:5 & 16:26 **15:19** [h]Acts 19:11 2 Cor. 12:12 **15:20** [i]2 Cor. 10:13,15, 16 **15:21** [j]Is. 52:15 **15:22** [k]ch. 1:13 1 Thes. 2:17 **15:23** [l]Acts 19:21 ch. 1:11 **15:24** [m]Acts 15:3 [n]ver. 32

15:25 [o]Acts 19:21 & 24:17 **15:26** [p]1 Cor. 16:1 2 Cor. 8:1 **15:27** [q]ch. 11:17 [r]1 Cor. 9:11 Gal. 6:6 **15:28** [s]Phil. 4:17 **15:29** [t]ch. 1:11 **15:30** [u]Phil. 2:1 [v]2 Cor. 1:11 Col. 4:12 **15:31** [w]2 Thes. 3:2 [x]2 Cor. 8:4 **15:32** [y]ch. 1:10 [z]Acts 18:21 1 Cor. 4:19 Jas. 4:15 [a]1 Cor. 16:18 2 Cor. 7:13 2 Tim. 1:16 Philem. 7,20 **15:33** [b]ch. 16:20 1 Cor. 14:33

25 But now [o]I go unto Jerusalem to minister unto the saints.

26 For [p]it hath pleased them of Macedonia and Achaia to make a certain contribution for the poor saints which are at Jerusalem.

27 It hath pleased them verily; and their debtors they are. For [q]if the Gentiles have been made partakers of their spiritual things, [r]their duty is also to minister unto them in carnal things.

28 When therefore I have performed this, and have sealed to them [s]this fruit, I will come by you into Spain.

29 [t]And I am sure that, when I come unto you, I shall come in the fulness of the blessing of the gospel of Christ.

30 Now I beseech you, brethren, for the Lord Jesus Christ's sake, and [u]for the love of the Spirit, [v]that ye strive together with me in *your* prayers to God for me;

Gal. 5:22-23

31 [w]That I may be delivered from them that [z]do not believe in Judaea; and that [x]my service which *I have* for Jerusalem may be accepted of the saints;

32 [y]That I may come unto you with joy [z]by the will of God, and may with you [a]be refreshed.

33 Now [b]the God of peace *be* with you all. Amen.

Commendations and greetings

16 I COMMEND unto you Phebe our sister, which is a servant of the church which is at [c]Cenchrea;

2 [d]That ye receive her in the Lord,

2 Cor. 13:11; Phil. 4:9; 1 Thes. 5:23; 2 Thes. 3:16; Heb. 13:20 **16:1** [c]Acts 18:18 **16:2** [d]Phil. 2:29; 3 John 5,6

[w] Or, *sacrificing* [x] Or, *many ways,* or, *oftentimes* [y] Gk. *with you* [z] Or, *are disobedient*

15:17 I MAY GLORY. It is not wrong to speak excitedly and joyfully about what God is doing through us if it is done in a spirit of humility and thankfulness to God. Glorying should not be in mere numbers, but in a ministry that produces the obedience of faith in word and deed and that issues from a genuine work and manifestation of the Holy Spirit in power (vv. 18–19).

15:20 NOT WHERE CHRIST WAS NAMED. Paul's policy of ministry was missionary-centered. He chose to direct his labors in areas where the gospel had not been preached sufficiently, thereby enabling those who had not heard to have a chance to accept Christ (v. 21).

15:29 THE FULNESS OF THE BLESSING . . . OF CHRIST. Paul's ministry was accompanied with the fullness of Christ's blessing, power, grace, and presence. Whenever he ministered, this blessing would be imparted to other believers. We who serve the Lord and the churches of Christ should seek the same fullness in our ministries.

16:1 PHEBE. Phebe was probably the one who delivered this letter to the Romans. She was a servant (or woman deacon) in the church at Cenchrea who ministered to the poor, the sick, and the needy as well as assisted missionaries such as Paul. Paul's greetings to no less than eight women in this chapter indicate that women performed distinguished service in the churches.

as becometh saints, and that ye assist
her in whatsoever business she hath
need of you: for she hath been a suc-
courer of many, and of myself also.
3 Greet [e]Priscilla and Aquila my
helpers in Christ Jesus:
4 Who have for my life laid down
their own necks: unto whom not only
I give thanks, but also all the churches
of the Gentiles.
5 Likewise *greet* [f]the church that
is in their house. Salute my well-
beloved Epaenetus, who is [g]the first-
fruits of Achaia unto Christ.
6 Greet Mary, who bestowed much
labour on us.
7 Salute Andronicus and Junia, my
kinsmen, and my fellowprisoners, who
are of note among the apostles, who
also [h]were in Christ before me.
8 Greet Amplias my beloved in the
Lord.
9 Salute Urbane, our helper in
Christ, and Stachys my beloved.
10 Salute Apelles approved in
Christ. Salute them which are of Aris-
tobulus' [a]*household*.
11 Salute Herodion my kinsman.
Greet them that be of the [a]*household*
of Narcissus, which are in the Lord.
12 Salute Tryphena and Tryphosa,
who labour in the Lord. Salute the be-
loved Persis, which laboured much in
the Lord.
13 Salute Rufus [i]chosen in the
Lord, and his mother and mine.
14 Salute Asyncritus, Phlegon,
Hermas, Patrobas, Hermes, and the
brethren which are with them.
15 Salute Philologus, and Julia, Ne-
reus, and his sister, and Olympas, and
all the saints which are with them.
16 [j]Salute one another with an
holy kiss. The churches of Christ sa-
lute you.
17 Now I beseech you, brethren,
mark them [k]which cause divisions
and offences contrary to the doctrine
which ye have learned; and [l]avoid
them.
18 For they that are such serve not
our Lord Jesus Christ, but [m]their own
belly; and [n]by good words and fair
speeches deceive the hearts of the sim-
ple.
19 For [o]your obedience is come
abroad unto all *men*. I am glad there-
fore on your behalf: but yet I would
have you [p]wise unto that which is
good, and [b]simple concerning evil.

16:3 [e]Acts 18:2,18,26
16:5 [f]1 Cor. 16:19 Col. 4:15 Philem. 2 [g]1 Cor. 16:15
16:7 [h]Gal. 1:22
16:13 [i]2 John 1
16:16 [j]1 Cor. 16:20 2 Cor. 13:12
16:17 [k]Acts 15:1 [l]1 Cor. 5:9 2 Tim. 3:5
16:18 [m]Phil. 3:19 1 Tim. 6:5 [n]Col. 2:4 2 Tim. 3:6
16:19 [o]ch. 1:8 [p]Mat. 10:16

[a] Or, friends [b] Or, *harmless*

16:7 WHO ARE OF NOTE AMONG THE APOSTLES. Andronicus and Junia are called apostles. The word "apostle" here is used in the general sense to refer to a traveling messenger or missionary rather than in the special sense of "apostle" (cf. Acts 14:4, note; 1 Cor. 9:1–2; 2 Cor. 8:23; 12:12; Phil. 2:25; see article on THE MINISTRY GIFTS OF THE CHURCH, p. 1852).

16:17–18 MARK THEM. At the end of his letter, Paul gives a strong warning to the church in Rome to be alert to all those who do damage to the church by corrupting and distorting the "doctrine" (teaching) of Paul and the other apostles. They are to "mark" the proponents of false doctrine and "avoid them" and their ministry. Those marked may have been antinomians (i.e., against the law), who taught that because salvation is by grace, saving faith does not necessarily include obedience to Christ Jesus (cf. 6:1–2; 2 Cor. 4:2; 11:3; Eph. 4:14; Rev. 2:4–5; see article on FALSE TEACHERS, p. 1508). They believed that a person could live in sin and reject God's moral law, and yet possess eternal salvation. These false teachers were eloquent orators, speaking with comforting words and flattering speeches (cf. Jude 16), but deceiving simple Christians.

16:19 SIMPLE CONCERNING EVIL. God wants believers to be innocent (Gk. *akeraios*) in what is evil; this word means "unmixed" or "pure," i.e., innocent like a child whose mind has not yet been exposed to evil or mixed with the values of the world (cf. 1 Cor. 14:20). (1) This Biblical principle is in direct opposition to the idea advocated by some that children of Christians should be exposed to sin, immorality, ungodliness, and the things of Satan in order to learn to confront temptation. Some suggest that children need not be guarded from ungodliness. However, according to Biblical revelation, this philosophy is not only against God's will for the believer, but also represents Satan's own desire that everyone be exposed to the knowledge of good and evil (Gen. 3:5).

(2) Knowledge of evil, along with continual exposure to Satan's ways, will lead many from the path of faith and obedience. Lot found this out to his deep sorrow, losing his entire family for this reason (Gen. 13:12–13; 19:1–38). Scripture warns that "evil communications [i.e., company] corrupt good manners" (1 Cor. 15:33), and that "Jesus Christ . . . gave himself . . . that he might deliver us from this present evil world" (Gal. 1:3–4). Those who advocate exposing innocent children to an ungodly environment and/or influence are in danger of violating Jesus' warning in Mat. 18:6.

(3) Believers should do all within their means and power to guard their children from being exposed to the deceitfulness of sin and the perverseness of this generation. To refuse to protect our children in this respect disregards the Holy Spirit's desire that they be innocent and babes regarding what is evil.

20 And [q]the God of peace [r]shall
[c]bruise Satan under your feet shortly.
[s]The grace of our Lord Jesus Christ *be*
with you. Amen.
21 [t]Timotheus my workfellow,
and [u]Lucius, and [v]Jason, and [w]Sosipater,
my kinsmen, salute you.
22 I Tertius, who wrote *this* epistle,
salute you in the Lord.
23 [x]Gaius mine host, and of the
whole church, saluteth you. [y]Erastus
the chamberlain of the city saluteth
you, and Quartus a brother.
24 [z]The grace of our Lord Jesus
Christ *be* with you all. Amen.
25 Now [a]to him that is of power to
stablish you [b]according to my gospel,
and the preaching of Jesus Christ, [c]according
to the revelation of the mystery,
[d]which was kept secret since the
world began,
26 But [e]now is made manifest, and
by the scriptures of the prophets, according
to the commandment of the
everlasting God, made known to all nations
for [f]the obedience of faith:
27 To [g]God only wise, *be* glory
through Jesus Christ for ever. Amen.

16:20 [q]ch. 15:33 [r]Gen. 3:15 [s]1 Cor. 16:23 **16:21** [t]Acts 16:1 Heb. 13:23 [u]Acts 13:1 [v]Acts 17:5 [w]Acts 20:4 **16:23** [x]1 Cor. 1:14 [y]Acts 19:22 **16:24** [z]1 Thes. 5:28 **16:25** [a]Eph. 3:20 [b]ch. 2:16 [c]Eph. 1:9 [d]Col. 1:26 **16:26** [e]Eph. 1:9 [f]Acts 6:7 **16:27** [g]Jude 25

[c] Or, *tread*

THE GIFTS OF THE HOLY SPIRIT

A. The Ministry Gifts of the Church

Gift	Definition	General References	Specific examples
Apostle (Specific)	Those specifically commissioned by the resurrected Lord to establish the church and the original message of the gospel	Acts 4:33–37; 5:12,18–42; 6:6; 8:14,18; 9:27; 11:1; 15:1–6,22–23; 16:4; 1 Cor. 9:5; 12:28–29; Gal. 1:17; Eph. 2:20; 4:11; Jude 17	12 apostles: Mat. 10:2; Mark 3:14; Luke 6:13; Acts 1:15–26; Rev. 21:14 Paul: Rom. 1:1; 11:13; 1 Cor. 1:1; 9:1–2; 15:9–10; 2 Cor. 1:1; Gal. 1:1; 1 Tim. 2:7 Peter: 1 Pet. 1:1; 2 Pet. 1:1
Apostle (General)	Any messenger commissioned as a missionary or for other special responsibilities	Acts 13:1–3; 1 Cor. 12:28–29; Eph. 4:11	Barnabas: Acts 14:4,14 Andronicus and Junias: Rom. 16:7 Titus and others: 2 Cor. 8:23 Epaphroditus: Phil. 2:25 James, Jesus' brother: Gal. 1:19
Prophet	Those who spoke under the inspiration of the Holy Spirit, bringing a message from God to the church, and whose main motivation and concern were with the spiritual life and purity of the church	Rom. 12:6; 1 Cor. 12:10; 14:1–33; Eph. 4:11; 1 Thes. 5:20–21; 1 Tim. 1:18; 1 Pet. 4:11; 1 John 4:1–3	Peter: Acts 2:14–40; 3:12–26; 4:8–12; 10:34–44 Paul: Acts 13:1,16–41 Barnabas: Acts 13:1 Simeon: Acts 13:1 Lucius: Acts 13:1 Manaen: Acts 13:1 Agabus: Acts 11:27–28; 21:10 Judas and Silas: Acts 15:32 John: Rev. 1:1,3; 10:8–11; 11:18
Evangelist	Those gifted by God to proclaim the gospel to the unsaved	Eph. 4:11	Philip: Acts 8:5–8,26–40; 21:8 Paul: Acts 26:16–18
Pastor (Elder or Overseer)	Those chosen and gifted to oversee the church and care for its spiritual needs	Acts 14:23; 15:1–6,22–23; 16:4; 20:17–38; Rom. 12:8; Eph. 4:11–12; Phil. 1:1; 1 Tim. 3:1–7; 5:17–20; Tit. 1:5–9; Heb. 13:17; 1 Pet. 5:1–5	Timothy: 1 Tim. 1:1–4; 4:12–16; 2 Tim. 1:1–6; 4:2,5 Titus: Tit. 1:4–5 Peter: 1 Pet. 5:1 John: 1 John 2:1,12–14 Gaius: 3 John 1–7

Gift	Definition	General References	Specific examples
Teacher	Those gifted to clarify and explain God's Word in order to build up the church	Rom. 12:7; Eph. 4:11–12; Col. 3:16; 1 Tim. 3:2; 5:17; 2 Tim. 2:2,24	Paul: Acts 15:35; 20:20; 28:31; Rom. 12:19–21; 13:8–10; 1 Cor. 4:17; 1 Tim. 1:5; 4:16; 2 Tim. 1:11 Barnabas: Acts 15:35 Apollos: Acts 18:25–28 Timothy: 1 Cor. 4:17; 1 Tim. 1:3–5; 4:11–13; 6:2; 2 Tim. 4:2 Titus: Tit. 2:1–3,9–10
Deacon	Those chosen and gifted to render practical assistance to members of the church	Acts 6:1–6; Rom. 12:7; Phil. 1:1; 1 Tim. 3:8–13; 1 Pet. 4:11	Seven deacons: Acts 6:5 Phoebe: Rom. 16:1–2
Helper	Those gifted for a variety of helpful deeds	1 Cor. 12:28	Paul: Acts 20:35 Lydia: Acts 16:14–15 Gaius: 3 John 5–8
Administrator	Those gifted to guide and oversee the various activities of the church	1 Cor. 12:7; Eph. 4:11–12; 1 Tim. 3:1–7; Heb. 13:7–17,24	Peter: Acts 6:3–4; 11:1–18 Paul: Acts 20:17–35; 1 Cor. 11:23–24; 14; 16:1–9
Exhorter	Those gifted to motivate other Christians to a deeper faith and dedication to Christ, a fuller manifestation of the fruit of the Holy Spirit, and a more complete separation from the world	Rom. 12:8; 1 Cor. 14:3; 1 Thes. 5:11,14–22; Heb. 10:24–25	Barnabas: Acts 11:23–24; 14:22 Paul: Acts 14:22; 16:40; 20:1; Rom. 8:26–39; 12:1–2; 2 Cor. 6:14–7:1; Gal. 5:16–26 Judas and Silas: Acts 15:32; 16:40 Timothy: 1 Thes. 3:2; 2 Tim. 4:2 Titus: Tit. 2:6,13 Peter: 1 Pet. 5:1–2 John: 1 John 2:15–17; 3:1–3
Giver	Those gifted to give freely of their resources to the needs of God's people	Acts 2:44–45; 4:34–35; 11:29–30; 1 Cor. 16:1–4; 2 Cor. 8–9; Eph. 4:28; 1 Tim. 6:17–19; Heb. 13:16; 1 John 3:16–18	Barnabas: Acts 4:36–37 Christians in Macedonia: Rom. 15:26–27; 2 Cor. 8:1–5 Christians in Achaia: Rom. 15:26–27; 2 Cor. 9:2

Gift	Definition	General References	Specific examples
Comforter	Those gifted to give comfort by acts of mercy to people in distress	Rom. 12:8; 2 Cor. 1:3–7	Paul: 2 Cor. 1:4 Hebrew Christians: Heb. 10:34 Various Christians: Col. 4:10–11 Dorcas: Acts 9:36–39

B. Manifestations of the Holy Spirit through Individual Believers

Gift	Definition	General References	Specific examples
Word of wisdom	An utterance from the Holy Spirit applying God's Word or wisdom to a specific situation	Acts 6:3; 1 Cor. 12:8; 13:2,9,12	Stephen: Acts 6:10 James: Acts 15:13–21
Word of knowledge	An utterance from the Holy Spirit revealing knowledge about people, circumstances, or Biblical truth	Acts 10:47–48; 13:2; 15:7–11; 1 Cor. 12:8; 13:2,9,12; 14:25	Peter: Acts 5:9–10
Faith	Supernatural faith imparted by the Holy Spirit, enabling a Christian to believe God for the miraculous	Mat. 21:21–22; Mark 9:23–24; 11:22–24; Luke 17:6; Acts 3:1–8; 6:5–8; 1 Cor. 12:9; 13:2; Jas. 5:14–15	A centurion: Mat. 8:5–10 A sick woman: Mat. 9:20–22 Two blind men: Mat. 9:27–29 A Canaanite woman: Mat. 15:22–28 A sinful woman: Luke 9:36–50 A leper: Luke 17:11–19
Healing	Restoring someone to physical health by divinely supernatural means	Mat. 4:23–24; 8:16; 9:35; 10:1,8; Mark 1:32–34; 6:13; 16:18; Luke 4:40–41; 9:1–2; John 6:2; 14:12; Acts 4:30; 5:15–16; 19:11–12; 1 Cor. 12:9,28,30	Jesus: see chart on THE MIRACLES OF JESUS, p. 1645 Apostles: see chart on THE MIRACLES OF THE APOSTLES, p. 1646
Miracles	Divine supernatural power to alter the course of nature, including casting out demons	Mat. 4:23–24; 8:16; 10:1,8; 13:54; Mark 1:32–33,39; 3:15; 6:13; 16:17; Luke 4:40–41; 9:1; 10:17; John 7:3; 10:25,32; 14:11; 15:24; Acts 2:22,43; 4:30; 5:15–16; 6:8; 8:6–7; 14:3; 15:12; 19:11–12; Rom. 15:19; 1 Cor. 12;10,29; 2 Cor. 12:12; Gal. 3:5	Jesus: see chart on THE MIRACLES OF JESUS, p. 1645 Apostles: see chart on THE MIRACLES OF THE APOSTLES, p. 1646

Gift	Definition	General References	Specific examples
Prophecy	A special temporary ability to bring a word, warning, exhortation, or revelation from God under the impulse of the Holy Spirit	Luke 12:12; Acts 2:17–18; 1 Cor. 12:10; 13:9; 14:1–33; Eph. 4:11; 1 Thes. 5:20–21; 2 Pet. 1:20–21; 1 John 4:1–3	Elizabeth: Luke 1:40–45 Mary: Luke 1:46–55 Zacharias: Luke 1:67–79 Peter: Acts 2:14–40; 4:8–12 Twelve men from Ephesus: Acts 19:6 Four daughters of Philip: Acts 21:9 Agabus: Acts 21:10–11
Discerning of spirits	Special ability to judge whether prophecies and utterances are from the Holy Spirit	1 Cor. 12:10; 14:29	Peter: Acts 8:18–24 Paul: Acts 13:8–12; 16:16–18
Speaking in tongues	Expressing oneself at the level of one's spirit under the direct influence of the Holy Spirit in a language he or she has not learned and does not know	1 Cor. 12:10,28,30; 13:1; 14:1–40	Disciples: Acts 2:4–11 Cornelius and his family: Acts 10:44–45; 11:17 Ephesian believers: Acts 19:2–7 Paul: 1 Cor. 14:6,15,18
Interpretation of tongues	Special ability to interpret what is spoken in tongues	1 Cor. 12:10,30; 14:5,13,26–28	

1 CORINTHIANS

Outline

Introduction (1:1–9)

I. Discussion of Problems About Which Paul Had Been Informed (1:10—6:20)

A. Divisions in the Church (1:10—4:21)

1. Four Factions (1:10–17)
2. Causes of the Divisions (1:18—4:5)
   a. A Wrong Conception of Wisdom (1:18—3:4)
   b. A Wrong Conception of Christian Ministry (3:5—4:5)
3. An Appeal for Reconciliation (4:6–21)

Principle: The church as the one body of Christ (cf. 12:12ff) should not be split into separate parts (1:10,13)

B. Moral Problems in the Church (5:1—6:20)

1. A Problem of Incest and Church Discipline (5:1–13)
2. The Problem of Secular Lawsuits Between Christians (6:1–11)
3. The Problem of Fornication (6:12–20)

Principle: You who are united with the Lord should conduct yourself so as to bring honor to Him (6:17,20)

II. Answers to Questions About Which the Corinthians Had Written (7:1—16:9)

A. Questions Concerning Marriage (7:1–40)

1. Marriage and Celibacy (7:1–9)
2. Christian Obligations in Marriage (7:10–16)
3. Principle of Contentment (7:17–24)
4. Counsel to the Unmarried (7:25–38)
5. Instruction About Remarriage (7:39–40)

Principle: God gives some the gift of a husband or wife; others he gives the gift of remaining single for the sake of the kingdom (7:7,32)

B. Questions Concerning the Use of Christian Liberty (8:1—11:1)

1. The Problem of Food Offered to Idols (8:1–13)
2. Paul's Disciplined Use of Liberty (9:1–27)
3. A Warning Against Presumptuous Overconfidence (10:1–13)
4. The Incompatibility of Pagan Feasts and the Lord's Table (10:14–23)
5. Some General Principles and Practical Advice (10:24—11:1)

Principle: Do everything to bring glory to God; do nothing that might make others stumble (10:31–32) or might disqualify yourself from the race (9:24–27)

C. Questions Concerning Public Worship (11:2—14:40)

1. Women's Head Covering in Church (11:2–16)
2. Behavior at the Lord's Supper (11:17–34)
3. Spiritual Gifts (12:1—14:40)

Principle: Let all things be done in a proper and orderly manner (14:40)

D. Questions Concerning the Resurrection (15:1–58)

1. Q. How Do Some Say There is No Resurrection of the Dead? (15:12)
   A. The Certainty of the Resurrection (15:1–34)
2. Q. How Are the Dead Raised? And with What Kind of Body Do They Come? (15:35)
   A. The Nature of the Resurrection Body (15:35–57)

3. Conclusion to the Question (15:58)
Principle: As Christ was raised from the dead, so will be all those who are Christ's when He comes back (15:22–23)
E. Questions Concerning the Collection for the Saints (16:1–9)
Final Instructions (16:10–24)

Author: Paul

Theme: Church Problems and Solutions

Date of Writing: A.D. 55/56

Background

Corinth, an ancient city of Greece, was in many ways the most prominent Greek metropolis of Paul's time. Like many of the prosperous cities of the world today, Corinth was intellectually arrogant, materially affluent, and morally corrupt. Sin of every kind flourished in this notoriously sensual city.

In conjunction with Priscilla and Aquila (16:19) and his own apostolic team (Acts 18:5), Paul founded the Corinthian church during his eighteen-month ministry at Corinth on his second missionary journey (Acts 18:1–17). The church was made up of some Jews but mostly of ex-pagan Gentiles. After Paul left Corinth, a variety of problems arose in the young church, requiring his apostolic authority and teaching by written correspondence and personal visits.

The first letter to the Corinthians was written during his three-year ministry at Ephesus (Acts 20:31) on his third missionary journey (Acts 18:23—21:16). Reports reached Paul at Ephesus about the problems at Corinth (1 Cor. 1:11); afterwards a delegation from the Corinthian congregation (16:17) delivered a letter to Paul, requesting his instruction on a variety of issues (7:1; cf. 8:1; 12:1; 16:1). In response to the reports and the letter from Corinth, Paul wrote this letter.

Purpose

Paul had two primary reasons in mind as he penned this epistle: (1) To reprove and correct the serious problems in the Corinthian church which had been reported to him. These were disorders which the Corinthians viewed lightly, but which Paul regarded as serious sin. (2) To provide counsel and instruction on a variety of questions about which the Corinthians had written. These included both issues of doctrine and personal and corporate conduct and purity.

Survey

This epistle addresses the kinds of problems that churches experience when members remain "carnal" (3:1–3) and do not decisively separate themselves from the pagan society around them (2 Cor. 6:17)—problems such as divisiveness (1:10–13; 11:17–22), tolerance of a sin like incest (5:1–13), sexual immorality in general (6:12–20), secular lawsuits between Christians (6:1–11), humanistic thinking about apostolic truth (ch. 15), and conflicts over "Christian liberty" (chs. 8; 10). Paul also instructs the Corinthians about matters related to celibacy and marriage (ch. 7), public worship, including the Lord's Supper (chs. 11—14), and the offering for the Jerusalem saints (16:1–4).

Among the most important contributions of 1 Corinthians is Paul's teaching on the manifestations and gifts of the Holy Spirit in the context of corporate worship (chs. 12—14). More than anywhere else in the N.T., these chapters provide insight into the character and components of worship in the early church (cf. 14:26–33). Paul indicates that God's purpose for the church includes a wide variety of the Spirit's manifestations occurring through faithful believers (12:4–10) and individuals called to certain ministries (12:28–30)—a diversity within unity analogous to the many functions of a human body (12:12–27). In providing guidelines for the corporate function of spiritual gifts, Paul makes an essential distinction between individual and corporate edification (14:2–6,12,16–19,26), insisting

that all public manifestations or gifts must flow from love (ch. 13) and exist for the edification of the gathered believers (12:7; 14:4–6,26).

Special Features

Five major features or emphases characterize 1 Corinthians. (1) It is the most problem-centered epistle in the N.T. In addressing the various problems and issues at Corinth, Paul gives clear and enduring spiritual principles (see the outline), each of which is applicable universally for the church (e.g. 1:10; 6:17,20; 7:7; 9:24–27; 10:31–32; 14:1–10; 15:22–23). (2) There is an overall emphasis on the oneness of the local church as the body of Christ, a focus which occurs in discussions about divisions, the Lord's Supper, and spiritual gifts. (3) This epistle contains the most extensive teaching in the N.T. on such important subjects as celibacy, marriage, and remarriage (ch. 7); the Lord's Supper (10:16–21; 11:17–34); tongues, prophecy, and spiritual gifts in corporate gatherings (chs. 12; 14); agape love (ch. 13); and the resurrection of the body (ch. 15). (4) It provides invaluable wisdom for pastoral oversight in relation to church discipline (ch. 5). (5) It emphasizes the real possibility of falling away from the faith by those who persist in unrighteous behavior and do not hold fast to Christ (6:9–10; 9:24–27; 10:5–12,20–21; 15:1–2).

Reading 1 Corinthians

In order to read the entire New Testament in one year, the book of 1 Corinthians should be read in 19 days, according to the following schedule:
☐ 1 ☐ 2 ☐ 3 ☐ 4 ☐ 5 ☐ 6 ☐ 7 ☐ 8 ☐ 9 ☐ 10:1–13 ☐ 10:14—11:1 ☐ 11:2–34 ☐ 12 ☐ 13 ☐ 14:1–25 ☐ 14:26–40 ☐ 15:1–34 ☐ 15:35–58 ☐ 16

NOTES

Paul's thanksgiving

1 PAUL, [a]CALLED *to be* an apostle
of Jesus Christ [b]through the will
of God, and Sosthenes *our* brother,
2 Unto the church of God which is at
Corinth, to them that [c]are sanctified
in Christ Jesus, [d]called *to be* saints,
with all that in every place call upon
the name of Jesus Christ [e]our Lord,
[f]both theirs and ours:
3 [g]Grace *be* unto you, and peace,
from God our Father, and *from* the Lord
Jesus Christ.
4 [h]I thank my God always on your
behalf, for the grace of God which is
given you by Jesus Christ;
5 That in every thing ye are enriched by him, [i]in all utterance, and *in*
all knowledge;
6 Even as [j]the testimony of Christ
was confirmed in you:
1 Cor. 12:1-31 7 So that ye come behind in no gift;
[k]waiting for the [a]coming of our Lord
Jesus Christ:
8 [l]Who shall also confirm you
unto the end, [m]*that ye may be* blameless in the day of our Lord Jesus
Christ.
9 [n]God *is* faithful, by whom ye were
called unto [o]the fellowship of his Son
Jesus Christ our Lord.

1:1 [a]Rom. 1:1 [b]2 Cor. 1:1
1:2 [c]Acts 15:9 [d]Rom. 1:7 [e]ch. 8:6 [f]Rom. 3:22
1:3 [g]Rom. 1:7 2 Cor. 1:2
1:4 [h]Rom. 1:8
1:5 [i]ch. 12:8
1:6 [j]2 Tim. 1:8 Rev. 1:2
1:7 [k]Phil. 3:20 Tit. 2:13 2 Pet. 3:12
1:8 [l]1 Thes. 3:13 [m]Col. 1:22
1:9 [n]Is. 49:7 1 Thes. 5:24 [o]John 15:4
1:10 [p]2 Cor. 13:11 1 Pet. 3:8
1:12 [q]ch. 3:4 [r]Acts 18:24 [s]John 1:42
1:13 [t]2 Cor. 11:4
1:14 [u]Acts 18:8 [v]Rom. 16:23
1:16 [w]ch. 16:15
1:17 [x]ch. 2:4

An appeal for unity

10 Now I beseech you, brethren, by
the name of our Lord Jesus Christ,
[p]that ye all speak the same thing, and
that there be no [b]divisions among you;
but *that* ye be perfectly joined together
in the same mind and in the same judgment.
11 For it hath been declared unto
me of you, my brethren, by them *which
are of the house* of Chloe, that there are
contentions among you.
12 Now this I say, [q]that every one
of you saith, I am of Paul; and I of
[r]Apollos; and I of [s]Cephas; and I of
Christ.
13 [t]Is Christ divided? was Paul
crucified for you? or were ye baptized
in the name of Paul?
14 I thank God that I baptized none
of you, but [u]Crispus and [v]Gaius;
15 Lest any should say that I had
baptized in mine own name.
16 And I baptized also the household of [w]Stephanas: besides, I know
not whether I baptized any other.
17 For Christ sent me not to baptize, but to preach the gospel: [x]not
with wisdom of [c]words, lest the cross
of Christ should be made of none effect.

[a] Gk. *revelation* [b] Gk. *schisms* [c] Or, *speech*

1:2 CALLED *TO BE* SAINTS. See Acts 9:13, note on the meaning of the term "saints."

1:7 YE COME BEHIND IN NO GIFT. Paul commends the Corinthians because God in His grace (v. 4) has bestowed upon them specific spiritual gifts. Such gifts are a valuable and indispensable accompaniment of the Holy Spirit's ministry in the church; without them believers fail to strengthen and help one another as God desires. Nowhere in this epistle does Paul seek to eliminate these gifts. Rather he seeks to change the attitude of the Corinthians toward spiritual gifts so that they use their gifts according to God's intention.

1:7 WAITING FOR THE COMING OF OUR LORD. The early Christians lived in expectation of the imminent return of Christ (see Mat. 24:42, note; John 14:3, note). They fixed their faith firmly on the fact of the Lord's coming, living every day in anticipation of that great hope. Note that the Christian's hope is for the personal return of the Lord Jesus Christ, not for the general complex of events that comprises the last days (cf. 1 Thes. 1:9–10; 4:13–17; Tit. 2:13; Heb. 9:28; see article on BIBLICAL HOPE, p. 834).

1:12 I AM OF PAUL . . . APOLLOS . . . CEPHAS. Division over leaders in the church was beginning to develop; some members in the church were becoming more attached to certain ministers of the gospel than to the gospel itself. Paul condemns this attitude, reminding them that neither he nor any other man was crucified for them. This same error is present today. Some believers become more attached to a pastor or evangelist than to Christ and His Word. This disposition can cause them to betray Christian principles and even divide the church. We must always be careful to center our love, devotion, and loyalty upon God and His Word, not on any minister or person.

1:12 I AM . . . OF CHRIST. The "Christ party" probably consisted of false teachers who were enemies of the apostle (4:18–19) and claimed to have a superior spirituality and "wisdom." They believed that their knowledge (8:1) brought freedom from the restraints of the law (6:12; 10:23) and from the demands of morality (5:2). They were attempting to win the church over to their own distorted gospel (2 Cor. 11:4,20–21). It is against them and their converts at Corinth that Paul mainly contends.

1:17 CHRIST SENT ME NOT TO BAPTIZE. Paul is not minimizing Jesus' teaching concerning baptism (Mat. 28:19). Rather, he makes it clear that he delegated the performing of baptism to his associates, as did Christ (John 4:1–2) and Peter (Acts 10:47–48). The apostle does not want to provide an opportunity for his converts to presume that they were "baptized in the name of Paul" (v. 13). For himself, Paul focused on preaching the gospel.

Christ, God's power and wisdom

18 For the preaching of the cross is to [y]them that perish [z]foolishness; but unto us [a]which are saved it is the [b]power of God.

19 For it is written, [c]I will destroy the wisdom of the wise, and will bring to nothing the understanding of the prudent.

20 [d]Where *is* the wise? where *is* the scribe? where *is* the disputer of this world? [e]hath not God made foolish the wisdom of this world?

21 [f]For after that in the wisdom of God the world by wisdom knew not God, it pleased God by the foolishness of preaching to save them that believe.

22 For the [g]Jews require a sign, and the Greeks seek after wisdom:

23 But we preach Christ crucified, [h]unto the Jews a stumblingblock, and unto the Greeks [i]foolishness;

24 But unto them which are called, both Jews and Greeks, Christ [j]the power of God, and [k]the wisdom of God.

25 Because the foolishness of God is wiser than men; and the weakness of God is stronger than men.

26 For ye see your calling, brethren, how that [l]not many wise men after the flesh, not many mighty, not many noble, *are called:*

27 But [m]God hath chosen the foolish things of the world to confound the wise; and God hath chosen the weak things of the world to confound the things which are mighty;

28 And base things of the world, and things which are despised, hath God chosen, *yea,* and [n]things which are not, [o]to bring to nought things that are:

29 [p]That no flesh should glory in his presence.

30 But of him are ye in Christ Jesus, who of God is made unto us [q]wisdom, and [r]righteousness, and [s]sanctification, and [t]redemption:

31 That, according as it is written, [u]He that glorieth, let him glory in the Lord.

The gospel in Spirit and power

2 AND I, brethren, when I came to you, [v]came not with excellency of speech or of wisdom, declaring unto you [w]the testimony of God.

1:18 [y]2 Cor. 2:15 [z]Acts 17:18 [a]ch. 15:2 [b]Rom. 1:16 **1:19** [c]Is. 29:14 **1:20** [d]Is. 33:18 [e]Job 12:17 Is. 44:25 Rom. 1:22 **1:21** [f]Mat. 11:25 Luke 10:21 Rom. 1:20 **1:22** [g]Mat. 12:38 Mark 8:11 John 4:48 **1:23** [h]Is. 8:14 Luke 2:34 John 6:60 Gal. 5:11 [i]ch. 2:14 **1:24** [j]Rom. 1:4 [k]Col. 2:3 **1:26** [l]John 7:48 **1:27** [m]Mat. 11:25 **1:28** [n]Rom. 4:17 [o]ch. 2:6 **1:29** [p]Rom. 3:27 Eph. 2:9 **1:30** [q]ver. 24 [r]Jer. 23:5 Rom. 4:25 2 Cor. 5:21 [s]John 17:19 [t]Eph. 1:7 **1:31** [u]Jer. 9:23 **2:1** [v]ch. 1:17 [w]ch. 1:6

1:18 IT IS THE POWER OF GOD. The message of the cross not only involves wisdom and truth, but the active power of God coming down to save, heal, cast out the demonic, and redeem from the power of sin (see article on THE KINGDOM OF GOD, p. 1428).

1:20 THE WISDOM OF THIS WORLD. The wisdom of this world is a wisdom that excludes God, emphasizes human self-sufficiency, makes man the highest authority, and refuses to recognize God's revelation in Jesus Christ. (1) This wisdom God calls foolishness (3:19–20), for through it humans have failed to find the truth or come to know their Creator (v. 21). (2) The believer must develop a godly contempt for both human wisdom and a secular world view (see vv. 18–31; 2:1–16; Acts 17:18; Rom. 1:20–32; Col. 2:8, note; 2 Thes. 2:10–12; 2 Tim. 3:1–9; 2 Pet. 2:1–3,7; Jude 4–19). The gospel and the message of the cross must never be accommodated to philosophy, science, or any other so-called wisdom of man (2:4–5; Gal. 6:14).

1:21 THE FOOLISHNESS OF PREACHING. The word translated "preaching" should be translated "what is preached." It is not the method of preaching that is considered foolish, but the message of the Lordship of the crucified and resurrected Christ.

1:27 GOD HATH CHOSEN THE FOOLISH THINGS. In vv. 25–29, Paul emphasizes that God's standards and values are different from those accepted by the world and that He is now in the process of overthrowing its false standards and wisdom.

1:28 BRING TO NOUGHT THINGS THAT ARE. Through the crucifixion and resurrection of Jesus (vv. 18,23) and through choosing the lowly things of this world (vv. 26–27), God nullifies the esteemed things of this present age. God is now in the process of bringing humanistic philosophies, psychologies, and all other worldly systems to an end.

1:30 CHRIST JESUS . . . IS MADE UNTO US. It is through Christ, in Christ, and with Christ that the believer receives wisdom from God and experiences righteousness (cf. Rom. 4), sanctification (2 Thes. 2:13–15) and redemption (Rom. 3:24; Eph. 4:30). As long as one is joined to Christ, He is the source of all these blessings (see John 15:1–6, notes on abiding in Christ).

2:1 I CAME . . . NOT WITH . . . WISDOM. The content of Paul's preaching was not according to the latest human "wisdom," either in the world or the church. Instead he concentrated on the central truth of the gospel (redemption through Christ) and on the power of the Holy Spirit (see next note). He was quite aware of his human limitations, his personal inadequacy, and his inner fear and trembling. Consequently, he did not rely on himself but on his message and on the Holy Spirit (v. 4). This resulted in a greater demonstration of the Spirit's work and power.

2 For I determined not to know any thing among you, [x]save Jesus Christ, and him crucified.

3 And [y]I was with you [z]in weakness, and in fear, and in much trembling.

4 And my speech and my preaching [a]*was* not with [d]enticing words of man's wisdom, [b]but in demonstration of the Spirit and of power:

5 That your faith should not [e]stand in the wisdom of men, but [c]in the power of God.

True wisdom the gift of God

6 Howbeit we speak wisdom among them [d]that are perfect: yet not [e]the wisdom of this world, nor of the princes of this world, [f]that come to nought:

7 But we speak the wisdom of God in a mystery, *even* the hidden *wisdom*, [g]which God ordained before the world unto our glory:

8 [h]Which none of the princes of this world knew: for [i]had they known *it*, they would not have crucified the Lord of glory.

9 But as it is written, [j]Eye hath not seen, nor ear heard, neither have entered into the heart of man, the things which God hath prepared for them that love him.

10 But [k]God hath revealed *them* unto us by his Spirit: for the Spirit searcheth all things, yea, the deep things of God.

11 For what man knoweth the things of a man, [l]save the spirit of man which is in him? [m]even so the things of God knoweth no man, but the Spirit of God.

12 Now we have received, not the spirit of the world, but [n]the spirit which is of God; that we might know the things that are freely given to us of God.

13 Which things also we speak, not in the words which man's wisdom teacheth, but which the Holy Ghost

2:2 [x]Gal. 6:14 Phil. 3:8
2:3 [y]Acts 18:1 [z]2 Cor. 4:7
2:4 [a]2 Pet. 1:16 [b]Rom. 15:19
2:5 [c]2 Cor. 4:7
2:6 [d]ch. 14:20 Heb. 5:14 [e]2 Cor. 1:12 [f]ch. 1:28
2:7 [g]Eph. 3:5 Col. 1:26
2:8 [h]Mat. 11:25 [i]Luke 23:34
2:9 [j]Is. 64:4
2:10 [k]Mat. 13:11
2:11 [l]Prov. 20:27 Jer. 17:9 [m]Rom. 11:33
2:12 [n]Rom. 8:15

[d] Or, *persuasible* [e] Gk. *be*

2:4 IN DEMONSTRATION OF THE SPIRIT AND OF POWER. (1) As a demonstration of the Holy Spirit's power (1:18,24), Paul's preaching included (a) the Holy Spirit's convicting people of sin, righteousness, and judgment, and His bearing witness to the saving power of the risen Christ (cf. chs. 5–6; see John 16:8, note; Acts 2:36–41); (b) the power to transform lives (1:26–27; cf. Acts 4:13); (c) the power to effect holiness in the believer (5:3–5); and (d) God's power manifested by signs and wonders (Acts 2:29–33; 4:29–30; 5:12; 14:3; 2 Cor. 12:12).

(2) Several other N.T. passages emphasize that the preaching of the gospel in N.T. times was accompanied by a special power of the Holy Spirit: 4:20; Mark 16:17–18; Luke 10:19; Acts 28:3–6; Rom. 15:19; 1 Thes. 1:5; Heb. 2:4.

(3) Every minister of the gospel should pray that through his ministry (a) souls will be saved (Acts 2:41; 11:21,24; 14:1), (b) new believers will be filled with the Holy Spirit (Acts 2:4; 4:31; 8:17; 19:6), (c) evil spirits will be cast out (Acts 5:16; 8:7; 16:18), (d) the sick will be healed (Acts 3:6; 4:29–30; 14:10), and (e) disciples will learn to obey Christ's righteous standards and teachings (Mat. 28:18–20; Acts 11:23,26; see article on SIGNS OF BELIEVERS, p. 1516).

2:12 THAT WE MIGHT KNOW. The things which God has prepared for those who love Him (v. 9) can be understood by the believer through the Spirit's revelation and illumination (vv. 10–16). As the believer reads and studies the Bible, the Holy Spirit illuminates his understanding of the truth. The Spirit also gives to the faithful believer a strong assurance of the divine origin of Scripture (John 16:13; Eph. 1:17).

2:13 WORDS . . . WHICH THE HOLY GHOST TEACHETH. Though Paul is writing about the divine origin of his preaching, vv. 9–13 suggest the steps by which the Holy Spirit also inspired the writing of Scripture.

Step 1: God desired to communicate His wisdom to mankind (vv. 7–9). This wisdom concerned our salvation, centering in Christ as the wisdom of God (cf. 1:30; 2:2,5).

Step 2: It is only through the Holy Spirit that God's truth and wisdom were revealed to humanity (v. 10). The Holy Spirit knows fully the thoughts of God (v. 11).

Step 3: God's revelation was given to chosen believers through the indwelling presence of the Spirit (v. 12; cf. Rom. 8:11,15).

Step 4: The writers of Scripture wrote with words taught by the Holy Spirit (v. 13); the Holy Spirit directed the writers in the choice of the words they used (cf. Ex. 24:4; Is. 51:16; Jer. 1:9; 36:28,32; Ezek. 2:7; Mat. 4:4). At the same time, the Spirit's guidance in the expression of divine truth was not mechanical; rather the Spirit used each writer's vocabulary and personal style.

Step 5: The divinely inspired Scripture is understood by spiritual believers as they examine its content through the illumination of the Holy Spirit (vv. 14–16).

Thus, both the thoughts and language of the Scriptures were inspired by the Spirit of God. Not a single writer uttered a false word or phrase. The Word of God was protected from error by the Holy Spirit (see articles on THE WORD OF GOD, p. 1064, and THE INSPIRATION AND AUTHORITY OF SCRIPTURE, p. 1924).

teacheth; comparing spiritual things with spiritual.

14 [o]But the natural man receiveth not the things of the Spirit of God: [p]for they are foolishness unto him: [q]neither can he know *them,* because they are spiritually discerned.

15 [r]But he that is spiritual [f]judgeth all things, yet he himself is [g]judged of no man.

16 [s]For who hath known the mind of the Lord, that he [h]may instruct him? [t]But we have the mind of Christ.

Immature believers

3 AND I, brethren, could not speak unto you as unto [u]spiritual, but as unto [v]carnal, *even* as unto [w]babes in Christ.

2 I have fed you with [x]milk, and not with meat: [y]for hitherto ye were not able *to bear it,* neither yet now are ye able.

3 For ye are yet carnal: for [z]whereas *there is* among you envying, and strife, and [i]divisions, are ye not carnal, and walk [j]as men?

4 For while one saith, I am of Paul; and another, I *am* of Apollos; are ye not carnal?

Fellow workers with God

5 Who then is Paul, and who *is* Apollos, but [a]ministers by whom ye believed, [b]even as the Lord gave to every man?

6 [c]I have planted, [d]Apollos watered; [e]but God gave the increase.

7 So then [f]neither is he that planteth any thing, neither he that watereth; but God that giveth the increase.

8 Now he that planteth and he that watereth are one: [g]and every man shall receive his own reward according to his own labour.

9 For [h]we are labourers together with God: ye are God's [k]husbandry, *ye are* [i]God's building.

Loss of reward with God

10 [j]According to the grace of God which is given unto me, as a wise masterbuilder, I have laid [k]the foundation, and another buildeth thereon. But let every man take heed how he buildeth thereupon.

11 For other foundation can no man lay than [l]that is laid, [m]which is Jesus Christ.

12 Now if any man build upon this foundation gold, silver, precious stones, wood, hay, stubble;

13 Every man's work shall be made manifest: for the day [n]shall declare it, because [o]it [l]shall be revealed by fire; and the fire shall try every man's work of what sort it is.

2:14 [o]Mat. 16:23 [p]ch. 1:18,23 [q]Jude 19
2:15 [r]1 John 4:1
2:16 [s]Job 15:8 [t]John 15:15
3:1 [u]ch. 2:15 [v]ch. 2:14 [w]Heb. 5:13
3:2 [x]Heb. 5:12 1 Pet. 2:2 [y]John 16:12
3:3 [z]Gal. 5:20 Jas. 3:16
3:5 [a]2 Cor. 3:3 [b]Rom. 12:3 1 Pet. 4:11
3:6 [c]Acts 18:4 2 Cor. 10:14 [d]Acts 18:24 & 19:1 [e]2 Cor. 3:5
3:7 [f]2 Cor. 12:11 Gal. 6:3
3:8 [g]Ps. 62:12 Rom. 2:6 Gal. 6:4,5
3:9 [h]Acts 15:4 2 Cor. 6:1 [i]Eph. 2:20 Col. 2:7 Heb. 3:3,4
3:10 [j]Rom. 1:5 & 12:3 [k]ch. 4:15
3:11 [l]Is. 28:16 Mat. 16:18 2 Cor. 11:4 [m]Eph. 2:20
3:13 [n]1 Pet. 1:7 [o]Luke 2:35

[f] Or, *discerneth* [g] Or, *discerned* [h] Gk. *shall* [i] Or, *factions* [j] Gk. *according to man?* [k] Or, *tillage* [l] Gk. *is revealed*

2:14–15 THE NATURAL MAN . . . HE THAT IS SPIRITUAL. For comments on this verse, see article on THREE KINDS OF PEOPLE, p. 1772.

2:16 WE HAVE THE MIND OF CHRIST. To have the mind of Christ means knowing His will and His redemptive plan and purpose (vv. 9–10). It means appraising and seeing things the way God sees them, valuing things the way He values them, loving what He loves, and hating what He hates (v. 15; Heb. 1:9). It means understanding the holiness of God and the awfulness of sin. Thus, receiving the Spirit and following the Spirit (v. 12) cause the believer's values and world view to become radically different from the ways and wisdom of this age (cf. Phil. 2:5–8).

3:1 NOT . . . SPIRITUAL. One of the major problems of the Corinthian church was its attempt to experience the blessings of God while refusing to separate itself from the evil ways of the world (see article on THE CHRISTIAN'S RELATIONSHIP TO THE WORLD, p. 2004). (1) The pastors and leaders of the Corinthian church were allowing professed converts to come into the congregations without forsaking many of their evil practices. The Corinthians were tolerating within their fellowship: selfish divisions (11:18), the world's philosophy (1:18–25; 3:19), jealousy and strife (3:3), pride (3:21; 4:7), immorality (5:1), trivial lawsuits (6:1–8), attendance at idolatrous festivals (chs. 8; 10), and the rejection of apostolic teaching (14:36–37). Because the Corinthians failed to see the absolute necessity of apostolic truth, love, and godly standards (6:9–10; 13), they abused the gifts of the Spirit (chs. 12; 14) and the "Lord's supper" (11:20–34), and distorted the message of the gospel (1:18–31).

(2) Jesus Himself warns that any church which tolerates within its fellowship the unrighteous practices of the world or the distortion of Biblical truth (see Rev. 2:20, note) will be rejected by Him and lose its place in the kingdom of God (see Rev. 2:5,16; 3:15–16). The Spirit calls such a church to true repentance (5:2), to separation from the world (2 Cor. 6:16–18), and to "perfecting holiness in the fear of God" (2 Cor. 7:1).

3:3 YE ARE YET CARNAL. For comments on the difference between carnal and spiritual Christians, see article on THREE KINDS OF PEOPLE, p. 1772.

THREE KINDS OF PEOPLE

***1 Cor. 2:14–15** "But the natural man receiveth not the things of the Spirit of God: for they are foolishness unto him: neither can he know* them, *because they are spiritually discerned. But he that is spiritual judgeth all things, yet he himself is judged of no man."*

BASIC DIVISION. Scripture normally divides all humans into two classes. (1) The natural man/woman (Gk. *psuchikos*, 1 Cor. 2:14) identifies the unregenerated or fleshly person, i.e., one governed by mere natural instincts (2 Pet. 2:12). This kind of person does not have the Holy Spirit (Rom. 8:9), is under the dominion of Satan (Acts 26:18), and is enslaved to the body and its passions (Eph. 2:3). He belongs to the world, is in sympathy with it (Jas. 4:4), and rejects the righteous ways of the Spirit (1 Cor. 2:14). The natural person is not able to understand God and His ways, but instead relies on human reasoning or emotions.

(2) The spiritual man/woman (Gk. *pneumatikos*, 1 Cor. 2:15; 3:1) identifies the regenerated person, i.e., one who has the Holy Spirit. This person is spiritually minded, thinks the thoughts of God (1 Cor. 2:11–13), and lives by the Spirit of God (Rom. 8:4–17; Gal. 5:16–26). Such an individual believes in Jesus Christ, endeavors to follow the leading of the indwelling Spirit, and resists sensual desires and the dominion of sin (Rom. 8:13–14).

How does one become a spiritual man/woman? When a person accepts by faith the salvation provided through Christ, he is regenerated; the Holy Spirit imparts to him or her a new nature by an infusion of divine life (2 Pet. 1:4; see article on REGENERATION, p. 1597). He is born again (John 3:3,5,7), renewed (Rom. 12:2), made a new creation (2 Cor. 5:17), and receives God's righteousness through faith in Christ (Phil. 3:9).

FURTHER DISTINCTION AMONG CHRISTIANS. Although regenerated believers receive the new life of the Spirit, they retain the sinful nature with its evil inclinations (Gal. 5:16–21). The sinful nature that remains in them cannot be made good; it must be put to death and overcome through the power and grace of the Holy Spirit (Rom. 8:13). They accomplish this by denying themselves daily (Mat. 16:24; Rom. 8:12–13; Tit. 2:12), removing every hindrance or sin (Heb. 12:1), and resisting all sinful inclinations (Rom. 13:14; Gal. 5:16; 1 Pet. 2:11). Believers themselves, by the power of the Spirit, must wage war against the sinful nature (Rom. 8:13–14; Gal. 5:16–18), crucify it (Gal. 5:24), and put it to death daily (Col. 3:5). By this process of self-denial and yielding to the Holy Spirit's sanctifying work, believers in Christ will experience liberation from the power of their sinful nature and live their lives as spiritual Christians (Rom. 6:13; Gal. 5:16).

Not all Christians put forth the required effort to overcome fully this sinful nature, however. In addressing the Corinthians, Paul notes (1 Cor. 3:1,3) that some of them were behaving in a carnal or fleshly way (Gk. *sarkikos*); that is, instead of consistently resisting the inclinations of their sinful nature, they yielded to at least some of them. Although they were not living in persistent disobedience, they were in the process of compromising with the world, the flesh, and the devil in some areas of their lives, while still wanting to remain a part of the people of God (10:21; 2 Cor. 6:14–18; 11:3; 13:5).

(1) The condition of carnal Christians. Although carnality and rebellion were not the rule in their lives, nor had they entered into the serious immorality and unrighteousness that would separate them from the kingdom of God (see 1 Cor. 6:9–11; cf. Gal. 5:19–21; Eph. 5:5), carnal Christians were behaving in such a way that they were no longer growing in grace and were acting as if they were new converts who did not yet understand the full implication of salvation in Christ (1 Cor. 3:1–2). Their carnality was

expressed in "envying, and strife" (3:3). They were indifferent to and tolerant of immorality within the church (5:1–13; 6:13–20). They did not take the Word of God or His apostle with utmost seriousness (4:18–19). They were going to law courts over trivial matters (6:7–8). However, it should be noted that the Corinthians who had entered into sexual immorality or other gross sins are considered by the apostle Paul as being excluded altogether from salvation in Christ (1 Cor. 5:1,9–11; 6:9–10).

(2) The perils of carnal Christians. The carnal Christians of Corinth were in danger of being led astray from sincere and pure devotion to Christ (2 Cor. 11:3) and being more and more conformed to the world (cf. 2 Cor. 6:14–18). Because of their carnality, they would be chastened and judged by the Lord, and if they continued to conform to the world, they would ultimately be excluded from the kingdom of God (1 Cor. 6:9–10; 11:31–32). In fact, spiritual death had already occurred for some of them who had committed flagrant sin heading to spiritual death (see 1 John 3:15, note; 5:17, note; cf. Rom. 8:13; 1 Cor. 5:5; 2 Cor. 12:21; 13:5).

(3) The warnings to carnal Christians. (a) Carnal Christians must realize that they are in danger of departing from the faith if they are unwilling to cleanse themselves from all that displeases God (Rom. 6:14–16; 1 Cor. 6:9–10; 2 Cor. 11:3; Gal. 6:7–9; Jas. 1:12–16). (b) They must take warnings from the tragic example of the children of Israel whom God destroyed because of sin (1 Cor. 10:5–12). (c) They must understand that it is impossible to partake of the things of the Lord and the things of Satan at the same time (Mat. 6:24; 1 Cor. 10:21). (d) They must separate themselves completely from the world (2 Cor. 6:14–18) and purify themselves from everything that contaminates body and spirit, perfecting holiness in the fear of the Lord (2 Cor. 7:1).

14 If any man's work abide which
he hath built thereupon, he shall re-
ceive a reward.
15 If any man's work shall be
burned, he shall suffer loss: but he
himself shall be saved; yet so as by
fire.
16 [p]Know ye not that ye are the
temple of God, and *that* the Spirit of
God dwelleth in you?
17 If any man [m]defile the temple of
God, him shall God destroy; for the
temple of God is holy, which *temple* ye
are.
18 [q]Let no man deceive himself. If
any man among you seemeth to be wise
in this world, let him become a fool,
that he may be wise.
19 For the wisdom of this world is
foolishness with God. For it is written,
[r]He taketh the wise in their own craft-
iness.
20 And again, [s]The Lord knoweth
the thoughts of the wise, that they are
vain.

3:16 [p]2 Cor. 6:16
3:18 [q]Prov. 3:7
3:19 [r]Job 5:13
3:20 [s]Ps. 94:11
3:21 [t]2 Cor. 4:5
3:23 [u]Rom. 14:8 2 Cor. 10:7 Gal. 3:29
4:1 [v]Mat. 24:45 Col. 1:25 [w]Luke 12:42 Tit. 1:7
4:5 [x]Mat. 7:1 Rom. 2:1 Rev. 20:12

21 Therefore let no man glory in
men. For [t]all things are yours;
22 Whether Paul, or Apollos, or Ce-
phas, or the world, or life, or death, or
things present, or things to come; all
are yours;
23 And [u]ye are Christ's; and Christ
is God's.

Apostles of Christ, the example

4 LET A man so account of us, as of
[v]the ministers of Christ, [w]and
stewards of the mysteries of God.
2 Moreover it is required in stew-
ards, that a man be found faithful.
3 But with me it is a very small
thing that I should be judged of you, or
of man's [n]judgment: yea, I judge not
mine own self.
4 For I know nothing by myself; yet
am I not hereby justified: but he that
judgeth me is the Lord.
5 [x]Therefore judge nothing before
the time, until the Lord come, who both

[m] Or, *destroy* [n] Gk. *day;* see ch. 3:13

3:15 HE SHALL SUFFER LOSS. The Bible asserts that all the redeemed are free from God's judgment of condemnation (John 5:24; Rom. 8:1; Heb. 10:14–17). However, there is a future judgment for believers (1 John 4:17) as to the degree of their faithfulness to God and the grace given unto them during this life on earth (v. 10; 4:2–5; 2 Cor. 5:10). In that judgment there is the possibility that a believer, although receiving salvation, may experience great loss (Gk. *zēmioō*, meaning "to suffer loss or damage").

The careless believer is in danger of suffering loss or damage in the following ways: (1) a feeling of shame at Christ's coming (2 Tim. 2:15; 1 John 2:28); (2) loss of his life's work for God (vv. 12–15); (3) loss of glory and honor before God (cf. Rom. 2:7); (4) loss of opportunity for service and authority in heaven (Mat. 25:14–30); (5) a low position in heaven (Mat. 5:19; 19:30); (6) loss of rewards (cf. vv. 14–15); and (7) repayment for the wrong done to others (Col. 3:24–25). These Scriptures should impress upon us the necessity of complete dedication, including faithful, self-sacrificing service to our Lord (cf. Rom. 12:1–2; Phil. 2:12; 4:3; see article on THE JUDGMENT OF BELIEVERS, p. 1811).

3:15 YET SO AS BY FIRE. Fire is probably an expression meaning "yet so only barely saved." God will evaluate the quality of life, influence, teaching, and work in the church of each person, and especially here, of each minister. If his work is judged unworthy, he will lose his reward, yet he himself may be saved. Note that this passage does not teach a doctrine of purgatory; it addresses a judgment of works, not the cleansing of a person from mortal sins.

3:16 YE ARE THE TEMPLE OF GOD. The emphasis here is on the entire congregation of believers as the temple of God and the dwelling place of the Holy Spirit (cf. v. 9; 2 Cor. 6:16; Eph. 2:21). As the temple of God in the midst of a perverse society, God's people in Corinth were not to participate in the evils prevalent in that society, but were to reject all forms of immorality. God's temple must be holy (v. 17) because God is holy (cf. 1 Pet. 1:14–16; see article on THE TEMPLE, p. 654).

3:17 HIM SHALL GOD DESTROY. Paul presents one of the strongest warnings in the N.T. to anyone responsible for building the church of Christ. This passage has special relevance to all those in teaching/leadership positions. If anyone defiles or corrupts God's temple (i.e., a local congregation or a group of congregations), God Himself will punish that individual with terrible ruin and eternal death. People corrupt and destroy the church of God by: (1) engaging in immorality (5:1); (2) fostering lies, deceptions, and selfish ambition (v. 3; Acts 5:1–11); (3) promoting false doctrine, rejecting apostolic revelation, and showing indifference to Scriptural truth (1 Tim. 4:1; Jude 4); (4) accepting sin and worldliness within the congregation (5:1–2,5–7; Rev. 3:17); (5) attempting to build the church by worldly wisdom or a distorted gospel (1:18—2:5; Phil. 1:15–16).

4:5 MANIFEST THE COUNSELS OF THE HEARTS. God will bring to light the secret acts of every person and expose his true thoughts and motives, good as well as bad (Mat. 6:3–4,6; 1 Tim. 5:24–25; see article on THE JUDGMENT OF BELIEVERS, p. 1811). In other words, the inner life of everyone will be revealed exactly as it was; nothing will be left hidden (Mark 4:22; Luke 12:2–3; Rom. 2:16).

will bring to light the hidden things of darkness, and will make manifest the counsels of the hearts: and [y]then shall every man have praise of God.

6 And these things, brethren, [z]I have in a figure transferred to myself and *to* Apollos for your sakes; [a]that ye might learn in us not to think *of men* above that which is written, that no one of you [b]be puffed up for one against another.

7 For who [o]maketh thee to differ *from another?* and [c]what hast thou that thou didst not receive? now if thou didst receive *it,* why dost thou glory, as if thou hadst not received *it?*

8 Now ye are full, [d]now ye are rich, ye have reigned as kings without us: and I would to God ye did reign, that we also might reign with you.

9 For I think that God hath set forth [p]us the apostles last, [e]as it were appointed to death: for [f]we are made a [q]spectacle unto the world, and to angels, and to men.

10 [g]We *are* [h]fools for Christ's sake, but ye *are* wise in Christ; [i]we *are* weak, but ye *are* strong; ye *are* honourable, but we *are* despised.

11 [j]Even unto this present hour we both hunger, and thirst, and [k]are naked, and [l]are buffeted, and have no certain dwellingplace;

12 [m]And labour, working with our own hands: [n]being reviled, we bless; being persecuted, we suffer it:

13 Being defamed, we entreat: [o]we are made as the filth of the world, *and are* the offscouring of all things unto this day.

4:5 [y]Rom. 2:29 2 Cor. 5:10 **4:6** [z]ch. 1:12 [a]Rom. 12:3 [b]ch. 3:21 **4:7** [c]John 3:27 **4:8** [d]Rev. 3:17 **4:9** [e]Ps. 44:22 [f]Heb. 10:33 **4:10** [g]ch. 2:3 [h]Acts 17:18 [i]2 Cor. 13:9 **4:11** [j]Phil. 4:12 [k]Rom. 8:35 [l]Acts 23:2 **4:12** [m]Acts 18:3 & 20:34 1 Thes. 2:9 2 Thes. 3:8 1 Tim. 4:10 [n]Mat. 5:44 Luke 6:28 & 23:34 Acts 7:60 Rom. 12:14 **4:13** [o]Lam. 3:45 **4:14** [p]1 Thes. 2:11 **4:15** [q]Acts 18:11 Gal. 4:19 Jas. 1:18 **4:16** [r]ch. 11:1 1 Thes. 1:6 **4:17** [s]Acts 19:22 Phil. 2:19 [t]1 Tim. 1:2 2 Tim. 1:2 [u]ch. 11:2 [v]ch. 7:17 [w]ch. 14:33 **4:18** [x]ch. 5:2 **4:19** [y]Acts 19:21 2 Cor. 1:15 [z]Acts 18:21; Heb. 6:3; Jas. 4:15 **4:20** [a]1 Thes. 1:5 **4:21** [b]2 Cor. 10:2

Paul's warning

14 I write not these things to shame you, but [p]as my beloved sons I warn *you.*

15 For though ye have ten thousand instructors in Christ, yet *have ye* not many fathers: for [q]in Christ Jesus I have begotten you through the gospel.

16 Wherefore I beseech you, [r]be ye followers of me.

17 For this cause have I sent unto you [s]Timotheus, [t]who is my beloved son, and faithful in the Lord, who shall bring you [u]into remembrance of my ways which be in Christ, as I [v]teach every where [w]in every church.

18 [x]Now some are puffed up, as though I would not come to you.

19 [y]But I will come to you shortly, [z]if the Lord will, and will know, not the speech of them which are puffed up, but the power.

20 For [a]the kingdom of God *is* not in word, but in power.

21 What will ye? [b]shall I come unto you with a rod, or in love, and *in* the spirit of meekness?

[o] Gk. *distinguisheth thee* [p] Or, *us the last apostles, as* [q] Gk. *theatre*

4:7 WHY DOST THOU GLORY. The basis for Christian humility is to realize that the native endowments or spiritual gifts that we possess are from God and thus furnish no basis for superiority, status, or pride. All that we have and all that we become are made possible by God and others. Consequently, there is no place for pride, only gratefulness to God and others.

4:8 YE ARE FULL . . . ARE RICH. Some at Corinth boasted of their wisdom, superior knowledge, and spiritual gifts. Already they had all they wanted; they were "full" and "rich" and "reigned as kings." Paul shows them that the true life of a faithful believer is the way of the cross and that suffering must precede glory (cf. Rom. 8:17).

4:9–13 THE APOSTLES . . . APPOINTED TO DEATH. In vv. 9–13 Paul lists the trials endured by the apostles. The verb "set forth" suggests that God has appointed the apostles to a life of suffering, to be seen by the world, by angels, and by the church.

(1) Paul lacks (even at that present time) such things as food, drink, and proper clothes. He is despised, roughly treated, and has no certain home. He labors night and day and is reviled, persecuted, slandered, and considered the scum of the world, "the offscouring of all things" (cf. 2 Cor. 4:8–9; 6:4–5,8–10; 11:23–29; 12:10).

(2) Although suffering was in one sense a special appointment of the apostolic ministry (cf. Acts 9:16), it is also the common lot of all believers who, united with Christ, are in opposition to sin, immorality, Satan, the evils of the world, and injustice. Their suffering is seen as a fellowship, a participation in the suffering of Christ (Rom. 8:17; Phil. 1:29; 3:10; 1 Thes. 3:3).

4:20 KINGDOM OF GOD . . . POWER. The "kingdom of God" reveals itself in power. Thus, members of that kingdom must have more than word and message; they must manifest the power of the Holy Spirit as well (2:4; Acts 1:8). In the N.T. this power consisted of a power to convince people of sin, righteousness, and judgment (John 16:8), to bring them into salvation (v. 15; Acts 26:16–18), to perform miracles (see 2:4, note; see article on THE KINGDOM OF GOD, p. 1428), and to live a righteous life (Rom. 14:17).

A case of immorality

5 IT IS reported commonly *that there is* fornication among you, and such fornication as is not so much as [c]named among the Gentiles, [d]that one should have his [e]father's wife.

2 [f]And ye are puffed up, and have not rather [g]mourned, that he that hath done this deed might be taken away from among you.

3 [h]For I verily, as absent in body, but present in spirit, have [r]judged already, as though I were present, *concerning* him that hath so done this deed,

4 In the name of our Lord Jesus Christ, when ye are gathered together, and my spirit, [i]with the power of our Lord Jesus Christ,

Expel the immoral person

5 [j]To deliver such an one unto [k]Satan for the destruction of the flesh, that the spirit may be saved in the day of the Lord Jesus.

6 [l]Your glorying *is* not good. Know ye not that [m]a little leaven leaveneth the whole lump?

7 Purge out therefore the old leaven, that ye may be a new lump, as ye are unleavened. For even [n]Christ our [o]passover [s]is sacrificed for us:

8 Therefore [p]let us keep [t]the feast, [q]not with old leaven, neither [r]with the leaven of malice and wick-

5:1 [c]Eph. 5:3 [d]Lev. 18:8 [e]2 Cor. 7:12
5:2 [f]ch. 4:18 [g]2 Cor. 7:7
5:3 [h]Col. 2:5
5:4 [i]Mat. 16:19 John 20:23 2 Cor. 2:10
5:5 [j]Ps. 109:6 1 Tim. 1:20 [k]Acts 26:18
5:6 [l]ch. 3:21 [m]Gal. 5:9 2 Tim. 2:17
5:7 [n]Is. 53:7 1 Pet. 1:19 [o]John 19:14
5:8 [p]Ex. 12:15 [q]Deut. 16:3

[r]Mat. 16:6; Mark 8:15; Luke 12:1

r Or, *determined* s Or, *is slain* t Or, *holyday*

5:1 FORNICATION AMONG YOU. Paul now writes about a report of immorality in the Corinthian church and the refusal of the leaders to deal with the offender (vv. 1–8). He declares that the church, as a holy people, must not permit or tolerate immorality among its members. He gives three reasons why the church should discipline an offending member: (1) For the good of the offender (v. 5). Excommunication might awaken him to the tragedy of his sin and his need for forgiveness and restoration.

(2) For the sake of the purity of the church (vv. 6–8). Tolerating evil within a church will gradually lower the moral standard of all.

(3) For the good of the world (cf. v. 1). The church cannot win men and women to Christ if it is like the world (cf. Mat. 5:13). For other N.T. passages on discipline in the church, see Mat. 5:22; 18:15–17; 2 Thes. 3:6,14–15; and Rev. 2:19–23.

5:1 HAVE HIS FATHER'S WIFE. The exact sin is not clear. Paul's reference to "his father's wife" probably means the offender was sexually involved with his stepmother. (1) Paul was dismayed and appalled that the church would tolerate such immorality in its midst. He sees this as much more serious than the actual transgression of the individual.

(2) The permissiveness of the Corinthians speaks to our situation today. Many churches today are tolerant of and silent about immorality among their members, including adultery and all forms of fornication. Premarital sexual intimacy, especially among church youth, is not only tolerated but at times justified on the pretense of love and commitment. More than a few leaders in the church fail to challenge in the name of Christ the immoral dating habits of today's youth. Like the Corinthian leaders, they refuse to mourn over the defilement of God's people as they become more and more like the society in which they live. In self-complacency these leaders permit sin because, so they claim, "we live in the modern day and must not be judgmental."

5:2 HAVE NOT RATHER MOURNED. Paul expresses what should be the normal reaction of a Spirit-filled church to the immorality found among its professing members. Those who embrace the Biblical view of God's holiness and His revulsion to sin will be moved to sorrow and regret (cf. Is. 6). They will remove wickedness from among themselves (vv. 2,4–5,7,13).

5:5 DELIVER SUCH AN ONE UNTO SATAN. To deliver one to Satan means that the church must remove the immoral person from its fellowship and to return him to Satan's domain. This will, in turn, expose him to the destructive influences of evil and the demonic (vv. 7,13). (1) This discipline has two purposes: (a) that the offender, by experiencing problems and physical suffering, may repent and ultimately be saved (cf. Luke 15:11–24); (b) that the church may "purge out therefore the old leaven" (v. 7; i.e., sinful influences), so that the people of God might become a new bread of "sincerity and truth" (v. 8). (2) The same action can be taken by the church today in seeking the salvation of one who has forsaken the Christian life and returned to the world (cf. 1 Tim. 1:20).

5:6 A LITTLE LEAVEN LEAVENETH THE WHOLE. In the Bible, "leaven" (i.e., yeast which produces fermentation) is a symbol of that which permeates the whole and corrupts truth, righteousness, and spiritual life (see Ex. 13:7, note; Mark 8:15, note; Gal. 5:7–9). Paul in this passage compares leaven with the process by which sin and wickedness slowly spread in a Christian community until many are corrupted by it. Any church that does not take radical action against sexual immorality among its members will find its evil influence spreading throughout the fellowship and infecting many. Sin must be expelled rigorously, or in time the entire Christian fellowship will be corrupted and the Holy Spirit banished from the church (see Rev. 2–3, notes).

edness; but with the unleavened *bread*
of sincerity and truth.

Reject evil members of the church

9 I wrote unto you in an epistle
[s]not to company with fornicators:
10 [t]Yet not altogether with the for-
nicators [u]of this world, or with the
covetous, or extortioners, or with idol-
aters; for then must ye needs go [v]out
of the world.
11 But now I have written unto you
not to keep company, [w]if any man that
is called a brother be a fornicator, or
covetous, or an idolater, or a railer, or
a drunkard, or an extortioner; with
such an one [x]no not to eat.
12 For what have I to do to judge
[y]them also that are without? do not ye
judge [z]them that are within?
13 But them that are without God
judgeth. Therefore [a]put away from
among yourselves that wicked person.

Lawsuits among brethren

6 DARE ANY of you, having a matter
against another, go to law before
the unjust, and not before the saints?
2 Do ye not know that [b]the saints
shall judge the world? and if the world
shall be judged by you, are ye unworthy
to judge the smallest matters?

5:9 [s]2 Cor. 6:14 Eph. 5:11
5:10 [t]ch. 10:27 [u]ch. 1:20 [v]John 17:15 1 John 5:19
5:11 [w]Mat. 18:17 Rom. 16:17 2 John 10 [x]Gal. 2:12
5:12 [y]Mark 4:11 Col. 4:5 1 Thes. 4:12 [z]ch. 6:1-4
5:13 [a]Deut. 13:5
6:2 [b]Ps. 49:14 Dan. 7:22 Mat. 19:28 Luke 22:30
6:3 [c]2 Pet. 2:4
6:4 [d]ch. 5:12
6:7 [e]Prov. 20:22 Mat. 5:39 Luke 6:29
6:8 [f]1 Thes. 4:6
6:9 [g]Gal. 5:21 Eph. 5:5 1 Tim. 1:9

3 Know ye not that we shall [c]judge
angels? how much more things that
pertain to this life?
4 [d]If then ye have judgments of
things pertaining to this life, set them
to judge who are least esteemed in the
church.
5 I speak to your shame. Is it so,
that there is not a wise man among
you? no, not one that shall be able to
judge between his brethren?
6 But brother goeth to law with
brother, and that before the unbeliev-
ers.
7 Now therefore there is utterly a
fault among you, because ye go to law
one with another. [e]Why do ye not
rather take wrong? why do ye not rath-
er *suffer yourselves to* be defrauded?
8 Nay, ye do wrong, and defraud,
[f]and that *your* brethren.

God to be glorified in the body

9 Know ye not that the unrighteous
shall not inherit the kingdom of God?
Be not deceived: [g]neither fornicators,
nor idolaters, nor adulterers, nor ef-
feminate, nor abusers of themselves
with mankind,
10 Nor thieves, nor covetous, nor
drunkards, nor revilers, nor extortion-
ers, shall inherit the kingdom of God.

5:12 JUDGE THEM THAT ARE WITHIN. Believers must not be involved in superficial or unjust criticism of another believer (cf. Mat. 7:1–5). However, Paul here does indicate that the church must judge its members according to God's Word and standards when serious sin, wrongdoing, immorality, or persistent ungodly conduct is the issue. Such wicked actions demand judging and discipline for the sake of the person involved, the purity of the church, and the witness of Christ in the world (see v. 1, note).

6:1 GO TO LAW BEFORE THE UNJUST. When trivial disputes (v. 2) between Christians occur, they should be settled within the church and not in courts of law. The church must judge the right or wrong involved, render a verdict, and discipline if needed (see Mat. 18:15, note). (1) This teaching does not mean that a believer may not use courts in serious cases with non-believers. Paul himself appealed to the judicial system more than once (see Acts 16:37–39; 25:10–12).

(2) Nor is Paul saying the church must allow its members to unlawfully abuse or mistreat the innocent, such as widows, children, or the weak. Rather, Paul was speaking of issues where there was no clear right or wrong. Blatant sinful actions must not be tolerated, but handled according to Christ's instruction in Mat. 18:15–17.

(3) Furthermore, in cases where a so-called "brother" has divorced or deserted his family and refuses to support his wife and children with alimony, a mother with the right motives and concern for her children may take recourse in the courts. Paul is not advocating that those who break the law be allowed to defraud and threaten the life or well-being of another. His statement in v. 8 indicates he is speaking of minor disputes where the wrong could be accepted and tolerated.

6:9 UNRIGHTEOUS SHALL NOT INHERIT THE KINGDOM. Some in Corinth were deceived into believing that if they broke fellowship with Christ, denied Him, and lived in immorality and injustice to others, their salvation and inheritance in the kingdom of God were still secure. (1) However, Paul declares that spiritual death is the inevitable consequence of habitual sinning, even for the Christian (cf. Rom. 8:13). No one can live for immoral gratification and inherit the kingdom of God (cf. Rom. 6:16; Jas. 1:15; see 1 John 2:4, note; 3:9, note). The apostle Paul repeats this cardinal teaching often (e.g., Gal. 5:21 and Eph. 5:5–6). Note that this principle was frequently proclaimed by the O.T. prophets (see Jer. 8:7, note; 23:17, note; Ezek. 13:10, note).

(2) Paul's warning is for the whole Christian community. We must not be deceived, for all who are "unrighteous shall not inherit the kingdom of God." Salvation without the regenerating and sanctifying work of the Holy Spirit has no place in Paul's theology.

11 And such were [h]some of you:
[i]but ye are washed, but ye are sancti-
fied, but ye are justified in the name of
the Lord Jesus, and by the Spirit of our
God.
12 [j]All things are lawful unto me,
but all things are not [u]expedient: all
things are lawful for me, but I will not
be brought under the power of any.
13 [k]Meats for the belly, and the
belly for meats: but God shall destroy
both it and them. Now the body *is* not
for fornication, but [l]for the Lord;
[m]and the Lord for the body.
14 And [n]God hath both raised up
the Lord, and will also raise up us [o]by
his own power.
15 Know ye not that [p]your bodies
are the members of Christ? shall I then
take the members of Christ, and make
them the members of an harlot? God
forbid.
16 What? know ye not that he which
is joined to an harlot is one body? for
[q]two, saith he, shall be one flesh.
17 [r]But he that is joined unto the
Lord is one spirit.
18 [s]Flee fornication. Every sin
that a man doeth is without the body;
but he that committeth fornication sin-
neth [t]against his own body.
19 What? [u]know ye not that your

6:11 [h]ch. 12:2 [i]Heb. 10:22
6:12 [j]ch. 10:23
6:13 [k]Mat. 15:17 Rom. 14:17 Col. 2:22 [l]1 Thes. 4:3 [m]Eph. 5:23
6:14 [n]Rom. 6:5,8 2 Cor. 4:14 [o]Eph. 1:19
6:15 [p]Rom. 12:5 Eph. 4:12 & 5:30
6:16 [q]Gen. 2:24 Mat. 19:5 Eph. 5:31
6:17 [r]John 17:21 Eph. 4:4
6:18 [s]Rom. 6:12 Heb. 13:4 [t]Rom. 1:24 1 Thes. 4:4
6:19 [u]2 Cor. 6:16
[v]Rom. 14:7
6:20 [w]Acts 20:28 Gal. 3:13 Heb. 9:12 1 Pet. 1:18 2 Pet. 2:1 Rev. 5:9
7:1 [x]ver. 8,26
7:3 [y]Ex. 21:10 1 Pet. 3:7
7:5 [z]Joel 2:16

body is the temple of the Holy Ghost
which is in you, which ye have of God,
[v]and ye are not your own?
20 For [w]ye are bought with a price:
therefore glorify God in your body, and
in your spirit, which are God's.

Marriage and its duties

7 NOW CONCERNING the things
whereof ye wrote unto me: [x]*It is*
good for a man not to touch a woman.
2 Nevertheless, *to avoid* fornication,
let every man have his own wife, and
let every woman have her own hus-
band.
3 [y]Let the husband render unto the
wife due benevolence: and likewise
also the wife unto the husband.
4 The wife hath not power of her
own body, but the husband: and like-
wise also the husband hath not power
of his own body, but the wife.
5 [z]Defraud ye not one the other,
except *it be* with consent for a time,
that ye may give yourselves to fasting
and prayer; and come together again,
that [a]Satan tempt you not for your in-
continency.

Zech. 7:3; See Ex. 19:15; 1 Sam. 21:4 [a]1 Thes. 3:5

[u] Or, *profitable*

6:11 JUSTIFIED ... BY THE SPIRIT. Justification involves not only the redeeming work of the Lord Jesus Christ, but also the work of the Spirit of God in the life of the believer (see article on BIBLICAL WORDS FOR SALVATION, p. 1726).

6:12 ALL THINGS ARE LAWFUL UNTO ME. This statement is clearly a quotation of the theological position of Paul's opponents. They thought they had the right to do anything they wished.

6:15 THE MEMBERS OF CHRIST. The apostle, warning against moral laxity, shows the terrible consequences of sexual immorality for the believer. Joining his body to an immoral woman causes him to become one with her, to come under her domination (v. 16; cf. Gen. 2:24), to desecrate what the cross has made holy (v. 15), and to sever himself from the kingdom of God (v. 9). In sexual immorality a person virtually removes himself from union with Christ by making his body a member of the immoral and ungodly person.

6:18 FLEE FORNICATION. Sexual immorality is particularly abhorrent to God. More than any other sinful act, it desecrates the body, which is the temple of the Spirit (vv. 15–20). Hence, Paul gives the admonition to "flee" sexual immorality. The use of the present tense here indicates that the Christian must repeatedly flee sexual immorality (cf. Gen. 39:12; see article on STANDARDS OF SEXUAL MORALITY, p. 1964).

6:19 YOUR BODY IS THE TEMPLE OF THE HOLY GHOST. Your body as a Christian is the personal dwelling place of the Holy Spirit (see also Rom. 8:11, where the Holy Spirit is God's mark on you that you belong to Him). Because He dwells in you and you belong to God, your body must never be defiled by any impurity or evil, whether by immoral thoughts, desires, deeds, films, books, or magazines. Rather, you must live in such a way as to glorify and please God in your body (v. 20).

7:1 A MAN NOT TO TOUCH A WOMAN. The entire seventh chapter is Paul's response to questions asked by the church in Corinth concerning marriage relations. His instructions must be read in light of v. 26, "This is good for the present distress." A time of great distress and persecution was coming for the early Christians, and in this situation the marriage relationship would be difficult. Note that "not to touch a woman" means not to marry.

7:3 THE HUSBAND RENDER UNTO THE WIFE. The commitment of marriage means that each partner relinquishes the exclusive right to his or her own body and gives the other a claim to it. That is, neither marriage partner may fail to submit to the normal sexual desires of the other. Such desires within marriage are natural and God-given, and to refuse to carry out one's responsibility in fulfilling the other's needs is to open the marriage up to Satan's temptation of adultery (v. 5).

6 But I speak this by permission, [b]*and* not of commandment.

7 For [c]I would that all men were [d]even as I myself. But [e]every man hath his proper gift of God, one after this manner, and another after that.

8 I say therefore to the unmarried and widows, [f]It is good for them if they abide even as I.

9 But [g]if they cannot contain, let them marry: for it is better to marry than to burn.

Marriage and separation

10 And unto the married I command, *yet* not I, but the Lord, [h]Let not the wife depart from *her* husband:

11 But and if she depart, let her remain unmarried, or be reconciled to *her* husband: and let not the husband put away *his* wife.

Mixed marriages

12 But to the rest speak I, not the Lord: If any brother hath a wife that believeth not, and she be pleased to dwell with him, let him not put her away.

13 And the woman which hath an husband that believeth not, and if he be pleased to dwell with her, let her not leave him.

14 For the unbelieving husband is sanctified by the wife, and the unbelieving wife is sanctified by the husband: else [i]were your children unclean; but now are they holy.

15 But if the unbelieving depart, let him depart. A brother or a sister is not under bondage in such *cases:* but God hath called us [j]to[v] peace.

16 For what knowest thou, O wife, whether thou shalt [k]save *thy* husband? or [w]how knowest thou, O man, whether thou shalt save *thy* wife?

Abiding in God's call

17 But as God hath distributed to every man, as the Lord hath called every one, so let him walk. And [l]so ordain I in all churches.

18 Is any man called being circumcised? let him not become uncircumcised. Is any called in uncircumcision? [m]let him not be circumcised.

19 [n]Circumcision is nothing, and uncircumcision is nothing, but [o]the keeping of the commandments of God.

20 Let every man abide in the same calling wherein he was called.

21 Art thou called *being* a servant? care not for it: but if thou mayest be made free, use *it* rather.

22 For he that is called in the Lord, *being* a servant, is [p]the Lord's [x]free-

7:6 [b]2 Cor. 8:8 & 11:17
7:7 [c]Acts 26:29 [d]ch. 9:5 [e]ch. 12:11
7:8 [f]ver. 1,26
7:9 [g]1 Tim. 5:14
7:10 [h]Mal. 2:14 Mat. 5:32 & 19:6,9 Mark 10:11 Luke 16:18
7:14 [i]Mal. 2:15
7:15 [j]Rom. 12:18 & 14:19 ch. 14:33
7:16 [k]1 Pet. 3:1
7:17 [l]ch. 4:17
7:18 [m]Acts 15:1 Gal. 5:2
7:19 [n]Gal. 5:6 [o]John 15:14 1 John 2:3 & 3:24
7:22 [p]John 8:36 Rom. 6:18 Philem. 16

[v]Gk. *in peace* [w]Gk. *what* [x]Gk. *made free*

7:11 IF SHE DEPART, LET HER REMAIN UNMARRIED. In v. 10 Paul recognizes that God wants marriage to be permanent. He also acknowledges, however, that sometimes a marriage relationship may become so unbearable that separation from the partner is necessary. In v. 11, therefore, Paul is not talking about divorce, permitted by God because of adultery (see Mat. 19:9, note) or the abandonment of a marriage partner (see v. 15, note). Rather, Paul is speaking of separation without legal divorce. He may be referring to situations where a marriage partner is acting in such a way as to endanger the physical or spiritual life of the wife and children. In such conditions, it may be best that one of the partners leave the home and neither partner remarry. It is inconceivable that Paul would advocate that a wife remain with a husband who repeatedly brought physical harm and abuse on her and the children.

7:12 SPEAK I, NOT THE LORD. Paul is not merely giving his own opinion here; rather he states that he does not have a saying of Jesus to confirm what he is about to write. However, he writes this as one who has apostolic authority and is under divine inspiration (cf. vv. 25,40; 14:37).

7:14 HUSBAND . . . WIFE . . . CHILDREN. When a believer is involved in a marriage with an unbeliever, the marriage as well as the children born to that union are legitimate before God. Therefore, the believer should live with the unbeliever and not seek to divide the marriage or the home. Furthermore, because the husband or wife is a believer, he/she may have a special influence so that the spouse is led to accept Christ (cf. 1 Pet. 3:1–2).

7:15 IS NOT UNDER BONDAGE. In the event that an unbelieving partner abandons or divorces a believer, the marriage relation is dissolved and the believer is freed from his or her former marital obligation. "Not under bondage in such *cases*" means that the believer is released from the marital contract. The word "bondage" (Gk. *douloō*) literally means "to enslave"; i.e., the faithful believer is no longer enslaved to his or her marriage vows. In this case, the abandoned believer would be free to remarry, provided he or she marries a Christian (v. 39; see Mat. 19:9, note on divorce).

7:19 KEEPING OF THE COMMANDMENTS OF GOD. How can Paul, who emphasized so strongly salvation by faith (Rom. 3–4), say that what really matters is the "keeping of the commandments of God"? Because salvation by faith must lead to obeying, loving, and serving God. Anything less than such obedience falls short of N.T. saving faith (cf. Gal. 5:6; 6:15).

man: likewise also he that is called, *being* free, is [q]Christ's servant.

23 [r]Ye are bought with a price; be not ye the servants of men.

24 Brethren, let every man, wherein he is called, therein abide with God.

Marriage and Christian service

25 Now concerning virgins [s]I have no commandment of the Lord: yet I give my judgment, as one [t]that hath obtained mercy of the Lord [u]to be faithful.

26 I suppose therefore that this is good for the present [y]distress, *I say,* [v]that *it is* good for a man so to be.

27 Art thou bound unto a wife? seek not to be loosed. Art thou loosed from a wife? seek not a wife.

28 But and if thou marry, thou hast not sinned; and if a virgin marry, she hath not sinned. Nevertheless such shall have trouble in the flesh: but I spare you.

29 But [w]this I say, brethren, the time *is* short: it remaineth, that both they that have wives be as though they had none;

30 And they that weep, as though they wept not; and they that rejoice, as though they rejoiced not; and they that buy, as though they possessed not;

31 And they that use this world, as not [x]abusing *it:* for [y]the fashion of this world passeth away.

32 But I would have you without carefulness. [z]He that is unmarried careth for the things [z]that belong to the Lord, how he may please the Lord:

33 But he that is married careth for the things that are of the world, how he may please *his* wife.

34 There is difference *also* between a wife and a virgin. The unmarried woman [a]careth for the things of the Lord, that she may be holy both in body and in spirit: but she that is married careth for the things of the world, how she may please *her* husband.

35 And this I speak for your own profit; not that I may cast a snare upon you, but for that which is comely, and that ye may attend upon the Lord without distraction.

36 But if any man think that he behaveth himself uncomely toward his virgin, if she pass the flower of *her* age, and need so require, let him do what he will, he sinneth not: let them marry.

37 Nevertheless he that standeth stedfast in his heart, having no necessity, but hath power over his own will, and hath so decreed in his heart that he will keep his virgin, doeth well.

38 [b]So then he that giveth *her* in marriage doeth well; but he that giveth *her* not in marriage doeth better.

39 [c]The wife is bound by the law as long as her husband liveth; but if her husband be dead, she is at liberty to be married to whom she will; [d]only in the Lord.

40 But she is happier if she so abide, [e]after my judgment: and [f]I think also that I have the Spirit of God.

Food offered to idols

8 NOW [g]AS touching things offered unto idols, we know that we

7:22 [q]ch. 9:21 Gal. 5:13 Eph. 6:6 1 Pet. 2:16
7:23 [r]1 Pet. 1:18 See Lev. 25:42
7:25 [s]2 Cor. 8:8 [t]1 Tim. 1:16 [u]1 Tim. 1:12
7:26 [v]ver. 1,8
7:29 [w]Rom. 13:11 1 Pet. 4:7 2 Pet. 3:8,9
7:31 [x]ch. 9:18 [y]Ps. 39:6 Jas. 1:10 & 4:14 1 Pet. 1:24 & 4:7 1 John 2:17
7:32 [z]1 Tim. 5:5
7:34 [a]Luke 10:40
7:38 [b]Heb. 13:4
7:39 [c]Rom. 7:2 [d]2 Cor. 6:14
7:40 [e]ver. 25 [f]1 Thes. 4:8
8:1 [g]Acts 15:20 ch. 10:19

[y] Or, *necessity* [z] Gk. *of the Lord* as ver. 34

7:31 THEY THAT USE THIS WORLD. We live in the period when all things of the world are hastening toward an end. For this reason life in this world should not be our utmost concern; we should direct our greatest attention toward our heavenly home (Heb. 11:13–16).

7:34 THE UNMARRIED WOMAN. Scripture maintains that the unmarried state is in no way inferior to the married. In fact it is better in the most important way of all—the possibility of offering undistracted service to God. The unmarried man (vv. 32–33) or woman (v. 34) can concentrate on the things that belong to the Lord in a greater way than the married. To be "holy both in body and in spirit" does not refer to ethical achievement, but to the possibility of a greater commitment to God unencumbered by family responsibilities, problems, and concerns. The unmarried can devote themselves with all their gifts to the Lord, free from care, totally occupied with the Lord and His Word.

8:1 THINGS OFFERED UNTO IDOLS. In chs. 8–10 Paul deals with the question of the Corinthians concerning meat offered to idols and whether it is right to buy and eat this meat and to participate in festivals at idol temples (v. 10). (1) In treating this subject he reveals an important principle by which Christians of all ages should live. This principle applies to any questionable activities that might tempt some believers to sin and lead them to spiritual ruin (v. 11). The Holy Spirit through Paul has given directions that a Christian must always act with a love toward other believers that may in fact require self-denial.

(2) Self-denial means limiting one's freedom and setting aside all questionable activities in order not to offend or weaken the sincere convictions of other Christians which they feel are based on Biblical principles. The opposite of self-denial is

all have [h]knowledge. [i]Knowledge puffeth up, but charity edifieth.

2 And [j]if any man think that he knoweth any thing, he knoweth nothing yet as he ought to know.

3 But if any man love God, [k]the same is known of him.

4 As concerning therefore the eating of those things that are offered in sacrifice unto idols, we know that [l]an idol *is* nothing in the world, [m]and that *there is* none other God but one.

5 For though there be that are [n]called gods, whether in heaven or in earth, (as there be gods many, and lords many,)

6 But [o]to us *there is but* one God, the Father, [p]of whom *are* all things, and we [a]in him; and [q]one Lord Jesus Christ, [r]by whom *are* all things, and we by him.

7 Howbeit *there is* not in every man that knowledge: for some [s]with conscience of the idol unto this hour eat *it* as a thing offered unto an idol; and their conscience being weak is [t]defiled.

8 But [u]meat commendeth us not to God: for neither, if we eat, [b]are we the better; neither, if we eat not, [c]are we the worse.

9 But [v]take heed lest by any means this [d]liberty of yours become [w]a stumblingblock to them that are weak.

10 For if any man see thee which hast knowledge sit at meat in the idol's temple, shall not [x]the conscience of him which is weak be [e]emboldened to eat those things which are offered to idols;

11 And [y]through thy knowledge shall the weak brother perish, for whom Christ died?

12 But [z]when ye sin so against the brethren, and wound their weak conscience, ye sin against Christ.

13 Wherefore, [a]if meat make my brother to offend, I will eat no flesh while the world standeth, lest I make my brother to offend.

Paul's Christian rights

9 AM[b] I not an apostle? am I not free? [c]have I not seen Jesus Christ our Lord? [d]are not ye my work in the Lord?

2 If I be not an apostle unto others, yet doubtless I am to you: for [e]the seal of mine apostleship are ye in the Lord.

3 Mine answer to them that do examine me is this,

4 [f]Have we not power to eat and to drink?

5 Have we not power to lead about a sister, a [f]wife, as well as other apostles, and *as* [g]the brethren of the Lord, and [h]Cephas?

6 Or I only and Barnabas, [i]have not we power to forbear working?

7 Who [j]goeth a warfare any time at his own charges? who [k]planteth a vineyard, and eateth not of the fruit thereof? or who [l]feedeth a flock, and eateth not of the milk of the flock?

8 Say I these things as a man? or saith not the law the same also?

9 For it is written in the law of Moses, [m]Thou shalt not muzzle the mouth of the ox that treadeth out the corn. Doth God take care for oxen?

10 Or saith he *it* altogether for our sakes? For our sakes, no doubt, *this* is

8:1 [h]Rom. 14:14 [i]Rom. 14:3 **8:2** [j]ch. 13:8,9 Gal. 6:3 1 Tim. 6:4 **8:3** [k]Ex. 33:12 Nah. 1:7 Mat. 7:23 Gal. 4:9 **8:4** [l]Is. 41:24 [m]Deut. 4:39 & 6:4 Is. 44:8 Mark 12:29 Eph. 4:6 1 Tim. 2:5 **8:5** [n]John 10:34 **8:6** [o]Mal. 2:10 Eph. 4:6 [p]Acts 17:28 Rom. 11:36 [q]John 13:13 Acts 2:36 Eph. 4:5 Phil. 2:11 [r]John 1:3 Col. 1:16 Heb. 1:2 **8:7** [s]ch. 10:28 [t]Rom. 14:14 **8:8** [u]Rom. 14:17 **8:9** [v]Gal. 5:13 [w]Rom. 14:13 **8:10** [x]ch. 10:28 **8:11** [y]Rom. 14:15 **8:12** [z]Mat. 25:40 **8:13** [a]Rom. 14:21 2 Cor. 11:29 **9:1** [b]Acts 9:15 & 13:2 & 26:17 2 Cor. 12:12 Gal. 2:7,8 1 Tim. 2:7 2 Tim. 1:11 [c]Acts 9:3,17 & 18:9 & 22:14,18 ch. 15:8 [d]ch. 3:6 **9:2** [e]2 Cor. 12:12 **9:4** [f]1 Thes. 2:6

9:5 [g]Mat. 13:55; Gal. 1:19 [h]Mat. 8:14 **9:6** [i]2 Thes. 3:8 **9:7** [j]2 Cor. 10:4; 1 Tim. 1:18 [k]Deut. 20:6 [l]John 21:15; 1 Pet. 5:2 **9:9** [m]Deut. 25:4; 1 Tim. 5:18

a Or, *for him* **b** Or, *have we the more* **c** Or, *have we the less* **d** Or, *power* **e** Gk. *edified* **f** Or, *woman*

defending one's own right to engage in a questionable activity, one that may entice others to follow—to their own hurt (cf. Rom. 14:1—15:3; Acts 15:29, note; 1 Cor. 9:19, note).

8:2 HE KNOWETH NOTHING. Those who base their right to partake of certain questionable things on their "knowledge" and "mature understanding" show that in reality they do not know as they ought. Our knowledge in this life is always incomplete and imperfect. Thus, our actions must first be based on love toward God and others. If love is our determining consideration, we will refuse to engage in or encourage any activity that might lead even one believer to stumble and head toward eternal ruin. Those who live by the rule of love are those who are "known of him [God]" (v. 3).

8:12 YE SIN AGAINST CHRIST. Those who by their example or inducement lead another believer into sin and spiritual ruin (v. 11), sin not only against that person, but also against Christ Himself. A great sin has been committed; the purpose for which Christ died is considered of little value in comparison to one's own self-centered desires (see Mat. 18:7, note).

9:1 AM I NOT AN APOSTLE? Paul personally illustrates the principle set forth in 8:13 (see 8:1, note) by willingly setting aside his own personal rights as an apostle in order not to hinder the gospel of Christ (v. 12; see v. 19, note).

written: that [n]he that ploweth should plow in hope; and that he that thresheth in hope should be partaker of his hope.

11 [o]If we have sown unto you spiritual things, *is it* a great thing if we shall reap your carnal things?

12 If others be partakers of *this* power over you, *are* not we rather? [p]Nevertheless we have not used this power; but suffer all things, [q]lest we should hinder the gospel of Christ.

13 [r]Do ye not know that they which minister about holy things [g]live *of the things* of the temple? and they which wait at the altar are partakers with the altar?

14 Even so [s]hath the Lord ordained [t]that they which preach the gospel should live of the gospel.

Paul gives up his rights

15 But [u]I have used none of these things: neither have I written these things, that it should be so done unto me: for [v]*it were* better for me to die, than that any man should make my glorying void.

16 For though I preach the gospel, I have nothing to glory of: for [w]necessity is laid upon me; yea, woe is unto me, if I preach not the gospel!

17 For if I do this thing willingly, [x]I have a reward: but if against my will, [y]a dispensation *of the gospel* is committed unto me.

18 What is my reward then? *Verily* that, [z]when I preach the gospel, I may

9:10 [n]2 Tim. 2:6
9:11 [o]Rom. 15:27 Gal. 6:6
9:12 [p]Acts 20:33 1 Thes. 2:6 [q]2 Cor. 11:12
9:13 [r]Lev. 6:16
9:14 [s]Mat. 10:10 Luke 10:7 [t]Gal. 6:6
9:15 [u]Acts 18:3 [v]2 Cor. 11:10
9:16 [w]Rom. 1:14
9:17 [x]ch. 3:8,14 [y]Gal. 2:7 Col. 1:25
9:18 [z]ch. 10:33 [a]ch. 7:31
9:19 [b]ver. 1 [c]Gal. 5:13 [d]Mat. 18:15 1 Pet. 3:1
9:20 [e]Acts 16:3 & 18:18
9:21 [f]Gal. 3:2 [g]Rom. 2:12 [h]ch. 7:22
9:22 [i]Rom. 15:1 2 Cor. 11:29 [j]ch. 10:33 [k]Rom. 11:14
9:24 [l]Gal. 2:2 2 Tim. 4:7
9:25 [m]Jas. 1:12 Rev. 2:10
9:26 [n]2 Tim. 2:5
9:27 [o]Rom. 8:13 Col. 3:5

make the gospel of Christ without charge, that I [a]abuse not my power in the gospel.

19 For though I be [b]free from all *men,* yet have [c]I made myself servant unto all, [d]that I might gain the more.

20 And [e]unto the Jews I became as a Jew, that I might gain the Jews; to them that are under the law, as under the law, that I might gain them that are under the law;

21 [f]To [g]them that are without law, as without law, ([h]being not without law to God, but under the law to Christ,) that I might gain them that are without law.

22 [i]To the weak became I as weak, that I might gain the weak: [j]I am made all things to all *men,* [k]that I might by all means save some.

23 And this I do for the gospel's sake, that I might be partaker thereof with *you.*

The Christian race

24 Know ye not that they which run in a race run all, but one receiveth the prize? [l]So run, that ye may obtain.

25 And every man that striveth for the mastery is temperate in all things. Now they *do it* to obtain a corruptible crown; but we [m]an incorruptible.

26 I therefore so run, [n]not as uncertainly; so fight I, not as one that beateth the air:

27 [o]But I keep under my body, and

[g] Or, *feed*

9:14 SHOULD LIVE OF THE GOSPEL. The Bible teaches in both the O.T. (Deut. 25:4; cf. Lev. 6:16,26; 7:6) and the N.T. (Mat. 10:10; Luke 10:7) that those who are engaged in proclaiming the Word of God should be supported by those who receive spiritual blessing from it (see Gal. 6:6–10, note; 1 Tim. 5:18).

9:19 I MADE MYSELF SERVANT UNTO ALL. Paul uses himself as an example of the principle of self-denial for the sake of others (see 8:1, note). He renounces his rights out of sympathetic consideration for the convictions of others (Rom. 14:15–21), in order not to limit his ministry or hinder the gospel (v. 12). This practice does not mean that Paul compromises Christian principles or seeks to please others for the purpose of winning their esteem (Gal. 1:8–10). What he affirms is that he is prepared to conform to the standards and convictions of those whom he is trying to help, provided it does not violate Christian principles. He understands that if he offends them by disregarding the conviction of their conscience, his ministry to them for the sake of Christ could be seriously hindered (vv.12,19–23; see 8:1, note).

9:24 THE PRIZE. The "prize," the "incorruptible" crown (v. 25), refers to the victory of gaining eternal salvation, the precious goal of the Christian life (cf. 1:8; 4:5; 6:2,9–10; 15:12–19). This goal can only be won by giving up some of our rights for the sake of others (8:7–13) and by renouncing those things that would take us out of the race altogether (10:5–22).

9:24–27 RUN, THAT YE MAY OBTAIN. Paul illustrates the principle that if one fails to exercise self-control, self-denial, and love with regard to others, he himself will be rejected by God, even if he is a gospel preacher (see next note).

9:27 I MYSELF SHOULD BE A CASTAWAY. "Be a castaway" (Gk. *adokimos*) conveys the idea of "failing the test," "being rejected." Paul uses this same term in 2 Cor. 13:5, where he states that Christ does not dwell in any who are "reprobates" (Gk. *adokimoi*). Paul is not referring merely to the loss of a ministerial reward. What he recognizes is the possibility that he may fail to obtain the prize (i.e., the inheritance) of final salvation (vv. 24–25)

[p]bring *it* into subjection: lest that by
any means, when I have preached to
others, I myself should be [q]a cast-
away.

The Israelites in the wilderness

10 MOREOVER, BRETHREN, I
would not that ye should be ig-
norant, how that all our fathers were
under [r]the cloud, and all passed
through [s]the sea;
2 And were all baptized unto Moses
in the cloud and in the sea;
3 And did all eat the same [t]spiritu-
al meat;
4 And did all drink the same [u]spiri-
tual drink: for they drank of that spiri-
tual Rock that [h]followed them: and
that Rock was Christ.
5 But with many of them God was
not well pleased: for they [v]were over-
thrown in the wilderness.
6 Now these things were [i]our ex-
amples, to the intent we should not
lust after evil things, as [w]they also
lusted.

9:27 [p]Rom. 6:18 [q]Jer. 6:30 2 Cor. 13:5 **10:1** [r]Ex. 13:21 [s]Ex. 14:22 Ps. 78:13 **10:3** [t]Ex. 16:15 Ps. 78:24 **10:4** [u]Ex. 17:6 Ps. 78:15 **10:5** [v]Num. 14:29 Ps. 106:26 **10:6** [w]Num. 11:4 **10:7** [x]ver. 14 [y]Ex. 32:6 **10:8** [z]Rev. 2:14 [a]Ps. 106:29 **10:9** [b]Ex. 17:2,7 [c]Num. 21:6 **10:10** [d]Ex. 16:2 [e]Num. 14:37 [f]Ex. 12:23 **10:11** [g]Rom. 15:4 [h]Phil. 4:5 Heb. 10:25 **10:12** [i]Rom. 11:20

7 [x]Neither be ye idolaters, as *were*
some of them; as it is written, [y]The
people sat down to eat and drink, and
rose up to play.
8 [z]Neither let us commit fornica-
tion, as some of them committed, and
[a]fell in one day three and twenty thou-
sand.
9 Neither let us tempt Christ, as
[b]some of them also tempted, and
[c]were destroyed of serpents.
10 Neither murmur ye, as [d]some of
them also murmured, and [e]were de-
stroyed of [f]the destroyer.
11 Now all these things happened
unto them for [j]examples: and [g]they
are written for our admonition, [h]upon
whom the ends of the world are come.
12 Wherefore [i]let him that
thinketh he standeth take heed lest he
fall.
13 There hath no temptation taken
you but such as is [k]common to man:

h Or, *went with them* **i** Gk. *our figures* **j** Or, *types* **k** Or, *moderate*

if he should cease living a holy life, exercising self-control, and enduring hardships for Christ (vv. 25–27).

10:1 I WOULD NOT THAT YE SHOULD BE IGNORANT. The fact that one may be redeemed, partake of divine grace, and yet later be rejected by God because of evil conduct (see 9:27, note), is now verified by examples from the experience of Israel (vv. 1–12).

10:5 THEY WERE OVERTHROWN IN THE WILDERNESS. The Israelites had experienced the grace of God in the exodus. They had been delivered from bondage (v. 1), baptized (v. 2), and divinely sustained in the wilderness, experiencing close fellowship with Christ (vv. 3–4). Yet in spite of these spiritual blessings, they failed to please God and were destroyed by Him in the wilderness; they forfeited their election and hence, failed to reach the promised land (cf. Num. 14:30; see article on GOD'S COVENANT WITH THE ISRAELITES, p. 314). Paul's point is that, as God did not tolerate Israel's idolatry, sin, and immorality, so He will not tolerate the sin of believers under the new covenant.

10:6 THESE THINGS WERE OUR EXAMPLES. The terrible judgment of God upon the disobedient Israelites serves as an example and a warning for those under the new covenant not to seek evil things. Paul warns the Corinthians that if they repeat Israel's unfaithfulness to God (vv. 7–10), they too will receive His judgment and fail to enter the promised heavenly country.

10:11 WRITTEN FOR OUR ADMONITION. The history of God's judgment of His people in the O.T. was written down in the Scriptures to provide those in the N.T. with ample warnings against sinning and falling from grace (v. 12; see Num. 14:29, note).

10:12 TAKE HEED LEST HE FALL. The Israelites, as God's elect, thought they could safely enter into sin, idolatry, and immorality; yet they met with condemnation. So also those who believe they can securely live in carnal gratification must realize that God's condemnation also awaits them.

10:13 GOD *IS* FAITHFUL. A professing believer may not justify sinning with excuses that he is simply human and thus imperfect, or that in this life all born-again believers continue sinning in word, thought, and deed (cf. Rom. 6:1). At the same time, Paul assures the Corinthians that no true believer need fall from the grace and mercy of God. (1) The Holy Spirit explicitly affirms that God provides His children with adequate grace to overcome every temptation and thus to resist sinning (cf. Rev. 2:7,17,26). God's faithfulness expresses itself in two ways: (a) He will not allow us to be tempted above that which we can bear, and (b) He will with each temptation provide a way by which we can endure the temptation and overcome sin (cf. 2 Thes. 3:3).

(2) The grace of God (Eph. 2:8–10; Tit. 2:11–14), the blood of Jesus Christ (Eph. 2:13; 1 Pet. 2:24), the Word of God (Eph. 6:17; 2 Tim. 3:16–17), the indwelling power of the Holy Spirit (Tit. 3:5–6; 1 Pet. 1:5), and the heavenly intercession of Christ bring sufficient power for the believer's warfare against sin and the spiritual forces of wickedness (Eph. 6:10–18; Heb. 7:25).

(3) If the Christian yields to sin, it is not because Christ's provision of grace is inadequate, but because the believer fails to resist his own sinful desires by the power of the Spirit (Rom. 8:13–14;

but [j]God *is* faithful, [k]who will not
suffer you to be tempted above that ye
are able; but will with the temptation
also make a way to escape, that ye may
be able to bear *it.*

Prohibition of idol feasts

14 Wherefore, my dearly beloved,
[l]flee from idolatry.
15 I speak as to [m]wise men; judge
ye what I say.
16 [n]The cup of blessing which we
bless, is it not the communion of the
blood of Christ? [o]The bread which we
break, is it not the communion of the
body of Christ?
17 For [p]we *being* many are one
bread, *and* one body: for we are all par-
takers of that one bread.
18 Behold [q]Israel [r]after the flesh:
[s]are not they which eat of the sacri-
fices partakers of the altar?
19 What say I then? [t]that the idol
is any thing, or that which is offered in
sacrifice to idols is any thing?
20 But *I say,* that the things which
the Gentiles [u]sacrifice, they sacrifice
to devils, and not to God: and I would
not that ye should have fellowship with
devils.
21 [v]Ye cannot drink the cup of the
Lord, and [w]the cup of devils: ye cannot
be partakers of the Lord's table, and of
the table of devils.
22 Do we [x]provoke the Lord to
jealousy? [y]are we stronger than he?

Do all to the glory of God

23 [z]All things are lawful for me,
but all things are not expedient: all
things are lawful for me, but all things
edify not.
24 [a]Let no man seek his own, but
every man another's *wealth.*
25 [b]Whatsoever is sold in the
shambles, *that* eat, asking no question
for conscience sake:
26 For [c]the earth *is* the Lord's, and
the fulness thereof.
27 If any of them that believe not
bid you *to a feast,* and ye be disposed to
go; [d]whatsoever is set before you, eat,
asking no question for conscience
sake.
28 But if any man say unto you,
This is offered in sacrifice unto idols,
eat not [e]for his sake that showed it,
and for conscience sake: for [f]the
earth *is* the Lord's, and the fulness
thereof:
29 Conscience, I say, not thine own,
but of the other: for [g]why is my liberty
judged of another *man's* conscience?
30 For if I by [1]grace be a partaker,
why am I evil spoken of for that [h]for
which I give thanks?
31 [i]Whether therefore ye eat, or
drink, or whatsoever ye do, do all to
the glory of God.

10:13 [j]ch. 1:9 [k]Ps. 125:3 2 Pet. 2:9
10:14 [l]2 Cor. 6:17
10:15 [m]ch. 8:1
10:16 [n]Mat. 26:26 [o]Acts 2:42
10:17 [p]ch. 12:27
10:18 [q]Rom. 4:12 [r]Rom. 4:1 2 Cor. 11:18 [s]Lev. 3:3
10:19 [t]ch. 8:4
10:20 [u]Lev. 17:7 Deut. 32:17 Ps. 106:37
10:21 [v]2 Cor. 6:15 [w]Deut. 32:38
10:22 [x]Deut. 32:21 [y]Ezek. 22:14
10:23 [z]ch. 6:12
10:24 [a]Rom. 15:1,2 ch. 13:5
10:25 [b]1 Tim. 4:4
10:26 [c]Ex. 19:5 Ps. 24:1
10:27 [d]Luke 10:7
10:28 [e]ch. 8:10,12 [f]Deut. 10:14 Ps. 24:1
10:29 [g]Rom. 14:16
10:30 [h]Rom. 14:6 1 Tim. 4:3,4
10:31 [i]Col. 3:17 1 Pet. 4:11

[1]Or, *thanksgiving*

Gal. 5:16,24; Jas. 1:13–15). God's "divine power hath given unto us all things that *pertain* unto life and godliness" (2 Pet. 1:3), and through the salvation provided by Christ we can "walk worthy of the Lord unto all pleasing, being fruitful in every good work, . . . strengthened with all might, according to his glorious power, unto all patience and longsuffering with joyfulness" (Col. 1:10–11; see Mat. 4:1, note on how to conquer temptation). We can "bear" every temptation and "escape" if we sincerely desire to and depend upon the faithfulness and power of God.

10:16 THE CUP OF BLESSING. The cup we take at the Lord's Supper typifies the death of Christ and his sacrificial suffering for sinful men and women. "Communion of the blood of Christ" refers to the believer sharing in the salvation provided by the death of Christ (cf. 11:25). Scripture does not teach that the bread and the fruit of the vine actually become the body and blood of Christ (see 11:24–25, note on the Lord's Supper).

10:20 THEY SACRIFICE TO DEVILS. Idolatry involves the worship of demons (cf. Deut. 32:17; Ps. 106:35–38; see article on THE NATURE OF IDOLATRY, p. 428) and is associated with greed or covetousness (see Col. 3:5, note). Therefore, demonic powers stand behind love for worldly possessions, honor, or position.

10:21 THE CUP OF THE LORD . . . THE CUP OF DEVILS. As partaking of the Lord's Supper is a sharing in the redemption of Christ, so the partaking in idolatrous feasts is a sharing or participation in demons (v. 20). The error of some members at Corinth was failing to distinguish between righteousness and unrighteousness, between that which is holy and that which is defiled, between that which is of Christ and that which is of the devil. They did not understand the holy jealousy of God (v. 22; cf. Ex. 20:5; Deut. 4:24; Josh. 24:19) and the seriousness of compromising with the world. Christ Himself spoke of this fatal error: "No man can serve two masters" (Mat. 6:24).

10:31 DO ALL TO THE GLORY OF GOD. The main object of the believer's life is to please God and promote His glory (see article on THE GLORY OF GOD, p. 1186). Thus what cannot be done for God's glory (i.e., in honor and thanksgiving to Him as our Lord, Creator, and Redeemer) should not be done at all. We honor Him by obedience, thankfulness, reliance, prayer, faith, and loyalty to Him. Living to the glory of God must be a primary direction of our lives, a guide for our

32 [j]Give none offence, neither to
the Jews, nor to the [m]Gentiles, nor to
[k]the church of God:
33 Even as [l]I please all *men* in all
things, [m]not seeking mine own profit,
but the *profit* of many, that they may be
saved.

The covering of women's heads

11 BE [n]YE followers of me, even
as I also *am* of Christ.
2 Now I praise you, brethren, [o]that
ye remember me in all things, and
[p]keep the [n]ordinances, as I delivered
them to you.
3 But I would have you know, that
[q]the head of every man is Christ; and
[r]the head of the woman *is* the man;
and [s]the head of Christ *is* God.
4 Every man praying or [t]prophesy-
ing, having *his* head covered, dishon-
oureth his head.
5 But [u]every woman that prayeth
or prophesieth with *her* head uncov-
ered dishonoureth her head: for that is
even all one as if she were [v]shaven.
6 For if the woman be not covered,
let her also be shorn: but if it be [w]a

10:32 [j]Rom. 14:13 ch. 8:13 [k]Acts 20:28 1 Tim. 3:5 **10:33** [l]Rom. 15:2 [m]ver. 24 **11:1** [n]Eph. 5:1 Phil. 3:17 **11:2** [o]ch. 4:17 [p]ch. 7:17 **11:3** [q]Eph. 5:23 [r]Gen. 3:16 1 Tim. 2:11 [s]John 14:28 Phil. 2:7-9 **11:4** [t]ch. 12:10 **11:5** [u]Acts 21:9 [v]Deut. 21:12 **11:6** [w]Num. 5:18

[m] Gk. *Greeks* [n] Or, *traditions*

---

conduct, and a test of our actions.

11:1 FOLLOWERS ... OF CHRIST. The believer, like Paul, is called upon to follow the example of Christ and become a Christlike person (cf. Rom. 13:14; Gal. 3:27). What is Christlikeness?

(1) Christlikeness is first and foremost love for God and for others (Mat. 22:37–39; Luke 10:27). The believer's love for God motivates and directs his love for others (1 John 4:20–21), just as Christ's love for God was always first and His love for others subordinate to and based on that love for the Father (cf. Mat. 22:37–39; John 17:23–24).

(2) Christ's love for His Father was revealed in His concern for God's glory (Mat. 6:9; John 12:28; 17:4), will (Mat. 26:42; John 4:34; Heb. 10:7–12), Word (Mat. 26:54; John 8:28; 17:14,17), and the nearness of His presence (Luke 5:16; John 17:21). We see this love in His faithfulness to God (Heb. 3:2) and His willingness to carry out God's will by sacrificing His life for our redemption (Mat. 26:42; John 3:16–17; Heb. 10:4–9). Christ's love for His Father is further revealed in His love for righteousness and a hatred of iniquity (see Heb. 1:9, note).

(3) Christ's love for humans is seen in His compassion (Mat. 9:36; 14:14; 15:32; 20:34; cf. Luke 15:11–24), kindness (Mat. 8:3,16–17; 9:22), tears (John 11:35), humility (Mat. 11:29), good deeds (Acts 10:38), gentleness (Mat. 11:29), forgiveness (Luke 23:34), patience (Luke 13:34), and mercy (Mat. 15:22–28; Jude 21). He also manifested love when He rebuked sin (Mat. 16:23; Mark 9:19; 10:13–14), expressed anger at those who were cruel, heartless, or insensitive to the suffering and needs of others (see Mark 3:5, note), warned us of hell (Mat. 5:29–30; Luke 12:5), and offered Himself as a sacrifice for our salvation (Mat. 26:38; John 10:11,17–18; 13:1).

11:2 ORDINANCES. Ordinances were instructions relating to doctrine, moral standards, and codes of conduct that Paul delivered to the churches by the authority of Christ. Note that the content and instruction of ch. 11 outlines God's will for His people in such matters as outward dress, modesty, appearance, and proper conduct. To teach that God is concerned only with inner attitudes and not with "externals" departs from God's clear revelation in Scripture. To dress properly and modestly is a Biblical principle of lasting validity (see 1 Tim. 2:9, note).

11:3 HEAD OF EVERY MAN. Paul is concerned about the proper relationship between men and women, and he seeks to uphold that relationship as ordained by God. (1) He maintains that in Christ a perfect spiritual equality exists among men and women as heirs of God's grace, yet it is an equality involving order and subordination with respect to authority (see Gal. 3:28, note). As God is the head of Christ, Christ is the head of man, and man the head of woman. The word "head" seems to express both authority and origination (cf. 3:23; 11:8,10; 15:28; Judg. 10:18; Eph. 1:21–22; 5:23–24; Col. 1:18; 2:10).

(2) Paul bases the husband's headship not on cultural considerations, but on God's creative activity and purpose in creating the woman to help the man (vv. 8–9; see Gen. 2:18, note; 1 Tim. 2:13, note).

(3) Subordination is not demeaning to one's person, for it does not imply suppression or oppression. Rather it states that the husband must recognize the worth God places upon the woman and that his responsibility involves protecting and leading her in such a way as to fulfill God's will for her in the home and the church.

(4) Just as Christ is not inferior or second-class because the Father is His Head, so the woman is not a second-class person because man is her "head." Furthermore, in the kingdom of God leadership never implies being "greater." Servanthood and obedience are greatness in the kingdom of God (Mat. 20:25–28; Phil. 2:5–9). Paul's treatment of the relationship of men and women should be studied in conjunction with his treatment of the wife's and husband's responsibilities in marriage (see Eph. 5:21–23, notes).

11:6 LET HER BE COVERED. The woman covered her head in Paul's day in order to show modesty and subordination to her husband and to demonstrate her dignity. The veil meant that she was to be respected and honored as a woman. Without a veil she had no dignity; men did not respect women without veils because they were in effect flaunting themselves publicly and shamefully. Thus, the veil served as a sign of the value, worth, and glory of womanhood as God created her.

The principle behind the wearing of veils is still

shame for a woman to be shorn or shaven, let her be covered.

7 For a man indeed ought not to cover *his* head, forasmuch as [x]he is the image and glory of God: but the woman is the glory of the man.

8 For [y]the man is not of the woman; but the woman of the man.

9 [z]Neither was the man created for the woman; but the woman for the man.

10 For this cause ought the woman [a]to have [o]power on *her* head [b]because of the angels.

11 Nevertheless [c]neither is the man without the woman, neither the woman without the man, in the Lord.

12 For as the woman *is* of the man, even so *is* the man also by the woman; but all things of God.

13 Judge in yourselves: is it comely that a woman pray unto God uncovered?

14 Doth not even nature itself teach you, that, if a man have long hair, it is a shame unto him?

15 But if a woman have long hair, it is a glory to her: for *her* hair is given her for a [p]covering.

16 But [d]if any man seem to be contentious, we have no such custom, [e]neither the churches of God.

The Lord's Supper

11:23–25pp — Mat. 26:26–28; Mark 14:22–24; Luke 22:17–20

17 Now in this that I declare *unto you* I praise *you* not, that ye come together not for the better, but for the worse.

18 For first of all, when ye come together in the church, [f]I hear that there be [q]divisions among you; and I partly believe it.

19 For [g]there must be also [r]heresies among you, [h]that they which are approved may be made manifest among you.

20 When ye come together there-

11:7 [x]Gen. 1:26
11:8 [y]Gen. 2:21
11:9 [z]Gen. 2:18
11:10 [a]Gen. 24:65 [b]Eccl. 5:6
11:11 [c]Gal. 3:28
11:16 [d]1 Tim. 6:4 [e]ch. 7:17
11:18 [f]ch. 1:10,11
11:19 [g]Mat. 18:7 Luke 17:1 1 Tim. 4:1 [h]Luke 2:35 1 John 2:19

[o] i.e. *a covering, in sign that she is under the power of her husband* [p] Or, *veil* [q] Or, *schisms* [r] Or, *sects*

needed today. A Christian woman should dress in a modest and careful way, with honorable and dignified dress that allows her to go anywhere with security and profound respect. When dressing modestly and properly for the glory of God, a woman enhances her own God-given place of dignity, worth, and honor.

11:10 POWER ON *HER* HEAD. Once again Paul emphasizes that women should be veiled in public, that is, have a symbol of "power" or authority on their heads (see vv. 3,6, notes). The phrase "because of the angels" may refer to the fact that angels are concerned with proper order and are shocked at conduct not according to God's will (cf. 4:9).

11:14 IF A MAN HAVE LONG HAIR. God desires that the physical differences between men and women be observed. (1) Paul uses hair as an example, stating that the length of the hair of men and women should be such as to distinguish between one or the other. A woman's hair should be long in comparison to the man's, symbolizing her acceptance of the dignity, value, and honor of her womanhood as God created her (see v. 6, note). A man's hair, in contrast to the woman's, should be short.

(2) In N.T. times, long hair was disgraceful and shunned by Jewish men as well as by those of first-century Corinth. Pictures portraying Jesus as having long hair are based wholly on the imagination of the artists from the Middle Ages, not on Biblical or historical evidence (thousands of paintings and sculptures from N.T. times prove this). The apostle would not have written, "if a man have long hair, it is a shame unto him," if Christ had worn his hair long as did women. Hence, Paul's statement is in conflict, not with the custom of Jesus, but with the invention of artists (cf. Ex. 20:4).

11:20 THE LORD'S SUPPER. The Lord's Supper is described in four passages: Mat. 26:26–29; Mark 14:22–25; Luke 22:15–20; 1 Cor. 11:23–25. Its significance relates to the past, the present, and the future.

(1) The past significance. (a) It is a remembrance (Gk. *anamnēsis*; vv. 24–26; Luke 22:19) of the death of Christ on Calvary for the believer's redemption from sin and condemnation. Through the Lord's Supper we are once again confronted with the saving death of Christ and its redemptive significance for our lives. The death of Christ is our ultimate motivation against falling into sin and for abstaining from all appearance of evil (1 Thes. 5:22). (b) It is a thanksgiving (Gk. *eucharistia*) for the blessings and salvation of God made available by the sacrifice of Jesus Christ on the cross (v. 24; Mat. 26:27–28; Mark 14:23; Luke 22:19).

(2) The present significance. (a) The Lord's Supper is a fellowship (Gk. *koinōnia*) with Christ and a participation in the benefits of His sacrificial death, as well as a fellowship with the other members of the body of Christ (10:16–17). In this supper with the risen Lord, He as the host becomes present in a special way (cf. Mat. 18:20; Luke 24:35). (b) It is a recognition and proclamation of the new covenant (Gk. *kainē diathēkē*) by which believers reaffirm the Lordship of Christ and our commitment to do His will, to remain loyal, to resist sin, and to identify ourselves with the mission of Christ (v. 25; Mat. 26:28; Mark 14:24; Luke 22:20; see article on THE OLD COVENANT AND THE NEW COVENANT, p. 1954).

(3) The future significance. (a) The Lord's Sup-

fore into one place, [s]*this* is not to eat
the Lord's supper.
21 For in eating every one taketh
before *other* his own supper: and one is
hungry, and [i]another is drunken.
22 What? have ye not houses to eat
and to drink in? or despise ye [j]the
church of God, and [k]shame [t]them
that have not? What shall I say to you?
shall I praise you in this? I praise *you*
not.
23 For [l]I have received of the Lord
that which also I delivered unto you,
[m]That the Lord Jesus the *same* night in
which he was betrayed took bread:
24 And when he had given thanks,
he brake *it*, and said Take, eat: this is
my body, which is broken for you: this
do [u]in remembrance of me.
25 After the same manner also *he*
took the cup, when he had supped, say-
ing, This cup is the new testament in
my blood: this do ye, as oft as ye drink
it, in remembrance of me.
26 For as often as ye eat this bread,
and drink this cup, [v]ye do show the
Lord's death [n]till he come.
27 [o]Wherefore whosoever shall
eat this bread, and drink *this* cup of the
Lord, unworthily, shall be guilty of the
body and blood of the Lord.
28 But [p]let a man examine him-
self, and so let him eat of *that* bread,
and drink of *that* cup.
29 For he that eateth and drinketh
unworthily, eateth and drinketh
[w]damnation to himself, not discerning
the Lord's body.
30 For this cause many *are* weak
and sickly among you, and many sleep.
31 For [q]if we would judge our-
selves, we should not be judged.
32 But when we are judged, [r]we
are chastened of the Lord, that we
should not be condemned with the
world.
33 Wherefore, my brethren, when
ye come together to eat, tarry one for
another.
34 And if any man hunger, let him
eat at home; that ye come not together
unto [w]condemnation. And the rest
[s]will I set in order when [t]I come.

11:21 [i]2 Pet. 2:13; Jude 12
11:22 [j]ch. 10:32; [k]Jas. 2:6
11:23 [l]ch. 15:3; [m]Mat. 26:26; Luke 22:19
11:26 [n]John 14:3; Acts 1:11
11:27 [o]John 6:51
11:28 [p]2 Cor. 13:5
11:31 [q]Ps. 32:5; 1 John 1:9
11:32 [r]Ps. 94:12
11:34 [s]Tit. 1:5; [t]ch. 4:19
12:1 [u]ch. 14:1,37

The diversities of spiritual gifts

12 NOW [u]CONCERNING spiritual
gifts, brethren, I would not have
you ignorant.

[s] Or, *ye cannot eat* [t] Or, *them that are poor?* [u] Or, *for a remembrance* [v] Or, *show ye* [w] Or, *judgment*

per is a foretaste of the future kingdom of God and the future messianic banquet when all believers will be present with the Lord (Mat. 8:11; 22:1–14; Mark 14:25; Luke 13:29; 22:17–18,30). (b) It looks forward to the imminent return of Christ for His people (v. 26) and dramatizes the prayer, "Thy kingdom come" (Mat. 6:10; cf. Rev. 22:20).

At the Lord's Supper all the above significances are made meaningful only if we come before the Lord in true faith, sincere prayer, and with commitment to God's Word and will.

11:21 ANOTHER IS DRUNKEN. "One is hungry, and another is drunken" can be translated, "One is hungry and another is filled to the full." This is a preferred translation for the following reasons. (1) The word "drunk" (Gk. *methuō*) carries two meanings. It can refer (a) to being drunk or (b) to being filled or satisfied without reference to intoxication (see John 2:10, note on the use of this word in relation to the wedding at Cana).

(2) The Scriptural context of this verse clearly relates to the meal in general. When the Corinthians gathered together for their fellowship meals before partaking of the Lord's Supper (cf. 2 Pet. 2:13; Jude 12), some gathered in small groups and ate their meals separately (vv. 18–19). The poor who could not contribute to the meal were ignored and left hungry. Paul was not referring to an issue of intoxication here; if he had been, he surely would have severely condemned it as he did elsewhere in the letter (cf. 6:10). He regarded drunkenness not merely as an issue of disregard for others, but also a condition so serious that it excludes one from the kingdom of God (6:10; Gal. 5:21).

11:24–25 MY BODY . . . MY BLOOD. These words refer to Christ's body given in death and his blood shed sacrificially on the cross. When Christ said of the bread, "This is my body," He meant that it represented His body. The "cup" represented the blood of Christ shed on Calvary for ratification of the "new testament." To eat the bread and drink the cup means to proclaim and accept the benefits of Christ's sacrificial death (v. 26).

11:27 EAT . . . DRINK . . . UNWORTHILY. To eat in an unworthy manner is to partake of the Lord's table in an indifferent, self-centered, careless, and irreverent spirit, without any intention or desire of departing from known sins and of accepting the covenant of grace with all its promises and obligations. One who participates in such an unworthy manner sins terribly against the Lord. He is guilty of recrucifying Christ and immediately comes under special judgment and retribution (vv. 29–32). Being "guilty of the body and blood of the Lord" means being held responsible for His death.

11:32 CHASTENED OF THE LORD. The purpose of the judgment and chastening of the Lord (cf. v. 30) is that we might not be condemned eternally with the world. This merciful purpose of God avails for all who repent of their sins and judge themselves rightly (v. 31).

12:1 CONCERNING SPIRITUAL *GIFTS*. In

2 Ye know [v]that ye were Gentiles,
carried away unto these [w]dumb idols,
even as ye were led.
3 Wherefore I give you to under-
stand, [x]that no man speaking by the
Spirit of God calleth Jesus [x]accursed:
and [y]*that* no man can say that Jesus
is the Lord, but by the Holy Ghost.
4 Now [z]there are diversities of
gifts, but [a]the same Spirit.
5 [b]And there are differences of
[y]administrations, but the same Lord.
6 And there are diversities of opera-
tions, but it is the same God [c]which
worketh all in all.

The manifestation of the Spirit

7 [d]But the manifestation of the
Spirit is given to every man to profit
withal.
8 For to one is given by the Spirit
[e]the word of wisdom; to another [f]the
word of knowledge by the same Spirit;

12:2 [v]Eph. 2:11 1 Thes. 1:9 1 Pet. 4:3 [w]Ps. 115:5 **12:3** [x]Mark 9:39 1 John 4:2 [y]Mat. 16:17 John 15:26 **12:4** [z]Rom. 12:4 1 Pet. 4:10 [a]Eph. 4:4 **12:5** [b]Rom. 12:6 Eph. 4:11 **12:6** [c]Eph. 1:23 **12:7** [d]Rom. 12:6 Eph. 4:7 **12:8** [e]ch. 2:6,7 [f]2 Cor. 8:7 **12:9** [g]Mat. 17:19 2 Cor. 4:13 [h]Mark 16:18 Jas. 5:14 **12:10** [i]Mark 16:17 Gal. 3:5 [j]Rom. 12:6

9 [g]To another faith by the same
Spirit; to another [h]the gifts of healing
by the same Spirit;
10 [i]To another the working of mir-
acles; to another [j]prophecy; [k]to an-
other discerning of spirits; to another
[l]*divers* kinds of tongues; to another
the interpretation of tongues:
11 But all these worketh that one
and the selfsame Spirit, [m]dividing to
every man severally [n]as he will.

The importance of all gifts

12 For [o]as the body is one, and
hath many members, and all the mem-
bers of that one body, being many, are
one body: [p]so also *is* Christ.
13 For [q]by one Spirit are we all

[k]1 John 4:1 [l]Acts 2:4 **12:11** [m]Rom. 12:6; 2 Cor. 10:13 [n]John 3:8 **12:12** [o]Rom. 12:4,5; Eph. 4:4 [p]Gal. 3:16 **12:13** [q]Rom. 6:5

[x]Or, *anathema* [y]Or, *ministries*

chs. 12–14 Paul deals with the gifts of the Holy Spirit given to the body of Christ. These gifts were an indispensable part of the early church's life and ministry. God intends that these gifts continue in operation until the return of Jesus Christ (see 1:7, note). His purposes for the spiritual gifts are as follows:

(1) To manifest the grace, power, and love of the Holy Spirit among His people in their public gatherings, homes, families, and individual lives (vv. 4–7; 14:25; Rom. 15:18–19; Eph. 4:8);

(2) To help make the preaching of the gospel to lost people effective by giving supernatural confirmation to the message (Mark 16:15–20; Acts 14:8–18; 16:16–18; 19:11–20; 28:1–10);

(3) To meet human needs and to strengthen and build up spiritually both the church (vv. 7,14–30; 14:3,12,26) and individual believers (14:4), i.e., to perfect believers in "charity out of a pure heart and *of* a good conscience, and *of* faith unfeigned" (1 Tim. 1:5; cf. 1 Cor. 13);

(4) To wage effective spiritual war against Satan and the forces of evil (Is. 61:1; Acts 8:5–7; 26:18; Eph. 6:11–12). Passages that deal with spiritual gifts are Rom. 12:3–8; 1 Cor. 1:7; 12–14; Eph. 4:4–16; 1 Pet. 4:10–11.

12:1–6 SPIRITUAL *GIFTS*. The terms that the Bible uses for spiritual gifts specify their nature. (1) "Spiritual *gifts*" (Gk. *pneumatika*, derived from *pneuma*, "Spirit") refer to supernatural manifestations which come as gifts from the Holy Spirit operating through believers for the common good (vv. 1,7; 14:1).

(2) "Gifts" or "grace gifts" (Gk. *charismata*, derived from *charis*, "grace") indicates that spiritual gifts involve both an inward motivation and the power to perform them (i.e., actualized enablement), received from the Holy Spirit; such gifts strengthen spiritually the body of Christ and those in need of spiritual help (v. 4; see Rom. 12:6, note; Eph. 4:11; 1 Pet. 4:10; see article on THE MINISTRY GIFTS OF THE CHURCH, p. 1852).

(3) "Administrations" or "ministries" (Gk. *diakoniai*, derived from *diakonia*, "service") emphasizes that there are different ways of service and that certain gifts involve being given the ability and power to help and assist others (vv. 4–5,27–31; Eph. 4:7,11–13). Paul indicates that the ministry aspect of the gifts reflects the "servant" ministry of the Lord Jesus. Thus the operation of the gifts are defined in terms of Christ's presence and operation in our midst (cf. 1:4; 12:3).

(4) "Operations" or "effects" (Gk. *energēmata*, from *energēs*, "active, energetic") signifies that spiritual gifts are direct operations of the power of God the Father and produce certain results (vv. 6,10).

(5) "The manifestation of the Spirit" (Gk. *phanerōsis*, from *phaneros*, "manifest") emphasizes that spiritual gifts are direct manifestations of the working and presence of the Holy Spirit in the congregation (vv. 7–11).

12:3 JESUS IS THE LORD. Paul begins the discussion on spiritual gifts with the truth that the gifts and manifestations of the Holy Spirit will exalt Jesus as Lord of the church. The ultimate criterion of the Spirit's activity is an ever-growing expression of the person, presence, power, love, and righteousness of the Lord Jesus Christ. In the manifestation of spiritual gifts Christ Himself ministers by the Spirit through His people to His people (see vv. 12–27; Mat. 25:40).

12:7 MANIFESTATION OF THE SPIRIT. For comments on spiritual gifts as manifestations of the Holy Spirit, as well as a description of the various gifts listed here, see article on SPIRITUAL GIFTS FOR BELIEVERS, p. 1790.

12:12 THE BODY . . . *IS* CHRIST. See v. 1, note on spiritual gifts and the body of Christ.

12:13 BY ONE SPIRIT ARE WE ALL BAP-

baptized into one body, [r]whether *we be* Jews or [z]Gentiles, whether *we be* bond or free; and [s]have been all made to drink into one Spirit.

14 For the body is not one member, but many.

15 If the foot shall say, Because I am not the hand, I am not of the body; is it therefore not of the body?

16 And if the ear shall say, Because I am not the eye, I am not of the body; is it therefore not of the body?

17 If the whole body *were* an eye, where *were* the hearing? If the whole *were* hearing, where *were* the smelling?

18 But now hath [t]God set the members every one of them in the body, [u]as it hath pleased him.

19 And if they were all one member, where *were* the body?

20 But now *are they* many members, yet but one body.

21 And the eye cannot say unto the hand, I have no need of thee: nor again the head to the feet, I have no need of you.

22 Nay, much more those members of the body, which seem to be more feeble, are necessary:

23 And those *members* of the body, which we think to be less honourable, upon these we [a]bestow more abundant honour; and our uncomely *parts* have more abundant comeliness.

24 For our comely *parts* have no need: but God hath tempered the body together, having given more abundant honour to that *part* which lacked:

25 That there should be no [b]schism in the body; but *that* the members should have the same care one for another.

26 And whether one member suffer, all the members suffer with it; or one member be honoured, all the members rejoice with it.

27 Now [v]ye are the body of Christ, and [w]members in particular.

28 And [x]God hath set some in the church, first [y]apostles, secondarily [z]prophets, thirdly teachers, after that [a]miracles, then [b]gifts of healings, [c]helps, [d]governments, [c]diversities of tongues.

29 *Are* all apostles? *are* all prophets? *are* all teachers? *are* all [d]workers of miracles?

30 Have all the gifts of healing? do all speak with tongues? do all interpret?

31 But [e]covet earnestly the best gifts: and yet show I unto you a more excellent way.

1 Cor. 14:1-40

12:13 [r]Gal. 3:28 Col. 3:11 [s]John 6:63
12:18 [t]ver. 28 [u]Rom. 12:3
12:27 [v]Rom. 12:5 Eph. 1:23 & 4:12 & 5:23,30 Col. 1:24 [w]Eph. 5:30
12:28 [x]Eph. 4:11 [y]Eph. 2:20 & 3:5 [z]Acts 13:1 Rom. 12:6 [a]ver. 10 [b]ver. 9 [c]Num. 11:17 [d]Rom. 12:8 1 Tim. 5:17 Heb. 13:17,24
12:31 [e]ch. 14:1,39

The relationship of gifts and love

13 THOUGH I speak with the tongues of men and of angels, and have not charity, I am become *as*

[z] Gk. *Greeks* [a] Or, *put on* [b] Or, *division* [c] Or, *kinds;* ver. 10 [d] Or, *powers*

TIZED. The baptism "by one Spirit" refers neither to water baptism nor to Christ's baptism of the believer in the Holy Spirit, such as occurred on the day of Pentecost (see Mark 1:8; Acts 2:4, note). Rather, it refers to the Holy Spirit's baptizing the believer into Christ's body, uniting him to the body of Christ and making him spiritually one with other believers. It is a spiritual transformation (i.e., regeneration) which occurs at conversion and puts the believer "in Christ" (see article on REGENERATION, p. 1597).

12:25 MEMBERS ... CARE ONE FOR ANOTHER. Spiritual gifts should not be the basis for honoring a person or considering one believer as more important than another (vv. 22–24). Rather each person is placed in Christ's body according to God's will (v. 18), and all the members are important for the spiritual well-being and proper functioning of the body. Spiritual gifts must be used, not in pride or for personal exaltation, but with the sincere desire to help others and with a heart which genuinely cares for one another (see ch. 13).

12:28 GOD HATH SET SOME IN THE CHURCH. Paul gives here a partial list of the ministry gifts (see Rom. 12:6–8 and Eph. 4:11–13 for other lists of ministry gifts). See article on THE MINISTRY GIFTS OF THE CHURCH, p. 1852, for the definition of apostles, prophets, evangelists, pastors, and teachers; see also John 6:2, note, for definition of "miracles"; Rom. 12:7–8, for notes on "helps" (the gift of mercy) and "governments" (the gift of ruling).

12:30 DO ALL SPEAK WITH TONGUES? Paul's rhetorical question here implies a negative answer. The context in ch. 12 shows that Paul is referring to the use of the gift of tongues and its companion gift of interpretation in public worship services. He is not attempting to limit the use of tongues in prayer and praise privately addressed to God (cf. 14:5). Most believers baptized in the Holy Spirit find it easy to pray in tongues as they yield themselves to the Spirit. On the day of Pentecost (Acts 2:4), in Caesarea (Acts 10:44–46), and at Ephesus (Acts 19:2–6), all who were filled with the Spirit spoke with tongues as a sign that they had received the fullness of the Spirit (see article on SPEAKING IN TONGUES, p. 1656).

13:1 AND HAVE NOT CHARITY. Ch. 13 is a continuation of Paul's discussion of the question of spiritual gifts. Here he emphasizes that to possess spiritual gifts without having love amounts to nothing (vv. 1–3). The "more excellent way"

SPIRITUAL GIFTS FOR BELIEVERS

1 Cor. 12:7 "But the manifestation of the Spirit is given to every man to profit withal."

GENERAL PERSPECTIVE. The Holy Spirit is manifested through a variety of spiritual gifts given to believers (1 Cor. 12:7–11). These manifestations of the Spirit are intended for the upbuilding and sanctification of the church (12:7; see 14:26, note). They are not the same as the gifts and ministries mentioned in Rom. 12:6–8 and Eph. 4:11, whereby a believer receives the power and ability to minister in a more permanent manner in the church. The list in 1 Cor. 12:8–10 is not necessarily exhaustive and the gifts may occur in various combinations.

(1) The manifestations of the Spirit are given according to the will of the Spirit (1 Cor. 12:11) when need arises and according to the earnest desire of the believer (12:31; 14:1).

(2) Some gifts may be manifested through an individual on a regular basis, and a believer may have more than one gift to minister to particular needs. The believer ought to desire "gifts," not just one gift (1 Cor. 12:31; 14:1).

(3) It is unscriptural and unwise to assume that because someone exercises a spectacular gift, that person is more spiritual than one who has less spectacular gifts. Furthermore, possessing a gift does not mean that God approves of all a person does or teaches. Spiritual gifts must not be confused with the fruit of the Spirit that relates more directly to Christian character and sanctification (Gal. 5:22–23).

(4) The Spirit's manifestation through gifts may be counterfeited by Satan or false workers disguising themselves as servants of Christ (Mat. 7:21–23; 24:11,24; 2 Cor. 11:13–15; 2 Thes. 2:8–10). The believer must not believe every spiritual manifestation, but ought to "try the spirits whether they are of God: because many false prophets are gone out into the world" (1 John 4:1; cf. 1 Thes. 5:20–21; see article on TESTING FOR GENUINE BAPTISM IN THE SPIRIT, p. 1682).

INDIVIDUAL GIFTS. In 1 Cor. 12:8–10, the apostle Paul lists a variety of the gifts that the Holy Spirit gives to believers. Though he does not define their characteristics here, we can glean from other passages of the Scriptures what they might be.

(1) *Word of wisdom*. This is a wise utterance spoken through the operation of the Holy Spirit. It applies the revelation of God's Word or the Holy Spirit's wisdom to a specific situation or problem (Acts 6:10; 15:13–22). It is not, however, the same as having the wisdom of God for daily living. The latter is obtained by diligent study and meditation on God's ways and Word, and by prayer (Jas. 1:5–6).

(2) *Word of knowledge*. This is an utterance inspired by the Holy Spirit that reveals knowledge about people, circumstances, or Biblical truth. It is often connected closely with prophecy (Acts 5:1–10; 1 Cor. 14:24–25).

(3) *Gift of faith*. This is not saving faith, but rather a special supernatural faith imparted by the Holy Spirit that enables the Christian to believe God for the extraordinary and miraculous. It is a faith that removes mountains (1 Cor. 13:2) and is often found in combination with other manifestations such as healings and miracles (see Mat. 17:20, note on true faith; Mark 11:22–24; Luke 17:6).

(4) *Gifts of healing*. These gifts are given to the church to restore physical health by divinely supernatural means (Mat. 4:23–25; 10:1; Acts 3:6–8; 4:30). The plural (gifts) indicates healing of various illnesses and suggests that every act of healing is a special gift of God. Although gifts of healing are not given to every member of the body in a special way (cf. 1 Cor. 12:11,30), all members may pray for the sick. When faith is present, the sick will be healed (see article on DIVINE HEALING, p. 1418.) Healing may also occur as a result of obedience to the instructions of Jas. 5:14–16 (see Jas. 5:15, notes).

(5) *Miracles*. These are deeds of supernatural power which alter the normal course of nature. They include divine acts in which God's kingdom is manifested against Satan and evil spirits (see John 6:2, note; see article on THE KINGDOM OF GOD, p. 1428).

(6) *Prophecy*. We must distinguish between prophecy listed in 1 Cor. 12:10 as a temporary manifestation of the Spirit from prophecy cited as a ministry gift of the church in Eph. 4:11. As a ministry gift, prophecy is given only to some believers, who must then function as prophets within the church (see article on THE MINISTRY GIFTS OF THE CHURCH, p. 1852). As a spiritual manifestation, prophecy is potentially available to every Spirit-filled Christian (Acts 2:17–18). Concerning the second of these two forms of prophecy, observe the following: (a) Prophecy is a special gift that enables a believer to bring a word or revelation directly from God under the impulse of the Holy Spirit (1 Cor. 14:24–25,29–31). It is not the delivery of a previously prepared sermon. (b) In both the O.T. and the N.T., prophecy is not primarily foretelling the future, but proclaiming the will of God and exhorting God's people to righteousness, faithfulness, endurance, and encouragement (14:3; see article on THE PROPHET IN THE OLD TESTAMENT, p. 1002). (c) The message may expose the condition of a person's heart (14:25) or offer edification, exhortation, comfort, warning, and judgment (14:3,25–26,31). (d) The church must not receive such prophecy as an infallible message, for many false prophets will enter the church (1 John 4:1). Therefore, all prophecies must be tested as to their genuineness and truth (1 Cor. 14:29,32; 1 Thes. 5:20–21) by whether they conform to the Word of God (1 John 4:1), by whether they promote godly living (1 Tim. 6:3), and by whether they are uttered by one who is sincerely living under the Lordship of Christ (1 Cor. 12:3). (e) Prophecy operates under the will of God and not man. The N.T. never indicates that the church actively sought revelation or direction from those who claimed they were prophets. Prophecy was given to the church only when God initiated the message (1 Cor. 12:11; 2 Pet. 1:21).

(7) *Discerning of spirits*. This gift is a special ability given by the Spirit to properly discern and judge prophecies and to distinguish whether an utterance is from the Holy Spirit or not (see 1 Cor. 14:29, note; 1 John 4:1). Towards the end of the age when false teachers (see Mat. 24:5, note) and distortion of Biblical Christianity will greatly increase (see 1 Tim. 4:1, note), this gift will be extremely important for the church.

(8) *Kinds of tongues*. Concerning "tongues" (Gk. *glōssa*, meaning language) as a supernatural manifestation of the Spirit, the following must be pointed out. (a) Tongues may be an existing spoken language (Acts 2:4–6) or a language unknown on earth, e.g., "tongues . . . of angels" (1 Cor. 13:1; see ch. 14, notes; see also article on SPEAKING IN TONGUES, p. 1656). Such speech has not been learned and is often unintelligible both to the speaker (14:14) and to the hearers (14:16). (b) Speaking in tongues involves the spirit of man and the Spirit of God intermingling so that the believer communicates directly to God (i.e., in prayer, praise, blessing, or thanksgiving), giving expression or utterance at the level of one's spirit rather than the mind (14:2,14) and praying for oneself or others under the direct influence of the Holy Spirit apart from the activity of the mind (cf. 1 Cor. 14:2,4,15,28; Jude 20). Speaking in tongues with interpretation may at times contain a revelation, knowledge, prophecy, or teaching for the assembly of believers (1 Cor. 14:6). (c) Tongues in the congregation must be accompanied by a Spirit-given interpretation that communicates the content and meaning of the utterance to the community of believers (1 Cor. 14:3,27–28). When interpreted to the congregation, they function either as a form and directive to worship and prayer or as prophecy. The entire body of believers can then participate in this Spirit-inspired revelation. Interpreted tongues can thus be a means of edification as the whole congregation responds to the utterance (cf. 14:6,13). (d) Speaking in tongues within the congregation must be regulated. The speaker may never be in "ecstasy" or "out of control" (1 Cor. 14:27–28; see article on SPEAKING IN TONGUES, p. 1656).

(9) *Interpretation of tongues*. This is the ability given by the Holy Spirit to understand and make known the meaning of an utterance given in tongues. The gift may be given to the one who speaks in tongues or to someone else. Those who speak in tongues should pray also for the gift of interpretation (1 Cor. 14:13).

sounding brass, or a tinkling cymbal.
2 And though I have *the gift of*
[f]prophecy, and understand all mys-
teries, and all knowledge; and though
I have all faith, [g]so that I could re-
1 Thes. 3:7 move mountains, and have not charity,
I am nothing.
3 And [h]though I bestow all my
goods to feed *the poor,* and though I
give my body to be burned, and have
not charity, it profiteth me nothing.
4 [i]Charity suffereth long, *and* is
kind; charity envieth not; charity
[e]vaunteth not itself, is not puffed up,
5 Doth not behave itself unseemly,
[j]seeketh not her own, is not easily
provoked, thinketh no evil;
6 [k]Rejoiceth not in iniquity, but
[l]rejoiceth [f]in the truth;
7 [m]Beareth all things, believeth all
things, hopeth all things, endureth all
things.
8 Charity never faileth: but whether
there be prophecies, they shall fail;
whether *there be* tongues, they shall
cease; whether *there be* knowledge, it
shall vanish away.

13:2 [f]ch. 12:8-10,28 & 14:1 See Mat. 7:22 [g]Mat. 17:20 Mark 11:23 Luke 17:6
13:3 [h]Mat. 6:1,2
13:4 [i]Prov. 10:12 1 Pet. 4:8
13:5 [j]ch. 10:24 Phil. 2:4
13:6 [k]Ps. 10:3 Rom. 1:32 [l]2 John 4
13:7 [m]Rom. 15:1 Gal. 6:2 2 Tim. 2:24
13:9 [n]ch. 8:2
13:12 [o]2 Cor. 3:18 & 5:7 Phil. 3:12 [p]Mat. 18:10 1 John 3:2
14:1 [q]ch. 12:31 [r]Num. 11:25,29
14:2 [s]Acts 2:4 & 10:46

9 [n]For we know in part, and we
prophesy in part.
10 But when that which is perfect is
come, then that which is in part shall
be done away.
11 When I was a child, I spake as a
child, I understood as a child, I
[g]thought as a child: but when I be-
came a man, I put away childish
things.
12 For [o]now we see through a
glass, [h]darkly; but then [p]face to
face: now I know in part; but then shall
I know even as also I am known.
13 And now abideth faith, hope,
charity, these three; but the greatest of
these *is* charity.

Prophecy and uninterpreted tongues

14 FOLLOW AFTER charity, and
[q]desire spiritual *gifts,* [r]but
rather that ye may prophesy.
2 For he that [s]speaketh in an *un-*
known tongue speaketh not unto men,

[e] Or, *is not rash* [f] Or, *with the truth* [g] Or, *reasoned* [h] Gk. *in a riddle*

(12:31) is the exercise of spiritual gifts in love (vv. 4–8). As the only context in which spiritual gifts can fulfill the will of God, love must be the governing principle of all spiritual manifestations. Paul therefore exhorts the Corinthians to "follow after charity [love], and desire spiritual gifts" (14:1). They must earnestly desire the things of the Spirit because they sincerely want to help, comfort, and bless others in this life.

13:2 I AM NOTHING. Those whose lives are filled with "religious activities" are not necessarily approved of God; in fact, they may not be believers at all. For example, those who speak in tongues, prophesy, have knowledge, or achieve great works of faith, yet at the same time lack Christlike love and righteousness, are "nothing" in the sight of God. In God's judgment their spirituality and profession of faith are empty (v. 1) and they have no real place in His kingdom (cf. 6:9–10). They are not only lacking in the Spirit's fullness, but are also void of His indwelling presence. The spiritual manifestations through them are not of God but of another spirit, i.e., an evil spirit (see Acts 8:21, note; 1 John 4:1, note; see article on TESTING FOR GENUINE BAPTISM IN THE SPIRIT, p. 1682). What is essential to true Christian faith is love expressed through an ethic which does no harm to others and perseveres in loyalty to Christ and His Word (see also v. 13, note).

13:4–7 CHARITY SUFFERETH LONG. This section describes love as an activity and a behavior, not just as an inner feeling or motivation. The various aspects of love included here characterize God the Father, Son, and Holy Spirit. Since this is so, every believer must seek to grow in this kind of love.

13:8 TONGUES, THEY SHALL CEASE. Spiritual gifts such as prophecy, tongues, and knowledge will cease at the end of this age. The time of this ceasing is described as "when that which is perfect is come" (v. 10)—that is, at the end of this present age, when the believer's knowledge and character become perfect in eternity after Christ's second coming (v. 12; 1:7). Until then, we need the Holy Spirit and His gifts in our churches. There is no indication here or elsewhere in Scripture that the manifestation of the Holy Spirit through His gifts was to cease at the end of the first century era.

13:13 THE GREATEST . . . *IS* CHARITY. It is clear from this chapter that God exalts Christlike character more than ministry, faith, or the possession of spiritual gifts. (1) God values and emphasizes character that acts in love, patience (v. 4), kindness (v. 4), unselfishness (v. 5), hatred for evil and love for the truth (v. 6), honesty (v. 6), and endurance in righteousness (v. 7) much more than faith to move mountains or to perform great achievements in the church (vv. 1–2,8,13).

(2) The greatest in God's kingdom will be those who are great in inward godliness and love to God, not necessarily those who are greatest in outward accomplishments (see Luke 22:24–30, note). The love of God poured out within the believer's heart through the Holy Spirit is always greater than faith, hope, or anything else (Rom. 5:5).

14:1 DESIRE SPIRITUAL *GIFTS.* Believers who possess genuine love for others in the body of Christ must desire spiritual gifts in order to be able to help, comfort, encourage, and strengthen those

but unto God: for no man [i]understandeth *him;* howbeit in the spirit he speaketh mysteries.

3 But he that prophesieth speaketh unto men *to* edification, and exhortation, and comfort.

4 He that speaketh in an *unknown* tongue edifieth himself; but he that prophesieth edifieth the church.

Prophecy and interpreted tongues equally important

5 I would that ye all spake with tongues, but rather that ye prophesied: for greater *is* he that prophesieth than he that speaketh with tongues, except he interpret, that the church may receive edifying.

Uninterpreted tongues no benefit to others

6 Now, brethren, if I come unto you speaking with tongues, what shall I profit you, except I shall speak to you

[i] Gk. *heareth;* see Acts 22:9

in need (cf. 12:17). They may not wait passively for God to give the gifts of the Holy Spirit (12:7–10). Instead, they must earnestly desire, seek, and pray for those gifts, especially those which serve to exhort, comfort, and edify (vv. 3,13,19,26).

14:2 SPEAKETH IN AN *UNKNOWN* TONGUE. The Corinthians had overestimated the importance of the gift of tongues in public worship (see article on SPIRITUAL GIFTS FOR BELIEVERS, p. 1790) and were emphasizing it at the expense of the other gifts. Furthermore, they were exercising this gift in the church without interpretation. Paul seeks to correct this abuse by pointing out the unprofitableness of tongues without interpretation in public services. An outline of this chapter is as follows:

(1) Prophecy edifies the church more than uninterpreted tongues (vv. 1–4).

(2) Prophecy and tongues with interpretation are equally important to the church (v. 5).

(3) Speaking in tongues in public worship services without interpretation is of no benefit to others (vv. 6–12).

(4) Those who speak or pray in tongues in the church should seek to edify the church by praying for the gift of interpretation (v. 13).

(5) In Paul's personal life speaking in tongues to God is an important means of worship and spiritual growth (vv. 14–19).

(6) Prophecy is more useful than uninterpreted tongues because prophecy brings conviction of sin and the knowledge of God's presence (vv. 20–25).

(7) Speaking in tongues and prophesying must be regulated so that order may be maintained in the church (vv. 26–40).

14:2 SPEAKETH NOT UNTO MEN, BUT UNTO GOD. There are basically two ways to understand this verse. (1) Some believe that this verse indicates that the principal use of tongues, whether in the church or in private, is to speak primarily unto God and not to men. When tongues are directed unto God, they involve communing with God by the Holy Spirit and can take the form of prayer, praise, singing, blessing, and thanksgiving. What is spoken are "mysteries," i.e., things not understandable to the speaker or hearers (cf. vv. 2,13–17). Interpretation of the utterance (vv. 5,13) in tongues allows the congregation to enter into this manifestation of the Spirit-directed worship and thus to say "Amen" (v. 16) to the Spirit-inspired prayer or praise (v. 16; see also v. 6, note).

(2) On the other hand Paul's statement may mean that only God understands a tongue unless it is interpreted (v. 5). The implication would be that tongues, when interpreted, *are* unto men. This view is supported by Paul's statement that the reason why tongue-speaking is not unto men is because "no man understandeth" it (see v. 6, note).

14:3 PROPHESIETH . . . EDIFICATION. The gift of prophecy in the church is motivated by the Holy Spirit, not primarily to foretell the future, but to strengthen the believer's faith, spiritual life, and moral resolve to remain faithful to Christ and His teachings. Prophecy is not, however, preaching a prepared sermon, but giving a spontaneous word under the impulse of the Holy Spirit for the edification of the congregation (see article on SPIRITUAL GIFTS FOR BELIEVERS, p. 1790).

14:4 EDIFIETH HIMSELF. Tongues without interpretation edify (i.e., build up one's faith and spiritual life; see v. 26, note) the speaker because it puts him in direct communion with God by the Spirit (cf. Eph. 3:16; Jude 20), bypassing the mind. Paul states that he prays and communes with God in this way as well as with the mind (vv. 14–15).

14:5 I WOULD THAT YE ALL SPAKE WITH TONGUES. Paul's wish here refers to tongue-speaking in private devotion to God. Clearly such tongues have value for the individual Christian's personal worship and prayer (vv. 2,4). Paul adds that authentic tongues accompanied with interpretation in the assembly bring edification to the church, just as prophecy does. Speaking in tongues without interpretation does nothing for the church (vv. 7–9).

14:6 SPEAKING WITH TONGUES . . . PROFIT YOU, EXCEPT. Speaking in tongues can at times be directed toward the Christian community. Paul describes the hypothetical situation of coming to the Corinthians and speaking in tongues in the worship service. Such speaking would be of no benefit to them "except" he brings some revelation or knowledge. The construction of this verse suggests that his speaking in tongues, when interpreted, would consist of a message containing revelation, knowledge, prophecy, or instruction to the congregation. This interpretation finds support in v. 8, where Paul gives the analogy of a trumpet which brings a message and warns to prepare for battle. In other words, speaking in tongues with interpretation can bring a message to God's people, such as a message to prepare for spiritual war-

either by [t]revelation, or by knowledge, or by prophesying, or by doctrine?

7 And even things without life giving sound, whether pipe or harp, except they give a distinction in the [j]sounds, how shall it be known what is piped or harped?

8 For if the trumpet give an uncertain sound, who shall prepare himself to the battle?

9 So likewise ye, except ye utter by the tongue words [k]easy to be understood, how shall it be known what is spoken? for ye shall speak into the air.

10 There are, it may be, so many kinds of voices in the world, and none of them *is* without signification.

11 Therefore if I know not the meaning of the voice, I shall be unto him that speaketh a barbarian, and he that speaketh *shall be* a barbarian unto me.

12 Even so ye, forasmuch as ye are zealous [l]of spiritual *gifts*, seek that ye may excel to the edifying of the church.

Pray to interpret

13 Wherefore let him that speaketh in an *unknown* tongue pray that he may interpret.

14 For if I pray in an *unknown* tongue, my spirit prayeth, but my understanding is unfruitful.

Paul's use of tongues

15 What is it then? I will pray with the spirit, and I will pray with the understanding also: [u]I will sing with the spirit, and I will sing [v]with the understanding also.

16 Else when thou shalt bless with the spirit, how shall he that occupieth the room of the unlearned say Amen [w]at thy giving of thanks, seeing he understandeth not what thou sayest?

17 For thou verily givest thanks well, but the other is not edified.

18 I thank my God, I speak with tongues more than ye all:

19 Yet in the church I had rather speak five words with my understanding, that *by my voice* I might teach others also, than ten thousand words in an *unknown* tongue.

Prophecy brings conviction of sin

20 Brethren, [x]be not children in understanding: howbeit in malice [y]be ye children, but in understanding be [m]men.

21 [z]In the law it is [a]written, With *men of* other tongues and other lips will I speak unto this people; and yet for all that will they not hear me, saith the Lord.

22 Wherefore tongues are for a

14:6 [t]ver. 26
14:15 [u]Eph. 5:19 Col. 3:16 [v]Ps. 47:7
14:16 [w]ch. 11:24
14:20 [x]Ps. 131:2 Mat. 11:25 & 18:3 & 19:14 Rom. 16:19 ch. 3:1 Eph. 4:14 Heb. 5:12,13 [y]Mat. 18:3 1 Pet. 2:2
14:21 [z]John 10:34 [a]Is. 28:11,12

j Or, *tunes* k Gk. *significant* l Gk. *of spirits* m Gk. *perfect*, or, *of a ripe age;* see ch. 2:6

fare with Satan, sin, and the ungodly elements of the world, or it can challenge us to be ready for the imminent return of Christ.

14:8 TRUMPET . . . PREPARE HIMSELF TO THE BATTLE. Speaking in tongues in the congregation is like music; those who speak should produce sounds easy to be identified (v. 7). Like a trumpet, they must convey a clear message. Thus the one speaking in a tongue must pray that he may interpret what he says for the edification of others (v. 12).

14:15 PRAY WITH THE SPIRIT . . . WITH THE UNDERSTANDING. Paul refers to his own experience, to his own private use of tongues unto God. "I will pray with the spirit" means to pray in tongues with one's own spirit under the impulse of the Holy Spirit. The believer's spirit prays as the Holy Spirit gives the utterance (cf. 12:7,11; Acts 2:4). Paul is speaking here of the private use of tongues unto God. Paul used tongues not only for praying, but also for singing, praising, and giving thanks unto God (vv. 14–16). To "pray with the understanding" means to pray and praise with one's own mind in a learned language, also under the impulse of the Spirit.

14:18 I SPEAK WITH TONGUES. Paul considered the gift of tongues an important part of his spiritual life, which was frequently given to praying, singing, praising, and giving thanks in tongues. He speaks with reverence and gratitude for this manifestation of the Holy Spirit. Some have interpreted this verse as meaning that Paul spoke more learned languages than the Corinthians. However, this interpretation is incorrect, for the word "more" (Gk. *mallon*) is not an adjective modifying the noun "tongues," but a comparative adverb, modifying the verb "speak." Thus, Paul did not say "I speak in more languages," but rather, "I speak in tongues more (i.e., more often) than all of you."

14:19 YET IN THE CHURCH. In the church Paul preferred to utter a few words that people could understand than to speak ten thousand words in tongues without an interpretation. Vv. 18–19 imply that Paul spoke in tongues more in private devotions than in public worship.

14:22 TONGUES ARE FOR A SIGN. Tongues within the congregation become a negative sign to unbelievers in that they signify that the unbeliever is separated from God and cannot understand what is occurring (vv. 21,23). Prophecy, however, is a sign to the believer, for he recognizes that it

sign, not to them that believe, but
to them that believe not: but prophe-
sying *serveth* not for them that
believe not, but for them which be-
lieve.
23 If therefore the whole church be
come together into one place, and all
speak with tongues, and there come in
those that are unlearned, or unbeliev-
ers, [b]will they not say that ye are
mad?
24 But if all prophesy, and there
come in one that believeth not, or *one*
unlearned, he is convinced of all, he is
judged of all:
25 And thus are the secrets of his
heart made manifest; and so falling
down on *his* face he will worship God,
and report [c]that God is in you of a
truth.

14:23 [b]Acts 2:13
14:25 [c]Is. 45:14 Zech. 8:23
14:26 [d]ver. 6 ch. 12:8-10 [e]ch. 12:7 2 Cor. 12:19 Eph. 4:12
14:29 [f]ch. 12:10
14:30 [g]1 Thes. 5:19,20

Regulating spiritual gifts

26 How is it then, brethren? when
ye come together, every one of you
hath a psalm, [d]hath a doctrine, hath
a tongue, hath a revelation, hath an in-
terpretation. [e]Let all things be done
unto edifying.
27 If any man speak in an *unknown*
tongue, *let it be* by two, or at the most
by three, and *that* by course; and let
one interpret.
28 But if there be no interpreter, let
him keep silence in the church; and let
him speak to himself, and to God.
29 Let the prophets speak two or
three, and [f]let the other judge.
30 If *any thing* be revealed to anoth-
er that sitteth by, [g]let the first hold
his peace.
31 For ye may all prophesy one by

---

is a supernatural work of the Holy Spirit and a proof that God is at work in the church (vv. 24–25). Tongues also may be a sign to believers indicating that the Holy Spirit is being poured out (cf. Acts 10:44–46; 11:15–17) and manifested among God's people (cf. 12:7,10).

14:24 BELIEVETH NOT ... JUDGED OF ALL. One of the surest signs that the Holy Spirit is present and at work in any congregation is His conviction of sin, righteousness, and judgment (see John 16:8, note). (1) Through the manifestation of the Spirit among God's people, sin will be exposed, repentance called for, and sinners convicted. Where there is no exposing of unrighteousness, no conviction of sin, or no plea for repentance, the Holy Spirit is clearly not at work according to the Biblical pattern. (2) The exposing of sin within a person's heart (v. 25) does not require a special gift of revelation or "mind reading." The word of prophecy and its moral truth when proclaimed under the impulse of the Holy Spirit is sufficient to convict the heart of a sinner (Heb. 4:12).

14:26 ALL THINGS ... UNTO EDIFYING. The principal purpose of all spiritual gifts is to edify the church and the individual (vv. 3–4,12,17,26). "Edifying" (Gk. *oikodomeō*) means to strengthen and promote spiritual life, maturity, and godly character in believers. It is a work of the Holy Spirit through spiritual gifts by which believers are increasingly spiritually transformed in order that they may not be conformed to this world (Rom. 12:2–8), but may be built up in sanctification, love for God, concern for others, purity of heart, a good conscience, and a sincere faith (see ch. 13; Rom. 8:13; 14:1–4,26; Gal. 5:16–26; Eph. 2:19–22; 4:11–16; Col. 3:16; 1 Thes. 5:11; Jude 20; see 1 Tim. 1:5, note).

14:27 TWO, OR . . . THREE . . . INTERPRET. In the use of spiritual gifts there must be order and balance. The Biblical guidelines for speaking in tongues within the church are: (1) In any one meeting there must not be more than two or three who speak, pray, or praise in tongues, and this must be done with interpretation (vv. 27–28). (2) Speaking in tongues must be done by one person at a time (v. 27). (3) All speaking in tongues must be judged by the church as to its authenticity (vv. 29,32). (4) If there is no interpreter present, a believer may speak in tongues privately in prayer to God (v. 28).

14:29 LET THE OTHER JUDGE. All prophecy must be evaluated and weighed carefully as to what is said. This shows that N.T. prophecy was less than infallible and might need to be corrected. (1) At times prophecy and speaking in tongues might not be a word from God (cf. 1 John 4:1). Even evil spirits, through the presence of false teachers or prophets, can work in the congregation. Prophesying, speaking in tongues, or possessing any supernatural gift is no guarantee that one is a true prophet or a true believer (see article on FALSE TEACHERS, p. 1508), for spiritual gifts may be counterfeited by Satan (Mat. 24:24; 2 Thes. 2:9–12; Rev. 13:13–14).

(2) If the church has not set up proper and orderly ways (cf. v. 40) to evaluate and judge prophecies, it has failed to follow Biblical guidelines. Note too that prophecy was not considered an irresistible impulse of the Spirit, for only one prophet could speak at a time (vv. 30–32).

(3) What should be the attitude of the church toward prophetic messages? (a) All prophecy must be tested according to the standard of Biblical truth (cf. Deut. 13:1–3). That means that believers should watch for its fulfillment (cf. Deut. 18:22), preparing themselves for the possibility that the prophecy may or may not be fulfilled. (b) If the word of prophecy is an exhortation, the congregation needs to ask, "What must we do to obey the will of the Spirit?"

14:31 YE MAY ALL PROPHESY. The distinction between prophecy as a spiritual gift and prophecy as part of Holy Scripture must be clearly maintained, even though in both cases a message is received from God. (1) The writers of the Scrip-

one, that all may learn, and all may be
comforted.
32 And [h]the spirits of the prophets
are subject to the prophets.
33 For God is not *the author* of
[n]confusion, but of peace, [i]as in all
churches of the saints.
34 [j]Let your women keep silence
in the churches: for it is not permitted
unto them to speak; but *they are commanded*
to be under obedience, as also
saith the [k]law.
35 And if they will learn any thing,
let them ask their husbands at home:
for it is a shame for women to speak in
the church.
36 What? came the word of God out
from you? or came it unto you only?
37 [l]If any man think himself to be
a prophet, or spiritual, let him acknowledge
that the things that I write
unto you are the commandments of the
Lord.
38 But if any man be ignorant, let
him be ignorant.
39 Wherefore, brethren, [m]covet to
prophesy, and forbid not to speak with
tongues.
Gal. 3:5 40 [n]Let all things be done decently
and in order.

The resurrection of Christ

15 MOREOVER, BRETHREN, I
declare unto you the gospel
[o]which I preached unto you, which
also ye have received, and [p]wherein
ye stand;
2 [q]By which also ye are saved, if ye
[o]keep in memory [p]what I preached
unto you, unless [r]ye have believed in
vain.
3 For [s]I delivered unto you first of
all that [t]which I also received, how
that Christ died for our sins [u]according
to the scriptures;
4 And that he was buried, and that
he rose again the third day [v]according
to the scriptures:
5 [w]And that he was seen of Cephas,
then [x]of the twelve:
6 After that, he was seen of above
five hundred brethren at once; of whom
the greater part remain unto this
present, but some are fallen asleep.
7 After that, he was seen of James;
then [y]of all the apostles.
8 [z]And last of all he was seen of

14:32 [h]1 John 4:1 **14:33** [i]ch. 11:16 **14:34** [j]1 Tim. 2:11,12 [k]Gen. 3:16 **14:37** [l]2 Cor. 10:7 1 John 4:6 **14:39** [m]ch. 12:31 1 Thes. 5:20 **14:40** [n]ver. 33
15:1 [o]Gal. 1:11 [p]Rom. 5:2 **15:2** [q]Rom. 1:16 ch. 1:21 [r]Gal. 3:4 **15:3** [s]ch. 11:2,23 [t]Gal. 1:12 [u]Ps. 22:15 Is. 53:5,6 Dan. 9:26 Zech. 13:7 Luke 24:26,46 Acts 3:18 & 26:23 1 Pet. 1:11 & 2:24 **15:4** [v]Ps. 16:10 Is. 53:10 Hos. 6:2 Luke 24:26 Acts 2:25 1 Pet. 1:11 **15:5** [w]Luke 24:34 [x]Mat. 28:17 Mark 16:14 Luke 24:36 John 20:19
15:7 [y]Luke 24:50; Acts 1:3,4 **15:8** [z]Acts 9:4 & 22:14, 18

[n] Gk. *tumult,* or, *unquietness* [o] Or, *hold fast*
[p] Gk. *by what speech*

tures received their messages by direct inspiration of the Holy Spirit and communicated it without error. The result was an infallible message (see article on THE INSPIRATION AND AUTHORITY OF SCRIPTURE, p. 1924).

(2) However, prophecy as described in chs. 12 and 14 may not be assigned the same authority or infallibility as the inspired Word of God (2 Tim. 3:16). Although coming from the impulse of the Spirit, this kind of prophecy may never be considered inerrant. Its message is always subject to human error. This is why prophecy today may never be equated with the Holy Scripture. Furthermore, present-day prophecy may not be accepted by the local church until other believers judge the content of the utterance in order to determine if it is valid (see v. 29, note; 12:10). The primary basis for judging is the written Word of God: does it conform to apostolic teaching? The written Word of God must always stand in judgment over all experiences and utterances.

14:34 LET YOUR WOMEN KEEP SILENCE. V. 34 may be interpreted by v. 35 in the sense of forbidding women to interrupt the service by asking questions which could be asked at home. In 11:5 Paul assumes that women pray and prophesy in public assemblies (cf. the "all" of 14:23–24,31).

14:39 PROPHESY, AND FORBID NOT ... TONGUES. This double injunction concludes Paul's discussion of prophecy and tongues. If the Corinthians refuse to recognize that his instructions are "the commandments of the Lord," then they prove they are neither prophets nor the people of the Holy Spirit (vv. 37–38). Churches today that claim to follow God's Word, yet forbid speaking in tongues and do not earnestly desire that their people prophesy, should ask themselves how vv. 37–38 might apply to them.

15:2 IF YE KEEP IN MEMORY WHAT I PREACHED. Believers are not those who merely have faith in Jesus Christ. Rather believers are those who have faith in Jesus Christ as He is revealed in the full message of the gospel (vv. 1–4). Their faith in Christ is always bound to God's Word and the doctrine of the apostles (11:2,23; 15:1,3; Rom. 6:17; Gal. 1:12). For this reason, believers can be described as people who submit to the Christ of the Bible as their Lord and Savior and who live under the Word of God. They submit without reservation to its authority, hold firmly to its teaching, trust its promises, heed its warnings, and follow its commands. They are a people captive to the Word of God, using the Scriptures to test all human ideas and accepting nothing that is contrary to the Bible.

15:8 AND LAST OF ALL. Paul's statement "last of all" must be taken absolutely. Paul was the last of the apostles defined in the sense of receiving a special commission through a personal meeting with the risen Lord in order to participate in forming the original and fundamental testimony of Jesus Christ (cf. Acts 9:3–8; 22:6–11; 26:12–18).

THE RESURRECTION OF THE BODY

***1 Cor. 15:35** "But some man will say, How are the dead raised up? and with what body do they come?"*

The resurrection of the body is an important and essential doctrine in the Scriptures. It refers to God's raising of a body from the dead and reuniting it with the person's soul and spirit, from which it was separated during the intermediate state.

(1) The Bible reveals at least three reasons why the resurrection of the body is necessary. (a) The body is essential to man's total personality; he is incomplete without a body. Thus, the redemption Christ offers applies to the whole person, including the body (Rom. 8:18–25; see article on HUMAN PERSONHOOD, p. 978). (b) The body is the temple of the Holy Spirit (1 Cor. 6:19); it will become once more a temple of the Spirit at the resurrection. (c) To undo the result of sin at all levels, man's final enemy (death of the body) must be conquered by the resurrection (1 Cor. 15:26).

(2) Both the O.T. Scriptures (compare Heb. 11:17–19 with Gen. 22:1–14; Ps. 16:10 with Acts 2:24ff; cf. Job 19:25–27; Is. 26:19; Dan. 12:2; Hosea 13:14) and the N.T. Scriptures (Luke 14:13–14; 20:35–36; John 5:21,28–29; 6:39–40,44,54; 1 Cor. 15:21–23; Phil. 3:11; 1 Thes. 4:14–16; Rev. 20:4–6,13) teach the future bodily resurrection.

(3) Our bodily resurrection is guaranteed by the resurrection of Christ (see Mat. 28:6, note; Acts 17:31; Rom. 8:11; 1 Cor. 15:12,20–23).

(4) In general terms, the believer's resurrected body will be like the Lord's own resurrected body (Rom. 8:29; 1 Cor. 15:20,42–44,49; Phil. 3:20–21; 1 John 3:2). More specifically, that means that the resurrected body will be: (a) a body possessing continuity and identity with the body of this life and therefore recognizable (Luke 16:19–31); (b) a body changed into a heavenly body adapted for the new heaven and new earth (1 Cor. 15:42–44,47–48; cf. Rev. 21:1); (c) an imperishable body, free from decay and death (1 Cor. 15:42); (d) a glorified body, like Christ's (1 Cor. 15:43; Phil. 3:20–21); (e) a powerful body not subject to disease or weakness (1 Cor. 15:43); (f) a spiritual (i.e., not natural, but supernatural) body, not bound by the laws of nature (Luke 24:31; John 20:19; 1 Cor. 15:44); (g) a body capable of eating and drinking (Luke 14:15; 22:14–18,30; 24:43).

(5) When believers receive their new bodies, they put on immortality (1 Cor. 15:53). Scripture indicates at least three purposes for this: (a) so that believers may become all that God intended for humans at creation (cf. 1 Cor. 2:9); (b) so that believers may come to know God as fully as He wants them to know Him (John 17:3); (c) so that God may express His love to His children as He desires (John 3:16; Eph. 2:7; 1 John 4:8–16).

(6) The faithful who are still alive at the return of Christ for His followers will experience the same bodily transformation as those who have died in Christ prior to the day of resurrection (1 Cor. 15:51–53). They will be given new bodies identical to the new bodies given to those raised from the dead at that time. They will never experience physical death (see article on THE RAPTURE, p. 1889).

(7) Jesus speaks of a resurrection of life for the believer and a resurrection of judgment for the wicked (John 5:28–29).

is written, [v]Death is swallowed up in victory.

55 [w]O death, where *is* thy sting? O [t]grave, where *is* thy victory?

56 The sting of death *is* sin; and [x]the strength of sin *is* the law.

57 [y]But thanks *be* to God, which giveth us [z]the victory through our Lord Jesus Christ.

58 [a]Therefore, my beloved brethren, be ye stedfast, unmoveable, always abounding in the work of the Lord, forasmuch as ye know [b]that your labour is not in vain in the Lord.

The collection for the poor

16 NOW CONCERNING [c]the collection for the saints, as I have given order to the churches of Galatia, even so do ye.

2 [d]Upon the first *day* of the week let every one of you lay by him in store, as *God* hath prospered him, that there be no gatherings when I come.

3 And when I come, [e]whomsoever ye shall approve by *your* letters, them will I send to bring your [u]liberality unto Jerusalem.

4 [f]And if it be meet that I go also, they shall go with me.

Paul's itinerary

5 Now I will come unto you, [g]when I shall pass through Macedonia: for I do pass through Macedonia.

6 And it may be that I will abide, yea, and winter with you, that ye may [h]bring me on my journey whithersoever I go.

7 For I will not see you now by the way; but I trust to tarry a while with you, [i]if the Lord permit.

8 But I will tarry at Ephesus until Pentecost.

9 For [j]a great door and effectual is opened unto me, and [k]*there are* many adversaries.

10 Now [l]if Timotheus come, see that he may be with you without fear: for [m]he worketh the work of the Lord, as I also *do*.

11 [n]Let no man therefore despise him: but conduct him forth [o]in peace, that he may come unto me: for I look for him with the brethren.

12 As touching *our* brother [p]Apollos, I greatly desired him to come unto you with the brethren: but his will was not at all to come at this time; but he will come when he shall have convenient time.

Concluding message

13 [q]Watch ye, [r]stand fast in the faith, quit you like men, [s]be strong.

14 [t]Let all your things be done with charity.

15 I beseech you, brethren, (ye know [u]the house of Stephanas, that it is [v]the firstfruits of Achaia, and *that* they have addicted themselves to [w]the ministry of the saints,)

16 [x]That ye submit yourselves unto such, and to every one that helpeth with *us*, and [y]laboureth.

17 I am glad of the coming of Stephanas and Fortunatus and Achaicus: [z]for that which was lacking on your part they have supplied.

18 [a]For they have refreshed my spirit and yours: therefore [b]acknowledge ye them that are such.

19 The churches of Asia salute you. Aquila and Priscilla salute you much in the Lord, [c]with the church that is in their house.

20 All the brethren greet you. [d]Greet ye one another with an holy kiss.

15:54 [v]Is. 25:8; Rev. 20:14
15:55 [w]Hos. 13:14
15:56 [x]Rom. 4:15
15:57 [y]Rom. 7:25 [z]1 John 5:4
15:58 [a]2 Pet. 3:14 [b]ch. 3:8
16:1 [c]Acts 11:29; Gal. 2:10
16:2 [d]Acts 20:7
16:3 [e]2 Cor. 8:19
16:4 [f]2 Cor. 8:19
16:5 [g]Acts 19:21; 2 Cor. 1:16
16:6 [h]Acts 15:3; Rom. 15:24
16:7 [i]Acts 18:21; Jas. 4:15
16:9 [j]Acts 14:27; 2 Cor. 2:12; Col. 4:3 [k]Acts 19:9
16:10 [l]Acts 19:22 [m]Phil. 2:20; 1 Thes. 3:2
16:11 [n]1 Tim. 4:12 [o]Acts 15:33
16:12 [p]ch. 1:12
16:13 [q]Mat. 24:42; 1 Thes. 5:6; 1 Pet. 5:8 [r]Phil. 1:27; 1 Thes. 3:8; 2 Thes. 2:15 [s]Eph. 6:10; Col. 1:11
16:14 [t]1 Pet. 4:8
16:15 [u]ch. 1:16 [v]Rom. 16:5 [w]2 Cor. 8:4; Heb. 6:10
16:16 [x]Heb. 13:17 [y]Heb. 6:10
16:17 [z]2 Cor. 11:9; Phil. 2:30
16:18 [a]Col. 4:8 [b]Phil. 2:29
16:19 [c]Rom. 16:5
16:20 [d]Rom. 16:16

[u] Gk. *gift;* see 2 Cor. 8:4

16:1 THE COLLECTION. In ch. 16 Paul gives direction for the collection for the poor believers at Jerusalem, describes his future plans, and speaks about his fellow workers in the Lord.

16:22 ANATHEMA. Paul ends this Corinthian letter by reminding all professing believers that to claim to be believers, yet to "love not the Lord," is to be "Anathema" (i.e., accursed, doomed). To "love not the Lord" means to fail to have a heartfelt love toward Him, to not obey Him (John 14:21), and to distort the apostolic gospel of N.T. revelation (see Gal. 1:9, note). To be accursed means being excluded from the true spiritual church on earth and finally from the heavenly kingdom of the age to come. Paul wants his readers to understand that the ultimate test of Christian discipleship is a personal, heartfelt loyalty to the Lord Jesus Christ (cf. Rom. 10:9).

21 [e]The salutation of *me* Paul with
mine own hand.
22 If any man [f]love not the Lord
Jesus Christ, [g]let him be Anathema
[h]Maranatha.
23 [i]The grace of our Lord Jesus
Christ *be* with you.
24 My love *be* with you all in Christ
Jesus. Amen.

16:21 [e]Col. 4:18
16:22 [f]Eph. 6:24 [g]Gal. 1:8,9 [h]Jude 14,15
16:23 [i]Rom. 16:20

16:22 MARANATHA. *Maranatha* is an Aramaic expression meaning "Come, Lord," and was probably used as a prayer or greeting among Christians. The early church was constantly praying that Christ might return soon. Christians are those who "love his appearing" (2 Tim. 4:8) and express this longing by word and life (1 Thes. 1:10; Rev. 22:20).

2 CORINTHIANS

Outline

Introduction (1:1–11)

I. Paul's Defense for the Sake of the Loyal Majority (1:12—7:16)
  A. Denial That He Has Been Fickle (1:12–22)
  B. Explanation of His Change in Travel Plans (1:23—2:17)
  C. Clarification Concerning the Character of His Ministry (3:1—6:10)
    1. It is in the Service of a New Covenant (3:1–18)
    2. It is in Openness and Truth (4:1–6)
    3. It is in Personal Suffering (4:7—5:10)
    4. It is in Compassionate Dedication (5:11—6:10)
  D. Personal Appeal to and Affectionate Regard for the Corinthians (6:11—7:16)

II. The Collection for Needy Christians in Jerusalem (8:1—9:15)
  A. The Grace of Christian Liberality (8:1–15)
  B. Titus to Head Up Arrangements for the Collection (8:16–24)
  C. An Appeal for a Ready Response (9:1–5)
  D. An Appeal for a Generous Response (9:6–15)

III. Paul's Reply to the Rebellious Minority (10:1—13:10)
  A. An Answer to Charges of Cowardice and Weakness (10:1–18)
  B. A Reluctant Self-Defense of His Apostleship (11:1—12:18)
    1. Apology for Boastful Tone (11:1–15)
    2. Affirms He is Not Inferior to the Judaizers (11:16—12:10)
    3. Legitimate Claims to Apostleship (12:11–18)
  C. An Upcoming Third Visit Mentioned as a Warning (12:19—13:10)
    1. Apprehensiveness Concerning the Corinthians (12:19–21)
    2. Determination to Be Firm (13:1–10)

Conclusion (13:11–14)

Author: Paul

Theme: Glory Through Suffering

Date of Writing: A.D. 55/56

Background

Paul wrote this epistle to the church at Corinth and to believers throughout Achaia (1:1), identifying himself twice by name (1:1; 10:1). Having founded the Corinthian church during his second missionary journey, Paul and the Corinthians had frequent contacts thereafter because of problems in the church (see Introduction to 1 Corinthians).

The sequence of these contacts and the setting for writing 2 Corinthians are as follows. (1) After some initial contacts and correspondence between Paul and the church (e.g. 1 Cor. 1:11; 5:9; 7:1), Paul wrote 1 Corinthians from Ephesus (spring A.D. 55 or 56). (2) Next, Paul made a trip across the Aegean Sea to Corinth to deal with further problems in the church. This visit between 1 and 2 Corinthians (cf. 13:1–2) was a painful one for Paul and the congregation (2:1–2). (3) After this painful visit, reports reached Paul at Ephesus that antagonists were still attacking him and his apostolic authority at Corinth, in hopes

of persuading a portion of the church to reject Paul. (4) In response to this report, Paul wrote 2 Corinthians from Macedonia (fall A.D. 55 or 56). (5) Shortly thereafter Paul traveled to Corinth again (13:1), where he remained for about three months (cf. Acts 20:1–3a) and from whence he wrote Romans.

Purpose

Paul wrote this epistle to address three categories of people at Corinth. (1) First, he wrote to encourage and settle the majority at Corinth who remained faithful to him as their spiritual father. (2) He wrote to challenge and expose the false apostles who continued to speak against him personally, hoping to undermine his authority and apostleship and to distort his message. (3) He also wrote to reprimand the minority in the church who were being influenced by Paul's opponents and who were resisting his authority and correction. Paul reaffirmed his integrity and apostolic authority in relation to them, clarified his motives, and warned them against further rebellion. 2 Corinthians served to prepare the church as a whole for his impending visit.

Survey

2 Corinthians has three main divisions. (1) In the first (chs. 1—7), Paul begins by thanking God for His comfort in the midst of suffering for the gospel, commends the Corinthians for disciplining a chief offender, and defends his integrity in changing his travel plans. In 3:1—6:10 Paul shares the most extensive insight in the N.T. on the true character of Christian ministry. He stresses the importance of separation from the world (6:11—7:1) and expresses joy in learning from Titus of the repentance of many in the Corinthian church who had previously rebelled against his authority (ch. 7).

(2) In chs. 8 and 9, Paul exhorts the Corinthians to match the wholehearted Christian generosity of the Macedonians in contributing to the offering he was raising for the poor saints at Jerusalem.

(3) The epistle's tone changes in chs. 10—13. Here Paul defends his apostleship by setting forth his calling, qualifications, and sufferings as a true apostle. By this Paul hopes the Corinthians will discern the false apostles among them and thereby be spared further discipline when he arrives again in person. Paul concludes 2 Corinthians with the only trinitarian benediction in the N.T. (13:14).

Special Features

Four major features or emphases characterize this epistle. (1) It is the most autobiographical of Paul's epistles. His many personal references are made with transparent humility, apology, and even embarrassment, but out of necessity because of the situation at Corinth. (2) It surpasses all other Pauline epistles in revealing the intensity and depth of Paul's love and concern for his spiritual children. (3) It contains the most developed theology in the N.T. about Christian suffering (1:3–11; 4:7–18; 6:3–10; 11:23–30; 12:1–10) and about Christian giving (chs. 8—9). (4) Key terms, such as weakness, grief, tears, perils, tribulation, suffering, comfort, boasting, truth, ministry, and glory, underscore the unique character of this letter.

Reading 2 Corinthians

In order to read the entire New Testament in one year, the book of 2 Corinthians should be read in 12 days, according to the following schedule:
☐ 1:1—2:4 ☐ 2:5—3:6 ☐ 3:7—4:18 ☐ 5:1—6:2 ☐ 6:3—7:1 ☐ 7:2–16 ☐ 8–9 ☐ 10 ☐ 11:1–15 ☐ 11:16–33 ☐ 12 ☐ 13

NOTES

[e]punishment, which *was inflicted* [k]of
many.
7 [l]So that contrariwise ye *ought*
rather to forgive *him,* and comfort *him,*
lest perhaps such a one should be
swallowed up with overmuch sorrow.
8 Wherefore I beseech you that ye
would confirm *your* love toward him.
9 For to this end also did I write,
that I might know the proof of you,
whether ye be [m]obedient in all things.
10 To whom ye forgive any thing, I
forgive also: for if I forgave any thing,
to whom I forgave *it,* for your sakes
forgave I it [f]in the person of Christ;
11 Lest Satan should get an advan-
tage of us: for we are not ignorant of
his devices.

The nature of the ministry

12 Furthermore, [n]when I came to
Troas to *preach* Christ's gospel, and [o]a
door was opened unto me of the Lord,
13 [p]I had no rest in my spirit, be-
cause I found not Titus my brother: but
taking my leave of them, I went from
thence into Macedonia.
14 Now thanks *be* unto God, which
always causeth us to triumph in Christ,
and maketh manifest [q]the savour of
his knowledge by us in every place.
15 For we are unto God a sweet sa-
vour of Christ, [r]in them that are
saved, and [s]in them that perish:
16 [t]To the one *we are* the savour of
death unto death; and to the other the
savour of life unto life. And [u]who *is*
sufficient for these things?
17 For we are not as many, which
[v]corrupt[g] the word of God: but as
[w]of sincerity, but as of God, in the
sight of God speak we [h]in Christ.
3 DO [x]WE begin again to commend
ourselves? or need we, as some
others, [y]epistles of commendation to
you, or *letters* of commendation from
you?
2 [z]Ye are our epistle written in our
hearts, known and read of all men:
3 *Forasmuch as ye are* manifestly de-
clared to be the epistle of Christ [a]min-
istered by us, written not with ink, but
with the Spirit of the living God; not
[b]in tables of stone, but [c]in fleshy ta-
bles of the heart.
4 And such trust have we through
Christ to God-ward:
5 [d]Not that we are sufficient of our-
selves to think any thing as of our-
selves; but [e]our sufficiency *is* of God;
6 Who also hath made us able
[f]ministers of [g]the new testament;
not [h]of the letter, but of the spirit: for
[i]the letter killeth, [j]but the spirit
[i]giveth life.

A new covenant of the Spirit

7 But if [k]the ministration of death,
[l]written *and* engraven in stones, was

[e] Or, *censure* [f] Or, *in the sight* [g] Or, *deal deceitfully with* [h] Or, *of* [i] Or, *quickeneth*

2:6 [k]1 Cor. 5:4,5; 1 Tim. 5:20
2:7 [l]Gal. 6:1
2:9 [m]ch. 10:6
2:12 [n]Acts 16:8; [o]1 Cor. 16:9
2:13 [p]ch. 7:5,6
2:14 [q]Sol. 1:3
2:15 [r]1 Cor. 1:18; [s]ch. 4:3
2:16 [t]Luke 2:34; John 9:39; 1 Pet. 2:7; [u]1 Cor. 15:10
2:17 [v]2 Pet. 2:3; [w]ch. 1:12
3:1 [x]ch. 5:12; [y]Acts 18:27
3:2 [z]1 Cor. 9:2
3:3 [a]1 Cor. 3:5; [b]Ex. 24:12; [c]Ps. 40:8; Ezek. 11:19; Heb. 8:10
3:5 [d]John 15:5; [e]1 Cor. 15:10
3:6 [f]1 Cor. 3:5; Eph. 3:7; Col. 1:25; [g]Jer. 31:31; Mat. 26:28; Heb. 8:6,8; [h]Rom. 2:27; [i]Rom. 3:20; Gal. 3:10; [j]John 6:63; Rom. 8:2
3:7 [k]Rom. 7:10; [l]Ex. 34:1; Deut. 10:1

Many churches today have abandoned N.T. church discipline. They advocate tolerance of sin, call for unconditional forgiveness, offer cheap grace, and refuse to hear what the Spirit says to the churches (see Rev. 2–3). As a result, sin is taken lightly and the fear of God is gone from their midst (see Mat. 18:15, note on church discipline).

2:11 SATAN . . . AN ADVANTAGE OF US. One of our key defenses against Satan's attack is being aware of the enemy's continual effort to gain an advantage over us and to lead us away from sincere devotion to Christ (see Eph. 6:11, note).

2:14 TRIUMPH IN CHRIST. Paul describes believers as being led in a triumphal procession behind Christ and being displayed by God to the world as a triumph and trophy of the redeeming grace of Christ. Through this triumphal procession, the knowledge of Christ and the redeemed lives of the believers are manifested as a sweet aroma before God and man. To God it is pleasing, to humans it results in life or death (vv. 15–16).

2:17 CORRUPT THE WORD OF GOD. Paul here describes preachers who were watering down the demands of the gospel for gain of money, acceptance, and success (cf. 11:4,12–15). They were talented and persuasive, yet secretly insincere. They were greedy for money and prominence (cf. John 10:12–13; Phil. 1:15,17; 1 Pet. 5:2; 2 Pet. 2:1–3,14–16).

3:3 WRITTEN . . . IN FLESHY TABLES OF THE HEART. Under the new covenant established by the blood of Christ (Mat. 26:28), the Holy Spirit writes the law of God, not in tablets of stone as at Sinai (Ex. 31:18), but in "tables of the heart" (see article on THE OLD COVENANT AND THE NEW COVENANT, p. 1954). Hence, believers have the law of God in their hearts, and through the power of the Spirit they are able to keep it (see Jer. 31:33, note; Ezek. 11:19, note). This internal law is made up of love to God and other people (cf. Mat. 22:34–40; Rom. 13:8–10).

3:6 THE LETTER KILLETH. It is not the law or written Word of God itself that destroys. Rather, it is the demands of the law without the life and power of the Spirit which brings condemnation (vv. 7,9; cf. Jer. 31:33; Rom. 3:31; see article on FAITH AND GRACE, p. 1738). Through salvation in Christ the Holy Spirit gives to the believer spiritual life and power in order to fulfill God's will. With the Holy Spirit the letter no longer kills.

glorious, [m]so that the children of Isra-
el could not stedfastly behold the face
of Moses for the glory of his counte-
nance; which *glory* was to be done
away:
8 How shall not [n]the ministration
of the spirit be rather glorious?
9 For if the ministration of condem-
nation *be* glory, much more doth the
ministration [o]of righteousness exceed
in glory.
10 For even that which was
made glorious had no glory in this re-
spect, by reason of the glory that ex-
celleth.
11 For if that which is done away
was glorious, much more that which re-
maineth *is* glorious.
12 Seeing then that we have such
hope, [p]we use great [j]plainness of
speech:
13 And not as Moses, [q]*which* put a
veil over his face, that the children of
Israel could not stedfastly look to
[r]the end of that which is abolished:
14 But [s]their minds were blinded:
for until this day remaineth the same
veil untaken away in the reading of the
old testament; which *veil* is done away
in Christ.
15 But even unto this day, when
Moses is read, the veil is upon their
heart.
16 Nevertheless [t]when it shall
turn to the Lord, [u]the veil shall be tak-
en away.
17 Now [v]the Lord is that Spirit:
and where the Spirit of the Lord *is*,
there *is* liberty.
18 But we all, with open face be-
holding [w]as in a glass [x]the glory of
the Lord, [y]are changed into the same
image from glory to glory, *even* as [k]by
the Spirit of the Lord.

The ministry and God's power

4 THEREFORE SEEING we have
[z]this ministry, [a]as we have re-
ceived mercy, we faint not;
2 But have renounced the hidden
things of [l]dishonesty, not walking in
craftiness, [b]nor handling the word of
God deceitfully; but [c]by manifestation
of the truth [d]commending ourselves
to every man's conscience in the sight
of God.
3 But if our gospel be hid, [e]it is hid
to them that are lost:
4 In whom [f]the god of this world

3:7 [m]Ex. 34:29
3:8 [n]Gal. 3:5
3:9 [o]Rom. 1:17
3:12 [p]ch. 7:4; Eph. 6:19
3:13 [q]Ex. 34:33; [r]Rom. 10:4; Gal. 3:23
3:14 [s]Is. 6:10; Acts 28:26
3:16 [t]Ex. 34:34; Rom. 11:23; [u]Is. 25:7
3:17 [v]1 Cor. 15:45
3:18 [w]1 Cor. 13:12; [x]ch. 4:4,6; [y]Rom. 8:29
4:1 [z]ch. 3:6; [a]1 Cor. 7:25
4:2 [b]ch. 2:17; [c]ch. 6:4,7; [d]ch. 5:11
4:3 [e]1 Cor. 1:18
4:4 [f]Eph. 6:12

[j] Or, *boldness* [k] Or, *of the Lord the Spirit*
[l] Gk. *shame*

3:8 THE MINISTRATION OF THE SPIRIT. Paul calls the "new testament" or new covenant here "the ministration of the spirit," meaning the ministration of the Holy Spirit. Through faith in Christ one receives the Holy Spirit, is born again (see article on REGENERATION, p. 1597), and is promised the baptism in the Spirit (Acts 1:8; 2:4). All the redemptive benefits in Christ come by way of the Holy Spirit. It is He who mediates the presence of Christ and all His blessings to us (v. 9; see article on THE DOCTRINE OF THE HOLY SPIRIT, p. 1668).

3:17 THE SPIRIT . . . THERE *IS* LIBERTY. The freedom which comes through Christ (Gal. 5:1) is, first and foremost, liberation from the condemnation and slavery of sin (vv. 7–9; Rom. 6:6, 14; 8:2; Eph. 4:22–24; Col. 3:9–10) and the whole dominion of Satan (Acts 26:18; Col. 1:13; 1 Pet. 5:8). (1) True liberation begins with the believer's union with Christ (Acts 4:12; Eph. 1:7) and his receiving the Holy Spirit (see article on REGENERATION, p. 1597). Liberation from spiritual bondage is maintained through the Holy Spirit's continued indwelling and the believer's obedience to His direction (Rom. 8:1ff; Gal. 5:18; cf. John 15:1–11).

(2) Freedom provided by Christ is not a freedom for the believer to do what he wants (1 Cor. 10:23–24), but to do what he should (Rom. 6:18–23). Spiritual freedom must never be used as a pretext for evil or as a rationale for conflict (Jas. 4:1–2; 1 Pet. 2:16–23). Christian liberation frees believers for service to God (1 Thes. 1:9) and other people (1 Cor. 9:19) in the way of righteousness (Rom. 6:18ff). We are now Christ's slaves (Rom. 1:1; 1 Cor. 7:22; Phil. 1:1), living by grace unto God (Rom. 5:21; 6:10–13).

3:18 BEHOLDING . . . THE GLORY OF THE LORD. This phrase means to behold the glory, truth, and person of Christ as He is revealed in the gospel. It means experiencing His nearness, love, righteousness, and power through prayer and the Holy Spirit while abiding in Him and His Word; it results in our being transformed into His likeness (4:6; cf. Col. 1:15; Heb. 1:3). In this age the transformation is progressive and partial. But when Christ returns, we shall behold Him face to face and our transformation will be complete (1 John 3:2; Rev. 22:4).

4:4 GOD OF THIS WORLD. The "god of this world" refers to Satan (cf. John 12:31; 14:30; 16:11; Eph. 2:2; 1 John 5:19), who holds power over and controls much of the activity of this present age. His rule is usurped, however, temporary and not absolute. He continues only by the permissive will of God until the end of history (Rev. 19:11—20:10). Those who do not submit themselves to Jesus Christ remain under Satan's sway. He blinds their eyes to the truth and glory of the gospel in order that they might not be saved. The solution to this fatal situation is to bind his activity through intercession and to preach the

[g]hath blinded the minds of them
which believe not, lest [h]the light of
the glorious gospel of Christ, [i]who is
the image of God, should shine unto
them.

5 [j]For we preach not ourselves,
but Christ Jesus the Lord; and [k]our-
selves your servants for Jesus' sake.
6 For God, [l]who commanded the
light to shine out of darkness, [m]hath
[m]shined in our hearts, to *give* [n]the
light of the knowledge of the glory of
God in the face of Jesus Christ.

7 But we have this treasure in
[o]earthen vessels, [p]that the excellen-
cy of the power may be of God, and not
of us.

The trials of ministry

8 *We are* [q]troubled on every side,
yet not distressed; *we are* perplexed,
but [n]not in despair;
9 Persecuted, but not forsaken;
[r]cast down, but not destroyed;
10 [s]Always bearing about in the
body the dying of the Lord Jesus, [t]that
the life also of Jesus might be made
manifest in our body.
11 For we which live [u]are always
delivered unto death for Jesus' sake,

4:4 [g]John 12:40 [h]ch. 3:8,9 [i]John 1:18 Heb. 1:3
4:5 [j]1 Cor. 1:13 & 10:33 [k]1 Cor. 9:19
4:6 [l]Gen. 1:3 [m]2 Pet. 1:19 [n]1 Pet. 2:9
4:7 [o]ch. 5:1 [p]1 Cor. 2:5
4:8 [q]ch. 7:5
4:9 [r]Ps. 37:24
4:10 [s]Phil. 3:10 [t]Rom. 8:17
4:11 [u]Rom. 8:36
4:12 [v]ch. 13:9
4:13 [w]2 Pet. 1:1 [x]Ps. 116:10
4:14 [y]Rom. 8:11 1 Cor. 6:14
4:15 [z]Col. 1:24 2 Tim. 2:10 [a]ch. 1:11
4:16 [b]Rom. 7:22 Col. 3:10
4:17 [c]Mat. 5:12 Rom. 8:18 1 Pet. 1:6
4:18 [d]Rom. 8:24 Heb. 11:1

that the life also of Jesus might be
made manifest in our mortal flesh.
12 So then [v]death worketh in us,
but life in you.
13 We having [w]the same spirit of
faith, according as it is written, [x]I be-
lieved, and therefore have I spoken; we
also believe, and therefore speak;
14 Knowing that [y]he which raised
up the Lord Jesus shall raise up us also
by Jesus, and shall present *us* with you.
15 For [z]all things *are* for your
sakes, that [a]the abundant grace
might through the thanksgiving of
many redound to the glory of God.

The eternal glory of the ministry

16 For which cause we faint not; but
though our outward man perish, yet
[b]the inward *man* is renewed day by
day.
17 For [c]our light affliction, which
is but for a moment, worketh for us a
far more exceeding *and* eternal weight
of glory;
18 [d]While we look not at the things
which are seen, but at the things which
are not seen: for the things which are

[m] Gk. is he *who hath* [n] Or, *not altogether without help,* or, *means*

gospel in the power of the Holy Spirit (Acts 1:8) in order that people may hear, understand, and choose to believe or disbelieve (vv. 5–6; see Mat. 4:10, note on Satan).

4:7 THIS TREASURE IN EARTHEN VESSELS. A Christian is an "earthen vessel" who at times experiences sadness, tears, afflictions, perplexities, weakness, and fears (cf. 1:4,8–9; 7:5). Yet because of the heavenly "treasure" within him, he is not defeated. Christianity is not the removal of weakness, nor is it merely the manifestation of divine power. Rather, it is the manifestation of divine power through human weakness (12:9). This means (1) that in every affliction we may be more than conquerors by the power and love of God (Rom. 8:37), and (2) that our weakness, troubles, and suffering open us up to the abundant grace of Christ and allow the life of Jesus to be manifested in our bodies (vv. 8–11; cf. 12:7–10).

4:8 TROUBLED . . . YET NOT DISTRESSED. If you experience the presence of Christ and His power in your life, absolutely no trouble, affliction, sickness, or tragedy will cause your spiritual defeat. When outward circumstances become unbearable and your human resources are exhausted, God's resources are given to enlarge and expand your faith, hope, and strength. Under no circumstances will God forsake His faithful children (Rom. 8:35–39; Heb. 13:5).

4:11–12 DELIVERED UNTO DEATH. If one Christian is to minister life to another, he must share the sufferings of Christ and experience the working of death in his own life (v. 12). Self-denial, affliction, disappointment, and suffering for Christ's sake will allow our lives to minister grace to others (cf. 11:23–29; Rom. 8:36–37; Phil. 1:29; 1 Pet. 4:14). Jesus taught this same great principle of brokenness in John 12:24–25.

4:16 OUTWARD MAN . . . INWARD *MAN*. The "outward man" is one's physical body, subject to decay and moving toward death because of mortality and the afflictions of life (v. 17). The "inward man" is the human spirit and inward person that has the spiritual life of Christ. Although our bodies age and decay, we experience ongoing renewal through the constant impartation of the life and power of Christ, the influence of which enables our minds, emotions, and wills to be conformed to His likeness and eternal purpose.

4:17 LIGHT AFFLICTION . . . GLORY. The afflictions and hardships endured in the lives of those who remain faithful to Christ are light in comparison to the abundance of glory which we have through Christ. This glory is already present in part, but will be fully experienced in the future (cf. Rom. 8:18). When we reach our inheritance in heaven, we shall say that the severest tribulations were as nothing compared with the glory of the eternal state. Therefore, we must not despair, lose hope, or diminish our faith in the midst of our problems.

seen *are* temporal; but the things which are not seen *are* eternal.

A confident ministry

5 FOR WE know that if [e]our earthly house of *this* tabernacle were dissolved, we have a building of God, an house not made with hands, eternal in the heavens.

2 For in this [f]we groan, earnestly desiring to be clothed upon with our house which is from heaven:

3 If so be that [g]being clothed we shall not be found naked.

4 For we that are in *this* tabernacle do groan, being burdened: not for that we would be unclothed, but [h]clothed upon, that mortality might be swallowed up of life.

5 Now [i]he that hath wrought us for the selfsame thing *is* God, who also [j]hath given unto us the earnest of the Spirit.

6 Therefore *we are* always confident, knowing that, whilst we are at home in the body, we are absent from the Lord:

7 (For [k]we walk by faith, not by sight:)

8 We are confident, *I say,* and [l]willing rather to be absent from the body, and to be present with the Lord.

9 Wherefore we [o]labour, that, whether present or absent, we may be accepted of him.

10 [m]For we must all appear before the judgment seat of Christ; [n]that every one may receive the things *done* in *his* body, according to that he hath done, whether *it be* good or bad.

A reconciling ministry

11 Knowing therefore [o]the terror of the Lord, we persuade men; but [p]we are made manifest unto God; and I trust also are made manifest in your consciences.

12 For [q]we commend not ourselves again unto you, but give you occasion [r]to glory on our behalf, that ye may have somewhat to *answer* them which glory [p]in appearance, and not in heart.

13 For [s]whether we be beside ourselves, *it is* to God: or whether we be sober, *it is* for your cause.

14 For the love of Christ constraineth us; because we thus judge, that [t]if one died for all, then were all dead:

15 And *that* he died for all, [u]that they which live should not henceforth live unto themselves, but unto him which died for them, and rose again.

16 [v]Wherefore henceforth know we no man after the flesh: yea, though we have known Christ after the flesh, [w]yet now henceforth know we *him* no more.

5:1 [e]Job 4:19
5:2 [f]Rom. 8:23
5:3 [g]Rev. 3:18
5:4 [h]1 Cor. 15:53
5:5 [i]Is. 29:23; Eph. 2:10; [j]Rom. 8:23; Eph. 1:14
5:7 [k]Rom. 8:24; Heb. 11:1
5:8 [l]Phil. 1:23
5:10 [m]Rom. 14:10; [n]Gal. 6:7; Eph. 6:8; Rev. 22:12
5:11 [o]Heb. 10:31; Jude 23; [p]ch. 4:2
5:12 [q]ch. 3:1; [r]ch. 1:14
5:13 [s]ch. 11:1,16
5:14 [t]Rom. 5:15
5:15 [u]Rom. 6:11; 1 Cor. 6:19; Gal. 2:20
5:16 [v]Mat. 12:50; Col. 3:11; [w]John 6:63

[o] Or, *endeavour* [p] Gk. *in the face*

5:1 IF OUR EARTHLY HOUSE. Paul uses the conditional clause, "if our earthly house . . . were dissolved," because he knows that Christ could return soon, in which case he would not experience death; rather, his body would be immediately transformed (see article on THE RAPTURE, p. 1889). This same double possibility, death or transformation, exists for believers today. Christ has stated we do not know the day nor the hour of His return (Mat. 24:36,42,44); therefore, this event is always imminent, offering a powerful motivation for holy living (see Mat. 24:42, notes; 1 John 3:2–3).

5:1 OUR EARTHLY HOUSE . . . A BUILDING. (1) The term "earthly house" refers either to the believer's earthly body or to the earthly life of the believer. (2) The "building of God, an house not made with hands, eternal in the heavens" likely refers either to a temporary body prepared for the believer in heaven while he awaits his resurrection body, or to the environment of the heavenly existence.

Some have used this difficult passage to teach that after death and while awaiting resurrection, believers exist as disembodied spirits, vague shadows, or naked souls without form. However, note that both Moses and Elijah on the Mount of Transfiguration appeared clothed with a heavenly body, even though they were awaiting their resurrection bodies (see article on THE RESURRECTION OF THE BODY, p. 1799). Furthermore, in Rev. 6:9–11 souls in heaven are described as capable of being seen, wearing white robes; they are not naked souls.

5:8 TO BE PRESENT WITH THE LORD. Clearly from this verse and others (e.g., Luke 23:42–43; Phil. 1:23), there is no lapse of time between death and the life to come (see article on DEATH, p. 782). The believer's death brings him immediately into Christ's presence (1 Cor. 13:12). Thus, to die is gain (Phil. 1:21). This does not mean that Christ is not present with believers now, for the Holy Spirit's work is to mediate the presence of Christ to the believer (see article on THE DOCTRINE OF THE HOLY SPIRIT, p. 1668). But it does indicate that we are now with the Lord by faith and not through appearance (Heb. 11:1).

5:10 THE JUDGMENT SEAT OF CHRIST. For comments on what happens to believers on the day of judgment, see article on THE JUDGMENT OF BELIEVERS, p. 1811.

THE JUDGMENT OF BELIEVERS

2 Cor. 5:10 "For we must all appear before the judgment seat of Christ; that every one may receive the things done *in* his *body, according to that he hath done, whether* it be *good or bad."*

The Bible teaches that believers will someday have to give an account at "the judgment seat of Christ" for all deeds done in the body, whether good or bad. Concerning the judgment of the believer, the following facts should be kept in mind.

(1) All Christians will be subject to judgment; there will be no exceptions (Rom. 14:12; 1 Cor. 3:12–15; 2 Cor. 5:10; see Eccl. 12:14, note).

(2) This judgment will occur when Christ returns for His church (see John 14:3, note; cf. 1 Thes. 4:14–17).

(3) The judge is Christ (John 5:22; 2 Tim. 4:8).

(4) The Bible speaks of the believer's judgment as something solemn and serious, especially since it includes the possibility of damage or "loss" (1 Cor. 3:15; cf. 2 John 8), of being ashamed before him "at his coming" (1 John 2:28), and of "burning" one's whole life's work (1 Cor. 3:13–15). The believer's judgment, however, will not involve a declaration of condemnation by God.

(5) Everything will be made manifest. The word "appear" (Gk. *phaneroō*, 2 Cor. 5:10) means "to be manifest openly or publicly." Hence, God will examine and openly reveal, in their true reality, (a) our secret acts (Mark 4:22; Rom. 2:16), (b) our character (Rom. 2:5–11), (c) our words (Mat. 12:36–37), (d) our good works (Eph. 6:8), (e) our attitudes (Mat. 5:22), (f) our motives (1 Cor. 4:5), (g) our lack of love (Col. 3:18—4:1), and (h) our work and ministry (1 Cor. 3:13).

(6) In sum, the believer will have to give an account of the degree of his faithfulness or unfaithfulness to God (Mat. 25:21,23; 1 Cor. 4:2–5) and of his deeds and actions in light of the grace, opportunity, and understanding made available to him (Luke 12:48; Rom. 8:1).

(7) The believer's bad deeds, when repented of, are forgiven in relation to eternal punishment (Rom. 8:1), but they are still taken into account when being judged for recompense: "He that doeth wrong shall receive for the wrong which he hath done" (Col. 3:25; cf. Eccl. 12:14; 1 Cor. 3:15; 2 Cor. 5:10). The believer's good deeds and love are remembered by God and rewarded (Heb. 6:10); "whatsoever good thing any man doeth, the same shall he receive of the Lord" (Eph. 6:8).

(8) The specific results of the believer's judgment will be varied. There will be either the gain or the loss of joy (1 John 2:28), divine approval (Mat. 25:21), tasks and authority (Mat. 25:14–30), position (Mat. 5:19; 19:30), rewards (1 Cor. 3:12–14; Phil. 3:14; 2 Tim. 4:8), and honor (Rom. 2:10; 1 Pet. 1:7).

(9) The anticipation of the Christian's judgment to come should perfect in him the fear of the Lord (2 Cor. 5:11; Phil. 2:12; 1 Pet. 1:17) and cause him to be sober, to watch and pray (1 Pet. 4:5,7), to live in holy conduct and godliness (2 Pet. 3:11), and to show mercy and kindness to all (Mat. 5:7; cf. 2 Tim. 1:16–18).

17 Therefore if any man [x]*be* in
Christ, [q]*he is* [y]a new creature: [z]old
things are passed away; behold, all
things are become new.
18 And all things *are* of God, [a]who
hath reconciled us to himself by Jesus
Christ, and hath given to us the minis-
try of reconciliation;
19 To wit, that [b]God was in Christ,
reconciling the world unto himself, not
imputing their trespasses unto them;
and hath [r]committed unto us the
word of reconciliation.
20 Now then we are [c]ambassadors
for Christ, as [d]though God did be-
seech *you* by us: we pray *you* in Christ's
stead, be ye reconciled to God.
21 For [e]he hath made him *to be* sin
for us, who knew no sin; that we might
be made [f]the righteousness of God in
him.

A suffering ministry

6 WE THEN, *as* [g]workers together
with him, [h]beseech *you* also [i]that
ye receive not the grace of God in vain. Gal. 2:16
2 (For he saith, [j]I have heard thee
in a time accepted, and in the day of
salvation have I succoured thee: be-
hold, now *is* the accepted time; behold,
now *is* the day of salvation.)
3 [k]Giving no offence in any thing,
that the ministry be not blamed:
4 But in all *things* [s]approving our-
selves [l]as the ministers of God, in
much patience, in afflictions, in neces-
sities, in distresses,
5 [m]In stripes, in imprisonments,
[t]in tumults, in labours, in watchings,
in fastings;
6 By pureness, by knowledge, by
longsuffering, by kindness, by the Holy
Ghost, by love unfeigned,
7 [n]By the word of truth, by [o]the
power of God, by [p]the armour of righ-

5:17 [x]Rom. 8:9 [y]Gal. 5:6 [z]Is. 65:17 Eph. 2:15 Rev. 21:5 **5:18** [a]Rom. 5:10 Eph. 2:16 Col. 1:20 **5:19** [b]Rom. 3:24 **5:20** [c]Job 33:23 Mal. 2:7 Eph. 6:20 [d]ch. 6:1 **5:21** [e]Is. 53:6,9 Gal. 3:13 1 Pet. 2:22 1 John 3:5 [f]Rom. 1:17 & 10:3 **6:1** [g]1 Cor. 3:9 [h]ch. 5:20 [i]Heb. 12:15 **6:2** [j]Is. 49:8 **6:3** [k]Rom. 14:13 1 Cor. 9:12 & 10:32 **6:4** [l]1 Cor. 4:1 **6:5** [m]ch. 11:23 **6:7** [n]ch. 7:14 [o]1 Cor. 2:4 [p]ch. 10:4; Eph. 6:11; 2 Tim. 4:7

[q]Or, let him be [r]Gk. *put in us* [s]Gk. *commending;* see ch. 4:2 [t]Or, *in tossings to and fro*

5:17 *HE IS* A NEW CREATURE. Through the creative command of God (4:6), those who accept Jesus Christ by faith are made a new creation that belongs to the totally new world of God in which the Spirit rules (Rom. 8:14; Gal. 5:25; Eph. 2:10). The believer becomes a new person (Gal. 6:15; Eph. 2:10,15; 4:24; Col. 3:10), renewed after God's image (4:16; 1 Cor. 15:49; Eph. 4:24; Col. 3:10), sharing His glory (3:18) with a renewed knowledge (Col. 3:10) and understanding (Rom. 12:2), and living a life of holiness (Eph. 4:24).

5:18 RECONCILED US TO HIMSELF. Reconciliation (Gk. *katallagē*) is one aspect of Christ's work of redemption. It refers to the restoration of the sinner to fellowship with God. (1) The sin and rebellion of the human race have resulted in hostility toward and alienation from God (Eph. 2:3; Col. 1:21). This rebellion calls forth God's wrath and judgment (Rom. 1:18,24–32; 1 Cor. 15:25–26; Eph 5:6).

(2) Through Christ's atoning death, God has removed the barrier of sin and opened a way for the sinner to return to God (v. 19; Rom. 3:25; 5:10; Eph. 2:15–16).

(3) Reconciliation becomes effective for each person through his or her personal repentance and faith in Christ (Mat. 3:2; Rom. 3:22).

(4) The church has been given the ministry of reconciliation, calling all people to be reconciled to God (v. 20; see Rom. 3:25, note).

5:21 MADE HIM *TO BE* SIN. Scripture nowhere states that Christ actually became a "sinner," for He remained the spotless Lamb of God. But Christ did take our sin upon Himself (see article on THE DAY OF ATONEMENT, p. 188), and God the Father made Him the object of His judgment when Christ became an offering for our sins on the cross (Is. 53:10). In taking our punishment on the cross, Jesus made it possible for God to justly forgive sinners (see Is. 53:5, note; Rom. 3:24–25, notes).

5:21 WE . . . THE RIGHTEOUSNESS OF GOD. (1) Righteousness here does not refer to a legal righteousness, but to the experiential righteousness of the child of God as a new creature, i.e., to his character and moral state which is founded on and flows from his faith in Christ (Phil. 3:9; see Rom. 3:21, note; 4:22, note). The whole context of the passage (vv. 14–21) is concerned with the believer living for Christ (v. 15), controlled by "the love of Christ" (v. 14), becoming a "new creature" (v. 17), and fulfilling the ministry of reconciliation as a representative of God and His righteousness in the world (vv. 18–20; see 1 Cor. 1:30, note on Jesus Christ as the righteousness of the believer).

(2) God's righteousness is manifested and experienced by the believer in this world by abiding in Christ. Only to the extent that we live in union and fellowship with Christ do we become the righteousness of God (see John 15:4–5; Gal. 2:20, note; 1 John 1:9).

6:1 RECEIVE NOT THE GRACE OF GOD IN VAIN. Paul unquestionably believed that a believer could receive the grace of God and experience salvation (v. 2), and afterwards, through spiritual carelessness or deliberate sin, abandon the faith and life of the gospel and again be lost. All people must be exhorted to be reconciled to God and to receive His grace (5:20). Those who receive God's grace must be exhorted not to receive it in vain (cf. vv. 14–18).

6:4 IN AFFLICTIONS . . . DISTRESSES. See 11:23, note on the suffering of Paul.

teousness on the right hand and on the left,

8 By honour and dishonour, by evil report and good report: as deceivers, and *yet* true;

9 As unknown, and [q]*yet* well known; [r]as dying, and, behold, we live; as [s]chastened, and not killed;

10 As sorrowful, yet always rejoicing; as poor, yet making many rich; as having nothing, and *yet* possessing all things.

11 O *ye* Corinthians, our mouth is open unto you, [t]our heart is enlarged.

12 Ye are not straitened in us, but [u]ye are straitened in your own bowels.

13 Now for a recompence in the same, ([v]I speak as unto *my* children,) be ye also enlarged.

The believer's separation from evil

14 [w]Be ye not unequally yoked together with unbelievers: for [x]what fellowship hath righteousness with unrighteousness? and what communion hath light with darkness?

15 And what concord hath Christ with Belial? or what part hath he that believeth with an infidel?

16 And what agreement hath the temple of God with idols? for [y]ye are the temple of the living God; as God hath said, [z]I will dwell in them, and walk in *them;* and I will be their God, and they shall be my people.

17 [a]Wherefore come out from among them, and be ye separate, saith the Lord, and touch not the unclean *thing;* and I will receive you,

18 [b]And will be a Father unto you, and ye shall be my sons and daughters, saith the Lord Almighty.

7 HAVING [c]THEREFORE these promises, dearly beloved, let us cleanse ourselves from all filthiness of the flesh and spirit, perfecting holiness in the fear of God. Gal. 6:14

2 Receive us; we have wronged no

6:9 [q]ch. 4:2 & 5:11 [r]1 Cor. 4:9 ch. 1:9 & 4:10,11 [s]Ps. 118:18
6:11 [t]ch. 7:3
6:12 [u]ch. 12:15
6:13 [v]1 Cor. 4:14
6:14 [w]Deut. 7:2,3 1 Cor. 5:9 [x]1 Sam. 5:2,3 1 Ki. 18:21 1 Cor. 10:21 Eph. 5:7,11
6:16 [y]1 Cor. 3:16 & 6:19 Eph. 2:21 Heb. 3:6 [z]Ex. 29:45 Lev. 26:12 Jer. 31:33 & 32:38 Ezek. 11:20 Zech. 13:9
6:17 [a]Is. 52:11 Rev. 18:4
6:18 [b]Jer. 31:1,9 Rev. 21:7
7:1 [c]1 John 3:3

6:10 AS POOR. It is not contradictory to the gospel for a truly dedicated Christian to be financially poor. Paul affirms he possessed little of this world's goods, yet he made others spiritually rich as a servant of God (cf. 8:9; Acts 3:1ff; Eph. 3:8).

6:14 UNEQUALLY YOKED . . . WITH UNBELIEVERS. The ultimate division of people before God is between those who are in Christ and those who are not (vv. 14–16; see article on THREE KINDS OF PEOPLE, p. 1772). Therefore, believers must not be in voluntary partnership or in intimate association with unbelievers, for such relationships can corrupt their relationship with Christ. This includes partnership in business, secret orders (lodges), dating, marriage, and close friendships. A Christian's association with unbelievers should be only such as is necessary for social or economic existence, or to show unbelievers the way of salvation (see article on SPIRITUAL SEPARATION FOR BELIEVERS, p. 1814).

6:15–16 THE TEMPLE OF GOD WITH IDOLS. Paul presents a strong argument that a born-again believer, as the temple of God and the Holy Spirit (John 14:23; 1 Cor. 6:19; see article on THE TEMPLE, p. 654), cannot be indwelt by a demon. (1) Idols both in the O.T. and in the N.T. represented demons (Deut. 32:17; 1 Cor. 10:20–21; see article on THE NATURE OF IDOLATRY, p. 428). Hence, the worst form of desecration in the O.T. was to erect idols in God's own temple (2 Ki. 21:7,11–14). Likewise, we may never desecrate our bodies as the habitation of the Holy Spirit by allowing access to demons (cf. v. 15, where "Belial" refers to Satan; see also Luke 10:19, note; 2 Tim. 2:25–26; 1 John 4:4; 5:18).

(2) Although an unclean spirit cannot dwell alongside of the Holy Spirit within the true believer, there may be circumstances in which an evil spirit dwells in an individual who is actively in the process of conversion, but has not yet been fully regenerated by the Holy Spirit (see article on REGENERATION, p. 1597). Conversion may at times require the casting out of demons from a person who sincerely desires to follow Christ, yet is undergoing problems with certain sins. Until the demonic power or stronghold is broken (see article on POWER OVER SATAN AND DEMONS, p. 1486), that person cannot experience a full and complete salvation and so become "the temple of the living God" (v. 16; Mat. 12:28–29).

6:17 BE YE SEPARATE. See article on SPIRITUAL SEPARATION FOR BELIEVERS, p. 1814.

7:1 HAVING THEREFORE THESE PROMISES. Paul makes it unmistakably clear that one cannot claim the wonderful and gracious promises of God listed in 6:16–18 without a life of separation and holiness (see article on SPIRITUAL SEPARATION FOR BELIEVERS, p. 1814). This explains why some have lost their Christian joy (John 15:11), divine protection (John 17:12,14–15), answered prayers (John 15:7,16), and the sense of the fatherly presence of God (John 14:21,23). To compromise with the world is to lose the presence and promises of God.

7:1 LET US CLEANSE OURSELVES. Believers must cleanse themselves from every sin of the body and spirit. This means making a clean break with every form of ungodly compromise and continually resisting the desires of the flesh. We must put to death the sinful deeds of the body, hate them more and more, and run away from them (vv. 9–11; Rom. 8:12–13; Gal. 5:16).

SPIRITUAL SEPARATION FOR BELIEVERS

2 Cor. 6:17–18 "Wherefore come out from among them, and be ye separate, saith the Lord, and touch not the unclean thing; and I will receive you, And will be a Father unto you, and ye shall be my sons and daughters, saith the Lord Almighty."

The concept of separation from all evil is fundamental to God's relationship with His people. According to the Bible, separation involves two dimensions, one negative and the other positive: (a) separating yourself morally and spiritually from sin and from everything that is contrary to Jesus Christ, righteousness, and the Word of God; (b) drawing near to God in a close and intimate fellowship through dedication, worship, and service unto Him. Separation in this twofold sense results in a relationship where God is our heavenly Father who abides with us and is our God, and we in turn are His sons and daughters (2 Cor. 6:16–18).

(1) In the O.T. separation was a continual requirement of God for His people (see Ex. 23:24, note; Lev. 11:44, note; Deut. 7:3, note; Ezra 9:2, note; see article on THE DESTRUCTION OF THE CANAANITES, p. 336). God's people were expected to be different, holy, and separated from all other peoples in order to belong to God as His very own. One of the main reasons why God punished His people with the exile in Assyria and Babylon was their persistent desire to accommodate themselves to the idolatry and lifestyles of the nations around them (see 2 Ki. 17:7–8, notes; 24:3, note; 2 Chr. 36:14, note; Hos. 7:8, note; Jer. 2:5,13, notes; Ezek. 23:2, note).

(2) In the N.T. God commanded separation of the believer (a) from the corrupt world system and unholy compromise (John 17:15–16; 2 Tim. 3:1–5; Jas. 1:27; 4:4; see article on THE CHRISTIAN'S RELATIONSHIP TO THE WORLD, p. 2004), (b) from those in the church who sin and refuse to repent (Mat. 18:15–17; 1 Cor. 5:9–11; 2 Thes. 3:6–15), and (c) from false teachers, churches, or cults who teach theological error and deny Biblical truths (see Mat. 7:15; Rom. 16:17; Gal. 1:9, note; Tit. 3:9–11; 2 Pet. 2:17–22; 1 John 4:1; 2 John 10–11; Jude 12–13).

(3) Our attitude in separation must be one of (a) hatred toward sin, unrighteousness, and the corrupt world system (Rom. 12:9; Heb. 1:9; 1 John 2:15), (b) opposition toward false doctrine (Gal. 1:9), (c) genuine love toward those from whom we must separate (John 3:16; 1 Cor. 5:5; Gal. 6:1; cf. Rom. 9:1–3; 2 Cor. 2:1–8; 11:28–29; Jude 22), and (d) fear of God as we perfect holiness (2 Cor. 7:1).

(4) The purpose of separation is that we as God's people might (a) persevere in salvation (1 Tim. 4:16; Rev. 2:14–17), faith (1 Tim. 1:19; 6:10,20–21), and holiness (John 17:14–21; 2 Cor. 7:1); (b) live wholly for God as our Lord and Father (Mat. 22:37; 2 Cor. 6:16–18); and (c) convince the unbelieving world of the truth and blessings of the gospel (John 17:21; Phil. 2:15).

(5) If we separate ourselves properly, God Himself rewards us by drawing near with His protection, blessing, and fatherly care. He promises to be everything that a good Father should be. He will be our counselor and guide; He will love and cherish us as His own children (2 Cor. 6:16–18).

(6) The refusal of believers to separate themselves from evil, the false, and the unclean, will inevitably result in the loss of their fellowship with God (2 Cor. 6:16), of their acceptance by the Father (6:17), and of their privileges of being children of God (6:18; cf. Rom. 8:15–16).

man, we have corrupted no man, [d]we
have defrauded no man.
3 I speak not *this* to condemn *you:*
for [e]I have said before, that ye are in
our hearts to die and live with *you.*
4 [f]Great *is* my boldness of speech
toward you, [g]great *is* my glorying of
you: [h]I am filled with comfort, I am
exceeding joyful in all our tribulation.

The joy of good news

5 For, [i]when we were come into
Macedonia, our flesh had no rest, but
[j]we were troubled on every side;
[k]without *were* fightings, within *were*
fears.
6 Nevertheless [l]God, that com-
forteth those that are cast down, com-
forted us by [m]the coming of Titus;
7 And not by his coming only, but by
the consolation wherewith he was
comforted in you, when he told us your
earnest desire, your mourning, your
fervent mind toward me; so that I re-
joiced the more.
8 For though I made you sorry with
a letter, I do not repent, [n]though I did
repent: for I perceive that the same
epistle hath made you sorry, though *it*
were but for a season.
9 Now I rejoice, not that ye were
made sorry, but that ye sorrowed to re-
pentance: for ye were made sorry [u]af-
ter a godly manner, that ye might re-
ceive damage by us in nothing.
10 For [o]godly sorrow worketh re-
pentance to salvation not to be repent-
ed of: [p]but the sorrow of the world
worketh death.
11 For behold this selfsame thing,
that ye sorrowed after a godly sort,
what carefulness it wrought in you,
yea, *what* clearing of yourselves, yea,
what indignation, yea, *what* fear, yea,
what vehement desire, yea, *what* zeal,
yea, *what* revenge! In all *things* ye have
approved yourselves to be clear in this
matter.
12 Wherefore, though I wrote unto
you, *I did it* not for his cause that had
done the wrong, nor for his cause that
suffered wrong, [q]but that our care for
you in the sight of God might appear
unto you.
13 Therefore we were comforted in
your comfort: yea, and exceedingly the
more joyed we for the joy of Titus, be-
cause his spirit [r]was refreshed by you
all.
14 For if I have boasted any thing to
him of you, I am not ashamed; but as
we spake all things to you in truth,
even so our boasting, which *I made* be-
fore Titus, is found a truth.
15 And his [v]inward affection is
more abundant toward you, whilst he
remembereth [s]the obedience of you
all, how with fear and trembling ye re-
ceived him.
16 I rejoice therefore that [t]I have
confidence in you in all *things.*

The giving of the Macedonians

8 MOREOVER, BRETHREN, we do
you to wit of the grace of God be-
stowed on the churches of Macedonia;
2 How that in a great trial of afflic-

7:2 [d]Acts 20:33 **7:3** [e]ch. 6:11,12 **7:4** [f]ch. 3:12 [g]1 Cor. 1:4 [h]Phil. 2:17 Col. 1:24 **7:5** [i]ch. 2:13 [j]ch. 4:8 [k]Deut. 32:35 **7:6** [l]ch. 1:4 [m]See ch. 2:13 **7:8** [n]ch. 2:4 **7:10** [o]2 Sam. 12:13 Mat. 26:75 [p]Prov. 17:22 **7:12** [q]ch. 2:4 **7:13** [r]Rom. 15:32 **7:15** [s]ch. 2:9 Phil. 2:12 **7:16** [t]2 Thes. 3:4 Philem. 8,21

[u] Or, *according to God* [v] Gk. *bowels;* see ch. 6:12

7:5 TROUBLED . . . FEARS. Once again Paul's words and experience remind us that outward problems and inward fears can be the experience of a truly dedicated, born-again believer.

7:6 COMFORTETH THOSE THAT ARE CAST DOWN. As a God of mercy and comfort (1:3), it is His nature to comfort those who are depressed and cast down. In fact, the more we are afflicted, the greater will be the comfort and nearness of Christ in our life. Note that it was through the agency of Titus that God comforted Paul. We should always be sensitive to the Holy Spirit's leading us to console and comfort a person in need.

7:10 GODLY SORROW . . . SORROW OF THE WORLD. Paul identifies two kinds of sorrow here. (1) There is a genuine sorrow for sin that leads to repentance, i.e., a change of heart that causes us to turn from sin unto God. This type of repentance leads to salvation. For Paul, repentance from sin and faith in Christ are the human responsibilities in salvation (see Mat. 3:2, note). (2) In contrast, the unrepentant often become sorry only for the consequences of their sin; such sorrow results in eternal death and judgment (Mat. 13:42,50; 25:30; Rom. 6:23).

8:1—9:15 THE CHURCHES OF MACEDONIA. These two chapters deal with instruction about the offering for the poor believers in Jerusalem. Paul's words contain the most extensive teaching about Christian giving found in the N.T. The principles given here are a guide for believers and churches for all time (see next note).

8:2 THE RICHES OF THEIR LIBERALITY. The principles and promises of Christian giving contained in these two chapters are as follows: (1) We belong to God; what we have is held as a trust for our Lord (v. 5). (2) We must make the basic decision within our hearts to serve God and not money (v. 5; Mat. 6:24). (3) Giving is done to help those in need (v. 14; 9:12; Prov. 19:17; Gal. 2:10; see article on THE CARE OF THE POOR AND NEEDY, p. 1312), to advance the kingdom of God

tion the abundance of their joy and [u]their deep poverty abounded unto the riches of their [w]liberality.

3 For to *their* power, I bear record, yea, and beyond *their* power *they were* willing of themselves;

4 Praying us with much entreaty that we would receive the gift, and *take upon us* [v]the fellowship of the ministering to the saints.

5 And *this they did,* not as we hoped, but first gave their own selves to the Lord, and unto us by the will of God.

6 Insomuch that [w]we desired Titus, that as he had begun, so he would also finish in you the same [x]grace also.

7 Therefore, as [x]ye abound in every *thing, in* faith, and utterance, and knowledge, and *in* all diligence, and *in* your love to us, *see* [y]that ye abound in this grace also.

The example of Jesus

8 [z]I speak not by commandment, but by occasion of the forwardness of others, and to prove the sincerity of your love.

9 For ye know the grace of our Lord Jesus Christ, [a]that, though he was rich, yet for your sakes he became poor, that ye through his poverty might be rich.

10 And herein [b]I give *my* advice: for [c]this is expedient for you, who have begun before, not only to do, but also to be [d]forward[y] a year ago.

11 Now therefore perform the doing *of it;* that as *there was* a readiness to will, so *there may be* a performance also out of that which ye have.

12 For [e]if there be first a willing mind, *it is* accepted according to that a man hath, *and* not according to that he hath not.

13 For *I mean* not that other men be eased, and ye burdened:

8:2 [u]Mark 12:44
8:4 [v]Acts 11:29 & 24:17 Rom. 15:25,26 1 Cor. 16:1,3,4 ch. 9:1
8:6 [w]ver. 17 ch. 12:18
8:7 [x]1 Cor. 1:5 & 12:13 [y]ch. 9:8
8:8 [z]1 Cor. 7:6
8:9 [a]Mat. 8:20 Luke 9:58 Phil. 2:6,7
8:10 [b]1 Cor. 7:25 [c]Prov. 19:17 Mat. 10:42 1 Tim. 6:18,19 Heb. 13:16 [d]ch. 9:2
8:12 [e]Mark 12:43,44 Luke 21:3
8:15 [f]Ex. 16:18
8:17 [g]ver. 6
8:18 [h]ch. 12:18
8:19 [i]1 Cor. 16:3,4 [j]ch. 4:15
8:21 [k]Rom. 12:17 Phil. 4:8 1 Pet. 2:12
8:23 [l]Phil. 2:25

14 But by an equality, *that* now at this time your abundance *may be a supply* for their want, that their abundance also may be *a supply* for your want: that there may be equality:

15 As it is written, [f]He that *had gathered* much had nothing over; and he that *had gathered* little had no lack.

Policies in giving

16 But thanks *be* to God, which put the same earnest care into the heart of Titus for you.

17 For indeed he accepted [g]the exhortation; but being more forward, of his own accord he went unto you.

18 And we have sent with him [h]the brother, whose praise *is* in the gospel throughout all the churches;

19 And not *that* only, but who was also [i]chosen of the churches to travel with us with this [z]grace, which is administered by us [j]to the glory of the same Lord, and *declaration of* your ready mind:

20 Avoiding this, that no man should blame us in this abundance which is administered by us:

21 [k]Providing for honest things, not only in the sight of the Lord, but also in the sight of men.

22 And we have sent with them our brother, whom we have oftentimes proved diligent in many things, but now much more diligent, upon the great confidence which [a]*I have* in you.

23 Whether *any do inquire* of Titus, *he is* my partner and fellow-helper concerning you: or our brethren *be inquired of, they are* [l]the messengers of the churches, *and* the glory of Christ.

24 Wherefore show ye to them, and before the churches, the proof of your

[w] Gk. *simplicity;* see also ch. 9:11 [x] Or, *gift;* also ver. 4,19 [y] Gk. *willing* [z] Or, *gift;* also ver. 4,6,7; ch. 9:8 [a] Or, he hath

(1 Cor. 9:14; Phil. 4:15–18), to lay up treasures in heaven (Mat. 6:20; Luke 6:32–35), and to learn to fear the Lord (Deut. 14:22–23). (4) Giving should be in proportion to our income (vv. 3,12; 1 Cor. 16:2). (5) Giving is seen as a proof of our love (v. 24) and should be done sacrificially (v. 3) and voluntarily (9:7). (6) By giving to God we sow not only money, but also faith, time, and service, thus reaping greater faith and blessing (v. 5; 9:6,10–12). (7) When God supplies an abundance, it is so that we may multiply our good works (9:8; Eph. 4:28). (8) Giving increases our dedication to God (Mat. 6:21) and activates the work of God in our financial affairs (Luke 6:38). For more on this, see article on TITHES AND OFFERINGS, p. 1388.

8:9 HE BECAME POOR. Sacrificial giving is essential to the nature and character of Jesus Christ. By His becoming poor, we now partake of His eternal riches. God wants the same attitude among believers as evidence of His grace working within us. All the gifts of grace and salvation, the kingdom of glory and heaven, and even the reproach of Christ, are the everlasting riches we have received in exchange for the rags of iniquity (Luke 12:15; Eph. 1:3; Phil. 4:11–13,18–19; Heb. 11:26; Rev. 3:17).

love, and of our [m]boasting on your behalf.

Encouragement to give

9 FOR AS touching [n]the ministering to the saints, it is superfluous for me to write to you:

2 For I know [o]the forwardness of your mind, [p]for which I boast of you to them of Macedonia, that [q]Achaia was ready a year ago; and your zeal hath provoked very many.

3 [r]Yet have I sent the brethren, lest our boasting of you should be in vain in this behalf; that, as I said, ye may be ready:

4 Lest haply if they of Macedonia come with me, and find you unprepared, we (that we say not, ye) should be ashamed in this same confident boasting.

5 Therefore I thought it necessary to exhort the brethren, that they would go before unto you, and make up beforehand your [b]bounty, [c]whereof ye had notice before, that the same might be ready, as *a matter of* bounty, and not as *of* covetousness.

Giving generously

6 [s]But this *I say,* He which soweth sparingly shall reap also sparingly; and he which soweth bountifully shall reap also bountifully.

7 Every man according as he purposeth in his heart, *so let him give;* [t]not grudgingly, or of necessity: for [u]God loveth a cheerful giver.

8 [v]And God *is* able to make all grace abound toward you; that ye, always having all sufficiency in all *things,* may abound to every good work:

9 (As it is written, [w]He hath dispersed abroad; he hath given to the poor: his righteousness remaineth for ever.

10 Now he that [x]ministereth seed to the sower both minister bread for *your* food, and multiply your seed sown, and increase the fruits of your [y]righteousness;)

11 Being enriched in every thing to all [d, e]bountifulness, [z]which causeth through us thanksgiving to God.

12 For the administration of this service not only [a]supplieth the want of the saints, but is abundant also by many thanksgivings unto God;

13 Whiles by the experiment of this ministration they [b]glorify God for your professed subjection unto the gospel of Christ, and for *your* liberal [c]distribution unto them, and unto all *men;*

14 And by their prayer for you, which long after you for the exceeding [d]grace of God in you.

15 Thanks *be* unto God [e]for his unspeakable gift.

Paul defends his ministry

10 NOW [f]I Paul myself beseech you by the meekness and gentleness of Christ, [g]who [f]in presence *am* base among you, but being absent am bold toward you:

2 But I beseech *you,* [h]that I may not be bold when I am present with that confidence, wherewith I think to

8:24 [m]ch. 7:14 & 9:2
9:1 [n]Acts 11:29 Rom. 15:26 1 Cor. 16:1 ch. 8:4 Gal. 2:10
9:2 [o]ch. 8:19 [p]ch. 8:24 [q]ch. 8:10
9:3 [r]ch. 8:6,17
9:6 [s]Prov. 11:24
9:7 [t]Deut. 15:7 [u]Ex. 35:5 Prov. 11:25 Rom. 12:8 ch. 8:12
9:8 [v]Prov. 11:24 Phil. 4:19
9:9 [w]Ps. 112:9
9:10 [x]Is. 55:10 [y]Hos. 10:12 Mat. 6:1
9:11 [z]ch. 1:11
9:12 [a]ch. 8:14
9:13 [b]Mat. 5:16 [c]Heb. 13:16
9:14 [d]ch. 8:1
9:15 [e]Jas. 1:17
10:1 [f]Rom. 12:1 [g]ch. 12:5
10:2 [h]1 Cor. 4:21 ch. 13:2,10

[b] Gk. *blessing;* see Gen. 33:11; 1 Sam. 25:27; 2 Ki. 5:15 [c] Or, *which hath been so much spoken of before* [d] Or, *liberality* [e] Gk. *simplicity* [f] Or, *in outward appearance*

9:6 SHALL REAP . . . SPARINGLY. Christians can give either generously or sparingly; God will reward them accordingly (Mat. 7:1–2). To Paul, giving is not a loss, but a form of saving; it results in substantial benefits for those who give (see 8:2, note; 9:11, note). He is not speaking primarily of the quantity given, but of the quality of our hearts' desires and motives. The poor widow gave little, but God considered it much because of the proportion she gave and the complete dedication she reflected (see Luke 21:1–4, note; cf. Prov. 11:24–25; 19:17; Mat. 10:41–42; Luke 6:38).

9:8 GRACE ABOUND TOWARD YOU. The believer who gives what he can to help those in need will find that the grace of God furnishes a sufficiency for his own needs, and even more, in order that he may abound in good works for others (cf. Eph. 4:28).

9:11 ENRICHED IN EVERY THING. In order for generosity to be outwardly expressed, the heart must already be enriched with sincere love and compassion for others. Giving of ourselves and our possessions results in (1) supplying the needs of poorer brethren, (2) praise and thanksgiving to God (v. 12), and (3) reciprocal love from those who receive the help (v. 14).

10:1 NOW I PAUL MYSELF BESEECH YOU. The majority of Corinthian believers had accepted Paul's authority and submitted to his teachings and apostleship (7:8–16). Yet there was a minority, led by false ministers undermining the gospel and doing Satan's work (11:13), who continued to resist him and to slander his person and character. In chs. 10–13 Paul addresses these false believers.

be bold against some, which [g]think of
us as if we walked according to the
flesh.
3 For though we walk in the flesh,
we do not war after the flesh:
4 ([i]For the weapons [j]of our war-
fare *are* not carnal, but [k]mighty
[h]through God [l]to the pulling down of
strong holds;)
5 [m]Casting down [i]imaginations,
and every high thing that exalteth it-
self against the knowledge of God, and
bringing into captivity every thought to
the obedience of Christ;
6 [n]And having in a readiness to re-
venge all disobedience, when [o]your
obedience is fulfilled.
7 [p]Do ye look on things after the
outward appearance? [q]If any man
trust to himself that he is Christ's, let
him of himself think this again, that, as
he *is* Christ's, even so *are* [r]we
Christ's.
8 For though I should boast some-
what more [s]of our authority, which
the Lord hath given us for edification,
and not for your destruction, [t]I should
not be ashamed:
9 That I may not seem as if I would
terrify you by letters.
10 For *his* letters, [j]say they, *are*
weighty and powerful; but [u]*his* bodily
presence *is* weak, and *his* [v]speech
contemptible.
11 Let such an one think this, that,
such as we are in word by letters when
we are absent, such *will we be* also in
deed when we are present.
12 [w]For we dare not make our-

10:4 [i]Eph. 6:13 1 Thes. 5:8 [j]1 Tim. 1:18 2 Tim. 2:3 [k]Acts 7:22 1 Cor. 2:5 [l]Jer. 1:10
10:5 [m]1 Cor. 1:19
10:6 [n]ch. 13:2,10 [o]ch. 7:15
10:7 [p]John 7:24 [q]1 Cor. 14:37 1 John 4:6 [r]1 Cor. 3:23 ch. 11:23
10:8 [s]ch. 13:10 [t]ch. 7:14
10:10 [u]1 Cor. 2:3,4 Gal. 4:13 [v]1 Cor. 1:17
10:12 [w]ch. 5:12

[g] Or, *reckon* [h] Or, *to God* [i] Or, *reasonings* [j] Gk. *saith he*

10:4 WEAPONS OF OUR WARFARE. Our warfare is against spiritual forces of wickedness (Eph. 6:12). Therefore, carnal weapons such as human ingenuity, talent, wealth, organizing ability, eloquence, propaganda, charisma, and personality are in themselves inadequate to pull down the strongholds of Satan. The only weapons adequate to destroy the fortresses of Satan, unrighteousness, and false teaching are those which God gives.

(1) These weapons are powerful because they are spiritual and come from God. Elsewhere Paul lists some of these weapons—commitment to truth, a life of righteousness, proclamation of the gospel, faith, love, hope of salvation, the Word of God, persevering prayer (Eph. 6:11–19; 1 Thes. 5:8). By using these weapons against the enemy, the church will come forth victorious. That is, the presence and kingdom of God will be powerfully manifested in order to save sinners, cast out demons, sanctify believers, baptize them in the Holy Spirit, and heal the sick (see article on SIGNS OF BELIEVERS, p. 1516).

(2) The church today is often tempted to meet the challenge of the world by carnal means and by the world's weapons, i.e., by humanistic wisdom, philosophy, psychology, exciting attractions, church performances focused on entertainment, etc. These all too often serve as a substitute for the basic N.T. practices of intense prayer, uncompromising commitment to the Word of God, and fervent proclamation of the gospel. But such weapons will not bring about a Holy Ghost revival, for they cannot possibly destroy the stronghold of sin, deliver us from the power of Satan, and overthrow the evil passions that are running rampant in the world today. If we use the world's weapons, we will only secularize the church and separate it from the weapons of faith, righteousness, and the power of the Holy Spirit. Tragically, the church itself will then be overshadowed by the power of darkness and its families be cast down and taken captive by the forces of the world.

10:5 BRINGING INTO CAPTIVITY EVERY THOUGHT. Christian warfare involves bringing all our thoughts into alignment with the will of Christ; failure to do so will lead to immorality and spiritual death (Rom. 6:16,23; 8:13). Use the following four steps to bring your thought life under the Lordship of Christ. (1) Be aware that God knows every thought and that nothing is hidden from Him (Ps. 94:11; 139:2,4,23–24). We will have to account to God for our thoughts as well as for our words and deeds (5:10; Eccl. 12:14; Mat. 12:35–37; Rom. 14:12).

(2) Be aware that the mind is a battleground. Some thoughts originate with us, while others come directly from the enemy. To bring every thought into captivity to Christ requires warfare against both our sinful nature and Satanic forces (Eph. 6:12–13; cf. Mat. 4:3–11). Regarding the latter, steadfastly resist and reject evil and unwholesome thoughts in the name of the Lord Jesus Christ (Phil. 4:7). Remember that we as believers overcome our adversary by the blood of the Lamb, by the word of our testimony, and by persistently saying "No!" to the devil, temptation, and sin (Tit. 2:11–12; Jas. 4:7; Rev. 12:11; cf. Mat. 4:3–11).

(3) Be resolute in focusing your mind on Christ and heavenly things rather than on earthly things (Phil. 3:19; Col. 3:2), for the mind set on the Spirit is life and peace (Rom. 8:6–7). Fill your mind with God's Word (Ps. 1:1–3; 19:7–14; 119) and with those things which are noble, excellent, and praiseworthy (Phil. 4:8).

(4) At all times be careful what your eyes see and your ears hear. Resolutely refuse (a) to let your eyes be an instrument for lust (Job 31:1; 1 John 2:16), or (b) to set any worthless or evil thing before your eyes, whether in books, magazines, pictures, television programs, or in real life (Ps. 101:3; Is. 33:14–15; Rom. 13:14).

10:12 MEASURING THEMSELVES BY THEMSELVES. To compare ourselves with the

selves of the number, or compare ourselves with some that commend themselves: but they measuring themselves by themselves, and comparing themselves among themselves, [k]are not wise.

13 [x]But we will not boast of things without *our* measure, but according to the measure of the [l]rule which God hath distributed to us, a measure to reach even unto you.

14 For we stretch not ourselves beyond *our measure,* as though we reached not unto you: [y]for we are come as far as to you also in *preaching* the gospel of Christ:

15 Not boasting of things without *our* measure, *that is,* [z]of other men's labours; but having hope, when your faith is increased, that we shall be [m]enlarged by you according to our rule abundantly,

16 To preach the gospel in the *regions* beyond you, *and* not to boast in another man's [n]line of things made ready to our hand.

17 [a]But he that glorieth, let him glory in the Lord.

18 For [b]not he that commendeth himself is approved, but [c]whom the Lord commendeth.

Paul and false apostles

11 WOULD TO God ye could bear with me a little in [d]*my* folly: and indeed [o]bear with me.

2 For I am [e]jealous over you with godly jealousy: for [f]I have espoused you to one husband, [g]that I may present *you* [h]*as* a chaste virgin to Christ.

3 But I fear, lest by any means, as [i]the serpent beguiled Eve through his subtlety, so your minds [j]should be corrupted from the simplicity that is in Christ.

4 For if he that cometh preacheth another Jesus, whom we have not preached, or *if* ye receive another spirit, which ye have not received, or [k]another gospel, which ye have not accepted, ye might well bear [p]with *him.*

5 For I suppose [l]I was not a whit behind the very chiefest apostles.

6 But though [m]*I be* rude in speech, yet not [n]in knowledge; but [o]we have been thoroughly made manifest among you in all things.

7 Have I committed an offence in abasing myself that ye might be exalted, because I have preached to you the gospel of God freely?

8 I robbed other churches, taking wages *of them,* to do you service.

9 And when I was present with you, and wanted, [p]I was chargeable to no man: for that which was lacking to me [q]the brethren which came from Macedonia supplied: and in all *things* I have kept myself [r]from being burdensome unto you, and *so* will I keep *myself.*

10 [s]As the truth of Christ is in me, [t]no[q] man shall stop me of this boasting in the regions of Achaia.

11 Wherefore? [u]because I love you not? God knoweth.

12 But what I do, that I will do, [v]that I may cut off occasion from them which desire occasion; that wherein they glory, they may be found even as we.

10:13 [x]ver. 15 **10:14** [y]1 Cor. 3:5 **10:15** [z]Rom. 15:20 **10:17** [a]Is. 65:16 Jer. 9:24 1 Cor. 1:31 **10:18** [b]Prov. 27:2 [c]Rom. 2:29 1 Cor. 4:5 **11:1** [d]ver. 16 ch. 5:13 **11:2** [e]Gal. 4:17 [f]Hos. 2:19 1 Cor. 4:15 [g]Col. 1:28 [h]Lev. 21:13 **11:3** [i]Gen. 3:4 John 8:44 [j]Eph. 6:24 Col. 2:4,8 1 Tim. 1:3 **11:4** [k]Gal. 1:7,8 **11:5** [l]1 Cor. 15:10 **11:6** [m]1 Cor. 1:17 [n]Eph. 3:4 [o]ch. 12:12 **11:9** [p]Acts 20:33 1 Thes. 2:9 [q]Phil. 4:10 [r]ch. 12:14 **11:10** [s]Rom. 9:1 [t]1 Cor. 9:15 **11:11** [u]ch. 6:11 **11:12** [v]1 Cor. 9:12

k Or, *understand it not* **l** Or, *line* **m** Or, *magnified in you* **n** Or, *rule* **o** Or, *ye do bear with me* **p** Or, *with me* **q** Gk. *this boasting shall not be stopped in me*

contemporary standards and lives of believers around us shows that we are yet without proper understanding of God's will. The standard by which we must measure ourselves is the standard revealed by Christ and the apostles in the N.T.

11:3 YOUR MINDS . . . CORRUPTED. Some at Corinth were in grave danger of being deceived by false preachers and accepting a distorted gospel (v. 4). By accepting the teachings of these "deceitful workers" (v. 13), they were in peril of having their minds led astray from wholehearted devotion to Christ. In the churches today there are also those who appear as ministers of righteousness, yet whose teachings contradict the Word of God and lead their followers to spiritual disaster (see next two notes; Mat. 23:13, note). We must be on our guard against them (see articles on FALSE TEACHERS, p. 1508, and OVERSEERS AND THEIR DUTIES, p. 1706).

11:4 PREACHETH . . . ANOTHER GOSPEL. False teachers may state that Biblical revelation is true, but at the same time allege that they possess extra-biblical revelations or knowledge equal in authority to Scripture and valid for the church as a whole. Such false teaching usually draws the Christian faith into a syncretism with other religions or philosophies. This results in the following errors: (1) The supposed new "revelation" is put on the same level of authority as the original apostolic Biblical revelation in Christ. (2) Scripture becomes less important and Christ takes second place to "saints" or to founders of a movement or church. (3) The false teachers claim to have deeper or exclusive understanding of so-called "hidden revelations" in Scripture.

13 For such [w]*are* false apostles,
[x]deceitful workers, transforming
themselves into the apostles of Christ.
14 And no marvel; for Satan himself
is transformed into [y]an angel of light.
15 Therefore *it is* no great thing if
his ministers also be transformed as
the ministers of righteousness;
2 Cor. 12:7-10 [z]whose end shall be according to their
works.

Paul's rightful boasting

16 I say again, Let no man think me
a fool; if otherwise, yet as a fool [r]re-
ceive me, that I may boast myself a lit-
tle.
17 That which I speak, [a]I speak
it not after the Lord, but as it were
foolishly, in this confidence of boast-
ing.
18 Seeing that many glory after the
flesh, I will glory also.
19 For ye suffer fools gladly, [b]see-
ing ye *yourselves* are wise.
20 For ye suffer, [c]if a man bring
you into bondage, if a man devour *you,*
if a man take *of you,* if a man exalt him-
self, if a man smite you on the face.
21 I speak as concerning reproach,
[d]as though we had been weak. How-
beit [e]whereinsoever any is bold, (I
speak foolishly,) I am bold also.

Paul's apostolic suffering

22 Are they Hebrews? [f]so *am* I.
Are they Israelites? so *am* I. Are they
the seed of Abraham? so *am* I.
23 Are they ministers of Christ? (I

11:13 [w]Acts 15:24 Rom. 16:18 Gal. 1:7 Phil. 1:15 2 Pet. 2:1 Rev. 2:2 [x]Phil. 3:2 Tit. 1:10 **11:14** [y]Gal. 1:8 **11:15** [z]Phil. 3:19 **11:17** [a]1 Cor. 7:6 **11:19** [b]1 Cor. 4:10 **11:20** [c]Gal. 2:4 **11:21** [d]ch. 10:10 [e]Phil. 3:4 **11:22** [f]Acts 22:3 Rom. 11:1 Phil. 3:5

[r] Or, *suffer*

11:13 DECEITFUL WORKERS, TRANSFORMING THEMSELVES. Satan the great deceiver (v. 3; John 8:44) uses evil men as his agents, transforming them into "false apostles, deceitful workers." (1) The Bible speaks of these deceitful ministers and leaders as people who, energized by Satan, (a) appear to accomplish great things for God (v. 15; Rev. 13:2), (b) preach attractive gospel messages (v. 4; see 1 Tim. 4:1, note), and (c) appear to be righteous, but in reality reject godliness and deny its power (2 Tim. 3:5).

(2) These people disguise themselves as "apostles of Christ" and "ministers of righteousness" (v. 15). Thus, they imitate real ministers of Christ, putting into their message every available "form of godliness" (2 Tim. 3:5). They may be sincerely caring and loving, and they may preach forgiveness, peace, fulfillment, brotherhood, and many other helpful things—but they live under the influence of Satan. Their gospel is often one of human reason and not a true interpretation of God's revelation found in the Scriptures (cf. Gal. 1:6–7; 1 Pet. 2:1–3). Their message deviates from the N.T. apostolic doctrine (see 1 John 4:1, note).

(3) All believers must beware of these misleading ministers and leaders (vv. 3–4; Mat. 7:15; 16:6) and not be deceived by their charisma, oratory, education, miracles, numerical success, philosophy, or popular message.

(4) All religious leaders must be judged according to their attitude and loyalty toward the blood redemption of Jesus Christ and the gospel as presented by Christ and the writers of the N.T. (see Gal. 1:9, note; see article on FALSE TEACHERS, p. 1508).

11:23 THE SUFFERINGS OF PAUL. The Holy Spirit, through the words of Paul, reveals to us the anguish and suffering of someone fully committed to Christ, His Word, and the cause for which He died (see article on THE SUFFERING OF THE RIGHTEOUS, p. 764). Paul was in fellowship with the feelings of God and in sympathy with the heart and pathos of Christ. The following are twenty ways Paul shared the sufferings of Christ. Paul speaks of: (1) "much tribulation" encountered in serving God (Acts 14:22);

(2) his torment of "spirit" because of the overwhelming sin in society (Acts 17:16);

(3) serving the Lord with "tears" (2:4);

(4) warning the church "night and day with tears" for a period of three years because of the destruction of souls brought about by the distortion of the gospel through teachers not faithful to Biblical apostolic faith (Acts 20:31; see article on OVERSEERS AND THEIR DUTIES, p. 1706);

(5) his grief in departing from beloved believers (Acts 20:17–38), and his broken heart at their sorrow (Acts 21:13);

(6) the "great heaviness and continual sorrow" in his heart because of the refusal of his "kinsmen" to accept the gospel of Christ (Rom. 9:2–3; 10:1);

(7) the many trials and troubles which came to him through his work for Christ (4:8–12; 11:23–29; 1 Cor. 4:11–13);

(8) his mourning and anguish of spirit over sin tolerated within the church (2:1–3; 12:21; 1 Cor. 5:1–2; 6:8–10);

(9) his "much affliction and anguish of heart" as he wrote to those who were forsaking Christ and the true gospel (2:4);

(10) his groaning and "being burdened" with the desire to be with Christ and free from the sin and concern of this world (5:1–4; cf. Phil. 1:23);

(11) his being "troubled on every side" because of his commitment to the moral and doctrinal purity of the church (7:5; 11:3–4);

(12) the daily "care" upon him because of concern for "all the churches" (11:28);

(13) his intense concern when a Christian was led into sin (11:29);

(14) his having to count "accursed" those who preached a different gospel from that of the revealed N.T. faith (Gal. 1:6–9);

(15) his "travail" to restore those fallen from grace (Gal. 4:19; 5:4);

(16) his "weeping" over enemies of the cross of

speak as a fool) I *am* more; [g]in labours
more abundant, [h]in stripes above
measure, in prisons more frequent,
[i]in deaths oft.

24 Of the Jews five times received I
[j]forty *stripes* save one.

25 Thrice was I [k]beaten with rods,
[l]once was I stoned, thrice I [m]suffered
shipwreck, a night and a day I have
been in the deep;

26 *In* journeyings often, *in* perils of
waters, *in* perils of robbers, [n]*in* perils
by *mine own* countrymen, [o]*in* perils by
the heathen, *in* perils in the city, *in*
perils in the wilderness, *in* perils in the
sea, *in* perils among false brethren;

27 In weariness and painfulness,
[p]in watchings often, [q]in hunger and
thirst, in fastings often, in cold and nakedness.

28 Beside those things that are
without, that which cometh upon me
daily, [r]the care of all the churches.

29 [s]Who is weak, and I am not
weak? who is offended, and I burn not?

30 If I must needs glory, [t]I will
glory of the things which concern mine
infirmities.

31 [u]The God and Father of our
Lord Jesus Christ, [v]which is blessed
for evermore, knoweth that I lie not.

32 [w]In Damascus the governor under Aretas the king kept the city of the
Damascenes with a garrison, desirous
to apprehend me:

33 And through a window in a basket was I let down by the wall, and escaped his hands.

11:23 [g]1 Cor. 15:10 [h]Acts 9:16 [i]1 Cor. 15:30
11:24 [j]Deut. 25:3
11:25 [k]Acts 16:22 [l]Acts 14:19 [m]Acts 27:41
11:26 [n]Acts 9:23 [o]Acts 14:5
11:27 [p]Acts 20:31 [q]1 Cor. 4:11
11:28 [r]Acts 20:18 Rom. 1:14
11:29 [s]1 Cor. 8:13
11:30 [t]ch. 12:5
11:31 [u]Rom. 1:9 Gal. 1:20 1 Thes. 2:5 [v]Rom. 9:5
11:32 [w]Acts 9:24

12:2 [x]Rom. 16:7 Gal. 1:22 [y]Acts 22:17
12:4 [z]Luke 23:43
12:5 [a]ch. 11:30
12:6 [b]ch. 11:16
12:7 [c]See Ezek. 28:24 Gal. 4:13 [d]Job 2:7 Luke 13:16
12:8 [e]Deut. 3:23 Mat. 26:44

Paul's visions of the Lord

12 IT IS not expedient for me
doubtless to glory. [s]I will
come to visions and revelations of the
Lord.

2 I knew a man [x]in Christ above
fourteen years ago, (whether in the
body, I cannot tell; or whether out of
the body, I cannot tell: God knoweth;)
such an one [y]caught up to the third
heaven.

3 And I knew such a man, (whether
in the body, or out of the body, I cannot
tell: God knoweth;)

4 How that he was caught up into
[z]paradise, and heard unspeakable
words, which it is not [t]lawful for a
man to utter.

5 Of such an one will I glory: [a]yet
of myself I will not glory, but in mine
infirmities.

6 For [b]though I would desire to
glory, I shall not be a fool; for I will say
the truth: but *now* I forbear, lest any
man should think of me above that
which he seeth me *to be,* or *that* he
heareth of me.

7 And lest I should be exalted above
measure through the abundance of the
revelations, there was given to me a
[c]thorn in the flesh, [d]the messenger
of Satan to buffet me, lest I should be
exalted above measure.

8 [e]For this thing I besought the
Lord thrice, that it might depart
from me.

[s] Gk. *For I will come* [t] Or, *possible*

Christ (Phil. 3:18);

(17) his "affliction and distress" in wondering whether some might fall from the faith (1 Thes. 3:5–8);

(18) his persecution because of his passion for righteousness and godliness (2 Tim. 3:12);

(19) his sorrowful plight at the defections of Asian believers (2 Tim. 1:15); and

(20) his anguished plea to Timothy to faithfully guard the true faith in light of the coming apostasy (1 Tim. 4:1; 6:20; 2 Tim. 1:14).

12:2 A MAN IN CHRIST. Paul refers to himself as "a man in Christ" who was taken up into heaven in order to receive revelations, probably concerning Christ's gospel and the unspeakable glories of heaven that are reserved for believers (v. 7; cf. Rom. 8:18; 2 Tim. 4:8). This great privilege and revelation granted to Paul strengthened him, enabling him to endure the long and severe sufferings that came to him during his apostolic ministry.

12:2 THIRD HEAVEN. The Scriptures indicate that there are three heavens. (1) The first heaven is the atmosphere which surrounds the earth (Hos. 2:18; Dan. 7:13). (2) The second heaven is that of the stars (Gen. 1:14–18). (3) The third heaven, also called paradise (vv. 3–4; Luke 23:43; Rev. 2:7), is the abode of God and the home of all departed believers (5:8; Phil. 1:23). Its location is not revealed.

12:7 A THORN IN THE FLESH. The word "thorn" communicates the idea of pain, trouble, sufferings, humiliation, or physical infirmities, but not temptation to sin (cf. Gal. 4:13–14). (1) Paul's thorn remains undefined, so that those with any "thorn" might readily apply the spiritual lesson of this passage to themselves. (2) Paul's thorn is attributed to demonic activity or origin, permitted yet limited by God (cf. Job 2:1ff). (3) At the same time, Paul's thorn was given to him to keep him from becoming proud over revelations that he had received. (4) Paul's thorn kept him dependent in greater measure on divine grace (v. 9, note; Heb. 12:10).

12:8 I BESOUGHT THE LORD THRICE. Many times when God answers a sincere prayer by a re-

9 And he said unto me, My grace is sufficient for thee: for my strength is made perfect in weakness. Most gladly therefore [f]will I rather glory in my infirmities, [g]that the power of Christ may rest upon me.

10 Therefore [h]I take pleasure in infirmities, in reproaches, in necessities, in persecutions, in distresses for Christ's sake: [i]for when I am weak, then am I strong.

Eph. 6:10-18

The signs of a true apostle

11 I am become [j]a fool in glorying; ye have compelled me: for I ought to have been commended of you: for [k]in nothing am I behind the very chiefest apostles, though [l]I be nothing.

12 [m]Truly the signs of an apostle were wrought among you in all patience, in signs, and wonders, and mighty deeds.

13 [n]For what is it wherein ye were inferior to other churches, except *it be* that [o]I myself was not burdensome to you? forgive me [p]this wrong.

14 [q]Behold, the third time I am ready to come to you; and I will not be burdensome to you: for [r]I seek not yours, but you: [s]for the children ought not to lay up for the parents, but the parents for the children.

15 And I will very gladly spend and be spent [t]for [u]you, though [u]the more abundantly I love you, the less I be loved.

16 But be it so, [v]I did not burden you: nevertheless, being crafty, I caught you with guile.

17 [w]Did I make a gain of you by any of them whom I sent unto you?

18 [x]I desired Titus, and with *him* I sent a [y]brother. Did Titus make a gain of you? walked we not in the same spirit? *walked we* not in the same steps?

The appeal for repentance

19 [z]Again, think ye that we excuse ourselves unto you? [a]we speak before God in Christ: [b]but *we do* all things, dearly beloved, for your edifying.

20 For I fear, lest, when I come, I shall not find you such as I would, and *that* [c]I shall be found unto you such as ye would not: lest *there be* debates, envyings, wraths, strifes, backbitings, whisperings, swellings, tumults:

21 *And* lest, when I come again, my God [d]will humble me among you, and *that* I shall bewail many [e]which have sinned already, and have not repented of the uncleanness and [f]fornication and lasciviousness which they have committed.

12:9 [f]ch. 11:30 [g]1 Pet. 4:14
12:10 [h]Rom. 5:3 ch. 7:4 [i]ch. 13:4
12:11 [j]ch. 11:1,16 [k]ch. 11:5 Gal. 2:6-8 [l]1 Cor. 3:7 Eph. 3:8
12:12 [m]Rom. 15:18 1 Cor. 9:2 ch. 4:2
12:13 [n]1 Cor. 1:7 [o]1 Cor. 9:12 ch. 11:9 [p]ch. 11:7
12:14 [q]ch. 13:1 [r]Acts 20:33 1 Cor. 10:33 [s]1 Cor. 4:14
12:15 [t]John 10:11 ch. 1:6 Col. 1:24 2 Tim. 2:10 [u]ch. 6:12,13
12:16 [v]ch. 11:9
12:17 [w]ch. 7:2
12:18 [x]ch. 8:6,16 [y]ch. 8:18
12:19 [z]ch. 5:12 [a]Rom. 9:1 ch. 11:31 [b]1 Cor. 10:33
12:20 [c]1 Cor. 4:21 ch. 13:2,10
12:21 [d]ch. 2:1,4 [e]ch. 13:2 [f]1 Cor. 5:1

[u] Gk. *your souls*

---

fusal, something much better is bestowed (see next note; Eph. 3:20).

12:9 MY GRACE IS SUFFICIENT FOR THEE. Grace is God's presence, favor, and power. It is a force, a heavenly strength bestowed on those who call upon God. This grace will descend upon the faithful believer who accepts his weaknesses and difficulties for the gospel's sake (Phil. 4:13; see article on FAITH AND GRACE, p. 1738). (1) The greater our weakness and trials for Christ, the more grace God will give us to accomplish His will. What he bestows on us is always sufficient for us to live our daily lives, to work for Him, and to endure our suffering and "thorns in the flesh" (cf. 1 Cor. 10:13). As long as we draw near to Christ, Christ will bestow His heavenly strength and comfort on us. (2) We should glory and see eternal value in our weaknesses, for they cause the power of Christ to descend on us and dwell within us as we walk through life toward our heavenly home.

12:15 SPEND AND BE SPENT FOR YOU. Paul's spirit of dedicated love toward those whom he is trying to help is an example for all pastors, teachers, missionaries, and ministers. It portrays a dedicated love (cf. 6:11–13; 7:1–4) like that of a father for his children. It is a love that is ready to be spent to the uttermost for the sake of their souls, a love that does not think of itself but bestows genuine concern for those under its care. Paul seeks nothing in return but the response of their hearts turned toward Christ. Every faithful minister of the gospel should have this type of love.

12:20 BACKBITINGS, WHISPERINGS. The Bible condemns sins of speech that harm other people as grave offenses against the Christian law of love. Any kind of disparaging speech defaming the character of another person must be resisted. The discussion or exposing of another's wrongdoings should be done only with a sincere motive to help that person or to protect others and the kingdom of God (Rom. 1:29; Eph. 4:31; 2 Tim. 4:10, 14–15; 1 Pet. 2:1).

12:21 I SHALL BEWAIL MANY WHICH HAVE SINNED. Christian ministers must mourn over those in the church who refuse to repent of and forsake their sin, for they are spiritually dead. The tragic message for them is Paul's word to the Corinthians (1 Cor. 6:9), the Galatians (Gal. 5:21), and the Ephesians (Eph. 5:5–6), a word pronouncing exclusion from the kingdom of God.

13 THIS *IS* [g]the third *time* I am
coming to you. [h]In the mouth
of two or three witnesses shall every
word be established.
2 [i]I told you before, and foretell
you, as if I were present, the second
time; and being absent now I write to
them [j]which heretofore have sinned,
and to all other, that, if I come again,
[k]I will not spare:
3 Since ye seek a proof of Christ
[l]speaking in me, which to you-ward is
not weak, but is mighty [m]in you.
4 [n]For though he was crucified
through weakness, yet [o]he liveth by
the power of God. For [p]we also are
weak ▼in him, but we shall live with
him by the power of God toward
you.
5 Examine yourselves, whether ye
be in the faith; prove your own selves.
Know ye not your own selves, [q]how
that Jesus Christ is in you, except ye be
[r]reprobates?
6 But I trust that ye shall know that
we are not reprobates.
7 Now I pray to God that ye do no
evil; not that we should appear ap-
proved, but that ye should do that
which is honest, though [s]we be as re-
probates.
8 For we can do nothing against the
truth, but for the truth.
9 For we are glad, [t]when we are
weak, and ye are strong: and this also
we wish, [u]*even* your perfection.
10 [v]Therefore I write these things
being absent, lest being present I
should use sharpness, according to the
power which the Lord hath given me to
edification, and not to destruction.

Farewell and benediction

11 Finally, brethren, farewell. Be
perfect, be of good comfort, [w]be of one
mind, live in peace; and the God of love
[x]and peace shall be with you.
12 [y]Greet one another with an holy
kiss.
13 All the saints salute you.
14 [z]The grace of the Lord Jesus
Christ, and the love of God, and [a]the
communion of the Holy Ghost, *be* with
you all. Amen.

▼Or, *with him*

13:1 [g]ch. 12:14 [h]Num. 35:30 Deut. 17:6 Mat. 18:16 John 8:17 Heb. 10:28
13:2 [i]ch. 10:2 [j]ch. 12:21 [k]ch. 1:23
13:3 [l]Mat. 10:20 1 Cor. 5:4 [m]1 Cor. 9:2
13:4 [n]Phil. 2:7,8 1 Pet. 3:18 [o]Rom. 6:4 [p]ch. 10:3,4
13:5 [q]Rom. 8:10 Gal. 4:19 [r]1 Cor. 9:27
13:7 [s]ch. 6:9
13:9 [t]1 Cor. 4:10 ch. 11:30 [u]1 Thes. 3:10
13:10 [v]1 Cor. 4:21 ch. 12:20,21
13:11 [w]Rom. 12:16,18 [x]Rom. 15:33
13:12 [y]Rom. 16:16 1 Cor. 16:20 1 Thes. 5:26 1 Pet. 5:14
13:14 [z]Rom. 16:24 [a]Phil. 2:1

13:2 I WILL NOT SPARE. A minister's love for his people (see 12:15, note) demands sternness as well as affection. There comes a time when patience runs its course and when, for the good of the church, offenders should no longer be spared. A holy righteousness, not indulgence, is required.

13:5 EXAMINE ... WHETHER YE BE IN THE FAITH. No knowledge is so important to believers as the certainty that they have eternal life (cf. 1 John 5:13; see John 17:3, note). All professing Christians should examine themselves to ascertain that their salvation is a present reality (see article on ASSURANCE OF SALVATION, p. 2010).

13:14 GRACE ... LOVE ... COMMUNION. Paul's benediction witnesses to the N.T. church's belief in the Trinity. Paul prays that the Corinthians may continually experience (1) the grace of Christ, i.e., His nearness, power, mercy, and comfort; (2) the fatherly love of God with all His blessings; and (3) a deepening fellowship with the Holy Spirit. If this threefold reality is our abiding blessing, then our everlasting salvation will be assured.

A. The Holy Spirit in Relation to Creation and Revelation

Task	References
1. Active in creation	Gen. 1:2; Job 33:4
2. Imparts life to God's creatures	Gen. 2:7; Job 33:4; Ps. 104:30
3. Inspired the prophets and apostles	Num. 11:29; Is. 59:21; Mic. 3:8; Zec. 7:12; 2 Tim. 3:16; 2 Pet. 1:21
4. Speaks through the Word	2 Sam. 23:1–2; Acts 1:16–20; Eph. 6:17; Heb. 3:7–11; 9:8; 10:15

B. The Holy Spirit in Relation to Jesus Christ

Task	References
1. Jesus was conceived in Mary by the Spirit	Mat. 1:18,20–23; Luke 1:34–35
2. Was filled with the Spirit	Mat. 3:16–17; Mark 1:12–13; Luke 3:21–22; Luke 4:1
3. Preached in the Spirit	Is. 11:2–4; 61:1–2; Luke 4:16–27
4. Performed miracles by the power of the Spirit	Is. 61:1; Mat. 12:28; Luke 11:20; Acts 10:38
5. Will baptize believers in the Holy Spirit	Mat. 3:11; Mark 1:8; Luke 3:16; John 1:33; Acts 1:4–5; 11:16
6. Promises the Holy Spirit as the Comforter	John 14:16–18,25–26; 15:26–27; 16:7–15
7. Promises the ministry of the Holy Spirit to flow through believers	John 7:37–39
8. Is revealed to believers by the Spirit	John 16:13–15
9. Offered Himself on the cross through the Spirit	Heb. 9:14
10. Was raised from the dead by the Spirit	Rom. 1:3–4; 8:11
11. Received the Spirit from the Father	John 16:5–14; Acts 2:33
12. Poured out the Spirit upon believers	Acts 2:33,38–39
13. Is glorified by the Spirit	John 16:13–14
14. Spirit prays for His return	Rev. 22:17

C. The Holy Spirit in Relation to the Church

Task	References
1. Dwells in the church as His temple	1 Cor. 3:16; Eph. 2:22; cf. Hag. 2:5
2. Is poured out like rain upon the church	Acts 1:5; 2:1–4,16–21; cf. Is. 32:15; 44:3; Hos. 6:3; Joel 2:23–32
3. Speaks to the church	Rev. 2:7,11,17,27; 3:6,13,22
4. Creates fellowship in the church	2 Cor. 13:14; Phil. 2:1
5. Unites the church	1 Cor. 12:13; Eph. 4:4
6. Gives gifts to the church	Rom. 12:6–8; Eph. 4:11; see chart on THE GIFTS OF THE HOLY SPIRIT, p. 0000
7. Strengthens the church through supernatural manifestations	Acts 4:30–33; 1 Cor. 12:7–13; 14:1–33

C. The Holy Spirit in Relation to the Church (cont.)

Task	References
8. Appoints leaders for the church	Acts 20:28; Eph. 4:11; see chart on THE GIFTS OF THE HOLY SPIRIT, p. 346
9. Works through Spirit-filled people	Acts 6:3,5,8; 8:6–12; 15:28,32; cf. Num. 27:18; Judg. 6:34; 1 Sam. 16:13; Zech. 4:6
10. Empowers preachers	1 Cor. 2:4
11. Commissions men of God	Acts 13:2–4
12. Directs the missionary enterprise	Acts 8:29,39; 16:6–7; 20:23
13. Guards the church against error	2 Tim. 1:14
14. Warns the church of apostasy	1 Tim. 4:1; cf. Neh. 9:30
15. Equips the church for spiritual warfare	Eph. 6:10–18
16. Glorifies Christ	John 16:13–15
17. Promotes righteousness	Rom. 14:17; Eph. 2:21–22; 3:16–21; 1 Thes. 4:7–8

D. The Holy Spirit in Relation to Individual Believers

Task	References
1. Lives in every believer	Rom. 8:11; 1 Cor. 6:15–20; 2 Cor. 3:3; Eph. 1:13; Heb. 6:4; 1 John 3:24; 4:13
2. Convicts us of sin	John 16:7–11; Acts 2:37
3. Regenerates us	John 3:5–6; 14:17; 20:22; Rom. 8:9; 2 Cor. 3:6; Tit. 3:5
4. Imparts God's love to us	Rom. 5:5
5. Makes us realize God is our Father	Rom. 8:14–16; Gal. 4:6
6. Enables us to say "Jesus is Lord"	1 Cor. 12:3
7. Reveals Christ to us	John 15:26; 16:14–15; 1 Cor. 2:10–11
8. Reveals God's truth to us	Neh. 9:20; John 14:16–17,26; 16:13–14; 1 Cor. 2:9–16
9. Enables us to distinguish truth from error	1 John 4:1–3
10. Incorporates us into the church	1 Cor. 12:13
11. Is given to all who ask	Luke 11:13
12. Baptizes us into the body of Christ	1 Cor. 12:13
13. Is the One into whom we are baptized by Christ	Mat. 3:11; Mark 1:8; Luke 3:16; John 1:33; Acts 1:4–5; 11:16
14. Fills us	Luke 1:15,41,67; Acts 2:4; 4:8,31; 6:3–5; 7:55; 11:24; 13:9,52; Eph. 5:18; cf. Ex. 31:3; Judg. 14:19; 1 Sam. 10:10
15. Gives us power and boldness to witness	Luke 1:15–17; 24:47–49; Acts 1:8; 4:31; 6:9–10; 19:6; Rom. 9:1–3
16. Gives us special gifts	Mark 16:17–18; 1 Cor. 1:7; 12:7–11; 1 Pet. 4:10–11; see chart on THE GIFTS OF THE HOLY SPIRIT

D. The Holy Spirit in Relation to Individual Believers (cont.)

Task	References
17. Gives visions and prophecy	Joel 2:28–29; Acts 2:17–18; 10:9–22; 1 Cor. 14:1–5,21–25
18. Develops His fruit in us	Rom. 14:17; 1 Cor. 13; Gal. 5:22–23; 1 Thes. 1:6
19. Enables us to live a holy life	Ps. 51:10–12; 143:10; Ezek. 11:19–20; 37:26; Rom. 8:4–10; 15:16; Gal. 5:16–18,25; Phil. 2:12–13; 2 Thes. 2:13; 1 Pet. 1:2
20. Frees us from the power of sin	Rom. 8:2; Eph. 3:16
21. Enables us to fight Satan with the Word	Eph. 6:17
22. Enables us to speak in difficult moments	Mat. 10:17–20; Mark 13:11; Luke 12:11–12
23. Gives us comfort and encouragement	John 14:17–18,26–27; Acts 9:31
24. Helps us to pray	Acts 4:23–24; Rom. 8:26; Eph. 6:18; Jude 20
25. Enables us to worship	John 4:23–24; Acts 10:46; Eph. 5:18–19; Phil. 3:3
26. Is grieved by our sin	Gen. 6:3; Eph. 4:30; cf. Mat. 12:31–32
27. Is our pledge of final redemption	2 Cor. 1:22; 5:5; Eph. 1:13–14
28. Makes us yearn for Christ's return	Rom. 8:23; Rev. 22:20
29. Gives life to our mortal bodies	Rom. 8:11

E. The Holy Spirit in Relation to Sinner

Task	References
1. Convicts of sin, righteousness, and judgment	John 16:7–11
2. Commissions believers to proclaim the gospel to sinners	Acts 1:8; 2:17,21; 4:31; 11:12–18; 13:1–4
3. Reveals the saving truth of the gospel	Luke 4:18–19; John 15:26–27; Acts 4:8; 11:15,18; 14:3; 1 Cor. 2:4,12; 1 Thes. 1:5

NOTES

Greeting

1 PAUL, AN apostle, (not of men, neither by man, but [a]by Jesus Christ, and God the Father, [b]who raised him from the dead;)

2 And all the brethren [c]which are with me, [d]unto the churches of Galatia:

3 [e]Grace *be* to you and peace from God the Father, and *from* our Lord Jesus Christ,

4 [f]Who gave himself for our sins, that he might deliver us [g]from this present evil world, according to the will of God and our Father:

5 To whom *be* glory for ever and ever. Amen.

1:1 [a]Acts 9:6 Tit. 1:3 [b]Acts 2:24 **1:2** [c]Phil. 2:22 [d]1 Cor. 16:1 **1:3** [e]1 Thes. 1:1 **1:4** [f]Mat. 20:28 Rom. 4:25 Tit. 2:14 [g]Heb. 2:5 1 John 5:19

1:6 [h]ch. 5:8 **1:7** [i]2 Cor. 11:4 [j]Acts 15:1 2 Cor. 2:17 **1:8** [k]1 Cor. 16:22

The Galatian falling away

6 I marvel that ye are so soon removed [h]from him that called you into the grace of Christ unto another gospel:

7 [i]Which is not another; but there be some [j]that trouble you, and would pervert the gospel of Christ.

Condemnation of false teachers

8 But though [k]we, or an angel from heaven, preach any other gospel unto you than that which we have preached unto you, let him be accursed.

9 As we said before, so say I now again, If any *man* preach any other gos-

1:4 DELIVER US FROM THIS PRESENT EVIL WORLD. This verse is probably an early confession of faith that was well known throughout the N.T. churches. It connects the death of Christ with the forgiveness of sin and deliverance from "this present evil world." Essential to the saving purpose of Christ is the deliverance of believers from the evil that dominates the societies of this world. The first gospel message preached after the Pentecostal outpouring of the Holy Spirit contained the words: "Save yourselves from this untoward generation" (Acts 2:40). Believers must live for God and refuse to be governed by the prevailing values, wisdom, opinions, corrupt desires, ambitions, and pleasures of the people of the world (Rom. 12:2, note; Tit. 2:14; see article on THE CHRISTIAN'S RELATIONSHIP TO THE WORLD, p. 2004).

1:6 ANOTHER GOSPEL. False teachers had come to the Galatians, attempting to persuade them to reject Paul's teaching and accept "another gospel." Their different gospel taught that salvation involved not only believing in Christ, but also being incorporated into the Jewish faith by circumcision (5:2), works of the law (3:5), and keeping Jewish holy days (4:10). (1) The Bible clearly affirms that there is only one gospel, "the gospel of Christ" (v. 7). It has come to us through "the revelation of Jesus Christ" (v. 12) and the inspiration of the Holy Spirit (see article on THE INSPIRATION AND AUTHORITY OF SCRIPTURE, p. 1924). The gospel is defined and revealed in the Bible, the Word of God. (2) Any teachings, doctrines, or ideas originating from persons, churches, or traditions and not expressed or implied in God's Word, may not be included in the gospel of Christ (v. 11). To mix them with the original content of the gospel is to "pervert the gospel of Christ" (v. 7).

1:9 LET HIM BE ACCURSED. The word "accursed" (Gk. *anathema*) means that one lies under the curse of God, is doomed to destruction, and will receive God's wrath and damnation. (1) The apostle Paul reveals the Holy Spirit's inspired attitude of judgment and indignation toward those who attempt to distort the original gospel of Christ (v. 7) and to change the truth of apostolic witness. This same attitude was evident in Jesus Christ (see Mat. 23:13, note), Peter (2 Pet. 2), John (2 John 7–11), and Jude (Jude 3–4,12–19), and will be found in the heart of every follower of Christ who loves the gospel of Christ as revealed in God's Word and who believes that it is the indispensable good news of salvation for a world lost in sin (Rom. 10:14–15).

(2) Accursed are all those who preach a gospel contrary to the message that Paul preached, as revealed to him by Christ (vv. 11–12; see v. 6, note). Anyone adding to or taking away from the original and fundamental gospel of Christ and the apostles stands under the curse of God; "God shall take away his part out of the book of life" (Rev. 22:18–19).

(3) God commands believers to defend the faith (see Jude 3, note), to correct in love (2 Tim. 2:25–26), and to separate themselves from teachers, ministers, and others in the church who deny fundamental Bible truths taught by Jesus and the apostles (vv. 8–9; Rom. 16:17–18; 2 Cor. 6:17). These truths include:

(a) The deity of Christ and His virgin birth (Mat. 1:23; see John 20:28, note);

(b) The full inspiration and authority of God's Word in all it teaches (see article on THE INSPIRATION AND AUTHORITY OF SCRIPTURE, p. 1924);

(c) The historicity of the fall of Adam (Rom. 5:12–19);

(d) The inherent corruption of human nature (Gen. 6:5; 8:21; Rom. 1:21–32; 3:10–18; 7:14,21);

(e) The lostness of mankind without Christ (see Acts 4:12, note; Rom. 1:16–32; 10:13–15);

(f) Salvation by faith in Christ as Lord and Savior through His death and blood atonement (Rom. 3:24–25; 5:10; see article on FAITH AND GRACE, p. 1738);

(g) The bodily resurrection of Christ (see Mat. 28:6, note; 1 Cor. 15:3–4);

(h) The historical reality of miracles in both the O.T. and N.T. (1 Cor. 10:1);

(i) The reality of Satan and demons as spiritual beings (Mat. 4:1; 8:28; 2 Cor. 4:4; Eph. 2:2;

pel unto you [l]than that ye have received, let him be accursed.

10 For [m]do I now [n]persuade men, or God? or [o]do I seek to please men? for if I yet pleased men, I should not be the servant of Christ.

Paul's authority of divine origin

11 [p]But I certify you, brethren, that the gospel which was preached of me is not after man.

12 For [q]I neither received it of man, neither was I taught *it,* but [r]by the revelation of Jesus Christ.

13 For ye have heard of my conversation in time past in the Jews' religion, how that [s]beyond measure I persecuted the church of God, and [t]wasted it:

14 And profited in the Jews' religion above many my [a]equals in mine own nation, [u]being more exceedingly zealous [v]of the traditions of my fathers.

15 But when it pleased God, [w]who separated me from my mother's womb, and called *me* by his grace,

16 [x]To reveal his Son in me, that [y]I might preach him among the heathen; immediately I conferred not with [z]flesh and blood:

17 Neither went I up to Jerusalem to them which were apostles before me; but I went into Arabia, and returned again unto Damascus.

18 Then after three years [a]I [b]went up to Jerusalem to see Peter, and abode with him fifteen days.

19 But [b]other of the apostles saw I none, save [c]James the Lord's brother.

20 Now the things which I write unto you, [d]behold, before God, I lie not.

21 [e]Afterwards I came into the regions of Syria, and Cilicia;

22 And was unknown by face [f]unto the churches of Judaea which [g]were in Christ:

23 But they had heard only, That he which persecuted us in times past now preacheth the faith which once he destroyed.

24 And they glorified God in me.

Paul accepted by the church

2 THEN FOURTEEN years after [h]I went up again to Jerusalem with Barnabas, and took Titus with *me* also.

2 And I went up by revelation, [i]and communicated unto them that gospel which I preach among the Gentiles, but [c]privately to them which were of reputation, lest by any means [j]I should run, or had run, in vain.

3 But neither Titus, who was with me, being a Greek, was compelled to be circumcised:

4 And that because of [k]false brethren unawares brought in, who came in privily to spy out our [l]liberty which we have in Christ Jesus, [m]that they might bring us into bondage:

5 To whom we gave place by subjec-

[a] Gk. *equals in years* [b] Or, *returned* [c] Or, *severally*

1:9 [l]Deut. 4:2 Prov. 30:6 Rev. 22:18
1:10 [m]1 Thes. 2:4 [n]1 Sam. 24:7 Mat. 28:14 [o]1 Thes. 2:4 Jas. 4:4
1:11 [p]1 Cor. 15:1
1:12 [q]1 Cor. 15:1 [r]Eph. 3:3
1:13 [s]Acts 9:1 1 Tim. 1:13 [t]Acts 8:3
1:14 [u]Acts 26:9 Phil. 3:6 [v]Jer. 9:14 Mat. 15:2 Mark 7:5
1:15 [w]Is. 49:1,5
1:16 [x]2 Cor. 4:6 [y]Acts 9:15 Eph. 3:8 [z]Mat. 16:17 Eph. 6:12
1:18 [a]Acts 9:26
1:19 [b]1 Cor. 9:5 [c]Mat. 13:55
1:20 [d]Rom. 9:1
1:21 [e]Acts 9:30
1:22 [f]1 Thes. 2:14 [g]Rom. 16:7
2:1 [h]Acts 15:2
2:2 [i]Acts 15:12 [j]Phil. 2:16 1 Thes. 3:5
2:4 [k]Acts 15:1 2 Cor. 11:26 [l]ch. 3:25 [m]ch. 4:3,9

6:11–18; 1 Pet. 5:8);

(j) The Biblical teaching about hell (see Mat. 10:28, note);

(k) The literal return of Jesus Christ to earth (John 14:3, note; Acts 1:11; 1 Cor. 1:7, note; Rev. 19:11, note).

(4) Similar passages warning against false teachers are found in Rom. 16:17; 2 Pet. 2:17–22; 2 John 9–11; Jude 12–13; see 2 Cor. 11:13, note; see article on FALSE TEACHERS, p. 1508.

1:10 FOR IF I YET PLEASED MEN. One cannot be a genuine minister of the gospel and attempt to please people by compromising the truths of the gospel (cf. 1 Cor. 4:3–6). Paul regarded it his duty to speak "not as pleasing men, but God, which trieth our hearts" (1 Thes. 2:4, note). All believers of the gospel of Christ must make it their aim, as did Paul, to please God even if it means displeasing some people (cf. Acts 5:29; Eph. 6:6; Col. 3:22).

1:15 GOD, WHO SEPARATED ME. Although Paul was primarily referring to his apostolic ministry, there is a sense in which each believer has been set apart by grace in order that God may reveal His Son in him or her. We have been separated from sin and the present evil world (see v. 4, note), that we might live in fellowship with God and witness to Jesus Christ before the world. Being a separated person means being a person with God, for God, and near God—living in faith and obedience for His glory and the manifestation of His Son (see article on SPIRITUAL SEPARATION FOR BELIEVERS, p. 1814).

2:5 WE GAVE PLACE BY SUBJECTION, NO. Paul was tolerant of and patient toward many things (cf. 1 Cor. 13:4–7), but unyielding and inflexible when it came to the "truth of the gospel." The revelation that he received from Christ (1:12) is the one and only gospel that possesses the power of salvation to all who believe (Rom. 1:16). Paul understood that that gospel may never be compromised for the sake of peace, unity, or current opinion. Both the glory of Jesus Christ and the salvation of the lost were at stake. Today if we relinquish any part of the gospel according to N.T. revelation, we begin to tear down the only mes-

tion, no, not for an hour; that [n]the truth of the gospel might continue with you.

6 But of these [o]who seemed to be somewhat, (whatsoever they were, it maketh no matter to me: [p]God accepteth no man's person:) for they who seemed *to be somewhat* [q]in conference added nothing to me:

7 But contrariwise, [r]when they saw that the gospel of the uncircumcision [s]was committed unto me, as *the gospel* of the circumcision *was* unto Peter;

8 (For he that wrought effectually in Peter to the apostleship of the circumcision, [t]the same was [u]mighty in me toward the Gentiles:)

9 And when James, Cephas, and John, who seemed to be [v]pillars, perceived [w]the grace that was given unto me, they gave to me and Barnabas the right hands of fellowship; that we *should go* unto the heathen, and they unto the circumcision.

Paul's rebuke of Peter

10 Only *they would* that we should remember the poor; [x]the same which I also was forward to do.

11 [y]But when Peter was come to Antioch, I withstood him to the face, because he was to be blamed.

12 For before that certain came from James, [z]he did eat with the Gentiles: but when they were come, he withdrew and separated himself, fearing them which were of the circumcision.

13 And the other Jews dissembled likewise with him; insomuch that Barnabas also was carried away with their dissimulation.

14 But when I saw that they walked not uprightly according to [a]the truth of the gospel, I said unto Peter [b]before *them* all, [c]If thou, being a Jew, livest after the manner of Gentiles, and not as do the Jews, why compellest thou the Gentiles to live as do the Jews?

15 [d]We *who are* Jews by nature, and not [e]sinners of the Gentiles,

16 [f]Knowing that a man is not justified by the works of the law, but [g]by the faith of Jesus Christ, even we have believed in Jesus Christ, that we might be justified by the faith of Christ, and not by the works of the law: for [h]by

2:5 [n]ver. 14
2:6 [o]ch. 6:3 [p]Acts 10:34 Rom. 2:11 [q]2 Cor. 12:11
2:7 [r]Acts 13:46 Rom. 11:13 2 Tim. 1:11 [s]1 Thes. 2:4
2:8 [t]Acts 9:15 1 Cor. 15:10 [u]ch. 3:5
2:9 [v]Mat. 16:18 Rev. 21:14 [w]Rom. 1:5 1 Cor. 15:10 Eph. 3:8
2:10 [x]Acts 11:30 Rom. 15:25
2:11 [y]Acts 15:35
2:12 [z]Acts 10:28
2:14 [a]ver. 5 [b]1 Tim. 5:20 [c]Acts 10:28
2:15 [d]Acts 15:10 [e]Mat. 9:11 Eph. 2:3
2:16 [f]Acts 13:38 [g]Rom. 1:17 ch. 3:24 [h]Ps. 143:2 Rom. 3:20

---

sage that saves us from eternal destruction (cf. Mat. 18:6).

2:6 GOD ACCEPTETH NO MAN'S PERSON. God does not show favoritism to any person because of his or her heritage, reputation, position, or accomplishment (cf. Lev. 19:15; Deut. 10:17; Job 34:19; Acts 10:34; Eph. 6:9). (1) God sees and evaluates the heart, the inner person, and His favor rests upon those whose hearts are sincerely turned toward Him in love, faith, and purity (cf. 1 Sam. 16:7; Mat. 23:28; Luke 16:15; John 7:24; 2 Cor. 10:7; see 1 Cor. 13:1, note). (2) This fundamental truth of the gospel means that God does not prefer the love, fellowship, and prayers of the educated more than the uneducated, the rich more than the poor, or the powerful more than the weak; God's eternal principle is that "in every nation he that feareth him, and worketh righteousness, is accepted with him" (Acts 10:35).

2:10 REMEMBER THE POOR. A repeated theme in Scripture is the special importance of helping the poor (Ex. 23:10–11; Deut. 15:7–11; Jer. 22:16; Amos 2:6–7; Mat. 6:2–4; John 13:29). There will always be those around us who need help. The poor, especially those of the household of faith (6:10), require both our material assistance and our prayers (see article on THE CARE OF THE POOR AND NEEDY, p. 1312).

2:11 I WITHSTOOD HIM TO THE FACE. Any minister or spiritual leader who is guilty of error and hypocrisy (v. 13) must be opposed and rebuked (cf. 1 Tim. 5:19). This must be applied without respect of persons; even a prominent person like the apostle Peter, who was used greatly by God, needed corrective rebuke (vv. 11–17; cf. 1 Tim. 5:20–21). Scripture indicates that Peter recognized his error and accepted Paul's reproof in a humble and repentant manner. He later refers to Paul as "our beloved brother Paul" (2 Pet. 3:15).

2:12 FEARING THEM . . . OF THE CIRCUMCISION. Those "of the circumcision" were Jewish Christians, especially in the Jerusalem church, who believed that circumcision was necessary for all believers. They also taught that Jewish believers should not eat with any Gentile believers who were not circumcised and did not observe Jewish customs and dietary restrictions. Peter, although knowing that God accepted Gentile believers without partiality (Acts 10:34–35), went against his own conviction out of fear of criticism and the possible loss of authority in the Jewish-Christian church in Jerusalem. His withdrawal of table fellowship with Gentile believers encouraged the error that there were two bodies of Christ, Jewish and Gentile.

2:16 JUSTIFIED BY . . . FAITH. Paul deals here with the question of how a sinner can be justified, i.e., be forgiven of his sins, accepted by God, and put in a right relationship with Him. This will happen not by "the works of the law," but by a living faith in Christ Jesus (see article on BIBLICAL WORDS FOR SALVATION, p. 1726).

the works of the law shall no flesh be
justified.
17 But if, while we seek to be justi-
fied by Christ, we ourselves also are
found [i]sinners, *is* therefore Christ the
minister of sin? God forbid.
18 For if I build again the things
which I destroyed, I make myself a
transgressor.
19 For I [j]through the law [k]am
dead to the law, that I might [l]live
unto God.
20 I am [m]crucified with Christ: nev-
ertheless I live; yet not I, but Christ
liveth in me: and the life which I now
live in the flesh [n]I live by the faith of
the Son of God, [o]who loved me, and
gave himself for me.
21 I do not frustrate the grace of
God: for [p]if righteousness *come* by the
law, then Christ is dead in vain.

2:17 [i]1 John 3:8
2:19 [j]Rom. 8:2 [k]Rom. 6:14 [l]Rom. 6:11 2 Cor. 5:15 Heb. 9:14
2:20 [m]Rom. 6:6 [n]2 Cor. 5:15 1 Pet. 4:2 [o]Eph. 5:2 Tit. 2:14
2:21 [p]Heb. 7:11 Rom. 11:6
3:1 [q]ch. 5:7 [r]ch. 2:14
3:2 [s]Acts 2:38 Eph. 1:13 Heb. 6:4 [t]Rom. 10:16
3:3 [u]ch. 4:9 [v]Heb. 7:16
3:4 [w]Heb. 10:35 2 John 8

Receiving the Spirit by faith

3 O FOOLISH Galatians, [q]who
hath bewitched you, that ye should
not obey [r]the truth, before whose
eyes Jesus Christ hath been evidently
set forth, crucified among you?
2 This only would I learn of you, Re-
ceived ye [s]the Spirit by the works of
the law, [t]or by the hearing of faith?
3 Are ye so foolish? [u]having begun
in the Spirit, are ye now made perfect
by [v]the flesh?
4 [w]Have ye suffered [d]so many
things in vain? if *it be* yet in vain.

The Spirit works miracles by faith

5 He therefore that ministereth to
you the Spirit, and worketh miracles

[d] Or, *so great*

2:19 DEAD TO THE LAW. See Rom. 7:4, note on the meaning of death to the law; Mat. 5:17, note on the believer's relation to the law; see article on THE OLD TESTAMENT LAW, p. 124.

2:20 I AM CRUCIFIED WITH CHRIST. Paul describes his relationship to Christ in terms of a profound personal attachment to and reliance upon his Lord. Those who have faith in Christ live their lives in intimate union with their Lord both in His death and resurrection. (1) All believers have been crucified with Christ on the cross. They have died to the law as a means of salvation and now live through Christ unto God (v. 19). Because of salvation in Christ, sin no longer has dominion over them (see Rom. 6:11, note; cf. Rom. 6:4,8,14; Gal. 5:24; 6:14; Col. 2:12,20).

(2) We who have been crucified with Christ now live with Him in His resurrection life. Christ and His strength dwell within us, becoming the source of all of life and the center of all our thoughts, words, and deeds (John 15:1–6; Eph. 3:17). It is through the Holy Spirit that the risen life of Christ is continually communicated to us (John 16:13–14; Rom. 8:10–11).

(3) Our sharing in Christ's death and resurrection is appropriated through faith, i.e., the belief, confidence, love, devotion, and loyalty we have in the Son of God, who loved us and gave Himself up for us (cf. John 3:16; see article on FAITH AND GRACE, p. 1738). This living by faith can be seen as living by the Spirit (3:3; 5:25; cf. Rom. 8:9–11).

2:21 RIGHTEOUSNESS. Paul's understanding of justification (vv. 16–17) and righteousness includes more than a mere legal declaration by God. The righteousness that comes by faith involves a moral change (v. 19), the grace of God (v. 21), and a relationship with Christ whereby we share His resurrected life (v. 20). This is confirmed in 3:21, where Paul makes it clear that the righteousness that comes through faith in Christ gives life, a life that is seen as receiving the Spirit (3:2–3,14; see article on BIBLICAL WORDS FOR SALVATION, p. 1726).

3:2 RECEIVED YE THE SPIRIT BY ... FAITH? Paul demonstrates the superiority of salvation through faith in Christ over the attempt to gain salvation through obedience to the law. Through faith in Christ we receive the Holy Spirit and all His blessings, including the gift of eternal life (vv. 2–3,5,14,21; 4:6). However, the person who relies on the law to gain salvation does not receive the Spirit and life, for mere law cannot impart life (v. 21).

3:5 THE SPIRIT. Paul's references to the Spirit (vv. 2,5,14; 4:6) include both the baptism in the Holy Spirit and the subsequent special operations of the Spirit (cf. Acts 1:4–5; 2:4; 8:14–17; 10:44–47; 11:16–17; 19:1–6; 1 Cor. 12:4–11). This is indicated by (1) the use of the term "miracles" (Gk. *dunamis*), which implies that the apostle is thinking of the charismatic manifestations of the Spirit and His coming with "power" (Gk. *dunamis*) at Pentecost (Acts 1:8; cf. 2:1–4); (2) the use of the present participles ("ministereth" and "worketh"), which indicate the continuous manifestation of the Spirit's gifts; (3) the use of the expression "the promise of the Spirit" (v. 14), which is identical to Peter's words in Acts 2:33 (cf. Luke 24:49; Acts 1:4); and (4) the affirmation in 4:6 that sonship occurred prior to and is the basis for sending forth the Spirit into the believer's heart.

3:5 THE SPIRIT ... WORKETH MIRACLES. The ongoing work of the Spirit in the Galatian churches involved miracles. For Paul, receiving the Holy Spirit was not just an invisible inward work, but an experience that manifested itself in divine power among believers. The gifts of the Spirit were a determinative norm for the Spirit's presence and authority (cf. 1 Cor. 12–14). Conversion and the baptism in the Holy Spirit should continually result in the demonstration of miracles and the other manifestations of the Holy Spirit.

Eph. 4:7-12 among you, *doeth he it* by the works of the law, or by the hearing of faith?

The blessing of Abraham

6 Even as [x]Abraham believed God, and it was [e]accounted to him for righteousness.

7 Know ye therefore that [y]they which are of faith, the same are the children of Abraham.

8 And [z]the scripture, foreseeing that God would justify the heathen through faith, preached before the gospel unto Abraham, *saying,* [a]In thee shall all nations be blessed.

9 So then they which be of faith are blessed with faithful Abraham.

10 For as many as are of the works of the law are under the curse: for it is written, [b]Cursed *is* every one that continueth not in all things which are written in the book of the law to do them.

11 But [c]that no man is justified by the law in the sight of God, *it is* evident: for, [d]The just shall live by faith.

12 And [e]the law is not of faith: but, [f]The man that doeth them shall live in them.

13 [g]Christ hath redeemed us from the curse of the law, being made a curse for us: for it is written, [h]Cursed *is* every one that hangeth on a tree:

14 [i]That the blessing of Abraham might come on the Gentiles through Jesus Christ; that we might receive [j]the promise of the Spirit through faith.

15 Brethren, I speak after the manner of men; [k]Though *it be* but a man's [f]covenant, yet *if it be* confirmed, no man disannulleth, or addeth thereto.

16 Now [l]to Abraham and his seed were the promises made. He saith not, And to seeds, as of many; but as of one, And to thy seed, which is [m]Christ.

17 And this I say, *that* the covenant, that was confirmed before of God in Christ, the law, [n]which was four hundred and thirty years after, cannot disannul, [o]that it should make the promise of none effect.

18 For if [p]the inheritance *be* of the law, [q]*it is* no more of promise: but God gave *it* to Abraham by promise.

The function of the law

19 Wherefore then *serveth* the law? [r]It was added because of transgressions, till the seed should come to whom the promise was made; *and it was* [s]ordained by angels in the hand [t]of a mediator.

20 Now a mediator is not *a mediator* of one, [u]but God is one.

21 *Is* the law then against the promises of God? God forbid: for if there had been a law given which could have giv-

3:6 [x]Gen. 15:6 Rom. 4:3,9 Jas. 2:23
3:7 [y]John 8:39
3:8 [z]Rom. 9:17 [a]Gen. 12:3 Acts 3:25
3:10 [b]Deut. 27:26 Jer. 11:3
3:11 [c]ch. 2:16 [d]Hab. 2:4 Rom. 1:17 Heb. 10:38
3:12 [e]Rom. 4:4,5 [f]Lev. 18:5 Rom. 10:5
3:13 [g]Rom. 8:3 2 Cor. 5:21 [h]Deut. 21:23
3:14 [i]Rom. 4:9 [j]Is. 32:15 Ezek. 11:19 Acts 2:33
3:15 [k]Heb. 9:17
3:16 [l]Gen. 12:3 [m]1 Cor. 12:12
3:17 [n]Ex. 12:40 [o]Rom. 4:13
3:18 [p]Rom. 8:17 [q]Rom. 4:14
3:19 [r]John 15:22 Rom. 4:15 [s]Acts 7:53 [t]Ex. 20:19 John 1:17
3:20 [u]Rom. 3:29

[e] Or, *imputed* [f] Or, *testament*

3:6 IT WAS ACCOUNTED ... FOR RIGHTEOUSNESS. See Rom. 4:3,5,22, notes.

3:11 THE JUST SHALL LIVE BY FAITH. Paul quotes Hab. 2:4 to illustrate justification by faith (cf. Rom. 1:17). Habakkuk emphasizes that one who is justified by faith possesses actual inward righteousness, for he contrasts the righteous person with the unrighteous person whose "soul . . . is not upright in him" (see Hab. 2:4, note). Thus, Paul believed justification involved an actual inner righteousness through the indwelling Holy Spirit (see article on BIBLICAL WORDS FOR SALVATION, p. 1726).

3:14 BLESSING OF ABRAHAM. The content of God's promise to Abraham (v. 8) is defined as "the promise of the Spirit through faith" (cf. Luke 24:49; Acts 1:4–5). To receive the Spirit is to have righteousness, life, and all the other spiritual blessings (see v. 5, note; 4:6, note).

3:19 WHEREFORE THEN *SERVETH* THE LAW? The word for "law" (Gk. *nomos*; Heb. *torah*) means "teaching" or "direction." The law can refer to the Ten Commandments, the Pentateuch, or any commandment in the O.T.; Paul's use of law here would include the sacrificial system of the Mosaic covenant. Concerning the law Paul states several things: (1) It was given by God "because of transgressions," i.e., in order to show sin as the violation of God's will and to awaken man's sense of need for God's mercy, grace, and salvation in Christ (v. 24; cf. Rom. 5:20; 8:2).

(2) Although the O.T. law was holy, good, and just (Rom. 7:12), it was inadequate in that it could not impart spiritual life or moral strength (v. 21; Rom. 8:3; Heb. 7:18–19).

(3) The law acted as a temporary "schoolmaster" or tutor for God's people until salvation by faith in Christ should come (vv. 22–26). As such, the law revealed God's will for His people's behavior (Ex. 19:4–6; 20:1–17; 21:1—24:8), provided for blood sacrifices to cover the sins of His people (see Lev. 1:5; 16:33), and pointed to Christ's atoning death (Heb. 9:14; 10:12–14).

(4) The law was given to lead us to Christ that we might be justified by faith (v. 24). But now that Christ has come, the supervisory function of the law has ended (v. 25). Therefore we no longer seek salvation through the old covenant and obedience to its laws and sacrificial system. Salvation now comes by belonging to Christ (vv. 27–29; see Mat. 5:17, note on the Christian's relation to the law; see article on THE OLD TESTAMENT LAW, p. 124).

en life, verily righteousness should
have been by the law.
22 But the scripture hath concluded
[v]all under sin, [w]that the promise by
faith of Jesus Christ might be given to
them that believe.
23 But before faith came, we were
kept under the law, shut up unto the
faith which should afterwards be re-
vealed.
24 Wherefore [x]the law was our
schoolmaster *to bring us* unto Christ,
[y]that we might be justified by faith.
25 But after that faith is come, we
are no longer under a schoolmaster.
26 For ye [z]are all the children of
God by faith in Christ Jesus.
27 For [a]as many of you as have
been baptized into Christ [b]have put on
Christ.
28 [c]There is neither Jew nor
Greek, there is neither bond nor free,
there is neither male nor female: for ye
are all [d]one in Christ Jesus.
29 And [e]if ye *be* Christ's, then are
ye Abraham's seed, and [f]heirs ac-
cording to the promise.

Do not return to bondage

4 NOW I say, *That* the heir, as long
as he is a child, differeth nothing
from a servant, though he be lord of all;
2 But is under tutors and governors
until the time appointed of the father.
3 Even so we, when we were chil-
dren, [g]were in bondage under the
[g]elements of the world:
4 But [h]when the fulness of the
time was come, God sent forth his Son,
[i]made [j]of a woman, [k]made under
the law,
5 [l]To redeem them that were un-
der the law, [m]that we might receive
the adoption of sons.
6 And because ye are sons, God
hath sent forth [n]the Spirit of his Son
into your hearts, crying, Abba, Father.
7 Wherefore thou art no more a ser-
vant, but a son; [o]and if a son, then an
heir of God through Christ.
8 Howbeit then, [p]when ye knew
not God, [q]ye did service unto them
which by nature are no gods.
9 But now, [r]after that ye have
known God, or rather are known of
God, [s]how turn ye [h]again to [t]the
weak and beggarly [g]elements, where-
unto ye desire again to be in bondage?
10 [u]Ye observe days, and months,
and times, and years.
11 I am afraid of you, [v]lest I have
bestowed upon you labour in vain.

Paul's concern for the Galatians

12 Brethren, I beseech you, be as I
am; for I *am* as ye *are:* [w]ye have not
injured me at all.

3:22 [v]Rom. 11:32 [w]Rom. 4:11 **3:24** [x]Rom. 10:4 [y]Acts 13:39 **3:26** [z]John 1:12 Rom. 8:14 **3:27** [a]Rom. 6:3 [b]Rom. 13:14 **3:28** [c]Rom. 10:12 [d]John 10:16 Eph. 2:14 **3:29** [e]Gen. 21:10 Heb. 11:18 [f]Rom. 8:17
4:3 [g]Col. 2:8 Heb. 9:10 **4:4** [h]Gen. 49:10 Mark 1:15 [i]John 1:14 Heb. 2:14 [j]Gen. 3:15 Is. 7:14 Mat. 1:23 [k]Mat. 5:17 Luke 2:27 **4:5** [l]Mat. 20:28 Heb. 9:12 [m]John 1:12 Eph. 1:5 **4:6** [n]Rom. 5:5 **4:7** [o]Rom. 8:16 **4:8** [p]Eph. 2:12 1 Thes. 4:5 [q]Rom. 1:25 1 Cor. 12:2 1 Thes. 1:9 **4:9** [r]1 Cor. 8:3 [s]Col. 2:20 [t]Heb. 7:18 **4:10** [u]Rom. 14:5 **4:11** [v]1 Thes. 3:5 **4:12** [w]2 Cor. 2:5

[g] Or, *rudiments* [h] Or, *back*

3:28 NEITHER MALE NOR FEMALE. Paul removes all ethnic, racial, national, social, or sexual distinctions with regard to one's spiritual relationship with Jesus Christ. All in Christ are equal heirs of the grace of life (1 Pet. 3:7), the promised Spirit (v. 14; 4:6), and renewal in the image of God (Col. 3:10–11). On the other hand, within the context of spiritual equality men remain men and women remain women (Gen. 1:27). Their God-assigned roles in marriage and society remain unchanged (1 Pet. 3:1–4; see Eph. 5:22–23, notes; 1 Tim. 2:13,15, notes).

4:2 TUTORS . . . APPOINTED OF THE FATHER. Paul's statement here, although primarily used to illustrate the situation of a believer in O.T. times, indicates that godly parents normally oversaw the instruction and education of their children (see Deut. 6:7, note). Such oversight would have been done through education in the home or by placing the children under godly teachers selected by them. Scripture clearly teaches that parents should do all they can to ensure that their children receive a holy and Christlike education and are guarded from the ungodly philosophies and unbiblical principles of the world (see Luke 1:17, note; see article on PARENTS AND CHILDREN, p. 1880).

4:6 THE SPIRIT . . . CRYING, ABBA, FATHER. One of the Holy Spirit's tasks is to create in the child of God a feeling of sonship and filial love that causes him to know God as his Father. (1) The term "Abba" is Aramaic, meaning "O Father." It was the word Jesus used when referring to the heavenly Father. The combining of the Aramaic term "Abba" with the Greek term for Father (Gk. *patēr*) expresses the depth of intimacy, deep emotion, earnestness, warmth, and confidence by which the Holy Spirit causes us to cry out to God (cf. Mark 14:36; Rom. 8:15,26–27). Two certain signs of the Spirit's work within us are the spontaneous cry to God as "Father" and the spontaneous obedience to Jesus as "Lord" (see 1 Cor. 12:3, note).

(2) In this passage, Paul may have in mind primarily the baptism in the Holy Spirit and His continual filling (cf. Acts 1:5; 2:4; Eph. 5:18), since he makes our sonship the cause for sending forth the Spirit. That is, because we are already "sons" through faith in Christ, God pours forth the Spirit into our hearts. The "adoption of sons" (v. 5) precedes the sending forth of the Spirit of His Son (see 3:5, notes).

13 Ye know how [x]through infirmi-
ty of the flesh I preached the gospel
unto you at the first.
14 And my temptation which was in
my flesh ye despised not, nor rejected;
but received me [y]as an angel of God,
[z]*even* as Christ Jesus.
15 [i]Where is then the blessedness
ye spake of? for I bear you record, that,
if *it had been* possible, ye would have
plucked out your own eyes, and have
given them to me.
16 Am I therefore become your ene-
my, because I tell you the truth?
17 They [a]zealously affect you, *but*
not well; yea, they would exclude
[j]you, that ye might affect them.
18 But *it is* good to be zealously af-
fected always in *a* good *thing,* and not
only when I am present with you.
19 [b]My little children, of whom I
travail in birth again until Christ be
formed in you,
20 I desire to be present with you
now, and to change my voice; for [k]I
stand in doubt of you.

Hagar and Sarah

21 Tell me, ye that desire to be un-
der the law, do ye not hear the law?
22 For it is written, that Abraham
had two sons, [c]the one by a bondmaid,
[d]the other by a freewoman.
23 But he *who was* of the bondwom-
an [e]was born after the flesh; [f]but he
of the freewoman *was* by promise.
24 Which things are an allegory: for
these are the two [l]covenants; the one
from the mount [g]Sinai,[m] which gen-
dereth to bondage, which is Agar.
25 For this Agar is mount Sinai in
Arabia, and [n]answereth to Jerusalem
which now is, and is in bondage with
her children.
26 But [h]Jerusalem which is above
is free, which is the mother of us all.
27 For it is written, [i]Rejoice, *thou*
barren that bearest not; break forth
and cry, thou that travailest not: for
the desolate hath many more children
than she which hath an husband.
28 Now we, brethren, as Isaac was,
are [j]the children of promise.
29 But as then [k]he that was born
after the flesh persecuted him *that was*
born after the Spirit, [l]even so *it is*
now.
30 Nevertheless what saith [m]the
scripture? [n]Cast out the bondwoman
and her son: for [o]the son of the bond-
woman shall not be heir with the son
of the freewoman.
31 So then, brethren, we are not
children of the bondwoman, [p]but of
the free.

The consequences of deserting Christ

5 STAND FAST therefore in [q]the
liberty wherewith Christ hath
made us free, and be not entangled
again [r]with the yoke of bondage.
2 Behold, I Paul say unto you, that
[s]if ye be circumcised, Christ shall
profit you nothing.
3 For I testify again to every man
that is circumcised, [t]that he is a debt-
or to do the whole law.
4 [u]Christ is become of no effect
unto you, whosoever of you are justi-

4:13 [x]1 Cor. 2:3 **4:14** [y]Mal. 2:7 [z]Luke 10:16 **4:17** [a]Rom. 10:2 **4:19** [b]1 Cor. 4:15 **4:22** [c]Gen. 16:15 [d]Gen. 21:2 **4:23** [e]Rom. 9:7,8 [f]Heb. 11:11 **4:24** [g]Deut. 33:2 **4:26** [h]Is. 2:2 **4:27** [i]Is. 54:1 **4:28** [j]Acts 3:25 **4:29** [k]Gen. 21:9 [l]ch. 5:11 **4:30** [m]ch. 3:8,22 [n]Gen. 21:10 [o]John 8:35 **4:31** [p]John 8:36 **5:1** [q]Rom. 6:18 [r]Acts 15:10 **5:2** [s]Acts 15:1 **5:3** [t]ch. 3:10 **5:4** [u]Rom. 9:31

[i] Or, *What was then perplexed for you* [j] Or, *us* [k] Or, *I am perplexed for you* [l] Or, *testaments* [m] Gk. *Sina* [n] Or, *is in the same rank with*

4:13 INFIRMITY OF THE FLESH. This may have been eye trouble (v. 15), malaria, Paul's thorn in the flesh (2 Cor. 12:7), or a physical disability due to stoning. Whatever it was, it seems to have involved some kind of physical problem. Note that a faithful believer who is in the will of the Lord and active in Christian service may at times be plagued by ill health, bodily pain, or weakness.

4:19 I TRAVAIL IN BIRTH. Travail (Gk. *ōdinō*), meaning "the pains of childbirth," expresses the heartache, affliction, pain, and yearning by which Paul desires the salvation of those Galatians who have become alienated from Christ and have "fallen from grace" (5:4). He represents them as needing a second spiritual birth and himself as a mother suffering once more with birth pangs in order that Christ might be formed in them.

4:22 ABRAHAM HAD TWO SONS. Paul uses an illustration to show the difference between the old and new covenants. Hagar represents the old covenant established at Mount Sinai (v. 25); her children now live under this covenant and are of the flesh, i.e., they do not have the Holy Spirit. Sarah, Abraham's other wife, represents the new covenant; her children, i.e., believers in Christ, possess the Spirit and are true children of God (see articles on GOD'S COVENANT WITH THE ISRAELITES, p. 314, and THE OLD COVENANT AND THE NEW COVENANT, p. 1954).

5:4 FALLEN FROM GRACE. Some Galatians had transferred their faith in Christ to faith in legalistic observances of the law (1:6–7; 5:3). Paul states they have fallen from grace. To fall from grace is to be alienated from Christ (cf. John 15:4–6) and to abandon the principle of God's grace that brings us life and salvation. It is to have

fied by the law; [v]ye are fallen from
grace.
5 For we through the Spirit [w]wait
for the hope of righteousness by faith.
6 For [x]in Jesus Christ neither cir-
cumcision availeth any thing, nor un-
circumcision; but [y]faith which
worketh by love.
7 Ye [z]did run well; [a]who [o]did
hinder you that ye should not obey the
truth?
8 This persuasion *cometh* not of him
[b]that calleth you.
9 [c]A little leaven leaveneth the
whole lump.
10 [d]I have confidence in you
through the Lord, that ye will be none
otherwise minded: but [e]he that trou-
bleth you [f]shall bear his judgment,
whosoever he be.
11 [g]And I, brethren, if I yet preach
circumcision, [h]why do I yet suffer per-
secution? then is [i]the offence of the
cross ceased.
12 [j]I would they were even cut off
[k]which trouble you.

Freedom from sin

13 For, brethren, ye have been
called unto liberty; only [l]*use* not liber-
ty for an occasion to the flesh, but [m]by
love serve one another.

5:4 [v]Heb. 12:15
5:5 [w]Rom. 8:24
5:6 [x]Col. 3:11 [y]1 Thes. 1:3
5:7 [z]1 Cor. 9:24 [a]ch. 3:1
5:8 [b]ch. 1:6
5:9 [c]1 Cor. 5:6
5:10 [d]2 Cor. 2:3 [e]ch. 1:7 [f]2 Cor. 10:6
5:11 [g]ch. 6:12 [h]1 Cor. 15:30 [i]1 Cor. 1:23
5:12 [j]Josh. 7:25 [k]Acts 15:1,2
5:13 [l]1 Cor. 8:9 1 Pet. 2:16 [m]1 Cor. 9:19
5:14 [n]Mat. 7:12 Jas. 2:8 [o]Mat. 22:39
5:16 [p]Rom. 6:12 1 Pet. 2:11
5:17 [q]Rom. 7:23 [r]Rom. 7:15
5:18 [s]Rom. 6:14
5:19 [t]Eph. 5:3

14 For [n]all the law is fulfilled in
one word, *even* in this; [o]Thou shalt
love thy neighbour as thyself.
15 But if ye bite and devour one an-
other, take heed that ye be not con-
sumed one of another.

Conflict between Spirit and flesh

16 *This* I say then, [p]Walk in the
Spirit, and [p]ye shall not fulfil the lust
of the flesh.
17 For [q]the flesh lusteth against
the Spirit, and the Spirit against the
flesh: and these are contrary the one to
the other: [r]so that ye cannot do the
things that ye would.
18 But [s]if ye be led of the Spirit, ye
are not under the law. Eph. 2:10

Works of the flesh

19 Now [t]the works of the flesh are
manifest, which are *these;* Adultery,
fornication, uncleanness, lascivious-
ness,
20 Idolatry, witchcraft, hatred, vari-
ance, emulations, wrath, strife, sedi-
tions, heresies,
21 Envyings, murders, drunken-
ness, revellings, and such like: of the
which I tell you before, as I have also

[o] Or, *who did drive you back* [p] Or, *fulfil not*

one's association with Christ nullified and to no longer "abide in Christ" (see John 15:6, note; 2 Pet. 2:15,20–22; see article on FAITH AND GRACE, p. 1738).

5:6 FAITH WHICH WORKETH BY LOVE. The Bible maintains that a person is saved by faith (2:15–16; Rom. 3:22; Eph. 2:8–9). (1) In this passage Paul defines the exact nature of that faith. Saving faith is a living faith in a living Savior, a faith so vital that it cannot avoid expression in deeds motivated by love. (2) Faith that does not sincerely love and obey Christ (cf. 1 John 2:3; 5:3), show a real concern for the work of God's kingdom (cf. Mat. 12:28), and actively resist sin and the world (vv. 16–17), does not qualify as saving faith (cf. Jas. 2:14–16; see article on FAITH AND GRACE, p. 1738).

5:7 NOT OBEY THE TRUTH. False teaching either takes the form of denying the cardinal truths of the Christian faith (see 1:9, note), or it states that something else besides what is found in the N.T. is required for a believer to be a complete Christian (cf. 1:6; 2:16; 5:2,6). (1) All Christian teaching must be tested by apostolic truth, i.e., does the teaching conform to the original message of Christ and the apostles found in the N.T. (cf. 1:11–12; 2:1–2,7–9; see Eph. 2:20, note)? We must ask: Does a teaching contain less than the apostolic message? Or does it add something unbiblical to the truth while acknowledging the apostolic message? (2) We must never test teaching solely by feelings, experience, results, miracles, or by what other people are saying. The N.T. is the ultimate standard for truth. (3) We must beware of any teaching that says the Scriptures are no longer sufficient and that the church needs modern scholarship, science, philosophy, psychology, or new revelations in order to reach its maturity in Christ.

5:13 CALLED UNTO LIBERTY. See 2 Cor. 3:17, note on Christian freedom.

5:17 THE SPIRIT AGAINST THE FLESH. The spiritual conflict within the believer involves the totality of his person as he struggles to determine whether he will wholly surrender to the inclinations of the "flesh" (i.e., the sinful nature) and return to the dominion of sin, or whether he will yield to the demands of the Holy Spirit and continue under the dominion of Christ (v. 16; Rom. 8:4–14). The battlefield is within the Christian himself, and the conflict must continue throughout his earthly life if he is to eventually reign with Christ (Rom. 7:7–25; 2 Tim. 2:12; Rev. 12:11; see Eph. 6:11, note).

5:19 WORKS OF THE FLESH. For comments on the individual works of the flesh, see article on THE WORKS OF THE FLESH AND THE FRUIT OF THE SPIRIT, p. 1840.

5:21 NOT INHERIT THE KINGDOM OF GOD. Although Paul maintains that it is impossible to inherit the kingdom of God by practicing the works

told *you* in time past, that [u]they which
do such things shall not inherit the
kingdom of God.

Fruit of the Spirit

22 But [v]the fruit of the Spirit is
love, joy, peace, longsuffering, [w]gen-
tleness, [x]goodness, [y]faith,
Eph. 3:17-21 23 Meekness, temperance:
[z]against such there is no law.
24 And they that are Christ's
[a]have crucified the flesh with the
[q]affections and lusts.
25 [b]If we live in the Spirit, let us
also walk in the Spirit.
26 [c]Let us not be desirous of vain
glory, provoking one another, envying
one another.

Doing good to all

6 BRETHREN, [d]IF[r] a man be
overtaken in a fault, ye [e]which
are spiritual, restore such an one [f]in
the spirit of meekness; considering
thyself, [g]lest thou also be tempted.
2 [h]Bear ye one another's burdens,
and so fulfil [i]the law of Christ.
3 For [j]if a man think himself to be
something, when [k]he is nothing, he
deceiveth himself.
4 But [l]let every man prove his own

5:21 [u]1 Cor. 6:9
5:22 [v]John 15:2; Eph. 5:9; [w]Col. 3:12; [x]Rom. 15:14; [y]1 Cor. 13:7
5:23 [z]1 Tim. 1:9
5:24 [a]Rom. 6:6; 1 Pet. 2:11
5:25 [b]Rom. 8:4,5
5:26 [c]Phil. 2:3
6:1 [d]Rom. 14:1; [e]1 Cor. 2:15; [f]1 Cor. 4:21; [g]1 Cor. 7:5
6:2 [h]Rom. 15:1; 1 Thes. 5:14; [i]Jas. 2:8
6:3 [j]Rom. 12:3; 1 Cor. 8:2; [k]2 Cor. 3:5
6:4 [l]1 Cor. 11:28; [m]Luke 18:11
6:5 [n]Rom. 2:6; 1 Cor. 3:8
6:6 [o]1 Cor. 9:11
6:7 [p]1 Cor. 6:9; [q]Job 13:9; [r]Rom. 2:6; 2 Cor. 9:6
6:8 [s]Job 4:8
6:9 [t]1 Cor. 15:58

work, and then shall he have rejoicing
in himself alone, and [m]not in another.
5 For [n]every man shall bear his
own burden.
6 [o]Let him that is taught in the
word communicate unto him that
teacheth in all good things.
7 [p]Be not deceived; [q]God is not
mocked: for [r]whatsoever a man
soweth, that shall he also reap.
8 [s]For he that soweth to his flesh
shall of the flesh reap corruption; but
he that soweth to the Spirit shall of the
Spirit reap life everlasting.
9 And [t]let us not be weary in well
doing: for in due season we shall reap,
[u]if we faint not.
10 [v]As we have therefore opportu-
nity, [w]let us do good unto all *men*, es-
pecially unto them who are of [x]the
household of faith.

Paul's personal conclusion

11 Ye see how large a letter I have
written unto you with mine own hand.
12 As many as desire to make a fair

[u]Mat. 24:13; Rev. 2:10 **6:10** [v]John 9:4 [w]Tit. 3:8 [x]Eph. 2:19

[q] Or, *passions* [r] Or, *although*

of the law (2:16; 5:4), he does teach it is possible to shut oneself out of the kingdom by engaging in evil practices (see 1 Cor. 6:9, note; cf. Mat. 25:41–46; Eph. 5:7–11).

5:22–23 THE FRUIT OF THE SPIRIT. For comments on the various aspects of the fruit of the Spirit, see article on THE WORKS OF THE FLESH AND THE FRUIT OF THE SPIRIT, p. 1840.

6:1 RESTORE SUCH AN ONE. The word "restore" (Gk. *katartizō*) is used in the N.T. for mending fishing nets (Mat. 4:21) or for perfecting human character (2 Cor. 13:11). Thus, to restore a person means to lead him back to true repentance for sin and to a full commitment to Jesus Christ and His ways. This may involve disciplinary action (see Mat. 13:30, note), undertaken in a "spirit of meekness."

(1) Paul here is not thinking of those serious sins that bring public disgrace to the congregation (cf. 1 Cor. 5:5). Such sins may require a temporary expulsion from the fellowship before restoration is granted (1 Cor. 5:11).

(2) The restoration that Paul mentions here does not refer to restoration to leadership positions or teaching roles within the church. Qualifications and standards for those desiring to serve in a ministerial position involve more than a person's present spiritual condition. They require a history of persevering faithfulness to God's principles for righteousness in order that they may be an example to those who believe (1 Tim. 4:12; see article on MORAL QUALIFICATIONS FOR OVERSEERS, p. 1908).

6:2 BEAR YE ONE ANOTHER'S BURDENS. To bear one another's burdens includes helping needy people in times of sickness, sorrow, and financial stress. Paul may have in mind the support of missionaries and teachers (see v. 6, note; cf. Rom. 15:1; 1 Cor. 9:14). To bear the burden of another is a divine quality (Ps. 55:22; 1 Pet. 5:7).

6:6–10 COMMUNICATE UNTO HIM. It is the duty of all who are taught God's Word to help provide material support for those who serve them in this respect (1 Cor. 9:14; 1 Tim. 5:18). Those who are worthy of support include faithful pastors, workers, teachers, evangelists, or missionaries (1 Cor. 9:14; 3 John 6–8). To refuse to give support, if means are available, is to sow selfishness in the flesh and to reap corruption (vv. 7–9). To give to those who minister in the Word is a part of doing good to those of the household of faith (v. 10); "in due season we shall reap" (v. 9) both reward (Mat. 10:41–42) and eternal life (v. 8).

6:7 GOD IS NOT MOCKED. Those who claim to be born-again followers of Christ and to possess the Holy Spirit (v. 3), while at the same time consciously sow to the flesh (5:19–21), are guilty of mocking and despising God. Let there be no deception: such persons will not reap "life everlasting" but "corruption" (v. 8) and eternal death (Rom. 6:20–23; see 1 Cor. 6:9, note).

show in the flesh, [y]they constrain you
to be circumcised; [z]only lest they
should [a]suffer persecution for the
cross of Christ.
13 For neither they themselves who
are circumcised keep the law; but de-
sire to have you circumcised, that they
may glory in your flesh.
14 [b]But God forbid that I should
glory, save in the cross of our Lord
Jesus Christ, [s]by whom the world is
[c]crucified unto me, and I unto the
Tim. :1-5 world.
15 For [d]in Christ Jesus neither cir-
cumcision availeth any thing, nor un-
circumcision, but [e]a new creature.
16 [f]And as many as walk [g]ac-
cording to this rule, peace *be* on them,
and mercy, and upon [h]the Israel of
God.
17 From henceforth let no man
trouble me: for [i]I bear in my body the
marks of the Lord Jesus.
18 Brethren, [j]the grace of our
Lord Jesus Christ *be* with your spirit.
Amen.

6:12 [y]ch. 2:3,14 [z]Phil. 3:18 [a]ch. 5:11 **6:14** [b]Phil. 3:3,7 [c]Rom. 6:6 **6:15** [d]1 Cor. 7:19 [e]2 Cor. 5:17 **6:16** [f]Ps. 125:5 [g]Phil. 3:16 [h]Rom. 2:29 **6:17** [i]2 Cor. 1:5 **6:18** [j]2 Tim. 4:22

[s] Or, *whereby*

6:14 THE WORLD IS CRUCIFIED UNTO ME. The cross of Christ, representing the horrible death that the Savior suffered for our eternal salvation, is now the barrier by which the world is fenced off from us and us from the world. The "world" means everything that is opposed to God, His kingdom, and His righteousness (cf. 4:3; John 3:16; 1 Cor. 2:12; 3:19; 1 John 2:15–17). (1) For those who make the cross their life, their glory, and their boast, the world with all its accepted standards, values, opinions, honors, and lifestyles is no longer cherished or loved. (2) For us to be "crucified with Christ" (2:20) includes our being crucified to the world. There is no sharing in the salvation and glory of His cross without turning our backs on all the earthly pleasures that draw our hearts away from Christ and His nearness.

6:16 ISRAEL OF GOD. This term refers to all God's people under the new covenant, i.e., both believing Jews and believing Gentiles. That is, all who through "the cross of our Lord Jesus Christ" are crucified to the world (v. 14) and become a "new creature" (v. 15) constitute the true "Israel of God" (cf. Rom. 2:28–29; 9:7–8; Eph. 2:14–22; Phil. 3:3; 1 Pet. 2:9).

THE WORKS OF THE FLESH AND THE FRUIT OF THE SPIRIT

Gal. 5:22–23 "But the fruit of the Spirit is love, joy, peace, longsuffering, gentleness, goodness, faith, Meekness, temperance: against such there is no law."

No passage in the Bible draws a clearer contrast between the lifestyle of the Spirit-filled believer and that of the sinful human nature than Gal. 5:16–26. Paul not only discusses the general difference in lifestyles by emphasizing that the Spirit and the flesh are at war with each other, but he includes a specific list both of the works of the flesh and of the fruit of the Spirit.

WORKS OF THE FLESH. "Flesh" (Gk. *sarx*) is the sinful element in human nature with its corrupt desires. It remains within the Christian after his conversion and is a deadly enemy to him (Rom. 8:6–8,13; Gal. 5:17,21). Those who practice the deeds of the flesh cannot inherit the kingdom of God (Gal. 5:21). Hence, they must be resisted and put to death in a continual warfare that the believer wages through the Holy Spirit (Rom. 8:4–14; see Gal. 5:17, note). The works of the flesh (Gal. 5:19–21) include:

(1) "Adultery" (Gk. *moicheia*), i.e., sexual relations of a married person with someone other than his or her spouse (cf. Ex. 20:14; Deut. 5:18; Mat. 5:31–32);

(2) "Fornication" (Gk. *porneia*), i.e., immoral sexual conduct and intercourse; it includes taking pleasure in pornographic pictures, films, or writing (cf. Mat. 5:32; 19:9; Acts 15:20,29; 21:25; 1 Cor. 5:1);

(3) "Uncleanness" (Gk. *akatharsia*), i.e., sexual sins, evil deeds, and vices, including thoughts and desires of the heart (Eph. 5:3; Col. 3:5);

(4) "Lasciviousness" (Gk. *aselgeia*), i.e., sensuality, following one's passions and desires to the point of having no shame or public decency (2 Cor. 12:21);

(5) "Idolatry" (Gk. *eidōlolatria*), i.e., worship of spirits, persons, or graven images, also trust in any person, institution, or thing as having equal or greater authority than God and His Word (Col. 3:5);

(6) "Witchcraft" (Gk. *pharmakeia*), i.e., sorcery, spiritism, black magic, worship of demons, and use of drugs to produce "spiritual" experiences (Ex. 7:11,22; 8:18; Rev. 9:21; 18:23);

(7) "Hatred" (Gk. *echthra*), i.e., intense, hostile intentions and acts, extreme dislike or enmity;

(8) "Variance" (Gk. *eris*), i.e., quarreling, antagonism, a struggle for superiority (Rom. 1:29; 1 Cor. 1:11; 3:3);

(9) "Emulations" (Gk. *zēlos*), i.e., resentfulness, envy of another's success (Rom. 13:13; 1 Cor. 3:3);

(10) "Wrath" (Gk. *thumos*), i.e., explosive anger or rage which flares into violent words and deeds (Col. 3:8);

(11) "Strife" (Gk. *eritheia*), i.e., selfish ambition and seeking of power (2 Cor. 12:20; Phil. 1:16–17);

(12) "Seditions" (Gk. *dichostasia*), i.e., introducing divisive teachings not supported by the Word of God (Rom. 16:17);

(13) "Heresies" (Gk. *hairesis*), i.e., division within the congregation into selfish groups or cliques, which destroy the unity of the church (1 Cor. 11:19);

(14) "Envyings" (Gk. *phthonos*), i.e., resentful dislike of another person who has something that one desires;

(15) "Murders" (Gk. *phonos*), i.e., killing a person unlawfully and with malice;

(16) "Drunkenness" (Gk. *methē*), i.e., impairing one's mental or physical control by alcoholic drink;

(17) "Revellings" (Gk. *kōmos*), i.e., excessive feasting, revelry, a party spirit involving alcohol, drugs, sex, or the like.

Paul's final comment on the works of the flesh is stern and forceful: any so-called Christians who engage in these types of activities shut themselves out of the kingdom of God, i.e., they do not possess eternal salvation (Gal. 5:21; see 1 Cor. 6:9, note).

THE FRUIT OF THE SPIRIT. Contrasted to the works of the flesh is a single-minded lifestyle called "the fruit of the Spirit." This is produced in God's children as they allow the Spirit to so direct and influence their lives that they destroy the power of sin, especially the works of the flesh, and walk in fellowship with God (see Rom. 8:5–14, note; 8:14, note; cf. 2 Cor. 6:6; Eph. 4:2–3; 5:9; Col. 3:12–15; 2 Pet. 1:4–9). The fruit of the Spirit includes:

(1) "Love" (Gk. *agapē*), i.e., a caring and seeking for the highest good of another person without motive for personal gain (Rom. 5:5; 1 Cor. 13; Eph. 5:2; Col. 3:14);

(2) "Joy" (Gk. *chara*), i.e., the feeling of gladness based on the love, grace, blessings, promises, and nearness of God that belong to those who believe in Christ (Ps. 119:16; 2 Cor. 6:10; 12:9; 1 Pet. 1:8; see Phil. 1:14, note);

(3) "Peace" (Gk. *eirēnē*), i.e., the quietness of heart and mind based on the knowledge that all is well between the believer and his or her heavenly Father (Rom. 15:33; Phil. 4:7; 1 Thes. 5:23; Heb. 13:20);

(4) "Longsuffering" (Gk. *makrothumia*), i.e., endurance, patience, being slow to anger or despair (Eph. 4:2; 2 Tim. 3:10; Heb. 12:1);

(5) "Gentleness" (Gk. *chrēstotēs*), i.e., not wanting to hurt someone or give him or her pain (Eph. 4:32; Col. 3:12);

(6) "Goodness" (Gk. *agathōsunē*), i.e., zeal for truth and righteousness and a hatred for evil; it can be expressed in acts of kindness (Luke 7:37–50) or in rebuking and correcting evil (Mat. 21:12–13);

(7) "Faith" (Gk. *pistis*), i.e., faithfulness, firm and unswerving loyalty and adherence to a person to whom one is united by promise, commitment, trustworthiness, and honesty (Mat. 23:23; Rom. 3:3; 1 Tim. 6:12; 2 Tim. 2:2; 4:7; Tit. 2:10);

(8) "Meekness" (Gk. *prautēs*), i.e., restraint coupled with strength and courage; it describes a person who can be angry when anger is needed and humbly submissive when submission is needed (2 Tim. 2:25; 1 Pet. 3:15; for meekness in Jesus, compare Mat. 11:29 with Mat. 23; Mark 3:5; in Paul, compare 2 Cor. 10:1 with 10:4–6; Gal. 1:9; in Moses, compare Num. 12:3 with Ex. 32:19–20);

(9) "Temperance" (Gk. *egkrateia*), i.e., having control or mastery over one's own desires and passions, including faithfulness to one's marriage vows; also purity, chastity (1 Cor. 9:25; Tit. 1:8; 2:5).

Paul's final comment on the fruit of the Spirit indicates that there are no restrictions to the lifestyle indicated here. Christians can—in fact, ought—to practice these virtues over and over again; they will never discover a law prohibiting them from living according to these principles.

EPHESIANS

Outline

Christian Greetings (1:1–2)

I. Powerful Doctrine—The Believer's Redemption (1:3—3:21)
  A. The Preeminence of Christ in Redemption (1:3–14)
    1. His Preeminence in the Father's Plan (1:3–6)
    2. His Preeminence in the Believer's Participation (1:7–12)
    3. His Preeminence in the Spirit's Application (1:13–14)
    Prayer: For the Believer's Spiritual Enlightenment (1:15–23)
  B. The Results of Redemption in Christ (2:1—3:21)
    1. Releases Us from Sin and Death to New Life in Christ (2:1–10)
    2. Reconciles Us to Others Who Are Being Saved (2:11–15)
    3. Unites Us in Christ in One Household (2:16–22)
    4. Reveals God's Wisdom through the Church (3:1–13)
    Prayer: For the Believer's Spiritual Fulfillment (3:14–19)

II. Practical Instruction—The Believer's Life (4:1—6:20)
  A. The Believer's New Life (4:1—5:21)
    1. In Harmony with God's Purpose for the Church (4:1–16)
    2. A New Life of Purity (4:17—5:7)
    3. Living as Children of Light (5:8–14)
    4. Careful and Spirit-Filled (5:15–21)
  B. The Believer's Domestic Relationships (5:22—6:9)
    1. Wives and Husbands (5:22–23)
    2. Children and Parents (6:1–4)
    3. Servants and Masters (6:5–9)
  C. The Believer's Spiritual Warfare (6:10–20)
    1. Our Ally—God (6:10–11a)
    2. Our Enemy—Satan and His Forces (6:11b–12)
    3. Our Equipment—Full Armor of God (6:13–20)

Conclusion (6:21–24)

Author: Paul

Theme: Christ and the Church

Date of Writing: c. A.D. 62

Background

Ephesians is one of the mountain peaks of Biblical revelation and has a unique place among Paul's letters. Rather than being hammered out on the anvil of doctrinal controversy or pastoral problems as Paul's other epistles were, Ephesians conveys the impression of a rich overflow of revelation growing out of Paul's personal prayer life. Paul wrote the letter while a prisoner on behalf of Christ (3:1; 4:1; 6:20), most likely at Rome. Ephesians has numerous affinities with Colossians and probably was penned shortly after Colossians. Both letters appear to have been carried simultaneously to their destination by a co-worker of Paul named Tychicus (6:21; cf. Col. 4:7).

It is commonly believed that Paul wrote Ephesians with a wider readership in mind than just the church in Ephesus—perhaps intending it to serve as a circular letter for churches throughout the province of Asia. Originally each church in Asia Minor may have inserted its own name in 1:1, testifying to the intense relevance of its profound message for all true churches of Jesus Christ. Many think Ephesians is the so-called letter to the Laodiceans, mentioned by Paul in Col. 4:16.

Purpose

Paul's immediate purpose for writing Ephesians is implied in 1:15–17. He prayerfully longs for his readers to advance in faith, love, wisdom, and revelation of the Father of glory. He earnestly desires them to live a life worthy of the Lord Jesus Christ (e.g., 4:1–3; 5:1–2). Paul, therefore, seeks to strengthen their faith and spiritual foundations by revealing the fulness of God's eternal purpose of redemption "in Christ" (1:3–14; 3:10–12) for the church (1:22–23; 2:11–22; 3:21; 4:11–16; 5:25–27) and for each individual (1:15–21; 2:1–10; 3:16–20; 4:1–3,17–32; 5:1—6:20).

Survey

In the simplest possible terms there are two basic themes in the N. T.: (1) how we are redeemed by God, and (2) how we as the redeemed are to live. Chs. 1–3 of Ephesians address largely the former theme, while chs. 4–6 focus on the latter.

(1) Chs. 1–3 are introduced by an opening paragraph that is one of the most profound passages in the Bible (1:3–14). This magnificent hymn of redemption offers praise for the Father's election, predestination, and adoption of us as His children (1:3–6), for the Son redeeming us through His blood (1:7–12), and for the Spirit as our seal and first installment of our inheritance (1:13–14). In these chapters Paul stresses that in redemption by grace through faith, God is reconciling us to Himself (2:1–10) and to others who are being saved (2:11–15), and is uniting us in Christ in one body, the church (2:16–22). The goal of redemption is "to gather together in one all things in Christ, both which are in heaven, and which are on earth" (1:10).

(2) Chs. 4–6 consist largely of practical instructions for the church about the demands which redemption in Christ makes upon our lives individually and corporately. Among the 35 directives given in Ephesians on how the redeemed ought to live, three broad categories are emphasized. (1) Believers are called to a new life of purity and separation from the world. They are called to "be holy and without blame before him" (1:4), grow "unto an holy temple" (2:21), "walk worthily of the vocation wherewith [they] are called" (4:1), become "a perfect man" (4:13), live "in righteousness and true holiness" (4:24), "walk in love" (5:2; cf. 3:17–19), and be holy "by the word" (5:26) in order that Christ may have a "church, not having spot, or wrinkle . . . holy and without blemish" (5:27). (2) Believers are called to a new way of life in family and vocational relationships (5:22—6:9). These relationships are to be governed by principles which mark believers as distinctly different from the secular society in which they live. (3) Finally, believers are called to stand firm against all the devil's schemes and against formidable "spiritual wickedness in high *places*" (6:10–20).

Special Features

Five major features or emphases characterize this epistle. (1) The unfolding of great theological truth in chs. 1–3 is interrupted by two of the most powerful apostolic prayers of the N.T.: one asks for wisdom and revelation in a knowledge of God (1:15–23); the other focuses on knowing the love, power, and glory of God (3:14–21). (2) "In Christ," a weighty Pauline expression (160 times in Paul's letters), is especially prominent in Ephesians (about 36 times). "Every spiritual blessing" and every practical issue of life relates to being "in Christ." (3) God's eternal purpose and goal for the church is emphasized in Ephesians. (4) There is a multifaceted emphasis on the role of the Holy Spirit in the Christian life (1:13–14,17; 2:18; 3:5,16,20; 4:3–4,30; 5:18; 6:17–18). (5) Ephesians is sometimes regarded as a "twin epistle" with Colossians, because the two have certain resemblances in content and were written about the same time (cf. the outlines to the two letters).

Reading Ephesians

In order to read the entire New Testament in one year, the book of Ephesians should be read in 9 days, according to the following schedule:
☐ 1:1–14 ☐ 1:15—2:10 ☐ 2:11–22 ☐ 3 ☐ 4:1–16 ☐ 4:17—5:2 ☐ 5:3–21 ☐ 5:22—6:9 ☐ 6:10–24

NOTES

1 PAUL, AN apostle of Jesus Christ [a]by the will of God, [b]to the saints which are at Ephesus, [c]and to the faithful in Christ Jesus:

2 [d]Grace *be* to you, and peace, from God our Father, and *from* the Lord Jesus Christ.

Spiritual blessings in Christ

3 [e]Blessed *be* the God and Father of our Lord Jesus Christ, who hath blessed us with all spiritual blessings in heavenly [a]*places* in Christ:

4 According as [f]he hath chosen us in him [g]before the foundation of the world, that we should [h]be holy and without blame before him in love:

5 [i]Having predestinated us unto [j]the adoption of children by Jesus Christ to himself, [k]according to the good pleasure of his will,

6 To the praise of the glory of his grace, [l]wherein he hath made us accepted in [m]the beloved.

7 [n]In whom we have redemption through his blood, the forgiveness of sins, according to [o]the riches of his grace;

8 Wherein he hath abounded toward us in all wisdom and prudence;

9 [p]Having made known unto us the mystery of his will, according to his good pleasure [q]which he hath purposed in himself:

10 That in the dispensation of [r]the fulness of times [s]he might gather together in one [t]all things in Christ, both which are in [b]heaven, and which are on earth; *even* in him:

11 [u]In whom also we have obtained an inheritance, [v]being predestinated according to [w]the purpose of him who worketh all things after the counsel of his own will:

Sealed with the Spirit

12 [x]That we should be to the praise of his glory, [y]who first [c]trusted in Christ.

13 In whom ye also *trusted,* after that ye heard [z]the word of truth, the gospel of your salvation: in whom also after that ye believed, [a]ye were sealed with that holy Spirit of promise,

14 [b]Which is the earnest of our in-

1:1 [a]2 Cor. 1:1 [b]Rom. 1:7; 2 Cor. 1:1 [c]1 Cor. 4:17
1:2 [d]Gal. 1:3
1:3 [e]2 Cor. 1:3
1:4 [f]Rom. 8:28 [g]1 Pet. 1:2 [h]Luke 1:75
1:5 [i]Rom. 8:29 [j]John 1:12 [k]1 Cor. 1:21
1:6 [l]Rom. 3:24 [m]Mat. 3:17
1:7 [n]Heb. 9:12 [o]Rom. 3:24
1:9 [p]Rom. 16:25 [q]2 Tim. 1:9
1:10 [r]Gal. 4:4 [s]1 Cor. 3:22 [t]Col. 1:20
1:11 [u]Rom. 8:17 [v]ver. 5 [w]Is. 46:10
1:12 [x]2 Thes. 2:13 [y]Jas. 1:18
1:13 [z]John 1:17 [a]2 Cor. 1:22
1:14 [b]2 Cor. 5:5

a Or, things b Gk. *the heavens* c Or, *hoped*

1:1 IN CHRIST JESUS. Every "faithful" believer has life only "in Christ Jesus." (1) The terms "in Christ Jesus," "in the Lord," "in Him," etc., occur 160 times in Paul's writings (36 times in Ephesians). "In Christ" means that the believer now lives and acts in the sphere of Christ Jesus. Union with Christ is the redeemed Christian's new environment. "In Christ" the believer has conscious communion with his Lord, and in this relationship his very life is seen as the life of Christ living in him (see Gal. 2:20, note). This personal fellowship with Christ is the most important thing in Christian experience. Union with Christ comes as a gift of God through faith.

(2) The Bible contrasts our new life "in Christ" with our old unregenerated life "in Adam." Whereas the old life is characterized by disobedience, sin, condemnation, and death, our new life "in Christ" is characterized by salvation, life in the Spirit, abundant grace, righteousness, and eternal life (see Rom. 5:12–21; 6; 8; 14:17–19; 1 Cor. 15:21–22,45–49; Phil. 2:1–5; 4:6–9; see article on FAITH AND GRACE, p. 1738).

1:4 HATH CHOSEN US. See article on ELECTION AND PREDESTINATION, p. 1846.

1:5 HAVING PREDESTINED US. See article on ELECTION AND PREDESTINATION, p. 1846.

1:5 ADOPTION. See 1 John 3:1, note.

1:13 SEALED . . . HOLY SPIRIT. The Holy Spirit is a "seal." As a "seal" the Holy Spirit is given to the believer as God's mark of ownership (see 2 Cor. 1:22). Hence, one has the evidence that he is God's adopted child and that his redemption is real when the Holy Spirit is present in his life (cf. Gal. 4:6). We can know that we really belong to God when the Holy Spirit regenerates and renews us (John 1:12–13; 3:3–6), delivers us from the power of sin (Rom. 8:1–17; Gal. 5:16–25), gives us a consciousness of God as our Father (v. 5; Rom. 8:15; Gal. 4:6), and fills us with power to witness for Him (Acts 1:8; 2:4).

1:13 HOLY SPIRIT. The Holy Spirit and His place in the believer's redemption is a central emphasis in the book of Ephesians. The Holy Spirit (1) is the mark or seal of God's ownership; (2) is the first installment of the believer's inheritance (v. 14); (3) is the Spirit of wisdom and revelation (v. 17); (4) helps the believer when he draws near to God (2:18); (5) builds the body of believers into a holy temple (2:21–22); (6) reveals the mystery of Christ (3:4–5); (7) strengthens the believer with might in the inner being (3:16); (8) motivates unity in the Christian faith in full Christlikeness (4:3, 13); (9) grieves when there is sin in the life of the believer (4:30); (10) desires to repeatedly fill and empower the believer (5:18); and (11) helps in prayer and spiritual warfare (6:18).

1:13–14 HOLY SPIRIT . . . THE EARNEST. The Holy Spirit is the "earnest" or deposit of our inheritance, i.e., a first installment or down payment. In this age the Holy Spirit is given to believers as a down payment of what we are going to have in greater fullness in the future. His presence and work in our lives is a pledge of our future inheritance (cf. Rom. 8:23; 2 Cor. 1:22; 5:5).

ELECTION AND PREDESTINATION

***Eph. 1:4–5** "According as he hath chosen us in him before the foundation of the world, that we should be holy and without blame before him in love; Having predestinated us unto the adoption of children by Jesus Christ to himself, according to the good pleasure of his will."*

ELECTION. God's choice of those who believe in Christ is an important doctrine to the apostle Paul (see Rom. 8:29–33; 9:6–26; 11:5,7,28; Col. 3:12; 1 Thes. 1:4; 2 Thes. 2:13; Tit. 1:1). Election (Gk. *eklegō*) refers to God's choice in Christ of a people for Himself in order that they should be holy and blameless before Him (cf. 2 Thes. 2:13). Paul sees this election as expressing the love of God as He receives as His own all who receive His Son, Jesus (John 1:12). The doctrine of election involves the following truths:

(1) Election is Christocentric, i.e., election of humans occurs only in union with Jesus Christ. "He hath chosen us in him" (Eph. 1:4; see v. 1, note). Jesus Himself is first of all the elect of God. Concerning Jesus, God states, "Behold my servant, whom I have chosen" (Mat. 12:18; cf. Is. 42:1,6; 1 Pet. 2:4). Christ, as the elect, is the foundation of our election. Only in union with Christ do we become members of the elect (Eph. 1:4,6–7,9–10,12–13). No one is elect apart from union with Christ through faith.

(2) Election is "in [him] . . . through his blood" (Eph. 1:7). God purposed before creation (Eph. 1:4) to have a people through Christ's redemptive death on the cross. Thus election is grounded on Christ's sacrificial death on Calvary to save us from our sins (Acts 20:28; Rom. 3:24–26).

(3) Election in Christ is primarily corporate, i.e., an election of a people (Eph. 1:4–5,7,9). The elected are called "the body of Christ" (4:12), "my church" (Mat. 16:18), God's special people (1 Pet. 2:9), and the "bride" of Christ (Rev. 21:9). Hence, election is corporate and embraces individual persons only as they identify and associate themselves with the body of Christ, the true church (Eph. 1:22–23; see Robert Shank, *Elect in the Son* [Minneapolis: Bethany House Publishers], pp. 45–55). This was true already of Israel in the O.T. (see Deut. 29:18–21, note; 2 Ki. 21:14, note; see article on GOD'S COVENANT WITH THE ISRAELITES, p. 314).

(4) The election to salvation and holiness of the body of Christ is always certain. But the certainty of election for individuals in the body remains conditional on their personal living faith in Jesus Christ and perseverance in union with Him. The apostle Paul demonstrates this as follows. (a) God's eternal purpose for the church is that we should "be holy and without blame before him" (Eph. 1:4). This refers both to forgiveness of sins (1:7) and to the church's sanctification and holiness. God's elect people are being led by the Holy Spirit toward sanctification and holiness (see Rom. 8:14; Gal. 5:16–25). The apostle repeatedly emphasizes this paramount purpose of God (see Eph. 2:10; 3:14–19; 4:1–3,13–24; 5:1–18). (b) Fulfillment of this purpose for the corporate church is certain: Christ will "present it to himself a glorious church . . . holy and without blemish" (5:27). (c) Fulfillment of this purpose for individuals in the church is conditional. Christ will present us "holy and without blame before him" (1:4) only if we continue in the faith. Paul states this clearly: Christ will "present you holy and unblameable . . . in his sight: If ye continue in the faith grounded and settled, and *be* not moved away from the hope of the gospel" (Col. 1:22–23).

(5) Election to salvation in Christ is offered to all (John 3:16–17; 1 Tim. 2:4–6; Tit. 2:11; Heb. 2:9) and becomes actual for particular persons contingent on their repentance and faith as they accept God's gift of salvation in Christ (Eph. 2:8; 3:17; cf. Acts 20:21; Rom. 1:16; 4:16). At the point of faith, the believer is incorporated into the elect body of Christ (the church) by the Holy Spirit (1 Cor. 12:13), thereby becoming one of the elect. Thus, both God and humans have a decision in election (see Rom. 8:29, note; 2 Pet. 1:1–11).

PREDESTINATION. Predestination (Gk. *proorizō*) means "to decide beforehand" and applies to God's purposes and objectives comprehended in election. Election is God's choice "in Christ" of a people (the true church) for Himself. Predestination comprehends what will happen to God's people (all genuine believers in Christ).

(1) God predestinates His elect to be: (a) called (Rom. 8:30); (b) justified (Rom. 3:24; 8:30); (c) glorified (Rom. 8:30); (d) conformed to the image of His Son (Rom. 8:29); (e) holy and without blame (Eph 1:4); (f) adopted as children (1:5); (g) redeemed (1:7); (h) recipients of an inheritance (1:14); (i) for the praise of His glory (Eph. 1:12; 1 Pet. 2:9); (j) recipients of the Holy Spirit (Eph. 1:13; Gal. 3:14); and (k) created for good works (Eph. 2:10).

(2) Predestination, like election, refers to the corporate body of Christ (i.e., the true spiritual church), and comprehends individuals only in association with that body through a present living faith in Jesus Christ (Eph. 1:5,7,13; cf. Acts 2:38–41; 16:31).

SUMMARY. Concerning election and predestination, we might use the analogy of a great ship on its way to heaven. The ship (the church) is chosen by God to be His very own vessel. Christ is the Captain and Pilot of this ship. All who desire to be a part of this elect ship and its Captain can do so through a living faith in Christ, by which they come on board the ship. As long as one is on the ship, in company with its Captain, he is among the elect. If he chooses to abandon the ship and Captain, he ceases to be one of the elect. Election is always only in union with the Captain and His ship. Predestination tells us about the ship's destination and what God has prepared for those remaining on it. God invites everyone to come aboard the elect ship through faith in Jesus Christ.

heritance [c]until the redemption of
[d]the purchased possession, [e]unto
the praise of his glory.

Prayer for spiritual understanding

15 Wherefore I also, [f]after I heard
of your faith in the Lord Jesus, and love
unto all the saints,
16 [g]Cease not to give thanks for
you, making mention of you in my
prayers;
17 That [h]the God of our Lord Jesus
Christ, the Father of glory, [i]may give
unto you the spirit of wisdom and reve-
lation **d**in the knowledge of him:
18 [j]The eyes of your understand-
ing being enlightened; that ye may
know what is [k]the hope of his calling,
and what the riches of the glory of his
inheritance in the saints,
19 And what *is* the exceeding great-
ness of his power to us-ward who be-
lieve, [l]according to the working **e**of
his mighty power,
20 Which he wrought in Christ,
when [m]he raised him from the dead,
and [n]set *him* at his own right hand in
the heavenly *places,*
21 [o]Far above all [p]principality,
and power, and might, and dominion,
and every name that is named, not only
in this world, but also in that which is
to come:
22 And [q]hath put all *things* under
his feet, and gave him [r]*to be* the head
over all *things* to the church,
23 [s]Which is his body, [t]the ful-
ness of him [u]that filleth all in all.

1:14 [c]Rom. 8:23 [d]Acts 20:28 [e]1 Pet. 2:9
1:15 [f]Col. 1:4
1:16 [g]Rom. 1:9
1:17 [h]John 20:17 [i]Col. 1:9
1:18 [j]Acts 26:18 [k]ch. 2:12
1:19 [l]Col. 2:12
1:20 [m]Acts 2:24 [n]Ps. 110:1
1:21 [o]Phil. 2:9,10 [p]Rom. 8:38
1:22 [q]Mat. 28:18 [r]Heb. 2:7
1:23 [s]Rom. 12:5 [t]Col. 2:9 [u]1 Cor. 12:6
2:1 [v]Col. 2:13 [w]ch. 4:18
2:2 [x]Col. 1:21 [y]ch. 6:12 [z]Col. 3:6
2:3 [a]1 Pet. 4:3 [b]Gal. 5:16 [c]Ps. 51:5
2:4 [d]Rom. 10:12
2:5 [e]Rom. 5:6,8 [f]Rom. 6:4,5
2:6 [g]ch. 1:20
2:7 [h]Tit. 3:4
2:8 [i]2 Tim. 1:9 [j]Rom. 4:16 [k]Mat. 16:17
2:10 [l]Is. 19:25

New life with Christ

2 AND [v]YOU *hath he quickened,*
[w]who were dead in trespasses and
sins;
2 [x]Wherein in time past ye walked
according to the course of this world,
according to [y]the prince of the power
of the air, the spirit that now worketh
in [z]the children of disobedience:
3 [a]Among whom also we all had
our conversation in times past in [b]the
lusts of our flesh, fulfilling **f**the de-
sires of the flesh and of the mind; and
[c]were by nature the children of wrath,
even as others.
4 But God, [d]who is rich in mercy,
for his great love wherewith he
loved us,
5 [e]Even when we were dead in
sins, hath [f]quickened us together
with Christ, (**g**by grace ye are saved;)
6 And hath raised *us* up together,
and made *us* sit together [g]in heavenly
places in Christ Jesus:
7 That in the ages to come he might
show the exceeding riches of his grace
in [h]*his* kindness toward us through
Christ Jesus.
8 [i]For by grace are ye saved
[j]through faith; and that not of your-
selves: [k]*it is* the gift of God:
9 Not of works, lest any man should
boast. 1 Th 5:8-
10 For we are [l]his workmanship,

d Or, *for the acknowledgment* **e** Gk. *of the might of his power* **f** Gk. *the wills* **g** Or, *by whose grace*

1:16–20 IN MY PRAYERS. Paul's prayer for the Ephesians reflects God's highest desire for every believer in Christ. He prays that the Spirit might work in them in greater measure (cf. 3:16). The reason for this increased measure of the Spirit's impartation is that believers may receive more wisdom, revelation, and knowledge concerning God's redemptive purposes for present and future salvation (vv. 17–18), and experience a more abundant "power" of the Holy Spirit in their lives (vv. 19–20).

1:19 HIS POWER. In order for the believer to advance in grace, achieve victory over Satan and sin, witness effectively for Christ, and gain final salvation, he must ever have God's power moving toward him (cf. 1 Pet. 1:5). This power is an activity, manifestation, and strength of the Holy Spirit working within the faithful believer. It is the same power and Spirit that raised Christ from the dead and seated Him at God's right hand (v. 20; Rom. 8:11–16, 26–27; Gal. 5:22–25).

2:2 THE CHILDREN OF DISOBEDIENCE. Vv. 1–4 reveal a major reason why the Christian should have great compassion and mercy for those still living in trespasses and sin. (1) All who are without Christ are controlled by "the prince of the power of the air," i.e., Satan. Their minds are blinded by Satan to the truth of God (cf. 2 Cor. 4:3–4). They are enslaved to sin and the lusts of the flesh (v. 3; Luke 4:18). (2) Because of the unregenerate person's spiritual condition, he cannot understand or accept the truth apart from the grace of God (vv. 5,8; 1 Cor. 1:18; Tit. 2:11–14). (3) The Christian must see everyone from the Biblical perspective. Those involved in immorality and pride are to be pitied because of their slavery to sin and Satan (vv. 1–2; cf. John 3:16). (4) The person without Christ is still responsible for his sin, for God gives every human being a measure of light and grace by which to seek God and escape the slavery of sin through faith in Christ (John 1:9; Rom. 1:18–32; 2:1–16).

2:8 BY GRACE . . . THROUGH FAITH. See article on FAITH AND GRACE, p. 1738.

2:9 NOT OF WORKS. One cannot be saved by works, good deeds of love, or trying to keep God's commandments. One must be saved by the grace

created in Christ Jesus unto good
works, which God hath before [h]or-
15 dained that we should walk in them.

The household of God

11 Wherefore remember, that ye *being* in time past Gentiles in the flesh, who are called Uncircumcision by that which is called [m]the Circumcision in the flesh made by hands;

12 [n]That at that time ye were without Christ, [o]being aliens from the commonwealth of Israel, and strangers from [p]the covenants of promise, [q]having no hope, [r]and without God in the world:

13 [s]But now in Christ Jesus ye who sometimes were [t]far off are made nigh by the blood of Christ.

14 For [u]he is our peace, [v]who hath made both one, and hath broken down the middle wall of partition *between us;*

15 [w]Having abolished [x]in his flesh the enmity, *even* the law of commandments *contained* in ordinances; for to make in himself of twain one [y]new man, *so* making peace;

16 And that he might [z]reconcile both unto God in one body by the cross, [a]having slain the enmity [i]thereby:

17 And came [b]and preached peace to you which were afar off, and to [c]them that were nigh.

18 For [d]through him we both have access [e]by one Spirit unto the Father.

Habitation of God

19 Now therefore ye are no more strangers and foreigners, but [f]fellowcitizens with the saints, and of [g]the household of God;

20 And are [h]built [i]upon the foundation of the [j]apostles and prophets,

2:11 [m]Col. 2:11
2:12 [n]Col. 1:21 [o]Ezek. 13:9 [p]Rom. 9:4,8 [q]1 Thes. 4:13 [r]Gal. 4:8
2:13 [s]Gal. 3:28 [t]Acts 2:39
2:14 [u]Mic. 5:5 [v]John 10:16
2:15 [w]Col. 2:14 [x]Col. 1:22 [y]Gal. 6:15
2:16 [z]Col. 1:20-22 [a]Rom. 6:6
2:17 [b]Is. 57:19 [c]Ps. 148:14
2:18 [d]John 10:9 [e]1 Cor. 12:13
2:19 [f]Phil. 3:20 [g]Gal. 6:10
2:20 [h]1 Pet. 2:4 [i]Mat. 16:18 [j]1 Cor. 12:28

h Or, *prepared* **i** Or, *in himself*

---

of God. The reasons for this are the following: (1) All the unsaved are spiritually dead (v. 1), under the dominion of Satan (v. 2), enslaved to sin (v. 3), and under the condemnation of God (v. 3).

(2) In order to be saved one must receive God's provision of salvation (vv. 4–5), be forgiven of sin (Rom. 4:7–8), be made spiritually alive (Col. 1:13), be delivered from the power of Satan and sin (Col. 1:13), be made a new creature (v. 10; 2 Cor. 5:17), and receive the Holy Spirit (John 7:37–39; 20:22). No amount of self-effort can accomplish the above.

(3) What brings salvation is God's grace through faith (vv. 5,8). God's gift of grace includes the following: (a) First comes the call to repentance and faith (Acts 2:38). With this call comes the work of the Holy Spirit within a person, giving him the power and ability to respond to God. (b) Those who respond in faith and repentance and accept Christ as Lord and Savior receive additional grace to be regenerated or born again by the Spirit (see article on REGENERATION, p. 1597) and to be filled with the Spirit (5:18; Acts 1:8; 2:38). (c) Those who are made new creatures in Christ receive continuing grace to live the Christian life, resist sin, and serve God (Rom. 8:13–14; 2 Cor. 9:8). The believer strives to live to God by the grace of God which works within him (1 Cor. 15:10). God's grace operates within the committed believer both to will and to work for God's good pleasure (Phil. 2:12–13). From beginning to end, salvation is by the grace of God (see article on FAITH AND GRACE, p. 1738).

2:18 ACCESS ... UNTO THE FATHER. Access to God the Father is through Jesus Christ by the Holy Spirit. "Access" means that we who have faith in Christ have the freedom and right to approach our heavenly Father with confidence that we will be accepted, loved, and welcomed. (1) This access is gained through Christ—His shed blood on the cross (v. 13; Rom. 5:1–2) and His heavenly intercession for all who come to Him (Heb. 7:25; cf. 4:14–16). (2) Access to God also necessitates the aid of the Holy Spirit. The Spirit's indwelling power makes it possible to pray and call on God according to His will and purpose (John 14:16–17; 16:13–14; Rom. 8:15–16,26–27).

2:20 FOUNDATION ... APOSTLES. The church can only be a true church if it is founded on the Christ-inspired infallible revelation to the first apostles. (1) The N.T. apostles were the original messengers, witnesses, and authorized representatives of the crucified and risen Lord. They were the foundation stones of the church, and their message is preserved in the writings of the N.T. as the original, fundamental testimony to the gospel of Christ, valid for all times.

(2) All believers and churches are dependent on the words, message, and faith of the first apostles as recorded in Acts and in the apostles' inspired writings. Their authority is retained in the N.T., and later generations of the church have the task of obeying the apostolic revelation and of witnessing to its truth. The gospel given to the N.T. apostles through the Holy Spirit is the enduring source of life, truth, and direction for the church.

(3) All believers and churches are true believers and true churches only so long as they do the following: (a) They must agree with and sincerely endeavor to follow the apostles' original teaching and revelation concerning the gospel as found in the N.T. (Acts 2:42). To reject the apostles' teachings is to reject the Lord Himself (John 16:13–15; 1 Cor. 14:36–38; Gal. 1:9–11). (b) They must continue the apostolic mission and ministry by communicating anew the apostolic message to the world and the church through faithful proclamation and teaching in the power of the Spirit (Acts 1:8; 2 Tim. 1:8–14; Tit. 1:7–9). (c) They must not only believe the apostolic message but also defend and guard it against all distortion or alter-

Jesus Christ himself being [k]the chief corner *stone;*

21 In whom all the building fitly framed together groweth unto [l]an holy temple in the Lord:

22 [m]In whom ye also are builded together for an habitation of God through the Spirit.

Paul, apostle to the Gentiles

3 FOR THIS cause I Paul, [n]the prisoner of Jesus Christ [o]for you Gentiles,

2 If ye have heard of [p]the dispensation of the grace of God [q]which is given me to you-ward:

3 [r]How that by revelation [s]he made known unto me the mystery; (as I wrote [j]afore in few words,

4 Whereby, when ye read, ye may understand my knowledge in the mystery of Christ)

5 [t]Which in other ages was not made known unto the sons of men, as it is now revealed unto his holy apostles and prophets by the Spirit;

6 That the Gentiles [u]should be fellowheirs, and of the same body, and partakers of his promise in Christ by the gospel:

7 [v]Whereof I was made a minister, [w]according to the gift of the grace of God given unto me by [x]the effectual working of his power.

2:20 [k]Ps. 118:22
2:21 [l]1 Cor. 3:17
2:22 [m]1 Pet. 2:5
3:1 [n]Acts 21:33 [o]Col. 1:24
3:2 [p]Rom. 1:5 [q]Acts 9:15
3:3 [r]Acts 22:17 [s]Rom. 16:25
3:5 [t]Rom. 16:25
3:6 [u]Gal. 3:28
3:7 [v]Rom. 15:16 [w]Rom. 1:5 [x]Rom. 15:18
3:8 [y]1 Cor. 15:9 [z]Col. 1:27
3:9 [a]Rom. 16:25 [b]Ps. 33:6
3:10 [c]1 Pet. 1:12 [d]Col. 1:16 [e]1 Tim. 3:16
3:12 [f]Heb. 4:16
3:13 [g]Phil. 1:14 [h]2 Cor. 1:6
3:15 [i]ch. 1:10
3:16 [j]Phil. 4:19 [k]Col. 1:11

8 Unto me, [y]who am less than the least of all saints, is this grace given, that I should preach among the Gentiles [z]the unsearchable riches of Christ;

9 And to make all *men* see what *is* the fellowship of the mystery, [a]which from the beginning of the world hath been hid in God, [b]who created all things by Jesus Christ:

10 [c]To the intent that now [d]unto the principalities and powers in heavenly *places* [e]might be known by the church the manifold wisdom of God,

11 According to the eternal purpose which he purposed in Christ Jesus our Lord:

12 In whom we have boldness and access [f]with confidence by the faith of him.

13 [g]Wherefore I desire that ye faint not at my tribulations for you, [h]which is your glory.

Strength through the Spirit

14 For this cause I bow my knees unto the Father of our Lord Jesus Christ,

15 Of whom [i]the whole family in heaven and earth is named,

16 That he would grant you, [j]according to the riches of his glory, [k]to

[j] Or, *a little before*

ation. The apostles' original revelation as found in the N.T. can never be replaced or made void by later revelation, testimony, or prophecy (Acts 20:27–31; 1 Tim. 6:20).

3:4 MYSTERY OF CHRIST. Paul speaks of the "mystery of Christ," hidden for ages in God (v. 9) and now made known by revelation (v. 3) through the Spirit to the apostles and prophets (v. 5). The mystery is God's purpose to "gather together in one all things in Christ, both which are in heaven, and which are on earth" (1:10), and to include people of all nations in the promise of life and salvation (v. 6; Rom. 16:25–26; 2 Tim. 1:1). From the Jews and the Gentile nations God created "in Christ" (v. 6) a new people for Himself (1:4–6; 2:16; 4:4,16; Mat. 16:18; Col. 1:24–28; 1 Pet. 2:9–10).

3:7 GRACE OF GOD. The grace of God, given to each believer to accomplish God's will, is an energizing strength that flows from the risen Christ and operates by the Holy Spirit indwelling the believer (1:19; 4:7; Acts 6:8; 11:23; 14:26; 1 Cor. 15:10; 2 Cor. 12:9; Phil. 2:13; Col. 1:29; Tit. 2:11–13; see article on FAITH AND GRACE, p. 1738).

3:10 PRINCIPALITIES AND POWERS. There are two possible interpretations of this verse. (1) The "principalities and powers in heavenly *places*" may refer to good angels (cf. Col. 1:16). They behold the astonishing wisdom of God as He demonstrates that wisdom through the church (1 Pet. 1:10–12). (2) The "principalities and powers in heavenly *places*" may refer to the ruling powers of darkness in the spiritual realm (cf. 6:12; Dan. 10:13,20–21) to whom God's "eternal purpose" (v. 11) is being made known through the church's proclamation of salvation and through spiritual warfare against Satan and his forces (cf. 6:12–18; Dan. 9:2–23; 10:12–13,20–21; 2 Cor. 10:4–5).

3:16–19 STRENGTHENED . . . INNER MAN. To have the "inner man" strengthened by the Spirit is to have our feelings, thoughts, and purposes placed more and more under His influence and direction so that the Spirit can manifest His power through us in greater measure. The purpose of this strengthening by the Spirit is fourfold: (1) that Christ may establish His presence in our hearts (vv. 16–17; cf. Rom. 8:9–10); (2) that we may be grounded in sincere love for God, Christ, and others (v. 17); (3) that we may comprehend with our minds and experience in our lives the love of Christ for us (vv. 18–19); (4) that we may "be filled with all the fulness of God" (v. 19), i.e., that God's presence may so fill us that we reflect and manifest from our innermost being the character and stature which belong to the Lord

be strengthened with might by his Spirit in [l]the inner man;

17 [m]That Christ may dwell in your hearts by faith; that ye, [n]being rooted and grounded in love,

18 [o]May be able to comprehend with all saints [p]what *is* the breadth, and length, and depth, and height;

19 And to know the love of Christ, which passeth knowledge, that ye might be filled [q]with all the fulness of God.

20 Now [r]unto him that is able to do exceeding abundantly [s]above all that we ask or think, [t]according to the power that worketh in us,

21 [u]Unto him *be* glory in the church by Christ Jesus throughout all ages, world without end. Amen. ol. :6-8

The unity of the Spirit

4 I THEREFORE, [v]the prisoner [k]of the Lord, beseech you that ye [w]walk worthy of the vocation wherewith ye are called,

2 [x]With all lowliness and meekness, with longsuffering, forbearing one another in love;

3 Endeavouring to keep the unity of the Spirit [y]in the bond of peace.

4 [z]*There is* one body, and one Spirit, even as ye are called in one hope of your calling;

5 [a]One Lord, [b]one faith, [c]one baptism,

6 [d]One God and Father of all, who *is* above all, and [e]through all, and in you all.

The ministry gifts

7 But [f]unto every one of us is given grace according to the measure of the gift of Christ.

8 Wherefore he saith, [g]When he ascended up on high, [h]he led [1]captivity captive, and gave gifts unto men.

9 [i](Now that he ascended, what is it but that he also descended first into the lower parts of the earth?

10 He that descended is the same also [j]that ascended up far above all heavens, [k]that he might [m]fill all things.)

11 [l]And he gave some, apostles; and some, prophets; and some, [m]evangelists; and some, [n]pastors and [o]teachers;

Purpose of the gifts

12 [p]For the perfecting of the saints, for the work of the ministry, [q]for the edifying of [r]the body of Christ: 1 Tim. 4:14

13 Till we all come [n]in the unity of

3:16 [l]Rom. 7:22
3:17 [m]John 14:23 [n]Col. 1:23
3:18 [o]ch. 1:18 [p]Rom. 10:3
3:19 [q]ch. 1:23
3:20 [r]Rom. 16:25 [s]1 Cor. 2:9 [t]Col. 1:29
3:21 [u]Rom. 11:36
4:1 [v]Philem. 1,9 [w]Phil. 1:27
4:2 [x]Acts 20:19
4:3 [y]Col. 3:14
4:4 [z]Rom. 12:5
4:5 [a]1 Cor. 1:13 [b]Jude 3 [c]Heb. 6:6
4:6 [d]Mal. 2:10 [e]Rom. 11:36
4:7 [f]1 Cor. 12:11
4:8 [g]Ps. 68:18 [h]Judg. 5:12
4:9 [i]John 3:13
4:10 [j]Acts 1:9 [k]Acts 2:33
4:11 [l]1 Cor. 12:28 [m]Acts 21:8 [n]Acts 20:28 [o]Rom. 12:7
4:12 [p]1 Cor. 12:7 [q]1 Cor. 14:26 [r]Col. 1:24

[k] Or, *in the Lord* [1] Or, *a multitude of captives* [m] Or, *fulfil* [n] Or, *into the unity*

Jesus Christ (cf. 4:13, 15).

3:20 EXCEEDING ABUNDANTLY ABOVE. God will do for us not only more than we ask and desire in prayer, but also even more than our imagination can perceive. This promise is conditioned and dependent upon the degree of the Holy Spirit's presence, power, and grace operating in our life (1:19; 3:16–19; Is. 65:24; John 15:7; Phil. 2:13).

4:3 KEEP THE UNITY. "The unity of the Spirit" cannot be created by any human being. It already exists for those who have believed the truth and received Christ, as the apostle proclaimed in chs. 1–3. The Ephesians are now to keep and preserve that unity, not through human efforts or organizations, but by walking "worthy of the vocation wherewith [they] are called" (v. 1). Spiritual unity is maintained by being loyal to the truth and by walking after the Spirit (vv. 1–3,14–15; Gal. 5:22–26). It cannot be attained "by the flesh" (Gal. 3:3).

4:5 ONE LORD. Essential to Christian faith and unity is the belief and confession that there is only "one Lord." (1) That there is only "one Lord" means that Jesus Christ and His work of redemption is perfect and sufficient, and no other redeemer or mediator is needed to give the believer complete salvation (1 Tim. 2:5–6; Heb. 9:15). The believer is to draw near to God through Christ alone (Heb. 7:25).

(2) "One Lord" also means that to profess equal or greater allegiance to any authority (secular or religious) other than God revealed in Christ and His inspired Word is the same as withdrawing oneself from the Lordship of Christ, and thus from the life that is in Him alone. There can be no Lordship of Christ or "unity of the Spirit" (v. 3) apart from the affirmation that the Lord Jesus is the ultimate authority for the believer and that His authority is communicated in the written Word of God.

4:11 AND HE GAVE. See article on THE MINISTRY GIFTS OF THE CHURCH, p. 1852.

4:13 UNITY OF THE FAITH. In ch. 4 Paul teaches that the "unity of the Spirit" (v. 3) and the "unity of the faith" are maintained and perfected by: (1) accepting only the faith and message of the N.T. apostles, prophets, evangelists, pastors, and teachers (vv. 11–12); (2) growing in grace, advancing toward spiritual maturity, and growing up in all aspects into Christ (v. 15), and being filled with all the fullness of Christ and God (v. 13; cf. 3:19); (3) being no longer children who accept "every wind of doctrine" but who instead have a knowledge of the truth by which to reject false teachers (vv. 14–15); (4) holding and speaking the revealed truth of Scripture in love (v. 15); and (5) walking in "righteousness and true

THE MINISTRY GIFTS OF THE CHURCH

***Eph. 4:11** "And he gave some, apostles; and some, prophets; and some, evangelists; and some, pastors and teachers."*

THE GIVER. Eph. 4:11 lists the ministry gifts which Christ gave to the church. Paul states that He gave these gifts (1) for equipping God's people for works of service (4:12), and (2) for the spiritual growth and development of the body of Christ as God intended (4:13–16; see article on SPIRITUAL GIFTS FOR BELIEVERS, p. 1790).

APOSTLES. The title "apostle" is applied to certain leaders in the N.T. The verb *apostellō* means to send someone on a special mission as a messenger and personal representative of the one who sends him. The title is used of Christ (Heb. 3:1), the twelve disciples (Mat. 10:2), the apostle Paul (Rom. 1:1; 2 Cor. 1:1; Gal. 1:1), and others (Acts 14:4,14; Rom. 16:7; Gal. 1:19; 2:8–9; 1 Thes. 2:6–7).

(1) The term "apostle" was used in the N.T. in a general sense for a commissioned representative of a church, such as the first Christian missionaries. Hence, in the N.T. the term referred to any messenger appointed and sent as a missionary or for some other special responsibility (see Acts 14:4,14; Rom. 16:7; cf. 2 Cor. 8:23; Phil. 2:25). They were men who manifested extraordinary spiritual leadership, were anointed with power to confront directly the powers of darkness and to confirm the gospel with miracles, and were dedicated to establishing churches according to apostolic truth and purity. They were itinerate, risking their lives for the name of our Lord Jesus Christ and the advancement of the gospel (Acts 11:21–26; 13:50; 14:19–22; 15:25–26). They were Spirit-filled men of faith and prayer (see Acts 11:23–25; 13:2–5; 46–52; 14:1–7,21–23).

(2) Apostles in this general sense remain essential to God's purpose in the church. If churches cease to send forth Spirit-filled people, then the spread of the gospel into all the world will be hindered. On the other hand, as long as the church produces and sends forth such people, it will fulfill its missionary task and remain faithful to the Lord's great commission (Mat. 28:18–20).

(3) The term "apostle" is also used in the N.T. in a special sense, referring to those who saw Jesus after His resurrection and were personally commissioned by the resurrected Lord to preach the gospel and establish the church (e.g., the twelve disciples and Paul). They possessed a unique authority within the church that relates to divine revelation and the original message of the gospel that can no longer exist in anyone today (see Eph. 2:20, note). Thus, the office of apostle in this specialized sense is unique and unrepeatable. These original apostles have no successors (see 1 Cor. 15:8, note).

(4) A primary task of the N.T. apostles was to establish churches and to ensure that they were founded on sincere devotion to Christ and the N.T. faith (cf. John 21:15–17; 1 Cor. 12:28; 2 Cor. 11:2–3; Eph. 4:11–13; Phil. 1:17). This task involved two main burdens: (a) An urgent God-given desire to maintain the purity of the church and its separation from sin and the world (1 Cor. 5:1–5; 2 Cor. 6:14–18; Jas. 2:14–26; 1 Pet. 2:11; 4:1–5; 1 John 2:1,15–17; 3:3–10). (b) A continuing burden to proclaim the N.T. gospel and to defend it against heresy and false teachers (Rom. 16:17; 1 Cor. 11:2; 2 Cor. 11:3–4,13, notes; Gal. 1:9, note; 2 Pet. 2:1–3; 1 John 4:1–6; 2 John 7–11; Jude 3–4,12–13; see article on OVERSEERS AND THEIR DUTIES, p. 1706).

(5) Although the first apostles who laid the foundation of the church have no successors, the church today is still dependent on their words, message, and faith. The church must obey and remain faithful to their original writings. To reject the inspired revelation of the apostles is to cease to be a church according to the Biblical pattern and to reject the Lord Himself (John 16:13–15; 1 Cor. 14:36–38; Gal. 1:9–11). On the other hand, to believe the apostolic message, obey it, and guard it against all distortion is to remain true to the Holy Spirit (Acts 20:28, 2 Tim. 1:14) and to guarantee the continued life, blessing, and presence of God within the church (see Eph. 2:20, note).

PROPHETS. Prophets were men in the church who spoke under the direct impulse of the

Holy Spirit and whose main motivation and concern were with the spiritual life and purity of the church. Under the new covenant they were raised up and empowered by the Holy Spirit to bring a message from God to His people (Acts 2:17; 4:8; 21:4).

(1) The O.T. prophet provides a basis for understanding the prophetic ministry in the early church. The O.T. prophet's primary task was to speak a word of God by the Spirit in order to encourage God's people to remain faithful to their covenant relationship. He also, at times, predicted the future as the Spirit revealed it to him (see article on THE PROPHET IN THE OLD TESTAMENT, p. 1002). Christ and the apostles serve as examples of the N.T. ideal (Acts 3:22–23; 13:1–2).

(2) The prophet's function within the church included the following: (a) He was a Spirit-filled proclaimer and interpreter of the Word of God, called by God to warn, exhort, comfort, and edify (Acts 2:14–36; 3:12–26; 1 Cor. 14:3). (b) He was to exercise the gift of prophecy (see article on SPIRITUAL GIFTS FOR BELIEVERS, p. 1790). (c) He was at times a seer (cf. 1 Chr. 29:29) who foretold the future (Acts 11:28; 21:10–11). (d) It was the N.T. prophet's task, just as it was the prophet's task in the O.T., to expose sin, proclaim righteousness, warn of judgment to come, and combat worldliness and lukewarmness among God's people (Luke 1:14–17). Because of their message of righteousness, the prophet and his ministry can expect rejection by many in the churches during any time of lukewarmness and apostasy.

(3) The prophet's character, burden, desire, and ability include: (a) a zeal for church purity (John 17:15–17; 1 Cor. 6:9–11; Gal. 5:22–25); (b) a deep sensitivity to evil and the capacity to identify, define, and hate unrighteousness (Rom. 12:9; Heb. 1:9); (c) a keen understanding of the danger of false teachings (Mat. 7:15; 24:11,24; Gal. 1:9; 2 Cor. 11:12–15); (d) an inherent dependence on the Word of God to validate his message (Luke 4:17–19; 1 Cor. 15:3–4; 2 Tim. 3:16); (e) a concern for the spiritual success of the kingdom of God and a sharing in the feelings of God (cf. Mat. 21:11–13; 23:37; Luke 13:34; John 2:14–17; Acts 20:27–31).

(4) The prophet's message is not to be regarded as infallible. His messages are subject to the evaluation of the church, other prophets, and the Word of God. The congregation is required to discern and test whether the prophet's witness is from God (1 Cor. 14:29–33; 1 John 4:1).

(5) Prophets continue to be essential to God's purpose for the church. A church that rejects God's prophets will be a declining church, drifting toward worldliness and the compromise of Biblical truth and standards (1 Cor. 14:3; cf. Mat. 23:31–38; Luke 11:49; Acts 7:51–52). If the prophet is not allowed to bring words of reproof and warning, words prompted by the Spirit, words exposing sin and unrighteousness (John 16:8–11), then the church will become a place where the Spirit can no longer be heard. Ecclesiastical politics and worldly power will replace the working of the Spirit (2 Tim. 3:1–9; 4:3–5; 2 Pet. 2:1–3,12–22). On the other hand, if the church, with its leaders, hears the voice of the prophets, it will be moved to renewed life and fellowship with Christ, sin will be forsaken, and the presence and holiness of the Spirit will be evident among the faithful (cf. 1 Cor. 14:3; 1 Thes. 5:19–21).

EVANGELISTS. In the N.T., evangelists were men of God who were gifted and commissioned by God to proclaim the gospel, i.e., the good news, of salvation to the unsaved and to help establish a new work in a city. When proclaimed, it always carries with it the offer and power of salvation.

(1) The ministry of Philip the "evangelist" (Acts 21:8) gives a clear picture of the work of an evangelist according to the N.T. pattern. (a) Philip preached the gospel of Christ (Acts 8:4–5,35). (b) Many were saved and baptized in water (Acts 8:6,12). (c) Signs, miracles, healings, and deliverance from evil spirits accompanied his preaching (Acts 8:6–7,13). (d) He was concerned that the new converts be filled with the Holy Spirit (Acts 8:12–17; cf. 2:38; 19:1–6).

(2) The evangelist is essential to God's purpose for the church. The church that fails to encourage and support the ministry of the evangelist will cease to gain converts as God desires. It will become a static church, void of growth and missionary outreach. The church that values the spiritual gift of the evangelist and maintains an earnest and

ongoing love and care for the lost will proclaim the message of salvation with convicting and saving power (Acts 2:14–41).

PASTORS. Pastors are those who oversee and care for the spiritual needs of a local congregation. They are also called "elders" (Acts 20:17; Tit. 1:5) and "bishops" or overseers (1 Tim. 3:1; Tit. 1:7).

(1) The task of pastors is to proclaim sound doctrine, refute heresy (Tit. 1:9–11), teach God's Word and exercise leadership in the local church (1 Thes. 5:12; 1 Tim. 3:1–5), be examples of purity and sound doctrine (Tit. 2:7–8), and take care to see that all believers remain in divine grace (Heb. 12:15; 13:17; 1 Pet. 5:2). Their task is described in Acts 20:28–31 as safeguarding apostolic truth and the flock of God by being on the alert for false doctrine and false teachers who arise within the church (see article on OVERSEERS AND THEIR DUTIES, p. 1706). They function as a shepherd of which Jesus as the good Shepherd is a model (John 10:11–16; 1 Pet. 2:25; 5:2–4).

(2) The N.T. pattern is a plurality of pastors directing the spiritual life of a local church (Acts 20:28; Phil. 1:1). Pastors were chosen, not through politics, but through the Spirit's wisdom given to the body as it examined the candidate's spiritual qualifications (see article on MORAL QUALIFICATIONS FOR OVERSEERS, p. 1908).

(3) The pastor is essential to God's purpose for His church. The church which fails to select godly and faithful pastors will cease to be governed according to the mind of the Spirit (see 1 Tim. 3:1–7). It will be a church left open to the destructive forces of Satan and the world (see Acts 20:28–31). The preaching of the Word will be distorted and the standards of the gospel lost (2 Tim. 1:13–14). Members and families of the church will not be cared for according to the purpose of God (1 Tim. 4:6,12–16; 6:20–21). Many will turn away from the truth and turn aside to fables (2 Tim. 4:4). On the other hand, if godly pastors are appointed, believers will be nourished on the words of faith and sound doctrine and disciplined for the purpose of godliness (1 Tim. 4:6–7). The church will be taught to persevere in the teaching of Christ and the apostles and thus ensure salvation for itself and those who hear (1 Tim. 4:16; 2 Tim. 2:2).

TEACHERS. Teachers are those who have a special, God-given gift to clarify, expound, and proclaim God's Word in order to build up the body of Christ (Eph. 4:12).

(1) The special task of teachers is to guard, by the help of the Holy Spirit, the gospel entrusted to them (2 Tim. 1:11–14). They are faithfully to point the church to Biblical revelation and to the original message of Christ and the apostles, and to persevere in this task.

(2) The principal purpose of Biblical teaching is to preserve truth and to produce holiness by leading the body of Christ into an uncompromising commitment to the godly lifestyle set forth in God's Word. Scripture states the goal of Christian instruction is love "out of a pure heart, and *of* a good conscience, and *of* faith unfeigned" (1 Tim. 1:5). Thus, the evidence of Christian learning is not just in what one knows, but how one lives—i.e., the manifestation of love, purity, faith, and sincere godliness.

(3) Teachers are essential to God's purpose for His church. The church that rejects or refuses to hear those teachers and theologians who remain faithful to Scriptural revelation will cease to be concerned about the genuineness of the Biblical message and the correct interpretation of the original teaching of Christ and the apostles. The church in which such teachers and theologians remain silent will not continue steadfast in the truth and holy faith. New winds of doctrine will be uncritically accepted and religious experience and human ideas, rather than revealed truth, will be the ultimate guide to the doctrine, standards, and practices of the church.

On the other hand, the church that listens to godly teachers and theologians will have its current teachings and practice measured by the fundamental testimony of the gospel, its false ideas exposed, and the purity of the original message of Christ handed down to its children. The inspired Word of God will become the test of all teaching and ideas, and the church will be ever reminded that the Holy Spirit's inspired Word is ultimate truth and authority, and as such, stands over the churches and their institutions.

the faith, and [s]of the knowledge of the
Son of God, unto [t]a perfect man, unto
the measure of the [o]stature of the ful-
ness of Christ:
14 That we *henceforth* be no more
[u]children, [v]tossed to and fro, and
carried about with every [w]wind of doc-
trine, by the sleight of men, *and* cun-
ning craftiness, [x]whereby they lie in
wait to deceive;
15 But [y]speaking[p] the truth in
love, [z]may grow up into him in all
things, [a]which is the head, *even*
Christ:
16 [b]From whom the whole body
fitly joined together and compacted by
that which every joint supplieth, ac-
cording to the effectual working in the
measure of every part, maketh in-
crease of the body unto the edifying of
itself in love.

Put away the old life

17 This I say therefore, and testify
in the Lord, that [c]ye henceforth walk
not as other Gentiles walk, [d]in the
vanity of their mind,
18 [e]Having the understanding
darkened, [f]being alienated from the
life of God through the ignorance that
is in them, because of the [g]blind-
ness[q] of their heart:
19 [h]Who being past feeling [i]have
given themselves over unto lascivious-
ness, to work all uncleanness with
greediness.
20 But ye have not so learned
Christ;

4:13
[s]Col. 2:2
[t]1 Cor. 14:20
4:14
[u]Is. 28:9
[v]Heb. 13:9
[w]Mat. 11:7
[x]Rom. 16:18
4:15
[y]2 Cor. 4:2
[z]ch. 1:22
[a]Col. 1:18
4:16
[b]Col. 2:19
4:17
[c]Col. 3:7
[d]Rom. 1:21
4:18
[e]Acts 26:18
[f]1 Thes. 4:5
[g]Rom. 1:21
4:19
[h]1 Tim. 4:2
[i]1 Pet. 4:3

4:22
[j]Col. 2:11
[k]Col. 3:7
4:23
[l]Col. 3:10
4:24
[m]Rom. 6:4
4:25
[n]Zech. 8:16
[o]Rom. 12:5
4:26
[p]Ps. 37:8
4:27
[q]1 Pet. 5:9
4:28
[r]Acts 20:35
[s]Luke 3:11
4:29
[t]Col. 3:8
[u]1 Thes. 5:11
[v]Col. 3:16
4:30
[w]Is. 7:13

21 If so be that ye have heard him,
and have been taught by him, as the
truth is in Jesus:
22 That ye [j]put off concerning
[k]the former conversation the old man,
which is corrupt according to the de-
ceitful lusts;

Put on the new life

23 And [l]be renewed in the spirit of
your mind;
24 And that ye [m]put on the new
man, which after God is created in righ-
teousness and [r]true holiness.
25 Wherefore putting away lying,
[n]speak every man truth with his
neighbour: for [o]we are members one
of another.
26 [p]Be ye angry, and sin not: let
not the sun go down upon your wrath:
27 [q]Neither give place to the devil.
28 Let him that stole steal no more:
but rather [r]let him labour, working
with *his* hands the thing which is good,
that he may have [s]to give [s]to him
that needeth.
29 [t]Let no corrupt communication
proceed out of your mouth, but [u]that
which is good [t]to the use of edifying,
[v]that it may minister grace unto the
hearers.

Grieve not the Spirit

30 And [w]grieve not the holy Spirit

[o] Or, *age* [p] Or, *being sincere* [q] Or, *hardness*
[r] Or, *holiness of truth* [s] Or, *to distribute*
[t] Or, *to edify profitably*

---

holiness" (v. 24; cf. vv. 17–32).

4:14 BE NO MORE CHILDREN. In vv. 13–15 Paul defines spiritually "perfect" or mature persons who possess the fullness of Christ. (1) To be spiritually mature means not being "children" who are unstable, easily deceived by false doctrines of men, and susceptible to crafty showmanship. People remain children if their understanding of and commitment to Biblical truth are inadequate (vv. 14–15). (2) To be spiritually mature involves "speaking the truth in love" (v. 15). The truth of the gospel as presented in the N.T. is to be held in love, presented in love, and contended for in a spirit of love. The love is first directed to "Christ" (v. 15), and then to the church (v. 16) and to one another (v. 32; cf. 1 Cor. 16:14).

4:15 TRUTH IN LOVE. Maintaining the unity of the faith (v. 13) must be based on an active love which seeks to resolve problems and reconcile differences by mutual loyalty and obedience to Christ and His Word. This means that holding and proclaiming N.T. truth in love have priority over loyalty to Christian institutions, traditions, individual people, or the visible church. Any endeavor to maintain fellowship or unity must never invalidate the Word of God or be based on the compromise of Biblical truth (v. 14). Faithfulness to Scripture may involve separation from a part of the visible church which has become unfaithful to Christ and apostolic doctrine (see 2:20, note). Subsequently the Holy Spirit will initiate the formation of a new visible church loyal to Christ and the original N.T. truth.

4:30 GRIEVE . . . THE HOLY SPIRIT. The Holy Spirit, who dwells within the believer (Rom. 8:9; 1 Cor. 6:19), is a Person who can experience intense grief or sorrow as Jesus Himself did when He wept over Jerusalem or grieved on other occasions (Mat. 23:37; Mark 3:5; Luke 19:41; John 11:35). (1) The believer causes the Holy Spirit grief or pain when he ignores His presence, voice, or leading (Rom. 8:5–17; Gal. 5:16–25; 6:7–9). (2) Grieving the Spirit leads to resisting the Holy Spirit (Acts 7:51); this, in turn, leads to quenching the Spirit (1 Thes. 5:19), and finally to despising the Spirit of grace (Heb. 10:29). This last activity

of God, whereby ye are sealed unto the
day of [x]redemption.
31 [y]Let all bitterness, and wrath,
and anger, and clamour, and [z]evil
speaking, be put away from you, [a]with
all malice:
32 And [b]be ye kind one to another,
tenderhearted, [c]forgiving one anoth-
er, even as God for Christ's sake hath
forgiven you.

Walk in love and purity

5 BE [d]YE therefore followers of
God, as dear children;
2 And [e]walk in love, [f]as Christ
also hath loved us, and hath given him-
self for us an offering and a sacrifice to
God [g]for a sweetsmelling savour.
3 But [h]fornication, and all un-
cleanness, or covetousness, [i]let it not
be once named among you, as
becometh saints;

The immoral are not in God's kingdom

4 [j]Neither filthiness, nor foolish
talking, nor jesting, [k]which are not
convenient: but rather giving of
thanks.
5 For this ye know, that [l]no whore-
monger, nor unclean person, nor covet-
ous man, [m]who is an idolater, [n]hath
any inheritance in the kingdom of
Christ and of God.
6 [o]Let no man deceive you with
vain words: for because of these things
[p]cometh the wrath of God upon the
children of [u]disobedience.

4:30 [x]Luke 21:28
4:31 [y]Col. 3:8,19 [z]Jas. 4:11 [a]Tit. 3:3
4:32 [b]2 Cor. 2:10 [c]Mark 11:25
5:1 [d]Luke 6:36
5:2 [e]1 Thes. 4:9 [f]Gal. 1:4 [g]2 Cor. 2:15
5:3 [h]Rom. 6:13 [i]1 Cor. 5:1
5:4 [j]Mat. 12:35 [k]Rom. 1:28
5:5 [l]1 Cor. 6:9 [m]Col. 3:5 [n]Rev. 22:15
5:6 [o]Jer. 29:8 [p]Rom. 1:18
5:8 [q]Is. 9:2 [r]2 Cor. 3:18 [s]Luke 16:8
5:9 [t]Gal. 5:22
5:10 [u]Rom. 12:2
5:11 [v]Rom. 6:21 [w]1 Tim. 5:20
5:12 [x]Rom. 1:24
5:13 [y]John 3:20
5:14 [z]Is. 60:1 [a]John 5:25
5:15 [b]Col. 4:5
5:16 [c]Col. 4:5 [d]Eccl. 11:2
5:17 [e]Col. 4:5 [f]Rom. 12:2 [g]1 Thes. 4:3
5:18 [h]Prov. 20:1

7 Be not ye therefore partakers
with them.
8 [q]For ye were sometimes dark-
ness, but now [r]*are ye* light in the Lord:
walk as [s]children of light:
9 (For [t]the fruit of the Spirit *is* in
all goodness and righteousness and
truth;)
10 [u]Proving what is acceptable
unto the Lord.
11 And have no fellowship with
[v]the unfruitful works of darkness, but
rather [w]reprove *them.*
12 [x]For it is a shame even to speak
of those things which are done of them
in secret.
13 But [y]all things that are [v]re-
proved are made manifest by the light:
for whatsoever doth make manifest is
light.
14 Wherefore [w]he saith, [z]Awake
thou that sleepest, and [a]arise from
the dead, and Christ shall give thee
light.
15 [b]See then that ye walk circum-
spectly, not as fools, but as wise,
Phi 2:12 16
16 [c]Redeeming the time, [d]be-
cause the days are evil.
17 [e]Wherefore be ye not unwise,
but [f]understanding [g]what the will of
the Lord *is.*

Be filled with the Spirit

18 And [h]be not drunk with wine,
wherein is excess; but be filled with the
Spirit;
End

[u] Or, *unbelief* [v] Or, *discovered* [w] Or, *it*

may be identified with blasphemy against the Holy Spirit, for which there is no forgiveness (see Mat. 12:31, note).

5:5 THIS YE KNOW. The apostle Paul as well as the Ephesians knew with unqualified certainty that all individuals (whether within or outside of the church) who were immoral, impure, or greedy (i.e., loved things more than God) were excluded from the kingdom of Christ. This was taught with strong conviction by the O.T. prophets (see Jer. 8:7, note; 23:17, note; Ezek. 13:10, note) and by the apostles and the N.T. church (see 1 Cor. 6:9, note; Gal. 5:21, note). People who committed such sins gave clear evidence of not being saved, of being devoid of the life of God, and of being separated from eternal life (see John 8:42, note; 1 John 3:15, note).

5:6 DECEIVE. Paul knew that some teachers would tell the Ephesians that they need not fear the wrath of God on them for their immorality. Thus he admonishes, "Let no man deceive you." It is apparent here that one may be deceived into believing that some immoral and impure persons do have an inheritance in the kingdom of Christ (see article on FALSE TEACHERS, p. 1508).

5:11 WORKS OF DARKNESS. The one whose allegiance belongs to Christ cannot be neutral or silent with respect to the "works of darkness" (v. 11) and immorality (vv. 3–6). He must be ever ready to expose, rebuke, and speak against wickedness in all forms. To cry out sincerely against unrighteousness is to hate sin (Heb. 1:9), to stand beside God against evil (Ps. 94:16), and to remain faithful to Christ, who also exposed deeds of evil (John 7:7; 15:18–20; cf. Luke 22:28).

5:18 WINE. The fullness of the Holy Spirit is contingent upon the believer's response to the grace given to him to attain and maintain sanctification. That is, a person cannot be "drunk with wine" and at the same time "filled with the Spirit." Paul warns all believers concerning the deeds of the flesh, that those who practice such things "shall not inherit the kingdom of God" (Gal. 5:19–21; cf. Eph. 5:3–7). Furthermore, those who "do such things" (Gal. 5:21) will have no part in the abiding presence and fullness of the Holy Spir-

19 Speaking to yourselves [i]in
psalms and hymns and spiritual songs,
singing and making melody in your
heart to the Lord;
20 [j]Giving thanks always for all
things unto God and the Father [k]in
the name of our Lord Jesus Christ;
21 [l]Submitting yourselves one to
another in the fear of God.

Wives and husbands

5:22–33pp — Col. 3:18–19

22 [m]Wives, submit yourselves unto
your own husbands, [n]as unto the
Lord.
23 For [o]the husband is the head of
the wife, even as [p]Christ is the head
of the church: and he is the saviour of
[q]the body.
24 Therefore as the church is sub-
ject unto Christ, so *let* the wives *be* to
their own husbands [r]in every thing.
25 [s]Husbands, love your wives,
even as Christ also loved the church,
and [t]gave himself for it;
26 That he might sanctify and
cleanse it [u]with the washing of water
by the word,
27 [v]That he might present it to
himself a glorious church, [w]not having
spot, or wrinkle, or any such thing; but
that it should be holy and without
blemish.
28 So ought men to love their wives
as their own bodies. He that loveth his
wife loveth himself.
29 For no man ever yet hated his
own flesh; but nourisheth and cherish-
eth it, even as the Lord the church:
30 For [x]we are members of his
body, of his flesh, and of his bones.
31 [y]For this cause shall a man

5:19 [i]Acts 16:25
5:20 [j]Ps. 34:1 [k]1 Pet. 2:5
5:21 [l]Phil. 2:3
5:22 [m]Gen. 3:16 [n]ch. 6:5
5:23 [o]1 Cor. 11:3 [p]Col. 1:18 [q]ch. 1:23
5:24 [r]Tit. 2:9
5:25 [s]Col. 3:19 [t]Acts 20:28
5:26 [u]John 3:5
5:27 [v]Col. 1:22 [w]Sol. 4:7
5:30 [x]Gen. 2:23
5:31 [y]Mat. 19:5

it. In other words, to lack "the fruit of the Spirit" (Gal. 5:22–23) is to lose the fullness of the Spirit (see Acts 8:21, note).

5:18 FILLED WITH THE SPIRIT. "Be filled" (present passive imperative) carries the meaning in Greek of "repeatedly being filled." The spiritual life of the child of God must experience constant renewal (3:14–19; 4:22–24; Rom. 12:2) by repeatedly being filled with the Holy Spirit. (1) The Christian is to be baptized in the Holy Spirit after conversion (see Acts 1:5; 2:4), yet he is to be filled with the Holy Spirit repeatedly for worship, service, and witness (see Acts 4:31–33, note; 6:3, note). (2) One experiences repeated fillings with the Holy Spirit by maintaining a living faith in Jesus Christ (Gal. 3:5), being filled with God's Word (Col. 3:16), praying, giving thanks, and singing to the Lord (vv. 19–20; 1 Cor. 14:15), serving others (v. 21), and doing what the Holy Spirit desires (4:30; Rom. 8:1–14; Gal. 5:16ff; 1 Thes. 5:19). (3) Several results of being filled with the Holy Spirit are noted here: (a) speaking with joy to God in psalms, hymns, and spiritual songs (v. 19), (b) giving thanks (v. 20), and (c) submitting to one another (v. 21).

5:19 SINGING . . . TO THE LORD. All our spiritual songs, both in the church and in private, should be first and foremost directed unto God as a prayer of praise or petition (Ps. 40:3; 77:6). (1) Singing praises or any spiritual song can be a manifestation of the Holy Spirit (vv. 18–20; 1 Cor. 14:15). (2) Singing spiritual songs is a means of edification, teaching, giving thanks, and praying (Col. 3:16). (3) Christian singing is an expression of joy. (4) The goal of singing hymns or spiritual songs is not for entertainment or individual aggrandizement, but for worship and praise of God (Rom. 15:9–11; Rev. 5:9–10).

5:21 SUBMITTING YOURSELVES ONE TO ANOTHER. Submission to one another in Christ is a general spiritual principle. This principle is to be applied first and foremost to the Christian family. Submission, humility, gentleness, patience, and forbearance must be characteristic of each member. The wife must submit (i.e., yield in love) to the husband's responsibility of leadership of the family (see next note). The husband must submit to the needs of the wife in an attitude of love and self-giving (see v. 23, note). Children must submit to the authority of the parents in obedience (see 6:1, note). And parents must submit to the needs of their children and bring them up in the godly instruction of the Lord (see 6:4, note).

5:22 WIVES, SUBMIT. The wife is given the God-appointed task of helping and submitting to her husband (vv. 22–24). Her duty to her husband includes love (Tit. 2:4), respect (v. 33; 1 Pet. 3:1–2), assistance (Gen. 2:18), purity (Tit. 2:5; 1 Pet. 3:2), submissiveness (v. 22; 1 Pet. 3:5), development of a gentle and quiet spirit (1 Pet. 3:4), and being a good mother (Tit. 2:4) and homemaker (1 Tim. 2:15; 5:14; Tit. 2:5). A wife's submissiveness to her husband is seen by God as an actual part of her obedience to Jesus, "as unto the Lord" (see also Gal. 3:28, note; 1 Tim. 2:13,15, notes; Tit. 2:4, note).

5:23 HUSBAND . . . HEAD. God has established the family as the most basic unit in society. Every family must have a leader. Hence, God has assigned to the husband the responsibility of being the head of his wife and family (vv. 23–33; 6:4). His headship must be exercised in love, gentleness, and consideration for his wife and family (vv. 25–30; 6:4). The husband's God-given responsibility as "head of the wife" includes: (1) leadership and provision for the family's spiritual and domestic needs (vv. 23–24; Gen. 3:16–19; 1 Tim. 5:8); (2) love, protection, security, and interest in her welfare in the same manner as Christ loves the church (vv. 25–33); (3) honor, understanding, appreciation, and thoughtfulness (Col. 3:19; 1 Pet. 3:7); (4) absolute faithfulness and fidelity to the marriage relationship (v. 31; Mt. 5:27–28).

leave his father and mother, and shall
be joined unto his wife, and they [z]two
shall be one flesh.
32 This is a great mystery: but I
speak concerning Christ and the
church.
33 Nevertheless [a]let every one of
you in particular so love his wife even
as himself; and the wife *see* that she
[b]reverence *her* husband.

Children and parents

6:1–4pp — Col. 3:20–21

6 CHILDREN, [c]OBEY your parents
in the Lord: for this is right.
2 [d]Honour thy father and mother;
which is the first commandment with
promise;
3 That it may be well with thee, and
thou mayest live long on the earth.
4 And, [e]ye fathers, provoke not
your children to wrath: but [f]bring
them up in the nurture and admonition
of the Lord.

Workers and masters

6:5–9pp — Col. 3:22–4:1

5 [g]Servants, be obedient to them
that are *your* masters according to the
flesh, [h]with fear and trembling, [i]in
singleness of your heart, as unto
Christ;
6 [j]Not with eyeservice, as men-
pleasers; but as the servants of Christ,
doing the will of God from the heart;
7 With good will doing service, as to
the Lord, and not to men:
8 [k]Knowing that whatsoever good
thing any man doeth, the same shall he
receive of the Lord, [l]whether *he be*
bond or free.
9 And, ye [m]masters, do the same
things unto them, [x]forbearing threat-
ening: knowing that [y]your Master
also is in heaven; [n]neither is there re-
spect of persons with him.

The whole armour of God

10 Finally, my brethren, be strong
in the Lord, and in the power of his
might.
11 [o]Put on the whole armour of
God, that ye may be able to stand
against the wiles of the devil.
12 For we wrestle not against

5:31 [z]1 Cor. 6:16
5:33 [a]Col. 3:19 [b]1 Pet. 3:6
6:1 [c]Col. 3:20
6:2 [d]Ex. 20:12
6:4 [e]Col. 3:21 [f]Gen. 18:19
6:5 [g]1 Tim. 6:1 [h]2 Cor. 7:15 Phil. 2:12 [i]1 Chr. 29:17 Col. 3:22
6:6 [j]Col. 3:22
6:8 [k]Rom. 2:6 Col. 3:24 [l]Gal. 3:28
6:9 [m]Col. 4:1 [n]Rom. 2:11
6:11 [o]2 Cor. 6:7

[x] Or, *moderating* [y] Some read, *both your and their Master*

6:1 CHILDREN, OBEY. Normally children of believers must remain under parental guidance until they become part of another family unit through marriage. (1) Small children must be taught to obey and honor their parents by being brought up in the discipline and instruction of the Lord (see next note; Prov. 13:24, note; 22:6, note). (2) Older children, even after marriage, must show respect for the counsel of their parents (v. 2) and honor them in old age through care and financial support if needed (Mat. 15:1–6). (3) Children who honor their parents will be blessed by God, here on earth and in eternity (v. 3).

6:4 FATHERS . . . YOUR CHILDREN. For an extended discussion of the parents' role in bringing up their children, see article on PARENTS AND CHILDREN, p. 1880.

6:11 AGAINST THE WILES OF THE DEVIL. The Christian is engaged in a spiritual conflict with evil. This spiritual conflict is described as a warfare of faith (2 Cor. 10:4; 1 Tim. 1:18–19; 6:12) that continues until he enters the life to come (2 Tim. 4:7–8; see Gal. 5:17, note). (1) The believer's victory has been secured by Christ Himself through His death on the cross. Jesus waged a triumphant battle against Satan, disarmed the evil powers and authorities of wickedness (Col. 2:15; cf. Mat. 12:29; Luke 10:18; John 12:31), led captive a host of captives (4:8), and redeemed the believer from Satan's dominion (1:7; Acts 26:18; Rom. 3:24; Col. 1:13–14).

(2) At the present time Christians are involved in a spiritual warfare that they wage by the power of the Holy Spirit (Rom. 8:13): (a) against the corrupt desires within themselves (1 Pet. 2:11; see Gal. 5:17, note), (b) against the ungodly pleasures of the world and temptations of every sort (Mat. 13:22; Gal. 1:4; Jas. 1:14–15; 1 John 2:16), and (c) against Satan and his forces (see next note). Believers are called upon to separate themselves from the present world system (see article on SPIRITUAL SEPARATION FOR BELIEVERS, p. 1814), hating its evil (cf. Heb. 1:9; see article on THE CHRISTIAN'S RELATIONSHIP TO THE WORLD, p. 2004), overcoming and dying to its temptations (Gal. 6:14; 1 John 5:4), and condemning openly its sin (cf. John 7:7).

(3) Christian soldiers must wage war against all evil, not in their own power (2 Cor. 10:3), but with spiritual weapons (vv. 10–18; 2 Cor. 10:4–5).

(4) In their warfare of faith Christians are called upon to endure hardships as good soldiers of Christ (2 Tim. 2:3), suffer for the gospel (Mat. 5:10–12; Rom. 8:17; 2 Cor. 11:23; 2 Tim. 1:8), fight the good fight of faith (1 Tim. 6:12; 2 Tim. 4:7), wage war (2 Cor. 10:3), persevere (v. 18), conquer (Rom. 8:37), be victorious (1 Cor. 15:57), triumph (2 Cor. 2:14), defend the gospel (Phil. 1:16), strive for the faith (Phil. 1:27), not be alarmed by opponents (Phil. 1:28), put on the full armor of God, stand firm (v. 14), destroy Satan's strongholds (2 Cor. 10:4), take captive every thought (2 Cor. 10:5), become mighty in war (Heb. 11:34), and contend for the faith (Jude 3).

6:12 AGAINST PRINCIPALITIES . . . POWERS . . . RULERS. The Christian faces a spiritual

[z]flesh and blood, but against [p]principalities, against powers, against [q]the rulers of the darkness of this world, against [a]spiritual wickedness in [b]high *places.*

13 [r]Wherefore take unto you the whole armour of God, that ye may be able to withstand [s]in the evil day, and [c]having done all, to stand.

14 Stand therefore, [t]having your loins girt about with truth, and [u]having on the breastplate of righteousness;

15 [v]And your feet shod with the preparation of the gospel of peace;

16 Above all, taking [w]the shield of faith, wherewith ye shall be able to quench all the fiery darts of the wicked.

17 And [x]take the helmet of salvation, and [y]the sword of the Spirit, which is the word of God:

Pray always

18 [z]Praying always with all prayer and supplication in the Spirit, and [a]watching thereunto with all perseverance and [b]supplication for all saints;

6:12 [p]Rom. 8:38 [q]Luke 22:53
6:13 [r]2 Cor. 10:4 [s]ch. 5:16
6:14 [t]Is. 11:5 1 Pet. 1:13 [u]Is. 59:17
6:15 [v]Is. 52:7
6:16 [w]1 John 5:4
6:17 [x]1 Thes. 5:8 [y]Heb. 4:12
6:18 [z]Luke 18:1 [a]Mat. 26:41 [b]Phil. 1:4
6:19 [c]Acts 4:29 [d]2 Cor. 3:12
6:20 [e]2 Cor. 5:20 [f]Phil. 1:20
6:21 [g]Acts 20:4
6:22 [h]Col. 4:8
6:23 [i]1 Pet. 5:14

19 [c]And for me, that utterance may be given unto me, that I may open my mouth [d]boldly, to make known the mystery of the gospel, 1 Thes. 1:5

20 For which [e]I am an ambassador [d]in bonds: that [e]therein [f]I may speak boldly, as I ought to speak.

Concluding benediction

21 But that ye also may know my affairs, *and* how I do, [g]Tychicus, a beloved brother and faithful minister in the Lord, shall make known to you all things:

22 [h]Whom I have sent unto you for the same purpose, that ye might know our affairs, and *that* he might comfort your hearts.

23 [i]Peace *be* to the brethren, and love with faith, from God the Father and the Lord Jesus Christ.

24 Grace *be* with all them that love our Lord Jesus Christ [f]in sincerity. Amen.

[z] Gk. *blood and flesh* [a] Or, *wicked spirits* [b] Or, *heavenly* [c] Or, *having overcome all* [d] Or, *in a chain* [e] Or, *thereof* [f] Or, *with incorruption*

---

conflict with Satan and a host of evil spirits (see Mat. 4:10, note on Satan; see article on POWER OVER SATAN AND DEMONS, p. 1486). (1) These powers of darkness are the spiritual rulers of the world (John 12:31; 14:30; 16:11; 2 Cor. 4:4; 1 Jn. 5:19) who energize the ungodly (2:2), oppose God's will (Gen. 3:1–7; Dan. 10:12–13; Mat. 13:38–39), and frequently attack the believers of this age (1 Pet. 5:8). (2) They constitute a vast multitude (Rev. 12:4,7) and are organized into a highly systematized empire of evil with rank and order (2:2; John 14:30).

6:17 THE SWORD OF THE SPIRIT. The "sword of the Spirit, which is the word of God," is the believer's offensive weapon to be used in his war against the power of evil. For this reason Satan will make every effort to undermine or destroy the Christian's confidence in that Word. The church must defend the inspired Scriptures against allegations that it is not God's Word in everything it teaches. To abandon the position and attitude of Christ and the apostles toward God's inspired Word is to destroy its power to convict or correct, to redeem, to heal, to drive out demons, and to overcome all evil. To deny its absolute trustworthiness in all it teaches is to deliver ourselves into the hand of Satan (see 2 Pet. 1:21, note; cf. Mat. 4:1–11; see article on THE INSPIRATION AND AUTHORITY OF SCRIPTURE, p. 1924).

6:18 PRAYING ... IN THE SPIRIT. The Christian's warfare against Satan's spiritual forces calls for an intensity in prayer, i.e., praying "in the Spirit," "always," "with all prayer and supplication," "for all saints," "with all perseverance." Prayer is not to be seen just as another weapon, but as part of the actual conflict itself, where the victory is won for ourselves and others by co-laboring with God Himself. To fail to pray diligently, with all kinds of prayer in all situations, is to surrender to the enemy and cease to fight (Luke 18:1; Rom. 12:12; Phil. 4:6; Col. 4:2; 1 Thes. 5:17).

PHILIPPIANS

Outline

Introduction (1:1–11)
- A. Christian Greetings (1:1–2)
- B. Thanksgiving and Prayer for the Philippians (1:3–11)

I. Paul's Present Circumstances (1:12–26)
- A. The Gospel Has Advanced Because of His Imprisonment (1:12–14)
- B. In Every Way Christ is Proclaimed (1:15–18)
- C. His Readiness for Life or Death (1:19–26)

II. Matters of Concern to the Church (1:27—4:9)
- A. Paul's Exhortation to the Philippians (1:27—2:18)
  - 1. To Steadfastness (1:27–30)
  - 2. To Unity (2:1–2)
  - 3. To Humility and Servanthood (2:3–11)
  - 4. To Obedience and Irreproachable Conduct (2:12–18)
- B. Paul's Messengers to the Church (2:19–30)
  - 1. Timothy (2:19–24)
  - 2. Epaphroditus (2:25–30)
- C. Paul's Warning Concerning Erroneous Teaching (3:1–21)
  - 1. The False Circumcision Versus the True (3:1–16)
  - 2. The Earthly-Minded Versus the Spiritual (3:17–21)
- D. Paul's Concluding Counsel (4:1–9)
  - 1. Stability and Harmony (4:1–3)
  - 2. Joy and Forbearance (4:4–5)
  - 3. Freedom from Anxiety (4:6–7)
  - 4. Control of the Mind and the Will (4:8–9)

Conclusion (4:10–23)
- A. Grateful Acknowledgment of Gifts Received (4:10–20)
- B. Final Greetings and Benediction (4:21–23)

Author: Paul

Theme: Joy in Living for Christ

Date of Writing: C. A.D. 62/63

Background

The city of Philippi in eastern Macedonia, ten miles inland from the Aegean Sea, was named after King Philip II of Macedon, father of Alexander the Great. In Paul's day, it was an honored Roman city and military post.

The church in Philippi was founded by Paul and his team of co-laborers (Silas, Timothy, Luke) on his second missionary journey in response to a God-given vision at Troas (Acts 16:9–40). A strong bond of friendship developed between the apostle and the Philippian church. Several times the church sent Paul financial help (2 Cor. 11:9; Phil. 4:15–16) and contributed generously to his offering for the poor saints in Jerusalem (cf. 2 Cor. 8—9). It appears that Paul visited the church twice on his third missionary journey (Acts 20:1,3,6).

Purpose

From prison (1:7,13–14), most likely in Rome (Acts 28:16–31), Paul wrote this letter to the Philippian believers to thank them for their recent generous gift carried to him by Epaphroditus (4:14–19) and to update them on his present circumstances. In addition, he wrote to assure the congregation of the triumph of God's purpose in his imprisonment (1:12–30), to reassure the church that their messenger (Epaphroditus) had fulfilled his charge faithfully and was not returning to them prematurely (2:25–30), and to encourage them to press on to know the Lord in unity, humility, fellowship, and peace.

Survey

Unlike many of Paul's letters, Philippians was not written primarily because of church problems or conflicts. Its basic tone is one of cordial affection and appreciation for the congregation. From salutation (1:1) to benediction (4:23), the letter focuses on Christ Jesus as the purpose for living and the believer's hope for eternal life. Within this epistle, Paul does address three minor problems at Philippi: (1) their *discouragement* over his prolonged imprisonment (1:12–26); (2) small seeds of *disunity* between two women in the church (4:2; cf. 2:2–4); and (3) the ever-present threat in the church of *disloyalty* because of Judaizers and the earthly-minded (ch. 3). In connection with these three potential problems, we have Paul's richest teaching about (1) joy in the midst of all life's circumstances (e.g., 1:4,12; 2:17–18; 4:4,11–13), (2) Christian humility and service (2:1–18), and (3) the surpassing value of knowing Christ (ch. 3).

Special Features

Five major features or emphases characterize this epistle. (1) It is highly personal and affectionate, reflecting Paul's close relationship to the Philippian believers. (2) It is highly Christocentric, reflecting Paul's close relationship with Christ (e.g. 1:21; 3:7–14). (3) It contains one of the most profound Christological statements in the Bible (2:5–11). (4) It is preeminently the N.T. "epistle of joy." (5) It presents an especially vigorous standard of the Christian life, including living in humility and as a servant (2:1–8), pressing earnestly toward the goal (3:13–14), rejoicing in the Lord always (4:4), experiencing freedom from anxiety (4:6), being content in all circumstances (4:11), and doing all things through the enabling grace of Christ (4:13).

Reading Philippians

In order to read the entire New Testament in one year, the book of Philippians should be read in 5 days, according to the following schedule:
☐ 1 ☐ 2:1–18 ☐ 2:19—3:11 ☐ 3:12—4:3 ☐ 4:4–23

NOTES

1 PAUL AND Timotheus, the servants of Jesus Christ, to all the saints [a]in Christ Jesus which are at Philippi, with the bishops and deacons:

2 [b]Grace *be* unto you, and peace, from God our Father, and *from* the Lord Jesus Christ.

Prayer of thankfulness

3 [c]I thank my God upon every [a]remembrance of you,

4 Always in every prayer of mine for you all making request with joy,

5 [d]For your fellowship in the gospel from the first day until now;

6 Being confident of this very thing, that he which hath begun [e]a good work in you [b]will perform *it* until the day of Jesus Christ:

7 Even as it is meet for me to think this of you all, because [c]I have you in my heart; inasmuch as both in my bonds, and in the defence and confirmation of the gospel, ye all are [d]partakers of my grace.

8 For [f]God is my record, how greatly I long after you all in the bowels of Jesus Christ.

9 And this I pray, that your love may abound yet more and more in knowledge and *in* all [e]judgment;

10 That [g]ye may [f]approve things that [g]are excellent; [h]that ye may be sincere and without offence [i]till the day of Christ;

11 Being filled with the fruits of righteousness, [j]which are by Jesus Christ, [k]unto the glory and praise of God.

Paul's suffering advances the gospel

12 But I would ye should understand, brethren, that the things *which happened* unto me have fallen out rather unto the furtherance of the gospel;

13 So that my bonds [h]in Christ are manifest [l]in all [i]the palace, and [j]in all other *places;*

14 And many of the brethren in the Lord, waxing confident by my bonds, are much more bold to speak the word without fear.

1:1 [a] 1 Cor. 1:2
1:2 [b] 1 Pet. 1:2
1:3 [c] 1 Cor. 1:4
1:5 [d] Rom. 12:13
1:6 [e] John 6:29
1:8 [f] Rom. 1:9 Gal. 1:20
1:10 [g] Rom. 12:2 [h] Acts 24:16 [i] 1 Cor. 1:8
1:11 [j] Eph. 2:10 Col. 1:6 [k] John 15:8
1:13 [l] ch. 4:22

[a] Or, *mention* [b] Or, *will finish* it [c] Or, *ye have me in your heart* [d] Or, *partakers with me of grace* [e] Or, *sense* [f] Or, *try* [g] Or, *differ* [h] Or, *for Christ* [i] Or, *Caesar's court* [j] Or, *to all others*

1:4 JOY. Joy is an integral part of our salvation in Christ. It is an inner peace and delight in God the Father, Son, and Holy Spirit, and in the blessing that flows from our relationship with them (cf. 2 Cor. 13:14). Scriptural teaching about joy includes the following: (1) Joy is associated with the salvation God provides in Christ (1 Pet. 1:3–6; cf. Ps. 5:11; 9:2; Is. 35:10) and with God's Word (Jer. 15:16; cf. Ps. 119:14).

(2) Joy flows from God as a gift of the Spirit (Ps. 16:11; Rom. 15:13; Gal. 5:22). Hence, it does not come to us automatically, but is experienced only as we maintain an abiding relationship with Christ (John 15:1–11). Our joy becomes greater when the Holy Spirit mediates a deep sense of the presence and nearness of God in our lives (cf. John 14:15–21; see 16:14, note). Jesus taught that the fullness of joy is inseparably connected to our abiding in His Word, loving others, obeying His commandments (John 15:7,10–11), and being separated from the world (John 17:13–17).

(3) Joy as a delight in God's nearness and His redemptive gifts cannot be destroyed by pain, suffering, weakness, or difficult circumstances (Mat. 5:12; Acts 16:23–25; 2 Cor. 12:9).

1:6 BEING CONFIDENT OF THIS. Paul's confidence in the Philippians is based not only on God's good work in them, but also on their zeal and sacrifice for the faith (vv. 5,7; 4:15–18). God's faithfulness always avails for faithful believers, but His faithfulness can do nothing for those who resist His grace (see 2:13, note; 2 Tim. 2:13, note).

1:9 LOVE MAY ABOUND ... IN KNOWLEDGE. Love, if it is to be Christian, must be based on Biblical revelation and knowledge. (1) In the N.T. "knowledge" (Gk. *epignōsis*) means a spiritual knowing in the heart, not merely head knowledge. It refers to God's revelation as experientially known and involves a personal relationship with God rather than intellectually knowing mere facts about God (vv. 10–11; Eph. 3:16–19; see article on BIBLE TRAINING FOR CHRISTIANS, p. 1920).

(2) Thus, to know God's Word (cf. Rom. 7:1) or to know God's will (Acts 22:14; Rom. 2:18) implies a knowledge that expresses itself in fellowship, obedience, life, and nearness to God (John 17:3; 1 John 4:8). Knowing theological truth (1 Tim. 6:3; Tit. 1:9; see Gal. 1:9, note) has as its objective love to God and freedom from sin (Rom. 6:6; see article on BIBLE TRAINING FOR CHRISTIANS, p. 1920). "*In* all judgment" means the believer through love and knowledge discerns what is good and evil.

1:10 SINCERE AND WITHOUT OFFENCE. "Sincere" means "without any mixture of evil," "completely pure"; "without offence" means "blameless," "not causing offense" to God or another person. Such holiness must be the ultimate aim of all believers in the light of the return of Christ. Only by an abounding love poured out within our hearts by the Holy Spirit (Rom. 5:5; cf. Tit. 3:5–6) and a full commitment to the Word of God will we be "sincere and without offence till the day of Christ."

15 Some indeed preach Christ even of envy and [m]strife; and some also of good will:

16 The one preach Christ of contention, not sincerely, supposing to add affliction to my bonds:

17 But the other of love, knowing that I am set for the defence of the gospel.

18 What then? notwithstanding, every way, whether in pretence, or in truth, Christ is preached; and I therein do rejoice, yea, and will rejoice.

19 For I know that this shall turn to my salvation [n]through your prayer, and the supply of the Spirit of Jesus Christ,

20 According to my [o]earnest expectation and *my* hope, that [p]in nothing I shall be ashamed, but *that* [q]with all boldness, as always, *so* now also Christ shall be magnified in my body, whether *it be* by life, or by death.

Christ's glory through life or death

21 For to me to live *is* Christ, and to die *is* gain.

22 But if I live in the flesh, this *is* the fruit of my labour: yet what I shall choose I wot not.

23 For [r]I am in a strait betwixt two, having a desire to [s]depart, and to be with Christ; which is far better:

24 Nevertheless to abide in the flesh *is* more needful for you.

25 And [t]having this confidence, I know that I shall abide and continue with you all for your furtherance and joy of faith;

26 That [u]your rejoicing may be more abundant in Jesus Christ for me by my coming to you again.

The privilege of suffering

27 Only [v]let your conversation be as it becometh the gospel of Christ: that whether I come and see you, or else be absent, I may hear of your affairs, that ye stand fast in one spirit, [w]with one mind striving together for the faith of the gospel;

28 And in nothing terrified by your adversaries: [x]which is to them an evident token of perdition, [y]but to you of salvation, and that of God.

29 For unto you [z]it is given in the behalf of Christ, [a]not only to believe on him, but also to suffer for his sake;

30 [b]Having the same conflict [c]which ye saw in me, and now hear *to be* in me.

Imitating Christ's humility

2 IF *THERE be* therefore any consolation in Christ, if any comfort of love, [d]if any fellowship of the Spirit, if any [e]bowels and mercies,

2 [f]Fulfil ye my joy, [g]that ye be likeminded, having the same love, *being* of one accord, of one mind.

3 [h]*Let* nothing *be done* through

1:15 [m]ch. 2:3
1:19 [n]2 Cor. 1:11
1:20 [o]Rom. 8:19 [p]Rom. 5:5 [q]Eph. 6:19
1:23 [r]2 Cor. 5:8 [s]2 Tim. 4:6
1:25 [t]ch. 2:24
1:26 [u]2 Cor. 1:14
1:27 [v]Eph. 4:1 1 Thes. 2:12 [w]1 Cor. 1:10 Acts 2:36
1:28 [x]2 Thes. 1:5 [y]Rom. 8:17
1:29 [z]Rom. 5:3 [a]Eph. 2:8
1:30 [b]Col. 2:1 [c]Acts 16:19 1 Thes. 2:2
2:1 [d]2 Cor. 13:14 [e]Col. 3:12
2:2 [f]John 3:29 [g]Rom. 12:16 1 Cor. 1:10
2:3 [h]Gal. 5:26 Jas. 3:14

1:17 THE DEFENCE OF THE GOSPEL. God gave Paul the important task of defending the content of the gospel as defined in Scripture. All believers are called upon to defend Biblical truth and to resist those who would distort the faith (v. 27; see Gal. 1:9, note; Jude 3, note; see article on THE MINISTRY GIFTS OF THE CHURCH, p. 1852). Paul's words seem foreign to those ministers today who feel no need to "earnestly contend for the faith which was once delivered unto the saints" (Jude 3).

1:19 THE SPIRIT OF JESUS CHRIST. The Holy Spirit who dwells in the believer is called the "Spirit of Jesus Christ" (cf. Acts 16:7; Rom. 8:9; Gal. 4:6) because it is Christ who imparts the Spirit to the believer at conversion (see article on THE REGENERATION OF THE DISCIPLES, p. 1638) and subsequently baptizes the believer in the Holy Spirit (see Acts 1:8, note; see article on BAPTISM IN THE HOLY SPIRIT, p. 1652). This Spirit is the same Spirit who anointed Jesus to bring redemption to the world (see Luke 4:18; see article on JESUS AND THE HOLY SPIRIT, p. 1550).

1:21 TO DIE *IS* GAIN. True believers, living in the center of God's will, do not need to fear death. They know God has a purpose for their living and that death, when it comes, is simply the end of their earthly mission and the beginning of a greater life with Christ (vv. 20–25; see Rom. 8:28, note; see article on DEATH, p. 782).

1:27 STAND FAST IN ONE SPIRIT. The true essence of the unity of the Spirit consists of living in a worthy manner (cf. Eph. 4:1–3), standing firm in one spirit and purpose (cf. Eph. 4:3), striving side by side like warriors for the advancement and defense of the gospel according to apostolic revelation (v. 17; cf. Eph. 4:13–15), and defending gospel truth together against those who are "enemies of the cross of Christ" (3:18, note).

2:3 IN LOWLINESS OF MIND. Due to fallen man's innate self-centeredness and preference for self-promotion, the world does not highly regard humility and lowliness of mind. Yet with the Bible's God-centered view of man and salvation, it places the utmost importance on humility. (1) Humility involves being conscious of our weaknesses and being disposed to ascribe credit to God and others for what we accomplish (John 3:27; 5:19; 14:10; Jas. 4:6).

(2) We must be humble because we are lowly

strife or vainglory; but [i]in lowliness of mind let each esteem other better than themselves.

4 [j]Look not every man on his own things, but every man also on the things of others.

5 [k]Let this mind be in you, which was also in Christ Jesus:

6 Who, [l]being in the form of God, thought it not robbery to be equal with God:

7 [m]But made himself of no reputation, and took upon him the form [n]of a servant, and [o]was made in the [k]likeness of men:

8 And being found in fashion as a man, he humbled himself, and [p]became obedient unto death, even the death of the cross.

9 Wherefore God also [q]hath highly exalted him, and [r]given him a name which is above every name:

10 [s]That at the name of Jesus every knee should bow, of *things* in heaven, and *things* in earth, and *things* under the earth;

11 And [t]*that* every tongue should confess that Jesus Christ *is* Lord, to the glory of God the Father.

Obligations of Christians

12 Wherefore, my beloved, [u]as ye have always obeyed, not as in my presence only, but now much more in my

2:3 [i]Rom. 12:10 1 Pet. 5:5 **2:4** [j]1 Cor. 13:5 **2:5** [k]Mat. 11:29 1 Pet. 2:21 **2:6** [l]2 Cor. 4:4 Col. 1:15 **2:7** [m]Ps. 22:6 Is. 53:3 Dan. 9:26 Mark 9:12 [n]Is. 42:1 Ezek. 34:23 Zech. 3:8 Mat. 20:28 Luke 22:27 [o]John 1:14 Rom. 1:3 Gal. 4:4 **2:8** [p]Mat. 26:39 Heb. 5:8 **2:9** [q]Acts 2:33 Heb. 2:9 [r]Heb. 1:4 **2:10** [s]Is. 45:23; Mat. 28:18 **2:11** [t]John 13:13; Acts 2:36 **2:12** [u]ch. 1:5

[k] Or, *habit*

creatures (Gen. 18:27) who are sinful apart from Christ (Luke 18:9–14) and can boast in nothing (Rom. 7:18; Gal. 6:3) except in the Lord (2 Cor. 10:17). Hence, we are dependent on God for our worth and fruitfulness and can accomplish nothing of lasting good without the help of God and others (Ps. 8:4–5; John 15:1–16).

(3) God's presence goes with those who walk humbly (Is. 57:15; Mic. 6:8). A greater grace is given to the humble, but God opposes the proud (Jas. 4:6; 1 Pet. 5:5). The most zealous of his children serve "the Lord with all humility" (Acts 20:19).

(4) As believers we must live in humility toward others, esteeming them as more important than ourselves (cf. Rom. 12:3).

(5) The opposite of humility is pride, an exaggerated feeling of self-importance and self-esteem in a person who believes in his own merit, superiority, and accomplishments. The inevitable tendency of human nature and the world is toward pride, not humility (1 John 2:16; cf. Is. 14:13–14; Ezek. 28:17; 1 Tim. 6:17).

2:5 LET THIS MIND BE IN YOU. Paul emphasizes how the Lord Jesus left incomparable glory in heaven and took upon Himself the humiliation of a servant, becoming obedient unto death to benefit others (vv. 5–8). Christ's humility of spirit and mind must be found in His followers. They too must live their lives in sacrifice, caring, doing good to others, and doing nothing out of selfishness.

2:6 BEING IN THE FORM OF GOD. Jesus Christ has always been God by nature, equal with the Father before, during, and after His time on earth (see John 1:1; 8:58; 17:24; Col. 1:15,17; see Mark 1:11, note; John 20:28, note). Christ, however, did not cling to his divine rights, but He let go of His privileges and glory in heaven in order that we on earth might be saved.

2:7 MADE HIMSELF OF NO REPUTATION. The Greek for this phrase literally says He "emptied himself," i.e., laid aside His heavenly glory (John 17:4), position (John 5:30; Heb. 5:8), riches (2 Cor. 8:9), rights (Luke 22:27; Mat. 20:28), and the use of His divine attributes (John 5:19; 8:28; 14:10). This "emptying himself" meant not only a voluntary restraint on His divine capacities and privileges, but also an acceptance of suffering, misunderstanding, ill-treatment, hatred, and finally death on the cross.

2:7 FORM OF A SERVANT ... THE LIKENESS OF MEN. For passages in the Bible that deal with Christ's taking the form of a servant, see Mark 13:32; Luke 2:40–52; Rom. 8:3; 2 Cor. 8:9; Heb. 2:7,14. Although He remained fully divine, Christ took on a human nature with its temptations, humiliations, and weaknesses, yet without sin (vv. 7–8; Heb. 4:15).

2:12 WORK OUT YOUR OWN SALVATION. As believers saved by grace, we must work out our salvation unto the end. If we fail to do this, we will lose the salvation bestowed on us. (1) We do not work out our salvation by mere human effort, but by means of the grace of God and the power of the Spirit given to us (see article on FAITH AND GRACE, p. 1738).

(2) In order to work out our salvation we must resist sin and follow the desires of the Holy Spirit within us. This involves a continual, sustained effort to use every God-appointed means for defeating evil and manifesting Christ's life. Thus, working out our salvation focuses on the importance of sanctification (see Gal. 5:17, note; see article on THE WORKS OF THE FLESH AND THE FRUIT OF THE SPIRIT, p. 1840).

(3) We work out our salvation by ever drawing near to Christ (see Heb. 7:25, note) and receiving His power to will and to work for God's good pleasure (see v. 13, note). Thus we are "labourers together with God" (1 Cor. 3:9) in bringing our salvation to completion in heaven.

(4) Working out our salvation is so vital that it must be performed "with fear and trembling" (see next note).

2:12 FEAR AND TREMBLING. In the salvation accomplished through Christ, Paul finds room for "fear and trembling." All children of God should possess a holy fear that trembles at God's Word

absence, work out your own salvation
with [v]fear and trembling.
13 For [w]it is God which worketh in
you both to will and to do of *his* good
pleasure.
14 Do all things [x]without murmur-
ings and [y]disputings:
15 That ye may be blameless and
[1]harmless, [z]the sons of God, without
rebuke, [a]in the midst of [b]a crooked
and perverse nation, among whom
[c]ye[m] shine as lights in the world;
16 Holding forth the word of life;
that [d]I may rejoice in the day of
Christ, that [e]I have not run in vain,
neither laboured in vain.
17 Yea, and if [f]I be [n]offered upon
the sacrifice [g]and service of your
faith, [h]I joy, and rejoice with you all.
18 For the same cause also do ye
joy, and rejoice with me.

Timothy's godly character

19 [o]But I trust in the Lord Jesus to
send [i]Timotheus shortly unto you,
that I also may be of good comfort,
when I know your state.

2:12 [v]Eph. 6:5 2:13 [w]2 Cor. 3:5 2:14 [x]1 Pet. 4:9 [y]Rom. 14:1 2:15 [z]Mat. 5:45 Eph. 5:1 [a]1 Pet. 2:12 [b]Deut. 32:5 [c]Eph. 5:8 2:16 [d]2 Cor. 1:14 1 Thes. 2:19 [e]Gal. 2:2 2:17 [f]2 Tim. 4:6 [g]Rom. 15:16 [h]2 Cor. 7:4 Col. 1:24 2:19 [i]Rom. 16:21 2:20 [j]Ps. 55:13 2:21 [k]1 Cor. 10:24 & 13:5 2 Tim. 4:10 2:22 [l]1 Cor. 4:17 1 Tim. 1:2 2:24 [m]ch. 1:25 2:25 [n]ch. 4:18 [o]Philem. 2

20 For I have no man [j]likemind-
ed,[p] who will naturally care for your
state.
21 For all [k]seek their own, not the
things which are Jesus Christ's.
22 But ye know the proof of him,
[l]that, as a son with the father, he hath
served with me in the gospel.
23 Him therefore I hope to send pre-
sently, so soon as I shall see how it will
go with me.
24 But [m]I trust in the Lord that I
also myself shall come shortly.

Epaphroditus's dedicated service

25 Yet I supposed it necessary to
send to you [n]Epaphroditus, my broth-
er, and companion in labour, and [o]fel-
lowsoldier, [p]but your messenger, and
[q]he that ministered to my wants.
26 [r]For he longed after you all,
and was full of heaviness, because that
ye had heard that he had been sick.

[p]2 Cor. 8:23 [q]2 Cor. 11:9 2:26 [r]ch. 1:8

[1] Or, *sincere* [m] Or, *shine ye* [n] Gk. *poured forth* [o] Or, *Moreover* [p] Or, *so dear unto me*

(Is. 66:2) and causes them to turn away from all evil (Prov. 3:7; 8:13). The fear (Gk. *phobos*) of the Lord is not, as is often defined, merely "reverential trust," but includes an awe of God's power, holiness, and righteous retribution, and a dread of sinning against Him and of the consequences that may follow (cf. Ex. 3:6; Ps. 119:120; Luke 12:4–5). It is not a destructive fear, but a controlling and redeeming fear that leads to moral purity, life, God's nearness and blessing, and salvation (cf. Ps. 5:7; 85:9; Prov. 14:27; 16:6; see article on THE FEAR OF THE LORD, p. 282).

2:13 GOD WHICH WORKETH IN YOU. God's grace is at work in His children to produce in them both the desire and power to do His will (see article on FAITH AND GRACE, p. 1738). However, God's work in us is not one of compulsion or irresistible grace. The work of grace within us (1:6; 1 Thes. 5:24; 2 Tim. 4:18; Tit. 3:5–7) is always dependent on our faithfulness and cooperation (vv. 12,14–16).

2:15 CROOKED AND PERVERSE NATION. Jesus and the apostles emphasized that the world in which we live is a "faithless and perverse generation" (Mat. 17:17; cf. 12:39; Acts 2:40). The people of the world hold wrong views, have corrupt values, follow an immoral way of life, and reject the norms and standards of the Word of God. Children of God must separate themselves from the world and be blameless, innocent, and above reproach in order to proclaim the glorious redemption of Christ to the lost world (cf. 1 John 2:15).

2:17 IF I BE OFFERED UPON THE SACRIFICE. Paul's love and concern for the Philippians was such that he was willing to give his life for them as if it were an offering to God. (1) Paul would not regret but rather rejoice in being the victim of sacrifice, if only it would deepen their faith in and love for Christ and make their life what it should be (cf. 2 Tim. 4:6).

(2) If Paul had such sacrificial love for his spiritual children in the faith, what sacrifice and suffering should we be willing to undergo for the faith of our own children? If, in order to make our children as complete as possible in the Lord, it became necessary for us to pour out our lives, strength, and even blood, as an offering to the Lord, then we ought to be prepared to make such a sacrifice (see article on PARENTS AND CHILDREN, p. 1880, giving fifteen steps parents should take to lead their children to a life of godliness in Christ).

2:19 TIMOTHEUS. Timothy was a good example of what a minister and missionary of God should be. He was an eager and obedient student of God's Word (2 Tim. 3:15), a persevering and worthy servant of Christ (1 Thes. 3:2), a man of good reputation (Acts 16:2), beloved and faithful (1 Cor. 4:17), genuinely concerned for others (v. 20), dependable (2 Tim. 4:9,21), and devoted to Paul and the gospel (v. 22; Rom. 16:21).

2:21 FOR ALL SEEK THEIR OWN. There are ministers who preach, teach, pastor, or write, not out of genuine concern for the furtherance of the gospel, but for their own interests, honor, glory, prestige, and selfish ambition. Rather than seeking to please the Lord Jesus, they seek instead to please men and gain their favor (vv. 20–21; 1:15; 2 Tim. 4:10,16). Such ministers are not true servants of the Lord.

27 For indeed he was sick nigh unto
death: but God had mercy on him; and
not on him only, but on me also, lest I
should have sorrow upon sorrow.
28 I sent him therefore the more
carefully, that, when ye see him again,
ye may rejoice, and that I may be the
less sorrowful.
29 Receive him therefore in the
Lord with all gladness; and [s]hold[q]
such in reputation:
30 Because for the work of Christ
he was nigh unto death, not regarding
his life, [t]to supply your lack of service
toward me.

No confidence in the flesh

3 FINALLY, MY brethren, [u]rejoice
in the Lord. To write the same
things to you, to me indeed *is* not grievous, but for you *it is* safe.
2 [v]Beware of dogs, beware of evil
workers, [w]beware of the concision.
3 For we are [x]the circumcision,
[y]which worship God in the spirit, and
[z]rejoice in Christ Jesus, and have no
confidence in the flesh.
4 Though [a]I might also have confidence in the flesh. If any other man
thinketh that he hath whereof he might
trust in the flesh, I more:
5 Circumcised the eighth day, of the
stock of Israel, [b]*of* the tribe of Benjamin, [c]an Hebrew of the Hebrews; as
touching the law, [d]a Pharisee;
6 [e]Concerning zeal, persecuting
the church; [f]touching the righteousness which is in the law, [g]blameless.
7 But [h]what things were gain to
me, those I counted loss for Christ.

Paul's desire to serve Christ

8 Yea doubtless, and I count all
things *but* loss [i]for the excellency of
the knowledge of Christ Jesus my Lord:
for whom I have suffered the loss of all
things, and do count them *but* dung,
that I may win Christ,
9 And be found in him, not having
[j]mine own righteousness, which is of
the law, but [k]that which is through
the faith of Christ, the righteousness
which is of God by faith:
10 That I may know him, and the

2:29 [s]1 Cor. 16:18; 1 Thes. 5:12; 1 Tim. 5:17
2:30 [t]1 Cor. 16:17
3:1 [u]2 Cor. 13:11; 1 Thes. 5:16
3:2 [v]Gal. 5:15 [w]Rom. 2:28
3:3 [x]Deut. 30:6; Jer. 4:4 [y]Rom. 7:6 [z]Gal. 6:14
3:4 [a]2 Cor. 11:18
3:5 [b]Rom. 11:1 [c]2 Cor. 11:22 [d]Acts 23:6
3:6 [e]Acts 22:3 [f]Rom. 10:5 [g]Luke 1:6
3:7 [h]Mat. 13:44
3:8 [i]Is. 53:11
3:9 [j]Rom. 10:3 [k]Rom. 1:17

[q]Or, *honour such*

3:2 DOGS ... EVIL WORKERS ... CONCISION. Paul's greatest trial was the grief he felt and experienced because of those who distorted the gospel of Christ. His love for Christ, the church, and redemptive truth was so strong that it drove him to oppose fervently those who perverted pure doctrine, describing them as "dogs" and "evil workers" (see 1:17, note; Gal. 1:9, note; cf. Mat. 23). The term "concision" means "mutilation" and is Paul's term for the rite of Jewish circumcision as taught by the Judaizers, who claimed it was necessary for salvation. Paul states that true circumcision is a work of the Spirit in the heart of a person when sin and evil are cut away (v. 3; Rom. 2:25–29; Col. 2:11).

3:8–11 THAT I MAY WIN CHRIST. These verses show the heart of the apostle and the essence of Christianity. Paul's greatest longing in life was to know Christ and to experience His personal fellowship and nearness in a more intimate way. His pursuit involved the following: (1) To know Christ personally as well as to know His ways, nature, and character as revealed in God's Word. True knowledge of Christ involves listening to His Word, following His Spirit, responding to His dealings with us in faith, truth, and obedience, and identifying with His concerns and purposes.

(2) To be found in Christ (v. 9), i.e., to have a union and fellowship with Christ that produces righteousness that can be experienced only as a gift from God (1:10–11; 1 Cor. 1:30, note; see article on BIBLICAL WORDS FOR SALVATION, p. 1726).

(3) To know the power of His resurrection (v. 10), i.e., to experience renewal of life, deliverance from sin (Rom. 6:4; Eph. 2:5–6), and the power of the Holy Spirit to bring about effective witness, healing, miracles, and finally one's own resurrection from the dead (v. 11; Eph. 1:18–20).

(4) To share in Christ's sufferings by self-denial, crucifixion of the flesh, and suffering for the sake of Christ and His cause in the world (cf. 1:29; Acts 9:16; Rom. 6:5–6; 1 Cor. 15:31; 2 Cor. 4:10; Gal. 2:20; Col. 1:24; 1 Pet. 4:13).

3:9 THE RIGHTEOUSNESS WHICH IS OF GOD. The righteousness of believers consists first of all in being forgiven of sin, justified, and accepted by God through faith (see Rom. 4:5, note). (1) However, our righteousness is more than this. God's Word states that our righteousness is Christ, the Lord Jesus Himself, dwelling within our hearts (cf. 1:20–21; Rom. 8:10; 1 Cor. 1:30; Gal. 2:20; Eph. 3:17; Col. 3:4); in the O.T. the Messiah is referred to as the "righteous Branch" and "THE LORD OUR RIGHTEOUSNESS" (see Jer. 23:5–6, note). In other words, the righteousness we have is not of ourselves but of Jesus, in whom we place our faith (1 Cor. 1:30, note; Gal. 2:20, note). Through this indwelling, we become "the righteousness of God in him" (2 Cor. 5:21, note).

(2) The ground for our salvation and our only hope of righteousness is the sacrificial death and shed blood of Christ on Calvary (Rom. 3:24; 4:25; 5:9; 8:3–4; 1 Cor. 15:3; Gal. 1:4; 2:20; Eph. 1:7; Heb. 9:14; 1 Pet. 1:18–19; 1 John 4:10) and His resurrection life within our hearts (Rom. 4:25; 5:9–10; 8:10–11; Gal. 2:20; Col. 3:1–3; see Rom. 4:22, note).

power of his resurrection, and [l]the
fellowship of his sufferings, being
made conformable unto his death;
11 If by any means I might [m]attain
unto the resurrection of the dead.

The high calling of God

12 Not as though I had already [n]at-
tained, either were already [o]perfect:
but I follow after, if that I may ap-
prehend that for which also I am appre-
hended of Christ Jesus.
13 Brethren, I count not myself to
have apprehended: but *this* one thing *I*
do, [p]forgetting those things which are
behind, and [q]reaching forth unto
those things which are before,
14 [r]I press toward the mark for
the prize of [s]the high calling of God in
Christ Jesus.
15 Let us therefore, as many as be
[t]perfect, [u]be thus minded: and if in
any thing ye be otherwise minded, God
shall reveal even this unto you.
16 Nevertheless, whereto we have
already attained, [v]let us walk [w]by the
same rule, let us mind the same thing.

Warning against false brethren

17 Brethren, [x]be followers togeth-
er of me, and mark them which walk so
as [y]ye have us for an example.

3:10 [l]Rom. 6:3-5 & 8:17 **3:11** [m]Acts 26:7 **3:12** [n]1 Tim. 6:12 [o]Heb. 12:23 **3:13** [p]Luke 9:62 [q]Heb. 6:1 **3:14** [r]2 Tim. 4:7 [s]Heb. 3:1 **3:15** [t]1 Cor. 2:6 [u]Gal. 5:10 **3:16** [v]Rom. 12:16 & 15:6 [w]Gal. 6:16 **3:17** [x]1 Cor. 11:1 1 Thes. 1:6 [y]1 Pet. 5:3 **3:18** [z]Gal. 1:7 & 2:21 **3:19** [a]2 Cor. 11:15 [b]1 Tim. 6:5 Tit. 1:11 [c]Hos. 4:7 Gal. 6:13 [d]Rom. 8:5 **3:20** [e]Eph. 2:6 Col. 3:1,3 [f]Acts 1:11 [g]1 Cor. 1:7 1 Thes. 1:10 **3:21** [h]1 Cor. 15:43 Col. 3:4 [i]Eph. 1:19 [j]1 Cor. 15:26 **4:1** [k]ch. 1:8

18 (For many walk, of whom I have
told you often, and now tell you even
weeping, *that they are* [z]the enemies of
the cross of Christ:
19 [a]Whose end *is* destruction,
[b]whose God *is their* belly, and [c]*whose*
glory *is* in their shame, [d]who mind
earthly things.)
20 For [e]our conversation is in
heaven; [f]from whence also we [g]look
for the Saviour, the Lord Jesus Christ:
21 [h]Who shall change our vile
body, that it may be fashioned like unto
his glorious body, [i]according to the
working whereby he is able [j]even to
subdue all things unto himself. 1 Thes. 1:10

Appeal to rejoice in the Lord

4 THEREFORE, MY brethren dearly
beloved and [k]longed for, [l]my joy
and crown, so [m]stand fast in the Lord,
my dearly beloved.
2 I beseech Euodias, and beseech
Syntyche, [n]that they be of the same
mind in the Lord.
3 And I entreat thee also, true yoke-
fellow, help those women which [o]la-
boured with me in the gospel, with

[l]2 Cor. 1:14; ch. 2:16 [m]ch. 1:27 **4:2** [n]ch. 3:16 **4:3** [o]Rom. 16:3

3:13 ***THIS* ONE THING *I DO*.** Paul sees himself as a runner in a race (cf. Heb. 12:1, note), exerting all his strength and pressing on with intense concentration in order not to fall short of the goal that Christ has set for his life — Paul's perfect oneness with Christ (vv. 8–10), his final salvation, and his resurrection from the dead (v. 11). (1) This was the motive of Paul's life. He had received a glimpse of the glory of heaven (2 Cor. 12:4) and had resolved that his whole life, by the grace of God, would be centered around his determination to press on and someday get to heaven and see Christ face to face (cf. 2 Tim. 4:8; Rev. 2:10; 22:4).

(2) Such determination is necessary for all of us. Throughout our lives there are all kinds of distractions and temptations, such as worldly cares, wealth, and evil desires, threatening to choke off our commitment to the Lord (cf. Mark 4:19; Luke 8:14). What is needed is a "forgetting those things which are behind," i.e., the perverse world and our old life of sin (cf. Gen. 19:17,26; Luke 17:32), and a "reaching forth" for complete and final salvation in Christ.

3:18 ENEMIES OF THE CROSS OF CHRIST. These enemies can best be understood as professed believers who were corrupting the gospel by immoral lives and false teaching. One key to Paul's greatness was that he was a man of intense feeling whose heart was stirred to its very depth when the gospel was distorted or when those whom he served were in danger (see v. 2, note; Gal. 1:9, note; see article OVERSEERS AND THEIR DUTIES, p. 1706).

3:20 OUR CONVERSATION IS IN HEAVEN. The term "conversation" (Gk. *politeuma*) means "citizenship" or "homeland." Paul emphasizes that Christians are no longer citizens of this world; they have become strangers and pilgrims on the earth (Rom. 8:22–24; Gal. 4:26; Heb. 11:13; 12:22–23; 13:14; 1 Pet. 1:17; 2:11; see article on THE CALL OF ABRAHAM, p. 25). (1) In regard to our walk, values, and direction in life, therefore, heaven is now our fatherland. We have been born from above (John 3:3), our names are written on heaven's register (4:3), our lives are guided by heavenly standards, and our rights and inheritance are reserved in heaven.

(2) It is to heaven that our prayers ascend (2 Chr. 6:21; 30:27) and our hope is directed. Many of our friends and family are already there, and we shall be there soon. Jesus is there also, preparing a place for us, and He has promised to return and take us unto Himself (see John 14:2–3, notes; cf. John 3:3; 14:1–4; Rom. 8:17; Eph. 2:6; Col. 3:1–3; Heb. 6:19–20; 12:22–24; 1 Pet. 1:4–5; Rev. 7:9–17). For these reasons we deeply desire a better country, i.e., a heavenly one. Therefore, God is not ashamed to be called our God, and He has prepared for us an eternal city (Heb. 11:16).

Clement also, and *with* other my fellowlabourers, whose names *are* in [p]the book of life.

4 [q]Rejoice in the Lord always: *and* again I say, Rejoice.

5 Let your moderation be known unto all men. [r]The Lord *is* at hand.

6 [s]Be careful for nothing; but in every thing by prayer and supplication with thanksgiving let your requests be made known unto God.

7 And [t]the peace of God, which passeth all understanding, shall keep your hearts and minds through Christ Jesus.

8 Finally, brethren, whatsoever things are true, whatsoever things *are* [r]honest, whatsoever things *are* just, whatsoever things *are* pure, whatsoever things *are* lovely, [u]whatsoever things *are* of good report; if *there be* any virtue, and if *there be* any praise, think on these things.

9 [v]Those things, which ye have both learned, and received, and heard, and seen in me, do: and [w]the God of peace shall be with you.

The Philippian gifts

10 But I rejoiced in the Lord greatly, that now at the last [x]your care of me [s]hath flourished again; wherein ye were also careful, but ye lacked opportunity.

11 Not that I speak in respect of want: for I have learned, in whatsoever state I am, [y]*therewith* to be content.

12 [z]I know both how to be abased, and I know how to abound: every where and in all things I am instructed both to be full and to be hungry, both to abound and to suffer need.

13 I can do all things [a]through Christ which strengtheneth me.

14 Notwithstanding ye have well done, that [b]ye did communicate with my affliction.

15 Now ye Philippians know also, that in the beginning of the gospel, when I departed from Macedonia, [c]no church communicated with me as concerning giving and receiving, but ye only.

4:3 [p]Ex. 32:32 Ps. 69:28 Dan. 12:1
4:4 [q]Rom. 12:12 1 Thes. 5:16 1 Pet. 4:13
4:5 [r]Heb. 10:25 1 Pet. 4:7
4:6 [s]Ps. 55:22 Prov. 16:3 Mat. 6:25
4:7 [t]John 14:27 Rom. 5:1 Col. 3:15
4:8 [u]1 Thes. 5:22
4:9 [v]ch. 3:17 [w]Rom. 15:33
4:10 [x]2 Cor. 11:9
4:11 [y]1 Tim. 6:6
4:12 [z]1 Cor. 4:11
4:13 [a]John 15:5
4:14 [b]ch. 1:7
4:15 [c]2 Cor. 11:8

[r] Or, *venerable* [s] Or, *is revived*

4:4 REJOICE IN THE LORD. The believer must rejoice and strengthen himself by recalling to mind the Lord's grace, nearness, and promises (see 1:4, note).

4:5 THE LORD *IS* AT HAND. We must believe the Lord may come at any time. The N.T. perspective is that the return of Jesus is imminent (see Luke 12:35–40, note); therefore, we must be ready, working, and watching at all times (Mat. 24:36; 25:1–13; Rom. 13:12–14).

4:6 BE CAREFUL FOR NOTHING. Paul instructs us not to be anxious or worried. The one essential cure for worry is prayer, for the following reasons. (1) Through prayer we renew our trust in the Lord's faithfulness by casting our anxieties and problems upon Him who cares for us (Mat. 6:25–34; 1 Pet. 5:7). (2) The peace of God comes to guard our hearts and minds as a result of our communion with Christ Jesus (vv. 6–7; Is. 26:3; Col. 3:15). (3) God strengthens us to do all things He desires of us (v. 13; 3:20, note; Eph. 3:16). (4) We receive mercy, grace, and help in time of need (Heb. 4:16). (5) We are assured that all things God allows to happen to us will work out for our good (see v. 11, note; Rom. 8:28, note).

4:7 PEACE OF GOD . . . SHALL KEEP YOUR HEARTS. When we call on God from hearts that sincerely endeavor to abide in His Word (John 15:7), then the peace of God will flood our troubled souls. (1) This peace is an inner tranquility mediated to us by the Holy Spirit (Rom. 8:15–16). It involves a firm conviction that Jesus is near and that God's love will be active in our lives for good (Rom. 8:28,32; cf. Is. 26:3). (2) When we lay our troubles before God in prayer, this peace will stand guard at the door of our hearts and minds, preventing the cares of life and the heartaches of disappointment from overthrowing our lives and hope in Christ (v. 6; Is. 26:3–4,12; 37:1–7; Rom. 8:35–39; 1 Pet. 5:7). (3) If fear and anxiety return, prayer, supplication, and thanksgiving will once again put us under the peace of God that guards our hearts. Once more we will feel safe and rejoice in the Lord (v. 4; see article on THE PEACE OF GOD, p. 1122).

4:8 WHATSOEVER THINGS *ARE* PURE. Believers must place their minds on those things which are true, pure, holy, righteous, etc. That this is a prerequisite for experiencing the peace of God and freedom from anxiety is clear from v. 9: if you do these things, "the God of peace shall be with you." The consequence of placing our minds on unholy things of the world is that the joy, nearness, and peace of God are lost and our hearts are no longer guarded.

4:11 I HAVE LEARNED . . . TO BE CONTENT. The key to contentment is realizing that God has given you in your present circumstances everything you need to remain victorious in Christ (1 Cor. 15:57; 2 Cor. 2:14; 1 John 5:4). Your ability to live triumphantly above changing circumstances is Christ's power flowing in and through you (v. 13; see 1 Tim. 6:8, note). This does not come naturally, however; it must be learned through dependence on Christ.

4:13 I CAN DO ALL THINGS THROUGH CHRIST. Christ's power and grace rest upon believers to enable them to do all that He has asked them to do (see article on FAITH AND GRACE, p. 1738).

16 For even in Thessalonica ye sent
once and again unto my necessity.
17 Not because I desire a gift: but I
desire [d]fruit that may abound to your
account.
18 But †I have all, and abound: I
am full, having received [e]of Epaphro-
ditus the things *which were sent* from
you, [f]an odour of a sweet smell, [g]a
sacrifice acceptable, wellpleasing to
God.
19 But my God [h]shall supply all
your need [i]according to his riches in
glory by Christ Jesus.

4:17 [d]Tit. 3:14
4:18 [e]ch. 2:25 [f]Heb. 13:16 [g]2 Cor. 9:12
4:19 [h]Ps. 23:1 [i]Eph. 1:7
4:20 [j]Rom. 16:27
4:21 [k]Gal. 1:2
4:22 [l]ch. 1:13
4:23 [m]Rom. 16:24

20 [j]Now unto God and our Father
be glory for ever and ever. Amen.

Concluding benediction

21 Salute every saint in Christ
Jesus. The brethren [k]which are with
me greet you.
22 All the saints salute you, [l]chief-
ly they that are of Caesar's household.
23 [m]The grace of our Lord Jesus
Christ *be* with you all. Amen.

† Or, *I have received all*

4:16 YE SENT ... UNTO MY NECESSITY. The Philippian church was a missionary church that ministered to Paul's needs during his travels (vv. 15–17; 1:4–5). The support of missionaries in their work for the gospel is honored and accepted by God as "an odour of a sweet smell, a sacrifice acceptable, well-pleasing" unto Him (v. 18). Thus, what we give to the support of a faithful missionary is regarded as an offering brought to God. What is done for one of the least of His brethren is done for the Lord Himself (Mat. 25:40).

4:19 SUPPLY ALL YOUR NEED. Paul emphasizes the loving care of God the Father for His children. He will supply all your needs (material and spiritual) as you present them to Him. The supply of our needs is "by Christ Jesus." Only in union with Christ and in His fellowship can we experience the provision of God. Among the many Scriptural promises that have given hope and encouragement to God's people concerning His care and help are: Gen. 28:15; 50:20; Ex. 33:14; Deut. 2:7; 32:7–14; 33:27; Josh. 1:9; 1 Sam. 7:12; 1 Ki. 17:6, 16; 2 Chr. 20:17; Ps. 18:35; 23; 121; Is. 25:4; 32:2; 40:11; 41:10; 43:1–2; 46:3–4; Joel 2:21–27; Mal. 3:10; Mat. 6:25–34; 14:20; 23:37; Luke 6:38; 12:7; 22:35; John 10:27–28; 17:11; Rom. 8:28, 31–39; 2 Tim. 1:12; 4:18; 1 Pet. 5:7; see article on THE PROVIDENCE OF GOD, p. 80).

COLOSSIANS

Outline

Introduction (1:1–12)
- A. Christian Greetings (1:1–2)
- B. Thanksgiving for Their Faith, Love, and Hope (1:3–8)
- C. Prayer for Their Spiritual Advancement (1:9–12)

I. Powerful Doctrine—The Believer's Redemption (1:13—2:23)
- A. The Absolute Preeminence of Christ (1:13–23)
  1. As Vicarious Redeemer (1:13–14; cf. 20,22)
  2. As Lord of Creation (1:15–17)
  3. As Head of the Church (1:18)
  4. As Reconciler of All Things (1:19–20)
  5. As Reconciler of the Colossians to God (1:21–23)
- B. Paul's Ministry of God's Mystery in Christ (1:24—2:7)
  1. Filling Up the Sufferings of Christ (1:24–25)
  2. Perfecting Believers in Christ (1:26—2:7)
- C. Warnings Against Erroneous Teaching (2:8–23)
  1. Problem: Teaching Not According to Christ (2:8)
     Solution: Made Complete in Christ (2:9–15)
  2. Problem: Religious Practices Not According to Christ (2:16–23)
     Solution: Crucified with Christ (2:20)

II. Practical Instructions—The Believer's Life (3:1—4:6)
- A. The Believer's Personal Conduct (3:1–17)
  1. When Christ is Our Life (3:1–4)
  2. Laying Aside the Old Life of Sin (3:5–9)
  3. Putting on the New Man in Christ (3:10–17)
- B. The Believer's Domestic Relationships (3:18—4:1)
  1. Wives and Husbands (3:18–19)
  2. Children and Parents (3:20–21)
  3. Servants and Masters (3:22—4:1)
- C. The Believer's Spiritual Influence (4:2–6)
  1. A Life Devoted to Prayer (4:2–4)
  2. Wise Conduct Toward Outsiders (4:5)
  3. Speech Seasoned with Grace (4:6)

Conclusion (4:7–18)

Author: Paul

Theme: Supremacy of Christ

Date of Writing: c. A.D. 62

Background

·losse was located near Laodicea (cf. 4:16) in southwest Asia Minor about 100
ast of Ephesus. The Colossian church appears to have been founded as a
xceptional three-year ministry at Ephesus (Acts 20:31), the effects of

which were so powerful and far-reaching that "all they which dwelt in Asia heard the word of the Lord Jesus" (Acts 19:10). Although Paul may never have visited Colosse in person (2:1), he had maintained contact with the church through Epaphras, one of his converts and associates from Colosse (1:7; 4:12).

The occasion for this epistle was the appearance of false teaching in the Colossian church that was threatening its spiritual future (2:8). When Epaphras, a leader in the Colossian church and perhaps its founder, traveled to visit Paul and to inform him about the situation at Colosse (1:8; 4:12), Paul responded by writing this letter. He was a prisoner at the time (4:3,10,18), most likely at Rome (Acts 28:16–31) awaiting his appeal before Caesar (Acts 25:11–12). Paul's co-worker, Tychicus, delivered the letter in person to Colosse on Paul's behalf (4:7).

The exact nature of the Colossian heresy is not described explicitly in the epistle, for the original readers knew it well. From Paul's statements made in opposition to the false teachings, however, it is apparent that the heresy, which was undermining and replacing the centrality of Jesus Christ, was a strange mixture of Christian teaching, certain extra-biblical Jewish traditions, and pagan philosophy (similar to the mixture of cults today).

Purpose

Paul wrote (1) to combat the dangerous false teaching at Colosse that was supplanting the centrality and supremacy of Jesus Christ in creation, revelation, redemption, and the church; and (2) to stress the true nature of new life in Christ and its demands upon the believer.

Survey

After greeting the church and expressing gratitude for their faith, love, and hope, and for their continued progress as believers, Paul focuses on two main issues: correct doctrine (1:13—2:23) and practical exhortations (3:1—4:6).

Theologically, Paul emphasizes the true character and glory of the Lord Jesus Christ. He is the image of the invisible God (1:15), the fullness of deity in bodily form (2:9), the Creator of all things (1:16–17), the Head of the church (1:18), and the all-sufficient Source of our salvation (1:14,20–22). Whereas Christ is completely adequate, the Colossian heresy is utterly inadequate—hollow, deceitful, and humanistic (2:8); superficially spiritual and arrogant (2:18); and without power against the flesh (2:23).

In his practical exhortations, Paul appeals for a life grounded in the complete sufficiency of Christ as the only way to progress in Christian living. The reality of the indwelling Christ (1:27) must be evident in Christian behavior (3:1–17), domestic relationships (3:18—4:1), and spiritual discipline (4:2–6).

Special Features

Three major features or emphases characterize this epistle. (1) More than any other N.T. book, Colossians focuses on the twofold truth of Christ's preeminence and the believer's completeness in Him. (2) It strongly affirms Christ's full deity (2:9) and contains one of the most exalted passages in the N.T. about His glory (1:15–23). (3) It is sometimes regarded as a "twin epistle" with Ephesians, because the two have certain resemblances in content and were written about the same time.

Reading Colossians

In order to read the entire New Testament in one year, the book of Colossians should be read in 5 days, according to the following schedule:
☐ 1:1–23 ☐ 1:24—2:5 ☐ 2:6–23 ☐ 3:1—4:1 ☐ 4:2–18

NOTES

Salutation and thanksgiving

1 PAUL, [a]AN apostle of Jesus Christ by the will of God, and Timotheus *our* brother,

2 To the saints [b]and faithful brethren in Christ which are at Colosse: [c]Grace *be* unto you, and peace, from God our Father and the Lord Jesus Christ.

3 [d]We give thanks to God and the Father of our Lord Jesus Christ, praying always for you,

4 [e]Since we heard of your faith in Christ Jesus, and of [f]the love *which ye have* to all the saints,

5 For the hope [g]which is laid up for you in heaven, whereof ye heard before in the word of the truth of the gospel;

6 Which is come unto you, [h]as *it is* in all the world; and bringeth forth fruit, as *it doth* also in you, since the day ye heard *of it,* and knew [i]the grace of God in truth:

7 As ye also learned of [j]Epaphras our dear fellowservant, who is for you [k]a faithful minister of Christ;

8 Who also declared unto us your [l]love in the Spirit.

Paul's prayer for the Colossians

9 [m]For this cause we also, since the day we heard *it,* do not cease to pray for you, and to desire [n]that ye might be filled with [o]the knowledge of his will [p]in all wisdom and spiritual understanding;

10 [q]That ye might walk worthy of the Lord [r]unto all pleasing, [s]being fruitful in every good work, and increasing in the knowledge of God;

11 [t]Strengthened with all might, according to his glorious power, [u]unto all patience and longsuffering [v]with joyfulness;

12 [w]Giving thanks unto the Father, which hath made us meet to be partakers of [x]the inheritance of the saints in light:

13 Who hath delivered us from [y]the power of darkness, [z]and hath translated *us* into the kingdom of [a]his dear Son:

14 [a]In whom we have redemption

1:1 [a]Eph. 1:1
1:2 [b]1 Cor. 4:17 [c]Gal. 1:3
1:3 [d]1 Cor. 1:4 Eph. 1:16 Phil. 1:3
1:4 [e]Eph. 1:15 [f]Heb. 6:10
1:5 [g]1 Pet. 1:4
1:6 [h]Mat. 24:14 [i]Eph. 3:2 Tit. 2:11
1:7 [j]Philem. 23 [k]2 Cor. 11:23 1 Tim. 4:6
1:8 [l]Rom. 15:30
1:9 [m]Eph. 1:15 [n]1 Cor. 1:5 [o]Rom. 12:2 [p]Eph. 1:8
1:10 [q]Phil. 1:27 [r]1 Thes. 4:1 [s]Heb. 13:21
1:11 [t]Eph. 3:16 [u]Eph. 4:2 [v]Acts 5:41
1:12 [w]Eph. 5:20 [x]Eph. 1:11
1:13 [y]Eph. 6:12 [z]2 Pet. 1:11
1:14 [a]Eph. 1:7

[a] Gk. *the Son of his love*

1:2 TO THE SAINTS . . . AT COLOSSE. Paul wrote this epistle because the church in Colosse was being infiltrated by false teachers who taught that apostolic doctrine and salvation in Christ were inadequate for full redemption. This false teaching mixed human "philosophy" and "tradition" with the gospel (2:8) and called for the worship of angels as intermediaries between God and man (2:18). The false teachers demanded observance of certain Jewish religious requirements (2:16,21–23) and justified their error by claiming revelation through visions (2:18). (1) The underlying philosophy behind these errors appears today in the teaching that Jesus Christ and the original gospel of the N.T. are not adequate to meet our spiritual needs (see 2 Pet. 1:3, note).

(2) Paul refutes this heresy by showing that Christ is not only our personal Savior, but the head of the church and Lord of the universe and creation. Hence, Jesus Christ and His power in our lives, not human philosophy or wisdom, redeems us and saves us eternally; intermediaries are unnecessary, and we must approach Him directly.

(3) Being a believer means believing in Christ and His gospel, trusting Him, loving Him, and living in His personal presence. We must not add anything to the gospel nor promote modern, humanistic wisdom or philosophy.

1:9 KNOWLEDGE OF HIS WILL. The knowledge of God's will results from prayer and abiding in His Word and in fellowship with Him. Only this kind of knowledge results in spiritual wisdom and understanding and transforms our hearts and lives (vv. 9–11; see Phil. 1:9, note).

1:9–12 WE . . . DO NOT CEASE TO PRAY FOR YOU. This is one of four great N.T. apostolic prayers by Paul, spoken under the inspiration of the Holy Spirit (the other three are Eph. 1:16–19; 3:14–19; Phil. 1:9–11). From these prayers we learn how to pray for others, such as our children, friends, fellow believers, missionaries, pastors, etc. We must pray that they may (1) understand God's will, (2) gain spiritual wisdom, (3) live a holy life pleasing unto the Lord, (4) bear fruit for Christ, (5) be strengthened spiritually by the Holy Spirit, (6) persevere in faith and righteousness, (7) be grateful to the Father, (8) continue in the hope of heaven, (9) experience the nearness of Christ, (10) know the love of Christ, (11) be filled with the fullness of God, (12) show love and kindness to others, (13) discern evil, (14) be sincere and blameless, and (15) eagerly await the return of the Lord.

1:11 STRENGTHENED WITH . . . HIS GLORIOUS POWER. In order to live in a manner worthy of the Lord (v. 10), we must be strengthened by His power. This impartation of power is an ongoing experience of receiving from God His own life. Nothing else can enable us to overcome sin, Satan, and the world (cf. Phil. 4:13; see article on FAITH AND GRACE, p. 1738).

1:13 FROM THE POWER OF DARKNESS. Central to redemption in Christ is deliverance from the dominion and power of darkness, i.e., from Satan (Mat. 4:8–11; Luke 22:52–53; Eph. 2:2; 6:12). We are now in the kingdom of Christ and under His rule (Rom. 6:17–22; see Acts 26:18, note).

through his blood, *even* the forgiveness of sins:

Christ's preeminence in creation

15 Who is [b]the image of the invisible God, [c]the firstborn of every creature:

16 For [d]by him were all things created, that are in heaven, and that are in earth, visible and invisible, whether *they be* thrones, or [e]dominions, or principalities, or powers: all things were created [f]by him, and for him:

17 [g]And he is before all things, and by him all things consist.

18 And [h]he is the head of the body, the church: who is the beginning, [i]the firstborn from the dead; that [b]in all *things* he might have the preeminence.

Christ's preeminence in redemption

19 For it pleased *the Father* that [j]in him should all fulness dwell;

20 And, [k]having[c] made peace through the blood of his cross, [l]by him to reconcile [m]all things unto himself; by him, *I say*, whether *they be* things in earth, or things in heaven.

21 And you, [n]that were sometime alienated and enemies [d]in *your* mind [o]by wicked works, yet now hath he reconciled

22 [p]In the body of his flesh through death, [q]to present you holy and unblameable and unreproveable in his sight:

23 If ye continue in the faith [r]grounded and settled, and *be* [s]not moved away from the hope of the gospel, which ye have heard, [t]*and* which was preached to every creature which is under heaven; [u]whereof I Paul am made a minister;

Paul's labor for the church

24 [v]Who now rejoice in my sufferings [w]for you, and fill up [x]that which is behind of the afflictions of Christ in my flesh for [y]his body's sake, which is the church:

25 Whereof I am made a minister, according to [z]the dispensation of God which is given to me for you, [e]to fulfil the word of God;

26 *Even* [a]the mystery which hath been hid from ages and from generations, [b]but now is made manifest to his saints:

27 [c]To whom God would make

1:15 [b]2 Cor. 4:4 [c]Rev. 3:14
1:16 [d]Heb. 1:2 [e]Eph. 1:21 [f]Heb. 2:10
1:17 [g]John 17:5
1:18 [h]1 Cor. 11:3 [i]Rev. 1:5
1:19 [j]John 1:16
1:20 [k]Eph. 2:14 [l]2 Cor. 5:18 [m]Eph. 1:10
1:21 [n]Eph. 2:1 [o]Tit. 1:15
1:22 [p]Eph. 2:15 [q]Eph. 5:27
1:23 [r]Eph. 3:17 [s]John 15:6 [t]Rom. 10:18 [u]Acts 1:17
1:24 [v]2 Cor. 7:4 [w]Eph. 3:1,13 [x]2 Cor. 1:5 [y]Eph. 1:23
1:25 [z]Gal. 2:7
1:26 [a]1 Cor. 2:7 [b]2 Tim. 1:10
1:27 [c]2 Cor. 2:14

[b] Or, *among* [c] Or, *making* [d] Or, *by* your *mind in* [e] Or, *fully to preach*

1:15 THE FIRSTBORN OF EVERY CREATURE. This phrase does not mean Christ was a created being. Rather, "firstborn" has the O.T. meaning: "first in position," "heir," or "supreme" (e.g., Ex. 4:22; Jer. 31:9; see also Ps. 89:27, where "firstborn" is used of David's rulership, although he was not a firstborn son). Christ is heir and ruler of all creation as the eternal Son (cf. v. 18; Heb. 1:1–2).

1:16 BY HIM WERE ALL THINGS CREATED. Paul affirms the creative activity of Christ. (1) All things, both material and spiritual, owe their existence to the work of Christ as the active agent in creation (John 1:3; Heb. 1:2). (2) All things hold together and are sustained by Him (v. 17; Heb. 1:3; see article on CREATION, p. 6).

1:18 FIRSTBORN FROM THE DEAD. Jesus Christ was the first to rise from the dead with a spiritual and immortal body (1 Cor. 15:20). On His resurrection day Jesus became head of the church. The N.T. church began on the day of Jesus' resurrection when the disciples received the Holy Spirit (see article on THE REGENERATION OF THE DISCIPLES, p. 1638). The fact that Christ is the "firstborn" from the dead implies the subsequent resurrection of all those for whom He died.

1:19 IN HIM . . . ALL FULNESS DWELL. Paul states the deity of Christ in the plainest of terms. The full and complete Godhead with all its powers and nature resides with Christ (2:9; cf. Heb. 1:8).

1:20 RECONCILE ALL THINGS. Mankind and everything in the universe are brought in unity and harmony under Christ (cf. vv. 16–18). It does not mean, however, that all people are reconciled irrespective of their wills. The person who rejects Christ's offer of reconciliation remains an enemy of God (Rom. 2:4–10).

1:23 IF YE CONTINUE IN THE FAITH. Notice the human responsibility and activity which Paul states are essential for the Christian to appear finally before Christ "holy and unblameable and unreproveable" (v. 22). We must (1) "continue in the faith," i.e., maintain a persevering faith in Jesus as Lord and Savior (see article on FAITH AND GRACE, p. 1738); (2) be "grounded and settled" in the teaching of Jesus and the apostles; and (3) be "not moved away from the hope of the gospel," i.e., we must not return to our former state of hopelessness with its soul-destroying vices (3:5–11; see Heb. 10:38, note).

1:24 MY SUFFERINGS FOR YOU. Paul sees Christ still suffering, not for our redemption, but in fellowship with His people as they carry the gospel to the lost (cf. Acts 9:4). Paul rejoices because he is allowed to share in His sufferings (Phil. 3:10; cf. 2 Cor. 1:4–5, notes; 4:7, note; 11:23, note on the sufferings of Paul).

1:27 CHRIST IN YOU, THE HOPE OF GLORY. Christ's living within us is our assurance of future glory and eternal life. Only His indwelling and our

known what *is* [d]the riches of the glory
of this mystery among the Gentiles;
which is Christ [f]in you, [e]the hope of
glory:
28 Whom we preach, [f]warning ev-
ery man, and teaching every man in all
wisdom; [g]that we may present every
man perfect in Christ Jesus:
29 [h]Whereunto I also labour,
[i]striving [j]according to his working,
which worketh in me mightily.

Paul's concern for the church

2 FOR I would that ye knew what
great [k]conflict[g] I have for you,
and *for* them at Laodicea, and *for* as
many as have not seen my face in the
flesh;
2 [l]That their hearts might be com-
forted, [m]being knit together in love,
and unto all riches of the full assur-
ance of understanding, [n]to the ac-
knowledgement of the mystery of God,
and of the Father, and of Christ;
3 [o]In[h] whom are hid all the trea-
sures of wisdom and knowledge.
4 And this I say, [p]lest any man
should beguile you with enticing
words.

1:27 [d]Rom. 9:23 [e]1 Tim. 1:1
1:28 [f]Acts 20:20 [g]Eph. 5:27
1:29 [h]1 Cor. 15:10 [i]ch. 2:1 [j]Eph. 1:19
2:1 [k]Phil. 1:30
2:2 [l]2 Cor. 1:6 [m]ch. 3:14 [n]Phil. 3:8
2:3 [o]1 Cor. 1:24
2:4 [p]Rom. 16:18
2:5 [q]1 Thes. 2:17 [r]1 Cor. 14:40 [s]1 Pet. 5:9
2:6 [t]1 Thes. 4:1
2:7 [u]Eph. 2:21
2:8 [v]Gal. 1:14 [w]Gal. 4:3,9
2:9 [x]John 1:14
2:10 [y]1 Pet. 3:22 [z]ch. 1:16
2:11 [a]Deut. 10:16

5 For [q]though I be absent in the
flesh, yet am I with you in the spirit,
joying and beholding [r]your order, and
the [s]stedfastness of your faith in
Christ.
6 [t]As ye have therefore received
Christ Jesus the Lord, *so* walk ye in
him:
7 [u]Rooted and built up in him, and
stablished in the faith, as ye have been
taught, abounding therein with thanks-
giving.

The sufficiency of Christ

8 Beware lest any man spoil you
through philosophy and vain deceit, af-
ter [v]the tradition of men, after the
[w]rudiments[i] of the world, and not af-
ter Christ.
9 For [x]in him dwelleth all the ful-
ness of the Godhead bodily.
10 And ye are complete in him,
[y]which is the head of all [z]principality
and power:
11 In whom also ye are [a]circum-
cised with the circumcision made with-

[f] Or, *among* [g] Or, *care* [h] Or, *Wherein* [i] Or, *elements*

continual close communion with Him can dispel any doubt about obtaining heaven. To have Him is to have life (cf. Rom. 8:11; Eph. 1:13–14; 1 John 5:11–12).

1:28 PERFECT IN CHRIST JESUS. See article on SANCTIFICATION, p. 1982.

2:8 PHILOSOPHY . . . NOT AFTER CHRIST. Paul warns us to be on guard against all philosophies, religions, and traditions that emphasize man functioning independently from God and His written revelation. Today one of the greatest philosophical threats to Biblically based Christianity is "secular humanism." This has become the underlying philosophy and accepted religion in most of secular education, government, and society in general, and is the established viewpoint of most of the news and entertainment media throughout the world.

(1) What does the philosophy of humanism teach? (a) It teaches that man, the universe, and all that exists consist only of matter and energy that have been shaped into their present form by impersonal chance. (b) It teaches that man has not been created by a personal God, but has resulted from a chance process of evolution. (c) It rejects belief in a personal, infinite God and denies that the Bible is God's inspired revelation to the human race. (d) It asserts that knowledge does not exist apart from man's discovery and that man's reason determines the appropriate ethics of society, thus making human beings the ultimate authority. (e) It seeks to modify or improve human behavior through education, economic redistribution, modern psychology, or human wisdom. (f) It believes that moral standards are not absolute but relative, determined by what makes people happy, brings them pleasure, or seems good for society according to the goals set by its leaders; Biblical values and morality are rejected. (g) It considers man's self-fulfillment, satisfaction, and pleasure to be the highest good of life. (h) It maintains that people should learn to cope with death and the difficulties in life without belief in or dependence upon God.

(2) The philosophy of humanism began with Satan and is an expression of the lie of Satan that man can be as God (Gen. 3:5). Scripture identifies humanists as those who have "changed the truth of God into a lie, and worshipped and served the creature more than the Creator . . ." (Rom. 1:25).

(3) All Christian leaders, pastors, and parents must do their utmost to protect their sons and daughters from humanistic indoctrination by exposing its error and instilling in their minds a godly contempt for its destructive influence (Rom. 1:20–32; 2 Cor. 10:4–5; 2 Tim. 3:1–10; Jude 4–20; see 1 Cor. 1:20, note; 2 Pet. 2:19, note).

2:11 CIRCUMCISION MADE WITHOUT HANDS. In the O.T. circumcision was the sign that the individual Israelite stood in a covenant relationship with God (see Gen. 17:11, note). It symbolized a cutting away or separation from sin and all that was unholy in the world. The believer under the N.T. covenant has undergone a spiritual circumcision, namely, the removal of "the body of the sins of the flesh." Such circumcision is a spiri-

out hands, in [b]putting off the body of
the sins of the flesh by the circumci-
sion of Christ:
12 Buried with him in baptism,
wherein also ye are risen with *him*
through [c]the faith of the operation of
God, [d]who hath raised him from the
dead.
13 And you, being dead in your sins
and the uncircumcision of your flesh,
hath he quickened together with him,
having forgiven you all trespasses;
14 [e]Blotting out the handwriting
of ordinances that was against us,
which was contrary to us, and took it
out of the way, nailing it to his cross;
15 *And* [f]having spoiled [g]prin-
cipalities and powers, he made a show
of them openly, triumphing over them
[j]in it.

Avoid human regulations

16 Let no man therefore [h]judge
you [i]in[k] meat, or in drink, or [l]in
respect [j]of an holyday, or of the new
moon, or of the sabbath *days:*
17 [k]Which are a shadow of things
to come; but the body *is* of Christ.
18 Let no man [m]beguile you of your
reward [n]in a voluntary humility and
worshipping of angels, intruding into
those things which he hath not seen,
vainly puffed up by his fleshly mind,
19 And not holding [l]the Head,
from which all the body by joints and
bands having nourishment ministered,
and knit together, increaseth with the
increase of God.
20 Wherefore if ye be [m]dead with
Christ from the [o]rudiments of the
world, [n]why, as though living in the
world, are ye subject to ordinances,
21 ([o]Touch not; taste not; handle
not;
22 Which all are to perish with the
using;) [p]after the commandments and
doctrines of men?
23 [q]Which things have indeed a
show of wisdom in will-worship. and
humility, and [p]neglecting of the body;
not in any honour to the satisfying of
the flesh.

The true center of Christian life

3 IF YE then be risen with Christ,
seek those things which are above,
where [r]Christ sitteth on the right
hand of God.
2 Set your [q]affection on things
above, not on things on the earth.

2:11 [b]Rom. 6:6
2:12 [c]Eph. 1:19 [d]Acts 2:24
2:14 [e]Eph. 2:15
2:15 [f]Is. 53:12 [g]Eph. 6:12
2:16 [h]Rom. 14:3 [i]Rom. 14:2 [j]Rom. 14:5
2:17 [k]Heb. 8:5
2:19 [l]Eph. 4:15
2:20 [m]Rom. 6:3,5 [n]Gal. 4:3,9
2:21 [o]1 Tim. 4:3
2:22 [p]Tit. 1:14
2:23 [q]1 Tim. 4:8
3:1 [r]Eph. 1:20

[j] Or, *in himself* [k] Or, *for eating and drinking* [l] Or, *in part* [m] Or, *judge against you* [n] Gk. *being a voluntary in humility* [o] Or, *elements* [p] Or, *punishing,* or, *not sparing* [q] Or, *mind*

tual act whereby Christ cuts away our old unregenerate nature of rebellion against God and imparts to us the spiritual or resurrection life of Christ (vv. 12–13); it is a circumcision of the heart (Deut. 10:16; 30:6; Jer. 4:4; 9:26; Rom. 2:29).

2:14 HANDWRITING OF ORDINANCES. This refers to the Law of Moses, i.e., to commandments which pointed to right conduct but could not give life and the power to obey God (Gal. 3:21). Salvation through the O.T. covenant has been nailed to the cross (i.e., abolished), and God has established a better covenant through Christ and by His Spirit (2 Cor. 3:6–9; Heb. 8:6–13; 10:16–17,29; 12:24; see article on THE OLD COVENANT AND THE NEW COVENANT, p. 1954).

2:15 SPOILED PRINCIPALITIES AND POWERS. Christ triumphed over all the demonic forces and satanic powers of the world through His death on the cross (cf. Eph. 6:12). He stripped them of their power to hold men and women captive to the dominion of evil against their will (cf. 1:13; Mat. 12:29; Luke 10:18; 11:20–22; Heb. 2:14; see article on POWER OVER SATAN AND DEMONS, p. 1486). The child of God shares in this triumph. We not only gain victory over the world and temptation (1 John 4:4), but also possess the power to wage war against the spiritual forces of evil (see Eph. 6:12, note; see article on SIGNS OF BELIEVERS, p. 1516).

2:16 MEAT . . . DRINK . . . SABBATH *DAYS*. The first two words probably refer to Jewish ascetic dietary rules of the O.T. that were urged upon the Colossians as necessary for salvation (cf. v. 17). "Holyday," "new moon," and "sabbath *days*" probably refer to certain required holy days of the Jewish calendar. The apostle Paul teaches that a Christian is freed from legal and ceremonial obligations of this kind (Gal. 4:4–11; 5:1; see Mat. 12:1, note on the Sabbath; Mark 7:6, note on legalism).

2:18 WORSHIPPING OF ANGELS. The false teachers were saying that angels should be called upon and worshiped as mediators in order for people to make contact with God. To Paul, calling upon angels would be displacing Jesus Christ as the supreme and sufficient head of the church (v. 19); consequently, he warns against this. Today the belief that Jesus Christ is not the only intermediary between God and man is promoted in the practice of worshiping and praying to dead saints, who act as patrons and mediators. This practice robs Christ of His supremacy and centrality in God's redemptive plan. Worship and prayer to anyone other than God the Father, God the Son, and God the Holy Spirit are unbiblical and must be rejected (see 1:2, note; see article on WORSHIP, p. 730).

3:2 SET YOUR AFFECTION ON THINGS ABOVE. Because our lives are hidden with Christ in heaven (v. 3), we must set our minds on, and let

3 [s]For ye are dead, [t]and your life is hid with Christ in God.

4 [u]When Christ, *who is* [v]our life, shall appear, then shall ye also appear with him [w]in glory.

Put off sin

5 [x]Mortify therefore [y]your members which are upon the earth; [z]fornication, uncleanness, inordinate affection, evil concupiscence, and covetousness, [a]which is idolatry:

6 [b]For which things' sake the wrath of God cometh on [c]the children of disobedience:

7 [d]In the which ye also walked some time, when ye lived in them.

8 [e]But now ye also put off all these; anger, wrath, malice, blasphemy, [f]filthy communication out of your mouth.

9 [g]Lie not one to another, [h]seeing that ye have put off the old man with his deeds;

10 And have put on the new *man*, which [i]is renewed in knowledge [j]after the image of him that [k]created him:

11 Where there is neither [l]Greek nor Jew, circumcision nor uncircumcision, Barbarian, Scythian, bond *nor* free: [m]but Christ *is* all, and in all.

Put on love, peace, and truth

12 Put on therefore, [n]as the elect of God, holy and beloved, [o]bowels of mercies, kindness, humbleness of mind, meekness, longsuffering;

13 [p]Forbearing one another, and forgiving one another, if any man have a [r]quarrel against any: even as Christ forgave you, so also *do* ye.

14 [q]And above all these things [r]*put on* charity, which is the [s]bond of perfectness. 1 Thes. 4:1-7

15 And let [t]the peace of God rule in your hearts, [u]to the which also ye are called [v]in one body; and be ye thankful.

16 Let the word of Christ dwell in you richly in all wisdom; teaching and admonishing one another [w]in psalms and hymns and spiritual songs, singing with grace in your hearts to the Lord.

17 And [x]whatsoever ye do in word or deed, *do* all in the name of the Lord Jesus, giving thanks to God and the Father by him. Heb. 13:15

3:3 [s]Rom. 6:2 [t]2 Cor. 5:7
3:4 [u]1 John 3:2 [v]John 14:6 [w]1 Cor. 15:43
3:5 [x]Rom. 8:13 [y]Rom. 6:13 [z]Eph. 5:3 [a]Eph. 5:5
3:6 [b]Rev. 22:15 [c]Eph. 2:2
3:7 [d]1 Cor. 6:11
3:8 [e]Eph. 4:22 [f]Eph. 4:29
3:9 [g]Eph. 4:25 [h]Eph. 4:22
3:10 [i]Rom. 12:2 [j]Eph. 4:23 [k]Eph. 2:10
3:11 [l]Gal. 3:28 [m]Eph. 1:23
3:12 [n]1 Pet. 1:2 [o]Gal. 5:22
3:13 [p]Mark 11:25
3:14 [q]1 Pet. 4:8 [r]1 Cor. 13 [s]Eph. 4:3
3:15 [t]Phil. 4:7 [u]1 Cor. 7:15 [v]Eph. 4:4
3:16 [w]Eph. 5:19
3:17 [x]1 Cor. 10:31

[r] Or, *complaint*

---

our attitudes be determined by, the things above. We must value, judge, view, and consider everything from an eternal and heavenly perspective. Our goals, pursuits, and ambitions should be to seek spiritual things (vv. 1–4), resist sin (vv. 5–11), and put on the character of Christ (vv. 12–17). Spiritual graces, power, experiences, and blessings are all with Christ in heaven. He bestows those things upon all who sincerely ask, diligently seek, and persistently knock (Luke 11:1–13; 1 Cor. 12:11; Eph. 1:3; 4:7–8).

3:4 CHRIST, *WHO IS* OUR LIFE. Although right doctrine (2 Tim. 1:13–14) and holy lives (vv. 5–17; John 14:15,21) are an essential part of redemption in Christ, it is fellowship with and love for Christ as a person that must always be kept central (cf. Rom. 3:22). Notice the emphasis on the believer's personal communion with Christ in this epistle (1:27; 2:6–7,10,20; 3:1,3–4).

3:5 COVETOUSNESS . . . IDOLATRY. What is idolatry? (1) It is allowing things to become the focus of a person's desires, values, and dependence, displacing reliance on and faith in God Himself (cf. Ex. 20:3–6; Deut. 7:25–26; Is. 40:18–23; see article on THE NATURE OF IDOLATRY, p. 428). For this reason covetousness (greed for worldly possessions) is called idolatry. (2) Idolatry can involve professing allegiance to God and His Word while at the same time giving equal or greater allegiance to persons, institutions, traditions, or authorities on earth. Nothing may be placed higher than one's faithful relationship to God and His Word as revealed in the Bible (Rom. 1:22–23; Eph. 5:5).

3:16 WORD OF CHRIST DWELL IN YOU. The word of Christ (i.e., the Scriptures, the Word of God) must be continually read, studied, meditated upon, and prayed over, until it richly dwells within us. When this is our experience, our thoughts, words, deeds, and motivation will be influenced and controlled by Christ (Ps. 119:11; John 15:7; see 1 Cor. 15:2, note). Psalms, hymns, and spiritual songs must be used to teach the Word and admonish believers to live a life of obedience to Christ (see Eph. 5:19, note on spiritual singing).

3:17 WHATSOEVER YE DO IN WORD OR DEED. The Bible presents general principles that permit the Spirit-led believer to determine the rightness or wrongness of actions not expressly mentioned in God's Word. In everything that we say, do, think, or enjoy, we must ask the following questions: (1) Can it be done to the glory of God (1 Cor. 10:31)? (2) Can it be done "in the name of the Lord Jesus," asking His blessing on the activity (see John 14:13, note)? (3) Can it be done while sincerely giving thanks to God? (4) Is it a Christlike action (1 John 2:6)? (5) Will it weaken the sincere convictions of other Christians (see 1 Cor. 8:1, note)? (6) Will it weaken my desire for spiritual things, God's Word, and prayer (Luke 8:14; see Mat. 5:6, note)? (7) Will it weaken or hinder my witness for Christ (Mat. 5:13–16)?

The Christian family

3:18—4:1pp — Eph. 5:22—6:9

18 [y]Wives, submit yourselves unto your own husbands, [z]as it is fit in the Lord.

19 [a]Husbands, love *your* wives, and be not [b]bitter against them.

20 [c]Children, obey *your* parents [d]in all things: for this is wellpleasing unto the Lord.

21 [e]Fathers, provoke not your children *to anger,* lest they be discouraged.

22 [f]Servants, obey [g]in all things *your* masters [h]according to the flesh; not with eyeservice, as menpleasers; but in singleness of heart, fearing God:

23 [i]And whatsoever ye do, do *it* heartily, as to the Lord, and not unto men;

24 [j]Knowing that of the Lord ye shall receive the reward of the inheritance: [k]for ye serve the Lord Christ.

25 But he that doeth wrong shall receive for the wrong which he hath done: and [l]there is no respect of persons.

4 MASTERS,[m] GIVE unto *your* servants that which is just and equal; knowing that ye also have a Master in heaven.

2 [n]Continue in prayer, and watch in the same [o]with thanksgiving;

3 [p]Withal praying also for us, that God would [q]open unto us a door of utterance, to speak [r]the mystery of Christ, [s]for which I am also in bonds:

4 That I may make it manifest, as I ought to speak.

5 [t]Walk in wisdom toward them that are without, [u]redeeming the time.

6 Let your speech *be* always [v]with

3:18 [y]1 Pet. 3:1 [z]Eph. 5:3 **3:19** [a]Eph. 5:25 [b]Eph. 4:31 **3:20** [c]Eph. 6:1 [d]Eph. 5:24 **3:21** [e]Eph. 6:4 **3:22** [f]Eph. 6:5 1 Tim. 6:1 Tit. 2:9 1 Pet. 2:18 [g]ver. 20 [h]Philem. 16 **3:23** [i]Eph. 6:6,7 **3:24** [j]Eph. 6:8 [k]1 Cor. 7:22 **3:25** [l]Rom. 2:11 Eph. 6:9 1 Pet. 1:17 Deut. 10:17 **4:1** [m]Eph. 6:9 **4:2** [n]Luke 18:1 Rom. 12:12 [o]ch. 2:7

4:3 [p]Eph. 6:19 [q]1 Cor. 16:9; 2 Cor. 2:12 [r]Eph. 6:19 [s]Eph. 6:20; Phil. 1:7 **4:5** [t]Eph. 5:15 [u]Eph. 5:16 **4:6** [v]Eccl. 10:12

3:18–19 WIVES, SUBMIT YOURSELVES. See Eph. 5:21–23, notes; 1 Tim. 2:13,15, notes on the responsibility of wives and husbands in the family relationship.

3:20 CHILDREN, OBEY *YOUR* PARENTS. See Eph. 6:1, note on the responsibility of children in the family relationship.

3:20 FATHERS, PROVOKE NOT YOUR CHILDREN. For a discussion of this passage, including fifteen steps on how parents can lead their children to Christ, see article on PARENTS AND CHILDREN, p. 1880.

3:22 SERVANTS . . . MASTERS. Paul instructs slaves how to live in a Christian way within their tragic situation. He never indicates that the slave-master relationship is ordained by God or should be perpetuated. Rather he sows the seeds for its abolition in Philem. 10,12,14–17,21, and in the meantime seeks to regulate it to the benefit of both masters and slaves (Eph. 6:5–9; 1 Tim. 6:1–2; Tit. 2:9–10; cf. 1 Pet. 2:18–19).

3:23 DO *IT* . . . AS TO THE LORD. Paul exhorts Christians to regard all labor as a service rendered to the Lord. We must work as though Christ were our employer, knowing that all work performed "as to the Lord" will someday be rewarded (v. 24: cf. Eph. 6:6–8).

3:25 HE THAT DOETH WRONG. Within family, church, and employment relationships (vv. 12–25), Paul is concerned about the demonstration of love, justice, and fairness to one another. If taken seriously, these verses would eliminate much of the unloving and unjust treatment of others within our homes and churches. Specifically, we learn that: (1) Mistreatment of others by Christians is a serious matter affecting our future glory in heaven (cf. 2 Cor. 5:10). (a) Those who treat others in love and goodness will receive a reward from the Lord (v. 24; Eph. 6:8). (b) Those who mistreat and do wrong to another believer "shall receive for the wrong" which they have done. Those guilty will carry that wrong to judgment and bear the consequences without partiality (Deut. 10:17; 2 Chr. 19:7; Acts 10:34; Rom. 2:11).

(2) The principle of future accountability to God should guide and help motivate our love, kindness, and mercy toward all human beings. Let all believers keep in mind that God will hold His children responsible for the way they have treated one another (Gal. 6:7; see Mat. 22:37,39, notes; John 13:34, note; see article on THE JUDGMENT OF BELIEVERS, p. 1811).

4:2 CONTINUE IN PRAYER . . . WATCH. "Continue" (Gk. *proskartereō*) means "devote," "continue steadfast," "persevere," implying strong persistence and fervor, a holding fast to prayer. "Watch" (Gk. *grēgoreō*) means to be spiritually awake or alert. (1) Thus, we must devote ourselves intensely to prayer and remain alert to the many things that would detour us from this purpose. Satan and the weakness of our human nature will attempt to cause us to neglect prayer itself or to distract our minds and thoughts while praying. Hence, we must discipline ourselves to achieve the prayer required for Christian victory.

(2) This was an essential practice of those in the N.T. church who were baptized in the Holy Spirit: "they continued stedfastly . . . in prayers" (Acts 2:42). This devotion to God in prayer must be characterized by thanksgiving to Christ for what He has done for us.

4:3 GOD WOULD OPEN UNTO US A DOOR. The apostle Paul was confident that God was working with him by opening and shutting doors in order to direct his life and ministry. The fruitfulness of our lives and our witness for Christ depends both on His providence and on His direct intervention. We should pray for God to open doors for us and to indicate where we ought to work (cf. Acts 16:6–10).

grace, [w]seasoned with salt, [x]that ye may know how ye ought to answer every man.

Tychicus and Onesimus

7 All my state shall Tychicus declare unto you, *who is* a beloved brother, and a faithful minister and fellowservant in the Lord:
8 [y]Whom I have sent unto you for the same purpose, that he might know your estate, and comfort your hearts;
9 With [z]Onesimus, a faithful and beloved brother, who is *one* of you. They shall make known unto you all things which *are done* here.

Greetings and final instructions

10 [a]Aristarchus my fellowprisoner saluteth you, and [b]Marcus, sister's son to Barnabas, (touching whom ye received commandments: if he come unto you, receive him;)
11 And Jesus, which is called Justus, who are of the circumcision. These only *are my* fellowworkers unto the kingdom of God, which have been a comfort unto me.
12 [c]Epaphras, who is *one* of you, a servant of Christ, saluteth you, always [d]labouring[s] fervently for you in prayers, that ye may stand [e]perfect and [t]complete in all the will of God.
13 For I bear him record, that he hath a great zeal for you, and them *that are* in Laodicea, and them in Hierapolis.
14 [f]Luke, the beloved physician, and [g]Demas, greet you.
15 Salute the brethren which are in Laodicea, and Nymphas, and [h]the church which is in his house.
16 And when [i]this epistle is read among you, cause that it be read also in the church of the Laodiceans; and that ye likewise read the *epistle* from Laodicea.
17 And say to [j]Archippus, Take heed to [k]the ministry which thou hast received in the Lord, that thou fulfil it.
18 [l]The salutation by the hand of me Paul. [m]Remember my bonds. [n]Grace *be* with you. Amen.

4:6 [w]Mark 9:50 [x]1 Pet. 3:15
4:8 [y]Eph. 6:22
4:9 [z]Philem. 10
4:10 [a]Acts 19:29 [b]Acts 15:37 2 Tim. 4:11
4:12 [c]Philem. 23 [d]Rom. 15:30 [e]Mat. 5:48 1 Cor. 2:6
4:14 [f]2 Tim. 4:11 [g]2 Tim. 4:10
4:15 [h]Rom. 16:5 1 Cor. 16:19
4:16 [i]1 Thes. 5:27
4:17 [j]Philem. 2 [k]1 Tim. 4:6
4:18 [l]1 Cor. 16:21 2 Thes. 3:17 [m]Heb. 13:3 [n]Heb. 13:25

[s] Or, *striving* [t] Or, *filled*

4:6 SPEECH . . . WITH GRACE . . . SALT. A believer's speech must be pleasant, winsome, kind, and gracious. It must be language that results from the operation of God's grace in our hearts and speaks the truth in love (Eph. 4:15). "Seasoned with salt" may mean conversation that is appropriate and marked by purity, not corruption (cf. Eph. 4:29). Speech with grace, however, does not exclude fervent and stern words when necessary, to oppose those false believers who are enemies of the cross (see Mat. 23; Acts 15:1–2; Gal. 1:9).

4:12 LABOURING FERVENTLY FOR YOU IN PRAYERS. "Labouring fervently" (Gk. *agōnizō*, from which we derive the English word "agonize") denotes an intense desire, an agonizing, a wrestling, or a striving in prayer. Faithful N.T. believers not only continued steadfast in prayer (v. 2), but *agonized* with strong pleading in their prayers. The needs of our families, churches, and the world are no less significant today. We ought to pray fervently, knowing that in our struggles Christ's power is working mightily within us (1:29).

4:16 WHEN THIS EPISTLE IS READ. Paul's letters were read out loud to the congregation when they assembled for worship. The Colossian Christians, after receiving this letter, would most likely have made a copy of it to keep for themselves and then sent one of the copies to the nearby Laodiceans. The letter which the Colossians were to receive from Laodicea was probably the one we call Ephesians (see Introduction to Ephesians).

4:18 REMEMBER MY BONDS. During Paul's first Roman imprisonment he wrote Colossians, Philemon, Ephesians, and Philippians. In spite of Paul's being unjustly confined to prison for four or more years, his letters are filled with "thanksgiving" (1:3,12; 2:7; 3:15; 4:2), "grace" (Eph. 1:2, 6–7; 2:5; 3:2; 4:7; 6:24), "joy" (Phil. 1:4,18; 2:2; 3:1; 4:1,4), and "love" (Philem. 5,7,9).

PARENTS AND CHILDREN

***Col. 3:21** "Fathers, provoke not your children* to anger, *lest they be discouraged."*

It is the solemn obligation of parents (Gk. *patēr*; the plural, *pateres*, can mean "fathers" or "father and mother") to give their children the instruction and correction that belong to a Christian upbringing. Parents should be examples of Christian life and conduct, caring more for the salvation of their children than for their jobs, professions, ministry in the church, or social standing (cf. Ps. 127:3).

(1) According to Paul's word in Eph. 6:4 and Col. 3:21, as well as God's instruction in many O.T. passages (see Gen. 18:19, note; Deut. 6:7, note; Ps. 78:5, note; Prov. 4:1–4, note; 6:20, note), it is the responsibility of the parents to give their children the upbringing that prepares them for lives pleasing to God. It is the family, not the church or church school, that is primarily responsible for the Biblical and spiritual training of the children. Church and Sunday school only assist parental training.

(2) The very heart of Christian nurture is this: The heart of the father must be turned to the heart of the child in order to bring the heart of the child to the heart of the Savior (see Luke 1:17, note).

(3) In raising their children, the parents should show no favoritism, encourage as well as correct, punish only intentional wrongdoing, instruct with patience, and dedicate their lives in love to them with a heart of compassion, kindness, humility, gentleness, and patience (Col. 3:12–14,21).

(4) Here are fifteen steps that you as parents should take to lead your children to a life of godliness in Christ:

(a) Dedicate your children to God at the beginning of their lives (1 Sam. 1:28; Luke 2:22).

(b) Teach your children to fear the Lord and turn away from evil, to love righteousness and to hate iniquity. Instill in them an awareness of God's attitude and judgment toward sin (see Heb. 1:9, note).

(c) Teach your children to obey you as parents through Biblical discipline (Deut. 8:5; Prov. 3:11–12; 13:24; 23:13–14; 29:15,17; Heb. 12:7).

(d) Protect your children from ungodly influences by being aware of Satan's attempts to destroy them spiritually through attraction to the world or through immoral companions (Prov. 13:20; 28:7; 1 John 2:15–17).

(e) Make your children aware that God is always observing and evaluating what they do, think, and say (Ps. 139:1–12).

(f) Bring your children early in life to personal faith, repentance, and water baptism in Christ (Mat. 19:14).

(g) Establish your children in a spiritual church where God's Word is proclaimed, His righteous standards honored, and the Holy Spirit is manifested. Teach them to follow the principle: "I *am* a companion of all *them* that fear thee" (Ps. 119:63; see Acts 12:5, note).

(h) Encourage your children to remain separated from the world and to witness and work for God (2 Cor. 6:14—7:1; Jas. 4:4). Teach them that they are strangers and pilgrims upon this earth (Heb. 11:13–16), that their real home and citizenship is in heaven with Christ (Phil. 3:20; Col. 3:1–3).

(i) Instruct them in the importance of the baptism in the Holy Spirit (Acts 1:4–5,8; 2:4,39).

(j) Teach your children that God loves them and has a specific purpose for their lives (Luke 1:13–17; Rom. 8:29–30; 1 Pet. 1:3–9).

(k) Instruct your children daily in the sacred Scriptures, both in conversation and family devotions (Deut. 4:9; 6:5–7; 2 Tim. 3:15).

(l) Through example and exhortation, encourage your children to devote themselves to prayer (Acts 6:4; Rom. 12:12; Eph. 6:18; Jas. 5:16).

(m) Prepare your children to suffer and endure persecution for the sake of righteousness (Mat. 5:10–12). They must know "all that will live godly in Christ Jesus shall suffer persecution" (2 Tim. 3:12).

(n) Lift your children up to God by constant and fervent intercession (cf. Eph. 6:18; Jas. 5:16; see John 17:1, note on Jesus' prayer for His disciples as a model of the parents' prayer for their children).

(o) Have such love and concern for your children that you would be willing to pour out your life as if it were a sacrifice unto the Lord, in order to deepen their faith and make their lives what they should be in the Lord (see Phil. 2:17, note).

1 THESSALONIANS

Outline

Christian Greetings (1:1)

I. Paul's Personal Gratitude for the Thessalonians (1:2—3:13)
   - A. Rejoices About Their New Life in Christ (1:2–10)
     1. Their Faith, Love, and Hope (1:2–3)
     2. Their Genuine Conversion (1:4–6)
     3. Their Good Example to Others (1:7–10)
   - B. Reminisces About His Role in Their Lives (2:1—3:8)
     1. Reviews His Labors (2:1–12)
     2. Recalls Their Response (2:13–16)
     3. Retains His Interest (2:17—3:8)
   - C. Prays for an Opportunity to Return, and for Their Spiritual Advancement and Establishment in Holiness (3:9–13)

II. Paul's Practical Instruction to the Thessalonians (4:1—5:22)
   - A. Concerning Sexual Purity (4:1–8)
   - B. Concerning Brotherly Love (4:9–10)
   - C. Concerning Honest Labor (4:11–12)
   - D. Concerning the Coming of Christ (4:13—5:11)
     1. The State of the Dead in Christ (4:13–18)
     2. The Readiness of the Living in Christ (5:1–11)
   - E. Concerning Esteem for Spiritual Leaders (5:12–13)
   - F. Concerning Christian Living (5:14–18)
   - G. Concerning Spiritual Discernment (5:19–22)

Conclusion (5:23–28)
   - A. Prayer for Their Sanctification and Preservation (5:23–24)
   - B. Final Requests and Benediction (5:25–28)

Author: Paul

Theme: The Return of Christ

Date of Writing: c. A.D. 51

Background

Thessalonica, located slightly less than a hundred miles southwest of Philippi, was the capital, foremost city, and harbor of the Roman province of Macedonia. Among the city's 200,000 population was a strong Jewish community. When Paul founded the Thessalonian church on his second missionary journey, his fruitful ministry there was prematurely terminated because of intense Jewish hostility (Acts 17:1–9).

Being forced to leave Thessalonica, therefore, Paul went to Berea where another brief but successful ministry was cut short by persecution stirred up by hostile Jews who followed him from Thessalonica (Acts 17:10–13). Paul then traveled to Athens (Acts 17:15–34), where Timothy joined him; afterward Paul sent Timothy back to Thessalonica to check on the infant church (3:1–5), while he went on to Corinth (Acts 18:1–17). Timothy, upon completing his assignment, traveled to Corinth with a report for Paul about the

4 But as [z]we were allowed of God
[a]to be put in trust with the gospel,
even so we speak; [b]not as pleasing
men, but God, [c]which trieth our
hearts.
5 For [d]neither at any time used we
flattering words, as ye know, nor a
cloak of covetousness; [e]God *is* witness:
6 [f]Nor of men sought we glory, neither of you, nor *yet* of others, when
[g]we might have [b]been [h]burdensome, [i]as the apostles of Christ.
7 But [j]we were gentle among you,
even as a nurse cherisheth her children:
8 So being affectionately desirous
of you, we were willing [k]to have imparted unto you, not the gospel of God
only, but also [l]our own souls, because
ye were dear unto us.
9 For ye remember, brethren, our
labour and travail: for [m]labouring
night and day, [n]because we would not
be chargeable unto any of you, we
preached unto you the gospel of God.
10 [o]Ye *are* witnesses, and God *also*,
[p]how holily and justly and unblameably we behaved ourselves among you
that believe:
11 As ye know how we exhorted
and comforted and charged every one
of you, as a father *doth* his children,
12 [q]That ye would walk worthy of
God, [r]who hath called you unto his
kingdom and glory.

Paul's reception in Thessalonica

13 For this cause also thank we God
[s]without ceasing, because, when ye
received the word of God which ye
heard of us, ye received *it* [t]not *as* the
word of men, but as it is in truth, the
word of God, which effectually worketh
also in you that believe.
14 For ye, brethren, became followers [u]of the churches of God which in
Judaea are in Christ Jesus: for [v]ye also
have suffered like things of your own
countrymen, even as they *have* of the
Jews:
15 [w]Who both killed the Lord
Jesus, and [x]their own prophets, and
have [c]persecuted us; and they please
not God, [y]and are contrary to all men:
16 [z]Forbidding us to speak to the
Gentiles that they might be saved, [a]to

2:4 [z]1 Cor. 7:25 [a]Tit. 1:3 [b]Gal. 1:10 [c]Prov. 17:3 **2:5** [d]2 Cor. 2:17 [e]Rom. 1:9 **2:6** [f]1 Tim. 5:17 [g]1 Cor. 9:4 [h]2 Cor. 11:9 [i]1 Cor. 9:1 **2:7** [j]1 Cor. 2:3 **2:8** [k]Rom. 1:11 & 15:29 [l]2 Cor. 12:15 **2:9** [m]Acts 20:34 2 Thes. 3:8 [n]2 Cor. 12:13 **2:10** [o]ch. 1:5 [p]2 Cor. 7:2 **2:12** [q]Col. 1:10 [r]1 Cor. 1:9 2 Thes. 2:14 **2:13** [s]ch. 1:3 [t]Gal. 4:14 **2:14** [u]Gal. 1:22 [v]Acts 17:5 **2:15** [w]Acts 2:23 [x]Mat. 5:12 [y]Esth. 3:8 **2:16** [z]Luke 11:52 Acts 13:50 [a]Gen. 15:16 Mat. 23:32

[b] Or, *used authority* [c] Or, *chased us out*

2:4 WE SPEAK; NOT AS PLEASING MEN. Every preacher of the gospel faces the temptation to please men, i.e., seek acceptance, approval, and glory from others (v. 6) by preaching only what will not offend. (1) Yielding to this temptation may take the form of tolerating sin and lukewarmness in the congregation (cf. Rev. 2:20; 3:15–16). It may also involve the use of flattering speech in order to gain financial offerings, numerical gain, political office, or praise from others (vv. 4–6). (2) If this occurs, irreparable damage is done to the righteousness and integrity of Christ's church. For this reason it is essential that our motive in preaching should always be to seek God's approval and not man's (1 Cor. 4:5; Gal. 1:9–10; see Luke 1:17, note; 2 Tim. 4:3–4, note).

2:7 AS A NURSE CHERISHETH HER CHILDREN. Paul and his helpers offer an example of the spiritual attitude that all missionaries, evangelists, and pastors should have as they preach the gospel. (1) As missionaries, they acted as a mother or nurse with little children. This implies that under great sacrifice, they made a special effort to nurture, protect, and provide for the spiritual needs of the new converts.

(2) Their gentleness implies they did not act like important or superior persons.

(3) The missionaries possessed such a yearning and love for the Thessalonians that they were willing to spend their very lives for the people (v. 8).

(4) They devoted long hours, even to the point of weariness, in order to give them the gospel (v. 9).

(5) They lived upright and blameless lives before the people, exhorting and correcting them as any good father would (vv. 10–12).

2:10 JUSTLY AND UNBLAMEABLY WE BEHAVED. Paul does not accept the erroneous view of "sinning Christianity," which says that the salvation provided by Christ and His atoning blood is not adequate to save us from the bondage and power of sin. This unbiblical doctrine maintains that all Christians must expect to sin against God daily in word, thought, and deed throughout their earthly life. Contrary to the above doctrine, (1) Paul affirms, with regard to his own conduct among the Thessalonians, that he behaved "holily and justly and unblameably." (2) Paul called both the church and God Himself as witnesses that the sufficient grace of God through Christ had enabled him, as he affirmed elsewhere, to cleanse himself "from all filthiness of the flesh and spirit, perfecting holiness in the fear of God" (2 Cor. 7:1; cf. 2 Cor. 1:12; 2:17; 6:3–10; 1 Thes. 1:5; 2 Tim. 1:3).

2:16 THE WRATH IS COME UPON THEM. Paul denounces the Jews who oppose the gospel (vv. 14–16) and speaks of God's wrath as already upon them. This wrath includes both God's turning the already hardened Jews of Israel over to blindness and a reprobate mind (cf. Rom. 1:21), and the future outpouring of His wrath foretold by Christ (Mat. 21:43; 23:38; 24:15–28; Luke 21:5–24; 23:27–31).

fill up their sins always: [b]for the wrath is come upon them to the uttermost.

Paul's concern for the Thessalonians

17 But we, brethren, being taken from you for a short time [c]in presence, not in heart, endeavoured the more abundantly [d]to see your face with great desire.

18 Wherefore we would have come unto you, even I Paul, once and again; but [e]Satan hindered us.

19 For [f]what *is* our hope, or joy, or [g]crown of [d]rejoicing? *Are* not even ye in the presence of our Lord Jesus Christ [h]at his coming?

20 For ye are our glory and joy.

Timothy's visit and report

3 WHEREFORE [i]WHEN we could no longer forbear, [j]we thought it good to be left at Athens alone;

2 And sent [k]Timotheus, our brother, and minister of God, and our fellowlabourer in the gospel of Christ, to establish you, and to comfort you concerning your faith:

3 [l]That no man should be moved by these afflictions: for yourselves know that [m]we are appointed thereunto.

4 [n]For verily, when we were with you, we told you before that we should suffer tribulation; even as it came to pass, and ye know.

2:16 [b]Mat. 24:6
2:17 [c]1 Cor. 5:3; Col. 2:5; [d]ch. 3:10
2:18 [e]Rom. 1:13
2:19 [f]2 Cor. 1:14; [g]Prov. 16:31; [h]1 Cor. 15:23
3:1 [i]ver. 5; [j]Acts 17:15
3:2 [k]Rom. 16:21; 1 Cor. 16:10
3:3 [l]Eph. 3:13; [m]Acts 9:16; 1 Cor. 4:9; 2 Tim. 3:12
3:4 [n]Acts 20:24
3:5 [o]ver. 1; [p]1 Cor. 7:5; 2 Cor. 11:3; [q]Gal. 2:2
3:6 [r]Acts 18:1; [s]Phil. 1:8
3:7 [t]2 Cor. 1:4
3:8 [u]Phil. 4:1
3:9 [v]ch. 1:2
3:10 [w]Acts 26:7; [x]Rom. 15:32; [y]ch. 2:17; [z]Col. 4:12
3:11 [a]Mark 1:3
3:12 [b]ch. 4:10
3:13 [c]1 Cor. 1:8; Phil. 1:10

5 For this cause, [o]when I could no longer forbear, I sent to know your faith, [p]lest by some means the tempter have tempted you, and [q]our labour be in vain.

6 [r]But now when Timotheus came from you unto us, and brought us good tidings of your faith and charity, and that ye have good remembrance of us always, desiring greatly to see us, [s]as we also *to see* you:

7 Therefore, brethren, [t]we were comforted over you in all our affliction and distress by your faith:

8 For now we live, if ye [u]stand fast in the Lord.

9 [v]For what thanks can we render to God again for you, for all the joy wherewith we joy for your sakes before our God;

10 [w]Night and day [x]praying exceedingly [y]that we might see your face, [z]and might perfect that which is lacking in your faith?

Paul's prayer for the church

11 Now God himself and our Father, and our Lord Jesus Christ, [a]direct[e] our way unto you.

12 And the Lord [b]make you to increase and abound in love one toward another, and toward all *men,* even as we *do* toward you:

13 To the end he may [c]stablish your hearts unblameable in holiness

[d] Or, *glorying?* [e] Or, *guide*

2:18 BUT SATAN HINDERED US. Paul's missionary endeavors had at times been frustrated by Satan. Scriptural truths concerning Satan's opposition to faithful believers include the following: (1) Satan is permitted by God to war against and hinder believers from doing what they sincerely desire to do for Christ (Eph. 6:11–12; cf. Dan. 10:13,20–21; Zech. 3:1; Mat. 4:1–10).

(2) Satan's power is, however, subject to God's overruling (Job 1:9–12; 2:6; see 1:12, note); He can overrule Satan's activities and turn them into good for His kingdom (2 Cor. 12:7–9).

(3) This hindering of Satan can be overcome and need not be permanent (cf. 3:11). To this end, we must pray daily for deliverance from his schemes and power (see 3:5, note; Mat. 4:10, note on Satan; 6:13; Eph. 6:12, note; see article on POWER OVER SATAN AND DEMONS, p. 1486).

3:3 AFFLICTIONS. The followers of Christ must not regard trouble, persecution, and affliction as alien to the Christian life. (1) True believers who refuse to conform to the prevailing characteristics of their world will "suffer tribulation" (v. 4; cf. Acts 14:22; Rom. 8:18; 2 Tim. 3:12; see Mat. 5:10, note). (2) These afflictions must not be identified with the end-time outpouring of God's wrath upon the ungodly (5:9; Mat. 24:21; 2 Thes. 1:6; Rev. 3:10, note).

3:5 THE TEMPTER HAVE TEMPTED YOU. This is the second time Paul has referred to the activity of Satan in this letter (cf. 2:18). Paul firmly believed in Satan and the realm of evil spirits (Eph. 2:2; 2 Thes. 2:9), as did Jesus Christ (Mat. 13:39; Mark 3:14–15; 4:15; Luke 4:1–13,33–41). Today many no longer believe in a personal Satan; he is seldom mentioned, exposed, or confronted directly in or by the church. The devil has tempted us to believe that he is somehow no longer a real enemy who takes people captive, and that we need no longer cast out evil spirits as Jesus and the early N.T. believers did. Many churches feel no need to challenge Satan directly with the power of the kingdom of Christ (see Mat. 4:10, note on Satan; see article on POWER OVER SATAN AND DEMONS, p. 1486).

3:13 UNBLAMEABLE IN HOLINESS ... AT THE COMING. Paul often prayed with the return of Christ in mind (cf. Phil. 1:10). He considered it

before God, even our Father, at the
coming of our Lord Jesus Christ [d]with
all his saints.

Living to please God

4 FURTHERMORE THEN we [f]be-
seech you, brethren, and [g]exhort
you by the Lord Jesus, [e]that as ye
have received of us [f]how ye ought to
walk [g]and to please God, *so* ye would
abound more and more.
2 For ye know what commandments
we gave you by the Lord Jesus.
3 For this is [h]the will of God, *even*
[i]your sanctification, [j]that ye should
abstain from fornication:
4 [k]That every one of you should
know how to possess his vessel in
sanctification and honour;
5 [l]Not in the lust of concupis-
cence, [m]even as the Gentiles [n]which
know not God:
6 That no *man* go beyond and [h]de-
fraud his brother [i]in *any* matter: be-
cause that the Lord [o]*is* the avenger of
all such, as we also have forewarned
you and testified.
7 For God hath not called us unto
uncleanness, [p]but unto holiness.
8 [q]He therefore that [j]despiseth,
despiseth not man, but God, [r]who
hath also given unto us his holy Spirit.
9 But as touching brotherly love
[s]ye need not that I write unto you: for
[t]ye yourselves are taught of God [u]to
love one another.
10 [v]And indeed ye do it toward all
the brethren which are in all Macedo-
nia: but we beseech you, brethren,
[w]that ye increase more and more;
11 And that ye study to be quiet,
and [x]to do your own business, and
[y]to work with your own hands, as we
commanded you;
12 [z]That ye may walk honestly to-
ward them that are without, and *that* ye
may have lack [k]of nothing.

The sudden coming of the Lord

13 But I would not have you to be

3:13 [d]Zech. 14:5
4:1 [e]Phil. 1:27 [f]ch. 2:12 [g]Col. 1:10
4:3 [h]Rom. 12:2 [i]Eph. 5:27 [j]Col. 3:5
4:4 [k]Rom 6:19
4:5 [l]Col. 3:5 [m]Eph. 4:17 [n]1 Cor. 15:34
4:6 [o]2 Thes. 1:8
4:7 [p]Lev. 11:44
4:8 [q]Luke 10:16 [r]1 Cor. 2:10
4:9 [s]ch. 5:1 [t]Jer. 31:34 [u]Mat. 22:39
4:10 [v]ch. 1:7 [w]ch. 3:12
4:11 [x]2 Thes. 3:11 [y]Acts 20:35 Eph. 4:28
4:12 [z]Rom. 13:13

Heb. 10:23-26

[f] Or, *request* [g] Or, *beseech* [h] Or, *oppress,* or, *overreach* [i] Or, *in the matter* [j] Or, *rejecteth* [k] Or, *of no man*

a tragedy if at the Lord's return some within the church were caught living in sin or lukewarmness. Jesus emphasized this same concern (Mat. 24:42–51; 25:1–13). In light of Christ's return, the Biblical standard is to be "unblameable in holiness." We must be wholeheartedly given over to the Lord and separated from all that offends Him. The phrase "with all his saints" refers to departed saints who are already with the Lord in heaven (see article on THE RAPTURE, p. 1889).

4:3 THIS IS THE WILL OF GOD. Although they lived in an age when sexual sin was accepted, the apostles did not compromise the truth and holiness of God. They would not lower their standards to accommodate the ideas or trends of their contemporary society. Whenever they found low standards in some of the churches (cf. Rev. 2:14–15,20), they rebuked and sought to correct them. In the light of the prevalent low morals of today, apostolic-type leaders are needed, as they were in N.T. times, to call the church to God's standards of righteousness.

4:3–7 ABSTAIN FROM FORNICATION. God imposes on all believers high standards of purity and sanctification in regard to all sexual matters. For a discussion of what these standards are, see article on STANDARDS OF SEXUAL MORALITY, p. 1964.

4:6 DEFRAUD HIS BROTHER. Sexual immorality defrauds another person, whether a believer or not. To defraud (Gk. *pleonokteō*) means "to go beyond what is right," "to transgress," "to overreach." All sexual activity or play outside of marriage is an act of terrible injustice against another individual. Adultery violates the rights of another married person. Sexual looseness before marriage defiles and robs another person of the holiness and chastity that God desires for him or her. It destroys the purity and virginity that must be brought into a marriage.

4:8 DESPISETH NOT MAN, BUT GOD. Those who reject the instructions of the apostle on sanctification and purity are rejecting God. (1) To disregard Paul's admonition is to stand squarely against the Holy Spirit, i.e., to sin against the purity that the Spirit desires. God will avenge and punish church members who disregard moral purity for the satisfaction of their own lusts (v. 6; cf. Heb. 13:4).

(2) All those in the world and within the visible church who reject the truth and take "pleasure in unrighteousness" (2 Thes. 2:12, note) will be abandoned by Christ when the faithful of His churches are caught up "to meet the Lord in the air" (v. 17; see article on THE RAPTURE, p. 1889). They will suffer destruction (5:3), wrath (5:9), retribution (2 Thes. 1:8), and judgment (2 Thes. 1:9; 2:12) at the final coming of Jesus Christ from heaven in flaming fire to judge all who "obey not the gospel" (2 Thes. 1:7–8).

4:13 CONCERNING THEM WHICH ARE ASLEEP. This phrase refers to Christians who had died and whose souls were in heaven; it does not mean that the dead are unconscious in a sort of soul-sleep (cf. Phil. 1:21, note). The Thessalonians did not understand how the resurrection of Christians who had already died related to the catching up of living Christians at the coming of Christ (see John 14:3, note). They apparently thought that those dying before Christ returns for

ignorant, brethren, concerning them
which are asleep, that ye sorrow not,
[a]even as others [b]which have no
hope.
14 For [c]if we believe that Jesus
died and rose again, even so [d]them
also which sleep in Jesus will God
bring with him.
15 For this we say unto you [e]by the
word of the Lord, that [f]we which are
alive *and* remain unto the coming of the
Lord shall not prevent them which are
asleep.
16 For [g]the Lord himself shall descend from heaven with a shout, with
the voice of the archangel, and with
[h]the trump of God: [i]and the dead in
Christ shall rise first:
17 [j]Then we which are alive *and*
remain shall be caught up together
with them [k]in the clouds, to meet the
Lord in the air: and so [l]shall we ever
be with the Lord.

4:13 [a]Lev. 19:28 2 Sam. 12:20 [b]Eph. 2:12
4:14 [c]1 Cor. 15:13 [d]1 Cor. 15:23
4:15 [e]1 Ki. 13:17 [f]1 Cor. 15:51
4:16 [g]Mat. 24:30 Acts 1:11 [h]1 Cor. 15:52 [i]1 Cor. 15:23
4:17 [j]1 Cor. 15:51 [k]Acts 1:9 [l]John 17:24
4:18 [m]ch. 5:11
5:1 [n]Mat. 24:3 [o]ch. 4:9
5:2 [p]2 Pet. 3:10
5:3 [q]Is. 13:6-9 [r]Hos. 13:13
5:4 [s]Rom. 13:12
5:5 [t]Eph. 5:8

18 [m]Wherefore [1]comfort one another with these words.

The day of the Lord

5 BUT OF [n]the times and the seasons, brethren, [o]ye have no need
that I write unto you.
2 For yourselves know perfectly
that [p]the day of the Lord so cometh as
a thief in the night.
3 For when they shall say, Peace
and safety; then [q]sudden destruction
cometh upon them, [r]as travail upon a
woman with child; and they shall not 2 T 1:7- 2:8
escape.
4 [s]But ye, brethren, are not in
darkness, that that day should overtake you as a thief.
5 Ye are all [t]the children of light,
and the children of the day: we are not
of the night, nor of darkness.

[1] Or, *exhort*

the church (vv. 16–17) would not be resurrected until a time much later. Paul tells them that the dead in Christ shall rise at the same time the Lord returns for the faithful of His churches (see article on THE RAPTURE, p. 1889).

4:14–18 THE LORD HIMSELF SHALL DESCEND. The event described by Paul in these verses is often referred to as "the rapture of the church." For a discussion of this future event, see article on THE RAPTURE, p. 1889.

4:18 COMFORT ONE ANOTHER. Paul inspires hope in the Thessalonians, not by telling them to prepare for martyrdom during the period of "the day of the Lord" (5:2–10), i.e., the tribulation (Rev. 6–19), but by informing them of the rapture (see vv. 14–17; John 14:3, note; 1 Cor. 15:51–58; see article on THE RAPTURE, p. 1889). With the knowledge of this doctrine they will be able to comfort one another.

5:1 THE TIMES AND THE SEASONS. Having spoken about the return of Christ to catch up His followers from the earth (4:13–18), Paul now turns to the subject of God's final judgment upon all those on earth who reject salvation in Christ in the final days, that terrible time called "the day of the Lord" (v. 2). The believers' rapture (4:17) must be simultaneous with the beginning of "the day of the Lord" in order for Christ's return to be imminent and unexpected, as He taught (see Mat. 24:42,44, notes).

5:2 THE DAY OF THE LORD. The "day of the Lord" normally refers not to a 24-hour day, but to an extended period of time when God's enemies are overthrown (Is. 2:12–21; 13:9–16; 34:1–4; Jer. 46:10; Joel 1:15—2:11,28; 3:9,12–17; Amos 5:18–20; Zech. 14:1–3), followed by the earthly reign of Christ (Zeph. 3:14–17; Rev. 20:4–7). (1) This day begins when direct divine judgment and tribulation fall upon the world toward the end of this age (v. 3). The tribulation period is included within the day of the Lord (Rev. 6–19; see 6:1, note). This wrath of God culminates with Christ's coming to destroy all the wicked (see Joel 1:14, note; 2:30–31, note; Zeph. 1:7, note; Rev. 16:16, note; 19:11–21).

(2) The day of the Lord apparently begins at a time when people are hoping for peace and safety (v. 3).

(3) The "day" will not overtake faithful believers like a thief, for they are destined for salvation, not wrath, and are alert, spiritually awake, living in faith, love, and righteousness (vv. 4–9).

(4) Believers are delivered from this "wrath to come" (1:10, note) through the Lord Jesus Christ (v. 9) when He comes in the clouds to catch up the faithful of His churches and take them to heaven (4:17; see John 14:3, note; Rev. 3:10, note; see article on THE RAPTURE, p. 1889).

(5) The day of the Lord will end after the millennial kingdom (Rev. 20:4–10) at the creation of the new heaven and new earth (cf. 2 Pet. 3:13; Rev. 21:1).

5:2 A THIEF IN THE NIGHT. The metaphor regarding a thief in the night means that the time when the day of the Lord begins is uncertain and unexpected. There is no way one can date it (see Mat. 24:42–44, notes on the Lord's teaching on the unexpected time of His coming for the church).

5:3 PEACE AND SAFETY. It is the unbeliever who will be saying, "Peace and safety." This could mean that the world will be expecting and hoping for peace. The day of the Lord and its worldwide tribulation will come upon them suddenly, destroying any hope for peace and security.

5:4 YE, BRETHREN, ARE NOT IN DARKNESS. Believers do not live in sin and rebellion toward God. They belong to the day that precedes the night and will not experience God's appointed night of wrath (vv. 8–9; see article on THE RAPTURE, p. 1889).

THE RAPTURE

***1 Thes. 4:16–17** "For the Lord himself shall descend from heaven with a shout, with the voice of the archangel, and with the trump of God: and the dead in Christ shall rise first: Then we which are alive and remain shall be caught up together with them in the clouds, to meet the Lord in the air: and so shall we ever be with the Lord."*

The term "rapture" is derived from the Latin word *raptus*, which means "caught away" or "caught up." This Latin word is equivalent to the Greek *harpazō*, translated as "caught up" in 1 Thes. 4:17. This event, described here and in 1 Cor. 15, refers to the catching up of the church from the earth to meet the Lord in the air. It involves only the faithful of Christ's churches.

(1) Just prior to the rapture, as Christ is descending from heaven for His church, the resurrection of the "dead in Christ" will occur (1 Thes. 4:16). This is not the same resurrection found in Rev. 20:4, for the latter is an event occurring after Christ returns to earth, destroys the wicked, and binds Satan (Rev. 19:11—20:3). The resurrection in Rev. 20:4 relates to the martyred dead of the tribulation and possibly to O.T. saints (see Rev. 20:6, note).

(2) As the dead in Christ are raised, living believers will be transfigured; their bodies will put on immortality (1 Cor. 15:51,53). Their transformation will happen in a very short time, "in the twinkling of an eye" (1 Cor. 15:52).

(3) Both the resurrected believers and the transfigured believers will be "caught up together" (1 Thes. 4:17) to meet Christ in the air, that is, in the atmosphere between earth and heaven.

(4) They will be visibly united with Christ (1 Thes. 4:16–17), taken to His Father's house in heaven (see John 14:2–3, notes), and united with loved ones who have died (1 Thes. 4:13–18).

(5) They will be removed from all distress (2 Cor. 5:2,4; Phil. 3:21), from all persecution and oppression (see Rev. 3:10, note), from the entire sphere of sin and from death (1 Cor. 15:51–57); the rapture delivers them from "the wrath to come" (see 1 Thes. 1:10, note; 5:9), that is, from the great tribulation.

(6) The hope that our Savior will soon return to take us out of the world to "ever be with the Lord" (1 Thes. 4:17) is the blessed hope of all the redeemed (Tit. 2:13). It is a major source of comfort for suffering believers (1 Thes. 4:17–18; 5:10).

(7) Paul uses "we" in 1 Thes. 4:17 because he knows the Lord's return was something that could have happened in his own lifetime, and he communicates this same anticipation to the Thessalonians. The Bible insists on a continual waiting with eagerness for the return of our Lord. Believers today must be ever watchful and hopeful for Christ's return to take them out of this world and unto Himself (cf. Rom. 13:11; 1 Cor. 7:29; 10:11; 15:51–52; Phil. 4:5).

(8) The portion of the professing church that fails to abstain from evil and is unfaithful to Christ will be left behind at the rapture (see Mat. 25:1, note; Luke 12:45, note). They will remain as part of the apostate church (see Rev. 17:1, note; see article on THE AGE OF THE ANTICHRIST, p. 1896), subject to God's wrath.

(9) Following the rapture is the day of the Lord, a time that brings tribulation and wrath to the ungodly (1 Thes. 5:2–10; see 5:2, note). That will be followed by the second stage of Christ's coming, when He comes to destroy the ungodly and to reign on earth (see Mat. 24:42,44 notes).

6 [u]Therefore let us not sleep, as *do* others; but [v]let us watch and be sober.

7 For [w]they that sleep sleep in the night; and they that be drunken [x]are drunken in the night.

✝ 8 But let us, who are of the day, be sober, [y]putting on the breastplate of faith and love; and for an helmet, the hope of salvation.

9 For [z]God hath not appointed us to wrath, [a]but to obtain salvation by our Lord Jesus Christ,

10 [b]Who died for us, that, whether we wake or sleep, we should live together with him.

2 Thes. 2:13

11 [c]Wherefore [m]comfort yourselves together, and edify one another, even as also ye do.

Final exhortation

12 And we beseech you, brethren, [d]to know them which labour among you, and are over you in the Lord, and admonish you;

13 And to esteem them very highly in love for their work's sake. [e]*And* be at peace among yourselves.

14 Now we [n]exhort you, brethren, [f]warn them that are [o]unruly, [g]comfort the feebleminded, [h]support the weak, [i]be patient toward all *men.*

15 [j]See that none render evil for evil unto any *man;* but ever [k]follow that which is good, both among yourselves, and to all *men.*

16 [l]Rejoice evermore.

17 [m]Pray without ceasing.

18 In every thing give thanks: for this is the will of God in Christ Jesus concerning you.

19 [n]Quench not the Spirit.

20 [o]Despise not prophesyings.

21 [p]Prove all things; [q]hold fast that which is good.

5:6 [u]Mat. 25:5 [v]1 Pet. 5:8 **5:7** [w]Luke 21:34 [x]Acts 2:15 **5:8** [y]Eph. 6:14 **5:9** [z]Rom. 9:22 [a]2 Thes. 2:13 **5:10** [b]2 Cor. 5:15 **5:11** [c]ch. 4:18 **5:12** [d]1 Cor. 16:18 **5:13** [e]Mark 9:50 **5:14** [f]2 Thes. 3:11 [g]Heb. 12:12 [h]Rom. 14:1 [i]Gal. 5:22 **5:15** [j]Lev. 19:18 [k]Gal. 6:10 **5:16** [l]2 Cor. 6:10 **5:17** [m]Eph. 6:18 **5:19** [n]Eph. 4:30 **5:20** [o]1 Cor. 14:1 **5:21** [p]1 John 4:1 [q]Phil. 4:8

[m] Or, *exhort* [n] Or, *beseech* [o] Or, *disorderly*

5:6 LET US WATCH. "Watch" (Gk. *grēgoreō*) means to "stay awake and keep alert." The context (vv. 4–9) indicates that Paul is not exhorting his readers to "watch" for the "day of the Lord" (v. 2), but rather to be spiritually prepared in order to escape the wrath of the day of the Lord (cf. 2:11–12; Luke 21:34–36). (1) If we wish to escape the wrath of God (v. 3), we must remain spiritually awake and morally alert, and we must continue in faith, love, and the hope of salvation (vv. 8–9; see Luke 21:36, note; Eph. 6:11, note). (2) Since the faithful will be protected from God's wrath through the rapture (see v. 2, note; see article on THE RAPTURE, p. 1889), they must not fear the day of the Lord, but must "wait for his Son from heaven . . . Jesus, which delivered us from the wrath to come" (1:10).

5:6 BE SOBER. The word "sober" (Gk. *nēphō*) had two meanings in N.T. times. (1) The primary and literal meaning, as given by various Greek lexicons, is "a state of abstinence from wine," "to drink no wine," "to abstain from wine," "to be completely unaffected by wine," or "to be sober, abstain from wine." It carries a secondary or metaphorical meaning of alertness, wakefulness, or self-control, i.e., to be alert spiritually and self-controlled, just as someone who does not drink alcoholic wine (see Tit. 2:2, note).

(2) The context of v. 6 supports the view that Paul was not excluding the literal meaning. The words "let us watch and be sober" are contrasted with the words of the following verse, "they that be drunken are drunken in the night" (v. 7). Thus, Paul's contrast of *nēphō* with physical drunkenness would indicate that he was including the literal meaning of "abstinence from wine." Compare with Jesus' statement about those who eat and drink with drunkards and are thus caught unaware by His return (Mat. 24:48–51).

5:9 NOT APPOINTED US TO WRATH. One reason why the hope of Christ's return is such a comfort to believers (4:17–18) is that He delivers us from the terrible wrath of God, i.e., the judgments of the day of the Lord (v. 2–3; cf. Rev. 6:16–17; 11:18; 14:10,19; 15:1,7; 16:1,19; 19:15).

5:10 LIVE TOGETHER WITH HIM. Paul identifies our deliverance from the day of God's wrath and our hope of salvation with Christ's sacrificial death and His return to take us to live together with Him.

5:17 PRAY WITHOUT CEASING. This means to abide in the presence of the Father, having a continual cry from the heart for His grace and blessing. "Without ceasing" does not mean to be constantly uttering formal prayers. Rather, it implies recurring prayer on all sorts of occasions throughout the day (Luke 18:1; Rom. 12:12; Eph. 6:18; Col. 4:2).

5:19–20 QUENCH NOT THE SPIRIT. (1) Paul equates quenching the Spirit's presence and activity with the depreciation and rejection of the Holy Spirit's supernatural manifestations such as prophesying. To repress or reject the right and orderly use of prophecy or other spiritual gifts will result in the loss of the manifestation of the Spirit among believers (1 Cor. 12:7–10,28–30). The Holy Spirit's ministry for believers is described in John 14:26; 15:26–27; 16:13–14; Acts 1:8; 13:2; Rom. 8:2,11,16,26; 1 Cor. 2:9–14; 12:1–11; Gal. 5:22–25. (2) The two verses clearly indicate that churches other than Corinth experienced spiritual gifts in public worship. Note that although prophetic utterances were not to be despised, they also were not to be accepted until they had been examined carefully (v. 21; see 1 Cor. 14:29, note.)

(i.e., a prophecy or a revelation), a "word" (verbal message), or a "letter" (supposedly from Paul), that the time of great tribulation and the day of the Lord had begun. Paul corrects this misunderstanding by stating that three significant events will signal that the day of the Lord has arrived (2:2): (1) a major apostasy and rebellion will occur (2:3), (2) God's appointed restraint against evil will be lifted (2:6–7), and (3) "the man of sin" will be revealed (2:3–4,8–12). Paul rebukes those in the church who were using the expectation of Christ's imminent return as an excuse for not working daily. He exhorts all believers to live diligent and disciplined lives (3:6–12).

Special Features

Three major features or emphases characterize this epistle. (1) It contains one of the most developed passages in the N.T. concerning unrestrained lawlessness and deception at the end of history (2:3–12). (2) God's righteous judgment that will accompany Christ's second coming is described here in apocalyptic terms, similar to the book of Revelation (1:6–10; 2:8). (3) It uses terms for the eschatological antichrist not found elsewhere in the Bible (2:3,8).

Reading 2 Thessalonians

In order to read the entire New Testament in one year, the book of 2 Thessalonians should be read in 3 days, according to the following schedule:
☐ 1 ☐ 2 ☐ 3

NOTES

Thanksgiving and prayer

1 PAUL, [a]AND Silvanus, and Timotheus, unto the church of the Thessalonians [b]in God our Father and the Lord Jesus Christ:

2 [c]Grace unto you, and peace, from God our Father and the Lord Jesus Christ.

3 [d]We are bound to thank God always for you, brethren, as it is meet, because that your faith groweth exceedingly, and the charity of every one of you all toward each other aboundeth;

Heb. 11:29-35

Encouragement in persecution

4 So that [e]we ourselves glory in you in the churches of God [f]for your patience and faith [g]in all your persecutions and tribulations that ye endure:

5 *Which is* [h]a manifest token of the righteous judgment of God, that ye may be counted worthy of the kingdom of God, [i]for which ye also suffer:

6 [j]Seeing *it is* a righteous thing with God to recompense tribulation to them that trouble you;

7 And to you who are troubled [k]rest with us, when [l]the Lord Jesus shall be revealed from heaven with [a]his mighty angels,

8 [m]In flaming fire [b]taking vengeance on them [n]that know not God, and [o]that obey not the gospel of our Lord Jesus Christ:

9 [p]Who shall be punished with everlasting destruction from the presence of the Lord, and [q]from the glory of his power;

10 [r]When he shall come to be glorified in his saints, [s]and to be admired in all them that believe (because our testimony among you was believed) in that day.

11 Wherefore also we pray always for you, that our God would [t]count[c] you worthy of *this* calling, and fulfil all the good pleasure of *his* goodness, and [u]the work of faith with power:

12 [v]That the name of our Lord Jesus Christ may be glorified in you, and ye in him, according to the grace of our God and the Lord Jesus Christ.

Instruction concerning the day of the Lord

2 NOW WE beseech you, brethren, [w]by the coming of our Lord Jesus Christ, [x]and *by* our gathering together unto him,

2 [y]That ye be not soon shaken in

1:1 [a]2 Cor. 1:19 [b]1 Thes. 1:1 **1:2** [c]1 Cor. 1:3 **1:3** [d]1 Thes. 1:2 ch. 2:13 **1:4** [e]2 Cor. 7:14 1 Thes. 2:19 [f]1 Thes. 1:3 [g]1 Thes. 2:14 **1:5** [h]Phil. 1:28 [i]1 Thes. 2:14 **1:6** [j]Rev. 6:10 **1:7** [k]Rev. 14:13 [l]1 Thes. 4:16 Jude 14 **1:8** [m]Heb. 12:29 2 Pet. 3:7 Rev. 21:8 [n]Ps. 79:6 [o]Rom. 2:8 **1:9** [p]Phil. 3:19 2 Pet. 3:7 [q]Deut. 33:2 Is. 2:19 **1:10** [r]Ps. 89:7 [s]Ps. 68:35 **1:11** [t]ver. 5 [u]1 Thes. 1:3 **1:12** [v]1 Pet. 1:7 **2:1** [w]1 Thes. 4:16 [x]Mat. 24:31 Mark 13:27 **2:2** [y]Mat. 24:4 Eph. 5:6

[a] Gk. *the angels of his power* [b] Or, *yielding* [c] Or, *vouchsafe*

1:5 THE RIGHTEOUS JUDGMENT OF GOD. The Thessalonians were persevering in faith amidst persecution and afflictions (v. 4). Their enduring attitude was a "token" or indication of God's righteous judgment, meaning that God judged the Thessalonians to be worthy of His grace and kingdom, for which they were suffering. Their unjust suffering was also a sign that those doing the persecuting opposed God's own people and would thus experience God's future retribution (vv. 5–9).

1:7 REST WITH US. Although God will begin to repay the wicked (v. 6) at the beginning of the tribulation (Rev. 6; see article on THE GREAT TRIBULATION, p. 1456), complete retribution and vengeance (vv. 6–9) will occur only at the end of the age when the Lord Jesus returns to earth in final judgment (vv. 7–10; Rev. 19:11–21). Similarly, partial relief will come to God's people when He removes them from earth to be with Him always (see article on THE RAPTURE, p. 1889), but complete rest will occur only when the Lord Jesus returns to earth with His saints to judge evil and govern the human race. Full rest means seeing Christ "glorified in you, and ye in him" at the final day (v. 12). The result is the total victory, when righteousness reigns, sin is defeated, and the faithful followers of Christ are vindicated.

1:9 EVERLASTING DESTRUCTION. This is the clearest statement in Paul's epistles concerning the eternal future punishment of the wicked (see Mat. 10:28, note on hell).

1:10 HE SHALL COME TO BE GLORIFIED. This passage is not speaking of the time when believers will be taken from earth to meet Christ in the air (John 14:2–3; 1 Thes. 4:17). Rather, it speaks of the revelation of Jesus Christ in power and great glory to destroy the present world system and inaugurate His thousand-year reign on earth (Rev. 19:11—20:4).

2:1 THE COMING OF OUR LORD JESUS. In his first letter to the Thessalonians, Paul gave assurance to all true believers that they would be caught up to meet the Lord in the air and thus would forever be with their Lord (1 Thes. 4:13–18). This event would deliver them from the coming wrath of God that was to fall upon the earth (1 Thes. 1:10; 5:9–10). Now, however, false teachers were teaching that the day of the Lord had already begun and that God's final wrath was being poured out upon the earth (see next note).

2:2 SHAKEN . . . TROUBLED. The Thessalonians were troubled and shaken because of what the false teachers were saying about the day of the Lord (see previous note). He tells them not to be alarmed, for the day of God's wrath has not yet arrived. Two things will signal its arrival: (1) There must come a specific "falling away," and (2)

mind, or be troubled, neither by spirit,
nor by word, nor by letter as from
us, as that the day of Christ is at
hand.

Its relation to apostasy

3 [z]Let no man deceive you by any
means: for *that day shall not come,* [a]except there come a falling away first,
and [b]that man of sin be revealed,
[c]the son of perdition;

Its relation to the man of sin

4 Who opposeth and [d]exalteth
himself [e]above all that is called God,
or that is worshipped; so that he as
God sitteth in the temple of God, shewing himself that he is God.
5 Remember ye not, that, when I
was yet with you, I told you these
things?

Its relation to the restrainer

6 And now ye know what [d]withholdeth that he might be revealed in
his time.
7 For [f]the mystery of iniquity doth
already work: only he who now letteth
will let, until he be taken out of the way.
8 And then shall that Wicked be revealed, [g]whom the Lord shall consume [h]with the spirit of his mouth,
and shall destroy [i]with the brightness
of his coming:
9 *Even him,* whose coming is [j]after
the working of Satan with all power
and [k]signs and lying wonders,

Its relation to unbelievers

10 And with all deceivableness of
unrighteousness in [l]them that perish;

1 Tim. 6:14-15

2:3 [z]Mat. 24:4 Eph. 5:6 [a]1 Tim. 4:1 [b]Dan. 7:25 Rev. 13:11 [c]John 17:12
2:4 [d]Is. 14:13 Rev. 13:6 [e]1 Cor. 8:5
2:7 [f]1 John 2:18
2:8 [g]Dan. 7:10 [h]Is. 11:4 [i]Heb. 10:27
2:9 [j]John 8:41 Rev. 18:23 [k]Deut. 13:1 Rev. 19:20
2:10 [l]2 Cor. 2:15

[d] Or, *holdeth*

the "man of sin" will be revealed (v. 3). Paul goes on to state that these two events will not reach fulfillment until that which "letteth . . . be taken out of the way" (v. 7).

Paul's words "by spirit, nor by word" may indicate that the false teaching was coming through tongues and interpretation or through prophecy (see 1 Cor. 14:29, note on judging tongues and prophecy).

2:3 *THAT DAY SHALL NOT COME,* EXCEPT. Paul explains the events that will signal the beginning of the day of the Lord and goes on to discuss the destruction of the man of sin and the unrighteous at the end of the age. The sequence of events is as follows: (1) Throughout the entire church age, a "mystery of iniquity" (v. 7) is at work, reminding us that the end is coming; evil will become progressively worse as history draws to a close. (2) As the "mystery of iniquity" becomes more prevalent, apostasy in the church will reach major proportions (v. 3; cf. Mat. 24:12; 2 Tim. 4:3–4). (3) The restrainer (i.e., "he who now letteth") of the man of lawlessness is then taken out of the way (vv. 6–7). (4) Next, the man of lawlessness is revealed (vv. 3–4,7,9–10). (5) The apostasy reaches its climax in total rebellion against God and His Word; God sends a deluding influence upon those who did not love the truth (vv. 9–11). (6) The man of lawlessness is then destroyed along with all who took pleasure in wickedness (v. 12); this occurs at Christ's coming after the tribulation, i.e., at the end of the age (v. 8; Rev. 19:20–21).

2:3 A FALLING AWAY FIRST ... MAN OF SIN BE REVEALED. For a discussion of the "falling away" and "the man of sin," see article on THE AGE OF THE ANTICHRIST, p. 1896.

2:6 WHAT WITHHOLDETH. Something or someone is holding back the man of sin. When he who holds him back is taken out of the way, then the day of the Lord will begin (see article on THE AGE OF THE ANTICHRIST, p. 1896, for a discussion of the restrainer).

2:7 MYSTERY OF INIQUITY DOTH ALREADY WORK. The "mystery of iniquity" is a secret or a behind-the-scenes activity of evil powers throughout the course of human history, preparing the way for the apostasy and the man of sin. (1) It is an insidious process that entraps unbelievers and prepares many within the church to turn from true faith and to accept the lie embodied in the apostate church. It involves a spirit or movement against true Biblical faith and divine law; it seeks to gain freedom from moral restraint and to take pleasure in sin (vv. 10–12; see v. 12, note). (2) Though this spirit existed already in Paul's day, it will be especially prevalent in the world and in Christianity toward the end of the age (see Mat. 24:11, note; 2 Tim. 4:3–4, note; see article on THE AGE OF THE ANTICHRIST, p. 1896).

2:8 WHOM THE LORD SHALL CONSUME. After Satan and the man of sin have done their work of deceit and evil (vv. 9–10), they will be overthrown by Christ's coming to earth at the end of the tribulation (see Rev. 19:20, note).

2:9 WITH ALL POWER AND SIGNS AND LYING WONDERS. For a discussion of the activities of "the man of sin," see article on THE AGE OF THE ANTICHRIST, p. 1896.

2:10 THE LOVE OF THE TRUTH. From the very beginning of creation the central issue in man's relationship with God has been either his disregard of the Word and truth of God or his love for them. This response to God's word is also a pivotal issue in the last days of this age. Salvation will be realized only by those who by faith in Christ maintain a fervent and sincere "love of the truth," who believe with unwavering conviction what God has said, and who reject all new "revelation" or teaching that conflicts with that truth (see Mat. 24:5,11, notes; see article on THE GREAT TRIBULATION, p. 1456).

THE AGE OF THE ANTICHRIST

2 Thes. 2:3–4 "Let no man deceive you by any means: for that *day shall not come, except there come a falling away first, and that man of sin be revealed, the son of perdition; Who opposeth and exalteth himself above all that is called God, or that is worshipped; so that he as God sitteth in the temple of God, showing himself that he is God."*

According to the Bible, the antichrist (cf. 1 John 2:18) is coming, the one who engineers the final onslaught of Satan against Christ and the saints just prior to the time when our Lord Jesus Christ establishes His kingdom on earth. Paul's terms for the antichrist are the "man of sin" and "the son of perdition" (2 Thes. 2:3). Other terms used in the Bible are the "beast [rising] up out of the sea" (Rev. 13:1–10), "a scarlet coloured beast" (Rev. 17:3), and "the beast" (Rev. 17:8,16; 19:19–20; 20:10).

SIGNS OF THE ANTICHRIST'S COMING. Unlike the rapture (see article on THE RAPTURE, p. 1889), the coming of the antichrist will not be without warning. Several signs point to his coming and his appearance. At least three events must occur before he makes his appearance on earth: (1) the "mystery of iniquity," already at work in the world, must intensify (2 Thes. 2:7); (2) the "falling away" must come (2:3); (3) "he who now letteth" must be removed (2:7).

(1) The "mystery of iniquity," that behind-the-scenes activity of evil powers evident throughout the world (see 2 Thes. 2:7, note), will increase until it reaches its climax in the complete ridicule of and disregard for any standards and commandments held sacred in the Bible. Because of a prevailing spirit of lawlessness, the love of many will grow cold (Mat. 24:10–12; cf. Luke 18:8). Yet a faithful remnant will remain loyal to the apostolic faith as revealed in the N.T. (Mat. 24:13; 25:10; Luke 18:7; see Rev. 2:7, note). Through these faithful people, the church will remain a warrior church, wielding the sword of the Spirit until it is taken out of the world (see Eph. 6:11, note).

(2) The "apostasy" (Gk. *apostasia*), literally meaning "departure," "falling away" (2 Thes. 2:3), or "abandonment and rebellion," will occur. In the last days, multitudes within the professing church will depart from Biblical truth.

(a) Both the apostle Paul and Christ depict a dismal picture of the condition of much of the visible church—morally, spiritually, and doctrinally—as the present age closes (cf. Mat. 24:5,10–13,24; 1 Tim. 4:1; 2 Tim. 4:3–4). Paul in particular stresses that the churches will be invaded by godless elements in the last days.

(b) This "falling away" within the church will have two dimensions. (i) *Theological apostasy* is the departure from and rejection of a part or all of the original teachings of Christ and the apostles (1 Tim. 4:1; 2 Tim. 4:3). False leaders will offer salvation and cheap grace and ignore Christ's demand for repentance, separation from immorality, and loyalty to God and His standards (2 Pet. 2:1–3,12–19). False gospels centering on human desires, needs, and goals of self-interest will become popular (see 2 Tim. 4:3–4, note). (ii) *Moral apostasy* is the severing of one's saving relationship with Christ and returning to sin and immorality. Apostates may proclaim right doctrine and N.T. teaching, yet abandon God's moral standards (Is. 29:13; Mat. 23:25–28; see article on PERSONAL APOSTASY, p. 1946). Many churches will tolerate almost anything for the sake of numbers, money, success, and honor (see 1 Tim. 4:1, note). The gospel of the cross with its call to suffer reproach from the world (Phil. 1:29), to radically renounce sin (Rom. 8:13), to sacrifice for the kingdom of God, and to deny one's self will become rare (Mat. 24:12; 2 Tim. 3:1–5; 4:3).

(c) Both the history of the church and the predicted apostasy of the last days warn all believers not to take for granted a continual progress of the kingdom of God through

all ages until the end. At some point in time in the worldwide history of the church, rebellion against God and His Word will reach astounding proportions. The day of the Lord will bring God's wrath upon those who reject His truth (1 Thes. 5:2–9).

(d) The ultimate triumph of God's kingdom and His righteousness in the world, therefore, depends not on the gradual increase of the success of the professing church, but on the final intervention of God when He breaks into the world with righteous judgment (Rev. 19–22; see 2 Thes. 2:7–8; 1 Tim. 4:1, note; 2 Pet. 3:10–13; and the book of Jude).

(3) A pivotal and decisive event must occur before the "man of sin" can be revealed and the day of the Lord and its tribulation begins (2 Thes. 2:2–3), namely, the taking "out of the way" of someone (2:7) or something that "letteth" the mystery of iniquity and the "man of sin" (2:3–6). "Letteth" is an old English word meaning "obstruct, hold back, restrain." When he who holds back the man of sin is taken out of the way, then the day of the Lord can begin (2:6–7).

(a) "He who now letteth [restraineth]" (2 Thes. 2:7) may best be understood as referring to the Holy Spirit, who alone has the power to hold back iniquity, the man of sin, and Satan (2 Thes. 2:9). The restrainer is referred to by both the masculine article ("he who now letteth," 2:7) and by the neuter article ("what withholdeth," 2:6). Likewise, the word for "Spirit" in the Greek language can be referred to by a masculine or neuter pronoun (see John 16:8, note; Rom. 8:13; see Gal. 5:17, note on the Holy Spirit's work of restraining sin).

(b) At the beginning of the final seven years of tribulation, the Holy Spirit will be "taken out of the way" (2 Thes. 2:7). This does not mean He is taken out of the world, but only that His restraining influence against lawlessness and the antichrist's entrance will cease. All restraints against sin will be removed and the satanically inspired rebellion will begin. However, the Holy Spirit will still remain on earth during the tribulation to convict people of their sins, convert them to Christ, and empower them (Rev. 7:9,14; 11:1–11; 14:6–7).

(c) The Holy Spirit's being taken out of the way enables the man of sin to come on the scene (2 Thes. 2:3–4). God will send a deluding influence upon all those who have refused to love the truth (see 2:11, note); they will accept the claims of the man of sin, and human society will degenerate to a depth of depravity never seen before.

(d) The Holy Spirit's sin-restraining ministry is carried on largely through the church, which is the temple of the Holy Spirit (1 Cor. 3:16; 6:19). Therefore, many interpreters believe the Holy Spirit's being taken out of the way is a strong indication that the rapture of the faithful will occur at the same time (1 Thes. 4:17). That is, the return of Christ to gather the overcomers of His churches unto Himself and to deliver them from the coming wrath (1 Thes. 1:10) will occur before the beginning of the day of the Lord and at the time when the man of sin is revealed (see article on THE RAPTURE, p. 1889).

(e) Some scholars believe that the restrainer of 2 Thes. 2:6 (neuter gender) refers to the Holy Spirit and His restraining ministry, while in 2:7 the "he who now letteth" (masculine gender) refers to the believers who are gathered together to Christ and taken out of the way, i.e., raptured to meet Christ in the air in order to be with the Lord (1 Thes. 4:17).

THE ANTICHRIST'S ACTIVITIES. As the day of the Lord begins, the "man of sin" is revealed. He will be a world ruler who will make a covenant with Israel seven years before the end of the age (see Dan. 9:27, note).

(1) His true identification will be confirmed three and one-half years later as he breaks his covenant with Israel, becomes the world ruler, declares himself to be God, desecrates the temple in Jerusalem (see article on THE GREAT TRIBULATION, p. 1456), forbids the worship of the Lord (see 2 Thes. 2:8–9), and devastates the land of Palestine (see Dan. 9:27, note; 11:36–45, note).

(2) The antichrist will declare himself to be God and will severely persecute those who remain loyal to God and Christ (see Dan. 7:8,24–25, notes; Rev. 11:6–7; 13:7,15–18). He will demand worship, evidently from a great temple that he uses as the center

of his pronouncements (cf. Dan. 7:8,25; 8:4; 11:31,36). Humans have sought this status since the beginning of creation (see 2 Thes. 2:8, note; Rev. 13:8,12, notes; see also article on THE GREAT TRIBULATION, p. 1456).

(3) The "man of sin" will demonstrate through the power of Satan great signs, wonders, and miracles in order to propagate error (2 Thes. 2:9). "Lying wonders" means that they are genuine supernatural miracles that deceive people into accepting a lie. (a) It is possible these demonstrations of the supernatural will be seen on television around the world. Millions will be impressed, deceived, and persuaded by this highly persuasive and popular leader because they have no deep commitment to or love for the truth of God's Word (2:9–12). (b) Both Paul's words (2 Thes. 2:9) and Jesus' (Mat. 24:24) should caution believers to not assume that everything that is miraculous comes from God. Apparent "manifestations of the Spirit" (1 Cor. 12:7–10) and alleged experiences from God or the Holy Spirit must be tested by the person's loyalty to Christ and Scripture.

THE DEFEAT OF THE ANTICHRIST. At the end of the tribulation, Satan will gather together many nations at Armageddon under the direction of the antichrist and make war against God and His people in a battle that will involve the entire world (see Rev. 16:16, note). When that occurs, Christ will return and supernaturally intervene to destroy the antichrist, his armies, and all who do not obey the gospel (see Dan. 11:45, note; Rev. 19:15–21, notes). Thereupon Christ will bind Satan and establish His kingdom on earth (20:1–6).

because they received not the love of the truth, that they might be saved.

11 And [m]for this cause God shall send them strong delusion, [n]that they should believe a lie:

12 That they all might be damned who believed not the truth, but [o]had pleasure in unrighteousness.

Its relation to believers

13 But [p]we are bound to give thanks always to God for you, brethren beloved of the Lord, because God [q]hath [r]from the beginning chosen you to salvation [s]through sanctification of the Spirit and belief of the truth:

14 Whereunto he called you by our gospel, to [t]the obtaining of the glory of our Lord Jesus Christ.

15 Therefore, brethren, [u]stand fast, and hold [v]the traditions which ye have been taught, whether by word, or our epistle.

16 [w]Now our Lord Jesus Christ himself, and God, even our Father, [x]which hath loved us, and hath given *us* everlasting consolation and [y]good hope through grace,

17 Comfort your hearts, [z]and stablish you in every good word and work.

Appeals for prayer

3 FINALLY, BRETHREN, [a]pray for us, that the word of the Lord [e]may have *free* course, and be glorified, even as *it is* with you:

2 And [b]that we may be delivered from [f]unreasonable and wicked men: [c]for all *men* have not faith.

3 But [d]the Lord is faithful, who shall stablish you, and [e]keep *you* from evil.

4 And [f]we have confidence in the Lord touching you, that ye both do and will do the things which we command you.

5 And [g]the Lord direct your hearts

2:11 [m]Rom. 1:24 [n]1 Tim. 4:1 **2:12** [o]Rom. 1:32 **2:13** [p]ch. 1:3 [q]1 Thes. 1:4 [r]Eph. 1:4 [s]1 Pet. 1:2 **2:14** [t]1 Pet. 5:10 **2:15** [u]1 Cor. 16:13 [v]1 Cor. 11:2 **2:16** [w]ch. 1:1,2 [x]Rev. 1:5 [y]1 Pet. 1:3 **2:17** [z]1 Cor. 1:8 **3:1** [a]Eph. 6:19 **3:2** [b]Rom. 15:31 [c]Acts 28:24 Rom. 10:16 **3:3** [d]1 Cor. 1:9 [e]John 17:15 2 Pet. 2:9 **3:4** [f]2 Cor. 7:16 **3:5** [g]1 Chr. 29:18

e Gk. *may run* f Gk. *absurd*

2:11 SEND THEM STRONG DELUSION. After the removal of the restrainer (see article on THE AGE OF THE ANTICHRIST, p. 1896) and the revealing of the man of sin, there will be no more opportunity for salvation for one particular group of people. (1) This group consists of all those inside or outside the church who, after adequately hearing the truth of God's Word, have willingly and intentionally refused to love that truth and chosen instead to take pleasure in the wickedness of the world (see vv. 10,12, notes).

(2) God will send those individuals a strong delusion so that they may never again have an opportunity to believe the truth they refused to love (v. 12). They are forever doomed to believe "a lie" (i.e., the claims of the man of sin).

(3) God's purpose in sending the "strong delusion" is that they "might be damned" (v. 12). Therefore, for those who have heard and understood God's Word, yet did not love and receive its truth but chose instead the pleasure of sin, "there remaineth no more sacrifice for sins, But a certain fearful looking for of judgment" (Heb. 10:26–27; see article on PERSONAL APOSTASY, p. 1946).

(4) Salvation during the days of the tribulation will be offered only to those who never had an adequate opportunity to receive the knowledge of the truth or to hear and understand the gospel (cf. Rev. 7:14; 11:3; 14:6–7). Those who proclaim the gospel during those days will include the 144,000 sons of Israel (see Rev. 7:4, note), the two witnesses (see Rev. 11:3, note), and angels (see Rev. 14:6, note).

2:12 HAD PLEASURE IN UNRIGHTEOUSNESS. Taking "pleasure in unrighteousness," while loving not the truth (v. 10), will be the deciding factor in God's judgment in the last days. (1) Those who are to experience the wrath and tribulation of God will be those who did not love the truth and therefore participated in, and entertained themselves with, evil and immorality (see 2 Tim. 3:1, note). They will be abandoned to demonic deception, the power of darkness, and divine justice (see Luke 23:35, note; Rom. 1:32, note; 1 Tim. 4:1, note).

(2) Those experiencing condemnation during the "day of the Lord" (see v. 2, note) will include not only unbelievers, but also those guilty of apostasy from the true faith. They chose to enjoy sin instead of enjoying God and refused to take a stand against the immorality of the last days (see vv. 3,7, notes; 2 Tim. 4:3–4, note).

3:1 PRAY FOR US. Paul was able to accomplish what he did for Christ partly because of the prayers of God's people. Therefore he often sought the prayers of those to whom he ministered, aware that God's will for his life and ministry would not be realized without the prayers and intercession of fellow believers (cf. Rom. 15:30–32; 2 Cor. 1:11; Phil. 1:19; Col. 4:2; 1 Thes. 5:25). This spiritual principle of God's kingdom is valid today. We need the prayers of other believers and they need our prayers. With faithful intercession in the churches, the desires of God will be accomplished, Satan's purposes frustrated (v. 3), and the full power of the Holy Spirit manifested (Acts 4:24–33).

3:3 KEEP *YOU* FROM EVIL. When believers earnestly pray, they can be assured that God will protect them from the evil of Satan. God will strengthen them to face any temptation that may assail them (1 Cor. 10:13; Heb. 2:18) and will protect them from the powerful forces of the demonic (see Eph. 6:12, note).

into the love of God, and into [g]the pa-
tient waiting for Christ.

Warning against idleness

6 Now we command you, brethren,
in the name of our Lord Jesus Christ,
[h]that ye withdraw yourselves [i]from
every brother that walketh [j]disor-
derly, and not after [k]the tradition
which he received of us.
7 For yourselves know [l]how ye
ought to follow us: for [m]we behaved
not ourselves disorderly among you;
8 Neither did we eat any man's
bread for nought; but [n]wrought with
labour and travail night and day, that
we might not be chargeable to any of
you:
9 [o]Not because we have not power,
but to make [p]ourselves an example
unto you to follow us.
10 For even when we were with you,
this we commanded you, [q]that if any
would not work, neither should he eat.
11 For we hear that there are some
[r]which walk among you disorderly,
[s]working not at all, but are busybod-
ies.
12 [t]Now them that are such we
command and exhort by our Lord Jesus
Christ, [u]that with quietness they
work, and eat their own bread.
13 But ye, brethren, [v]be[h] not
weary in well doing.
14 And if any man obey not our
word [i]by this epistle, note that man,
and [w]have no company with him, that
he may be ashamed.
15 [x]Yet count *him* not as an enemy,
[y]but admonish *him* as a brother.

Benediction

16 Now [z]the Lord of peace himself
give you peace always by all means.
The Lord *be* with you all.
17 [a]The salutation of Paul with
mine own hand, which is the token in
every epistle: so I write.
18 [b]The grace of our Lord Jesus
Christ *be* with you all. Amen.

3:6 [h]Rom. 16:17 [i]1 Cor. 5:11 [j]1 Thes. 4:11 [k]ch. 2:15
3:7 [l]1 Cor. 4:16 [m]1 Thes. 2:10
3:8 [n]Acts 18:3 2 Cor. 11:9
3:9 [o]1 Cor. 9:6 [p]ver. 7
3:10 [q]1 Thes. 4:11
3:11 [r]ver. 6 [s]1 Tim. 5:13
3:12 [t]1 Thes. 4:11 [u]Eph. 4:28
3:13 [v]Gal. 6:9
3:14 [w]Mat. 18:17
3:15 [x]Lev. 19:17 [y]Tit. 3:10
3:16 [z]Rom. 15:33
3:17 [a]1 Cor. 16:21
3:18 [b]Rom. 16:24

[g] Or, *the patience of Christ* [h] Or, *faint not*
[i] Or, *signify that man by an epistle*

3:6 WALKETH DISORDERLY. Those who were walking disorderly were people who were loafing, idle, and unwilling to work. They were taking advantage of the generosity of the church (cf. 1 Thes. 4:9–10) and receiving support from brethren who made a living by ordinary occupations (vv. 6–15). (1) Paul says that such people must be disciplined by refusing to support them and by withdrawing fellowship from them (vv. 6,14). (2) Although Paul advocates that help must be given to those in real need, he nowhere teaches that believers ought to give food or money to able-bodied people who refuse to work steadily for a living (cf. v. 10).

3:12 WITH QUIETNESS THEY WORK. Christians must not be loafers, but must work hard and steadily in order to provide for themselves and their families and to have enough to help others in need (1 Cor. 16:1; 2 Cor. 8:1–15; Eph. 4:28).

1 TIMOTHY

Outline

Introduction (1:1–20)

I. Directions Concerning the Church's Ministry (2:1—4:5)
  - A. The Prominence of Prayer (2:1–8)
  - B. The Appropriate Conduct of Women (2:9–15)
  - C. Qualifications for Overseers (Elders) (3:1–7)
    1. Personal
       - a. Above Reproach (3:2)
       - b. Temperate (3:2)
       - c. Prudent (3:2)
       - d. Respectable (3:2)
       - e. Hospitable (3:2)
       - f. Able to Teach (3:2)
       - g. Not Given to Wine (3:3)
       - h. Not Belligerent (3:3)
       - i. Gentle (3:3)
       - j. Not Contentious (3:3)
       - k. Not a Lover of Money (3:3)
       - l. Not a Recent Convert (3:6)
       - m. Good Reputation Outside the Church (3:7)
    2. Family
       - a. Husband of One Wife (3:2)
       - b. Manages His Own Household Well (3:4–5)
       - c. Has Obedient and Respectful Children (3:4)
  - D. Qualifications for Deacons (3:8–12)
    1. Personal
       - a. Worthy of Respect (3:8)
       - b. Sincere (3:8)
       - c. Not Given to Wine (3:8)
       - d. Free from Covetousness (3:8)
       - e. Holds to the Faith with a Clear Conscience (3:9)
       - f. Tested and Above Reproach (3:10)
    2. Family
       - a. Husband of One Wife (3:12)
       - b. A Godly and Trustworthy Wife (3:11)
       - c. Manages His Children and Household Well (3:12)
  - E. Reasons the Church Must Require High Qualifications for Leaders (3:13—4:5)

II. Directions Concerning Timothy's Ministry (4:6—6:19)
  - A. His Personal Life (4:6–16)
  - B. His Relationship to Persons in the Church (5:1—6:19)
    1. Older and Younger Men (5:1)
    2. Older and Younger Women (5:2)
    3. Widows (5:3–16)
    4. Elders and Prospective Elders (5:17–25)
    5. Servants (6:1–2)
    6. False Teachers (6:3–10)
       Parenthesis: Exhortation to Timothy Himself (6:11–16)
    7. The Rich (6:17–19)

Conclusion (6:20–21)

Author: Paul

Theme: Sound Doctrine and Godliness

Date of Writing: c. A.D. 65

Background

1 and 2 Timothy and Titus—commonly referred to as "The Pastoral Epistles"—are letters from Paul (1 Tim. 1:1; 2 Tim. 1:1; Tit. 1:1) to Timothy (at Ephesus) and Titus (at Crete) concerning pastoral care of the churches. Some critics have questioned Paul's authorship of these letters, but the early church emphatically placed them among Paul's authentic epistles. Although differences in style and vocabulary do exist in the Pastoral Epistles when compared with Paul's other letters, these differences may be adequately and convincingly accounted for within the context of Paul's advanced years and his personal concerns for the ministries of Timothy and Titus.

Paul wrote 1 Timothy after the events recorded at the end of Acts. Paul's first Roman imprisonment (Acts 28) apparently ended in his freedom (2 Tim. 4:16–17). Afterwards, according to Clement of Rome (c. A.D. 96) and the Muratorian Canon (c. A.D. 170), Paul went from Rome westward to Spain and fulfilled a long-desired ministry there (cf. Rom. 15:23–24,28). Based on data in the Pastoral Epistles, Paul then returned to the Aegean Sea region (especially Crete, Macedonia, and Greece) for further ministry. During this time (c. A.D. 64–65), Paul commissioned Timothy as his apostolic representative to minister in Ephesus, and Titus to do the same at Crete. From Macedonia Paul wrote his first letter to Timothy, and a short time later he wrote to Titus. Afterwards, Paul again became a prisoner in Rome, during which time he wrote a second letter to Timothy, shortly before his martyrdom in A.D. 67/68 (see 2 Tim. 4:6–8; see also Introduction to 2 Timothy).

Purpose

Paul had a threefold purpose in writing 1 Timothy: (1) to exhort Timothy himself about his ministry and personal life; (2) to exhort Timothy to defend the purity of the gospel and its holy standards from corruption by false teachers; and (3) to give Timothy instructions concerning various church matters and problems at Ephesus.

Survey

One of the foremost concerns that Paul communicates to his younger assistant is that Timothy earnestly contend for the faith and refute the false teachings that were diluting the saving power of the gospel (1:3–7; 4:1–8; 6:3–5,20–21). Paul also instructs Timothy about the spiritual and character qualifications for church leadership; he provides a composite picture of the kind of persons who are permitted to become spiritual leaders of the churches (see the detailed list of qualifications for overseers and deacons in the above outline).

Among other things, Paul instructs Timothy how to relate to various groups within the church, such as women (2:9–15; 5:2), widows (5:3–16), older and younger men (5:1), elders (5:17–25), slaves (6:1–2), false teachers (6:3–10), and the rich (6:17–19). Paul gives Timothy five clear charges to fulfill (1:18–20; 3:14–16; 4:11–16; 5:21–25; 6:20–21). Through the epistle Paul conveys affection for Timothy as his convert and son in the faith and sets forth a high standard of godliness for his life and for the church.

Special Features

Four major features or emphases characterize this epistle. (1) Addressed directly to Timothy as Paul's representative to the church at Ephesus, the letter is very personal and written with deep emotion and feeling. (2) Along with 2 Timothy, it stresses more than any other N.T. epistle the pastoral responsibility of keeping the gospel pure and free from false teachings that would weaken its saving power. (3) It emphasizes the supreme value of the gospel, the demonic influence behind its corruption, the holy calling of the church, and the high qualifications God requires for its leaders. (4) It provides the most specific direction in the N.T. about how a pastor is to relate properly to both sexes and to all age and social groups in the church.

Reading 1 Timothy

In order to read the entire New Testament in one year, the book of 1 Timothy should be read in 6 days, according to the following schedule:

□ 1 □ 2 □ 3 □ 4 □ 5 □ 6

NOTES

1 PAUL, AN apostle of Jesus Christ
[a]by the commandment [b]of God
our Saviour, and Lord Jesus Christ,
[c]*which is* our hope;
2 Unto [d]Timothy, [e]*my* own son in
the faith: [f]Grace, mercy, *and* peace,
from God our Father and Jesus Christ
our Lord.

Warning against false teachers

3 As I besought thee to abide still at
Ephesus, [g]when I went into Macedo-
nia, that thou mightest charge some
[h]that they teach no other doctrine,
4 [i]Neither give heed to fables and
endless genealogies, [j]which minister
questions, rather than godly edifying
which is in faith: *so do.*
5 Now [k]the end of the command-
ment is charity [l]out of a pure heart,
and *of* a good conscience, and *of* faith
unfeigned:
6 From which some [a]having
swerved have turned aside unto [m]vain
jangling;
7 Desiring to be teachers of the law;
[n]understanding neither what they
say, nor whereof they affirm.
8 But we know that [o]the law *is*
good, if a man use it lawfully;
9 [p]Knowing this, that the law is
not made for a righteous man, but for
the lawless and disobedient, for the un-
godly and for sinners, for unholy and
profane, for murderers of fathers and
murderers of mothers, for manslayers,
10 For whoremongers, for them
that defile themselves with mankind,
for menstealers, for liars, for perjured
persons, and if there be any other thing
that is contrary [q]to sound doctrine;
11 According to the glorious gospel
of the blessed God, [r]which was com-
mitted to my trust.

The Lord's grace to Paul

12 And I thank Christ Jesus our
Lord, [s]who hath enabled me, [t]for
that he counted me faithful, [u]putting
me into the ministry;
13 [v]Who was before a blasphemer,
and a persecutor, and injurious: but I
obtained mercy, because [w]I did *it* igno-
rantly in unbelief.
14 [x]And the grace of our Lord was
exceeding abundant [y]with faith [z]and
love which is in Christ Jesus.
15 [a]This *is* a faithful saying, and
worthy of all acceptation, that [b]Christ
Jesus came into the world to save sin-
ners; of whom I am chief.
16 Howbeit for this cause [c]I ob-
tained mercy, that in me first Jesus
Christ might show forth all longsuffer-
ing, [d]for a pattern to them which
should hereafter believe on him to life
everlasting.
17 Now unto [e]the King eternal,
[f]immortal, [g]invisible, [h]the only
wise God, [i]*be* honour and glory for
ever and ever. Amen.

Paul's charge to Timothy

18 This charge [j]I commit unto

1:1 [a]Acts 9:15 [b]Tit. 1:3 [c]Col. 1:27
1:2 [d]Acts 16:1 [e]Tit. 1:4 [f]Gal. 1:3
1:3 [g]Acts 20:1 [h]Gal. 1:6,7
1:4 [i]Tit. 1:14 [j]ch. 6:4
1:5 [k]Rom. 13:8 Gal. 5:14 [l]2 Tim. 2:22
1:6 [m]ch. 6:4,20
1:7 [n]ch. 6:4
1:8 [o]Rom. 7:12
1:9 [p]Gal. 3:19
1:10 [q]2 Tim. 4:3 Tit. 1:9
1:11 [r]1 Cor. 9:17 Gal. 2:7 Col. 1:25
1:12 [s]2 Cor. 12:9 [t]1 Cor. 7:25 [u]2 Cor. 3:5
1:13 [v]Acts 8:3 [w]John 4:21
1:14 [x]Rom. 5:20 [y]2 Tim. 1:13 [z]Luke 7:47
1:15 [a]2 Tim. 2:11 [b]Mat. 9:13
1:16 [c]2 Cor. 4:1 [d]Acts 13:39
1:17 [e]Ps. 10:16 [f]Rom. 1:23 [g]Heb. 11:27 [h]Rom. 16:27 [i]1 Chr. 29:11
1:18 [j]2 Tim. 2:2

[a] Or, *not aiming at*

1:3 TEACH NO OTHER DOCTRINE. Seven years before Paul wrote this letter he warned the elders of Ephesus that false teachers would attempt to distort the true message of Christ (see Acts 20:29, note). Now that this was happening, Paul exhorts Timothy to confront them boldly. This young pastor must not compromise with these false teachings that were corrupting both the law and the gospel. He must faithfully wage a good warfare against them (v. 18) by proclaiming the original faith taught by Christ and the apostles (2 Tim. 1:13–14).

1:5 THE END OF THE COMMANDMENT. The supreme goal of all instruction from God's Word is not Bible knowledge in itself, but an inward moral transformation that expresses itself in love, purity of heart, a clear conscience, and faith without hypocrisy (see Acts 24:16, note on a good conscience; see article on BIBLE TRAINING FOR CHRISTIANS, p. 1920). Concerning this truth two important facts must be kept in mind. (1) The Biblical concept of teaching and learning is not primarily to impart knowledge or to prepare oneself academically. It is to produce holiness and a righteous lifestyle, conforming to the ways of God (cf. 2 Tim. 1:13). (2) The teacher of God's Word must be someone whose life illustrates perseverance in truth, faith, and holiness (3:1–13).

1:8 THE LAW *IS* GOOD. See Mat. 5:17, note on the law and the Christian; cf. Rom. 7:12; see article on THE OLD TESTAMENT LAW, p. 124.

1:13 A BLASPHEMER ... PERSECUTOR. Before his conversion, Paul was a violent persecutor of believers in Christ (cf. Acts 8:3; 9:1–2,4–5; 22:4–5; 26:9–11; Gal. 1:13). His terrible crimes against God's people were sufficient reason for ranking himself as the foremost of sinners (vv. 14–15; cf. 1 Cor. 15:9; Eph. 3:8). Yet, because he sincerely believed he was serving God (Acts 23:1; 26:9), he was shown mercy and great patience, and was given the opportunity to repent and accept Christ as Lord (Acts 9:1–19). God's mercy toward Paul should encourage us to present the gospel to sinners, confident that the power and grace of God can redeem and change their lives.

1:18 ACCORDING TO THE PROPHECIES.

thee, son Timothy, [k]according to the
prophecies which went before on thee,
that thou by them mightest [l]war a
good warfare;
19 Holding faith, and a good con-
science; which some having put away
concerning faith have made shipwreck:
20 Of whom is [m]Hymenaeus and
[n]Alexander; whom I have [o]delivered
unto Satan, that they may learn not to
[p]blaspheme.

Instruction concerning prayer

2 I [b]EXHORT therefore, that, first
of all, supplications, prayers, in-
tercessions, *and* giving of thanks, be
made for all men;
2 [q]For kings, and [r]*for* all that are
in [c]authority; that we may lead a qui-
et and peaceable life in all godliness
and honesty.
3 For this *is* [s]good and acceptable
in the sight [t]of God our Saviour;
4 [u]Who will have all men to be
saved, [v]and to come unto the knowl-
edge of the truth.
5 [w]For *there is* one God, and [x]one
mediator between God and men, the
man Christ Jesus;
6 [y]Who gave himself a ransom for
all, [z]to[d] be testified [a]in due time. 2 Tim. 3:15
7 [b]Whereunto I am ordained a
preacher, and an apostle, ([c]I speak
the truth in Christ, *and* lie not;) [d]a
teacher of the Gentiles in faith and ver-
ity.
8 I will therefore that men pray
[e]every where, [f]lifting up holy hands,
without wrath and doubting.

The godly conduct of women

9 In like manner also, that [g]wom-
en adorn themselves in modest appar-

1:18 [k]ch. 4:14 [l]2 Tim. 2:3
1:20 [m]2 Tim. 2:17 [n]2 Tim. 4:14 [o]1 Cor. 5:5 [p]Acts 13:45
2:2 [q]Ezra 6:10 [r]Rom. 13:1
2:3 [s]Rom. 12:2 [t]2 Tim. 1:9
2:4 [u]Ezek. 18:23 Tit. 2:11 [v]John 17:3 2 Tim. 2:25
2:5 [w]Gal. 3:20 [x]Heb. 9:15
2:6 [y]Mark 10:45 [z]1 Cor. 1:6 2 Tim. 1:8 [a]Rom. 5:6 Eph. 1:9
2:7 [b]Eph. 3:7,8 [c]Rom. 9:1 [d]Gal. 1:16
2:8 [e]Luke 23:34 [f]Ps. 134:2
2:9 [g]1 Pet. 3:3

[b] Or, *desire* [c] Or, *eminent place* [d] Or, *a testimony*

Evidently prophecies had been made regarding the will of God for Timothy's ministry in the church (see 1 Cor. 14:29, note; see article on SPIRITUAL GIFTS FOR BELIEVERS, p. 1790). Paul exhorts Timothy to remain faithful to that revealed will for his life. As a pastor and overseer of the church, he must remain loyal to the true apostolic faith and wage warfare against the false doctrines that were creeping into the church.

1:19 CONCERNING FAITH HAVE MADE SHIPWRECK. Paul warns Timothy several times of the terrible possibility of apostasy (4:1; 5:11–15; 6:9–10; see article on PERSONAL APOSTASY, p. 1946).

1:20 DELIVERED UNTO SATAN. Paul's action probably means that these two men were excommunicated from the church. Salvation and union with the body of Christ (the church) protect us from Satan's power. To be expelled from the church, on the other hand, exposes one's life to destructive, satanic attacks (cf. Job 2:6–7; 1 Cor. 5:5; Rev. 2:22). Church discipline serves to bring the individual back to repentance, true faith, and salvation in Christ (see 1 Cor. 5:5, note).

2:4 WHO WILL HAVE ALL MEN TO BE SAVED. The Bible reveals two aspects of the will of God for humankind with regard to salvation: God's perfect will (which says that He desires everyone to be saved) and His permissive will (which acknowledges that He permits many to refuse to come to Christ and receive His salvation; see Mat. 7:21; Luke 7:30; 13:34; John 7:17; Acts 7:51; see article on THE WILL OF GOD, p. 1060).

2:5 ONE MEDIATOR . . . CHRIST JESUS. We must draw near to God only through Jesus Christ (Heb. 7:25), relying on His sacrificial death to cover our sins and praying in faith for strength and divine mercy to help us with all of our needs (Heb. 4:14–16). We must not allow any other created being to take Christ's place by praying to him or her (see Heb. 8:6; 9:15; 12:24).

2:6 A RANSOM FOR ALL. See Mat. 20:28, note.

2:8 MEN PRAY . . . LIFTING UP HOLY HANDS. In the N.T. church's public worship, it was apparently customary for all the worshipers to offer prayers aloud (see Acts 4:24–31; cf. Ezra 3:12–13). To be acceptable, prayer had to be offered by those who were living holy and righteous lives toward others, i.e., with "holy hands."

2:9 WOMEN . . . IN MODEST APPAREL, WITH SHAMEFACEDNESS. It is God's will that Christian women be committed to dressing modestly and discreetly. (1) The word "shamefacedness" (Gk. *aidos*) implies a certain shame in exposing the body. It involves a refusal to dress in such a way as to draw attention to the body and to pass the boundaries of proper reserve. The source of modesty is in a person's heart or inner character. In other words, modesty is the outward manifestation of an inward chastity or purity.

(2) Dressing in an immodest manner that may excite impure desires in others is as wrong as the immoral desire it provokes. No activity or condition justifies the wearing of immodest apparel that exposes the body in such a way as to cause immoral desire or lust in someone else (cf. Gal. 5:13; Eph. 4:27; Tit. 2:11–12; see Mat. 5:28, note).

(3) It is a sad commentary on any church when the Biblical standard for modest dress is ignored and the world's customs are passively adopted. In a day of sexual permissiveness, the church should act and dress differently from a corrupt society that casts aside and ridicules the Holy Spirit's desire for modesty and purity (cf. Rom. 12:1–2).

2:9 BRAIDED HAIR, OR GOLD. This possibly means the braiding of hair with gold or other articles of luxury.

el, with shamefacedness and sobriety;
not with [e]braided hair, or gold, or
pearls, or costly array;
10 [h]But (which becometh women
professing godliness) with good works.
11 Let the woman learn in silence
with all subjection.
12 But [i]I suffer not a woman to
teach, nor to usurp authority over the
man, but to be in silence.
13 For [j]Adam was first formed,
then Eve.
14 And [k]Adam was not deceived,
but the woman being deceived was in
the transgression.
15 Notwithstanding she shall be
saved in childbearing, if they continue
in faith and charity and holiness with
sobriety.

2:10 [h]1 Pet. 3:4
2:12 [i]1 Cor. 14:34
2:13 [j]Gen. 1:27 1 Cor. 11:8
2:14 [k]Gen. 3:6 2 Cor. 11:3
3:2 [l]Tit. 1:6 [m]2 Tim. 2:24
3:3 [n]2 Tim. 2:24

The spiritual qualifications for overseers

3:2–4Ref — Tit. 1:6–8

3 THIS *IS* a true saying, If a man de-
sire the office of a bishop, he
desireth a good work.
2 [l]A bishop then must be blame-
less, the husband of one wife, vigilant,
sober, [f]of good behaviour, given to
hospitality, [m]apt to teach;
3 [g]Not given to wine, [n]no striker,

[e] Or, *plaited* [f] Or, *modest* [g] Or, *Not ready to quarrel, and offer wrong, as one in wine*

2:13 ADAM WAS FIRST FORMED. Paul's argument for man's responsibility as head and spiritual leader in the home and church (see Eph. 5:23, note; see article on PARENTS AND CHILDREN, p. 1880) has two bases. (1) It is based on God's purpose in creation. God created man first, thus revealing God's intention that man was to direct and give leadership to the woman and family. The woman, created after man, was designed to be his companion and helper in fulfilling God's desire for their lives (Gen. 2:18; 1 Cor. 11:8–9; 14:34). (2) It is also based on the disastrous consequences when man and woman abandoned their God-given roles in the Garden of Eden. Eve, by acting independently of her husband as head, ate the forbidden fruit. Adam, by neglecting his responsibility of leadership under God, consented to Eve's transgression. As a result he too fell and brought sin and death into the human race (v. 14; Gen. 3:6,12; Rom. 5:12).

2:15 SHE SHALL BE SAVED IN CHILDBEARING. Paul says that women in general will be saved by faith in God and by accepting the sphere of activity assigned to them by their Creator. (1) Woman's highest position and true dignity are in the home as a godly wife and mother. No greater joy, inner delight, blessing, or honor can come to her than when, as a Christian wife and mother, she bears children (5:14), loves them (Tit. 2:4), raises them to live Christlike lives for God's glory (cf. 2 Tim. 1:5; 3:14–15; see article on PARENTS AND CHILDREN, p. 1880), and continues ever faithful to her Savior (v. 15b).

(2) The honor and dignity of childbearing must not be depreciated by a Christian. It was the childbearing of Mary that became the channel of salvation to the world (Gen. 3:15; Mat. 1:18–25).

(3) Those societies, cultures, and churches that compromise or reject God's purpose for women and thereby depreciate the Christian family, home, and motherhood, will increasingly experience disintegration in their marriages, families, and societies (see 2 Tim. 3:3, note).

(4) Paul's address to Christian women is not intended to demean women who are not married or who are unable to have children. The faith, love, and sanctity of such women can be as great as those with a family (see 1 Cor. 7:34, note).

3:1–7 IF A MAN DESIRE THE OFFICE OF A BISHOP. For comments on the important qualifications for being an overseer or pastor, see article on MORAL QUALIFICATIONS FOR OVERSEERS, p. 1908.

3:2 MUST BE BLAMELESS. The prospective overseer *must* be "blameless" (Gk. *anepilēmptos*, literally meaning "not to be laid hold of"). This has to do with proven observable conduct which is above reproach in his marital life, family life, social life, and business life. No overseer should have a justifiable charge of immorality or misdoing alleged against him. Rather, he is one who has a blameless reputation with those inside as well as those outside the church (see v. 7, note), because he has not marred his Christian life with serious sin or immorality by habit or incident. He can serve as a model for all believers to follow (see 4:12, note).

3:3 NOT GIVEN TO WINE. This phrase (Gk. *mē paroinon*, from *mē*, meaning "not," and *paroinos*, a compound meaning "at, by, near, next to, or with wine") literally translates "not by, near, or with wine," "not being beside wine." The Bible here requires that no overseer or elder may "sit beside wine" or "be with wine." In other words, he should not drink intoxicating wine, be tempted or enticed by it, nor "eat and drink with the drunken" (Mat. 24:49).

(1) Total abstinence from fermented wine was the standard for kings, princes, and judges in the O.T. (Prov. 31:4–7). It was also the standard for all who sought the highest level of consecration to God (Lev. 10:8–11; Num. 6:1–5; Judg. 13:4–7; 1 Sam. 1:14–15; Jer. 35:2–6; see Prov. 23:31, note; see article on WINE IN THE OLD TESTAMENT, p. 220).

(2) Those who rule in the church of Jesus Christ certainly should not have a lower standard. Furthermore, all believers in the church are called priests and kings (1 Pet. 2:9; Rev. 1:6) and as such should live by God's highest standard (John 2:3, note; Eph. 5:18, note; 1 Thes. 5:6, note; Tit. 2:2,

[o]not greedy of filthy lucre; but patient, not a brawler, not covetous;

4 One that ruleth well his own house, [p]having his children in subjection with all gravity;

5 (For if a man know not how to rule his own house, how shall he take care of the church of God?)

6 Not [h]a novice, lest being lifted up with pride he fall into the condemnation of the devil.

7 Moreover he must have a good report [q]of them which are without; lest he fall into reproach [r]and the snare of the devil.

For deacons

8 Likewise *must* [s]the deacons *be* grave, not doubletongued, [t]not given to much wine, not greedy of filthy lucre;

9 [u]Holding the mystery of the faith in a pure conscience.

10 And let these also first be proved; then let them use the office of a deacon, being *found* blameless.

11 [v]Even so *must their* wives *be* grave, not slanderers, sober, faithful in all things.

12 Let the deacons be the husbands of one wife, ruling their children and their own houses well.

13 For [w]they that have [i]used the office of a deacon well purchase to themselves a good degree, and great boldness in the faith which is in Christ Jesus.

14 These things write I unto thee, hoping to come unto thee shortly:

15 But if I tarry long, that thou mayest know how thou oughtest to behave thyself [x]in the house of God, which is the church of the living God, the pillar and [j]ground of the truth.

16 And without controversy great is the mystery of godliness: [y]God was

3:3 [o]1 Pet. 5:2
3:4 [p]Tit. 1:6
3:7 [q]Acts 22:12; 1 Cor. 5:12 [r]2 Tim. 2:26
3:8 [s]Acts 6:3 [t]Ezek. 44:21
3:9 [u]ch. 1:19
3:11 [v]Tit. 2:3
3:13 [w]Mat. 25:21
3:15 [x]Eph. 2:21; 2 Tim. 2:20
3:16 [y]John 1:14; 1 John 1:2

[h] Or, *one newly come to the faith* [i] Or, *ministered* [j] Or, *stay*

note; see articles on WINE IN NEW TESTAMENT TIMES (1) and (2), p. 1538 and p. 1594).

3:4 RULETH WELL HIS OWN HOUSE. A foremost qualification for the candidate desiring the office of overseer is faithfulness in marriage and family relationships. For more on this, see MORAL QUALIFICATIONS FOR OVERSEERS, p. 1908.

3:7 HE MUST HAVE A GOOD REPORT. The overseer or prospective overseer must "have a good report" with two groups: (a) insiders, i.e., church members (vv. 1–6), and (b) outsiders, i.e., those outside of the church (v. 7). He must have a past and ongoing reputation of a righteous lifestyle according to the gospel of Christ.

3:8 THE DEACONS. Deacon (Gk. *diakonos*) means "servant." One of their functions in the N.T. church is suggested in Acts 6:1–6. They were to assist the pastors by administrating the temporal and material affairs of the church so that the pastors might give themselves to prayer and the ministry of the Word (Acts 6:4). The spiritual qualifications for deacons are essentially the same as for pastors (compare vv. 1–7 with vv. 8–13; see Acts 6:3).

3:8 NOT GIVEN TO MUCH WINE. Concerning this qualification, the following should be noted (see also v. 3, note). (1) It is morally unthinkable that the apostle was approving the moderate use of all the kinds of wine available in his day. Many wines were drugged and dangerous (cf. Prov. 23:29–35).

(2) Some interpret Paul to be saying that deacons must not be habitual drunkards, implicitly condoning moderate alcoholic drinking. However, Paul states that drunkenness is such a terrible sin that it excludes one from the kingdom of God (1 Cor. 6:10). It is absurd, therefore, that Paul would actually require, as one of his high standards for deacons (cf. v. 2), that they not be habitual drunkards (i.e., someone who is unsaved). He must have a different meaning in mind for "wine" than intoxicating wine.

(3) Rather than condoning "moderate" alcoholic drinking, Paul was most likely warning against the excessive desire and use, within a pagan society, of legitimate unfermented types of wines (see article on WINE IN NEW TESTAMENT TIMES (1), p. 1538). Addiction even to nonintoxicating wine was a vice prevalent in pagan societies and corresponded to gluttony (see Pliny, *Natural History*, 14.28.139). Paul was emphasizing self-control in all areas of life, even in something good; note Prov. 25:27, which states that one must not eat or be given to "much honey."

(4) The apostle Paul was not alone in this kind of admonition. Rabbinic literature contains warnings about the excessive use of the sweet unfermented juice of the grape. This literature states concerning *tirosh*, a grape drink which includes "all kinds of sweet juices and must, and does not include fermented wine" (Tosef., Ned. IV.3), that "if drunk in moderation it gives leadership; . . . if drunk in excess it leads to poverty" (Yoma, 76b). "One that drinks it habitually is certain to become poor" (*The Jewish Encyclopedia*, 12.533; see article on WINE IN NEW TESTAMENT TIMES (1), p. 1538).

3:15 CHURCH . . . PILLAR AND GROUND OF THE TRUTH. The church must be the foundation of the truth of the gospel. It upholds and preserves the truth revealed by Christ and the apostles by receiving and obeying it (Mat. 13:23), hiding it in the heart (Ps. 119:11), proclaiming it as "the word of life" (Phil. 2:16), defending it (Phil. 1:17), and demonstrating its power in the Holy Spirit (Mark 16:15–20; Acts 1:8; 4:29–33; 6:8).

MORAL QUALIFICATIONS FOR OVERSEERS

***1 Tim. 3:1–2** "This is a true saying, If a man desire the office of a bishop, he desireth a good work. A bishop then must be blameless, the husband of one wife, vigilant, sober, of good behavior, given to hospitality, apt to teach."*

If a man wants to be a "bishop" (Gk. *episkopos*, i.e., one who has pastoral oversight, an overseer or pastor), he desires a noble and important work (1 Tim. 3:1). However, such people must have that desire confirmed by the Word of God (3:1–10; 4:12) and the church (3:10), for God has established for the church certain specific qualifications. This means that the church must not endorse any person for ministerial work based solely on his desire, education, burden, vision, or call. For those seeking the office of an overseer, any professed call of God to do the work of a pastor, teacher, or missionary must be tested by the members of the church according to the Biblical standards of 1 Tim. 3:1–13; 4:12; Tit. 1:5–9 (see article on THE MINISTRY GIFTS OF THE CHURCH, p. 1852). The church today has no right to diminish these requirements which God has set forth by the Holy Spirit. They stand as absolutes and must be followed for the sake of God's name, His kingdom, and the honor and credibility of the high office of overseer.

(1) The Biblical standards listed for overseers are primarily moral and spiritual. The proven character of those who seek leadership in the church is more important than personality, preaching gifts, administrative abilities, or academic accomplishment. The focal point of the qualifications falls upon behavior that has persevered in godly wisdom and right choices. Thus, the spiritual history of the person who desires the office of overseer has to "first be proved" (cf. 1 Tim. 3:10). Thus, the Holy Spirit sets forth the high standard that the candidate must be a believer who has steadfastly adhered to Jesus Christ and His principles of righteousness, and who can therefore serve as a role model of faithfulness, truth, honesty, and chastity. In other words, his character must reflect Christ's teaching in Mat. 25:21, that being faithful over a few things leads to a position of being ruler over many things.

(2) A Christian leader must be first and foremost "an example of the believers" (1 Tim. 4:12; cf. 1 Pet. 5:3). That is, his Christian life and steadfastness in the faith can be set before the congregation as preeminently worthy of imitation.

(a) Overseers must manifest the highest example of perseverance in godliness, faithfulness, purity in the face of temptation, and loyalty and love toward Christ and the gospel (1 Tim. 4:12,15).

(b) The people of God must learn Christian ethics and true godliness, not only from the Word of God, but also from the example of pastors who live according to apostolic standards. A pastor whose quality of life is an illustration of the faith is absolutely essential in God's plan for Christian leadership. To cast aside the principle of having godly leadership that has set an unblemished pattern for those of the church to follow is to ignore the clear teaching of Scripture. The pastor must be one whose faithfulness to Christ can be set forth as a pattern, model, or example (cf. 1 Cor. 11:1; Phil. 3:17; 1 Thes. 1:6; 2 Thes. 3:7,9; 2 Tim. 1:13).

(3) The Holy Spirit regards the person's leadership in home, marriage, and family relationships as of the highest importance (1 Tim. 3:2,4–5; Tit. 1:6). That is, the overseer must be an example to the family of God *especially* in his faithfulness to his wife and children. After all, if he has failed in this realm, "how shall he take care of the church of God?" (1 Tim. 3:5). He must be "the husband of one wife" (1 Tim. 3:2). The phrase defends the position that a candidate for the office of an overseer should be a believer who has remained morally faithful to his wife. The literal translation of the Greek (*mias gunaikos*, an attributive genitive) is "a one-woman man," i.e., the faithful husband of his

wife. This means that the candidate must be a person who gives evidence of being true and faithful in this all-important area. It is evident that persevering moral faithfulness to one's wife and family is required of those desiring to be a leader and an example in the church.

(4) Consequently, persons within the church who become guilty of serious sin or moral transgressions have disqualified themselves from the office of pastor and from any position of high leadership in the local church (cf. 1 Tim. 3:8–12). Such persons may be abundantly pardoned by the grace of God, but they have lost the ability to serve as models of unfailing perseverance in faith, love, and purity (4:11–16; Tit. 1:9). As candidates for leadership, they cannot be called blameless (3:2). Already in the O.T. God had made it clear that those who were leaders among God's people were expected to maintain high moral and spiritual standards; and if they did not, others would be put in their place (see Gen. 49:4, note; Lev. 10:2, note; 21:7,17, notes; Num. 20:12, note; 1 Sam. 2:23, note; Jer. 23:14, note; 29:23, note).

(5) Furthermore, these principles in 1 Tim. 3:2,7 set forth the principle that any overseer who casts aside his steadfast loyalty to God and His Word and his fidelity to his wife and family, must be removed from the office of an overseer. Such a person cannot, therefore, be regarded as "blameless," i.e., above reproach. The Word of God states concerning one among God's people who commits adultery, that "his reproach shall not be wiped away" (see Prov. 6:32–33, note).

(6) This does not mean that God or the church will not forgive. God will indeed forgive any sin listed in 1 Tim. 3:1–3, if there is godly sorrow and repentance for that sin. Let it be clear that such a person may be mercifully forgiven and restored in his relation to God and the church. However, what the Holy Spirit is stating is that there are some sins so grave that the disgrace and shame (i.e., reproach) of that sin will remain with the individual even after forgiveness and for the rest of their lives (cf. 2 Sam. 12:9–14).

(7) But what about King David? His continuation as Israel's king in spite of his sins of adultery and murder (2 Sam. 11:1–21; 12:9–15) is sometimes viewed as Biblical justification for one's continuance as an overseer in God's church even though he has violated the above-mentioned standards. This comparison, however, is faulty on several counts.

(a) The office of the king of Israel under the old covenant and that of spiritual overseer of the church of Jesus Christ under the new covenant are two entirely different things. God not only allowed David, but also many kings who were exceptionally evil and wicked to remain as kings of national Israel. Leadership of the N.T. church, purchased with the blood of Jesus Christ, requires much higher spiritual standards.

(b) According to God's revelation and requirements in the N.T., David would not have qualified for the office of an overseer in a N.T. church. He had multiple wives, was guilty of marital unfaithfulness, greatly failed to manage his own household, and was a murderer and a violent man of bloodshed. Note that because of his sin, David remained under the punishment of God for the rest of his life (see 2 Sam. 12:9–12, notes).

(8) The churches of today must not turn from the righteous requirements for an overseer which God has set forth in the original revelation of the apostles. The church must instead require from its leaders the highest standard of holiness, perseverance in faithfulness to God and His Word, and a godly life. They are to be earnestly prayed for, encouraged, and supported, while they serve as "an example of the believers, in word, in conversation, in charity, in spirit, in faith, in purity" (1 Tim. 4:12).

[k]manifest in the flesh, [z]justified in the Spirit, [a]seen of angels, [b]preached unto the Gentiles, [c]believed on in the world, [d]received up into glory.

The danger of false teachers

4 NOW THE Spirit [e]speaketh expressly, that [f]in the latter times some shall depart from the faith, giving heed [g]to seducing spirits, [h]and doctrines of devils;

2 [i]Speaking lies in hypocrisy; [j]having their conscience seared with a hot iron;

3 [k]Forbidding to marry, [l]*and commanding* to abstain from meats, which God hath created [m]to be received [n]with thanksgiving of them which believe and know the truth.

4 For [o]every creature of God *is* good, and nothing to be refused, if it be received with thanksgiving:

5 For it is sanctified by the word of God and prayer.

Warn the church

6 If thou put the brethren in remembrance of these things, thou shalt be a good minister of Jesus Christ, [p]nourished up in the words of faith and of good doctrine, whereunto thou hast attained.

7 But [q]refuse profane and old wives' fables, and [r]exercise thyself *rather* unto godliness.

8 For [s]bodily exercise profiteth [1]little: [t]but godliness is profitable unto all things, [u]having promise of the life that now is, and of that which is to come.

9 This *is* a faithful saying and worthy of all acceptation.

10 For therefore [v]we both labour and suffer reproach, because we trust in the living God, [w]who is the Saviour of all men, specially of those that believe.

Teach the Word

11 These things command and teach.

12 Let no man despise thy youth; but [x]be thou an example of the believers, in word, in conversation, in charity, in spirit, in faith, in purity.

13 Till I come, give attendance to reading, to exhortation, to doctrine.

3:16 [z]Mat. 3:16; Rom. 1:4 [a]Mat. 28:2; Mark 16:5 [b]Acts 10:34; Rom. 10:18 [c]Col. 1:6,23 [d]Luke 24:51
4:1 [e]John 16:13; 2 Thes. 2:3; 2 Tim. 3:1 [f]1 Pet. 1:20 [g]2 Tim. 3:13; Rev. 16:14 [h]Dan. 11:35; Rev. 9:20
4:2 [i]Mat. 7:15 [j]Eph. 4:19
4:3 [k]1 Cor. 7:28 [l]Rom. 14:3 [m]Gen. 1:29 [n]Rom. 14:6
4:4 [o]Rom. 14:14
4:6 [p]2 Tim. 3:14
4:7 [q]2 Tim. 2:16; Tit. 1:14 [r]Heb. 5:14
4:8 [s]1 Cor. 8:8 [t]ch. 6:6 [u]Ps. 37:4
4:10 [v]1 Cor. 4:11 [w]Ps. 36:6
4:12 [x]Tit. 2:7

[k] Gk. *manifested* [1] Or, *for a little time*

4:1 SOME SHALL DEPART FROM THE FAITH. The Holy Spirit has explicitly revealed that in the latter times, there will be a falling away both from a personal faith in Jesus Christ (see article on PERSONAL APOSTASY, p. 1946) and from Scriptural truth (cf. 2 Thes. 2:3; Jude 3–4). (1) There will appear within the church ministers who are highly gifted and mightily anointed by God. Some will accomplish great things for God and preach gospel truth effectively, but they will depart from the faith and gradually turn to seducing spirits and false doctrines. Because of their former anointing and zeal for God, they will mislead many (see article on THE GREAT TRIBULATION, p. 1456).

(2) Many believers will fall away from the faith because they will fail to love the truth (2 Thes. 2:10) and resist the sinful trends of the last days (cf. Mat. 24:5,10–12; see 2 Tim. 3:2–3, notes). Thus, the distorted gospel of compromising ministers and educators will find little resistance in many churches (4:1; 2 Tim. 3:5; 4:3; see 2 Cor. 11:13, note).

(3) The popularity of unbiblical teaching will be primarily the result of Satan's directing his demonic hosts in a more intensified opposition to God's work. The second coming of Christ will be preceded by a greater intensity of satanism, spiritism, the occult, demon possession, and demonic deception in the world and in the church (Eph. 6:11–12; see articles on POWER OVER SATAN AND DEMONS, p. 1486, and THE AGE OF THE ANTICHRIST, p. 1896).

(4) The believer's protection against such deception involves utter loyalty to God and His inspired Word, and the knowledge that men of great charisma and anointing can be deceived and then deceive others with their mixture of truth and error. This awareness must be accompanied by a true desire within the believer's heart to do the will of God (John 7:17) and to walk in righteousness and the fear of God (Ps. 25:4–5,12–15).

(5) Faithful believers must not think that because apostasy is prevalent within Christianity during the last days that authentic revival cannot occur or evangelism according to the N.T. pattern cannot be successful. God has promised that during the "last days" He will save all who call upon His name and separate themselves from this perverse generation (Acts 2:16–21,33,38–40; 3:19), and He will pour forth His Spirit on them (Acts 2:16–21,33,38–40; 3:19).

4:12 BE THOU AN EXAMPLE. This is one of the most important qualifications for a church leader. The word translated "example" (Gk. *tupos*) means "model, image, ideal, or pattern." A pastor must be a model of faithfulness, purity, and perseverance in godly living. Only those may be placed in the office of an overseer of whom the church can say to its members, "This leader has lived a godly life worthy of example." For more on this, see MORAL QUALIFICATIONS FOR OVERSEERS, p. 1908.

strifes of words, whereof cometh envy,
strife, railings, evil surmisings,
5 [k]Perverse[x] disputings of men of
corrupt minds, and destitute of the
truth, [l]supposing that gain is godli-
ness: [m]from such withdraw thyself.

The love of money

6 But [n]godliness with contentment
is great gain.
7 For [o]we brought nothing into *this*
world, *and it is* certain we can carry
nothing out.
8 And [p]having food and raiment let
us be therewith content.
9 But [q]they that will be rich fall
into temptation and a snare, and *into*
many foolish and hurtful lusts, [r]which
drown men in destruction and perdi-
tion.
10 [s]For the love of money is the
root of all evil: which while some covet-
ed after, they have [y]erred from the
faith, and pierced themselves through
with many sorrows.

The good fight of faith

11 [t]But thou, [u]O man of God, flee
these things; and follow after righ-
teousness, godliness, faith, love, pa-
tience, meekness.
12 [v]Fight the good fight of faith,
[w]lay hold on eternal life, whereunto
thou art also called, [x]and hast pro-
fessed a good profession before many
witnesses.
13 [y]I give thee charge in the sight
of God, [z]who quickeneth all things,
and *before* Christ Jesus, [a]who before
Pontius Pilate witnessed a good [z]con-
fession;
14 That thou keep *this* command-
ment without spot, unrebukeable,
[b]until the appearing of our Lord Jesus
Christ:
15 Which in his times he shall
show, *who is* [c]the blessed and only Po-
tentate, the King of kings, and Lord of
lords; 2 Tim. 4:8
16 Who only hath immortality,
dwelling in the light which no man can
approach unto; [d]whom no man hath
seen, nor can see: [e]to whom *be* honour
and power everlasting. Amen.

6:5 [k]1 Cor. 11:16 [l]2 Pet. 2:3 [m]Rom. 16:17
6:6 [n]Ps. 37:16 Heb. 13:5
6:7 [o]Job 1:21
6:8 [p]Gen. 28:20 Heb. 13:5
6:9 [q]Prov. 15:27 [r]ch. 1:19
6:10 [s]Deut. 16:19
6:11 [t]2 Tim. 2:22 [u]Deut. 33:1
6:12 [v]ch. 1:18 [w]Phil. 3:12 [x]Heb. 13:23
6:13 [y]ch. 5:21 [z]1 Sam. 2:6 [a]John 18:37
6:14 [b]Phil. 1:6
6:15 [c]ch. 1:11,17
6:16 [d]John 6:46 [e]Eph. 3:21

[x] Or, *Gallings one of another* [y] Or, *been seduced* [z] Or, *profession*

6:5 MEN OF CORRUPT MINDS. Paul returns to the discussion of false teachers (cf. ch. 1), informing Timothy what his judgment upon such men must be. Modern indifference to extrabiblical doctrine is unapostolic and ignores the clear admonitions in this and other N.T. epistles (cf. Gal. 1:9).

6:6 GODLINESS ... IS GREAT GAIN. The false teachers at Ephesus outwardly practiced "godliness" in order to gain an abundance of riches. They were driven by an underlying motivation of greed and taught that their wealth was a sign of God's approval on their teachings.

6:8 LET US BE THEREWITH CONTENT. Believers should be content with the basics of food, clothing, and shelter. If special financial needs should arise, we must look to God to provide (Ps. 50:15), while we continue to work (2 Thes. 3:7–8), help those in need (2 Cor. 8:2–3), and serve God with offerings (2 Cor. 8:3; 9:6–7). We must not desire to get rich (vv. 9–11).

6:9 RICH FALL INTO TEMPTATION. See article on RICHES AND POVERTY, p. 1568.

6:12 FIGHT THE GOOD FIGHT OF FAITH. The word "fight" is from the Greek word meaning "agonize." Paul sees the Christian life as a fight, an intense struggle that requires persevering in loyalty to Christ and contending with adversaries of the gospel. All of us are called to defend the gospel in whatever occupation God has placed us (see Eph. 6:11–12, notes).

6:14 UNTIL THE APPEARING. Paul's admonition to Timothy clearly reveals that he believes that Christ's appearing could occur within his lifetime. The N.T. apostles repeatedly encouraged believers in their generation to expect and hope for the Lord's return in their lifetime (Phil. 3:20; 1 Thes. 1:9–10; Tit. 2:13; Heb. 9:28). Loving the Lord and longing for His return and immediate presence must be a basic motivation in our lives (see Rev. 21:1—22:15).

6:16 WHO ONLY HATH IMMORTALITY. This term expresses the transcendence of God, that God is different and independent from His creation—whether man, angel, spirit, or physical or material things (Ex. 24:9–18; Is. 6:1–3; 40:12–26; 55:8–9; Ezek. 1). (1) God must not be placed on the same level with humans or any other being He has created. His being and existence are in a totally different realm. He dwells in perfect and pure existence, far above His creation. He is not part of His creation nor is His creation a part of Him. Furthermore, believers are not God and will never be "gods." We shall always be limited and dependent beings, even in the age to come.

(2) Although a radical division exists between God and all creation, God is also present and active throughout the world. He lives and manifests Himself in His people who repent of their sins and live by faith in Christ (Ex. 33:17–23; Is. 57:15; see Mat. 10:31, note; Rom. 8:28, note; Gal. 2:20, note; see article on THE ATTRIBUTES OF GOD, p. 912).

17 Charge them that are rich in this
world, that they be not highminded,
[f]nor trust in [g]uncertain[a] riches, but
in [h]the living God, [i]who giveth us
richly all things to enjoy;
18 That they do good, that [j]they be
rich in good works, [k]ready to distribute,
[l]willing[b] to communicate;
19 [m]Laying up in store for themselves
a good foundation against the
time to come, that they may lay hold on
eternal life.

6:17 [f]Luke 12:21 [g]Prov. 23:5 [h]1 Thes. 1:9 [i]Acts 14:17
6:18 [j]Jas. 2:5 [k]Rom. 12:13 [l]Gal. 6:6
6:19 [m]Mat. 6:20
6:20 [n]2 Tim. 1:14 [o]Tit. 1:14
6:21 [p]2 Tim. 2:18

Final charge and benediction

20 O Timothy, [n]keep that which is
committed to thy trust, [o]avoiding profane
and vain babblings, and oppositions
of science falsely so called:
21 Which some professing [p]have
erred concerning the faith. Grace *be*
with thee. Amen.

[a] Gk. *uncertainty of riches* [b] Or, *sociable*

6:20 KEEP ... THY TRUST. For the fourth time, Paul charges Timothy to guard the faith that has been entrusted to him (1:18–19; 4:6–11; 6:13–16; 6:20). The Greek literally means "keep the deposit" and refers to the solemn and sacred obligation of keeping safe a treasured possession committed to one's care. The gospel of Christ has been committed to us by the Holy Spirit (2 Tim. 1:14; 3:16). We must proclaim the pure and full gospel in the Pentecostal power of the Holy Spirit (Acts 2:4), ever ready to defend the precious truths when they are attacked, distorted, or denied.

2 TIMOTHY

Outline

Introduction (1:1–4)

I. Paul's Charge to Timothy (1:5–18)
   A. Kindle Afresh the Gift of God (1:5–7)
   B. Be Willing to Suffer for the Gospel (1:8–10)
   C. Paul's Example (1:11–12)
   D. Retain and Guard the Truth (1:13–14)
   E. Disloyal and Loyal Friends of Paul in Rome (1:15–18)

II. Requirements for a Faithful Minister (2:1–26)
   A. Be Strong in Grace (2:1)
   B. Pass On the Message to Faithful Men (2:2)
   C. Manifest Endurance (2:3–7)
      1. Like a Good Soldier (2:3–4)
      2. Like a Disciplined Athlete (2:5)
      3. Like a Hardworking Farmer (2:6–7)
   D. Die with and Suffer for Jesus Christ (2:8–13)
   E. Avoid Senseless Controversy and Defend the Gospel in an Irreproachable Manner (2:14–26)

III. The Approaching Final Upsurge of Evil (3:1–9)

IV. Steadfastness in the Truth (3:10–17)
   A. As Learned from Paul (3:10–14)
   B. As Learned from the Scriptures (3:15–17)

V. Preach the Word (4:1–5)

VI. Paul's Testimony and Instructions (4:6–18)
   A. Paul's Farewell Testimony (4:6–8)
   B. Personal Instruction to Timothy (4:9–13)
   C. A Word of Caution (4:14–15)
   D. The Assurance of God's Faithfulness (4:16–18)

Conclusion (4:19–22)

Author: Paul

Theme: Steadfast Endurance

Date of Writing: c. A.D. 67

Background

This is Paul's last letter. At the time of writing, the emperor Nero was attempting to stop the spread of the Christian faith in Rome by severely persecuting believers; Paul was again the emperor's prisoner in Rome (1:16–17). He was suffering deprivation as a common criminal (2:9), deserted by most of his friends (1:15) and aware that his ministry was over and his death near (4:6–8,18; see Introduction to 1 Timothy for a fuller discussion of authorship and background).

Paul writes to Timothy as a "beloved son" (1:2) and faithful co-worker (cf. Rom. 16:21). His closeness to and reliance on Timothy is seen in naming him a co-sender of six epistles,

in Timothy's remaining with Paul during his first imprisonment (Phil. 1:1; Col. 1:1; Philem. 1), and in Paul's writing to him two personal letters. As Paul faces the imminent prospect of execution, he twice requests Timothy to join him in Rome again (4:9,21). Timothy was still at Ephesus (1:18; 4:19) when Paul wrote him this second epistle.

Purpose

Knowing that Timothy was timid and facing hardship, and realizing the prospect of severe persecution from without the church and false teachers from within, Paul exhorts Timothy to guard the gospel, preach the Word, endure hardship, and fulfill his charge.

Survey

In ch. 1 Paul assures Timothy of his continuing love and prayers and exhorts him to remain uncompromisingly faithful to the gospel, to guard the truth diligently, and to follow Paul's example.

In ch. 2 Paul charges his spiritual son to preserve the faith by passing on its truths to faithful men who will teach it to others also (2:2). He admonishes the young pastor to suffer hardship as a good soldier (2:3), to serve God diligently and handle the word of truth accurately (2:15), to separate himself from those who depart from apostolic truth (2:18–21), to keep himself pure (2:22), and to labor patiently as a teacher (2:23–26).

In the next chapter Paul informs Timothy that evil and apostasy will increase (3:1–9), but that he must be unwaveringly faithful to his heritage and to the Scriptures (3:10–17).

In the final chapter Paul charges Timothy to preach the Word and make full proof of his ministry (4:1–5). He concludes by updating Timothy on his present circumstances as he faces the end, urging him to come soon (4:6–22).

Special Features

Five major features or emphases characterize this epistle. (1) It contains the last recorded words of Paul before his execution by Nero in Rome almost 35 years after his Damascus road conversion to Christ. (2) It contains one of the clearest statements in the Bible about the divine inspiration and purpose of the Scriptures (3:16–17); Paul emphasizes that Scripture be accurately interpreted by ministers of the Word (2:15) and urges the commitment of God's Word to faithful men who can then teach others also (2:2). (3) Terse exhortations occur throughout the letter; e.g., "stir up the gift of God" (1:6), "be not ashamed" (1:8), suffer for the gospel (1:8), "hold fast the [standard] of sound words" (1:13), guard the truth (1:14), "be strong in the grace" (2:1), pass on the message (2:2), "endure [hardship]" (2:3), be diligent in the Word (2:15), "shun" (2:16), "flee . . . follow" (2:22), beware of approaching apostasy (3:1–9), "continue" in the truth (3:14), "preach the word" (4:2), "do the work of an evangelist" (4:5), and "make full proof of thy ministry" (4:5). (4) The recurring themes of its many exhortations are to hold fast to the faith (Jesus Christ and the original apostolic gospel), guard it from distortion and corruption, oppose false teachers, and preach the true gospel with unswerving perseverance. (5) Paul's farewell testimony is a moving example of courage and hope in the face of certain martyrdom (4:6–8).

Reading 2 Timothy

In order to read the entire New Testament in one year, the book of 2 Timothy should be read in 4 days, according to the following schedule:
☐ 1 ☐ 2 ☐ 3 ☐ 4

NOTES

1 PAUL, [a]AN apostle of Jesus Christ by the will of God, according to [b]the promise of life which is in Christ Jesus,

2 [c]To Timothy, *my* dearly beloved son: Grace, mercy, *and* peace, from God the Father and Christ Jesus our Lord.

Timothy's godly background

3 [d]I thank God, [e]whom I serve from *my* forefathers with pure conscience, that [f]without ceasing I have remembrance of thee in my prayers night and day;

4 [g]Greatly desiring to see thee, being mindful of thy tears, that I may be filled with joy;

5 When I call to remembrance [h]the unfeigned faith that is in thee, which dwelt first in thy grandmother Lois, and [i]thy mother Eunice; and I am persuaded that in thee also.

6 Wherefore I put thee in remembrance [j]that thou stir up the gift of God, which is in thee by the putting on of my hands. (Heb. 2:4)

7 For [k]God hath not given us the spirit of fear; [l]but of power, and of love, and of a sound mind.

Timothy charged to guard the gospel

8 [m]Be not thou therefore ashamed of [n]the testimony of our Lord, nor of me [o]his prisoner: [p]but be thou partaker of the afflictions of the gospel according to the power of God;

9 [q]Who hath saved us, and [r]called *us* with an holy calling, [s]not according to our works, but [t]according to his own purpose and grace, which was given us in Christ Jesus [u]before the world began,

10 But [v]is now made manifest by the appearing of our Saviour Jesus Christ, [w]who hath abolished death, and hath brought life and immortality to light through the gospel:

11 [x]Whereunto I am appointed a preacher, and an apostle, and a teacher of the Gentiles.

12 [y]For the which cause I also suffer these things: nevertheless I am not ashamed: [z]for I know whom I have [a]believed, and am persuaded that he is able to [a]keep that which I have committed unto him against that day.

13 [b]Hold fast [c]the form of [d]sound words, which thou hast heard of me, [e]in faith and love which is in Christ Jesus.

14 That good thing which was committed unto thee keep by the Holy Ghost [f]which dwelleth in us.

15 This thou knowest, that [g]all they which are in Asia be turned away from me; of whom are Phygellus and Hermogenes.

1:1 [a]2 Cor. 1:1 [b]Eph. 3:6 Heb. 9:15 **1:2** [c]1 Tim. 1:2 **1:3** [d]Rom. 1:8 Eph. 1:16 [e]Acts 22:3 Rom. 1:9 [f]1 Thes. 1:2 **1:4** [g]ch. 4:9,21 **1:5** [h]1 Tim. 1:5 [i]Acts 16:1 **1:6** [j]1 Tim. 4:14 **1:7** [k]Rom. 8:15 [l]Acts 1:8 **1:8** [m]Rom. 1:16 [n]1 Tim. 2:6 [o]Eph. 3:1 [p]Col. 1:24 **1:9** [q]1 Tim. 1:1 [r]Heb. 3:1 [s]Rom. 3:20 [t]Rom. 8:28 [u]Rom. 16:25 **1:10** [v]Eph. 1:9 [w]1 Cor. 15:54 **1:11** [x]Acts 9:15 1 Tim. 2:7 **1:12** [y]Eph. 3:1 [z]1 Pet. 4:19 [a]1 Tim. 6:20 **1:13** [b]Tit. 1:9 Heb. 10:23 [c]Rom. 2:20 [d]1 Tim. 6:3 [e]1 Tim. 1:14 **1:14** [f]Rom. 8:11 **1:15** [g]Acts 19:10

[a] Or, *trusted*

1:4 GREATLY DESIRING TO SEE THEE. Now a prisoner in Rome awaiting death and forsaken by many of his friends (v. 15; 4:16), Paul longs to see Timothy once more. He begs his faithful co-worker to remain faithful to the truth of the gospel and to hurry to come to him during his last days on earth (4:21).

1:6 STIR UP THE GIFT OF GOD. The "gift" (Gk. *charisma*) given to Timothy is compared to a fire (cf. 1 Thes. 5:19) that he must stir or fan into flames. The "gift" was probably a special gift and power from the Holy Spirit to fulfill his ministry. Note that the gifts and power bestowed on us by the Holy Spirit do not automatically remain strong and vital. They must be fueled by the grace of God through our prayer, faith, obedience, and diligence.

1:12 TO KEEP THAT WHICH I HAVE COMMITTED. Paul does not define that which he has committed unto God. It may refer to his apostolic work, teaching, or even his life.

1:13 HOLD FAST ... SOUND WORDS. The "sound words" are the original and fundamental revelation of Christ and the apostles, the doctrines taught to Timothy by Paul. Timothy must hold these truths fast in faith and love toward Jesus Christ, never depart from them, and not compromise them even if it means suffering, rejection, and disgrace. Today it is popular in some churches to emphasize that experience, not doctrine, is the most important thing. This is firmly contradicted in the Pastoral Epistles of Paul (cf. 4:3; 1 Tim. 1:10; 6:3; Tit. 1:9,13; 2:1–2,8).

1:14 KEEP BY THE HOLY GHOST. A pastoral leader must guard and defend the gospel committed to him even in a day when many depart from the N.T. faith (3:13–15; 4:2–5; 1 Tim. 4:1). (1) He must defend it against attack and challenge the church if it is tempted to lay aside the truth. This duty is essential to ensure salvation for himself and for those under his charge (see 3:14–15; 1 Tim. 4:16, note; see article on OVERSEERS AND THEIR DUTIES, p. 1706). (2) Guarding of the deposit of faith must be done with the help of the Holy Spirit. It is He who inspired the infallible truths of Scripture (see 3:16; 2 Pet. 1:21) and it is He who is the great guide and defender of the truth (John 16:13). Defending the ancient faith once delivered unto the saints (Jude 3) means standing faithfully beside the Holy Spirit (John 14:17; 15:26–27; 16:13).

1:15 ALL ... TURNED AWAY FROM ME.

16 The Lord [h]give mercy unto the house of Onesiphorus; [i]for he oft refreshed me, and was not ashamed of [j]my chain:

17 But, when he was in Rome, he sought me out very diligently, and found *me.*

18 The Lord grant unto him that he may find mercy of the Lord [k]in that day: and in how many things he [l]ministered unto me at Ephesus, thou knowest very well.

Encouragement to determination and endurance

2 THOU THEREFORE, [m]my son, [n]be strong in the grace that is in Christ Jesus.

2 And the things that thou hast heard of me [b]among many witnesses, the same commit thou to faithful men, who shall be able to teach others also.

3 Thou therefore endure hardness, [o]as a good soldier of Jesus Christ.

4 [p]No man that warreth entangleth himself with the affairs of *this* life; that he may please him who hath chosen him to be a soldier.

5 And [q]if a man also strive for masteries, *yet* is he not crowned, except he strive lawfully.

6 [c]The husbandman that laboureth must be first partaker of the fruits.

1:16 [h]Mat. 5:7 [i]Philem. 7 [j]Acts 28:20
1:18 [k]2 Thes. 1:10 [l]Heb. 6:10
2:1 [m]1 Tim. 1:2 [n]Eph. 6:10
2:3 [o]1 Tim. 1:18
2:4 [p]1 Cor. 9:25
2:5 [q]1 Cor. 9:25
2:8 [r]Rom. 1:3,4 [s]1 Cor. 15:1 [t]Rom. 2:16
2:9 [u]Acts 9:16 [v]Eph. 3:1 [w]Acts 28:31 Eph. 6:19
2:10 [x]Eph. 3:13 [y]2 Cor. 1:6
2:11 [z]Rom. 6:5,8
2:12 [a]Rom. 8:17 1 Pet. 4:13 [b]Mat. 10:33 Mark 8:38
2:13 [c]Rom. 3:3 [d]Num. 23:19
2:14 [e]1 Tim. 5:21

7 Consider what I say; and the Lord give thee understanding in all things.

8 Remember that Jesus Christ [r]of the seed of David [s]was raised from the dead [t]according to my gospel:

9 [u]Wherein I suffer trouble, as an evildoer, [v]*even* unto bonds; [w]but the word of God is not bound.

10 Therefore [x]I endure all things for the elect's sakes, [y]that they may also obtain the salvation which is in Christ Jesus with eternal glory.

11 *It is* a faithful saying: For [z]if we be dead with *him,* we shall also live with *him:*

12 [a]If we suffer, we shall also reign with *him:* [b]if we deny *him,* he also will deny us:

13 [c]If we believe not, *yet* he abideth faithful: [d]he cannot deny himself.

A workman approved unto God

14 Of these things put *them* in remembrance, [e]charging *them* before the Lord that they strive not about words to no profit, *but* to the subverting of the hearers.

15 Study to show thyself approved unto God, a workman that needeth not

[b] Or, *by* [c] Or, *The husbandman, labouring first, must be partaker of the fruits*

This is one of the saddest times in Paul's life. He is in prison in Rome with no hope of freedom. He sees the gospel, for which he had given his life, undergoing persecution and desertion at Rome (4:6–7). He is also experiencing such a staggering defection from him and his gospel in the east that he states that everyone in Asia has turned away from him (cf. 4:4,16; Tit. 1:14).

(1) Yet in this terrible trial of suffering and apostasy, Paul maintains his faith in God. He is assured that Christ will guard the true gospel and his ministry (v. 12), that there will always be people such as Timothy who will keep and proclaim it (v. 14; 2:2), and that at his death the Lord will bring him safely to His heavenly kingdom (4:6,8,18).

(2) This sorrowful plight of Paul will be the experience of many of the faithful in the last days before the end. Those loyal to the N.T. gospel will suffer similar grief as they see many abandon the true Biblical faith (Mat. 24:10; see 1 Tim. 4:1, note) and as they find their ministry rejected by those seeking to be in harmony with the prevailing spirit of this evil age (see 4:3–4, note). As was happening to Paul, many will turn away from the true child of God who remains loyal to the N.T. gospel.

2:2 COMMIT THOU TO FAITHFUL MEN. For comments on the church's responsibility in instructing Christians in the faith, see article on BIBLE TRAINING FOR CHRISTIANS, p. 1920.

2:3 ENDURE HARDNESS. A minister of the gospel who remains loyal to Christ and the gospel will be called upon to endure hardship (cf. 1:8; 2:9; 2 Cor. 11:23–29). Like a soldier, he must be willing to undergo difficulties and suffering and to wage spiritual warfare in wholehearted devotion to his Lord (Eph. 6:10–18); like an athlete, he must be willing to sacrifice and live a life of strict discipline (v. 5); like a farmer, he must be committed to hard work and long hours (v. 6).

2:12 IF WE SUFFER. The word "suffer" (Gk. *hupomenō*) means to endure or persevere. Those who persevere and remain steadfast in the faith to the end shall live (v. 11; Mat. 10:22; 24:13) and reign with Christ (4:18; Rev. 20:4). Christ will deny on the day of judgment those who cease to endure and deny Him either by word or deed (cf. Mat. 10:33; 25:1–12; see article on PERSONAL APOSTASY, p. 1946).

2:13 HE ABIDETH FAITHFUL. Christ will most certainly carry out both His promises to us (cf. Mat. 10:32) and His warnings (cf. Mat. 10:33). Divine faithfulness is a comfort for those who remain loyal (1 Thes. 5:24; 2 Thes. 3:3; Heb. 10:23) and a solemn warning for those who depart from the faith. God must remain faithful to His Word (2 Sam. 7:28; Jer. 10:10; Tit. 1:2; Rev. 3:7).

BIBLE TRAINING FOR CHRISTIANS

2 Tim. 2:2 "And the things that thou hast heard of me among many witnesses, the same commit thou to faithful men, who shall be able to teach others also."

The church has the responsibility to safeguard the true and original apostolic doctrine found in Scripture and commit it to others without compromise or corruption. This implies the necessity of Biblical instruction within the church.

(1) The Bible gives the following reasons for Biblical or theological training, whether in the home, church, or school: (a) to entrust the gospel of Christ to faithful believers in order that they may know (2 Tim. 3:15; see Jer. 2:8, note), guard (see 2 Tim. 1:14, note), and teach the true Biblical faith (1 Tim. 4:6,11; 2 Tim. 2:2) and righteous standards (see Rom. 6:17, note; 1 Tim. 6:3);

(b) to show students the vital necessity to "earnestly contend for the faith which was once delivered unto the saints" (see Jude 3, note), and to give them the means by which to defend it against all false theologies (see Acts 20:31, note; Gal. 1:9, note; 1 Tim. 4:1, note; 6:3–4; Tit. 1:9; see article on FALSE TEACHERS, p. 1508);

(c) to lead students into continual growth in character by teaching "doctrine which is according to godliness" (1 Tim. 6:3; cf. Josh. 1:8; Ps. 1:2–3; 119:97–100; Mat. 28:20; John 17:14–18; 1 Thes. 4:1; 1 Tim. 1:5, note; 4:7,16; 2 Tim. 3:16);

(d) to equip students to strengthen and bring to maturity other believers, so that together they may reflect the image of Christ in the home, the local church, and the body of Christ (Eph. 4:11–16);

(e) to bring students to a deeper understanding and experience of the kingdom of God on earth and its conflict with the power of Satan (Eph. 6:10–18; see article on THE KINGDOM OF GOD, p. 1428);

(f) to motivate students, through the eternal truths of the gospel, to be committed unreservedly to evangelizing the lost and preaching the gospel to all nations in the power of the Holy Spirit (Mat. 28:18–20; Mark 16:15–20);

(g) to deepen students' experience of Christ's love, personal fellowship, and gift of the Spirit (John 17:3,21,26; Eph. 3:18–19) by exhorting them to follow the leading of the indwelling Holy Spirit (Rom. 8:14), by encouraging them to experience the baptism in the Holy Spirit (see Acts 2:4; see article on BAPTISM IN THE HOLY SPIRIT, p. 1652), and by teaching them to pray (Mat. 6:9, note), fast (Mat. 6:16, note), and worship, as they long for the blessed appearing of Jesus Christ with the spiritual intensity of N.T. saints (2 Tim. 4:8; Tit. 2:13).

(2) It is obvious from these purposes of Biblical training that instruction must be done only by those who are fervently loyal to Scripture as the fully inspired Word of God (see Ezra 7:10, note; 2 Tim. 1:13–14; see article on THE INSPIRATION AND AUTHORITY OF SCRIPTURE, p. 1924) and to the Holy Spirit and His ministry of truth, righteousness, and power (1:14).

(3) Note that true Biblical training emphasizes true righteousness (i.e., knowing, being, *and* doing) rather than mere apprehension of Biblical facts or truths. The great doctrines revealed in the Scriptures are redemptive truths, not academic ones. As issues involving life or death, they demand a personal response and decision from both the teacher and the student (Jas. 2:17; see Phil. 1:9, note).

to be ashamed, rightly dividing the word of truth.

16 But [f]shun profane *and* vain babblings: for they will increase unto more ungodliness.

17 And their word will eat as doth a [d]canker: of whom is Hymenaeus and Philetus;

18 Who concerning the truth have erred, [g]saying that the resurrection is past already; and overthrow the faith of some.

19 Nevertheless [h]the foundation of God standeth [e]sure, having this seal, The Lord [i]knoweth them that are his. And, Let every one that nameth the name of Christ depart from iniquity.

20 But in a great house there are not only vessels of gold and of silver, but also of wood and of earth; [j]and some to honour, and some to dishonour.

21 [k]If a man therefore purge himself from these, he shall be a vessel unto honour, sanctified, and meet for the master's use, *and* [l]prepared unto every good work.

22 Flee also youthful lusts: but follow righteousness, faith, charity, peace, with them that [m]call on the Lord [n]out of a pure heart.

23 But [o]foolish and unlearned questions avoid, knowing that they do gender strifes.

24 And [p]the servant of the Lord must not strive; but be gentle unto all *men,* [q]apt to teach, [f]patient,

25 [r]In meekness instructing those that oppose themselves; [s]if God peradventure will give them repentance [t]to the acknowledging of the truth;

26 And *that* they may [g]recover themselves [u]out of the snare of the devil, who are [h]taken captive by him at his will.

The coming apostasy

3 THIS KNOW also, that [v]in the last days perilous times shall come. 

2 For men shall be [w]lovers of their own selves, [x]covetous, [y]boasters, [z]proud, [a]blasphemers, [b]disobedient to parents, unthankful, unholy,

3 [c]Without natural affection,

2:16 [f]1 Tim. 4:7
2:18 [g]1 Cor. 15:12
2:19 [h]Mat. 24:24 [i]Nah. 1:7 John 10:14
2:20 [j]Rom. 9:21
2:21 [k]Is. 52:11 [l]ch. 3:17
2:22 [m]Acts 9:14 1 Cor. 1:2 [n]1 Tim. 1:5
2:23 [o]1 Tim. 1:4
2:24 [p]Tit. 3:2 [q]Tit. 1:9
2:25 [r]Gal. 6:1 1 Tim. 6:11 [s]Acts 8:22 [t]1 Tim. 2:4
2:26 [u]1 Tim. 3:7
3:1 [v]1 Tim. 4:1
3:2 [w]Phil. 2:21 [x]2 Pet. 2:3 [y]Jude 16 [z]1 Tim. 6:4 [a]1 Tim. 1:20 [b]Rom. 1:30
3:3 [c]Rom. 1:31

[d] Or, *gangrene* [e] Or, *steady* [f] Or, *forbearing* [g] Gk. *awake* [h] Gk. *taken alive*

2:19 FOUNDATION OF GOD STANDETH SURE. Although many may stray from the truth (Mat. 24:11) and false teachers make inroads into the church (vv. 14–18), God's purpose for His faithful followers cannot be thwarted. The "foundation of God," i.e., the true church, cannot be destroyed. On this foundation is a "seal" with two truths inscribed, referring to those who belong to Christ's church. (1) God unerringly knows those who remain true to His original gospel and those who compromise its truths (cf. Gen. 18:19; Ex. 33:12,17; Num. 16:5; 1 Cor. 8:1–3); (2) those who really belong to God turn away from iniquity and false teaching (cf. 1 Tim. 6:3–5,11).

2:21 PURGE HIMSELF FROM THESE. In God's external or visible church on earth there are many vessels. There are vessels of "honour," i.e., faithful believers who separate from evil and hold fast to the true gospel according to Biblical revelation, and vessels of "dishonour," i.e., false believers who stray from the truth (vv. 14–19). Those among the faithful who desire to be useful to the Master must keep themselves separate from all religions and professed believers who advocate doctrines contrary to Scripture (v. 19). Any contact with those who teach unbiblical doctrine may only be made for the purpose of correction in love, in order that they might repent and turn to the truth (v. 25).

3:1 IN THE LAST DAYS PERILOUS TIMES. The last days include the entire Christian era. Yet Paul prophesies through the Holy Spirit (cf. 1 Tim. 4:1) that things will become worse as the end approaches (2 Pet. 3:3; 1 John 2:18; Jude 17–18). (1) The last days will be marked by ever-increasing wickedness in the world, a collapse of moral standards, and the multiplying of false believers and churches within the kingdom of God (Mat. 24:11–12; see 1 Tim. 4:1, note; see article on THE AGE OF THE ANTICHRIST, p. 1896). These times will be especially grievous and trying for God's true servants.

(2) Paul issues this warning in order to fortify those ministers and their churches who remain loyal to Christ and His revelation. The full blessing of salvation in Christ and the mighty outpouring of the Holy Spirit will still be available for those who remain true to N.T. faith and practice. The church in apostasy only means greater grace and power for those who hold fast to the original faith delivered to the saints (Acts 4:33; Rom. 5:20).

3:2 LOVERS OF THEIR OWN SELVES. Paul gives a list of sins that all have their root in self-love (vv. 2–4). Today some teach that a lack of love for oneself is the root of sin. Apostolic revelation teaches the opposite.

3:3 WITHOUT NATURAL AFFECTION. In the last days the believer must be prepared to face an overwhelming deluge of ungodliness. (1) The apostle prophesies that Satan will bring great destruction upon the family. Children will be "disobedient to parents" (v. 2), and men and women will be "without natural affection" (Gk. *astorgoi*). This denotes "without family affection" and refers to a

[d]trucebreakers, [i]false accusers, [e]incon-
tinent, fierce, despisers of those that
are good,
4 [f]Traitors, heady, highminded,
[g]lovers of pleasures more than lovers
of God;
5 Having a form of godliness, but
Tit. 2:11-12 [h]denying the power thereof: [i]from
such turn away.
6 For [j]of this sort are they which
creep into houses, and lead captive sil-
ly women laden with sins, led away
with divers lusts,
7 Ever learning, and never able [k]to
come to the knowledge of the truth.
8 [l]Now as Jannes and Jambres
withstood Moses, so do these also re-
sist the truth: [m]men of corrupt minds,
[n]reprobate[j] concerning the faith.
9 But they shall proceed no further:
for their folly shall be manifest unto all
men, [o]as theirs also was.

Paul's defence of the faith

10 [p]But [k]thou hast fully known
my doctrine, manner of life, purpose,
faith, longsuffering, charity, patience,
11 Persecutions, afflictions, which
came unto me [q]at Antioch, [r]at Iconi-
um, [s]at Lystra; what persecutions I
endured: but [t]out of *them* all the Lord
delivered me.
12 Yea, and [u]all that will live godly
in Christ Jesus shall suffer persecu-
tion.
13 [v]But evil men and seducers
shall wax worse and worse, deceiving,
and being deceived.
14 But [w]continue thou in the
things which thou hast learned and
hast been assured of, knowing of
whom thou hast learned *them;*
15 And that from a child thou hast
known [x]the holy scriptures, which are
able to make thee wise unto salvation
through faith which is in Christ Jesus. Tit. 3:3-
16 [y]All scripture *is* given by inspi-
ration of God, [z]and *is* profitable for
doctrine, for reproof, for correction, for
instruction in righteousness:
17 [a]That the man of God may be
perfect, [b]thoroughly[l] furnished unto
all good works.

3:3 [d]Rom. 1:31 [e]2 Pet. 3:3
3:4 [f]2 Pet. 2:10 [g]Phil. 3:19
3:5 [h]1 Tim. 5:8 [i]1 Tim. 6:5
3:6 [j]Mat. 23:14 Tit. 1:11
3:7 [k]1 Tim. 2:4
3:8 [l]Ex. 7:11 [m]1 Tim. 6:5 [n]Rom. 1:28
3:9 [o]Ex. 7:12
3:10 [p]1 Tim. 4:6
3:11 [q]Acts 13:45 [r]Acts 14:2 [s]Acts 14:19 [t]Ps. 34:19
3:12 [u]Ps. 34:19
3:13 [v]2 Thes. 2:11
3:14 [w]ch. 1:13
3:15 [x]John 5:39
3:16 [y]2 Pet. 1:20 [z]Rom. 15:4
3:17 [a]1 Tim. 6:11 [b]ch. 2:21

[i] Or, *troublemakers* [j] Or, *of no judgment*
[k] Or, *thou hast been a diligent follower of*
[l] Or, *perfected*

lack of the feelings of natural tenderness and love, as demonstrated by a mother who rejects her children or kills her baby, a father who abandons his family, or children who neglect to care for their aging parents (see Luke 1:17, note).

(2) Men and women will become lovers of money and pleasure and will pursue their own selfish desires (v. 2). Parenthood, sacrificial love, and care for children will no longer be considered a worthy or dignified task (vv. 2–4). Loving parents will be replaced more and more by those who are selfish and brutal and who abandon their children (cf. Ps. 113:9; 127:3–5; Prov. 17:6; Mat. 24:12; Tit. 2:4–5; see 2 Tim. 4:3–4, note).

(3) If Christian parents are to save their families in the difficult times of the last days, they must shield them against the corrupt values of the society in which they live (John 21:15–17; Acts 20:28–30), separate them from the world's ways and customs, and refuse to let the ungodly influence their children (Acts 2:40; Rom. 12:1–2; see article on SPIRITUAL SEPARATION FOR BELIEVERS, p. 1814). They must accept God's plan for the family (see Eph. 5:21–25, notes; see article on PARENTS AND CHILDREN, p. 1880) and not walk as the ungodly do (Lev. 18:3–5; Eph. 4:17). They and their families must indeed become as strangers and pilgrims on the earth (Heb. 11:13–16).

3:5 HAVING A FORM OF GODLINESS. Paul refers to those who profess to be Christians and appear to be religious, yet do not manifest the power of God that can save them from sin, selfishness, and immorality. Such people tolerate immorality within their churches and teach that a person may practice the sins listed in vv. 2–4 and yet inherit salvation and the kingdom of God (cf. vv. 5–9; 4:3–4; 2 Pet. 2:12–19; see 1 Cor. 6:9, note).

3:8 RESIST THE TRUTH. False teachers in the church can many times be identified by their opposition or indifference to the essential truths of the gospel (see 1 Tim. 4:1, note).

3:12 ALL THAT WILL LIVE GODLY . . . PERSECUTION. Persecution in one form or another is inevitable for those who desire to live a godly life in Christ (Mat. 5:10–12; 10:22; Acts 14:22; Phil. 1:29; 1 Pet. 4:12; see Mat. 5:10, note). Loyalty to Christ, His truth, and His righteous standards involves a constant resolve not to compromise our faith or yield to the deluge of voices calling for believers to conform to the world and to lay aside Scriptural truth. Because of their godly standards, the faithful will be deprived of privilege and advantage and be ridiculed; they will experience grief at seeing godliness rejected by the majority. We should all ask ourselves: have I suffered persecution because of my commitment to live in a godly manner? Or is my lack of suffering a sign that I have not stood firmly for the righteousness for which Christ died?

3:16–17 ALL SCRIPTURE *IS* GIVEN BY INSPIRATION OF GOD. A discussion of the inspiration and authority of Scripture can be found in the article THE INSPIRATION AND AUTHORITY OF SCRIPTURE, p. 1924.

Charge to preach the Word

4 I [c]CHARGE *thee* therefore before God, and the Lord Jesus Christ, [d]who shall judge the quick and the dead at his appearing and his kingdom;

2 Preach the word; be instant in season, out of season; reprove, [e]rebuke, [f]exhort with all longsuffering and doctrine.

3 [g]For the time will come when they will not endure [h]sound doctrine; [i]but after their own lusts shall they heap to themselves teachers, having itching ears;

4 And they shall turn away *their* ears from the truth, and [j]shall be turned unto fables.

5 But watch thou in all things, [k]endure afflictions, do the work of [l]an evangelist, [m]make[m] full proof of thy ministry.

Paul's confidence while facing death

6 For [n]I am now ready to be offered, and the time of [o]my departure is at hand.

7 [p]I have fought a good fight, I have finished *my* course, I have kept the faith:

8 Henceforth there is laid up for me [q]a crown of righteousness, which the

4:1 [c]1 Tim. 5:21 [d]Acts 10:42 **4:2** [e]1 Tim. 5:20 Tit. 1:13 [f]1 Tim. 4:13 **4:3** [g]ch. 3:1 [h]1 Tim. 1:10 [i]ch. 3:6 **4:4** [j]1 Tim. 1:4 **4:5** [k]ch. 1:8 [l]Acts 21:8 [m]Rom. 15:19 **4:6** [n]Phil. 2:17 [o]Phil. 1:23 2 Pet. 1:14 **4:7** [p]Phil. 3:14 Heb. 12:1 **4:8** [q]Jas. 1:12

[m] Or, *fulfil*

4:3–4 THEY WILL NOT ENDURE SOUND DOCTRINE. Throughout the history of the church some have always refused to love sound doctrine; yet as the end draws near, the situation will grow worse (cf. 3:1–5; 1 Tim. 4:1). (1) "They will not endure sound doctrine" (v. 3). Many will profess to be Christians, gather at churches, appear to reverence God, but will not tolerate the original N.T. apostolic faith or the Biblical demand to separate from unrighteousness (3:5; cf. Rom. 1:16; see article on SPIRITUAL SEPARATION FOR BELIEVERS, p. 1814).

(2) "They shall turn away *their* ears from the truth" (v. 4). Sound Biblical preaching from a man of God will no longer be endured or tolerated by many within the churches. Those who will turn from the truth will want sermons that demand less than the true gospel (cf. 2:18; 3:7–8; 1 Tim. 6:5; Tit. 1:14). They will not accept God's Word when it speaks of repentance, sin, damnation, and the necessity of holiness and separation from the world (cf. 3:15–17; Jer. 5:31; Ezek. 33:32).

(3) "After their own lusts shall they heap to themselves teachers" (v. 3). These professing believers will not seek pastors according to the standards of God's Word (cf. 1:13–14; 1 Tim. 3:1–10), but will seek those who conform to their own self-seeking and worldly desires. They will choose preachers with gifts of oratory, the ability to entertain, and a message that reassures them that they can remain a Christian while living according to the flesh (cf. Rom. 8:4–13; 2 Pet. 2).

(4) The Holy Spirit warns all those who remain faithful to God and submit themselves to His Word to expect persecution and suffering for righteousness' sake (3:10–12; Mat. 5:10–12). Furthermore, they must separate from people, churches, and institutions who deny the power of God in salvation and who preach a compromising gospel (3:5; see Gal. 1:9, note; 1 Tim. 4:1–2; 2 Pet. 2:1; Jude 3; Rev. 2:24). We must ever be loyal to the N.T. gospel and to God's faithful ministers who proclaim it. Doing this, we can be assured of the close fellowship of Christ (Rev. 3:20–22) and times of refreshing from the presence of the Lord (Acts 3:19–20).

4:4 THE TRUTH. God's written Word must be our ultimate guide to truth and practice. (1) We must use God's Word, given by the Holy Spirit, as our full and sufficient guide by which to judge what we believe and do. (2) The tendency within some churches to form doctrine, practice, or new truth on subjective experiences, miracles, success, man-centered goals, or man-made theories without solid Scriptural authentication will be one of Satan's chief means of deception in the apostasy of the last days (see Mat. 24:5,11, notes; 2 Thes. 2:11, note; see article on THE GREAT TRIBULATION, p. 1456).

4:7 I HAVE FOUGHT A GOOD FIGHT. In reviewing his life for God, Paul knows death is imminent (v. 6) and describes his Christian life in the following terms. (1) He considers the Christian life as a "good fight," the only fight worth fighting. He fought against Satan (Eph. 6:12), Jewish and pagan vices (3:1–5; Rom. 1:21–32; Gal. 5:19–21), Judaism (Acts 14:19; 20:19; Gal. 5:1–6), antinomianism and immorality in the church (3:5; 4:3; Rom. 6; 1 Cor. 5:1; 6:9–10; 2 Cor. 12:20–21), false teachers (4:3–5; Acts 20:28–31; Rom. 16:17–18), the distortion of the gospel (Gal. 1:6–12), worldliness (Rom. 12:2), and sin (Rom. 6; 8:13; 1 Cor. 9:24–27).

(2) He has finished his course amidst trials, difficulties, and temptations, and has remained faithful to his Lord and Savior throughout his life (cf. 2:12; Heb. 10:23; 11; 12:1–2).

(3) He has kept the faith in times of severe testing, great discouragement, and much affliction, both when forsaken by friends and opposed by false teachers. He never compromised the original truth of the gospel (1:13–14; 2:2; 3:14–16; 1 Tim. 6:12).

4:8 CROWN OF RIGHTEOUSNESS. Because Paul remained faithful to his Lord and the gospel entrusted to him, the Spirit witnessed to him that the loving approval of God and the "crown of righteousness" was awaiting him in heaven. God has reserved in heaven rewards for all those who keep the faith in righteousness (cf. Mat. 19:27–29; 2 Cor. 5:10).

4:8 THEM . . . THAT LOVE HIS APPEARING. The N.T. Christians possessed an intense

THE INSPIRATION AND AUTHORITY OF SCRIPTURE

2 Tim. 3:16–17 "All scripture is given by inspiration of God, and is profitable for doctrine, for reproof, for correction, for instruction in righteousness: That the man of God may be perfect, thoroughly furnished unto all good works."

"Scripture" as used in 2 Tim. 3:16 refers primarily to the O.T. writings (3:15). There is indication, however, that some N.T. writings were already being viewed as inspired and authoritative Scripture at about the time Paul wrote 2 Timothy (1 Tim. 5:18, which quotes Luke 10:7; 2 Pet. 3:15–16). For us today, Scripture refers to the authoritative writings of both the O.T. and N.T., i.e., "the Bible." They are the original message of God to humankind and the only infallible witness to God's saving activity for all people.

(1) Paul affirms that all Scripture is inspired by God. The word "inspired" (Gk. *theopneustos*) comes from two Greek words: *theos*, meaning "God," and *pneō*, meaning "to breathe." Thus, "inspired" means "God-breathed." All Scripture is therefore God-breathed; it is the very life and Word of God. Down to the very words of the original manuscripts, the Bible is without error, absolutely true, trustworthy, and infallible. This is true not only when it speaks of salvation, ethical values, and morality, but it is also without error on all subjects about which it speaks, including history and the cosmos (cf. 2 Pet. 1:20–21; note also the attitude of the psalmist toward Scripture in Ps. 119).

(2) The writers of the O.T. were conscious of the fact that what they said to the people and wrote down was God's word to them (see Deut. 18:18; 2 Sam. 23:2; see articles on THE PROPHET IN THE OLD TESTAMENT, p. 1002, and THE WORD OF GOD, p. 1064). Over and over the prophets prefaced their comments with, "Thus saith the LORD."

(3) Jesus Christ Himself taught that Scripture is the inspired Word of God to even the smallest detail (Mat. 5:18). He also affirmed that all He said He received from the Father and is true (John 5:19,30–31; 7:16; 8:26). He further spoke of revelation that was to come (i.e., the truth revealed in the N.T.) from the Holy Spirit through the apostles (John 16:13; cf. 14:16–17; 15:26–27).

(4) To deny the full inspiration of Holy Scripture, therefore, is to set aside the fundamental witness of Jesus Christ (Mat. 5:18; 15:3–6; Luke 16:17; 24:25–27,44–45; John 10:35), the Holy Spirit (John 15:26; 16:13; 1 Cor. 2:12–13), and the apostles (2 Tim. 3:16; 2 Pet. 1:20–21). Furthermore, to limit or disregard its inerrancy is to impair its divine authority.

(5) In His work of inspiration by His Spirit, God, while not violating the personality of the writers, moved upon them in such a way that they wrote without error (2 Tim. 3:16; 2 Pet. 1:20–21; see 1 Cor. 2:12–13, notes).

(6) The inspired Word of God is the expression of God's wisdom and character and is therefore able to give wisdom and spiritual life through faith in Christ (Mat. 4:4; John 6:63; 2 Tim. 3:15; 1 Pet. 2:2).

(7) The Holy Scriptures are God's infallible, true witness to His saving activity for humankind in Christ Jesus. For this reason Scripture is incomparable, forever finished, and uniquely binding. No word of man or religious institution is equal to its authority.

(8) All doctrines, commentaries, interpretations, explanations, and traditions must be judged and legitimized by the words and message in Holy Scripture (see Deut. 13:3, note; see article on FALSE TEACHERS, p. 1508).

(9) The Holy Scriptures as the Word of God must be received, believed, and obeyed as the final authority in all things that pertain to life and godliness (Mat. 5:17–19; John 14:21; 15:10; 2 Tim. 3:15–16; 2 Pet. 1:3; see Ex. 20:3, note). It must be used in the church as the final authority in all matters for teaching, reproof, correction, doctrine, and instruction in righteous living (2 Tim. 3:16–17). One cannot submit to the Lordship of Christ without submitting to God and His Word as ultimate and final authority (John 8:31–32,37).

(10) The Holy Scriptures can only be understood when we are in a right relation to the Holy Spirit. It is He who opens our minds to understand its meaning and gives us the inward witness of its authority (see 1 Cor. 2:12, note; see article on THREE KINDS OF PEOPLE, p. 1772).

(11) We must use the inspired Word of God to conquer the power of sin, Satan, and the world in our lives (Mat. 4:4; Eph. 6:12,17; Jas. 1:21).

(12) The Scriptures must be loved, treasured, and guarded by all those of the church who see it as God's only truth for a lost and dying world. We must safeguard its doctrines by faithfully adhering to its teaching, proclaiming its saving message, entrusting it to faithful men, and defending it against all those who would destroy or distort its eternal truths (see Phil. 1:17; 2 Tim. 1:13–14, notes; 2:2; Jude 3). No one may add anything to the Scriptures or take anything away (see Deut. 4:2, note; Rev. 22:19, note).

(13) One final thing should be noted here. Inerrant inspiration applies only to the original writing of the Biblical books. Thus, whenever one finds in Scripture something that appears to be in error, rather than assuming that the writer of the Scripture made a mistake, one should remember that three possibilities exist in regard to any apparent problem: (a) the existing copies of the original manuscript may not be totally accurate; (b) the present-day translation of the Hebrew or Greek Biblical text may be faulty; or (c) one's understanding of the Biblical text may be inadequate or incorrect.

Lord, the righteous judge, shall give
me [r]at that day: and not to me only,
but unto all them also that love his ap-
Tit. 2:13 pearing.

Greetings and benediction

9 Do thy diligence to come shortly
unto me:
10 For [s]Demas hath forsaken me,
[t]having loved this present world, and
is departed unto Thessalonica; Cres-
cens to Galatia, Titus unto Dalmatia.
11 [u]Only [v]Luke is with me. Take
[w]Mark, and bring him with thee: for he
is profitable to me for the ministry.
12 And [x]Tychicus have I sent to
Ephesus.
13 The cloak that I left at Troas
with Carpus, when thou comest, bring
with thee, and the books, *but* especially
the parchments.
14 [y]Alexander the coppersmith did
me much evil: [z]the Lord reward him
according to his works:
15 Of whom be thou ware also; for
he hath greatly withstood [n]our words.
16 At my first answer no man stood
with me, but all *men* forsook me: [a]*I
pray God* that it may not be laid to their
charge.
17 [b]Notwithstanding the Lord
stood with me, and strengthened me;
[c]that by me the preaching might be
fully known, and *that* all the Gentiles
might hear: and I was delivered [d]out
of the mouth of the lion.
18 [e]And the Lord shall deliver me
from every evil work, and will preserve
me unto his heavenly kingdom: [f]to
whom *be* glory for ever and ever. Amen.
19 Salute [g]Prisca and Aquila, and
the household of Onesiphorus.
20 [h]Erastus abode at Corinth: but
[i]Trophimus have I left at Miletum
sick.
21 [j]Do thy diligence to come be-
fore winter. Eubulus greeteth thee, and
Pudens, and Linus, and Claudia, and
all the brethren.
22 [k]The Lord Jesus Christ *be* with
thy spirit. Grace *be* with you. Amen.

4:8 [r]ch. 1:12 **4:10** [s]Col. 4:14 [t]1 John 2:15 **4:11** [u]ch. 1:15 [v]Col. 4:14 [w]Acts 12:25 **4:12** [x]Acts 20:4 Eph. 6:21 **4:14** [y]Acts 19:33 [z]2 Sam. 3:39 Ps. 28:4 **4:16** [a]Acts 7:60 **4:17** [b]Acts 23:11 [c]Acts 9:15 [d]Ps. 22:21 **4:18** [e]Ps. 121:7 [f]Rom. 11:36 Gal. 1:5 Heb. 13:21 **4:19** [g]Acts 18:2 Rom. 16:3 **4:20** [h]Acts 19:22 Rom. 16:23 [i]Acts 20:4 **4:21** [j]ver. 9 **4:22** [k]Gal. 6:18 Philem. 25

[n] Or, *our preachings*

longing for the return of the Lord to take them from earth to be with Him forever (see 1 Thes. 5:13–18; cf. Phil. 3:20–21; Tit. 2:13; see article on THE RAPTURE, p. 1889). A distinctive mark of God's people is that they do not feel at home in this world and are looking forward to their heavenly home (cf. Heb. 11:13–16).

4:17 THE LORD STOOD WITH ME. Because of the severe persecution against the Christians in Rome, no one dared to identify himself with the faithful and outspoken apostle (v. 16). He was deeply disappointed and felt deserted. But in such times he experienced the Lord's special nearness as He stood by him and strengthened him (cf. Acts 23:11; 27:23; Rom. 4:20; 2 Cor. 1:3–5; Eph. 6:10; Phil. 4:13).

4:22 GRACE *BE* WITH YOU. These are the last words of Paul recorded in Scripture, written while awaiting martyrdom in a Roman prison. From the world's perspective, the apostle's life was about to end in tragic failure. (1) For thirty years he had given up everything for Christ; he had gained little but persecution, disgrace, and hatred from his own countrymen. His mission and preaching to the Gentiles had resulted in the establishment of a good number of churches, yet many of these churches were falling away from loyalty to him and the apostolic faith (1:15). And now in prison, with all his loyal friends gone except for Luke (vv. 11, 16), he awaits death. These circumstances point to apparent failure with regard to his mission to the Gentiles. Yet, the battle-scarred apostle of the cross shows no regrets as he lays down his life for his Lord.

(2) Now, 2,000 years later, Paul's influence surpasses that of all God's servants in the kingdom. His writings are a crucial part of Holy Scripture and have led countless numbers to faith in Christ. Let no one who has remained loyal and faithful to Jesus Christ, though he or she seems to have accomplished little for God, think that death terminates the results. God takes our faithful efforts and multiplies them far beyond what we would have imagined or ever hoped for. Even our apparent failure may be sown seed that will be reaped bountifully by others (John 4:37–38).

TITUS

Outline

Introduction (1:1–4)
- I. Instruction About Appointing Elders (1:5–9)
  - A. Appoint Elders in Every Town (1:5)
  - B. Various Qualifications for Elders (1:6–9)
    - 1. Personal
      - a. Above Reproach (1:6)
      - b. A Trustworthy Steward (1:7)
      - c. Not Self-willed (1:7)
      - d. Not Quick-tempered (1:7)
      - e. Not Given to Wine (1:7)
      - f. Not Belligerent (1:7)
      - g. Not Greedy (1:7)
      - h. Hospitable (1:8)
      - i. Loves What is Good (1:8)
      - j. Just (1:8)
      - k. Devout/Holy (1:8)
      - l. Self-controlled (1:18)
      - m. Holding Fast to the Faithful Word (1:9)
      - n. Able to Exhort from the Word (1:9)
      - o. Able to Refute Those who Contradict the Word (1:9)
    - 2. Family
      - a. Husband of One Wife (1:6)
      - b. Has Believing Children (1:6)
      - c. His Children are not Wild or Rebellious (1:6)
- II. Instruction Concerning False Teachers (1:10–16)
  - A. Their Character (1:10)
  - B. Their Conduct (1:11–12)
  - C. Their Correction (1:13–16)
- III. Instruction Concerning Various Groups in the Churches (2:1–15)
  - A. The Scope of the Instruction (2:1–10)
  - B. The Foundation for the Instruction (2:11–14)
  - C. The Responsibility of Titus (2:15)
- IV. Exhortations Concerning Good Works (3:1–11)
  - A. Our Conduct Toward Others (3:1–2)
  - B. God's Mercy Toward Us (3:3–7)
  - C. Discerning What is Profitable and Unprofitable (3:8–11)

Conclusion (3:12–15)

Author: Paul

Theme: Sound Doctrine and Good Works

Date of Writing: c. A.D. 65/66

Background

Like 1 and 2 Timothy, Titus is a personal letter from Paul to one of his younger assistants. It is called a "Pastoral Epistle" because it deals with matters relating to church order and ministry. Titus, a Gentile convert (Gal. 2:3), became a close companion of Paul in the apostolic ministry. Although not mentioned by name in Acts (perhaps because he was Luke's brother), Titus's closeness to the apostle Paul is indicated by (1) the thirteen

references to Titus in Paul's epistles, (2) his being one of Paul's converts and sons (1:4) in the ministry (like Timothy) and a trustworthy co-worker (2 Cor. 8:23), (3) his serving as Paul's representative on at least one important mission to Corinth during Paul's third missionary journey (2 Cor. 2:12–13; 7:6–15; 8:6,16–24), and (4) his working as a co-laborer with Paul at Crete (1:5).

Paul and Titus worked together briefly on the island of Crete (southwest of Asia Minor in the Mediterranean Sea) between Paul's first and second Roman imprisonments (see Introduction to 1 Timothy). Paul commissioned Titus to continue working with the Cretans (1:5) while he traveled on to Macedonia (cf. 1 Tim. 1:3). Sometime thereafter Paul wrote this letter to Titus, instructing him to complete the task at Crete which the two of them had begun. It is probable that Paul sent the letter with Zenas and Apollos who were traveling through Crete (3:13).

In this letter Paul conveys his plans to send either Artemas or Tychicus soon to replace Titus, at which time Titus was to join Paul at Nicopolis (Greece), where the apostle planned to remain during the winter (3:12). We know that this did occur, since Paul later reassigned Titus to Dalmatia (modern Yugoslavia) (2 Tim. 4:10).

Purpose

Paul wrote primarily to instruct Titus in his task of (1) setting in order what Paul had left unfinished in the churches of Crete, including the appointment of elders (1:5); (2) helping the churches grow in faith, in knowledge of the truth, and in godly living (1:1); (3) silencing false teachers (1:11); and (4) coming to Paul after he is relieved by Artemas or Tychicus (3:12).

Survey

Paul discusses four main issues in this epistle. (1) He instructs Titus about the character and spiritual qualifications necessary for all those who are to be selected as elders (or overseers) in the church. Elders must be godly men of proven character who have succeeded as leaders in their own homes (1:5–9). (2) Paul directs Titus to teach sound doctrine and to rebuke and silence false teachers (1:10—2:1). In the course of the letter, Paul gives two succinct summaries of sound doctrine (2:11–14; 3:4–7). (3) Paul delineates for Titus (cf. 1 Tim. 5:1—6:2) the proper role of older men (2:1–2), older women (2:3–4), young women (2:4–5), young men (2:6–8), and servants (2:9–10). (4) Finally, Paul emphasizes that good works and a righteous life are the necessary fruit of genuine faith (1:16; 2:7,14; 3:1,8,14; cf. Jas. 2:14–26).

Special Features

Three major features or emphases characterize this epistle. (1) It contains two short classic summaries of the true nature of salvation in Christ Jesus (2:11–14; 3:4–7). (2) It emphasizes that the church and its ministry must be built on strong spiritual, theological, and ethical foundations. (3) It contains one of two N.T. lists enumerating the required qualifications for leadership in the church's ministry (1:5–9; cf. 1 Tim. 3:1–13).

Reading Titus

In order to read the entire New Testament in one year, the book of Titus should be read in 2 days, according to the following schedule:
☐ 1–2 ☐ 3

NOTES

1 PAUL, A servant of God, and an
apostle of Jesus Christ, according
to the faith of God's elect, and [a]the
acknowledging of the truth [b]which is
after godliness;
2 [c]In[a] hope of eternal life, which
God, [d]that cannot lie, promised [e]be-
fore the world began;
3 [f]But hath in due times mani-
fested his word through preaching,
[g]which is committed unto me accord-
ing to the commandment of God our
Saviour;
4 To [h]Titus, *mine* own son after the
common faith: [i]Grace, mercy, *and*
peace, from God the Father and the
Lord Jesus Christ our Saviour.

Qualifications for elders

1:6–8Ref – 1 Ti. 3:2–4

5 For this cause left I thee in Crete,
that thou shouldest [j]set in order the
things that are [b]wanting, and ordain
elders in every city, as I had appointed
thee:
6 [k]If any be blameless, the hus-
band of one wife, [l]having faithful chil-
dren not accused of riot or unruly.
7 For a bishop must be blameless,
as [m]the steward of God; not self-
willed, not soon angry, [n]not given to
wine, no striker, not given to filthy
lucre;
8 [o]But a lover of hospitality, a lov-
er of [c]good men, sober, just, holy,
temperate;
9 Holding fast the faithful word
[d]as he hath been taught, that he may
be able [p]by sound doctrine both to ex-
hort and to convince the gainsayers.

Dealing with false teachers

10 For [q]there are many unruly and
vain talkers and deceivers, [r]specially
they of the circumcision:
11 Whose mouths must be stopped,
[s]who subvert whole houses, teaching
things which they ought not, [t]for
filthy lucre's sake.
12 [u]One of themselves, *even* a
prophet of their own, said, The Cre-
tians *are* always liars, evil beasts, slow
bellies.
13 This witness is true. [v]Where-
fore rebuke them sharply, that they
may be [w]sound in the faith;
14 [x]Not giving heed to Jewish fa-
bles, and [y]commandments of men,
that turn from the truth.
15 [z]Unto the pure all things *are*

1:1 [a]2 Tim. 2:25 [b]1 Tim. 3:16
1:2 [c]2 Tim. 1:1 [d]2 Tim. 2:13 [e]Rom. 16:25
1:3 [f]2 Tim. 1:10 [g]1 Thes. 2:4
1:4 [h]2 Cor. 2:13 [i]Eph. 1:2
1:5 [j]1 Cor. 11:34
1:6 [k]1 Tim. 3:2 [l]1 Tim. 3:4
1:7 [m]Mat. 24:45 [n]Lev. 10:9
1:8 [o]1 Tim. 3:2
1:9 [p]1 Tim. 1:10
1:10 [q]1 Tim. 1:6 [r]Acts 15:1
1:11 [s]2 Tim. 3:6 [t]1 Tim. 6:5
1:12 [u]Acts 17:28
1:13 [v]2 Cor. 13:10 [w]ch. 2:2
1:14 [x]1 Tim. 1:4 [y]Is. 29:13
1:15 [z]1 Cor. 6:12

[a] Or, *For* [b] Or, *left undone* [c] Or, *good things* [d] Or, *in teaching*

1:1 TRUTH WHICH IS AFTER GODLINESS. Those who say they proclaim the true gospel must be ready to have their message judged by whether it produces godliness in the lives of those who accept it. No church or denomination has the right to claim that its message or doctrine agrees with the "sound doctrine" of the apostles (v. 9; 2 Tim. 1:11–14; 2:2; 3:10–12) and "the words of our Lord Jesus Christ" (1 Tim. 6:3), if that message or doctrine does not lead its adherents to a life of godliness (v. 16, note; 1 Tim. 6:3; Heb. 1:9; see 1 Cor. 13:1, note).

1:2 GOD, THAT CANNOT LIE. See Heb. 6:18, note.

1:5 ORDAIN ELDERS ... AS I HAD APPOINTED. All pastoral ministries must refer back to and be based on the message of Jesus Christ as proclaimed by the apostles; i.e., they must be founded on the apostolic standard of vv. 5–9 and 1 Tim. 3:1–7. Such ministry is valid only as long as it holds fast to the faithful Word in accordance with the teaching, the ministry, and the writings of the N.T. (v. 9; Acts 14:23; see Eph. 2:20, note).

1:6 BLAMELESS, THE HUSBAND OF ONE WIFE. See article on MORAL QUALIFICATIONS FOR OVERSEERS, p. 1908.

1:7 BISHOP. The terms "elder" (Gk. *presbuteros*, v. 5) and "bishop" (Gk. *episkopos*, v. 7) are interchangeable and refer to the same church office. The former points to the spiritual maturity and dignity required for the office; the latter refers to the task of overseeing the church as a steward of God's house.

1:7 BISHOP MUST BE BLAMELESS. God insists on the highest moral standards for overseers in the church. God knows that if the leaders are not blameless, then the church will depart from righteousness because of the lack of godly role models. For more on this, see article on MORAL QUALIFICATIONS FOR OVERSEERS, p. 1908.

1:9 HOLDING FAST THE FAITHFUL WORD. An elder must not only meet the moral and spiritual standards listed in vv. 6–8, but he must also be committed to hold fast to the original apostolic testimony about the saving work of Jesus Christ, love it, know it, and give his life for it. This kind of commitment is essential for two reasons. (1) He must be able to teach, encourage, and exhort from the Word of God, in order to lead the hearts and minds of God's people to wholehearted devotion to Christ, truth, and righteousness (cf. 2 Tim. 4:2). (2) He must be able to correct those who teach things contrary to Scripture, in order to lead them to the truth (2 Tim. 2:24–26). If they refuse correction, then he must convince other believers of the error of their teachings (see articles on THE MINISTRY GIFTS OF THE CHURCH, p. 1852, and OVERSEERS AND THEIR DUTIES, p. 1706).

1:15 ALL THINGS *ARE* PURE. Paul is probably speaking about the ritual purity of Jewish food

pure: but unto them that are defiled and unbelieving *is* nothing pure; but even their mind and conscience is defiled.

16 They profess that they know God; but [a]in works they deny *him*, being abominable, and disobedient, [b]and unto every good work [e]reprobate.

Christian doctrine and conduct

2 BUT SPEAK thou the things which become [c]sound doctrine:

2 That the aged men be [f]sober, grave, temperate, sound in faith, in charity, in patience.

3 The aged women likewise, that *they be* in behaviour as becometh [g]holiness, not [h]false accusers, not given to much wine, teachers of good things;

4 That they may teach the young women to be [i]sober, to love their husbands, to love their children,

5 *To be* discreet, chaste, keepers at home, good, [d]obedient to their own husbands, [e]that the word of God be not blasphemed.

6 Young men likewise exhort to be [j]sober minded.

7 [f]In all things showing thyself a

1:16 [a]2 Tim. 3:5 [b]Rom. 1:28
2:1 [c]1 Tim. 1:10
2:5 [d]1 Cor. 14:34 [e]Rom. 2:24
2:7 [f]1 Tim. 4:12

[e] Or, *void of judgment* [f] Or, *vigilant* [g] Or, *holy women* [h] Or, *troublemakers* [i] Or, *wise* [j] Or, *discreet*

---

laws (cf. Mat. 15:10–11; Mark 7:15; 1 Tim. 4:3–5). Some teachers were obsessed with the distinction between pure and impure food, teaching that proper observance in these things was the essence of true righteousness. They ignored true moral character, inward purity, and outward righteousness (v. 16). Paul emphasizes that if a person's moral condition is pure, then distinction between unclean and clean foods has no moral meaning for him. Paul is not referring to things or actions that are morally wrong, but only to ceremonial purity.

1:16 THEY PROFESS ... THEY DENY *HIM*. One of the greatest abominations in the eyes of God is to profess faith in Christ and have hope of eternal life (v. 2), while at the same time living in disobedience to Him and His Word (cf. Luke 6:46; John 14:12; 15:10–14; 1 John 2:4).

2:2 AGED MEN BE SOBER. The clear intent of this text is that older men must be an example to all believers of presenting themselves to God as living sacrifices without the use of intoxicating wine (see 1 Tim. 3:2,11, where this word is used in reference to pastors and women). This is supported by the following facts.

(1) "Sober" (Gk. *nēphalios*) is defined in N.T. Greek lexicons as having the primary meaning of abstaining from wine. Consider the following definitions: "The word originally connotes abstinence from alcohol" (Reinecher and Rogers); "one who does not drink wine" (*Greek Dictionary of Byzantius*, Athens, 1839); "not with wine, wineless" (Liddell and Scott); "free from all infusion of wine" (Moulton-Milligan); "holding no wine" (Kittel and Friedrich); "not mixed with wine" (G. Abbott-Smith); "literally, of a state of abstinence from wine" (Brown, *Dictionary of New Testament Theology*, Vol. 1). Brown adds: "*Nēphalios* occurs only in the Pastoral Epistles and denotes the abstinence style of life required of bishops (1 Tim. 3:2), women (1 Tim. 3:11), and elders (Tit. 2:2)." R. Laird Harris states that "it is used regularly in the classical authors meaning free from all wine" (*The Bible Today*, p. 139).

(2) Jewish writers, contemporaries of Paul and Peter, confirm the common use of the primary definition. Josephus states in reference to Jewish priests that "they are in all respects pure and abstinent (*nēphalioi*), being forbidden to drink wine while they wear the priestly robe" (*Antiquities*, 3.12.2). Philo states that the regenerate soul "abstains (*nēphein*) continually and during the whole of its life" (*Drunkedness*, 37).

(3) In the light of the foregoing, it cannot be reasonably supposed that Paul used this term without knowledge of its principal and dominant meaning (see 1 Thes. 5:6, note).

2:3 NOT GIVEN TO MUCH WINE. See 1 Tim. 3:8, note.

2:4–5 WOMEN ... LOVE THEIR HUSBANDS ... CHILDREN. God has a distinct purpose for the woman in relation to family, home, and motherhood. (1) God's desire and purpose for a wife and mother are that her attention and devotion be focused on her family. The home, husband, and children must be the center of a Christian mother's world; this is her divinely appointed way of honoring the Word of God (cf. Deut. 6:7; Prov. 31:27; 1 Tim. 5:14).

(2) The woman's specific God-given tasks as they relate to the family include: (a) caring for the children God has entrusted to her (v. 4; 1 Tim. 5:14) as unto the Lord (Ps. 127:3; Mat. 18:5; Luke 9:48); (b) being a helper and faithful companion to her husband (vv. 4–5; see Gen. 2:18, note); (c) helping the father train the children in godly character and practical life skills (Deut. 6:7; Prov. 1:8–9; Col. 3:20; 1 Tim. 5:10; see article on PARENTS AND CHILDREN, p. 1880); (d) providing hospitality (Is. 58:6–8; Luke 14:12–14; 1 Tim. 5:10); (e) using her skill to furnish the needs of the home (Prov. 31:13,15–16,18–19,22,24); (f) caring in her home for elderly parents (1 Tim. 5:8; Jas. 1:27).

(3) Mothers who desire to fulfill God's plan for their lives and their families, but because of economic necessity must seek employment away from the children, should commit their circumstances unto the Lord while praying to God to make a way for her to fulfill her God-given place and function in the home with her children (Prov. 3:5–6; 1 Tim. 5:3; see also Eph. 5:21–23, notes).

2:7 SHOWING THYSELF A PATTERN. See

pattern of good works: in doctrine *showing* uncorruptness, gravity, [g]sincerity,

8 [h]Sound speech, that cannot be condemned; [i]that he that is of the contrary part may be ashamed, having no evil thing to say of you.

9 *Exhort* [j]servants to be obedient unto their own masters, *and* to please *them* well [k]in all *things;* not [k]answering again;

10 Not purloining, but showing all good fidelity; [l]that they may adorn the doctrine of God our Saviour in all things.

11 For [m]the grace of God [l]that bringeth salvation [n]hath appeared to all men,

12 Teaching us [o]that, denying ungodliness [p]and worldly lusts, we should live soberly, righteously, and godly, in this present world;

Heb. 11:13-16

13 [q]Looking for that blessed [r]hope, and the glorious [s]appearing of the great God and our Saviour Jesus Christ;

Heb. 9:28

14 [t]Who gave himself for us, that he might redeem us from all iniquity, [u]and purify unto himself [v]a peculiar people, [w]zealous of good works.

15 These things speak, and [x]exhort, and rebuke with all authority. Let no man despise thee.

Doing what is good

3 PUT THEM in mind [y]to be subject to principalities and powers, to obey magistrates, [z]to be ready to every good work,

2 [a]To speak evil of no man, [b]to be no brawlers, *but* [c]gentle, showing all [d]meekness unto all men.

3 For [e]we ourselves also were sometimes foolish, disobedient, deceived, serving divers lusts and pleasures, living in malice and envy, hateful, *and* hating one another.

4 But after that [f]the kindness and [m]love of [g]God our Saviour toward man appeared,

5 [h]Not by works of righteousness which we have done, but according to his mercy he saved us, by [i]the washing of regeneration, and renewing of the Holy Ghost;

6 [j]Which he shed on us [n]abundantly through Jesus Christ our Saviour;

2:7 [g]Eph. 6:24 **2:8** [h]1 Tim. 6:3 [i]Neh. 5:9 **2:9** [j]Eph. 6:5 [k]Eph. 5:24 **2:10** [l]Mat. 5:16 **2:11** [m]Rom. 5:15 [n]Luke 3:6 **2:12** [o]Luke 1:75 [p]1 Pet. 4:2 **2:13** [q]1 Cor. 1:7 [r]Acts 24:15 [s]Col. 3:4 **2:14** [t]Gal. 1:4 [u]Heb. 9:14 [v]Ex. 15:16 [w]Eph. 2:10 **2:15** [x]2 Tim. 4:2

3:1 [y]1 Pet. 2:13 [z]Col. 1:10 Heb. 13:21 **3:2** [a]Eph. 4:31 [b]2 Tim. 2:24 [c]Phil. 4:5 [d]Eph. 4:2 Col. 3:12 **3:3** [e]1 Cor. 6:11 1 Pet. 4:3 **3:4** [f]ch. 2:11 [g]1 Tim. 2:3 **3:5** [h]Rom. 3:20 2 Tim. 1:9 [i]John 3:3 1 Pet. 3:21 **3:6** [j]Ezek. 36:25; Joel 2:28

k Or, *gainsaying* **l** Or, *that bringeth salvation to all men, hath appeared* **m** Or, *pity* **n** Gk. *richly*

article on MORAL QUALIFICATIONS FOR OVERSEERS, p. 1908.

2:11 THE GRACE OF GOD. Vv. 11–14 describe the character and purpose of God's saving grace. According to Paul, saving grace (1) instructs the believer to decisively reject the ungodly passions, pleasures, and values of the present age and regard them as abominable (v. 12; cf. Rom. 1:18–32; 2 Tim. 2:22; 1 John 2:15–17); and (2) commands and gives power to the believer to live "righteously and godly," while waiting expectantly for the blessed hope and appearing of Christ Jesus (v. 13; Gal. 5:5; Col. 1:5; 2 Tim. 4:8; see article on FAITH AND GRACE, p. 1738).

2:13 THAT BLESSED HOPE. The "blessed hope" for which every Christian should long is "the glorious appearing of the great God and our Saviour, Jesus Christ" and our union with Him for eternity (see John 14:3, note; see article on THE RAPTURE, p. 1889). This hope is capable of being realized at any time (cf. Mat. 24:42; Luke 12:36–40; Jas. 5:7–9). Thus, Christians should never surrender their prayerful hope that perhaps today the trumpet will sound and the Lord will return.

2:14 GAVE HIMSELF FOR US, THAT. Christ shed His blood on the cross (1 Pet. 1:18–19) in order (1) to redeem us from all iniquity and the desire to defy God's law and holy standards (cf. 1 John 3:4), and (2) to make us a holy people, separated from sin and the world to be God's own special possession. "Peculiar" means "special," one's very own. Those struggling with sin and the power of Satan should know that if Christ died for their redemption, how much more will He now give adequate grace to live victoriously over the power of sin and evil (Rom. 5:9–11).

3:1 SUBJECT TO PRINCIPALITIES. Since it is important for the ongoing witness and furtherance of the gospel, believers must be obedient to civil and governmental authorities, obey civil law, be good citizens, and act as respectful neighbors (cf. Mat. 17:24–27; 22:15–22; Rom. 13:1–7; 1 Pet. 2:13–17). The only exception occurs when governmental law conflicts with Biblical teaching (cf. Acts 5:29).

3:5 WASHING OF REGENERATION. This refers to the new birth of the believer, symbolically pictured in Christian baptism (see article on REGENERATION, p. 1597). "Renewing of the Holy Ghost" points to the constant impartation of divine life to believers as they surrender their lives to God (cf. Rom. 12:2).

3:6 SHED ON US ABUNDANTLY. Paul's reference to the Holy Spirit's work points back to the outpouring of the Holy Spirit on the day of Pentecost and afterward (cf. Acts 2:33; 11:15). God supplies an abundant and adequate supply of His grace and power as a result of the new birth and the Holy Spirit's work in us.

7 [k]That being justified by his
grace, [l]we should be made heirs [m]ac-
cording to the hope of eternal life.
8 [n]*This is* a faithful saying, and
these things I will that thou affirm con-
stantly, that they which have believed
in God might be careful [o]to maintain
good works. These things are good and
profitable unto men.
9 But [p]avoid foolish questions, and
genealogies, and contentions, and
strivings about the law; [q]for they are
unprofitable and vain.
10 A man that is an heretic [r]after
the first and second admonition [s]re-
ject;
11 Knowing that he that is such is
subverted, and sinneth, [t]being con-
demned of himself.

3:7 [k]Rom. 3:24 [l]Rom. 8:23 [m]ch. 1:2
3:8 [n]1 Tim. 1:15 [o]ch. 2:14
3:9 [p]1 Tim. 1:4 [q]2 Tim. 2:14
3:10 [r]2 Cor. 13:2 [s]Mat. 18:17
3:11 [t]Acts 13:46
3:12 [u]Acts 20:4
3:13 [v]Acts 18:24
3:14 [w]ver. 8 [x]Rom. 15:28 Phil. 1:11

Closing instruction, benediction

12 When I shall send Artemas unto
thee, or [u]Tychicus, be diligent to
come unto me to Nicopolis: for I have
determined there to winter.
13 Bring Zenas the lawyer and
[v]Apollos on their journey diligently,
that nothing be wanting unto them.
14 And let ours also learn [w]to
°maintain good works for necessary
uses, that they be [x]not unfruitful.
15 All that are with me salute thee.
Greet them that love us in the faith.
Grace *be* with you all. Amen.

° Or, *profess honest trades*

3:10 HERETIC . . . REJECT. Heretics are false teachers who teach opinions and doctrines that have no Biblical basis and that create division. After a second admonition proves ineffective in dealing with such persons, they must be rejected, i.e., expelled from church membership. Those who reject Biblical truth and substitute their own ideas and opinions are perverted and sinning (v. 11).

3:14 GOOD WORKS. Paul emphasizes that "good works" are the result of the believer's conversion and life in the Holy Spirit (vv. 4–8). Believers must be "a pattern of good works" (2:7), "zealous of good works" (2:14), "ready [for] every good work" (v. 1), and "careful to maintain good works" (v. 8), and they must "learn to maintain good works."

PHILEMON

Outline

Christian Greetings (1–3)
- I. Appreciation for Philemon (4–7)
  - A. An Object of Thankful Prayer (4–6)
  - B. An Occasion of Great Joy (7)
- II. Appeal for Onesimus (8–21)
  - A. An Entreaty Rather Than a Command (8–11)
  - B. Motives for Sending Onesimus Back (12–16)
  - C. A Substitutionary Appeal (17–19)
  - D. A Positive Response Expected from Philemon (20–21)

Closing Matters (22–25)
- A. Hopes to Make a Visit Soon (22)
- B. Greetings from Paul's Companions (23–24)
- C. Benediction (25)

Author: Paul

Theme: Reconciliation

Date of Writing: c. A.D. 62

Background

Paul wrote this "prison epistle" (vv. 1,9) as a personal letter to a man named Philemon, most likely during Paul's first imprisonment at Rome (Acts 28:16–31). The identical names mentioned in Philemon (vv. 1–2,10,23–24) and Colossians (Col. 4:9–10,12,14,17) indicate that Philemon lived at Colosse and that both letters were written and delivered at the same time.

Philemon was a slaveowner (v. 16) and church member at Colosse (compare vv. 1–2 with Col. 4:17), perhaps a convert of Paul (v. 19). Onesimus was Philemon's slave, who had run away to Rome; there he came into contact with Paul, who led him to Christ. A strong bond of friendship developed between the two of them (vv. 9–13). Paul now reluctantly sends Onesimus back to Philemon, accompanied by Paul's co-worker Tychicus and this letter (cf. Col. 4:7–9).

Purpose

Paul wrote Philemon to deal with the specific problem of his runaway slave Onesimus. According to Roman law, a runaway slave could be punished by death. Paul intercedes on Onesimus's behalf with Philemon and petitions him to graciously receive Onesimus back as a fellow believer and as Paul's companion, with the same love with which he would receive Paul himself.

Survey

Paul's appeal to Philemon goes as follows: (1) He entreats Philemon as a Christian brother (vv. 8–9,20–21) to receive Onesimus back, not as a slave but as a brother in Christ (vv. 15–16). (2) In a wordplay Paul observes that Onesimus (whose name means "useful") was

formerly "useless," but now is "useful" to both Paul and Philemon (vv. 10–12). (3) Paul wishes Onesimus could remain with him in Rome but sends him back instead to his lawful master (vv. 13–14). (4) Paul offers himself as a substitute for Onesimus's debt and reminds Philemon of his indebtedness to Paul (vv. 17–19). The letter concludes with greetings from some of Paul's co-workers in Rome (vv. 23–24) and with a benediction (v. 25).

Special Features

Three major features or emphases characterize this epistle. (1) This is the shortest of all Paul's letters. (2) More than any other portion of the N.T., it illustrates how Paul and the early church dealt with the problem of Roman slavery. Rather than attacking it directly or stirring up armed rebellion, Paul set forth Christian principles which removed the harshness of Roman slavery and eventually led to its banishment altogether within Christianity. (3) It provides unique insight into the inner life of Paul, for he identifies himself with a slave so closely that he calls Onesimus "mine own bowels" (v. 12).

Reading Philemon

In order to read the entire New Testament in one year, the book of Philemon should be read in 1 day: ☐ Philemon

NOTES

1 PAUL, [a]A prisoner of Jesus Christ, and Timothy *our* brother, unto Philemon our dearly beloved, [b]and fellowlabourer,

2 And to *our* beloved Apphia, and [c]Archippus [d]our fellowsoldier, and to [e]the church in thy house:

3 [f]Grace to you, and peace, from God our Father and the Lord Jesus Christ.

Thanksgiving and prayer

4 [g]I thank my God, making mention of thee always in my prayers,

5 [h]Hearing of thy love and faith, which thou hast toward the Lord Jesus, and toward all saints;

6 That the communication of thy faith may become effectual [i]by the acknowledging of every good thing which is in you in Christ Jesus.

7 For we have great joy and consolation in thy love, because the bowels of the saints [j]are refreshed by thee, brother.

Appeal for Onesimus

8 Wherefore, [k]though I might be much bold in Christ to enjoin thee that which is convenient,

9 Yet for love's sake I rather beseech *thee,* being such an one as Paul the aged, [l]and now also a prisoner of Jesus Christ.

10 I beseech thee for my son [m]Onesimus, [n]whom I have begotten in my bonds:

11 Which in time past was to thee unprofitable, but now profitable to thee and to me:

12 Whom I have sent again: thou therefore receive him, that is, mine own bowels:

13 Whom I would have retained with me, [o]that in thy stead he might have ministered unto me in the bonds of the gospel:

14 But without thy mind would I do nothing; [p]that thy benefit should not be as it were of necessity, but willingly.

15 [q]For perhaps he therefore departed for a season, that thou shouldest receive him for ever;

16 Not now as a servant, but above a servant, [r]a brother beloved, specially to me, but how much more unto thee, [s]both in the flesh, and in the Lord?

Promise to Philemon

17 If thou count me therefore [t]a partner, receive him as myself.

18 If he hath wronged thee, or oweth *thee* aught, put that on mine account;

19 I Paul have written *it* with mine own hand, I will repay *it:* albeit I do not say to thee how thou owest unto me even thine own self besides.

20 Yea, brother, let me have joy of thee in the Lord: [u]refresh my bowels in the Lord.

21 [v]Having confidence in thy obedience I wrote unto thee, knowing that thou wilt also do more than I say.

22 But withal prepare me also a lodging: for [w]I trust that [x]through

1:1 [a]ver. 9 Eph. 3:1 & 4:1 2 Tim. 1:8 [b]Phil. 2:25
1:2 [c]Col. 4:17 [d]Phil. 2:25 [e]Rom. 16:5 1 Cor. 16:19
1:3 [f]Eph. 1:2
1:4 [g]Eph. 1:16 1 Thes. 1:2 2 Thes. 1:3
1:5 [h]Eph. 1:15 Col. 1:4
1:6 [i]Phil. 1:9
1:7 [j]ver. 20 2 Cor. 7:13 2 Tim. 1:16
1:8 [k]1 Thes. 2:6
1:9 [l]ver. 1
1:10 [m]Col. 4:9 [n]1 Cor. 4:15 Gal. 4:19
1:13 [o]1 Cor. 16:17 Phil. 2:30
1:14 [p]2 Cor. 9:7
1:15 [q]Gen. 45:5,8
1:16 [r]Mat. 23:8 1 Tim. 6:2 [s]Col. 3:22
1:17 [t]2 Cor. 8:23
1:20 [u]ver. 7
1:21 [v]2 Cor. 7:16
1:22 [w]Phil. 1:25 & 2:24 [x]2 Cor. 1:11

---

1 A PRISONER OF JESUS CHRIST. Paul wrote this letter to Philemon during his two-year imprisonment in Rome (vv. 1,9; cf. Acts 28:30).

2 THE CHURCH IN THY HOUSE. Philemon evidently made his home available as a place of worship for the believers in Colosse. There were many "house churches" in N.T. times (cf. Rom. 16:5; 1 Cor. 16:19; Col. 4:15). It is not until the third century that records appear of separate church buildings.

10 ONESIMUS. Onesimus, a slave belonging to Philemon, had run away, possibly taking with him some of his master's goods (vv. 15–16,18–19). Somehow he reached Rome, came into contact with Paul, and was converted to Christ under Paul's ministry. Paul now writes this letter, asking Philemon to take Onesimus back with kindness, love, and forgiveness.

12 WHOM I HAVE SENT AGAIN. The N.T. did not advocate a direct movement to free the slaves, even Christian slaves. To have initiated such an effort in the socio-political conditions of N.T. times would have destroyed the church and the cause of Christ. Instead of direct confrontation, guidelines were laid down for both the Christian slave and master that would undermine slavery from within and eventually bring about its abolition (vv. 10,12, 14–17,21; see v. 16, note).

14 NOT . . . OF NECESSITY, BUT WILLINGLY. Onesimus should be set free if he so desires. The ethics and love demanded in the gospel of Christ all point to this fact. Yet, Paul does not state it directly. He wanted Philemon and all masters to do it voluntarily.

16 A BROTHER BELOVED. Slavery cannot exist among believers who have seen the truth of Christian brotherhood. Onesimus must no longer be treated as a slave, but as a fellow believer and beloved brother, one who in God's sight is equal with the apostle Paul and Philemon (see Col. 3:22, note).

your prayers I shall be given unto
you.
23 There salute thee [y]Epaphras,
my fellowprisoner in Christ Jesus;
24 [z]Marcus, [a]Aristarchus, [b]Demas,
[c]Lucas, my fellowlabourers.

25 [d]The grace of our Lord Jesus
Christ *be* with your spirit. Amen.

1:23 [y]Col. 1:7 & 4:12 **1:24** [z]Acts 12:12,25 [a]Acts 19:29 & 27:2 Col. 4:10 [b]Col. 4:14 [c]2 Tim. 4:11 **1:25** [d]2 Tim. 4:22

HEBREWS

Outline

I. The Argument: Christ and the Christian Faith are Superior to Judaism (1:1—10:18)
  A. In Revelation (1:1—4:13)
    Jesus Christ is the Full and Final Revelation of God to Mankind
    1. Superior to the Prophets (1:1–3)
    2. Superior to the Angels (1:4—2:18)
       Exhortation: the Peril of Neglect (2:1–4)
    3. Superior to Moses (3:1–6)
       Exhortation: the Peril of Unbelief (3:7–19)
    4. Superior to Joshua (4:1–13)
  B. In Mediation (4:14—10:18)
    As Our Great High Priest Jesus Far Surpasses the O.T. Levitical Priesthood
    1. Superior in His Qualifications (4:14—7:25)
       Exhortation: Danger of Remaining Spiritually Immature (5:11—6:3)
       Exhortation: Danger of Falling Away (6:4–20)
    2. Superior in His Character (7:26–28)
    3. Superior in His Ministry (8:1—10:18)
       a. Located in a Better Sanctuary (8:1–5)
       b. Based on a Better Covenant (8:6–13)
       c. Performed Through a Better Service (9:1–22)
       d. Fulfilled by a Better Sacrifice (9:23—10:18)
II. The Application: Exhortation to Steadfastness (10:19—13:17)
  A. In the Realm of Salvation (10:19–38)
  B. In the Realm of Faith (10:39—11:40)
    1. The Nature of Faith (10:39—11:3)
    2. Examples of Faith from the Old Testament (11:4–38)
    3. The Vindication of Faith: Completed in Christ (11:39–40)
  C. In the Realm of Endurance (12:1–13)
  D. In the Realm of Holiness (12:14—13:17)
    1. The Priority of Holiness (12:14–29)
    2. The Practice of Holiness (13:1–17)
Conclusion (13:18–25)

Author: Undesignated

Theme: The Better Covenant

Date of Writing: A.D. 67–69 (uncertain)

Background

The destination of this epistle is uncertain, though Rome is a likely possibility. The book's title in the oldest Greek manuscripts is simply "To the Hebrews." However, its content reveals that the letter was written to Jewish Christians. The author's use of the Septuagint (Greek translation of the O.T.) when quoting from the O.T. indicates that the readers were

probably Greek-speaking Jews outside of Palestine. The phrase "they of Italy salute you" (13:24) most likely means that the author was writing to Rome and was including greetings from Italian believers living away from their homeland. The recipients may have consisted of house churches within the larger church community at Rome, some of whom were on the verge of forsaking their faith in Jesus and turning back to their former Jewish faith because of persecution and discouragement.

The author of Hebrews is not identified in its original title nor in the book, though he was well known to his readers (13:18–24). For some reason, his identity was lost by the end of the first century. Subsequently in early church tradition (second to fourth centuries) many different opinions were expressed about who may have written Hebrews. The opinion that Paul wrote Hebrews did not prevail until the fifth century.

Many conservative Bible scholars today believe Paul's authorship is unlikely, since the author's polished and Alexandrian writing style, reliance on the Septuagint, manner of introducing O.T. quotations, method of argument and teaching, structure of the argumentation, and exclusion of personal identification are all distinctly different from that of Paul. Moreover, while Paul always appeals to his firsthand revelation from Christ (cf. Gal. 1:11–12), this writer places himself among the second-generation Christians to whom the gospel was confirmed by eyewitnesses of Jesus' ministry (2:3). Among the men mentioned by name in the N.T., Luke's description of Apollos in Acts 18:24–28 most perfectly fits the profile of the author of Hebrews.

Regardless of who wrote Hebrews, this much is certain: the author wrote with the apostolic fullness of the Spirit and with apostolic insight, revelation, and authority. The absence of any reference in Hebrews to the destruction of the Jerusalem temple and its Levitical worship strongly suggests the author wrote before A.D. 70.

Purpose

Hebrews was written primarily to Jewish Christians who were undergoing persecution and discouragement. The writer endeavors to strengthen their faith in Christ by carefully explaining the superiority and finality of God's revelation and redemption in Jesus Christ. He shows that God's redemptive provisions under the old covenant have been fulfilled and made obsolete by the coming of Jesus and the establishment of the new covenant through His atoning death. The writer challenges his readers (1) to hold fast their confession of Christ firm until the end, (2) to go on to spiritual maturity, and (3) not to turn back to condemnation by abandoning faith in Jesus Christ.

Survey

Hebrews is more like a sermon than an epistle. The author describes his work as a "word of exhortation" (13:22). It has three major divisions. (1) First, Jesus as the powerful Son of God (1:1–3) is declared to be God's full revelation to mankind—greater than the prophets (1:1–3), angels (1:4—2:18), Moses (3:1–6), and Joshua (4:1–11). A solemn warning occurs in this division about the consequences of spiritually drifting from the faith or hardening one's heart in unbelief (2:1–3; 3:7—4:2). (2) The second division presents Jesus as the high priest whose qualifications (4:14—5:10, 6:19—7:25), character (7:26–28), and ministry (8:1—10:18) are perfect and everlasting. A solemn warning is given about remaining spiritually immature or even "falling away" after becoming partakers of Christ (5:11—6:12). (3) The final division (10:19—13:17) strongly exhorts believers to persevere in salvation, faith, suffering, and holiness.

Special Features

Eight major features or emphases characterize this epistle. (1) It is unique among N.T. epistles in its format: "it begins like a treatise, proceeds like a sermon, and concludes like a letter" (Origen). (2) It is the most polished book in the N.T., approaching classical Greek style more nearly than any other N.T. writer (except perhaps for Luke in Luke 1:1–4). (3) It is the only N.T. writing that develops the concept of Jesus' high priestly ministry. (4) Its Christology is richly varied, with more than twenty names and titles for Christ being used.

(5) Its key word is "better" (13 times). Jesus is better than the angels and all O.T. mediators. He offers a better rest, covenant, hope, priesthood, sacrifice/blood atonement, and promises. (6) It contains the foremost chapter in the Bible on faith (ch. 11). (7) It is saturated with O.T. references and allusions that provide a rich insight into early Christian interpretation of O.T. history and worship, particularly in the realm of typology. (8) It warns about the dangers of spiritual apostasy more than any other N.T. writing.

Reading Hebrews

In order to read the entire New Testament in one year, the book of Hebrews should be read in 17 days, according to the following schedule:
☐ 1 ☐ 2 ☐ 3 ☐ 4:1–13 ☐ 4:14—5:10 ☐ 5:11—6:20 ☐ 7 ☐ 8 ☐ 9:1–10 ☐ 9:11–28 ☐ 10:1–18 ☐ 10:19–39 ☐ 11:1–16 ☐ 11:17–40 ☐ 12:1–13 ☐ 12:14–29 ☐ 13

NOTES

The Son superior to prophets

1 GOD, WHO at sundry times and
[a]in divers manners spake in time
past unto the fathers by the prophets,
2 Hath [b]in these last days [c]spo-
ken unto us by *his* Son, [d]whom he
hath appointed heir of all things, [e]by
whom also he made the worlds;
3 [f]Who being the brightness of *his*
glory, and the express image of his per-
son, and [g]upholding all things by the
word of his power, [h]when he had by
himself purged our sins, [i]sat down on
the right hand of the Majesty on
high;

The Son superior to angels

4 Being made so much better than
the angels, as [j]he hath by inheritance
obtained a more excellent name than
they.
5 For unto which of the angels said
he at any time, [k]Thou art my Son, this
day have I begotten thee? And again,
[l]I will be to him a Father, and he shall
be to me a Son?
6 [a]And again, when he bringeth in
[m]the first begotten into the world, he
saith, [n]And let all the angels of God
worship him.
7 And [b]of the angels he saith,
[o]Who maketh his angels spirits, and
his ministers a flame of fire.
8 But unto the Son *he saith,* [p]Thy
throne, O God, *is* for ever and ever: a
sceptre of [c]righteousness *is* the scep-
tre of thy kingdom.
9 Thou hast loved righteousness,
and hated iniquity; therefore God, *even*
thy God, [q]hath anointed thee with the
oil of gladness above thy fellows.
10 And, [r]Thou, Lord, in the begin-
ning hast laid the foundation of the
earth; and the heavens are the works
of thine hands:
11 [s]They shall perish; but thou re-
mainest; and they all shall wax old as
doth a garment;
12 And as a vesture shalt thou fold
them up, and they shall be changed:
but thou art the same, and thy years
shall not fail.
13 But to which of the angels said
he at any time, [t]Sit on my right hand,
until I make thine enemies thy foot-
stool?
14 [u]Are they not all ministering
spirits, sent forth to minister for them
who shall be [v]heirs of salvation?

1:1 [a]Num. 12:6 **1:2** [b]Eph. 1:10 [c]John 1:17 [d]Ps. 2:8 [e]John 1:3 **1:3** [f]John 1:14 [g]John 1:4 Rev. 4:11 [h]ch. 7:27 [i]Ps. 110:1 **1:4** [j]Phil. 2:9,10 **1:5** [k]Ps. 2:7 Acts 13:33 [l]2 Sam. 7:14 **1:6** [m]Rom. 8:29 [n]Deut. 32:43 LXX **1:7** [o]Ps. 104:4 **1:8** [p]Ps. 45:6,7 **1:9** [q]Is. 61:1 **1:10** [r]Ps. 102:25 **1:11** [s]Is. 34:4 **1:13** [t]Ps. 110:1 Luke 20:42 **1:14** [u]Ps. 103:20 Mat. 18:10 [v]Rom. 8:17

[a] Or, *When he bringeth again* [b] Gk. *unto* [c] Gk. *rightness,* or, *straightness*

1:1–2 SPOKEN UNTO US BY *HIS* SON. These verses establish a major theme of this epistle: in the past God spoke through the prophets, but now He has spoken to us in His Son Jesus Christ, who is supreme over all things. God's Word through His Son is final; it fulfills and transcends all previous words by God (see article on THE WORD OF GOD, p. 1064). Absolutely nothing, neither prophets (v. 1) nor angels (v. 4), has greater authority than Christ. He is the only way to eternal salvation and the only mediator between God and man. The author confirms Christ's supremacy by listing seven great revelations about Christ (vv. 2–3).

1:3 SAT DOWN ON THE RIGHT HAND. After Christ provided the forgiveness of our sins by His death on the cross, He took His place of authority at the right hand of God. Christ's redeeming activity in heaven involves His ministry as divine mediator (8:6; 13:15; 1 John 2:1–2), high priest (2:17–18; 4:14–16; 8:1–3), intercessor (7:25), and baptizer in the Spirit (Acts 2:33).

1:4 BETTER THAN THE ANGELS. Just as Jesus is superior to the prophets because He is the Son, so He is superior to angels because He is the Son (vv. 4–14). Angels had played an important part in the giving of the O.T. covenant (Deut. 33:2; Acts 7:53; Gal. 3:19). The author, writing to Jewish believers, establishes Christ's superiority to the angels by quoting from the O.T. For more on angels, see article on ANGELS AND THE ANGEL OF THE LORD, p. 368.

1:5 THIS DAY HAVE I BEGOTTEN THEE. See John 1:14, note.

1:8 UNTO THE SON . . . O GOD. The author is here pointing out the deity of Christ (see John 1:1, note).

1:9 LOVED RIGHTEOUSNESS, AND HATED INIQUITY. It is not enough for the child of God to love righteousness; he must also hate evil. We see this clearly in Christ's devotion to righteousness (Is. 11:5) and His hatred of iniquity in His life, ministry, and death (see John 3:19, note; 11:33, note). (1) Christ's faithfulness to His Father while on earth, as demonstrated by His love of righteousness and hatred of wickedness, is the basis for God's anointing of His Son. In the same way, the Christian's anointing will come only as he identifies with his Master's attitude toward righteousness and evil (Ps. 45:7).

(2) The believer's love of righteousness and hatred of evil will increase by two means: (a) by growing in heartfelt love and compassion for those whose lives are being destroyed by sin, and (b) by experiencing more and more oneness with his God and Savior, who "loved righteousness, and hated iniquity" (see Ps. 94:16; 97:10; Prov. 8:13; Amos 5:15; Rom. 12:9; 1 John 2:15; Rev. 2:6).

1:13 THE ANGELS. For a discussion of the role that angels have in our lives, see article on ANGELS AND THE ANGEL OF THE LORD, p. 368.

Warning against drifting from the faith

2 THEREFORE WE ought to give
the more earnest heed to the
things which we have heard, lest at any
time we should [d]let *them* slip.
2 For if the word [w]spoken by an-
gels was stedfast, and [x]every trans-
gression and disobedience received a
just recompence of reward;
3 [y]How shall we escape, if we ne-
glect so great salvation; [z]which at the
first began to be spoken by the Lord,
and was [a]confirmed unto us by them
Heb. 5:9 that heard *him;*
4 [b]God also bearing *them* witness,
[c]both with signs and wonders, and
with divers miracles, and [d]gifts[e] of
1 Pet. 4:10-11 the Holy Ghost, [e]according to his own
will?

The Son over all

5 For unto the angels hath he not
put in subjection [f]the world to come,
whereof we speak.
6 But one in a certain place testi-
fied, saying, [g]What is man, that thou
art mindful of him? or the son of man,
that thou visitest him?
7 Thou madest him [f]a little lower
than the angels; thou crownedst him
with glory and honour, and didst set
him over the works of thy hands:
8 [h]Thou hast put all things in sub-
jection under his feet. For in that he
put all in subjection under him, he left
nothing *that is* not put under him. But
now [i]we see not yet all things put un-
der him.
9 But we see Jesus, [j]who was
made a little lower than the angels
[g]for the suffering of death, [k]crowned
with glory and honour; that he by the
grace of God should taste death [l]for
every man.

The captain of our salvation

10 [m]For it became him, [n]for whom
are all things, and by whom *are* all

2:2 [w]Deut. 33:2 Acts 7:53 [x]Num. 15:30 **2:3** [y]ch. 10:28 [z]Mat. 4:17 [a]Luke 1:2 **2:4** [b]Mark 16:20 [c]Acts 2:22 [d]1 Cor. 12:4,7,11 [e]Eph. 1:5,9 **2:5** [f]2 Pet. 3:13 **2:6** [g]Job 7:17 **2:8** [h]Mat. 28:18 Eph. 1:22 [i]1 Cor. 15:25 **2:9** [j]Phil. 2:7-9 [k]Acts 2:33 [l]John 3:16 2 Cor. 5:15 1 John 2:2 Rev. 5:9 **2:10** [m]Luke 24:46 [n]Rom. 11:36

[d] Gk. *run out as leaking vessels* [e] Or, *distributions* [f] Or, *a little while inferior to* [g] Or, *by*

2:1–3 LEST ... WE SHOULD LET *THEM* SLIP. One reason the writer of Hebrews emphasizes the superiority of God's Son and His revelation over that of prophets and angels is to stress to those who have experienced salvation that they must take with intense seriousness the original witness and doctrine of Christ and the apostles. Therefore, we must give close attention to God's Word, our relation to Christ, and the leading of the Holy Spirit (Gal. 5:16–25). (1) Neglect, carelessness, or unconcern is fatal. A believer who, because of negligence, allows the truth and teachings of the gospel to slip, is in great peril of being swept along downstream past a fixed landing place and of failing to gain its security.

(2) Like the recipients of this letter, all Christians are tempted to become indifferent to God's Word. Because of carelessness and unconcern, we may easily begin to pay less attention to God's warnings (v. 2), cease to persevere in our struggle against sin (12:4; 1 Pet. 2:11), and slowly drift away from God's Son, Jesus Christ (vv. 1–3; 6:4–8; 10:31–32; see Rom. 8:13, note).

2:3 CONFIMRED UNTO US. The apostolic gospel was first announced by the Lord Jesus Christ and then confirmed by: (1) the firsthand testimony of those who had actually heard and known Jesus during His earthly life (cf. Acts 1:4; 1 John 1:1), and (2) the testimony of God Himself, who bore witness to the authenticity of the gospel proclamation of salvation by signs, wonders, and miracles and by spiritual gifts (see next note; cf. 1 Cor. 12:4–11). Thus the early church did not proclaim the gospel in word only, but also "in power, and in the Holy Ghost, and in much assurance" (1 Thes. 1:5).

2:4 GOD ALSO BEARING *THEM* WITNESS. The Holy Spirit through the writer of Hebrews reaffirms that God confirmed and supported the gospel message with signs, wonders, miracles, and gifts of the Holy Spirit (Acts 2:22). After His resurrection Christ promised that miraculous confirmation of the gospel message would accompany all who believe (see article on SIGNS OF BELIEVERS, p. 1516). God desires that the believer's witness be more than simply words (Mark 16:20; John 10:25; Acts 2:22,43; 1 Cor. 2:4–5; Gal. 3:5; 1 Thes. 1:5; 1 Pet. 1:12; see Acts 4:30, note).

2:8 NOT YET ALL THINGS PUT UNDER HIM. In this fallen world dominated by Satan, we do not yet see everything in subjection to Christ. Yet Jesus is already crowned with glory and honor in heaven (v. 9), and this means that all the evil powers in the world are doomed to defeat and judgment.

2:9 TASTE DEATH FOR EVERY MAN. Christ experienced the humiliation and suffering of death for all people. His death was not, as some claim, a "limited atonement." Since He bore the punishment of the sins of all mankind, His death avails for all who accept Him (see Rom. 3:25, note).

2:10 PERFECT THROUGH SUFFERINGS. This does not mean that Christ needed to be made morally and spiritually perfect. What was perfected was his role as "captain" or leader — one who goes before to make a way for others to follow. He could only be the perfect Savior of all those who believe if He first endured suffering and death as a human. His obedience and death on the cross qualified Him to be the perfect representative of fallen humanity and to suffer in their place.

things, in bringing many sons unto glo-
ry, to make [o]the captain of their salva-
tion [p]perfect through sufferings.
11 For [q]both he that sanctifieth
and they who are sanctified [r]*are* all of
one: for which cause [s]he is not
ashamed to call them brethren,
12 Saying, [t]I will declare thy name
unto my brethren, in the midst of the
church will I sing praise unto thee.
13 And again, [u]I will put my trust
in him. And again, [v]Behold I and the
children [w]which God hath given me.

Christ the high priest

14 Forasmuch then as the children
are partakers of flesh and blood, he
[x]also himself likewise took part of the
same; [y]that through death he might
destroy him that had the power of
death, that is, the devil;
15 And deliver them who [z]through
fear of death were all their lifetime sub-
ject to bondage.
16 For verily [h]he took not on *him*
the nature of angels; but he took on *him*
the seed of Abraham.
17 Wherefore in all things it be-
hooved him [a]to be made like unto *his*
brethren, that he might be [b]a merciful
and faithful high priest in things *per-*

2:10 [o]Acts 5:31 [p]Luke 13:32 **2:11** [q]ch. 10:10 [r]Acts 17:26 [s]Mat. 28:10 John 20:17 **2:12** [t]Ps. 22:22 **2:13** [u]Ps. 18:2 Is. 12:2 [v]Is. 8:18 [w]John 10:29 **2:14** [x]John 1:14 Phil. 2:7 [y]1 Cor. 15:54 Col. 2:15 **2:15** [z]Luke 1:74 2 Tim. 1:7 **2:17** [a]Phil. 2:7 [b]ch. 4:15 **2:18** [c]ch. 4:15,16 **3:1** [d]Rom. 1:7 1 Cor. 1:2 Phil. 3:14 2 Pet. 1:10 [e]Rom. 15:8 **3:2** [f]Num. 12:7 **3:3** [g]Zech. 6:12 Mat. 16:18 **3:4** [h]Eph. 2:10 ch. 1:2 **3:5** [i]ver. 2

taining to God, to make reconciliation
for the sins of the people.
18 [c]For in that he himself hath suf-
fered being tempted, he is able to suc-
cour them that are tempted.

Christ superior to Moses

3 WHEREFORE, HOLY brethren,
partakers of [d]the heavenly call-
ing, consider [e]the Apostle and High
Priest of our profession, Christ Jesus;
2 Who was faithful to him that [i]ap-
pointed him, as also [f]Moses *was faith-*
ful in all his house.
3 For this *man* was counted worthy
of more glory than Moses, inasmuch as
[g]he who hath builded the house hath
more honour than the house.
4 For every house is builded by
some *man;* but [h]he that built all things
is God.
5 [i]And Moses verily *was* faithful in
all his house, as [j]a servant, [k]for a
testimony of those things which were
to be spoken after;
6 But Christ as [l]a son over his own

[j]Ex. 14:31; Deut. 3:24 [k]Deut. 18:19 **3:6** [l]ch. 1:2

[h] Gk. *he taketh not hold of angels, but of the seed of Abraham he taketh hold* [i] Gk. *made*

2:11 HE THAT SANCTIFIETH. "He that sanctifieth" is Christ (cf. 10:10,14,29; 13:12) and the "sanctified" are those who have been redeemed from the guilt and power of sin and set apart as the people of God. Christ's consecration of Himself to die for us provides the way for our sanctification (see article on SANCTIFICATION, p. 1982).

2:14 PARTAKERS OF FLESH AND BLOOD. Because those whom Jesus came to redeem are flesh and blood (i.e., human), He also had to take on humanity. For only as a true human being could He qualify to redeem the human race from Satan's power. Christ died to destroy Satan's control and power over those who believe (cf. 1 John 3:8) and to deliver them from the fear of death (Rev. 1:18) by promising eternal life with God (John 17:3; Rev. 21–22).

2:17 MERCIFUL AND FAITHFUL HIGH PRIEST. Christ became one with mankind in order to become a high priest and so to represent believers before God. (1) In this ministry, the Son's death propitiates (i.e., makes atonement) by removing God's wrath against us because of our sins (cf. Rom. 1:18; 5:10). As a result we can now approach God in confidence. (2) The Son mercifully sympathizes with us when we are tempted and comes to our aid because He, as a human, has experienced suffering, trials, and temptations, yet did not sin (cf. 4:14–15; 2 Cor. 6:2).

2:18 HE IS ABLE TO SUCCOUR. When we are tempted to be disloyal to God and give in to sin, we must pray to Christ, who triumphed over temptation and now, as our high priest, promises to give us the strength and grace to resist sin. Our responsibility is to draw near to Him in time of trouble; His responsibility is to give help in every time of need (see 4:16, note).

3:1 HOLY BRETHREN. This epistle was probably written to a group of Jewish Christians who, after their conversion to Christ, had been exposed to persecution and discouragement (10:32–39). That the readers were true born-again Christians is apparent from the following: (1) 2:1–4, which speaks of the danger of their drifting away from salvation; (2) 3:1, where the readers are called "holy brethren, partakers of the heavenly calling"; (3) 3:6, where they are called God's house. For further evidence that the readers were saved by Christ, see 3:12–19; 4:14–16; 6:9–12,18–20; 10:19–25,32–36; 12:1–29; 13:1–6,10–14,20–21.

3:1 APOSTLE AND HIGH PRIEST. Under the old covenant Moses (vv. 2–5) was the apostle (i.e., one sent by God with His authority) and Aaron (5:1–5) the high priest of God's people. Now under the new covenant, these two offices of apostleship and high priesthood are combined in the person of Jesus.

3:6 IF WE HOLD FAST . . . FIRM UNTO THE END. The conditional statements in the book of Hebrews deserve special attention (see 2:3; 3:6, 14; 10:26), for they warn that salvation is conditional. (1) The believer's security in Christ is main-

house; [m]whose house are we, [n]if we
hold fast the confidence and the rejoic-
ing of the hope firm unto the end.

The danger of an unbelieving heart

7 Wherefore (as [o]the Holy Ghost
saith, [p]Today if ye will hear his voice,
8 Harden not your hearts, as in the
provocation, in the day of temptation in
the wilderness:
9 When your fathers tempted me,
proved me, and saw my works forty
years.
10 Wherefore I was grieved with
that generation, and said, They do al-
ways err in *their* heart; and they have
not known my ways.
11 So I sware in my wrath, [j]They
shall not enter into my rest.)
12 Take heed, brethren, lest there
be in any of you an evil heart of unbe-
lief, in departing from the living God.
13 But exhort one another daily,
while it is called Today; lest any of you
be hardened through the deceitfulness
of sin.

Hold firmly until the end

14 For we are made partakers of
Christ, [q]if we hold the beginning of
our confidence stedfast unto the end;
15 While it is said, [r]Today if ye will
hear his voice, harden not your hearts,
as in the provocation.
16 [s]For some, when they had
heard, did provoke: howbeit not all
that came out of Egypt by Moses.
17 But with whom was he grieved
forty years? *was it* not with them that
had sinned, [t]whose carcases fell in
the wilderness?
18 And [u]to whom sware he that
they should not enter into his rest, but
to them that believed not?

3:6 [m] 1 Cor. 3:16 [n] Mat. 10:22 Rom. 5:2 Col. 1:23 **3:7** [o] Acts 1:16 [p] Ps. 95:7 **3:14** [q] ver. 6 **3:15** [r] ver. 7 **3:16** [s] Num. 14:2 **3:17** [t] Num. 14:22 Ps. 106:26 **3:18** [u] Num. 14:30

j Gk. *If they shall enter*

tained only as he cooperates with God's grace by persevering in faith and holiness unto the end of his earthly existence. This truth was emphasized by Christ (John 8:31; Rev. 2:7,11,17,25–26; 3:5, 11–12,21) and is a repeated admonition in the epistle to the Hebrews (2:1; 3:6,14; 4:16; 7:25; 10:34–38; 12:1–4,14). (2) The reassurance of salvation for church members who willfully sin, so prevalent in some circles today, finds no place in the N.T. (Rev. 3:14–16; see Luke 12:42–48, note; John 15:6, note).

3:7 THE HOLY GHOST SAITH. Along with other writers of the N.T., the writer of Hebrews regards Scripture in the ultimate and truest sense as the words of the Holy Spirit rather than the mere words of men (cf. 9:8; 10:15; 2 Tim. 3:16; 2 Pet. 1:21; see article on THE INSPIRATION AND AUTHORITY OF SCRIPTURE, p. 1924). When we read the Bible, we should not think that we are reading merely the opinions of Matthew, Paul, Peter, John, etc., but the very words of the Holy Spirit revealing God's will for the church and for our lives.

3:7–11 TODAY IF YE WILL HEAR HIS VOICE. Quoting Ps. 95:7–11, the writer refers to the disobedience of Israel in the wilderness after their exodus from Egypt as a warning for believers under the new covenant. Because of the Israelites' failure to resist sin and remain loyal to God, they were barred from entering into the promised land (see Num. 14:29,43, notes; Ps. 95:7–10, notes). Likewise, believers must realize that they too may fail to enter into God's rest in heaven if they disobey and allow their hearts to grow hard.

3:8 HARDEN NOT YOUR HEARTS. The Holy Spirit speaks to us concerning sin, righteousness, and judgment (John 16:8–11; Rom. 8:11–14; Gal. 5:16–25). If we ignore His voice, our hearts will increasingly grow hard and unyielding until they are no longer sensitive to the Word of God or the desires of the Holy Spirit (v. 7). Truth and righteous living will no longer be priorities for us, but we will more and more seek pleasure in the ways of the world rather than the ways of God (v. 10). The Holy Spirit warns us that God will not go on pleading with us indefinitely if we harden our hearts in rebellion (vv. 7–11; Gen. 6:3). There is a point of no return (vv. 10–11; 6:6; 10:26).

3:12 DEPARTING FROM THE LIVING GOD. At regular intervals throughout his epistle, the author of Hebrews warns his readers about the danger of falling away from the faith. For more on this subject, see article on PERSONAL APOSTASY, p. 1946.

3:13 EXHORT ONE ANOTHER DAILY. Many ministers fail to "exhort" or admonish believers to continue in the faith. Such ministers do not preach the urgent warnings of the apostles (Col. 1:21–23; 1 Tim. 4:1,16; Jas. 5:19–20; 2 Pet. 1:8–11; 1 John 2:23–25), the writer of Hebrews (2:3; 3:6–19), or Jesus Himself (Mat. 24:11–13; John 15:1–6).

3:18 THEY SHOULD NOT ENTER INTO HIS REST. The possibility of the believer missing God's promised rest is illustrated by the Israelites, who failed to enter the promised land after Moses had led them out of Egypt (see Num. 14:29, note; Deut. 1:26, note). The writer points out two things: (1) The Israelites had experienced the redemptive power of God (v. 16), seen God's mighty works (v. 9), yet become disobedient because they would not believe God's promises or heed His warnings (vv. 18–19). Therefore, they were destroyed in the wilderness (v. 17) and failed to enter the promised land. (2) The Israelites' initial experiences with God did not guarantee their safe arrival in Canaan. By failing to persevere, they cast aside their only source of security: the grace, mercy, and presence of "the living God" (v. 12).

19 So we see that they could not enter in because of unbelief.

The promise of rest

4 LET [v]US therefore fear, lest, a promise being left *us* of entering into his rest, any of you should seem to come short of it.

2 For unto us was the gospel preached, as well as unto them: but [k]the word preached did not profit them, [l]not being mixed with faith in them that heard *it.*

3 [w]For we which have believed do enter into rest, as he said, [x]As I have sworn in my wrath, if they shall enter into my rest: although the works were finished from the foundation of the world.

4 For he spake in a certain place of the seventh *day* on this wise, [y]And God did rest the seventh day from all his works.

5 And in this *place* again, If they shall enter into my rest.

6 Seeing therefore it remaineth that some must enter therein, [z]and they to whom [m]it was first preached entered not in because of unbelief:

7 Again, he limiteth a certain day, saying in David, Today, after so long a time; as it is said, [a]Today if ye will hear his voice, harden not your hearts.

8 For if [n]Jesus had given them rest, then would he not afterward have spoken of another day.

4:1 [v]ch. 12:15
4:3 [w]ch. 3:14 [x]Ps. 95:11
4:4 [y]Ex. 20:11
4:6 [z]ch. 3:19
4:7 [a]Ps. 95:7
4:12 [b]Ps. 147:15 Jer. 23:29 [c]Is. 49:2 [d]Eph. 6:17 Rev. 1:16 [e]1 Cor. 14:25
4:13 [f]Ps. 90:8 [g]Job 26:6
4:14 [h]ch. 7:26 [i]ch. 10:23
4:15 [j]Is. 53:3 [k]Luke 22:28 [l]2 Cor. 5:21 1 Pet. 2:22
4:16 [m]Eph. 2:18

9 There remaineth therefore a [o]rest to the people of God.

10 For he that is entered into his rest, he also hath ceased from his own works, as God *did* from his.

11 Let us labour therefore to enter into that rest, lest any man fall after the same example of [p]unbelief.

12 For the word of God *is* [b]quick, and powerful, and [c]sharper than any [d]twoedged sword, piercing even to the dividing asunder of soul and spirit, and of the joints and marrow, and *is* [e]a discerner of the thoughts and intents of the heart.

13 [f]Neither is there any creature that is not manifest in his sight: but all things *are* naked [g]and opened unto the eyes of him with whom we have to do.

Jesus the great high priest

14 Seeing then that we have a great high priest, [h]that is passed into the heavens, Jesus the Son of God, [i]let us hold fast *our* profession.

15 For [j]we have not an high priest which cannot be touched with the feeling of our infirmities; but [k]was in all points tempted like as *we are,* [l]yet without sin.

16 [m]Let us therefore come boldly

[k] Gk. *the word of hearing* [l] Or, *because they were not united by faith to* [m] Or, *the gospel was first preached* [n] i.e. *Joshua* [o] Or, *keeping of a sabbath* [p] Or, *disobedience*

4:1 HIS REST . . . COME SHORT OF IT. Ceasing to persevere in faith and obedience to Jesus results in the failure to reach the eternal promised rest of heaven (cf. 11:16; 12:22–24). (1) The phrase "let us therefore fear" is spoken in the light of this terrible possibility and of the judgment of God. (2) Perseverance in faith requires that we continue to draw near to God through Christ with uttermost determination (v. 16; 7:25).

4:3 ENTER INTO REST. Only we who have believed the saving message of Christ enter into God's spiritual rest. Christ takes our burdens and sins and gives us the "rest" of His forgiveness, salvation, and the Holy Spirit (Mat. 11:28). However, in this life our rest is only partial, for we are like pilgrims plodding through a harsh world. One by one, as we die in the Lord, we enter into His perfect rest in heaven (see next note).

4:9 REMAINETH . . . A REST. God's promised rest is not only earthly, but heavenly as well (vv. 7–8; cf. 13:14). For believers, there remains an eternal rest in heaven (John 14:1–3; cf. Heb. 11:10,16). Entering this final rest means ceasing from the labors, sufferings, and persecution common to our lives on this earth (cf. Rev. 14:13), participating in God's own rest, and experiencing unending joy, delight, love, and fellowship with God and other redeemed saints. It will be a seventh day without end (Rev. 21–22).

4:11 LABOUR THEREFORE TO ENTER. In light of the glorious blessing of the eternal state and the terrible fate of those who fail to enter it, believers must diligently strive to arrive at the heavenly home of God's people. This requires pressing on toward the heavenly goal (Phil. 3:13–14) and clinging to the Word (v. 12) in devotion to prayer (v. 16).

4:12 THE WORD OF GOD. The Word of God determines who will enter into God's rest. It is a sharp sword that cuts into our innermost being in order to discern whether our thoughts and motives are spiritual or fleshly. It has two edges, either cutting to save our lives or judging us unto eternal death (cf. John 6:63; 12:48). Therefore, our response to God's Word should be to draw near to Jesus as our high priest (vv. 14–16; see article on THE WORD OF GOD, p. 1064).

4:14 WE HAVE A GREAT HIGH PRIEST. See 8:1, note on Jesus' ministry as high priest.

4:16 COME BOLDLY UNTO THE THRONE.

PERSONAL APOSTASY

Heb. 3:12 "Take heed, brethren, lest there be in any of you an evil heart of unbelief, in departing from the living God."

Apostasy (Gk. *apostasia*) appears twice in the N.T. as a noun (Acts 21:21; 2 Thes. 2:3) and here in Heb. 3:12 as a verb (Gk. *aphistēmi*, translated "depart"). The Greek term is defined as a falling away, defection, withdrawal, or turning from what one has formerly turned to.

(1) To apostatize means to sever one's saving relationship with Christ or to withdraw from vital union with and true faith in Him (see article on FAITH AND GRACE, p. 1738). Thus, individual apostasy is possible only for those who have first experienced salvation, regeneration, and renewing by the Holy Spirit (cf. Luke 8:13; Heb. 6:4–6); it is not a mere denial of N.T. doctrine by the unsaved within the visible church. Apostasy may involve two separate, though related, aspects: (a) theological apostasy, i.e., a rejection of all or some of the original teachings of Christ and the apostles (1 Tim. 4:1; 2 Tim. 4:3), and (b) moral apostasy, i.e., the former believer ceases to abide in Christ and instead becomes enslaved again to sin and immorality (Is. 29:13; Mat. 23:25–28; Rom. 6:15–23; 8:6–13).

(2) The Bible issues urgent warnings concerning the possibility of apostasy, designed both to alert us to the deadly peril of abandoning our union with Christ and to motivate us to persevere in faith and obedience. The divine purpose of these warning passages must not be weakened by the view that states, "the warnings are real, but the possibility of actual apostasy is not." Rather, we must see these warnings as speaking to the reality of our probationary period, and we should regard them with sincere alarm if we want to attain final salvation. A few of the many N.T. warning passages are: Mat. 24:4–5,11–13; John 15:1–6; Acts 11:21–23; 14:21–22; 1 Cor. 15:1–2; Col. 1:21–23; 1 Tim. 4:1,16; 6:10–12; 2 Tim. 4:2–5; Heb. 2:1–3; 3:6–8,12–14; 6:4–6; Jas. 5:19–20; 2 Pet. 1:8–11; 1 John 2:23–25.

(3) Examples of actual apostasy can be found in Ex. 32; 2 Ki. 17:7–23; Ps. 106; Is. 1:2–4; Jer. 2:1–9; Acts 1:25; Gal. 5:4; 1 Tim. 1:18–20; 2 Pet. 2:1,15,20–22; Jude 4,11–13; see article on THE AGE OF THE ANTICHRIST, p. 1896, for comments on apostasy predicted to occur within the professing church in the last days of this age.

(4) The steps which lead to apostasy are as follows: (a) The believer, through unbelief, fails to take the truths, exhortations, warnings, promises, and teachings of God's Word with utmost seriousness (Mark 1:15; Luke 8:13; John 5:44,47; 8:46).

(b) As the realities of the world become greater than the realities of God's heavenly kingdom, the believer gradually ceases to draw near to God through Christ (Heb. 4:16; 7:19,25; 11:6).

(c) Through the deceitfulness of sin, the believer becomes increasingly tolerant of sin in his own life (1 Cor. 6:9–10; Eph. 5:5; Heb. 3:13) and no longer loves righteousness and hates iniquity (see Heb. 1:9, note).

(d) Through hardness of heart (Heb. 3:8,13) and rejecting God's way (v. 10), the believer ignores the repeated voice and rebuke of the Holy Spirit (Eph. 4:30; 1 Thes. 5:19–22; Heb. 3:7–11).

(e) The Holy Spirit is grieved (Eph. 4:30; cf. Heb. 3:7–8) and quenched (1 Thes. 5:19), and His temple violated (1 Cor. 3:16). He eventually departs from the former believer (Judg. 16:20; Ps. 51:11; Rom. 8:13; 1 Cor. 3:16–17; Heb. 3:14).

(5) If apostasy continues on its course unchecked, an individual may eventually reach the point when no second beginning is possible. (a) That is, a person who once had a saving experience with Christ but deliberately and continually hardens his or her heart to the Holy Spirit's voice (Heb. 3:7–19), continues to sin willfully (Heb. 10:26), and refuses to repent and return to God, may reach a point of no return where repentance and salvation is no longer possible (Heb. 6:4–6; cf. Deut. 29:18–21, note; 1 Sam. 2:25, note; Prov. 29:1, note). There is a limit to the patience of God (see 1 Sam. 3:11–14; Mat. 12:31–32; 2 Thes. 2:9–11; Heb. 10:26–29,31; 1 John 5:16). (b) This point of no return cannot be defined in advance. Hence, the only safeguard against the peril of ultimate apostasy is found in the admonition: "Today, if ye will hear his voice, harden not your hearts" (Heb. 3:7–8,15; 4:7).

(6) It must be emphasized that while apostasy is a danger for all who drift from the faith (Heb. 2:1–3) and fall away from God (6:6), it is not made complete without constant and willful sinning against the voice of the Holy Spirit (see Mat. 12:31, note on the sin against the Holy Spirit).

(7) Those who by an unbelieving heart depart from God (Heb. 3:12) may yet think they are Christians, but their indifference to the demands of Christ and the Holy Spirit and to the warnings of Scripture points otherwise. Because of the possibility of self-deception, Paul exhorts all those claiming salvation to "examine yourselves, whether ye be in the faith; prove your own selves" (see 2 Cor. 13:5, note).

(8) Persons who become sincerely concerned about their spiritual condition and find in their hearts the desire to return to God in repentance, have sure evidence they have not committed unpardonable apostasy. The Scriptures clearly affirm that God is "not willing that any should perish" (2 Pet. 3:9; cf. Is. 1:18–19; 55:6–7) and declare that God will receive all who were once under saving grace if they repent and return to Him (compare Gal. 5:4 with 4:19; 1 Cor. 5:1–5 with 2 Cor. 2:5–11; see also Luke 15:11–24; Rom. 11:20–23; Jas. 5:19–20; Rev. 3:14–20; note the example of Peter, Mat. 16:16; 26:74–75; John 21:15–22).

unto the throne of grace, that we may obtain mercy, and find grace to help in time of need.

Christ the perfect high priest

5 FOR EVERY high priest taken from among men [n]is ordained for men in things *pertaining* to God, that he may offer both gifts and sacrifices for sins:

2 Who [q]can have compassion on the ignorant, and on them that are out of the way; for that he himself also is compassed with infirmity.

3 And [o]by reason hereof he ought, as for the people, so also for himself, to offer for sins.

4 [p]And no man taketh this honour unto himself, but he that is called of God, as [q]*was* Aaron.

5 [r]So also Christ glorified not himself to be made an high priest; but he that said unto him, [s]Thou art my Son, today have I begotten thee.

6 As he saith also in another *place*, [t]Thou *art* a priest for ever after the order of Melchisedec.

7 Who in the days of his flesh, when he had [u]offered up prayers and supplications [v]with strong crying and tears unto him [w]that was able to save him from death, and was heard [x]in[r] that he feared;

8 [y]Though he were a Son, yet learned he [z]obedience by the things which he suffered;

9 And being made perfect, he became the author of eternal salvation unto all them that obey him; Heb 7:25

10 Called of God an high priest after the order of Melchisedec.

Reproved for immaturity

11 Of whom [a]we have many things to say, and hard to be uttered, seeing ye are [b]dull of hearing.

12 For when for the time ye ought to be teachers, ye have need that one teach you again which *be* the first principles of the oracles of God; and are become such as have need of [c]milk, and not of strong meat.

13 For every one that useth milk [s]*is* unskilful in the word of righteousness: for he is [d]a babe.

14 But strong meat belongeth to

5:1 [n]ch. 8:3
5:3 [o]Lev. 4:3
5:4 [p]2 Chr. 26:18 John 3:27 [q]Ex. 28:1
5:5 [r]John 8:54 [s]Ps. 2:7
5:6 [t]Ps. 110:4
5:7 [u]Mat. 26:39 Mark 14:36 John 17:1 [v]Ps. 22:1 Mat. 27:46
[w]Mat. 26:53 Mark 14:36 [x]Mat. 26:37 Mark 14:33 Luke 22:43 John 12:27
5:8 [y]ch. 3:6 [z]Phil. 2:8
5:11 [a]John 16:12 2 Pet. 3:16 [b]Mat. 13:15
5:12 [c]1 Cor. 3:1
5:13 [d]1 Cor. 13:11 Eph. 4:14 1 Pet. 2:2

[q] Or, *can reasonably bear with* [r] Or, *for his piety* [s] Gk. *hath no experience*

Because Christ sympathizes with our weaknesses (v. 15), we can confidently approach the heavenly throne, knowing that our prayers and petitions are welcomed and desired by our heavenly Father (cf. 10:19–20). It is called the "throne of grace" because from it flow God's love, help, mercy, forgiveness, spiritual power, the outpouring of the Holy Spirit, His spiritual gifts, the fruit of the Holy Spirit, and all that we need under any circumstances. One of the greatest blessings of salvation is that Christ is now our high priest, opening a way to His personal presence whereby we can always seek the help we need.

5:1 EVERY HIGH PRIEST. Two qualifications are necessary for a valid priesthood: (1) He must be sympathetic, gentle, and patient with those who go astray through ignorance, unintentional sin, or weakness (v. 2; 4:15; cf. Lev. 4; Num. 15:27–29). (2) He must be appointed by God (vv. 4–6). Christ qualified in both ways (see Lev. 8:2, note).

5:6 THE ORDER OF MELCHISEDEC. Melchisedec is a mysterious O.T. figure who appears in Gen. 14 as God's priest of Salem (perhaps Jerusalem, 7:1; Gen. 14:18; Ps. 110:1–4) before the time of the Levitical priesthood. Christ's priesthood is of the same kind as Melchisedec's (see 7:1–3, notes).

5:7 STRONG CRYING AND TEARS. This passage probably refers to the intensity of Jesus' prayer in the Garden of Gethsemane. Jesus' prayer was "heard" not in the sense that God removed all that was involved in death, but in the sense that He received God's aid to undergo His appointed suffering. There will be times when we too face trials and our fervent prayers seem unanswered. In such times, we must remember that Jesus was tested in the same way and that God will give us sufficient grace to undergo what He allows for our lives (see Mat. 26:39, note).

5:8 LEARNED HE OBEDIENCE. Christ learned by experience the suffering, cost, and hardship that often result from faithful obedience to God in a corrupt world (cf. 12:2; Is. 50:4–6; Phil. 2:8). He became a perfect Savior and high priest because His suffering and death on the cross were accomplished without sin. Therefore, He was qualified in every way (vv. 1–6) to bring us eternal salvation (v. 9; see 2:10, note).

5:9 SALVATION UNTO ALL THEM THAT OBEY HIM. The eternal salvation that was gained by the suffering of Jesus (v. 8) is made available only to those who are obedient to Him through faith. The faith that saves is an obedient faith (John 8:31; Rom. 1:5; 16:26; Jas. 2:17–26).

5:12 MILK, AND NOT OF STRONG MEAT. See article on THREE KINDS OF PEOPLE, p. 1772.

5:14 DISCERN BOTH GOOD AND EVIL. Those who are weak and immature in the faith lack spiritual sensitivity and discernment with regard to what is good and what is evil in this life. Mature believers, because of their strong commitment to God and His Word, practice righteousness and thereby possess a sensitivity to all that brings

them that are [t]of full age, *even* those
who by reason [u]of use have their
senses exercised [e]to discern both
good and evil.

Warning against apostasy

6:4–6Ref — Heb. 10:26–31

6 THEREFORE [f]LEAVING [v]the
principles of the doctrine of Christ,
let us go on unto perfection; not laying
again the foundation of repentance
[g]from dead works, and of faith toward
God,
2 [h]Of the doctrine of baptisms,
[i]and of laying on of hands, [j]and of
resurrection of the dead, [k]and of eter-
nal judgment.
3 And this will we do, [l]if God per-
mit.
4 For [m]*it is* impossible for those
[n]who were once enlightened, and
have tasted of [o]the heavenly gift, and
[p]were made partakers of the Holy
Ghost,
5 And have tasted the good word of
God, and the powers of [q]the world to
come,
6 If they shall fall away, to renew
them again unto repentance; [r]seeing
they crucify to themselves the Son of
God afresh, and put *him* to an open
shame.
7 For the earth which drinketh in
the rain that cometh oft upon it, and
bringeth forth herbs meet for them
[w]by whom it is dressed, [s]receiveth
blessing from God:
8 [t]But that which beareth thorns
and briers *is* rejected, and *is* nigh
unto cursing; whose end *is* to be
burned.

5:14 [e]Is. 7:15 1 Cor. 2:14 **6:1** [f]Phil. 3:12-14 ch. 5:12 [g]ch. 9:14 **6:2** [h]Acts 19:4,5 [i]Acts 8:14 & 19:6 [j]Acts 17:31 [k]Acts 24:25 Rom. 2:16 **6:3** [l]Acts 18:21 **6:4** [m]Mat. 12:31 ch. 10:26 2 Pet. 2:20 1 John 5:16 [n]ch. 10:32 [o]John 4:10 & 6:32 Eph. 2:8 [p]Gal. 3:2,5 ch. 2:4 **6:5** [q]ch. 2:5 **6:6** [r]ch. 10:29 **6:7** [s]Ps. 65:10 **6:8** [t]Is. 5:6 **6:10** [u]Prov. 14:31 Mat. 10:42 & 25:40 John 13:20 [v]Rom. 3:4 2 Thes. 1:6,7 [w]1 Thes. 1:3 [x]Rom. 15:25 2 Cor. 8:4 2 Tim. 1:18 **6:11** [y]ch. 3:6,14 [z]Col. 2:2 **6:12** [a]ch. 10:36 **6:13** [b]Gen. 22:16,17 Ps. 105:9 Luke 1:73 **6:16** [c]Ex. 22:11 **6:17** [d]ch. 11:9 [e]Rom. 11:29

Encouragement to the faithful

9 But, beloved, we are persuaded
better things of you, and things that
accompany salvation, though we thus
speak.
10 [u]For [v]God *is* not unrighteous
to forget [w]your work and labour of
love, which ye have shown toward his
name, in that ye have [x]ministered to
the saints, and do minister.
11 And we desire that [y]every one
of you do show the same diligence [z]to
the full assurance of hope unto the
end:
12 That ye be not slothful, but fol-
lowers of them who through faith and
patience [a]inherit the promises.

God's oath unchanging

13 For when God made promise to
Abraham, because he could swear by
no greater, [b]he sware by himself,
14 Saying, Surely blessing I will
bless thee, and multiplying I will multi-
ply thee.
15 And so, after he had patiently en-
dured, he obtained the promise.
16 For men verily swear by the
greater: and [c]an oath for confirmation
is to them an end of all strife.
17 Wherein God, willing more abun-
dantly to show unto [d]the heirs of
promise [e]the immutability of his coun-
sel, [x]confirmed *it* by an oath:
18 That by two immutable things, in
which *it was* impossible for God to lie,
we might have a strong consolation,

[t] Or, *perfect;* see 1 Cor. 2:6 [u] Or, *of an habit, or, perfection* [v] Or, *the word of the beginning of Christ* [w] Or, *for* [x] Gk. *interposed himself by an oath*

---

dishonor to God. They have learned to love righteousness and hate iniquity (see 1:9, note), their minds are renewed with principles of righteousness (Rom. 12:1–2), and they are enabled by the Holy Spirit to see things from God's point of view.

6:4–6 IT IS IMPOSSIBLE . . . TO RENEW THEM AGAIN. Here the author of Hebrews discusses the consequences of apostasy (falling away from the faith). For more on this, see article on PERSONAL APOSTASY, p. 1946.

6:6 IF THEY SHALL FALL AWAY. This phrase (Gk. *parapesontas*, from *parapiptō*) is an aorist participle and should be rendered in the past tense—literally, "having fallen away." The word "if" does not appear in any Greek text.

6:9–20 BUT, BELOVED. The writer is confident that his readers have not entered into the apostasy described in vv. 4–8. He assures them that for those who remain loyal to Christ in faith and love (vv. 10–12), their hope of eternal salvation is certain and unchangeable, because God cannot lie and His promises remain steadfast (vv. 13–20).

6:18 IMPOSSIBLE FOR GOD TO LIE. Because it is "impossible for God to lie," His Word and promises to Abraham are true (v. 14). This truthfulness of God applies not only to His Word to Abraham, but also to His Word in all Scripture. That is, because Scripture is the inspired Word of God, it is completely true and trustworthy. The truth of God's Word is inherent in the very words and sentences of Scripture. Its authors were guided by the Holy Spirit to write the original manuscripts in such a way that the transmission of God's message to mankind was communicated without error (see articles on THE WORD OF GOD, p. 1064, and THE INSPIRATION AND AUTHORITY OF SCRIPTURE, p. 1924).

who have fled for refuge to lay hold upon the hope [f]set before us:

19 Which *hope* we have as an anchor of the soul, both sure and stedfast, [g]and which entereth into that within the veil;

20 [h]Whither the forerunner is for us entered, *even* Jesus, [i]made an high priest for ever after the order of Melchisedec.

The priesthood of Melchisedec

7 FOR THIS [j]Melchisedec, king of Salem, priest of the most high God, who met Abraham returning from the slaughter of the kings, and blessed him;

2 To whom also Abraham gave a tenth part of all; first being by interpretation King of righteousness, and after that also King of Salem, which is, King of peace;

3 Without father, without mother, [y]without descent, having neither beginning of days, nor end of life; but made like unto the Son of God; abideth a priest continually.

4 Now consider how great this man *was,* [k]unto whom even the patriarch Abraham gave the tenth of the spoils.

5 And verily [l]they that are of the sons of Levi, who receive the office of the priesthood, have a commandment to take tithes of the people according to the law, that is, of their brethren, though they come out of the loins of Abraham:

6 But he whose [z]descent is not counted from them received tithes of Abraham, [m]and blessed [n]him that had the promises.

7 And without all contradiction the less is blessed of the better.

8 And here men that die receive tithes; but there he *receiveth them,* [o]of whom it is witnessed that he liveth.

9 And as I may so say, Levi also, who receiveth tithes, paid tithes in Abraham.

10 For he was yet in the loins of his father, when Melchisedec met him.

11 [p]If therefore perfection were by the Levitical priesthood, (for under it the people received the law,) what further need *was there* that another priest should rise after the order of Melchisedec, and not be called after the order of Aaron?

12 For the priesthood being changed, there is made of necessity a change also of the law.

13 For he of whom these things are spoken pertaineth to another tribe, of which no man gave attendance at the altar.

14 For *it is* evident that [q]our Lord sprang out of Judah; of which tribe Moses spake nothing concerning priesthood.

Christ's priesthood superior

15 And it is yet far more evident: for that after the similitude of Melchisedec there ariseth another priest,

16 Who is made, not after the law of a carnal commandment, but after the power of an endless life.

17 For he testifieth, [r]Thou *art* a priest for ever after the order of Melchisedec.

18 For there is verily a disannulling of the commandment going before for [s]the weakness and unprofitableness thereof.

19 For [t]the law made nothing per-

6:18 [f]ch. 12:1
6:19 [g]Lev. 16:15 ch. 9:7
6:20 [h]ch. 4:14 & 8:1 & 9:24 [i]ch. 3:1 & 5:6,10 & 7:17
7:1 [j]Gen. 14:18
7:4 [k]Gen. 14:20
7:5 [l]Num. 18:21,26
7:6 [m]Gen. 14:19 [n]Rom. 4:13
7:8 [o]ch. 5:6 & 6:20
7:11 [p]ver. 18,19 Gal. 2:21 ch. 8:7
7:14 [q]Is. 11:1 Mat. 1:3 Luke 3:33 Rom. 1:3 Rev. 5:5
7:17 [r]Ps. 110:4 ch. 6:20
7:18 [s]Rom. 8:3 Gal. 4:9
7:19 [t]Acts 13:39 Rom. 3:20,21,28

[y]Gk. *without pedigree* [z]Or, *pedigree*

7:1 MELCHISEDEC. Melchisedec was a Canaanite king of Salem and a priest of God (Gen. 14:18). He was superior to Abraham because Abraham paid tithes to him and was blessed by him (vv. 2–7). The author of Hebrews considered him a type of Jesus Christ, who was both priest and king (v. 3). Christ's priesthood is "after the order of Melchisedec" (6:20), meaning that He is greater than Abraham, Levi, and the Levitical priests.

7:3 WITHOUT FATHER, WITHOUT MOTHER. This does not mean that Melchisedec literally had no parents or family or that he was an angel. It simply means that the Scriptures do not record his genealogy and say nothing of his beginning and end. Therefore, he serves as a type of the eternal Christ, whose priesthood will never end (vv. 24–25).

7:11 IF THEREFORE PERFECTION WERE. Because the Levitical priesthood was imperfect (cf. 10:4) and administered by sinful men (vv. 27–28), it was replaced by the perfect priest, the Son of God. Christ is a perfect priest because He is wholly righteous, had to die only once as a sacrifice for our sins, serves as our eternal priest before God in heaven, and lives forever (vv. 24–28). Therefore, He is able to save completely and forever all those who draw near to God through Him (see v. 25, note).

7:19 THE LAW MADE NOTHING PERFECT. The O.T. law was imperfect because it could not impart divine life and the power to fulfill its demands, nor did it offer complete and perfect access to God (v. 25; see Gal. 3:19, note; see article on THE OLD TESTAMENT LAW, p. 124).

fect, [a]but the bringing in of [u]a better hope *did;* by the which [v]we draw nigh unto God.

20 And inasmuch as not without an oath *he was made priest:*

21 (For those priests were made [b]without an oath; but this with an oath by him that said unto him, [w]The Lord sware and will not repent, Thou *art* a priest for ever after the order of Melchisedec:)

22 By so much [x]was Jesus made a surety of a better testament.

23 And they truly were many priests, because they were not suffered to continue by reason of death:

24 But this *man,* because he continueth ever, hath [c]an unchangeable priesthood.

Christ our interceding priest

25 Wherefore he is able also to save them [d]to the uttermost that come unto God by him, seeing he ever liveth [y]to make intercession for them.

26 For such an high priest became us, [z]*who is* holy, harmless, undefiled, separate from sinners, [a]and made higher than the heavens;

27 Who needeth not daily, as those high priests, to offer up sacrifice, [b]first for his own sins, [c]and then for the people's: for [d]this he did once, when he offered up himself.

28 For the law maketh [e]men high priests which have infirmity; but the word of the oath, which was since the law, *maketh* the Son, [f]who is [e]consecrated for evermore.

Superiority of the new covenant

8 NOW OF the things which we have spoken *this is* the sum: We have such an high priest, [g]who is set on the

7:19 [u]ch. 6:18 [v]Rom. 5:2 Eph. 2:18 ch. 4:16 **7:21** [w]Ps. 110:4 **7:22** [x]ch. 8:6 **7:25** [y]Rom. 8:34 1 Tim. 2:5 1 John 2:1 **7:26** [z]ch. 4:15 [a]Eph. 1:20 & 4:10 **7:27** [b]Lev. 9:7 [c]Lev. 16:15 [d]Rom. 6:10 **7:28** [e]ch. 5:1,2 [f]ch. 2:10 & 5:9 **8:1** [g]Eph. 1:20 Col. 3:1 ch. 10:12

[a] Or, *but* it was *the bringing in;* see Gal. 3:24 [b] Or, *without swearing of an oath* [c] Or, *which passeth not from one to another* [d] Or, *evermore* [e] Gk. *perfected*

7:25 LIVETH TO MAKE INTERCESSION. Christ lives in heaven in His Father's presence (8:1), interceding for each and every one of His followers according to the Father's will (cf. Rom. 8:33–34; 1 Tim. 2:5; 1 John 2:1; see article on INTERCESSION, p. 1268). (1) Through Christ's ministry of intercession, we experience God's love and presence, and find mercy and grace to help in any kind of need (4:16), temptation (Luke 22:32), weakness (4:15; 5:2), sin (1 John 1:9; 2:1), and trial (Rom. 8:31–39).

(2) Christ's high-priestly prayer for His people (John 17), as well as His desire to pour forth the Holy Spirit upon all believers (Acts 2:33), help us understand the content of Christ's intercessory ministry (see John 17:1, note).

(3) Through Christ's intercession, the one who draws near (i.e., continually draws near, for the Greek participle is present tense, emphasizing continual activity) to God may receive grace to be saved "to the uttermost." Christ's intercession as our high priest is essential to our salvation. Without that and without His grace, mercy, and help mediated to us through that intercession, we would fall away from God, once again be enslaved to sin and the dominion of Satan, and incur just condemnation. Our only hope is to draw near to God through Christ in faith (see 1 Pet. 1:5, note).

(4) Note that Christ does not remain an advocate and intercessor for those who refuse to confess and forsake sin and who depart from fellowship with God (cf. 1 John 1:5–7,9; 3:10). His intercession to save "to the uttermost" is only for those who "come unto God by him" (cf. 4:16). There is no safety and security for those who deliberately sin and cease to draw near to God through Him (10:21–31; see 3:6, note; see article on PERSONAL APOSTASY, p. 1946).

(5) Since Christ is our only mediator and intercessor in heaven, any attempt to treat angels or dead saints as mediators and to offer prayers to the Father through them is both futile and unbiblical (see Col. 1:2, note; 2:18, note).

8:1 WE HAVE ... AN HIGH PRIEST. After Christ took upon Himself the punishment for our sins by giving His life as a sacrifice, He entered heaven, where He serves in the presence of God on behalf of us who believe. Jesus' ministry as "high priest" (cf. 2:17) embraces six areas: (1) Jesus was both the priest and the sacrifice itself. He offered Himself for all people as a perfect sacrifice for sin by shedding His blood and dying in the sinner's place (2:17–18; 4:15; 7:26–28; Mark 10:45; 1 Cor. 15:3; 1 Pet. 1:18–19; 2:22–24; 3:18; see article on THE DAY OF ATONEMENT, p. 188).

(2) Jesus mediates the new and better covenant in order that all who are "called might receive the promise of the eternal inheritance" (9:15–22; see article on THE OLD COVENANT AND THE NEW COVENANT, p. 1954), and with confidence might have continual access to God (4:16; 6:19–20; 7:25; 10:19–22; see John 17:1, note on the high-priestly prayer of Jesus).

(3) He is in heaven in the presence of God to bestow the grace of God upon us who believe (4:14–16). By this grace mediated to us by Him, Christ regenerates us (John 3:3) and pours out the Holy Spirit upon us (Acts 1:4; 2:4,33).

(4) Jesus acts as a mediator between God and all those who have broken God's law and seek forgiveness and reconciliation (1 John 2:1–2).

(5) Jesus holds His priesthood permanently, sympathizing with believers' temptations and aiding them in their needs (2:18; 4:15–16).

(6) Jesus lives forever to "make intercession" continually in heaven for all those who in faith

right hand of the throne of the Majesty in the heavens;

2 A minister [f]of [h]the sanctuary, and of [i]the true tabernacle, which the Lord pitched, and not man.

3 For [j]every high priest is ordained to offer gifts and sacrifices: wherefore [k]*it is* of necessity that this man have somewhat also to offer.

4 For if he were on earth, he should not be a priest, seeing that [g]there are priests that offer gifts according to the law:

5 Who serve unto the example and [l]shadow of heavenly things, as Moses was admonished of God when he was about to make the tabernacle: [m]for, See, saith he, *that* thou make all things according to the pattern shown to thee in the mount.

6 But now [n]hath he obtained a more excellent ministry, by how much also he is the mediator of a better [h]covenant, which was established upon better promises.

7 [o]For if that first *covenant* had been faultless, then should no place have been sought for the second.

8 For finding fault with them, he saith, [p]Behold, the days come, saith the Lord, when I will make a new covenant with the house of Israel and with the house of Judah:

9 Not according to the covenant that I made with their fathers in the day when I took them by the hand to lead them out of the land of Egypt; because they continued not in my covenant, and I regarded them not, saith the Lord.

10 For [q]this *is* the covenant that I will make with the house of Israel after those days, saith the Lord; I will [i]put my laws into their mind, and write them [j]in their hearts: and [r]I will be to them a God, and they shall be to me a people:

11 And [s]they shall not teach every man his neighbour, and every man his brother, saying, Know the Lord: for all shall know me, from the least to the greatest.

12 For I will be merciful to their unrighteousness, [t]and their sins and their iniquities will I remember no more.

13 [u]In that he saith, A new *covenant*, he hath made the first old. Now that which decayeth and waxeth old *is* ready to vanish away.

8:2 [h]ch. 9:8,12 [i]ch. 9:11 **8:3** [j]ch. 5:1 [k]Eph. 5:2 ch. 9:14 **8:5** [l]Col. 2:17 ch. 9:23 [m]Ex. 25:40 Num. 8:4 Acts 7:44 **8:6** [n]2 Cor. 3:6,8 ch. 7:22 **8:7** [o]ch. 7:11,18 **8:8** [p]Jer. 31:31 **8:10** [q]ch. 10:16 [r]Zech. 8:8 **8:11** [s]Is. 54:13 John 6:45 1 John 2:27 **8:12** [t]Rom. 11:27 **8:13** [u]2 Cor. 5:17 **9:1** [v]Ex. 25:8 **9:2** [w]Ex. 26:1 [x]Ex. 26:35 [y]Ex. 25:31 [z]Ex. 25:23 **9:3** [a]Ex. 26:31 **9:4** [b]Ex. 25:10 [c]Ex. 16:33 [d]Num. 17:10 [e]Ex. 25:16 Deut. 10:2 **9:5** [f]Lev. 16:2

Temporary sacrifices by Levites

9 THEN VERILY the first *covenant* had also [k]ordinances of divine service, and [v]a worldly sanctuary.

2 [w]For there was a tabernacle made; the first, [x]wherein *was* [y]the candlestick, and [z]the table, and the showbread; which is called [l]the sanctuary.

3 [a]And after the second veil, the tabernacle which is called the Holiest of all;

4 Which had the golden censer, and [b]the ark of the covenant overlaid round about with gold, wherein *was* [c]the golden pot that had manna, and [d]Aaron's rod that budded, and [e]the tables of the covenant;

5 And [f]over it the cherubims of glory shadowing the mercyseat; of which we cannot now speak particularly.

[f] Or, *of holy things* [g] Or, *they are priests* [h] Or, *testament* [i] Gk. *give* [j] Or, *upon* [k] Or, *ceremonies* [l] Or, *holy*

"come unto God by him" (7:25). He will eventually bring the believer's salvation to final fulfillment (see 7:25, note; 9:28, note).

8:6–13 A BETTER COVENANT. A significant theme of chs. 8–10 is the contrast between the old covenant that was centered around the law of Moses and the new covenant that was instituted by Jesus Christ. See article on THE OLD COVENANT AND THE NEW COVENANT, p. 1954.

9:1–7 THE FIRST *COVENANT*. In his discussion on how the new covenant is so much better than the old (or first) covenant, the writer to the Hebrews analyzes the major features of worship and sacrifice in Israel's religion. See article on THE OLD COVENANT AND THE NEW COVENANT, p. 1954.

9:4 THE ARK OF THE COVENANT. The ark of the covenant was a sacred box or chest containing the two stone tablets on which were written the Ten Commandments (Ex. 25:16,21); this demonstrated how important the law was as the standard of holiness that God required for His covenant people in the O.T. The lid of the ark was a golden plate called the mercyseat (see next note).

9:5 THE MERCYSEAT. On the Day of Atonement, both the blood of the bull which made atonement for the high priest and his family and the blood of the goat which served as a sin offering for the nation were sprinkled on the mercyseat before God (Lev. 16:2,14; see article on THE DAY OF ATONEMENT, p. 188). The earthly mercyseat is a figure or type of the heavenly throne of grace, to which believers draw near in order to receive grace and help (4:16).

6 Now when these things were thus
ordained, [g]the priests went always
into the first tabernacle, accomplish-
ing the service *of God*.
7 But into the second *went* the high
priest alone [h]once every year, not
without blood, [i]which he offered for
himself, and *for* the errors of the peo-
ple:
8 [j]The Holy Ghost this signifying,
that [k]the way into the holiest of all
was not yet made manifest, while as
the first tabernacle was yet standing:
9 Which *was* a figure for the time
then present, in which were offered
both gifts and sacrifices, [l]that could
not make him that did the service per-
fect, as pertaining to the conscience;
10 *Which stood* only in [m]meats and
drinks, and [n]divers washings, [o]and
carnal [m]ordinances, imposed *on them*
until the time of reformation.

The eternal sacrifice of Christ

11 But Christ being come [p]an high
priest [q]of good things to come, [r]by a
greater and more perfect tabernacle,
not made with hands, that is to say, not
of this building;
12 Neither [s]by the blood of goats
and calves, but [t]by his own blood he
entered in [u]once into the holy place,
[v]having obtained eternal redemption
for us.
13 For if [w]the blood of bulls and of
goats, and [x]the ashes of an heifer
sprinkling the unclean, sanctifieth to
the purifying of the flesh:
14 How much more [y]shall the
blood of Christ, [z]who through the
eternal Spirit offered himself without
[n]spot to God, [a]purge your con-
science from [b]dead works [c]to serve
the living God?
15 [d]And for this cause [e]he is the
mediator of the new testament, [f]that
by means of death, for the redemption
of the transgressions *that were* under
the first testament, [g]they which are
called might receive the promise of
eternal inheritance.
16 For where a testament *is*, there
must also of necessity [o]be the death
of the testator.
17 For [h]a testament *is* of force af-
ter men are dead: otherwise it is of no
strength at all while the testator liveth.
18 [i]Whereupon neither the first
testament was [p]dedicated without
blood.
19 For when Moses had spoken ev-
ery precept to all the people according
to the law, [j]he took the blood of
calves and of goats, [k]with water, and
[q]scarlet wool, and hyssop, and sprin-
kled both the book, and all the people,
20 Saying, [l]This *is* the blood of the
testament which God hath enjoined
unto you.
21 Moreover [m]he sprinkled with
blood both the tabernacle, and all the
vessels of the ministry.
22 And almost all things are by the
law purged with blood; and [n]without
shedding of blood is no remission.

9:6 [g]Num. 28:3
9:7 [h]Ex. 30:10 [i]ch. 7:27
9:8 [j]ch. 10:19 [k]John 14:6
9:9 [l]Gal. 3:21
9:10 [m]Col. 2:16 [n]Num. 19:7 [o]Eph. 2:15
9:11 [p]ch. 3:1 [q]ch. 10:1 [r]ch. 8:2
9:12 [s]ch. 10:4 [t]Eph. 1:7 Col. 1:14 [u]Zech. 3:9 [v]Dan. 9:24
9:13 [w]Lev. 16:14 [x]Num. 19:2
9:14 [y]1 John 1:7 [z]Rom. 1:4 [a]ch. 10:22 [b]ch. 6:1 [c]Luke 1:74
9:15 [d]1 Tim. 2:5 [e]ch. 7:22 [f]Rom. 3:25 [g]ch. 3:1
9:17 [h]Gal. 3:15
9:18 [i]Ex. 24:6
9:19 [j]Ex. 24:5,6 [k]Lev. 14:4
9:20 [l]Ex. 24:8 Mat. 26:28
9:21 [m]Ex. 29:12 Lev. 8:15
9:22 [n]Lev. 17:11

[m]Or, *rites*, or, *ceremonies* [n]Or, *fault* [o]Or, *be brought in* [p]Or, *purified* [q]Or, *purple*

9:7 THE SECOND. The second room in the tabernacle was the inner sanctuary, called the holy of holies; it symbolized the presence of God. The high priest was strictly forbidden to enter the holy of holies more than once a year. The Holy Spirit was teaching that under the old covenant, unimpeded access to the presence of God was not yet possible because close communion with Him could exist only when a person's inward conscience had been cleansed perfectly (vv. 8–9). This cleansing was provided for when Christ died as an eternal sacrifice for sin.

9:14 THE BLOOD OF CHRIST. The blood of Jesus Christ is central to the N.T. concept of redemption (1 Cor. 10:16; 11:27; Eph. 2:13; 1 Pet. 1:2; Rev. 7:14; 12:11). At His death on the cross Christ gave His innocent blood in order to remove our sins and to reconcile us with God (5:8; Rom. 5:19; Phil. 2:8; cf. Lev. 16).

By His blood Christ accomplished the following: (1) His blood forgives the sins of all who repent and believe (Mat. 26:28). (2) His blood ransoms all believers from the power of Satan and evil powers (Acts 20:28; Eph. 1:7; 1 Pet. 1:18–19; Rev. 5:9; 12:11). (3) His blood justifies all who believe in Him (Rom. 3:24–25). (4) His blood cleanses the believer's conscience that he might serve God without guilt in full assurance (9:14; 10:22; 13:18). (5) His blood sanctifies the people of God (13:12; 1 John 1:7–10). (6) His blood opens the way for believers to come directly before God through Christ in order to find grace, mercy, help, and salvation (7:25; 10:19; Eph. 2:13,18). (7) His blood is a guarantee of all the promises of the new covenant. (10:29; 13:20; Mat. 26:28; 1 Cor. 11:25). (8) The saving, reconciling, and purifying power of the blood of Christ is continually appropriated to the believer as he draws near to God through Christ (7:25; 10:22; 1 John 1:7).

9:15 MEDIATOR OF THE NEW TESTAMENT. For comments on Jesus' function as the mediator of the new covenant, see article on THE OLD COVENANT AND THE NEW COVENANT, p. 1954.

THE OLD COVENANT AND THE NEW COVENANT

***Heb. 8:6** "But now hath he obtained a more excellent ministry, by how much also he is the mediator of a better covenant, which was established upon better promises."*

Heb. 8–10 describes numerous aspects of the old covenant, such as the worship, regulations, and sacrificial ritual in the tabernacle; it discusses the various rooms and furniture of this O.T. worship center. The author's purpose is twofold: (1) to contrast the service of the high priest in the earthly sanctuary under the old covenant with the ministry of Christ as high priest in the heavenly sanctuary under the new covenant; (2) to show how these various aspects in the old covenant foreshadow or serve as a type of the ministry of Christ, the One who inaugurated the new covenant. This article summarizes the relationship between these two covenants.

(1) Under the old covenant, salvation and a right relationship with God came through a faith relationship with God expressed through obedience to His law and its sacrificial system (see article on GOD'S COVENANT WITH THE ISRAELITES, p. 314). Sacrifices in the O.T. had three main purposes: (a) They taught the people of God the gravity of sin. Sin separated sinners from a holy God, and they could be reconciled to God and find forgiveness only through the shedding of blood (Ex. 12:3–14; Lev. 16; 17:11; Heb. 9:22; see Lev. 1:2–3, note; 4:3, note; 9:8, note). (b) The sacrifices provided a way for Israel to come to God through faith, obedience, and love (cf. Heb. 4:16; 7:25; 10:1). (c) They pointed forward to or foreshadowed (Heb. 8:5; 10:1) the perfect sacrifice of Christ for the sins of the human race (cf. John 1:29; 1 Pet. 1:18–19; see Ex. 12:3–14; Lev. 16; see Gal. 3:19, note; see article on THE DAY OF ATONEMENT, p. 188).

(2) Jeremiah prophesied that at some time in the future, God would make a new covenant, a better one, with his people (see Jer. 31:31–34, notes; cf. Heb. 8:8–12). It is a better covenant than the old (cf. Rom. 7) because it completely forgives the sins of the repentant (Heb. 8:12), makes them children of God (Rom. 8:15–16), gives them a new heart and nature so that they can spontaneously love and obey God (Heb. 8:10; cf. Ezek. 11:19–20), brings them into a close personal relationship with Jesus Christ and the Father (Heb. 8:11), and provides a greater experience in the Holy Spirit (Joel 2:28; Acts 1:5,8; 2:16–17,33,38–39; Rom. 8:14–15,26).

(3) Jesus is the one who instituted the new covenant or new testament (both ideas are present in the Greek word *diathēkē*), and His heavenly ministry is far superior to the ministry of O.T. earthly priests. The new covenant is an agreement, promise, last will and testament, and a statement of intention to bestow divine grace and blessing on those who respond to God in obedient faith. Specifically, it is a covenant of promise for those who by faith accept Christ as God's Son, receive His promises, and commit themselves personally to Him and to the obligations of the new covenant.

(a) Jesus Christ's position as mediator of the new covenant (Heb. 8:6; 9:15; 12:24) is based on His sacrificial death (Mat. 26:28; Mark 14:24; Heb. 9:14–15; 10:29; 12:24). The promises and obligations of this new covenant are embodied in the entire N.T. Its purpose is (i) to save from guilt and condemnation of the law all those who believe in Christ and commit their lives to the truths and obligations of his testament (Heb. 9:16–17; cf. Mark 14:24; 1 Cor. 11:25), and (ii) to form them into a people for God's own possession (8:10; cf. Ezek. 11:19–20; 1 Pet. 2:9).

(b) Jesus' sacrifice is better than the sacrifices of the old covenant because it was a voluntary and obedient sacrifice of a righteous person (Jesus Christ) rather than the involuntary sacrifice of an animal. Jesus' sacrifice was perfect and thus made a way for complete forgiveness, reconciliation to God, and sanctification (Heb. 10:10,15–17; see Lev. 9:8, note).

(c) The new covenant can be called the new covenant of the Spirit, for it is the Holy Spirit who ministers life and power to those who accept God's covenant (2 Cor. 3:1–6; see John 17:3, note; see articles on BIBLICAL WORDS FOR SALVATION, p. 1726, and FAITH AND GRACE, p. 1738).

(4) All who participate in the new covenant through Jesus Christ receive its blessings and salvation only as they persevere in faith and obedience (see Heb. 3:6, note). The faithless are excluded from its blessing (see 3:18, note; see article on PERSONAL APOSTASY, p. 1946).

(5) With the institution of the new covenant through Christ, the old covenant became obsolete (Heb. 8:13). The new covenant, however, does not render the entire body of Scripture in the O.T. obsolete, but only the Mosaic covenant whereby salvation was obtained by obedience to the law and by the sacrificial system. The O.T. is not obsolete; much of its revelation points toward Christ (see article on CHRIST IN THE OLD TESTAMENT, p. 562) and, as God's inspired Word, is still profitable for teaching, reproof, correction, and training in righteous living (see article on THE INSPIRATION AND AUTHORITY OF SCRIPTURE, p. 1924).

Christ's one time sacrifice

23 *It was* therefore necessary that [o]the patterns of things in the heavens should be purified with these; but the heavenly things themselves with better sacrifices than these.

24 For [p]Christ is not entered into the holy places made with hands, *which are* the figures of [q]the true; but into heaven itself, now [r]to appear in the presence of God for us:

25 Nor yet that he should offer himself often, as [s]the high priest entereth into the holy place every year with blood of others;

26 For then must he often have suffered since the foundation of the world: but now [t]once [u]in the end of the world hath he appeared to put away sin by the sacrifice of himself.

27 [v]And as it is appointed unto men once to die, [w]but after this the judgment:

28 So [x]Christ was once [y]offered to bear the sins [z]of many; and unto them that [a]look for him shall he appear the second time without sin unto salvation.

1 Pet. 5:4

Christ a better sacrifice

10 FOR THE law having [b]a shadow [c]of good things to come, *and* not the very image of the things, [d]can never with those sacrifices which they offered year by year continually make the comers thereunto [e]perfect.

2 For then [r]would they not have ceased to be offered? because that the worshippers once purged should have had no more conscience of sins.

3 [f]But in those *sacrifices there is* a remembrance again *made* of sins every year.

4 For [g]*it is* not possible that the blood of bulls and of goats should take away sins.

5 Wherefore when he cometh into the world, he saith, [h]Sacrifice and offering thou wouldest not, but a body [s]hast thou prepared me:

6 In burnt offerings and *sacrifices* for sin thou hast had no pleasure.

7 Then said I, Lo, I come (in the volume of the book it is written of me,) to do thy will, O God.

8 Above when he said, Sacrifice and offering and burnt offerings and *offering* for sin thou wouldest not, neither hadst pleasure *therein;* which are offered by the law;

9 Then said he, Lo, I come to do thy will, O God. He taketh away the first, that he may establish the second.

10 [i]By the which will we are sanctified [j]through the offering of the body of Jesus Christ once *for all.*

11 And every priest standeth [k]daily ministering and offering oftentimes the same sacrifices, [l]which can never take away sins:

12 [m]But this man, after he had offered one sacrifice for sins for ever, sat down on the right hand of God;

13 From henceforth expecting [n]till his enemies be made his footstool.

14 For by one offering [o]he hath

9:23 [o]ch. 8:5
9:24 [p]ch. 6:20 [q]ch. 8:2 [r]Rom. 8:34 1 John 2:1
9:25 [s]ver. 7
9:26 [t]ch. 7:27 [u]1 Cor. 10:11
9:27 [v]Gen. 3:19 Eccl. 3:20 [w]2 Cor. 5:10
9:28 [x]Rom. 6:10 1 Pet. 3:18 [y]1 Pet. 2:24 1 John 3:5 [z]Mat. 26:28 Rom. 5:15 [a]Tit. 2:13
10:1 [b]Col. 2:17 [c]ch. 9:11 [d]ch. 9:9 [e]ver. 14
10:3 [f]ch. 9:7
10:4 [g]Mic. 6:6,7
10:5 [h]Ps. 40:6
10:10 [i]John 17:19 [j]ch. 9:12
10:11 [k]Num. 28:3 [l]ver. 4
10:12 [m]Col. 3:1
10:13 [n]Ps. 110:1 Acts 2:35
10:14 [o]ver. 1

[r] Or, *they would have ceased to be offered, because* [s] Or, *thou hast fitted me*

9:28 SHALL ... APPEAR THE SECOND TIME. Under the old covenant, the Israelites watched intensely for the reappearance of their high priest after he had gone into the sanctuary to make atonement. Likewise believers, knowing that their high priest has entered the heavenly sanctuary as their advocate, wait with earnest hope for His reappearing to bring a full and complete salvation (see John 14:3, note; 2 Tim. 4:8; see article on THE RAPTURE, p. 1889).

10:1 THOSE SACRIFICES WHICH THEY OFFERED. For comments on the purposes of sacrifices in the O.T., see article on THE OLD COVENANT AND THE NEW COVENANT, p. 1954.

10:4 THE BLOOD OF BULLS. The blood of animals was only a temporary provision or atonement for the sins of the people; ultimately, a man was needed to serve as a substitute for humankind (see article on THE DAY OF ATONEMENT, p. 188). Hence, Christ came to earth and was born as a man so that He might offer Himself in our place (2:9,14, notes). Furthermore, only a man who was free from sin could take our punishment for sin (2:14–18; 4:15) and thus adequately and perfectly satisfy the demands of God's holiness (cf. Rom. 3:25–26).

10:5–10 SACRIFICE AND OFFERING. Ps. 40:6–8 is cited to prove that the voluntary and obedient sacrifice of Jesus Christ is better than the involuntary animal sacrifices in the O.T.; see article on THE OLD COVENANT AND THE NEW COVENANT, p. 1954.

10:14 PERFECTED FOR EVER ... SANCTIFIED. The one offering of Christ on the cross and its benefit (i.e., perfect salvation) are eternally efficacious. Perfect salvation in Christ is imparted to all who are being sanctified as they draw near to God through Christ (v. 22; 7:25). Note that the Greek word "sanctify" here and in v. 10 is a

perfected for ever them that are sanctified.

15 *Whereof* the Holy Ghost also is a witness to us: for after that he had said before,

16 [p]This *is* the covenant that I will make with them after those days, saith the Lord, I will put my laws into their hearts, and in their minds will I write them;

17 [t]And their sins and iniquities will I remember no more.

18 Now where remission of these *is, there is* no more offering for sin.

Boldness to approach God

19 Having therefore, brethren, [q]boldness[u] to enter [r]into the holiest by the blood of Jesus,

20 By [s]a new and living way, which he hath [v]consecrated for us, [t]through the veil, that is to say, his flesh;

21 And *having* [u]an high priest over [v]the house of God;

22 [w]Let us draw near with a true heart [x]in full assurance of faith, having our hearts sprinkled [y]from an evil conscience, and [z]our bodies washed with pure water.

The appeal to hold fast

23 [a]Let us hold fast the profession of *our* faith without wavering; (for [b]he *is* faithful that promised;)

24 And let us consider one another to provoke unto love and to good works:

25 [c]Not forsaking the assembling of ourselves together, as the manner of some *is;* but exhorting *one another:* and [d]so much the more, as ye see [e]the day approaching.

The consequences of persistent sin

26 For [f]if we sin wilfully [g]after that we have received the knowledge of the truth, there remaineth no more sacrifice for sins, Heb. 12:1

27 But a certain fearful looking for of judgment and [h]fiery indignation, which shall devour the adversaries.

28 [i]He that despised Moses' law died without mercy [j]under two or three witnesses:

29 [k]Of how much sorer punishment, suppose ye, shall he be thought worthy, who hath trodden under foot the Son of God, and [l]hath counted the blood of the covenant, wherewith he was sanctified, an unholy thing, [m]and hath done despite unto the Spirit of grace?

30 For we know him that hath said, [n]Vengeance *belongeth* unto me, I will recompense, saith the Lord. And again, [o]The Lord shall judge his people.

31 [p]*It is* a fearful thing to fall into the hands of the living God.

Encouragement to persevere in the faith

32 But [q]call to remembrance the former days, in which, [r]after ye were

10:16 [p]ch. 8:10,12 **10:19** [q]Eph. 2:18 [r]ch. 9:8,12 **10:20** [s]John 10:9 [t]ch. 9:3 **10:21** [u]ch. 4:14 [v]1 Tim. 3:15 **10:22** [w]ch. 4:16 [x]Eph. 3:12 [y]ch. 9:14 [z]Ezek. 36:25 **10:23** [a]ch. 4:14 [b]1 Cor. 1:9 2 Thes. 3:3 **10:25** [c]Acts 2:42 [d]Rom. 13:11 [e]Phil. 4:5 2 Pet. 3:9 **10:26** [f]Num. 15:30 [g]2 Pet. 2:20 **10:27** [h]Zeph. 1:18 2 Thes. 1:8 **10:28** [i]ch. 2:2 [j]Mat. 18:16 **10:29** [k]ch. 2:3 [l]1 Cor. 11:29 [m]Mat. 12:31 Eph. 4:30 **10:30** [n]Deut. 32:35 [o]Deut. 32:36 **10:31** [p]Luke 12:5 **10:32** [q]Gal. 3:4 [r]ch. 6:4

[t] Some copies have, *Then he said, And their* [u] Or, *liberty* [v] Or, *new made*

present participle, emphasizing continuous action in the present.

10:19 HAVING THEREFORE. In contrast to the limited access to God which the Israelites had, Christ, by giving His life as a perfect sacrifice, has opened up a way into the very presence of God and the throne of grace. Therefore, we as believers may in gratefulness constantly draw near to God in prayer.

10:22 LET US DRAW NEAR. Faith and drawing near to God through Jesus Christ are inseparable. (1) Faith is defined as sincerely coming to God and believing in His goodness (11:6). By drawing near to God through Christ, one finds mercy, grace, help (v. 1; 4:16; 7:19), salvation (7:25), sanctification (v. 14), and cleansing (v. 22). (2) Clearly this implies that where there is no drawing near to God in prayer and fellowship with Christ, there is no saving faith (cf. v. 38). Jesus Himself equates faith with earnest prayer to God (Luke 18:8).

10:25 AS YE SEE THE DAY APPROACHING. The day of Christ's return for His faithful is approaching (see article on THE RAPTURE, p. 1889). As it does, we will face many spiritual trials and persecutions, and much doctrinal deception. We must meet together regularly in order to encourage one another to hold fast to Christ and the apostolic faith of the new covenant.

10:26 IF WE SIN WILFULLY. The author of Hebrews here speaks of the "falling away" from Christ about which he warned his readers in 6:4–8 (see article on PERSONAL APOSTASY, p. 1946).

10:29 TRODDEN UNDER FOOT. To keep on sinning deliberately after we have received the knowledge of the truth (v. 26) is (1) to be guilty of trampling underfoot Jesus Christ, treating Him with contempt, and despising His life and death; (2) to count the blood of Christ as unworthy of our loyalty; and (3) to insult and rebel against the Holy Spirit, who brings the grace of God to our hearts (see article on PERSONAL APOSTASY, p. 1946).

illuminated, ye endured [s]a great fight of afflictions;

33 Partly, whilst ye were made [t]a gazingstock both by reproaches and afflictions; and partly, whilst [u]ye became companions of them that were so used.

34 For ye had compassion of me [v]in my bonds, and [w]took joyfully the spoiling of your goods, knowing [w]in yourselves that [x]ye have in heaven a better and an enduring substance.

35 Cast not away therefore your confidence, [y]which hath great recompence of reward.

36 [z]For ye have need of patience, that, after ye have done the will of God, [a]ye might receive the promise.

37 For [b]yet a little while, and [c]he that shall come will come, and will not tarry.

38 Now [d]the just shall live by faith: but if *any man* draw back, my soul shall have no pleasure in him.

39 But we are not of them [e]who draw back unto perdition; but of them that [f]believe to the saving of the soul.

Faith defined

11 NOW FAITH is the [x]substance of things hoped for, the evidence [g]of things not seen.

2 For [h]by it the elders obtained a good report.

3 Through faith we understand that [i]the worlds were framed by the word of God, so that things which are seen were not made of things which do appear.

Examples of faith: the patriarchs

4 By faith [j]Abel offered unto God a more excellent sacrifice than Cain, by which he obtained witness that he was righteous, God testifying of his gifts: and by it he being dead yet [y]speaketh.

5 By faith [k]Enoch was translated that he should not see death; and was not found, because God had translated him: for before his translation he had this testimony, that he pleased God.

6 But without faith *it is* impossible to please *him:* for he that cometh to God must believe that he is, and *that* he is a rewarder of them that diligently seek him.

7 By faith [l]Noah, being warned of God of things not seen as yet, [z]moved with fear, [m]prepared an ark to the saving of his house; by the which he condemned the world, and became heir of [n]the righteousness which is by faith.

Abraham and his family

8 By faith [o]Abraham, when he was

10:32 [s]Phil. 1:29 Col. 2:1
10:33 [t]1 Cor. 4:9 [u]Phil. 1:7
10:34 [v]2 Tim. 1:16 [w]Mat. 5:12 [x]Mat. 6:20
10:35 [y]Mat. 5:12
10:36 [z]Luke 21:19 [a]Col. 3:24
10:37 [b]Luke 18:8 [c]Hab. 2:3,4
10:38 [d]Rom. 1:17 Gal. 3:11
10:39 [e]2 Pet. 2:20 [f]Acts 16:31 1 Thes. 5:9 2 Thes. 2:14
11:1 [g]Rom. 8:24 2 Cor. 4:18
11:2 [h]ver. 39
11:3 [i]Gen. 1:1 Ps. 33:6 John 1:3 2 Pet. 3:5
11:4 [j]Gen. 4:4 1 John 3:12
11:5 [k]Gen. 5:22
11:7 [l]Gen. 6:13 [m]1 Pet. 3:20 [n]Rom. 3:22 Phil. 3:9
11:8 [o]Gen. 12:1 Acts 7:2-4

w Or, *that ye have in yourselves,* or, *for yourselves* x Or, *ground,* or, *confidence*
y Or, *is yet spoken of* z Or, *being wary*

10:38 THE JUST SHALL LIVE BY FAITH. This fundamental principle, affirmed four times in Scripture (Hab. 2:4; Rom. 1:17; Gal. 3:11; Heb. 10:38), governs our relationship to God and our participation in the salvation provided through Jesus Christ. (1) This cardinal truth affirms that the just shall obtain eternal life by faithfully drawing near to God with a sincere believing heart (see v. 22, note). (2) For anyone who draws back from Christ and deliberately keeps on sinning, God "shall have no pleasure in him" and he will incur eternal damnation.

11:1 NOW FAITH IS. Ch. 11 demonstrates the nature of the only kind of faith that is acceptable before God and that will triumph in the worst of situations. It is a faith that believes in spiritual realities (v. 1), leads to righteousness (v. 4), seeks God (v. 6), believes in His goodness (v. 6), has confidence in His Word (vv. 7,11), obeys His commands (v. 8), regulates life on the promises of God (vv. 13,39), rejects the spirit of this present evil age (v. 13), seeks a heavenly home (vv. 14–16; cf. 13:14), perseveres in testing (vv. 17–19), blesses the next generation (v. 21), refuses the pleasures of sin (v. 25), endures persecution (v. 27), performs mighty acts of righteousness (vv. 33–35), suffers for God (vv. 25,35–38), and does not return to "that *country* from whence they came out," i.e., the world (vv. 15–16; see article on FAITH AND GRACE, p. 1738).

11:3 THE WORLDS . . . BY THE WORD. The faith by which we understand that God created the world is faith in the divinely inspired revelation found in Gen. 1 and other passages (cf. Ps. 33:6,9; Is. 55:11).

11:4 A MORE EXCELLENT SACRIFICE. God accepted the sacrifice of Abel because Abel was righteous, devoted, and obedient to Him (cf. Prov. 15:8; Mat. 23:35; 1 John 3:12).

11:6 BELIEVE THAT HE IS. This verse describes the convictions that are a part of saving faith. (1) We must believe in the existence of a personal, infinite, holy God who cares for us. (2) We must believe that He will reward us when we earnestly seek Him, knowing that our greatest reward is the joy and presence of God Himself. He is our shield and our exceeding great reward (Gen. 15:1; Deut. 4:29; Mat. 7:7–8, note; John 14:21, note). (3) We must diligently seek God and earnestly desire His presence, nearness, and grace.

11:8 BY FAITH ABRAHAM . . . OBEYED. Faith and obedience are inseparable, just as unbelief and disobedience are inseparable (3:18–19; see John 3:36, note).

called to go out into a place which he
should after receive for an inheritance,
obeyed; and he went out, not knowing
whither he went.

9 By faith he sojourned in the land
of promise, as *in* a strange country,
[p]dwelling in tabernacles with Isaac
and Jacob, [q]the heirs with him of the
same promise:

10 For he looked for [r]a city which
hath foundations, [s]whose builder and
maker *is* God.

11 Through faith also [t]Sarah her-
self received strength to conceive
seed, and [u]was delivered of a child
when she was past age, because she
judged him [v]faithful who had prom-
ised.

12 Therefore sprang there even of
one, and [w]him as good as dead, [x]*so
many* as the stars of the sky in multi-
tude, and as the sand which is by the
sea shore innumerable.

13 These all died [a]in faith, [y]not
having received the promises, but
[z]having seen them afar off, and were
persuaded of *them,* and embraced *them,*
and [a]confessed that they were strang-
ers and pilgrims on the earth.

14 For they that say such things
[b]declare plainly that they seek a
country.

15 And truly, if they had been mind-
ful of that *country* from whence they
came out, they might have had oppor-
tunity to have returned.

16 But now they desire a better
country, that is, an heavenly: wherefore
God is not ashamed [c]to be called their
God: for [d]he hath prepared for them a
city.

17 By faith [e]Abraham, when he
was tried, offered up Isaac: and he that
had received the promises [f]offered up
his only begotten *son,*

18 [b]Of whom it was said, [g]That in
Isaac shall thy seed be called:

19 Accounting that God [h]*was* able
to raise *him* up, even from the dead;
from whence also he received him in a
figure.

20 By faith [i]Isaac blessed Jacob
and Esau concerning things to come.

21 By faith Jacob, when he was a-
dying, [j]blessed both the sons of Jo-
seph; and [k]worshipped, *leaning* upon
the top of his staff.

22 By faith [l]Joseph, when he died,
[c]made mention of the departing of the
children of Israel; and gave command-
ment concerning his bones.

Moses

23 By faith [m]Moses, when he was
born, was hid three months of his par-
ents, because they saw *he was* a proper
child; and they were not afraid of the
king's [n]commandment.

24 By faith [o]Moses, when he was
come to years, refused to be called the
son of Pharaoh's daughter;

25 [p]Choosing rather to suffer af-
fliction with the people of God, than to
enjoy the pleasures of sin for a season;

26 Esteeming [q]the reproach [d]of
Christ greater riches than the trea-

11:9 [p]Gen. 12:8 [q]ch. 6:17 **11:10** [r]ch. 12:22 [s]Rev. 21:10 **11:11** [t]Gen. 17:19 & 18:11,14 [u]Luke 1:36 [v]Rom. 4:21 **11:12** [w]Rom. 4:19 [x]Rom. 4:18 **11:13** [y]ver. 39 [z]John 8:56 [a]Gen. 23:4 1 Chr. 29:15 Ps. 39:12 1 Pet. 1:17 **11:14** [b]ch. 13:14 **11:16** [c]Ex. 3:6,15 Mat. 22:32 Acts 7:32 [d]ch. 13:14 **11:17** [e]Gen. 22:1 [f]Jas 2:21 **11:18** [g]Gen. 21:12 Rom. 9:7 **11:19** [h]Rom. 4:17 **11:20** [i]Gen. 27:27 **11:21** [j]Gen. 48:5 [k]Gen. 47:31 **11:22** [l]Gen. 50:24 **11:23** [m]Ex. 2:2 [n]Ex. 1:16 **11:24** [o]Ex. 2:10 **11:25** [p]Ps. 84:10 **11:26** [q]ch. 13:13

Jas. 1:27

[a] Gk. *according to faith* [b] Or, *To* [c] Or, *remembered* [d] Or, *for Christ*

11:10 FOR HE LOOKED FOR A CITY. Abraham knew that the earthly land of promise was not the end of his pilgrimage. Rather, it pointed beyond to the heavenly city that God had prepared for His faithful servants (see article on THE CALL OF ABRAHAM, p. 25). Abraham serves as an example of all God's people; we must realize that we are only traveling through this world on our way to our true home in heaven. In this life we must not seek ultimate security in or be fascinated with this present world (vv. 14,16; 13:14). We must see ourselves as strangers and exiles on the earth. This is not our homeland, but foreign territory; the end of our pilgrimage will be "a better country" (v. 16), "the heavenly Jerusalem" (12:22), and the "city . . . to come" (13:14).

11:13 NOT HAVING RECEIVED THE PROMISES. These O.T. saints died with the faith that God had something better in store for them. In their lifetime they did not see the final promised blessing of the redeemed. Their basic hope was for eternal life with God in a heavenly homeland, and they fixed their eyes on their citizenship in the new heaven and the new earth (vv. 13–16; cf. Is. 65:17; 66:22; Phil. 3:20; Rev. 21:1). Believers today must likewise persevere in faith and trust in God, even when they do not see all the promises of God fulfilled in their lives. The faith that God approves of is a faith that is able to surrender God's promises back to Him for their fulfillment according to His will.

11:16 GOD IS NOT ASHAMED. For those who honor God by living as "strangers and pilgrims" (1 Pet. 2:11) and by desiring a better country, God will honor them by calling Himself their God. He will not be ashamed to acknowledge them as His very own children (cf. Ex. 3:6).

11:25 ENJOY THE PLEASURES OF SIN. Every believer faces the recurring choice either of enjoying the passing pleasures of sin or of suffering as he or she continues in obedience to the will of God (see Gal. 5:17, note).

sures in Egypt: for he had respect unto [r]the recompence of the reward.

27 By faith [s]he forsook Egypt, not fearing the wrath of the king: for he endured, as [t]seeing him who is invisible.

28 Through faith [u]he kept the passover, and the sprinkling of blood, lest he that destroyed the firstborn should touch them.

Israelites and Rahab

29 By faith [v]they passed through the Red sea as by dry *land:* which the Egyptians assaying to do were drowned.

30 By faith [w]the walls of Jericho fell down, after they were compassed about seven days.

31 By faith [x]the harlot Rahab perished not with them [e]that believed not, when [y]she had received the spies with peace.

Judges and prophets

32 And what shall I more say? for the time would fail me to tell of [z]Gedeon, and *of* Barak, and *of* [a]Samson, and *of* [b]Jephthae; *of* [c]David also, and [d]Samuel, and *of* the prophets:

33 Who through faith subdued kingdoms, wrought righteousness, [e]obtained promises, [f]stopped the mouths of lions,

11:26 [r]ch. 10:35
11:27 [s]Ex. 10:28 [t]ver. 13
11:28 [u]Ex. 12:21
11:29 [v]Ex. 14:22
11:30 [w]Josh. 6:20
11:31 [x]Josh. 6:23 [y]Josh. 2:1
11:32 [z]Judg. 6:11 [a]Judg. 13:24 [b]Judg. 12:7 [c]1 Sam. 16:1 [d]1 Sam. 1:20
11:33 [e]2 Sam. 7:11 [f]Judg. 14:5 1 Sam. 17:34
11:34 [g]Dan. 3:25 [h]1 Sam. 20:1 [i]2 Ki. 20:7 [j]Judg. 15:8
11:35 [k]1 Ki. 17:22 [l]Acts 22:25
11:36 [m]Gen. 39:20 Jer. 20:2
11:37 [n]1 Ki. 21:13 Acts 7:58 [o]2 Ki. 1:8 Mat. 3:4 [p]Zech. 13:4
11:38 [q]1 Ki. 18:4
11:39 [r]ver. 2,13
11:40 [s]ch. 5:9

34 [g]Quenched the violence of fire, [h]escaped the edge of the sword, [i]out of weakness were made strong, waxed valiant in fight, [j]turned to flight the armies of the aliens.

35 [k]Women received their dead raised to life again: and others were [l]tortured, not accepting deliverance; that they might obtain a better resurrection:

36 And others had trial of *cruel* mockings and scourgings, yea, moreover [m]of bonds and imprisonment:

37 [n]They were stoned, they were sawn asunder, were tempted, were slain with the sword: [o]they wandered about [p]in sheepskins and goatskins; being destitute, afflicted, tormented;

38 (Of whom the world was not worthy:) they wandered in deserts, and *in* mountains, and [q]*in* dens and caves of the earth.

39 And these all, [r]having obtained a good report through faith, received not the promise:

40 God having [f]provided some better thing for us, that they without us should not be [s]made perfect.

Christ our example

12 WHEREFORE SEEING we also are compassed about with so

[e] Or, *that were disobedient* [f] Or, *foreseen*

11:35 OTHERS WERE TORTURED. God permitted some of His faithful children to experience great suffering and trouble (see article on THE SUFFERING OF THE RIGHTEOUS, p. 764). Though they enjoyed divine companionship, He did not deliver all of them from suffering and death (vv. 35–39). (1) Notice that by faith some "escaped the edge of the sword" (v. 34) and by faith some "were slain with the sword" (v. 37). By faith one was delivered and by faith another died (cf. 1 Ki. 19:10; Jer. 26:23; Acts 12:2). Sincere faith will not only lead believers to do great exploits for God (vv. 33–35), but will also at times bring them into suffering, persecution, hardship, and destitution (vv. 35–39; cf. Ps. 44:22; Rom. 8:36; see Mat. 5:10, note).

(2) Faithfulness to God does not guarantee comfort or deliverance from persecution in this world. But it does assure us of God's grace, help, and strength in times of persecution, trials, or suffering (cf. 12:2; Jer. 20:1,7–8; 37:13–15; 38:5; 2 Cor. 6:9).

11:38 THEY WANDERED IN DESERTS . . . CAVES. God's faithful saints refused to conform to the world's low standards or to enjoy its immoral pleasures, and in return they received scorn and affliction from the world. Because they rejected the world, they were rejected by the world. Even though blessings were promised for the faithful in the O.T. (Deut. 29:9; Josh. 1:8), they had to endure affliction and destitution (vv. 35–39). In the N.T. the faithful are taught to expect adversity (see 2 Tim. 3:12, note), be identified with the cross (see Mat. 10:38, note; Gal. 2:20, note), and follow the "man of sorrows" (Isa. 53:3; cf. Heb. 12:2).

11:40 THEY WITHOUT US. All the saints of the O.T. died without receiving the full blessings and promises of God. But at the death and resurrection of Christ, He procured perfect salvation for them, and they will receive their full inheritance with us in the new heaven and earth (Rev. 21–22).

12:1 THE RACE THAT IS SET BEFORE US. This race is the lifelong test of faith in this world (10:23,38; 11; 12:25; 13:13). (1) The race must be run with "patience" (Gk. *hupomonē*), i.e., with perseverance and endurance (cf. 10:36; Phil. 3:12–14). The way of victory is the same as that of the saints in ch. 11—pressing on to the finish (cf. 6:11–12; Luke 21:19; 1 Cor. 9:24–25; Phil. 3:11–14; Rev. 3:21).

(2) The race must be run by laying aside the sins that impede or slow us down (v. 1) and by fixing our eyes, lives, and hearts on Jesus and the example of persevering obedience He set on earth (vv. 1–4).

(3) The race must be run with an awareness that

great a cloud of witnesses, [t]let us lay
aside every weight, and the sin which
doth so easily beset *us,* and [u]let us run
[v]with patience the race that is set be-
fore us,
2 Looking unto Jesus the [g]author
and finisher of *our* faith; [w]who for the
joy that was set before him endured the
cross, despising the shame, and [x]is
set down at the right hand of the
throne of God.

God disciplines His sons

3 [y]For consider him that endured
such contradiction of sinners against
himself, [z]lest ye be wearied and faint
in your minds.
4 [a]Ye have not yet resisted unto
blood, striving against sin.
5 And ye have forgotten the exhor-
tation which speaketh unto you as unto
children, [b]My son, despise not thou
the chastening of the Lord, nor faint
when thou art rebuked of him:
6 For [c]whom the Lord loveth he
chasteneth, and scourgeth every son
whom he receiveth.
7 [d]If ye endure chastening, God
dealeth with you as with sons; for what
son is he whom the father chasteneth
not?

12:1 [t]Col. 3:8 [u]1 Cor. 9:24 [v]Rom. 12:12
12:2 [w]Luke 24:26 Phil. 2:8 [x]Ps. 110:1 1 Pet. 3:22
12:3 [y]Mat. 10:24 John 15:20 [z]Gal. 6:9
12:4 [a]1 Cor. 10:13
12:5 [b]Job 5:17
12:6 [c]Ps. 94:12 Jas. 1:12
12:7 [d]Deut. 8:5
12:8 [e]1 Pet. 5:9
12:9 [f]Job 12:10
12:10 [g]Lev. 11:44
12:11 [h]Jas. 3:18
12:12 [i]Job 4:3,4
12:13 [j]Prov. 4:26 [k]Gal. 6:1
12:14 [l]Ps. 34:14 2 Tim. 2:22

8 But if ye be without chastisement,
[e]whereof all are partakers, then are
ye bastards, and not sons.
9 Furthermore we have had fathers
of our flesh which corrected *us,* and we
gave *them* reverence: shall we not
much rather be in subjection unto
[f]the Father of spirits, and live?
10 For they verily for a few days
chastened *us* [h]after their own plea-
sure; but he for *our* profit, [g]that *we*
might be partakers of his holiness.
11 Now no chastening for the
present seemeth to be joyous, but
grievous: nevertheless afterward it
yieldeth [h]the peaceable fruit of righ-
teousness unto them which are exer- Jas. 3:17-18
cised thereby.

An appeal for holiness

12 Wherefore [i]lift up the hands
which hang down, and the feeble
knees;
13 [j]And make [i]straight paths for
your feet, lest that which is lame be
turned out of the way; [k]but let it rath-
er be healed.
14 [l]Follow peace with all *men,* and

[g] Or, *beginner* [h] Or, *as seemed good,* or, *meet to them* [i] Or, *even*

the greatest peril confronting us is the temptation to yield to sin (vv. 1,4), to return to "that *country* from whence [we] came out" (11:15; Jas. 1:12), and to become once more citizens of the world (11:13; Jas. 4:4; 1 John 2:15; see Heb. 11:10, note).

12:2 LOOKING UNTO JESUS. In our race of faith we look to Jesus as (1) our example of trust in God (2:13), of commitment to His will (10:7–10; Mark 14:36), of prayer (5:7; Mark 1:35; John 17), of overcoming temptation and suffering (2:10; 4:15), of endurance in loyalty to the Father (vv. 2–3), and of seeking the joy of completing the work to which God has called us (v. 2; cf. Luke 15:6,24,32; John 15:11); (2) our source of strength, love, grace, mercy, and help (4:16; 7:25; 10:22; Rev. 3:21).

12:5 THE CHASTENING OF THE LORD. Note several facts about God's discipline of believers and the hardships and troubles He allows us to suffer. (1) They are a sign that we are children of God (vv. 7–8).

(2) They are an assurance of God's love and concern for us (v. 6).

(3) The Lord's discipline has two purposes: (a) that we might not be finally condemned with the world (1 Cor. 11:31–32), and (b) that we might share God's holiness and continue to live sanctified lives without which we will never see the Lord (vv. 10–11,14).

(4) There are two possible consequences of the Lord's discipline. (a) We may endure the hardships God leads us through, submit to God's will, and continue to remain faithful (vv. 5–6). By doing this we will continue to live as God's spiritual children (vv. 7–9) and to share His holiness (v. 10); it will yield the fruit of righteousness (v. 11). (b) We may "despise" the discipline of our Father (v. 5), rebel against God because of suffering and hardship, and thereby fall away from God (v. 25; 3:12–14).

(5) Under God's will, adversity may come (a) as a result of our spiritual warfare with Satan (Eph. 6:11–18), (b) as a test to strengthen our faith (1 Pet. 1:6–7) and our works (Mat. 7:24–27; 1 Cor. 3:13–15), or (c) as a preparation for us to comfort others (2 Cor. 1:3–5) and to manifest the life of Christ (2 Cor. 4:8–10,12,16).

(6) In all kinds of adversity we must seek God, examine our lives (2 Chr. 26:5; Ps. 3:4; 9:12; 34:17), and forsake all that is contrary to His holiness (vv. 10,14; see Ps. 60:1–12, note; 66:18, note; see article on THE SUFFERING OF THE RIGHTEOUS, p. 764).

12:14 FOLLOW . . . HOLINESS. Holiness is being separated from sin and being set apart for God. It is being close to God, being like Him, and seeking His presence, righteousness, and fellowship with all our hearts. Above all things, holiness is God's priority for His followers (Eph. 4:21–24). (1) Holiness was God's purpose for His people when He planned their salvation in Christ (Eph. 1:4).

holiness, [m]without which no man shall see the Lord:

15 Looking diligently [n]lest any man [j]fail of the grace of God; [o]lest any root of bitterness springing up trouble *you,* and thereby many be defiled;

16 [p]Lest there *be* any fornicator, or profane person, as Esau, [q]who for one morsel of meat sold his birthright.

17 For ye know how that afterward, [r]when he would have inherited the blessing, he was rejected: for he found no [k]place of repentance, though he sought it carefully with tears.

Warning against turning away from God

18 For ye are not come unto [s]the mount that might be touched, and that burned with fire, nor unto blackness, and darkness, and tempest,

19 And the sound of a trumpet, and the voice of words; which *voice* they that heard [t]entreated that the word should not be spoken to them any more:

20 (For they could not endure that which was commanded, [u]And if so much as a beast touch the mountain, it shall be stoned, or thrust through with a dart:

21 [v]And so terrible was the sight, *that* Moses said, I exceedingly fear and quake:)

22 But ye are come [w]unto mount Zion, [x]and unto the city of the living God, the heavenly Jerusalem, [y]and to an innumerable company of angels,

12:14 [m]Mat. 5:8 2 Cor. 7:1
12:15 [n]Gal. 5:4 [o]ch. 3:12
12:16 [p]Eph. 5:3 [q]Gen. 25:33
12:17 [r]Gen. 27:34
12:18 [s]Deut. 4:11
12:19 [t]Ex. 20:19 Deut. 5:5
12:20 [u]Ex. 19:13
12:21 [v]Ex. 19:16
12:22 [w]Gal. 4:26 Rev. 3:12 [x]Phil. 3:20 [y]Deut. 33:2 Ps. 68:17
12:23 [z]Jas. 1:18 [a]Luke 10:20 [b]Ps. 94:2 [c]Phil. 3:12
12:24 [d]ch. 9:15 [e]Ex. 24:8 [f]Gen. 4:10
12:25 [g]ch. 2:2,3
12:26 [h]Ex. 19:18 [i]Hag. 2:6
12:27 [j]2 Pet. 3:10
12:29 [k]Ex. 24:17 Deut. 4:24
13:1 [l]Rom. 12:10 1 Pet. 1:22
13:2 [m]Mat. 25:35 1 Tim. 3:2

23 To the general assembly and church of [z]the firstborn, [a]which are [l]written in heaven, and to God [b]the Judge of all, and to the spirits of just men [c]made perfect,

24 And to Jesus [d]the mediator of the new [m]covenant, and to [e]the blood of sprinkling, that speaketh better things [f]than *that of* Abel.

25 See that ye refuse not him that speaketh. For [g]if they escaped not who refused him that spake on earth, much more *shall not* we *escape,* if we turn away from him that *speaketh* from heaven:

26 [h]Whose voice then shook the earth: but now he hath promised, saying, [i]Yet once more I shake not the earth only, but also heaven.

27 And this *word,* Yet once more, signifieth [j]the removing of those things that [n]are shaken, as of things that are made, that those things which cannot be shaken may remain.

28 Wherefore we receiving a kingdom which cannot be moved, [o]let us have grace, whereby we may serve God acceptably with reverence and godly fear:

29 For [k]our God *is* a consuming fire.

Concluding exhortations

13 LET [l]BROTHERLY love continue.

2 [m]Be not forgetful to entertain

[j] Or, *fall from* [k] Or, *way to change his mind* [l] Or, *enrolled* [m] Or, *testament* [n] Or, *may be shaken* [o] Or, *let us hold fast*

(2) Holiness was Christ's purpose for His people when He came to this earth (Mat. 1:21; 1 Cor. 1:2, 30).

(3) Holiness was Christ's purpose for His people when He gave Himself up for them on the cross (Eph. 5:25–27).

(4) Holiness is God's purpose in making us a new creation and in giving us the Holy Spirit (Rom. 8:2–15; Gal. 5:16–25; Eph. 2:10).

(5) Without holiness no one can be useful to God (2 Tim. 2:20–21).

(6) Without holiness there is no nearness to or fellowship with God (Ps. 15:1–2).

(7) Without holiness no one will see the Lord (v. 14; Mat. 5:8; see article on SANCTIFICATION, p. 1982).

12:15 ROOT OF BITTERNESS. A "root of bitterness" refers to a spirit and attitude that is characterized by intense animosity and resentment. Here it may refer to an attitude of bitter resentment toward God's discipline instead of humble submission to His will for our lives. Bitterness can also be directed toward persons in the church. It results in defiling the person who is bitter, i.e., making him or her unfit to approach God in prayer. Bitterness in the community of believers can spread and defile many, destroying the "holiness without which no man shall see the Lord" (v. 14).

12:18–25 THE MOUNT THAT MIGHT BE TOUCHED. The awesome circumstances of the giving of the law (cf. Ex. 19:10–25; Deut. 4:11–12; 5:22–26) and the features of the gospel are contrasted. The consequences of turning away from the gospel are far more dreadful than were the consequences of rejecting the law.

12:26–29 SHOOK THE EARTH. God will one day put down the present world order and shake to pieces the whole material universe (see Hag. 2:6–9,21, notes). The present form of the world is not eternal; it will be destroyed by fire and replaced by a new heaven and earth (Rev. 20:11; 21:1; cf. 2 Pet. 3:10–13). The only thing that will survive in its present form will be the kingdom of God and those who belong to it (v. 28).

strangers: for thereby [n]some have en-
tertained angels unawares.
3 [o]Remember them that are in
bonds, as bound with them; *and* them
which suffer adversity, as being your-
selves also in the body.
4 Marriage *is* honourable in all, and
the bed undefiled: [p]but whoremong-
ers and adulterers God will judge.
5 *Let your* conversation *be* without
covetousness; *and* [q]*be* content with
such things as ye have: for he hath
said, [r]I will never leave thee, nor for-
sake thee.
6 So that we may boldly say, [s]The
Lord *is* my helper, and I will not fear
what man shall do unto me.
7 [t]Remember them which [p]have
the rule over you, who have spoken
unto you the word of God: [u]whose
faith follow, considering the end of
their conversation.
8 Jesus Christ [v]the same yester-
day, and today, and for ever.
9 [w]Be not carried about with divers
and strange doctrines. For *it is* a good
thing that the heart be established
with grace; [x]not with meats, which

13:2 [n]Gen. 18:3
13:3 [o]Mat. 25:26
13:4 [p]1 Cor. 6:9
13:5 [q]Phil. 4:11 [r]Gen. 28:15
13:6 [s]Ps. 27:1
13:7 [t]ver. 17 [u]ch. 6:12
13:8 [v]John 8:58
13:9 [w]Eph. 4:14 Col. 2:4,8 [x]Rom. 14:17 1 Tim. 4:3
13:10 [y]1 Cor. 9:13
13:11 [z]Ex. 29:14
13:12 [a]Acts 7:58
13:13 [b]1 Pet. 4:14
13:14 [c]Mic. 2:10 Phil. 3:20
13:15 [d]Eph. 5:20 [e]Lev. 7:12 [f]Hos. 14:2
13:16 [g]Rom. 12:13 [h]2 Cor. 9:12 Phil. 4:18
13:17 [i]Phil. 2:29 1 Tim. 5:17

have not profited them that have been
occupied therein.
10 [y]We have an altar, whereof they
have no right to eat which serve the
tabernacle.
11 For [z]the bodies of those beasts,
whose blood is brought into the sanctu-
ary by the high priest for sin, are
burned without the camp.
12 Wherefore Jesus also, that he
might sanctify the people with his own
blood, [a]suffered without the gate.
13 Let us go forth therefore unto
him without the camp, bearing [b]his re-
proach.
14 [c]For here have we no continu-
ing city, but we seek one to come.
15 [d]By him therefore let us offer
[e]the sacrifice of praise to God contin-
ually, that is, [f]the fruit of *our* lips 1 Pet.
[q]giving thanks to his name. 2:9
16 [g]But to do good and to commu-
nicate forget not: for [h]with such sacri-
fices God is well pleased.
17 [i]Obey them that [r]have the
rule over you, and submit yourselves:

[p] Or, *are the guides* [q] Gk. *confessing to*
[r] Or, *guide*

13:1 BROTHERLY LOVE. In the N.T. church believers thought of and addressed each other as brothers and sisters in Christ (cf. 1 Thes. 4:9–10; 1 Pet. 1:22; 2 Pet. 1:7). Christian brotherhood comes from our mutual relationship with the Father and His only Son (1:2). As we participate in the grace of Christ, we are all made sons and daughters with Him and fellow heirs of the Father's blessings (1:2; John 1:12–13; Rom. 8:14–17; Eph. 1:5–7). Because of this brotherhood, we are taught by the Father to love one another (1 Thes. 4:9; 1 John 4:11; see John 13:34–35, notes).

13:4 MARRIAGE IS HONOURABLE. God has high standards for His people in marriage and sexuality. For a discussion of this important issue, see article on STANDARDS OF SEXUAL MORALITY, p. 1964.

13:5 WITHOUT COVETOUSNESS. Notice that the exhortation to remain free from the love of money follows the warning against immorality (v. 4). Greed and immorality are closely connected in the N.T. (1 Cor. 5:11; 6:9–10; Eph. 5:3; Col. 3:5). All too often the love of abundance and luxury and the constant desire for wealth open up a person to sexual sins (see 1 Tim. 6:6–10).

13:6 THE LORD *IS* MY HELPER. No matter how limited our earthly possessions may be or how trying our circumstances, we never need fear that God will desert or forsake us (see Josh. 1:5, note). Scripture declares that the heavenly Father cares for us. Thus, we can say with the author of Hebrews, who echoes the psalmist, "The Lord *is* my helper, and I will not fear." This can be affirmed with confidence in times of want, distress, trials, or trouble (see Mat. 6:30,33 notes).

13:8 JESUS CHRIST THE SAME. The truth that Jesus Christ does not change provides a sure anchor for our faith. It means that present-day believers must not be content until they experience the same salvation, communion with God, baptism in the Holy Spirit, and kingdom power that the N.T. believers experienced in their service to God through Christ Jesus (see article on THE KINGDOM OF GOD, p. 1428).

13:12 SANCTIFY THE PEOPLE. Jesus suffered on the cross outside the city gate of Jerusalem in order that we might be sanctified, i.e., separated from the old sinful life and dedicated to the service of God (see articles on SPIRITUAL SEPARATION FOR BELIEVERS, p. 1814, and SANCTIFICATION, p. 1982).

13:13 LET US GO FORTH. To be a follower of Christ involves going forth outside "the camp." For these Jewish Christians the camp represented Judaism. For us it represents the world with all its sinful pleasures, ungodly values, and temporal goals. We must bear the reproach of Christ in order to follow Him, sympathize with Him, be His friend, identify with Him, and announce to the world our commitment to His standards and purposes. In going forth outside the gate we find ourselves strangers and exiles on the earth (v. 14; 11:13). Yet we are not without a city, for we seek a city which is to come, a city which has a foundation, "whose builder and maker *is* God" (11:10,14,16).

13:17 OBEY THEM. Obedience and faithfulness to Christian leaders, pastors, and teachers

STANDARDS OF SEXUAL MORALITY

Heb. 13:4 "Marriage* is *honourable in all, and the bed undefiled: but whoremongers and adulterers God will judge."

Believers, first and foremost, must be morally and sexually pure (cf. 2 Cor. 11:2; Tit. 2:5; 1 Pet. 3:2). The word "pure" or "chaste" (Gk. *hagnos*) means to be free from all taint of that which is lewd. It suggests refraining from all acts and thoughts that incite desire not in accordance with one's virginity or one's marriage vows. It stresses restraint and avoidance of all sexual actions and excitements that would defile, debase, or cheapen one's purity before God. It includes controlling one's own body "in sanctification and honour" (1 Thes. 4:4), and not in "lust" (4:5). This instruction of Scripture is for both those who are single and those married. With regard to the Biblical teaching concerning sexual morality, note the following:

(1) Sexual intimacy is reserved for the marriage relationship and is approved and blessed by God only in that state (see Gen. 2:24, note; Sol. 2:7, note; 4:12, note). Through marriage the husband and wife become one flesh according to God's will. The physical and emotional pleasures resulting from a faithful marriage relationship are ordained by God and held in honor by Him.

(2) Adultery, fornication, homosexuality, sensuality, impure desire, and degrading passions are considered grave sins in the sight of God since they are a transgression of His law (see Ex. 20:14, note) and a defiling of the marriage relationship. Such sins are severely condemned in Scripture (see Prov. 5:3, note) and exclude the guilty from the kingdom of God (Rom. 1:24–32; 1 Cor. 6:9–10; Gal. 5:19–21).

(3) Sexual immorality and impurity include not only forbidden intercourse or consummated acts, but also involve any act of sexual gratification with another person other than one's marriage partner, achieved by uncovering or exploring the nakedness of that person. The contemporary teaching that sexual intimacy among "committed" unmarried youth and adults is acceptable as long as it stops short of full sexual union is contrary to the holiness of God and the Biblical standard of purity. God explicitly prohibits the "uncovering of the nakedness" or "seeing the nakedness" of anyone who is not a lawful wife or husband (Lev. 18:6–30; 20:11,17,19–21; see 18:6, note).

(4) The believer must exercise self-control and steadfast restraint with reference to all sexual matters before marriage. To justify premarital intimacy in the name of Christ merely on the ground of a real or a felt "commitment" to another flagrantly compromises God's holy standards with the world's impure ways and, in effect, justifies immorality. After marriage, sexual intimacy must be confined to one's marriage partner. The Bible names self-control as an aspect of the Spirit's fruit, the positive and pure behavior that is in contrast to immoral sexual play, gratification, fornication, adultery, and impurity. One's faith commitment to God's will opens the way to receiving this gift of self-control (Gal. 5:22–24).

(5) Biblical terms used for sexual immorality, describing the breadth of its evil, are as follows: (a) Fornication (Gk. *porneia*) describes a wide variety of sexual activities before or outside of marriage. Any intimate sexual activity or play outside the marriage relationship, including the touching of the intimate parts of the body or viewing the nakedness of another person, is included in this term and is clearly a transgression of God's moral standards for His people (see Lev. 18:6–30; 20:11–12,17,19–21; 1 Cor. 6:18; 1 Thes. 4:3). (b) Lasciviousness (Gk. *aselgeia*) denotes the absence of clear moral principles, specifically, disregard of sexual reserve and restraint that maintains pure and chaste behavior (see 1 Tim. 2:9, note on modesty). It includes the inclination toward indulging in or arousing sinful lust, and thus is a partaking in Biblically unjustifiable conduct (Gal. 5:19; Eph. 4:19; 1 Pet. 4:3; 2 Pet. 2:2,18). (c) Defraud (Gk. *pleonekteō*) means to deprive another of the moral purity and chastity that God desires for that person in order to satisfy one's own self-centered desires. To arouse sexual desires in someone which cannot be righteously fulfilled is defrauding that person (1 Thes. 4:6; cf. Eph. 4:19). (d) Lust (Gk. *epithumia*) is having an immoral desire which one would fulfill if the opportunity arose (see Mat. 5:28, note; Eph. 4:19,22; 1 Pet. 4:3; 2 Pet. 2:18).

for [j]they watch for your souls, as they
that must give account, that they may
do it with joy, and not with grief: for
that *is* unprofitable for you.
18 [k]Pray for us: for we trust we
have [l]a good conscience, in all things
willing to live honestly.
19 But I beseech *you* the rather to
do this, that I may be restored to you
the sooner.
20 Now [m]the God of peace, [n]that
brought again from the dead our Lord
Jesus, [o]that great shepherd of the
sheep, [p]through the blood of the ever-
lasting [s]covenant,
21 [q]Make you perfect in every
good work to do his will, [r]working[t]
in you that which is wellpleasing in his
sight, through Jesus Christ; [s]to whom
be glory for ever and ever. Amen.
22 And I beseech you, brethren, suf-
fer the word of exhortation: for [t]I
have written a letter unto you in few
words.
23 Know ye that [u]*our* brother Tim-
othy [v]is set at liberty; with whom, if
he come shortly, I will see you.
24 Salute all them [w]that have the
rule over you, and all the saints. They
of Italy salute you.
25 [x]Grace *be* with you all. Amen.

13:17 [j]Ezek. 3:17
13:18 [k]Eph. 6:19 [l]Acts 23:1
13:20 [m]Rom. 15:33 [n]Rom. 4:24 Gal. 1:1 [o]1 Pet. 2:25 [p]Zech. 9:11
13:21 [q]1 Pet. 5:10 [r]Phil. 2:13 [s]Gal. 1:5
13:22 [t]1 Pet. 5:12
13:23 [u]1 Thes. 3:2 [v]1 Tim. 6:12
13:24 [w]ver. 7,17
13:25 [x]Tit. 3:15

[s] Or, *testament* [t] Or, *doing*

must be based on a higher loyalty to God. The believer's loyalty on a descending scale is as follows: (1) first, to God in a person-to-person relationship (see Mat. 22:37, note), including faithfulness to the truth and principles of His Word (see article on THE INSPIRATION AND AUTHORITY OF SCRIPTURE, p. 1924); (2) second, to the visible church as it remains faithful to God and His written Word (John 15:12; Gal. 6:10); (3) third, to human leaders within the church, as long as they remain faithful and loyal to God, to Holy Scripture, and to His purpose for the church.

JAMES

Outline

Christian Greetings (1:1)

I. Facing Trials and Benefiting from Them (1:2–18)
   A. Accept Them as a Means of Growth (1:2–4)
   B. Pray for Wisdom in Coping with Them (1:5–8)
   C. Rejoice in Their Leveling Action (1:9–12)
   D. Recognize the Difference Between Trials and Temptations (1:13–18)

II. Hearing the Word and Doing It (1:19–27)

III. Being Impartial and Showing It (2:1–13)

IV. Professing Faith and Proving It (2:14–26)

V. Recognizing Pitfalls and Avoiding Them (3:1—5:6)
   A. The Unruly Tongue (3:1–12)
   B. Unspiritual Wisdom (3:13–18)
   C. Sinful Behavior (4:1–10)
   D. Speaking Against a Brother (4:11–12)
   E. Presumptuous Living (4:13–17)
   F. Selfish Wealth (5:1–6)

VI. Christian Virtues and Living by Them (5:7–20)
   A. Patience and Endurance (5:7–11)
   B. Simple Honesty (5:12)
   C. Prevailing Prayers for the Sick (5:13–18)
   D. Reclaiming the Wayward (5:19–20)

Author: James

Theme: Faith that Works

Date of Writing: A.D. 45–49

Background

James is classified as a "general epistle" because it was originally addressed to a wider audience than a local church. The salutation, "to the twelve tribes which are scattered abroad" (1:1), along with other references (2:19,21), indicate that the epistle was written initially to Jewish Christians living outside Palestine. It is possible that the recipients of the letter were among the first converts in Jerusalem who, after Stephen's martyrdom, were scattered by persecution (Acts 8:1) as far as Phoenicia, Cyprus, Syrian Antioch, and beyond (Acts 11:19). This would explain (1) the letter's opening emphasis on joyfully enduring trials which test faith and require perseverance (1:2–12), (2) James' personal knowledge of the "scattered" believers, and (3) the authoritative tone of the letter. As leader of the Jerusalem church, James was writing to his scattered sheep.

The author's prominence is indicated by the way he identifies himself simply as "James" (1:1). James, the half-brother of Jesus and the leader of the Jerusalem church, is generally regarded as the author. His speech at the Jerusalem Council (Acts 15:13–21) as well as descriptions of him elsewhere in the N.T. (e.g. Acts 12:17; 21:18; Gal. 1:19; 2:9,12; 1 Cor. 15:7) correspond perfectly with what is known about the author of this epistle. James most

likely wrote his epistle during the 40s. This early date for writing is indicated by several factors, such as the fact that James uses the Greek word *synagōgē* (literally, synagogue) to refer to the Christians' place of meeting (2:2). According to the Jewish historian Josephus, James, the Lord's brother, was martyred at Jerusalem in A.D. 62.

Purpose

James wrote (1) to encourage Jewish believers who were suffering various trials that were testing their faith, (2) to correct erroneous ideas about the nature of saving faith, and (3) to exhort and instruct the readers about the practical outworkings of their faith in righteous living and good works.

Survey

This epistle covers a wide variety of topics related to living a genuine Christian life. James exhorts believers to endure their trials joyfully and benefit from them (1:2–11); to resist temptations (1:12–18); to be doers of the Word, not just hearers (1:19–27); and to demonstrate an active faith, not an empty profession (2:14–26). He solemnly warns about the sinfulness of an unruly tongue (3:1–12; 4:11–12), carnal wisdom (3:13–16), sinful behavior (4:1–10), presumptuous living (4:13–17), and self-centered wealth (5:1–6). James concludes with an emphasis on patience, prayer, and reclaiming the wayward (5:7–20).

Throughout its five chapters, the relationship between true faith and godly living is emphasized. Genuine faith is a tested faith (1:2–16), is an active faith (1:19–27), loves one's neighbor as oneself (2:1–13), manifests itself in good works (2:14–26), keeps a tight rein on the tongue (3:1–12), seeks God's wisdom (3:13–18), submits to God as the righteous judge (4:1–12), trusts God in daily living (4:13–17), is not self-centered or self-indulgent (5:1–6), is patient in suffering (5:7–12), and is diligent in prayer (5:13–20).

Special Features

Seven major features or emphases characterize this epistle. (1) It is most likely the first book written in the N.T. (2) Although it contains only two references to Christ by name, there are more reminiscences of Jesus' teaching in this epistle, including at least fifteen allusions to the Sermon on the Mount, than in all the other N.T. epistles combined. (3) More than half of its 108 verses are imperatives or commands. (4) In many ways it is the Proverbs of the N.T., for (a) it is full of godly wisdom and practical instructions for living a genuine Christian life, and (b) it is written in crisp commands, terse style, and vivid analogies. (5) James is an astute observer of the operations of nature and of fallen human nature. He often draws lessons from the former to expose the latter (e.g., 3:1–12). (6) It emphasizes more than any other N.T. book the necessary relation between faith and works (esp. 2:14–26). (7) James is sometimes called the Amos of the N.T., because he vigorously addresses issues of social injustice and inequality.

Reading James

In order to read the entire New Testament in one year, the book of James should be read in 4 days, according to the following schedule:
☐ 1 ☐ 2:1–3:13 ☐ 3:14–4:12 ☐ 4:13–5:20

NOTES

The purpose of trials

1 JAMES,[a] [b]A servant of God and of the Lord Jesus Christ, [c]to the twelve tribes [d]which are scattered abroad, greeting.

2 My brethren, [e]count it all joy [f]when ye fall into divers temptations;

3 [g]Knowing *this,* that the trying of your faith worketh patience.

4 But let patience have *her* perfect work, that ye may be perfect and entire, wanting nothing.

5 [h]If any of you lack wisdom, [i]let him ask of God, that giveth to all *men* liberally, and upbraideth not; and [j]it shall be given him.

6 [k]But let him ask in faith, nothing wavering. For he that wavereth is like a wave of the sea driven with the wind and tossed.

7 For let not that man think that he shall receive any thing of the Lord.

8 [l]A double minded man *is* unstable in all his ways.

9 Let the brother of low degree [a]rejoice in that he is exalted:

10 But the rich, in that he is made low: because [m]as the flower of the grass he shall pass away.

11 For the sun is no sooner risen with a burning heat, but it withereth the grass, and the flower thereof falleth, and the grace of the fashion of it perisheth: so also shall the rich man fade away in his ways.

12 [n]Blessed *is* the man that endureth temptation: for when he is tried, he shall receive [o]the crown of life, [p]which the Lord hath promised to them that love him.

The source of sin

13 Let no man say when he is tempted, I am tempted of God: for God cannot be tempted with [b]evil, neither tempteth he any man:

14 But every man is tempted, when he is drawn away of his own lust, and enticed.

15 Then [q]when lust hath conceived, it bringeth forth sin: and sin, when it is finished, [r]bringeth forth death.

16 Do not err, my beloved brethren.

17 [s]Every good gift and every perfect gift is from above, and cometh down from the Father of lights, [t]with whom is no variableness, neither shadow of turning.

18 [u]Of his own will begat he us with the word of truth, [v]that we should be a kind of [w]firstfruits of his creatures.

True faith obeys God's Word

19 Wherefore, my beloved brethren, [x]let every man be swift to hear, [y]slow to speak, [z]slow to wrath:

20 For the wrath of man worketh not the righteousness of God.

21 Wherefore [a]lay apart all filthiness and superfluity of naughtiness,

1:1 [a]Acts 12:17 [b]Tit. 1:1 [c]Acts 26:7 [d]Deut. 32:26 John 7:35 Acts 2:5 1 Pet. 1:1
1:2 [e]Acts 5:41 [f]1 Pet. 1:6
1:3 [g]Rom. 5:3
1:5 [h]1 Ki. 3:9 Prov. 2:3 [i]Mat. 7:7 Luke 11:9 John 14:13 [j]Jer. 29:12 1 John 5:14
1:6 [k]Mark 11:24 1 Tim. 2:8
1:8 [l]ch. 4:8
1:10 [m]Job 14:2 Ps. 37:2 1 Cor. 7:31
1:12 [n]Job 5:17 Prov. 3:11 [o]1 Cor. 9:25 2 Tim. 4:8 [p]Mat. 10:22
1:15 [q]Job 15:35 Ps. 7:14 [r]Rom. 6:21
1:17 [s]John 3:27 [t]Num. 23:19
1:18 [u]John 1:13 1 Cor. 4:15 [v]Eph. 1:12 [w]Rev. 14:4
1:19 [x]Eccl. 5:1 [y]Prov. 10:19 Eccl. 5:2 [z]Prov. 14:17
1:21 [a]Col. 3:8 1 Pet. 2:1

[a] Or, *glory* [b] Or, *evils*

1:2 TEMPTATIONS. The word "temptation" (Gk. *peirasmoi*) does not refer to enticements to sin, but to trials, persecution, and afflictions from the world or Satan. (1) The believer must meet these trials with joy (cf. Mat. 5:11–12; Rom. 5:3; 1 Pet. 1:6), for they will develop patience (i.e., perseverance, endurance). Our faith can only reach full maturity when faced with difficulties and opposition (vv. 3–4). (2) James calls these trials a "trying of your faith" (v. 3). Trials are sometimes brought into a believer's life so that God can test his faith. Scripture nowhere teaches that troubles in life are always an indication that God is displeased with us. They can be a sign that He recognizes our firm commitment to Him (cf. Job 1–2).

1:4 YE MAY BE PERFECT. "Perfect" (Gk. *teleios*) reflects the Biblical idea of perfection, defined as a right relationship with God that bears fruit in a sincere endeavor to love Him with all one's heart in undivided devotion, obedience, and a blameless life (Deut. 6:5; 18:13; Mat. 22:37; see 1 Thes. 2:10, note; see article on SANCTIFICATION, p. 1982).

1:5 IF ANY OF YOU LACK WISDOM. Wisdom means the spiritual capacity to see and evaluate life and conduct from God's point of view (see Prov. 1:2, note). It involves making right choices and doing right things according to both the will of God revealed in His Word and the leading of the Holy Spirit (Rom. 8:4–17). We can receive wisdom by drawing near to God and asking for it in faith (vv. 6–8; cf. Prov. 2:6; 1 Cor. 1:30).

1:9–10 THE BROTHER OF LOW DEGREE . . . THE RICH. See article on RICHES AND POVERTY, p. 1568.

1:13 TEMPTED. No person who sins can evade guilt by throwing the blame on God. God may test us in order to strengthen our faith, but never with the intent of leading us to sin. The nature of God demonstrates that He cannot be a source of temptation (see article on THE ATTRIBUTES OF GOD, p. 912).

1:14 DRAWN AWAY OF HIS OWN LUST. Temptation basically comes from our own inward desires or inclinations (cf. Mat. 15:19). If evil desire is not resisted and purged by the Holy Spirit, it leads to sin and then to spiritual death (v. 15; Rom. 6:23; 7:5,10,13).

and receive with meekness the en-
grafted word, [b]which is able to save
your souls.
22 But [c]be ye doers of the word,
and not hearers only, deceiving your
own selves.
23 For [d]if any be a hearer of the
word, and not a doer, he is like unto a
man beholding his natural face in a
glass:
24 For he beholdeth himself, and
goeth his way, and straightway for-
getteth what manner of man he was.
25 But [e]whoso looketh into the
perfect [f]law of liberty, and continueth
therein, he being not a forgetful hearer,
but a doer of the work, [g]this man shall
be blessed in his [c]deed.
26 If any man among you seem to be
religious, and [h]bridleth not his

1:21 [b]Acts 13:26 Rom. 1:16 Eph. 1:13 Tit. 2:11
1:22 [c]Mat. 7:21 Rom. 2:13 1 John 3:7
1:23 [d]Luke 6:47
1:25 [e]2 Cor. 3:18 [f]ch. 2:12 [g]John 13:17
1:26 [h]Ps. 34:13 1 Pet. 3:10
1:27 [i]Is. 1:16 Mat. 25:36 [j]Rom. 12:2 1 John 5:18
2:1 [k]1 Cor. 2:8 [l]Lev. 19:15 Deut. 1:17 Mat. 22:16 Jude 16

tongue, but deceiveth his own heart,
this man's religion *is* vain.
27 Pure religion and undefiled be-
fore God and the Father is this, [i]To
visit the fatherless and widows in their
affliction, [j]*and* to keep himself un-
spotted from the world.

Jas. 4:4-6

True faith impartial

2 MY BRETHREN, have not the
faith of our Lord Jesus Christ, [k]*the
Lord* of glory, with [l]respect of per-
sons.
2 For if there come unto your [d]as-
sembly a man with a gold ring, in good-
ly apparel, and there come in also a
poor man in vile raiment;
3 And ye have respect to him that

[c] Or, *doing* [d] Gk. *synagogue*

1:21 LAY APART ALL FILTHINESS. The Word of God, either preached or written, cannot effectively take hold of a person's life if he or she is not separated from moral filth and evil. (1) God commands the believer to set aside all the ungodly filth that permeates an unregenerate and corrupt society and seeks to influence him and his family. This filth defiles one's soul and spirit and blights his life (cf. Eph. 4:22,25,31; Col. 3:8; 1 Pet. 2:1).

(2) Scripture tells us what is improper for God's holy people. Accordingly, we must not engage in any kind of impurity or obscenity (Eph. 5:3–4). Furthermore, we must be aware that allowing *any kind* of moral filth into our lives or homes, including filthy language or obscenity through videos or T.V., grieves the Holy Spirit and violates the holy standards of God for His people. God's Word warns us, "Let no man deceive you with vain words: for because of these things cometh the wrath of God. . . Be not ye therefore partakers with them" (Eph. 5:6–7).

(3) We as believers must take righteousness and holiness seriously. Our houses must be swept clean and filled with the Word of God and the holiness of Christ (cf. Mat. 12:43–45; see article on SANCTIFICATION, p. 1982).

1:21 THE ENGRAFTED WORD. Christians begin their new life in Christ by being born again by the "word of truth" (v. 18; see article on REGENERATION, p. 1597). New life in Christ demands that we get rid of all moral filth that offends the Holy Spirit (see previous note), and that we be constant in receiving the Word of God into our hearts. The term "engrafted" (Gk. *emphutos*) means "implanted," implying that the Word must become a part of our very nature. The implanted Word brings us to our final salvation (cf. Mat. 13:3–23; Rom. 1:16; 1 Cor. 15:2; Eph. 1:13; see John 6:54, note).

1:25 LAW OF LIBERTY. This law (cf. 2:12) is the will of God internalized in our hearts by the indwelling Holy Spirit (cf. Ezek. 11:19–20). Through faith in Christ we receive not only mercy and forgiveness (2:12–13), but also the power and freedom to obey the law of God (Rom. 3:31; see 8:4, note). It is called the "law of liberty" because the believer desires to do the will of God: "I will walk at liberty: for I seek thy precepts" (Ps. 119:45). It must never be viewed as a freedom to violate the commandments of Christ, but rather as the freedom and power to obey them.

1:27 PURE RELIGION AND UNDEFILED. James gives two principles that define the content of true Christianity. (1) Genuine love for those in need. In N.T. days, orphans and widows had few ways to support themselves; they often had no guardian or helper. Believers were expected to show them the same care and love that God exercises toward the fatherless and widows (see Deut. 10:18; 24:17, note; Ps. 68:5, note; 146:9). Today among our brothers and sisters in Christ are those who need help and care. We should seek to alleviate their distress and sufferings and thereby show them that God cares for them (see Luke 7:13, note; cf. Gal. 6:10; see article on THE CARE OF THE POOR AND NEEDY, p. 1312).

(2) Keeping ourselves holy before God. James says that love for others must be accompanied by a love for God that is expressed in separation from the sinful ways of the world. Love to others must be accompanied by holiness before God or it is not Christian love.

2:1 RESPECT OF PERSONS. This phrase means showing special attention or favoritism toward a person because of his wealth, clothing, or position. To do so is wrong for several reasons. (1) It displeases God, who looks not on outward appearance but on the heart (1 Sam. 16:7). (2) It is not motivated by genuine love for all (v. 8). The admiration of social status is a sin against the law of love. (3) It makes us "judges of evil thoughts" (v. 4); i.e., instead of honoring "*the Lord* of glory" and accepting persons on the basis of their faith in Christ, we unjustly favor the rich or influential in the world from an evil motive of gain or honor that we might receive.

weareth the gay clothing, and say unto
him, Sit thou here [e]in a good place;
and say to the poor, Stand thou there,
or sit here under my footstool:
4 Are ye not then partial in your-
selves, and are become judges of evil
thoughts?
5 Hearken, my beloved brethren,
[m]Hath not God chosen the poor of this
world [n]rich in faith, and heirs of [f]the
kingdom [o]which he hath promised to
them that love him?
6 But [p]ye have despised the poor.
Do not rich men oppress you, [q]and
draw you before the judgment seats?
7 Do not they blaspheme that wor-
thy name by the which ye are called?
8 If ye fulfil the royal law according
to the scripture, [r]Thou shalt love thy
neighbour as thyself, ye do well:
9 But [s]if ye have respect to per-
sons, ye commit sin, and are convinced
of the law as transgressors.
10 For whosoever shall keep the
whole law, and yet offend in one *point*,
[t]he is guilty of all.
11 For [g]he that said, [u]Do not
commit adultery, said also, Do not kill.

2:5
[m]John 7:48
[n]Luke 12:21
[o]Ex. 20:6
Prov. 8:17
2:6
[p]1 Cor. 11:22
[q]Acts 13:50
2:8
[r]Lev. 19:18
Mat. 22:39
2:9
[s]ver. 1
2:10
[t]Deut. 27:26
Mat. 5:19
Gal. 3:10
2:11
[u]Ex. 20:13
2:12
[v]ch. 1:25
2:13
[w]Job 22:6
[x]1 John 4:17
2:14
[y]Mat. 7:26
Mat. 15:11
2:15
[z]Luke 3:11
2:16
[a]1 John 3:18

Now if thou commit no adultery, yet if
thou kill, thou art become a transgres-
sor of the law.
12 So speak ye, and so do, as they
that shall be judged by [v]the law of lib-
erty.
13 For [w]he shall have judgment
without mercy, that hath shown no
mercy; and [x]mercy [h]rejoiceth
against judgment.

True faith evidenced by works

14 [y]What *doth it* profit, my breth-
ren, though a man say he hath faith,
and have not works? can faith save
him?
15 [z]If a brother or sister be naked,
and destitute of daily food,
16 And [a]one of you say unto them,
Depart in peace, be *ye* warmed and
filled; notwithstanding ye give them
not those things which are needful to
the body; what *doth it* profit?
17 Even so faith, if it hath not
works, is dead, being [i]alone.
18 Yea, a man may say, Thou hast

[e] Or, *well*, or, *seemly* [f] Or, *that* [g] Or, *that* law *which said* [h] Or, *glorieth* [i] Gk. *by itself*

2:5 HATH NOT GOD CHOSEN THE POOR. The poor are special and precious to God (cf. Is. 61:1; Luke 4:18; 6:20; 7:22). Often it is the poor in this world who are the richest in faith and spiritual gifts and who, in their need, cry out most intensely to God in sincere hunger for His presence, mercy, and help (Luke 6:20–21). The economically depressed around the world learn that they cannot put their trust in material possessions. Therefore, they respond more readily to Jesus' invitation to "come unto me, all *ye* that labour and are heavy laden, and I will give you rest" (Mat. 11:28; see article on RICHES AND POVERTY, p. 1568).

2:12 SO SPEAK YE. We must speak and act from the perspective of those who will be judged by God and the "law of liberty," i.e., the law and love of God poured forth into our hearts by God's Spirit. God will condemn all showing of partiality, for it transgresses the law of love (see v. 1, note; see article on THE JUDGMENT OF BELIEVERS, p. 1811).

2:14 FAITH, AND HAVE NOT WORKS. Vv. 14–26 treat the ever-present problem of those in the church who profess to have saving faith in the Lord Jesus Christ, yet at the same time show no evidence of sincere devotion to Him and His Word. (1) Saving faith is always a living faith that does not stop with mere confession of Christ as Savior, but also prompts obedience to Him as Lord. Thus, obedience is an essential aspect of faith. Only those who obey can believe, and only those who believe can obey (see v. 24, note; Rom. 1:5, note on "obedience to the faith"; see article on FAITH AND GRACE, p. 1738).

(2) Note that there is no contradiction between Paul and James in regard to the matter of saving faith. Normally Paul emphasizes faith as the means by which we accept Christ as Savior (Rom. 3:22). James calls attention to the fact that true faith must be an enduring faith which shapes our very existence.

2:17 FAITH, IF IT HATH NOT WORKS, IS DEAD. (1) True saving faith is so vital that it cannot but express itself in godly action and devotion to Jesus Christ. Works without faith are dead works. Faith without works is dead faith. True faith always manifests itself in obedience toward God and compassionate deeds toward needy people (see v. 22, note; Rom. 1:5, note; see articles on THE CARE OF THE POOR AND NEEDY, p. 1312, and FAITH AND GRACE, p. 1738).

(2) James is directing his teaching against those in the church who professed faith in Christ and His blood atonement and believed that such profession was all that was necessary for salvation. They believed that a personal, obedient relationship with Christ as Lord was not essential. James says that such faith is dead and will produce neither salvation nor anything good (vv. 14–16,20–24). The only kind of faith that saves is "faith which worketh by love" (Gal. 5:6).

(3) On the other hand, we must not think that we maintain a living faith solely by our own effort. The grace of God, the indwelling Holy Spirit, and the intercession of Christ (see Heb. 7:25, note) work in our lives to enable us to respond to God by faith from first to last (cf. Rom. 1:17). If we ever cease to be receptive to God's grace and the lead-

faith, and I have works: show me thy
faith [j]without thy works, [b]and I will
show thee my faith by my works.
19 Thou believest that there is one
God; thou doest well: the devils also
believe, and tremble.
20 But wilt thou know, O vain man,
that faith without works is dead?
21 Was not Abraham our father justified by works, [c]when he had offered
Isaac his son upon the altar?
22 [k]Seest thou [d]how faith
wrought with his works, and by works
was faith made perfect?
23 And the scripture was fulfilled
which saith, [e]Abraham believed God,
and it was imputed unto him for righteousness: and he was called [f]the
Friend of God.
24 Ye see then how that by works a
man is justified, and not by faith only.
25 Likewise also [g]was not Rahab
the harlot justified by works, when she
had received the messengers, and had
sent *them* out another way?
26 For as the body without the
[l]spirit is dead, so faith without works
is dead also.

True faith evidenced by words

3 MY BRETHREN, [h]be not many
masters, [i]knowing that we shall
receive the greater [m]condemnation.
2 For [j]in many things we offend
all. [k]If any man offend not in word,
[l]the same *is* a perfect man, *and* able
also to bridle the whole body.
3 Behold, [m]we put bits in the
horses' mouths, that they may obey us;
and we turn about their whole body.
4 Behold also the ships, which
though *they be* so great, and *are* driven
of fierce winds, yet are they turned
about with a very small helm, whithersoever the governor listeth.
5 Even so [n]the tongue is a little
member, and [o]boasteth great things.
Behold, how great [n]a matter a little
fire kindleth!
6 And [p]the tongue *is* a fire, a world
of iniquity: so is the tongue among our
members, that [q]it defileth the whole
body, and setteth on fire the [o]course
of nature; and it is set on fire of hell.
7 For every [p]kind of beasts, and of
birds, and of serpents, and of things in
the sea, is tamed, and hath been tamed
of [q]mankind:
8 But the tongue can no man tame;
it is an unruly evil, [r]full of deadly poison.
9 Therewith bless we God, even the
Father; and therewith curse we men,

2:18 [b]ch. 3:13
2:21 [c]Gen. 22:9
2:22 [d]Heb. 11:17
2:23 [e]Gen. 15:6 Rom. 4:3 Gal. 3:6 [f]2 Chr. 20:7 Is. 41:8
2:25 [g]Heb. 11:31
3:1 [h]Mat. 23:8 [i]Luke 6:37
3:2 [j]1 Ki. 8:46 2 Chr. 6:36 Prov. 20:9 [k]Ps. 34:13 1 Pet. 3:10 [l]Mat. 12:37
3:3 [m]Ps. 32:9
3:5 [n]Prov. 12:18 [o]Ps. 12:3
3:6 [p]Prov. 16:27 [q]Mat. 15:11
3:8 [r]Ps. 140:3

[j]Some copies read, *by thy works* [k]Or, *Thou seest* [l]Or, *breath* [m]Or, *Judgment* [n]Or, *wood* [o]Gk. *wheel* [p]Gk. *nature* [q]Gk. *nature of man*

ing of the Holy Spirit, then our faith will die.
2:21 ABRAHAM . . . JUSTIFIED BY WORKS. The works by which Abraham was justified were not "deeds of the law" (Rom. 3:28), but works of faith and love. His willingness to sacrifice Isaac was an expression of his faith in and commitment to God (see Gen. 15:6, note; 22:1, note). James uses the example of Abraham to demolish the belief that faith can exist without commitment to and love for God. The apostle Paul uses the example of Abraham's faith to destroy the view that salvation rests on the merit of one's own works rather than the grace of God (Rom. 4:3; Gal. 3:6).
2:22 FAITH WROUGHT WITH HIS WORKS. James is not saying that faith *and* works save us. This separates faith from works. James contends instead for faith at work. Thus, faith and works can never be separated; the latter flows naturally from the former (see Gal. 5:6, note).
2:24 BY WORKS A MAN IS JUSTIFIED. The term "works" as used by James has a different meaning than it did for Paul in Rom. 3:28. (1) For James "works" refers to our obligations to God and man that are commanded in Scripture and that proceed from a sincere faith, a pure heart, the grace of God, and the desire to please Christ. (2) For Paul "works" refers to a desire to gain merit and salvation by obeying the law through one's own effort rather than through repentance and faith in Christ. (3) Note that both Paul and James state emphatically that true saving faith will inevitably produce works of love (1:27; 2:8; Gal. 5:6; 1 Cor. 13; cf. John 14:15).
3:1 MASTERS. This word means "teachers" and includes pastors, church leaders, missionaries, preachers of the Word, or anyone who gives instruction to a congregation. The teacher must understand that no one has a more solemn responsibility than those who teach the sacred Scriptures. In the future judgment, Christian teachers will be judged more strictly than other believers.
3:6 THE TONGUE *IS* A FIRE. James emphasizes our inclination to sin in our speaking. Sins of speech include harsh and unkind words, lying, exaggeration, teaching false doctrine, slander, gossiping, and boasting. The mature believer keeps his tongue under control by the guidance of the Holy Spirit, who brings "into captivity every thought to the obedience of Christ" (2 Cor. 10:5) and makes us aware when we are transgressing the law of love and thus offending both God and others. Because of the tendency to sin with the tongue, James exhorts every person to "be swift to hear, slow to speak, slow to wrath" (1:19).

[s]which are made after the similitude of God.

10 Out of the same mouth proceedeth blessing and cursing. My brethren, these things ought not so to be.

11 Doth a fountain send forth at the same [r]place sweet *water* and bitter?

12 Can the fig tree, my brethren, bear olive berries? either a vine, figs? so *can* no fountain both yield salt water and fresh.

True and false wisdom

13 [t]Who *is* a wise man and endued with knowledge among you? let him show out of a good conversation [u]his works [v]with meekness of wisdom.

14 But if ye have [w]bitter envying and strife in your hearts, [x]glory not, and lie not against the truth.

15 [y]This wisdom descendeth not from above, but *is* earthly, [s]sensual, devilish.

16 For [z]where envying and strife *is,* there *is* [t]confusion and every evil work.

17 But [a]the wisdom that is from above is first pure, then peaceable, gentle, *and* easy to be entreated, full of mercy and good fruits, [u]without partiality, [b]and without hypocrisy.

18 [c]And the fruit of righteousness is sown in peace of them that make peace.

Selfishness and greed

4 FROM WHENCE *come* wars and [v]fightings among you? *come they* not hence, *even* of your [w]lusts [d]that war in your members?

2 Ye lust, and have not: ye [x]kill, and desire to have, and cannot obtain: ye fight and war, yet ye have not, because ye ask not.

3 [e]Ye ask, and receive not, [f]because ye ask amiss, that ye may consume *it* upon your [w]lusts.

Friendship with the world

4 [g]Ye adulterers and adulteresses, know ye not that [h]the friendship of the world is enmity with God? [i]whosoever therefore will be a friend of the world is the enemy of God.

5 Do ye think that the scripture

3:9 [s]Gen. 1:26
3:13 [t]Gal. 6:4 [u]ch. 2:18 [v]ch. 1:21
3:14 [w]Rom. 13:13 [x]Rom. 2:17
3:15 [y]Phil. 3:19
3:16 [z]1 Cor. 3:3 Gal. 5:20
3:17 [a]1 Cor. 2:6 [b]Rom. 12:9 1 Pet. 1:22
3:18 [c]Prov. 11:18
4:1 [d]Rom. 7:23 Gal. 5:17
4:3 [e]Job 27:9 Ps. 18:41 [f]Ps. 66:18
4:4 [g]Ps. 73:27 [h]1 John 2:15 [i]John 15:19 Gal. 1:10

[r] Or, *hole* [s] Or, *natural* [t] Gk. *tumult,* or, *unquietness* [u] Or, *without wrangling* [v] Or, *brawlings* [w] Or, *pleasures* [x] Or, *envy*

3:14–15 STRIFE. "Strife" is related to envy and refers to the vice of selfish ambition that prompts us to promote our own interests. Selfish ambition in the church is (1) "earthly," i.e., defiles that which is holy and of the Spirit; (2) "sensual" or unspiritual, i.e., without the Holy Spirit; and (3) "devilish," i.e., it is inspired by demons (see 1 Tim. 4:1, note).

4:1 WHENCE *COME* WARS AND FIGHTINGS AMONG YOU? The major source of quarrels and conflicts in the church centers in a desire for recognition, honor, glory, power, pleasure, money, and superiority. The satisfaction of selfish desires becomes more important than righteousness and the will of God (cf. Mark 4:19; Luke 8:14; Gal. 5:16–20). When this occurs, self-centered conflicts are created in the fellowship. Those responsible show themselves void of the Spirit and outside of the kingdom of God (Gal. 5:19–21; Jude 16–19).

4:2 YE KILL. This phrase may be used figuratively in the sense of hate (cf. Mat. 5:21–22).

4:3 YE ASK, AND RECEIVE NOT. God refuses to answer the prayers of those who are selfishly ambitious, love pleasure, and desire honor, power, or riches (see v. 1, note). All of us should take note, for God will not listen to our prayers if we have a heart filled with selfish desires (see article on EFFECTIVE PRAYING, p. 540). Scripture tells us God accepts only the prayers of the righteous (Ps. 34:13–15; 66:18–19), of those who call upon Him in truth (Ps. 145:18), of the genuinely repentant and humble (Luke 18:14–15), and of those who ask anything according to His will (1 John 5:14).

4:4 FRIENDSHIP OF THE WORLD . . . ENMITY WITH GOD. "Friendship of the world" is spiritual adultery, i.e., unfaithfulness to God and our pledge of commitment to Him (1 John 2:15–17; cf. Is. 54:5; Jer. 3:20). It involves embracing the world's sin, values, and evil pleasures (see article on THE CHRISTIAN'S RELATIONSHIP TO THE WORLD, p. 2004). God will not accept such friendship (Mat. 6:24), for He is a jealous God (Ex. 20:5; Deut. 5:9).

One example of such friendship is participation in secret orders (e.g., lodge membership) that demand unscriptural religious oaths and a strong binding together with unbelievers, both of which are forbidden in God's Word (Mat. 5:33–37; 2 Cor. 6:14). Believers cannot belong to such orders without compromising Christian doctrine (cf. 2 Pet. 3:16), godly standards, and their loyalty to Christ (Mat. 6:24).

4:5 THE SPIRIT . . . LUSTETH TO ENVY. The construction of v. 5 in the Greek is unclear. It may mean that the natural tendency of man's spirit is to hate God and his neighbor and to desire the sinful pleasures of the world (v. 4). Yet this tendency can be changed by the grace of God that comes to all who humbly accept salvation in Christ (v. 6).

saith in vain, [j]The spirit that dwelleth
in us lusteth [y]to envy?
6 But he giveth more grace. Where-
fore he saith, [k]God resisteth the
proud, but giveth grace unto the hum-
ble.
7 Submit yourselves therefore to
God. [l]Resist the devil, and he will flee
from you.
8 [m]Draw nigh to God, and he will
draw nigh to you. [n]Cleanse *your*
hands, *ye* sinners; and [o]purify *your*
hearts, *ye* [p]double minded.
9 [q]Be afflicted, and mourn, and
weep: let your laughter be turned to
mourning, and *your* joy to heaviness.
10 [r]Humble yourselves in the
sight of the Lord, and he shall lift
you up.

Slander and false confidence

11 [s]Speak not evil one of another,
brethren. He that speaketh evil of *his*
brother, [t]and judgeth his brother,
speaketh evil of the law, and judgeth
the law: but if thou judge the law, thou
art not a doer of the law, but a judge.
12 There is one lawgiver, [u]who is
able to save and to destroy: [v]who art
thou that judgest another?

Dependence on God

13 [w]Go to now, ye that say, Today
or tomorrow we will go into such a city,
and continue there a year, and buy and
sell, and get gain:
14 Whereas ye know not what *shall*
be on the morrow. For what *is* your life?
[x]It[z] is even a vapour, that appeareth
for a little time, and then vanisheth
away.
15 For that ye *ought* to say, [y]If the
Lord will, we shall live, and do this, or
that.
16 But now ye rejoice in your boast-
ings: [z]all such rejoicing is evil.
17 Therefore [a]to him that knoweth
to do good, and doeth *it* not, to him it
is sin.

Warning to rich oppressors

5 GO [b]TO now, *ye* rich men, weep
and howl for your miseries that
shall come upon *you*.
2 Your riches are corrupted, and
[c]your garments are motheaten.
3 Your gold and silver is cankered;
and the rust of them shall be a witness
against you, and shall eat your flesh as
it were fire. [d]Ye have heaped treasure
together for the last days.
4 Behold, [e]the hire of the labour-
ers who have reaped down your fields,
which is of you kept back by fraud,
crieth: and [f]the cries of them which
have reaped are entered into the ears
of the Lord of sabaoth.
5 [g]Ye have lived in pleasure on the
earth, and been wanton; ye have nour-
ished your hearts, as in a day of
slaughter.

4:5 [j]Gen. 6:5 Num. 11:29
4:6 [k]Job 22:29 Ps. 138:6 Prov. 3:34 Mat. 23:12
4:7 [l]Eph. 4:27 1 Pet. 5:9
4:8 [m]2 Chr. 15:2 [n]Is. 1:16 [o]1 Pet. 1:22 1 John 3:3 [p]ch. 1:8
4:9 [q]Mat. 5:4
4:10 [r]Job 22:29
4:11 [s]1 Pet. 2:1 [t]Mat. 7:1
4:12 [u]Mat. 10:28 [v]Rom. 14:4
4:13 [w]Prov. 27:1
4:14 [x]Job 7:7
4:15 [y]Acts 18:21
4:16 [z]1 Cor. 5:6
4:17 [a]Luke 12:47 John 9:41
5:1 [b]Prov. 11:28 Luke 6:24
5:2 [c]Job 13:28 Mat. 6:20
5:3 [d]Rom. 2:5
5:4 [e]Lev. 19:13 [f]Deut. 24:15
5:5 [g]Job 21:13 Amos 6:1

[y] Or, *enviously?* [z] Or, *For it is*

4:6 GOD RESISTETH THE PROUD. It should be impressed upon our hearts and minds how much God hates pride. Pride in our lives will cause God to turn from our prayers and withhold His presence and grace from us. To be exalted in our own minds and to seek honor and the esteem of others in order to satisfy our pride is to shut out the help of God. But for those who humbly submit themselves to God and draw near to Him, there is abundant grace, mercy, and help in every situation of life (see Phil. 2:3, note; Heb. 4:16; 7:25).

4:8 DRAW NIGH TO GOD. God promises to draw near to all those who turn from sin, purify their hearts, and call upon Him in true repentance. God's nearness will bring His presence, grace, blessings, and love.

4:11 SPEAK NOT EVIL. By neglecting to learn all the facts about a situation, by failing to speak to an accused person about a problem, and by slandering him or her, we set aside God's law of love.

4:15 IF THE LORD WILL. In making goals and plans for the future, believers must always consider God and His will. We must not act like the rich fool (Luke 12:16–21); rather we must recognize that true happiness and useful lives are completely dependent on God. The principle by which we live must be, "If the Lord will." If our prayer is truly "Thy will be done" (Mat. 26:42), then we have the assurance that our present and future are in the protective care of our heavenly Father (cf. Acts 18:21; 1 Cor. 4:19; 16:7; Heb. 6:3; see article on THE WILL OF GOD, p. 1060).

4:16 BOASTINGS. For those who have set goals and have succeeded, the temptation is to boast. Boasting is based on the false assumption that whatever we accomplished, we did by ourselves and not with the help of God and others. The N.T. exhorts us to boast in our weaknesses and our dependence on God (2 Cor. 11:30; 12:5,9).

5:1 *YE* RICH . . . WEEP AND HOWL. The Bible does not teach that all the rich are ungodly people. Nevertheless, what James is describing is characteristic of many people with wealth (vv. 1–6; 2:1–3). The exception is the rich person who is not possessed by his wealth and uses it instead to advance the gospel and to help those in need (see article on RICHES AND POVERTY, p. 1568).

6 [h]Ye have condemned *and* killed the just; *and* he doth not resist you.

Patience in suffering

7 [a]Be patient therefore, brethren, unto the coming of the Lord. Behold, the husbandman waiteth for the precious fruit of the earth, and hath long patience for it, until he receive [i]the early and latter rain.

8 Be ye also patient; stablish your hearts: [j]for the coming of the Lord draweth nigh.

9 [k]Grudge[b] not one against another, brethren, lest ye be condemned: behold, the judge [l]standeth before the door.

10 [m]Take, my brethren, the prophets, who have spoken in the name of the Lord, for an example of suffering affliction, and of patience.

11 Behold, [n]we count them happy which endure. Ye have heard of [o]the patience of Job, and have seen [p]the end of the Lord; that [q]the Lord is very pitiful, and of tender mercy.

12 But above all things, my brethren, [r]swear not, neither by heaven, neither by the earth, neither by any other oath: but let your yea be yea; and *your* nay, nay; lest ye fall into condemnation.

Prayer for the sick

13 Is any among you afflicted? let him pray. Is any merry? [s]let him sing psalms.

14 Is any sick among you? let him call for the elders of the church; and let them pray over him, [t]anointing him with oil in the name of the Lord:

15 And the prayer of faith shall save the sick, and the Lord shall raise him up; [u]and if he have committed sins, they shall be forgiven him.

16 Confess *your* faults one to anoth-

5:6 [h]ch. 2:6
5:7 [i]Deut. 11:14; Hos. 6:3
5:8 [j]Phil. 4:5; 1 Pet. 4:7
5:9 [k]ch. 4:11; [l]Mat. 24:33
5:10 [m]Mat. 5:12
5:11 [n]Ps. 94:12; [o]Job 2:10; [p]Job 42:10; [q]Num. 14:18
5:12 [r]Mat. 5:34
5:13 [s]Eph. 5:19
5:14 [t]Mark 6:13
5:15 [u]Is. 33:24

[a] Or, *Be long patient*, or, *Suffer with long patience* [b] Or, *Groan*, or, *Grieve not*

5:7 BE PATIENT . . . UNTO THE COMING OF THE LORD. James speaks of the return of Christ as drawing nigh (v. 8). He will come as judge to punish the wicked and to both reward the righteous and deliver them from wrongs they have suffered (v. 9). We must exercise patience until He comes. Patience is the virtue of enduring injustice, suffering, trouble, etc., while committing our lives to God in the faith that He will make all things right at His coming (Deut. 32:35; Rom. 12:12; Heb. 10:30; 12:1–2; see Job 2:3, note; Ps. 73:17, note).

5:9 STANDETH BEFORE THE DOOR. The motive for patience and perseverance in the faith is the imminent coming of the Lord (v. 8). He "standeth before the door." The door may not open until tomorrow, or next week, or next year, but it could open at any time.

5:11 THE PATIENCE OF JOB. The word translated "patience" (Gk. *hupomonē*) is better rendered "endurance" or "perseverance." It indicates endurance in whatever trials we may face without losing our faith in God. It is born of a faith that triumphs to the end in the midst of sufferings (Job 13:15). The outcome of the Lord's dealings with Job reveals that in all his affliction, God cared deeply about him and mercifully sustained him. James wants us to know that God is concerned about all His people and that, in suffering, He will sustain them in love and mercy (see Job 6:4, note; 42:10, note).

5:13 IS ANY AMONG YOU AFFLICTED . . . MERRY? When you are experiencing poverty, affliction, or distress, Scripture invites you to seek strength from God through prayer. Draw near to your mediator, Jesus Christ. He will represent you before God, make intercession for you (Heb. 7:25), and give mercy and grace to help in time of need (Heb. 4:16). Take seriously God's Word: "casting all your care upon him; for he careth for you" (1 Pet. 5:7). If we are happy in the Lord, we must sing songs of praise to Him (cf. Ps. 33:2–3; 81:1–2; 92:1–3; 98:4–6; 144:9; 149:1–5; 150).

5:15 PRAYER OF FAITH SHALL SAVE THE SICK. James is speaking of physical sickness. We may deal with illness by sending for the elders or leaders of the church. (1) It is the duty of pastors and elders to pray for the sick and to anoint them with oil. Note that the responsibility to pray the prayer of faith is on them, not on the sick person. The N.T. places the major burden for healing on the church and its leaders.

(2) The oil probably represents the healing power of the Holy Spirit and was used as an aid to faith (cf. Mark 6:13).

(3) It is prayer that James emphasizes as most important. Effective prayer must be offered in faith if the sick are to be healed. The Lord will give faith according to His will (see Mat. 17:20, note; see article on DIVINE HEALING, p. 1418).

(4) People may or may not always be healed; nevertheless, God promises to be with all those who cry unto Him in fervent prayer.

5:15 IF HE HAVE COMMITTED SINS. James recognizes that sickness may be due to sin (v. 16). Hence, whenever sickness occurs, one should examine himself before the Lord in prayer to determine if his sickness is due to personal sin. The word "if" makes it clear that sickness is not always the result of personal sin (see article on DIVINE HEALING, p. 1418).

5:16 CONFESS . . . PRAY . . . BE HEALED. This verse gives us an important reason why healing is often lacking in the Christian community. Sin must be confessed to others, and fervent

er, and pray one for another, that ye
may be healed. [v]The effectual fervent
prayer of a righteous man availeth
much.
17 Elias was a man [w]subject to like
passions as we are, and [x]he prayed
[c]earnestly that it might not rain:
[y]and it rained not on the earth by
the space of three years and six
months.
18 And [z]he prayed again, and the
heaven gave rain, and the earth
brought forth her fruit.
19 Brethren, [a]if any of you do err
from the truth, and one convert him;
20 Let him know, that he which
converteth the sinner from the error of
his way [b]shall save a soul from death,
and [c]shall hide a multitude of sins.

5:16 [v]Num. 11:2 John 9:31
5:17 [w]Acts 14:15 [x]1 Ki. 17:1 [y]Luke 4:25
5:18 [z]1 Ki. 18:42,45
5:19 [a]Mat. 18:15
5:20 [b]Rom. 11:14 [c]Prov. 10:12 1 Pet. 4:8

[c] Or, *in his prayer*

prayer for one another be made unto God. Sin in the church hinders the prayers of believers and blocks the healing power of God from being manifested in the congregation.

5:16 FERVENT PRAYER ... AVAILETH MUCH. The prayer of a man who is righteous accomplishes much. A righteous man's prayer: (1) draws him near to God (Heb. 7:25); (2) opens the way to a Spirit-filled life (Luke 11:13; Acts 1:14); (3) brings him power for ministry (Acts 1:8; 4:31, 33) and Christian devotion (Eph. 1:19); (4) builds him up spiritually (Jude 20); (5) gives him insight into Christ's provision for him (Eph. 1:16–19); (6) helps him overcome Satan (Dan. 10:12–13; Eph. 6:12–13,18); (7) clarifies the will of God for him (Ps. 32:6–8; Prov. 3:5–6; Mark 1:35–39); (8) enables him to receive spiritual gifts (1 Cor. 14:1); (9) brings him into fellowship with God (Mat. 6:9; John 7:37; 14:16); (10) brings him grace, mercy, and peace (Phil. 4:6–7; Heb. 4:16); (11) brings the lost to Christ (v. 20); (12) brings him the wisdom, revelation, and knowledge of Christ (Eph. 1:16–17); (13) brings him healing (v. 15); (14) brings him deliverance from trouble (Ps. 34:4–7; Phil. 1:19); (15) glorifies God with praise and thanksgiving (Ps. 100:4); (16) makes the presence of Christ real to him (cf. Rev. 3:20); (17) ensures him of his final salvation and of Christ's intercession for him (Heb. 7:25; see article on EFFECTIVE PRAYING, p. 540).

5:18 HE PRAYED ... THE HEAVEN GAVE RAIN. Elijah was a man who had faith that his prayers to God would accomplish much, even to the point of God's intervention in the course of nature. He believed that prayer by a righteous man does change things and circumstances (vv. 13–16; Ps. 34:6; Is. 38:1–5; Mat. 17:21; 26:41,53; Mark 11:24; 2 Thes. 3:1; see 1 Ki. 17:22, note; 18:42, note).

(1) We must be careful not to accept any teaching that undermines our faith in the power of prayer to bring about God's intervention in our lives. One such teaching is the concept of "fate," the pagan notion that everything we do and everything that happens to us is fixed unchangeably in advance, long before it occurs. Belief in fate is contrary to Scripture and causes one to assume that both good and bad are absolutely determined and unalterable, and that nothing is really changed by fervent, believing prayer.

(2) Scripture teaches that God deals with His children, not through absolute determinism, but by divine providence, whereby He interacts with and responds to the prayers of the righteous. Our prayers and faith in God do cause many good things to happen which would otherwise not occur (Ex. 32:9–14).

5:19–20 IF ANY OF YOU DO ERR. Believers should do everything possible to turn back to God those who stray from the truth (e.g., Gal. 4:19; 6:1; 2 Tim. 2:18,25–26; Jude 22–23). The salvation of a wandering brother or sister should always be a high priority in the Christian community. If the backslider returns to Christ, the one who converts him or her will have saved the soul of the sinner "from death," i.e., spiritual death and eternal separation from God (cf. Rom. 6:23; Gal. 6:8; Rev. 20:14).

1 PETER

Outline

Christian Greetings (1:1–2)

I. The Believer's Relationship to God (1:3—2:10)
   A. Salvation through Faith (1:3–12)
   B. Holiness through Obedience (1:13—2:10)

II. The Believer's Relationship to Others (2:11—3:12)
   A. Public Responsibilities (2:11–17)
   B. Domestic Responsibilities (2:18—3:7)
      1. Servants' Responsibility to Their Masters (2:18–25)
      2. Wives' Responsibility to Their Husbands (3:1–6)
      3. Husbands' Responsibility to Their Wives (3:7)
   C. Summary of Principles Governing the Believer's Relationship to Others (3:8–12)

III. The Believer's Relationship to Suffering (3:13—5:11)
   A. Endurance in the Face of Suffering (3:13—4:11)
      1. Because of the Blessing of Suffering Unjustly (3:13–17)
      2. Because of the Powerful Example of Christ (3:18—4:6)
      3. Because of the Urgency of the End-Time (4:7–11)
   B. Rejoicing in the Face of Suffering (4:12–19)
      1. Because it Tests the Reality of Our Faith (4:12)
      2. Because it is a Sharing in Christ's Sufferings (4:13a,14–16)
      3. Because it Prepares Us for the Glory of His Coming (4:13b,17–19)
   C. Exhortations in the Face of Suffering (5:1–11)
      1. To Elders — Shepherd the Flock (5:1–4)
      2. To Younger Men (5:5–11)

Conclusion (5:12–14)

Author: Peter

Theme: Suffering for Christ

Date of Writing: A.D. 60–63

Background

This is the first of two letters in the N.T. written by the apostle Peter (1:1; 2 Pet. 1:1). Peter testifies that he wrote his first letter with the assistance of Silvanus (Gk. name for Silas) as his scribe (5:12). Silas's fluent Greek and writing style are reflected here, while possibly Peter's own less polished Greek appears in his second epistle. The tone and content of 1 Peter is consistent with what we know about Simon Peter. His years of close fellowship with the Lord Jesus underlie his recalling of Jesus' death (1:11,19; 2:21–24; 3:18; 5:1) and resurrection (1:3,21; 3:21); indirectly he seems to refer even to Jesus' post-resurrection appearance to him in Galilee (2:25; 5:2a; cf. John 21:15–23). In addition, many similarities occur between this letter and Peter's sermons recorded in Acts.

Peter addresses this letter to "strangers scattered" throughout the Roman provinces of Asia Minor (1:1). Some of these may have been converts who had responded to Peter's

message on the day of Pentecost and had returned to their respective cities with their newfound faith (cf. Acts 2:9–11). These believers are called "strangers and pilgrims" (2:11) to remind them that their Christian pilgrimage is in a world which is hostile to Jesus Christ and from which they can expect persecution. Peter probably wrote this letter in response to reports from believers in Asia Minor of growing opposition to them (4:12–16) that did not yet have official governmental sanction (2:12–17).

Peter wrote from "Babylon" (5:13). This may be understood literally as the city of Babylon in Mesopotamia or as a figurative expression for Rome, the supreme center of anti-God power in the first century. Scripturally, we can only account for Mark (5:13) being at Rome (Col. 4:10) in the early 60s. Although Peter may have visited at some point the large colony of orthodox Jews in Babylon, we can more readily account for Peter, Silas (5:12), and Mark (5:13) being together at Rome (Col. 4:10; cf. Papias' comments about Peter and Mark at Rome) in the early 60s rather than at literal Babylon. Peter wrote most likely between A.D. 60–63, surely before the terrible bloodbath of Nero in Rome (A.D. 64).

Purpose

Peter wrote this epistle of joyful hope to provide believers with a divine and eternal perspective on their earthly life and to give practical guidance to those who were beginning to experience a fiery trial of suffering as Christians in a pagan environment. Peter was concerned that believers should not provoke governmental structures unnecessarily and that they should follow Jesus' example in suffering innocently, righteously, and nobly.

Survey

1 Peter begins by reminding believers (1) that they have a glorious calling and heavenly inheritance in Jesus Christ (1:2–5), (2) that their faith and love in this life will be subjected to testing and refining and will result in praise, glory, and honor at the Lord's appearing (1:6–9), (3) that this great salvation was foreseen by the O.T. prophets (1:10–12), and (4) that believers must live holy lives, clearly different from the unregenerate world around them (1:13–21). Believers, chosen and sanctified (1:2), are growing infants who need the pure milk of the Word (2:1–3), living stones who are being built into a spiritual house (2:4–10), and pilgrims who are passing through a foreign land (2:11–12); they must live honorably and humbly in their relations with all people during their sojourning (2:13—3:12).

The preeminent message of 1 Peter concerns submission and suffering righteously for Christ's sake and according to His own example (2:18–24; 3:9—5:11). Peter assures believers that for righteous suffering they will obtain God's favor and reward. In the context of this teaching concerning suffering for Christ, Peter stresses the interrelated themes of salvation, hope, love, joy, faith, holiness, humility, fear of God, obedience, and submission.

Special Features

Five major features or emphases characterize this epistle. (1) Along with Hebrews and Revelation, its message revolves around believers who are facing the prospect of severe persecution because of their identity with Jesus Christ. (2) More than any other N.T. epistle, it provides instruction on how to respond as a Christian to unjust persecution and suffering (3:9—5:11). (3) Peter stresses the truth that believers are strangers and pilgrims on earth (1:1; 2:11). (4) Many O.T. titles for God's people are applied to N.T. believers (e.g., 2:5,9–10). (5) It contains one of the most difficult passages in the N.T. to interpret: when, where, and how Jesus "preached unto the spirits in prison; which sometime were disobedient . . . in the days of Noah" (3:19–20).

Reading 1 Peter

In order to read the entire New Testament in one year, the book of 1 Peter should be read in 5 days, according to the following schedule:

☐ 1:1–21 ☐ 1:22—2:25 ☐ 3 ☐ 4 ☐ 5

NOTES

1 PETER, AN apostle of Jesus
Christ, to the strangers [a]scat-
tered throughout Pontus, Galatia, Cap-
padocia, Asia, and Bithynia,
2 [b]Elect [c]according to the fore-
knowledge of God the Father,
[d]through sanctification of the Spirit,
unto obedience and [e]sprinkling of the
blood of Jesus Christ: [f]Grace unto
you, and peace, be multiplied.

A future hope

3 [g]Blessed *be* the God and Father
of our Lord Jesus Christ, which [h]ac-
cording to his [a]abundant mercy
[i]hath begotten us again unto a lively
hope [j]by the resurrection of Jesus
Christ from the dead,
4 To an inheritance incorruptible,
and undefiled, and that fadeth not
away, [k]reserved in heaven [b]for you,
5 [l]Who are kept by the power of
God through faith unto salvation ready
to be revealed in the last time.

1:1 [a]John 7:35; Acts 2:5,9; Jas. 1:1
1:2 [b]Eph. 1:4; [c]Rom. 8:29; [d]2 Thes. 2:13; [e]Heb. 12:24; [f]Rom. 1:7
1:3 [g]Eph. 1:3; [h]Tit. 3:5; [i]John 3:3,5; Jas. 1:18; [j]1 Cor. 15:20
1:4 [k]Col. 1:5
1:5 [l]John 10:28
1:6 [m]Mat. 5:12; [n]2 Cor. 4:17; [o]Jas. 1:2
1:7 [p]Jas. 1:3; [q]Job 23:10; Prov. 17:3; [r]Rom. 2:7
1:8 [s]1 John 4:20; [t]John 20:29
1:9 [u]Rom. 6:22
1:10 [v]Gen. 49:10

Present trials

6 [m]Wherein ye greatly rejoice,
though now [n]for a season, if need be,
[o]ye are in heaviness through manifold
temptations:
7 That [p]the trial of your faith, be-
ing much more precious than of gold
that perisheth, though [q]it be tried
with fire, [r]might be found unto praise
and honour and glory at the appearing
of Jesus Christ:
8 [s]Whom having not seen, ye love;
[t]in whom, though now ye see *him* not,
yet believing, ye rejoice with joy un-
speakable and full of glory:
9 Receiving [u]the end of your faith,
even the salvation of *your* souls.
10 [v]Of which salvation the proph-
ets have inquired and searched dili-
gently, who prophesied of the grace
that should come unto you:
11 Searching what, or what manner

[a] Gk. *much* [b] Or, *for us*

1:2 THE FOREKNOWLEDGE OF GOD. Divine foreknowledge must be understood as God's eternal intention and love for His people, the church (see Rom. 8:29, note). The "elect" are the chosen company of true believers, chosen in harmony with God's determination to redeem the church by the "blood of Jesus Christ" through the "sanctification of the Spirit" (see article on ELECTION AND PREDESTINATION, p. 1846). All believers must participate in their election by giving diligence to make their calling and election sure (see 2 Pet. 1:5,10, notes).

1:2 SANCTIFICATION OF THE SPIRIT. For a discussion of the Christian's life of sanctification, see article on SANCTIFICATION, p. 1982.

1:3 BEGOTTEN US AGAIN. See article on REGENERATION, p. 1597.

1:5 KEPT BY THE POWER OF GOD THROUGH FAITH. This verse presents three truths concerning the security of believers, a message of particular relevance for Peter's audience since many of them were experiencing intense persecution. (1) Believers are "kept" (i.e., protected) against all the forces of evil that would destroy their lives and salvation in Christ (2 Tim. 4:18; Jude 1,24) "by the power of God" (cf. Rom. 8:31–39).

(2) The essential condition required for God's protection is "faith" (see article on FAITH AND GRACE, p. 1738). God's keeping of us by His grace does not work arbitrarily, for only "through faith" are believers protected by the power of God, just as only "through faith" are believers saved (Eph. 2:8). Thus, a living faith in Christ as Lord and Savior is our present responsibility in maintaining God's continued protection (v. 9; John 15:4,6; Col. 1:23; 2 Tim. 3:14–15; 4:7; Rev. 3:8,10).

(3) The ultimate goal of God's protection through the believer's faith is "salvation." Here salvation refers to the future final salvation, i.e., the obtaining of an inheritance in heaven (v. 4) and "the salvation of *your* souls" (v. 9).

1:7 TRIAL OF YOUR FAITH. The theme of suffering is emphasized throughout this epistle (2:19–23; 3:14–17; 4:1–4,12–19; 5:10). We must rejoice in our various trials (v. 6) because remaining faithful to Christ in the midst of them will purify our faith and result in praise, glory, and honor both to us and to the Lord Jesus Christ at His coming. The Lord considers our perseverance through trial and our faith in Christ precious and invaluable to Him throughout eternity.

1:8 HAVING NOT SEEN, YE LOVE. God considers the faith of believers today as greater than the faith of those who knew Jesus in the beginning. They saw and heard Jesus personally, even after His resurrection. Believers now, although they have never seen Him, love Him and believe in Him. According to Jesus, there is a special blessing for those who "have not seen, and *yet* have believed" (John 20:29). In our life of faith we are given joy as God's gift to us (Ps. 16:11; John 16:24; Rom. 15:13; Gal. 5:22).

1:11 SPIRIT OF CHRIST ... IN THEM. Our faith is based not only on the Word of God in the N.T., but also on God's Word in the O.T. The Holy Spirit through the prophets predicted the sufferings of Christ and the glories to follow (e.g., Gen. 49:10; Ps. 22; Is. 52:13—53:12; Dan. 2:44; Zech. 9:9–10; 13:7; cf. Luke 24:26–27; see 2 Pet. 1:21, note; see article on CHRIST IN THE OLD TESTAMENT, p. 562). He is called "the Spirit of Christ" because He spoke about Christ through the prophets and He was sent from Christ (vv. 11–12; cf. John 16:7; 20:22; Acts 2:33).

SANCTIFICATION

1 Pet. 1:2 "Elect according to the foreknowledge of God the Father, through sanctification of the Spirit, unto obedience and sprinkling of the blood of Jesus Christ: Grace unto you, and peace, be multiplied."

Sanctification (Gk. *hagiasmos*) as used in the Scriptures means to make holy, to consecrate, to separate from the world, and be set apart from sin in order that we may have close fellowship with God and serve Him (see also article on SPIRITUAL SEPARATION FOR BELIEVERS, p. 1814).

(1) In addition to the actual word "sanctify" (cf. 1 Thes. 5:23), the Scriptural standard of sanctification is expressed in such terms as "love the Lord thy God with all thy heart . . . soul . . . mind" (Mat. 22:37), "unblameable in holiness" (1 Thes. 3:13), "perfecting holiness" (2 Cor. 7:1), "charity out of a pure heart, and of a good conscience, and of faith unfeigned" (1 Tim. 1:5), "sincere and without offence" (Phil. 1:10), "made free from sin" (Rom. 6:18), "dead to sin" (Rom. 6:2), "servants to righteousness unto holiness" (Rom. 6:19), "keep his commandments" (1 John 3:22), and "overcometh the world" (1 John 5:4). Such terms describe the operation of the Holy Spirit through salvation in Christ by which He delivers us from the slavery and power of sin (Rom. 6:1–14), separates us from the sinful practices of this present world, renews our nature according to the image of Christ, produces in us the fruit of the Spirit, and enables us to live a holy and victorious life of dedication to God (John 17:15–19,23; Rom. 6:5,13,16,19; 12:1; Gal. 5:16,22–23; see 2 Cor. 5:17, note).

(2) These terms do not imply an absolute perfection, but an ethical righteousness of unblemished character demonstrated in purity before God, obedience to His law, and blamelessness before the world (Phil. 2:14–15; Col. 1:22; 1 Thes. 2:10; cf. Luke 1:6). The Christian, by the grace of God, has died with Christ and is set free from the power and dominion of sin (Rom. 6:18); therefore, believers need not and ought not sin, but can find adequate victory in their Savior Jesus Christ. Through the Holy Spirit we are able not to sin (1 John 3:6), even though we never come to the place where we are free from temptation and the possibility of sin.

(3) Sanctification was God's will for the Israelites in the O.T.; they were to live holy or sanctified lives, separate from the lifestyles of the nations around them (see Ex. 19:6, note; Lev. 11:44, note; 19:2, note; 2 Chr. 29:5, note). Likewise, it is a requirement for believers in Christ. The Scriptures teach that we must maintain a life of "holiness, without which no man shall see the Lord" (Heb. 12:14).

(4) God's children achieve sanctification by faith (Acts 26:18), by union with Christ in His death and resurrection (John 15:4–10; Rom. 6:1–11; 1 Cor. 1:30), by the blood of Christ (1 John 1:7–9), by the Word (John 17:17), and by the regenerating and sanctifying work of the Holy Spirit in their hearts (Jer. 31:31–34; Rom. 8:13; 1 Cor. 6:11; Phil. 2:12–13; 2 Thes. 2:13).

(5) Sanctification is both a work of God and a work of His people (Phil. 2:12–13). In order to accomplish God's will in sanctification, believers must respond to the sanctifying work of the Holy Spirit by ceasing to do evil (Rom. 6:1–2), cleansing themselves "from all filthiness of the flesh and spirit" (2 Cor. 7:1; cf. Rom. 6:12; Gal. 5:16–25), and keeping themselves unspotted from the world (Jas. 1:27; cf. Rom. 6:13,19; 8:13; 12:1–2; 13:14; Eph. 4:31; 5:18; Col. 3:5,10; Heb. 6:1; Jas. 4:8).

(6) True sanctification requires that believers maintain intimate communion with Christ (see John 15:4, note), engage in fellowship with believers (Eph. 4:15–16), devote themselves to prayer (Mat. 6:5–13; Col. 4:2) obey God's Word (John 17:17), be sensitive to the presence and care of God (Mat. 6:25–34), love righteousness and hate iniquity (Heb. 1:9), put sin to death (Rom. 6), submit to God's discipline (Heb. 12:5–11), continue to obey, and be filled with the Holy Spirit (Rom. 8:14; Eph. 5:18).

(7) In the N.T., sanctification is not seen as a slow process of forsaking sin little by little. Rather, it is presented as a definitive act by which the believer by grace is freed from Satan's bondage and makes a clear break with sin in order to live unto God (Rom. 6:18; 2 Cor. 5:17; Eph. 2:4–6; Col. 3:1–3). At the same time, however, sanctification is described as a lifelong process by which we continue to put to death the sinful desires of the flesh (Rom. 8:1–17), are progressively transformed into the likeness of Christ (2 Cor. 3:18), grow in grace (2 Pet. 3:18), and exercise a greater love for God and others (Mat. 22:37–39; 1 John 4:7–8,11,20–21).

(8) Sanctification can involve a definite crisis experience after initial salvation. Believers may receive a clear revelation of the holiness of God as well as a consciousness that God is calling them to separate themselves from sin and the world and to walk closer to God (2 Cor. 6:16–18). Through this consciousness, believers present themselves to God as living and holy sacrifices and receive from the Holy Spirit grace, purity, power, and victory to live holy lives, acceptable to God (Rom. 6:19–22; 12:1–2).

of time [w]the Spirit of Christ which was in them did signify, when it testified beforehand the sufferings of Christ, and the glory that should follow.

12 [x]Unto whom it was revealed, that [y]not unto themselves, but unto us they did minister the things, which are now reported unto you by them that have preached the gospel unto you with [z]the Holy Ghost sent down from heaven; [a]which things the angels desire to look into.

An appeal for a holy life

13 Wherefore [b]gird up the loins of your mind, [c]be sober, and hope [c]to the end for the grace that is to be brought unto you [d]at the revelation of Jesus Christ;

14 As obedient children, [e]not fashioning yourselves according to the former lusts [f]in your ignorance:

15 [g]But as he which hath called you is holy, so be ye holy in all manner of conversation;

2 Pet. 1:3-11 16 Because it is written, [h]Be ye holy; for I am holy.

17 And if ye call on the Father, [i]who without respect of persons judgeth according to every man's work, [j]pass the time of your [k]sojourning *here* in fear:

18 Forasmuch as ye know [l]that ye were not redeemed with corruptible things, *as* silver and gold, from your vain conversation [m]*received* by tradition from your fathers;

19 But [n]with the precious blood of Christ, [o]as of a lamb without blemish and without spot:

20 [p]Who verily was foreordained before the foundation of the world, but was manifest [q]in these last times for you,

21 Who by him do believe in God, [r]that raised him up from the dead, and [s]gave him glory; that your faith and hope might be in God.

22 Seeing ye [t]have purified your souls in obeying the truth through the Spirit unto unfeigned [u]love of the brethren, *see that ye* love one another with a pure heart fervently:

23 [v]Being born again, not of corruptible seed, but of incorruptible, [w]by the word of God, which liveth and abideth for ever.

24 [d]For [x]all flesh *is* as grass, and all the glory of man as the flower of grass. The grass withereth, and the flower thereof falleth away:

25 [y]But the word of the Lord endureth for ever. [z]And this is the word which by the gospel is preached unto you.

1:11 [w]2 Pet. 1:21
1:12 [x]Dan. 9:24 [y]Heb. 11:13 [z]Acts 2:4 [a]Dan. 8:13
1:13 [b]Eph. 6:14 [c]Luke 21:34 Rom. 13:13 [d]1 Cor. 1:7
1:14 [e]Rom. 12:2 [f]Acts 17:30
1:15 [g]2 Cor. 7:1
1:16 [h]Lev. 11:44
1:17 [i]Deut. 10:17 [j]Heb. 12:28 [k]Heb. 11:13
1:18 [l]1 Cor. 6:20 [m]Ezek. 20:18
1:19 [n]Acts 20:28 [o]Ex. 12:5
1:20 [p]Rom. 3:25 [q]Gal. 4:4
1:21 [r]Acts 2:24 [s]Acts 2:33
1:22 [t]Acts 15:9 [u]Heb. 13:1
1:23 [v]John 1:13 [w]Jas. 1:18
1:24 [x]Is. 40:6
1:25 [y]Is. 40:8 [z]John 1:1

[c] Gk. *perfectly* [d] Or, *For that*

1:12 PREACHED ... WITH THE HOLY GHOST. The same Spirit who inspired the prophets of the O.T. (v. 11) has inspired the truth of the gospel; thus, the message originates from God, not from humans. On the day of Pentecost, the same Spirit who inspired the truth of the gospel began to give power to all believers to proclaim the message (Acts 1:8; 2:4).

1:14 NOT FASHIONING YOURSELVES. See Rom. 12:2, note.

1:16 BE YE HOLY. God is holy, and what is true of God must be true of His people. Holiness carries the thought of being separated from the ungodly ways of the world and set apart for love, service, and worship toward God (see Lev. 11:44, note). Holiness is the goal and purpose of our election in Christ (Eph. 1:4); it means being like God, dedicated to God, and living to please God (Rom. 12:1; Eph. 1:4; 2:10; see Heb. 12:14, note). It is accomplished by the Spirit of God, who cleanses our souls and spirits from sin, renews us in the image of Christ, and enables us by the infusion of grace to obey God according to His Word (Gal. 5:16, 22–23,25; Col. 3:10). For more on holiness as a way of life, see article on SANCTIFICATION, p. 1982.

1:17 JUDGETH. See article on THE JUDGMENT OF BELIEVERS, p. 1811.

1:17 PASS THE TIME . . . IN FEAR. See Acts 5:11, note; 9:31, note; Rom. 3:18, note; Phil. 2:12, note.

1:18 REDEEMED. See article on BIBLICAL WORDS FOR SALVATION, p. 1726.

1:19 THE PRECIOUS BLOOD OF CHRIST. Scripture plainly sets forth the sacrificial death of Christ on the cross as that which procures the believer's redemption, i.e., release from the bondage and slavery to sin (cf. Eph. 1:7; see Heb. 9:14, note).

1:22 LOVE ONE ANOTHER . . . FERVENTLY. See John 13:34–35, notes; Rom. 12:10, note.

1:25 THE WORD OF THE LORD ENDURETH. Peter's quotation of Is. 40:6–8 indicates that all human glory and attainments (such as culture, science, philosophy), like the earth itself, are in constant change. But God's Word abides forever. Hence, all human endeavors and the current spirit of the world must be constantly judged by the Bible, rather than the Bible being judged by them. Those who bend the Word of God to conform to the intellectual trends and diluted standards of their generation betray the "word of God, which liveth and abideth for ever" (v. 23).

Desire the Word

2 WHEREFORE [a]LAYING aside all
malice, and all guile, and hypocri-
sies, and envies, and all evil speakings,
2 [b]As newborn babes, desire the
sincere [c]milk of the word, that ye may
grow thereby:
3 If so be ye have [d]tasted that the
Lord *is* gracious.

Christ our sure foundation

4 To whom coming, *as unto* a living
stone, [e]disallowed indeed of men, but
chosen of God, *and* precious,
5 [f]Ye also, as lively stones, [e]are
built up [g]a spiritual house, [h]an holy
priesthood, to offer up [i]spiritual sac-
rifices, [j]acceptable to God by Jesus
Christ.
6 Wherefore also it is contained in
the scripture, [k]Behold, I lay in Zion a
chief corner stone, elect, precious: and
he that believeth on him shall not be
confounded.
7 Unto you therefore which believe
he is [f]precious: but unto them which
be disobedient, [l]the stone which the
builders disallowed, the same is made
the head of the corner,
8 [m]And a stone of stumbling, and a
rock of offence, [n]*even to them* which
stumble at the word, being disobedi-
ent: [o]whereunto also they were ap-
pointed.
9 But ye *are* [p]a chosen generation,
[q]a royal priesthood, [r]an holy nation,
[s]a[g] peculiar people; that ye should
show forth the [h]praises of him who
hath called you out of [t]darkness into
his marvellous light: Rev. 5:9-14
10 [u]Which in time past *were* not a
people, but *are* now the people of God:
which had not obtained mercy, but now
have obtained mercy.
11 Dearly beloved, I beseech *you*
[v]as strangers and pilgrims, [w]abstain
from fleshly lusts, [x]which war against
the soul;
12 [y]Having your conversation hon-
est among the Gentiles: that,
[i]whereas they speak against you as
evildoers, [z]they may by *your* good
works, which they shall behold, glorify
God in the day of visitation. 1 John 2:15-17

Christian submission

13 [a]Submit yourselves to every or-
dinance of man for the Lord's sake:
whether it be to the king, as supreme;
14 Or unto governors, as unto them

2:1 [a]Heb. 12:1 **2:2** [b]Mat. 18:3 [c]1 Cor. 3:2 **2:3** [d]Heb. 6:5 **2:4** [e]Ps. 118:22 Acts 4:11 **2:5** [f]Eph. 2:21 [g]Heb. 3:6 [h]Is. 61:6 [i]Hos. 14:2 Mal. 1:11 [j]Phil. 4:18 **2:6** [k]Is. 28:16 **2:7** [l]Ps. 118:22 **2:8** [m]Is. 8:14 [n]1 Cor. 1:23 [o]Rom. 9:22 **2:9** [p]Deut. 10:15 [q]Rev. 5:10 [r]Is. 62:12 [s]Deut. 4:20 [t]Acts 26:18 **2:10** [u]Hos. 1:9 **2:11** [v]Ps. 39:12 [w]Gal. 5:16 [x]Jas. 4:1 **2:12** [y]Phil. 2:15 [z]Mat. 5:16 **2:13** [a]Rom. 13:1

[e] Or, *be ye built* [f] Or, *an honour* [g] Or, *a purchased people* [h] Or, *virtues* [i] Or, *wherein*

2:2 DESIRE . . . THE WORD. As born-again children of God (1 Cor. 6:19; Gal. 4:6), we should long for and crave the pure milk of God's Word (1:23–25). A sure sign of our spiritual growth is a strong desire to feed on the living and abiding Word of God. Thus, we must be alert to the loss of hunger and thirst for God's Word, a yearning that we can destroy through wrong attitudes toward others (v. 1) and through the cares and riches of the world (Luke 8:14; see Mat. 5:6, note; 1 Cor. 15:2, note).

2:5 AN HOLY PRIESTHOOD. In the O.T. the priesthood was restricted to a qualified minority. Their distinctive activity was to offer sacrifices to God on behalf of His people and to communicate directly with God (Ex. 28:1; 2 Chr. 29:11). Now through Jesus Christ, every Christian has been made a priest before God (Rev. 1:6; 5:10; 20:6). The priesthood of all believers means the following: (1) All believers have direct access to God through Christ (3:18; John 14:6; Eph. 2:18).

(2) All believers are under obligation to live a holy life (1:14–17; 2:5,9).

(3) All believers must offer up "spiritual sacrifices" to God, including: (a) living in obedience to God and nonconformity to the world (Rom. 12:1–2); (b) praying to and praising God (Ps. 50:14; Heb. 13:15; see article on PRAISE, p. 816); (c) serving with whole hearts and willing minds (1 Chr. 28:9; Eph. 5:1–2; Phil. 2:17); (d) performing good deeds (Heb. 13:16); (e) giving of our material possessions (Rom. 12:13; Phil. 4:18); and (f) presenting our bodies to God as instruments of righteousness (Rom. 6:13,19).

(4) All believers must intercede and pray for one another and for all people (Col. 4:12; 1 Tim. 2:1; Rev. 8:3; see article on INTERCESSION, p. 1268).

(5) All believers must declare the Word and pray for its success (3:15; Acts 4:31; 1 Cor. 14:26; 2 Thes. 3:1).

(6) All believers may administer baptism and the Lord's Supper (Mat. 28:19; Luke 22:19).

2:9 AN HOLY NATION. Believers are set apart from the world in order to belong completely to God (cf. Acts 20:28; Tit. 2:14) and to proclaim the gospel of salvation to His glory and praise (see Ex. 19:6, note; Is. 42:1, notes).

2:11 STRANGERS AND PILGRIMS. Our new position as God's own possession sets us apart from the people of this world to become pilgrims in this world. We now live in a country to which we do not belong, and our true citizenship is with Christ in heaven (cf. Phil. 3:20; Heb. 11:9–16). Because we are foreigners upon this earth, we must abstain from the evil pleasures of this world which seek to destroy our souls (see article on THE WORKS OF THE FLESH AND THE FRUIT OF THE SPIRIT, p. 1840).

2:13 SUBMIT . . . TO EVERY ORDINANCE. See Rom. 13:1, note.

that are sent by him [b]for the punishment of evildoers, and [c]for the praise of them that do well.

15 For so is the will of God, that [d]with well doing ye may put to silence the ignorance of foolish men:

16 [e]As free, and not [j]using *your* liberty for a cloak of maliciousness, but as [f]the servants of God.

17 [g]Honour[k] all *men.* [h]Love the brotherhood. [i]Fear God. Honour the king.

18 [j]Servants, *be* subject to *your* masters with all fear; not only to the good and gentle, but also to the froward.

19 For this *is* [k]thankworthy,[l] if a man for conscience toward God endure grief, suffering wrongfully.

20 For what glory *is it,* if, when ye be buffeted for your faults, ye shall take it patiently? but if, when ye do well, and suffer *for it,* ye take it patiently, this *is* [l]acceptable with God.

Christ our great example

21 For [l]even hereunto were ye called: because Christ also suffered [m]for us, [m]leaving us an example, that ye should follow his steps:

22 [n]Who did no sin, neither was guile found in his mouth:

23 [o]Who, when he was reviled, reviled not again; when he suffered, he threatened not; but [p]committed[n] *himself* to him that judgeth righteously:

24 [q]Who his own self bare our sins in his own body [o]on the tree, [r]that we, being dead to sins, should live unto righteousness: [s]by whose stripes ye were healed.

End

25 For [t]ye were as sheep going astray; but are now returned [u]unto the Shepherd and Bishop of your souls.

The husband and the wife

3 LIKEWISE, [v]YE wives, *be* in subjection to your own husbands; that, if any obey not the word, [w]they also may without the word [x]be won by the conversation of the wives;

2 [y]While they behold your chaste conversation *coupled* with fear.

3 [z]Whose adorning let it not be

2:14 [b]Rom. 13:4 [c]Rom. 13:3
2:15 [d]Tit. 2:8
2:16 [e]Gal. 5:1 [f]1 Cor. 7:22
2:17 [g]Rom. 12:10 [h]Heb. 13:1 [i]Rom. 13:7
2:18 [j]Eph. 6:5
2:19 [k]Mat. 5:10
2:21 [l]Mat. 16:24 [m]1 John 2:6
2:22 [n]Is. 53:9
2:23 [o]Is. 53:7 [p]Luke 23:46
2:24 [q]Heb. 9:28 [r]Rom. 7:6 [s]Is. 53:5
2:25 [t]Is. 53:6 [u]Ezek. 34:23 Heb. 13:20
3:1 [v]1 Cor. 14:34 [w]1 Cor. 7:16 [x]Mat. 18:15
3:2 [y]ch. 2:12
3:3 [z]1 Tim. 2:9

[j] Gk. *having* [k] Or, *Esteem* [l] Or, *thank*
[m] Some read, *for you* [n] Or, *committed* his cause [o] Or, *to*

2:21 CHRIST ALSO SUFFERED . . . FOLLOW HIS STEPS. The highest glory and privilege of any believer is to suffer for Christ and the gospel (see Mat. 5:10, note). In suffering, the believer follows the example of Christ and the apostles (Is. 53; Mat. 16:21; 20:28; Acts 9:16, note; Heb. 5:8).

(1) Christians must be willing to suffer (4:1; 2 Cor. 11:23–29), i.e., to share in the sufferings of Christ (4:13; 2 Cor. 1:5; Phil. 3:10), and must expect suffering to be a part of their ministry (2 Cor. 4:10–12; cf. 1 Cor. 11:1).

(2) Suffering for Christ is called suffering "according to the will of God" (4:19), for His "name's sake" (Acts 9:16), for "the gospel" (2 Tim. 1:8), "for righteousness' sake" (3:14), and for "the kingdom of God" (2 Thes. 1:5).

(3) Suffering for Christ is a way to arrive at spiritual maturity (Heb. 2:10), to obtain the blessing of God (4:14), and to minister life to others (2 Cor. 4:10–12). Sharing in Christ's suffering is a prerequisite for being glorified with Christ (Rom. 8:17) and attaining eternal "glory" (Rom. 8:18). In this sense it may be regarded as a precious gift from God (v. 19; Phil. 1:29).

(4) In living for Christ and the gospel, suffering must not be sought, but believers must be willing to undergo it out of devotion to Christ.

2:24 BARE OUR SINS. Christ bore our sins on the cross (cf. Is. 53:4,11–12) in that He became our substitute by taking upon Himself the penalty for our sins (John 1:29; Heb. 9:28; 10:10; see article on THE DAY OF ATONEMENT, p. 188). The purpose of this substitutionary death was that we might be totally separated from sin's guilt, power, and influence. By His death Christ removed our guilt and the punishment for our sins, opening a way whereby we might justly return to God (Rom. 3:24–26) and receive grace to live righteously before Him (Rom. 6:2–3; 2 Cor. 5:15; Gal. 2:20). Peter uses the word "healed" in relation to salvation with all its benefits (cf. Is. 53:5; Mat. 8:16–17).

3:1 HUSBANDS . . . MAY . . . BE WON. Peter instructs a wife how she ought to act in order to win her unsaved husband to Christ. (1) She must be subject to her husband and recognize his leadership of the family (see Eph. 5:22, note). (2) She must conduct herself in a holy and respectful manner with a gentle and quiet spirit (vv. 2–4; see 1 Tim. 2:13,15, notes). (3) She must endeavor to win her husband more by her behavior than by her words.

3:3–4 ADORNING . . . OF THE HEART. Gaudy, showy, or expensive adornment is contrary to the spirit of modesty that God desires for the Christian wife (see 1 Tim. 2:9, note). (1) What God highly values and exalts in a Christian wife is a gentle and quiet disposition (cf. Mat. 11:29; 21:5) that seeks to honor Him by giving herself to help her husband and family achieve God's will for their lives. (a) The adjective "meek" describes a bearing which is gentle and unassuming and expresses itself in gracious submissiveness and a concern for others (cf. Mat. 5:5; 2 Cor. 10:1; Gal. 5:23). (b) The adjective "quiet" refers to a quiet disposition which is not boisterous and does not create disturbances. In other words, God declares that true

that outward *adorning* of plaiting the hair, and of wearing of gold, or of putting on of apparel;

4 But *let it be* [a]the hidden man of the heart, in that which is not corruptible, *even the ornament* of a meek and quiet spirit, which is in the sight of God of great price.

5 For after this manner in the old time the holy women also, who trusted in God, adorned themselves, being in subjection unto their own husbands:

6 Even as Sarah obeyed Abraham, [b]calling him lord: whose [p]daughters ye are, as long as ye do well, and are not afraid with any amazement.

7 [c]Likewise, ye husbands, dwell with *them* according to knowledge, giving honour unto the wife, [d]as unto the weaker vessel, and as being heirs together of the grace of life; [e]that your prayers be not hindered.

Christian conduct

8 Finally, [f]*be ye* all of one mind, having compassion one of another, [g]love[q] as brethren, [h]*be* pitiful, *be* courteous:

9 [i]Not rendering evil for evil, or railing for railing: but contrariwise blessing; knowing that ye are thereunto called, [j]that ye should inherit a blessing.

10 For [k]he that will love life, and see good days, [l]let him refrain his tongue from evil, and his lips that they speak no guile:

3:4 [a]Rom. 2:29
3:6 [b]Gen. 18:12
3:7 [c]1 Cor. 7:3 [d]1 Cor. 12:23 [e]Job 42:8 Mat. 18:19
3:8 [f]Rom. 12:16 [g]Rom. 12:10 Heb. 13:1 [h]Eph. 4:32
3:9 [i]Prov. 17:13 [j]Mat. 25:34
3:10 [k]Ps. 34:12 [l]Jas. 1:26 Rev. 14:5
3:11 [m]Ps. 37:27 3 John 11 [n]Rom. 12:18 Heb. 12:14
3:12 [o]John 9:31 Jas. 5:16
3:13 [p]Prov. 16:7
3:14 [q]Jas. 1:12 ch. 2:19 [r]Is. 8:12,13
3:15 [s]Ps. 119:46 Col. 4:6 2 Tim. 2:25
3:16 [t]Heb. 13:18 [u]Tit. 2:8
3:18 [v]Rom. 5:6 [w]2 Cor. 13:4 [x]Col. 1:21 [y]Rom. 1:4

11 Let him [m]eschew evil, and do good; [n]let him seek peace, and ensue it.

12 For the eyes of the Lord *are* over the righteous, [o]and his ears *are open* unto their prayers: but the face of the Lord *is* [r]against them that do evil.

Suffering for doing good

13 [p]And who *is* he that will harm you, if ye be followers of that which is good?

14 [q]But and if ye suffer for righteousness' sake, happy *are ye:* and [r]be not afraid of their terror, neither be troubled;

15 But sanctify the Lord God in your hearts: and [s]*be* ready always to *give* an answer to every man that asketh you a reason of the hope that is in you with meekness and [s]fear: 1 John 1:2

16 [t]Having a good conscience; [u]that, whereas they speak evil of you, as of evildoers, they may be ashamed that falsely accuse your good conversation in Christ.

17 For *it is* better, if the will of God be so, that ye suffer for well doing, than for evil doing.

18 For Christ also hath [v]once suffered for sins, the just for the unjust, that he might bring us to God, [w]being put to death [x]in the flesh, but [y]quickened by the Spirit:

19 By which also he went and

[p] Gk. *children* [q] Or, *loving to the brethren* [r] Gk. *upon* [s] Or, *reverence*

beauty is a matter of character and not a matter of decoration.

(2) Christian wives today must remain loyal to Christ and His Word in a world governed by materialism, manipulative fashions, self-assertion, sexual obsession, and contempt for the values of the home and family.

3:7 YE HUSBANDS. Peter mentions three things that husbands must be concerned about with regard to their wives. (1) They must be considerate and understanding, living with their wives in love and in harmony with God's Word (Eph. 5:25–33; Col. 3:19).

(2) They must show respect to them as equal heirs of the grace of God and salvation. This requires that wives be honored, provided for, helped, and protected according to their needs. "Weaker" probably refers to the woman's physical strength. A husband must praise and highly treasure his wife as she endeavors to love and help him according to God's will (vv. 1–6; see Eph. 5:23, note).

(3) They must be concerned about unjust and improper treatment of their wives. Peter indicates that a husband who fails to live with his wife in an understanding way and to give her honor as a fellow child of God will damage his relation with God by creating a barrier between his prayers and God (cf. Col. 3:19).

3:10 LOVE LIFE . . GOOD DAYS. Peter quotes Ps. 34:12–16 to emphasize that the one who turns away from evil in both word and deed and pursues peace will experience (1) a life full of God's blessing and favor, (2) the close presence of God with His help and grace (v. 12), and (3) God's answer to his prayers (cf. Jas. 5:16; 1 John 3:21–22).

3:15 SANCTIFY THE LORD GOD IN YOUR HEARTS. Peter calls for an inner reverence for and commitment to Christ as Lord that is always ready to speak for Him and to explain the gospel to others (cf. Is. 8:13). Thus, we must know God's Word and truth in order to rightly witness for Christ and lead others to Him (cf. John 4:4–26).

3:19 PREACHED UNTO THE SPIRITS. Vv. 18–20 have long been difficult for interpreters. (1) One view is that Christ, after His death and resurrection (v. 18), went to imprisoned angels who had sinned in Noah's day (v. 19–20; cf. 2 Pet. 2:4–5) and proclaimed to them His victory over death and

[z]preached unto the spirits [a]in prison;

20 Which sometime were disobedient, [b]when once the longsuffering of God waited in the days of Noah, while [c]the ark was a-preparing, [d]wherein few, that is, eight souls were saved by water.

21 [e]The like figure whereunto *even* baptism doth also now save us (not the putting away of [f]the filth of the flesh, [g]but the answer of a good conscience toward God,) [h]by the resurrection of Jesus Christ:

22 Who is gone into heaven, and [i]is on the right hand of God; [j]angels and authorities and powers being made subject unto him.

Determine not to sin

4 FORASMUCH THEN [k]as Christ hath suffered for us in the flesh, arm yourselves likewise with the same mind: for [l]he that hath suffered in the flesh hath ceased from sin;

2 [m]That he no longer [n]should live the rest of *his* time in the flesh to the lusts of men, [o]but to the will of God.

3 [p]For the time past of *our* life may suffice us [q]to have wrought the will of the Gentiles, when we walked in lasciviousness, lusts, excess of wine, revellings, banquetings, and abominable idolatries:

4 Wherein they think it strange that ye run not with *them* to the same excess of riot, [r]speaking evil of *you:*

5 Who shall give account to him that is ready [s]to judge the quick and the dead.

6 For for this cause [t]was the gospel preached also to them that are dead, that they might be judged according to men in the flesh, but live according to God in the spirit.

7 But [u]the end of all things is at hand: [v]be ye therefore sober, and watch unto prayer.

8 [w]And above all things have fervent charity among yourselves: for [x]charity †shall cover the multitude of sins.

9 [y]Use hospitality one to another [z]without grudging.

10 [a]As every man hath received

3:19 [z]ch. 1:12 [a]Is. 42:7 **3:20** [b]Gen. 6:3,5 [c]Heb. 11:7 [d]Gen. 7:7 **3:21** [e]Eph. 5:26 [f]Tit. 3:5 [g]Rom. 10:10 [h]ch. 1:3 **3:22** [i]Ps. 110:1 Rom. 8:34 [j]Rom. 8:38 1 Cor. 15:24 **4:1** [k]ch. 3:18 [l]Gal. 5:24 **4:2** [m]Rom. 14:7 [n]Gal. 2:20 [o]John 1:13 **4:3** [p]Ezek. 44:6 [q]Eph. 2:2 1 Thes. 4:5 Tit. 3:3 **4:4** [r]Acts 13:45 **4:5** [s]Acts 10:42 Rom. 14:10 2 Tim. 4:1 **4:6** [t]ch. 3:19 **4:7** [u]Rom. 13:12 [v]Mat. 26:41 Luke 21:34 **4:8** [w]Col. 3:14 Heb. 13:1

[x]Prov. 10:12; 1 Cor. 13:7 **4:9** [y]Heb. 13:2 [z]2 Cor. 9:7 **4:10** [a]Rom. 12:6

† Or, *will*

Satan (v. 22). Another interpretation is that Christ by the Holy Spirit proclaimed through the mouth of Noah (cf. 2 Pet. 2:5) a message of warning to his disobedient generation, who are now in Hades awaiting final judgment. This interpretation fits best with the context, which speaks of the disobedient and unsaved people of Noah's day. It would be in harmony with Peter's statement that the Spirit of Christ spoke in times past through the prophets (2 Pet. 1:20–21).

(2) Neither this passage nor 4:6 teaches that unregenerate sinners will have a second chance to accept salvation after death. After death comes judgment (see Heb. 9:27) and one's fixed destiny in eternity (Luke 16:26).

3:21 BAPTISM DOTH . . . NOW SAVE US. Water baptism saves us in the sense that it is an obedient expression of our repentance and faith in Christ and of our commitment to come out of the world. It is our confession and pledge that we belong to Christ and have died and risen with Him (Rom. 6:3–5; Gal. 3:27; Col. 2:12; cf. Acts 2:38–39). Note the comparison with the flood (v. 20): just as Noah's observing God's instructions regarding the flood was a testimony to his faith before the flood, so going through the waters of baptism is a testimony to our faith that brought salvation through Christ before we were baptized.

4:1 HE THAT HATH SUFFERED. Those who willingly suffer for the cause of Christ find it easier to resist sin and to follow God's will. They have united themselves with Christ and shared His cross. As a result the pull of sin is made insignificant and the will of God paramount (v. 2). This spiritual principle will work in the lives of all believers. Obeying God when it means suffering, ridicule, or rejection will strengthen the believer morally and spiritually, and he will receive from God a greater grace (v. 14).

4:6 TO THEM THAT ARE DEAD. This term is best understood as referring to those to whom the gospel was preached while they were still living on earth, but are now dead. They heard the gospel and believed, and although they have died (i.e., have been "judged according to men in the flesh"), they now live with God. The verse could be paraphrased to read, "the gospel was preached to those who believed and later died, that they might have eternal life with God."

4:7 END OF ALL THINGS IS AT HAND. We should view our present lives in light of Christ's imminent coming and the end of the world (cf. Heb. 10:25; Jas. 5:8–9; 1 John 2:18). To Peter, this calls for the following commitments: (1) to pray to God fervently and daily (see Acts 10:9, note; 12:5, note; Col. 4:2,12, notes); (2) to love one another sincerely and fervently from the heart (v. 8; cf. 1:22; Mat. 22:37–39; 1 Thes. 4:9–10; 2 Pet. 1:7); (3) to be hospitable and kind to those in need (v. 9); (4) to serve other believers through the use of spiritual gifts given to us by the Holy Spirit (v. 10; see article on SPIRITUAL GIFTS FOR BELIEVERS, p. 1790); (5) to witness for Christ and serve God in the power of the Holy Spirit (v. 11; Acts 1:5–8); (6) to praise God (v. 11); and (7) to remain loyal to Christ in trials (vv. 12–19).

the gift, *even so* minister the same one to another, [b]as good stewards of [c]the manifold grace of God.

11 [d]If any man speak, *let him speak* as the oracles of God; [e]if any man minister, *let him do it* as of the ability which God giveth: that [f]God in all things may be glorified through Jesus Christ, [g]to whom be praise and domin-
1 ion for ever and ever. Amen.

The Christian and suffering

12 Beloved, think it not strange concerning [h]the fiery trial which is to try you, as though some strange thing happened unto you:

13 [i]But rejoice, inasmuch as [j]ye are partakers of Christ's sufferings; that, when his glory shall be revealed, ye may be glad also with exceeding joy.

14 [k]If ye be reproached for the name of Christ, happy *are ye;* for the spirit of glory and of God resteth upon you: on their part he is evil spoken of, but on your part he is glorified.

15 But [l]let none of you suffer as a murderer, or *as* a thief, or *as* an evildoer, [m]or as a busybody in other men's matters.

16 Yet if *any man suffer* as a Christian, let him not be ashamed; [n]but let him glorify God on this behalf.

17 For the time *is come* [o]that judgment must begin at the house of God: and [p]if *it* first *begin* at us, [q]what shall the end *be* of them that obey not the gospel of God?

18 [r]And if the righteous scarcely be saved, where shall the ungodly and the sinner appear?

19 Wherefore let them that suffer according to the will of God [s]commit the keeping of their souls *to him* in well doing, as unto a faithful Creator.

Christian life in God's care

5 THE ELDERS which are among you I exhort, who am also [t]an elder, and [u]a witness of the sufferings of Christ, and also [v]a partaker of the glory that shall be revealed:

2 [w]Feed the flock of God [u]which is

4:10 [b]Mat. 24:45 Tit. 1:7 [c]1 Cor. 12:4 Eph. 4:11 **4:11** [d]Jer. 23:22 [e]1 Cor. 3:10 [f]Eph. 5:20 [g]1 Tim. 6:16 **4:12** [h]1 Cor. 3:13 **4:13** [i]Acts 5:41 [j]Rom. 8:17 **4:14** [k]2 Cor. 12:10 Jas. 1:12 **4:15** [l]ch. 2:20 [m]1 Thes. 4:11 **4:16** [n]Acts 5:41 **4:17** [o]Is. 10:12 [p]Luke 23:31 [q]Luke 10:12 **4:18** [r]Luke 23:31 **4:19** [s]2 Tim. 1:12 **5:1** [t]Philem. 9 [u]Luke 24:48 Acts 1:8 [v]Rev. 1:9 **5:2** [w]Acts 20:28

[u] Or, *as much as in you is*

4:12 THE FIERY TRIAL. The N.T. emphasizes that troubles and afflictions are the inevitable experience of faithful believers in an ungodly world controlled by Satan and opposed to the gospel (see article on THE SUFFERING OF THE RIGHTEOUS, p. 764). Those who are committed to Jesus Christ with a devoted and loyal faith, who walk after the Spirit, and who love the truth of the gospel will experience trouble and sorrow. In fact, suffering for righteousness' sake is an evidence of the genuineness of our devotion to Christ (cf. Mat. 5:10–12; Acts 14:22; Rom. 8:17–18; 2 Tim. 2:12). For this reason problems in your life may be a sign that you are pleasing God and are faithful to Him. They frequently accompany your warfare of faith against sin, the ungodly world, and Satan (1:6–9; Eph. 6:12). Through fiery trials God allows you to share in His suffering and forms within you the quality of character He desires (Rom. 5:3–5; 2 Cor. 1:3–7; Jas. 1:2–4). Yet when you suffer and remain faithful to Christ, you will be considered blessed, for "the spirit of glory and of God resteth upon you" (see v. 14, note; cf. 2:21, note).

4:13 REJOICE ... CHRIST'S SUFFERINGS. It is a principle within the kingdom of God that suffering for the cause of Christ will increase the depth of the believer's joy in the Lord (see Mat. 5:10–12; Acts 5:41; 16:25; Rom. 5:3; Col. 1:24; Heb. 10:34; see next note). This being so, those involved in little or no suffering for the Lord are not to be envied.

4:14 THE SPIRIT OF GLORY AND OF GOD. Those who suffer because of their loyalty to Christ are blessed (cf. v. 13; 3:14; Mat. 5:11–12), for the Holy Spirit will rest upon them in a special way. Their lives will be full of the presence of the Holy Spirit to work in them, bless them, help them, and provide them with a foretaste of heaven's glory (cf. Is. 11:1–2; John 1:29–34; Acts 6:9–15).

4:17 JUDGMENT ... HOUSE OF GOD. See article on THE JUDGMENT OF BELIEVERS, p. 1811.

5:2 FEED THE FLOCK OF GOD. Elders (overseers or pastors) have the responsibility of caring for believers, discipling them, feeding them with the Word, and protecting them (see articles on THE MINISTRY GIFTS OF THE CHURCH, p. 1852; OVERSEERS AND THEIR DUTIES, p. 1706).

5:2 NOT FOR FILTHY LUCRE. Pastors and church leaders must beware of two dangerous sins. (1) The first is greed for money (see 1 Tim. 3:3,8; Tit. 1:7). The N.T. standard for those who oversee God's work is to receive adequate support from the church (Luke 10:7; 1 Cor. 9:14; 1 Tim. 5:17) and to be content with basic and necessary provisions for themselves and their families. No minister ought to make himself rich from God's work. Those who fall into this temptation open themselves up to sins of greed, compromise, and theft. For the sake of money, they compromise God's Word, righteous standards, and kingdom principles.

(2) The second sin is desire for power. Those greedy for power will dominate those whom they are to serve by excessively using their authority. Instead, the pastor must lead the church by being an example to the flock in devotion to Christ, humble service, perseverance in righteousness, steadfastness in prayer, and love for the Word.

among you, taking the oversight *thereof*, [x]not by constraint, but willingly; [y]not for filthy lucre, but of a ready mind;

3 Neither as [z]being[v] lords over [a]*God's* heritage, but [b]being examples to the flock.

2 Pet. 3:8-14 4 And when [c]the chief Shepherd shall appear, ye shall receive [d]a crown of glory that fadeth not away.

5 Likewise, ye younger, submit yourselves unto the elder. Yea, [e]all *of you* be subject one to another, and be clothed with humility: for [f]God resisteth the proud, and [g]giveth grace to the humble.

6 [h]Humble yourselves therefore under the mighty hand of God, that he may exalt you in due time:

7 [i]Casting all your care upon him; for he careth for you.

8 [j]Be sober, be vigilant; because [k]your adversary the devil, as a roaring lion, walketh about, seeking whom he may devour:

9 [l]Whom resist stedfast in the faith, [m]knowing that the same afflictions are accomplished in your brethren that are in the world.

10 But the God of all grace, [n]who hath called us unto his eternal glory by Christ Jesus, after that ye have suffered [o]a while, [p]make you perfect, [q]stablish, strengthen, settle *you*.

11 [r]To him *be* glory and dominion for ever and ever. Amen.

Conclusion and benediction

12 [s]By Silvanus, a faithful brother unto you, as I suppose, I have [t]written briefly, exhorting, and testifying [u]that this is the true grace of God wherein ye stand.

13 The *church that is* at Babylon, elected together with *you*, saluteth you; and *so doth* [v]Marcus my son.

14 [w]Greet ye one another with a kiss of charity. [x]Peace *be* with you all that are in Christ Jesus. Amen.

5:2 [x]1 Cor. 9:17 [y]1 Tim. 3:3
5:3 [z]Ezek. 34:4 [a]Ps. 33:12 [b]Phil. 3:17
5:4 [c]Heb. 13:20 [d]2 Tim. 4:8
5:5 [e]Rom. 12:10 [f]Jas. 4:6 [g]Is. 57:15
5:6 [h]Jas. 4:10
5:7 [i]Ps. 37:5 Heb. 13:5
5:8 [j]Luke 21:34 [k]Job 1:7
5:9 [l]Eph. 6:11 [m]Acts 14:22
5:10 [n]1 Cor. 1:9 [o]2 Cor. 4:17 [p]Heb. 13:21 [q]2 Thes. 2:17
5:11 [r]Rev. 1:6
5:12 [s]2 Cor. 1:19 [t]Heb. 13:22 [u]Acts 20:24
5:13 [v]Acts 12:12
5:14 [w]Rom. 16:16 [x]Eph. 6:23

[v] Or, *overruling*

5:5 BE CLOTHED WITH HUMILITY. Humility must be the mark of all God's people. It means an absence of pride in oneself, a consciousness of one's weaknesses, and the disposition to ascribe to God and others the credit for what one is achieving or has accomplished (cf. Mat. 11:29; Phil. 2:3–4; Col. 3:12). The word "clothe" (Gk. *egkomboomai*) means to attach a piece of clothing to oneself. In N.T. times slaves used to fasten a white piece of cloth or apron over their clothing so that others would know that they were slaves. Peter exhorts us to tie the cloth of humility on ourselves in order (1) to be identified as believers in Christ as we act humbly toward others, and (2) to receive God's grace and help (vv. 5–7). Peter may have had in mind Jesus' action of tying on a towel and washing the disciples' feet (John 13:4–5).

5:7 HE CARETH FOR YOU. God's care for the afflictions of every one of His children is a truth emphasized throughout His Word (see Ps. 27:10; 37:5; 40:17; 55:22; Mat. 6:25–34; 10:29–31; 11:28–30; Phil. 4:6, note). All your fears, cares, and concerns must be decisively cast upon God (cf. Ps. 55:22; Luke 12:11–12; see article on THE PROVIDENCE OF GOD, p. 80).

5:8 YOUR ADVERSARY THE DEVIL. When man sinned, Satan became the ruler of the world (John 12:31; 14:30; 16:11). He dominates the whole world (1 John 5:19), patrols this earth, and is commander of a host of evil spirits through whom he enslaves and keeps captive those without Christ (Eph. 2:2; see article on POWER OVER SATAN AND DEMONS, p. 1486). Only the believer has been delivered from his power (see article on THE KINGDOM OF GOD, p. 1428). Yet, as a roaring lion, he remains a threat to believers (cf. Ps. 22:13; Ezek. 22:25) and seeks to destroy them, especially through experiences of suffering (vv. 8–10). He will spiritually destroy anyone who abandons the protection of God. Through our faith in the blood of Christ (Rev. 12:11), our spiritual warfare by the Spirit (Eph. 6:11–18) and our prayers to God (Mat. 6:13), we are fully equipped to defeat Satan's schemes (Eph. 6:11), to resist him, and to stand firm in the faith (v. 9). Greater is he who is in you, than he that is in the world (1 John 4:4).

2 PETER

Outline

Christian Greetings (1:1–2)

- I. The Commendation of True Knowledge (1:2b-21)
  - A. The Transforming Power of a True Knowledge of God (1:2b-4)
  - B. The Progressive Character of Christian Growth (1:5–11)
  - C. The Apostle's Attestation of the Word of Truth (1:12–21)
    - 1. His Motive (1:12–15)
    - 2. His Method (1:16–21)
      - a. Eyewitness of the Prophetic Word (1:16–19)
      - b. Inspiration of the Prophetic Scripture (1:20–21)
- II. The Condemnation of False Teachers (2:1–22)
  - A. What to Expect from False Teachers (2:1–3)
  - B. What They May Expect from God (2:4–10a)
  - C. Some Characteristics of False Teachers (2:10b-19)
  - D. The Perils of Relapse from the Truth (2:20–22)
- III. The Certainty of the Lord's Coming (3:1–18a)
  - A. Denial of His Coming (3:1–7)
  - B. Assurance of His Coming (3:8–10)
  - C. Living for His Coming (3:11–18a)

Benediction (3:18b)

Author: Peter

Theme: Faithful Truth vs. False Teachers

Date of Writing: c. A.D. 66–68

Background

In the salutation, Simon Peter identifies himself as author of this letter; he later remarks that this is his second epistle to the readers (3:1), indicating that he is writing the same believers in Asia Minor who had received his first epistle (1 Pet. 1:1). Since Peter, like Paul, was put to death by an edict of the wicked Nero (who himself died in June, A.D. 68), it is most likely that Peter wrote this epistle between A.D. 66–68, shortly before his martyrdom in Rome (1:13–15).

Some scholars in ancient and modern times, ignoring certain remarkable similarities between 1 and 2 Peter and stressing instead the differences between them, have assumed that Peter was not the author of this letter. However, the differences in content, vocabulary, emphases, and literary style between the two epistles can be accounted for adequately by the different circumstances of both Peter and his readers in the two letters. (1) The original circumstances of the recipients had changed from serious persecution inflicted by their surrounding society to serious assault from within by false teachers that threatened the churches' foundations of truth and righteousness. (2) Peter's circumstances were also different. Whereas he had the skilled assistance of Silas when writing his first epistle (1 Pet. 5:12), it appears that Silas was not available when writing this one. He may have used his own rough Galilean Greek or relied on a less capable scribe than Silas.

Purpose

Peter wrote (1) to exhort believers to diligently pursue godliness and a true knowledge of Christ, and (2) to expose and repudiate the insidious activity of false prophets and teachers among the churches in Asia Minor who were undermining apostolic truth. Peter summarizes his purpose in 3:17–18, where he exhorts true believers (1) to "beware lest" they be "led away with the error" of unprincipled men (3:17), and (2) to "grow in grace, and *in* the knowledge of our Lord and Saviour Jesus Christ" (3:18).

Survey

This short epistle earnestly instructs believers to take hold of life and godliness through a true knowledge of Christ. The first chapter emphasizes the importance of Christian growth. Having begun by faith, the believer must diligently pursue moral excellence, knowledge, self-control, perseverance, godliness, brotherly kindness, and selfless love, resulting in a mature faith and true knowledge of the Lord Jesus (1:3–11).

The next chapter solemnly warns about false prophets and teachers who are arising among the churches. Peter denounces them as unprincipled men (2:1,3; 3:17) who indulge the flesh and its lust (2:2,7,10,13–14,18–19), who are covetous (2:3,14–15), arrogant (2:18), and self-willed (2:10), and who despise authority (2:10–12). Peter seeks to protect true believers against their destructive heresies (2:1) by exposing their evil motives and conduct.

In ch. 3, Peter refutes the skepticism of these teachers about the Lord's coming (3:3–4). As Noah's generation mistakenly scoffed at the idea of the judgment of a great flood from God, these scoffers are equally blind concerning the promises of Christ's return. But with the same decisive action as the judgment of the flood (3:5–6), Christ will return and dissolve the present earth by fire (3:7–12) and create a righteous new order (3:13). In view of this, believers must live holy and godly lives in this present age (3:11,14).

Special Features

Four major features or emphases characterize this epistle. (1) It contains one of the strongest statements in the Bible about the inspiration, reliability, and authority of the Holy Scriptures (1:19–21). (2) 2 Pet. 2 and Jude's epistle are remarkably similar in their denunciation of false teachers. Perhaps Jude, facing at a later date the same problem of false teachers, utilized portions of Peter's inspired teaching to make the same point (see Introduction to Jude). (3) Ch. 3 is one of the great chapters in the N.T. on the second coming of Christ. (4) Peter indirectly refers to Paul's writings as Scripture by mentioning them in relation to "the other Scriptures" (3:15–16).

Reading 2 Peter

In order to read the entire New Testament in one year, the book of 2 Peter should be read in 3 days, according to the following schedule:
☐ 1 ☐ 2 ☐ 3

NOTES

1 SIMON[a] PETER, a servant and
an apostle of Jesus Christ, to them
that have obtained [a]like precious faith
with us through the righteousness [b]of
God and our Saviour Jesus Christ:
2 [b]Grace and peace be multiplied
unto you through the knowledge of
God, and of Jesus our Lord,

Making our calling and election sure

3 According as his divine power
hath given unto us all things that *per-
tain* unto life and godliness, through
the knowledge of him [c]that hath
called us [c]to glory and virtue:
4 [d]Whereby are given unto us ex-
ceeding great and precious promises:
that by these ye might be [e]partakers
of the divine nature, having escaped
the corruption that is in the world
through lust.
5 And beside this, [f]giving all dili-
gence, add to your faith virtue; and to
virtue [g]knowledge;
6 And to knowledge temperance;
and to temperance patience; and to pa-
tience godliness;
7 And to godliness brotherly kind-
ness; and [h]to brotherly kindness
charity.
8 For if these things be in you, and
abound, they make *you that ye shall* nei-
ther *be* [d]barren [i]nor unfruitful in the
knowledge of our Lord Jesus Christ.
9 But he that lacketh these things
[j]is blind, and cannot see afar off, and
hath forgotten that he was [k]purged
from his old sins.
10 Wherefore the rather, brethren,
give diligence [l]to make your calling
and election sure: for if ye do these
things, ye shall never fall:
11 For so an entrance shall be min-
istered unto you abundantly into the
everlasting kingdom of our Lord and
Saviour Jesus Christ. 1 John 2:3-6

The basis of true knowledge

12 Wherefore [m]I will not be negli-
gent to put you always in remembrance
of these things, [n]though ye know
them, and be established in the present
truth.
13 Yea, I think it meet, [o]as long as
I am in this tabernacle, to stir you up
by putting *you* in remembrance;
14 [p]Knowing that shortly I must
put off *this* my tabernacle, even as
[q]our Lord Jesus Christ hath
shown me.
15 Moreover I will endeavour that

1:1 [a]Eph. 4:5 **1:2** [b]Dan. 4:1 **1:3** [c]1 Thes. 2:12 **1:4** [d]2 Cor. 7:1 [e]2 Cor. 3:18 Heb. 12:10 **1:5** [f]ch. 3:18 [g]1 Pet. 3:7 **1:7** [h]Gal. 6:10 1 Thes. 3:12 **1:8** [i]John 15:2 Tit. 3:14 **1:9** [j]1 John 2:9 [k]Eph. 5:26 Heb. 9:14 **1:10** [l]1 John 3:19 **1:12** [m]Phil. 3:1 1 John 2:21 [n]1 Pet. 5:12 **1:13** [o]2 Cor. 5:1 **1:14** [p]2 Tim. 4:6 [q]John 21:18,19

[a] Or, *Simeon,* as in Acts 15:14 [b] Gk. *of our God and Saviour* [c] Or, *by* [d] Gk. *idle*

1:3 ALL THINGS THAT *PERTAIN* UNTO LIFE AND GODLINESS. The love of our heavenly Father, salvation through Jesus Christ, His intercession for us in heaven, the indwelling of and baptism in the Holy Spirit, the communion of the saints, and the inspired Word of God are all sufficient to meet the needs of believers as those things "that *pertain* unto life and godliness" (Mat. 11:28–30; Heb. 4:16; 7:25; 9:14).

(1) No additional human wisdom, technique, or theory is needed to complete the sufficiency of God's Word that reveals our perfect salvation in Christ. The words of Jesus, the N.T. apostolic faith, and the grace of God were adequate in the early days of the church to meet the needs of the lost, and they are just as adequate today. Absolutely nothing can offer more height, depth, strength, and help than what Jesus Himself proclaimed and provided and what the apostles testified to in Biblical revelation. Jesus Christ alone is "the way, the truth, and the life" (John 14:6).

(2) If the gospel we hold is found wanting in these days, it is because our gospel is something less than the gospel of Christ and the apostles.

1:4 PARTAKERS OF THE DIVINE NATURE. As believers we partake of the very nature of God. Our sharing in His nature is another description of the new birth by which we receive the life of God (see article on REGENERATION, p. 1597). We share God's nature in order to conform to God and His holiness (cf. 1 Cor. 6:19–20; Eph. 4:24).

1:5 ADD TO YOUR FAITH. Peter lists the virtues a Christian must develop in order to be spiritually victorious and fruitful before God (v. 8). The phrase "giving all diligence" demonstrates that believers must be actively involved in their Christian growth (cf. Phil. 2:12–13). Those who become Christians must immediately put forth every possible effort to add to their faith these seven qualities (vv. 5–8). Note that godly characteristics do not automatically grow without our diligent effort to cultivate them (see article on THE WORKS OF THE FLESH AND THE FRUIT OF THE SPIRIT, p. 1840).

1:10 MAKE YOUR CALLING AND ELECTION SURE. Our faith and salvation must not be taken for granted. We will continue faithful to the end only if we sincerely endeavor by God's grace to add to our faith the spiritual qualities listed in vv. 5–9 (see article on ELECTION AND PREDESTINATION, p. 1846).

1:11 ABUNDANTLY INTO THE ... KINGDOM. Some believers, because of negligence, will barely make it into the kingdom (1 Cor. 3:15), while others who remain steadfast in holiness will be welcomed richly with honor (Mat. 25:21; Acts 7:55–56; 2 Tim. 4:7–8,18).

ye may be able after my decease to have these things always in remembrance.

16 For we have not followed [r]cunningly devised fables, when we made known unto you the power and coming of our Lord Jesus Christ, but [s]were eyewitnesses of his majesty.

17 For he received from God the Father honour and glory, when there came such a voice to him from the excellent glory, [t]This is my beloved Son, in whom I am well pleased.

18 And this voice which came from heaven we heard, when we were with him in [u]the holy mount.

Prophecy of Scripture

19 We have also a more sure word of prophecy; whereunto ye do well that ye take heed, as unto [v]a light that shineth in a dark place, until the day dawn, and [w]the day star arise in your hearts:

20 Knowing this first, that [x]no prophecy of the scripture is of any private interpretation.

21 For [y]the prophecy came not [e]in old time by the will of man: [z]but holy men of God spake *as they were* moved by the Holy Ghost.

False teachers in the church

2 BUT [a]THERE were false prophets also among the people, even as [b]there shall be false teachers among you, who privily shall bring in damnable heresies, even [c]denying the Lord [d]that bought them, [e]and bring upon themselves swift destruction.

2 And many shall follow their [f]pernicious

1:16 [r]1 Cor. 1:17 [s]Mark 9:2 1 John 1:1
1:17 [t]Mat. 3:17 Luke 9:35
1:18 [u]Mat. 17:6
1:19 [v]Ps. 119:105 John 5:35 [w]Rev. 22:16
1:20 [x]Rom. 12:6
1:21 [y]2 Tim. 3:16 1 Pet. 1:11 [z]2 Sam. 23:2 Acts 1:16
2:1 [a]Deut. 13:1 [b]Mat. 24:11 1 John 4:1 [c]Jude 4 [d]1 Cor. 6:20 Heb. 10:29 Rev. 5:9 [e]Phil. 3:19

[e] Or, *at any time*

[f] Or, *lascivious ways,* as some copies read

1:19 A MORE SURE WORD OF PROPHECY. Peter contrasts humanistic ideas with God's Word (v. 16). He goes on to attest to the divine origin of Scripture and affirms that all prophecy originated from God, not from humans (cf. v. 21). This assures us that God's message is infallible (incapable of mistakes or errors) and inerrant (free from error, falsehood, or deceit). Infallibility and inerrancy cannot be separated, for the inerrancy of Scripture is the result of the infallibility of God's own Word. Scripture in its entirety is true and reliable in all its teaching (cf. 2 Sam. 23:2; Jer. 1:7–9; 1 Cor. 14:37; see article on THE INSPIRATION AND AUTHORITY OF SCRIPTURE, p. 1924).

1:20 NO PROPHECY OF THE SCRIPTURE. This probably means that no prophecy in Scripture came about by the writer's own interpretation, ideas, or reasoning, but it came from the Holy Spirit.

1:21 MEN OF GOD SPAKE ... MOVED BY THE HOLY GHOST. Peter affirms the divine origin and authority of prophecy in Scripture (see article on THE PROPHET IN THE OLD TESTAMENT, p. 1002). All believers must likewise maintain a strong uncompromising view of the Holy Scriptures as inspired and authoritative. There are several reasons for this. (1) It is the only way to be faithful to what Jesus Christ, the apostles, and the Bible itself teach about Scripture (see Ps. 119; John 5:47, note; see article on THE INSPIRATION AND AUTHORITY OF SCRIPTURE, p. 1924).

(2) Without a strong view of holy Scripture, the church has no true and sure foundation for its faith, no certainty of salvation, no moral absolutes, no message to preach without doubt, no sure expectancy for the baptism in the Holy Spirit and the working of miracles, and no hope for the imminent return of Jesus Christ.

(3) Without a strong view of holy Scripture, Bible-believing Christians have no absolute and objective truth based on the authority of God Himself by which to judge and reject the ever-changing values of this world, human philosophies, and the ungodly practices of their culture (Ps. 119:160).

(4) Without a strong view of holy Scripture, the Christian will not be ready to withstand the extreme difficulties of the last days to come (see 1 Thes. 2:1–12; 1 Tim. 4:1, note; 2 Tim. 3:1, note).

(5) Without a strong view of holy Scripture, the full authority and teaching of the Bible are weakened; the Bible will subsequently be replaced by human subjective religious experience or by independent and critical reasoning (2:1–3).

2:1 THERE SHALL BE FALSE TEACHERS AMONG YOU. The Holy Spirit repeatedly warns in Scripture that there will be many false teachers within the churches. The warnings concerning teachers and leaders who introduce destructive heresies among God's people began with Jesus (see Mat. 24:11, note; 24:24–25) and were continued by the Holy Spirit through Paul (see 2 Thes. 2:7, note; 1 Tim. 4:1, note; 2 Tim. 3:1–5), Peter (vv. 1–22), John (1 John 2:18; 4:1; 2 John 7–11); Jude (Jude 3–4,12,18), and Christ's letters to the seven churches (see Rev. 2:2,6, notes; see article on FALSE TEACHERS, p. 1508).

2:1 DENYING THE LORD THAT BOUGHT THEM. According to Peter, the false teachers within the church who were "denying [Gk. *arneomai*, meaning to disown or renounce] the Lord that bought them" had forsaken the right way, gone astray (v. 15), and become "wells without water" (v. 17). At one time they had escaped the wickedness of the world through Jesus Christ, but now were again entangled in sin (v. 20).

2:2 WAY OF TRUTH EVIL SPOKEN OF. Many professed believers will follow these false preachers and their "pernicious" (i.e., sexually immoral) ways. Because of the sinful lifestyles of the leaders and their followers, God and His gospel will be put to shame (see 2 Tim. 4:3–4, note).

nicious ways; by reason of whom the
way of truth shall be evil spoken of.
3 And [f]through covetousness
shall they with feigned words [g]make
merchandise of you: [h]whose judgment
now of a long time lingereth not, and
their damnation slumbereth not.

The destruction of false teachers

4 For if God spared not [i]the angels
[j]that sinned, but [k]cast *them* down to
hell, and delivered *them* into chains of
darkness, to be reserved unto judg-
ment;
5 And spared not the old world, but
saved [l]Noah the eighth *person,* [m]a
preacher of righteousness, [n]bringing
in the flood upon the world of the un-
godly;
6 And [o]turning the cities of Sodom
and Gomorrha into ashes condemned
them with an overthrow, [p]making *them*
an example unto those that after
should live ungodly;
7 And [q]delivered just Lot, vexed
with the filthy conversation of the
wicked:
8 (For that righteous man dwelling
among them, [r]in seeing and hearing,
vexed *his* righteous soul from day to
day with *their* unlawful deeds;)
9 [s]The Lord knoweth how to deliv-
er the godly out of temptations, and to

2:3 [f]Rom. 16:18 Tit. 1:11 [g]2 Cor. 2:17 [h]Deut. 32:35 Jude 4,15
2:4 [i]Job 4:18 Jude 6 [j]John 8:44 [k]Luke 8:31 Rev. 20:2
2:5 [l]Gen. 7:1 Heb. 11:7 1 Pet. 3:20 [m]1 Pet. 3:19 [n]ch. 3:6
2:6 [o]Gen. 19:24 Deut. 29:23 [p]Num. 26:10
2:7 [q]Gen. 19:16
2:8 [r]Ps. 119:139 Ezek. 9:4
2:9 [s]Ps. 34:17 1 Cor. 10:13
2:10 [t]Jude 4,7,8 [u]Jude 8
2:11 [v]Jude 9
2:12 [w]Jude 10
2:13 [x]Phil. 3:19 [y]Rom. 13:13 [z]Jude 12 [a]1 Cor. 11:20
2:14 [b]Jude 11

reserve the unjust unto the day of judg-
ment to be punished:
10 But chiefly [t]them that walk af-
ter the flesh in the lust of uncleanness,
and despise [g]government. [u]Pre-
sumptuous *are they,* self-willed, they
are not afraid to speak evil of dignities.
11 Whereas [v]angels, which are
greater in power and might, bring not
railing accusation [h]against them be-
fore the Lord.

The character of false teachers

12 But these, [w]as natural brute
beasts, made to be taken and de-
stroyed, speak evil of the things that
they understand not; and shall utterly
perish in their own corruption;
13 [x]And shall receive the reward
of unrighteousness, *as* they that count
it pleasure [y]to riot in the day time.
[z]Spots *they are* and blemishes, sport-
ing themselves with their own deceiv-
ings while [a]they feast with you;
14 Having eyes full of [i]adultery,
and that cannot cease from sin; beguil-
ing unstable souls: [b]an heart they
have exercised with covetous prac-
tices; cursed children:
15 Which have forsaken the right

[g] Or, *dominion* [h] Some read, *against themselves* [i] Gk. *an adulteress*

2:3 FEIGNED WORDS. The false teachers will commercialize the gospel, being experts in greed and in getting money from believers to enhance their ministries and affluent lifestyles. (1) Believers must be aware that one of the chief methods of false ministers is to use "feigned words," i.e., to tell impressive stories that are not true, or to give exaggerated statistics in order to inspire God's people to give money. They glorify themselves and enhance their ministries with these fabricated stories (cf. 2 Cor. 2:17). Thus, the unwary and sincere child of God becomes an object of exploitation. (2) Because these ministers defile God's truth and people with greed and deceit, they are assigned to doom and destruction.

2:4 ANGELS . . . CAST *THEM* DOWN TO HELL. This probably refers to the angels who rebelled with Satan against God (see Ezek. 28:12, note), becoming the wicked spirits spoken of in the N.T. Why some of the wicked spirits are in prison and some are free to work with Satan on earth is not explained in Scripture (cf. Jude 6; see article on POWER OVER SATAN AND DEMONS, p. 1486).

2:8 VEXED *HIS* RIGHTEOUS SOUL. An essential characteristic of a truly righteous man is that he loves righteousness and hates evil (see Heb. 1:9, note). His soul is distressed and tormented (vv. 7–8) by the sin, immorality, and ungodliness in the world (e.g., see Ezek. 9:4, note; John 2:13–17; Acts 17:16).

2:9 DELIVER THE GODLY. Lot's response to the evil and immorality around him (v. 8) became a test that determined both his own deliverance and his destiny in eternity. (1) God rescued Lot because he rejected evil and was repulsed in his soul at the "filthy conversation of the wicked" (v. 7; see previous note).

(2) When Christ returns to receive His people (see John 14:3, note) and to pour out His wrath upon the ungodly (3:10–12), He will gather together to Himself those in the visible church who, because of their faith in and love for Him, are, like Lot, tormented by the sensual conduct, filthy lives, and sin of their surrounding society (see article on THE RAPTURE, p. 1889).

(3) We can be sure that God knows how to deliver His faithful believers from immoral and corrupt people in every generation (cf. Mat. 6:13; 2 Tim. 4:18; Rev. 3:10).

2:10 DESPISE GOVERNMENT . . . DIGNITIES. Peter speaks of unrighteous and immoral people who, like the homosexuals of Sodom (v. 8; cf. Gen. 19:4–11), despise all manner of authority which restrains evil, including Christ and His Word.

way, and are gone astray, following the way of [c]Balaam *the son* of Bosor, who loved the wages of unrighteousness;

16 But was rebuked for his iniquity: the dumb ass speaking with man's voice forbad the madness of the prophet.

17 [d]These are wells without water, clouds that are carried with a tempest; to whom the mist of darkness is reserved for ever.

18 For when [e]they speak great swelling *words* of vanity, they allure through the lusts of the flesh, *through much* wantonness, those that [f]were [j]clean escaped from them who live in error.

19 While they promise them [g]liberty, they themselves are [h]the servants of corruption: for of whom a man is overcome, of the same is he brought in bondage.

20 For [i]if after they [j]have escaped the pollutions of the world [k]through the knowledge of the Lord and Saviour Jesus Christ, they are again entangled therein, and overcome, the latter end is worse with them than the beginning.

21 For [l]it had been better for them not to have known the way of righteousness, than, after they have known *it*, to turn from the holy commandment delivered unto them.

22 But it is happened unto them according to the true proverb, [m]The dog *is* turned to his own vomit again; and the sow that was washed to her wallowing in the mire.

The day of the Lord

3 THIS SECOND epistle, beloved, I now write unto you; in *both* which [n]I stir up your pure minds by way of remembrance:

2 That ye may be mindful of the words which were spoken before by the holy prophets, [o]and of the commandment of us the apostles of the Lord and Saviour:

3 Knowing this first, that there shall come in the last days scoffers, [p]walking after their own lusts,

4 And saying, [q]Where is the promise of his coming? for since the fathers fell asleep, all things continue as *they were* from the beginning of the creation.

5 For this they willingly are ignorant of, that [r]by the word of God the heavens were of old, and the earth [s]standing[k] out of the water and in the water:

6 [t]Whereby the world that then was, being overflowed with water, perished:

7 But [u]the heavens and the earth, which are now, by the same word are kept in store, reserved unto [v]fire against the day of judgment and perdition of ungodly men.

2:15 [c]Num. 22:5 Jude 11 **2:17** [d]Jude 12,13 **2:18** [e]Jude 16 [f]Acts 2:40 **2:19** [g]Gal. 5:13 [h]John 8:34 Rom. 6:16 **2:20** [i]Mat. 12:45 Luke 11:26 Heb. 6:4 [j]ver. 18 [k]ch. 1:2 **2:21** [l]Luke 12:47 **2:22** [m]Prov. 26:11

3:1 [n]ch. 1:13 **3:2** [o]Jude 17 **3:3** [p]ch. 2:10 **3:4** [q]Is. 5:19 Jer. 17:15 Ezek. 12:22 Mat. 24:48 Luke 12:45 **3:5** [r]Gen. 1:6,9 Ps. 33:6 Heb. 11:3 [s]Ps. 24:2 Col. 1:17 **3:6** [t]Gen. 7:11 **3:7** [u]ver. 10 [v]Mat. 25:41 2 Thes. 1:8

j Or, *for a little*, or, *a while*, as some read
k Gk. *consisting*

2:15 WAY OF BALAAM. This refers to a love for personal honor and material gain at the expense of God's people (cf. Num. 31:16; Rev. 2:14; see Num. 25:2, note). Peter emphasizes that sexual immorality, love of honor, and greed for money characterize false teachers and preachers.

2:16 SPEAKING WITH MAN'S VOICE. Peter clearly believes in the miracles recorded in the O.T. Today self-appointed critics within the church arrogantly scoff at the miracles recorded in God's Word and regard those who believe in them as being unenlightened or naive. The genuine child of God, however, believes in God and accepts all the miracles of the Bible. He also believes that God performs miracles today in response to the prayers and faith of His people (see John 6:2, note).

2:19 THEY PROMISE THEM LIBERTY. The spirit of lawlessness that promises freedom from godly restraint will be especially prevalent in society and in the church in the last days before the coming of Christ (see 1 Tim. 4:1, note; 2 Tim. 3:1, note). God's moral absolutes will be considered outdated and mere legalistic restraint to one's personal autonomy, self-fulfillment, and happiness. As people set themselves up as the ultimate authority, they become slaves to moral corruption (v. 19b; see Rom. 1:24,27, notes).

2:20 HAVE ESCAPED . . . AGAIN ENTANGLED. Vv. 20–22 obviously mean that some of the false teachers were once saved and redeemed from the power of sin, and then forfeited salvation (cf. vv. 1,15).

3:4 WHERE IS THE PROMISE OF HIS COMING? In the last days, the period between Christ's first and second coming, false teachers will deny that Christ will return to destroy the ungodly and the world (cf. Rev. 19:11–21).

3:7 RESERVED UNTO FIRE. Because sin has contaminated the earth and the universe, God has determined to completely destroy them by fire (vv. 7,10,12). This day will come as surely as the universal flood did in Noah's time. God's intervention to purify the earth by fire signifies that He will not allow sin to go unpunished forever.

Events connected with that day

8 But, beloved, be not ignorant of this one thing, that one day *is* with the Lord as a thousand years, and [w]a thousand years as one day.

9 [x]The Lord is not slack concerning his promise, as some men count slackness; but [y]is longsuffering to us-ward, [z]not willing that any should perish, but [a]that all should come to repentance.

10 But [b]the day of the Lord will come as a thief in the night; in the which [c]the heavens shall pass away with a great noise, and the elements shall melt with fervent heat, the earth also and the works that are therein shall be burned up.

11 *Seeing* then *that* all these things shall be dissolved, what manner *of persons* ought ye to be [d]in *all* holy conversation and godliness,

12 [e]Looking for and [1]hasting unto the coming of the day of God, wherein the heavens being on fire shall [f]be dissolved, and the elements shall [g]melt with fervent heat?

13 Nevertheless we, according to his promise, look for [h]new heavens and a new earth, wherein dwelleth righteousness.

Holy living until that day

14 Wherefore, beloved, seeing that ye look for such things, be diligent [i]that ye may be found of him in peace, without spot, and blameless. 1 John 3:2

15 And account *that* [j]the longsuffering of our Lord *is* salvation; even as our beloved brother Paul also according to the wisdom given unto him hath written unto you;

16 As also in all *his* epistles, [k]speaking in them of these things; in which are some things hard to be understood, which they that are unlearned and unstable wrest, as *they do* also the other scriptures, unto their own destruction.

17 Ye therefore, beloved, [l]seeing ye know *these things* before, [m]beware lest ye also, being led away with the error of the wicked, fall from your own stedfastness.

18 [n]But grow in grace, and *in* the knowledge of our Lord and Saviour Jesus Christ. [o]To him *be* glory both now and for ever. Amen.

3:8 [w]Ps. 90:4
3:9 [x]Hab. 2:3; Heb. 10:37 [y]Is. 30:18; 1 Pet. 3:20 [z]Ezek. 33:11 [a]Rom. 2:4; 1 Tim. 2:4
3:10 [b]Mat. 24:43; Luke 12:39; 1 Thes. 5:2 [c]Ps. 102:26; Is. 51:6; Mat. 24:35; Rom. 8:12
3:11 [d]1 Pet. 1:15
3:12 [e]1 Cor. 1:7; Tit. 2:13 [f]Ps. 50:3; Is. 34:4 [g]Mic. 1:4
3:13 [h]Is. 65:17 & 66:22; Rev. 21:1
3:14 [i]1 Cor. 1:8 & 15:58; Phil. 1:10; 1 Thes. 3:13
3:15 [j]Rom. 2:4; 1 Pet. 3:20
3:16 [k]Rom. 8:19; 1 Cor. 15:24; 1 Thes. 4:15
3:17 [l]Mark 13:23 [m]Eph. 4:14
3:18 [n]Eph. 4:15; 1 Pet. 2:2 [o]2 Tim. 4:18; Rev. 1:6

[1] Or, *hasting the coming*

3:8 ONE DAY . . . A THOUSAND YEARS. God views time from the perspective of eternity (cf. Ps. 90:4). "A thousand years" looks different to God than to humans. He can accomplish in one day what we might expect would take a thousand years, or He can take a thousand years to accomplish what we would like to see done in a day.

3:9 NOT WILLING THAT ANY SHOULD PERISH. The delay of Christ's return is related to the preaching of the gospel of the kingdom to the whole world (Mat. 24:14). God wants everyone to hear the gospel and does not desire anyone to perish eternally (1 Tim. 2:4; see Ezek. 33:11, note; Jonah 3:10, note). This truth does not mean that all will be saved, for if a person rejects God's grace and salvation, then he or she remains lost.

3:10 THE DAY OF THE LORD. The day of the Lord refers to the events that begin with Christ's return to catch up the faithful of His churches to meet Him in the air (see article on THE RAPTURE, p. 1889) and culminates with the destruction of the present heavens and earth and the creation of the new heaven and the new earth (Rev. 21—22; see Joel 1:14, note; Zeph. 1:7, note; 1 Thes. 5:2, note). The beginning of the day of the Lord is unknown and will be marked by an unexpected suddenness (see Mat. 24:42,44, notes).

3:11 HOLY CONVERSATION AND GODLINESS. Because God will soon destroy the world and judge the unrighteous, we must not become attached to this world's system or things within it. Our values, goals, and purposes in life must be centered around God and the hope of a new heaven and earth (v. 13; see articles on SPIRITUAL SEPARATION FOR BELIEVERS, p. 1814, and SANCTIFICATION, p. 1982).

3:12 HASTING UNTO THE COMING OF THE DAY OF GOD. Believers are able to hasten the coming of the day of God. That is, the church can help shorten the time before Christ's return by (1) committing themselves to evangelism and missionary work throughout the whole world (v. 9; Mat. 24:14), and (2) eagerly desiring His return by praying, "Come, Lord Jesus" (Rev. 22:20; cf. Mat. 6:10).

3:13 LOOK FOR NEW HEAVENS. See Heb. 11:10, note.

3:16 *HIS* EPISTLES . . . OTHER SCRIPTURES. Peter speaks of Paul's epistles as being on the same level as other Scripture, i.e., the O.T.

1 JOHN

Outline

Introduction (1:1–4)

I. Fellowship with God (1:5—2:28)
   A. The Principles of Fellowship with God (1:5—2:2)
      1. No "Darkness" in God (1:5)
      2. No Fellowship in the Darkness (1:6)
      3. Fellowship in the Light (1:7)
      4. Fellowship in the Cleansing of Sin (1:8—2:2)
   B. The Manifestations of Fellowship with God (2:3–28)
      1. Obedience (2:3–5)
      2. Christlikeness (2:6)
      3. Love (2:7–11)
      4. Separation from the World (2:12–17)
      5. Loyalty to the Truth (2:18–28)

II. Children of God (2:29—3:24)
   A. Characteristics of God's Children (2:29—3:18)
   B. Confidence of God's Children (3:19–24)

III. Spirit of Truth (4:1–6)
   A. Recognizing the Spirit of Error (4:1,3,5)
   B. Affirming the Spirit of Truth (4:2,4,6)

IV. Love of God (4:7—5:3)
   A. Divine Origin of Love (4:7–10)
   B. Proper Response to God's Love (4:11–13,19–21)
   C. Abiding in God's Love (4:14–16)
   D. Perfection of Love (4:17–18)
   E. Obedience of Love (5:1–3)

V. Assurances from God (5:4–20)
   A. About Overcoming the World (5:4–5)
   B. About the Trustworthiness of the Gospel (5:6–10)
   C. About Eternal Life in His Son (5:11–13)
   D. About Answers to Prayer (5:14–17)
   E. About Three Great Certainties (5:18–20)

Conclusion (5:21)

Author: John

Theme: Truth and Righteousness

Date of Writing: A.D. 85–95

Background

Five N.T. books are associated with the name John: a Gospel, three epistles, and Revelation. Although John does not identify himself by name in this epistle, second-century witnesses (e.g., Papias, Irenaeus, Tertullian, Clement of Alexandria) affirm that it was written by the apostle John, one of Jesus' original twelve disciples. Strong similarities in style,

vocabulary, and themes between 1 John and the Gospel of John substantiate the reliable testimony of ancient Christianity that both books were written by the apostle John (see Introduction to John's Gospel).

The recipients of this letter are undesignated. There are no greetings or mention of persons, places, or events in the letter. The most likely explanation for this uncommon format is that John wrote from his residence at Ephesus to a number of churches in the province of Asia over which he had apostolic responsibility (cf. Rev. 1:11). Since the congregations shared a common problem and similar needs, John wrote this as a circular epistle and dispatched it by a personal emissary along with his verbal greetings.

The foremost background issue in this epistle is the problem of false teaching about salvation in Christ and its operation in the believer. Certain people, formerly associated with the readers, had left the congregations (2:19), but the results of their false teaching were still distorting the gospel as to how they might "know" that they had eternal life. Doctrinally, their heresy denied that Jesus is the Christ (2:22; cf. 5:1) or that Christ came in the flesh (4:2–3); ethically, they taught that obeying the commandments of Christ (2:3–4; 5:3) and living a holy life separated from sin (3:7–12) and from the world (2:15–17) were not necessary for saving faith (cf. 1:6; 5:4–5).

Purpose

John's purpose in writing this epistle was twofold: (1) to expose and repudiate the doctrinal and ethical errors of the false teachers, and (2) to exhort his spiritual children to pursue a life of holy fellowship with God in truth and righteousness, in the full joy (1:4) and assurance (5:13) of eternal life, through an obedient faith in Jesus as the Son of God (4:15; 5:3–5,12), and by the abiding presence of the Holy Spirit (2:20; 4:4,13). Some believe that it was also intended as a letter accompanying the Gospel of John.

Survey

Belief and behavior are inseparably woven together in this letter. The false teachers, whom John calls "antichrists" (2:18–22), were departing from the apostolic teaching about Christ and righteous living. Similar to 2 Peter and Jude, 1 John vigorously repudiates and condemns the false teachers (e.g., 2:18–19,22–23,26; 4:1,3,5) with their destructive beliefs and behavior.

On the positive side, 1 John sets forth the characteristics of true fellowship with God (e.g., 1:3—2:2) and reveals five specific tests by which believers may "know" with confidence and assurance that they have eternal life: (1) the test of apostolic truth about Christ (1:1–3; 2:21–23; 4:2–3,15; 5:1,5,10,20); (2) the test of an obedient faith that keeps Christ's commandments (2:3–11; 5:3–4); (3) the test of holy living, i.e., turning from sin to fellowship with God (1:6–9; 2:3–6,15–17,29; 3:1–10; 5:2–3); (4) the test of love toward God and other believers (2:9–11; 3:10–11,14,16–18; 4:7–12,18–21); and (5) the test of the Spirit's witness (2:20,27; 4:13; 5:7–12). John concludes that a person may know with confidence that he has eternal life (5:13) when the fruit of these five areas is evident in his life.

Special Features

Five major features or emphases characterize this epistle. (1) It defines the Christian life by using contrasting terms and by seeming to allow no middle ground between light and darkness, truth and lies, righteousness and sin, love and hate, loving God and loving the world, children of God and children of the devil, etc. (2) Significantly, it is the only N.T. writing to speak of Jesus as our "advocate [Gk. *paraklētos*] with the Father" when we sin as sincere believers (2:1–2; cf. John 14:16–17,26; 15:26; 16:7–8). (3) Its message is grounded almost entirely in the apostolic witness rather than in prior O.T. revelation; references to O.T. Scripture are noticeably absent. (4) Since it presents Christology in connection with the refutation of a particular kind of heresy, it focuses on the incarnation and blood (i.e., the cross) of Jesus without making specific mention of His resurrection. (5) Its style is simple and repetitive as John discusses certain leading terms such as "light,"

"truth," "believe," "abide," "know," "love," "righteousness," "witness," "born of God," and "eternal life."

Reading 1 John

In order to read the entire New Testament in one year, the book of 1 John should be read in 5 days, according to the following schedule:
☐ 1:1—2:14 ☐ 2:15—3:10 ☐ 3:11–24 ☐ 4 ☐ 5

NOTES

The Word of life

1 THAT [a]WHICH was from the beginning, which we have heard, which we have seen with our eyes, [b]which we have looked upon, and [c]our hands have handled, of the Word of life;

2 (For [d]the life [e]was manifested, and we have seen *it,* [f]and bear witness, [g]and show unto you that eternal life, [h]which was with the Father, and was manifested unto us;)

3 That which we have seen and heard declare we unto you, that ye also may have fellowship with us: and truly [i]our fellowship *is* with the Father, and with his Son Jesus Christ.

4 And these things write we unto you, [j]that your joy may be full.

The test of fellowship

5 [k]This then is the message which we have heard of him, and declare unto you, that [l]God is light, and in him is no darkness at all.

6 [m]If we say that we have fellowship with him, and walk in darkness, we lie, and do not the truth:

7 But if we walk in the light, as he is in the light, we have fellowship one with another, and [n]the blood of Jesus Christ his Son cleanseth us from all sin.

8 [o]If we say that we have no sin, we deceive ourselves, [p]and the truth is not in us.

9 [q]If we confess our sins, he is faithful and just to forgive us *our* sins, and to [r]cleanse us from all unrighteousness.

10 If we say that we have not sinned, we make him a liar, and his word is not in us.

Jesus Christ our advocate

2 MY LITTLE children, these things write I unto you, that ye sin not. And if any man sin, [s]we have an advocate

1:1 [a]John 1:1 [b]John 1:14 2 Pet. 1:16 [c]Luke 24:39 John 20:27
1:2 [d]John 1:4 & 14:6 [e]Rom. 16:26 1 Tim. 3:16 [f]John 21:24 [g]ch. 5:20 [h]John 1:1
1:3 [i]John 17:21 1 Cor. 1:9
1:4 [j]John 16:24
1:5 [k]ch. 3:11 [l]John 1:9
1:6 [m]2 Cor. 6:14
1:7 [n]1 Cor. 6:11 Eph. 1:7 Heb. 9:14 1 Pet. 1:19 Rev. 1:5
1:8 [o]Job 9:2 Eccl. 7:20 Jas. 3:2 [p]ch. 2:4
1:9 [q]Ps. 32:5 [r]Ps. 51:2
2:1 [s]Heb. 7:25

1:2 ETERNAL LIFE. John defines eternal life in terms of Christ. It can be found only through faith in and fellowship with Jesus Christ (vv. 2,6–7; 2:22–25; 5:20).

1:3 FELLOWSHIP WITH US. "Fellowship" (Gk. *koinōnia*) literally means "having in common" and involves sharing and participation. Christians have fellowship because they have a common faith (Tit. 1:4; Jude 3), common grace of God in Christ (1 Cor. 1:9; Phil. 1:7), common indwelling of the Spirit (John 20:22; Rom. 8:9,11), common gifts of the Spirit (Rom. 15:27), and a common enemy (2:15–18; 1 Pet. 5:8). There can be no true fellowship with those who reject the teaching of N.T. faith (2 John 7–11; see Gal. 1:9, note).

1:6 FELLOWSHIP WITH HIM. To "walk in darkness" means to live in sin and immoral pleasure. Such people do not "have fellowship with him," i.e., they are not born of God (cf. 3:7–9; John 3:19; 2 Cor. 6:14). Those who have fellowship with God experience God's grace and live a life of holiness in the presence of God (v. 7; 2:4; 3:10).

1:7 WALK IN THE LIGHT. This means to believe the truth of God as revealed in His Word and to make a sincere and sustained effort by His grace to follow it in word and deed. "The blood of Jesus Christ his Son cleanseth us from all sin" refers to the ongoing work of sanctification within the believer and the continual cleansing through the blood of Christ for our inadvertent sins. John is probably not thinking here of deliberate sin against God, since he speaks of walking in the light. This continual cleansing allows us to have intimate fellowship with God (see article on SANCTIFICATION, p. 1982).

1:8 IF WE SAY THAT WE HAVE NO SIN. John uses the noun "sin" rather than a verb ("we do not sin") to emphasize sin as a principle in human nature. (1) John is probably arguing against those who affirm that sin does not exist as a principle or power in human nature, or those who say the evil actions they commit are not really sin. This heresy is with us today in those who deny the fact of sin and interpret evil in terms of deterministic, psychological, or social causes (see Rom. 6:1, note; 7:9–11, note). (2) Believers must be aware that the flesh or sinful nature is a constant threat in their lives and that they must ever be putting to death its evil deeds through the Holy Spirit who dwells within (Rom. 8:13; Gal. 5:16–25).

1:9 CONFESS OUR SINS. We must admit our sins and seek forgiveness and cleansing from God. The two results are (1) forgiveness by and reconciliation with God, and (2) the cleansing (i.e., removal) of guilt and the destruction of the power of sin in order to live lives of holiness (Ps. 32:1–5; Prov. 28:13; Jer. 31:34; Luke 15:18; Rom. 6:2–14).

1:10 WE HAVE NOT SINNED. If we claim that we have never sinned and therefore do not need the saving efficacy of Christ's death, we are making God a liar (cf. Rom. 3:23).

2:1 THAT YE SIN NOT. John believed that born-again Christians are still capable of some kinds of sin. However, he does not teach that the Christian *must* sin; instead he exhorts his readers to live without sin (cf. Rom. 6:15, note; 1 Thes. 2:10, note). For those who do fall into sin, the remedy is to confess and forsake that sin (see 1:9, note). The assurance of forgiveness lies in the blood of Jesus Christ (1:7; 2:2) and His heavenly ministry as "advocate." Advocate (Gk. *paraklētos*) in this context means that Jesus intercedes before God on our behalf on the basis of His atoning

cate with the Father, Jesus Christ the
righteous:
2 And [t]he is the propitiation for
our sins: and not for ours only, but
[u]also for *the sins of* the whole world.

The test of knowing Christ

3 And hereby we do know that we
know him, if we keep his command-
ments.
4 [v]He that saith, I know him, and
keepeth not his commandments, [w]is a
liar, and the truth is not in him.
5 But [x]whoso keepeth his word,
[y]in him verily is the love of God per-
fected: [z]hereby know we that we are
in him.
6 [a]He that saith he abideth in him
[b]ought himself also so to walk, even
as he walked.

1 John 3:9-18

Love one another

7 Brethren, [c]I write no new com-
mandment unto you, but an old com-
mandment [d]which ye had from the be-
ginning. The old commandment is the
word which ye have heard from the be-
ginning.
8 Again, [e]a new commandment I
write unto you, which thing is true in
him and in you: [f]because the dark-
ness is past, and [g]the true light now
shineth.
9 [h]He that saith he is in the light,
and hateth his brother, is in darkness
even until now.
10 [i]He that loveth his brother
abideth in the light, and [j]there is none
[a]occasion of stumbling in him.
11 But he that hateth his brother is
in darkness, and walketh in darkness,
and knoweth not whither he goeth, be-
cause that darkness hath blinded his
eyes.
12 I write unto you, little children,
because [k]your sins are forgiven you
for his name's sake.
13 I write unto you, fathers, be-
cause ye have known him [l]*that is* from
the beginning. I write unto you, young
men, because ye have overcome the
wicked one. I write unto you, little chil-
dren, because ye have known the Fa-
ther.
14 I have written unto you, fathers,
because ye have known him *that is*
from the beginning. I have written unto
you, young men, because [m]ye are
strong, and the word of God abideth in
you, and ye have overcome the wicked
one.

Love not the world

15 [n]Love not the world, neither the
things *that are* in the world. [o]If any
man love the world, the love of the Fa-
ther is not in him.
16 For all that *is* in the world, the
lust of the flesh, [p]and the lust of the
eyes, and the pride of life, is not of
the Father, but is of the world.
17 And [q]the world passeth away,
and the lust thereof: but he that doeth
the will of God abideth for ever.

1 John 5:4-5

The spirit of the antichrist

18 [r]Little children, [s]it is the last
time: and as ye have heard that [t]anti-

2:2 [t]Rom. 3:25; 2 Cor. 5:18 [u]John 1:29
2:4 [v]ch. 1:6 [w]ch. 1:8
2:5 [x]John 14:21,23 [y]ch. 4:12 [z]ch. 4:13
2:6 [a]John 15:4 [b]Mat. 11:29; 1 Pet. 2:21
2:7 [c]2 John 5 [d]2 John 5
2:8 [e]John 13:34 [f]Rom. 13:12 [g]John 1:9
2:9 [h]1 Cor. 13:2; 2 Pet. 1:9
2:10 [i]ch. 3:14 [j]2 Pet. 1:10
2:12 [k]Luke 24:47
2:13 [l]ch. 1:1
2:14 [m]Eph. 6:10
2:15 [n]Rom. 12:2 [o]Mat. 6:24
2:16 [p]Eccl. 5:11
2:17 [q]1 Cor. 7:31; 1 Pet. 1:24
2:18 [r]John 21:5 [s]Heb. 1:2 [t]2 Thes. 2:3

[a] Gk. *scandal*

death, our repentance of sin, and our faith in Him (cf. Rom. 8:34; Heb. 7:25, note; see also 1 John 3:15, note; see article on INTERCESSION, p. 1268).

2:2 PROPITIATION. "Propitiation" means that Jesus took on Himself the punishment for our sins and satisfied God's righteous judgment against sin. Forgiveness is now offered to everyone throughout the world and is received by those who turn to Christ in repentance and faith (4:9,14; John 1:29; 3:16; 5:24; see article on BIBLICAL WORDS FOR SALVATION, p. 1726).

2:4 KEEPETH NOT HIS COMMANDMENTS. John was contending against a misunderstanding of the doctrine of grace and salvation. He opposed antinomian teachers who taught that forsaking a sinful life was optional for the believer. (1) They declared that one can legitimately claim to "know" God in a saving relationship and at the same time be indifferent to the commandments and will of God and disobey them (see John 17:3, note). (2) Those who make such a claim, John states, are liars and do not have the truth of God in them. The attempt to be justified through faith in Christ without a commitment to follow Christ is doomed to failure.

2:10 LOVETH HIS BROTHER. See John 13:34–35, notes.

2:15–16 THE WORLD. See article on THE CHRISTIAN'S RELATIONSHIP TO THE WORLD, p. 2004.

2:18 MANY ANTICHRISTS. An antichrist or false Christ will come toward the end of the age to rule the world and to lead a great rebellion against Christ and the N.T. faith (see Rev. 13:1,8,18, notes; 19:20; 20:10; see article on THE AGE OF THE ANTICHRIST, p. 1896). Yet John says that "many antichrists" have already entered into the church. These are professed believers who love the world and its sinful pleasures and distort the gospel and its message of the cross, thus placing themselves against Christ and His righteousness.

christ shall come, [u]even now are there
many antichrists; whereby we know
[v]that it is the last time.
19 [w]They went out from us, but
they were not of us; for [x]if they had
been of us, they would *no doubt* have
continued with us: but *they went out*,
[y]that they might be made manifest
that they were not all of us.
20 But [z]ye have an unction [a]from
the Holy One, and [b]ye know all things.
21 I have not written unto you be-
cause ye know not the truth, but be-
cause ye know it, and that no lie is of
the truth.
22 [c]Who is a liar but he that de-
nieth that Jesus is the Christ? He is an-
tichrist, that denieth the Father and
the Son.
23 [d]Whosoever denieth the Son,
the same hath not the Father: *[but]*
[e]*he that acknowledgeth the Son hath the*
Father also.
24 Let that therefore abide in you,
[f]which ye have heard from the begin-
ning. If that which ye have heard from
the beginning shall remain in you, [g]ye
also shall continue in the Son, and in
the Father.
25 [h]And this is the promise that

2:18 [u]Mat. 24:5 2 John 7 [v]1 Tim. 4:1 2 Tim. 3:1
2:19 [w]Deut. 13:13 [x]Mat. 24:24 John 6:37 [y]1 Cor. 11:19
2:20 [z]2 Cor. 1:21 Heb. 1:9 [a]Acts 3:14 [b]John 16:13
2:22 [c]2 John 7
2:23 [d]John 15:23 2 John 9 [e]ch. 4:15
2:24 [f]2 John 6 [g]John 14:23
2:25 [h]John 17:3
2:26 [i]2 John 7
2:27 [j]ver. 20 [k]ver. 21 [l]John 14:26
2:28 [m]ch. 3:2 [n]ch. 4:17
2:29 [o]Acts 22:14 [p]ch. 3:7,10
3:1 [q]John 1:12 [r]John 16:3
3:2 [s]Is. 56:5 Rom. 8:15

he hath promised us, *even* eternal
life.
26 These *things* have I written unto
you [i]concerning them that seduce
you.
27 But [j]the anointing which ye
have received of him abideth in you,
and [k]ye need not that any man teach
you: but as the same anointing
[l]teacheth you of all things, and is
truth, and is no lie, and even as it hath
taught you, ye shall abide in [b]him.
28 And now, little children, abide in
him; that, [m]when he shall appear, we
may have confidence, [n]and not be
ashamed before him at his coming.
29 [o]If ye know that he is righteous,
[c]ye know that [p]every one that doeth
righteousness is born of him.

Children of God

3 BEHOLD, WHAT manner of love
the Father hath bestowed upon us,
that [q]we should be called the sons of
God: therefore the world knoweth us
not, [r]because it knew him not.
2 Beloved, [s]now are we the sons of

[b] Or, *it* [c] Or, *know ye*

2:19 THEY WENT OUT FROM US. When the antichrists departed from their fellowship with true believers, they were not in a saving relationship with Christ. This allows for two possibilities: (1) They were never true believers to begin with, or (2) they had once been in a saving relationship with Christ but afterward abandoned their faith in Christ (see article on PERSONAL APOSTASY, p. 1946).

2:20 AN UNCTION. The believer has received an anointing from Christ, namely, the Holy Spirit (cf. 2 Cor. 1:21–22). Through the Holy Spirit we know "all things," i.e., the truth (see v. 27, note).

2:24 HEARD FROM THE BEGINNING. A believer will abide in Christ and experience salvation only as long as he abides in the original teaching of Christ and the apostles (see Eph. 2:20, note). This suggests two things: (1) To abandon the original gospel of N.T. faith is spiritually fatal and separates one from Jesus Christ (cf. Gal. 1:6–8; 5:1–4). Believers must remain Biblical in their theology in the sense of always adhering to the teachings of the N.T. (2) It is perilous to run after new teachings or teachers who preach new things not found in the Christian faith (cf. Jude 3). For this reason, it is important to study and hold fast to the Word of God; our very souls and eternal destiny depend on it.

2:27 THE SAME ANOINTING TEACHETH. Every child of God is given the "anointing" (i.e., the Holy Spirit) to help lead him into truth (John 14:26; 16:13). As believers abide in Christ and read the Word of God, the Holy Spirit helps them understand its redemptive truths. (1) All believers may study and know God's truth and learn from each other through mutual teaching and exhorting (Mat. 28:20; Eph. 3:18; Col. 3:16). (2) Thus, believers have two safeguards against doctrinal error — Biblical revelation (cf. v. 24) and the Holy Spirit. (3) Believers do not need those who teach extrabiblical doctrine. This is the meaning of John's words, "ye need not that any man teach you."

3:1 THE SONS OF GOD. The truth that God is our heavenly Father and we are His children is one of the greatest revelations in the N.T. (1) Being a child of God is the highest privilege of our salvation (John 1:12; Gal. 4:7). (2) Being a child of God is the basis for our faith and trust in God (Mat. 6:25–34) and our hope of glory for the future. As children of God, we are heirs of God and co-heirs with Christ (Rom. 8:16–17; Gal. 4:7). (3) God wants us to be increasingly made aware through the Holy Spirit, the "Spirit of adoption" (Rom. 8:15), that we are His children. The Spirit produces the cry "Abba" (Father) in our hearts (see Gal. 4:6, note) and gives us the desire to be "led by the Spirit" (Rom. 8:14). (4) Being a child of God is the basis for our discipline by the Father (Heb. 12:6–7,11) and the reason we live to please God (v. 9; 4:17–19). God's ultimate goal in making us His children is to save us forever (John 3:16) and to conform us to the image of His Son (Rom. 8:29).

THE CHRISTIAN'S RELATIONSHIP TO THE WORLD

***1 John 2:15–16** "Love not the world, neither the things* that are *in the world. If any man love the world, the love of the Father is not in him. For all that* is *in the world, the lust of the flesh, and the lust of the eyes, and the pride of life, is not of the Father, but is of the world."*

The term "world" (Gk. *kosmos*) often refers to the vast system of this age which Satan promotes and which exists independent of God. It consists not only in the obviously evil, immoral, and sinful pleasures of the world, but also refers to a spirit of rebellion, resistance, or indifference to God and His revelation that exists within all human enterprises that are not under the Lordship of Christ. In this age Satan uses the world's ideas, morality, philosophies, psychology, desires, governments, culture, education, science, art, medicine, music, economic systems, entertainment, mass media, religions, sports, agriculture, etc., to oppose God, His people, His Word and His righteous standards (Mat. 16:26; 1 Cor. 2:12; 3:19; Tit. 2:12; 1 John 2:15–16). For example, Satan will use the medical profession to advocate and promote the killing of unborn babies, agriculture to produce life-destroying drugs such as alcohol and narcotics, education to promote ungodly and humanistic philosophy, and the entertainment media to destroy godly standards. Believers must be aware that behind all human enterprises there is a spirit, force, or power that moves against God and His Word, some to a lesser degree, some to a greater degree. Finally, the "world" also includes all man-made religious systems and all unbiblical, worldly, or lukewarm "Christian" organizations and churches.

(1) Satan (see Mat. 4:10, note on Satan) is the god of the present world system (see John 12:31, note; 14:30; 16:11; 2 Cor. 4:4; cf. 1 John 5:19). He controls it along with a host of subordinate evil spirits (Dan. 10:13; Luke 4:5–7; Eph. 6:12–13; see article on POWER OVER SATAN AND DEMONS, p. 1486).

(2) Satan has organized the world into political, cultural, economic, and religious systems that are hostile toward God and His people (John 7:7; 15:18; Jas. 4:4; 1 John 2:16,18) and that refuse to submit to His truth which exposes its wrongdoing (John 7:7).

(3) The world and the true church are two distinct groups of people. The world is under the dominion of Satan (see John 12:31, note); the church belongs exclusively to God (Eph. 5:23–24; Rev. 21:2; see article on THREE KINDS OF PEOPLE, p. 1772). Thus, believers must separate themselves from the world (see articles on SPIRITUAL SEPARATION FOR BELIEVERS, p. 1814, and SANCTIFICATION, p. 1982).

(4) In the world believers are strangers and pilgrims (Heb. 11:13; 1 Pet. 2:11). (a) They must come out of the world (John 15:19), not be conformed to the world (see Rom. 12:2, note), not love the world (1 John 2:15), overcome the world (1 John 5:4), hate the world (see Heb. 1:9, note), die to the world (Gal. 6:14), and be delivered from the world (Col. 1:13–14).

(b) Loving the world (cf. 1 John 2:15) defiles our fellowship with God and leads to spiritual destruction. It is impossible to love the world and the Father at the same time (Mat. 6:24; Luke 16:13; see Jas. 4:4, note). To love the world means being in intimate fellowship with and devotion to its values, interest, ways, and pleasures; it means taking pleasure in or enjoying what is offensive and opposed to God (see Luke 23:35, note). Note, of course, that the terms "world" and "earth" are not synonymous; God does not forbid a love for the created earth, i.e., nature, mountains, forests, etc.

(c) According to 1 John 2:16, three aspects of the sinful world create open hostility to God: (i) "The lust of the flesh": this includes impure desires, sinful pleasures, and sensual gratification (1 Cor. 6:18; Jas. 1:14; cf. Phil. 3:19). (ii) "The lust of the eyes": this refers to coveting or lusting for things which are attractive to the eye but forbidden by God, including the desire to watch that which gives sinful pleasure (Ex. 20:17; Rom. 7:7). In the present modern age this includes the desire to entertain oneself by viewing pornography, violence, ungodliness, and immorality in the theater, television, movies, or magazines (Gen. 3:6; Josh. 7:21; 2 Sam. 11:2; Mat. 5:28). (iii) "The pride of life": this means the spirit of arrogance, pride, and self-sufficient independence that does not recognize God as Lord or His Word as final authority. It is seeking to exalt, glorify, and promote oneself as the center of life (Jas. 4:16).

(5) Believers must have no close or intimate fellowship with those who participate in the world's evil system (see Mat. 9:11, note; 2 Cor. 6:14, note), must condemn openly their sin (John 7:7; Eph. 5:11, note), must be light and salt to them (Mat. 5:13–14), must love them (John 3:16), and must attempt to win them to Christ (Mark 16:15; Jude 22–23).

(6) From the world the true Christian will experience tribulation (John 16:2–3), hatred (John 15:19), persecution (Mat. 5:10–12), and suffering (Rom. 8:22–23; 1 Pet. 2:19–21). Using the lures of the world, Satan makes an unceasing effort to destroy the life of God in the Christian (2 Cor. 11:3; 1 Pet. 5:8).

(7) The world system is temporary and will be destroyed by God (Dan. 2:34–35,44; 2 Thes. 1:7–10; 1 Cor. 7:31; 2 Pet. 3:10, note; Rev. 18:2). Even now it is passing away (1 John 2:17).

God, and [t]it doth not yet appear what
we shall be: but we know that, when he
Jude 14-15 shall appear, [u]we shall be like him; for
[v]we shall see him as he is.
3 [w]And every man that hath this
hope in him purifieth himself, even as
he is pure.

Those who disobey, children of Satan

4 Whosoever committeth sin trans-
gresseth also the law: for [x]sin is the
transgression of the law.
5 And ye know [y]that he was mani-
fested [z]to take away our sins; and
[a]in him is no sin.
6 Whosoever abideth in him sinneth
not: [b]whosoever sinneth hath not
seen him, neither known him.
7 Little children, [c]let no man de-
ceive you: [d]he that doeth righteous-
ness is righteous, even as he is righ-
teous.
8 [e]He that committeth sin is of the
devil; for the devil sinneth from the be-
ginning. For this purpose the Son of
God was manifested, [f]that he might
Jude 9 destroy the works of the devil.

3:2 [t]Rom 8:18 2 Cor. 4:17 [u]Rom. 8:29 2 Pet. 1:4 [v]Ps. 16:11 Mat. 5:8
3:3 [w]ch. 4:17
3:4 [x]Rom. 4:15
3:5 [y]ch. 1:2 [z]Is. 53:5,6 [a]2 Cor. 5:21 Heb. 4:15 1 Pet. 2:22
3:6 [b]ch. 2:4
3:7 [c]ch. 2:26 [d]Rom. 2:13
3:8 [e]Mat. 13:38 John 8:44 [f]Luke 10:18 John 16:11
3:9 [g]ch. 5:18 [h]1 Pet. 1:23
3:10 [i]ch. 2:29 [j]ch. 4:8
3:11 [k]ch. 1:5 [l]John 13:34 2 John 5
3:12 [m]Gen. 4:4,8 Heb. 11:4

Those who practice righteousness, children of God

9 [g]Whosoever is born of God doth
not commit sin; for [h]his seed re-
maineth in him: and he cannot sin, be-
cause he is born of God.
10 In this the children of God are
manifest, and the children of the devil:
[i]whosoever doeth not righteousness
is not of God, [j]neither he that loveth
not his brother.
11 For [k]this is the [d]message that
ye heard from the beginning, [l]that we
should love one another.
12 Not as [m]Cain, *who* was of that
wicked one, and slew his brother. And
wherefore slew he him? Because his
own works were evil, and his brother's
righteous.

Salvation and the test of love

13 Marvel not, my brethren, if [n]the
world hate you.
14 [o]We know that we have passed

3:13 [n]John 17:14 **3:14** [o]ch. 2:10

[d] Or, *commandment*

3:6 ABIDETH IN HIM. The terms "abideth in him" and "born of God" (v. 9) are equivalent expressions. Only those who continue to abide in God continue to be born of God (see John 15:4, note; see article on REGENERATION, p. 1597).

3:6 HATH NOT SEEN . . . KNOWN HIM. The verbs "seen" and "known" are in the perfect tense (the Greek perfect tense refers to action that occurred in the past and its results continue to the present moment). Hence, John says that no one who sins (i.e., is living in sin) has seen and continues to see Him, nor has he known and continues to know Him. Thus, this can be applied either to those who have never had real faith in Christ or to apostates who knew God in the past but have not continued knowing Him to the present.

3:9 DOTH NOT COMMIT SIN. This means that no one who is born of God "continues to sin," "practices sin," or "keeps on sinning." "Sin" (Gk. *hamartanō*) is a present active infinitive, implying continued action. John emphasizes that one truly born of God cannot make sin his way of life because the life of God cannot exist in one who practices sin (cf. 1:5–7; 2:3–11,15–17,24–29; 3:6–24; 4:7–8,20).

(1) The new birth produces spiritual life resulting in an ever-present relationship with God. In this epistle, every time John speaks of the new birth of the believer, he uses the Greek perfect tense to emphasize the continued and sustained relationship which the new birth began (2:29; 3:9; 4:7; 5:1,4,18; see article on REGENERATION, p. 1597).

(2) For one to have God's life in him (i.e., born of God) and to go on sinning is a spiritual impossibility. A believer may occasionally lapse from God's high standard, but he will not continue in sin (vv. 6,10).

(3) That which keeps the faithful from sinning is God's "seed" in him. The "seed" is God's very life, Spirit, and nature dwelling within the believer (5:11–12; John 15:4; 2 Pet. 1:4).

(4) By faith (5:4), the indwelling Christ, the power of the Holy Spirit, and the written Word (see 1 Thes. 2:10, note), all believers can live moment by moment free from offense and sin against God.

3:10 CHILDREN OF GOD . . . CHILDREN OF THE DEVIL. This is the heart and conclusion of John's teaching in 2:28—3:10. He has warned the reader not to be deceived about the nature of salvation (v. 7). Consequently, the believer must reject any theology or teaching which alleges that one can be out of fellowship with God (1:3), continue to sin, do the works of the devil (v. 8), love the world (2:15), do harm to others (vv. 14–18), and yet be a child of God who is saved and destined for heaven.

Contrary to this false teaching, John clearly believed that anyone who continues in sin (see v. 9, note) "is of the devil" (v. 8) and "is not of God" (v. 10). If the one who habitually practices sin claims to possess eternal life and be God's child, he is deceived and "is a liar" (2:4). Furthermore, what characterizes a true child of God is a love for God manifested in keeping His commandments (5:2) and showing genuine concern for the spiritual and physical needs of other believers (vv. 16–17).

from death unto life, because we love
the brethren. [p]He that loveth not *his*
brother abideth in death.
15 [q]Whosoever hateth his brother
is a murderer: and ye know that [r]no
murderer hath eternal life abiding in
him.
16 [s]Hereby perceive we the love *of*
God, because he laid down his life for
us: and we ought to lay down *our* lives
for the brethren.
17 But [t]whoso hath this world's
good, and seeth his brother have need,
and shutteth up his bowels *of compas-*
sion from him, [u]how dwelleth the love
of God in him?
18 My little children, [v]let us not
love in word, neither in tongue; but in
4 deed and in truth.
19 And hereby we know [w]that we
are of the truth, and shall [e]assure our
hearts before him.
20 [x]For if our heart condemn us,
God is greater than our heart, and
knoweth all things.

3:14 [p]ch. 2:9,11
3:15 [q]Mat. 5:21 [r]Gal. 5:21
3:16 [s]John 3:16
3:17 [t]Deut. 15:7 Luke 3:11 [u]ch. 4:20
3:18 [v]Ezek. 33:31 Rom. 12:9 Eph. 4:15
3:19 [w]John 18:37
3:20 [x]1 Cor. 4:4
3:21 [y]Job 22:26 [z]Heb. 10:22
3:22 [a]Ps. 34:15 Prov. 15:29 Jer. 29:12 Mat. 7:8 [b]John 8:29
3:23 [c]John 6:29 [d]Mat. 22:39 John 13:34 Eph. 5:2 [e]ch. 2:8,10
3:24 [f]John 14:23 [g]John 17:21 [h]Rom. 8:9

21 [y]Beloved, if our heart condemn
us not, [z]*then* have we confidence to-
ward God.
22 And [a]whatsoever we ask, we re-
ceive of him, because we keep his com-
mandments, [b]and do those things that
are pleasing in his sight.
23 [c]And this is his commandment,
That we should believe on the name of
his Son Jesus Christ, [d]and love one
another, [e]as he gave us command-
ment.
24 And [f]he that keepeth his com-
mandments [g]dwelleth in him, and he
in him. And [h]hereby we know that he
abideth in us, by the Spirit which
he hath given us.

Test the spirits

4 BELOVED, [i]BELIEVE not every
spirit, but [j]try the spirits whether

4:1 [i]Jer. 29:8; Mat. 24:4 [j]1 Cor. 14:29; 1 Thes. 5:21; Rev. 2:2

[e] Gk. *persuade*

3:15 NO MURDERER HATH ETERNAL LIFE. The Bible generally distinguishes between different kinds of sins: unintentional sins (Lev. 4:2,13,22; 5:4–6; see 4:2, note; Num. 15:31, note), less serious sins (Mat. 5:19), deliberate sins (cf. 1 John 5:16–17), and sins bringing spiritual death (5:16). John emphasizes that there are certain sins that a true born-again believer will not commit because of the eternal life of Christ abiding in him (cf. 2:11,15–16; 3:6–10,14–15; 4:20; 5:2; 2 John 9). These sins, because of their gravity and their origin in the very center of one's spirit, indicate an intense rebellion against God, a severing from Christ, a falling from grace, and a separation from the vital life of salvation (Gal. 5:4).

(1) Examples of sins in Scripture which give conclusive evidence that one is yet in the bondage of iniquity or has fallen from grace and eternal life are apostasy (2:19; 4:6; Heb. 10:26–31), murder (v. 15; 2:11), sexual impurity or immorality (Rom. 1:21–27; 1 Cor. 5; Eph. 5:5; Rev. 21:8), abandonment of one's family (1 Tim. 5:8), leading others into sin (Mat. 18:6–10), and cruelty (Mat. 24:48–51). These abominable sins manifest utter rejection of honor toward God and loving care for others (cf. 2:9–10; 3:6–10; 1 Cor. 6:9–11; Gal. 5:19–21; 1 Thes. 4:5; 2 Tim. 3:1–5; Heb. 3:7–19). Hence, anyone who says, "I have fellowship with Jesus Christ, am indwelt by the Spirit, and am in a saving relationship with Him," yet partakes in the above-mentioned sins, is deceiving himself and "is a liar, and the truth is not in him" (2:4; cf. 1:6; 3:7–8).

(2) Believers must keep in mind, however, that all sins, even the less serious ones, can lead to a weakening of spiritual life, to a rejection of the Holy Spirit's leading, and thus, to spiritual death (Rom. 6:15–23; 8:5–13).

3:17 HIS BROTHER HAVE NEED. Love is expressed by sincerely helping persons in need, i.e., by sharing our earthly possessions with them (cf. Jas. 2:14–17). To refuse to give of our food, clothing, or money to help others in real need is to close our hearts to them (cf. Deut. 15:7–11). This also includes giving our money to help spread the gospel to those who have not heard (4:9–10).

3:22 BECAUSE WE KEEP HIS COMMANDMENTS. Why are some prayers answered and others are not? John declares that an effective prayer life is related to our devotion to God. Obeying God's commandments, loving Him, and pleasing Him (John 8:29; 2 Cor. 5:9; Eph. 5:10; Heb. 13:21) are indispensable conditions in order to receive what we ask for in prayer (see Ps. 50:14–15; Prov. 15:29; Is. 59:1–2; Mat. 6:15; Mark 11:25; Jas. 5:16; see article on EFFECTIVE PRAYING, p. 540).

4:1 TRY THE SPIRITS. The reason for testing every spirit (i.e., a person moved or inspired by a spirit) is that "many false prophets" will enter the church (see article on FALSE TEACHERS, p. 1508). This will be especially true as tolerance for unbiblical doctrine increases toward the end of the age (see Mat. 24:11, note; 1 Tim. 4:1, note; 2 Tim. 4:3–4, note; 2 Pet. 2:1–2). Christians are commanded to test all professed Christian teachers, writers, preachers, and prophets, in fact, any individual who claims his work or message comes from the Holy Spirit. Believers may never assume that a ministry or spiritual experience is of God merely because one claims it is. Furthermore, no teaching or doctrine may be accepted as true solely on the basis of success, miracles, or apparent anointing (Mat. 7:22; 1 Cor. 14:29;

they are of God: because [k]many false
prophets are gone out into the world.
2 Hereby know ye the Spirit of God:
[l]Every spirit that confesseth that
Jesus Christ is come in the flesh is of
God:
3 And [m]every spirit that confesseth
not that Jesus Christ is come in the
flesh is not of God: and this is that *spir-
it* of antichrist, whereof ye have heard
that it should come; and [n]even now
already is it in the world.
4 [o]Ye are of God, little children,
and have overcome them: because
greater is he that is in you, than [p]he
that is in the world.
5 [q]They are of the world: therefore
speak they of the world, and [r]the
world heareth them.
6 We are of God: [s]he that knoweth
God heareth us; he that is not of God
heareth not us. Hereby know we [t]the
spirit of truth, and the spirit of error.

The source of love

7 [u]Beloved, let us love one anoth-
er: for love is of God; and every one
that loveth is born of God, and knoweth
God.
8 He that loveth not [v]knoweth not
God; for [w]God is love.
9 [x]In this was manifested the love
of God toward us, because that God
sent his only begotten Son into the
world, [y]that we might live through
him.
10 Herein is love, [z]not that we
loved God, but that he loved us, and
sent his Son [a]*to be* the propitiation for
our sins.
11 Beloved, [b]if God so loved us, we
ought also to love one another.
12 [c]No man hath seen God at any
time. If we love one another, God
dwelleth in us, and [d]his love is per-
fected in us.
13 [e]Hereby know we that we dwell
in him, and he in us, because he hath
given us of his Spirit.
14 And [f]we have seen and do testi-
fy that [g]the Father sent the Son *to be*
the Saviour of the world.
15 [h]Whosoever shall confess that
Jesus is the Son of God, God dwelleth
in him, and he in God.
16 And we have known and believed
the love that God hath to us. [i]God is
love; and [j]he that dwelleth in love
dwelleth in God, and God in him.
17 Herein is [f]our love made per-

4:1 [k]Mat. 24:5 Acts 20:30 1 Tim. 4:1 2 Pet. 2:1
4:2 [l]1 Cor. 12:3
4:3 [m]2 John 7 [n]2 Thes. 2:7
4:4 [o]ch. 5:4 [p]John 12:31 Eph. 2:2
4:5 [q]John 3:31 [r]John 15:19
4:6 [s]John 8:47 [t]Is. 8:20
4:7 [u]ch. 3:10,11
4:8 [v]ch. 2:4 [w]ver. 16
4:9 [x]John 3:16 [y]ch. 5:11
4:10 [z]John 15:16 Rom. 5:8 Tit. 3:4 [a]ch. 2:2
4:11 [b]Mat. 18:33 ch. 3:16
4:12 [c]John 1:18 1 Tim. 6:16 [d]ch. 2:5
4:13 [e]John 14:20
4:14 [f]John 1:14 [g]John 3:17
4:15 [h]Rom. 10:9
4:16 [i]ver. 8 [j]ch. 3:24

[f] Gk. *love with us*

2 Thes. 2:8–10; 2 John 7; Rev. 13:4; 16:14; 19:20).

(1) All teaching must be tested against the revelation of God's truth in Scripture (see Gal. 1:9, note).

(2) It is the "spirit" of the teaching that must be tested. Does the teaching bear the same kind of spirit and emphasis as N.T. apostolic teaching? Beware of any teaching that a person claims to have received from the Holy Spirit or an angel that cannot be supported by sound Biblical exegesis.

(3) The teacher's life must be tested as to his relation to the ungodly world (see v. 5; see article on THE CHRISTIAN'S RELATIONSHIP TO THE WORLD, p. 2004) and to the Lordship of Christ (vv. 2,6; Rom. 10:9, note; see article on TESTING FOR GENUINE BAPTISM IN THE SPIRIT, p. 1682).

4:2 JESUS CHRIST IS COME IN THE FLESH. Theological liberalism and religious cults betray themselves as "antichrist" (v. 3) when they deny the full deity of Jesus Christ (see John 1:1, note), His virgin birth (see Mat. 1:23, note), or His redemptive death and resurrection for our salvation (vv. 9–10; 2:2; see article on BIBLICAL WORDS FOR SALVATION, p. 1726). Every departure from Biblical revelation concerning Christ opens itself up to demonic "spirits" of deception (v. 1) because it sets aside the authority and complete trustworthiness of God's Word (see 2 Pet. 1:3, note; see article on THE INSPIRATION AND AUTHORITY OF SCRIPTURE, p. 1924).

4:4 GREATER IS HE THAT IS IN YOU. Scripture emphasizes that the Holy Spirit dwells within the believer (1 Cor. 6:19). Through the Holy Spirit, we can overcome the evil in the world, including sin, Satan, trials, temptation, sorrow, persecution, and false teaching, and we can victoriously achieve God's will for our lives.

4:7 LET US LOVE ONE ANOTHER. Although love is an aspect of the Spirit's fruit (Gal. 5:22–23) and an evidence of the new birth (2:29; 3:9–10; 5:1), it is also something that we are responsible to develop. For this reason John exhorts us to love others, to be concerned about them, and to seek their welfare. John is not talking about a feeling of goodwill, but a decision and disposition to help people in their needs (3:16–18; cf. Luke 6:31). John admonishes us to demonstrate love for three reasons: (1) Love is the very nature of God (vv. 7–9), which He showed by giving His own Son for us (vv. 9–10). We share His nature because we are born of Him (v. 7). (2) Because God loved us, we who have experienced His love, forgiveness, and help are under obligation to help others, even at great personal cost. (3) If we love one another, God continues to dwell in us and His love is perfected in us (v. 12).

4:17 BOLDNESS IN THE DAY OF JUDGMENT. If we abide in Christ, have fellowship with

fect, that [k]we may have boldness in
the day of judgment: [l]because as he
is, so are we in this world.
18 There is no fear in love; but per-
fect love casteth out fear: because fear
hath torment. He that feareth [m]is not
made perfect in love.
19 We love him, because he first
loved us.
20 [n]If a man say, I love God, and
hateth his brother, he is a liar: for he
that loveth not his brother whom he
hath seen, how can he love God
[o]whom he hath not seen?
21 And [p]this commandment have
we from him, That he who loveth God
love his brother also.

Faith overcomes the world

5 WHOSOEVER [q]BELIEVETH that
[r]Jesus is the Christ is [s]born of
God: [t]and every one that loveth him
that begat loveth him also that is be-
gotten of him.
2 By this we know that we love the
children of God, when we love God, and
keep his commandments.
3 [u]For this is the love of God, that
we keep his commandments: and [v]his
commandments are not grievous.
4 For [w]whatsoever is born of God
overcometh the world: and this is the
victory that overcometh the world, *even*
our faith.
5 Who is he that overcometh the
world, but [x]he that believeth that
Jesus is the Son of God?

Life only in the Son

6 This is he that came [y]by water
and blood, *even* Jesus Christ; not by wa-
ter only, but by water and blood. [z]And
it is the Spirit that beareth witness, be-
cause the Spirit is truth.
7 For there are three that bear
record in heaven, the Father, [a]the
Word, and the Holy Ghost: [b]and these
three are one.
8 And there are three that bear wit-
ness in earth, the spirit, and the water,
and the blood: and these three agree in
one.
9 If we receive [c]the witness of
men, the witness of God is greater:
[d]for this is the witness of God which
he hath testified of his Son.
10 He that believeth on the Son of
God [e]hath the witness in himself: he
that believeth not God [f]hath made
him a liar; because he believeth not the
record that God gave of his Son.
11 [g]And this is the record, that
God hath given to us eternal life, and
[h]this life is in his Son.
12 [i]He that hath the Son hath life;
and he that hath not the Son of God
hath not life.

The certainties of faith

13 [j]These things have I written
unto you that believe on the name of

4:17 [k]Jas. 2:13 [l]ch. 3:3 **4:18** [m]ver. 12 **4:20** [n]ch. 2:4 [o]ver. 12 **4:21** [p]Mat. 22:37 John 13:34 **5:1** [q]John 1:12 [r]ch. 2:22,23 [s]John 1:13 [t]John 15:23 **5:3** [u]John 14:15 2 John 6 [v]Mic. 6:8 **5:4** [w]John 16:33 **5:5** [x]1 Cor. 15:57 **5:6** [y]John 19:34 [z]John 14:17 1 Tim. 3:16 **5:7** [a]John 1:1 Rev. 19:13 [b]John 10:30 **5:9** [c]John 8:17 [d]Mat. 3:16 **5:10** [e]Rom. 8:16 [f]John 3:33 **5:11** [g]ch. 2:25 [h]ch. 4:9 **5:12** [i]John 3:36 **5:13** [j]John 20:31

Rev. 2:7

Rev. 3:20

the Father (1:3), endeavor to keep His commandments (2:3), remain separate from the world (2:15–17), abide in the truth (2:24), and love others (vv. 7–12), then we can have confidence that we will not be condemned in the day of judgment (vv. 17–18; see article on ASSURANCE OF SALVATION, p. 2010).

5:1 BELIEVETH . . . LOVETH. Genuine faith will manifest gratitude to and love for the Father and Jesus Christ His Son. Faith and love are inseparable, for when we are born of God, the Holy Spirit pours forth the love of God into our hearts (Rom. 5:5).

5:2 BY THIS WE KNOW. Love for others is genuine Christian love only if it is accompanied by love for God and observance of His commandments (cf. 2:3; 3:23; John 15:10; see Mat. 22:37, note; John 14:21, note).

5:4 OVERCOMETH THE WORLD . . . OUR FAITH. The faith that overcomes the world is a faith that sees eternal realities, experiences the power of God, and loves Christ to such an extent that the sinful pleasures, secular values, ungodly ways, and selfish materialism of the world not only lose their attraction for us, but also are looked upon with disgust, aversion, and grief (see Rev. 2:7, note).

5:6 WATER AND BLOOD. This phrase probably refers to Jesus' baptism at the beginning of His ministry and to His death on the cross. John may have written this because some were teaching that the divine Christ did not experience death. He maintains that Jesus Christ died as the God-man and is thereby fully able to make atonement for our sins. The Spirit also bears witness to this truth (vv. 7–8).

5:12 HE THAT HATH THE SON HATH LIFE. All people should hear the gospel because eternal life is in God's Son and cannot be received or possessed in any other way. He is the only "way . . . and the life" (John 14:6). Eternal life is Christ's life in us. We have it as we maintain a vital faith relationship with Him (John 15:4; see John 17:3, note; Col. 3:4).

5:13 THAT YE MAY KNOW THAT YE HAVE ETERNAL LIFE. John declares his purpose in writing this epistle: to furnish God's people with the Biblical standard for assurance of salvation. For a discussion of this, see article on ASSURANCE OF SALVATION, p. 2010.

ASSURANCE OF SALVATION

***1 John 5:13** "These things have I written unto you that believe on the name of the Son of God; that ye may know that ye have eternal life, and that ye may believe on the name of the Son of God."*

Every Christian desires to have assurance of salvation, that is, the certainty that when Christ returns or death comes, he or she will go to be with the Lord Jesus in heaven (Phil. 1:23). John's purpose in writing his first epistle is that God's people may have that assurance (1 John 5:13). Note that nowhere in the letter does John state that a past experience of conversion constitutes an assurance or guarantee of salvation. To assume we possess eternal life based solely on a past experience or a faith that is no longer vital is a grave error. This epistle puts forth nine ways for us to know that we are in a saving relationship with Jesus Christ.

(1) We have assurance of eternal life if we believe "on the name of the Son of God" (1 John 5:13; cf. 4:15; 5:1,5). There is no eternal life or assurance of salvation without an earnest faith in Jesus Christ that confesses Him as God's Son, sent to be our Lord and Savior (see article on FAITH AND GRACE, p. 1738).

(2) We have assurance of eternal life if we are honoring Christ as Lord of our lives and are sincerely seeking to keep His commandments. "And hereby we do know that we know him, if we keep his commandments. He that saith, I know him, and keepeth not his commandments, is a liar, and the truth is not in him. But whoso keepeth his word, in him verily is the love of God perfected: hereby know we that we are in him" (1 John 2:3–5; cf. 3:24; 5:2; John 8:31,51; 14:21–24; 15:9–14; Heb. 5:9).

(3) We have assurance of eternal life if we love the Father and the Son rather than the world, and if we overcome the influence of the world. "Love not the world, neither the things *that are* in the world. If any man love the world, the love of the Father is not in him" (1 John 2:15; cf. 4:4–6; 5:4; see article on THE CHRISTIAN'S RELATIONSHIP TO THE WORLD, p. 2004).

(4) We have assurance of eternal life if we habitually and persistently practice righteousness rather than sin. "If ye know that he is righteous, ye know that every one that doeth righteousness is born of him" (1 John 2:29). On the other hand, "He that committeth sin is of the devil" (3:7–10; see 3:9, note).

(5) We have assurance of eternal life if we love the brethren. "We know that we have passed from death unto life, because we love the brethren . . . And hereby we know that we are of the truth, and shall assure our hearts before him" (1 John 3:14,19; cf. 2:9–11; 3:23; 4:8,11–12,16,20; 5:1; John 13:34–35).

(6) We have assurance of eternal life if we are conscious of the Holy Spirit dwelling within us. "And hereby we know that he [Jesus Christ] abideth in us, by the Spirit which he hath given us" (1 John 3:24; cf. 4:13).

(7) We have assurance of eternal life if we are endeavoring to follow the example of Jesus and live as He lived. "He that saith he abideth in him ought himself also so to walk, even as he walked" (1 John 2:6; cf. John 8:12; 13:15).

(8) We have assurance of eternal life if we believe, accept, and abide in the "Word of life," i.e., the living Christ (1 John 1:1), and in the original message of Christ and the apostles. "If that which ye have heard from the beginning shall remain in you, ye also shall continue in the Son, and in the Father" (2:24; cf. 1:1–5; 4:6).

(9) We have assurance of eternal life if we have an earnest longing and a certain hope for the return of Jesus Christ to receive us to Himself. "Beloved, now are we the sons of God, and it doth not yet appear what we shall be: but we know that, when he shall appear, we shall be like him; for we shall see him as he is. And every man that hath this hope in him purifieth himself, even as he is pure" (1 John 3:2–3; cf. John 14:1–3).

the Son of God; [k]that ye may know that ye have eternal life, and that ye may believe on the name of the Son of God.

14 And this is the confidence that we have [g]in him, that, [l]if we ask any thing according to his will, he heareth us:

15 And if we know that he hear us, whatsoever we ask, we know that we have the petitions that we desired of him.

16 If any man see his brother sin a sin *which is* not unto death, he shall ask, and [m]he shall give him life for them that sin not unto death. [n]There is a sin unto death: [o]I do not say that he shall pray for it.

17 [p]All unrighteousness is sin: and there is a sin not unto death.

18 We know that [q]whosoever is born of God sinneth not; but he that is begotten of God [r]keepeth himself, and that wicked one toucheth him not.

19 *And* we know that we are of God, and [s]the whole world lieth in wickedness.

5:13 [k]ch. 1:1,2
5:14 [l]ch. 3:22
5:16 [m]Job 42:8 Jas. 5:14 [n]Mat. 12:31 Mark 3:29 Heb. 6:4,6 [o]Jer. 7:16 John 17:9
5:17 [p]ch. 3:4
5:18 [q]1 Pet. 1:23 [r]Jas. 1:27
5:19 [s]Gal. 1:4

[g] Or, *concerning him*

5:14 ASK . . . ACCORDING TO HIS WILL. In our prayers we must submit to God and pray that His will may be done in our lives (John 14:13). We know God's will in many instances because it is revealed in Scripture. At other times it becomes clear only as we earnestly seek His will. Once we know His will about any given issue, then we can ask in confidence and faith. When we do this, we know that He hears us and that His purposes for us will be accomplished (see 3:22, note; see article on EFFECTIVE PRAYING, p. 540).

5:16 HE SHALL ASK . . . GIVE HIM LIFE. John refers to a type of prayer according to God's will that we can have confidence that He will answer (cf. vv. 14–15), i.e., prayer for spiritually weak believers who need the prayers of God's people to minister life and grace to them. The conditions guiding such a prayer are the following: (1) The person needing prayer must be a "brother," i.e., a believer who has committed sin unintentionally, and whose sin did not involve deliberate rebellion against God's will (see next note). Thus, he has not committed sin to the point of spiritual death (cf. Rom. 8:13). The brother still has spiritual life, but he is weak spiritually; he is repentant and desires to be free from all that displeases God, yet needs help in conquering the power of Satan and sin.

(2) For such a person the church must pray that God will give him "life." "Life" here means a restoration of spiritual strength and the grace of God (see article on FAITH AND GRACE, p. 1738), which is being threatened by sin (cf. Rom. 8:6; 2 Cor. 3:6; 1 Pet. 3:7). God promises to answer that prayer.

(3) For a former believer who has committed a "sin unto death" (i.e., spiritual death), the church cannot pray with assurance that God will give more grace and life. This type of sin involves willful transgression which comes from a deliberate refusal to obey God (see article on THE WORKS OF THE FLESH AND THE FRUIT OF THE SPIRIT, p. 1840). Such persons, having died spiritually, can only be given life if they repent of sin and turn to God (see Rom. 8:13, note). We must pray that God will so direct the circumstances of their lives that they may have an adequate opportunity to accept once more the salvation of God in Christ.

5:17 SIN NOT UNTO DEATH. John distinguishes between two types of sins: (1) Less serious sins that occur unconsciously or inadvertently and do not immediately lead to spiritual death; and (2) sins so terrible that they indicate a purposeful rebellion against God and His Word, resulting from or leading to spiritual death and separation from the life of God (see 3:15, note; Num. 15:31, note; Rom. 8:13; Gal. 5:4, note).

5:19 WHOLE WORLD LIETH IN WICKEDNESS. We will never adequately understand the N.T. unless we recognize its underlying conviction that Satan is the god of this world. He is the evil one and his power controls the present evil age (cf. Luke 13:16; 2 Cor. 4:4; Gal. 1:4; Eph. 6:12; Heb. 2:14; see Mat. 4:10, note; see article on THE KINGDOM OF GOD, p. 1428).

(1) Scripture does not teach that God is now in direct control of the ungodly world, involving sinful people, evil, cruelty, injustice, and wickedness. In no way does God desire or cause all the suffering in the world, nor is everything that occurs the perfect will of God (see Mat. 23:37; Luke 13:34; 19:41–44; see article on THE WILL OF GOD, p. 1060). The Bible indicates that at the present time the world is not under God's dominion, but is in rebellion against His rule and is enslaved to Satan. Because of this condition Christ came to die (John 3:16) and to reconcile the world unto God (2 Cor. 5:18–19). We should never allege that "God is in control" in order to free ourselves from the responsibility of seriously battling sin, evil, or spiritual lukewarmness.

(2) However, there is a sense in which God *is* in control of the ungodly world. God is sovereign and thus all things happen under His permissive will and oversight, or at times through His direct involvement according to His purpose. Nevertheless, at this time in history God has limited His supreme power and rule over the world. Yet this self-limitation is only temporary, for at the time determined by His wisdom, He will destroy all evil and Satan (Rev. 19–20). Only then will "the kingdoms of this world . . . become *the kingdoms* of our Lord, and of his Christ; and he shall reign for ever and ever" (Rev. 11:15).

20 And we know that the Son of God
is come, and [t]hath given us an understanding,
[u]that we may know him
that is true, and we are in him that is
true, *even* in his Son Jesus Christ.
[v]This is the true God, [w]and eternal
life.
21 Little children, [x]keep yourselves
from idols. Amen.

5:20 [t]Luke 24:45 [u]John 17:3 [v]Is. 9:6 Acts 20:28 Tit. 2:13 [w]ver. 11,12 **5:21** [x]1 Cor. 10:14

2 JOHN

Outline

Christian Greetings (1–3)
- A. To the Elect Lady and Her Children (1)
- B. On Behalf of the Truth (2–3)

I. Commendation and Commandment (4–6)
- A. Past Loyalty to Truth Commended (4)
- B. Love and Obedience Commanded (5–6)

II. Counsel and Warning (7–11)
- A. Recognize False Teachers (7)
- B. Beware of Being Influenced by Them (8–9)
- C. Refuse Them the Use of Your Home (10–11)

Conclusion (12–13)

Author: John

Theme: Walking in Truth

Date of Writing: A.D. 85–95

Background

The author identifies himself as "the elder" (v. 1). This was probably a title of honor widely ascribed to the apostle John during the last two decades of the first century because of his advanced age and his venerated position of authority as the only surviving original apostle.

John addresses this letter to "the elect lady and her children" (v. 1). Some interpret "the elect lady" figuratively as a local church, "her children" as the members, and her "elect sister" (v. 13) as a sister congregation. Others interpret the addressee literally as a prominent Christian widow of John's acquaintance in one of the nearby church communities in Asia Minor over which he had spiritual authority. Her family (v. 1) and her sister's children (v. 13) are persons of prominence among the churches in that region. As with John's other epistles, 2 John was probably written from Ephesus in the late 80s or early 90s.

Purpose

John wrote this letter to caution "the elect lady" about extending hospitality, greetings, or support to traveling ministers (teachers, evangelists, and prophets) who departed from the apostolic truth and propagated false teaching, lest she help spread their error and share their guilt. It repudiates the same false teaching that is denounced in 1 John.

Survey

This epistle underscores a warning also found in 1 John about the danger of false teachers who deny the incarnation of Jesus Christ and depart from the apostolic message (vv. 7–8). John commends "the elect lady" and her children for "walking in truth" (v. 4). True love involves obeying Christ's commandments and loving the brethren (v. 6). Christian love must discern between truth and error and not provide an open door to false teachers (vv. 7–9). To cordially receive false teachers is to participate in their error (vv. 10–11). The letter is brief because John plans soon to visit the lady "face to face" (v. 12).

Special Features

Three major features or emphases characterize this epistle. (1) It is the shortest book in the N.T. (2) It is strikingly similar to 1 and 3 John in its message, vocabulary, and simple writing style. (3) It provides an important balance to the message of 3 John by advising caution concerning the support of ministers not belonging to one's own congregation. It urges careful discernment in the light of the teachings of Christ and the apostles before supporting such ministers.

Reading 2 John

In order to read the entire New Testament in one year, the book of 2 John should be read in 1 day: □ 2 John

NOTES

1 THE ELDER unto the elect lady
and her children, [a]whom I love in the
truth; and not I only, but also all they
that have known [b]the truth;
2 For the truth's sake, which
dwelleth in us, and shall be with us for
ever.
3 [c]Grace [a]be with you, mercy, *and*
peace, from God the Father, and from
the Lord Jesus Christ, the Son of the
Father, in truth and love.

Walk in love

4 I rejoiced greatly that I found of
thy children [d]walking in truth, as we
have received a commandment from
the Father.
5 And now I beseech thee, lady,
[e]not as though I wrote a new commandment
unto thee, but that which
we had from the beginning, [f]that we
love one another.
6 And [g]this is love, that we walk
after his commandments. This is the
commandment, That, as [h]ye have
heard from the beginning, ye should
walk in it.

Reject false brethren

7 For [i]many deceivers are entered
into the world, [j]who confess not that
Jesus Christ is come in the flesh.
[k]This is a deceiver and an antichrist.
8 [l]Look to yourselves, [m]that we
lose not those things which we have
[b]wrought, but that we receive a full
reward.
9 [n]Whosoever transgresseth, and
abideth not in the doctrine of Christ,
hath not God. He that abideth in the
doctrine of Christ, he hath both the Father
and the Son.
10 If there come any unto you, and
bring not this doctrine, receive him not

1:1 [a]3 John 1 [b]Col. 1:5 **1:3** [c]1 Tim. 1:2 **1:4** [d]3 John 3 **1:5** [e]1 John 3:11 [f]John 13:34 **1:6** [g]1 John 2:5 [h]1 John 2:24 **1:7** [i]1 John 4:1 [j]1 John 4:2 [k]1 John 2:22 **1:8** [l]Mark 13:9 [m]Gal. 3:4 **1:9** [n]1 John 2:23

[a] Gk. *shall be* [b] Or, *gained:* Some copies read, *which ye have gained, but that ye receive*

---

1 ELECT LADY. Some take this to mean John's letter was addressed to a lady named Electa and her family. However, the term "elect lady and her children" is most likely a figurative way of saying "the church and its members" (cf. 1 Pet. 5:13).

1 I LOVE IN THE TRUTH. John loves and cares for others in a way consistent with N.T. revelation about Christ. It is possible to show love toward others, yet not be committed to the truth of God's Word. Such persons place love, acceptance, friendship, and unity above the truth and commandments of God (vv. 5–6). On the other hand, it is also possible for a person in the church to promote Biblical truth and defend its doctrines, yet not show love and concern for others. What God requires is that we demonstrate both love for His truth and love for others. We must speak the truth in love (Eph. 4:15; cf. 1 Cor. 13:6).

3 GRACE . . . MERCY . . . PEACE. The conditions for receiving God's grace, mercy, and peace are to guard the truth (vv. 7–11) and to love the brethren (vv. 5–6). To fail to do either will cause the church to lose God's blessings.

5 LOVE ONE ANOTHER. See John 13:34–35, notes.

6 HIS COMMANDMENTS. See John 14:21, note.

7 MANY DECEIVERS. John warns that many deceivers and false teachers are perverting God's Word and attempting to persuade Christians to accept their views. Their false teaching concerns the person of Jesus Christ. They deny that Jesus Christ was the eternal Son of God, born of the virgin (Mat. 1:18; Luke 1:27), whose blood provides forgiveness for the sins of all who believe (1 John 2:2; 4:9–10) and who is "the true God, and eternal life" (1 John 5:20).

9 ABIDETH NOT IN THE DOCTRINE OF CHRIST. Those who reject the original revelation of Christ and the apostles do not have God. Although they may claim to know God (1 John 2:4), they are deceived if they do not abide in the teaching of Christ; those who forsake Christ's doctrine forsake Christ. All theology that does not hold to the truth and righteousness revealed in the N.T. is not Christian theology and must be rejected (see Eph. 2:20, note).

10 RECEIVE HIM NOT. The believer's love for and loyalty to Christ and the Word of God must lead him to reject and count as an enemy of the gospel of Christ any professed believer (minister or layman) who is not fully committed to the "doctrine of Christ" and the apostles (v. 9). All who distort and oppose the N.T. faith must not be received into the fellowship of believers. (1) God warns the true believer to watch lest he himself accept false teaching (v. 8). He must be aware that "many deceivers are entered into the world" (v. 7).

(2) The believer must consider all supposed Christian teachers who do not abide in the doctrine of Christ as teachers who do not have God (v. 9) and who are accursed of God (see Gal. 1:9, note).

(3) God commands the believer not to give encouragement or financial support to, or to remain under, the ministry of such teachers. To do so is to join them in opposing God and His Word and to come under the same condemnation as the compromising teachers (v. 11).

(4) These authoritative words of John, inspired by the Holy Spirit, are an offense to many in the church today. They feel John's admonition lacks a loving attitude or a spirit of unity. However, John's instruction will seem wrong only to those who have little concern for the glory of Christ, the authority of God's Word, and people whose eternal souls are destroyed by casting aside God's truth.

into *your* house, [o]neither bid him God
speed:
11 For he that biddeth him God
speed is partaker of his evil deeds.
12 [p]Having many things to write
unto you, I would not *write* with paper
and ink: but I trust to come unto you,
and speak [c]face to face, [q]that [d]our
joy may be full.
13 [r]The children of thy elect sister
greet thee. Amen.

1:10 [o]Rom. 16:17
1:12 [p]3 John 13
[q]John 17:13
1:13 [r]1 Pet. 5:13

[c] Gk. *mouth to mouth* [d] Or, *your*

3 JOHN

Outline

Christian Greetings (1)
- I. Commendation of Gaius (2–8)
  - A. For His Spiritual Health (2)
  - B. For His Walking in the Truth (3–4)
  - C. For His Hospitality to Traveling Brethren (5–8)
- II. Counsel to Gaius (9–12)
  - A. Concerning the Bad Example of Diotrephes (9–11)
  - B. Concerning the Good Example of Demetrius (12)

Conclusion (13–14)

Author: John

Theme: Acting Faithfully

Date of Writing: A.D. 85–95

Background

John, the beloved apostle, again identifies himself by the title of "the elder" (v. 1; see Introduction to 2 John). This personal letter is addressed to a loyal believer named Gaius (v. 1), probably in one of the church communities in Asia Minor. As with John's other epistles, 3 John was most likely written from Ephesus in the late 80s or early 90s.

Toward the end of the first century, itinerant ministers who traveled from city to city were commonly supported by believers who received them into their homes and helped them on their way (vv. 5–8; cf. 2 John 10). Gaius was one of many faithful Christians who graciously hosted and supported trustworthy traveling ministers (vv. 1–8). However, a leader named Diotrephes arrogantly resisted John's authority and refused to receive traveling brethren whom he had sent.

Purpose

John wrote to commend Gaius for his faithful hospitality and support of trustworthy traveling ministers, to indirectly warn the rebellious leader Diotrephes, and to prepare the way for his own personal visit.

Survey

Three men are mentioned by name in 3 John. (1) Gaius is warmly commended for his godly walk in truth (v. 3–4) and his exemplary hospitality to traveling brethren (vv. 5–8). (2) Diotrephes, a dictatorial leader, is denounced for his pride ("loveth to have preeminence," v. 9) and its manifestations: rejecting a former letter by John (v. 9), slandering John, refusing to receive John's messengers, and threatening to excommunicate those who do (v. 10). (3) Demetrius, perhaps the bearer of this letter or a pastor in a nearby community, is commended as a man of good reputation and loyalty to the truth (v. 12).

Special Features

Two major features or emphases characterize this epistle. (1) Though brief, it provides insight into several important facets of early church history toward the end of the first century. (2) There are remarkable similarities between 3 John and 2 John. Nevertheless, the two epistles differ in one important aspect: 3 John commends hospitality and support for trustworthy traveling ministers, while 2 John urges that hospitality and support not be given to untrustworthy ministers lest one be found promoting their error or evil deeds.

Reading 3 John

In order to read the entire New Testament in one year, the book of 3 John should be read in 1 day: ☐ 3 John

NOTES

The faithfulness of Gaius

1 THE ELDER unto the wellbeloved
Gaius, [a]whom I love [a]in the truth.
2 Beloved, I [b]wish above all things
that thou mayest prosper and be in
health, even as thy soul prospereth.
3 For I rejoiced greatly, when the
brethren came and testified of the
truth that is in thee, even as [b]thou
walkest in the truth.
4 I have no greater joy than to hear
that [c]my children walk in truth.
5 Beloved, thou doest faithfully
whatsoever thou doest to the brethren,
and to strangers;
6 Which have borne witness of thy
charity before the church: whom if
thou bring forward on their journey
[c]after a godly sort, thou shalt do well:
7 Because that for his name's sake
they went forth, [d]taking nothing of
the Gentiles.
8 We therefore ought to receive

1:1 [a]2 John 1
1:3 [b]2 John 4
1:4 [c]1 Cor. 4:15 Philem. 10
1:7 [d]1 Cor. 9:12,15

[a] Or, *truly* [b] Or, *pray* [c] Gk. *worthy of God*

2 THOU MAYEST PROSPER. It is normally God's will that believers be healthy and that our lives be accompanied by His blessings. He wants us to prosper, i.e., that our work, plans, purposes, ministry, families, etc., go according to God's will and direction. Thus, God's blessings that come to us through the redemption of Christ include both physical and spiritual needs.

Concerning prosperity, both physical and spiritual, Scripture teaches the following: (1) The word "prosper" (Gk. *euodoō*) literally means "to have a good journey." According to that meaning, John's primary prayer was that as believers walk the road of salvation, they may abide in God's will and His truth and enjoy His blessing (cf. vv. 3–4).

(2) It is God's will that we earn enough to provide shelter, food, and clothing for ourselves and our families, and have sufficient to help others and to further the cause of Christ (Phil. 4:15–19). We know that God is able to give us enough for our needs (2 Cor. 9:8–12) and that He promises to supply us according to His riches in glory (Phil. 4:19; see article on THE PROVIDENCE OF GOD, p. 80).

(3) Although we may pray that God will supply all our needs materially, we must recognize the Bible's teaching that there will be times when God allows a true child of His to experience want or lack. This can occur because of the following: (a) God may allow us to experience times of need in order to encourage us to trust Him more and to develop our faith, spiritual endurance, and ministry (Rom. 8:35–39; 2 Cor. 4:7–12; 6:4–10; 12:7–10; 1 Pet. 1:6–7). (b) We may experience poverty due to national or natural circumstances, such as war, famine, drought, or poor economic or social conditions (Acts 11:28–30; 2 Cor. 8:2, 12–14). (c) We may experience want and need due to persecution and oppression from the world because of our testimony and service to Christ (Luke 6:20–23; Heb. 10:32–34; 1 Pet. 2:19–21; Rev. 2:9–10; see article on THE SUFFERING OF THE RIGHTEOUS, p. 764).

(4) God's presence, help, and blessing in our physical lives is related to the prosperity of our spiritual lives. We must seek God's will (Mat. 6:10; 26:39; Heb. 10:7–9), obey the Holy Spirit (Rom. 8:14), remain separated from the world (Rom. 12:1–2; 2 Cor. 6:16–18), love God's Word (Jas. 1:21; 1 Pet. 2:2), seek His help in prayer (Mat. 6:9–13; Heb. 4:16), work hard (2 Thes. 3:6–12), trust Him to supply our needs (Mat. 6:25–34; 1 Pet. 5:7), and live by the principle of seeking first the kingdom of God and His righteousness (Mat. 6:33; see Mat. 6:11, note; Luke 11:3, note; Col. 4:12, note; see article on DIVINE HEALING, p. 1418).

(5) Although things may be going well with our souls, we will not automatically be exempt from difficulties in other areas of our lives. Adversity, troubles, and needs must be faced by prayer and trust in God.

5 THOU DOEST FAITHFULLY. John praises Gaius for one particular aspect of his walking in the truth (vv. 3–4), namely, that he had been faithful in helping traveling missionaries (vv. 5–8). He supplied them with lodging, food, money, and whatever other help they needed for their journey (cf. Tit. 3:13). His commitment to the missionary cause of Christ was so impressive that missionaries had specifically mentioned it to John (v. 6). Gaius's action toward these preachers of the gospel came from his love for them, for the gospel, and for those without Christ.

7 FOR HIS NAME'S SAKE THEY WENT FORTH. Vv. 5–8 refer to traveling messengers of the gospel of Christ. It is a duty and privilege of God's people to contribute to missionary needs and work. (1) Receiving, sending, and supporting missionaries must be done in a manner worthy of God (v. 6; 1 Cor. 9:14; Phil. 4:10–18). They must not be treated like beggars, but must be received as the Lord (Mat. 10:40) and as His servants carrying the gospel to all the world (see Mat. 28:19, note).

(2) The sending of missionaries in the early church consisted of providing for their journey and supplying them with food and money to pay expenses and live adequately (see Gal. 6:6–10, note; Phil. 4:16, note; Tit. 3:13). By supporting missionaries God's people became "fellow helpers" in spreading the truth (v. 8).

7 TAKING NOTHING OF THE GENTILES. Missionaries who leave their homes and go to other places to proclaim the name of the Lord Jesus Christ should refuse help from the unbelievers they are trying to win to Christ. To accept help from an unbeliever might hinder the gospel and expose the missionary to charges of preaching for financial gain (cf. 1 Cor. 9:12). Therefore, missionaries should receive help from individual believers

such, that we might be fellowhelpers to the truth.

The pride of Diotrephes

9 I wrote unto the church: but Diotrephes, who loveth to have the preeminence among them, receiveth us not.
10 Wherefore, if I come, I will remember his deeds which he doeth, prating against us with malicious words: and not content therewith, neither doth he himself receive the brethren, and forbiddeth them that would, and casteth *them* out of the church.

The good reputation of Demetrius

11 Beloved, [e]follow not that which is evil, but that which is good. [f]He that doeth good is of God: but he that doeth evil hath not seen God.
12 Demetrius [g]hath good report of all *men*, and of the truth itself: yea, and we *also* bear record; [h]and ye know that our record is true.
13 [i]I had many things to write, but I will not with ink and pen write unto thee:
14 But I trust I shall shortly see thee, and we shall speak [d]face to face. Peace *be* to thee. *Our* friends salute thee. Greet the friends by name.

1:11 [e]Ps. 37:27 Is. 1:16,17 1 Pet. 3:11 [f]1 John 2:29 & 3:6,9 **1:12** [g]1 Tim. 3:7 [h]John 21:24 **1:13** [i]2 John 12

[d] Gk. *mouth to mouth*

and from the church (Luke 10:7; 1 Cor. 9:14; 1 Tim. 5:18). In contributing to the missionary endeavor of our church, we must remember the words of Christ, "He that receiveth a prophet in the name of a prophet shall receive a prophet's reward; and he that receiveth a righteous man in the name of a righteous man shall receive a righteous man's reward" (see Mat. 10:41, note).

JUDE

Outline

Christian Greetings (1–2)

- I. An Explanation for Writing the Letter (3–4)
- II. Exposing the False Teachers (5–16)
  - A. Their Doom Illustrated from the Past (5–7)
    1. The Experience of Israel (5)
    2. The Experience of Unbelieving Rebellious Angels (6)
    3. The Experience of Sodom and Gomorrah (7)
  - B. Their Description in the Present (8–16)
    1. Reviling Speech (8–10)
    2. Unholy Character (11)
    3. Blameworthy Conduct (12–16)
- III. Exhorting the True Believers (17–23)
  - A. Remember the Predictions of the Apostles (17–19)
  - B. Keep Yourselves in God's Love (20–21)
  - C. Help Others in Mercy with Fear (22–23)

Doxology (24–25)

Author: Jude

Theme: Contending for the Faith

Date of Writing: A.D. 70–80

Background

Jude identifies himself simply as the "brother of James" (v. 1). The only brothers in the N.T. by the names of Jude (Judas) and James are the half-brothers of Jesus (Mat. 13:55; Mark 6:3). Perhaps Jude mentioned James because his brother's prominence as leader of the Jerusalem church would serve to clarify his own identity and authority.

This brief but hard-hitting epistle was written against false teachers who were blatantly antinomian (i.e., they taught that salvation by grace allowed them to sin without condemnation) and who were contemptuously denying the original apostolic revelation about the person and nature of Jesus Christ (v. 4). Thus they were dividing the churches on what to believe (vv. 19a,22) and how to behave (vv. 4,8,16). Jude describes these unprincipled men as "ungodly" (v. 15) and as "having not the Spirit" (v. 19).

The probable relationship between Jude and 2 Peter 2:1—3:4 has a bearing on when Jude was written. Most likely Jude was familiar with 2 Peter (vv. 17–18) and therefore wrote after Peter, i.e., sometime between A.D. 70–80. The recipients are not identified specifically but may have been the same as those addressed in 2 Peter (see Introduction to 2 Peter).

Purpose

Jude wrote this letter (1) to urgently warn believers about the serious threat of false teachers and their subversive influence within the churches, and (2) to forcefully challenge

all true believers to rise up and "earnestly contend for the faith which was once delivered unto the saints" (v. 3).

Survey

After his greetings (vv. 1–2), Jude reveals that his original intention was to write about the nature of salvation (v. 3a). However, he was constrained instead to write this letter because of the apostate teachers who were perverting the grace of God and in so doing were undermining truth and righteousness in the churches (v. 4). Jude indicts them as sexually impure (vv. 4,8,16,18), compromising like Cain (v. 11), covetous like Balaam (v. 11), rebellious like Korah (Core, v. 11), arrogant (vv. 8,16), deceptive (vv. 4a,12), sensual (v. 19), and divisive (v. 19). He declares the certainty of God's judgment on all who commit such sins and illustrates the same by six O.T. examples (vv. 5–11). A twelvefold description of their lives reveals their ripeness for God's wrath (vv. 12–16). Believers are exhorted to guard themselves and to have compassion mixed with fear for those who are wavering (vv. 20–23). Jude concludes with a crescendo of inspiration in his benediction (vv. 24–25).

Special Features

Four major features or emphases characterize this epistle. (1) It contains the most direct and vigorous denunciation of false teachers in the N.T. It underscores for all generations the seriousness of the threat which false teaching always poses to genuine faith and holy living. (2) It demonstrates a fondness for illustrating in series of threes—e.g., three O.T. examples of judgment (vv. 5–7), a threefold description of the false teachers (v. 8), and three O.T. examples of unholy men (v. 11). (3) Under the full influence of the Holy Spirit, Jude freely refers to written sources: (a) O.T. Scriptures (vv. 5–7,11), (b) Jewish traditions (vv. 9,14–15), and (c) 2 Peter, quoting directly from 3:3, which he acknowledges as being from the apostles (vv. 17–18). (4) It contains the most majestic benediction in the N.T.

Reading Jude

In order to read the entire New Testament in one year, the book of Jude should be read in 1 day: ☐ Jude

NOTES

Earnestly contend for the faith

1 JUDE, THE servant of Jesus
Christ, and [a]brother of James, to them
that are sanctified by God the Father,
and [b]preserved in Jesus Christ, *and*
[c]called:
2 Mercy unto you, and [d]peace, and
love, be multiplied.
3 Beloved, when I gave all diligence
to write unto you [e]of the common sal-
vation, it was needful for me to write
unto you, and exhort *you* that [f]ye
should earnestly contend for the faith
which was once delivered unto the
saints.
4 [g]For there are certain men crept
in unawares, [h]who were before of old
ordained to this condemnation, ungod-
ly men, [i]turning [j]the grace of our
God into lasciviousness, and [k]denying
the only Lord God, and our Lord Jesus
Christ.

The doom of false teachers

5 I will therefore put you in remem-
brance, though ye once knew this, how
that [l]the Lord, having saved the peo-
ple out of the land of Egypt, afterward
[m]destroyed them that believed not.
6 And [n]the angels which kept not
their [a]first estate, but left their own
habitation, [o]he hath reserved in ever-
lasting chains under darkness [p]unto
the judgment of the great day.
7 Even as [q]Sodom and Gomorrha,
and the cities about them in like man-
ner, giving themselves over to fornica-
tion, and going after [b]strange flesh,
are set forth for an example, suffering
the vengeance of eternal fire.
8 [r]Likewise also these *filthy*
dreamers defile the flesh, despise do-
minion, and [s]speak evil of dignities.
9 Yet [t]Michael the archangel,
when contending with the devil he dis-
puted about the body of Moses, [u]durst
not bring against him a railing accusa- Rev. 12:7-11
tion, but said, [v]The Lord rebuke thee.
10 [w]But these speak evil of those
things which they know not: but what

[a] Or, *principality* [b] Gk. *other*

1:1 [a]Acts 1:13 [b]John 17:11 1 Pet. 1:5 [c]Rom. 1:7 **1:2** [d]1 Pet. 1:2 2 Pet. 1:2 **1:3** [e]Tit. 1:4 [f]Phil. 1:27 2 Tim. 1:13 **1:4** [g]Gal. 2:4 2 Pet. 2:1 [h]Rom. 9:22 [i]2 Pet. 2:10 [j]Tit. 2:11 [k]Tit. 1:16 **1:5** [l]1 Cor. 10:9 [m]Num. 14:29 Ps. 106:26 **1:6** [n]John 8:44 [o]2 Pet. 2:4 [p]Rev. 20:10 **1:7** [q]Gen. 19:24 2 Pet. 2:6 **1:8** [r]2 Pet. 2:10 [s]Ex. 22:28 **1:9** [t]Dan. 10:13 [u]2 Pet. 2:11 [v]Zech. 3:2 **1:10** [w]2 Pet. 2:12

2 MERCY ... BE MULTIPLIED. As we draw near to God, His mercy, peace, and love can be doubled, tripled, or even quadrupled unto us.

3 THE FAITH ... ONCE DELIVERED UNTO THE SAINTS. Those faithful to Christ are placed under the solemn obligation to "earnestly contend" for the faith which God delivered to the apostles and saints (Phil. 1:27; cf. 1 Tim. 1:18–19; 6:12). (1) "The faith" consists of the gospel proclaimed by Christ and the apostles. It is the fixed and unalterable truth, given by the Holy Spirit and embodied in the N.T. However, "the faith" is more than objective truth. It is also a way of life to be lived in love and purity (Col. 1:9–11; 1 Tim. 1:5). It is a kingdom which comes in power to baptize all believers in the Holy Spirit (see articles on THE KINGDOM OF GOD, p. 1428, and BAPTISM IN THE HOLY SPIRIT, p. 1652), that they may proclaim the gospel to all nations (Mark 16:15–17; see 1 Thes. 1:5, note) with signs and miracles and gifts of the Holy Spirit (see Acts 2:22; 14:3; Rom. 15:19; Heb. 2:4, note; see article on SIGNS OF BELIEVERS, p. 1516).

(2) The words "earnestly contend" (Gk. *epagonizomai*) describe the battle that the faithful believer must fight in the defense of the faith. It means literally to "struggle," "suffer," "be under great stress," or "fight a fight." We must exert ourselves to the utmost in the defense of God's Word and the N.T. faith, even though it may be costly and agonizing. We must deny ourselves and, if need be, accept martyrdom in behalf of the gospel (cf. 2 Tim. 4:7).

(3) Contending for the faith means taking a direct stand against those within the visible church who deny the authority of the Bible or distort the ancient faith as presented by Christ and the apostles, and proclaiming it as redemptive truth to all people (see John 5:47, note; see article on THE INSPIRATION AND AUTHORITY OF SCRIPTURE, p. 1924). Those whose allegiance is to Christ and the full N.T. faith must never allow its message to be weakened by compromising its authority, distorting its truth, or explaining away its power and promises.

4 GRACE OF OUR GOD INTO LASCIVIOUSNESS. Lasciviousness means unrestrained vice or sexual freedom. Jude denounces certain persons who teach that salvation by grace allows professed believers to indulge in serious sin and yet not be condemned by God. They may have taught that God will freely forgive those who continually engage in sexual lust, or that those who presently live in moral filth are eternally secure if they have trusted in Christ sometime in the past (cf. Rom. 5:20; 6:1–2). They preached pardon for sin but not the imperative of holiness.

6 THE ANGELS. Jude refers to angels who did not remain in their first position of authority, but who rebelled against God, broke His law, and are now in prison awaiting judgment. However, not all fallen angels are locked up, for Satan and many demons are on the earth right now (see 2 Pet. 2:4, note; 1 John 5:19, note).

8 DESPISE DOMINION. See 2 Pet. 2:10, note.

9 MICHAEL ... CONTENDING WITH THE DEVIL. If the greatest archangel Michael refused to rebuke Satan but relied on the power of God, how much more should we as humans refrain from challenging and speaking abusively against all things, including evil spirits (see 2 Pet. 2:11).

they know naturally, as brute beasts, in those things they corrupt themselves.

11 Woe unto them! for they have gone in the way [x]of Cain, and [y]ran greedily after the error of Balaam for reward, and perished [z]in the gainsaying of Core.

12 [a]These are spots in your [b]feasts of charity, when they feast with you, feeding themselves without fear: [c]clouds *they are* without water, [d]carried about of winds; trees whose fruit withereth, without fruit, twice dead, [e]plucked up by the roots;

13 [f]Raging waves of the sea, [g]foaming out their own shame; wandering stars, [h]to whom is reserved the blackness of darkness for ever.

14 And Enoch also, [i]the seventh from Adam, prophesied of these, saying, Behold, [j]the Lord cometh with ten thousands of his saints,

15 To execute judgment upon all, and to convince all that are ungodly among them of all their ungodly deeds which they have ungodly committed, and of all their [k]hard *speeches* which ungodly sinners have spoken against him.

Rev. 1:7

16 These are murmurers, complainers, walking after their own lusts; and [l]their mouth speaketh great swelling *words,* [m]having men's persons in admiration because of advantage.

1:11 [x]1 John 3:12 [y]2 Pet. 2:15 [z]Num. 16:1
1:12 [a]2 Pet. 2:13 [b]1 Cor. 11:21 [c]Prov. 25:14 2 Pet. 2:17 [d]Eph. 4:14 [e]Mat. 15:13
1:13 [f]Is. 57:20 [g]Phil. 3:19 [h]2 Pet. 2:17
1:14 [i]Gen. 5:18 [j]Deut. 33:2
1:15 [k]1 Sam. 2:3 Ps. 31:18
1:16 [l]2 Pet. 2:18 [m]Prov. 28:21
1:17 [n]2 Pet. 3:2
1:18 [o]1 Tim. 4:1 2 Pet. 2:1
1:19 [p]Prov. 18:1 [q]Jas. 3:15
1:20 [r]Col. 2:7 [s]Rom. 8:26
1:21 [t]Tit. 2:13 2 Pet. 3:12
1:23 [u]Rom. 11:14 [v]Amos 4:11 Zech. 3:2 [w]Zech. 3:4,5
1:24 [x]Eph. 3:20 [y]Col. 1:22
1:25 [z]Rom. 16:27

A call to persevere in true faith

17 [n]But, beloved, remember ye the words which were spoken before of the apostles of our Lord Jesus Christ;

18 How that they told you [o]there should be mockers in the last time, who should walk after their own ungodly lusts.

19 These be they [p]who separate themselves, [q]sensual, having not the Spirit.

20 But ye, beloved, [r]building up yourselves on your most holy faith, [s]praying in the Holy Ghost,

21 Keep yourselves in the love of God, [t]looking for the mercy of our Lord Jesus Christ unto eternal life.

22 And of some have compassion, making a difference:

23 And others [u]save with fear, [v]pulling *them* out of the fire; hating even [w]the garment spotted by the flesh.

Benediction

24 [x]Now unto him that is able to keep you from falling, and [y]to present *you* faultless before the presence of his glory with exceeding joy,

25 [z]To the only wise God our Saviour, *be* glory and majesty, dominion and power, both now and ever. Amen.

---

12 TWICE DEAD. The apostate teachers among Jude's readers are "twice dead" (literally, "twice having died"). The false teachers were once believers in Christ who had "passed from death unto life" (John 5:24) but had sometime afterward severed their union with Christ and passed out of life back into death (cf. Eph. 2:1; see Rom. 8:13, note). The previous verse gives the reason for their spiritual death.

14 ENOCH . . . PROPHESIED. Jude may be quoting from the book of Enoch, written prior to 110 B.C., or simply from Jewish tradition. Jude's use of this passage confirms only the truth of the prophecy; it does not mean that he endorses the entire book of Enoch.

18 IN THE LAST TIME. See 1 Tim. 4:1, note; 2 Tim. 3:1, note.

20 BUILDING UP YOURSELVES. Believers must defend and propagate the faith and resist false teaching in four ways. (1) By building ourselves up in the most holy faith. The holy faith is the N.T. revelation handed down by Christ and the apostles (v. 3). This requires study of God's Word and a determined effort to know the truth and teachings of Scripture (cf. Acts 2:42; 20:27; Heb. 5:12; 2 Tim. 2:15).

(2) By praying in the Spirit. We must pray by the enabling power of the Holy Spirit, i.e., by looking to the Holy Spirit to inspire, guide, energize, sustain, and help us to do battle in our praying (see Rom. 8:26, note; cf. Gal. 4:6; Eph. 6:18). Praying in the Spirit includes both praying with one's mind and praying with one's spirit (see 1 Cor. 14:15, note).

(3) By remaining in the sphere of God's love for us. This involves loyal obedience to God and His Word (John 15:9–10).

(4) By looking for and awaiting the return of our Lord and the eternal glory that will accompany His return (see John 14:2, note).

Event	Description	References
Last Days of Preparation	Increase of false prophets and religious compromise within the church	Mat. 24:4–5,10–11,24; Luke 18:8; 2 Thes. 2:3; 1 Tim. 4:1; 2 Tim. 3:1,13; 4:3–4; 2 Pet. 2:1–3; 3:3–4
	Increase of crime and disregard of God's law	Mat. 24:12,37–39; Luke 17:26–30; 18:8; 1 Tim. 4:1; 2 Tim. 3:1–8
	Increase of wars, famines, and earthquakes	Mat. 24:6–8; Mark 13:7–8; Luke 21:9
	Decrease in love and family affection	Mat. 10:21; 24:12; Mark 13:12; 2 Tim. 3:1–3
	More severe persecution of God's people	Mat. 10:22–23; 24:9–10; Mark 13:13; John 15:19–20; 16:33; Acts 14:22; Rom. 5:3
	Those who stand firm will be saved	Mat. 24:13; Mark 13:13
	Gospel will be preached to the whole world	Mat. 24:14; Mark 13:10
	The Spirit will be poured forth upon God's people	Acts 2:17–21,38–39

Event	Description	References
The Rapture	Believers must be prepared and wait constantly for this imminent event	Mat. 24:42,44; 25:1–13; Mark 13:33–37; Luke 12:35; 21:19,34–36; Rom. 13:11; Phil. 4:5; 1 Thes. 1:10; 4:16–18; 5:6–11; 2 Tim. 4:8; Tit. 2:13
	Christ will come unexpectedly, since the time cannot be calculated	Mat. 24:36,42,44; 25:5–7,13; Mark 13:32–37; Luke 12:35–46
	Christ will come to catch up believers living on earth at this time	Luke 21:36; John 14:3; 1 Thes. 1:10; 4:15–17; 2 Thes. 2:1; Rev. 3:10–11
	Believers will be delivered from the wrath to come	Luke 21:36; 1 Thes. 1:10; 5:2–9; Rev. 3:10–11
	Believers living at this time will receive transformed bodies	Rom. 8:23; 1 Cor. 15:51–54; 1 Thes. 4:16–17
	Believers who died before this event will rise and be caught up with Christ	1 Cor. 15:50–55; 1 Thes. 4:16–17
	All raptured saints will be judged by Christ	John 5:22; Rom. 14:12; 1 Cor. 3:12–15; 2 Cor. 5:10; 2 Tim. 4:8
	Believers will be judged according to their deeds	Eccl. 12:14; Mat. 5:22; 12:36–37; Mark 4:22; Rom. 2:5–11,16; 1 Cor. 4:5; 2 Cor. 5:10; Eph. 6:8; Col. 3:23–25

Event	Description	References
The Rapture (cont.)	Faithful believers will receive rewards	Mat. 5:11–12; 25:14–23; Luke 19:12–19; 22:28–30; Gal. 6:8–10; 1 Cor. 3:12–14; 9:25–27; 13:3; Eph. 6:8; 2 Tim. 4:8; Heb. 6:10; 1 Pet. 5:4; Rev. 2:7,11,17, 26–28; 3:4–5,12,21
	Less faithful believers will not be condemned, but will receive little or no reward	Eccl. 12:14; Mat. 5:19; 1 Cor. 2:13–15; 2 Cor. 5:10; Col. 3:25; 1 John 2:28

Event	Description	References
The Tribulation	The faithful in Christ's churches will be kept from the time of trial	Luke 21:36; John 14:1–3; 2 Cor. 5:2,4; Phil. 3:20–21; 1 Thes. 1:10; 4:16–18; 5:8–10; Rev. 3:10
	Will begin after the restrainer is taken out of the way	2 Thes. 2:6–8
	Will begin after the secret power lawlessness intensifies	2 Thes. 2:7–8
	Will begin after a great rebellion against the faith occurs	2 Thes.2:3
	The antichrist (the man of lawlessness) will appear	Dan. 9:26–27; 2 Thes. 2:3–10; Rev. 13:1–18; 16:2; 17:9–18; 19:19–20
	Will begin with the opening of seven seals	Rev. 6:1
	A time of worldwide distress	Mat. 24:21–22; Rev. 6—19
	Will last for seven years	Dan. 9:27
	False prophets will perform great signs and wonders	Mat. 24:24; 2 Thes. 2:8–10; Rev. 13:13; 16:14; 19:20
	The gospel will be preached by angels and possibly Jews	Rev. 7:1–4; 11:3–6; 14:6–7
	People will be saved during these days	Deut. 4:30–31; Rev. 7:9–17; 14:6–7; 11:13
	Many Jews will turn to Christ	Rom. 11:25–26; Rev. 7:1–8
	Those who had opportunity to believe in Jesus before the rapture will have no further opportunity to repent	Mat. 25:1–12; Luke 12:45–46; 2 Thes. 2:10–12
	Will be a time of persecution for all who are faithful to Jesus	Dan. 12:10; Mat. 24:15–21; Rev. 6:9–11; 7:9–17; 9:3–5; 12:12,17; 13:7,15–17; 14:6,13; 17:6; 18:24; 20:4

Event	Description	References
The Great Tribulation	Last three and one half years of "The Tribulation"	Dan. 9:27; Rev. 11:1–2; 12:6; 13:5–7
	Will begin with the abomination that causes desolation standing in the holy place (the temple)	Dan. 9:27; 12:11; Mat. 24:15; Mark 13:14; 2 Thes. 2:4; Rev. 13:14–15
	Demonic activity will increase greatly	Rev. 9:3–11,14–19; 16:12–14
	Sorcery and witchcraft will increase greatly	1 Tim. 4:1; Rev. 9:21; 18:23; 22:15
	Cosmic events related to sun, moon, stars will occur	Is. 13:9–11; Mat. 24:29; Mark 13:24–25; Luke 21:25; Rev. 6:12–14; 8:10,12; 9:2
	Religious deceit will be widespread	Mat. 24:24; Mark 13:6,21–22; 2 Thes. 2:9–11
	Time of terrible suffering for Jews	Jer. 30:5–7; Rev. 11:2; 12:12–17
	The world's worst and most intense time of worldwide distress	Dan. 12:1; Mat. 24:21; Mark 13:15–19; Rev. 6:9–17; 9:1—9:21; 16:1–21
	God will extend His wrath on the ungodly	Is. 13:6–13; Jer. 30:4–11; Dan. 12:1; Zech. 14:1–4; Rev. 3:10; 6:17; 9:1–6,18–21; 14:9–11; 19:15
	The apostate church will be destroyed	Rev. 17:16–17
	Two witnesses who preached the gospel and were killed will be resurrected	Rev. 11:11–12
	End of great tribulation can be known by definite signs	Mat. 24:15–29,32–33; Mark 13:28–29; Luke 21:28
	Will end with the battle of Armageddon and God's full wrath on the ungodly	Jer. 25:29–38; Ezek. 39:17–20; Joel 3:2,9–17; Zeph. 3:8; Zech. 14:2–5; Rev. 14:9–11,14–20; 16:12–21; 19:17–18
	Christ will triumph over the antichrist and his armies	Mat. 24:30–31; 2 Pet. 3:10–13; Rev. 19:11–21

Event	Description	References
The Antichrist	Ruler during the tribulation who controls the entire world	Dan. 7:2–7,24–27; 8:4; 11:36; Rev. 13:1–18; 17:11–17
	An incredibly wicked person, a "man of sin" and lawlessness	Dan. 9:27; 2 Thes. 2:3; Rev. 13:12
	Described as a beast	Rev. 13:1–18; 17:3,8,16; 19:19–20; 20:10

Event	Description	References
The Antichrist (cont.)	Will set up an image of himself in the temple and will demand worship	Dan. 7:8,25; 11:31,36; Mat. 24:15; Mark 13:14; 2 Thes. 2:3–4; Rev. 13:4,8,12,14–15; 14:9; 16:2
	Will exercise miracles through the power of Satan	Mat. 24:24; 2 Thes. 2:9–10; Rev. 13:3,12–14; 16:14; 17:8
	Will have ability to deceive the nations	1 Thes. 2:9–10; 1 John 2:18; Rev. 20:3
	Will be assisted by the false prophet (the beast of the earth)	Rev. 13:11–17; 16:13; 19:20; 20:10
	Will kill the two witnesses who proclaimed the gospel	Rev. 11:7–10
	Will attempt to kill all who do not have the mark of the beast	Rev. 6:9; 13:15–17; 14:12–13
	Will eventually destroy the religious system with which he was aligned	Rev. 17:16–17
	Will be defeated by Christ when He returns to earth to establish his kingdom	2 Thes. 2:8; Rev. 16:16; 19:15–21

Event	Description	References
Christ's Glorious Appearing from Heaven to Judge and to Wage War	Christ will return with believers and His angels	2 Thes. 1:7–10; Jude 14–15; Rev. 19:14
	Christ will gather the tribulation saints	Mat. 24:31; 25:31–40,46; Mark 13:27; Rev. 20:4
	Unbelievers will be unprepared for this event	Mat. 24:38–39,43
	Christ will separate peoples on earth	Mat. 13:40–41,47–50; 25:31–46
	Nations will be enraged at this event	Rev. 11:18
	Saints will rejoice at this event	Rev. 19:1–8
	Christ will judge and destroy the ungodly, including the antichrist and Satan	Is. 13:6–12; Ezek. 20:34–38; Mat. 13:41–50; 24:30; 25:41–46; Luke 19:11–27; 1 Thes. 5:1–11; 2 Thes. 2:7–10,12; Rev. 6:16–17; 11:18; 17:14; 18:1–24; 19:11—20:3
	Tribulation saints will receive rewards	Mat. 5:11–12; 1 Cor. 3:12–14; 9:25–27; Gal. 6:9–10; 2 Tim. 4:8; Rev. 20:4
	Tribulation saints will share in Christ's glory and kingdom	Mat. 25:31–40; Rom. 8:29; 2 Thes. 2:13–14; Rev. 20:4

Event	Description	References
The Millennium	Satan will be bound	Rev. 20:2–3
	Tribulation saints (and possibly O.T. saints) will rise from the dead	Rev. 20:4
	The church and all martyred tribulation saints will reign with Christ	Rev. 2:26–27; 3:21; 5:9–10; 11:15–18; 20:4–6
	Christ will reign on earth over the tribulation saints alive at His coming	Is. 9:6–7; Mic. 4:1–8; Dan. 2:44; Zech. 14:6–9; Rev. 5:10; 11:15–18; 20:4–6
	Time span of reign will be a thousand years	Rev. 20:4–7
	God's children will have rest	2 Thes. 1:7
	Nature will be restored to its original order and perfection	Ps. 96:11–13; 98:7–9; Is. 14:7–8; 35:1–2,6–7; 51:3; 55:12–13; Ezek. 34:25; Rom. 8:18–23
	Satan will be loosed for a brief time at the end of Millennium	Rev. 20:7
	Will end with Christ turning over the kingdom to the Father	1 Cor.15:24

Event	Description	References
The Final Judgment	Final battle of Gog and Magog	Rev. 20:7–9
	All the wicked will be raised from the dead to face judgment	Is. 26:19–21; Dan. 12:2; John 5:28–29; Rev. 20:12–15
	The great white throne judgment	Rev. 20:11–15
	All God's enemies will be put into the lake of fire	2 Thes. 1:9; Rev. 20:10,12–15; 21:8

Event	Description	References
The New Heavens and New Earth	God will destroy the present earth	Ps. 102:25–26; Is. 34:4; 51:6; Hag. 2:6; Heb. 12:26–28; 2 Pet. 3:7,10,12
	God will create a new heaven and a new earth	Is. 51:6; 65:17; 66:22; Rom. 8:19–21; 2 Pet. 3:10–13; Rev. 21:1—22:6
	God will wipe away all effects of sin	2 Pet. 3:13; Rev. 21:4; 22:3,15
	New earth will become headquarters of God	Rev. 21:1–3

REVELATION

Outline

The Prologue (1:1–8)

I. The Exalted Lord and His Churches (1:9—3:22)
   - A. Vision of the Exalted Lord Among the Lampstands (1:9–20)
   - B. His Messages to the Seven Churches (2:1—3:22)

II. The Worthy Lamb and His Role in the Outcome of History (4:1—11:19)
   - A. Vision of the Majestic Court of Heaven (4:1—5:14)
     1. The Creator-God on His Throne in Awesome Holiness (4:1–11)
     2. The Sealed Scroll and the Worthy Lamb (5:1–14)
   - B. Vision of the Lamb in Relation to the Seven Seals and Seven Trumpets (6:1—11:19)
     1. Opening the First Six Seals (6:1–17)
        FIRST INTERLUDE: The Two Multitudes (7:1–17)
     2. Opening the Seventh Seal: Seven Angels with Seven Trumpets (8:1–6)
     3. The First Six Trumpets (8:7—9:21)
        SECOND INTERLUDE: The Little Scroll (10:1–11)
        The Two Witnesses (11:1–14)
     4. The Seventh Trumpet (11:15–19)

III. The Lord God and His Christ in the Great Conflict with Satan (12:1—22:5)
   - A. Perspective of the Conflict (12:1—15:8)
     1. From the Viewpoint of the Earth's Enemies (12:1—13:18)
        - a. The Dragon (12:1–17)
        - b. The Sea Beast (13:1–10)
        - c. The Earth Beast (13:11–18)
     2. From the Viewpoint of Heaven (14:1–20)
        THIRD INTERLUDE: Seven Angels with Seven Plagues (15:1–8)
   - B. Final Progression of the Conflict (16:1—19:10)
     1. The Seven Bowls of God's Wrath (16:1–21)
     2. Judgment of the Great Harlot (17:1–18)
     3. The Fall of Babylon the Great (18:1–24)
     4. Rejoicing in Heaven (19:1–10)
   - C. Climax of the Conflict (19:11—20:10)
     1. The Return and Triumph of Christ (19:11–18)
     2. The Defeat of the Beast and His Allies (19:19–21)
     3. Binding, Loosing, and Finally Defeating Satan (20:1–10)
   - D. Aftermath of the Conflict (20:11–22:5)
     1. Great White Throne Judgment (20:11–15)
     2. The Doom of the Unrighteous (20:14–15; 21:8)
     3. New Heaven and New Earth (21:1–22:5)

The Epilogue (22:6–21)

Author: John

Theme: Conflict and Consummation

Date of Writing: c. A.D. 90–96

Background

Revelation is the last N.T. book and the most unusual. It is at once an apocalypse (1:1–2,20), a prophecy (1:3; 22:7,10,18–19), and a composite of seven letters (1:4,11; 2:1—3:22). ("Apocalypse" is derived from the Greek word *apocalupsis*, translated "revelation" in 1:1.) The book is an apocalypse with regard to the nature of its content, a prophecy in respect to its message, and an epistle in relation to its addressees.

Five important facts about the book's background are revealed in ch. 1. (1) It is "the revelation of Jesus Christ" (1:1). (2) This revelation was communicated supernaturally to the author by the exalted Christ, angels, and visions (1:1,10–18). (3) The communication was to God's servant John (1:1,4,9; cf. 22:8). (4) John received the visions and apocalyptic message while exiled on the island of Patmos (50 miles southwest of Ephesus), because of God's Word and John's own testimony (1:9). (5) The original recipients were seven churches in the province of Asia (1:4,11).

Historical and internal evidence point to John the apostle as the author. Irenaeus verifies that Polycarp (Irenaeus knew Polycarp, and Polycarp knew the apostle John) spoke about John writing Revelation near the end of Domitian's reign as Roman emperor (A.D. 81–96).

The book's content reflects the historical circumstances of Domitian's reign, when he demanded all his subjects to address him as "Lord and God." The emperor's decree undoubtedly created a confrontation between those willing to worship the emperor and the faithful Christians who confessed that only Jesus was "Lord and God." Thus the book was written at a time when believers were undergoing a measure of serious persecution because of the word of their testimony, a situation that obviously forms the background to Revelation itself (1:19; 2:10,13; 6:9–11; 7:14–17; 11:7; 12:11,17; 17:6; 18:24; 19:2; 20:4).

Purpose

The purpose of the book is threefold. (1) The letters to the seven churches reveal that serious deviation from the N.T. apostolic standard of truth and righteousness was occurring among many churches in Asia. John writes on Christ's behalf to rebuke their compromise and sin, and to call them to repent and return to their first love. (2) In view of persecution resulting from Domitian's self-deification, Revelation was given to the churches to strengthen their faith, resolve, and loyalty to Jesus Christ, and to inspire them to be overcomers and remain faithful even unto death. (3) Finally, it was written to provide believers of all generations with God's perspective on their fierce conflict with Satan's combined forces by revealing the future outcome of history. It particularly discloses the events during the last seven years preceding Christ's second coming, that God will prevail and vindicate the saints by pouring out His wrath on Satan's kingdom; this will be followed by the second coming of Christ.

Survey

The prophetic message of this book is communicated through dramatic apocalyptic images and symbolism, depicting the consummation of the whole Biblical message of redemption. It features Christ's role as the worthy Lamb who was slain (ch. 5) and the wrathful Lamb who is coming to judge the world and purge it of evil (chs. 6–19). The other major symbolic images in the book are the dragon (Satan), the sea beast (the antichrist), the earth beast (the false prophet), and Babylon the Great (the center of satanic deception and world power).

After the Prologue (1:1–8), there are three main sections in the book. In the first section (1:9—3:22), John has an awesome vision of the exalted Christ in the midst of the lampstands (churches), who commissions John to write letters to seven churches in Asia Minor (1:11,19). Each letter (2:1—3:22) includes a symbolic description of the exalted Lord from the opening vision, an evaluation of the church, words of commendation or rebuke or both, words of warning to five churches, an exhortation to hear and repent, and a promise to all overcomers. Emphasis on the number seven in this section indicates that the letters rep-

resent a collective fullness of what the exalted Lord says to the church in every city and generation.

The book's second main section (4:1—11:19) contains visions of things in heaven and on earth concerning the Lamb and His role in the outcome of history. It begins with a vision of the majestic court of heaven where God sits enthroned in holiness and unapproachable light (ch. 4). Ch. 5 focuses on a sealed scroll of destiny in God's right hand and on the Lamb, who alone is worthy to break its seals and disclose its contents. The opening of the first six seals (ch. 6) continues the vision begun in chs. 4–5, except now the scene shifts to events on earth. The first five seals unveil God's judgments in the last days that lead up to the end. The sixth seal announces the coming wrath of God. The book's "First Interlude" occurs in ch. 7, describing the sealing of the 144,000 on the threshold of the great tribulation (7:1–8) and the reward of the saints in heaven after the great tribulation (7:9–17). Chs. 8–9 reveal the opening of the seventh seal, unveiling another series of judgments, i.e., the seven trumpets. A "Second Interlude" occurs between the sixth and seventh trumpets, involving John, a little scroll (10:1–11), and two mighty prophetic witnesses in the great city (11:1–14). Finally, the seventh trumpet (11:15–19) serves as a preview of the consummation (v. 15) and a prelude to the final scenes of God's unfolding mystery (chs. 12–22).

The third main section (12:1—22:5) provides a detailed picture of the great end-time conflict between God and His adversary, Satan. Chs. 12–13 reveal that the saints on earth must face a terrible conspiracy and triad of evil, consisting of (1) the dragon (ch. 12), (2) the sea beast (13:1–10), and (3) the earth beast (13:11–18). Chs. 14–15 contain visions to reassure the tribulation saints that justice will prevail as God is about to pour out His final wrath on the civilization of the antichrist. A full disclosure of God's wrath then occurs in the series of seven vials or bowl judgments (ch. 16), the judgment of the great harlot (ch. 17), and the fall of Babylon the Great (ch. 18). At this point, great rejoicing bursts forth in heaven, and the marriage supper of the Lamb and His bride is announced (19:1–10).

However, the grand finale is yet to occur. John then sees heaven opened and Christ riding forth on the white horse as the King of kings and Lord of lords to defeat the beast and all his allies (19:11–21). Satan's final defeat is preceded by his being bound for a thousand years (20:1–6), during which Christ reigns with the saints (20:4) and after which Satan is loosed for a short time (20:7–9) and then cast into "the lake of fire" forever (20:10). The apocalyptic prophecy concludes with the great white throne judgment scene (20:11–15), the just doom of the wicked (20:14–15; 21:8), and the new heaven and new earth as the destiny of the saints (21:1—22:5). The book ends with warnings about heeding its message and entering into eternal life (22:6–21).

Special Features

Eight major features or emphases characterize this book. (1) Revelation is the only N.T. book classified as prophecy and apocalyptic. (2) As an apocalyptic book, its message is conveyed in symbols that represent realities about future times and events while preserving a certain enigma or mystery. (3) Numbers are used prolifically, including 2; 3; 3 and 1/2; 4; 5; 6; 7; 10; 12; 24; 42; 144; 666; 1000; 1260; 7000; 12,000; 144,000; 100,000,000; and 200,000,000. The book especially features the number seven, which occurs no less than 54 times and symbolizes perfect completeness or fullness. (4) Visions are prominent, with the scenes often shifting in locale from earth to heaven and back to earth. (5) Angels are prominently associated with the visions and the heavenly decrees. (6) It is a polemical book that (a) exposes the demonic character of any earthly ruler's claim to deity and (b) reveals Jesus Christ as the exalted Lord and the Ruler of the kings of the earth (1:5; 19:16). (7) It is a dramatic book that makes the truth of its message as vivid and forceful as possible. (8) It breathes the spirit of O.T. prophecy without any formal O.T. quotations.

Interpretation

This is the most difficult book in the N.T. to interpret. Although the original readers probably understood its message without excessive perplexity, in subsequent centuries

varying opinions about the book have resulted in four major schools of interpretation. (1) The *preterist* interpretation views the book and its prophecies as having been fulfilled in the original historical setting of the Roman Empire, except for chs. 19–22 which await future fulfillment. (2) The *historicist* interpretation views Revelation as a prophetic forecast of the entire sweep of church history from John's day to the end of the age. (3) The *idealist* interpretation regards the book's symbolism as conveying certain timeless spiritual principles about good and evil in history generally, without reference to actual historical events. (4) The *futurist* interpretation approaches chs. 4–22 as prophecy concerning events in history that will occur only at the end of this age. This study Bible interprets Revelation primarily from the futurist point of view.

Reading Revelation

In order to read the entire New Testament in one year, the book of Revelation should be read in 24 days, according to the following schedule:
☐ 1 ☐ 2:1–17 ☐ 2:18—3:6 ☐ 3:7–22 ☐ 4 ☐ 5 ☐ 6 ☐ 7 ☐ 8 ☐ 9 ☐ 10 ☐ 11 ☐ 12 ☐ 13:1–10 ☐ 13:11—14:20 ☐ 15 ☐ 16 ☐ 17 ☐ 18 ☐ 19:1–10 ☐ 19:11–21 ☐ 20 ☐ 21 ☐ 22

NOTES

The revelation of Jesus Christ

1 THE REVELATION of Jesus
Christ, [a]which God gave unto
him, to show unto his servants things
which must shortly come to pass; and
[b]he sent and signified *it* by his angel
unto his servant John:
2 [c]Who bare record of the word of
God, and of the testimony of Jesus
Christ, and of all things [d]that he saw.
3 [e]Blessed *is* he that readeth, and
they that hear the words of this proph-
ecy, and keep those things which are
written therein: for [f]the time *is* at
hand.

The salutation

4 John to the seven churches which
are in Asia: Grace *be* unto you, and
peace, from him [g]which is, and
[h]which was, and which is to come;
[i]and from the seven Spirits which are
before his throne;
5 And from Jesus Christ, [j]*who is*
the faithful witness, *and* the [k]first be-
gotten of the dead, and [l]the prince of
the kings of the earth. Unto him [m]that
loved us, [n]and washed us from our
sins in his own blood,
6 And hath [o]made us kings and
priests unto God and his Father; [p]to
him *be* glory and dominion for ever and
ever. Amen.
7 [q]Behold, he cometh with clouds;
and every eye shall see him, and [r]they
also which pierced him: and all kin-
dreds of the earth shall wail because of
him. Even so, Amen.

The voice and the vision

8 [s]I am Alpha and Omega, the be-
ginning and the ending, saith the Lord,
[t]which is, and which was, and which
is to come, the Almighty.
9 I John, who also am your brother,
and [u]companion in tribulation, and
[v]in the kingdom and patience of Jesus
Christ, was in the isle that is called
Patmos, [w]for the word of God, and for
the testimony of Jesus Christ.
10 [x]I was in the Spirit on [y]the
Lord's day, and heard behind me [z]a
great voice, as of a trumpet,
11 Saying, [a]I am Alpha and Ome-
ga, [b]the first and the last: and, What
thou seest, write in a book, and send *it*
unto the seven churches which are in
Asia; unto Ephesus, and unto Smyrna,
and unto Pergamos, and unto Thyatira,
and unto Sardis, and unto Philadel-
phia, and unto Laodicea.
12 And I turned to see the voice

1:1 [a]John 3:32 [b]ch. 22:16
1:2 [c]1 Cor. 1:6 [d]1 John 1:1
1:3 [e]Luke 11:28 [f]Jas. 5:8
1:4 [g]Ex. 3:14 [h]John 1:1 [i]Zech. 3:9
1:5 [j]John 8:14 1 Tim. 6:13 [k]Col. 1:18 [l]ch. 17:14 [m]John 13:34 Gal. 2:20 [n]Heb. 9:14 1 John 1:7
1:6 [o]1 Pet. 2:5 [p]1 Tim. 6:16
1:7 [q]Dan. 7:13 [r]Zech. 12:10
1:8 [s]Is. 41:4 [t]ch. 4:8
1:9 [u]Phil. 1:7 [v]Rom. 8:17 2 Tim. 2:12 [w]ch. 6:9
1:10 [x]Acts 10:10 2 Cor. 12:2 [y]John 20:26 [z]ch. 4:1
1:11 [a]ver. 8 [b]ver. 17

1:1 REVELATION OF JESUS CHRIST. This book is a revelation from Jesus Christ about Himself. This is extremely important, for (1) it reveals Jesus' evaluation of His churches 60 to 65 years after His resurrection and ascension to heaven, and (2) it discloses future events concerning the tribulation, God's triumph over evil, the return of Christ to reign on earth, and the blessedness of God's eternal kingdom.

1:3 BLESSED *IS* HE THAT READETH. This is the first of seven "beatitudes" or blessings found in Revelation, given to those who read, hear, and obey the things written in the book. The other six blessings are found in 14:13; 16:15; 19:9; 20:6; 22:7; 22:14 (cf. Luke 11:28). That believers must keep the commands of Revelation indicates that this is a practical book with moral instructions and not a mere prophecy of the future. We should read the book not only to understand God's future program for the world and His people, but also to learn and apply the great spiritual principles emphasized in it. Above all it should draw us nearer to Jesus Christ in faith, hope, and love.

1:4 TO THE SEVEN CHURCHES. Revelation is addressed to seven churches in Asia (located in what is now part of western Turkey). Each particular church was comprised of various congregations. These churches were probably selected because they represented the totality of churches of that day, for the word "seven" stands for completion. What was said to them is meant for the church today. In other words, the "seven churches" represent all the churches of all ages. The "seven Spirits" may represent the perfection and ministry of the Holy Spirit to the church (cf. 4:5; 5:6; Is. 11:2–3).

1:7 HE COMETH. The primary purpose of the book of Revelation is to describe the return of Christ to establish His kingdom on earth and the end-time events surrounding that coming (cf. Dan. 7:13; Mat. 24:29–30). It presents an eschatology of victory for the faithful, teaching that history will end in the judgment of Satan's system in this world (chs. 17–18) and in the eternal reign of Christ and His people (20:4; 21:1—22:5).

1:8 ALPHA AND OMEGA. Alpha is the first letter of the Greek alphabet and Omega is the last letter. God is eternal, and from creation to consummation He is Lord over all. To Him belong the final victory over evil and the rulership over all things (cf. 22:13).

1:9 ISLE . . . PATMOS. Patmos is a small island in the Aegean Sea, about 50 miles southwest of Ephesus. John was a prisoner there because he faithfully proclaimed the gospel and remained loyal to Christ and His Word.

1:10 IN THE SPIRIT. This expression refers to a special intensity of spiritual sensitivity to the communication of the Holy Spirit by which visions may be received (cf. Acts 10:10).

that spake with me. And being turned,
[c]I saw seven golden candlesticks;
13 [d]And in the midst of the seven
candlesticks [e]*one* like unto the Son of
man, [f]clothed with a garment down to
the foot, and [g]girt about the paps with
a golden girdle.
14 His head and [h]*his* hairs *were*
white like wool, as white as snow; and
[i]his eyes *were* as a flame of fire;
15 [j]And his feet like unto fine
brass, as if they burned in a furnace;
and [k]his voice as the sound of many
waters.
16 [l]And he had in his right hand
seven stars: and [m]out of his mouth
went a sharp twoedged sword: [n]and
his countenance *was* as the sun
shineth in his strength.
17 And [o]when I saw him, I fell at
his feet as dead. And [p]he laid his right
hand upon me, saying unto me, Fear
not; [q]I am the first and the last:
18 [r]*I am* he that liveth, and was
dead; and, behold, [s]I am alive for
evermore, Amen; and [t]have the keys
of hell and of death.
19 Write the things which thou hast
seen, [u]and the things which are,
[v]and the things which shall be hereaf-
ter;
20 The mystery of the seven stars
which thou sawest in my right hand,
and the seven golden candlesticks.
The seven stars are [w]the angels of the
seven churches: and [x]the seven
candlesticks which thou sawest are
the seven churches.

The message to Ephesus

2 UNTO THE angel of the church of
Ephesus write; These things saith
[y]he that holdeth the seven stars in his
right hand, [z]who walketh in the midst
of the seven golden candlesticks;
2 [a]I know thy works, and thy la-
bour, and thy patience, and how thou
canst not bear them which are evil: and
[b]thou hast tried them [c]which say
they are apostles, and are not, and hast
found them liars:
3 And hast borne, and hast pa-
tience, and for my name's sake hast
laboured, and hast [d]not fainted.
4 Nevertheless I have *somewhat*
against thee, because thou hast left thy
first love.
5 Remember therefore from whence
thou art fallen, and repent, and do the
first works; [e]or else I will come unto
thee quickly, and will remove thy
candlestick out of his place, except
thou repent.
6 But this thou hast, that thou hat-

1:12 [c]Ex. 25:37 Zech. 4:2 **1:13** [d]ch. 2:1 [e]Ezek. 1:26 Dan. 7:13 & 10:16 [f]Dan. 10:5 [g]ch. 15:6 **1:14** [h]Dan. 7:9 [i]Dan. 10:6 **1:15** [j]Ezek. 1:7 Dan. 10:6 [k]Ezek. 43:2 Dan. 10:6 ch. 14:2 **1:16** [l]ch. 2:1 [m]Is. 49:2 Eph. 6:17 Heb. 4:12 [n]Acts 26:13 **1:17** [o]Ezek. 1:28 [p]Dan. 8:18 & 10:10 [q]Is. 41:4 & 44:6 & 48:12 ch. 22:13 **1:18** [r]Rom. 6:9 [s]ch. 4:9 [t]Ps. 68:20 ch. 20:1 **1:19** [u]ch. 2:1 [v]ch. 4:1 **1:20** [w]Mal. 2:7 ch. 2:1 [x]Zech. 4:2 Mat. 5:15 Phil. 2:15 **2:1** [y]ch. 1:16 [z]ch. 1:13

2:2 [a]Ps. 1:6; ch. 3:1,8 [b]1 John 4:1 [c]2 Cor. 11:13; 2 Pet. 2:1 **2:3** [d]Gal. 6:9; Heb. 12:3,5 **2:5** [e]Mat. 21:41

1:12 SEVEN GOLDEN CANDLESTICKS. These are actually stands that hold oil lamps, not candles (see Zech. 4:2, note); they represent the seven churches mentioned in v. 11 (cf. v. 20).

1:13 THE SON OF MAN. This term refers to the exalted Christ, a term also used by the O.T. prophet Daniel (see Dan. 7:13, note; 10:16). In this vision, Christ is described as king, priest, and judge of His churches (cf. vv. 13–16).

1:16 SEVEN STARS. The seven stars represent either angels who are assigned, each to a church, to assist it in its spiritual warfare (see v. 20; cf. Mat. 18:10), or the pastors of these churches. The "twoedged sword" represents the Word of God, which either cuts away sin from the churches and brings God's grace, or cuts a church away from the kingdom of God in judgment (3:14–22).

1:19 THINGS . . . SEEN . . . ARE . . . SHALL BE. Here we have an outline of the book of Revelation: (1) the things which John saw (ch. 1); (2) the things which are (chs. 2–3); (3) the things which will take place in the future (i.e., events preceding and following Christ's coming to earth, chs. 4–22).

1:20 THE SEVEN CHURCHES. See article on CHRIST'S MESSAGE TO THE SEVEN CHURCHES, p. 2036.

2:2 WHICH SAY THEY ARE APOSTLES. One of Christ's major concerns as He gave His final message to the seven churches was that they not fall into apostasy by tolerating false teachers, prophets, or apostles who were distorting His Word or weakening its power and authority. (1) Christ instructs the churches to test all who claim spiritual authority. (2) Note Christ's condemnation of the churches in Pergamos (vv. 14–16) and Thyatira (v. 20) for accepting rather than withstanding those disloyal to the truth and the standards of God's Word (see article on OVERSEERS AND THEIR DUTIES, p. 1706).

2:4 LEFT THY FIRST LOVE. This refers to the Ephesians' first deep love for and devotion to Christ and His Word (John 14:15,21; 15:10). (1) This warning teaches us that knowing correct doctrine, obeying some of the commandments, and worshiping in the church are not enough. The church must have above all a heartfelt love for Jesus Christ and all His Word (2 Cor. 11:3; cf. Deut. 10:12). (2) Sincere love for Christ results in single-hearted devotion to Him, purity of life, and a love of the truth (2 Cor. 11:3; see 2 Chr. 30:6, note; Mat. 22:37,39, notes; John 21:15, note).

2:5 REMOVE THY CANDLESTICK. Christ will reject any congregation or church and remove it from His kingdom if it does not repent of its declining love for and obedience to the Lord Jesus Christ.

CHRIST'S MESSAGE TO THE SEVEN CHURCHES

***Rev. 1:19–20** "Write the things which thou hast seen, and the things which are, and the things which shall be hereafter; The mystery of the seven stars which thou sawest in my right hand, and the seven golden candlesticks. The seven stars are the angels of the seven churches: and the seven candlesticks which thou sawest are the seven churches."*

Christ's messages to seven local churches in western Asia Minor (see Rev. 1:4, note) are intended for the exhortation, warning, and edification of believers and churches throughout this entire age (cf. 2:7,11,17,29; 3:6,13,22). The relevance of these messages for churches today include: (1) a revelation of what Jesus Christ Himself loves and values in His churches as well as what He hates and condemns; (2) a clear statement from Christ regarding (a) the consequences of disobedience and spiritual neglect and (b) the rewards for spiritual vigilance and faithfulness to Christ; (3) a standard by which any church or individual may judge his or her true spiritual state before God; (4) an example of the methods that Satan uses to attack the church or the individual Christian (see also Judg. 3:7, note). This article examines each of these aspects by using a question and answer format.

(1) What does Christ praise? Christ praises a church for not bearing with evil persons (Rev. 2:2); for testing the life, doctrine, and claims of Christian leaders (2:2); for persevering in faith, love, witness, service, and suffering for Christ (2:3,10,13,19,26); for hating what God hates (2:6); for overcoming sin, Satan, and the ungodly world (2:7,11,17,26; 3:5,12,21); for refusing to conform to immorality in the world and worldliness in the church (2:24; 3:4); and for keeping the Word of God (3:8,10).

(2) How does Christ reward churches that persevere and remain loyal to Him and His Word? He rewards such churches (a) by delivering them from the time of trial that will come upon the whole world (3:10), (b) by giving them His love, presence, and close fellowship (3:20), and (c) by blessing them with eternal life with God (Rev. 2:11,17,26; 3:5,12; 21:7).

(3) What does Christ condemn? He condemns a church for failing to maintain a close personal relationship to Himself and God (Rev. 2:4); for departing from Biblical faith; for tolerating immoral church leaders, teachers, or laypersons (2:14–15,20); for becoming spiritually dead (3:1) or lukewarm (3:15–16); and for substituting outward success and affluence (3:17) for real spirituality, i.e., purity, righteousness, and spiritual wisdom (3:18).

(4) How does Christ punish churches that decline spiritually and tolerate immorality within their midst? He punishes such churches (a) by removing them from their place in the kingdom of God (Rev. 2:5; 3:16); (b) by causing them to lose the presence of God, the genuine power of the Holy Spirit, the true Biblical message of salvation, and the protection of their members from Satan's destruction (Rev. 2:5,16,22–23; 3:16; see Mat. 13, notes concerning the good and the evil within the kingdom of heaven during this age); and (c) by placing their leaders under the judgment of God (Rev. 2:20–23).

(5) What does Christ's message reveal about the natural trend of churches toward spiritual stagnation, decline, and apostasy? (a) The seven letters suggest that it is the inherent tendency of churches to err, to accept false teaching, and to adapt to the evil, anti-God elements of the world (see Gal. 5:17, note). (b) In addition, we see that churches are often affected by apostate, evil, and unfaithful people (Rev. 2:2,14–15,20). For this reason the present spiritual state of a church can never be taken as a valid test

of God's will or as an ultimate justification for determining truth and doctrine. The gospel, i.e., the original message of Christ and the apostles, is the ultimate authority by which to measure the true and the false.

(6) How may churches avoid spiritual decline and subsequent judgment by Christ? These letters reveal several ways. (a) First and foremost, all churches must be willing to "hear what the Spirit saith unto the churches" (Rev. 2:5–7,16–17,21). The Word of Jesus Christ must always be the church's guide (Rev. 1:1–5), for His Word, as revealed to the N.T. apostles through the Holy Spirit, is the guide by which churches must examine their beliefs and activities and renew their spiritual lives (2:7,11,17,29; 3:6,13,22). (b) Churches must continually examine their spiritual condition before God and, if necessary, correct their degree of toleration of worldliness and immorality among their members (Rev. 2:4,14–15,20; 3:1–2,14–17). (c) Spiritual decline can be halted in any church or group only if there is sincere repentance from sin and a diligent return to the original love, truth, purity, and power of Jesus Christ and of Biblical revelation (2:5–7,16–17; 3:1–3,15–22).

THE SEVEN CHURCHES OF REVELATION

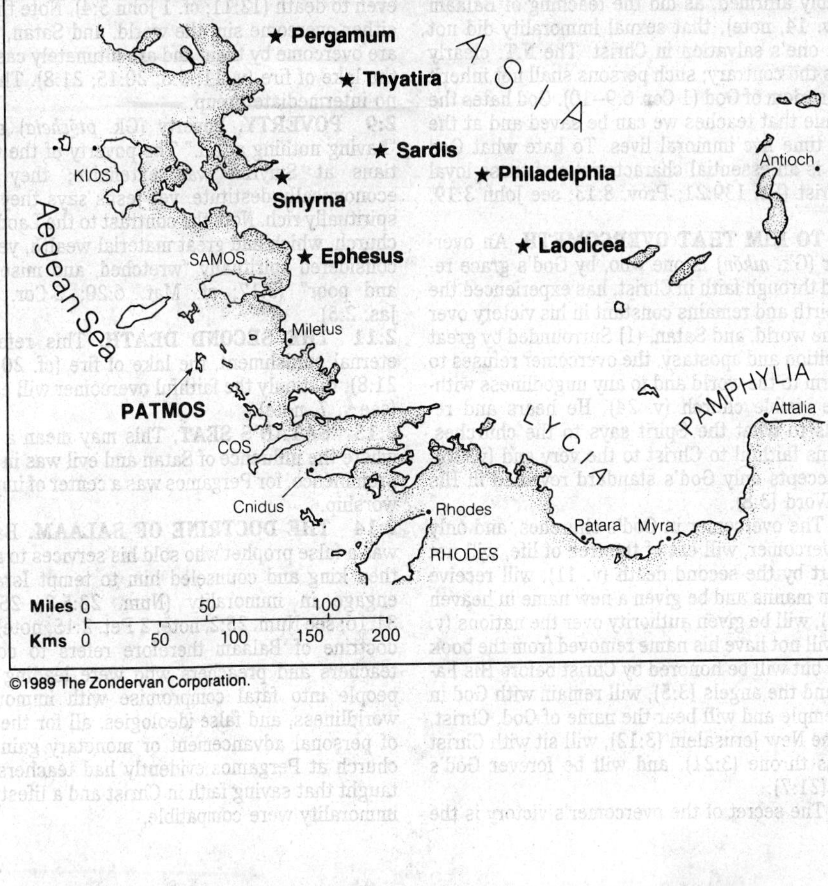

est the deeds of the Nicolaitans, which I also hate.

7 [f]He that hath an ear, let him hear what the Spirit saith unto the churches; To him that overcometh will I give [g]to eat of [h]the tree of life, which is in the midst of the paradise of God.

Rev. 2:12-17

The message to Smyrna

8 And unto the angel of the church in Smyrna write; These things saith [i]the first and the last, which was dead, and is alive;

9 I know thy works, and tribulation, and poverty, (but thou art [j]rich) and *I know* the blasphemy of [k]them which say they are Jews, and are not, [l]but *are* the synagogue of Satan.

10 [m]Fear none of those things which thou shalt suffer: behold, the devil shall cast *some* of you into prison, that ye may be tried; and ye shall have tribulation ten days: [n]be thou faithful unto death, and I will give thee [o]a crown of life.

11 [p]He that hath an ear, let him hear what the Spirit saith unto the churches; He that overcometh shall not be hurt of [q]the second death.

The message to Pergamos

12 And to the angel of the church in Pergamos write; These things saith [r]he which hath the sharp sword with two edges;

13 I know thy works, and where thou dwellest, *even* where Satan's seat *is:* and thou holdest fast my name, and hast not denied my faith, even in those days wherein Antipas *was* my faithful martyr, who was slain among you, where Satan dwelleth.

14 But I have a few things against thee, because thou hast there them that hold the doctrine of [s]Balaam, who taught Balac to cast a stumblingblock before the children of Israel, [t]to

2:7 [f]Mat. 11:15 & 13:9,43 ch. 3:6,13 [g]ch. 22:2,14 [h]Gen. 2:9
2:8 [i]ch. 1:8,17
2:9 [j]Luke 12:21 1 Tim. 6:18 Jas. 2:5 [k]Rom. 2:17 [l]ch. 3:9
2:10 [m]Mat. 10:22 [n]Mat. 24:13 [o]Jas. 1:12 ch. 3:11
2:11 [p]ch. 13:9 [q]ch. 20:1 & 21:8
2:12 [r]ch. 1:16
2:14 [s]Num. 24:14 & 25:1 & 31:16 2 Pet. 2:15 Jude 11 [t]Acts 15:29 1 Cor. 8:9 & 10:19,20

2:6 THOU HATEST . . . THE NICOLAITANS, WHICH I ALSO HATE. The Nicolaitans (cf. v. 15) probably affirmed, as did the teaching of Balaam (see v. 14, note), that sexual immorality did not affect one's salvation in Christ. The N.T. clearly states the contrary; such persons shall not inherit the kingdom of God (1 Cor. 6:9–10). God hates the doctrine that teaches we can be saved and at the same time live immoral lives. To hate what God hates is an essential characteristic of those loyal to Christ (Ps. 139:21; Prov. 8:13; see John 3:19, note).

2:7 TO HIM THAT OVERCOMETH. An overcomer (Gk. *nikōn*) is one who, by God's grace received through faith in Christ, has experienced the new birth and remains constant in his victory over sin, the world, and Satan. (1) Surrounded by great opposition and apostasy, the overcomer refuses to conform to the world and to any ungodliness within the visible church (v. 24). He hears and responds to what the Spirit says to the churches, remains faithful to Christ to the very end (v. 26), and accepts only God's standard revealed in His holy Word (3:8).

(2) The overcomer in God's churches, and only the overcomer, will eat of the tree of life, will not be hurt by the second death (v. 11), will receive hidden manna and be given a new name in heaven (v. 17), will be given authority over the nations (v. 26), will not have his name removed from the book of life but will be honored by Christ before His Father and the angels (3:5), will remain with God in His temple and will bear the name of God, Christ, and the New Jerusalem (3:12), will sit with Christ on His throne (3:21), and will be forever God's child (21:7).

(3) The secret of the overcomer's victory is the atoning death of Christ, his own faithful testimony about Jesus, and his perseverance in love to Christ even to death (12:11; cf. 1 John 5:4). Note that we either overcome sin, the world, and Satan, or we are overcome by them and are ultimately cast into the lake of fire (v. 11; 3:5; 20:15; 21:8). There is no intermediate group.

2:9 POVERTY. Poverty (Gk. *ptōcheia*) means "having nothing at all." The poverty of the Christians at Smyrna was extensive; they were economically destitute, yet Jesus says they were spiritually rich. Note the contrast to the Laodicean church, which had great material wealth, yet was considered spiritually "wretched, and miserable, and poor" (3:17; cf. Mat. 6:20; 2 Cor. 6:10; Jas. 2:5).

2:11 THE SECOND DEATH. This refers to eternal punishment, the lake of fire (cf. 20:6,14; 21:8), that only the faithful overcomer will escape (see v. 7, note).

2:13 SATAN'S SEAT. This may mean a place where the influence of Satan and evil was in great prominence, for Pergamos was a center of imperial worship.

2:14 THE DOCTRINE OF BALAAM. Balaam was a false prophet who sold his services to a heathen king and counseled him to tempt Israel to engage in immorality (Num. 22:5,7; 25:1–2; 31:16; see Num. 25:2, note; 2 Pet. 2:15, note). The doctrine of Balaam therefore refers to corrupt teachers and preachers who were leading their people into fatal compromise with immorality, worldliness, and false ideologies, all for the sake of personal advancement or monetary gain. The church at Pergamos evidently had teachers who taught that saving faith in Christ and a lifestyle of immorality were compatible.

eat things sacrificed unto idols, [u]and to commit fornication.

15 So hast thou also them that hold the doctrine of the Nicolaitans, which thing I hate.

16 Repent; or else I will come unto thee quickly, and [v]will fight against them with the sword of my mouth.

17 He that hath an ear, let him hear what the Spirit saith unto the churches; To him that overcometh will I give to eat of the hidden manna, and will give him a white stone, and in the stone [w]a new name written, which no man knoweth saving he that receiveth *it.*

The message to Thyatira

18 And unto the angel of the church in Thyatira write; These things saith the Son of God, [x]who hath his eyes like unto a flame of fire, and his feet *are* like fine brass;

19 [y]I know thy works, and charity, and service, and faith, and thy patience, and thy works; and the last *to be* more than the first.

20 Notwithstanding I have a few things against thee, because thou sufferest that woman [z]Jezebel, which calleth herself a prophetess, to teach and to seduce my servants [a]to commit fornication, and to eat things sacrificed unto idols.

21 And I gave her space [b]to repent of her fornication; and she repented not.

22 Behold, I will cast her into a bed, and them that commit adultery with her into great tribulation, except they repent of their deeds.

23 And I will kill her children with death; and all the churches shall know that [c]I am he which searcheth the reins and hearts: and [d]I will give unto every one of you according to your works.

24 But unto you I say, and unto the rest in Thyatira, as many as have not this doctrine, and which have not known the depths of Satan, as they speak; [e]I will put upon you none other burden.

25 But [f]that which ye have *already* hold fast till I come.

26 And he that overcometh, and keepeth [g]my works unto the end, [h]to him will I give power over the nations:

27 [i]And he shall rule them with a rod of iron; as the vessels of a potter shall they be broken to shivers: even as I received of my Father.

28 And I will give him [j]the morning star.

29 [k]He that hath an ear, let him

2:14 [u]1 Cor. 6:13
2:16 [v]Is. 11:4; 2 Thes. 2:8; ch. 1:16
2:17 [w]ch. 3:12 & 19:12
2:18 [x]ch. 1:14,15
2:19 [y]ver. 2
2:20 [z]1 Ki. 16:31 & 21:25; 2 Ki. 9:7; [a]Ex. 34:15; Acts 15:20
2:21 [b]ch. 9:20
2:23 [c]1 Sam. 16:7; Jer. 11:20; John 2:24; Acts 1:24; Rom. 8:27; [d]Ps. 62:12; 2 Cor. 5:10
2:24 [e]Acts 15:28
2:25 [f]ch. 3:11
2:26 [g]John 6:29; 1 John 3:23; [h]Mat. 19:28; Luke 22:29; 1 Cor. 6:3
2:27 [i]Ps. 2:8,9; Dan. 7:22
2:28 [j]2 Pet. 1:19
2:29 [k]ver. 7

2:16 I . . . WILL FIGHT AGAINST THEM. Jesus will oppose any within His churches who promote a tolerant attitude toward sin (v. 15; see v. 6, note; 1 Cor. 5:2, note; Gal. 5:21, note); He promises to make war against immoral professing believers if they do not repent.

2:17 HEAR WHAT THE SPIRIT SAITH. We must heed the warnings of the Holy Spirit today. He continues to speak the same words Christ spoke to the seven churches of Asia, commanding us to overcome sin in the world and not to tolerate immorality in our midst. If we fail to overcome in this important area, we lose the presence of God and the power of the Holy Spirit and become enemies of the kingdom of God. If, on the other hand, we overcome, we receive the hidden manna of spiritual life and a "white stone," signifying the triumph of our faith over all that sought to destroy our devotion to Christ.

2:20 THOU SUFFEREST THAT WOMAN JEZEBEL, WHICH CALLETH HERSELF A PROPHETESS. A prevalent sin within the church in Thyatira was the tendency to tolerate sin, unrighteousness, or unbiblical teaching in its leaders (vv. 14,20). (1) John calls one particular person Jezebel, a name derived from the O.T. Jezebel and synonymous with idolatry and persecution (1 Ki. 16:31; 19:1–3; 21:1–15; see 21:25, note). Some at Thyatira probably accepted false teachers because they claimed to speak for God and because they manifested great talents, power, position, success, and influence. Christ condemns the sin of tolerance.

(2) We must reject all spokespersons who put their own words above Biblical revelation (see 1 Cor. 14:29, note) and who state that God accepts within the church any who commit acts of immorality and participate in the evil pleasures of the world. Some in the church often tolerate such false teaching because of indifference, fear of confrontation, or personal friendship, or because of a desire for peace, harmony, personal advancement, or money; God will destroy such a church with its leaders (vv. 20–23; see also Luke 17:3–4, note).

2:24 THE REST. There were those in Thyatira who had held fast to Christ's Word and His righteous standards. God knows them and promises that they will rule with Him over the nations (v. 26). "The depths of Satan" may refer to the false teaching that says in order to fully experience the grace and salvation of God, one must enter into the depths of sin and become acquainted with all kinds of evil.

2:25 HOLD FAST TILL I COME. Christ's words "till I come" and "unto the end" (v. 26) make it clear that His messages, warnings, and promises to the seven churches apply also to all churches until the end.

hear what the Spirit saith unto the churches.

The message to Sardis

3 AND UNTO the angel of the church in Sardis write; These things saith he [l]that hath the seven Spirits of God, and the seven stars; [m]I know thy works, that thou hast a name that thou livest, [n]and art dead.

2 Be watchful, and strengthen the things which remain, that are ready to die: for I have not found thy works perfect before God.

3 [o]Remember therefore how thou hast received and heard, and hold fast, and [p]repent. [q]If therefore thou shalt not watch, I will come on thee as a thief, and thou shalt not know what hour I will come upon thee.

4 Thou hast [r]a few names even in Sardis which have not [s]defiled their garments; and they shall walk with me [t]in white: for they are worthy.

Rev. 21:8

5 He that overcometh, [u]the same shall be clothed in white raiment; and I will not [v]blot out his name out of the [w]book of life, but [x]I will confess his name before my Father, and before his angels.

6 [y]He that hath an ear, let him hear what the Spirit saith unto the churches.

The message to Philadelphia

7 And to the angel of the church in Philadelphia write; These things saith [z]he that is holy, [a]he that is true, he that hath [b]the key of David, [c]he that openeth, and no man shutteth; and [d]shutteth, and no man openeth;

8 [e]I know thy works: behold, I have set before thee [f]an open door, and no man can shut it: for thou hast a little strength, and hast kept my word, and hast not denied my name.

9 Behold, I will make [g]them of the synagogue of Satan, which say they are Jews, and are not, but do lie; behold, [h]I will make them to come and worship before thy feet, and to know that I have loved thee.

10 Because thou hast kept the word of my patience, [i]I also will keep thee

3:1 [l]ch. 1:4,16 [m]ch. 2:2 [n]Eph. 2:1,5
3:3 [o]1 Tim. 6:20 2 Tim. 1:13 [p]ver. 19 [q]Mat. 24:42 Mark 13:33 Luke 12:39 1 Thes. 5:2,6 2 Pet. 3:10
3:4 [r]Acts 1:15 [s]Jude 23 [t]ch. 4:4 & 6:11
3:5 [u]ch. 19:8 [v]Ex. 32:32 [w]Phil. 4:3 [x]Luke 12:8
3:6 [y]ch. 2:7
3:7 [z]Acts 3:14 [a]1 John 5:20 [b]Is. 22:22 Luke 1:32 [c]Mat. 16:19 [d]Job 12:14
3:8 [e]ver. 1 [f]1 Cor. 16:9
3:9 [g]ch. 2:9 [h]Is. 49:23
3:10 [i]2 Pet. 2:9

3:1 THOU . . . ART DEAD. The church of Sardis was spiritually dead, with only a few of its members remaining faithful to the gospel. Outwardly it appeared alive and active and had a reputation of success and spirituality. It may have had an exciting form of worship, but not the true power and righteousness of the Holy Spirit. But Jesus saw the inner lives and hearts of the people.

3:4 A FEW . . . EVEN IN SARDIS. Throughout church history, there have always been a few (i.e., a remnant) who have not "defiled their garments" and who have sought to return to the simplicity and purity of devotion to Christ which the apostles and many others in the N.T. knew (2 Cor. 11:3).

3:5 BLOT OUT HIS NAME. Clearly any person who experiences the new birth, but later refuses to persevere in faith and to overcome, will have his name taken out of the book of life (see 2:7, note). To have one's name blotted out of the book of life is to lose eternal life itself (2:7,10–11) and to be condemned to the lake of fire in the end (20:15). This is what the Spirit says to the churches (v. 6; 13:8; 17:8; 20:12; 21:27; cf. Ex. 32:32).

3:7 PHILADELPHIA. Philadelphia was a faithful church that kept Christ's Word and did not deny Him. They had endured opposition from the world and resisted conforming to the evil trends of other churches, yet had persevered in loyalty to Christ and the truth of the N.T. gospel (vv. 7–10). Because of their persevering faithfulness, God promises to deliver them from the hour of trial (see next note).

3:10 THE HOUR OF TEMPTATION. Christ's promise to deliver the faithful in Philadelphia from the hour of trial is identical to Paul's promise to the Thessalonians that they would be delivered from the "wrath to come" (1 Thes. 1:10); it extends to all of God's faithful throughout the ages (vv. 13,22). This hour includes the divinely appointed time of trial, wrath, and tribulation that will come on "all the world" in the last years of this age, just prior to the establishment of Christ's kingdom on earth (5:10; 6—19; 20:4). Concerning this time, the Bible reveals the following truths.

(1) This time of trial involves the wrath of God upon the ungodly (chs. 6–19; Is. 13:6–13; 17:4–11; Dan. 9:27; 12:1; Zech. 14:1–4; Mat. 24:9–31; see 1 Thes. 5:2, note; see article on THE GREAT TRIBULATION, p. 1456).

(2) Also included in this time of trial, however, is the wrath of Satan on the godly, i.e., on those accepting Christ during this terrible time. For them there will be hunger, thirst, exposure to elements (7:16), and great suffering and tears (7:9–17; Dan. 12:10; Mat. 24:15–21). They will experience indirectly the natural catastrophes of war, famine, and death. They will be persecuted, tortured, and in all probability will suffer martyrdom (6:11; 13:7; 14:13). They will undergo the ravages of Satan and demonic forces (9:3–5; 12:12), evil and violence from wicked men, and persecution by the antichrist (6:9; 12:17; 13:15–17). They will suffer loss of home and will need to flee in fear (Mat. 24:15–21). It will be an especially disastrous time for those with families and children (Mat. 24:19), so terrible that the tribulation saints who die are counted blessed, for they rest from their labors and are free from persecution (14:13).

(3) For those who are overcomers before that

from the hour of temptation, which shall come upon [j]all the world, to try them that dwell [k]upon the earth.

11 Behold, [l]I come quickly: [m]hold that fast which thou hast, that no man take [n]thy crown.

12 Him that overcometh will I make [o]a pillar in the temple of my God, and he shall go no more out: and [p]I will write upon him the name of my God, and the name of the city of my God, *which is* [q]new Jerusalem, which cometh down out of heaven from my God: [r]and *I will write upon him* my new name.

13 [s]He that hath an ear, let him hear what the Spirit saith unto the churches.

The message to Laodicea

14 And unto the angel of the church [a]of the Laodiceans write; [t]These things saith the Amen, [u]the faithful and true witness, [v]the beginning of the creation of God;

15 [w]I know thy works, that thou art neither cold nor hot: I would thou wert cold or hot.

16 So then because thou art lukewarm, and neither cold nor hot, I will spew thee out of my mouth.

17 Because thou sayest, [x]I am rich, and increased with goods, and have need of nothing; and knowest not that thou art wretched, and miserable, and poor, and blind, and naked:

18 I counsel thee [y]to buy of me gold tried in the fire, that thou mayest be rich; and [z]white raiment, that thou mayest be clothed, and *that* the shame of thy nakedness do not appear; and anoint thine eyes with eyesalve, that thou mayest see.

19 [a]As many as I love, I rebuke and chasten: be zealous therefore, and repent.

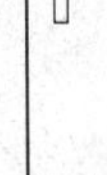

20 Behold, [b]I stand at the door, and knock: [c]if any man hear my voice, and open the door, [d]I will come in to him, and will sup with him, and he with me.

End

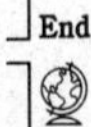

21 To him that overcometh [e]will I grant to sit with me in my throne, even as I also overcame, and am set down with my Father in his throne.

22 [f]He that hath an ear, let him

3:10 [j]Luke 2:1 [k]Is. 24:17
3:11 [l]Phil. 4:5 [m]ch. 2:25 [n]ch. 2:10
3:12 [o]1 Ki. 7:21 Gal. 2:9 [p]ch. 14:1 [q]Heb. 12:22 [r]ch. 22:4
3:13 [s]ch. 2:7
3:14 [t]Is. 65:16 [u]ch. 19:11 [v]Col. 1:15
3:15 [w]ver. 1
3:17 [x]Hos. 12:8 1 Cor. 4:8
3:18 [y]Is. 55:1 Mat. 13:44 [z]2 Cor. 5:3 ch. 7:13
3:19 [a]Job 5:17 Prov. 3:11 Heb. 12:5,6
3:20 [b]Sol. 5:2 [c]Luke 12:37 [d]John 14:23
3:21 [e]Mat. 19:28 Luke 22:30 2 Tim. 2:12
3:22 [f]ch. 2:7

[a] Or, *in Laodicea*

day arrives (see 2:7, note; Luke 21:36, note), God will keep them from that hour of trial, most likely through the rapture, i.e., the catching up of the faithful to meet Christ in the air before God pours out His wrath (see John 14:3, note; see article on THE RAPTURE, p. 1889). This deliverance is a reward for those who persevere in keeping God's Word in true faith.

(4) Present-day believers who hope to escape all these things that are about to come upon the world will do so only by faithfulness to Christ and His Word and by constant vigilance in prayer (see Luke 21:36, note), lest they be deceived (see Mat. 24:5, note).

3:11 BEHOLD, I COME QUICKLY. The close connection of this verse with v. 10 indicates (1) that Christ's coming to take up His church from the earth will be the means of their deliverance (cf. 1 Thes. 1:10; 4:14–18), and (2) that deliverance from the hour of trial and tribulation will come only to those faithful of the churches who hold fast to Christ and His Word (v. 8).

3:15–16 LUKEWARM . . . NEITHER COLD NOR HOT. This describes the spiritual condition of the church of Laodicea. (1) A lukewarm church is one that compromises with the world and resembles its surrounding society; it professes Christianity, yet in reality is spiritually "wretched and miserable" (vv. 17–18). It would be better for the kingdom of God if that church would deny Christ completely. Christ warns such churches that He will reject them (cf. Luke 13:25–28).

(2) In the midst of a lukewarm church age, the promises of Christ to overcoming churches remain valid. He will come to them in blessing and in the power of the Holy Spirit (vv. 20–22), opening a door that no one can shut, so that they may glorify His name and proclaim the everlasting gospel (v. 8).

3:20 IF ANY MAN HEAR MY VOICE. In its self-sufficient prosperity and worldliness (vv. 15–18), the church of Laodicea has excluded the Lord Jesus Christ from their congregations. Christ's invitation, spoken from outside the door, is a request for fellowship with any individual who will repent of and overcome the spiritual lukewarmness of the church (v. 21).

3:22 THE SPIRIT . . . THE CHURCHES. The distinction between the churches and the Holy Spirit must be continually affirmed. Churches are subordinate to the Spirit of God and to His inspired Word (2 Tim. 3:15–16; 1 Pet. 1:24–25; 2 Pet. 1:20–21). This distinction between the Spirit and the churches can be expressed by the following Biblical truths. (1) The Spirit is not the possession of the churches or any human institution. He is the Spirit of God and of Christ, not the Spirit of the churches (v. 1). The Spirit remains free to come and leave according to God's righteous standards (cf. John 1:33; 7:39; 14:17).

(2) The Holy Spirit represents the present Lordship of Christ over the churches. The Spirit and His Word are the ultimate authority. Churches must constantly judge their beliefs and actions by the Spirit. They must never trust in, obey, and listen to themselves alone. The Spirit and the in-

Rev. 21:7 hear what the Spirit saith unto the
churches.

The heavenly worship

4 AFTER THIS I looked, and, be-
hold, a door *was* opened in heaven:
and [g]the first voice which I heard *was*
as it were of a trumpet talking with me;
which said, [h]Come up hither, [i]and I
will show thee things which must be
hereafter.
2 And immediately [j]I was in the
spirit: and, behold, [k]a throne was set
in heaven, and *one* sat on the throne.
3 And he that sat was to look upon
like a jasper and a sardine stone: [l]and
there was a rainbow round about the
throne, in sight like unto an emerald.
4 [m]And round about the throne
were four and twenty seats: and upon
the seats I saw four and twenty elders
sitting, [n]clothed in white raiment; and
they had on their heads crowns of gold.
5 And out of the throne proceeded
[o]lightnings and thunderings and
voices: [p]and *there were* seven lamps of
fire burning before the throne, which
are [q]the seven Spirits of God.
6 And before the throne *there was*
[r]a sea of glass like unto crystal: [s]and
in the midst of the throne, and round
about the throne, *were* four beasts full
of eyes before and behind.

4:1 [g]ch. 1:10 [h]ch. 11:12 [i]ch. 1:19
4:2 [j]ch. 1:10 [k]Is. 6:1 Ezek. 1:26 Dan. 7:9
4:3 [l]Ezek. 1:28
4:4 [m]ch. 11:16 [n]ch. 3:4,5
4:5 [o]ch. 8:5 [p]Ex. 37:23 2 Chr. 4:20 Ezek. 1:13 Zech. 4:2 [q]ch. 1:4
4:6 [r]Ex. 38:8 ch. 15:2 [s]Ezek. 1:5
4:7 [t]Num. 2:2 Ezek. 1:10
4:8 [u]Is. 6:2 [v]Is. 6:3 [w]ch. 1:8 [x]ch. 1:4
4:9 [y]ch. 1:18
4:10 [z]ch. 5:8,14
4:11 [a]ch. 5:12 [b]Gen. 1:1 Acts 17:24 Eph. 3:9
5:1 [c]Ezek. 2:9 [d]Is. 29:11 Dan. 12:4

7 [t]And the first beast *was* like a
lion, and the second beast like a calf,
and the third beast had a face as a man,
and the fourth beast *was* like a flying
eagle.
8 And the four beasts had each of
them [u]six wings about *him;* and *they*
were full of eyes within: and [b]they rest
not day and night, saying, [v]Holy, holy,
holy, [w]Lord God Almighty, [x]which
was, and is, and is to come.
9 And when those beasts give glory
and honour and thanks to him that sat
on the throne, [y]who liveth for ever
and ever,
10 [z]The four and twenty elders fall
down before him that sat on the throne,
and worship him that liveth for ever
and ever, and cast their crowns before
the throne, saying,
11 [a]Thou art worthy, O Lord, to re-
ceive glory and honour and power:
[b]for thou hast created all things, and
for thy pleasure they are and were cre-
ated.

The book and the Lamb

5 AND I saw in the right hand of him
that sat on the throne [c]a book
written within and on the backside,
[d]sealed with seven seals.

[b] Gk. *they have no rest*

spired Word are greater than the churches of history.

(3) The Holy Spirit will remain with any church only as long as it remains faithful to Christ and His Word and hears what the Spirit says to the churches (2:5,16,22–23; 3:3,15–16).

4:1 AFTER THIS. Many Bible expositors believe that at this point in Revelation, Christ has already taken the faithful overcomers of His churches out of the world. Thus, the catching away of the true church (see John 14:3, note; see article on THE RAPTURE, p. 1889) precedes the tribulation period (chs. 6–18). This is believed for the following reasons: (1) Beginning with 4:1, the terms "church" or "churches" disappear until 22:16. (2) The bride of Christ (i.e., the church) appears in ch. 19 already with Christ in heaven before He returns to earth to judge the wicked and to reign in the millennial kingdom (see 20:4, note). (3) The promise given to the Philadelphia church to keep it from the hour of worldwide trial pertains to all believers who stand true to Christ before the tribulation (see 3:10, note).

4:4 FOUR AND TWENTY ELDERS. Who are these elders? Some believe they represent the entire church in heaven (see John 14:3, note; 2 Tim. 4:8; 1 Pet. 5:4). Others believe they may be ruling angels; note, however, that angels stand around the elders (7:11; cf. 5:8–10). Still others believe they represent Israel and the church joined in worship to God and the Lamb, i.e., the combining of 12 (Israel) and 12 (the church) equals 24 (God's people of both ages).

4:5 SEVEN SPIRITS OF GOD. The seven Spirits of God represent the presence of the Holy Spirit at the throne of God. The language may come from the sevenfold expression of the spirit in Is. 11:2. The Holy Spirit is like a burning fire filled with judgment against sin and with the purity of God (cf. Is. 4:4; John 16:8).

4:6 FOUR BEASTS. These four creatures probably represent the entire living creation (v. 7). All of God's living creatures will bring glory and honor to Him in heaven and will be redeemed from the curse of sin (vv. 8–11).

4:8 HOLY, HOLY, HOLY. The entire creation emphasizes and praises God's holiness (see article on PRAISE, p. 816). To be holy means to be separated from sin, unrighteousness, and all evil, and to be dedicated to righteousness, goodness, justice, and purity. Holiness is an eternal attribute of God; His holiness will never change (see Is. 6:1,3, notes; see article on THE ATTRIBUTES OF GOD, p. 912).

5:1 A BOOK. This "book" or scroll is of utmost importance, for it contains the revelation of what God has determined for the future course of the world and mankind. It describes how the world

2 And I saw a strong angel proclaiming with a loud voice, Who is worthy to open the book, and to loose the seals thereof?

3 And no man in heaven, nor in earth, neither under the earth, was able to open the book, neither to look thereon.

4 And I wept much, because no man was found worthy to open and to read the book, neither to look thereon.

5 And one of the elders saith unto me, Weep not: behold, [e]the Lion of the tribe of Judah, [f]the Root of David, hath prevailed to open the book, [g]and to loose the seven seals thereof.

6 And I beheld, and, lo, in the midst of the throne and of the four beasts, and in the midst of the elders, stood [h]a Lamb as it had been slain, having seven horns and [i]seven eyes, which are [j]the seven Spirits of God sent forth into all the earth.

7 And he came and took the book out of the right hand [k]of him that sat upon the throne.

8 And when he had taken the book, [l]the four beasts and four *and* twenty elders fell down before the Lamb, having every one of them [m]harps, and golden vials full of [c]odours, [n]which are the prayers of saints.

9 And [o]they sung a new song, saying, [p]Thou art worthy to take the book, and to open the seals thereof: for thou wast slain, and [q]hast redeemed us to God by thy blood [r]out of every kindred, and tongue, and people, and nation;

10 [s]And hast made us unto our God kings and priests: and we shall reign on the earth.

11 And I beheld, and I heard the voice of many angels round about the throne and the beasts and the elders: and the number of them was [t]ten thousand times ten thousand, and thousands of thousands;

12 Saying with a loud voice, [u]Worthy is the Lamb that was slain to receive power, and riches, and wisdom, and strength, and honour, and glory, and blessing.

13 And [v]every creature which is in heaven, and on the earth, and under the earth, and such as are in the sea, and all that are in them, heard I saying, [w]Blessing, and honour, and glory, and power, *be* unto him [x]that sitteth upon the throne, and unto the Lamb for ever and ever.

14 [y]And the four beasts said, Amen. And the four *and* twenty elders fell down and worshipped him [z]that liveth for ever and ever. Rev. 7:9-12

The white horse

6 AND [a]I saw when the Lamb opened one of the seals, and I

5:5 [e]Gen. 49:9 Heb. 7:14 [f]Is. 11:1,10 ch. 22:16 [g]ch. 6:1
5:6 [h]Is. 53:7 John 1:29 1 Pet. 1:19 [i]Zech. 3:9 [j]ch. 4:5
5:7 [k]ch. 4:2
5:8 [l]ch. 4:8,10 [m]ch. 14:2 [n]Ps. 141:2
5:9 [o]Ps. 40:3 [p]ch. 4:11 [q]Acts 20:28 Rom. 3:24 1 Cor. 6:20 Eph. 1:7 Col. 1:14 Heb. 9:12 1 Pet. 1:18 2 Pet. 2:1 1 John 1:7 [r]Dan. 4:1
5:10 [s]Ex. 19:6 1 Pet. 2:5
5:11 [t]Ps. 68:17 Dan. 7:10 Heb. 12:22
5:12 [u]ch. 4:11
5:13 [v]Phil. 2:10 [w]1 Chr. 29:11 Rom. 9:5 & 16:27 1 Tim. 6:16 1 Pet. 4:11 & 5:11 [x]ch. 6:16
5:14 [y]ch. 19:4 [z]ch. 4:9,10
6:1 [a]ch. 5:5-7

[c] Or, *incense*

will be judged and portrays the final triumph of God and His people over all evil. When each seal is broken, a portion of the book's content is revealed in a vision (ch. 6; compare Ezek. 2:9–10).

5:4 I WEPT MUCH. John weeps because he knows that if a worthy person is not found to open the book, God's purpose of judgment and blessing for the world will remain unfulfilled (see John 12:31, note).

5:5 THE LION OF THE TRIBE OF JUDAH. Christ is pictured as a Lion, indicating He will rule all the earth. He is from the tribe of Judah and the family of David. These titles of Jesus as the conquering Messiah (Gen. 49:9–10) and eternal king accord with the promises made to David (Is. 11:1, 10).

5:6 LAMB AS IT HAD BEEN SLAIN. Christ, appearing as a Lamb that bears the marks of having been slain, represents His giving of Himself on Calvary for the sins of the human race. It signifies that Christ's worthiness, power, authority, and victory come from His sacrificial death on the cross (vv. 9–14). "Lamb" is Revelation's foremost symbol for Christ (e.g., vv. 6–7; 12:11; 15:3; 17:14; 21:22; 22:1,3). Christ's judgment is on those who rejected His sacrifice as the Lamb of God (6:16–17). The "seven horns" represent the power and strength of a ruler (1 Ki. 22:11; Dan. 7:24); for "seven Spirits," see 4:5, note.

5:8 THE PRAYERS OF SAINTS. This refers to the intercession of the saints for the coming of the kingdom when they shall reign on earth (vv. 9–10). Their prayer is, "Thy kingdom come. Thy will be done in earth, as *it is* in heaven" (Mat. 6:10; see 6:6, note; 2 Pet. 3:12, note; cf. Ps. 141:2).

6:1 THE LAMB OPENED. Jesus Christ Himself (i.e., the Lamb) breaks all the seals, which disclose the devastating judgments of God upon the world (vv. 1,3,5,7,9,12). This indicates that the judgments are divine in origin, for they have been given into Christ's hands (5:1,7; cf. John 5:22). Throughout the book of Revelation, the plague judgments are called the wrath of God (vv. 16–17; 11:18; 14:10,19; 15:1,7; 16:1,19; 19:15).

6:1 OPENED ONE OF THE SEALS. Some interpreters understand the breaking of the first seal as the beginning of the seven-year tribulation, that future time of unprecedented suffering and judgment leading up to the second coming of Christ to earth (see Dan. 9:27; cf. Jer. 30:7; Dan. 12:1; Rev. 6:17; 7:14; see article on THE GREAT TRIBULATION, p. 1456). Others believe the seals describe

heard, as it were the noise of thunder,
[b]one of the four beasts saying, Come
and see.
2 And I saw, and behold [c]a white
horse: [d]and he that sat on him had a
bow; [e]and a crown was given unto
him: and he went forth conquering, and
to conquer.

The red horse

3 And when he had opened the sec-
ond seal, [f]I heard the second beast
say, Come and see.
4 [g]And there went out another
horse *that was* red: and *power* was giv-
en to him that sat thereon to take
peace from the earth, and that they
should kill one another: and there was
given unto him a great sword.

The black horse

5 And when he had opened the third
seal, [h]I heard the third beast say,
Come and see. And I beheld, and lo [i]a
black horse; and he that sat on him had
a pair of balances in his hand.
6 And I heard a voice in the midst of
the four beasts say, [d]A measure of
wheat for a penny, and three measures
of barley for a penny; and [j]see thou
hurt not the oil and the wine.

The pale horse

7 And when he had opened the
fourth seal, [k]I heard the voice of the
fourth beast say, Come and see.
8 [l]And I looked, and behold a pale
horse: and his name that sat on him
was Death, and Hell followed with him.
And power was given [e]unto them over
the fourth part of the earth, [m]to kill
with sword, and with hunger, and with
death, [n]and with the beasts of the
earth.

The souls of the martyrs

9 And when he had opened the fifth
seal, I saw under [o]the altar [p]the
souls of them that were slain [q]for the
word of God, and for [r]the testimony
which they held:
10 And they cried with a loud voice,
saying, [s]How long, O Lord, [t]holy

6:1 [b]ch. 4:7
6:2 [c]Zech. 6:3; ch. 19:11 [d]Ps. 45:4,5 LXX [e]Zech. 6:11; ch. 14:14
6:3 [f]ch. 4:7
6:4 [g]Zech. 6:2
6:5 [h]ch. 4:7 [i]Zech. 6:2
6:6 [j]ch. 9:4
6:7 [k]ch. 4:7
6:8 [l]Zech. 6:3 [m]Ezek. 14:21 [n]Lev. 26:22
6:9 [o]ch. 8:3 & 14:18 [p]ch. 20:4 [q]ch. 1:9 [r]2 Tim. 1:8; ch. 19:10
6:10 [s]See Zech. 1:12 [t]ch. 3:7

[d] The word *choenix* signifies a measure containing one wine quart, and the twelfth part of a quart [e] Or, *to him*

---

the final three and one-half years of the seven-year tribulation, often called the great tribulation. Still others see them as the beginning of God's judgment toward the end of the age. The judgments of God are revealed in successive series. The first series is the seven seals (ch. 6); the second, the seven trumpet judgments (chs. 8–9; 11:15–19); and the third, the seven "vials of the wrath of God" (ch. 16; see 8:1, note).

6:2 A WHITE HORSE. Four horsemen come forth as the first four seals are broken (cf. Zech. 1:8–17; 6:1–8), representing God's judgment on the corrupt and evil world system and the ungodly. The rider of the white horse is thought by many Bible interpreters to be the antichrist (1 John 2:18), the future world ruler who is to begin his activity at the beginning of the last seven years (see article on THE AGE OF THE ANTICHRIST, p. 1896). He is allowed by God to deceive all who oppose Christ. His initial conquest will be accomplished without open warfare, for peace is taken from the earth beginning with the second horseman (v. 4; cf. Dan. 9:26–27; 1 Thes. 5:3). On the other hand, all the other horsemen are personifications, so the rider on the white horse may simply represent conquest or a strong spirit of antichrist let loose in the end time.

6:4 HORSE *THAT WAS* RED. The red horse and its rider represent war and violent death, which God will allow in bringing His wrath upon the world (cf. Zech. 1:8; 6:2). The tribulation will be a time of violence, murder, and war.

6:5–6 A BLACK HORSE. The black horse and its rider symbolize great famine (cf. Jer. 4:26–28; Lam. 4:8–9; 5:10). Basic necessities of life will be scarce and prices extremely high; hunger will spread throughout the world. The "oil and the wine" refer to the olive tree and grapevine, which are not hurt as much by drought as grain. Though famines have occurred throughout the church age (Mat. 24:7), this passage is dealing with a specific famine during the tribulation.

6:8 A PALE HORSE. The pale horse and its rider named Death symbolize a terrible intensification of war, famine, death, plagues, disease, and evil beasts. This judgment will be so terrible that one-fourth of the human race will be killed.

6:9 SLAIN FOR THE WORD OF GOD. When the fifth seal is opened, John sees what is happening in heaven. Those "slain for the word of God" are those who are martyred for their faith in Christ and the truth of His Word. (1) They are told to have patience, for many more will yet die for their faith in Christ (cf. 7:13–14; 13:15; 18:24; 20:4). (2) The period of tribulation will be a terrible time of persecution for those who accept the gospel and remain faithful to God and His Word (see 3:10, note; 7:9, note; 14:6, note). Perhaps all the martyrs of past ages are included among those underneath the altar.

6:10 JUDGE AND AVENGE OUR BLOOD. Those in heaven pray that the wicked who have rejected God and killed His followers will receive divine justice. There are times when God leads His people to pray for justice to prevail, for evil to be destroyed, for righteousness to be established on earth, and for Christ to be exalted above all those who oppose Him. The prayer is not for personal

and true, [u]dost thou not judge and
avenge our blood on them that dwell on
the earth?
11 And [v]white robes were given
unto every one of them; and it was said
unto them, [w]that they should rest yet
for a little season, until their fellowser-
vants also and their brethren, that
should be killed as they *were*, should be
fulfilled.

The signs in heaven

12 And I beheld when he had
opened the sixth seal, [x]and, lo, there
was a great earthquake; and [y]the sun
became black as sackcloth of hair, and
the moon became as blood;
13 [z]And the stars of heaven fell
unto the earth, even as a fig tree
casteth her [f]untimely figs, when she
is shaken of a mighty wind.
14 [a]And the heaven departed as a
scroll when it is rolled together; and
[b]every mountain and island were
moved out of their places.
15 And the kings of the earth, and
the great men, and the rich men, and
the chief captains, and the mighty men,
and every bondman, and every free
man, [c]hid themselves in the dens and
in the rocks of the mountains;
16 [d]And said to the mountains and
rocks, Fall on us, and hide us from the
face of him that sitteth on the throne,
and from the wrath of the Lamb:
17 [e]For the great day of his wrath
is come; [f]and who shall be able to
stand?

Interlude: 144,000 sealed

7 AND AFTER these things I saw
four angels standing on the four
corners of the earth, [g]holding the four
winds of the earth, [h]that the wind
should not blow on the earth, nor on
the sea, nor on any tree.
2 And I saw another angel ascend-
ing from the east, having the seal of the
living God: and he cried with a loud
voice to the four angels, to whom it
was given to hurt the earth and the
sea,
3 Saying, [i]Hurt not the earth, nei-
ther the sea, nor the trees, till we have
sealed the servants of our God [j]in
their foreheads.
4 [k]And I heard the number of them

6:10 [u]ch. 11:18
6:11 [v]ch. 3:4,5 [w]Heb. 11:40
6:12 [x]ch. 16:18 [y]Joel 2:10 & 3:15 Mat. 24:29 Acts 2:20
6:13 [z]ch. 8:10 & 9:1
6:14 [a]Ps. 102:26 Is. 34:4 Heb. 1:12 [b]Jer. 3:23 & 4:24 ch. 16:20
6:15 [c]Is. 2:19
6:16 [d]Hos. 10:8 Luke 23:30
6:17 [e]Is. 13:6 Zeph. 1:14 ch. 16:14 [f]Ps. 76:7
7:1 [g]Dan. 7:2 [h]ch. 9:4
7:3 [i]ch. 6:6 [j]ch. 22:4
7:4 [k]ch. 9:16

[f] Or, *green figs*

vengeance, for it comes out of a concern for God, righteousness, and the suffering of His people.

6:11 BRETHREN, THAT SHOULD BE KILLED. Some people will be given the opportunity to be saved during the tribulation, namely, those on earth who had never adequately heard or understood the gospel. But those who heard the gospel before the rapture of the church and yet continued to live in sin will be given no further opportunity for salvation after the church is taken out of the world (see article on THE RAPTURE, p. 1889). God will send them a strong delusion, that they may never believe again (see 2 Thes. 2:10–12, notes).

6:12 GREAT EARTHQUAKE. The catastrophic judgments of God portrayed here involve a physical shaking of the world, cosmic upheaval, and great darkness and terror for the inhabitants of the earth (vv. 15–17; cf. Is. 34:4; Joel 2:30–31; Hag. 2:6; Mat. 24:29). This is not the end of the tribulation. There is yet a seventh seal (ch. 8).

6:16 FALL ON US. All those left behind after believers are caught up from the earth to meet the Lord in the air (1 Thes. 4:17) will experience intense fear and despair as they attempt to run and hide.

6:16 THE WRATH OF THE LAMB. The wrath of the Lamb portrayed in chs. 6–19 should alert all readers as to the extent that God hates sin, immorality, and impenitent wickedness. It is identical with the wrath of God (cf. 15:7; see Rom. 1:18, note; Heb. 1:9, note). The faithful of Christ's churches are not appointed for the day of God's wrath (1 Thes. 5:9), for Jesus has promised to come and deliver them from the wrath to come (see 3:10, note; 1 Thes. 1:10, note; see article on THE RAPTURE, p. 1889).

7:1 I SAW FOUR ANGELS. Ch. 7 is an interlude between the sixth and seventh seals, revealing those who became faithful to Christ during the great tribulation. Those who take their stand for God (6:17) are both Jew (vv. 3–8) and non-Jew (vv. 9–10,13–15). They accept the everlasting gospel proclaimed by angels (14:6).

7:2 SEAL OF THE LIVING GOD. The seal was a tool or ring that stamped an owner's mark of identification on something. The seal of God on a person identifies that person as belonging to God and under His care (Eph. 1:13).

7:4 HUNDRED *AND* FORTY *AND* FOUR THOUSAND. The 144,000 are described as bondservants of God (v. 3) from the tribes of the sons of Israel (vv. 4–8). God will set a seal or mark upon their foreheads to indicate consecration and ownership (cf. 9:4; Ezek. 9:1–6; 2 Tim. 2:19). (1) Some Bible interpreters believe these new believers from among the sons of Israel will be commissioned and empowered by the Holy Spirit to preach the gospel during the tribulation days.

(2) Their being sealed by God does not mean they are protected from physical death or from martyrdom coming from Satan's persecution (v. 14). However, they are protected from the direct judgment of God and from demonic affliction (9:4).

which were sealed: *and there were* sealed [l]an hundred *and* forty *and* four thousand of all the tribes of the children of Israel.

5 Of the tribe of Judah *were* sealed twelve thousand. Of the tribe of Reuben *were* sealed twelve thousand. Of the tribe of Gad *were* sealed twelve thousand.

6 Of the tribe of Aser *were* sealed twelve thousand. Of the tribe of Nepthalim *were* sealed twelve thousand. Of the tribe of Manasses *were* sealed twelve thousand.

7 Of the tribe of Simeon *were* sealed twelve thousand. Of the tribe of Levi *were* sealed twelve thousand. Of the tribe of Issachar *were* sealed twelve thousand.

8 Of the tribe of Zabulon *were* sealed twelve thousand. Of the tribe of Joseph *were* sealed twelve thousand. Of the tribe of Benjamin *were* sealed twelve thousand.

The saints in white robes

9 After this I beheld, and, lo, [m]a great multitude, which no man could number, [n]of all nations, and kindreds, and people, and tongues, stood before the throne, and before the Lamb, [o]clothed with white robes, and palms in their hands;

10 And cried with a loud voice, saying, [p]Salvation to our God [q]which sitteth upon the throne, and unto the Lamb.

11 [r]And all the angels stood round about the throne, and *about* the elders and the four beasts, and fell before the throne on their faces, and worshipped God,

12 [s]Saying, Amen: Blessing, and glory, and wisdom, and thanksgiving, and honour, and power, and might, *be* unto our God for ever and ever. Amen.

13 And one of the elders answered, saying unto me, What are these which are arrayed in [t]white robes? and whence came they?

14 And I said unto him, Sir, thou knowest. And he said to me, [u]These are they which came out of great tribulation, and have [v]washed their robes, and made them white in the blood of the Lamb.

15 Therefore are they before the throne of God, and serve him day and night in his temple: and he that sitteth on the throne shall [w]dwell among them.

16 [x]They shall hunger no more, neither thirst any more; [y]neither shall the sun light on them, nor any heat.

17 For the Lamb which is in the midst of the throne [z]shall feed them, and shall lead them unto living fountains of waters: [a]and God shall wipe away all tears from their eyes.

The seventh seal: the prayers of the saints

8 AND [b]WHEN he had opened the seventh seal, there was silence in heaven about the space of half an hour.

2 [c]And I saw the seven angels which stood before God; [d]and to them were given seven trumpets.

3 And another angel came and stood at the altar, having a golden cen-

7:4 [l]ch. 14:1
7:9 [m]Rom. 11:25 [n]ch. 5:9 [o]ver. 14 ch. 3:5,18 & 4:4 & 6:11
7:10 [p]Ps. 3:8 Is. 43:11 Jer. 3:23 Hos. 13:4 ch. 19:1 [q]ch. 5:13
7:11 [r]ch. 4:6
7:12 [s]ch. 5:13,14
7:13 [t]ver. 9
7:14 [u]ch. 6:9 & 17:6 [v]Is. 1:18 See Zech. 3:3-5
7:15 [w]Is. 4:5,6 ch. 21:3
7:16 [x]Is. 49:10 [y]Ps. 121:6 ch. 21:4
7:17 [z]Ps. 23:1 & 36:8 John 10:11,14 [a]Is. 25:8 ch. 21:4
8:1 [b]ch. 6:1
8:2 [c]Mat. 18:10 Luke 1:19 [d]2 Chr. 29:25-28

7:9 A GREAT MULTITUDE. John describes a scene in heaven of a great multitude of people from all nations who come to salvation through faith in Christ. They will be with God (v. 15), free from pain and sorrow (vv. 16–17; see 6:9, note). Many believe that this multitude saved by the "blood of the Lamb" (v. 14) are tribulation saints, because John states that they "came out of great tribulation" (v. 14). Those who accept Christ are special objects of persecution from Satan and evil men (cf. 12:9–17).

7:14 GREAT TRIBULATION. The great tribulation is a time of divine judgment on an ungodly world that has rejected Christ, but it is also a time of satanic wrath and persecution against those who receive Christ and His Word during the tribulation (12:12). During this period, many saints will suffer terribly as objects of the wrath of Satan and the ungodly (6:9–11; 7:9–17; 20:4; cf. 14:13; see article on THE GREAT TRIBULATION, p. 1456). So intense is the conflict between righteousness and evil that it can only be called "great tribulation." This phrase in the Greek literally reads "the tribulation, the great"; in the Greek language repeating the article "the" makes a statement emphatic.

7:17 SHALL WIPE AWAY ALL TEARS. This promise may refer to the removal of any memory that might cause us suffering, regret, or remorse. In heaven nothing that involves deprivation, suffering, or sorrow remains (v. 16).

8:1 THE SEVENTH SEAL. The breaking of the seventh seal initiates the seven trumpets of judgment; hence, the trumpet judgments are the seventh seal. The trumpet judgments are partial judgments (chs. 8–9; 11:15–19), while the judgments of the seven bowls (ch. 16) are more severe. The seventh trumpet judgment will announce the seven bowls of judgment (16:1–21). The silence in heaven is due to the horror of the coming judgments against sin.

ser; and there was given unto him
much incense, that he should [g]offer *it*
with [e]the prayers of all saints upon
[f]the golden altar which was before
the throne.
4 And [g]the smoke of the incense,
which came with the prayers of the
saints, ascended up before God out of
the angel's hand.
5 And the angel took the censer,
and filled it with fire of the altar, and
cast *it* [h]into the earth: and [h]there
were voices, and thunderings, and
lightnings, [i]and an earthquake.

The seven trumpets

6 And the seven angels which had
the seven trumpets prepared them-
selves to sound.

Hail, fire, and blood

7 The first angel sounded, [j]and
there followed hail and fire mingled
with blood, and they were cast [k]upon
the earth: and the third part [l]of trees
was burnt up, and all green grass was
burnt up.

The sea turned into blood

8 And the second angel sounded,
[m]and as it were a great mountain
burning with fire was cast into the sea:
[n]and the third part of the sea [o]be-
came blood;
9 [p]And the third part of the crea-
tures which were in the sea, and had
life, died; and the third part of the ships
were destroyed.

The pollution of waters

10 And the third angel sounded,
[q]and there fell a great star from heav-
en, burning as it were a lamp, [r]and it
fell upon the third part of the rivers,
and upon the fountains of waters;
11 [s]And the name of the star is
called Wormwood: [t]and the third part
of the waters became wormwood; and
many men died of the waters, because
they were made bitter.

Sun, moon, and stars darkened

12 [u]And the fourth angel sounded,
and the third part of the sun was smit-
ten, and the third part of the moon, and
the third part of the stars; so as the
third part of them was darkened, and
the day shone not for a third part of it,
and the night likewise.
13 And I beheld, [v]and heard an an-
gel flying through the midst of heaven,
saying with a loud voice, [w]Woe, woe,
woe, to the inhabiters of the earth by
reason of the other voices of the trum-
pet of the three angels, which are yet
to sound!

The opening of the bottomless pit

9 AND THE fifth angel sounded,
[x]and I saw a star fall from heaven

8:3 [e]ch. 5:8 [f]Ex. 30:1 ch. 6:9 **8:4** [g]Ps. 141:2 Luke 1:10 **8:5** [h]ch. 16:18 [i]2 Sam. 22:8 1 Ki. 19:11 Acts 4:31 **8:7** [j]Ezek. 38:22 [k]ch. 16:2 [l]Is. 2:13 ch. 9:4 **8:8** [m]Jer. 51:25 Amos 7:4 [n]ch. 16:3 [o]Ezek. 14:19 **8:9** [p]ch. 16:3 **8:10** [q]Is. 14:12 ch. 9:1 [r]ch. 16:4 **8:11** [s]Ruth 1:20 [t]Ex. 15:23 **8:12** [u]Is. 13:10 Amos 8:9 **8:13** [v]ch. 14:6 & 19:17 [w]ch. 9:12 & 11:14 **9:1** [x]Luke 10:18 ch. 8:10

[g] Or, *add it to the prayers* [h] Or, *upon*

8:3 PRAYERS OF ALL SAINTS. The repeated mentioning of the prayers of the saints (5:8; 8:3–4) indicates that the intercessory prayers of believers are extremely important in the destruction of evil and the establishment of righteousness upon the earth (see 5:8, note). (1) John mentions the prayers of *all* the saints. Thus, the prayers of tribulation saints on earth are joined by the intercession of all the saints in heaven (cf. 6:9–11). The saints in heaven are vitally concerned about the events on earth. (2) Note that God in some sense stores up our prayers. Although the Lord may not answer all our prayers immediately, He does not cast them aside, but keeps them for the proper time of fulfillment.

8:7 HAIL AND FIRE . . . BLOOD. The first four trumpet judgments begin. (1) One-third of the earth's vegetation is destroyed by fire and hail; one-third of the sea and rivers is polluted; the heavens, sun, moon, and stars are darkened for a third part of both day and night (vv. 7–13). (2) The judgments affect humans also, for many are killed (v. 11). The judgment is limited to one-third of the world, because the purpose is partially to warn people and bring them to repentance (9:20–21).

8:8 A GREAT MOUNTAIN BURNING. This may be a great burning meteor, which falls into the sea and kills one-third of the sea creatures and destroys many ships.

8:11 WORMWOOD. "Wormwood" is a bitter plant, representing God's judgment and human sorrow (see Deut. 29:18; Prov. 5:4; Jer. 9:15; Amos 5:7).

8:13 AN ANGEL FLYING. The angel's threefold cry of woe is to warn that the next three trumpet judgments will be much more intense and devastating than those that preceded. The fifth and sixth judgments will involve horrible demonic forces (ch. 9).

9:1 A STAR . . . BOTTOMLESS PIT. The star falling from heaven is probably an angel who carries out God's judgment; it is referred to as "he" in v. 2. The bottomless pit is the abyss, i.e., the place of imprisonment for demons (cf. vv. 1–2; 11:7; 17:8; 20:1,3; 2 Pet. 2:4; Jude 6). The beast, who is the antichrist, comes out of the abyss (11:7), and Satan will be imprisoned there for one thousand years (20:3).

unto the earth: and to him was given
the key of [y]the bottomless pit.
2 And he opened the bottomless pit;
and there arose a smoke out of the pit,
as the smoke of a great furnace; and
the sun and the air were darkened by
reason of the smoke of the pit.
3 And there came out of the smoke
[z]locusts upon the earth: and unto
them was given power, [a]as the scorpi-
ons of the earth have power.
4 And it was commanded them
[b]that they should not hurt [c]the grass
of the earth, neither any green thing,
neither any tree; but only those men
which have not [d]the seal of God in
their foreheads.
5 And to them it was given that they
should not kill them, [e]but that they
should be tormented five months:
and their torment *was* as the torment
of a scorpion, when he striketh a
man.
6 And in those days [f]shall men
seek death, and shall not find it; and
shall desire to die, and death shall flee
from them.
7 And [g]the shapes of the locusts
were like unto horses prepared unto
battle; [h]and on their heads *were* as it
were crowns like gold, [i]and their
faces *were* as the faces of men.
8 And they had hair as the hair of
women, and [j]their teeth were as *the*
teeth of lions.
9 And they had breastplates, as it
were breastplates of iron; and the
sound of their wings *was* [k]as the
sound of chariots of many horses run-
ning to battle.
10 And they had tails like unto scor-
pions, and there were stings in their
tails: [l]and their power *was* to hurt
men five months.
11 [m]And they had a king over
them, *which is* [n]the angel of the bot-
tomless pit, whose name in the Hebrew
tongue *is* Abaddon, but in the Greek
tongue hath *his* name [i]Apollyon.
12 [o]One woe is past; *and,* behold,
there come two woes more hereafter.

The four angels released

13 And the sixth angel sounded,
and I heard a voice from the four horns
of the golden altar which is before God,
14 Saying to the sixth angel which
had the trumpet, Loose the four angels
which are bound [p]in the great river
Euphrates.
15 And the four angels were loosed,
which were prepared [j]for an hour,
and a day, and a month, and a year, for
to slay the third part of men.
16 And [q]the number of the army
[r]of the horsemen *were* two hundred
thousand thousand: [s]and I heard the
number of them.
17 And thus I saw the horses in the
vision, and them that sat on them, hav-
ing breastplates of fire, and of jacinth,
and brimstone: [t]and the heads of the
horses *were* as the heads of lions; and

9:1 [y]ver. 2,11 Luke 8:31 ch. 17:8 & 20:1
9:3 [z]Ex. 10:4 Judg. 7:12 [a]ver. 10
9:4 [b]ch. 6:6 & 7:3 [c]ch. 8:7 [d]See Ex. 12:23 Ezek. 9:4 ch. 7:3
9:5 [e]ver. 10 ch. 11:7
9:6 [f]Job 3:21 Is. 2:19 Jer. 8:3 ch. 6:16
9:7 [g]Joel 2:4 [h]Nah. 3:17 [i]Dan. 7:8
9:8 [j]Joel 1:6
9:9 [k]Joel 2:5-7
9:10 [l]ver. 5
9:11 [m]Eph. 2:2 [n]ver. 1
9:12 [o]ch. 8:13
9:14 [p]ch. 16:12
9:16 [q]Ps. 68:17 Dan. 7:10 [r]Ezek. 38:4 [s]ch. 7:4
9:17 [t]1 Chr. 12:8 Is. 5:28,29

[i] That is to say, *A destroyer* [j] Or, *at*

9:3 CAME OUT ... LOCUSTS. These locusts represent an increased number of demons and demonic activity released upon the earth toward the end of history (see previous note; see Mat. 25:41, note on fallen angels). They have the power of scorpions to cause pain and misery (v. 10). Their assault is directed against the wicked upon the earth for a time period of five months (vv. 5,10), though they are not permitted to torment believers (v. 4).

9:6 SEEK DEATH, AND SHALL NOT FIND IT. The pain inflicted by the demonic locusts is so severe that people desire to die, but will not be able to (vv. 5–6). This judgment reveals (1) that evil and impenitence will most certainly receive divine retribution (see Rom. 1:18, note), and (2) that when people oppose God and His truth and seek evil, they become the prey of the demonic. Evil forces will possess their very nature, soul, and life (see 1 Tim. 4:1, note; see article on POWER OVER SATAN AND DEMONS, p. 1486).

9:7 SHAPES OF THE LOCUSTS. The appearance and sound of the demons will be terrifying (vv. 7–9). Their "breastplates" (v. 9) may indicate that man-made weapons cannot destroy them.

9:11 A KING OVER THEM. The leading angel of the demonic locusts is called "Abaddon," which means "destruction" (cf. Job 26:6; Prov. 15:11). "Apollyon" means "the destroyer."

9:14 LOOSE THE FOUR ANGELS. The sixth angel releases four angels; these must be evil angels or demons, since holy angels are not bound. They are let loose to kill one-third of the world's population (v. 15). They are released from the river Euphrates, because in O.T. history, the Euphrates area symbolized a military invasion by which God brings judgment (cf. Is. 8:5–8; 10:5–7).

9:16 TWO HUNDRED THOUSAND THOUSAND. Bible interpreters differ widely as to the meaning of the two hundred million horsemen. (1) Some say they represent demonlike evil spirits from the bottomless pit under the leadership of the four angels (v. 14; see v. 3, note). (2) Others see the mounted troops as representing many armies gathered for battle.

out of their mouths issued fire and
smoke and brimstone.
18 By these three was the third part
of men killed, by the fire, and by the
smoke, and by the brimstone, which is-
sued out of their mouths.
19 For their power is in their mouth,
and in their tails: [u]for their tails *were*
like unto serpents, and had heads, and
with them they do hurt.
20 And the rest of the men which
were not killed by these plagues [v]yet
repented not of the works of their
hands, that they should not worship
[w]devils, [x]and idols of gold, and silver,
and brass, and stone, and of wood:
which neither can see, nor hear, nor
walk:
21 Neither repented they of their
murders, [y]nor of their sorceries, nor
of their fornication, nor of their thefts.

Interlude: John eats the book

10 AND I saw another mighty an-
gel come down from heaven,
clothed with a cloud: [z]and a rainbow
was upon his head, and [a]his face *was*
as it were the sun, and [b]his feet as
pillars of fire:
2 And he had in his hand a little
book open: [c]and he set his right foot
upon the sea, and *his* left *foot* on the
earth,
3 And cried with a loud voice, as
when a lion roareth: and when he had
cried, [d]seven thunders uttered their
voices.
4 And when the seven thunders had
uttered their voices, I was about to
write: and I heard a voice from heaven
saying unto me, [e]Seal up those things
which the seven thunders uttered, and
write them not.
5 And the angel which I saw stand
upon the sea and upon the earth [f]lift-
ed up his hand to heaven,
6 And sware by him that liveth for
ever and ever, [g]who created heaven,
and the things that therein are, and the
earth, and the things that therein are,
and the sea, and the things which are
therein, [h]that there should be time no
longer:
7 But [i]in the days of the voice of
the seventh angel, when he shall begin
to sound, the mystery of God should be
finished, as he hath declared to his ser-
vants the prophets.
8 And [j]the voice which I heard
from heaven spake unto me again, and
said, Go *and* take the little book which
is open in the hand of the angel which
standeth upon the sea and upon the
earth.
9 And I went unto the angel, and
said unto him, Give me the little book.

9:19 [u]Is. 9:15 **9:20** [v]Deut. 31:29 [w]Lev. 17:7 Deut. 32:17 Ps. 106:37 1 Cor. 10:20 [x]Ps. 115:4 & 135:15 Dan. 5:23 **9:21** [y]ch. 22:15 **10:1** [z]Ezek. 1:28 [a]Mat. 17:2 ch. 1:16 [b]ch. 1:15 **10:2** [c]Mat. 28:18 **10:3** [d]ch. 8:5 **10:4** [e]Dan. 8:26 & 12:4,9 **10:5** [f]Ex. 6:8 Dan. 12:7 **10:6** [g]Neh. 9:6 ch. 4:11 & 14:7 [h]Dan. 12:7 ch. 16:17 **10:7** [i]ch. 11:15 **10:8** [j]ver. 4

9:18 FIRE ... SMOKE ... BRIMSTONE. What John saw is a reminder of God's judgment on Sodom and Gomorrah (Gen. 19:24,28; cf. Jude 7). These words are God's warning that those who indulge in the sinful ways of Sodom will most surely experience the judgment of Sodom (Gen. 19:14).
9:20 YET REPENTED NOT. Even God's judgment does not bring people to repentance. This demonstrates the depth of human depravity and its love for sinful pleasure (cf. Jer. 17:9). The most prominent sins of the last days and the tribulation period are (vv. 20–21): (1) the worship of or consorting with demons and the participating in spiritism, the occult, and magic (Deut. 32:17; 1 Cor. 10:20); (2) murder and violence; (3) sorcery (Gk. *pharmekeia*), which involves drugs, occult worship, and witchcraft (18:23; 21:8; 22:15; Gal. 5:20; see next note); (4) immorality, sexual lust, and pornography; (5) thefts and lawlessness (cf. Rom. 1:24, 28–31).
9:21 THEIR SORCERIES. Sorcery will be greatly revived in the last days before and during the tribulation period (18:23; 21:8; 22:15; 1 Tim. 4:1). Sorcery is connected with the occult, which includes contact with the dead, supernatural powers, paranormal energies, or demonic forces in order to acquire power to manipulate or influence things or people. The use of drugs may be involved with sorcery.
10:1 ANOTHER MIGHTY ANGEL. Ch. 10 reveals the vision of the angel with the little book. It is an interlude between the sixth trumpet (blown in 9:13) and the seventh trumpet (blown in 11:15).
10:2 A LITTLE BOOK. The angel placing his right foot upon the sea and his left foot on the earth signifies that this little book contains a message that affects the destiny of the whole world.
10:3 SEVEN TRUMPETS. These signify certain aspects of God's coming wrath and judgment (cf. 8:5; 11:19; 16:18), though John is forbidden to disclose the message of the seven peals of thunder (v. 4). This indicates that during the tribulation period, judgments not revealed in the seals, trumpets, and bowls will occur. Therefore, no one knows in advance everything that will happen. Thus we should not be dogmatic about the sequence of events in the book of Revelation.
10:6 TIME NO LONGER. The word "time" can also be translated as "delay." In other words, there will be no more delay before the seventh trumpet is sounded.
10:7 MYSTERY OF GOD. Within the period of time following the sound of the seventh trumpet (11:15), all the prophecies that God revealed to His prophets concerning the final days will come to pass. This concerns the fulfillment of God's purpose in the return of Christ to earth and the establishment of His kingdom (11:15).

And he said unto me, [k]Take *it,* and eat
it up; and it shall make thy belly bitter,
but it shall be in thy mouth sweet as
honey.
10 And I took the little book out of
the angel's hand, and ate it up; [l]and
it was in my mouth sweet as honey:
and as soon as I had eaten it, [m]my bel-
ly was bitter.
11 And he said unto me, Thou must
prophesy again before many peoples,
and nations, and tongues, and kings.

The two witnesses

11 AND THERE was given me [n]a
reed like unto a rod: and the an-
gel stood, saying, [o]Rise, and measure
the temple of God, and the altar, and
them that worship therein.
2 But [p]the court which is without
the temple [k]leave out, and measure it
not; [q]for it is given unto the Gentiles:
and the holy city shall they [r]tread un-
der foot [s]forty *and* two months.
3 And [1]I will give *power* unto my
two [t]witnesses, [u]and they shall
prophesy [v]a thousand two hundred
and threescore days, clothed in sack-
cloth.
4 These are the [w]two olive trees,
and the two candlesticks standing be-
fore the God of the earth.
5 And if any man will hurt them,
[x]fire proceedeth out of their mouth,
and devoureth their enemies: [y]and if
any man will hurt them, he must in this
manner be killed.
6 These [z]have power to shut heav-
en, that it rain not in the days of their
prophecy: and have power over waters
to turn them to blood, and to smite the
earth with all plagues, as often as they
will.
7 And when they [a]shall have fin-
ished their testimony, [b]the beast that
ascendeth [c]out of the bottomless pit
[d]shall make war against them, and
shall overcome them, and kill them.
8 And their dead bodies *shall lie* in
the street of [e]the great city, which
spiritually is called Sodom and Egypt,
[f]where also our Lord was crucified.
9 [g]And they of the people and kin-
dreds and tongues and nations shall
see their dead bodies three days and an
half, [h]and shall not suffer their dead
bodies to be put in graves.
10 [i]And they that dwell upon the
earth shall rejoice over them, and
make merry, [j]and shall send gifts one
to another; [k]because these two proph-
ets tormented them that dwelt on the
earth.

10:9 [k]Jer. 15:16 Ezek. 2:8 **10:10** [l]Ezek. 3:3 [m]Ezek. 2:10 **11:1** [n]Ezek. 40:3 ch. 21:15 [o]Num. 23:18 **11:2** [p]Ezek. 40:17 [q]Ps. 79:1 Luke 21:24 [r]Dan. 8:10 [s]ch. 13:5 **11:3** [t]ch. 20:4 [u]ch. 19:10 [v]ch. 12:6 **11:4** [w]Ps. 52:8 Jer. 11:16 Zech. 4:3 **11:5** [x]2 Ki. 1:10 Jer. 1:10 Ezek. 43:3 Hos. 6:5 [y]Num. 16:29 **11:6** [z]1 Ki. 17:1 Jas. 5:16 **11:7** [a]Luke 13:32 [b]ch. 13:1,11 [c]ch. 9:2 [d]Dan. 7:21 Zech. 14:2 **11:8** [e]ch. 14:8 [f]Heb. 13:12 **11:9** [g]ch. 17:15 [h]Ps. 79:2,3 **11:10** [i]ch. 12:12 [j]Esth. 9:19 [k]ch. 16:10

[k] Gk. *cast out* [1] Or, *I will give unto my two witnesses that they may prophesy*

10:9 TAKE *IT*, AND EAT IT UP. The "little book," tasting as sweet as honey but turning bitter in John's stomach, refers to the books's mixture of blessing and curse. God's word is sweet, both to hear and to keep for His servants (Ps. 19:9–10; cf. Jer. 15:16; Ezek. 3:1–3), but it also pronounces the judgment on sin and evil that unbelievers must face (cf. Luke 19:41–44; cf. Jer. 20:8–9; Amos 5:10).

11:1 MEASURE THE TEMPLE. Ch. 11 continues an interlude (begun in ch. 10) that discusses Israel and the temple and gives an appraisal of her spiritual life. The events recorded here occur in the city where the "Lord was crucified," i.e., Jerusalem (v. 8). Israel is basically still in unbelief during this part of the tribulation. The "temple of God" may imply the existence of a temple in Jerusalem at this time; it will be desecrated by the antichrist (see 13:14–15; Dan. 9:27; 12:11; 2 Thes. 2:4; see article on THE GREAT TRIBULATION, p. 1456). The measuring of the temple signifies God measuring the spiritual condition of the Jewish people (cf. Ezek. 40; Zech. 2).

11:2 TREAD UNDER FOOT. During the tribulation, Israel and the "holy city" will be oppressed by the Gentiles and suffer greatly for 42 months (see Luke 21:24, note). Israel will be severely judged because of her rejection of Christ and her immorality like that of "Sodom" (vv. 8,13). The 42 months probably refer to the final three and one-half years of the tribulation (see Dan. 9:27, note; cf. 7:25; 12:7).

11:3 MY TWO WITNESSES. God will send two witnesses to preach the gospel and prophesy about the future; they will possess great supernatural power (vv. 5–6) and perform their ministry in the power of the Spirit. They will be a great threat to the antichrist and the entire wicked world for a period of 1260 days and counteract the signs and wonders of the prophets of the antichrist (13:13–14). The two witnesses have the power of both Moses and Elijah (see Mal. 4:5, note).

11:4 OLIVE TREES . . . CANDLESTICKS. By using this language John says that the two witnesses will be empowered by the Holy Spirit, in order to reveal the light or truth of God (see Zech. 4:2–14, notes).

11:7 THE BEAST . . . KILL THEM. The two witnesses are killed because they brought the truth of the gospel and faithfully cried out against the sins of the people. Jerusalem is called "Sodom" because of its immorality and "Egypt" because of its worldliness (v. 8). The beast is the antichrist (cf. 13:1; 14:9,11; 15:2; 16:2; 17:3,13; 19:20; 20:10) or the "man of sin" (2 Thes. 2:3–10). Note that the two witnesses could not be killed until they finished their work. This is true of all of God's servants who remain faithful to Him.

11 [l]And after three days and an
half [m]the Spirit of life from God en-
tered into them, and they stood upon
their feet; and great fear fell upon them
which saw them.
12 And they heard a great voice
from heaven saying unto them, Come
up hither. [n]And they ascended up to
heaven [o]in a cloud; [p]and their ene-
mies beheld them.
13 And the same hour [q]was there
a great earthquake, [r]and the tenth
part of the city fell, and in the earth-
quake were slain [m]of men seven thou-
sand: and the remnant were affrighted,
[s]and gave glory to the God of heaven.
14 [t]The second woe is past; *and,*
behold, the third woe cometh quickly.

The seventh trumpet

15 And [u]the seventh angel sound-
ed; [v]and there were great voices in
heaven, saying, [w]The kingdoms of this
world are become *the kingdoms* of our
Lord, and of his Christ; [x]and he shall
reign for ever and ever.
16 And [y]the four and twenty el-
ders, which sat before God on their
seats, fell upon their faces, and wor-
shipped God,
17 Saying, We give thee thanks,
O Lord God Almighty, [z]which art, and
wast, and art to come; because thou
hast taken to thee thy great power,
[a]and hast reigned.
18 [b]And the nations were angry,
and thy wrath is come, [c]and the time
of the dead, that they should be judged,
and that thou shouldest give reward
unto thy servants the prophets, and to
the saints, and them that fear thy
name, [d]small and great; [e]and should-
est destroy them which [n]destroy the
earth.
19 And [f]the temple of God was
opened in heaven, and there was seen
in his temple the ark of his testament:
and [g]there were lightnings, and
voices, and thunderings, and an earth-
quake, [h]and great hail.

The woman and the dragon

12 AND THERE appeared a great
[o]wonder in heaven; a woman
clothed with the sun, and the moon un-
der her feet, and upon her head a
crown of twelve stars:
2 And she being with child cried,
[i]travailing in birth, and pained to be
delivered.
3 And there appeared another
[o]wonder in heaven; and behold [j]a
great red dragon, [k]having seven
heads and ten horns, [l]and seven
crowns upon his heads.
4 And [m]his tail drew the third part
[n]of the stars of heaven, [o]and did cast
them to the earth: and the dragon
stood [p]before the woman which was
ready to be delivered, [q]for to devour
her child as soon as it was born.
5 And she brought forth a man

11:11 [l]ver. 9 [m]Ezek. 37:5 **11:12** [n]Is. 14:13 [o]Is. 60:8 Acts 1:9 [p]2 Ki. 2:1 **11:13** [q]ch. 6:12 [r]ch. 16:19 [s]Josh. 7:19 **11:14** [t]ch. 8:13 **11:15** [u]ch. 10:7 [v]Is. 27:13 [w]ch. 12:10 [x]Dan. 2:44 **11:16** [y]ch. 4:4 **11:17** [z]ch. 16:5 [a]ch. 19:6 **11:18** [b]ver. 2,9 [c]Dan. 7:9 [d]ch. 19:5 [e]ch. 13:10 **11:19** [f]ch. 15:5,8 [g]ch. 8:5 [h]ch. 16:21 **12:2** [i]Is. 66:7 Gal. 4:19 **12:3** [j]ch. 17:3 [k]ch. 17:9,10 [l]ch. 13:1 **12:4** [m]ch. 9:10,19 [n]ch. 17:18 [o]Dan. 8:10 [p]ver. 2 [q]Ex. 1:16

[m]Gk. *names of men* [n]Or, *corrupt* [o]Or, *sign*

11:11 GREAT FEAR FELL UPON THEM. Because of the resurrection of the two witnesses (vv. 11–12) and the judgment of God (v. 13), a remnant in Jerusalem will receive the message of the two witnesses and give glory to God (v. 13).

11:15 THE SEVENTH ANGEL SOUNDED. The sounding of the seventh trumpet brings an announcement that the world has become the kingdom of Christ, and He will reign forever (see 20:4, note; Ezek. 21:26–27; Dan. 2:44; 4:3; 6:26; Zech. 14:9). In other words, the seventh trumpet involves events extending to Christ's return, including therefore the judgments of the seven bowls (beginning in ch. 16). The sound of the seventh trumpet is followed by a parenthetical passage that reveals some events related to the tribulation period (12:1—15:4).

11:16 FOUR AND TWENTY ELDERS. The twenty-four elders prophesy what will happen at the coming of Christ. The nations will be enraged (v. 18), the dead will be judged (v. 18), and God will destroy those who destroy the earth, i.e., those who are evil (cf. 19:20–21).

12:1 AND THERE APPEARED. Ch. 12 presents four great conflicts between God and Satan: (1) Satan's conflict with Christ and His work of redemption (vv. 1–5), (2) Satan's conflict with the faithful of Israel (vv. 6, 13–16), (3) Satan's conflict with heaven (vv. 7–9), and (4) Satan's conflict with believers (vv. 10–11,17).

12:1 A WOMAN. This woman refers to the faithful of Israel through whom the Messiah (i.e., the Christ child, vv. 2,4–5) came into the world (cf. Rom. 9:5). This is indicated not only by the birth of the child, but also by the reference to the sun and the moon (see Gen. 37:9–11) and the twelve stars, which would naturally refer to the twelve tribes of Israel.

12:3 A GREAT RED DRAGON. This dragon is Satan (see v. 9). The seven heads, horns, and crowns may represent his great power.

12:4 THIRD PART OF THE STARS. This may refer to the original fall of Satan from heaven and the angels who fell with him (2 Pet. 2:4; Jude 6), or to the great power that Satan has in the universe over those who oppose his power. Satan attempts to destroy the Christ child.

12:5 A MAN CHILD. The man child is Jesus

child, [r]who was to rule all nations with a rod of iron: and her child was caught up unto God, and *to* his throne.

6 And [s]the woman fled into the wilderness, where she hath a place prepared of God, that they should feed her there [t]a thousand two hundred *and* threescore days.

War in heaven

7 And there was war in heaven: [u]Michael and his angels fought [v]against the dragon; and the dragon fought and his angels,

8 And prevailed not; neither was their place found any more in heaven.

9 And [w]the great dragon was cast out, [x]that old serpent, called the Devil, and Satan, [y]which deceiveth the whole world: [z]he was cast out into the earth, and his angels were cast out with him.

10 And I heard a loud voice saying in heaven, [a]Now is come salvation, and strength, and the kingdom of our God, and the power of his Christ: for the accuser of our brethren is cast down, [b]which accused them before our God day and night.

11 And [c]they overcame him by the blood of the Lamb, and by the word of their testimony; [d]and they loved not their lives unto the death.

12 Therefore [e]rejoice, *ye* heavens, and ye that dwell in them. [f]Woe to the inhabiters of the earth and of the sea! for the devil is come down unto you, having great wrath, [g]because he knoweth that he hath but a short time.

War on earth

13 And when the dragon saw that he was cast unto the earth, he persecuted [h]the woman which brought forth the man *child*.

14 [i]And to the woman were given two wings of a great eagle, [j]that she might fly [k]into the wilderness, into her place, where she is nourished [l]for a time, and times, and half a time, from the face of the serpent.

15 And the serpent [m]cast out of his mouth water as a flood after the woman, that he might cause her to be carried away of the flood.

16 And the earth helped the woman, and the earth opened her mouth, and swallowed up the flood which the dragon cast out of his mouth.

17 And the dragon was wroth with the woman, [n]and went to make war with the remnant of her seed, [o]which keep the commandments of God,

12:5 [r]Ps. 2:9; ch. 19:15
12:6 [s]ver. 4; [t]ch. 11:3
12:7 [u]Dan. 10:13; [v]ch. 20:2
12:9 [w]Luke 10:18; John 12:31; [x]Gen. 3:1,4; ch. 20:2; [y]ch. 20:3; [z]ch. 9:1
12:10 [a]ch. 11:15; [b]Job 1:9; Zech. 3:1
12:11 [c]Rom. 16:20; [d]Luke 14:26
12:12 [e]Ps. 96:11; Is. 49:13; ch. 18:20; [f]ch. 8:13; [g]ch. 10:6
12:13 [h]ver. 5
12:14 [i]Ex. 19:4; [j]ver. 6; [k]ch. 17:3; [l]Dan. 7:25
12:15 [m]Is. 59:19
12:17 [n]Gen. 3:15; ch. 11:7; [o]ch. 14:12

Christ (19:15), and the catching up of the child refers to His ascension into heaven after His resurrection (Luke 24:51; Acts 1:9–11).

12:6 THE WOMAN FLED. Here the woman refers to the persecuted faithful ones of Israel during the last half of the tribulation (cf. the 1260 days, exactly half of the length of the tribulation period). (1) During the tribulation, the faithful of Israel are God-fearing Jews who oppose the religion of the antichrist. Sincerely searching the Scriptures, they accept the truth about Jesus Christ as the Messiah (Deut. 4:30–31; Zech. 13:8–9). They receive help from God during the last three and one-half years of the tribulation, and Satan will not be allowed to overcome them completely (see vv. 13–16).

(2) Those of Israel who accept the religion of the antichrist and reject the Scriptural truth of the Messiah will be judged and destroyed in the days of the great tribulation (see Ezek. 11:17–21; 20:34–38; Zech. 13:8–9).

12:7–9 WAR IN HEAVEN. The tribulation will involve not only great spiritual conflict on earth, but also war in heaven. Satan and his angels will put forth a supreme effort to defeat God and His angels in heaven. (1) Satan is defeated, cast down to earth (cf. Luke 10:18), and allowed no more access to heaven. (2) Heaven rejoices (vv. 10–12), for Satan is no longer a spiritual force in heavenly places (see Eph. 6:12, note). At the same time it causes "woe" to those on earth (vv. 12–13). This fall of Satan may begin the great tribulation.

12:10 ACCUSER OF OUR BRETHREN. Satan accuses believers before God of serving Him for personal advantage (cf. Job 1:6–11; Zech. 3:1).

12:11 THEY OVERCAME HIM. Faithful believers on earth overcome Satan by being freed from his power by the blood of the Lamb, by determining to speak for Christ, and by showing a willingness to serve Christ at any cost.

12:12 DEVIL . . . HAVING GREAT WRATH. Satan, knowing he is doomed and will shortly be defeated, has power only upon the earth. The "short time" refers to the tribulation period. His great wrath results in widespread suffering for the saints (v. 11).

12:13 PERSECUTED THE WOMAN. Satan attempts to destroy the woman (see v. 6, note). Those of Israel who accept Christ will be hunted and persecuted by Satan and the followers of the antichrist (cf. Mat. 24:15–21). God will give supernatural protection for the saints of Israel during this time (vv. 14–16).

12:17 DRAGON . . . WENT TO MAKE WAR. Satan, confined to earth, knows he has only a short time to persecute the woman (see v. 6, note) and the rest of her seed. The "woman" may refer to the faithful of Israel in Judea and "the remnant of her seed" to believing Jews elsewhere in the world.

and have [p]the testimony of Jesus
Christ.

The beast from the sea

13 AND I stood upon the sand of
the sea, and saw [q]a beast rise
up out of the sea, [r]having seven heads
and ten horns, and upon his horns ten
crowns, and upon his heads the
[p]name of blasphemy.
2 [s]And the beast which I saw was
like unto a leopard, [t]and his feet were
as *the feet* of a bear, [u]and his mouth as
the mouth of a lion: and [v]the dragon
gave him his power, and his seat, [w]and
great authority.
3 And I saw one of his heads [x]as it
were [q]wounded to death; and his
deadly wound was healed: and [y]all the
world wondered after the beast.
4 And they worshipped the dragon
which gave power unto the beast: and
they worshipped the beast, saying,
[z]Who *is* like unto the beast? who is
able to make war with him?
5 And there was given unto him [a]a
mouth speaking great things and blas-
phemies; and power was given unto
him [r]to continue [b]forty *and* two
months.
6 And he opened his mouth in blas-
phemy against God, to blaspheme his
name, [c]and his tabernacle, and them
that dwell in heaven.
7 And it was given unto him [d]to
make war with the saints, and to over-
come them: [e]and power was given
him over all kindreds, and tongues,
and nations.
8 And all that dwell upon the earth
shall worship him, [f]whose names are
not written in the book of life of the
Lamb slain [g]from the foundation of
the world.
9 [h]If any man have an ear, let him
hear.
10 [i]He that leadeth into captivity
shall go into captivity: [j]he that killeth
with the sword must be killed with the
sword. [k]Here is the patience and the
faith of the saints.

The beast from the earth

11 And I beheld another beast

12:17 [p]1 Cor. 2:1 1 John 5:10
13:1 [q]Dan. 7:2,7 [r]ch. 12:3
13:2 [s]Dan. 7:6 [t]Dan. 7:5 [u]Dan. 7:4 [v]ch. 12:9 [w]ch. 12:4
13:3 [x]ver. 12,14 [y]ch. 17:8
13:4 [z]ch. 18:18
13:5 [a]Dan. 7:8 [b]ch. 11:2
13:6 [c]John 1:14 Col. 2:9
13:7 [d]Dan. 7:21 ch. 11:7 [e]ch. 11:18
13:8 [f]Ex. 32:32 Dan. 12:1 Phil. 4:3 ch. 3:5 [g]ch. 17:8
13:9 [h]ch. 2:7
13:10 [i]Is. 33:1 [j]Gen. 9:6 Mat. 26:52 [k]ch. 14:12

[p] Or, *names;* see ch. 17:3 [q] Gk. *slain* [r] Or, *to make war*

13:1 A BEAST RISE UP OUT OF THE SEA. Ch. 13 describes the conflict between the antichrist and God and His people during the tribulation. The beast that rises out of the sea is history's final great world government, consisting of ten kingdoms under the control of the antichrist (see 17:12, note; Dan. 2:40–45, notes; 7:24–25, note; 11:36–45, note), note). The sea represents many nations (cf. 17:15). Satan gives his power to this government and uses it against God and His people (v. 2). See 17:8–11 for the angel's explanation of the beast.

13:2 BEAST . . . LEOPARD. The beast in v. 2 is the same beast of v. 1, representing not only the end-time Gentile world kingdom, but also the king of that kingdom. The beast is a person, as cruel as a beast, who will gain the political and religious power of the world at that time (see 17:13; Dan. 7:4–6; 8:25; 9:27). He is called the "man of sin" in 2 Thes. 2:3–4 and the "antichrist" in 1 John 2:18 ("anti" means "instead of"; thus the antichrist may claim he is the real Christ, the true Messiah, Mat. 24:24–25; 2 Thes. 2:3–4). He will make a covenant with the nation of Israel (see Dan. 9:27, note; see article on THE AGE OF THE ANTICHRIST, p. 1896).

13:3 WOUNDED TO DEATH. It appears to the whole earth that the antichrist has suffered a fatal wound, but is brought back to life again by the supernatural power of Satan (vv. 2,14; cf. 2 Thes. 2:9; see Rev. 17:8, note). Evidently God will permit Satan to try to duplicate the power of Christ. This may be his chief means of deceiving the human race (cf. 2 Thes. 2:9–10).

13:7 MAKE WAR WITH THE SAINTS. During the tribulation, people will have to choose whether to follow the easy and popular way of the new religion or to believe in Christ and remain faithful to Him. (1) Those who remain faithful to God and His Word will be persecuted and possibly die (see 6:9, note; 7:9, note). (2) Satan will "overcome them," not in the sense that their faith is destroyed, but in the martyrdom of many (6:9–11). For "forty *and* two months" the antichrist will make war against the saints (v. 5).

13:8 ALL . . . SHALL WORSHIP HIM. The antichrist declares himself to be deity and possesses the supernatural power of the demonic world (2 Thes. 2:4,9). Accordingly, he will be worshiped (vv. 4,8,12; 14:9; 16:2). The religion of the antichrist, in other words, teaches the doctrine of the divinity of man, (cf. Gen. 3:5). Instead of the truth that in Christ God became man (John 1:14), he speaks the lie that in himself humanity has and can become God (2 Thes. 2:4). New Age teaching presently emphasizes this doctrine of the antichrist and may be preparing the masses for its ultimate acceptance.

13:8 LAMB SLAIN FROM THE FOUNDATION. The redemptive death of Christ for the salvation of humanity was decreed from the very beginning of the creation of the world (see 17:8, note; Gen. 3:15; 1 Pet. 1:18–20).

13:11 ANOTHER BEAST. This other beast will assist the first beast (see v. 2, note), directing the world to worship the antichrist (v. 12) and misleading mankind by working great miracles (vv. 13–14; cf. Deut. 13:1–3; 2 Thes. 2:9–12). He is

[l]coming up out of the earth; and he
had two horns like a lamb, and he
spake as a dragon.
12 And he exerciseth all the power
of the first beast before him, and
causeth the earth and them which
dwell therein to worship the first
beast, [m]whose deadly wound was
healed.
13 And [n]he doeth great wonders,
[o]so that he maketh fire come down
from heaven on the earth in the sight
of men,
14 [p]And deceiveth them that dwell
on the earth [q]by *the means of* those
miracles which he had power to do in
the sight of the beast; saying to them
that dwell on the earth, that they
should make an image to the beast,
which had the wound by a sword, [r]and
did live.
15 And he had power to give [s]life
unto the image of the beast, that the
image of the beast should both speak,
[s]and cause that as many as would not
worship the image of the beast should
be killed.
16 And he causeth all, both small
and great, rich and poor, free and bond,
[t]to[t] receive a mark in their right
hand, or in their foreheads:

13:11 [l]ch. 11:7
13:12 [m]ver. 3
13:13 [n]Deut. 13:1 Mat. 24:24 2 Thes. 2:9 ch. 16:14 [o]1 Ki. 18:38 2 Ki. 1:10
13:14 [p]ch. 12:9 [q]2 Thes. 2:9 [r]2 Ki. 20:7
13:15 [s]ch. 16:2
13:16 [t]ch. 14:9
13:17 [u]ch. 14:11 [v]ch. 15:2
13:18 [w]ch. 17:9 [x]ch. 15:2 [y]ch. 21:17
14:1 [z]ch. 5:6 [a]ch. 7:4 [b]ch. 13:16
14:2 [c]ch. 1:15 [d]ch. 5:8
14:3 [e]ch. 5:9 [f]ver. 1

17 And that no man might buy or
sell, save he that had the mark, or
[u]the name of the beast, [v]or the num-
ber of his name.
18 [w]Here is wisdom. Let him that
hath understanding count [x]the num-
ber of the beast: [y]for it is the number
of a man; and his number *is* Six hun-
dred threescore *and* six.

Interlude: the Lamb and the 144,000

14 AND I looked, and, lo, [z]a
Lamb stood on the mount Zion,
and with him [a]an hundred forty *and*
four thousand, [b]having his Father's
name written in their foreheads.
2 And I heard a voice from heaven,
[c]as the voice of many waters, and as
the voice of a great thunder: and I
heard the voice of [d]harpers harping
with their harps:
3 And [e]they sung as it were a new
song before the throne, and before the
four beasts, and the elders: and no man
could learn that song [f]but the hun-
dred *and* forty *and* four thousand,
which were redeemed from the earth.
4 These are they which were not de-

[s] Gk. *breath* [t] Gk. *to give them*

also referred to as "the false prophet" (19:20; 20:10). An image of the antichrist will probably be placed in the temple of God (Dan. 9:27; Mat. 24:15; 2 Thes. 2:4). His "two horns like a lamb" signify his attempt to deceive by portraying himself as a loving, gentle, and caring person. In reality, however, his character is not like that of a lamb but of the dragon (cf. Mat. 7:15).

13:12 TO WORSHIP THE FIRST BEAST. The second beast will promote an ecumenical false church that will worship the antichrist. He will accomplish this in large measure by performing great signs and wonders (vv. 13–14). His ministry will in some ways counterfeit the supernatural ministry of the Holy Spirit (cf. 2 Thes. 2:9–10).

13:15 WORSHIP THE IMAGE OF THE BEAST. A decree will be given to kill all who refuse to worship the world ruler and his images. In other words, many who resist the antichrist and remain faithful to Jesus will pay for their faith with their lives (see 6:9, note; 14:12–13).

13:16 A MARK. The antichrist will seek to gain total economic control of the world. All people must worship him and receive a mark on their hands or foreheads in order to buy or sell (vv. 16–17), identifying the followers of the world religion promoted by the antichrist. Those who refuse to take the mark will be hunted down in order to be killed (v. 15).

13:18 SIX HUNDRED THREESCORE *AND* SIX. Although the antichrist is called "the beast" throughout Revelation, his number is 666. Many commentators believe that six is the number for man in Scripture and three is the number for God. Therefore, the three sixes could very well refer to a man who makes himself god. Like the Roman emperors and many both before and after them, he believes he is a god (see v. 8, note; 2 Thes. 2:4).

14:1 AN HUNDRED FORTY *AND* FOUR THOUSAND. Chs. 14 and 15 introduce the judgments of chs. 16–18, showing the reward awaiting those who persevere in their faith in Jesus (v. 12; 15:2–4). Ch. 14 begins by describing the scene of 144,000 outstanding believers appearing in heaven close to the Lamb. They probably represent the most consecrated and faithful of God's people of all time, who enjoy a special position and favor in heaven (see next note). The number 144,000 does not mean they are limited to that number. Any believer may be among this group by consecrated and devoted faith, love, and service to God.

14:4 WERE NOT DEFILED WITH WOMEN. This phrase is best understood in a spiritual sense. The 144,000 overcomers remained pure by refusing to conform to the pagan world system (see article on THE CHRISTIAN'S RELATIONSHIP TO THE WORLD, p. 2004) or to become a part of the apostate church of the last days (see 17:1, notes). Note the character of those who will be close to Christ in heaven. (1) They are separated from the world and the apostate church (see article on SPIRITUAL SEPARATION FOR BELIEVERS, p.

filed with women; [g]for they are vir-
gins. These are they [h]which follow the
Lamb whithersoever he goeth. These
[i]were[u] redeemed from among men,
[j]*being* the firstfruits unto God and to
the Lamb.
5 And [k]in their mouth was found
no guile: for [l]they are without fault
before the throne of God.

Angels proclaiming the gospel

6 And I saw another angel [m]fly in
the midst of heaven, [n]having the ever-
lasting gospel to preach unto them that
dwell on the earth, [o]and to every na-
tion, and kindred, and tongue, and peo-
ple,
7 Saying with a loud voice, [p]Fear
God, and give glory to him; for the hour
of his judgment is come: [q]and worship
him that made heaven, and earth, and
the sea, and the fountains of waters.
8 And there followed another angel,
saying, [r]Babylon is fallen, is fallen,
[s]that great city, because she made all
nations drink of the wine of the wrath
of her fornication.
9 And the third angel followed
them, saying with a loud voice, [t]If any
man worship the beast and his image,
and receive *his* mark in his forehead, or
in his hand,
10 The same [u]shall drink of the
wine of the wrath of God, which is
[v]poured out without mixture into
[w]the cup of his indignation; and [x]he
shall be tormented with [y]fire and
brimstone in the presence of the holy
angels, and in the presence of the
Lamb:

14:4 [g]2 Cor. 11:2 [h]ch. 3:4 [i]ch. 5:9 [j]Jas. 1:18
14:5 [k]Ps. 32:2 Zeph. 3:13 [l]Eph. 5:27 Jude 24
14:6 [m]ch. 8:13 [n]Eph. 3:9 Tit. 1:2 [o]ch. 13:7
14:7 [p]ch. 11:18 [q]Neh. 9:6 Ps. 33:6 & 124:8 & 146:5,6 Acts 14:15 & 17:24
14:8 [r]Is. 21:9 ch. 18:2 [s]Jer. 51:7 ch. 16:19 & 17:2,5 & 18:3,10
14:9 [t]ch. 13:14
14:10 [u]Ps. 75:8 Is. 51:17 Jer. 25:15 [v]ch. 18:6 [w]ch. 16:19 [x]ch. 20:10 [y]ch. 19:20
14:11 [z]Is. 34:10
14:12 [a]ch. 13:10 [b]ch. 12:17
14:13 [c]Eccl. 4:1,2 [d]1 Cor. 15:18 1 Thes. 4:16 [e]2 Thes. 1:7 Heb. 4:9,10
14:14 [f]Ezek. 1:26 Dan. 7:13 [g]ch. 6:2
14:15 [h]ch. 16:17 [i]Joel 3:13 Mat. 13:39

11 And [z]the smoke of their tor-
ment ascendeth up for ever and ever:
and they have no rest day nor night,
who worship the beast and his image,
and whosoever receiveth the mark of
his name.
12 [a]Here is the patience of the
saints: [b]here *are* they that keep the
commandments of God, and the faith of
Jesus.
13 And I heard a voice from heaven
saying unto me, Write, [c]Blessed *are*
the dead [d]which die in the Lord
[v]from henceforth: Yea, saith the Spir-
it, [e]that they may rest from their la-
bours; and their works do follow them.
14 And I looked, and behold a white
cloud, and upon the cloud *one* sat
[f]like unto the Son of man, [g]having on
his head a golden crown, and in his
hand a sharp sickle.
15 And another angel [h]came out of
the temple, crying with a loud voice to
him that sat on the cloud, [i]Thrust in
thy sickle, and reap: for the time is
come for thee to reap; for the harvest
[j]of the earth is [w]ripe.
16 And he that sat on the cloud
thrust in his sickle on the earth; and
the earth was reaped.
17 And another angel came out of
the temple which is in heaven, he also
having a sharp sickle.
18 And another angel came out
from the altar, [k]which had power over
fire; and cried with a loud cry to him

[j]Jer. 51:33; ch. 13:12 **14:18** [k]ch. 16:8

[u] Gk. *were bought* [v] Or, *from henceforth saith the Spirit, Yea* [w] Or, *dried*

1814). (2) They follow Christ (cf. Mark 8:34; John 14:21, note). (3) They give themselves to God and Christ (v. 4). (4) They do not speak lies (v. 5; cf. 21:27—22:15). (5) They are morally blameless (see article on SANCTIFICATION, p. 1982).

14:6 THE EVERLASTING GOSPEL TO PREACH. During the last half of the tribulation the gospel of Jesus will be proclaimed by an angel (or angels) to the entire world in clarity, power, and warning. It is a call for people to fear God, give Him glory, and worship Him rather than the antichrist (vv. 7–10).

14:8 BABYLON IS FALLEN. Babylon represents the political, religious, and commercial system of the whole world in the time of the end (see 17:1, note), and its fall is foretold here (see chs. 17–18 for more details).

14:9 IF ANY MAN WORSHIP THE BEAST. Those who worship the beast and receive his mark (see 13:16, note) will seal their doom, suffer severe judgments from God, and be tormented forever and ever (9:4,13–21; 14:9–11; 16:2; see Mat. 10:28, note). The warning is directed to unbelievers (v. 6) and to saints who will be tempted to deny their faith in view of the great danger of martyrdom (vv. 12–13).

14:12 KEEP THE COMMANDMENTS. The fate of the followers of the beast is awful (vv. 9–11). Therefore, the saints must continue to "keep the commandments of God, and the faith of Jesus." For their allegiance to Christ they will probably die (see next note).

14:13 BLESSED ... DIE IN THE LORD. Those dying for their faith in Christ during the tribulation are especially blessed. They are released from persecution, torture, and suffering, and are taken to be with Christ.

14:14–16 SON OF MAN. In v. 14 the Son of man (i.e., Christ) is pictured as ready to wield the sickle of judgment on a world ripe with iniquity (vv. 14–20). Vv. 14–16 are a prediction or preview of the events of 16:12–16 and 19:11–21.

that had the sharp sickle, saying,
[l]Thrust in thy sharp sickle, and gath-
er the clusters of the vine of the earth;
for her grapes are fully ripe.
19 And the angel thrust in his sickle
into the earth, and gathered the vine of
the earth, and cast *it* into [m]the great
winepress of the wrath of God.
20 And [n]the winepress was trod-
den [o]without the city, and blood came
out of the winepress, [p]even unto the
horse bridles, by the space of a thou-
sand *and* six hundred furlongs.

Visions in heaven

15 AND [q]I saw another sign in
heaven, great and marvellous,
[r]seven angels having the seven last
plagues; [s]for in them is filled up the
wrath of God.
2 And I saw as it were [t]a sea of
glass [u]mingled with fire: and them
that had gotten the victory over the
beast, [v]and over his image, and over
his mark, *and* over the number of his
name, stand on the sea of glass, [w]hav-
ing the harps of God.
3 And they sing [x]the song of Mo-
ses the servant of God, and the song of
the Lamb, saying, [y]Great and marvel-
lous *are* thy works, Lord God Almighty;
[z]just and true *are* thy ways, thou King
of [×]saints.
4 [a]Who shall not fear thee, O Lord,
and glorify thy name? for *thou* only *art*
holy: for [b]all nations shall come and
worship before thee; for thy judgments
are made manifest.
5 And after that I looked, and, be-
hold, [c]the temple of the tabernacle of
the testimony in heaven was opened:
6 [d]And the seven angels came out
of the temple, having the seven
plagues, [e]clothed in pure and white
linen, and having their breasts girded
with golden girdles.
7 [f]And one of the four beasts gave
unto the seven angels seven golden vi-
als full of the wrath of God, [g]who
liveth for ever and ever.
8 And [h]the temple was filled with
smoke [i]from the glory of God, and
from his power; and no man was able
to enter into the temple, till the seven
plagues of the seven angels were ful-
filled.

The seven vials of God's wrath

16 AND I heard a great voice out
of the temple saying [j]to the
seven angels, Go your ways, and pour
out the vials [k]of the wrath of God
upon the earth.

Sores on men

2 And the first went, and poured out
his vial [l]upon the earth; and [m]there
fell a noisome and grievous sore upon
the men [n]which had the mark of the

14:18 [l]Joel 3:13
14:19 [m]ch. 19:15
14:20 [n]Is. 63:3; Lam. 1:15; [o]Heb. 13:12; [p]ch. 19:14
15:1 [q]ch. 12:1,3; [r]ch. 21:9; [s]ch. 14:10
15:2 [t]ch. 4:6; [u]Mat. 3:11; [v]ch. 13:15; [w]ch. 5:8
15:3 [x]Ex. 15:1; [y]Deut. 32:4; Ps. 111:2; [z]Ps. 145:17; Hos. 14:9
15:4 [a]Ex. 15:14; Jer. 10:7; [b]Is. 66:23
15:5 [c]Num. 1:50
15:6 [d]ver. 1; [e]Ex. 28:6; Ezek. 44:17
15:7 [f]ch. 4:6; [g]1 Thes. 1:9
15:8 [h]Ex. 40:34; 2 Chr. 5:14; [i]2 Thes. 1:9
16:1 [j]ch. 15:1; [k]ch. 14:10
16:2 [l]ch. 8:7; [m]Ex. 9:9-11; [n]ch. 13:16

[×] Or, *nations*, or, *ages*

14:19 THE GREAT WINEPRESS. In Biblical days grapes were put in a trough and trampled by foot to remove the wine (i.e., the juice of the grape). The treading of grapes was used in the O.T. as a figure for the execution of divine wrath upon the ungodly (Is. 63:3, note; cf. Rev. 19:15). At Christ's return at the end of the tribulation, all unbelievers in the world will be gathered and judged in the valley of Jehoshaphat (see Ps. 110:6, note; Joel 3:2, note; Mat. 25:32, note) and then killed (see Mat. 13:40; Luke 17:37, note; cf. Ps. 97:3–5; Prov. 2:22; Is. 63:1–6; 66:15–17; Jer. 25:30–33; Rev. 19:15).

14:20 BLOOD CAME OUT. A great slaughter occurs in the last days of the tribulation. This probably refers to the battle of Armageddon (Zech. 14:1–4; see Rev. 16:16, note; 19:17–19).

15:1 SEVEN LAST PLAGUES. These plagues contain the final judgments of God on the earth during the tribulation. They are called judgments of the "seven golden vials" (v. 7) and begin in ch. 16. The seven bowls of judgment may be the unfolding of the seventh trumpet judgment (see 11:15, note).

15:2 VICTORY OVER THE BEAST. Standing on a crystal surface (cf. 4:6) are those who did not abandon their faith in Christ when persecuted, threatened, or killed by the antichrist (cf. 13:7–10).

15:5 THE TABERNACLE OF THE TESTIMONY. John saw a temple in heaven like the tabernacle in the O.T. that contained the Ten Commandments (cf. Ex. 32:15; 40:34–35). This signifies that the judgments are the result of God's opposition to sin and of human rejection of His law and Word.

15:7 FULL OF THE WRATH OF GOD. This will be the last divine judgment on a wicked world before the reign of Christ. The fact that no one can enter the temple of God until the plagues are finished means that no one can intercede to stop the judgment (v. 8). God has declared the end; His judgment will be complete and without mercy.

16:1 WRATH OF GOD. Pouring out the seven bowls of the wrath of God now begins, at a point just before Christ's return to earth. A great world war will occur toward the end of these judgments (v. 14; see v. 16, note; Dan. 11:36–45, note), judgments more intense and severe than the preceding ones.

beast, and *upon* them [o]which wor-
shipped his image.

Sea becomes like blood

3 And the second angel poured out
his vial [p]upon the sea; and [q]it be-
came as the blood of a dead *man:* [r]and
every living soul died in the sea.

Rivers and forestation become blood

4 And the third angel poured out his
vial [s]upon the rivers and fountains of
waters; [t]and they became blood.
5 And I heard the angel of the wa-
ters say, [u]Thou art righteous, O Lord,
[v]which art, and wast, and shalt be, be-
cause thou hast judged thus.
6 For [w]they have shed the blood
[x]of saints and prophets, [y]and thou
hast given them blood to drink; for they
are worthy.
7 And I heard another out of the al-
tar say, Even so, [z]Lord God Almighty,
[a]true and righteous *are* thy judg-
ments.

Firece heat of the sun

8 And the fourth angel poured out
his vial [b]upon the sun; [c]and power
was given unto him to scorch men with
fire.
9 And men were [y]scorched with
great heat, and [d]blasphemed the
name of God, which hath power over
these plagues: [e]and they repented not
[f]to give him glory.

16:2 [o]ch. 13:14
16:3 [p]ch. 8:8 [q]Ex. 7:17 [r]ch. 8:9
16:4 [s]ch. 8:10 [t]Ex. 7:20
16:5 [u]ch. 15:3 [v]ch. 1:4,8
16:6 [w]Mat. 23:34 ch. 13:15 [x]ch. 11:18 [y]Is. 49:26
16:7 [z]ch. 15:3 [a]ch. 13:10
16:8 [b]ch. 8:12 [c]ch. 9:17,18
16:9 [d]ver. 11,21 [e]Dan. 5:22 [f]ch. 11:13
16:10 [g]ch. 13:2 [h]ch. 9:2 [i]ch. 11:10
16:11 [j]ver. 9,21 [k]ver. 2 [l]ver. 9
16:12 [m]ch. 9:14 [n]Jer. 50:38 [o]Is. 41:2,25
16:13 [p]1 John 4:1 [q]ch. 12:3,9 [r]ch. 19:20
16:14 [s]1 Tim. 4:1 Jas. 3:15 [t]2 Thes. 2:9 [u]Luke 2:1 [v]ch. 17:14
16:15 [w]Mat. 24:43 [x]2 Cor. 5:3
16:16 [y]ch. 19:19

Darkness

10 And the fifth angel poured out
his vial [g]upon the seat of the beast;
[h]and his kingdom was full of dark-
ness; [i]and they gnawed their tongues
for pain,
11 And [j]blasphemed the God of
heaven because of their pains and
[k]their sores, [l]and repented not of
their deeds.

Demonic spirits

12 And the sixth angel poured out
his vial [m]upon the great river Euphra-
tes; [n]and the water thereof was dried
up, [o]that the way of the kings of the
east might be prepared.
13 And I saw three unclean [p]spir-
its like frogs *come* out of the mouth of
[q]the dragon, and out of the mouth of
the beast, and out of the mouth of [r]the
false prophet.
14 [s]For they are the spirits of
devils, [t]working miracles, *which* go
forth unto the kings of the earth [u]and
of the whole world, to gather them to
[v]the battle of that great day of God
Almighty.
15 [w]Behold, I come as a thief.
Blessed *is* he that watcheth, and
keepeth his garments, [x]lest he walk
naked, and they see his shame.
16 [y]And he gathered them togeth-
er into a place called in the Hebrew
tongue Armageddon.

Rev. 19:11-16

[y] Or, *burned*

16:3 BLOOD. The sea becomes so corrupt that every living creature in it dies and its polluted color looks like blood (Ex. 7:20–25). This also happens with the streams and rivers (v. 4).

16:7 RIGHTEOUS *ARE* THY JUDGMENTS. Those who question God's righteousness in His judgments do not understand sin's terrible evil or God's intense hatred of it. A holy and righteous God must of necessity oppose and punish evil (see John 3:19, note; Heb. 1:9, note; cf. Ps. 119:137).

16:9 GREAT HEAT. A great heat wave will spread across the earth, so unbearable that people will blaspheme God (cf. Mal. 4:1). Their hearts are so hardened that they refuse to repent (see v. 11, note). Compare this with the condition of those in heaven, of whom it is said, "neither shall the sun light on them, nor any heat" (7:16).

16:10 THE SEAT OF THE BEAST. The fifth bowl begins to throw the world dominion of the antichrist into confusion. This special judgment centers on his headquarters and followers.

16:11 REPENTED NOT. Amid the terrible judgment of God, men and women will choose to live in sin and to persist in their rebellion against righteousness. Repentance is the only act that will stop the judgments of God (cf. 2:21; 9:21; 16:9), but that act they refuse to do.

16:12 KINGS OF THE EAST. These are nations from the Orient that will participate in a great conflict, driven by satanic power to the war of Armageddon (see v. 16, note; 19:17–21). The sixth angel prepares the way for the final war of the age by a drying up of the river Euphrates, allowing armies from the east to approach the vicinity of Israel (Is. 11:15).

16:13 FROGS. These unclean spirits are demons who can work miracles and thus deceive the nations in order to support evil, sin, and the antichrist. The "dragon" must be identified with Satan (12:9), the "beast" with the antichrist (see ch. 13).

16:14 DEVILS, WORKING MIRACLES. During the tribulation rulers of the nations will be demonized. Deceived by Satan through miracles, they will enter into an insane scheme that will plunge the entire world into a great holocaust (see article on THE GREAT TRIBULATION, p. 1456, and THE AGE OF THE ANTICHRIST, p. 1896).

16:16 ARMAGEDDON. Armageddon (Gk. *har-*

Earthquake

17 And the seventh angel poured
out his vial into the air; and there came
a great voice out of the temple of heav-
en, from the throne, saying, [z]It is
done.
18 And [a]there were voices, and
thunders, and lightnings; [b]and there
was a great earthquake, [c]such as was
not since men were upon the earth,
so mighty an earthquake, *and* so
great.
19 And [d]the great city was divided
into three parts, and the cities of the
nations fell: and great Babylon [e]came
in remembrance before God, [f]to give
unto her the cup of the wine of the
fierceness of his wrath.
20 And [g]every island fled away,
and the mountains were not found.
21 [h]And there fell upon men a
great hail out of heaven, *every stone*
about the weight of a talent: and [i]men
blasphemed God because of [j]the
plague of the hail; for the plague there-
of was exceeding great.

The great harlot

17 AND THERE came [k]one of the
seven angels which had the
seven vials, and talked with me, saying
unto me, Come hither; [l]I will show
unto thee the judgment of [m]the great
whore [n]that sitteth upon many wa-
ters:
2 [o]With whom the kings of the
earth have committed fornication, and
[p]the inhabitants of the earth have

16:17 [z]ch. 21:6
16:18 [a]ch. 4:5 [b]ch. 11:13 [c]Dan. 12:1
16:19 [d]ch. 14:8 & 17:18 [e]ch. 18:5 [f]Is. 51:17 ch. 14:10
16:20 [g]ch. 6:14
16:21 [h]ch. 11:19 [i]ver. 9,11 [j]Ex. 9:23
17:1 [k]ch. 21:9 [l]ch. 16:19 [m]Nah. 3:4 ch. 19:2 [n]Jer. 51:13
17:2 [o]ch. 18:3 [p]Jer. 51:7 ch. 18:3

---

magedōn), located in north-central Palestine, means "the mountain of Megiddo"; it will be the center of "the battle of that great day of God Almighty" (v. 14). This war will occur toward the end of the tribulation and terminate when Christ returns to destroy the wicked (see 14:19, note), to deliver His people, and to inaugurate His Messianic kingdom. Note the following concerning this event. (1) The prophets of the O.T. prophesied the event (Deut. 32:43; Jer. 25:31; Joel 3:2,9–17; Zeph. 3:8; Zech. 14:2–5).

(2) Satan and demons will gather together many nations under the direction of the antichrist in order to make war against God, His armies, and His people, and to destroy Jerusalem (vv. 13–14,16; 17:14; 19:14,19; see also Ezek. 38–39, Zech. 14:2). Although the focal point will be in the land of Israel, the event of Armageddon will involve the whole world (Jer. 25:29–38).

(3) Christ will return and supernaturally intervene to destroy the antichrist and his armies (19:19–21; Zech. 14:1–5) and all who disobey the gospel (Ps. 110:5; Is. 66:15–16; 2 Thes. 1:7–10). God will also send destruction and earthquakes upon the whole world at this time (vv. 18–19; Jer. 25:29–33).

16:19 GREAT BABYLON. See next note.

17:1 SAYING UNTO ME. Chs. 17–18 portray the fall of the great Babylon (16:19; 17:5). (1) Babylon is the symbol for the whole world system dominated by Satan and manifesting wickedness politically, religiously, and commercially (see Jer. 50:1, note; 51:1–64, note). (2) Babylon will be completely destroyed during the last three and one-half years of this age. Religious Babylon (i.e., the harlot) will be destroyed by the antichrist (vv. 16–17), while political Babylon will be destroyed by Christ at His coming (19:11–21).

17:1 THE GREAT WHORE. This represents religious Babylon and encompasses all false religions, including apostate Christianity. In the Bible prostitution and adultery, when used figuratively, normally denote religious apostasy and unfaithfulness to God (Is. 1:21; Jer. 3:9; Ezek. 16:14–18,32; Jas. 4:4), and signify a people who profess to serve God while actually worshiping and serving other gods. Note the sharp contrast between the great harlot and the bride of the Lamb (see 19:7–8). The harlot is subject to Satan; the bride is subject to Christ. Satan clothes the one (v. 4); God clothes the other (19:8). Eternal death is the portion of the harlot; eternal glory the lot of the bride.

Concerning this false religion, (1) the harlot will reject the gospel of Christ and the apostles, the power of godliness, and the basic doctrines of Christianity (Mat. 24:24; 2 Tim. 3:5; 4:3).

(2) She will enter into partnership with the powers and philosophy of "Babylon" (v. 5), i.e., the world system with its immorality (17:2). Religious and political power will be combined to take spiritual control of the nations (v. 18).

(3) Her leaders will persecute the true followers of Christ (v. 6). She will be a melting pot for many faiths and creeds, and doctrine will not be of primary importance. Her chief concern will be fellowship and oneness with her religious system, values, and goals. She will become a "habitation of devils, and the hold of every foul spirit" (18:2; cf. Is. 47:12–13).

(4) All true believers are commanded to come out of her or they will be condemned with her (18:4).

(5) God will cause the antichrist to destroy her (see v. 16, note).

17:2 INHABITANTS OF THE EARTH. The true kinship of the great harlot (see previous note) is not with Christ but with the world. (1) Hypocrites and false prophets achieve worldly success as a result of her doctrine, for she encourages worldly people to join her. The false religious system allows her members to profess to be of God, yet at the same time to commit fornication. (2) Compromise with political power and toleration of unrighteousness is her trademark. As a whore the apostate church sells her favor to the world at every opportunity (18:3).

been made drunk with the wine of her
fornication.
3 So he carried me away in the spirit
[q]into the wilderness: and I saw a
woman sit [r]upon a scarlet coloured
beast, full of [s]names of blasphemy,
[t]having seven heads and [u]ten horns.
4 And the woman [v]was arrayed in
purple and scarlet colour, [w]and
[z]decked with gold and precious
stones and pearls, [x]having a golden
cup in her hand [y]full of abominations
and filthiness of her fornication:
5 And upon her forehead *was* a
name written, [z]MYSTERY, BAB-
YLON THE GREAT, THE MOTHER OF
[a]HARLOTS AND ABOMINATIONS
OF THE EARTH.
6 And I saw [a]the woman drunken
[b]with the blood of the saints, and with
the blood of [c]the martyrs of Jesus: and
when I saw her, I wondered with great
admiration.

The great harlot explained

7 And the angel said unto me,
Wherefore didst thou marvel? I will tell
thee the mystery of the woman, and of
the beast that carrieth her, which hath
the seven heads and ten horns.
8 The beast that thou sawest was,
and is not; and [d]shall ascend out of
the bottomless pit, and [e]go into perdi-
tion: and they that dwell on the earth
[f]shall wonder, [g]whose names were
not written in the book of life from the
foundation of the world, when they be-
hold the beast that was, and is not, and
yet is.
9 And [h]here *is* the mind which hath
wisdom. [i]The seven heads are seven
mountains, on which the woman
sitteth.
10 And there are seven kings: five
are fallen, and one is, *and* the other is
not yet come; and when he cometh, he
must continue a short space.
11 And the beast that was, and is
not, even he is the eighth, and is of the
seven, [j]and goeth into perdition.
12 And [k]the ten horns which thou
sawest are ten kings, which have re-
ceived no kingdom as yet; but receive
power as kings one hour with the
beast.
13 These have one mind, and shall
give their power and strength unto the
beast.

17:3 [q]ch. 12:6,14 [r]ch. 12:3 [s]ch. 13:1 [t]ver. 9 [u]ver. 12
17:4 [v]ch. 18:12 [w]Dan. 11:38 [x]Jer. 51:7 ch. 18:6 [y]ch. 14:8
17:5 [z]2 Thes. 2:7
17:6 [a]ch. 18:24 [b]ch. 13:15 [c]ch. 6:9,10
17:8 [d]ch. 11:7 [e]ch. 13:10 [f]ch. 13:3 [g]ch. 13:8
17:9 [h]ch. 13:18 [i]ch. 13:1
17:11 [j]ver. 8
17:12 [k]Dan. 7:20 Zech. 1:18

[z] Gk. *gilded* [a] Or, *fornications*

17:3 A SCARLET COLOURED BEAST. This beast is the world government or political Babylon, which supports the apostate spiritual power. For comments on the "seven heads," see v. 10, note; on the "ten horns," see v. 12, note.

17:4 A GOLDEN CUP. This cup, filled with "abominations" but beautiful on the outside, reveals the spiritual condition of the apostate church of the last days (cf. Mat. 23:27–28). The church that holds the golden cup will offer people both God and carnal satisfaction, i.e., a perverted Christianity that assures its members they can enjoy immorality and still be accepted by God.

17:5 BABYLON. The origin of the name "Babylon" is from "Babel," which symbolizes false religion, sorcery, astrology, and rebellion against God (Gen. 10:8–10; 11:4; Is. 47:13).

17:6 THE BLOOD OF THE SAINTS. The false religion in league with the world system will persecute everyone truly devoted to Christ and the Biblical faith.

17:8 BEAST . . . WAS . . . YET IS. Some interpret this verse to mean the antichrist is a person who once lived in history, but is now dead, and in the future will come up out of the abyss, remain on earth for a period, and then finally be destroyed (cf. vv. 8–11; 19:20). Others relate it to John's statement in 13:3 (see note).

17:8 WRITTEN IN THE BOOK OF LIFE FROM THE FOUNDATION OF THE WORLD. These words cannot be used to prove a predetermined individual election to salvation or damnation, for according to John, a person's name may be erased out of the book of life by disloyalty and a failure to overcome (3:5; see 13:8, note; cf. Ps. 69:28).

17:10 SEVEN KINGS. Some believe the seven kings represent seven secular kingdoms of the world (the five fallen kingdoms are most likely Egyptian, Assyrian, Babylonian, Medo-Persian, Greek). John informs his readers that the Roman empire is part of this sequence (i.e., the one that "is"). The one yet to come refers to the feet of iron and clay on the image pictured in Dan. 2 (see Dan. 2:41–43, note). This kingdom represents the nationalistic states that have followed the fall of the Roman Empire, up to and including the present time. The next kingdom, the eighth (v. 11), will be that of the antichrist.

17:11 HE IS THE EIGHTH. The beast, i.e., the antichrist (ch. 13), will be the head of the final world empire. He is one "of the seven" (see previous note), but also an "eighth." This may mean that he belongs to the same ungodly world system as did the first seven, yet he is not a part of them (see v. 8, note). The antichrist will be destroyed at the end of the tribulation.

17:12 TEN HORNS . . . TEN KINGS. These kings are ten nations that will have great political power and support the future world ruler (v. 13). They make up a world confederacy of nations that will oppose Christ and the true Biblical faith (cf. Dan. 7:23–25).

14 [l]These shall make war with the
Lamb, and the Lamb shall overcome
them: [m]for he is Lord of lords, and
King of kings: [n]and they that are with
him *are* called, and chosen, and faith-
ful.

15 And he saith unto me, [o]The wa-
ters which thou sawest, where the
whore sitteth, [p]are peoples, and mul-
titudes, and nations, and tongues.

The great harlot destroyed

16 And the ten horns which thou
sawest upon the beast, [q]these shall
hate the whore, and shall make her
desolate [r]and naked, and shall eat her
flesh, and [s]burn her with fire.
17 [t]For God hath put in their
hearts to fulfil his will, and to agree,
and give their kingdom unto the beast,
[u]until the words of God shall be ful-
filled.
18 And the woman which thou saw-
est [v]is that great city, [w]which
reigneth over the kings of the earth.

The doom of Babylon

18 AND [x]AFTER these things I
saw another angel come down
from heaven, having great power;
[y]and the earth was lightened with his
glory.
2 And he cried mightily with a
strong voice, saying, [z]Babylon the
great is fallen, is fallen, and [a]is be-
come the habitation of devils, and the
hold of every foul spirit, and [b]a cage
of every unclean and hateful bird.
3 For all nations [c]have drunk of
the wine of the wrath of her fornica-
tion, and the kings of the earth have
committed fornication with her, [d]and
the merchants of the earth are waxed
rich through the [b]abundance of her
delicacies.

The call to come out of Babylon

4 And I heard another voice from
heaven, saying, [e]Come out of her, my
people, that ye be not partakers of her
sins, and that ye receive not of her
plagues.
5 [f]For her sins have reached unto
heaven, and [g]God hath remembered
her iniquities.
6 [h]Reward her even as she reward-
ed you, and double unto her double ac-
cording to her works: [i]in the cup
which she hath filled [j]fill to her dou-
ble.
7 [k]How much she hath glorified
herself, and lived deliciously, so much
torment and sorrow give her: for she
saith in her heart, I sit a [l]queen, and
am no widow, and shall see no sorrow.

17:14 [l]ch. 16:14 [m]Deut. 10:17 1 Tim. 6:15 ch. 19:16 [n]Jer. 50:44 ch. 14:4 **17:15** [o]Is. 8:7 [p]ch. 13:7 **17:16** [q]Jer. 50:41 ch. 16:12 [r]Ezek. 16:37 ch. 18:16 [s]ch. 18:8 **17:17** [t]2 Thes. 2:11 [u]ch. 10:7 **17:18** [v]ch. 16:19 [w]ch. 12:4 **18:1** [x]ch. 17:1 [y]Ezek. 43:2 **18:2** [z]Is. 13:19 Jer. 51:8 [a]Is. 13:21 Jer. 50:39 [b]Is. 14:23 Mark 5:2 **18:3** [c]ch. 14:8 [d]Is. 47:15 **18:4** [e]Is. 48:20 Jer. 50:8 2 Cor. 6:17 **18:5** [f]Gen. 18:20 Jer. 51:9 Jonah 1:2 [g]ch. 16:19 **18:6** [h]Ps. 137:8 Jer. 50:15 [i]ch. 14:10 [j]ch. 16:19

18:7 [k]Ezek. 28:2 [l]Is. 47:7,8; Zeph. 2:15

[b] Or, *power*

17:14 MAKE WAR WITH THE LAMB. Christ will overthrow the antichrist and those who align themselves with him at the final battle (see 16:14,16, notes).

17:15 WATERS. The whore sitting on many waters indicates that there will be one ecumenical, universal, apostate religious system in the first part of the tribulation. This will be replaced by the religion of the antichrist when he gains great political power (Mat. 24:15; 2 Thes. 2:3–4).

17:16 THESE SHALL HATE THE WHORE. Sometime during the antichrist's rule, the whore (see v. 1, note) will be hated by the antichrist and his supporters, and they will utterly destroy her and her institutions. This is God's judgment against the world religious system that rejected God's truth in Christ. This may occur at the midpoint of the seven-year tribulation, when the beast professes to be god and demands that all worship him (13:8,15; see Dan. 9:27; 11:36–38; see article on THE GREAT TRIBULATION, p. 1456, and THE AGE OF THE ANTICHRIST, p. 1896).

18:2 BABLYON THE GREAT IS FALLEN. In ch. 18, Babylon the great is portrayed primarily in its commercial and political aspect. (1) Some believe Babylon here represents a literal city or nation that embodies the ungodly aspects of the city described in the chapter. (2) Others believe it represents the whole ungodly world system brought under the antichrist's rule. Here her commercial system is destroyed; in ch. 19 her political system is judged by God at the end of the tribulation (cf. 19:17–21; Is. 13:1–11).

18:4 COME OUT OF HER, MY PEOPLE. This is God's prophetic call to the last generation of believers to come out of Babylon the great (v. 2), because those of God's people who remain in the ungodly system will inevitably become "partakers of her sins" and therefore "receive . . . her plagues." The call to be separate from the world and false religious institutions has been an essential aspect of salvation throughout redemptive history (cf. Is. 52:11; Jer. 51:45; 1 Cor. 11:32; see article on SPIRITUAL SEPARATION FOR BELIEVERS, p. 1814).

18:7 GLORIFIED HERSELF . . . LIVED DELICIOUSLY. The suffering and misery to fall on commercial Babylon will be in proportion to the self-glorification and luxurious lifestyle she lived. The rich, powerful, and unscrupulous enterprisers who rejected God and piled up wealth to the injury of others will be stripped of their wealth in one day (v. 8; cf. Jas. 5:1–6).

8 Therefore shall her plagues come [m]in one day, death, and mourning, and famine; and [n]she shall be utterly burned with fire: [o]for strong *is* the Lord God who judgeth her.

The world laments over Babylon

9 And [p]the kings of the earth, who have committed fornication and lived deliciously with her, [q]shall bewail her, and lament for her, [r]when they shall see the smoke of her burning,

10 Standing afar off for the fear of her torment, saying, [s]Alas, alas, that great city Babylon, that mighty city! [t]for in one hour is thy judgment come.

11 And [u]the merchants of the earth shall weep and mourn over her; for no man buyeth their merchandise any more:

12 [v]The merchandise of gold, and silver, and precious stones, and of pearls, and fine linen, and purple, and silk, and scarlet, and all [c]thyine wood, and all manner vessels of ivory, and all manner vessels of most precious wood, and of brass, and iron, and marble,

13 And cinnamon, and odours, and ointments, and frankincense, and wine, and oil, and fine flour, and wheat, and beasts, and sheep, and horses, and chariots, and [d]slaves, and [w]souls of men.

14 And the fruits that thy soul lusted after are departed from thee, and all things which were dainty and goodly are departed from thee, and thou shalt find them no more at all.

15 [x]The merchants of these things, which were made rich by her, shall stand afar off for the fear of her torment, weeping and wailing,

16 And saying, Alas, alas, that great city, [y]that was clothed in fine linen, and purple, and scarlet, and decked with gold, and precious stones, and pearls!

17 [z]For in one hour so great riches is come to nought. And [a]every shipmaster, and all the company in ships, and sailors, and as many as trade by sea, stood afar off,

18 [b]And cried when they saw the smoke of her burning, saying, [c]What *city is* like unto this great city!

19 And [d]they cast dust on their heads, and cried, weeping and wailing, saying, Alas, alas, that great city, wherein were made rich all that had ships in the sea by reason of her costliness! [e]for in one hour is she made desolate.

Heaven rejoices over Babylon's fall

20 [f]Rejoice over her, *thou* heaven, and *ye* holy apostles and prophets; for [g]God hath avenged you on her.

21 And a mighty angel took up a stone like a great millstone, and cast *it* into the sea, saying, [h]Thus with violence shall that great city Babylon be thrown down, and [i]shall be found no more at all.

22 [j]And the voice of harpers, and musicians, and of pipers, and trumpeters, shall be heard no more at all in thee; and no craftsman, of whatsoever craft *he be*, shall be found any more in thee; and the sound of a millstone shall be heard no more at all in thee;

18:8 [m]ver. 10 Is. 47:9 [n]ch. 17:16 [o]Jer. 50:34 ch. 11:17
18:9 [p]Ezek. 26:16 [q]Jer. 50:46 [r]ch. 19:3
18:10 [s]Is. 21:9 ch. 14:8 [t]ver. 17,19
18:11 [u]Ezek. 27:27
18:12 [v]ch. 17:4
18:13 [w]Ezek. 27:13
18:15 [x]ver. 3,11
18:16 [y]ch. 17:4
18:17 [z]ver. 10 [a]Is. 23:14 Ezek. 27:29
18:18 [b]Ezek. 27:30 [c]ch. 13:4
18:19 [d]Josh. 7:6 1 Sam. 4:12 Job 2:12 Ezek. 27:30 [e]ver. 8
18:20 [f]Is. 44:23 & 49:13 Jer. 51:48 [g]Luke 11:49 ch. 19:2
18:21 [h]Jer. 51:64 [i]ch. 12:8 & 16:20
18:22 [j]Jer. 7:34 & 16:9 & 25:10 Ezek. 26:13

[c] Or, *sweet* [d] Or, *bodies*

18:9 KINGS . . . LAMENT FOR HER. All those whose main concern was money, luxury, and gratification of pleasure will weep and mourn, for the god of their life is destroyed. They can no longer profit in merchandise since their great riches are gone (cf. Jas. 5:1–6). God clearly indicates here his hatred for businesses and governments that are founded on greed and oppressive power. He stands against individuals who seek riches, status, and pleasure instead of the humble values of Jesus Christ. Those who live in selfish luxury and pleasure will be brought down by the wrath of God.

18:20 REJOICE OVER HER. All the godly in heaven and earth rejoice at God's righteous judgment on the great satanic system of evil with all its wicked manifestations, sinful pleasures, self-centered luxury, humanistic government, and godless commerce. The exuberant celebration of the saints in heaven, described in 19:1–10, is proportionate to their present grief at the triumph of evil in this world. The mark of a true child of God is his distress at the immoral conduct around him. He will be tormented day after day by the lawless deeds he sees and about which he hears (2 Pet. 2:7–8). Nevertheless, he is assured by God that in the future he will rejoice at the triumph of righteousness.

18:21 BABYLON . . . SHALL BE FOUND NO MORE. An angel declares the final fall of political Babylon. The antichrist and his ungodly world system will be totally destroyed at "the battle of that great day of God Almighty," when Christ returns to earth (16:14; see 14:8; 16:14,16, notes; 19:11–21; cf. the fall of Babylon in Dan. 5).

23 [k]And the light of a candle shall
shine no more at all in thee; [l]and the
voice of the bridegroom and of the
bride shall be heard no more at all in
thee: for [m]thy merchants were the
great men of the earth; [n]for by thy sor-
ceries were all nations deceived.
24 And [o]in her was found the blood
of prophets, and of saints, and of all
that [p]were slain upon the earth.

Praise to God for His judgment

19 AND AFTER these things [q]I
heard a great voice of much
people in heaven, saying, Alleluia;
[r]Salvation, and glory, and honour,
and power, unto the Lord our God:
2 For [s]true and righteous *are* his
judgments: for he hath judged the
great whore, which did corrupt the
earth with her fornication, and [t]hath
avenged the blood of his servants at
her hand.
3 And again they said, Alleluia. And
[u]her smoke rose up for ever and ever.
4 And [v]the four and twenty elders
and the four beasts fell down and wor-
shipped God that sat on the throne,
saying, [w]Amen; Alleluia.
5 And a voice came out of the
throne, saying, [x]Praise our God, all ye
his servants, and ye that fear him,
[y]both small and great.
6 [z]And I heard as it were the voice
of a great multitude, and as the voice
of many waters, and as the voice of
mighty thunderings, saying, Alleluia:
for [a]the Lord God omnipotent
reigneth.

18:23 [k]Jer. 25:10 [l]Jer. 7:34 & 16:9 & 25:10 & 33:11 [m]Is. 23:8 [n]2 Ki. 9:22 ch. 17:2,5 **18:24** [o]ch. 17:6 [p]Jer. 51:49 **19:1** [q]ch. 11:15 [r]ch. 4:11 & 7:10,12 **19:2** [s]ch. 15:3 [t]Deut. 32:43 **19:3** [u]Is. 34:10 ch. 14:11 **19:4** [v]ch. 4:4,6 [w]1 Chr. 16:36 Neh. 5:13 & 8:6 ch. 5:14 **19:5** [x]Ps. 134:1 [y]ch. 11:18 & 20:12 **19:6** [z]Ezek. 1:24 ch. 14:2 [a]ch. 11:15 **19:7** [b]Mat. 22:2 & 25:10 2 Cor. 11:2 Eph. 5:32 ch. 21:2,9 **19:8** [c]Ps. 45:13 Ezek. 16:10 ch. 3:18 [d]Ps. 132:9 **19:9** [e]Mat. 22:2 Luke 14:15 [f]ch. 22:6 **19:10** [g]ch. 22:8 [h]Acts 10:26 ch. 22:9 [i]1 John 5:10 ch. 12:17

Marriage supper of the Lamb

7 Let us be glad and rejoice, and
give honour to him: for [b]the marriage
of the Lamb is come, and his wife hath
made herself ready.
8 And [c]to her was granted that she
should be arrayed in fine linen, clean
and [e]white: [d]for the fine linen is the
righteousness of saints.
9 And he saith unto me, Write,
[e]Blessed *are* they which are called
unto the marriage supper of the Lamb.
And he saith unto me, [f]These are the
true sayings of God.
10 And [g]I fell at his feet to worship
him. And he said unto me, [h]See *thou
do it* not: I am thy fellowservant, and
of thy brethren [i]that have the testi-
mony of Jesus: worship God: for the
testimony of Jesus is the spirit of
prophecy.

The coming of Christ

11 [j]And I saw heaven opened, and
behold [k]a white horse; and he that sat
upon him *was* called [l]Faithful and
True, and [m]in righteousness he doth
judge and make war.
12 [n]His eyes *were* as a flame of fire,
[o]and on his head *were* many crowns;
[p]and he had a name written, that no
man knew, but he himself.
13 [q]And he *was* clothed with a ves-

19:11 [j]ch. 15:5 [k]ch. 6:2 [l]ch. 3:14 [m]Is. 11:4 **19:12** [n]ch. 1:14 [o]ch. 6:2 [p]ch. 2:17 **19:13** [q]Is. 63:2,3

[e] Or, *bright*

19:1 AFTER THESE THINGS. Ch. 19 deals with the end of the tribulation and the glorious second coming of Christ to earth to destroy the ungodly and reign with His people.

19:1 ALLELUIA. This is the first of four times the word "Alleluia" (or "Hallelujah") occurs in the N.T. (see vv. 1,3–4,6). It is derived from two Hebrew words: *halal*, meaning "praise," and *jah*, meaning "Yahweh" or "LORD"; thus, it means "Praise the Lord." The people in heaven praise the Lord because God has judged the world and avenged the saints who suffered at its hand, and because Jesus Christ is returning to earth to reign (vv. 6,11; 20:4). This is heaven's "Hallelujah Chorus."

19:7 HIS WIFE HATH MADE HERSELF READY. The chronology of ch. 19 places the "wife" (i.e., the church, 2 Cor. 11:2) already in heaven before Christ's coming to earth. Many interpreters believe this indicates the church has already been caught up to heaven before Christ's coming pictured in vv. 11–21 (see article on THE RAPTURE, p. 1889). Two reasons are given: (1) The bride (cf. 21:2) is entirely dressed and ready in heaven for the "marriage of the Lamb"; hence, the church must already be raptured and in heaven. (2) The bride who is already in heaven is fully clothed in "the righteousness of saints," i.e., their righteous acts (v. 8). For the righteous acts of the saints to be complete, they must be in heaven and delivered from all impurity.

19:10 JESUS IS THE SPIRIT OF PROPHECY. Ultimately, all prophecy is related to Jesus and His redemptive work and exalts Him.

19:11 I SAW HEAVEN OPENED. This verse sets forth the beginning of the second coming of Jesus Christ to earth as King of kings and Lord of lords (v. 16). He comes from heaven as the Warrior-Messiah (cf. 2 Thes. 1:7–9) to establish truth and justice (Ps. 96:13), to judge the nations, and to make war against evil (cf. John 5:30). This is the event for which the faithful of all generations have waited.

ture dipped in blood: and his name is called [r]The Word of God.

14 [s]And the armies *which were* in heaven followed him upon white horses, [t]clothed in fine linen, white and clean.

15 And [u]out of his mouth goeth a sharp sword, that with it he should smite the nations: and [v]he shall rule them with a rod of iron: and [w]he treadeth the winepress of the fierceness and wrath of Almighty God.

16 And [x]he hath on *his* vesture and on his thigh a name written, [y]KING OF KINGS, AND LORD OF LORDS.

The defeat of the ungodly

17 And I saw an angel standing in the sun; and he cried with a loud voice, saying [z]to all the fowls that fly in the midst of heaven, [a]Come and gather yourselves together unto the supper of the great God;

18 [b]That ye may eat the flesh of kings, and the flesh of captains, and the flesh of mighty men, and the flesh of horses, and of them that sit on them, and the flesh of all *men, both* free and bond, both small and great.

19 [c]And I saw the beast, and the kings of the earth, and their armies, gathered together to make war against him that sat on the horse, and against his army.

20 [d]And the beast was taken, and with him the false prophet that wrought miracles before him, with which he deceived them that had received the mark of the beast, and [e]them that worshipped his image. [f]These both were cast alive into a lake of fire [g]burning with brimstone.

21 And the remnant [h]were slain with the sword of him that sat upon the horse, which *sword* proceeded out of his mouth: [i]and all the fowls [j]were filled with their flesh.

The binding of Satan

20 AND I saw an angel come down from heaven, [k]having the key of the bottomless pit and a great chain in his hand.

2 And he laid hold on [l]the dragon, that old serpent, which is the Devil,

19:13 [r]John 1:1; 1 John 5:7
19:14 [s]ch. 14:20; [t]Mat. 28:3; ch. 4:4
19:15 [u]Is. 11:4; 2 Thes. 2:8; ch. 1:16; [v]Ps. 2:9; ch. 2:27; [w]Is. 63:3; ch. 14:19
19:16 [x]ver. 12; [y]Dan. 2:47; 1 Tim. 6:15; ch. 17:14
19:17 [z]ver. 21; [a]Ezek. 39:17
19:18 [b]Ezek. 39:18
19:19 [c]ch. 16:16
19:20 [d]ch. 16:13; [e]ch. 13:12; [f]Dan. 7:11; ch. 20:10; [g]ch. 14:10
19:21 [h]ver. 15; [i]ver. 17,18; [j]ch. 17:16
20:1 [k]ch. 1:18
20:2 [l]2 Pet. 2:4; Jude 6; ch. 12:9

19:14 ARMIES. The armies who return with Christ include all the saints who are already in heaven (cf. 17:14). Their white clothing confirms this.

19:15 SMITE THE NATIONS. When Christ returns to earth, He will punish the wicked nations. To "rule them with a rod of iron" means to destroy them (cf. Ps. 2:9). "He treadeth the winepress" indicates the awfulness of His judgment (cf. Is. 64:1–2; Zech. 14:3–4; Mat. 24:29–30; cf. Rev. 14:19, note).

19:15 THE FIERCENESS AND WRATH OF ALMIGHTY GOD. This is a stern reminder that God hates sin. The sentimental view that Christ tolerates sin and immorality because of His love finds no place in Christ's own revelation of Himself in this book (see next note).

19:17 THE SUPPER OF THE GREAT GOD. This supper refers to the battle of Armageddon (see 16:16, note). (1) The destruction of God's enemies on earth will be so great that it will require a multitude of birds to clean up the battlefield. It is called the "supper of the great God," for God will provide it for the birds of prey. (2) The scene is one of judgment against the terrible cruelty and evil of this world. Other prophecies which in all probability refer to this coming event are 14:14–20; 16:13–16; 17:14; Jer. 51:27–44; Ezek. 39:17–20; Joel 3:9–16; Zeph. 3:8; Zech. 14:2–5.

19:19 TO MAKE WAR. In preparation for the war, God through demonic forces will gather the nations together in the vicinity of Armageddon (see 16:16, note; Joel 3:2; Zeph. 3:8; Zech. 14:2–3). (1) The war will end swiftly with the destruction of the antichrist and all the ungodly (vv. 19–21). (2) God's judgment not only includes the gathered armies but extends to the entire world (Jer. 25:29–33).

19:20 FALSE PROPHET THAT WROUGHT MIRACLES. John again describes the false prophet and his religion by one outstanding characteristic: he deceived many by performing signs, wonders, and miracles (cf. 13:13–15; cf. 2 Thes. 2:9–10). The conclusion is obvious: in the last days those who seek to persevere in faithfulness to Christ and His commandments (cf. 14:12) must not base their evaluation of truth solely on success or miracles. The Lord Himself solemnly warns: "For there shall arise false Christs, and false prophets, and shall show great signs and wonders; insomuch that, if *it were* possible, they shall deceive the very elect" (Mat. 24:24; see article on THE GREAT TRIBULATION, p. 1456).

19:21 THE REMNANT WERE SLAIN. God destroys the wicked throughout the whole earth (see Jer. 25:29–33). Therefore no unsaved or unrighteous person will enter the thousand-year kingdom of God (20:4). During the tribulation, the gospel was adequately presented by angels from the skies to everyone living on earth. Those who rejected the truth were given a "strong delusion, that they should believe a lie: that they all might be damned who believed not the truth" (2 Thes. 2:11–12). Note that the unrighteous "shall not inherit the kingdom of God" (1 Cor. 6:9–11; cf. Gal. 5:19–21). They will be separated from the righteous after Christ returns in glory and will be consigned to eternal punishment (Mat. 25:31–46).

and Satan, and bound him a thousand
years,
3 And cast him into the bottomless
pit, and shut him up, and [m]set a seal
upon him, [n]that he should deceive the
nations no more, till the thousand
Rev. 20:7-10 years should be fulfilled: and after that
he must be loosed a little season.

The 1,000-year reign of Christ

4 And I saw [o]thrones, and they sat
upon them, and [p]judgment was given
unto them: and *I saw* [q]the souls of
them that were beheaded for the wit-
ness of Jesus, and for the word of God,
and [r]which had not worshipped the
beast, [s]neither his image, neither had
received *his* mark upon their fore-
heads, or in their hands; and they lived
and [t]reigned with Christ a thousand
years.
5 But the rest of the dead lived not
again until the thousand years were
finished. This *is* the first resurrec-
tion.
6 Blessed and holy *is* he that hath
part in the first resurrection: on such
[u]the second death hath no power, but
they shall be [v]priests of God and of
Christ, [w]and shall reign with him a
thousand years.

The release of Satan

7 And when the thousand years are

20:3 [m]Dan. 6:17 [n]ch. 12:9
20:4 [o]Dan. 7:9 Mat. 19:28 Luke 22:30 [p]1 Cor. 6:2,3 [q]ch. 6:9 [r]ch. 13:12 [s]ch. 13:15 [t]Rom. 8:17 2 Tim. 2:12 ch. 5:10
20:6 [u]ch. 2:11 [v]Is. 61:6 1 Pet. 2:9 ch. 1:6 [w]ver. 4

20:2 DRAGON . . . BOUND HIM A THOUSAND YEARS. After the return of Christ and the events of ch. 19, Satan will be bound and imprisoned for a thousand years, in order that he may not deceive the nations. This implies a complete cessation of his influence during this time. After the thousand years, he will be loosed for a short time in order to deceive those who rebel against God's rule (vv. 3,7–9). Satan's most characteristic work is to deceive (see Gen. 3:13; Mat. 24:24; 2 Thes. 2:9–10).

20:3 DECEIVE THE NATIONS NO MORE. The nations that will exist during the reign of Christ on earth are formed from those believers who are alive at the end of the tribulation (see 19:21, note; 20:4, note). Although at times the term "nations" is used specifically of the ungodly, John also uses it to represent the saved (21:24; 22:2).

20:4 THRONES . . . THEY SAT UPON THEM. Those who sit on the thrones are probably the overcomers from all the churches of all time (cf. 2:7, note), possibly including the O.T. saints (see Ezek. 37:11–14; Eph. 2:14–22; 3:6; Heb. 11:39–40). Those who "lived" (i.e., came to life) after Christ's return are said to be those faithful to Him who died during the tribulation (6:9; 12:17). John does not mention the resurrection of the church saints who have died, for this occurred when Christ removed His church from earth and took it to heaven (i.e., the rapture; see John 14:3, note; 1 Cor. 15:51, note; see article on THE RAPTURE, p. 1889).

20:4 REIGNED WITH CHRIST A THOUSAND YEARS. This thousand-year reign of Christ is sometimes called "the millennium," meaning "a thousand years" (*mille* is a Latin word meaning "thousand," and *annus* a Latin word meaning "year"). The characteristics of this reign are the following: (1) It was predicted in the O.T. (Is. 9:6; 65:19–25; Dan. 7:13–14; Mic. 4:1–8; Zech. 14:1–9; cf. Rev. 2:25–28).

(2) Satan will be bound (see vv. 2–3, notes).

(3) Christ's reign will be shared by the faithful of His churches (2:26–27; 3:21; 5:10; 20:4), and possibly also by the resurrected O.T. saints (see Ezek. 37:11–14; Eph. 2:14–22; 3:6; Heb. 11:39–40) and martyred tribulation saints (see previous note).

(4) The people ruled by Christ will consist of those on earth who were faithful to Christ during the tribulation and who survived until the Lord's coming and those born during the millennium (14:12; 18:4; Is. 65:20–23; see Mat. 25:1, note).

(5) No unsaved will enter the kingdom (see 19:21, note).

(6) Those reigning with Christ stand far above all the nations, for they will minister to and rule both Israel and the other nations (3:21; 5:10; 20:6; Mat. 19:28; see Zeph. 3:9–20, note).

(7) There will be peace, safety, prosperity, and righteousness throughout the earth (Is. 2:2–4; Mic. 4:4; Zech. 9:10; see Zech. 2:5, note; 9:8, note).

(8) Nature will be restored to its original order, perfection, and beauty (Ps. 96:11–13; 98:7–9; Is. 14:7–8; 35:1–2,6–7; 51:3; 55:12–13; 65:25; Ezek. 34:25; Rom. 8:18–23; see Is. 65:17–25, note; Ezek. 36:8–15, note; Zech. 14:8, note).

(9) The nations during this reign are obliged to continue in faith in and obedience to Christ and His rule. However, some will choose the way of rebellion and disobedience and will be punished (vv. 7–10).

(10) At the end of the thousand years, the kingdom will be delivered up by Jesus to the Father (1 Cor. 15:24); then will begin the final and everlasting kingdom of God and the Lamb (21:1—22:5).

20:6 THE FIRST RESURRECTION. This term includes the resurrection of Christ and all God's people, in contrast to the resurrection of the wicked at the end of the millennium (vv. 12–13; Is. 26:19–21; Dan. 12:2,13; Mat. 27:52–53; John 11:25–26; 14:19; 1 Cor. 15:20,52; see article on THE RAPTURE, p. 1889).

20:7 SATAN SHALL BE LOOSED. At the close of Christ's reign, Satan will be released. (1) Satan himself, deceived in believing he can yet defeat God, will be allowed to deceive those who desire to rebel against Christ's rule of righteousness and will gather a multitude of such rebels together. (2)

expired, [x]Satan shall be loosed out of his prison,

8 And shall go out [y]to deceive the nations which are in the four quarters of the earth, [z]Gog and Magog, [a]to gather them together to battle: the number of whom *is* as the sand of the sea.

9 [b]And they went up on the breadth of the earth, and compassed the camp of the saints about, and the beloved city: and fire came down from God out of heaven, and devoured them.

Satan punished forever

10 [c]And the devil that deceived them was cast into the lake of fire and brimstone, [d]where the beast and the false prophet *are,* and [e]shall be tormented day and night for ever and ever.

The great white throne judgment

11 And I saw a great white throne, and him that sat on it, from whose face [f]the earth and the heaven fled away; [g]and there was found no place for them.

12 And I saw the dead, [h]small and great, stand before God; [i]and the books were opened: and another [j]book was opened, which is *the book* of life: and the dead were judged out of those things which were written in the books, [k]according to their works.

13 And the sea gave up the dead which were in it; [l]and death and [f]hell delivered up the dead which were in them: [m]and they were judged every man according to their works.

14 And [n]death and hell were cast into the lake of fire. [o]This is the second death.

15 And whosoever was not found written in the book of life [p]was cast into the lake of fire.

The new heaven and the new earth

21 AND [q]I saw a new heaven and a new earth: [r]for the first heaven and the first earth were passed away; and there was no more sea.

20:7 [x]ver. 2
20:8 [y]ver. 3,10 [z]Ezek. 38:2 & 39:1 [a]ch. 16:14
20:9 [b]Is. 8:8 Ezek. 38:9
20:10 [c]ver. 8 [d]ch. 19:20 [e]ch. 14:10
20:11 [f]2 Pet. 3:7 ch. 21:1 [g]Dan. 2:35
20:12 [h]ch. 19:5 [i]Dan. 7:10 [j]Ps. 69:28 Dan. 12:1 Phil. 4:3 ch. 3:5 [k]Jer. 17:10 & 32:19 Mat. 16:27 Rom. 2:6 ch. 2:23
20:13 [l]ch. 6:8 [m]ver. 12
20:14 [n]1 Cor. 15:26 [o]ch. 21:8
20:15 [p]ch. 19:20
21:1 [q]Is. 65:17 2 Pet. 3:13 [r]ch. 20:11

[f] Or, *the grave*

"Gog and Magog" (v. 8; derived from Ezek. 38–39) represent all the nations of the world and their spirit of rebellion against God and righteousness.

20:8 DECEIVE THE NATIONS. This is the last rebellion against God in history. Many of those born during the millennium evidently choose to reject the visible Lordship of Christ and choose instead Satan and his lie. God's judgment is total destruction and ruin (v. 9).

20:10 THE DEVIL . . . THE LAKE OF FIRE. Satan's power will not last forever, for he will be taken by God and cast forever into the lake of fire (see Is. 14:9–17). There he will not rule, but will be tormented day and night forever.

20:11–13 GREAT WHITE THRONE. The judgment described here is called the "Great White Throne Judgment" and includes the lost of all ages. Some believe that those saved during Christ's thousand-year reign on earth will be included in this judgment.

20:11 EARTH AND THE HEAVEN FLED AWAY. This may refer to the destruction of the universe and the creation of a new heaven and earth (21:1; cf. Is. 51:6; 2 Pet. 3:7,10–12).

20:14 THE LAKE OF FIRE. The Bible portrays a terrible picture of the destiny of the lost. (1) It speaks of "tribulation and anguish" (Rom. 2:9), "weeping and gnashing of teeth" (Mat. 22:13; 25:30), "everlasting destruction" (2 Thes. 1:9), and a "furnace of fire" (Mat. 13:42,50). It speaks of "chains of darkness" (2 Pet. 2:4), "everlasting punishment" (Mat. 25:46), a "hell" and a "fire that never shall be quenched" (Mark 9:43), a "lake of fire burning with brimstone" (19:20), and "the smoke of their torment ascendeth up for ever and ever: and they have no rest day nor night" (14:11). Indeed, "*It is* a fearful thing to fall into the hands of the living God" (Heb. 10:31); "It had been good for that man if he had not been born" (Mat. 26:24; see also Mat. 10:28, note).

(2) The believers of the N.T. church lived in the consciousness of the fate of those who lived in sin. It was for this reason they preached with tears (see Acts 20:19, note) and defended God's infallible Word and saving gospel against all distortion and false doctrine (see Phil. 1:17, note; 2 Tim. 1:14, note; see article on OVERSEERS AND THEIR DUTIES, p. 1706).

(3) The solemn fact of eternal punishment for the wicked is the greatest motivation for carrying the gospel to all the world and doing everything possible to persuade people to repent and receive Christ before it is too late (see John 3:16, note).

20:15 BOOK OF LIFE. See 3:5, note.

21:1 NEW HEAVEN AND A NEW EARTH. The final goal and expectation of the N.T. faith is a new, transformed, and redeemed world where Christ abides with His people and righteousness dwells in holy perfection (cf. Ps. 102:25–26; Is. 65:17; 66:22; Rom. 8:19–22; Heb. 1:12; 12:27; 2 Pet. 3:13). To erase all traces of sin, there will be a destruction of the earth, stars, and galaxies. Heaven and earth will be shattered (Hag. 2:6; Heb. 12:26–28) and will disappear like smoke (Is. 51:6); the stars will melt and the elements dissolve (Is. 34:4; 2 Pet. 3:7,10,12). The renewed earth will become the dwelling place of both man and God (vv. 2–3; 22:3–5). All the redeemed will

2 And I John saw [s]the holy city, new Jerusalem, coming down from God out of heaven, prepared [t]as a bride adorned for her husband.

3 And I heard a great voice out of heaven saying, Behold, [u]the tabernacle of God *is* with men, and he will dwell with them, and they shall be his people, and God himself shall be with them, *and be* their God.

4 [v]And God shall wipe away all tears from their eyes; and [w]there shall be no more death, [x]neither sorrow, nor crying, neither shall there be any more pain: for the former things are passed away.

5 And [y]he that sat upon the throne said, [z]Behold, I make all things new. And he said unto me, Write: for [a]these words are true and faithful.

6 And he said unto me, [b]It is done. [c]I am Alpha and Omega, the beginning and the end. [d]I will give unto him that is athirst of the fountain of the water of life freely.

7 He that overcometh shall inherit [g]all things; and [e]I will be his God, and he shall be my son.

End

8 [f]But the fearful, and unbelieving, and the abominable, and murderers, and whoremongers, and sorcerers, and idolaters, and all liars, shall have their part in [g]the lake which burneth with fire and brimstone: which is the second death.

21:2 [s]Is. 52:1 Gal. 4:26 Heb. 11:10 & 12:22 ch. 3:12 [t]Is. 54:5 2 Cor. 11:2
21:3 [u]Lev. 26:11 Ezek. 43:7 2 Cor. 6:16
21:4 [v]Is. 25:8 [w]1 Cor. 15:26 ch. 20:14 [x]Is. 35:10 & 61:3 & 65:19
21:5 [y]ch. 4:2,9 & 20:11 [z]Is. 43:19 2 Cor. 5:17 [a]ch. 19:9
21:6 [b]ch. 16:17 [c]ch. 1:8 [d]Is. 12:3 John 4:10 & 7:37
21:7 [e]Zech. 8:8 Heb. 8:10
21:8 [f]1 Cor. 6:9 Gal. 5:19 Eph. 5:5 1 Tim. 1:9 Heb. 12:14 [g]ch. 20:14
21:9 [h]ch. 15:1 [i]ch. 19:7
21:10 [j]ch. 1:10 [k]Ezek. 48

The new Jerusalem

9 And there came unto me one of [h]the seven angels which had the seven vials full of the seven last plagues, and talked with me, saying, Come hither, I will show thee [i]the bride, the Lamb's wife.

10 And he carried me away [j]in the spirit to a great and high mountain, and showed me [k]that great city, the holy Jerusalem, descending out of heaven from God,

11 [l]Having the glory of God: and her light *was* like unto a stone most precious, even like a jasper stone, clear as crystal;

12 And had a wall great and high, *and* had [m]twelve gates, and at the gates twelve angels, and names written thereon, which are *the names* of the twelve tribes of the children of Israel:

13 [n]On the east three gates; on the north three gates; on the south three gates; and on the west three gates.

21:11 [l]ch. 22:5 **21:12** [m]Ezek. 48:31-34 **21:13** [n]Ezek. 48:31-34

g Or, *these things*

---

possess a body like Christ's resurrection body, one that is real, visible, and tangible, but incorruptible and immortal (Rom. 8:23; 1 Cor. 15:51–54).

21:2 NEW JERUSALEM. The new Jerusalem already exists in heaven (Gal. 4:26); it will soon come to earth as the city of God for which Abraham and all of God's faithful waited and of which God is architect and builder (Phil. 3:20; Heb. 11:10, 13,16; see article on THE CITY OF JERUSALEM, p. 622). The new earth will become the headquarters of God and He will remain with His people forever (cf. Lev. 26:11–12; Jer. 31:33; Ezek. 37:27; Zech. 8:8).

21:4 WIPE AWAY ALL TEARS. The effects of sin, such as sorrow, pain, unhappiness, and death (7:16–17; Gen. 3; Is. 35:10; 65:19; Rom. 5:12), are gone forever, for the evil things of the first heaven and earth have completely passed away. Believers, although remembering all things worth remembering, will evidently not remember that which would cause them sorrow (Is. 65:17).

21:7 HE THAT OVERCOMETH. God Himself declares who shall inherit the blessings of the new heaven and the new earth—those who faithfully persevere as Christ's overcomers (see 2:7, note). Those who do not overcome sin and ungodliness will be cast into the lake of fire (see next note).

21:8 THE FEARFUL, AND UNBELIEVING. God mentions several classes of people who will have a part in the lake that burns with fire and brimstone. (1) The "fearful" are those who fear the disapproval and threat of humans more than they value loyalty to Christ and the truth of His Word. Their personal safety and status among others mean more than faithfulness to Christ. They include the compromisers among God's people who give up the fight and do not conquer (cf. Mark 8:35; 1 Thes. 2:4, note; 2 Tim. 2:12–13, notes).

(2) The "unbelieving" include former believers in Christ who were overcome by various sins, such as those listed here. To profess Christ and then practice such evil is an abomination unto God.

(3) Many churches today proclaim that it is possible for a person to be simultaneously a true child of God and an immoral person, liar, adulterer, homosexual, or murderer. Such people contradict the clear words of God here (cf. 1 Cor. 6:9–10; Gal. 5:19–21; Eph. 5:5–7).

21:9 THE BRIDE, THE LAMB'S WIFE. This metaphor for the new city means that God's people dwell within it. John uses symbolic language to describe the holy city whose glory cannot be totally comprehended by human understanding (see 21:9—22:5).

21:12–14 TWELVE GATES. The wall of the city suggests the security which the saved have in the new city. The twelve gates represent Israel (v. 12) and the twelve foundations represent the church (v. 14). This emphasizes the unity of God's people of O.T. and N.T. times.

14 And the wall of the city had twelve foundations, and [o]in them the names of the twelve apostles of the Lamb.

Its measurements

15 And he that talked with me [p]had a golden reed to measure the city, and the gates thereof, and the wall thereof.

16 And the city lieth foursquare, and the length is as large as the breadth: and he measured the city with the reed, twelve thousand furlongs. The length and the breadth and the height of it are equal.

17 And he measured the wall thereof, an hundred *and* forty *and* four cubits, *according to* the measure of a man, that is, of the angel.

18 And the building of the wall of it was *of* jasper: and the city *was* pure gold, like unto clear glass.

19 [q]And the foundations of the wall of the city *were* garnished with all manner of precious stones. The first foundation *was* jasper; the second, sapphire; the third, a chalcedony; the fourth, an emerald;

20 The fifth, sardonyx; the sixth, sardius; the seventh, chrysolite; the eighth, beryl; the ninth, a topaz; the tenth, a chrysoprasus; the eleventh, a jacinth; the twelfth, an amethyst.

21 And the twelve gates *were* twelve pearls; every several gate was of one pearl: [r]and the street of the city *was* pure gold, as it were transparent glass.

21:14 [o]Mat. 16:18 Gal. 2:9 Eph. 2:20
21:15 [p]Ezek. 40:3 Zech. 2:1
21:19 [q]Is. 54:11
21:21 [r]ch. 22:2
21:22 [s]John 4:23
21:23 [t]Is. 24:23 & 60:19,20
21:24 [u]Is. 60:3 & 66:12
21:25 [v]Is. 60:11 [w]Is. 60:20 Zech. 14:7 ch. 22:5
21:26 [x]ver. 24
21:27 [y]Is. 35:8 & 52:1 & 60:21 Joel 3:17 ch. 22:14 [z]Phil. 4:3
22:1 [a]Ezek. 47:1 Zech. 14:8
22:2 [b]Ezek. 47:12 ch. 21:21 [c]Gen. 2:9 ch. 2:7 [d]ch. 21:24
22:3 [e]Zech. 14:11 [f]Ezek. 48:35
22:4 [g]Mat. 5:8 1 Cor. 13:12 1 John 3:2

Its light

22 [s]And I saw no temple therein: for the Lord God Almighty and the Lamb are the temple of it.

23 [t]And the city had no need of the sun, neither of the moon, to shine in it: for the glory of God did lighten it, and the Lamb *is* the light thereof.

24 [u]And the nations of them which are saved shall walk in the light of it: and the kings of the earth do bring their glory and honour into it.

25 [v]And the gates of it shall not be shut at all by day: for [w]there shall be no night there.

26 [x]And they shall bring the glory and honour of the nations into it.

27 And [y]there shall in no wise enter into it any thing that defileth, neither *whatsoever* worketh abomination, or *maketh* a lie: but they which are written in the Lamb's [z]book of life.

Its blessings

22 AND HE showed me [a]a pure river of water of life, clear as crystal, proceeding out of the throne of God and of the Lamb.

2 [b]In the midst of the street of it, and on either side of the river, *was there* [c]the tree of life, which bare twelve *manner of* fruits, *and* yielded her fruit every month: and the leaves of the tree *were* [d]for the healing of the nations.

3 And [e]there shall be no more curse: [f]but the throne of God and of the Lamb shall be in it; and his servants shall serve him:

4 And [g]they shall see his face;

21:16 THE CITY LIETH FOURSQUARE. The size of the city indicates that it will have sufficient space for the believers of all ages. "Twelve thousand furlongs" is approximately 1,350 miles. The city is portrayed as a cube. In the O.T. the holy of holies where God met His people was a perfect cube. The entire city will be filled with God's glory and holiness.

21:22 GOD ... LAMB ARE THE TEMPLE. God's presence and nearness will permeate the entire holy city, not just a temple.

21:24–26 THEM WHICH ARE SAVED. The new Jerusalem does not include the whole new earth, for the city has gates through which the righteous may enter and leave. The new Jerusalem may be the capital of the new earth.

21:25 NO NIGHT THERE. This refers only to the holy city, for John does not say there is no night on the new earth. Some believe that there will be night outside the city, for God has promised that day and night will never pass away (cf. Ps. 148:3–6; Is. 66:22–23; Jer. 33:20–21,25).

22:1 RIVER OF WATER OF LIFE. This could be a literal river symbolizing the Holy Spirit and the life, blessing, and spiritual power that He gives (cf. 7:17; 21:6; 22:17; Is. 44:3; John 7:37–39).

22:2 THE TREE OF LIFE. This tree refers to the eternal life given to all who populate the new city (Gen. 2:9; 3:22). The healing leaves indicate the absence of anything that brings physical or spiritual harm (cf. Ezek. 47:12); note that even in our new bodies we will be dependent on the Lord for life, strength, and health.

22:4 THEY SHALL SEE HIS FACE. This is the final goal of redemptive history: God dwelling in the midst of His faithful people on an earth purged from all evil. On this new earth the saints will see and dwell with Jesus, the Lamb of God, who through love redeemed them by His death on the cross. Their greatest happiness will be: "Blessed are the pure in heart; for they shall see God" (Mat. 5:8; cf. Ex. 33:20,23; Is. 33:17; John 14:9; 1 John 3:2).

and [h]his name *shall be* in their fore-
heads.
5 [i]And there shall be no night
there; and they need no candle, neither
light of the sun; for [j]the Lord God
giveth them light: [k]and they shall
reign for ever and ever.

The truth of revelation

6 And he said unto me, [l]These say-
ings *are* faithful and true: and the Lord
God of the holy prophets [m]sent his an-
gel to show unto his servants the
things which must shortly be done.
7 [n]Behold, I come quickly:
[o]blessed *is* he that keepeth the say-
ings of the prophecy of this book.
8 And I John saw these things, and
heard *them.* And when I had heard and
seen, [p]I fell down to worship before
the feet of the angel which showed me
these things.
9 Then saith he unto me, [q]See *thou*
do it not: for I am thy fellowservant,
and of thy brethren the prophets, and
of them which keep the sayings of this
book: worship God.

Distinction between the good and the evil

10 [r]And he saith unto me, Seal not
the sayings of the prophecy of this
book: [s]for the time is at hand.
11 [t]He that is unjust, let him be
unjust still: and he which is filthy, let
him be filthy still: and he that is righ-
teous, let him be righteous still: and he
that is holy, let him be holy still.
12 [u]And, behold, I come quickly;
and [v]my reward *is* with me, [w]to give
every man according as his work
shall be.
13 [x]I am Alpha and Omega, the be-
ginning and the end, the first and the
last.
14 [y]Blessed *are* they that do his
commandments, that they may have
right [z]to the tree of life, [a]and may
enter in through the gates into the city.
15 For [b]without *are* [c]dogs, and
sorcerers, and whoremongers, and
murderers, and idolaters, and whoso-
ever loveth and maketh a lie.

Invitation to salvation

16 [d]I Jesus have sent mine angel to
testify unto you these things in the
churches. [e]I am the root and the off-
spring of David, *and* [f]the bright and
morning star.
17 And the Spirit and [g]the bride
say, Come. And let him that heareth
say, Come. [h]And let him that is athirst
come. And whosoever will, let him take
the water of life freely.
18 For I testify unto every man that
heareth the words of the prophecy of
this book, [i]If any man shall add unto
these things, God shall add unto him
the plagues that are written in this
book:
19 And if any man shall take away
from the words of the book of this

22:4 [h]ch. 14:1
22:5 [i]ch. 21:23 [j]Ps. 36:9 [k]Dan. 7:27 Rom. 5:17 2 Tim. 2:12
22:6 [l]ch. 19:9 [m]ch. 1:1
22:7 [n]ch. 3:11 [o]ch. 1:3
22:8 [p]ch. 19:10
22:9 [q]ch. 19:10
22:10 [r]Dan. 8:26 [s]ch. 1:3
22:11 [t]Ezek. 3:27 Dan. 12:10 2 Tim. 3:13
22:12 [u]ver. 7 [v]Is. 40:10 [w]ch. 20:12
22:13 [x]Is. 41:4
22:14 [y]Dan. 12:12 1 John 3:24 [z]ch. 2:7 [a]ch. 21:27
22:15 [b]1 Cor. 6:9 Gal. 5:19 Col. 3:6 [c]Phil. 3:2
22:16 [d]ch. 1:1 [e]ch. 5:5 [f]Num. 24:17 Zech. 6:12 2 Pet. 1:19
22:17 [g]ch. 21:2,9 [h]Is. 55:1 John 7:37
22:18 [i]Deut. 4:2 Prov. 30:6

22:7 I COME QUICKLY. See 1 Cor. 15:51, note on the N.T. time perspective related to the return of Christ (see also Rom. 13:12, note).

22:10 SEAL NOT THE SAYINGS. The message and prophecy of the book must be proclaimed to all believers and all churches (cf. Dan. 12:4).

22:11 LET HIM BE UNJUST STILL. This may mean that those who reject John's prophecy will continue in their sins. Believers, however, must persevere in righteousness and holiness until Christ's return.

22:12 ACCORDING AS HIS WORK. See 1 Cor. 3:15, note; see article on THE JUDGMENT OF BELIEVERS, p. 1811.

22:15 WHOSOEVER LOVETH AND MAKETH A LIE. Notice how the Bible's last two chapters focus on the issue of lying. Those who practice lying are mentioned three times: (1) All liars "shall have their part in the lake which burneth with fire" (21:8); (2) he who "*maketh* a lie" will not enter the eternal city of God (21:27); (3) those who love and practice lying will be outside of God's eternal kingdom. Lying is the last sin condemned in the Bible, possibly because it was a lie that brought the fall of the human race (Gen. 3:1–5; cf. John 8:44). These solemn words should be a warning for all in the churches who feel that God tolerates lying and deceit.

22:17 THE SPIRIT AND THE BRIDE SAY, COME. The last mention of the Holy Spirit in the Bible shows Him inspiring the bride (i.e., the church) to invite all who want salvation to come to Christ. The church is now empowered by the Holy Spirit to accomplish the evangelism of the world (Acts 1:5–8; 2:4).

22:19 GOD SHALL TAKE AWAY. John ends this Revelation of Christ by warning about the terrible possibility of losing one's share in the tree of life and the holy city. We may not have a careless attitude toward this book or any part of God's holy Scripture. Such an attitude is manifested if we choose to believe only certain parts of God's revelation and reject other parts that we do not like, or if we teach our own ideas as if they were part of God's Word itself (v. 18). As at the beginning of the sojourn of the human race on earth, failure to take God's Word with absolute seriousness is a matter of life and death (see Gen. 3:3–4).

prophecy, [j]God shall take away his
part [h]out of the book of life, and out
of [k]the holy city, and *from* the things
which are written in this book.

22:19 [j]Ex. 32:33 Ps. 69:28 [k]ch. 21:2
22:20 [l]ver. 12 [m]John 21:25 [n]2 Tim. 4:8
22:21 [o]Rom. 16:20

Come, Lord Jesus

20 He which testifieth these things
saith, [l]Surely I come quickly.
[m]Amen. [n]Even so, come, Lord Jesus. End
21 [o]The grace of our Lord Jesus
Christ *be* with you all. Amen.

[h] Or, *from the tree of life*

22:20 COME, LORD JESUS. The Bible ends with Jesus' promise that He is coming quickly, to which John responds, "Come, Lord Jesus." This longing is shared by all true Christians. (1) This prayer is a confession that until He comes, our redemption remains incomplete, evil and sin are not yet overthrown, and this world is not yet renewed.

(2) We have every reason to believe that the day is fast approaching when He who is called "The Word of God" (19:13) and "the bright and morning star" (v. 16) will come down from heaven to take His faithful away from the earth to His Father's house (John 14:1–3; 1 Thes. 4:16–18), after which He will return in glory and triumph to reign forever as "KING OF KINGS, AND LORD OF LORDS" (19:16). This is our unfailing hope and joyful expectation (2 Pet. 1:19).

Table of Weights and Measures

BIBLICAL UNIT		APPROXIMATE AMERICAN EQUIVALENT	APPROXIMATE METRIC EQUIVALENT
		WEIGHTS	
talent	*(60 minas)*	75 pounds	34 kilograms
mina	*(50 shekels)*	1 1/4 pounds	0.6 kilogram
shekel	*(2 bekas)*	2/5 ounce	11.5 grams
pim	*(2/3 shekel)*	1/3 ounce	7.6 grams
beka	*(10 gerahs)*	1/5 ounce	5.5 grams
gerah		1/50 ounce	0.6 gram
		LENGTH	
cubit		18 inches	0.5 meter
span		9 inches	23 centimeters
handbreadth		3 inches	8 centimeters
		CAPACITY	
		Dry Measure	
cor [homer]	*(10 ephahs)*	6 bushels	220 liters
lethek	*(5 ephahs)*	3 bushels	110 liters
ephah	*(10 omers)*	3/5 bushel	22 liters
seah	*(1/3 ephah)*	7 quarts	7.3 liters
omer	*(1/10 ephah)*	2 quarts	2 liters
cab	*(1/18 ephah)*	1 quart	1 liter
		Liquid Measure	
bath	*(1 ephah)*	6 gallons	22 liters
hin	*(1/6 bath)*	4 quarts	4 liters
log	*(1/72 bath)*	1/3 quart	0.3 liter

The figures of the table are calculated on the basis of a shekel equaling 11.5 grams, a cubit equaling 18 inches and an ephah equaling 22 liters. The quart referred to is either a dry quart (slightly larger than a liter) or a liquid quart (slightly smaller than a liter), whichever is applicable. The ton referred to in the footnotes is the American ton of 2,000 pounds.

This table is based upon the best available information, but it is not intended to be mathematically precise; like the measurement equivalents in the footnotes, it merely gives approximate amounts and distances. Weights and measures differed somewhat at various times and places in the ancient world. There is uncertainty particularly about the ephah and the bath; further discoveries may give more light on these units of capacity.

SUBJECT INDEX

This subject index will enable you to locate where various topics are discussed in the study notes and articles. Page numbers are given in boldface type.

Themefinder™ Index

This Themefinder™ Index will provide an "at-a-glance" listing of the passages assigned to a particular theme of importance in the Pentecostal tradition. Themefinders link the most significant texts on crucial Bible topics.

Baptized in/Filled with the Holy Spirit

Exodus 31:1–6
Numbers 27:18
Judges 3:9–10
Judges 6:34
Judges 11:29
Judges 15:14–15
1 Samuel 11:6–7
1 Samuel 16:13
1 Chronicles 12:18
2 Chronicles 24:20–21
Psalm 51:10–12
Isaiah 11:1–3a
Isaiah 32:15
Isaiah 42:1
Isaiah 44:3
Isaiah 59:21
Ezekiel 2:1–2
Ezekiel 11:19–20
Ezekiel 36:26–27
Ezekiel 37:14
Ezekiel 39:29
Joel 2:28–29
Micah 3:8
Zechariah 4:6
Matthew 3:11
Mark 1:7–8
Luke 1:15
Luke 1:41
Luke 1:67
Luke 3:16
Luke 4:1
Luke 24:49
John 1:32–33
John 7:38–39
Acts 1:4–5
Acts 2:4–13
Acts 2:38–39
Acts 4:8
Acts 4:31
Acts 6:3
Acts 7:55
Acts 8:14–17
Acts 9:17
Acts 10:44–47
Acts 11:15–17
Acts 13:9
Acts 15:8
Acts 19:1–7
Ephesians 5:18

Gifts of the Holy Spirit

Exodus 35:30–35
Numbers 11:24–29
Judges 4:4
1 Samuel 10:5–11
2 Samuel 23:1–2
Nehemiah 9:30
Isaiah 61:1–3
Ezekiel 8:3–4
Zechariah 7:12
Mark 16:17–18
Acts 6:8
Acts 11:27–28
Acts 14:3
Acts 15:32
Acts 21:9–12
Romans 1:11
Romans 12:6–8
Romans 15:19
1 Corinthians 1:7
1 Corinthians 12:1–31
1 Corinthians 14:1–40
Galatians 3:5
Ephesians 4:7–12
1 Timothy 4:14
2 Timothy 1:6
Hebrews 2:4
1 Peter 4:10–11

Fruit of the Holy Spirit

Genesis 50:19–21
Numbers 6:24–26
Numbers 12:3–7
Ruth 3:10–11
2 Samuel 9:1–7
Psalm 1:3
Isaiah 3:10
Isaiah 27:6
Isaiah 32:16–18
Ezekiel 17:22–24
Hosea 6:1–3
Hosea 14:4–8
Matthew 7:16–20
Matthew 12:33
Luke 6:43–44
John 15:1–8
Acts 13:52
Romans 5:5
Romans 8:6
Romans 14:17
Romans 15:30
Galatians 5:22–23
Ephesians 3:17–21
Colossians 1:6–8
1 Thessalonians 1:6
Hebrews 12:11
James 3:17–18

Healing

Faith that moves mountains

Witnessing

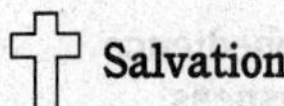

Salvation

Genesis 12:1–3
Exodus 12:29–42
Exodus 14:13–14
Leviticus 16:15–22
Deuteronomy 26:6–9
1 Samuel 2:1–2
Psalm 13:5–6
Psalm 18:1–3
Psalm 27:1
Psalm 37:39–40
Psalm 62:1–8
Psalm 85:4–7
Psalm 98:1–3
Psalm 116:1–13
Isaiah 12:1–3
Isaiah 25:9
Isaiah 43:11–13
Isaiah 51:4–6
Isaiah 53:6–12
Isaiah 55:6–7
Isaiah 59:15–17
Isaiah 61:10
Isaiah 63:1–6
Jeremiah 23:5–6
Ezekiel 3:16–21
Ezekiel 18:21–23
Ezekiel 33:14–16
Joel 2:32
Micah 7:7
Matthew 1:21
Luke 1:76–79
Luke 19:10
John 1:12
John 3:14–17
John 11:25–26
John 20:31
Acts 4:12
Acts 13:38–39
Romans 1:16
Romans 3:21–26
Romans 10:4–13
1 Corinthians 15:1–8
2 Corinthians 5:17—6:1
Galatians 2:16
Ephesians 2:4–9
1 Thessalonians 5:8–10
2 Thessalonians 2:13
1 Timothy 1:15–16
1 Timothy 2:3–6
2 Timothy 3:15
Titus 3:3–7
Hebrews 2:3
Hebrews 5:9
Hebrews 7:25
1 John 5:11–12
Revelation 3:20

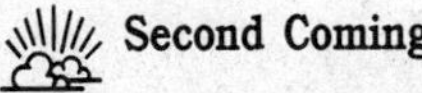

Second Coming

Psalm 98:8–9
Isaiah 11:3b–4
Isaiah 35:3–5
Isaiah 40:10–11
Isaiah 62:11–12
Isaiah 66:15–16
Ezekiel 43:2
Joel 1:15
Zechariah 8:3–15
Zechariah 9:10
Zechariah 14:3–9
Malachi 4:2–3
Matthew 16:27–28
Matthew 24:15–51
Matthew 25:31–46
Matthew 26:64
Mark 13:1–37
Luke 17:22–37
John 14:3
Acts 1:11
1 Corinthians 4:5
1 Corinthians 15:23
Philippians 3:20–21
1 Thessalonians 1:10
1 Thessalonians 4:15—5:3
2 Thessalonians 1:7—2:8
1 Timothy 6:14–15
2 Timothy 4:8
Titus 2:13
Hebrews 9:28
1 Peter 5:4
2 Peter 3:8–14
1 John 3:2
Jude 14–15
Revelation 1:7
Revelation 16:15
Revelation 19:11–16
Revelation 22:12
Revelation 22:20

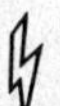

Victory over Satan and demons

Genesis 3:15
Exodus 7:10–12
Judges 6:25–32
Judges 16:23–30
1 Samuel 16:22–23
1 Kings 18:21–39
Job 1:6–22
Psalm 91:1–13
Isaiah 14:12–20
Isaiah 24:21–23
Daniel 10:11
Matthew 4:1–11
Matthew 8:28–33
Matthew 17:14–18
Mark 1:23–28
Mark 3:10–15
Mark 3:20–27
Mark 5:1–16
Luke 4:2–13
Luke 4:33–36
Luke 10:17–19
Luke 11:20–26
Acts 5:3–5
Acts 16:16–18
Acts 19:13–20
Romans 8:38–38
2 Corinthians 11:12–15
2 Corinthians 12:7–10
Ephesians 6:10–18
James 4:7
1 Peter 5:8–9
1 John 3:8
Jude 9
Revelation 12:7–11
Revelation 20:2–3
Revelation 20:7–10

Overcoming the world and worldliness

Genesis 19:15–26
Exodus 23:23–24
Leviticus 11:44–45
Leviticus 18:1–5
Deuteronomy 7:1–6
Joshua 23:11–13
1 Kings 19:18
2 Chronicles 30:6–9
Ezra 4:1–5
Nehemiah 2:18–20
Psalm 2
Psalm 18:37–40
Psalm 37:1–6
Psalm 49:13–15
Psalm 144
Proverbs 16:7
Isaiah 44:24–25
Jeremiah 1:18–19
Ezekiel 9:4
Daniel 1:8–20
Matthew 5:3–16
Matthew 6:19–24
John 15:18–20
John 16:33
John 17:14–18
John 18:36–37
Romans 12:1–2
1 Corinthians 2:6–16
2 Corinthians 6:14–7:1
Galatians 6:14
2 Timothy 3:1–5
Titus 2:11–12
Hebrews 11:13–16
James 1:27
James 4:4–6
1 Peter 2:11–12
1 John 2:15–17
1 John 5:4–5
Revelation 2:7
Revelation 2:12–17
Revelation 3:21–22
Revelation 21:7

Praise

Exodus 15:1–21
Deuteronomy 8:10
Judges 5:1–2
2 Samuel 22:47–50
1 Chronicles 16:7–43
1 Chronicles 29:20
Ezra 3:10–13
Psalm 9:1–2
Psalm 34:1–3
Psalm 92:1–4
Psalm 100
Psalm 113
Psalm 135:1–4
Psalm 146
Psalm 150
Isaiah 12:4–6
Isaiah 26:1–4
Isaiah 42:10–12
Jeremiah 20:13
Jeremiah 31:7
Daniel 2:20–23
Joel 2:23–27
Habakkuk 3:3
Zephaniah 3:19–20
Matthew 9:8
Matthew 21:15–16
Luke 1:42–47
Luke 2:13–14
Luke 2:20
Luke 18:43
Luke 19:36–40
Acts 2:46–47
Romans 15:5–11
Ephesians 1:3–6
Ephesians 5:19–20
Colossians 3:16–17
Hebrews 13:15
1 Peter 2:9
Revelation 5:9–14
Revelation 7:9–12
Revelation 19:1–6

Walking in obedience and righteousness

Genesis 5:22
Genesis 6:9–10
Genesis 17:1–2
Genesis 26:2–6
Exodus 19:3–6
Exodus 20:1–17
Leviticus 20:26
Deuteronomy 10:12–13
Deuteronomy 11:26–28
Joshua 1:7–8
Joshua 22:5
1 Samuel 12:14–15
1 Samuel 15:22–23
1 Kings 2:2–4
1 Kings 9:3–8
1 Chronicles 28:6–9
2 Chronicles 13:4–12
Ezra 7:10
Nehemiah 10:28–39
Job 1:1–5
Job 23:10–12
Psalm 1:1–2
Psalm 40:6–8
Psalm 78:1–8
Psalm 119:1–16
Proverbs 3:1–6
Ecclesiastes 12:13–14
Isaiah 2:3–5
Isaiah 35:8–9
Isaiah 58:1–8
Jeremiah 11:1–5
Ezekiel 20:39–44
Daniel 9:4–6
Micah 6:8
Malachi 2:5–6
Matthew 7:21–23
Matthew 19:16–26
Mark 9:42–48
Luke 6:46–49
Luke 10:25–37
Luke 12:42–48
John 8:31
John 14:21–24
Acts 10:34–35
Romans 6:1–14
Romans 8:1–5
Romans 13:12–14
Galatians 5:13–18
Ephesians 2:10
Ephesians 5:1–15
Philippians 2:12–16
Colossians 3:5–14
1 Thessalonians 4:1–7
Hebrews 10:23–26
Hebrews 12:1
James 2:14–26
1 Peter 1:13–16
2 Peter 1:3–11
1 John 2:3–6
1 John 3:9–18
Revelation 3:1–4
Revelation 21:8

READING PLAN

The Entire Bible in a Year

This reading plan gives you a structured pattern for reading through the entire Bible in one year. There are two readings for each day, one in the Old Testament, the other in the New Testament. If you feel bogged down by so much reading each day, an alternative plan is to read the Old Testament passages the first year and the New Testament passages the second year, completing the entire Bible in two years rather than one.

JANUARY	A.M.	P.M.
1	Gen 1–2	Matt 1
2	Gen 3–5	Matt 2
3	Gen 6–8	Matt 3
4	Gen 9–11	Matt 4
5	Gen 12–14	Matt 5:1–20
6	Gen 15–17	Matt 5:21–48
7	Gen 18–19	Matt 6:1–18
8	Gen 20–22	Matt 6:19–7:6
9	Gen 23–24	Matt 7:7–29
10	Gen 25–26	Matt 8:1–27
11	Gen 27–28	Matt 8:28–9:17
12	Gen 29–30	Matt 9:18–38
13	Gen 31–33	Matt 10:1–23
14	Gen 34–35	Matt 10:24–42
15	Gen 36–37	Matt 11:1–30
16	Gen 38–39	Matt 12:1–21
17	Gen 40–41	Matt 12:22–50
18	Gen 42–43	Matt 13:1–23
19	Gen 44–45	Matt 13:24–43
20	Gen 46–48	Matt 13:44–14:12
21	Gen 49–50	Matt 14:13–36
22	Exod 1–2	Matt 15:1–28
23	Exod 3–5	Matt 15:29–16:12
24	Exod 6–7	Matt 16:13–17:13
25	Exod 8–9	Matt 17:14–18:14
26	Exod 10–12	Matt 18:15–35
27	Exod 13–14	Matt 19:1–15
28	Exod 15	Matt 19:16–20:16
29	Exod 16–17	Matt 20:17–34
30	Exod 18–19	Matt 21:1–32
31	Exod 20–21	Matt 21:33–22:14

FEBRUARY	A.M.	P.M.
1	Exod 22–23	Matt 22:15–46
2	Exod 24–25	Matt 23
3	Exod 26–27	Matt 24:1–35
4	Exod 28	Matt 24:36–51
5	Exod 29–30	Matt 25:1–30
6	Exod 31	Matt 25:31–46
7	Exod 32–33	Matt 26:1–30
8	Exod 34–35	Matt 26:31–56
9	Exod 36–37	Matt 26:57–75
10	Exod 38–39	Matt 27:1–26
11	Exod 40	Matt 27:27–44
12	Lev 1–3	Matt 27:45–66
13	Lev 4–5	Matt 28
14	Lev 6–7	Acts 1
15	Lev 8	Acts 2:1–21
16	Lev 9–10	Acts 2:22–47
17	Lev 11–12	Acts 3
18	Lev 13–14	Acts 4:1–31
19	Lev 15	Acts 4:32–5:11
20	Lev 16–18	Acts 5:12–42
21	Lev 19–21	Acts 6
22	Lev 22–23	Acts 7:1–53
23	Lev 24	Acts 7:54–8:8
24	Lev 25	Acts 8:9–40
25	Lev 26–27	Acts 9:1–31
26	Num 1–2	Acts 9:32–43
27	Num 3–4	Acts 10:1–23
28	Num 5–6	Acts 10:24–48
29	John 17	Heb 13

MARCH	A.M.	P.M.
1	Num 7–8	Acts 11:1–18
2	Num 9–10	Acts 11:19–30
3	Num 11–13	Acts 12
4	Num 14–15	Acts 13:1–12
5	Num 16–17	Acts 13:13–52
6	Num 18–19	Acts 14
7	Num 20–21	Acts 15:1–21
8	Num 22–23	Acts 15:22–35
9	Num 24–26	Acts 15:36–16:15
10	Num 27–28	Acts 16:16–40
11	Num 29–31	Acts 17:1–15
12	Num 32–33	Acts 17:16–34
13	Num 34–36	Acts 18:1–23
14	Deut 1–2	Acts 18:24–19:7
15	Deut 3–4	Acts 19:8–41
16	Deut 5–7	Acts 20:1–16
17	Deut 8–10	Acts 20:17–38
18	Deut 11–12	Acts 21:1–16
19	Deut 13–15	Acts 21:17–36
20	Deut 16–17	Acts 21:37–22:21
21	Deut 18–21	Acts 22:22–23:11
22	Deut 22–24	Acts 23:12–35
23	Deut 25–27	Acts 24
24	Deut 28	Acts 25:1–12
25	Deut 29–30	Acts 25:13–26:1
26	Deut 31–32	Acts 26:2–18
27	Deut 33–34	Acts 26:19–32
28	Josh 1–2	Acts 27:1–26
29	Josh 3–4	Acts 27:27–44
30	Josh 5–6	Acts 28:1–16
31	Josh 7–9	Acts 28:17–31

APRIL	A.M.	P.M.
1	Josh 10–12	Mark 1:1–20
2	Josh 13–15	Mark 1:21–45
3	Josh 16–19	Mark 2:1–22
4	Josh 20–22	Mark 2:23–3:12
5	Josh 23–24	Mark 3:13–35
6	Judg 1–2	Mark 4:1–20
7	Judg 3–4	Mark 4:21–41
8	Judg 5–6	Mark 5:1–20
9	Judg 7–8	Mark 5:21–43
10	Judg 9	Mark 6:1–29
11	Judg 10–11	Mark 6:30–56
12	Judg 12–13	Mark 7:1–23
13	Judg 14–16	Mark 7:24–8:13
14	Judg 17–18	Mark 8:14–26
15	Judg 19–21	Mark 8:27–9:13
16	Ruth	Mark 9:14–32
17	1 Sam 1–2	Mark 9:33–50
18	1 Sam 3–7	Mark 10:1–31
19	1 Sam 8–10	Mark 10:32–52
20	1 Sam 11–13	Mark 11:1–26
21	1 Sam 14–15	Mark 11:27–12:17
22	1 Sam 16–17	Mark 12:18–44
23	1 Sam 18–19	Mark 13
24	1 Sam 20–22	Mark 14:1–26
25	1 Sam 23–25	Mark 14:27–52
26	1 Sam 26–28	Mark 14:53–72
27	1 Sam 29–31	Mark 15:1–20
28	2 Sam 1–3	Mark 15:21–47
29	2 Sam 4–6	Mark 16
30	2 Sam 7–8	Jude

MAY	A.M.	P.M.
1	2 Sam 9–11	1 Pet 1:1–21
2	2 Sam 12–14	1 Pet 1:22–2:25
3	2 Sam 15–17	1 Pet 3
4	2 Sam 18–19	1 Pet 4
5	2 Sam 20–21	1 Pet 5
6	2 Sam 22	2 Pet 1
7	2 Sam 23–24	2 Pet 2
8	1 Kings 1	2 Pet 3
9	1 Kings 2–3	Jas 1
10	1 Kings 4–6	Jas 2–3:13
11	1 Kings 7–8	Jas 3:14–4:12
12	1 Kings 9	Jas 4:13–5:20
13	1 Kings 10–11	Luke 1:1–25
14	1 Kings 12–14	Luke 1:26–56
15	1 Kings 15–17	Luke 1:57–80
16	1 Kings 18–19	Luke 2:1–20
17	1 Kings 20–21	Luke 2:21–52
18	1 Kings 22	Luke 3
19	2 Kings 1–3	Luke 4:1–13
20	2 Kings 4–5	Luke 4:14–44
21	2 Kings 6–7	Luke 5:1–16
22	2 Kings 8–9	Luke 5:17–39
23	2 Kings 10–12	Luke 6:1–16
24	2 Kings 13–15	Luke 6:17–49
25	2 Kings 16–17	Luke 7:1–35
26	2 Kings 18–19	Luke 7:36–50
27	2 Kings 20–22	Luke 8:1–21
28	2 Kings 23–25	Luke 8:22–39
29	1 Chron 1–2	Luke 8:40–56
30	1 Chron 3–4	Luke 9:1–17
31	1 Chron 5–6	Luke 9:18–36

JUNE	A.M.	P.M.
1	1 Chron 7–8	Luke 9:37–62
2	1 Chron 9–10	Luke 10:1–24
3	1 Chron 11–13	Luke 10:25–42
4	1 Chron 14–16	Luke 11:1–13
5	1 Chron 17–19	Luke 11:14–36
6	1 Chron 20–22	Luke 11:37–54
7	1 Chron 23–25	Luke 12:1–21
8	1 Chron 26–29	Luke 12:22–48
9	2 Chron 1–4	Luke 12:49–59
10	2 Chron 5–7	Luke 13:1–21
11	2 Chron 8–11	Luke 13:22–35
12	2 Chron 12–15	Luke 14:1–24
13	2 Chron 16–19	Luke 14:25–15:10
14	2 Chron 20–22	Luke 15:11–32
15	2 Chron 23–25	Luke 16
16	2 Chron 26–28	Luke 17:1–19
17	2 Chron 29–30	Luke 17:20–18:14
18	2 Chron 31–32	Luke 18:15–43
19	2 Chron 33–34	Luke 19:1–27
20	2 Chron 35–36	Luke 19:28–48
21	Ezra 1–3	Luke 20:1–19
22	Ezra 4–6	Luke 20:20–21:4
23	Ezra 7–8	Luke 21:5–38
24	Ezra 9–10	Luke 22:1–38
25	Neh 1–3	Luke 22:39–65
26	Neh 4–6	Luke 22:66–23:25
27	Neh 7–8	Luke 23:26–49
28	Neh 9–10	Luke 23:50–24:12
29	Neh 11–13	Luke 24:13–35
30	Est 1–4	Luke 24:36–53

JULY	A.M.	P.M.
1	Est 5–7	1 Thess 1–2:16
2	Est 8–10	1 Thess 2:17–3:13
3	Job 1–2	1 Thess 4
4	Job 3–5	1 Thess 5
5	Job 6–8	2 Thess 1
6	Job 9–11	2 Thess 2
7	Job 12–14	2 Thess 3
8	Job 15–18	1 Cor 1
9	Job 19–21	1 Cor 2
10	Job 22–24	1 Cor 3
11	Job 25–28	1 Cor 4
12	Job 29–31	1 Cor 5
13	Job 32–35	1 Cor 6
14	Job 36–39	1 Cor 7
15	Job 40–42	1 Cor 8
16	Psa 1–6	1 Cor 9
17	Psa 7–10	1 Cor 10:1–13
18	Psa 11–16	1 Cor 10:14–11:1
19	Psa 17–18	1 Cor 11:2–34
20	Psa 19–20	1 Cor 12
21	Psa 21–22	1 Cor 13
22	Psa 23–25	1 Cor 14
23	Psa 26–29	1 Cor 15:1–34
24	Psa 30–31	1 Cor 15:35–58
25	Psa 32–34	1 Cor 16
26	Psa 35–37	2 Cor 1–2:4
27	Psa 38–41	2 Cor 2:5–3:6
28	Psa 42–44	2 Cor 3:7–4:18
29	Psa 45–48	2 Cor 5:1–6:2
30	Psa 49–51	2 Cor 6:3–7:1
31	Psa 52–55	2 Cor 7:2–16

AUGUST	A.M.	P.M.
1	Psa 56–59	2 Cor 8–9
2	Psa 60–63	2 Cor 10
3	Psa 64–67	2 Cor 11:1–15
4	Psa 68–69	2 Cor 11:16–33
5	Psa 70–73	2 Cor 12
6	Psa 74–77	2 Cor 13
7	Psa 78	Rom 1:1–17
8	Psa 79–81	Rom 1:18–32
9	Psa 82–84	Rom 2
10	Psa 85–88	Rom 3
11	Psa 89	Rom 4
12	Psa 90–93	Rom 5:1–11
13	Psa 94–98	Rom 5:12–21
14	Psa 99–101	Rom 6:1–14
15	Psa 102–103	Rom 6:15–7:6
16	Psa 104–106	Rom 7:7–25
17	Psa 107–108	Rom 8:1–17
18	Psa 109–112	Rom 8:18–39
19	Psa 113–116	Rom 9:1–29
20	Psa 117–118	Rom 9:30–10:21
21	Psa 119:1–112	Rom 11:1–24
22	Psa 119:113–176	Rom 11:25–36
23	Psa 120–127	Rom 12:1–16
24	Psa 128–134	Rom 12:17–13:14
25	Psa 135–138	Rom 14–15:4
26	Psa 139–141	Rom 15:5–13
27	Psa 142–145	Rom 15:14–33
28	Psa 146–150	Rom 16
29	Prov 1–2	Gal 1
30	Prov 3–4	Gal 2
31	Prov 5–7	Gal 3:1–14

SEPTEMBER	A.M.	P.M.
1	Prov 8–9	Gal 3:15–25
2	Prov 10–11	Gal 3:26–4:20
3	Prov 12–13	Gal 4:21–5:15
4	Prov 14–15	Gal 5:16–26
5	Prov 16–17	Gal 6
6	Prov 18–19	Eph 1:1–14
7	Prov 20–21	Eph 1:15–2:10
8	Prov 22–23	Eph 2:11–22
9	Prov 24–26	Eph 3
10	Prov 27–28	Eph 4:1–16
11	Prov 29–31	Eph 4:17–5:2
12	Ecc 1–2	Eph 5:3–21
13	Ecc 3–5	Eph 5:22–6:9
14	Ecc 6–8	Eph 6:10–24
15	Ecc 9–12	Php 1
16	S of S 1–2	Php 2:1–18
17	S of S 3–5	Php 2:19–3:11
18	S of S 6–8	Php 3:12–4:3
19	Obadiah	Php 4:4–23
20	Joel	Col 1:1–23
21	Jonah	Col 1:24–2:5
22	Amos 1–4	Col 2:6–23
23	Amos 5–9	Col 3:1–4:1
24	Hos 1–2	Col 4:2–18
25	Hos 3–6	Philemon
26	Hos 7–10	Heb 1
27	Hos 11–14	Heb 2
28	Isa 1–2	Heb 3
29	Isa 3–5	Heb 4:1–13
30	Isa 6–8	Heb 4:14–5:10

OCTOBER	A.M.	P.M.
1	Isa 9–10	Heb 5:11–6:20
2	Isa 11–12	Heb 7
3	Isa 13–14	Heb 8
4	Isa 15–18	Heb 9:1–10
5	Isa 19–22	Heb 9:11–28
6	Isa 23–24	Heb 10:1–18
7	Isa 25–26	Heb 10:19–39
8	Isa 27–28	Heb 11:1–16
9	Isa 29–30	Heb 11:17–40
10	Isa 31–32	Heb 12:1–13
11	Isa 33–34	Heb 12:14–29
12	Isa 35–37	Heb 13
13	Isa 38–39	Titus 1–2
14	Isa 40–41	Titus 3
15	Isa 42–43	1 Tim 1
16	Isa 44–45	1 Tim 2
17	Isa 46–47	1 Tim 3
18	Isa 48–49	1 Tim 4
19	Isa 50–51	1 Tim 5
20	Isa 52–53	1 Tim 6
21	Isa 54–56	2 Tim 1
22	Isa 57–58	2 Tim 2
23	Isa 59–60	2 Tim 3
24	Isa 61–63	2 Tim 4
25	Isa 64–66	John 1:1–18
26	Mic 1–3	John 1:19–51
27	Mic 4–5	John 2
28	Mic 6–7	John 3:1–21
29	Nahum	John 3:22–36
30	Habakkuk	John 4:1–26
31	Zephaniah	John 4:27–54

NOVEMBER	A.M.	P.M.
1	Jer 1–2	John 5:1–30
2	Jer 3–4	John 5:31–47
3	Jer 5–6	John 6:1–24
4	Jer 7–8	John 6:25–59
5	Jer 9–10	John 6:60–71
6	Jer 11–12	John 7:1–24
7	Jer 13–14	John 7:25–8:11
8	Jer 15–16	John 8:12–30
9	Jer 17–18	John 8:31–47
10	Jer 19–22	John 8:48–59
11	Jer 23–25	John 9
12	Jer 26–28	John 10:1–21
13	Jer 29–30	John 10:22–42
14	Jer 31–32	John 11:1–16
15	Jer 33	John 11:17–57
16	Jer 34–35	John 12:1–19
17	Jer 36–37	John 12:20–50
18	Jer 38–40	John 13:1–30
19	Jer 41–43	John 13:31–14:14
20	Jer 44–47	John 14:15–31
21	Jer 48–49	John 15:1–17
22	Jer 50–51	John 15:18–16:16
23	Jer 52	John 16:17–33
24	Lam 1–2	John 17
25	Lam 3–5	John 18:1–27
26	Ezek 1–2	John 18:28–19:16
27	Ezek 3–4	John 19:17–42
28	Ezek 5–7	John 20:1–18
29	Ezek 8–10	John 20:19–31
30	Ezek 11–12	John 21

DECEMBER	A.M.	P.M.
1	Ezek 13–15	1 John 1–2:14
2	Ezek 16	1 John 2:15–3:10
3	Ezek 17–19	1 John 3:11–24
4	Ezek 20–21	1 John 4
5	Ezek 22–23	1 John 5
6	Ezek 24–26	2 John
7	Ezek 27–28	3 John
8	Ezek 29–30	Rev 1
9	Ezek 31–32	Rev 2:1–17
10	Ezek 33–34	Rev 2:18–3:6
11	Ezek 35–36	Rev 3:7–22
12	Ezek 37–38	Rev 4
13	Ezek 39–40	Rev 5
14	Ezek 41–42	Rev 6
15	Ezek 43–44	Rev 7
16	Ezek 45–46	Rev 8
17	Ezek 47–48	Rev 9
18	Dan 1–2	Rev 10
19	Dan 3–4	Rev 11
20	Dan 5–6	Rev 12
21	Dan 7–8	Rev 13:1–10
22	Dan 9–10	Rev 13:11–14:20
23	Dan 11–12	Rev 15
24	Haggai	Rev 16
25	Zech 1–3	Rev 17
26	Zech 4–6	Rev 18
27	Zech 7–8	Rev 19:1–10
28	Zech 9–11	Rev 19:11–21
29	Zech 12–14	Rev 20
30	Mal 1–2	Rev 21
31	Mal 3–4	Rev 22

CONCORDANCE

CONCORDANCE

TO THE OLD AND NEW TESTAMENTS

For each verse quoted in this concordance, an italicized single letter followed by a period is used to designate the word entry. The texts chosen for each word are in Bible book order under the entry. Occasionally the verses under a word entry contain different forms of that entry (for example, under the word ABASE, entries may contain "abased" or "abasing"). Those alternate forms of the word have been placed in parentheses after the key word. The context of each verse will help the reader understand which form of the word fits the italicized letter.

A

ABASE (ABASED, ABASING)
Job 40:11 every one that is proud, and *a.*
Is. 31: 4 nor *a.* himself for the noise of them
Ezek. 21:26 *a.* him that is high
Dan. 4:37 walk in pride he is able to *a.*
Mat. 23:12 exalt himself shall be *a.*
2 Cor. 11: 7 offence in *a.* myself

ABATED
Gen. 8: 3 fifty days the waters were *a.*
Lev. 27:18 shall be *a.* from thy estimation
Deut. 34: 7 nor his natural force *a.*
Judg. 8: 3 their anger was *a.* towards

ABHOR (ABHORRED, ABHORREST, ABHORRETH, ABHORRING)
Ex. 5:21 made our savour to be *a.*
Lev. 26:11 my soul shall not *a.* you
26:15 if your soul *a.* my judgments
26:30 my soul shall *a.* you
26:43 their soul *a.* my statutes
26:44 neither will I *a.* them
Deut. 23: 7 shalt not *a.* an Edomite
32:19 when the Lord saw it he *a.* them
1 Sam. 2:17 for men *a.* the offering
27:12 made his people to *a.* him
Job 19:19 my inward friends *a.* me
30:10 they *a.* me, they flee
33:20 so that his life *a.* bread
42: 6 I *a.* myself, and repent
Ps. 5: 6 Lord will *a.* the bloody
10: 3 covetous, whom the Lord *a.*
22:24 nor *a.* the affliction of the afflicted
36: 4 he *a.* not evil
89:38 cast off and *a.* . . . thine anointed
106: 40 he *a.* his own inheritance
107: 18 their soul *a.* all manner of meat
119:163 I hate and *a.* lying
Prov. 22:14 *a.* of the Lord shall fall
Is. 49: 7 him whom the nation *a.*
66:24 be an *a.* unto all flesh
Jer. 14:21 do not *a.* us for thy name's sake
Lam. 2: 7 Lord hath *a.* his sanctuary
Amos 5:10 they *a.* him that speaketh
6: 8 I *a.* the excellency of Jacob
Mic. 3: 9 house of Israel that *a.* judgment
Zech. 11: 8 their soul also *a.* me
Rom. 2:22 thou that *a.* idols

ABIDE
Ex. 16:29 *a.* ye every man in his place
Num. 35:25 *a.* in it unto the death of the high
2 Sam. 11:11 Israel, and Judah, *a.* in tents
Ps. 15: 1 who shall *a.* in thy tabernacle
61: 4 I will *a.* in thy tabernacle
61: 7 he shall *a.* before God for ever
91: 1 *a.* under the shadow of the Almighty
Prov. 7:11 her feet *a.* not in her house
19:23 that hath it shall *a.* satisfied
Hos. 3: 3 shall *a.* for me many days
3: 4 Israel shall *a.* without a king
Joel 2:11 terrible; who can *a.* it
Mal. 3: 2 who may *a.* the day of his
Mat. 10:11 there *a.* till ye go thence
Luke 19: 5 I must *a.* at thy house
24:29 *a.* with us; for it is toward
John 14:16 Comforter, that he may *a.* with you
15: 4 *a.* in me and I in you
15:10 ye shall *a.* in my love, *a.* in his
Acts 20:23 bonds and afflictions *a.* me
1 Cor. 3:14 if any man's work *a.*
7: 8 good for them if they *a.* even as I
7:20 every man *a.* in the same
7:24 is called therein *a.* with God
Phil. 1:24 to *a.* in the flesh is needful
1:25 know that I shall *a.* with you
1 John 2:24 let that therefore *a.* in you
2:27 ye shall *a.* in him
2:28 little children *a.* in him

ABIDETH (ABIDING)
Ps. 49:12 man being in honour *a.* not
55:19 even he that *a.* of old
Eccl. 1: 4 the earth *a.* for ever
John 3:36 wrath of God *a.* on him
5:38 not his word *a.* in you
8:35 but the Son *a.* for ever
12:24 except it die it *a.* alone
12:34 Christ *a.* for ever
15: 5 he that *a.* in me bringeth forth
2 Tim. 2:13 yet he *a.* faithful
1 Pet. 1:23 word of God *a.* for ever
1 John 3: 6 whoso *a.* in him sinneth not
3:15 no murderer hath eternal life *a.*
3:24 hereby we know he *a.* in us

ABODE
John 14:23 make our *a.* with him

ABILITY
Mat. 25:15 every man according to his several *a.*
1 Pet. 4:11 as of the *a.* God giveth

ABLE
Ex. 18:21 *a.* men, such as fear God,
Lev. 14:22 such as he is *a.* to get
Deut. 16:17 every man give as he is *a.*
2 Chr. 20: 6 none is *a.* to withstand
Dan. 3:17 God is *a.* to deliver
4:37 walk in pride he is *a.* to abase
Mat. 3: 9 God is *a.* of these stones to raise
9:28 believe ye I am *a.* to do this?
10:28 are not *a.* to kill the soul
19:12 he that is *a.* to receive it, let
Mark 4:33 as they were *a.* to hear
John 10:29 no man is *a.* to pluck them
Rom. 4:21 he was *a.* to perform
14: 4 God is *a.* to make him stand
1 Cor. 3: 2 neither yet now are ye *a.*
10:13 tempted above that ye are *a.*
2 Cor. 9: 8 *a.* to make all grace abound
Phil. 3:21 *a.* to subdue all to himself
2 Tim. 1:12 *a.* to keep that which
3:15 which are *a.* to make thee wise
Heb. 2:18 *a.* to succour the tempted
5: 7 *a.* to save him from death
7:25 *a.* to save to the uttermost
11:19 *a.* to raise him from dead
Jas. 1:21 *a.* to save your souls
4:12 *a.* to save and to destroy
Jude 1:24 *a.* to keep you from falling

ABOLISH (ABOLISHED)
Is. 2:18 idols he shall utterly *a.*
51: 6 righteousness shall not be *a.*
Ezek. 6: 6 your works may be *a.*
2 Cor. 3:13 to the end of that which is *a.*
Eph. 2:15 having *a.* in his flesh
2 Tim. 1:10 Jesus Christ hath *a.* death

ABOMINABLE
Lev. 7:21 or any *a.* unclean thing
18:30 commit not any one of these *a.* customs
1 Chr. 21: 6 king's word was *a.* to Joab
Job 15:16 how much more *a.* is man
Ps. 14: 1 have done *a.* works
Is. 14:19 thy grave like an *a.* branch
Jer. 16:18 carcases of their detestable and *a.* things
44: 4 do not this *a.* thing that I hate
Nah. 3: 6 I will cast *a.* filth on thee
Tit. 1:16 in works deny him being *a.*
1 Pet. 4: 3 walked in *a.* idolatries
Rev. 21: 8 unbelieving and *a.* shall

ABOMINATION (ABOMINATIONS)
2 Ki. 21: 2 the *a.* of the heathen
Ezra 9:14 join people of these *a.*
Prov. 6:16 seven things are an *a.* to Lord
11: 1 a false balance is *a.* to the Lord
11:20 they of a froward heart are *a.*
12:22 lying lips are *a.* to the Lord
15: 8 sacrifice of wicked is an *a.*
15:26 thoughts of wicked are an *a.*
16: 5 proud in heart is an *a.* to Lord
20:23 divers weights are an *a.* to the Lord
26:25 seven *a.* in his heart
28: 9 even his prayer shall be *a.*
Is. 1:13 incense is an *a.* unto me
Jer. 7:10 delivered to do all these *a.*
Ezek. 16: 2 cause Jerusalem to know her *a.*
18:13 hath done all these *a.* shall die
Dan. 9:27 for the overspreading of *a.*
11:31 place the *a.* that maketh desolate
12:11 *a.* that maketh desolate set up
Mat. 24:15 see the *a.* of desolation
Luke 16:15 is *a.* in the sight of God
Rev. 17: 5 mother of harlots and *a.*

ABOUND (ABOUNDED, ABOUNDING)
Prov. 28:20 faithful shall *a.* with blessings
Mat. 24:12 because iniquity shall *a.*
Rom. 3: 7 truth of God hath more *a.*
5:20 that the offence might *a.*
6: 1 in sin that grace may *a.*
1 Cor. 15:58 always *a.* in the work
Eph. 1: 8 wherein he hath *a.* toward us
Phil. 1: 9 that your love may *a.* yet more
4:12 both to *a.* and to suffer need
4:17 fruit that may *a.* to your account
4:18 I have all and *a.*
Col. 2: 7 *a.* therein with thanksgiving
1 Thes. 3:12 the Lord make you *a.* in love
2 Pet. 1: 8 these things be in you and *a.*

ABOVE
Ex. 20: 4 that is in the heaven *a.*
John 3:31 cometh from *a.* is *a.* all
8:23 I am from *a.*; ye are of this world
19:11 power given thee from *a.*
Gal. 4:26 Jerusalem which is *a.* is free
Eph. 4: 6 one God who is *a.* all
Col. 3: 1 seek those things which are *a.*
3: 2 set your affection on things *a.*
Jas. 1:17 every perfect gift is from *a.*
3:15 wisdom from *a.* is pure

ABSENT
2 Cor. 5: 6 in body we are *a.* from the Lord
5: 8 willing rather to be *a.* from the body
5: 9 that whether present or *a.*
Col. 2: 5 though I be *a.* in the flesh

ABSTAIN
Acts 15:20 that they *a.* from pollutions of idols

1 Thes. 4: 3 ye should *a.* from fornication
5:22 *a.* from all appearance of evil
1 Tim. 4: 3 commanding to *a.* from meats
1 Pet. 2:11 *a.* from fleshly lusts

ABUNDANCE
Deut. 28:47 for the *a.* of all things
Eccl. 5:10 he that loveth *a.* with increase
5:12 *a.* of the rich not suffer him to
Mat. 12:34 out of the *a.* of the heart the mouth
13:12 and he shall have more *a.*
Mark 12:44 cast in of their *a.*
Luke 12:15 life consisteth not in *a.*
2 Cor. 8: 2 *a.* of their joy abounded
12: 7 through *a.* of revelations

ABUNDANT (ABUNDANTLY)
Ex. 34: 6 *a.* in goodness and truth
Job 12: 6 whose hand God bringeth *a.*
Ps. 36: 8 shall be *a.* satisfied
Sol. 5: 1 yea, drink *a.* O beloved
Is. 55: 7 he will *a.* pardon
John 10:10 might have life more *a.*
1 Cor. 15:10 laboured more *a.* than all
2 Cor. 4:15 for your sakes, that the *a.* grace
9:12 is *a.* also by many thanksgivings
11:23 in labours more *a.*
1 Tim. 1:14 grace of our Lord exceeding *a.*
Tit. 3: 6 shed on us *a.* through Jesus
1 Pet. 1: 3 his *a.* mercy hath begotten
2 Pet. 1:11 shall be ministered unto you *a.*

ABUSE (ABUSING)
1 Cor. 7:31 use this world as not *a.* it
9:18 that I *a.* not my power

ACCEPT (ACCEPTED, ACCEPTEST, ACCEPTETH, ACCEPTING)
Gen. 4: 7 shalt thou not be *a.*
19:21 *a.* thee concerning this thing
32:20 peradventure he will *a.* of me
Lev. 26:41 *a.* of the punishment of their
Deut. 33:11 *a.* the work of his hands
2 Sam. 24:23 Lord thy God *a.* thee
Job 13: 8 will ye *a.* his person
32:21 not *a.* any man's person
34:19 *a.* not the persons of princes
42: 8 servant Job, him will I *a.*
Ps. 119:108 *a.* freewill offerings
Prov. 18: 5 not good to *a.* the person
Eccl. 9: 7 God now *a.* thy works
Ezek. 43:27 I will *a.* you, saith the Lord
Hos. 8:13 but the Lord *a.* them not
Mal. 1:13 should I *a.* this of your
Luke 4:24 no prophet is *a.* in his own
20:21 neither *a.* thou the person
Acts 10:35 worketh righteousness is *a.*
24: 3 we *a.* it always
2 Cor. 5: 9 we may be *a.* of him
6: 2 behold, now is the *a.* time
Gal. 2: 6 God *a.* no man's person
Eph. 1: 6 made us *a.* in the beloved
Heb. 11:35 were tortured not *a.* deliverance

ACCEPTABLE (ACCEPTABLY)
Ps. 19:14 meditation of my heart, be *a.*
Eccl. 12:10 sought out to find *a.* words
Is. 49: 8 in an *a.* time I heard thee
58: 5 and an *a.* day to the Lord
61: 2 proclaim the *a.* year of the Lord
Dan. 4:27 let my counsel be *a.*
Rom. 12: 1 sacrifice holy *a.* to God
Eph. 5:10 proving what is *a.* to Lord
Phil. 4:18 a sacrifice *a.* wellpleasing
Heb. 12:28 serve God *a.* with reverence
1 Pet. 2: 5 *a.* to God by Jesus Christ

ACCEPTATION
1 Tim. 1:15 worthy of all *a.*

ACCESS
Rom. 5: 2 we have *a.* by faith
Eph. 2:18 we both have *a.* by one Spirit
3:12 boldness and *a.* with confidence

ACCOMPLISH (ACCOMPLISHED, ACCOMPLISHING)
Ps. 64: 6 they *a.* a diligent search
Prov. 13:19 desire *a.* is sweet
Is. 40: 2 her warfare is *a.* that her
55:11 it shall *a.* that which I please
Ezek. 6:12 thus will I *a.* my fury
Dan. 9: 2 he would *a.* seventy years
Luke 9:31 he should *a.* at Jerusalem
John 19:28 all things were now *a.*
Heb. 9: 6 *a.* the service of God
1 Pet. 5: 9 same afflictions are *a.*

ACCORD
Acts 1:14 continued with one *a.* in prayer
2: 1 with one *a.* in one place
2:46 continuing daily with one *a.*
4:24 voice to God with one *a.*
15:25 being assembled with one *a.*

ACCOUNT (ACCOUNTED)
Job 33:13 not *a.* of any of his matters
Ps. 22:30 it shall be *a.* to the Lord
144: 3 that thou makest *a.* of him
Eccl. 7:27 one by one to find out the *a.*
Is. 2:22 wherein is he to be *a.* of
Mat. 12:36 give *a.* thereof in the day of judgment
18:23 would take *a.* of his servants
Luke 16: 2 give an *a.* of thy stewardship
20:35 they which shall be *a.* worthy to obtain that world
21:36 you may be *a.* worthy to escape
22:24 which should be *a.* the greatest
Rom. 14:12 give *a.* of himself to God
Gal. 3: 6 *a.* to him for righteousness
Phil. 4:17 fruit that may abound to your *a.*
Heb. 13:17 as they that must give *a.*
1 Pet. 4: 5 shall give *a.* to him that

ACCURSED
Deut. 21:23 hanged is *a.* of God.
Josh. 6:18 keep from the *a.* thing
Is. 65:20 one hundred years old shall be *a.*
Rom. 9: 3 wish myself *a.* from Christ
1 Cor. 12: 3 the Spirit of God calleth Jesus *a.*
Gal. 1: 8 unto him, let him be *a.*

ACCUSATION
Ezra 4: 6 wrote they unto him an *a.*
Mat. 27:37 over his head his *a.*
Luke 6: 7 might find an *a.* against him
19: 8 from any man by false *a.*
John 18:29 What *a.* bring ye against this man
Acts 25:18 they brought none *a.* of such things
2 Pet. 2:11 bring not a railing *a.*

ACCUSE (ACCUSETH, ACCUSING)
Prov. 30:10 *a.* not a servant unto his master
Luke 3:14 neither *a.* any falsely
John 5:45 that I will *a.* you to the Father
Rom. 2:15 their thoughts the meanwhile *a.*
Tit. 1: 6 not *a.* of riot or unruly
1 Pet. 3:16 falsely *a.* your good conversation
Rev. 12:10 which *a.* them before our God

ACCUSERS
Acts 25:16 have the *a.* face to face
2 Tim. 3: 3 trucebreakers, false *a.*
Tit. 2: 3 becometh holiness not false *a.*

ACKNOWLEDGE (ACKNOWLEDGING)
Deut. 33: 9 neither did he *a.* his brethren
Ps. 32: 5 I *a.* my sin unto thee, and mine
51: 3 For I *a.* my transgression
Prov. 3: 6 in all thy ways *a.* him
Is. 33:13 ye that are near *a.* my might
63:16 though Israel *a.* us not
Jer. 3:13 only *a.* thine iniquity
14:20 we *a.* our wickedness
Hos. 5:15 till they *a.* their offence
1 Cor. 16:18 *a.* them that are such
2 Tim. 2:25 to the *a.* of the truth
Tit. 1: 1 and the *a.* of the truth

ACKNOWLEDGMENT
Col. 2: 2 to the *a.* of the mystery of God and of the Father

ACQUAINT (ACQUAINTED)
Job 22:21 *a.* now thyself with him
Ps. 139: 3 art *a.* with all my ways
Is. 53: 3 man of sorrows, and *a.* with grief

ACQUAINTANCE
Job 19:13 mine *a.* are verily estranged from me
Ps. 31:11 a fear to my *a.*
55:13 my guide, and mine *a.*
88: 8 put away mine *a.* far from me
88:18 mine *a.* into the darkness

ACQUIT
Job 10:14 wilt not *a.* me from mine iniquity
Nah. 1: 3 will not at all *a.* the wicked

ACT (ACTS)
Deut. 11: 3 his miracles, and his *a.*
11: 7 great *a.* of the Lord
Judg. 5:11 rehearse the righteous *a.*
1 Sam. 12: 7 reason of all righteous *a.*
Ps. 106: 2 who can utter the mighty *a.*
145: 4 declare thy mighty *a.*

Is. 28:21 to pass his *a.* his strange *a.*
John 8: 4 taken in adultery in the very *a.*
speak of thy mighty *a.*

ADD (ADDED, ADDETH)
Lev. 5:16 shall *a.* the fifth part thereto
6: 5 shall *a.* the fifth part more thereto
Deut. 4: 2 shall not *a.* unto the word
5:22 and he *a.* no more
29:19 *a.* drunkenness to thirst
1 Sam. 12:19 *a.* to all our sins this evil
Ps. 69:27 *a.* iniquity to their iniquity
Prov. 10:22 he *a.* no sorrow with it
30: 6 *a.* not unto his words
Is. 30: 1 that they may *a.* sin to sin
Jer. 36:32 were *a.* many like words
45: 3 Lord *a.* grief to my sorrow
Mat. 6:27 can *a.* one cubit unto his stature
Acts 2:41 there were *a.* unto them about
2:47 Lord *a.* to the church daily
5:14 believers were the more *a.*
11:24 much people was *a.* to the Lord
Phil. 1:16 *a.* affliction to bonds
2 Pet. 1: 5 *a.* to your faith virtue
Rev. 22:18 if any man *a.* unto these things

ADDER
Gen. 49:17 an *a.* in the path
Ps. 91:13 tread upon the lion and *a.*

ADJURE
1 Ki. 22:16 how many times shall I *a.* thee
2 Chr. 18:15 How many times shall I *a.* thee
Mat. 26:63 I *a.* thee by the living God
Mark 5: 7 I *a.* thee by God
Acts 19:13 We *a.* you by Jesus

ADMINISTRATION
1 Cor. 12: 5 there are differences of *a.*
2 Cor. 9:12 the *a.* of this service not only

ADMINISTERED
2 Cor. 8:19 this grace, which is *a.* to us
8:20 this abundance which is *a.* by us

ADMONISH (ADMONISHED, ADMONISHING)
Eccl. 4:13 foolish king will no more be *a.*
12:12 by these, my son be *a.*
Jer. 42:19 know that I have *a.* you
Rom. 15:14 able to *a.* one another
Col. 3:16 *a.* one another in psalms
1 Thes. 5:12 over you and *a.* you
2 Thes. 3:15 *a.* him as a brother
Heb. 8: 5 as Moses was *a.* of God

ADMONITION
1 Cor. 10:11 they were written for our *a.*
Eph. 6: 4 up in the nurture and *a.* of the Lord
Tit. 3:10 after first and second *a.* reject

ADOPTION
Rom. 8:15 ye have received the Spirit of *a.*
8:23 *a.*, to wit, the redemption of our body
Gal. 4: 5 we might receive the *a.* of sons
Eph. 1: 5 us unto the *a.* of children

ADORN (ADORNED, ADORNETH)
Is. 61:10 as a bride *a.* herself
Jer. 31: 4 again be *a.* with thy tabrets
Luke 21: 5 it was *a.* with goodly stones
1 Tim. 2: 9 women *a.* themselves in modest
Tit. 2:10 *a.* the doctrine of God our
1 Pet. 3: 5 holy women *a.* themselves
Rev. 21: 2 as a bride *a.* for her husband

ADULTERER (ADULTERERS)
Lev. 20:10 the *a.* and adulteress shall surely
Job 24:15 eye also of the *a.* waits for twilight
Is. 57: 3 seed of the *a.* and the whore
Jer. 23:10 For the land is full of *a.*
9: 2 for they be all *a.*
Hos. 7: 4 they are all *a.*
Mal. 3: 5 the sorcerers and against *a.*
Heb. 13: 4 whoremongers and *a.* God will judge
Jas. 4: 4 ye *a.* and adulteresses know ye

ADULTERESS (ADULTERESSES)
Prov. 6:26 *a.* hunt for the precious life
Jas. 4: 4 ye adulterers and *a.* know ye

ADULTERY (ADULTERIES)
Prov. 6:32 committeth *a.* with a woman lacks
Mat. 5:28 committed *a.* in his heart
15:19 out of the heart proceed *a.*
2 Pet. 2:14 having eyes full of *a.*

ADULTEROUS
Prov. 30:20 such is the way of an *a.* woman
Mat. 12:39 *a.* generation seeketh after a sign
16: 4 A wicked and *a.* generation seeketh
Mark 8:38 this *a.* and sinful generation

ADVANTAGE (ADVANTAGED)
Luke 9:25 what is a man *a.*
Rom. 3: 1 What *a.* then hath the Jew
2 Cor. 2:11 lest Satan get an *a.*

ADVERSARY (ADVERSARIES)
Ex. 23:22 I will be an *a.* to thy *a.*
1 Sam. 2:10 *a.* of the Lord shall be broken
1 Ki. 5: 4 is neither *a.* nor evil
Job 31:35 my *a.* had written a book
Lam. 1: 5 her *a.* are the chief, her
Mat. 5:25 agree with thine *a.*
Luke 21:15 all your *a.* shall not be able
1 Cor. 16: 9 and there are many *a.*
Phil. 1:28 in nothing terrified by your *a.*
1 Tim. 5:14 give no occasion to *a.*
Heb. 10:27 shall devour the *a.*
1 Pet. 5: 8 your *a.* the devil as a

ADVERSITY
1 Sam. 10:19 saved you out of all *a.*
2 Sam. 4: 9 redeemed my soul from all *a.*
2 Chr. 15: 6 God did vex with all *a.*
Ps. 10: 6 I shall never be in *a.*
31: 7 thou hast known my soul in *a.*
94:13 give rest from days of *a.*
Prov. 17:17 brother is born for *a.*
Eccl. 7:14 in the day of *a.* consider
Is. 30:20 give you the bread of *a.*

ADVOCATE
1 John 2: 1 we have an *a.* with the Father

AFAR
Gen. 22: 4 saw the place *a.* off
37:18 when they saw him *a.* off
Ps. 65: 5 of them that are *a.* off
138: 6 proud he knoweth *a.*
139: 2 understandest thoughts *a.* off
Jer. 23:23 Lord, and not a God *a.* off
Eph. 2:17 preached peace to you *a.*
Heb. 11:13 having seen promises *a.*
2 Pet. 1: 9 blind and cannot see *a.*

AFFECT (AFFECTED, AFFECTETH)
Lam. 3:51 mine eye *a.* my heart
Gal. 4:17 they zealously *a.* you
4:18 good to be zealously *a.*

AFFECTION (AFFECTIONED)
Rom. 12:10 be kindly *a.* one to another
Col. 3: 5 mortify therefore your members . . . inordinate *a.*

AFFECTIONS
Rom. 1:26 gave them up to vile *a.*
Gal. 5:24 have crucified flesh with the *a.*

AFFLICT (AFFLICTED)
Gen. 15:13 they shall *a.* them four hundred years
Ex. 1:11 taskmasters to *a.* them
22:22 You shall not *a.* any widow
Num. 30:13 every binding oath to *a.* the soul
2 Sam. 22:28 *a.* people thou wilt save
Ezra 8:21 that we might *a.* ourselves
Job 6:14 to him that is *a.* pity should be showed
34:28 heareth the cry of the *a.*
Ps. 22:24 nor abhorred the affliction of the *a.*
119: 67 before I was *a.* I went astray
119: 71 it is good that I have been *a.*
119: 75 thou in faithfulness hast *a.* me
119:107 I am *a.* very much; quicken
140: 12 wilt maintain the cause of the *a.*
Prov. 15:15 all days of the *a.* are evil
Is. 49:13 and will have mercy upon his *a.*
53: 4 smitten of God and *a.*
53: 7 he was oppressed and he was *a.*
58: 5 day for man to *a.* his soul
58:10 satisfy the *a.* soul
Lam. 3:33 doth not *a.* willingly
Mic. 4: 6 driven out, and her that I have *a.*

AFFLICTION (AFFLICTIONS)
Ex. 3: 7 seen the *a.* of my people
2 Ki. 14:26 For the Lord saw the *a.* of Israel
Job 5: 6 *a.* cometh not forth of dust
36: 8 and be holden in cords of *a.*
36:15 He delivereth the poor in his *a.*
36:21 this hast thou chosen rather than *a.*
Ps. 25:18 look upon my *a.* and pain
34:19 many are the *a.* of the righteous
107: 10 being bound in *a.* and iron
107: 39 brought low through oppression, *a.*
119: 92 should have perished in *a.*
132: 1 remember David and all his *a.*
Is. 48:10 chosen thee in the furnace of *a.*
63: 9 in all their *a.* he was afflicted
Hos. 5:15 in their *a.* they will seek
Amos 6: 6 not grieved for the *a.* of Joseph
Obad. 1:13 not have looked on their *a.*
Nah. 1: 9 *a.* shall not rise up the second time
Zech. 1:15 and they helped forward the *a.*
Acts 7:10 delivered him out of all his *a.*
20:23 bonds and *a.* abide me
2 Cor. 4:17 our light *a.* which is
Phil. 4:14 communicate with my *a.*
1 Thes. 1: 6 received word in much *a.*
3: 3 should be moved by these *a.*
2 Tim. 1: 8 partaker of the *a.* of the gospel
Heb. 10:32 endured a great fight of *a.*
11:25 choosing rather to suffer *a.*
Jas. 1:27 to visit the fatherless and widows in *a.*
1 Pet. 5: 9 the same *a.* accomplished

AFRAID
Lev. 26: 6 and none shall make you *a.*
Num. 12: 8 were ye not *a.* to speak against
Job 13:21 let not thy dread make me *a.*
Ps. 56: 3 What time I am *a.*
56:11 Not be *a.* what man can do
119:120 I am *a.* of thy judgments
Is. 12: 2 I will trust, and not be *a.*
Mat. 14:27 it is I; be not *a.*
Mark 5:36 Be not *a.*, only believe
Luke 12: 4 Be not *a.* of them that kill
Heb. 11:23 they were not *a.* of the king's commandment
1 Pet. 3: 6 ye do well, and are not *a.*
3:14 be not *a.* of their terror

AGE
Job 5:26 come to thy grave in a full *a.*
Ps. 39: 5 mine *a.* is as nothing before thee
John 9:21 he is of *a.* ask him
Heb. 5:14 meat to those of full *a.*

AGED
Tit. 2: 2 that the *a.* men be sober, grave

AGES
Eph. 2: 7 that in the *a.* to come he might
3: 5 which in other *a.* was not made known
3:21 Christ Jesus throughout all *a.*
Col. 1:26 mystery which hath been hid from *a.*

AGREE (AGREED)
Amos 3: 3 walk together, except they be *a.*?
Mat. 5:25 *a.* with thine adversary quickly
18:19 if two shall *a.* on earth
Acts 5: 9 that ye have *a.* together
1 John 5: 8 these three *a.* in one

AGREEMENT
Is. 28:15 and with hell are we at *a.*
2 Cor. 6:16 *a.* hath the temple of God with idols

ALIEN, (ALIENS)
Ex. 18: 3 been an *a.* in a strange land
Deut. 14:21 thou mayest sell it unto an *a.*
Ps. 69: 8 an *a.* unto my mother's children
Is. 61: 5 sons of the *a.* shall be
Lam. 5: 2 to strangers our houses to *a.*
Eph. 2:12 being *a.* from the commonwealth
Heb. 11:34 turned to fight the armies of the *a.*

ALIENATED
Eph. 4:18 being *a.* from the life of God
Col. 1:21 you, that were sometime *a.*

ALIVE
Num. 22:33 had slain thee, and saved her *a.*
1 Sam. 2: 6 The Lord killeth and maketh *a.*
15: 8 he took Agag *a.*
Luke 15:24 my son was dead and is *a.*
Rom. 6:11 *a.* unto God through Jesus
6:13 as those *a.* from the dead
7: 9 I was *a.* without the law once
1 Cor. 15:22 in Christ shall all be made *a.*
1 Thes. 4:15 we which are *a.* and remain
Rev. 1:18 I am *a.* for evermore
2: 8 which was dead and is *a.*

ALLOW (ALLOWED, ALLOWETH)
Luke 11:48 *a.* the deeds of your fathers
Acts 24:15 which they themselves also *a.*
Rom. 7:15 that which I do I *a.* not
14:22 in that thing which he *a.*
1 Thes. 2: 4 as we were *a.* of God

ALMIGHTY
Gen. 17: 1 I am the *A.* God; walk before
35:11 I am God *A.*: be fruitful and
Ex. 6: 3 by the name of God *A.*
Num. 24: 4 which saw the vision of the *A.*
Ruth 1:20 the *A.* hath dealt very bitterly
Job 21:15 what is the *A.*, that we should
22:25 *A.* shall be thy defence
27:10 delight himself in the *A.*
Ps. 91: 1 under the shadow of the *A.*
Ezek. 1:24 as the voice of the *A.*
2 Cor. 6:18 sons and daughters, saith the Lord *A.*
Rev. 1: 8 and which is to come, the *A.*
4: 8 Holy, holy, holy, Lord God *A.*
19:15 fierceness and wrath of *A.* God
21:22 for the Lord God *A.* and the Lamb

ALMOST
Ex. 17: 4 they be *a.* ready to stone me
Ps. 73: 2 as for me, my feet were *a.* gone
94:17 my soul had *a.* dwelt in silence
Prov. 5:14 I was *a.* in all evil in the midst
Acts 26:28 *a.* thou persuadest me to be a Christian

ALMS
Mat. 6: 1 do not your *a.* before men
Luke 11:41 rather give *a.* of such things
12:33 sell that ye have, give *a.*
Acts 3: 2 to ask *a.* of them that entered
10: 2 which gave much *a.* to people
10: 4 thine *a.* are come up for memorial
24:17 I came to bring *a.* to my nation

ALONE
Gen. 32:24 and Jacob was left *a.*
2:18 not good for man to be *a.*
Ex. 32:10 let me *a.* that my wrath
Num. 23: 9 lo, the people shall dwell *a.*
Deut. 32:12 So the Lord *a.* did lead him
Ps. 136: 4 to him *a.* who doeth great wonders
Eccl. 4:10 woe to him that is *a.*
Is. 5: 8 that they may be placed *a.*
Hos. 4:17 Ephraim is joined to idols, let him *a.*
Mat. 15:14 let them *a.*
John 8:16 for I am not *a.* but I and
17:20 neither pray I for these *a.*
Gal. 6: 4 rejoicing in himself *a.*

ALTAR (ALTARS)
Gen. 8:20 builded an *a.* unto the Lord
12: 7 there builded he an *a.*
13: 4 unto the place of the *a.*
26:25 builded an *a.* there
35: 1 make there an *a.* unto God
35: 3 I will make there an *a.*
Ex. 17:15 Moses built an *a.*
40:10 anoint the *a.* of the burnt offering
Deut. 7: 5 ye shall destroy their *a.*
12: 3 ye shall overthrow their *a.*
Josh. 22:10 built there an *a.* by Jordan
Judg. 6:25 throw down the *a.* of Baal
1 Ki. 13: 2 cried against the *a.* in the word
Ps. 26: 6 so will I compass thine *a.*
43: 4 then will I go to the *a.* of God
Mat. 5:23 if thou bring thy gift to the *a.*
5:24 leave there thy gift before the *a.*
Acts 17:23 found an *a.* with the inscription
1 Cor. 9:13 they that wait at the *a.* are partakers
10:18 of the sacrifices partakers of the *a.*?
Heb. 13:10 we have an *a.* whereof
Rev. 9:13 the golden *a.* which is before God

ALWAYS
Gen. 6: 3 my spirit shall not *a.* strive
Deut. 14:23 learn to fear the Lord *a.*
1 Chr. 16:15 mindful *a.* of the covenant
Job 27:10 will he *a.* call on God
32: 9 great men are not *a.* wise
Ps. 9:18 needy shall not *a.* be forgotten
16: 8 I set the Lord *a.* before me
Prov. 5:19 ravished *a.* with her love
28:14 happy is man that feareth *a.*
Is. 57:16 neither will I be *a.* wroth
Mat. 26:11 have the poor *a.* with you
28:20 I am with you *a.*, to the end
Luke 18: 1 men ought *a.* to pray
John 8:29 I do *a.* things that please

Acts 10: 2 Cornelius prayed to God *a.*
2 Cor. 6:10 yet *a.* rejoicing; as poor, yet
Eph. 6:18 praying *a.* with all prayer
Phil. 4: 4 rejoice in the Lord *a.*
Col. 4: 6 your speech be *a.* with grace

AMBASSADOR (AMBASSADORS)
Prov. 13:17 a faithful *a.* is health
Is. 33: 7 the *a.* of peace shall weep bitterly
2 Cor. 5:20 we are *a.* for Christ
Eph. 6:20 I am an *a.* in bonds

AMEN
2 Cor. 1:20 promises of God in him *a.*
Rev. 3:14 these things saith the *A.*
22:20 *A.* Even so, come, Lord Jesus

AMEND
Jer. 26:13 *a.* your ways and your doings
35:15 *a.* your doings, and go not

ANCHOR (ANCHORS)
Acts 27:30 they would have cast *a.* out
Heb. 6:19 as an *a.* of the soul

ANCIENT (ANCIENTS)
Job 12:12 with the *a.* is wisdom
Ps. 119:100 I understand more than the *a.*
Dan. 7: 9 the *a.* of days did sit

ANGEL
Gen. 24: 7 send his *a.* before thee
48:16 the *a.* which redeemed me
Ex. 23:23 my *a.* shall go before thee
Ps. 34: 7 *a.* of the Lord encampeth round
Is. 63: 9 *a.* of his presence saved
Dan. 3:28 sent his *a.* and delivered
6:22 sent his *a.* and shut the lions' mouths
Zech. 12: 8 as the *a.* of the Lord before them
John 5: 4 *a.* went down at a certain
Acts 5:19 *a.* of the Lord by night opened
6:15 his face as the face of an *a.*
12: 7 *a.* of the Lord came upon him
12:23 *a.* of the Lord smote him
23: 8 Sadducees say that there is no . . . *a.*

ANGELS (ANGELS')
Gen. 28:12 *a.* of God ascending and
Job 4:18 *a.* he charged with folly
Ps. 8: 5 a little lower than the *a.*
68:17 even thousands of *a.*
78:25 man did eat *a.* food
104: 4 maketh his *a.* spirits
Mat. 4:11 *a.* came and ministered
13:39 and the reapers are the *a.*
18:10 their *a.* do always behold the face of
22:30 are as the *a.* of God in heaven
24:31 send his *a.* with a great sound
24:36 no, not the *a.* of heaven
25:31 all the holy *a.* with him
Mark 12:25 are as the *a.* in heaven
Luke 15:10 joy in the presence of the *a.*
20:36 equal unto the *a.*
John 1:51 the *a.* of God ascending and
Acts 7:53 the law by the disposition of *a.*
1 Cor. 6: 3 ye not that we shall judge *a.*
Col. 2:18 beguile worshipping of *a.*
2 Thes. 1: 7 with his mighty *a.*
1 Tim. 3:16 seen of *a.*, preached unto
Heb. 2:16 took not the nature of *a.*
12:22 an innumerable company of *a.*
13: 2 entertained *a.* unawares
1 Pet. 1:12 *a.* desire to look into
2 Pet. 2:11 *a.* which are greater in power
Jude 1: 6 *a.* which kept not their first estate
Rev. 1:20 *a.* of the seven churches

ANGER
Ex. 32:22 let not the *a.* of my lord wax
Deut. 29:24 meaneth the heat of this great *a.*
Josh. 7:26 from fierceness of his *a.*
Neh. 9:17 slow to *a.*, and of great kindness
Job 9:13 if God will not withdraw his *a.*
Ps. 27: 9 put not thy servant away in *a.*
30: 5 his *a.* endureth but a moment
77: 9 hath he in *a.* shut up
78:38 turned he his *a.* away
78:50 he made a way to his *a.*
85: 4 cause *a.* towards us to cease
90: 7 we are consumed by thine *a.*
90:11 who knoweth power of thine *a.*
103: 8 slow to *a.*, and plenteous in mercy
103: 9 will he keep his *a.* for ever
Prov. 15: 1 grievous words stir up *a.*
Eccl. 7: 9 *a.* resteth in the bosom of fools
Hos. 11: 9 execute the fierceness of mine *a.*
14: 4 my *a.* is turned away from him
Joel 2:13 slow to *a.*, and of great kindness
Jonah 4: 2 slow to *a.*, and of great kindness
Mic. 7:18 retaineth not his *a.* for ever
Nah. 1: 3 slow to *a.*, and great in power
1: 6 who can abide his *a.*
Eph. 4:31 let all *a.* be put away
Col. 3: 8 put off all these; *a.*, wrath
Jas. 1:19 slow to *a.*, slow to wrath

ANGERED
Ps. 106: 32 they *a.* him also at the waters

ANGRY
Gen. 18:30 let not the Lord be *a.*
Deut. 1:37 Also the Lord was *a.* with me
9:20 Lord was very *a.* with Aaron
1 Ki. 11: 9 Lord was *a.* with Solomon
Ps. 2:12 kiss the Son lest he be *a.*
7:11 God is *a.* with the wicked every day
76: 7 in thy sight when once thou art *a.*
Prov. 14:17 He that is soon *a.* dealeth foolishly
22:24 no friendship with an *a.* man
29:22 an *a.* man stirreth up strife
Eccl. 7: 9 be not hasty to be *a.*
Is. 12: 1 though thou wast *a.* with
Jonah 4: 9 I do well to be *a.* even
Mat. 5:22 whosoever is *a.* with his brother
Eph. 4:26 be ye *a.* and sin not
Tit. 1: 7 bishop must not be soon *a.*

ANGUISH
Gen. 42:21 saw the *a.* of his soul
Ex. 6: 9 hearkened not for *a.* of spirit
Ps. 119:143 trouble and *a.* take hold
Jer. 6:24 *a.* hath taken hold of us
John 16:21 remembereth no more the *a.*, for joy
Rom. 2: 9 tribulation and *a.* upon every soul

ANOINT
Ex. 28:41 shalt *a.* them and consecrate them
Ps. 23: 5 thou *a.* my head with oil
Dan. 9:24 to *a.* the most holy
Amos 6: 6 *a.* with chief ointments
Mat. 6:17 when thou fastest, *a.* thy head
Jas. 5:14 *a.* him with oil
1 John 2:27 same *a.* teacheth you of all things
Rev. 3:18 *a.* thine eyes with eyesalve

ANOINTED
1 Sam. 2:10 exalt the horn of his *a.*
24: 6 seeing he is the *a.* of the Lord
1 Chr. 16:22 touch not my *a.*
2 Chr. 6:42 turn not away the face of thine *a.*
Ps. 2: 2 against the Lord and his *a.*
18:50 mercy to his *a.*, to David
20: 6 the Lord saveth his *a.*
28: 8 Lord is the saving strength of his *a.*
45: 7 *a.* thee with the oil of gladness
84: 9 look upon face of thine *a.*
89:38 hast been wroth with thine *a.*
132: 17 ordained a lamp for mine *a.*
Hab. 3:13 salvation with thine *a.*
Zech. 4:14 two *a.* ones, that stand by the Lord
Acts 4:27 Jesus, whom thou hast *a.*
10:38 how God *a.* Jesus of Nazareth
2 Cor. 1:21 who hath *a.* us is God

ANSWER
Gen. 41:16 God shall give Pharaoh an *a.* of peace
Deut. 20:11 if it make thee *a.* of peace
Job 9: 3 he cannot *a.* him one of a thousand
14:15 thou shalt call and I will *a.*
19:16 he gave me no *a.*; I entreated
40: 4 I am vile, what shall I *a.* thee
40: 5 once have I spoken, but I will not *a.*
Ps. 91:15 call upon me and I will *a.* him
102: 2 when I call, *a.* me speedily
143: 1 in thy faithfulness *a.* me
Prov. 15: 1 soft *a.* turneth away wrath
16: 1 *a.* of the tongue is from the Lord
26: 4 *a.* a fool according to his folly
Is. 14:32 what shall one then *a.* the messengers
58: 9 shalt thou call, and the Lord shall *a.*
65:24 before they call, I will *a.*
66: 4 when I called none did *a.*
Jer. 33: 3 Call unto me, and I will *a.* thee
Ezek. 14: 7 I the Lord will *a.* him by myself
Mic. 3: 7 there is no *a.* of God
Mat. 25:37 then shall the righteous *a.*
Luke 12:11 what thing ye shall *a.*
13:25 he shall *a.*, I know you not
21:14 meditate not what to *a.*
Rom. 11: 4 what saith the *a.* of God
2 Cor. 5:12 somewhat to *a.* them
Col. 4: 6 know how to *a.* every man
2 Tim. 4:16 at my first *a.* no man stood
1 Pet. 3:15 ready to give an *a.* to
3:21 the *a.* of a good conscience

ANSWERED (ANSWERETH, ANSWERING)
Ps. 18:41 to the Lord, but he *a.* not
81: 7 I *a.* thee in the secret place
99: 6 called on the Lord and he *a.*
Prov. 18:23 but the rich *a.* roughly
18:13 he that *a.* a matter before he
27:19 As in water face *a.* to face
Eccl. 10:19 money *a.* all things
Tit. 2: 9 in all things, not *a.* again

ANT (ANTS)
Prov. 6: 6 Go to the *a.*, thou sluggard
30:25 the *a.* are a people not strong

ANTICHRIST (ANTICHRISTS)
1 John 2:18 even now are there many *a.*
2:22 he is *a.*, that denieth the Father
4: 3 this is that spirit of *a.*
2 John 1: 7 this is a deceiver and an *a.*

APOSTLE (APOSTLES)
Mat. 10: 2 names of the twelve *a.*
Luke 11:49 I will send prophets and *a.*
Acts 1:26 numbered with the eleven *a.*
Rom. 11:13 I am an *a.* of Gentiles
1 Cor. 4: 9 God hath set forth us the *a.*
9: 1 am I not an *a.*? Am I not free
15: 9 I am the least of the *a.*
2 Cor. 11:13 such are false *a.*; deceitful workers
12:12 signs of an *a.* were wrought
Eph. 2:20 built upon the foundation of the *a.*
4:11 gave some *a.*, some prophets
Heb. 3: 1 consider the *a.* and high priest
Rev. 2: 2 say they are *a.* and are not
18:20 and ye holy *a.* and prophets
21:14 names of the twelve *a.* of the Lamb

APOSTLESHIP
Acts 1:25 part of this ministry and *a.*
Rom. 1: 5 we have received grace and *a.*
1 Cor. 9: 2 seal of mine *a.* are ye
Gal. 2: 8 to the *a.* of the circumcision

APPAREL
Is. 63: 1 that is glorious in his *a.*
Zeph. 1: 8 such as are clothed with strange *a.*
1 Tim. 2: 9 adorn themselves in modest *a.*

ADORNING
1 Pet. 3: 3 let it not be that outward *a.*

APPEAR (APPEARED)
Ex. 23:15 none shall *a.* before me empty
Deut. 16:16 all thy males *a.* before the Lord
1 Sam. 2:27 plainly *a.* unto the house of thy father
2 Chr. 1: 7 did God *a.* to Solomon
Ps. 42: 2 when shall I *a.* before God
Is. 1:12 when ye come to *a.* before me
66: 5 shall *a.* to your joy, but they
Mat. 6:16 they may *a.* to men to fast
23:27 which indeed *a.* beautiful outward
Rom. 7:13 sin that it might *a.* sin
2 Cor. 5:10 we must all *a.* before the judgment
Col. 3: 4 shall *a.*, then shall ye also *a.*
1 Tim. 4:15 that thy profiting may *a.* to all
Tit. 2:11 bringeth salvation hath *a.* to all men
Heb. 9:24 to *a.* in the presence of God
9:26 he *a.* to put away sin
9:28 *a.* the second time without sin to
11: 3 were not made of things which do *a.*
1 Pet. 5: 4 when the chief shepherd shall *a.*
1 John 3: 2 not yet *a.* what we shall be

APPEARANCE
1 Sam. 16: 7 man looketh on the outward *a.* but the Lord
John 7:24 judge not according to *a.*
1 Thes. 5:22 abstain from all *a.* of evil

APPEARING
2 Tim. 1:10 manifest by the *a.* of Jesus
4: 1 judge the quick and the dead at his *a.*
4: 8 all them that love his *a.*
Tit. 2:13 the glorious *a.* of the great God
1 Pet. 1: 7 unto praise at the *a.* of Jesus

APPLE
Deut. 32:10 kept him as the *a.* of his eye
Ps. 17: 8 keep me as the *a.* of the eye
Prov. 7: 2 my law as the *a.* of thine eye
Zech. 2: 8 toucheth the *a.* of his eye

APPOINT (APPOINTED)
Gen. 30:28 *a.* me thy wages, and I will give
Job 7: 1 an *a.* time to man upon earth
14:14 all the days of my *a.* time
30:23 to the house *a.* for all living
Ps. 79:11 preserve those *a.* to die
Is. 26: 1 salvation will God *a.* for walls
61: 3 *a.* to them that mourn in Zion
Jer. 5:24 the *a.* weeks of the harvest
Hab. 2: 3 vision is yet for an *a.* time
Mat. 24:51 *a.* him his portion with the hypocrites
Luke 22:29 I *a.* unto you a kingdom
1 Thes. 5: 9 God hath not *a.* us to wrath
Heb. 9:27 *a.* unto men once to die

APPREHEND (APPREHENDED)
Acts 12: 4 when he had *a.* him, he put him in
2 Cor. 11:32 a garrison, desirous to *a.* me
Phil. 3:12 which also I am *a.* of Christ Jesus
3:13 I count myself not to have *a.*

APPROACH (APPROACHING)
Lev. 18: 6 none of you shall *a.* to any
Ps. 65: 4 the man whom thou . . . causest to *a.*
Is. 58: 2 take delight in *a.* to God
Jer. 30:21 engaged his heart to *a.* unto me
1 Tim. 6:16 light which none can *a.* unto
Heb. 10:25 as ye see the day *a.*

APPROVE (APPROVED, APPROVEST, APPROVETH, APPROVING)
Ps. 49:13 posterity *a.* their sayings
Lam. 3:36 man in his cause, the Lord *a.* not
Acts 2:22 a man *a.* of God among you
Rom. 2:18 *a.* the things that are more excellent
14:18 acceptable to God, and *a.* of men
16:10 Salute Apelles *a.* in Christ
1 Cor. 11:19 *a.* may be made manifest among
2 Cor. 6: 4 in all things *a.* ourselves
Phil. 1:10 may *a.* things that are excellent

ARE
Gen. 41:27 came up after them *a.* seven years
1 Cor. 1:28 things which *a.* not
1:30 of him *a.* ye in Christ Jesus
8: 6 of whom *a.* all things
Heb. 2:10 and by whom *a.* all things
Rev. 1:19 write the things . . . which *a.*

ARIGHT
Ps. 50:23 ordereth his conversation *a.*
78: 8 that set not their heart *a.*
Jer. 8: 6 but they spake not *a.*

ARISE (ARISETH)
1 Chr. 22:16 *a.* therefore and be doing
Ps. 44:26 *A.* for our help, and redeem
68: 1 let God *a.*, let his enemies be
112: 4 Unto the upright there *a.* light
Amos 7: 2 by whom shall Jacob *a.*
Mic. 7: 8 when I fall, I shall *a.*
Mal. 4: 2 shall the Sun of righteousness *a.*
Mat. 13:21 persecution *a.* because

ARM (ARMS)
Gen. 49:24 *a.* of his hands were made strong
Ex. 15:16 by the greatness of thine *a.*
Deut. 33:27 underneath are the everlasting *a.*
2 Chr. 32: 8 with him is an *a.* of flesh
Job 40: 9 hast thou an *a.* like God
Ps. 44: 3 never did their own *a.* save them
89:13 Thou hast a mighty *a.*: strong
98: 1 his holy *a.*, hath gotten him victory
Is. 33: 2 be thou their *a.* every morning
40:10 his *a.* shall rule for him
40:11 gather the lambs with his *a.*
51: 5 on my *a.* shall they trust
51: 9 put on strength, O *a.* of the Lord
53: 1 is the *a.* of the Lord revealed
62: 8 Lord hath sworn . . . by the *a.*
63:12 led them by his glorious *a.*
Jer. 17: 5 maketh flesh his *a.*
Luke 1:51 he hath shown strength with his *a.*
Acts 13:17 with a high *a.* brought he them
1 Pet. 4: 1 *a.* yourselves likewise with with same

ARMED
Luke 11:21 when a strong man *a.* keepeth

ARMIES
1 Sam. 17:26 defy the *a.* of the living God
Job 25: 3 Is there any number of his *a.*
Ps. 44: 9 goest not forth with our *a.*
Sol. 6:13 it were the company of two *a.*
Rev. 19:14 *a.* which were in heaven followed

ARMOUR
Rom. 13:12 put on the *a.* of light
2 Cor. 6: 7 by the *a.* of righteousness
Eph. 6:11 put on the whole *a.* of God

ARROGANCY
1 Sam. 2: 3 let not *a.* come out of your mouth
Prov. 8:13 pride and *a.*, and the evil way
Is. 13:11 cause the *a.* of the proud to cease

ARROW (ARROWS)
Deut. 32:23 I will spend mine *a.* upon
2 Ki. 13:17 the *a.* of Lord's deliverance
Job 6: 4 the *a.* of the Almighty
Ps. 38: 2 thine *a.* stick fast in me
45: 5 thine *a.* are sharp in the heart
91: 5 nor for the *a.* that flieth by day
Lam. 3:12 set me as a mark for the *a.*

ASCEND (ASCENDED, ASCENDING)
Gen. 28:12 angels *a.* and descending
Ps. 24: 3 shall *a.* into the hill of the Lord
139: 8 if I *a.* up into heaven
Prov. 30: 4 who hath *a.* into heaven
John 1:51 *a.* and descending upon the Son of man
3:13 no man hath *a.* to heaven
20:17 I *a.* unto my Father and your
Eph. 4: 8 when he *a.* up on high
Rev. 8: 4 the smoke of the incense . . . *a.*
11:12 *a.* up to heaven in a cloud

ASCRIBE
Deut. 32: 3 *a.* ye greatness unto our God
Job 36: 3 *a.* righteousness to my Maker

ASHAMED
Gen. 2:25 man and his wife, and were not *a.*
Ezra 9: 6 I am *a.* and blush to lift
Ps. 25: 2 let me not be *a.*
Is. 49:23 not be *a.* that wait for me
Ezek. 16:61 shalt remember thy ways and be *a.*
Mark 8:38 be *a.* of me and my word
Rom. 1:16 I am not *a.* of the gospel
6:21 whereof ye are now *a.*
9:33 believeth on him shall not be *a.*
2 Tim. 2:15 workman that needeth not to be *a.*

ASHES
Gen. 18:27 which am but dust and *a.*
Job 2: 8 sat down among the *a.*
13:12 remembrances are like unto *a.*
42: 6 repent in dust and *a.*
Ps. 102: 9 I have eaten *a.* like bread
Is. 61: 3 give unto them beauty for *a.*
Ezek. 28:18 I will bring thee to *a.*
Mal. 4: 3 *a.* under the soles of your feet

ASK (ASKETH)
Jer. 50: 5 They shall *a.* the way to Zion
6:16 *a.* for the old paths, where is
Mat. 7: 7 *a.* and it shall be given
7: 8 For everyone that *a.* receiveth
7:11 give good things to them that *a.* him
20:22 ye know not what ye *a.*
Luke 12:48 of him they will *a.* more
John 14:14 whatsoever ye *a.* in my name
16:24 *a.* and ye shall receive
Eph. 3:20 above all that we *a.* or think
Jas. 1: 5 wisdom let him *a.* of God
1: 6 let him *a.* in faith, not wavering
4: 2 ye have not, because ye *a.* not
1 John 3:22 whatsoever we *a.* we receive
5:14 *a.* anything according to his will

ASLEEP
1 Cor. 15: 6 but some are fallen *a.*
15:18 are fallen *a.* in Christ
1 Thes. 4:13 concerning them which are *a.*

ASP (ASPS)
Deut. 32:33 dragons, and cruel venom of *a.*
Job 20:14 it is the gall of *a.* within him
20:16 suck the poison of *a.*
Is. 11: 8 play on the hole of the *a.*
Rom. 3:13 poison of *a.* is under their lips

ASS
Is. 1: 3 the *a.* his master's crib: but Israel
Zech. 9: 9 lowly, and riding upon an *a.*
Mat. 21: 5 meek, and sitting upon an *a.*

ASSEMBLY (ASSEMBLIES)
Ps. 22:16 the *a.* of the wicked have inclosed me
89: 7 to be feared in the *a.* of the saints
Is. 4: 5 and upon her *a.*, a cloud
Heb. 12:23 general *a.* of the firstborn

ASSEMBLING
Heb. 10:25 forsake not the *a.* of ourselves

ASSURANCE
Is. 32:17 effect of righteousness quietness and *a.*
Col. 2: 2 riches of the full *a.* of understanding
1 Thes. 1: 5 gospel came in much *a.*
Heb. 6:11 the full *a.* of hope unto the end

ASSURE
1 John 3:19 and shall *a.* our hearts before him

ASTRAY
Ps. 119:176 gone *a.* like a lost sheep
Is. 53: 6 all we like sheep have gone *a.*
Mat. 18:12 one of them be gone *a.*
1 Pet. 2:25 ye were as sheep going *a.*

ATHIRST
Judg. 15:18 he was sore *a.*, and called on
Rev. 21: 6 give to him that is *a.*

ATONEMENT
Ex. 30:16 take the *a.* money
Lev. 16:11 make an *a.* for himself
23:27 brought in to make *a.*
Num. 8:19 make an *a.* for the children

ATTAIN (ATTAINED)
Ps. 139: 6 high, I cannot *a.* unto it
Prov. 1: 5 man of understanding shall *a.*
Ezek. 46: 7 according as his hand shall *a.*
Phil. 3:11 *a.* unto the resurrection of dead
3:12 as though I had already *a.*

ATTEND (ATTENDED)
Ps. 55: 2 *a.* unto me, and hear me
86: 6 *a.* to the voice of my supplication
142: 6 *a.* unto my cry; for I am
Prov. 4: 1 *a.* to know understanding
4:20 my son, *a.* to my words
Acts 16:14 she *a.* to things spoken

ATTENT (ATTENTIVE)
2 Chr. 6:40 ears be *a.* unto the prayer
Neh. 1: 6 let thine ear now be *a.*
Ps. 130: 2 thine ears be *a.* to the voice
Luke 19:48 were very *a.* to hear him

AUTHOR
1 Cor. 14:33 God is not the *a.* of confusion
Heb. 5: 9 *a.* of eternal salvation
12: 2 Jesus the *a.* and finisher of our faith

AUTHORITY (AUTHORITIES)
Mat. 7:29 taught as one having *a.*
John 5:27 *a.* to execute judgment
1 Cor. 15:24 put down all rule and all *a.*
Tit. 2:15 exhort, and rebuke with all *a.*
1 Pet. 3:22 *a.* and powers being made . . .
Rev. 13: 2 dragon gave him . . . great *a.*

AVAILETH
Esth. 5:13 yet all this *a.* me nothing
Gal. 5: 6 neither circumcision *a.* any thing
Jas. 5ı6. prayer of a righteous man *a.* much

AVENGE (AVENGED, AVENGETH, AVENGING)
Lev. 19:18 thou shalt not *a.*, nor bear
26:25 *a.* the quarrel of my covenant
Deut. 32:43 he will *a.* the blood of his
Judg. 5: 2 praise the Lord for the *a.* of Israel
2 Sam. 22:48 It is God that *a.* me
Is. 1:24 I will *a.* me of my enemies

Jer. 5: 9 not my soul be *a.* on such a nation
9: 9 shall not my soul be *a.* on such a
Luke 18: 7 shall not God *a.* his elect
Rom. 12:19 *a.* not yourselves, but rather
Rev. 6:10 dost thou not *a.* our blood
18:20 God hath *a.* you on her

AVENGER
Num. 35:12 cities for refuge from the *a.*
Ps. 8: 2 still the enemy and the *a.*
44:16 by reason of the enemy and *a.*
1 Thes. 4: 6 the Lord is the *a.* of all

AVOID
Prov. 4:15 *a.* it, pass not by it
Rom. 16:17 which ye have learned and *a.* them

AWAKE (AWAKED, AWAKEST)
Job 8: 6 surely now he would *a.* for thee
Ps. 35:23 *a.* to my judgment, even unto my
73:20 when thou *a.* thou shalt despise
78:65 Lord *a.* as one out of sleep
139: 18 when I *a.* I am still with
1 Cor. 15:34 *a.* to righteousness; and sin not
Eph. 5:14 *a.* thou that sleepest; and arise

AWE
Ps. 4: 4 stand in *a.*, and sin not
33: 8 of the world stand in *a.* of him

AXE (AXES)
Deut. 19: 5 a stroke with the *a.* to cut down
2 Sam. 12:31 under *a.* of iron, and made them
1 Ki. 6: 7 neither hammer nor *a.* nor any tool
2 Ki. 6: 5 the *a.* head fell into the water
Ps. 74: 5 according as he had lifted up *a.*
Is. 10:15 the *a.* boast itself against him
Jer. 46:22 come against her with *a.*
51:20 thou art my battle *a.*
Mat. 3:10 *a.* laid to root of trees

B

BABE (BABES)
Ps. 8: 2 out of the mouth of *b.*
17:14 rest of their substance to their *b.*
Is. 3: 4 princes and *b.* shall rule over them
Luke 1:41 the *b.* leaped in her womb
1 Cor. 3: 1 as unto *b.* in Christ
1 Pet. 2: 2 as newborn *b.*, desire the sincere

BACK (BACKS)
Ex. 33:23 shalt see my *b.* parts
1 Sam. 10: 9 turned his *b.* to go from Samuel
1 Ki. 14: 9 cast me behind thy *b.*
Neh. 9:26 cast thy law behind their *b.*
Ps. 19:13 keep *b.* thy servant from
53: 6 when God bringeth *b.* captivity
129: 3 plowers plowed on my *b.*
Prov. 26: 3 rod for the fool's *b.*
Is. 38:17 cast my sins behind thy *b.*
50: 6 gave my *b.* to smiters
Jer. 2:27 they have turned their *b.* unto me
18:17 show them the *b.* and not the face
Acts 20:20 kept *b.* nothing profitable

BACKBITERS (BACKBITETH, BACKBITINGS)
Ps. 15: 3 He that *b.* not with his tongue
Rom. 1:30 *b.*, haters of God, despiteful
2 Cor. 12:20 strifes, *b.*, whisperings, swellings

BACKSLIDER
Prov. 14:14 *b.* in heart shall be filled

BACKSLIDING (BACKSLIDINGS)
Jer. 2:19 thy *b.* shall reprove thee
3:12 return thou *b.* Israel
5: 6 and their *b.* are increased
8: 5 slidden back by perpetual *b.*
Hos. 11: 7 my people are bent to *b.*
14: 4 I will heal their *b.*

BACKWARD
Gen. 9:23 went *b.* and covered the nakedness
Is. 1: 4 into anger they are gone away *b.*
59:14 judgment is turned away *b.*
John 18: 6 went *b.* and fell to ground

BAG (BAGS)
Deut. 25:13 have in thy *b.* divers measures
Prov. 16:11 weights of his *b.* are his work
Mic. 6:11 *b.* of deceitful weights
Hag. 1: 6 earneth wages to put it into a *b.*
Luke 12:33 provide yourselves *b.* which wax not old
John 13:29 because Judas had the *b.*

BALANCE
Job 31: 6 be weighed in an even *b.*
Ps. 62: 9 to be laid in the *b.*
Prov. 11: 1 false *b.* is abomination to
Is. 40:12 and the hills in a *b.*
40:15 as the small dust of the *b.*
46: 6 weigh silver in the *b.*
Dan. 5:27 art weighed in the *b.*
Hos. 12: 7 *b.* of deceit are in hand
Mic. 6:11 count pure with wicked *b.*

BALD
2 Ki. 2:23 go up, thou *b.* head
Jer. 16: 6 nor make themselves *b.* for them

BALDNESS
Lev. 21: 5 not make *b.* upon their head
Deut. 14: 1 nor make any *b.* between your eyes
Is. 3:24 instead of well set hair *b.*
22:12 to mourning, and to *b.*
Ezek. 7:18 *b.* upon all their heads

BALM
Gen. 37:25 bearing spicery and *b.* and myrhh
43:11 a little *b.* and a little honey
Jer. 8:22 is there no *b.* in Gilead
51: 8 take *b.* for her pain if so be
Ezek. 27:17 and honey, and oil, and *b.*

BANNER (BANNERS)
Ps. 20: 5 we will set up our *b.*
60: 4 *b.* to them that fear thee
Sol. 2: 4 his *b.* over me was love
6: 4 terrible as an army with *b.*
Is. 13: 2. Lift ye up a *b.* upon the high

BANQUET
Esth. 5: 4. come this day unto the *b.*
Dan. 5:10 came into the *b.* house: and the queen

BAPTISM (BAPTISMS)
Mat. 20:22 be baptized with the *b.* that I am
21:25 the *b.* of John, whence was it
Mark 1: 4 preach the *b.* of repentance
10:38 be baptized with the *b.* that I am
11:30 the *b.* of John, was it from heaven
Luke 7:29 being baptized with the *b.* of John
20: 4 The *b.* of John, was it from heaven
Acts 1:22 Beginning from the *b.* of John
10:37 after the *b.* which John preached
13:24 before his coming the *b.* of repentance
18:25 knowing only the *b.* of John
19: 3 they said unto John's *b.*
19: 4 verily baptized with the *b.* of repentance
Rom. 6: 4 buried with him by *b.*
Eph. 4: 5 One Lord, one faith, one *b.*
Heb. 6: 2 doctrine of *b.* and of laying
1 Pet. 3:21 even *b.* doth also now save us by

BAPTIZE
Mat. 3:11 I indeed *b.* you with water
Mark 1: 4 John did *b.* in wilderness
1: 8 he shall *b.* you with the Holy Ghost
Luke 3:16 he shall *b.* you with the Holy Ghost
12:50 I have a *b.* to be baptized with
John 1:26 I *b.* with water: but there
1:33 he that sent me to *b.* with

BAPTIZED (BAPTIZING)
Mat. 28:19 all nations *b.* them in the name
Mark 1: 5 were all *b.* of him in the river
1: 8 I indeed have *b.* you with water
1: 9 Jesus was *b.* of John
16:16 he that believeth and is *b.*
Luke 3: 7 came forth to be *b.* of him
3:21 when all the people were *b.*
7:29 publicans, justified God, being *b.*
John 4: 1 Jesus *b.* more disciples
Acts 1: 5 ye shall be *b.* with the Holy Ghost
2:38 repent and be *b.* every one
2:41 received his word were *b.*
8:13 Simon believed and was *b.*
8:48 Peter commanded them to be *b.*
16:15 she was *b.* and her household
16:33 was *b.* he and all his straight way
18: 8 Corinthians believed and were *b.*
22:16 arise and be *b.* wash away
Rom. 6: 3 Jesus Christ were *b.* into his death
1 Cor. 1:13 were ye *b.* in the name of Paul
10: 2 were all *b.* unto Moses in the cloud
12:13 are all *b.* into one body
15:29 do which are *b.* for the dead
Gal. 3:27 as have been *b.* into Christ

BARE
Ex. 19: 4 how I *b.* you on eagles' wings
Is. 53:12 he *b.* the sin of many
1 Pet. 2:24 *b.* our sins in his own body

BARN (BARNS)
Prov. 3:10 shall thy *b.* be filled with plenty
Mat. 6:26 neither do they reap, nor gather into *b.*
13:30 gather the wheat into my *b.*
Luke 12:24 which neither have storehouse nor *b.*
12:18 I will pull down my *b.*

BARREN
Gen. 11:30 But Sarai was *b.*; she had no child
25:21 for his wife because she was *b.*
29:31 opened her womb; but Rachel was *b.*
Ex. 23:26 cast their young nor be *b.*
Judg. 13: 2 his wife was *b.* and bare not
1 Sam. 2: 5 so that the *b.* hath borne seven
Ps. 113: 9 maketh the *b.* woman to keep house
Sol. 4: 2 none is *b.* among them
Is. 54: 1 sing, O *b.*, thou that didst not bear
Luke 1: 7 because that Elisabeth was *b.*
2 Pet. 1: 8 neither *b.* nor unfruitful

BASE (BASEST)
2 Sam. 6:22 and will be *b.* in mine own sight
Ezek. 29:15 It shall be the *b.* of kingdoms
Dan. 4:17 setteth up over it the *b.* of men
1 Cor. 1:28 *b.* things of this world
2 Cor. 10: 1 who in presence am *b.* among you

BASTARD (BASTARDS)
Deut. 23: 2 A *b.* shall not enter into the congregation
Zech. 9: 6 And a *b.* shall dwell in Ashdod
Heb. 12: 8 Then are ye *b.* and not sons

BATTLE
Gen. 14: 8 *b.* of four kings against five
Josh. 8:14 men of Ai against Israel to *b.*
Judg. 8:13 Gideon returned from *b.*
20:14 to *b.* against the children of Israel
2 Sam. 2:17 there was a very sore *b.* that day
10: 8 Ammon put the *b.* in array
2 Chr. 13: 3 Abijah set the *b.* in array
14:10 Asa set the *b.* in array
25: 8 be strong for the *b.*: God shall
Ps. 140: 7 covered my head in the day of *b.*
Eccl. 9:11 not the *b.* to the strong neither
Jer. 8: 6 as the horse rusheth into the *b.*
Rev. 16:14 *b.* of the great day of God

BEAM (BEAMS)
Sol. 1:17 *b.* of our house are cedar
Hab. 2:11 *b.* out of the timber shall answer it
Mat. 7: 3 the *b.* that is in thine own eye

BEAR
Gen. 4:13 punishment greater than I can *b.*
49:15 bowed his shoulder to *b.*
Num. 11:14 not able to *b.* all this people
Deut. 1: 9 not able to *b.* you myself alone
Ps. 75: 3 I *b.* up the pillars of it
91:12 *b.* thee up in their hands
Prov. 18:14 wounded spirit who can *b.*
30:21 for four which it cannot *b.*
Lam. 3:27 he *b.* the yoke in his youth
Ezek. 17: 8 that it might *b.* fruit
Hos. 9:16 they shall *b.* no fruit
Amos 7:10 land not able to *b.* words
Mic. 7: 9 I will *b.* the indignation of Lord
Luke 13: 9 and if it *b.* fruit, well
14:27 whosoever doth not *b.* his cross
John 15: 8 that ye *b.* much fruit
16:12 ye cannot *b.* them now
Rom. 15: 1 strong *b.* the infirmities of the weak
1 Cor. 3: 2 hitherto ye were not able to *b.*
10:13 that ye may be able to *b.* it
Gal. 6: 2 *b.* ye one another's burdens
6: 5 every man *b.* his own burden
6:17 I *b.* in my body the marks

Heb. 9:28 offered to *b.* the sins of many

BEAREST (BEARETH, BEARING)

Ps. 106: 4 favour that thou *b.* unto thy people
126: 6 *b.* precious seed, shall doubtless
Joel 2:22 for the tree *b.* her fruit
Mat. 13:23 which also *b.* fruit, and bringeth
John 15: 2 every branch that *b.* fruit
Rom. 2:15 conscience also *b.* witness
11:18 Thou *b.* not the root but the root
13: 4 *b.* the not sword in vain
1 Cor. 13: 7 *b.* all things, believeth all things
Heb. 13:13 without the camp, *b.* his reproach

BEARD (BEARDS)

2 Sam. 10: 4 shaved off one half of their *b.*
2 Sam 19:24 nor trimmed his *b.*, nor washed his
20: 9 Joab took Amasa by the *b.*
Ezra 9: 3. off the hair of my head and of my *b.*
Ps. 133: 2 that ran down upon the *b.*
Is. 15: 2 be baldness and every *b.* cut off
Jer. 41: 5 having their *b.* shaven
48:37 shall be bald and every *b.* clipped

BEAR (BEARS)

2 Ki. 2:24 there came forth two she *b.*
Prov. 1712. Let a *b.* be robbed of her whelps
Is. 59:11 We roar all like *b.*, and mourn
Dan. 7: 5 beast a second, like to a *b.*
Hos. 13: 8 *b.* that is bereaved of her whelps
Amos 5:19 from a lion and a *b.* met him
Rev. 13: 2 were as the feet of a *b.*

BEAST (BEASTS)

Gen. 1:24 and *b.* of the earth after his kind
Ps. 49:12 like the *b.* that perish
73:22 I was as a *b.* before thee
Prov. 9: 2 she hath killed her *b.*; she hath
Dan. 7: 3 four great *b.* came up from the sea
7:11 I beheld even till the *b.* was slain
1 Cor. 15:32 I fought with the *b.* at Ephesus
Rev. 4: 6 were four *b.* full of eyes before and
11: 7 the *b.* that ascendeth out
13: 1 saw a *b.* rise up out of the sea
14: 3 and before the four *b.*
16:13 out of the mouth of the *b.* Rev.
17: 8 the *b.* that thou sawest was
19: 4 four *b.* fell down and worshipped God
20:10 where the *b.* and the false prophet are

BEAT (BEATEN, BEATETH)

Prov. 23:14 Thou shalt *b.* him with the rod
Is. 3:15 that ye *b.* my people to pieces
Luke 12:47 shall be *b.* with many stripes
1 Cor. 9:26 not as one who *b.* the air

BEAUTY

Ex. 28: 2 thy brother for glory and for *b.*
2 Chr. 20:21 praise the *b.* of holiness
Ps. 29: 2 the Lord in the *b.* of holiness
27: 4 to behold the *b.* of the Lord
39:11 makest his *b.* to consume
96: 9 the Lord in the *b.* of holiness
Prov. 20:29 *b.* of old men is the gray head
31:30 favour is deceitful and *b.* is vain
Is. 3:24 sackcloth; and burning instead of *b.*
33:17 eyes shall see the king in his *b.*
61: 3 to give unto them *b.* for ashes
Zech. 11: 7 two staves: the one I called *B.*

BEAUTIFY

Ps. 149: 4 he will *b.* the meek with salvation
Is. 60:13 to *b.* the place of my sanctuary

BEAUTIFUL

Eccl. 3:11 every thing *b.* in his time
Sol. 6: 4 Thou art *b.*, O my love
Is. 52: 1 put on thy *b.* garments, O Jerusalem
64:11 Our holy and our *b.* house
Jer. 13:20 that was given thee, thy *b.* flock
Ezek. 16:13 thou was exceeding *b.*
Mat. 23:27 which indeed appear *b.* outside
Acts 3: 2 temple which is called *b.*
Rom. 10:15 How *b.* are the feet of them

BED (BEDS)

2 Ki. 4:10 let us set for him there a *b.*
Ps. 41: 3 make his *b.* in sickness
Sol. 3: 1 on my *b.* I sought him
Is. 28:20 *b.* is shorter than that a man
Amos 6: 4 lie on *b.* of ivory
Heb. 13: 4 and the *b.* undefiled but whoremongers
Rev. 2:22 I will cast her into a *b.*

BEFORE

Gen. 31: 2 behold, it was not toward him as *b.*
43:15 to Egypt and stood *b.* Joseph
Josh. 8:10 of Israel *b.* the people to Ai
2 Sam. 6:21 unto Michal, it was *b.* the Lord
1 Ki. 17: 1 God of Israel liveth *b.* whom I stand
2 Ki. 3:14 Lord of hosts liveth, *b.* whom I stand
Luke 22:47 one of the twelve went *b.* them
John 1:15 cometh after me is preferred *b.* me
Phil. 3:13 those things which are *b.*
Col. 1:17 he is *b.* all things, and by him

BEG (BEGGED, BEGGING)

Ps. 37:25 forsaken, nor his seed *b.* bread
109: 10 children be continually vagabonds and *b.*
Prov. 20: 4 therefore shall he *b.* in harvest
Luke 16: 3 I cannot dig; to *b.* I am ashamed
John 9: 8 Is not this he that sat and *b.*

BEGGAR

1 Sam. 2: 8 and lifteth up the *b.* from the
Luke 16:20 a certain *b.* named Lazarus

BEGIN

Ezek. 9: 6 and *b.* at my sanctuary

BEGINNING

Gen. 49: 3 my might and the *b.* of strength
Ex. 12: 2 the *b.* of months
Deut. 21:17 for he is the *b.* of his strength
Ps. 111: 10 fear of the Lord is the *b.* of wisdom
Eccl. 7: 8 better the end than the *b.*
Mat. 24: 8 all these are the *b.* of sorrows
Col. 1:18 who is the *b.*, the firstborn
2 Pet. 2:20 end is worse than the *b.*
Rev. 1: 8 Alpha and the Omega, the *b.* and the
3:14 saith the *b.* of the creation of God

BEGOTTEN

Job 38:28 who hath *b.* the drops of dew
Ps. 2: 7 this day have I *b.* thee
John 1:14 as of the only *b.* of the Father
3:16 that he gave his only *b.* Son
1 Pet. 1: 3 *b.* us again unto a lively hope
1 John 4: 9 sent his only *b.* Son into the world
5: 1 loveth him that is *b.* of him
Rev. 1: 5 Christ the first *b.* of the dead

BEGUILE (BEGUILED, BEGUILING)

Gen. 3:13 The serpent *b.* me, and I did eat
2 Cor. 11: 3 as the serpent *b.* Eve
Col. 2: 4 lest any man should *b.* you
2 Pet. 2:14 cannot cease from sin: *b.* unstable souls

BEHELD

Num. 23:21 He hath not *b.* iniquity in Jacob
Luke 10:18 I *b.* Satan as lightning fall
John 1:14 we *b.* his glory, the glory as of
Rev. 11:12 in a cloud and their enemies *b.* them

BEHIND

Ex. 10:26 shall not an hoof left *b.*
Neh. 9:26 cast thy law *b.* their backs
Ps. 139: 5 thou hast beset me *b.* and before
Is. 38:17 cast my sins *b.* thy back
Phil. 3:13 forgetting those things which are *b.*
Col. 1:24 fill up that which is *b.* of the afflictions

BEHOLD

Deut. 3:27 *b.* it with thine eyes: for thou shalt
Job 19:27 mine eyes shall *b.* and not another
40: 4 *b.* I am vile; what shall I
Ps. 11: 4 his eyes *b.* his eyelids try
11: 7 his countenance doth *b.* the upright
17:15 I will *b.* thy face in righteousness
27: 4 desired to *b.* the beauty of Lord
37:37 the perfect man and *b.* the upright
113: 6 he who humbleth himself to *b.*
133: 1 *b.* how good and how pleasant it is
Eccl. 11: 7 it is pleasant to *b.* the sun
Is. 24: 1 *b.* the Lord maketh the earth empty
32: 1 *b.* a king shall reign in righteousness
37: 7 *b.* I will send a blast upon him
40:10 *b.* the Lord will come with strong hand
42: 1 *b.* my servant, whom I uphold; mine
48:10 *b.* I have refined thee but not with
49: 1 *b.* Lord's hand is not shortened
Hab. 1:13 of purer eyes than to *b.*
Mat. 18:10 their angels do always *b.* the face of
John 17:24 they may *b.* my glory
19: 5 Pilate saith unto them, *b.* the man
19:26 unto his mother, Woman *b.* thy son
1 Pet. 3: 2 while they *b.* your chaste conversation
Rev. 1: 7 *b.* he cometh with clouds
1:18 *b.* I am alive for evermore
3: 8 *b.* I set before thee an open door
3:11 *b.* I come quickly hold that fast
3:20 *b.* I stand at the door, and knock
4: 2 *b.* a throne was set in heaven
9:12 *b.* there come two woes more
11:14 *b.* a third woe cometh quickly
21: 5 *b.* I make all things new

BEHOLDETH (BEHOLDING)

Ps. 33:13 from heaven; he *b.* all the sons of men
119: 37 turn away mine eyes from *b.* vanity
Prov. 15: 3 *b.* the evil and the good
2 Cor. 3:18 open face *b.* as in a glass
Col. 2: 5 joying and *b.* your order
Jas. 1:23 like unto a man *b.* his natural face
1:24 he *b.* himself and goeth his way

BEING

Ps. 104: 33 to my God while I have my *b.*
146: 2 unto my God while I have any *b.*
Acts 17:28 and move, and have our *b.*

BELIAL

Deut. 13:13 the children of *B.* are gone out
Judg. 19:22 men of the city, certain sons of *B.*
20:13 children of *B.* which are in Gibeah
1 Sam. 2:12 sons of Eli were sons of *B.*
10:27 but the children of *B.* said
25:17 for he is such a son of *B.*
2 Sam. 16: 7 bloody man, and thou man of *B.*
23: 6 the sons of *B.* shall be all
1 Ki. 21:10 set two men, sons of *B.*, before him
2 Chr. 13: 7 vain men, the children of *B.*
2 Cor. 6:15 what concord hath Christ with *B.*

BELIEVE

Ex. 4: 1 behold, they will not *b.* me
Num. 14:11 how long will it be ere they *b.*
Deut. 1:32 ye did not *b.* the Lord
2 Chr. 20:20 *b.* in the Lord your God
Is. 7: 9 if ye will not *b.*, surely ye shall
Mat. 9:28 *b.* ye that I am able to do this
Mark 1:15 repent and *b.* the gospel
9:24 Lord, I *b.* help thou mine unbelief
11:24 *b.* that ye receive them
Luke 8:13 which for a while *b.* and in time
24:25 slow of heart to *b.* all
John 4:48 signs and wonders, ye will not *b.*
6:69 we *b.* and are sure thou art that Christ
7:39 that *b.* on him should receive
8:24 if ye *b.* not I am he, ye die
10:26 ye *b.* not, because ye are not
11:27 I *b.* that thou art the Christ
11:40 if thou wouldst *b.* thou shouldst see
11:42 they may *b.* that thou hast sent me
12:36 *b.* in the light while ye have
12:39 they could not *b.* because that Esaias
14: 1 ye *b.* in God, *b.* also in me
17:20 pray for them who shall *b.*
20:25 hand into his side, I will not *b.*
20:31 written that ye might *b.*
Acts 8:37 I *b.* Jesus Christ is the Son
13:39 all that *b.* are justified
16:31 *b.* on the Lord Jesus Christ
Rom. 3: 3 for what if some did not *b.*

Rom. 3:22 Jesus Christ unto all them that *b.*
10: 9 shalt *b.* in thine heart
10:14 how shall they *b.* on him
2 Cor. 4: 4 blinded the mind of them that *b.* not
4:13 we *b.* and therefore speak
Phil. 1:29 not only to *b.* but suffer
2 Thes. 2:11 they should *b.* a lie
2:13 worketh also in you that *b.*
1 Tim. 4:10 especially those that *b.*
2 Tim. 2:13 we *b.* not, yet he abideth faithful
Heb. 10:39 *b.* to the saving of the soul
11: 6 cometh to God must *b.* that he is
Jas. 2:19 devils also *b.* and tremble
1 John 3:23 *b.* on the name of his Son Jesus Christ
4: 1 beloved, *b.* not every spirit

BELIEVED
Gen. 15: 6 *b.* in Lord, and he counted
Num. 20:12 because ye *b.* me not to sanctify
Ps. 27:13 I had fainted unless I had *b.*
78:32 and *b.* not for his wondrous works
106: 24 they *b.* not his word
116: 10 I *b.* therefore have I spoken
119: 66 for I *b.* thy commandments
Is. 53: 1 who hath *b.* our report
Jonah 3: 5 people of Nineveh *b.* God
Mat. 8:13 as thou hast *b.* so be it
21:32 publicans and harlots *b.* him
John 4:53 himself *b.* and his house
7:48 have any of the Pharisees *b.* on
17: 8 have *b.* that thou didst send me
Acts 4:32 that *b.* were of one heart
8:13 Simon *b.* and was baptized
11:21 great number *b.* and turned
13:48 were ordained to eternal life *b.*
Rom. 4:18 against hope *b.* in hope
10:14 in whom they have not *b.*
13:11 salvation nearer than when we *b.*
Eph. 1:13 after that ye *b.* ye were sealed
2 Thes. 2:12 who *b.* not the truth
1 Tim. 3:16 *b.* on in the world, recieved up
2 Tim. 1:12 for I know whom I have *b.*
Heb. 3:18 but to them that *b.* not

BELIEVERS
Acts 5:14 and *b.* were the more added
1 Tim. 4:12 be thou an example of the *b.*

BELIEVEST (BELIEVING)
Luke 1:20 because thou *b.* not my words
John 1:50 I saw thee under the fig tree, *b.* thou
11:26 shall never die. *b.* thou this
14:10 *b.* thou not that I am in the Father
20:27 be not faithless, but *b.*
20:31 that *b.* ye might have life
Acts 8:37 if thou *b.* with all thine heart
16:34 *b.* in God with all his house
26:27 I know that thou *b.*
Rom. 15:13 all joy and peace in *b.*
1 Tim. 6: 2 And they that have *b.* masters
Jas. 2:19 Thou *b.* that there is one God
1 Pet. 1: 8 yet *b.* ye rejoice with joy

BELIEVETH
Prov. 14:15 the simple *b.* every word
Is. 28:16 he that *b.* shall not make haste
Mark 9:23 things possible to him that *b.*
16:16 he that *b.* shall be saved
Luke 24:41 while they yet *b.* not for joy
John 3:15 *b.* in him shall not perish
3:18 that *b.* not is condemned already
3:36 *b.* on the Son hath everlasting life
5:24 *b.* on him that sent me
6:35 *b.* on me shall never thirst
6:40 and *b.* on him, may have everlasting life
7:38 that *b.* on me out of his belly shall flow
11:25 *b.* in me though he were dead
11:26 he that *b.* in me shall never die
12:44 *b.* in me, *b.* not on me, but
12:46 *b.* on me should not abide in darkness
14:12 *b.* on me the works that I do
Rom. 1:16 unto salvation to every one that *b.*
3:26 justifier of him that *b.* in Jesus
4: 5 worketh not, but *b.* on him
9:33 *b.* on him shall not be ashamed
10: 4 for righteousness to every one that *b.*
14: 2 one *b.* that he may eat all things
1 Cor. 7:12 brother hath a wife that *b.* not
13: 7 *b.* all things, hopeth all things
14:24 come in one that *b.* not, or one
2 Cor. 6:15 he that *b.* with an infidel
1 Tim. 5:16 that *b.* have widows, let them relieve
1 Pet. 2: 6 *b.* on him shall not be confounded
1 John 5: 1 whosoever *b.* that Jesus is the Christ
5: 5 overcometh the world, but he that *b.*

BELLY (BELLIES)
Gen. 3:14 upon thy *b.* shalt thou go
Num. 5:21 thy thigh to rot, and thy *b.* to swell
25: 8 thrust them through the *b.*
Job 3:11 when I came out of the *b.*
15: 2 fill his *b.* with the east wind
15:35 their *b.* prepareth deceit
20:15 God cast them out of his *b.*
Ps. 17:14 whose *b.* thou fillest with
22:10 art my God from my mother's *b.*
44:25 our *b.* cleaveth to the earth
Is. 46: 3 borne by me from the *b.*
Jonah 1:17 was in the *b.* of fish
2: 1 prayed to God out of the fish's *b.*
2: 2 out of the *b.* of hell cried I
Hab. 3:16 when I heard my *b.* trembled
Luke 15:16 fill his *b.* with husks
John 7:38 out of his *b.* shall flow
1 Cor. 6:13 meats for the *b.* and the *b.* for
Phil. 3:19 whose god is their *b.*, and whose glory
Tit. 1:12 Cretians are always liars . . . slow *b.*
Rev. 10: 9 it shall make thy *b.* bitter

BELONG (BELONGETH)
Gen. 40: 8 interpretations *b.* to God
Deut. 29:29 secret things *b.* to the Lord
Ezra 10: 4 for this matter *b.* unto thee
Ps. 3: 8 salvation *b.* to the Lord
47: 9 shields of the earth *b.* to God
62:11 heard this; that power *b.* unto God
68:20 to God *b.* the issues from death
Dan. 9: 8 to us *b.* confusion of face
9: 9 to the Lord *b.* mercies and forgivenesses
Mark 9:41 because ye *b.* to Christ
Luke 19:42 things that *b.* to thy peace
1 Cor. 7:32 for the things that *b.* to the Lord
Heb. 5:14 strong meat *b.* to them

BELOVED
Deut. 21:15 two wives, one *b.* and another hated
Neh. 13:26 who was *b.* of his God
Ps. 60: 5 thy *b.* may be delivered
127: 2 Lord giveth his *b.* sleep
Sol. 1:14 my *b.* is unto me as a cluster
4:16 let my *b.* come into his garden
5: 2 it is the voice of my *b.*
5: 9 thy *b.* more than another *b.*
6: 2 my *b.* is gone down into his garden
Is. 5: 1 of my *b.* touching his vineyard
Dan. 10:11 O Daniel, a man, greatly *b.*
Mat. 3:17 this is my *b.* Son, in whom
17: 5 this is my *b.* Son, in whom
Rom. 9:25 and her *b.* which was not *b.*
11:28 they are *b.* for the fathers' sake
16: 8 Amplias my *b.* in the Lord
Eph. 1: 6 made us accepted in the *b.*
Col. 3:12 as the elect of God holy and *b.*
4:14 Luke the *b.* physician
2 Pet. 3:15 even as our *b.* brother Paul
Rev. 20: 9 and the *b.* city: and fire came

BEND (BENDETH, BENDING, BENT)
Ps. 11: 2 the wicked *b.* their bow
37:14 and have *b.* their bow, to cast
58: 7 when he *b.* his bow to shoot
Is. 5:28 and all their bows *b.*
60:14 afflicted thee come *b.*
Jer. 9: 3 *b.* their tongues like a bow
Lam. 3:12 he hath *b.* his bow, and set
Zech. 9:13 I have *b.* Judah for me

BENEFACTORS
Luke 22:25 authority upon them are called *b.*

BENEFITS
Ps. 68:19 who daily loadeth us with *b.*
103: 2 forget not all his *b.*
116: 12 render to Lord for all his *b.*

BEREAVED
Gen. 43:14 If I be *b.* of my children
Eccl. 4: 8 do I labor and *b.* my soul
Jer. 15: 7 I will *b.* them of children
Jer. 18:21 let their wives be *b.* of their children
Ezek. 5:17 evil beasts, and they shall *b.* thee
36:12 henceforth *b.* them of men
Hos. 13: 8 a bear that is *b.* of her whelps

BEREAVETH
Lam. 1:20 abroad the sword *b.*, at home

BESEECH (BESOUGHT)
Deut. 3:23 I *b.* the Lord at that time
2 Sam. 12:16 David therefore *b.* God for the child
1 Ki. 13: 6 the man of God *b.* the Lord
2 Ki. 13: 4 Jehoahaz *b.* the Lord
2 Chr. 33:12 he *b.* the Lord his God
Ezra 8:23 we fasted and *b.* our God for this
Mal. 1: 9 *b.* God that he will be gracious
2 Cor. 5:20 as though God did *b.* you by us
12: 8 I *b.* the Lord thrice

BESET
Ps. 139: 5 Thou hast *b.* me behind and before
Hos. 7: 2 own doings have *b.* them about
Heb. 12: 1 sin which doth so easily *b.* us

BESIDE
Ps. 23: 2 leadeth me *b.* the still waters
Is. 32:20 ye that sow *b.* all waters
Sol. 1: 8 feed thy kids *b.* the shepherds' tents
Is. 56: 8 *b.* those that are gathered

BESOM
Is. 14:23 sweep it with the *b.* of destruction

BEST
Ps. 39: 5 man at his *b.* state is altogether vanity
Luke 15:22 bring forth the *b.* robe
1 Cor. 12:31 covet earnestly the *b.* gifts

BESTOW (BESTOWED)
Ex. 32:29 that he may *b.* upon you a blessing
Luke 12:17 room to *b.* my fruits
John 4:38 whereon ye *b.* no labour
1 Cor. 12:23 *b.* more abundant honour
13: 3 *b.* all my goods to feed the poor
15:10 his grace which was *b.* on me
2 Cor. 1:11 gift *b.* upon us by the means
8: 1 grace of God *b.* on the churches
Gal. 4:11 have *b.* upon you labour in vain
1 John 3: 1 love the Father hath *b.* on us

BETRAY (BETRAYETH)
Mat. 24:10 be offended, and shall *b.* one another
26:21 one of you shall *b.* me
Mark 13:12 brother shall *b.* the brother to death
14:18 which eateth with me shall *b.* me
Luke 22:21 the hand of him that *b.* me is with me
John 13:21 one of you shall *b.* me

BETROTH
Deut. 28:30 Thou shalt *b.* a wife
Hos. 2:19 I will *b.* thee unto me for ever
2:20 even *b.* thee unto me in faithfulness

BETTER
Judg. 8: 2 grapes of Ephraim *b.* than the vintage
1 Sam. 1: 8 am I not *b.* to thee than ten sons
Prov. 15:16 *b.* is little with fear of the Lord
15:17 *b.* is a dinner of herbs where love
16: 8 *b.* is a little with righteousness
16:16 much *b.* to get wisdom than gold
17: 1 *b.* is a dry morsel, and quietness
27:10 *b.* is a neighbour near than
Eccl. 4: 9 two are *b.* than one
4:13 *b.* is a poor and wise child than
7: 1 *b.* is a good name than precious
7: 2 *b.* to go to the house of mourning
7: 3 *b.* is sorrow than laughter
7: 5 *b.* to hear the rebuke of the wise than
7: 8 the patient in spirit is *b.* than
9:16 wisdom is *b.* than strength
9:18 wisdom is *b.* than weapons of
Sol. 1: 2 for thy love is *b.* than wine
Rom. 3: 9 are we *b.* than they? No, in no
1 Cor. 9:15 for it were *b.* for me to die
11:17 come not for the *b.* but worse
Phil. 1:23 with Christ; which is far *b.*
2: 3 esteem others *b.* than themselves
Heb. 1: 4 made so much *b.* than the angels

Heb. 6: 9 we are persuaded *b.* things of you
7:19 bringing in of a *b.* hope did
7:22 Jesus made a surety of a *b.* testament
8: 6 mediator of a *b.* covenant
10:34 a *b.* and an enduring substance
11:16 now they desire a *b.* country
11:35 might obtain a *b.* resurrection
11:40 God having provided some *b.* thing
12:24 blood speaketh *b.* than Abel
2 Pet. 2:21 *b.* for them not to have known

BETWEEN
Gen. 3:15 put enmity *b.* thee and the woman
1 Ki. 3: 9 discern *b.* good and bad
18:21 how long halt ye *b.* two opinions
1 Tim. 2: 5 one mediator *b.* God and men

BETWIXT
Phil. 1:23 for I am in a strait *b.* two

BEWARE
Mat. 7:15 *b.* of false prophets, which come
10:17 But *b.* of men: for they will
16: 6 *b.* of the leaven of Pharisees
Luke 12:15 *b.* of covetousness: for a man's life
Phil. 3: 2 *b.* of dogs, *b.* of evil workers
Col. 2: 8 *b.* lest any man spoil you
2 Pet. 3:17 *b.* lest ye also being led away

BID (BIDDEN)
Mat. 22: 9 as ye shall find, *b.* to the marriage
23: 3 whatsoever they *b.* you observe
Luke 14:10 but when thou art *b.* of any man

BILL
Deut. 24: 1 let him write her a *b.* of divorcement
Is. 50: 1 the *b.* of your mother's divorcement
Jer. 3: 8 and given her a *b.* of divorcement
Mark 10: 4 write a *b.* of divorcement
Luke 16: 6 take thy *b.*, and sit down
16: 7 take thy *b.* and write fourscore

BILLOWS
Ps. 42: 7 thy *b.* are gone over me
Jonah 2: 3 all thy *b.* and thy waves

BIND
Job 38:31 canst thou *b.* the sweet influences
31:36 I would *b.* it as a crown
Ps. 105: 22 *b.* his princes at pleasure
149: 8 to *b.* their kings with chains
Prov. 3: 3 *b.* them about thy neck
Is. 8:16 *b.* up the testimony, seal the law
Hos. 6: 1 smitten, and will *b.* us up
Mat. 12:29 first *b.* the strong man and
13:30 *b.* them in bundles to burn
16:19 thou shalt *b.* on earth
22:13 *b.* him hand and foot, and cast

BIRD (BIRDS)
Gen. 15:10 but the *b.* divided he not
2 Sam. 21:10 neither the *b.* of the air to rest
Ps. 104: 17 where the *b.* make their nests
124: 7 soul is escaped as a *b.*
Prov. 7:23 as a *b.* hasteth to the snare
Eccl. 9:12 as the *b.* that are caught
10:20 *b.* of the air shall carry the voice
Sol. 2:12 the time of the singing of the *b.*
Is. 31: 5 as *b.* flying so will the Lord
46:11 ravenous *b.* from the east
Jer. 5:27 as a cage is full of *b.*
12: 9 the *b.* round about are against her
Mat. 8:20 the *b.* of the air have nests

BIRTH
2 Ki. 19: 3 for the children are come to the *b.*
Eccl. 7: 1 of death than the day of one's *b.*
Is. 66: 9 shall I bring to the *b.*, and not
Ezek. 16: 3 thy *b.* and thy nativity
Gal. 4:19 whom I travail in *b.* again

BIRTHDAY
Gen. 40:20 the third day, which was Pharaoh's *b.*
Mat. 14: 6 when Herod's *b.* was kept

BIRTHRIGHT
Gen. 25:31 sell me this day thy *b.*
27:36 he took away my *b.*; and behold
43:33 the firstborn according to his *b.*
1 Chr. 5: 1 the *b.* was given unto the sons

Heb. 12:16 for one morsel of meat sold his *b.*

BISHOP (BISHOPS)
Phil. 1: 1 at Philippi, with *b.* and deacons
1 Tim. 3: 1 desire the office of *b.*
Tit. 1: 7 for a *b.* must be blameless
1 Pet. 2:25 returned unto the shepherd and *b.* of souls

BITE (BITETH, BITTEN)
Num. 21: 9 if a serpent had *b.* any man
Prov. 23:32 at last it *b.* like a serpent
Eccl. 10:11 the serpent will *b.* without enchantment
Jer. 8:17 not be charmed and they shall *b.* you
Amos 9: 3 command the serpent, and he shall *b.* thee
Mic. 3: 5 prophets *b.* with their teeth
Hab. 2: 7 rise up suddenly that shall *b.* thee
Gal. 5:15 if ye *b.* and devour one another

BITTER
Ex. 1:14 made their lives *b.* with hard bondage
12: 8 with *b.* herbs they shall eat it
Deut. 32:24 devoured with *b.* destruction
32:32 grapes of gall, their clusters are *b.*
2 Ki. 14:26 of Israel, that it was very *b.*
Job 3:20 life given to the *b.* in soul
13:26 write *b.* things against me
Ps. 64: 3 to shoot their arrows even *b.* words
Prov. 27: 7 every *b.* thing is sweet
Is. 5:20 woe to them that put *b.* for sweet
Jer. 2:19 it is an evil thing and *b.* that
Col. 3:19 wives and be not *b.* against them
Jas. 3:14 if ye have *b.* envying and strife
Rev. 8:11 because they were made *b.*
10: 9 and it shall make thy belly *b.*

BITTERLY
Judg. 5:23 curse ye *b.* inhabitants thereof
Is. 22: 4 I will weep *b.*, labour not to comfort
Ezek. 27:30 heard against thee, and shall cry *b.*
Hos. 12:14 provoked him most *b.*
Mat. 26:75 went out and wept *b.*

BITTERNESS
1 Sam. 1:10 she was in *b.* of soul, and prayed
15:32 surely the *b.* of death is past
2 Sam. 2:26 it will be *b.* in the end
Prov. 14:10 heart knows its own *b.*
Acts 8:23 in gall of *b.* and bond of
Rom. 3:14 whose mouth full of cursing and *b.*
Eph. 4:31 let all *b.* . . . be put away from you
Heb. 12:15 root of *b.* springing up trouble you

BLACK
1 Ki. 18:45 the heaven was *b.* with clouds
Sol. 1: 5 look not upon me because I am *b.*
Mat. 5:36 canst not make one hair white or *b.*

BLACKNESS
Heb. 12:18 burned with fire nor unto *b.* and darkness
Jude 1:13 reserved the *b.* of darkness for ever

BLAME (BLAMED)
Gen. 43: 9 let me bear the *b.* forever
2 Cor. 6: 3 that the ministry be not *b.*
8:20 no man should *b.* us in this abundance
Gal. 2:11 because he was to be *b.*
Eph. 1: 4 we should be holy and without *b.*

BLAMELESS
Gen. 44:10 and ye shall be found *b.*
Josh. 2:17 we will be *b.* of this thine oath
Judg. 15: 3 now shall I be more *b.*
Mat. 12: 5 profane the sabbath, and are *b.*
Luke 1: 6 in ordinances of the Lord *b.*
1 Cor. 1: 8 be *b.* in the day of our Lord
Phil. 3: 6 righteous which is in the law *b.*
1 Thes. 5:23 soul and body be preserved *b.* unto the
1 Tim. 3: 2 bishop then must be *b.*, the husband
3:10 office of a deacon being found *b.*
5: 7 give in charge, that they may be *b.*

Tit. 1: 7 for a bishop must be *b.*
2 Pet. 3:14 of him in peace, without spot and *b.*

BLASPHEME (BLASPHEMED, BLASPHEMETH)
Lev. 24:16 *b.* the name of the Lord
2 Ki. 19: 6 of Assyria have *b.* me
Ps. 44:16 voice of him that reproacheth and *b.*
74:10 shall the enemy *b.* thy name forever
74:18 foolish people have *b.* thy name
Is. 52: 5 my name continually every day is *b.*
Mat. 9: 3 scribes said this man *b.*
Mark 3:29 *b.* against Holy Ghost hath never
Luke 12:10 unto him that *b.* against the Holy
Acts 26:11 compelled them to *b.*
Rom. 2:24 is *b.* among the Gentiles through you
1 Tim. 1:20 that they may learn not to *b.*
6: 1 name of God and his doctrine be not *b.*
Jas. 2: 7 do they not *b.* that name
Rev. 16:11 and *b.* the God of heaven because

BLASPHEMER (BLASPHEMERS)
1 Tim. 1:13 who was before a *b.*, and a persecutor
2 Tim. 3: 2 covetous, boasters, proud, *b.*

BLASPHEMY
2 Ki. 19: 3 day of trouble, and of rebuke, and *b.*
Is. 37: 3 day of trouble, and of rebuke, and of *b.*
Mat. 12:31 and *b.* shall be forgiven unto men
Mark 7:22 an evil eye, *b.*, pride, foolishness
Col. 3: 8 off all these; anger, wrath, malice, *b.*
Rev. 2: 9 I know the *b.* of them which say

BLEMISH
Ex. 12: 5 Your lamb shall be without *b.*
29: 1 and two rams without *b.*
Lev. 1: 3 let him offer a male without *b.*
4:23 of the goats a male without *b.*
Dan. 1: 4 children in whom was no *b.*
Eph. 5:27 that it should be holy and without *b.*
1 Pet. 1:19 as of a lamb without *b.* and without

BLESS
Gen. 12: 2 and I will *b.* thee
12: 3 I will *b.* them that *b.* thee
22:17 in blessing I will *b.* thee
Ex. 23:25 God, and he shall *b.* thy bread and water
24: 1 pleased the Lord to *b.* Israel
Num. 6:24 Lord *b.* thee and keep thee
Deut. 8:10 thou shalt *b.* the Lord thy God
Judg. 5: 9 among the people *b.* ye the Lord
Ps. 5:12 Thou, Lord wilt *b.* the righteous
16: 7 I will *b.* the Lord
28: 9 *b.* thine inheritance and feed
29:11 will *b.* his people with peace
63: 4 Thus will I *b.* thee while I live
67: 1 be merciful to us and *b.* us
103: 1 *b.* the Lord, O my soul
104: 35 *b.* the Lord, O my soul
115: 13 he will *b.* them that fear
132: 15 I will abundantly *b.* her
134: 3 the Lord *b.* thee out of Zion
145: 2 Every day will I *b.* thee
Hag. 2:19 from this day will I *b.*
Rom. 12:14 *b.* them that persecute
Acts 3:26 sent him to *b.* you
1 Cor. 4:12 being reviled we *b.*

BLESSED
Gen. 1:22 God *b.* them, saying, Be fruitful
2: 3 God *b.* the seventh day
Ex. 20:11 the Lord *b.* the sabbath day
Num. 24: 9 *b.* is he that blesseth
Ps. 1: 1 *b.* is the man that walketh not in the counsel
32: 1 *b.* is he whose transgression is
32: 2 *b.* is the man unto whom the Lord imputeth
33:12 *b.* is the nation whose God is
34: 8 *b.* is the man that trusteth in him
41: 1 *b.* is he that considereth the poor
65: 4 *b.* is the man whom thou choosest
84: 5 *b.* is the man whose strength is in thee
94:12 *b.* is the man whom thou chastenest

Ps. 112: 1 *b.* is the man *that* feareth the Lord
Prov. 8:32 *b.* are they that keep my ways
8:34 *b.* is the man that heareth me
10: 7 memory of the just is *b.*
Is. 30:18 *b.* are all they that wait for him
56: 2 *b.* is the man that doeth this,
Jer. 17: 7 *b.* is the man that trusteth in the Lord
Dan. 12:12 *b.* is he that waiteth and cometh
Mat. 5: 3 *b.* are the poor in spirit
5: 4 *b.* are they that mourn
5: 5 *b.* are the meek: for they shall
5: 6 *b.* are they which do hunger and thirst
5: 7 *b.* are the merciful: for they
5: 8 *b.* are the pure in heart
5: 9 *b.* are the peacemakers
5:10 *b.* are they which are persecuted
5:11 *b.* are ye, when men shall revile you
11: 6 *b.* is he whosoever not offended in me
13:16 *b.* are your eyes for they see
21: 9 *b.* is he that cometh in the name of the Lord
24:46 *b.* is that servant whom his lord
Mark 10:16 in his arms and *b.* them
11: 9 *b.* is he that cometh in the name of the Lord
Luke 1:28 *b.* art thou among women
1:48 all generations shall call me *b.*
11:28 *b.* are they that hear the word
John 12:13 *b.* is he that cometh in
20:29 *b.* are they that have not seen, and
Acts 20:35 it is more *b.* to give
Rom. 1:25 the Creator who is *b.* for ever
4: 7 *b.* are they whose iniquities are . . .
1 Tim. 1:11 glorious gospel of the *b.* God
6:15 *b.* and only Potentate
Jas. 1:12 *b.* is the man that endureth temptation
Rev. 1: 3 *b.* is he that readeth this prophecy
14:13 *b.* are the dead which die in the Lord
19: 9 *b.* are they which are called unto the marriage supper
20: 6 *b.* and holy is he that hath part
22: 7 *b.* is he that keepeth the sayings of this book
22:14 *b.* are they that do his commandments

BLESSEDNESS
Rom. 4: 6 describeth the *b.* of the man, unto whom God
Gal. 4:15 where is then the *b.* ye spake of

BLESSING (BLESSINGS)
Gen. 12: 2 name great; and thou shalt be a *b.*
27:36 now he hath taken away my *b.*
28: 4 give thee *b.* of Abraham
49:25 who shall bless thee with *b.* of heaven above
Deut. 11:26 set before you a *b.* and a curse
23: 5 turned curse into a *b.* unto thee
Josh. 8:34 words of the law, the *b.* and the cursings
Neh. 9: 5 name, which is exalted above all *b.*
Job 29:13 *b.* of him that was ready to perish
Ps. 3: 8 thy *b.* is upon thy people
21: 3 preventest him with *b.* of goodness
109: 17 as he delighted not in *b.*
129: 8 the *b.* of the Lord be upon you
Prov. 28:20 faithful man shall abound with *b.*
Is. 65: 8 destroy it not, for a *b.* is in it
Joel 2:14 repent and leave a *b.* behind him
Mal. 2: 2 I will curse your *b.*: yea I have
1 Cor. 10:16 cup of *b.* which we bless
Gal. 3:14 *b.* of Abraham come on Gentiles
Eph. 1: 3 hath blessed us with all spiritual *b.*
Jas. 3:10 out of the same mouth proceedeth *b.* and cursing

BLIND
Lev. 21:18 not approach, a *b.* man, or a lame
Job 29:15 I was eyes to the *b.*, and feet
Ps. 146: 8 openeth the eyes of the *b.*
Is. 42: 7 to open the *b.* eyes, to bring out
42:19 who is *b.* but my servant
43: 8 bring the *b.* people that have eyes
Mat. 11: 5 the *b.* receive their sight
Mat. 23:16 woe unto you ye *b.* guides
Luke 4:18 recovery of sight to the *b.*
2 Pet. 1: 9 lacketh these things is *b.*
Rev. 3:17 not that thou art . . . *b.* and naked

BLINDED
John 12:40 he hath *b.* their eyes and hardened
Rom. 11: 7 obtained it, and the rest were *b.*
2 Cor. 4: 4 god of this world *b.* the minds
1 John 2:11 that darkness hath *b.* his eyes

BLOOD
Gen. 4:11 receive thy brother's *b.* from thy hand
49:11 his clothes in the *b.* of grapes
Job 16:18 cover thou not my *b.*, and let
Ps. 9:12 when he maketh inquisition for *b.*
72:14 precious is their *b.* in his sight
Is. 26:21 earth shall disclose her *b.*
Ezek. 3:18 his *b.* will I require at thine hand
9: 9 land is full of *b.* and the city full
16: 6 polluted in thine own *b.*
Mic. 3:10 they build up Zion with *b.*
Mat. 26:28 This is my *b.* of the new testament
27: 8 that field was called the field of *b.*
27:25 his *b.* be on us and on our children
Luke 13: 1 whose *b.* Pilate had mingled with
22:44 as it were great drops of *b.*
John 1:13 born not of *b.* nor of flesh
6:54 drinketh my *b.* hath eternal life
6:55 my *b.* is drink indeed
6:56 drinketh my *b.* dwelleth in me
Acts 17:26 made of one *b.* all nations
18: 6 your *b.* be on your own heads
20:26 pure from the *b.* of all men
20:28 hath purchased with his own *b.*
Rom. 3:25 through faith in his *b.*
1 Cor. 11:27 guilty of the body and *b.* of the Lord
Eph. 1: 7 redemption through his *b.* even forgiveness
Col. 1:20 peace through the *b.* of the cross
Heb. 9:20 This is the *b.* of the testament
10:19 into the holiest by the *b.* of Jesus
12: 4 ye have not yet resisted unto *b.*
12:24 *b.* of sprinkling that speaketh
1 Pet. 1: 2 sprinkling of the *b.* of Jesus
1:19 with the precious *b.* of Christ
1 John 1: 7 *b.* of Jesus Christ cleanseth us
5: 6 he that came by water and *b.*
Rev. 1: 5 washed us in his own *b.*
6:10 dost thou not avenge our *b.*
8: 7 hail and fire mingled with *b.*
16: 6 thou hast given them *b.* to drink
17: 6 drunken with the *b.* of saints

BLOODGUILTINESS
Ps. 51:14 deliver me from *b.*, O God

BLOSSOM (BLOSSOMED)
Num. 17: 5 man's rod, whom I shall choose, shall *b.*
Is. 5:24 their *b.* shall go up as dust
27: 6 Israel shall *b.* and bud
35: 1 the desert shall *b.* as the rose
35: 2 it shall *b.* abundantly and rejoice
Ezek. 7:10 rod hath *b.*, pride hath budded
Hab. 3:17 the fig tree shall not *b.*

BLOT (BLOTTED, BLOTTETH, BLOTTING)
Ex. 32:32 *b.* me out of thy book
Deut. 9:14 and *b.* out their name from under heaven
2 Ki. 14:27 he would *b.* out the name of Israel
Neh. 4: 5 let not their sin be *b.* out
Job 31: 7 if any *b.* hath cleaved to mine hands
Ps. 51: 1 *b.* out my transgressions
109: 13 let their name be *b.* out
Prov. 9: 7 rebuketh a wicked man getteth himself a *b.*
Is. 43:25 I am he that *b.* out thy transgressions
Jer. 18:23 neither *b.* out their sin from thy sight
Acts 3:19 that your sins may be *b.* out
Col. 2:14 *b.* out handwriting of ordinances

BLUSH
Ezra 9: 6 and *b.* to lift up my face
Jer. 6:15 ashamed neither could they *b.*

BOAST (BOASTETH)
Ps. 34: 2 my soul shall make her *b.* in the Lord
52: 1 why *b.* thou thyself in mischief
Prov. 20:14 he is gone his way, then he *b.*
27: 1 *b.* not thyself of tomorrow
Rom. 1:30 despiteful, proud, *b.*, inventors of
11:18 *b.* not against the branches, but if thou *b.*
Eph. 2: 9 not of works lest any man should *b.*
Jas. 3: 5 *b.* as he that putteth it off

BOASTERS
2 Tim. 3: 2 covetous, *b.* proud, blasphemers

BOASTING (BOASTINGS)
Acts 5:36 rose up Theudas, *b.* himself to be
Rom. 3:27 where is *b.* then? It is excluded
Jas. 4:16 now ye rejoice in your *b.*

BODY
Ex. 24:10 as it were the *b.* of heaven
Deut. 28:11 in the fruit of thy *b.*, and in
Job 19:26 after my skin worms destroy this *b.*
Mic. 6: 7 fruit of my *b.* for the sin of
Mat. 6:22 light of the body is the eye
10:28 fear not them which kill the *b.*
26:26 take, eat: this is my *b.*
John 2:21 spake of the temple of his *b.*
Rom. 6: 6 *b.* of sin might be destroyed
7: 4 dead to the law by the *b.* of Christ
7:24 me from the *b.* of this death
8:10 *b.* is dead because of sin
8:13 do mortify the deeds of the *b.*
8:23 the redemption of our *b.*
1 Cor. 5: 3 absent in *b.*, but present in spirit
6:18 sin that a man doeth is without the *b.*
6:19 *b.* is the temple of Holy Ghost
7: 4 wife hath not power of her own *b.*
9:27 I keep under my *b.* and bring
10:16 communion of the *b.* of Christ
11:29 not discerning the Lord's *b.*
12:14 the *b.* is not one member, but many
12:27 ye are the *b.* of Christ
15:44 it is raised a spiritual *b.*
2 Cor. 5: 6 home in *b.* absent from the Lord
5: 8 to be absent from the *b.*
5:10 receive things done in his *b.*
12: 2 whether in *b.* or out I cannot
Eph. 3: 6 fellowheirs of the same *b.*
4:12 for edifying the *b.* of Christ
5:23 he is the saviour of the *b.*
Phil. 1:20 Christ magnified in my *b.*
3:21 shall change our vile *b.*
Col. 1:18 head of the *b.* the church
2:11 putting off the *b.* of sins of flesh
2:23 humility, and neglecting of the *b.*
Heb. 10: 5 but a *b.* hast thou prepared
13: 3 being yourselves also in the *b.*
Jas. 3: 6 tongue defileth the whole *b.*
1 Pet. 2:24 bare our sins in his own *b.*
Jude 1: 9 disputed about the *b.* of Moses

BODIES
Rom. 8:11 quicken your mortal *b.* by your spirit
12: 1 present your *b.* a living sacrifice
1 Cor. 6:15 your *b.* are the members of Christ
Eph. 5:28 love wives as their own *b.*
Heb. 10:22 our *b.* washed with pure water

BODILY
Luke 3:22 Holy Ghost in a *b.* shape
2 Cor. 10:10 his *b.* presence is weak
Col. 2: 9 the fulness of Godhead *b.*
1 Tim. 4: 8 *b.* exercise profiteth little

BOLD (BOLDLY)
Prov. 28: 1 righteous are *b.* as a lion
Mark 15:43 went in *b.* unto Pilate and craved
2 Cor. 10: 1 being absent am *b.* toward you
11:21 if any is *b.* I am *b.* also
Phil. 1:14 are much more *b.* to speak
Heb. 4:16 come *b.* to throne of grace

BOLDNESS
2 Cor. 7: 4 Great is my *b.* of speech toward
Eph. 3:12 in whom we have *b.* and
Heb. 10:19 *b.* to enter into the holiest
1 John 4:17 may have *b.* in the day of judgment

BOND (BONDS)
Job 12:18 He looseth looseth the *b.* of kings
Ps. 116: 16 handmaid: thou hast loosed my *b.*

Ezek. 20:37 bring you into the *b.* of the covenant
Acts 20:23 *b.* and afflictions abide me
23:29 worthy of death or of *b.*
1 Cor. 12:13 whether we be *b.* or free
Gal. 3:28 there is neither *b.* nor free
Eph. 4: 3 unity of Spirit in the *b.* of peace
6: 8 whether he be *b.* or free
6:20 I am an ambassador in *b.*
Phil. 1:16 to add affliction to my *b.*
Col. 3:11 *b.* nor free but Christ is all
3:14 charity which is the *b.* of perfectness

BONDMAN (BONDWOMAN)
Gen. 21:10 cash out this *b.* and her son
Gal. 4:23 but he who was of the *b.* was born
Rev. 6:15 and every *b.*, and every free man

BONDAGE
Ex. 13: 3 out of the of *b.*
1:14 their lives bitter with hard *b.*
2:23 sighed by reason of the *b.*
Rom. 8:15 spirit of *b.* again to fear
1 Cor. 7:15 brother or a sister is not under *b.*
Gal. 4:24 Sinai which gendereth to *b.*
5: 1 entangled with the yoke of *b.*

BONE (BONES)
Gen. 2:23 this is now *b.* of my bones
Ex. 12:46 neither shall ye break a *b.* thereof
Judg. 9: 2 remember also that I am your *b.*
2 Sam. 19:13 art thou not of my *b.*
1 Chr. 11: 1 behold we are thy *b.* and thy flesh
Ps. 6: 2 heal me, my *b.* are vexed
22:14 all my *b.* are out of joint
32: 3 my *b.* waxed old through my roaring
34:20 he keepeth all his *b.*: not one of
35:10 All my *b.* shall say, Lord, who is like
38: 3 neither is there any rest in my *b.*
51: 8 *b.* which thou hast broken may
102: 3 my *b.* are burned as an hearth
102: 5 my *b.* cleave to my skin
Eccl. 11: 5 how the *b.* do grow in the womb
Ezek. 37: 1 valley which was full of dry *b.*
37: 3 Son of man, can these *b.* live
Mat. 23:27 are within full of dead men's *b.*
John 19:36 *b.* of him shall not be broken
Eph. 5:30 of his flesh, and of his *b.*

BOOK (BOOKS)
Gen. 5: 1 This is the *b.* of the generations
Ex. 32:32 blot me out of thy *b.*
Esth. 6: 1 to bring the *b.* of the records
Job 19:23 O that they were printed in a *b.*
Ps. 40: 7 in the volume of the *b.*
56: 8 tears, are they not in thy *b.*
139: 16 in thy *b.* all my members were written
Eccl. 12:12 of making many *b.* there is no end
Dan. 7:10 judgment was set, and the *b.* were opened
John 21:25 could not contain the *b.* that should be
Phil. 4: 3 whose names are in the *b.* of life
2 Tim. 4:13 bring with thee, and the *b.*
Heb. 10: 7 the volume of the *b.* it is written
Rev. 3: 5 name out of the *b.* of life
13: 8 names are not written in the *b.*
20:12 and the *b.* were opened
20:15 not found written in the *b.* of life
22:19 words of the *b.* of this prophecy

BORN
Job 5: 7 Yet man is *b.* unto trouble
14: 1 man that is *b.* of a woman
Ps. 58: 3 go astray as soon as they be *b.*
87: 4 with Ethiopia this man was *b.* there
Prov. 17:17 brother is *b.* for adversity
Eccl. 3: 2 a time to be *b.* and a time to die
Is. 9: 6 unto us a child is *b.* unto us
66: 8 shall a nation be *b.* at once
Mat. 11:11 among them that are *b.* of women
26:24 better if he had not been *b.*
Luke 7:28 among those that are *b.* of women
John 3: 3 except a man be *b.* again
3: 4 can man be *b.* when he is old
3: 5 *b.* of water and of the Spirit
3: 6 which is *b.* of the flesh is flesh
3: 7 said unto thee ye must be *b.* again
Rom. 9:11 children being not yet *b.*
1 Cor. 15: 8 as of one *b.* out of due time
Gal. 4:23 bond woman was *b.* after the flesh
1 Pet. 2: 2 as new *b.* babes desire milk of
1 John 3: 9 is *b.* of God doth not commit
4: 7 everyone that loveth if *b.* of God

BORNE
Jer. 15:10 that thou hast *b.* me a man of strife

BORROW (BORROWED)
Ex. 3:22 every woman shall *b.* of her neighbor
12:35 they *b.* of the Egyptians
22:14 if a man *b.* aught of his neighbour
Deut. 15: 6 but thou shalt not *b.*: and thou
28:12 many nations, and thou shalt not *b.*
Mat. 5:42 would *b.* of thee turn thou not away

BORROWER
Prov. 22: 7 the *b.* is servant to the lender
Is. 24: 2 as with the lender so with the *b.*

BOSOM
Gen. 16: 5 I have given my maid into thy *b.*
Ex. 4: 6 he put his hand into his *b.*
Num. 11:12 carry them in thy *b.* as a
Deut. 13: 6 wife of thy *b.*; or thy friend
Ps. 35:13 my prayer returned into my own *b.*
74:11 pluck thy hand out of thy *b.*
79:12 sevenfold into their *b.* their reproach
89:50 how I do bear in my *b.*
Prov. 5:20 and embrace the *b.* of a stranger
17:23 taketh a gift out of the *b.* to pervert
19:24 hideth his hands in his *b.*
Eccl. 7: 9 anger resteth in the *b.* of fools
Is. 40:11 his arm, and carry them in his *b.*
65: 6 recompense even recompense into their *b.*
Jer. 32:18 fathers into the *b.* of their children
Mic. 7: 5 her that lieth in thy *b.*
Luke 6:38 running over, shall men give into your *b.*
16:22 carried by the angels into Abraham's *b.*
John 13:23 leaning on Jesus' *b.* one of his disciples

BOTTLE (BOTTLES)
Gen. 21:14 took bread, and a *b.* of water
Job 38:37 who can stay the *b.* of heaven
Ps. 56: 8 put thou my tears into thy *b.*
119: 83 I am become like a *b.* in the smoke
Jer. 13:12 every *b.* filled with wine
Mat. 9:17 do men put new wine into old *b.*
Mark 2:22 no man putteth new wine into new *b.*

BOUGHT
Gen. 17:13 he that is *b.* with thy money
33:19 he *b.* a parcel of a field
Deut. 32: 6 is not he thy father that hath *b.* thee?
Mat. 13:46 sold all that he had and *b.* it
1 Cor. 6:20 For ye are *b.* with a price
7:23 Ye are *b.* with a price
2 Pet. 2: 1 denying the Lord that *b.* them

BOUND
Gen. 22: 9 *b.* Isaac his son, and laid him
Job 36: 8 if they be *b.* in fetters
Ps. 107: 10 shadow of death being *b.* in affliction
Prov. 22:15 foolishness is *b.* in the heart
Is. 1: 6 have not been closed neither *b.* up
61: 1 prison to them that are *b.*
Ezek. 30:21 it shall not be *b.* up to be healed
34: 4 neither have ye *b.* up that which
Hos. 13:12 iniquity of Ephraim is *b.* up
Mat. 16:19 bind on earth shall be *b.* in heaven
Acts 20:22 I go *b.* in the spirit
21:13 ready not to be *b.* only, but
Rom. 7: 2 wife is *b.* to her husband
1 Cor. 7:39 the wife is *b.* by law so long
2 Tim. 2: 9 the word of God is not *b.*
Heb. 13: 3 remember them in bonds as *b.* with them

BOW (BOWS)
Gen. 9:13 I do set my *b.* in the clouds
49:24 his *b.* abode in strength, and the arms
Josh. 24:12 not with thy sword nor with thy *b.*
1 Sam. 2: 4 the *b.* of the mighty men are broken
2 Sam. 1:18 children of Judah the use of the *b.*
Ps. 7:12 hath bent his *b.* and made
11: 2 lo, the wicked bend their *b.*
37:15 their *b.* shall be broken
44: 6 I will not trust in my *b.*
78:57 turned aside like a deceitful *b.*
Jer. 9: 3 bend their tongue like their *b.* for lies
Lam. 2: 4 bent his *b.* like an enemy
3:12 bent his *b.* and set me as a mark
Hos. 1: 5 break the *b.* of Israel
1: 7 I will not save them by *b.*
7:16 turned like a deceitful *b.*

BOW (BOWED, BOWETH)
Gen. 23:12 Abraham *b.* down himself before the
Judg. 7: 5 every one that *b.* down upon his knees
2 Ki. 19:16 Lord, *b.* down thine ear
Job 31:10 let others *b.* down upon her
Ps. 31: 2 *b.* down thine ear to me
38: 6 I am *b.* down greatly; I go mourning
95: 6 let us worship and *b.* down
145: 14 raiseth up all that be *b.* down
Prov. 22:17 *b.* down thine ear, and hear
Is. 2:11 haughtiness of men shall be *b.* down

BOWELS
Gen. 43:30 for his *b.* did yearn upon his brother
1 Ki. 3:26 for her *b.* yearned upon her son
2 Chr. 21:18 the Lord smote him in his *b.*
Ps. 71: 6 took me out of my mother's *b.*
Is. 63:15 the sounding of thy *b.* and of thy
Jer. 4:19 my *b.* my *b.* I am pained
31:20 my *b.* are troubled for him
Acts 1:18 in the midst and, all his *b.* gushed out
2 Cor. 6:12 you are straitened in your own *b.*
Phil. 1: 8 I long after you in the *b.* of Christ
Col. 3:12 put on the *b.* of mercies
Philem. 1: 7 *b.* of the saints are refreshed
1:20 refresh my *b.* in the Lord
1 John 3:17 shutteth up his *b.* of compassion

BRAKE
Ex. 32:19 and *b.* them beneath the mount
1 Sam. 4:18 Eli *b.* his neck and died
1 Ki. 19:11 and *b.* into pieces the rocks
2 Ki. 10:27 they *b.* down the images of Baal
11:18 and *b.* it down, his altars
23:14 *b.* into pieces the images
25:10 *b.* down the walls of Jerusalem
2 Chr. 14: 3 and *b.* down the images, and cut down
25:23 and *b.* down the wall of Jerusalem
Job 29:17 *b.* the jaws of the wicked
Ps. 76: 3 *b.* the arrows of the bow
105: 16 *b.* the whole staff of bread
107: 14 *b.* their bands in sunder
Jer. 31:32 my covenant they *b.* although I was
39: 8 and *b.* down the walls of Jerusalem
52:14 *b.* down all the walls of Jerusalem
Ezek. 17:16 and whose covenant he *b.*, even with him
Dan. 2: 1 troubled, and his sleep *b.* from him
6:24 *b.* all their bones to pieces
Mat. 14:19 he blessed and *b.*, and gave the loaves
15:36 and gave thanks, and *b.* them
26:26 blessed it, and *b.* it and gave it
Mark 6:41 and blessed, and *b.* the loaves
14: 3 she *b.* the box and poured it on his
14:22 took bread, and blessed and *b.* it
Luke 22:19 took bread, and gave thanks, and *b.* it
24:30 took bread, and blessed it, and *b.*
1 Cor. 11:24 he *b.* it and said, Take, eat

BRAMBLE
Judg. 9:14 said all the trees unto the *b.*, Come
Luke 6:44 nor of a *b.* bush gather they grapes

BRANCH
Num. 13:23 a *b.* with one cluster of grapes
Job 14: 7 the tender *b.* thereof will not cease
18:16 and above shall his *b.* be cut off
Prov. 11:28 righteous shall flourish as a *b.*
Is. 4: 2 shall the *b.* of the Lord be beautiful
9:14 cut off from head to tail, *b.*
11: 1 a *B.* shall grow out of
14:19 cast out like an abominable *b.*
25: 5 *b.* of the terrible ones shall be
60:21 *b.* of my planting, the work of my
Jer. 23: 5 I will raise unto David a righteous *B.*
Ezek. 8:17 they put the *b.* to their nose
Zech. 3: 8 bring forth my servant the *B.*
6:12 behold the man whose name is the *B.*
Mal. 4: 1 leave neither root nor *b.*
Mat. 24:32 fig tree; when his *b.* is yet tender
John 15: 4 As the *b.* cannot bear fruit of itself
15: 6 cast forth as a *b.* and is withered

BRANCHES
Lev. 23:40 *b.* of palm trees, and the boughs
Neh. 8:15 fetch olive *b.*, and pine *b.*,
Job 15:30 flame shall dry up his *b.*
Ps. 80:11 sent her *b.* unto the river
104: 12 habitation, which sing among the *b.*
Is. 16: 8 her *b.* are stretched out, they are gone
17: 6 four or five in the outmost fruitful *b.*
18: 5 take away and cut down the *b.*
Jer. 11:16 the *b.* of it are broken
Ezek. 17: 6 whose *b.* turned toward him
19:11 exalted among the thick *b.*
Dan. 4:14 hew down the tree, and cut off his *b.*
Hos. 14: 6 his *b.* shall spread and his beauty
Zech. 4:12 what be these two olive *b.*
John 15: 5 I am the vine, ye are the *b.*
Rom. 11:16 root be holy, so are the *b.*
11:17 if some of the *b.* be broken off
11:21 God spared not the natural *b.*

BRASEN
Num. 16:39 Eleazar the priest took the *b.* censers
2 Ki. 18: 4 brake in pieces the *b.* serpent
2 Chr. 6:13 Solomon had made a *b.* scaffold
Jer. 1:18 and *b.* walls against the whole land
Mark 7: 4 washing of cups, and pots, *b.* vessels

BRASS
Gen. 4:22 instructor of every artificer in *b.* and iron
Num. 21: 9 And Moses made a serpent of *b.*
Deut. 8: 9 out of whose hills thou mayest dig *b.*
28:23 that is over thy head shall be *b.*
Job 6:12 strength of stones or is my flesh *b.*
41:27 he esteemeth *b.* as rotten wood
Ps. 107: 16 broken the gates of *b.*, and cut
Is. 48: 4 thy neck iron, and thy brow *b.*
Dan. 2:32 his belly and his thighs of *b.*
5: 4 of silver, of *b.*, of iron, of wood
Zech. 6: 1 the mountains were mountains of *b.*
1 Cor. 13: 1 I am become as sounding *b.* and
Rev. 1:15 his feet like unto fine *b.*
2:18 his feet are like fine *b.*

BREACH (BREACHES)
Gen. 38:29 this *b.* be upon thee: therefore his
Num. 14:34 ye shall know my *b.* of promise
Judg. 21:15 Lord had made a *b.* in the tribes
2 Sam. 6: 8 Lord had made a *b.* upon Uzzah
Job 16:14 He breaketh me with *b.* upon *b.*
Ps. 60: 2 heal the *b.* thereof; for it shaketh
106: 23 his chosen stood before him in the *b.*
Is. 30:13 this iniquity shall be to you as *b.*
58:12 shalt be called the repairer of the *b.*
Lam. 2:13 thy *b.* is great like the sea

BREAD
Gen. 3:19 sweat of thy face shalt thou eat *b.*
19: 3 and did bake unleavened *b.*
28:20 will give me *b.* to eat
49:20 Out of Asher his *b.* shall be fat
Ex. 12:15 shall ye eat unleavened *b.*
Ex. 16: 4 I will rain *b.* from heaven
23:25 he will bless thy *b.* and water
Lev. 21: 6 *b.* of their God they do offer
26:26 I have broken the staff of your *b.*
Num. 14: 9 they are *b.* for us: their defense
21: 5 soul loatheth this light *b.*
Deut. 8: 3 man doth not live by *b.* only
16: 3 *b.* therewith even the *b.* of affliction
Ruth 1: 6 visited his people giving *b.*
1 Sam. 2: 5 hired themselves for *b.*
25:11 take my *b.* and my water
1 Ki. 18: 4 fed them with *b.* and water
Neh. 5:14 not eaten *b.* of the governor
9:15 gavest them *b.* from heaven
Ps. 37:25 nor his seed begging *b.*
78:20 can he give *b.* also
80: 5 feedest them with *b.* of tears
102: 9 I have eaten ashes like *b.*
105: 16 he brake the whole staff of *b.*
127: 2 to eat the *b.* of sorrows
132: 15 satisfy her poor with *b.*
Prov. 9:17 *b.* eaten in secret is pleasant
20:17 *b.* of deceit is sweet to a man
22: 9 giveth of his *b.* to the poor
25:21 be hungry, give him *b.* to eat
31:27 she eateth not *b.* of idleness
Eccl. 9:11 neither yet *b.* to the wise
11: 1 cast thy *b.* upon the waters
Is. 3: 1 the staff whole stay of *b.*
30:20 Lord give you *b.* of adversity
55: 2 money for that which is not *b.*
55:10 seed to the sower, *b.* to the eater
58: 7 deal thy *b.* to the hungry
Lam. 4: 4 the young children ask *b.*
Ezek. 4:16 I will break the staff of *b.*
18: 7 hath given his *b.* to the hungry
Hos. 2: 5 give me my *b.* and water
Amos 4: 6 want of *b.* in all your places
Mal. 1: 7 ye offer polluted *b.* on mine
Mat. 4:3 these stones be made *b.*
4: 4 not live by *b.* alone
6:11 Give us this day our daily *b.*
7: 9 son ask *b.* will he give a stone
15:26 meet to take the children's *b.*
26:26 took *b.* and blessed it
Mark 7: 5 but eat *b.* with unwashen hands
8: 4 satisfy these men with *b.*
14:12 the first day of unleavened *b.*
Luke 7:33 neither eating *b.* nor drinking wine
15:17 servants of my father's have *b.* enough
22: 7 then came the day of unleavened *b.*
24:35 known to them in breaking of *b.*
John 6:32 Moses gave you not that *b.*
6:33 the *b.* of God is he that cometh
6:34 evermore give us this *b.*
6:35 I am the *b.* of life
6:50 this is the *b.* that cometh down
13:18 he that eateth *b.* with me
Acts 2:42 breaking *b.* and in prayer
2:46 breaking *b.* from house to house
20: 6 after the days of unleavened *b.*
20: 7 came together to break *b.*
27:35 he took *b.* and gave thanks
1 Cor. 10:16 *b.* we break is it not the communion
5: 8 with the unleavened *b.* of sincerity and truth
10:17 we many are one *b.* and one body
11:26 for as often as ye eat this *b.*
2 Cor. 9:10 both minister *b.* for your food
2 Thes. 3:12 they work, and eat their own *b.*

BREAK
Ex. 19:21 lest they *b.* through to come up
19:22 lest the Lord *b.* forth upon them
23:24 and quite *b.* down their images
34:13 destroy their altars, *b.* their images,
Deut. 7: 5 and *b.* down their images, and cut down
Ezra 9:14 should we again *b.* thy commandments
Job 19: 2 and *b.* me in pieces with words
Ps. 2: 3 let us *b.* their bands asunder
2: 9 shalt *b.* them with a rod of iron
10:15 *b.* thou the arm of the wicked
58: 6 *b.* their teeth in their mouth
72: 4 and shall *b.* into pieces the oppressor
89:31 if they *b.* my statutes
89:34 my covenant will I not *b.* nor
94: 5 they *b.* into pieces thy people
Eccl. 3: 3 a time to *b.* down, and a time to
Sol. 2:17 till the day *b.* and the shadow
Is. 14: 7 they *b.* forth into singing
Is. 38:13 as a lion so will he *b.* all
42: 3 bruised reed shall be not *b.*
45: 2 I will *b.* into pieces the gates
55:12 the hills shall *b.* forth before you
Jer. 1:14 an evil shall *b.* forth upon all
14:21 *b.* not thy covenant with us
15:12 shall iron *b.* northern iron
33:20 if ye can *b.* my covenant of the day
51:22 I will *b.* into pieces the horse
Ezek. 17:15 *b.* the covenant and be delivered
Dan. 2:44 but it shall *b.* into pieces
7:23 tread it down, and *b.* it into pieces
Hos. 1: 5 that I will *b.* the bow of Israel
10: 2 he shall *b.* down their altars
Zech. 11:10 that I might *b.* my covenant which I
Mat. 5:19 *b.* one of these least commandments
6:19 thieves *b.* through and steal
Acts 21:13 mean ye to weep and to *b.* mine heart?
1 Cor. 10:16 bread which we *b.*, is not the
Gal. 4:27 *b.* forth and cry, that travailest

BREAKETH (BREAKING)
Gen. 32:26 let me go, for the day *b.*
Job 9:17 he *b.* me with a tempest
Ps. 29: 5 voice of the Lord *b.* the cedars
46: 9 *b.* the bow and cutteth the spear
119: 20 my soul *b.* for the longing
Prov. 25:15 a soft tongue *b.* the bone
Eccl. 10: 8 *b.* an hedge, a serpent shall bite
Jer. 19:11 as one *b.* a potter's vessel
23:29 like a hammer that *b.* rocks
Luke 24:35 known of them in *b.* of bread
Acts 2:42 and in *b.* of bread, and in prayer
Rom. 2:23 through *b.* the law dishonourest thou God?

BREAST (BREASTS)
Gen. 49:25 blessings of the *b.*, and of the womb
Job 3:12 why *b.* that I should suck
21:24 his *b.* are full of milk
Ps. 22: 9 I was upon my mother's *b.*
Prov. 5:19 let her *b.* satisfy thee at
Sol. 1:13 all night between my *b.*
4: 5 thy *b.* are like two roes
7: 7 thy *b.* to clusters of grapes
8: 1 sucked the *b.* of my mother
8: 8 a little sister, and she hath no *b.*
8:10 I am a wall, and my *b.* like towers
Is. 28: 9 from the milk and drawn from the *b.*
60:16 and shalt suck the *b.* of kings
66:11 satisfied with the *b.* of her consolation
Lam. 4: 3 sea monsters draw out the *b.*
Ezek. 16: 7 thy *b.* are fashioned, and thine hair
23: 3 there were their *b.* pressed
23: 8 they bruised the *b.* of her virginity
Hos. 2: 2 adulteries from between her *b.*
9:14 given them a miscarrying womb and dry *b.*
Joel 2:16 the children, and those that suck *b.*
Luke 23:48 smote their *b.* and returned
John 13:25 He then lying on Jesus' *b.*
21:20 which also leaned on his *b.* at supper
Rev. 15: 6 their *b.* girded with golden girdles

BREASTPLATE (BREASTPLATE)
Ex. 28: 4 garments which they shall make; a *b.*
Eph. 6:14 having on the *b.* of righteousness
1 Thes. 5: 8 putting on the *b.* of faith and love
Rev. 9:17 having *b.* of fire and of jacinth

BREATH
Gen. 2: 7 into his nostrils the *b.* of life
Job 12:10 the *b.* of all mankind
15:30 by the *b.* of his mouth
17: 1 my *b.* is corrupt, my days are extinct
33: 4 *b.* of the Almighty hath given me life
34:14 if he gather his spirit and *b.*
37:10 by the *b.* of God frost is given
41:21 his *b.* kindleth coals
Ps. 33: 6 host of them, by the *b.* of his mouth
104: 29 thou takest away their *b.*
135: 17 neither any *b.* in their mouths
146: 4 *b.* goeth forth, he returneth

Eccl. 3:19 the other; yea they have all one *b.*
Is. 2:22 whose *b.* is in his nostrils
11: 4 the *b.* of his lips shall he slay
30:28 his *b.*, as an overflowing stream
30:33 the *b.* of the Lord doth kindle it
33:11 your *b.* as fire shall devour you
42: 5 giveth *b.* unto the people
Jer. 10:14 and there is no *b.* in them
Lam. 4:20 the *b.* of our nostrils
Dan. 5:23 in whose hand thy *b.* is
Hab. 2:19 no *b.* at all in the midst
Acts 17:25 giveth to all life and *b.*

BREATHE (BREATHED, BREATHING)
Ps. 27:12 such as *b.* out cruelty
Ezek. 37: 9 come *b.* upon these slain
John 20:22 he *b.* on them, and saith unto
Acts 9: 1 *b.* out threatenings and slaughter

BREED (BRED, BREEDING)
Gen. 8:17 that they may *b.* abundantly
Ex. 16:20 *b.* worms and stank; and Moses was wroth
Deut. 32:14 lambs and rams of the *b.* of Bashan
Zeph. 2: 9 even the *b.* of nettles, and salt pits

BRETHREN
Gen. 13: 8 and thy headmen for we be *b.*
19: 7 I pray you *b.* do not so wickedly
24:27 me to the house of my master's *b.*
42: 3 Joseph's ten *b.* went to buy corn
42: 6 *b.* bowed down themselves before him
45:16 Joseph's *b.* are come: and it pleased
49: 5 Simeon and Levi are *b.*
49:26 of him that was separate from his *b.*
50:15 Joseph's *b.* saw their father was dead
Num. 27: 4 give therefore a possession among the *b.*
27:10 if he have no *b.*, they ye shall give
Deut. 17:20 be not lifted up above his *b.*
25: 5 if *b.* dwell together, and one of them die
33: 9 neither did he acknowledge his *b.*
33:24 let him be acceptable to his *b.*
Josh. 6:23 brought out Rahab . . . and her *b.*
Judg. 9: 1 went to Shechem unto his mother's *b.*
2 Ki. 10:13 we are *b.* of Ahaziah
1 Chr. 4: 9 more honourable than his *b.*
5: 2 prevailed above his *b.*
12: 2 Saul's *b.* of Benjamin
26: 7 whose *b.* were strong men, Elihu and
27:18 Elihu one of the *b.* of David
2 Chr. 21: 2 he had *b.* the sons of Jehoshaphat
22: 8 the sons of the *b.* of Ahaziah
Job 6:15 my *b.* dealt deceitfully
19:13 put my *b.* far from me
Ps. 22:22 declare thy name unto my *b.*
69: 8 become a stranger to my *b.*
122: 8 for my *b.* and companions' sakes
133: 1 for *b.* to dwell in unity
Prov. 6:19 soweth discord among *b.*
17: 2 part of the inheritance of *b.*
Hos. 13:15 though he be fruitful among his *b.*
Mat. 4:18 Jesus . . . saw two *b.*, Simon called
12:48 my mother, who are my *b.*
19:29 forsaken houses, or *b.* or sisters
20:24 moved against the two *b.*
22:25 now there were with us seven *b.*
23: 8 even Christ and all ye are *b.*
25:40 the least of these my *b.* ye have
28:10 go tell my *b.* that they go
Mark 10:29 man that hath left house or *b.*
Luke 14:26 hate not . . . *b.*, sisters, yea,
16:28 for I have five *b.*; that he may
21:16 betrayed by both by parents and *b.*
John 7: 5 neither did his *b.* believe
20:17 go to my *b.* and say, I ascend
Acts 6: 3 *b.* look ye out among you seven men
7:26 sirs, ye are *b.* why do ye
9:30 when the *b.* knew, they brought him
10:23 certain *b.* from Joppa accompanied
11:12 these six *b.* accompanied me
11:29 determined send relief to the *b.*
Acts 12:17 show these things to James and to the *b.*
14: 2 evil affected against the *b.*
15: 3 caused great joy to all the *b.*
15:22 chief men among the *b.*
15:32 exhorted the *b.* with many words
15:40 by the *b.* unto the grace of God
17: 6 drew Jason and certain *b.*
17:10 *b.* sent away Paul and Silas
18:18 Paul took leave of the *b.*
18:27 *b.* wrote exhorting the disciples
20:32 now *b.* I commend you to God
23: 6 men and *b.* I am a Pharisee
Rom. 8:29 the firstborn among many *b.*
9: 3 accursed from Christ for my *b.*
1 Cor. 6: 5 to judge between his *b.*
8:12 when ye sin so against the *b.*
15: 6 seen of above five hundred *b.* at once
Gal. 2: 4 false *b.* unawares brought in
1 Tim. 4: 6 If thou put the *b.* in remembrance
5: 1 a father and the younger men as *b.*
Heb. 2:11 is not ashamed to call them *b.*
1 Pet. 1:22 the Spirit unto unfeigned love of the *b.*
3: 8 love as *b.* be pitiful, courteous
1 John 3:14 unto life because we love the *b.*
3:16 to lay down our lives for the *b.*
3 John 1:10 neither doth receive the *b.*

BRIBE (BRIBES)
1 Sam. 8: 3 turned aside after lucre, and took *b.*
12: 3 have I received any *b.* to blind
Ps. 26:10 and their right hand is full of *b.*
Is. 33:15 that shaketh his hands from holding *b.*
Amos 5:12 they take a *b.*, and they turn aside

BRIBERY
Job 15:34 fire shall consume the tabernacles of *b.*

BRICK (BRICKS)
Gen. 11: 3 and they had *b.* for stone
Ex. 1:14 hard bondage, in mortar and in *b.*
5: 7 give the people straw to make *b.*
Is. 9:10 the *b.* are fallen down
65: 3 burneth incense upon altars of *b.*

BRIDE
Is. 49:18 bind them on thee, as a *b.* doeth
61:10 as a *b.* adorneth herself
Jer. 2:32 can a *b.* forget her attire
Joel 2:16 of his chamber, and the *b.* out of her closet
John 3:29 hath *b.* is the bridegroom
Rev. 21: 2 as a *b.* adorned for her husband
21: 9 I will show thee the *b.* the Lamb's wife

BRIDEGROOM
Ps. 19: 5 as *b.* coming out of the chamber
Is. 61:10 as a *b.* decketh himself
62: 5 as a *b.* rejoiceth over the bride
Jer. 7:34 I cause to cease the voice of the *b.*
33:11 the voice of the *b.*, and the voice of
Joel 2:16 let the *b.* go forth of his chamber
Mat. 9:15 as long as the *b.* is with them
25: 1 went forth to meet the *b.*
John 2: 9 the governor of the feast called the *b.*
3:29 friend of *b.* rejoiceth
Rev. 18:23 and the voice of the *b.* and of the

BRIDLE
Job 30:11 let loose the *b.* before me
Ps. 32: 9 must be held in with bit and *b.*
39: 1 I will keep my mouth as with a *b.*
Prov. 26: 3 a *b.* for the ass, and a rod for
Is. 37:29 put my *b.* in thy lips
Jas. 3: 2 able to *b.* the whole body

BRIDLES
Rev. 14:20 even unto the horse *b.*, by thy space

BRIDLETH
Jas. 1:26 *b.* not his tongue, but deceiveth

BRIER (BRIERS)
Judg. 8:16 and thorns of the wilderness and *b.*
Is. 5: 6 come up *b.* and thorns
7:23 it shall even be for *b.* and thorns
9:18 it shall devour the *b.* and thorns
Is. 27: 4 set *b.* against me in battle
55:13 instead of *b.* shall come up myrtle
Ezek. 2: 6 though *b.* and thorns be with thee
28:24 no more a pricking *b.* unto
Mic. 7: 4 the best of them is as a *b.*
Heb. 6: 8 that which beareth thorns and *b.* is rejected

BRIGHT
Lev. 13: 2 a scab, or *b.* spot and it be in
Job 37:11 he scattereth his *b.* cloud
Sol. 5:14 his belly is as *b.* ivory
Jer. 51:11 make *b.* the arrows; gather the shields
Ezek. 1:13 the fire was *b.* and out of
21:15 it is made *b.*, it is wrapped
Nah. 3: 3 up both the *b.* sword and the glittering
Zech. 10: 1 the Lord shall make *b.* clouds
Mat. 17: 5 a *b.* cloud overshadowed them
Luke 11:36 *b.* shining of a candle doth give thee
Acts 10:30 a man stood in *b.* clothing
Rev. 22:16 of David, and the *b.* and morning star

BRIGHTNESS
2 Sam. 22:13 through the *b.* before him were
Job 31:26 beheld the moon walking in *b.*
Is. 59: 9 for *b.* but we walk in darkness
Ezek. 1:28 the appearance of the *b.* round about
8: 2 as the appearance of *b.*
10: 4 full of the *b.* of the Lord's glory
28: 7 they shall defile thy *b.*
28:17 corrupted thy wisdom by reason of thy *b.*
Dan. 4:36 mine honour and *b.* returned unto me
12: 3 shine as the *b.* of the firmament
Amos 5:20 even very dark and no *b.* in it?
Hab. 3: 4 and his *b.* was as the light
Acts 26:13 a light above the *b.* of the sun
2 Thes. 2: 8 Lord with the *b.* of his coming
Heb. 1: 3 being the *b.* of his glory

BRIMSTONE
Gen. 19:24 Lord rained upon Sodom and upon Gomorrah .
Deut. 29:23 the whole land thereof is *b.*
Ps. 11: 6 rain snares, fire, and *b.*
Is. 30:33 of the Lord like a stream of *b.*
34: 9 dust thereof into *b.*, land burning
Ezek. 38:22 great hailstones, fire, and *b.*
Luke 17:29 it rained fire and *b.* from heaven
Rev. 9:17 issued fire and smoke and *b.*
19:20 cast into a lake of fire and *b.*

BRING
Gen. 1:11 let the earth *b.* forth grass
1:24 the earth *b.* forth the living creature
6:17 even I, do *b.* a flood of waters
Josh. 23:15 *b.* upon you all the evil
1 Ki. 8:32 to *b.* his way on his head
2 Ki. 19: 3 there is not strength to *b.* forth
Job 14: 4 who can *b.* a clean thing
15:35 and *b.* forth vanity
33:30 to *b.* back his soul from the pit
Ps. 37: 6 he shall *b.* forth thy righteousness
60: 9 who will *b.* me into the strong city
92:14 they shall still bring forth fruit in old age
Prov. 27: 1 knowest not what a day may *b.* forth
Eccl. 11: 9 God will *b.* thee into judgment
Sol. 8: 2 *b.* thee to my mother's house
Is. 1:13 *b.* no more vain oblations
41:21 *b.* forth your strong reasons
42: 1 *b.* forth judgment to the Gentiles
43: 5 I will *b.* thy seed from the east
43: 6 *b.* my sons from afar, and
46:13 I *b.* near my righteousness
66: 8 shall earth be made to *b.* forth in one day?
66: 9 *b.* to the birth and not cause
Hos. 2:14 *b.* her into wilderness and speak
Zeph. 2: 2 before the decree *b.* forth
3: 5 every morning doth he *b.* his judgment
Mat. 1:21 she shall *b.* forth a son
Mark 4:20 *b.* forth fruit some thirtyfold
Luke 2:10 I *b.* you good tidings of great joy
3: 8 *b.* forth fruits worthy of repentance
8:14 this life, and *b.* no fruit to perfection
John 12:24 if it die it *b.* much fruit
14:26 and *b.* all to your remembrance

John 15: 2 that it may *b.* forth more fruit
Acts 5:28 intend to *b.* this man's blood on us
1 Cor. 1:28 *b.* to nought things that are
4: 5 *b.* to light the hidden things
1 Thes. 4:14 will God *b.* with him
1 Pet. 3:18 that he might *b.* us to God

BRINGETH
Ps. 1: 3 *b.* forth fruit in his season
Hos. 10: 1 He *b.* forth fruit unto himself
Mat. 3:10 every tree which *b.* not forth good fruit
7:19 every tree that *b.* not forth good fruit
Luke 6:43 a good tree *b.* not forth corrupt fruit
Jas. 1:15 when lust hath conceived, it *b.* forth sin

BROAD
Num. 16:39 they were made *b.* plates for a covering
Job 36:16 out of the strait into a *b.* place
Ps. 119: 96 but thy commandment is exceeding *b.*
Is. 33:21 be unto us a place of *b.* rivers
Nah. 2: 4 one against another in the *b.* ways
Mat. 7:13 *b.* is the way that leadeth to destruction
23: 5 they make *b.* their phylacteries

BROKEN
Gen. 17:14 he hath *b.* my covenant
Ps. 34:18 nigh unto them that are of a *b.* heart
44:19 sore *b.* us in the place of dragons
51: 8 bones which thou hast *b.* rejoice
51:17 a *b.* spirit, a *b.* and a contrite heart
55:20 he hath *b.* his covenant
147: 3 He healeth the *b.* in heart, and bindeth
Prov. 17:22 but a *b.* spirit drieth the bones
Eccl. 4:12 a threefold cord is not quickly *b.*
Is. 24: 5 the ordinance *b.* the everlasting covenant
61: 1 sent me to bind up the *b.* hearted
Jer. 2:13 hewed them out cisterns, *b.* cisterns
5: 5 these have altogether *b.* the yoke
33:21 then may also my covenant be *b.*
Ezek. 44: 7 they have *b.* my covenant
Dan. 2:42 partly strong and partly *b.*
Hos. 5:11 Ephraim is oppressed and *b.* in judgment
Mat. 21:44 fall on this stone shall be *b.*

BROOK (BROOKS)
Job 20:17 the floods, the *b.* of honey and butter
Ps. 110: 7 drink of the *b.* in the way
Is. 19: 6 the *b.* of defence shall be emptied

BROTHER
Prov. 17:17 a *b.* is born for adversity
18:19 a *b.* offended is harder to be won
18:24 a friend that sticketh closer than a *b.*
27:10 neighbour that is near, than a *b.* far off
Jer. 9: 4 trust ye not in any *b.* for every *b.*
Mat. 10:21 *b.* shall deliver up *b.* to death
Mark 13:12 *b.* shall betray the *b.* to death
Acts 9:17 on him said, *b.* Saul, the Lord, even Jesus
1 Cor. 5:11 *b.* be a fornicator or
7:15 A *b.* or sister is not under bondage
8:11 though thy knowledge shall the weak *b.* perish
1 Thes. 4: 6 no man go beyond and defraud his *b.*
2 Thes. 3:15 as an enemy, but admonish him as a *b.*
Jas. 1: 9 let the *b.* of low degree rejoice

BROTHERHOOD
Zech. 11:14 I might break the *b.* between Judah and
1 Pet. 2:17 Love the *b.*. Fear God.

BROTHERLY
Amos 1: 9 and remembered not the *b.* covenant
Rom. 12:10 affectioned one to another with *b.* love
1 Thes. 4: 9 as touching *b.* love, ye need not that

Heb. 13: 1 let *b.* love continue
2 Pet. 1: 7 to godliness *b.* kindness; and to *b.*

BROUGHT
Deut. 33:14 precious fruits *b.* forth by the sun
2 Sam. 7:18 that thou hast *b.* me hitherto
Neh. 4:15 God had *b.* their counsel to nought
9:33 thou art just in all that is *b.* on
Ps. 45:14 be *b.* unto the king in raiment
79: 8 mercies prevent us: we are *b.* low
90: 2 before the mountains were *b.* forth
106: 43 *b.* low for their iniquities
107: 39 *b.* low through oppression
Is. 1: 2 nourished and *b.* up children
66: 7 before she travailed, she *b.* forth
Mat. 10:18 ye shall *b.* before governors and kings
Luke 12:16 ground of a certain rich man *b.* forth
1 Cor. 6:12 I will not be *b.* under the power of any
Gal. 2: 4 because of false brethren unawares *b.* in
1 Tim. 6: 7 we *b.* nothing into this world, and it
Jas. 5:18 the earth *b.* forth her fruit

BRUISE (BRUISED)
Gen. 3:15 it shall *b.* thy head, and thou shalt
2 Ki. 18:21 trustest upon the staff of this *b.* reed
Is. 42: 3 a *b.* reed shall he not break
53: 5 He was *b.* for our iniquities
53:10 it pleased the Lord to *b.* him.
Ezek. 23: 3 there they *b.* the teats of their virginity
Luke 4:18 to set at liberty them that are *b.*
Rom. 16:20 God of peace shall *b.* Satan

BRUTISH
Ps. 92: 6 a *b.* man knoweth not; neither doth a
94: 8 understand ye *b.* among the people
Prov. 12: 1 but he that hateth reproof is *b.*
Jer. 10:14 every man is *b.* in his knowledge

BUCKET (BUCKETS)
Num. 24: 7 He shall pour the water out of his *b.*
Is. 40:15 the nations are as a drop of a *b.*

BUCKLER
1 Chr. 5:18 men able to bear *b.* and sword
Job 15:26 upon the thick bosses of his *b.*
Ps. 91: 4 his truth shall be thy shield and *b.*
Sol. 4: 4 where on there hang a thousand *b.*

BUILD (BUILDETH)
Josh. 6:26 cursed be the man that . . . *b.* this city
Ps. 51:18 *b.* thou the walls of Jerusalem
102: 16 when the Lord shall *b.* up Zion, he shall
127: 1 except the Lord *b.* the house they labour
Prov. 14: 1 Every wise woman *b.* her house: but
Eccl. 3: 3 break down and a time to *b.* up
Jer. 22:13 woe to him that *b.* the house
Amos 9: 6 that *b.* his stories in heaven
Mic. 3:10 they *b.* up Zion with blood
Hab. 2:12 him that *b.* a town with blood
Acts 20:32 his grace, which is able to *b.* you up
1 Cor. 3:10 the foundations and another *b.* thereon

BUILDER
Ps. 118: 22 stone which the *b.* refused is become head
Mat. 21:42 stone which the *b.* rejected
Mark 12:10 stone which the *b.* rejected
Acts 4:11 stone which was set at nought of you *b.*
Heb. 11:10 foundations whose *b.* and maker is God
1 Pet. 2: 7 the stone which the *b.* disallowed

BUILDING
1 Cor. 3: 9 God's husbandry, ye are God's *b.*
2 Cor. 5: 1 we have a *b.* of God, an house
Eph. 2:21 all the *b.* fitly framed together

BUILT
Job 22:23 to the Almighty, thou shalt be *b.* up
Ps. 89: 2 mercy shall be *b.* up for ever
Mat. 7:24 wise man which *b.* his house upon a rock
Eph. 2:20 ye are *b.* on the foundation of
Heb. 3: 4 he that *b.* all things is God
1 Pet. 2: 5 *b.* up a spiritual house, an holy

BULLS
Ps. 22:12 many *b.* have compassed me: strong *b.*
50:13 will I eat the flesh of *b.*, or drink
68:30 rebuke the multitude of *b.*
Heb. 9:13 if the blood of *b.* and goats

BULLOCK (BULLOCKS)
Ps. 51:19 they offer *b.* on thine altar
69:31 better than an ox or *b.* that hath horns
Is. 1:11 delight not in the blood of *b.*
Jer. 31:18 as a *b.* unaccustomed to the yoke: turn

BULRUSH (BULRUSHES)
Ex. 2: 3 took for him an ark of *b.*
Is. 18: 2 even in vessels of *b.*
58: 5 Is it to bow down his head as a *b.*

BULWARKS
Ps. 48:13 mark ye well her *b.*
Is. 26: 1 salvation will God appoint for walls and *b.*

BURDEN
Ex. 18:22 shall bear the *b.* with thee
23: 5 ass lying under his *b.*
Deut. 1:12 how can I bear your *b.*
2 Sam. 15:33 thou shalt be a *b.* unto
19:35 servant be yet a *b.* unto my lord
2 Ki. 5:17 two mules' *b.* of earth
9:25 the Lord laid this *b.* upon him
2 Chr. 35: 3 not be a *b.* on your shoulders
Neh. 13:19 no *b.* brought in on the sabbath day
Job 7:20 so that I am a *b.* to myself
Ps. 38: 4 a *b.* they are too heavy for me
55:22 cast thy *b.* upon the Lord
81: 6 I removed his shoulder from the *b.*
Eccl. 12: 5 grasshopper shall be a *b.*
Is. 9: 4 thou hast broken the yoke of his *b.*
13: 1 the *b.* of Babylon, which Isaiah
30:27 the *b.* thereof is heavy: his lips full
Ezek. 12:10 this *b.* concerneth the prince in Jerusalem
Nah. 1: 1 the *b.* of Nineveh. The book of
Hab. 1: 1 the *b.* which Habakkuk the prophet
Zeph. 3:18 reproach of it was a *b.*
Zech. 9: 1 the *b.* of the word of the Lord
12: 3 all that *b.* themselves with it shall
Mal. 1: 1 *b.* of the word of the Lord
Mat. 11:30 my yoke is easy, my *b.* is light
Acts 15:28 no greater *b.* than necessary
2 Cor. 12:16 But be it so, I did not *b.* you
Gal. 6: 5 every man bear his own *b.*
Rev. 2:24 put on you no other *b.*

BURDENED
2 Cor. 5: 4 in this tabernacle do groan being *b.*
8:13 not that other men be eased and ye *b.*

BURDENS
Gen. 49:14 couching down between two *b.*
Ex. 1:11 taskmasters to afflict them with their *b.*
Is. 58: 6 to undo the heavy *b.* and let the
Lam. 2:14 seen for thee false *b.* and causes of
Mat. 23: 4 bind heavy *b.* and grievous to be born
Gal. 6: 2 bear one another's *b.* and fulfil

BURN (BURNED, BURNETH)
Gen. 44:18 let not thine anger *b.*
Ex. 3: 2 the bush *b.* with fire
29:13 and *b.* them upon the altar
Lev. 1: 9 the priest shall *b.* all on the altar
6:15 *b.* it upon the altar for a sweet
Deut. 9:15 the mount *b.* with fire
32:22 shall *b.* unto the lowest hell
Ps. 46: 9 *b.* the chariot in the fire

Ps. 74: 8 they have *b.* up all the synagogues of God
Is. 9:18 wickedness *b.* as the fire
27: 4 go through them, I would *b.* them
Mal. 4: 1 day cometh shall *b.* as an oven
Luke 3:17 chaff he will *b.* with fire
24:32 did not our heart *b.* within us?
1 Cor. 3:15 if man's work shall be *b.*, he shall
7: 9 it is better to marry than to *b.*
13: 3 though I give my body to be *b.* and
2 Cor. 11:29 who is offended and I *b.* not?
Heb. 6: 8 whose end is to be *b.*
12:18 not come to the mount that *b.*
Rev. 21: 8 lake which *b.* with fire

BURNING (BURNINGS)
Gen. 15:17 a *b.* lamp that passed between
Ex. 21:25 *b.* for *b.*, wound for wound
Deut. 28:22 smite thee with extreme *b.*
Is. 3:24 of sackcloth and *b.* instead of beauty
4: 4 judgment and by the spirit of *b.*
33:14 shall dwell with everlasting *b.*
Jer. 20: 9 word was in mine heart as a *b.* fire
Ezek. 1:13 their appearance was like *b.* coals of fire
Amos 4:11 as a firebrand plucked out of the *b.*
Luke 12:35 loins be girded about, and your lights *b.*
John 5:35 He was a *b.* and a shining light
Rev. 4: 5 there were seven lamps of fire *b.*

BURNT
Gen. 8:20 and offered *b.* offerings on the altar
Deut. 12: 6 hither shall ye bring your *b.* offerings
1 Sam 15:22 great delight in *b.* offerings and sacrifices
Ps. 51:16 thou delightest not in *b.* offering
Is. 1:11 I am full of the *b.* offerings
64:11 is *b.* up with fire
Jer. 7:21 put your *b.* offerings unto your sacrifices
Hos. 6: 6 knowledge of God more than *b.* offerings
Mic. 6: 6 shall I come before him with *b.* offerings
Mat. 22: 7 and *b.* up their city
Mark 12:33 is more than all *b.* offerings
Heb. 10: 6 In *b.* offerings and sacrifices
2 Pet. 3:10 works that are therein shall be *b.*

BURST
Jer. 2:20 broken thy yoke, and *b.* thy bands
5: 5 broken the yoke and *b.* the bonds
Mark 2:22 new wine doth *b.* the bottles
Acts 1:18 he *b.* asunder in the midst

BURY (BURIED, BURYING)
Gen. 23: 4 *b.* my dead out of my sight
47:30 bury me in their *b.* place
49:29 *b.* me with my fathers in the cave
Ps. 79: 3 there was none to *b.* them
Mat. 8:21 first to go and *b.* my father
8:22 let the dead *b.* their dead
Rom. 6: 4 we are *b.* with him by baptism into death
1 Cor. 15: 4 he was *b.* and rose again
Col. 2:12 *b.* with him in baptism, wherein

BUSHEL
Mat. 5:15 and put it under a *b.*; but on a
Luke 11:33 neither under a *b.*, but on a

BUSINESS
Gen. 39:11 went into the house to do his *b.*
Deut. 24: 5 neither shall he be charged with any *b.*
Ps. 107: 23 in ships, that do *b.* in great waters
Dan. 8:27 rose up and did the king's *b.*
Luke 2:49 must be about my Father's *b.*
Rom. 12:11 not slothful in *b.*; fervent
1 Thes. 4:11 study to be quiet, and to do your own *b.*

BUTTER
Gen. 18: 8 and he took *b.*, and milk, and the calf
2 Sam. 17:29 and honey, and *b.* and sheep
Job 20:17 the brooks of honey and *b.*
Ps. 55:21 words were smoother than *b.*
Is. 7:15 *b.* and honey shall he eat

BUY (BUYETH)
Prov. 23:23 *b.* the truth, and sell it not
Is. 55: 1 *b.* and eat, yea, *b.* wine
Mat. 13:44 selleth all and *b.* that field
Jas. 4:13 *b.* and sell, and get gain
Rev. 3:18 I counsel thee to *b.* gold
13:17 no man might *b.* or sell
18:11 no man *b.* their merchandise

BUYER
Prov. 20:14 it is naught, saith the *b.*
Is. 24: 2 as with *b.* so with seller
Ezek. 7:12 let not the *b.* rejoice, nor

BYWORD
Deut. 28:37 and a *b.* among all nations
1 Ki. 9: 7 Israel shall be a . . . *b.* among
Job 17: 6 he hath made me also a *b.* of the prophet
Ps. 44:14 makest us a *b.* among the heathen

C

CAKE (CAKES)
Gen. 18: 6 make *c.* upon the hearth
Lev. 24: 5 flour and bake twelve *c.* thereof
Judg. 7:13 *c.* of barley tumbled into the host
1 Ki. 17:12 I have not a *c.* but meal
Jer. 7:18 make *c.* to the queen of heaven
Hos. 7: 8 Ephraim is a *c.* not turned

CALAMITY (CALAMITIES)
Deut. 32:35 the day of their *c.* is at hand
Job 6: 2 my *c.* laid in the balances
Ps. 18:18 prevented me in the day of my *c.*
57: 1 until these *c.* be overpast
141: 5 my prayer shall be in their *c.*
Prov. 1:26 I will laugh at your *c.*
17: 5 glad at *c.* shall not be unpunished
19:13 a foolish son is the *c.* of his
27:10 brother's house in the day of thy *c.*
Jer. 18:17 not the face in the day of their *c.*
46:21 day of their *c.* is come
Ezek. 35: 5 the sword in the day of their *c.*
Obad. 1:13 my people in the day of their *c.*

CALF (CALVES)
Gen. 18: 7 fetched a *c.* tender and good
Ex. 32: 4 made a molten *c.*
Lev. 9: 2 thee a young *c.* for a sin offering
Deut. 9:16 had made a molten *c.*
1 Ki. 12:28 made two *c.* of gold for you
Neh. 9:18 they had made them a molten *c.*
Job 21:10 calveth and casteth not her *c.*
Ps. 29: 6 them also to skip like a *c.*
106: 19 They made a *c.* in Horeb
Is. 11: 6 *c.* and the young lion
27:10 there shall the *c.* feed
Jer. 34:18 they cut the *c.* in twain
Hos. 8: 5 thy *c.*, O Samaria, hath cast thee
14: 2 we will render the *c.* of our lips
Mic. 6: 6 come with *c.* of a year old
Mal. 4: 2 grow up as *c.* of the stall
Luke 15:23 bring hither the fatted *c.*
Heb. 9:12 blood of goats and *c.*, but by his
Rev. 4: 7 the second beast like a *c.*

CALL
Gen. 2:19 to see what he would *c.* them
4:26 began men to *c.* upon the name of the Lord
12: 8 and *c.* upon the name of the Lord
24:57 we will *c.* the damsel and inquire
30:13 daughters will *c.* me blessed
Deut. 4: 7 God is in all things that we *c.* upon
4:26 I *c.* heaven and earth to witness
1 Sam. 3: 6 for thou didst *c.* me
1 Ki. 8:52 in all that they *c.* for
18:24 and I will *c.* on the name of the Lord
2 Ki. 5:11 and *c.* on the name of the Lord
Job 5: 1 *C.* now if there be any to answer
13:22 *c.* thou, and I will answer
27:10 will he always *c.* upon God
Ps. 4: 1 hear me when I *c.*, O God
14: 4 they *c.* not upon the Lord
49:11 *c.* their lands after their own names
50:15 And *c.* upon me in the day of trouble
91:15 He shall *c.* upon me
77: 6 I *c.* to remembrance my song
80:18 quicken us and we will *c.* on thy name
86: 5 plenteous in mercy to all that *c.*
116: 4 then I *c.* upon the name of the Lord
145: 18 nigh to all that *c.* upon him
Prov. 1:28 then shall they *c.* upon me
Is. 5:20 woe unto them that *c.* evil good
22:12 Lord God of hosts *c.* to weeping
58: 9 thou shalt *c.* and Lord will answer
65:24 before they *c.* I will answer
Jer. 25:29 I will *c.* for a sword upon all
29:12 then shall ye *c.* upon me
Joel 2:32 whosoever shall *c.* on the name
Jonah 1: 6 arise, *c.* upon thy God
Zeph. 3: 9 that all may *c.* upon the name of the Lord
Zech. 13: 9 shall *c.* upon thy name
Mal. 3:12 all nations shall *c.* you blessed
3:15 and now we *c.* the proud happy
Mat. 9:13 I am not come to *c.* the righteous
22: 3 *c.* them that were bidden
23: 9 *c.* no man your father on earth
Luke 1:48 all generations will *c.* me blessed
6:46 why *c.* ye me Lord, Lord and
14:12 a supper *c.* not thy friends
14:13 a feast *c.* the poor, the maimed
John 4:16 *c.* thy husband and come hither
13:13 ye *c.* me Master and Lord
15:15 I *c.* you not servants, but friends
Acts 2:21 shall *c.* on the name of the Lord
2:39 as many as the Lord shall *c.*
24:14 after the way which they *c.* heresy
Rom. 9:25 I will *c.* them my people
10:12 rich in mercy to all that *c.* on him
10:13 shall *c.* upon the name of the Lord
1 Cor. 1: 2 *c.* upon the name of Jesus Christ
2 Cor. 1:23 I *c.* God for a record upon my soul
Heb. 2:11 not ashamed to *c.* them brethren
Jas. 5:14 *c.* for the elders of the church
1 Pet. 1:17 if ye *c.* on the Father

CALLED
Gen. 21:17 angel of God *c.* to Hagar
22:11 angel of Lord *c.* to Abraham
Ex. 3: 4 God *c.* him out of the bush
Judg. 15:18 sore athirst and *c.* on the Lord
2 Ki. 8: 1 Lord hath *c.* for a famine
1 Chr. 4:10 Jabez *c.* on the God of Israel
21:26 David *c.* upon the Lord and he
2 Chr. 6:33 have built is *c.* by my name
7:14 which are *c.* by my name
Ps. 17: 6 I have *c.* upon thee
18: 6 in my distress I *c.* upon the Lord
79: 6 that have not *c.* on thy name
88: 9 I have *c.* daily upon thee
118: 5 I *c.* on the Lord in my distress
Prov. 1:24 I have *c.* and ye refused
Sol. 5: 6 I *c.* him, he gave no answer
Is. 41: 2 who *c.* him to his foot
42: 6 I the Lord *c.* thee in righteousness
43: 1 I have *c.* thee by thy name
43: 7 that is *c.* by my name
48: 1 *c.* by the name of Israel
49: 1 the Lord *c.* me from the womb
50: 2 when I *c.*, was there none to answer
51: 2 I *c.* him alone, and blessed him
61: 3 might be *c.* trees of righteousness
62: 4 thou shalt be *c.* Hephzibah
65:12 when I *c.* ye did not answer
Jer. 7:11 which is *c.* by my name
15:16 I am *c.* by thy name
25:29 city which is *c.* by my name
34:15 House which is *c.* by my name
Lam. 1:19 I *c.* for my lovers
3:55 I *c.* upon thy name, O Lord
Dan. 9:19 people are *c.* by thy name
Hos. 11: 1 I *c.* my son out of Egypt
Amos 7: 4 the Lord *c.* to contend by fire
9:12 heathen which are *c.* by my name
Hag. 1:11 I *c.* for a drought on the land
Mark 14:72 Peter *c.* to mind the word
Luke 15:19 not worthy to be *c.* thy son
John 1:48 before that Philip *c.* thee
10:35 if he *c.* them gods to whom
15:15 but I have *c.* you friends
Acts 9:21 destroy them which *c.* on this name
9:41 when he had *c.* the saints
10:24 *c.* together his kinsmen and near friends
11:26 disciples were *c.* Christians first
13: 2 for the work whereto I *c.* them
15:17 Gentiles upon whom my name is *c.*
19:40 we are in danger to be *c.* in question
24:21 of the dead I am *c.* in question
Rom. 1: 1 *c.* to be an apostle
1: 6 ye also the *c.* of Jesus Christ

Rom 1: 7 beloved of God *c.* to be saints
Rom. 2:17 art *c.* a Jew, and restest in the law
8:28 the *c.* according to his purpose
8:30 predestinate, them he also *c.*
9:24 whom he *c.*, not of Jews only
1 Cor. 1: 9 ye were *c.* unto the fellowship
1:26 not many wise, not many noble are *c.*
5:11 if any man that is *c.* a brother
7:17 as the Lord hath *c.* every one,
7:18 any man *c.* being circumcised?
7:24 wherein he is *c.* therein abide
15: 9 not meet to be *c.* an apostle
Gal. 1: 6 *c.* you into the grace of Christ
1:15 God who *c.* me by his grace
5:13 ye have been *c.* to liberty
Eph. 2:11 who are *c.* uncircumcision
4: 4 are *c.* in one hope of your calling
Col. 3:15 peace of God to which ye are *c.*
1 Thes. 2:12 who hath *c.* you unto his Kingdom
4: 7 God hath not *c.* us to uncleanness
2 Thes. 2: 4 above all that is *c.* God
2:14 he *c.* you by our gospel
1 Tim. 6:12 life, whereunto thou art *c.*
2 Tim. 1: 9 *c.* us with holy calling
Heb. 3:13 while it is *c.* today
5: 4 *c.* of God, as was Aaron
11:16 not ashamed to be *c.* their God
11:24 be *c.* the son of Pharaoh's daughter
Jas. 2: 7 name by the which ye are *c.*
1 Pet. 1:15 as he that *c.* you is holy
2: 9 who *c.* you out of darkness
2:21 For even hereunto were ye *c.*
5:10 God *c.* us to his eternal glory
2 Pet. 1: 3 *c.* us to glory and virtue
1 John 3: 1 we should be *c.* sons of God
Jude 1: 1 preserved in Christ Jesus and *c.*
Rev. 17:14 that are with him are *c.* and chosen
19: 9 are *c.* unto the marriage supper

CALLETH
1 Ki. 8:43 that the stranger *c.* to thee
Ps. 42: 7 deep *c.* unto deep at the noise
147: 4 stars, he *c.* them by all their
Is. 59: 4 none *c.* for justice nor for truth
64: 7 none that *c.* upon thy name
Hos. 7: 7 none among them that *c.* unto me
Amos 5: 8 that *c.* for waters of the sea
Luke 15: 6 home, he *c.* together his friends
John 10: 3 he *c.* his own sheep by name
Rom. 4:17 *c.* those things which be not
9:11 not of works but of him that *c.*
Gal. 5: 8 cometh not of him that *c.* you
1 Thes. 5:24 faithful is he that *c.* you

CALLING
Is. 41: 4 *c.* the generations from the beginning
Mat. 11:16 children sitting in the markets, and *c.*
Mark 11:21 Peter *c.* to remembrance saith unto
Acts 7:59 they stoned Stephen, *c.* upon God
22:16 *c.* on the name of the Lord
Rom. 11:29 the gifts and *c.* of God
1 Cor. 1:26 ye see your *c.*, brethren
7:20 let every man abide in the same *c.*
Eph. 1:18 know what is the hope of his *c.*
4: 4 called in one hope of your *c.*
Phil. 3:14 prize of the high *c.* of God
2 Thes. 1:11 count worthy of this *c.*
2 Tim. 1: 9 and called us with a holy *c.*
Heb. 3: 1 partakers of the heavenly *c.*
1 Pet. 3: 6 obeyed Abraham, *c.* him lord
2 Pet. 1:10 make your *c.* and election sure

CALM
Ps. 107: 29 he maketh the storm a *c.*, so that
Jonah 1:11 sea may be *c.* unto us
Mat. 8:26 there was a great *c.*
Mark 4:39 and there was a great *c.*
Luke 8:24 and there was a great *c.*

CAME
2 Chr. 7: 3 how the fire *c.* down
Mat. 20:28 Son of man *c.* not to be ministered
John 1:11 He *c.* unto his own and his own
1:17 grace and truth *c.* by Jesus Christ
3:13 he that *c.* down from heaven
6:38 I *c.* down from heaven not to do
6:51 bread which *c.* down from heaven
16:28 I *c.* forth from the Father
18:37 for this cause *c.* I into the world
Rom. 9: 5 concerning the flesh Christ *c.*
1 Tim. 1:15 Christ Jesus *c.* into the world
1 John 5: 6 he that *c.* by water and blood
Rev. 20: 9 fire *c.* down from God out of heaven

CAMEL
Mat. 3: 4 John had his raiment of *c.*'s hair
19:24 it is easier for a *c.* to go through
23:24 strain at a gnat, and swallow a *c.*

CAMP
Ex. 14:19 angel of God which went before the *c.*
16:13 quails came up and covered the *c.*
32:17 noise of war in the *c.*
36: 6 proclaimed throughout the *c.*
Num. 11:26 and they prophesied in the *c.*
11:31 let the quails fall by the *c.*
Deut. 23:14 therefore shall thy *c.* be holy
Judg. 13:25 began to move him at times in the *c.*
Heb. 13:13 go unto him without the *c.*
Rev. 20: 9 compassed the *c.* of the saints

CAN
Gen. 41:38 *c.* we find such a one as this is
Deut. 1:12 how *c.* I myself alone bear your
32:39 neither is there any that *c.* deliver
2 Sam. 7:20 what *c.* David say more unto thee
2 Chr. 1:10 for who *c.* judge this thy people
Esth. 8: 6 how *c.* I endure to see the evil
Job 8:11 *c.* the rush grow up without mire
25: 4 how *c.* man be justified with God?
34:29 who then *c.* make trouble?
Eccl. 4:11 but how *c.* one be warm alone
Is. 49:15 *c.* a woman forget her sucking child
Jer. 2:32 *c.* the maid forget her ornaments
Ezek. 22:14 *c.* thine heart endure or can thine
37: 3 Son of man, *c.* these bones live?
Amos 3: 3 *c.* two walk together except
Mat. 12:34 how *c.* ye speak good things?
19:25 amazed, saying who then *c.* be saved?
Mark 2: 7 who *c.* forgive sins but God?
2:19 *c.* the children of the bridechamber
3:27 no man *c.* enter into a strong man's
10:38 *c.* ye drink of the cup that I
John 3: 4 how *c.* man be born when old?
3: 9 said unto him how *c.* these things be
5:19 the Son *c.* do nothing of himself
6:44 no man *c.* come to me except
6:60 an hard saying who *c.* hear it?
9: 4 night cometh, when no man *c.* work
14: 5 how *c.* we know the way?
15: 4 no more *c.* ye, except ye abide
1 Cor. 12: 3 no man *c.* say that Jesus is Lord
2 Cor. 13: 8 *c.* do nothing against the truth
1 Tim. 6: 7 is certain we *c.* carry nothing out
Heb. 10:11 sacrifices which *c.* never take away sins
Jas. 2:14 have not works, *c.* faith save him?

CANNOT
Gen. 32:12 which *c.* be numbered for multitude
Num. 23:20 blessed, I *c.* reverse it
Josh. 24:19 ye *c.* serve the Lord; for he
1 Sam. 12:21 after vain things which *c.* profit
1 Ki. 8:27 heaven of heavens *c.* contain thee
2 Chr. 6:18 heaven of heavens *c.* contain thee
Ezra 9:15 we *c.* stand before thee
Job 9: 3 contend with him he *c.* answer him
12:14 he breaketh down and it *c.* be
14: 5 appointed his bounds that he *c.* pass
28:15 it *c.* be gotten for gold
36:18 a great ransom *c.* deliver thee
Ps. 40: 5 they *c.* be reckoned up in order
77: 4 I am so troubled that I *c.* speak
93: 1 stablished, that it *c.* be moved
139: 6 it is high I *c.* attain unto it
Is. 38:18 the grave *c.* praise thee death *c.*
44:18 they *c.* see; they *c.* understand
44:20 he *c.* deliver his soul, nor say
45:20 pray unto a god that *c.* save
56:11 they are shepherds that *c.* understand
59: 1 is not shortened that it *c.* save
Jer. 4:19 I *c.* hold my peace because thou
6:10 uncircumcised and they *c.* hearken
7: 8 trust in lying words that *c.* profit
Jer. 14: 9 as a mighty man that *c.* save
18: 6 *c.* I do with you as this potter?
29:17 like the vile figs that *c.* be
33:22 the host of heaven *c.* be numbered
Lam. 3: 7 hedged me about that I *c.* get out
Mat. 6:24 ye *c.* serve God and mammon
7:18 a good tree *c.* bring forth evil fruit
19:11 all men *c.* receive this saying
26:53 thinkest thou I *c.* now pray to
27:42 saved others himself he *c.* save
Luke 14:26 life also, he *c.* be my disciple
John 3: 3 he *c.* see the kingdom of God
7:34 where I am thither ye *c.* come
8:43 because ye *c.* hear my word
14:17 spirit of truth whom the world *c.* receive
15: 4 branch *c.* bear fruit of itself
16:12 say to you but ye *c.* bear them now
Acts 4:20 we *c.* but speak the things
5:39 if it be of God ye *c.* overthrow it
Rom. 8: 8 in the flesh *c.* please God
8:26 with groanings which *c.* be uttered
1 Cor. 10:21 ye *c.* drink the cup of the Lord
15:50 flesh and blood *c.* inherit the kingdom
2 Cor. 12: 2 or whether out of the body I *c.* tell
Gal. 5:17 ye *c.* do the things that ye would
2 Tim. 2:13 faithful: he *c.* deny himself
Tit. 1: 2 which God, that *c.* lie, promised
2: 8 sound speech, that *c.* be condemned
Heb. 4:15 high priest which *c.* be touched
9: 5 we *c.* now speak particularly
12:27 things which *c.* be shaken may remain
12:28 receiving a kingdom which *c.* be moved
Jas. 1:13 God *c.* be tempted with evil
1 John 3: 9 he *c.* sin because he is born of

CANST
Ex. 33:20 thou *c.* not see my face: for there
Deut. 28:27 itch, whereof thou *c.* not be healed
Job 11: 7 *c.* thou by searching find out God
Mat. 8: 2 if thou wilt, thou *c.* make me clean
Mark 9:22 if thou *c.* do any thing, have
John 3: 8 but *c.* not tell whence it cometh
13:36 thou *c.* not follow me now

CANDLE (CANDLES, CANDLESTICK, CANDLESTICKS)
Ex. 25:31 shalt make a *c.* of pure gold
Num. 8: 2 give light over against the *c.*
2 Ki. 4:10 a stool, and a *c.* and it shall be
Job 18: 6 his *c.* shall be put with him
29: 3 when his *c.* shined on my head
Ps. 18:28 the Lord will light my *c.*
Prov. 20:27 spirit of man is the *c.* of the Lord
24:20 *c.* of the wicked shall be put out
31:18 her *c.* goeth not out by night
Dan. 5: 5 wrote over against the *c.* upon the plaster
Zeph. 1:12 I will search Jerusalem with *c.*
Zech. 4: 2 behold a *c.*, all of gold
Mat. 5:15 do men light a *c.* and put it
Luke 15: 8 light a *c.* and sweep the house
Rev. 1:20 seven *c.* are the seven churches
2: 5 I will remove thy *c.* out of his
18:23 light of the *c.* shine no more
22: 5 they need no *c.*, neither light

CAPTAIN
Num. 2: 3 shall be *c.* of the children of Judah
Josh. 5:14 as *c.* of the Lord's host am I
2 Chr. 13:12 God himself is our *c.*
Heb. 2:10 make the *c.* of their salvation perfect

CAPTIVE
Gen. 14:14 his brother was taken *c.*
Judg. 5:12 arise, Barak, lead thy captivity *c.*
Is. 49:24 mighty, or the lawful *c.* delivered
51:14 The *c.* exile hasteneth that he may
Jer. 22:12 whither they have led him *c.*
Amos 7:11 Israel shall surely be led away *c.*
2 Tim. 2:26 are taken *c.* by him at his will
3: 6 lead *c.* silly women laden with

CAPTIVITY
Deut. 30: 3 Lord thy God will turn thy *c.*
Job 42:10 the Lord turned the *c.* of Job

Ps. 14: 7 Lord bringeth back the *c.*
68:18 thou hast led *c.* captive
78:61 delivered his strength into *c.*
126: 1 turned again the *c.* of Zion
126: 4 turn again our *c.* as streams in south
Jer. 15: 2 such as are for *c.*, to the *c.*
29:14 I will turn away your *c.*
30: 3 bring again the *c.* of my people
Hos. 6:11 returned the *c.* of my people
Zeph. 2: 7 shall visit them and turn away their *c.*
Rom. 7:23 bringing me into *c.* to the law of sin
2 Cor. 10: 5 bringing into *c.* every thought
Eph. 4: 8 he led *c.* captive and gave gifts
Rev. 13:10 he that leadeth into *c.* shall go

CARE (CARED, CARETH)
Deut. 11:12 land which the Lord thy God *c.* for
Ps. 142: 4 no man *c.* for my soul
Mat. 13:22 and the *c.* of this world and the
Luke 10:40 dost thou not *c.* that my sister
John 10:13 hireling *c.* not for the sheep
12: 6 not that he *c.* for the poor
1 Cor. 7:21 *c.* not for it but if thou mayest
7:32 is unmarried *c.* for things of the Lord
9: 9 doth God take *c.* for oxen
2 Cor. 11:28 daily, the *c.* of all the churches
1 Tim. 3: 5 how shall he take *c.* of the church
1 Pet. 5: 7 *c.* upon him for he *c.* for you

CAREFUL
2 Ki. 4:13 thou hast been *c.* for us
Jer. 17: 8 shall not be *c.* in year of drought
Dan. 3:16 we are not *c.* to answer thee
Luke 10:41 Martha, thou art *c.* and troubled
Phil. 4: 6 be *c.* for nothing; but in every thing
4:10 were *c.* but ye lacked opportunity
Tit. 3: 8 might be *c.* to maintain good works

CARELESS
Is. 32: 9 hear my voice, ye *c.* daughters

CARNAL
Rom. 7:14 law is spiritual, but I am *c.*
8: 7 the *c.* mind is enmity against God
15:27 minister to them in *c.* things
1 Cor. 3: 1 as unto spiritual, but as unto *c.*
9:11 if we shall reap your *c.* things?
2 Cor. 10: 4 weapons of our warfare are not *c.*
Heb. 7:16 not after the law of a *c.* commandment
9:10 *c.* ordinances imposed on them until

CARNALLY
Rom. 8: 6 to be *c.* minded is death

CARPENTER (CARPENTERS, CARPENTER'S)
2 Sam. 5:11 and *c.*, and masons and they built David
Is. 41: 7 so the *c.* encouraged the goldsmith
Jer. 24: 1 with the *c.* and smiths from Jerusalem
Zech. 1:20 and the Lord showed me four *c.*
Mat. 13:55 Is not this the *c.* son?
Mark 6: 3 Is not this the *c.*, the son of Mary

CARRY (CARRIED)
Ex. 33:15 not with me *c.* us not up hence
Num. 11:12 say unto me *c.* them in thy bosom
Eccl. 10:20 bird of the air shall *c.* the voice
Is. 40:11 *c.* them in his bosom and shall gently
46: 4 even to hoar hairs will I *c.* you
Luke 10: 4 *c.* neither purse nor scrip, nor shoes
16:22 *c.* by the angels into Abraham's bosom
John 21:18 *c.* thee whither thou wouldest not
Eph. 4:14 *c.* about with every wind
1 Tim. 6: 7 it is certain we can *c.* nothing out
Heb. 13: 9 *c.* about with divers doctrines
Rev. 17: 3 *c.* me away in the spirit

CAST
Gen. 21:10 *c.* out this bondwoman and her son
Ex. 34:24 I will *c.* out the nations before thee
Lev. 18:24 which I *c.* out before thee
26:44 I will not *c.* away
Deut. 7: 1 *c.* out many nations before thee
2 Sam. 1:21 shield is vilely *c.* away
Neh. 9:26 *c.* thy law behind their backs
Job 8:20 God will not *c.* away perfect man
22:29 when men are *c.* down then
Ps. 2: 3 let us *c.* away their cords from us
22:10 *c.* upon thee from the womb
37:24 not be utterly *c.* down
42: 5 why art thou *c.* down
44: 9 but thou has *c.* off
55:22 *c.* thy burden on the Lord
71: 9 *c.* me not off in the time of old age
78:55 he *c.* out heathen also before them
80: 8 *c.* out the heathen
89:38 thou hast *c.* off and abhorred
94:14 the Lord will not *c.* his people
Prov. 1:14 *c.* in thy lot among us
16:33 the lot is *c.* into the lap
Eccl. 11: 1 *c.* thy bread upon the waters
Is. 2:20 man *c.* his idols of silver
14:19 thou art *c.* out of thy grave
26:19 the earth shall *c.* out the dead
38:17 hast *c.* all my sins behind thy back
41: 9 I will not *c.* thee away
58: 7 poor that are *c.* out to thy house
66: 5 *c.* you out for my name's sake
Jer. 7:15 I will *c.* you out of my sight
16:13 I will *c.* you out of this land
31:37 I will *c.* off all the seed of Israel
Lam. 3:31 the Lord will not *c.* off for ever
Ezek. 18:31 *c.* away all your transgressions
23:35 *c.* me behind thy back
Dan. 3:20 *c.* into the fiery furnace
Jonah 2: 4 I am *c.* out of thy sight
Mic. 7:19 *c.* all their sins into the sea
Nah. 3: 6 *c.* abominable filth on thee
Mal. 3:11 vine shall not *c.* her fruit
Mat. 3:10 hewn down and *c.* into the fire
5:25 thou be *c.* into prison
5:29 pluck it out *c.* it from thee
7: 5 *c.* the beam out of thine own eye
7: 6 neither *c.* pearls before swine
8:12 children of the kingdom shall be *c.* out
12:24 *c.* out devils but by Beelzebub
13:42 *c.* them into a furnace of fire
18:30 went and *c.* him into prison
21:12 *c.* out them that sold and bought
22:13 *c.* him into outer darkness
25:30 *c.* the unprofitable servant into
Mark 9:28 why could not we *c.* him out?
11:23 be thou *c.* into the sea
12: 8 *c.* him out of the vineyard
12:44 she of her want *c.* in all
16:17 in my name shall they *c.* out devils
Luke 1:29 she *c.* in her mind what
6:22 *c.* out your name as evil
12: 5 power to *c.* into hell
12:58 lest the officer *c.* thee into prison
John 6:37 I will in no wise *c.* out
8: 7 let him first *c.* a stone at her
12:31 prince of this world be *c.* out
Acts 16:23 they *c.* them into prison
Rom. 11: 1 hath God *c.* away his people
13:12 let us *c.* off the works of darkness
2 Cor. 4: 9 *c.* down but not destroyed
7: 6 comforteth those that are *c.* down
Gal. 4:30 *c.* out this bondwoman and her son
Heb. 10:35 *c.* not away your confidence
1 Tim. 5:12 they *c.* off their first faith
Rev. 2:10 *c.* some of you into prison
2:22 I will *c.* her into a bed, and them
12: 9 and the great dragon was *c.* out
20: 3 *c.* him into the bottomless pit

CASTETH
Job 21:10 cow *c.* not her calf
Ps. 147: 6 *c.* the wicked to the ground
Jer. 6: 7 so she *c.* out wickedness
Mat. 9:34 he *c.* out devils through Beelzebub
Mark 3:22 of the devils *c.* he out devils
Luke 11:15 *c.* out devils through Beelzebub
1 John 4:18 perfect love *c.* out fear
3 John 1:10 *c.* them out of the church

CASTING
Job 6:21 ye see my *c.* down and are afraid
Rom. 11:15 if the *c.* away of them be
2 Cor. 10: 5 *c.* down imaginations and every high
1 Pet. 5: 7 *c.* all your care upon him

CATTLE
Ps. 50:10 the *c.* upon a thousand hills
104: 14 grass to grow for the *c.*
Ezek. 34:17 I judge between *c.* and *c.*
John 4:12 drank thereof and his *c.*

CATCH (CAUGHT)
Judg. 21:21 and *c.* you every man his wife
Ps. 10: 9 he lieth in wait to *c.* the poor
35: 8 his net that he hid *c.* himself
109: 11 let the extortioner *c.* all he hath
Prov. 7:13 so she *c.* him and kissed him
Jer. 5:26 they set a trap, they *c.* men
Mark 12:13 they *c.* him in his words
Luke 5:10 henceforth thou shalt *c.* men
John 21: 3 that night they *c.* nothing
Acts 8:39 Spirit of the Lord *c.* away Philip
2 Cor. 12: 4 he was *c.* up into paradise
1 Thes. 4:17 remain shall be *c.* up together with
Rev. 12: 5 her child was *c.* up unto God

CAUSE
Ex. 9:16 for this *c.* have I raised thee up
22: 9 *c.* of both parties shall come before
23: 2 shalt thou speak in a *c.* to decline
23: 3 countenance a poor man in his *c.*
23: 6 wrest judgment of thy poor in his *c.*
Deut. 1:17 the *c.* that is too hard for you
Job 5: 8 to God would I commit my *c.*
6:24 *c.* me to understand wherein I
Ps. 9: 4 maintained my right and my *c.*
10:17 wilt *c.* thine ear to hear
35:23 judgment even unto my *c.*, my God
85: 4 *c.* thine anger towards us to cease
143: 8 *c.* me to know the way
Prov. 3:30 with a man without *c.*
18:17 that is first in his own *c.*
25: 9 debate thy *c.* with thy neighbour
Eccl. 7:10 the *c.* that is former days
Is. 3:12 which lead thee, *c.* thee to err
51:22 pleadeth the *c.* of his people
58:14 I will *c.* thee to ride
66: 9 and not *c.* to bring forth
Jer. 3:12 not *c.* my anger to fall
5:28 the *c.* of the fatherless
7: 3 *c.* you to dwell in this place
15: 4 *c.* them to be removed
15:11 *c.* the enemy to treat thee well
18: 2 I will *c.* thee to hear my words
32:37 I will *c.* them to dwell safely
Lam. 3:32 though he *c.* grief
3:36 to subvert a man in his *c.*
Ezek. 36:27 *c.* you to walk in statutes
37: 5 *c.* breath to enter into you
Dan. 9:17 *c.* thy face to shine upon thy
Mat. 5:22 without *c.* shall be in danger
19: 3 put away his wife for every *c.*
19: 5 For this *c.* shall a man
John 15:25 hated me without *c.*
1 Cor. 11:30 this *c.* many are weak and sickly
2 Cor. 4:16 for which *c.* we faint not
5:13 if we be sober it is for your *c.*
Eph. 5:31 For this *c.* shall a man
1 Tim. 9: 1 for this *c.* I obtained mercy

CAUSED (CAUSETH)
Prov. 7:21 fair speech *c.* him to yield
10: 5 in harvest is a son *c.* shame
18:18 the lot *c.* contentions to cease
19:27 cease instruction that *c.* to err
Mat. 5:32 *c.* her to commit adultery
2 Cor. 2:14 always *c.* us to triumph

CAVE (CAVES)
Gen. 19:30 he dwelt in a *c.*, he and his
23:19 buried Sarah his wife in the *c.*
25: 9 buried Abraham in the *c.*
49:29 bury me with my fathers in the *c.*
Josh. 10:16 hid themselves in a *c.*
Is. 2:19 go to *c.* for fear of the Lord
Ezek. 33:27 be in the *c.* shall die of pestilence
John 11:38 to the grave. It was a *c.*
Heb. 11:38 wandered in the *c.* of the earth

CEASE (CEASETH)
Gen. 8:22 day and night shall not *c.*
Neh. 6: 3 why should the work *c.*
Job 3:17 wicked *c.* from troubling
Ps. 12: 1 Help, Lord; for the godly man *c.*
37: 8 *c.* from anger and wrath
46: 9 he maketh wars to *c.* unto the end
Prov. 19:27 *c.* to hear instruction
23: 4 *c.* from thine own wisdom

Prov. 26:20 where there is no talebearer, the strife *c.*
Acts 13:10 wilt thou not *c.* to pervert
1 Cor. 13: 8 tongues, they shall *c.*
Eph. 1:16 *c.* not to give thanks for
Col. 1: 9 *c.* not to pray for you
2 Pet. 2:14 that cannot *c.* from sin

CEASING
Rom 1: 9 without *c.* I make mention
1 Thes. 5:17 pray without *c.*
2:13 thank we God without *c.*.
2 Tim. 1: 3 without *c.* I have remembrance

CEDAR (CEDARS)
Lev. 14: 4 and *c.* wood and scarlet
2 Ki. 14: 9 sent to *c.* that was in Lebanon
Ps. 29: 5 voice of the Lord breaketh *c.*
92:12 grow like a *c.* in Lebanon
Sol. 1:17 beams of our house are *c.*
5:15 countenance excellent as *c.*
Is. 9:10 we will change them into *c.*
Ezek. 17: 3 took the highest branch of the *c.*
31: 3 the Assyrian was a *c.* in Lebanon

CHAFF
Job 21:18 as *c.* that the storm carrieth away
Ps. 1: 4 the *c.* which the wind driveth away
35: 5 be as *c.* before the wind
Is. 5:24 the flame consumeth the *c.*
17:13 chased as the *c.* of mountains
33:11 ye shall conceive *c.*
41:15 make the hills as *c.*
Jer. 23:28 what is the *c.* to the wheat
Dan. 2:35 became like *c.* of the summer
Hos. 13: 3 as the *c.* that is driven
Zeph. 2: 2 before the day pass as the *c.*
Mat. 3:12 burn up the *c.* in unquenchable
Luke 3:17 the *c.* he will burn with fire

CHAIN (CHAINS)
Gen. 41:42 gold *c.* about his neck
Ps. 73: 6 compasseth them as a *c.*
149: 8 to bind their kings with *c.*
Prov. 1: 9 thy head and *c.* about thy neck
Is. 3:19 Lord will take away thy *c.*
Ezek. 7:23 Make a *c.* for the land is full
16:11 I put a *c.* on thy neck
Dan. 5: 7 have a gold *c.* about his neck
Acts 12: 7 Peter's *c.* fell from his hands
28:20 I am bound with this *c.*
2 Tim. 1:16 was not ashamed of my *c.*
2 Pet. 2: 4 delivered into the *c.* of darkness
Jude 1: 6 reserved in everlasting *c.*
Rev. 20: 1. a great *c.* in his hand

CHAMBER (CHAMBERS)
Gen. 43:30 Joseph entered into his *c.* and wept
Job 9: 9 Pleiades, and the *c.* of the south
Ps. 19: 5 bridegroom coming out of his *c.*
104: 3 beams of his *c.* in the waters
Prov. 7:27 going down to the *c.* of death
Sol. 1: 4 the king brought me to his *c.*
Is. 26:20 enter thou into thy *c.* and shut
Joel 2:16 bridegroom go forth of his *c.*
Dan. 6:10 windows being open in his *c.* toward Jerusalem
Mat. 24:26 he is in the secret *c.*

CHANCE
1 Sam. 6: 9 it was a *c.* that happened
2 Sam. 1: 6 I happened by *c.* upon Mount Gilboa
Eccl. 9:11 time and *c.* happeneth to them all
Luke 10:31 by *c.* there came down a certain priest

CHANGE (CHANGED, CHANGETH)
Job 14:14 time will I wait till my *c.* come
17:12 *c.* the night into day
Ps. 102: 26 as a vesture shalt thou *c.* them
Prov. 24:21 with them that are given to *c.*
Jer. 13:23 can the Ethiopian *c.* his skin
Dan. 2:21 he *c.* times and seasons
3:27 neither were their coats *c.*
7:25 think to *c.* times and laws
Mal. 3: 6 I am the Lord, I *c.* not
Rom. 1:23 *c.* the glory of the uncorruptible God
1:25 *c.* the truth of God into a lie
1:26 women did *c.* the natural use
2 Cor. 3:18 *c.* into the same image into glory
Phil. 3:21 Christ shall *c.* our vile bodies
Heb. 1:12 they shall be *c.*: but thou art
7:12 necessity a *c.* also of the law

CHANGES
Job 10:17 *c.* and war are against me

Ps. 55:19 they have no *c.*, therefore they fear

CHARGE (CHARGED)
Gen. 26: 5 obeyed my voice and kept my *c.*
28: 6 as he blessed him he gave him a *c.*
Ex. 6:13 gave them a *c.* unto the children
Job 1:22 nor *c.* God foolishly
4:18 *c.* his angels with folly
Ps. 35:11 to my *c.* things that I knew not
91:11 give his angels *c.* over thee
Sol. 2: 7 I *c.* you, O daughters of Jerusalem
8: 4 I *c.* you, O daughters of Jerusalem
Mat. 4: 6 He shall give his angels *c.*
Luke 4:10 He shall give his angels *c.*
9:21 and he straightly *c.* them
Acts 7:60 lay not to their *c.*
16:24 such a *c.* thrust into the inner prison
23:29 nothing laid to his *c.* worthy of
Rom. 8:33 lay to the *c.* of God's elect
1 Cor. 9:18 make the gospel without *c.*
1 Thes. 2:11 *c.* every one as a father
1 Tim. 1:18 this *c.* I commit to thee
6:13 I give thee *c.* in the sight of God
6:17 *c.* them that are rich
2 Tim. 4:16 be laid to their *c.*

CHARIOT (CHARIOTS)
Gen. 41:43 the second *c.* which he had
Ex. 14: 6 made ready his *c.*
14:25 and took off their *c.* wheels
Josh. 17:16 of the valley have *c.* of iron
1 Sam. 8:11 take sons for his *c.*
2 Sam. 8: 4 took from him a thousands *c.*
1 Ki. 10:26 Solomon gathered together *c.* and horsemen
6:17 mountain full of *c.* and horses
2 Ki. 14: 2 *c.* of fire
13:14 the *c.* of Israel
Ps. 20: 7 some trust in *c.*,
68:17 the *c.* of God are twenty thousand
104: 3 who maketh the clouds his *c.*
Sol. 1: 9 a company of horses in Pharaoh's *c.*
6:12 like the *c.* of Amminadib
Is. 21: 7 a *c.* of asses, and a *c.* of
22:18 there the *c.* of thy glory
31: 1 stay on horses and trust in *c.*
Hab. 3: 8 and thy *c.* of salvation
Zech. 6: 1 four *c.* between two mountains
Acts 8:28 sitting in his *c.* read Esaias
Rev. 9: 9 sound of wings as of *c.*

CHARITY
1 Cor. 8: 1 knowledge puffeth up but *c.* edifieth
13: 2 have not *c.* I am nothing
13:13 faith, hope, *c.* . . . but the greatest is *c.*
Col. 3:14 above all these things put on *c.*
1 Thes. 3: 6 tidings of your faith and *c.*
2 Thes. 1: 3 *c.* of every one aboundeth
1 Tim. 1: 5 end of commandment is *c.*
2:15 if they continue in faith and *c.*
4:12 be thou an example in *c.*
2 Tim. 2:22 follow righteousness, faith, *c.*
3:10 known my doctrine, faith, *c.*
Tit. 2: 2 aged men be sound in *c.*
1 Pet. 4: 8 fervent *c.* among yourselves for *c.*
5:14 greet one another with a kiss of *c.*
2 Pet. 1: 7 to brotherly kindness, *c.*
3 John 1: 6 borne witness of thy *c.*
Jude 1:12 spots in your feasts of *c.*
Rev. 2:19 I know thy works and *c.*

CHARITABLY
Rom. 14:15 now walkest thou not *c.*

CHASTE
2 Cor. 11: 2 as a *c.* virgin to Christ
Tit. 2: 5 young women discreet, *c.*
1 Pet. 3: 2 they behold your *c.* conversation

CHASTEN (CHASTENED, CHASTENEST)
Deut. 8: 5 as man *c.* his son so the Lord
2 Sam. 7:14 I will *c.* him with the rod
Ps. 6: 1 neither *c.* me in thy
69:10 *c.* my soul with fasting
94:12 blessed is the man whom thou *c.*
118: 18 the Lord hath *c.* me sore
Prov. 13:24 loveth him *c.* him betimes
19:18 *c.* thy son while there is hope
Dan. 10:12 to *c.* thyself before God
1 Cor. 11:32 we are *c.* of the Lord
2 Cor. 6: 9 as *c.* and not killed

Heb. 12: 6 whom the Lord loveth he *c.*
12:10 fathers for few days *c.* us
Rev. 3:19 as many as I love, I *c.*

CHASTENING
Job 5:17 despise not thou *c.* of the Lord
Prov. 3:11 despise not the *c.* of
Is. 26:16 when thy *c.* was upon them
Heb. 12: 5 despise not thou *c.* of the Lord
12: 7 if ye endure *c.*, God dealeth
12:11 no *c.* for present seemeth joyous

CHASTISE
Lev. 26:28 will *c.* you seven times
Deut. 22:18 the elders shall *c.* him
Hos. 7:12 I will *c.* as their congregation
10:10 my desire that I should *c.* them
Luke 23:16 *c.* him and release him

CHASTISEMENT
Job 34:31 I have borne *c.*, I will not
Is. 53: 5 *c.* of our peace was upon him
Jer. 30:14 with the *c.* of a cruel one
Heb. 12: 8 without *c.* then are ye bastards

CHEEK
1 Ki. 22:24 smote Micaiah on the *c.*
Job 16:10 smitten me upon the *c.* reproachfully
Mic. 5: 1 judge of Israel, with a rod upon the *c.*
Mat. 5:39 smite thee on the right *c.*, turn
Luke 6:29 smiteth thee on the one *c.* offer

CHEER (CHEERETH)
Deut. 24: 5 and shall *c.* up his wife
Judg. 9:13 leave my wine, which *c.* God and man
Eccl. 11: 9 let thy heart *c.* thee
Mat. 9: 2 Son, be of good *c.*; thy sins be
14:27 Be of good *c.*; it is I; be
John 16:33 be of good *c.*, I have overcome
Acts 23:11 Be of good *c.*, Paul
27:25 be of good *c.*, for I believe

CHERISHETH
Eph. 5:29 own flesh but nourisheth and *c.* it
1 Thes. 2: 7 as a nurse *c.* her children

CHICKENS
Mat. 23:37 gathereth her *c.* under her wings

CHIEF
Num. 31:26 the *c.* fathers of the congregation
2 Ki. 25:18 took Seraiah the *c.* priest
1 Chr. 7: 3 all of them *c.* men
Job 40:19 he is the *c.* of the ways of God
Ps. 78:51 the *c.* of their strength
Mat. 16:21 the elders and *c.* priests and scribes
20:27 whoso will be *c.* among you
Luke 22:26 is *c.*, as he that serveth
Eph. 2:20 himself being the *c.* corner stone
1 Tim. 1:15 sinners, of whom I am *c.*
1 Pet. 2: 6 in Sion a *c.* corner stone

CHILD
2 Sam. 12:16 David besought God for a *c.*
1 Ki. 3: 7 I am not but a little *c.*
3:25 divide the living *c.* in two
2 Ki. 5:14 like unto the flesh of a little *c.*
Job 33:25 shall be fresher than a *c.*
Ps. 131: 2 quieted as a *c.* that is weaned
Prov. 20:11 even a *c.* is known by his doings
22: 6 train up a *c.* in the way he
22:15 bound in the heart of the *c.*
Eccl. 4:13 better is as poor and wise *c.*
10:16 woe when thy king is a *c.*
Is. 7:16 before the *c.* shall know to refuse
9: 6 for unto us a *c.* is born
11: 6 and a little *c.* shall lead them
11: 8 and the sucking *c.* shall play
65:20 for the *c.* shall die an hundred
Jer. 31:20 is he a pleasant *c.*?
Hos. 11: 1 when Israel was a *c.* I loved
Mat. 18: 5 receive one such little *c.* in my name
Luke 2:34 this *c.* is set for the fall
9:48 shall receive this *c.* in my name
18:17 as a little *c.* shall in no wise
Gal. 4: 1 as long as he is a *c.*
Rev. 12: 5 a man *c.* who was to rule

CHILDBEARING
1 Tim. 2:15 she shall be saved in *c.* if

CHILDISH
1 Cor. 13:11 a man, I put away *c.* things

CHILDLESS

Gen. 15: 2 seeing I go *c.*, and the steward
Jer. 22:30 write ye this man *c.*

CHILDREN

Gen. 3:16 thou shalt bring forth *c.*
18:19 he will command his *c.*
30: 1 give me *c.* or else I die
50:25 an oath of the *c.* of Israel
Ex. 1: 7 *c.* of Israel were fruitful
13:15 firstborn of my *c.* I redeem
20: 5 iniquity of the fathers upon the *c.*
29:45 dwell among the *c.* of Israel
34: 7 upon the *c.* and the children's *c.*
Lev. 25:45 *c.* of the strangers that do sojourn
Num. 14:33 your *c.* shall wander forty years
Deut. 6: 7 teach them diligently unto thy *c.*
24:16 to death for the *c.*, neither shall the *c.*
32: 5 their spot is not the spot of his *c.*
1 Ki. 2: 4 thy *c.* take heed to their way
6:13 dwell among the *c.* of Israel
9:20 were not of the *c.* of Israel
2 Ki. 17:31 Sepharvites burnt their *c.*
2 Chr. 33: 6 cause his *c.* to pass through
Ps. 17:14 they are full of *c.* and leave
69: 8 an alien to my mother's *c.*
72: 4 he shall save the *c.* of the needy
82: 6 all of you are *c.* of the Most High
89:30 If his *c.* forsake my law
103: 17 righteousness unto children's *c.*
127: 4 mighty men so are *c.* of the youth
128: 3 thy *c.* like olive plants
128: 6 thou shalt see thy children's *c.*
147: 13 hath blessed thy *c.* within thee
Prov. 17: 6 glory of *c.* are their fathers
20: 7 his *c.* are blessed after him
31:28 her *c.* rise and call her blessed
Is. 1: 2 I brought up *c.* and they rebelled
2: 6 in the *c.* of strangers
8:18 I and the *c.* whom the Lord hath
54:13 thy *c.* shall be taught of the Lord
57: 5 slaying the *c.* in the valleys
Jer. 3:14 backsliding *c.*, wise to evil
7:18 *c.* gather wood, and the fathers
31:15 Rahel weeping for her *c.*
Lam. 4: 4 the young *c.* ask for bread
Ezek. 16:21 that thou hast slain my *c.*
Dan. 5:13 of the *c.* of the captivity of Judah
Nah. 3:10 her young *c.* also were dashed in pieces
Mal. 4: 6 turn the hearts of fathers to the *c.*
Mat. 2:18 Rachel weeping for her *c.*,
3: 9 raise up the *c.* unto Abraham
5: 9 be called the *c.* of God
5:45 *c.* of the Father in heaven
8:12 but the *c.* of the kingdom
11:19 wisdom is justified of her *c.*
21:15 the *c.* crying in the temple
23:31 the *c.* of them which killed
23:37 have gathered thy *c.* together
Luke 6:32 *c.* sitting in the marketplace
6:35 ye shall be *c.* of the Highest
11: 7 my *c.* are with me in bed
16: 8 for the *c.* of this world are in
20:34 the *c.* of this world marry
20:36 *c.* of God being the *c.* of the resurrection
John 11:52 together in one the *c.* of God
12:36 ye may be the *c.* of light
Acts 2:39 promise unto you and to your *c.*
3:25 ye are the *c.* of the prophets
Rom. 8:16 we are the *c.* of God
8:17 if *c.* then heirs; heirs of God
8:21 liberty of the *c.* of God
9: 7 seed of Abraham, are they all *c.*
9: 8 *c.* of the promise are counted
9:26 they shall be called *c.* of the
1 Cor. 14:20 in malice be ye *c.* in understanding
2 Cor. 12:14 *c.* ought not to lay up for the
Gal. 3: 7 same are the *c.* of Abraham
3:26 all the *c.* of God by
4: 3 we, when we were *c.*, were in bondage
4:28 are the *c.* of the promise
Eph. 1: 5 unto the adoption of *c.* by Jesus
2: 3 by nature the *c.* of wrath
4:14 no more *c.* tossed to and fro
5: 6 upon the *c.* of disobedience
5: 8 walk as *c.* of light
6: 1 *c.*, obey your parents
6: 4 fathers provoke not your *c.*
Col. 3: 6 on the *c.* of disobedience
3:20 *c.*, obey your parents
3:21 provoke not your *c.* to anger
1 Thes. 5: 5 ye are all *c.* of light
1 Tim. 5: 4 if any widow have *c.* or
Heb. 2:14 as the *c.* are partakers of flesh
12: 5 speaketh unto you as unto *c.*
1 Pet 1:14 as obedient *c.*; not fashioning
1 John 3:10 *c.* of God are manifest, and the *c.*
5: 2 that we love the *c.* of God

CHOKE (CHOKED)

Mat. 13: 7 thorns sprung up and *c.* them
Mark 4:19 things entering in *c.* the word
5:13 and were *c.* in the sea
Luke 8:14 and are *c.* with cares and riches

CHOOSE (CHOOSEST, CHOOSING, CHOSE)

Gen. 13:11 Lot *c.* the plain of
Num. 17: 5 the man's rod whom I shall *c.*
Deut. 12: 5 place the Lord God shall *c.*
17:10 the Lord shall *c.* shall show
17:15 whom the Lord thy God shall *c.*
30:19 therefore *c.* life, that both thou
Josh. 24:15 *c.* you this day whom ye will serve
2 Sam. 24:12 three things, *c.* thee one of them
Neh. 9: 7 Lord God didst *c.* Abraham
Ps. 65: 4 blessed is the man whom thou *c.*
Prov. 1:29 did not *c.* the fear of the Lord
Is. 7:15 refuse evil and *c.* good
14: 1 the Lord will yet *c.* Israel
56: 4 *c.* the things that please me
Zech. 1:17 I shall yet *c.* Jerusalem
Luke 6:13 he *c.* twelve, whom
Phil. 1:22 what I shall *c.* I wot not
Heb. 11:25 *c.* rather to suffer affliction with the

CHOSEN

Judg. 10:14 unto the gods which you have *c.*
1 Sam. 16: 8 neither hath the Lord *c.* this
1 Ki. 8:48 city which thou hast *c.*
Job 36:21 iniquity *c.* rather than affliction
Ps. 105: 43 with joy and his *c.* with gladness
119: 30 I have *c.* the way of truth
119: 73 I have *c.* his precepts
Prov. 16:16 rather to be *c.* than silver
Is. 41: 8 Jacob, whom I have *c.*, the seed
41: 9 my servant, I have *c.* thee
43:20 give drink to my people, my *c.*
44: 1 Israel, whom I have *c.*
48:10 I have *c.* thee in the furnace of
58: 5 is it such a fast that I have *c.*
65:15 for a curse unto my *c.*
Jer. 8: 3 death shall be *c.* rather than
33:24 families which the Lord hath *c.*
49:19 who is a *c.* man that I may
Mat. 20:16 many be called, but few *c.*
Mark 13:20 elect's sake, whom he hath *c.*
Luke 10:42 Mary hath *c.* that good part
23:35 Christ the *c.* of God
John 13:18 I know whom I have *c.*
15:16 Ye have not *c.* me
Acts 9:15 for he is a *c.* vessel unto me
1 Cor. 1:27 God hath *c.* the foolish
Eph. 1: 4 *c.* us in him before the foundation
1 Pet. 2: 4 *c.* of God, and precious
Rev. 17:14 called, and *c.* and faithful

CHRIST

Mat. 2: 4 where *C.* should be born
16:16 thou art the *C.* the Son
23: 8 one is your master, even *C.*,
Mark 9:41 because ye belong to *C.*
Luke 2:26 not die before seeing *C.*
4:41 the devils knew he was *C.*
24:26 ought not *C.* to have suffered
24:46 it behooved *C.* to suffer and rise
John 4:25 Messias cometh which is called *C.*
7:26 that this is the very *C.*
7:27 when *C.* cometh, no man knoweth
7:41 shall *C.* come out of Galilee?
7:42 *C.* cometh of the seed of David
11:27 I believe that thou art the *C.*
12:34 that *C.* abideth for ever
Acts 8: 5 Samaria, and preached *C.* unto them
Rom. 5: 6 *C.* died for the ungodly
5: 8 while yet sinners, *C.* died for us
6: 8 if we be dead with *C.*
8: 1 them which are in *C.* Jesus
8: 2 law of the spirit of life in *C.* Jesus
8: 9 have not the Spirit of *C.*, he is none of
8:10 if *C.* be not in you, the body is dead
8:17 heirs of God and joint heirs with *C.*
12: 5 many, one body in *C.*
15: 3 for *C.* pleased not himself; but
1 Cor. 1:24 *C.* the power of God and
1:30 but of him are ye in *C.* Jesus
2: 2 save Jesus *C.*, and him crucified
3:23 ye are *C.*'s, and *C.* is God's
5: 7 *C.* our passover is sacrificed
15:14 if *C.* be not risen, then is
15:16 if dead rise not, *C.* is not raised
15:18 fallen asleep in *C.* are perished
15:19 if in this life only we have hope in *C.*
2 Cor. 5:17 if any man be in *C.*
5:19 God was in *C.* reconciling the world
6:16 though we have known *C.* after
12: 2 I knew a man in *C.* above fourteen years
13: 5 know ye not *C.* Jesus is in you?
Gal. 1:22 churches which were in *C.*
2:20 I am crucified with *C.*
3:13 *C.* hath redeemed us from the curse
3:28 ye are all one in *C.* Jesus
4:19 travail till *C.* be formed in you
5: 6 in *C.* Jesus neither circumcision nor
Eph. 1: 1 faithful in *C.* Jesus
2: 5 quickened us together with *C.*
2:10 created in *C.* Jesus unto good works
2:12 ye were without *C.*, aliens
3:17 that *C.* dwell in your hearts
4:20 ye have not so learned *C.*, if so
5:14 dead, and *C.* shall give thee light
5:23 wife, as *C.* is head of the church
6: 5 in singleness of heart, as unto *C.*
Phil. 1:13 so that my bonds in *C.* are manifest in all
1:21 to live is *C.* and to die
1:23 desire to depart and be with *C.*
2: 1 if there be any consolation in *C.*
2:11 confess that *C.* Jesus is Lord
3: 3 rejoice in *C.* Jesus
3: 8 that I may win *C.*
3:12 for which I am apprehended of *C.* Jesus
4:13 I can do all things through *C.*
Col. 1: 2 saints and faithful in *C.*
1:27 *C.* in you hope of glory
2: 6 received *C.* Jesus the Lord
2:20 if ye be dead with *C.* from the
3: 3 and your life is hid with *C.* in God
1 Thes. 4:16 the dead in *C.* shall rise first
1 Tim. 1:15 *C.* Jesus came into world to save
2 Tim. 2: 3 as a good soldier of *C.* Jesus
3:12 will live godly in *C.* Jesus shall suffer
Heb. 13: 8 *C.* Jesus the same yesterday, and
Rev. 20: 4 reigned with *C.* a thousand years

CHRISTIAN (CHRISTIANS)

Acts 11:26 were called *C.* first at Antioch
26:28 persuadest me to be a *C.*

CHURCH

Mat. 16:18 this rock I will build my *c.*
18:17 tell it unto the *c.*
Acts 2:47 the Lord added to the *c.* daily
5:11 great fear came on all the *c.*
8: 1 great persecution against the *c.*
11:26 assembled themselves with the *c.*
14:27 and had gathered the *c.* together
15: 3 brought on their way by the *c.*
15:22 pleased elders, with the whole *c.*
20:28 to feed the *c.* of God
1 Cor. 1: 2 *c.* of God which is at Corinth
4:17 teach every where in the *c.*
10:32 nor to the *c.* of God
14: 4 he that prophesieth edifieth the *c.*
16:19 *c.* that is in their house,
2 Cor. 1: 1 unto the *c.* of God
Eph. 1:22 head over all things to the *c.*
3:10 heavenly places known by the *c.*
5:24 as the *c.* is subject unto Christ
5:25 as Christ loved the *c.* and gave
5:27 present to himself a glorious *c.*
5:32 I speak concerning Christ and the *c.*
Phil. 3: 6 Concerning zeal, persecuting the *c.*
4:15 no *c.* communicated with me
Col. 1:18 he is head of the body, the *c.*
1:24 for his body's sake, which is the *c.*
4:15 the *c.* which is in his house
1 Tim. 3: 5 take care of the *c.* of God
5:16 let not the *c.* be charged
Heb. 12:23 assembly and *c.* of the firstborn
3 John 1: 6 witness of thy charity before the *c.*
1: 9 I wrote unto the *c.*: but

CHURCHES
Acts 9:31 then had the *c.* rest throughout
15:41 and Cilicia, confirming the *c.*
16: 5 the *c.* established in faith
Rom. 16:16 *c.* of Christ salute you
1 Cor. 7:17 and so ordain I in all *c.*
14:33 as in all *c.* of the saints
14:34 women keep silence in the *c.*
1 Thes. 2:14 became followers of the *c.* of God
2 Thes. 1: 4 glory in you in the *c.* of God
Rev. 1: 4 seven *c.* which are in Asia
2: 7 hear what the Spirit saith unto the *c.*
22:16 testify these things in the *c.*

CIRCUMCISE (CIRCUMCISED)
Gen. 17:10 every male shall be *c.*
17:11 ye shall *c.* the flesh
21: 4 Abraham *c.* his son Isaac, being eight
Deut. 30: 6 the Lord will *c.* thy heart
10:16 *c.* therefore the foreskin
Josh. 5: 2 *c.* again the children of Israel
5: 4 the cause why Joshua did *c.*
Jer. 4: 4 *c.* yourselves to the Lord
9:25 all which are *c.* with uncircumcised
Acts 15: 1 except the *c.* cannot be saved
15:24 ye must be *c.* and keep the law
16: 3 *c.* him because of the Jews
Gal. 2: 3 Titus...was compelled to be *c.*
Phil. 3: 5 *c.* the eighth day, of the stock
Col. 2:11 in whom also ye are *c.*

CIRCUMCISION
John 7:22 Moses therefore gave unto you *c.*
Acts 7: 8 God gave the covenant of *c.*
Rom. 2:25 *c.* verily profiteth if thou keep the
2:29 *c.* is that of the heart, in the spirit
3: 1 what profit is there of *c.*?
3:30 which shall justify the *c.* by faith
4: 9 cometh this blessedness on the *c.* only?
4:11 he received the sign of *c.*
15: 8 Christ was minister of the *c.*
1 Cor. 7:19 *c.* is nothing, but the keeping
Gal. 2: 7 as the gospel of *c.* was unto Peter
5: 6 neither *c.* availeth nor uncircumcision
Phil. 3: 3 we are the *c.* which worship
Col. 2:11 with the *c.* made without hands
Tit. 1:10 deceivers, specially of the *c.*

CISTERN (CISTERNS)
2 Ki. 18:31 every one the waters of his *c.*
Prov. 5:15 waters out of thine own *c.*
Jer. 2:13 hewed them out *c.*, broken *c.*

CITY
Gen. 4:17 he builded a *c.*, and called the name
Josh. 21:13 to be a *c.* of refuge
Neh. 11: 1 to dwell in Jerusalem the holy *c.*
Ps. 48: 2 the *c.* of the great King
107: 4 they found no *c.* to dwell in
127: 1 except the Lord keep the *c.*
Prov. 16:32 than he that taketh a *c.*
Sol. 3: 2 I will go about the *c.* in
Is. 1:21 is the faithful *c.* become a harlot
22: 2 a tumultuous *c.* a joyous *c.*
26: 1 We have a strong *c.*, salvation
33:20 look on Zion, *c.* of our solemnities
48: 2 call themselves of the holy *c.*
62:12 sought out, a *c.* not forsaken
Jer. 3:14 take you one of a *c.*, two of a
29: 7 seek the peace of the *c.*
Lam. 1: 1 How doth the *c.* sit solitary
Dan. 9:24 upon thy holy *c.* to finish
Amos 4: 7 to rain on one *c.* not on
Zeph. 2:15 this is the rejoicing *c.*
Zech. 8: 3 shall be called the *c.* of truth
Mat. 4: 5 devil taketh him into the holy *c.*
5:14 *c.* on a hill cannot be hid
5:35 the *c.* of the great king
9: 1 and came into his own *c.*
27:53 resurrections and went into the holy *c.*
Luke 10: 8 whatsoever *c.* ye enter
10:12 tolerable for Sodom than for that *c.*
19:41 he beheld the *c.* and wept over it
Heb. 11:10 he looked for a *c.* which
11:16 he hath prepared for them a *c.*
12:22 to the *c.* of the living God
13:14 have here no continuing *c.*
Rev. 3:12 name of the *c.* of my God
11: 2 holy *c.* shall they tread
21: 2 John saw the holy *c.*
21:18 the *c.* was pure gold, like unto
21:23 *c.* had no need of the sun
22:19 and out of the holy *c.*

CITIES
Num. 35:15 these six *c.* shall be refuge
Luke 19:17 have thou authority over ten *c.*
Rev. 16:19 the *c.* of the nations fell

CITIZEN (CITIZENS)
Luke 15:15 joined himself to a *c.*
19:14 but his *c.* hated him
Acts 21:39 a *c.* of no mean city
Eph. 2:19 fellow *c.* with the saints

CLAY
Job 10: 9 that thou hast made me as *c.*
4:19 them tat dwell in houses of *c.*
38:14 it is turned as *c.* to the seal
Is. 41:25 as the potter treadeth *c.*
45: 9 shall the *c.* say to him
64: 8 we are the *c.*, thou our potter
Jer. 18: 4 that he made of *c.* was marred
18: 6 the *c.* is in the potter's hands
43: 9 hide them in the *c.* in the kiln
Dan. 2:33 feet part of iron, part of *c.*
John 9: 6 made *c.* of spittle and anointed
Rom. 9:21 power over the *c.*

CLEAN
Gen. 7: 2 of every *c.* beast thou shalt
8:20 took of every *c.* beast
Lev. 10:10 unholy and between unclean and *c.*
Job 14: 4 bring a *c.* thing out of unclean
17: 9 he that hath *c.* hands shall be
25: 4 how can he be *c.* that is born
Ps. 19: 9 the fear of the Lord is *c.*
22:15 my tongue *c.* to my jaws
24: 4 that hath *c.* hands and
44:25 our belly *c.* unto the earth
51:10 in me a *c.* heart, O God
73: 1 such as are of a *c.* heart
Prov. 16: 2 ways of man are *c.* in his own
Is. 1:16 wash you, make you *c.*; put
52:11 be ye *c.* that bear the vessels
Jer. 13:27 wilt thou not be made *c.*
Ezek. 22:26 between unclean and *c.*
36:25 *c.* water upon you, and ye shall be *c.*
44:23 discern between the unclean and the *c.*
Mat. 8: 3 I will, be thou *c.*
23:25 make *c.* the outside of the cup
Luke 11:41 all things are *c.* to you
John 13:11 said he, Ye are not all *c.*
Rev. 19: 8 fine linen, *c.* and white

CLEANNESS
Ps. 18:24 according to the *c.* of my hands
Amos 4: 6 given you *c.* of teeth

CLEANSE (CLEANSED, CLEANSETH)
2 Chr. 30:19 though he be not *c.* according
Ps. 19:12 *c.* me from secret faults
51: 2 *c.* me from my sin
73:13 I have *c.* my heart in vain
119: 9 shall a young man *c.* his way
Jer. 33: 8 I will *c.* them from all sin
Ezek. 36:25 from idols will I *c.* you
36:33 *c.* you from all iniquities
Mat. 10: 8 heal the sick, *c.* the lepers
11: 5 lame walk, the lepers are *c.*
Luke 17:17 were there not ten *c.*
Acts 10:15 what God hath *c.*, that call not
2 Cor. 7: 1 let us *c.* ourselves from
Eph. 5:26 *c.* with washing of water
Jas. 4: 8 *c.* your hands, ye sinners
1 John 1: 7 blood of Jesus Christ *c.* us from all

CLEAR
Ex. 34: 7 no means *c.* the guilty
Ps. 51: 4 be *c.* when thou judgest
Sol. 6:10 *c.* as the sun, and terrible as
Zech. 14: 6 light shall not be *c.* nor dark

CLEAVE (CLEAVETH)
Gen. 2:24 and shall *c.* unto his wife
Deut. 4: 4 ye that did *c.* to the Lord
11:22 his ways, and to *c.* unto him
Josh. 23: 8 but *c.* unto the Lord your God
Ps. 137: 6 tongue *c.* to the roof of my mouth
Mat. 19: 5 and shall *c.* to his wife
Mark 10: 7 mother and *c.* to his wife
Rom. 12: 9 *c.* to that which is good

CLOAK
Is. 59:17 and was clad with zeal as a *c.*
Mat. 5:40 let him have thy *c.* also
John 15:22 have no *c.* for their sin
2 Tim. 4:13 the *c.* that I left at Troas
1 Pet. 2:16 liberty for a *c.* of maliciousness

CLOSET
Joel 2:16 and the bride out of her *c.*
Mat. 6: 6 when thou prayest, enter thy *c.*

CLOTHE (CLOTHED)
Gen. 3:21 God make coats of skins and *c.* them
Job 10:11 *c.* me with skin and flesh
Ps. 35:26 let them be *c.* with shame
104: 1 *c.* with honour and majesty
109: 18 he *c.* himself with cursing
132: 9 priests be *c.* with righteousness
132: 18 his enemies will I *c.* with shame
Is. 61:10 *c.* with garments of salvation
Ezek. 16:10 I *c.* thee with broidered
Zeph. 1: 8 *c.* with strange apparel
Zech. 3: 3 Joshua was *c.* with filthy garments
Mat. 6:30 God so *c.* the grass of the
11: 8 a man *c.* in soft raiment
25:36 naked, and ye *c.* me: I was
2 Cor. 5: 2 desiring to be *c.* upon with
5: 4 not unclothed, but *c.* upon
1 Pet. 5: 5 be *c.* with humility: for
Rev. 3: 5 be *c.* with white raiment
12: 1 a woman *c.* with the sun
19:13 *c.* in vesture dipped in blood
19:14 *c.* in fine linen, clean and white

CLOTHING
Job 22: 6 stripped naked of their *c.*
Ps. 45:13 her *c.* is of wrought gold
Prov. 31:25 strength and honour are her *c.*
Is. 59:17 garment of vengeance for *c.*
Mat. 7:15 which come to you in sheep's *c.*
Mark 12:38 love to go in long *c.*
Acts 10:30 stood before me in bright *c.*
Jas. 2: 3 to him that weareth the gay *c.*

CLOUD (CLOUDS)
Gen. 9:13 set my bow in the *c.*
Ex. 14:20 it was a *c.* and darkness to them
19: 9 I come unto thee in a thick *c.*
Judg. 5: 4 the *c.* also dropped water
2 Sam. 23: 4 even a morning without *c.*
Ps. 36: 5 faithfulness reacheth to the *c.*
57:10 and thy truth unto the *c.*
104: 3 who maketh *c.* his chariot
Eccl. 11: 4 regardeth the *c.* shall not reap
Is. 44:22 blotted out as a thick *c.*
Mat. 24:30 coming in the *c.* of heaven
Mark 14:62 coming in the *c.* of heaven
1 Cor. 10: 1 our fathers were under the *c.*
1 Thes. 4:17 with them in the *c.*, to meet
Heb. 12: 1 so great a *c.* of witnesses
2 Pet. 2:17 *c.* that are carried with a tempest
Jude 1:12 *c.* without water, carried about
Rev. 1: 7 he cometh with the *c.*
11:12 ascended up to heaven in a *c.*

COAL (COALS)
2 Sam. 14: 7 shall quench my *c.* which
Job 41:21 his breath kindleth *c.*
Ps. 18: 8 *c.* were kindled by it
140: 10 let burning *c.* fall upon them
Prov. 6:28 can one go upon hot *c.*
25:22 heap *c.* of fire on his head
26:21 as *c.* are to burning *c.*
Sol. 8: 6 thereof are *c.* of fire
Is. 6: 6 a live *c.* in his hands
47:14 shall not be a *c.* to warm
Lam. 4: 8 visage is blacker than *c.*
John 18:18 who had made a fire of *c.*
21: 9 they saw a fire of *c.* there
Rom. 12:20 heap *c.* of fire on his head

COAT (COATS)
Gen. 37: 3 made him a *c.* of many colors
Ex. 28: 4 and a broidered *c.*, a mitre
Sol. 5: 3 put off my *c.*; how shall I
John 19:23 the *c.* was without seam
21: 7 Peter girt his fisher's *c.*

COLD
Gen. 3:21 God make *c.* of skin and clothe
8:22 and *c.* and heat, and summer and
Job 24: 7 have no covering in the *c.*
Mat. 10:10 neither two *c.*, neither shoes
24:12 the love of many shall wax *c.*
Luke 3:11 he that hath two *c.* let him
Acts 9:39 *c.* and garments which Dorcas made
Rev. 3:15 thou art neither *c.* nor hot

COLLECTION
1 Cor. 16: 1 the *c.* for the saints

COME
Gen. 49: 6 my soul, *c.* not thou into
Ex. 20:24 where I record my name, I will *c.*
1 Sam. 17:45 I *c.* to thee in the name of
1 Chr. 29:14 all things *c.* of thee
Job 22:21 good shall *c.* unto thee
38:11 hitherto shalt thou *c.*, but no
Ps. 40: 7 lo I *c.*: in the volume of the
65: 2 to thee shall all flesh *c.*
Eccl. 9: 2 all things *c.* alike to all
Sol. 4:16 north wind; and *c.*, thou south
Is. 1:18 *c.* let us reason together
35: 4 your God will *c.* and save you
55: 1 that thirsteth *c.* ye to the waters
55: 3 incline your ear, and *c.* unto me
Jer. 3:22 we *c.* to thee for thou art Lord
Hos. 6: 1 *C.* let us return unto the Lord
Mic. 6: 6 wherewith shall I *c.* before
Hab. 2: 3 it will surely *c.* it will not tarry
Mal. 3: 1 Lord shall suddenly *c.* to his temple
4: 6 lest I *c.* and smite the earth
Mat. 8:11 many shall *c.* from east and west
11: 3 art thou he that should *c.* or look we
11:28 *c.* unto me all ye that labour and
16:24 if any man will *c.* after me
17:10 say scribes Elias must first *c.*
22: 4 all things ready, *c.* to marriage
Luke 7: 8 I say *c.* and he cometh
14:20 married a wife, I cannot *c.*
John 1:39 saith unto them *c.* and see
4:29 *C.* see a man, which told me all
5:40 ye will not *c.* to me
6:44 no man can *c.* to me, except
7:37 if any man thirst, let him *c.*
14:18 leave you comfortless, I will *c.* to
Acts 1:11 this Jesus shall so *c.* as
16: 9 *C.* over into Macedonia
1 Cor. 11:26 Lord's death till he *c.*
2 Cor. 6:17 *c.* out from among them
1 Tim. 4: 8 promise of the life to *c.*
Heb. 4:16 *c.* boldly unto the throne of
7:25 save them that *c.* to God by him
10:37 he that shall *c.* will *c.*
Rev. 6: 1 four beasts, saying *c.* and see
17: 1 saying unto me *c.* hither
18: 4 *c.* out of her, my people
21: 9 *C.* hither, I will show thee
22:17 the Spirit and the bride say, *c.*

COMETH
Ps. 118: 26 *c.* in the name of the Lord
Is. 63: 1 who is this that *c.* from Edom
Mat. 3:11 he that *c.* after me is
Luke 6:47 whoso *c.*, heareth, doeth, is
John 3:31 he that *c.* from above
6:35 *c.* to me shall never hunger
6:37 *c.* to me, I will in no wise cast out
6:45 hath learned of the Father *c.* unto me
Heb. 11: 6 that *c.* to God must believe
Jas. 1:17 gift *c.* down from the Father

COMING
Ps. 19: 5 as a bridegroom *c.* out of his
121: 8 the Lord shall preserve thy *c.* in
Mal. 3: 2 who may abide the day of his *c.*
Mat. 24: 3 what is the sign of thy *c.*
John 1:27 *c.* after me is preferred before
1 Cor. 1: 7 waiting for the *c.* of our
15:23 that are Christ's at his *c.*
1 Thes. 2:19 presence of Jesus Christ at his *c.*
3:13 at the *c.* of our Lord
5:23 unto the *c.* of our Lord Jesus
2 Thes. 2: 1 by the *c.* of our Lord
Jas. 5: 8 for the *c.* of the Lord
1 Pet. 2: 4 to whom *c.* as unto a living stone
2 Pet. 1:16 power and *c.* of the Lord
3:12 hasting unto the *c.* of the day of God

COMELY
1 Sam. 16:18 and a *c.* person, and the Lord
Job 41:12 his power, nor his *c.* proportion
Ps. 33: 1 praise is *c.* for the upright
Prov. 30:29 yea, four are *c.* in going
Sol. 1: 5 I am black but *c.*
6: 4 *c.* as Jerusalem, terrible as an
Jer. 6: 2 Zion to a *c.* and delicate woman
1 Cor. 12:24 our *c.* parts have no need

COMELINESS
Is. 53: 2 he hath no form nor *c.*
Ezek. 16:14 it was perfect through my *c.*

COMFORT (COMFORTED)
Gen. 5:29 this same shall *c.* us concerning
24:67 Isaac was *c.* after his mother's
37:35 but he refused to be *c.*
Job 7:13 my bed shall *c.* me
Ps. 23: 4 thy rod and thy staff they *c.* me
119: 50 is my *c.* in my affliction
Is. 40: 1 *c.* ye *c.* ye my people
49:13 Lord hath *c.* his people
51: 3 for the Lord shall *c.* Zion
51:12 I, even I am he that *c.*
54:11 tossed with tempest, and not *c.*
61: 2 to *c.* all that mourn
Jer. 31:13 I will *c.* and make them rejoice
31:15 Rahel weeping . . . refused to be *c.*
Lam. 1: 2 she hath none to *c.* her
Mat. 9:22 be of good *c.*, thy faith hath
Luke 16:25 he is *c.* thou art tormented
Acts 9:31 walking in the *c.* of the Holy Ghost
Rom. 1:12 I may be *c.* together with you
1 Cor. 14: 3 edification and exhortation and *c.*
14:31 all prophesy one by one all be *c.*
2 Cor. 1: 4 we may be able to *c.* them
7:13 we were *c.* in your comfort
Phil. 2: 1 if any *c.* of love, if any
Col. 4:11 which have been a *c.* unto me
1 Thes. 3: 7 *c.* over you by your faith
4:18 *c.* one another with these
5:11 *c.* selves together, and edify one
5:14 *c.* the feeble minded, support the weak
2 Thes. 2:17 Lord Jesus *c.* your hearts and

COMFORTABLY
2 Sam. 19: 7 speak *c.* unto thy servants
2 Chr. 30:22 spake *c.* unto all the Levites
32: 6 spake *c.* to them, saying
Is. 40: 2 speak ye *c.* to Jerusalem
Hos. 2:14 wilderness and speak *c.* unto her

COMFORTERS
Job 16: 2 miserable *c.* are ye all
Ps. 69:20 and for *c.*, but I found none

COMFORTLESS
John 14:18 I will not leave you *c.*

COMMAND (COMMANDETH, COMMANDING)
Gen. 18:19 Abraham will *c.* his children
Deut. 28: 8 Lord shall *c.* thy blessing upon thee
Ps. 42: 8 Lord will *c.* his lovingkindness
Is. 45:11 work of my hands, *c.* me
Lam. 3:37 when the Lord *c.* it not
Mat. 4: 3 *c.* these stones be made bread
John 15:14 if ye do whatsoever I *c.*
Acts 17:30 now *c.* all men to repent
1 Cor. 7:10 unto the married I *c.*
1 Tim. 4: 3 *c.* to abstain from meats, which God
4:11 these things I *c.* and teach

COMMANDED
Ps. 111: 9 he hath *c.* his covenant for ever
119: 4 hast *c.* us to keep thy precepts
133: 3 Lord *c.* the blessing, even life
148: 5 Lord *c.* and they were created
Mat. 28:20 whatsoever I have *c.* you
2 Cor. 4: 6 God who *c.* the light to
Heb. 12:20 not endure that which was *c.*

COMMANDMENT
Num. 23:20 I have received *c.* to bless
Ps. 119: 96 thy *c.* is exceeding broad
Prov. 6:23 the *c.* is a lamp; and law is light
8:29 waters should not pass his *c.*
Hos. 5:11 willingly walked after the *c.*
Mat. 22:38 is the first and great *c.*
Mark 7: 9 reject the *c.* of God
John 10:18 this *c.* I received of my Father
12:50 his *c.* is life everlasting
13:34 a new *c.* give I unto you
15:12 this is my *c.* that ye love one
Rom. 7: 8 sin taking occasion by the *c.*
7: 9 when the *c.* came, sin revived
1 Tim. 1: 5 end of the *c.* is charity
Heb. 7:16 not after the law of a carnal *c.*
2 Pet. 2:21 turn from the holy *c.*
1 John 2: 7 an old *c.* which ye had
3:23 this is his *c.* that we believe

COMMANDMENTS
Ex. 34:28 words of the covenant the ten *c.*
Ps. 111: 7 all his *c.* are sure
112: 1 delighteth greatly in his *c.*
119: 6 I have respect unto all thy *c.*
119: 19 hide not thy *c.* from me
119: 21 which do err from thy *c.*
Ps. 119: 35 make me to go in the path of thy *c.*
119: 48 thy *c.* which I have loved
119: 66 I have believed thy *c.*
119: 73 give understanding to learn thy *c.*
119:127 I love thy *c.* above gold
119:131 I longed for thy *c.*
119:172 all thy *c.* are righteousness
Mat. 15: 9 for doctrines the *c.* of men
22:40 on these two *c.* hang all the law
Mark 10:19 thou knowest the *c.*, do not commit
Luke 1: 6 walking in all the *c.* and ordinances
Col. 2:22 after the *c.* and doctrines of men
1 John 3:24 he that keepeth his *c.* dwelleth
2 John 1: 6 that we walk after his *c.*

COMMEND (COMMENDED, COMMENDETH)
Gen. 12:15 and *c.* her before pharaoh
Luke 23:46 to thy hands I *c.* my spirit
Acts 14:23 *c.* them to the Lord on whom
Rom. 3: 5 if our unrighteousness *c.* the righteousness
5: 8 God *c.* his love toward us
16: 1 I *c.* unto you Phebe our sister
1 Cor. 8: 8 meat *c.* us not to God
2 Cor. 5:12 we *c.* not ourselves again unto
10:12 ourselves with some that *c.* themselves
10:18 not he that *c.* self is approved

COMMENDATION
2 Cor. 3: 1 as some others epistles of *c.*

COMMIT (COMMITTED, COMMITTETH)
Ex. 20:14 thou shalt not *c.* adultery
Job 5: 8 to God would I *c.* my cause
Ps. 10:14 the poor *c.* himself unto thee
31: 5 to thy hand I *c.* my spirit
37: 5 *c.* thy way unto the Lord
Prov. 16: 3 *c.* thy works unto the Lord
Mat. 5:27 thou shalt not *c.* adultery
19:18 thou shalt not *c.* adultery
Luke 12:48 to whom men have *c.* much
16:11 who will *c.* to your trust
John 2:24 did not *c.* himself unto them
5:22 *c.* all judgment to the Son
8:34 who *c.* sin is servant of sin
Rom. 1:32 *c.* such things are worthy of death
1 Cor. 9:17 dispensation of the gospel is *c.* unto
Gal. 2: 7 uncircumcision was *c.* unto me
1 Tim. 1:11 God's which was *c.* to my trust
1:18 this charge I *c.* unto thee
2 Tim. 1:12 which I have *c.* unto him against
1 Pet. 2:23 *c.* himself to him that judgeth
4:19 *c.* the keeping of their souls
1 John 3: 8 who *c.* sin is of the devil
3: 9 born of God doth not *c.* sin
Jude 1:15 which they have ungodly *c.*

COMMON
Lev. 4:27 one of the *c.* people sin through
Num. 16:29 the *c.* death of all men
Jer. 31: 5 and shall eat them as *c.* things
Ezek. 23:42 men of the *c.* sort were brought
Mark 12:37 the *c.* people heard him gladly
Acts 2:44 together and had all things *c.*
10:15 God hath cleansed, that call not *c.*
1 Cor. 10:13 such as is *c.* to man
Jude 1: 3 write unto you of the *c.* salvation

COMMONLY
Mat. 28:15 this saying is *c.* reported

COMMONWEALTH
Eph. 2:12 from the *c.* of Israel

COMMUNE (COMMUNED)
Ex. 25:22 I will *c.* with thee from above
Ps. 4: 4 *c.* with your own heart
Luke 6:11 they *c.* one with another

COMMUNICATE (COMMUNICATED)
Gal. 2: 2 *c.* unto them that gospel which
6: 6 taught in the word *c.* unto him
Phil. 4:14 ye did *c.* with my affliction
4:15 no church *c.* with me in
1 Tim. 6:18 ready to distribute, willing to *c.*
Heb. 13:16 do good and to *c.* forget not

COMMUNICATION (COMMUNICATIONS)
Luke 24:17 what manner of *c.* are these
1 Cor. 15:33 evil *c.* corrupt good manners
Eph. 4:29 let no corrupt *c.* proceed
Col. 3: 8 filthy *c.* out of your mouth

COMMUNION
1 Cor. 10:16 is it not the *c.* of the blood of
2 Cor. 6:14 what *c.* hath light with darkness?
13:14 *c.* of the Holy Ghost be with you

COMPANY
Gen. 32:21 lodged that night in the *c.*
Ps. 55:14 to the house of God in *c.*
Prov. 29: 3 keepeth *c.* with harlots
Sol. 6:13 as it were the *c.* of two armies
Acts 6: 7 a great *c.* of the priests
Rom. 15:24 first filled with your *c.*
1 Cor. 5:11 not to keep *c.*, if any man
2 Thes. 3:14 have no *c.* with him, that he may
Heb. 12:22 an innumerable *c.* of angels

COMPANION (COMPANIONS)
Ps. 119: 63 I am a *c.* of all them that
45:14 the virgins, her *c.* that follow
122: 8 for my brethren and *c.* sakes
Prov. 13:20 *c.* of fools shall be destroyed
Is. 1:23 are rebellious and *c.* of thieves
Mal. 2:14 thy *c.* and thy wife of the covenant
Phil. 2:25 Epaphroditus my *c.* in labour
Rev. 1: 9 your brother and *c.* in tribulation

COMPARE (COMPARED, COMPARING)
Ps. 89: 6 who in heaven can be *c.*
Prov. 3:15 desire are not to be *c.* unto her
Sol. 1: 9 *c.* thee, O my love to a company
Is. 40:18 what likeness will ye *c.* unto him
46: 5 *c.* me, that we may be like
Rom. 8:18 not worthy to be *c.* with the glory
1 Cor. 2:13 *c.* spiritual things with spiritual
2 Cor. 10:12 *c.* ourselves with some that commend

COMPASS (COMPASSED, COMPASSEST, COMPASSETH)
Ps. 5:12 with favour *c.* him as with
18: 4 the sorrows of death *c.* me
26: 6 innocency: so will I *c.* thy altar
32:10 mercy shall *c.* him about
73: 6 pride *c.* them about as a chain
116: 3 sorrows of death *c.* me
118: 10 all nations *c.* me about
139: 3 thou *c.* my path and my lying
Is. 50:11 *c.* yourselves with sparks
Jer. 31:22 a woman shall *c.* a man
Hos. 11:12 Ephraim *c.* me with lies
Jonah 2: 3 and the floods *c.* me about
Hab. 1: 4 wicked doth *c.* the righteous
Mat. 23:15 ye *c.* sea and land to

COMPASSION (COMPASSIONS)
Ex. 2: 6 babe wept. And she had *c.*
Deut. 30: 3 Lord turn captivity and have *c.*
1 Ki. 8:50 give them *c.* before them who
Ps. 78:38 being full of *c.* forgave their
111: 4 Lord is gracious and full of *c.*
145: 8 and full of *c.*
Jer. 12:15 return and have *c.* on them
Lam. 3:22 consumed because his *c.* fail not
3:32 cause grief, yet will he have *c.*
Mic. 7:19 he will have *c.* on us
Zech. 7: 9 and show mercy and *c.* every man
Mat. 9:36 he was moved with *c.* on them
14:14 was moved with *c.* toward them
15:32 I have *c.* on the multitude
18:27 servant was moved with *c.*
20:34 So Jesus had *c.* on them
Mark 1:41 Jesus, moved with *c.* put forth
5:19 friends, tell how the Lord had *c.* on
9:22 canst do any thing have *c.* on us
Luke 7:13 Lord had *c.* and said, Weep not
15:20 off, his father saw him, and had *c.*
Rom. 9:15 will have *c.* on whom I will have *c.*
Heb. 5: 2 who can have *c.* on the ignorant
1 Pet. 3: 8 having *c.* one of another
1 John 3:17 shutteth up his bowels of *c.*
Jude 1:22 And of some have *c.*, making a

COMPEL (COMPELLED, COMPELLEST)
2 Chr. 21:11 fornication and *c.* Judah thereto
Mat. 5:41 shall *c.* thee to go a mile
Mark 15:21 they *c.* one Simon a Cyrenian
Luke 14:23 and *c.* them to come in
Acts 26:11 I *c.* them to blaspheme
2 Cor. 12:11 I am a fool ye *c.* me
Gal. 2: 3 not *c.* to be circumcised
2:14 *c.* Gentiles to live as Jews

COMPREHEND (COMPREHENDED)
Job 37: 5 doeth he which we cannot *c.*
John 1: 5 and the darkness *c.* it not

Rom. 13: 9 it is briefly *c.* in this saying
Eph. 3:18 be able to *c.* with all saints

CONCEAL (CONCEALETH, CONCEALED)
Gen. 37:26 slay our brother and *c.* his blood
Job 6:10 not *c.* words of the Holy One
27:11 the Almighty will I not *c.*
Ps. 40:10 not *c.* thy lovingkindness and thy
Prov. 12:23 a prudent man *c.* knowledge

CONCEIT (CONCEITS)
Prov. 18:11 and as an high wall in his own *c.*
26: 5 lest he be wise in his own *c.*
28:11 rich man is wise in his own *c.*
Rom. 11:25 should be wise in your own *c.*

CONCEIVE (CONCEIVED)
Gen. 30:38 should *c.* when they came to drink
Num. 11:12 have I *c.* all this people?
Job 3: 3 there is a man child *c.*
15:35 they *c.* mischief, and bring forth
Ps. 7:14 hath *c.* mischief, and brought forth
51: 5 in sin did my mother *c.* me
Is. 59: 4 they *c.* mischief, and bring forth
7:14 a virgin shall *c.* and bear a son
Jer. 49:30 *c.* a purpose against you
Mat. 1:20 *c.* in her is of the Holy Ghost
Luke 1:31 thou shalt *c.* in thy womb
1:36 Elizabeth, she hath also *c.* a son
2:21 so named before he was *c.*
Acts 5: 4 why hast thou *c.* in thy heart
Heb. 11:11 Sara also received strength to *c.*
Jas. 1:15 when lust hath *c.* it bringeth

CONCORD
2 Cor. 6:15 what *c.* hath Christ with Belial

CONCUBINE (CONCUBINES)
Judg. 19: 1 a *c.* out of Bethleham-Judah
2 Sam. 16:21 go in unto thy father's *c.*
1 Ki. 11: 3 and three hundred *c.*: and his wives
1 Chr. 1:32 Keturah, Abraham's *c.*: she bare
Dan. 5: 2 and his *c.* might drink therein

CONCUPISCENCE
Rom. 7: 8 in me all manner of *c.*
Col. 3: 5 affection, evil *c.*, and covetousness
1 Thes. 4: 5 not in the lust of *c.*, even

CONDEMN (CONDEMNED, CONDEMNETH)
2 Chr. 36: 3 *c.* the land in a hundred talents
Job 9:20 my own mouth shall *c.* me
10: 2 I will say to God, do not *c.* me
Ps. 37:33 nor *c.* him when judged
94:21 righteous and *c.* the innocent blood
Is. 50: 9 Lord will help me, who shall *c.*?
Prov. 17:15 he that *c.* the just, even they
Mat. 12:37 by thy words thou shalt be *c.*
12:41 this generation and shall *c.* it
Luke 6:37 *c.* not and ye shall not be condemned
John 3:17 into the world to *c.* the world
8:11 neither do I *c.* thee, go and sin
Rom. 8: 3 for sin, *c.* sin in the flesh
8:34 who is he that *c.*? It is Christ
14:22 Happy is he that *c.* not himself
1 Cor. 11:32 we should not be *c.* with the world
Tit. 2: 8 sound speech cannot be *c.*

CONDEMNATION
Luke 23:40 seeing thou art in the same *c.*
John 3:19 this is the *c.*, that light is
5:24 shall not come into *c.* but is
Rom. 5:16 judgment by one to *c.*, but free
8: 1 no *c.* to them which are in
2 Cor. 3: 9 the ministration of *c.* be glory
1 Tim. 3: 6 fall into *c.* of the devil
Jas. 3: 1 we shall receive the greater *c.*
5:12 swear not, lest ye fall into *c.*
Jude 1: 4 of old ordained to this *c.*

CONFESS (CONFESSED, CONFESSETH, CONFESSING)
Lev. 5: 5 he shall *c.* that he hath
26:40 if they *c.* their iniquity
1 Ki. 8:35 and *c.* thy name, and turn from
Neh. 1: 6 *c.* the sins of the children
Ps. 32: 5 I will *c.* my transgressions unto
Prov. 28:13 whoso *c.* and forsaketh them shall
Dan. 9:20 *c.* my sin and the sin of my
Mat. 3: 6 baptized in the Jordan *c.* their sins
10:32 shall *c.* me before men

Luke 12: 8 him will the Son of Man also *c.*
Rom. 10: 9 *c.* with thy mouth the Lord Jesus;
Heb. 11:13 *c.* that they were strangers
Jas. 5:16 *c.* your faults one to another
1 John 1: 9 if we *c.* our sins, he is faithful
4:15 *c.* Jesus is the Son of God
2 John 1: 7 *c.* not that Jesus Christ is come

CONFESSION
Josh. 7:19 make *c.* unto him; and tell me
2 Chr. 30:22 making *c.* to the Lord God
Ezra 10:11 make *c.* unto the Lord God of
Dan. 9: 4 made my *c.* and said, O Lord
Rom. 10:10 mouth *c.* is made unto salvation
1 Tim. 6:13 Pontius Pilate witnessed a good *c.*

CONFIDENCE (CONFIDENCES)
Ps. 65: 5 *c.* of all the ends of the earth
118: 8 than to put *c.* in man
Prov. 3:26 the Lord shall be thy *c.*
Jer. 2:37 the Lord hath rejected thy *c.*
48:13 Israel ashamed of Beth-el, their *c.*
Ezek. 29:16 no more the *c.* of Israel
Mic. 7: 5 put ye not *c.* in a guide,
Eph. 3:12 in whom we have access with *c.*
Phil. 3: 3 we have no *c.* in the flesh
Heb. 3: 6 if we hold fast the *c.*
1 John 3:21 then have we *c.* toward God
2:28 we may have *c.*, and not

CONFIRM (CONFIRMED, CONFIRMING)
Is. 35: 3 and *c.* the feeble knees
44:26 that *c.* the word of his servant
Dan. 9:27 he shall *c.* the covenant
Mark 16:20 and *c.* the word with the signs
Rom. 15: 8 to *c.* the promises made unto
1 Cor. 1: 8 shall also *c.* you unto the end
2 Cor. 2: 8 *c.* your love toward him
Heb. 6:17 of his counsel *c.* it by an oath

CONFORMED
Rom. 8:29 predestined to be *c.* to the image
12: 2 be not *c.* to this world

CONFOUND (CONFOUNDED)
Gen. 11: 7 and there *c.* their language
Ps. 97: 7 *c.* be all they that serve graven
Jer. 1:17 lest I *c.* thee before them
17:18 but let not me be *c.*: let them
Ezek. 16:52 be thou *c.* also and bear thy shame
Mic. 3: 7 and the diviners *c.*: yea, they
7:16 nations shall see and be *c.*
Acts 2: 6 multitude came together and were *c.*
9:22 *c.* the Jews which dwelt at
1 Cor. 1:27 foolish things of the world to *c.*
1 Pet. 2: 6 believeth shall not be *c.*

CONFUSION
Ezra 9: 7 to a spoil and to *c.* of face
Ps. 44:15 my *c.* is continually before
71: 1 let me never be put to *c.*
Is. 24:10 the city of *c.* is broken
1 Cor. 14:33 God is not the author of *c.*

CONGREGATION
Ex. 16: 2 the whole *c.* of the children
16:22 the rulers of the *c.* came
27:21 tabernacle of the *c.* without the
40: 2 tabernacle of the tent of the *c.*
Lev. 4:15 elders of the *c.* shall lay their hands
Num. 4:34 chief of the *c.* numbered
14:27 I bear with this evil *c.*
16: 2 famous in the *c.*, men of renown
31:26 chief fathers of the *c.*
Josh. 9:15 princes of the *c.* sware
22:30 princes of the *c.* and heads
Judg. 21:13 whole *c.* sent some to speak
21:16 elders of the *c.* said
Neh. 13: 1 into the *c.* of God forever
Ps. 22:25 be of thee in the great *c.*
Is. 14:13 the mount of the *c.* in the sides
Lam. 1:10 heathen not enter the *c.*,
Mic. 2: 5 cast a cord by lot in the *c.*

CONQUER (CONQUERING)
Rev. 6: 2 he went forth *c.* and to *c.*

CONQUERORS
Rom. 8:37 we are more than *c.* through him

CONSCIENCE
John 8: 9 convicted by their own *c.*
Acts 23: 1 in all good *c.* before God
24:16 a *c.* void of offence
Rom. 2:15 their *c.* also bearing witness
9: 1 my *c.* also bearing me witness
13: 5 also for *c.* sake

1 Cor. 8: 7 some with *c.* of the idol
10:28 and for *c.* sake
2 Cor. 1:12 testimony of our *c.*
1 Tim. 3: 9 of faith in a pure *c.*
4: 2 having their *c.* seared with hot
2 Tim. 1: 3 my forefathers with pure *c.*
Tit. 1:15 their mind and *c.* is defiled
Heb. 9:14 purge *c.* from dead works
10: 2 *c.* of sins
13:18 we have a good *c.*
1 Pet. 3:21 answer of a good *c.* toward God

CONSENT (CONSENTING)
Gen. 34:15 we will *c.* unto you
Prov. 1:10 entice thee, *c.* thou not
Hos. 6: 9 murder in the way by *c.*
Luke 14:18 all with one *c.* began
Acts 8: 1 was *c.* unto his death
22:20 and *c.* unto his death
Rom. 7:16 I *c.* unto the law
1 Tim. 6: 3 and *c.* not to wholesome

CONSIDER (CONSIDERED, CONSIDEREST)
Deut. 4:39 *c.* it in thy heart
32:29 would *c.* their latter end
1 Sam. 12:24 *c.* how great things he
Job 1: 8 hast thou *c.* my servant Job
Ps. 8: 3 when I *c.* thy heavens
31: 7 thou hast *c.* my trouble
41: 1 blessed is he that *c.* the poor
77: 5 have *c.* days of old, the years
Eccl. 7:13 *c.* the work of God
Is. 1: 3 my people doth not *c.*
5:12 neither *c.* operation of his hands
Hag. 1: 5 saith the Lord, *c.* your ways
Mat. 6:28 *c.* the lilies of the field
7: 3 *c.* not the beam
Mark 6:52 *c.* not the miracle of the loaves
Rom. 4:19 *c.* not his own body dead
2 Tim. 2: 7 *c.* what I say, and Lord give
Heb. 3: 1 *c.* the Apostle and the High Priest
10:24 *c.* one another to provoke to
12: 3 *c.* him that endured such

CONSOLATION (CONSOLATIONS)
Job 15:11 are the *c.* of God small
Is. 66:11 with the breasts of her *c.*
Luke 2:25 waiting for the *c.* of Israel
6:24 woe are rich, have received your *c.*
Acts 4:36 being interpreted the son of *c.*
Rom. 15: 5 God of *c.* grant you to
2 Cor. 1: 5 our *c.* aboundeth by Christ
Phil. 2: 1 if therefore any *c.* in Christ
Heb. 6:18 might have a strong *c.*

CONSTRAIN (CONSTRAINED)
Acts 16:15 abide there and she *c.* us
2 Cor. 5:14 for the love of Christ *c.*
Gal. 6:12 they *c.* you to be circumcised

CONSTRAINT
1 Pet. 5: 2 not by *c.* but willingly

CONSUME (CONSUMED)
Ex. 3: 2 bush was not *c.*
33: 3 lest I *c.* thee in the way
Deut. 5:25 this great fire will *c.* us
Ps. 37:20 they shall *c.*; into smoke
78:33 their days did he *c.* in vanity
90: 7 we are *c.* by thine anger
119:139 my zeal hath *c.* me, because
Prov. 5:11 thy flesh and body are *c.*
Lam. 3:22 of the Lord's mercies not *c.*
Ezek. 4:17 *c.* for the iniquity
Gal. 5:15 not *c.* one of another
2 Thes. 2: 8 Lord shall *c.* with the spirit of
Jas. 4: 3 *c.* it upon your lusts

CONSUMING
Deut. 4:24 thy God is a *c.* fire
Heb. 12:29 our God is a *c.* fire

CONTAIN (CONTAINED, CONTAINING)
1 Ki. 8:27 heaven of heavens cannot *c.*
John 2: 6 *c.* two or three firkins
21:25 itself could not *c.* the books
Rom. 2:14 the things *c.* in the law
1 Cor. 7: 9 if they cannot *c.*, let them marry

CONTEMN
Ps. 10:13 doth the wicked *c.* God
Ezek. 21:13 if sword *c.* the rod

CONTEMNED
Ps. 15: 4 a vile person is *c.*

CONTEMPT
Ps. 123: 3 we are filled with *c.*
Dan. 12: 2 shame and everlasting *c.*

CONTEMPTIBLE
Mal. 1: 7 table of the Lord *c.*
2: 9 have I made you *c.* before all
2 Cor. 10:10 weak, his speech *c.*

CONTEND (CONTENDETH)
Deut. 2: 9 neither *c.* with them in battle
Job 40: 2 he that *c.* with the Almighty
Is. 49:25 I will *c.* with them that *c.*
50: 8 who will *c.* with me
57:16 I will not *c.* for ever
Jer. 12: 5 then how canst thou *c.* with horses?
Amos 7: 4 the Lord God called to *c.* by fire
Jude 1: 3 earnestly *c.* for the faith

CONTENTION (CONTENTIONS)
Prov. 13:10 only by pride cometh before *c.*
17:14 water, leave off *c.* before it be
18: 6 A fool's lips enter into *c.* and
22:10 out the scorner, and *c.* shall go out
Jer. 15:10 borne me a man of *c.* to
Hab. 1: 3 raise up strife and *c.*
Acts 15:39 and the *c.* was so sharp between them
Phil. 1:16 the one preach Christ of *c.*
1 Thes. 2: 2 gospel of God with much *c.*

CONTENTIOUS
Prov. 18:18 lot causeth *c.* to cease
19:13 and the *c.* of a wife are a
21:19 than with a *c.* and an angry woman
26:21 so is a *c.* man to kindle
27:15 rainy day and a *c.* woman are alike
Rom. 2: 8 them that are *c.*, and do not obey
1 Cor. 1:11 there are *c.* among you
11:16 but if any man seem to be *c.*
Tit. 3: 9 and *c.* and strivings about the law

CONTENT
Josh. 7: 7 would to God we had been *c.*
Prov. 6:35 neither will he rest *c.*
Luke 3:14 be *c.* with your wages
Phil. 4:11 therewith to be *c.*
1 Tim. 6: 8 food and raiment let us be *c.*
Heb. 13: 5 be *c.* with such things

CONTENTMENT
1 Tim. 6: 6 but godliness with *c.* is great gain

CONTINUAL (CONTINUALLY)
Gen. 6: 5 heart was only evil *c.*
Ex. 28:30 upon his heart before the Lord *c.*
29:42 there shall be a *c.* burnt offering
Ps. 34: 1 his praise *c.* in my mouth
52: 1 goodness of God endureth *c.*
71: 3 habitation whereto I may *c.* resort
71:14 I will hope *c.*, and will yet
73:23 I am *c.* with thee
Prov. 6:21 bind *c.* upon thine heart
Is. 58:11 the Lord shall guide thee *c.*
Hos. 12: 6 turn and wait on thy God *c.*
Acts 6: 4 give ourselves *c.* to prayer
Rom. 9: 2 great heaviness and *c.* sorrow in my heart
Heb. 13:15 sacrifice of praise to God *c.*

CONTINUANCE
Ps. 139: 16 which in *c.* were fashioned
Rom. 2: 7 to them who by patient *c.* in well doing

CONTINUE
1 Sam. 12:14 *c.* following the Lord your God
Ps. 36:10 O *c.* thy lovingkindness unto
102: 28 children of thy servants shall *c.*
119: 91 *c.* according to thine ordinances
Mat. 15:32 because they *c.* with me
John 8:31 *c.* in my word, then are ye my disciples
15: 9 *c.* ye in my love
Acts 13:43 to *c.* in the grace of God
14:22 exhorting them to *c.* in the faith
26:22 I *c.* unto this day, witnessing
Rom. 6: 1 shall we *c.* in sin that grace
Col. 1:23 if ye *c.* in faith grounded
4: 2 *c.* in prayer, and watch
1 Tim. 2:15 if they *c.* in faith and charity
4:16 doctrine; *c.* in them: for
2 Tim. 3:14 *c.* thou in things learned
Heb. 13: 1 let brotherly love *c.*
Rev. 13: 5 to *c.* forty-two months

CONTINUED (CONTINUETH, CONTINUING)
Neh. 5:16 I *c.* in the work of this wall
Jer. 30:23 with fury, a *c.* whirlwind
Dan. 1:21 Daniel *c.* even unto the first year

Luke 6:12 *c.* all night in prayer
22:28 *c.* with me in my temptations
Acts 1:14 *c.* with one accord in prayer
2:42 *c.* stedfastly in the apostles' doctrine
2:46 *c.* daily with one accord
20: 7 *c.* his speech till midnight
Rom. 12:12 patient in tribulation, *c.* instant in prayer
Gal. 3:10 that *c.* not in all things
1 Tim. 5: 5 *c.* in supplication and prayer
Heb. 7:24 this man, because he *c.* ever
8: 9 because they *c.* not in my covenant
13:14 for here have we no *c.* city
Jas. 1:25 law of liberty, and *c.* therein
1 John 2:19 would have *c.* with us

CONTRARY
Lev. 26:21 if ye walk *c.* unto me
Ezek. 16:34 therefore thou art *c.*
Mat. 14:24 for the wind was *c.*
Acts 18:13 to worship God *c.* to the law
26: 9 things *c.* to the name of Jesus
27: 4 because the winds were *c.*
Rom. 11:24 and wert grafted *c.* to nature
Gal. 5:17 these are *c.* the one to another
Col. 2:14 against us, which was *c.* to us
1 Thes. 2:15 not God, and are *c.* to all men
1 Tim. 1:10 other thing that is *c.* to sound doctrine

CONVENIENT
Prov. 30: 8 feed with food *c.* for me
Acts 24:25 I have a *c.* season I will call
Rom. 1:28 over to do things not *c.*
Eph. 5: 4 nor jesting which are not *c.*
Philem. 1: 8 that which is *c.*

CONVERSATION
Ps. 37:14 such as be of upright *c.*
50:23 ordereth his *c.* aright will I
2 Cor. 1:12 we have had our *c.* in the world
Gal. 1:13 ye have heard of my *c.* in times
Eph. 2: 3 we all had our *c.* in times past
4:22 the former *c.* the old man
Phil. 1:27 *c.* be as becometh the gospel
3:20 our *c.* is in heaven
1 Tim. 4:12 an example of believers in *c.*
Heb. 13: 5 let your *c.* be without covetousness
Jas. 3:13 show out of good *c.* his works
1 Pet. 1:15 holy in all manner of *c.*
2:12 *c.* honest among the Gentiles
3: 1 won by *c.* of the wives
3:16 accuse your good *c.* in Christ
2 Pet. 2: 7 with the filthy *c.* of the wicked
3:11 in all holy *c.* and godliness

CONVERT (CONVERTED)
Ps. 51:13 sinners be *c.* to thee
Is. 6:10 understand with their heart and *c.* and be healed
60: 5 abundance of sea, *c.* to thee
Mat. 13:15 be *c.* and I should heal them
18: 3 except ye be *c.* and become as
Luke 22:32 when thou art *c.* strengthen
Acts 3:19 be *c.* and your sins blotted out
Jas. 5:19 err from the truth, and one *c.* him

CONVERTS
Is. 1:27 her *c.* with rightousness

CORD (CORDS)
Josh. 2:15 let them down by a *c.*
Job 30:11 he hath loosed my *c.*, and afflicted me

CORDS
Job 36: 8 be holden in *c.* of affliction
Ps. 118: 27 bind the sacrifice with *c.*
2: 3 cast away their *c.* from us
129: 4 asunder of *c.* of the wicked
Prov. 5:22 holden with the *c.* of his sins
Eccl. 4:12 threefold *c.* not quickly broken
Is. 54: 2 spare not, lengthen thy *c.*, and strengthen
Jer. 10:20 all my *c.* are broken
Hos. 11: 4 *c.* of a man, bands of love
Mic. 2: 5 shall cast a *c.* by lot
John 2:15 made a scourge of small *c.*

CORN
Gen. 41:49 gathered *c.* as the sand of the sea
Deut. 7:13 thy *c.*, and thy wine, and thine oil
25: 4 ox that treadeth out *c.*
Josh. 5:11 eat of the old *c.* of the land
Neh. 13: 5 the tithes of the *c.*, the new wine
Job 5:26 as a shock of *c.* cometh in
Ps. 65: 9 thou preparest them *c.*

Ps. 72:16 handful of *c.* in the earth
78:24 given them *c.* of heaven to eat
Is. 62: 8 no more than give *c.* to enemies
Ezek. 36:29 call for *c.* and increase
Hos. 2: 8 did not know that I gave her *c.*
Zech. 9:17 *c.* shall make the young men
Mat. 12: 1 began to pluck the ears of *c.*
John 12:24 except a *c.* of wheat fall
1 Cor. 9: 9 ox that treadeth out the *c.*
1 Tim. 5:18 ox that treadeth out the *c.*

CORNER (CORNERS)
Lev. 19: 9 shalt not reap the *c.* of thy field
19:27 mar the *c.* of thy beard
Job 38: 6 who laid the *c.* stone thereof
Ps. 118: 22 is become the head of the *c.*
144: 12 daughters may be as *c.* stones
Prov. 7: 8 through the street near her *c.*
21: 9 it is better to dwell in a *c.*
Is. 28:16 a precious *c.* stone
30:20 not thy teachers be removed into a *c.*
Zech. 10: 4 out of him came forth the *c.*
Mat. 6: 5 synagogues and in *c.* of the streets
21:42 same has become the head of the *c.*
Acts 4:11 has become the head of the *c.*
Eph. 2:20 himself being the chief *c.* stone
1 Pet. 2: 6 in Sion a chief *c.* stone

CORRECT (CORRECTED, CORRECTETH)
Job 5:17 happy is the man whom God *c.*
Ps. 39:11 with rebukes dost *c.* man
94:10 chastiseth the heathen, shall not he *c.*?
Prov. 3:12 whom the Lord loveth he *c.*
29:17 *c.* thy son, and he shall give
Jer. 2:19 thine own wickedness shall *c.* thee
10:24 *c.* me, but with judgment
Heb. 12: 9 our flesh which *c.* us

CORRECTION
Job 37:13 whether for *c.*, or for his land
Prov. 3:11 but be not weary of his *c.*
22:15 rod of *c.* shall drive foolishness
23:13 withhold not *c.* from the child
Hab. 1:12 established them for *c.*
2 Tim. 3:16 Scripture profitable for *c.*

CORRUPT
Job 17: 1 My breath is *c.*, my days
Ps. 14: 1 they are *c.*, they have done
38: 5 wounds stink and are *c.*
Mat. 6:19 moth and rust doth *c.*
7:17 but a *c.* tree bringeth forth
12:33 or else make the tree *c.*
1 Cor. 15:33 evil communications *c.* good manners
2 Cor. 2:17 not as many which *c.* word
Eph. 4:22 the old man which is *c.*
1 Tim. 6: 5 men of *c.* minds and destitute
2 Tim. 3: 8 men of *c.* minds, reprobate
Jude 1:10 in those they *c.* themselves

CORRUPTED
Ex. 32: 7 Egypt, have *c.* themselves
Hos. 9: 9 have deeply *c.* themselves
Mal. 2: 8 ye have *c.* the covenant of Levi
2 Cor. 7: 2 we have *c.* no man, we have

CORRUPTIBLE
1 Cor. 9:25 do it to obtain a *c.* crown
15:53 For this *c.* must put in
1 Pet. 1:18 redeemed with *c.* things

CORRUPTION
Job 17:14 I have said to *c.*
Ps. 16:10 Holy one to see *c.*
Is. 38:17 from the pit of *c.*
Dan. 10: 8 turned in me into *c.*
Jonah 2: 6 brought up my life from *c.*
Acts 2:31 his flesh did see *c.*
13:34 now no more to return to *c.*
Rom. 8:21 from the bondage of *c.*
1 Cor. 15:42 It is sown in *c.*, it is raised
Gal. 6: 8 shall of the flesh reap *c.*
2 Pet. 1: 4 having escaped through *c.*

COST
2 Sam. 19:42 eaten all of the king's *c.*
24:24 of that which doth *c.* me nothing
1 Chr. 21:24 offer burnt offering without *c.*
Luke 14:28 and counteth the *c.*, whether we

COUNCIL
Ps. 68:27 princes of Judah and their *c.*
Mat. 5:22 shall be in danger of the *c.*
10:17 they will deliver you up to the *c.*
26:59 and all the *c.* sought false witness
Mark 15: 1 scribes and the whole *c.*, and bound
Acts 4:15 them to go aside out of the *c.*

COUNSEL
Num. 27:21 who shall ask *c.* for him
31:16 through the *c.* of Balaam
1 Ki. 12: 8 forsook the *c.* of the old men
Job 5:13 *c.* of froward is carried headlong
12:13 he hath *c.* and understanding
21:16 *c.* of the wicked far from me
38: 2 who is this that darkeneth *c.*
Ps. 1: 1 walketh not in the *c.* of the ungodly
14: 6 ye have shamed the *c.* of the poor
33:10 *c.* of the Lord stands for ever
55:14 we took sweet *c.* together
83: 3 taken crafty *c.* against thy people
Prov. 1:25 set at nought all my *c.*
8:14 *c.* is mine and sound wisdom
11:14 where no *c.* is the people fall
20:18 purpose established by *c.*
21:30 nor *c.* against the Lord
24: 6 by wise *c.* make war, in multitude
27: 9 a man's friend by hearty *c.*
Is. 11: 2 the spirit of *c.* and might
28:29 which is wonderful in *c.* and
40:14 with whom took he *c.* and who
Jer. 32:19 great in thy *c.* and mighty in thy work
Zech. 6:13 *c.* of peace between them
Luke 7:30 rejected the *c.* of God against
Acts 2:23 delivered by the determinate *c.*
5:38 if this *c.* be of men it will come
20:27 declare to you all the *c.* of God
Eph. 1:11 after the *c.* of his own will

COUNSELLOR (COUNSELLORS)
2 Sam. 15:12 Ahithophel the Gilonite, David's *c.*
1 Chr. 26:14 Zechariah his son, a wise *c.*
2 Chr. 22: 3 mother was his *c.* to do wickedly
Ezra 4: 5 and hired *c.* against them
Ps. 119: 24 thy testimonies are my *c.*
Prov. 11:14 in a multitude of the *c.* safety
Is. 1:26 restore the *c.* as at the beginning
9: 6 called Wonderful, *C.*, the mighty God
Dan. 3:24 spake and said unto his *c.*
Mark 15:43 Joseph of Arimathaea, an honourable *c.*
Rom. 11:34 who has been his *c.*

COUNT (COUNTED)
Gen. 15: 6 *c.* to him for righteousness
Ex. 12: 4 shall make your *c.* for the lamb
Num. 23:10 who can *c.* the dust of Jacob
Job 31: 4 doth not he *c.* all my steps
Ps. 106: 31 and that was *c.* unto him for
139: 18 if I should *c.* them, they are more
Is. 40:17 *c.* to him less than nothing
Hos. 8:12 law *c.* as a strange thing
10:29 *c.* the blood of the covenant unholy
Acts 20:24 neither *c.* I my life dear
Rom. 4: 3 it was *c.* unto him for rightousness
Phil. 3: 7 those I *c.* loss for Christ
3:13 I *c.* not to have apprehended
Jas. 1: 2 *c.* it all joy when ye fall

COUNTENANCE
Gen. 4: 5 Cain was very wroth and his *c.* fell
31: 2 and Jacob beheld the *c.* of Laban
Num. 6:26 Lord lift up his *c.* upon thee
1 Sam. 1:18 and her *c.* was no more sad
16: 7 look not on his *c.* or height
Neh. 2: 2 why is thy *c.* sad, seeing thou art
Job 29:24 the light of my *c.* they cast not
Ps. 4: 6 the light of thy *c.* upon us
90: 8 secret sins in the light of thy *c.*
Sol. 2:14 let me see thy *c.*, let me hear
Mat. 6:16 as hypocrites of a sad *c.*
Acts 2:28 full of joy with thy *c.*

COUNTRY
Prov. 25:25 good news from a far *c.*
Mat. 21:33 and went into a far *c.*
25:14 a man traveling into a far *c.*
Luke 15:13 his journey into a far *c.*
20: 9 into a far *c.* for a long time
Heb. 11:14 declare plainly they seek a *c.*
11:16 they desire a better *c.*

COURAGE
Num. 13:20 and be ye of good *c.*
Deut. 31: 6 be strong and of good *c.*
Josh. 1: 6 be strong and of good *c.*
2:11 any more *c.* in any man
2 Sam. 10:12 be of good *c.*, and let us
1 Chr. 28:20 be strong and of good *c.*
Ezra 10: 4 be of good *c.* and do it
Ps. 27:14 Wait on the Lord: be of good *c.*
Is. 41: 6 Be of good *c.*
Acts 28:15 he thanked God, and took *c.*

COURAGEOUS
Josh. 23: 6 be ye therefore very *c.*
2 Sam. 13:28 be *c.* and be valiant

COURSE (COURSES)
1 Chr. 23: 6 divided them into *c.* among the sons
Ps. 82: 5 foundations of the earth are out of *c.*
Acts 20:24 finish my *c.* with joy
1 Cor. 14:27 at most by three, and that by *c.*
Eph. 2: 2 according to the *c.* of this world
2 Thes. 3: 1 word may have free *c.* and
2 Tim. 4: 7 I have finished my *c.*
Jas. 3: 6 setteth on fire the *c.* of nature

COURT (COURTS)
Ex. 27: 9 make the *c.* of tabernacle
Ps. 65: 4 that he may dwell in thy *c.*
84:10 for a day in thy *c.* is better
100: 4 enter his *c.* with praise
Is. 1:12 who required, to tread my *c.*
34:13 for dragons and a *c.* for owls
62: 9 drink it in the *c.* of my holiness
Amos 7:13 and it is the king's *c.*
Rev. 11: 2 *c.* without the temple leave

COVENANT
Gen. 9: 9 I establish my *c.* with you
9:12 this is the token of the *c.*
9:15 and I will remember my *c.*
15:18 Lord made a *c.* with Abraham
17: 7 will establish my *c.* between me and thee
17: 9 thou shalt keep my *c.* therefore
17:11 token of the *c.* betwixt me and you
Ex. 2:24 God remembered his *c.* with Abraham
6: 4 have established my *c.* with them
6: 5 I have remembered my *c.*
19: 5 obey my voice indeed, and keep my *c.*
24: 7 he took the book of the *c.*
34:27 I have made a *c.* with thee
34:28 wrote upon the tables the words of the *c.*
Num. 10:33 the ark of the *c.* of the Lord
25:13 *c.* of an everlasting priesthood
Deut. 5: 2 made a *c.* with us in Horeb
7: 9 which keepeth *c.* and mercy
9:15 tables of the *c.* were in my two
Josh. 7:11 also transgressed my *c.*
Judg. 2: 1 never brake the *c.* with you
2:20 people hath transgressed my *c.*
2 Sam. 23: 5 made with me an everlasting *c.*
1 Ki. 8:23 who keepest *c.* and mercy
11:11 thou hast kept my *c.* and statues
2 Ki. 18:12 but transgressed his *c.*, and all
23: 3 made a *c.* before the Lord
1 Chr. 16:15 be ye mindful always of his *c.*
16:17 Even of the *c.* which he made
2 Chr. 6:14 the earth; which keepest my *c.*
Neh. 1: 5 that keepeth *c.* and mercy for them
9:32 who keepest *c.* and mercy
Job 31: 1 I made a *c.* with mine eyes
Ps. 25:10 keep his *c.* and testimonies
25:14 he will shew them his *c.*
50: 5 made a *c.* with me by sacrifice
74:20 Have respect to the *c.*: for the
89: 3 I have made a *c.* with my chosen
103: 18 to such as keep his *c.*
105: 10 to Israel for an everlasting *c.*
106: 45 he remembered for them his *c.*
132: 12 if thy children keep my *c.*
Prov. 2:17 forgetteth the *c.* of her God
Is. 28:15 we have made a *c.* with death
42: 6 give thee for a *c.* of the people
54:10 nor the *c.* of my peace be removed
55: 3 I will make an everlasting *c.* with
61: 8 will make an everlasting *c.* with them
Jer. 14:21 break not the *c.* with us
31:31 will make a new *c.* with the house
32:40 I will make an everlasting *c.* with them
34:18 men that have transgressed my *c.*
50: 5 to the Lord in a perpetual *c.*

Ezek. 16:60 I will remember my *c.*
20:37 bring into the bond of the *c.*
Dan. 9: 4 keeping the *c.* and mercy to them
9:27 confirm the *c.* with many for one
Hos. 8: 1 they have transgressed my *c.*
6: 7 like men, have transgressed the *c.*
10: 4 swearing falsely in making a *c.*
Amos 1: 9 remember not thy brotherly *c.*
Mal. 2: 4 that my *c.* might be with Levi
2:14 thy companion, the wife of the *c.*
Luke 1:72 to remember his holy *c.*
Acts 3:25 ye the children of the *c.*
Rom. 9: 4 adoption, and glory and *c.*
Eph. 2:12 strangers from the *c.* of promise
Heb. 8: 6 the mediator of a better *c.*
8:13 A new *c.*, he hath made the first
12:24 the mediator of the new *c.*
13:20 through the blood of an everlasting *c.*

COVER (COVERED, COVEREST, COVERETH)
Ex. 21:33 dig a pit and not *c.* it
33:22 I will *c.* thee with my hand
Deut. 33:12 Lord shall *c.* him all day
1 Sam. 24: 3 went in to *c.* his feet
Job 16:18 O earth *c.* not my blood
31:33 if I *c.* my transgressions
Ps. 32: 1 is forgiven whose sin is *c.*
73: 6 violence *c.* them as a garment
91: 4 *c.* thee with his feathers
104: 2 *c.* thyself with light as with
Prov. 10:12 but love *c.* all sins
Is. 11: 9 as the waters *c.* the sea
58: 7 seest the naked that thou *c.* him
Lam. 3:44 *c.* thyself with a cloud
Hos. 10: 8 say to the mountains, *c.* us
Rom. 4: 7 and whose sins are *c.*
1 Cor. 11: 7 man ought not to *c.* his head
1 Pet. 4: 8 charity shall *c.* a multitude of

COVET (COVETED)
Ex. 20:17 thou shalt not *c.* thy neighbor's house
Acts 20:33 I have *c.* no man's silver, or gold
1 Cor. 12:31 *c.* earnestly the best gifts
14:39 *c.* to prophesy and forbid not
1 Tim. 6:10 which while some *c.* after, they

COVETOUS
Ps. 10: 3 blesseth the *c.*, whom the Lord
Luke 16:14 Pharisees also who were *c.*, heard
1 Cor. 5:10 of this world or with *c.*, or
6:10 nor the *c.* inherit the kingdom of God
Eph. 5: 5 Person, nor *c.* man, who is an
1 Tim. 3: 3 but patient, not a brawler, not *c.*
2 Tim. 3: 2 lovers of their own selves, covetous
2 Pet. 2:14 heart they have exercised with *c.*

COVETOUSNESS
Ex. 18:21 fear God, men of truth, hating *c.*
Ps. 119: 36 thy testimonies and not to *c.*
Ezek. 33:31 their heart goeth after their *c.*
Luke 12:15 and beware of *c.*: for man's life
Col. 3: 5 and *c.* which is idolatry
Heb. 13: 5 let your conversation be without *c.*

CRAFTY
Job 5:12 disappoint devices of the *c*
15: 5 choosest the tongue of the *c.*

CRAFTINESS
Job 5:13 in their own *c.*
Luke 20:23 but he perceived their *c.*, and said
1 Cor. 3:19 taketh the wise in their own *c.*
2 Cor. 4: 2 not walking in *c.*, nor handling
Eph. 4:14 and cunning *c.*, whereby

CREATE (CREATED)
Gen. 1: 1 God *c.* the heavens and the earth
Ps. 51:10 *c.* in me a clean heart
102: 18 people which shall be *c.* shall
104: 30 forth thy spirit, they are *c.*
Is. 4: 5 will *c.* upon every dwelling place
43: 7 I have *c.* him for my glory
45: 7 I form light and *c.* darkness
57:19 I *c.* the fruit of the lips, peace
65:18 rejoice for ever in that which I *c.*
Jer. 31:22 *c.* a new thing in the earth
Mal. 2:10 hath not one God *c.* us
Eph. 2:10 *c.* in Christ Jesus to good works
3: 9 *c.* all things by Jesus Christ
Col. 1:16 all things were *c.* by him
3:10 after the image of him that *c.* him
1 Tim. 4: 3 which God *c.* to be received
Rev. 4:11 thou hast *c.* all things
10: 6 *c.* heaven and things therein

CREATION
Mark 10: 6 from the beginning of the *c.*
13:19 from the beginning of the *c.*
Rom. 1:20 of him from the *c.* of the world
8:22 the whole *c.* groaneth
Rev. 3:14 beginning of the *c.* of God

CREATOR
Eccl. 12: 1 remember now thy *C.* in the days
Is. 40:28 the Lord is the *C.* of ends of earth
43:15 *C.* of Israel, your king
Rom. 1:25 more than the blessed *C.*
1 Pet. 4:19 in well doing as unto a faithful *C.*

CREATURE
Gen. 1:20 moving *c.* that hath life
Lev. 11:46 of every living *c.* that moveth
Mark 16:15 preach the gospel to every *c.*
Rom. 8:20 *c.* was made subject to vanity
8:21 *c.* itself also shall be delivered
2 Cor. 5:17 man in Christ is a new *c.*
Gal. 6:15 availeth anything but a new *c.*
Col. 1:15 the firstborn of every *c.*
1 Tim. 4: 4 for every *c.* of God is good
Heb. 4:13 neither is there any *c.* that

CRIB
Job 39: 9 to serve thee or abide by thy *c.*
Prov. 14: 4 no oxen are, the *c.* is clean
Is. 1: 3 and the ass his master's *c.*

CROOKED
Deut. 32: 5 are a perverse and *c.* generation
Job 26:13 hand hath formed the *c.* serpent
Ps. 125: 5 their *c.* ways
Eccl. 1:15 *c.* cannot be made straight
Is. 27: 1 leviathan that *c.* serpent
40: 4 the *c.* shall be made straight
Luke 3: 5 the *c.* shall be made straight
Phil. 2:15 a *c.* and perverse generation

CROSS
Mat. 10:38 taketh not up his *c.* and followeth
Luke 14:27 whosoever doth not bear his *c.*
23:26 on him they laid the *c.*
John 19:17 bearing his *c.* went forth
19:31 should not remain upon the *c.*
1 Cor. 1:17 lest the *c.* of Christ be of none
Gal. 5:11 is the offence of the *c.* ceased
6:14 glory save in the *c.* of Lord Jesus
Phil. 2: 8 even death on the *c.*
3:18 enemies of the *c.* of Christ
Col. 1:20 peace through the blood of his *c.*
2:14 nailing it to his *c.*
Heb. 12: 2 before him endured the *c.*

CROWN (CROWNS)
Lev. 8: 9 the golden plate, the holy *c.*
Esth. 1:11 the king with the *c.* royal
Ps. 89:39 thou hast profaned his *c.*
Prov. 12: 4 virtuous woman is a *c.*
14:24 *c.* of the wise is their riches: but
14:17 children's children are the *c.* of
Sol. 3:11 behold king Solomon with the *c.*
Is. 28: 5 Lord of hosts for the *c.* of glory
62: 3 a *c.* of glory in hand of the Lord
Zech. 6:11 silver and gold and make *c.*
1 Cor. 9:25 to obtain a corruptible *c.*
Phil. 4: 1 my joy and *c.*, so stand fast
1 Thes. 2:19 or joy or *c.* of rejoicing
2 Tim. 4: 8 laid up for me a *c.* of righteousness
Jas. 1:12 receive the *c.* of life which Lord
Rev. 2:10 I will give thee a *c.* of life
3:11 that no man take thy *c.*
4: 4 on their heads *c.* of gold
9: 7 as it were like *c.* of gold
12: 3 seven *c.* upon his heads
13: 1 upon his horns ten *c.*
19:12 on his head were many *c.*

CROWNED (CROWNETH)
Ps. 8: 5 and hast *c.* him with glory
103: 4 *c.* thee with lovingkindness
Prov. 14:18 prudent are *c.* with knowledge
Heb. 2: 9 *c.* with glory and honor

CRUCIFY (CRUCIFIED)
Mat. 20:19 to scourge and to *c.* him
23:34 ye shall kill and *c.*
27:31 led him away to *c.* him
28: 5 ye seek Jesus, which was *c.*
Rom. 6: 6 the old man is *c.* with him
1 Cor. 1:13 was Paul *c.* for you?
1:23 but we preach Christ *c.*
2 Cor. 13: 4 though he was *c.* through weakness
Gal. 2:20 I am *c.* with Christ, I live
5:24 that are Christ's have *c.* the flesh
6:14 world is *c.* to me, I to world
Heb. 6: 6 they *c.* the Son of God afresh
Rev. 11: 8 where also our Lord was *c.*

CRUEL
Gen. 49: 7 and their wrath, for it was *c.*
Ps. 71: 4 of the unrighteous and *c.* man
Prov. 11:17 he that is *c.* troubleth
12:10 mercies of the wicked are *c.*
Sol. 8: 6 jealousy is *c.* as the grave
Is. 13: 9 *c.* both with wrath and fierce anger
19: 4 into the hand of a *c.* lord
Jer. 6:23 they are *c.* and have no mercy
Heb. 11:36 had a trial of *c.* mockings

CRUMBS
Mat. 15:27 dogs eat the *c.* which fall
Luke 16:21 with the *c.* which fell

CRY (CRIED, CRIEST, CRIETH)
Gen. 4:10 brother's blood *c.* unto me
18:20 Because the *c.* of Sodom and Gomorrah
27:34 great and exceeding bitter *c.*
Ex. 2:23 their *c.* came up to God
22:23 I will surely hear their *c.*
Ps. 9:12 forgetteth not the *c.* of the humble
22: 5 *c.* to thee and were delivered
34: 6 this poor man *c.* and the Lord heard
138: 3 I *c.* thou answeredst me
Prov. 1:20 wisdom *c.* without; she uttereth
2: 3 if thou *c.* after knowledge
Is. 42: 2 not *c.* nor lift up his voice
58: 1 *c.* aloud, spare not, show my
Jer. 7:16 neither lift up *c.* nor prayer
Lam. 2:18 their heart *c.* unto the Lord
Ezek. 9: 4 men that sigh and *c.* for
Hos. 7:14 not *c.* unto me with their heart
Jonah 3: 8 and *c.* mightily to God
Mic. 6: 9 Lord's voice *c.* to the city
Mat. 25: 6 at midnight there was a *c.* made
Luke 18: 7 *c.* day and night to him
19:40 peace, the stones would *c.* out
Rom. 8:15 where by we *c.*, Abba Father

CRYING
Prov. 19:18 thy soul spare for his *c.*
Mat. 3: 3 voice of one *c.* in the wilderness
Heb. 5: 7 with strong *c.* and tears
Rev. 21: 4 neither sorrow nor *c.*, neither

CUP
Gen. 40:11 Pharaoh's *c.* was in my hand
44: 2 my *c.* the silver *c.* in the
Ps. 16: 5 mine inheritance and of my *c.*
23: 5 with oil; my *c.* runneth over
73:10 waters of a full *c.* are wrung
116: 13 take the *c.* of salvation
Prov. 23:31 when it giveth colour in the *c.*
Is. 51:17 the dregs of the *c.* of trembling
Jer. 16: 7 give them the *c.* of salvation
25:15 the wine *c.* of this fury
51: 7 Babylon hath been a golden *c.*
Lam. 4:21 the *c.* also shall pass through
Ezek. 23:31 give her *c.* into her hand
23:33 *c.* of thy sister Samaria
Hab. 2:16 *c.* of the Lord's right hand
Mat. 10:42 a *c.* of cold water only
20:22 able to drink of the *c.* that I
23:25 make clean outside of the *c.* and
26:39 let this *c.* pass from me
John 18:11 *c.* which the Father hath given
1 Cor. 10:16 *c.* of blessing which we
10:21 drink the *c.* of the Lord and the *c.* of devils
11:25 this *c.* is the new testament
Rev. 16:19 give unto her the *c.* of the wine

CURSE
Gen. 8:21 not again *c.* the ground
27:13 Upon me be thy *c.*, my son
Ex. 22:28 nor *c.* the ruler of thy people
Lev. 19:14 thou shalt not *c.* the deaf
Num. 22: 6 I pray thee *c.* me this people
Deut. 11:26 before you a blessing and a *c.*
23: 5 turned the *c.* into a blessing
30: 1 the blessing and the *c.*
Judg. 5:23 *c.* ye Meroz, *c.* bitterly
2 Sam. 16:10 let him *c.* because the Lord
Job 1:11 he will *c.* thee to thy face
2: 9 retain integrity? *c.* God and die
Ps. 109: 28 let them not *c.* but bless
Prov. 3:33 *c.* of the Lord is in the house
11:26 the people shall *c.* him
26: 2 so the *c.* causeless shall not come
Eccl. 10:20 *c.* not the king in his chamber

Is. 65:15 for a *c.* unto my chosen
Jer. 15:10 every one of them doth *c.* me
26: 6 city a *c.* to all the nations
42:18 and a *c.* and a reproach
Mal. 2: 2 I will *c.* your blessings
3: 9 ye are cursed with a *c.*
Mat. 5:44 bless them that *c.* you,
Rom. 12:14 bless, and do not *c.*

CURSED (CURSING)
Gen. 49: 7 *c.* be their anger, for it
Deut. 30:19 life and death, blessing and *c.*
Job 3: 1 opened Job his mouth and *c.* his day
Ps. 119: 21 proud *c.* which do err from
Jer. 11: 3 *c.* be man that obeyeth not
48:10 *c.* be he that doeth the work of the

CURTAIN (CURTAINS)
Ex. 26: 1 ten *c.* of fine twined linen
2 Sam. 7: 2 God dwelleth within the *c.*
Ps. 104: 2 stretchest out the heavens like a *c.*

CUSTOM (CUSTOMS)
Gen. 31:35 the *c.* of the women is upon me
Jer. 10: 3 the *c.* of the people are vain
Luke 4:16 as his *c.* was, he went
Rom. 13: 7 *c.* to whom *c.*; fear to
1 Cor. 11:16 we have no such *c.*

CUT
Lev. 22:24 or crushed, of broken, of *c.*
Job 4: 7 were the righteous *c.* off
22:20 substance is not *c.* down
Ps. 37:28 the wicked shall be *c.* off
76:12 He shall *c.* off the spirit
129: 4 he hath *c.* asunder the cords
Prov. 2:22 but the wicked shall be *c.* off
Jer. 48: 2 also thou shalt be *c.* down
Zech. 11:10 *c.* it asunder that I might break
Mat. 5:30 hand offend thee, *c.* it off
18: 8 thy foot offend thee, *c.* it off
24:51 and shall *c.* him asunder
Luke 12:46 and will *c.* him in sunder
13: 7 and find none: *c.* it down
Acts 7:54 they were *c.* to the heart
Rom. 11:22 thou also shalt be *c.* off
Gal. 5:12 they were even *c.* off which trouble you

CYMBAL (CYMBALS)
2 Sam. 6: 5 and on cornets and on *c.*
Ps. 150: 5 Praise him upon the loud *c.*
Ezra 3:10 with *c.* to praise the Lord
1 Cor. 13: 1 as sounding brass, or a tinkling *c.*

D

DAMNED
Mark 16:16 believeth not shall be *d.*
Rom. 14:23 doubteth, is *d.* if he eat
2 Thes. 2:12 they all might be *d.*

DAMNATION
Mat. 23:14 ye shall receive the greater *d.*
23:33 can ye escape the *d.* of hell
Mark 3:29 is in danger of eternal *d.*
John 5:29 forth to resurrection of *d.*
1 Cor. 11:29 eateth and drinketh *d.*
1 Tim. 5:12 having *d.* because they cast off
2 Pet. 2: 3 their *d.* slumbereth not

DANCE (DANCED, DANCES)
Ex. 15:20 with timbrels and with *d.*
Judg. 11:34 with timbrels and with *d.*
21:21 come out to *d.* in *d.*
2 Sam. 6:14 And David *d.* before the Lord
Ps. 149: 3 let them praise his name in the *d.*
Is. 13:21 the satyrs shall *d.* there
Mat. 14: 6 the daughter of Herodias *d.*

DARE
Rom. 5: 7 some would even *d.* to die
1 Cor. 6: 1 *D.* any of you, having a matter
2 Cor. 10:12 we *d.* not make ourselves

DARK
Num. 12: 8 and not in *d.* speeches
2 Sam. 22:12 *d.* waters, and thick clouds of the
Job 24:16 in the *d.* dig through houses
Ps. 18:11 *d.* waters and thick clouds of the
74:20 for the *d.* places of the earth
78: 2 I will utter *d.* sayings
88:12 thy wonders known in the *d.*?
Prov. 1: 6 of the wise and their *d.* sayings
Is. 45:19 in a *d.* place of the earth
Lam. 3: 6 set me in the *d.* places
Dan. 8:23 and understanding *d.* sentences
John 6:17 And it was now *d.*, and Jesus

DARKENED
Ex. 10:15 so that the land was *d.*
Ps. 69:23 let eyes be *d.* that they see not
Mat. 24:29 shall the sun be *d.*
Rom. 1:21 their foolish heart was *d.*
11:10 Let their eyes be *d.* that they may
Eph. 4:18 having the understanding *d.*

DARKLY
1 Cor. 13:12 now we see through a glass *d.*

DARKNESS
Gen. 1: 2 *d.* was upon the face of the deep
Deut. 28:29 as the blind gropeth in *d.*
1 Sam. 2: 9 wicked shall be silent in *d.*
2 Sam. 22:29 Lord will lighten my *d.*
Job 34:22 no *d.* nor shadow of death
Ps. 104: 20 makest *d.*, and it is night
107: 10 such as sit in *d.* and in the
Is. 5:20 *d.* for light, and light for *d.*
9: 2 that walked in *d.* have seen
29:18 out of obscurity and out of *d.*
45: 7 I form light and create *d.*
Mat. 4:16 sat in *d.* saw a great light
6:23 whole body full of *d.*
8:12 cast out into outer *d.*
John 1: 5 light shineth in the *d.*
3:19 men loved *d.* rather than light
12:35 light lest *d.* come upon you
Acts 26:18 turn them from *d.* to light
Rom. 13:12 cast off the works of *d.*
1 Cor. 4: 5 the hidden things of *d.*
2 Cor. 4: 6 light to shine out of *d.*
Eph. 5: 8 ye were sometimes *d.* but
5:11 the unfruitful works of *d.*
6:12 the rulers of the *d.* of this world
1 Thes. 5: 4 but ye brethren are not in *d.*
1 Pet. 2: 9 called you out of the *d.*
2 Pet. 2: 4 delivered into chains of *d.*
1 John 1: 5 in him is no *d.* at all
2: 8 *d.* is past, and the true light shineth
2:11 because *d.* hath blinded his eyes
Jude 1:13 blackness of *d.* for ever

DARTS
Eph. 6:16 quench all the fiery *d.* of the wicked

DASH (DASHED, DASHETH)
Ex. 15: 6 hath *d.* in pieces the enemy
2 Ki. 8:12 wilt *d.* their children, and rip up
Ps. 2: 9 *d.* in pieces like a potter's vessel
91:12 lest thou *d.* thy foot against a stone
137: 9 *d.* thy little ones against the stones
Is. 13:18 bows shall *d.* the young men
Jer. 13:14 will *d.* them one against another
Hos. 10:14 the mother was *d.* in pieces

DAY
Gen. 1: 5 and God called the light *d.*
Ps. 19: 2 *d.* unto *d.* uttereth speech
20: 1 Lord hear in the *d.* of trouble
50:15 call on me in the *d.* of trouble
59:16 my defence and refuge in the *d.* of trouble
77: 2 in the *d.* of trouble I sought the
84:10 a *d.* in thy courts is better than
118: 24 this is the *d.* which the Lord
Prov. 27: 1 what a *d.* may bring forth
Is. 2:12 *d.* of the Lord of Hosts
13: 9 the *d.* of the Lord cometh
34: 8 the *d.* of the Lord's vengeance
37: 3 This *d.* is a *d.* of trouble and
Jer. 46:10 the *d.* of the Lord of Hosts
Lam. 2:22 a solemn *d.* my terrors round
Ezek. 7: 7 time is come, the *d.* of trouble is near
30: 3 For the *d.* is near, even the day
Joel 1:15 the *d.* of the Lord is at hand
3:14 the *d.* of the Lord is near
Amos 5:18 that desire the *d.* of the Lord
6: 3 put far away the evil *d.*
Obad. 1:15 the *d.* of the Lord is near
Nah. 1: 7 a strong hold in the *d.* of trouble
Hab. 3:16 I might rest in the *d.* of trouble
Zeph. 1:15 a *d.* of trouble and distress
2: 3 be hid in the *d.* of the Lord's anger
Zech. 4:10 despised the *d.* of small things
14: 1 the *d.* of the Lord cometh
Mal. 4: 5 the great and dreadful *d.*
Mat. 6:34 sufficient to the *d.* is the evil
10:15 in the *d.* of judgment than for
12:36 thereof in the *d.* of judgment
Mark 6:11 in the *d.* of judgment than for
John 8:56 Abraham rejoiced to see my *d.*
1 Cor. 1: 8 blameless in the *d.* of our Lord
3:13 the *d.* shall declare it
5: 5 the *d.* of the Lord Jesus
2 Cor. 1:14 in the *d.* of the Lord Jesus
Phil. 1: 6 the *d.* of Jesus Christ
1 Thes. 5: 5 children of the *d.*
5: 2 the *d.* of the Lord so cometh
2 Thes. 2: 2 as that the *d.* of Christ
2 Pet. 1:19 *d.* star arise in your hearts
2: 9 unto the *d.* of judgment
3: 7 the *d.* of judgment and perdition
3:10 *d.* of the Lord will come
Rev. 1:10 the Spirit on the Lord's *d.*

DAYS
Gen. 49: 1 which shall befall you in the last *d.*
Num. 24:14 to thy people in the latter *d.*
Deut. 31:29 befall you in the latter *d.*
Job 7: 6 my *d.* are swifter than a
7:16 let me alone, my *d.* are vanity
8: 9 *d.* on earth as a shadow
14: 1 of few *d.* and full of trouble
32: 7 *d.* should speak, and multitude
Ps. 39: 4 to know the end, and measure of my *d.*
90:12 teach us to number our *d.*
102: 3 my *d.* are consumed like smoke
102: 23 in the way; he shortened my *d.*
Prov. 3:16 length of *d.* is in her right
Eccl. 7:10 former *d.* better than these
11: 8 remember the *d.* of darkness; many
12: 1 while the evil *d.* come not
Is. 2: 2 it shall come to pass in the last *d.*
39: 8 peace and truth in my *d.*
Jer. 2:32 forgotten me *d.* without number
20:18 my *d.* are consumed with shame
23:20 in the latter *d.* ye shall
30:24 in the latter *d.* ye shall consider
Dan. 10:14 befall thy people in the latter *d.*
Hos. 3: 5 his goodness in the latter *d.*
Mic. 4: 1 in the last *d.* it shall
Acts 2:17 come to pass in the last *d.*
Gal. 4:10 observe the *d.*, months, and years
Eph. 5:16 time because the *d.* are evil
2 Tim. 3: 1 that in the last *d.* perilous
Heb. 1: 2 in these last *d.* spoken unto us
Jas. 5: 3 treasure together in the last *d.*
1 Pet. 3:10 love life and see good *d.*
2 Pet. 3: 3 come in the last *d.* scoffers

DAILY
Ps. 61: 8 I may *d.* perform my vows
Prov. 8:34 watching *d.* at my gates
Is. 58: 2 seek me *d.* and delight in
Acts 2:47 the Lord added to the church *d.*
Heb. 3:13 but exhort one another *d.*, while

DEACONS
Phil. 1: 1 at Philippi with the bishops and *d.*
1 Tim. 3: 8 likewise must the *d.* be grave

DEAD
Gen. 20: 3 behold thou art but a *d.* man
23: 3 up from before his *d.*
Num. 16:48 stood between *d.* and living
1 Sam. 24:14 after a *d.* dog, after a flea
Ps. 88:10 shall the *d.* arise and praise
115: 17 the *d.* praise not the Lord
Eccl. 9: 5 the *d.* know not any thing
10: 1 *d.* flies cause the ointment to
Mat. 8:22 let the *d.* bury their own *d.*
22:32 not the God of the *d.* but of the
Luke 8:52 she is not *d.* but sleepeth
John 5:25 *d.* hear the voice of the Son of God
11:25 though *d.* yet shall he live
Rom. 6: 8 now if we be *d.* with Christ
6:11 *d.* indeed unto sin, but alive
Gal. 2:19 I through the law am *d.* to the law
Eph. 2: 1 who were *d.* in trespasses and sins
Col. 2:13 being *d.* in your sins and the
1 Thes. 4:16 *d.* in Christ rise first
2 Tim. 2:11 *d.* with him, we shall live
Heb. 11: 4 by it he being *d.* yet speaketh
Rev. 14:13 blessed are the *d.* which die

DEAF
Ex. 4:11 who maketh the dumb or *d.*
Lev. 19:14 thou shalt not curse the *d.*
Ps. 38:13 I, as a *d.* man, heard not
Is. 35: 5 ears of the *d.* shall be unstopped
42:18 hear, ye *d.* and look, ye blind

Is. 42:19 or *d.* as my messenger that I sent?
43: 8 and the *d.* people that have ears
Mic. 7:16 their mouth, their ears shall be *d.*
Mat. 11: 5 the *d.* hear, the dead are raised up
Mark 7:32 unto him the one that was *d.*

DEATH
Gen. 21:16 not see the *d.* of the child
Num. 23:10 let me die the *d.* of the righteous
Deut. 30:15 set before you life and *d.*
Ps. 6: 5 in *d.* no remembrance of thee
68:20 to the Lord belong issues from *d.*
73: 4 have no bands in their *d.*: but
89:48 liveth and shall not see *d.*
116: 15 Lord is the *d.* of his saints
118: 18 he hath not given me over unto *d.*
Prov. 2:18 her house inclineth to *d.*
8:36 all they that hate me love *d.*
18:21 *d.* and life in the power of the tongue
Eccl. 7:26 more bitter than *d.* the woman
8: 8 hath power in the day of *d.*
Is. 25: 8 he will swallow up *d.* in victory
28:15 we have made a covenant with *d.*
38:18 *d.* cannot celebrate thee
Jer. 8: 3 *d.* chosen rather than life
21: 8 you a way of life, a way of *d.*
Hos. 13:14 O *d.*, I will be thy plagues
Mat. 16:28 which shall not taste of *d.*
26:38 exceeding sorrowful even unto *d.*
John 5:24 is passed from *d.* unto life
8:51 he shall never see *d.*,
12:33 what *d.* he should die
Acts 2:24 having loosed the pains of *d.*
Rom. 5:12 sin entered, and *d.* by sin
6: 5 planted in the likeness of his *d.*
6: 9 *d.* hath no more dominion over
6:21 for the end of those things is *d.*
7: 5 to bring forth fruit unto *d.*
8: 2 free from the law of sin and *d.*
8: 6 for to be carnally minded is *d.*
8:38 *d.* nor life shall separate us from
1 Cor. 3:22 or life, or *d.* or things
11:26 ye show the Lord's *d.* till he come
15:21 by man came *d.* by man also
15:54 *d.* is swallowed up in victory
15:55 O *d.*, where is thy sting
15:56 sting of *d.* is sin, and strength
2 Cor. 1: 9 sentence of *d.* in ourselves
1:10 deliver from so great a *d.* and doth
2:16 we are the savour of *d.* unto *d.*
4:11 delivered to *d.* for Jesus' sake
4:12 *d.* worketh in us, but life in you
Phil. 2: 8 *d.* even the *d.* of the cross
Heb. 2: 9 should taste *d.* for every man
2:15 through fear of *d.* are subject to
11: 5 should not see *d.*,
Jas. 1:15 sin finished bringeth *d.*
1 Pet. 3:18 put to *d.* in the flesh
1 John 3:14 but is passed from *d.* unto life
5:16 there is a sin unto *d.*: I do not
Rev. 1:18 I have the keys of hell and *d.*
2:10 be faithful unto *d.* and I will
20: 6 on such second *d.* hath no power
21: 4 there shall be no more *d.* nor

DEBATE
Prov. 25: 9 *d.* thy cause with thy neighbour
Is. 27: 8 thou wilt *d.* with it he stayeth
58: 4 fast for strife and *d.*
Rom. 1:29 full of envy, murder, *d.*
2 Cor. 12:20 lest there be *d.* envyings

DEBT (DEBTS)
Mat. 6:12 forgive us our *d.*
18:27 and forgave him the *d.*
Rom. 4: 4 reckoned of grace, but of *d.*

DEBTOR (DEBTORS)
Ezek. 18: 7 restored the *d.* his pledge
Luke 7:41 creditor which had two *d.*
Rom. 1:14 I am *d.* both to the Greeks
8:12 brethren, we are *d.*; not to the
15:27 verily; and their *d.* they are
Gal. 5: 3 he is a *d.* to do the whole law

DECEIT
Ps. 72:14 redeem thy soul from *d.*
101: 7 worketh *d.* shall not dwell
Prov. 20:17 bread of *d.* is sweet to man
Is. 53: 9 neither was any *d.* in his mouth
Jer. 5:27 their houses full of *d.*
8: 5 they hold fast *d.* they refuse
9: 8 an arrow shot out; it speaketh *d.*
Col. 2: 8 spoil through philosophy and vain *d.*

DECEITFUL (DECEITFULLY)
Job 13: 7 and talk *d.* for him
Ps. 5: 6 abhor the bloody and *d.* man
24: 4 unto vanity, nor sworn *d.*
35:20 they devise *d.* matters against
55:23 *d.* men shall not live half their days
78:57 turned aside like a *d.* bow
109: 2 mouth of the *d.* are opened
Prov. 11:18 wicked worketh a *d.* work
14:25 but a *d.* witness speaketh lies
27: 6 kisses of an enemy are *d.*
Jer. 17: 9 heart *d.* above all things
48:10 the work of the lord *d.*
Hos. 7:16 they are like a *d.* bow
2 Cor. 4: 2 handling the word of God *d.*
Eph. 4:22 corrupt according to the *d.* lusts

DECEITFULNESS
Mat. 13:22 *d.* of riches, choke the word

DECEIVE (DECEIVED, DECEIVING, DECEIVETH)
Deut. 11:16 that your heart be not *d.*
2 Ki. 4:28 did I not say Do not *d.* me
18:29 Let not Hezekiah *d.* you
Job 12:16 *d.* and the deceiver are
Prov. 24:28 and *d.* not with thy lips
26:19 the man that *d.* his neighbor
Is. 44:20 a *d.* heart hath turned
Jer. 20: 7 O Lord, thou hast *d.* me
Ezek. 14: 9 I, Lord, have *d.* that prophet
Obad. 1: 3 pride of thine heart hath *d.* thee
Mat. 24: 4 take heed no man *d.* you
24:24 if possible *d.* the very elect
Rom. 7:11 sin *d.* me, and by it slew me
1 Cor. 3:18 let no man *d.* himself
Gal. 6: 3 when he is nothing, he *d.* himself
1 Tim. 2:14 and Adam was not *d.* but the woman
2 Tim. 3:13 and worse, *d.* and being *d.*
Jas. 1:26 but *d.* his own heart, this man's
1 John 1: 8 no sin, we *d.* ourselves
Rev. 12: 9 which *d.* the whole world

DECEIVER (DECEIVERS)
Gen. 27:12 shall seem to him as a *d.*
Mal. 1:14 but cursed be the *d.*, which hath
Mat. 27:63 remember that the *d.* said
2 Cor. 6: 8 as *d.* and yet true
Tit. 1:10 and vain talkers and *d.*, specially
2 John 1: 7 many *d.* are entered into the world

DECLARE (DECLARED, DECLARETH)
Gen. 41:24 there was none that could *d.* it
Ps. 22:22 I will *d.* thy name unto brethren
38:18 I will *d.* my iniquity and
50:16 to do to *d.* my statutes
78: 6 may *d.* them to their children
145: 4 shall *d.* thy mighty acts
Is. 3: 9 they *d.* their sin as Sodom
42: 9 and new things do I *d.*
53: 8 who shall *d.* his generation
Amos 4:13 *d.* to man his thought
Acts 17:23 worship him *d.* I unto you
20:27 not shunned to *d.* all counsel
Rom. 1: 4 *d.* to be the Son of God
3:25 to *d.* his righteousness for the
Heb. 11:14 say such things *d.* plainly
1 John 1: 3 seen and heard *d.* we unto you

DECREE (DECREED, DECREES)
Job 28:26 he made a *d.* for rain
Ps. 2: 7 I will declare the *d.*
Prov. 8:15 reign, and princes *d.* justice
8:29 gave to the sea his *d.*
Is. 10: 1 unto them that *d.* unrighteous *d.*
10:22 the consumption *d.* shall overflow
Jer. 5:22 bound of the sea by a perpetual *d.*
Dan. 4:17 by the *d.* of the watchers
Zeph. 2: 2 before the *d.* bring forth
Luke 2: 1 went out a *d.* from Caesar
Acts 17: 7 contrary to the *d.* of Caesar
1 Cor. 7:37 and hath *d.* in his heart

DEDICATE (DEDICATED)
Deut. 20: 5 and another man *d.* it
2 Sam. 8:11 King David did *d.* unto the Lord
1 Chr. 26:20 the treasures of the *d.* things
26:27 battles did they *d.* to maintain
Ezek. 44:29 and every *d.* thing in Israel

DEDICATION
Num. 7:84 this was the *d.* of the altar
2 Chr. 7: 9 they kept the *d.* of the altar
Ezra 6:17 at the *d.* of this house
Neh. 12:27 the *d.* of the wall of Jerusalem
John 10:22 the feast of the *d.*, and it was

DEED (DEEDS)
Judg. 19:30 no such *d.* done nor seen
2 Sam. 12:14 by this *d.* thou hast
Neh. 13:14 wipe not out my good *d.*
Ps. 28: 4 give them according to their *d.*
Jer. 25:14 them according to their *d.*
John 3:19 because their *d.* were evil
Rom. 2: 6 every man according to his *d.*
3:20 by *d.* of law no flesh justified
8:13 do mortify the *d.* of the body
15:18 obedient by word and *d.*
Col. 3: 9 the old man with his *d.*
3:17 whatsoever ye do in word or *d.*
1 John 3:18 in tongue but in *d.* and in truth
2 John 1:11 partaker of his evil *d.*

DEEP
Gen. 1: 2 was upon the face of the *d.*
7:11 fountains of the great *d.*
Job 38:30 the face of the *d.* is frozen
Ps. 36: 6 thy judgments are a great *d.*
42: 7 *d.* calleth unto *d.* at the noise
1 Cor. 2:10 yea, the *d.* things of God
2 Cor. 11:25 I have been in the *d.*

DEEPLY
Is. 31: 6 children of Israel have *d.* revolted
Hos. 9: 9 they have *d.* corrupted themselves
Mark 8:12 sighed *d.* in spirit, and saith

DEFENCE
2 Chr. 11: 5 built cities for *d.* in Judah
Num. 14: 9 their *d.* is departed from them
Job 22:25 the Almighty shall be thy *d.*
Ps. 59: 9 upon thee; for God is my *d.*
62: 2 he is my *d.*, I shall not
89:18 for the Lord is our *d.*
94:22 but the Lord is my *d.*
Eccl. 7:12 for wisdom is a *d.*, and money
Is. 4: 5 on all the glory shall be the *d.*
19: 6 brooks of *d.* shall be emptied
33:16 place of *d.* shall be the munitions

DEFER (DEFERRED, DEFERRETH)
Prov. 13:12 hope *d.* maketh the heart sick
19:11 discretion of a man *d.* his anger
Eccl. 5: 4 *D.* not to pay it, for he
Is. 48: 9 name's sake will I defer my anger
Dan. 9:19 *d.* not for thine own sake

DEFILE (DEFILED, DEFILETH)
Lev. 18:25 and the land is *d.*, therefore
Is. 24: 5 the earth also is *d.*
Dan. 1: 8 he would not *d.* himself
Mat. 15:18 and they *d.* the man
Mark 7: 2 his disciples eat bread with *d.*
1 Cor. 3:17 if any *d.* the temple of God
Tit. 1:15 mind and conscience is *d.*
Heb. 12:15 and thereby many be *d.*
Rev. 3: 4 have not *d.* their garments
21:27 not enter any thing that *d.*

DEFRAUD (DEFRAUDED)
Lev. 19:13 thou shalt not *d.* thy neighbor
1 Sam. 12: 3 or whom have I *d.*? whom have I
1 Cor. 6: 7 why not rather be *d.*
2 Cor. 7: 2 we have *d.* no man

DELAY (DELAYED, DELAYETH)
Ex. 22:29 not *d.* to offer the first
32: 1 Moses *d.* to come down
Ps. 119: 60 I *d.* not to keep thy commandments
Mat. 24:48 my lord *d.* his coming
Acts 9:38 he would not *d.* to come

DELICATE (DELICATES)
Deut. 28:56 tender and *d.* woman among you
Is. 47: 1 no more be called tender and *d.*
Jer. 6: 2 a comely and *d.* woman
51:34 filled his belly with my *d.*
Mic. 1:16 poll thee for thy *d.* children

DELICATELY
1 Sam. 15:32 Agag came unto him *d.*
Prov. 29:21 he that *d.* bringeth up his servant
Lam. 4: 5 that did feed *d.* are desolate
Luke 7:25 gorgeously apparelled, and live *d.*

DELIGHT (DELIGHTED, DELIGHTETH)
Gen. 34:19 he had *d.* in Jacob's daughter
Num. 14: 8 If the Lord *d.* in us
Deut. 10:15 Lord had a *d.* in thy fathers
1 Sam. 15:22 as great *d.* in burnt offerings
2 Sam. 22:20 because he *d.* in me
24: 3 Why doth the king *d.* in this thing?
Esth. 2:14 except the king *d.* in her
6: 6 whom the king *d.* to honour

Job 22:26 thy *d.* in the Almighty
27:10 will he *d.* himself in
Ps. 1: 2 his *d.* is in the law
16: 3 saints in whom is all my *d.*
22: 8 deliver him, seeing he *d.* in him
40: 8 I *d.* to do thy will, O my God
94:19 thy comforts *d.* my soul
109: 17 he *d.* not in blessing, so let
147: 10 he *d.* not in the strength of the horse
Prov. 3:12 the son in whom he *d.*
11: 1 just weight is his *d.*
11:20 in their way is his *d.*
15: 8 prayer of the upright is his *d.*
Sol. 2: 3 under his shadow with *d.*
Is. 1:11 I *d.* not in the blood of bullocks
42: 1 elect in whom my soul *d.*
55: 2 let your soul *d.* itself in
58: 2 take *d.* in approaching to God
62: 4 Beulah: for the Lord *d.* in thee
Jer. 9:24 in these things I *d.* saith Lord
Mic. 7:18 for ever, because he *d.* in mercy
Rom. 7:22 I *d.* in the law of God

DELIGHTS
Ps. 119: 92 thy law had been my *d.*
Prov. 8:31 my *d.* were with sons of men
Sol. 7: 6 how pleasant, O love, for *d.*

DELIGHTSOME
Mal. 3:12 ye shall be a *d.* land

DELIVER
Ex. 3: 8 come down to *d.* them
5:18 ye shall *d.* the tale
Job 5:19 *d.* thee in six troubles
10: 7 none can *d.* out of thy hand
Ps. 33:19 to *d.* their soul from death
50:15 I will *d.* thee, and thou
91:15 I will *d.* him and honour him
56:13 wilt thou not *d.* my feet
74:19 *d.* not the soul of thy turtledove
Eccl. 8: 8 shall wickedness *d.* those that are
Ezek. 14:14 should *d.* but their own souls
34:10 I will *d.* my flock from their mouth
Dan. 3:17 our God is able to *d.* us
Hos. 11: 8 how shall I *d.* thee, Israel
Rom. 7:24 shall *d.* me from the body
1 Cor. 5: 5 to *d.* such a one to Satan
2 Tim. 4:18 Lord shall *d.* me from every evil
Heb. 2:15 *d.* them who through fear
2 Pet. 2: 9 Lord knoweth how to *d.* the godly

DELIVERED
Prov. 28:26 walketh wisely shall and be *d.*
Is. 38:17 *d.* it from the pit of corruption
49:24 or the lawful captive *d.*?
Jer. 7:10 *d.* to do all abominations
Ezek. 3:19 but thou hast *d.* thy soul
33: 9 but thou hast *d.* thy soul
Dan. 12: 1 at that time thy people shall be *d.*
Joel 2:32 name of the Lord shall be *d.*
Mic. 4:10 Babylon, there shalt thou be *d.*
Mat. 11:27 all *d.* to me of my Father
Acts 2:23 *d.* by the determinate counsel
Rom. 4:25 who was *d.* for our offences
7: 6 now we are *d.* from the law, that
8:32 *d.* him up for us all
2 Cor. 1:10 who *d.* us from so great a death
4:11 *d.* to death for Jesus' sake
1 Thes. 1:10 *d.* us from the wrath to come
1 Tim. 1:20 whom I have *d.* to Satan
Jude 1: 3 faith once *d.* to the saints

DELIVERANCE
Gen. 45: 7 save your lives by a great *d.*
Judg. 15:18 this great *d.* into the hand
2 Ki. 5: 1 had given *d.* to Syria
13:17 the arrow of the Lord's *d.*
1 Chr. 11:14 saved them by a great *d.*
Ezra 9:13 given us such *d.* as this
Esth. 4:14 *d.* arise to the Jews from another
Ps. 18:50 great *d.* giveth he to
32: 7 about with songs of *d.*
Joel 2:32 and in Jerusalem shall be *d.*
Obad. 1:17 upon mount Zion shall be *d.*
Luke 4:18 to preach *d.* to the captives
Heb. 11:35 tortured, not accepting *d.*

DELUSION (DELUSIONS)
Is. 66: 4 I also will choose their *d.*
2 Thes. 2:11 God shall send them a strong *d.*

DEN (DENS)
Judg. 6: 2 the *d.* which are in the mountains
Job 37:17 beasts go into *d.*, and remain
Ps. 10: 9 as a lion in his *d.*
104: 22 lay them down in their *d.*
Sol. 4: 8 from the lion's *d.*, from the
Jer. 7:11 become a *d.* of robbers in your eyes
9:11 and a *d.* of dragons, and I
10:22 desolate and a *d.* of dragons
Dan. 6:24 cast them into the *d.* of lions
Amos 3: 4 young lion cry out of his *d.*
Nah. 2:12 and his *d.* with ravin
Mat. 21:13 have made it a *d.* of thieves
Heb. 11:38 in *d.* and caves of the earth
Rev. 6:15 hid themselves in the *d.* and in the

DENY (DENIED, DENYING)
1 Ki. 2:16 one petition of thee, *d.* me not
Job 8:18 then it shall *d.* him
Prov. 30: 9 lest I be full, and *d.* thee
Mat. 10:33 shall *d.* me before men
16:24 let him *d.* himself and take up
26:34 cock crow thou shalt *d.* me
26:35 yet will I not *d.* thee
Mark 14:30 thou shalt *d.* me thrice
1 Tim. 5: 8 he hath *d.* the faith
2 Tim. 2:12 if we *d.* him, he will *d.* us
Tit. 1:16 but in works they *d.* him
2:12 *d.* ungodliness and the worldly
2 Pet. 2: 1 *d.* the Lord that bought them
Rev. 2:13 and hast not *d.* my faith

DEPART (DEPARTED, DEPARTETH, DEPARTING, DEPARTS)
2 Sam. 22:22 have not wickedly *d.* from my God
Job 21:14 they say unto God, *d.* from us
28:28 *d.* from evil is understanding
Ps. 18:21 not wickedly *d.* from my God
34:14 *d.* from evil and do good
37:27 *d.* from evil and do good
119:102 have *d.* from thy judgments
Prov. 14:16 feareth and *d.* from evil
3: 7 fear the Lord and *d.* from evil
16:17 the upright is to *d.* from evil
Is. 59:15 that *d.* from evil makes himself prey
Hos. 9:12 woe also to them when I *d.*
Mat. 7:23 *d.* from me, ye that work
25:41 *d.* from me, ye cursed, into
Luke 2:29 lettest thy servant *d.* in peace
5: 8 saying, *d.* from me, for I am a
Acts 20:29 after my *d.* shall grievous wolves
Phil. 1:23 having a desire to *d.* and
Heb. 3:12 unbelief, in *d.* from the living God
1 Tim. 4: 1 some shall *d.* from faith

DEPARTURE
Ezek. 26:18 shall be trouble at thy *d.*
2 Tim. 4: 6 time of my *d.* is at hand

DEPTH (DEPTHS)
Ex. 15: 5 the *d.* have covered them
Job 38:16 walked in search of the *d.*
Ps. 68:22 from the *d.* of the sea
130: 1 out of the *d.* have I cried
Prov. 8:27 upon the face of the *d.*
9:18 are in the *d.* of hell
Mic. 7:19 cast all their sins into the *d.*
Mat. 18: 6 drowned in the *d.* of the sea
Mark 4: 5 because it had no *d.* of earth
Rom. 8:39 neither height nor *d.* nor any other
Eph. 3:18 breadth, length, *d.* and height
Rev. 2:24 have not known the *d.* of Satan

DERISION
Job 30: 1 younger than I have me in *d.*
Ps. 2: 4 Lord shall have them in *d.*
44:13 a scorn and *d.* to them
119: 51 have had me greatly in *d.*
Jer. 20: 8 reproach unto me, and a *d.* daily

DESCEND (DESCENDED, DESCENDING)
Gen. 28:12 angels of God ascending and *d.*
Ex. 19:18 Lord *d.* upon it in fire
33: 9 the cloudy pillar *d.*, and stood
Ps. 49:17 glory not *d.* after him
Is. 5:14 rejoiceth shall *d.* into it
Mat. 3:16 the Spirit of God *d.* like a dove
Mark 1:10 like a dove *d.* upon him
John 1:32 saw the spirit *d.* from heaven
1:51 angels of God ascending and *d.*
1 Thes. 4:16 Lord shall *d.* from heaven

DESERT (DESERTS)
Ex. 3: 1 to the backside or the *d.*
5: 3 three days journey into the *d.*
2 Chr. 26:10 also he built towers in the *d.*
Job 24: 5 as wild asses in the *d.*
Ps. 78:40 and grieve him in the *d.*
102: 6 like an owl of the *d.*
Is. 13:21 wild beasts of the *d.* shall lie
21: 1 the burden of the *d.* of the sea
35: 1 and the *d.* shall rejoice
35: 6 break out and streams in the *d.*
40: 3 in the *d.* a highway for our God
41:19 set in the *d.* the fir tree
43:19 and rivers in the *d.*
51: 3 her *d.* like the garden
Jer. 2: 6 through a land of *d.* and of pits
Ezek. 13: 4 like the foxes in the *d.*
Mark 1:45 but was without in *d.* places
Luke 1:80 in *d.* till the day of showing
John 6:31 fathers did eat manna in the *d.*
Heb. 11:38 wandered in *d.* and mountains

DESIRE
Gen. 3:16 *d.* shall be to thy husband
Ex. 34:24 nor any man *d.* thy land
Deut. 18: 6 come with all the *d.* of his mind
2 Chr. 15:15 and sought him with their whole *d.*
Neh. 1:11 who *d.* to fear thy name
Job 14:15 wilt have a *d.* to the work of
21:14 we *d.* not knowledge of thy ways
Ps. 38: 9 all my *d.* is before thee
145: 16 satisfieth the *d.* of every living
Prov. 10:24 *d.* of righteous shall be granted
11:23 *d.* of the righteous is only good
13:19 *d.* accomplished is sweet
Eccl. 12: 5 *d.* shall fail because man goeth
Is. 26: 8 *d.* of our soul is to thy name
Hag. 2: 7 the *d.* of all nations shall
Luke 22:15 with *d.* I have desired to eat
Jas. 4: 2 *d.* to have and cannot obtain
Rev. 9: 6 *d.* to die, and death shall flee

DESIRED (DESIRES, DESIREST, DESIRETH)
Job 7: 2 servant earnestly *d.* the shadow
Ps. 19:10 more to be *d.* are they than gold
27: 4 one thing have I *d.* of the Lord
34:12 what man *d.* life and loveth
37: 4 give thee the *d.* of thine heart
51: 6 thou *d.* truth in the inward parts
51:16 thou *d.* not sacrifice, else would
68:16 hill which God *d.* to dwell in
Prov. 12:12 wicked *d.* the net of evil men
13: 4 soul of the sluggard *d.* and hath
21:10 soul of wicked *d.* evil
Is. 26: 9 with my soul have I *d.* thee
Jer. 17:16 neither have I *d.* the woeful day
Hos. 6: 6 I *d.* mercy, not sacrifice
Eph. 2: 3 fulfilling *d.* of the flesh

DESOLATE
2 Sam. 13:20 Tamar remained *d.* in her brother
Job 15:28 he dwelleth in *d.* cities and in
16: 7 thou hast made *d.* all my company
Ps. 25:16 I am *d.* and afflicted
Is. 49:21 I have lost my children, and am *d.*
54: 1 for more are the children of the *d.*
Mat. 23:38 behold your house is left unto you *d.*
Rev. 1716. and shall make her *d.* and naked

DESOLATIONS
Jer. 25:12 and will make it perpetual *d.*
Ezek. 35: 9 I will make thee perpetual *d.*
Dan. 9: 2 seventy years in the *d.* of Jerusalem

DESPAIR
Eccl. 2:20 to cause my heart to *d.*
2 Cor. 4: 8 we are perplexed, but not in *d.*

DESPERATE (DESPERATELY)
Job 6:26 speeches of one that is *d.*
Is. 17:11 in the day of grief and of *d.* sorrow
Jer. 17: 9 deceitful above all things and *d.* wicked

DESPISE (DESPISED, DESPISEST, DESPISETH, DESPISING)
Gen. 16: 4 her mistress was *d.* in her eyes
Lev. 26:15 if ye shall *d.* my statutes
1 Sam. 2:30 they that *d.* me be lightly
2 Sam. 6:16 she *d.* him in her heart
Job 5:17 *d.* not the chastening of the Almighty
36: 5 God is mighty and *d.* not any
Ps. 102: 17 destitute and will not *d.* their
Prov. 11:12 void of wisdom *d.* his neighbour
12: 9 he that is *d.* and hath a servant
13:13 whoso *d.* the word shall be destroyed
15:32 refuseth instruction *d.* his soul
19:16 he that *d.* his ways shall die

Prov. 23:22 *d.* not thy mother when she is old
30:17 and *d.* to obey his mother
Is. 33:15 he that *d.* the gain of oppression
53: 3 he is *d.* and rejected
Amos 5:21 I *d.* your feast days
Zech. 4:10 who *d.* the day of small things
Mat. 6:24 hold to one, and *d.* the other
Luke 10:16 he that *d.* you, *d.* me, and he that
18: 9 they were righteous and *d.* others
Rom. 2: 4 *d.* thou the riches of goodness
14: 3 that eateth *d.* him that eateth not
1 Thes. 4: 8 *d.* not man but God who hath also
1 Tim. 4:12 no man *d.* thy youth
Heb. 10:28 he that *d.* Moses' law died without
12: 2 *d.* the shame, and is set down

DESPISERS
Acts 13:41 behold, ye *d.*, and wonder, and perish
2 Tim. 3: 3 *d.* of those that are good

DESPITE
Heb. 10:29 done *d.* unto the Spirit of grace

DESTROY (DESTROYED)
Gen. 19:13 for we will *d.* this place
Esth. 4:14 thy father's house shall be *d.*
Ps. 37:38 transgressors shall be *d.* together
101: 8 I will *d.* the wicked of the land
Prov. 1:32 prosperity of fools shall *d.* them
13:20 a companion of fools shall be *d.*
Eccl. 7:16 why shouldest thou *d.* thyself
Dan. 2:44 kingdom which shall never be *d.*
Hos. 4: 6 are *d.* for lack of knowledge
13: 9 Israel, thou hast *d.* thyself
10: 8 the sin of Israel, shall be *d.*
Mat. 5:17 not come to *d.* but to fulfil
21:41 miserably *d.* those wicked men
John 2:19 *d.* this temple, and in three days
Rom. 14:15 *d.* not him with thy meat
14:20 for meat *d.* not the work of God
1 Cor. 3:17 defile the temple of God shall God *d.*
6:13 God shall *d.* both it and them
15:26 that shall be *d.* is death
2 Cor. 4: 9 cast down, but not *d.*
Jas. 4:12 who is able to save and to *d.*
1 John 3: 8 might *d.* the works of the devil

DESTROYER
Job 15:21 in prosperity the *d.* shall come upon
Ps. 17: 4 kept me from the paths of the *d.*
Prov. 28:24 same is the companion of a *d.*
Jer. 4: 7 *d.* of the Gentiles is on his way
1 Cor. 10:10 and were destroyed of the *d.*

DESTRUCTION
Deut. 7:23 shall destroy them with a mighty *d.*
Job 5:22 at *d.* and famine shall laugh
21:30 wicked is reserved to the day of *d.*
26: 6 *d.* before him hath no covering
31:23 *d.* from God was a terror to me
Ps. 90: 3 thou turnest man to *d.*
91: 6 *d.* that wasteth at noonday
Prov. 10:29 *d.* shall be to workers of iniquity
15:11 Hell and *d.* are before the Lord
16:18 pride goeth before *d.*, and an
18:12 before *d.* the heart of man is haughty
27:20 hell and *d.* are never full
Jer. 4:20 *d.* upon *d.* is cried, for
Hos. 13:14 O grave, I will be thy *d.*
Mat. 7:13 the way, that leadeth to *d.*
Rom. 3:16 *d.* and misery are in their ways
1 Cor. 5: 5 for the *d.* of the flesh
2 Cor. 10: 8 and not for your *d.*, I should
1 Thes. 5: 3 sudden *d.* cometh on them
2 Pet. 2: 1 bring upon themselves swift *d.*
3:16 scriptures unto their own *d.*

DETERMINED
2 Chr. 25:16 God hath *d.* to destroy thee
Is. 10:23 even *d.*, in the midst of all the land
Dan. 9:24 seventy weeks are *d.* upon thy people
Acts 4:28 thy counsel *d.* before to be done
17:26 hath *d.* the times before appointed
1 Cor. 2: 2 I *d.* not to know any thing among you

DEVICE (DEVICES)
Job 5:12 he disappointeth the *d.* of the crafty
Ps. 33:10 he maketh the *d.* of the people
Prov. 1:31 and be filled with their own *d.*
14:17 a man of wicked *d.* is hated
Eccl. 9:10 for there is no work nor *d.*
Jer. 18:12 we will walk after our own *d.*
2 Cor. 2:11 we are not ignorant of his *d.*

DEVIL
Mat. 4: 1 wilderness to be tempted of the *d.*
13:39 the enemy that sowed is the *d.*
John 6:70 twelve, and one of you is a *d.*
7:20 thou hast a *d.*: who goeth about
8:44 ye are of your father the *d.*
13: 2 *d.* having now put into the heart
Eph. 4:27 neither give place to the *d.*
1 Tim. 3: 6 fall into condemnation of the *d.*
2 Tim. 2:26 recover out of the snare of the *d.*
Jas. 4: 7 resist the *d.* and he will flee
1 Pet. 5: 8 because your adversary the *d.*
1 John 3: 8 to destroy the works of the *d.*
3:10 children of God and children of the *d.*
Rev. 2:10 the *d.* shall cast some of you

DEVILS
Lev. 17: 7 offer their sacrifices unto *d.*
2 Chr. 11:15 the high places and for the *d.*
Ps. 106: 37 sacrificed their sons to *d.*
Mat. 4:24 which were possessed with *d.*
10: 8 raise the dead, cast out *d.*
Mark 16: 9 out of whom he had cast seven *d.*
Luke 8:36 he that was possessed of the *d.*
10:17 even *d.* are subject to us
1 Tim. 4: 1 to seducing spirits and doctrines of *d.*
Jas. 2:19 the *d.* also believe and tremble

DEVISE (DEVISETH)
Prov. 3:29 *d.* not evil against thy neighbour
14:22 do they not err that *d.* evil
16: 9 a man's heart *d.* his ways
Jer. 18:18 *d.* devices against Jeremiah
Mic. 2: 1 woe to them that *d.* iniquity

DEVOUR (DEVOURED)
Gen. 49:27 he shall *d.* the prey
Is. 9:12 they shall *d.* Israel with open mouth
Prov. 30:14 to *d.* the poor off the earth
Is. 24: 6 hath curse *d.* the earth
Jer. 3:24 shame hath *d.* the labour
50:17 Israel the king of Assyria hath *d.*
Hos. 7: 7 and have *d.* their judges
Mat. 23:14 for ye *d.* widows' houses, and
2 Cor. 11:20 if a man *d.* you, if a man take
Gal. 5:15 if ye bite and *d.* one another
Heb. 10:27 which shall *d.* the adversaries
1 Pet. 5: 8 seeking whom he may *d.*

DEVOURING
Ex. 24:17 like *d.* fire on top of the mount
Ps. 52: 4 thou lovest all *d.* words
Is. 29: 6 and the flame of *d.* fire
33:14 shall dwell with the *d.* fire

DEVOUT
Luke 2:25 the same man was just and *d.*
Acts 2: 5 dwelling at Jerusalem Jews, *d.* men
8: 2 and *d.* men carried Stephen
10: 2 a *d.* man, and one that feared God
13:50 Jews stirred up the *d.* and honourable women
17: 4 and of the *d.* Greeks a great multitude
22:12 Ananias, a *d.* man according to the law

DEW
Gen. 27:28 God give thee of the *d.* of heaven
Deut. 32: 2 my speech shall distill as the *d.*
Ps. 110: 3 thou hast the *d.* of thy youth
Is. 26:19 thy *d.* is as the *d.* of herbs
Hos. 6: 4 goodness is as the early *d.*
14: 5 I will be as *d.* to Israel
Mic. 5: 7 many people as a *d.* from the Lord

DIE
Gen. 2:17 thereof thou shalt surely *d.*
3: 4 ye shall not surely *d.*
6:17 everything that is in the earth shall *d.*
Ex. 20:19 let not God speak with us, lest we *d.*
1 Sam. 14:44 for thou shalt surely *d.*, Jonathan
1 Ki. 2:42 that thou shalt surely *d.*
Job 14:14 if a man *d.* shall he live again?
Ps. 82: 7 but ye shall *d.* like men
Prov. 23:13 with the rod, he shall not *d.*
Eccl. 3: 2 born and a time to *d.*
7:17 why shouldst thou *d.* before thy time
Is. 22:13 for tomorrow we shall *d.*
Jer. 26: 8. him, saying Thou shalt surely *d.*
31:30 *d.* for his own iniquity
Ezek. 3:18 wicked man shall *d.* in his iniquity
3:19 he shall *d.* in his iniquity
18:31 why will ye *d.* O house of Israel
Jonah 4: 3 better for me to *d.* than to live
Mat. 26:35 though I should *d.* with thee
Luke 20:36 neither can they *d.* any more
John 8:21 ye shall *d.* in your sins
11:50 that one man should *d.* for the people
Rom. 14: 8 we *d.* we *d.* unto the Lord
1 Cor. 9:15 better for me to *d.* than
Phil. 1:21 to live is Christ, to *d.* is gain
Heb. 9:27 appointed unto men once to *d.*
Rev. 3: 2 which remain that are ready to *d.*

DIED (DIETH)
Rom. 5: 6 Christ *d.* for the ungodly
5: 8 while we were yet sinners, Christ *d.*
6: 9 being raised from the dead *d.* no more
6:10 for in that he *d.* he *d.* unto sin
7: 9 sin revived and I *d.*
14: 7 no man *d.* to himself
14: 9 to this end Christ *d.* and rose
1 Cor. 15: 3 Christ *d.* for our sins
2 Cor. 5:15 he *d.* for all, that they
1 Thes. 5:10 who *d.* for us that whether
Heb. 11:13 these all *d.* in faith, not

DYING
2 Cor. 4:10 the *d.* of the Lord Jesus
6: 9 yet well known as *d.* and, behold
Heb. 11:21 By faith, Jacob, when he was *d.*

DILIGENCE
Prov. 4:23 keep thy heart with all *d.*
Luke 12:58 give *d.* that thou mayest be delivered
Rom. 12: 8 he that ruleth, with *d.*
2 Cor. 8: 7 in all *d.* and in your love to us
2 Tim. 4: 9 Do thy *d.* to come shortly unto me
4:21 do thy *d.* to come before winter
2 Pet. 1: 5 giving all *d.*, add to your faith
1:10 give *d.* to make your calling
Jude 1: 3 when I gave all *d.* to write

DILIGENT (DILIGENTLY)
Ex. 15:26 if thou wilt *d.* hearken to
Deut. 4: 9 keep thy soul *d.*, lest thou forget
6:17 *d.* keep the commandments of the Lord
19:18 judges shall make *d.* inquisition
28: 1 thou shalt hearken *d.* unto the voice
Ps. 37:10 thou shalt *d.* consider his place
64: 6 they accomplish a *d.* search
Prov. 10: 4 hand of the *d.* maketh rich
12:24 hand of the *d.* shall bear rule
13: 4 soul of the *d.* shall be made fat
21: 5 thoughts of the *d.* tend to plenty
22:29 man *d.* in his business
Jer. 17:24 if ye *d.* hearken unto me
Zech. 6:15 if ye will *d.* obey the voice
Luke 15: 8 seek *d.* till she find it
1 Pet. 1:10 prophets have inquired and searched *d.*
2 Pet. 3:14 be *d.* to be found of him

DINNER
Prov. 15:17 better is a *d.* of herbs
Luke 14:12 when thou makest a *d.* or a supper

DIP (DIPPED)
Ruth 2:14 and *d.* thy morsel in the vinegar
Ps. 68:23 thy foot may be *d.* in the blood
John 13:26 when he had *d.* the sop

DIRECT (DIRECTED)
Ps. 5: 3 will I *d.* my prayer to thee
119: 5 my ways were *d.* to keep
Prov. 3: 6 he shall *d.* thy paths
16: 9 the Lord *d.* his steps
Eccl. 10:10 but wisdom is profitable to *d.*
Is. 40:13 who hath *d.* the spirit of the Lord
45:13 and I will *d.* all his ways
61: 8 I will *d.* their work in truth
Jer. 10:23 walketh to *d.* his steps

DISCERN (DISCERNED, DISCERNETH, DISCERNING)

2 Sam. 14:17 the king to *d.* good and bad
Eccl. 8: 5 a wise man's heart *d.* both time
Mal. 3:18 *d.* between the righteous and the
1 Cor. 2:14 because they are spiritually *d.*
11:29 not *d.* the Lord's body
12:10 to another *d.* of spirits
Heb. 5:14 to *d.* both good and evil

DISCIPLE (DISCIPLES)

Mat. 10:24 *d.* is not above his master
10:42 cup of water in the name of a *d.*
Luke 14:26 life also he cannot be my *d.*
John 8:31 then are ye my *d.* indeed
9:28 thou art his *d.*; but we are
19:38 Joseph of Arimathaea, being a *d.*
Acts 21:16 an old *d.* with whom

DISEASED

John 6: 2 he did on them that were *d.*

DISEASES

Ex. 15:26 I will put none of these *d.*
2 Chr. 16:12 in his *d.* he sought not the Lord
Ps. 38: 7 are filled with a loathsome *d.*
103: 3 who healeth all thy *d.*
Eccl. 6: 2 and it is an evil *d.*
Mat. 4:23 and all manner of *d.* among the people

DISHONOUR (DISHONOURETH)

Ezra 4:14 not meet for us to see the king's *d.*
Ps. 35:26 clothed with shame and *d.*
Prov. 6:33 a wound and *d.* shall he get
Mic. 7: 6 for the son *d.* his father
Rom. 1:24 to *d.* their own bodies
1 Cor. 15:43 it is sown in *d.* it is raised
2 Cor. 6: 8 by honour and *d.*, by evil report

DISOBEDIENCE

Rom. 5:19 by one man's *d.* many were made
2 Cor. 10: 6 readiness to revenge all *d.*
Eph. 2: 2 worketh in the children of *d.*
5: 6 wrath of God upon the children of *d.*
Col. 3: 6 cometh upon the children of *d.*
Heb. 2: 2 if every *d.* received just

DISOBEDIENT

1 Ki. 13:26 who was *d.* unto the word of God
Neh. 9:26 nevertheless they were against *d.*
Luke 1:17 *d.* to the wisdom of the just
Rom. 1:30 of evil things *d.* to parents
1 Tim. 1: 9 law made for lawless and *d.*
2 Tim. 3: 2 *d.* to parents, unthankful, unholy
Tit. 1:16 deny him being abominable, and *d.*
1 Pet. 3:20 which sometime were *d.* which once

DISPENSATION

1 Cor. 9:17 a *d.* of the gospel is committed
Eph. 1:10 in the *d.* of the fulness of time
3: 2 the *d.* of the grace of God
Col. 1:25 according to the *d.* of God

DISPLEASED

Gen. 38:10 the thing which he did *d.* the Lord
2 Sam. 11:27 that David had done *d.* the Lord
1 Chr. 21: 7 God was *d.* with this thing
Zech. 1:15 I am very sore *d.* with the heathen
Mark 10:14 he was much *d.*, and said

DISPLEASURE

Deut. 9:19 afraid of the anger and hot *d.*
Ps. 2: 5 and vex them in his sore *d.*

DISPUTE (DISPUTED, DISPUTING)

Job 23: 7 there the righteous might *d.* with him
Mark 9:33 what was it that ye *d.* among yourselves
Acts 6: 9 Cilicia and of Asia, *d.* with Stephen
9:29 and *d.* against the Grecians
17:17 therefore *d.* he in the synagogue
19: 9 disciples, *d.* daily in the school

DISPUTATIONS

Rom. 14: 1 but not to doubtful *d.*

DISSENSION

Acts 15: 2 Paul and Barnabas had no small *d.*
23:10 when there arose a great *d.*

DISSOLVED (DISSOLVEST)

Job 30:22 upon it and *d.* my substance
Ps. 75: 3 all the inhabitants thereof are *d.*
Is. 24:19 the earth is clean *d.*
2 Cor. 5: 1 house of this tabernacle were *d.*
2 Pet. 3:11 all these things shall be *d.*

DISTRESS

Gen. 35: 3 answered me in the day of my *d.*
42:21 therefore is this *d.* come upon us
2 Sam. 22: 7 in my *d.* I called upon the Lord
1 Ki. 1:29 redeemed thy soul out of *d.*
Neh. 9:37 and we are in great *d.*
Ps. 4: 1 enlarged me when I was in *d.*
18: 6 in my *d.* I called upon the Lord
120: 1 In my *d.* I cried unto the Lord
Prov. 1:27 when *d.* and anguish cometh
Is. 25: 4 strength to the needy in his *d.*
Zeph. 1:15 day of trouble and *d.*, a day of
Luke 21:25 upon the earth *d.* of nations
Rom. 8:35 shall tribulation, or *d.*, or persecution

DISTRESSED

Gen. 32: 7 Then Jacob was greatly afraid and *d.*
2 Sam. 1:26 I am *d.* for thee, my brother Jonathan
2 Chr. 28:20 and *d.* him, but strengthened him not

DISTRIBUTE (DISTRIBUTING, DISTRIBUTETH)

Job 21:17 God *d.* sorrows in anger
Luke 18:22 and *d.* unto the poor, and thou
Rom. 12:13 *d.* to the necessity of saints
1 Tim. 6:18 ready to *d.*, willing to communicate

DISTRIBUTION

Acts 4:35 *d.* was made to every man
2 Cor. 9:13 for your liberal *d.* unto them

DITCH (DITCHES)

2 Ki. 3:16 make this valley full of *d.*
Job 9:31 shalt thou plunge me in the *d.*
Ps. 7:15 and is fallen into the *d.*
Prov. 23:27 for a whore is a deep *d.*
Is. 22:11 made also a *d.* between the two walls
Mat. 15:14 both shall fall into the *d.*

DIVIDE (DIVIDED, DIVIDING)

Gen. 1: 6 *d.* the waters from the waters
1:14 to *d.* the day from the night
10:25 isles of the Gentiles *d.* in their
Ex. 14:16 thine hand over the sea, and *d.* it
Josh. 19:51 *d.* for an inheritance land by lot
Ps. 55: 9 destroy O Lord and *d.* their tongues
Is. 53:12 will I *d.* him a portion
Dan. 2:41 the kingdom shall be *d.*
Mat. 12:25 city or house *d.* against itself
Luke 12:13 to *d.* the inheritance with me
1 Cor. 1:13 is Christ *d.*? was Paul
12:11 *d.* to every man severally as he will
2 Tim. 2:15 rightly *d.* the word of truth
Heb. 4:12 to the *d.* asunder of soul and spirit

DIVISION (DIVISIONS)

Judg. 5:16 for the *d.* of Reuben there were
Luke 12:51 I tell you Nay, but rather *d.*

DIVINE

1 Sam. 28: 8 *d.* unto me by the familiar spirit
Prov. 16:10 a *d.* sentence is in the lips
Mic. 3:11 prophets thereof *d.* for money
Heb. 9: 1 had also ordinances of *d.* service
2 Pet. 1: 3 his *d.* power hath given

DIVINATION

Num. 22: 7 the rewards of *d.* in their hand
Deut. 18:10 or that useth *d.* or an observer
Ezek. 21:21 of the two ways, to use *d.*
Acts 16:16 possessed with a spirit of *d.*

DIVINERS

1 Sam. 6: 2 called for the priests and the *d.*
Is. 44:25 and maketh *d.* mad, that turneth
Mic. 3: 7 and the *d.* confounded: yea, they
Zech. 10: 2 and the *d.* have seen a lie

DIVORCE (DIVORCED)

Lev. 22:13 Priest's daughter be a widow, or *d.*
Num. 30: 9 and of her that is *d.*
Jer. 3: 8 and given her a bill of *d.*

DIVORCEMENT

Deut. 24: 1 let him write her a bill of *d.*
Is. 50: 1 where is the bill of your mother's *d.*
Mat. 5:31 let him give her a writing of *d.*

DO

Gen. 18:25 not the Judge of all the earth *d.* right
Mat. 7:12 men *d.* to you, *d.* ye even so
John 15: 5 without me ye can *d.* nothing
Rom. 7:15 what I would that *d.* I not
Phil. 4:13 I can *d.* all things all through Christ
Heb. 4:13 with whom we have to *d.*
Rev. 19:10 see thou *d.* it not

DOERS

Rom. 2:13 *d.* of it shall be justified
Jas. 1:22 be ye *d.* of word and not

DOING (DOINGS)

Lev. 18: 3 after the *d.* of the land of Canaan
Ps. 64: 9 they shall wisely consider of his *d.*
118: 23 this is the Lord's *d.*
Prov. 20:11 even a child is known by his *d.*
Jer. 7: 3 amend your ways and your *d.*
Acts 10:38 who went about *d.* good
Rom. 2: 7 by patient continuance in well *d.*
Gal. 6: 9 let us not be weary in well *d.*
Eph. 6: 6 *d.* the will of God from the heart
2 Thes. 3:13 brethren, be not weary in well *d.*
1 Pet. 2:15 that with well *d.* ye may put
3:17 that ye suffer for well *d.*
4:19 of their souls to him in well *d.*

DOCTOR (DOCTORS)

Luke 2:46 sitting in the midst of the *d.*
5:17 there were Pharisees and *d.* of the law
Acts 5:34 Gamaliel, a *d.* of the law

DOCTRINE

Deut. 32: 2 my *d.* shall drop as the rain
Is. 28: 9 whom shall he make to understand *d.*?
Jer. 10: 8 the stock is a *d.* of vanities
Mat. 7:28 the people were astonished at his *d.*
Mark 1:27 what new *d.* is this? for
John 7:17 he shall know of the *d.*
Acts 2:42 in the apostles' *d.* and fellowship
Rom. 6:17 form of *d.* which was delivered
16:17 contrary to the *d.* ye have learned
Eph. 4:14 about with every wind of *d.*
1 Tim. 5:17 they who labour in word and *d.*
6: 3 *d.* which is according to godliness
2 Tim. 3:16 and is profitable for *d.*, for
Tit. 2: 7 in *d.* showing uncorruptness, gravity
2:10 may adorn the *d.* of God our Saviour
Heb. 6: 1 principles of the *d.* of Christ
6: 2 *d.* of baptisms and laying on of hands
Rev. 2:14 that hold the *d.* of Balaam

DOCTRINES

Mat. 15: 9 teaching for *d.* the commandments of men
Col. 2:22 after the commandments and *d.* of men
1 Tim. 4: 1 giving heed to the *d.* of the devils
Heb. 13: 9 carried about with divers strange *d.*

DOG (DOGS)

Ex. 11: 7 shall not a *d.* move his tongue
1 Sam. 17:43 am I a *d.* that thou comest
Prov. 26:11 as a *d.* to his vomit
Eccl. 9: 4 living *d.* better than a dead lion
Is. 56:10 they are all dumb *d.*
Mat. 7: 6 give not that which is holy to *d.*
15:27 the *d.* eat of the crumbs
Phil. 3: 2 beware of *d.*, beware of evil
2 Pet. 2:22 the *d.* is turned to his own vomit
Rev. 22:15 for without are *d.* and sorcerers

DOMINION

Gen. 1:26 let them have *d.* over
37: 8 shalt thou indeed have *d.* over us
Num. 24:19 he that shall have *d.*
Job 25: 2 *d.* and fear are with him
Ps. 8: 6 *d.* over the works of thy hands
49:14 upright shall have *d.* over them
72: 8 shall have *d.* from sea to sea
145: 13 thy *d.* endureth through all
Is. 26:13 other lords had *d.* over us

Dan. 4: 3 his *d.* is from generation to generation
Zech. 9:10 his *d.* shall be from sea even to sea
Rom. 6: 9 death hath no more *d.* over
2 Cor. 1:24 not have *d.* over your faith
Jude 1: 8 despise *d.* and speak evil of
1:25 our Saviour, be glory and majesty *d.*

DOMINIONS
Dan. 7:27 all *d.* shall serve and obey him
Col. 1:16 thrones or *d.* or principalities

DOOR (DOORS)
Gen. 4: 7 sin lieth at the *d.*
Ex. 12: 7 and on the upper *d.* post
12:23 Lord will pass over the *d.*
Deut. 11:20 thou shalt write them upon the *d.* posts
15:17 thrust it through his ear unto the *d.*
Ps. 24: 7 be ye lift up ye everlasting *d.*
84:10 *d.* keeper in the house of my God
141: 3 keep the *d.* of my lips
Prov. 26:14 as the *d.* turneth upon his hinges
Is. 6: 4 and the posts of the *d.* moved
Hos. 2:15 valley of Achor for a *d.* of hope
Mal. 1:10 would shut the *d.* for nought
Mat. 6: 6 when thou hast shut thy *d.*
John 10: 1 entereth not by the *d.*
10: 7 I am the *d.* of the sheep
Acts 14:27 opened the *d.* of faith to the Gentiles
Col. 4: 3 would open unto us a *d.* of utterance
Jas. 5: 9 judge standeth before the *d.*
Rev. 3: 8 set before thee an open *d.*

DOUBLE
Gen. 43:12 and take *d.* money in your hand
Ex. 22: 4 or sheep he shall restore *d.*
Deut. 21:17 giving him a *d.* portion of all
2 Ki. 2: 9 *d.* portion of thy spirit be upon me
1 Chr. 12:33 they were not of *d.* heart
Job 11: 6 secrets of wisdom that they are *d.* to
Is. 40: 2 Lord's hand *d.* for her sins
Jer. 17:18 destroy them with *d.* destruction
1 Tim. 3: 8 deacons not *d.* tongued, not given
5:17 be counted worthy of *d.* honour
Jas. 1: 8 *d.* minded man is unstable in all
Rev. 18: 6 *d.* to her, fill to her *d.*

DOUBT (DOUBTETH)
Deut. 28:66 thy life shall hang in *d.*
Mat. 14:31 wherefore didst thou *d.*
21:21 have faith and *d.* not
John 10:24 how long dost thou make us to *d.*
Rom. 14:23 he that *d.* is damned
Gal. 4:20 for I stand in *d.* of you

DOUBTFUL
Luke 12:29 neither be ye of *d.* mind
Rom. 14: 1 but not to *d.* disputations

DOVE (DOVES)
Ps. 55: 6 that I had wings like a *d.*
74:19 deliver not the soul of thy turtle*d.*
Sol. 1:15 thou hast *d.* eyes
Is. 38:14 I did mourn as a *d.*
60: 8 fly as *d.* to their windows
Ezek. 7:16 mountains, like *d.* of the valleys
Hos. 7:11 Ephraim is like a silly *d.*
Mat. 3:16 the Spirit of God descending like a *d.*
10:16 wise as serpents and harmless as *d.*
John 1:32 Spirit descending from heaven like a *d.*

DRAGON (DRAGONS)
Deut. 32:33 their wine is the poison of *d.*
Ps. 44:19 broken us in the place of *d.*
74:13 thou brakest the heads of the *d.*
91:13 the *d.* shalt thou trample under foot
Is. 13:22 and *d.* in their pleasant palaces
27: 1 shall slay the *d.* that is in the sea
51: 9 cut Rahab and wounded the *d.*
Jer. 9:11 and a den of *d.*, and I will
51:34 hath swallowed me up like a *d.*
Ezek. 29: 3 the great *d.* that lieth in the midst
Mic. 1: 8 I will make a wailing like the *d.*
Mal. 1: 3 waste for the *d.* of the wilderness
Rev. 13: 2 the *d.* gave him his power
20: 2 the *d.*, that old serpent

DRAW (DRAWN, DREW)
Job 21:33 every man *d.* after him
Ps. 18:16 *d.* me out of many waters
28: 3 *d.* me not away with the wicked
73:28 good for me to *d.* near to God
Eccl. 12: 1 years *d.* nigh when thou shalt say
Sol. 1: 4 *d.* me, we will run after thee
Is. 5:18 woe unto them that *d.* iniquity with
29:13 *d.* near me with their mouth
Jer. 31: 3 with lovingkindness have I *d.* thee
Hos. 11: 4 *d.* them with cords of a man
John 6:44 the Father which hath sent me *d.* him
Heb. 7:19 by which we *d.* nigh to God
10:38 if any man *d.* back
Jas. 4: 8 *d.* nigh to God, he will *d.*

DREAD
Gen. 9: 2 the *d.* of you shall be upon
Ex. 15:16 fear and *d.* shall fall upon them
Deut. 1:29 *d.* not, neither be afraid
2:25 I put the *d.* of thee and the fear
Is. 8:13 and let him be your *d.*

DREADFUL
Gen. 28:17 how *d.* is this place
Dan. 9: 4 the great and *d.* God
Mal. 1:14 my name is *d.* among the heathen
4: 5 great and *d.* day of the Lord

DREAM
Gen. 20: 3 God came to Abimelech in a *d.*
31:11 spake unto me in a *d.*
37: 5 and Joseph dreamed a *d.*
40: 5 and they dreamed a *d.* both of them
Num. 12: 6 will speak unto him in a *d.*
Job 20: 8 fly away as a *d.*
33:15 in a *d.* in a vision of the night
Ps. 126: 1 we were like them that *d.*
Eccl. 5: 3 *d.* cometh through the multitude of business
5: 7 in multitude of *d.* there are
Is. 29: 7 shall be as a *d.* of night vision
Jer. 23:28 hath a *d.* let him tell a *d.*
Dan. 2:28 thy *d.* and the visions of thy head
Joel 2:28 your old men shall *d.* dreams
Mat. 1:20 angel appeared in a *d.*
2:12 warned of God in a *d.*
27:19 suffered many things in a *d.*
Acts 2:17 your old men shall *d.* dreams

DRINK
Ex. 15:24 saying what shall we *d.*
Lev. 10: 9 not *d.* wine nor strong *d.*
Judg. 7: 5 boweth down upon his knees to *d.*
Job 21:20 *d.* of the wrath of the Almighty
Ps. 36: 8 *d.* of the river of thy pleasures
60: 3 *d.* the wine of astonishment
69:21 they gave me vinegar to *d.*
80: 5 givest them tears to *d.*
110: 7 *d.* of the brook in the way
Prov. 4:17 *d.* the wine of violence
5:15 *d.* out of thine own cistern
31: 5 lest they *d.* and forget the law
Sol. 5: 1 *d.*, yea, *d.* abundantly
Is. 22:13 let us eat and *d.*, for tomorrow
65:13 my servants shall *d.* but ye
Hos. 4:18 their *d.* is sour: they have
Amos 4: 1 Bring, and let us *d.*
Mic. 2:11 unto thee of wine and of strong *d.*
Mat. 10:42 *d.* to one of these little ones
20:22 able to *d.* of the cup that I shall
25:35 thirsty, and ye gave me *d.*
26:27 *d.* ye all of it
26:29 I will not *d.* henceforth of this fruit
27:34 gave him vinegar to *d.*
Luke 1:15 shall *d.* neither wine nor strong *d.*
John 6:55 and my blood is *d.* indeed
7:37 let him come unto me and *d.*, for in
Rom. 12:20 if he thirst give him *d.*
14:17 kingdom of God is not meat and *d.*
1 Cor. 10: 4 did all *d.* the same spiritual *d.*
10:21 cannot *d.* the cup of Lord and devils
11:25 as often as ye *d.* it in remembrance
15:32 let us eat and *d.*: for tomorrow

DRINKETH
Job 15:16 which *d.* iniquity like water
John 6:54 *d.* my blood hath eternal life
1 Cor. 11:29 eateth and *d.* unworthily
Heb. 6: 7 earth which *d.* in rain

DRUNKARD (DRUNKARDS)
Deut. 21:20 he is a glutton and *d.*
Ps. 69:12 I was the song of the *d.*
Prov. 23:21 *d.* and glutton shall come to poverty
26: 9 thorn goeth up into the hand of a *d.*
Is. 24:20 earth shall reel like a *d.*
Joel 1: 5 Awake, ye *d.*, and weep
Nah. 1:10 and while they are drunken as *d.*
1 Cor. 5:11 idolator, or a railer, or a *d.*
6:10 nor *d.*, nor revilers nor

DRUNK (DRUNKEN)
Job 12:25 stagger like a *d.* man
Ps. 107: 27 stagger like a *d.* man
Is. 19:14 a *d.* man staggereth in his vomit
29: 9 they are *d.* but not with wine
1 Cor. 11:21 one is hungry, another *d.*
1 Thes. 5: 7 be *d.* are *d.* in the night
Rev. 17: 2 *d.* with the wine of her fornication

DRUNKENNESS
Deut. 29:19 to add *d.* to thirst
Eccl. 10:17 for strength, and not for *d.*
Ezek. 23:33 thou shalt be filled with *d.*
Luke 21:34 be overcharged with surfeiting, and *d.*
Rom. 13:13 not in rioting and *d.*
Gal. 5:21 murders, *d.*, revelling, and such like

DROP (DROPPED)
Ps. 65:11 goodness; and thy paths *d.* fatness
Prov. 5: 3 *d.* as an honeycomb, and her mouth
Sol. 4:11 O my spouse, *d.* as the honeycomb
5: 5 my hands *d.* with myrrh
Is. 40:15 nations as a *d.* of a bucket

DROPS
Job 36:27 he maketh small the *d.* of water
38:28 who hath begotten the *d.* of dew
Sol. 5: 2 my locks with the *d.* of the night
Luke 22:44 as it were great *d.* of blood

DROSS
Ps. 119:119 all the wicked of the earth like *d.*
Is. 1:25 purely purge away thy *d.*
Ezek. 22:18 the house of Israel is to me become *d.*

DRY
Judg. 6:37 if it be *d.* upon all the earth
Prov. 17: 1 better is a *d.* morsel
Is. 44: 3 and floods upon the *d.* ground
56: 3 behold, I am a *d.* tree
Jer. 4:11 a *d.* wind of the high places
Ezek. 17:24 have made the *d.* tree to flourish
Hos. 9:14 a miscarrying womb and *d.* breasts

DUE
Deut. 32:35 foot shall slide in *d.* time
1 Chr. 15:13 sought him not after *d.* order
Ps. 104: 27 meat in *d.* season
Prov. 3:27 good from them to whom it is *d.*
15:23 a word spoken in *d.* season
Eccl. 10:17 thy princes eat in *d.* season
Mat. 18:34 pay all that was *d.* unto him
24:45 to give them their meat in *d.* season
Luke 12:42 their portion of meat in *d.* season
23:41 we receive the *d.* reward of our deeds
Rom. 13: 7 tribute to whom tribute is *d.*
Gal. 6: 9 in *d.* season we shall reap
1 Cor. 15: 8 as one born out of *d.* time
1 Tim. 2: 6 to be testified in *d.* time

DUMB
Ps. 38:13 I was as a *d.* man
Prov. 31: 8 open thy mouth for the *d.*
Is. 35: 6 tongue of the *d.* to sing
53: 7 as a sheep before her shearers is *d.*
56:10 watchmen are all *d.* dogs
Ezek. 3:26 that thou shalt be *d.*, and shalt
Hab. 2:18 therein to make *d.* idols
Mat. 9:33 devil was cast out, the *d.* spake
Mark 9:25 thou *d.* and deaf spirit
Luke 1:20 behold, thou shalt be *d.*
1 Cor. 12: 2 carried away unto these *d.* idols

2 Pet. 2:16 the *d.* ass speaking with man's voice

DUNG
Mal. 2: 3 even the *d.* of your solemn feasts
Phil. 3: 8 I count them but *d.*

DUST
Gen. 3:19 unto *d.* thou shalt return
13:16 thy seed as the *d.* of the earth
18:27 which am but *d.* and ashes
28:14 seed shall be as the *d.* of the earth
Ex. 8:17 smote the *d.* of the land
Num. 23:10 who can count the *d.* of Jacob
Deut. 28:24 make the rain of thy land powder and *d.*
2 Chr. 1: 9 like the *d.* of the earth in multitude
Job 10: 9 wilt thou bring me into *d.* again
30:19 I am become like *d.* and ashes
42: 6 repent in *d.* and ashes
Ps. 7: 5 lay mine honour in the *d.*
18:42 beat them small as the *d.* before
22:15 brought me into the *d.* of death
30: 9 shall the *d.* praise thee
102: 14 stones and favour the *d.* thereof
103: 14 remembereth that we are *d.*
104: 29 they die, and return to their *d.*
Eccl. 12: 7 shall the *d.* return to the earth
Is. 26:19 awake and sing, ye that dwell in *d.*
41: 2 he gave them as the *d.* to his sword
Lam. 3:29 he putteth his mouth in the *d.*
Dan. 12: 2 sleep in the *d.* of the earth
Amos 2: 7 that pant after the *d.* of the earth
Mat. 10:14 shake off the *d.* of your feet
Acts 13:51 they shook off the *d.* of their feet
Rev. 18:19 they cast *d.* on their heads

DUTY
Ex. 21:10 and her *d.* of marriage shall he not
2 Chr. 8:14 as the *d.* of every day required
Eccl. 12:13 this is the whole *d.* of man
Luke 17:10 which was our *d.* to do

DWELL (DWELLETH, DWELT)
Ps. 15: 1 who shall *d.* in thy holy hill
23: 6 *d.* in house of Lord for ever
84:10 than to *d.* in the tents of wickedness
120: 5 that I *d.* in the tents of Kedar
132: 14 here will I *d.* for I desired
Is. 33:14 who *d.* with devouring fire
33:16 he shall *d.* on high
Ezek. 43: 7 I will *d.* in the midst of the children
John 1:14 Word made flesh and *d.*
6:56 *d.* in me, and I in him
14:10 Father that *d.* in me, he doeth
14:17 ye know him for he *d.* with you
Acts 7:48 *d.* not in temples made with hands
13:17 they *d.* as strangers in the land of
Rom. 7:17 sin that *d.* in me
7:18 in my flesh *d.* no good thing
8: 9 Spirit of God *d.* in you
2 Cor. 6:16 I will *d.* in them, and walk in
Eph. 3:17 that Christ may *d.* in your hearts
Col. 1:19 that in him should all fulness *d.*
2: 9 in Christ *d.* all the fulness of
3:16 let the word of Christ *d.* in you richly
2 Tim. 1: 5 which *d.* first in thy grandmother
1:14 Holy Ghost which *d.* in us
Jas. 4: 5 spirit which *d.* in us lusteth
2 Pet. 3:13 wherein *d.* righteousness
1 John 3:17 how *d.* the love of God in him
4:12 God *d.* in us, and his love is
4:13 know that we *d.* in him
4:15 God *d.* in him, and he in God
2 John 1: 2 truth's sake which *d.* in us
Rev. 21: 3 he will *d.* with them, and

DWELLING (DWELLINGS)
Ps. 87: 2 more than all the *d.* of Jacob
1 Tim. 6:16 *d.* in the light which no man
Heb. 11: 9 *d.* in tabernacles with Isaac
2 Pet. 2: 8 righteous man *d.* among them

E

EAGLE (EAGLES)
Ex. 19: 4 I bare you on *e.* wings
Deut. 28:49 as swift as the *e.* flieth
2 Sam. 1:23 they were swifter than *e.*, stronger
Job 9:26 *e.* that hasteth to the prey
39:27 doth the *e.* mount up
Ps. 103: 5 thy youth is renewed like the *e.*
Prov. 30:17 the young *e.* shall eat it
30:19 way of an *e.* in the air
Is. 40:31 they shall mount up with wings as *e.*
Jer. 49:16 thy nest as high as the *e.*
Lam. 4:19 persecutors swifter than *e.*
Ezek. 10:14 the fourth the face of an *e.*
17: 3 a great *e.* with great wings
Dan. 7: 4 like a lion and had *e.* wings
Hos. 8: 1 he shall come as an *e.* against the house
Obad. 1: 4 thou exalt thyself as the *e.*
Mic. 1:16 enlarge thy baldness as the *e.*
Hab. 1: 8 they shall fly as the *e.* that
Rev. 4: 7 beast was like a flying *e.*
12:14 given two wings of a great *e.*

EAR
Ex. 21: 6 shall bore his *e.* through with an awl
29:20 blood upon the tip of the right *e.*
Deut. 32: 1 Give *e.* O ye heavens
Judg. 5: 3 give *e.*, o ye princes
2 Ki. 19:16 bow down thine *e.*, and hear
Neh. 1: 6 let thine *e.* now be attentive
Job 4:12 mine *e.* received a little thereof
36:10 God openeth man's *e.*
42: 5 heard of thee by hearing of the *e.*
Ps. 5: 1 give *e.* to my words, O Lord
10: 17 cause thine *e.* to hear
17: 6 incline thine *e.* unto me
49: 1 give *e.*, all ye inhabitants
54: 2 give *e.* to the words of my mouth
78: 1 give *e.*, O my people, to my law
86: 6 give *e.*, O Lord, unto my prayer
94: 9 He that planted the *e.* shall
130: 2 let thine *e.* be attentive
Prov. 15:31 *e.* that heareth reproof
20:12 The hearing *e.* and seeing eye
25:12 wise reprover on an obedient *e.*
Is. 1: 2 hear, O heavens, and give *e.*
8: 9 give *e.*, all ye of far countries
37:17 incline thine *e.*, O Lord
48: 8 time thine *e.* was not opened
50: 5 Lord God hath opened mine *e.* and
Jer. 6:10 *e.* is uncircumcised and they cannot
Joel 1: 2 hear this, ye old men, and give *e.*
Amos 3:12 two legs or a piece of an *e.*
Luke 12: 3 which ye have spoken in the *e.*
1 Cor. 2: 9 eye hath not seen nor *e.* heard

EARS
Deut. 29: 4 eyes to see and *e.* to hear
2 Sam. 7:22 all that we have heard with our *e.*
22: 7 my cry did enter into his *e.*
2 Chr. 6:40 let thine *e.* be attent
Job 15:21 a dreadful sound in his *e.*
33:16 He openeth the *e.* of men
Ps. 34:15 his *e.* are open unto their cry
40: 6 my *e.* hast thou opened
44: 1 we have heard with our *e.*
49: 4 I will incline mine *e.* to a parable
78: 1 incline your *e.* to the words
115: 6 they have *e.* but they hear not
Prov. 23:12 apply thine *e.* to words of knowledge
Is. 30:21 thine *e.* shall hear a word behind
32: 3 *e.* of hearers shall hearken
35: 5 the *e.* of the deaf shall be unstopped
43: 8 and the deaf that have *e.*
55: 3 incline your *e.* and come unto me
Jer. 5:21 which have *e.*, and hear not
Ezek. 3:10 and hear with thine *e.*
23:25 shall take away thy nose and thine *e.*
Zech. 7:11 and stopped their *e.* that they
Mat. 11:15 *e.* to hear, let him hear
13: 9 who hath *e.* to hear, let him hear
Mark 7:33 Jesus put his fingers into his *e.*
8:18 having *e.* hear ye not?
Luke 9:44 let sayings sink into your *e.*
Rev. 2: 7 he that hath an *e.*, let him hear

EARLY
Gen. 19:27 Abraham gat up *e.* in the morning
Ps. 46: 5 God shall help her and that right *e.*
57: 8 I myself will awake *e.*
90:14 satisfy us *e.* with thy mercy
Prov. 1:28 seek me *e.* and not find
8:17 that seek me *e.* shall find me
Is. 26: 9 within me will I seek thee *e.*
Jer. 26: 5 both rising up *e.*, and sending them
Hos. 5:15 in affliction will seek me *e.*
John 18:28 hall of judgment and it was *e.*
20: 1 cometh Mary Magdalene *e.*
Jas. 5: 7 receive *e.* and latter rain

EARNEST (EARNESTLY)
Job 7: 2 servant *e.* desireth shadow
Jer. 11: 7 I *e.* protested unto your fathers
Mic. 7: 3 do evil with both hands *e.*
Luke 22:44 in agony, he prayed more *e.*
Rom. 8:19 for the *e.* expectation of
1 Cor. 12:31 covet *e.* the best gifts
2 Cor. 1:22 given the *e.* of the Spirit in our hearts
5: 2 in this we groan, *e.* desiring
5: 5 given unto us the *e.* of the Spirit
7: 7 told us of your *e.* desire
Eph. 1:14 which is the *e.* of our inheritance
Phil. 1:20 according to my *e.* expectation
Heb. 2: 1 we ought to give the more *e.* heed
Jas. 5:17 prayed *e.* that it might not rain
Jude 1: 3 ye should *e.* contend for the faith

EARRINGS
Gen. 35: 4 and all their *e.* which were in
Ex. 32: 2 break off the golden *e.*
Num. 31:50 bracelets, rings, *e.*, and tablets
Judg. 8:24 every man the *e.* of his prey
Ezek. 16:12 and *e.* in thine ears
Hos. 2:13 decked herself with her *e.*

EARTH
Gen. 6:11 the *e.* also was corrupt
11: 1 whole *e.* of one language
41:47 *e.* brought forth by handfuls
Ex. 9:29 that the *e.* is the Lord's
Num. 16:32 *e.* opened her mouth
Deut. 10:14 the *e.* also, with all that therein is
28:23 *e.* under thee be iron
32: 1 hear O *e.* the words of my mouth
Judg. 5: 4 the *e.* trembled and the heavens
1 Sam. 2: 8 pillars of the *e.* are the Lord's
1 Chr. 16:31 and let the *e.* rejoice: and let
Job 9: 6 shaketh the *e.* out of her place
11: 9 longer than the *e.*, broader than the sea
16:18 O *e.* cover not thou my blood
26: 7 and hangeth the *e.* upon nothing
30: 8 base men, viler than the *e.*
38: 4 I laid the foundations of the *e.*
Ps. 24: 1 the *e.* is the Lord's
33: 5 *e.* is full of the goodness of the Lord
65: 9 visitest the *e.* and waterest it
67: 2 way be known upon the *e.*, thy saving
67: 6 shall thee*.* yield her increase
72:19 let the whole *e.* be filled
73:25 none upon the *e.* that I desire
78:69 like the *e.* established for ever
89:11 are thine, the *e.* also is thine
97: 4 the world: the *e.* saw and trembled
104: 24 the *e.* is full of thy riches
106: 17 the *e.* opened and swallowed up Dathan
115: 16 *e.* hath he given to the children
139: 15 in lowest parts of the *e.*
Prov. 25: 3 heaven for height and *e.* for depth
Eccl. 1: 4 but the *e.* abideth for ever
5: 2 God is in heaven and thou upon *e.*
7:20 not a just man upon *e.* that doeth good
10: 7 princes walking as servants upon the *e.*
Is. 6: 3 the whole *e.* is full of his glory
11: 4 smite the *e.* with the rod
11: 9 *e.* shall be full of the knowledge
13:13 *e.* shall remove out of her place
24: 1 Lord maketh the *e.* empty
24: 4 the *e.* mourneth and fadeth away
24: 5 the *e.* also is defiled under the
24:19 the *e.* is utterly broken down
24:20 *e.* shall reel to and fro like a
26:19 *e.* shall cast out the dead
66: 1 *e.* is my footstool, where is
Jer. 22:29 O *e. e. e.* hear the word
Ezek. 34:27 *e.* shall yield her increase
43: 2 the *e.* shined with his glory
Hos. 2:22 *e.* shall hear the corn, and
Hab. 2:14 for the *e.* shall be filled
3: 3 and *e.* was full of his praise
Mat. 13: 5 where they had not much *e.*
Luke 5:24 Son of man power upon *e.* to forgive

John 3:31 he that is of *e.* is earthly
1 Cor. 10:28 the *e.* is the Lord's
Col. 3: 5 mortify your members which are upon the *e.*
Heb. 6: 7 *e.* which drinketh in the rain that
Rev. 12:16 and the *e.* helped the woman

EARTHEN
Jer. 19: 1 get a potter's *e.* bottle
Lam. 4: 2 how they are esteemed as *e.* pitchers

EARTHLY
John 3:31 he that is of the earth is *e.*
2 Cor. 4: 7 we have this treasure in *e.* vessels
5: 1 if our *e.* house of this tabernacle
Phil. 3:19 their shame who mind *e.* things

EARTHQUAKE (EARTHQUAKES)
1 Ki. 19:12 and after the *e.* a fire
Is. 29: 6 with thunder, and with *e.*
Amos 1: 1 two years before the *e.*
Zech. 14: 5 as ye fled from before the *e.*
Mat. 24: 7 and *e.* in divers places
27:54 with him, watching Jesus, saw the *e.*
28: 2 behold, there was a great *e.*
Acts 16:26 suddenly there was a great *e.*
Rev. 11:19 and an *e.*, and great hail
16: 8 and there was a great *e.*

EASE
Job 12: 5 the thought of him that is at *e.*
Ps. 25:13 his soul shall dwell at *e.*
Is. 1:24 I will *e.* me of adversaries
32:11 tremble, ye women that are at *e.*
Jer. 46:27 and be in rest and at *e.*
Ezek. 23:42 and a voice of a multitude being at *e.*
Amos 6: 1 woe to them that are at *e.*
Zech. 1:15 with the heathen that are at *e.*
Luke 12:19 take thine *e.* and be merry

EASY (EASIER, EASILY)
Prov. 14: 6 knowledge is *e.* to him
Mat. 9: 5 for whether is *e.*, to say
11:30 my yoke is *e.*, and my burden
Luke 16:17 *e.* for heaven and earth to pass
1 Cor. 14: 9 words *e.* to be understood
Heb. 12: 1 sin which doth so *e.* beset
Jas. 3:17 gentle, *e.* to be entreated

EAST
Gen. 28:14 abroad to the west and to the *e.*
41: 6 blasted with the *e.* wind
Ex. 14:21 go back by a strong *e.* wind
Ps. 48: 7 ships of Tarshish with an *e.* wind
103: 12 as far as the *e.* is from the west
Is. 27: 8 in the day of the *e.* wind
43: 5 bring thy seed from the *e.*
Hos. 13:15 an *e.* wind shall come
Hab. 1: 9 faces shall sup up as the *e.* wind
Mat. 2: 1 there came wise men from the *e.*
8:11 many shall come from the *e.*

EAT
Gen. 2:16 tree of the garden thou mayest freely *e.*
2:17 good and evil thou shalt not *e.*
3:14 dust shalt thou *e.* all the days
3:19 thy face shalt thou *e.* bread
9: 4 the blood thereof, shall ye not *e.*
18: 8 by them under the tree and they did *e.*
27: 4 bring it to me that I may *e.*
Ex. 10: 5 shall *e.* the residue of that
12:48 no uncircumcised person shall *e.* thereof
16:35 Israel did *e.* manna forty years, until
32: 6 people sat down to *e.* and to drink
Lev. 7:21 and *e.* of the flesh of the sacrifice
11: 2 are the beasts which ye shall *e.*
11:22 of them ye may *e.*, the locusts
17:14 *e.* the blood of no manner of flesh
19:25 shall ye *e.* of the fruit thereof
26:38 land of your enemies shall *e.* you up
Num. 6: 3 nor *e.* moist grapes, or dried
11: 5 fish we *e.* in Egypt, melons, leeks
Deut. 4:28 gods which neither *e.* nor
14:21 shall not *e.* anything that dieth
14:23 *e.* before Lord God tithe, firstlings
28:55 flesh of his children whom he shall *e.*
1 Sam. 14:32 the people did *e.* them with the blood
1 Ki. 13: 9 *e.* no bread, drink no water
19: 5 and said unto him Arise and *e.*
21:23 dogs shall *e.* Jezebel
2 Ki. 4:43 give the people that they may *e.*
6:29 boiled my son, and did *e.* him
Neh. 8:10 *e.* the fat, drink the sweet
Ps. 22:26 meek shall *e.* and be satisfied
53: 4 *e.* up my people as bread
78:25 man did *e.* angels' food
128: 2 *e.* the labour of thine hands
Prov. 1:31 *e.* the fruit of their own way
13: 2 *e.* good by the fruit of his mouth
25:16 *e.* so much as is sufficient
Eccl. 3:13 every man should *e.* and drink
9: 7 *e.* thy bread with joy
Sol. 5: 1 *e.* O friends; drink, yea
Is. 1:19 if obedient ye shall *e.*
3:10 shall *e.* the fruit of their doings
4: 1 we will *e.* our own bread, only let
7:15 butter and honey shall he *e.*
9:20 *e.* every man the flesh of his own
11: 7 and the lion shall *e.* straw
30:24 young asses that ear the ground shall *e.*
37:30 *e.* this year such as groweth of itself
51: 8 worm shall *e.* them as wool
55: 1 buy and *e.*, yea, come buy
55: 2 *e.* that is good, let your soul delight
61: 6 ye shall *e.* the riches of the Gentiles
62: 9 they that have gathered it shall *e.* it
65: 4 which *e.* swine's flesh, and broth of
Jer. 15:16 words were found and I did *e.*
Ezek. 3: 1 *e.* this roll, and go speak
4:13 Israel *e.* their defiled bread among the Gentiles
4:16 *e.* bread by weight, and with care
5:10 fathers shall *e.* the sons
22: 9 they *e.* upon the mountains
Dan. 1:12 let them give us pulse to *e.*
4:33 and did *e.* grass as oxen
Hos. 4:10 *e.* and not have enough
Amos 7:12 there *e.* bread, and prophesy
9:14 gardens, and *e.* the fruit of them
Mic. 3: 3 *e.* the flesh of my people
Zech. 7: 6 did not ye *e.* for yourselves?
Mat. 6:25 no thought what ye shall *e.*
26:26 Jesus said, Take *e.* this is my body
Mark 1: 6 *e.* locusts and wild honey
7: 5 *e.* bread with unwashen hands
7:28 dogs *e.* of the children's crumbs
14:22 as they did *e.*, Jesus took bread
Luke 10: 8 *e.* such things as are set before you
15:23 let us *e.*, and be merry
22:30 ye may *e.* and drink at my table
John 4:31 I have meat to *e.* that ye
6:26 because ye did *e.* of the loaves
6:53 except ye *e.* the flesh of the Son
Acts 2:46 did *e.* their meat with gladness
1 Cor. 5:11 with such an one, no not to *e.*
8: 7 *e.* it as a thing offered unto an idol
10: 7 the people sat down to *e.* and drink
10:31 whether therefore ye *e.* or drink
11:24 take, *e.*: this is my body
2 Thes. 3:10 not work, neither should he *e.*
Jas. 5: 3 *e.* your flesh as it were fire
Rev. 2: 7 will I give to *e.* of the tree
10: 9 take it and *e.* it up
17:16 shall *e.* her flesh, and burn

EATEN (EATETH, EATING)
Num. 13:32 is a land that *e.* up the inhabitants
Deut. 26:14 not *e.* thereof in my mourning
1 Sam. 30:16 *e.* and drinking, and dancing,
Ps. 69: 9 zeal of thine house hath *e.* me up
Prov. 9:17 bread *e.* in secret is pleasant
Eccl. 4: 5 together and *e.* his own flesh
Hos. 10:13 having *e.* the fruit of lies
Joel 1: 4 hath the locust *e.*, and that
Amos 7: 2 end of *e.* the grass of the land
Mat. 9:11 why *e.* your master with publicans and
11:18 John came neither *e.* nor drinking.
14:21 *e.* were about five thousand
24:38 were *e.* and drinking, marrying and
26:26 as they were *e.* Jesus took
Luke 13:26 *e.* and drunk in thy presence
John 2:17 the zeal of thine house hath *e.* me up
6:54 whoso *e.* my flesh and drinketh
6:58 he that *e.* this bread shall live
Acts 12:23 he was *e.* of worms
Rom. 14: 6 he that *e.* *e.* to the Lord
14:20 for that man who *e.* with offence
1 Cor. 11:29 *e.* and drinketh unworthily, *e.* and

EATER
Judg. 14:14 out of the *e.* came forth meat
Is. 55:10 seed to the sower, bread to the *e.*
Nah. 3:12 fall into the mouth of the *e.*

EDIFY (EDIFIED, EDIFIETH)
Acts 9:31 and were *e.*, and walking in the fear
Rom. 14:19 wherewith one may *e.* another
1 Cor. 8: 1 knowledge puffeth up, but charity *e.*
10:23 but all things *e.* not
14:17 but the other is not *e.*
1 Thes. 5:11 yourselves together, and *e.* one

EDIFICATION
Rom. 15: 2 please his neighbour for his good to *e.*
1 Cor. 14: 3 speaketh unto men to *e.*
2 Cor. 10: 8 which the Lord hath given us for *e.*

EDIFYING
1 Cor. 14:12 may excel to the *e.* of the church
2 Cor. 12:19 we do all for your *e.*
Eph. 4:12 for the *e.* of the body of Christ
4:16 body unto the *e.* of itself in love
4:29 but that which is good to the use of *e.*
1 Tim. 1: 4 questions rather than godly *e.*

EFFECT
Is. 32:17 *e.* of righteousness quietness
Mat. 15: 6 commandment of God of none *e.*
Mark 7:13 making the word of God of none *e.*
Rom. 3: 3 make the faith of God without *e.*
9: 6 word of God had taken none *e.*
1 Cor. 1:17 cross of Christ be made of none *e.*
Gal. 5: 4 Christ is become of no *e.* to you

EFFECTUAL
1 Cor. 16: 9 great door and *e.* is opened unto
2 Cor. 1: 6 which is *e.* in the enduring
Eph. 3: 7 by the *e.* working of his power
Philem. 1: 6 thy faith may become *e.* by the
Jas. 5:16 *e.* fervent prayer of a righteous

EFFEMINATE
1 Cor. 6: 9 nor adulterers, nor *e.*, nor abusers

EGG (EGGS)
Deut. 22: 6 whether they be young ones, or *e.*
Job 6: 6 any taste in the white of an *e.*
Is. 10:14 as one gathereth *e.* that are left
Jer. 17:11 as the partridge sitteth on *e.*
Luke 11:12 or if he shall ask an *e.*

ELDER (ELDERS)
Gen. 10:21 the brother of Japheth the *e.*
25:23 the *e.* shall serve the younger
Deut. 32: 7 thy *e.* and they will tell thee
Ezra 10: 8 according to the counsel of the *e.*
Joel 2:16 assemble the *e.*, gather the
Acts 14:23 ordained them *e.* in every church
15:23 *e.* and brethren send greeting
20:17 Ephesus, and called the *e.* of the church
Rom. 9:12 the *e.* shall serve the younger
1 Tim. 5: 1 rebuke not an *e.* but entreat
5: 2 the *e.* women as mothers
5:17 *e.* that rule well be counted
Tit. 1: 5 ordain *e.* in every city
Heb. 11: 2 *e.* obtained a good report
Jas. 5:14 let him call for the *e.* of the church
1 Pet. 5: 1 *e.* which are among you I exhort
5: 5 younger, submit yourselves unto the *e.*
2 John 1: 1 the *e.* unto the elect lady
3 John 1: 1 the *e.* unto the well-beloved Gaius
Rev. 4: 4 four and twenty *e.* sitting
11:16 and the four and twenty *e.*, which sat

ELECT
Is. 42: 1 *e.* in whom my soul delighteth
65: 9 mine *e.* shall inherit it
Mat. 24:22 for the *e.*'s sake those days shall shortened
24:24 if possible deceive the very *e.*
24:31 gather his *e.* from the four winds
Luke 18: 7 God avenge his own *e.*

Rom. 8:33 to the charge of God's *e.*
Col. 3:12 put on as the *e.* of God
1 Tim. 5:21 the *e.* angels, that thou observe
2 Tim. 2:10 I endure all things for the *e.*'s sake
Tit. 1: 1 according to the faith of God's *e.*
1 Pet. 1: 2 *e.* according to the foreknowledge of God
2: 6 corner stone, *e.*, precious
2 John 1: 1 the elder unto the *e.* lady

ELECTED
1 Pet. 5:13 *e.* together with you, saluteth you

ELECTION
Rom. 9:11 according to *e.* might stand
11: 5 remnant according to the *e.* of grace
11: 7 but the *e.* hath obtained it
1 Thes. 1: 4 brethren beloved, your *e.* of God
2 Pet. 1:10 make your calling and *e.* sure

ELEMENTS
Gal. 4: 9 again to the weak and beggarly *e.*

EMPTY
Gen. 37:24 into a pit: and the pit was *e.*
41:27 the seven *e.* ears blasted with
Ex. 23:15 and none shall appear before me *e.*
Deut. 15:13 shalt not let him go away *e.*
16:16 they shall not appear before the Lord *e.*
Judg. 7:16 in every man's hand, with *e.* pitchers
2 Sam. 1:22 sword of Saul returned not *e.*
2 Ki. 4: 3 even *e.* vessels; borrow not a few
Hos. 10: 1 Israel is an *e.* vine, he bringeth
Luke 1:53 the rich he hath sent *e.* away

EMPTINESS
Is. 34:11 confusion and the stones of *e.*

END
Gen. 6:13 the *e.* of all flesh is come
Num. 23:10 let my last *e.* be like his
Deut. 8:16 to do thee good at thy latter *e.*
32:20 see what their *e.* shall be
Job 42:12 Lord blessed the latter *e.* of Job more
Ps. 37:37 the *e.* of that man is peace
39: 4 make me to know mine *e.*
73:17 then understood I their *e.*
102: 27 and thy years shall have no *e.*
119: 33 I shall keep it unto the *e.*
119: 96 seen an *e.* of all perfection
Prov. 5: 4 her *e.* is bitter as wormwood
19:20 thou mayest be wise in thy latter *e.*
Eccl. 4: 8 there is no *e.* of his labour
7: 2 for that is the *e.* of all men
7: 8 better is the *e.* of a thing
Is. 9: 7 of his government there shall be no *e.*
Jer. 4:27 yet will I not make a full *e.*
5:31 what will ye do in the *e.*
12: 4 he shall not see our last *e.*
17:11 days, and at his *e.* shall be a fool
31:17 and there is hope in thine *e.*
Lam. 4:18 our *e.* is come, our *e.* is near
Ezek. 11:13 wilt thou make a full *e.* of the remnant
21:25 when iniquity shall have an *e.*
Dan. 6:26 dominion shall be even unto the *e.*
8:19 at the time appointed the *e.* shall
Amos 8: 2 *e.* is come upon my people of Israel
Hab. 2: 3 at the *e.* it shall speak
Mat. 13:39 harvest is the *e.* of the world
24: 3 and of the *e.* of the world
24: 6 but the *e.* is not yet
24:13 he that shall endure unto the *e.*
28:20 even unto the *e.* of the world
Luke 21: 9 but the *e.* is not by and by
John 13: 1 he loved them unto the *e.*
Rom. 6:21 the *e.* of those things is death
6:22 and the *e.* everlasting life
14: 9 to this *e.* Christ both died and rose
1 Cor. 1: 8 who shall also confirm you unto the *e.*
1 Tim. 1: 5 *e.* of the commandment is charity
Heb. 3:14 beginning of our confidence stedfast unto the *e.*
6: 8 whose *e.* is to be burned
6:11 assurance of hope unto the *e.*
6:16 is to them an *e.* of all strife
7: 3 beginning of days, nor *e.* of life
Jas. 5:11 seen the *e.* of the Lord

1 Pet. 1: 9 receiving the *e.* of your faith
4: 7 the *e.* of all things is at hand
4:17 *e.* of those that obey not the gospel
2 Pet. 2:20 the latter *e.* is worse with them
Rev. 1: 8 Alpha and Omega, the beginning and the *e.*
2:26 overcometh, and keepeth my works unto the *e.*
21: 6 Omega, the beginning and the *e.*
22:13 Alpha and Omega, the beginning and the *e.*

ENDS
Ps. 22:27 the *e.* of the world shall remember
67: 7 all the *e.* of the earth shall fear him
Is. 45:22 be ye saved, all the *e.* of the earth
52:10 all the *e.* of the earth shall see
Zech. 9:10 even to the *e.* of the earth
Acts 13:47 salvation unto the *e.* of the earth
1 Cor. 10:11 upon whom the *e.* of the world are come

ENDURE (ENDURED)
Gen. 33:14 as children are able to *e.*
Ps. 9: 7 the Lord shall *e.* forever
30: 5 weeping may *e.* for a night
72:17 His name shall *e.* forever
81:15 time should have *e.* for ever
89:36 his seed shall *e.* forever,
102: 26 they shall perish, but thou shalt *e.*
Prov. 27:24 crown *e.* to every generation
Ezek. 22:14 can thine heart *e.* or can thine
Mat. 24:13 he that shall *e.* to the end
Mark 4:17 no root, and *e.* but for a time
13:13 that shall *e.* unto the end shall
Rom. 9:22 *e.* with much longsuffering
2 Tim. 2: 3 *e.* hardness as a good soldier
2:10 *e.* all things for the elect's sake
3:11 what persecutions I *e.*, but out of
4: 5 watch thou, *e.* afflictions, do the
Heb. 6:15 he had patiently *e.*, he obtained
11:27 *e.* as seeing him who is invisible
12: 2 that was set before him *e.* the cross
12: 7 if ye *e.* chastening, God dealeth
Jas. 5:11 we count them happy which *e.*

ENDURETH
1 Chr. 16:34 for his mercy *e.* for ever
2 Chr. 5:13 for his mercy *e.* forever
Ezra 3:11 for his mercy *e.* forever toward Israel
Ps. 30: 5 his anger *e.* but a moment
100: 5 his truth *e.* to all generations
106: 1 for his mercy *e.* forever
111: 10 his praise *e.* for ever
112: 3 his righteousness *e.* for ever
117: 2 the truth of the Lord *e.* for ever
119:160 thy righteous judgments *e.* for ever
135: 13 thy name, O Lord, *e.* for ever
136: 1 for his mercy *e.* forever
138: 8 thy mercy, O Lord, *e.* forever
145: 13 and thy dominion *e.* throughout all
Mat. 10:22 that *e.* to end shall be saved
John 6:27 meat which *e.* unto life
1 Cor. 13: 7 hopeth all things, *e.* all things
Jas. 1:12 blessed is the man that *e.* temptation
1 Pet. 1:25 the word of the Lord *e.* for ever

ENEMY
Ex. 23:22 I will be an *e.* unto thine enemies
Deut. 32:27 not that I feared the wrath of the *e.*
1 Sam. 24:19 find his *e.* will he let him go
1 Ki. 21:20 hast thou found me, O mine *e.*
Job 33:10 he counteth me for his *e.*
Ps. 7: 5 let the *e.* persecute my soul
8: 2 mightest still the *e.* and avenger
Prov. 27: 6 kisses of an *e.* are deceitful
Mic. 7: 8 rejoice not against me, O mine *e.*
1 Cor. 15:26 the last *e.* destroyed is death
Gal. 4:16 am I therefore become your *e.*
2 Thes. 3:15 count him not as an *e.*, but
Jas. 4: 4 friend of the world is the *e.* of God

ENEMIES
Gen. 22:17 seed shall possess the gate of his *e.*
Ex. 23:22 I will be an enemy unto thine *e.*
Deut. 28:48 therefore shalt thou serve thine *e.*
Judg. 5:31 let all thine *e.* perish, O Lord

Ps. 68: 1 let his *e.* be scattered
92: 9 for lo, thine *e.* shall perish
132: 18 his *e.* will I clothe with shame
Prov. 16: 7 he maketh even his *e.* to be at peace
Is. 66: 6 that rendereth recompence to his *e.*
Mic. 7: 6 man's *e.* are the men of his own house
Mat. 22:44 till I make thine *e.* thy footstool
Rom. 5:10 if when we were *e.* we were reconciled
1 Cor. 15:25 put all *e.* under his feet
Col. 1:21 *e.* in your mind by wicked works
Heb. 1:13 until I make thine *e.* thy footstool
10:13 till his *e.* be made his footstool

ENMITY
Gen. 3:15 I will put *e.* between thee and
Rom. 8: 7 carnal mind is *e.* against God
Eph. 2:15 abolished in his flesh the *e.*

ENJOY
Lev. 26:34 shall the land *e.* her sabbaths
Num. 36: 8 children of Israel may *e.* every man
Deut. 28:41 thou shalt not *e.* them; for they
Acts 24: 2 we *e.* great quietness
Heb. 11:25 *e.* the pleasures of sin for a season

ENLARGE (ENLARGED, ENLARGETH)
Gen. 9:27 God shall *e.* Japheth and he
Deut. 33:20 blessed be he that *e.* Gad
2 Sam. 22:37 thou hast *e.* my steps under me
Ps. 4: 1 thou hast *e.* me when in distress
25:17 troubles of my heart are *e.*
Is. 5:14 hell hath *e.* herself, and opened
54: 2 *e.* the place of thy tent, and let
Hab. 2: 5 *e.* his desire as hell and is as
2 Cor. 6:11 unto you our heart is *e.*

ENLIGHTEN (ENLIGHTENED)
Ps. 18:28 the Lord my God will *e.* my darkness
Eph. 1:18 eyes of your understanding being *e.*
Heb. 6: 4 impossible for those who were once *e.*

ENOUGH
Gen. 33:11 with me and because I have *e.*
45:28 is *e.* Joseph my son is yet alive
Ex. 36: 5 people bring more than *e.* for the
2 Sam. 24:16 Lord said to the angel, It is *e.*
1 Ki. 19: 4 it is *e.* now, O Lord
Prov. 30:15 say not, it is *e.*
Mat. 10:25 it is *e.* for the disciple that
Mark 14:41 it is *e.* the hour is come
Luke 15:17 bread *e.* and to spare

ENSIGN (ENSIGNS)
Ps. 74: 4 set up their *e.* for signs
Is. 5:26 he will lift up an *e.* to the nations
11:10 stand for an *e.* to the people
Zech. 9:16 lifted up as an *e.* upon his land

ENTER
Num. 20:24 for he shall not *e.* into the land
Job 22: 4 will he *e.* with thee into judgment
Ps. 100: 4 *e.* his gates with thanksgiving
118: 20 gate into which the righteous shall *e.*
Prov. 4:14 *e.* not into the path of the wicked
23:10 *e.* not into the fields of the fatherless
Is. 2:10 *e.* into the rock and hide
26:20 *e.* into thy chambers, and shut
57: 2 he shall *e.* into peace
Dan. 11:17 set his face to *e.* with the strength
Mat. 5:20 no case *e.* into the kingdom
6: 6 when thou prayest, *e.* into thy closet
7:21 shall *e.* into the kingdom of heaven
18: 8 it is better to *e.* into life halt
19:24 than for rich men to *e.* into the kingdom
25:21 *e.* thou into the joy of thy Lord
26:41 that ye *e.* not into temptation
Mark 14:38 watch and pray, lest ye *e.* into temptation
Luke 13:24 seek to *e.* but not able
24:26 things and to *e.* into his glory
John 3: 4 can he *e.* the second time into his
3: 5 he cannot *e.* into the kingdom of God
10: 9 I am the door; by me if any man *e.*

Acts 14:22 tribulation *e.* into the kingdom of God
Heb. 4: 3 believed do *e.* into rest
10:19 *e.* into the holiest by the blood of Jesus
Rev. 15: 8 no man was able to *e.* the temple
22:14 *e.* through the gates into the city

ENTERED (ENTERETH)
Gen. 19:23 the earth when Lot *e.* into Zoar
Ex. 33: 9 as Moses *e.* into the tabernacle
Luke 11:52 ye *e.* not in yourselves, and them
John 4:38 ye are *e.* into their labours
10: 1 *e.* not by the door, but climbeth up
Rom. 5:12 by one man sin *e.* into the world
5:20 law *e.* that offence might abound
Heb. 4: 6 *e.* not because of unbelief

ENTERTAIN
Heb. 13: 2 be not forgetful to *e.* strangers

ENTREAT (ENTREATED)
Gen. 12:16 and he *e.* Abram well for her sake
Ex. 9:28 *e.* the Lord (for it is enough)
1 Sam. 2:25 if a man sin who shall *e.*
Jer. 15:11 I will cause the enemy to *e.* thee well
1 Cor. 4:13 being defamed, we *e.*: we are made
1 Tim. 5: 1 not an elder but *e.* him as a father
Jas. 3:17 easy to be *e.*, full of mercy

ENTREATY (ENTREATIES)
Prov. 18:23 the poor useth *e.*, but the rich
2 Cor. 8: 4 praying us with much *e.* that we

ENVY (ENVIES)
Job 5: 2 and *e.* slayeth the silly one
Prov. 3:31 *e.* thou not the oppressor, and
14:30 *e.* is the rottenness of bones
23:17 let not thy heart *e.* sinners
27: 4 who is able to stand before *e.*
Is. 11:13 *e.* also of Ephraim shall depart
Ezek. 35:11 and according to thine *e.* which thou
Mat. 27:18 for *e.* they delivered him
Acts 7: 9 moved with *e.* sold Joseph into
17: 5 which believed not, moved with *e.*
Phil. 1:15 some indeed preach Christ even of *e.*
1 Tim. 6: 4 whereof cometh *e.*, strife, railings
Tit. 3: 3 living in malice, *e.*, hateful and
Jas. 4: 5 spirit in us lusteth to *e.*
1 Pet. 2: 1 hypocrisies and *e.* and all evil

ENVIED (ENVIEST, ENVYING)
Gen. 26:14 the Philistines *e.* him
Num. 11:29 *e.* thou for my sake? would God
Ps. 106: 16 they *e.* Moses also in the camp
Eccl. 4: 4 work, that for this a man is *e.*
Rom. 13:13 wantonness, not in strife and *e.*
1 Cor. 3: 3 *e.* and strife, and divisions, are ye
Gal. 5:26 provoking one another, *e.* one another

ENVIOUS
Ps. 37: 1 neither be thou *e.*
Prov. 24: 1 be not thou *e.* against the workers

EPHOD
Ex. 39: 2 made the *e.* of gold, blue, and purple
Judg. 8:27 and Gideon made an *e.* thereof
17: 5 and made an *e.*, and teraphim
1 Sam. 2:18 girded with a linen *e.*
21: 9 wrapped in a cloth behind the *e.*
23: 9 the priest, bring hither the *e.*
30: 7 pray thee, bring me hither the *e.*
2 Sam. 6:14 David was girded with a linen *e.*
Hos. 3: 4 without an image, and without an *e.*

EPISTLE
Acts 15:30 together they delivered the *e.*
Rom. 16:22 I Tertius, who wrote this *e.*
1 Cor. 5: 9 I wrote unto you in an *e.*
2 Cor. 3: 2 *e.* written in our hearts
7: 8 the same *e.* hath made you sorry
Col. 4:16 ye likewise read the *e.* from Laodicea
1 Thes. 5:27 this *e.* be read unto all
2 Thes. 2:15 whether by word, or our *e.*
2 Pet. 3: 1 this second *e.*, beloved, I now write

EQUAL (EQUALS)
Is. 40:25 Or shall I be *e.*? saith the Holy

Ezek. 18:25 ye say, the way of the Lord is not *e.*
Mat. 20:12 thou hast made them *e.* unto us
Luke 20:36 for they are *e.* unto the angels
John 5:18 making himself *e.* with God
Gal. 1:14 my *e.* in mine own nation
Phil. 2: 6 it not robbery to be *e.* with God
Col. 4: 1 servants that which is just and *e.*
Rev. 21:16 breadth, and the height of it are *e.*

EQUALITY
2 Cor. 8:14 but by an *e.*, that now

EQUITY
Ps. 98: 9 and the people with *e.*
99: 4 thou dost establish *e.*, thou
Prov. 1: 3 wisdom, justice, judgment, *e.*
17:26 nor to strike princes for *e.*
Eccl. 2:21 labour is in wisdom, knowledge, *e.*
Is. 11: 4 reprove with *e.* for the meek
59:14 truth fallen, *e.* cannot enter
Mic. 3: 9 princes that pervert all *e.*
Mal. 2: 6 Levi walked with me in *e.*

ERR (ERRED)
Num. 15:22 and if ye have *e.*, and not
1 Sam. 26:21 the fool, and have *e.* exceedingly
Job 6:24 understand wherein I have *e.*
Ps. 95:10 do *e.* in their heart
119: 21 which do *e.* from thy commandments
119:110 I *e.* not from thy precepts
Prov. 14:22 do they not *e.* that devise evil
Is. 9:16 leaders of this people cause them to *e.*
30:28 jaws of the people, causing them to *e.*
28: 7 and prophet have *e.* through strong drink
35: 8 wayfaring men, though fools, shall not *e.*
63:17 why hast thou made us to *e.* from thy
Jer. 23:13 and caused my people Israel to *e.*
Mic. 3: 5 prophets that make my people *e.*
Mat. 22:29 ye do *e.* not knowing the scripture
1 Tim. 6:10 have *e.* from the faith, and pierced
6:21 professing have *e.* concerning the faith
2 Tim. 2:18 who concerning the truth have *e.*
Jas. 5:19 if any of you *e.* from the truth

ERROR (ERRORS)
2 Sam. 6: 7 God smote him there for his *e.*
Job 19: 4 mine *e.* remaineth with myself
Ps. 19:12 who can understand his *e.*
Eccl. 10: 5 as an *e.* which proceedeth from the ruler
Is. 32: 6 utter *e.* against the Lord
Jer. 10:15 are vanity and the work of *e.*
Dan. 6: 4 neither was any *e.* or fault
Rom. 1:27 recompence of their *e.* which was
Heb. 9: 7 and for the *e.* of the people
Jas. 5:20 sinner from the *e.* of his way
2 Pet. 2:18 from them who live in *e.*
1 John 4: 6 spirit of truth and the spirit of *e.*
Jude 1:11 after the *e.* of Balaam for reward

ESCAPE (ESCAPED)
Gen. 19:22 haste thee, *e.* thither, for I cannot
32: 8 the other company which is left shall *e.*
Ezra 9: 8 to leave us a remnant to *e.*
9:15 for we remain yet *e.*, as it
Esth. 4:13 think not that thou shalt *e.*
Job 1:15 I only alone am *e.* to tell
11:20 fail, and they shall not *e.*
Ps. 56: 7 shall they *e.* by iniquity
71: 2 deliver me and cause me to *e.*
124: 7 our soul is *e.* as a bird
141: 10 own nets, whilst I withal *e.*
Prov. 19: 5 that speaketh lies shall not *e.*
Eccl. 7:26 pleaseth God shall *e.* from her
Is. 20: 6 Assyria: and how shall we *e.*
45:20 that are *e.* of the nations
Jer. 11:11 which they shall not be able to *e.*
Ezek. 17:15 shall he *e.* that doeth such things
Mat. 23:33 can ye *e.* the damnation of hell
Luke 21:36 accounted worthy to *e.* all these
John 10:39 he *e.* out of their hand
Rom. 2: 3 thou shalt *e.* the judgment of God
1 Cor. 10:13 temptation also make a way to *e.*
1 Thes. 5: 3 child; and they shall not *e.*
Heb. 2: 3 how shall we *e.* if we neglect
12:25 *e.* not who refused him that spake
2 Pet. 1: 4 *e.* the corruption that is in the

2 Pet. 2:18 allure those that were clean *e.*

ESTABLISH
Gen. 9: 9 I *e.* my covenant with you, and
17: 7 I will *e.* my covenant between me and
Lev. 26: 9 and *e.* my covenant with you
Deut. 8:18 that he may *e.* his covenant which he sware
1 Sam. 1:23 only the Lord *e.* his word
2 Sam. 7:12 and I will *e.* his kingdom
2 Chr. 9: 8 God loved Israel to *e.* them
Ps. 7: 9 but *e.* the just: for the righteous
48: 8 our God: God will *e.* it for ever
89: 2 faithfulness shalt thou *e.* in heaven
89: 4 thy seed will I *e.* for ever
90:17 *e.* the work of our hands
99: 4 thou dost *e.* equity, thou
Prov. 15:25 will *e.* the border of the widow
Is. 9: 7 order it, and to *e.* it with judgment
49: 8 to *e.* the earth, to cause to
62: 7 no rest till he *e.* Jerusalem
Ezek. 16:60 I will *e.* unto thee an everlasting covenant
Rom. 3:31 God forbid: yea, we *e.* the law
3:10 to *e.* their own righteousness
1 Thes. 3:13 *e.* your hearts

ESTABLISHED
Gen. 41:32 the thing is *e.* by God
Ex. 6: 4 I have also *e.* my covenant with them
15:17 which thy hands have *e.*
Ps. 40: 2 upon a rock, he *e.* my goings
78: 5 he *e.* a testimony in Jacob
93: 2 thy throne is *e.* of old
119: 90 hast *e.* the earth, and it abideth
Prov. 3:19 by understanding hath he *e.* the heavens
4:26 let all thy ways be *e.*
12: 3 man not be *e.* by wickedness
16:12 throne is *e.* by righteousness
20:18 every purpose is *e.* by counsel
Is. 7: 9 surely, ye shall not be *e.*
16: 5 in mercy shall the throne be *e.*
Jer. 10:12 hath *e.* the world by his wisdom
Hab. 1:12 thou hast *e.* them for correction
Mat. 18:16 or three witnesses every word may be *e.*
Acts 16: 5 so were the churches *e.* in the faith
Rom. 1:11 gift to the end ye may be *e.*
Heb. 8: 6 *e.* upon better promises
13: 9 that the heart be *e.* with grace
2 Pet. 1:12 and be *e.* in the present truth

ESTATE
Ps. 136: 23 who remembered us in our low *e.*
Prov. 27:23 know the *e.* of thy flocks
Luke 1:48 the low *e.* of his handmaiden
Jude 1: 6 angels that kept not their first *e.*

ESTEEM (ESTEEMED, ESTEEMETH, ESTEEMING)
Deut. 32:15 and lightly *e.* the rock of his salvation
1 Sam. 2:30 they that despise me shall be lightly *e.*
Job 23:12 *e.* the words of his mouth more than
Ps. 119:128 I *e.* all thy precepts concerning
Is. 53: 4 we did *e.* him stricken of God
Luke 16:15 which is highly *e.* among men is
Rom. 14: 5 one man *e.* one day above another
14:14 to him that *e.* it, it is unclean
Phil. 2: 3 *e.* each other better than themselves
1 Thes. 5:13 *e.* them very highly in love for
Heb. 11:26 *e.* the reproach of Christ

ESTRANGED
Ps. 58: 3 wicked are *e.* from the womb
78:30 not *e.* from their lusts
Ezek. 78:14 they are all *e.* from me

ETERNAL
Deut. 33:27 the *e.* God is thy refuge
Is. 60:15 make thee an *e.* excellency
Mat. 19:16 that I may have *e.* life
25:46 the righteous into life *e.*
Mark 3:29 is in danger of *e.* damnation
10:17 that I may inherit *e.* life
10:30 and in the world to come *e.* life
Luke 10:25 what shall I do to inherit *e.* life
John 3:15 should not perish but have *e.* life
4:36 wages, gathereth fruit unto *e.* life
6:54 hath *e.* life and I will raise him up

John 6:68 we go? thou hast the words of *e.* life
10:28 and I give unto them *e.* life
12:25 shall keep it unto *e.* life
17: 3 this is life *e.*, that they might
Acts 13:48 ordained to *e.* life believed
Rom. 1:20 even his *e.* power and Godhead
2: 7 honour, immortality, and *e.* life
6:23 the gift of God is *e.* through Jesus
2 Cor. 4:17 exceeding and *e.* weight of glory
4:18 the things which are not seen are *e.*
5: 1 hands, *e.* in the heavens
Eph. 3:11 according to the *e.* purpose
1 Tim. 1:17 unto the King *e.* immortal, invisible
6:12 lay hold on *e.* life
2 Tim. 2:10 which is in Christ Jesus with *e.* glory
Tit. 1: 2 in hope of *e.* life which God
3: 7 heirs according to the hope of *e.* life
Heb. 5: 9 author of *e.* salvation unto all
9:12 obtained *e.* redemption for us
9:14 through the *e.* Spirit offered himself
1 Pet. 5:10 called us unto his *e.* glory
1 John 1: 2 *e.* life which was with the Father
3:15 ye know that no murderer hath *e.* life
5:11 God has given to us *e.* life
Jude 1:21 our Lord Jesus Christ unto *e.* life

EUNUCH (EUNUCHS)
2 Ki. 9:32 looked out to him two or three *e.*
20:18 they shall be *e.* in the palace
Is. 56: 3 neither *e.* say, I am a dry tree
Mat. 19:12 themselves *e.* for the kingdom of heaven's sake
Acts 8:27 *e.* of great authority under Candace

EVEN *or* **EVENING**
Gen. 1: 5 the *e.* and the morning were the first
19: 1 there came two angels to Sodom at *e.*
1 Ki. 18:29 offering of the *e.* sacrifice
Ezra 9: 5 at the *e.* sacrifice I arose
Ps. 141: 2 my hands as the *e.* sacrifice
Dan. 9:21 about the time of the *e.* oblation
Hab. 1: 8 horses more fierce than *e.* wolves
Zeph. 3: 3 her judges are *e.* wolves
Zech. 14: 7 at *e.* time it shall be light

EVER
Gen. 3:22 and eat and live for *e.*
Ex. 15:18 Lord reigneth for *e.* and *e.*
Deut. 19: 9 to walk *e.* in his way
32:40 to heaven and say, I live for *e.*
Josh. 4:24 fear the Lord your God for *e.*
1 Ki. 10: 9 because the Lord loved Israel for *e.*
11:39 afflict seed of David, but not for *e.*
Ps. 5:11 let them *e.* shout for joy
9: 7 for the Lord shall endure for *e.*
10:16 the Lord is king for *e.*
12: 7 them from this generation for *e.*
22:26 your heart shall live for *e.*
23: 6 dwell in the house of the Lord for *e.*
25:15 my eyes are *e.* towards the Lord
25:37 he is *e.* merciful and lendeth
30:12 I will give thanks unto thee for *e.*
33:11 counsel of the Lord standeth for *e.*
37:18 their inheritance shall be for *e.*
45: 6 thy throne, O God, is for *e.*
48:14 this God is our God for *e.*
49: 9 he should still live for *e.*
51: 3 and my sin is *e.* before me
73:26 my heart and my portion for *e.*
74:19 the congregation of thy poor for *e.*
81:15 their time should have endured for *e.*
92: 7 that they shall be destroyed for *e.*
103: 9 neither will he keep his anger for *e.*
105: 8 hath remembered his covenant for *e.*
111: 8 commandments stand fast for *e.*
119: 44 I will keep thy law for *e.*
119:111 have I taken as an heritage for *e.*
119:145 I will bless thy name for *e.*
146: 6 which keepeth truth for *e.*
Prov. 27:24 riches are not for *e.*
Eccl. 1: 4 the earth abideth for *e.*
Is. 26: 4 trust in the Lord for *e.*
32:17 quietness and assurance for *e.*
40: 8 the word of our God shall stand for *e.*
57:16 I will not contend for *e.*
Jer. 3: 5 will he reserve anger for *e.*
32:39 that they may fear me for *e.*
Lam. 3:31 the Lord will not cast off for *e.*
Mic. 4: 5 the Lord our God for *e.* and *e.*
7:18 retaineth not his anger for *e.*
Zech. 1: 5 prophets, do they live for *e.*
Luke 15:31 son, thou art *e.* with me
John 6:51 of this bread, he shall live for *e.*
8:35 but the son abideth *e.*
Rom. 1:25 the Creator who is blessed for *e.*
9: 5 who is over all, God blessed for *e.*
2 Cor. 9: 9 his righteousness remaineth for *e.*
Gal. 1: 5 to whom be glory for *e.* and *e.*
Phil. 4:20 our Father be glory for *e.* and *e.*
1 Thes. 4: 5 *e.* follow that which is good
4:17 shall we *e.* be with the Lord
1 Tim. 1:17 be honour and glory and *e.* and *e.*
2 Tim. 3: 7 *e.* learning, and never able to
Heb. 7:24 this man, because he continueth *e.*
7:25 he *e.* liveth to make intercession
13: 8 the same, yesterday today and for *e.*
13:21 to whom be glory for *e.* and *e.*
1 Pet. 1:23 the word of God abideth for *e.*
1:25 word of the Lord endureth for *e.*
4:11 be praise and dominion for *e.* and *e.*
1 John 2:17 doeth the will of God abideth for *e.*
Jude 1:25 to God be glory now and *e.*
Rev. 1: 6 to him be glory and dominion for *e.* and *e.*
4: 9 who liveth for *e.* and *e.*

EVERLASTING
Gen. 17: 8 land of Canaan, an *e.* possession
21:33 on the name of the Lord, the *e.* God
49:26 unto the utmost bound of the *e.* hills
Ex. 40:15 *e.* priesthood throughout their generations
Deut. 33:27 and underneath are the *e.* arms
Ps. 24: 7 be ye lift up ye *e.* doors
41:13 blessed be God from *e.* to *e.*
90: 2 even from *e.* to *e.* thou art
103: 17 mercy of Lord from *e.* to *e.*
112: 6 the righteous shall be in *e.* remembrance
139: 24 lead me in the way *e.*
145: 13 thy kingdom is an *e.* kingdom
Prov. 10:25 righteous is an *e.* foundation
Is. 9: 6 The mighty God, the *e.* Father
26: 4 in the Lord Jehovah is *e.* strength
33:14 who dwell with *e.* burnings
35:10 songs and *e.* joy upon their heads
40:28 the *e.* God, the Lord, the Creator
45:17 Israel saved with *e.* salvation
55:13 to the Lord for a name, an *e.* sign
56: 5 I will give them an *e.* name
60:19 the Lord shall be an *e.* light
Jer. 10:10 he is the living God, and an *e.* King
20:11 *e.* confusion shall never be forgotten
23:40 I will bring an *e.* reproach
31: 3 I have loved thee with an *e.* love
Dan. 4:34 whose dominion is an *e.* dominion
12: 2 awake some to *e.* life, and some
Mic. 5: 2 goings forth of old, from *e.*
Hab. 1:12 art thou not from *e.*, O Lord my God
3: 6 the *e.* mountains were scattered
Mat. 18: 8 to be cast into *e.* fire
19:29 and shall inherit *e.* life
25:46 shall go into *e.* punishment.
Luke 16: 9 may receive you into *e.* habitations
18:30 in the world to come *e.* life
John 3:16 not perish but have *e.* life
3:36 believeth on the Son hath *e.* life
4:14 well of water springing up into *e.* life
5:24 that heareth my word hath *e.* life
6:27 meat which endureth to *e.* life
6:40 whoso believeth may have *e.* life
12:50 his commandment is *e.* life
Acts 13:46 yourselves unworthy of *e.* life
Rom. 6:22 holiness and the end *e.* life
Gal. 6: 8 shall of the Spirit reap *e.* life
2 Thes. 1: 9 shall be punished with *e.* destruction
1 Tim. 1:16 believe on him to life *e.*
6:16 to whom be honour and power *e.*
2 Pet. 1:11 *e.* kingdom of our Lord Jesus Christ
Jude 1: 6 hath reserved in *e.* chains under
Rev. 14: 6 having the *e.* gospel to preach unto

EVIL
Gen. 6: 5 thoughts of his heart only *e.*
Deut. 29:21 I will separate him to *e.*
30:15 life and good, death and *e.*
Josh. 24:15 if it seem *e.* unto you to serve the
Job 2:10 shall we not receive *e.*
5:19 there shall no *e.* touch thee
30:26 looked for good then *e.* came
Ps. 23: 4 I will fear no *e.* for thou
34:21 *e.* shall slay the wicked, and they
51: 4 have done this *e.* in thy sight
52: 3 thou lovest *e.* more than good
91:10 shall no *e.* befall thee, neither
97:10 ye that love the Lord, hate *e.*
Prov. 5:14 I was almost in all *e.* in the midst
12:21 there shall no *e.* happen to the just
14:19 the *e.* bow before the good
15: 3 beholding the *e.* and the good
15:15 all the days of the afflicted are *e.*
31:12 will do him good and not *e.*
Eccl. 5:13 sore *e.* which I have seen
9: 3 heart of the sons of men is full of *e.*
Is. 1: 4 a seed of *e.* doers, children that
5:20 them that call *e.* good, and good *e.*
7:15 know to refuse the *e.*, and choose
45: 7 I make peace and create *e.*
57: 1 taken away from the *e.* to come
59: 7 feet run to *e.* and make haste
Jer. 17:17 art my hope in the day of *e.*
18:11 I frame *e.* against you, and devise
29:11 thoughts of peace and not of *e.*
44:27 I will watch over them for *e.*
Lam. 3:38 most High proceedeth not *e.* and good
Ezek. 7: 5 an *e.*, an only *e.*, behold is come
Dan. 9:12 bringing upon us a great *e.*
Amos 3: 6 shall there be *e.* in a city
5:14 seek good and not *e.*, that ye may
9: 4 set eyes on them for *e.*, and not for
Hab. 1:13 purer eyes than to behold *e.*, and
Mat. 5:11 all manner of *e.* against you falsely
5:45 his sun to rise on the *e.* and the
6:34 sufficient to the day is the *e.* thereof
7:11 if ye, being *e.*, know how to give
Luke 6:35 kind to the unthankful and to the *e.*
John 3:19 light because their deeds were *e.*
Rom. 2: 9 on every soul that doeth *e.*
7:19 *e.* which I would not that I do
7:21 I would do good *e.* is present with me
12:17 recompense to no man *e.* for *e.*
12:21 be not overcome of *e.* but overcome *e.*
1 Cor. 13: 5 not easily provoked, thinketh no *e.*
Eph. 5:16 time because the days are *e.*
1 Thes. 5:15 none render *e.* for *e.* unto any man
5:22 abstain from all appearance of *e.*
1 Tim. 6:10 love of money is the root of all *e.*
Tit. 3: 2 to speak *e.* of no man, to be no
Heb. 5:14 exercised discern both good and *e.*
3 John 1:11 follow not that which is *e.*
Jude 1:10 speak *e.* of those things which they

EXALT (EXALTED, EXALTETH)
Ex. 15: 2 my father's God, I will *e.*
Num. 24: 7 and his kingdom shall be *e.*
1 Sam. 2:10 *e.* the horn of his anointed
2 Sam. 22:47 *e.* be the God of my salvation
Neh. 9: 5 *e.* above all blessing and praise
Job 5:11 which mourn may be *e.* to safety
Ps. 34: 3 let us *e.* his name together
89:16 in righteousness shall be *e.*
99: 5 *e.* ye the Lord our God
118: 28 my God, I will *e.* thee
Prov. 11:11 blessing of the upright, the city is *e.*
14:34 righteousness *e.* a nation, but sin
Is. 2: 2 and shall be *e.* above the hills
2:11 Lord alone shall be *e.* in that day
40: 4 every valley shall be *e.*

Ezek. 21:26 *e.* him that is low, and abase
Hos. 13: 1 Ephraim was *e.* in Israel
Mat. 11:23 Capernaum, which art *e.* to heaven
23:12 humbleth himself shall be *e.*
Luke 1:52 their seats and *e.* them of low degree
14:11 *e.* himself shall be abased
18:14 for every one that *e.* himself shall be
Acts 2:33 by right hand of God *e.*
5:31 Him hath God *e.* with his right hand
2 Cor. 12: 7 I should be *e.* above measure through
Phil. 2: 9 God hath highly *e.* him
2 Thes. 2: 4 *e.* himself above all that is called
1 Pet. 5: 6 that he may *e.* you in due time

EXAMINE (EXAMINED)
Ps. 26: 2 *e.* me, O Lord, and prove me
Luke 23:14 having *e.* him before you, have found
Acts 4: 9 this day be *e.* of the good deed
1 Cor. 11:28 and so let a man *e.* himself
2 Cor. 13: 5 *e.* yourselves, whether ye be in the faith

EXAMPLE (EXAMPLES)
Mat. 1:19 not make her a public *e.*
John 13:15 I have given you an *e.*
1 Cor. 10: 6 these things were our *e.*
10:11 happened unto them for *e.*
Phil. 3:17 as ye have us for an *e.*
1 Thes. 1: 7 ye were *e.* to all that believe
2 Thes. 3: 9 to make ourselves an *e.*
1 Tim. 4:12 an *e.* of the believers in word
Heb. 4:11 after the same *e.* of unbelief
8: 5 serve unto the *e.* and shadow
Jas. 5:10 for an *e.* of suffering affliction
1 Pet. 2:21 suffered for us leaving us an *e.*
5: 3 but being *e.* to the flock
2 Pet. 2: 6 making them an *e.* unto those
Jude 1: 7 for an *e.* suffering the vengeance

EXCEED
Mat. 5:20 your righteousness shall *e.* the
2 Cor. 3: 9 ministration of righteousness *e.*

EXCEEDING (EXCEEDINGLY)
Gen. 13:13 wicked and sinners before the Lord *e.*
17: 6 I will make thee *e.* fruitful
27:34 Esau cried with a great and *e.* bitter
Num. 14: 7 search it, it is an *e.* good land
1 Sam. 2: 3 talk no more so *e.* proudly
1 Ki. 4:29 gave Solomon wisdom *e.* much
1 Chr. 22: 5 builded for the Lord must be *e.* magnifical
Ps. 43: 4 I will go to God my *e.* joy
68: 3 yea, let them *e.* rejoice
119:167 thy testimonies I love *e.*
Mat. 5:12 rejoice and be *e.* glad
Rom. 7:13 commandment might become *e.* sinful
2 Cor. 4:17 a far more *e.* and eternal weight
7: 4 I am *e.* joyful in all tribulation
Eph. 1:19 *e.* greatness of his power to us-ward
2: 7 might show *e.* riches of his grace
3:20 him that is able to do *e.* abundantly
1 Thes. 3:10 praying *e.* that we might see your face
2 Thes. 1: 3 that your faith groweth *e.*
1 Tim. 1:14 grace was *e.* abundant with faith
2 Pet. 1: 4 *e.* great and precious promises
Jude 1:24 presence of his glory with *e.* joy

EXCEL (EXCELLEST, EXCELLETH)
Ps. 103: 20 angels that *e.* in strength
Prov. 31:29 virtuously but thou *e.* them all
Eccl. 2:13 wisdom *e.* folly, as far as light
1 Cor. 14:12 seek that ye may *e.* to the edifying
2 Cor. 3:10 respect by reason of glory that *e.*

EXCELLENCY
Gen. 49: 3 the *e.* of dignity and the *e.* of
Ex. 15: 7 in the greatness of thine *e.*
Deut. 33:26 rideth in his *e.* on sky
Job 13:11 shall not his *e.* make you afraid
37: 4 thunders with the voice of his *e.*
40:10 deck thyself now with *e.*
Ps. 47: 4 *e.* of Jacob, whom he loved
68:34 his *e.* is over Israel, and his
Is. 35: 2 see glory and *e.* of our God
Amos 6: 8 I abhor the *e.* of Jacob, and hate
1 Cor. 2: 1 not with *e.* of speech or of wisdom
2 Cor. 4: 7 *e.* of the power may be of God, and
Phil. 3: 8 loss for the *e.* of the knowledge of Christ

EXCELLENT
Esth. 1: 4 the honour of his *e.* majesty
Ps. 8: 1 how *e.* is thy name in all the earth
16: 3 saints, *e.* in whom my delight
36: 7 how *e.* is thy lovingkindness
148: 13 the Lord, for his name alone is *e.*
Prov. 12:26 the righteous is more *e.* than his
17:27 man of understanding is of *e.* spirit
Is. 12: 5 Lord hath done *e.* things
Ezek. 16: 7 and thou art come to *e.* ornaments
Dan. 5:12 an *e.* spirit and knowledge and
Rom. 2:18 the things that are more *e.*
1 Cor. 12:31 I show unto you a more *e.* way
Phil. 1:10 approve things that are *e.*
Heb. 1: 4 obtained a more *e.* name than they
11: 4 offered a more *e.* sacrifice
2 Pet. 1:17 such a voice from the *e.* glory

EXCUSE (EXCUSING)
Luke 14:18 with one consent began to make *e.*
Rom. 1:20 so that they are without *e.*
2:15 while accusing or else *e.* one another

EXECUTE
Ex. 12:12 I will *e.* judgment; I am the Lord
Num. 5:30 priest shall *e.* upon her all this law
8:11 they may *e.* the service of the Lord
Deut. 10:18 he doth *e.* the judgment of the
Ps. 119: 84 when wilt thou *e.* judgment on them
149: 7 *e.* vengeance upon the heathen
Is. 16: 3 take counsel, *e.* judgment; make thy
Jer. 7: 5 if ye thoroughly *e.* judgment
Hos. 11: 9 not *e.* the fierceness of mine anger
Mic. 7: 9 plead my cause, and *e.* judgment for me
Zech. 8:16 *e.* the judgment of truth and peace
John 5:27 hath given him authority to *e.* judgment
Rom. 13: 4 a revenger to *e.* wrath upon him that
Jude 1:15 to *e.* judgment upon all

EXHORT (EXHORTED, EXHORTING)
Acts 2:40 did he testify and *e.*, saying
11:23 was glad, and *e.* them all
2 Cor. 9: 5 thought it necessary to *e.* the brethren
1 Thes. 2:11 how we *e.* and comforted and charged
5:14 now we *e.* you, brethren
2 Thes. 3:12 *e.* by our Lord Jesus Christ
1 Tim. 2: 1 I *e.* therefore, that, first of all
2 Tim. 4: 2 *e.* with all longsuffering and doctrine
Tit. 1: 9 both to *e.* and to convince the gainsayers
Heb. 3:13 *e.* one another daily while it
10:25 but *e.* one another, and so much the
1 Pet. 5: 1 I *e.*, who am also an elder
Jude 1: 3 and *e.* you that ye should earnestly contend

EXHORTATION
Luke 3:18 in his *e.* preached he unto the people
Acts 13:15 if ye have any word of *e.* for the
20: 2 and had given them much *e.*
Rom. 12: 8 or he that exhorteth, on *e.*
1 Cor. 14: 3 to edification, and *e.*, and comfort
2 Cor. 8:17 for indeed he accepted the *e.*
1 Thes. 2: 3 for our *e.* was not of deceit
1 Tim. 4:13 give attendance to reading, to *e.*, to doctrine
Heb. 12: 5 ye have forgotten the *e.* which
13:22 suffer the word of *e.*: for I have

EXPECTATION
Ps. 9:18 *e.* of the poor shall not perish for
62: 5 on God; for my *e.* is from him
Prov. 10:28 but the *e.* of the wicked shall perish
11:23 but the *e.* of the wicked is wrath
23:18 thine *e.* shall not be cut off
Is. 20: 5 and ashamed of Ethiopia, their *e.*
Luke 3:15 as the people were in *e.*
Acts 12:11 from all the *e.* of the people
Rom. 8:19 *e.* of the creature waiteth for the
Phil. 1:20 according to my earnest *e.* and my

EXPEDIENT
John 11:50 nor consider that it is *e.* for us
16: 7 *e.* for you that I go away
1 Cor. 6:12 but all things are not *e.*
12: 1 it is not *e.* for me to glory

EXTEND (EXTENDED, EXTENDETH)
Ezra 9: 9 but hath *e.* mercy unto us
Ps. 16: 2 my goodness *e.* not to thee
109: 12 none to *e.* mercy unto him
Is. 66:12 *e.* peace to her like a river

EXTOL (EXTOLLED)
Ps. 30: 1 I will *e.* thee, O Lord
68: 4 *e.* him that rideth upon the heavens
145: 1 I will *e.* thee, my God, O king
Is. 52:13 he shall be exalted and *e.*
Dan. 4:37 I Nebuchadnezzar praise and *e.* and honour

EXTORTION
Ezek. 22:12 gained of thy neighbors by *e.*
Mat. 23:25 within they are full of *e.*

EXTORTIONER
Ps. 109: 11 Let the *e.* catch all that he hath
Is. 16: 4 for the *e.* is at an end, the spoiler
1 Cor. 5:11 or a drunkard, or an *e.*; with such a

EXTORTIONERS
Luke 18:11 not as other men are, *e.*, unjust
1 Cor. 6:10 nor revilers, nor *e.*, shall inherit

EYE
Ex. 21:24 *e.* for *e.*, tooth for tooth
Deut. 32:10 kept him as the apple of his *e.*
Job 24:15 no *e.* shall see me, and disguiseth
Ps. 17: 8 keep me as the apple of thine *e.*
33:18 the *e.* of the Lord is upon them
Prov. 20:12 the seeing *e.*, the Lord hath
23: 6 bread of him that hath an evil *e.*
Eccl. 1: 8 the *e.* is not satisfied with seeing
Is. 64: 4 neither hath the *e.* seen, O God
Jer. 13:17 mine *e.* shall weep sore, because
Mat. 5:38 an *e.* for an *e.*, and a tooth
6:22 light of the body is the *e.*
18: 9 if thine *e.* offend thee, pluck it out
Mark 7:22 an evil *e.*, blasphemy, pride
Luke 11:34 the light of the body is the *e.*
1 Cor. 2: 9 *e.* hath not seen nor ear heard
Rev. 1: 7 and every *e.* shall see him, and they

EYELIDS
Job 16:16 on my *e.* is the shadow of death
Ps. 11: 4 his eyes behold, his *e.* try
Prov. 4:25 let thine *e.* look straight before thee
30:13 and their *e.* are lifted up
Jer. 9:18 our *e.* gush out with waters

EYEWITNESSES
Luke 1: 2 from the beginning were *e.*
2 Pet. 1:16 but were *e.* of his majesty

EYES
Gen. 3: 5 then your *e.* shall be opened and ye
6: 8 Noah found grace in the *e.* of the Lord
Deut. 12: 8 whatsoever is right in his own *e.*
13:18 right in the *e.* of the Lord
Judg. 17: 6 which was right in his own *e.*
21:25 that which was right in his own *e.*
1 Sam. 26:24 be much set by in the *e.* of the Lord
2 Sam. 15:25 find favour in the *e.* of the Lord
1 Ki. 15:11 was right in the *e.* of the Lord
1 Ki 22:43 which was right in the *e.* of the Lord
2 Chr. 16: 9 *e.* of the Lord run to and fro
Job 10: 4 hast thou *e.* of flesh or seest thou
32: 1 he was righteous in his own *e.*
Ps. 15: 4 whose *e.* a vile person is condemned
25:15 mine *e.* are ever towards the Lord

Ps. 34:15 *e.* of the Lord are upon the righteous
101: 6 mine *e.* shall be upon the faithful
119:148 mine *e.* prevent the night watches
123: 2 our *e.* wait on the Lord
139: 16 thine *e.* did see my substance
141: 8 mine *e.* are unto thee, O God
145: 15 the *e.* of all wait upon thee and thou
Prov. 5:21 ways of man before the *e.* of the Lord
15: 3 the *e.* of the Lord are in every place
22:12 the *e.* of the Lord preserve knowledge
23: 5 set thine *e.* on that which is not
Eccl. 2:14 wise man's *e.* are in his head
11: 7 for the *e.* to behold the sun
Is. 1:15 I will hide mine *e.* from you
3:16 stretched forth necks and wanton *e.*
29:18 *e.* of the blind see out of obscurity
29:32 *e.* of them that see shall not dim
30:20 thine *e.* shall see thy teachers
35: 5 *e.* of the blind shall be opened
43: 8 Blind people that have *e.*
49: 5 be glorious in the *e.* of the Lord
65:12 did evil before mine *e.*
Jer. 5: 3 are not thine *e.* upon the truth
5:21 have *e.* and see not; which have
9: 1 that mine *e.* were a fountain of tears
14:17 let mine *e.* run down with tears
24: 6 set mine *e.* upon them for good
Ezek. 24:16 take away the desire of thine *e.*
Amos 9: 4 set mine *e.* upon them for evil
9: 8 the *e.* of the Lord God are upon
Hab. 1:13 art of purer *e.* than to behold evil
Zech. 3: 9 on one stone shall be seven *e.*
Mat. 13:16 blessed are your *e.* for they see
18: 9 having two *e.* to be cast into hell fire
20:33 that our *e.* may be opened
Mark 8:18 having *e.* see ye not
Luke 2:30 mine *e.* have seen thy salvation
4:20 *e.* of all were fastened on him
10:23 blessed are the *e.* which see
John 9: 6 anointed the *e.* of blind man
Rom. 11: 8 *e.* that they should not see, and ears
Eph. 1:18 *e.* of your understanding being
Heb. 4:13 all open unto the *e.* of him
2 Pet. 2:14 *e.* full of adultery, and that cannot
1 John 1: 1 which we have seen with our *e.*
2:16 lust of the *e.* and pride
Rev. 1:14 his *e.* were as a flame of fire
2:18 who hath his *e.* like unto a flame
3:18 and anoint thine *e.* with eyesalve
4: 6 four beasts full of *e.* before and behind
19:12 His *e.* were as a flame of fire

F

FABLES
1 Tim. 4: 7 refuse profane and old wives' *f.*
2 Tim. 4: 4 and shall be turned unto *f.*
Tit. 1:14 not giving heed to Jewish *f.*
2 Pet. 1:16 not followed cunningly devised *f.*

FACE
Lev. 19:32 honour the *f.* of the old man
Num. 6:25 the Lord make his *f.* shine upon thee
2 Chr. 6:42 turn not the *f.* of thine anointed
Ps. 17:15 behold thy *f.* in righteousness
31:16 make thy *f.* to shine upon
84: 9 behold the *f.* of the anointed
119:135 make thy *f.* to shine upon thy
Ezek. 1:10 *f.* of a man, and the *f.* of a lion
Dan. 9:17 cause thy *f.* to shine upon
Hos. 5: 5 Israel doth testify to his *f.*
Mat. 11:10 my messenger before thy *f.*
Luke 9:52 sent messengers before his *f.*
Acts 2:25 foresaw the Lord always before my *f.*
1 Cor. 13:12 glass darkly but then *f.* to *f.*
2 Cor. 3:18 with open *f.* beholding as in a glass
Jas. 1:23 his natural *f.* in a glass
Rev. 4: 7 third beast had a *f.* like a man

FADE (FADETH)
Is. 64: 6 we all do *f.* as a leaf
Jas. 1:11 rich man *f.* away in his ways
1 Pet. 1: 4 inheritance that *f.* not away
5: 4 crown of glory that *f.* not away

FAIL (FAILED, FAILETH)
Deut. 31: 6 Lord will not *f.* nor forsake
Josh. 1: 5 not *f.* thee, nor forsake thee
1 Chr. 28:20 he will not *f.* thee, nor forsake
Ps. 12: 1 faithful *f.* from among the children of men
31:10 strength *f.* because of mine iniquity
40:12 therefore my heart *f.* me
71: 9 forsake me not when my strength *f.*
77: 8 doth his promise *f.* for evermore
143: 7 my spirit *f.*; hide not thy face
Sol. 5: 6 soul *f.* when he spake, I sought
Lam. 3:22 because his compassions *f.* not
Luke 12:33 treasure in heaven that *f.* not
16: 9 when ye *f.* they may receive you
16:17 than one tittle of the law to *f.*
22:32 prayed that thy faith *f.* not
1 Cor. 13: 8 charity never *f.*, but whether there
Heb. 12:15 lest any *f.* of the grace

FAINT (FAINTED, FAINTETH)
Ps. 27:13 *f.* unless I believed to see the
84: 2 even *f.* for the courts of the Lord
119: 81 my soul *f.* for thy salvation
Is. 1: 5 head is sick, and the whole heart *f.*
40:28 of the ends of the earth *f.* not
40:29 he giveth power to the *f.*
40:30 youths shall *f.* and be weary
40:31 wait on the Lord shall walk and not *f.*
2 Cor. 4: 1 we have received mercy we *f.* not
Gal. 6: 9 we shall reap if we *f.* not
Heb. 12: 5 nor *f.* when thou art rebuked of him
Rev. 2: 3 hast laboured and hast not *f.*

FAIR (FAIRER)
Ps. 45: 2 *f.* than the children of men
Prov. 7:21 with her much *f.* speech, she caused
Sol. 1:15 behold thou art *f.*; thou hast
Jer. 12: 6 they speak *f.* words unto thee
Dan. 1:15 their countenances appeared *f.* and fatter
Acts 7:20 Moses was born and was exceeding *f.*
Gal. 6:12 desire to make a *f.* show in

FAITH
Deut. 32:20 children in whom is no *f.*
Hab. 2: 4 just shall live by *f.*
Mat. 6:30 clothe you, O ye of little *f.*
8:10 not found so great *f.*
8:26 are ye fearful, O ye of little *f.*
9: 2 Jesus seeing their *f.* said unto
9:22 thy *f.* hath made thee whole
14:31 O thou of little *f.*, wherefore didst
15:28 O woman, great is thy *f.* be it unto
17:20 *f.* as a grain of mustard seed
21:21 have *f.* and doubt not, ye shall not
23:23 omitted judgment, mercy, and *f.*
Mark 4:40 how is it ye have no *f.*
Luke 7: 9 I have not found so great *f.*
7:50 thy *f.* hath saved thee
8:25 where is your *f.*
17: 5 unto the Lord, increase our *f.*
17: 6 if ye had *f.* ye might say to this
18: 8 shall he find *f.* on the earth
22:32 I have prayed that thy *f.* fail not
Acts 3:16 the *f.* which is by him hath given him
6: 5 Stephen, a man full of *f.*
6: 7 company of priests obedient to the *f.*
11:24 man, full of the Holy Ghost and of *f.*
14: 9 that he had *f.* to be healed
15: 9 purifying their hearts by *f.*
16: 5 churches established in the *f.*
20:21 *f.* toward our Lord Jesus Christ
Rom. 1: 5 for obedience to the *f.* among all
1: 8 your *f.* is spoken of through
1:12 by the mutual *f.* both of you and me
1:17 righteousness of God revealed from *f.* to *f.*
2:19 I know thy works and *f.*
3: 3 make the *f.* of God without effect
3:25 propitiation through *f.* in his blood
3:27 Nay, but by the law of *f.*
3:28 conclude a man is justified by *f.*

Rom. 3:30 which shall justify circumcision by *f.*
4: 5 his *f.* is counted for righteousness
4:11 circumcision, a seal of righteousness
4:13 through the righteousness of *f.*
4:14 law be heirs, *f.* is made void
4:19 not weak in *f.*, he considered not
4:20 strong in *f.* giving glory to God
5: 1 being justified by *f.* we have peace
9:32 not by *f.* but by the works of the law
10: 8 the word of *f.* which we preach
10:17 *f.* cometh by hearing, and hearing
11:20 broken off, and thou standest by *f.*
12: 3 to every man the measure of *f.*
12: 6 according to the proportion of *f.*
14:22 hast thou *f.*? have it to thyself before God
16:26 nations for the obedience of *f.*
1 Cor. 2: 5 that your *f.* not stand in wisdom
12: 9 to another *f.* by the same spirit
13: 2 though I have all *f.* to remove
13:13 now abideth *f.*, hope, charity
15:14 your *f.* is also vain
16:13 stand fast in the *f.*, quit you like men
2 Cor. 1:24 of your joy; for by *f.* ye stand
4:13 having the same Spirit of *f.*
5: 7 we walk by *f.* and not by sight
8: 7 ye abound in *f.* and utterance
10:15 when your *f.* is increased, we
13: 5 examine whether ye be in *f.*
Gal. 1:23 preacheth the *f.* which once he
2:16 by the works of the law, but by *f.*
2:20 I live by the *f.* of the Son of God
3: 2 Spirit by the hearing of *f.*
3: 8 God would justify the heathen through *f.*
3:11 The just shall live by *f.*
3:12 the law is not of *f.* but the man
3:14 receive the promise of the Spirit through *f.*
3:22 the promise by *f.* of Jesus Christ be given
3:23 before *f.* came, we were under the law
3:25 after that *f.* is come, we are no
3:26 children of God by *f.* in Jesus Christ
5: 5 for hope of righteousness by *f.*
5: 6 but *f.* which worketh by love
5:22 but the fruit of the Spirit is . . . *f.*
Eph. 1:15 heard of your *f.* in the Lord Jesus
2: 8 by grace ye are saved through *f.*
3:12 with confidence by the *f.* of him
3:17 Christ dwell in your hearts by *f.*
4: 5 one Lord, one *f.*, one baptism
6:16 above all taking the shield of *f.*
6:23 love with *f.* from God the Father
Phil. 1:25 for your furtherance and joy of the *f.*
1:27 striving together for *f.* of the gospel
2:17 sacrifice and service of your *f.*
3: 9 which is through the *f.* of Christ
Col. 1: 4 since we heard of your *f.* in Christ Jesus
1:23 if ye continue in *f.* grounded
2: 5 the stedfastness of your *f.*
2:12 through the *f.* of the operation of God
1 Thes. 1: 3 remember your work of *f.*
1: 8 your *f.* to God-ward is spread
3: 2 comfort you concerning your *f.*
3: 5 I sent to know your *f.*, lest
3: 6 brought us good tidings of your *f.*
3: 7 comforted in affliction by your *f.*
3:10 perfect that which is lacking in your *f.*
5: 8 putting on the breastplate of *f.*
2 Thes. 1: 3 your *f.* groweth exceedingly
1: 4 for your patience and *f.* in all
3: 2 for all men have not *f.*
1 Tim. 1: 2 Timothy, my own son in the *f.*
1: 4 godly edifying which is in *f.*
1: 5 charity out of *f.* unfeigned
1:14 exceeding abundant with *f.* and love
2: 7 teacher of the Gentiles in *f.*
2:15 if they continue in *f.* and charity
3: 9 holding the mystery of the *f.*
3:13 great boldness in the *f.* which is in
4: 1 some shall depart from the *f.*
4: 6 nourished up in the words of *f.*

1 Tim. 5: 8 he hath denied the *f.* and is worse
5:12 because they have cast off their first *f.*
6:12 fight the good fight of *f.*
2 Tim. 1: 5 unfeigned *f.* that is in thee
1:13 in *f.* and love which is in Christ Jesus
2:18 and overthrow the *f.* of some
2:22 follow righteousness, *f.*, charity
3: 8 reprobate concerning the *f.*
3:10 fully known my doctrine, manner of life, *f.*
3:15 salvation through *f.* in Jesus
4: 7 I have kept the *f.*
Tit. 1: 1 according to the *f.* of God's elect
1:13 that they may be sound in *f.*
3:15 greet them that love us in *f.*
Philem. 1: 6 that the communication of thy *f.*
Heb. 4: 2 not being mixed with *f.* in them
6: 1 dead works and of *f.* toward God
6:12 through *f.* and patience inherit promises
10:22 draw near in assurance of *f.*
10:23 hold fast the profession of our *f.*
11: 1 *f.* is the substance of things hoped
11: 3 through *f.* we understand the worlds
11: 4 by *f.* Abel offered unto God
11: 6 without *f.* it is impossible to please him
11:13 these died in *f.* not having
11:28 through *f.* Moses kept the passover
11:33 through *f.* subdued kingdoms
11:39 obtained a good report through *f.*
12: 2 Jesus the finisher of our *f.*
13: 7 whose *f.* follow, considering the end
Jas. 1: 1 like precious *f.* with us through
1: 3 trying of your *f.* worketh patience
1: 6 ask in *f.*, nothing wavering
2: 1 have not the *f.* of our Lord Jesus
2: 5 poor of this world rich in *f.*
2:17 *f.* if it hath not works, is dead
2:18 show me thy *f.* without thy works
2:22 how *f.* wrought with his works
2:24 justified by works, not by *f.*
5:15 prayer of *f.* shall save the sick
1 Pet. 1: 5 kept by the power of God through *f.*
1: 7 trial of your *f.* being precious
1: 9 receiving the end of your *f.*
1:21 that your *f.* and hope might be in God
5: 9 whom resist, stedfast in the *f.*
2 Pet. 1: 5 add to your *f.* virtue, and to virtue
1 John 5: 4 overcometh the world, even our *f.*
Jude 1: 3 contend earnestly for the *f.*
1:20 building up yourselves on holy *f.*
Rev. 2:13 hast not denied my *f.*
13:10 here is the *f.* of the saints
14:12 which keep the *f.* of Jesus

FAITHLESS

Mat. 17:17 O *f.* and perverse generation
John 20:27 be not *f.* but believing

FAITHFUL

Num. 12: 7 who is *f.* in all my house
Deut. 7: 9 God, the *f.* God which keepeth covenant
1 Sam. 2:35 I will raise me up a *f.* priest
2 Sam. 20:19 that are peaceable and *f.* in Israel
Neh. 7: 2 a *f.* man, and feared God
9: 8 foundest his heart *f.* before thee
13:13 for they were counted *f.*
Ps. 12: 1 *f.* fail from among the children of
31:23 Lord preserveth the *f.*, and
89:37 and as a *f.* witness in heaven
101: 6 mine eyes be upon the *f.* of the land
119: 86 all thy commandments are *f.*: they
Prov. 11:13 He that is of a *f.* spirit
13:17 a *f.* ambassador is health
14: 5 a *f.* witness will not lie
20: 6 a *f.* man who can find?
27: 6 *f.* are the wounds of a friend
28:20 *f.* man shall abound with blessings
Is. 1:21 the *f.* city become an harlot
1:26 city of righteousness, *f.* city
8: 2 I took *f.* witnesses to record
49: 7 Lord is *f.* and the Holy One of Israel
Jer. 42: 5 the Lord be a *f.* witness
Hos. 11:12 and is *f.* with the saints
Dan. 6: 4 forasmuch as he was *f.*
Mat. 25:21 well done thou good and *f.* servant
25:23 *f.* over a few things, I will
Luke 12:42 who is that *f.* steward
16:10 *f.* in least is *f.* also in much
16:12 not *f.* in what is another man's
Acts 16:15 judged me *f.* to the Lord
1 Cor. 1: 9 God is *f.* by whom ye were called
4: 2 required in stewards, a man *f.*
4:17 Timothy who is *f.* in the Lord
10:13 God is *f.* who will not suffer
Eph. 1: 1 *f.* in Christ Jesus
6:21 *f.* minister in the Lord, shall make
1 Thes. 5:24 *f.* is he that calleth you who
2 Thes. 3: 3 but the Lord is *f.* who will
1 Tim. 1:12 for he counted me *f.*, putting me
1:15 a *f.* saying and worthy of all acceptation
3:11 slanderers, sober, *f.* in all things
6: 2 because they are *f.* and beloved
2 Tim. 2: 2 same commit thou to *f.* men, who shall
2:11 it is a *f.* saying: for if we be
2:13 abideth *f.* he cannot deny himself
Tit. 1: 6 one wife, having *f.* children
1: 9 holding fast the *f.* word as taught
3: 8 this is a *f.* saying, and these things
Heb. 2:17 might be a merciful and *f.* high priest
3: 2 Moses was *f.* in all his house
10:23 *f.* is he that promised
1 Pet. 4:19 well doing as unto a *f.* Creator
5:12 by Silvanus, a *f.* brother
1 John 1: 9 he is *f.* and just to forgive
Rev. 1: 5 *f.* witness and the first begotten
17:14 are called, they are chosen and *f.*
21: 5 for these words are true and *f.*

FAITHFULNESS

1 Sam. 26:23 his righteousness and his *f.*
Ps. 5: 9 no *f.* in their mouth
36: 5 thy *f.* reacheth to the clouds
40:10 I have declared thy *f.* and thy
88:11 or thy *f.* in destruction?
89: 1 make known thy *f.* to all generations
89: 5 praise thy *f.* in the congregation
89: 8 who is like to thy *f.* round about thee
89:24 my *f.* shall be with him
89:33 nor suffer my *f.* to fail
92: 2 to show forth thy *f.* every night
119: 75 thou in *f.* hast afflicted me
119: 90 thy *f.* is unto all generations
143: 1 in thy *f.* answer me, and in thy
Is. 11: 5 *f.* the girdle of his reins
Lam. 3:23 new every morning, great is thy *f.*
Hos. 2:20 I will betroth thee to me in *f.*

FALL

Gen. 45:24 *f.* not out by the way
2 Sam. 24:14 *f.* into the hand of Lord
Ps. 37:24 though he *f.* he shall not
45: 5 whereby people *f.* under thee
141: 10 let the wicked *f.* into their own nets
145: 14 the Lord upholdeth all that *f.*
Prov. 11: 5 wicked shall *f.* by his own wickedness
24:16 wicked shall *f.* into mischief
26:27 whoso diggeth a pit shall *f.* therein
28:14 hardeneth his heart shall *f.*
Eccl. 4:10 if they *f.* one will lift up
Is. 8:15 many shall stumble and *f.*
Dan. 11:35 them of understanding shall *f.*
Hos. 10: 8 and to the hills *f.* on us
Mic. 7: 8 rejoice not when I *f.*
Mat. 7:27 great was the *f.* of it
10:29 sparrow not *f.* on the ground
15:14 blind lead the blind, both shall *f.* into
Luke 2:34 set for the *f.* and rising of many
23:30 say to the mountains, *f.* on us
Rom. 11:11 stumbled that they should *f.*
11:11 through their *f.* salvation is come
1 Cor. 10:12 take heed lest he *f.*
1 Tim. 3: 6 *f.* into the condemnation of the devil
6: 9 will be rich *f.* into temptation
Heb. 4:11 *f.* after the same example of unbelief
6: 6 if they shall *f.* away, to renew them
10:31 *f.* into the hands of the living God
Jas. 1: 2 when ye *f.* into divers temptations
2 Pet. 1:10 ye do these things, ye shall never *f.*
3:17 lest ye *f.* from stedfastness
Rev. 6:16 *f.* on us and hide us from the face

FALLEN (FALLING)

Ps. 16: 6 *f.* unto me in pleasant places
56:13 wilt thou not deliver my feet from *f.*
116: 8 from tears and my feet from *f.*
Hos. 14: 1 thou hast *f.* by thine iniquity
Gal. 5: 4 by the law, ye are *f.* from grace
2 Thes. 2: 3 there come a *f.* away first
Jude 1:24 able to keep you from *f.*
Rev. 2: 5 remember whence thou art *f.*

FALSE

Ex. 20:16 not bear *f.* witness against thy neighbour
23: 1 thou shalt not raise a *f.* report
23: 7 keep thee far from a *f.* matter
Deut. 5:20 shalt thou bear *f.* witness
Ps. 119:104 therefore I hate every *f.* way
Prov. 6:19 a *f.* witness that speaketh lies
11: 1 a *f.* balance is abomination to the
21:28 a *f.* witness shall perish
25:18 a man that beareth *f.* witness against
Jer. 14:14 prophesy unto you a *f.* vision and
23:32 against them that prophesy *f.* dreams
Zech. 8:17 love no *f.* oath: for all these
Mal. 3: 5 against *f.* swearers, and against
Mat. 7:15 beware of *f.* prophets which come to
15:19 fornications, thefts, *f.* witnesses, blasphemies
19:18 thou shalt not bear *f.* witness
24:24 arise *f.* Christs and *f.* prophets
Luke 6:26 so did their fathers to the *f.* prophets
Rom. 13: 9 thou shalt not bear *f.* witness
1 Cor. 15:15 and we are found *f.* witnesses of God
2 Cor. 11:13 for such are *f.* apostles, deceitful
Gal. 2: 4 because of *f.* brethren unawares brought in
2 Tim. 3: 3 affection, trucebreakers, *f.* accusers
2 Pet. 2: 1 there were *f.* prophets also among the people
1 John 4: 1 many *f.* prophets are gone out

FALSEHOOD

Ps. 119:118 their deceit is *f.*
144: 8 hand is a right hand of *f.*
Is. 57: 4 children of transgression, a seed of *f.*
59:13 from the heart words of *f.*
Jer. 10:14 for his molten image is *f.*

FALSELY

Lev. 6: 3 and lieth concerning it, and sweareth *f.*
19:12 ye shall not swear by my name *f.*
Ps. 44:17 neither have we dealt *f.* in thy covenant
Jer. 6:13 unto the priest, every one dealeth *f.*
Zech. 5: 4 house of him that sweareth *f.*
Mat. 5:11 evil against you *f.* for my sake
Luke 3:14 neither accuse any *f.*, and be content
1 Pet. 3:16 be ashamed that *f.* accuse

FAMILY (FAMILIES)

Gen. 10: 5 after their *f.*, in their nations
Lev. 20: 5 against that man, and against his *f.*
Ps. 68: 6 God setteth the solitary in *f.*
Amos 3: 2 known of all the *f.* of the earth
Zech. 12:12 mourn, every *f.* apart
Eph. 3:15 whole *f.* in heaven and earth is named

FAMINE

Gen. 12:10 and there was a *f.* in the land
41:27 shall be seven years of *f.*
Job 5:20 in *f.* he shall redeem thee
Ps. 33:19 keep them alive in *f.*
37:19 the days of *f.* they shall be satisfied
Ezek. 5:16 evil arrows of *f.*, which shall be
Amos 8:11 not a *f.* of bread, nor a thirst for

FAR

Ex. 23: 7 keep thee *f.* from a false matter
Ps. 73:27 that are *f.* from thee shall perish
Mark 12:34 not *f.* from the kingdom of God

Eph. 2:13 were *f.* off are made nigh by the
Phil. 1:23 to be with Christ; which is *f.* better

FASHION (FASHIONED, FASHIONETH, FASHIONING)

Job 10: 8 made me and *f.* me together
Ps. 33:15 he *f.* their hearts alike, he
119: 73 thy hands have made me and *f.* me
139: 16 which in continuance were *f.*
Ezek. 16: 7 thy breasts are *f.*, and thine hair
1 Cor. 7:31 for the *f.* of this world passeth away
Phil. 2: 8 being found in *f.* as a man
3:21 be *f.* like his glorious body
1 Pet. 1:14 as obedient children, not *f.* yourselves

FAST

2 Sam. 12:21 thou didst *f.* and weep for the child
1 Ki. 21: 9 saying, proclaim a *f.*, and set Naboth
2 Chr. 20: 3 proclaimed a *f.* throughout all Judah
Ezra 8:21 then I proclaimed a *f.* there
Esth. 4:16 and *f.* ye for me and neither eat
Is. 58: 4 ye *f.* for strife and debate
58: 5 is it such a *f.* that I have chosen
Jer. 14:12 when they *f.* I will not hear
36: 9 they proclaimed a *f.* before the Lord
Joel 1:14 sanctify ye a *f.*, call a solemn
Jonah 3: 5 Nineveh believed God, and proclaimed a *f.*
Zech. 7: 5 did ye at all *f.* unto me
8:19 the *f.* of the fourth month
Mat. 6:16 ye *f.* be not as the hypocrites
9:14 why do we *f.* but thy disciples *f.* not
9:15 taken from them and then shall they *f.*
Luke 18:12 I *f.* twice in the week
Acts 27: 9 because the *f.* was now already past

FASTED

Judg. 20:26 and *f* that day until even
2 Sam. 1:12 wept and *f.* till even for Saul and
12:16 David *f.* and lay all night on
Ezra 8:23 we *f.* and besought the Lord
Is. 58: 3 why have we *f.* and thou
Mat. 4: 2 when he had *f.* forty days
Acts 13: 2 ministered to the Lord, and *f.* and

FASTING (FASTINGS)

Neh. 9: 1 of Israel were assembled with *f.*
Esth. 4: 3 great mourning among the Jews and *f.*
Ps. 109: 24 my knees are weak through *f.*
Jer. 36: 6 in the Lord's house upon the *f.* day
Dan. 6:18 palace and passed the night *f.*
9: 3 to seek by prayer and supplication with *f.*
Joel 2:12 with all your hearts and *f.*
Mat. 15:32 not send them away *f.*
Luke 2:37 with *f.* and prayers night and day
Acts 10:30 days ago I was *f.* till this hour
14:23 and had prayed with *f.*, they commended
1 Cor. 7: 5 give yourselves to *f.* and prayer
2 Cor. 6: 5 in tumults, in labours, in watchings, in *f.*
11:27 in hunger and thirst, in *f.* often

FAT

Lev. 3:16 all the *f.* is the Lord's
4: 8 *f.* of the bullock for the sin offering
Prov. 11:25 liberal soul shall be made *f.*
13: 4 soul of the diligent shall be made *f.*
15:30 good report maketh the bones *f.*
28:25 trust in the Lord shall be made *f.*
Is. 25: 6 *f.* things full of marrow

FATNESS

Job 36:16 on thy table should be full of *f.*
Ps. 36: 8 satisfied with the *f.* of thy house
63: 5 satisfied as with marrow and *f.*
65:11 goodness, and thy paths drop *f.*
Is. 55: 2 let your soul delight in *f.*
Jer. 31:14 satiate the soul of the priests with *f.*
Rom. 11:17 root and *f.* of the olive tree

FATHER

Gen. 2:24 a man shall leave his *f.*
4:21 he was the *f.* of all such
17: 4 be a *f.* of many nations
Ex. 15: 2 my *f.*'s God, and I will exalt
Num. 11:12 as a nursing *f.* beareth the sucking child
2 Sam. 7:14 I will be his *f.*, and he shall be
Job 29:16 I was a *f.* to the poor, and the cause
31:18 brought up with me as with a *f.*
38:28 hath the rain a *f.* or who
Ps. 68: 5 a *f.* of the fatherless and a judge
103: 13 as a *f.* pitieth his children
Is. 9: 6 the everlasting *F.*, prince of
Jer. 31: 9 I am a *f.* to Israel and
Mal. 1: 6 if I be a *f.* where is my honour
2:10 Have we not all one *f.*?
Mat. 5:16 glorify your *F.* in heaven
23: 9 call no man your *f.* on earth
John 5:17 my *F.* worketh hitherto and I work
5:19 what he seeth the *F.* do
5:20 the *F.* loveth the Son
5:21 as the *F.* raiseth up the dead and
5:22 the *F.* judgeth no man
5:26 as the *F.* hath life in himself
8:18 *F.* that sent me beareth witness of me
8:29 *F.* hath not left me alone
8:41 ye do the deeds of your *f.*
10:30 I and my *f.* are one
14:20 that I am in my *F.* and ye in me
14:28 I go unto the *F.*, for my *F.* is
16:32 I am not alone, because the *F.* is
20:17 I ascend to my *F.* and your *f.*
Acts 1: 4 wait for the promise of the *F.*
1: 7 the *F.* hath put in his own power
Rom. 4:11 the *f.* of all that believe
4:12 and the *f.* of circumcision
1 Cor. 8: 6 *F.* of whom are all things, and we
2 Cor. 1: 3 be God even the *F.* of our Lord
6:18 I will be a *F.* to you and ye
Eph. 1: 3 Blessed be the God and *f.*
1 Tim. 5: 1 intreat him as a *f.*
Heb. 1: 5 I will be to him a *f.*
12: 9 subjection to the *F.* of spirits
Jas. 1:17 and cometh down from the *F.* of lights
1 Pet. 1: 3 the God and *F.* of our Lord Jesus

FATHERS

Neh. 9:16 our *f.* dealt proudly, and hardened
Ps. 22: 4 our *f.* trusted in thee, they trusted
39:12 sojourner, as all my *f.* were
Lam. 5: 7 our *f.* have sinned, and are not
Acts 15:10 our *f.* nor we were able to bear

FATHERLESS

Ex. 22:22 not afflict any widow, or *f.* child
Deut. 10:18 execute judgment of the *f.*
Ps. 10:14 thou art the helper of the *f.*
68: 5 a father of the *f.*, and a judge
146: 9 he relieveth the *f.* and widow
Is. 1:17 judge the *f.*, plead for the widow
Hos. 14: 3 in thee the *f.* findeth mercy
Jas. 1:27 visit the *f.* in affliction

FAULT (FAULTS)

Ps. 19:12 cleanse thou me from secret *f.*
Mat. 18:15 tell him his *f.* between thee and him
Luke 23: 4 I find no *f.* in this man
John 18:38 I find in him no *f.* at all
19: 6 for I find no *f.* in him
1 Cor. 6: 7 there is utterly a *f.* among you
Gal. 6: 1 if a man be overtaken in a *f.*
1 Pet. 2:20 if when ye be buffeted for your *f.*

FAVOUR

1 Sam. 2:26 and was in *f.* both with the Lord
Job 10:12 thou hast granted me life and *f.*
Ps. 5:12 with *f.* wilt thou compass him as
30: 5 in his *f.* is life; weeping may endure
Prov. 31:30 *f.* is deceitful, and beauty is vain
Luke 2:52 in *f.* with God and man

FEAR

Gen. 9: 2 and the *f.* of you and the dread
15: 1 *f.* not I am thy shield
20:11 *f.* of God is not in this place
42:18 this do and live, for I *f.* God
Ex. 15:16 *f.* and dread shall fall upon them
18:21 such as *f.* God, men of truth
Num. 14: 9 Lord is with us, *f.* not them
Deut. 1:21 *f.* not, neither be discouraged
4:10 learn to *f.* me all the days that
5:29 such a heart that would *f.* me
6: 2 mightest *f.* the Lord, thy God, to
6:13 thou shalt *f.* the Lord thy God
6:24 to *f.* the Lord our God for our good
10:12 but to *f.* the Lord thy God, to walk
14:23 learn to *f.* the Lord thy God
28:58 mayest *f.* this glorious name
Josh. 4:24 ye might *f.* the Lord your God
8: 1 *f.* not, neither be thou dismayed
24:14 therefore *f.* the Lord and serve him
1 Sam. 12:14 if ye will *f.* the Lord and serve
12:24 *f.* the Lord and serve him in truth
2 Sam. 23: 3 must be just ruling in the *f.* of God
1 Ki. 18:12 thy servant did *f.* the Lord
2 Ki. 17:28 how they should *f.* the Lord
1 Chr. 16:30 *f.* before him, all the earth
2 Chr. 6:31 that they may *f.* thee, to walk in
Neh. 1:11 servants, desire to *f.* thy name
5:15 not I because of the *f.* of God
Job 28:28 the *f.* of the Lord, that is wisdom
37:24 therefore men do *f.* him
Ps. 2:11 serve the Lord with *f.*, and rejoice
15: 4 he honoureth them that *f.* the Lord
19: 9 the *f.* of the Lord is clean, enduring
22:23 ye that *f.* the Lord trust in him
23: 4 I will *f.* no evil, for thou
25:14 of the Lord is with them that *f.* him
31:19 goodness laid up for those that *f.*
33: 8 let all the earth *f.* the Lord
33:18 the Lord is upon them that *f.* him
34:11 children, I will teach you the *f.* of the Lord
36: 1 there is no *f.* of God before his eyes
53: 5 in great *f.* where no *f.* was
56: 4 I will not *f.* what flesh can do
61: 5 heritage of them that *f.* thy name
66:16 come and hear, all that *f.* God
85: 9 salvation is nigh them that *f.* him
86:11 unite my heart to *f.* thy name
90:11 according to thy *f.* so is wrath
103: 13 Lord pitieth them that *f.* him
115: 13 he will bless them that *f.* the Lord
118: 4 let them that *f.* the Lord say
119: 38 servant who is devoted to thy *f.*
119:120 flesh trembleth for *f.* of thee
135: 20 ye that *f.* the Lord, bless the Lord
147: 11 Lord taketh pleasure in them that *f.*
Prov. 1:26 I will mock when *f.* cometh
1:29 they did not choose the *f.* of the Lord
3: 7 *f.* the Lord and depart from evil
8:13 the *f.* of the Lord is to hate evil
10:27 the *f.* of the Lord prolongeth days
14:26 the *f.* of the Lord is strong confidence
15:33 the *f.* of the Lord is instruction of wisdom
16: 6 by the *f.* of the Lord men depart
19:23 the *f.* of the Lord tendeth to life
22: 4 by the *f.* of the Lord are riches
23:17 be thou in the *f.* of the Lord all
24:21 my son, *f.* the Lord and meddle not
29:25 the *f.* of man bringeth a snare
Eccl. 5: 7 vanities, *f.* thou God
8:12 shall be well with them that *f.* God
12:13 *f.* God and keep his commandments
Is. 8:12 neither *f.* ye their *f.* nor be afraid
29:13 their *f.* toward me is taught
33: 6 the *f.* of the Lord is his treasure
41:10 *f.* thou not for I am with thee
43: 5 *f.* not; for I am with thee
63:17 hardened our heart from thy *f.*
Jer. 5:22 *f.* ye not me, saith the Lord
5:24 let us *f.* the Lord that giveth rain
10: 7 who would not *f.* thee, O king of
26:19 did not he *f.* the Lord
30:10 *f.* thou not, O my servant Jacob
32:39 heart that may *f.* me for ever
32:40 but I put my *f.* in their hearts
Hos. 3: 5 and shall *f.* the Lord and his goodness
Jonah 1: 9 I *f.* the Lord the God of heaven
Mal. 1: 6 if I be a master where is my *f.*
Mat. 10:28 *f.* thou not them that kill the body
Luke 1:50 his mercy on them that *f.* him from
12: 5 *f.* him, which after he hath killed
12:32 *f.* not little flock, for it is your

Acts 9:31 walking in the *f.* of the Lord and comfort
Rom. 8:15 the spirit of bondage again to *f.*
11:20 be not highminded, but *f.*
13: 7 render *f.* to whom *f.*, honour to
2 Cor. 7: 1 perfecting holiness in the *f.* of God
Phil. 2:12 work out your own salvation with *f.*
2 Tim. 1: 7 spirit of *f.* but of power and of
Heb. 2:15 who through *f.* of death were all
4: 1 *f.* lest a promise being left us
12:21 Moses said, I exceedingly *f.* and quake
12:28 with reverence and godly *f.*
13: 6 I will not *f.* what man shall do
1 Pet. 1:17 time of sojourning here in *f.*
1 John 4:18 there is no *f.* in love, but perfect
Rev. 2:10 *f.* none of those things which thou
11:18 saints and them that *f.* thy name

FEARED (FEAREST, FEARETH)
Gen. 22:12 I know that thou *f.* God
Ex. 1:17 midwives *f.* God and did not
14:31 people *f.* the Lord and believed
1 Sam. 12:18 all the people greatly *f.* the Lord
Neh. 7: 2 faithful man and *f.* God above many
Job 1: 1 that *f.* God and eschewed evil
1: 8 one that *f.* God and escheweth
Ps. 25:12 what man is he that *f.* the Lord
76: 7 thou, even thou art to be *f.*
89: 7 God is greatly to be *f.* in the
96: 4 Lord is to be *f.* above all gods
112: 1 blessed is the man that *f.* the Lord
Prov. 28:14 happy man that *f.* always
Is. 50:10 who is among you that *f.* the Lord
Mal. 3:16 they that *f.* the Lord spake often
Acts 10: 2 one that *f.* God with all his house
10:22 one that *f.* God and of good report
10:35 that *f.* God and worketh righteousness
13:26 whosoever among you *f.* God to you is
Heb. 5: 7 and was heard in that he *f.*

FEARFUL (FEARFULLY)
Ex. 15:11 glorious in holiness, *f.* in praises
Ps. 139: 14 I am *f.* and wonderfully made
Mat. 8:26 why are ye *f.*, O ye of little faith
Heb. 10:27 certain *f.* looking for of judgment
10:31 *f.* thing to fall into the hands
Rev. 21: 8 *f.* and unbelieving shall have their part

FEARFULNESS
Ps. 55: 5 *f.* and trembling are come upon me
Is. 33:14 *f.* hath surprised the hypocrites

FEAST
Prov. 15:15 merry heart hath a continual *f.*
Eccl. 10:19 a *f.* is made for laughter, and wine
Is. 25: 6 unto all people a *f.* of fat things
1 Cor. 5: 8 let us keep the *f.*, not with

FEEBLE
Ps. 105: 37 not one *f.* person among
Is. 35: 3 weak hands and confirm the *f.* knees
Zech. 12: 8 he that is *f.* shall be as David
1 Thes. 5:14 comfort the *f.* minded, support the
Heb. 12:12 hang down and lift up the *f.* knees

FEED (FEEDETH, FED)
Ps. 28: 9 *f.* them also and lift them up for
37: 3 verily thou shalt be *f.*
49:14 death shall *f.* on them; and the
Prov. 10:21 lips of the righteous *f.* many
30: 8 *f.* me with food convenient for me
Sol. 1: 8 *f.* thy kids beside the shepherds' tents
2:16 I am his; he *f.* among the lilies
Is. 44:20 he *f.* on ashes: a deceived heart
58:14 *f.* thee with the heritage of Jacob
Jer. 3:15 pastors *f.* you with knowledge
Hos. 12: 1 Ephraim *f.* on the wind and followeth
Mic. 7:14 *f.* thy people with thy rod
John 21:15 he saith unto him *f.* my lambs
Rom. 12:20 if thine enemy hunger, *f.* him
Acts 20:28 to *f.* the church of God, which he
1 Cor. 3: 2 I have *f.* you with milk, and
9: 7 who *f.* a flock and eateth not
13: 3 give my goods to *f.* the poor
1 Pet. 5: 2 *f.* the flock of God among

FEET
1 Sam. 2: 9 keep the *f.* of his saints
Neh. 9:21 and their *f.* swelled not
Job 12: 5 is ready to slip with his *f.*
29:15 and *f.* was I to the lame
Ps. 73: 2 as for me, my *f.* were almost gone
116: 8 delivered my *f.* from falling
119:101 refrained my *f.* from every evil
119:105 thy word is a lamp to my *f.*
Prov. 4:26 ponder the path of thy *f.*
Is. 59: 7 their *f.* run to evil, and
Luke 1:79 guide our *f.* into the way of
Eph. 6:15 *f.* shod with the preparation of
Heb. 12:13 and make straight paths for your *f.*
Rev. 11:11 they stood upon their *f.*

FELLOW
Eccl. 4:10 if they fall, one will lift up his *f.*
Acts 24: 5 found this man a pestilent *f.*
Rom. 16: 7 my kinsmen and *f.* prisoners
2 Cor. 8:23 he is my partner and *f.* helper
Eph. 2:19 *f.* citizens with the saints, and of
Phil. 2:25 companion in labour, and *f.* soldier
4: 3 I entreat thee also, true yoke *f.*
Col. 1: 7 of Epaphras our dear *f.* servant
4:10 Aristarchus my *f.* prisoner
1 Thes. 3: 2 our *f.* labourer in the gospel
3 John 1: 8 that we might be *f.* helpers
Rev. 6:11 until their *f.* servants also and their
22: 9 for I am thy *f.* servant

FELLOWSHIP
Ps. 94:20 throne of iniquity have *f.* with thee
Acts 2:42 stedfastly in the apostles' doctrine and *f.*
1 Cor. 1: 9 called unto the *f.* of his Son
10:20 should have *f.* with devils
2 Cor. 6:14 what *f.* hath righteousness with unrighteousness
8: 4 *f.* of the ministering to the saints
Gal. 2: 9 gave us right hands of *f.* that we
Eph. 5:11 and have no *f.* with works of
Phil. 1: 5 for your *f.* in the gospel
2: 1 if there be any *f.* of the spirit
3:10 know him and the *f.* of his sufferings
1 John 1: 3 ye also may have *f.* with us: and
1: 6 if we say we have *f.* with him

FERVENT (FERVENTLY)
Acts 18:25 and being *f.* in the spirit
Rom. 12:11 *f.* in spirit, serving the Lord
2 Cor. 7: 7 your *f.* mind toward me; so that I
Col. 4:12 Epaphras always labouring *f.* for you
Jas. 5:16 *f.* prayer of a righteous man availeth
1 Pet. 1:22 love one another with a pure heart *f.*
4: 8 have *f.* charity among yourselves
2 Pet. 3:10 the elements shall melt with *f.* heat

FEW
Gen. 29:20 seemed unto him but a *f.* days
Ps. 105: 12 when they were but a *f.* men
Mat. 7:14 *f.* there be that find it
20:16 many be called, but *f.* chosen
1 Pet. 3:20 *f.* that is, eight souls were saved
Rev. 2:14 I have a *f.* things against you
3: 4 thou hast a *f.* names in Sardis

FIERY
Deut. 33: 2 from his right hand went a *f.* law
Num. 21: 6 Lord sent *f.* serpents among the people
Ps. 21: 9 thou shalt make them as a *f.* oven
Eph. 6:16 quench all the *f.* darts of the wicked
Heb. 10:27 *f.* indignation which shall devour
1 Pet. 4:12 not strange concerning the *f.* trial

FIGHT
Ex. 14:14 the Lord shall *f.* for you
1 Sam. 17:20 as the host was going forth to the *f.*
Acts 5:39 found to *f.* against God
23: 9 let us not *f.* against God
1 Tim. 6:12 *f.* the good *f.* of faith
2 Tim. 4: 7 I have fought a good *f.*
Heb. 10:32 a great *f.* of afflictions

FIG (FIGS)
Gen. 3: 7 they sewed *f.* leaves together
Judg. 9:10 to the *f.* tree, come thou and
1 Ki. 4:25 under his vine and under his *f.* tree
Is. 34: 4 as a falling *f.* from the *f.* tree
36:16 and every one of his *f.* tree

FIGS
Jer. 24: 2 one basket had very good *f.*
Nah. 3:12 strong holds shall be like *f.* trees
Zech. 3:10 the vine and under the *f.* tree
Mat. 7:16 grapes of thorns or *f.* of thistles?
21:19 presently the *f.* tree withered away
Luke 13: 7 I come seeking fruit on this *f.* tree
John 1:50 I saw thee under the *f.* tree
Jas. 3:12 can the *f.* tree, my brethren, bear
Rev. 6:13 even as a *f.* tree casteth her

FILL (FILLED)
Job 8:21 till he *f.* thy mouth with laughing
Ps. 72:19 earth be *f.* with his glory
81:10 open thy mouth wide, and I will *f.* it
Jer. 23:24 do I not *f.* heaven and earth
Luke 1:15 and he shall be *f.* with the Holy Ghost
1:53 hath *f.* the hungry with good things
Acts 9:17 and be *f.* with the Holy Ghost
2: 4 they were all *f.* with the Holy Ghost
4:31 they were all *f.* with the Holy Ghost
13: 9 *f.* with the Holy Ghost, set his eyes
Rom. 15:13 God *f.* you with all joy
15:14 *f.* with all knowledge, able also to
2 Cor. 7: 4 I am *f.* with comfort; I am exceeding
Eph. 3:19 be *f.* with all fulness of God
4:10 that he might *f.* all things
Phil. 1:11 *f.* with the fruits of righteousness
Col. 1: 9 *f.* with the knowledge of his will
2 Tim. 1: 4 that I may be *f.* with joy

FILTHINESS
Ezek. 36:25 from all *f.* will I cleanse you
2 Cor. 7: 1 cleanse ourselves from all *f.* of
Jas. 1:21 lay apart all *f.* and superfluity of

FILTHY
Job 15:16 more abominable and *f.* is man
Ps. 14: 3 they are altogether become *f.*
Is. 64: 6 our righteousness as *f.* rags
Col. 3: 8 *f.* communication out of your mouth
1 Tim. 3: 3 not greedy of *f.* lucre
Tit. 1:11 they ought not, for *f.* lucre's sake
1 Pet. 5: 2 but willingly, not for *f.* lucre
2 Pet. 2: 7 vexed with the *f.* conversation of the
Rev. 22:11 that is *f.* let him be *f.*

FINALLY
2 Cor. 13:11 *f.*, brethren, farewell. Be perfect
Eph. 6:10 *f.*, my brethren, be strong in the Lord
Phil. 3: 1 *f.*, my brethren, rejoice in the Lord
2 Thes. 3: 1 *f.*, brethren, pray for us
1 Pet. 3: 8 *f.*, be ye all of one mind

FIND (FINDETH)
Num. 32:23 your sin will *f.* you out
Prov. 1:28 me early but they shall not *f.* me
8:35 whoso *f.* me *f.* life
18:22 whoso *f.* a wife *f.* a good thing
Eccl. 9:10 whatsoever thy hand *f.* to do
Sol. 5: 6 I sought but could not *f.*
Jer. 6:16 ye shall *f.* rest for your souls
29:13 shall seek me and *f.* me, when ye
Mat. 7: 7 seek and ye shall *f.*, knock and it
7: 8 and he that seeketh *f.*; and to him
7:14 way to life, few there be that *f.* it
10:39 that *f.* his life shall lose it: and
11:29 ye shall *f.* rest unto your souls
Luke 11:10 receiveth and he that seeketh *f.*
11:25 when he cometh, he *f.* it swept
John 7:34 shall seek me, and shall not *f.* me
2 Tim. 1:18 he may *f.* mercy of the Lord in that
Heb. 4:16 *f.* grace to help in time of need
Rev. 9: 6 seek death and shall not *f.* it

FINGER (FINGERS)
Ex. 8:19 this is the *f.* of God
31:18 written with the *f.* of God
Deut. 9:10 written with the *f.* of God
1 Ki. 12:10 my little *f.* shall be thicker
Ps. 8: 3 the work of thy *fingers*
Prov. 6:13 he teacheth with his *f.*
Luke 11:20 with the *f.* of God cast out
11:46 the burdens with one of your *f.*
John 20:27 reach hither thy *f.*

FINISH (FINISHED)
Dan. 9:24 to *f.* the transgression, and to make
John 17: 4 I have *f.* the work which thou
19:30 he said, It is *f.*
Acts 20:24 I might *f.* my course with joy
2 Cor. 8: 6 he would *f.* in you the same grace
2 Tim. 4: 7 I have *f.* my course
Jas. 1:15 sin when it is *f.* bringeth death

FINISHER
Heb. 12: 2 author and *f.* of faith

FIRE
Gen. 19:24 Lord rained brimstone and *f.*
Ex. 3: 2 unto him in a flame of *f.*
9:24 and *f.* mingles with hail
40:38 *f.* was on it by night
Lev. 10: 1 offered a strange *f.* before the Lord
Ps. 11: 6 rain *f.* and brimstone on the wicked
39: 3 while I was musing the *f.* burned
Prov. 6:27 can man take *f.* in his bosom
25:22 heap coals of *f.* on head
Sol. 8: 6 coals thereof are coals of *f.*
Is. 9:18 wickedness burneth as a *f.*
10:17 light of Israel for a *f.*
31: 9 Lord whose *f.* is in Zion
43: 2 walkest through the *f.* thou shalt
Jer. 23:29 is not my word like *f.*
Amos 5: 6 lest the Lord break out like *f.*
7: 4 Lord God called to contend by *f.*
Hab. 2:13 people shall labour in the very *f.*
Zech. 2: 5 I will be a wall of *f.*
Mal. 3: 2 he is like a refiner's *f.*
Mat. 3:10 hewn down, and cast into the *f.*
Mark 9:43 into the *f.* that never shall be quenched
Luke 3:17 he will burn with *f.* unquenchable
9:54 command *f.* to come down
12:49 am come to send *f.* on earth
Rom 12:20 thou shalt heap coals of *f.* on his head
1 Cor. 3:13 revealed by *f.* and *f.* shall try
Heb. 12:29 our God is a consuming *f.*
Jude 1:23 pulling them out of the *f.*

FIRST
Is. 41: 4 the Lord is the *f.* and the last
44: 6 I am the *f.* and I am the last
Mat. 6:33 seek ye *f.* the kingdom of God
7: 5 hypocrite *f.* cast out the beam
19:30 many that are *f.* shall be last
Acts 26:23 Christ should be the *f.* to rise
Rom. 11:35 who hath *f.* given to him
1 Cor. 15:45 *f.* Adam was made a living soul
2 Cor. 8: 5 *f.* gave their own selves to the Lord
8:12 if there be *f.* a willing mind
1 Pet. 4:17 if it *f.* begin at us, what shall
1 John 4:19 because he *f.* loved us
Rev. 2: 4 because thou hast left thy love *f.*
20: 5 this is the *f.* resurrection

FIRSTBORN
Mat. 1:25 brought forth her *f.* son
Luke 2: 7 brought forth her *f.* son
Rom. 8:29 might be the *f.* among many brethren
Col. 1:15 God, the *f.* of every creature
1:18 beginning the *f.* from the dead
Heb. 12:23 assembly and church of the *f.*

FIRSTFRUIT (FIRSTFRUITS)
Prov. 3: 9 with the *f.* of all thine increase
Rom. 8:23 which have the *f.* of the Spirit
11:16 if the *f.* be holy the lump also
1 Cor. 15:20 Christ is the *f.* of them that slept
Jas. 1:18 we should be a kind of *f.*
Rev. 14: 4 being the *f.* unto God

FISH
Ezek. 29: 5 all the *f.* of thy rivers
47:10 their *f.* shall be according to

FISHERS
Jer. 16:16 I will send for many *f.*
Ezek. 47:10 the *f.* shall stand upon it

Mat. 4:19 I will make you *f.* of men
John 21: 7 he girt his *f.* coat

FLAME
Ex. 3: 2 appeared unto him in a *f.*
Judg. 13:20 ascended in the *f.* of the altar
Is. 10:17 his Holy One for a *f.*
Heb. 1: 7 his ministers a *f.* of fire

FLAMING
2 Thes. 1: 8 in *f.* fire taking on them that

FLATTER (FLATTERETH, FLATTERING)
Job 32:22 I know not to give *f.* titles
Ps. 78:36 they did *f.* him with
Prov. 2:16 the stranger which *f.*
20:19 not with him that *f.* with his lips
1 Thes. 2: 5 at any time used we *f.* words

FLEE (FLED)
Prov. 28: 1 wicked *f.* when no man
Is. 10: 3 will ye *f.* for help
Mat. 3: 7 who warned you to *f.* from the wrath
1 Cor. 6:18 my dearly beloved *f.* from fornication
10:14 dearly beloved *f.* from idolatry
2 Tim. 2:22 *f.* also youthful lusts
Heb. 6:18 who have *f.* for refuge
Jas. 4: 7 resist the devil, he will *f.*

FLESH
Gen. 2:23 and *f.* of my *f.*: she shall
2:24 they shall be one *f.*
Job 10:11 clothed with skin and *f.*
19:26 in my *f.* shall I see God
Ps. 56: 4 not fear what *f.* can do to me
65: 2 to thee shall all *f.* come
63: 1 my *f.* longeth for thee in a day
78:39 remember they are but *f.*
Is. 40: 6 all *f.* is grass, and all the
49:26 all *f.* know I am thy Redeemer
Jer. 17: 5 in man and maketh *f.* his arm
32:27 I am the Lord, God of all *f.*
Joel 2:28 I will pour my Spirit on all *f.*
Mat. 16:17 *f.* and blood hath not revealed
19: 5 they twain shall be one *f.*
26:41 is willing, but the *f.* is weak
Luke 3: 6 all *f.* shall see the salvation of God
John 1:13 born not of will but of the *f.*
1:14 the Word was made *f.*
3: 6 which is born of the *f.* is *f.*
6:53 eat the *f.* of the Son of man
6:63 *f.* profiteth nothing, words are
8:15 ye judge after the *f.*
17: 2 given him power over all *f.*
Rom. 7: 5 when we were in the *f.*
7:18 that is, in my *f.*
7:25 with the *f.* the law of sin
8: 1 walk not after the *f.*
8: 5 the *f.* mind things of the *f.*
8: 8 are in the *f.* cannot please God
8:13 if ye live after the *f.* ye shall die
9: 5 of whom concerning the *f.* Christ
9: 8 which are the children of the *f.*
13:14 make not provision for the *f.*
1 Cor. 1:26 not many wise men after the *f.*
1:29 that no *f.* should glory
6:16 saith he, shall be one *f.*
10:18 Israel after the *f.*, are not they
15:50 *f.* and blood cannot inherit the
2 Cor. 1:17 purpose according to the *f.*
5:16 we have known Christ after the *f.*
10: 2 walked according to the *f.*
Gal. 5:19 works of the *f.* are manifest
5:24 crucified the *f.* with affections
6: 8 shall of the *f.* reap corruption
6:13 they may glory in your *f.*
Eph. 2: 3 *f.* fulfilling the desires of the *f.*
5:30 members of his body, of his *f.*
5:31 they two shall be one *f.*
6: 5 masters according to the *f.*
6:12 we wrestle not against *f.* and blood
Heb. 2:14 partakers of *f.* and blood
12: 9 we had fathers of our *f.*
1 Pet. 1:24 for all *f.* is as grass, and all
3:18 he was put to death in the *f.*
3:21 not putting away filth of the *f.*
2 Pet. 2:10 after the *f.* in lust of uncleanness
1 John 2:16 lust of the *f.* lust of the eyes
Jude 1: 7 going after strange *f.*
1:23 hating the garment spotted by *f.*

FLESHLY
2 Cor. 1:12 not with *f.* wisdom but by
Col. 2:18 puffed up by his *f.* mind
1 Pet. 2:11 abstain from *f.* lusts

FLOCK (FLOCKS)
Gen. 32: 5 I have oxen, and asses, *f.*
Ps. 77:20 leddest thy people like a *f.*
Is. 40:11 he shall feed his *f.* like
63:11 with the shepherd of his *f.*
Jer. 13:20 given thee, thy beautiful *f.*
Zech. 11: 4 feed the *f.* of slaughter
Acts 20:28 to yourselves and to all the *f.*
1 Pet. 5: 2 feed the *f.* of God among you

FOLLOW (FOLLOWED)
Ex. 23: 2 thou shalt not *f.* a multitude
Num. 14:24 hath *f.* me fully, him I will bring
32:12 for they have wholly *f.* the Lord
Deut. 16:20 is altogether just shalt thou *f.*
Josh. 14: 8 I wholly *f.* the Lord
Ps. 23: 6 goodness and mercy shall *f.* me
Is. 51: 1 that *f.* after righteousness
Hos. 6: 3 if we *f.* on to know the Lord
Mat. 4:19 *f.* me and I will make you
9: 9 saith unto him, *f.* me
16:24 take up his cross and *f.* me
Luke 18:22 sell all thou hast, and *f.* me
John 1:43 saith unto him, *f.* me
12:26 if any serve me let him *f.* me
21:19 saith unto him, *f.* me
Rom. 9:30 *f.* not after, have attained to righteousness
14:19 *f.* things that make for peace
1 Cor. 14: 1 *F.* after charity, and desire spiritual
Phil. 3:12 but I *f.* that I may apprehend
1 Thes. 5:15 *f.* that which is good
1 Tim. 6:11 *f.* after righteousness, godliness, faith
2 Tim. 2:22 *f.* righteousness, faith, charity, peace
Heb. 12:14 *f.* peace with all men, and holiness
13: 7 whose faith *f.* considering the end
1 Pet. 2:21 example that ye *f.* his steps
Rev. 14:13 their works do *f.* them

FOLLY
Gen. 34: 7 had wrought *f.* in Israel
Josh. 7:15 hath wrought *f.* in Israel
Job 4:18 angels he charged with *f.*
Ps. 49:13 their way is their *f.*
Prov. 26: 5 answer a fool according to his *f.*
2 Tim. 3: 9 their *f.* shall be manifest

FOOD
Gen. 3: 6 saw that the tree was good for *f.*
Deut. 10:18 in giving him *f.* and raiment
Job 23:12 his mouth more than my necessary *f.*
Ps. 78:25 men did eat the angels' *f.*
146: 7 which giveth *f.* to the hungry
Prov. 30: 8 feed me with *f.* convenient for me
Acts 14:17 filling our hearts with *f.*
2 Cor. 9:10 ministered bread for your *f.*, and
1 Tim. 6: 8 having *f.* and raiment let us be

FOOL (FOOLS)
Ps. 14: 1 the *f.* hath said in his heart
75: 4 *f.* deal not foolishly: and to the
94: 8 and ye *f.* when will ye be wise
Prov. 13:20 companion of *f.* shall be destroyed
14: 8 folly of the *f.* is deceitful
14: 9 *f.* make a mock at sin: but among
Eccl. 5: 4 he hath no pleasure in *f.*
Jer. 17:11 at his end shall be a *f.*
Mat. 5:22 say to brother, Thou *f.*
23:17 ye *f.* and blind, for whether is greater
Luke 12:20 thou *f.* this night thy soul
Rom. 1:22 professing to be wise became *f.*
1 Cor. 3:18 let him become a *f.* that
4:10 we are *f.* for Christ's sake
2 Cor. 11:16 let no man think me a *f.*
Eph. 5:15 circumspectly, not as *f.*, but as wise

FOOLISH (FOOLISHLY)
Gen. 31:28 thou hast done *f.* in so doing
Num. 12:11 wherein we have done *f.*
Deut. 32: 6 Lord, requite *f.* people and unwise
1 Sam. 13:13 to Saul, thou hast done *f.*
2 Sam. 24:10 I have done very *f.*
Job 1:22 not nor charged God *f.*
Ps. 5: 5 *f.* shall not stand in thy sight
73:22 so *f.* was I and ignorant
Prov. 14:17 He that is soon angry dealeth *f.*
Mat. 7:26 likened unto a *f.* man which built
25: 2 them were wise and five were *f.*
Rom. 1:21 and their *f.* heart darkened
2 Cor. 11:21 (I speak *f.*,) I am bold also
Gal. 3: 1 O *f.* Galatians, who hath

Eph. 5: 4 neither filthiness, nor *f.* talking
Tit. 3: 3 we ourselves also were sometimes *f.*

FOOLISHNESS
2 Sam. 15:31 counsel of Ahithophel into *f.*
Prov. 12:23 heart of fools proclaimeth *f.*
14:24 *f.* of fools is their folly
15:14 mouth of fools feedeth on *f.*
22:15 *f.* is bound in the heart of a child
24: 9 the thought of *f.* is sin; and the
27:22 yet will not his *f.* depart
1 Cor. 1:18 cross to them that perish *f.*
1:21 God by the *f.* of preaching to save
2:14 they are *f.* to him; neither can he
3:19 wisdom of this world is *f.* with God

FOOT
Prov. 3:23 thy *f.* shall not stumble
Eccl. 5: 1 keep thy *f.* when thou goest to
Is. 58:13 turn away thy *f.* from the sabbath
Mat. 18: 8 if thy *f.* offend thee, cut
1 Cor. 12:15 if *f.* shall say, because I am not
Heb. 10:29 trodden under *f.* the Son of God

FORBID (FORBIDDING)
Mark 10:14 and *f.* them not: for of such is
Luke 18:16 and *f.* them not: for of such is
Acts 24:23 that he should *f.* none
28:31 all confidence no man *f.* him
1 Thes. 2:16 *f.* us to speak to the Gentiles
1 Tim. 4: 3 *f.* to marry, and commanding to abstain

FOREHEAD (FOREHEADS)
Ex. 28:38 it shall be on Aaron's *f.*
Jer. 3: 3 thou hast a whore's *f.*
Ezek. 3: 8 thy *f.* strong against their foreheads
Rev. 7: 3 sealed in their *f.*
9: 4 the seal of God on their *f.*
22: 4 his name shall be in their *f.*

FOREIGNER (FOREIGNERS)
Ex. 12:45 a *f.* and a hired servant
Deut. 15: 3 of a *f.* thou mayest exact it
Obad. 1:11 the *f.* entered into his gates
Eph. 2:19 ye are no more strangers and *f.*

FOREKNOW (FOREKNEW)
Rom. 8:29 whom he did *f.*, he also did
11: 2 cast away his people which he *f.*

FOREKNOWLEDGE
Acts 2:23 determinate counsel, and *f.* of God
1 Pet. 1: 2 according to the *f.* of God

FOREORDAINED
1 Pet. 1:20 who was verily *f.* before the foundation

FORGET (FORGETTETH, FORGETTING, FORGOTTEN)
Deut. 9: 7 *f.* not, how thou provokedst the
32:18 thou hast *f.* God that formed
Job 8:13 paths of all that *f.* God
Ps. 9:12 he *f.* not the cry of the humble
10:11 God hath *f.*: he hideth his face
42: 9 why hast thou *f.* me
45:10 *f.* also thine own people, and thy
50:22 consider this, ye that *f.* God
77: 9 hath God *f.* to be gracious
103: 2 and *f.* not all his benefits
119: 16 I will not *f.* thy words
119: 61 I have not *f.* thy law
Prov. 2:17 *f.* the covenant of her God
3: 1 my son *f.* not my law
Is. 17:10 *f.* the God of thy salvation
49:14 Zion said, my Lord hath *f.* me
49:15 can a woman *f.* her sucking child
Jer. 2:32 can a maid *f.* her ornaments or a
3:21 have *f.* the Lord their God
50: 5 covenant that shall not be *f.*
Phil. 3:13 *f.* those things which are behind
Heb. 6:10 unrighteous to *f.* your labour of love
12: 5 ye have *f.* the exhortation which
13:16 to do good and to communicate *f.* not
Jas. 1:24 straightway *f.* what manner of man

FORGIVE (FORGAVE, FORGAVEST, FORGIVEN, FORGIVETH, FORGIVING)
Ex. 32:32 if thou wilt *f.* their sin
34: 7 *f.* iniquity and transgression and sin, and
Ps. 32: 1 transgression is *f.*, whose sin is
32: 5 thou *f.* the iniquity of my sin
78:38 *f.* their iniquity, and destroyed
85: 2 *f.* the iniquity of thy people
86: 5 art good and ready to *f.*
99: 8 thou wast a God that *f.* them
103: 3 *f.* thine iniquities; who healeth
Is. 2: 9 humbleth himself therefore *f.* them not
33:24 people shall be *f.* their iniquity
Jer. 31:34 for I will *f.* their iniquity
Mat. 6:12 *f.* us our debts, as we *f.*
6:14 if ye *f.* men their trespasses
9: 6 Son of man hath power on earth to *f.*
18:27 and loosed him, *f.* him the debt
Luke 6:37 *f.* and ye shall be forgiven
7:42 frankly *f.* them both tell me therefore
7:43 that he, to whom the *f.* most
7:47 to whom little is *f.* the same loveth
17: 3 if he repent, *f.* him
23:34 Father, *f.* them, they know not
Rom. 4: 7 are those whose iniquities are *f.*
2 Cor. 2:10 to whom ye *f.* any thing
Eph. 4:32 as God for Christ's sake hath *f.* you
Col. 3:13 as Christ *f.* you, so also do ye
Jas. 5:15 sins, they shall be *f.* him
1 John 1: 9 faithful to *f.* us our sins
2:12 because your sins are *f.* you

FORGIVENESS (FORGIVENESSES)
Dan. 9: 9 to the Lord our God belong mercies and *f.*
Acts 5:31 repentance to Israel and *f.* of sins
26:18 may receive *f.* of sins by faith
Col. 1:14 redemption, even the *f.* of sins

FORM
Gen. 1: 2 the earth was without *f.*
1 Sam. 28:14 said unto her what *f.* is he of
Is. 45: 7 I *f.* the light and create darkness
53: 2 hath no *f.* nor comeliness
Rom. 2:20 which hast the *f.* of knowledge
6:17 from the heart that *f.* of doctrine
Phil. 2: 6 who being in the *f.* of God
2: 7 took upon him the *f.* of a servant
2 Tim. 1:13 hold the *f.* of sound words
3: 5 having the *f.* of godliness

FORMED
Ps. 94: 9 that *f.* the eye shall he not see?
Prov. 26:10 great God that *f.* all things both
Is. 27:11 *f.* them will show them no favour
43:21 this people I *f.* for myself
44: 2 thee and *f.* thee from the womb
54:17 no weapon *f.* against thee shall prosper
Rom. 9:20 thing *f.* say to him that *f.*
Gal. 4:19 till Christ be *f.* in you

FORNICATION (FORNICATIONS)
2 Chr. 21:11 inhabitants of Jerusalem to commit *f.*
Is. 23:17 shall commit *f.* with all the kingdoms
Ezek. 16:15 pouredst out thy *f.* on everyone
16:26 committed *f.* with the Egyptians
Mat. 15:19 adulteries, *f.*, thefts
John 8:41 we be not born of *f.*
Acts 15:20 from *f.*, and from things strangled
Rom. 1:29 filled with *f.*, wickedness
1 Cor. 5: 1 there is *f.* among you, and such *f.* as
6:13 Now the body not for *f.*, but
6:18 *f.*. Every sin that a man doeth
7: 2 to avoid *f.* have thy own wife
10: 8 neither let us commit *f.*
2 Cor. 12:21 not repented of their *f.*
Gal. 5:19 works of flesh, adultery, *f.*
Eph. 5: 3 But *f.* and all uncleanness, or covetousness
Col. 3: 5 *f.*, uncleanliness, inordinate affection
1 Thes. 4: 3 should abstain from *f.*
Jude 1: 7 giving themselves to *f.*
Rev. 2:14 sacrificed unto idols and to commit *f.*
2:21 I gave her space to repent her *f.*
9:21 neither repented of their *f.*
14: 8 the wine of the wrath of her *f.*
17: 4 abominations and filthiness of her *f.*
18: 3 the earth have committed *f.* with her
19: 2 did corrupt the earth with her *f.*

FORNICATORS
1 Cor. 5: 9 an epistle not to company with *f.*
6: 9 be not deceived: neither *f.*, nor

Heb. 12:16 Lest there be any *f.* or profane

FORSAKE (FORSAKEN, FORSAKETH, FORSOOK)
Deut. 4:31 will not *f.* thee neither destroy thee
12:19 thou *f.* not the Levite as long
31:16 will *f.* me, and break my covenant
32:15 then he *f.* God which made him
Josh. 1: 5 I will not fail thee nor *f.* thee
1 Sam. 8:57 let him not leave nor *f.* us
12:22 Lord will not *f.* his people
1 Chr. 28:20 will not fail thee, nor *f.* thee
Ps. 22: 1 my God, why hast thou *f.* me
27:10 when my father and my mother *f.* me
71:11 God hath *f.* him: persecute and take
94:14 neither will he *f.* the inheritance
119: 87 I *f.* not thy precepts
Prov. 2:17 which *f.* the guide of her youth
28:13 and *f.* them shall have mercy
Is. 41:17 God of Israel will not *f.* them
49:14 But Zion said, the Lord hath *f.* me
54: 7 for a small moment have I *f.* thee
55: 7 let the wicked *f.* his way
Jer. 2:13 *f.* me the fountain of living waters
17:13 that *f.* thee shall be ashamed
Jonah 2: 8 lying vanities *f.* their own mercy
Mat. 19:27 we have *f.* all, and followed thee
27:46 my God, why hast thou *f.* me
2 Cor. 4: 9 Persecuted but not *f.*; cast down
2 Tim. 4:16 stood with me, but all men *f.* me
Heb. 13: 5 never leave thee, nor *f.* thee

FORTRESS
2 Sam. 22: 2 my rock, and my *f.*
Ps. 18: 2 The Lord is my rock and my *f.*
31: 3 for thou art my rock and my *f.*
71: 3 for thou art my rock and my *f.*
91: 2 He is my refuge and my *f.*: my God
144: 2 my goodness, and my *f.*; my high tower
Jer. 16:19 my strength, and my *f.*, and my refuge

FOUND
Gen. 26:19 and *f.* there a well of springing
31:37 thou *f.* of all thy household
Eccl. 7:27 this have I *f.* that
Sol. 3: 1 I sought him, but I *f.* him not
3: 4 I *f.* him whom my soul
Is. 55: 6 seek the Lord while he may be *f.*
65: 1 *f.* of them that sought me not
Ezek. 22:30 I sought a man and *f.* none
Dan. 5:27 in the balance and *f.* wanting
2 Pet. 3:14 be *f.* of him in peace

FOUNDED
Ps. 24: 2 hath *f.* it upon the seas
Is. 14:32 the Lord hath *f.* Zion
Mat. 7:25 For it was *f.* on a rock

FOUNDATION (FOUNDATIONS)
Job 4:19 whose *f.* is in the dust
Ps. 11: 3 if the *f.* be destroyed
104: 5 Who laid the *f.* of the earth
Prov. 8:29 appointed the *f.* of the earth
10:25 righteous is an everlasting *f.*
Is. 28:16 I lay in Zion a sure *f.*
51:16 and lay the *f.* of the earth
John 17:24 before the *f.* of the world
Rom. 15:20 build on another man's *f.*
1 Cor. 3:10 I have laid the *f.*
Eph. 1: 4 before the *f.* of the world
2:20 built on the *f.* of prophets
1 Tim. 6:19 a good *f.* against the time to come
2 Tim. 2:19 the *f.* of God standeth sure
Heb. 11:10 looked for a city which hath *f.*
1 Pet. 1:20 before the *f.* of the world
Rev. 13: 8 from the *f.* of the world
21:14 the city hath twelve *f.*

FOUNTAIN (FOUNTAINS)
Gen. 7:11 the *f.* of the great deep broken up
Deut. 8: 7 of *f.* and depths that spring
33:28 *f.* of Jacob shall be upon a land
Ps. 36: 9 with thee is the *f.* of life
68:26 bless the Lord from the *f.* of Israel
Prov. 5:18 let thy *f.* be blessed
13:14 law of the wise is a *f.* of life
14:27 fear of the Lord is a *f.* of life
Eccl. 12: 6 a pitcher broken at the *f.*
Sol. 4:12 a spring shut up, a *f.* sealed
Jer. 2:13 forsaken me, the *f.* of living waters

Jer. 9: 1 that my eyes were a *f.* of tears
Joel 3:18 a *f.* out of the house of the Lord
Zech. 13: 1 a *f.* opened to the house of David
Jas. 3:12 can a *f.* both yield salt
Rev. 21: 6 the *f.* of the water of life

FOX (FOXES)
Judg. 15: 4 caught three hundred *f.*
Ps. 63:10 they shall be a portion for *f.*
Sol. 2:15 take us the *f.*, the little foxes
Lam. 5:18 the *f.* walk upon it
Ezek. 13: 4 prophets are like *f.* in the deserts
Mat. 8:20 The *f.* have holes, and the birds of
Luke 13:32 Go ye, and tell that *f.*

FRAME (FRAMED)
Ps. 103: 14 For he knoweth our *f.*
Is. 29:16 thing *f.* say of him that *f.*
Jer. 18:11 I *f.* evil against you, and devise
Eph. 2:21 the building fitly *f.* together
Heb. 11: 3 the worlds were *f.* by the word

FREE
Ex. 21: 2 he shall go out *f.* for nothing
Lev. 19:20 because she was not *f.*
2 Chr. 29:31 as many as were of a *f.* heart
Ps. 51:12 uphold with thy *f.* spirit
88: 5 *f.* among the dead, like the slain
John 8:32 truth shall make you *f.*
8:36 Son make you *f.* you shall be *f.* indeed
Rom. 5:15 so also is a *f.* gift
5:18 the *f.* gift came on all men
1 Cor. 7:22 he that is called, being *f.*
Gal. 3:28 There is neither bond nor *f.*
Col. 3:11 bond nor *f.*, but Christ is all
2 Thes. 3: 1 word of Lord may have *f.* course
1 Pet. 2:16 *f.* and not using liberty

FREELY
Hos. 14: 4 I will love them *f.*
Mat. 10: 8 *f.* ye have received, *f.* give
Rom. 3:24 justified *f.* by his grace
8:32 with him *f.* give us all things
1 Cor. 2:12 things *f.* given us of God
Rev. 21: 6 fountain of the water of life *f.*

FRIEND (FRIENDS)
Ex. 33:11 as a man speaketh to his *f.*
Deut. 13: 6 *f.* which is as his own soul
2 Sam. 16:17 is this kindness to thy *f.*
2 Chr. 20: 7 the seed of Abraham thy *f.* forever
Prov. 17:17 *f.* loveth at all times
18:24 a *f.* closer than a brother
27:10 own *f.* and thy father's *f.*
Sol. 5:16 and this is my *f.*, O daughters
Jer. 6:21 neighbor and his *f.* shall perish
Hos. 3: 1 beloved of her *f.*, yet an adulteress
Mic. 7: 5 trust ye not in a *f.*
John 15:13 lay down his life for his *f.*
Jas. 2:23 he was called the *f.* of God

FRIENDSHIP
Prov. 22:24 make no *f.* with an angry man
Jas. 4: 4 *f.* of the world is enmity with God

FROWARD (FROWARDLY)
Deut. 32:20 for they are a very *f.* generation
Job 5:13 counsel of the *f.* is carried
Ps. 18:26 *f.* wilt show thyself *f.*
101: 4 *f.* heart shall depart from
Prov. 4:24 put away from thee a *f.* mouth
10:31 the *f.* tongue shall be cut
11:20 are of a *f.* heart are abomination
17:20 hath a *f.* heart findeth no good
Is. 57:17 he went on *f.* in the way
1 Pet. 2:18 good and gentle, but also to the *f.*

FRUIT
Gen. 4: 3 brought of the *f.* of the ground
30: 2 withheld from thee the *f.* of the womb
Ex. 21:22 hurt so that the *f.* depart
Lev. 19:24 all the *f.* thereof shall be holy
2 Ki. 19:30 downward, and bear the *f.* upward
Ps. 92:14 shall bring forth *f.* in old age
127: 3 the *f.* of the womb is his reward
Prov. 11:30 *f.* of the righteous tree of life
Sol. 2: 3 his *f.* was sweet to taste
Is. 3:10 eat the *f.* of their doings
27: 9 all the *f.* to take away sin
57:19 I create the *f.* of the lips
Hos. 10: 1 he bringeth *f.* unto himself
Mic. 6: 7 *f.* of my body for the sin of my soul
Mat. 7:17 good tree bringeth forth good *f.*
Mat. 12:33 make his tree corrupt and his *f.* corrupt
26:29 drink henceforth of this *f.* of the vine
Luke 1:42 blessed is the *f.* of thy womb
John 4:36 gathereth *f.* to life eternal
15: 2 branch beareth not *f.* he taketh away
Rom. 6:21 what *f.* had ye then
7: 4 should bring forth *f.* unto God
15:28 have sealed to them this *f.*
Gal. 5:22 *f.* of the Spirit is love, joy
Eph. 5: 9 *f.* of Spirit is in all goodness
Phil. 4:17 I desire *f.* that may abound
Heb. 12:11 peaceable *f.* of righteousness
Jas. 3:18 *f.* of righteousness sown
Rev. 22: 2 and yielded her *f.* every month

FRUITS
Sol. 4:13 with pleasant *f.*; camphire
7:13 all manner of pleasant *f.*
Mat. 3: 8 therefore *f.* meet for repentance
2 Cor. 9:10 increase the *f.* of your righteousness
Phil. 1:11 filled with the *f.* of righteousness
Jas. 3:17 full of mercy and good *f.*

FULL
Deut. 34: 9 Nun was *f.* of the spirit of wisdom
Ruth 1:21 I went out *f.*, and the Lord hath
1 Sam. 2: 5 that were *f.* have hired
Job 5:26 come to the grave in *f.* age
Ps. 17:14 they are *f.* of children, and leave
Prov. 27: 7 the *f.* soul loatheth an honeycomb
30: 9 lest I be *f.* and deny thee
Luke 4: 1 Jesus *f.* of the Holy Ghost
6:25 woe to you that are *f.*
John 1:14 was made flesh, *f.* of grace and truth
Phil. 4:12 know both to be *f.* and
Col. 2: 2 and unto all riches of the *f.* assurance
2 Tim. 4: 5 make *f.* proof of thy ministry
Heb. 6:11 to the *f.* assurance of hope
10:22 near in *f.* assurance of faith

FULFILL (FULFILLED, FULFILLING)
Gen. 29:27 He will *f.* her week, and we will
Ps. 145: 19 *f.* the desire of them
Mat. 3:15 us to *f.* all righteousness
Luke 21:24 until the times of the Gentiles be *f.*
Acts 13:22 which shall *f.* all my will
Gal. 5:14 all the law is *f.* in one word
5:16 shall not *f.* the lust of the flesh
6: 2 bear the burden and so *f.* the law of
Eph. 2: 3 *f.* the desires of the flesh, mind
Phil. 2: 2 *f.* ye my joy, that ye be
Col. 4:17 in the Lord that thou *f.* it
Jas. 2: 8 if ye *f.* the royal law
Rev. 17:17 put in their hearts to *f.* his will

FULNESS
Job 20:22 in the *f.* of his sufficiency
John 1:16 of his *f.* have we received
Rom. 11:25 till the *f.* of the Gentiles become
15:29 *f.* of the blessing of the Gospel
Gal. 4: 4 when the *f.* of the time was come
Eph. 1:10 dispensation of the *f.* of times
1:23 *f.* of him that filleth all in all
3:19 filled with the *f.* of God
4:13 to the stature of the *f.* of Christ
Col. 1:19 in him should all *f.* dwell
2: 9 all the *f.* of the Godhead

FURNACE
Deut. 4:20 you forth out of the iron *f.*
Ps. 12: 6 tried in a *f.* of the earth
Is. 31: 9 fire is in Zion, his *f.* in Jerusalem
48:10 chosen thee in a *f.* of affliction
Dan. 3:11 into the midst of a burning fiery *f.*
Mat. 13:50 cast them into the *f.*
Rev. 1:15 if they burned in a *f.*

G

GAIN (GAINED)
Job 27: 8 hope of the hypocrite though he hath *g.*
Is. 33:15 despiseth the *g.* of oppressions
Mat. 16:26 if he shall *g.* the whole world
18:15 thou hast *g.* thy brother
Luke 19:16 Lord, thy pound hath *g.* ten pounds
1 Cor. 9:19 servant to all, that I might *g.*
Phil. 1:21 to live is Christ, to die is *g.*
1 Tim. 6: 5 supposing that *g.* godliness

GALL
Deut. 29:18 root beareth *g.* and wormwood
Job 16:13 poureth out my *g.* upon the earth
20:25 sword cometh out of his *g.*
Ps. 69:21 gave me *g.* for meat
Jer. 8:14 given us water of *g.*
Lam. 3:19 my misery, wormwood and the *g.*
Mat. 27:34 vinegar drink mixed with *g.*
Acts 8:23 in the *g.* of bitterness

GARDEN
Gen. 2:15 took the man, and put him in the *g.*
3:23 sent him forth from the *g.*
13:10 as the *g.* of the Lord
Sol. 4:12 a *g.* enclosed is my sister
Is. 58:11 thou shalt be like a watered *g.*
Jer. 31:12 their soul shall be as a watered *g.*

GARMENT (GARMENTS)
Josh. 7:21 a goodly Babylonish *g.*
Ezra 9: 3 rent my *g.*, and my mantle
Job 37:17 How thy *g.* are warm, when he
Ps. 22:18 part my *g.* among them
Is. 9: 5 and *g.* rolled in blood
59:17 put on *g.* of vengeance
Joel 2:13 rend your hearts not *g.*
Mat. 21: 8 spread their *g.* in the way
Acts 9:39 coats and *g.* Dorcas made
Rev. 3: 4 have not defiled their *g.*
16:15 watcheth and keepeth his *g.*

GATE (GATES)
Gen. 19: 1 sat at the *g.* of Sodom
22:17 shall possess the *g.* of his enemies
28:17 and this is the *g.* of heaven
34:24 went out of the *g.* of his city
Job 29: 7 I went out to the *g.* through
Ps. 9:13 lifteth me up from the *g.* of death
24: 7 lift up your heads, O ye *g.*
100: 4 enter his *g.* with thanksgiving
118: 19 open to me the *g.* of righteousness
118: 20 this *g.* of the Lord, into which the
Is. 38:10 go to the *g.* of the grave
Mat. 7:13 enter ye at the strait *g.*
16:18 the *g.* of hell shall not prevail
Heb. 13:12 suffered without the *g.*

GATHER (GATHERED, GATHERETH)
Deut. 30: 3 *g.* thee from all the nations
Neh. 1: 9 yet will I *g.* them from thence
Ps. 26: 9 *g.* not my soul with sinners
Jer. 29:14 I will *g.* you from all the nations
Zeph. 3:18 *g.* them that are sorrowful
Mat. 3:12 *g.* his wheat into garner
7:16 do men *g.* grapes of thorns
23:37 would I have *g.* thy children together
John 4:36 *g.* fruit unto life eternal
Eph. 1:10 *g.* in one all things in Christ

GAVE (GAVEST)
Gen. 14:20 and *g.* him tithes of all
Ex. 11: 3 the Lord *g.* the people favour
Ps. 21: 4 asked life of thee, thou *g.* it
81:12 *g.* them up unto their own hearts' lust
Is. 42:24 who *g.* Jacob for a spoil and Israel
John 1:12 *g.* he power to become the sons
3:16 God *g.* his only begotten Son
17: 4 The work which thou *g.* me to do
17:22 And the glory which thou *g.* me
18: 9 of them which thou *g.* me
1 Cor. 3: 6 Apollos watered; but God *g.* the increase
2 Cor. 8: 5 first *g.* their own selves to the
Gal. 1: 4 who *g.* himself for our sins
2:20 who loved me *g.* himself for me
Eph. 4: 8 captive, and *g.* gifts unto men
4:11 *g.* some apostles; and some, prophets
1 Tim. 2: 6 *g.* himself a ransom for all
Tit. 2:14 who *g.* himself for us

GENEALOGIES
1 Tim. 1: 4 heed to fables and endless *g.*
Tit. 3: 9 avoid foolish questions and *g.*

GENERATION (GENERATIONS)
Gen. 2: 4 these are the *g.* of the heavens
6: 9 These are the *g.* of Noah
Deut. 32: 5 perverse and crooked *g.*
32:20 a very froward *g.* in whom
Ps. 14: 5 God is in the *g.* of righteous
22:30 the accounted to the Lord for a *g.*
24: 6 this is the *g.* of them that seek

Ps. 33:11 the thoughts of his heart to all *g.*
45:17 name to be remembered in all *g.*
72: 5 sun and moon endure, throughout all *g.*
79:13 show forth thy praise to all *g.*
89: 4 build thy throne to all *g.*
90: 1 our dwelling place in all *g.*
100: 5 his truth endureth to all *g.*
102: 18 written for the *g.* to come
102: 24 thy years are throughout all *g.*
112: 2 *g.* of upright shall be blessed
119: 90 thy faithfulness is to all *g.*
145: 4 one *g.* shall praise thy works
145: 13 dominion endureth to all *g.*
Mat. 3: 7 O *g.* of vipers, who hath warned
Acts 13:36 had served his own *g.* by the will
Col. 1:26 mystery hid from ages and *g.*
1 Pet. 2: 9 ye are a chosen *g.* a royal

GENTILES
Gen. 10: 5 the isles of the *G.* divided
Is. 11:10 to it shall the *G.* seek
42: 6 the people, for a light of the *G.*
49: 6 give a light to the *G.*
60: 3 *g.* shall come to thy light
60:62 *g.* shall see thy righteousness
Mat. 6:32 after these things do the *g.* seek
Luke 2:32 A light to lighten the *G.*
21:24 till the times of the *g.* be
John 7:35 dispersed among the *g.*, teach the *g.*
Acts 13:46 everlasting life, lo, we turn to the *g.*
13:47 set thee to be a light to the *G.*
14:27 opened the door of faith unto the *g.*
Rom. 2:14 *g.* which have not the law
3:29 is he not also of the *g.*?
11:25 until the fulness of the *g.* become
15:10 rejoice, ye *g.*, with his people
15:12 reign over the *g.*; in him shall *g.* trust
Eph. 3: 6 that the *g.* should be fellowheirs
1 Tim. 2: 7 teacher of the *g.* in faith
3:16 God in flesh, preached to the *g.*

GENTLE (GENTLY)
Is. 40:11 *g.* lead those with young
1 Thes. 2: 7 we were *g.* among you even as a
2 Tim. 2:24 servant of the Lord must be *g.*
Tit. 3: 2 be *g.* showing all meekness
Jas. 3:17 wisdom from above is *g.*
1 Pet. 2:18 not only to the *g.* but to

GENTLENESS
Ps. 18:35 thy *g.* made me great
2 Cor. 10: 1 by the meekness and *g.* of Christ
Gal. 5:22 longsuffering, *g.*, goodness

GIFT (GIFTS)
Ex. 23: 8 take no *g.* for a *g.* blindeth the wise
Ps. 68:18 thou hast received *g.* for men
Prov. 17: 8 A *g.* is as a precious stone
18:16 a man's *g.* maketh room for
21:14 a *g.* in secret pacifieth anger
Eccl. 7: 7 a *g.* destroyeth the heart
Mat. 7:11 to give good *g.* unto your children
John 4:10 if thou knewest the *g.* of God
Rom. 6:23 *g.* of God is eternal life
11:29 for the *g.* and calling of God are
1 Cor. 1: 7 ye come behind in no *g.*
7:7 every man hath his proper *g.*
Eph. 2: 8 it is the *g.* of God
4: 8 captivity captive gave *g.* to men
Phil. 4:17 not because I desire a *g.*
1 Tim. 4:14 neglect not the *g.* that
Heb. 6: 4 have tasted of the heavenly *g.*

GIRD (GIRDED, GIRDETH, GIRT)
Ps. 18:32 God that *g.* me with strength
30:11 sackcloth, and *g.* me with gladness
Luke 12:35 let your loins be *g.*
Eph. 6:14 have your loins *g.* about with truth
1 Pet. 1:13 *g.* up the loins of the mind

GIRDLE (GIRDLES)
Is. 11: 5 shall be the *g.* of his loins
Mat. 3: 4 leathern *g.* about his loins
Rev. 1:13 the paps with a golden *g.*
15: 6 their breasts girded with golden *g.*

GIVE (GIVEN, GIVETH)
Gen. 12: 7 unto thy seed will I *g.* this land
30:31 thou shalt not *g.* me anything
1 Ki. 3: 5 ask what I shall *g.* thee
Ps. 2: 8 I shall *g.* thee the heathen
29:11 Lord will *g.* strength to his
37:21 righteous showeth mercy and *g.*
84:11 Lord will *g.* grace and glory
104: 27 mayest *g.* them their meat
109: 4 I *g.* myself unto prayer
Prov. 28:27 he that *g.* to the poor shall
Is. 40:29 He *g.* power to the faint
42: 5 he that *g.* breath unto the people on earth
Jer. 17:10 to *g.* every man according to his works
32:19 to *g.* everyone according to his ways
Hos. 11: 8 how shall I *g.* thee up
Mat. 13:12 whosoever hath, to him shall be *g.*
13:11 it is *g.* to you to know mysteries
Luke 6:38 *g.* and it shall be given
12:48 to whomsoever much is *g.*
John 10:28 I *g.* to them eternal life
Acts 3: 6 such as I have *g.* I thee
20:35 more blessed to *g.* than to receive
Rom. 8:32 not with him also freely *g.* us all
11:35 Or who hath first *g.* to him
1 Cor. 2:12 know things freely *g.* of God
Eph. 4:28 have to *g.* to him that needeth
1 Tim. 4:15 *g.* thyself wholly to them
6:17 *g.* us richly all things to enjoy
Jas. 1: 5 that *g.* to all men liberally
Rev. 22:12 to *g.* every man according to his work

GIVER
2 Cor. 9: 7 God loveth the cheerful *g.*

GLAD (GLADLY)
Ps. 16: 9 therefore, my heart is *g.*
31: 7 I will be *g.* and rejoice in
64:10 righteous shall be *g.* in the Lord
104: 34 I will be *g.* in the Lord
122: 1 I was *g.* when they said unto me
Mark 6:20 many things; and heard him *g.*
Luke 8:40 was returned, the people *g.* received him
Acts 2:41 that *g.* received his word
2 Cor. 12:15 I will very *g.* spend and be spent

GLADNESS
Ps. 4: 7 thou hast put *g.* in my heart
30:11 sackcloth and girded me with *g.*
45: 7 anointed thee with the oil of *g.*
51: 8 make me to hear joy and *g.* come before
100: 2 serve the Lord with *g.*, and sorrow
106: 5 rejoice in the *g.* of thy nation
Is. 35:10 obtain joy and *g.*
Acts 2:46 eat their meat with *g.*
14:17 filling our hearts with food and *g.*

GLASS
1 Cor. 13:12 now we see through a *g.*, darkly
2 Cor. 3:18 beholding as in a *g.* the glory
Jas. 1:23 beholding a natural face in *g.*
Rev. 4: 6 a sea of *g.* like unto crystal
21:18 the city of pure gold like clear *g.*

GLORY
Ex. 16: 7 ye shall see the *g.* of the Lord
1 Sam. 4:21 saying the *g.* departed from Israel
1 Chr. 16:10 *G.* ye in his holy name: let the heart
29:11 and the power and the *g.*
Job 29:20 my *g.* was fresh in me
Ps. 8: 5 crowned him with *g.* and honour
19: 1 declare the *g.* of God
29: 9 every one speak of his *g.*
57: 8 Awake up my *g.*; awake, psaltery
64:10 upright in heart shall *g.*
72:19 filled with his *g.*; Amen, and Amen
73:24 afterward receive me to *g.*
89:17 art the *g.* of their strength
104: 31 *g.* of the Lord shall endure forever
145: 11 speak of the *g.* of thy kingdom
Prov. 3:35 the wise shall inherit *g.*
16:31 hoary head is a crown of *g.*
25:27 to search their own *g.* is not *g.*
Is. 4: 5 upon all the *g.* shall be a defence
6: 3 the whole earth is full of his *g.*
23: 9 to stain the pride of all *g.*
24:16 heard songs, even *g.* to the righteous
28: 5 Lord shall be for a crown of *g.*
40: 5 *g.* of the Lord shall be revealed
41:16 shalt *g.* in the Holy One of
42: 8 my *g.* will I not give
45:25 seed of Israel be justified, and *g.*
48:11 not give my *g.* unto another
60: 1 the *g.* of the Lord is risen
60: 7 I will glorify the house of my *g.*
Jer. 2:11 my people have changed their *g.*
Ezek. 1:28 likeness of the *g.* of the Lord
20: 6 which is the *g.* of all lands
43: 5 the *g.* of the Lord filled the house
Hos. 4: 7 will I change their *g.* into shame
Hab. 3: 3 his *g.* covered the heavens
Hag. 2: 7 I will fill this house with *g.*
Zech. 2: 5 will be the *g.* in the midst
6:13 build the temple and bear the *g.*
Mat. 6: 2 that they may have *g.* of men
6:13 thine is the kingdom, the power the *g.*
25:31 son of man shall come in his *g.*
Luke 2: 9 the *g.* of the Lord shone round
2:14 *g.* to God in the highest
2:32 light of Gentiles, *g.* of thy people
John 1:14 his *g.*, *g.* as of the only begotten Son
2:11 manifested forth his *g.*; and his disciples
17:22 *g.* which thou gavest me I have
17:24 I am; that they may behold my *g.*
Rom. 2: 7 seek for *g.* and honour and immortality
4: 2 hath whereof to *g.* but not
5: 2 rejoice in the hope and *g.* of God
5: 3 we *g.* in tribulations also
11:36 to whom be *g.* for ever, Amen
16:27 wise be the *g.* through Christ
1 Cor. 10:31 do all to the *g.* of God
11: 7 is the image and *g.* of God
15:43 sown in dishonour, raised in *g.*
2 Cor. 3:18 as in a glass, the *g.* of the Lord
4:17 exceeding and eternal weight of *g.*
5:12 occasion to *g.* on our behalf
11:18 many *g.* after the flesh, I *g.* also
12: 1 it is not expedient for me to *g.*
12: 9 will I rather *g.* in my infirmities
Gal. 6:14 God forbid I should *g.*
Eph. 1: 6 praise of the *g.* of his grace
1:12 to the praise of his *g.*
3:21 to him be *g.* in the church
3:13 my tribulation for you is your *g.*
Phil. 3:19 whose *g.* is in their shame
Col. 1:27 Christ in you, the hope of *g.*
3: 4 ye also appear with him in *g.*
1 Thes. 2:12 called you to his kingdom and *g.*
2:20 ye are our *g.* and joy
1 Tim. 3:16 The world received up into *g.*
Heb. 1: 3 who, being the brightness of his *g.*
13:21 to whom be *g.* for ever and ever
1 Pet. 1: 8 joy unspeakable, full of *g.*
1:11 the sufferings of Christ, and the *g.* that
4:13 when his *g.* shall be revealed
5: 1 partaker of the *g.* to be revealed
5: 4 ye shall receive a crown of *g.*
5:10 called us to eternal *g.* by Christ
2 Pet. 1: 3 called us to *g.* and virtue
1:17 came a voice from excellent *g.*
Rev. 4:11 and worthy, O lord, to receive *g.*
5:12 and honour, and *g.*, and blessing
21:11 having the *g.* of God

GLORIFY (GLORIFIED)
Lev. 10: 3 before all I will be *g.*
Is. 25: 3 shall the strong people *g.* thee
60: 7 I will *g.* the house of my glory
Mat. 5:16 *g.* your Father in heaven
John 7:39 Jesus was not yet *g.*
12:23 Son of man should be *g.*
12:28 Father, *g.* thy name
15: 8 herein is my Father *g.*
17: 1 *g.* thy Son that the Son *g.* thee
17:10 all mine are thine, I am *g.*
21:19 by what death he should *g.* God
Acts 3:13 God of our fathers hath *g.* his Son
4:21 all men *g.* God for that which was
Rom. 1:21 they *g.* him not as God
1 Cor. 6:20 *g.* God in your body and
Gal. 1:24 they *g.* God in me
2 Thes. 1:10 come to be *g.* in his saints
3: 1 word have free course and be *g.*
Heb. 5: 5 even Christ *g.* not himself
1 Pet. 2:12 *g.* God in the day of visitation
Rev. 15: 4 who shall not fear thee, and *g.*
18: 7 how she hath *g.* herself

GLORIOUS
Ex. 15: 6 Lord, is become *g.* in power
15:11 who is like thee, *g.* in holiness
Deut. 28:58 fear this *g.* and fearful name

1 Chr. 29:13 thank thee, and praise thy *g.* name
Ps. 45:13 king's daughter is all *g.* within
66: 2 make his praise be *g.*
72:19 blessed be his *g.* name
87: 3 *g.* things spoken of thee
111: 3 his work is honourable and *g.*
145: 5 speak of the *g.* honour of thy
145: 12 the *g.* majesty of his kingdom
Is. 4: 2 branch of Lord shall be *g.*
11:10 his rest shall be *g.*
22:23 be for a *g.* throne to his father's house
30:30 cause his *g.* voice to be heard
49: 5 I be *g.* in eyes of the Lord
60:13 make the place of my feet *g.*
63:12 hand of Moses with his *g.* arm
Jer. 17:12 a *g.* high throne from the beginning
Rom. 8:21 *g.* liberty of the children of God
2 Cor. 3: 7 written and engraves in stone, was *g.*
4: 4 light of the *g.* gospel should shine
Eph. 5:27 present it to himself a *g.* church
Phil. 3:21 fashioned like unto his *g.* body
Col. 1:11 according to his *g.* power
1 Tim. 1:11 according to the *g.* gospel of
Tit. 2:13 and the *g.* appearing of the great

GLUTTON
Deut. 21:20 he is a *g.* and a drunkard
Prov. 23:21 the drunkard and the *g.*

GLUTTONOUS
Mat. 11:19 and they say behold a man *g.*
Luke 7:34 and ye say behold a *g.* man

GOINGS
Job 34:21 and he seeth all his *g.*
Ps. 17: 5 hold up my *g.* in thy paths
40: 2 rock, and established my *g.*
68:24 they have seen thy *g.*, O God
Prov. 5:21 he pondereth all his *g.*
20:24 man's *g.* are of the Lord
Mic. 5: 2 whose *g.* are of old, from

GOAT (GOATS)
Lev. 3:12 if his offering be a *g.*, then
16:21 hands upon the head of the live *g.*
Is. 1:11 of bullocks or of lambs, or of he *g.*
Ezek. 34:17 judge between rams and *g.*
Zech. 10: 3 I punished the *g.*: for the Lord
Mat. 25:32 set *g.* on his left hand
Heb. 9:12 Neither by the blood of *g.*
10: 4 blood of bulls and of *g.*

GOD
Job 33:12 *G.* is greater than man
Ps. 18:31 who is *G.* save the Lord
86:10 wondrous things, thou art *G.* alone
Dan. 11:36 marvelous things against the *G.* of gods
Mic. 7:18 who a *G.* like thee
Mat. 6:24 cannot serve *G.* and mammon
19:17 none good but one, that is *G.*
Mark 12:32 one *G.* and none other
John 1: 1 with *G.*, and the Word was *G.*
1:18 hath seen *G.* at anytime
17: 3 know thee the only true *G.*
Acts 7: 2 *G.* of glory appeared to Abraham
Rom. 3: 4 *G.* forbid: yea, let *G.* be true
8:31 if *G.* be for us, who can be against
9: 5 over all, *G.* blessed for ever
15: 5 *G.* of patience and consolation
15:13 *G.* of hope fill you with all joy
1 Cor. 15:28 that *G.* may be all in all
2 Cor. 1: 3 mercies, and the *G.* of all comfort
2 Thes. 2: 4 above all that is called *G.*
1 Tim. 3:16 *G.* was manifest in the flesh
1 Pet. 5:10 *G.* of all grace, who hath called
1 John 4:12 no man hath seen *G.* at any time
5:20 This is the true *G.*

GODHEAD
Acts 17:29 *G.* is like unto gold
Rom. 1:20 his eternal power and *G.*
Col. 2: 9 the fulness of the *G.* bodily

GODLY
Ps. 4: 3 that is *g.* for himself
32: 6 every one that is *g.* pray
Mal. 2:15 he might seek a *g.* seed
2 Cor. 1:12 in simplicity and *g.* sincerity
7: 9 sorrow after a *g.* manner
Tit. 2:12 live soberly, righteously and *g.*
Heb. 12:28 with reverence and *g.* fear
2 Pet. 2: 9 deliver the *g.* out of
3 John 1: 6 journey after a *g.* sort

GODLINESS
1 Tim. 2: 2 quiet and peaceable life in all *g.*
3:16 great is the mystery of *g.*
4: 7 exercise thyself rather unto *g.*
4: 8 *g.* is profitable to all things
6: 3 doctrine which is according to *g.*
6: 6 *g.* with contentment is great gain
6:11 follow after righteousness, *g.*
2 Tim. 3: 5 having a form of *g.* but
Tit. 1: 1 truth which is after *g.*
2 Pet. 1: 3 all that pertain to life and *g.*
1: 6 Patience; and to patience and *g.*
3:11 in all holy conversation and *g.*

GOLD
Gen. 2:11 land of Havilah where there is *g.*
13: 2 in silver, and in *g.*
Job 23:10 I shall come forth as *g.*
31:24 if I have made *g.* my hope, or
Ps. 19:10 more desired than *g.*, yea
119:127 love thy commandments above *g.*
Prov. 8:19 my fruit is better than *g.*
Is. 2: 7 full of silver and *g.*
13:12 man more precious than fine *g.*
Zech. 13: 9 and will try them as *g.* is tried
1 Cor. 3:12 build on this foundation, *g.*
1 Tim. 2: 9 not with braided hair, or *g.*
1 Pet. 1: 7 trial of faith more precious than *g.*
3: 3 the hair and of wearing of *g.*
Rev. 3:18 buy of me *g.* tried in the fire

GOOD
Gen. 1:31 every thing was very *g.*
2:18 not *g.* for man to be alone
32:12 thou saidst, I will do thee *g.*
50:20 God meant it unto *g.*
2 Ki. 20:19 *g.* is the word of the Lord
Neh. 2:18 their hands for this *g.* work
Ps. 34: 8 taste and see that the Lord is *g.*
73: 1 truly God is *g.* to Israel
86: 5 Lord, art *g.*, ready to forgive
106: 5 may see the *g.* of thy chosen
145: 9 Lord is *g.* to all; and his tender
Lam. 3:25 Lord *g.* to them that wait
Mic. 6: 8 shown thee what is *g.*
Mat. 19:17 Why callest thou me *g.*?
26:10 she has wrought a *g.* work upon me
John 10:32 many *g.* works have I shown you
10:33 for a *g.* work we stone thee not
Acts 9:36 Dorcas was full of *g.* works
Rom. 3: 8 do evil that *g.* may come
7:18 that which is *g.* I find not
13: 3 not a terror to *g.* works
2 Cor. 9: 8 abound to every *g.* work
Eph. 2:10 in Jesus Christ unto *g.* works
Phil. 1: 6 begun a *g.* work will finish it
Col. 1:10 being fruitful in every *g.* work
1 Thes. 5:15 follow that which is *g.*
2 Thes. 2:17 establish you in every *g.* work
1 Tim. 2:10 (women professing godliness) with *g.* works
5:10 have diligently followed every *g.* work
5:25 the *g.* works of some are manifest
Tit. 1:16 and unto every *g.* work reprobate
3: 1 to be ready to every *g.* work
3: 8 careful to maintain *g.* works
Heb. 10:24 provoke unto love and to *g.* works
13:21 perfect in every *g.* work
1 Pet. 2:12 may by your *g.* works which

GOODNESS
Ex. 33:19 I will make my *g.* pass
34: 6 God abundant in *g.* and truth
2 Chr. 6:41 let saints rejoice in *g.*
Neh. 9:25 delight themselves in *g.*
9:35 not served thee in thy great *g.*
Ps. 16: 2 my *g.* extendeth not to
23: 6 *g.* and mercy shall follow me
27:13 believed to see the *g.* of the Lord
31:19 how great is thy *g.*, which thou
33: 5 earth full of the *g.* of the Lord
52: 1 the *g.* of God endureth continually
65: 4 satisfied with the *g.* of thy house
65:11 crownest the year with thy *g.*
Is. 63: 7 great *g.* bestowed on Israel
Hos. 3: 5 fear the Lord and his *g.*
Rom. 2: 4 *g.* of God leadeth to repentance
11:22 behold the *g.* and severity of God
Gal. 5:22 longsuffering, gentleness, *g.*
Eph. 5: 9 fruit of Spirit in all *g.*

GOSPEL
Mat. 4:23 preaching the *g.* of the kingdom
Mark 1: 1 the beginning of the *g.*
8:35 for my sake, and the *g.*
16:15 preach the *g.* to every creature
Acts 20:24 testify the *g.* of the grace of God
Rom. 1: 1 separated unto *g.* of God
1 Cor. 1:17 but to preach the *g.*
4:15 begotten you through the *g.*
2 Cor. 4: 3 if our *g.* hid, it is hid
11: 4 another *g.* which ye have not accepted
Eph. 1:13 truth, the *g.* of your salvation
6:15 preparation of the *g.* of peace
Phil. 1: 5 For your fellowship in the *g.*
1:27 as it becometh the *g.* of Christ
Col. 1: 5 the word of truth of the *g.*
1 Thes. 1: 5 our *g.* came to you not only
1 Tim. 1:11 according to the glorious *g.*
Heb. 4: 2 unto us was the *g.* preached
1 Pet. 4: 6 *g.* was preached to the dead
Rev. 14: 6 having the everlasting *g.* to preach

GOVERNMENT (GOVERNMENTS)
Is. 9: 6 *g.* shall be upon his shoulder
22:21 commit thy *g.* into his hand
1 Cor. 12:28 gifts of healing, helps *g.*
2 Pet. 2:10 uncleanliness, and despise *g.*

GRACE
Ezra 9: 8 for a little space *g.* hath been
Esth. 2:17 she obtained *g.* and favor
Ps. 84:11 Lord will give *g.* and glory
Prov. 3:34 but he giveth *g.* to the lowly
Zech. 4: 7 with shoutings, crying, *g. g.* unto it
12:10 spirit of *g.* and supplications
Luke 2:40 *g.* of God was upon him
Acts 15:11 *g.* of our Lord Jesus Christ
18:27 which we had believed through *g.*
Rom. 1: 7 *g.* and peace to you
3:24 justified freely by his *g.*
5:20 *g.* did much more abound
6:14 not under law, but *g.*
11: 5 according to the election of *g.*
11: 6 if by *g.* then not of works
16:20 *g.* of our Lord Jesus Christ
1 Cor. 16:23 *g.* of our Lord Jesus Christ
2 Cor. 1:12 by the *g.* of God our conversation
6: 1 receive not the *g.* of God in vain
8: 1 *g.* of God bestowed on the churches
9:14 for the exceeding *g.* of God in you
12: 9 my *g.* sufficient for thee
13:14 *g.* of the Lord Jesus Christ
Gal. 2:21 I do not frustrate the *g.* of God
6:18 *g.* of our Lord Jesus Christ
Eph. 2: 5 by *g.* ye are saved
2: 7 show exceeding riches of his *g.*
2: 8 by *g.* are ye saved
4:29 minister *g.* to the hearers
Phil. 4:23 *g.* of our Lord Jesus Christ
Col. 1: 6 knew the *g.* of God in truth
1 Thes. 5:28 *g.* of our Lord Jesus Christ
2 Thes. 3:18 *g.* of our Lord Jesus Christ
Tit. 3: 7 justified by his *g.*
Heb. 4:16 come boldly to the throne of *g.*
13: 9 heart be established with *g.*
Jas. 4: 6 he giveth more *g.* unto the humble
1 Pet. 3: 7 heirs of the *g.* of life
4:10 stewards of the manifold *g.* of God
5: 5 and giveth *g.* to the humble
5:12 this the true *g.* of God wherein ye stand
2 Pet. 3:18 grow in *g.* and knowledge
Jude 1: 4 turning the *g.* of God into lasciviousness
Rev. 22:21 *g.* of our Lord Jesus Christ

GRACIOUS (GRACIOUSLY)
Gen. 33: 5 which God hath *g.* given thy servant
43:29 God be *g.* unto thee my son
Ex. 22:27 I will hear, for I am *g.*
22:19 I will be *g.* to whom I will be *g.*
34: 6 Lord God merciful and *g.*
Num. 6:25 and be *g.* unto thee
2 Chr. 30: 9 God is *g.* and merciful
Neh. 9:31 thou art a *g.* and merciful God
Job 33:24 then he is *g.* to him
Ps. 77: 9 hath God forgotten to be *g.*
86:15 full of compassion and *g.*
103: 8 Lord is merciful and *g.*
119: 29 grant me thy law *g.*
Hos. 14: 2 all iniquity, and receive us *g.*
Joel 2:13 for he is *g.* and merciful

Amos 5:15 the Lord God of hosts will be *g.*
Jonah 4: 2 knew thou art a *g.* God
Mal. 1: 9 he will be *g.* unto us
1 Pet. 2: 3 tasted that the Lord is *g.*

GRAPES
Deut. 32:32 their *g.* are *g.* of gall
Sol. 2:13 the tender *g.* give a good smell
Is. 5: 4 brought it forth wild *g.*
Ezek. 18: 2 fathers have eaten sour *g.*
Mic. 7: 1 fruits, as the *g.* gleanings of vintage

GRASS
Ps. 37: 2 soon be cut down like the *g.*
90: 5 like the *g.* which groweth up
103: 15 as for man his days are like *g.*
Is. 40: 6 shall I cry? All flesh is *g.*
51:12 shall be made as *g.*
Mat. 6:30 if God so clothe the *g.*
Jas. 1:11 but it withereth the *g.*
1 Pet. 1:24 for all flesh is as *g.*
Rev. 8: 7 all green *g.* was burnt up

GRAVE
1 Sam. 2: 6 Lord bringeth down to the *g.*
Job 5:26 come to thy *g.* in full age
14:13 hide me in the *g.*
Ps. 6: 5 in the *g.* who shall give thanks
Prov. 1:12 swallow alive, as the *g.*
Eccl. 9:10 nor wisdom in the *g.*
Is. 38:18 the *g.* cannot praise thee
Hos. 13:14 ransom them from the power of the *g.*
1 Cor. 15:55 O *g.* where is thy victory

GRAVEN
Job 19:24 they were *g.* with an iron
Is. 49:16 have *g.* thee on the palms
Jer. 17: 1 it is sin *g.* upon table of their heart

GREAT
Gen. 6: 5 wickedness of man was *g.*
12: 2 make of thee a *g.* nation
30: 8 with *g.* wrestlings have I wrestled
Ex. 32:11 land of Egypt with a *g.* power
Deut. 29:24 the heat of this *g.* anger
1 Sam. 6: 9 he hath done us this *g.* evil
Neh. 13:27 to do all this *g.* evil
Job 5: 9 *g.* things and unsearchable
Ps. 47: 2 a *g.* king over all the earth
48: 2 the city of the *g.* king
147: 5 *g.* is our Lord, and of *g.* power
Eccl. 2:21 vanity and a *g.* evil
Jer. 45: 5 seekest thou *g.* things for thyself
Dan. 9:12 bringing upon us a *g.* evil
Hos. 8:12 written to him the *g.* things
Joel 3:13 for their wickedness is *g.*
Nah. 1: 3 slow to anger and *g.* in power
Mal. 1:14 I am a *g.* king
Luke 1:49 hath done to me *g.* things
Acts 4:33 with *g.* power gave the apostles
Rev. 11:17 taken to thee thy *g.* power

GREATER
Job 33:12 God is *g.* than man
Mat. 12:42 *g.* than Solomon is here
John 1:50 see *g.* things than these
4:12 art thou *g.* than our father Jacob
10:29 gave them me, is *g.* than all
14:28 my father is *g.* than I
1 Cor. 14: 5 *g.* is he that prophesieth
1 John 3:20 God *g.* than our heart
4: 4 *g.* he that is in you
5: 9 witness of God is *g.*

GREATLY
1 Sam. 30: 6 David was *g.* distressed
2 Sam. 24:10 I have sinned *g.* in that I
1 Ki. 18: 3 Obadiah feared the Lord *g.*
1 Chr. 16:25 great is the Lord and *g.* to be praised
2 Chr. 33:12 humbled himself *g.* before the God
Job 3:25 thing I *g.* feared is come
Ps. 28: 7 therefore my heart *g.* rejoiceth
89: 7 God is *g.* to be feared in the assembly
116: 10 have I spoken I was *g.* afflicted
145: 3 great is the Lord, and *g.* to be praised
Dan. 9:23 O man, *g.* beloved
Mark 12:27 ye therefore do *g.* err

GREATNESS
Ex. 15: 7 *g.* of thy excellency
Num. 14:19 according to the *g.* of thy mercy
Deut. 32: 3 ascribe ye *g.* to our God
Ps. 66: 3 through the *g.* of thy power
Ps. 145: 3 and his *g.* is unsearchable
Is. 63: 1 travelling in *g.* of strength
Eph. 1:19 the exceeding *g.* of his power

GREEDY
Prov. 1:19 every one that is *g.* of gain
15:27 he that is *g.* of gain troubleth
Is. 56:11 they are *g.* dogs, never
1 Tim. 3: 3 not *g.* of filthy lucre

GREEDINESS
Eph. 4:19 to work all uncleanness with *g.*

GRIEF
Is. 53: 3 sorrows, and acquainted with *g.*
Heb. 13:17 with joy, and not with *g.*

GRIEVE (GRIEVED)
Gen. 6: 6 earth, and it *g.* him at his heart
Judg. 10:16 his soul was *g.* for misery
Ps. 95:10 forty years long was I *g.*
119:158 I beheld transgressors and was *g.*
139: 21 *g.* with those that rise up
Is. 54: 6 called thee as a woman forsaken and *g.*
Jer. 5: 3 stricken, they have not *g.*
Lam. 3:33 nor *g.* the children of men
Amos 6: 6 they are not *g.* for affliction
Mark 3: 5 *g.* for hardness of their hearts
Rom. 14:15 if thy brother be *g.* with thy meat

GRIEVIOUS
Ps. 10: 5 His ways are always *g.*; thy judgments
Mat. 8: 6 sick of the palsy, *g.* tormented
23: 4 burdens *g.* to be borne
Acts 20:29 shall *g.* wolves enter
1 John 5: 3 his commandments are not *g.*

GROAN (GROANED, GROANETH)
John 11:33 *g.* in spirit, and was troubled
Rom. 8:22 whole creation *g.* and travaileth
2 Cor. 5: 4 we that are in this tabernacle do *g.*

GROANING (GROANINGS)
Ps. 6: 6 I was weary with my *g.*
38: 9 my *g.* is not hid from thee
102: 20 to hear the *g.* of the prisoner
Rom. 8:26 *g.* which cannot be uttered

GROW (GROWETH)
Gen. 48:16 let them *g.* into a multitude
2 Sam. 23: 5 although he make it not to *g.*
Ps. 92:12 *g.* like a cedar in Lebanon
Hos. 14: 5 he shall *g.* as a lily
Eph. 2:21 *g.* unto an holy temple in the Lord
4:15 *g.* up into him in all things
1 Pet. 2: 2 milk of word that ye may *g.*
2 Pet. 3:18 *g.* in grace, and in knowledge

GUIDE
Ps. 48:14 he will be our *g.* even unto death
73:24 *g.* me with thy counsel
Prov. 2:17 forsaketh the *g.* of youth
Is. 58:11 Lord shall *g.* thee continually
Jer. 3: 4 Father, thou art the *g.* of my youth
Luke 1:79 *g.* our feet into the way of peace
John 16:13 he will *g.* you into all truth
1 Tim. 5:14 bear children, *g.* the house

GUILE
Ex. 21:14 to slay him with *g.*
Ps. 32: 2 in whose spirit is no *g.*
34:13 keep thy lips from speaking *g.*
55:11 deceit and *g.* depart not from her
John 1:47 Israelite indeed in whom is no *g.*
2 Cor. 12:16 I caught you with *g.*
1 Thes. 2: 3 nor of uncleanliness, nor in *g.*
1 Pet. 2: 1 laying aside malice and *g.*

GUILTY
Ex. 34: 7 will by no means clear the *g.*
Lev. 4:13 not be done, and are *g.*
Num. 14:18 by no means clearing the *g.*
Rom. 3:19 all the world may become *g.* before
1 Cor. 11:27 *g.* of the body and blood of
Jas. 2:10 offend in one point, *g.* of all

GUILTLESS
Ex. 20: 7 not hold him *g.* that taketh

H

HABITATION (HABITATIONS)
Deut. 26:15 look down from thy holy *h.*
2 Chr. 29: 6 from the *h.* of the Lord
Ps. 26: 8 loved the *h.* of thy house
Ps. 68: 5 God in his holy *h.*
71: 3 be thou my strong *h.* whereunto
74:20 earth full of *h.* of cruelty
89:14 are the *h.* of thy throne
91: 9 hast made the Most High thy *h.*
Prov. 3:33 he blesseth the *h.* of the just
Is. 33:20 see Jerusalem a quiet *h.*
63:15 behold from the *h.* of thy holiness
Jer. 31:23 Lord bless thee, O *h.* of justice
Zech. 2:13 out of his holy *h.*
Luke 16: 9 receive into everlasting *h.*
Jude 1: 6 angels which left their own *h.*
Rev. 18: 2 Babylon is become the *h.* of

HAIR (HAIRS)
Ps. 40:12 more than the *h.* of mine head
Hos. 7: 9 gray *h.* are here and there
Mat. 5:36 not make one *h.* white or
10:30 *h.* of your head are all numbered
1 Cor. 11:14 if a man hath long *h.*
1 Tim. 2: 9 not with braided *h.*, or gold
1 Pet. 3: 3 plaiting the *h.*, and wearing of gold

HAND
Gen. 3:22 he put forth his hand
16:12 every man's *h.* against him
Num. 11:23 is the Lord's *h.* waxed short
Deut. 33: 3 all his saints are in thy *h.*
2 Sam. 24:14 fall now into the *h.* of the Lord
Ezra 7: 9 good *h.* of his God on him
8:22 *h.* of our God is upon all
Job 2:10 good at the *h.* of God and not evil
12: 6 into whose *h.* God bringeth
12: 9 *h.* of the Lord hath wrought this
Ps. 16: 8 he is at my right *h.*
16:11 at thy right *h.* are pleasures for
18:35 thy right *h.* hath holden me up
31: 5 into thy *h.* I commend my spirit
48:10 thy right *h.* is full of righteousness
73:23 hast holden me by my right *h.*
110: 5 Lord at thy right *h.* shall strike
137: 5 let my right *h.* forget her cunning
139: 10 thy *h.* lead and thy right *h.*
145: 16 thou openest thy *h.* and satisfiest
Prov. 3:16 length of days is in her right *h.*
10: 4 *h.* of the diligent maketh rich
11:21 though *h.* join in *h.*
30:32 lay thy *h.* upon thy mouth
Eccl. 9: 1 wise and their works in the *h.* of God
9:10 whatsoever thy *h.* findeth to do
10: 2 wise man's heart at his right *h.*
Sol. 2: 6 his right *h.* doth embrace me
Is. 1:12 who required this at your *h.*
26:11 when thy *h.* is lifted up, they
40: 2 received of the *h.* of the Lord double
59: 1 *h.* of the Lord is not shortened
Mat. 5:30 if thy right *h.* offend thee
6: 3 left *h.* know what thy right *h.*
18: 8 if thy *h.* or thy foot offend
20:21 one on the right *h.*, the other on
22:13 bind him *h.* and foot
25:33 sheep on the right *h.*, goats on left
Mark 14:62 sitting on right *h.* of power
16:19 sat on the right *h.* of God
Luke 1:74 out of the *h.* of our enemies
Acts 2:33 the right *h.* of God exalted
4:28 to do whatsoever thy *h.* and
7:55 Jesus standing on the right *h.*
Rom. 8:34 even at the right *h.* of God
Col. 3: 1 sitteth on the right *h.* of God
Heb. 1: 3 sat down on the right *h.*
8: 1 who is set on the right *h.*
10:12 sat down on the right *h.*
1 Pet. 3:22 is on the right *h.* of God
5: 6 under the mighty *h.* of God

HANDS
Gen. 27:22 *h.* are the *h.* of Esau
Ex. 17:12 Moses' *h.* were heavy, and they
Job 17: 9 clean *h.* shall be stronger
Ps. 24: 4 clean *h.* and a pure heart
119: 73 thy *h.* have made me and fashioned
Prov. 31:20 reacheth thy *h.* to the needy
31:31 give her of the fruit of her *h.*
Is. 1:15 when ye spread forth your *h.*
Mic. 7: 3 do evil with both *h.*
Mat. 9:44 delivered into the *h.* of men
18: 8 having two *h.* or feet
Luke 23:46 into thy *h.* I commend my spirit
John 13: 3 given all things into his *h.*
13: 9 but also my *h.* and head
2 Cor. 5: 1 house not made with *h.*

Eph. 4:28 let him labour, working with his *h*.
1 Tim. 2: 8 pray every where, lifting up holy *h*.
Heb. 9:11 tabernacle, not made with *h*.
10:31 fall into the *h*. of the living God
Jas. 4: 8 cleanse your *h*. ye sinners
1 John 1: 1 and our *h*. have handled of the

HANG (HANGED, HANGETH)
Deut. 21:23 that is *h*. is accursed of God
28:66 thy life shall *h*. in doubt
Josh. 8:29 he *h*. on a tree until eventide
Job 26: 7 he *h*. the earth on nothing
Ps. 137: 2 we *h*. our harps upon the willows
Mat. 18: 6 millstone were *h*. about his neck
22:40 commandments *h*. all the law and the prophets
Gal. 3:13 everyone that *h*. on a tree
Heb. 12:12 lift up the hands which *h*. down

HAPPY
Gen. 30:13 *H*. am I for the daughters
Deut. 33:29 *h*. art thou, O Israel
1 Ki. 10: 8 *h*. are thy men, *h*. are these
Job 5:17 *h*. the man whom God correcteth
Ps. 127: 5 *h*. the man who hath his quiver
128: 2 *h*. shalt thou be, and be well
144: 15 *h*. is that people, that is in such
146: 5 *h*. is he that hath the God
Prov. 3:13 *h*. is the man that findeth wisdom
14:21 that hath mercy on poor, *h*. is he
16:20 who trusteth in Lord, *h*. is he
28:14 *h*. is man that feareth always
29:18 he that keepeth the law, *h*. is he
Mal. 3:15 now we call the proud *h*.
John 13:17 *h*. are ye if ye do them
Rom. 14:22 *h*. is he that condemneth not
1 Pet. 3:14 suffer for righteousness' sake, *h*. are ye
4:14 reproached for the name of Christ, *h*. are ye

HARD
Gen. 18:14 any thing too *h*. for the Lord
35:17 she was in *h*. labour
Ex. 1:14 made their lives bitter with *h*. bondage
18:26 the *h*. causes they brought unto Moses
2 Sam. 13: 2 thought it *h*. for him to do anything
2 Ki. 2:10 thou hast asked a *h*. thing
Ps. 60: 3 shown thy people *h*. things
88: 7 wrath lieth *h*. upon me
Prov. 13:15 way of transgressors is *h*.
Jer. 32:17 nothing too *h*. for thee
Mark 10:24 how *h*. is it for them that trust
Acts 9: 5 *h*. for thee to kick against the pricks
26:14 it is *h*. for thee to kick
2 Pet. 3:16 things too *h*. to be understood
Jude 1:15 of all their *h*. speeches which ungodly

HARDEN (HARDENED)
Ex. 4:21 I will *h*. his heart
Deut. 15: 7 thou shalt not *h*. thy heart
Josh. 11:20 was of the Lord to *h*. their hearts
Job 9: 4 hath *h*. himself against him
Ps. 95: 8 *h*. not your heart, as in the provocation
Is. 63:17 *h*. our heart from thy fear
Mark 6:52 loaves; for their heart was *h*.
Heb. 3: 8 *h*. not your hearts, as in the
3:13 *h*. through the deceitfulness of sin

HARDNESS
Mat. 19: 8 *h*. of your hearts suffered you
Mark 3: 5 grieved for the *h*. of their
Rom. 2: 5 after thy *h*. and impenitent
2 Tim. 2: 3 endure *h*. as a good soldier

HARLOT (HARLOTS)
Gen. 34:31 sister as with a *h*.
Josh. 2: 1 came into an *h*. house named Rahab
Judg. 11: 1 was the son of a *h*.
Prov. 7:10 woman with the attire of an *h*.
Is. 1:21 the faithful city become as an *h*.
23:15 Tyre sing as a *h*.
Jer. 2:20 thou wanderest, playing the *h*.
Ezek. 16:15 own beauty, and playedst the *h*.
Hos. 2: 5 mother hath played the *h*.
4:15 though thou Israel, play the *h*.
Mat. 21:31 *h*. into the kingdom of God
1 Cor. 6:16 joined to a *h*. is one body
Heb. 11:31 by faith the *h*. Rahab
Jas. 2:25 Rahab the *h*. justified by works
Rev. 17: 5 mother of *h*. and abominations

HARM
Gen. 31:52 pillar unto me, for *h*.
1 Chr. 16:22 do my prophets no *h*.
Ps. 105: 15 do my prophets no *h*.
Prov. 3:30 have done thee no *h*.
Jer. 39:12 look well to him and do him no *h*.
Acts 28: 5 into the fire and felt no *h*.
1 Pet. 3:13 who is he that will *h*. you

HARMLESS
Mat. 10:16 as serpents and *h*. as doves
Phil. 2:15 ye may be blameless and *h*.

HARVEST
Gen. 8:22 remaineth, seedtime and *h*.
30:14 went in the days of wheat *h*.
Ex. 34:21 in *h*. thou shalt rest
Is. 9: 3 according to the joy in *h*.
Jer. 5:24 unto us the appointed weeks of the *h*.
8:20 *h*. is past, summer is ended
51:33 time of her *h*. shall come
Joel 3:13 sickle for the *h*. is ripe
Mat. 9: 3 pray ye the Lord of the *h*.
13:39 *h*. is the end of the world
Rev. 14:15 for the *h*. of earth is ripe

HASTE
Ex. 12:33 out of the land in *h*.
Ps. 31:22 I said in my *h*., I am cut off
38:22 make *h*. to help me, O Lord
40:13 O Lord, make *h*. to help me
71:12 O my God, make *h*. for my help
119: 60 I made *h*. and delayed not
141: 1 make *h*. unto me; give ear unto
Sol. 8:14 make *h*., my beloved and be thou
Is. 28:16 believeth shall not make *h*.
49:17 thy children shall make *h*.
52:12 ye shall not go out with *h*.

HASTEN
Ps. 16: 4 multiplied that *h*. after another god
Is. 5:19 let him make speed and *h*.
60:22 I the Lord will *h*. it in his time
Jer. 1:12 I will *h*. my word to perform it

HASTY (HASTILY)
Prov. 20:21 inheritance may be gotten *h*.
29:20 a man that is *h*. in words?

HATE
Gen. 24:60 the gate of those which *h*. them
Lev. 19:17 shall not *h*. thy brother
Deut. 7:10 repayeth them that *h*. him
Ps. 68: 1 let them that *h*. him flee
97:10 ye that love the Lord, *h*. evil
119:104 I *h*. every false way
119:113 I *h*. vain thoughts
139: 21 do not I *h*. them that *h*.
Prov. 8:13 fear of Lord is to *h*. evil
8:36 all they that *h*. me love death
Jer. 44: 4 abominable thing that I *h*.
Amos 5:15 *h*. the evil, and love the good
Luke 14:26 and *h*. not his father
Rom. 7:15 what I *h*. that do I
1 John 3:13 marvel not if the world *h*.
Rev. 2: 6 *h*. deeds, which I *h*.
17:16 these shall *h*. the whore

HATED (HATEST, HATETH)
Ex. 23: 5 ass of him that *h*. thee lying
Deut. 21:15 one beloved, and another *h*.
Ps. 5: 5 thou *h*. all workers of iniquity
50:17 seeing thou *h*. instruction
Prov. 1:29 for that they *h*. knowledge
5:12 how have I *h*. instruction
13:24 spareth rod, *h*. his son
Is. 66: 5 your brethren that *h*. you
Mal. 1: 3 I *h*. Esau, and laid his mountains
Mat. 10:22 shall be *h*. of all men
Luke 19:14 his citizens *h*. him, and sent
John 12:25 *h*. his life in this world
15:24 *h*. both seen, and me and my Father
Rom. 9:13 loved, but Esau have I *h*.
Eph. 5:29 no man *h*. his own flesh
1 John 2: 9 *h*. his brother is in darkness
3:15 *h*. his brother is a murderer
4:20 and *h*. his brother

HATEFUL
Tit. 3: 3 living in malice and envy, *h*.
Jude 1:23 *h*. garment spotted by flesh

HATERS
Rom. 1:30 backbiters, *h*. of God

HAUGHTY
Ps. 131: 1 Lord, my heart is not *h*.
Prov. 16:18 and an *h*. spirit before a fall
21:24 proud and *h*. scorner is his name
Zeph. 3:11 thou shalt no more be *h*. because

HAUGHTINESS
Is. 2:11 *h*. of men shall be bowed down
13:11 will lay low the *h*. of the
16: 6 he is very proud: even of his *h*.

HEAD
Gen. 3:15 it shall bruise thy *h*. and
49:26 blessings on Joseph's *h*.
Ezra 9: 6 iniquity increased over thy *h*.
Ps. 38: 4 iniquities gone over my *h*.
Prov. 16:31 hoary *h*. is a crown of glory
20:29 beauty of the old men is a gray *h*.
25:22 heap coals of fire upon his *h*.
Eccl. 2:14 wise man's eyes are in his *h*.
9: 8 let thy *h*. lack no ointment
Sol. 5: 2 my *h*. is filled with dew
5:11 his *h*. is as most fine gold
Is. 1: 5 whole *h*. is sick and the whole
1: 6 the sole of the foot even unto the *h*.
Jer. 9: 1 Oh that my *h*. were waters
48:37 every *h*. shall be bald
Ezek. 9:10 their way on their *h*.
16:43 thy way upon thy *h*.
Dan. 2:28 visions of thy *h*. on a bed
2:38 thou art this *h*. of gold
Zech. 4: 7 bring forth the *h*. stone
Mat. 8:20 where to lay his *h*.
14: 8 give me the *h*. of John Baptist
Rom. 12:20 coals of fire on his *h*.
Eph. 1:22 gave him to be *h*. over all
4:15 which is the *h*. even Christ
5:23 husband is the *h*. of the wife
Col. 1:18 he is the *h*. of the body
2:19 holding the *h*. from which all
Rev. 19:12 on his *h*. were many crowns

HEADS
Gen. 2:10 was parted and became into four *h*.
Ps. 24: 7 lift up your *h*, O ye gates
Is. 35:10 everlasting joy upon their *h*.
Luke 21:28 look up, and lift up your *h*.
Rev. 13: 1 having seven *h*. and ten horns

HEAL (HEALED, HEALETH)
Ex. 15:26 I the Lord that *h*. thee
Num. 12:13 Lord, saying, *h*. her now, O God
Deut. 32:39 I make alive; I wound, and I *h*.
2 Chr. 7:14 and will *h*. their land
30:20 Hezekiah, and *h*. the people
Ps. 6: 2 *h*. me, for my bones are
30: 2 unto thee and thou hast *h*. me
41: 4 *h*. my soul, for I have sinned
103: 3 who *h*. all thy diseases
147: 3 he *h*. the broken in heart
Is. 6:10 with their heart, and convert and be *h*.
30:26 *h*. the stroke of their wound
53: 5 with his stripes we are *h*.
57:18 seen his ways and will *h*. him
Jer. 3:22 I will *h*. your backslidings
6:14 *h*. the hurt of the daughter
15:18 which refuseth to be *h*.
17:14 *h*. me, and I shall be healed
Hos. 6: 1 hath torn and he will *h*. us
7: 1 I would have *h*. Israel
Mat. 4:24 had the palsy, and he *h*. them
12:15 followed him, and he *h*. them all
Luke 4:18 sent me to *h*. the brokenhearted
4:23 will say, Physician, *h*. thyself
John 12:40 converted and I should *h*.
Acts 28:27 and I should *h*. them
Heb. 12:13 let it rather be *h*.
Jas. 5:16 pray that ye may be *h*.
1 Pet. 2:24 by whose stripes ye were *h*.
Rev. 13: 3 his deadly wound was *h*.

HEALING
Jer. 14:19 for the time of *h*., and behold
30:13 thou hast no *h*. medicine
Mal. 4: 2 righteousness arise with *h*. in his wings
Mat. 4:23 *h*. all manner of sickness
1 Cor. 12: 9 to another the gifts of *h*.
Rev. 22: 2 tree were for the *h*. of the nations

HEALTH
Ps. 42:11 *h*. of countenance, and my God
Prov. 3: 8 shall be *h*. to thy navel, and marrow
12:18 the tongue of the wise is *h*.
Jer. 8:15 looked for a time of *h*.
30:17 I will restore *h*. and heal

HEAP (HEAPED, HEAPETH)
Deut. 32:23 I will *h.* mischiefs upon
Job 36:13 hypocrites in heart *h.* up wrath
Ps. 39: 6 he *h.* up riches, and knoweth not
Prov. 25:22 shalt *h.* coals of fire on
2 Tim. 4: 3 shall they *h.* to themselves teachers
Jas. 5: 3 ye have *h.* treasure together for

HEAPS
Judg. 15:16 *h.* upon *h.* with the jaw of an

HEAR
Deut. 30:17 if thou wilt not *h.*
1 Ki. 8:30 *h.* thou in heaven thy dwellingplace
2 Ki. 19:16 bow thine ear, and *h.*
2 Chr. 6:21 *h.* from thy dwelling
Job 5:27 *h.* it and know it for good
Ps. 4: 1 mercy upon me, and *h.* my prayer
10:17 thou wilt cause thine ear to *h.*
39:12 mercy upon me, and *h.* my prayer oh Lord
51: 8 make me to *h.* joy and gladness
59: 7 who, say they, doth *h.*
66:16 come and *h.* all ye that
84: 8 Lord God of hosts, *h.* my prayer
115: 6 they have ears, but *h.* not
143: 1 *h.* my prayer, O Lord, give ear
Prov. 19:27 cease to *h.* instruction
Eccl. 5: 1 be more ready to *h.* than
Sol. 2:14 let me *h.* thy voice
Is. 1: 2 *h.* O heavens, and give ear
6:10 lest they *h.* with ears
55: 3 *h.* and your soul shall live
Dan. 9:19 O Lord, *h.*; oh Lord forgive
Zech. 10: 6 the Lord their God, and will *h.* them
Mat. 10:27 what ye *h.* in the ear
13:17 to *h.* those things which ye *h.*
17: 5 I am well pleased, *h.* ye him
18:17 if he neglect to *h.* them
Mark 4:24 take heed in what ye *h.*
4:33 as they were able to *h.*
Luke 8:18 take heed therefore how ye *h.*
John 5:25 they that *h.* shall live
Acts 10:33 to *h.* all things that are commanded
Jas. 1:19 every man be swift to *h.*
Rev. 3:20 if any *h.* my voice, and open

HEARD
Ex. 2:24 God *h.* their groaning, and God remembered
Ps. 6: 9 Lord hath *h.* my supplication
10:17 hast *h.* the desire of the humble
34: 4 I sought the Lord, and he *h.*
61: 5 thou O God, hast *h.* my vows
66:19 verily God hath *h.* me
118: 21 I will praise thee, for thou hast *h.* me
120: 1 I cried to Lord, and he *h.*
Is. 40:28 hast thou not *h.* that God
Jer. 8: 6 I hearkened and *h.*, but they spake
Jonah 2: 2 I cried to Lord and he *h.*
Mal. 3:16 and the Lord hearkened and *h.* it
Mat. 6: 7 be *h.* for much speaking
Luke 1:13 thy prayer is *h.* and thy
John 3:32 what he hath seen and *h.*
8: 6 wrote as though he *h.* them not
Rom. 10:14 of whom they have not *h.*
1 Cor. 2: 9 eye hath not seen nor ear *h.*
Phil. 4: 9 learned and received and *h.*
Heb. 4: 2 with faith in them that *h.*
5: 7 was *h.* in that he feared
Jas. 5:11 ye have *h.* of the patience of Job
Rev. 3: 3 how thou hast received and *h.*

HEARER (HEARERS)
Rom. 2:13 not the *h.* of the law are just
Eph. 4:29 minister grace unto the *h.*
Jas. 1:22 doers of the word, and not *h.* only
1:25 not a forgetful *h.* but a doer

HEAREST (HEARETH)

HEARETH
1 Sam. 3: 9 speak, Lord; for thy servant *h.*
Ps. 65: 2 O thou that *h.* prayer, unto thee
Prov. 8:34 blessed the man that *h.* me
Mat. 7:24 whoso *h.* these sayings of mine
Luke 10:16 he that *h.* you *h.* me
John 9:31 God *h.* not sinners, but
11:42 I knew thou *h.* me always
1 John 5:14 ask according to his will he *h.*
Rev. 22:17 let him that *h.* say, Come

HEARING
Job 42: 5 of thee by the *h.* of the ear
Prov. 20:12 the *h.* ear, and the seeing eye
28: 9 turneth away his ear from *h.*
Rom. 10:17 faith cometh by *h.* and *h.* by
Heb. 5:11 seeing ye are dull of *h.*
2 Pet. 2: 8 in seeing and *h.* vexed his

HEARKEN
Deut. 28: 1 if thou *h.* diligently
28:15 if thou wilt not *h.* unto the voice
1 Sam. 15:22 to *h.* better than the fat of rams
Ps. 103: 20 angels *h.* to the voice of his word
Is. 46:12 *h.* unto me, ye stouthearted
51: 1 *h.* unto me, ye that follow
55: 2 *h.* diligently unto me, eat

HEART
Ex. 35: 5 whosoever is of a willing *h.*
Deut. 6: 5 love God with all thy *h.* and soul
11:13 serve him with all your *h.* and soul
26:16 keep and do them with all thy *h.* and
Josh. 22: 5 serve him with all your *h.*
1 Sam. 1:13 she spake in her *h.* only
10: 9 God gave him another *h.*
16: 7 but the Lord looketh on the *h.*
24: 5 David's *h.* smote him because
2 Ki. 20: 3 thee in truth and with perfect *h.*
1 Chr. 16:10 let the *h.* of them rejoice
22:19 now set your *h.* and your soul
28: 9 serve him with a perfect *h.*
2 Chr. 17: 6 *h.* lifted up in the Lord's ways
30:19 prepareth his *h.* to seek God
Ps. 22:26 your *h.* shall live for ever
24: 4 clean hands and a pure *h.*
37:31 law of his God is in his *h.*
45: 1 my *h.* is inditing a good
51:17 a broken and contrite *h.*, O God
57: 7 my *h.* is fixed, O God
64: 6 every one of them, and the *h.*, is deep
73:26 my flesh and my *h.* faileth, but
78:37 their *h.* was not right with
84: 2 my *h.* and my flesh crieth for the
Prov. 3: 5 trust in Lord with all thy *h.*
4:23 keep thy *h.* with diligence
10:20 *h.* of the wicked is little worth
14:10 *h.* knoweth its own bitterness
16: 9 a man's *h.* deviseth his way
27:19 so the *h.* of man to man
Eccl. 7: 4 *h.* of the wise is in the house
10: 2 wise man's *h.* at his right hand
Sol. 3:11 day of the gladness of his *h.*
5: 2 I sleep, but my *h.* waketh
Is. 6:10 make the *h.* of this people fat
57:15 to revive the *h.* of the contrite ones
Jer. 3:15 give pastors according to my *h.*
11:20 triest reins and the *h.* let me see
12:11 no man layeth it to *h.*
17: 9 *h.* is deceitful above all things
24: 7 I will give them an *h.* to know
29:13 search for me with all your *h.*
32:39 And I will give them one *h.*
Lam. 3:41 lift up our *h.* with hands
Ezek. 11:19 I will give them an *h.* of flesh
18:31 make you a new *h.*, and a new spirit
36:26 I will take away the stony *h.*
Joel 2:13 rend your *h.* not garments
Mal. 4: 6 turn the *h.* of the fathers
Mat. 5: 8 blessed are the pure in *h.*
6:21 there will your *h.* be also
12:35 of good treasure of the *h.*
15:19 out of the *h.* proceed evil thoughts
22:37 Lord thy God with all thy *h.*
Luke 2:19 pondered them in her *h.*
2:51 mother kept all these sayings in her *h.*
10:27 love the Lord thy God, with all thy *h.*
24:25 O fools, slow of *h.* to believe
24:32 did not our *h.* burn within us
John 14: 1 let not your *h.* be troubled
Acts 5:33 that they were cut to the *h.*
11:23 with the purpose of *h.* they would cleave
13:22 found a man after mine own *h.*
Rom. 10:10 with the *h.* man believeth
1 Cor. 2: 9 nor entered into the *h.* of man
2 Cor. 3: 3 in fleshy tables of the *h.*
1 Tim. 1: 5 charity out of a pure *h.*
2 Tim. 2:22 call on the Lord out of a pure *h.*
1 Pet. 1:22 love one another with pure *h.*
3: 4 the hidden man of the *h.*
1 John 3:20 if the *h.* condemn us, God

HEATHEN
Lev. 25:44 shall be of the *h.* that are round
26:45 in the sight of the *h.*
Ps. 2: 1 why do the *h.* rage
2: 8 give thee the *h.* for thine
Acts. 4:25 why did the *h.* rage
Gal. 3: 8 justify the *h.* through faith

HEAVEN
1 Ki. 8:27 the *h.* and the *h.* of heavens
2 Chr. 6:18 behold, *h.*, and the *h.* of heavens
Ps. 73:25 whom have I in *h.* but thee
103: 11 as *h.* is high above the
115: 16 *h.* even the heavens are the Lord's
Prov. 25: 3 *h.* for height, and earth
Eccl. 5: 2 God is in *h.* thou upon earth
Is. 66: 1 *h.* is my throne, and the earth
Jer. 31:37 if *h.* can be measured
Hag. 1:10 *h.* is stayed from dew
Luke 15:18 sinned against *h.*, and before thee
John 1:51 you shall see *h.* open and angels
Acts 3:21 the *h.* must receive until the times
7:49 *h.* is my throne, and the earth
Heb. 10:34 have in *h.* a better substance
1 Pet. 1: 4 inheritance reserved in *h.*
Rev. 21: 1 saw a new *h.* and a new earth

HEAVENS
Ps. 8: 3 when I consider thy *h.*
19: 1 the *h.* declare the glory of God
89:11 the *h.* are thine, and earth also
Is. 65:17 I create new *h.* and a new earth
66:22 for as the new *h.* and the new earth
2 Cor. 5: 1 a house eternal in the *h.*
Eph. 4:10 ascended far above all *h.*
2 Pet. 3:12 *h.* being on fire shall be dissolved

HEAVENLY
Mat. 6:14 your *h.* Father will also
18:35 likewise shall my *h.* Father do
Luke 11:13 your *h.* father give the
John 3:12 if I tell you of *h.* things
1 Cor. 15:48 and as is the *h.* such are they
Eph. 1: 3 all spiritual blessings in *h.* places
2: 6 in *h.* places in Christ Jesus
2 Tim. 4:18 will preserve me unto his *h.* kingdom
Heb. 3: 1 partakers of the *h.* calling

HEAVY
Prov. 31: 6 wine to those of *h.* hearts
Is. 6:10 make their ears *h.* lest
58: 6 to undo the *h.* burdens, and to let
Mat. 11:28 that labour and are *h.* laden
23: 4 bind *h.* burdens and grievous

HEAVINESS
Ps. 69:20 I am full of *h.*: and I looked
119: 28 my soul melteth for *h.*
Prov. 12:25 *h.* in the heart maketh it stoop
14:13 end of that mirth is *h.*
Rom. 9: 2 I have great *h.* and sorrow
1 Pet. 1: 6 in *h.* through manifold temptations

HEED
Deut. 2: 4 take good *h.* to yourselves
Josh. 22: 5 take diligent *h.* to do the
2 Sam. 20:10 But Amasa took no *h.* to the sword
2 Ki. 10:31 took no *g.* to walk in the law
Ps. 119: 9 by taking *h.* thereto according to
Jer. 18:18 not give *h.* to any of his

HEEL (HEELS)
Gen. 3:15 thou shalt bruise his heel
Ps. 41: 9 lifted his *h.* against me
49: 5 iniquity of *h.* shall compass
Hos. 12: 3 he took his brother by the *h.*
John 13:18 lifted up his *h.* against me

HEIFER
Num. 19: 2 that they bring thee a red *h.*
Jer. 46:20 Egypt is like a fair *h.*
Hos. 4:16 slideth back as a backsliding *h.*
Heb. 9:13 the ashes of an *h.* sprinkling

HEIR (HEIRS)
Gen. 15: 4 own bowels shall be thine *h.*
21:10 bondwoman shall not be *h.*
Jer. 49: 1 Israel no sons? Hath he no *h.*
Rom. 4:13 should be *h.* of the world
8:17 *h.* of God, joint *h.* with Christ
Gal. 3:29 Abraham's seed and *h.* according to
4: 7 if a son, then an *h.* of God
Eph. 3: 6 Gentiles should be fellow *h.*

Heb. 1: 2 whom he hath appointed *h.* of all
6:17 willing to show *h.* of promise
11: 7 became *h.* of the righteousness
1 Pet. 3: 7 *h.* together of the grace of life

HELL
Deut. 32:22 shall burn to the lowest *h.*
2 Sam. 22: 6 the sorrows of *h.* compassed me
Job 11: 8 it is deeper than *h.*; what
26: 6 *h.* is naked before him and
Ps. 9:17 wicked shall be turned into *h.*
16:10 not leave my soul in *h.*
55:15 let them go down quick into *h.*
86:13 delivered my soul from lowest *h.*
139: 8 make my bed in *h.* thou art
Prov. 5: 5 her steps take hold on *h.*
7:27 her house is the way to *h.*
9:18 her guests are in the depths of *h.*
15:11 *h.* and destruction before the Lord
15:24 that he may depart from *h.*
23:14 shalt deliver his soul from *h.*
27:20 *h.* and destruction are never full
Is. 5:14 *h.* hath enlarged herself, and opened
14: 9 *h.* from beneath is moved for thee
14:15 thou shalt be brought down to *h.*
57: 9 debase thyself even to *h.*
Amos 9: 2 though they dig into *h.*
Jonah 2: 2 out of the belly of *h.* cried I
Hab. 2: 5 enlargeth his desire as *h.*
Mat. 5:22 be in danger of *h.* fire
5:29 body should be cast into *h.*
10:28 destroy soul and body in *h.*
11:23 heaven shalt be brought down to *h.*
16:18 gates of *h.* shall not prevail
18: 9 to be cast into *h.* fire
23:15 twofold more than the child of *h.*
Mark 9:45 to be cast into *h.*
Luke 12: 5 power to cast into *h.*
16:23 in *h.* he lift up his eyes
Acts 2:27 wilt not leave my soul in *h.*
2:31 his soul not left in *h.*
Jas. 3: 6 tongue set on the fire of *h.*
2 Pet. 2: 4 cast them down to *h.*
Rev. 1:18 have the keys of *h.* and
6: 8 Death, and *H.* followed with
20:13 death and *h.* delivered up the dead
20:14 death and *h.* were cast into

HELMET
1 Sam. 17: 5 he had an *h.* of brass
2 Chr. 26:14 and spears, and *h.*, and habergeons
Eph. 6:17 take the *h.* of salvation
1 Thes. 5: 8 an *h.*, hope of salvation

HELP
Gen. 2:18 make him an *h.* meet for him
Deut. 33:29 Lord, the shield of thy *h.*
Judg. 5:23 came not to the *h.* of the Lord
2 Chr. 14:11 nothing with thee to *h.*
Ps. 27: 9 thou hast been my *h.*
33:20 he is our *h.* and shield
40:13 make haste to *h.* me
40:17 thou art my *h.* and my deliverer
46: 1 God a very present *h.* in trouble
60:11 vain is the *h.* of man
71:12 my God, make haste for my *h.*
89:19 laid *h.* on one that is mighty
115: 9 Lord is our *h.* and shield
124: 8 our *h.* is in the name of Lord
Is. 41:10 I will *h.* thee
63: 5 I looked and there was none to *h.*
Hos. 13: 9 but in me is thy *h.*
Acts 16: 9 come to Macedonia, and *h.* us
26:22 having obtained the *h.* of God
Heb. 4:16 find grace to *h.* in time

HELPED (HELPETH)
1 Sam. 7:12 hitherto hath the Lord *h.* us
Is. 49: 8 in the day of salvation I *h.*
Zech. 1:15 and they *h.* forward the affliction
Acts 18:27 *h.* them much which believed
Rom. 8:26 the Spirit also *h.* our infirmities
Rev. 12:16 the earth *h.* the woman

HELPER (HELPERS)
Job 9:13 proud *h.* do stoop under him
Ps. 10:14 art the *h.* of the fatherless
2 Cor. 1:24 faith, but are the *h.* of your joy
3 John 1: 8 we might be fellow *h.* to the truth

HEM
Mat. 9:20 touched the *h.* of his garment
14:36 touch the *h.* of his garment

HEN
Mat. 23:37 even as a *h.* gathereth
Luke 13:34 as a *h.* gathereth her brood

HERESY (HERESIES)
Acts 24:14 way which they call *h.*
Gal. 5:20 strife, seditions, *h.*
1 Cor. 11:19 there must also be *h.*
2 Pet. 2: 1 shall bring in damnable *h.*

HERITAGE
Job 20:29 and the *h.* appointed unto him
Ps. 16: 6 I have a goodly *h.*
61: 5 *h.* of those that fear thy name
119:111 testimonies taken as *h.* for
Is. 54:17 *h.* of the servant of the Lord's
Jer. 3:19 goodly *h.* of the hosts of nations
Joel 2:17 give not thine *h.* to reproach
1 Pet. 5: 3 not as lords over God's *h.*

HEW
Ex. 34: 1 *h.* thee two tables of stone
Deut. 12: 3 ye shall *h.* the graven images

HEWED
Jer. 2:13 *h.* them out cisterns, broken cisterns
Hos. 6: 5 have I *h.* them by the prophets

HIDE (HID, HIDDEN, HIDEST, HIDETH)
Gen. 3: 8 Adam and his wife *h.* themselves
18:17 shall I *h.* from Abraham that thing
Job 13:24 why *h.* thou thy face
33:17 and *h.* thy pride from man
34:29 when he *h.* his face
42: 3 who is he that *h.* counsel
Ps. 17: 8 *h.* me under the shadow
27: 5 in time of trouble he shall *h.* me
30: 7 didst *h.* thy face and I was troubled
31:20 shalt *h.* them in the secret
44:24 wherefore *h.* thou thy face
51: 9 *h.* thy face from my sins
88:14 why *h.* thou thy face
119: 11 thy word have I *h.* in mine heart
139: 12 the darkness *h.* not from thee
143: 7 *h.* not thy face from me
Is. 8:17 I will wait on the Lord that *h.*
26:20 *h.* thyself as it were for a little
45:15 thou art a God that *h.* thyself
Mat. 10:26 and *h.* that shall not be known
11:25 hast *h.* these things from the wise
1 Cor. 4: 5 bring to light *h.* things
2 Cor. 4: 3 if the gospel be *h.* it is *h.* to
Col. 2: 3 in whom are *h.* all the treasures
3: 3 your life is *h.* with Christ in God
Jas. 5:20 and shall *h.* a multitude of sins
1 Pet. 3: 4 let it be the *h.* man of heart
Rev. 2:17 give to eat of the *h.* manna
6:16 *h.* us from the face of him

HIGH
Num. 24:16 the knowledge of the most *h.*
Deut. 12: 2 served their Gods upon the *h.* mountains
26:19 make thee *h.* above all
32: 8 when the most *h.* divided
2 Sam. 22:14 the most *h.* uttered
1 Ki. 9: 8 at this house which is *h.*
1 Chr. 17:17 estate of a man of *h.* degree
Job 5:11 set on *h.* those that be
11: 8 It is as *h.* as heaven, what canst
16:19 and my record is on *h.*
Ps. 49: 2 both low and *h.*, rich and
56: 2 O thou most *h.*
47: 2 the Lord most *h.* is terrible
83:18 Jehovah art most *h.* over all earth
89:13 strong hand, and *h.* is his right hand
97: 9 Lord art *h.* above all the earth
103: 11 as heaven is *h.* above the earth and my record is on *h.*
107: 41 setteth the poor on *h.*
113: 5 like our God who dwelleth on *h.*
131: 1 or in things too *h.* for me
138: 6 though the Lord be *h.* yet hath
Eccl. 12: 5 afraid of that which is *h.*
Is. 14:14 I will be like the most *h.*
26: 5 bringeth down those that dwell on *h.*
57:15 I dwell in the *h.* and holy place
Ezek. 21:26 is low, and abase him that is *h.*
Hos. 11: 7 called them to the most *h.*
Luke 24:49 be endued with power from on *h.*
Acts 7:48 most *h.* dwelleth not in temples
Rom. 12:16 mind not *h.* things, but condescend
2 Cor. 10: 5 every *h.* thing that exalteth itself

Phil. 3:14 the prize of the *h.* calling of God

HIGHER (HIGHEST)
Ps. 18:13 *H.* gave his voice; hail stones and
Eccl. 5: 8 he that is *h.* than the *h.*
Is. 55: 9 as the heavens are *h.* then
Luke 1:35 power of the *H.* shall overshadow
2:14 glory to God in the *h.*
6:35 shall be the children of the *H.*
Heb. 7:26 made *h.* than the heavens

HIGHLY
Luke 1:28 thou that art *h.* favoured
16:15 is *h.* esteemed among men
Rom. 12: 3 not to think of himself more *h.*
1 Thes. 5:13 to esteem them very *h.* in love

HEIGHT
Job 22:12 Is not God in the *h.*
Rom. 8:39 nor *h.* nor depth nor any other creature
Eph. 3:18 length, and depth and *h.*, nor any other

HILL (HILLS)
Gen. 7:19 all the high *h.* covered
49:26 utmost bound of everlasting *h.*
Ex. 24: 4 and builded an altar under the *h.*
Num. 23: 9 from the *h.* I beheld him
Ps. 2: 6 set the King on the holy *h.* of Zion
65:12 little *h.* rejoice on every side
68:15 is as the *h.* of Bashan
68:16 why leap ye, ye high *h.*
98: 8 let the *h.* be joyful together
99: 9 worship at his holy *h.*
114: 4 little *h.* skipped like lambs
Hos. 10: 8 and to the *h.* fall on us
Hab. 3: 6 the perpetual *h.* did bow
Luke 23:30 and to the *h.*, cover us

HOLD (HOLDETH, HOLDING)
Ex. 20: 7 will not *h.* him guiltless
Judg. 9:46 *h.* of the house of the god Berith
Job 2: 3 still he *h.* fast integrity
17: 9 righteous shall *h.* on to the way
Ps. 66: 9 which *h.* our soul in life
Prov. 17:28 fool when he *h.* his peace counted wise
Is. 41:13 God will *h.* thy right hand
62: 1 for Zion's sake will I not *h.* my peace
Jer. 2:13 cisterns that can *h.* no water
6:11 I am weary with *h.* in; I will
Mat. 6:24 *h.* to one, despise the other
Phil. 2:16 *h.* forth the word of life
2:29 gladness; and *h.* such in reputation
Col. 2:19 not *h.* the Head, from which all
1 Thes. 5:21 *h.* fast to that which is good
1 Tim. 1:19 *h.* faith and a good conscience
3: 9 *h.* mystery of faith in a pure conscience
2 Tim. 1:13 *h.* fast to the form of sound words
Tit. 1: 9 *h.* fast the faithful word
Heb. 3: 6 if we *h.* fast the confidence
3:14 if we *h.* the beginning of our confidence
4:14 let us *h.* fast our profession, 10:23.
Rev. 2:25 what ye have *h.* fast till I come
3: 3 received and heard *h.* fast and repent
3:11 *h.* fast that which thou hast

HOLY
Ex. 3: 5 thou standest is *h.* ground
19: 6 of priests, and an *h.* nation
26:33 the *h.* place, and the most *h.*
28:38 bear the iniquity of *h.* things
29: 6 the *h.* crown upon the mitre
30:25 make it an oil of *h.* ointment
31:15 Sabbath of rest *h.* to the Lord
Lev. 11:45 be *h.* for I am *h.*
16:33 an atonement for the *h.* sanctuary
20: 3 to profane my *h.* name
21:22 both of the most *h.* and the *h.*
27:14 sanctify his house to be *h.*
27:30 it is *h.* unto the Lord
Num. 5:17 priest shall take *h.* water
31: 6 the war with the *h.* instruments
Deut. 7: 6 for thou art an *h.* people
28: 9 an *h.* people unto himself
33: 8 Urim be with the *h.* one
1 Sam. 2: 2 there is none *h.* as Lord
21: 5 vessels of the young men are *h.*
1 Ki. 6:16 for the most *h.* place
1 Chr. 16:35 my give thanks to my *h.* name
2 Chr. 3: 8 made the most *h.* house

Ps. 5: 7 I worship toward the *h.* temple
16:10 thou suffer thine *H.* one
22: 3 but thou art *h.*, O thou
33:21 trusted in his *h.* name
87: 1 foundation is in the *h.* mountains
99: 5 worship at his footstool, for he is *h.*
138: 2 will worship toward thy *h.* temple
145: 17 *h.* in all his works
Prov. 20:25 man who devoureth that which is *h.*
Is. 11: 9 nor destroy in all my *h.* mountain
49: 7 redeemer of Israel, and his *H.* one
62:12 the *h.* people, the redeemed
Ezek. 22:26 no difference between the *h.*
36:20 they profaned my *h.* name
43:12 whole limit shall be most *h.*
Dan. 4:13 an *h.* one came down from heaven
12: 7 scatter the power of the *h.* people
Hos. 11: 9 the *H.* one in the midst of thee
Joel 2: 1 an alarm in my *h.* mountain
Obad. 1:16 drunk upon my *h.* mountain
Jonah 2: 7 in unto thee, into thine *h.* temple
Mic. 1: 2 the Lord from his *h.* temple
Hab. 1:12 O Lord my God, mine *H.* one
2:20 the Lord is in his *h.* temple
Mat. 7: 6 give not that which is *h.* unto the dogs
Luke 1:35 *h.* thing which shall be born
Acts 3:14 denied the *H.*, and the Just
4:27 truth against thy *h.* child Jesus
Rom. 7:12 wherefore the law is *h.*
11:16 for if the firstfruit is *h.*
12: 1 sacrifice, *h.*, acceptable to God
1 Cor. 7:14 children unclean, now *h.*
Eph. 2:21 unto an *h.* temple in the Lord
2 Tim. 1: 9 called us with *h.* calling
3:15 hast known the *h.* scriptures
Tit. 1: 8 sober, just, *h.*, temperate
1 Pet. 1:15 be ye *h.* in all manner of conversation
2: 5 a *h.* priesthood, to offer up
2: 9 an *h.* nation, a peculiar
2 Pet. 1:21 *h.* men of God spake as
1 John 2:20 have an unction from the *H.* one
Jude 1:20 building yourselves in most *h.* faith
Rev. 3: 7 he that is *h.*. he that is true
4: 8 *h. h. h.* Lord God Almighty
15: 4 fear thee for thou only art *h.*
22:11 he that is *h.* let him be *h.* still

HOLINESS
Ex. 15:11 like thee glorious in *h.*
28:36 *h.* to the Lord
1 Chr. 16:29 worship the Lord in the beauty of *h.*
2 Chr. 20:21 praise the beauty of his *h.*
31:18 sanctified themselves in *h.*
Ps. 29: 2 worship the Lord in the beauty of *h.*
30: 4 thanks at the remembrance of his *h.*
47: 8 God sitteth upon the throne of his *h.*
60: 6 God hath spoken in his *h.*
89:35 I have sworn by my *h.*
93: 5 *h.* becometh thine house, O Lord
110: 3 in the beauties of *h.*; from the
Is. 23:18 shall be *h.* to the Lord
35: 8 shall be called the way of *h.*
62: 9 drink it in the courts of my *h.*
63:18 the people of thy *h.* have possessed
Jer. 2: 3 Israel was *h.* unto the Lord
23: 9 because of the Lord and words of his *h.*
Amos 4: 2 Lord hath sworn by his *h.*
Obad. 1:17 deliverance and there shall be *h.*
Zech. 14:20 on horse bells, *h.* to Lord
Mal. 2:11 Judah profaned the *h.* of the Lord
Luke 1:75 in *h.* and righteousness
Acts 3:12 by your own power or *h.*
Rom. 1: 4 according to the Spirit of *h.*
6:22 ye have your fruit unto *h.*
2 Cor. 7: 1 perfecting *h.* in the fear of God
Eph. 4:24 in righteousness and true *h.*
1 Thes. 3:13 unblameable in *h.* before God
1 Tim. 2:15 charity, *h.* with sobriety
Tit. 2: 3 behaviour as becometh *h.*
Heb. 12:10 we might be partakers of his *h.*
12:14 follow peace with all men, and *h.*

HOLY GHOST
Mat. 1:18 was found with child of the *H.*
3:11 ye shall be baptize you with the *H.*
3:12 blasphemy against the *H.*
Mark 12:36 for David himself said by the *H.*
13:11 not ye that speak, but the *H.*
Luke 1:15 *H.* shall come upon thee
1:26 revealed unto him by the *H.*
3:22 *H.* descended in bodily shape
12:12 *H.* shall teach you what to say
John 7:39 for the *H.* was not yet given
14:26 Comforter, which is the *H.*
20:22 unto them receive ye the *H.*
Acts 1: 2 through the *H.* had given commandment
1: 5 baptized with the *H.*
1: 8 after that the *H.* is come upon you
2:38 receive the gift of the *H.*
5: 3 filled thine heart to lie to the *H.*
5:32 and so is also the *H.*
7:51 ye do always resist the *H.*
8:15 they might receive the *H.*
9:31 walking in the comfort of the *H.*
10:38 with the *H.*, and with power
10:44 the *H.* fell on all them which
11:16 be baptized with the *H.*
13: 2 and fasted, the *H.* said; Separate me
13: 4 they being sent forth by the *H.*
15:28 it seemed good to the *H.* and us
16: 6 forbidden of the *H.* to preach in
20:23 save that the *H.* witnesseth
20:28 flock over which the *H.* made you overseers
21:11 thus saith the *H.* so shall the Jews
Rom. 5: 5 by the *H.* which is given
9: 1 conscience bearing witness in the *H.*
14:17 righteousness, peace, joy in the *H.*
15:16 being sanctified by the *H.*
1 Cor. 2:13 in words the *H.* teacheth
6:19 your body is the temple of the *H.*
2 Cor. 6: 6 by the *H.* by love unfeigned
13:14 communion of the *H.* be with you
1 Thes. 1: 5 in power and in the *H.*
2 Tim. 1:14 keep by the *H.* which
Tit. 3: 5 by the renewing of the *H.*
Heb. 2: 4 with gifts of the *H.*
3: 7 as the *H.* saith, today if
9: 8 *H.* this signifying, that the way
1 Pet. 1:12 preached gospel with the *H.*
2 Pet. 1:21 they were moved by the *H.*
1 John 5: 7 Father, Word, and the *H.*
Jude 1:20 holy faith praying in the *H.*

HOLY SPIRIT
Ps. 51:11 take not thy *H.* from me
Is. 63:10 rebelled and vexed his *H.*
63:11 where is he that put his *H.* within
Luke 11:13 give the *H.* to them that ask
Eph. 1:13 sealed with the *H.*
4:30 grieve not the *H.* of God
1 Thes. 4: 8 God, who hath given his *H.*

HOME
Ruth 1:21 Lord hath brought me *h.* again empty
Job 39:12 he will bring *h.* thy seed
Ps. 68:12 tarried at *h.* divided the spoil
Eccl. 12: 5 man goeth to his long *h.*
2 Cor. 5: 6 whilst at *h.* in body, absent
Tit. 2: 5 chaste, keepers at *h.*, good

HONEST (HONESTLY)
Luke 8:15 which in an *h.* and good heart
Acts 6: 3 seven men of *h.* report, full
Rom. 12:17 provide things *h.* in the sight
13:13 let us walk *h.* as in the day
2 Cor. 8:21 Providing for *h.* things not only
13: 7 should do that which is *h.*
Phil. 4: 8 are true whatsoever things are *h.*
1 Thes. 4:12 ye may walk *h.* toward them
Heb. 13:18 in all things willing to live *h.*
1 Pet. 2:12 having your conversation *h.* among

HONEY
Gen. 43:11 and a little *h.*, spices myrrh
Ex. 16:31 taste was like wafers made with *h.*
Judg. 14:18 what is sweeter than *h.*
1 Ki. 14: 3 and a cruse of *h.*, and go to him
Ps. 19:10 fine gold sweeter also than *h.*
81:16 with *h.* out of the rock should I
Sol. 4:11 *h.* and milk under thy tongue
Is. 7:15 butter and *h.* shall he eat
Ezek. 27:17 Pannag, and *h.*, and oil, and balm
Mat. 3: 4 his meat locusts and wild *h.*
Rev. 10: 9 shall be in thy mouth sweet as *h.*

HONEYCOMB
1 Sam. 14:27 and dipped it in an *h.*

HONOUR
Gen. 49: 6 to their assembly, mine *h.*
Ex. 14:17 I will get me *h.* upon Pharaoh
Judg. 4: 9 shall not be for thine *h.*
1 Sam. 2:30 that *h.* me I will *h.*
15:30 *h.* me before the elders
1 Chr. 29:12 both riches and *h.* come of thee
2 Chr. 26:18 shall it be for thine *h.*
Ps. 7: 5 lay mine *h.* in the dust
8: 5 crowned him with glory and *h.*
26: 8 place where thine *h.* dwelleth
49:20 man in *h.* understandeth not
149: 9 this *h.* have all his saints
Prov. 3: 9 *h.* the Lord with substance
3:16 her left hand riches and *h.*
14:28 the people is the king's *h.*
15:33 wisdom: and before *h.* is humility
20: 3 it is an *h.* to cease from strife
21:21 findeth life, righteousness, and *h.*
25: 2 *h.* of kings to search a matter
26: 1 *h.* is not seemly for a fool
29:23 *h.* shall uphold the humble
Is. 29:13 with their lips do *h.* me
Mat. 13:57 prophet is not without *h.*
John 5:41 I receive not *h.* from men
5:23 *h.* the Son as they *h.* the Father
12:26 serve me, him will my Father *h.*
Rom. 2: 7 in well doing seek glory, *h.*
9:21 make one vessel to *h.*, and another
12:10 in *h.* preferring one another
2 Cor. 6: 8 by *h.* and dishonour, by evil report
1 Tim. 5: 3 *h.* widows that are widows indeed
Heb. 5: 4 taketh this *h.* to himself
1 Pet. 1: 7 found unto praise and *h.*
2:17 *h.* all men. Love thy brotherhood
3: 7 giving *h.* unto the wife

HOPE
Ezra 10: 2 now there is *h.* in Israel
Job 11:20 *h.* shall be as giving up
17:15 where is now my *h.*? as for my *h.*
31:24 if I have made gold my *h.*
Ps. 16: 9 my flesh shall rest in *h.*
22: 9 didst make me *h* on my mother's
33:18 them that *h.* in his mercy
39: 7 wait I for my *h.* is in thee
42: 5 *h.* thou in God, for I shall
78: 7 might set their *h.* in God
119: 49 thou hast caused me to *h.*
119: 81 I *h.* in thy word
Prov. 10:28 *h.* of the righteous shall be gladness
11: 7 *h.* of unjust men perisheth
14:32 righteous hath *h.* in his death
19:18 chasten thy son while there is *h.*
26:12 more *h.* of a fool than of him
Is. 57:10 saidst thou not, There is no *h.*
Jer. 14: 8 the *h.* of Israel, the Saviour
17: 7 blessed whose *h.* the Lord is
18:12 they said, there is no *h.*
50: 7 the *h.* of their fathers
Lam. 3:26 good that a man should *h.*
3:29 if so be there be *h.*
Ezek. 37:11 bones are dried and our *h.* is lost
Hos. 2:15 valley of Achor for the door of *h.*
Joel 3:16 Lord will be the *h.* of his people
Zech. 9:12 to the strong hold, ye prisoners of *h.*
Acts 24:15 have *h.* towards God, which they
28:20 for the *h.* of Israel I am bound
Rom. 5: 4 patience experience; experience, *h.*
5: 5 *h.* maketh not ashamed; because
8:24 we are saved by *h.*: but *h.*
8:25 if we *h.* for that we see not
15: 4 comfort of scriptures, have *h.*
1 Cor. 13:13 now abideth faith, *h.*, charity
15:19 in this life only we have *h.*
Gal. 5: 5 wait for the *h.* of righteousness
Eph. 2:12 having no *h.* and without God
Col. 1:23 away from the *h.* of the gospel
1 Thes. 4:13 as others which have no *h.*
5: 8 for the helmet, the *h.* of salvation
1 Tim. 1: 1 Jesus Christ who is our *h.*
Tit. 2:13 looking for that blessed *h.*
Heb. 6:11 to the full assurance of *h.*
6:19 which *h.* we have as an anchor
1 Pet. 1: 3 begotten again to lively *h.*
1:13 be sober and *h.* to the end
3:15 asketh a reason of *h.* in you
1 John 3: 3 every man that hath this *h.*

HORN (HORNS)
1 Sam. 2: 1 my *h.* is exalted in the Lord

Ps. 18: 2 and the *h.* of my salvation
92:10 my *h.* is as the *h.* of a unicorn
148: 14 he exalteth the *h.* of his
Mic. 4:13 I will make thy *h.* iron
Rev. 5: 6 as it had been slain having seven *h.*
13: 1 having seven heads and ten *h.*

HORSE (HORSES)
Ex. 15:21 the *h.* and his rider hath he thrown
Ps. 32: 9 be ye not as the *h.* or mule
33:17 *h.* is a vain thing for safety
147: 10 delighteth not in the strength of the *h.*
Eccl. 10: 7 have seen servants on *h.*
Jer. 8: 6 as the *h.* rusheth into battle
12: 5 canst thou contend with *h.*
Hos. 14: 3 we will not ride upon *h.*
Zech. 1: 8 there red *h.* speckled and white
6: 6 black *h.* which are there
Rev. 6: 8 and behold a pale *h.*

HOSPITALITY
Rom. 12:13 necessity of saints; given to *h.*
1 Tim. 3: 2 of good behavior, given to *h.*
Tit. 1: 8 but a lover of *h.*, a lover of
1 Pet. 4: 9 use *h.* one to another

HOST (HOSTS)
Ps. 27: 3 an *h.* should encamp against me
33:16 by the multitude of an *h.*
148: 2 praise ye him, all his *h.*
103: 21 Bless ye the Lord, all ye his *h.*
Is. 40:26 bringeth out their *h.* by number
Jer. 3:19 a goodly heritage of the *h.*
Luke 2:13 multitude of the heavenly *h.*
10:35 and gave them to the *h.*
Rom. 16:23 Gaius, mine *h.*, and of the whole

HOT
Ps. 38: 1 chasten me in thy *h.* displeasure
39: 3 my heart was *h.* within me
Prov. 6:28 can one go upon *h.* coals
Hos. 7: 7 they are all *h.* as an oven
1 Tim. 4: 2 seared with a *h.* iron
Rev. 3:15 thou art neither cold nor *h.*

HOUR
Dan. 3:15 shall be cast the same *h.*
4:33 the same *h.* was the thing
Mat. 10:19 given you in that same *h.*
24:36 day and *h.* knoweth no man
25:13 know neither day nor *h.*
Luke 12:12 Holy Ghost shall teach you that same *h.*
22:53 this is your *h.* and power
John 2: 4 mine *h.* is not yet come
4:23 *h.* cometh, and now is when
7:30 his *h.* was not yet come
Rev. 3: 3 not know what *h.* I come
3:10 keep from the *h.* of temptation
17:12 power as kings one *h.* with the beast
18:10 in one *h.* is thy judgment

HOUSE
Gen. 28:17 is none other but the *h.* of God
Ex. 12:30 not a *h.* where there was not one
Deut. 6: 7 when thou sittest in thine *h.*
Josh. 24:15 as for me and my *h.*
2 Sam. 23: 5 although my *h.* be not so with God
Job 21:28 where is the *h.* of the prince
30:23 *h.* appointed for all living
Ps. 23: 6 in the *h.* of the Lord
26: 8 I loved the habitation of thine *h.*
36: 8 satisfied with the fatness of thine *h.*
55:14 unto the *h.* of God in company
101: 2 I will walk within my *h.* with
105: 21 him lord of all his *h.*
112: 3 wealth and riches shall be in his *h.*
Prov. 3:33 curse of the Lord is in the *h.* of
7:27 her *h.* is the way to hell
12: 7 *h.* of the righteous shall stand
Eccl. 5: 1 goest to the *h.* of God
7: 2 go to the *h.* of mourning
12: 3 when keepers of the *h.* tremble
Sol. 2: 4 brought me to the banqueting *h.*
Is. 2: 3 to the *h.* of the God of Jacob
5: 8 woe to them that join *h.* to *h.*
38: 1 set thine *h.* in order, for thou
60: 7 I will glorify the *h.* of my
64:11 our holy and beautiful *h.*
Mic. 4: 2 to the *h.* of the God of Jacob
Mat. 10:13 if the *h.* be worthy, let your peace
12:25 a *h.* divided against itself shall not
12:44 I will return into my *h.* from
23:38 *h.* is left unto you desolate
Luke 11:17 and a *h.* divided against a *h.*
11:24 I will return unto my *h.*
12: 3 proclaimed upon the *h.* tops
John 4:53 believed and his whole *h.*
14: 2 in my Father's *h.* are many
Acts 10: 2 feared God with all his *h.*
11:14 thou and all thine *h.* saved
16:31 thou shalt be saved, and thy *h.*
16:34 believing in God with all his *h.*
Rom. 16: 5 greet the church that is in their *h.*
1 Cor. 16:19 church that is in their *h.*
Col. 4:15 the church which is in his *h.*
1 Tim. 3:15 behave thyself in the *h.* of God
5: 8 specially for those of his own *h.*
2 Tim. 1:16 mercy to the *h.* of Onesiphorus
Philem. 1: 2 to the church in thy *h.*
Heb. 3: 2 faithful in all his *h.*
3: 3 *h.* more honour than the *h.*
1 Pet. 4:17 must begin at the *h.* of God
2 John 1:10 receive him not to your *h.*

HOUSES
Job 4:19 dwell in *h.* of clay
Ps. 49:11 *h.* shall continue for ever
Prov. 19:14 *h.* and riches are the inheritance
Mat. 11: 8 wear soft clothing are in king's *h.*
19:29 everyone that hath forsaken *h.*
23:14 hypocrites! for ye devour widows' *h.*
Mark 10:29 no man that hath left the *h.*
Luke 16: 4 may receive me into their *h.*
20:47 which devour widows *h.*, and for a show
1 Cor. 11:22 have ye not *h.* to eat and drink in
1 Tim. 3:12 their children and their own *h.* well
2 Tim. 3: 6 they which creep into *h.* and lead
Tit. 1:11 subvert whole *h.* teaching things

HOUSEHOLD
Acts 16:15 baptized and her whole *h.*
Gal. 6:10 who are of the *h.* of faith
Eph. 2:19 saints of the *h.* of God

HUMBLE (HUMBLED)
Ex. 10: 3 thou refuse to *h.* thyself
Lev. 26:41 if uncircumcised hearts be *h.*
Deut. 8: 2 to *h.* thee, and prove
2 Ki. 22:19 hast *h.* thyself before the Lord
2 Chr. 7:14 shall *h.* themselves
12: 6 Israel and the kings *h.* themselves
12:12 And when he *h.* himself the wrath
33:23 *h.* not himself before the Lord
34:27 didst *h.* thyself before God
Ps. 9:12 forgetteth not the cry of the *h.*
10:12 up thine hand: forget not the *h.*
34: 2 *h.* shall hear thereof, and be glad
35:13 I *h.* my soul with fasting
Prov. 6: 3 *h.* thyself, make sure thy friend
16:19 to be of an *h.* spirit
Is. 2:11 lofty looks of man shall be *h.*
5:15 *h.* and eyes of the lofty shall be *h.*
10:33 haughty shall be *h.*
57:15 *h.* spirit, to revive the spirit of
Jer. 13:18 to the queen, *h.* yourselves
44:10 they are not *h.* unto this day
Lam. 3:20 my soul is *h.* in me
Dan. 5:22 hast not *h.* thy heart
Mat. 18: 4 whosoever therefore shall *h.* himself
23:12 he that shall *h.* himself
2 Cor. 12:21 my God will *h.* me
Phil. 2: 8 *h.* himself and became obedient
Jas. 4: 6 But giveth grace unto the *h.*
4:10 *h.* yourselves in the sight of Lord
1 Pet. 5: 5 giveth grace to the *h.*
5: 6 *h.* yourselves under the mighty hand

HUMILITY
Prov. 15:33 wisdom: and before honour is *h.*
18:12 man is haughty, and before honour is *h.*
22: 4 by *h.* are riches and honour
Acts 20:19 serving the Lord with all *h.*
Col. 2:18 of your reward in a voluntary *h.*
1 Pet. 5: 5 be clothed with *h.*: For God resisteth

HUNGER
Deut. 8: 3 suffered thee to *h.*, and fed thee
Ps. 34:10 do lack, and suffer *h.*
Prov. 19:15 idle soul shall suffer *h.*
Is. 49:10 shall not *h.* nor thirst
Lam. 4: 9 sword better than slain with *h.*
Mat. 5: 6 blessed are they which do *h.*
Luke 6:21 blessed are ye that *h.* now
6:25 unto you that are full! Ye shall *h.*
John 6:35 cometh to me shall never *h.*
Rom. 12:20 Therefore if thine enemy *h.* feed
1 Cor. 4:11 we both *h.* and thirst, and are naked
11:34 if any man *h.* let him eat at

HUNGRY
Ps. 107: 9 filleth the *h.* soul with goodness
146: 7 God giveth food to the *h.*
Prov. 25:21 if thine enemy be *h.* give him
27: 7 to the *h.* soul every bitter thing is sweet
Is. 58: 7 to deal thy bread to the *h.*
58:10 if thou draw out thy soul to the *h.*
65:13 shall eat; but ye shall be *h.*
Ezek. 18: 7 hath given his bread to the *h.*
Luke 1:53 filled the *h.* with good things
Phil. 4:12 how to be full and to be *h.*

HURT
Gen. 4:23 and a young man to my *h.*
26:29 thou wilt do us no *h.*
Josh. 24:20 will turn and do you *h.*
Ps. 15: 4 sweareth to his own *h.*
Eccl. 5:13 owners thereof to their *h.*
Jer. 6:14 healed the *h.* of the daughter
8:11 they have healed the *h.*
Rev. 2:11 shall not be *h.* of second death

HUSBAND (HUSBANDS)
Gen. 3:16 to thy *h.*, and he shall rule over
29:32 therefore my *h.* will love me
Ex. 4:25 surely a bloody *h.* art thou to me
Is. 54: 5 for thy Maker is thine *h.*
Mark 10:12 if a woman put away her *h.*
John 4:17 I have no *h.*. Jesus said unto
4:18 thou hast had five *h.*
1 Cor. 7:14 unbelieving *h.* is sanctified by
7:34 careth how she may please her *h.*
14:35 let them ask the *h.* at home
2 Cor. 11: 2 I have espoused you to one *h.*
Eph. 5:22 wives, submit to your *h.*
5:23 the *h.* is the head of wife
5:33 wife see that she reverence her *h.*
5:25 *h.*, love your wives, as Christ
Col. 3:19 *h.* love your wives, and be not bitter
3:18 wives, submit to your *h.*
1 Pet. 3: 1 ye wives be in subjection to your own *h.*
3: 7 likewise ye *h.*, dwell with them

HUSBANDMAN
John 15: 1 my father is the *h.*
Jas. 5: 7 *h.* waiteth for the precious fruit

HUSBANDRY
1 Cor. 3: 9 together with God: ye are God's *h.*

HYMN (HYMNS)
Mat. 26:30 when they had sung a *h.*
Eph. 5:19 in psalms and *h.*, and spiritual psalms
Col. 3:16 admonishing one another in psalms and *h.*

HYPOCRISY
Is. 32: 6 to practice *h.* and to utter
Mat. 23:28 within ye are full of *h.*
Mark 12:15 knowing their *h.*, said unto them
Luke 12: 1 the pharisees, which is *h.*
1 Tim. 4: 2 speaking lies in *h.* having their conscience
Jas. 3:17 without partiality and without *h.*
1 Pet. 2: 1 and all guile and *h.*

HYPOCRITE (HYPOCRITES)
Job 8:13 the *h's.* hope shall perish
15:34 congregation of *h.* shall be desolate
20: 5 joy of the *h.* for a moment
27: 8 what is the hope of the *h.*
Is. 9:17 every one is a *h.* and evil
33:14 fearfulness hath surprised the *h.*
Mat. 6: 2 as the *h.* do in the synagogues
7: 5 thou *h.*, first cast out the beam
15: 7 ye *h.*, well did Esaias
16: 3 oh ye *h.*, ye can discern
23:13 scribes and pharisees, *h.*!
24:51 appoint him portion with *h.*
Luke 6:42 thou *h.* cast out first the beam out
13:15 thou *h.*. doth not each one

I

IDLE
Prov. 19:15 an *i.* soul shall suffer
Mat. 12:36 every *i.* word that men shall speak
20: 6 ye stand here all the day *i.*
Luke 24:11 words seemed as *i.* tales

IDLENESS
Prov. 31:27 eateth not the bread of *i.*
Eccl. 10:18 and through *i.* of hands
Ezek. 16:49 abundance of *i.* was in her

IDOL (IDOLS)
Ps. 96: 5 gods of nations are *i.*
Is. 2: 8 land is full of *i.*; they worship
66: 3 as if he blessed an *i.*
Jer. 50:38 they are mad upon *i.*
Hos. 4:17 Ephraim is joined to *i.*
Zech. 11:17 woe to the *i.* shepherd
Acts 15:20 abstain from the pollutions of *i.*
Rom. 2:22 thou that abhorrest *i.* dost thou commit
1 Cor. 8: 1 touching things offered to *i.*
8: 4 an *i.* is nothing in the world
1 John 5:21 keep yourselves from *i.*
Rev. 2:14 eat things sacrificed to *i.*
9:20 not worship devils and *i.* of gold

IDOLATER (IDOLATERS)
1 Cor. 5:11 or an *i.*, or a railer
6: 9 nor *i.*, nor adulterers
10: 7 neither be ye *i.*, as were some
Eph. 5: 5 covetous man, who is an *i.*
Rev. 21: 8 and sorcerers, and *i.*, and all liars
22:15 and *i.*, and whosoever loveth

IDOLATRY
Acts 17:16 city wholly given to *i.*
1 Cor. 10:14 dearly beloved, flee from *i.*
Gal. 5:20 *i.*, witchcraft, hatred, variance
Col. 3: 5 concupiscence, and covetousness, which is *i.*

IGNORANCE
Lev. 4:13 congregation of Israel sin through *i.*
Num. 15:25 be forgiven them for it is *i.*
Acts 3:17 I wot that through *i.* ye did it
17:30 the times of this *i.* God winked at
Eph. 4:18 alienated from God through *i.*

IGNORANT (IGNORANTLY)
Is. 63:16 our father, though Abraham be *i.* of
Rom. 10: 3 for being *i.* of God's righteousness
Acts 17:23 whom therefore ye *i.* worship
1 Cor. 14:38 if man be *i.* let him be *i.*
1 Tim. 1:13 I did it *i.* in unbelief
Heb. 5: 2 can have compassion on the *i.*

IMAGE
Gen. 1:26 let us make man in our *i.*
5: 3 in his own likeness after his *i.*
9: 6 for in the *i.* of God
Lev. 26: 1 set up any *i.* of stone
Ps. 73:20 thou shalt despise their *i.*
Dan. 2:31 this great *i.* whose brightness
Mat. 22:20 whose is this *i.* and superscription
Rom. 8:29 conformed to the *i.* of the Son
1 Cor. 15:49 *i.* of earthy shall also bear *i.*
2 Cor. 4: 4 Christ who is the *i.* of God
Col. 1:15 the *i.* of the invisible God
3:10 after the *i.* of him that
Heb. 1: 3 express the *i.* of his person
Rev. 13:14 make an *i.* to the beast

IMMORTAL
1 Tim. 1:17 the King *i.*, invisible

IMMORTALITY
Rom. 2: 7 seek for glory, honour, *i.*
1 Cor. 15:53 this mortal must put on *i.*
2 Tim. 1:10 brought life and *i.* to light

IMPOSSIBLE
Mat. 17:20 nothing shall be *i.* unto you
19:26 with men this is *i.* but with God
Luke 1:37 with God nothing shall be *i.*
17: 1 it is *i.* but offences will come
Heb. 6: 4 *i.* for those once enlightened
6:18 in two things it was *i.* for God to
11: 6 without faith it is *i.* to please

IMPUTED (IMPUTETH, IMPUTING)
Lev. 7:18 shall it be *i.* unto him that offereth
17: 4 blood shall be *i.* unto that man
Ps. 32: 2 whom the Lord *i.* not iniquity
Rom. 4: 6 God *i.* righteousness without work
4:11 righteousness might be *i.*
4:22 *i.* to him for righteousness
5:13 sin is not *i.* when there is no law
2 Cor. 5:19 not *i.* their trespasses unto them
Jas. 2:23 *i.* unto him for righteousness

INCLINE (INCLINED)
Josh. 24:23 *i.* your heart unto the God
Judg. 9: 3 their hearts *i.* to follow Abimelech
1 Ki. 8:58 that he may *i.* our hearts unto him
Ps. 40: 1 he *i.* unto me and heard
78: 1 *i.* your ears to the words
116: 2 he hath *i.* his ear unto me
119: 36 *i.* my heart unto thy testimonies
Prov. 2: 2 *i.* thine ear unto wisdom
5:13 nor *i.* mine ear to them
Is. 55: 3 *i.* your ear and come unto me
Jer. 7:26 nor *i.* their ear, but hardened
17:23 obeyed not, neither *i.* their ear
34:14 not unto me neither *i.* their ear
44: 5 nor *i.* their ear to turn

INCORRUPTIBLE (UN-)
Rom. 1:23 the glory of the *i.* God
1 Cor. 9:25 corruptible crown; but we an *i.*
15:52 dead shall be raised *i.*, and we shall
1 Pet. 1: 4 to an inheritance *i.* and undefiled
1:23 not of corruptible seed, but of *i.*

INCORRUPTION
1 Cor. 15:50 neither doth corruption inherit *i.*

INCREASE (INCREASED)
Lev. 19:25 yield unto you the *i.* thereof
25:36 take no usury of him nor *i.*
Num. 32:14 your father's stead an *i.* of sinful men
Deut. 16:15 bless thee in all thine *i.*
Ezra 9: 6 iniquities are *i.* over our head
Ps. 62:10 if riches *i.* set not your heart
67: 6 shall the earth yield her *i.*
Prov. 1: 5 will hear, and will *i.* learning
Eccl. 5:11 when goods *i.* they are
Is. 9: 3 and not *i.* the joy: they joy before
9: 7 of the *i.* of his government
29:19 the meek shall also *i.* their joy
Ezek. 18: 8 neither taken any *i.* that hath
Luke 2:52 Jesus *i.* in wisdom and
17: 5 said unto the Lord, *i.* our faith
John 3:30 he must *i.* but I decrease
Acts 6: 7 the word of God *i.* and the
1 Cor. 3: 6 Apollos watered; but God gave the *i.*
Col. 2:19 increaseth with the *i.* of God
1 Thes. 3:12 Lord make you to *i.* and abound
2 Tim. 2:16 for they will *i.* to more ungodliness
Rev. 3:17 I am rich and *i.* with goods

INDIGNATION
Neh 4: 1 took great *i.* and mocked the Jews
Esth. 5: 9 full of *i.* against Mordecai
Ps. 78:49 his anger, wrath, and *i.*, and trouble
102: 10 thine *i.*, and thy wrath
Is. 10: 5 staff in their hand is mine *i.*
Mic. 7: 9 I will bear the *i.* of the Lord
Nah. 1: 6 who can stand before his *i.*
Mat. 20:24 moved with *i.* against the two
26: 8 when disciples saw it, they had *i.*
Rom. 2: 8 *i.* and wrath, tribulation
2 Cor. 7:11 yea, what *i.*, yea, what fear
Heb. 10:27 fiery *i.* which shall devour
Rev. 14:10 poured into the cup of his *i.*

INFINITE
Job 22: 5 and thine iniquities, *i.*
Ps. 147: 5 of great power: his understanding is *i.*
Nah. 3: 9 her strength, and it was *i.*

INFIRMITY (INFIRMITIES)
Ps. 77:10 this is my *i.*: but
Prov. 18:14 spirit of man will sustain *i.*
Mat. 8:17 himself took our *i.*, and bare our
Rom. 8:26 the Spirit helpeth our *i.*
2 Cor. 12: 9 will I rather glory in my *i.*
12:10 pleasure in *i.*, in reproaches
1 Tim. 5:23 stomach's sake and thine often *i.*
Heb. 4:15 with the feeling of our *i.*
5: 2 himself is compassed with *i.*
7:28 maketh men high priests which have *i.*

INHERIT
Gen 15: 8 shall I know that I shall *i.* it
1 Sam. 2: 8 make them *i.* the throne of glory
Ps. 25:13 his seed shall *i.* the earth
37:11 the meek shall *i.* the earth
37:29 the righteous shall *i.* the land
82: 8 O God, thou shalt *i.* all nations
Prov. 3:35 wise shall *i.* glory; but
8:21 that love me to *i.* substance
Mat. 5: 5 they shall *i.* the earth
25:34 *i.* the kingdom prepared for you
Mark 10:17 what shall I do that I may *i.* eternal
1 Cor. 6: 9 unrighteous shall not *i.* the kingdom
15:50 flesh and blood cannot *i.* the kingdom
Gal. 5:21 shall not *i.* the kingdom of God
Heb. 6:12 faith and patience *i.* the promises
1 Pet. 3: 9 that ye should *i.* a blessing
Rev. 21: 7 overcometh shall *i.* all things

INHERITANCE
Num. 18:20 I am thy part and thine *i.*
Deut. 4:20 a people of *i.*, as ye are this day
10: 9 no part nor *i.* with his brethren
18: 2 the Lord is their *i.*
1 Ki. 8:36 hast given to thy people for an *i.*
Ps. 16: 5 Lord is a portion of mine *i.*
28: 9 save thy people and bless thine *i.*
78:62 and was wroth with his *i.*
94:14 neither will he forsake his *i.*
106: 40 that he abhorred his own *i.*
Prov. 19:14 riches are the *i.* of fathers
Eccl. 7:11 wisdom is good with an *i.*
Is. 19:25 and Israel mine *i.*
Jer. 51:19 Israel is the rod of his *i.*
Ezek. 44:28 *i.*: I am their *i.*: and ye shall
Acts 20:32 and to give you an *i.*
Eph. 1:11 in whom we obtained an *i.*
1:14 earnest of our *i.* until the
5: 5 any *i.* in the kingdom of Christ
Col. 1:12 partakers of the *i.* of saints
3:24 shall receive the reward of *i.*
Heb. 9:15 the promise of eternal *i.*
1 Pet. 1: 4 to an *i.* incorruptible and undefiled

INIQUITY
Gen. 15:16 for the *i.* of the Amorites
Ex. 20: 5 visiting the *i.* of the fathers upon
34: 7 forgiving *i.*, and transgression
Lev. 26:41 accept the punishment of their *i.*
Num. 23:21 hath not beheld *i.* in Jacob
Job 4: 8 they that plow *i.* and sow wickedness
5:16 and *i.* stoppeth her mouth
15:16 man which drinketh *i.* like water
22:23 put away *i.* far from thy tabernacles
34:22 workers of *i.* may hide
34:32 if I have done *i.* I will do no
Ps. 5: 5 thou hatest all workers of *i.*
18:23 kept myself from mine *i.*
32: 5 mine *i.* have I not hid
39:11 dost correct man for his *i.*
51: 5 behold, I was shapen in *i.*
66:18 if I regard *i.* in my heart
69:27 add *i.* unto their *i.*: and let them
92: 7 workers of *i.* do flourish
119: 3 they also do no *i.*: they walk
119:133 let not any *i.* have dominion
Prov. 21:15 shall be to the workers of *i.*
Eccl. 3:16 place of righteousness there *i.* was
Is. 1: 4 people laden with *i.*, a seed
5:18 woe to them that draw *i.* with
27: 9 by this shall the *i.* of Jacob be purged
33:24 people shall be forgiven their *i.*
53: 6 Lord laid on him the *i.* of us all
57:17 for the *i.* of his covetousness
59: 3 your fingers with *i.*; your lips have
Jer. 2: 5 what *i.* have fathers found
3:13 only acknowledge thine *i.*
31:30 every one shall die for his own *i.*
50:20 *i.* of Israel shall be sought for
Ezek. 3:18 he shall die in his *i.*
18:30 so *i.* shall not be your ruin
33: 8 that wicked man shall die in his *i.*
Dan. 9:24 make reconciliation for *i.*
Hos. 14: 2 take away all *i.* and receive us
Mic. 7:18 that pardoneth *i.* and passeth by the
Hab. 1:13 canst not look on *i.*: wherefore
Mat. 7:23 depart from me, ye that work *i.*

Mat. 24:12 because *i.* shall abound, the love of
Luke 13:27 all ye workers of *i.*
Acts 8:23 and in the bond of *i.*
Rom. 6:19 uncleanness and to *i.* unto *i.*
1 Cor. 13: 6 rejoiceth not in *i.* but rejoices in
2 Thes. 2: 7 mystery of *i.* doth already work
2 Tim. 2:19 the name of Christ depart from *i.*
Tit. 2:14 he might redeem us from all *i.*
Jas. 3: 6 tongue is a fire, a world of *i.*

INIQUITIES
Lev. 16:21 confess over him all *i.*
26:39 and also in the *i.* of their fathers
Ezra 9: 6 our *i.* are increased over our head
9:13 punished less than our *i.* deserve
Neh. 9: 2 confessed *i.* of the fathers
Job 13:26 to possess the *i.* of my youth
Ps. 38: 4 mine *i.* are gone over my head
40:12 mine *i.* have taken hold upon
51: 9 my sins, and blot out all mine *i.*
65: 3 *i.* prevail against me: as for
79: 8 remember not against us former *i.*
90: 8 thou hast set our *i.* before thee
107: 17 because of their *i.* are afflicted
130: 3 if thou, Lord, mark *i.*
130: 8 he shall redeem Israel from all *i.*
Prov. 5:22 his own *i.* shall take the wicked
Is. 43:24 hast wearied me with thine *i.*
Jer. 14: 7 our *i.* testify against us
Dan. 4:27 thine *i.* by showing mercy to the
Mic. 7:19 he will subdue our *i.* and
Acts 3:26 every one of you from his *i.*
Rom. 4: 7 blessed are they whose *i.* are forgiven
Rev. 18: 5 God hath remembered her *i.*

INK
2 John 1:12 would not write with paper and *i.*
3 John 1:13 will not with *i.* and pen write

INNOCENT
Ps. 19:13 and I shall be *i.* from the great
Prov. 28:20 to be rich shall not be *i.*

INNOCENCY
Gen. 20: 5 *i.* of my hands have I done
Ps. 26: 6 I will wash my hands in *i.*
73:13 washed my hands in *i.*
Dan. 6:22 before him the *i.* found in me
Hos. 8: 5 how long ere they attain *i.*

INNUMERABLE
Job 21:33 as there are *i.* before him
Ps. 40:12 *i.* evils have compassed me
Luke 12: 1 together an *i.* multitude of people
Heb. 11:12 which is by the sea shore *i.*
12:22 an *i.* company of angels

INQUIRE (INQUIRED, INQUIREST)
Judg. 20:27 children of Israel *i.* of the Lord
1 Sam. 30: 8 David *i.* at the Lord, saying
2 Sam. 2: 1 David *i.* of the Lord, saying
5:23 when David *i.* of the Lord
Job 10: 6 that thou *i.* after mine iniquity
Ps. 78:34 returned and *i.* early after God
27: 4 Lord and to *i.* in his temple
Eccl. 7:10 thou dost not *i.* wisely concerning
Is. 21:12 if ye will *i. i.* ye: return
Jer. 21: 2 *i.* I pray thee of the Lord
Ezek. 36:37 be *i.* of by the house of Israel
Zeph. 1: 6 have not sought the Lord, nor *i.* for him
Mat. 2: 7 *i.* of them diligently what time the
1 Pet. 1:10 of which salvation prophets have *i.*

INQUIRY
Prov. 20:25 is holy and after vows to make *i.*

INSPIRATION
Job 32: 8 the *i.* of the Almighty giveth them
2 Tim. 3:16 scripture is given by *i.*

INSTANT (INSTANTLY)
Is. 29: 5 shall be at an *i.* suddenly
30:13 cometh suddenly at an *i.*
Jer. 18: 7 at what *i.* shall I speak
Luke 7: 4 they besought him *i.*, saying
Acts 26: 7 *i.* serving God day and night, hope
Rom. 12:12 tribulation continuing *i.* in prayer
2 Tim. 4: 2 be *i.* in season, out of season

INSTRUCT (INSTRUCTED)
Deut. 4:36 hear his voice that he might *i.* thee
32:10 led him about, he *i.* him
Neh. 9:20 thy good spirit to *i.* them
Job 40: 2 contendeth with the Almighty *i.* him
Ps. 16: 7 my reins *i.* me in the night
Sol. 8: 2 mother's house who would *i.* me
Is. 8:11 *i.* me that I should not walk
28:26 his God doth *i.* him to discretion
1 Cor. 2:16 Lord that he may *i.* him
Phil. 4:12 in all things I am *i.* both

INSTRUCTION
Job 33:16 men and sealeth their *i.*
Ps. 50:17 hatest *i.* and castest my words
Prov. 4:13 take fast hold of *i.*; let her not
5:12 how have I hated *i.* and
19:27 cease to hear *i.* that causeth
23:12 apply thine heart to *i.* and
2 Tim. 3:16 correction, for *i.* in righteousness

INSTRUCTOR (INSTRUCTORS)
Rom. 2:20 an *i.* of the foolish, a teacher
1 Cor. 4:15 ye have ten thousand *i.* in Christ

INSTRUMENTS
Gen. 49: 5 *i.* of cruelty are in their habitations
Ps. 7:13 prepared for him *i.* of death
Is. 32: 7 the *i.* also of the churl are evil
Rom. 6:13 neither yield members as *i.* of unrighteousness
6:13 as *i.* of righteousness unto sin

INTEGRITY
Gen. 20: 5 didst this in the *i.* of my heart
Job 2: 3 still he holdeth fast his *i.*
27: 5 I will not remove mine *i.*
Ps. 7: 8 according to my *i.* that is
25:21 let *i.* and uprightness preserve me
26: 1 I have walked in mine *i.*
Prov. 11: 3 *i.* of upright shall guide

INTERCESSION
Is. 53:12 and made *i.* for the transgressors
Jer. 7:16 neither make *i.* for me
27:18 now make *i.* to the Lord
Rom. 8:26 Spirit maketh *i.* for us
8:34 who also maketh *i.* for us
11: 2 maketh *i.* to God against Israel
Heb. 7:25 he ever liveth to make *i.*

INTERCESSOR
Is. 59:16 there was no *i.*: therefore his

INTERPRETATION
Gen. 40: 5 according to the *i.* of his dream
Judg. 7:15 dream, and the *i.* thereof
Dan. 2:36 we will tell the *i.* thereof
1 Cor. 12:10 another the *i.* of tongues
14:26 revelation, hath an *i.*
2 Pet. 1:20 scripture is of any private *i.*

INTERPRETER
Job 33:23 *i.* one among a thousand to show unto

INVENT
Amos 6: 5 *i.* themselves instruments of music

INVENTIONS
Ps. 99: 8 tookest vengeance of their *i.*
106: 29 provoked him with their *i.*
106: 39 went a-whoring with their *i.*
Prov. 8:12 find out knowledge of witty *i.*
Eccl. 7:29 but they have sought many *i.*

INVENTORS
Rom. 1:30 *i.* of evil things, disobedient to

INVISIBLE
Rom. 1:20 the *i.* things of him from the
Col. 1:16 visible, and *i.*, whether they be
1 Tim. 1:17 King eternal, immortal, *i.*
Heb. 11:27 endured as seeing him who is *i.*

INWARD (INWARDLY)
Job 19:19 my *i.* friends abhorred me
Ps. 5: 9 their *i.* part is very wickedness
51: 6 desireth truth in the *i.* parts
62: 4 but they curse *i.* Selah
Prov. 20:27 the *i.* parts of the belly
Jer. 31:33 my law in their *i.* parts
Mat. 7:15 *i.* they are ravening wolves
Luke 11:39 your *i.* part is full of ravening
Rom. 2:29 he is a Jew which is one *i.*
7:22 Law of God after the *i.* man
2 Cor. 4:16 the *i.* man is renewed day by day

IRON
Prov. 27:17 *i.* sharpeneth *i.*; so a man
Eccl. 10:10 if the *i.* be blunt, and he do not
Is. 48: 4 neck is an *i.* sinew, and
Jer. 15:12 shall *i.* break northern *i.*
Dan. 2:33 legs of *i.*, his feet part *i.*
4:23 even with a band of *i.* and
5:23 gods of silver, and gold, of brass, *i.*
1 Tim. 4: 2 conscience seared with a hot *i.*

ISSUES
Ps. 68:20 belong the *i.* from death
Prov. 4:23 for out of it are the *i.* of life

IVORY
1 Ki. 10:18 made a great throne of *i.*
22:39 *i.* house which he made, and all the
Ps. 45: 8 out of the *i.* palaces, whereby
Sol. 5:14 belly is as bright *i.*
Ezek. 27: 6 have made benches of *i.*
Amos 6: 4 that lie upon beds of *i.*
Rev. 18:12 all manner vessels of *i.*

J

JEALOUS (JEALOUSY)
Ex. 20: 5 am a *j.* God, visiting the iniquity
34:14 name is *j.*, is a *j.* God
Deut. 6:15 thy God is a *j.* God among you
29:20 *j.* shall smoke against that man
Josh. 24:19 he is a *j.* God; he will not forgive
Ps. 79: 5 shall thy *j.* burn like fire
Prov. 6:34 *j.* is the rage of a man
Sol. 8: 6 *j.* is cruel as the grave
Ezek. 39:25 be *j.* for my holy name
Joel 2:18 Lord be *j.* for his land
Nah. 1: 2 God is *j.* and the Lord
Zech. 1:14 I am *j.* for Jerusalem and for Zion
Rom. 10:19 provoke you to *j.* by them that are
11:11 for to provoke them to *j.*
1 Cor. 10:22 we provoke the Lord to *j.*
2 Cor. 11: 2 *j.* over you with godly jealousy

JERUSALEM
Is. 24:23 reign in mount Zion, and in *J.*
62: 1 *J.* sake I will not rest
Jer. 3:17 the name of the Lord to *J.*
Joel 2:32 in mount Zion, and in *J.*
Zech. 12:10 upon the inhabitants of *J.*
Gal. 4:26 *J.* which is above is free
Heb. 12:22 living God, the heavenly *J.*
Rev. 3:12 which is new *J.*, which cometh down
21: 2 the holy city, new *J.*

JESUS
Mat. 1:21 thou shalt call his name *J.*
2: 1 *J.* was born in Bethlehem
8:29 do with thee *J.* thou Son of God
14: 1 tetrarch heard of the fame of *J.*
27:37 This is *J.* the King of the Jews
1 Cor. 12: 3 Spirit of God calleth *J.* accursed
2 Cor. 4: 5 but Christ *J.* the Lord, and ourselves
Eph. 4:21 taught by him as the truth is in *J.*
Heb. 2: 9 But we see *J.*, who was made a little
12: 2 looking unto *J.* the author and
Rev. 22:16 I *J.* have sent my angel

JEW (JEWS)
Rom. 1:16 the *J.* first, and also to the Greek
2:10 *J.* first, and also to the Gentile
2:28 *J.* which is one outwardly, but a *J.*
10:12 no difference between *J.* and Greek
1 Cor. 9:20 to Jews I became as a *J.*
Gal. 3:28 there is neither *J.* nor Greek, there
Col. 3:11 there is neither Greek nor *J.*
Rev. 2: 9 say they are *J* and are not
3: 9 say they are *J.*, and are not

JOIN (JOINED)
Ex. 1:10 they *j.* also unto our enemies
Num. 25: 3 Israel *j.* himself to Baal-Peor
Ezra 9:14 and *j.* in affinity with the people
Prov. 11:21 hand *j.* in hand, the wicked shall
Eccl. 9: 4 for him that is *j.* to the living
Is. 5: 8 woe to them that *j.* house to house
Jer. 50: 5 let us *j.* ourselves to the Lord
Hos. 4:17 Ephraim is *j.* to idols
Zech. 2:11 nations shall be *j.* to the Lord
Mat. 19: 6 what God hath *j.* together let not
Acts 5:13 durst no man *j.* himself
1 Cor. 1:10 that ye be perfectly *j.* together
Eph. 5:31 shall be *j.* to his wife

JOINTS
Col. 2:19 which all the body by *j.* and bands
Heb. 4:12 and of the *j.* and marrow

JOY
1 Chr. 12:40 there was *j.* in Israel
2 Chr. 20:27 go again to Jerusalem with *j.*
Neh. 8:10 *j.* of the Lord is your strength
Esth. 8:17 Jews had *j.* and gladness
Job 20: 5 *j.* of the hypocrite but for
Ps. 16:11 thy presence is fulness of *j.*
43: 4 unto God my exceeding *j.*
51: 8 make me hear *j.* and gladness
51:12 restore to me the *j.* of thy salvation
126: 5 that sow in tears shall reap in *j.*
Eccl. 9: 7 eat thy bread with *j.*
Is. 9: 3 according to the *j.* in harvest
12: 3 with *j.* shall ye draw water out
35:10 with songs and everlasting *j.*
61: 3 give them the oil of *j.* for mourning
61: 7 everlasting *j.* shall be to them
66: 5 he shall appear to your *j.*
Zeph. 3:17 will *j.* over thee with singing
Mat. 2:10 rejoiced with great *j.*
13:20 hear the word, and with *j.*
Luke 1:44 babe leaped in the womb for *j.*
15: 7 *j.* shall be in heaven over one
John 15:11 and that your *j.* might be full
16:20 your sorrow be turned into *j.*
16:22 your *j.* no man taketh from you
16:24 that your *j.* may be full
17:13 my *j.* fulfilled in themselves
Acts 20:24 finish my course with *j.*
Rom. 15:13 fill you with all *j.* and peace
2 Cor. 1:24 but are helpers of your *j.*
2: 3 my *j.* is the *j.* of you all
Gal. 5:22 fruit of the Spirit is love, *j.*
Phil. 4: 1 my *j.* and crown, so stand fast in
1 Thes. 1: 6 receive the word with *j.* of
Heb. 12: 2 who for the *j.* set before
Jas. 1: 2 count it all *j.* when ye
1 Pet. 1: 8 rejoice with *j.* unspeakable
4:13 be glad with exceeding *j.*
1 John 1: 4 write that your *j.* may be full

JOYFUL (JOYFULLY)
Ezra 6:22 the Lord hath made them *j.*
Ps. 35: 9 my soul shall be *j.* in the Lord
63: 5 I will praise thee with *j.* lips
89:15 people that know the *j.* sound
Eccl. 7:14 in the day of prosperity be *j.*
9: 9 live *j.* with the wife whom thou
Is. 56: 7 make them *j.* in my house
61:10 my soul shall be *j.* in God
2 Cor. 7: 4 exceeding *j.* in all our tribulation
Heb. 10:34 took *j.* the spoiling of goods

JOYFULNESS
Deut. 28:47 servedst not the Lord thy God with *j.*
Col. 1:11 all patience longsuffering with *j.*

JOYING
Col. 2: 5 *j.* and beholding your order, and the

JOYOUS
Heb. 12:11 for the present seemeth to be *j.*

JUDGE
Gen. 16: 5 Lord *j.* between me and thee
18:25 shall not the *J.* of the earth
Ex. 2:14 thee a prince and a *j.* over us
Deut. 32:36 the Lord shall *j.* his people
1 Sam. 2:25 the *j.* shall *j.* him; but
24:12 Lord *j.* between me and thee
Ps. 7: 8 Lord shall *j.* the people
9: 8 Lord shall *j.* the world in righteousness
68: 5 father of the fatherless and *j.* of widows
75: 7 God is the *j.*: he putteth down
98: 9 with righteousness shall he *j.*
Is. 33:22 The Lord is our *j.*, the Lord is our
Mic. 3:11 heads thereof *j.* for reward
Mat. 7: 1 *j.* not, that ye be not judged
Luke 12:14 who made me a *j.* or a divider
John 5:30 as I hear I *j.* and my judgment
12:47 I came not to *j.* the world
Acts 7:27 made thee ruler and a *j.*
10:42 to be the *J.* of the quick and dead
17:31 in which he will *j.* the world in
23: 3 sittest thou to *j.* me after the law
Rom. 2:16 when God shall *j.* the secrets of men
3: 6 then how shall God *j.* the world
14:10 why dost thou *j.* thy brother
1 Cor. 4: 3 I *j.* not mine own self
4: 5 *j.* nothing before the time
6: 3 know ye not that we shall *j.* angels
11:31 if we would *j.* ourselves, we
14:29 two or three and let the other *j.*
Col. 2:16 let no man *j.* you in meat
2 Tim. 4: 1 who shall *j.* the quick and the dead
4: 8 Lord the righteous *j.*, shall give me
Heb. 10:30 Lord shall *j.* his people
12:23 are come to God the *J.*
Jas. 4:11 if thou *j.* the law thou art not a
5: 9 the *J.* standeth before the door

JUDGETH (JUDGING)
Deut. 1:17 ye shall not respect persons in *j.*
Ps. 7:11 God *j.* the righteous and God is
58:11 he is a God that *j.* in earth
Mat. 19:28 *j.* the twelve tribes of Israel
Luke 22:30 sit on thrones, *j.* the twelve
1 Cor. 2:15 but he that is spiritual *j.* all things
4: 4 he that *j.* me is the Lord

JUDGMENT
Deut. 1:17 for the *j.* is God's: and the cause
Ps. 1: 5 ungodly not stand in the *j.*
9:16 Lord is known by the *j.* he executeth
101: 1 I will sing of mercy and *j.*
143: 2 enter not into *j.* with thy servant
149: 9 to execute upon them the *j.*
Prov. 21:15 it is joy to the just to do *j.*
29:26 every man's *j.* cometh from the Lord
Eccl. 11: 9 God will bring thee into *j.*
Is. 1:27 Zion shall be redeemed with *j.*
28:17 *j.* also will I lay to the line
30:18 for the Lord is a God of *j.*
42: 1 he shall bring *j.* to the Gentiles
53: 8 he was taken from prison and *j.*
61: 8 I the Lord love *j.*, I hate
Jer. 5: 1 if there be any that executeth *j.*
8: 7 people know not the *j.* of the Lord
10:24 correct me, but with *j.*; not in
Dan. 4:37 whose works are truth and his ways *j.*
7:22 and *j.* was given to the saints
Hos. 12: 6 keep mercy and *j.*, wait on
Amos 5: 7 who turn *j.* to wormwood
5:24 let *j.* run down as waters, and
Mat. 5:21 kill shall be in danger of the *j.*
12:20 till he send *j.* unto victory
John 5:27 and given him authority to execute *j.*
9:39 for *j.* I am come into the world
16: 8 and of righteousness, and of *j.*
Acts 24:25 temperance, and *j.* to come
Rom. 5:18 *j.* came upon all men to condemnation
14:10 must all stand before the *j.* seat
1 Pet. 4:17 *j.* begin at the house of God
Jude 1:15 execute *j.* upon all, and to convince
Rev. 17: 1 show thee *j.* of a great whore

JUDGMENTS
Ps. 19: 9 *j.* of the Lord are true and righteous
36: 6 thy *j.* are a great deep
119: 75 I know, O Lord, that thy *j.* are right
119:108 O Lord, teach me thy *j.*
119:120 and I am afraid of thy *j.*
Is. 26: 8 in the way of thy *j.*, O Lord, have
26: 9 when thy *j.* are in the earth
Jer. 12: 1 let me talk with thee of thy *j.*
Rom. 11:33 how unsearchable are his *j.*, and his

JUST
Gen. 6: 9 Noah was a *j.* man and perfect
Lev. 19:36 *j.* balance, *j.* weights, a *j.* ephah
Deut. 16:20 that which is *j.* shalt thou follow
25:15 shalt have a perfect and *j.* weight
32: 4 without iniquity *j.* and right is he
2 Sam. 23: 3 he that ruleth men must be *j.*
Neh. 9:33 art *j.* in all that is brought upon us
Prov. 4:18 path of the *j.* is as a shining
10: 6 blessings are on the head of the *j.*
11: 1 but a *j.* weight is his delight
12:21 no evil shall happen to the *j.*
17:26 to punish the *j.* is not good
18:17 in his own cause seemeth *j.*
Prov. 20: 7 the *j.* man walketh in his integrity
24:16 *j.* man falleth seven times
Eccl. 7:15 there is a *j.* man that perisheth
7:20 there is not a *j.* man on earth
8:14 be *j.* men, to whom it happeneth
Is. 26: 7 way of the *j.* is uprightness
45:21 no God beside me; a *j.* God
Ezek. 18: 9 he is *j.*, he shall live
Hab. 2: 4 *j.* shall live by his faith
Zeph. 3: 5 the *j.* Lord is in the midst
Luke 15: 7 more than over ninety-nine *j.* persons
20:20 who should feign themselves *j.*
John 5:30 I judge and my judgment is *j.*
Acts 7:52 the coming of the *J.* One
24:15 both of the *j.* and the unjust
Rom. 1:17 *j.* shall live by faith
2:13 not hearers of the law are *j.*
3:26 he might be *j.* and the justifier
7:12 commandment holy, *j.* and
Gal. 3:11 *j.* shall live by faith
Phil. 4: 8 whatsoever things are *j.*
Col. 4: 1 that which is *j.* and
Heb. 2: 2 received a *j.* recompence
10:38 *j.* shall live by faith
12:23 spirits of *j.* men made perfect
1 Pet. 3:18 once suffered for sins, the *j.*
Rev. 15: 3 *j.* and true are thy ways

JUSTLY
Mic. 6: 8 to do *j.* and love kindness
Luke 23:41 we indeed *j.* for we receive the due
1 Thes. 2:10 how holily and *j.* we behaved

JUSTICE
Gen. 18:19 to do *j.* and judgment, that the
Job 37:23 judgment, and in plenty of *j.*
Ps. 89:14 *j.* and judgment are the habitation
Prov. 8:15 kings reign, and princes decree *j.*
Jer. 31:23 O habitation of *j.*
50: 7 O habitation of *j.*, and mountain of

JUSTIFICATION
Rom. 4:25 was raised again for our *j.*
5:16 gift is of many offences unto *j.*

JUSTIFIED
Job 11: 2 should a man full of talk be *j.*
13:18 I know that I shall be *j.*
25: 4 how can man be *j.* with God?
32: 2 he *j.* himself rather than God
Ps. 51: 4 mightest be *j.* when thou speakest
Is. 43: 9 that they may be *j.*
45:25 the seed of Israel be *j.*
Jer. 3:11 hath *j.* herself more than Judah
Ezek. 16:51 hast *j.* thy sisters in all thine
Mat. 11:19 wisdom is *j.* of her children
12:37 by thy words thou shalt be *j.*
Luke 7:29 *j.* God, being baptized of
Rom. 2:13 doers of the law shall be *j.*
3: 4 thou mightest be *j.* in thy sayings
3:20 there shall no flesh be *j.* in his
3:24 being *j.* freely by his grace
3:28 man is *j.* by faith without deeds
4: 2 if Abraham were *j.* by works
5: 1 being *j.* by faith, we have
5: 9 being now *j.* by his blood
8:30 whom he *j.* them he also
1 Cor. 4: 4 yet am I not hereby *j.*
6:11 ye are *j.* in the name of the Lord
Gal. 2:16 not *j.* by the works of law
2:17 we seek to be *j.* by Christ
3:11 no man is *j.* by the law
3:24 that we might be *j.* by faith
5: 4 *j.* by the law, ye are fallen
1 Tim. 3:16 in flesh, *j.* in spirit
Tit. 3: 7 that being *j.* by his grace
Jas. 2:21 Abraham *j.* by works when
2:25 not Rahab the harlot *j.* by works

JUSTIFY (JUSTIFIETH)
Ex. 23: 7 will not *j.* the wicked
Deut. 25: 1 they shall *j.* the righteous
Job 9:20 if I *j.* myself, mine own mouth
27: 5 God forbid that I should *j.*
33:32 speak, for I desire to *j.* thee
Prov. 17:15 he that *j.* the wicked
Is. 5:23 them which *j.* the wicked
53:11 shall my servant *j.* many
50: 8 he is near that *j.* me
Luke 10:29 he, willing to *j.* himself
16:15 ye are they which *j.* yourselves
Rom. 3:30 God shall *j.* circumcision
4: 5 him that *j.* the ungodly
8:33 it is God that *j.*
Gal. 3: 8 God would *j.* the heathen

K

KEEP
Gen. 2:15 to dress it and to *k.* it
18:19 *k.* the way of the Lord
28:15 I am with thee and will *k.* thee
28:20 if God will be with me, and *k.* me
Ex. 23: 7 *k.* thee far from a false matter
23:20 I send an angel to *k.* thee in
Num. 6:24 Lord bless thee and *k.* thee
Deut. 23: 9 *k.* thee from every wicked thing
29: 9 *k.* the words of this covenant
Judg. 3:19 who said *k.* silence. And all that
1 Sam. 2: 9 he will *k.* the feet of his
1 Chr. 4:10 that thou wouldest *k.* me from evil
Ps. 17: 8 *k.* me as the apple of the eye
25:10 to such as *k.* his covenant
25:20 O *k.* my soul, and deliver me: let me
35:22 *k.* not silent: oh Lord
39: 1 *k.* my mouth with a bridle
89:28 my mercy will I *k.* for him
91:11 angels to *k.* thee in all thy ways
103: 18 such as *k.* his covenant
106: 3 blessed are they that *k.* judgment
119: 2 are they that *k.* his testimonies
119: 4 commanded us to *k.* thy precepts
119: 17 that I may live and *k.* thy word
119: 33 and I shall *k.* it unto the end
127: 1 except the Lord *k.* the city
140: 4 *k.* me, O Lord, from the hands of the
141: 3 before my mouth; *k.* the door of my
Eccl. 3: 7 a time to *k.* silence, and a time
5: 1 *k.* thy foot when thou goest
Is. 26: 3 thou wilt *k.* him in perfect
41: 1 *k.* silence before me, O islands
62: 6 of the Lord, *k.* not silence
Jer. 3:12 I will not *k.* anger for ever
Lam. 2:10 and *k.* silence: they have cast up
Hos. 12: 6 *k.* mercy and judgment, and wait on
Mic. 7: 5 *k.* the doors of thy mouth
Hab. 2:20 let the earth *k.* silence
Mal. 2: 7 priest's lips should *k.* knowledge
Luke 11:28 hear the word of God and *k.* it
1 Cor. 5: 8 let us *k.* the feast, not with old
5:11 not to *k.* company with such
9:27 I *k.* under my body, and bring it
14:34 let your women *k.* silence
Eph. 4: 3 endeavouring to *k.* unity of the
Phil. 4: 7 shall *k.* your hearts and minds through
2 Thes. 3: 3 Lord shall stablish you and *k.* you
1 Tim. 5:22 other men's sins *k.* thyself pure
6:20 *k.* that which is committed
2 Tim. 1:12 able to *k.* that which I have
1:14 *k.* by the Holy Ghost which dwelleth
Jas. 1:27 *k.* himself unspotted from the world
2:10 *k.* the whole law and yet offend
Jude 1:21 *k.* yourselves in the love of God
1:24 that is able to *k.* you from
Rev. 1: 3 and *k.* those things which
3:10 I will *k.* thee from the hour of
22: 9 them which *k.* the sayings

KEEPEST (KEEPETH, KEEPING)
Ex. 34: 7 *k.* mercy for thousands, forgiving
1 Ki. 8:23 who *k.* covenant and mercy
2 Chr. 6:14 nor in the earth: which *k.* covenant
Neh. 9:32 who *k.* covenant and mercy
Ps. 19:11 in *k.* of them is great reward
121: 3 he that *k.* thee will not slumber
146: 6 therein is which *k.* truth for ever
Prov. 13: 3 he that *k.* his mouth *k.* his life
29:18 he that *k.* the law is happy
Dan. 9: 4 *k.* the covenant and mercy to them
1 Pet. 4:19 *k.* of their souls to him in well
1 John 5:18 that is begotten of God *k.* himself
Rev. 16:15 that watcheth and *k.* his garments
22: 7 blessed is he that *k.* the sayings

KEEPER (KEEPERS)
Ps. 121: 5 the Lord is thy *k.*: the Lord
Eccl. 5: 7 *k.* took away my veil from me
12: 3 when *k.* of the house shall
Sol. 1: 6 made me the *k.* of vineyards
Tit. 2: 5 chaste, *k.* at home, good, obedient

KEPT
Deut. 33: 9 thy word and *k.* thy covenant
Josh. 14:10 Lord hath *k.* me alive
2 Sam. 22:22 *k.* the ways of the Lord and have
Job 23:11 his way have I *k.* and
Ps. 17: 4 *k.* me from the paths of the
18:23 *k.* myself from mine iniquity
50:21 and I *k.* silence; thou thoughtest
30: 3 *k.* me alive, that I should not go
Sol. 1: 6 mine own vineyard not *k.*
Mat. 19:20 all these things have I *k.* from my
Luke 2:19 Mary *k.* all these things
John 15:20 if they have *k.* my sayings
17: 6 they have *k.* thy word
17:12 that thou gavest me I have *k.*
Rom. 16:25 *k.* secret since the world
2 Tim. 4: 7 I have *k.* the faith
1 Pet. 1: 5 who are *k.* by the power of God
Rev. 3: 8 hast *k.* my word, and not

KEY (KEYS)
Is. 22:22 the *k.* of the house of David
Mat. 16:19 the *k.* of the kingdom of heaven
Rev. 1:18 have the *k.* of hell and of death
3: 7 he that hath the *k.* of David
9: 1 *k.* of the bottomless pit
20: 1 the *k.* of the bottomless pit

KILL (KILLED, KILLETH)
Ex. 20:13 thou shalt not *k.*
1 Sam. 2: 6 the Lord *k.* and maketh
1 Ki. 21:19 hast thou *k.* and also taken
Ps. 44:22 are we *k.* all day long
Eccl. 3: 3 time to *k.* and a time to heal
Mat. 10:28 *k.* the body, but are not able to *k.*
Mark 3: 4 lawful to save life, or *k.*
Luke 12: 5 after he hath *k.* hath power
John 16: 2 who *k.* you will think he doeth
Acts 3:15 *k.* the Prince of life whom God
2 Cor. 3: 6 letter *k.* but the spirit giveth life
6: 9 we live as chastened, and not *k.*
1 Thes. 2:15 *k.* the Lord Jesus and their own
Rev. 13:10 that *k.* with sword must be *k.*

KIND
Gen. 1:11 yielding fruit after his *k.*
Luke 6:35 he is *k.* to the unthankful
1 Cor. 13: 4 charity suffereth long and is *k.*

KINDNESS
1 Sam. 20:14 I live show me the *k.* of the Lord
2 Sam. 9: 3 may show the *k.* of God
16:17 is this thy *k.* to thy friend
Neh. 9:17 slow to anger and of great *k.*
Ps. 117: 2 his merciful *k.* is great toward
141: 5 smite me; it shall be a *k.*
Prov. 19:22 the desire of a man is his *k.*
31:26 in her tongue is the law of *k.*
Is. 54: 8 with everlasting *k.* will I have mercy
54:10 my *k.* shall not depart from thee
Jer. 2: 2 I remember thee, the *k.* of
Joel 2:13 to anger and of great *k.*
Jonah 4: 2 and of great *k.* and repentest thou
Col. 3:12 put on bowels of mercies, *k.*
2 Pet. 1: 7 brotherly *k.* to brotherly *k.* charity

KINDLE (KINDLED)
2 Sam. 22: 9 devoured: coals were *k.* by it
Ps. 2:12 when his wrath is *k.* but a little
Prov. 26:21 a contentious man to *k.* strife
Is. 10:16 he shall *k.* a burning
30:33 stream of brimstone, doth *k.* it
50:11 sparks that ye have *k.*
Hos. 11: 8 my repentings are *k.*
Luke 12:49 will I, if it be already *k.*

KING
Gen. 14:18 Melchizedek *k.* of Salem
36:31 any *k.* over the children
Job 18:14 bring him to the *k.* of terrors
Ps. 10:16 the Lord is *k.* forever
24: 7 *K.* of glory shall come in
33:16 no *k.* saved by the multitude of
47: 7 God is *K.* of all the earth
74:12 God is my *k.* of old
Prov. 30:31 a *k.* against whom there is no
Eccl. 5: 9 *k.* himself is served by the field
8: 4 where the word of the *k.* is there
Sol. 1: 4 *k.* brought me into his chambers
1:12 while the *k.* sitteth at his table
7: 5 the *k.* is held in the galleries
Is. 32: 1 a *k.* shall reign in righteousness
33:22 the Lord is our *k.* he will save
43:15 Creator of Israel, your *K.*
Hos. 3: 5 Lord their God and David their *k.*
7: 5 in the day of our *k.* the princes
13:11 I gave thee a *k.* in mine anger
Zech. 9: 9 behold, thy *K.* cometh
Luke 23: 2 he himself is Christ, a *k.*
John 6:15 by force to make him *k.*
1 Tim. 1:17 now unto the *K.* eternal
6:15 *K.* of kings, and Lord of lords
1 Pet. 2:17 fear God, honour thy *k.*
Rev. 15: 3 thy ways, thou *k.* of saints
17:14 Lord of Lords, and *k.* of kings
19:16 *k.* of kings, and Lord of Lords

KINGS (KINGS')
Ps. 72:11 *k.* shall fall before him
76:12 terrible to the *k.* of earth
102: 15 *k.* of the earth be thy glory
144: 10 that giveth salvation to *k.*
149: 8 to bind their *k.* with chains
Prov. 8:15 by me *k.* reign, and princes
Is. 62: 2 and all *k.* thy glory: and thou
Hos. 8: 4 they set up *k.* but not by
Mat. 11: 8 soft clothing in *k.* houses
Luke 22:25 *k.* of Gentiles exercise authority
1 Cor. 4: 8 reigned as *k.* without us
1 Tim. 2: 2 *k.* and for all that are in authority
Rev. 1: 6 made us *k.* and priests to God
5:10 unto our God, *k.* and priests

KINGDOM
Ex. 19: 6 be a *k.* of priests, and an
1 Sam. 10:25 people the manner of the *k.*
1 Chr. 29:11 thine is the *k.*, O Lord
Ps. 22:28 for the *k.* is the Lord's
Dan. 2:44 God of heaven set up a *k.*
4:17 High ruleth in the *k.* of men
7:27 whose *k.* is an everlasting *k.*
Mat. 3: 2 for the *k.* of heaven is at hand
4:17 for the *k.* of heaven is at hand
5: 3 theirs is the *k.* of heaven
6:13 for thine is the *k.* and the
6:33 seek ye first the *k.* of God
11:12 *k.* of heaven suffereth violence
12:25 every *k.* divided against itself
12:28 the *k.* of God is come unto you
13:19 heareth the word of the *k.*
13:38 good seed are the children of the *k.*
16:19 the keys of the *k.* of heaven
23:13 shut up the *k.* of heaven against men
25: 1 *k.* of heaven be likened unto ten
25:34 inherit the *k.* prepared for you
Mark 1:15 the *k.* of God is at hand
11:10 blessed be the *k.* of our father David
Luke 10:11 *k.* of God is come nigh unto you
12:32 good pleasure to give you the *k.*
17:21 *k.* of God is within you
19:12 to receive for himself a *k.*
21:31 *k.* of God is nigh at hand
22:29 I appoint unto you a *k.* as my
John 3: 3 he cannot see the *k.* of God
18:36 my *k.* is not of this world
Rom. 14:17 *k.* of God is not meat and drink
1 Cor. 4:20 *k.* of God is not in word
6: 9 shall not inherit the *k.* of God
15:24 delivered up the *k.* to God
Eph. 5: 5 hath any inheritance in the *k.* of God
Col. 1:13 translated us into the *k.* of
2 Thes. 1: 5 be counted worthy of the *k.* of God
2 Tim. 4:18 preserve me to the heavenly *k.*
Jas. 2: 5 rich in faith, heirs of the *k.*
2 Pet. 1:11 into the everlasting *k.* of our Lord
Rev. 1: 9 in the *k.* and patience of Jesus
12:10 strength and the *k.* of our God
17:17 to give their *k.* to the beast

KINGDOMS
Rev. 11:15 *k.* of this world are become the *k.*

KISS (KISSED)
Ps. 2:12 *k.* the son lest he be angry
85:10 peace have *k.* each other
Sol. 1: 2 let him *k.* me with the kisses
Luke 7:38 *k.* his feet and anointed
Rom. 16:16 salute one another with an holy *k.*
1 Pet. 5:14 with the *k.* of charity

KISSES
Prov. 27: 6 *k.* of an enemy are deceitful

KNEE (KNEES)
Gen. 30: 3 she shall bear upon my *k.*
41:43 bow the *k.*: and he made him
Is. 35: 3 confirm the feeble *k.*
45:23 to God every *k.* shall bow
Dan. 5: 6 *k.* smote one against another
Nah. 2:10 the *k.* smite together and much pain
Mat. 27:29 they bowed the *k.* before him

Rom. 14:11 every *k.* shall bow to me
Eph. 3:14 I bow my *k.* unto the Lord
Phil. 2:10 of Jesus every *k.* should bow
Heb. 12:12 which hang down and the feeble *k.*

KNOCK
Mat. 7: 7 *k.* and it shall be opened
Rev. 3:20 I stand at the door and *k.*

KNEW (KNEWEST)
Gen. 3: 7 they *k.* they were naked
4: 1 Adam *k.* Eve his wife, and she
28:16 Lord in this place, I *k.* it not
Deut. 34:10 whom the Lord *k.* face to face
Jer. 1: 5 in the belly I *k.* thee
Mat. 7:23 I never *k.* you: depart ye
John 4:10 if thou *k.* the gift of God
Rom. 1:21 *k.* God they glorified him not
1 John 3: 1 us not, because it *k.* him not

KNOW
Gen. 18:19 *k.* him that he will command
22:12 now I *k.* that thou fearest God
Ex. 4:14 I *k.* that he can speak
Deut. 8: 2 to *k.* what was in thy
Josh. 22:22 Israel he shall *k.*; if it be in
1 Sam. 3: 7 Samuel did not yet *k.* Lord
1 Ki. 8:38 shall *k.* every man the plague of
2 Ki. 19:27 I *k.* thy abode and thy going
1 Chr. 28: 9 *k.* thou the God of thy father
Job 5:27 *k.* thou it for thy good
8: 9 are but of yesterday, and *k.* nothing
13:23 make me to *k.* my transgression
19:25 I *k.* that my Redeemer liveth
22:13 how doth God *k.*? can he judge
Ps. 4: 3 *k.* that Lord doth set apart the godly
9:10 that *k.* thy name will trust in
41:11 by this I *k.* thou favourest
46:10 be still, and *k.* that I am God
51: 6 thou shalt make me to *k.* wisdom
73:16 when I thought to *k.* this
139: 23 search me O God and *k.* my heart
Eccl. 11: 9 *k.* thou that for all these
Is. 58: 2 seek me daily and delight to *k.*
Jer. 10:23 I *k.* that the way of man is not
17: 9 desperately wicked, who can *k.* it
22:16 was not this to *k.* me, saith Lord
24: 7 I will give them a heart to *k.*
29:11 I *k.* the thoughts that I think
31:34 *k.* the Lord, for they shall all *k.*
44:28 shall *k.* whose words shall
Ezek. 2: 5 shall *k.* that there hath been a
Hos. 2:20 faithfulness, and thou shalt *k.* the
Mic. 3: 1 is it not for you to *k.* judgment
Mat. 6: 3 let not the left hand *k.* what
7:11 *k.* how to give good gifts
25:12 say unto ye, I *k.* you not
John 4:42 we *k.* this is the Christ
7:17 he shall *k.* of the doctrine
10: 4 sheep follow him, for they *k.*
10:14 and *k.* my sheep and am known
13: 7 knowest not now, but thou shalt *k.*
13:17 if ye *k.* these things, happy are
13:18 I *k.* whom I have chosen
13:35 by this shall all men *k.*
Acts 1: 7 it is not for you to *k.* the times
26:27 I *k.* that thou believest
Rom. 7:18 I *k.* that in me, that is in my
1 Cor. 2:14 neither can he *k.* them
4: 4 for I *k.* nothing by myself
4:19 and will *k.* not the speech
8: 2 knoweth nothing as he ought to *k.*
13:12 now I *k.* in part; but then
Eph. 3:19 to *k.* the love of Christ
Phil. 4:12 I *k.* both how to be abased
2 Tim. 1:12 I *k.* whom I have believed
Tit. 1:16 profess they *k.* God, but
1 John 2: 4 he that saith I *k.* him, and keepeth
Rev. 2: 2 I *k.* thy works and thy labor
3: 1 I *k.* thy works, that thou hast

KNOWETH (KNOWN)
Ps. 1: 6 Lord *k.* the way of the righteous
9:16 Lord is *k.* by judgment which he
31: 7 hast *k.* my soul in adversities
67: 2 that thy way may be *k.* on earth
94:11 Lord *k.* the thoughts of man that
103: 14 he *k.* our frame, that we
138: 6 the proud he *k.* afar off
139: 14 my soul *k.* right well
Eccl. 9: 1 no man *k.* either love or
Is. 1: 3 ox *k.* his owner, and ass his
45: 4 thou hast not *k.* me
Jer. 8: 7 stork *k.* her appointed times
Zeph. 3: 5 the unjust *k.* no shame
Mat. 6: 8 Father *k.* things ye have need of
10:26 hid that shall not be *k.*
24:36 of that day and hour *k.* no man
Luke 19:42 if thou hadst *k.*, even thou, at
Acts 15:18 *k.* to God are all his works
Rom. 1:19 that which may be *k.* of God
7: 7 I had not *k.* sin but by the law
1 Cor. 8: 3 love God, the same is *k.* of him
13:12 even as I am also *k.*
Gal. 4: 9 *k.* God, or rather are *k.* of God
2 Tim. 2:19 Lord *k.* them that are his
3:15 from a child thou hast *k.*
2 Pet. 2: 9 Lord *k.* how to deliver
1 John 3: 1 the world *k.* us not
Rev. 2:17 a name which no man *k.*
2:24 have not *k.* the depths of Satan

KNOWLEDGE
Gen. 2:17 of the tree of *k.* of good and evil
1 Sam. 2: 3 the Lord is a God of *k.*
Ps. 19: 2 night unto night showeth *k.*
73:11 is there *k.* in the Most High
139: 6 such *k.* is too wonderful
Prov. 8:12 I find out *k.* of witty inventions
9:10 *k.* of the holy is understanding
14: 6 *k.* is easy to him that understandeth
19: 2 soul be without *k.* is not good
30: 3 nor have the *k.* of the holy
Eccl. 9:10 nor device nor *k.* nor wisdom
Is. 28: 9 whom shall he teach *k.*
53:11 by his *k.* shall my righteous
Jer. 3:15 feed you with *k.* and understanding
Dan. 12: 4 and *k.* shall be increased
Hos. 4: 6 are destroyed for lack of *k.*
Hab. 2:14 earth shall be filled with the *k.* of
Mal. 2: 7 priest's lips should keep *k.*
Rom. 2:20 hast the form of *k.* and of the
3:20 for by the law is the *k.* of sin
10: 2 a zeal of God, but not according to *k.*
1 Cor. 8: 1 all have *k.* *K.* puffeth up
Eph. 3:19 love of Christ which passeth *k.*
Phil. 3: 8 loss for excellency of the *k.* of
Col. 2: 3 treasures of wisdom and *k.*
3:10 renewed in *k.* after the image
1 Pet. 3: 7 dwell with them according to their *k.*
2 Pet. 1: 5 faith virtue and to virtue *k.*
3:18 grow in grace and in the *k.* of the

L

LABOUR
Gen. 31:42 and the *l.* of my hands
35:16 and she had hard *l.*
Ps. 90:10 yet is their strength *l.*
104: 23 work to his *l.* until
128: 2 thou shalt eat the *l.* of thine
Prov. 14:23 in all *l.* there is profit
23: 4 *l.* not to be rich; cease
Eccl. 1: 8 all things are full of *l.*
4: 8 yet is there no end of all his *l.*
Is. 55: 2 ye spend your *l.* for that which
Mat. 11:28 ye that *l.* and are heavy laden
John 4:38 reap that whereon ye bestowed no *l.*
6:27 *l.* not for the meat that
1 Cor. 15:58 your *l.* is not in vain in
1 Thes. 1: 3 work of faith, *l.* of love
5:12 know them which *l.* among you, and
Heb. 4:11 let us *l.* to enter into

LABOURED
Is. 49: 4 I have *l.* in vain
John 4:38 other men *l.* and ye are entered
1 Cor. 15:10 I *l.* more abundantly that they
Phil. 2:16 not run in vain, neither *l.* in vain

LABOURER (LABOURERS)
Mat. 9:37 plenteous but the *l.* are few
Luke 10: 2 send forth *l.* into his harvest
10: 7 the *l.* is worthy of his hire
1 Cor. 3: 9 for we are *l.* together with God
1 Tim. 5:18 the *l.* is worthy of his reward

LABOURS
Rev. 14:13 that they may rest from their *l.*

LACK (LACKING)
Hos. 4: 6 for *l.* of knowledge: because thou
Mat. 19:20 my youth up: what I *l.* yet
2 Cor. 11: 9 that which was *l.* to me
1 Thes. 3:10 which is *l.* in your faith
Jas. 1: 5 If any of you *l.* wisdom

LADY (LADIES)
Judg. 5:29 her wise *l.* answered her
Esth. 1:18 *l.* of Persia and Media say this
Is. 47: 5 no more be called the *l.* of kingdoms
47: 7 I shall be a *l.* for ever
2 John 1: 1 unto the elect *l.* and her children

LAMB (LAMBS)
Gen. 22: 7 where is the *l.* for a burnt offering
22: 8 God will provide himself a *l.*
Ex. 12: 3 to them every man a *l.*
2 Sam. 12: 3 had nothing save one little ewe *l.*
Is. 11: 6 wolf shall dwell with the *l.*
53: 7 brought as a *l.* to slaughter
John 1:29 behold the *L.* of God
21:15 Jesus said to Peter, Feed my *l.*
1 Pet. 1:19 as a *l.* without blemish
Rev. 5:12 worthy is the *L.* that was slain
7:14 white in the blood of the *L.*
7:17 *L.* in the midst of the throne
13: 8 *L.* slain from the foundation

LAME
Lev. 21:18 a blind man, or a *l.*, or he
Job 29:15 eyes to the blind, feet to the *l.*
Prov. 26: 7 legs of the *l.* are not equal
Is. 35: 6 shall the *l.* man leap as an hart
Mal. 1:13 that which was torn, and the *l.*
Heb. 12:13 *l.* be turned out of the way

LAMP
Ex. 25:37 make the seven *l.* thereof
27:20 to cause the *l.* to burn
Num. 8: 2 the *l.*, the seven *l.* shall
2 Sam. 22:29 thou art my *l.* O Lord
1 Ki. 15: 4 give him a *l.* in Jerusalem
Job 12: 5 is as a *l.* despised in the thought
Ps. 119:105 thy word a *l.* to my feet
132: 17 I have ordained a *l.* for mine
Prov. 6:23 the commandment is a *l.* and the law
13: 9 *l.* of wicked shall be put out
Is. 62: 1 salvation as the *l.* that burneth
Zech. 4: 2 and his seven *l.* thereon, and seven
Mat. 25: 1 which took their *l.* went forth
Rev. 4: 5 were seven *l.* of fire

LANGUAGE
Gen. 11: 1 earth was of one *l.*
Neh. 13:24 could not speak in the Jew's *l.*
Ps. 81: 5 I heard a *l.* that I understood not
Is. 19:18 speak the *l.* of Canaan
Zeph. 3: 9 I turn to the people a pure *l.*

LASCIVIOUSNESS
Mark 7:22 deceit, *l.*, an evil eye
2 Cor. 12:21 fornication and *l.*, which they have
Gal. 5:19 fornication, uncleanness, *l.*
Eph. 4:19 given themselves over to *l.*
1 Pet. 4: 3 when we walked in *l.*
Jude 1: 4 turning the grace of God into *l.*

LATTER
Job 19:25 stand at the *l.* upon earth
Prov. 19:20 be wise in the *l.* end
Hag. 2: 9 glory of this *l.* house
1 Tim. 4: 1 that in the *l.* times

LAUGH (LAUGHING)
Gen. 17:17 upon his face and *l.*
18:15 he said, Nay, but thou didst *l.*
Job 5:22 thou shalt *l.* neither shalt thou be
8:21 till he fill thy mouth with *l.*
Ps. 2: 4 he that sitteth in heavens shall *l.*
37:13 Lord shall *l.* at him for he seeth
52: 6 righteous shall see and fear and *l.*
Prov. 1:26 I will *l.* at your calamity
Luke 6:21 weep now for ye shall *l.*
6:25 woe to you that *l.*

LAUGHTER
Ps. 126: 2 was our mouth filled with *l.*
Prov. 14:13 in *l.* the heart is sorrowful
Eccl. 2: 2 I said of *l.*, It is mad
7: 3 sorrow is better than *l.*
Jas. 4: 9 let *l.* be turned to mourning

LAW
Gen. 47:26 made it a *l.* over the land
Deut. 33: 2 from his right hand went a fiery *l.*
Neh. 8: 7 caused people to understand the *l.*
9:26 cast thy *l.* behind their backs
10:28 of the lands unto the *l.* of God
Job 22:22 *l.* from his mouth and lay up his

Ps. 19: 7 *l.* of the Lord is perfect
37:31 *l.* of his God is in his heart
40: 8 thy *l.* is within my heart
78: 5 appointed a *l.* in Israel
94:12 teachest him out of thy *l.*
119: 18 wondrous things out of thy *l.*
119: 70 I delight in thy *l.*
119: 72 *l.* of thy mouth is better
119: 97 how I love thy *l.*
Prov. 6:23 the *l.* is the light: and reproofs
7: 2 keep my *l.* as the apple of thine eye
13:14 the *l.* of the wise is a fountain
28: 9 away his ear from hearing the *l.*
29:18 keepeth the *l.* happy is he
Is. 2: 3 out of Zion shall go forth the *l.*
8:16 seal the *l.* among my disciples
8:20 to the *l.* and the testimony
42:21 magnify the *l.* and make it
51: 7 people in whose heart is my *l.*
Jer. 18:18 *l.* shall not perish from the priest
31:33 I will put the *l.* in inward parts
Hos. 8:12 great things of my *l.*, but they were
Mal. 2: 7 they should seek the *l.* at his mouth
Luke 16:16 *l.* and prophets were until John
John 1:17 *l.* was given by Moses
19: 7 we have a *l.* and by our *l.* he
Acts 13:39 not justified by the *l.* of Moses
Rom. 2:12 without the *l.* perish without the *l.*
2:13 not hearers of the *l.*
2:14 having not the *l.* are a *l.*
3:20 *l.* shall no flesh be justified
3:31 do we make void the *l.*?
4:15 *l.* worketh wrath; where no *l.*
5:13 sin is not imputed where no *l.*
7: 7 known sin but by the *l.*
7: 8 for without the *l.* sin was dead
7: 9 I was alive without the *l.*
7:12 the *l.* is holy, just, and good
7:14 *l.* is spiritual, but I am carnal
7:22 I delight in the *l.* of God
7:23 warring against the *l.* of my mind
8: 2 made me free from the *l.* of sin
10: 5 righteousness which is of the *l.*
1 Cor. 6: 1 go to *l.* before the unjust
6: 7 brother goeth to the *l.* with brother
Gal. 2:16 man not justified by works of the *l.*
2:19 I through the *l.* am dead to the *l.*
3:10 of works of the *l.* are under a curse
3:12 the *l.* is not of faith, but the
3:13 us from the curse of the *l.*
5:23 love, faith, against such is no *l.*
Phil. 3: 9 righteousness which is of the *l.*
1 Tim. 1: 8 the *l.* is good, if a man use
1: 9 that *l.* is not made for the righteous
Heb. 7:19 for the *l.* made nothing perfect
Jas. 1:25 whoso looketh into the perfect *l.*
1 John 3: 4 sin transgresseth the *l.*

LAWFUL
Ezek. 18: 5 do that which is *l.* and right
33:19 do that which is *l.* and right
1 Cor. 6:12 all things are *l.* unto me
10:23 All things are *l.* for me

LAY
Gen. 19:35 perceived when she *l.* down
Eccl. 7: 2 the living will *l.* it to heart
Is. 28:16 I *l.* in Zion for a foundation
Mal. 2: 2 ye do not *l.* it to heart
Mat. 6:20 *l.* up for yourselves treasure
8:20 hath not where to *l.* his head
John 10:15 I *l.* down my life for the sheep
Acts 7:60 *l.* not this sin to their charge
15:28 *l.* on you no greater burden
1 Tim. 5:22 *l.* hands suddenly on no man
6:12 *l.* hold on eternal life
Heb. 6:18 *l.* hold upon the hope set before
12: 1 *l.* aside every weight
Jas. 1:21 *l.* apart all filthiness and superfluity
1 John 3:16 we ought to *l.* down our lives

LAID (LAYETH, LAYING)
1 Sam. 21:12 David *l.* up these words in his
Job 21:19 God *l.* up his iniquity
Ps. 31:19 *l.* up for them that fear
62: 9 to be *l.* in the balance
89:19 I *l.* help on one that is
Prov. 2: 7 *l.* up sound wisdom for the righteous
26:24 and *l.* up deceit within him
Sol. 7:13 *l.* up for thee O my beloved
Is. 53: 6 Lord hath *l.* on him the iniquity
56: 2 that *l.* hold on it
57: 1 no man *l.* it to heart
Jer. 12:11 because no man *l.* it to heart
Luke 1:66 *l.* up in their hearts
12:19 much goods *l.* up for many years
1 Cor. 3:10 I have *l.* the foundation
Col. 1: 5 hope which is *l.* up for you
2 Tim. 4: 8 *l.* up for me a crown of
Heb. 6: 1 not *l.* again the foundation
6: 2 *l.* on of hands, and of resurrection
1 Pet. 2: 1 *l.* aside all malice and all guile
1 Tim. 6:19 *l.* up in store for themselves

LEAD (LEADETH, LED)
Ex. 15:10 sank as *l.* in the mighty waters
Ps. 5: 8 *l.* me O Lord in thy righteousness
23: 2 *l.* me beside still waters
25: 5 *l.* me in thy truth and teach
61: 2 *l.* me to the rock that is higher
139: 24 *l.* me in the way everlasting
Sol. 8: 2 I would *l.* thee and bring thee
Is. 11: 6 a little child shall *l.* them
40:11 gently *l.* those with young
Zech. 5: 8 weight of *l.* upon the mouth
Mat. 7:13 broad is the way that *l.* to
7:14 narrow is the way that *l.* to life
15:14 blind *l.* the blind, both shall fall
John 10: 3 calleth sheep and *l.* them out
Rom. 8:14 as are *l.* by the spirit
Gal. 5:18 ye be *l.* of the spirit
1 Tim. 2: 2 may *l.* a quiet and peaceable life
Rev. 7:17 and shall *l.* them unto living

LEAN (LEANING, LEANED)
Job 8:15 he shall *l.* upon his house
Prov. 3: 5 *l.* not unto thine own understanding
Sol. 8: 5 wilderness *l.* on her beloved
Mic. 3:11 yet will they *l.* on the Lord
John 13:23 *l.* on Jesus' bosom one of his
21:20 which also *l.* on his breast

LEAP (LEAPED, LEAPING)
Sol. 2: 8 cometh *l.* upon the mountains
Is. 35: 6 shall the lame man *l.*
Zeph. 1: 9 I punish all those that *l.*
Luke 1:41 the babe *l.* in her womb
6:23 rejoice in that day and *l.* for joy

LEARN (LEARNED)
Deut. 4:10 that they may *l.* to fear
31:13 and *l.* to fear the Lord
Ps. 106: 35 among the heathen *l.* their works
119: 71 that I might *l.* thy statutes
Prov. 22:25 lest thou *l.* his ways
Is. 1:17 *l.* to do well, seek
26:10 yet will he not *l.* righteousness
50: 4 given me the tongue of the *l.*
Jer. 10: 2 *l.* not the way of the heathen
Mat. 9:13 *l.* what that meaneth, I will have
11:29 *l.* of me, for I am meek
John 6:45 hath *l.* of Father cometh unto me
Acts 7:22 Moses was *l.* in all wisdom
Eph. 4:20 ye have not so *l.* Christ
Tit. 3:14 also *l.* to maintain good
Heb. 5: 8 he were a Son, yet *l.* he obedience
Rev. 14: 3 no man could *l.* that song

LEARNING
Acts 26:24 much *l.* doth make thee mad
Rom. 15: 4 were written for our *l.*
2 Tim. 3: 7 ever *l.* and never able to

LEAST
Gen. 32:10 not worthy of the *l.* of all the
Jer. 31:34 shall know me from the *l.* of them
Luke 16:10 in that which is *l.* is faithful
1 Cor. 6: 4 them to judge who are *l.* esteemed
15: 9 I am the *l.* of the apostles
Eph. 3: 8 less than the *l.* of all saints

LEAVE
Gen. 2:24 man shall *l.* his father and mother
1 Ki. 8:57 let him not *l.* us, nor
Ps. 16:10 not *l.* my soul in hell
27: 9 *l.* me not, neither forsake me
Mat. 5:24 *l.* there thy gift before the altar
19: 5 shall a man *l.* father and mother
23:23 and not to *l.* the other undone
Mark 10: 7 man *l.* his father and mother
John 14:18 will not *l.* you comfortless
14:27 peace I *l.* with you, my peace
Acts 2:27 not *l.* my soul in hell
Eph. 5:31 man *l.* his father and mother
Heb. 13: 5 I will never *l.* thee, nor forsake

LEAVEN
Ex. 12:15 put away *l.* our of your houses
Lev. 2:11 ye shall burn no *l.*, nor any honey
Mat. 13:33 heaven is like unto *l.* which a woman
16: 6 beware of the *l.* of the Pharisees
Luke 12: 1 beware ye of the *l.* of the Pharisees
1 Cor. 5: 6 a little *l.* leaveneth a whole lump
5: 8 not with old *l.*, neither with the

LEND (LENDETH, LENT)
Ex. 22:25 *l.* money to any of my people
Deut. 23:20 stranger thou mayest *l.* upon usury
1 Sam. 1:28 I have *l.* him to the Lord
Ps. 37:26 merciful and *l.*, and his seed is
112: 5 showeth favour and *l.*, he will guide
Prov. 19:17 hath pity upon the poor *l.* to Lord
Jer. 15:10 I have neither *l.* on usury, nor

LENDER
Prov. 22: 7 borrower is servant to the *l.*

LEOPARD (LEOPARDS)
Sol. 4: 8 the mountains of the *l.*
Is. 11: 6 *l.* shall lie down with the kid
Jer. 5: 6 a *l.* shall watch over their cities
13:23 or the *l.* his spots; then may ye
Hos. 13: 7 as a *l.* by the way will I
Hab. 1: 8 also are swifter than the *l.*

LEVIATHAN
Job 41: 1 draw out *l.* with an hook
Ps. 74:14 breakest the heads of *l.*

LIAR (LIARS)
Ps. 116: 11 All men are *l.*
Is. 44:25 frustrateth the tokens of *l.*
John 8:44 he is a *l.* and the father
Rom. 3: 4 let God be true, every man a *l.*
Tit. 1:12 the Cretians are always *l.*
1 John 1:10 we make him a *l.*, and his word
5:10 hath made him a *l.* because he
2: 4 keepeth not his commandments is a *l.*
Rev. 2: 2 not and hast found them *l.*

LIBERAL (LIBERALLY)
Prov. 11:25 *l.* soul shall be made fat
Is. 32: 8 the *l.* deviseth *l.* things
2 Cor. 9:13 your *l.* distribution unto them
Jas. 1: 5 giveth to all men *l.*, and upbraideth

LIBERALITY
1 Cor. 16: 3 bring your *l.* into Jerusalem
2 Cor. 8: 2 unto the riches of their *l.*

LIBERTY
Lev. 25:10 and proclaim *l.* throughout all the land
Ps. 119: 45 I will walk at *l.* for I seek
Is. 61: 1 proclaim *l.* to the captives
Jer. 34: 8 to proclaim *l.* unto them
Luke 4:18 to set at *l.* the bruised
Rom. 8:21 glorious *l.* of the children of God
Gal. 5: 1 stand fast in the *l.* wherewith Christ
5:13 use not *l.* for an occasion to
Jas. 1:25 looketh into the perfect law of *l.*
2:12 be judged by the law of *l.*

LIE
Ps. 62: 9 men of high degree are a *l.*
Num. 23:19 God is not a man, that he should *l.*
Is. 63: 8 children that will not *l.*
Hab. 2: 3 it shall speak and not *l.*
Col. 3: 9 *l.* not one to another, seeing
2 Thes. 2:11 they should believe a *l.*
Tit. 1: 2 God that cannot *l.* hath promised
Heb. 6:18 it was impossible for God to *l.*

LIES
Job 11: 3 should thy *l.* make men hold
Ps. 58: 3 as they are born, speaking *l.*
101: 7 that telleth *l.* shall not tarry
Hos. 11:12 compasseth me about with *l.*
1 Tim. 4: 2 speaking *l.* in hypocrisy

LYING
Ps. 119: 29 remove from me the way of *l.*
119:163 I hate and abhor *l.* but love thy law
Prov. 12:19 a *l.* tongue is but for a moment
Jer. 7: 4 trust ye not in *l.* words, saying
Hos. 4: 2 by swearing and *l.* and killing and

Jonah 2: 8 observe l. vanities forsake their own
Eph. 4:25 wherefore putting away l.

LIFE
Gen. 2: 9 tree of l. also in the midst
44:30 is bound up in the lad's l.
Deut. 30:15 before thee this day, l. and good
32:47 because it is your l.: and
1 Sam. 25:29 bound in the bundle of l.
1 Ki. 19: 4 O Lord, take away my l.
Job 2: 4 hath will he give for his l.
10:12 granted me l. and favour
Ps. 16:11 show me the path of l.
21: 4 asked l. of thee and thou gavest
36: 9 with thee is the fountain of l.
63: 3 lovingkindness better than l.
66: 9 God holdeth our soul in l.
91:16 with long l. will I satisfy
Prov. 8:35 whoso findeth me findeth l.
15:24 way of l. is above to the wise
18:21 death and l. are in the power of the
Is. 57:10 thou hast found the l. of thine hand
Mat. 6:25 take no thought for your l.
10:39 findeth his l. shall loose it
20:28 to give his l. a ransom for many
John 1: 4 in him was l. and the l. was
3:36 believeth on the Son hath everlasting l.
5:40 come to me, that ye might have l.
6:35 I am the bread of l.
6:51 flesh which I will give for the l.
6:63 are spirit, and they are l.
8:12 but shall have the light of l.
10:10 I am come that they might have l.
11:25 I am the resurrection and the l.
14: 6 I am the way, the truth, and the l.
Rom. 5:10 reconciled shall be saved by his l.
5:17 reign in l. by one, Jesus Christ
8: 2 law of the Spirit of l. in Christ
8: 6 to be spiritually minded is l. and
2 Cor. 2:16 to the other, the savour of l. unto l.
3: 6 letter killeth, the spirit giveth l.
4:11 l. of Jesus might be manifest
5: 4 mortality swallowed up of l.
Gal. 2:20 the l. which I now live in the flesh
Eph. 4:18 alienated from a l. of God
Col. 3: 3 your l. is hid with Christ
3: 4 when Christ our l. shall appear
1 Tim. 2: 2 a peaceable l. in all godliness
4: 8 having the promise of the l. that
2 Tim. 1:10 brought l. and immortality to light
2 Pet. 1: 3 that pertain unto l. and godliness
1 John 5:12 he that hath the Son hath l.

LIFT UP (LIFTED, LIFTING)
Num. 6:26 l. his countenance upon thee
2 Chr. 17: 6 heart l. in ways of the Lord
Ps. 4: 6 Lord l. the light of countenance
7: 6 Lord l. thyself because of rage
24: 7 l. up your heads, O ye gates
25: 1 to thee I l. my soul
75: 4 wicked l. not the horn
83: 2 they that hate thee l. the head
102: 10 thou hast l. and cast me down
121: 1 l. mine eyes unto the hills
141: 2 l. of my hands as the evening
Eccl. 4:10 one will l. his fellow
Is. 33:10 now will I l. myself
26:11 Lord, when thy hand is l.
42: 2 he shall not cry, nor l.
Jer. 7:16 neither l. cry nor prayer for them
Lam. 3:41 let us l. our hearts with
Hab. 2: 4 his soul which is l. is not upright
John 3:14 so must the Son of man be l.
8:28 when ye have l. the Son of man
12:32 if I be l. will draw all men
1 Tim. 2: 8 l. holy hands, without wrath
Heb. 12:12 l. the hands which hang
Jas. 4:10 Lord and he shall l. you up

LIGHT
Gen. 1: 3 let there be l.
Num. 21: 5 our soul loatheth this l. bread
Judg. 9: 4 vain and l. persons which followed
1 Ki. 16:31 it had been a l. thing
Job 18: 5 l. of the wicked put out
25: 3 on whom doth not his l. arise
33:30 enlightened with the l. of the living
Ps. 4: 6 lift up the l. of thy countenance
36: 9 in thy l. shall we see l.
43: 3 O send out thy l. and thy truth
90: 8 sins in the l. of thy countenance
97:11 l. is sown for the righteous
104: 2 coverest thyself with l. as a
112: 4 to the upright ariseth l. in
119:105 and a l. unto my path
Prov. 4:18 path of the just is as shining l.
6:23 and the law is l., and reproofs
15:30 l. of the eyes rejoiceth the
Eccl. 11: 7 l. is sweet and a pleasant
Is. 5:20 darkness for l. and l. for
5:30 the l. is darkened in the heavens
8:20 because there is no l. in them
9: 2 in darkness have seen a great l.
30:26 l. of the moon shall be as the l.
42: 6 a l. of the Gentiles
45: 7 I form l. and create darkness
49: 6 it is a l. thing
50:10 walketh in darkness and hath no l.
58: 8 thy l. break forth as morning
58:60 shine; for thy l. is come
Ezek. 8:17 Is it a l. thing
Zeph. 3: 4 her prophets are l. and
Zech. 14: 6 l. shall not be clear nor
14: 7 evening time it shall be l.
Mat. 5:14 ye are the l. of the world
5:16 let your l. so shine before men
11:30 my yoke easy, my burden l.
Luke 2:32 a l. to lighten the Gentiles
16: 8 wiser than the children of l.
John 1: 4 the life was the l. of men
1: 7 came to bear witness of the l.
1: 9 true l. that lighteth every man
3:19 loved darkness rather than l.
3:20 neither cometh to the l., lest
5:35 a burning and a shining l.
8:12 I am the l. of the world
8:12 shall have the l. of life
12:35 walk while ye have the l.
Acts 13:47 I have set thee for a l.
26:18 turn them from darkness to l.
Rom. 13:12 put on the armour of l.
2 Cor. 4: 4 the l. of the glorious gospel
4:17 our l. affliction which is
6:14 what communion hath l. with darkness
Eph. 5: 8 walk as children of l.
5:14 Christ shall give thee l.
1 Thes. 5: 5 ye are the children of l.
1 Pet. 2: 9 to his marvellous l.
1 John 1: 5 God is l. and in him is
Rev. 21:23 the Lamb is the l. thereof

LIGHTS
Ps. 136: 7 to him that made great l.; for his
Ezek. 32: 8 all the bright l. of heaven
Luke 12:35 girded about and your l. burning
Phil. 2:15 ye shine as l. in the world
Jas. 1:17 down from the father of l.

LIGHTEN (LIGHTENED)
2 Sam. 22:29 Lord will l. my darkness
Ezra 9: 8 God may l. our eyes
Ps. 13: 3 God: l. mine eyes lest I sleep
34: 5 looked unto him, and were l.
Rev. 21:23 glory of God did l. it

LIGHTNING (LIGHTNINGS)
Ex. 19:16 there were thunders and l.
Ps. 18:14 and he shot out l.
Mat. 24:27 as the l. cometh out of the
28: 3 his countenance was like l.
Luke 10:18 Satan as l. fall from heaven

LIKE
1 Cor. 16:13 quit you l. men, be strong
Heb. 2:17 be made l. his brethren
1 John 3: 2 we shall be l. him

LIKENESS
Gen. 1:26 in our image, after our l.
5: 3 begat a son in his own l.
Ps. 17:15 when I awake with thy l.
Rom. 6: 5 together in the l. of his death
8: 3 in the l. of sinful flesh
Phil. 2: 7 made in the l. of men

LINE (LINES)
Ps. 16: 6 l. are fallen unto me in pleasant
Is. 28:13 l. upon l., l. upon l.
28:17 judgment will I lay to the l.
34:11 stretch out on it a l. of confusion
2 Cor. 10:16 boast in another man's l. of things

LION (LIONS)
Gen. 49: 9 Judah is a l. whelp
Judg. 14:18 what is stronger than a l.
Job 4:11 l. should perish for lack of prey
28: 8 the l. whelps have not trodden
Ps. 7: 2 tear my soul like a l.
22:13 ravening and a roaring l.
Prov. 22:13 there is a l. without
28: 1 righteous are bold as a l.
Is. 11: 6 calf and young l. and the fatling
35: 9 no l. shall be there, nor
38:13 as a l. so will he break all my
65:25 l. shall eat straw like the bullock
Ezek. 1:10 face of a l., on the right side
Hos. 5:14 and as a young l. to the house
2 Tim. 4:17 delivered out of the mouth of the l.
1 Pet. 5: 8 the devil as a roaring l. walketh
Rev. 4: 7 beast was like a l.
5: 5 L. of the tribe of Judah

LIPS
Ex. 6:30 I am of uncircumcised l.
Ps. 12: 3 cut off all flattering l.
17: 1 goeth not out of feigned l.
17: 4 by the word or thy l. I have kept me
31:18 lying l. be put to silence
45: 2 grace is poured into thy l.
51:15 open thou my l.
63: 3 my l. shall praise thee
63: 5 praise thee with joyful l.
141: 3 keep the door of my l.
Prov. 10:18 hideth hatred with lying l.
10:21 l. of the righteous feed many
16:10 in the l. of the king
17: 4 giveth heed to false l.
26:23 burning l. and a wicked heart
Sol. 7: 9 l. of those that are asleep to speak
Is. 6: 5 I am a man of unclean l.
57:19 I create the fruit of the l.
59: 3 your l. have spoken lies
Mal. 2: 7 priest's l. should keep knowledge

LITTLE
Ezra 9: 8 now for a l. space grace hath
Neh. 9:32 trouble seem l. before thee
Ps. 2:12 his wrath is kindled but a l.
8: 5 a l. lower than the angels
37:16 a l. that a righteous man hath
Prov. 6:10 a l. sleep, a l. slumber, a l.
15:16 better is a l. with fear
16: 8 better is a l. with righteousness
Is. 28:10 here a l. and there a l.
54: 8 in a l. wrath I hid my face
Ezek. 11:16 will I be to them as a l. sanctuary
Mat. 6:30 O ye of l. faith
14:31 O thou of l. faith
Luke 12:32 fear not, l. flock, it is
19:17 been faithful in a very l.
1 Tim. 4: 8 bodily exercise profiteth l.
Heb. 2: 7 a l. lower then the angels
Rev. 3: 8 hast a l. strength, and hast kept

LIVE
Gen. 3:22 of life and eat and l. forever
17:18 Ishmael might l. before thee
Lev. 18: 5 if a man do, he shall l.
Job 14:14 if a man die, shall he l. again
Ps. 55:23 men shall not l. out half their days
63: 4 will I bless thee while I l.
118: 17 I shall not die, but l. and
146: 2 while I l. will I praise
Is. 38:16 recover me and make me to l.
55: 3 hear, and your soul shall l.
Ezek. 3:21 he shall surely l., because he is
16: 6 wast in thy blood, L.; yea, I said
18:32 turn yourselves and l.
33:16 lawful and right, he shall surely l.
Hab. 2: 4 the just shall l. by faith
Mat. 4: 4 man shall not l. by bread alone
Acts 17:28 in him we l. and move and have
Rom. 8:13 if ye l. after the flesh, ye
10: 5 those things shall l. by them
14: 8 whether we l., we l. unto the Lord
1 Cor. 9:14 they which preach the gospel l. of
2 Cor. 5:15 which l. should not l. to themselves
6: 9 as dying, and behold we l.
13:11 be of one mind, l. in peace
Gal. 2:20 l. in the flesh, I l. by the faith
3:12 shall l. in them
5:25 if we l. in Spirit, walk in
Phil. 1:21 to l. is Christ, and to die is
2 Tim. 3:12 all that will l. godly in Christ
Tit. 2:12 we should l. soberly
Heb. 13:18 willing to l. honestly
1 Pet. 2:24 should l. unto righteousness, by
1 John 4: 9 would that we might l. through him

LIVED (LIVETH)
Job 19:25 for I know that my Redeemer *l.*
Acts 23: 1 *l.* in all good conscience before God
Rom. 6:10 in that he *l.*, he *l.* unto God
1 Tim. 5: 6 *l.* in pleasure is dead while she *l.*
Heb. 7:25 he ever *l.* to make intercession
Jas. 5: 5 ye have *l.* in pleasure on the earth
Rev. 1:18 he that *l.* and was dead
18: 9 *l.* deliciously with her, shall bewail

LIVELY
Acts 7:38 received the *l.* oracles to give unto
1 Pet. 1: 3 begotten again to a *l.* hope
2: 5 ye, as *l.* stones, are built up a

LIVING
Eccl. 7: 2 *l.* will lay it to heart
Is. 38:19 the *l.*, the *l.* shall praise
Jer. 2:13 fountain of *l.* waters, and hewed them
Mat. 22:32 God of the dead, but of the *l.*
John 7:38 shall flow rivers of *l.* water
Rom. 12: 1 present your bodies a *l.* sacrifice
14: 9 Lord both of the dead and *l.*
1 Cor. 15:45 first man Adam made a *l.* soul
Heb. 10:20 by a new and *l.* way, which he hath
1 Pet. 2: 4 coming as to a *l.* stone, disallowed
Rev. 7:17 lead them to *l.* fountains

LOFTY
Ps. 131: 1 not haughty nor mine eyes *l.*
Prov. 30:13 how *l.* are their eyes
Is. 2:11 *l.* looks of man shall be humbled
57:15 *l.* One that inhabiteth eternity

LOINS
Prov. 31:17 she girdeth her *l.* with strength
Is. 11: 5 shall be the girdle of his *l.*
Luke 12:35 let your *l.* be girded
Eph. 6:14 *l.* girt about with truth
1 Pet. 1:13 gird up the *l.* of your mind

LONG (LONGED, LONGETH, LONGING)
Job 6: 8 the thing that I *l.* for
Ps. 63: 1 my flesh *l.* for thee
84: 2 my soul *l.*, yea, even fainteth
107: 9 he satisfieth the *l.* soul
119: 20 my soul breaketh for the *l.*
119: 40 I have *l.* after thy precepts
119:131 I have *l.* for thy commandments
119:174 I have *l.* for thy salvation
Rom. 1:11 for I *l.* to see you

LONGSUFFERING
Ex. 34: 6 gracious, *l.*, and abundant
Num. 14:18 the Lord is *l.* and of great mercy
Ps. 86:15 compassion, and gracious, *l.*
Jer. 15:15 take me not away in thy *l.*
Rom. 2: 4 goodness, and forbearance, and *l.*
9:22 endured with much *l.* the vessels
Gal. 5:22 joy peace, *l.*, gentleness
Eph. 4: 2 meekness, with *l.*, forbearing one
Col. 1:11 unto all patience, and *l.*
3:12 humbleness of mind, meekness, and *l.*
1 Tim. 1:16 Christ might show forth all *l.*
2 Tim. 3:10 purpose, faith, *l.*, charity, patience
4: 2 exhort with all *l.* and doctrine
1 Pet. 3:20 when once the *l.* of God waited in
2 Pet. 3; 9 but is *l.* to us-ward

LOOK (LOOKED)
Gen. 13:14 and *l.* from the place where
29:32 the Lord *l.* on my affliction
Ex. 2:25 God *l.* upon the children
4:31 he had *l.* upon their affliction
10:10 *l.* to it; for evil is before you
Ps. 34: 5 they *l.* to him and were lightened
Sol. 1: 6 *l.* not upon me, because I am black
Is. 5: 7 he *l.* for judgment, but behold
8:17 of Jacob, and I will *l.* for him
22:11 ye have not *l.* to the maker of
45:22 *l.* unto me and be saved
64: 3 didst terrible things we *l.* not for
66: 2 to this man will I *l.*
Jer. 8:15 we *l.* for peace, but no good came
Mic. 7: 7 I will *l.* unto the Lord
Hag. 1: 9 ye *l.* for much and lo, it came to
Luke 2:38 that *l.* for redemption in Jerusalem
7:19 or *l.* we for another
22:61 the Lord turned and *l.* upon Peter
2 Cor. 4:18 we *l.* not at things seen
Phil. 2: 4 *l.* not every man on his own
3:20 heaven, from whence also we *l.* for
Heb. 9:28 unto them that *l.* for him he shall
11:10 for he *l.* for a city which hath
1 Pet. 1:12 things the angels desire to *l.* into
1 John 1: 1 that which we have *l.* on

LOOKETH (LOOKING)
1 Sam. 16: 7 *l.* on outward appearance, but the
Ps. 33:13 the Lord *l.* from heaven
Prov. 14:15 prudent man *l.* well to his
Sol. 2: 9 he *l.* forth at the windows, showing
Is. 38:14 mine eyes fail with *l.* upward
Mat. 5:28 whosoever *l.* on a woman to lust after
24:50 come in a day he *l.* not for
Luke 9:62 *l.* back is fit for the kingdom of God
Tit. 2:13 *l.* for that blessed hope
Heb. 10:27 a certain fearful *l.* for
12: 2 *l.* to Jesus, the author and
Jas. 1:25 *l.* into the perfect law of
2 Pet. 3:12 *l.* for and hasting unto the coming
Jude 1:21 *l.* for the mercy of our Lord

LOOKS
Ps. 18:27 wilt bring down high *l.*

LOOSE (LOOSED, LOOSETH)
Deut. 25: 9 and *l.* his shoe from his foot
Josh. 5:15 *l.* thy shoe from thy foot
Ps. 102: 20 to *l.* those appointed to death
146: 7 Lord *l.* the prisoners
Eccl. 12: 6 or ever the silver cord be *l.*
Acts 2:24 *l.* the pains of death
1 Cor. 7:27 seek not to be *l.* Art thou *l.*

LORD
Gen. 15: 6 he believed in the *L.*
Ex. 34: 6 *L.*, the *L.* God, merciful
Deut. 4:35 *L.* he is God; there is none else
6: 4 O Israel, the *L.* our God is one *L.*
10:17 the *L.* your God is God of gods
1 Sam. 2: 1 heart rejoiced in the *L.*
1 Ki. 18:39 the *L.*, he is the God
2 Ki. 18: 5 he trusted in the *L.* God
Neh. 9: 6 art thou, even thou *L.* alone; thou
Ps. 4: 5 put your trust in the *L.*
31:24 hope in the *L.*
34: 2 soul make her boast in the *L.*
37: 3 Trust in the *L.*
37: 4 delight thyself in the *L.*
97:12 rejoice in the *L.*, ye righteous
100: 3 the *L.*, he is God, it is he that
104: 34 will be glad in the *L.*
118: 27 God is the *L.*, which hath shown
Prov. 3: 5 trust in the *L.* with
Is. 26: 4 trust ye in the *L.*
37:20 therefore, oh *L.* our God
45:17 Israel shall be saved in the *L.*
45:24 in the *L.* have I righteousness
45:25 in the *L.* all the seed of Israel
61:10 greatly rejoice in the *L.*
Dan. 2:47 and a *L.* of kings, and a revealer
Joel 2:23 rejoice in the *L.* your God
Zeph. 3: 2 she trusted not in the *L.*
Zech. 10: 7 heart shall rejoice in the *L.*
Mark 2:28 Son of man is *L.* of the sabbath
Acts 2:36 crucified, both *L.* and Christ
Rom. 10:12 same *L.* over all is rich
14: 9 *L.* of the dead and of the living
16:12 labour in the *L.*
1 Cor. 2: 8 have crucified the *L.* of glory
8: 6 one God, one *L.* Jesus Christ
15:47 second man is the *L.* from heaven
15:58 abounding in the work of the *L.*
Eph. 4: 5 one *L.*, one faith, one baptism
Phil. 3: 1 rejoice in the *L.*
Col. 4: 7 fellow servant in the *L.*
1 Thes. 5:12 over you in the *L.*
1 Tim. 6:15 king of kings and *L.* of lords
Rev. 14:13 dead which die in the *L.*
17:14 he is the *L.* of lords, and king
19:16 and *L.* of lords

LOSE (LOST)
Ps. 119:176 astray like *l.* sheep
Prov. 23: 8 and *l.* thy sweet words
Eccl. 3: 6 and a time to *l.*; a time to
Ezek. 37:11 our hope is *l.*, we are cut
Mat. 5:13 if salt have *l.* his savour
10: 6 to the *l.* sheep of the house of
10:42 in no wise *l.* his reward
16:26 and *l.* his own soul
18:11 save that which was *l.*
Luke 15: 4 hundred sheep, if he *l.* one
Luke 19:10 save that which is *l.*
15:32 thy brother was *l.* and is found
John 6:39 I should *l.* nothing
2 Cor. 4: 3 gospel be hid, hid to them that are *l.*
2 John 1: 8 that we *l.* not those things

LOSS
1 Cor. 3:15 he shall suffer *l.*
Phil. 3: 8 I have suffered the *l.*

LOT (LOTS)
Lev. 16:10 on which the *l.* fell
Josh. 15: 1 the *l.* of the tribe
1 Sam. 14:41 Give a perfect *l.*
Ps. 16: 5 thou maintainest my *l.*
22:18 cast *l.* upon my vesture
125: 3 not rest upon the *l.* of the righteous
Prov. 16:33 the *l.* is cast into the lap
18:18 *l.* causeth contentions to cease
Mat. 27:35 parted his garments, casting *l.*
Mark 15:24 casting *l.* upon them
Acts 1:26 the *l.* fell on Matthias

LOVE
Gen. 27: 4 meat, such as I *l.*
Lev. 19:18 thou shalt *l.* thy neighbour as thyself
Deut. 6: 5 shalt *l.* the Lord thy God with all
7: 7 Lord did not set his *l.* upon you
10:12 to *l.* him and to serve
2 Sam. 1:26 passing the *l.* of women
Ps. 18: 1 I will *l.* thee, oh Lord
31:23 *l.* the Lord, all ye his saints
116: 1 I *l.* the Lord because
119: 97 O, how *l.* I thy law. It is
145: 20 Lord preserveth them that *l.* him
Eccl. 9: 1 no man knoweth either *l.*
Sol. 1: 4 the upright *l.* thee
2: 5 I am sick of *l.*
8: 6 *l.* is strong as death
Jer. 2: 2 the *l.* of thine espousals
31: 3 loved thee with everlasting *l.*
Ezek. 16: 8 thy time was the time of *l.*
33:31 their mouth they show much *l.*
Zech. 8:19 *l.* the truth and peace
Mat. 5:44 *l.* your enemies, bless
19:19 *l.* thy neighbor as thyself
22:37 *l.* the Lord thy God
22:39 *l.* thy neighbor as thyself
24:12 *l.* of many shall wax cold
Luke 11:42 over judgment, and the *l.* of God
John 5:42 have not the *l.* of God
13:34 that ye also *l.* one another
14:23 if a man *l.* me, he will keep
15: 9 continue ye in my *l.*
15:13 greater *l.* hath no man than this
15:17 that ye *l.* one another
Rom. 5: 5 *l.* of God is shed abroad in our
8:35 separate us from the *l.* of Christ
12: 9 let *l.* be without dissimulation
13: 8 but to *l.* one another
13:10 *l.* is the fulfilling of the law
15:30 Christ's sake, and the *l.* of Spirit
1 Cor. 16:22 if any man *l.* not the Lord
2 Cor. 5:14 *l.* of Christ constraineth
13:14 and the *l.* of God, and the communion
Gal. 5: 6 faith which worketh by *l.*
5:13 by *l.* serve one another
5:14 *l.* thy neighbor as thyself
5:22 fruit of the Spirit is *l.*, joy, peace
Eph. 1: 4 without blame before him in *l.*
3:17 rooted and grounded in *l.*
4: 2 forbearing one another in *l.*
4:15 speaking truth in *l.*
5: 2 walk in *l.* as Christ hath loved
5:25 *l.* your wives, even as Christ
Col. 2: 2 knit together in *l.* and
3:19 Husbands, *l.* your wives
1 Thes. 1: 3 your labour of *l.*, and patience of
3:12 abound in *l.* toward one another
5: 8 breastplate of faith and *l.*
5:13 esteem very highly in *l.*
2 Thes. 2:10 received not the *l.* of truth
3: 5 hearts into the *l.* of God
2 Tim. 4: 8 unto them also that *l.* his appearing
Heb. 13: 1 let brotherly *l.* continue
Jas. 2: 8 *l.* thy neighbor as thyself
1 Pet. 1: 8 having not seen, ye *l.*
1:22 see that ye *l.* one another
2:17 *l.* the brotherhood
1 John 2: 5 in him is the *l.* of God perfected
2:15 *l.* not the world, neither the things
3: 1 what manner of *l.* the Father hath
3:16 perceive we the *l.* of God

1 John 3:23 and *l.* one another
4: 7 for *l.* is of God
4: 8 knoweth not God, for God is *l.*
4: 9 in this was manifested the *l.* of God
4:12 If we *l.* one another
4:18 there is no fear in *l.*
4:19 we *l.* him because he first
4:21 who loveth God *l.* his brother
5: 3 the *l.* of God that we keep his commandments
2 John 1: 1 whom I *l.* in the truth, and
Rev. 2: 4 thou hast left thy first *l.*
3:19 as many as I *l.* I rebuke

LOVED
Deut. 7: 8 because the Lord *l.* you
33: 3 he *l.* the people, all his saints
1 Sam. 18: 1 *l.* him as his own soul
2 Sam. 12:24 and the Lord *l.* him.
1 Ki. 3: 3 Solomon *l.* the Lord
10: 9 the Lord *l.* Israel for ever
Hos. 11: 1 Israel was a child, then I *l.* him
Mal. 1: 2 yet I have *l.* Jacob
Mark 10:21 Jesus beholding him, *l.* him
Luke 7:47 are forgiven, for she *l.* much
John 3:16 God so *l.* the world that
3:19 men *l.* darkness rather than
12:43 *l.* the praise of men more
13: 1 having *l.* his own, which were in
13:23 one of his disciples whom Jesus *l.*
14:28 if ye *l.* me, ye would rejoice
15: 9 as my Father *l.* me, so have I *l.*
16:27 Father loveth you because ye *l.* me
17:23 hast *l.* them as thou hast *l.* me
17:26 wherewith thou hast *l.* me
21: 7 whom Jesus *l.* saith unto Peter
Rom. 8:37 conquerors through him that *l.* us
9:13 Jacob I *l.*, Esau I hated
Gal. 2:20 Son of God, who *l.* me
Eph. 2: 4 great love wherewith he *l.* us
5: 2 walk in love, as Christ *l.* us
5:25 wives as Christ *l.* the church
2 Thes. 2:16 Father, which hath *l.* us
2 Tim. 4:10 *l.* this present world, and is
Heb. 1: 9 hast *l.* righteousness and hated
2 Pet. 2:15 who *l.* the wages of unrighteousness
1 John 4:10 that we *l.* God, but that he *l.* us
Rev. 1: 5 that *l.* us and washed us
12:11 *l.* not their lives unto death

LOVETH
Ps. 146: 8 the Lord *l.* the righteous
Prov. 3:12 whom the Lord *l.* he correcteth
17:17 a friend *l.* at all times
21:17 he that *l.* pleasure shall be poor
Sol. 1: 7 whom my soul *l.*, where thou
Mat. 10:37 *l.* father or mother more than me
John 3:35 Father *l.* the Son and hath
2 Cor. 9: 7 God *l.* a cheerful giver
Heb. 12: 6 whom the Lord *l.*, he chasteneth
3 John 1: 9 Diotrephes, who *l.* to have the
Rev. 22:15 whosoever *l.* and maketh a lie

LOVINGKINDNESS
Ps. 36: 7 how excellent is thy *l.*
36:10 O continue thy *l.* unto them
63: 3 thy *l.* is better than life
103: 4 who crowneth thee with *l.*
Is. 63: 7 I will mention the *l.* of the Lord
Jer. 9:24 the Lord which exercise *l.*
31: 3 with *l.* have I drawn thee
32:18 thou showest *l.* to thousands
Hos. 2:19 in *l.* and in mercies

LOW
Deut. 28:43 shalt come down very *l.*
Job 40:12 that is proud and bring him *l.*
Ps. 49: 2 both *l.* and high, rich and
136: 23 remembered us in our *l.* estate
Prov. 29:23 man's pride shall bring him *l.*
Is. 26: 5 the lofty city, he layeth it *l.*
32:19 city shall be *l.* in a *l.* place
Luke 1:48 he hath regarded the *l.* estate
3: 5 every mountain and hill shall be brought *l.*

LOWLINESS
Eph. 4: 2 with all *l.* and meekness
Phil. 2: 3 but in *l.* of mind let each

LOWLY
Ps. 138: 6 yet hath he respect to the *l.*
Prov. 3:34 he giveth grace unto the *l.*
11: 2 with the *l.* is wisdom
Mat. 11:29 learn of me, I am meek and *l.*

LUCRE
1 Tim. 3: 3 not greed of filthy *l.*
3: 8 not greedy of filthy *l.*
Tit. 1: 7 not given to filthy *l.*
1 Pet. 5: 2 not for filthy *l.*, but of a ready

LUKEWARM
Rev. 3:16 then because thou art *l.*

LUST (LUSTETH)
Ex. 15: 9 my *l.* shall be satisfied
Ps. 78:18 asking meat for their *l.*
81:12 up to their own hearts' *l.*
Mat. 5:28 looketh on a woman to *l.* after her
Rom. 7: 7 I had not known *l.* except the law
1 Cor. 10: 6 not *l.* after evil things
Gal. 5:16 shall not fulfil the *l.* of the flesh
5:17 flesh *l.* against the Spirit
1 Thes. 4: 5 not in the *l.* of concupiscence
Jas. 4: 2 Ye *l.* and have not: ye kill
1 John 2:16 *l.* of the flesh, and *l.* of

LUSTS
Mark 4:19 *l.* of other things entering in
John 8:44 *l.* of your father ye will do
Rom. 6:12 ye should obey it in the *l.* thereof
13:14 for the flesh, to fulfil the *l.*
13:24 crucified flesh with affections and *l.*
1 Tim. 6: 9 foolish and hurtful *l.*
2 Tim. 2:22 flee also youthful *l.*: but follow
3: 6 laden with sins, led away with *l.*
Tit. 2:12 denying ungodliness and worldly *l.*
3: 3 serving divers *l.* and pleasures
Jas. 4: 3 ye may consume it upon your *l.*
1 Pet. 2:11 abstain from fleshly *l.*
4: 2 no longer live to the *l.* of men
2 Pet. 3: 3 walking after their own *l.*
Jude 1:18 walk after their own ungodly *l.*

M

MAD
Deut. 28:34 thou shalt be *m.* for the sight
1 Sam. 21:13 feigned himself *m.* in their hands
Jer. 50:38 they are *m.* upon idols
Hos. 9: 7 prophet is a fool, spiritual man is *m.*
John 10:20 he hath a devil and is *m.*
Acts 26:11 being exceedingly *m.* against them, I
26:24 much learning doth make thee *m.*

MADNESS
Deut. 28:28 Lord shall smite thee with *m.*
Eccl. 1:17 and to know *m.* and folly
2:12 myself to behold wisdom and *m.*
Zech. 12: 4 astonishment, and his horse with *m.*
Luke 6:11 they were filled with *m.*
2 Pet. 2:16 forbad the *m.* of the prophet

MAGNIFY (MAGNIFIED)
Gen. 19:19 thou hast *m.* thy mercy
Josh. 3: 7 I begin to *m.* thee
2 Sam. 7:26 let thy name be *m.* for
1 Chr. 29:25 the Lord *m.* Solomon exceedingly
Job 7:17 man, that thou shouldest *m.* him
Ps. 34: 3 *m.* the Lord with me
35:27 let the Lord be *m.*
69:30 *m.* him with thanksgiving
138: 2 hast *m.* thy word above
Is. 42:21 *m.* the law, and make it
Luke 1:46 my soul doth *m.* the Lord
Acts 10:46 spake with tongues, *m.* God
19:17 name of Lord Jesus was *m.*
Phil. 1:20 Christ be *m.* in my body

MAJESTY
1 Chr. 29:11 victory and the *m.*: for all that is
Job 40:10 deck thyself now with *m.*
Ps. 21: 5 honour and *m.* hast thou laid
29: 4 voice of the Lord is full of *m.*
45: 4 in thy *m.* ride prosperously
93: 1 he is clothed with *m.*; the Lord
145: 5 of the glorious honour of thy *m.*
145: 12 and the glorious *m.* of his kingdom
Is. 2:10 for glory of his *m.*
Dan. 4:36 excellent *m.* was added unto
Heb. 1: 3 right hand of the *M.* on high
8: 1 throne of the *M.* in the heavens
2 Pet. 1:16 but were eyewitnesses of his *m.*
Jude 1:25 be glory and *m.*, dominion and power

MAINTAIN (MAINTAINED)
1 Ki. 8:45 their supplication and *m.* their cause
Job 13:15 I will *m.* mine own ways
Ps. 9: 4 of my cup thou hast *m.* my right
140: 12 the Lord will *m.* the cause
Tit. 3: 8 might be careful to *m.* good works

MAINTAINEST
Ps. 16: 5 thou *m.* my lot

MAKE (MADE)
Gen. 1:26 Let us *m.* man in our
3: 6 desired to *m.* one wise
Ex. 2:14 who *m.* thee a prince
Deut. 32:35 come upon them *m.* haste
1 Sam. 20:38 *m.* speed, haste, stay not
2 Sam. 13: 6 and *m.* himself sick
Ps. 104: 24 in wisdom hast thou *m.* them all
139: 14 fearfully and wonderfully *m.*
Prov. 16: 4 Lord hath *m.* all things for himself
John 1: 3 all things were *m.* by him
Rom. 1: 3 Christ, *m.* of the seed of David
1:20 being understood by things that are *m.*
1 Cor. 1:30 who of God is *m.* unto us
4: 5 will *m.* manifest the counsels
9:22 *m.* all things to all men
Gal. 4: 4 *m.* of a woman, *m.* under the law
Phil. 2: 7 *m.* in the likeness of men

MAKER
Job 4:17 more pure than his *m.*?
32:22 my *m.* would soon take me
35:10 where is God my *m.*
36: 3 ascribe righteousness to my *m.*
Prov. 14:31 the poor, reproacheth his *m.*
22: 2 Lord is the *m.* of them all
Is. 17: 7 day shall man look to his *m.*
22:11 looked to the *m.* thereof
45: 9 unto him that striveth with his *m.*
51:13 forgettest the Lord thy *m.*
54: 5 thy *m.* is thy husband; the
Heb. 11:10 whose builder and *m.* is God

MALE
Gen. 1:27 *m.* and female created he them
Num. 5: 3 both *m.* and female shall ye put out
Mal. 1:14 hath in his flock a *m.*
Mat. 19: 4 made them *m.* and female
Gal. 3:28 there is neither *m.* nor female

MALICE
1 Cor. 5: 8 with the leaven of *m.*
14:20 in *m.* be children, but in
Eph. 4:31 away from you, with all *m.*
Col. 3: 8 anger, wrath, *m.*, blasphemy
Tit. 3: 3 living in *m.* and envy
1 Pet. 2: 1 laying aside all *m.*

MAMMON
Mat. 6:24 you cannot serve God and *m.*
Luke 16: 9 friends of the *m.* of righteousness

MAN (MAN'S)
Gen. 1:27 God created *m.* in his own image
Ex. 15: 3 the Lord is a *m.* of war
Num. 23:19 God is not a *m.* that he
Deut. 33: 1 Moses the *m.* of God blessed the
Judg. 13: 8 let the *m.* of God which thou didst
2 Ki. 1:13 said unto him, O *m.* of God
9:11 know the *m.*, and his communication
Job 4:17 *m.* be more just than God?
7:17 what is *m.* that thou shouldest be
11:12 for vain *m.* would be wise
14: 1 *m.* born of woman is of few days
15:14 What is *m.*, that he should be clean?
25: 4 How can *m.* be justified with God?
25: 6 much less *m.* that is a worm
Ps. 8: 4 what is *m.* that thou art mindful
10:18 *m.* of the earth may no more oppress
25:12 what *m.* is he that feareth the Lord
49:12 *m.* being in honour abideth not
90: 3 thou turnest *m.* to destruction
104: 23 *m.* goeth forth to his work
118: 6 not fear; what can *m.* do
Prov. 1: 5 a wise *m.* will hear, and will
9: 8 rebuke a wise *m.* and he will love thee
14:16 a wise *m.* feareth and departeth
20:24 *m.* goings are of the Lord

Eccl. 2:14 a wise *m.* eyes are in his head
6:10 it is known that it is *m.*
7:29 God made *m.* upright, but
10: 2 a wise *m.* heart is at his right hand
12: 5 *m.* goeth to his long home
Is. 2:22 cease ye from *m.* whose breath
47: 3 I will not meet thee as a *m.*
53: 3 a *m.* of sorrows and acquainted
Jer. 9:23 let not the wise *m.* glory in wisdom
15:10 borne me a *m.* of strife and
31:22 a woman shall compass a *m.*
Zech. 13: 7 awake against the *m.* that
Mat. 4: 4 *m.* shall not live by bread
8: 9 I am a *m.* under the authority
16:26 what shall a *m.* give in exchange
26:72 I know not the *m.*
John 3: 3 except a *m.* be born again
7:46 never *m.* spake like this *m.*
Acts 10:26 I myself also am a *m.*
Rom. 6: 6 old *m.* crucified with him
7:22 in the law of God after the inward *m.*
1 Cor. 2:11 *m.* knoweth the things of a *m.*
2:14 natural *m.* receiveth not things
11: 8 *m.* is not of the woman, but the
15:47 first *m.* is of the earth earthy; the
2 Cor. 4:16 though outward *m.* perish, yet inward *m.* is renewed
12: 2 I knew a *m.* in Christ
Eph. 4:22 the old *m.* which is corrupt
4:24 put on the new *m.*
Phil. 2: 8 in fashion as a *m.* he humbled
Col. 3:10 put on the new *m.*
1 Tim. 6:11 O *m.* of God, flee these things
2 Tim. 3:17 the *m.* of God may be perfect
Jas. 3:13 who is a wise *m.* and endued with
1 Pet. 3: 4 be the hidden *m.* of the heart

MANIFEST (MANIFESTED)
Eccl. 3:18 that God might *m.* them
Mark 4:22 which shall not be *m.*
John 2:11 *m.* forth his glory, and his
14:21 love him and will *m.* myself to him
17: 6 I have *m.* thy name unto men
1 Cor. 4: 5 make *m.* the counsels of the hearts
15:27 it is *m.* that he is excepted
Gal. 5:19 works of the flesh are *m.*
1 Tim. 3:16 God was *m.* in the flesh
1 John 3: 5 was *m.* to take away sin
3:10 in this children of God are *m.*
4: 9 in this was *m.* the love of God

MANIFESTATION
Rom. 8:19 *m.* of the sons of God
1 Cor. 12: 7 *m.* of the Spirit is given

MANIFOLD
Neh. 9:27 according to thy *m.* mercies
Ps. 104: 24 how *m.* are thy works
Amos 5:12 I know your *m.* transgressions
Luke 18:30 receive *m.* more in this present time
Eph. 3:10 known by the church the *m.* wisdom of God
1 Pet. 1: 6 in heaviness through *m.* temptations
4:10 good stewards of the *m.* grace of God

MANNA
Ex. 16:15 It is *m.*; for they wist not
Num. 11: 6 this *m.* before our eyes
Deut. 8: 3 and fed thee with *m.* which thou
8:16 fed thee in the wilderness with *m.*
Josh. 5:12 the *m.* ceased on the morrow
Neh. 9:20 withheldest not thy *m.* from their
Ps. 78:24 rained down *m.* upon them
John 6:31 fathers did eat *m.* in
Rev. 2:17 will I give to eat of the hidden *m.*

MARK (MARKED, MARKS)
Job 7:20 set me as a *m.* against thee
Ps. 37:37 *m.* the perfect man and behold
130: 3 if thou shouldest *m.* iniquity
Jer. 2:22 thine iniquity is *m.* before me
Ezek. 9: 4 set thy *m.* on the foreheads
Rom. 16:17 *m.* them which cause divisions
Gal. 6:17 I bear in my body the *m.* of
Phil. 3:14 I press toward the *m.*
Rev. 13:17 save he that had the *m.*

MARRIAGE
Mat. 22: 2 king made a *m.* for his son
25:10 that were ready went into the *m.*
John 2: 1 there was a *m.* in Cana
Heb. 13: 4 *m.* is honourable in all
Rev. 19: 7 *m.* of Lamb is come

MARROW
Job 21:24 bones moistened with *m.*
Ps. 63: 5 soul is satisfied as with *m.*
Prov. 3: 8 health to thy naval and *m.*
Is. 25: 6 feast of fat things full of *m.*
Heb. 4:12 joints and *m.*, and is a discerner

MARRY (MARRIED, MARRIETH)
Gen. 38: 8 thy brother's wife, and *m.* her
Deut. 25: 5 the wife of the dead shall not *m.*
Is. 62: 5 as a young man *m.* a virgin
Jer. 3:14 I am *m.* to you, saith Lord
Luke 14:20 I have *m.* a wife, and
1 Cor. 7: 9 better to *m.* than to burn
1 Tim. 4: 3 forbidding to *m.* and commanding
5:14 that younger women *m.* and

MARTYR (MARTYRS)
Acts 22:20 the blood of thy *m.* Stephen
Rev. 2:13 Antipas was my faithful *m.*
17: 6 the blood of the *m.* of Jesus

MARVEL (MARVELLED)
Ps. 48: 5 they saw it and so they *m.*
Eccl. 5: 8 *m.* not at the matter
Mat. 8:10 when Jesus heard it, he *m.*
8:27 but the men *m.*, saying, What
21:20 disciples saw it they *m.*
Mark 6: 6 he *m.* because of their unbelief
Luke 1:63 name is John And they *m.* all
John 3: 7 *M.* not that I said unto thee
5:28 *M.* not at this: for the hour
Acts 3:12 why *m.* ye at this
2: 7 were all amazed and *m.*
4:13 unlearned and ignorant men, they *m.*
1 John 3:13 *M.* not my brethren, if

MARVELLOUS
1 Chr. 16:12 remember his *m.* works
Job 5: 9 unsearchable *m.* things without number
10:16 showed thyself *m.* upon me
Ps. 17: 7 show thy *m.* kindness
98: 1 for he hath done *m.* things
105: 5 remember his *m.* works
139: 14 *m.* are thy works; and that my soul
Mic. 7:15 show unto him *m.* things
1 Pet. 2: 9 out of darkness into his *m.* light
Rev. 15: 3 Great and *m.* are thy works

MASTER (MASTERS)
Eccl. 12:11 by the *m.* of assemblies
Is. 24: 2 the servant so with his *m.*
Mal. 1: 6 and a servant his *m.*
Mat. 6:24 no man can serve two *m.*
23:10 neither be ye called *m.*
John 3:10 art thou a *m.* of Israel
13:13 ye call me *M.* and Lord
13:14 your Lord and *M.* have washed your
Rom. 14: 4 to his own *m.* he standeth
Eph. 6: 9 ye *m.* do the same thing unto them
Col. 4: 1 *m.* give unto your servants that
Jas. 3: 1 be not many *m.*, knowing we shall

MATTER (MATTERS)
Ex. 18:22 that every great *m.* they bring
1 Sam. 10:16 of the *m.* of the kingdom
Job 32:18 for I am full of *m.*
33:13 account of any of his *m.*
Ps. 45: 1 my heart is inditing a good *m.*
131: 1 exercise myself in great *m.*
Dan. 7:28 I kept the *m.* in my heart
Acts 8:21 part nor lot in this *m.*
2 Cor. 9: 5 be ready as a *m.* of bounty
1 Pet. 4:15 busybody in other men's *m.*

MEAN (MEANT)
Gen. 50:20 but God *m.* it unto good
Ex. 12:26 what *m.* you by this service
Deut. 6:20 what *m.* the testimonies
Josh. 4:21 What *m.* these stones
Ezek. 17:12 Know ye not what these things *m.*
Acts 17:20 know therefore what these things *m.*
21:13 what *m.* ye to weep and to break

MEANEST
Ezek. 37:18 what thou *m.* by these
Jonah 1: 6 what *m.* thou O sleeper

MEANS
Ps. 49: 7 by any *m.* redeem his brother
Jer. 5:31 priests bear rule by their *m.*
1 Cor. 9:22 might by all *m.* save some
Phil. 3:11 If by any *m.* I might attain
1 Thes. 3: 5 lest by some *m.* the tempter

MEASURE
Lev. 19:35 in weight or in *m.*
Deut. 25:15 perfect and just *m.* shalt
Job 11: 9 the *m.* is longer than the earth
Ps. 39: 4 the *m.* of my days, what it is
Is. 27: 8 in *m.* when it shooteth forth
Jer. 30:11 I will correct thee in *m.*
Mat. 7: 2 with what *m.* ye mete
23:32 fill up the *m.* of your fathers
John 3:34 giveth not the Spirit by *m.*
2 Cor. 1: 8 that we were pressed out of *m.*
12: 7 lest I be exalted above *m.*
Eph. 4: 7 according to the *m.* of the gift of
4:13 unto the *m.* of the stature of
Rev. 11: 1 Rise, and *m.* the temple of God

MEAT (MEATS)
Job 6: 7 are as my sorrowful *m.*
Ps. 42: 3 my tears have been my *m.*
104: 27 give them their *m.* in due season
111: 5 given *m.* to them that fear him
Prov. 6: 8 provideth her *m.* in the summer
Hos. 11: 4 I laid *m.* unto them
Hab. 1:16 is fat and their *m.* plenteous
3:17 the fields shall yield no *m.*
Hag. 2:12 or wine, or oil, of any *m.*
Mal. 1:12 even his *m.* is contemptible
Mat. 6:25 is not life more than *m.*
John 4:32 I have *m.* to eat ye know
4:34 my *m.* is to do the will of him
6:27 labour not for *m.* which perisheth
6:55 my flesh is *m.* indeed
Rom. 14:15 destroy not him with thy *m.*
14:17 kingdom of God is not *m.* and drink
1 Cor. 6:13 *m.* for the belly, and the belly
8: 8 *m.* commendeth us not to God
10: 3 did all eat the same spiritual *m.*

MEDIATOR
Gal. 3:19 by angels in the hand of a *m.*
3:20 a *m.* is not a *m.* of one
1 Tim. 2: 5 one *m.* between God and men
Heb. 8: 6 he is the *m.* of a better covenant
9:15 he is the *m.* of a new testament
12:24 to Jesus the *m.* of a new covenant

MEDICINE (MEDICINES)
Prov. 17:22 merry heart doeth good like a *m.*
Jer. 30:13 thou hast no healing *m.*
46:11 in vain shalt thou use many *m.*
Ezek. 47:12 the leaf thereof, for *m.*

MEDITATE
Gen. 24:63 Issac went out to *m.* in
Josh. 1: 8 shalt *m.* therein, day and
Ps. 1: 2 in his law doth he *m.* day and night
63: 6 *m.* on thee in the night watches
77:12 I will *m.* also of all thy work
119: 15 I will *m.* in thy precepts
Is. 33:18 thine heart shall *m.* terror
Luke 21:14 not *m.* before what ye shall answer
1 Tim. 4:15 *m.* upon these things

MEDITATION
Ps. 5: 1 words, O Lord, consider my *m.*
49: 3 *m.* of my heart shall be of understanding
104: 34 my *m.* of him shall be sweet
119: 97 thy law! It is my *m.* all the day
119: 99 thy testimonies are my *m.*

MEEK
Num. 12: 3 Moses was very *m.* above all
Ps. 22:26 *m.* shall eat and be satisfied
25: 9 *m.* will he guide in judgment
37:11 *m.* shall inherit the earth
147: 6 the Lord lifteth up the *m.*
149: 4 beautify the *m.* with salvation
Is. 11: 4 reprove with equity for the *m.*
29:19 *m.* shall increase their joy
61: 1 preach good tidings to the *m.*
Amos 2: 7 turn aside the way of the *m.*
Mat. 5: 5 blessed are the *m.*: for they shall
11:29 I am *m.* and lowly in heart
1 Pet. 3: 4 ornament of the *m.* and quiet spirit

MEEKNESS
Ps. 45: 4 because of truth and *m.*
Zeph. 2: 3 seek righteousness, seek *m.*
1 Cor. 4:21 love, and in the spirit of *m.*
2 Cor. 10: 1 beseech you by the *m.* and gentleness

Gal. 5:23 *m.*, temperance, against such
6: 1 one in the spirit of *m.*
Eph. 4: 2 walk with lowliness, *m.*
1 Tim. 6:11 follow after love, patience, *m.*
2 Tim. 2:25 in *m.* instructing those that oppose
Tit. 3: 2 showing all *m.* unto all men
Jas. 1:21 receive with *m.* the engrafted word
3:13 works with *m.* of wisdom
1 Pet. 3:15 hope that is in you with *m.* and fear

MEET (MEETEST)
Gen. 2:18 make him an help *m.* for him
Job 34:31 it is *m.* to be said to God
Is. 47: 3 I will not *m.* thee as a man
64: 5 thou *m.* him that rejoiceth
Hos. 13: 8 I will *m.* them as a bear
Amos 4:12 prepare to *m.* thy God
Mat. 3: 8 therefore fruits *m.* for repentance
Acts 26:20 do works *m.* for repentance
1 Cor. 15: 9 not *m.* to be called an apostle
Col. 1:12 *m.* to be partakers of the inheritance
1 Thes. 4:17 caught up to *m.* the Lord
2 Tim. 2:21 *m.* for the master's use, and prepared
Heb. 6: 7 herbs *m.* for them by whom it is dressed

MEMBER (MEMBERS)
Ps. 139: 16 book all my *m.* were written
Mat. 5:29 that one of thy *m.* should perish
Rom. 6:13 neither yield ye your *m.* as
7:23 I see another law in my *m.*
12: 5 every one *m.* one of another
1 Cor. 6:15 your bodies *m.* of Christ
12:12 body is one, and hath many *m.*
12:14 the body is not one *m.*, but many
Jas. 3: 5 tongue is a little *m.* and
Eph. 4:25 we are *m.* one of another
5:30 *m.* of his body, his flesh and
Col. 3: 5 mortify your *m.* on earth

MEMORY
Ps. 109: 15 he may cut off the *m.* of them
145: 7 utter the *m.* of thy great goodness
Prov. 10: 7 *m.* of the just is blessed
Eccl. 9: 5 for the *m.* of them is forgotten
Is. 26:14 made all their *m.* to perish
1 Cor. 15: 2 if ye keep in *m.* what I

MEMORIAL
Ex. 3:15 this is my *m.* to all generations
13: 9 for a *m.* between thine eyes
17:14 write this for a *m.* in the book
Hos. 12: 5 God of hosts; the Lord is his *m.*
Mat. 26:13 hath done, be told for a *m.* of her
Acts 10: 4 alms are come up for a *m.* before God

MEN
Gen. 32:28 with *m.*, and hast prevailed
42:11 we are true *m.*, thy servants
Ps. 9:20 know themselves to be but *m.*
17:14 *m.* which are thy hand, O Lord
82: 7 ye shall die like *m.* and fall
Eccl. 12: 3 strong *m.* shall bow
Is. 31: 3 Egyptians are *m.*, not God
Hos. 6: 7 they like *m.* have transgressed
Mat. 7:12 ye would that *m.* should do to you
Eph. 6: 6 with eyeservice, as *m.* pleasers
Col. 3:22 not with eyeservice as with *m.* pleasers
1 Thes. 2: 4 not as pleasing *m.*, but God

MENTION
Ex. 23:13 make no *m.* of the name
Job 28:18 no *m.* shall be made of coral
Ps. 71:16 make *m.* of thy righteousness
Is. 26:13 by thee only will we make *m.* of
62: 6 ye that make *m.* of the Lord
Rom. 1: 9 make *m.* of you in my prayers
Eph. 1:16 making *m.* of you in my prayers
1 Thes. 1: 2 making *m.* of you in my prayers
Philem. 1: 4 *m.* of thee always in my prayers

MERCY
Gen. 19:19 thou hast magnified thy *m.*
Ex. 34: 7 keeping *m.* for thousands, forgiving
Num. 14:18 and of great *m.*, forgiving iniquity
Deut. 7: 9 which keepeth covenant and *m.*
1 Ki. 8:23 who keepest covenant and *m.*
Neh. 9:32 who keepest covenant and *m.*
Ps. 23: 6 goodness and *m.* shall follow me
25:10 all paths of the Lord are *m.* and
Ps. 33:18 them that hope in his *m.*
52: 8 I trust in the *m.* of God
57: 3 God shall send forth his *m.*
66:20 prayer nor his *m.* from me
69:13 in the multitude of thy *m.*, hear me
86: 5 plenteous in *m.* to all
101: 1 I will sing of his *m.* and
103: 8 slow to anger and plenteous in *m.*
103: 17 *m.* of the Lord is from everlasting
106: 1 his *m.* endureth for ever
107: 1 his *m.* endureth forever
Prov. 16: 6 by *m.* and truth iniquity is purged
20:28 *m.* and truth preserve the king and
Dan. 9: 4 keeping the covenant and *m.* to them
Hos. 6: 6 I desired *m.* and not sacrifice
14: 3 in thee the fatherless findeth *m.*
Jonah 2: 8 vanities forsake their own *m.*
Mic. 6: 8 to do justly, and love *m.*
7:18 because he delighteth in *m.*
7:20 and the *m.* to Abraham which thou
Luke 1:50 his *m.* is on them that fear him
1:78 through the tender *m.* of our God
Rom. 9:15 *m.* on whom I will have *m.*
9:23 on vessels of *m.* prepared
11:31 through your *m.* they obtain *m.*
15: 9 might glorify God for his *m.*
2 Cor. 4: 1 as we have received *m.*
1 Tim. 1: 2 Grace *m.* and peace from God
1:13 I obtained *m.* because I did it
2 Tim. 1:18 that he may find *m.* in
Heb. 4:16 we may obtain *m.* and
Jas. 2:13 shall have judgment without *m.*
3:17 full of *m.* and good fruits
5:11 Lord is very pitiful and of tender *m.*
2 John 1: 3 Grace be with you, *m.*
Jude 1: 2 *m.* unto you, and peace

MERCIES
Gen. 32:10 not worthy of the least of all the *m.*
1 Chr. 21:13 for very great are his *m.*
Ps. 25: 6 thy tender *m.* and thy lovingkindness
40:11 not thou thy tender *m.* from me
51: 1 the multitude of thy tender *m.*
145: 9 his tender *m.* are over all his
Is. 55: 3 even the sure *m.* of David
Dan. 9: 9 to the Lord our God belong *m.* and
Acts 13:34 will give you the sure *m.*
Rom. 12: 1 I beseech you by the *m.* of God
2 Cor. 1: 3 Father of *m.* and God of
Col. 3:12 put on bowels of *m.*

MERCIFUL
Ex. 34: 6 Lord God *m.* and gracious
2 Chr. 30: 9 God is *m.* and gracious
Neh. 9:31 art a *m.* and gracious God
Ps. 18:25 thou wilt show thyself *m.*
37:26 he is ever *m.* and lendeth
103: 8 The Lord is *m.* and gracious
117: 2 his *m.* kindness is great toward us
Is. 57: 1 *m.* men are taken away
Jer. 3:12 I am *m.*, saith the Lord
Joel 2:13 for he is gracious and *m.*
Jonah 4: 2 thou art a gracious God, and *m.*
Mat. 5: 7 blessed are the *m.*, for they shall
Luke 6:36 *m.*, as your Father also is *m.*
Heb. 2:17 a *m.* and faithful high priest
8:12 I will be *m.* to their unrighteousness

MESSAGE
Judg. 3:20 I have a *m.* from God
Hag. 1:13 Lord's *m.* unto the people
1 John 1: 5 the *m.* which ye have heard

MESSENGER (MESSENGERS)
Job 33:23 if there be a *m.* with him, an
Is. 14:32 answer the *m.* of a nation
42:19 who is blind or deaf, as my *m.*
44:26 that performeth counsel of his *m.*
Mal. 2: 7 he is the *m.* of the Lord

MIDST
Ps. 22:14 in the *m.* of my bowels
46: 5 God is in the *m.* of her, she
110: 2 in the *m.* of thine enemies
Prov. 4:21 in the *m.* of thine heart
Is. 41:18 in the *m.* of the valleys
Ezek. 43: 9 dwell in the *m.* of them
Joel 2:27 I am in the *m.* of Israel
Zeph. 3: 5 Lord is in the *m.* thereof
Phil. 2:15 in the *m.* of a crooked and
Rev. 1:13 in the *m.* of seven candlesticks
5: 6 in the *m.* of the elders
7:17 Lamb in the *m.* of the throne

MIGHT
Gen. 49: 3 firstborn, my *m.*, and the beginning
Num. 14:13 this people in thy *m.* from among them
Deut. 6: 5 all thy soul, and with all thy *m.*
2 Ki. 23:25 turned to the Lord with *m.*
2 Chr. 20:12 no *m.* against this great company
Ps. 76: 5 none of the men of *m.* found
145: 6 speak of the *m.* of thy terrible acts
Eccl. 9:10 do it with thy *m.*
Is. 40:29 to them that have no *m.*
Zech. 4: 6 not by *m.*, nor by power, but
Eph. 3:16 strengthened with *m.* by his Spirit
6:10 and in the power of his *m.*
Col. 1:11 strengthened with all *m.*, according

MIGHTY (MIGHTILY)
Deut. 7:23 with a *m.* destruction, until they
10:17 a great God, a *m.* and a
Judg. 5:23 help of the Lord against the *m.*
Ps. 24: 8 Lord strong and *m.*, the Lord *m.*
Is. 5:22 *m.* to drink wine, men of strength
Jer. 32:19 great in counsel, *m.* in work
Acts 18:28 he *m.* convinced the Jews
19:20 so *m.* grew the word of God
1 Cor. 1:26 many *m.*, not many noble are called
2 Cor. 10: 4 but *m.* through God to the pulling
Col. 1:29 which worketh in me *m.*

MILK
Gen. 18: 8 and he took butter and *m.*
49:12 and his teeth white with *m.*
Job 10:10 hast poured me out as *m.*
Sol. 4:11 and *m.* under thy tongue
5: 1 drunk my wine with my *m.*
Is. 55: 1 buy wine and *m.* without
Joel 3:18 the hills shall flow with *m.*
Heb. 5:12 such as have need of *m.*
1 Pet. 2: 2 desire the sincere *m.* of the word

MIND
Gen. 26:35 a grief of *m.* unto Isaac and to
Lev. 24:12 the *m.* of the Lord might be shown
1 Chr. 28: 9 heart and with a willing *m.*
Neh. 4: 6 people had a *m.* to work
Is. 26: 3 whose *m.* is stayed on thee
Luke 12:29 neither be ye of doubtful *m.*
Acts 17:11 with readiness of *m.*, and searched
20:19 serving Lord with all humility of *m.*
Rom. 7:25 with *m.* I serve the law of God
8: 5 of the flesh do *m.* things of
8: 7 carnal *m.* is enmity against
11:34 who hath known the *m.* of the Lord
12:16 *m.* not high things, but condescend
1 Cor. 1:10 joined together in the same *m.*
2:16 we have the *m.* of Christ
2 Cor. 8:12 if there be first a willing *m.*
13:11 be of one *m.*, live in peace
Phil. 2: 2 being of one accord, of one *m.*
3:16 by the same rule, *m.* the same thing
3:19 glory in their shame, *m.* earthly things
2 Tim. 1: 7 of love and of sound *m.*
Tit. 1:15 their *m.* and conscience is defiled
1 Pet. 3: 8 be ye all of one *m.*
5: 2 not for filthy lucre, but ready *m.*

MINDS
2 Cor. 3:14 their *m.* were blinded: for until
Phil. 4: 7 keep your hearts and *m.* through
Heb. 10:16 in their *m.* will I write
12: 3 wearied and faint in your *m.*
2 Pet. 3: 1 stir up your pure *m.* by

MINDED
Rom. 8: 6 to be carnally *m.* is death

MINDFUL
1 Chr. 16:15 be ye *m.* always of his covenant
Ps. 8: 4 man that thou art *m.* of him?
111: 5 he will be ever *m.* of his covenant

MINISTER (MINISTERS)
Josh. 1: 1 Joshua, the son of Nun, Moses' *m.*
Ps. 103: 21 *m.* of his that do his pleasure

Ps. 104: 4 his *m.* a flaming fire
Joel 1: 9 the priests, the Lord's *m.*
Mat. 20:26 among you, let him be your *m.*
Luke 1: 2 eyewitnesses and *m.* of the
4:20 he gave it again to the *m.*
Acts 26:16 to make thee a *m.* and
Rom. 13: 4 he is the *m.* of God to thee
13: 6 they are God's *m.*, attending
15: 8 Christ was the *m.* of circumcision
15:16 *m.* of Jesus Christ to the Gentiles
15:25 to *m.* unto the saints
15:27 *m.* unto them in carnal things
1 Cor. 3: 5 Apollos, but *m.* by whom ye believed
4: 1 account of us as *m.* of Christ
2 Cor. 3: 6 made us able *m.* of the new testament
6: 4 approved ourselves as *m.* of God
9:10 *m.* bread for your food
11:23 are they *m.* of Christ?
Eph. 3: 7 was made a *m.* according to the gift
4:29 may *m.* grace unto the hearers
1 Tim. 4: 6 shalt be a good *m.* of Jesus
Heb. 1: 7 his *m.* a flame of fire
6:10 ministered to the saints and do *m.*
8: 2 *m.* of the sanctuary, and of the
1 Pet. 4:11 if any man *m.*, let him do it

MINISTERED (MINISTERING)
Mat. 4:11 angels came and *m.* unto him
Luke 8: 3 which *m.* unto him of their
Gal. 3: 5 he that *m.* to you the spirit
Heb. 1:14 all *m.* spirits sent forth to
6:10 ye have *m.* to the saints
2 Pet. 1:11 entrance shall be *m.* unto you

MINISTRATIONS
Luke 1:23 days of his *m.* were accomplished
Acts 6: 1 were neglected in the daily *m.*
2 Cor. 3: 8 the *m.* of the spirit be rather
9:13 the experiment of this *m.* they glorify

MINISTRY
Acts 6: 4 to prayer and to the *m.* of the word
20:24 finish the *m.* which I have received
2 Cor. 4: 1 seeing we have this *m.*
5:18 given to us the *m.* of reconciliation
6: 3 that the *m.* be not blamed
Col. 4:17 take heed to the *m.* which thou hast
1 Tim. 1:12 faithful putting me into the *m.*
2 Tim. 4: 5 make full proof of thy *m.*
Heb. 8: 6 obtained more excellent *m.*

MIRACLE (MIRACLES)
Mark 6:52 they considered not the *m.*
9:39 shall do a *m.* in my name
Luke 23: 8 seen some *m.* done by him
John 2:11 this beginning of *m.* did Jesus in
10:41 John did no *m.*, but all things
11:47 this man doeth many *m.*
Acts 2:22 by *m.* and wonders and signs
4:16 a notable *m.* hath been done by
19:11 special *m.* by the hands of Paul
1 Cor. 12:10 to another the working of *m.*
12:29 are all workers of *m.*
Gal. 3: 5 worketh *m.* among you, doeth he it
Heb. 2: 4 and with divers *m.*, and gifts of

MISCHIEF
Gen. 42: 4 peradventure *m.* fall on him
Job 15:35 they conceive *m.* and bring forth
Ps. 10:14 thou beholdest *m.* and spite, to
10:23 *m.* is in their hearts
36: 4 he deviseth *m.* upon his bed
94:20 which frameth *m.* by a law
Prov. 10:23 sport to a fool to do *m.*
11:27 he that seeketh *m.* it shall
24:16 wicked shall fall into *m.*

MISERY
Judg. 10:16 his soul grieved for *m.*
Job 3:20 to him that is in *m.*
Prov. 31: 7 drink and remember his *m.* no more
Eccl. 8: 6 the *m.* of man is great
Lam. 3:19 mine affliction and my *m.*
Rom. 3:16 destruction and *m.* are in their ways

MISERABLE
Job 16: 2 *m.* comforters are ye all
1 Cor. 15:19 we are of all men most *m.*

Rev. 3:17 thou art wretched and *m.*

MOCK (MOCKED, MOCKETH)
1 Ki. 18:27 that Elijah *m.* them, and said
2 Chr. 36:16 *m.* the messengers of God
Prov. 1:26 I will *m.* when your fear cometh
14: 9 fools make a *m.* at sin
17: 5 whoso *m.* the poor reproacheth his
30:17 the eye that *m.* at his father

MOCKER (MOCKERS)
Prov. 20: 1 wine is a *m.*, strong drink
Is. 28:22 be not *m.* lest your bands
Jude 1:18 there should be *m.* in the last

MOMENT
Ex. 33: 5 the midst of thee in a *m.*
Num. 16:21 consume them in a *m.*
16:45 consume them as in a *m.*
Job 20: 5 joy of the hypocrite but for a *m.*
Ps. 30: 5 his anger endureth but a *m.*
Is. 26:20 hide thyself, as it were, for a little *m.*
27: 3 I will water it every *m.*
54: 7 for a small *m.* have I forsaken
1 Cor. 15:52 in a *m.*, in the twinkling

MONEY
Gen. 23: 9 as much *m.* as it was worth
31:15 hath quite devoured also our *m.*
Eccl. 7:12 wisdom is defence, and *m.*
10:19 merry, but *m.* answereth all things
Is. 55: 1 he that hath no *m.*, come
55: 2 wherefore do ye spend *m.*
Mic. 3:11 the prophets divine for *m.*
Acts 8:20 thy *m.* perish with thee because
1 Tim. 6:10 love of *m.* is the root of all

MORTAL
Job 4:17 shall *m.* man be more just than
Rom. 6:12 let not sin reign in your *m.* body
8:11 quicken your *m.* bodies by his
1 Cor. 15:53 this *m.* must put on immortality

MORTALITY
2 Cor. 5: 4 *m.* might be swallowed up of life

MORTIFY
Col. 3: 5 *m.* your members on earth

MOTH
Job 4:19 are crushed before the *m.*
Ps. 39:11 beauty to consume away like a *m.*
Is. 50: 9 the *m.* shall eat them up
Hos. 5:12 unto Ephraim as a *m.*, and to the
Mat. 6:20 where neither *m.* nor rust doth corrupt
Luke 12:33 thief approacheth, neither *m.* corrupteth

MOTHER (MOTHER'S)
Gen. 3:20 she was the *m.* of all living
21:21 his *m.* took him a wife
Judg. 5: 7 that I arose a *m.* in Israel
2 Sam. 20:19 destroy a city and a *m.* in Israel
1 Ki. 3:27 she is the *m.* thereof
Ps. 27:10 when father and *m.* forsake me
71: 6 out of my *m.* bowels
139: 13 covered me in my *m.* womb
Mat. 12:49 behold my *m.* and my brethren
Gal. 4:26 which is the *m.* of us all

MOVE (MOVED)
Ex. 11: 7 not a dog *m.* his tongue
Ps. 15: 5 doeth these things shall never be *m.*
46: 5 she shall not be *m.*: God shall help
62: 6 my defense: I shall not be *m.*
121: 3 will not suffer thy foot to be *m.*
Prov. 12: 3 the righteous shall not be *m.*
Acts 17:28 in him we live and *m.*
20:24 none of these things *m.* me
Col. 1:23 be not *m.* away from hope
1 Thes. 3: 3 no man be *m.* by these
Heb. 12:28 kingdom which cannot be *m.*
2 Pet. 1:21 as they were *m.* by the Holy Ghost

MOURN (MOURNED)
Neh. 8: 9 *m.* not nor weep. For all the
Is. 61: 2 to comfort all that *m.*
Mat. 5: 4 blessed are they that *m.*
11:17 we have *m.* unto you
1 Cor. 5: 2 and have not rather *m.*
Jas. 4: 9 be afflicted and *m.* and

MOURNERS
Eccl. 12: 5 *m.* go about the streets

Is. 57:18 restore comforts to him and to his *m.*

MOURNING
Ps. 30:11 for me my *m.* into dancing
Is. 61: 3 the oil of joy for *m.*, the garment
Jer. 9:17 call for the *m.* women, that they
31:13 I will turn their *m.* into joy
Joel 2:12 with fasting and with weeping and with *m.*
Jas. 4: 9 laughter be turned to *m.*

MOUTH
Ps. 8: 2 out of the *m.* of babes
17: 3 that my *m.* shall not transgress
37:30 *m.* of righteous speaketh wisdom
81:10 open thy *m.* wide, and I will
103: 5 who satisfieth thy *m.* with good
Prov. 10:14 *m.* of the foolish is near destruction
10:31 *m.* of the just bringeth forth wisdom
12: 6 *m.* of the upright shall deliver
14: 3 in the *m.* of fools is a rod of pride
15: 2 *m.* of fools poureth out foolishness
18: 7 a fool's *m.* is his destruction
22:14 *m.* of strange women is a pit
31: 8 open thy *m.* for the dumb in
Eccl. 5: 6 suffer not thy *m.* to cause thy flesh
Lam. 3:29 putteth his *m.* in dust
3:38 out of the *m.* of the Most High
Mal. 2: 7 they should seek law at his *m.*
Mat. 12:34 out of abundance of heart the *m.* speaketh
21:16 out of the *m.* of babes
Luke 21:15 will give you a *m.* and
Rom. 10:10 with the *m.* confession is made

MULTIPLY
Gen. 16:10 I will *m.* thy seed

MULTITUDE
Ex. 12:38 a mixed *m.* went up
Num. 11: 4 mixed *m.* that was among them
Job 32: 7 *m.* of years should teach wisdom
Ps. 5: 7 in the *m.* of thy mercy
5:10 cast them out in the *m.* of their
33:16 no king saved by the *m.* of
51: 1 unto the *m.* of thy tender mercies
94:19 in the *m.* of my thoughts
106: 45 to the *m.* of his mercies
Prov. 10:19 in *m.* of words wanteth not sin
11:14 in *m.* of counsellors safety
15:22 in the *m.* of counsellors
24: 6 in *m.* of counsellors there is
Eccl. 5: 3 voice is known by *m.* of words
Jas. 5:20 and shall hide a *m.* of sins
1 Pet. 4: 8 shall cover the *m.* of sins

MURDER (MURDERS)
Mat. 15:19 proceed evil thoughts, *m.*
Rom. 1:29 full of envy, *m.*, debate
Gal. 5:21 envyings, *m.*, drunkenness
Rev. 9:21 repented they of their *m.*

MURDERER
Job 24:14 *m.* rising with the light killeth
Hos. 9:13 forth his children to the *m.*
John 8:44 was a *m.* from the beginning
1 Pet. 4:15 none suffer as a *m.*, or as an

MURMURED
Deut. 1:27 ye *m.* in your tents
Ps. 106: 25 but *m.* in their tents an hearkened

MURMURERS
Jude 1:16 these are *m.*, complainers

MURMURINGS
Ex. 16: 7 he heareth your *m.* against the
Phil. 2:14 without *m.* and disputings

MYSTERY (MYSTERIES)
Mark 4:11 know the *m.* of the kingdom
Rom. 11:25 ye should be ignorant of this *m.*
16:25 according to revelation of the *m.*
1 Cor. 2: 7 wisdom of God in a *m.*, even the
4: 1 stewards of the *m.* of God
13: 2 prophecy and understand all *m.*
14: 2 in the spirit he speaketh *m.*
Eph. 1: 9 made known the *m.* of
3: 4 my knowledge in the *m.* of Christ
3: 9 what is the fellowship of the *m.*
6:19 make known the *m.* of the gospel
Col. 1:26 *m.* which hath been hid
1:27 glory of this *m.* among Gentiles
2: 2 acknowledgement of the *m.* of God

Col. 4: 3 to speak the *m.* of Christ
2 Thes. 2: 7 *m.* of iniquity doth already work
1 Tim. 3: 9 holding the *m.* of the faith
3:16 great is the *m.* of godliness
Rev. 1:20 write the *m.* of seven stars
10: 7 *m.* of God should be finished

N

NAIL (NAILS)
Judg. 5:26 put her hand to the *n.*
Eccl. 12:11 *n.* fastened by the masters
Is. 22:23 fasten him as a *n.* in a
Zech. 10: 4 out of him the *n.*, out of him

NAKED
Gen. 2:25 they were both *n.*, the man and
3: 7 knew that they were *n.*
3:11 told thee that thou wast *n.*
Ex. 32:25 when Moses saw the people were *n.*
2 Chr. 28:19 he made Judah *n.*, and transgressed
Job 1:21 *n.* came I out of my mother's womb
Mat. 25:36 *n.* and ye clothed me: I was
1 Cor. 4:11 hunger and thirst and are *n.*
2 Cor. 5: 3 clothed we shall not be found *n.*
Heb. 4:13 all things are *n.* and open
Rev. 16:15 keepeth his garments, lest he walk *n.*

NAME (NAME'S)
Ex. 23:13 no mention of the *n.* of other gods
23:21 for my *n.* is in him
28:12 Aaron bear their *n.* before the Lord
34:14 whose *n.* is jealous, is a jealous
Lev. 18:21 profane the *n.* of thy God
2 Chr. 14:11 in thy *n.* we go against this
Ps. 8: 1 how excellent is thy *n.* in all
20: 1 the *n.* of the God of Jacob
48:10 according to thy *n.* so is thy
72:17 his *n.* shall endure for ever
75: 1 thy *n.* is near, thy wondrous works declare
76: 1 his *n.* is great in Israel
106: 8 he saved them for his *n.* sake
109: 13 let their *n.* be blotted
138: 2 praise thy *n.* for thy lovingkindness
Prov. 10: 7 the *n.* of the wicked shall rot
22: 1 a good *n.* is rather to be chosen
30: 3 what is his *n.* and what is his
Eccl. 7: 1 good *n.* better than precious ointment
Sol. 1: 3 thy *n.* is as ointment poured
Is. 9: 6 his *n.* shall be called Wonderful
26: 8 desire of our soul is to thy *n.*
48: 9 for my *n.* sake I defer anger
55:13 shall be to the Lord for a *n.*
56: 5 a *n.* better than of sons and
62: 2 thou shalt be called by a new *n.*
64: 7 none that calleth on thy *n.*
Jer. 13:11 for a people, and for a *n.*
32:20 made thee a *n.* as at this day
33: 9 shall be to me a *n.* of joy
Ezek. 20: 9 wrought for my *n.* sake
Mic. 4: 5 walk in the *n.* of the Lord
6: 9 man of wisdom shall see thy *n.*
Zech. 14: 9 shall be one Lord and his *n.*
Mal. 1:14 my *n.* is dreadful among the
2: 2 lay it to heart, to give glory to my *n.*
Mat. 10:22 hated of all for my *n.* sake
10:41 receive prophet in the *n.* of
Luke 6:22 cast out your *n.* as evil
John 14:13 ask in my *n.*, that will I do
15:16 ask of the father in my *n.*
16:24 asked nothing in my *n.*
16:26 ye shall ask in my *n.*
17:12 I kept them in thy *n.*
20:31 ye might have life through his *n.*
Acts 9:15 a chosen vessel to bear my *n.*
Rom. 2:24 *n.* of God is blasphemed
Eph. 1:21 every *n.* that is named
Phil. 2: 9 a *n.* above every *n.*
Col. 3:17 do all in the *n.* of the Lord
2 Tim. 2:19 that nameth the *n.* of Christ
Heb. 1: 4 obtained a more excellent *n.*
1 Pet. 4:14 reproached for the *n.* of Christ
1 John 3:23 believe on the *n.* of the Son
Rev. 2: 3 for my *n.* sake hast laboured, and
2:13 holdest fast my *n.*, and hast not
2:17 new *n.* written, which no man
3: 1 thou hast a *n.* that thou livest
3: 5 confess his *n.* before my father
3: 8 and hast not denied my *n.*
Rev. 3:12 write on him the *n.* of my God
14: 1 his Father's *n.* written in their

NAMES
Deut. 12: 3 destroy the *n.* of them
Ps. 16: 4 nor take up their *n.* into my
49:11 call lands after their *n.*
Luke 10:20 your *n.* are written in heaven
Rev. 3: 4 hast a few *n.* in Sardis which have

NARROW (NARROWER)
1 Ki. 6: 4 made windows of *n.* slits
Prov. 23:27 strange woman is a *n.* pit
Is. 28:20 covering *n.* then that he can wrap
49:19 now be too *n.* by reason of the
Mat. 7:14 and *n.* is the way which leadeth

NATION (NATIONS)
Gen. 10:32 after their generations in their *n.*
15:14 and also that *n.*, whom they
17: 6 I will make *n.* of thee and kings
20: 4 wilt slay a righteous *n.*
21:13 the bondwoman will I make a *n.*
Ex. 19: 6 priests, and an holy *n.*
Num. 14:12 make of thee a greater *n.*
2 Sam. 7:23 what one *n.* in the earth
Ps. 9:20 *n.* may know themselves to be but
33:12 *n.* whose God is the Lord
113: 4 Lord high above all *n.*, and his
147: 20 not dealt so with any *n.*
Is. 1: 4 Ah sinful *n.*, a people laden
2: 2 all *n.* shall flow unto it
2: 4 *n.* shall not lift the sword against *n.*
40:17 *n.* before him are as nothing
49: 7 him whom the *n.* abhorreth
55: 5 *n.* that knew thee not shall
66: 8 shall a *n.* be born at once
Jer. 4: 2 *n.* shall bless themselves in
Zech. 2:11 many *n.* be joined to the Lord
Mat. 25:32 before him be gathered all *n.*
24: 7 *n.* shall rise against *n.*
Luke 7: 5 he loveth our *n.* and he hath built
Acts 10:35 in every *n.* he that feareth
14:16 suffered all *n.* to walk in
Rom. 10:19 by a foolish *n.* I will
Phil. 2:15 midst of a crooked and perverse *n.*
1 Pet. 2: 9 ye are an holy *n.*, a peculiar people
Rev. 5: 9 kindred and tongue, and people and *n.*
21:24 *n.* of them that are saved

NATURAL (NATURALLY)
Deut. 34: 7 nor his *n.* force abated
Rom. 1:27 the *n.* use of the women
11:24 would be the *n.* branches
1 Cor. 2:14 the *n.* man receiveth not
15:46 but that which is *n.*
Phil. 2:20 who will *n.* care for your state
2 Tim. 3: 3 without *n.* affection, trucebreakers
Jas. 1:23 beholding his *n.* face in a glass
2 Pet. 2:12 as *n.* brute beasts, made to be
Jude 1:10 they know *n.* as brute beasts

NATURE
Rom. 1:26 that which is against *n.*
2:14 do by *n.* things contained in
2:27 uncircumcision, which is by *n.*
1 Cor. 11:14 doth not even *n.* itself teach
Gal. 4: 8 them which by *n.* are no gods
Eph. 2: 3 by *n.* the children of wrath
Heb. 2:16 on him the *n.* of angels
Jas. 3: 6 setteth on fire the course of *n.*
2 Pet. 1: 4 might be partakers of the divine *n.*

NECK (NECKS)
2 Ki. 17:14 but hardened their *n.*; like to the
Neh. 9:29 and hardened their *n.*, and would
Sol. 1:10 thy *n.* with chains of gold
Is. 48: 4 thy *n.* is an iron sinew
Jer. 7:26 but hardened their *n.*, they did worse
Acts 15:10 upon the *n.* of the disciples
Rom. 16: 4 laid down their own *n.*

NEED (NEEDETH)
Mat. 6:32 ye have *n.* of all these things
9:12 they that are whole *n.* not
Luke 15: 7 just persons which *n.* no repentance
Eph. 4:28 give to him that *n.*
Heb. 4:16 grace to help in time of *n.*
1 Pet. 1: 6 if *n.* be, ye are in heaviness
1 John 2:27 *n.* not that any man teach you
Rev. 3:17 and have *n.* of nothing
21:23 the city had no *n.* of sun
22: 5 and they *n.* no candle

NEEDFUL
Luke 10:42 one thing is *n.*, and Mary hath

NEEDY
Ps. 9:18 *n.* shall not always be forgotten
72:12 he shall deliver the *n.*
113: 7 lifteth the *n.* out of the dunghill
Is. 14:30 *n.* shall lie down in safety

NEGLECT
Mat. 18:17 he shall *n.* to hear them
1 Tim. 4:14 *n.* not the gift that is in thee
Heb. 2: 3 if we *n.* so great a salvation

NEIGHBOUR
Ex. 3:22 every woman shall borrow of her *n.*
11: 2 every woman of her *n.* jewels of
20:16 not bear false witness against thy *n.*
Lev. 19:13 thou shalt not defraud thy *n.*
19:17 thou shalt in any wise rebuke thy *n.*
19:18 shalt love thy *n.* as thyself
Ps. 15: 3 nor doeth evil to his *n.*
Prov. 27:10 better is a *n.* that is near
Jer. 31:34 teach no more every man his *n.*
Mat. 19:19 love thy *n.* as thyself
22:39 love thy *n.* as thyself
Luke 10:29 Jesus, and who is my *n.*
Rom. 13: 9 love thy *n.* as thyself
13:10 love worketh no ill to his *n.*
15: 2 let every one of us please his *n.*
Gal. 5:14 love thy *n.* as thyself
Jas. 2: 8 love thy *n.* as thyself

NEST (NESTS)
Job 29:18 I shall die in my *n.*
Ps. 84: 3 the swallow a *n.* for herself
Prov. 27: 8 bird that wandereth from her *n.*
Is. 10:14 my hand has found as a *n.* the riches
Hab. 2: 9 set his *n.* on high, that he may
Mat. 8:20 birds of the air have *n.*

NET (NETS)
Job 19: 6 hath compassed me with his *n.*
Ps. 9:15 in the *n.* which they hid
31: 4 Pull me out of the *n.*
35: 8 his *n.* that he hath hid
66:11 broughtest us into the *n.*
Eccl. 7:26 woman whose heart is snares and *n.*
Is. 51:20 as a wild bull in a *n.*
Hab. 1:16 they sacrifice unto their *n.*
Mat. 13:47 heaven in like unto a *n.*

NEW
Num. 16:30 Lord make a *n.* thing, and the
Deut. 32:17 to *n.* gods that came newly up
Judg. 5: 8 chose *n.* gods: then there was
Ps. 33: 3 sing unto him a *n.* song
Eccl. 1: 9 there is no *n.* thing under the sun
Is. 42:10 sing unto the Lord a *n.* song
62: 2 be called by a *n.* name
65:17 *n.* heavens and a *n.* earth
66:22 *n.* heavens and the *n.* earth
Jer. 31:22 created a *n.* thing in the earth
Ezek. 11:19 put a *n.* spirit within you
36:26 a *n.* heart also will I give
Mat. 9:16 putteth *n.* cloth unto an old garment
9:17 neither put *n.* wine in old bottles
13:52 his treasure things *n.* and old
Mark 1:27 what *n.* doctrine is this
John 13:34 a *n.* commandment I give unto you
Acts 17:19 we know what this *n.* doctrine
17:21 to tell or to hear some *n.* thing
1 Cor. 5: 7 that ye may be a *n.* lump
2 Cor. 5:17 *n.* creature; behold, all things are become *n.*
Gal. 6:15 nor uncircumcision, but a *n.* creature
Eph. 4:24 put on the *n.* man
Col. 3:10 put on the *n.* man
2 Pet. 3:13 *n.* heavens and a *n.* earth
1 John 2: 8 a *n.* commandment I write unto you
Rev. 2:17 a *n.* name written, which
5: 9 they sung a *n.* song, saying
21: 1 a *n.* heaven and a *n.* earth

NEWNESS
Rom. 6: 4 should walk in the *n.* of life
7: 6 should serve in the *n.* of spirit

NIGH
Deut. 4: 7 who hath God so *n.* unto
30:14 word is very *n.* to thee
Ps. 34:18 Lord is *n.* unto them that are
145: 18 Lord is *n.* them that call on
Mat. 15: 8 draweth *n.* unto me with their mouth
Rom. 10: 8 the word is *n.* thee
Eph. 2:13 made *n.* by the blood of Christ
2:17 and to them that were *n.*

NIGHT
Gen. 1: 5 and the darkness he called *n.*
26:24 appeared unto him the same *n.*
Ex. 12:42 this is that *n.* of the Lord
Job 35:10 giveth songs in the *n.*
Ps. 16: 7 instruct me in the *n.* seasons
19: 2 *n.* unto *n.* showeth knowledge
30: 5 weeping may endure for a *n.*
42: 8 in the *n.* his song shall be
77: 6 I call to remembrance my song in the *n.*
119: 55 in the *n.*, and have kept thy law
134: 1 which by *n.* stand in the house
139: 11 *n.* shall be light about me
Is. 21:11 Watchman, what of *n.*?
30:29 ye shall have a song as in the *n.*
59:10 stumble at noonday as in the *n.*
Jer. 14: 8 turneth aside to tarry for a *n.*
Luke 6:12 continued all *n.* in prayer
12:20 this *n.* thy soul shall be required
John 3: 2 the same came to Jesus by *n.*
9: 4 *n.* cometh when no man can work
11:10 if a man walk in the *n.* he stumbleth
19:39 first came to Jesus by *n.*
Rom. 13:12 *n.* is far spent; the day is at hand
1 Thes. 5: 7 sleep in the *n.* and they that
Rev. 21:25 shall be no *n.* there

NOBLE (NOBLES)
Ex. 24:11 upon the *n.* of the children
Ezra 4:10 whom the great *n.* Asnapper brought
Neh. 13:17 contended with the *n.* of Judah
Esth. 6: 9 the king's most *n.* princes
Ps. 149: 8 their *n.* with fetters of iron
Prov. 8:16 by me princes rule, and *n.*
Eccl. 10:17 when thy king is a son of *n.*
Jer. 2:21 planted thee a *n.* vine
Acts 17:11 these were more *n.* than those
1 Cor. 1:26 not many *n.* are called

NOBLEMAN
Luke 19:12 *n.* went into a far country
John 4:49 the *n.* saith unto him, Sir, come

NOSE
Prov. 30:33 the wringing of the *n.*
Is. 65: 5 these are a smoke in my *n.*

NOSTRILS
Is. 2:22 man, whose breath is in his *n.*
Lam. 4:20 the breath of our *n.*, the anointed

NOTHING
Gen. 11: 6 now *n.* will be restrained
Ex. 12:10 let *n.* of it remain
Num. 6: 4 eat *n.* that is made of
Josh. 11:15 he left *n.* undone, of all
2 Sam. 24:24 which doth cost me *n.*
1 Ki. 8: 9 *n.* in the ark save the two tables
Neh. 8:10 send to them for whom *n.* is prepared
Job 6:21 for now ye are *n.*; ye see my
8: 9 of yesterday, and know *n.*
26: 7 and hangeth the earth upon *n.*
34: 9 it profiteth a man *n.*
Ps. 17: 3 tried me, and shalt find *n.*
49:17 when he dieth, shall carry *n.* away
119:165 *n.* shall offend them
Prov. 13: 4 sluggard desireth and hath *n.*
13: 7 maketh himself rich, yet hath *n.*
Is. 40:17 all nations before him are as *n.*
Jer. 10:24 lest thou bring me to *n.*
Lam. 1:12 is it *n.* to you, all ye that
Luke 1:37 with God *n.* shall be impossible
John 14:30 cometh and hath *n.* in me
15: 5 without me ye can do *n.*
1 Cor. 1:19 bring to *n.* the understanding
13: 2 and have not charity, I am *n.*
2 Cor. 6:10 having *n.* yet possessing all
1 Tim. 6: 7 we brought *n.* into world

NUMBER (NUMBERED, NUMBEREST, NUMBERS)
Job 14:16 for now thou *n.* my steps
Ps. 71:15 I know not the *n.* thereof
90:12 teach us to *n.* our days
Is. 53:12 *n.* with the transgressors, and he
65:12 I will *n.* you to the sword
Jer. 33:22 host of heaven cannot be *n.*
Hos. 1:10 which cannot be measured nor *n.*
Rev. 7: 9 multitude no man could *n.*
13:17 beast, or the *n.* of his name

NURSE (NURSING)
Is. 49:23 *n.* fathers and their queens *n.* mothers
1 Thes. 2: 7 a *n.* cherisheth her children

O

OATH
Gen. 24: 8 thou shalt be clear from this my *o.*
1 Sam. 14:26 people feared the *o.*
2 Sam. 21: 7 Lord's *o.* that was between
2 Chr. 15:15 all Judah rejoiced at the *o.*
Eccl. 8: 2 in regard of the *o.* of God
Ezek. 16:59 which hast despised the *o.*
Luke 1:73 *o.* which he sware to our
Heb. 6:16 and an *o.* for confirmation is
Jas. 5:12 neither by any other *o.*

OBEY (OBEYED)
Gen. 27: 8 therefore, my son, *o.* my voice
Ex. 5: 2 the Lord, that I should *o.* his voice
Deut. 11:27 blessing if ye *o.*
13: 4 keep his commandments and *o.* his voice
Josh. 24:24 his voice will we *o.*
1 Sam. 12:14 serve him and *o.* his voice
15:22 to *o.* is better than sacrifice
Jer. 7:23 *o.* my voice and I will be your God
Acts 5:29 ought to *o.* God rather than men
Rom. 2: 8 contentious, and do not *o.* truth
6:16 servants ye are to whom ye *o.*
6:17 but ye have *o.* from the heart
Eph. 6: 1 children, *o.* your parents in the Lord
Col. 3:20 Children, *o.* your parents in all things
3:22 servants, *o.* in all things
2 Thes. 1: 8 that *o.* not the gospel
3:14 if any man *o.* not our word
Tit. 3: 1 to *o.* magistrates, to be ready to
Heb. 5: 9 salvation to all them that *o.*
13:17 *o.* them that have rule over
1 Pet. 3: 1 if any *o.* not the word
3: 6 even as Sarah *o.* Abraham

OBEDIENCE
Rom. 1: 5 for *o.* to the faith among all nations
5:19 by the *o.* of one shall many be
16:19 your *o.* is come abroad
16:26 to all nations for the *o.* of faith
1 Cor. 14:34 they are commanded to be under *o.*
2 Cor. 7:15 he remembereth the *o.* of you
10: 5 every thought to the *o.* of Christ
10: 6 when your *o.* is fulfilled
Heb. 5: 8 learned *o.* by things suffered
1 Pet. 1: 2 sanctification of the Spirit to *o.*

OBEDIENT
Ex. 24: 7 will we do, and be *o.*
Num. 27:20 children of Israel may be *o.*
Deut. 4:30 turn and be *o.* to his voice
8:20 perish; because ye would not be *o.*
2 Sam. 22:45 they shall be *o.* unto me
Prov. 25:12 the wise reprover upon an *o.* ear
Is. 1:19 if ye be willing and *o.*
42:24 neither were they *o.* to his law
Acts 6: 7 priests were *o.* to the faith
Rom. 15:18 to make Gentiles *o.* by word
2 Cor. 2: 9 whether ye be *o.* in all
Eph. 6: 5 servants, be *o.* to them
Phil. 2: 8 he became *o.* unto death
Tit. 2: 9 exhort servants to be *o.*
1 Pet. 1:14 as *o.* children, not fashioning

OBSERVE (OBSERVED)
Ex. 12:17 *o.* the feast of unleavened bread
12:42 it is a night to be much *o.*
34:11 *o.* thou that which I command thee
Ps. 107: 43 who is wise and will *o.*
119: 34 *o.* it with my whole heart
Prov. 23:26 let thine eyes *o.* my ways
Jonah 2: 8 they that *o.* lying vanities
Mat. 28:20 teaching them to *o.* all things
Mark 6:20 man and an holy, and *o.* him
10:20 all these I *o.* from my youth
Gal. 4:10 ye *o.* days and months and times

OBSERVATION
Luke 17:20 kingdom of God cometh not with *o.*

OBTAIN (OBTAINED)
Prov. 8:35 and shall *o.* favour of the Lord
Is. 35:10 they shall *o.* joy and gladness, and
Hos. 2:23 her that had not *o.* mercy
Luke 20:35 worthy to *o.* that world
Acts 26:22 having therefore *o.* help of God
Rom. 11: 7 the election hath *o.* it
1 Cor. 9:24 so run, that ye may *o.*
Eph. 1:11 whom also we have *o.* an inheritance
1 Tim. 1:13 but I *o.* mercy, because I did
Heb. 1: 4 inheritance *o.* a more excellent name
4:16 we may *o.* mercy and find grace
6:15 patiently endured, he *o.* the promise
8: 6 hath he *o.* a more excellent ministry
9:12 *o.* eternal redemption for us
11:35 they might *o.* a better resurrection
Jas. 4: 2 ye desire to have, and cannot *o.*

OCCASION (OCCASIONS)
2 Sam. 12:14 given great *o.* to the enemies
Job 33:10 he findeth *o.* against me
Jer. 2:24 in her *o.* who can turn
Rom. 7: 8 sin, taking *o.* by the commandment
14:13 *o.* to fall in his brother's way
2 Cor. 11:12 I may cut off *o.* from them
Gal. 5:13 use not liberty for *o.* to the flesh
1 Tim. 5:14 give none *o.* to the adversary
1 John 2:10 there is none *o.* of stumbling in him

OFFENCE (OFFENCES)
1 Sam. 25:31 nor *o.* of heart unto my lord
Eccl. 10: 4 yielding pacifieth great *o.*
Is. 8:14 rock of *o.* to both the houses of Israel
Mat. 16:23 thou art an *o.* unto me
Acts 24:16 conscience void of *o.*
Rom. 4:25 who was delivered for our *o.* and
5:15 the *o.* so also is the free gift
5:17 by one man's *o.* death reigned
9:33 a stumblingstone and rock of *o.*
14:20 for him that eateth with *o.*
16:17 cause divisions and *o.* contrary to
2 Cor. 6: 3 giving no *o.* in any thing
11: 7 have I committed an *o.* in abasing
Gal. 5:11 then is the *o.* of the cross ceased
Phil. 1:10 without *o.* till the day of Christ
1 Pet. 2: 8 and a rock of *o.*, even to them

OFFEND (OFFENDED)
Job 34:31 I will not *o.* any more
Ps. 73:15 I should *o.* against the generation
119:165 law: and nothing shall *o.* them
Prov. 18:19 a brother *o.* is harder to be won
Jer. 2: 3 all that devour him shall *o.*
50: 7 we *o.* not because they have
Hos. 4:15 harlot, yet let not Judah *o.*
Mat. 5:29 if thy right eye *o.* thee
11: 6 whosoever shall not be *o.* in me
13:41 of his kingdom all things that *o.*
17:27 yet lest we should *o.* them, go
18: 6 shall *o.* one of these little ones
26:33 yet will I never be *o.*
Mark 4:17 immediately they are *o.*
9:43 if thy hand *o.* thee, cut it off
Rom. 14:21 thy brother stumbleth or is *o.*
2 Cor. 11:29 who is *o.* and I burn not
Jas. 2:10 yet *o.* in one point he is guilty
3: 2 in many things we *o.* all

OFFER (OFFERED)
Gen. 31:54 then Jacob *o.* sacrifice upon the mount
Lev. 1: 3 he shall *o.* it of his own voluntary
Mat. 5:24 then come and *o.* thy gift
Phil. 2:17 *o.* upon the sacrifice and service
2 Tim. 4: 6 I am now ready to be *o.*, and the time
Heb. 9:14 Spirit *o.* himself without spot to God
9:28 Christ was once *o.* to bear sins
11: 4 by faith Abel *o.* unto God a more
11:17 Abraham, when he was tried, *o.* up Isaac
13:15 let us *o.* the sacrifice of praise
Rev. 8: 3 *o.* it with the prayers of all saints

OFFERING
Eph. 5: 2 an *o.* and a sacrifice to God

Heb. 10: 5 sacrifice and *o.* thou wouldest not
10:14 by one *o.* he hath perfected for ever

OFFSCOURING
Lam. 3:45 thou hast made us as the *o.*
1 Cor. 4:13 we are the *o.* of all things

OFTEN
Prov. 29: 1 he, that being *o.* reproved
Mal. 3:16 the Lord spake *o.* one to another
Mat. 23:37 how *o.* would I have gathered
1 Cor. 11:26 as *o.* as ye eat this bread
Phil. 3:18 many walk, of whom I have told you *o.*
Heb. 9:25 yet that he should offer himself *o.*

OIL
Gen. 28:18 and poured *o.* upon the top of it
Ex. 25: 6 *o.* for the light, spices for anointing
Ps. 45: 7 anointed thee with the *o.* of gladness
89:20 with my holy *o.* have I anointed
92:10 I shall be anointed with fresh *o.*
104: 15 *o.* to make his face to shine
141: 5 it shall be an excellent *o.*
Is. 61: 3 *o.* of joy for mourning, the garment
Mic. 6: 7 with ten thousands of rivers of *o.*
Mat. 25: 3 and took no *o.* with them
25: 4 wise took *o.* in their vessels
25: 8 give us of your *o.* for our lamps
Luke 7:46 head with *o.* didst not anoint
10:34 pouring in *o.* and wine, and set him
Heb. 1: 9 anointed thee with the *o.* of gladness

OINTMENT (OINTMENTS)
Ps. 133: 2 it is like precious *o.* upon the head
Prov. 27:16 and the *o.* of his right hand
Eccl. 7: 1 good name is better than precious *o.*
Sol. 1: 3 the savour of thy good *o.*
Is. 1: 6 bound up neither mollified with *o.*
Amos 6: 6 anoint themselves with chief *o.*
Mat. 26:12 she hath poured this *o.* on my body
Luke 7:37 brought an alabaster box of *o.*
John 12: 5 why was not this *o.* sold

OLD
Gen. 5:32 and Noah was five hundred years *o.*
18:13 of a surety bear a child, which am *o.*
25: 8 and died in a good *o.* age
Ps. 37:25 I have been young, and now am *o.*
71: 9 me not off in the time of *o.* age
92:14 still bring forth fruit in *o.* age
Prov. 22: 6 when he is *o.* he will not depart from
Jer. 6:16 ask for the *o.* paths, where is the
Rom. 6: 6 our *o.* man is crucified with him
1 Cor. 5: 7 purge out the *o.* leaven
2 Cor. 5:17 *o.* things are passed away
Eph. 4:22 concerning the former conversation the *o.* man
Col. 3: 9 ye have put off the *o.* man
2 Pet. 1: 9 purged from his *o.* sins

OMEGA
Rev. 1: 8 I am the Alpha and the *O.*
1:11 Alpha and *O.*, the first and the last
21: 6 Alpha and *O.*, the beginning and the end
22:13 Alpha and *O.*, the beginning and the end

ONE
Gen 2:24 and they shall be *o.* flesh
Ps. 89:19 laid help upon *o.* that is mighty
Eccl. 4: 9 two are better than *o.*
Jer. 3:14 *o.* of a city, and two of a
Mat. 19: 5 and they twain shall be *o.* flesh
19:17 none good but *o.*, that is God
Luke 10:42 but *o.* thing is needful: and Mary
John 10:30 I and my Father are *o.*
1 Cor. 8: 4 there is none other God but *o.*
10:17 we being many are *o.* bread and *o.* body
Gal. 3:20 not mediator of *o.*, but God is *o.*
Phil. 3:13 this *o.* thing I do, forgetting
1 John 5: 7 Ghost: and these three are *o.*

OPEN (OPENED, OPENEST)
Gen. 3: 7 eyes of them both were *o.*
Ps. 51:15 O Lord, *o.* thou my lips: and my
81:10 *o.* thy mouth wide, and I will fill
104: 28 thou *o.* thine hand, they are
119: 18 *o.* thou mine eyes, that I may
145: 16 thou *o.* thine hand, and satisfiest
Prov. 31: 8 *o.* thy mouth for the dumb in the
Sol. 5: 2 *o.* to me, my sister, my love
Is. 22:22 shall *o.* and none shall shut
35: 5 eyes of the blind shall be *o.*
42: 7 to *o.* the blind eyes, to bring out
53: 7 yet he *o.* not his mouth
Ezek. 16:63 never *o.* thy mouth any more because
Mat. 7: 7 knock, and it shall be *o.*
25:11 saying, Lord, Lord, *o.* to us
Acts 14:27 *o.* the door of faith to the Gentiles
16:14 whose heart the Lord *o.*
26:18 to *o.* their eyes, and to turn them
1 Cor. 16: 9 great door and effectual is *o.*
2 Cor. 2:12 door *o.* unto me of the Lord
Col. 4: 3 *o.* to us a door of utterance
Heb. 4:13 naked and *o.* unto the eyes of
Rev. 5: 2 who is worthy to *o.* the book

OPPORTUNITY
Mat. 26:16 he sought *o.* to betray him
Gal. 6:10 as we have therefore *o.*, let us do good
Phil. 4:10 were also careful, but ye lacked *o.*
Heb. 11:15 they might have had *o.* to have returned

OPPRESS (OPPRESSED)
Ex. 3: 9 wherewith the Egyptians *o.* them
22:21 neither vex a stranger nor *o.* him
Lev. 25:14 ye shall not *o.* one another
Judg. 10:12 and the Maonites did *o.* you
Job 10: 3 good unto thee that thou shouldest *o.*
Ps. 9: 9 Lord also will be a refuge for the *o.*
10:18 that man of the earth may no more *o.*
Prov. 22:22 neither *o.* the afflicted in the gate
Eccl. 4: 1 tears of such as were *o.*
Is. 1:17 relieve the *o.*, judge the fatherless
58: 6 and to let the *o.* go free
Zech. 7:10 *o.* not the widow, nor the fatherless
Mal. 3: 5 witness against those that *o.*
Acts 10:38 healing all that were *o.* of the devil
Jas. 2: 6 do not rich men *o.* you?

OPPRESSION (OPPRESSIONS)
Deut. 26: 7 looked on our labour and our *o.*
2 Ki. 13: 4 for he saw the *o.* of Israel
Ps. 12: 5 for the *o.* of the poor, for the
62:10 trust not in *o.* and become
Eccl. 4: 1. considered all the *o.* that are done
7: 7 *o.* maketh a wise man mad
Is. 5: 7 judgment, but behold *o.*; for
33:15 he that despiseth gain of *o.*

OPPRESSOR (OPPRESSORS)
Ps. 54: 3 and *o.* seek after my soul
72: 4 shall break in pieces the *o.*
Prov. 3:31 envy thou not the *o.*
28:16 is also a great *o.*; but he
Is. 3:12 children are their *o.*, and women
51:13 because of the fury of the *o.*

ORACLES
Acts 7:38 who received the lively *o.* to give
Rom. 3: 2 unto them were committed the *o.* of God
Heb. 5:12 first principles of the *o.* of God
1 Pet. 4:11 let him speak as the *o.* of God

ORDAIN (ORDAINED)
Ps. 8: 2 hast thou *o.* strength because of
132: 17 *o.* a lamp for mine anointed
Is. 26:12 Lord, thou wilt *o.* peace for us
30:33 Tophet is *o.* of old, for
Jer. 1: 5 *o.* thee a prophet to the nations
Hab. 1:12 Lord, thou hast *o.* them for judgment
Acts 13:48 as many as were *o.* to eternal life
14:23 *o.* them elders in every church
17:31 judge by that man whom he *o.*
Rom. 7:10 the commandment which was *o.* to life
13: 1 powers that be are *o.* of God
Gal. 3:19 *o.* by angels in the hand of

Eph. 2:10 God hath before *o.* that we should
1 Tim. 2: 7 *o.* a preacher and an apostle
Tit. 1: 5 and *o.* elders in every city
Heb. 5: 1 *o.* for men in things pertaining to
Jude 1: 4 before of old *o.* to this condemnation

ORDER
Gen. 22: 9 laid the wood in *o.*, and bound Isaac
Job 23: 4 I would *o.* my cause before him
33: 5 set thy words in *o.* before me
Ps. 40: 5 be reckoned up in *o.* unto thee
50:21 set them in *o.* before thine eyes
1 Cor. 14:40 things be done decently and in *o.*
Col. 2: 5 joying and beholding your *o.*
Tit. 1: 5 set in *o.* things wanting

ORDINANCE (ORDINANCES)
Lev. 22: 9 they shall therefore keep mine *o.*
Neh. 10:32 also we made *o.* for us
Is. 58: 2 ask of me the *o.* of justice
Jer. 31:35 *o.* of the moon and of the stars
Ezek. 11:20 keep mine *o.* and do them
Luke 1: 6 in all commandments and *o.* of the Lord
Rom. 13: 2 resisteth the *o.* of God
1 Cor. 11: 2 remember me in all things, and keep the *o.*
Eph. 2:15 law of commandments contained in *o.*
Col. 2:14 out the handwriting of *o.* that was
Heb. 9: 1 had also *o.* of divine service, and a
1 Pet. 2:13 submit to every *o.* of man

OUTSIDE
Ezek. 40: 5. a wall on the *o.* of the house
Mat. 23:25 make clean the *o.* of the cup

OUTSTRETCHED
Deut. 26: 8 and with an *o.* arm and with
Jer. 21: 5 fight against you with an *o.* hand
27: 5 my great power and by my *o.* arm

OUTWARD (OUTWARDLY)
1 Sam. 16: 7 man looketh on the *o.* appearance
Mat. 23:28 even so ye also *o.* appear righteous
Rom. 2:28 not a Jew, which is one *o.*
2 Cor. 4:16 though our *o.* man perish
1 Pet. 3: 3. let it not be that *o.* adorning

OVERCOME (OVERCOMETH)
Gen. 49:19 he shall *o.* at the last
Num. 13:30 for we are well able to *o.* it
Sol. 6: 5 for they have *o.* me: thy hair
John 16:33 good cheer, I have *o.* the world
1 John 2:13 ye have *o.* the wicked one
2:14 ye have *o.* the wicked one
4: 4 are of God, little children, and have *o.*
5: 4 born of God *o.* the world
Rev. 2: 7 to him that *o.* I will give
2:11 he that *o.* shall not be hurt of
3: 5 he that *o.* shall be clothed
3:12 him that *o.* will I make a pillar
3:21 him that *o.* will I grant to sit
17:14 the Lamb shall *o.* them: for he is

OVERSEER (OVERSEERS)
Prov. 6: 7 which having no guide, *o.*, or ruler
Acts 20:28 the Holy Ghost hath made you *o.*

OVERSIGHT
Gen. 43:12 peradventure it was an *o.*
1 Pet. 5: 2 taking the *o.* thereof, not by constraint

OVERTHROW (OVERTHROWETH, OVERTHROWN)
Deut. 12: 3 ye shall *o.* their altars
Job 12:19 princes away spoiled, and *o.* the mighty
Ps. 140: 11 hunt the violent man to *o.* him
Prov. 13: 6 but wickedness *o.* the sinner
21:12 God *o.* the wicked for their wickedness
Amos 4:11 I have *o.* some of you, as God
Acts 5:39 be of God, ye cannot *o.* it
2 Tim. 2:18 and *o.* the faith of some

OWE (OWED)
Mat. 18:24 which *o.* him ten thousand talents
Rom. 13: 8 *o.* no man anything, but to love

OWN
Deut. 24:16 be put to death for his *o.* sin

Judg. 7: 2 mine o. hand hath saved me
John 1:11 his o. and his o. received him not
1 Cor. 6:19 and ye are not your o.
10:24 let no man seek his o., but
Phil. 2: 4 look not every man on his o. things

OX (OXEN)
Ps. 144: 14 that our o. may be strong to labour
Prov. 7:22 as an o. goeth to the slaughter
15:17 than a stalled o. and hatred therewith
Is. 1: 3 the o. knoweth his owner
22:13 behold joy and gladness, slaying o.
Mat. 22: 4 my o. and my fatlings are killed
Luke 14:19 I have bought five yoke of o.
John 2:14 in the temple those that sold o.
1 Cor. 9: 9 doth God take care for o.

P

PAIN (PAINS)
Ps. 116: 3 p. of hell gat hold on me
Is. 21: 3 are my loins filled with p.
66: 7 before her p. came, she was delivered
Jer. 6:24 and p., as of a woman in travail
Mic. 4:10 be in p. and labour to bring forth
Acts 2:24 loosed the p. of death
Rev. 21: 4 neither shall there be any more p.

PAINED
Ps. 55: 4 my heart is sore p.
Is. 23: 5 they be sorely p. at the report of Tyre
Jer. 4:19 I am p. at my very heart
Joel 2: 6 the people shall be much p.
Rev. 12: 2 travailing in birth and p.

PALACE
1 Chr. 29:19 and to build the p., for which
Ps. 45:15 they shall enter into the king's p.
Sol. 8: 9 will build upon her a p. of silver
Is. 25: 2 a p. of strangers to be no city
Phil. 1:13 in Christ are manifest in all the p.

PARABLE (PARABLES)
Ps. 49: 4 incline mine ear to a p.
78: 2 I will open my mouth in a p.
Prov. 26: 9 is a p. in the mouth of fools
Ezek. 20:49 doth he not speak p.
Mic. 2: 4 shall one take up a p. against you
Mat. 13: 3 spake many things unto them in p.
Luke 5:36 spake also a p. unto them; no man
13: 6 he spake also this p.; a certain man
21:29 and he spake to them a p.

PARADISE
Luke 23:43 today shalt thou be with me in p.
2 Cor. 12: 4 he was caught up into p.
Rev. 2: 7 in the midst of the p. of God

PARDON (PARDONED, PARDONETH)
Ex. 34: 9 p. our iniquity, and our sin
23:21 he will not p. your transgressions
Num. 14:19 p. the iniquity of the people
1 Sam. 15:25 p. my sin and turn again with me
2 Ki. 24: 4 which the Lord would not p.
2 Chr. 30:18 the good Lord p. every one
Neh. 9:17 thou art a God ready to p.
Job 7:21 why dost thou not p. my transgression
Ps. 25:11 thy name's sake O Lord p. my iniquity
Is. 40: 2 that her iniquity is p.
55: 7 to our God, for he will abundantly p.
Jer. 5: 7 how shall I p. thee for this
33: 8 I will p. all their iniquities
50:20 I will p. them whom I reserve
Mic. 7:18 who is God like unto thee that p.

PARENTS
Mat. 10:21 children rise up against their p.
Luke 2:27 when the p. brought in the child Jesus
8:56 and her p. were astonished
18:29 no man hath left house, or p.
21:16 ye shall be betrayed both by p.
Rom. 1:30 of evil things, disobedient to p.
2 Cor. 12:14 the p. but the p. for the children
1 Tim. 5: 4 to requite their p.: for that
2 Tim. 3: 2 disobedient to p., unthankful, unholy

PART
Ex. 29:26 the Lord: and it shall be thy p.
Num. 18:20 thy p. and thine inheritance among
Ps. 5: 9 their inward p. is very wickedness
118: 7 Lord taketh my p. with them
Luke 10:42 Mary hath chosen that good p.
Acts 8:21 neither p. nor lot in this matter
1 Cor. 13: 9 know in p. and we prophesy in p.

PARTAKER (PARTAKERS)
Ps. 50:18 thou hast been p. with adulterers
Rom. 15:27 made p. of their spiritual things
1 Cor. 9:10 in hope should be p. of his hope
9:13 wait at the altar are p. with the altar
10:17 we are all p. of that one bread
10:21 cannot be p. of the Lord's table
10:30 if I by grace be a p. why am I
Eph. 5: 7 be ye not therefore p. with them
1 Tim. 5:22 be not p. of other men's sins
Heb. 3:14 for we are made p. of Christ
6: 4 and were made p. of the Holy Ghost
12:10 might be p. of his holiness
1 Pet. 5: 1 a p. of the glory that shall be revealed
2 John 1:11 God speed is p. of his evil deeds

PARTIAL
Mal. 2: 9 but have been p. in the law
Jas. 2: 4 are ye not then p. in yourselves

PARTIALITY
1 Tim. 5:21 before another, doing nothing by p.
Jas. 3:17 without p., and without hypocrisy

PASS (PASSED, PASSEST, PASSETH)
Is. 43: 2 when thou p. through the waters
Mic. 7:18 p. by the transgression of the remnant
Mark 14:35 the hour might p. from him
Luke 16:17 easier for heaven and earth to p.
John 5:24 but is p. from death unto life
1 Cor. 7:31 fashion of this world p. away
Phil. 4: 7 peace of God p. all understanding
1 John 2:17 world p. away and the lust thereof

PASSOVER
Ex. 12:11 it is the Lord's p.
Deut. 16: 2. therefore sacrifice the p. unto the Lord
Josh. 5:11 on the morrow after the p.
2 Chr. 30:15 killed the p. on the fourteenth day
35:11 they killed the p., and the priests
1 Cor. 5: 7 Christ our p. is sacrificed
Heb. 11:28 through faith he kept the p.

PASTOR (PASTORS)
Jer. 3:15 I will give you p. according
17:16 have not hastened from being a p.
Eph. 4:11 and some, p. and teachers

PASTURE (PASTURES)
Ps. 23: 2 maketh me to lie down in green p.
74: 1 against the sheep of thy p.
95: 7 we are the people of his p.
100: 3 his people and the sheep of his p.
Is. 49: 9 their p. shall be in all high places
Ezek. 34:18 to have eaten up the good p.
John 10: 9 shall go in and out, and find p.

PATH (PATHS)
Num. 22:24 angel of the Lord stood in a p.
Job 28: 7 there is a p. which no fowl knoweth
Ps. 16:11 wilt show me the p. of life
17: 4 kept me from the p. of the destroyer
17: 5 hold up my goings in thy p.
25:10 all p. of the Lord are mercy
27:11 lead me in a plain p.
65:11 and thy p. drop fatness
119: 35 go in the p. of thy commandments
139: 3 thou compassest my p., and my lying
Prov. 3:17 all her p. are peace
4:18 p. of just is as a shining light
4:26 ponder the p. of thy feet
5: 6 lest thou ponder the p. of life
Is. 26: 7 thou dost weigh the p. of the just
59: 7 destruction are in their p.
59: 8 they have made them crooked p.
Hos. 2: 6 she shall not find her p.
Mat. 3: 3 way of the Lord make his p. straight
Heb. 12:13 make straight p. for your feet

PATIENCE
Mat. 18:29 have p. with me, and I will pray
Luke 8:15 bring forth fruit with p.
21:19 in your p. possess ye your souls
Rom. 5: 3 knowing that tribulation worketh p.
15: 4 that we through p. and comfort of
15: 5 now the God of p. and consolation
2 Cor. 12:12 wrought among you in all p.
Col. 1:11 unto all p. and longsuffering
1 Thes. 1: 3 p. of hope in our Lord Jesus
2 Thes. 1: 4 for your p. and faith in all your
1 Tim. 6:11 godliness, faith, love p. meekness
2 Tim. 3:10 purpose, faith, longsuffering, charity, p.
Tit. 2: 2 sound in faith, in charity, in p.
Heb. 6:12 through faith and p. inherit the promises
10:36 have need of p., that after ye have
12: 1 run with p. the race that is set before us
Jas. 1: 3 trying of your faith worketh p.
1: 4 let p. have her perfect work
5:10 for an example of suffering affliction and of p.
5:11 ye have heard of the p. of Job
2 Pet. 1: 6 and to temperance p., and to p.
Rev. 1: 9 in the kingdom and p. of Jesus
2: 2 I know thy works and thy labour, and thy p.
13:10 here is the p. of saints

PATIENT
Eccl. 7: 8 the p. in spirit better than the proud
Rom. 2: 7 by p. continuance in well doing
12:12 p. in tribulation, instant in
2 Thes. 3: 5 into the p. waiting for Christ
1 Tim. 3: 3 not greedy of filthy lucre, but p.
2 Tim. 2:24 gentle unto all men, apt to teach, p.
Jas. 5: 7 p. therefore, brethren, unto the coming of the Lord

PATIENTLY
Ps. 37: 7 in the Lord, and wait p. for him
40: 1 I waited p. for the Lord
Heb. 6:15 after he had p. endured, he obtained
1 Pet. 2:20 for your faults, ye shall take it p.

PATTERN (PATTERNS)
Ezek. 43:10 and let them measure the p.
1 Tim. 1:16 show forth all longsuffering, for a p.
Tit. 2: 7 showing thyself a p. of good works
Heb. 8: 5 make all things according to the p.
9:23 that the p. of things in the heavens

PEACE
Num. 6:26 countenance upon thee, and give thee p.
Job 22:21 acquaint now thyself with him and be at p.
Ps. 34:14 do good; seek p. and pursue it
37:37 the end of that man is p.
85: 8 he will speak p. unto his people
119:165 great p. have they which love
120: 7 I am for p.: but when I speak
122: 6 pray for the p. of Jerusalem
125: 5 but p. shall be upon Israel
Prov. 16: 7 his enemies to be at p. with him
Is. 9: 6 everlasting Father, Prince of P.
26: 3 thou wilt keep him in perfect p.
27: 5 that he may make p. with me
45: 7 I make p. and create evil
48:18 had thy p. been as a river
48:22 there is no p., saith the Lord
57:19 p., p. to him that is far off
59: 8 way of p. they know not
60:17 I will also make thy officers p.
66:12 extend p. to her like a river
Jer. 6:14 saying p., p. when there is no p.
8:15 looked for p. but no good came
29: 7 seek the p. of the city
29:11 thoughts of p. and not of evil
Ezek. 13:10 saying p., and there was no p.
Mic. 5: 5 this man shall be the p.
Zech. 8:19 therefore love the truth and p.
Mat. 10:34 I came not to send p. but a sword
Mark 9:50 have p. one with another

Luke 2:14 on earth *p.*, good will towards
2:29 lettest thou thy servant depart in *p.*
19:42 things that belong to thy *p.*
John 14:27 *p.* I leave with you; my *p.* I give
16:33 that in me ye might have *p.*
Rom. 5:1 we have *p.* with God through Jesus Christ
8:6 spiritually minded is life and *p.*
14:17 righteousness, and *p.* and joy in the
1 Cor. 7:15 God hath called us to *p.*
2 Cor. 13:11 live in *p.*, and the God of
Gal. 5:22 fruit of the Spirit is love, joy, *p.*
Eph. 2:14 he is our *p.*, who hath made both
Phil. 4:7 the *p.* of God, which passeth all
1 Thes. 5:13 and be at *p.* among yourselves
Heb. 12:14 follow *p.* with all men and holiness
Jas. 3:18 fruit of righteousness is sown in *p.*
1 Pet. 3:11 let him seek *p.* and ensue
2 Pet. 3:14 ye may be found of him in *p.*

PEACEABLE (PEACEABLY)
Rom. 12:18 lieth in you live *p.* with all men
1 Tim. 2:2 that we may lead a quiet and *p.* life
Jas. 3:17 from above is first pure, then *p.*

PEACEMAKERS
Mat. 5:9 blessed are the *p.*: for they

PEARL (PEARLS)
Mat. 7:6 cast not *p.* before swine
13:46 found one *p.* of great price
Rev. 21:21 the twelve gates were twelve *p.*

PECULIAR
Ex. 19:5 ye shall be a *p.* treasure unto me
Deut. 14:2 chosen thee to be a *p.* people
26:18 thee this day to be his *p.* people
Ps. 135:4 Israel for his *p.* treasure
Eccl. 2:8 *p.* treasure of kings, and of the
Tit. 2:14 purify unto himself a *p.* people
1 Pet. 2:9 an holy nation, a *p.* people

PEOPLE
Gen. 27:29 let *p.* serve thee, and nations bow
Ex. 6:7 I will take you to me for a *p.*
Ps. 50:7 hear, O my *p.* and I will speak
100:3 we are his *p.* and the sheep of his
144:15 happy is that *p.* whose God
148:14 the children of Israel a *p.* near unto
Is. 1:4 a *p.* laden with iniquity, a seed of
10:6 against the *p.* of my wrath
27:11 a *p.* of no understanding
34:5 upon the *p.* of my curse
63:8 they are my *p.* that will not lie
Jer. 30:22 ye shall be my *p.*, and I will be
31:33 their God, and they shall be my *p.*
Ezek. 36:28 and ye shall be my *p.*, and I will
Hos. 1:9 Lo-ammi: for ye are not my *p.*
4:9 there shall be like *p.* like priest
Zech. 8:8 they shall be my *p.*, and I will
Mat. 1:21 Jesus shall save his *p.* from their sins
Rom. 11:2 God hath not cast away his *p.*
2 Cor. 6:16 their God and they shall be my *p.*
Heb. 4:9 remaineth a rest to the *p.* of God
11:25 suffer affliction with the *p.* of God
1 Pet. 2:10 but are now the *p.* of God

PERDITION
John 17:12 is lost but the son of *p.*
Phil. 1:28 to them an evident token of *p.*
2 Thes. 2:3 be revealed, the son of *p.*
1 Tim. 6:9 drown men in destruction and *p.*
Heb. 10:39 of them who draw back unto *p.*
2 Pet. 3:7 judgment and *p.* of ungodly men
Rev. 17:11 of the seven, and goeth into *p.*

PERFECT
Gen. 6:9 Noah was a just man and *p.*
17:1 walk before me, and be *p.*
Deut. 18:13 shalt be *p.* with the Lord thy God
2 Sam. 22:31 As for God, his way is *p.*
Job 1:1 and that man was *p.* and upright
Ps. 19:7 law of the Lord is *p.*
37:37 mark the *p.* man, and behold
Mat. 5:48 *p.* even as your Father which is in
19:21 if thou wilt be *p.* go and sell
1 Cor. 2:6 among them that are *p.*
2 Cor. 12:9 my strength is made *p.* in weakness
13:11 farewell be *p.*, be of good comfort
Eph. 4:13 a *p.* man, unto the measure of
Phil. 3:12 either were already *p.*: but I follow
Col. 1:28 present every man *p.* in Christ
4:12 may stand *p.* and complete
2 Tim. 3:17 man of God may be *p.*
Heb. 2:10 make the captain of their salvation *p.*
7:19 the law made nothing *p.*
12:23 spirits of just men made *p.*
13:21 make you *p.* in every good work
Jas. 1:4 let patience have her *p.* work
1:17 good gift and every *p.* gift is from above
1 John 4:18 *p.* love casteth out fear
Rev. 3:2 I have not found thy works *p.*

PERFECTING
2 Cor. 7:1 *p.* holiness in the fear of God
Eph. 4:12 for the *p.* of the saints

PERFECTION
Job 11:7 thou find out the Almighty unto *p.*
Ps. 119:96 have seen an end of all *p.*
Luke 8:14 bring no fruit to *p.*
2 Cor. 13:9 this also we wish, even your *p.*
Heb. 6:1 let us go on unto *p.*

PERFORM (PERFORMED, PERFORMETH)
Ruth 3:13 that if he will *p.* unto thee
Neh. 9:8 hast *p.* thy words; for thou art
Job 5:12 hands cannot *p.* their enterprise
Ps. 57:2 God that *p.* all things
119:106 have sworn and will *p.* it
119:112 inclined mine heart to *p.* thy statutes
Is. 9:7 zeal of the Lord of hosts will *p.*
10:12 Lord *p.* his whole work
44:26 and *p.* the counsel of his messengers
44:28 shall *p.* all my pleasure
Jer. 51:29 purpose of the Lord shall be *p.*
Mic. 7:20 thou wilt *p.* truth to Jacob
Rom. 4:21 promised, was able to *p.*
7:18 how to *p.* that which is good
Phil. 1:6 *p.* it until day of Jesus Christ

PERISH (PERISHED)
Gen. 41:36 land *p.* not through the famine
Lev. 26:38 ye shall *p.* among the heathen
Num. 17:12 we die, we *p.*, we all *p.*
Esth. 4:16 if I *p.*, I *p.*
Ps. 2:12 ye *p.* from the way, when his wrath
119:92 should then have *p.* in my affliction
Prov. 29:18 there is no vision, the people *p.*
Mat. 8:25 him, saying Lord, save us, we *p.*
John 3:15 believeth in him should not *p.*
3:16 should not *p.* but have everlasting life
10:28 they shall never *p.*; neither shall
1 Cor. 8:11 the weak *p.* for whom Christ died
2 Pet. 3:9 not willing that any *p.*

PERSECUTES (PERSECUTED, PERSECUTEST)
Job 19:22 why *p.* me as God
Ps. 10:2 wicked in his pride doth *p.* the poor
35:6 let the angel of the Lord *p.* them
83:15 *p.* them with thy tempest
109:16 *p.* the poor and needy man
119:161 princes *p.* me without cause
143:3 the enemy hath *p.* my soul
Mat. 5:11 when men shall revile you and *p.* you
5:44 despitefully use you and *p.* you
10:23 when they *p.* you in this city
John 15:20 they *p.* me they will persecute you
Acts 9:4 Saul, Saul, why *p.* thou me?
22:4 I *p.* this way unto the death
26:11 I *p.* them to strange cities
Rom. 12:14 bless them which *p.* you: bless and
1 Cor. 4:12 we bless; being *p.* we suffer it
15:9 because I *p.* the church of God
2 Cor. 4:9 *p.* but not forsaken, cast
Gal. 1:13 I *p.* the church of God
4:29 *p.* him born after the Spirit

PERSECUTION
2 Tim. 3:12 godly in Christ Jesus shall suffer *p.*

PERSECUTOR
1 Tim. 1:13 who was before a blasphemer and a *p.*

PERSEVERANCE
Eph. 6:18 watching thereunto with all *p.*

PERSON (PERSONS)
Lev. 19:15 nor honour the *p.* of the mighty
Deut. 10:17 which regardeth not *p.*, nor taketh
Mal. 1:8 will he accept thy *p.*
Mat. 22:16 thou regardest not the *p.* of men
Acts 10:34 God is no respecter of *p.*
Gal. 2:6 God accepteth no man's *p.*
Eph. 6:9 neither is there respect of *p.* with him
Col. 3:25 and there is no respect of *p.*
Heb. 1:3 and the express image of his *p.*
1 Pet. 1:17 who without respect of *p.* judgeth
2 Pet. 3:11 what manner of *p.* ought ye to be
Jude 1:16 men's *p.* in admiration because of

PERSUADE (PERSUADED)
Acts 13:43 *p.* them to continue in the grace
21:14 when he would not be *p.*
Rom. 8:38 I am *p.* that neither death
2 Cor. 5:11 we *p.* men, but we are made manifest
Gal. 1:10 do I *p.* men, or God
Heb. 6:9 are *p.* better things of you
11:13 were *p.* of them, and embraced them

PERSUASION
Gal. 5:8 this *p.* cometh not of him that calleth

PERVERSE
Num. 22:32 because thy way is *p.* before me
Deut. 32:5 they are a *p.* and crooked generation
Job 6:30 cannot my taste discern *p.* things
Prov. 4:24 and *p.* lips put far from thee
17:20 he that hath a *p.* tongue falleth
Is. 19:14 the Lord hath mingled a *p.* spirit
Mat. 17:17 O faithless and *p.* generation
Acts 20:30 shall men arise, speaking *p.* things
Phil. 2:15 in the midst of a crooked and *p.* nation
1 Tim. 6:5 *p.* disputings of men or corrupt minds

PERVERT (PERVERTED, PERVERTING)
Deut. 24:17 thou shalt not *p.* the judgment
1 Sam. 8:3 and took bribes, and *p.* judgment
Job 33:27 sinned and *p.* that which was right
34:12 neither will the Almighty *p.* judgment
Prov. 17:23 to *p.* the ways of judgment
Jer. 3:21 they have *p.* their way
Mic. 3:9 that abhor judgment, and *p.* all equity
Luke 23:2 this fellow *p.* the nation
Acts 13:10 not cease to *p.* the right

PESTILENCE (PESTILENCES)
2 Sam. 24:15 so the Lord sent a *p.* upon Israel
1 Ki. 8:37 if there be *p.*, blasting, mildew
Ps. 78:50 but gave their life over to the *p.*
Jer. 14:12 by the famine, and by the *p.*
Ezek. 5:12 part of thee shall die with the *p.*
Amos 4:10 I have sent among you the *p.*
Hab. 3:5 before him went the *p.*
Mat. 24:7 there shall be famines, and *p.*

PETITION (PETITIONS)
1 Sam. 1:17 grant thee thy *p.*, that thou hast
Esth. 5:6 what is thy *p.*? and it shall
Ps. 20:5 the Lord fulfil all thy *p.*
1 John 5:15 we have the *p.* that we desired

PHYSICIAN
Job 13:4 ye are all *p.* of no value
Jer. 8:22 is there no *p.* there
Mat. 9:12 that be whole need not a *p.*
Luke 4:23 say unto me, *P.* heal thyself
Col. 4:14 Luke the beloved *p.* and Demas

PIECE
Prov. 6:26 is brought to a *p.* of bread
28:21 for a *p.* of bread that man will
Mat. 9:16 no man putteth a *p.* of new cloth
Luke 14:18 I have bought a *p.* of ground

PIERCE (PIERCED, PIERCING)
Num. 24:8 and *p.* them through with his arrows
2 Ki. 18:21 go into his hand and *p.* it
Ps. 22:16 they *p.* my hands and my feet
Luke 2:35 sword shall *p.* through thy
1 Tim. 6:10 *p.* themselves through with many sorrows

Heb. 4:12 *p.* even to the dividing asunder of
Rev. 1: 7 they also which *p.* him

PILGRIMS
Heb. 11:13 were strangers and *p.* on the earth
1 Pet. 2:11 I beseech you as strangers and *p.*

PILGRIMAGE
Gen. 47: 9 the years of my *p.* are an hundred
Ex. 6: 4 the land of their *p.*, wherein they
Ps. 119: 54 my songs in the house of my *p.*

PILLAR (PILLARS)
Gen. 19:26 she became a *p.* of salt
Ex. 13:21 by day in a *p.* of cloud
Num. 14:14 and in a *p.* of fire by night
Deut. 31:15 tabernacle in a *p.* of a cloud
Neh. 9:12 in the night by a *p.* of fire
Job 9: 6 the *p.* thereof tremble
26:11 the *p.* of heaven tremble
Ps. 75: 3 I bear up the *p.* of it
99: 7 spake unto them in the cloudy *p.*
Prov. 9: 1 hath hewn out her seven *p.*
Sol. 3: 6 *p.* of smoke perfumed with myrrh
3:10 made the *p.* thereof of silver
5:15 his legs are as *p.* of marble
Is. 19:19 *p.* at the border thereof to the Lord
Jer. 1:18 I made thee an iron *p.*
1 Tim. 3:15 God the *p.* and ground of the truth
Rev. 3:12 make a *p.* in the temple

PILLOW
Gen. 28:11 put them for his *p.*, and lay down
Ezek. 13:18 the women that sew *p.* to all armholes

PIT
Gen. 37:20 cast him into some *p.*, and we will
Ex. 21:33 if a man shall dig a *p.*, and not
Job 33:24 deliver him from going down to the *p.*
Ps. 9:15 sunk down in the *p.* they had made
28: 1 like them that go down to the *p.*
40: 2 out of an horrible *p.*
55:23 bring them down into the *p.* of destruction
88: 4 them that go down into the *p.*
143: 7 unto them that go down into the *p.*
Prov. 1:12 as those that go down into the *p.*
22:14 mouth of strange women is a deep *p.*
23:27 and a strange woman is a narrow *p.*
Is. 38:17 it from the *p.* of corruption
38:18 they that go down into the *p.*
51: 1 hole of the *p.* whence ye are digged
Zech. 9:11 sent prisoners out of the *p.*
Rev. 20: 1 having the key of the bottomless *p.*

PITS
Ps. 119: 85 proud digged *p.* for me, which are
Jer. 14: 3 came to the *p.* and found no water

PITY
Deut. 7:16 thine eye shall have no *p.* upon them
Job 6:14 *p.* should be shown from his friend
19:21 have *p.* on me, have *p.*
Is. 63: 9 in his *p.* he redeemed them
Ezek. 36:21 had *p.* for my holy name
Mat. 18:33 even as I had *p.* on thee

PITIETH
Ps. 103: 13 *p.* his children, so the Lord *p.*

PITIFUL
Jas. 5:11 that the Lord is very *p.*
1 Pet. 3: 8 as brethren be *p.*, be courteous

PLACE (PLACES)
Ex. 3: 5 the *p.* whereon thou standest is holy
Deut. 12:14 in the *p.* which the Lord shall choose
Job 7:10 neither shall his *p.* know him any more
Ps. 16: 6 lines fallen unto me in pleasant *p.*
26: 8 the *p.* where thine honour dwelleth
32: 7 thou art my hiding *p.*; thou shalt
90: 1 Lord, thou hast been our dwelling *p.*
Prov. 8: 2 she standeth in the top of high *p.*
15: 3 eyes of the Lord are in every *p.*
Is. 40: 4 and the rough *p.* plain
66: 1 where is the *p.* of my rest
Hos. 5:15 will go and return to my *p.*
10: 8 the high *p.* also of Aven
Amos 4:13 treadeth upon the high *p.* of the earth
Hab. 3:19 make me to walk upon mine high *p.*
John 8:37 my word hath no *p.* in you
11:48 take away both our *p.* and nation
Rom. 12:19 avenge not, but rather give *p.*
1 Cor. 4:11 and have no certain dwelling *p.*
11:20 ye come together into one *p.*
Eph. 1: 3 all spiritual blessings in heavenly *p.*
2: 6 in heavenly *p.* in Christ Jesus
3:10 principalities and powers in heavenly *p.*
4:27 neither give *p.* to the devil
6:12 against spiritual wickedness in high *p.*
Rev. 12: 6 she hath a *p.* prepared of God

PLAGUE (PLAGUES)
1 Ki. 8:38 every man the *p.* of his own heart
Ps. 89:23 and *p.* them that hate him
Hos. 13:14 O death, I will be thy *p.*
Rev. 16: 9 which hath power over these *p.*
18: 8 therefore shall her *p.* come in one day
22:18 God shall add unto him the *p.*

PLAIN (PLAINLY)
Gen. 25:27 Jacob was a *p.* man
Ps. 27:11 lead me in a *p.* path
Prov. 8: 9 they are all *p.* to him
Zech. 4: 7 thou shalt become a *p.*
John 16:29 unto him, Lo now speakest thou *p.*

PLAINNESS
2 Cor. 3:12 we use great *p.* of speech

PLANT (PLANTED, PLANTETH, PLANTS)
Gen. 2: 5 and every *p.* of the field
Job 14: 9 bring forth boughs like a *p.*
Ps. 1: 3 a tree *p.* by the rivers
92:13 *p.* in the house of the Lord
128: 3 thy children like olive *p.* around
Is. 40:24 yea, they shall not be *p.*
Jer. 2:21 I *p.* thee a noble vine
18: 9 kingdom, to build it and to *p.* it
24: 6 *p.* them and not pluck
17: 8 as a tree *p.* by the waters
Ezek. 34:29 raise up for them a *p.* of renown
Mat. 15:13 my heavenly Father hath not *p.*
21:33 *p.* a vineyard and hedged it
Rom. 6: 5 we have been *p.* together
1 Cor. 3: 6 I have *p.*, Apollos watered
9: 7 who *p.* a vineyard and eateth not

PLANTING
Is. 60:21 the branch of my *p.*, the work of
61: 3 trees of righteousness, the *p.* of the Lord

PLAY
Ex. 32: 6 and to drink, and rose up to *p.*
2 Sam. 2:14 now arise and *p.* before us
Ezek. 33:32 can *p.* well on an instrument
1 Cor. 10: 7 eat and drink, and rose up to *p.*

PLEAD
Judg. 6:31 he that will *p.* for him
Job 13:19 who will *p.* with me
16:21 might *p.* for man with God
23: 6 will he *p.* against me with great power
Is. 1:17 the fatherless; *p.* for the widow
43:26 let us *p.* together: declare thou
66:16 by fire and sword will the Lord *p.*
Jer. 2:29 wherefore will ye *p.* with me
12: 1 righteous art thou, Lord, when I *p.*
25:31 he will *p.* with all flesh
Hos. 2: 2 *p.* with your mother, *p.*
Joel 3: 2 I will *p.* for them there

PLEASE
2 Sam. 7:29 now let it *p.* thee to bless
Ps. 69:31 this also shall *p.* the Lord
Prov. 16: 7 when man's ways *p.* the Lord
Is. 55:11 accomplish that which I *p.*
56: 4 choose the things that *p.* me
Rom. 8: 8 that are in flesh cannot *p.* God
15: 1 and not to *p.* ourselves
15: 2 let every one of us *p.* his neighbour
1 Cor. 7:32 how he may *p.* the Lord
10:33 I *p.* men in all things
Gal. 1:10 do I seek to *p.* men
1 Thes. 4: 1 how ye ought to walk, and to *p.* him
Heb. 11: 6 without faith it is impossible to *p.*

PLEASED (PLEASETH, PLEASING)
Ps. 115: 3 God hath done whatsoever he *p.*
Eccl. 7:26 whoso *p.* God shall escape
8: 3 he doeth whatsoever *p.* him
Is. 42:21 Lord is well *p.* for his
53:10 it *p.* the Lord to bruise him
Mic. 6: 7 will the Lord be *p.* with thousands
Mat. 3:17 Son, in whom I am well *p.*
17: 5 in whom I am well *p.*, hear ye him
Rom. 15: 3 for even Christ *p.* not himself
Col. 1:10 worthy of the Lord unto all *p.*
1:19 it *p.* the Father that in him should
1 Thes. 2: 4 not as *p.* men, but God
Heb. 11: 5 he had this testimony, that he *p.* God
13:16 with such sacrifices God is well *p.*
13:21 working in you that which is well *p.*
1 John 3:22 do things *p.* in his sight

PLEASANT
Gen. 2: 9 every tree that is *p.* to the sight
3: 6 that it was *p.* to the eyes
2 Sam. 1:23 Saul and Jonathan were lovely and *p.*
Ps. 16: 6 lines fallen to me in *p.* places
133: 1 how *p.* for brethren to dwell
Prov. 2:10 knowledge is *p.* to the soul
5:19 as a loving hind and *p.* roe
9:17 bread eaten in secret is *p.*
Eccl. 11: 7 *p.* for the eyes to behold the sun
Sol. 1:16 thou art fair, my beloved, yea, *p.*
7: 6 how *p.* art thou, O love, for delights
Jer. 31:20 dear son? is he a *p.* child
Mic. 2: 9 have ye cast out from their *p.* houses

PLEASANTNESS
Prov. 3:17 her ways are ways of *p.*

PLEASURE
Gen. 18:12 shall I have *p.*, my lord being old
1 Chr. 29:17 and hast *p.* in uprightness. As for
Ps. 5: 4 not a God that hath *p.* in
35:27 hath *p.* in the prosperity of his
51:18 do good in thy good *p.* unto Zion
102: 14 servants take *p.* in her stones
103: 21 ministers of his that do his *p.*
147: 11 Lord taketh *p.* in them
Prov. 21:17 he that loveth *p.* shall be poor
Eccl. 5: 4 for he hath no *p.* in fools
12: 1 say, I have no *p.* in them
Is. 44:28 shall perform all my *p.*
53:10 the *p.* of the Lord shall prosper in
Jer. 22:28 is he a vessel wherein is no *p.*
Ezek. 18:32 no *p.* in the death of him that dieth
Mal. 1:10 I have no *p.* in you, saith the Lord
Luke 12:32 it is your Father's good *p.*
2 Cor. 12:10 I take *p.* in infirmities
Eph. 1: 5 according to the good *p.* of
Phil. 2:13 and to do of his good *p.*
2 Thes. 1:11 fulfil all good *p.* of his
Heb. 10:38 my soul shall have no *p.*
12:10 chastened us after their own *p.*
Rev. 4:11 for thy *p.* they are and were created

PLEASURES
Ps. 16:11 at thy right hand *p.* for evermore
36: 8 drink of the river of thy *p.*
2 Tim. 3: 4 lovers of *p.* more than lovers of God
Tit. 3: 3 serving divers lusts and *p.*
Heb. 11:25 than to enjoy the *p.* of sin

PLENTY
Job 37:23 in judgment, and in *p.* of justice

PLENTEOUS
Ps. 86: 5 *p.* in mercy unto all them that call
103: 8 slow to anger, and *p.* in mercy
130: 7 with him is *p.* redemption
Mat. 9:37 harvest is *p.*, but the labourers

PLOUGH (PLOW, PLOWED, PLOWETH)
Deut. 22:10 thou shalt not *p.* with an ox and an
Judg. 14:18 if ye had not *p.* with my heifer
Job 4: 8 they that *p.* iniquity, and
Ps. 129: 3 the plowers *p.* on my back: they made
Prov. 20: 4 sluggard will not *p.* by reason of
Is. 28:24 doth plowman *p.* all day
Jer. 26:18 Zion shall be *p.* like a field
Hos. 10:13 ye have *p.* wickedness, ye have
Luke 9:62 having put his hand to the *p.*
1 Cor. 9:10 he that *p.* should plow in hope; and

PLOWMAN
Is. 61: 5 shall be your *p.* and your vinedressers
Amos 9:13 the *p.* shall overtake the reaper

PLOWSHARES
Is. 2: 4 they shall beat their swords into *p.*
Joel 3:10 beat your *p.* into swords
Mic. 4: 3 shall beat their swords into *p.*

POLLUTE (POLLUTED)
Num. 18:32 neither shall ye *p.* the holy things
Ezek. 7:21 for a spoil; and they shall *p.* it
Mic. 2:10 because it is *p.*, it shall destroy you
Zeph. 3: 1 woe to her that is filthy and *p.*
Mal. 1:12 the table of the Lord is *p.*

POLLUTIONS
Acts 15:20 they abstain from *p.* of idols
2 Pet. 2:20 they have escaped the *p.* of the world

PONDER (PONDERED, PONDERETH)
Prov. 4:26 *p.* the way of thy feet and let
21: 2 but the Lord *p.* the hearts
24:12 he that *p.* the heart consider it
Luke 2:19 *p.* them in her heart

POOR
Ex. 23:11 that the *p.* of thy people may eat
30:15 the *p.* shall not give less
Lev. 19:15 not respect the person of the *p.*
Deut. 15:11 for the *p.* shall never cease out
1 Sam. 2: 7 Lord maketh *p.* and maketh rich
2: 8 raiseth the *p.* out of dust
Job 5:16 so the *p.* hath hope, and iniquity
36:15 deliver the *p.* in affliction
Ps. 10:14 *p.* committeth himself to thee
69:33 the Lord heareth the *p.* and
72: 4 he shall judge the *p.* of the
132: 15 satisfy her *p.* with bread
140: 12 and the right of the *p.*
Prov. 13: 7 there is that maketh himself *p.*
14:20 *p.* is hated of his neighbour
14:31 oppresseth the *p.* reproacheth his Maker
19: 4 *p.* is separated from his neighbour
19: 7 all brethren of the *p.* do hate him
22:22 rob not the *p.* because he is *p.*
30: 9 lest I be *p.* and steal
Is. 14:32 *p.* of his people shall trust
29:19 *p.* among men shall rejoice
41:17 when the *p.* and needy seek water
58: 7 bring the *p.* that are cast out to thy
66: 2 that is *p.* and of a contrite
Jer. 5: 4 surely these are *p.*; they are foolish
Amos 2: 6 and the *p.* for a pair of shoes
Zeph. 3:12 an afflicted and *p.* people
Zech. 11:11 *p.* of the flock waited on me
Mat. 5: 3 blessed are the *p.* in spirit
11: 5 *p.* have the gospel preached to
26:11 ye have the *p.* always with you
Luke 6:20 blessed be ye *p.*: for yours is the
2 Cor. 6:10 as *p.*, yet making many rich
8: 9 for your sakes he became *p.*
9: 9 he hath given to the *p.*
Gal. 2:10 we should remember the *p.*
Jas. 2: 5 God chosen the *p.* of this world
Rev. 3:17 thou art wretched, and miserable and *p.*

PORTION
Deut. 21:17 by giving him a double *p.* of all
33:21 in a *p.* of the lawgiver, was he
32: 9 Lord's *p.* is his people
2 Ki. 2: 9 double *p.* of thy spirit
Job 24:18 their *p.* is cursed in earth
26:14 how little a *p.* is heard
31: 2 what *p.* of God is from above
Ps. 16: 5 Lord is the *p.* of mine inheritance
17:14 have their *p.* in this life
63:10 they shall be a *p.* for foxes
73:26 of my heart and my *p.* for ever
142: 5 art my *p.* in him a *p.* with the
Is. 61: 7 they shall rejoice in their *p.*
Jer. 10:16 the *p.* of Jacob not like them
Hab. 1:16 because by them their *p.* is fat
Zech. 2:12 Lord shall inherit Judah his *p.*

POSSESS (POSSESSED, POSSESSING)
Gen. 22:17 thy seed shall *p.* the gate of his
Judg. 11:24 wilt thou not *p.* that which Chemosh
Job 7: 3 made to *p.* months of vanity
13:26 *p.* the iniquities of my youth
Ps. 139: 13 for thou hast *p.* my reins: thou
Prov. 8:22 Lord *p.* me in the beginning
Is. 63:18 people of thy holiness *p.* it a little
Luke 21:19 in your patience *p.* ye your souls
1 Cor. 7:30 they that buy as though they *p.* not
2 Cor. 6:10 as having nothing yet *p.* all
1 Thes. 4: 4 you should know how to *p.* his vessel

POSSESSION
Eph. 1:14 until the redemption of the purchased *p.*

POSSIBLE
Mat. 19:26 with God all things are *p.*
24:24 if *p.* shall deceive the very elect
Mark 9:23 all things are *p.* to him that
14:36 Father, all things are *p.* to thee
Luke 18:27 impossible with men are *p.* with God
Rom. 12:18 if it be *p.*, as much as lieth in you
Heb. 10: 4 not *p.* that the blood of bulls

POT (POTS)
Ex. 16:33 take a *p.* and put an omer full
Ps. 68:13 though you have lain among the *p.*
Jer. 1:13 I said, I see a seething *p.*
Zech. 14:21 every *p.* in Jerusalem and in Judah

POTTER (POTTER'S)
Is. 29:16 shall be esteemed as the *p.* clay
64: 8 and thou our *p.*, ad we all are
Jer. 18: 6 cannot I do with you as this *p.*
Lam. 4: 2 the work of the hands of the *p.*
Rom. 9:21 hath not the *p.* power over the clay
Rev. 2:27 as the vessels of the *p.* shall they

POUR (POURED, POURETH)
Job 10:10 hast thou not *p.* me out as milk
12:21 he *p.* contempt upon princes
16:20 mine eye *p.* out tears unto God
30:16 my soul is *p.* out upon me
Ps. 45: 2 grace is *p.* into thy lips
62: 8 *p.* out your heart before him
79: 6 *p.* out thy wrath on the heathen
107: 40 he *p.* contempt upon princes
Prov. 1:23 I will *p.* out my Spirit
Sol. 1: 3 name is as ointment *p.* forth
Is. 32:15 the Spirit be *p.* upon us from on high
42:25 he hath *p.* upon him the fury
44: 3 *p.* water on him that is thirsty
53:12 *p.* out his soul unto death
Jer. 7:20 my fury shall be *p.* out
10:25 *p.* out thy fury upon the heathen
Lam. 2:19 *p.* thine heart like water before
Ezek. 20: 8 I will *p.* out my fury upon them
30:15 I will *p.* my fury upon Sin
Zeph. 3: 8 to *p.* upon them my indignation
Rev. 16: 1 *p.* vials of the wrath of God

POVERTY
Gen. 45:11 all that thou hast, come to *p.*
Prov. 6:11 so shall thy *p.* come as one
10:15 destruction of the poor is their *p.*
11:24 but it tendeth to *p.*
20:13 love not sleep lest thou come to *p.*
30: 8 give me neither *p.* nor riches
2 Cor. 8: 2 their deep *p.* abounded unto the
8: 9 ye through his *p.* might be rich
Rev. 2: 9 I know thy works, and tribulation, and *p.*

POWER
Gen. 32:28 for as a prince hast thou *p.* with God
49: 3 dignity and excellency of *p.*
Deut. 8:18 giveth thee *p.* to get wealth
32:36 when he seeth that their *p.* is gone
2 Sam. 22:33 God is my strength and *p.*
1 Chr. 29:11 is the greatness, and the *p.* and
Ezra 8:22 *p.* and his wrath is against all them
Job 26: 2 thou helped him that is without *p.*
26:14 thunder of his *p.* who can
Ps. 62:11 that the *p.* belongeth unto God
Prov. 3:27 when it is in the *p.* of thine hand
18:21 and life are in the *p.* of the tongue
Eccl. 8: 4 the word of the king is, there is *p.*
8: 8 no man that hath *p.* over the spirit to
Is. 40:29 he giveth *p.* to the faint
Jer. 10:12 he hath made the earth by his *p.*
Hos. 12: 3 by strength he had *p.* with God
Mic. 3: 8 I am full of *p.* by the Spirit
Hab. 1:11 imputing *p.* to his God
3: 4 there was the hiding of his *p.*
Zech. 4: 6 not by might, nor by *p.* but by
Mat. 9: 6 hath *p.* on earth to forgive sins
9: 8 glorified God which had given such *p.*
22:29 the scriptures nor the *p.* of God
28:18 all *p.* is given unto me in heaven
Mark 9: 1 kingdom of God come with *p.*
Luke 1:35 *p.* of the Highest shall overshadow
5:17 *p.* of the Lord to heal them
22:53 this is your hour and *p.* of
24:49 till ye be endued with *p.*
John 1:12 gave he *p.* to become the sons of God
10:18 *p.* to lay it down and *p.* to
17: 2 given him *p.* over all flesh
19:10 that I have *p.* to crucify thee
Acts 26:18 them from the *p.* of Satan to God
Rom. 1:16 gospel is the *p.* of God unto salvation
1:20 even his eternal *p.* and Godhead
9:22 to make his *p.* known, endured with
13: 1 there is no *p.* but of God
1 Cor. 1:24 Christ the *p.* of God, and the wisdom
2: 4 demonstration of the Spirit and *p.*
4:19 which are puffed up, but the *p.*
5: 4 together with the *p.* of our Lord
6:12 not be brought under the *p.* of
9: 4 have we not *p.* to eat and
2 Cor. 4: 7 excellency of the *p.* may be of God
13:10 according to the *p.* which the Lord hath given
Eph. 1:19 exceeding greatness of his *p.*
2: 2 to the prince of the *p.* of the air
Phil. 3:10 know the *p.* of his resurrection
Col. 1:11 according to his glorious *p.*
1:13 delivered from the *p.* of darkness
2:10 head of all principality and *p.*
2 Thes. 1: 9 and from the glory of his *p.*
1 Tim. 6:16 to whom be honour and *p.* everlasting
2 Tim. 1: 7 Spirit of *p.* and of love
3: 5 form of godliness, denying *p.*
Heb. 1: 3 all things by the word of his *p.*
2:14 destroy him that had the *p.* of death
6: 5 the good word of God and the *p.*
1 Pet. 1: 5 kept by the *p.* of God through faith
2 Pet. 1: 3 his divine *p.* hath given
Jude 1:25 be glory and majesty, dominion and *p.*
Rev. 2:26 him will I give *p.* over nations
4:11 to receive glory and honour and *p.*
5:13 blessing and honour and glory and *p.*
7:12 and *p.* and might be unto our God
11: 3 I give *p.* unto my two witnesses
11:17 hast taken to thee thy great *p.*
12:10 of our God and the *p.* of his Christ
16: 9 hath *p.* over these plagues
19: 1 honour and *p.*, unto the Lord our God

POWERS
Eph. 6:12 against principalities, against *p.*
Col. 1:16 or dominions or principalities, or *p.*
1 Pet. 3:22 authorities and *p.* being made subject unto him

PRAISE (PRAISED)
Deut. 10:21 he is thy *p.* and thy God
Judg. 5: 3 I will sing *p.* to the Lord God
2 Sam. 22: 4 who is worthy to be *p.*: so shall
1 Chr. 16:25 greatly to be *p.*: he also is to
Neh. 9: 5 above all blessing and *p.*
Ps. 7:17 I will *p.* the Lord according to his
9: 1 I will *p.* thee, O Lord, with my
22:25 my *p.* shall be of thee
30: 9 shall the dust *p.* thee? shall it
33: 1 *p.* is comely for the upright
42: 5 shall *p.* him for the help of his
48: 1 greatly to be *p.* in the city of
63: 3 my lips shall *p.* thee
65: 1 *p.* waiteth for thee, O God
88:10 shall the dead arise and *p.*
96: 4 great and greatly to be *p.*
109: 1 hold not peace, God of my *p.*
119:164 seven times a day do I *p.* thee
145: 3 Lord, and greatly to be *p.*
145: 10 all thy works shall *p.* thee
Prov. 27: 2 let another man *p.* thee, and not
27:21 so is a man to his *p.*
31:31 her own works *p.* her in the gates
Is. 38:18 the grave cannot *p.* thee
38:19 the living shall *p.* thee as I do
60:18 walls Salvation and thy gates *P.*
62: 7 make Jerusalem a *p.* in the earth
Jer. 13:11 for a *p.* and for a glory
17:14 be saved: for thou art my *p.*
Joel 2:26 eat in plenty and be satisfied and *p.*
Hab. 3: 3 earth was full of his *p.*
John 12:43 *p.* of men more than the *p.* of God
Rom. 2:29 whose *p.* is not of men
Eph. 1: 6 *p.* of the glory of his grace
Phil. 4: 8 if there be any *p.*, think on
Heb. 13:15 offer the sacrifice of *p.* to God
1 Pet. 2:14 for the *p.* of them that do well

PRAISES (PRAISING)
Ex. 15:11 glorious in holiness, fearful in *p.*
2 Chr. 5:13 to be heard in *p.*, and thanking thee
Ezra 3:11 sang together by course in *p.*
Ps. 22: 3 that inhabitest the *p.* of Israel
78: 4 generation to come the *p.* of the
84: 4 they will still be *p.* thee
149: 6 high *p.* of God be in their mouth
Is. 60: 6 shall show forth the *p.* of the Lord
63: 7 and the *p.* of the Lord, according
Luke 2:13 multitude of the heavenly host *p.* God
Acts 2:47 *p.* God, and having favour with all
1 Pet. 2: 9 ye should show forth the *p.* of him

PRAY
Gen. 20: 7 *p.* for thee and thou shalt live
1 Sam. 7: 5 I will *p.* for you to the Lord
2 Sam. 7:27 found in his heart to *p.* this
Job 21:15 profit shall we have, if we *p.*
42: 8 my servant Job shall *p.* for
Ps. 5: 2 my God: to thee will I *p.*
55:17 morning and noon will I *p.*
122: 6 *p.* for the peace of Jerusalem
Jer. 7:16 therefore *p.* not for this people
Mat. 5:44 *p.* for them which despitefully
26:41 watch and *p.* that ye enter not
Mark 11:24 things ye desire when ye *p.*
Luke 11: 1 teach us to *p.* as John also
16:27 I *p.* thee therefore, father
18: 1 end, that men ought always to *p.*
21:36 watch ye and *p.* always
John 16:26 I will *p.* the Father for
17: 9 I *p.* for them: I *p.* not
17:20 neither *p.* I for these alone
Acts 8:22 *p.* God, if perhaps the thought of
10: 9 Peter went on the housetop to *p.*
Rom. 8:26 know not what we should *p.* for
1 Cor. 14:15 I will *p.* with the spirit
2 Cor. 5:20 we *p.* you in Christ's stead
Col. 1: 9 do not cease to *p.* for you
1 Thes. 5:17 *p.* without ceasing
5:25 brethren, *p.* for us
2 Thes. 3: 1 finally, brethren, *p.* for us
1 Tim. 2: 8 that men *p.* every where lifting up
Heb. 13:18 *p.* for us, for we trust we have
Jas. 5:13 any afflicted? let him *p.*
5:16 *p.* one for another, that ye may

PRAYING (PRAYED)
Luke 22:32 I have *p.* for thee that thy faith
22:44 in an agony he *p.* more earnestly
Acts 10: 2 gave much alms to people and *p.* to God
20:36 he kneeled down and *p.* with them all
Eph. 6:18 *p.* always with all prayer and supplication
Jas. 5:17 he *p.* earnestly that it might not rain

PRAYER
2 Sam. 7:27 to pray this *p.* to thee
1 Ki. 8:28 respect unto the *p.* of thy servant
8:38 what *p.* and supplication soever be
8:45 hear thou in heaven their *p.*
Neh. 1: 6 mayest hear the *p.* of thy servant
4: 9 we made our *p.* to our God
Job 15: 4 off fear, and restrainest *p.* before God
Ps. 65: 2 thou that hearest *p.* unto thee
102: 17 he will regard the *p.* of the destitute
109: 4 but I give myself unto *p.*
Prov. 15: 8 *p.* of the upright is his delight
15:29 Lord heareth the *p.* of the righteous
28: 9 even his *p.* shall be abomination
Is. 26:16 they poured out a *p.* when thy
56: 7 an house of *p.* for all people
Lam. 3:44 our *p.* should not pass through
Dan. 9: 3 to seek by *p.* and supplications
Mat. 17:21 this kind goeth not out but by *p.*
23:14 for a pretence, make long *p.*
Luke 6:12 continued all night in *p.* to God
Acts 1:14 continued with one accord in *p.* and
3: 1 to the temple at the hour of *p.*
6: 4 give ourselves continually to *p.*
12: 5 *p.* was made without ceasing
16:13 where *p.* was wont to be made
Rom. 12:12 continuing instant in *p.*
1 Cor. 7: 5 may give yourselves to *p.*
2 Cor. 1:11 ye also helping together by *p.* for us
Phil. 4: 6 in every thing by *p.* and supplication
Col. 4: 2 continue in *p.*, and watch
1 Tim. 4: 5 sanctified by the word of God and *p.*
Jas. 5:15 *p.* of faith shall save the sick
5:16 effectual fervent *p.* of a righteous
1 Pet. 4: 7 be ye therefore sober and watch unto *p.*

PRAYERS
Ps. 72:20 *p.* of David the son of Jesse are
Acts 10: 4 thy *p.* and thine alms are
1 Tim. 2: 1 first of all that supplications, *p.*
1 Pet. 3: 7 that your *p.* be not hindered
3:12 his ears are open to their *p.*
Rev. 5: 8 which are the *p.* of saints

PREACH
Neh. 6: 7 appointed prophets to *p.* of thee
Jonah 3: 2 *p.* unto it the preaching that I bid
Mat. 4:17 Jesus began to *p.* and to say
10:27 what ye hear in thine ear, that *p.* ye
Mark 1: 4 and *p.* the baptism of repentance for
Luke 4:18 to *p.* deliverance to the captives
9:60 go and *p.* the kingdom of God
Acts 10:42 commanded us to *p.* unto the people
15:21 in every city them that *p.* him
Rom. 10: 8 word of faith which we *p.*
10:15 how shall they *p.* except they
1 Cor. 1:23 we *p.* Christ crucified, unto the
15:11 so we *p.* and so ye believed
2 Cor. 4: 5 we *p.* not ourselves but Christ
Phil. 1:15 some indeed *p.* Christ even of envy
2 Tim. 4: 2 *p.* the word; be instant in season

PREACHED (PREACHETH, PREACHING)
Ps. 40: 9 I have *p.* righteousness in the great
Mark 2: 2 he *p.* the word unto them
6:12 he *p.* that men should repent
16:20 *p.* everywhere, the Lord working with
Luke 4:44 he *p.* in the synagogues of Galilee
24:47 remission of sins should be *p.* in his
Acts 8: 5 Samaria, and *p.* Christ unto them
9:20 he *p.* Christ in the synagogues
10:36 *p.* peace by Jesus Christ: (he is Lord)
11:19 *p.* the word to none but Jews
13:38 through this man is *p.* unto you
1 Cor. 1:18 *p.* of the cross is to them
1:21 by foolishness of *p.* to save them
2: 4 my *p.* was not with enticing words
1 Cor. 9:27 when I have *p.* to others, I myself
15: 1 gospel which I *p.* unto you
15: 2 keep in memory what I *p.*
15:12 if Christ be *p.* that he rose
15:14 then is our *p.* vain, and faith
Gal. 1:23 *p.* the faith he once destroyed
Col. 1:23 which was *p.* to every creature
1 Tim. 3:16 *p.* unto the Gentiles believed on
Heb. 4: 2 the word *p.* did not profit them
1 Pet. 3:19 went and *p.* unto the spirits in prison

PREACHER
Eccl. 1: 1 the words of the *p.*, the son of
12: 9 because the *p.* was wise, he still
1 Tim. 2: 7 ordained a *p.*, and an apostle
2 Tim. 1:11 whereunto I am appointed a *p.*

PRECEPTS
Neh. 9:14 commandedst them *p.*, statutes, and laws
Ps. 119: 4 commanded us to keep thy *p.*
119: 15 I will meditate in thy *p.*
119: 27 to understand the way of thy *p.*
119: 45 at liberty: for I seek thy *p.*
119: 56 had, because I kept thy *p.*
119:110 I erred not from thy *p.*
119:128 I esteem all thy *p.* to be right
119:141 I do not forget thy *p.*
119:159 consider I love thy *p.*: quicken
Is. 28:10 *p.* upon *p.* upon *p.*
29:13 fear is taught by *p.* of men

PRECIOUS
1 Sam. 3: 1 word of the Lord was *p.*
26:21 my soul was *p.* in thine eyes
Ps. 49: 8 redemption of the soul is *p.*
116: 15 *p.* in the sight of the Lord
126: 6 goeth forth and weepeth, bearing *p.* seed
139: 17 how *p.* are thy thoughts
Eccl. 7: 1 good name is better than *p.* ointment
Is. 13:12 I will make a man more *p.* than gold
28:16 a tried stone, a *p.* corner stone
43: 4 since thou wast *p.* in my sight
Jer. 15:19 if thou take *p.* from vile
Lam. 4: 2 *p.* sons of Zion are comparable to
Jas. 5: 7 husbandman waiteth for the *p.* fruit
1 Pet. 1: 7 the trial of your faith is more *p.*
1:19 redeemed with the *p.* blood of Christ
2: 4 stone chosen of God and *p.*
2 Pet. 1: 1 obtained like *p.* faith with us
1: 4 exceeding great and *p.* promises

PREDESTINATE (PREDESTINATED)
Rom. 8:30 whom he did *p.* them he also called
Eph. 1: 5 having *p.* us unto the adoption

PREFER (PREFERRED, PREFERRING)
Ps. 137: 6 if I *p.* not Jerusalem above my chief
John 1:15 cometh after me is *p.* before me
Rom. 12:10 in honour *p.* one another
1 Tim. 5:21 without *p.* one before another

PREPARATION (PREPARATIONS)
Prov. 16: 1 the *p.* of the heart in man
Mark 15:42 it was the *p.*, that is, the day

PREPARE
Ex. 15: 2 I will *p.* him an habitation
1 Sam. 7: 3 *p.* your hearts to the Lord
1 Chr. 29:18 *p.* their heart unto thee
2 Chr. 35: 6 sanctify yourselves, and *p.* your brethren
Job 11:13 if thou *p.* thy heart and
Ps. 10:17 thou wilt *p.* their heart
61: 7 O *p.* mercy and truth, which may
Prov. 24:27 *p.* thy work without, and make it
Is. 40: 3 *p.* ye the way of the Lord
Amos 4:12 *p.* to meet thy God, O Israel
Mic. 3: 5 they even *p.* war against him
Mat. 11:10 shall *p.* thy way before thee
John 14: 2 I go to *p.* a place for you

PREPARED (PREPAREST, PREPARETH)
2 Chr. 19: 3 hast *p.* thine heart to seek God
27: 6 he *p.* his ways before the Lord
29:36 God had *p.* the people: for the thing
30:19 that *p.* his heart to seek God
Neh. 8:10 unto them for whom nothing is *p.*
Ps. 23: 5 thou *p.* a table before me in the
65: 9 thou *p.* them corn, when thou hast

Ps. 68:10 *p.* of thy goodness for the poor
147: 8 who *p.* rain for the earth
Is. 64: 4 what he hath *p.* for him
Hos. 6: 3 his going forth is *p.* as the
Mat. 20:23 to them for whom it is *p.*
22: 4 I have *p.* my dinner; my oxen
25:34 inherit the kingdom *p.* for you
Luke 1:17 ready a people *p.* for the Lord
12:47 knew his lord's will, and *p.* not
Rom. 9:23 of mercy which he had afore *p.* to
2 Tim. 2:21 *p.* and unto every good work
Heb. 10: 5 but a body hast thou *p.* me
11:16 for he hath *p.* for them a city
Rev. 12: 6 where she hath a place *p.* of God
21: 2 *p.* as a bride adorned for her husband

PRESENT
Ps. 46: 1 a very *p.* help in trouble
Acts 10:33 all here *p.* before God
Rom. 7:18 for to will is *p.* with me
8:38 nor things *p.* nor things to come
12: 1 *p.* your bodies a living sacrifice
1 Cor. 3:22 or thing *p.*, or things to come
5: 3 absent in body, but *p.* in spirit
2 Cor. 5: 8 to be *p.* with the Lord
11: 2 *p.* you as a chaste virgin
Gal. 1: 4 deliver us from this *p.* evil world
Col. 1:22 to *p.* you holy and unblameable and
1:28 *p.* every man perfect in Christ
2 Tim. 4:10 having loved this *p.* world
2 Pet. 1:12 and be established in the *p.* truth
Jude 1:24 *p.* you faultless before the presence

PRESENCE
Gen. 3: 8 themselves from the *p.* of the Lord
4:16 Cain went from the *p.* of the Lord
Job 1:12 Satan went forth from the *p.* of the
23:15 I am troubled at his *p.*: when I
Ps. 16:11 in thy *p.* is fulness of joy
31:20 hide them in the secret of thy *p.*
51:11 cast me not away from thy *p.*
100: 2 come before his *p.* with singing
114: 7 thou earth, at the *p.* of the Lord
139: 7 whither shall I flee from thy *p.*
140: 13 upright shall dwell in thy *p.*
Is. 63: 9 angel of his *p.* saved them
Jer. 4:26 broken down at the *p.* of the Lord
5:22 will ye not tremble at my *p.*
Jonah 1:10 fled from the *p.* of the Lord
1 Cor. 1:29 no flesh glory in his *p.*
2 Cor. 10: 1 who in *p.* am base among you
Jude 1:24 present you faultless before the *p.*
Rev. 14:10 *p.* of the holy angels and in *p.* of

PRESERVE (PRESERVED, PRESERVETH)
Gen. 45: 7 sent me before you to *p.* you a posterity
2 Sam. 8: 6 the Lord *p.* David whithersoever he
Job 10:12 and thy visitation hath *p.* my spirit
Ps. 12: 7 thou shalt *p.* them from this generation
16: 1 *p.* me, O God, for in thee
25:21 let integrity and uprightness *p.* me
32: 7 thou shalt *p.* me from trouble
41: 2 Lord will *p.* and keep him alive
61: 7 mercy and truth may *p.* him
64: 1 *p.* my life from fear of the enemy
86: 2 *p.* my soul, for I am holy
97:10 he *p.* the souls of his saints
116: 6 the Lord *p.* the simple: I was brought
121: 7 Lord shall *p.* thee from all evil
140: 1 *p.* me from the violent man
145: 20 Lord *p.* all them that love him
146: 9 Lord *p.* the stranger; he relieveth
Prov. 2: 8 he *p.* the way of his saints
2:11 discretion shall *p.* thee
Luke 17:33 shall lose his life shall *p.* it
1 Thes. 5:23 soul and body be *p.* blameless unto
2 Tim. 4:18 *p.* me to his heavenly kingdom
Jude 1: 1 and *p.* in Jesus Christ, and called

PRESERVER
Job 7:20 O thou *p.* of men? why hast thou

PRESS (PRESSED, PRESSETH)
Gen. 40:11 and *p.* them into Pharaoh's cup
Judg. 16:16 she *p.* him daily with her words
Ps. 38: 2 me, and thy hand *p.* me sore
Amos 2:13 *p.* under you as a cart is *p.*
Luke 6:38 good measure, *p.* down, and shaken
Acts 18: 5 Paul was *p.* in the spirit and
2 Cor. 1: 8 were *p.* out of measure, above strength
Phil. 3:14 I *p.* towards the mark for

PRETENCE
Mat. 23:14 and for a *p.* make long prayer
Phil. 1:18 whether in *p.*, or in truth, Christ is

PREVAIL (PREVAILED, PREVAILEST)
Gen. 7:20 fifteen cubits upward did the waters *p.*
32:28 power with God and men, and hast *p.*
Ex. 17:11 held up his hand, Israel *p.*
Judg. 16: 5 by what means we may *p.* against him
1 Sam. 2: 9 by strength shall no man *p.*
Job 14:20 thou *p.* for ever against him
Ps. 9:19 arise, O Lord, let not man *p.*
65: 3 iniquities *p.* against me
Eccl. 4:12 if one *p.* against him, two shall
Hos. 12: 4 power over the angel, and *p.*: he wept
Mat. 16:18 gates of hell shall not *p.*
Acts 19:20 mightily grew the word of God and *p.*

PREY
Gen. 49:27 the morning he shall devour the *p.*
Esth. 9:16 they laid not their hands on the *p.*
Ps. 124: 6 not given us a *p.* to their teeth
Is. 49:24 *p.* be taken from the mighty
59:15 departeth from evil maketh himself a *p.*
Jer. 21: 9 life shall be unto him for a *p.*

PRICE
Lev. 25:16 thou shalt increase the *p.* thereof
Deut. 23:18 or the *p.* of a dog, into the house
Job 28:13 man knoweth not the *p.* thereof
Prov. 17:16 a *p.* in the hand of a fool
Is. 55: 1 and milk without money and without *p.*
Mat. 13:46 pearl of great *p.*, went and sold
Acts 5: 2 kept back part of the *p.*, his wife
1 Cor. 6:20 for ye are bought with a *p.*
1 Pet. 3: 4 in the sight of God of great *p.*

PRICKS (PRICKED)
Ps. 73:21 I was *p.* in my reins
Acts 2:37 they were *p.* in their heart
9: 5 for thee to kick against the *p.*
26:14 for thee to kick against the *p.*

PRIDE
2 Chr. 32:26 humbled himself for the *p.* of his
Job 33:17 hide purpose, and *p.* from man
Ps. 10: 2 wicked in his *p.* doth persecute
31:20 hide them from the *p.* of man
73: 6 *p.* compasseth them about as a chain
Prov. 8:13 hate evil, *p.* and arrogancy
11: 2 when *p.* cometh, then cometh shame
13:10 by *p.* cometh contention: but with the
16:18 *p.* goeth before destruction
29:23 man's *p.* shall bring him low
Jer. 13:17 weep in secret for your *p.*
Ezek. 7:10 rod hath blossomed, *p.* hath budded
16:49 iniquity of Sodom, *p.*, fulness of bread
Dan. 4:37 those that walk in *p.*
Hos. 5: 5 *p.* of Israel doth testify to his
Obad. 1: 3 *p.* of thine heart hath deceived thee
1 Tim. 3: 6 lest being lifted up with *p.* he fall
1 John 2:16 lust of the eyes, and the *p.* of life

PRIEST
Gen. 14:18 he was the *p.* of the most high God
Ex. 2:16 the *p.* of Midian had seven daughters
Lev. 5: 6 the *p.* shall make an atonement
21:10 is the high *p.* among his brethren
Is. 24: 2 as with people, so with the *p.*
28: 7 *p.* and prophet have erred through
Jer. 23:11 prophet and *p.* are profane; yea
Ezek. 7:26 law shall perish from the *p.*
Hos. 4: 4 they that strive with the *p.*
Hos. 4: 9 and there shall be like people, like *p.*
Heb. 2:17 a merciful and faithful high *p.*
3: 1 consider the Apostle and High *p.* of
5: 1 every high *p.* taken from among men
5: 6 thou art a *p.* for ever after the
6:20 Jesus, made an high *p.* for ever
7:26 for such an high *p.* became us
8: 3 every high *p.* is ordained to offer
9:11 Christ being come an high *p.* of good
10:21 having an high *p.* over the house of God

PRIESTS
Ps. 132: 9 thy *p.* be clothed with righteousness
Is. 61: 6 ye be named *P.* of the Lord
Jer. 5:31 *p.* bear rule by their means
31:14 satiate the soul of the *p.* with fatness
Ezek. 22:26 her *p.* have violated my law
Joel 1: 9 the *p.*, the Lord's ministers, mourn
Mat. 12: 5 *p.* in the temple profane the sabbath
Acts 6: 7 company of the *p.* were obedient to
Rev. 1: 6 kings and *p.* unto God and his Father
5:10 made us unto our God kings and *p.*

PRIESTHOOD
Ex. 40:15 everlasting *p.* throughout their generations
Heb. 7:24 ever hath an unchangeable *p.*
1 Pet. 2: 5 an holy *p.*, to offer up spiritual
2: 9 ye are a chosen generation, a royal *p.*

PRINCE
Gen. 23: 6 thou art a mighty *p.* among us
32:28 as a *p.* hast thou power with
34: 2 *p.* of the country saw her, he took
Ex. 2:14 who made thee a *p.* and judge over
2 Sam. 3:38 *p.* and great man fallen this day
Job 31:37 as a *p.* would I go near
Is. 9: 6 everlasting Father, *P.* of Peace
Ezek. 34:24 my servant David, a *p.* among them
Dan. 10:21 in these things but Michael your *p.*
12: 1 Michael stand up, the great *p.*
Hos. 3: 4 asking, and without a *p.*
John 12:31 now shall the *p.* of this world
14:30 *p.* of this world cometh and hath
16:11 the *p.* of this world is judged
Acts 3:15 And killed the *P.* of life, whom God
5:31 to be a *P.* and a Saviour
Eph. 2: 2 *p.* of the power of the air
Rev. 1: 5 the *p.* of the kings of the earth

PRINCES
Job 12:19 he leadeth *p.* away spoiled
12:21 he poureth contempt upon *p.*
34:19 that accepteth not persons of *p.*
Ps. 45:16 thou mayest make *p.* in earth
76:12 he shall cut off the spirit of *p.*
82: 7 shall fall like one of the *p.*
118: 9 than to put confidence in *p.*
119: 23 *p.* did sit and speak against me
119:161 *p.* persecuted me without cause
Prov. 8:15 kings reign, and *p.* decree justice
17:26 not good, nor to strike *p.* for equity
28: 2 of a land many are the *p.* thereof
31: 4 drank wine; nor for *p.* strong drink
Is. 3: 4 give children to be their *p.*
Hos. 7: 5 *p.* have made him sick with bottles
8: 4 made *p.* and I knew it not
Mat. 20:25 *p.* of Gentiles exercise dominion over
1 Cor. 2: 6 nor of the *p.* of this world

PRINCIPALITY (PRINCIPALITIES)
Jer. 13:18 for your *p.* shall come down
Rom. 8:38 nor angels, nor *p.*, nor powers
Eph. 1:21 far above all *p.*, and power and might
6:12 but against *p.*, against powers
Col. 2:10 which is the head of all *p.* and power
Tit. 3: 1 be subject to *p.* and powers

PRISON
Gen. 39:20 put him into the *p.*, a place where
Is. 42: 7 bring out the prisoners from the *p.*
53: 8 he was taken from *p.* and from
61: 1 opening of *p.* to them that are bound
Mat. 5:25 and thou be cast into *p.*
18:30 cast into *p.* till he should pay
25:36 I was in *p.* and ye came
1 Pet. 3:19 preached unto the spirits in *p.*
Rev. 2:10 devil cast some of you into *p.*

PRISONER (PRISONERS)
Ps. 69:33 hungry. The Lord despiseth not his *p.*
79:11 let the sighing of the *p.* come before
102: 20 to hear the groaning of the *p.*
146: 7 the Lord looseth the *p.*
Zech. 9:11 sent forth thy *p.* out of the pit
9:12 turn to the stronghold, ye *p.* of hope
Eph. 4: 1 I a *p.* of the Lord beseech you

PRIVATE (PRIVATELY)
Gal. 2: 2. but *p.* to them which were of reputation
2 Pet. 1:20 scripture is of any *p.* interpretation

PRIZE
1 Cor. 9:24 run all, but one receiveth the *p.*
Phil. 3:14 for the *p.* of the high calling

PROCEED (PROCEEDED, PROCEEDETH)
Gen. 24:50 thing *p.* from the Lord: we cannot
Deut. 8: 3 by every word that *p.* out of the mouth
1 Sam. 24:13 wickedness *p.* from the wicked
Is. 29:14 I will *p.* to do a marvellous work
51: 4 a law shall *p.* from me
Jer. 9: 3 they *p.* from evil to evil
Lam. 3:38 mouth of the most High *p.* not evil
Mat. 4: 4 word that *p.* out of the mouth of God
15:19 out of the heart *p.* evil thoughts
Luke 4:22 gracious words which *p.* out of his mouth
John 8:42 I *p.* forth and came from God
15:26 Spirit of truth, which *p.* from the
Eph. 4:29 no corrupt communication *p.* out of
2 Tim. 3: 9 they shall *p.* no further
Jas. 3:10 out of the same mouth *p.* blessing
Rev. 11: 5 fire *p.* out of their mouth

PROCLAIM (PROCLAIMED)
Ex. 33:19 I will *p.* the name of the Lord
34: 6 Lord passed before him and *p.*
Lev. 23: 2 which ye shall *p.* to be holy
Deut. 20:10 then *p.* peace unto it
Prov. 20: 6 men *p.* every one his own goodness
Is. 61: 2 to *p.* the acceptable year of the Lord

PROFANE (PROFANED, PROFANING)
Lev. 18:21 shalt thou *p.* the name of thy God
19:12 shalt thou *p.* the name of thy God
21: 6 and not *p.* the name of their God
Neh. 13:17 that ye do and *p.* the sabbath day
Ezek. 22: 8 things, and hast *p.* my sabbaths
22:26 no difference between the holy and *p.*
Mal. 1:12 have *p.* it, in that ye say
2:10 *p.* the covenant of our fathers
2:11 Judah *p.* the holiness of the Lord
Mat. 12: 5 priests in the temple *p.* the sabbath
1 Tim. 1: 9 law is for the unholy and *p.*
4: 7 refuse *p.* and old wives' fables
6:20 avoiding *p.* and vain babblings
Heb. 12:16 there be any fornicator or *p.* person

PROFESS
Deut. 26: 3 I *p.* this day unto the Lord thy God
Tit. 1:16 they *p.* that they know God

PROFESSION
1 Tim. 6:12 and hast professed a good *p.*
Heb. 3: 1 High Priest of our *p.*, Christ Jesus
4:14 Son of God, let us hold fast our *p.*
10:23 let us hold fast the *p.* of our faith

PROFIT (PROFITETH)
1 Sam. 12:21 which cannot *p.* nor deliver
Job 34: 9 it *p.* a man nothing that he should
Prov. 10: 2 treasures of wickedness *p.* nothing
11: 4 riches *p.* not in the day of wrath
14:23 in all labour there is *p.*
Eccl. 7:11 by it there is *p.* to them that
Is. 30: 5 not *p.* then nor be an help nor *p.*
57:12 for they shall not *p.* thee
Jer. 2: 8 walked after things that do not *p.*
16:19 wherein there is no *p.*
23:32 they shall not *p.* this people at all
John 6:63 the flesh *p.* nothing: the words that
1 Cor. 13: 3 have not charity, it *p.* me nothing
Gal. 5: 2 Christ shall *p.* you nothing
2 Tim. 2:14 they strive not about words to no *p.*
Heb. 4: 2 the word preached did not *p.* them
12:10 but he for our *p.* that we might
Jas. 2:14 what doth it *p.* my brethren

PROFITABLE
Job 22: 2 is wise may be *p.* unto himself
Eccl. 10:10 strength: but wisdom is *p.* to direct
Acts 20:20 kept back nothing that was *p.* unto
1 Tim. 4: 8 godliness is *p.* unto all things
2 Tim. 3:16 inspiration of God, and is *p.* for doctrine
Tit. 3: 8 these things are good and *p.* unto men
Philem. 1:11 now *p.* to thee and to me

PROFITING
1 Tim. 4:15 that thy *p.* may appear to all

PROMISE (PROMISES)
Num. 14:34 ye shall know my breach of *p.*
Neh. 5:12 that they should do according to this *p.*
Ps. 77: 8 doth his *p.* fail for evermore
Luke 24:49 the *p.* of my Father upon you
Acts 1: 4 wait for the *p.* of the Father
Rom. 4:16 *p.* might be sure to all the seed
9: 4 the service of God and the *p.*
9: 8 children of the *p.* are counted for
15: 8 confirm the *p.* made unto the fathers
2 Cor. 1:20 all the *p.* of God in him are yea
7: 1 having therefore these *p.*
Gal. 3:21 is the law against the *p.*
4:28 as Isaac was, are the children of *p.*
Eph. 1:13 with that holy Spirit of *p.*
6: 2 the first commandment with *p.*
1 Tim. 4: 8 *p.* of the life that now is, and
Heb. 4: 1 lest a *p.* being left us of
6:12 through faith and patience inherit the *p.*
6:17 willing to show unto the heirs of *p.*
8: 6 which was established upon better *p.*
9:15 receive the *p.* of eternal inheritance
11:17 he that had received *p.*
2 Pet. 1: 4 us exceeding great and precious *p.*
3: 4 where is the *p.* of his coming?
1 John 2:25 *p.* that he promised us, even eternal

PROMISED
Rom. 1: 2 which he had *p.* afore by his prophets
Tit. 1: 2 which God, that cannot lie, *p.* before
Heb. 10:23 for he is faithful that *p.*
11:11 she judged him faithful who had *p.*
12:26 but now he hath *p.* saying

PROPHECY
1 Cor. 12:10 the working of miracles; to another *p.*
1 Tim. 4:14 which was given thee by *p.*
2 Pet. 1:20 no *p.* of the scripture is of any
Rev. 1: 3 they that hear the words of this *p.*
11: 6 it rain not in the days of their *p.*
19:10 testimony of Jesus is the spirit of *p.*
22: 7 keepeth the sayings of the *p.* of

PROPHESY (PROPHESIED)
Num. 11:25 them, they *p.* and did not cease
1 Ki. 22: 8 doth not *p.* good concerning me
Is. 30:10 *p.* not right things *p.* deceits
Jer. 23:21 I have not spoken to them, yet they *p.*
Joel 2:28 thy sons and thy daughters shall *p.*
Amos 2:12 commanded the prophets, saying *p.* not
3: 8 Lord God hath spoken, who can but *p.*
Mat. 7:22 have we not *p.* in thy name
11:13 prophets and the law *p.* until John
John 11:51 *p.* that Jesus should die
1 Cor. 13: 9 know in part and we *p.* in part
14: 1 but rather that ye may *p.*
14:31 for ye may all *p.* one by one
14:39 covet to *p.* and forbid not to
1 Pet. 1:10 *p.* of the grace that should come
Jude 1:14 Enoch also the seventh from Adam *p.*
Rev. 10:11 thou must *p.* again before many

PROPHET
Gen. 20: 7 he is a *p.* and shall pray for thee
Ex. 7: 1 and Aaron thy brother shall be thy *p.*
Deut. 18:15 raise up unto thee a *p.*
18:18 raise them up a *p.* from among
2 Ki. 5:13 if the *p.* had bid thee do some
Ezek. 33:33 know that a *p.* hath been among them
Hos. 9: 7 *p.* is a fool, the spiritual man
12:13 by a *p.* was he preserved
Mat. 10:41 he that receiveth a *p.* in the name
13:57 a *p.* is not without honour save in
Luke 7:28 there is not a greater *p.*
13:33 a *p.* perish out of Jerusalem
24:19 *p.* mighty in deed and word
John 7:40 said, Of a truth this is the *P.*
7:52 out of Galilee ariseth no *p.*
Acts 3:22 a *p.* shall the Lord raise
3:23 will not hear the *p.* shall be destroyed
Tit. 1:12 even a *p.* of their own, said
2 Pet. 2:16 forbad the madness of the *p.*

PROPHETS
Num. 11:29 all the Lord's people were *p.*, and
Ps. 105: 15 anointed, and do my *p.* no harm
Jer. 5:13 the *p.* shall become wind, and the
23:26 are *p.* of the deceit of their
Lam. 2:14 *p.* have seen vain and foolish things
Hos. 6: 5 I hewed them by the *p.*
Mic. 3:11 *p.* thereof divine for money: yet
Zeph. 3: 4 her *p.* are light and treacherous
Mat. 5:17 come to destroy the law, or *p.*
7:12 this is the law and the *p.*
13:17 many *p.* and righteous men have desired
22:40 on these hang all the law and the *p.*
23:34 I send you *p.* and wise men
Luke 1:70 spake by the mouth of his holy *p.*
6:23 so did their fathers unto the *p.*
16:29 they have Moses and the *p.*
16:31 if they hear not Moses and the *p.*
24:25 to believe all that the *p.* have spoken
24:44 *p.*, and in the psalms, concerning me
John 8:52 Abraham is dead, and the *p.*
Acts 3:18 by the mouth of all his *p.*
3:25 ye are children of the *p.*
10:43 to him give all the *p.* witness
13:27 knew him not nor yet voices of *p.*
26:22 things which the *p.* and Moses
26:27 believest thou the *p.*?
Rom. 1: 2 which he had promised afore by his *p.*
3:21 being witnessed by the law and the *p.*
1 Cor. 12:28 first apostles, secondarily *p.*
14:32 spirits of the *p.* are subject to the *p.*
Eph. 2:20 the foundation of the apostles and *p.*
1 Thes. 2:15 killed the Lord Jesus and their own *p.*
Heb. 1: 1 spake in the past unto the fathers by the *p.*
Jas. 5:10 take, my brethren, the *p.* who have spoken
Rev. 18:20 rejoice, ye apostles and *p.*
22: 6 Lord God of the holy *p.* sent his
22: 9 and of thy brethren the *p.*

PROPITIATION
Rom. 3:25 God hath set forth to be a *p.*
1 John 2: 2 he is the *p.* for our sins
4:10 his Son to be the *p.* for our sins

PROSPER (PROSPERED)
Gen. 24:40 and *p.* thy way; and thou shalt
39: 3 Lord made all that he did to *p.*
Deut. 29: 9 that ye may *p.* in that all ye do
Josh. 1: 7 thou mayest *p.* whithersoever thou goest
Neh. 1:11 and *p.*, I pray thee, thy servant
Job 12: 6 tabernacles of robbers *p.* and they
Ps. 1: 3 whatsoever he doeth shall *p.*
122: 6 they shall *p.* that love thee
Is. 53:10 the pleasure of the Lord shall *p.*
54:17 no weapon against thee shall *p.*
55:11 shall *p.* in the thing whereto
Jer. 12: 1 Wherefore doth the way of the wicked *p.*
23: 5 a King shall reign and *p.*
1 Cor. 16: 2 as God hath *p.* him, that there be

PROSPERITY
1 Ki. 10: 7 thy wisdom and *p.* exceedeth the fame
Job 36:11 spend their days in *p.*
Ps. 30: 6 in my *p.* I said I shall never
73: 3 when I saw the *p.* of the wicked
118: 25 Lord, I beseech thee, send now *p.*
122: 7 walls, and *p.* be in thy palaces
Prov. 1:32 *p.* of fools shall destroy them
Eccl. 7:14 in the day of *p.* be joyful
Jer. 22:21 I spake to thee in thy *p.*

PROUD
Job 9:13 the *p.* helpers do stoop under him
Ps. 12: 3 the tongue that speaketh *p.* things
40: 4 respecteth not the *p.* nor
138: 6 the *p.* he knoweth afar off
Prov. 6:17 *p.* look, a lying tongue, and hands
21: 4 high look and a *p.* heart, and the
Eccl. 7: 8 patient in spirit is better than the *p.*
Mal. 3:15 now we call the *p.* happy; yea
Luke 1:51 the *p.* in the imagination of their
Jas. 4: 6 God resisteth the *p.*, but giveth grace
1 Pet. 5: 5 for God resisteth the *p.*, and giveth

PROUDLY
Ex. 18:11 wherein they dealt *p.* he was above
1 Sam. 2: 3 talk no more so exceeding *p.*
Neh. 9:10 knewest that they dealt *p.* against
Ps. 17:10 with their mouth they speak *p.*
Is. 3: 5 child behave *p.* against ancient

PROVE (PROVED)
Ex. 16: 4 that I may *p.* them, whether they will
20:20 fear not, for God is come to *p.* you
Deut. 8:16 and that he might *p.* thee
33: 8 whom thou didst *p.* at Massah
1 Ki. 10: 1 she came to *p.* him with hard
Job 9:20 mouth shall *p.* me perverse
Ps. 17: 3 thou hast *p.* mine heart
26: 2 examine me, O Lord, *p.* me
66:10 thou, O God, hast *p.* us as
95: 9 tempted me, *p.* me, and saw my work
Mal. 3:10 *p.* me now herewith, saith the Lord
Rom. 12: 2 that ye may *p.* what is that good and
2 Cor. 8: 8 to *p.* the sincerity of your love
13: 5 *p.* your own selves, know ye not
Gal. 6: 4 let every man *p.* his work
1 Thes. 5:21 *p.* all things; hold fast
Heb. 3: 9 your father tempted me, *p.* me

PROVERB (PROVERBS)
Deut. 28:37 thou shalt become an astonishment, a *p.*
1 Ki. 4:32 he spake three thousand *p.*
9: 7 and Israel shall be a *p.*
Ps. 69:11 and I became a *p.* to them
Prov. 1: 1 the *p.* of Solomon, the son of David
10: 1 the *p.* of Solomon. A wise son
25: 1 these are also *p.* of Solomon
Eccl. 12: 9 he set in order many *p.*
Is. 14: 4 thou shalt take up this *p.* against
Jer. 24: 9 to be a reproach and a *p.*
Ezek. 14: 8 will make him a sign and a *p.*
John 16:25 things have I spoken unto you in *p.*
2 Pet. 2:22 unto them according to the true *p.*

PROVIDE (PROVIDETH)
Gen. 22: 8 God will *p.* himself a lamb
Job 38:41 who *p.* for the raven his food
Ps. 78:20 can he *p.* flesh for people
Prov. 6: 8 *p.* her meat in the summer
Mat. 10: 9 *p.* neither gold nor silver nor brass
Luke 12:33 *p.* bags which wax not old
Rom. 12:17 *p.* things honest in the sight of all
1 Tim. 5: 8 if any *p.* not for his own

PROVOKE (PROVOKED)
Ex. 23:21 obey his voice, *p.* him not
Num. 14:11 how long will this people *p.* me
14:23 neither any of them that *p.* me
16:30 these men have *p.* the Lord
Deut. 9: 8 ye *p.* the Lord to wrath
31:20 and *p.* me, and break my covenant
1 Ki. 14:22 *p.* him to jealousy with their sins
2 Ki. 23:26 that Manasseh *p.* him withal
1 Chr. 21: 1 and *p.* David to number Israel
Ezra 5:12 our fathers had *p.* God to
Ps. 78:40 how oft did they *p.* him
78:56 and *p.* the most high God, and
106: 7 *p.* him at the sea, even at the Red
106: 33 because they *p.* his spirit, so that
106: 43 they *p.* him with their counsel
Is. 3: 8 to *p.* the eyes of his glory
Jer. 7:19 do they *p.* me to anger
44: 8 ye *p.* me to wrath with your
Zech. 8:14 when your fathers *p.* me to wrath
Luke 11:53 to *p.* him to speak of many things
Rom. 10:19 I will *p.* you to jealousy
1 Cor. 10:22 do we *p.* the Lord to jealousy
2 Cor. 9: 2 and your zeal hath *p.* very many
Heb. 3:16 for some when they heard, did *p.*
10:24 to *p.* unto love and good works

PRUDENT
1 Sam. 16:18 a man of war, and *p.* in matters
Prov. 12:16 known but a *p.* man covereth shame
12:23 *p.* man concealeth knowledge: but the
13:16 *p.* man dealeth with knowledge
14: 8 wisdom of the *p.* is to understand
14:15 the *p.* man looketh well to his
14:18 the *p.* are crowned with knowledge
15: 5 he that regardeth reproof is *p.*
16:21 wise in heart shall be called *p.*
18:15 heart of the *p.* getteth knowledge
19:14 a *p.* wife is from the Lord
22: 3 a *p.* man foreseeth the evil
Is. 5:21 and *p.* in their own sight
Hos. 14: 9 is *p.* and he shall know them? for
Mat. 11:25 hid these things from the wise and *p.*
1 Cor. 1:19 to nothing the understanding of the *p.*

PRUDENCE
2 Chr. 2:12 endued with *p.* and understanding
Prov. 8:12 I wisdom dwell with *p.*
Eph. 1: 8 abounded toward us in all wisdom and *p.*

PRUDENTLY
Is. 52:13 my servant shall deal *p.*

PSALM (PSALMS)
1 Chr. 16: 7 David delivered first this *p.* to thank
16: 9 sing *p.* unto him, talk ye of all
Ps. 81: 2 take a *p.*, and bring hither the timbrel
95: 2 joyful noise unto him with *p.*
98: 5 and with the voice of a *p.*
Acts 13:33 it is also written in the second *p.*
1 Cor. 14:26 every one of you hath a *p.*
Eph. 5:19 speaking to yourselves in *p.*
Jas. 5:13 merry? let him sing *p.*

PUBLICAN (PUBLICANS)
Mat. 5:46 do not even the *p.* the same
11:19 a friend of *p.* and sinners
18:17 unto thee as an heathen man and a *p.*
21:31 *p.* and harlots go into the kingdom
21:32 *p.* and harlots believed him
Luke 3:12 came also *p.* to be baptized
7:29 the *p.*, justified God, being baptized
18:13 and the *p.*, standing afar off

PUBLISH (PUBLISHED)
Deut. 32: 3 I will *p.* the name of the Lord
2 Sam. 1:20 *p.* it not in the streets
Ps. 26: 7 *p.* with a voice of thanksgiving
Is. 52: 7 bringeth good tidings, that *p.* peace
Jer. 4:15 and *p.* affliction from mount Ephraim
Acts 13:49 word of the Lord was *p.*

PUFFED (PUFFETH)
1 Cor. 4:19 the speech of them which are *p.* up
5: 2 and ye are *p.* up, and have not
8: 1 knowledge *p.* up, but charity edifieth
13: 4 charity vaunteth not itself, is not *p.* up
Col. 2:18 vainly *p.* up by his fleshly mind

PUNISH (PUNISHED)
Lev. 26:18 I will *p.* you seven times more
Ezra 9:13 God hast *p.* us less than we deserve
Is. 10:12 *p.* the fruit of the stout heart
13:11 I will *p.* the world for their
Jer. 9:25 *p.* all them which are circumcised with
Hos. 4:14 I will not *p.* your daughters
12: 2 will *p.* Jacob according to his ways
2 Thes. 1: 9 be *p.* with everlasting destruction
2 Pet. 2: 9 unto the day of judgment to be *p.*

PUNISHMENT
Gen. 4:13 my *p.* is greater than I can
Lev. 26:41 accept the *p.* of their iniquity
Lam. 3:39 a man for the *p.* of his sins
Amos 1: 3 I will not turn away the *p.*
Mat. 25:46 go into everlasting *p.*
2 Cor. 2: 6 sufficient to such a man is this *p.*
Heb. 10:29 of how much sorer *p.*, suppose
1 Pet. 2:14 sent by him, for the *p.* of

PURCHASED
Ps. 74: 2 thy congregation, which thou hast *p.*
Acts 8:20 the gift of God may be *p.* with money
20:28 which he hath *p.* with his own blood
Eph. 1:14 until the redemption of the *p.* possession

PURE
Ex. 27:20 they bring thee *p.* olive oil
30:34 these sweet spices with *p.* frankincense
2 Sam. 22:27 with the *p.* thou wilt show thyself *p.*
Job 4:17 man can be more *p.* than his Maker
25: 5 stars are not *p.* in his sight
Ps. 12: 6 words of the Lord are *p.* words
19: 8 commandment of the Lord is *p.*
24: 4 clean hands and a *p.* heart
Prov. 15:26 words of the *p.* are pleasant
30: 5 every word of God is *p.*
30:12 generation that are *p.* in their own eyes
Zeph. 3: 9 turn to the people a *p.* language
Acts 20:26 I am *p.* from the blood of all
Rom. 14:20 all things indeed are *p.*; but it is
Phil. 4: 8 are just, whatsoever things are *p.*
1 Tim. 3: 9 faith in a *p.* conscience
5:22 other men's sins: keep thyself *p.*
Tit. 1:15 to the *p.* all things are *p.*
Heb. 10:22 our bodies washed with *p.* water
Jas. 1:27 *p.* religion and undefiled before God
3:17 wisdom from above is first *p.*
2 Pet. 3: 1 I stir up your *p.* minds

PURITY
1 Tim. 4:12 in charity, in spirit, in faith, in *p.*

PURGE (PURGED)
Ps. 51: 7 *p.* me with hyssop, and I shall be
65: 3 transgressions, thou shalt *p.*
79: 9 *p.* away our sins for thy name's
Is. 6: 7 iniquity is taken, and sin *p.*
27: 9 shall the iniquity of Jacob be *p.*
Mal. 3: 3 purify and *p.* them as gold
Mat. 3:12 he will thoroughly *p.* his floor, and
1 Cor. 5: 7 *p.* out therefore the old leaven

2 Tim. 2:21 if a man therefore *p.* himself from
Heb. 1:3 had by himself *p.* our sins
9:14 *p.* your conscience from dead works
2 Pet. 1:9 he was *p.* from old sins

PURIFY (PURIFIED, PURIFIETH, PURIFYING)
Ps. 12:6 in a furnace of earth *p.* seven times
Dan. 12:10 many shall be *p.* and made white
Mal. 3:3 and he shall *p.* the sons of Levi
Acts 15:9 *p.* their hearts by faith
Heb. 9:13 sanctifieth to the *p.* of the flesh
Tit. 2:14 *p.* unto himself a peculiar
Jas. 4:8 *p.* your hearts, ye double
1 Pet. 1:22 *p.* your souls in obeying the truth
1 John 3:3 *p.* himself, even as he is pure

PURPOSE (PURPOSED)
Job 33:17 withdraw man from his *p.*
Prov. 20:18 every *p.* is established by counsel
Eccl. 3:17 a time there for every *p.* and for
Is. 14:26 the *p.* that is purposed upon the whole
Jer. 51:29 *p.* of the Lord shall be performed
Acts 11:23 with *p.* of heart they would cleave
Rom. 8:28 called according to his *p.*
Eph. 1:9 which he hath *p.* in himself
1:11 according to the *p.* of him who
3:11 according to the eternal *p.* which
2 Tim. 1:9 according to his own *p.* and grace
1 John 3:8 for this *p.* the Son of God

PUT
Gen. 2:8 there he *p.* the man whom he had formed
3:15 I will *p.* enmity between thee and
28:20 bread to eat and raiment to *p.* on
Ezra 7:27 which hath *p.* such a thing as this
Neh. 2:12 what God *p.* in the heart
3:5 nobles *p.* not their necks
Job 4:18 he *p.* no trust in his servants
29:14 I *p.* on righteousness and it
38:36 hath *p.* wisdom in inward parts
Ps. 4:7 hast *p.* gladness in my heart
8:6 *p.* all things under his feet
9:20 *p.* them in fear, that they may
Eccl. 10:10 then must he *p.* to more strength
Sol. 5:3 *p.* off my coat, how shall I *p.* it on?
Is. 5:20 woe to them that *p.* darkness for light
42:1 I have *p.* my Spirit upon him
43:26 *p.* me in remembrance: let us plead
51:9 awake, *p.* on strength, O arm of
59:17 *p.* on righteousness as a breastplate
63:11 who *p.* his holy spirit within him
Jer. 31:33 *p.* my law in their inward parts
32:40 I will *p.* my fear in their hearts
Ezek. 11:19 *p.* a new spirit within you
36:27 I will *p.* my Spirit in you
Mic. 7:5 *p.* ye not confidence in a guide
Mat. 5:15 *p.* it under a bushel, but on a
6:25 nor for body, what ye shall *p.* on
19:6 let not man *p.* asunder
Luke 1:52 *p.* down the mighty from their seats
Acts 1:7 Father hath *p.* in his own power
15:9 *p.* no difference between us
Rom. 13:12 *p.* on the armour of light
13:14 *p.* on the Lord Jesus Christ
Gal. 3:27 baptized into Christ have *p.* on Christ
Eph. 4:22 *p.* off concerning the former conversation
6:11 *p.* on the whole armour of God
Col. 3:9 that ye have *p.* off the old man
3:12 *p.* on therefore as the elect
3:14 above all things *p.* on charity
2 Pet. 1:14 I must *p.* off this tabernacle
Rev. 17:17 God hath *p.* in their hearts

PUTTETH (PUTTING)
Num. 22:38 word that God *p.* in my mouth
Job 15:15 he *p.* no trust in saints
Ps. 15:5 that *p.* not out his money
75:7 God *p.* down one, and setteth
Sol. 2:13 the fig tree *p.* forth her green figs
Lam. 3:29 he *p.* his mouth in the dust; if so be
Mal. 2:16 saith that he hateth *p.* away
Eph. 4:25 *p.* away lying, speak every man truth
Col. 2:11 in *p.* off the body of sins
1 Thes. 5:8 *p.* on the breastplate of faith
1 Pet. 3:3 wearing of gold or *p.* on of
3:21 not *p.* away of the filth of the flesh

Q

QUAKE (QUAKED, QUAKING)
Ex. 19:18 the whole mount *q.* greatly
Ezek. 12:18 eat thy bread with *q.*
Dan. 10:7 but a great *q.* fell upon them
Mat. 27:51 the bottom; and the earth did *q.*

QUEEN (QUEENS)
1 Ki. 10:1 the *q.* of Sheba heard of the fame
Ps. 45:9 did stand the *q.* in gold of Ophir
Sol. 6:8 there are threescore *q.* and fourscore
Jer. 44:25 to burn incense to the *q.* of heaven
Mat. 12:42 the *q.* of the south shall rise up
Rev. 18:7 I sit a *q.*, and am no widow

QUENCH (QUENCHED)
2 Sam. 14:7 so they shall *q.* my coal
21:17 that thou *q.* not the light of Israel
Sol. 8:7 many waters cannot *q.* love
Is. 42:3 smoking flax shall he not *q.*
Mark 9:43 fire that never shall be *q.*
Eph. 6:16 to *q.* the fiery darts of wicked
1 Thes. 5:19 *q.* not the Spirit

QUESTION (QUESTIONS)
1 Ki. 10:1 came to prove him with hard *q.*
Mark 12:34 no man after that durst ask him any *q.*
Luke 2:46 hearing them, and asking them *q.*
1 Cor. 10:25 asking no *q.* for conscience sake
1 Tim. 1:4 which minister *q.*, rather than godly
2 Tim. 2:23 but foolish and unlearned *q.* avoid

QUICK (QUICKLY)
Ex. 32:8 turned aside *q.* out of the way
Num. 16:30 they go down *q.* into the pit
Deut. 11:17 lest ye perish *q.* from off the good
Ps. 55:15 let them go down *q.* into hell
Eccl. 4:12 threefold cord is not *q.* broken
Is. 11:3 of *q.* understanding in fear
Mat. 5:25 agree with thine adversary *q.*
Acts 10:42 to be the Judge of *q.* and dead
2 Tim. 4:1 who shall judge the *q.* and dead
Rev. 3:11 behold, I come *q.*: hold that

QUICKEN (QUICKENED, QUICKENETH, QUICKENING)
Ps. 71:20 *q.* me again and shalt bring me
80:18 *q.* us, and we will call on thy name
119:25 *q.* thou me according to thy word
119:37 *q.* thou me in thy way
119:40 *q.* me in thy righteousness
119:50 for thy word hath *q.* me
119:149 *q.* me according to thy judgment
John 5:21 even so the Son *q.* whom he will
6:63 it is the Spirit that *q.*
Rom. 8:11 *q.* your mortal bodies by his
1 Cor. 15:45 last Adam was made a *q.* spirit
Col. 2:13 hath he *q.* together with him
1 Pet. 3:18 in the flesh, but *q.* by the Spirit

QUIET
Eccl. 9:17 words of the wise are heard in *q.*
Is. 7:4 take heed and be *q.*, fear not
1 Thes. 4:11 study to be *q.* and to do your own
1 Tim. 2:2 lead a *q.* and peaceable life in all
1 Pet. 3:4 ornament of a meek and *q.* spirit

QUIETNESS
1 Chr. 22:9 shall give peace and *q.* to Israel
Job 2020. he shall not feel *q.* in his belly
34:29 when he giveth *q.* who then can make
Eccl. 4:6 better is a handful with *q.*
Is. 30:15 in *q.* and confidence shall be your
32:17 effect of righteousness shall be *q.*
2 Thes. 3:12 exhort that with *q.* they work

QUIVER
Ps. 127:5 the man that hath his *q.* full of them
Is. 49:2 in his *q.* hath he hid me
Jer. 5:16 *q.* is as an open sepulchre

R

RACE
Ps. 19:5 strong man to run a *r.*
Eccl. 9:11 that the *r.* is not to the swift
1 Cor. 9:24 they which run in a *r.* run all
Heb. 12:1 run with patience the *r.* that is set

RAGE (RAGED, RAGETH, RAGING)
2 Ki. 5:12 he turned and went away in a *r.*
2 Chr. 16:10 for he was in a *r.* with him
28:9 ye have slain them in a *r.*
Ps. 46:6 the heathen *r.*, the kingdoms were
89:9 rulest the *r.* of the sea
Prov. 6:34 jealousy is the *r.* of a man
14:16 the fool *r.* and is confident
20:1 wine is a mocker, strong drink is *r.*
29:9 whether he *r.* or laugh is no
Jude 1:13 *r.* waves of the sea, foaming out

RAGS
Prov. 23:21 drowsiness shall clothe a man with *r.*
Is. 64:6 our righteousnesses are as filthy *r.*

RAIMENT
Gen. 28:20 bread to eat and *r.* to put on
Ex. 21:10 *r.* and her duty of marriage, shall he
Deut. 8:4 thy *r.* waxed not old upon
24:17 not take the widow's *r.* to
Zech. 3:4 clothe thee with change of *r.*
Mat. 6:25 meat, and the body more than *r.*
11:8 man clothed in soft *r.*? Behold
17:2 his *r.* was white as the light
1 Tim. 6:8 having food and *r.* let us be therewith
Rev. 3:5 shall be clothed in white *r.*

RAIN
Lev. 26:4 I will give you *r.* in due season
Deut. 32:2 my doctrine shall drop as the *r.*
2 Sam. 23:4 by clear shining after *r.*
1 Ki. 8:35 no *r.* because they have sinned
2 Chr. 7:13 that there be no *r.*, or if I command
Job 5:10 who giveth *r.* on the earth
28:26 he made a decree for the *r.*
38:26 cause it to *r.* on the earth
Ps. 11:6 upon the wicked he shall *r.* snares
68:9 didst send a plentiful *r.*
72:6 he shall come down like *r.*
147:8 who prepareth *r.* for the earth
Prov. 16:15 favour is as a cloud of the latter *r.*
Eccl. 12:2 nor clouds return after *r.*
Sol. 2:11 winter is past; the *r.* is over
Is. 4:6 a covert from storm and from *r.*
5:6 clouds that they *r.* no *r.* upon
55:10 as the *r.* cometh down from
Jer. 5:24 Lord our God, that giveth *r.*
Hos. 10:12 till he come and *r.* righteousness
Amos 4:7 withholden the *r.* from you, when
Zech. 10:1 ask ye of the Lord *r.* in the time of
14:17 even upon them shall be no *r.*
Mat. 5:45 sendeth *r.* on the just and on
Heb. 6:7 earth which drinketh in *r.*
Jas. 5:18 prayed again, the heaven gave *r.*

RAISE (RAISED, RAISETH)
Ex. 9:16 for this cause I have *r.* thee up
Deut. 18:18 I will *r.* them up a Prophet
2 Sam. 12:11 I will *r.* up evil against thee
Ps. 113:7 he *r.* up the poor out of dust
145:14 *r.* up those that are bowed down
Is. 44:26 *r.* up the decayed places thereof
58:12 *r.* up the foundations of many
Hos. 6:2 third day he will *r.* us up
Amos 9:11 I will *r.* up the tabernacle of
Mat. 11:5 deaf hear, the dead are *r.* up
Luke 1:69 *r.* up an horn of salvation
John 6:40 I will *r.* him up at the last day
Rom. 4:25 *r.* again for our justification
6:4 as Christ was *r.* from the dead
1 Cor. 6:14 God hath both *r.* up the Lord
2 Cor. 4:14 he which *r.* up the Lord Jesus
Eph. 2:6 hath *r.* us up together and made us

RANSOM
Ex. 21:30 he shall give for the *r.* of his life
30:12 give every man a *r.* for
Job 33:24 to the pit. I have found a *r.*
36:18 great *r.* cannot deliver thee
Ps. 49:7 nor give to God a *r.* for him
Prov. 6:35 he will not regard any *r.*
13:8 *r.* of man's life are his riches
21:18 the wicked shall be a *r.* for the
Is. 43:3 I gave Egypt for thy *r.*
Mat. 20:28 to give his life a *r.* for
1 Tim. 2:6 gave himself a *r.* for all

READ (READEST, READETH)
Ex. 24: 7 and *r.* in the audience of the people
Deut. 17:19 *r.* therein all the days of his life
Neh. 13: 1 they *r.* in the book of Moses
Acts 8:30 understandest thou what thou *r.*
15:21 *r.* in the synagogues every Sabbath
2 Cor. 3: 2 known and *r.* of all men
Col. 4:16 that ye likewise *r.* the epistle from
1 Thes. 5:27 epistle be *r.* unto all
Rev. 1: 3 blessed is he that *r.*

READY
Neh. 9:17 thou art a God *r.* to pardon
Ps. 45: 1 tongue is the pen of a *r.* writer
Eccl. 5: 1 more *r.* to hear, than
Mat. 24:44 be ye also *r.* for in such an
Mark 14:38 spirit is *r.* but the flesh
Acts 21:13 *r.* not to be bound only
1 Tim. 6:18 do good, *r.* to distribute
2 Tim. 4: 6 for I am now *r.* to be offered
Tit. 3: 1 to be *r.* to every good work
Rev. 3: 2 that are *r.* to die: for I have

REAP (REAPED, REAPETH)
Lev. 19: 9 when ye *r.* the harvest of your land
Hos. 10:12 *r.* in mercy, break up your fallow
10:13 plowed wickedness, ye have *r.* iniquity
Mat. 6:26 sow not, neither do they *r.*
John 4:36 he that *r.* receiveth wages
1 Cor. 9:11 a great thing if we *r.*
Gal. 6: 7 man soweth, that shall he also *r.*
6: 8 shall of the Spirit *r.* life everlasting
6: 9 shall *r.* if we faint not
Rev. 14:16 earth; and the earth was *r.*

REAPERS
Mat. 13:39 world; and the *r.* are the angels

REASON
Prov. 26:16 seven men that can render a *r.*
Dan. 4:36 my *r.* returned unto me, and for the
1 Pet. 3:15 asketh a *r.* of the hope

REASONABLE
Rom. 12: 1 which is your *r.* service

REBEL (REBELLED)
Num. 14: 9 only *r.* not ye against the Lord
Josh. 22:19 but *r.* not against the Lord
Neh. 9:26 and *r.* against thee, and cast thy
Job 24:13 of those that *r.* against the light
Is. 63:10 *r.* and vexed his holy Spirit

REBELLION
1 Sam. 15:23 *r.* is as the sin of witchcraft

REBELLIOUS
Deut. 9: 7 ye have been *r.* against the Lord
Is. 30: 9 this is a *r.* people, lying
50: 5 I was not *r.* neither turned away
65: 2 all the day unto a *r.* people
Jer. 4:17 she hath been *r.* against me
5:23 people hath a revolting and *r.* heart
Ezek. 2: 5 for they are a *r.* house
12: 3 though they be a *r.* house
44: 6 thou shalt say to the *r.*

REBELS
Num. 20:10 hear now, ye *r.*; must we fetch
Ezek. 20:38 purge out from you the *r.*

REBUKE
Lev. 19:17 shalt in any wise *r.* thy neighbour
2 Ki. 19: 3 a day of trouble, *r.* and blasphemy
Ps. 6: 1 *r.* me not in thine anger, nor
Prov. 9: 8 *r.* a wise man, he will love
27: 5 open *r.* is better than secret love
Zech. 3: 2 Lord said to Satan, The Lord *r.* thee
Mat. 16:22 Peter took him and began to *r.* him
Luke 17: 3 brother trespass against thee *r.* him
Phil. 2:15 sons of God, without *r.*
1 Tim. 5: 1 *r.* not an elder, entreat
5:20 them that sin *r.* before all
Tit. 1:13 wherefore *r.* them sharply that

RECEIVE
Job 2:10 shall we *r.* good at the hand of God
22:22 *r.* I pray thee the law from his mouth
Ps. 6: 9 the Lord will *r.* my prayer
49:15 grave: for he shall *r.* me
73:24 and afterward *r.* me to glory
75: 2 when I shall *r.* the congregation
Mat. 10:41 shall *r.* a prophet's reward; and he
18: 5 *r.* one such little child in my name
19:11 all men cannot *r.* this saying
21:22 ask in prayer, believing, ye shall *r.*
Mark 4:16 heard the word, immediately *r.* it with
11:24 believe that ye *r.* them, and ye shall
Luke 16: 9 *r.* you into everlasting habitations
John 3:27 man can *r.* nothing except
5:44 which *r.* honour one of another
16:24 ask, and ye shall *r.*, that your joy
Acts 2:38 shall *r.* the gift of the Holy Ghost
7:59 Lord Jesus, *r.* my spirit
10:43 whosoever believeth shall *r.* remission
20:35 more blessed to give than to *r.*
26:18 may *r.* forgiveness of sins
Rom. 14: 1 him that is weak in faith *r.* ye
1 Cor. 3: 8 every man *r.* his own reward
2 Cor. 5:10 may *r.* things done in the body
6: 1 *r.* not the grace of God in vain
Gal. 3:14 *r.* the promise of the Spirit
Eph. 6: 8 same shall he *r.* of the Lord
Col. 3:24 *r.* the reward of inheritance
Jas. 1:21 *r.* with meekness the engrafted word
3: 1 we shall *r.* the greater condemnation
1 Pet. 5: 4 shall *r.* a crown of glory
1 John 3:22 whatsoever we ask, we *r.*
2 John 1: 8 but that we *r.* a full reward

RECEIVED (RECEIVETH, RECEIVING)
Job 4:12 mine ear *r.* a little thereof
Ps. 68:18 thou hast *r.* gifts for men
Jer. 7:28 nor *r.* correction, truth is perished
Mat. 7: 8 every one that asketh *r.*
10: 8 freely ye have *r.*, freely give
10:40 he that *r.* you *r.* me
Luke 6:24 ye have *r.* your consolation
John 1:11 own, and his own *r.* him not
3:32 no man *r.* his testimony
12:48 rejecteth me, and *r.* not my words
Acts 8:17 them, and they *r.* the Holy Ghost
17:11 *r.* the word with all readiness
20:24 ministry which I *r.* of the Lord
Rom. 5:11 by whom we have *r.* atonement
8:15 have *r.* the spirit of adoption
14: 3 him that eateth, for God hath *r.* him
15: 7 ye one another, as Christ also *r.* us
1 Cor. 2:14 natural man *r.* not the things
11:23 For I have *r.* of the Lord
Phil. 4:15 as concerning giving and *r.*, but ye
1 Tim. 3:16 in the world *r.* up into glory
4: 3 meats which God hath created to be *r.*
Heb. 11:13 in faith not having *r.* promises
12:28 wherefore we *r.* a kingdom
1 Pet. 1: 9 *r.* the end of your faith

RECOMPEN(C)SE
Deut. 32:35 to me belongeth vengeance and *r.*
Job 15:31 vanity shall be his *r.*
Prov. 12:14 and the *r.* of a man's hands
Is. 35: 4 even God with a *r.*; he will come
66: 6 render *r.* to his enemies
Jer. 25:14 *r.* them according to their deeds
Hos. 9: 7 the days of *r.* are come
Luke 14:12 again and a *r.* be made thee
14:14 they cannot *r.* thee: for thou shalt
Rom. 12:17 *r.* to no man evil for evil
Heb. 2: 2 disobedience received just *r.* of reward
10:35 confidence, which hath great *r.* of
11:26 he had respect unto *r.* of

RECOMPENSED
2 Sam. 22:21 cleanness of my hands hath he *r.* me
Prov. 11:31 the righteous shall be *r.*
Jer. 18:20 shall evil be *r.* for good
Rom. 11:35 it shall be *r.* unto him again

RECONCILE (RECONCILED, RECONCILING)
Lev. 6:30 to *r.* withal in the holy place
Mat. 5:24 first be *r.* to thy brother
Rom. 5:10 when we were enemies we were *r.*
2 Cor. 5:18 God, who hath *r.* us to himself
5:19 God was in Christ *r.* the world
5:20 in Christ's stead, be ye *r.* to God
Col. 1:20 to *r.* all things to himself

RECONCILIATION
Lev. 8:15 sanctified it, to make *r.* upon it
2 Chr. 29:24 they made *r.* with their blood
Ezek. 45:17 to make *r.* for the house of Israel
Dan. 9:24 and to make *r.* for iniquity
2 Cor. 5:18 given to us the ministry of *r.*
5:19 committed to us the word of *r.*
Heb. 2:17 make *r.* for the sins of the people

RECORD
Ex. 20:24 in all places where I *r.* my name
Deut. 30:19 I call heaven and earth to *r.* this day
Job 16:19 in heaven and my *r.* is on high
John 1:32 And John bare *r.* saying, I saw
12:17 and raised him from the dead, bare *r.*
19:35 and he that saw it bare *r.*
Rom. 10: 2 for I bear them *r.* that they have
Gal. 4:15 for I bear ye *r.*, that if it had
2 Cor. 1:23 I call God for a *r.* upon my
Phil. 1: 8 for God is my *r.*, how greatly
1 John 5: 7 three bear *r.* in heaven
Rev. 1: 2 bare *r.* of the word of God

RED
Ps. 75: 8 and the wine is *r.*; it is full of
Is. 1:18 though they be *r.* like crimson
27: 2 a vineyard of *r.* wine
63: 2 wherefore art thou *r.* in thine apparel
Zech. 1: 8 a man riding upon a *r.* horse
Rev. 6: 4 went out another horse that was *r.*
12: 3 behold a great *r.* dragon

REDEEM (REDEEMED, REDEEMETH)
Gen. 48:16 angel which *r.* me from all evil
Ex. 6: 6 I will *r.* you with a stretched out arm
2 Sam. 4: 9 *r.* my soul out of adversity
7:23 Israel whom God went to *r.*
Job 5:20 in famine he shall *r.* thee
Ps. 34:22 the Lord *r.* the soul of his servants
49:15 God will *r.* my soul from power
103: 4 who *r.* thy life from destruction
130: 8 *r.* Israel from all his iniquities
136: 24 *r.* us from our enemies: for his
Is. 1:27 Zion shall be *r.* with judgment
52: 3 shall be *r.* without money
63: 9 love and in his pity he *r.* them
Hos. 13:14 I will *r.* them from death
Luke 1:68 he hath visited and *r.* his people
24:21 which should have *r.* Israel
Gal. 3:13 Christ hath *r.* us from the curse of
Eph. 5:16 *r.* the time because the days are evil
Col. 4: 5 that are without, *r.* the time
Tit. 2:14 might *r.* us from all iniquity
1 Pet. 1:18 not *r.* with corruptible things as
Rev. 5: 9 hast *r.* us to God by thy blood
14: 4 these were *r.* from among men

REDEEMER
Job 19:25 I know that my *r.* liveth
Ps. 19:14 O Lord, my strength and my *r.*
Prov. 23:11 their *r.* is mighty
Is. 63:16 our father and *r.*; he shall plead
Jer. 50:34 their *R.* is strong; the Lord of hosts

REDEMPTION
Lev. 25:24 ye shall grant a *r.* for the land
Num. 3:49 Moses took the *r.* money of them
Ps. 49: 8 *r.* of their soul is precious
111: 9 he sent *r.* unto his people
Luke 2:38 looked for *r.* in Jerusalem
21:28 heads, for your *r.* draweth nigh
Rom. 3:24 through *r.* that is in Christ Jesus
8:23 waiting for the *r.* of our body
1 Cor. 1:30 righteousness, and sanctification, and *r.*
Eph. 1: 7 in whom we have *r.* through his blood
1:14 until the *r.* of the purchased possession
4:30 sealed unto the day of *r.*
Col. 1:14 in whom we have *r.* through his blood
Heb. 9:12 obtained eternal *r.* for us

REFINE (REFINED)

Is. 25: 6 of wines on the lees well *r.*
48:10 behold, I have *r.* thee, but not
Zech. 13: 9 and will *r.* them as silver is refined

REFINER

Mal. 3: 3 he shall sit as a *r.* and purifier

REFRESHING

Is. 28:12 this is the *r.*, yet they would not hear
Acts 3:19 when the times of *r.* shall come from

REFUGE

Num. 35:13 six cities shall ye have for *r.*
Deut. 33:27 the eternal God is thy *r.*
Josh. 20: 3 they shall be your *r.* from the avenger
Ps. 9: 9 the Lord also will be a *r.*
46: 1 God is our *r.* and strength; a
57: 1 thy wings will I make my *r.*, until
59:16 hast been my defence and *r.* in the
62: 7 my strength and my *r.* is in God
Is. 4: 6 and for a place of *r.*, and for a
28:15 we have made lies our *r.*
Jer. 16:19 Lord my strength my fortress and my *r.*
Heb. 6:18 fled for *r.* to lay hold on

REFUSE (REFUSED)

Neh. 9:17 *r.* to obey, neither were mindful
Ps. 77: 2 my soul *r.* to be comforted
118: 22 the stone which the builders *r.*
Jer. 5: 3 have *r.* to receive correction
8: 5 hold fast deceit, they *r.* to return
31:15 *r.* to be comforted for her children
Lam. 3:45 made us as the offscouring and *r.*
Amos 8: 6 and sell the *r.* of the wheat
1 Tim. 4: 4 nothing to be *r.* if it be received
4: 7 *r.* profane and old wives' fables
Heb. 12:25 *r.* him that spake on earth

REGARD (REGARDED, REGARDEST, REGARDETH)

Deut. 10:17 which *r.* not persons nor taketh
Job 34:19 nor *r.* the rich more than the
Ps. 28: 5 they *r.* not the works of the Lord
66:18 if I *r.* iniquity in my heart
102: 17 will *r.* the prayer of the destitute
106: 44 he *r.* their affliction and
Prov. 12:10 righteous *r.* the life of the beast
13:18 he that *r.* reproof shall be
15: 5 he that *r.* reproof is prudent
Is. 5:12 that *r.* not the work of the Lord
Mat. 22:16 thou *r.* not the person of men
Luke 1:48 *r.* the low estate of his handmaiden
Rom. 14: 6 he that *r.* the day *r.* it
Heb. 8: 9 I *r.* them not saith the Lord

REGENERATION

Mat. 19:28 in the *r.* when the Son of man shall sit
Tit. 3: 5 saved us by the washing of *r.*

REIGN (REIGNED, REIGNEST, REIGNETH)

Gen. 37: 8 shalt thou indeed *r.* over us
Ex. 15:18 Lord shall *r.* for ever and ever
Lev. 26:17 they that hate you shall *r.* over you
1 Chr. 29:12 thou *r.* over all; and in thine
Ps. 93: 1 the Lord *r.*, he is clothed with majesty
99: 1 the Lord *r.*, let the people tremble
146: 10 the Lord shall *r.* for ever
Prov. 8:15 by me kings *r.* and princes
Is. 52: 7 saith unto Zion, Thy God *r.*
Jer. 23: 5 a King shall *r.* and prosper
Luke 19:14 not have this man to *r.* over us
Rom. 5:14 nevertheless death *r.* from Adam to Moses
5:17 *r.* in life by one, Jesus
5:21 that as sin *r.* unto death so
1 Cor. 4: 8 I would to God ye did *r.*
2 Tim. 2:12 if we suffer, we shall *r.*
Rev. 5:10 we shall *r.* on the earth
19: 6 for the Lord God omnipotent *r.*
20: 4 *r.* with Christ a thousand years
22: 5 they shall *r.* for ever and ever

REINS

Ps. 7: 9 God trieth the hearts and *r.*
16: 7 my *r.* also instruct me in the night
73:21 I was pricked in my *r.*
Prov. 23:16 my *r.* shall rejoice, when thy lips
Jer. 12: 2 mouth, and far from their *r.*
Jer. 17:10 search the heart, I try the *r.*
Rev. 2:23 I am he which searcheth the *r.* and

REJECT (REJECTED)

1 Sam. 8: 7 have not *r.* thee, but they have
2 Ki. 17:20 and the Lord *r.* all the seed of Israel
Is. 53: 3 is despised and *r.* of men
Jer. 6:19 nor to my law, but *r.* it
6:30 because the Lord hath *r.* them
8: 9 they *r.* the word of the Lord
Lam. 5:22 thou hast utterly *r.* us
Hos. 4: 6 because thou hast *r.* knowledge
Mark 6:26 sat with him, he would not *r.* her
7: 9 ye *r.* the commandment of God
Luke 7:30 *r.* the counsel of God
John 12:48 he that *r.* me, and receiveth not
Gal. 4:14 ye despised not, nor *r.*
Heb. 12:17 he was *r.* for he found no
Tit. 3:10 after the first and second admonition *r.*

REJOICE

Deut. 28:63 Lord will *r.* over you
1 Sam. 2: 1 because I *r.* in thy salvation
2 Chr. 6:41 let thy saints *r.* in goodness
20:27 the Lord made them to *r.*
Neh. 12:43 God made them *r.* with
Ps. 2:11 Lord with fear and *r.* with trembling
5:11 put their trust in thee *r.*
9:14 I will *r.* in thy salvation
33: 1 *r.* in the Lord, O ye righteous
51: 8 bones which thou hast broken may *r.*
58:10 righteous shall *r.* when he
65: 8 morning and evening to *r.*
68: 3 let them *r.* before God
85: 6 that thy people may *r.* in thee
86: 4 *r.* the soul of thy servant
104: 31 Lord shall *r.* in his works
105: 3 heart of them *r.* that seek the
119:162 I *r.* at thy word as one
Prov. 5:18 *r.* with the wife of thy youth
24:17 *r.* not when thine enemy falleth
Is. 29:19 poor among men shall *r.* in the Holy One
41:16 thou shalt *r.* in the Lord
62: 5 shall thy God *r.* over thee
65:13 my servants shall *r.*, but ye shall
Jer. 32:41 I will *r.* over them to do
Joel 2:23 and *r.* in the Lord your God
Hab. 3:18 Yet I will *r.* in the Lord
Zeph. 3:17 *r.* over thee with joy
Zech. 10: 7 their heart shall *r.* as through wine
Luke 6:23 *r.* ye in that day; leap
10:20 rather *r.* because your names
John 5:35 for a season to *r.* in his light
14:28 if ye loved me ye would *r.*
Rom. 5: 2 *r.* in hope of the glory of God
12:15 *r.* with them that do *r.*
1 Cor. 7:30 that *r.*, as though they rejoiced not
Phil. 3: 3 and *r.* in Christ Jesus, and have no
4: 4 *r.* in the Lord always: and again
Col. 1:24 *r.* in my sufferings for you
1 Thes. 5:16 *r.* evermore
Jas. 1: 9 brother of low degree *r.* in that he
1 Pet. 1: 8 *r.* with joy unspeakable and full of

REJOICED (REJOICETH)

Ex. 18: 9 and Jethro *r.* for all the goodness
Ps. 28: 7 my heart greatly *r.*: and with my
119: 14 I have *r.* in the way of thy
Prov. 13: 9 the light of the righteous *r.*
15:30 light of the eyes *r.* the heart
Is. 62: 5 bridegroom *r.* over the bride
64: 5 thou meetest him that *r.*
Luke 1:47 my spirit hath *r.* in God my
10:21 Jesus *r.* in spirit and said
John 8:56 father Abraham *r.* to see my day
1 Cor. 7:30 as though they *r.* not; and they that
13: 6 *r.* not in iniquity but *r.* in
Jas. 2:13 mercy; and mercy *r.* against judgment

REJOICING

Ps. 19: 8 statutes of Lord are right, *r.* the heart
119:111 for they are the *r.* of my heart
Prov. 8:31 *r.* in the habitable part
Jer. 15:16 thy word was the joy and *r.* of my
Acts 5:41 *r.* that they were counted worthy
8:39 he went on his way *r.*
2 Cor. 1:12 our *r.* is this, the testimony
Gal. 6: 4 shall he have *r.* in himself
Heb. 3: 6 *r.* of hope firm unto the end

RELIGION

Acts 26: 5 straitest sect of our *r.* I lived
Gal. 1:14 and profited in the Jews' *r.*
Jas. 1:27 pure *r.* and undefiled before God and

RELIGIOUS

Acts 13:43 Jews and *r.* proselytes followed Paul
Jas. 1:26 any man among you seem to be *r.*

REMEMBER

Gen. 9:16 look upon it that I may *r.*
40:23 yet did not the chief butler *r.* Joseph
Ex. 13: 3 *r.* this day in which ye came out of Egypt
Lev. 26:42 will I *r.* my covenant with Jacob
Deut. 5:15 *r.* that thou wast a servant in
7:18 shalt well *r.* what the Lord thy God did
8:18 thou shalt *r.* the Lord thy God
9: 7 *r.* and forget not how thou provokedst
2 Ki. 20: 3 *r.* now how I walked before thee
Neh. 1: 8 *r.*, I beseech thee, the word that thou
13:14 *r.* me O my God, concerning
Ps. 20: 7 we will *r.* the name of the Lord
25: 6 *r.* O Lord thy tender mercies
63: 6 when I *r.* thee upon my bed
74: 2 *r.* thy congregation, which thou hast
77:11 I will *r.* the works of the Lord
79: 8 O *r.* not against us former iniquities
89:47 *r.* how short my time is
119: 49 *r.* thy word unto thy servant
132: 1 *r.* David and all his afflictions
Eccl. 12: 1 *r.* now thy Creator in days of
Sol. 1: 4 we will *r.* thy love more
Is. 43:25 I will not *r.* thy sins
46: 8 *r.* this, show yourselves men
Jer. 2: 2 for I *r.* thee, the kindness of thy youth
31:20 I do earnestly *r.* him still
31:34 I will *r.* their sin no more
Ezek. 16:60 I will *r.* my covenant with thee
16:61 shalt *r.* thy ways, and be ashamed
36:31 shall ye *r.* your own evil ways
Mic. 6: 5 *r.* now what Balak king of Moab consulted
Hab. 3: 2 in wrath *r.* mercy
Luke 1:72 to *r.* his holy covenant
17:32 *r.* Lot's wife
Gal. 2:10 that we should *r.* the poor
Col. 4:18 *r.* my bonds. Grace be with you
Heb. 8:12 iniquities will I *r.* no more
13: 3 *r.* them that are in bonds

REMEMBERED (REMEMBERETH)

Gen. 8: 1 God *r.* Noah and every living thing
19:29 God *r.* Abraham and sent Lot
30:22 God *r.* Rachel, and God hearkened to her
Ex. 2:24 and God *r.* his covenant with Abraham
Num. 10: 9 ye shall be *r.* before the Lord
Ps. 77: 3 I *r.* God and was troubled
78:39 he *r.* they were but flesh
98: 3 hath *r.* his mercy and truth
119: 52 I *r.* thy judgments of old
119: 55 I have *r.* thy name, O Lord, in the
136: 23 who *r.* us in our low estate
137: 1 we wept when we *r.* Zion
Lam. 1: 9 she *r.* not her last end
Mat. 26:75 Peter *r.* the word of Jesus
Luke 24: 8 and they *r.* his words
John 2:17 disciples *r.* that it was written
Rev. 18: 5 God hath *r.* her iniquities

REMEMBRANCE

1 Ki. 17:18 unto me to call my sin to *r.*
Ps. 6: 5 in death is no *r.* of
Is. 26: 8 to thy name, and to the *r.* of thee
Lam. 3:20 my soul hath them still in *r.*
Mal. 3:16 a book of *r.* was written
Luke 1:54 Israel in *r.* of his mercy
22:19 for you: this do in *r.* of me
John 14:26 bring all things to your *r.*
Acts 10:31 thine alms are had in *r.*
1 Cor. 11:25 ye drink it, in *r.* of me
2 Tim. 1: 6 wherefore I put thee in *r.*

2 Pet. 3: 1 stir up your pure minds by way of *r.*
Jude 1: 5 I will therefore put you in *r.*
Rev. 16:19 Babylon came in *r.* before God

REMIT (REMITTED)
John 20:23 whosesoever sins ye *r.* they are *r.*

REMISSION
Mat. 26:28 shed for many for the *r.* of sins
Mark 1: 4 baptism of repentance for the *r.* of
Luke 1:77 by the *r.* of their sins
Acts 2:38 of Jesus Christ for the *r.* of sins
10:43 shall receive *r.* of sins
Rom. 3:25 his righteousness for the *r.* of sins
Heb. 9:22 without shedding of blood is no *r.*
10:18 where *r.* of these is, there is no

REMNANT
Lev. 2: 3 the *r.* of the meat offering
Deut. 3:11 king of Bashan remained of the *r.* of giants
2 Ki. 19: 4 lift up thy prayer for the *r.*
Ezra 9: 8 leave us a *r.* to escape
Is. 1: 9 left unto us a very small *r.*
10:21 the *r.* shall return, even the *r.* of
Jer. 23: 3 I will gather the *r.* of my flock
Ezek. 6: 8 yet will I leave a *r.*
Rom. 9:27 a *r.* shall be saved
11: 5 *r.* according to the election of grace

REMOVE (REMOVED)
Ps. 39:10 *r.* thy stroke away from me
103: 12 so far hath he *r.* our transgressions
119: 22 *r.* from me reproach and
119: 29 *r.* from me the way of lying
Prov. 4:27 nor the left: *r.* thy foot from evil
10:30 righteous shall never be *r.*
30: 8 *r.* far from me vanity and lies
Eccl. 11:10 *r.* sorrow from thy heart
Is. 30:20 shall not thy teachers be *r.*
Ezek. 36:17 as the uncleanness of a *r.* woman
Mat. 17:20 to yonder place; and it shall *r.*
Luke 22:42 if thou be willing, *r.* this cup
Rev. 2: 5 I will *r.* thy candlestick out of

REND
Is. 64: 1 thou wouldest *r.* the heavens
Joel 2:13 *r.* your heart and not your garments

RENDER
Deut. 32:43 will *r.* vengeance to his adversaries
2 Chr. 6:30 *r.* to every man according to his ways
Job 33:26 he will *r.* to man his righteousness
34:11 work of a man shall he *r.* to
Ps. 116: 12 what shall I *r.* to the Lord
Prov. 26:16 seven men that can *r.* a reason
Hos. 14: 2 we will *r.* the calves of our lips
Mat. 22:21 *r.* therefore unto Caesar the things
Rom. 13: 7 *r.* therefore to all their dues
1 Thes. 5:15 that none *r.* evil for evil

RENEW (RENEWED, RENEWEST, RENEWING)
Ps. 51:10 *r.* a right spirit in me
103: 5 thy youth is *r.* like the eagle's
104: 30 *r.* the face of the earth
Is. 40:31 upon the Lord shall *r.* their strength
Rom. 12: 2 transformed by the *r.* of your mind
2 Cor. 4:16 inward man is *r.* day by day
Eph. 4:23 be *r.* in the spirit of your mind
Tit. 3: 5 the *r.* of the Holy Ghost
Heb. 6: 6 *r.* them again unto repentance

REPAY (REPAID)
Deut. 7:10 he will *r.* him to his face
Job 41:11 that I should *r.* him
Prov. 13:21 to the righteous good shall be *r.*
Is. 59:18 to their deeds accordingly he will *r.*
Rom. 12:19 I will *r.*, saith the Lord

REPENT
Ex. 32:12 *r.* of this evil against my
Num. 23:19 neither the son of man that he should *r.*
Deut. 32:36 shall judge his people and *r.* himself
1 Ki. 8:47 *r.*, and make supplication unto thee
Job 42: 6 I abhor myself and *r.* in dust
Ps. 90:13 let it *r.* thee concerning
135: 14 will *r.* himself concerning
Jer. 18: 8 I will *r.* of the evil I thought
Ezek. 14: 6 *r.* and turn yourselves from your
Jonah 3: 9 if God will turn and *r.*
Mat. 3: 2 *r.* ye, for the kingdom of heaven is
Mark 1:15 *r.* and believe the gospel
6:12 preached that men should *r.*
Luke 13: 3 except ye *r.* ye shall all likewise
16:30 went unto them from dead, they will *r.*
17: 3 if he *r.* forgive him
Acts 2:38 *r.* and be baptized everyone
3:19 *r.* and be converted, that
8:22 *r.* of this thy wickedness
17:30 commandeth all men everywhere to *r.*
26:20 should *r.* and turn to God
Rev. 2: 5 whence thou art fallen, and *r.*
2:16 *r.*; or I will come unto thee
3:19 be zealous therefore, and *r.*

REPENTANCE
Hos. 13:14 *r.* shall be hid from mine eyes
Mat. 3: 8 fruits meet for *r.*
3:11 baptize you with water unto *r.*
9:13 not righteous but sinners to *r.*
Mark 1: 4 and preach the baptism of *r.*
Luke 15: 7 just persons which need no *r.*
24:47 that *r.* and remission of sins be
Acts 5:31 give *r.* to Israel and forgiveness of
11:18 God also to the Gentiles granted *r.*
13:24 preached the baptism of *r.* to all
Rom. 2: 4 goodness of God leadeth to *r.*
11:29 gifts and calling of God without *r.*
2 Cor. 7:10 godly sorrow worketh *r.* to salvation
Heb. 6: 1 not laying again the foundation of *r.*
12:17 found no place of *r.*, though he
2 Pet. 3: 9 that all should come to *r.*

REPENTED (REPENTETH)
Gen. 6: 6 and it *r.* the Lord that he had
Ex. 32:14 the Lord *r.* of the evil which he
Judg. 2:18 it *r.* the Lord because of their groanings
2 Sam. 24:16 the Lord *r.* him of the evil
Jer. 8: 6 no man *r.* him of his wickedness
Mat. 21:29 but afterward he *r.* and went
27: 3 *r.* himself, and brought again the
Luke 15: 7 one sinner that *r.*, more than over

REPORT
Gen. 37: 2 brought unto his father their evil *r.*
Ex. 23: 1 shalt not raise a false *r.*
Num. 13:32 brought up an evil *r.* of the land
Neh. 6:13 they might have matter for an evil *r.*
Is. 53: 1 who hath believed our *r.*
John 12:38 Lord, who hath believed our *r.*
Rom. 10:16 Esaias saith Lord, who hath believed our *r.*
2 Cor. 6: 8 by evil *r.* and good *r.*
Heb. 11: 2 by it the elders obtained a good *r.*

REPROACH (REPROACHED, REPROACHES)
Josh. 5: 9 have I rolled away the *r.* of Egypt
Neh. 1: 3 are in great affliction and *r.*
Job 27: 6 my heart shall not *r.* me
Ps. 15: 3 up a *r.* against his neighbour
69: 7 for thy sake I have borne *r.*
69: 9 *r.* of them that reproached
69:20 *r.* hath broken my heart
Prov. 14:34 sin is a *r.* to any people
18: 3 also contempt, and with ignominy *r.*
Is. 51: 7 fear ye not the *r.* of men
54: 4 not remember the *r.* of thy widowhood
Jer. 31:19 I did bear the *r.* of my youth
Zeph. 3:18 the *r.* of it was a burden
2 Cor. 12:10 I take pleasure in infirmities, in *r.*
Heb. 11:26 esteeming the *r.* of Christ greater riches
13:13 without the camp, bearing his *r.*
1 Pet. 4:14 if ye be *r.* for the name of Christ

REPROBATE (REPROBATES)
Jer. 6:30 *r.* silver shall men call them
Rom. 1:28 God gave them over to a *r.* mind
2 Cor. 13: 6 ye shall know we are not *r.*
2 Tim. 3: 8 corrupt minds, *r.* concerning the faith
Tit. 1:16 unto every good work *r.*

REPROOF
Job 26:11 are astonished at his *r.*
Prov. 1:23 turn you at my *r.*: behold I will
1:25 counsel, and would none of my *r.*
10:17 he that refuseth *r.* erreth
12: 1 he that hateth *r.* is brutish
13:18 he that regardeth *r.* shall be honoured
15: 5 he that regardeth *r.* is prudent
15:31 heareth *r.* of life abideth among the wise
15:32 heareth *r.* getteth understanding
17:10 *r.* entereth more into a wise
29:15 the rod and *r.* give wisdom
2 Tim. 3:16 is profitable for doctrine, for *r.*

REPROVE (REPROVED, REPROVETH)
Ps. 50:21 I will *r.* thee, and set them
105: 14 he *r.* kings for their sakes
141: 5 let him *r.* me, it shall be an
Prov. 9: 7 that *r.* a scorner getteth
9: 8 *r.* not a scorner, lest he
15:12 a scorner loveth not one that *r.*
29: 1 he that being often *r.* hardeneth
Is. 29:21 that *r.* in the gate, and turn aside
Hos. 4: 4 let no man strive nor *r.*
John 16: 8 *r.* the world of sin, righteousness
3:20 lest his deeds should be *r.*
Eph. 5:13 all things that are *r.* are

REPUTATION
Eccl. 10: 1 that is in *r.* for wisdom and honour
Acts 5:34 had in *r.* among all the people
Gal. 2: 2 privately to them which were of *r.*
Phil. 2: 7 made himself of no *r.*, and took

REQUEST (REQUESTS)
Ps. 106: 15 he gave them their *r.*; but sent
Phil. 4: 6 let your *r.* be made known unto God

REQUIRE (REQUIRED)
Gen. 9: 5 hand of every beast will I *r.*
42:22 behold also his blood is *r.*
Deut. 10:12 what doth the Lord *r.*
1 Ki. 8:59 maintain as the matter shall *r.*
1 Chr. 4: 2 it is *r.* in stewards, that
Prov. 30: 7 two things have I *r.* of thee
Is. 1:12 who *r.* this at your hand
Ezek. 3:20 his blood will I *r.* at thine
33: 8 his blood will I *r.* at thine
Mic. 6: 8 what doth the Lord *r.*
Luke 12:20 thy soul shall be *r.* of thee
12:48 of him shall much be *r.*

REQUITE (REQUITING)
Gen. 50:15 will certainly *r.* us all
Deut. 32: 6 do ye thus *r.* the Lord
2 Sam. 16:12 Lord will *r.* me good for his
2 Chr. 6:23 by *r.* the wicked, by recompensing
1 Tim. 5: 4 and to *r.* their parents: for that is

RESERVE (RESERVED, RESERVETH)
Job 21:30 wicked is *r.* to the day of
Jer. 3: 5 will he *r.* his anger for ever
50:20 will pardon them whom I *r.*
Nah. 1: 2 and he *r.* wrath for his enemies
1 Pet. 1: 4 not away, *r.* in heaven for you
2 Pet. 2: 9 and to *r.* the unjust unto the day
Jude 1: 6 *r.* in everlasting chains under

RESIST (RESISTED, RESISTETH)
Zech. 3: 1 at his right hand to *r.* him
Mat. 5:39 I say unto you that ye *r.* not evil
Acts 7:51 ye do always *r.* the Holy Ghost
Rom. 9:19 who hath *r.* his will?
13: 2 therefore *r.* the power *r.* the
2 Tim. 3: 8 so do these *r.* the truth
Heb. 12: 4 have not yet *r.* unto blood
Jas. 4: 6 God *r.* the proud, but giveth grace
4: 7 *r.* the devil, and he will
1 Pet. 5: 5 God *r.* the proud, and giveth grace
5: 9 whom *r.* stedfast in the faith

RESPECT (RESPECTETH)
Gen. 4: 4 Lord had *r.* unto Abel and to his
Ex. 2:25 Israel, and God had *r.* unto them
Lev. 19:15 thou shalt not *r.* the person
26: 9 I will have *r.* unto you
2 Ki. 13:23 and had *r.* unto them, because of his
2 Chr. 19: 7 nor *r.* of persons, nor taking of
Ps. 40: 4 *r.* not the proud, nor such
119: 6 *r.* to all thy commandments

Ps. 138: 6 yet hath he *r.* unto the lowly
Prov. 24:23 not good to have *r.* of persons
Rom. 2:11 there is no *r.* of persons
Eph. 6: 9 neither is there *r.* of persons
Col. 3:25 there is no *r.* of persons
Heb. 11:26 he had *r.* unto the recompence of the
Jas. 2: 1 Lord of glory, with *r.* of persons
2: 9 if ye have *r.* to persons, ye commit
1 Pet. 1:17 who without *r.* of persons

RESPECTER
Acts 10:34 God is no *r.* of persons

REST
Ex. 16:23 the *r.* of the holy sabbath
Deut. 12: 9 as yet come to the *r.* and to the
Ps. 16: 9 my flesh shall *r.* in hope
95:11 they should not enter into my *r.*
125: 3 rod of the wicked shall not *r.*
132: 14 this is my *r.* for ever: here will I
Is. 11:10 his *r.* shall be glorious
30:15 in returning and *r.* shall ye be saved
57: 2 he shall *r.* in their beds
57:20 the troubled sea, when it cannot *r.*
62: 7 give him no *r.* till he establish
Jer. 6:16 ye shall find *r.* for your souls
Mic. 2:10 this is not your *r.*: because it is
Hab. 3:16 I might *r.* in the day of trouble
Acts 9:31 then had the churches *r.* throughout
2 Thes. 1: 7 to you who are troubled *r.* with us
Heb. 4: 9 a *r.* to the people of God
4:10 entered into his *r.*, he also hath
Rev. 14:11 they have no *r.* day nor night
14:13 they may *r.* from their labours

RESTEST (RESTETH)
Prov. 14:33 wisdom *r.* in the heart of him
Eccl. 7: 9 anger *r.* in bosom of fools
Rom. 2:17 art called a Jew, and *r.* in
1 Pet. 4:14 glory and of God *r.* upon you

RESTING
Num. 10:33 search out a *r.* place for them
2 Chr. 6:41 into thy *r.* place, thou, and the ark
Prov. 24:15 spoil not his *r.* place
Is. 32:18 and in quiet *r.* places
Jer. 50: 6 they have forgotten their *r.* place

RESTORE (RESTORED, RESTORETH)
Ps. 23: 3 He *r.* my soul: he leadeth me
51:12 *R.* unto me the joy of thy
69: 4 I *r.* that which I took not away
Luke 19: 8 accusation, I *r.* him fourfold
Gal. 6: 1 *r.* such an one in the spirit

RESTORER
Is. 58:12 the *r.* of paths to dwell in

RESTITUTION
Ex. 22: 3 he should make full *r.*; as if he have
Acts 3:21 until the times of *r.* of all things

RESURRECTION
Mat. 22:23 Sadducees which say that there is no *r.*
Luke 20:36 being the children of the *r.*
John 5:29 done good unto the *r.* of life
11:25 I am the *r.* and the life
Acts 17:18 preached unto them Jesus and the *r.*
23: 8 Sadducees say that there is no *r.*
24:15 there shall be a *r.* of the dead
Rom. 6: 5 together in the likeness of his *r.*
1 Cor. 15:12 there is no *r.* of the dead
Phil. 3:10 and the power of his *r.*, and the
Heb. 6: 2 and of *r.* of the dead, and of
11:35 that they might obtain a better *r.*
Rev. 20: 5 This is the first *r.*

RETURN
Gen. 3:19 till thou *r.* unto the ground
1 Ki. 8:48 *r.* to thee with all their heart
Job 1:21 naked shall I *r.* thither
Ps. 73:10 his people *r.* hither; and waters
116: 7 *r.* unto thy rest, O my soul
Eccl. 12: 7 dust shall *r.* to the earth
Sol. 6:13 *r. r.* O Shulamite; *r. r.*
Is. 10:21 remnant shall *r.*, even the remnant
35:10 the ransomed of the Lord shall *r.*
55:11 shall not *r.* unto me void
Jer. 3:12 *r.*, thou backsliding Israel, saith
4: 1 if thou wilt *r.*, O Israel, saith
5: 3 they have refused to *r.*
15:19 let them *r.* unto thee, but *r.*
Hos. 2: 7 I will go and *r.* to my first husband
5:15 I will go and *r.* to my place
7:16 they *r.*, but not to the Most High
11: 5 *r.* into the land of Egypt
11: 9 I will not *r.* to destroy Ephraim
Mal. 3: 7 *r.* to me, and I will *r.* to
3:18 then shall ye *r.* and discern

RETURNED (RETURNING)
Ps. 35:13 my prayer *r.* into my bosom
78:34 they *r.* and inquired early after God
Is. 30:15 in *r.* and rest shall ye be
Amos 4: 6 yet have ye not *r.* unto me
1 Pet. 2:25 but are now *r.* unto the Shepherd

REVEAL (REVEALED, REVEALETH)
Deut. 29:29 things which are *r.* belong unto us
Job 20:27 heaven shall *r.* his iniquity
Prov. 11:13 talebearer *r.* secrets: but he that is
Is. 22:14 it was *r.* in mine ears
53: 1 whom is the arm of the Lord *r.*
Dan. 2:19 then was the secret *r.* unto Daniel
Amos 3: 7 *r.* his secret to his servants
Mat. 10:26 covered that shall not be *r.*
11:25 and hast *r.* them unto babes
16:17 flesh and blood hath not *r.*
Rom. 1:17 righteousness of God *r.* from faith to
8:18 glory which shall be *r.* in us
1 Cor. 2:10 God hath *r.* them to us
Gal. 1:16 To *r.* his Son in me, that I
2 Thes. 1: 7 when the Lord Jesus shall be *r.*
2: 3 and that man of sin be *r.*; the Son

REVELATION (REVELATIONS)
Rom. 2: 5 wrath and *r.* of the righteous
16:25 according to the *r.* of the mystery
2 Cor. 12: 1 I will come to visions and *r.*
Gal. 1:12 taught it, but by the *r.* of Jesus
Eph. 1:17 the spirit of wisdom and *r.* in the
3: 3 by *r.* he made known unto me the
1 Pet. 1:13 unto you at the *r.* of Jesus Christ
Rev. 1: 1 the *r.* of Jesus Christ, which God

REVENGE (REVENGETH)
Jer. 15:15 *r.* me of my persecutors; take me not
Nah. 1: 2 the Lord *r.* and is furious
2 Cor. 7:11 yea, what zeal, yea, what *r.*
10: 6 readiness to *r.* all disobedience

REVENGER
Num. 35:19 the *r.* of blood himself shall slay
Rom. 13: 4 a *r.* to execute wrath upon him that

REVERENCE
Lev. 19:30 my sabbaths, and *r.* my sanctuary
Ps. 89: 7 to be had in *r.* of all them
Eph. 5:33 wife see that she *r.* her
Heb. 12:28 serve God acceptably with *r.*

REVEREND
Ps. 111: 9 holy and *r.* is his name

REVILE (REVILED)
Ex. 22:28 shalt not *r.* the gods, nor curse the
Mat. 5:11 when men shall *r.* you, and persecute
1 Cor. 4:12 being *r.* we bless; being persecuted
1 Pet. 2:23 when he was *r. r.* not

REVILERS
1 Cor. 6:10 nor drunkards, nor *r.*, nor

REVILINGS
Is. 51: 7 be ye afraid of their *r.*
Zeph. 2: 8 and the *r.* of the children

REVIVE (REVIVED)
Ps. 85: 6 wilt thou not *r.* us again
Is. 57:15 *r.* the spirit of the humble, to *r.*
Hos. 6: 2 after two days will he *r.* us
14: 7 they shall *r.* as the corn, and
Rom. 7: 9 commandment came, sin *r.* and I died
14: 9 Christ both died and rose, and *r.*

REVOLT (REVOLTED, REVOLTING)
Is. 1: 5 ye will *r.* more and more
31: 6 children of Israel have deeply *r.*
Jer. 5:23 hath a *r.* and a rebellious heart

REVOLTERS
Jer. 6:28 they are all grievious *r.*
Hos. 5: 2 And the *r.* are profound to make
9:15 no more: all their princes are *r.*

REWARD
Gen. 15: 1 thy exceeding great *r.*
Deut. 10:17 regardeth not persons, nor taketh *r.*
Ps. 19:11 in keeping them is great *r.*
58:11 there is a *r.* for the righteous
127: 3 fruit of the womb is his *r.*
Prov. 11:18 righteousness shall be sure *r.*
Is. 3:11 *r.* of his hands shall be
Mic. 7: 3 the judge asketh for a *r.*
Mat. 5:12 great is your *r.* in heaven
6: 2 I say unto you, They have their *r.*
6: 4 secret himself shall *r.* thee openly
10:41 shall receive a prophet's *r.*
Rom. 4: 4 is the *r.* not reckoned of
1 Cor. 3: 8 every man shall receive his own *r.*
Col. 2:18 no man beguile you of your *r.*
3:24 receive the *r.* of inheritance
1 Tim. 5:18 labourer is worthy of his *r.*
2 Tim. 4:14 Lord *r.* him according to his works
Heb. 2: 2 received a just recompence of *r.*
2 John 1: 8 but that we receive a full *r.*
Rev. 18: 6 *r.* her as she rewarded you
22:12 I come quickly; and my *r.* is with

REWARDED (REWARDETH)
Ps. 31:23 and plentifully *r.* the proud doer
103: 10 nor *r.* us according to our iniquities
Is. 3: 9 have *r.* evil to themselves

REWARDER
Heb. 11: 6 *r.* of them that diligently seek

RICH
Gen. 13: 2 Abram was very *r.* in cattle
14:23 I have made Abram *r.*
Ex. 30:15 the *r.* shall not give more
Prov. 10: 4 hand of the diligent maketh *r.*
10:22 blessing of the Lord, it maketh *r.*
14:20 but the *r.* hath many friends
18:11 *r.* man's wealth is his strong city
22: 2 *r.* and poor meet together
23: 4 labour not to be *r.*: cease from
28:11 *r.* man wise in his own conceit
28:20 that maketh haste to be *r.* shall
Eccl. 5:12 abundance of the *r.* will not suffer
10:20 curse not the *r.* in thy bedchamber
Jer. 9:23 let not the *r.* man glory in his
Mat. 19:23 *r.* man shall hardly enter into the
Luke 1:53 *r.* he hath sent empty away
6:24 woe unto you that are *r.*
16: 1 certain *r.* man which had
18:23 sorrowful: for he was very *r.*
2 Cor. 6:10 as poor yet making many *r.*
8: 9 though he was *r.* yet for your sakes
Eph. 2: 4 God, who is *r.* in mercy, for his
1 Tim. 6: 9 they that will be *r.* fall into
6:17 charge them that are *r.* in this
6:18 that they be *r.* in good works
Jas. 2: 5 poor of this world *r.* in faith
Rev. 2: 9 thy poverty, (but thou art *r.*)
3:17 because thou sayest, I am *r.*

RICHES
1 Chr. 29:12 both *r.* and honour come of thee
Ps. 39: 6 he heapeth up *r.*, and knoweth not
49: 6 boast themselves in multitude of their *r.*
52: 7 trusted in the abundance of his *r.*
62:10 if *r.* increase, set not your heart
104: 24 the earth is full of thy *r.*
112: 3 wealth and *r.* shall be in his house
Prov. 3:16 in her left hand *r.* and
11: 4 *r.* profit not in the day of wrath
11:28 that trusteth in his *r.* shall fall
13: 8 ransom of man's life are his *r.*
14:24 crown of the wise is their *r.*
23: 5 *r.* certainly make themselves wings
27:24 *r.* are not for ever, nor the
30: 8 give me neither poverty nor *r.*
Jer. 17:11 so he that getteth *r.* and
Mat. 13:22 deceitfulness of *r.*, choke the word
Luke 16:11 to your trust the true *r.*
Rom. 2: 4 despisest thou the *r.*

Rom. 11:12 the fall of them be the *r.* of
2 Cor. 8: 2 unto the *r.* of their liberality
Eph. 1: 7 according to the *r.* of his
2: 7 show exceeding *r.* of grace
Col. 1:27 the *r.* of the glory of this mystery
2: 2 unto all *r.* of the full assurance
1 Tim. 6:17 not trust in uncertain *r.*
Jas. 5: 2 your *r.* are corrupted, and your

RICHLY
Col. 3:16 word of Christ dwell in you *r.*
1 Tim. 6:17 who giveth us *r.* all things to enjoy

RIDE (RIDETH)
Deut. 33:26 who *r.* upon thy heaven
Ps. 45: 4 *r.* prosperously because of truth
66:12 caused men to *r.* over our heads
68: 4 extol him that *r.* upon thy
68:33 that *r.* upon the heavens of heavens
Is. 19: 1 Lord *r.* upon a stiff cloud
Hab. 3: 8 thou didst ride upon thin horses

RIGHT
Gen. 18:25 Judge of all the earth do *r.*
Num. 27: 7 Zelophehad speak *r.*: thou shalt
Deut. 21:17 the *r.* of the firstborn is his
Ezra 8:21 seek of him a *r.* way for
Job 34:23 not lay upon man more than *r.*
Ps. 19: 8 the statutes of the Lord are *r.*
51:10 renew a *r.* spirit within me
119:128 concerning all things to be *r.*
Prov. 4:11 I have led thee in *r.* paths
8: 9 *r.* to them that find knowledge
12: 5 thoughts of the righteous are *r.*
14:12 a way which seemeth *r.* to
21: 2 way of man is *r.* in his own eyes
Is. 30:10 prophesy not unto us *r.* things
Ezek. 18: 5 do that which is lawful and *r.*
Hos. 14: 9 ways of the Lord are *r.*
Amos 3:10 they know not to do *r.*
Mark 5:15 and in his *r.* mind: and they were
Luke 12:57 judge ye not what is *r.*
Acts 4:19 whether it be *r.* in the sight of God
8:21 heart is not *r.* in the sight of
13:10 not cease to pervert *r.* ways
Eph. 6: 1 parents in the Lord: for this is *r.*
2 Pet. 2:15 forsaken the *r.* way, and are gone
Rev. 22:14 have a *r.* to the tree of life

RIGHTLY
2 Tim. 2:15 *r.* dividing the word of truth

RIGHTEOUS
Gen. 7: 1 thee have I seen *r.* before me
18:23 also destroy the *r.* with the wicked
Num. 23:10 let me die the death of the *r.*
Deut. 25: 1 shall justify the *r.* and condemn
Job 4: 7 where were the *r.* cut off?
17: 9 the *r.* shall hold on his way
Ps. 1: 6 Lord knoweth the way of the *r.*
5:12 thou, Lord, wilt bless the *r.*
7:11 God judgeth the *r.* and God is angry
32:11 glad in the Lord and rejoice, ye *r.*
34:17 *r.* cry, and the Lord heareth
34:19 many are the afflictions of the *r.*
37:25 have I not seen the *r.* forsaken
37:29 the *r.* shall inherit the land
55:22 never suffer the *r.* to be moved
58:11 there is a reward for the *r.*
64:10 *r.* shall be glad in the Lord
68: 3 let the *r.* be glad; let them rejoice
92:12 the *r.* shall flourish like a palm tree
97:11 light is sown for the *r.*, and gladness
112: 6 the *r.* shall be in everlasting
125: 3 shall not rest on the lot of the *r.*
145: 17 the Lord is *r.* in all his ways
146: 8 the Lord loveth the *r.*
Prov. 3:32 his secret is with the *r.*
10: 3 the soul of the *r.* to famish
10:21 the lips of the *r.* feed many
10:24 desire of the *r.* shall be granted
10:25 *r.* is an everlasting foundation
10:28 the hope of the *r.* shall be gladness
10:30 the *r.* shall never be removed
10:32 lips of the *r.* know what is acceptable
11: 8 *r.* is delivered out of trouble
11:21 seed of the *r.* shall be delivered
11:28 the *r.* shall flourish as a branch
11:30 fruit of the *r.* is a tree of life
11:31 the *r.* shall be recompensed in
12: 3 root of the *r.* shall not be moved
Prov. 12: 5 the thoughts of the *r.* are *r.*
12: 7 the house of the *r.* shall stand
12:10 *r.* man regardeth the life of his beast
12:12 root of the *r.* yieldeth fruit
12:26 *r.* is more excellent than his
13: 9 the light of the *r.* rejoiceth
13:25 *r.* eateth to the satisfying of his
14:32 *r.* hath hope in his death
15: 6 in the house of the *r.* is
15:19 the way of the *r.* is made plain
15:29 he heareth the prayer of the *r.*
28: 1 the *r.* are bold as a lion
Eccl. 7:16 be not *r.* over much, nor
9: 2 one event to the *r.* and to the wicked
Is. 3:10 say ye to *r.*, it shall be well
41: 2 who raised up the *r.* man from the east
57: 1 the *r.* perisheth, and no man layeth
60:21 thy people also shall be all *r.*
Ezek. 3:20 when a *r.* man doth turn
Mal. 3:18 discern between the *r.* and the
Mat. 9:13 not come to call the *r.*, but
10:41 shall receive the *r.* man's reward
25:46 but the *r.* into life eternal
Luke 1: 6 they were both *r.* before God
18: 9 that they were *r.* and despised
Rom. 3:10 there is none *r.*, no not one
5: 7 scarcely for a *r.* man will one
2 Thes. 1: 5 a token of the *r.* judgment of God
1 Tim. 1: 9 law is not made for a *r.*
Jas. 5:16 fervent prayer of the *r.* man
1 Pet. 4:18 and if the *r.* scarcely be saved
Rev. 22:11 he that is *r.* let him be *r.*

RIGHTEOUSLY
Tit. 2:12 live soberly, *r.*, and godly, in this

RIGHTEOUSNESS
Gen. 15: 6 and he counted it to him for *r.*
Deut. 6:25 it shall be our *r.* if
9: 5 nor for thy *r.*, or for the
33:19 offer sacrifices of *r.*
1 Ki. 8:32 give him according to his *r.*
Job 29:14 I put on *r.* and it clothed
36: 3 and will ascribe *r.* to my Maker
Ps. 11: 7 righteous Lord loveth *r.*
15: 2 walketh uprightly and worketh *r.*
40:10 I have not hid thy *r.* within my
50: 6 heavens shall declare his *r.*
51:14 tongue shall sing aloud of thy *r.*
85:10 *r.* and peace have kissed each other
97: 2 *r.* and judgment are the habitation
106: 3 he that doeth *r.* at all times
106: 31 that was counted unto him for *r.*
Prov. 10: 2 nothing but *r.* delivereth from death
11: 5 *r.* of the perfect shall direct his way
11: 6 *r.* of the upright shall deliver them
11:18 to him that soweth *r.* a sure
11:19 as *r.* tendeth to life; so he that
12:28 in the way of *r.* is life
13: 6 *r.* keepeth him that is upright in
14:34 *r.* exalteth a nation: but sin
15: 9 he loveth him that followeth *r.*
16:12 the throne is established by *r.*
16:31 if it be found in the way of *r.*
Is. 11: 5 *r.* shall be the girdle of his loins
26: 9 inhabitants of the world will learn *r.*
28:17 to line and *r.* to the plummet
32:17 work of *r.* shall be peace
45:24 in the Lord have I *r.* and
46:12 stouthearted, that are far from *r.*
46:13 I bring near my *r.*; it shall not
54:17 their *r.* is of me, saith the Lord
57:12 I will declare thy *r.*, and the works
61: 3 might be called trees of *r.*
61:10 covered me with the robe of *r.*
62: 2 Gentiles shall see thy *r.*, and all
64: 5 that rejoiceth and worketh *r.*
64: 6 and all our *r.* are as filthy rags
Jer. 23: 6 be called THE LORD OUR *R.*
Dan. 4:27 break off thy sins by *r.*
9: 7 O Lord, *r.* belongeth unto thee
9:24 to bring in everlasting *r.*
12: 3 they that turn many to *r.*
Zeph. 2: 3 seek *r.*, seek meekness: it may be
Mal. 4: 2 Sun of *r.* arise with healing
Mat. 3:15 it becometh us to fulfil all *r.*
5: 6 which do hunger and thirst after *r.*
Mat. 5:20 except your *r.* exceed the *r.* of
6:33 God, and his *r.*; and all these
21:32 came unto you in the way of *r.*
Luke 1:75 in holiness and *r.* before
John 16: 8 the world of sin, and of *r.*
Acts 10:35 worketh *r.*, is accepted, wilt thou
13:10 thou enemy of all *r.*
Rom. 1:17 therein is the *r.* of God revealed
3:22 even *r.* of God which is by faith of
3:25 his *r.* for the remission of sins
4: 5 his faith is counted for *r.*
4: 6 man to whom God imputeth *r.*
4:22 it was imputed to him for *r.*
5:18 by the *r.* of one the free gift came
5:21 grace reign through *r.* unto eternal
6:13 members as instruments of *r.*
6:19 members servants to *r.* unto holiness
8: 4 that the *r.* of the law might
9:30 have attained to *r.*, even *r.*, 31.
10: 3 ignorant of God's *r.*, and going about
10: 4 the end of the law for *r.* to every
10: 6 *r.* which is of faith speaketh
10:10 heart of man believeth unto *r.*
14:17 but *r.*, and peace, and joy
1 Cor. 1:30 made unto us wisdom and *r.*
15:34 awake to *r.* and sin not
2 Cor. 5:21 might be made the *r.* of God in him
6: 7 armour of *r.* on the right hand
9:10 increase the fruits of your *r.*
11:15 transformed as ministers of *r.*
Gal. 2:21 if *r.* come by the law, then
3: 6 and it was accounted to him for *r.*
Eph. 6:14 having on the breastplate of *r.*
Phil. 1:11 being filled with fruits of *r.*
3: 6 *r.* which is in the law blameless
3: 9 not mine own *r.* but the *r.* which
1 Tim. 6:11 follow after *r.*, godliness, faith
Heb. 12:11 peaceable fruit of *r.* unto them
Jas. 1:20 man worketh not the *r.* of God
3:18 fruit of *r.* is sown in peace
1 Pet. 3:14 if ye suffer for *r.* sake
2 Pet. 1: 1 through the *r.* of God and our
3:13 new earth, wherein dwelleth *r.*
1 John 2:29 one that doeth *r.* is born of him
Rev. 19: 8 fine linen is the *r.* of saints

RIOT
Tit. 1: 6 not accused or *r.* or unruly
1 Pet. 4: 4 to the same excess of *r.*, speaking
2 Pet. 2:13 it pleasure to *r.* in the daytime

RIOTING
Rom. 13:13 not in *r.* and drunkenness, not in

RIOTOUS
Prov. 23:20 winebibbers; among *r.* eaters of flesh
Luke 15:13 wasted his substance with *r.* living

RIPE
Gen. 40:10 thereof brought forth *r.* grapes
Ex. 22:29 to offer the first of thy *r.* fruits
Num. 18:13 whatsoever is first *r.* in the land
Jer. 24: 2 like the figs that are first *r.*
Hos. 9:10 saw your fathers as the first *r.*
Joel 3:13 the sickle, for the harvest is *r.*
Mic. 7: 1 my soul desired the first *r.* fruit
Nah. 3:12 fig trees with the first *r.* figs
Rev. 14:15 harvest of the earth is *r.*

RIPENING
Is. 18: 5 sour grape is *r.* in the flower

RISE
Sol. 3: 2 I will *r.* now, and go about
Is. 14:21 that they do not *r.*, nor possess the
26:14 deceased, they shall not *r.*
43:17 together, they shall not *r.*
54:17 every tongue that shall *r.* against thee
58:10 then shall thy light *r.* in obscurity
1 Thes. 4:16 dead in Christ shall *r.* first

RISING
Prov. 30:31 king against whom there is no *r.*
Luke 2:34 set for the fall and *r.* again

RIVER (RIVERS)
Ex. 1:22 is born ye shall cast into the *r.*
Job 20:17 he shall not see the *r.*
40:23 he drinketh up a *r.*, and hasteth not
Ps. 36: 8 drink of the *r.* of thy pleasures

Ps. 46: 4 There is a *r.*, the streams whereof
65: 9 enrichest it with the *r.* of God
119:136 *R.* of water run down mine eyes
Prov. 21: 1 of the Lord, as the *r.* of water
Is. 33:21 a place of broad *r.* and streams
48:18 then had thy peace been as a *r.*
66:12 I will extend peace to her like a *r.*
Mic. 6: 7 or with ten thousands of *r.* of oil
John 7:38 belly shall flow *r.* of living water
Rev. 22: 2 on either side of the *r.*

ROAR
Is. 42:13 he shall cry, yea *r.*; he shall
Jer. 25:30 mightily *r.* upon his habitation
Hos. 11:10 *r.*, then the children shall tremble
Joel 3:16 Lord also shall *r.* out of Zion
Amos 1: 2 Lord will *r.* from Zion, and utter

ROB (ROBBED)
Lev. 19:13 defraud thy neighbour neither *r.*
Prov. 22:22 *R.* not the poor, because he is poor
Is. 42:22 this is a people *r.* and spoiled
Mal. 3: 8 Will a man *r.* God? Yet ye have
2 Cor. 11: 8 I *r.* other churches, taking wages of

ROBBER
Job 5: 5 the *r.* swalloweth up their substance
John 10: 1 other way is a thief and a *r.*

ROBBERY
Ps. 62:10 become not vain in *r.*: if riches
Prov. 21: 7 *r.* of the wicked shall destroy
Is. 61: 8 I hate *r.* for burnt offering
Amos 3:10 who store up violence and *r.*
Phil. 2: 6 thought it not *r.* to be equal

ROBE (ROBES)
Is. 61:10 covered me with the *r.* of righteousness
Rev. 7: 9 clothed with white *r.*, and palms in
7:14 and have washed their *r.*

ROCK (ROCKS)
Ex. 17: 6 thou shalt smite the *r.*
Num. 20:11 with his rod he smote the *r.* twice
Deut. 32: 4 He is the *R.*, his work is perfect
Ps. 18: 2 the Lord is my *r.*
31: 3 thou art my *r.* and my fortress
61: 2 lead me to the *r.* that is higher than
62: 2 he only is my *r.* and my salvation
89:26 and the *r.* of my salvation
94:22 God is the *r.* of my refuge
Mat. 7:24 wise man, which built his house on a *r.*
16:18 on this *r.* I will build my church
1 Cor. 10: 4 them: and that *R.* was Christ
Rev. 6:16 said to the mountains and *r.*

ROD
Ex. 4:20 Moses took the *r.* of God
Num. 17: 8 the *r.* of Aaron for the house
Ps. 23: 4 thy *r.* and staff they comfort
125: 3 *r.* of the wicked shall not rest upon
Prov. 13:24 spareth his *r.* hateth his son
23:14 shalt beat him with the *r.*
29:15 *r.* and reproof give wisdom
Ezek. 20:37 cause to pass under the *r.*
Mic. 6: 9 hear ye the *r.* and who hath
7:14 feed thy people with thy *r.*
Rev. 2:27 he shall rule with a *r.* of iron
12: 5 rule all nations with a *r.*

ROOT
Deut. 29:18 among you a *r.* that beareth gall
Job 19:28 seeing the *r.* of the matter
Ps. 52: 5 *r.* thee out of the land of the living
Is. 11:10 there shall be *r.* of Jesse
37:31 take the *r.* downward, and bear fruit
Mat. 3:10 laid to the *r.* of the trees
13: 6 because they had no *r.*, they
Luke 17: 6 be thou plucked up by the *r.*
Rom. 11:16 if the *r.* be holy, so are the
1 Tim. 6:10 love of money is the *r.* of all

ROOTED
Mat. 15:13 not planted, shall be *r.* up
Eph. 3:17 being *r.* and grounded in love
Col. 2: 7 *r.* and built up in him, and

ROSE
Sol. 2: 1 I am the *r.* of Sharon

Is. 35: 1 shall rejoice and blossom as the *r.*

ROYAL
Is. 62: 3 and a *r.* diadem in the hand
Jas. 2: 8 if ye fulfil the *r.* law according
1 Pet. 2: 9 a *r.* priesthood, an holy nation

RUBIES
Job 28:18 Price of wisdom is above *r.*
Prov. 3:15 she is more precious than *r.*
8:11 for wisdom is better than *r.*
31:10 for her price is far above *r.*

RULE (RULETH)
Esth. 9: 1 Jews had *r.* over them that hated them
Ps. 103: 19 his kingdom *r.* over all
Prov. 16:23 he that *r.* his spirit than
17: 2 wise servant shall have *r.* over a
25:28 that hath no *r.* over his own spirit
Hos. 11:12 deceit: but Judah yet *r.* with God
Gal. 6:16 walk according to this *r.*
Phil. 3:16 let us walk by the same *r.*
Col. 3:15 let the peace of God *r.* in
1 Tim. 3: 5 man know not how to *r.* his own house
5:17 elders that *r.* well be counted worthy
Heb. 13: 7 remember them which have *r.* over you
Rev. 12: 5 man child who was to *r.* all

RULER (RULERS)
Mic. 5: 2 unto me that is to be *r.* in Israel
Mat. 25:21 I will make thee *r.* over many things
Rom. 13: 3 *r.* are not a terror to good works
Eph. 6:12 *r.* of the darkness of this world

RUN (RUNNETH)
Gen. 49:22 whose branches *r.* over the wall
Lev. 15: 3 whether his flesh *r.* with his issue
1 Sam. 8:11 some shall *r.* before his chariots
2 Chr. 16: 9 eyes of the Lord *r.* to and fro
Ps. 19: 5 rejoiceth as a strong man to *r.* a race
23: 5 my head with oil; my cup *r.* over
119: 32 I will *r.* the way of thy commandments
Eccl. 1: 7 all the rivers *r.* into the sea
Sol. 1: 4 draw me, we will *r.* after
Is. 40:31 shall *r.* and not be weary
Dan. 12: 4 many shall *r.* to and fro
Rom. 9:16 nor of him that *r.* but of God
Gal. 2: 2 *r.*, or had *r.* in vain
Heb. 12: 1 *r.* with patience the race
1 Pet. 4: 4 *r.* not with them to the same excess

S

SABBATH (SABBATHS)
Ex. 16:29 Lord hath given your the *s.*
20: 8 Remember the *s.* day, to keep it holy
Lev. 19: 3 and his father, and keep my *s.*
23: 3 seventh day is the *s.* of rest
26: 2 Ye shall keep my *s.*, and reverence
Neh. 9:14 known unto them thy holy *s.*
13:18 upon Israel by profaning the *s.*
Is. 56: 2 keepeth the *s.* from polluting it
56: 4 Eunuchs that keep my *s.*
56: 6 everyone that keepeth the *s.*
58:13 call the *s.* a delight, the holy
Ezek. 20:13 my *s.* they greatly polluted
23:38 and have profaned my *s.*
46: 3 in the *s.* and in the new moons
Mat. 12: 5 priests in the temple profane the *s.*
28: 1 end of the *s.*, as it began to dawn
Acts 13:42 preached to them the next *s.*
18: 4 reasoned in the synagogue every *s.*

SACKCLOTH
Gen. 37:34 put *s.* upon his loins, and mourned
Job 16:15 I have sewed *s.* upon my skin
Ps. 30:11 thou hast put off my *s.*, and
35:13 were sick, my clothing was *s.*
Is. 22:12 to baldness and to girding with *s.*
Rev. 11: 3 threescore days, clothed in *s.*

SACRIFICE
Gen. 31:54 then Jacob offered *s.* upon the mount
Ex. 8:25 *s.* to your God in the land
1 Sam. 2:29 wherefore kick ye at my *s.*
1 Sam. 3:14 Eli's house not purged with *s.*
15:22 to obey is better than *s.*
Ps. 50: 5 made covenant with me by *s.*
107: 22 *s.* the sacrifices of thanksgiving
141: 2 up of my hands as the evening *s.*
Prov. 15: 8 *s.* of the wicked is abomination
21: 3 more acceptable to Lord than *s.*
Eccl. 5: 1 than to give the *s.* of fools
Dan. 8:11 by him the daily *s.* was taken away
9:27 cause *s.* and oblation to cease
11:31 take away daily *s.*
Hos. 6: 6 for I desired mercy and not *s.*
Mat. 9:13 I will have mercy, and not *s.*
Mark 9:49 and every *s.* be salted with salt
Rom. 12: 1 present your bodies a living *s.*
Eph. 5: 2 a *s.* to God for a sweetsmelling
Phil. 2:17 offered on the *s.* and service of
4:18 a *s.* acceptable, wellpleasing to God
Heb. 9:26 put away sin by *s.* of himself

SACRIFICED (SACRIFICES)
Ps. 4: 5 offer the *s.* of righteousness
51:17 *s.* of God are a broken spirit
1 Cor. 5: 7 Christ our passover is *s.* for us
Heb. 13:15 offer the *s.* of praise to God
1 Pet. 2: 5 priesthood, to offer up spiritual *s.*

SAD
1 Sam. 1:18 and her countenance was no more *s.*
Ezek. 13:22 whom I have not made *s.*; and
Mark 10:22 he was *s.* at that saying, and went

SADNESS
Eccl. 7: 3 *s.* of the countenance the heart

SAINTS
Deut. 33: 2 came with ten thousands of the *s.*
33: 3 all his *s.* are in thy hand
1 Sam. 2: 9 he will keep the feet of his *s.*
Job 15:15 he putteth no trust in his *s.*
Ps. 16: 3 to the *s.* that are in the earth
50: 5 gather my *s.* together unto me
52: 9 it is good before thy *s.*
89: 5 in the congregation of the *s.*
97:10 he preserveth the souls of his *s.*
116: 15 is the death of his *s.*
Prov. 2: 8 preserveth the way of his *s.*
Dan. 7:18 *s.* of most High shall take
Hos. 11:12 and is faithful with the *s.*
Zech. 14: 5 Lord shall come, and all *s.*
Rom. 1: 7 beloved of God, called to be *s.*
8:27 intercession for the *s.*, according
12:13 to the necessity of the *s.*
15:25 Jerusalem, to minister unto the *s.*
1 Cor. 1: 2 called to be *s.*, with all that
6: 2 that the *s.* shall judge the world
16: 1 concerning the collection for the *s.*
2 Cor. 1: 1 *s.* which are in all Achaia
8: 4 of the ministering to the *s.*
9:12 supplieth the want of the *s.*
Eph. 1: 1 the *s.* which are at Ephesus
3: 8 less than the least of all *s.*
6:18 supplication for all *s.*
Col. 1: 2 to the *s.* and faithful brethren
1 Thes. 3:13 Lord Jesus Christ, with all his *s.*
2 Thes. 1:10 to be glorified in his *s.*
Heb. 6:10 ye have ministered to the *s.*
Jude 1: 14 cometh with ten thousand of his *s.*
Rev. 5: 8 which are the prayers of the *s.*
11:18 to the *s.* and them that fear
13: 7 to make war with the *s.*
14:12 here is the patience of the *s.*
15: 3 thy ways, thou King of *s.*
16: 6 shed the blood of the *s.* and prophets
19: 8 fine linen is the righteousness of *s.*
20: 9 compassed the camp of the *s.*

SALT
Gen. 19:26 she became a pillar of *s.*
Lev. 2:13 offerings thou shalt offer *s.*
Mat. 5:13 ye are the *s.* of the earth: but if
Mark 9:50 Have *s.* in yourselves, and have peace
Col. 4: 6 grace, seasoned with *s.*, that ye may

SALVATION
Ex. 14:13 see the *s.* of the Lord
15: 2 he is become my *s.*: he is my
2 Sam. 23: 5 this is all my *s.*, and all my
2 Chr. 20:17 see the *s.* of the Lord with you

Ps. 3: 8 *s.* belongeth to the Lord
14: 7 that the *s.* of Israel were come out
18: 2 the horn of my *s.*, and my high
27: 1 my light and my *s.*; whom shall I
37:39 *s.* of the righteous is of the Lord
50:23 I will show him the *s.* of God
51:14 thou God of my *s.*, and my tongue
53: 6 *s.* of Israel were come out of Zion
68:20 God is the God of *s.*
85: 9 his *s.* is nigh them that fear him
88: 1 O Lord God of my *s.*, I have cried
89:26 God, and the rock of my *s.*
118: 14 and song, and is become my *s.*
119:155 *s.* is far from the wicked
132: 16 I will also clothe her priests with *s.*
140: 7 Lord, the strength of my *s.*
149: 4 will beautify the meek with *s.*
Is. 12: 2 Behold, God is my *s.*; I will trust
25: 9 be glad and rejoice in his *s.*
26: 1 *s.* will God appoint for walls
33: 2 be our *s.* also in the time
33: 6 thy times, and strength of *s.*
45:17 Lord with an everlasting *s.*
46:13 I will place *s.* in Zion for
52:10 shall see the *s.* of our God
59:16 his arm brought *s.* unto him
59:17 for an helmet of *s.* upon his
60:18 call thy walls *S.*, thy gates
61:10 clothed me with garments of *s.*
62: 1 *s.* thereof as a lamp that burneth
Jer. 3:23 in vain is *s.* hoped for
Lam. 3:26 quietly wait for the *s.* of the Lord
Jonah 2: 9 have vowed *S.* is of the Lord
Mic. 7: 7 I will wait for the God of my *s.*
Hab. 3: 8 thine horses and thy chariots of *s.*
3:18 I will joy in the God of my *s.*
Zech. 9: 9 he is just and having *s.*
Luke 19: 9 this day is *s.* come to this house
John 4:22 worship: for *s.* is of the Jews
Acts 4:12 neither is there *s.* in any
13:26 is the word of this *s.* sent
Rom. 1:16 it is the power of God to *s.*
11:11 through their fall *s.* is come
13:11 now is our *s.* nearer than
2 Cor. 1: 6 it is for your consolation and *s.*
6: 2 behold, now is the day of *s.*
Eph. 6:17 take the helmet of *s.*
Phil. 2:12 work out your own *s.* with
1 Thes. 5: 8 for an helmet, the hope of *s.*
2 Thes. 2:13 from the beginning chosen you to *s.*
2 Tim. 2:10 to obtain *s.* which is in Christ
3:15 able to make thee wise unto *s.*
Tit. 2:11 grace of God that bringeth *s.*
Heb. 1:14 who shall be heirs of *s.*
2: 3 escape, if we neglect so great *s.*
5: 9 he became the author of eternal *s.*
6: 9 things that accompany *s.*, though we
9:28 second time without sin unto *s.*
1 Pet. 1: 5 through faith to *s.*, ready to be
Jude 1: 3 write unto you of common *s.*
Rev. 7:10 *S.* to our God, which sitteth upon
12:10 Now is come *s.*, and strength, and
19: 1 *S.*, and glory, and honour

SANCTIFY

Ex. 13: 2 *s.* unto me all the firstborn
19:10 *s.* them today and tomorrow
31:13 I am the Lord that doth *s.*
Lev. 20: 7 *s.* yourselves therefore and be ye holy
Is. 8:13 *s.* the Lord of hosts himself
Ezek. 38:23 I magnify myself and *s.* myself
Joel 1:14 *s.* ye a fast, call a solemn assembly
2:16 *s.* the congregation, assemble the
John 17:17 *s.* them through thy truth
17:19 for their sakes I *s.* myself
1 Thes. 5:23 very God of peace *s.* you wholly
Heb. 13:12 that he might *s.* the people
1 Pet. 3:15 *s.* the Lord God in your hearts

SANCTIFIED (SANCTIFIETH)

Gen. 2: 3 blessed seventh day and *s.* it
Lev. 10: 3 I will be *s.* in them that
Deut. 32:51 ye *s.* me not in the midst of
Job 1: 5 Job sent and *s.* them and
Is. 5:16 God that is holy shall be *s.*
Jer. 1: 5 I *s.* thee, and I ordained thee
Ezek. 20:41 *s.* in you before the heathen
Mat. 23:17 or the temple that *s.* the gold
John 10:36 him whom the Father hath *s.*
Acts 20:32 among all them which are *s.*
Rom. 15:16 being *s.* by the holy ghost
1 Cor. 1: 2 to them that are *s.* in Christ Jesus
6:11 ye are washed, but ye are *s.*
7:14 unbelieving husband is *s.* by the wife
1 Tim. 4: 5 *s.* by the word of God
Heb. 2:11 they who are *s.* are all of one
10:14 perfected for ever them that are *s.*

SANCTIFICATION

1 Cor. 1:30 righteousness, and *s.*, and redemption
1 Thes. 4: 4 possess his vessel in *s.* and honour
2 Thes. 2:13 chosen you to salvation through *s.*
1 Pet. 1: 2 *s.* of the spirit, unto obedience

SANCTUARY

Ps. 63: 2 seen thee in the *s.*
73:17 I went into the *s.* of God
Is. 8:14 he shall be for a *s.*
Ezek. 11:16 be to them as a little *s.*
Dan. 9:17 thy face to shine upon thy *s.*
Heb. 9: 2 the showbread; which is called the *s.*

SAND

Gen. 22:17 *s.* which is upon the seashore
32:12 thy seed as the *s.* of the sea
Job 6: 3 heavier than the *s.* of the sea
29:18 multiply my days as the *s.*
Is. 10:22 Israel be as the *s.* of the sea
Mat. 7:26 built his house upon the *s.*

SATAN

1 Chr. 21: 1 *S.* stood up against Israel
Job 1: 6 *S.* came also among them
Ps. 109: 6 let *S.* stand at his right
Mat. 4:10 get thee hence, *S.*: for it is
16:23 unto Peter, Get thee behind me *S.*
Luke 10:18 I beheld *S.* as lightning fall
22: 3 then entered *S.* into Judas
Acts 26:18 turn from the power of *S.*
Rom. 16:20 God of peace shall bruise *S.*
1 Cor. 5: 5 deliver such an one to *S.*
7: 5 *S.* tempt you not for your incontinency
2 Cor. 2:11 lest *S.* should get an advantage
11:14 *S.* is linen formed into an angel
12: 7 messenger of *S.* to buffet me
1 Tim. 1:20 I have delivered unto *S.*, that they
Rev. 2: 9 but are the synagogue of *S.*
2:24 have not known the depths of *S.*

SATISFY (SATISFIETH, SATISFIED)

Job 38:27 to *s.* the desolate and waste ground
Ps. 17:15 when I awake *s.* with thy likeness
22:26 The meek shall eat and be *s.*
63: 5 my soul shall be *s.* as with marrow
65: 4 *s.* with the goodness of thy house
90:14 O *s.* us early with thy mercy
91:16 with long life will I *s.* him
103: 5 who *s.* thy mouth with good
107: 9 he *s.* the longing soul and filleth
132: 15 I will *s.* her poor with bread
Prov. 5:19 let her breasts *s.* thee at all times
14:14 good man shall be *s.* from himself
27:20 so the eyes of man are never *s.*
30:15 there are three things never *s.*
Eccl. 5:10 loveth silver shall not be *s.*
Is. 55: 2 labour for that which *s.* not
9:20 and they shall not be *s.*
53:11 see travail of his soul and be *s.*
66:11 be *s.* the with the breasts of her
Jer. 31:14 people shall be *s.* with my goodness
Ezek. 16:28 and yet couldest not be *s.*
Hab. 2: 5 and cannot be *s.*, but gathereth

SATISFACTION

Num. 35:31 shall take no *s.* for the life

SAVE

Gen. 45: 7 *s.* your lives by a great deliverance
50:20 is this day, to *s.* much people alive
Job 22:29 he shall *s.* the humble person
Ps. 6: 4 *s.* me for thy mercies' sake
18:27 wilt *s.* the afflicted people; but
69:35 God will *s.* Zion and build the
72: 4 shall *s.* the children of the needy
72:13 and shall *s.* the souls of needy
Ps. 86: 2 *s.* thy servant that trusteth
86:16 *s.* the son of thine handmaid
109: 31 those that condemn to *s.* him from
118: 25 *s.* now; I beseech thee, O Lord
145: 19 hear their cry and will *s.* them
Prov. 20:22 wait on the Lord, and he shall *s.* thee
Is. 25: 9 waited for him and he will *s.* us
35: 4 he will come and *s.* you
45:20 pray unto a god that cannot *s.*
Jer. 17:14 *s.* me and I shall be saved
Ezek. 3:18 wicked way, to *s.* his life
18:27 he shall *s.* his soul alive
36:29 *s.* you from all your uncleanness
Hos. 14: 3 Asshur shall not *s.* us; we will
Zeph. 3:17 of thee is mighty; he will *s.*
3:19 and I will *s.* her that halteth
Zech. 8: 7 I will *s.* my people from the east
Mat. 1:21 *s.* his people from their sins
8:25 Lord, *s.* us: we perish
16:25 whosoever will *s.* his life shall lose
18:11 Son of man is come to *s.* that which
Mark 3: 4 to *s.* life or to kill? But they
John 12:27 *s.* me from this hour
12:47 judge the world but to *s.* the world
Acts 2:40 *s.* yourselves from this untoward
1 Cor. 1:21 preaching to *s.* them that believe
9:22 that I might by all means *s.* some
1 Tim. 1:15 to *s.* sinners, of whom I am chief
Heb. 7:25 able to *s.* them to the uttermost
Jas. 1:21 word which is able to *s.*
2:14 not works? can faith *s.* him?
5:15 prayer of faith shall *s.* the sick
5:20 shall *s.* a soul from death
1 Pet. 3:21 baptism doth also now *s.* us
Jude 1:23 others *s.* with fear, pulling

SAVED

Ps. 44: 7 thou hast *s.* us from our enemies
80: 3 face to shine, we shall be *s.*
106: 8 *s.* them for his name's sake
Is. 45:17 Israel shall be *s.* in the Lord
45:22 look unto me and be ye *s.*
Jer. 4:14 that thou mayest be *s.*
8:20 is ended, and we are not *s.*
23: 6 In his days, Judah shall be *s.*
Mat. 19:25 saying, who then can be *s.*
24:13 the end, the same shall be *s.*
Mark 16:16 believeth and is baptized shall be *s.*
Luke 1:71 be *s.* from our enemies
7:50 woman, thy faith hath *s.* thee
18:26 heard it said, Who then can be *s.*
18:42 thy sight: thy faith hath *s.* thee
23:35 he *s.* others, let him save himself
John 3:17 world through him might be *s.*
Acts 2:47 daily such as should be *s.*
4:12 none other name whereby we must be *s.*
16:30 what must I do to be *s.*
16:31 thou shalt be *s.*, and thy house
Rom. 5:10 we shall be *s.* by his life
8:24 we are *s.* by hope: but hope that
10: 1 for Israel is that they might be *s.*
11:26 all Israel shall be *s.*: as it is
1 Cor. 1:18 to us which are *s.* it is the power
5: 5 the spirit may be *s.* in the day of
Eph. 2: 5 by grace ye are *s.*
1 Tim. 2:15 she shall be *s.* in childbearing
Tit. 3: 5 according to his mercy he *s.* us
1 Pet. 4:18 if the righteous scarcely be *s.*
Rev. 21:24 nations of them which are *s.*

SAVIOUR

2 Sam. 22: 3 my refuge, my *s.*; thou savest
2 Ki. 13: 5 Lord gave Israel a *s.* so that
Is. 43: 3 I am thy *S.*: I gave Egypt for
43:11 beside me there is no *s.*
45:15 O God of Israel, the *S.*
60:16 am thy *s.* and thy Redeemer
Jer. 14: 8 the *s.* thereof in time of trouble
Hos. 13: 4 there is no *s.* beside me
Luke 1:47 my spirit hath rejoiced in God my *S.*
2:11 a *S.* which is Christ the Lord
Acts 5:31 to be a prince and a *s.*
Eph. 5:23 and he is the *s.* of the body
1 Tim. 1: 1 the commandment of God our *S.*
4:10 who is the *s.* of all men
Tit. 1: 4 Father and the Lord Jesus our *S.*
2:13 God and our *s.* Jesus Christ
3: 4 love of God our *S.* toward man
2 Pet. 1:11 our Lord and *s.* Jesus Christ
2:20 knowledge of the Lord and *S.*
Jude 1:25 only wise God our *S.* be glory

SAVIOURS
Neh. 9:27 thou gavest them *s.* who saved

SAVOUR (SAVOUREST)
Gen. 8:21 and the Lord smelled a sweet *s.*
Ex. 29:18 it is a sweet *s.*, an offering
Lev. 1: 9 by fire, a sweet *s.* unto the Lord
3:16 offering made by fire for a sweet *s.*
Sol. 1: 3 of the *s.* of thy good ointments thy
Mat. 16:23 thou *s.* not the things that be
2 Cor. 2:14 the *s.* of his knowledge by us
2:15 are to God a sweet *s.* of Christ
Eph. 5: 2 sacrifice to God for a sweetsmelling *s.*

SCATTER (SCATTERED, SCATTERETH)
Gen. 49: 7 in Judah, and *s.* them in Israel
Num. 10:35 let thine enemies be *s.*; and let
Prov. 11:24 there is that *s.*, and yet increaseth
Ezek. 34: 5 *s.*, because there is no shepherd
Mat. 9:36 *s.* abroad as sheep, having no shepherd
Luke 1:51 *s.* the proud in the imagination of

SCEPTRE
Gen. 49:10 *s.* shall not depart from Judah
Num. 24:17 *S.* shall rise out of Israel
Ps. 45: 6 *s.* of thy kingdom is a right *s.*
Zech. 10:11 *s.* of Egypt shall depart away
Heb. 1: 8 righteousness is the *s.* of thy kingdom

SCOFF
Hab. 1:10 they shall *s.* at the kings

SCOFFERS
2 Pet. 3: 3 come in the last days of *s.*

SCORN (SCORNEST)
Job 16:20 My friends *s.* me: but mine eye
Ps. 44:13 a *s.* and a derision to them
Prov. 9:12 if thou *s.* thou shalt bear it

SCORNER (SCORNERS)
Prov. 1:22 the *s.* delight in their scorning
9: 8 reprove not a *s.*, lest he hate
14: 6 a *s.* seeketh wisdom and findeth
15:12 *s.* loveth not one that reproveth
19:29 judgments are prepared for *s.*

SCORNFUL
Ps. 1: 1 sitteth in the seat of the *s.*
Prov. 29: 8 *S.* men bring a city into a snare
Is. 28:14 *s.* men, that rule this people

SCRIPTURE (SCRIPTURES)
Dan. 10:21 which is noted in the *s.* of truth
Mat. 22:29 ye do err not knowing the *s.*
John 5:39 Search the *s.*; for in them
Acts 17:11 and searched the *s.* daily
18:24 man, and mighty in the *s.*
Rom. 15: 4 through the comfort of the *s.*
2 Tim. 3:15 thou hast known the holy *s.*
3:16 all *s.* is given by inspiration
2 Pet. 1:20 no prophecy of the *s.* is of
3:16 wrest, as they do also other *s.*

SEA
Ps. 33: 7 gathereth the waters of the *s.* together
72: 8 dominion also from *s.* to *s.*
Prov. 8:29 gave to the *s.* his decree
Is. 48:18 righteousness as the waves of the *s.*
57:20 wicked are like the troubled *s.*
Zech. 9:10 his dominion shall be from *s.* to *s.*
Rev. 4: 6 there was a *s.* of glass
10: 2 set his right foot upon the *s.*
15: 2 a *s.* of glass mingled with fire
21: 1 and there was no more *s.*

SEAL
Sol. 8: 6 Set me as a *s.* upon thine heart
John 3:33 set to his *s.* that God is true
Rom. 4:11 *s.* of the righteousness of the faith
1 Cor. 9: 2 *s.* of my apostleship are ye
Rev. 7: 2 having the *s.* of the living God

SEALED
Job 14:17 my transgression is *s.* up in a
Sol. 4:12 spring shut up, a fountain *s.*
John 6:27 for him hath God the Father *s.*
2 Cor. 1:22 who hath also *s.* us and given the
Eph. 1:13 ye were *s.* with that Holy Spirit
Rev. 5: 1 a book *s.* with seven seals
7: 3 *s.* the servants of our God
7: 4 were *s.* an hundred and forty and four

SEARCH (SEARCHED, SEARCHEST, SEARCHETH)
Num. 10:33 to *s.* out a resting place
1 Chr. 28: 9 the Lord *s.* all hearts
Job 10: 6 iniquity, and *s.* after my sin
Ps. 139: 23 *s.* me, O God, and know
Prov. 2: 4 *s.* for her as for hid treasure
18:17 his neighbour cometh and *s.* him
25:27 men to *s.* their own glory is
Jer. 17:10 I the Lord *s.* the heart
29:13 when ye shall *s.* for me with
Zeph. 1:12 I will *s.* Jerusalem with candles
John 5:39 *s.* the scriptures; for in them ye
Acts 17:11 these *s.* the scriptures daily
1 Cor. 2:10 for the spirit *s.* all things, yea
Rev. 2:23 I am he which *s.* the reins

SEASON (SEASONS)
Gen. 40: 4 and they continued a *s.* in ward
Ex. 13:10 keep this ordinance in his *s.*
Ps. 1: 3 bringeth forth his fruit in his *s.*
Is. 50: 4 know how to speak a word in *s.*
Luke 4:13 he departed from him for a *s.*
John 5:35 willing for a *s.* to rejoice
Acts 1: 7 for you to know the times or *s.*
14:17 and fruitful *s.*, filling our hearts
1 Thes. 5: 1 of times and *s.* brethren ye have
2 Tim. 4: 2 be instant in *s.*, out of *s.*
Heb. 11:25 enjoy the pleasures of sin for a *s.*
1 Pet. 1: 6 greatly rejoice, though now for a *s.*

SEASONED
Col. 4: 6 speech be always with grace *s.*

SECRET (SECRETS)
Gen. 49: 6 come not thou into their *s.*
Job 11: 6 he would show thee the *s.* of wisdom
15: 8 hast thou heard the *s.* of God
29: 4 *s.* of God was on my tabernacle
40:13 and bind their faces in *s.*
Ps. 25:14 *s.* of the Lord is with them that
27: 5 in the *s.* of his tabernacle
44:21 he knoweth the *s.* of the heart
139: 15 when I was made in *s.*, and curiously
Prov. 3:32 his *s.* is with the righteous
9:17 bread eaten in *s.* is pleasant
11:13 A talebearer revealeth *s.*, but he
Dan. 2:28 God in heaven that revealeth *s.*
Amos 3: 7 revealeth his *s.* to his servants
Mat. 6: 4 thine alms may be in *s.*: and thy
John 18:20 in *s.* have I said nothing
Rom. 2:16 God shall judge the *s.* of men by

SECRETLY
John 19:38 but *s.* for fear of the Jews

SEE (SEEN, SEETH)
Ps. 34: 8 O taste and *s.* that the Lord is good
Mat. 5: 8 in heart: for they shall *s.* God
6: 1 before men to be *s.* of them
13:17 which ye *s.* and have not *s.* them
23: 5 their works they do to be *s.* of men
John 1:18 no man hath *s.* God at any time
12:45 he that *s.* me *s.* him that
14: 9 he that hath *s.* me hath *s.* the Father
14:17 because it *s.* him not, neither
14:19 the world *s.* me no more; but ye
16:22 I will *s.* you again, and your heart
20:29 blessed are they that have not *s.* and
2 Cor. 4:18 things which are *s.* are temporal
1 Tim. 6:16 whom no man hath *s.*, nor can *s.*
11: 1 the evidence of things not *s.*
1 Pet. 1: 8 whom not having *s.*, ye love
1 John 1: 1 that which we have *s.* and
3: 2 we shall *s.* him as he is
4:12 no man hath *s.* God at any time
Rev. 1: 7 and every eye shall *s.* him
22: 4 they shall *s.* his face: and his

SEED (SEEDS)
Gen. 1:11 whose *s.* is in itself upon the earth
17: 7 between me and thee and thy *s.*
38: 9 that the *s.* should not be his
Ps. 37:28 *s.* of wicked shall be cut off
69:36 *s.* of his servants shall inherit it
126: 6 bearing precious *s.* shall doubtless
Prov. 11:21 *s.* of righteous shall be
Eccl. 11: 6 in the morning, sow thy *s.*
Is. 1: 4 laden with iniquity, *s.* of evildoers
45:25 all the *s.* of Israel be justified
53:10 see his *s.*, he shall prolong his days
55:10 that it may give *s.* to the sower
Mal. 2:15 he might seek a godly *s.*
Mat. 13:38 good *s.* are the children of the kingdom
Luke 8:11 the *s.* is the word of God
Rom. 9: 8 children of promise are counted for *s.*
9:29 Lord of Sabaoth had left us a *s.*
Gal. 3:16 And to *s.*, as of many; but as
1 John 3: 9 his *s.* remaineth in him

SEEK
Deut. 4:29 thou *s.* him with all thy heart
1 Chr. 28: 9 thou *s.* him, he will be found
2 Chr. 15: 2 be with him: and if ye *s.* him
Ezra 8:21 to *s.* of him a right way
8:22 upon them for good that *s.* him
Job 5: 8 I would *s.* unto God, and unto God
Ps. 9:10 not forsake them that *s.*
10:15 *s.* out his wickedness till thou
63: 1 my God, early will I *s.* thee
69:32 heart shall live that *s.* God
119: 2 blessed are they that *s.* him
119:176 *s.* thy servant, for I do not forget
Prov. 8:17 that *s.* me early shall find
Sol. 3: 2 *s.* him whom my soul loveth
Is. 26: 9 within me will I *s.* thee early
45:19 *s.* ye me in vain: I the Lord
Jer. 29:13 ye shall *s.* me and find
Amos 5: 4 *s.* ye me, ye shall live
Zeph. 2: 3 *s.* righteousness, *s.* meekness
Mal. 2: 7 should *s.* the law at his mouth
2:15 that he might *s.* the godly seed
Mat. 6:33 *s.* ye first the kingdom of God
7: 7 *s.* and ye shall find; knock
Luke 13:24 many will *s.* to enter in
19:10 *s.* and to save that which was lost
John 8:21 ye shall *s.* me and shall die in your
Rom. 2: 7 *s.* for glory and honour and
1 Cor. 10:24 let no man *s.* his own but
Phil. 2:21 all *s.* their own, not the things
Col. 3: 1 *s.* those things which are above
1 Pet. 3:11 let him *s.* peace, and ensue it

SEEKETH (SEEKING)
John 4:23 Father *s.* such to worship
1 Cor. 13: 5 *s.* not her own, is not easily
1 Pet. 5: 8 walketh about *s.* whom he may devour

SELL (SELLETH)
Gen. 25:31 *S.* me this day thy birthright
Prov. 23:23 buy truth and *s.* it not
Mat. 13:44 *s.* all that he hath and buyeth
19:21 go, and *s.* that thou hast

SEND
Ps. 20: 2 *S.* thee help from the sanctuary
43: 3 O *s.* out thy light and
57: 3 he shall *s.* from heaven and
Mat. 9:38 *s.* forth labourers into his harvest
John 14:26 whom the Father will *s.* in my name
16: 7 if I depart I will *s.* him unto
2 Thes. 2:11 God shall *s.* them strong delusion

SENTENCE (SENTENCES)
Deut. 17: 9 show thee the *s.* of judgment
Prov. 16:10 a divine *s.* is in the lips
Eccl. 8:11 because the *s.* is not executed
Dan. 5:12 of dreams, and showing of hard *s.*
2 Cor. 1: 9 we had the *s.* of death in

SEPARATE (SEPARATED)
Gen. 13: 9 *s.* thyself, I pray thee, from me
49:26 him that was *s.* from his brethren
Ex. 33:16 so shall we be *s.*, I and thy
Deut. 29:21 Lord shall *s.* him unto evil
Is. 59: 2 iniquities have *s.* between you and
Acts 13: 2 *s.* me Barnabas and Saul for the work
19: 9 departed from them and *s.* the disciples
Rom. 8:35 who shall *s.* us from love of Christ
8:39 *s.* us from the love of God
2 Cor. 6:17 and be ye *s.*, saith the Lord
Gal. 1:15 who *s.* me from my mother's womb
Heb. 7:26 *s.* from sinners, and made higher

SERAPHIMS
Is. 6: 2 above it stood the s.
6: 6 flew one of the s. unto me

SERPENT (SERPENTS)
Gen. 3: 1 the s. was more subtle
49:17 Dan shall be a s. by the way
Num. 21: 6 Lord sent fiery s. among the people
Prov. 23:32 at last it biteth like a s.
Mat. 7:10 will he give him a s.
10:16 be ye wise as s., harmless as
John 3:14 as Moses lifted up the s. in the
2 Cor. 11: 3 as the s. beguiled Eve through his
Rev. 12: 9 that old s., called the Devil

SERVE
Deut. 10:20 him thou shalt s., and to him
11:13 s. him with all your heart
13: 4 shall s. him, and cleave
Josh. 22: 5 s. him with all your heart
24:14 fear the Lord, s. him
24:15 choose you this day whom ye will s.
1 Sam. 12:20 s. the Lord with all your heart
1 Chr. 28: 9 s. him with a perfect heart
Job 21:15 Almighty that we should s. him
Ps. 2:11 s. Lord with fear, rejoice
Mat. 6:24 ye cannot s. God and mammon
Luke 1:74 s. him without fear in
12:37 will come forth and s. them
John 12:26 if any man s. me let him
Acts 6: 2 leave the word of God and s. the tables
27:23 whose I am, and whom I s.
Rom. 1: 9 whom I s. with my spirit
7: 6 we should s. in newness of spirit
7:25 I myself s. the law of God
16:18 they s. not the Lord Jesus Christ
Gal. 5:13 but by love s. one another
Col. 3:24 for ye s. the Lord Christ
1 Thes. 1: 9 to s. the living and true God
Heb. 9:14 from dead works to s. the living God
12:28 whereby we may s. God acceptably
Rev. 7:15 s. him day and night in his temple

SERVANT (SERVANTS)
Ezra 5:11 are the s. of the God of heaven
Is. 24: 2 with the s. so with his master
42: 1 behold my s. whom I uphold
49: 3 thou art my s., O Israel, in
52:13 my s. shall deal prudently
Dan. 3:26 ye s. of the most high God
Mat. 20:27 among you, let him be your s.
25:21 well done, good and faithful s.
John 8:34 committeth sin is the s. of sin
13:16 s. not greater than the lord
Acts 16:17 s. of the most high God
Rom. 6:16 yield yourselves s. to obey
6:17 ye were the s. of sin
6:18 ye became s. of righteousness
1 Cor. 7:21 art thou called, being a s.
7:23 be not ye the s. of men
9:19 have I made myself a s. to all
Gal. 1:10 should not be the s. of Christ
Phil. 1: 1 the s. of Jesus Christ, to all the
2: 7 took on him the form of a s.
2 Tim. 2:24 the s. of the Lord must not strive
1 Pet. 2:16 but as the s. of God
2 Pet. 2:19 themselves are the s. of corruption
Rev. 7: 3 we have sealed the s. of our God
22: 3 and his s. shall serve him

SERVICE
Jer. 22:13 useth his neighbour's s. without
Rom. 12: 1 which is your reasonable s.

SERVING
Luke 10:40 Martha was cumbered about much s.
Acts 20:19 s. the Lord with all humility
26: 7 twelve tribes instantly s. God
Rom. 12:11 fervent in spirit; s. the Lord
Tit. 3: 3 s. divers lusts and pleasures

SETTLE (SETTLED)
Luke 21:14 S. it therefore in your hearts
Col. 1:23 in faith grounded and s.
1 Pet. 5:10 stablish, strengthen, s. you

SEVERITY
Rom. 11:22 the goodness and s. of God

SHADE
Ps. 121: 5 the Lord is thy s. upon thy

SHADOW (SHADOWS)
1 Chr. 29:15 days on the earth are as a s.
Job 8: 9 days upon earth are a s.
Ps. 17: 8 under the s. of thy wings
57: 1 in the s. of thy wings
109: 23 I am gone like the s. when it
144: 4 his days are as a s. that passeth
Eccl. 8:13 his days which are as a s.
Sol. 2: 3 I sat down under his s. with
Is. 4: 6 tabernacle for a s. in the daytime
32: 2 as the s. of the great rock
49: 2 in the s. of his hand hath he hid
Jer. 6: 4 s. of the evening are stretched
Acts 5:15 the s. of Peter passing by
Jas. 1:17 no variableness, neither s. of

SHAKE (SHAKEN)
Hag. 2: 7 I will s. all nations and
2:21 I will s. the heavens and
Mat. 10:14 s. off the dust of your feet
11: 7 a reed s. with the wind
Luke 6:38 measure, pressed down and s. together
Heb. 12:27 things which cannot be s.

SHAME
Ex. 32:25 made them naked to their s.
1 Sam. 20:34 his father had done him s.
2 Sam. 13:13 whither shall I cause my s. to go
Ps. 119: 31 O Lord, put me not to s.
Prov. 3:35 s. shall be the promotion of fools
11: 2 when pride cometh, then cometh s.
14:35 is against him that causeth s.
18:13 it is folly and s. unto him
25: 8 neighbor hath put thee to s.
Is. 22:18 thy glory shall be the s.
50: 6 I hid not my face from s.
Hos. 4: 7 change their glory to s.
Zeph. 3: 5 the unjust knoweth no s.
Acts 5:41 worthy to suffer s. for his
Heb. 12: 2 endured the cross, despising the s.
Rev. 3:18 s. of thy nakedness do not
16:15 naked, and they see his s.

SHAMEFACEDNESS
1 Tim. 2: 9 apparel, with s. and sobriety

SHARP (SHARPER)
Is. 41:15 a new s. threshing instrument
49: 2 my mouth like a s. sword
Mic. 7: 4 upright is s. then a thorn hedge
Heb. 4:12 s. then any twoedged sword
Rev. 1:16 went a s. two edged sword

SHARPENETH
Job 16: 9 s. his eyes upon me
Prov. 27:17 Iron s. iron; so a man

SHARPLY
Judg. 8: 1 they did chide with him s.
Tit. 1:13 Wherefore, rebuke them s.

SHARPNESS
2 Cor. 13:10 being present I should use s.

SHED
Mat. 26:28 which is s. for many for the
Rom. 5: 5 love of God is s. abroad
Tit. 3: 6 Which he s. on us abundantly

SHEEP
Ps. 44:22 are counted as s. for slaughter
49:14 s. they are laid in the grave
78:52 people to go forth like s.
79:13 s. of thy pasture will give thee
95: 7 pasture, and the s. of his hand
100: 3 people, and the s. of his pasture
119:176 gone astray like a lost s.
Is. 53: 6 all we like s. have gone astray
Zech. 13: 7 smite the shepherd, and the s. shall
Mat. 9:36 as s. having no shepherd
10: 6 to the lost s. of the house of Israel
18:12 If a man have an hundred s.
25:32 divideth his s. from the goats
John 10:27 My s. hear my voice
21:16 unto him, feed my s.
1 Pet. 2:25 were as s. going astray

SHEPHERD
Gen. 46:34 every s. is an abomination
49:24 the s., the stone of Israel
Num. 27:17 as sheep that have no s.
1 Ki. 22:17 as sheep that have no s.
Ps. 23: 1 the Lord is my s.' I shall
80: 1 give ear, O S. of Israel
Ezek. 34: 5 were scattered because there is no s.
34:12 s. seeketh out his flock
34:23 set up one s. over them, and
37:24 they all shall have one s.
Zech. 13: 7 awake, O sword, against my s.
Mark 6:34 as sheep not having a s.
John 10:11 I am the good s.: the good s.
Heb. 13:20 Lord Jesus, that great s.
1 Pet. 2:25 returned unto the S. and bishop
5: 4 when the chief S. shall appear

SHEPHERDS (SHEPHERDS')
Ex. 2:17 s. came and drove them away
Sol. 1: 8 feed thy kids before the s. tents
Ezek. 34: 2 prophesy against the s. of Israel
34: 7 ye s., hear the word of the Lord
Mic. 5: 5 raise against him seven s.

SHIELD
Gen. 15: 1 I am thy s., and thy exceeding
Deut. 33:29 Lord the s. of thy help
Ps. 3: 3 thou, O Lord art a s. for me
18:35 given me the s. of thy salvation
33:20 he is our help and our s.
59:11 bring them down, O Lord our s.
115: 9 he is their help and their s.
Eph. 6:16 above all, taking the s. of faith

SHINE
Num. 6:25 Lord make his face s. upon thee
Job 10: 3 s. on the counsel of the wicked
22:28 light shall s. upon thy ways
37:15 the lights of his cloud to s.
Ps. 31:16 face to s. upon thy servant
Eccl. 8: 1 man's wisdom maketh his face s.
Mat. 5:16 let your light so s. before
13:43 righteous s. forth as the sun
2 Cor. 4: 6 who commanded light to s.
Phil. 2:15 among whom ye s. as lights

SHIPWRECK
2 Cor. 11:25 thrice I suffered s.
1 Tim. 1:19 concerning faith have made s.

SHORT
Num. 11:23 Lord's hand waxed s.
Ps. 89:47 remember how s. my time is
Rom. 3:23 and come s. of the glory of God

SHORTENED
Ps. 102: 23 the way; he s. my days
Prov. 10:27 years of the wicked shall be s.
Is. 50: 2 is my hand s. at all, that it
Mat. 24:22 except those days be s.

SHOUT
Num. 23:21 the s. of a king is among them
Ps. 47: 5 God is gone up with a s.
Is. 12: 6 s., thou inhabitant of Zion
44:23 s., ye lower parts of the earth
Zeph. 3:14 s., Oh Israel; be glad
Zech. 9: 9 s., oh daughter of Jerusalem
1 Thes. 4:16 Lord shall descend with a s.

SHOW (SHOWETH, SHOWING)
Ps. 4: 6 who will s. us any good?
16:11 thou wilt s. me the path
39: 6 man walketh in a vain s.
91:16 I will s. him my salvation
92:15 to s. that the Lord is upright
Luke 20:47 for a s. make long prayers
John 5:20 and s. him all things
1 Cor. 11:26 s. the Lord's death till he come
Col. 2:23 things have indeed a s. of wisdom
Tit. 2: 7 s. thyself a pattern of good works
1 Pet. 2: 9 s. forth the praises of him
Rev. 22: 6 sent his angel to s. to his servants

SHUT (SHUTTETH)
Deut. 32:36 there is none s. up or left
1 Sam. 6:10 s. up their calves at home
Is. 22:22 shall s., and he shall s.
Mat. 23:13 ye s. up the kingdom of heaven
Gal. 3:23 s. up unto the faith which
Rev. 3: 7 that openeth, and no man s.

SICK
Sol. 2: 5 apples: for I am s. of love
5: 8 tell him, that I am s. of love
Is. 1: 5 whole head is s. and whole heart
John 11: 1 a certain man was s. named Lazarus
Jas. 5:14 is any s. among you? let him
5:15 prayer of faith shall save the s.

SICKLY
1 Cor. 11:30 many are weak and s. among you

SICKNESS (SICKNESSES)
Ex. 23:25 I will take s. away
Mat. 8:17 infirmities, and bare our s.

SIFT
Is. 30:28 to *s.* the nations with a sieve
Amos 9: 9 I will *s.* the house of Israel
Luke 22:31 that he may *s.* you as wheat

SIGHT
Ex. 3: 3 and see this great *s.*
2 Cor. 5: 7 we walk by faith, not by *s.*

SIGN (SIGNS)
Ex. 4:17 wherewith thou shalt do *s.*
Is. 8:18 Lord hath given me are for *s.*
Rom. 4:11 received the *s.* of circumcision
15:19 Through mighty *s.* and wonders

SILENT
1 Sam. 2: 9 wicked shall be *s.* in darkness
Ps. 28: 1 be not *s.* to me: lest, if thou
30:12 praise to thee, and not be *s.*

SILENCE
Ps. 31:18 lying lips be put to *s.*
50:21 hast thou done, and I kept *s.*
83: 1 Keep not thou *s.*, O God
Jer. 8:14 God hath put us to *s.*
Amos 5:13 the prudent shall keep *s.*
1 Cor. 14:34 Let your women keep *s.* in the
1 Tim. 2:12 over the man, but to be in *s.*
1 Pet. 2:15 ye may put to *s.* the ignorance
Rev. 8: 1 there was *s.* in heaven

SIMPLE
Ps. 19: 7 sure, making wise the *s.*
116: 6 Lord preserveth the *s.*
119:130 giveth understanding to the *s.*
Prov. 1: 4 to give subtlety to the *s.*
1:32 the turning away of the *s.*
8: 5 O ye *s.*, understand wisdom
9:13 she is *s.*, and knoweth nothing
14:15 the *s.* believeth every word: but the
14:18 The *s.* inherit folly: but the prudent
21:11 is punished, the *s.* is made wise
Rom. 16:18 deceive the hearts of the *s.*
16:19 which is good, and *s.* concerning evil

SIN
Gen. 4: 7 doest not well, *s.* lieth at the door
Job 10: 6 iniquity, and searchest after my *s.*
Ps. 4: 4 stand in awe and *s.* not
32: 1 is forgiven, whose *s.* is covered
32: 5 I acknowledged my *s.* unto thee
38:18 I will be sorry for my *s.*
51: 3 my *s.* is ever before me
51: 5 in *s.* did my mother conceive me
Prov. 14:34 *s.* is a reproach to any
Is. 30: 1 that they may add *s.* to *s.*
53:10 make his soul an offering for *s.*
53:12 and he bare the *s.* of many
John 1:29 taketh away the *s.* of the world
5:14 *s.* no more lest a worse thing
Rom. 5:12 by one man *s.* entered into the world
6:14 *s.* shall not have dominion
7: 9 *s.* revived, and I died
7:13 but *s.*, that it might appear *s.*
7:14 I am carnal, sold under *s.*
7:17 but *s.* that dwelleth in me
7:25 with the flesh the law of *s.*
8: 2 made me free from the law of *s.*
2 Cor. 5:21 him to be *s.* for us, who knew no *s.*
Eph. 4:26 be ye angry and *s.* not
Jas. 1:15 lust bringeth forth *s.*, and *s.*
1 Pet. 2:22 who did no *s.*, neither was guile
1 John 1: 8 if we say we have no *s.*
2: 1 ye *s.* not; if any man *s.* we have
3: 9 he cannot *s.* because he is born of God
5:16 there is *s.* unto death

SINS
Josh. 24:19 your transgressions, nor your *s.*
Ps. 19:13 thy servant from presumptuous *s.*
90: 8 our secret *s.* in the light
103: 10 dwelt with us after our *s.*
Is. 43:25 and will not remember thy *s.*
59: 2 your *s.* have hid his face
59:12 our *s.* testify against us
Jer. 5:25 *s.* have withholden good things
Ezek. 33:16 none of his *s.* that he hath committed
Dan. 9:16 for our *s.*, and for the iniquities
9:24 to make an end of *s.*
John 8:21 shall die in your *s.*: whither I go
1 Cor. 15: 3 Christ died for our *s.*
15:17 ye are yet in your *s.*
Gal. 1: 4 gave himself for our *s.*
1 Tim. 5:22 partaker of other men's *s.*
2 Tim. 3: 6 silly women laden with *s.*
Heb. 1: 3 had by himself purged our *s.*
1 Pet. 2:24 bare our *s.* in his own body
1 John 2: 2 he is the propitiation for our *s.*
Rev. 1: 5 and washed us from our *s.*

SINNED (SINNETH)
Ex. 9:27 I have *s.* this time: the Lord
32:33 whosoever hath *s.* against me, him
Num. 22:34 angel of the Lord, I have *s.*
Josh. 7:20 I have *s.* against the Lord God
Judg. 10:10 We have *s.* against thee
2 Sam. 12:13 I have *s.* against the Lord
Job 1:22 in all this Job *s.* not
33:27 I have *s.* and perverted
Ps. 51: 4 thee only have I *s.*, and done this evil
106: 6 we have *s.* with our fathers
Prov. 8:36 but he that *s.* against me wrongeth
Eccl. 7:20 man that doeth good, and *s.* not
Is. 42:24 he against whom we have *s.*
Jer. 3:25 we have *s.* against the Lord
Lam. 1: 8 Jerusalem hath grievously *s.*
5:16 woe unto us, that we have *s.*
Ezek. 18: 4 soul that *s.* it shall die
Dan. 9: 5 We have *s.*, and have committed iniquity
Mic. 7: 9 because I have *s.* against him
Mat. 27: 4 *s.* in that I have betrayed
Luke 15:18 Father, I have *s.* against heaven
15:21 I have *s.* against heaven
Rom. 2:12 many as *s.* without the law
3:23 all have *s.* and come short
1 John 1:10 if we say we have not *s.*
5:18 whosoever is born of God *s.* not

SINNER (SINNERS)
Gen. 13:13 wicked and *s.* before the Lord
Ps. 1: 1 nor standeth in the way of *s.*
25: 8 therefore will he teach *s.* in the way
Eccl. 7:26 the *s.* shall be taken by her
9:18 one *s.* destroyeth much good
Is. 33:14 the *s.* in Zion are afraid
Mat. 9:13 I am not come to call righteous, but *s.*
Luke 13: 2 were *s.* above all the Galilaeans
13: 4 think ye that they were *s.*
15: 7 joy in heaven over one *s.* that
18:13 God be merciful to me a *s.*
John 9:31 we know that God heareth not *s.*
Rom. 5: 8 while we were yet *s.* Christ died
5:19 disobedience many were made *s.*
Gal. 2:15 and not the *s.* of the Gentiles
1 Tim. 1:15 came into world to save *s.*
Heb. 7:26 separate from *s.*, and made higher
Jas. 4: 8 cleanse your hands, ye *s.*
5:20 converteth the *s.* from the error
1 Pet. 4:18 shall the ungodly and the *s.* appear
Jude 1:15 speeches which ungodly *s.* have spoken

SINCERE
Phil. 1:10 that ye may be *s.* and without
1 Pet. 2: 2 desire the *s.* milk of the word

SINCERITY
Josh. 24:14 serve him in *s.* and in truth
1 Cor. 5: 8 with the unleavened bread of *s.*
2 Cor. 1:12 in simplicity and godly *s.* we have
8: 8 to prove the *s.* of your love
Eph. 6:24 that love our Lord Jesus Christ in *s.*
Tit. 2: 7 showing uncorruptness, gravity, *s.*

SINEW (SINEWS)
Job 10:11 fenced me with bones and *s.*
Is. 48: 4 thy neck is an iron *s.*

SING
Ex. 15: 1 I will *s.* unto the Lord
15:21 *S.* ye to the Lord for he hath
Judg. 5: 3 I will *s.* praise to the Lord
1 Chr. 16:23 *S.* unto the Lord all the earth
Job 29:13 I caused the widows heart to *s.*
Ps. 9:11 *S.* praises to the Lord which
27: 6 I will *s.*, yea, I will *s.*
30: 4 *S.* unto the Lord O ye saints
47: 7 of all the earth: *s.* ye praises
57: 7 I will *s.* and give praise
68: 4 *s.* unto God, *s.* praises to his
92: 1 *s.* praises unto thy name, O most
95: 1 let us *s.* unto the Lord
101: 1 I will *s.* of mercy and judgment
135: 3 *s.* praises unto his name; for it is
144: 9 I will *s.* a new song unto thee
145: 7 and shall *s.* of thy righteousness
147: 1 it is good to *s.* praises
147: 7 *S.* unto the Lord with thanksgiving
Prov. 29: 6 the righteous doth *s.* and rejoice
Is. 5: 1 I will *s.* to my wellbeloved
12: 5 *S.* unto the Lord; for he hath
35: 6 and the tongue of the dumb *s.*
65:14 my servants shall *s.* for joy
1 Cor. 14:15 I will *s.* with the spirit
Jas. 5:13 is any merry? let him *s.*

SINGING
Eph. 5:19 *s.* and making melody in your heart

SINGLE
Mat. 6:22 therefore thine eye be *s.*
Luke 11:34 when thine eye is *s.*, thy whole

SINGLENESS
Acts 2:46 with gladness and *s.* of heart
Eph. 6: 5 trembling, in *s.* of your heart
Col. 3:22 in *s.* of heart, fearing God

SKIN (SKINS)
Job 2: 4 *s.* for *s.*, yea all that a man
10:11 clothed me with *s.* and flesh
19:26 after my *s.*, worms destroy this body
Jer. 13:23 Can the Ethiopian change his *s.*
Heb. 11:37 in sheep *s.* and goat *s.*

SKIP (SKIPPED, SKIPPING)
Ps. 29: 6 them also to *s.* like a calf
114: 4 mountains *s.* like rams, and the
Sol. 2: 8 upon the mountains, *s.* upon the hills

SLACK (SLACKED)
Deut. 7:10 will not be *s.* to him that hateth
Prov. 10: 4 poor that dealeth with a *s.* hand
Hab. 1: 4 Therefore, the law is *s.*
Zeph. 3:16 Let not thine hands be *s.*
2 Pet. 3: 9 The Lord is not *s.* concerning

SLAY (SLAIN)
Lev. 14:13 he shall *s.* the lamb in the place
Job 13:15 Though he *s.* me, yet will I
Ps. 139: 19 thou wilt *s.* the wicked
Eph. 2:16 having *s.* in his flesh the enmity
Rev. 5: 9 wast *s.* and hast redeemed
13: 8 of the Lamb *s.* from the foundation

SLEEP
Gen. 2:21 caused a deep *s.* to fall upon
15:12 a deep *s.* fell upon Abraham
1 Sam. 26:12 a deep *s.* from the Lord
Job 4:13 deep *s.* falleth on men
Ps. 76: 6 are cast into a dead *s.*
90: 5 they are as a *s.*: in the morning
127: 2 he giveth his beloved *s.*
132: 4 will not give *s.* to mine eyes
Prov. 3:24 and thy *s.* shall be sweet
6: 4 give not *s.* to thine eyes, nor
19:15 Slothfulness casteth into a deep *s.*
20:13 love not *s.* lest thou come to poverty
Eccl. 5:12 *s.* of the labouring man is sweet
Sol. 5: 2 I *s.* but my heart waketh
Is. 29:10 upon you the spirit of deep *s.*
Jer. 31:26 beheld: and my *s.* was sweet to me
51:39 *s.* a perpetual *s.*, and not wake
Luke 9:32 with him were heavy with *s.*
Rom. 13:11 time to awake out of *s.*
1 Cor. 11:30 sickly among you, and many *s.*
15:51 we shall not all *s.* but shall
1 Thes. 4:14 them also which *s.* in Jesus died
5: 6 let us not *s.* as others; but
5: 7 they that *s.* *s.* in the night
5:10 whether we wake or *s.* we should

SLEEPEST (SLEPT)
Ps. 3: 5 I laid me down and *s.*; I awaked
76: 5 they have *s.* their sleep: and none
1 Cor. 15:20 firstfruits of them that *s.*
Eph. 5:14 he saith, awake, thou that *s.*

SLING
1 Sam. 25:29 them shall he *s.* out as out of
Jer. 10:18 I will *s.* out the inhabitants

SLIP (SLIPPETH)
Ps. 18:36 under me, that my feet did not *s.*
94:18 I said, My foot *s.*; thy mercy
Heb. 2: 1 at any time we should let them *s.*

SLIPPERY
Ps. 35: 6 Let their way be dark and *s.*
73:18 thou didst send them into *s.* places
Jer. 23:12 unto them as *s.* ways in the darkness

SLOTHFUL (SLOTHFULNESS)
Prov. 12:24 but the *s.* shall be under tribute
12:27 *s.* man roasteth not that which he
15:19 way of the *s.* man is as a hedge of
18: 9 *s.* in his work is the brother to
19:15 *s.* casteth into a deep sleep
21:25 desire of the *s.* killeth him
24:30 I went by the field of the *s.*
26:14 door turneth on hinges, so doth the *s.*
Heb. 6:12 be not *s.* but followers of them

SLOW
Prov. 14:29 He that is *s.* to wrath is of great
Luke 24:25 fools *s.* of heart to believe
Jas. 1:19 *s.* to speak, *s.* to wrath

SLUGGARD
Prov. 6: 6 Go to the ant, thou *s.*
6: 9 how long wilt thou sleep, O *s.*
13: 4 the soul of the *s.* desireth
20: 4 *s.* will not plow by reason
26:16 *s.* is wiser in his own conceit

SLUMBER (SLUMBERED, SLUMBERETH)
Ps. 132: 4 mine eyes, or *s.* to mine eyelids
Mat. 25: 5 tarried, they all *s.* and
Rom. 11: 8 given them the spirit of *s.*
2 Pet. 2: 3 not, and their damnation *s.* not

SMITE (SMITEST, SMITTEN)
Deut. 28:22 The Lord shall *s.* thee with a
Ps. 141: 5 let the righteous *s.* me; it shall
Is. 53: 4 him stricken, *s.* of God, and
Jer. 18:18 let us *s.* him with the tongue
Hos. 6: 1 hath *s.* and he will bind us up
Mat. 5:39 *s.* thee on thy right cheek
John 18:23 but if well, why *s.* thou me

SMOKE (SMOKING)
Gen. 19:28 the *s.* of the country went up
Ex. 19:18 Sinai was altogether on a *s.*
Deut. 29:20 his jealousy shall *s.* against
Ps. 74: 1 why doth thine anger *s.* against
Is. 42: 3 *s.* flax shall he not quench
Rev. 14:11 *s.* of their torment ascendeth

SNARE (SNARES)
Ex. 23:33 it will surely be a *s.*
Judg. 2: 3 gods shall be a *s.* unto you
Ps. 11: 6 on the wicked he will rain *s.*
18: 5 the *s.* of death prevented me
69:22 let their table become a *s.*
91: 3 deliver thee from the *s.* of
119:110 wicked have laid a *s.* for me
124: 7 *s.* is broken, and we are escaped
Prov. 13:14 depart from the *s.* of death
29:25 fear of man bringeth a *s.*: but whoso
2 Tim. 2:26 out of the *s.* of the devil

SNOW
Ps. 51: 7 shall be whiter than *s.*
68:14 it was white as *s.* in Salmon
Is. 1:18 they shall be as white as *s.*
Dan. 7: 9 did sit, whose garment was white as *s.*
Mat. 28: 3 lightning, and his raiment white as *s.*
Rev. 1:14 white like wool, as white as *s.*

SOBER
2 Cor. 5:13 whether we be *s.*, it is for you
1 Thes. 5: 6 let us watch and be *s.*
1 Tim. 3: 2 vigilant, *s.*, of good behavior
3:11 wives be grave, not slanderers, *s.*
Tit. 1: 8 *s.*, just, holy, temperate
2: 2 that the aged men be *s.*, grave
2: 4 teach young women to be *s.*
1 Pet. 1:13 up the loins of your mind, be *s.*
4: 7 be ye therefore *s.* and watch unto prayer
5: 8 be *s.*, be vigilant: because your

SOBERLY
Rom. 12: 3 but to think *s.*, according as God
Tit. 2:12 worldly lusts, we should live *s.*

SOBERNESS
Acts 26:25 forth the words of truth and *s.*

SOFT
Job 23:16 for God maketh my heart *s.*
Prov. 15: 1 *s.* answer turneth away wrath: but
25:15 and a *s.* tongue breaketh the bone
Mat. 11: 8 to see? A man clothed in *s.* raiment

SOJOURN (SOJOURNING)
Gen. 12:10 went down into Egypt to *s.* there
Ex. 12:40 the *s.* of the children of Israel
Ps. 120: 5 I *s.* in Mesech, that I dwell
1 Pet. 1:17 the time of your *s.* here in fear

SOJOURNER (SOJOURNERS)
Lev. 25:23 are strangers and *s.* with me
1 Chr. 29:15 strangers before thee, and *s.*
Ps. 39:12 stranger with thee, and a *s.*

SOLD
1 Ki. 21:20 hast *s.* thyself to work evil
2 Ki. 17:17 *s.* themselves to do evil
Rom. 7:14 I am carnal, *s.* under sin

SOLDIER
2 Tim. 2: 3 as a good *s.* of Jesus Christ
2: 4 him who hath chosen him to be a *s.*

SON
Num. 23:19 neither the *s.* of man, that he
2 Sam. 18:33 O Absalom, my *s.*, my *s.*
Job 25: 6 *s.* of man, which is a worm
Ps. 2:12 kiss the *S.* lest he be angry
8: 4 *s.* of man, that thou visitest
80:17 upon the *s.* of man whom thou
Prov. 10: 1 a wise *s.* maketh a glad father
Dan. 3:25 is like the *S.* of God
7:13 one like the *S.* of man came
Mal. 3:17 as a man spareth his own *s.*
Mat. 4: 3 thou be the *S.* of God
11:27 no man knoweth the *S.*, but the Father
16:16 the *S.* of the living God
17: 5 this is my beloved *S.*, in whom
Luke 10: 6 if the *s.* of peace be there
John 1:18 only begotten *S.*, which is in the
3:16 gave his only begotten *s.*
5:21 *S.* quickeneth whom he will
5:23 men should honour the *S.*
8:35 but the *S.* abideth ever
8:36 if the *S.* shall make you free
Acts 3:13 hath glorified his *S.* Jesus
Rom. 1: 3 concerning his *S.* Jesus
5:10 by the death of his *s.*
8: 3 sending his own *S.* in the likeness
8:32 spared not his own *S.*
1 Cor. 1: 9 fellowship of his *S.* Jesus
Gal. 1:16 To reveal his *S.* in me, that I
4: 4 God sent forth his *S.*, made of a
4: 7 if a *s.* then an heir of God
1 Thes. 1:10 wait for his *S.* from heaven
Heb. 1: 2 spoken unto us by his *S.*
5: 8 though he were a *S.* yet learned he
1 John 1: 7 blood of Jesus Christ his *S.*
2:22 that denieth the father the *S.*
3:23 believe on the name of his *S.*
5:11 and this life is in his *S.*
5:12 *S.* hath life, hath not the *S.*

SONS
Gen. 6: 2 *s.* of God saw the daughters
Job 1: 6 *s.* of God came to present themselves
38: 7 all the *s.* of God shouted for joy
Ps. 144: 12 that our *s.* may be as plants
Sol. 2: 3 so is my beloved among *s.*
Hos. 1:10 Ye are the *s.* of the living God
Mal. 3: 3 purify the *s.* of Levi
Mark 3:17 Boanerges, which is, The *s.* of
John 1:12 become the *s.* of God, even to them
Rom. 8:14 of God, they are the *s.* of God
1 Cor. 4:14 as my beloved *s.* I warn
Gal. 4: 6 because ye are *s.*, God hath sent
Phil. 2:15 *s.* of God without rebuke, in the midst
Heb. 2:10 bringing many *s.* to glory
12: 7 God dealeth with you as with *s.*
1 John 3: 1 we should be called the *s.* of God
3: 2 Beloved, now are we the *s.* of God

SONG (SONGS)
Ex. 15: 2 Lord is my strength and my *s.*
Job 30: 9 And now am I their *s.*, yea
35:10 who giveth *s.* in the night
Ps. 32: 7 me about with *s.* of deliverance
33: 3 sing unto him a new *s.*
42: 8 his *s.* shall be with me and my
96: 1 sing unto the Lord a new *s.*
119: 54 *s.* in house of my pilgrimage
149: 1 Sing unto the Lord a new *s.*
Is. 30:29 Ye shall have a *s.*, as in the
42:10 Sing unto the Lord a new *s.*
Ezek. 33:32 to them as a very lovely *s.*
Eph. 5:19 in psalms and hymns and spiritual *s.*
Rev. 5: 9 they sung a new *s.* saying, Thou
14: 3 no man could learn that *s.*
15: 3 sing the *s.* of Moses the servant of

SORCERER (SORCERERS)
Jer. 27: 9 nor to your *s.*, which speak unto
Mal. 3: 5 swift witness against the *s.*
Acts 13: 8 But Elymas the *s.* (for so is his
Rev. 21: 8 whoremongers, and *s.*, and idolaters

SORCERIES
Acts 8:11 he had bewitched them with *s.*

SORRY
Ps. 38:18 I will be *s.* for my sin
2 Cor. 2: 2 if I make you *s.*, who is he then
7: 8 the same epistle hath made you *s.*

SORROW (SORROWS)
Ps. 18: 4 *s.* of death compassed me
18: 5 the *s.* of hell compassed me
90:10 is their strength, labour and *s.*
127: 2 sit up late to eat the bread of *s.*
Prov. 15:13 by *s.* of the heart the spirit
Eccl. 1:18 increaseth knowledge increaseth *s.*
7: 3 *s.* is better than laughter
Is. 35:10 *s.* and sighing shall flee away
50:11 ye shall lie down in *s.*
53: 3 man of *s.*, and acquainted with
53: 4 carried our *s.*: yet we did esteem
Jer. 31:12 shall not *s.* any more at all
Lam. 1:12 there be any *s.* like unto my *s.*
Mat. 24: 8 all these are the beginning of *s.*
John 16: 6 *s.* hath filled your heart
16:20 your *s.* shall be turned into joy
2 Cor. 2: 7 swallowed up with overmuch *s.*
7:10 for godly *s.* worketh repentance
Phil. 2:27 lest I should have *s.* upon *s.*
1 Thes. 4:13 *s.* not, as others which have no hope
1 Tim. 6:10 and pierced through with many *s.*
Rev. 21: 4 no more death, neither *s.*

SORROWED
2 Cor. 7: 9 but that ye *s.* to repentance: for

SORROWFUL
Job 6: 7 to touch are as my *s.* meat
Prov. 14:13 in laughter the heart is *s.*
Jer. 31:25 replenished the *s.* soul
Zeph. 3:18 gather them that are *s.*
Mat. 19:22 that saying, he went away *s.*
26:22 they were exceeding *s.*, and began

SOUGHT
Ex. 33: 7 every one which *s.* the Lord
1 Chr. 15:13 *s.* him not after the due
2 Chr. 14: 7 because we have *s.* the Lord
16:12 *s.* not to the Lord, but to the
Ps. 34: 4 I *s.* the Lord, and he heard
78:34 then they *s.* him: and they returned
111: 2 *s.* out of all them that have
119: 10 with my whole heart have I *s.* thee
Eccl. 7:29 they have *s.* out many inventions
Sol. 5: 6 I *s.* him, but I could not
Is. 62:12 shall be called, *S.* out, a city not
65: 1 found of them that *s.* me not
Jer. 8: 2 and whom they have *s.*, and whom they
Rom. 9:32 *s.* it not by faith, but by

SOUL
Ex. 30:12 every man a ransom for his *s.*
Lev. 26:15 your *s.* abhor my judgments
Deut. 6: 5 and with all thy *s.*, and with all
11:13 heart and with all your *s.*
13: 3 your heart and with your *s.*
Josh. 22: 5 your heart and with all your *s.*
Judg. 10:16 his *s.* was grieved for misery
1 Sam. 18: 1 *s.* of Jonathan knit with the *s.*
1 Ki. 8:48 and with all their *s.*, in the land of
2 Ki. 23:25 with all his *s.*, and with all
1 Chr. 22:19 *s.* to seek the Lord your God

Job 27: 8 when God taketh away his *s.*
Ps. 16:10 not leave my *s.* in hell
19: 7 Lord is perfect, converting the *s.*
31: 7 hast known my *s.* in adversities
34:22 Lord redeemeth the *s.* of his servants
35: 3 say to my *s.* I am thy salvation
35: 9 my *s.* shall be joyful in the Lord
42: 5 why cast down, O my *s.*
49: 8 redemption of their *s.* is precious
62: 1 Truly my *s.* waiteth upon God
62: 5: My *s.*, wait thou only upon God
63: 1 my *s.* thirsteth for thee, my flesh
63: 8 my *s.* followeth hard after thee
74:19 deliver not the *s.* of thy turtledove
107: 9 filleth the hungry *s.* with goodness
Prov. 10: 3 not suffer the *s.* of the righteous
19: 2 that *s.* be without knowledge
27: 7 the full *s.* loatheth an honeycomb
Is. 26: 8 the desire of our *s.* is to thy
26: 9 with my *s.* have I desired thee
55: 2 let your *s.* delight in fatness
55: 3 hear and your *s.* shall live
58:10 and satisfy the afflicted *s.*
61:10 my *s.* shall be joyful in my God
Jer. 31:25 I have satiated the weary *s.*
38:16 Lord liveth, that made us this *s.*
Ezek. 3:19 but thou hast delivered thy *s.*
Hab. 2: 4 his *s.* lifted up is not upright
Mat. 10:28 not able to kill the *s.*: but rather
16:26 gain the whole world, and lose his *s.*
22:37 and with all thy *s.*, and with all
26:38 My *s.* is exceedingly sorrowful
Mark 12:33 and with all the *s.*, and with all
Luke 1:46 my *s.* doth magnify the Lord
12:20 this night thy *s.* shall be
John 12:27 Now is my *s.* troubled; and what
Rom. 13: 1 let every *s.* be subject to
1 Thes. 5:23 *s.* and body be preserved blameless
Heb. 4:12 dividing asunder of *s.* and spirit
10:39 believe to the saving of the *s.*
3 John 1: 2 be in health even as thy *s.* prospereth

SOULS
Josh. 23:14 all your hearts and in all your *s.*
Prov. 11:30 and he that winneth *s.* is wise
Is. 57:16 and the *s.* which I have made
Jer. 6:16 ye shall find rest for your *s.*
Ezek. 14:14 they should deliver but their own *s.*
Mat. 11:29 ye shall find rest unto your *s.*
Luke 21:19 your patience possess ye your *s.*
Heb. 13:17 they watch for your *s.*, as they that
1 Pet. 1:22 ye have purified your *s.* in obeying
2:25 Shepherd and Bishop of your *s.*
4:19 commit the keeping of their *s.* to him
2 Pet. 2:14 beguiling unstable *s.*: an heart they
Rev. 6: 9 *s.* of them that were slain for the
20: 4 *s.* of them that were beheaded for

SOUND
Job 15:21 dreadful *s.* is in his ears
Ps. 47: 5 Lord with the *s.* of a trumpet
89:15 people that know joyful *s.*
119: 80 let my heart be *s.* in thy statutes
Prov. 2: 7 he layeth up *s.* wisdom
Eccl. 12: 4 *s.* of the grinding is low
Amos 6: 5 that chant to the *s.* of the viol
Rom. 10:18 *s.* went into all the earth
1 Tim. 1:10 thing that is contrary to *s.* doctrine
2 Tim. 1: 7 and of love and of a *s.* mind
1:13 hold fast the form of *s.* words
Tit. 2: 2 temperate, *s.* in faith, in charity

SOUNDNESS
Ps. 38: 3 there is no *s.* in my flesh
Is. 1: 6 there is no *s.* in it

SOW (SOWETH, SOWN)
Job 4: 8 *s.* wickedly, reap the same
Ps. 97:11 light is *s.* for the righteous, and
126: 5 *s.* in tears shall reap in joy
Prov. 11:18 to him that *s.* righteousness
22: 8 *s.* iniquity shall reap vanity
Eccl. 11: 4 observeth the wind shall not *s.*
Jer. 4: 3 fallow ground, and *s.* not among thorns
31:27 I will *s.* the house of Israel
Hos. 8: 7 *s.* wind, they shall reap whirlwind
10:12 *s.* to yourselves in righteousness, reap
Mic. 6:15 thou shalt *s.* but thou shalt not
Mat. 13: 3 Behold, a sower went forth to *s.*
Luke 12:24 the ravens; for they neither *s.* nor
19:22 reaping that I did not *s.*
John 4:37 true, and one *s.*, another reapeth
1 Cor. 9:11 have *s.* to you spiritual things
15:42 it is *s.* in corruption; it is raised
15:43 *s.* in dishonour, it is raised
2 Cor. 9: 6 *s.* sparingly shall reap also
9:10 multiply your seed *s.*, and increase
Gal. 6: 7 whatsoever a man *s.*, that shall
Jas. 3:18 fruit of righteousness *s.* in peace

SOWER
Is. 55:10 it may give seed to the *s.*

SPARE (SPARED, SPARETH)
Gen. 18:26 I will *s.* all the place
Neh. 13:22 *s.* me according to the greatness of
Ps. 39:13 *s.* me that I may recover strength
Prov. 13:24 he that *s.* the rod hateth his
Joel 2:17 *s.* thy people O Lord and give not
Mal. 3:17 I will *s.* them, as a man spareth
Rom. 8:32 He that *s.* not his own Son, but
11:21 if God *s.* not the natural branches
2 Pet. 2: 4 God *s.* not angels that sinned

SPARKS
Job 5: 7 trouble, as the *s.* fly upward
Is. 50:11 that compass yourself about with *s.*

SPARROW (SPARROWS)
Ps. 102: 7 am as a *s.* along upon the house
Mat. 10:29 two *s.* sold for a farthing

SPEAK
Gen. 18:27 taken on me to *s.* to the Lord
Ex. 4:14 I know he can *s.* well
34:35 went in to *s.* with him
1 Sam. 3: 9 *S.*, Lord, for thy servant heareth
Ps. 85: 8 he will *s.* peace to his people
Is. 50: 4 how to *s.* a word in season
Jer. 18: 7 at what instant I shall *s.*
Mat. 10:19 how or what ye shall *s.*
Luke 6:26 when all men *s.* well of
John 3:11 we *s.* that we do know and testify
Acts 4:20 cannot but *s.* the things which we
1 Cor. 1:10 ye all *s.* the same thing
Tit. 3: 2 to *s.* evil of no man to be no
Jas. 1:19 swift to hear, slow to *s.*
2 Pet. 2:10 not afraid to *s.* evil of dignities
Jude 1:10 *s.* evil of things which they

SPEAKETH (SPEAKING)
Is. 58:13 pleasure, nor *s.* thine own words
65:24 while they are *s.* I will hear
Dan. 9:20 whiles I was *s.* and praying, and
Mat. 6: 7 shall be heard for their much *s.*
12:32 *s.* a word against the Son of man
12:34 abundance of the heart the mouth *s.*
Eph. 4:15 But *s.* the truth in love may
4:31 evil *s.*, be put away from you, with
5:19 *s.* to yourselves in psalms
1 Tim. 4: 2 *s.* lies in hypocrisy
Heb. 11: 4 he being dead yet *s.*
12:24 *s.* better things than that of Abel
12:25 refuse not him that *s.*
Rev. 13: 5 a mouth *s.* great things

SPEECH (SPEECHES)
Gen. 11: 1 one language and of one *s.*
Mat. 26:73 them; for thy *s.* betrayeth thee
Rom. 16:18 by fair *s.* deceive the hearts
1 Cor. 2: 1 not with excellency of *s.*
2 Cor. 3:12 use great plainness of *s.*
10:10 weak, and his *s.* contemptible
Col. 4: 6 let your *s.* be always with grace
Tit. 2: 8 sound *s.*, that cannot be condemned
Jude 1:15 of all their hard *s.* which ungodly

SPEECHLESS
Mat. 22:12 garment? And he was *s.*

SPEND (SPENT)
Job 21:13 they *s.* their days in wealth
Ps. 90: 9 *s.* our years as a tale that
Is. 49: 4 have *s.* my strength for nought
55: 2 *s.* money for that which is
Rom. 13:12 night is far *s.*, the day is at
2 Cor. 12:15 gladly spend and be *s.* for you

SPEW (SPEWING)
Lev. 18:28 the land *s.* not you out also
Jer. 25:27 be drunken, and *s.* and fall
Hab. 2:16 shameful *s.* shall be on thy glory
Rev. 3:16 I will *s.* thee out

SPIRIT
Gen. 1: 2 the *s.* of God moved upon the face
6: 3 my *s.* shall not always strive
Ex. 35:21 everyone whom his *s.* made willing
Num. 11:17 take of the *s.* which is on
14:24 Caleb had another *s.* with
2 Ki. 2: 9 double portion of thy *s.*
2 Chr. 15: 1 *s.* of God came upon Azariah
Ezra 1: 5 whose *s.* God had raised, to go up to
Neh. 9:20 gavest also thy good *s.* to instruct
Job 26:13 by his *s.* he garnished the
32:18 the *s.* within constraineth me
Ps. 31: 5 to thine hand I commit my *s.*
32: 2 in whose *s.* there is no guile
34:18 such as be of a contrite *s.*
51:10 renew a right *s.* within me
51:11 take not thy holy *s.* from me
51:12 uphold me with thy free *s.*
51:17 sacrifices of God are a broken *s.*
76:12 he shall cut off the *s.* of princes
78: 8 *s.* was not stedfast with God
139: 7 whither should I go from thy *s.*
142: 3 when my *s.* was overwhelmed within
143: 7 O Lord, my *s.* faileth
Prov. 14:29 hasty of *s.* exalteth folly
15:13 by sorrow of heart the *s.* is broken
16:18 and an haughty *s.* before a fall
16:32 he that ruleth his *s.* than he
18:14 a wounded *s.* who can bear?
20:27 *s.* of man is the candle of the Lord
Eccl. 3:21 who knoweth the *s.* of man
8: 8 power over the *s.* to retain the *s.*
12: 7 the *s.* shall return to God
Is. 32:15 until the *s.* be poured upon us
34:16 his *s.* it hath gathered them
38:16 these things is the life of my *s.*
57:15 to revive the *s.* of the humble
57:16 the *s.* should fail before me
61: 3 garment of praise for the *s.* of
66: 2 that is poor and of a contrite *s.*
Ezek. 11:24 Afterwards the *s.* took me up
36:27 I will put my *s.* within you
Mic. 2:11 walking in *s.* and falsehood
Zech. 4: 6 but by my *s.*, saith the Lord
12: 1 formeth the *s.* of man within
12:10 *s.* of grace and supplication
13: 2 the prophets of the unclean *s.*
Mat. 3:16 *S.* of God descending like a dove
12:28 cast out devils by the *s.*
12:43 when the unclean *s.* is gone out of a
22:43 doth in *s.* call him Lord
26:41 *s.* is willing, but the flesh weak
Luke 1:47 my *s.* hath rejoiced in God my
1:80 child grew, and waxed strong in *s.*
2:27 he came by the *S.* into the temple
8:55 *s.* came again and she arose
9:55 know not what manner of *s.* ye are
23:46 into thy hands I commend my *s.*
24:39 *s.* hath not flesh and bones
John 3: 5 born of water and of *s.* he cannot
3: 6 that which is born of the *S.* is *s.*
4:24 God is a *S.*: and they that
6:63 it is the *s.* that quickeneth
Acts 6:10 resist the wisdom and the *s.*
7:59 Lord Jesus, receive my *s.*
16: 7 the *S.* suffered them not
17:16 *s.* was stirred in him when he saw
18: 5 Paul was pressed in *s.* and
Rom. 1: 9 whom I serve with my *s.* in the
8: 1 not after flesh, but after the *S.*
8: 2 *S.* of the life in Christ Jesus made
8: 9 if any have not the *S.* of Christ, he
8:13 through the *S.* do mortify the deeds
8:14 as many as are led by the *S.* of God
8:15 ye have received the *S.* of adoption
8:16 *S.* beareth witness with our *s.*
1 Cor. 2:10 *s.*: for the *S.* searcheth all things
2:14 the things of the *S.* of God
3:16 the *S.* of God dwelleth in you

1 Cor. 5: 5 the s. may be saved in the day of
6:11 Jesus, and by the S. of our God
6:17 joined unto the Lord is one s.
12: 3 speaking by the S. of God
12:13 all made to drink into one S.
14:14 unknown tongue, my s. prayeth
2 Cor. 3: 3 with the S. of the living God
3: 6 not of the letter but of the s.
3:17 S. of the Lord is, there is liberty
7: 1 from filthiness of flesh and s.
Gal. 3: 3 begun in S. are ye now perfect
4: 6 sent forth the S. of his Son into your
5:17 flesh lusteth against S. and S.
5:18 led of the S. ye are not under the
5:22 fruit of the S. is love, joy, peace
5:25 live in the S. let us also walk in
6:18 Lord Jesus Christ be with your s.
Eph. 1:13 sealed with that holy S. of promise
4: 4 there is one body, and one S. even
4:23 be renewed in the s. of your mind
4:30 grieve not the holy S. of God
5: 9 fruit of S. is in all goodness
6:18 prayer and supplication in the s.
Col. 2: 5 yet am I with you in the s.
1 Thes. 5:23 whole s. be preserved blameless unto
Heb. 4:12 diving asunder of soul and s.
9:14 through the eternal S. offered himself
Jas. 4: 5 s. that dwelleth in us lusteth
1 Pet. 3: 4 the ornament of a meek and quiet s.
3:18 in flesh, but quickened by the S.
4:14 s. of glory and of God resteth
1 John 4: 1 believe not every s., but try
4: 2 Hereby know ye the s. of God
Jude 1:19 themselves sensual, having not the S.
Rev. 1:10 I was in the S. on the Lord's day
11:11 S. of life from God entered
14:13 yea, saith the S., that they may

SPIRITS
Num. 16:22 God of the s. of all flesh
Prov. 16: 2 but the Lord weigheth the s.
Mat. 10: 1 gave them power against unclean s.
Luke 10:20 rejoice not that the s. are subject to you
Acts 5:16 them which were vexed with unclean s.
8: 7 unclean s., crying with loud voice
1 Cor. 14:32 s. of the prophets are subject
Heb. 12:23 to the s. of just men made
1 Pet. 3:19 preached unto the s. in prison
1 John 4: 1 believe not every spirit but try the s.
Rev. 16:14 they are the s. of devils

SPIRITUAL
Hos. 9: 7 the s. man is mad for the multitude
Rom. 1:11 impart unto you some s. gift
7:14 that the law is s., but I am carnal
15:27 partakers of their s. things
1 Cor. 2:13 comparing s. things with s.
2:15 he that is s. judgeth all things
3: 1 not speak unto you as unto the s.
9:11 if we have sown unto you s. things
10: 3 did all eat the same s. meat
10: 4 of that s. Rock that followed them
15:44 natural body, it is raised a s. body
Gal. 6: 1 ye which are s. restore
Eph. 1: 3 blessed us with all s. blessings
5:19 psalms and hymns and s. songs
6:12 against s. wickedness in high places
Col. 3:16 psalms and hymns and s. songs
1 Pet. 2: 5 are built up a s. house, an holy

SPIRITUALLY
Rom. 8: 6 to be s. minded is life and peace
1 Cor. 2:14 because they are s. discerned
Rev. 11: 8 which s. is called Sodom and Egypt

SPOIL (SPOILED, SPOILING)
Gen. 49:27 at night he shall divide the s.
Ex. 12:36 And they s. the Egyptians
Ps. 68:12 tarried at home divided the s.
Is. 53:12 divide the s. with the strong
Mat. 12:29 and then he will s. his house
Col. 2: 8 beware lest any man s. you
Col. 2:15 having s. principalities and powers
Heb. 10:34 took joyfully the s. of your goods

SPOT
Num. 19: 2 bring thee a red heifer without s.
Deut. 32: 5 s. is not the s. of his children
Job 11:15 shalt thou lift up thy face without s.
Sol. 4: 7 there is no s. in thee
1 Tim. 6:14 keep this commandment without s.
Heb. 9:14 offered himself without s. to God
1 Pet. 1:19 lamb without blemish and without s.
2 Pet. 3:14 peace, without s., and blameless

SPRING (SPRINGING, SPRUNG)
Ps. 65:10 thou blesses the s. thereof
85:11 Truth shall s. out of the earth
Mat. 13: 5 forthwith they s. up because they
13: 7 and the thorns s. up, and choked
John 4:14 s. up into everlasting life
Heb. 12:15 root of bitterness s. up trouble you

SPRINKLE (SPRINKLED, SPRINKLING)
Lev. 14: 7 he shall s. upon him that is to
Is. 52:15 so shall he s. many nations
Ezek. 36:25 then will I s. clean water upon you
Heb. 10:22 hearts s. from an evil conscience
12:24 to blood of s., that speaketh
1 Pet. 1: 2 s. of the blood of Jesus Christ

SPY
Num. 13:16 which Moses sent out to s. the land
Josh. 2: 1 two men to s. secretly, saying, Go
Gal. 2: 4 to s. out our liberty

STAFF
Gen. 32:10 with my s. I passed over
Ps. 23: 4 thy rod and thy s. they comfort me
Is. 3: 1 from Judah the stay and the s.
9: 4 burden, and the s. of his shoulder
10: 5 s. in their hand is mine indignation
Zech. 11:10 And I took my s., even Beauty, and

STAND
Ex. 9:11 magicians could not s. before Moses
14:13 s. still, and see the salvation of
Josh. 10:12 s. thou still upon Gibeon
1 Sam. 6:20 is able to s. before his holy Lord
2 Chr. 20:17 set yourselves, s. ye still
Job 19:25 s. at the latter day upon the earth
Ps. 76: 7 who may s. in thy sight
130: 3 iniquities, O Lord, who shall s.
Prov. 19:21 the counsel of the Lord, that shall s.
Is. 46:10 my counsel shall s., and I will
Ezek. 29: 7 their loins to be at a s.
Nah. 1: 6 who can s. before his indignation
Mal. 3: 2 who shall s. when he appeareth?
Mat. 12:25 against itself shall not s.
Luke 21:36 s. before the Son of man
Rom. 5: 2 this grace wherein we s.
14:10 shall all s. before the judgment seat
1 Cor. 16:13 s. fast in the faith quit you
2 Cor. 1:24 your joy: for by faith ye s.
Gal. 5: 1 s. fast in liberty wherewith
Phil. 1: 4 s. fast in the Lord, dearly beloved
1:27 that ye s. fast in one spirit
1 Thes. 3: 8 we live, if ye s. fast in Lord
2 Thes. 2:15 s. fast, and hold the traditions
1 Pet. 5:12 grace of God wherein ye s.
Rev. 3:20 I s. at the door and knock
20:12 small and great, s. before God

STANDETH
Ps. 1: 1 nor s. in the way of sinners
33:11 counsel of the Lord s. forever
Prov. 8: 2 She s. in the top of high
Is. 3:13 The Lord s. up to plead, and s.
Rom. 14: 4 to his own master he s. or falleth
1 Cor. 10:12 s. take heed lest he fall
2 Tim. 2:19 the foundation of God s. sure, having
Jas. 5: 9 the Judge s. before the door

STAR (STARS)
Num. 24:17 there shall come a S. out of Jacob
Judg. 5:20 the s. in their courses fought
Job 25: 5 s. are not pure in his sight
38: 7 the morning s. sang together
Dan. 12: 3 to righteousness as the s. for ever
Mat. 2: 2 we have seen his s. in the east
Rev. 12: 1 on her head a crown of twelve s.

STATURE
Mat. 6:27 can add one cubit unto his s.
Eph. 4:13 measure of the s. of the fulness of

STATUTES
Ex. 15:26 and keep all his s., I will put
Deut. 6:17 his testimonies and his s.
2 Ki. 17:15 they rejected his s., and his
Neh. 9:14 precepts, s., and laws, by the hand
Ps. 18:22 not put away his s. from me
19: 8 s. of the Lord are right
105: 45 that they might observe his s.
Ezek. 20:24 had despised my s. and had polluted
33:15 walk in the s. of life without
Mic. 6:16 the s. of Omri are kept

STEAL (STOLE, STOLEN)
Ex. 20:15 Thou shalt not s.
Prov. 6:30 thief, if he s. to satisfy his soul
9:17 s. waters are sweet, and bread
Jer. 23:30 saith the Lord, that s. my words
Mat. 6:19 thieves break through and s.
27:64 come by night, and s. him away
Eph. 4:28 let him that s., steal no more

STEDFAST
Job 11:15 yea, thou shalt be s., and shalt
Ps. 78: 8 whose spirit was not s. with God
Dan. 6:26 living God, and s. forever
1 Cor. 15:58 be ye s. unmoveable, always abounding
Heb. 3:14 of our confidence s. to the end
1 Pet. 5: 9 whom resist s. in the faith, knowing

STEADFASTNESS
Col. 2: 5 the s. of your faith in Christ
2 Pet. 3:17 of the wicked fall from your own s.

STEPS
Ex. 20:26 thou go up by s. unto mine altar
Ps. 18:36 thou hast enlarged my s. under me
37:23 s. of a good man are ordered
37:31 none of his s. shall slide
119:133 order my s. in thy word
Prov. 16: 9 but the Lord directeth his s.
Jer. 10:23 man that walketh to direct his s.
Rom. 4:12 who also walk in the s. of that faith
1 Pet. 2:21 that ye should follow his s.

STEWARD (STEWARDS)
Luke 12:42 that faithful and wise s.
16: 2 for thou mayest be no longer s.
1 Cor. 4: 1 and s. of the mysteries of God
Tit. 1: 7 must be blameless, as the s. of God
1 Pet. 4:10 as good s. of the manifold grace

STIFF (STIFFENETH)
Deut. 31:27 I know thy rebellion, and thy s. neck
2 Chr. 36:13 he s. his neck, and hardened his
Jer. 17:23 made their neck s., that they might

STIFFNECKED
Ex. 32: 9 and, behold, it is a s. people
34: 9 it is a s. people; and pardon
Deut. 9:13 and, behold, it is a s. people
10:16 heart, and be no more s.
Acts 7:51 s. and uncircumcised in heart

STILL (STILLETH)
Ex. 15:16 they shall be as s. as a stone
Ps. 4: 4 own heart upon your bed, and be s.
8: 2 s. the enemy and the avenger
46:10 be s. and know that I am God
65: 7 which s. the noise of the seas
83: 1 thy peace, be not s. O God
89: 9 thereof arise, thou s. them
139: 18 I awake, I am s. with thee
Is. 30: 7 their strength is to sit s.
Mark 4:39 Peace, be s. And the wind

STIR
Num. 24: 9 great lion: who shall s. him up
Ps. 35:23 s. up thyself, and awake to my
78:38 away, and did not s. up all his wrath

Sol. 2: 7 that ye *s.* not up, nor awake
2 Tim. 1: 6 *s.* up the gift of God that is

STONE (STONES)
Gen. 49:24 is the shepherd, the *s.* of Israel
Ps. 118: 22 *s.* which the builders refused
Is. 8:14 *s.* of stumbling and for a rock
28:16 a *s.*, a tried *s.*, a precious corner *s.*
Dan. 2:34 *s.* cut out without hands
Hab. 2:11 *s.* shall cry out of the wall
Zech. 3: 9 on one *s.* shall be seven eyes
Mat. 3: 9 God is able of these *s.* to raise
7: 9 ask for bread, will he give him a *s.*
Luke 19:40 the *s.* would immediately cry out
Rom. 9:33 lay in Zion, a stumbling *s.*
1 Pet. 2: 4 whom coming, as unto a living *s.*
2: 6 chief corner *s.*, elect, precious

STORM
Ps. 55: 8 escape from the windy *s.*
83:15 make them afraid with thy *s.*
107: 29 he maketh the *s.* a calm
Is. 4: 6 for a covert from *s.* and from
25: 4 refuge from the *s.*, a shadow
Nah. 1: 3 his way in the whirlwind, and in the *s.*
Mark 4:37 arose a great *s.* of wind

STORMY
Ps. 148: 8 *s.* wind fulfilling his word

STRAIGHT
Josh. 6: 5 ascend up every man *s.*
Ps. 5: 8 thy way *s.* before my face
Eccl. 1:15 which is crooked cannot be made *s.*
Is. 40: 3 make *s.* in the desert a highway for our
45: 2 make the crooked places *s.*
Jer. 31: 9 rivers of waters in a *s.* way
Luke 3: 4 way of Lord, make his paths *s.*
3: 5 crooked shall be made *s.*
Heb. 12:13 make *s.* paths for your feet

STRAIT
2 Sam. 24:14 I am in a great *s.*: let us fall
Job 36:16 removed thee out of the *s.*
Is. 49:20 place is too *s.* for me
Mat. 7:13 enter in at the *s.* gate
Phil. 1:23 I am in a *s.* betwixt two

STRAITENED
Mic. 2: 7 is the spirit of Lord *s.*?
Luke 12:50 how am I *s.* till it be accomplished
2 Cor. 6:12 not *s.* in us, but ye are *s.* in

STRANGE
Ex. 21: 8 sell her unto a *s.* nation
Lev. 10: 1 and offered *s.* fire before
Judg. 11: 2 for thou art the son of a *s.* woman
Ezra 10:11 the land, and from the *s.* wives
Ps. 81: 9 there shall no *s.* god be in thee
Prov. 2:16 deliver thee from the *s.* woman
Is. 28:21 do his *s.* work; and bring to pass
Jer. 2:21 plant of a *s.* vine unto me
Hos. 8:12 they were counted as a *s.* thing
Zeph. 1: 8 such as are clothed with *s.* apparel
Luke 5:26 we have seen *s.* things today
Heb. 11: 9 of promise, as in a *s.* country
13: 9 about with divers and *s.* doctrines
1 Pet. 4: 4 think it *s.* that ye run not
4:12 think it not *s.* concerning the fiery
Jude 1: 7 going after *s.* flesh are set forth

STRANGER (STRANGERS)
Gen. 23: 4 *s.* and a sojourner with you
1 Chr. 29:15 For we are *s.* before thee
Ps. 39:12 for I am a *s.* with thee, and
105: 12 yea, very few and *s.* in it
119: 19 I am a *s.* in the earth
146: 9 the Lord preserveth the *s.*
Jer. 14: 8 why shouldest thou be as a *s.*
Mat. 25:35 I was a *s.* and ye took me in
Luke 17:18 glory to God, save this *s.*
John 10: 5 a *s.* will they not follow
Eph. 2:19 are no more *s.* and foreigners
Heb. 11:13 confessed that they were *s.* and
13: 2 be not forgetful to entertain *s.*
1 Pet. 2:11 beseech you as *s.* and

STREAM (STREAMS)
Ps. 46: 4 There is a river the *s.* whereof
126: 4 as the *s.* in the south
Sol. 4:15 living waters and *s.* from Lebanon
Is. 30:25 rivers and *s.* of waters in the day
30:33 like a *s.* of brimstone doth kindle
33:21 a place of broad rivers and *s.*
35: 6 break out, and *s.* in the desert
66:12 Gentiles like a flowing *s.*
Dan. 7:10 fiery *s.* issued and came forth
Amos 5:24 and righteousness as a mighty *s.*
Luke 6:48 the *s.* beat vehemently upon that

STREET (STREETS)
Prov. 1:20 uttereth her voice in the *s.*
Sol. 3: 2 go about the city in the *s.* and in
Luke 14:21 Go out quickly into the *s.*
Rev. 11: 8 bodies shall lie in the *s.*
21:21 *s.* of the city was pure gold
22: 2 In the midst of the *s.* of it

STRENGTH
Gen. 49: 3 and the beginning of my *s.*, the
49:24 But his bow abode in *s.*, and
Ex. 15: 2 The Lord is my *s.* and song
1 Sam. 2: 9 by *s.* shall no man prevail
15:29 the *S.* of Israel will not lie
Job 6:12 Is my *s.* the *s.* of stones
9:19 if I speak of *s.* lo, he is
12:13 with him is wisdom and *s.*
Ps. 18: 2 my *s.*, in whom I will trust
18:32 It is God that girdeth me with *s.*
27: 1 the Lord is the *s.* of my life
28: 7 Lord is my *s.* and my shield
29:11 Lord will give *s.* to his people
33:16 mighty not delivered by much *s.*
39:13 spare me that I recover *s.*
43: 2 For thou art the God of my *s.*
46: 1 God is our refuge and *s.*, a very
68:35 he that giveth *s.* and power unto his
73:26 God is the *s.* of my heart
84: 5 blessed is the man whose *s.* is in
84: 7 they go from *s.* to *s.*, every one
93: 1 the Lord is clothed with *s.*
96: 6 *s.* and beauty are in his sanctuary
102: 23 He weakened my *s.* in the way
118: 14 The Lord is my *s.* and song, and
138: 3 strengthenedst me with *s.* in my soul
140: 7 Lord, the *s.* of my salvation
Eccl. 9:16 wisdom is better than *s.*
10:10 then must he put to more *s.*
Is. 12: 2 Jehovah is my *s.* and my song
25: 4 a *s.* to the poor, a *s.* to the needy
26: 4 the Lord Jehovah is everlasting *s.*
40:29 that have no might he increaseth *s.*
45:24 in the Lord have I righteousness and *s.*
49: 5 my God shall be my *s.*
Jer. 16:19 O Lord, my *s.*, and my fortress
Hab. 3:19 the Lord God is my *s.*, and he will
Joel 3:16 and the *s.* of the children of Israel
Luke 1:51 he hath shown *s.* with his arm
Rom. 5: 6 when we were without *s.*
1 Cor. 15:56 is sin; and *s.* of sin is the law
2 Cor. 12: 9 my *s.* is made perfect in weakness
Rev. 3: 8 thou hast a little *s.* and
5:12 wisdom, and *s.*, and honour
12:10 now is come salvation and *s.*

STRENGTHEN (STRENGTHENED, STRENGTHENEDST, STRENGTHENETH)
1 Sam. 23:16 wood, and *s.* his hand in God
Ps. 20: 2 sanctuary, and *s.* thee out of Zion
27:14 he shall *s.* thine heart
41: 3 *s.* him on the bed of languishing
104: 15 bread which *s.* man's heart
138: 3 *s.* me with strength in my soul
Ezek. 34: 4 diseased have ye not *s.*
Is. 35: 3 *s.* ye the weak hands, and confirm
41:10 I will *s.* thee, yea, I will
54: 2 lengthen thy cords, and *s.* thy stakes
Dan. 11: 1 stood to confirm and *s.* him
Zech. 10:12 I will *s.* them in the Lord
Luke 22:32 thou art converted, *s.* thy brethren
Eph. 3:16 to be *s.* with might by his
Phil. 4:13 through Christ which *s.* me
Col. 1:11 *s.* with all might according to
2 Tim. 4:17 Lord stood with me and *s.* me
1 Pet. 5:10 make you perfect, stablish, *s.*
Rev. 3: 2 watchful and *s.* the things which remain

STRETCH (STRETCHED, STRETCHETH)
Gen. 22:10 Abraham *s.* forth his hand
1 Ki. 17:21 *s.* himself upon the child three times
1 Chr. 21:16 sword *s.* out over Jerusalem
Job 11:13 *s.* out thine hands towards him
15:25 he *s.* out his hand against God
Prov. 31:20 she *s.* out her hand to the poor
Is. 5:25 but his hand is *s.* out still
40:22 *s.* out the heavens as a curtain
45:12 hands, have *s.* out the heavens
51:13 that hath *s.* forth the heavens
Jer. 10:12 hath *s.* out the heavens by his
Amos 6: 4 *s.* themselves on their couches
Zech. 12: 1 which *s.* forth the heavens
Mat. 12:13 *s.* forth thy hand. And he *s.*
John 21:18 thou shalt *s.* forth thy hands
Rom. 10:21 all day I have *s.* forth my hands

STRIFE (STRIFES)
Gen. 13: 8 there be no *s.* between me and thee
Ps. 80: 6 makest us a *s.* to our neighbours
Prov. 10:12 hatred stirreth up *s.*, but love
15:18 wrathful man stirreth up *s.*
16:28 A froward man soweth *s.*: and a
20: 3 honour for a man to cease from *s.*
28:25 a proud heart stirreth up *s.*
29:22 an angry man stirreth up *s.*
30:33 forcing of wrath bringeth *s.*
Is. 58: 4 ye fast for *s.* and debate
Jer. 15:10 hast borne me a man of *s.*
Luke 22:24 there was also a *s.* among them
1 Cor. 3: 3 there is among you envying, *s.*
Gal. 5:20 wrath, *s.*, seditions, heresies
Phil. 1:15 preach Christ even of envy and *s.*
2: 3 let nothing be done through *s.*
1 Tim. 6: 4 whereof cometh envy, *s.*, railings
2 Tim. 2:23 that they do gender *s.*
Jas. 3:14 if ye have bitter envying and *s.*

STRIPES
Prov. 17:10 than an hundred *s.* into a fool
20:30 so do *s.* the inward parts of the
Is. 53: 5 with his *s.* we are healed
Luke 12:48 commit things worthy of *s.*
1 Pet. 2:24 by whose *s.* ye were healed

STRIVE (STRIVETH, STRIVING)
Gen. 6: 3 Spirit shall not always *s.*
Ex. 21:22 men *s.*, and hurt a woman
Job 33:13 why dost thou *s.* against him
Prov. 3:30 *s.* not with a man without cause
Is. 45: 9 woe to him that *s.* with his Maker
Mat. 12:19 he shall not *s.* nor cry
Luke 13:24 *s.* to enter in at the strait gate
Phil. 1:27 one mind *s.* together for the faith
2 Tim. 2:24 the servant of Lord must not *s.*
Heb. 12: 4 resisted unto blood, *s.* against sin

STRONG
Josh. 14:11 I am as *s.* this day as I was in
Ps. 24: 8 The Lord *s.* and mighty, the Lord
30: 7 made my mountain to stand *s.*
31: 2 be thou my *s.* rock, for an house
71: 7 but thou art my *s.* refuge
Prov. 10:15 rich man's wealth is his *s.* city
14:26 fear of the Lord is *s.* confidence
18:10 name of the Lord is a *s.* tower
24: 5 a wise man is *s.*; yea, a man of
Eccl. 9:11 the swift, nor the battle to the *s.*
12: 3 and the *s.* men shall bow themselves
Sol. 8: 6 love is *s.* as death; jealousy
Is. 1:31 the *s.* shall be as tow, and the maker
26: 1 we have a *s.* city
35: 4 Be *s.*, fear not: behold, your God
53:12 shall divide the spoil with the *s.*
Jer. 50:34 their Redeemer is *s.*, the Lord of
Joel 3:10 let the weak say, I am *s.*
Hag. 2: 4 now, be *s.*, o Zerubbabel
Luke 11:21 *s.* man armed keepeth his palace
Rom. 4:20 but was *s.* in faith, giving
15: 1 we that are *s.* ought to bear the infirmities
1 Cor. 16:13 quit you like men, be *s.*
2 Cor. 12:10 when I am weak, then am I *s.*
Eph. 6:10 be *s.* in the Lord, and in the
2 Tim. 2: 1 be *s.* in the grace that is in
Heb. 11:34 out of weakness were made *s.*

STRONGER
Job 17: 9 clean hands shall be *s.* and *s.*
Jer. 20: 7 thou art *s.* than I and hast
1 Cor. 1:25 weakness of God is *s.* than men

STUBBORN (STUBBORNNESS)
Deut. 9:27 look not unto the *s.* of this people
21:18 a man have a *s.* and rebellious son
1 Sam. 15:23 and *s.* is as iniquity and idolatry

Ps. 78: 8 a *s.* and rebellious generation

STUDY (STUDIETH)
Prov. 15:28 heart of the righteous *s.*
24: 2 their heart *s.* destruction and their
Eccl. 12:12 much *s.* is a weariness of the flesh
1 Thes. 4:11 that ye *s.* to be quiet and to do
2 Tim. 2:15 *S.* to show thyself approved

STUMBLE (STUMBLED, STUMBLETH)
Prov. 3:23 thy foot shall not *s.*
4:12 runnest, thou shalt not *s.*
4:19 they know not at what they *s.*
Is. 5:27 none shall be weary nor *s.*
8:15 many among them shall *s.* and fall
28: 7 err in vision, *s.* in judgment
John 11: 9 if a man walk in the day he *s.* not
Rom. 9:32 they *s.* at that stumblingstone
14:21 whereby thy brother *s.* or is offended
1 Pet. 2: 8 even to them which *s.* at the word

STUMBLING
Is. 8:14 but for a stone of *s.* and for a
Rom. 9:32 stumbled at the *s.* stone
1 Pet. 2: 8 stone of *s.*, and a rock of offense
1 John 2:10 there is none occasion of *s.* in him

STUMBLINGBLOCK (STUMBLINGBLOCKS)
Lev. 19:14 put a *s.* before the blind
Is. 57:14 take up the *s.* out of the way
Jer. 6:21 I will lay *s.* before this people
Ezek. 3:20 I lay a *s.* before him
Rom. 11: 9 a trap, snare, and a *s.*, and a
14:13 put a *s.* or an occasion to fall in
1 Cor. 1:23 unto the Jews a *s.*, and unto the
Rev. 2:14 taught Balac to cast a *s.*

SUBDUE (SUBDUED)
Mic. 7:19 upon us; he will *s.* our iniquities
Phil. 3:21 able to *s.* all things unto himself
Heb. 11:33 who through faith *s.* kingdoms

SUBJECT
Luke 10:20 spirits are *s.* unto you; but rather
Rom. 8: 7 it is not *s.* to the law of God
8:20 creature was made *s.* to vanity
13: 1 every soul be *s.* unto the higher powers
1 Cor. 14:32 spirits of the prophets are *s.* to
15:28 shall be *s.* unto him that put all
Eph. 5:24 as the church is *s.* to Christ
Heb. 2:15 all their lifetime *s.* to bondage
Jas. 5:17 Elias was a man *s.* to like passions
1 Pet. 2:18 servants be *s.* to your masters
5: 5 all of you be *s.* one to another

SUBJECTION
1 Cor. 9:27 under my body, and bring it into *s.*
1 Tim. 2:11 woman learn in silence with all *s.*
3: 4 having his children in *s.*
Heb. 2: 8 put all in *s.* under him
12: 9 be in *s.* unto the father
1 Pet. 3: 5 in *s.* unto their own husbands

SUBMIT (SUBMITTED, SUBMITTING)
Gen. 16: 9 and *s.* thyself under her hands
Ps. 18:44 strangers shall *s.* themselves unto
68:30 till everyone *s.* himself
Rom. 10: 3 have not *s.* unto the righteousness of
1 Cor. 16:16 that ye *s.* yourselves unto such
Eph. 5:21 *s.* yourselves one to another
Col. 3:18 *s.* yourselves unto your own
Heb. 13:17 rule over you, and *s.* yourselves
Jas. 4: 7 *S.* yourselves therefore to God
1 Pet. 2:13 *S.* yourselves to every ordinance
5: 5 *s.* yourselves unto the elder

SUBSTANCE
Gen. 7: 4 every living *s.* that I have made
15:14 they come out with great *s.*
Deut. 33:11 bless, Lord, his *s.* and accept
Job 30:22 upon it and dissolvest my *s.*
Ps. 139: 15 my *s.* was not hid from thee
Prov. 3: 9 honour the Lord with thy *s.*
Hos. 12: 8 I have found me out *s.*: in all my
Luke 8: 3 ministered to him of their *s.*
Heb. 10:34 a better and an enduring *s.*
11: 1 faith is the *s.* of things hoped for

SUBTLE
Gen. 3: 1 serpent was more *s.* than any beast
Prov. 7:10 attire of an harlot, and *s.* of heart

SUBTLETY
Prov. 1: 4 to give *s.* to the simple
Acts 13:10 full of all *s.* and mischief
2 Cor. 11: 3 beguiled Eve through his *s.*

SUCK (SUCKED, SUCKING)
Gen. 21: 7 should have given children *s.*
Deut. 32:13 made him to *s.* honey out of
33:19 they shall *s.* of the abundance
Job 20:16 he shall *s.* the poison of asps
Is. 11: 8 the *s.* child shall play on the hole
49:15 can a woman forget her *s.* child
60:16 *s.* the milk of the Gentiles
Lam. 4: 4 the tongue of the *s.* child cleaveth
Mat. 24:19 to them that give *s.* in those
Luke 11:27 blessed are paps which thou hast *s.*
23:29 paps which never gave *s.*

SUFFER
Ex. 12:23 will not *s.* the destroyer
Lev. 19:17 neighbour, and not *s.* sin upon him
Ps. 55:22 never *s.* the righteous to be moved
89:33 nor *s.* my faithfulness to fail
121: 3 not *s.* thy foot to be moved
Prov. 10: 3 not *s.* the soul of righteous to famish
Mat. 16:21 *s.* many things of the elders and
17:17 how long shall I *s.* you?
19:14 *s.* little children, and forbid them
1 Cor. 4:12 being persecuted, we *s.* it
10:13 God will not *s.* you to be tempted
Phil. 1:29 but also to *s.* for his sake
2 Tim. 2:12 if we *s.* we shall also reign
Heb. 11:25 choosing rather to *s.* affliction
13:22 *s.* the word of exhortation
1 Pet. 4:15 none of you *s.* as a murderer
4:19 that *s.* according to the will of God

SUFFERED (SUFFERETH)
Ps. 105: 14 he *s.* no man to do them wrong
Mat. 11:12 kingdom of heaven *s.* violence
Acts 14:16 *s.* all nations to walk in their own
16: 7 the Spirit *s.* them not
1 Cor. 13: 4 Charity *s.* long, and is kind
Phil. 3: 8 for whom I *s.* loss of all
Heb. 5: 8 obedience by the things which he *s.*
1 Pet. 2:21 Christ also *s.* for us, leaving us
5:10 after that ye have *s.* a while

SUFFERINGS
Rom. 8:18 the *s.* of this present times
2 Cor. 1: 6 enduring of the same *s.*
Phil. 3:10 the fellowship of his *s.*
Col. 1:24 now rejoice in my *s.* for you
Heb. 2:10 of their salvation perfect through *s.*
1 Pet. 1:11 testified beforehand the *s.* of Christ
4:13 ye are partakers of Christ's *s.*

SUFFICIENT
Mat. 6:34 *s.* unto the day is the evil
2 Cor. 2:16 who is *s.* for these things?
3: 5 not that we are *s.* of ourselves
12: 8 my grace is *s.* for thee

SUMMER
Gen. 8:22 heat, and *s.* and winter, and day
Ps. 74:17 thou hast made *s.* and winter
Prov. 6: 8 provideth her meat in the *s.*
10: 5 that gathereth in the *s.* is a wise son
Is. 18: 6 fowls shall *s.* upon them
Zech. 14: 8 in *s.* and in winter shall it be

SUN
Josh. 10:12 *s.*, stand thou still upon Gibeon
Ps. 19: 4 he set a tabernacle for the *s.*
74:16 prepared the light and the *s.*
104: 19 *s.* knoweth his going down
121: 6 *s.* shall not smite thee by day
136: 8 *s.* to rule the day: for his mercy
Sol. 1: 6 because the *s.* looked on me
6:10 fair as the moon, clear as the *s.*
Is. 30:26 light of the *s.* shall be sevenfold
60:19 *s.* shall be no more thy light by day
60:20 thy *s.* shall no more go down
Jer. 31:35 giveth *s.* for a light by day
Mal. 4: 2 *S.* of righteousness arise

Mat. 5:45 his *s.* to rise on evil and
13:43 shine forth as the *s.* in the kingdom
1 Cor. 15:41 there is one glory of the *s.*
Eph. 4:26 let not the *s.* go down upon
Rev. 7:16 neither shall the *s.* light on them
10: 1 his face was as it the *s.*
21:23 city had no need of the *s.*

SUP
Hab. 1: 9 their faces shall *s.* up as the east
Luke 17: 8 make ready wherewith I may *s.*, and
Rev. 3:20 and will *s.* with him, and he with

SUPPER
Luke 14:16 A certain man made a great *s.*
22:20 also the cup after *s.*, saying
1 Cor. 11:20 is not to eat the Lord's *s.*
Rev. 19: 9 the marriage *s.* of the Lamb

SUPERSTITION (SUPERSTITIOUS)
Acts 17:22 in all things ye are too *s.*
25:19 against him of their own *s.*

SUPPLICATION (SUPPLICATIONS)
1 Ki. 8:28 thy servant and to his *s.*, O Lord
Job 8: 5 and make thy *s.* to the almighty
Ps. 6: 9 Lord hath heard my *s.*; the Lord
55: 1 hide not thyself from my *s.*
119:170 Let my *s.* come before thee
Dan. 6:11 making *s.* before his God
Hos. 12: 4 wept, and made *s.* unto him
Zech. 12:10 the spirit of grace and of *s.*
Eph. 6:18 prayer and *s.* in the spirit
Phil. 4: 6 prayer and *s.* with thanksgiving
1 Tim. 5: 5 continueth in *s.* and prayers
2: 1 first of all *s.*, prayers, intercessions
Heb. 5: 7 offered up prayers and *s.*

SUPPLY (SUPPLIETH)
2 Cor. 9:12 only *s.* the want of the saints
Eph. 4:16 by that which every joint *s.*
Phil. 1:19 the *s.* of the Spirit of Jesus
4:19 my God shall *s.* all your need

SURE
Gen. 23:17 borders round about, were made *s.*
2 Sam. 23: 5 ordered in all things, and *s.*
Ps. 19: 7 testimony of the Lord is *s.*
93: 5 thy testimonies are very *s.*
111: 7 all his commandments are *s.*
Prov. 11:15 he that hateth suretyship is *s.*
11:18 righteousness shall be a *s.* reward
Is. 22:25 nail that is fastened in a *s.* place
28:16 a *s.* foundation: he that believeth
33:16 given him; his waters shall be *s.*
55: 3 even the *s.* mercies of David
John 6:69 are *s.* that thou art that Christ
Acts 13:34 give you the *s.* mercies of David
Rom. 4:16 promise might be *s.* to all
2 Tim. 2:19 foundation of God standeth *s.*
2 Pet. 1:10 to make your calling and election *s.*
1:19 a more *s.* word of prophecy

SWALLOW (SWALLOWED)
Ex. 15:12 thy right hand, the earth *s.* them
Num. 16:32 opened her mouth, and *s.* them up
Ps. 84: 3 the *s.* a nest for herself
Jer. 8: 7 the *s.* observe the time of their
Is. 25: 8 will *s.* up death in victory
Mat. 23:24 strain at a gnat, *s.* a camel
2 Cor. 2: 7 should be *s.* up with overmuch sorrow
5: 4 mortality be *s.* up of life

SWEAR (SWEARETH, SWEARING)
Num. 30: 2 *s.* an oath to bind his soul
Deut. 6:13 and shalt *s.* by his name
Ps. 15: 4 he that *s.* to his own hurt
Eccl. 9: 2 that *s.* as he that feareth
Is. 45:23 shall bow, every tongue shall *s.*
65:16 shall *s.* by the God of truth
Jer. 4: 2 shalt *s.*, The Lord liveth
23:10 because of *s.* the land mourneth
Hos. 4: 2 by *s.*, and lying, and killing
10: 4 *s.* falsely in making a covenant
Zeph. 1: 5 Lord, and that *s.* by Malcham
Zech. 5: 3 every one that *s.* shall be cut off
Mat. 5:34 *s.* not at all; neither by
Jas. 5:12 *s.* not, neither by heaven, neither

SWEARERS
Mal. 3: 5 and against false *s.*, and against

SWEAT
Gen. 3:19 In the *s.* of thy face shalt thou
Luke 22:44 *s.* was as it were great drops

SWEET
Job 20:12 wickedness be *s.* in his mouth
Ps. 55:14 We took *s.* counsel together
104: 34 meditation of him shall be *s.*
119:103 how *s.* are thy words unto my taste
Prov. 3:24 thy sleep shall be *s.*
9:17 stolen waters are *s.*, and bread
27: 7 hungry soul every bitter thing is *s.*
Eccl. 5:12 sleep of the labouring man is *s.*
Sol. 2: 3 his fruit was *s.* to my taste
2:14 *s.* is thy voice and thy countenance
5:16 his mouth is most *s.*; yea, he is
Is. 5:20 put bitter for *s.* and *s.* for bitter
Phil. 4:18 an odour of a *s.* smell a sacrifice
Rev. 10: 9 in thy mouth *s.* as honey

SWEETER
Ps. 19:10 much fine gold *s.* also than honey

SWIFT
Deut. 28:49 as *s.* as the eagle flieth
Job 9:26 passed away as the *s.* ships
Eccl. 9:11 the race is not to the *s.*
Rom. 3:15 their feet are *s.* to shed blood
Jas. 1:19 *s.* to hear, slow to speak
2 Pet. 2: 1 bring on themselves *s.* destruction

SWIFTER
Job 7: 6 days *s.* than a weaver's shuttle
9:25 my days are *s.* than a post

SWIFTLY
Ps. 147: 15 his word runneth very *s.*
Joel 3: 4 if ye recompense me, *s.* and speedily

SWIM
2 Ki. 6: 6 in thither, and the iron did *s.*
Ps. 6: 6 make I my bed to *s.*; I water my
Ezek. 47: 5 waters to *s.* in, a river

SWORD (SWORDS)
Gen. 3:24 cherubims and a flaming *s.*
Ex. 32:27 put man his *s.* by his side
Lev. 26: 6 shall the *s.* go through your land
26:25 I will bring a *s.* upon you
Judg. 7:20 the *s.* of the Lord and of Gideon
2 Sam. 12:10 *s.* shall never depart from thine
Ps. 17:13 from the wicked, which is thy *s.*
55:21 yet were they drawn *s.*
59: 7 *s.* are in their lips: for who
Prov. 30:14 whose teeth are as *s.*
Sol. 3: 8 every man hath his *s.* on
Is. 2: 4 beat their *s.* into plowshares
Jer. 9:16 I will send a *s.* after them
15: 2 such as are for the *s.* to the *s.*
Ezek. 21:13 what if the *s.* contemn even the rod
32:27 they have laid their *s.* under their
Joel 3:10 Beat your plowshares into *s.*
Zech. 11:17 *s.* shall be upon his arm
Mat. 10:34 not to send peace, but the *s.*
Luke 2:35 a *s.* shall pierce through
Rom. 13: 4 he beareth not the *s.* in vain
Eph. 6:17 *s.* of the Spirit which is the word
Heb. 4:12 sharper than any twoedged *s.*
Rev. 1:16 mouth went a sharp twoedged *s.*
19:15 out of his mouth goeth a sharp *s.*

SYNAGOGUE (SYNAGOGUES)
Ps. 74: 8 they have burned up all the *s.*
Mat. 6: 5 love to pray standing in the *s.*
23: 6 and the chief seats in the *s.*
Luke 7: 5 he hath built us a *s.*
John 9:22 should be put out of the *s.*
18:20 I ever taught in the *s.* and in
Acts 15:21 read in the *s.* every sabbath day
Rev. 2: 9 are not but are the *s.* of Satan
3: 9 will make them of the *s.* of Satan

T

TABERNACLE (TABERNACLES)
Ex. 26: 1 make the *t.* with ten curtains
29:43 the *t.* shall be sanctified
Job 5:24 thy *t.* shall be in peace
12: 6 the *t.* of robbers prosper
Ps. 15: 1 who shall abide in thy *t.*
84: 1 how amiable are thy *t.*
118: 15 salvation is in the *t.* of the
Prov. 14:11 *t.* of the upright shall flourish
Is. 33:20 a *t.* that shall not be taken down
Amos 9:11 will I raise up the *t.* of David
Acts. 15:16 will build again the *t.* of David
2 Cor. 5: 1 if our earthly house of this *t.*
5: 4 we that are in this *t.* do groan
Heb. 8: 2 sanctuary and the true *t.*, which the
11: 9 dwelling in *t.* with Isaac and
2 Pet. 1:13 as long as I am in this *t.*
1:14 knowing I must put off this my *t.*
Rev. 21: 3 the *t.* of God is with men

TABLE (TABLES)
Ex. 25:23 make a *t.* of shittim wood
Deut. 10: 4 he wrote on the *t.* according to
2 Chr. 4:19 *t.* whereon the showbread was set
Job 36:16 on thy *t.* should be full of fatness
Ps. 23: 5 Thou preparest a *t.* before me
69:22 let their *t.* become a snare
128: 3 like olive plants round about thy *t.*
Prov. 3: 3 write them on the *t.* of thy heart
Sol. 1:12 while the king sitteth at his *t.*
Is. 28: 8 for all *t.* are full of vomit, and
Jer. 17: 1 is graven on the *t.* of their heart
Ezek. 40:41 Four *t.* were on this side
Hab. 2: 2 make it plain upon the *t.*
Mal. 1: 7 *t.* of Lord is contemptible
Mat. 15:27 which fall from the masters' *t.*
Acts 6: 2 hear the word of God and serve *t.*
1 Cor. 10:21 partakers of the Lord's *t.*
2 Cor. 3: 3 not in *t.* of stone, but fleshy *t.*
Heb. 9: 4 budded, and the *t.* of the covenant

TAKE
Ex. 6: 7 I will *t.* you to me for a people
20: 7 not *t.* the name of the Lord in vain
34: 9 *t.* us for thine inheritance
Ps. 27:10 the Lord will *t.* me up
51:11 *t.* not thy holy spirit from me
116: 13 I will *t.* the cup of salvation
119: 43 *t.* not the word of truth out
Hos. 14: 2 *t.* with you words, and turn to
Mat. 16:24 *t.* up his cross and follow
18:16 *t.* with thee one or two more
18:23 would *t.* account of his servants
20:14 *T.*, that thine is, and go
26:26 said *T.*, eat; this is my body
Luke 12:19 *t.* thine ease, eat, drink
John 10:17 my life, that I might *t.* it again
1 Cor. 11:24 *T.* eat, this is my body
Eph. 6:13 *t.* unto you the whole armour
6:17 *t.* the helmet of salvation
Rev. 3:11 that no man *t.* thy crown

TAKEN (TAKING)
Ps. 40:12 my iniquities have *t.* hold
83: 3 *t.* crafty counsel against thy people
119: 9 by *t.* heed thereto according to
119:111 thy testimonies have I *t.*
119:143 trouble and anguish have *t.* hold of
Is. 6: 7 thine iniquity is *t.* away and thy sin
16:10 gladness is *t.* away and joy out of
53: 8 he was *t.* from prison and
57: 1 and merciful men are *t.* away
Lam. 4:20 was *t.* in their pits of whom we
Mat. 6:27 which of you by *t.* thought can
21:43 kingdom of God shall be *t.* from
24:40 one shall be *t.*, the other left
Mark 4:25 shall be *t.* even that which he hath
Luke 10:42 good part not be *t.* away from
Acts 1: 9 he was *t.* up; and a cloud
Rom. 7: 8 sin, *t.* occasion by the commandment
2 Cor. 3:16 Lord, the veil shall be *t.* away
Eph. 6:16 above all *t.* the shield of faith
2 Tim. 2:26 *t.* captive by him at his will

TALE (TALES)
Ps. 90: 9 our years as a *t.* that is told
Ezek. 22: 9 that carry *t.* to shed blood
Luke 24:11 seemed to them as idle *t.*

TALEBEARER
Lev. 19:16 go up and down as a *t.*
Prov. 11:13 A *t.* revealeth secrets: but he that
18: 8 The words of a *t.* are as wounds
20:19 goeth about as a *t.* revealeth secrets
26:22 words of a *t.* are as wounds

TALENT (TALENTS)
Mat. 18:24 which owed him ten thousand *t.*
25:25 hid thy *t.* in the earth

TALK (TALKETH, TALKING)
Deut. 6: 7 *t.* of them when thou sittest
1 Sam. 2: 3 *t.* no more so exceeding proudly
Job 13: 7 for God? and *t.* deceitfully for him
Ps. 37:30 his tongue *t.* of judgment
71:24 my tongue shall *t.* righteousness
105: 2 *t.* ye of all his wondrous works
145: 11 glory of thy kingdom and *t.* of thy
Jer. 12: 1 *t.* with thee of thy judgments
John 14:30 I will not *t.* much with
Eph. 5: 4 nor foolish *t.*, nor jesting

TALKERS
Tit. 1:10 are many unruly and vain *t.*

TARRY (TARRIED)
2 Ki. 14:10 glory of this and *t.* at home
1 Chr. 19: 5 *T.* at Jericho until your beards
Ps. 68:12 she that *t.* at home divided the spoil
101: 7 telleth lies shall not *t.* in my sight
Prov. 23:30 that *t.* long at wine; they that
Jer. 14: 8 turneth aside to *t.* for a night
Hab. 2: 3 though it *t.* wait for it
Mat. 25: 5 bridegroom *t.*, they all slumbered
26:38 *t.* ye here and watch with me
Luke 2:43 child Jesus *t.* behind in Jerusalem
John 21:22 that he *t.* till I come what is that
1 Cor. 11:33 together to eat, *t.* one for another

TASTE (TASTED)
Ex. 16:31 the *t.* was like wafers
1 Sam. 14:43 I did but *t.* a little honey
Job 6: 6 *t.* in the white of an egg?
Ps. 34: 8 O *t.* and see that the Lord is good
Sol. 2: 3 his fruit was sweet to my *t.*
Jer. 48:11 therefore his *t.* remained in him
Mat. 16:28 shall not *t.* of death till they see
Luke 14:24 were bidden shall *t.* of my supper
John 8:52 keep my saying shall never *t.* death
Col. 2:21 touch not, *t.* not, handle not
Heb. 2: 9 of God should *t.* death for every man
6: 4 have *t.* of the heavenly gift
1 Pet. 2: 3 if ye have *t.* that the Lord is gracious

TAUGHT
2 Chr. 30:22 *t.* the good knowledge of the Lord
Ps. 71:17 hast *t.* me from my youth
Eccl. 12: 9 wise, he still *t.* the people knowledge
Is. 54:13 children shall be *t.* of the Lord
John 6:45 they shall be all *t.* of God
Acts 20:20 *t.* you publicly, and from house to
Gal. 6: 6 let him that is *t.* in the word
1 Thes. 4: 9 yourselves are *t.* of God to love

TEACH
Ex. 4:12 *t.* thee what thou shalt say
Lev. 10:11 ye may *t.* the children of Israel
Deut. 4: 9 *t.* them thy sons, and thy sons' sons
33:10 They shall *t.* Jacob thy judgments
1 Sam. 12:23 I will *t.* you the good and the
2 Chr. 17: 7 to *t.* in the cities of Judah
Job 21:22 shall any *t.* God knowledge
34:32 that which I see not *teach* thou me
Ps. 25: 5 lead me in thy truth, and *t.* me
25: 8 will he *t.* sinners in the way
27:11 *T.* me thy way, O Lord
34:11 I will *t.* you the fear of the Lord
51:13 will I *t.* transgressors thy ways
90:12 so *t.* us to number our days
119: 12 thou O Lord: *t.* my thy statutes
119: 66 *T.* me good judgment and knowledge
119:108 O Lord, *t.* me thy judgments
143: 10 *T.* me to do thy will; for thou
Is. 2: 3 and he will *t.* us of his ways
Jer. 31:34 *t.* no more every man his neighbour
Mat. 28:19 go ye therefore and *t.* all nations
John 9:34 and dost thou *t.* us?
14:26 he shall *t.* you all things
1 Cor. 4:17 as I *t.* every where in every church
1 Tim. 2:12 I suffer not a woman to *t.*
3: 2 given to hospitality, apt to *t.*
2 Tim. 2: 2 be able to *t.* others also
Heb. 5:12 have need that one *t.* you
1 John 2:27 need not that any man *t.* you

TEACHER (TEACHERS)
Ps. 119: 99 more understanding than all my *t.*
Is. 30:20 shall not thy *t.* be removed
Hab. 2:18 and a *t.* of lies, that the maker

John 3: 2 thou art a t. come from God
Rom. 2:20 a t. of babes which hast the
1 Tim. 2: 7 a t. of the Gentiles in faith
2 Tim. 1:11 and a t. of the Gentiles
4: 3 heap to themselves t., having itching
Tit. 2: 3 to much wine t. of good things
Heb. 5:12 ye ought to be t. ye have need

TEACHEST (TEACHETH, TEACHING)
2 Chr. 15: 3 and without a t. priest
Job 35:11 who t. us more than beasts
36:22 his power: who t. like him
Ps. 18:34 t. my hands to war so that a
94:12 O Lord, and t. him out of thy law
Is. 48:17 Lord thy God which t. thee to profit
Mat. 15: 9 t. for doctrines the commandments
22:16 t. the way of God in truth
28:20 t. them to observe all things
Rom. 2:21 t. another, t. thou not thyself
1 Cor. 2:13 wisdom t. but which the Holy Ghost t.
Col. 1:28 t. every man in all wisdom
Tit. 2:12 t. us that denying ungodliness
1 John 2:27 same anointing t. you of all things

TEARS
Job 16:20 mine eye poureth out t.
Ps. 6: 6 water my couch with my t.
56: 8 put thou my t. in thy bottle
80: 5 feedest them with the bread of t.
126: 5 they that sow in t. shall reap in joy
Is. 25: 8 wipe away all t. from off all faces
Jer. 9: 1 mine eyes were a fountain of t.
Luke 7:38 to wash his feet with t.
Acts 20:19 with many t. and temptations
20:31 warn everyone night and day with t.
2 Cor. 2: 4 I wrote unto you with many t.
2 Tim. 1: 4 being mindful of thy t., that I may
Heb. 5: 7 with strong crying and t. unto him
Rev. 7:17 wipe all t. from their eyes

TEETH
Gen 49:12 his t. white with milk
Job 4:10 the t. of the young lions
Ps. 3: 7 broken the t. of the ungodly
112: 10 he shall gnash with his t.
Sol. 4: 2 t. like a flock of sheep
Jer. 31:29 his t. shall be set on edge
Ezek. 18: 2 children's t. are set on edge
Amos 4: 6 cleanness of the t. in all cities
Mat. 8:12 shall be weeping and gnashing of t.
24:51 shall be weeping and gnashing of t.
25:30 shall be weeping and gnashing of t.

TELL
2 Sam. 1:20 T. it not in Gath, publish it
Ps. 48:13 t. it to the generation following
Prov. 30: 4 name, if thou canst t.
Mat. 8: 4 see thou t. no man; but go
18:15 go and t. him his fault
John 3: 8 not t. whence it cometh, and whither
4:25 when he is come he will t. us all
8:14 ye cannot t. whence I come
2 Cor. 12: 2 out of the body, I cannot t.
Gal. 4:16 because I t. you the truth
Phil. 3:18 now t. you even weeping that they

TEMPERANCE
Acts 24:25 as he reasoned of righteousness, t.
Gal. 5:23 t.: against such there is no law
2 Pet. 1: 6 And to knowledge t., and to t.

TEMPERATE
1 Cor. 9:25 mastery is to t. in all things
Tit. 1: 8 sober, just, holy, t.
2: 2 men be sober, grave, t.

TEMPLE (TEMPLES)
1 Sam. 1: 9 by a post of the t. of the Lord
1 Ki. 6: 5 of the t. and the oracle
Ps. 29: 9 in his t. doth every one speak of
Sol. 4: 3 thy t. are like a piece of a
Jer. 7: 4 The t. of the Lord are these
Mal. 3: 1 suddenly come to his t., even the
Mat. 12: 6 place is one greater than the t. is
John 2:19 destroy this t. and in three days
2:21 he spake of the t. of his body
Acts 7:48 most High dwelleth not in t.
1 Cor. 3:16 ye are the t. of God
6:19 body is the t. of the Holy Ghost
9:13 live of the things of the t.
2 Cor. 6:16 hath the t. of God with idols
Rev. 7:15 serve him day and night in the t.
11:19 t. of God was opened in heaven
21:22 God and the Lamb are the t.

TEMPT (TEMPTED, TEMPTING)
Gen. 22: 1 God did t. Abraham, and said unto
Ex. 17: 7 because they t. the Lord
Num. 14:22 t. me now these ten times
Deut. 6:16 ye shall not t. the Lord
Ps. 78:18 they t. God in their heart by asking
78:56 t. and provoked the most high God
95: 9 when your fathers t. me
Is. 7:12 not ask, neither will I t. the Lord
Mal. 3:15 they that t. God are even delivered
Mat. 4: 1 to be t. of the devil
4: 7 thou shalt not t. the Lord
16: 1 t. desired him that he would
22:18 why t. ye me, ye hypocrites
22:35 asked him a question, t. him
Luke 10:25 stood up, and t. him, saying
11:16 others, t. him, sought of him
John 8: 6 This they said, t. him
Acts 5: 9 have agreed together to t. the Spirit
15:10 why t. ye God to put a yoke
1 Cor. 7: 5 that Satan t. you not for
10:13 not suffer you to be t.
Gal. 6: 1 lest thou also be t.
1 Thes. 3: 5 the tempter have t. you
Heb. 2:18 being t. he is able to succour
4:15 in all points t. as we are
Jas. 1:13 is t., I am t. of God
1:14 say when is he t. when he is drawn

TEMPTATION (TEMPTATIONS)
Deut. 4:34 by t., by signs, and by wonders
Ps. 95: 8 as in the day of t. in the wilderness
Mat. 6:13 lead us not into t., but deliver us
Luke 4:13 the devil had ended all t.
8:13 in time of t. fall away
22:28 have continued with me in my t.
Acts. 20:19 with many tears and t.
1 Cor. 10:13 no t. taken you but such
Gal. 4:14 t. which was in my flesh
Heb. 3: 8 day of t. in the wilderness
Jas. 1: 2 when ye fall into diver's t.
1:12 blessed is man that endureth t.
1 Pet. 1: 6 heaviness through manifold t.
2 Pet. 2: 9 deliver the godly out of t.
Rev. 3:10 keep thee from the hour of t.

TEMPTER
Mat. 4: 3 when the t. came to him, he said
1 Thes. 3: 5 the t. have tempted you, and our labour

TENDER
2 Ki. 22:19 Because thine heart was t.
Luke 1:78 Through the t. mercy of our God
Jas. 5:11 pitiful, and of t. mercy

TENDERHEARTED
Eph. 4:32 be ye kind to one another, t.

TENTS
Gen. 9:27 he shall dwell in the t.
Num. 24: 5 how goodly are thy t., O Jacob
1 Ki. 12:16 to your t., O Israel: now see to
Ps. 84:10 dwell in the t. of wickedness
120: 5 I dwell in the t. of Kedar
Sol. 1: 8 feed thy kids beside shepherds' t.

TERRIBLE
Ex. 34:10 it is a t. thing that I will
Deut. 1:19 that great and t. wilderness
7:21 is among you, a mighty God and t.
10:21 for thee these great and t. things
Neh. 1: 5 the great and t. God
9:32 the great and mighty and t. God
Job 37:22 with God is t. majesty
Ps. 45: 4 hand shall teach thee t. things
47: 2 for the Lord most high is t.
66: 3 how t. art thou in thy works
66: 5 God is t. in his doing
76:12 he is t. to the kings of the earth
99: 3 praise thy great and t. name
Sol. 6: 4 t. as an army with banners
Jer. 20:11 is with me as a mighty t. one
Joel 2:11 Lord is great and very t.
Zeph. 2:11 The Lord will be t. unto them: for
Heb. 12:21 so t. was the sight that Moses

TERROR
Gen. 35: 5 t. of God was upon the cities
Deut. 32:25 sword without, and t. within
Job 31:23 destruction from God was a t.
Jer. 17:17 be not a t. unto me: thou art my
20: 4 make thee a t. to thyself, and to
Ezek. 26:21 I will make thee a t., and thou
Rom. 13: 3 rulers are not a t. to good
2 Cor. 5: 1 knowing therefore the t. of the Lord

TESTAMENT
Mat. 26:28 my blood of the new t.
Luke 22:20 This cup is the new t.
1 Cor. 11:25 This cup is the new t.
2 Cor. 3:14 the reading of the old t.
Heb. 7:22 Jesus made a surety of a better t.
9:16 where a t. is, there must also
Rev. 11:19 in his temple the ark of his t.

TESTATOR
Heb. 9:16 necessity be death of the t.
9:17 no strength at all while the t liveth

TESTIFY (TESTIFIED. TESTIFYING)
Num. 35:30 one witness shall not t.
Deut. 8:19 I t. against you this day
2 Chr. 24:19 they t. against them: but they
Neh. 9:34 thou didst t. against them
13:15 and I t. against them in the day
Ps. 50: 7 I will t. against thee
81: 8 I will t. unto thee: O Israel
Is. 59:12 our sins t. against us: for our
Jer. 14: 7 our iniquities t. against us
Hos. 5: 5 pride of Israel t. to his face
John 3:11 do know and t. that we have seen
Acts 20:24 t. the gospel of the grace of God
23:11 thou hast t. of me in Jerusalem
1 Tim. 2: 6 for all, to be t. in due time
Heb. 11: 4 God t. of his gifts
1 Pet. 5:12 t. that it is the true grace
1 John 4:14 t. that the Father sent
5: 9 he hath t. of his son

TESTIMONY (TESTIMONIES)
2 Ki. 11:12 upon him, and gave him the t.
Ps. 25:10 keep his covenant and his t.
78: 5 for he established a t. in Jacob
93: 5 Thy t. are very sure: holiness
119: 2 Blessed are they that keep his t.
119: 14 rejoiced in the way of thy t.
Is. 8:16 bind up the t., seal the law
Mat. 10:18 for a t. against them and the
John 3:32 testifieth, and no man receiveth his t.
Acts 14: 3 t. to the word of his grace
2 Cor. 1:12 the t. of our conscience
Heb. 11: 5 before his translation he had this t.
Rev. 1: 9 God, and for the t. of Jesus Christ
11: 7 shall have finished their t.
19:10 the t. of Jesus is the spirit

THANK
1 Chr. 16: 4 to t. and praise the Lord
Mat. 11:25 I t. thee, O Father, Lord of heaven
Luke 6:33 good to you, what t. have ye
17: 9 Doth he t. that servant because he
18:11 God, I t. thee, that I am not
John 11:41 I t. thee that thou hast heard
Rom. 1: 8 I t. my God through Jesus Christ
7:25 I t. God through Jesus Christ
1 Cor. 1: 4 I t. my God always on your behalf
1 Tim. 1:12 I t. Jesus Christ our Lord

THANKFUL
Ps. 100: 4 be t. unto him, and bless his
Rom. 1:21 as God, neither were t.
Col. 3:15 in one body, and be ye t.

THANKS
Dan. 6:10 gave t. before his God, as he did
Mat. 26:27 took the cup and gave t.
Mark 8: 6 seven loaves, and gave t.
Luke 22:17 took the cup and gave t.
1 Cor. 15:57 But t. be to God which giveth
2 Cor. 8:16 But t. be to God which put
9:15 t. be to God for his unspeakable
Eph. 1:16 Cease not to give t. for you
5: 4 but rather giving of t.
1 Thes. 3: 9 what t. can we render to God
5:18 In every thing, give t.
2 Thes. 2:13 we are bound to give t.
1 Tim. 2: 1 giving of t., be made for all men

Heb. 13:15 our lips giving *t.* to his name

THANKSGIVING
Lev. 7:12 If he offer it for a *t.*
Neh. 11:17 the principal to begin the *t.*
Ps. 26: 7 publish with the voice of *t.*
100: 4 Enter his gates with *t.*
116: 17 offer to thee the sacrifice of *t.*
Is. 51: 3 *t.*, and the voice of melody
Phil. 4: 6 by prayer and supplication with *t.*
1 Tim. 4: 3 created to be received with *t.*
Rev. 7:12 wisdom, and *t.*, and honour

THINK
Neh. 5:19 *T.* upon me, my God, for good
Jer. 29:11 thoughts that I *t.* toward you
Rom. 12: 3 *t.* of himself more highly
1 Cor. 8: 2 if any man *t.* that he knoweth
Gal. 6: 3 if a man *t.* himself to be something
Eph. 3:20 above all that we ask or *t.*
Phil. 4: 8 be any praise, *t.* on these things

THOUGHT
Gen. 50:20 As for you, ye *t.* evil against me
Ps. 48: 9 we have *t.* of thy lovingkindness
119: 59 I *t.* on my ways and turned
139: 2 understandest my *t.* afar
Prov. 24: 9 the *t.* of foolishness is sin
Eccl. 10:20 curse not the king, no not in thy *t.*
Mal. 3:16 and that *t.* on his name
Mat. 6:25 take no *t.* for your life
6:34 take therefore no *t.* for the morrow
Mark 13:11 take no *t.* beforehand what ye
14:72 when he *t.* thereon he wept
Luke 12:22 take no *t.* for your life
1 Cor. 13:11 I *t.* as a child, but when
2 Cor. 10: 5 bringeth into captivity every *t.*
Phil. 2: 6 *t.* it not robbery to be equal

THOUGHTS
Gen. 6: 5 imagination of the *t.* of his heart
Judg. 5:15 were great *t.* of the heart
1 Chr. 28: 9 the imaginations of the *t.*
29:18 keep for ever in imagination of *t.*
Ps. 10: 4 God is not in all his *t.*
33:11 the *t.* of his heart to all
40: 5 thy *t.* which are to us-ward
94:11 Lord knoweth the *t.* of man
94:19 in the multitude of my *t.* within me
139: 17 how precious are thy *t.* to me
139: 23 know my heart, try me, and know my *t.*
Prov. 12: 5 The *t.* of the righteous are right
15:26 *t.* of the wicked are the abomination
16: 3 thy *t.* shall be established
Is. 55: 7 way, and the unrighteous man his *t.*
55: 8 my *t.* are not your *t.*
59: 7 their *t.* are *t.* of iniquity
66:18 I know their works and their *t.*
Jer. 4:14 how long shall thy vain *t.*
Mic. 4:12 know not the *t.* of the Lord
Mat. 15:19 out of heart proceed evil *t.*
Luke 2:35 the *t.* of many hearts may be revealed
Rom. 2:15 witness and their *t.* the mean while
1 Cor. 3:20 the Lord knoweth the *t.* of the wise
Heb. 4:12 a discerner of the *t.* and intents
Jas. 2: 4 and are become judges of evil *t.*

THIRST (THIRSTETH)
Deut. 28:48 hunger, and in *t.*, and in nakedness
Ps. 42: 2 my soul *t.* for God, for the living
Is. 49:10 they shall not hunger nor *t.*
55: 1 Ho, every one that *t.*, come ye
Mat. 5: 6 do hunger and *t.* after righteousness
John 4:14 shall never *t.*, but the water that
6:35 believeth on me shall never *t.*
7:37 if any man *t.*, let him come unto me
Rom. 12:20 feed him; if he *t.* give him drink
Rev. 7:16 neither *t.* any more; neither shall

THORNS
Gen. 3:18 *T.* also thistles shall it bring
Num. 33:55 and *t.* in your sides, and shall vex
Josh. 23:13 and *t.* in your eyes, until ye perish
Judg. 2: 3 be as *t.* in your sides
2 Sam. 23: 6 as *t.* thrust away, because they
Jer. 4: 3 ground, and sow not among *t.*
Jer. 12:13 sown wheat, but shall reap *t.*
Mat. 7:16 do men gather grapes of *t.*?
13: 7 some fell among *t.*; and the *t.*

THREE
2 Sam. 24:12 I offer thee *t.* things; choose thee
Prov. 30:15 *t.* things that are never satisfied
30:21 *t.* things the earth is disquieted
30:29 *t.* things which go well, yea, four
Amos. 1: 3 For *t.* transgressions of Damascus
2: 1 For *t.* transgressions of Moab
1 Cor. 14:27 or at the most by *t.*, and that
1 John 5: 7 For there are *t.* that bear record in
Rev. 16:13 *t.* unclean spirits like frogs

THRESH (THRESHETH, THRESHING)
Lev. 26: 5 and your *t.* shall reach
Is. 21:10 my *t.*, and the corn
41:15 thou shalt *t.* the mountains
Mic. 4:13 Arise and *t.*, O daughter of Zion
Hab. 3:12 thou didst *t.* the heathen in anger
1 Cor. 9:10 that he that *t.* in hope

THRESHINGFLOOR
2 Sam. 24:18 the *t.* of Araunah, the Jebusite
24:21 To buy the *t.* of thee to build
24:24 So David bought the *t.*
Jer. 51:33 Babylon is like a *t.*, it is time

THROAT
Ps. 5: 9 their *t.* is an open sepulchre; they
69: 3 weary of my crying, my *t.* is dried
Prov. 23: 2 put a knife to thy *t.*

THRONE
Ps. 11: 4 the Lord's *t.* is heaven: his eyes
45: 6 Thy *t.*, O God, is for ever
89:14 are the habitation of thy *t.*
94:20 *t.* of iniquity have fellowship
Prov. 25: 5 *t.* shall be established in righteousness
Is. 22:23 a glorious *t.* to his father's house
Jer. 14:21 do not disgrace the *t.* of thy glory
17:12 A glorious high *t.* from
Lam. 5:19 thy *t.* from generation to
Dan. 7: 9 his *t.* was like a fiery flame
Mat. 19:28 shall sit in the *t.* of his glory
25:31 shall sit on the *t.* of his glory
Heb. 1: 8 Thy *t.*, O God, is for ever
4:16 boldly to the *t.* of grace
Rev. 3:21 with my Father in his *t.*
20:11 And I saw a great white *t.*
22: 3 *t.* of God and the Lamb shall be in

THUNDER (THUNDERETH)
Job 26:14 but the *t.* of his power who can
40: 9 canst thou *t.* with a voice
Ps. 29: 3 the God of glory *t.*: the Lord is
81: 7 in the secret place of *t.*
Mark 3:17 Boanerges, which is, The sons of *t.*

THUNDERINGS
Rev. 4: 5 lightnings and *t.*, and voices
8: 5 voices, and *t.*, and lightnings
11:19 voices, and *t.*, and an earthquake
19: 6 as the voice of mighty *t.*

TIDINGS
Ex. 33: 4 people heard these evil *t.*
Ps. 112: 7 not be afraid of evil *t.*
Luke 1:19 and to show thee these glad *t.*
2:10 I bring you good *t.* of great joy
8: 1 preaching and showing the glad *t.*
Acts 13:32 we declare unto you glad *t.*
Rom. 10:15 bring glad *t.* of good things

TIME
Ps. 32: 6 in a *t.* when thou mayest be found
37:19 be ashamed in the evil *t.*
41: 1 deliver him in *t.* of trouble
69:13 in an acceptable *t.*
89:47 remember how short my *t.* is
Eccl. 3: 1 and a *t.* to every purpose
3: 8 a *t.* of war and a *t.* of peace
9:11 *t.* and chance happeneth to them all
Ezek. 16: 8 thy *t.* was the *t.* of love
Dan. 7:25 till a *t.* and times
12: 7 that it shall be for a *t.*
Amos 5:13 keep silent in that *t.*
Luke 19:44 knewest not the *t.* of thy visitation
John 7: 6 my *t.* is not yet come: your *t.*
Acts 17:21 spent their *t.* in nothing else
Rom. 13:11 it is high *t.* to awake out of sleep
2 Cor. 6: 2 Behold, now is the accepted *t.*
Eph. 5:16 redeeming the *t.*, because the days
Col. 4: 5 are without, redeeming the *t.*
1 Pet. 1:17 pass the *t.* of your sojourning
Rev. 10: 6 there should be *t.* no longer
12:14 times, and a half *t.*

TIMES
Ps. 31:15 my *t.* are in thy hand
34: 1 bless the Lord at all *t.*
62: 8 trust in him at all *t.*; ye people
106: 3 that doeth righteousness at all *t.*
119: 20 unto thy judgments at all *t.*
Prov. 5:19 let her breasts satisfy thee at all *t.*
17:17 a friend loveth at all *t.*
Luke 21:24 till the *t.* of the Gentiles
Acts 1: 7 not for you to know the *t.*
3:19 *t.* of refreshing shall come
17:26 determined the *t.* before appointed
1 Tim. 4: 1 that in the latter *t.* some shall
2 Tim. 3: 1 in the last days perilous *t.*

TITHE (TITHES)
Gen. 14:20 he gave him *t.* of all
Amos 4: 4 and your *t.* after three years
Mal. 3: 8 we robbed thee? In *t.* and offerings
Mat. 23:23 ye pay *t.* of mint and anise and cummin
Luke 18:12 I give *t.* of all that I

TOGETHER
Ps. 2: 2 rulers take counsel *t.* against
Prov. 22: 2 rich and poor meet *t.*: the Lord is
Rom. 8:28 all things work *t.* for good
1 Cor. 3: 9 we are labourers *t.* with God
2 Cor. 6: 1 as workers *t.* with him, beseech
Eph. 2: 5 quickened us *t.* with Christ
2: 6 raised us up *t.* and made us sit *t.*

TOKEN (TOKENS)
Gen. 9:13 shall be for a *t.* of a covenant
17:11 it shall be a *t.* of the covenant
Ps. 65: 8 uttermost parts are afraid at thy *t.*
86:17 show me a *t.* for good; that they
135: 9 who sent *t.* and wonders into the midst
Phil. 1:28 to them an evident *t.* of perdition
2 Thes. 1: 5 a manifest *t.* of righteous judgment

TONGUE
Ex. 11: 7 shall not a dog move his *t.* against
Josh. 10:21 none moved his *t.* against any
Job 5:21 be hid from the scourge of the *t.*
20:12 though he hide it under his *t.*
Ps. 34:13 keep thy *t.* from evil, and thy lips
35:28 *t.* shall speak of thy righteousness
45: 1 my *t.* is the pen of a ready
137: 6 let my *t.* cleave to the roof
Prov. 10:20 *t.* of the just is as choice silver
12:18 but the *t.* of the wise is health
15: 4 wholesome *t.* is a tree of life
18:21 death and life are in power of the *t.*
21: 6 getting of treasures by a lying *t.*
21:23 keepeth his *t.* keepeth his soul
25:15 a soft *t.* breaketh the bone
Is. 30:27 his *t.* as a devouring fire
50: 4 Lord hath given me the *t.* of the learned
Jer. 9: 5 taught their *t.* to speak lies
Acts 2:26 heart rejoice and my *t.* was glad
Jas. 1:26 and bridleth not his *t.*
3: 5 *t.* is a little member and boasteth
3: 8 the *t.* can no man tame; it is an
1 Pet. 3:10 refrain his *t.* from evil

TONGUES
Ps. 31:20 pavilion from the strife of *t.*
55: 9 O Lord, and divide their *t.*
Mark 16:17 they shall speak with new *t.*
Acts 19: 6 spake with *t.* and prophesied
1 Cor. 12:10 to another divers kinds of *t.*
14:23 and all speak with *t.*, another come

TOOK
Ps. 22: 9 he that *t.* me out of the womb
Phil. 2: 7 *t.* on him the form of a servant
Heb. 10:34 *t.* joyfully the spoiling of your

TORMENT (TORMENTED)
Mat. 8:29 art thou come hither to *t.* us
Luke 16:24 for I am *t.* in this flame

Luke 16:28 come to this place of *t.*
Heb. 11:37 being destitute, afflicted, *t.*
Rev. 14:11 smoke of their *t.* ascendeth up for
18: 7 so much *t.* and sorrow give her: for

TOSS (TOSSED)
Ps. 109: 23 I am *t.* up and down like a locust
Is. 22:18 violently turn and *t.* thee like a
Jer. 5:22 though the waves thereof *t.* themselves
Jas. 1: 6 driven with the wind and *t.*
Eph. 4:14 be no more children *t.* to and fro

TOUCH (TOUCHED, TOUCHETH)
1 Sam. 10:26 men whose hearts God had *t.*
Job 5:19 in seven there shall no evil *t.*
19:21 hand of God hath *t.* me
Ps. 105: 15 *T.* not mine anointed and do my
Is. 52:11 *t.* no unclean thing; go ye out of
Zech. 2: 8 he that *t.* you *t.* the apple
Mat. 9:21 If I may but *t.* his garment
14:36 only *t.* the hem of his garment
Mark 10:13 that he should *t.* them: and his
Luke 11:46 *t.* not the burdens with one of your
John 20:17 *t.* me not, for I am not yet
1 Cor. 7: 1 good for a man not to *t.* a woman
2 Cor. 6:17 *t.* not the unclean thing; and I
Col. 2:21 *t.* not, taste not, handle not
1 John 5:18 that wicked one *t.* him not

TOWER
Ps. 61: 3 a strong *t.* from the enemy
144: 2 my high *t.*, and my deliverer
Sol. 4: 4 thy neck like the *t.* of David
7: 4 thy neck is as a *t.* of ivory
Is. 5: 2 built a *t.* in the midst of
Mat. 21:33 winepress in it, and built a *t.*

TRADITION (TRADITIONS)
Mat. 15: 3 commandment of God by your *t.*
Gal. 1:14 exceedingly jealous of the *t.*
Col. 2: 8 after the *t.* of men after the
2 Thes. 2:15 hold the *t.* which ye have been taught
3: 6 disorderly, and not after the *t.*
1 Pet. 1:18 received by *t.* from your fathers

TRAIN
Prov. 22: 6 *T.* up a child in the way
Is. 6: 1 up, and his *t.* filled the temple

TRANCE
Num. 24: 4 falling into a *t.*, but having
Acts 10:10 they made ready, he fell into a *t.*
11: 5 in a *t.*, I saw a vision
22:17 prayed in the temple, I was in a *t.*

TRANSFIGURED
Mat. 17: 2 And was *t.* before them: and his
Mark 9: 2 themselves: and he was *t.* before them

TRANSFORMED
Rom. 12: 2 be ye *t.* by the renewing of your
2 Cor. 11:15 *t.* as the ministers of rightousness

TRANSGRESS (TRANSGRESSED, TRANSGRESSETH)
Num. 14:41 now do ye *t.* the commandments
Deut. 26:13 I have not *t.* thy commandments
Josh. 7:11 they have also *t.* my covenant
1 Sam. 2:24 make the Lord's people to *t.*
2 Chr. 24:20 why *t.* ye the commandments of the Lord?
Neh. 1: 8 if ye *t.* I will scatter you
Ps. 17: 3 my mouth shall not *t.*
25: 3 be ashamed which *t.* without cause
Prov. 28:21 piece of bread that man will *t.*
Is. 43:27 teachers have *t.* against
Jer. 2: 8 pastors also *t.* against me
Lam. 3:42 we have *t.* and have rebelled
Ezek. 2: 3 they and their fathers have *t.*
Dan. 9:11 all Israel have *t.* thy law, even
Hos. 6: 7 they like men have *t.* the covenant
Amos 4: 4 come to Bethel and *t.*; at Gilgal
Hab. 2: 5 Yea, also, because he *t.* by wine
Mat. 15: 2 do thy disciples *t.* the traditions
Rom. 2:27 and circumcision dost *t.* the law
1 John 3: 4 whosoever committeth sin *t.*

TRANSGRESSION
Ex. 34: 7 forgiving iniquity, *t.*, and sin
Num. 14:18 great mercy, forgiving iniquity and *t.*
1 Chr. 10:13 Saul died for his *t.*
Job 13:23 make me to know my *t.*
Ps. 19:13 innocent from the great *t.*
32: 1 blessed he whose *t.* is forgiven
89:32 I will visit their *t.* with the rod
107: 17 Fools because of their *t.* are afflicted
Prov. 17: 9 that covereth *t.* seeketh love
Is. 53: 8 the *t.* of my people was he stricken
58: 1 show my people their *t.*, and the house
59:20 them that turn from *t.* in Jacob
Dan. 9:24 to finish the *t.* and make an end
Amos 4: 4 at Gilgal multiply *t.*; and bring your
Mic. 3: 8 to declare to Jacob his *t.*
6: 7 shall I give my firstborn for my *t.*
Rom. 4:15 where no law is, there is no *t.*
1 John 3: 4 sin is the *t.* of the law

TRANSGRESSIONS
Ex. 23:21 for he will not pardon your *t.*
Lev. 16:21 all their *t.* in all their sins
Josh. 24:19 will not forgive your *t.* nor your
Job 31:33 If I covered my *t.* as Adam, by
Ps. 25: 7 sins of my youth, nor my *t.*
32: 5 I said, I will confess my *t.*
39: 8 deliver me from all my *t.*
51: 1 tender mercies blot out my *t.*
51: 3 I acknowledge my *t.* and my sin is
103: 12 so far hath he removed our *t.*
Is. 43:25 I am he that blotteth out thy *t.*
44:22 blotted out as a thick cloud thy *t.*
53: 5 he was wounded for our *t.*, he was
59:12 our *t.* are multiplied before thee
Ezek. 18:31 cast away from you all *t.*
Heb. 9:15 for the redemption of the *t.*

TRANSGRESSOR (TRANSGRESSORS)
Ps. 51:13 Then will I teach *t.* thy ways
59: 5 be not merciful to any wicked *t.*
119:158 I beheld the *t.* and was grieved
Prov. 13:15 the way of the *t.* is hard
Is. 48: 8 called a *t.* from the womb
53:12 made intercession for the *t.*
Hos. 14: 9 the *t.* shall fall therein
Jas. 2: 9 convinced of the law as *t.*
2:11 if thou kill, thou art become a *t.*

TRAVAIL (TRAVAILED, TRAVAILETH, TRAVAILING)
Job 15:20 wicked man *t.* with pain all his
Eccl. 1:13 this sore *t.* hath God given
4: 4 I considered all *t.*, and every
5:14 those riches perish by evil *t.*
Is. 13: 8 be in pain as a woman that *t.*
53:11 He shall see of the *t.*
66: 7 before she *t.*, she brought forth
66: 8 as soon as Zion *t.*, she brought
Jer. 31: 8 her that *t.* with child together
Hos. 13:13 The sorrows of a *t.* woman
Gal. 4:19 children, of whom I *t.*
2 Thes. 3: 8 labour and *t.* night and day
Rev. 12: 2 being with child, *t.* in birth

TREACHEROUS (TREACHEROUSLY)
Is. 21: 2 treacherous dealer dealeth *t.*
24:16 *t.* dealers have dealt *t.*
Jer. 9: 2 an assembly of *t.* men
3:20 wife *t.* departeth from her husband
Hos. 5: 7 they have dealt *t.* against Lord
Mal. 2:15 none deal *t.* against the wife

TREAD (TREADETH)
Deut. 25: 4 not muzzle the ox when he *t.* out
Job 40:12 and *t.* down the wicked
Ps. 7: 5 let him *t.* down my life
44: 5 through thy name will we *t.* them under
Is. 1:12 of your hand, to *t.* my courts?
63: 3 I will *t.* them in mine anger
1 Cor. 9: 9 the ox that *t.* out the corn
1 Tim. 5:18 ox that *t.* out the corn
Rev. 11: 2 holy city shall they *t.*

TREASURE (TREASURES)
Ex. 19: 5 shall ye be a peculiar *t.* unto me
Deut. 28:12 Lord shall open to thee his good *t.*
32:34 sealed up among my *t.*
Ps. 135: 4 and Israel for his peculiar *t.*
Prov. 2: 4 searchest for her as for hid *t.*
10: 2 *t.* of wickedness profit nothing
21: 6 getting *t.* by a lying tongue
15: 6 house of the righteous is much *t.*
21:20 there is *t.* to be desired and oil
Is. 33: 6 fear of the Lord is his *t.*
Mat. 6:19 not up for yourselves *t.* on earth
6:20 lay up for yourselves *t.* in heaven
6:21 where your *t.* is, there will
12:35 a good man out of the good *t.* of
13:52 bringeth forth out of his *t.*
19:21 thou shalt have *t.* in heaven
Luke 12:21 layeth up *t.* for himself, and is not
2 Cor. 4: 7 we have this *t.* in earthen vessels
Col. 2: 3 hid all the *t.* of wisdom
Heb. 11:26 greater riches than *t.* in

TREE (TREES)
Gen. 2:16 Of every *t.* of the garden
3:22 take also the *t.* of life
Ps. 1: 3 like a *t.* planted by rivers
37:35 spreading himself like a bay *t.*
52: 8 I am like a green olive *t.*
104: 16 *t.* of the Lord are full of sap
Prov. 3:18 she is a *t.* of life to them
11:30 fruit of the righteous is the *t.* of
Is. 6:13 shall be eaten: as a teil *t.*
61: 3 might be called *t.* of righteousness
Jer. 17: 8 a *t.* planted by the waters
Ezek. 47:12 grow all *t.* for meat whose leaf
Mat. 3:10 every *t.* which bringeth not forth
7:17 good *t.* bringeth forth good fruit
12:33 the *t.* is known by his fruit
Mark 8:24 I see men as *t.* walking
1 Pet. 2:24 in his own body on the *t.*
Jude 1:12 *t.* whose fruit withereth without
Rev. 2: 7 will I give to eat of the *t.* of life
22: 2 in midst of street was the *t.* of life
22:14 may have right to the *t.* of life

TREMBLE (TREMBLED, TREMBLING)
Deut. 28:65 give thee there a *t.* heart
1 Sam. 4:13 for his heart *t.* for the ark of God
13: 7 all the people followed him *t.*
Ezra 9: 4 every one that *t.* at the words of God
10: 9 of God *t.* because of this matter
10: 3 those that *t.* at the commandment
Ps. 2:11 Lord with fear, and rejoice with *t.*
Eccl. 12: 3 keepers of the house shall *t.*
Is. 66: 5 ye that *t.* at his word
Jer. 5:22 will ye not *t.* at my presence?
10:10 at his wrath the earth shall *t.*
Ezek. 12:18 drink thy water with *t.*, and with
26:16 clothe themselves with *t.*
Dan. 6:26 men *t.* and fear before the God
Hos. 13: 1 when Ephraim spake *t.*, he exalted
Zech. 12: 2 make Jerusalem a cup of *t.*
Acts 24:25 as he reasoned Felix *t.*
1 Cor. 2: 3 in fear, in weakness, and in much *t.*
Phil. 2:12 your own salvation with fear and *t.*
Jas. 2:19 devils also believe and *t.*

TRESPASS (TRESPASSES)
Lev. 26:40 with their *t.* which the trespassed
1 Ki. 8:31 any man *t.* against his neighbor
Ezra 9: 6 our *t.* is grown up unto the heavens
9:15 we are before thee in our *t.*
Ezek. 39:26 and all their *t.* whereby they have
Mat. 6:14 if ye forgive men their *t.*
6:15 if ye forgive not men their *t.*
18:15 thy brother shall *t.* against thee
18:35 every one his brother their *t.*
Luke 17: 3 If thy brother *t.* against thee, rebuke
2 Cor. 5:19 not imputing their *t.* to
Eph. 2: 1 who were dead in *t.* and sins
Col. 2:13 having forgiven you all *t.*

TRIAL
Job 9:23 laugh at the *t.* of the innocent
Ezek. 21:13 Because it is a *t.*, and what if the
2 Cor. 8: 2 in a great *t.* of affliction
Heb. 11:36 others had a *t.* of cruel mockings
1 Pet. 1: 7 That the *t.* of your faith, being much
4:12 strange concerning the fiery *t.*

TRIBES
Num. 24: 2 in his tents according to their *t.*
Ps. 105: 37 not one feeble person among their *t.*
122: 4 whither the *t.* go up, the *t.* of
Mat. 24:30 shall all the *t.* of the earth
Acts 26: 7 promise our twelve *t.* instantly

TRIBULATION
Deut. 4:30 When thou art in *t.*, and all these
Judg. 10:14 in the time of your *t.*

1 Sam. 26:24 deliver me out of all *t.*
Mat. 13:21 when *t.* or persecution ariseth, because
24:29 immediately after the *t.* of those days
John 16:33 in the world ye shall have *t.*
Acts 14:22 we must through much *t.* enter into
Rom. 2: 9 *t.* and anguish upon every soul
5: 3 knowing that *t.* worketh patience
8:35 from the love of Christ? shall *t.*
12:12 rejoicing in hope, patient in *t.*
2 Cor. 1: 4 comforteth us in all our *t.*
7: 4 exceeding joyful in all our *t.*
2 Thes. 1: 6 to recompense *t.* to them that trouble
Rev. 1: 9 brother and companion in *t.*
2: 9 I know thy works and *t.*
2:10 ye shall have *t.* ten days
2:22 into great *t.* except they repent
7:14 which came out of great *t.*

TRIBULATIONS
1 Sam. 10:19 of all your adversities and your *t.*
Rom. 5: 3 glory in *t.* also: knowing that *t.*
Eph. 3:13 faint not at my *t.* for you
2 Thes. 1: 4 persecutions and *t.* that ye endure

TRIBUTE
Gen. 49:15 bear, and became a servant unto *t.*
Num. 31:28 levy a *t.* unto the Lord of the men
Prov. 12:24 slothful shall be under *t.*
Mat. 17:24 doth not the master pay *t.*
22:17 is it lawful to give *t.* to Caesar
Rom. 13: 7 *t.* to whom *t.* is due; custom

TRIUMPH (TRIUMPHED, TRIUMPHING)
Ex. 15: 1 he hath *t.* gloriously: the horse
15:21 for he hath *t.* gloriously: the horse
2 Sam. 1:20 daughters of the uncircumcised *t.*
Job 20: 5 the *t.* of the wicked is short
Ps. 25: 2 let not mine enemies *t.* over me
92: 4 *t.* in the works of thy hands
2 Cor. 2:14 God, which always causeth us to *t.*
Col. 2:15 of them openly, *t.* over them in it

TRODDEN
Judg. 5:21 thou hast *t.* down strength
Ps. 119:118 *t.* down all them that err
Is. 63: 3 I have *t.* the winepress alone
Luke 21:24 Jerusalem shall be *t.* down of the
Heb. 10:29 who hath *t.* under foot the Son of God

TROUBLE (TROUBLES)
Job 5: 6 neither doth *t.* spring out of the
5: 7 man is born to *t.* as sparks fly
14: 1 is of few days and full of *t.*
Ps. 9: 9 the oppressed a refuge in times of *t.*
25:17 *t.* of my heart are enlarged
27: 5 in time of *t.* he shall hide me
34:17 deliver them out of all their *t.*
37:39 their strength in the time of *t.*
46: 1 a very present help in *t.*
60:11 give us help from *t.*: for vain
71:20 shown me great and sore *t.*
88: 3 my soul is full of *t.*
91:15 I will be with him in *t.*
119:143 *t.* and anguish have taken hold
143: 11 bring my soul out of *t.*
Prov. 11: 8 righteous delivered out of *t.*
Is. 26:16 Lord, in *t.* have they visited
33: 2 our salvation also in time of *t.*
Jer. 8:15 time of health, and behold *t.*
14: 8 saviour thereof in time of *t.*
14:19 for a time of healing, and behold *t.*
Dan. 12: 1 there shall be a time of *t.*
1 Cor. 7:28 shall have *t.* in the flesh

TROUBLED (TROUBLETH)
Ex. 14:24 Lord *t.* the host of Egypt
1 Ki. 18:17 Art thou he that *t.* Israel
Job 23:16 soft, and the Almighty *t.* me
Ps. 30: 7 hide thy face, and I was *t.*
77: 3 I remembered God, and was *t.*
Prov. 11:17 he that is cruel *t.* his own flesh
11:29 he that *t.* his own house shall
Is. 57:20 wicked are like the *t.* sea
Luke 18: 5 because this widow *t.* me, I will
John 5: 4 *t.* the water: whosoever then first
12:27 now is my soul *t.*; and what shall
14: 1 let not your heart be *t.*
Gal. 5:10 he that *t.* you shall bear his judgment

2 Thes. 1: 7 to you who are *t.* rest

TRUE
Gen. 42:11 we are *t.* men, thy servants are
2 Sam. 7:28 thy words be *t.*, and thou hast
Ps. 19: 9 the judgments of the Lord are *t.*
119:160 thy word is *t.* from beginning
Prov. 14:25 A *t.* witness delivereth souls
Ezek. 18: 8 hath executed *t.* judgment between
Mat. 22:16 we know that thou art *t.* and
Luke 16:11 commit to your trust *t.* riches
John 1: 9 That was the *t.* Light, which lighteth
4:23 *t.* worshippers worship the Father
6:32 giveth you *t.* bread from heaven
7:28 but he that sent me is *t.*
15: 1 I am the *t.* vine, and my Father
2 Cor. 1:18 But as God is *t.*, our word toward
6: 8 as deceivers and yet *t.*
Phil. 4: 8 whatsoever things are *t.*
1 John 5:20 may know him that is *t.*
Rev. 3: 7 saith he that is holy, he that is *t.*
3:14 the faithful and *t.* witness
19:11 upon him was called Faithful and *T.*

TRUMPET (TRUMPETS)
Ex. 19:16 voice of the *t.* exceeding loud
Num. 10: 2 Make thee two *t.* of silver
Josh. 6: 4 bear before the ark seven *t.*
Ps. 81: 3 Blow up the *t.* in the new moon
98: 6 With *t.* and sound of cornet
Is. 27:13 that the great *t.* shall be blown
58: 1 lift up thy voice like a *t.*
Mat. 6: 2 do not sound a *t.* before thee
Rev. 8: 6 which had seven *t.* prepared

TRUST
1 Chr. 5:20 they put their *t.* in him
Job 4:18 put no *t.* in his servants
8:14 whose *t.* shall be a spider's web
13:15 though he slay me, yet will I *t.*
Ps. 4: 5 put your *t.* in the Lord
9:10 that know thy name will put their *t.*
37: 3 *t.* in the Lord, and do good
37: 5 *t.* also in him; and he shall bring it
37:40 save them because they *t.* in him
40: 4 that maketh the Lord his *t.*
55:23 but I will *t.* in thee
62: 8 *t.* in him at all times, ye
71: 5 thou art my *t.* from my youth
115: 9 *t.* thou in the Lord: he is their
118: 8 it is better to *t.* in the Lord
118: 9 it is better to *t.* in the Lord
119: 42 for I *t.* in thy word
125: 1 they that *t.* in the Lord shall
Prov. 22:19 thy *t.* may be in the Lord
Is. 26: 4 *t.* ye in the Lord for ever
50:10 *t.* in the name of the Lord
Jer. 7: 4 *t.* ye not in lying words
9: 4 and *t.* ye not in any brother
Mic. 7: 5 *t.* ye not in a friend, put ye
Mark 10:24 hard for them that *t.* in riches
2 Cor. 1: 9 should not *t.* in ourselves
Phil. 3: 4 he might *t.* in the flesh, I more

TRUSTED (TRUSTETH)
Ps. 22: 4 our fathers *t.* in thee: they *t.*
28: 7 my heart *t.* in him, and I am
32:10 he that *t.* in the Lord, mercy shall
34: 8 blessed is the man that *t.* in him
52: 7 *t.* in the abundance of his riches
57: 1 for my soul *t.* in thee
84:12 blessed is man that *t.* in thee
86: 2 save thy servant that *t.* in thee
Jer. 17: 5 cursed be man that *t.* in man
17: 7 blessed is man that *t.* in the Lord
Luke 18: 9 who certainly which *t.* in themselves
1 Tim. 5: 5 widow indeed, and desolate, and *t.* in God

TRUSTING
Ps. 112: 7 his heart is fixed, *t.* in the Lord

TRUTH
Gen. 24:27 my master of his mercy and his *t.*
Ex. 18:21 such as fear God, men of *t.*
34: 6 abundant in goodness and *t.*
Deut. 32: 4 a God of *t.* and without iniquity
Ps. 15: 2 and speaketh the *t.* in his heart
25: 5 Lead me in thy *t.*, and teach me
25:10 paths of the Lord are mercy and *t.*
51: 6 desirest *t.* in the inward parts
91: 4 his *t.* shall be thy shield
108: 4 thy *t.* reacheth unto the clouds

Ps. 117: 2 *t.* of the Lord endureth for ever
119: 30 I have chosen the way of *t.*
119:142 righteousness, and thy law is *t.*
119:151 all thy commandments are *t.*
Prov. 12:19 lip of *t.* shall be established
16: 6 by mercy and *t.* iniquity is purged
23:23 buy the *t.*, and sell it not, also
Is. 59:14 for *t.* is fallen in the street
Jer. 4: 2 swear, The Lord liveth, in *t.*
Dan. 4:37 all whose works are *t.*
Zech. 8:16 speak every man *t.* to his
John 1:14 full of grace and *t.*
8:32 know the *t.*, and the *t.* shall
14: 6 I am the way, the *t.*, and the life
14:17 Spirit of *t.*; whom the world
16:13 guide you into all *t.*
17:17 through thy *t.*: thy word is *t.*
17:19 might be sanctified through the *t.*
18:37 I should bear witness unto the *t.*
Acts 26:25 forth the words of *t.* and soberness
Rom. 1:18 who hold the *t.* in unrighteousness
1:25 changed the *t.* of God into a lie
2: 2 judgment of God is according to *t.*
1 Cor. 5: 8 bread of sincerity and *t.*
2 Cor. 13: 8 do nothing against the *t.*, but for
Gal. 3: 1 should not obey the *t.*, before whose
Eph. 4:15 but speaking the *t.* in love
4:21 taught by him, as *t.* is in Jesus
5: 9 goodness, and rightousness, and *t.*
6:14 having your loins girt about with *t.*
2 Thes. 2:10 received not the love of *t.*
1 Tim. 3:15 God, the pillar and ground of the *t.*
6: 5 destitute of the *t.*, supposing that
2 Tim. 2:18 who concerning the *t.* have erred
2:25 to the acknowledging of the *t.*
3: 7 come to the knowledge of the *t.*
3: 8 do these also resist the *t.*
4: 4 turn away their ears from *t.*
Jas. 3:14 lie not against the *t.*
1 Pet. 1:22 purified your souls in obeying the *t.*
2 Pet. 1:12 and be established in the present *t.*
1 John 1: 8 and the *t.* is not in us
5: 6 because the Spirit is *t.*

TRY
2 Chr. 32:31 God left him, to *t.* him
Job 7:18 morning, and *t.* him every moment
Ps. 11: 4 his eyelids *t.* the children of men
139: 23 *t.* me, and know my thoughts
Jer. 9: 7 will melt them, and *t.* them
Lam. 3:40 search and *t.* our ways, and turn
Dan. 11:35 shall fall, to *t.* them, and to
Zech. 13: 9 will *t.* them as gold is tried
1 Cor. 3:13 fire shall *t.* every man's work
1 Pet. 4:12 fiery trial which is to *t.* you
1 John 4: 1 *t.* the spirits whether they are of
Rev. 3:10 to *t.* them which dwell on the earth

TRIED (TRIEST, TRIETH, TRYING)
2 Sam. 22:31 word of the Lord is *t.*: he is a
1 Chr. 29:17 my God, that thou *t.* the heart
Ps. 7: 9 the righteous God *t.* the heart
11: 5 The Lord *t.* the righteous: but the
12: 6 as silver *t.* in a furnace of earth
66:10 thou hast *t.* us as silver is *t.*
105: 19 word of the Lord *t.* him
Jer. 11:20 that *t.* the reins and the heart
Dan. 12:10 many shall be purified and *t.*
1 Thes. 2: 4 but God, which *t.* our hearts
Heb. 11:17 by faith, Abraham, when he was *t.*
Jas. 1: 3 *t.* of your faith worketh patience
1:12 when he is *t.* he shall receive the
1 Pet. 1: 7 though it be *t.* with fire
Rev. 2: 2 hast *t.* them which say they are
2:10 into prison, that ye may be *t.*
3:18 buy of me gold *t.* in the fire

TURN
Deut. 4:30 if thou *t.* to the Lord thy God
1 Ki. 8:35 and *t.* from their sin, when thou
2 Ki. 17:13 *t.* ye from your evil ways
2 Chr. 15: 4 they in their trouble did *t.*
30: 6 *t.* again unto the Lord God of Abraham
Ps. 22:27 remember, and *t.* unto the Lord
80: 3 *T.* us again, O God, and cause thy
119: 37 *t.* away mine eyes from beholding vanity

Prov. 1:23 *T.* you at my reproof: behold, I
Sol. 2:17 *t.*, my beloved, and be thou like
Is. 31: 6 *t.* ye not unto him from
58:13 If thou *t.* away thy foot
Jer. 18: 8 *t.* from their evil, I will repent
31:18 *t.* thou me and I shall be turned
Lam. 3:40 and *t.* again to the Lord
5:21 *t.* us unto thee, O Lord, and
Ezek. 3:19 and he *t.* not from his wickedness
18:32 wherefore *t.* yourselves, and live ye
Hos. 12: 6 *t.* thou to thy God; keep mercy
14: 2 *t.* to the Lord: say unto
Joel 2:12 *t.* ye even to me with all your
2:13 and *t.* unto the Lord your God
Mic. 7:19 he will *t.* again, he will have compassion
Zech. 1: 3 and I will *t.* to you saith the
9:12 *T.* you to the strong hold
10: 9 live with their children, and *t.* again
Luke 1:16 children of Israel shall he *t.*
Acts 26:18 *t.* them from darkness
26:20 should repent, and *t.* to God
2 Cor. 3:16 when it shall *t.* to the Lord
Gal. 4: 9 how *t.* ye again to the weak
2 Tim. 3: 5 power thereof: from such *t.* away
Heb. 12:25 if we *t.* away from him that speaketh
2 Pet. 2:21 to *t.* from the holy commandment

TURNED
Deut. 9:12 they are quickly *t.* aside
Ps. 9:17 the wicked shall be *t.* into hell
30:11 *t.* for me my mourning into dancing
44:18 Our heart is not *t.* back
119: 59 *t.* my feet to thy testimonies
Is. 42:17 They shall be *t.* back, they shall
44:20 a deceived heart hath *t.* him
53: 6 *t.* every one to his own way
Jer. 2:27 for they have *t.* their back unto me
4: 8 anger of the Lord is not *t.* back
8: 6 every one *t.* to his course
Hos. 7: 8 Ephraim is a cake not *t.*
Zeph. 1: 6 them that are *t.* back
John 16:20 sorrow shall be *t.* to joy
1 Thes. 1: 9 how ye *t.* to God from idols to serve
Jas. 4: 9 let your laughter be *t.* to mourning
2 Pet. 2:22 dog is *t.* to his own vomit again

TURNETH (TURNING)
Ps. 146: 9 way of wicked he *t.* upside down
Prov. 15: 1 A soft answer *t.* away wrath
Is. 9:13 the people *t.* not unto him
Jer. 14: 8 *t.* aside to tarry for a night
Jas. 1:17 variableness, neither shadow of *t.*
Jude 1: 4 *t.* the grace of God into lasciviousness

TURTLE
Sol. 2:12 the voice of the *t.* is heard

TURTLEDOVES
Lev. 1:14 bring his offering of young *t.*
5: 7 two *t.* or two young pigeons unto
5:11 be not able to bring two *t.*
12: 6 and a young pigeon or a *t.*
Ps. 74:19 deliver not the soul of thy *t.*
Jer. 8: 7 the *t.* and the crane and the swallow

TWINKLING
1 Cor. 15:52 in the *t.* of an eye, at the last

U

UNAWARES
Deut. 4:42 which should kill his neighbor *u.*
Ps. 35: 8 destruction come upon him at *u.*
Luke 21:34 that day come upon you *u.*
Heb. 13: 2 some have entertained angels *u.*
Jude 1: 4 certain men crept in *u.*

UNBELIEF
Mat. 13:58 works there because of their *u.*
Mark 6: 6 marvelled because of their *u.*
9:24 I believe; help thou mine *u.*
16:14 upbraided them with their *u.*
Rom. 4:20 promise of God through *u.*
11:20 because of *u.* they were broken off
11:32 hath concluded them all in *u.*
1 Tim. 1:13 I did it ignorantly in *u.*
Heb. 3:12 you an evil heart of *u.*, in departing

UNBELIEVERS
Luke 12:46 his portion with the *u.*
1 Cor. 6: 6 and that before the *u.*
14:23 are unlearned or *u.*, will they not
2 Cor. 6:14 unequally yoked together with *u.*

UNBELIEVING
Acts 14: 2 *u.* Jews stirred up the Gentiles
1 Cor. 7:14 the *u.* husband is sanctified by the
7:15 But if the *u.* depart, let him depart
Tit. 1:15 defiled and *u.* is nothing pure
Rev. 21: 8 fearful, and *u.*, and the abominable

UNCIRCUMCISED
Ex. 6:30 I am of *u.* lips, and how shall
Jer. 6:10 behold, their ear is *u.*
9:26 all these nations are *u.*
Acts 7:51 Ye stiffnecked and *u.* in heart

UNCIRCUMCISION
Rom. 2:26 if the *u.* keep the righteous
3:30 by faith, and *u.* through faith
4:10 he was in circumcision, or in *u.*
1 Cor. 7:19 and *u.* is nothing, but the keeping
Gal. 2: 7 gospel of *u.* was committed
5: 6 availeth any thing, nor *u.*
6:15 availeth any thing, nor *u.*
Col. 2:13 dead in your sins and the *u.*
3:11 Jew, circumcision nor *u.*, Barbarian

UNCLEAN
Lev. 5: 2 a soul touch any *u.* thing
10:10 difference between *u.* and clean
11: 4 not the hoof; he is *u.* unto you
13:15 the raw flesh is *u.*: it is a
Num. 19:19 person shall sprinkle on the *u.*
Is. 6: 5 I am a man of *u.* lips
Lam. 4:15 depart ye; it is *u.*; depart
Ezek. 44:23 discern between *u.* and clean
Hag. 2:13 *u.* by a dead body touch any of
Rom. 14:14 there is nothing *u.* of itself
1 Cor. 7:14 else were your children *u.*
Eph. 5: 5 nor *u.* person, nor covetous man

UNCLEANNESS
Num. 5:19 hast not gone aside to *u.*
Ezra 9:11 to another with their *u.*
Mat. 23:27 dead men's bones, and of all *u.*
Rom. 6:19 members servants to *u.*, and to
Eph. 4:19 to work all *u.* with greediness
5: 3 all *u.* let it not once be named
1 Thes. 4: 7 hath not called us to *u.*

UNCTION
1 John 2:20 but ye have an *u.* from the Holy One

UNDEFILED
Ps. 119: 1 Blessed are the *u.*, in the way
Sol. 5: 2 my dove, my *u.*: for my head is
Heb. 7:26 holy, harmless, *u.*, separate from
13: 4 honourable in all, and the bed *u.*
Jas. 1:27 pure religion and *u.* before God and
1 Pet. 1: 4 to an inheritance incorruptible, *u.*

UNDERSTAND (UNDERSTANDEST, UNDERSTANDETH, UNDERSTOOD)
Gen. 11: 7 they may not *u.* one another's speech
Deut. 32:29 they were wise that they *u.* this
1 Chr. 28: 9 *u.* all the imaginations of the thoughts
Neh. 8: 7 caused people to *u.* the law
Ps. 19:12 who can *u.* his errors?
73:17 then *u.* I their end
107: 43 shalt *u.* the lovingkindness of the Lord
119:100 I *u.* more than the ancients
139: 2 thou *u.* my thought afar off
Prov. 2: 5 shalt thou *u.* the fear of the Lord
8: 5 O ye simple, *u.* wisdom: and, ye
8: 9 are all plain to him that *u.*
19:25 understanding and he will *u.* knowledge
28: 5 that seek the Lord *u.* all things
Is. 32: 4 heart also of the rash shall *u.*
Jer. 9:24 glory in this, that he *u.*
Mat. 13:19 and *u.* it not, then cometh the
13:51 have ye *u.* all these things
John 12:16 *u.* not his disciples at the first
Acts 8:30 *u.* thou what thou readest?
Rom. 3:11 none that *u.*, none that seeketh
1 Cor. 13: 2 prophecy, and to *u.* all mysteries
13:11 I *u.* as a child, I thought as a
2 Pet. 3:16 are some things hard to be *u.*

UNDERSTANDING
Ex. 31: 3 wisdom and in *u.*, and in knowledge
Deut. 4: 6 is your wisdom and your *u.*
1 Ki. 3:11 hast asked for thyself *u.* to discern
4:29 gave Solomon wisdom and *u.*
7:14 filled with wisdom and *u.*
1 Chr. 12:32 were men that had *u.* of the time
2 Chr. 26: 5 who had *u.* in the visions of God
Job 12:13 and strength, he hath counsel and *u.*
12:20 he taketh away the *u.* of the aged
17: 4 hast hid their heart from *u.*
28:28 to depart from evil is *u.*
32: 8 the Almighty giveth them *u.*
38:36 who hath given *u.* to the heart
39:17 neither imparted to her *u.*
Ps. 47: 7 sing ye praises with *u.*
49: 3 meditation of my heart be of *u.*
119: 34 give me *u.* and I shall keep
119: 99 have more *u.* than all my teachers
119:104 through thy precepts I get *u.*
119:130 it giveth *u.* unto the simple
147: 5 great power; his *u.* is infinite
Prov. 2: 2 apply thine heart to *u.*
2:11 preserve thee, *u.* shall keep thee
3: 5 lean not unto thine own *u.*
3:13 happy is the man that getteth *u.*
4: 5 get wisdom, get *u.*,: forget it
8: 1 *u.* put forth her voice
8: 5 ye fools, be ye of an *u.* heart
8:14 I am *u.*; I have strength
9: 6 and go in the way of *u.*
9:10 knowledge of the holy is *u.*
14:29 slow to wrath is of great *u.*
16:22 *u.* is a wellspring of life
19: 8 keepeth *u.* shall find good
21:30 *u.* nor counsel against the Lord
23:23 all wisdom, and instruction, and *u.*
30: 2 I have not the *u.* of a man
Eccl. 9:11 nor yet riches to men of *u.*
Is. 11: 2 spirit of wisdom and *u.*, the spirit
11: 3 make him of quick *u.* in the fear
27:11 it is a people of no *u.*
40:28 is no searching of his *u.*
Jer. 51:15 stretched out heaven by his *u.*
Mark 12:33 with all the heart and with all the *u.*
Luke 2:47 were astonished at his *u.* and answers
24:45 then opened he their *u.*
1 Cor. 1:19 bring to nothing the *u.* of the prudent
14:14 spirit prayeth, but *u.* is unfruitful
14:15 I will sing with the *u.* also
14:20 Brethren, be not children in *u.*
Eph. 1:18 eyes of your *u.* being enlightened
4:18 the *u.* darkened, being alienated
Phil. 4: 7 peace of God which passeth all *u.*
Col. 1: 9 in all wisdom and spiritual *u.*
2: 2 riches of the full assurance of *u.*
2 Tim. 2: 7 give thee *u.* in all things

UNDONE
Is. 6: 5 Woe is me! for I am *u.*
Mat. 23:23 not to leave the other *u.*

UNFEIGNED
2 Cor. 6: 6 by the Holy Ghost, by love *u.*
1 Tim. 1: 5 conscience, and of faith *u.*
2 Tim. 1: 5 the *u.* faith that is in thee
1 Pet. 1:22 through the Spirit unto *u.* love

UNFRUITFUL
Mat. 13:22 choke the word, and he becometh *u.*
1 Cor. 14:14 my understanding is *u.*
Eph. 5:11 fellowship with the *u.* works
Tit. 3:14 that they be not *u.*
2 Pet. 1: 8 barren nor *u.* in the knowledge

UNGODLY
2 Sam. 22: 5 *u.* men made me afraid
2 Chr. 19: 2 shouldest thou help the *u.*, and love
Job 16:11 God hath delivered me to the *u.*
Ps. 1: 1 walketh not in the counsel of the *u.*
1: 4 the *u.* are not so, but are like
1: 5 *u.* shall not stand in the judgment
1: 6 way of the *u.* shall perish
3: 7 hast broken the teeth of the *u.*
43: 1 plead my cause against an *u.* nation
Prov. 16:27 An *u.* man diggeth up evil
19:28 an *u.* witness scorneth judgment
Rom. 4: 5 him that justifieth the *u.*

Rom. 5: 6 in due time Christ died for the *u.*
1 Tim. 1: 9 disobedient for the *u.* and for sinners
1 Pet. 4:18 where shall the *u* and the sinner
2 Pet. 2: 5 the flood upon the world of the *u.*
2: 6 those that after should live *u.*
3: 7 day of judgment and perdition of *u.* men
Jude 1: 4 *u.* men, turning the grace of God
1:15 all their *u.* deeds, which they have
1:18 walk after their own *u.* lusts

UNGODLINESS
Rom. 1:18 against all *u.* and unrighteousness
11:26 turn away the *u.* from Jacob
Tit. 2:12 denying *u.* and worldly lusts

UNITE (UNITED)
Gen. 49: 6 honour, be not thou *u.*: for in their
Ps. 86:11 *u.* my heart to fear thy name

UNITY
Ps. 133: 1 brethren to dwell together in *u.*
Eph. 4: 3 Endeavouring to keep *u.* of the Spirit
4:13 till we all come in *u.* of faith

UNJUST
Ps. 43: 1 from the deceitful and *u.* man
Prov. 11: 7 hope of *u.* men perisheth
28: 8 by usury and *u.* gain increaseth his
29:27 *u.* man is an abomination to
Zeph. 3: 5 the *u.* knoweth no shame
Mat. 5:45 rain on the just and the *u.*
Luke 16: 8 lord commended the *u.* steward
18: 6 hear what the *u.* judge saith
18:11 other men are, extortioners, *u.*, adulterers
Acts 24:15 both of the just and *u.*
1 Pet. 3:18 suffered for sins, the just the for *u.*
2 Pet. 2: 9 reserve the *u.* to the day of
Rev. 22:11 that is *u.* let him be *u.*

UNJUSTLY
Ps. 82: 2 how long will ye judge *u.*, and
Is. 26:10 in land of uprightness will he deal *u.*

UNKNOWN
Acts 17:23 this inscription, To the *u.* god
Gal. 1:22 And was *u.* by face unto the churches
1 Cor. 14: 2 he that speaketh in an *u.* tongue
14: 4 he that speaketh in an *u.* tongue
14:27 If any man speak in an *u.* tongue
2 Cor. 6: 9 as *u.* and yet well known

UNLEARNED
Acts 4:13 perceived that they were *u.*
1 Cor. 14:16 he that occupieth the room of the *u.*
14:23 those that are *u.*, of unbelievers
14:24 believeth not, or one *u.*
2 Tim. 2:23 But foolish and *u.* questions
2 Pet. 3:16 they that are *u.* and unstable wrest

UNLEAVENED
Ex. 12:39 and they baked *u.* cakes
1 Cor. 5: 7 be a new lump, as ye are *u.*

UNPROFITABLE
Job 15: 3 should he reason with *u.* talk
Mat. 25:30 cast ye the *u.* servant to the outer
Luke 17:10 you say, we are *u.* servants
Rom. 3:12 they are together become *u.*
Tit. 3: 9 for they are *u.* and vain
Heb. 13:17 for that is *u.* for you

UNRIGHTEOUS
Is. 10: 1 unto them that decree *u.* decrees
Luke 16:11 not been faithful in *u.* mammon
Rom. 3: 5 is God *u.* who taketh vengeance?
1 Cor. 6: 9 *u.* shall not inherit the kingdom
Heb. 6:10 God is not *u.* to forget

UNRIGHTEOUSNESS
Lev. 19:15 Ye shall do no *u.* in
Jer. 22:13 woe to him that buildeth his house by *u.*
Luke 16: 9 friends of the mammon of *u.*
John 7:18 is true, and no *u.* in him
Rom. 1:18 who hold the truth in *u.*
6:13 members as instruments of *u.*
9:14 is there *u.* with God? God forbid
2 Cor. 6:14 what fellowship hath righteousness with *u.*
2 Thes. 2:10 all deceivableness of *u.*
2:12 believed not the truth, but had pleasure in *u.*
Heb. 8:12 will be merciful to their *u.*
2 Pet. 2:15 loved the wages of *u.*
1 John 1: 9 to cleanse us from all *u.*
5:17 all *u.* is sin

UNSEARCHABLE
Job 5: 9 doeth great things and *u.*
Ps. 145: 3 praised; and his greatness is *u.*
Prov. 25: 3 and the heart of kings is *u.*
Eph. 3: 8 Gentiles the *u.* riches of Christ

UNSPEAKABLE
2 Cor. 9:15 unto God for his *u.* gift
12: 4 and heard *u.* words, which it is
1 Pet. 1: 8 rejoice with joy *u.* and full of

UNSPOTTED
Jas. 1:27 keep himself *u.* from the world

UNSTABLE
Gen. 49: 4 *U.* as water, thou shalt not excel
Jas. 1: 8 man is *u.* in all his ways
2 Pet. 2:14 beguiling *u.* souls: an heart
3:16 they that are unlearned and *u.* wrest

UNWISE
Deut. 32: 6 O foolish people and *u.*
Hos. 13:13 he is an *u.* son; for he should
Rom. 1:14 to the wise and to the *u.*
Eph. 5:17 Wherefore be ye not *u.*

UNWORTHY (UNWORTHILY)
Acts 13:46 judge yourselves *u.* of everlasting
1 Cor. 6: 2 are ye *u.* to judge the smallest
11:27 drink this cup of the Lord *u.*

UPBRAID (UPBRAIDED, UPBRAIDETH)
Judg. 8:15 with whom ye did *u.* me
Mat. 11:20 Then began he to *u.* the cities
Mark 16:14 and *u.* them with their unbelief
Jas. 1: 5 to all men liberally, and *u.* not

UPHOLD (UPHOLDEST, UPHOLDETH, UPHOLDING)
Ps. 37:17 but the Lord *u.* the righteous
41:12 thou *u.* me in my integrity
51:12 *u.* me with thy free spirit
63: 8 thy right hand *u.* me
119:116 *u.* me according unto thy word
145: 14 The Lord *u.* all that fall
Prov. 29:23 honour shall *u.* the humble
Is. 41:10 I will *u.* thee with the right hand
Heb. 1: 3 *u.* all things by word of

UPRIGHT
Ps. 7:10 saveth the *u.* in heart
11: 7 his countenance doth behold the *u.*
18:23 I was also *u.* before him
18:25 *u.* man thou wilt show thyself *u.*
25: 8 good and *u.* is the Lord
37:37 perfect man, and behold the *u.*
64:10 all the *u.* in heart shall glory
112: 2 generation of the *u.* shall be blessed
112: 4 to the *u.* there ariseth light
140: 13 *u.* shall dwell in thy presence
Prov. 2:21 *u.* shall dwell in the land
10:29 way of Lord is strength to the *u.*
11: 3 integrity of the *u.* shall guide
11: 6 righteousness of the *u.* shall deliver
12: 6 mouth of the *u.* shall deliver
13: 6 righteousness keepeth him that is *u.*
14:11 tabernacle of the *u.* shall flourish
28:10 *u.* shall have good things
Eccl. 7:29 found, that God hath made man *u.*
Sol. 1: 4 more than wine: the *u.* love thee
Hab. 2: 4 is lifted up is not *u.* in him

UPRIGHTLY
Ps. 15: 2 He that walketh *u.*, and worketh
58: 1 do ye judge *u.*, O ye sons of
84:11 from them that walk *u.*
Prov. 2: 7 buckler to them that walk *u.*
15:21 man of understanding walketh *u.*
Is. 33:15 righteously, and speaketh *u.*,
Mic. 2: 7 to him that walketh *u.*
Gal. 2:14 I saw they walked not *u.*

UPRIGHTNESS
Deut. 9: 5 or for the *u.* of thine heart
1 Chr. 29:17 heart, and hast pleasure in *u.*
Job 33:23 to show unto man his *u.*
Ps. 25:21 let integrity and *u.* preserve me
143: 10 lead me into the land of *u.*
Is. 26: 7 the way of the just is *u.*

URIM
Ex. 28:30 breastplate of judgment the *U.*
Lev. 8: 8 in the breastplate the *U.*
Num. 27:21 for him after the judgment of *U.*
Deut. 33: 8 Thummim and thy *U.* be with
1 Sam. 28: 6 neither by dreams nor by *U.*
Ezra 2:63 a priest with *U.* and Thummim
Neh. 7:65 there stood up a priest with *U.*

USE (USES)
Rom. 1:26 natural *u.* into that which is
1 Cor. 7:31 *u.* this world, as not abusing
Gal. 5:13 *u.* not liberty for the occasion
Eph. 4:29 good to the *u.* of edifying
1 Tim. 1: 8 if a man *u.* it lawfully
Tit. 3:14 good works for necessary *u.*
Heb. 5:14 by reason of *u.* have their senses

USURY
Ex. 22:25 neither shalt thou lay upon him *u.*
Lev. 25:37 give him thy money upon *u.*
Deut. 23:20 thou mayest lend upon *u.*
Neh. 5:10 let us leave off this *u.*
Ps. 15: 5 putteth not out his money to *u.*
Prov. 28: 8 by *u.* and unjust gain increaseth
Is. 24: 2 as with the taker of *u.*, so with
Jer. 15:10 men have lent to me on *u.*
Ezek. 18:13 Hath given forth upon *u.*
22:12 thou hast taken *u.* and increase
Mat. 25:27 should have received mine own with *u.*
Luke 19:23 required mine own with *u.*

UTTER (UTTERED, UTTERETH)
Ps. 19: 2 day to day *u.* speech, and
78: 2 I will *u.* dark sayings
94: 4 they *u.* and speak hard things
Rom. 8:26 groanings which cannot be *u.*
2 Cor. 12: 4 words not lawful for man to *u.*
Heb. 5:11 things to say and hard to be *u.*

UTTERANCE
Acts 2: 4 as Spirit gave them *u.*
Eph. 6:19 that *u.* may be given me
Col. 4: 3 God would open unto us the door of *u.*

UTTERMOST
1 Thes. 2:16 wrath is come upon them to the *u.*
Heb. 7:25 save them to the *u.* that come

V

VAIN
Ex. 5: 9 let them not regard *v.* words
20: 7 the name of the Lord thy God in *v.*
Deut. 32:47 it is not a *v.* thing for
1 Sam. 12:21 should ye go after *v.* things
Job 11:12 for a *v.* man would be wise
Ps. 39: 6 they are disquieted in *v.*
60:11 for *v.* is the help of man
73:13 cleansed my heart in *v.*
89:47 why hast thou made all men in *v.*
119:113 I hate *v.* thoughts, but thy law
127: 1 the watchman waketh but in *v.*
127: 2 it is *v.* for you to rise up early
Is. 45:19 seek ye me in *v.*: I the Lord
Jer. 3:23 in *v.* is salvation hoped for from
4:14 how long shall thy *v.* thoughts
Mat. 6: 7 use not *v.* repetitions
15: 9 in *v.* do they worship me
Rom. 1:21 but became *v.* in their imaginations
13: 4 beareth not the sword in *v.*
1 Cor. 3:20 thoughts of the wise are *v.*
15:58 your labour is not in *v.*
2 Cor. 6: 1 receive not the grace of God in *v.*
Eph. 5: 6 deceive you with *v.* words
Phil. 2:16 run in *v.* neither laboured in *v.*
Jas. 1:26 this man's religion is *v.*
1 Pet. 1:18 from your *v.* conversation received

VANITY (VANITIES)
2 Ki. 17:15 they followed *v.*, and became vain
Job 7: 3 made to possess months of *v.*
7:16 let me along; for my days are *v.*
Ps. 12: 2 speak *v.* every one with his neighbour
24: 4 hath not lifted up his soul to *v.*
31: 6 hated them that regard lying *v.*
39: 5 his best state is altogether *v.*

Ps. 39:11 surely every man is *v.*
62: 9 men of low degree are *v.*
94:11 thoughts of man that they are *v.*
119: 37 turn away mine eyes from beholding *v.*
144: 4 man is like to *v.*: his days as a
144: 8 whose mouth speaketh *v.*
Prov. 22: 8 soweth iniquity shall reap *v.*
Eccl. 1: 2 *v.* of *v.*, all is *v.*
3:19 above a beast: for all is *v.*
12: 8 saith the preacher; all is *v.*
11:10 childhood and youth are *v.*
Is. 5:18 draw iniquity with cords of *v.*
40:17 less than nothing and *v.*
Jer. 10: 8 the stock is a doctrine of *v.*
Jonah 2: 8 that observe lying *v.*
Hab. 2:13 weary themselves for very *v.*
Acts 14:15 turn from these *v.* unto the
Rom. 8:20 creature was made subject to *v.*
Eph. 4:17 walk in the *v.* of their mind
2 Pet. 2:18 great swelling worlds of *v.*

VALIANT (VALIANTLY)
Num. 24:18 and Israel shall do *v.*
Ps. 60:12 Through God we shall do *v.*
108: 13 Through God we shall do *v.*
118: 16 hand of the Lord doeth *v.*
Sol. 3: 7 threescore *v.* men are about it
Is. 10:13 put down the inhabitants like a *v.* man
Jer. 9: 3 they are not *v.* for the truth
Heb. 11:34 waxed *v.* in fight, turned to

VALUE
Job 13: 4 are all physicians of no *v.*
Mat. 10:31 Ye are of more *v.* than many sparrows

VEIL
Gen. 24:65 therefore she took a *v.*
Sol. 5: 7 took away my *v.* from me
Is. 25: 7 the *v.* that is spread over all
Mat. 27:51 *v.* of the temple was rent
2 Cor. 3:13 Moses put a *v.* over his
Heb. 6:19 entereth into that within the *v.*
10:20 the *v.*, that is to say, his flesh

VENGEANCE
Gen. 4:15 *v.* shall be taken on him
Deut. 32:35 to me belongeth *v.* and recompence
Ps. 58:10 rejoice when he seeth *v.*
94: 1 God, to whom *v.* belongeth
Is. 34: 8 the day of the Lord's *v.*
Jer. 11:20 let me see thy *v.*
51: 6 time of the Lord's *v.*
Luke 21:22 these be days of *v.*, that all
Rom. 12:19 *V.* is mine; I will repay, saith
2 Thes. 1: 8 in flaming fire taking *v.*
Heb. 10:30 *V.* belongeth unto me, I will recompense
Jude 1: 7 suffering the *v.* of eternal fire

VESSEL (VESSELS)
Ps. 2: 9 pieces like a potter's *v.*
31:12 I am like a broken *v.*
Jer. 18: 4 *v.* that he made of clay
22:28 a *v.* wherein is no pleasure
48:11 not been emptied from *v.* to *v.*
Acts 9:15 he is a chosen *v.* unto me
Rom. 9:21 make one *v.* unto honour and another
9:22 *v.* of wrath fitted to destruction
2 Cor. 4: 7 we have this treasure in earthen *v.*
1 Thes. 4: 4 possess his *v.* in sanctification
2 Tim. 2:21 be a *v.* unto honour, sanctified
1 Pet. 3: 7 honour to the wife as to the weaker *v.*

VEXED
Job 27: 2 The Almighty who hath *v.* my soul
Ps. 6: 2 heal me; for my bones are *v.*
6: 3 soul is also sore *v.*
6:10 enemies be ashamed and sore *v.*
Is. 63:10 they rebelled and *v.* his holy spirit
2 Pet. 2: 7 Lot, *v.* with filthy conversation

VICTORY
1 Chr. 29:11 glory, and the *v.*, and the majesty
Ps. 98: 1 his holy arm hath gotten him *v.*
Is. 25: 8 He will swallow up death in *v.*
1 Cor. 15:15 death is swallowed up in *v.*
15:55 O grave, where is thy *v.*?
15:57 thanks to God, who giveth us *v.*
1 John 5: 4 the *v.* that overcometh the world, even

VIGILANT
1 Tim. 3: 2 husband of one wife, *v.*, sober
1 Pet. 5: 8 Be sober, be *v.*, because your

VILE
Deut. 25: 3 brother should seem *v.* unto thee
1 Sam. 3:13 sons made themselves *v.*
2 Sam. 6:22 I will yet be more *v.*
Ps. 15: 4 whose eyes a *v.* person is contemned
Is. 32: 6 *v.* person will speak villany
Jer. 15:19 take forth the precious from the *v.*
Rom. 1:26 gave them up to *v.* affections
Phil. 3:21 shall change our *v.* body

VINE
Deut. 32:32 for their *v.* is the *v.* of Sodom
1 Ki. 4:25 every man under his *v.* and under
Ps. 128: 3 wife shall be as a fruitful *v.*
Jer. 2:21 I planted thee a noble *v.*
Hos. 10: 1 Israel is an empty *v.*
Mic. 4: 4 sit every man under his *v.*
Mat. 26:29 not drink of this fruit of the *v.*
John 15: 1 I am the true *v.* and my Father
15: 5 I am the *v.*, ye are the branches

VINEYARD
Ps. 80:15 *v.* which thy right hand hath planted
Prov. 24:30 and by the *v.* of the man
Sol. 1: 6 mine own *v.* have I not kept
8:12 My *v.* which is mine
Is. 5: 1 My wellbeloved hath a *v.*
Mat. 20: 1 hire labourers into his *v.*
21:33 householder which planted a *v.*
Luke 13: 6 planted in his *v.*; and he came
1 Cor. 9: 7 who planteth a *v.*, and eateth not

VIOLENCE
Gen. 6:11 earth was filled with *v.*
Lev. 6: 2 a thing taken away by *v.*
2 Sam. 22: 3 thou savest me from *v.*
Ps. 72:14 redeem their soul from deceit and *v.*
73: 6 *v.* covereth them as a garment
Hab. 1: 2 cry out unto thee of *v.*
Mat. 11:12 kingdom of heaven suffereth *v.*
Luke 3:14 do *v.* to no man, and be
Heb. 11:34 quenched the *v.* of fire

VIRGIN (VIRGINS)
Sol. 1: 3 therefore do the *v.* love thee
Is. 7:14 Behold a *v.* shall conceive
Mat. 1:23 Behold, a *v.* shall be with child
2 Cor. 11: 2 present you as a chaste *v.*
Rev. 14: 4 for they are *v.*. These are they

VIRTUE
Mark 5:30 *v.* had gone out of him
Luke 6:19 there went *v.* out of him
Phil. 4: 8 if there be any *v.*, think
2 Pet. 1: 3 called us to glory and *v.*

VIRTUOUS
Prov. 12: 4 A *v.* woman is a crown
31:10 Who can find a *v.* woman

VISION
1 Sam. 3: 1 in those days there was no open *v.*
Ps. 89:19 Then thou spakest in *v.* to thy holy
Prov. 29:18 where there is no *v.* the people perish
Ezek. 13:16 see *v.* of peace for her, and
Hos. 12:10 I have multiplied *v.*, and used
Joel 2:28 young men shall see *v.*
Hab. 2: 2 write the *v.*, and make it plain
2: 3 the *v.* is yet for an appointed time
Mat. 17: 9 Tell the *v.* to no man
Acts 2:17 your young men shall see *v.*
10:19 Peter thought on the *v.*
16: 9 a *v.* appeared to Paul in the night

VISIT (VISITED, VISITING)
Gen. 50:25 God will surely *v.* you
Ex. 13:19 God will surely *v.* you
20: 5 *v.* the iniquity of the fathers
34: 7 *v.* the iniquity of the fathers
Num. 14:18 *v.* the iniquity of the fathers
Deut. 5: 9 *v.* the iniquity of the fathers
Job 7:18 thou shouldest *v.* him every
Ps. 17: 3 thou hast *v.* me in the night
106: 4 *v.* me with thy salvation
Jer. 5: 9 shall I not *v.* for these things?
Lam. 4:22 he will *v.* thine iniquity
Hos. 2:13 I will *v.* upon her the days of
8:13 and *v.* their sins: they shall return

Mat. 25:36 I was sick and ye *v.*
Luke 1:68 he hath *v.* and redeemed his people
1:78 dayspring from on high hath *v.* us
Acts 7:23 to *v.* his brethren the children of
15:36 *v.* our brethren in every city
15:14 did *v.* the Gentiles, to take out of
Jas. 1:27 to *v.* the fatherless and

VOICE
Gen. 4:10 *v.* of thy brother's blood
27:22 The *v.* is Jacob's *v.*, but the hands
Ex. 5: 2 the Lord that I should obey his *v.*?
Ps. 5: 3 my *v.* shalt thou hear in the morning
18:13 the Highest gave his *v.*
42: 4 to the house of God, with the *v.* of
95: 7 today, if ye will hear his *v.*
103: 20 hearkening to the *v.* of his word
Sol. 2:14 let me hear thy *v.*; for sweet is
Is. 30:19 unto thee at the *v.* of thy cry
50:10 obeyeth the *v.* of his servant
Ezek. 33:32 that hath a pleasant *v.*
John 5:25 dead shall hear the *v.* of
10: 3 sheep hear his *v.*: and he calleth
Gal. 4:20 to change my *v.*; for I stand in
1 Thes. 4:16 with the *v.* of the archangel
Rev. 3:20 if any man hear my *v.*

VOID
Deut. 32:28 a nation *v.* of counsel
Ps. 89:39 made *v.* the covenant of thy servant
119:126 for they have made *v.* thy law
Is. 55:11 it shall not return to me *v.*
Acts 24:16 conscience *v.* of offence toward
1 Cor. 9:15 man should make my glorying *v.*

VOMIT
Job 20:15 he shall *v.* them up again
Prov. 23: 8 thou hast eaten shalt thou *v.* up
26:11 dog returneth to his *v.*
Is. 19:14 drunken man staggereth in his *v.*
2 Pet. 2:22 dog is turned to his own *v.*

VOW (VOWED, VOWS, VOWEDST)
Gen. 28:20 Jacob *v.* a *v.*, saying, if God
31:13 thou *v.* a *v.* unto me
Deut. 23:21 when thou shalt *v.* a *v.*,
Num. 6: 2 to *v.* a *v.* of a Nazarite
30: 2 man *v.* a *v.* unto the Lord
1 Sam. 1:11 And she *v.* a *v.*, and said, O
2 Sam. 15: 8 thy servant *v.* a *v.*
Job 22:27 thou shalt pay thy *v.*
Ps. 50:14 pay thy *v.* to the most High
56:12 thy *v.* are upon me, O God
61: 5 for thou, O God, hast heard my *v.*
61: 8 I may daily perform my *v.*
65: 1 unto thee shall the *v.* be performed
76:11 *v.*, and pay unto the Lord
Prov. 20:25 after *v.* to make inquiry
31: 2 and what, the son of my *v.*
Eccl. 5: 4 a *v.* to God, defer not to pay
Is. 19:21 they shall *v.* a *v.* unto the Lord
Jonah 1:16 to the Lord, and made *v.*
2: 9 I will pay that that I have *v.*

W

WAGES
Lev. 19:13 the *w.* of him that is hired
Ezek. 29:18 yet had he no *w.*, nor his army
Hag. 1: 6 earneth *w.* to put into the bag
Mal. 3: 5 oppress the hireling in his *w.*
Luke 3:14 be content with your *w.*
Rom. 6:23 the *w.* of sin is death

WAIT
Job 14:14 my appointed time will I *w.*
Ps. 25: 5 on thee do I *w.* all the day
27:14 *w.* on the Lord: be of good
37:34 *w.* on the Lord and keep his way
62: 5 *w.* thou only upon God
104: 27 these *w.* all upon thee; that thou
130: 5 I *w.* for the Lord, my soul doth *w.*
145: 15 eyes of all *w.* upon thee
Prov. 20:22 *w.* on the Lord and he will save
Is. 8:17 I will *w.* upon the Lord
30:18 blessed are all they that *w.* for him
40:31 that *w.* on Lord shall renew
Lam. 3:25 good to them that *w.* for
3:26 quietly *w.* for the salvation of the
Hos. 12: 6 *w.* on thy God continually
Mic. 7: 7 *w.* for the God of my salvation
Hab. 2: 3 *w.* for it, because it will surely
Zeph. 3: 8 *w.* ye on me

Luke 12:36 men that *w.* for their lord
1 Thes. 1:10 to *w.* for his Son from heaven

WAITED (WAITETH, WAITING)
Gen. 49:18 I have *w.* for thy salvation
Ps. 33:20 our soul *w.* for the Lord
40: 1 I *w.* patiently for the Lord
130: 6 my soul *w.* for the Lord more
Prov. 8:34 *w.* at the posts of my doors
Is. 25: 9 our God, we have *w.* for him
26: 8 O Lord, have we *w.* for thee
33: 2 O Lord, we have *w.* for thee
64: 4 prepared for him that *w.* for him
Zech. 11:11 poor of the flock that *w.* upon me
Mark 15:43 which also *w.* for the kingdom of God
Luke 2:25 *w.* for the consolation of Israel
Rom. 8:23 within ourselves *w.* for the adoption
1 Cor. 1: 7 *w.* for the coming of our Lord
2 Thes. 3: 5 into the patient *w.* for Christ
1 Pet. 3:20 longsuffering of God *w.* in the days

WAKETH (WAKENETH, WAKENED)
Ps. 127: 1 watchman *w.* but in vain
Sol. 5: 2 but my heart *w.*: it is the voice
Is. 50: 4 he *w.* morning by morning, he *w.* my
Joel 3:12 let the heathen be *w.*

WALK
Gen. 17: 1 *w.* before me and be thou perfect
24:40 Lord before whom I *w.* will send
Ex. 16: 4 they will *w.* in my law or no
Lev. 26:12 I will *w.* among you and will be
26:21 if ye *w.* contrary unto me
26:23 but will *w.* contrary unto me
26:24 will I also *w.* contrary unto you
Deut. 5:33 *w.* in all the ways which the Lord
13: 4 ye shall *w.* after the Lord
Ps. 23: 4 though I *w.* through the valley
84:11 withhold from them that *w.* uprightly
116: 9 I will *w.* before the Lord
119: 3 do no iniquity, they *w.* in his ways
Eccl. 11: 9 *w.* in the ways of thine heart
Is. 2: 3 and we will *w.* in his paths
2: 5 let us *w.* in the light of the Lord
30:21 this is the way, *w.* ye in it
40:31 they shall *w.* and not faint
Jer. 23:14 they commit adultery and *w.* in lies
Dan. 4:37 those that *w.* in pride he is able
Hos. 14: 9 just shall *w.* in them
Amos 3: 3 can two *w.* together except they
Mic. 6: 8 *w.* humbly with thy God
Zech. 10:12 *w.* up and down in his name
John 8:12 not *w.* in darkness, but shall have
11: 9 *w.* in day he stumbleth not
12:35 *w.* while ye have light
Rom. 4:12 *w.* in the steps of that faith
6: 4 should *w.* in newness of life
8: 1 *w.* not after the flesh but after
13:13 let us *w.* honestly as in the day
2 Cor. 5: 7 we *w.* by faith, not by sight
10: 3 though we *w.* in the flesh, we do not war
Gal. 5:16 *w.* in the Spirit, and not fulfil the
5:25 if we live in the Spirit, let us *w.* in
6:16 as many as *w.* according to this rule
Eph. 2:10 ordained that we should *w.* in
4: 1 that ye *w.* worthy of the vocation
5: 2 *w.* in love, as Christ also hath loved
5: 8 *w.* as children of light
5:15 *w.* circumspectly, not as fools
Phil. 3:16 let us *w.* by the same rule
Col. 1:10 that ye might *w.* worthy
2: 6 Jesus the Lord, so *w.* ye in him
4: 5 *w.* in wisdom toward them that
1 Thes. 2:12 ye would *w.* worthy of God, who
4: 1 how ye ought to *w.* and to please
1 John 1: 7 if we *w.* in the light, as he is
2: 6 so to *w.* as he walked
3 John 1: 4 my children *w.* in truth
Rev. 3: 4 shall *w.* with me in white
16:15 lest he *w.* naked and they see his
21:24 shall *w.* in the light of

WALKED (WALKEST, WALKETH, WALKING)
Gen. 3: 8 voice of Lord God *w.* in the garden
Ps. 15: 2 he that *w.* uprightly and worketh
39: 6 every man *w.* in a vain show
55:14 we *w.* unto the house of God
81:12 *w.* in their own counsels
81:13 and Israel had *w.* in my ways
Is. 9: 2 people that *w.* in darkness
57: 2 each one *w.* in his uprightness
Jer. 6:28 revolters *w.* with slanders
Mic. 2:11 a man *w.* in the spirit and falsehood
2: 7 do good to him that *w.* uprightly
Luke 1: 6 God, *w.* in all the commandments and
Acts 9:31 *w.* in the fear of the Lord
Rom. 14:15 thy meat, now *w.* thou not charitably
2 Cor. 4: 2 not *w.* in craftiness, nor handling the
10: 2 as if we *w.* according to the flesh
12:18 *w.* we not in the same spirit
Gal. 2:14 saw they *w.* not uprightly
Eph. 2: 2 in time past ye *w.* according to the
Col. 3: 7 ye also *w.* some time, when ye lived
2 Thes. 3: 6 from every brother that *w.* disorderly
1 Pet. 4: 3 when we *w.* in lasciviousness
5: 8 *w.* about, seeking whom he may
2 Pet. 3: 3 *w.* after their own lusts
Rev. 2: 1 *w.* in the midst of seven golden

WANT
Deut. 28:48 and in *w.* of all things
Job 31:19 any perish for *w.* of clothing
Ps. 23: 1 is my shepherd; I shall not *w.*
34: 9 no *w.* to them that fear him
2 Cor. 8:14 a supply for your *w.*: that there may
Phil. 4:11 not that I speak in respect of *w.*

WAR
Ex. 13:17 people repent when they see *w.*
17:16 Lord will have *w.* with Amalek
Job 10:17 changes and *w.* are against me
Ps. 18:34 He teacheth my hands to *w.*
27: 3 though *w.* should rise against me
120: 7 when I speak, they are for *w.*
Prov. 20:18 with good advice make *w.*
Eccl. 8: 8 is no discharge in that *w.*
Is. 2: 4 neither shall they learn *w.* any more
Mic. 3: 5 they even prepare *w.* against him
2 Cor. 10: 3 we do not *w.* after the flesh
1 Tim. 1:18 them mightest *w.* a good warfare
1 Pet. 2:11 fleshly lusts which *w.* against the
Rev. 11: 7 pit shall make *w.* against them, and
12: 7 there was *w.* in heaven: Michael
17:14 these shall make *w.* with the Lamb
19:11 he doth judge and make *w.*

WARS (WARRETH)
Num. 21:14 in the book of the *w.* of the Lord
Ps. 46: 9 he maketh *w.* to cease unto the end
Mat. 24: 6 hear of *w.* and rumours of *w.*
2 Tim. 2: 4 no man that *w.* entangleth himself
Jas. 4: 1 from whence come *w.* and fightings

WARFARE
Is. 40: 2 that her *w.* is accomplished
1 Cor. 9: 7 Who goeth a *w.* any time at his
2 Cor. 10: 4 weapons of *w.* are not carnal
1 Tim. 1:18 by them mightest war a good *w.*

WARN (WARNED, WARNING)
2 Chr. 19:10 ye shall even *w.* them
Ps. 19:11 by them is thy servant *w.*
Jer. 6:10 to whom shall I speak, and give *w.*
Ezek. 3:19 if thou *w.* the wicked
33: 3 blow trumpet, *w.* the people
Mat. 3: 7 who hath *w.* you to flee
Acts 10:22 *w.* from God by an holy angel
20:31 I ceased not to *w.* every one night
1 Cor. 4:14 my beloved sons I *w.* you
Col. 1:28 whom we preach, *w.* every man, and
1 Thes. 5:14 *w.* them that are unruly comfort
Heb. 11: 7 Noah being *w.* of God

WASH (WASHED, WASHING)
Lev. 6:27 thou shalt *w.* that whereon
15:16 he shall *w.* all his flesh in water
Job 9:30 if I *w.* myself with snow water
29: 6 when I *w.* my steps with butter
Ps. 26: 6 *w.* my hands in innocency
51: 2 *w.* me thoroughly from mine iniquity
51: 7 *w.* me and I shall be whiter than
58:10 he shall *w.* his feet in blood
Sol. 5: 3 I have *w.* my feet; how shall I
Is. 1:16 *w.* you, make you clean
4: 4 *w.* away the filth of thy daughters
Jer. 2:22 thou *w.* thee with nitre
4:14 *w.* thy heart from wickedness
Ezek. 16: 4 neither wast thou *w.* in water
Luke 7:38 to *w.* his feet with tears
John 13: 5 began to *w.* the disciples' feet
13: 8 I *w.* thee not, thou hast no part
13:14 ought to *w.* one another's feet
Acts 22:16 be baptized and *w.* away
Eph. 5:26 *w.* of water by the word
Tit. 3: 5 saved us, by the *w.* of regeneration
Heb. 10:22 our bodies *w.* with pure water
Rev. 1: 5 *w.* us from our sins in his own blood
7:14 *w.* their robes, and made them white

WATCH
Neh. 4: 9 and set a *w.* against them
Job 7:12 thou settest a *w.* over me
14:16 dost thou not *w.* over my sin?
Ps. 102: 7 I *w.* and am as a sparrow
130: 6 they that *w.* for morning
141: 3 set a *w.*, O Lord, before my mouth
Jer. 44:27 I will *w.* over them for evil
Mat. 24:42 *w.* therefore, for ye know not
Mark 13:33 take ye heed, *w.* and pray
1 Cor. 16:13 *w.* ye, stand fast in the
Col. 4: 2 *w.* in the same with thanksgiving
1 Thes. 5: 6 let us *w.* and be sober
2 Tim. 4: 5 *w.* thou in all things endure
Heb. 13:17 for they *w.* for your souls
1 Pet. 4: 7 be sober, *w.* unto prayer
Rev. 3: 3 if therefore thou shalt not *w.* I will

WATCHED (WATCHES, WATCHETH, WATCHING)
Ps. 37:32 the wicked *w.* the righteous, and
63: 6 meditate on thee in the night *w.*
Prov. 8:34 *w.* daily at my gates, waiting
Lam. 2:19 in the beginning of the *w.*
Ezek. 7: 6 the end is come; it *w.* for thee
Jer. 20:10 familiars *w.* for my halting
31:28 like as I have *w.* over them
Mat. 24:43 he would have *w.*, and would not
Eph. 6:18 *w.* thereunto with all perseverance
Rev. 16:15 blessed is he that *w.* and

WATCHFUL
Rev. 3: 2 be *w.*, and strengthen the things which

WATCHINGS
2 Cor. 6: 5 tumults in labours, in *w.*, in fastings
11:27 painfulness, in *w.* often in hunger

WATCHMAN (WATCHMEN)
Sol. 3: 3 The *w.* that go about the city
Is. 21:11 *W.*, what of the night
52: 8 Thy *w.* shall lift up thy voice
62: 6 I have set *w.* upon thy walls
Jer. 31: 6 that the *w.* upon the mount
Ezek. 3:17 I have made thee a *w.*
33: 7 I have set thee a *w.*

WATER
Gen. 49: 4 Unstable as *w.*, thou shalt not excel
Ex. 12: 9 nor sodden at all with *w.*
17: 6 come *w.* out of it, that the people
2 Sam. 14:14 we are as *w.* spilt on the ground
Job 15:16 drinketh iniquity like *w.*
Ps. 22:14 I am poured out like *w.*
Is. 12: 3 draw *w.* out of wells of salvation
27: 3 I will *w.* it every moment
30:20 *w.* of affliction, yet shall not thy
41:17 when the poor and needy seek *w.* and
44: 3 pour *w.* on him that is thirsty
58:11 a spring of *w.*, whose waters fail
Lam. 1:16 eye runneth down with *w.*
Ezek. 36:25 will I sprinkle clean *w.* upon you
Amos 8:11 nor a thirst for *w.*, but of hearing
Mat. 3:11 I indeed baptize you with *w.*
10:42 cup of cold *w.* only in the name of a
Luke 16:24 dip the tip of his finger in *w.*
John 3: 5 except a man be born of *w.*
3:23 baptized because there was much *w.*
4:14 shall be in him a well of *w.*

John 7:38 flow rivers of living *w.*
19:34 came there out blood and *w.*
Acts 8:38 went down both into the *w.*
10:47 can any man forbid *w.*, that these
Eph. 5:26 cleanse it with the washing of *w.*
1 John 5: 6 he that came by *w.* and blood, even
5: 8 witness in earth, spirit, *w.* and
Jude 1:12 clouds they are without *w.*
Rev. 21: 6 fountain of the *w.* of life
22:17 take the *w.* of life freely

WATERED
Is. 58:11 thou shalt be like a *w.* garden
1 Cor. 3: 6 I have planted, Apollos *w.*

WATERS
Ps. 23: 2 leadeth me beside still *w.*
124: 4 *w.* had overwhelmed us
Prov. 5:15 drink *w.* out of thine own cistern
9:17 stolen *w.* are sweet, and bread
Eccl. 11: 1 cast thy bread upon the *w.*
Sol. 4:15 a well of living *w.*, and streams
Is. 32:20 are ye that sow beside all *w.*
33:16 given him; his *w.* shall be sure
35: 6 in the wilderness shall *w.* break forth
43:20 I give *w.* in the wilderness
54: 9 this is as the *w.* of Noah unto me
58:11 a spring of water, whose *w.* fail not
Jer. 2:13 fountain of living *w.*
9: 1 O that my head were *w.*
Ezek. 47: 1 *w.* issued out from under
Hab. 2:14 Lord, as the *w.* cover the sea
Zech. 14: 8 *w.* shall go out from Jerusalem
Rev. 1:15 sound of many *w.*
19: 6 his voice as the sound of many *w.*
7:17 lead them unto living fountains of *w.*

WAY
Ex. 13:21 to lead them the *w.*; and by night
32: 8 turned aside quickly out of the *w.*
1 Sam. 12:23 teach you the good and right *w.*
1 Ki. 2: 2 I go the *w.* of all the earth
8:32 bring his *w.* on his head
Ezra 8:21 seek of him a right *w.*
Job 17: 9 righteous shall hold on his *w.*
Ps. 1: 6 *w.* of the ungodly shall perish
2:12 and ye perish from the *w.*
18:30 as for God, his *w.* is perfect
25: 8 teach sinners in the *w.*
37:23 delighteth in his *w.*
49:13 their *w.* is their folly
67: 2 that thy *w.* may be known
78:50 He made a *w.* to his anger
119: 9 shall a young man cleanse his *w.*
119: 14 I rejoiced in the *w.* of thy testimonies
119: 30 I have chosen the *w.* of truth
119: 32 run the *w.* of thy commandments
139: 24 lead me in the *w.* everlasting
Prov. 2: 8 Lord preserveth the *w.* of his saints
10:29 *w.* of the Lord is strength
14: 8 prudent is to understand his *w.*
14:12 a *w.* which seemeth right
15: 9 *w.* of the wicked is abomination
15:24 *w.* of life is above to the wise
16: 9 man's heart deviseth his *w.*
Eccl. 11: 5 knowest not what is the *w.* of the
Is. 26: 7 *w.* of the just is uprightness
26: 8 in the *w.* of thy judgments
30:21 this is the *w.*, walk ye in it
35: 8 shall be called The *w.* of holiness
43:19 make a *w.* in the wilderness
55: 7 let the wicked forsake his *w.*
59: 8 *w.* of peace they know not
Jer. 6:16 where is the good *w.* and
10:23 *w.* of man is not in himself
21: 8 the *w.* of life and the *w.* of death
32:39 give them one heart and one *w.*
50: 5 shall ask the *w.* to Zion
Mat. 5:25 whiles thou art in the *w.* with him
7:13 broad is the *w.*, that leadeth
21:32 John came in the *w.* of righteousness
Luke 1:79 guide our feet in the *w.* of peace
John 1:23 straight is the *w.* of the Lord
14: 4 ye know, and the *w.* ye know
14: 6 I am the *w.*, the truth, and
Acts 16:17 show unto us the *w.* of salvation
18:25 instructed in the *w.* of the Lord
1 Cor. 10:13 make a *w.* to escape, that ye may
12:31 show I unto you a more excellent *w.*

2 Pet. 2: 2 the *w.* of truth shall be evil spoken

WAYS
Deut. 32: 4 all his *w.* are judgment
Job 21:14 desire not the knowledge of thy *w.*
40:19 he is chief of the *w.* of God
Ps. 84: 5 in whose heart are the *w.* of
91:11 keep thee in all thy *w.*
145: 17 Lord is righteous in all his *w.*
Prov. 3:17 Her *w.* are *w.* of pleasantness
4:26 let all thy *w.* be established
5:21 *w.* of man are before the eyes of the
16: 2 *w.* of a man are clean in his own
16: 7 when a man's *w.* please the Lord
Is. 2: 3 he will teach us of his *w.*
63:17 made us err from thy *w.*
Jer. 7: 3 amend your *w.* and your doings
Lam. 1: 4 the *w.* of Zion do mourn
3:40 let us search and try our *w.*
Ezek. 16:61 thou shalt remember thy *w.*
Dan. 5:23 whose are all thy *w.* hast thou
Mic. 4: 2 he will teach us of his *w.*
Rom. 11:33 and his *w.* past finding out
Rev. 15: 3 just and true are thy *w.*

WEAK
2 Chr. 15: 7 let not your hands be *w.*
Job 4: 3 thou hast strengthened the *w.* hands
Ps. 6: 2 O Lord; for I am *w.*: O Lord heal
Is. 35: 3 strengthen ye the *w.* hands
Ezek. 16:30 how *w.* is thine heart, saith the
Mat. 26:41 willing, but the flesh is *w.*
Rom. 4:19 and being not *w.* in faith
14: 1 him that is *w.* in the faith receive
1 Cor. 4:10 we are *w.* but ye are strong
9:22 to the *w.* became I as *w.*
11:30 for this cause many are *w.* and sickly
12:10 I am *w.* then am I strong
1 Thes. 5:14 support the *w.*, be patient toward

WEAKEN (WEAKENED, WEAKENETH)
Job 12:21 and *w.* the strength of the mighty
Ps. 102: 23 He *w.* my strength in the way
Is. 14:12 thou didst *w.* the nations

WEAKER
2 Sam. 3: 1 house of Saul waxed *w.* and *w.*
1 Pet. 3: 7 the wife, as unto the *w.* vessel

WEAKNESS
1 Cor. 1:25 the *w.* of God is stronger
2: 3 I was in you with *w.*
15:43 it is sown in *w.*; it is raised
2 Cor. 12: 9 my strength is made perfect in *w.*
13: 4 he was crucified through *w.*
Heb. 11:34 out of *w.* were made strong

WEALTH
Gen. 34:29 And all their *w.*, and all their
Deut. 8:17 mine hand hath gotten me this *w.*
8:18 giveth thee power to get *w.*
Job 21:13 They spend their days in *w.*
Ps. 49: 6 They that trust in their *w.*
49:10 and leave their *w.* to others
112: 3 *w.* and riches shall be in his
Prov. 10:15 rich man's *w.* is his strong city
13:11 *w.* gotten by vanity shall be
13:22 *w.* of the sinner is laid up for
19: 4 *w.* maketh many friends
1 Cor. 10:24 but every man another's *w.*

WEAPON (WEAPONS)
Deut. 23:13 have a paddle upon thy *w.*
Neh. 4:17 the other hand held a *w.*
Job 20:24 He shall flee from the iron *w.*
Is. 13: 5 the *w.* of his indignation
54:17 No *w.* that is formed against thee
2 Cor. 10: 4 *w.* of warfare are not carnal

WEARY
Gen. 27:46 I am *w.* of my life because
Job 3:17 there the *w.* be at rest
10: 1 my soul is *w.* of my life; I will
Prov. 3:11 nor be *w.* of his correction
Is. 7:13 *w.* men, will ye *w.* my God
40:28 fainteth not, neither is *w.*
40:31 shall run and not be *w.*
50: 4 word in season to him that is *w.*
Jer. 6:11 I am *w.* with holding in: I will
9: 5 *w.* themselves to commit iniquity
20: 9 I was *w.* with forbearing
31:25 I have satiated the *w.* soul
Gal. 6: 9 let us not be *w.* in well doing
2 Thes. 3:13 brethren, be not *w.* in well doing

WEDDING
Mat. 22: 3 them that were bidden to the *w.*
Luke 14: 8 any man to a *w.*, sit not down in

WEEK (WEEKS)
Dan. 9:24 Seventy *w.* are determined
9:27 covenant with many for one *w.*
10: 2 Daniel was mourning three full *w.*
Mat. 28: 1 toward the first day of the *w.*
Luke 18:12 I fast twice in the *w.*
Acts 20: 7 upon the first day of the *w.*
1 Cor. 16: 2 Upon the first day of the *w.*
Jer. 5:24 reserveth unto us the appointed *w.*

WEEP (WEEPEST, WEEPETH)
1 Sam. 1: 8 why *w.* thou? and why eatest thou
Job 30:25 Did not I *w.* for him
Ps. 126: 6 he that goeth forth and *w.*
Is. 30:19 thou shalt *w.* no more
Jer. 9: 1 I might *w.* day and night
13:17 my soul shall *w.* in secret
Lam. 1: 2 she *w.* sore in the night
Joel 2:17 *w.* between the porch and the altar
Luke 6:21 blessed are ye that *w.* now: for ye
23:28 *w.* not for me, but *w.* for yourselves
John 20:13 say unto her Woman, why *w.* thou
Rom. 12:15 *w.* with them that *w.*
1 Cor. 7:30 that *w.* as though they wept not
Jas. 5: 1 rich men, *w.* and howl

WEEPING
Ps. 30: 5 *w.* may endure for a night
Is. 22:12 Lord God of hosts call to *w.* and
Joel 2:12 with fasting and with *w.*
Mal. 2:13 covering the altar of the Lord with *w.*
Mat. 8:12 *w.* and gnashing of teeth
22:13 be *w.* and gnashing of teeth
25:30 be *w.* and gnashing of teeth

WEIGH (WEIGHED, WEIGHETH)
Job 31: 6 let me be *w.* in an even balance
Prov. 16: 2 but the Lord *w.* the spirits
Is. 26: 7 doth *w.* the path of the just
Dan. 5:27 art *w.* in the balances

WEIGHT (WEIGHTS)
Lev. 19:36 balances, just *w.*, a just ephah
Deut. 25:13 not have in thy bag divers *w.*
Prov. 11: 1 just *w.* is his delight
16:11 just *w.* and balance are the Lord's
20:23 Divers *w.* are an abomination
2 Cor. 4:17 exceeding and eternal *w.* of glory
Heb. 12: 1 let us lay aside every *w.*

WELL
Gen. 4: 7 if thou doest *w.* shalt
Ex. 1:20 God dealt *w.* with the midwives
Ps. 119: 65 hast dealt *w.* with thy servant
128: 2 it shall be *w.* with thee
Eccl. 8:12 it shall be *w.* with them
Is. 3:10 shall be *w.* with him
Rom. 2: 7 patient continuance in *w.* doing
Gal. 6: 9 not be weary in *w.* doing
2 Thes. 3:13 be not weary in *w.* doing
1 Pet. 2:15 with *w.* doing ye may put to silence
3:17 ye suffer for *w.* doing
4:19 their souls to him in *w.* doing

WELLS (WELLS)
Ps. 84: 6 valley of Baca make it a *w.*
Prov. 5:15 running waters out of thine own *w.*
10:11 righteous man is a *w.* of life
Sol. 4:15 a *w.* of living waters and streams
Is. 12: 3 ye draw water out of *w.*
John 4:14 a *w.* of water springing up
2 Pet. 2:17 These are *w.* without water

WEPT
Neh. 1: 4 I sat down and *w.*, and mourned
Ps. 69:10 When I *w.*, and chastened
Hos. 12: 4 he *w.*, and made supplication
Mat. 26:75 went out and *w.* bitterly
Luke 19:41 beheld the city, and *w.* over it
John 11:35 Jesus *w.*

WHEAT
Ps. 81:16 with the finest of the *w.*
Prov. 27:22 among *w.* with a pestle yet will
Sol. 7: 2 heap of *w.* set about with lilies
Jer. 12:13 they have sown *w.*, but shall reap
Amos 8: 5 we may set forth *w.*, making
Mat. 3:12 gather his *w.* into the garner

Luke 22:31 that he may sift you as *w.*
John 12:24 except a corn of *w.* fall

WHEEL (WHEELS)
Ex. 14:25 took off their chariot *w.*
Judg. 5:28 why tarry the *w.* of his chariot
Ps. 83:13 my God, make them like a *w.*
Prov. 20:26 bringeth the *w.* over them
Ezek. 1:16 appearance of the *w.* and their work
10:13 it was cried unto them, O *w.*
Dan. 7: 9 and his *w.* as burning fire
Nah. 3: 2 the rattling of the *w.*

WHIRLWIND (WHIRLWINDS)
2 Ki. 2:11 went up by a *w.* into heaven
Prov. 1:27 destruction cometh as a *w.*
10:25 As the *w.* passeth, so is the wicked
Is. 66:15 his chariots like a *w.*
Hos. 8: 7 they shall reap the *w.*
13: 3 the *w.* out of the floor
Nah. 1: 3 Lord hath his way in the *w.*
Hab. 3:14 came out as a *w.* to scatter me
Zech. 7:14 I scatter them with a *w.*
9:14 shall go with *w.* of the south

WHITE (WHITER)
Lev. 13: 4 spot be *w.* in the skin
Num. 12:10 Miriam became leprous, *w.* as snow
Job 6: 6 any taste in the *w.* of an egg
Ps. 51: 7 and I shall be *w.* than snow
68:14 it was *w.* as snow in Salmon
Eccl. 9: 8 thy garments be always *w.*
Sol. 5:10 my beloved is *w.* and ruddy
Is. 1:18 they shall be as *w.* as snow; though
Lam. 4: 7 they were *w.* than milk
Dan. 11:35 to purge and to make them *w.*
12:10 many shall be purified and be made *w.*
Mat. 17: 2 his raiment was *w.* as the light
Rev. 2:17 and will give him a *w.* stone
3: 4 they shall walk with me in *w.*
4: 4 elders sitting clothed in *w.* raiment
15: 6 clothed in pure and *w.* linen
19:14 clothed in fine linen, *w.* and clean

WHOLE
Job 5:18 he woundeth and his hands make *w.*
Ps. 9: 1 with my *w.* heart; I will show
119: 10 with my *w.* heart have I sought thee
Is. 54: 5 The God of the *w.* earth
Mic. 4:13 the Lord of the *w.* earth
Zech. 4:14 Lord of the *w.* earth
Mat. 9:21 touch his garment, I shall be *w.*
Mark 5:34 thy faith hath made thee *w.*
John 5: 4 *w.* of whatsoever disease
5: 6 unto him wilt thou be made *w.*
Acts 9:34 Jesus Christ maketh thee *w.*: arise
1 John 2: 2 for the sins of the *w.* world
5:19 the *w.* world lieth in wickedness

WHOLESOME
Prov. 15: 4 A *w.* tongue is a tree
1 Tim. 6: 3 consent not to *w.* words

WHOLLY
Num. 32:11 they have not *w.* followed me
Deut. 1:36 he hath *w.* followed the Lord
Jer. 46:28 not leave thee *w.* unpunished
1 Thes. 5:23 God of peace sanctify you *w.*
1 Tim. 4:15 give thyself *w.* to them

WHORE
Lev. 19:29 cause her to be a *w.*
21: 9 profane herself by playing the *w.*
Deut. 22:21 the *w.* in her father's house
23:18 not bring the hire of a *w.*
Prov. 23:27 a *w.* is a deep ditch; and a strange
Ezek. 16:28 thou hast played the *w.* also with
Rev. 17: 1 judgment of the great *w.* that sitteth
17:16 these shall hate the *w.*

WHOREDOM (WHOREDOMS)
Jer. 3: 9 through the lightness of her *w.*
Ezek. 16:26 hast increased thy *w.* to provoke
Hos. 2: 2 put away her *w.* out of her
2: 4 they be the children of *w.*
4:12 spirit of *w.* hath caused them to
5: 4 spirit of *w.* is in the midst

WHOREMONGER (WHOREMONGERS)
Eph. 5: 5 no *w.*, nor unclean person
1 Tim. 1:10 *w.*, for them that defile themselves
Heb. 13: 4 *w.* and adulterers God will judge
Rev. 21: 8 murderers, and *w.*, and sorcerers
22:15 sorcerers, and *w.*, and murderers

WICKED
Gen. 18:25 slay the righteous with the *w.*
Ex. 23: 7 I will not justify the *w.*
Deut. 15: 9 a thought in thy *w.* heart
25: 1 righteous, and condemn the *w.*
1 Sam. 2: 9 the *w.* shall be silent in
Job 21:30 that the *w.* is reserved to the day
Ps. 7:11 God is angry with the *w.*
9:17 *w.* shall be turned into hell
11: 6 on the *w.* he shall rain snares
58: 3 *w.* are estranged from the womb
119:155 salvation is far from the *w.*
145: 20 but all the *w.* will he destroy
Prov. 11: 5 *w.* shall fall by his own wickedness
21:12 God overthroweth the *w.* for their
28: 1 *w.* flee when no man pursueth
Eccl. 7:17 be not overmuch *w.*, neither be
Is. 55: 7 let the *w.* forsake his way
Jer. 17: 9 heart is deceitful and desperately *w.*
25:31 them that are *w.* to the sword
Ezek. 3:18 warn the *w.* from his *w.* way
33: 9 if thou warn the *w.* of his way to
Dan. 12:10 *w.* shall do wickedly: and none of

WICKEDLY
Gen. 19: 7 pray you, brethren, do not so *w.*
1 Sam. 12:25 if ye shall still do *w.*
Job 13: 7 will ye speak *w.* for God?
Ps. 18:21 have not *w.* departed

WICKEDNESS
Gen. 6: 5 God saw that the *w.*
39: 9 how can I do this great *w.*
1 Sam. 24:13 *w.* proceedeth from the wicked
Job 4: 8 and sow *w.* shall reap same
Ps. 7: 9 *w.* of the wicked come to an end
45: 7 righteousness, and hatest *w.*
Prov. 8: 7 *w.* is an abomination to my lips
10: 2 treasures of *w.* profit nothing
Eccl. 8: 8 neither shall *w.* deliver those
Is. 9:18 *w.* burneth as the fire: it shall
Jer. 2:19 thine own *w.* shall correct thee
4:14 O Jerusalem, wash thy heart from *w.*
14:20 we acknowledge, O Lord, our *w.*
Hos. 10:13 ye have plowed *w.*, ye have reaped
Acts 8:22 repent therefore of this thy *w.*
1 John 4:19 whole world lieth in *w.*

WIDOW (WIDOWS)
Deut. 10:18 judgment of the fatherless and *w.*, and
Ps. 68: 5 a judge of the *w.*, is God in his
146: 9 he relieveth the fatherless and *w.*
Jer. 49:11 and let the *w.* trust in me
Mat. 23:14 for ye devour *w.* houses
Mark 12:42 there came a certain poor *w.*
Luke 18: 3 there was a *w.* in that city
18: 5 yet because this *w.* troubleth me
1 Tim. 5: 3 honour *w.* that are *w.* indeed
5: 5 now she that is a *w.* indeed
Jas. 1:27 fatherless and *w.* in their affliction

WIFE (WIVES)
Ex. 20:17 not covet thy neighbor's *w.*
Lev. 21:13 take a *w.* in her virginity
Prov. 5:18 rejoice with the *w.* of thy youth
18:22 findeth a *w.* findeth a good thing
19:14 a prudent *w.* is from the Lord
Eccl. 9: 9 live joyfully with the *w.*
Mal. 2:15 against the *w.* of his youth
Luke 17:32 remember Lot's *w.*
1 Cor. 7:29 *w.* be as though they have none
Eph. 5:28 love their *w.* their own bodies
5:33 love his *w.* even as
Col. 3:19 Husbands, love your *w.*
1 Tim. 3:11 even so must their *w.* be grave
1 Pet. 3: 1 ye *w.*, be in subjection to your
Rev. 19: 7 his *w.* hath made herself ready
21: 9 show thee the bride, the Lamb's *w.*

WILDERNESS
Deut. 32:10 land, and in the waste howling *w.*
Prov. 21:19 better to dwell in the *w.*
Is. 35: 6 in the *w.* shall waters break out
41:19 I will plant in the *w.*
42:11 Let the *w.* and the cities

Rev. 12: 6 woman fled into the *w.*

WILES
Num. 25:18 vex you with their *w.*
Eph. 6:11 against the *w.* of the devil

WILL
Lev. 1: 3 of his own voluntary *w.*
22:19 ye shall offer at your own *w.*
Deut. 33:16 the good *w.* of him that
Ezra 7:18 do after the *w.* of your God
Ps. 40: 8 I delight to do thy *w.*, O my God
Mat. 7:21 doeth the *w.* of my Father
6:10 Thy *w.* be done in earth
26:42 I drink it, thy *w.* be done
Mark 3:35 shall do the *w.* of God
Luke 22:42 not my *w.*, but thine, be done
John 1:13 *w.* of flesh, nor of the *w.* of man
4:34 my meat is to do the *w.* of him that
6:40 this is the *w.* of him that sent
7:17 any man *w.* do his *w.*
15: 7 ask what ye *w.* and it
17:24 I *w.* that they also, whom thou hast
Acts 13:22 which shall fulfil all my *w.*
21:14 the *w.* of the Lord be done
22:14 thou shouldest know his *w.*
Rom. 1:10 journey by the *w.* of God
2:18 And knowest his *w.*, and approvest
7:18 to *w.* is present with me
8:27 according to the *w.* of God
9:18 on whom he *w.* have mercy
12: 2 and perfect, *w.* of God
1 Cor. 1: 1 through the *w.* of God
2 Cor. 8: 5 unto us by the *w.* of God
Gal. 1: 4 according to the *w.* of God
Eph. 1: 9 known unto us, the mystery of his *w.*
6: 6 doing the *w.* of God
Phil. 2:13 worketh both to *w.* and to do
Col. 1: 9 knowledge of his *w.* in all wisdom
4:12 complete in all the *w.* of God
1 Thes. 4: 3 this is the *w.* of God
2 Tim. 2:26 captive by him at his *w.*
Heb. 10: 9 I come to do thy *w.*, O God
10:36 ye have done the *w.* of God
13:21 in every good work to do his *w.*
1 Pet. 4:19 according to the *w.* of God
1 John 2:17 doeth the *w.* of God abideth for ever
5:14 any thing according to his *w.*
Rev. 17:17 in their hearts to fulfil his *w.*
22:17 whosoever *w.*, let him take the water of

WILLING (WILLINGLY)
Ex. 35: 5 whosoever is of a *w.* heart
35:22 as many as were *w.* hearted.
Judg. 5: 2 people *w.* offered themselves
1 Chr. 28: 9 with a perfect heart and with a *w.* mind
Ps. 110: 3 thy people shall be *w.* in the day
Lam. 3:33 he doth not afflict *w.* nor grieve thee
Hos. 5:11 he *w.* walked after the commandment
Mat. 26:41 spirit is indeed *w.* but the flesh
Luke 22:42 if thou be *w.*, remove this cup
John 5:35 *w.* for a season to rejoice in his
2 Cor. 5: 8 *w.* rather to be absent from the body
1 Tim. 6:18 ready to distribute, *w.* to communicate
Heb. 13:18 in all things *w.* to live
1 Pet. 5: 2 not by constraint, but *w.*
2 Pet. 3: 9 not *w.* that any should perish

WILL-WORSHIP
Col. 2:23 of wisdom in *w.*, and humility, and

WIN (WINNETH)
Prov. 11:30 and he that *w.* souls is wise
Phil. 3: 8 them but dung, that I may *w.* Christ

WIND (WINDS)
Job 7: 7 O remember that my life is *w.*
30:15 pursue my soul as the *w.*
Ps. 103: 16 *w.* passeth over it, and it is gone
135: 7 he bringeth the *w.* out of
Prov. 11:29 house shall inherit the *w.*
Eccl. 11: 4 he that observeth the *w.*
Is. 26:18 we have as it were brought forth *w.*
27: 8 he stayeth his rough *w.* in
Jer. 5:13 prophets shall become *w.*, and the

Jer. 10:13 forth the *w.* out of his treasures
Ezek. 37: 9 come from the four *w.*. O breath
Hos. 8: 7 sown the *w.*, and they shall reap
12: 1 feedeth on *w.*, and followeth after the
Mat. 8:26 rebuked the *w.* and the sea
Luke 8:25 commandeth even the *w.* and the water
John 3: 8 *w.* bloweth where it listeth
Eph. 4:14 about with every *w.* of doctrine, by

WINDOWS
Gen. 7:11 *w.* of heaven were opened
Eccl. 12: 3 that look out of the *w.* be darkened
Sol. 2: 9 he looketh forth at the *w.*, showing
Is. 60: 8 and as the doves to their *w.*
Jer. 9:21 death is come up into your *w.*

WINE
Ps. 104: 15 *w.* maketh glad the heart
Prov. 20: 1 *w.* is a mocker, strong drink is
21:17 loveth *w.* and oil shall not be rich
23:31 look not thou upon the *w.* when it is red
31: 6 and *w.* to those that be of heavy heart
Sol. 1: 2 love is better than *w.*
Is. 5:11 until night, till *w.* inflame them
5:12 pipe and *w.* are in their feasts
28: 7 they have erred through *w.*
55: 1 buy *w.* and milk without money and
Hos. 2: 9 and my *w.* in the season thereof, and
3: 1 look to other gods, love flagons of *w.*
Hab. 2: 5 he transgresseth by *w.*, he is a proud
Eph. 5:18 be not drunk with *w.* wherein is
1 Tim. 3: 3 not given to *w.*, no striker, not
3: 8 Not given to much *w.*, not greedy of
5:23 use a little *w.* for thy stomach's sake
Tit. 1: 7 not given to *w.*, no striker

WINEBIBBER (WINEBIBBERS)
Prov. 23:20 Be not among *w.*
Mat. 11:19 a man gluttonous, and a *w.*

WINGS
Ruth 2:12 under whose *w.* thou art come to trust
2 Sam. 22:11 seen upon the *w.* of wind
Ps. 17: 8 hide me under the shadow of thy *w.*
18:10 fly upon the *w.* of the wind
36: 7 trust under the shadow of thy *w.*
91: 4 under his *w.* shalt thou trust
Prov. 23: 5 riches certainly make themselves *w.*
Is. 6: 2 seraphims, each one had six *w.*
Mal. 4: 2 with healing in his *w.*

WINTER
Sol. 2:11 For, lo, the *w.* is past, the rain
Zech. 14: 8 summer and in *w.* it shall be

WISE
Gen. 41:39 discreet and *w.* as thou art
Ex. 23: 8 gift blindeth the *w.*, and perverteth
Deut. 16:19 doth blind the eyes of the *w.*
Job 11:12 vain man would be *w.*, though man be
32: 9 great men are not always *w.*
Ps. 2:10 Be *w.*, now therefore, O ye kings
19: 7 Lord is sure, making *w.* the simple
107: 43 whoso is *w.* and will observe
Prov. 3: 7 be not *w.* in thine own eyes
3:35 the *w.* shall inherit glory
13:20 walketh with *w.* men shall be *w.*
26:12 a man *w.* in his own conceit
Eccl. 7: 4 heart of the *w.* is in the house of
9: 1 the *w.* and their work are
Is. 5:21 are *w.* in their own eyes, and prudent
Jer. 4:22 they are *w.* to do evil, but to do
Dan. 12: 3 *w.* shall shine as brightness
Hos. 14: 9 who is *w.* and he shall understand
Mat. 10:16 be ye therefore *w.* as serpents
10:42 in no *w.* lose his reward
11:25 hid these things from the *w.*
Luke 18:17 shall in no *w.* enter therein
John 6:37 cometh to me I will in no *w.* cast
Rom. 1:22 professing themselves to be *w.*
16:19 be *w.* to that which is good
1 Cor. 3:18 seemeth to be *w.* in this world
4:10 but ye are *w.* in Christ
Eph. 5:15 circumspectly not as fools but as *w.*
Rev. 21:27 shall in no *w.* enter into it

WISDOM
Deut. 4: 6 is your *w.*, and your understanding
1 Ki. 4:29 God gave Solomon *w.*, and understanding
Job 28:28 the fear of the Lord, that is *w.*
Ps. 111: 10 Lord is the beginning of *w.*
Prov. 4: 5 get *w.*, get understanding: forget
4: 7 *w.* is the principal thing
9:10 Lord is the begining of *w.*
16:16 better is it to get *w.* than gold
19: 8 he that getteth *w.* loveth his own soul
23: 4 cease from thine own *w.*
23:23 sell it not; also *w.*, and instruction
Eccl. 1:18 in much *w.* is much grief
8: 1 a man's *w.* maketh his face
Mat. 11:19 But *w.* is justified of her children
1 Cor. 1:17 not with *w.* of words, lest the
1:24 power of God, and the *w.* of God
1:30 who of God is made unto us *w.*
2: 6 we speak *w.* among them that are perfect
3:19 *w.* of this world is foolishness
2 Cor. 1:12 not with fleshly *w.*, but by the grace
Col. 1: 9 in all *w.* and spiritual understanding
Jas. 1: 5 you lack *w.* let him ask of God
3:17 *w.* from above is first pure
Rev. 5:12 worthy is the Lamb to receive *w.*
13:18 here is *w.*: Let him that hath
17: 9 is the mind which hath *w.*

WITCH
Ex. 22:18 not suffer a *w.* to live
Deut. 18:10 of times, or an enchanter or a *w.*

WITCHCRAFT
1 Sam. 15:23 rebellion is as the sin of *w.*
Gal. 5:20 Idolatry, *w.*, hatred, variance

WITHHOLD (WITHHOLDETH, WITHHELD)
Gen. 20: 6 I also *w.* thee from sinning
22:12 thou hast not *w.* thy son
Job 31:16 If I have *w.* the poor from their
Ps. 40:11 *W.* not thou thy tender mercies
84:11 no good thing will he *w.*
Prov. 3:27 *w.* no good from them to whom it is
11:24 *w.* more than is meet but it tendeth
23:13 *w.* not correction from child
2 Thes. 2: 6 now ye know what *w.* that he might

WITHSTAND (WITHSTOOD)
Eccl. 4:12 two shall *w.* him, and a threefold
Acts 11:17 who was I, that I could *w.* God
Gal. 2:11 I *w.* him to the face, because he was
Eph. 6:13 able to *w.* in the evil day
2 Tim. 4:15 for he hath greatly *w.* our words

WITNESS
Gen. 31:48 This heap is a *w.* between me and thee
Lev. 5: 1 swearing, and is a *w.*, whether he hath
Num. 35:30 one *w.* shall not testify
Deut. 17: 6 at the mouth of one *w.*
Judg. 11:10 Lord be *w.*, between us
1 Sam. 12: 5 The Lord is *w.* against you
Job 16:19 my *w.* is in heaven, and my record is
Ps. 89:37 as a faithful *w.* in heaven
Is. 55: 4 him for a *w.* to the people
Jer. 42: 5 true and faithful *w.* between us
Mic. 1: 2 the Lord God be *w.* against you
Mal. 2:14 Lord hath been *w.* between thee
3: 4 I will be a swift *w.* against
John 3:11 seen; and ye receive not our *w.*
5:37 sent me hath borne *w.* of me
Acts 14:17 left not himself without *w.*
1 John 5:10 believeth on the Son of God hath *w.*
Rev. 1: 5 Christ, who is the faithful *w.*
20: 4 beheaded for the *w.* of Jesus

WITNESSES
Num. 35:30 put to death by the mouth of *w.*
Deut. 17: 6 At the mouth of two *w.*
Josh. 24:22 *w.* against yourselves that ye have
Is. 43:10 ye are my *w.*, saith the Lord
Mat. 18:16 mouth of two or three *w.*
2 Cor. 13: 1 two or three *w.* shall every word be
1 Thes. 2:10 ye are *w.* and God also
1 Tim. 5:19 but before two or three *w.*
6:12 a good profession before many *w.*
Heb. 10:28 without mercy, under two or three *w.*
12: 1 so great a cloud of *w.*
Rev. 11: 3 power unto my two *w.*, and they share

WOMAN
Gen. 2:23 she shall be called *W.*
3:15 enmity between thee and the *w.*
Lev. 18:23 any *w.* stand before a beast
20:13 as he lieth with a *w.* both of
Num. 30: 3 If a *w.* also vow a vow also
Prov. 11:16 gracious *w.* retaineth honour
12: 4 a virtuous *w.* is a crown to her
14: 1 every wise *w.* buildeth her house
31:10 who can find a virtuous *w.*
31:30 a *w.* that feareth the Lord, she shall
Eccl. 7:26 *w.* whose heart is snares and nets
7:28 *w.* among all those have I not found
Is. 49:15 can a *w.* forget her sucking child
54: 6 called thee as a *w.* forsaken
Jer. 31:22 the earth. A *w.* shall compass a man
Mat. 5:28 looketh on a *w.* to lust
John 2: 4 *w.*, what have I to do with thee
8: 3 brought unto him a *w.* taken in adultery
19:26 his mother, *w.*, behold thy son
Rom. 1:27 the natural use of *w.*
1 Cor. 11: 7 the *w.* is the glory of the man
Gal. 4: 4 sent forth his Son, made of a *w.*
1 Tim. 2:11 let *w.* learn in silence with
2:12 I suffer not a *w.* to teach
Rev. 12: 1 *w.* clothed with the sun, and the moon
17:18 *w.* which thou sawest is that great city

WOMEN
Judg. 5:24 blessed above *w.* shall Jael the wife
Prov. 31: 3 give not thy strength to *w.*
Sol. 1: 8 O thou fairest among *w.*, go thy
Is. 3:12 their oppressors, and *w.* rule over
32:11 tremble, ye *w.* that are at ease
Jer. 9:17 call for the mourning *w.*, that they
Lam. 4:10 *w.* have sodden their own children
Mat. 11:11 born of *w.*, there hath not risen
Luke 1:28 blessed art thou among *w.*
Rom. 1:26 *w.* did change the natural use
1 Cor. 14:34 let your *w.* keep silence in the
1 Tim. 2: 9 *w.* adorn themselves in modest apparel
5:14 therefore that the younger *w.* marry
2 Tim. 3: 6 lead captive silly *w.* laden with sins
1 Pet. 3: 5 in the old time holy *w.* also, who
Rev. 14: 4 were not defiled with *w.*

WOMB (WOMBS)
Gen. 25:23 Two nations are in thy *w.*
29:31 he opened her *w.*: but Rachel was
49:25 of the breasts, and of the *w.*
Ps. 22: 9 he that took me out of the *w.*
22:10 I was cast upon thee from the *w.*
127: 3 fruit of the *w.* is his reward
139: 13 covered me in my mother's *w.*
Eccl. 11: 5 how the bones do grow in the *w.*
Is. 44: 2 formed thee from the *w.*, which will
66: 9 to bring forth, and shut the *w.*
Hos. 9:14 give them a miscarrying *w.*
Luke 1:42 blessed is fruit of thy *w.*
11:27 blessed is *w.* that bare thee
23:29 barren, and the *w.* that never bare

WONDER (WONDERED)
Deut. 13: 1 giveth thee a sign of *w.*
Ps. 71: 7 I am as a *w.* unto many; but thou
Is. 29:14 marvelous work and a *w.*
59:16 *w.* that there was no intercessor
Zech. 3: 8 they are men *w.* at: for, behold, I
Luke 4:22 *w.* at the gracious words

Acts 13:41 ye despisers, and *w.* and perish
Rev. 12: 1 And there appeared a great *w.*

WONDERFUL
Deut. 28:59 the Lord will make thy plagues *w.*
Job 42: 3 things too *w.* for me, which I knew
Ps. 119:129 thy testimonies are *w.*: therefore doth
139: 6 such knowledge is too *w.* for me
Prov. 30:18 three things which are too *w.* for
Is. 9: 6 his name shall be called *W.*
25: 1 thou hast done *w.* things
Jer. 5:30 a *w.* and horrible thing is committed

WONDERS
Ex. 3:20 smite Egypt with all thy *w.*
7: 3 multiply my signs and my *w.*
15:11 holiness, fearful in praises, doing *w.*
Job 9:10 out yea, and *w.* without numbers
Ps. 77:14 thou art the God that doest *w.*
78:11 his *w.* that he had shown them
88:10 wilt thou show *w.* to the dead?
136: 4 who alone doeth great *w.*
Dan. 12: 6 shall it be to the end of these *w.*?
Joel 2:30 And I will show *w.* in the heavens
John 4:48 except ye see signs and *w.*
Acts 2:43 many *w.* and signs were done
Rom. 15:19 mighty signs and *w.* by the power of
Rev. 13:13 he doeth great *w.*, so that he

WORD
Num. 23: 5 put a *w.* in Balaam's mouth
Deut. 4: 2 Ye shall not add unto the *w.*
8: 3 every *w.* that proceedeth out
30:14 But the *w.* is very nigh unto thee
2 Ki. 20:19 *w.* of the Lord which thou hast spoken
Ps. 18:30 *w.* of the Lord is tried: he is a
68:11 the Lord gave the *w.*: great was
119: 11 thy *w.* have I hid in mine heart
119: 49 remember the *w.* to thy servant
119:105 thy *w.* is a lamp unto my feet
119:160 thy *w.* is true from the beginning
130: 5 in his *w.* do I hope
147: 19 showeth his *w.* unto Jacob
Prov. 15:23 *w.* spoken in due season, how good it
25:11 a *w.* fitly spoken is like apples
30: 5 Every *w.* of God is pure
Is. 29:21 make a man an offender for a *w.*
30:21 shall hear a *w.* behind thee
40: 8 the *w.* of our God shall stand
44:26 confirmeth the *w.* of his servant
50: 4 how to speak a *w.* in season
Jer. 5:13 the *w.* is not in them
15:16 thy *w.* was unto me joy and
20: 9 his *w.* was in mine heart as fire
Mat. 8: 8 speak the *w.* only and my
12:36 every idle *w.* that men shall speak
Mark 7:13 Making the *w.* of God of none effect
Luke 4:36 what a *w.* is this? for with authority
John 1: 1 in the beginning was the *W.*
1:14 the *W.* was made flesh, and dwelt
5:38 have not his *w.* abiding in you
8:31 If ye continue in my *w.*, then
15: 3 ye are clean through the *w.*
17: 6 they have kept thy *w.*
17:17 through thy truth: thy *w.* is truth
Acts 2:41 that gladly received his *w.*
13:15 any *w.* of exhortation for the people
13:26 to you is the *w.* of this salvation sent
17:11 received the *w.* with all readiness
20:32 and to the *w.* of his grace
Rom. 10:17 hearing by the *w.* of God
1 Cor. 4:20 kingdom of God is not in *w.*, but
Gal. 6: 6 taught in the *w.* communicate unto
Eph. 5:26 washing of water by the *w.*
Col. 3:16 let the *w.* of Christ dwell in
3:17 whatsoever ye do in *w.* or deed
1 Thes. 2:13 truth, the *w.* of God, which effectually
2 Thes. 2:17 stablish you in every good *w.*
3: 1 *w.* of the Lord may have free course
3:14 if any obey not our *w.*
1 Tim. 5:17 labour in *w.* and doctrine
Tit. 1: 9 holding fast the faithful *w.*
Heb. 4: 2 the *w.* preached did not profit
4:12 For the *w.* of God is quick
5:13 is unskilful in the *w.* of righteousness
13:22 suffer the *w.* of exhortation
Jas. 1:21 receive with meekness the engrafted *w.*
3: 2 if any man offend not in *w.*
1 Pet. 1:23 incorruptible, by the *w.* of God
1:25 *w.* of the Lord endureth forever
3: 1 if any obey not the *w.* they also
2 Pet. 1:19 also a more sure *w.* of prophecy
1 John 1: 1 hands have handled of the *W.*
Rev. 3: 8 and hast kept my *w.*, and hast not
3:10 kept the *w.* of my patience
12:11 overcame by the *w.* of their testimony
19:13 name is called the *W.* of God

WORDS
Job 23:12 I have esteemed the *w.* of his mouth
Ps. 50:17 instruction, and castest my *w.* behind
Prov. 15:26 *w.* of the pure are pleasant *w.*
19: 7 he pursueth them with *w.*
22:17 bow down thine ear, hear the *w.*
Eccl. 10:12 the *w.* of a wise man's mouth
12:10 to find out acceptable *w.*
12:11 *w.* of the wise are as goads
Is. 59:21 *w.* which I have put in thy mouth
Jer. 5:14 I will make thy *w.* in thy mouth
7: 4 trust ye not in lying *w.*
44:28 know whose *w.* shall stand
Dan. 7:25 speak great *w.* against the most High
Hos. 6: 5 slain them by the *w.* of my mouth
14: 2 take with you *w.*, and turn to
Mic. 2: 7 do not my *w.* do good
Zech. 1:13 good *w.* and comfortable *w.*
Mat. 26:44 the third time, saying the same *w.*
Mark 8:38 ashamed of me and of my *w.*
13:31 my *w.* shall not pass away
Luke 4:22 the gracious *w.* which proceeded
John 5:47 how shall ye believe my *w.*
15: 7 my *w.* abide in you, ye shall ask
Acts 7:22 was mighty in *w.* and in deeds
15:24 troubled you with *w.*, subverting
20:35 remember the *w.* of the Lord
26:25 speak forth the *w.* of truth and soberness
1 Cor. 2: 4 not with enticing *w.* of
2 Tim. 1:13 hold fast the form of sound *w.*
2:14 strive not about *w.* to no profit
Rev. 1: 3 hear the *w.* of this prophecy
22:18 the *w.* of the prophesy of this book

WORK
Gen. 2: 3 rested from all his *w.* which God
Ex. 20:10 in it thou shalt not do any *w.*
31:14 whosoever doeth any *w.* therein
Deut. 33:11 and accept the *w.* of his hands
1 Sam. 14: 6 the Lord will *w.* for us
Job 1:10 thou hast blessed the *w.* of his hands
10: 3 shouldest despise the *w.* of thine hands
14:15 a desire to the *w.* of thine hands
36: 9 he showeth them their *w.*
Ps. 8: 3 heavens, the *w.* of thy fingers
9:16 wicked is snared in the *w.* of his own
101: 3 I hate the *w.* of them that turn
119:126 time for thee, O Lord, to *w.*
143: 5 muse on the *w.* of thy hands
Eccl. 8:14 according to the *w.* of the wicked
8:17 I beheld all the *w.* of God
12:14 God shall bring every *w.* into judgment
Is. 10:12 performed his whole *w.* upon mount Zion
28:21 do his *w.*, his strange *w.*
29:16 shall the *w.* say of him that made it
43:13 I will *w.* and who shall
45:11 concerning the *w.* of my hands
49: 4 the Lord, and my *w.* with my God
64: 8 we all are the *w.* of thy hand
Jer. 10:15 vanity and the *w.* of errors
18: 3 potter wrought a *w.* on the
John 6:28 might *w.* the works of God
9: 4 I must *w.* the works of him
17: 4 finished the *w.* which thou gavest
Acts 5:38 if this *w.* be of men it will come
13: 2 for the *w.* whereto I have called
Rom. 2:15 show the *w.* of the law written
11: 6 otherwise the *w.* is no more *w.*
1 Cor. 3:13 every man's *w.* shall be made
9: 1 are not ye my *w.* in the Lord?
Eph. 4:12 for the *w.* of the ministry
1 Thes. 4:11 and to *w.* with your own hands, as we
2 Thes. 1:11 goodness, and the *w.* of faith with
2: 7 iniquity doth already *w.*
2:17 stablish you in every good *w.*
3:10 if any would not *w.*, neither should he eat
2 Tim. 4: 5 do the *w.* of an evangelist
Jas. 1: 4 let patience have her perfect *w.*
1:25 doer of the *w.* this man shall be blessed
1 Pet. 1:17 judgeth according to every man's *w.*

WORKS (WORKS)
Job 37:14 consider the wondrous *w.* of God
Ps. 17: 4 concerning the *w.* of men
40: 5 are thy wonderful *w.* which thou hast
46: 8 *w.* of the Lord, what desolations he
78: 4 wonderful *w.* that he hath done
78: 7 not forget the *w.* of God but keep
92: 4 triumph in the *w.* of thy hands
107: 8 wonderful *w.* to the children
111: 7 *w.* of his hands are verity
138: 8 forsake not the *w.* of thine own hands
Prov. 31:31 let her own *w.* praise
Eccl. 11: 5 knowest not the *w.* of God
Is. 26:12 wrought all our *w.* in us
Dan. 4:37 all whose *w.* are truth
Mat. 7:22 thy name done many wonderful *w.*
John 5:20 will show him greater *w.* than these
9: 3 *w.* of God should be made manifest in
10:32 of those *w.* do ye stone me?
10:38 believe the *w.*: that ye may know
14:11 believe me for the very *w.* sake
14:12 greater *w.* than these shall he do
Acts 2:11 our tongues the wonderful *w.* of God
26:20 God, and do *w.* meet for repentance
Rom. 3:27 of *w.*? nay: but by the law of faith
4: 6 God imputeth righteousness without *w.*
9:11 not of *w.* but of him that calleth
9:32 but as it were by the *w.* of the law
11: 6 then is it no more of *w.*
Gal. 2:16 by the *w.* of the law shall no flesh be
3:10 as many as are of the *w.* of the law
5:19 *w.* of the flesh are manifest
Eph. 2: 9 not of *w.*, lest any man should
2:10 Jesus unto good *w.*, which God hath
5:11 with the unfruitful *w.* of darkness
Col. 1:21 enemies in your mind by wicked *w.*
1 Thes. 5:13 highly in love for their *w.* sake
2 Tim. 1: 9 not according to our *w.*, but according
Tit. 1:16 in *w.* they deny him, being abominable
3: 5 not by *w.* or righteousness which
Heb. 6: 1 repentance from dead *w.*
9:14 conscience from dead *w.* to serve the
Jas. 2:14 and have not *w.*? can faith save
2:21 Abraham our father justified by *w.*
2:22 by *w.* was faith made perfect
2:24 by *w.* a man is justified
2:25 harlot justified by *w.*, when she had
1 John 3: 8 he might destroy the *w.* of the devil
Rev. 9:20 repented not of the *w.* of their
18: 6 her double according to her *w.*
20:12 in the books according to their *w.*
20:13 judged every man according to their *w.*

WORKETH
Prov. 11:18 wicked *w.* a deceitful *work*
Is. 64: 5 that rejoiceth and *w.* righteousness
John 5:17 my Father *w.* hitherto, and I *w.*
Acts 10:35 and *w.* righteousness, is accepted with
Rom. 4: 4 to him that *w.* is the reward not

1 Cor. 12: 6 same God which *w.* all in all
2 Cor. 4:17 *w.* for us a far more exceeding
Gal. 5: 6 but faith which *w.* by love
Eph. 1:11 *w.* all things after the counsel of
Phil. 2:13 it is God which *w.* in you
1 Thes. 2:13 effectually *w.* also in you that

WORKING
Is. 28:29 wonderful in counsel, excellent in *w.*
Rom. 7:13 sin, *w.* death in me by that which
Eph. 1:19 according to the *w.* of his mighty
3: 7 by effectual *w.* of his power
4:28 *w.* with his hands the thing
Phil. 3:21 according to *w.* whereby he is able
2 Thes. 3:11 *w.* not at all, but are busybodies
Heb. 13:21 *w.* in you that which is well pleasing

WORKERS
2 Cor. 6: 1 as *w.* together with him beseech you
11:13 are false apostles, deceitful *w.*
Phil. 3: 2 beware of evil *w.*, beware of the

WORKMAN
Mat. 10:10 for the *w.* is worthy of his meat
2 Tim. 2:15 *w.* that needeth not to be ashamed

WORKMAMSHIP
Ex. 31: 3 knowledge, and in all manner of *w.*
Eph. 2:10 we are his *w.*, created in Christ

WORLD
1 Sam. 2: 8 he hath set the *w.* upon them
1 Chr. 16:30 *w.* also shall be stable, that it
Ps. 17:14 from men of the *w.*, which have their
50:12 *w.* is mine and the fulness
93: 1 *w.* also is stablished that it
96:10 *w.* also shall be established
Eccl. 3:11 hath set the *w.* in their heart
Is. 26: 9 inhabitants of the *w.* will learn
Jer. 10:12 established the *w.* by his wisdom
Mat. 12:32 neither in the *w.* to come
16:26 gain the whole *w.* and lose his
18: 7 woe to the *w.* because of offences
24: 3 coming, and of the end of the *w.*
Mark 16:15 go ye into all the *w.* and
Luke 20:35 accounted worthy to obtain that *w.*
John 1:29 which taketh away the sin of the *w.*
3:16 God so loved the *w.* that he gave
3:17 *w.* through him might be saved
7: 7 the *w.* cannot hate you, but
8:23 ye are of this *w.*; I am not
12:47 to judge the *w.* but to save the *w.*
14:17 whom the *w.* cannot receive
14:19 *w.* seeth me no more; but ye see
14:31 *w.* may know that I love the Father
15:18 if the *w.* hate you, ye know that it
15:19 chosen you out of the *w.*
16:28 I leave the *w.* and go to the Father
17: 9 I pray not for the *w.*, but for them
17:11 I am no more in the *w.*, but these
17:16 not of the *w.*, even as I am not
17:18 thou hast sent me into the *w.*
17:23 *w.* may know that thou hast sent
Rom. 3:19 all the *w.* may become guilty
12: 2 But be not conformed to this *w.*
1 Cor. 1:21 *w.* by wisdom knew not God, it
Gal. 6:14 *w.* is crucified unto me, and I unto
Col. 1: 6 as it is in all the *w.*; and bringeth
1 Tim. 6: 7 brought nothing into this *w.*
Tit. 1: 2 promised before the *w.* began
Heb. 2: 5 put in subjection the *w.* to come
11:38 of whom the *w.* was not worthy
1 John 2: 2 for the sins of the whole *w.*
2:17 *w.* passeth away and the lust
3: 1 the *w.* knoweth us not, because it knew
4: 5 *w.* therefore speak they of the *w.* and the
5:19 the whole *w.* lieth in wickedness
Rev. 3:10 temptation shall come on all the *w.*
13: 3 all the *w.* wondered after the beast

WORLDS
Heb. 1: 2 by whom also he made the *w.*
11: 3 the *w.* were framed by the word of

WORM (WORMS)
Ex. 16:20 and it bred *w.*, and stank: and
Job 25: 6 How much less man, that is a *w.*
Ps. 22: 6 I am a *w.* and no man
Is. 41:14 fear not, thou *w.* Jacob
51: 8 *w.* shall eat them like wool
66:24 their *w.* shall not die, neither shall
Mark 9:48 their *w.* dieth not, and the fire

WORMWOOD
Deut. 29:18 a root that beareth gall and *w.*
Prov. 5: 4 But her end is bitter as *w.*
Lam. 3:19 my misery, the *w.* and the gall
Amos 5: 7 ye who turn judgment to *w.*
Rev. 8:11 the name of the star is called *W.*

WORSHIP (WORSHIPPED)
Ex. 4:31 bowed their heads and *w.*
32: 8 them a molten calf, and have *w.* it
1 Chr. 16:29 *w.* the Lord in the beauty of holiness
29:20 *w.* the Lord, and the king
Ps. 29: 2 *w.* the Lord in the beauty of holiness
96: 9 *w.* the Lord in the beauty of holiness
99: 5 *w.* at his footstool; for he is
Jer. 1:16 *w.* the works of their own hands
Mat. 4:10 Thou shalt *w.* the Lord thy God, and
15: 9 in vain do they *w.* me, teaching for
John 4:24 *w.* him must *w.* him in spirit
Acts 17:23 whom therefore ye ignorantly *w.*
24:14 so *w.* I the God of my fathers
Rom. 1:25 and *w.* and served the creature
2 Thes. 2: 4 all that is called God, or that is *w.*
Rev. 3: 9 to come and *w.* before thy feet
5:14 fell down and *w.* him that liveth for
7:11 on their faces, and *w.* God
13: 4 they *w.* the dragon which gave power
13:12 to *w.* first the beast
19:10 to *w.* God: for the testimony of
22: 9 sayings of this book: *w.* God

WORTHY
Gen. 32:10 I am not *w.* of the least
Mat. 8: 8 not *w.* that thou shouldest come
10:10 workman is *w.* of his meat
10:13 if the house be *w.* let your peace
22: 8 which were bidden were not *w.*
Luke 3: 8 forth therefore fruits *w.* of repentance
7: 4 *w.* for whom he should do this
10: 7 labourer is *w.* of his hire
15:19 no more *w.* to be called thy son
15:21 no more *w.* to be called thy son
20:35 accounted *w.* to obtain that world
21:36 *w.* to escape all these things
Acts 5:41 counted *w.* to suffer shame
Rom. 8:18 not *w.* to be compared with the glory
Eph. 4: 1 walk *w.* of the vocation wherewith
1 Thes. 2:12 walk *w.* of God, who hath called you
2 Thes. 1: 5 *w.* of the kingdom of God
1:11 God would count you *w.* of this calling
1 Tim. 1:15 *w.* of all acceptation, that Christ
5:18 labourer is *w.* of his reward
6: 1 count their masters *w.* of all honour
Heb. 3: 3 *w.* of more glory than Moses
10:29 sorer punishment shall he be thought *w.*
Rev. 3: 4 in white, for they are *w.*
5:12 *w.* is the Lamb that was slain
16: 6 blood to drink; for they are *w.*

WOULD
Neh. 9:30 yet *w.* they not give ear: therefore
Ps. 81:11 voice, and Israel *w.* none of me
Prov. 1:25 counsel, and *w.* none of my reproof
1:30 they *w.* none of my counsel
Is. 30:15 your strength: and ye *w.* not
Mat. 7:12 whatsoever ye *w.* that men should do
18:30 And he *w.* not: but went and
23:37 *w.* have gathered thy children
Rom. 7:15 what I *w.*, that I do not
11:25 For I *w.* not, brethren
Gal. 5:17 cannot do the things ye *w.*
Rev. 3:15 I *w.* thou wert cold or hot

WOUND (WOUNDED, WOUNDETH, WOUNDS)
Ex. 21:25 *w.* for *w.*, stripe for stripe
Deut. 32:39 I *w.* and I heal: neither is there
Job 5:18 he *w.* and his hands make whole
Ps. 69:26 grief of those whom thou hast *w.*
109: 22 my heart is *w.* within me
Prov. 6:33 A *w.* and dishonour shall he get
18:14 a *w.* spirit who can bear?
27: 6 Faithful are the *w.* of a friend
Sol. 5: 7 they smote me, they *w.* me
Is. 1: 6 *w.*, and bruises, and putrifying sores
53: 5 But he was *w.* for our transgressions
Jer. 10:19 my *w.* is grievous: but I said
15:18 pain perpetual, and my *w.* incurable
30:14 with the *w.* of an enemy, with the
30:17 heal thee of thy *w.*, saith the
Mic. 1: 9 For her *w.* is incurable
1 Cor. 8:12 and *w.* their weak conscience, ye sin
Rev. 13: 3 his deadly *w.* was healed: and all the

WRATH
Gen. 49: 7 their *w.*, for it was cruel
Ex. 32:11 Lord, why doth thy *w.* wax
Num. 16:46 *w.* gone out from the Lord
25:11 hath turned my *w.* away
Deut. 32:27 feared the *w.* of the enemy
Ezra 8:22 power and his *w.* is against all
Neh. 13:18 bring more *w.* on Israel
Job 5: 2 *w.* killeth the foolish man
Ps. 76:10 *w.* of man shall praise thee
78:38 did not stir up all his *w.*
95:11 I sware in my *w.* that they should
Is. 10: 6 against the people of my *w.*
54: 8 in a little *w.* I hid my face
60:10 in my *w.* I smote thee, but in my
Jer. 10:10 at his *w.*, the earth shall tremble
Ezek. 7:14 my *w.* is upon all the multitude
Hos. 5:10 pour out my *w.* upon them
Hab. 3: 2 make known; in *w.* remember mercy
Mat. 3: 7 flee from the *w.* to come
Rom. 2: 5 *w.* against the day of *w.*
5: 9 saved from *w.* through him
12:19 but rather give place unto *w.*
13: 5 for *w.* but also for conscience
Eph. 2: 3 by nature children of *w.*
4:26 let not the sun go down on your *w.*
1 Thes. 1:10 delivered us from the *w.* to come
5: 9 For God hath not appointed us to *w.*
1 Tim. 2: 8 holy hands without *w.* and doubting
Heb. 11:27 not fearing the *w.* of the king
Jas. 1:19 slow to speak, slow to *w.*
1:20 *w.* of man worketh not the righteousness
Rev. 6:16 from the *w.* of the Lamb
6:17 great day of his *w.* is come; and
14: 8 wine of *w.* of her fornication

WRESTLE (WRESTLED)
Gen. 32:25 out of joint as he *w.* with him
32:24 and there *w.* with a man
Eph. 6:12 we *w.* not against flesh and blood

WRETCHED
Rom. 7:24 O *w.* man that I am! who shall
Rev. 3:17 thou art *w.*, and miserable, and poor

WRINKLE (WRINKLES)
Job 16: 8 thou hast filled me with *w.*
Eph. 5:27 spot, or *w.*, or any such thing

WRITE (WRITTEN)
Ex. 34:27 *W.* thou these words: for after the
Deut. 6: 9 *w.* them upon the posts of thy house
27: 3 thou shalt *w.* upon them all the words
Ps. 69:28 and not be *w.* with the righteous
102: 18 shall be *w.* for the generation to come
Prov. 3: 3 *w.* them on table of thine heart
22:20 have not I *w.* to thee
Eccl. 12:10 and that which was *w.* was upright
Is. 8: 1 *w.* in it with a man's pen concerning
Jer. 30: 2 *W.* thee all the words that I have

Hab. 2: 2 *w.* the vision, and make it plain
1 Cor. 10:11 and they are *w.* for our admonition
2 Cor. 3: 2 ye are our epistle *w.* in our hearts
3: 3 *w.* not with ink but with the Spirit
Heb. 12:23 are *w.* in heaven, and to God
1 John 2: 1 these things *w.* I unto you that ye
2: 7 I *w.* no new commandment unto you
2: 8 a new commandment I *w.* unto you
2:13 I *w.* unto you, fathers
2:14 I have *w.* to you, fathers
2:21 I have not *w.* unto you because ye
2:26 these things have I *w.* unto you

WRONG (WRONGED, WRONGETH)
Ps. 105:14 suffered no man to do them *w.*
Prov. 8:36 *w.* his own soul: all they that
Jer. 22: 3 and do no *w.*, do no violence
22:13 and his chambers by *w.*; that useth
1 Cor. 6: 7 why do ye not rather take *w.*
2 Cor. 7: 2 we have *w.* no man, we have corrupted
Col. 3:25 he that doeth *w.* shall receive
Philem. 1:18 If he hath *w.* thee or oweth thee

WROUGHT
1 Sam. 6: 6 he had *w.* wonderfully among them
14:45 hath *w.* this great salvation
Ps. 139: 15 curiously *w.* in the lowest parts
Is. 26:12 thou also hast *w.* all our works in us
Ezek. 20: 9 I *w.* for my name's sake that it
John 3:21 that they are *w.* in God
Rom. 7: 8 *w.* in me all manner of concupiscence
2 Cor. 5: 5 that hath *w.* us for the selfsame
1 Pet. 4: 3 have *w.* the will of Gentiles

Y

YEA
Mat. 5:37 communication be *y.*, *y.*; Nay, nay
2 Cor. 1:18 toward you was not *y.* and nay
1:20 *y.* and in him Amen unto the glory

YEAR (YEARS)
Job 10: 5 are thy *y.* as man's days
Ps. 90: 4 a thousand *y.* in thy sight are but
Is. 61: 2 proclaim the acceptable *y.* of the Lord
63: 4 *y.* of my redeemed is come
Jer. 11:23 even the *y.* of their visitation
Luke 4:19 preach the acceptable *y.* of the Lord
2 Pet. 3: 8 a thousand *y.* as one day
Rev. 20: 2 Satan, and bound him a thousand *y.*

YESTERDAY
Job 8: 9 we are but of *y.*, and know
Heb. 13: 8 the same *y.*, and today, and for ever

YIELD (YIELDED, YIELDETH)
2 Chr. 30: 8 but *y.* yourselves unto the Lord
Ps. 67: 6 shall the earth *y.* her increase
Rom. 6:13 *y.* ye your members as instruments
6:16 whom ye *y.* yourselves servants to
6:19 ye have *y.* your members servants to
Heb. 12:11 *y.* the peaceable fruit of righteousness

YOKE (YOKED)
Deut. 28:48 shall put a *y.* of iron upon thy neck
1 Ki. 12: 4 Thy father made our *y.* grievous
Is. 9: 4 broken the *y.* of his burden
10:27 the *y.* shall be destroyed
Lam. 1:14 *y.* of my transgressions is bound by
Mat. 11:29 take my *y.* upon you, and learn of
11:30 my *y.* is easy and my burden is light
2 Cor. 6:14 be ye not unequally *y.* together with
Gal. 5: 1 entangled again with the *y.* of bondage

YOUNG
Ps. 37:25 I have been *y.*, and now am
Is. 40:11 gently lead those that are with *y.*

YOUNGER
1 Tim. 5: 1 and the *y.* men as brethren
5:14 I will therefore that *y.* women marry
1 Pet. 5: 5 ye *y.* submit yourselves to the elder

YOUTH
Gen. 8:21 imagination of man is evil from his *y.*
1 Ki. 18:12 fear the Lord from my *y.*
Job 13:26 possess iniquities of my *y.*
Ps. 25: 7 sins of my *y.*, nor my transgressions
Eccl. 11: 9 Rejoice, O young man, in thy *y.*
11:10 childhood and *y.* are vanity
Jer. 2: 2 the kindness of thy *y.*, the love of
1 Tim. 4:12 let no man despise thy *y.*

YOUTHFUL
2 Tim. 2:22 flee also *y.* lusts: but follow

Z

ZEAL
2 Ki. 10:16 with me, and see my *z.* for the Lord
Ps. 69: 9 the *z.* of thine house hath
119:139 my *z.* hath consumed me because
Is. 9: 7 *z.* of the Lord of hosts will perform
59:17 and was clad with *z.* as a cloak
63:15 where is thy *z.* and thy strength
Rom. 10: 2 record that they have a *z.* of God
Phil. 3: 6 concerning *z.*, persecuting the church

ZEALOUS (ZEALOUSLY)
Num. 25:13 because he was *z.* for his God
Acts 22: 3 and was *z.* toward God as ye all are
Gal. 4:18 *z.* affected always in a good thing
Tit. 2:14 peculiar people *z.* of good works
Rev. 3:19 be *z.* therefore and repent

ZION (ZION'S)
2 Sam. 5: 7 David took the stronghold of *Z.*
1 Ki. 8: 1 city of David, which is *Z.*
2 Ki. 19:31 they that escape out of mount *Z.*
Ps. 2: 6 my king upon my holy hill of *Z.*
9:11 to the Lord, which dwelleth in *Z.*
48: 2 joy of the whole earth is mount *Z.*
146:10 even thy God, O *Z.*, unto all
147: 12 O Jerusalem; praise thy God, O *Z.*
Is. 1:27 *Z.* shall be redeemed with judgment
60:14 The *Z.* of the Holy One of Israel
62: 1 For *Z.* sake will I not hold my peace
Heb. 12:22 But ye are come unto mount *Z.*

INDEX TO COLOR MAPS

Index to Color Maps

Map 1: **WORLD OF THE PATRIARCHS**

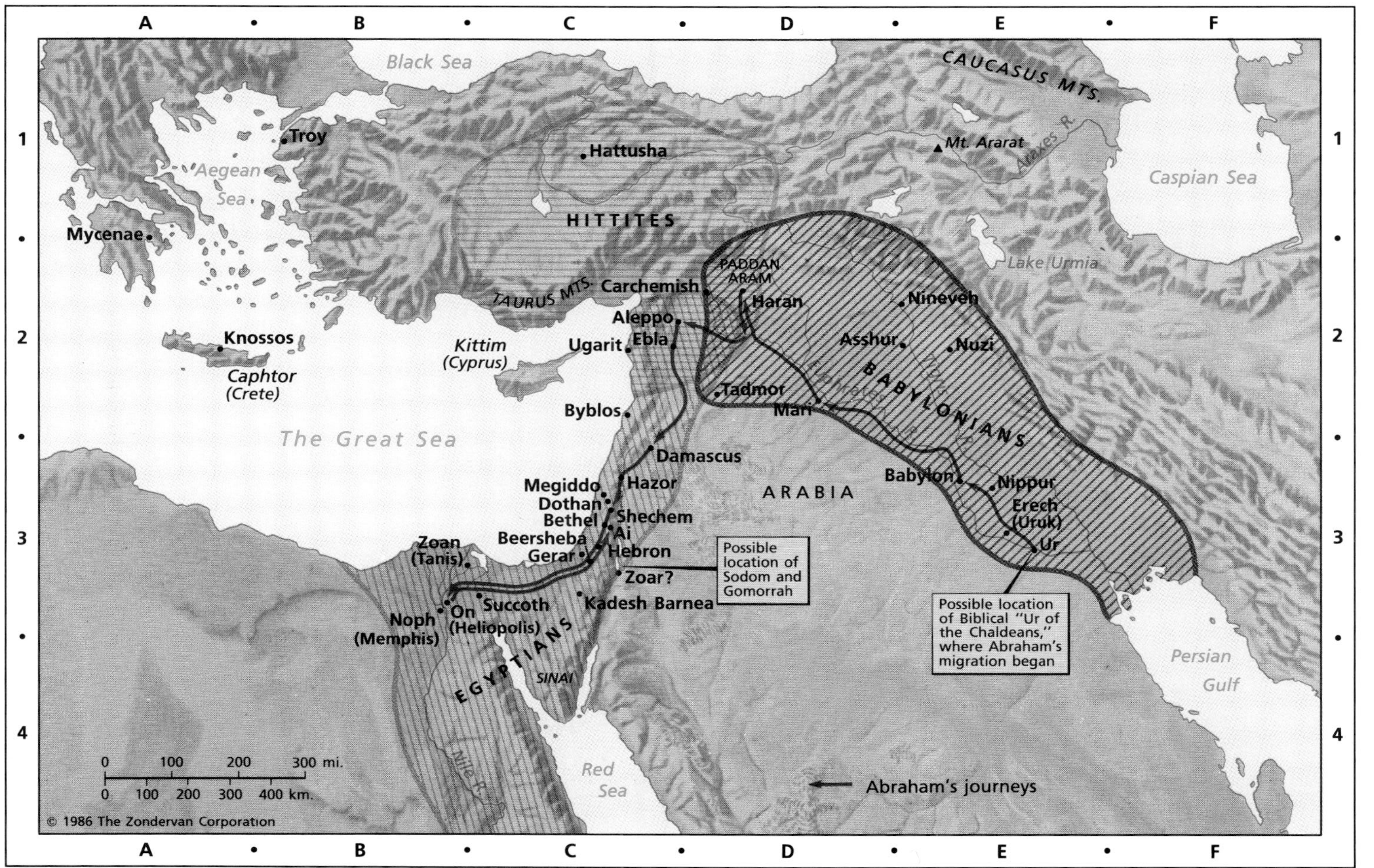

Map 2: **PALESTINE AND SINAI**

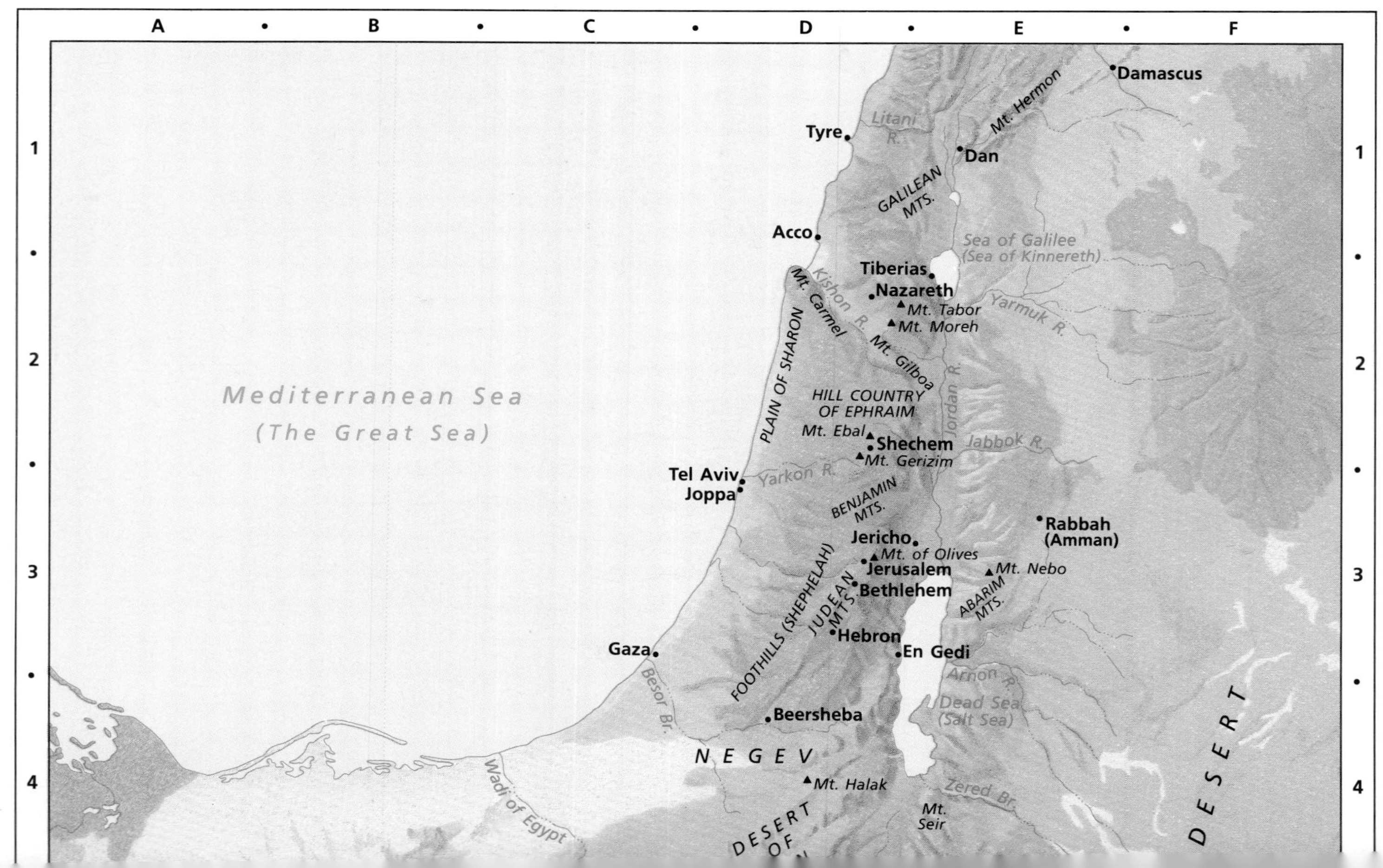

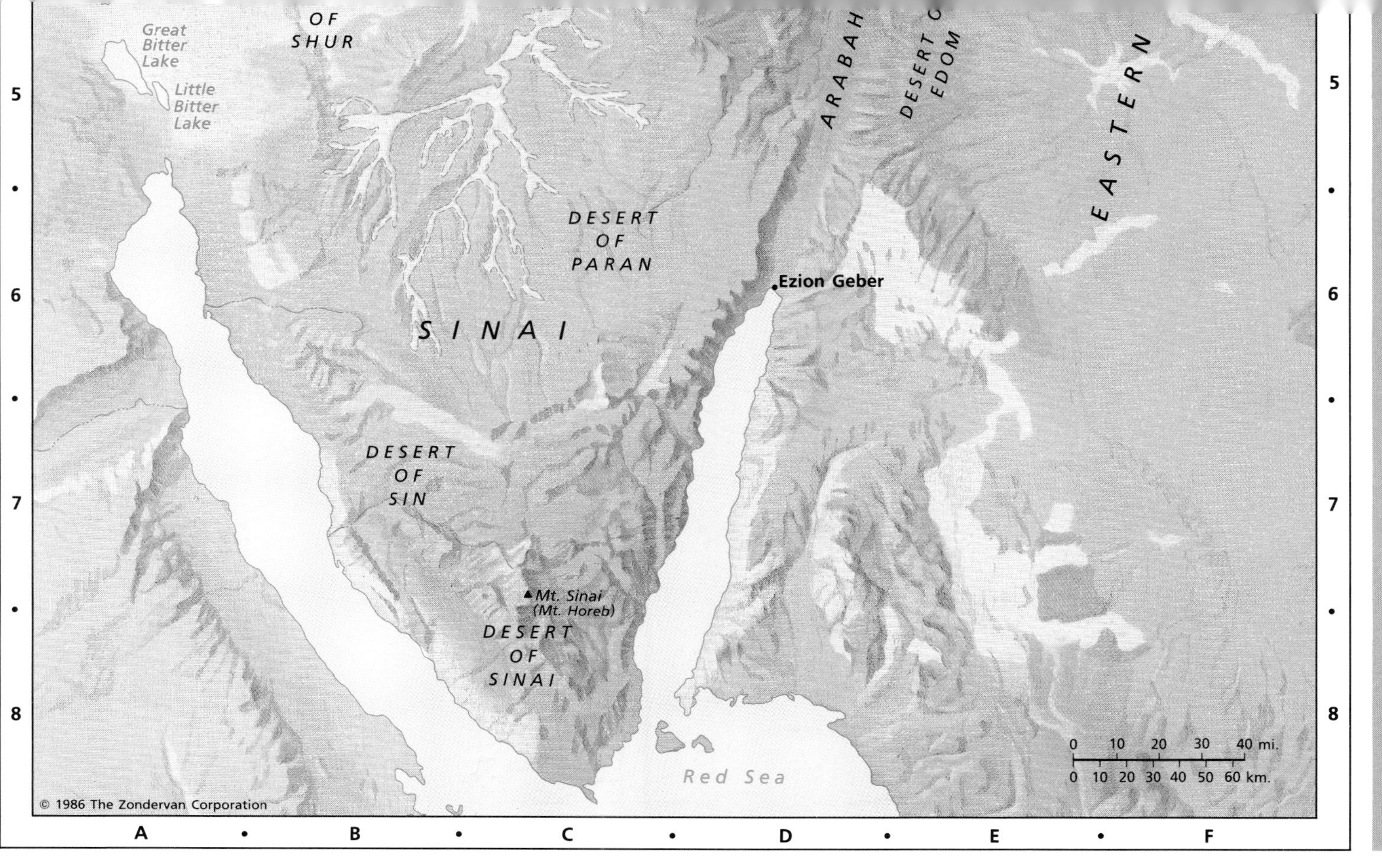

OF SHUR
Great Bitter Lake
Little Bitter Lake
DESERT OF PARAN
SINAI
ARABAH
DESERT O
EDOM
EASTERN
Ezion Geber
DESERT OF SIN
Mt. Sinai (Mt. Horeb)
DESERT OF SINAI
Red Sea
0 10 20 30 40 mi.
0 10 20 30 40 50 60 km.
A B C D E F
5 6 7 8

Map 3: **EXODUS AND CONQUEST OF CANAAN**

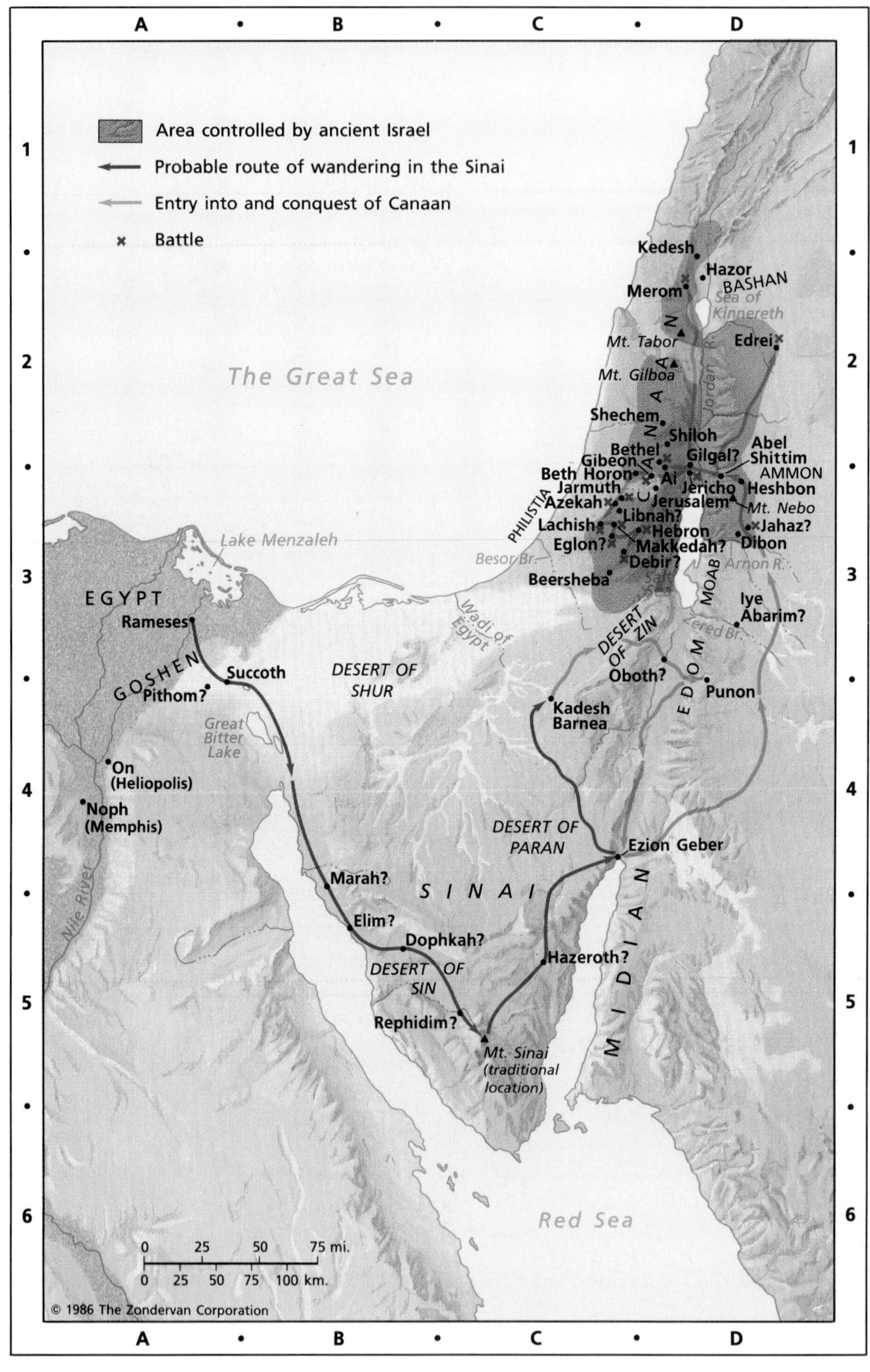

Map 4: **LAND OF THE TWELVE TRIBES**

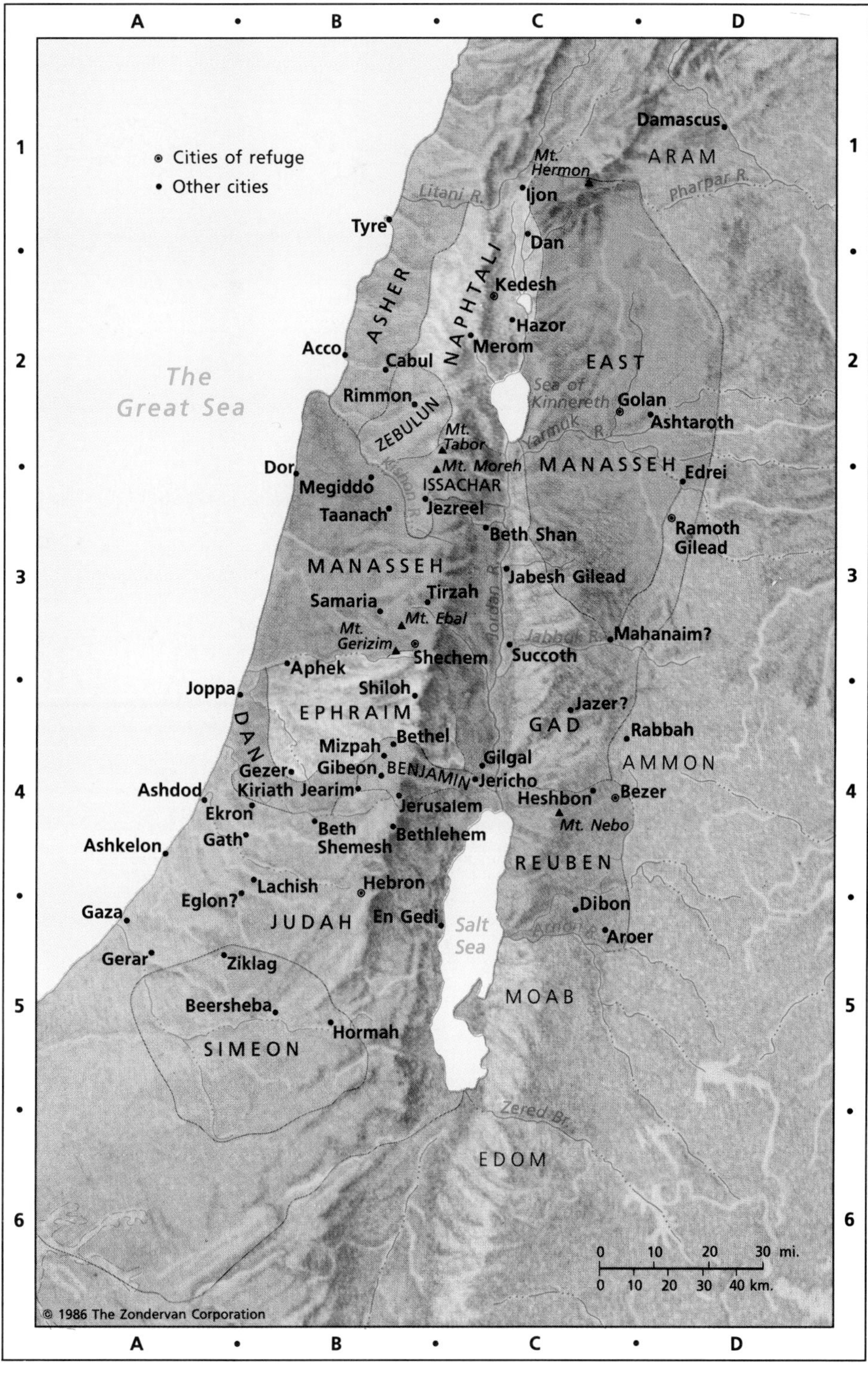

Map 5: **KINGDOM OF DAVID AND SOLOMON**

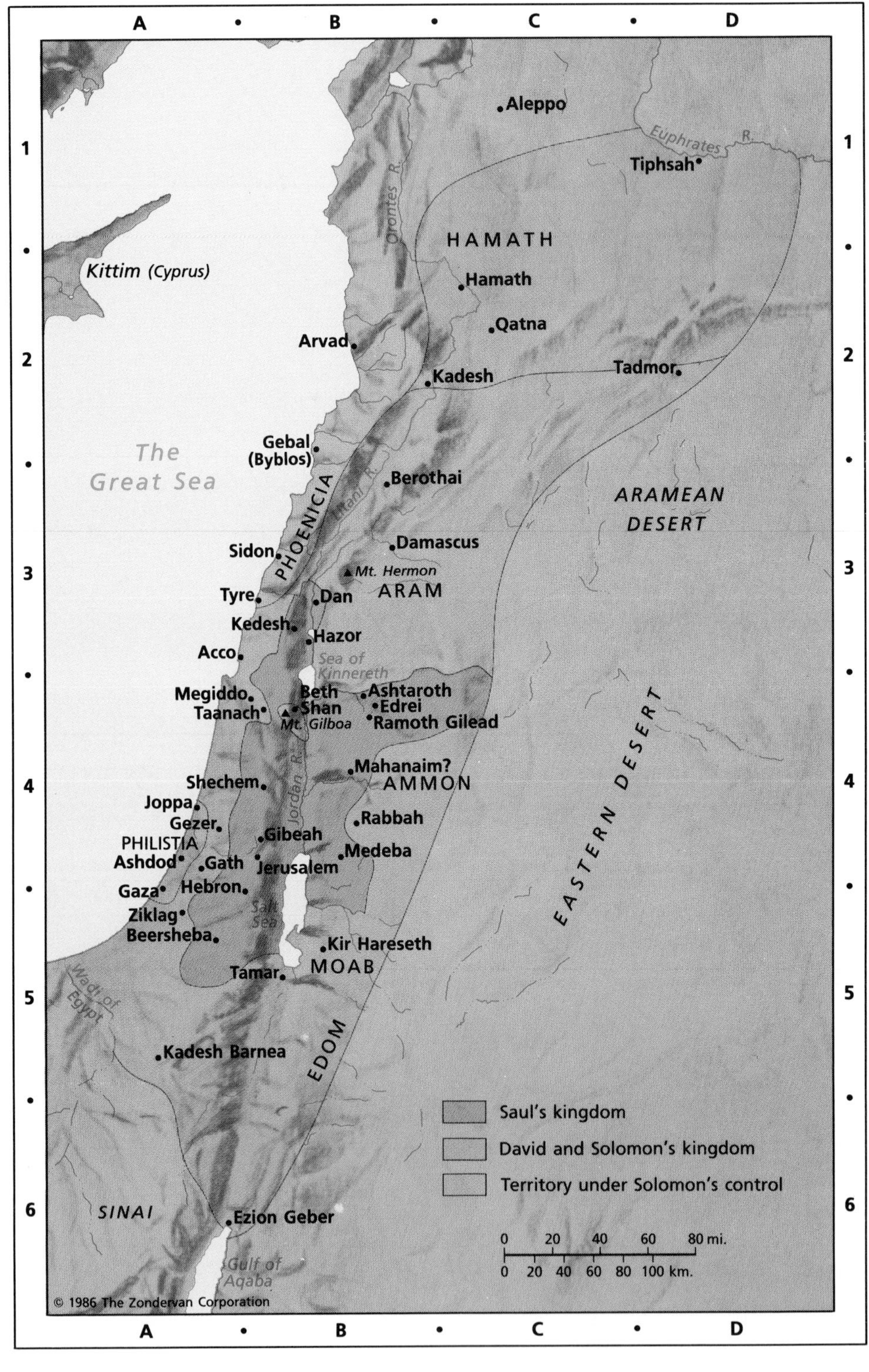

Map 6: **PROPHETS IN ISRAEL AND JUDAH**

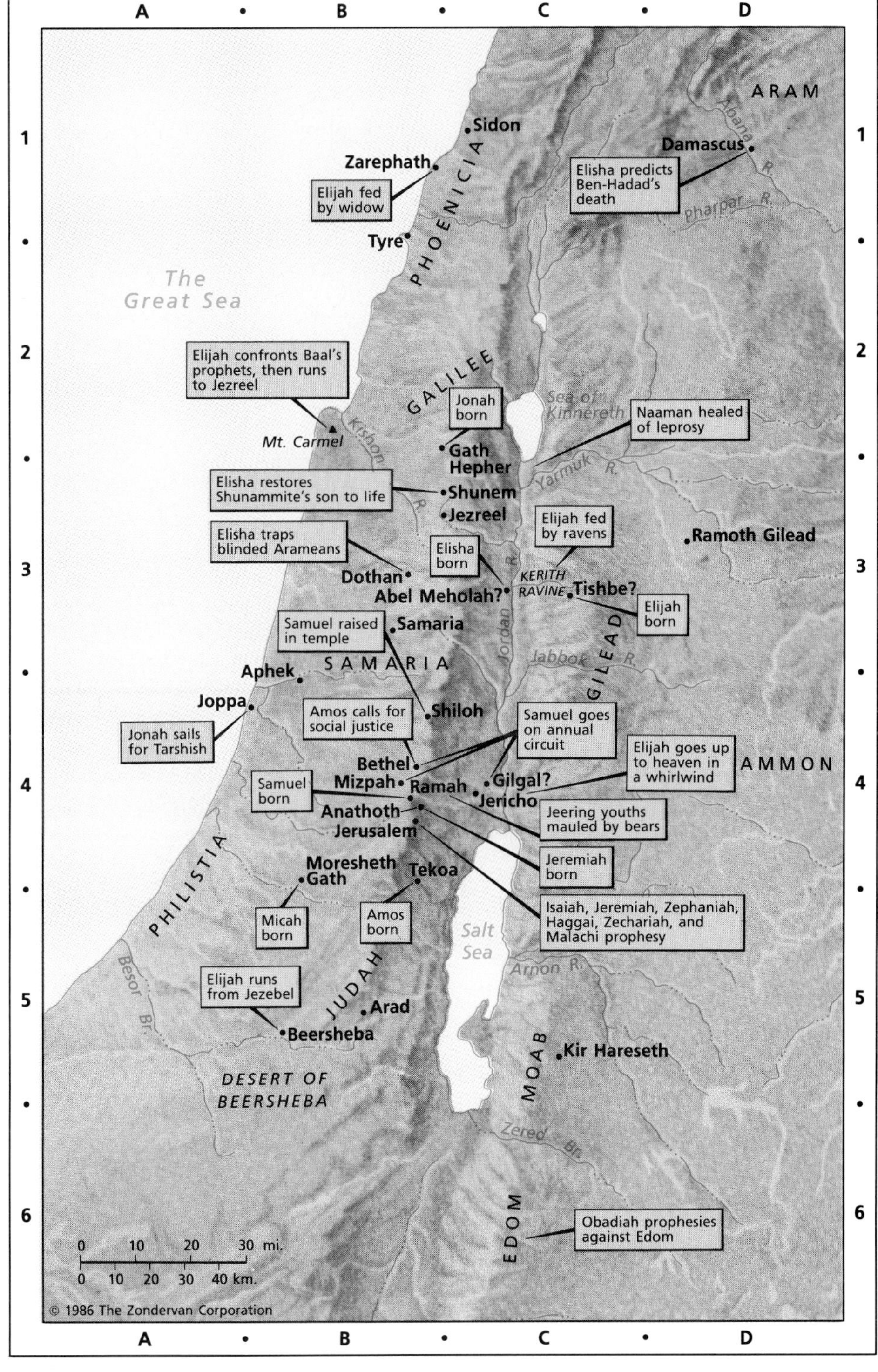

Map 7: ASSYRIAN AND BABYLONIAN EMPIRES

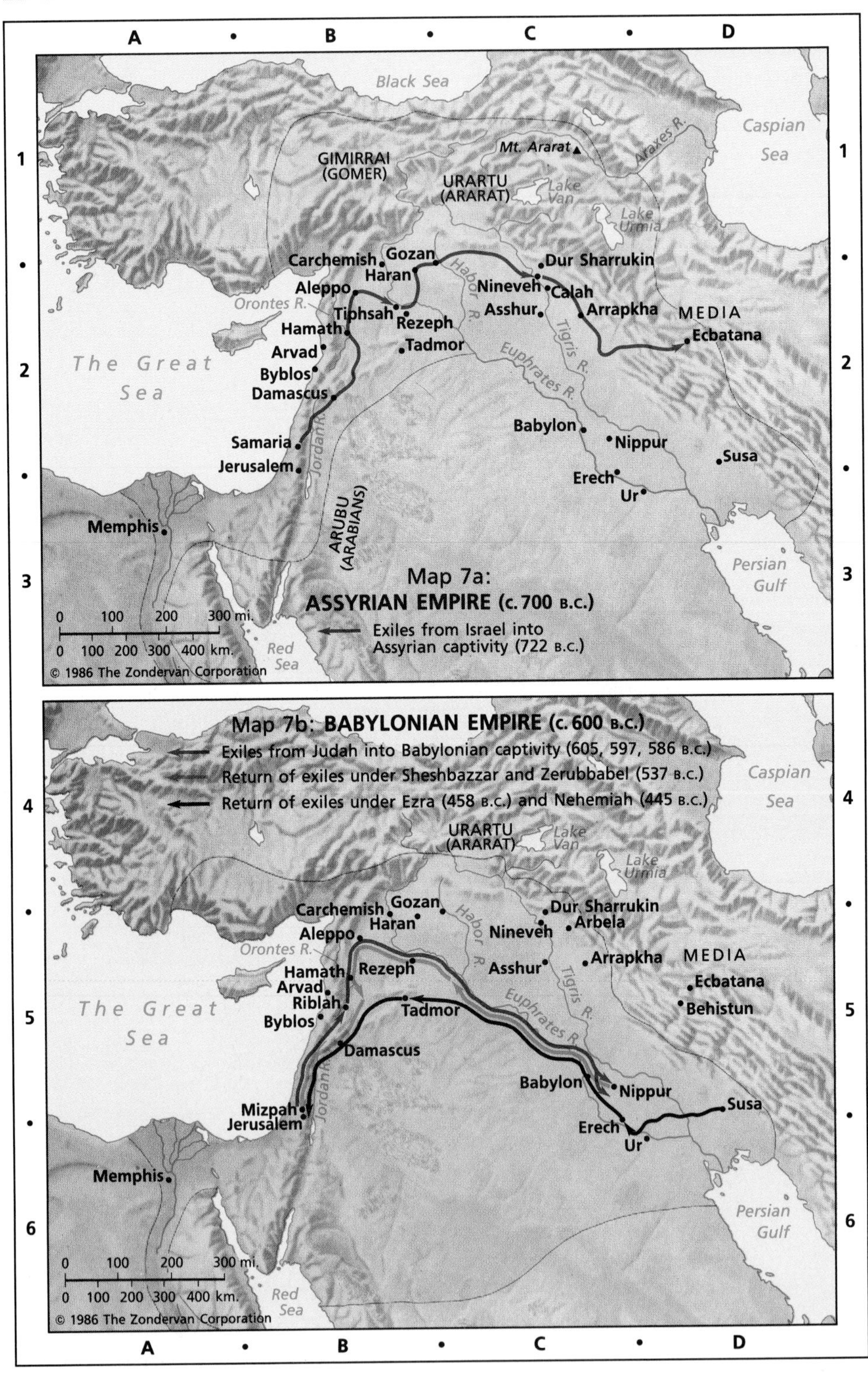

Map 8: **JERUSALEM IN JESUS' TIME**

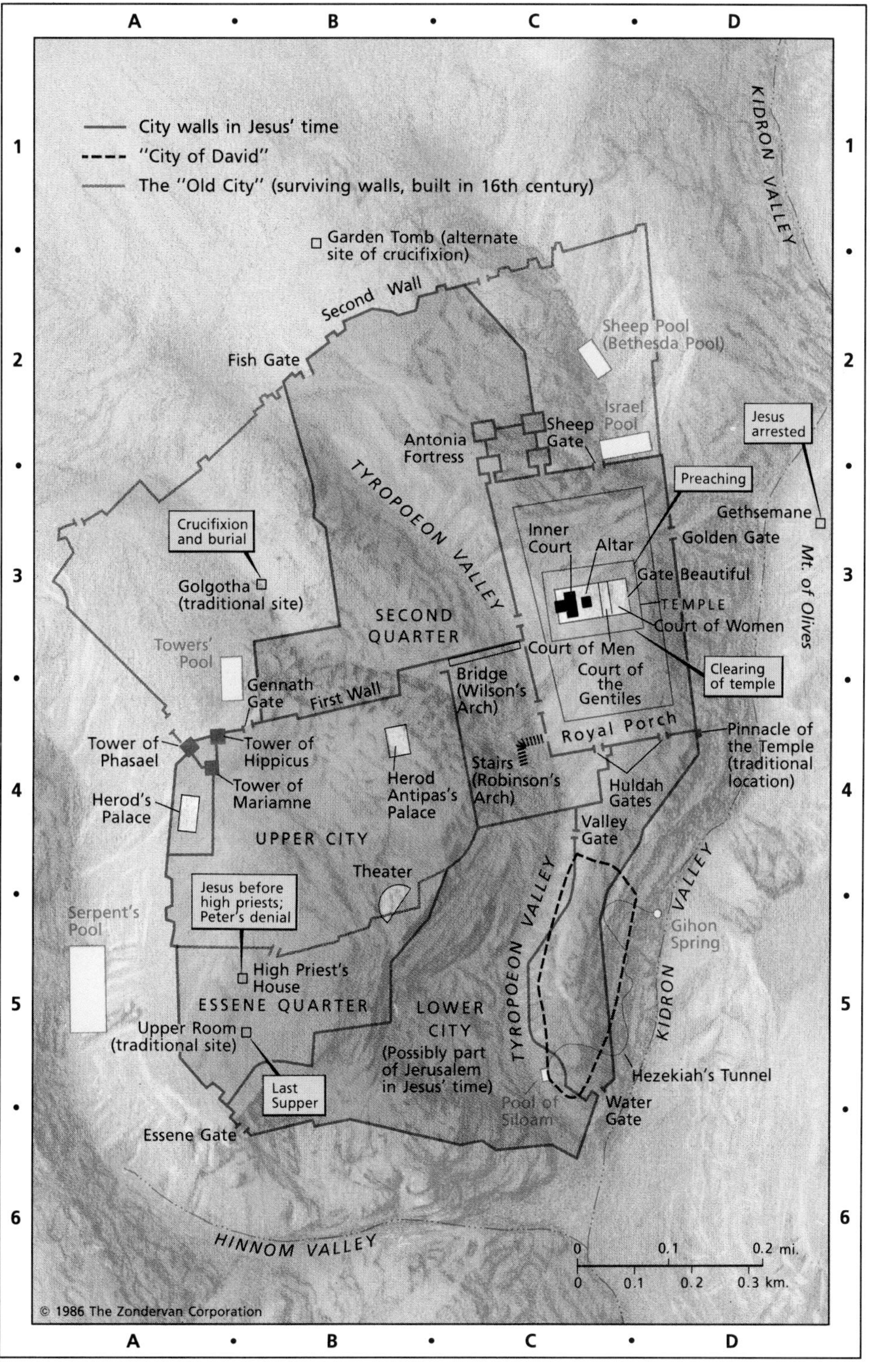

Map 9: JESUS' MINISTRY

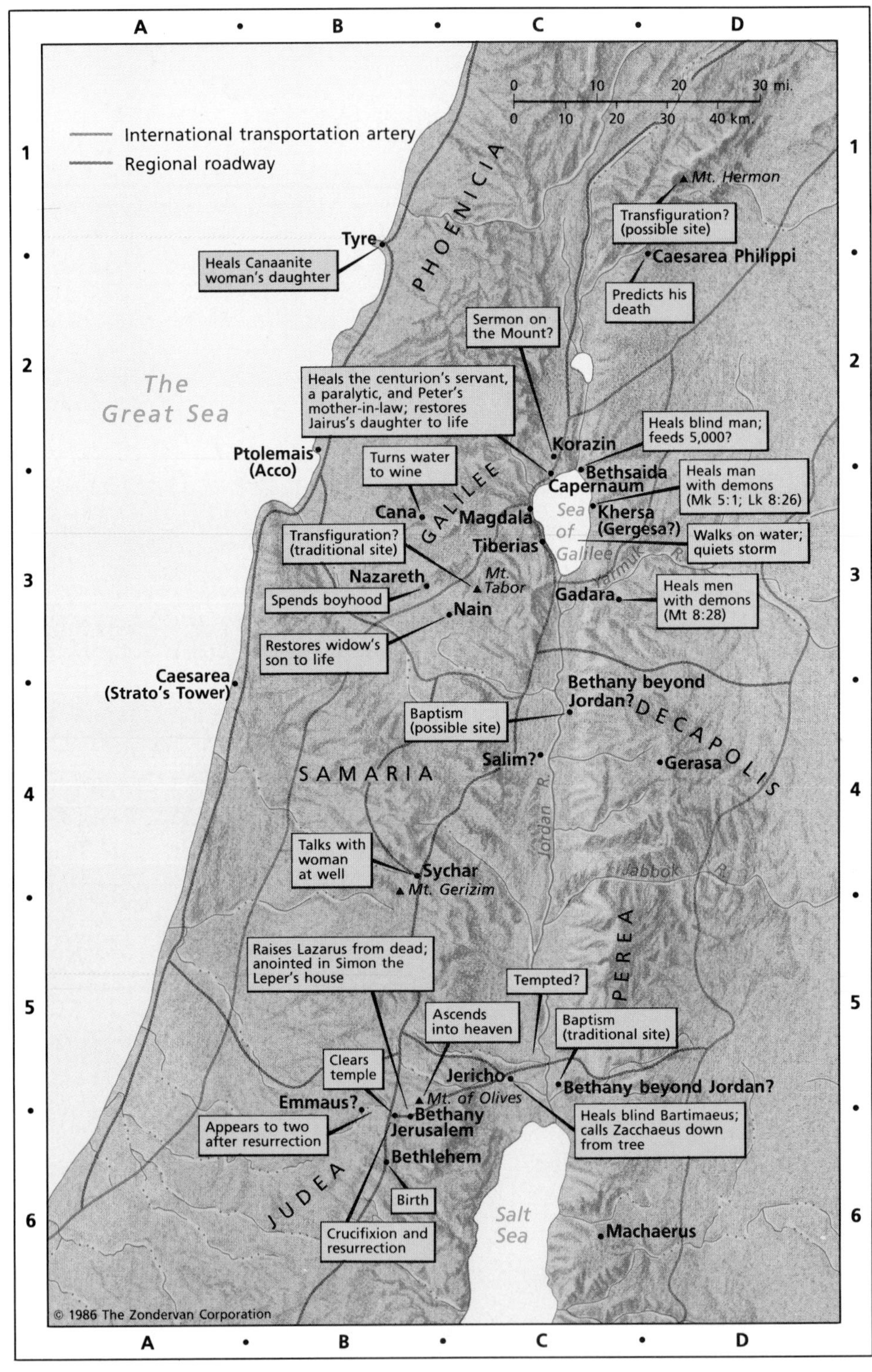

Map 10: **APOSTLES' EARLY TRAVELS**

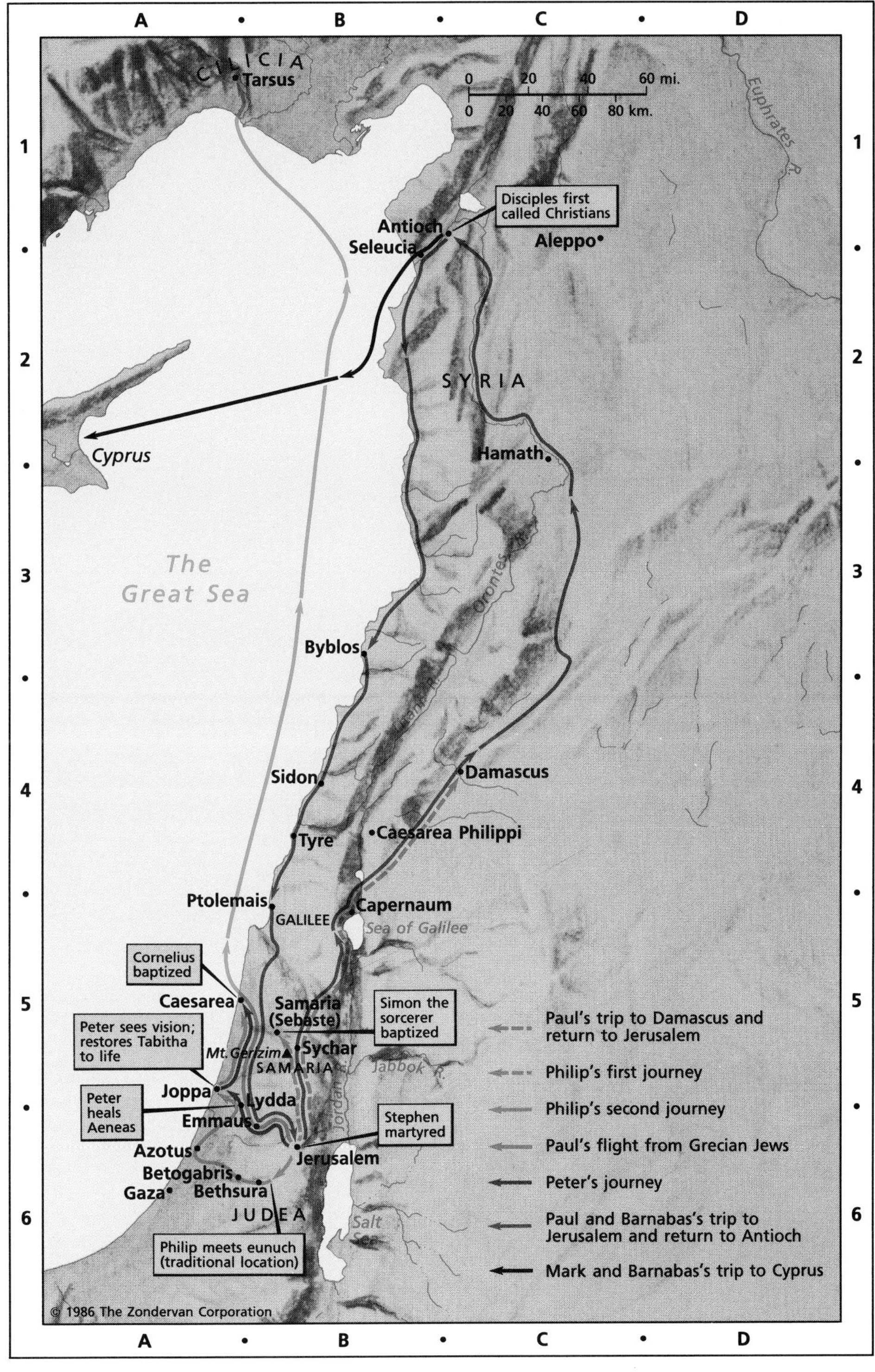

Map 11: **PAUL'S MISSIONARY JOURNEYS**

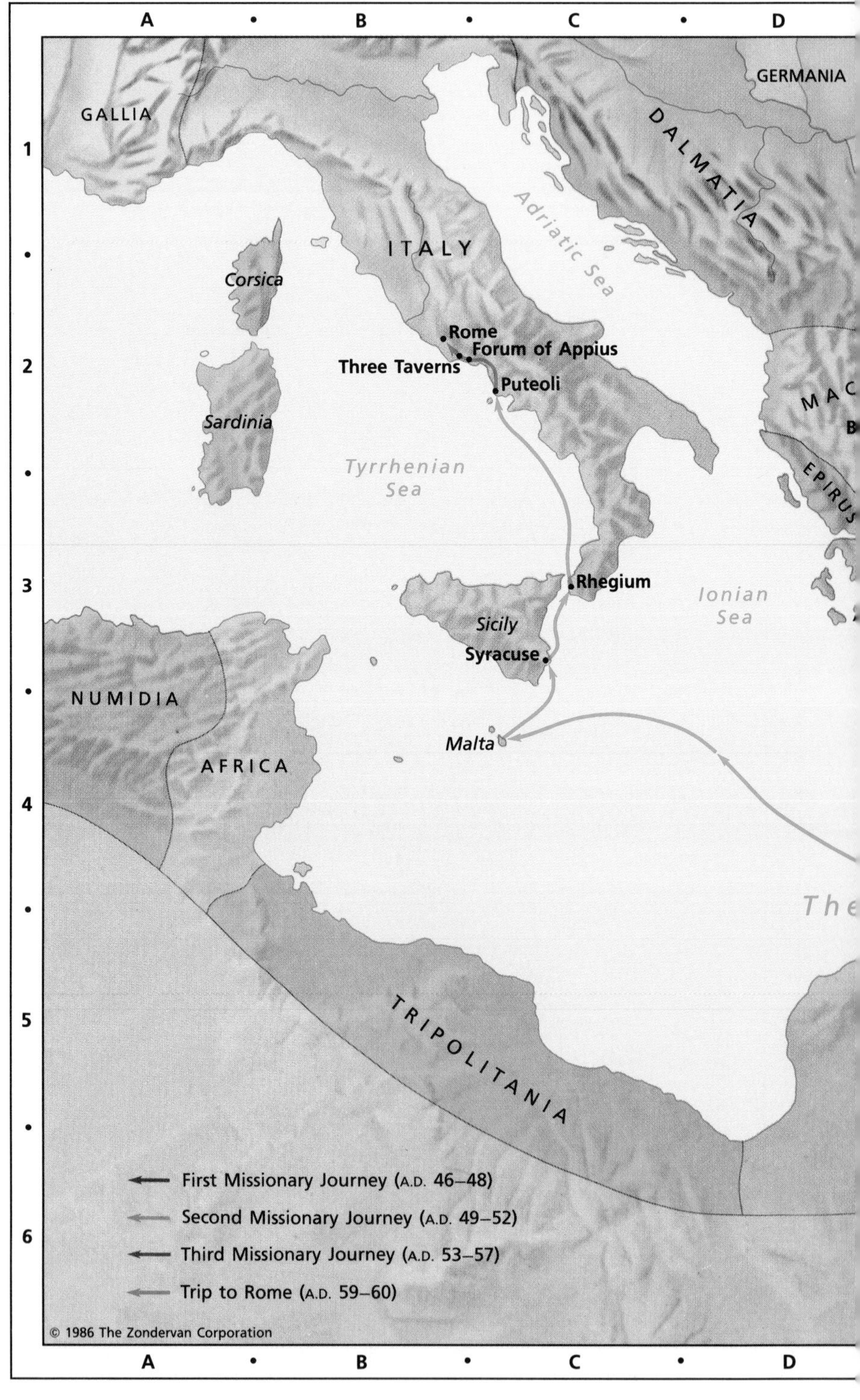

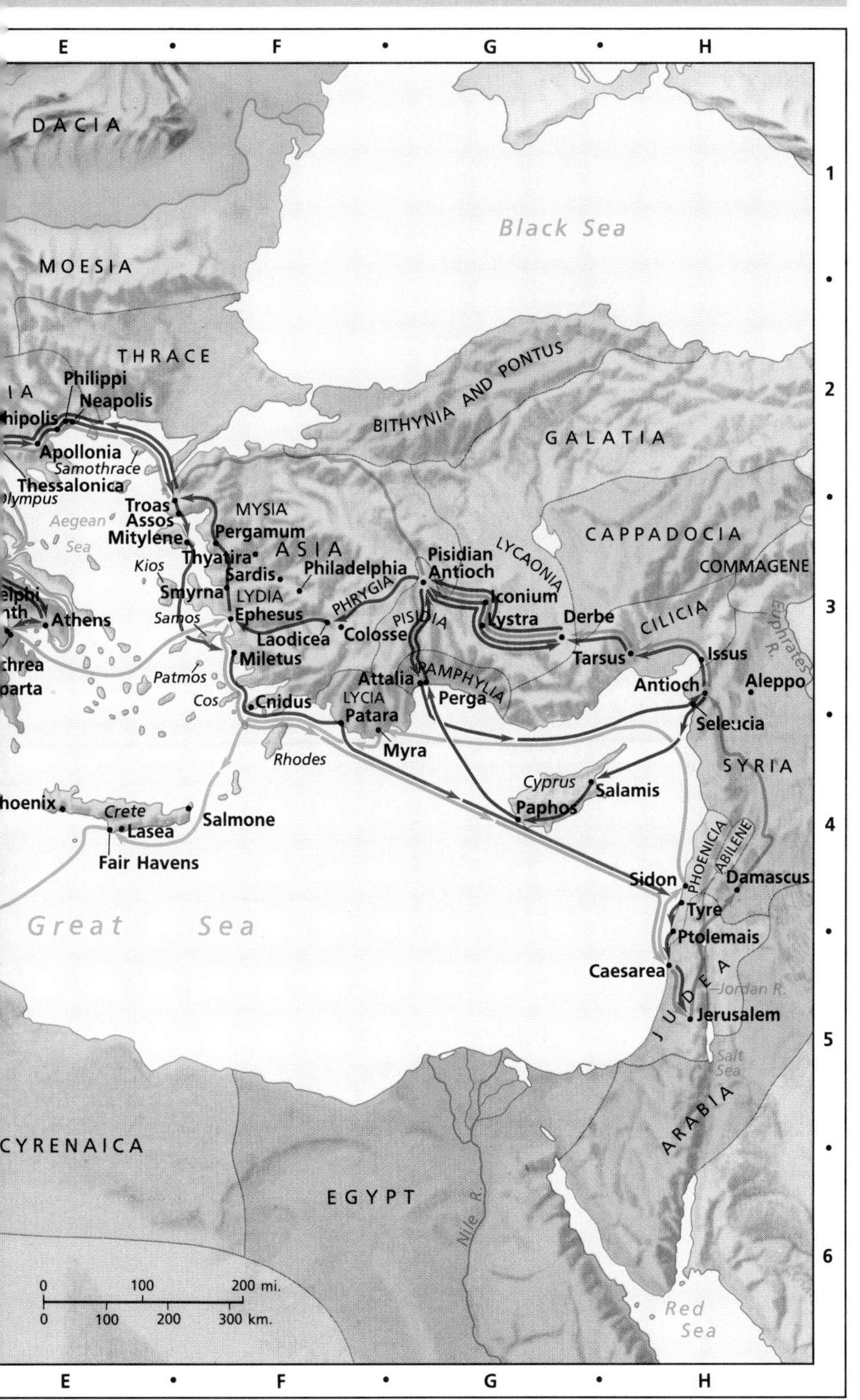
E
F
G
H
1
2
3
4
5
6
DACIA
MOESIA
THRACE
Black Sea
Philippi
Neapolis
Apollonia
Samothrace
Thessalonica
Troas
Assos
Mitylene
Aegean
Sea
MYSIA
Pergamum
Thyatira
Sardis
ASIA
Philadelphia
Kios
Smyrna
LYDIA
Athens
Samos
Ephesus
Laodicea
Colosse
PHRYGIA
Miletus
Patmos
Cos
Cnidus
Rhodes
LYCIA
Patara
Myra
Attalia
PAMPHYLIA
Perga
PISIDIA
Pisidian
Antioch
LYCAONIA
Iconium
Lystra
Derbe
BITHYNIA AND PONTUS
GALATIA
CAPPADOCIA
COMMAGENE
CILICIA
Tarsus
Issus
Antioch
Aleppo
Seleucia
Euphrates R.
SYRIA
Cyprus
Salamis
Paphos
Crete
Lasea
Fair Havens
Salmone
Great Sea
PHOENICIA
ABILENE
Sidon
Damascus
Tyre
Ptolemais
Caesarea
Jordan R.
JUDEA
Jerusalem
Salt
Sea
ARABIA
CYRENAICA
EGYPT
Nile R.
Red
Sea
0 100 200 mi.
0 100 200 300 km.

Map 12: THE WORLD TODAY

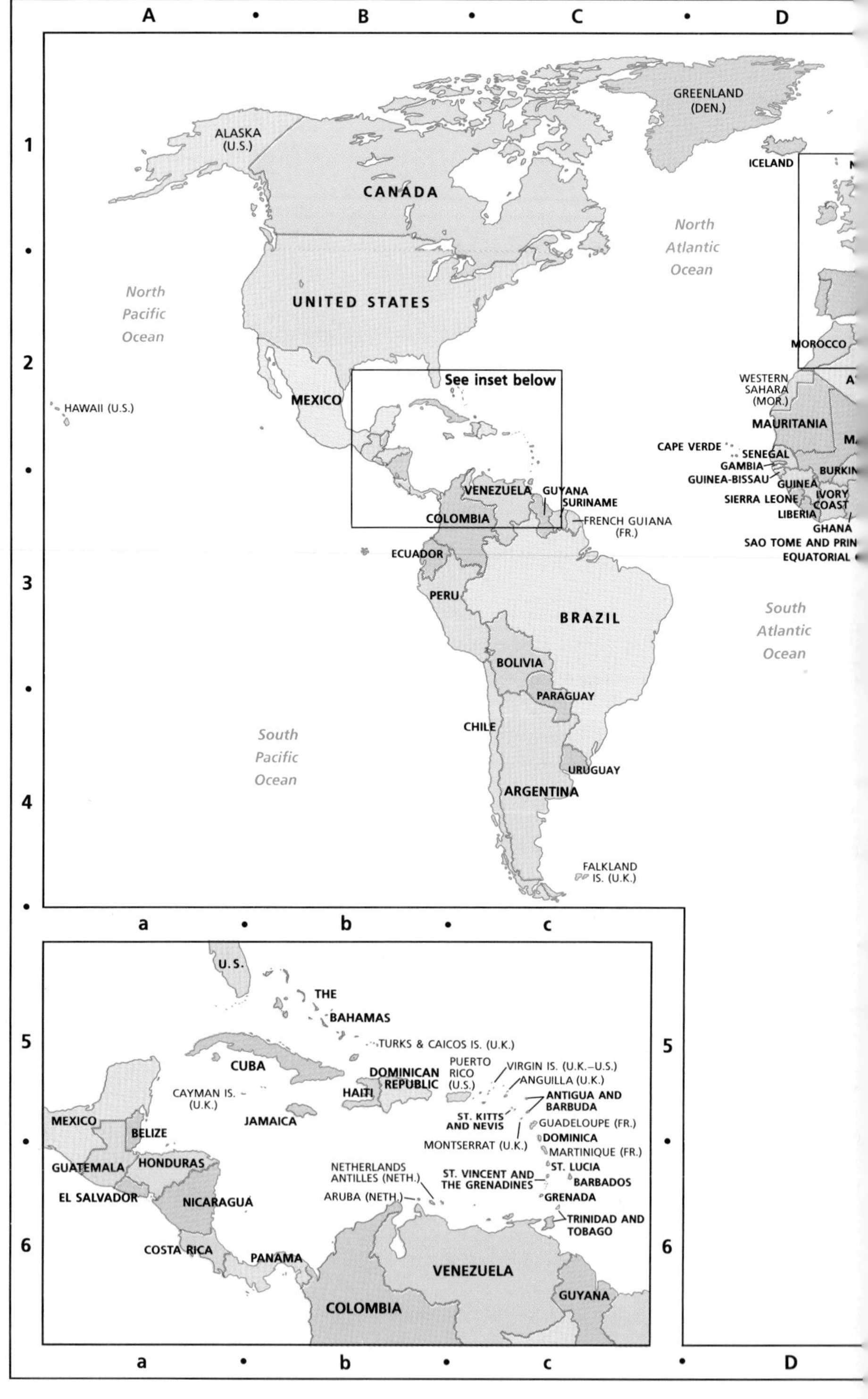

E
F
G
H
1
2
3
4
SVALBARD (NOR.)
See inset below
RUSSIA
North Pacific Ocean
KAZAKSTAN
MONGOLIA
UZBEKISTAN
KYRGYZSTAN
TURKMENISTAN
TAJIKISTAN
NORTH KOREA
SOUTH KOREA
JAPAN
TURKEY
IRAQ
AFGHANISTAN
IRAN
CHINA
NEPAL
BHUTAN
PAKISTAN
QATAR
EGYPT
SAUDI ARABIA
BANGLADESH
INDIA
TAIWAN
UNITED ARAB EMIRATES
OMAN
BURMA (MYANMAR)
LAOS
CHAD
ERITREA
YEMEN
THAILAND
SUDAN
CAMBODIA
PHILIPPINES
DJIBOUTI
VIETNAM
CENTRAL AFRICAN REPUBLIC
ETHIOPIA
SRI LANKA
BRUNEI
SOMALIA
MALDIVES
MALAYSIA
UGANDA
CONGO
KENYA
SINGAPORE
RWANDA
BURUNDI
SEYCHELLES
INDONESIA
PAPUA NEW GUINEA
ZAIRE
TANZANIA
Indian Ocean
COMOROS
SOLOMON ISLANDS
MALAWI
ZAMBIA
MOZAMBIQUE
VANUATU
ZIMBABWE
MAURITIUS
BOTSWANA
MADAGASCAR
RÉUNION (FR.)
NEW CALEDONIA (FR.)
AUSTRALIA
SWAZILAND
SOUTH AFRICA
LESOTHO
NEW ZEALAND
© 1996 The Zondervan Corporation
f
g
h
5
6
FAEROE IS. (DEN.)
NORWAY
FINLAND
SWEDEN
EST.
LATVIA
DENMARK
LITH.
RUSSIA
UNITED KINGDOM
IRELAND
BELARUS
NETHERLANDS
BELGIUM
GERMANY
POLAND
CZECH REPUBLIC
UKRAINE
KAZAKSTAN
LUXEMBOURG
SLOVAKIA
AUSTRIA
MOLDOVA
SWITZERLAND
HUNGARY
FRANCE
LIECH.
SLOV.
ROMANIA
CROATIA
BOS.& HERZ.
MONACO
SAN MARINO
YUGO.
BULGARIA
ANDORRA
ITALY
GEORGIA
PORTUGAL
ALBANIA
F.Y.R. MACED.
ARMENIA
SPAIN
GREECE
TURKEY
AZERBAIJAN
GIBRALTAR (U.K.)
MALTA
SYRIA
CYPRUS
TUNISIA
LEBANON
MOROCCO
WEST BANK
IRAQ
ALGERIA
LIBYA
ISRAEL
JORDAN
KUWAIT
EGYPT

Map 13: **ROMAN EMPIRE**

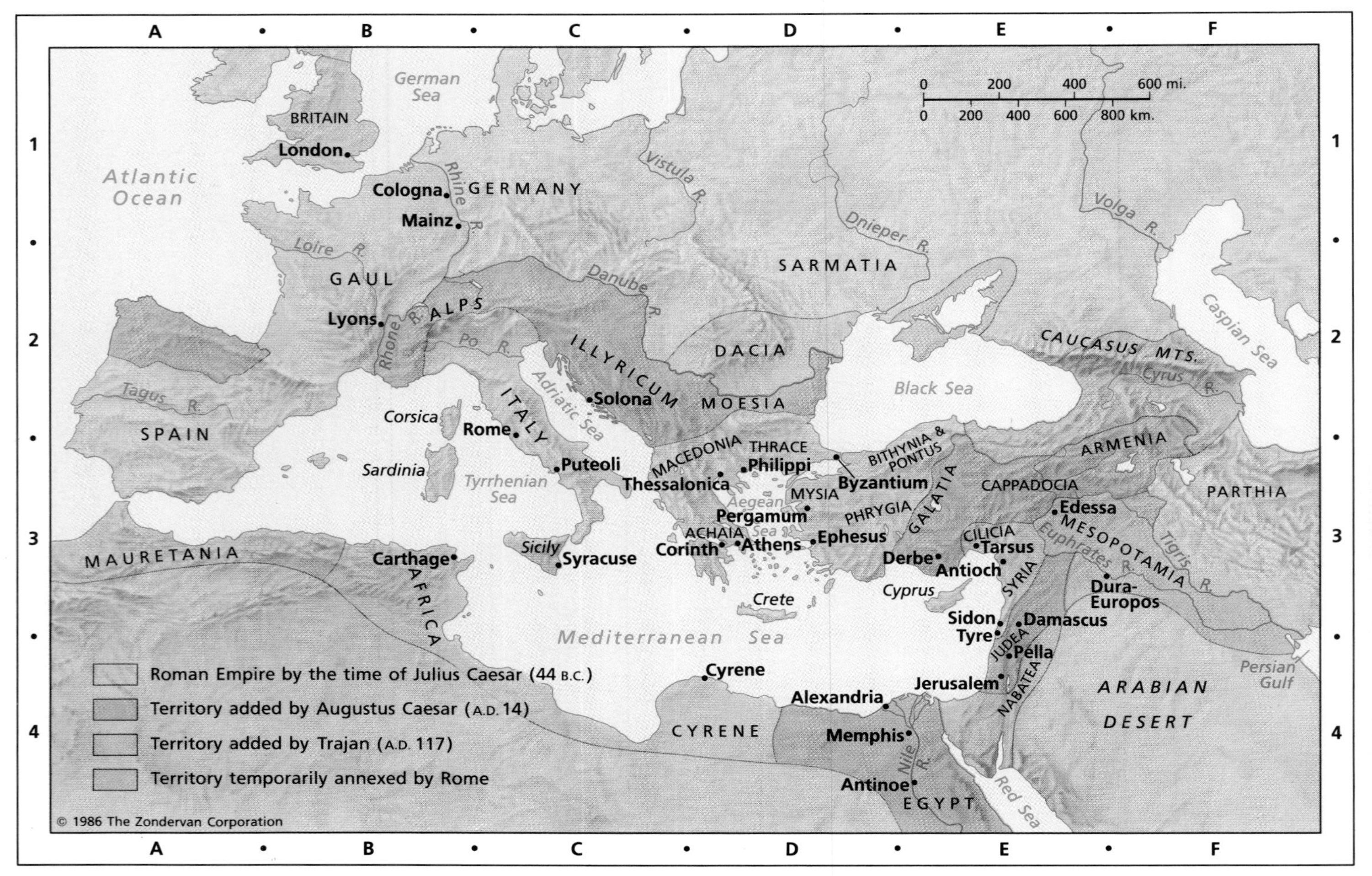